ESSAY

AND

GENERAL LITERATURE

INDEX

1975-1979

PERMANENT CUMULATIONS

ESSAY
AND
GENERAL LITERATURE
INDEX

1975-1979

EDITED BY
NORMA FREEDMAN

NEW YORK
THE H. W. WILSON COMPANY
1980

International Standard Serial Number 0014-083X

Library of Congress Catalog Card Number 34-14581

Printed in the United States of America

PREFATORY NOTE

ESSAY AND GENERAL LITERATURE INDEX is an author and subject index to collections of essays, with particular emphasis on materials in the humanities and social sciences. It is published semi-annually, with a paper issue in June, and an annual cumulation. A permanent cumulation, of which this is the ninth, is published every five years. Entries cover philosophy, religion, social and political science, economics, law, education, linguistics, science, the various arts, literature, and history. The Index also analyzes *Festschriften*. A full explanation of how to use ESSAY AND GENERAL LITERATURE INDEX will be found below.

This 1975-1979 cumulation includes a total of 20,125 essays analyzed in 1501 collections.

Directions for Use

Information for each entry includes the author and title of the essay, followed by an "In" reference (with inclusive paging) to the collection where the essay will be found.

Material under a person is arranged as follows:

1. Person's own works

2. Works about the person's life, or overall discussion of his work, are listed under the subdivision *About*

3. Criticism of an individual work is listed under the subdivision *About individual works*

For example:

Auden, Wystan Hugh
Introduction to The art of eating by M. F. K. Fisher. *In* Praise from famous men: an anthology of introductions p 1-9

About
Fraser, G. S. Auden in midstream. *In* Fraser, G. S. Essays on twentieth-century poets p136-45

About individual works
A certain world
Edel, L. The poetics of biography. *In* Contemporary approaches to English studies p38-58

In the case of authors about whom a great deal of biographical and critical material exists, there are additional specific subdivisions.

For examples, see the entries under Shakespeare.

Where the same essay is available in more than one collection, consecutive listings are made. If an essay appears under a varying title, the phrase *Same as*, followed by the variant title, is used.

Although it is basically an author and subject index, some title entries are made in "Essay Index," particularly for pseudonymous and anonymous works. Supreme Court cases are also listed under title, and there are occasional entries under the catchword or significant phrase of a title. Motion picture and theatre reviews are listed under the name of the film or play reviewed, followed by the phrase *Motion picture* or *Criticism* in parentheses.

CONTENTS

Essay and General Literature Index
1975-1979

A.B., pseud.
The direction of change. *In* From under the rubble p144-50

ABM (Antiballistic missiles) See Antimissile missiles

ACAN. See Agencia Controamericana de Noticias

ACP. See Communist Party of Albania

A.C.P.S. See Great Britain. Advisory Council on the Penal System

A.C.T.O. See Great Britain. Advisory Council on the Treatment of Offenders

A.E., pseud. See Russell, George William

AFL-CIO. See American Federation of Labor and Congress of Industrial Organizations

APA. See United States—Laws, statutes, etc.

ASEAN. See Association of South East Asian Nations

ASW. See Anti-submarine warfare

Aaron, Daniel
An approach to the thirties. *In* Luedtke, L. S. ed. The study of American culture p 1-17
The South in American history. *In* The South and Faulkner's Yoknapatawpha p3-21

Abailard, Pierre

About individual works
Historia calamitatum
Benton, J. B. and Ercoli, F. P. The style of the "Historia calamitatum": a preliminary test of the authenticity of the correspondence attributed to Abelard and Heloise. *In* Viator: medieval and Renaissance studies v6 p59-86
Hanning, R. W. Individuality in two twelfth-century personal histories. *In* Hanning, R. W. The individual in twelfth-century romance p17-52

Abandoned children
Paris
Delasselle, C. Abandoned children in eighteenth-century Paris. *In* Deviants and the abandoned in French society p47-82

Abbey church of Saint-Gilles. See Saint-Gilles, France (Gard). Abbey church of Saint-Gilles

Abbiateci, André
Arsonists in eighteenth-century France: an essay in the typology of crime. *In* Deviants and the abandoned in French society p157-79

Abbott, Daniel J. See Clinard, M. B. jt. auth.

Abbott, Keith
Blue Suede Shoes, issue 379 (the Babe Ruth essay). *In* Anderson, E. and Kinzie, M. eds. The little magazine in America: a documentary history p473-81

Abbott, Kenneth Morgan
Satira and satiricus in late Latin. *In* Illinois classical studies v4, 1979 p192-99

Abbott, Richard H.
Massachusetts and the recruitment of Southern Negroes, 1863-1865. *In* Hubbell, J. T. ed. Battles lost and won p157-70

Abbs, Peter
The mechanical world-picture. *In* Abbs, P. ed. The black rainbow p211-38

'Abd al-Nasir, Jamal. See Nasser, Gamal Abdel, President United Arab Republic

'Abd al-Raḥman al Kawākibi. See al-Kawākibi, 'Abd-al Raḥman

Abduction
Bassiouni, M. C. Unlawful seizures of persons by states as alternatives to extradition. *In* International terrorism and political crimes p343-68
O'Higgins, P. Unlawful seizure of persons by states. *In* International terrorism and political crimes p336-42
See also Kidnapping

Great Britain—History
Ives, E. W. 'Agaynst taking awaye of woman': the inception and operation of the Abduction Act of 1487. *In* Wealth and power in Tudor England p21-44

Abdul-Kasim Mansur. See Firdawsī

Abe, Kōbō
About
Rimer, J. T. Tradition and contemporary consciousness: Ibuse, Endō, Kaiko, Abe. *In* Rimer, J. T. Modern Japanese fiction and its traditions p245-70
Yamanouchi, H. Abe Kōbō and Oe Kenzaburō: the search for identity in contemporary Japanese literature. *In* Modern Japan p166-86
Yamanouchi, H. In search of identity: Abé Kōbo and Ōe Kenzaburō. *In* Yamanouchi, H. The search for authenticity in modern Japanese literature p153-74

About individual works
The ruined map
Tsuruta, K. An interpretation of The ruined map by Kōbō Abe. *In* Postwar trends in Japan p169-93

The woman in the dunes
Hyman, S. E. A trap named Hope. *In* Hyman, S. E. The critic's credentials p222-26

Abel, John Jacob
About
Harvey, A. M. Pharmacology's giant: John Jacob Abel. *In* Harvey, A. M. Adventures in medical research p49-59

Abel in fiction, drama, poetry, etc.
Brockman, B. A. Cain and Abel in the Chester creation: narrative tradition and dramatic potential. *In* Medievalia et humanistica no. 5 p169-82

Abelam (New Guinea tribe) painting. See Painting, Abelam (New Guinea tribe)

Abelard, Pierre. See Abailard, Pierre

Aberlee, Kathleen Gough
The origin of the family. *In* Reiter, R. R. ed. Toward an anthropology of women p51-76

Aberration, Chromatic and spherical. See Achromatism

Abers, Ernest S. and Kennel, Charles Frederick
Commentary: the role of error in ancient methods for determining the solar distance. *In* The Copernican achievement p130-36

Abesamis, Carlos H.
Doing theological reflection in a Philippine context. *In* The Emergent gospel p112-23

Abgarus. See Bible. New Testament. Apocryphal books. Abgar letters

Abgarus-Jesus Epistles in England in the Middle Ages, The Apocryphal. Lutz, C. E. *In* Essays on manuscripts and rare books p57-62

Ability

Testing
See Mental tests

Ability, Influence of age on
Tibbles, L. W. Medical and legal aspects of competency as affected by old age *In* Spicker, S. F.; Woodward, K. M. and Van Tassel, D. D. eds. Aging and the elderly p127-51

Abler, Ronald
The telephone and the evolution of the American metropolitan system. *In* The Social impact of the telephone p318-41

Abnormalities, Human
Smith, D. H. On letting some babies die. *In* Death inside out p129-38

Abolition of slavery. See Abolitionists

Abolitionists
Stewart, J. B. The aim and impact of Garrisonian abolitionism, 1840-1860. *In* Swierenga, R. P. ed. Beyond the Civil War synthesis p329-41
Wyatt-Brown, B. William Lloyd Garrison and antislavery unity: a reappraisal. *In* Swierenga, R. P. ed. Beyond the Civil War synthesis p309-28

Aborigines, Australian. See Australian aborigines

Abortion
Brody, B. A. Fetal humanity and the theory of essentialism. *In* Baker, R. and Elliston, F. A. eds. Philosophy & sex p338-55
Callahan, D. J. Abortion: a summary of the arguments. *In* Population policy and ethics p431-43
Cohen, H. Abortion and the quality of life. *In* Feminism and philosophy p429-40
English, J. Abortion and the concept of a person. *In* Feminism and philosophy p417-28
Fletcher, J. F. Abortion. *In* Fletcher, J. F. Humanhood: essays in biomedical ethics p132-39
Foot, P. The problem of abortion and the doctrine of the double effect. *In* Foot, P. Virtues and vices, and other essays in moral philosophy p19-32
Gordon, R. M. The abortion issue. *In* The Abdication of philosophy: philosophy and the public good p267-77
Hare, R. M. Abortion and the Golden Rule. *In* Baker, R. and Elliston, F. A. eds. Philosophy & sex p356-75

Jaggar, A. M. Abortion and a woman's right to decide. *In* Baker, R. and Elliston, F. A. eds. Philosophy & sex p324-37
Also in Gould, C. C. and Wartofsky, M. W. eds. Women and philosophy p347-60
Rapaport, E. and Sagal, P. T. One step forward, two steps backward: abortion and ethical theory. *In* Feminism and philosophy p408-16
Thomson, J. J. A defense of abortion. *In* Baker, R. and Elliston, F. A. eds. Philosophy & sex p305-23

Law and legislation—
United States
O'Meara, J. Abortion: the court decides a non-case. *In* The Supreme Court review, 1974 p337-60

Religious aspects—Catholic Church
Foot, P. The problem of abortion and the doctrine of the double effect. *In* Foot, P. Virtues and vices, and other essays in moral philosophy p19-32
Nicholson, S. T. The Roman Catholic doctrine of therapeutic abortion. *In* Feminism and philosophy p385-407

Abortion, Therapeutic
Nicholson, S. T. The Roman Catholic doctrine of therapeutic abortion. *In* Feminism and philosophy p385-407

Aboth de Rabbi Nathan
Goldin, J. A short note on the archangel Gabriel. *In* Law, church, and society p 1-4

Abraham, Henry Julian
The Supreme Court in the evolving political process. *In* Essays on the Constitution of the United States p61-73

Abrahams, Cecil A.
George Lamming and Chinua Achebe: tradition and the literary chroniclers. *In* Narasimhaiah, C. D. ed. Awakened conscience p294-306

Abrahams, Peter

About individual works
Mine boy
Wade, M. South Africa's first proletarian writer. *In* Parker, K. ed. The South African novel in English p95-113

A wreath for Udomo
Gakwandi, S. A. Nationalism: Abrahams' A wreath for Udomo. *In* Gakwandi, S. A. The novel and contemporary experience in Africa p43-56

Abrahams, Roger D.
The complex relations of simple forms. *In* Folklore genres p193-214
See also Szwed, J. F. jt. auth.

Abrahams, Roger D. and Bauman, Richard
Ranges of festival behavior. *In* Babcock, B. A. ed. The reversible world p193-208

Abrahams, William Miller. See Stansky, P. jt. auth.

Abrams, Howard B. and Abrams, Robert H.
Goldstein v. California: sound, fury, and significance. *In* The Supreme Court review, 1975 p147-87

Abrams, John Werner
The development of medieval astronomy. *In* Jeffrey, D. L. ed. By things seen: reference and recognition in medieval thought p187-209

Abrams, Meyer Howard

Belief and the suspension of disbelief. *In* Wimsatt, W. K. ed. Literary criticism: idea and act p149-69

Coleridge, Baudelaire, and modernist poetics. *In* Amacher, R. E. and Lange, V. eds. New perspectives in German literary criticism p150-81

The language and methods of humanism. *In* Hook, S.; Kurtz, P. W. and Todorovich, M. eds. The philosophy of the curriculum: the need for general education p89-97

A note on Wittgenstein and literary criticism. *In* ELH essays for Earl R. Wasserman p248-61

Abrams, Philip

Towns and economic growth: some theories and problems. *In* Towns in societies p9-33

Abrams, Robert H. See Abrams, H. B. jt. auth.

Abrams v. United States. *In* Stanford legal essays p195-249

Abramsky, Chimen

Tribute to E. H. Carr. *In* Essays in honour of E. H. Carr p vii-viii

Abramson, Ronald

Structure and meaning in the cinema. *In* Nichols, B. ed. Movies and methods p558-68

Absent object, Language and the genealogy of the. Smith, J. H. *In* Psychiatry and the humanities v 1 p145-70

Absolute, The. See One (The One in philosophy)

Absolute rights. See Natural law

Abstract art. See Art, Abstract

Abstract expressionism

Osborne, H. Expressive abstraction and abstract expressionism. *In* Osborne, H. Abstraction and artifice in twentieth-century art p111-24

Abstract paintings. See Art, Abstract

Absurd (Philosophy)

Nagel, T. The Absurd. *In* Donnelly, J. P. ed. Language, mataphysics, and death p106-15

Also in Nagel, T. Mortal questions p11-23

Absurd (Philosophy) in literature

Glicksberg, C. I. The politics of the Absurd. *In* Glicksberg, C. I. The literature of commitment p186-93

Glicksberg, C. I. The universe of the Absurd. *In* Glicksberg, C. I. The literature of nihilism p119-23

Kellogg, G. Albert Camus and the world of the Absurd. *In* Kellogg, G. Dark prophets of hope p89-100

Ketterer, D. Take-off to cosmic irony: science-fiction humor and the Absurd. *In* Cohen, S. B. ed. Comic relief p70-86

MacLeish, A. Return from the excursion. *In* MacLeish, A. Riders on the earth p3-12

Peyre, H. The motion of the Absurd in contemporary French literature. *In* Peyre, H. French literary imagination and Doestoevsky and other essays p57-73

Sayre, R. F. La chute: the egocentric individual. *In* Sayre, R. F. Solitude in society p155-75

White, H. V. The Absurdist moment in contemporary literary theory. *In* Krieger, M. and Dembo, L.S. eds. Directions for criticism p85-110

Also in White, H.V. Tropics of discoure p261-82

See also Black humor (Literature)

Absurd person singular (criticism) Ayckbourn, A. *In* Kauffmann, S. Persons of the drama p245-48

Absurdity (Philosophy) See Absurd (Philosophy)

Abu Ali Al-Hasan Ibn. See Alhazen

Abu-Bakr Muhammad ibn-Yaḥya ibn-Bājjah. See Avempace

Abū Isḥāq de Elvira. See Ibrāhīm ibn Masʿūd, Abū Ishak, al-Ilbīrī

Abū Isḥāq Ibrāhīm ibn Masʿūd al-Ilbīrī. See Ibrāhīm ibn Masʿūd, Abū Ishak, al-Ilbīrī

Abū-Lūghd, Jānit

The legitimacy of comparisons in comparative urban studies: a theoretical position and an application to North African studies. *In* Walton, J. and Massotti, L. H. eds. The city in comparative perspective p17-39

Moroccan cities: apartheid and the serendipity of conservation. *In* African themes p77-111

Recent migrations in the Arab world. *In* Human migration p224-38

Abu-Lughod, Janet. See Abū Lughd, Jānit

Abusir, Egypt

Antiquities

el Fakharani, F. The "Lighthouse" of Abusir in Egypt. *In* Harvard Studies in classical philology v78 p257-72

Academic freedom. See Teaching, Freedom of; University autonomy

Academie française, Paris

Racevskis, K. The French Academy as a proponent of egalitarianism. *In* Studies in eighteenth-century culture v7 p105-16

Academy of Natural Sciences of Philadelphia

Gerstner, P. A. The Academy of Natural Sciences of Philadelphia 1812-1850. *In* Oleson, A. and Brown, S. C. eds. The pursuit of knowledge in the early American Republic p174-93

Acadians

Louisiana

See Cajuns

Accad, Evelyne

The theme of sexual oppression in the North African novel. *In* Beck, L. and Keddie, N. R. eds. Women in the Muslim world p617-28

Accademia Olimpica, Vicenza

Gordon, D. J. Academicians build a theatre and give a play: the Accademia Olimpica. *In* Gordon, D. J. The Renaissance imagination p247-65

Accawai Indians

Colson, A. B. Birth customs of the Akawaio. *In* Studies in Social anthropology p285-309

Acceleration (Mechanics)

Costabel, P. Mathematics and Galileo's inclined plane experiments. *In* Bonelli, M. L. R. and Shea, W. R. eds. Reason, experiment, and mysticism in the scientific revolution p177-87

Acceleration principle (Economics)
Baumol, W. J. Acceleration incentives and x-efficiency. *In* Econometrics and economic theory p167-75

Acciaiuoli family
Krekić, B. Four Florentine commercial companies in Dubrovnik (Ragusa) in the first half of the fourteenth century. *In* The Medieval city p25-41

Accident law. See Personal injuries

Accidents
Franklin, M. A. Personal injury accidents in New Zealand and the United States: some striking similarities. *In* Stanford legal essays p129-48

Accidents (Philosophy)
Miller, J. W. Accidents will happen. *In* Miller, J. W. The paradox of cause, and other essays p42-55

Acclimatization. See Man—Influence of climate

Acculturation
Boulding, E. Adolescent culture: reflections of divergence. *In* Social forces and schooling p187-220
Dubos, R. J. Old World and New World. *In* Dubos, R. J. Beast or angel? p11-15
Spindler, L.S. Researching the psychology of culture change and urbanization. *In* Spindler, G. D. ed. The making of psychological anthropology p176-200
Wax, M. L. Cultural pluralism, political power, and ethnic studies. *In* Smithsonian Institution. The cultural drama p107-20
See also Assimilation (Sociology); Detribalization; Socialization

Acedia—its evolution from deadly sin to psychiatric syndrome. Altschule, M.D. *In* Altschule, M. D. Origins of concepts in human behavior p75-83

Achaeus

About
Hanfmann, G. M. A. The crucified donkey man: Achaios and Jesus. *In* Studies in classical art and archaeology p205-07

Achaios. See Achaeus

Achebe, Chinua
Morning yet on creation day
Contents
Africa and her writers
The African writer and the Biafran cause
The African writer and the English language
Chi in Igbo cosmology
Colonialist criticism
Language and the destiny of man
Named for Victoria, Queen of England
The novelist as teacher
Onitsha, gift of the Niger
Publishing in Africa: a writer's view
Tanganyika—jottings of a tourist
Thoughts on the African novel
Also in Exile and tradition p1-6
What do African intellectuals read?
Where angels fear to tread

About
Achebe, C. Named for Victoria, Queen of England. *In* Achebe, C. Morning yet on creation day p115-24
Echeruo, M. J. C. Chinua Achebe. *In* King, B. A. and Ogungbesan, K. eds. A celebration of Black and African writing p150-63

Lindfors, B. The blind men and the elephant. *In* African literature today no. 7: Focus on criticism p53-64
Taiwo, O. Chinua Achebe. *In* Taiwo, O. Culture and the Nigerian novel p11-48

About individual works
Arrow of God
Killam, D. Notions of religion, alienation and archetype in Arrow of God. *In* Exile and tradition p152-65
Vargo, E. P. Struggling with a bugaboo: the priest-character in Achebe and Greene and Keneally. *In* Narasimhaiah, C. D. ed. Awakened conscience p284-93
Wren, R. M. 'Mister Johnson' and the complexity of 'Arrow of God.' *In* Narasimhaiah, C. D. ed. Awakened conscience p50-62

A man of the people
Gakwandi, S. A. Disenchantment: Soyinka's The interpreters and Achebe's A man of the people. *In* Gakwandi, S. A. The novel and contemporary experience in Africa p66-86

No longer at ease
Gakwandi, S. A. The illusion of progress: Achebe's No longer at ease. *In* Gakwandi, S. A. The novel and contemporary experience in Africa p27-36

Things fall apart
Abrahams, C. A. George Lamming and Chinua Achebe: tradition and the literary chroniclers. *In* Narasimhaiah, C. D. ed. Awakened conscience p294-306

Achilles Tatius

About individual works
Leucippe and Clitophon
Heiserman, A. R. Antonine comedy. *In* Heiserman, A. R. The novel before the novel p117-66
Smith, M. On the Wine God in Palestine (Gen. 18, Jn. 2, and Achilles Tatius) *In* Salo Wittmayer Baron v2 p815-29

Achillini, Alessandro

About
Matsen, H. S. Giovanni Garzoni (1419-1505) to Alessandro Achillini (1463-1512): an unpublished letter and defense. *In* Philosophy and humanism p518-30

Achin, Indonesia. See Atjeh, Indonesia

Achromatism
Beck, J. Dimensions of an achromatic surface color. *In* Perception p166-84
Flock, H. R. Stimulus structure in lightness and brightness experiments. *In* Perception p185-208
Metelli, F. Achromatic color conditions in the perception of transparency. *In* Perception p95-116

Achtemeier, Paul J.
Jesus and the disciples as miracle workers in the Apocryphal New Testament. *In* Aspects of religious propaganda in Judaism and early Christianity p149-86

Ackerley, Joe Randolph

About
Fone, B. R. S. Sons and lovers: three English portraits. *In* Crew, L. ed. The gay academic p200-15

Ackerley, Joe R.—*Continued*

About individual works
My father and myself

Trilling, D. Our uncomplaining homosexuals. *In* Trilling, D. We must march my darlings p157-71

Ackley, Randall

The Navajo college-level-literacy program: a holistic response to language development for the "outsider." *In* Minority language and literature p99-106

Acmeism

Mandel'shtam, O. E. The morning of acmeism. *In* Mandel'shtam, O. E. Selected essays p128-32

Tjalsma, H. W. The Petersburg poets. *In* Gibian, G. and Tjalsma, H. W. eds. Russian modernism p65-84

Acmeist literary movement. See Acmeism

Acosta, Uriel

Authorship

Eisenstein-Barzilay, I. Finalizing an issue: Modena's authorship of the Qol sakhal. *In* Salo Wittmayer Baron v 1 p135-66

Acquired characters, Heredity of. See Inheritance of acquired characters

Acquired characters, Inheritance of. See Inheritance of acquired characters

Acquisition of language. See Children—Language

Acrostics

Levitan, W. Plexed artistry: Aratean acrostics. *In* Glyph 5 p55-68

Act (Philosophy)

Fay, B. C. How people change themselves: the relationship between critical theory and its audience. *In* Political theory and praxis p200-33

Garfinkel, H. The rational properties of scientific and common-sense activities. *In* Giddens, A. ed. Positivism and sociology p53-73

Nichols, R. L. Rebels, beginners, and buffoons: politics as action. *In* Political theory and praxis p159-99

Pettit, P. Rational man theory. *In* Hookway, C. and Pettit, P. eds. Action and interpretations p43-63

Ryan, A. Maximising, moralising and dramatising. *In* Hookway, C. and Pettit, P. eds. Action and interpretation p65-81

Weber, M. Subjectivity and determinism. *In* Giddens, A. ed. Positivism and sociology p23-31

Act psychology. See Intentionalism

Actaeon

Nagy, G. J. On the death of Actaeon. *In* Harvard Studies in classical philology v77 p179-80

• Steadman, J. M. "The merry wives of Windsor:" Falstaff as Actaeon. A dramatic emblem. *In* Steadman, J. M. Nature into myth p117-30

Actaeon in literature

Perrin, J. The Actaeon myth in Shelley's poetry. *In* English Association. Essays and studies, 1975 p29-46

Acting

Lindsay, N. V. Thirty differences between the photoplays and the stage; excerpt from "The art of the moving picture." *In* Denby, D. ed. Awake in the dark p9-18

Simon, J. I. Charm: indefinable but indispensable. *In* Simon, J. I. Singularities p216-18

Simon, J. I. In praise of professionalism. *In* Simon, J. I. Singularities p219-21

See also Actors; Actresses; Drama Pantomine; Theater

History

Bevington, D. M. Discontinuity in medieval acting traditions. *In* The Elizabethan theatre, V p 1-16

Weimann, R. The folk play and social custom. *In* Weimann, R. Shakespeare and the popular tradition in the theater: studies in the social dimension of dramatic form and function p15-48

Weimann, R. Moralities and interludes. *In* Weimann, R. Shakespeare and the popular tradition in the theater: studies in the social dimension of dramatic form and function p98-160

Weimann, R. The mystery cycles. *In* Weimann, R. Shakespeare and the popular tradition in the theater: studies in the social dimension of dramatic form and function p49-97

Actinide elements

Seaborg, G. T. From Mendeleev to Mendelevium—and beyond. *In* Neyman, J. ed. The heritage of Copernicus: theories "pleasing to the mind" p267-96

Actinide series. See Actinide elements

Actinides. See Actinide elements

Action, (Nonsymbolic) motion/ (symbolic). Burke, K. *In* Roland, A. Psychoanalysis, creativity, and literature p117-43

Action and desires, Reasons for. Foot, P. *In* Foot, P. Virtues and vices, and other essays in moral philosophy p148-56

Action in art

Osborne, H. Futurism and the representation of movement. *In* Osborne, H. Abstraction and artifice in twentieth-century art p77-93

See also Futurism (Art)

Actions and defenses. See Civil procedure; Class actions (Civil procedure); Evidence (Law)

Actions and defenses (Canon law)

Chodorow, S. A. Dishonest litigation in the Church courts, 1140-98. *In* Law, church, and society p187-206

Acton, Sir Harold Mario Mitchell

Max Beerbohm: a dandy among English classics. *In* Royal Society of Literature of the United Kingdom, London. Essays by divers hands v38 p 1-14

Acton, Harry Burrows

Kant's moral philosophy. *In* New studies in ethics v 1 p305-77

Acton, John Emerich Edward Dalberg Acton, Baron

About

Watson, G. Acton's 'History of liberty.' *In* Watson, G. Politics and literature in modern Britain p153-72

About individual works
Inaugural lecture on the study of history

Schoeck, R. J. The historian as dissenter: the function of criticism in Lord Acton's "Inaugural lecture on the study of history." *In* The Dissenting tradition p262-69

Acton, Lord. See Acton, John Emerich Edward Dalberg Acton, Baron

Actors

See also Acting; Actresses

Great Britain

Booth, M. R. Going on stage. *In* Altholz, J. L. ed. The mind and art of Victorian England p107-23

Actors, Afro-American. See Afro-American actors

Actors, American

Brustein, R. S. Acting in England and America. *In* Brustein, R. S. The culture watch p84-89

Brustein, R. S. The profession is not supporting the profession! *In* Brustein, R. S. The culture watch p125-30

Actors, English

Brustein, R. S. Acting in England and America. *In* Brustein, R. S. The culture watch p84-89

Actresses

Simon, J. I. The aesthetics of the actor's appearance. *In* Simon, J. I. Singularities p195-209

See also Acting; Actors; Moving picture actors and actresses

Great Britain

Kent, C. Image and reality: the actress and society. *In* Vicinus, M. ed. A widening sphere p94-116

Acts, Administrative. See Administrative acts

Actus Silvestri, Libri Carolini, and the Constantine Donation: the solution of a pseudo-problem. Wallach, L. *In* Wallach, L. Diplomatic studies in Latin and Greek documents from the Carolingian Age p152-59

Acuerdo de Cartagena

Milenky, E. S. The Cartagena Agreement in transition. *In* The Year book of world affairs, 1979 p167-79

Nelson, L. D. M. The Andean common market. *In* The Year book of world affairs, 1975 p208-21

Acuerdo de Cartagena countries

Economic policy

Nelson, L. D. M. The Andean common market. *In* The Year book of world affairs, 1975 p208-21

Acupuncture

History

Altschule, M. D. Acupuncture in the Western world up to a century ago. *In* Altschule, M. D. Origins of concepts in human behavior p153-63

Ad Herennium. See Rhetorica ad Herennium

Ad Hoc Committee of the Harvard Medical School to Examine the Definition of Brain Death

A definition of irreversible coma. *In* Weir, R. F. ed. Ethical issues in death and dying p82-89

Adages. See Maxims; Proverbs

Adair, Douglass G.

"That politics may be reduced to a science": David Hume, James Madison, and the tenth Federalist. *In* Livingston, D. W. and King, J. T. eds. Hume p404-17

Adam, Heribert

Internal constellations and potentials for change. *In* Thompson, L. M. and Butler, J. eds. Change in contemporary South Africa p303-26

Adamolekun, 'Ladipo

The foreign policy of Guinea. *In* Aluko, O. ed. The foreign policies of African states p98-117

Adamovich, Georgii Viktorovich

Vladimir Nabokov. *In* Erlich, V. ed. Twentieth-century Russian literary criticism p219-31

Adamovich, Georgij. See Adamovich, Georgii Viktorovich

Adams, Abigail Quincy (Smith) See Adams, Abigail (Smith)

Adams, Abigail (Smith)

About

Ketcham, R. L. The Puritan ethic in the Revolutionary era: Abigail Adams and Thomas Jefferson. *In* "Remember the ladies": new perspectives on women in American history p49-65

Adams, Andy

About

Dobie, J. F. Andy Adams, cowboy chronicler. *In* Dobie, J. F. Prefaces p3-13

About individual works
The log of a cowboy

Dobie, J. F. "Andy Adams, cowboy chronicler." *In* Praise from famous men: an anthology of introductions p60-68

Adams, Bert N. See Nahemow, N. jt. auth.

Adams, Charles J.

Islām. *In* Adams, C. J. ed. A reader's guide to the great religions p407-66

Islamic faith. *In* Savory, R. M. ed. Introduction to Islamic civilisation p33-45

Adams, Charles Phythian-. See Phythian-Adams, Charles

Adams, Eleanor Burnham

History of the Spanish Southwest: personalities and discoveries. *In* Voices from the Southwest p3-12

Adams, Hazard

Contemporary ideas of literature: terrible beauty or rough beast? *In* Krieger, M. and Dembo, L. S. eds. Directions for criticism p55-83

Revisiting Reynold's [sic] Discourses and Blake's annotations. *In* Essick, R. N. and Pearce, D. R. eds. Blake in his time p128-44

Adams, Henry

About

Auchincloss, L. Henry Adams. *In* Ross, R. G. ed. Makers of American thought p13-48

Auchincloss, L. In search of innocence: Henry Adams and John LaFarge in the South Seas. *In* Auchincloss, L. Life, law and letters p131-40

Donoghue, D. The American style of failure. *In* Donoghue, D. The sovereign ghost p103-27

Harbert, E. N. Henry Adams and the critics of his time. *In* Tulane Studies in English, v23 p71-84

Nevins, A. Henry Adams. *In* Nevins, A. Allan Nevins on history p373-92

Trilling, L. Adams at ease. *In* Trilling, L. A gathering of fugitives p126-34

Adams, Henry—Continued
About individual works
Democracy

Stineback, D. C. Visiting the "engine-room": Henry Adams's Democracy. *In* Stineback, D. C. Shifting world p61-74

The education of Henry Adams

Blasing, M. K. Henry Adams, connoisseur of chaos. *In* Blasing, M. K. The art of life p77-111

Cooley, T. The dissolving man: Henry Adams. *In* Cooley, T. Educated lives: the rise of modern autobiography in America p27-49

Couser, G. T. Henry Adams: heretic and prophet. *In* Couser, G. T. American autobiography p101-19

Harbert, E. N. Henry Adams's Education and autobiographical tradition. *In* Tulane studies in English v22 p133-41

Adams, John, President U.S.
About

Meyer, D. H. John Adams and the scenery of politics. *In* Meyer, D. H. The democratic Enlightenment p129-48

Smith, J. M. John Adams and the coming of the Revolution. *In* Suggs, G. G. ed. Perspectives on the American Revolution p75-98

Stinchcombe, W. C. John Adams and the Model Treaty. *In* The American Revolution and "a candid world" p69-84

Tichi, C. Worried celebrants of the American Revolution. *In* Emerson, E. H. ed. American literature, 1764-1789 p275-91

Adams, Léonie
About individual works
Poems: a selection

Olson, E. Louise Bogan and Léonie Adams. *In* Olson, E. On value judgments in the arts, and other essays p36-49

Adams, Mark B.

From "gene fund" to "gene pool": on the evolution of evolutionary language. *In* Studies in history of biology v3 p241-85

Adams, Maurianne

Family disintegration and creative reintegration: the case of Charlotte Brontë and Jane Eyre. *In* Wohl, A. S. ed. The Victorian family p148-79

Jane Eyre: woman's estate. *In* Diamond, A. and Edwards, L. R. eds. The authority of experience p137-59

Adams, Percy Guy

Benjamin Franklin and the travel-writing tradition. *In* Lemay, J. A. L. ed. The oldest revolutionary p33-50

Graces of harmony

Contents

The continuing echo
Definitions and the tradition
Graces of harmony in varied verse
James Thomson's luxuriant language
John Dryden's heavenly harmony
"Music resembles poetry": the auditory appeal of Pope's meter

Adams, Richard E. W.

Rio Bec archaeology and the rise of Maya civilization. *In* The Origins of Maya civilization p77-99

A trial estimation of classic Maya palace populations at Uaxactun. *In* Mesoamerican archaeology p285-96

Adams, Richard E. W. and Culbert, T. Patrick

The origins of civilization in the Maya Lowlands. *In* The Origins of Maya civilization p3-24

Adams, Richard George

Some ingredients of Watership Down. *In* Blishen, E. ed. The thorny paradise p163-73

About individual works
Watership Down

Adams, R. G. Some ingredients of Watership Down. *In* Blishen, E. ed. The thorny paradise p163-73

Chambers, A. Letter from England: Great leaping lapins! *In* Horn Book Magazine. Crosscurrents of criticism p308-10

Thomas, J. R. Old worlds and new: antifeminism in "Watership Down." *In* Horn Book Magazine. Crosscurrents of criticism p311-14

Adams, Richard Newbold

Rural collective action and the state: a discussion. *In* Forging nations: a comparative view of rural ferment and revolt p150-67

Adams, Richard Perrill

Faulkner: the European roots. *In* Faulkner: fiifty years after The marble faun p21-41

Pure poetry: Wallace Stevens' "Sea surface full of clouds." *In* Tulane Studies in English v21 p91-122

Sunrise out of The waste land. *In* Wagner, L. W. ed. Ernest Hemingway p241-51

See also Part 2 under title: Tulane Studies in English v23

Adams, Robert Lynn, and Fox, Robert Jon

Mainlining Jesus: the new trip. *In* Henslin, J. M. ed. Deviant life-style p87-100

Adams, Robert Martin

Afterjoyce

Contents

Carlo Emilio Gadda
Counterparts
Döblin, Broch
Joyce
The Joyce era?
Samuel Beckett
Three thematic interludes
Vladimir Nabokov
Woolf and Faulkner: streams of consciousness

Religion of man, religion of woman. *In* Art, politics, and will p173-90

Adams, Robert Pardie

Opposed Tudor myths of power: Machiavellian tyrants and Christian kings. *In* Studies in the continental background of Renaissance English literature: essays presented to John L. Lievsay p67-90

Adams, Stuart Nicholas

Evaluative research in corrections: status and prospects. *In* Riedel, M. and Chappell, D. eds. Issues in criminal justice: planning and evaluation p9-23

Adams, Thomas Randolph

Some bibliographical observations on and questions about the relationship between the discovery of America and the invention of printing. *In* First images of America p529-36

Adams, Walter
The contribution of economics to public policy formulation. *In* Major social issues p358-69

Adams family
Vidal, G. The four generations of the Adams family. *In* Vidal, G. Matters of fact and of fiction p153-74

Adaptability (Psychology). See Adaptation-level (Psychology)

Adaptation (Biology)
Dubos, R. J. Social adaptations. *In* Dubos, R. J. Beast or angel? p33-38
Ospovat, D. Perfect adaptation and teleological explanation: approaches to the problem of the history of life in the mid-nineteenth century. *In* Studies in history of biology, v2 p33-56
Stebbins, G. L. Adaptive shift and evolutionary novelty: a compositionist approach. *In* Ayala, F. J. and Dobzhansky, T. G. eds. Studies in the philosophy of biology p285-306
See also Bergmann's rule; Genetics; Man—Influence of environment

Adaptation-level (Psychology)
Flock, H. R. Stimulus structure in lightness and brightness experiments. *In* Perception p185-208

Adaptations, Film. See Film adaptations

Adaptations, Stage. See Stage adaptations

Addams, Jane
About
Goist, P. D. Social workers, reformers, and the city: Jane Addams and Jacob Riis. *In* Goist, P. D. From Main Street to State Street p80-93

Addison, Joseph
About
Albrecht, W. P. Addison. *In* Albrecht, W. P. The sublime pleasures of tragedy p25-38
Bloom, L. D. Addison's popular aesthetic: the rhetoric of the Paradise lost papers. *In* Martz, L. L. and Williams, A. L. eds. The author in his work p263-81

Addison, Paul
Journey to the centre: Churchill and Labour on coalition, 1940-5. *In* Crisis and controversy p165-93
Patriotism under pressure: Lord Rothermere and British foreign policy. *In* Peele, G. and Cook, C. eds The politics of reappraisal, 1918-1939 p189-208

Ade, Femi Ojo-. See Ojo-Ade, Femi

Ade, George
About
Farrell, J. T. George Ade: creator of "Artie" and "Pink Marsh". *In* Farrell, J. T. Literary essays, 1954-1974 p 44-49

Adelman, Irma, and Morris, Cynthia Taft
The derivation of cardinal scales from ordinal data: an application of multidimensional scaling to measure levels of national development. *In* Economic development and planning p 1-39

Adelman, Janet
Creation and the place of the poet in Paradise lost. *In* Martz, L. L. and Williams, A. L. eds. The author in his work p51-69

Adelman, Morris Albert
The hinge of energy policy: relations between energy markets in the United States and abroad. *In* Eppen, G. D. ed. Energy: the policy issues p71-81

Adelugba, Dapo
Language and drama: Ama Ata Aidoo. *In* African literature today no. 8: Drama in Africa p72-84

Adey, Lionel
Enjoyment, contemplation, and hierarchy in Hamlet. *In* Evolution of consciousness p149-67

Adib Ishaq. See Ishāq, Adīb

Adjustment (Psychology). See Adaptation-level (Psychology)

Adjustment, Social. See Social adjustment

Adkins, Arthur W. H.
Callinus 1 and Tyrtaeus 10 as poetry. *In* Harvard Studies in classical philology v81 p59-97

Adler, Irene, pseud. See Storr, Catherine

Adler, Jacob Henry
Tennessee Williams' South: the culture and the power. *In* Tennessee Williams: a tribute p30-52

Adler, Joyce
Wilson Harris's Tumatumari and the family of man. *In* Baugh, E. ed. Critics on Caribbean literature p113-20

Adler, Mortimer Jerome
Teaching and learning. *In* From Parnassus p57-65
About individual works
The difference of man and the difference it makes
Economos, J. J. Identity and "the difference." *In* Philosophical aspects of the mind-body problem p154-61

Adler, Nathan
Ritual, release, and orientation: maintenance of the self in the antinomian personality. *In* Zaretsky, I. I. and Leone, M. P. eds. Religious movements in contemporary America p283-97

Adler, Richard
Introduction: A context for criticism. *In* Television as a cultural force p 1-16
Understanding television: an overview of the literature of the medium as a social and cultural force. *In* Television as a social force: new approaches to TV criticism p23-47

Administration. See Civil service; Management; Political science; State, The

Administration, Public. See Public administration

Administration des bâtiments royaux. See France. Administration des bâtiments royaux

Administration of criminal justice. See Criminal justice, Administration of

Administration of juvenile justice. See Juvenile justice, Administration of

Administrative acts
United States
Scalia, A. Vermont Yankee: the A P A, the D.C. Circuit, and the Supreme Court. *In* The Supreme Court review, 1978 p345-409

Administrative agencies

Bardach, E. Reason, responsibility, and the new social regulation. *In* Burnham, W. D. and Weinberg, M. W. eds. American politics and public policy p364-90

See also Independent regulatory commissions

Management

Harris, K. L. Organizing to overhaul a mess. *In* Managing nonprofit organizations p229-43

Malek, F. V. Managing for results in the Federal government. *In* Managing nonprofit organizations p48-56

Schaffner, R. M. Can a scientific/technical executive from industry find happiness in a government agency? *In* Managing nonprofit organizations p32-37

United States

Wilson, J. Q. The politics of regulation. *In* McKie, J. W. ed. Social responsibility and the business predicament p135-68

Wise, D. Covert operations abroad: an overview. *In* Borosage, R. L. and Marks, J. D. eds. The CIA file p3-27

Administrative discretion

Davis, K. C. The inquiry—the subject, objectives, background, and method. *In* Davis, K. C. Discretionary justice in Europe and America p 1-15

Copenhagen—Case studies

Busck, L. The Family Guidance Center in Copenhagen. *In* Davis, K. C. Discretionary justice in Europe and America p115-31

France—Case studies

Merlin, C. Tax relief contracts in France. *In* Davis, K. C. Discretionary justice in Europe and America p161-78

Italy—Case studies

Cassese, S. State grants for the south of Italy. *In* Davis, K. C. Discretionary justice in Europe and America p149-60

Netherlands—Case studies

Staatsen, A. A. M. F. General assistance in the Netherlands. *In* Davis, K. C. Discretionary justice in Europe and America p133-48

Administrative law. See Administrative acts; Rule of law

Administrative procedure

United States

Scalia, A. Vermont Yankee: the A P A, the D.C. Circuit, and the Supreme Court. *In* The Supreme Court review, 1978 p345-409

Administrative Procedure Act. See United States—Laws, statutes, etc.

Administrative Reform Association, London

Anderson, O. The Administrative Reform Association, 1855-1857. *In* Hollis, P. ed. Pressure from without p262-88

Administrative responsibility. See Impeachments

Administrator-teacher relationships. See Teacher-administrator relationships

Admission to college. See Universities and colleges—United States—Admission

Admission to the bar

United States—History

Tabachnik, L. Licensing in the legal and medical professions, 1820-1860: a historical case study. *In* Gerstl, J. E. and Jacobs, G. eds. Professions for the people p25-42

Adolescence

Delors, J. The attitudes of adolescents to education and work. *In* Adolescence and youth in prospect p201-12

Eisenstadt, S. N. Cultural settings and adolescence and youth around the year 2000. *In* Adolescence and youth in prospect p114-24

Hartup, W. W. Adolescents peer relations: a look to the future. *In* Adolescence and youth in prospect p171-85

Hebbelinck, M. Biological aspects of development at adolescence. *In* Adolescence and youth in prospect p148-58

Hill, J. P. and Mönks, F. J. Overview and outcomes. *In* Adolescence and youth in prospect p 1-12

Hill, J. P. and Mönks, F. J. Some perspectives on adolescence in modern societies. *In* Adolescence and youth in prospect p28-78

Hill, J. P. and others. Summary record and conclusions. *In* Adolescence and youth in prospect p13-27

Husén, T. The adolescent and the school in Europe. *In* Adolescence and youth in prospect p186-200

Mahler, F. Adolescents' ethics and morals in the year 2000. *In* Adolescence and youth in prospect p79-94

Milani-Comparetti, M. Genetics and adolescent development: perspectives for the future. *In* Adolescence and youth in prospect p137-47

Piotrowski, J. Family and adolescents in the near future. *In* Adolescence and youth in prospect p159-70

See also Youth

Psychology

See Adolescent psychology

Adolescent boys in literature

Sarotte, G. M. Four archetypes of the homosexual couple: Adolescents. *In* Sarotte, G. M. Like a brother, like a lover p37-60

Adolescent psychology

Bettelheim, B. Obsolete youth. *In* Bettelheim, B. Surviving, and other essays p350-69

Clark, T. The oppression of youth; excerpt. *In* Gross, B. and Gross, R. eds. The children's rights movement p158-65

Elkind, D. Borderline retardation in low- and middle-income adolescents. *In* Elkind, D. The child and society p175-201

Elkind, D. Understanding the young adolescent. *In* Elkind, D. The child and society p90-100

Schwartz, S. K. Patterns of cynicism: differential political socialization among adolescents. *In* Schwartz, D. C. and Schwartz, S. K. eds. New directions in political socialization p188-202

Adolescent psychotherapy

Wittenberg, D. Art therapy for adolescent drug abusers. *In* Ulman, E. and Dachinger, P. eds. Art therapy p150-58

Adoption

Formosa

Wolf, A. P. Marriage and adoption in northern Taiwan. *In* Social organization and the applications of anthropology p128-60

Ador (The word)

Watkins, C. An Indo-European agricultural term: Latin ador, Hittite hat-. *In* Harvard Studies in classical philology v77 p187-93

Watkins, C. Latin ador, Hittite hat- again: addenda to HSCP 77 (1973) 187-193. *In* Harvard Studies in classical philology v79 p181-87

Adorno, Theodor W.

See also Horkheimer, M. jt. auth.

About

Agger, B. On happiness and the damaged life. *In* O'Neill, J. ed. On critical theory p12-33

Hughes, H. S. The critique of mass society. *In* Hughes, H. S. The sea change p134-88

Adrian I, Pope. See Hadrianus I, Pope

Adrian, Arthur Allen, and Adrian, Vonna H.

Frederick the Great: "That unutterable horror of a Prussian book." *In* Fielding, K. J. and Tarr, R. L. eds. Carlyle past and present p177-97

Adrian, Vonna H. See Adrian, A. A. jt. auth.

Adsit, Charles

In favor of house calls. *In* Home care p98-100

Adult education

See also Education of the aged

Evaluation

Hickey, T. and Hodgson, J. W. Contextual and developmental issues in the evaluation of adult learning: training in applied gerontology as an example. *In* Gubrium, J. F. ed. Late life p235-55

United States

Spear, G. E. The university and adult education. *In* Murphy, T. P. ed. Universities in the urban crisis p181-96

Adult education and libraries. See Libraries and adult education

Adultery

Framo, J. L. and others. How does an affair affect a marriage? *In* Gross, L. ed. Sexual issues in marriage p187-98

Myers, L. and Leggitt, H. A positive view of adultery. *In* Gross, L. ed. Sexual issues in marriage p165-80

Peterson, J. A. The office wife. *In* Gross, L. ed. Sexual issues in marriage p199-206

Sprey, J. Extramarital relationships. *In* Gross, L. ed. Sexual issues in marriage p131-43

Adulthood

Bellah, R. N. To kill and survive or to die and become: the active life and the contemplative life as ways of being adult. *In* Erikson, E. H. ed. Adulthood p61-80

Bouwsma, W. J. Christian adulthood. *In* Erikson, E. H. ed. Adulthood p81-96

Coles, R. Work and self-respect. *In* Erikson, E. H. ed. Adulthood p217-26

Jordan, W. D. Searching for adulthood in America. *In* Erikson, E. H. ed. Adulthood p189-99

Katchadourian, H. A. Medical perspectives on adulthood. *In* Erikson, E. H. ed. Adulthood p33-60

Lapidus, I. M. Adulthood in Islam: religious maturity in the Islamic tradition. *In* Erikson, E. H. ed. Adulthood p97-112

Malia, M. E. Adulthood refracted: Russia and Leo Tolstoi. *In* Erikson, E. H. ed. Adulthood p173-87

Rohlen, T. P. The promise of adulthood in Japanese spiritualism. *In* Erikson, E. H. ed. Adulthood p129-47

Rudolph, S. H. and Rudolph, L. I. Rajput adulthood: reflections on the Amar Singh Diary. *In* Erikson, E. H. ed. Adulthood p149-71

Stegner, W. E. The writer and the concept of adulthood. *In* Erikson, E. H. ed. Adulthood p227-36

Tu, Wei-ming. The Confucian perception of adulthood. *In* Erikson, E. H. ed. Adulthood p113-27

See also Aged

Law and legislation

Goldstein, J. On being adult and being an adult in secular law. *In* Erikson, E. H. ed. Adulthood p249-67

Adulthood in literature

Lynn, K. S. Adulthood in American literature. *In* Erikson, E. H. ed. Adulthood p237-47

Adults, Education of. See Adult education

Advaita

Mahadevan, T. M. P. Śankara. *In* Bishop, D. H. ed. Indian thought p283-300

Adventists

History

Butler, J. M. Adventism and the American experience. *In* The Rise of Adventism p173-206

Adventure stories. See Detective and mystery stories; Western stories

Adventure and adventurers. See Frontier and pioneer life

The Adventurer

Griffith, P. M. "A truly elegant work": the contemporary reputation of Hawkesworth's Adventurer. *In* The Dress of words p199-208

The adventures of Arsène Lupin (Motion picture)

Truffaut, F. Jacques Becker: Arsène Lupin. *In* Truffaut, F. The films in my life p180-83

The Adventurous history of Hsi Men and his six wives. See Chin p'ing mei

Adversaria. See Commonplace-books

Adversary system, Legal ethics and the. Dorsey G. L. *In* Hook, S.; Kurtz, P. and Todorovich, M. eds. The ethics of teaching and scientific research p99-115

Advertising

Dunn, S. W. The international language of advertising. *In* Fischer, H. D. and Merrill, J. C. eds. International and intercultural communication p308-15

Kramer, R. L. International advertising media. *In* Fischer, H. D. and Merrill, J. C. eds. International and intercultural communication p297-307

Pollard, B. International advertising: practical considerations. *In* Fischer, H. D. and Merrill, J. C. eds. International and intercultural communication p286-96

Advertising—*Continued*

Law
See Advertising—Lawyers

Lawyers
Freedman. M. H. Advertising and soliciting: the case for ambulance chasing. *In* Nader, R. and Green, M. J. eds. Verdicts on lawyers p94-104

Psychological aspects
Victoroff, D. The ludenic function of advertising. *In* Fischer, H. D. and Melnik, S. R. eds. Entertainment: a cross-cultural examination p115-19

Great Britain—History
Buck, J. D. C. The motives of puffing: John Newbery's advertisements 1742-1767. *In* Virginia. University. Bibliographical Society. Studies in bibliography v30 p196-210

Advertising, Newspaper
Lee, J. A. Meeting males by mail. *In* Crew, L. ed. The gay academic p415-27

Advertising, Political. See Television in politics

Advisory committees in education, Parents'. See Parents' advisory committees in education

Aelfric, abbot of Eynsham

About
Buckalew, R. E. Leland's transcript of Ælfric's Glossary. *In* Anglo-Saxon England 7 p149-64

Godden, M. R. Old English composite homilies from Winchester. *In* Anglo-Saxon England 4 p57-65

About individual works
Aelfric's Lives of saints
Waterhouse, R. Ælfric's use of discourse in some saints' lives. *In* Anglo-Saxon England 5 p83-103

Waterhouse, R. Affective language, especially alliterating qualifiers, in Ælfric's Life of St Alban. *In* Anglo-Saxon England 7 p131-48

Colloquy
Anderson, E. R. Social idealism in Ælfric's Colloquy. *In* Anglo-Saxon England 3 p153-62

Aeolian harp
Barfield, O. The harp and the camera. *In* Barfield, O. The rediscovery of meaning, and other essays p65-78

Aerial photography in archaeology
Cheyette, F. L. The castles of the Trencavels: a preliminary aerial survey. *In* Order and innovation in the Middle Ages p255-72

Aerial warfare. See Air warfare

Aerology. See Meteorology

Aeronautics
See also Air-ships

History
Stever, H. G. Man takes wings. *In* Neyman, J. ed. The heritage of Copernicus: theories "pleasing to the mind" p467-86

Aeschines

About
Diller, A. The manuscript tradition of Aeschines' orations. *In* Illinois classical studies v4, 1979 p34-64

Aeschylus

About
Else, G. F. Ritual and drama in Aischyleian tragedy. *In* Illinois classical studies, v2 1977 p70-87

Finley, J. H. Politics and early Attic tragedy. *In* Harvard Studies in classical philology v71 p 1-13

Havelock, E. A. The justice of Aeschylus. *In* Havelock, E. A. The Greek concept of justice p272-95

Hermassi, K. C. Political education through tragedy. *In* Hermassi, K. C. Polity and theater in historical perspective p43-64

Nicoll, A. The first dramatist: Æschylus. *In* Nicoll, A. World drama p3-25

Taplin, O. Aeschylean silences and silences in Aeschylus. *In* Harvard Studies in classical philology v76 p57-97

About individual works
Agamemnon
Brower, R. A. Seven Agamemnons. *In* Brower, R. A. Mirror on mirror p159-80

Fogelmark, S. Two cases of ΑΔΥΝΑΤΟΝ: AG. 612 and Theodoridas AP XIII.21. *In* Harvard Studies in classical philology v79 p149-63

Lloyd-Jones, H. Agamemnonea. *In* Harvard Studies in classical philology v73 p97-104

The Oresteia
Cole, J. R. The Oresteia and Cimon. *In* Harvard Studies in classical philology v81 p99-111

Holahan, M. N. The Oresteia. *In* Seidel, M. A. and Mendelson, E. eds. Homer to Brecht p143-70

Kauffmann, S. The Oresteia. *In* Kauffmann, S. Persons of the drama p102-04

Simon, B. Mental life in Greek tragedy. *In* Simon, B. Mind and madness in ancient Greece p89-121

Vellacott, P. Has good prevailed? A further study of The Oresteia. *In* Harvard Studies in classical philology v81 p113-22

Prometheus bound
Hermassi, K. C. Theatre of political memory. *In* Hermassi, K. C. Polity and theater in historical perspective p65-94

Prometheus bound (Lines 114-117)
Donovan, B. E. Prometheus bound 114-117 reconsidered. *In* Harvard Studies in classical philology v77 p125-27

Tracy, S. V. Prometheus bound 114-117. *In* Harvard Studies in classical philology v75 p59-62

The seven against Thebes
Winnington-Ingram, R. P. Septem contra Thebas. *In* Yale classical studies v25 p 1-45

Criticism, Textual
Lloyd-Jones, H. Agamemnonea. *In* Harvard Studies in classical philology v73 p97-104

Translations, English
Brower, R. A. Seven Agamemnons. *In* Brower, R. A. Mirror on mirror p159-80

Aesop. See Aesopus

Aesopus

About
Noel, T. Aesop as a popular figure and the fable in England. *In* Noel, T. Theories of the fable in the eighteenth century p25-37

Aesopus—*Continued*
About individual works
Fables
Downs, R. B. Famed fabulist. *In* Downs, R. B. Books that changed the world p44-48

Æstel (The word)
Harbert, B. King Alfred's 'æstel'. *In* Anglo-Saxon England 3 p103-10

Aesthetic form. *See* Form (Aesthetics)

Aesthetic movement (British art)
Williamson, A. Whistler, Wilde and the aesthetic influence. *In* Williamson, A. Artists and writers in revolt p182-96

Aesthetics
Alexander, H. G. On defining in aesthetics. *In* Aagaard-Mogensen, L. ed. Culture and art p110-18

Beardsley, M. C. The aesthetic point of view. *In* Margolis, J. Z. ed. Philosophy looks at the arts p6-24

Binkley, T. Deciding about art. *In* Aagaard-Mogensen, L. ed. Culture and art p90-109

Binkley, T. Piece: contra aesthetics. *In* Margolis, J. Z. ed. Philosophy looks at the arts p25-44

Bronowski, J. The shape of things. *In* Bronowski, J. The visionary eye p33-44

Brown, L. B. Animadversions on the autonomy of art. *In* Viva Vivas! p183-223

Brunius, T. Theory and ideologies in aesthetics. *In* Aagaard-Mogensen, L. ed. Culture and art p66-77

Cassirer, E. The educational value of art. *In* Cassirer, E. Symbol, myth, and culture p196-215

Cassirer, E. Language and art I. *In* Cassirer, E. Symbol, myth, and culture p145-65

Cassirer, E. Language and art II. *In* Cassirer, E. Symbol, myth, and culture p166-95

Cavell, S. Aesthetic problems of modern philosophy. *In* Cavell, S. Must we mean what we say? p73-96

Cavell, S. A matter of meaning it. *In* Cavell, S. Must we mean what we say? p213-37

Coomaraswamy, A. K. A figure of speech or a figure of thought? Excerpt from "Figures of speech or figures of thought: collected essays on the traditional or 'normal' view of art." *In* Coomaraswamy, A. K. Selected papers v 1 p13-42

Coomaraswamy, A. K. Samvega: aesthetic shock; excerpt from "Figures of speech or figures of thought: collected essays on the traditional or 'normal' view of art." *In* Coomaraswamy, A. K. Selected papers v 1 p179-85

Dark, P. J. C. What is art for anthropologists? *In* Greenhalgh, M. and Megaw, J. V. S. eds. Art in society p31-50

Davies, J. Time, aesthetics, and critical theory. *In* O'Neill, J. ed. On critical theory p58-77

Derrida, J. The theater of cruelty and the closure of representation. *In* Derrida, J. Writing and difference p232-50

Edelman, N. The case against Gothicism. *In* Edelman, N. The eye of the beholder p86-106

Elliott, R. K. Aesthetic theory and the experience of art. *In* Margolis, J. Z. ed. Philosophy looks at the arts p45-87

Faris, J. C. The productive basis of aesthetic traditions: some African examples. *In* Greenhalgh, M. and Megaw, J. V. S. eds. Art in society p317-39

Greene, M. The artistic-aesthetic and curriculum. *In* Greene, M. Landscapes of learning p168-84

Greene, M. Significant landscapes: an approach to the arts in interrelationship. *In* Greene, M. Landscapes of learning p198-210

Gruber, H. E. Darwin's "tree of nature" and other images of wide scope. *In* Wechsler, J. ed. On aesthetics in science p121-40

Hough, G. G. The aesthetic of pre-Raphaelitism; excerpt from "The last romantics". *In* Sambrook, J. ed. Pre-Raphaelitism p133-52

Iseminger, G. Appreciation, the artworld, and the aesthetic. *In* Aagaard-Mogensen, L. ed. Culture and art p118-30

Jauss, H. R. Theses on the transition from the aesthetics of literary works to a theory of aesthetic experience. *In* Valdés, M. J. and Miller, O. J. eds. Interpretation of narrative p137-47

Koestler, A. Literature and the law of diminishing returns. *In* Koestler, A. The heel of Achilles p119-37

Korn, S. M. The formal analysis of visual systems as exemplified by a study of Abelam (Papua New Guinea) paintings. *In* Greenhalgh, M. and Megaw, J. V. S. eds. Art in society p161-73

Malraux, A. Anti-critique. *In* Courcel, M. H. de, ed. Malraux p223-57

Margolis, J. Z. The ontological peculiarity of works of art. *In* Margolis, J. Z. ed. Philosophy looks at the arts p213-24

Margolis, J. Z. Robust relativism. *In* Margolis, J. Z. Philosophy looks at the arts p387-437

Martin, J. National development and ethnic poetics: the function of literature in the liberation of peoples. *In* Luedtke, L. S. ed. The study of American culture p219-40

Meyer, L. B. Forgery and the anthropology of art, excerpt from "Music, the arts, and ideas." *In* Aagaard-Mogensen, L. ed. Culture and art p53-66

Mitchell, C. 'Very like a whale': the spectator's role in modern art. *In* Concerning contemporary art p35-88

Mukařovský, J. The aesthetic norm. *In* Mukařovský, J. Structure, sign, and function p49-56

Mukařovský, J. Can there be a universal aesthetic value in art. *In* Mukařovský, J. Structure, sign, and function p57-69

Mukařovský, J. The essence of the visual arts. *In* Mukařovský, J. Structure, sign, and function p220-35

Mukařovský, J. On the problem of functions in architecture. *In* Mukařovský, J. Structure, sign, and function p236-50

Mukařovský, J. The place of the aesthetic function among the other functions. *In* Mukařovský, J. Structure, sign, and function p31-48

Mukařovský, J. The significance of aesthetics. *In* Mukařovský, J. Structure, sign, and function p17-30

Olson, E. On value judgments in the arts. *In* Olson, E. On value judgments in the arts, and other essays p307-26

Aesthetics—*Continued*

Papert, S. A. The mathematical unconscious. *In* Wechsler, J. ed. On aesthetics in science p105-19

Roaf, M. A mathematical analysis of the styles of the Persepolis reliefs. *In* Greenhalgh, M. and Megaw, J. V. S. eds. Art in society p133-45

Sabin, M. Beauty and taste. *In* Sabin, M. English romanticism and the French tradition p181-201

Sayers, D. L. Toward a Christian esthetic; excerpt from "Unpopular opinions." *In* Sayers, D. L. The whimsical Christian p73-91

Simon, J. I. What is taste? *In* Simon, J. I. Singularities p92-98

Smith, C. S. Structural hierarchy in science, art, and history. *In* Weschsler, J. ed. On aesthetics in science p9-53

Tilghman, B. R. Artistic puzzlement. *In* Aagaard-Mogensen, L. ed. Culture and art p77-90

Tormey, A. Art and expression: a critique; excerpt from "The concept of expression: a study in philosophical psychology and aesthetics." *In* Margolis, J. Z. ed. Philosophy looks at the arts p346-69

Trilling, L. Criticism and aesthetics. *In* Trilling, L. A gathering of fugitives p143-52

Walton, K. L. Categories of art. *In* Margolis, J. Z. ed. Philosophy looks at the arts p88-131

Weber, S. M. Aesthetic experience and self-reflection as emancipatory processes: two complementary aspects of critical theory. *In* O'Neill, J. ed. On critical theory p78-103

Wollheim, R. Aesthetics, anthropology and style: some programmatic remarks. *In* Greenhalgh, M. and Megaw, J. V. S. eds. Art in society p3-14

Wollheim, R. Art and its objects; excerpt. *In* Margolis, J. Z. ed. Philosophy looks at the arts p169-88

Wollheim, R. Style now. *In* Concerning contemporary art p133-53

Wolterstorff, N. Toward an ontology of art works. *In* Margolis, J. Z. ed. Philosophy looks at the arts p189-212

See also Art; Art—Philosophy; Art and literature; Avant-garde (Aesthetics); Classicism; Criticism; Cubism; Dadaism Expressionism (Art); Form (Aesthetics); Futurism (Art); Idealism in literature; Literature—Aesthetics; Modernism (Art); Moving-pictures—Aesthetics; Music—Philosophy and aesthetics; Naturalism in literature; Painting; Poetry; Realism in art; Realism in literature; Romanticism; Sublime, The; Surrealism; Symmetry; Ugliness; Ut pictura poesis (Aesthetics)

Aesthetics, American

Graburn, N. H. 'I like things to look more different than that stuff did': an experiment in cross-cultural art appreciation. *In* Greenhalgh, M. and Megaw, J. V. S. eds. Art in society p51-70

Aesthetics, British. See Aesthetic movement (British art)

Aesthetics, Communist. See Communist aesthetics

Aesthetics, Czech

Mukařovský, J. On structuralism. *In* Mukařovský, J. Structure, sign, and function p17-30

Aesthetics, Eskimo

Swinton, G. S. Touch and the real: contemporary Inuit aesthetics—theory, usage and relevance. *In* Greenhalgh, M. and Megaw, J. V. S. eds. Art in society p71-88

Aesthetics, French

History

Dieckmann, H. The transformation of the concept of imitation in eighteenth-century French esthetics. *In* Amacher, R. E. and Lange, V. eds. New perspectives in German literary criticism p49-85

Aesthetics, Medieval

Coomaraswamy, A. K. The mediaeval theory of beauty. *In* Coomaraswamy, A. K. Selected papers v 1 p189-228

Jones, C. W. Carolingian aesthetics: why modular verse? *In* Viator: medieval and Renaissance studies v6 p309-40

Schapiro, M. On the aesthetic attitude in Romanesque art. *In* Schapiro, M. Selected papers v 1 p 1-27

Aesthetics, Modern

Osborne, H. Art and information theory. *In* Osborne, H. Abstraction and artifice in twentieth-century art p6-21

Osborne, H. Epilogue. *In* Osborne, H. Abstraction and artifice in twentieth-century art p181-86

Peckham, M. The deplorable consequences of the idea of creativity. *In* Peckham, M. Romanticism and behavior p206-21

Peckham, M. Iconography and iconology in the arts of the nineteenth and twentieth centuries. *In* Peckham, M. Romanticism and behavior p90-108

16th century

Greenhalgh, M. European interest in the non-European: the sixteenth century and pre-Columbian art and architecture. *In* Greenhalgh, M. and Megaw, J. V. S. eds. Art in society p89-103

20th century

Binkley, T. Piece: contra aesthetics. *In* Margolis, J. Z. ed. Philosophy looks at the arts p25-44

Brustein, R. S. On the new cultural conservatism. *In* Brustein, R. S. The culture watch p26-31

Cavell, S. Music discomposed. *In* Cavell, S. Must we mean what we say? p180-212

Danto, A. C. The artworld. *In* Margolis, J. Z. ed. Philosophy looks at the arts p132-44

Herman, J. The modern artist in modern society. *In* Greenhalgh, M. and Megaw, J. V. S. eds. Art in society p121-30

Imdahl, M. Overstepping esthetic limits in visual art: four aspects of the problem. *In* Amacher, R. E. and Lange, V. eds. New perspectives in German literary criticism p279-92

Kaufmann, E. A profitable art. *In* The Uneasy coalition: design in corporate America p31-39

Kjørup, S. Art broadly and wholly conceived. *In* Aagaard-Mogensen, L. ed. Culture and art p45-53

Aesticampianus, Johannes Rhagius

About

Lutz, D. E. Aesticampianus' edition of the Tabula attributed to Cebes. *In* Lutz, C. E. Essays on manuscripts and rare books p79-86

Africa—*Continued*

Foreign relations—United States

Obatala, J. K. Black consciousness and American policy in Africa. *In* Said, A. A. and Simmons, L. R. eds. Ethnicity in an international context p64-75

Historical geography

Lamphear, J. Two basic themes in African history: migration and state formation. *In* Martin, P. M. and O'Meara, P. eds. Africa p83-97

Historiography

Ajayi, J. F. Ade. and Alagoa, E. J. Black Africa: the historians' perspective. *In* Mintz, S. W. ed. Slavery, colonialism, and racism p125-34

Hodgkin, T. L. Where the paths began. *In* African studies since 1945 p6-16

Ranger, T. O. Towards a usable African past. *In* African studies since 1945 p17-30

Wheatley, P. Analecta Sino-Africana recensa. *In* Chittick, H. N. and Rotberg, R. I. eds. East Africa and the Orient p76-114

History

Curtin, P. D. The Black experience of colonialism and imperialism. *In* Mintz, S. W. ed. Slavery, colonialism, and racism p17-29

History—Sources

Lamphear, J. Reconstructing the African past. *In* Martin, P. M. and O'Meara, P. eds. Africa p53-61

History—Study and teaching

Coquery-Vidrovitch, C. Changes in African historical studies in France. *In* African studies since 1945 p200-08

Geiss, I. The study of African history in Germany. *In* African studies since 1945 p209-19

History—To 1884

Brooks, G. E. European relations with Africa before 1870. *In* Martin, P. M. and O'Meara, P. eds. Africa p114-31

History—1884-1960

Gellar, S. The colonial era. *In* Martin, P. M. and O'Meara, P. eds. Africa p132-49

Keller, E. J. Decolonization and the struggle for independence. *In* Martin, P. M. and O'Meara, P. eds. Africa p150-65

Morris-Hale, W. From empire to nation: the African experience. *In* Aftermath of empire p85-101

History—1960-

Keller, E. J. Decolonization and the struggle for independence. *In* Martin, P. M. and O'Meara, P. eds. Africa p150-65

Morris-Hale, W. From empire to nation: the African experience. *In* Aftermath of empire p85-101

International status

Liebenow, J. G. Africa in world affairs. *In* Martin, P. M. and O'Meara, P. eds. Africa p395-414

Maps

Lane-Pool, E. H. The discovery of Africa: a history of the exploration of Africa as reflected in the maps in the collection of the Rhodes-Livingstone Museum. *In* The Occasional papers of the Rhodes-Livingstone Museum p215-48

McNulty, M. L. The contemporary map of Africa. *In* Martin, P. M. and O'Meara, P. eds. Africa p24-49

Politics and government

Chazan, N. Myths and realities in African socialism. *In* Eisenstadt, S. N. and Azmon, Y. eds. Socialism and tradition p141-71

Collier, R. B. Political change and authoritarian rule. *In* Martin, P. M. and O'Meara, P. P. eds. Africa p295-310

Dei-Anang, M. Foreign policy of the independent African states. *In* African studies since 1945 p66-76

Masanja, P. Neocolonialism and revolution in Africa. *In* The Emergent gospel p 9-21

Owusu, M. Comparative politics, history, and political anthropology. *In* Colonialism and change p25-65

Vaughan, J. H. Social and political organization in traditional societies. *In* Martin, P. M and O'Meara, P. eds. Africa p169-88

Politics and government 1960-

Thompson, W. S. and Zartman, I. W. The development of norms in the African system. *In* El-Ayouty, Y. ed. The Organization of African Unity after ten years p3-46

Population

Vaughan, J. H. Environment, population, and traditional society. *In* Martin, P. M. and O'Meara, P. eds. Africa p 9-23

Regionalism

See Regionalism—Africa

Relations (general) with China

Wheatley, P. Analecta Sino-Africana recensa. *In* Chittick, H. N. and Rotberg, R. I. eds. East Africa and the Orient p76-114

Relations (general) with Europe

Brooks, G. E. European relations with Africa before 1870. *In* Martin, P. M. and O'Meara, P. eds. Africa p114-31

Religion

Booth, N. S. An approach to African religion. *In* African religions: a symposium p 1-11

El-Shamy, H. African world view and religion. *In* Martin, P. M. and O'Meara, P. eds. Africa p208-20

Koech, K. African mythology: a key to understanding African religion. *In* African religions: a symposium p117-39

Sieber, R. Some aspects of religion and art in Africa. *In* African religions: a symposium p141-57

Religion—History

Martin, B. G. The spread of Islam. *In* Martin, P. M. and O'Meara, P. eds. Africa p98-113

Religion—Study and teaching

Brown, C. S. and Chappelle, Y. J. R. African religions and the quest for Afro-American heritage. *In* African religions: a symposium p241-54

Religious life and customs

Boshier, A. The religions of Africa. *In* Life after death p54-66

Rural conditions

Aluko, S. A. Rural economic development. *In* Colonialism and change p231-54

Africa—*Continued*

Social conditions

Aluko, S. A. Rural economic development. *In* Colonialism and change p231-54

Armer, M. J. and Gewirtz, M. Sociocultural change in contemporary Africa. *In* Martin, P. M. and O'Meara, P. eds. Africa p280-94

Carr, B. Africa's moral imperatives: liberation, identity, humanness. *In* World change and world security p103-16

Fortes, M. The plural society in Africa. *In* Leftwich, A. ed. South Africa: economic growth and political change p 1-27

Karefa-Smart, J. A. M. Doctors, development, and demons in Africa. *In* Disguises of the demonic p150-56

Masanja, P. Neocolonialism and revolution in Africa. *In* The Emergent gospel p 9-21

Shack, W. A. Open systems and closed boundaries: the ritual process of stranger relations in new African states. *In* Shack, W. A. and Skinner, E. P. eds. Strangers in African societies p37-47

Young, C. Nationalism and separatism in Africa. *In* Kilson, M. ed. New states in the modern world p57-74

Social life and customs

Vaughan, J. H. Environment, population, and traditional society. *In* Martin, P. M. and O'Meara, P. eds. Africa p 9-23

Vaughan, J. H. Social and political organization in traditional societies. *In* Martin, P. M. and O'Meara, P. eds. Africa p169-88

Study and teaching

Hodgkin, T. L. Where the paths began. *In* African studies since 1945 p6-16

Kirk-Greene, A. H. M. Public administration and African studies. *In* African studies since 1945 p125-35

Lienhardt, G. Social anthropology of Africa. *In* African studies since 1945 p179-85

Ranger, T. O. Towards a usable African past. *In* African studies since 1945 p17-30

Shula, M. South African studies since World War Two. *In* African studies since 1945 p186-99

Study and teaching—France

Coquery-Vidrovitch, C. Changes in African historical studies in France. *In* African studies since 1945 p200-08

Study and teaching—Germany

Geiss, I. The study of African history in Germany. *In* African studies since 1945 p209-19

Africa, Black. See Africa, Sub-Saharan

Africa, East

Antiquities

Posnansky, M. Connections between the Lacustrine peoples and the coast. *In* Chittick, H. N. and Rotberg, R. I. eds. East Africa and the Orient p216-25

Commerce—History

Quiggin, A. H. Trade routes, trade and currency in East Africa. *In* The Occasional papers of the Rhodes-Livingstone Museum p145-65

Description and travel

Connolly, C. On safari. *In* Connolly, C. The evening colonnade p60-72

Economic policy

Letiche, J. M. Dependent monetary systems and economic development: the case of sterling East Africa. *In* Economic development and planning p186-236

Politics and government

Vincent, J. Room for manœuvre: the political role of small towns in East Africa. *In* Colonialism and change p115-44

Social conditions

Vincent, J. Room for manœuvre: the political role of small towns in East Africa. *In* Colonialism and change p115-44

Africa, Eastern

History

Chittick, H. N. The peopling of the East African coast. *In* Chittick, H. N. and Rotberg, R. I. eds. East Africa and the Orient p16-43

Africa, French speaking west

Challenor, H. S. Strangers as colonial intermediaries: the Dahomeyans in Francophone Africa. *In* Shack, W. A. and Skinner, E. P. eds. Strangers in African societies p67-83

Africa, North

History—647-1517

Brett, M. The military interest of the Battle of Haydarān. *In* War, technology and society in the Middle East p78-88

Africa, South. See South Africa

Africa, Southern

Bibliography

Gosebrink, J. E. M. Sources for contemporary Southern Africa. *In* Carter, G. M. and O'Meara, P. eds. Southern Africa: the continuing crisis p363-81

Economic conditions

Gervasi, S. The politics of "accelerated economic growth." *In* Thompson, L. M. and Butler, J. eds. Change in contemporary South Africa p349-68

Grundy, K. W. Economic patterns in the new Southern African balance. *In* Carter, G. M. and O'Meara, P. eds. Southern Africa: the continuing crisis p291-312

Foreign relations

Legum, C. International rivalries in the Southern African conflict. *In* Carter, G. M. and O'Meara, P. eds. Southern Africa: the continuing crisis p3-17

Legum, C. Introduction: The international dimension of the crisis in Southern Africa. *In* Carter, G. M. and O'Meara, P. eds. Southern Africa in crisis p3-13

Politics and government

Bissell, R. E. Southern Africa: testing détente. *In* Kirk, G. L. and Wessell, N. H. eds. The Soviet threat p88-98

Gutteridge, W. F. Southern Africa: a study in conflict. *In* The Dynamics of the arms race p231-39

Kapungu, L. T. The OAU's support for the liberation of Southern Africa. *In* El-Ayouty, Y. ed. The Organization of African Unity after ten years p135-51

Legum, C. International rivalries in the Southern African conflict. *In* Carter, G. M. and O'Meara, P. eds. Southern Africa: the continuing crisis p3-17

Africa, Southern—Politics and government
—*Continued*

Legum, C. Introduction: The international dimension of the crisis in Southern Africa. *In* Carter, G. M. and O'Meara, P. eds. Southern Africa in crisis p3-13

Legum, C. Southern Africa: the politics of detente. *In* The Year book of world affairs, 1976 p14-29

Shaw, T. M. Southern Africa: from détente to deluge? *In* The Year book of world affairs, 1978 p117-38

Relations (general) with
South Africa

Potholm, C. P. The effects on South Africa of changes in contiguous territories. *In* Thompson, L. M. and Butler, J. eds. Change in contemporary South Africa p329-48

Social conditions

Gervasi, S. The politics of "accelerated economic growth." *In* Thompson, L. M. and Butler, J. eds. Change in contemporary South Africa p349-68

Potholm, C. P. The effects on South Africa of changes in contiguous territories. *In* Thompson, L. M. and Butler, J. eds. Change in contemporary South Africa p329-48

Africa, Southwest. See Namibia

Africa, Sub-Saharan

Emigration and immigration

Curtin, P. D. Postwar migrations in sub-Saharan Africa. *In* Human migration p188-98

History

Curtin, P. D. Postwar migrations in sub-Saharan Africa. *In* Human migration p188-98

Africa, West

Economic integration

Elias, T. O. The economic community of West Africa. *In* The Year book of world affairs, 1978 p93-116

Population

Ardener, E. Language, ethnicity, and population. *In* Studies in social anthropology p343-53

Africa in literature

Brathwaite, E. K. The African presence in Caribbean literature. *In* Mintz, S. W. ed. Slavery, colonialism, and racism p73-109

Brown, L. W. The African heritage and the Harlem Renaissance: a re-evaluation. *In* African literature no. 9: Africa, America and the Caribbean p 1-9

Gottlieb, L. C. and Keitner, W. Colonialism as metaphor and experience in 'The grass is singing' and 'Surfacing.' *In* Narasimhaiah, C. D. ed. Awakened conscience p307-14

Lindfors, B. "East is East and West is West": points of divergence in African literary history. *In* Narasimhaiah, C. D. ed. Awakened conscience p42-49

Snyder, E. Modern Africa in literature. *In* Martin, P. M. and O'Meara, P. eds. Africa p331-47

Taiwo, O. Historical and cultural influences on the Nigerian novelists. *In* Taiwo, O. Culture and the Nigerian novel p 1-33

Wren, R. M. 'Mister Johnson' and the complexity of 'Arrow of God.' *In* Narasimhaiah, C. D. ed. Awakened conscience p50-62

African Americans. See Afro-Americans

African art. See Art, African

African cooperation

Boutros-Ghali, B. The League of Arab States and the Organization of African Unity. *In* El-Ayouty, Y. ed. The Organization of African Unity after ten years p47-61

African didactic fiction. See Didactic fiction, African

African drama

History and criticism

De Graft, J. C. Roots in African drama and theatre. *In* African literature today no. 8: Drama in Africa p 1-25

Nkosi, L. Post-war drama in Africa. *In* Nicoll, A. World drama p895-99

Owomoyela, O. Drama. *In* Owomoyela, O. African literatures: an introduction p113-32

Soyinka, W. Drama and the African world-view. *In* Exile and tradition p173-90

African epic poetry. See Epic poetry, African

African fiction

See also Didactic fiction, African

History and criticism

Achebe, C. Thoughts on the African novel. *In* Exile and tradition p 1-6

Also in Achebe, C. Morning yet on creation day p81-90

Owomoyela, O. The novel. *In* Owomoyela, O. African literatures: an introduction p73-111

African fiction (English)

History and criticism

Gakwandi, S. A. Conclusion: realism and the African novel. *In* Gakwandi, S. A. The novel and contemporary experience in Africa p126-30

Gakwandi, S. A. Introduction: historical and literary background. *In* Gakwandi, S. A. The novel and contemporary experience in Africa p 1-11

African folk-lore. See Folk-lore, African

African languages

Ong, W. J. African talking drums and oral noetics. *In* Ong, W. J. Interfaces of the word p92-120

African literature

Snyder, E. Modern Africa in literature. *In* Martin, P. M. and O'Meara, P. eds. Africa p331-47

History and criticism

Achebe, C. Africa and her writers. *In* Achebe, C. Morning yet on creation day p29-45

Achebe, C. The African writer and the Biafran cause. *In* Achebe, C. Morning yet on creation day p137-47

Achebe, C. The African writer and the English language. *In* Achebe, C. Morning yet on creation day p91-103

Achebe, C. Colonialist criticism. *In* Achebe, C. Morning yet on creation day p3-28

Awoonor, K. Tradition and continuity in African literature. *In* Exile and tradition p166-72

Dorsinville, M. Senghor or the song of exile. *In* Exile and tradition p62-73

Edwards, P. G. West African literature and English studies. *In* African studies since 1945 p91-95

Afro-American churches—*Continued*

Richardson, H. V. Afro-American religion: the origin and development of the established churches. *In* The Black American reference book p492-506

History

Jones, L. The organized church: its historic significance and changing role in contemporary Black experiences. *In* Johnson, H. A. ed. Negotiating the mainstream p103-40

Mississippi

Welty, E. A pageant of birds. *In* Welty, E. The eye of the story p315-20

Afro-American coil basketry in Charleston County, South Carolina. *In* Yoder, D. American folklife p151-84

Afro-American college students

Gates, H. L. They think you're an airplane, but you're really a bird: the education of an Afro-American. *In* Hurdles p193-211

Sowell, T The plight of Black students in the United States *In* Mintz, S. W. ed. Slavery, colonialism, and racism p179-96

Afro-American colleges. See Afro-American universities and colleges

Afro-American dialect. See Black English

Afro-American drama (English) See American drama—Afro-American authors

Afro-American education. See Afro-Americans—Education

Afro-American English. See Black English

Afro-American entertainers. See Afro-American actors

Afro-American families

Douglass, J. H. and Smythe, M. M. The Black family. *In* The Black American reference book p316-40

Solomon, B. B. and Mendes, H. A. Black families: a social welfare perspective. *In* Tufte, V. and Myerhoff, B. G. eds. Changing images of the family p271-95

Afro-American farmers

Beale, C. L. The Black American in agriculture. *In* The Black American reference book p284-315

Afro-American fiction (English) See American fiction—Afro-American authors

Afro-American folk-lore

Dorson, R. M. The African connection: comments on African folklore in the New World. *In* Crowley, D. J. ed. African folklore in the New World p87-91

Dundes, A. African and Afro-American tales. *In* Crowley, D. J. ed. African folklore in the New World p35-53

Jackson, B. The other kind of doctor: conjure and magic in Black American folk medicine. *In* American folk medicine p259-72

Influence

Hemenway, R. Are you a flying lark or a setting dove? *In* Fisher, D. and Stepto, R. B. eds. Afro-American literature p122-52

Afro-American folk-lore in literature

Hemenway, R. Are you a flying lark or a setting dove? *In* Fisher, D. and Stepto, R. B. eds. Afro-American literature p122-52

O'Meally, R. G. Riffs and rituals: folk-lore in the work of Ralph Ellison. *In* Fisher, D. and Stepto, R. B. eds. Afro-American literature p153-69

Afro-American folk-songs. See Afro-American songs

Afro-American humor

Nichols, C. H. Comic modes in Black America (a ramble through Afro-American humor). *In* Cohen, S. B. ed. Comic relief p105-26

Afro-American intelligence. See Intelligence levels—Afro-Americans

Afro-American journalists

Jackson, L. P. The popular media: Part I, The mission of Black newsmen. *In* The Black American reference book p846-74

Afro-American leadership

Brisbane, R. H. Black protest in America. *In* The Black American reference book p537-79

Huggins, N. I. Afro-Americans. *In* Ethnic leadership in America p91-118

Afro-American literature (English) See American literature—Afro-American authors

Afro-American militant organizations. See Black militant organizations—United States

Afro-American military personnel. See United States—Armed Forces—Afro-Americans

Afro-American minstrel shows. See Minstrel shows

Afro-American music

Marks, M. A. Uncovering ritual structures in Afro-American music *In* Zaretsky, I.I. and Leone, M. P. eds. Religious movements in contemporary America p60-134

Reed, I. Music: Black, white and blue. *In* Reed, I. Shrovetide in old New Orleans p100-04

Reed, I. The old music. *In* Reed, I. Shrovetide in old New Orleans p64-66

Whalum, W.; Baker, D. N. and Long, R. A. Afro-American music. *In* The Black American reference book p791-826

Afro-American periodicals

Redmond, E. Stridency and the sword: literary and cultural emphasis in Afro-American magazines. *In* Anderson, E. and Kinzie, M. eds. The little magazine in America: a modern documentary history p538-73

Afro-American poetry (English) See American poetry—Afro-American authors

Afro-American press. See Afro-American journalists

Afro-American satirical songs. See Satirical songs, Afro-American

Afro-American scientists

Pearson, W. Race and universalism in the scientific community. *In* Gaston, J. ed. Sociology of science p38-53

Afro-American short stories (English) See Short stories, American—Afro-American authors

Afro-American soldiers. See United States—History—Revolution, 1775-1783—Afro-American troops; United States—History—Civil War, 1861-1865—Afro-American troops

Afro-American songs

Whalum, W.; Baker, D. N. and Long, R. A. Afro-American music. *In* The Black American reference book p791-826

See also Blues (Songs, etc.)

Afro-American spirituals. See Spirituals (Songs)

Afro-American studies

Brower, A. Black studies and changing times. *In* Fairfield, R. P. ed. Humanistic frontiers in American education p134-38

Lerner, A. P. Black studies: the universities in moral crisis. *In* Fairfield, R. P. ed. Humanistic frontiers in American education p127-33

Washington, M. H. Politics of the outsider: Black studies in the university, 1976. *In* Minority language and literature p130-33

Latin America

Bastide, R. The present status of Afro-American research in Latin America. *In* Mintz, S. W. ed. Slavery, colonialism, and racism p111-23

Afro-American suffrage. See Afro-Americans —Politics and suffrage

Afro-American universities and colleges

Kaiser, E. Blacks and American foundations: a historical survey. *In* The Black American reference book p480-85

McPherson, J. M. The new Puritanism: values and goals of freedmen's education in America *In* The University in society v2 p611-42

Afro-American university students. See Afro-American college students

Afro-American voting rights. See Afro-Americans—Politics and suffrage

Afro-American women

Harrison, D. D. Black women in the blues tradition. *In* Harley, S. and Terborg-Penn, R. eds. The Afro-American woman p58-73

Neverdon-Morton, C. The Black woman's struggle for equality in the South, 1895-1925. *In* Harley, S. and Terborg-Penn, R. eds. The Afro-American woman p43-57

Rich, A. C. Disloyal to civilization: feminism, racism, gynephobia. *In* Rich, A. C. On lies, secrets, and silence p275-310

Schultz, E. A. "Free in fact and at last": the image of the Black woman in Black American fiction. *In* Springer, M. A. ed. What manner of woman p316-44

Terborg-Penn, R. Black male perspectives on the nineteenth-century woman. *In* Harley, S. and Terborg-Penn, R. eds. The Afro-American woman p28-42

Terborg-Penn, R. Discrimination against Afro-American women in the woman's movement, 1830-1920. *In* Harley, S. and Terborg-Penn, R. eds. The Afro-American woman p17-27

Walker, E. The Black woman. *In* The Black American reference book p341-77

Education

Barnett, E. B. Nannie Burroughs and the education of Black women. *In* Harley, S. and Terborg-Penn, R. eds. The Afro-American woman p97-108

Employment

Harley, S. Northern Black female workers: Jacksonian era. *In* Harley, S. and Terborg-Penn, R. eds. The Afro-American woman p5-16

Sexual behavior

Gossett, R. R. Black widows. *In* Gochros, H. L. and Gochros, J. S. eds. The sexually oppressed p84-95

Afro-American women in fiction, drama, poetry, etc.

Rushing, A. B. Images of Black women in Afro-American poetry. *In* Harley, S. and Terborg-Penn, R. eds. The Afro-American woman p74-84

Afro-American youth

Clark, C. P. Young Black Americans. *In* The Black American reference book p378-409

Afro-Americans

Clarke, J. H. Black Americans: immigrants against their will. *In* The Immigrant experience in America p172-91

Huggins, N. I. Afro-Americans. *In* Ethnic leadership in America p91-118

Jordan, V. E. Blacks and American foundations: attitudes and outlook. *In* The Black American reference book p485-91

Reid, I. S. Black Americans and Africa. *In* The Black American reference book p648-83

Smythe, H. H. and Skinner, E. P. Black participation in U.S. foreign relations. *In* The Black American reference book p638-47

Staples, R. Black sexuality *In* Sexuality and human values p62-70

See also Freedmen; Missions to Afro-Americans; Slavery in the United States

Civil rights

Bennett, L. Have we overcome? *In* Have we overcome? Race relations since Brown p189-200

Bittker, B. I. Identifying the beneficiaries; excerpt from "The case for Black reparations." *In* Gross, B. R. ed. Reverse discrimination p279-87

Boxhill, B. The morality of reparation. *In* Gross, B. R. ed. Reverse discrimination p270-78

Brisbane, R. H. Black protest in America. *In* The Black American reference book p537-79

Chasteen, E. Legal change. *In* Lauer, R. H. ed. Social movements and social change p156-73

Crowe, C. R. Indians and Blacks in white America. *In* Hudson, C. M. ed. Four centuries of Southern Indians p148-69

Eschen, D. von; Kirk, J. R. and Pinard, M. The problems of success—violence legitimized. *In* Lauer, R. H. ed. Social movement and social change p203-26

Harding, V. So much history, so much future: Martin Luther King, Jr., and the Second Coming of America. *In* Have we overcome? Race relations since Brown p31-78

Henderson, E. W. The Federal government and the fight for basic human rights. *In* Johnson, H. A. ed. Negotiating the mainstream p141-63

Jackson, M. Broad societal changes. *In* Lauer, R. H. ed. Social movements and social change p174-89

Leuchtenburg, W. E. The White House and Black America: from Eisenhower to Carter. *In* Have we overcome? Race relations since Brown p121-45

Levin, H. M. Education and earnings of Blacks and the Brown decision. *In* Have we overcome? Race relations since Brown p79-119

Afro-Americans—*Continued*

History—1877-1964

Wolters, R. The New Deal and the Negro. *In* Braeman, J.; Bremner, R. H. and Brody, D. eds. The New Deal v 1 p170-217

Housing

Norton, D. G. Residential environment and Black self-image. *In* The Diverse society: implications for social policy p75-89

Intelligence

See Intelligence levels—Afro-Americans

Languages

See Black English

Legal status, laws, etc.

Bell, D. A. The racial imperative in American law. *In* The Age of segregation: race relations in the South, 1890-1945 p3-28

Henderson, E. W. The Federal government and the fight for basic human rights. *In* Johnson, H. A. ed. Negotiating the mainstream p141-63

Horwitz, M. J. The jurisprudence of Brown and the dilemmas of liberalism. *In* Have we overcome? Race relations since Brown p173-87

Leuchtenburg, W. E. The White House and Black America: from Eisenhower to Carter. *In* Have we overcome? Race relations since Brown p121-45

Motley, C. B. The legal status of the Black American. *In* The Black American reference book p90-127

Occupations

See Afro-Americans—Employment

Politics and suffrage

Cook, S. D. Democracy and tyranny in America: the radical paradox of the Bicentennial and Blacks in the American political system. *In* Havard, W. C. and Bernd, J. L. eds. 200 years of the Republic in retrospect p276-94

Field, P. F. Republicans and Black suffrage in New York State: the grass roots response. *In* Swierenga, R. P. ed. Beyond the Civil War synthesis p149-62

Grantham, D. W. Ralph J. Bunche and the making of a documentary classic. *In* Grantham, D. W. The regional imagination p133-52

Jones, M. H. Black politics: from civil rights to benign neglect. *In* Johnson, H. A. ed. Negotiating the mainstream p164-95

Kilson, M. L. The political status of American Negroes in the twentieth century. *In* Kilson, M. L. and Rotberg, R. I. eds. The African diaspora p459-84

Terborg-Penn, R. Black male perspectives on the nineteenth-century woman. *In* Harley, S. and Terborg-Penn, R. eds. The Afro-American woman p28-42

See also Afro-Americans—Civil rights

Politics and suffrage—History

Fleming, G. J. The Black role in American politics: Part II, The past. *In* The Black American reference book p622-37

Smythe, H. H. and Stokes, C. B. The Black role in American politics: Part I, The present. *In* The Black American reference book p580-621

Psychology

Pinderhughes, C. A. Black personality in American society. *In* The Black American reference book p128-58

Race identity

Brown, C. S. and Chappelle, Y. J. R. African religions and the quest for Afro-American heritage. *In* African religions: a symposium p241-54

Chestang, L. Environmental influences on social functioning: the Black experience. *In* The Diverse society: implications for social policy p59-74

Dixon, M. Rivers remembering their source: comparative studies in Black literary history—Langston Hughes, Jacques Roumain, and négritude. *In* Fisher, D. and Stepto, R. B. eds. Afro-American literature p25-43

Gates, H. L. Preface to Blackness: text and pretext. *In* Fisher, D. and Stepto, R. B. eds. Afro-American literature p44-69

Gilmore, A. The Black Southerner's response to the Southern system of race relations: 1900 to post—World War II. *In* The Age of segregation: race relations in the South, 1890-1945 p67-88

Horton, J. E. Time and cool people. *In* Henslin, J. M. ed. Deviant life-styles p59-72

Kilson, M. Blacks and neo-ethnicity in American political life. *In* Glazer, N. and Moynihan, D. P. eds. Ethnicity p236-66

Norton, D. G. Residential environment and Black self-image. *In* The Diverse society: implications for social policy p75-89

Obatala, J. K. Black consciousness and American policy in Africa. *In* Said, A. A. and Simmons, L. R. eds. Ethnicity in an international context p64-75

Williamson, J. W. E. B. Du Bois as a Hegelian. *In* What was freedom's price? p21-49

See also Afro-American studies; Black nationalism

Relations with Indians

Bolt, C. Red, Black and white in nineteenth-century America. *In* Hepburn, A. C. ed. Minorities in history p116-34

Relations with whites

See United States—Race question

Religion

Bentley, W. H. Bible believers in the Black community. *In* Wells, D. F. and Woodbridge, J. D. eds. The evangelicals p108-21

Brown, C. S. and Chappelle, Y. J. R. African religions and the quest for Afro-American heritage. *In* African religions: a symposium p241-54

Jones, L. The organized church: its historic significance and changing role in contemporary Black experiences. *In* Johnson, H. A. ed. Negotiating the mainstream p103-40

Smith, A. Black reflections on the study of new religious consciousness. *In* Needleman, J. and Baker, G. eds. Understanding the new religions p209-19

Afro-Americans—Southern States—History
—*Continued*

Berry, M. F. Repression of Blacks in the South, 1890-1945: enforcing the system of segregation. *In* The Age of segregation: race relations in the South, 1890-1945 p29-43

Southern States—Politics and suffrage

Carter, D. T. Southern political style. *In* The Age of segregation: race relations in the South, 1890-1945 p45-66

United States

See Afro-Americans

Afro-Americans in art. See Afro-American art

Afro-Americans in fiction. See Afro-Americans in literature

Afro-Americans in literature

Alexander, M. A. W. Faulkner & race. *In* The Maker and the myth: Faulkner and Yoknapatawpha, 1977 p105-21

Alter, R. Updike, Malamud, and the fire this time. *In* Alter, R. Defenses of the imagination p233-48

Bruck, P. Langston Hughes, The blues I'm playing. *In* Bruck, P. ed. The Black American short story in the 20th century p71-83

Elkind, D. Ethnicity and reading: three avoidable dangers. *In* Elkind, D. The child and society p41-47

Feuser, W. Prophet of violence: Chester Himes. *In* African literature today no. 9: Africa, America and the Caribbean p58-76

Freese, P. James Baldwin, Going to meet the Man. *In* Bruck, P. ed. The Black American short story in the 20th century p171-85

Freese, P. John A. Williams, Son in the afternoon. *In* Bruck, P. ed. The Black American short story in the 20th century p141-55

Galloway, D. William Melvin Kelley, The poker party. *In* Bruck, P. ed. The Black American short story in the 20th century p129-40

Gates, H. L. Preface to Blackness: text and pretext. *In* Fisher, D. and Stepto, R. B. eds. Afro-American literature p44-69

Hamilton, V. High John is risen again. *In* Horn Book Magazine. Crosscurrents of criticism p159-67

Howe, I. A Negro in America. *In* Howe, I. Celebrations and attacks p29-31

Jackson, B. The ghetto of the Negro novel: a theme with variations. *In* Jackson, B. The waiting years p179-88

Jackson, B. The Negro's image of his universe as reflected in his fiction. *In* Jackson, B. The waiting years p92-102

Jung, U. O. H. Jean Toomer, Fern. *In* Bruck, P. ed. The Black American short story in the 20th century p53-69

Karrer, W. Richard Wright, Fire and cloud. *In* Bruck, P. ed. The Black American short story in the 20th century p99-110

Liston, M. Chester Himes, A Nigger. *In* Bruck, P. ed. The Black American short story in the 20th century p85-97

Ogunyemi, C. O. Iconoclasts both: Wole Soyinka and LeRoi Jones. *In* African literature today no. 9: Africa, America and the Caribbean p25-38

Pryse, M. Faulkner's "Dry September" and "Red leaves": caste and outcast. *In* Pryse, M. The mark and the knowledge p92-107

Pryse, M. Invisible man: the world in a man-of-war. *In* Pryse, M. The mark and the knowledge p143-67

Pryse, M. Light in August: violence and excommunity. *In* Pryse, M. The mark and the knowledge p108-42

Puschmann-Nalenz, B. Ernest J. Gaines, A long day in November. *In* Bruck, P. ed. The Black American short story in the 20th century p157-69

Real, W. Ralph Ellison, King of the bingo game. *In* Bruck, P. ed. The Black American short story in the 20th century p111-27

Riggio, T. P. Uncle Tom reconstructed: a neglected chapter in the history of a book. *In* Zenderland, L. ed. Recycling the past p66-80

Rose, A. H. Blackness in the fantastic world of old Southwestern humor. *In* Rose, A. H. Demonic vision p19-38

Rose, A. H. Demonic vision and the conventions of antebellum Southern fiction. *In* Rose, A. H. Demonic vision p39-62

Rose, A. H. Recent American writings: the leveling of racial vision. *In* Rose, A. H. Demonic vision p119-36

Sarotte, G. M. Four archetypes of the homosexual couple: the white and the Black. *In* Sarotte, G. M. Like a brother, like a lover p92-104

Sullivan, W. Southern literature: the last twenty years. *In* Two decades of change p55-66

Turner, D. T. Faulkner and slavery. *In* The South and Faulkner's Yoknapatawpha p62-85

Wakefield, J. Paul Laurence Dunbar, The scapegoat. *In* Bruck, P. ed. The Black American short story in the 20th century p39-51

See also American literature—Afro-American authors

Afro-Americans in military service. See United States—Armed Forces—Afro-Americans

Afro-Americans in motion pictures

Cripps, T. R. "Race movies" as voices of the Black bourgeoisie: The scar of shame. *In* O'Connor, J. E. and Jackson, M. A. eds. American history/American film p39-55

Afro-Americans in Puerto Rico

Mathews, T. G. The question of color in Puerto Rico. *In* Toplin, R. B. ed. Slavery and race relations in Latin America p299-323

Afro-Americans in the Armed Forces. See United States—Armed Forces—Afro-Americans

Afro-Americans in the performing arts

Hughes, L. Black influences in the American theater: Part I. *In* The Black American reference book p684-704

Norford, G. E. The popular media: Part II, The Black role in radio and television. *In* The Black American reference book p875-88

See also Afro-American actors

History

Cruse, H. The creative and performing arts and the struggle for identity and credibility. *In* Johnson, H. A. ed. Negotiating the mainstream p47-102

Afro-Amerirans in the radio industry

Norford, G. E. The popular media: Part II, The Black role in radio and television. *In* The Black American reference book p875-88

After-images. *See* Eidetic imagery

Agassiz, Louis

About

Gould, S. J. Agassiz's marginalia in Lyell's Principles, or the perils of uniformity and the ambiguity of heroes. *In* Studies in history of biology v3 p119-38

Winsor, M. P. Louis Agassiz and the species question. *In* Studies in history of biology v3 p89-117

Age. See Age groups; Old age

Age (Law)

Goldstein, J. On being adult and being an adult in secular law. *In* Erikson, E. H. ed. Adulthood p249-67

Age (Psychology) See Adulthood

Age and employment. See Children—Employment

Age and intelligence

LaRue, A. and Jarvik, L. F. Aging and intellectual functioning: great expectations? *In* Jarvik, L. F. ed. Aging into the 21st century p79-96

Age and mental ability. See Age and intelligence

Age factors in disease

Katchadourian, H. A. Medical perspectives on adulthood. *In* Erikson, E. H. ed. Adulthood p33-60

Age groups

Cutler, N. E. Toward a generational conception of political socialization. *In* Schwartz, D. C. and Schwartz, S. K. eds. New directions in political socialization p254-88

O'Rourke, J. F. and Chevan, A. A factorial ecology of age groups in the United States, 1960. *In* Gubrium, J. F. ed. Late life p32-58

Stauf, R. Young meet old. *In* Gross, B. and Gross, R. eds. The children's rights movement p300-06

See also Conflict of generations

Aged

Gaitz, C. M. Aged patients, their families and physicians. *In* Aging: the process and the people p206-39

Halper, T. Paternalism and the elderly. *In* Spicker, S. F.; Woodward, K. M. and Van Tassel, D. D. eds. Aging and the elderly p321-39

Marquis, D. B. Ethics and the elderly: some problems. *In* Spicker, S. F.; Woodward, K. M. and Van Tassel, D. O. eds. Aging and the elderly p341-55

Stahmer, H. M. The aged in two ancient oral cultures: the ancient Hebrews and Homeric Greece. *In* Spicker, S. F.; Woodward, K. M. and Van Tassel, D. D. eds. Aging and the elderly p23-36

See also Aging

Care and hygiene

Rosenkrantz, B. G. and Vinovskis, M. A. The invisible lunatics: old age and insanity in mid-nineteenth-century Massachusetts. *In* Spicker, S. F.; Woodward, K. M. and Van Tassel, D. D. eds. Aging and the elderly p95-125

Spicker, S. F. Gerontogenetic mentation: memory, dementia and medicine in the penultimate years. *In* Spicker, S. F.; Woodward, K. M. and Van Tassel, D. D. eds. Aging and the elderly p153-80

See also Aged—Home care; Community health services for the aged; Nursing homes

Dwellings

Ross, J. K. Life goes on: social organization in a French retirement residence. *In* Gubrium, J. F. ed. Late life p99-120

Education

See Education of the aged

Home care—United States

Wilson, M. G. and Sugrue, R. Senior companion program. *In* Home care p178-84

Legal status, laws, etc.

Tibbles, L. W. Medical and legal aspects of competency as affected by old age. *In* Spicker, S. F.; Woodward, K. M. and Van Tassel, D. D. eds. Aging and the elderly p127-51

Medical care

See Community health services for the aged

Medical care—United States

Densen, P. M. Public accountability and reporting systems in Medicare and other health programs. *In* Smith, B. L. R. ed. The new political economy: the public use of the private sector p229-44

Nutrition

Alfin-Slater, R. B. and Friedman, R. Nutrition and aging: are we what we've eaten? *In* Jarvik, L. F. ed. Aging into the 21st century p61-76

Personality

See Aged—Psychology

Political activity

Maddox, G. L. Will senior power become a reality? *In* Jarvik, L. F. ed. Aging into the 21st century p185-96

Psychiatric care

See Geriatric psychiatry

Psychology

Bultena, G. L. Structural effects on the morale of the aged: a comparison of age-segregated and age-integrated communities. *In* Gubrium, J. F. ed. Late life p18-31

Eisdorfer, C. Psychophysiologic and cognitive studies in the aged. *In* Aging: the process and the people p96-128

Erikson, E. H. and Erikson, J. M. Introduction: reflections on aging. *In* Spicker, S. F.; Woodward, K. M. and Van Tassel, D. D. eds. Aging and the elderly p 1-8

Grotjahn, M. Group communication and group therapy with the aged: a promising project. *In* Jarvik, L. F. ed. Aging into the 21st century p113-21

Kahana, E. Matching environments to needs of the aged: a conceptual scheme. *In* Gubrium, J. F. ed. Late life p201-14

Tallmer, M. A societal response. *In* Anticipatory grief p19-25

See also Aging—Psychological aspects

Aged—*Continued*

Public opinion

Butler, R. N. Afterword: humanistic perspectives in gerontology. *In* Spicker, S. F.; Woodward, K. M. and Van Tassel, D. D. eds. Aging and the elderly p389-91

Eisdorfer, C. Societal response to aging: some possible consequences. *In* Jarvik, L. F. ed. Aging into the 21st century p123-35

Ganschow, T. W. The aged in a revolutionary milieu: China. *In* Spicker, S. F.; Woodward, K. M. and Van Tassel, D. D. eds. Aging and the elderly p303-20

Gruman, G. J. Cultural origins of present-day "age-ism": the modernization of the life cycle. *In* Spicker, S. F.; Woodward, K. M. and Van Tassel, D. D. eds. Aging and the elderly p359-87

Smith, D. S. Old age and the 'great transformation': a New England case study. *In* Spicker, S. F.; Woodward, K. M. and Van Tassel, D. D. eds. Aging and the elderly p285-302

Stannard, D. E. Growing up and growing old: dilemmas of aging in bureaucratic America. *In* Spicker, S. F.; Woodward, K. M. and Van Tassel, D. D. eds. Aging and the elderly p9-20

Religious life

Moberg, D. O. Spiritual well-being in late life. *In* Gubrium, J. F. ed. Late life p256-79

Research

See Old-age—Research

Sexual behavior

Pfeiffer, E. Sex and aging. *In* Gross, L. ed. Sexual issues in marriage p43-47

Social conditions

Birren, J. E. A gerontologist's overview. *In* Jarvik, L. F. ed. Aging into the 21st century p197-208

Eisdorfer, C. Societal response to aging: some possible consequences. *In* Jarvik, L. F. ed. Aging into the 21st century p123-35

Lindheim, R. Designs for living. *In* Jarvik, L. F. ed. Aging into the 21st century p153-68

Maddox, G. L. The social and cultural context of aging. *In* Aging: the process and the people p20-46

Neugarten, B. L. The future and the young-old. *In* Jarvik, L. F. ed. Aging into the 21st century p137-52

Societies and clubs

Hildebrandt, H. The community center in the life of a dying person with no family involvement. *In* Home care p215-22

China

Ganschow, T. W. The aged in a revolutionary milieu: China. *In* Spicker, S. F.; Woodward, K. M. and Van Tassel, D. D. eds. Aging and the elderly p303-20

Great Britain

Smith, S. R. Death, dying and the elderly in seventeenth-century England. *In* Spicker, S. F.; Woodward, K. M. and Van Tassel, D. D. eds. Aging and the elderly p205-19

Uganda

Nahemow, N. and Adams, B. N. Old age among the Baganda: continuity and change. *In* Gubrium, J. F. ed. Late life p147-66

United States

Butler, R. N. Overview on aging. *In* Aging: the process and the people p 1-19

Hareven, T. K. The last stage: historical adulthood and old age. *In* Erikson, E. H. ed. Adulthood p201-15

Stannard, D. E. Growing up and growing old: dilemmas of aging in bureaucratic America. *In* Spicker, S. F.; Woodward, K. M. and Van Tassel, D. D. eds. Aging and the elderly p9-20

United States—Conduct of life

Kelly, J The aging male homosexual. *In* Gochros, H. L. and Gochros, J. S. eds. The sexually oppressed p160-69

United States—Sexual behavior

Wasow, M. and Loeb, M. B. The aged. *In* Gochros, H. L. and Gochros, J. S. eds. The sexually oppressed p54-68

Aged and architecture. See Architecture and the aged

Aged in literature. See Old age in literature

Aged in politics. See Aged—Political activity

Agee, James

Comedy's greatest era; excerpt from "Agee on film v 1." *In* Denby, D. ed. Awake in the dark p230-48

David Wark Griffith; excerpt from "Agee on film v 1." *In* Denby, D. ed. Awake in the dark p60-65

Three short reviews; excerpt from "Agee on film v 1." *In* Denby, D. ed. Awake in the dark p378-82

Undirectable director: John Huston; excerpt from "Agee on film v 1." *In* Denby, D. ed. Awake in the dark p293-305

About

Murray, E. James Agee, "amateur critic." *In* Murray, E. Nine American film critics p5-23

About individual works

A death in the family

Milner, J. O. Autonomy and communion in A death in the family. *In* Tennessee Studies in literature v21 p105-13

Let us now praise famous men

Morris, W. James Agee. *In* Morris, W. Earthly delights, unearthly adornments p155-61

Rewak, W. J. James Agee's Let us now praise famous men: the shadow over America. *In* Tennessee Studies in literature v 21 p91-104

Ward, J. A. James Agee's aesthetic of silence: Let us now praise famous men. *In* Tulane Studies in English, v23 p193-206

Ageing. See Aging

Agencia Centroamericana de Noticias

Fernandez, G. ACACAN [sic]: a solution to the problem of news flow in the Third World. *In* Horton, P. C. ed. The Third World and press freedom p155-55

Agency (Law) See Proxy

Agent (Philosophy). See Act (Philosophy)

Ages, Arnold

Lamartine and the philosophes. *In* Literature and history in the age of ideas p321-40

Aggarwala, Narinder K.

News with Third World perspectives: a practical suggestion. *In* Horton, P. C. ed. The Third World and press freedom p197-209

Agger, Ben
On happiness and the damaged life. *In* O'Neill, J. ed. On critical theory p12-33
Aggregates. See Set theory
Aggressive behavior. See Aggressiveness (Psychology)
Aggressiveness (Child psychology)
Patterson, G. R. The aggressive child: victim and architect of a coercive system. *In* Behavior modification and families p267-316
Aggressiveness (Psychology)
Berndt, C. H. In aboriginal Australia. *In* Montague, A. ed. Learning non-aggression p144-60
Briggs, J. L. The origins of nonviolence: Inuit management of aggression. *In* Montagu, A. ed. Learning non-aggression p54-93
Dentan, R. K. Notes on childhood in a nonviolent context: the Semai case. *In* Montagu, A. ed. Learning non-aggression p94-143
Draper, P. The learning environment for aggression and anti-social behavior among the !Kung. *In* Montagu. A. ed. Learning non-aggression p31-53
Faulkner, R. R. Making violence by doing work: selves, situations, and the world of professional hockey. *In* Social problems in athletics p93-112
Hamburg, D. A. Human aggressiveness and conflict resolution. *In* World change and world security p39-60
Levy, R. I. Tahitian gentleness and redundant controls. *In* Montagu, A. ed. Learning non-aggression p222-35
Montagu, A. Introduction. *In* Montagu, A. ed. Learning non-aggression p 3-11
Turnbull, C. M. The politics of non-aggression. *In* Montagu, A. ed. Learning non-aggression p161-221
See also Violence
Aging
Birren, J. E. A gerontologist's overview. *In* Jarvik, L. F. ed. Aging into the 21st century p197-208
Butler, R. N. Overview on aging. *In* Aging: the process and the people p 1-19
Cowgill, D. O. Aging and modernization: a revision of the theory. *In* Gubrium, J. F. ed. Late life p123-46
Erikson, E. H. and Erikson, J. M. Introduction: reflections on aging. *In* Spicker, S. F.; Woodward, K. M. and Van Tassel, D. D. eds. Aging and the elderly p 1-8
Kiefer, C. W. Lessons from the issei. *In* Gubrium, J. F. ed. Late life p167-97
Maddox, G. L. The social and cultural context of aging. *In* Aging: the process and the people p20-46
Maddox, G. L. Sociology, aging, and guided social change: relating alternative organization of helping resources to well-being. *In* Major social issues p323-37
Whitehead, E. E. Religious images of aging: an examination of themes in contemporary Christian thought. *In* Spicker, S. F.; Woodward, K. M. and Van Tassel, D. D. eds. Aging and the elderly p37-48
See also Age factors in disease

Nutritional aspects
Alfin-Slater, R. B. and Friedman, R. Nutrition and aging: are we what we've eaten? *In* Jarvik, L. F. ed. Aging into the 21st century p61-76

Psychological aspects
Berg, G. and Gadow, S. Toward more human meanings of aging: ideals and images from philosophy and art. *In* Spicker, S. F.; Woodward, K. M. and Van Tassel, D. D. eds. Aging and the elderly p83-92
Fiske, M. The reality of psychological change. *In* Jarvik, L. F. ed. Aging into the 21st century p97-111
Freedman, R. Sufficiently decayed: gerontophobia in English literature. *In* Spicker, S. F.; Woodward, K. M. and Van Tassel, D. D. eds. Aging and the elderly p49-61
Gruman, G. J. Cultural origins of present-day "age-ism": the modernization of the life cycle. *In* Spicker, S. F.; Woodward, K. M. and Van Tassel, D. D. eds. Aging and the elderly p359-87
Lipton, M. A. and Nemeroff, C. B. The biology of aging and its role in depression. *In* Aging: the process and the people p47-95
Standard, D. E. Growing up and growing old: dilemmas of aging in bureaucratic America. *In* Spicker, S. F.; Woodward, K. M. and Van Tassel, D. D. eds. Aging and the elderly p9-20
See also Adulthood; Aged—Psychology

Research
Busse, E. W. Aging research: a review and critique. *In* Aging: the process and the people p129-65
Comfort, A. A. A biologist laments and exhorts. *In* Jarvik, L. F. ed. Aging into the 21st century p41-60
De Duve, C. R. Cells age: are lysosomes among the villains? *In* Jarvik, L. F. ed. Aging into the 21st century p25-31
Tomkins, G. M. The "metabolic code"—a key to prolonging life? *In* Jarvik, L. F. ed. Aging into the 21st century p33-40
Agnon, Samuel Joseph

About individual works
Betrothed
Alter, R. Agnon's Mediterranean fable. *In* Alter, R. Defenses of the imagination p187-98
Shira
Alter, R. A novel of the post-tragic world. *In* Alter, R. Defenses of the imagination p169-86
Agnosticism. See Belief and doubt; Positivism
Agnosticism in literature
Davie, D. Dissent and the agnostics, 1850-1900. *In* Davie, D. A gathered Church p73-90
Agostino di Duccio
About
Paoletti, J. T. The Bargello David and public sculpture in fifteenth-century Florence. *In* Collaboration in Italian Renaissance art p99-111
Agrarian question. See Agriculture—Economic aspects; Agriculture and state; Land tenure
Agrarian reform. See Land reform
Agrest, Diana, and Gandelsonas, Mario
Semiotics and the limits of architecture. *In* Sebeok, T. A. ed. A perfusion of signs p90-120

Agriculture—*Continued*

Germany—History

Lee, J. Administrators and agriculture: aspects of German agricultural policy in the First World War. *In* War and economic development p229-38

Great Britain—History

Kershaw, I. The great famine and agrarian crisis in England, 1315-1322. *In* Peasants, knights and heretics p85-132

Thirsk, J. The common fields. *In* Peasants, knights and heretics p10-32

Thirsk, J. The origin of the common fields. *In* Peasants, knights and heretics p51-56

Titow, J. Z. Medieval England and the open-field system. *In* Peasants, knights and heretics p33-50

Massachusetts—History

Rutman, D. B. Governor Winthrop's garden crop: the significance of agriculture in the early commerce of Massachusetts Bay. *In* Vaughan, A. T. and Bremer, F. J. eds. Puritan New England p155-71

Netherlands—Friesland

De Vries, J. Peasant demand patterns and economic development: Friesland, 1550-1750. *In* Parker, W. N. and Jones, E. L. eds. European peasants and their markets p205-66

Prussia—History

Dickler, R. A. Organization and change in productivity in Eastern Prussia. *In* Parker, W. N. and Jones, E. L. eds. European peasants and their markets p269-92

Russia

Holsti, O. R. Global food problems and Soviet agriculture. *In* Orr, D. W. and Soroos, M. S. eds. The global predicament p150-75

Russia—History

Davies, R. W. The Soviet rural economy in 1929-1930: the size of the kolkhoz. *In* Essays in honour of E. H. Carr p255-80

Lewin, M. 'Taking grain': Soviet policies of agricultural procurements before the War. *In* Essays in honour of E. H. Carr p281-323

United States

Carstensen, V. R. The Land of Plenty. *In* Alderson, W. T. ed. American issues p17-31

Paarlberg, D. Agriculture—stumbling block or stepping stone? *In* Prochnow, H. V. ed. Dilemmas facing the nation p179-201

United States—History

Rossiter, M. W. The organization of agricultural improvement in the United States, 1785-1865. *In* Oleson, A. and Brown, S. C. eds. The pursuit of knowledge in the early American Republic p279-98

Rossiter, M. W. The organization of the agricultural sciences. *In* Oleson, A. and Voss, J. eds. The organization of knowledge in modern America, 1860-1920 p211-48

Agriculture, Cooperative. See Collective farms

Agriculture, Primitive

Bender, B. The first revolution. *In* Goodall, V. M. ed. The quest for man p105-28

Nigeria

Netting, R. M. Maya subsistence: mythologies, analogies, possibilities. *In* The Origins of Maya civilization p299-333

Agriculture and state

See also Land reform

Germany—History

Lee, J. Administrators and agriculture: aspects of German agricultural policy in the First World War. *In* War and economic development p229-38

Russia

Holsti, O. R. Global food problems and Soviet agriculture. *In* Orr, D. W. and Soroos, M. S. eds. The global predicament p150-75

Lewin, M. 'Taking grain': Soviet policies of agricultural procurements before the War. *In* Essays in honour of E. H. Carr p281-323

Mills, R. M. The virgin lands since Khrushchev: choices and decisions in Soviet policy making. *In* Cocks, P.; Daniels, R. V. and Heer, N. W. eds. The dynamics of Soviet politics p178-92

Nove, A. Agriculture. *In* Brown, A. H. and Kaser, M. eds. The Soviet Union since the fall of Khrushchev p 1-15

Spain

Sevilla-Guzman, E. The peasantry and the Franco régime. *In* Preston, P. ed. Spain in crisis p101-24

United States

Kirkendall, R. S. The New Deal and agriculture. *In* Braeman, J.; Bremner, R. H. and Brody, D. eds. The New Deal v 1 p83-109

Paarlberg, D. Agriculture—stumbling block or stepping stone? *In* Prochnow, H. V. ed. Dilemmas facing the nation p179-201

Rossiter, M. W. The organization of the agricultural sciences. *In* Oleson, A. and Voss, J. eds. The organization of knowledge in modern America, 1860-1920 p211-48

Sloan, T. J. A look at America's potential roles in a global food crisis. *In* Orr, D. W. and Soroos, M. S. eds. The global predicament p110-30

Agursky, Mikhail

Contemporary socioeconomic systems and their future prospects. *In* From under the rubble p67-87

The Soviet legitimacy crisis and its international implications. *In* Kaplan, M. A. ed. The many faces of communism p146-93

Agus, Jacob Bernard

About

Kaufman, W. E. Arthur A. Cohen and Jacob B. Agus: the supernatural and the absolute self. *In* Kaufman, W. E. Contemporary Jewish philosophies p217-50

Ah, wilderness! (criticism) O'Neill, E. G. *In* Kauffmann, S. Persons of the drama p136-39

Ahafo, Ghana

Politics and government

Dunn, J. M. The eligible and the elect: Arminian thoughts on the social predestination of Ahafo leaders. *In* The Making of politicians: studies from Africa and Asia p49-65

Ahlstrom, Sydney E.
Diversity in religion as a force for liberty: a quadricentennial view of the problem. *In* Aspects of American liberty p56-67

From Puritanism to evangelicalism: a critical perspective. *In* Wells, D. F. and Woodbridge, J. D. eds. The evangelicals p269-89

From Sinai to the Golden Gate: the liberation of religion in the Occident. *In* Needleman, J. and Baker, G. eds. Understanding the new religions p3-22

National trauma and changing religious values. *In* A New America? p13-29

The radical turn in theology and ethics: why it occurred in the 1960s. *In* Mulder, J. M. and Wilson, J. F. eds. Religion in American history p445-56

The religious dimensions of American aspirations. *In* An Almost chosen people p39-49

Thought and social change: reflections on cultural studies. *In* Luedtke, L. S. ed. The study of American culture p63-75

Ahokas, Jaakko A.
The short story in Finnish literature. *In* Dauenhauer, R. and Binham, P. eds. Snow in May p29-40

Aid to underdeveloped areas. See Technical assistance

Aidoo, Ama Ata. See Aidoo, Christina Ama Ata

Aidoo, Christina Ama Ata

About

Adelugba, D. Language and drama: Ama Ata Aidoo. *In* African literature today no. 8: Drama in Africa p72-84

Aiex, Anoar
Graça Aranha and Brazilian modernism. *In* Forster, M. H. ed. Tradition and renewal p51-67

Aiken, Conrad Potter

About

Cowley, M. Conrad Aiken: from Savannah to Emerson. *In* Cowley, M.—And I worked at the writer's trade p231-48

Kunitz, S. J. The vaudeville of the mind. *In* Kunitz, S. J. A kind of order, a kind of folly p173-79

About individual works
Time in the rock

Kunitz, S. J. Learned in violence. *In* Kunitz, S. J. A kind of order, a kind of folly p180-82

Aiken, Joan
A free gift. *In* Blishen, E. ed. The thorny paradise p36-52

Aiken, Michael T.
Urban social structure and political competition: a comparative study of local politics in four European nations. *In* Walton, J. and Masotti, L. H. eds. The city in comparative perspective p119-53

Aiken, William
The right to be saved from starvation. *In* Aiken, W. and La Follette, H. eds. World hunger and moral obligation p85-102

Ainsworth, William Harrison

About

Sutherland, J. A. Lever and Ainsworth: missing the first rank. *In* Sutherland, J. A. Victorian novelists and publishers p152-65

About individual works
The Tower of London

Sanders, A. A Gothic revival: William Harrison Ainsworth's The Tower of London. *In* Sanders, A. The Victorian historical novel, 1840-1880 p32-46

Air, Ionized

Therapeutic use

Krueger, A. P. and Sobel, D. S. Air ions and health. *In* Sobel, D. S. ed. Ways of health p413-33

Air defenses. See Antimissile missiles

Air Force law

United States

Eisenhart, T. S. Rehabilitation: one man's opinion. *In* Henderson, G. ed. Human relations in the military p177-86

Ford, B. L. Justice is more than a word. *In* Henderson, G. ed. Human relations in the military p127-44

Air navigation. See Aeronautics

Air piracy. See Hijacking of aircraft

Air-ships
Wuellenkemper, T. Innovative transport technologies: the airship. *In* Strategies for human settlements: habitat and environment p164-69

Air warfare
Watt, D. C. Restraints on war in the air before 1945. *In* Howard, M. Restraints on war p57-77

See also Atomic warfare

Airlines

Hijacking

See Hijacking of aircraft

Airships. See Air-ships

Ajayi, J. F. Ade, and Alagoa, Ebiegberi Joe
Black Africa: the historians' perspective. *In* Mintz, S. W. ed. Slavery, colonialism, and racism p125-34

Akans (African people) See Ashantis

Akatziroi. See Khazars

Akavais Indians. See Accawai Indians

Akawaio Indians. See Accawai Indians

Akenten, Nana Wiafe

About

Crook, R. Political centralization and local politics in Ghana: the careers of Nana Wiafe Akenten II and E. K. Duncan-Williams of Offinso (Ashanti) *In* The Making of politicians: studies from Africa and Asia p28-48

Akerman, Sune
Towards an understanding of emigrational processes. *In* Human migration p287-306

Akerman, Sune, and Norberg, Anders
Employment opportunities, family-building and internal migration in the late nineteenth century: some Swedish case studies. *In* Economic factors in population growth p453-86

Akha people. See Kaw people

Akhavi, Shahrough
Egypt: neo-patrimonial elite. *In* Political elites and political development in the Middle East p69-113

Akhmatova, Anna Andreevna

About

Kunitz, S. J. On translating Akhmatova. *In* Kunitz, S. J. A kind of order, a kind of folly p39-46

Slonim, M. L. The fate of poets: Mandelstam, Akhmatova, Tsvetayeva. *In* Slonim, M. L. Soviet Russian literature p248-67

Akin Rabibhadana, M. R.

Clientship and class structure in the Early Bangkok period. *In* Change and persistence in Thai society p93-123

Akins, James E.

The oil crisis: this time the wolf is here. *In* Bundy, W. P. ed. The world economic crisis p21-49

Akinyemi, A. Bolaji

National unity within the context of regional relations: the Nigerian experience. *In* Smock, D. R. and Bentsi-Enchill, K. eds. The search for national integration in Africa p68-76

Akiwowo, Akinsola A.

Contemporary sociology in Nigeria. *In* Mohan, R. P. and Martindale, D. A. eds. Handbook of contemporary developments in world sociology p391-407

Akmeism. See Acmeism

Akrabova-Jandova, Ivanka. See Akrabova-Zhandova, Ivanka

Akrabova-Zhandova, Ivanka

Preslav inlaid ceramics. *In* Studies in memory of David Talbot Rice p25-33

Akrigg, G. Philip V.

Shakespeare the king-maker. *In* English Renaissance drama p46-58

Aksenov, Michael Meerson- See Meerson-Aksenov, Mikhail Georgievich

Aktaion. See Actaeon

Akula, William G. and Vora, Jay A.

Systems planning tomorrow's hospitals today. *In* Managing nonprofit organizations p118-23

Akutagawa, Ryūnosuke

About

Ueda, M. Akutagawa Ryūnosuke. *In* Ueda, M. Modern Japanese writers p111-44

Yamanouchi, H. The rivals: Shiga Naoya and Akutagawa Ryūnosuke. *In* Yamanouchi, H. The search for authenticity in modern Japanese literature p82-106

Alabama

Economic conditions

Thompson, A. A. Alabama's five economies. *In* The Rising South v2 p29-47

Alabama. University

Mathews, D. A Southern university and the South. *In* The Rising South v2 p178-86

Alabama in literature

Going, W. T. Alabama geography in Shirley Ann Grau's The keepers of the house. *In* Going, W. T. Essays on Alabama literature p32-38

Going, W. T. Alabama in the short story: notes for an anthology. *In* Going, W. T. Essays on Alabama literature p39-60

Going, W. T. The Prestons of Talladega and the Hubbards of Bowen: a dramatic note. *In* Going, W. T. Essays on Alabama literature p142-55

Going, W. T. Store and Mockingbird: two Pulitzer novels about Alabama. *In* Going, W. T. Essays on Alabama literature p9-31

Going, W. T. William March's Alabama. *In* Going, W. T. Essays on Alabama literature p97-113

Alagez, Armenia

Mandel'shtam, O. E. Alagez. *In* Mandel'shtam, O. E. Selected essays p204-08

Alagoa, Ebiegberi Joe. See Ajayi, J. F. Ade. jt. auth.

Alain-Fournier. See Fournier, Alain

Alain de Lille. See Alanus de Insulis

Alani

Bosworth, A. B. Arrian and the Alani. *In* Harvard Studies in classical philology v81 p217-55

Alans. See Alani

Alanus, Bp. of Auxerre. See Alanus de Insulis

Alanus de Insulis

About individual works

Liber de planctu naturae

Wetherbee, W. The theme of imagination in medieval poetry and the allegorical figure "Genius." *In* Medievalia et humanistica no.7 p45-64

Alapuro, Risto, and Allardt, Erik

The Lapua movement: the threat of rightist takeover in Finland, 1930-32. *In* The Breakdown of democratic regimes pt. 2 p122-41

Al-Ash'arī, Abu al-Hasan. See Al-Ash'arī, Alī ibn Ismā'īl

Al-Ash'arī, Alī ibn Ismā'īl

About

Alon, I. Between fatalism and causality: Al-Ash'ari and Spinoza. *In* Philosophy East/philosophy West p218-34

Alaska

Description and travel

White, E. B. The years of wonder. *In* White, E. B. Essays of E. B. White p169-96

Alban, J. R. and Allmand, C. T.

Spies and spying in the fourteenth century. *In* War, literature, and politics in the late Middle Ages p73-101

Albanese, Catherine L.

King Crockett: nature and civility on the American frontier. *In* American Antiquarian Society. Proceedings v88 pt2 p225-49

Albania

History

Peters, S. Ingredients of the Communist takeover in Albania. *In* Hammond, T. T. ed. The anatomy of Communist takeover p273-92

Albanian Communist Party. See Communist Party of Albania

Albany Institute, Albany, N.Y.

Hobbins, J. M. Shaping a provincial learned society: the early history of the Albany Institute. *In* Oleson, A. and Brown, S. C. eds. The pursuit of knowledge in the early American Republic p117-50

Albas

Shields, H. The grey cock: dawn song or revenant ballad? *In* Ballad studies p67-92

Albee, Edward

About

Sarotte, G. M. Homosexuality and the theater: Edward Albee: homosexual playwright in spite of himself. *In* Sarotte, G. M. Like a brother, like a lover p134-49

About individual works

All over

Kauffmann, S. All over. *In* Kauffmann, S. Persons of the drama p219-22

A delicate balance

Simon, J. I. Should Albee have said "No, thanks"? *In* Simon, J. I. Singularities p58-64

Seascape

Kauffmann, S. Seascape. *In* Kauffmann, S. Persons of the drama p222-24

Who's afraid of Virginia Woolf?

Schlueter, J. Albee's Martha and George. *In* Schlueter, J. Metafictional characters in modern drama p79-87

Characters

Schlueter, J. Albee's Martha and George. *In* Schlueter, J. Metafictional characters in modern drama p79-87

Albert, Consort of Queen Victoria

About

Sanders, C. R. Carlyle's pen portraits of Queen Victoria and Prince Albert. *In* Fielding, K. J. and Tarr, R. L. eds. Carlyle past and present p216-38

Albert, the Pious, Archduke of Austria, 1559-1621

Art patronage

Trevor-Roper, H. R. The Archdukes and Rubens. *In* Trevor-Roper, H. R. Princes and artists p127-63

Albert, Hans

The myth of total reason: dialectical claims in the light of undialectical criticism. *In* Giddens, A. ed. Positivism and sociology p157-94

About individual works

The myth of total reason: dialectical claims in the light of undialectical criticism

Habermaas, J. Rationalism divided in two: a reply to Albert. *In* Giddens, A. ed. Positivism and sociology p195-223

Alberti, Leone Battista

About

Vena, M. Alberti's linguistic innovations. *In* Italian literature: roots and branches p243-63

About individual works

Della pittura e della statua

Gilman, E. B. The Albertian perspective and the curious perspective. *In* Gilman, E. B. The curious perspective p16-49

Alberti, Rafael

About individual works

Selected poems (Translated by Ben Belitt)

Belitt, B. Translator's preface: The selected poems of Rafael Alberti. *In* Belitt, B. Adam's dream p91-97

Albertus Magnus, Saint, Bp. of Ratisbon

About

Shaw, J. R. Albertus Magnus and the rise of an empirical approach in medieval philosophy and science. *In* Jeffrey, D. L. ed. By things seen: reference and recognition in medieval thought p175-85

Albinski, Henry Stephen

Organized politics and political temper: predisposing factors and outcomes. *In* Perspectives on revolution and evolution p66-102

Albrecht, the Pious, Archduke of Austria

See Albert, the Pious, Archduke of Austria, 1559-1621

Albrecht, Erich A.

Eduard Dorsch and the Civil War. *In* The German contribution to the building of the Americas p275-87

Albrecht, William Price

The sublime pleasures of tragedy

Contents

Addison
Alison
Burke
Dennis
"The fierce dispute"
Gerard
Hazlitt
Introduction: The sublime and the tragic
Keats
Knight
The sublime of vision

Albury, William Randall

Experiment and explanation in the physiology of Bichat and Magendie. *In* Studies in history of biology, v 1 p47-131

Albus, L. Antonius

About

Bowersock, G. W. The proconsulate of Albus. *In* Harvard Studies in classical philology v72 p289-94

Alchemy

Casini, P. Newton, a sceptical alchemist? *In* Bonelli, M. L. R. and Shea, W. R. eds. Reason, experiment, and mysticism in the scientific revolution p233-38

Hall, M. B. Newton's voyage in the strange seas of alchemy. *In* Bonelli, M. L. R. and Shea, W. R. eds. Reason, experiment, and mysticism in the scientific revolution p239-46

Needham, J. Alchemy and early chemistry in China. *In* The Frontiers of human knowledge p171-81

Rossi, P. Hermeticism, rationality and the scientific revolution. *In* Bonelli, M. L. R. and Shea, W. R. eds. Reason, experiment, and mysticism in the scientific revolution p247-73

Westfall, R. S. The role of alchemy in Newton's career. *In* Bonelli, M. L. R. and Shea, W. R. eds. Reason, experiment, and mysticism in the scientific revolution p189-232

See also Elixir of life

History

Vasoli, C. Alchemy in the seventeenth century: the European and Italian scene. *In* Bonelli, M. L. R. and Shea, W. R. eds. Reason, experiment, and mysticism in the scientific revoltion p49-58

Alchemy—*Continued*
China
Strickmann, M. On the alchemy of T'ao Hung-ching. *In* Welch, H. and Seidel, A. K. eds. Facets of Taoism p123-92

Alchemy in literature
Salingar, L. Comic form in Ben Jonson: Volpone and the philosopher's stone. *In* English drama: forms and development p48-68

Alcidamas, of Elaea
About
Koniaris, G. L. Michigan papyrus 2754 and the Certamen. *In* Harvard Studies in classical philology v75 p107-29

Renehan, R. The Michigan Alcidamas-papyrus: a problem in methodology. *In* Harvard Studies in classical philology v75 p85-105

Alcmaeon
Mansfeld, J. Alcmaeon: 'physikos' or physician? With some remarks on Calcidius' 'On vision' compared to Galen's Plac. Hipp. Plat. VII. *In* Kephalaion p26-38

Alcock, Antony Evelyn
The development of governmental attitudes to cultural minorities in Western industrial states. *In* Alcock, A. E.; Taylor, B. K. and Welton, J. M. eds. The future of cultural minorities p102-19

A reappraisal of existing theory and practice in the protection of minorities. *In* Hepburn, A. C. ed. Minorities in history p226-41

Three case-studies in minority protection: South Tyrol, Cyprus, Quebec. *In* Hepburn, A. C. ed. Minorities in history p189-225

Alcock, Antony Evelyn; Taylor, Brian K. and Welton, John M.
Conclusions. *In* Alcock, A. E.; Taylor, B. K. and Welton, J. M. eds. The future of cultural minorities p177-99

Alcock, Nathaniel Warren
Vernacular architecture: historical evidence and historical problems. *In* Material culture and the study of American life p109-20

Alcock, Peter
James K. Baxter and the terror of history: the de-colonisation of a New Zealander. *In* Narasimhaiah, C. D. ed. Awakened conscience p92-110

Alcoholic beverages. See Temperance.

Alcoholics Anonymous
Trice, H. M. and Roman, P. M. Delabeling, relabeling and Alcoholics Anonymous. *In* Davis, F. J. and Stivers, R. eds. The collective definition of deviance p360-75

Alcoholism
Robins, L. N. Alcoholism and labelling theory. *In* Gove, W. R. ed. The labelling of deviance p21-33

Alcorn, John
The nature novel from Hardy to Lawrence
Contents
Butler: the new spirit
Epilogue: Is Great Pan dead?
Hardy: a better world
Hardy and Lawrence
Lawrence: a version of pastoral
Spirit of place: The novel
Spirit of place: The travel book
Toward Freud

Alcott, Amos Bronson
About
Richardson, R. D. Parker and Alcott. *In* Richardson, R. D. Myth and literature in the American renaissance p34-64

Alcott, Louisa May
About individual works
Little women
Auerbach, N. Austen and Alcott on matriarchy: new women or new wives. *In* Spilka, M. ed. Towards a poetics of fiction p266-86

Auerbach, N. Waiting together: two families. *In* Auerbach, N. Communities of women p33-73

Alcuin
About
Thomson, R. M. William of Malmesbury and the letters of Alcuin. *In* Medievalia et humanistica no. 8 p147-61

About individual works
De divinis officiis
Reynolds, R. E. Marginalia on a tenth-century text on the ecclesiastical officers. *In* Law, church, and society p115-29

Authorship
Wallach, L. Alcuin as the author of the Libri Carolini: epilogue to Part III. *In* Wallach, L. Diplomatic studies in Latin and Greek documents from the Carolingian age p287-94

Aldanov, Mark, pseud. See Landau, Mark Aleksandrovich

Aldcroft, Derek Howard
Investment in and utilisation of manpower: Great Britain and her rivals, 1870-1914. *In* Great Britain and her world, 1750-1914 p287-307

Aldecoa, Ignacio
About individual works
Parte de una historia
Schwartz, R. Ignacio Aldecoa and Parte de una historia (Part of a story) (1967). *In* Schwartz, R. Spain's New Wave novelists, 1950-1974 p217-32

Alderman, Harold Gordon
Heidegger's critique of science and technology. *In* Murray, M. E. ed. Heidegger and modern philosophy p35-50

Aldhelm, Saint, Bp. of Sherborne
About
Winterbottom, M. Aldhelm's prose style and its origins. *In* Anglo-Saxon England 6 p39-76

Aldington, Hilda Doolittle. See Doolittle, Hilda

Aldington, Richard
About individual works
Death of a hero
Morris, J. Richard Aldington and Death of a hero—or life of an anti-hero? *In* Klein, H. M. ed. The First World War in fiction p183-92

Life for life's sake
Connolly, C. Richard Aldington. *In* Connolly, C. The evening colonnade p233-36

Aldiss, Brian Wilson
   Pilgrim fathers: Lucian and all that; excerpt from "Billion year spree." *In* Knight, D. F. ed. Turning points p73-95
Aldrich, C. Knight
   Some dynamics of anticipatory grief. *In* Anticipatory grief p3-9
Aldrich, Duncan M.
   Frontier militias: militia laws on the North American and South African frontiers. *In* The Frontier v2 p153-66
Aldrich, Robert

About individual works
Kiss me deadly
   Truffaut, F. Robert Aldrich: Kiss me deadly. *In* Truffaut, F. The films in my life p93-94
Vera Cruz
   Truffaut, F. Robert Aldrich: Vera Cruz. *In* Truffaut, F. The films in my life p95-98
Aldridge, Alfred Owen
   Feijoo, Voltaire, and the mathematics of procreation. *In* Studies in eighteenth-century culture v4 p131-38
Aldridge, Robert
   Two planetary systems. *In* Peary, G. and Shatzkin, R. eds. The modern American novel and the movies p119-30
Aldus. See Manuzio, Aldo Pio
Aleichem, Sholom. See Rabinowitz, Shalom
Alejandro, Carlos Federico Diaz. See Diaz Alejandro, Carlos Federico
Alemán, Mateo

About individual works
Guzmán de Alfarache
   Bjornson, R. The dissemination of the picaresque: Guzmán de Alfarache and the converso problem. *In* Bjornson, R. The picaresque hero in European fiction p43-65
Alembert, Jean Lerond d'
   See also Diderot, Denis jt. auth.

About
   Voegelin, E. Positivism and its antecedents. *In* Voegelin, E. From Enlightenment to revolution p74-109
Aleramo, Sibilla, pseud. See Faccio, Rina
Aleut language
   Krauss, M. E. Eskimo-Aleut. *In* Sebeok, T. A. ed. Native languages of the Americas v 1 p175-281
Bibliography
   Krauss, M. E. Eskimo-Aleut. *In* Sebeok, T. A. ed. Native languages of the Americas v 1 p175-281
Aleutian language. See Aleut language
Alexander II, Emperor of Russia

Assassination
   Parry, A. Hunting the Tsar. *In* Parry, A. Terrorism: from Robespierre to Arafat p107-19
Alexander III, Pope

About
   Grayzel, S. Pope Alexander III and the Jews. *In* Salo Wittmayer Baron v2 p555-72

About individual works
The sentences of Rolandus
   Noonan, J. T. Who was Rolandus? *In* Law, church, and society p21-48

Stroma Rolandi ex decretorum corpore carptum
   Noonan, J. T. Who was Rolandus? *In* Law, church, and society p21-48
Alexander VI, Pope

About
   Weckmann-Muñoz, L. The Alexandrine bulls of 1493: pseudo-Asiatic documents. *In* First images of America p201-09
Alexander the Great

About
   Badian, E. A king's notebooks. *In* Harvard Studies in classical philology v72 p183-204

Art
   Demus, O. Elijah and Alexander. *In* Studies in memory of David Talbot Rice p64-67
Alexander the Great (Romances)
   Duggan, H. N. The role of formulas in the dissemination of a middle English alliterative romance. *In* Virginia. University. Bibliographical Society. Studies in bibliography v29 p265-88
Alexander, Gina
   Victim or spendthrift? The Bishop of London and his income in the sixteenth century. *In* Wealth and power in Tudor England p128-45
Alexander, Hubert Griggs
   On defining in aesthetics. *In* Aagaard-Mogensen, L. ed. Culture and art p110-18
Alexander, Jonathan James Graham
   Some aesthetic principles in the use of colour in Anglo-Saxon art. *In* Anglo-Saxon England 4 p145-54
Alexander, Lloyd
   High fantasy and heroic romance. *In* Horn Book Magazine. Crosscurrents of criticism p170-77
Alexander, Margaret Abigail Walker
   Faulkner & race. *In* The Maker and the myth: Faulkner and Yoknapatawpha, 1977 p105-21
Alexander, Michael J.
   Hardy among the poets. *In* Butler. L. S. ed. Thomas Hardy after fifty years p49-63
Alexander, Nigel
   English drama, edited by Marie Axton and Raymond Williams and Judith Weil's Christopher Marlowe. *In* Drama and society p279-89
   Past, present and Pinter. *In* English Association. Essays and studies, 1974 p 1-17
   Shakespeare's life, times, and stage. *In* Shakespeare survey 26 p168-76
   Shakespeare's life, times, and stage. (another essay) *In* Shakespearre survey 27 p172-79
Alexander, Richard D.
   Sexuality and sociality in humans and other primates. *In* Katchadourian, H. A. ed. Human sexuality p81-97
Alexander, William

About individual works
Johnny Gibb of Gushetneuk, in the parish of Pyketillim
   Hart, F. R. Victorian modes and models. *In* Hart, F. R. The Scottish novel p87-92
Alexander, Yonah
   From terrorism to war: the anatomy of the birth of Israel. *In* International terrorism p211-57

Alexander Nevsky (Motion picture)
Taylor, R. Alexander Nevsky. *In* Taylor, R. Film propaganda p116-30

Alexandria, Egypt

Commerce—History

Udovitch, A. L. A tale of two cities: commercial relations between Cairo and Alexandria during the second half of the eleventh century. *In* The Medieval city p143-62

History

Turner, E. G. Oxyrhynchus and Rome. *In* Harvard Studies in classical philology v79 p 1-24

Alexandrian school
Temkin, O. Studies on late Alexandrian medicine. *In* Temkin, O. The double face of Janus p178-97

al-Fārābī

About individual works
The attainment of happiness

Mahdi, M. Remarks on Alfarabi's Attainment of happiness. *In* Essays on Islamic philosophy and science p47-66

Alfārābī. See al-Fārābī

Alfarabius. See al-Fārābī

al-Fatah. See Fath

Alfin-Slater, Roslyn Bernice, and Friedman, Ruth
Nutrition and aging: are we what we've eaten? *In* Jarvik, L. F. ed. Aging into the 21st century p61-76

Alföldi, András

About individual works
Early Rome and the Latins

Momigliano, A. Did Fabius Pictor lie? *In* Momigliano, A. Essays in ancient and modern historiography p99-105

Alfred the Great, King of England

About individual works
Preface to Gregorius' Pastoral care

Harbert, B. King Alfred's 'æstel'. *In* Anglo-Saxon England 3 p103-10

Alfred of Sareshel. See Alfredus Anglicus, philosopher

Alfred, Randall H.
The Church of Satan. *In* The New religious consciousness p180-202

Alfredus Anglicus, philosopher

About

Otte, J. K. The role of Alfred of Sareshel (Alfredus Anglicus) and his commentary on the Metheora in the reacquisition of Aristotle. *In* Viator: medieval and Renaissance studies v7 p197-209

Alfvén, Hannes
Cosmology: myth or science? *In* Cosmology, history, and theology p 1-14

Algar, Hamid
Bibliographical notes on the Naqshbandi tariqat. *In* Essays on Islamic philosophy science p254-59

Algebra
See also Groups, Theory of; Numbers, Theory of

History

Hankins, T. L. Algebra as pure time: William Rowan Hamilton and the foundations of algebra. *In* Motion and time, space and matter p327-59

Algebra, Abstract. See Logic, Symbolic and mathematical

Algebra, Homological. See Functor theory

Algebra of logic. See Logic, Symbolic and mathematical

Algeo, John
Grammatical usage: modern shibboleths. *In* James B. McMillan: essays in linguistics by his friends and colleagues p53-71

Alger, Horatio

About

Kenner, H. The Promised Land. *In* Kenner, H. A homemade world p20-49

Algeria

Foreign relations

Ogunsanwo, A. The foreign policy of Algeria. *In* Aluko, O. ed. The foreign policies of African states p24-40

Politics and government

Zartman, I. W. Algeria: a post-revolutionary elite. *In* Political elites and political development in the Middle East p255-92

Al-Ghazzālī

About

Marmura, M. E. Ghazali's attitude to the secular sciences and logic. *In* Essays on Islamic philosophy and science p100-11

Algíc languages. See Algonquian languages

Algonkian Indians. See Algonquian Indians

Algonquian Indians
Steward, J. H. Tappers and trappers: parallel processes in acculturation. *In* Steward, J. H. Evolution and ecology p151-79
See also Chippewa Indians; Lumbee Indians

Algonquian languages
Teeter, K. V. Algonquian. *In* Sebeok, T. A. ed. Native languages of the Americas v 1 p505-25
See also Cree language

Algren, Nelson

About individual works
The man with the golden arm

Rosen, R. C. Anatomy of a junkie movie. *In* Peary, G. and Shatzkin, R. eds. The modern American novel and the movies p189-98

A walk on the wild side

Farrell, J. T. Nelson Algren's A walk on the wild side. *In* Farrell, J. T. Literary essays, 1954-1974 p101-03

Alhambra
Rosenthal, E. S. Plus Oultre: the idea imperial of Charles V in his columnar device on the Alhambra. *In* Enggass, R. C. and Stokstad, M. eds. Hortus imaginum p85-93

Alhasen. See Alhazen

Alhazen

About individual works
Opticae thesaurus Alhazeni libri vii

Sabra, A. E. Sensation and inference in Alhazen's theory of visual perception. *In* Studies in perception p160-85

Ali, Muhammad. See Muhammad Ali

'Alī, pasha of Janina

About

Skiotis, D. N. Mountain warriors and the Greek revolution. *In* War, technology and society in the Middle East p308-29

Ali, S. Matlub. See Matlub Ali, S.

Aliber, Robert Z.
Oil and the money crunch. *In* Eppen, G. D. ed. Energy: the policy issues p82-95

U.S. economic policies and the costs of national security. *In* Isolation or interdependence? p131-48

Alien plants. See Plant introduction

Alien property. See Eminent domain (International law)

Alienation (Social psychology)
Bettelheim, B. Alienation and autonomy. *In* Bettelheim, B. Surviving, and other essays p333-49

Bronfenbrenner, M. A harder look at alienation. *In* Capitalism and freedom p197-218

Letman, S. T. Some sociological aspects of terror-violence in a colonial setting. *In* International terrorism and political crimes p33-42

Mihajlov, M. Djilas versus Marx: the theory of alienation. *In* Mihajlov, M. Underground notes p105-24

Ong, W. J. Transformations of the word and alienation. *In* Ong, W. J. Interfaces of the word p17-49

Peckham, M. Arts for the cultivation of radical sensitivity. *In* Peckham, M. Romanticism and behavior p285-312

Peckham, M. Rebellion and deviance. *In* Peckham, M. Romanticism and behavior p67-89

Werkmeister, W. H. Reflections on our times. *In* The Abdication of philosophy: philosophy and the public good p243-49

West, E. G. Adam Smith and alienation: wealth increases, men decay? *In* Skinner, A. S. and Wilson, T. eds. Essays on Adam Smith p540-52

See also Social isolation

Alienation (Social psychology) in literature
Biasin, G. P. Strategies of the anti-hero: Svevo, Pirandello, and Montale. *In* Italian literature: roots and branches p363-81

Gill, J. E. Discovery and alienation, nature and reason in Gulliver's Travels, Parts I-III. *In* Tennessee Studies in literature v22 p85-104

Percy, W. The man on the train. *In* Percy, W. The messsage in the bottle p83-100

Robinson, C. The idealist revolt. *In* Robinson, C. French literature in the nineteenth century p13-49

Sayre, R. F. La chute: the egocentric individual. *In* Sayre, R. F. Solitude in society p155-75

Sayre, R. F. Le planétarium: solitude in the world of commodities. *In* Sayre, R. F. Solitude in society p176-94

Schwarz, L. W. Mutations of Jewish values in contemporary American fiction. *In* Tradition and change in Jewish experience p184-97

Simpson, L. P. The symbolism of literary alienation in the Revolutionary age. *In* Havard, W. C. and Bernd, J. L. eds. 200 years of the Republic in retrospect p79-100

Alienation, Social. See Alienation (Social psychology)

Aliens
See also Diplomatic protection; Refugees, Political—Legal status, laws, etc.

Ghana
Peil, M. Host reactions: aliens in Ghana. *In* Shack, W. A. and Skinner, E. P. eds. Strangers in African societies p123-40

Sudarkasa, N. From stranger to alien: the socio-political history of the Nigerian Yoruba in Ghana, 1900-1970. *In* Shack, W. A. and Skinner, E. P. eds. Strangers in African societies p141-67

Great Britain—History
Thrupp, S. L. Aliens in and around London in the fifteenth century. *In* Thrupp, S. L. Society and history p101-27

Thrupp, S. L. A survey of the alien population of England in 1440. *In* Thrupp, S. L. Society and history p133-49

United States
Rosberg, G. M. Legal regulation of the migration process: the "crisis" of illegal immigration. *In* Human migration p336-76

United States—Law and legislation
Rosberg, G. M. The protection of aliens from discriminatory treatment by the national government. *In* The Supreme Court review, 1977 p275-339

Aliens (Roman law)
Kirshner, J. "Ars imitatur naturam": a consilium of Baldus on naturalization in Florence. *In* Viator: medieval and Renaissance studies v5 p289-331

Aliens in literature
Hunter, G. K. Elizabethans and foreigners. *In* Hunter, G. K. Dramatic identities and cultural tradition p3-30

Alinsky, Saul David
The double revolution. *In* Smithsonian Institution. The cultural drama p289-303

Alison. See Alisoun

Alison, Archibald

About individual works
Essays on the nature and principles of taste
Albrecht, W. P. Alison. *In* Albrecht, W. P. The sublime pleasures of tragedy p69-82

Alisoun
Stemmler, T. An intepretation of Alysoun. *In* Chaucer and Middle English studies in honour of Rossell Hope Robbins p111-18

Alitto, Guy
The conservative as sage: Liang Shuming. *In* The Limits of change p213-41

al-Kātibī, 'Ali ibn'Umar

About individual works
Sun epistle
Rescher, N. and Vander Nat, A. The Arabic theory of temporal modal syllogistic. *In* Essays on Islamic philosophy and science p189-221

al-Kindī

About individual works
De aspectibus
Lindberg, D. C. The intromission-extramission controversy in Islamic visual theory: Alkindi versus Avicenna. *In* Studies in perception p137-59

al-Kindi—About individual works—*Cont.*

On first philosophy

Ivry, A. L. al-Kindī's On first philosophy and Aristotle's Metaphysics. *In* Essays on Islamic philosophy and science p15-24

al-Kindī, Ya'qūb ibn Ishāq. See al-Kindī

All in the family (Television program)

DeMott, B. The viewer's experience: notes on TV criticism and public health. *In* Television as a social force: new approaches to TV criticism p49-60

Pierce, K. M. The Bunkers, the critics and the news. *In* Television as a cultural force p59-75

All over (criticism) Albee, E. *In* Kauffmann, S. Persons of the drama p219-22

All that heaven allows (Motion picture)

French, B. Oppression in sheep's clothing. *In* French, B. On the verge of revolt p92-104

All the king's men (Motion picture)

Waling, W. In which Humpty Dumpty becomes king. *In* Peary, G. and Shatzkin, R. eds. The modern American novel and the movies p168-77

Allah. See God (Islam)

Allardt, Erik

Contemporary sociology in Finland. *In* Mohan, R. P. and Martindale, D. A. eds. Handbook of contemporary developments in world sociology p107-25

See also Alapuro, R. jt. auth.

Allardt, Erik. See Alapuro, R. jt. auth.

Allchin, Frank Raymond

Religious symbols and Indian thought. *In* Symbols of power p 1-34

Allegiance

United States

Bloomfield, M. H. Peter Van Schaack and the problem of allegiance. *In* Bloomfield, M. H. American lawyers in a changing society, 1776-1876 p 1-31

Allegories

Richter, D. H. Allegory versus fable: Golding's Lord of the flies. *In* Richter, D. H. Fable's end p61-82

See also Apocalyptic art; Fables

Allegory

Barfield, O. The rediscovery of allegory (I) *In* Barfield, O. The rediscovery of meaning, and other essays p93-100

Barfield, O. The rediscovery of allegory (II) *In* Barfield, O. The rediscovery of meaning, and other essays p101-10

Scholes, R. E. Modern allegory. *In* Scholes, R. E. Fabulation and metafiction p47-102

See also Apocalyptic literature; Symbolism in literature

History and criticism

Barney, S. A. Conclusion. *In* Barney, S. A. Allegories of history, allegories of love p310-15

Barney, S. A. Introduction: characteristics of allegories. *In* Barney, S. A. Allegories of history, allegories of love p13-55

Mazzeo, J. A. New wine in old bottles: reflections on historicity and the problem of allegory. *In* Mazzeo, J. A. Varieties of interpretation p47-69

Sayers, D. L. The writing and reading of allegory; excerpt from "The poetry of search and the poetry of statement and other posthumous essays on literature, religion, and language." *In* Sayers, D. L. The whimsical Christian p205-34

Starobinski, J. André Chénier and the allegory of poetry. *In* Kroeber, K. and Walling, W. eds. Images of romanticism p39-60

Allegory (Art) See Symbolism in art

Allen, David Grayson

A tale of two towns: persistent English localism in seventeenth-century Massachusetts. *In* Allen, H. C. and Thompson, R. eds. Contrast and connection p 1-35

Allen, Don Cameron

John Donne's knowledge of Renaissance medicine. *In* Roberts, J. R. ed. Essential articles for the study of John Donne's poetry p93-106

Allen, Dwight William

Urban education: hope and prospect. *In* Wagschal, P. H. ed. Learning tomorrows p131-45

Allen, Garland E.

Naturalists and experimentalists: the genotype and the phenotype. *In* Studies in history of biology v3 p179-209

The transformation of a science: T. H. Morgan and the emergence of a new American biology. *In* Oleson, A. and Voss, J. eds. The organization of knowledge in modern America, 1860-1920 p173-210

Allen, Gay Wilson

A new look at Emerson and science. *In* Literature and ideas in America p58-78

Walt Whitman and stoicism. *In* The Stoic strain in American literature p43-60

William James. *In* Ross, R. G. ed. Makers of American thought p49-84

Allen, Grace M.

Senora Carrar's rifles: dramatic means and didactic ends. *In* Mews, S. and Knust, H. eds. Essays on Brecht p156-73

Allen, Harold Byron

The Linguistic atlas of the Upper Midwest as a source of sociolinguistic information. *In* James B. McMillan: essays in linguistics by his friends and colleagues p3-19

Allen, Harry Cranbrook

The American Revolution and the Anglo-American relationship in historical perspective. *In* Allen, H. C. and Thompson, R. eds. Contrast and connection p149-77

The cultural tie; excerpt from "Conflict and concord, the Anglo-American relationship since 1783." *In* Burton, D. H. ed. American history—British historians p75-91

Allen, Horace T.

The life and ministry of Paul L. Lehmann: a personal tribute. *In* The Context of contemporary theology p15-22

Allen, Irving Lewis

Social integration as an organizing principle. *In* Gerbner, G. ed. Mass media policies in changing cultures p235-50

Allen, John Alexander

The other way to live: demigods in Eudora Welty's fiction. *In* Prenshaw, P. W. ed. Eudora Welty p26-55

Alpha particles. See Alpha rays

Alpha rays
Trenn, T. J. Rutherford and recoil atoms: the metamorphosis and success of a once stillborn theory. *In* Historical studies in the physical sciences v6 p513-47

Alphabet. See subdivision Alphabet or Writing under groups of languages or under particular language, e.g. Greek language—Alphabet

Alphand, Nicole Merenda
Escorting the Mona Lisa. *In* Courcel, M. H. de, ed. Malraux p95-99

Alpine Club, London
Robertson, D. A. Mid-Victorians amongst the Alps. *In* Knoepflmacher, U. C. and Tennyson, G. B. eds. Nature and the Victorian imagination p113-36

The **Alpine** frontiers and early medieval Italy to the middle of the seventh century. Burns, T. S. *In* The Frontier v2 p51-68

Alps

Antiquities, Roman
Burns, T. S. The Alpine frontiers and early medieval Italy to the middle of the seventh century. *In* The Frontier v2 p51-68

al-Qazwini al-Kātibī. See al-Kātibī, 'Ali ibn 'Umar

al-Rāzī, Abu Bakr Muhammad ibn Zakarīyā

About
Iskandar, A. Z. The medical bibliography of al-Rāzī. *In* Essays on Islamic philosophy and science p41-46

al-Rāzī, Fākhr al-Din Muhammad ibn'Umar

About
Goodman, L. E. Rāzī's myth of the fall of soul: its function in his philosophy. *In* Essays on Islamic philosophy and science p25-40

Alroy, Gil Carl
Military capabilities in the Middle East. *In* The New world balance and peace in the Middle East: reality or mirage? p50-60

Als y yod on ay Mounday (Ballad)
Lyle, E. B. The Wee wee man and Als y yod on ay Mounday. *In* Ballad studies p21-28

al-Shirwānī, Muhammad ibn Fayḍ Allāh ibn Muhammad Amīn

About
Rescher, N. and Vander Nat, A. The Arabic theory of temporal modal syllogistic. *In* Essays on Islamic philosophy and science p189-221

Alston, William P.
Self-intervention and the structure of motivation. *In* Mischel, T. ed. The self p65-102

Alstyne, Carol van. See Van Alstyne, Carol

Alstyne, William W. van. See Van Alstyne, William W.

Alt, Arthur Tilo
Escape and transformation: an inquiry into the nature of Storm's realism. *In* Creative encounter p117-32

Altar de los Sacrificios site, Guatemala. See Altar de Sacrificios site, Guatemala

Altar de Sacrificios site, Guatemala
Willey, G. R. The rise of classic Maya civilization: a Passión Valley perspective. *In* The Origins of Maya civilization p133-57

Altbach, Philip G.
Literary colonialism: books in the Third world. *In* Altbach, P. G. and McVey, S. eds. Perspectives on publishing p83-101

Publishing and the intellectual system. *In* Altbach, P. G. and McVey, S. eds. Perspectives on publishing p3-15

Publishing in a transitional society: the case of India. *In* Altbach, P. G. and McVey, S. eds. Perspectives on publishing p141-55

Altbach, Philip G. and Peterson, Patti McGill
Movement goals and fortunes. *In* Lauer, R. H. ed. Social movement and social change p29-45

Altenbernd, Lynn A.
The idea of national character: inspiration or fallacy? *In* Kagle, S. E. ed. America: exploration and travel p9-17

Alter, George. See Laurie, B. jt. auth.

Alter, Robert
Defenses of the imagination
Contents
Agnon's Mediterranean fable
Charles Reznikoff: between present and past
Defenses of the imagination
Eliot, Lawrence, and the Jews: two versions of Europe
Fiction in a state of siege
Gershom Scholem: history and the abyss
Jewish humor and the domestication of myth
Lea Goldberg: poetry in dark times
A novel of the post-tragic world
Osip Mandelstam: the poet as witness
A problem of horizons
Shtetl and revolution
Updike, Malamud, and the fire this time
Uri Zvi Greenberg: a poet of the Holocaust
Walter Benjamin: the aura of the past
Mimesis and the motive for fiction. *In* Images and ideas in American culture p99-123
Partial magic
Contents
Diderot's Jacques: this is and is not a story
The inexhaustible genre
The mirror of knighthood and the world of mirrors
The modernist revival of self-conscious fiction
Nabokov's game of worlds
The self-conscious novel in eclipse
Sterne and the nostalgia for reality

Alternative schools. See Free schools

Altheide, David L.
The sociology of Alfred Schutz. *In* Douglas, J. D. and Johnson, J. M. [eds.] Existential sociology p133-52

Altholz, Josef Lewis
The warfare of conscience with theology. *In* Altholz, J. L. ed. The mind and art of Victorian England p58-77

Altick, Richard Daniel
Past and present: topicality as technique. *In* Carlyle and his contemporaries p112-28

This will never do. *In* Review, v 1 1979 p47-60

Altieri, Charles F.
Enlarging the temple
Contents
Denise Levertov and the limits of the aesthetics of presence
Modern and post modern: symbolist and immanentist modes of poetic thought
Process as plenitude: the poetry of Gary Snyder and Robert Duncan
Robert Lowell and the difficulties of escaping modernism
The struggle with absence: Robert Creely and W. S. Merwin
Varieties of immanentist experience: Robert Bly, Charles Olson, and Frank O'Hara
A procedural definition of literature. *In* Hernadi, P. ed. What is literature? p62-78

Alting von Geusau, Frans A. M.
Détente after Helsinki. *In* The Year book of world affairs, 1978 p8-22

Altman, Albert A.
Shinbunshi: the early Meiji adaptation of the Western-style newspaper. *In* Modern Japan p52-66

Altman, Charles Frederick
Two types of opposition and the structure of Latin saints' lives. *In* Medievalia et humanistica no. 6 p 1-11

Altman, Joel Barrett
The Tudor play of mind
Contents
Conclusion
Demonstrative and explorative: two paradigms
"If words might serve": Marlowe's supposes
Inventing answers in English comedy
The method staged: debate plays by Heywood and Rastell
The moral cultivation of ambivalence
Propaedeutic for drama: questions as fiction
Quaestiones copiosae: pastoral and courtly in John Lyly
Seneca and the declamatory structure of tragedy
Terence and the mimesis of wit
Tragic perspectives among the Elizabethans

Altmann, Alexander
Letters from Dohm to Mendelssohn. *In* Salo Wittmayer Baron v 1 p39-62

Alto Adige. See Bolzano (Province)

Altruism
Blum, L. and others. Altruism and women's oppression. *In* Gould, C. C. and Wartofsky, M. W. eds. Women and philosophy p222-47
Jencks, C. S. The social basis of unselfishness. *In* On the making of Americans p63-86
Thomas, L. The Tucson zoo. *In* Thomas, L. The medusa and the snail p7-11
See also Self-sacrifice

Altschul, Michael
Culture and community in the Italian Renaissance: four recent studies. *In* Medievalia et humanistica no. 5 p247-52

Altschule, Mark David
Origins of concepts in human behavior
Contents
Acedia—its evolution from deadly sin to psychiatric syndrome
Acupuncture in the Western world up to a century ago
The calcified pineal gland: nature mimics art—almost

The early history of psychiatric treatment
George Cheyne and his English malady
The ideas of the Huron Indians about the unconscious mind
Miscellanea
The pneuma concept of the soul
St Isidore of Seville and his depressing ideas about depression
The singular case of James Tilly Matthews, a clear paranoid
Swedenborg and Stahl: opposite—and wrong—sides of the same coin

al-Tūsī, Nasīr al-Din Muhammad ibn Muhammad
About individual works
Principles of inference
Morewedge, P. The analysis of "substance" in Tūsī's Logic and in the ibn Sīnian tradition. *In* Essays on Islamic philosophy and science p158-88

Aluko, Olajide
The determinants of the foreign policies of African states. *In* Aluko, O. ed. The foreign policies of African states p 1-23
Ghana's foreign policy. *In* Aluko, O. ed. The foreign policies of African states p72-97
Nigerian foreign policy. *In* Aluko, O. ed. The foreign policies of African states p163-95

Aluko, Samuel A.
Rural economic development. *In* Colonialism and change p231-54

Aluko, T. MofOlorunso
About
Taiwo, O. T. M. Aluko. *In* Taiwo, O. Culture and the Nigerian novel p149-80

About individual works
One man, one matchet
Gakwandi, S. A. Nationalism: Aluko's One man one matchet. *In* Gakwandi, S. A. The novel and contemporary experience in Africa p56-65

Alvarez, Alfred
About individual works
The savage god
Gass, W. H. The doomed in their sinking. *In* Gass, W. H. The world within the word p3-15
Sheed, W. A. Alvarez: the savage god. *In* Sheed, W. The good word & other words p68-72

Alvaro, Corrado
About
Pacifici, S. The "southern" novel. *In* Pacifici, S. The modern Italian novel: from Pea to Moravia p47-78

Alvernia, Pier d'. See Peire d'Auvergne

Alysoun. See Alisoun

Amadi, Elechi
About
Taiwo, O. Onuora Nzekwu and Elechi Amadi. *In* Taiwo, O. Culture and the Nigerian novel p181-209

Amaguaco Indians. See Amahuaca Indians

Amahuaca Indians
Women
Dole, G. E. The marriages of Pacho: a woman's life among the Amahuaca. *In* Matthiasson, C. J. Many sisters; women in cross-cultural perspective p3-35

Amajuaco Indians. See Amahuaca Indians

Amalorpavadass, D. S.

The Indian universe of a new theology. *In* The Emergent gospel p137-56

Amanuddin, Syed

Toward a view of Commonwealth poetic tradition. *In* Narasimhaiah, C. D. ed. Awakened conscience p423-32

Amar Singh. See Singh, Amar

Amateur theatricals. See College theater

Amawaka Indians. See Amahuaca Indians

Amazon Valley

Colonization

Thompson, S. I. The cultural ecology of pioneer agriculture in contemporary South America. *In* Miller, D. H. and Steffen, J. O. eds. The frontier p297-316

Economic conditions

MacLachlan, C. M. African slave trade and economic development in Amazonia, 1700-1800. *In* Toplin, R. B. ed. Slavery and race relations in Latin America p112-45

Ambacher, Bruce I.

Urban response to Jacksonian democracy: Philadelphia Democrats and the Bank War, 1832-1834. *In* Essays on urban America p55-87

Ambassadors. See Legates, Papal

Ambiguity

Psychological aspects

Davis, L. J. Tolerance of ambiguity in interpersonal bargaining. *In* International terrorism and world security p314-24

Ambler, Eric

About

Lambert, G. The thin protection: Eric Ambler. *In* Lambert, G. The dangerous edge p104-31

Ambo (African people)

Stefaniszyn, B. The material culture of the Ambo of Northern Rhodesia. *In* The Occasional papers of the Rhodes-Livingstone Museum p721-826

Ambrose, Saint, Bp. of Milan

Manuscripts

Wallach, L. The textual history of a Greek Ambrose text: Libri Carolini II.15. *In* Wallach, L. Diplomatic studies in Latin and Greek documents from the Carolingian age p123-39

Ambrose of Milan. See Ambrose, Saint, Bp. of Milan

Ambrosiaster

Manuscripts

Wallach, L. Ambrosiaster and the Libri Carolini. *In* Wallach, L. Diplomatic studies in Latin and Greek documents from the Carolingian age p140-51

Ambrosius, Saint. See Ambrose, Saint, Bp. of Milan

Ambrosius Flandinus. See Flandino, Ambrogio

Amelinckx, Frans C.

Exploration and creativity: Chateaubriand's travels in America. *In* Kagle, S. E. ed. America: exploration and travel p40-49

Amen (Egyptian deity). See Amon (Egyptian deity)

Amenorrhea

Le Roy Ladurie, E. Amenorrhoea in time of famine (seventeenth to twentieth century). *In* Le Roy Ladurie, E. The territory of the historian p255-71

Same as: Le Roy Ladurie, E. Famine amenorrhoea (seventeenth-twentieth centuries) *In* Biology of man in history p163-78

Amerasinghe, Hamilton Shirley

Key issues in the Third United Nations Conference on the Law of the Sea. *In* Borgese, E. M. and Krieger, D. eds. The tides of change p328-39

America

Civilization—African influences

Szwed, J. F. and Abrahams, R. D. After the myth: studying Afro-American cultural patterns in the plantation literature. *In* Crowley, D. J. ed. African folklore in the New World p65-86

Discovery and exploration

Allen, J. L. Lands of myth, waters of wonder: the place of the imagination in the history of geographical exploration. *In* Geographies of the mind p41-61

Carew, J. The origins of racism in the Americas. *In* African themes p3-23

Carter, C. H. The New World as a factor in international relations, 1492-1739. *In* First images of America p231-63

Ewan, J. A. The Columbian discoveries and the growth of botanical ideas with special reference to the sixteenth century. *In* First images of America p807-12

Franklin, W. Speaking and touching: the problem of inexpressibility in American travel books. *In* Kagle, S. E. ed. America: exploration and travel p18-38

Hand, W. D. The effect of the discovery on ethnological and folklore studies in Europe. *In* First images of America p45-55

Kagle, S. E. Unaccustomed earth: the movement of Americans from travel to exploration. *In* Kagle, S. E. ed. America: exploration and travel p3-7

Discovery and exploration—Bibliography

Hirsch, R. Printed reports on the early discoveries and their reception. *In* First images of America p537-59

Discovery and exploration—Historiography

Gerbi, A. The earliest accounts on the New World. *In* First images of America p37-43

Gilmore, M. P. The New World in French and English historians of the sixteenth century. *In* First images of America p519-27

Jantz, H. E. S. Images of America in the German Renaissance. *In* First images of America p91-106

Discovery and exploration—Spanish

Cutter, D. C. Spanish scientific exploration along the Pacific Coast. *In* Weber, D. J. ed. New Spain's far northern frontier p35-47

Emigration and immigration

Borah, W. W. The mixing of populations. *In* First images of America p707-22

Literatures

See Spanish American literature

Politics

See Pan-Americanism

America in literature

Evans, E. J. The established self: the American episodes of Martin Chuzzlewit. *In* Dickens Studies Annual v5 p59-73

Jantz, H. E. S. German men of letters in the early United States. *In* The German contribution to the building of the Americas p75-95

American Academy of Arts and Letters

Cowley, M. "Sir: I have the honor." *In* Cowley, M.—And I worked at the writer's trade p161-75

American Academy of Arts and Sciences, Boston

Whitehill, W. M. Early learned societies in Boston and vicinity. *In* Oleson, A. and Brown, S. C. eds. The pursuit of knowledge in the early American Republic p151-73

American actors. See Actors, American

American aesthetics. See Aesthetics, American

American anatomists. See Anatomists, American

American Antiquarian Society, Worcester, Mass.

McCorison, M. A. The nature of humanistic societies in early America. *In* Oleson, A. and Brown, S. C. eds. The pursuit of knowledge in the early American Republic p248-60

American architecture. See Architecture, American

American artists. See Artists, American

American Association for the Advancement of Science

Kohlstedt, S. G. Savants and professionals: the American Association for the Advancement of Science, 1848-1860. *In* Oleson, A. and Brown, S. C. eds. The pursuit of knowledge in the early American Republic p299-325

American authors. See Authors, American

American ballads. See Ballads, American

American Bar Association

Green, M. J. The ABA as trade association. *In* Nader, R. and Green, M. J. eds. Verdicts on lawyers p 3-19

MacKenzie, J. P. Of judges and the ABA. *In* Nader, R. and Green, M. J. eds. Verdicts on lawyers p33-46

American black dialect. See Black English

American books abroad

Celli, A. Italian perspectives. *In* The Art of Willa Cather p103-20

Johnson, C. and Johnson, I. D. Introduction. *In* Johnson, I. D. and Johnson, C. [eds.] Les américanistes p 3-15

Sato, H. Willa Cather in Japan. *In* The Art of Willa Cather p84-102

American Booksellers Association

Anderson, C. B. Mark Twain at ABA. *In* Bookselling in America and the world p195-98

Grannis, C. B. More than merchants: seventy-five years of the ABA. *In* Bookselling in America and the world p65-108

American children's literature. See Children's literature, American

American Civil War. See United States—History—Civil War, 1861-1865

American Conservatory Theater. See San Francisco. American Conservatory Theater

American detective and mystery stories. See Detective and mystery stories, American

American detective stories. See Detective and mystery stories, American

American drama

Bibliography

Frazer, W. L. Drama. *In* American literary scholarship, 1976 p355-68

Frazer, W. Drama [another essay] *In* American literary scholarship, 1977 p389-403

Meserve, W. J. Drama. *In* American literary scholarship, 1973 p369-81

Miller, J. Y. Drama. *In* American literary scholarship, 1974 p373-86

Miller, J. Y. Drama [another essay] *In* American literary scholarship, 1975 p399-416

Afro-American authors—History and criticism

Johnson, H. A. Black influences in the American theater: Part II, 1960 and after. *In* The Black American reference book p705-40

Simon, J. I. Black plays, white reviewers. *In* Simon, J. I. Singularities p213-15

19th century—History and criticism

Watson, C. S. Conclusions: Charleston dramatists and American drama. *In* Watson, C. S. Antebellum Charleston dramatists p143-50

20th century—History and criticism

Brustein, R. S. The crack in the chimney: reflections on contemporary American playwriting. *In* Images and ideas in American culture p141-57

Cohn, R. Camp, cruelty, colloquialism. *In* Cohen, S. B. ed. Comic relief p281-303

Miller, A. Many writers: few plays. *In* Miller, A. The theater essays of Arthur Miller p22-26

Miller, A. The shadows of the gods. *In* Miller, A. The theater essays of Arthur Miller p175-94

Miller, J. Y. Expressionism: The waste land enacted. *In* French, W. G. ed. The twenties p439-54

Nicoll, A. The American advent and dramatic revolution in Poland. *In* Nicoll, A. World drama p647-53

Nicoll, A. Realism, social and otherwise. *In* Nicoll, A. World drama p689-710

Sarotte, G. M. The homosexual character on the stage. *In* Sarotte, G. M. Like a brother, like a lover p30-33

Simon, J. I. Is this the right way to rebel? *In* Simon, J. I. Singularities p84-91

Wilmurt, A. Post-war drama in the U.S.A. *In* Nicoll, A. World drama p797-805

Charleston, S.C.—History and criticism

Watson, C. S. Dramatic writing, 1797 to the Civil War. *In* Watson, C. S. Antebellum Charleston dramatists p27-51

England

Brustein, R. S. The great American tragedy. *In* Brustein, R. S. The culture watch p63-68

American economists. See Economists, American

American English. See English language in the United States

American epic poetry. See Epic poetry, American

American essays

History and criticism

Granger, B. I. Conclusion. *In* Granger, B. I. American essay serials from Franklin to Irving p228-32

American Federation of Labor and Congress of Industrial Organizations

Meany, G. Challenges to the labor movement. *In* Prochnow, H. V. ed. Dilemmas facing the nation p166-78

American fiction

Roth, P. Writing American fiction. *In* Roth, P. Reading myself and others p117-35

See also Detective and mystery stories, American; Dime novels; Science fiction, American; Short stories, American; Western stories

History and criticism

Cawelti, J. G. The best-selling social melodrama. *In* Cawelti, J. G. Adventure, mystery, and romance p260-95

Farrell, J. T. The development of the American novel. *In* Farrell, J. T. Literary essays, 1954-1974 p139-41

Harris, N. Utopian fiction and its discontents. *In* Uprooted Americans p209-44

Holman, C. H. Literary realism: an American mode. *In* Holman, C. H. Windows on the world p3-16

Lander, D. Eve among the Indians. *In* Diamond, A. and Edwards, L. R. eds. The authority of experience p194-211

Milne, G. Conclusion. *In* Milne, G. The sense of society p272-76

Milne, G. Introduction. *In* Milne, G. The sense of society p11-18

Pryse, M. Postscript. *In* Pryse, M. The mark and the knowledge p168-71

Pryse, M. The transcendental imagination: the mark as focus. *In* Pryse, M. The mark and the knowledge p 1-14

Rahv, P. The cult of experience in American writing. *In* Rahv, P. Essays on literature and politics, 1932-1977 p8-22

Sarotte, G. M. Four archetypes of the homosexual couple: Teacher and pupil. *In* Sarotte, G. M. Like a brother, like a lover p61-69

Sarotte, G. M. Four archetypes of the homosexual couple: The captain and the soldier. *In* Sarotte, G. M. Like a brother, like a lover p70-91

Sarotte, G. M. Four archetypes of the homosexual couple: The white and the Black. *In* Sarotte, G. M. Like a brother, like a lover p92-104

Sheed, W. The novel of manners. *In* Sheed, W. The good word & other words p28-32

Stineback, D. C. Conclusion: The present situation. *In* Stineback, D. C. Shifting world p171-76

Watkins, F. C. A void New World. *In* Watkins, F. C. In time and place p217-21

Afro-American authors

Bone, R. A. The Harlem Renaissance: a reappraisal. *In* Bone, R. A. Down home p109-38

Bone, R. A. Literary forebears. *In* Bone, R. A. Down home p3-18

Donald, M. The minorities. *In* Donald, M. The American novel in the twentieth century p141-75

Jackson, B. The ghetto of the Negro novel: a theme with variations. *In* Jackson, B. The waiting years p179-88

Jackson, B. The Negro's image of his universe as reflected in his fiction. *In* Jackson, B. The waiting years p92-102

Schultz, E. A. "Free in fact and at last": the image of the Black woman in Black American fiction. *In* Springer, M. A. ed. What manner of woman p316-44

Indian authors—History and criticism

Larson, C. R. The emergence of American Indian fiction. *In* Larson, C. R. American Indian fiction p 1-16

Larson, C. R. The figure in the dark forest. *In* Larson, C. R. American Indian fiction p165-72

Jewish authors

Alter, R. Jewish humor and the domestication of myth. *In* Alter, R. Defenses of the imagination p155-67

Cohen, S. B. The Jewish literary comediennes. *In* Cohen, S. B. ed. Comic relief p172-86

Donald, M. The minorities. *In* Donald, M. The American novel in the twentieth century p141-75

Field, L. A. Bernard Malamud and the marginal Jew. *In* The Fiction of Bernard Malamud p97-116

Sarotte, G. M. Latent homosexuality: short of and beyond true heterosexuality: The feminine-masochist temperament in certain Jewish characters. *In* Sarotte, G. M. Like a brother, like a lover p229-39

Schwarz, L. W. Mutations of Jewish values in contemporary American fiction. *In* Tradition and change in Jewish experience p184-97

Women authors

Baym, N. Z. Catharine Sedgwick and other early novelists. *In* Baym, N. Z. Woman's fiction p31-85

Baym, N. Z. The form and ideology of woman's fiction. *In* Baym, N. Z. Woman's fiction p22-50

Baym, N. Z. Introduction and conclusions. *In* Baym, N. Z. Woman's fiction p11-21

Baym, N. Z. Other novelists of the fifties. *In* Baym, N. Z. Woman's fiction p231-75

Cohen, S. B. The Jewish literary comediennes. *In* Cohen, S. B. ed. Comic relief p172-86

Howard, M. Introduction. *In* Howard, M. ed. Seven American women writers of the twentieth century p3-27

Mickelson, A. Z. Introduction. *In* Mickelson, A. Z. Reaching out: sensitivity and order in recent American fiction by women p 1-14

19th century—Bibliography

Inge, M. T. Nineteenth-century fiction. *In* American literary scholarship, 1973 p208-23

19th century—History and criticism

Auerbach, N. Introduction: the communal eye. *In* Auerbach, N. Communities of women p 1-32

Baym, N. Z. Catharine Sedgwick and other early novelists. *In* Baym, N. Z. Woman's fiction p31-85

Baym, N. Z. The form and ideology of woman's fiction. *In* Baym, N. Z. Woman's fiction p22-50

American fiction—20th century—History and criticism—Continued

Masinton, M. and Masinton, C. G. Second-class citizenship: the status of women in contemporary American fiction. In Springer, M. A. ed. What manner of woman p297-315

May, K. M. Attack on the unconscious. In May, K. M. Out of the maelstrom p78-97

Milne, G. Recent exemplars. In Milne, G. The sense of society p254-71

Milne, G. Turn-of-the-century figures. In Milne, G. The sense of society p100-15

Morris, W. The ghostly rumble among the drums. In Morris, W. Earthly delights, unearthly adornments p113-16

Mudrick, M. Fiction and truth. In Mudrick, M. Books are not life but then what is? p276-99

Ohmann, R. M. The social definition of literature. In Hernadi, P. ed. What is literature? p89-101

Pinsker, S. The urban tall tale: frontier humor in a contemporary key. In Cohen, S. B. ed. Comic relief p249-62

Sale, R. H. The golden age of the American novel. In Sale, R. H. On not being good enough p110-25

Sale, R. H. Novelists, readers, critics. In Sale, R. H. On not being good enough p53-66

Sale, R. H. Unknown novels. In Sale, R. H. On not being good enough p3-21

Sarotte, G. M. The circumstances of the homosexual as reflected in the novel and theater: Between the American woman and the American virile ideal. In Sarotte, G. M. Like a brother, like a lover p185-92

Sarotte, G. M. The circumstances of the homosexual as reflected in the novel and theater: Small town and big city. In Sarotte, G. M. Like a brother, like a lover p153-63

Sarotte, G. M. The circumstances of the homosexual as reflected in the novel and theater: Three categories of homosexuals. In Sarotte, G. M. Like a brother, like a lover p164-84

Sarotte, G. M. The evolution of the homosexual in the American novel—Melville to Baldwin. In Sarotte, G. M. Like a brother, like a lover p12-29

Sarotte, G. M. Four archetypes of the homosexual couple: Adolescents. In Sarotte, G. M. Like a brother, like a lover p37-60

Scholes, R. E. Metafiction. In Scholes, R. E. Fabulation and metafiction p103-38

Solomon, E. Fiction and the New Deal. In Braeman, J.; Bremner, R. H. and Brody, D. eds. The New Deal v 1 p310-25

Stevick, P. Prolegomena to the study of fictional dreck. In Cohen, S. B. ed. Comic relief p263-80

Tuttleton, J. W. "Combat in the erogenous zone": women in the American novel between the two world wars. In Springer, M. A. ed. What manner of woman p271-96

Vidal, G. The top ten best sellers according to the Sunday New York Times as of January 7, 1973. In Vidal, G. Matters of fact and of fiction p3-26

Wallace, R. H. Never mind that the nag's a pile of bones: the contemporary American comic novel and the comic tradition. In Wallace, H. The last laugh p 1-25

Wallace, R. H. No more happy endings. In Wallace, R. H. The last laugh p136-43

Watkins, F. C. The makings of American fiction. In Watkins, F. C. In time and place p 3-15

Southern States—History and criticism

Collins, C. E. Faulkner and certain earlier Southern fiction. In Inge, M. T. ed. The frontier humorists p259-65

Holman, C. H. Detached laughter in the South. In Cohen, S. B. ed. Comic relief p87-104

Rose, A. H. Demonic vision and the conventions of antebellum Southern fiction. In Rose, A. H. Demonic vision p39-62

Rose, A. H. Recent American writings: the leveling of racial vision. In Rose, A. H. Demonic vision p119-36

Simpson, L. P. The Southern aesthetic of memory. In Tulane Studies in English, v23 p207-27

Thorp, W. Suggs and Sut in modern dress: the latest chapter in Southern humor. In Inge, M. T. ed. The frontier humorists p292-99

American folk-lore. See Folk-lore, American

American freeman (Periodical)

Green, J. R. The "salesmen-soldiers" of the "appeal army": a profile of rank-and-file Socialist agitators. In Stave, B. M. ed. Socialism and the cities p13-40

American graffiti (Motion picture)

Kauffmann, S. American graffiti. In Kauffmann, S. Living images p218-20

American humorous poetry. See Humorous poetry, American

American Indians. See Indians of North America

American language. See English language in the United States

American Law Institute

Meyers, C. J. The covenant of habitability and the American Law Institute. In Stanford legal essays p355-79

American Legion

Lisio, D. J. United States: bread and butter politics. In The War generation p38-58

American Library Association

Holley, E. G. Library issues in the seventies. In As much to learn as to teach p25-37

American Library Association. Task Force on Gay Liberation

Gittings, B. Combatting the lies in the libraries. In Crew, L. ed. The gay academic p107-18

American literature

See also Christian literature, American; German-American literature; Spanish American literature; and similar headings

Bibliography

Anzilotti, R. Foreign scholarship: Italian contributions. In American literary scholarship, 1975 p487-94

Anzilotti, R. Foreign scholarship: Italian contributions [another essay] In American literary scholarship, 1976 p446-55

Anzilotti, R. Foreign scholarship: Italian contributions [another essay] In American literary scholarship, 1977 p493-98

American literature—Bibliography—*Continued*

Arner, R. D. Literature to 1800. *In* American literary scholarship, 1974 p167-91

Arner, R. D. Literature to 1800 [another essay] *In* American literary scholarship, 1975 p203-29

Arner, R. D. Literature to 1800 [another essay] *In* American literary scholarship, 1976 p169-94

Arner, R. D. Literature to 1800 [another essay] *In* American literary scholarship, 1977 p189-206

Beppu, K. Foreign scholarship: Japanese contributions. *In* American literary scholarship, 1975 p494-97

Beppu, K. Foreign scholarship: Japanese contributions [another essay] *In* American literary scholarship, 1976 p455-59

Beppu, K. Foreign scholarship: Japanese contributions [another essay] *In* American literary scholarship, 1977 p499-504

Couturier, M. Foreign scholarship: French contributions. *In* American literary scholarship, 1977 p467-74

Galinsky, H. Foreign scholarship: German contributions. *In* American literary scholarship, 1975 p476-87

Galinsky, H. Foreign scholarship: German contributions [another essay] *In* American literary scholarship, 1976 p435-46

Galinsky, H. Foreign scholarship: German contributions [another essay] *In* American literary scholarship, 1977 p474-92

Jarrett, D. and Jarrett, M. American literature to 1900. *In* English Association. The year's work in English studies v55 p482-504

Jarrett, M. American literature to 1900. *In* English Association. The year's work in English studies v56 p393-412

Jarrett, M. American literature to 1900 [another essay] *In* English Association. The year's work in English studies v57 p382-97

Lemay, J. A. L. Literature to 1800. *In* American literary scholarship, 1973 p179-207

Lundén, R. Foreign scholarship: Scandinavian contributions. *In* American literary scholarship, 1975 p498-501

Lundén, R. Foreign scholarship; Scandinavian contributions [another essay] *In* American literary scholarship, 1976 p459-62

Lundén, R. Foreign scholarship: Scandinavian contributions [another essay] *In* American literary scholarship, 1977 p505-15

Lyra, F. Foreign scholarship: East European contributions. *In* American literary scholarship, 1977 p463-67

Rivière, J. Foreign scholarship: French contributions. *In* American literary scholarship, 1975 p473-76

Rivière, J. Foreign scholarship: French contributions [another essay] *In* American literary scholarship, 1976 p431-34

Rivière, J. and others. Foreign contributions. *In* American literary scholarship, 1973 p439-57

Rivière, J. and others. Foreign scholarship. *In* American literary scholarship, 1974 p433-58

Welland, D. S. R. and Walker, I. M. American literature to 1900. *In* English Association. The year's work in English studies v53 p410-33

Welland, D. S. R. and Walker, I. M. American literature to 1900 [another essay] *In* English Association. The year's work in English studies v54 p406-24

Bibliography—First editions

Matheson, W. American literary bibliography—FPAA style. *In* Review, v 1 1979 p173-81

Criticism, Textual

Tanselle, G. T. Greg's theory of copytext and the editing of American literature. *In* Virginia. University. Bibliographical Society. Studies in bibliography v28 p167-229

History and criticism

Blasing, M. K. Coda: new life in a New World. *In* Blasing, M. K. The art of life p157-60

Buitenhuis, P. The stoic strain in American literature. *In* The Stoic strain in American literature p3-16

Couser, G. T. Epilogue: prophetic autobiography and prophetic behavior. *In* Couser, G. T. American autobiography p197-201

Cowley, M. "And Jesse begat . . ." a note on literary generations. *In* Cowley, M. —And I worked at the writer's trade p 1-20

Donaldson, S. and Massa, A. Individual and society. *In* Donaldson, S. and Massa, A. American literature: nineteenth and early twentieth centuries p120-51

Echeruo, M. J. C. The conditioned imagination. *In* Echeruo, M. J. C. The conditioned imagination from Shakespeare to Conrad p 1-23

French, W. G. Frost country. *In* Frost: centennial essays II p5-20

Greene, J. L. Black literature and the American literary mainstream. *In* Minority language and literature p20-28

Guillory, D. L. The mystique of childhood in American literature. *In* Tulane Studies in English, v23 p229-47

Howe, I. Literature and liberalism. *In* Howe, I. Celebrations and attacks p239-54

Kagle, S. E. Unaccustomed earth: the movement of Americans from travel to exploration. *In* Kagle, S. E. ed. America: exploration and travel p3-7

Kazin, A. The drama of good and evil in American writing. *In* An Almost chosen people p51-66

Lynn, K. S. Adulthood in American literature. *In* Erikson, E. H. ed. Adulthood p237-47

Madden, D. The American writer as public icon. *In* Browne, R. B. and Fishwick, M. W. eds. Icons of America p87-99

May, J. R. American literary variations on the demonic. *In* Disguises of the demonic p31-47

Pilkington, J. Nature's legacy to William Faulkner. *In* The South and Faulkner's Yoknapatawpha p104-27

Rahv, P. Paleface and Redskin. *In* Rahv, P. Essays on literature and politics, 1932-1972 p3-7

Schneider, D. J. The Manichean vision and the reading of symbolist works. *In* Schneider, D. J. Symbolism: the Manichean vision p 1-39

Shapiro, K. J. The decolonization of American literature. *In* Shapiro, K. J. The poetry wreck p201-23

Smith, A. J. M. Evolution and revolution as aspects of English-Canadian and American literature. *In* Perspectives on revolution and evolution p213-37

Spencer, B. T. Gertrude Stein: non-expatriate. *In* Literature and ideas in America p204-27

American literature—20th century—History and criticism—*Continued*

Thurley, G. Conclusion: towards decadence *In* Thurley, G. The American moment p229-34

Tichi, C. Epilogue. *In* Tichi, C. New World, new earth p250-58

Widmer, K. The waste land and the American breakdown. *In* French, W. G. ed. The twenties p475-96

New England—History and criticism

Grabo, N. S. Colonial American theology: holiness and the lyric impulse. *In* Essays in honor of Russel B. Nye p74-91

Northwest, Pacific—History and criticism

Venn, G. Continuity in Northwest literature. *In* Bingham, E. R. and Love, G. A. eds. Northwest perspectives p99-118

Southern States—History and criticism

Gray, R. J. Aftermath: Southern literature since World War II. *In* Gray, R. J. The literature of memory p257-305

Gray, R. J. The Nashville Agrarians. *In* Gray, R. J. The literature of memory p40-105

Gray, R. J. The social and historical context. *In* Gray, R. J. The literature of memory p 1-39

Holman, C. H. Her rue with a difference: Flannery O'Connor and the Southern literary tradition. *In* Friedman, M. J. and Lawson, L. A. eds. The added dimension p73-87

Howe, I. Southern Agrarians and American culture. *In* Howe, I. Celebrations and attacks p161-65

Rubin, L. D. Fugitives as Agrarians: the impulse behind I'll take my stand. *In* Rubin, L. D. William Elliott shoots a bear p145-63

Rubin, L. D. Is the Southern literary renascence over?: a sort of cautionary epistle. *In* The Rising South v 1 p72-91

Rubin, L. D. Second thoughts on the Old Gray Mare. *In* Rubin, L. D. William Elliott shoots a bear p250-69

Rubin, L. D. Southern literature: a Piedmont art. *In* Rubin, L. D. William Elliott shoots a bear p195-212

Simpson, L. P. The Southern Review and a post-Southern American letters. *In* Anderson, E. and Kinzie, M. eds. The little magazine in America: a documentary history p78-99

Stewart, R. Tidewater and frontier. *In* Inge, M. T. ed. The frontier humorists p281-91

Sullivan, W. Southern literature: the last twenty years. *In* Two decades of change p55-66

American loyalists

Ferguson, C. R. Carolina and Georgia patriot and loyalist militia in action, 1778-1783. *In* The Southern experience in the American Revolution p174-99

Modlin, C. E. The loyalists' reply. *In* Emerson, E. H. ed. American literature, 1764-1789 p59-71

Shay, J. W. Armed loyalism: the case of the lower Hudson Valley. *In* Shy, J. W. A people numerous and armed p181-92

Wright, E. The loyalists. *In* Allen, H. C. and Thompson, R. eds. Contrast and connection p113-48

Bibliography

Leventhal, H. and Mooney, J. E. eds. A bibliography of loyalist source material in the United States. Part I. *In* American Antiquarian Society. Proceedings v85 pt 1 p73-308

Leventhal, H. and Mooney, J. E. eds A bibliography of loyalist source material in the United States, Part II. *In* American Antiquarian Society. Proceedings v85 pt.2 p405-60

Leventhal, H. and Mooney, J. E. eds. A bibliography of loyalist source material in the United States, Part III. *In* American Antiquarian Society. Proceedings v86 pt2 p343-90

Mooney, J. E. Loyalist imprints printed in America, 1774-1785. *In* American Antiquarian Society. Proceedings v84 pt 1 p105-218

American medical assistance. See Medical assistance, American

American missionaries. See Missionaries, American

American mystery stories. See Detective and mystery stories, American

American national characteristics. See National characteristics, American

American newspapers

Oakes, J. B. The responsibility of the press. *In* Tomorrow's American p171-88

Weaver, P. H. Newspaper news and television news. *In* Television as a social force: new approaches to TV criticism p81-94

Social aspects

Street, D. and Street, W. P. Print media in urban society. *In* Handbook of contemporary urban life p428-67

Southern States

Jenkins, R. Mass media changes in the South since World War II. *In* The Rising South v2 p126-40

American opinion of China. See China—Foreign opinion, American

American opinion of Japan. See Japan—Foreign opinion, American

American Party

Bennett, D. H. Women and the Nativist movement. *In* "Remember the ladies": new perspectives on women in American history p71-89

American periodicals

Circulation

Street, D. and Street, W. P. Print media in urban society. *In* Handbook of contemporary urban life p428-67

History

Granger, B. I. Conclusion. *In* Granger, B. I. American essay serials from Franklin to Irving p228-32

Boston—History

Granger, B. I. Early Boston serials. *In* Granger, B. I. American essay serials from Franklin to Irving p13-40

Philadelphia—History

Granger, B. I. Early Philadelphia serials. *In* Granger, B. I. American essay serials from Franklin to Irving p41-69

Southern States—History

Granger, B. I. Early Southern serials. *In* Granger, B. I. American essay serials from Franklin to Irving p70-96

American philosophy. See Philosophy, American

American poetry

History and criticism

Adams, P. G. The continuing echo. *In* Adams, P. G. Graces of harmony p164-89

Coxe, L. O. Poetry and—religion? *In* Coxe, L. O. Enabling acts p96-113

Shapiro, K. J. American poet? *In* Shapiro, K. J. The poetry wreck p323-52

Shapiro, K. J. Is poetry an American art? *In* Shapiro, K. J. The poetry wreck p224-44

Thurley, G. American poetry: sketch of a theory. *In* Thurley, G. The American moment p3-32

Thurley, G. The intellectualist position. *In* Thurley, G. The ironic harvest p 1-22

Wilbur, R. Poetry and happiness. *In* Wilbur, R. Responses p91-114

Afro-American authors

Hull, G. T. Afro-American women poets: a bio-critical survey. *In* Gilbert, S. M. and Gubar, S. eds. Shakespeare's sisters p165-82

Rushing, A. B. Images of Black women in Afro-American poetry. *In* Harley, S. and Terborg-Penn, R. eds. The Afro-American woman p74-84

Williams, S. A. The blues roots of contemporary Afro-American poetry. *In* Fisher, D. and Stepto, R. B. eds. Afro-American literature p72-87

Women authors—History and criticism

Gelpi, B. C. A common language: the American poet. *In* Gilbert, S. M. and Gubar, S. eds. Shakespeare's sisters p269-79

Gilbert, S. M. and Gubar, S. Introduction: gender, creativity, and the woman poet. *In* Gilbert, S. M. and Gubar, S. eds. Shakespeare's sisters p xv-xxvi

Colonial period, ca. 1600-1775— History and criticism

Daly, R. J. Ars poetica. *In* Daly, R. J. God's altar p40-81

Daly, R. J. Gnostics and naturalists. *In* Daly, R. J. God's altar p128-61

Daly, R. J. The world's body. *In* Daly, R. J. God's altar p6-39

Colonial period, ca. 1600-1775— History and criticism—Bibliography

Daly, R. J. Appendix: In critic's hands: a bibliographical essay. *In* Daly, R. J. God's altar p201-23

20th century—Bibliography

Breslin, J. E. Poetry: the 1930s to the present. *In* American literary scholarship, 1977 p365-87

Crowder, R. Poetry: 1900 to the 1930s. *In* American literary scholarship, 1973 p304-28

Crowder, R. Poetry: 1900 to the 1930s [another essay] *In* American literary scholarship, 1974 p321-44

Crowder, R. Poetry: 1900 to the 1930s [another essay] *In* American literary scholarship,, 1975 p363-78

Crowder, R. Poetry: 1900 to the 1930s [another essay] *In* American literary scholarship, 1976 p319-37

Crowder, R. Poetry: 1900 to the 1930s [another essay] *In* American literary scholarship, 1977 p343-64

Wagner, L. W. Poetry: the 1930s to the present. *In* American literary scholarship, 1973 p329-68

Wagner, L. W. Poetry: the 1930s to the present [another essay] *In* American literary scholarship 1974 p345-71

Wagner, L. W. Poetry: the 1930s to the present [another essay] *In* American literary scholarship, 1975 p379-98

Wagner, L. W. Poetry: the 1930s to the present [another essay] *In* American literary scholarship, 1976 p339-54

20th century—History and criticism

Altieri, C. F. Introduction. *In* Altieri, C. F. Enlarging the temple p15-26

Berry, W. The specialization of poetry. *In* Gibbons, R. ed. The poet's work: 29 masters of 20th century poetry on the origins and practice of their art p139-56

Berryman, J. From the middle and senior generations. *In* Berryman, J. The freedom of the poet p310-15

Berryman, J. Poetry chronicle, 1948: waiting for the end, boys. *In* Berryman, J. The freedom of the poets p297-309

Eberhart, R. On Theodore Roethke's poetry. *In* Eberhart, R. Of poetry and poets p172-78

Eberhart, R. West coast rhythms. *In* Eberhart, R. Of poetry and poets p144-47

Kalstone, D. Introduction: Imagined lives. *In* Kalstone, D. Five temperaments p3-11

Kenner, H. Classroom accuracies. *In* Kenner, H. A homemade world p158-93

Kunitz, S. J. Quick studies. *In* Kunitz, S. J. A kind of order, a kind of folly p251-61

Miller, J. E. Bards of the great idea: seekers of the supreme fiction. *In* Miller, J. E. The American quest for a supreme fiction p318-32

Miller, J. E. The care & feeding of long poems: the American epic from Barlow to Berryman. *In* Miller, J. E. The American quest for a supreme fiction p12-29

Mills, R. J. Creation's very self: on the personal element in recent American poetry. *In* Mills, R. J. Cry of the human p1-47

Rosenthal, M. L. Some thoughts on American poetry today. *In* Boyers, R. ed. Contemporary poetry in America p16-29

Scannell, V. American poets of the Second World War. *In* Scannell, V. Not without glory p172-237

Shapiro, K. J. The poetry wreck. *In* Shapiro, K. J. The poetry wreck p353-65

Snodgrass, W. D. Tact and the poet's force. *In* Snodgrass, W. D. In radical pursuit p3-22

Thurley, G. American poetry: sketch of a theory. *In* Thurley, G. The American moment p3-32

Vernon, J. E. Fresh air: humor in contemporary American poetry. *In* Cohen, S. B. ed. Comic relief p304-23

Webber, J. Walking on water: Milton, Stevens, and contemporary American poetry. *In* Wittreich, J. A. ed. Milton and the line of vision p231-68

Zweig, P. The new surrealism. *In* Boyers, R. ed. Contemporary poetry in America p314-29

American prose literature

History and criticism

Spengemann, W. C. The poetics of adventure. *In* Spengemann, W. C. The adventurous muse p6-67

American Revolution. See United States—History—Revolution, 1775-1783

American Revolution Bicentennial, 1776-1976
Collier, A. T. On celebrating American independence. *In* Warner, S. B. ed. The American experiment p 1-10

MacLeish. A. The ghost of Thomas Jefferson. *In* MacLeish, A. Riders on the earth p57-65

American satire. See Satire, American

American science fiction. See Science fiction, American

American tales. See Tales, American

American Telephone and Telegraph Company
Debutts, J. D. The management of complexity. *In* Benton, L. R. ed. Management for the future p77-86

American University of Beirut
Kedourie, E. The American University of Beirut. *In* Kedourie, E. Arabic political memoirs and other studies p59-72

American wit and humor
Cohen, S. B. Introduction: the variety of humors. *In* Cohen, S. B. ed. Comic relief p 1-13

Cohn, R. Camp, cruelty, colloquialism. *In* Cohen, S. B. ed. Comic relief p281-303

Garrett, G. P. Ladies in Boston have their hats: notes on WASP humor. *In* Cohen, S. B. ed. Comic relief p207-37

Pinsker, S. The urban tall tale: frontier humor in a contemporary key. *In* Cohen, S. B. ed. Comic relief p249-62

Stevick, P. Prolegomena to the study of fictional dreck. *In* Cohen, S. B. ed. Comic relief p263-80

White, E. B. Some remarks on humor. *In* White, E. B. Essays of E. B. White p243-49

See also Humorous poetry, American

Middle West—History and criticism
McCann, W. Kin Hubbard and journalistic humor in the Midwest. *In* Essays in honor of Russel B. Nye p129-40

Southern States—Bibliography
Davis, C. E. and Hudson, M. B. Humor of the Old Southwest: a checklist of criticism. *In* Inge, M. T. ed. The frontier humorists p303-23

Southern States—History and criticism
Blair, W. Humor of the Old Southwest; excerpt from "Native American humor." *In* Inge, M. T. ed. The frontier humorists p45-82

Collins, C. E. Faulkner and certain earlier Southern fiction. *In* Inge, M. T. ed. The frontier humorists p259-65

Covici, P. Mark Twain and the humor of the Old Southwest; excerpt from "Mark Twain's humor: the image of a world." *In* Inge, M. T. ed. The frontier humorists p233-58

Holman, C. H. Detached laughter in the South. *In* Cohen, S. B. ed. Comic relief p87-104

Also in Holman, C. H. Windows on the world p27-47

Meine, F. J. Tall tales of the Southwest. *In* Inge, M. T. ed. The frontier humorists p15-31

Rose, A. H. Blackness in the fantastic world of old Southwestern humor. *In* Rose, A. H. Demonic vision p19-38

Thorp, W. Suggs and Sut in modern dress: the latest chapter in Southern humor. *In* Inge, M. T. ed. The frontier humorists p292-99

Wade, J. D. Southern humor. *In* Inge, M. T. ed. The frontier humorists p32-44

American women poets. See Women poets, American

Americanisms
Crystal, D. American English in Europe. *In* Bigsby, C. W. E. Superculture p57-68

Americanization
Mann, A. The melting pot. *In* Uprooted Americans p288-318

Rolle, A. F. The American Italians: psychological and social adjustments. *In* Studies in Italian American social history p105-17

Valletta, C. L. Family life: the question of independence. *In* Studies in Italian American social history p153-63

Americans in foreign countries
Smelstor, M. R. Expatriation and exploration: the exiled artists of the 1920s. *In* Kagle, S. E. ed. America: exploration and travel p136-52

Americans in France
MacLeish, A. Autobiographical information. *In* MacLeish, A. Riders on the earth p69-81

MacLeish, A. Expatriates in Paris. *In* MacLeish, A. Riders on the earth p89-93

Tate, A. Miss Toklas' American cake. *In* Tate, A. Memoirs and opinions, 1926-1974 p46-66

Americans in literature
Falk, R. Henry James's The American as a centennial novel. *In* Essays in honor of Russel B. Nye p31-41

Fraser, R. The American background in Why are we so blest? *In* African literature today no. 9: Africa, America and the Caribbean p39-46

Ames, Dianne Sigler
Strawberry Hill: architecture of the "as if." *In* Studies in eighteenth-century culture v8 p351-63

Ameuhaque Indians. See Amahuaca Indians

Amharas

Social life and customs
Reminick, R. A. The evil eye belief among the Amhara. *In* The Evil eye p85-101

Amiel, Henri Frédéric

About
Arnold, M. Amiel. *In* Arnold, M. The last word p265-81

Amin, Idi

About
Mazrui, A. A. The de-Indianization of Uganda: who is a citizen? *In* Smock, D. R. and Bentsi-Enchill, K. eds. The search for national integration in Africa p77-90

Mazrui, A. A. Ethnic stratification and the military-agrarian complex: the Uganda case. *In* Glazer, N. and Moynihan, D. P. eds. Ethnicity p420-49

Welch, C. E. The OAU and international recognition: lessons from Uganda. *In* El-Ayouty, Y. ed. The Organization of African Unity after ten years p103-17

Amino acid synthesis

Cohen, S. S. On the origins of cells: the development of a Copernican revolution. *In* Neyman, J. ed. The heritage of Copernicus: theories "pleasing to the mind" p207-27

Amino acids

Margoliash, E. Informational macromolecules and biological evolution. *In* Neyman, J. ed. The heritage of Copernicus: theories "pleasing to the mind" p184-206

Miller, S. L. The first laboratory synthesis of organic compounds under primitive earth conditions. *In* Neyman, J. ed. The heritage of Copernicus: theories "pleasing to the mind" p228-42

Amirthanayagam, Guy

Literature as culture. *In* Narasimhaiah, C. D. ed. Awakened conscience p433-40

Amis, Kingsley

The situation today; excerpt from "New maps of hell." *In* Knight, D. F. ed. Turning points p100-16

Amish

Hostetler, J. A. Folk medicine and sympathy healing among the Amish. *In* American folk medicine p249-58

MacLeish, A. News from the horse and wagon. *In* MacLeish, A. Riders on the earth p48-56

Ammerman, Albert J.; Cavalli-Sforza, Luigi Luca, and Wagener, Diane K.

Toward the estimation of population growth in Old World prehistory. *In* Zubrow, E. B. W. ed. Demographic anthropology p27-61

Ammianus Marcellinus

About

Momigliano, A. The lonely historian Ammianus Marcellinus. *In* Momigliano, A. Essays in ancient and modern historiography p127-40

Ammon (Egyptian deity). See Amon (Egyptian deity)

Ammonius

About

Jones, C. P. The teacher of Plutarch. *In* Harvard Studies in classical philology v71 p205-13

Ammons, A. R.

About

Lieberman, L. A. R. Ammons: of mind and world. *In* Lieberman, L. Unassigned frequencies p62-73

Lieberman, L. M. B. Tolson and A. R. Ammons: book-length poems. *In* Lieberman, L. Unassigned frequencies p252-56

Waggoner, H. H. The poetry of A. R. Ammons: some notes and reflections. *In* Boyers, R. ed. Contemporary poetry in America p330-38

Amnesia. See Aphasia

Amon (Egyptian deity)

Lawal, B. Yoruba-Sango ram symbolism: from ancient Sahara or dynastic Egypt? *In* African images p225-51

Amory, Anne. See Parry, Anne

Amos, Dan Ben- See Ben-Amos, Dan

Amos, Paula Ben- See Ben-Amos, Paula

Amphoras

Grace, V. R. Exceptional amphora stamps. *In* Studies in classical art and archaeology p115-27

Amputees

Psychology

Price, D. B. Miraculous restoration of lost body parts: relationship to the phantom limb phenomenon and to limb-burial superstitions and practices. *In* American folk medicine p49-71

Amsterdam, Anthony G.

Speedy criminal trial: rights and remedies. *In* Stanford legal essays p 1-19

Amulets

Hole, C. Protective symbols in the home. *In* Symbols of power p121-30

See also Charms

Amur, G. S.

Peter Nazareth's 'In a brown mantle': novel as revolutionary art. *In* Narasimhaiah, C. D. ed. Awakened conscience p111-17

Amusements. See Play; Riddles

Amuzegar, Jahangir

The oil story: facts, fiction and fair play. *In* Bundy, W. P. ed. The world economic crisis p69-82

Anacreontea. See Cicada (Greek Anacreontic poem)

Anagogy, aevum and two later medieval visionary arts. Nolan, B. *In* Nolan, B. The Gothic visionary perspective p35-83

Analogy (Linguistics)

Wicker, B. Metaphor and 'analogy.' *In* Wicker, B. The story-shaped world p11-32

Wicker, B. Metaphor and 'God.' *In* Wicker, B. The story-shaped world p71-106

Analogy (Religion) See Anthropomorphism

Analysis (Philosophy)

Durfee, H. A. Analytic philosophy, phenomenology, and the concept of consciousness. *In* Thought, consciousness, and reality p111-30

Keenan, E. L. Logic and language. *In* Bloomfield, M. W. and Haugen, E. I. eds. Language as a human problem p187-96

Pivčević, E. Concepts, phenomenology and philosophical understanding. *In* Pivčević, E. ed. Phenomenology and philosophical understanding p271-86

Tugendhat, E. Phenomenology and linguistic analysis. *In* Elliston, F. A. and McCormick, P. eds. Husserl p325-37

Weinberg, J. R. Logic and the laws of nature. *In* Weinberg, J. R. Ockham, Descartes, and Hume p151-62

See also Linguistic analysis (Linguistics); Logical positivism; Semantics (Philosophy)

Analysis, Linguistic (Linguistics) See Linguistic analysis (Linguistics)

Analysis, Philosophical. See Analysis (Philosophy)

Anand, Mulk Raj

Variety of ways: is there a shared tradition in Commonwealth literature? *In* Narasimhaiah, C. D. ed. Awakened conscience p441-46

About

Singh, R. S. From resentment to social protest: Mulk Raj Anand. *In* Singh, R. S. Indian novel in English p38-54

Anang, Michael Dei-. See Dei-Anang, Michael

Anania, Michael
Of living belfry and rampart: on American literary magazines since 1950. *In* Anderson, E. and Kenzie, M. eds. The little magazine in America: a modern documentary history p6-23

Anaphora (Linguistics)
Stenning, K. Anaphora as an approach to pragmatics. *In* Linguistic theory and psychological reality p162-200

Anarchism and anarchists
Greene, M. Paul Goodman and anarchistic education. *In* Social forces and schooling p313-36
Parry, A. Anarchists: philosophers with bombs. *In* Parry, A. Terrorism from Robespierre to Arafat p78-91
Voegelin, E. Bakunin: the anarchist. *In* Voegelin, E. From Enlightenment to revolution p217-39
See also Liberty; Socialism; Terrorism

Russia
Parry, A. Hunting the Tsar. *In* Parry, A. Terrorism: from Robespierre to Arafat p107-19

United States
DeLeon, D. Old visions of the New World. *In* DeLeon, D. The American as anarchist p125-33

United States—History
DeLeon, D. Left libertarianism. *In* DeLeon, D. The American as anarchist p85-101
DeLeon, D. Overview. *In* DeLeon, D. The American as anarchist p3-13
DeLeon, D. Right libertarianism. *In* DeLeon, D. The American as anarchist p61-84
Parry, A. America's pie. *In* Parry, A. Terrorism: from Robespierre to Arafat p92-106

Anarchy. See Anarchism and anarchists

Anātman. See Ātman

Anatomists, American
Harvey, A. M. A new school of anatomy: the story of Franklin P. Mall, Florence R. Sabin, and John B. MacCallum. *In* Harvey, A. M. Adventures in medical research p97-113

Anatomy
See also Histology

Terminology
Temkin, O. The Byzantine origin of the names for the basilic and cephalic veins. *In* Temkin, O. The double face of Janus p198-201

Anatomy, Comparative. See Morphology (Animals)

Anatomy, Microscopic. See Histology

Ancel, Marc
The relationship between criminology and 'politique criminelle.' *In* Crime, criminology and public policy p269-80

Ancestry. See Heredity

Ancient geography. See Geography, Ancient

Ancient sculpture. See Sculpture, Ancient

Ancona, Leonardo
Considerations on Christian vocations seen from the point of view of psychoanalysis. *In* Wolman, B. B. ed. Psychoanalysis and Catholicism p65-96

Ancourt, Florent Carton, sieur d', called Dancourt. See Dancourt, Florent Carton, sieur d'Ancourt, called

Ancren riwle
Raw, B. C. The prayers and devotions in the Ancrene wisse. *In* Chaucer and Middle English studies in honour of Rossell Hope Robbins p260-71

Ancrene wisse. See Ancren riwle

And God created woman (Motion picture)
Trufaut, F. Roger Vadim: Et Dieu créa la femme. *In* Truffaut, F. The films in my life p311-12

Andemicael, Berhanykun
OAU collaboration with the United Nations in economic and social development. *In* El-Ayouty, Y. ed. The Organization of African Unity after ten years p213-36

Andersen, Hans Christian

About
Haugaard, E. C. Random thoughts by a translator of Andersen. *In* Horn Book Magazine. Crosscurrents of criticism p277-82

About individual works
The complete fairy tales and stories
Mudrick, M. The ugly duck. *In* Mudrick, M. Books are not life but then what is? p87-97

Anderson, Alan B. and others
Sociology in Canada: a developmental overview. *In* Mohan, R. P. and Martindale, D. A. eds. Handbook of contemporary developments in world sociology p159-71

Anderson, Anne
The home of We-sake-cha. *In* Egoff, S. A. ed. One ocean touching p181-85

Anderson, B. L.
Law, finance and economic growth in England: some long-term influences. *In* Great Britain and her world, 1750-1914 p99-124

Anderson, Barbara Gallatin
The changing Frenchwoman: her challenged world. *In* Matthiasson, C. J. ed. Many sisters p59-75

Anderson, Charles Arnold, and Bowman, Mary Jean
Education and economic modernization in historical perspective. *In* Schooling and society p3-19

Anderson, Charles B.
Mark Twain at ABA. *In* Bookselling in America and the world p195-98

Anderson, Chester G.
Baby Tuckoo: Joyce's "features of infancy." *In* Staley, T. F. and Benstock, B. eds. Approaches to Joyce's Portrait p135-68

Anderson, David D.
Anderson and myth. *In* Anderson, D. D. ed. Sherwood Anderson: dimensions of his literary art p118-41

Anderson, Earl Robert
Social idealism in Ælfric's Colloquy. *In* Anglo-Saxon England 3 p153-62

Anderson, George Lester
Land-grant universities and their continuing challenge. *In* Land-grant universities and their continuing challege p 1-10

Anderson, George Lester, and Mortimer, Kenneth Paul
Governance and control of tomorrow's university: whose values? *In* Land-grant universities and their continuing challenge p326-49

Anderson, George Lincoln

Mr. Abel Boyer stops the press. *In* Virginia. University. Bibliographical Society. Studies in bibliography v29 p292-95

Anderson, Gerald Harry

The Philippines: reluctant beneficiary of the missionary impulse in Europe. *In* First images of America p391-403

Religion as a problem for the Christian mission. *In* Christian faith in a religiously plural world p104-16

Anderson, James Douglas

Education as a vehicle for the manipulation of Black workers. *In* Feinberg, W. and Rosemont, H. eds. Work, technology, and education p15-40

Anderson, John P.

Practical reasoning in action. *In* Douglas, J. D. and Johnson, J. M. [eds.] Existential sociology p174-98

Anderson, John Q.

Mike Hooter—the making of a myth. *In* Inge, M. T. ed. The frontier humorists p197-207

Texas and Southwest medical lore in the Anderson Collection, University of Houston. *In* American folk medicine p315-19

Anderson, Lindsay

About

Taylor, J. R. Lindsay Anderson. *In* Taylor, J. R. Directors and directions p69-99

Anderson, Malcolm

Power and inflation. *In* The Political economy of inflation p240-62

Anderson, Maxwell

About

Nicoll, A. The vogue of the historical play. *In* Nicoll, A. World drama p727-40

Anderson, Michael John

The comedy of Greece and Rome. *In* Howarth, W. D. ed. Comic drama p22-39

Anderson, Odin Waldemar

The model health service—a search for utopia. *In* The Frontiers of human knowledge p29-43

Anderson, Olive

The Administrative Reform Association, 1855-1857. *In* Hollis, P. ed. Pressure from without p262-88

Anderson, Poul

How to build a planet. *In* Knight, D. F. ed. Turning points p205-14

Anderson, Quentin

On The middle of the journey. *In* Art, politics, and will p254-64

About individual works

The American Henry James

Howe, I. Henry James as latter-day saint. *In* Howe, I. Celebrations and attacks p72-79

The imperial self

Gonnaud, M. Emerson and the imperial self: a European critique. *In* Levin, D. ed. Emerson: prophecy, metamorphosis, and influence p107-28

Anderson, Robert Fendel

The location, extension, shape, and size of Hume's perceptions. *In* Livingston, D. W. and King, J. T. eds. Hume p153-71

Anderson, Sherwood

About

Anderson, D. D. Anderson and myth. *In* Anderson, D. D. ed. Sherwood Anderson: dimensions of his literary art p118-41

Baldeshwiler, E. Sherwood Anderson and the lyric story. *In* French, W. G. ed. The twenties p65-74

Curry, M. M. Anderson's theories on writing fiction. *In* Anderson, D. D. ed. Sherwood Anderson: dimensions of his literary art p90-109

Goist, P. D. The ideal questioned but not abandoned: Sherwood Anderson, Sinclair Lewis, and Floyd Dell. *In* Goist, P. D. From Main Street to State Street p21-34

Miller, W. V. Portraits of the artist: Anderson's fictional storytellers. *In* Anderson, D. D. ed. Sherwood Anderson: dimensions of his literary art p 1-23

Morris, W. Sherwood Anderson. *In* Morris, W. Earthly delights, unearthly adornments p81-88

Sutton, W. A. Anderson's letters to Marietta D. Finley Hahn: a literary chronicle. *In* Anderson, D. D. ed. Sherwood Anderson: dimensions of his literary art p110-17

Tanner, T. Sherwood Anderson's little things. *In* Tanner, T. The reign of wonder p205-27

Taylor, W. D. Anderson and the problem of belonging. *In* Anderson, D. D. ed. Sherwood Anderson: dimensions of his literary art p61-74

Wagner L. W. Sherwood, Stein, the sentence, and grape sugar and oranges. *In* Anderson, D. D. ed. Sherwood Anderson: dimensions of his literary art p75-89

Weber, B. Sherwood Anderson. *In* Walcutt, C. C. ed. Seven novelists in the American naturalist tradition p168-204

White, R. L. The warmth of desire: sex in Anderson's novels. *In* Anderson, D. D. ed. Sherwood Anderson: dimensions of his literary art p24-40

About individual works

Dark laughter

Lewis, W. Sherwood Anderson; excerpt from "Paleface." *In* Lewis, W. Enemy salvoes p127-31

I want to know why

Fetterley, J. Palpable designs: four American short stories: Growing up male in America:: "I want to know why." *In* Fetterley, J. The resisting reader p12-22

Mary Cochran

Pfeiffer, W. S. Mary Cochran: Sherwood Anderson's ten-year novel. *In* Virginia. University. Bibliographical Society. Studies in bibliography v31 p248-57

A story teller's story

Cooley, T. The next generation; then as now: Sherwood Anderson. *In* Cooley, T. Educated lives: the rise of modern autobiography in America p138-56

Talbot Whittingham

Rideout, W. B. Talbot Whittingham and Anderson: a passage to Winesburg, Ohio. *In* Anderson, D. D. ed. Sherwood Anderson: dimensions of his literary art p41-60

Anderson Sherwood—About individual works
—*Continued*

Winesburg, Ohio

Weber, B. Sherwood Anderson. *In* Walcutt, C. C. ed. Seven novelists in the American naturalist tradition p168-204

Bibliography

White, R. L. Sherwood Anderson: fugitive pamphlets and broadsides, 1918-1940. *In* Virginia. University. Bibliographical Society. Studies in bibliography v31 p257-63

Criticism and interpretation

Meriwether, J. B. Faulkner's essays on Anderson. *In* Faulkner: fifty years after The marble faun p159-81

Anderson, Victor Elving

Evangelicals and science: fifty years after the Scopes trial (1925-75). *In* Wells, D. F. and Woodbridge, J. D. eds. The evangelicals p249-68

Anderson, Wallace E.

Cartesian motion. *In* Motion and time, space and matter p200-23

Anderson, Warren D.

Arnold and the classics. *In* Allott, K. ed. Matthew Arnold p259-85

Menander and Molière. *In* Johnson, R. B.; Neumann, E. S. and Trail, G. T. eds. Molière and the commonwealth of letters: patrimony and posterity p413-16

Anderson, William Scovil

Autobiography and art in Horace. *In* Perspectives of Roman poetry p33-56

Studies on the Naples Ms. IV F 3 of Ovid's Metamorphoses. *In* Illinois classical studies, v2 1977 p255-79

Andersson, Theodore Murdock

The Icelandic sagas. *In* Oinas, F. J. ed. Heroic epic and saga p144-71

Andhra Pradesh, India

Politics and government

Gray, H. Konda Lakshman Bapuji: a backward classes leader of the Telengana (Andhra Pradesh). *In* The Making of politicians: studies from Africa and Asia p156-65

Andrade, Jorge

About

Mazzara, R. A. The theater of Jorge Andrade. *In* Lyday, L. F. and Woodyard, G. W. eds. Dramatists in revolt p205-20

Andrae, Walter

About individual works

Die ionische Säule: Bauform oder Symbol?

Coomaraswamy, A. K. Walter Andrae's Die ionische Säule: Bauform oder Symbol?: a review; excerpt from "Figures of thought or figures of speech: collected essays on the traditional or 'normal' view of art." *In* Coomaraswamy, A. K. Selected papers v 1 p341-49

Andre, John and Fröschle, Hartmut

The American expedition of Emperor Joseph II and Bernhard Moll's silhouettes. *In* The German contribution to the building of the Americas p135-72

Andre le Chapelain

About individual works

The art of courtly love

Bowden, B. The art of courtly copulation. *In* Medievalia et humanistica; new ser. no. 9 p67-85

Andrea, John de. See De Andrea, John

Andreas (Anglo-Saxon poem)

Hamilton, D. B. Andreas and Beowulf: placing the hero. *In* Anglo-Saxon poetry: essays in appreciation p81-98

Stevick, R. D. Arithmetical design of the Old English Andreas. *In* Anglo-Saxon poetry: essays in appreciation p99-115

Andreas Capellanus. See Andre le Chapelain

Andreas-Salomé, Lou

About individual works

The Freud journal of Lou Andreas-Salomé

Hamburger, M. Psycho-analysis and art. *In* Hamburger, M. Art as second nature p42-44

Andreasen, N. J. C.

Theme and structure in Donne's Satyres. *In* Roberts, J. R. ed. Essential articles for the study of John Donne's poetry p411-23

Andreev, German

The Christianity of L. N. Tolstoy and of the contributors to "From under the rubble." *In* Medvedev, R. A. ed. The Samizdat register p267-314

Andreev, Leonid Nikolaevich

About

Nicoll, A. The theatre symbolic and theatrical. *In* Nicoll, A. World drama p608-15

Andreski, Stanislav

Imperialism: past and future. *In* The Year book of world affairs, 1975 p313-19

Andrew, Edward

The unity of theory and practice: the science of Marx and Nietzsche. *In* Political theory and praxis p117-37

Andrewes, Lancelot, Bp. of Winchester

About

Eliot, T. S. Lancelot Andrewes. *In* Eliot, T. S. Selected prose of T. S. Eliot p179-88

Andrews, Edward Deming, and Andrews, Faith

About individual works

Shaker furniture, the craftsmanship of an American commercial set

Coomaraswamy, A. K. Shaker furniture; excerpt from "Figures of speech or figures of thought: collected essays on the traditional or 'normal' view of art." *In* Coomaraswamy, A. K. Selected papers v 1 p255-59

Andrews, Faith. See Andrews, E. D. jt. auth.

Andrews, Kevin

Time and the will lie sidestepped: Athens, the interval. *In* Time was away p103-09

Andrews, Richard M.

The justices of the peace of Revolutionary Paris, September 1792-November 1794 (Frimaire Year III). *In* French society and the Revolution p167-216

Andrews, William David

Philip Freneau and Francis Hopkinson. *In* Emerson, E. H. ed. American literature, 1764-1789 p127-44

Andreyev, Leonid. See Andreev, Leonid Nikolaevich

Andreyev, Nikolay

Appanage and Muscovite Russia. *In* Auty, R. and Obolensky, D. eds. An introduction to Russian history p78-120

Andreyev, Nikolay—*Continued*

Literature in the Muscovite period (1300-1700). *In* Auty, R. and Obolensky, D. eds. An introduction to Russian language and literature p90-110

Andringa, Robert C.

A view from Capitol Hill. *In* Hook, S.; Kurtz, P. W. and Todorovich, M. eds. The university and the state: what role for government in higher education? p133-36

Androgynous behavior. See Androgyny (Psychology)

Androgyny (Psychology)

Ferguson, A. Androgyny as an ideal for human development. *In* Feminism and philosophy p45-69

Trebilcot, J. Two forms of androgynism. *In* Feminism and philosophy p70-78

Androgyny (Psychology) in literature

Harrison, A. H. The aesthetics of androgyny in Swinburne's early poetry. *In* Tennessee Studies in literature v23 p87-99

Showalter, E. Virginia Woolf and the flight into androgyny. *In* Showalter, E. A literature of their own p263-97

Anes de Soverosa, Vataça. See Soverosa, Vataça Anes de

Anfortas. See Fisher King

Angel, J. R.

Indonesian foreign policy since independence: changing preoccupations in pursuit of progress. *In* The Year book of world affairs, 1977 p46-63

Angel of Philadelphia. See Guiard of Cressonessart

Angelico, Fra. See Fiesole, Giovanni da, called Fra Angelico

Angels

Art

Winternitz, E. On angel concerts in the 15th century: a critical approach to realism and symbolism in sacred painting. *In* Winternitz, E. Musical instruments and their symbolism in Western art p137-49

Angermann, Erich

The impact of the American Revolution on Germany—a comment. *In* The Impact of the American Revolution abroad p160-63

Anglican Church. See Church of England

Anglin, Douglas George. See Shaw, T. M. jt. auth.

Anglo-American law. See Common law

Anglo-French War, 1294-1298

Strayer, J. R. The costs and profits of war: the Anglo-French conflict of 1294-1303. *In* The Medieval city p269-91

Anglo-Norman literature

History and criticism

Legge, M. D. Anglo-Norman hagiography and the romances. *In* Medievalia et humanistica no.6 p41-49

Anglo-Saxon architecture. See Architecture, Anglo-Saxon

Anglo-Saxon art. See Art, Anglo-Saxon

Anglo-Saxon chronicle

Parkes, M. B. The palaeography of the Parker manuscript of the Chronicle, laws and Sedulius, and historiography at Winchester in the late ninth and tenth centuries. *In* Anglo-Saxon England 5 p149-71

Anglo-Saxon civilization

Bibliography

See Civilization, Anglo-Saxon—Bibliography

Anglo-Saxon coins. See Coins, Anglo-Saxon

Anglo-Saxon illumination of books and manuscripts. See Illumination of books and manuscripts, Anglo-Saxon

Anglo-Saxon language

Derolez, R. L. M. Cross-Channel language ties. *In* Anglo-Saxon England 3 p 1-14

Etymology—Names

Gelling, M. Latin loan-words in Old English place-names. *In* Anglo-Saxon England 6 p 1-13

Glossaries, vocabularies, etc.

Law, V. The Latin and Old English glosses in the Ars Tatuini. *In* Anglo-Saxon England 6 p77-89

Terms and phrases

Barley, N. F. Old English colour classification: where do matters stand? *In* Anglo-Saxon England 3 p15-28

Rahtz, P. and Bullough, D. A. The parts of an Anglo-Saxon mill. *In* Anglo-Saxon England 6 p15-37

Anglo-Saxon literature

Bibliography

Mitchell, B. C.; Ball, C. and Cameron, A. F. Short titles of Old English texts. *In* Anglo-Saxon England 4 p207-21

Scragg, D. G. Old English literature. *In* English Association. The year's work in English studies v53 p67-83

Scragg, D. G. Old English literature [another essay] *In* English Association. The year's work in English studies v54 p69-82

Scragg, D. G. Old English literature [another essay] *In* English Association. The year's work in English studies v55 p76-91

Shippey, T. A. Old English literature. *In* English Association. The year's work in English studies v56 p63-80

Shippey, T. A. Old Engllish literature [another essay] *In* English Association. The year's work in English studies v57 p43-59

History and criticism

Day, V. The influence of the catechetical narratio on Old English and some other medieval literature. *In* Anglo-Saxon England 3 p51-61

Gatch, M. M. Old English literature and the liturgy: problems and potential. *In* Anglo-Saxon England 6 p237-47

Grant, R. J. S. Laurence Nowell's transcript of BM Cotton Otho B. xi. *In* Anglo-Saxon England 3 p111-24

Swanton, M. Heroes, heroism and heroic literature. *In* English Association. Essays and studies, 1977 p 1-21

Trahern, J. B. Caesarius of Arles and Old English literature: some contributions and a recapitulation. *In* Anglo-Saxon England 5 p105-19

History and criticism—Bibliography

Theiner, P. F. Medieval English literature. *In* Powell, J. M. ed. Medieval studies p239-75

Anglo-Saxon literature—*Continued*
Study and teaching
Quirk, R. The 'language' of language and literature. *In* Quirk, R. The linguist and the English language p65-76

Anglo-Saxon magic. See Magic, Anglo-Saxon

Anglo-Saxon manuscripts. See Manuscripts, Anglo-Saxon

Anglo-Saxon numismatics. See Numismatics, Anglo-Saxon

Anglo-Saxon poetry
Blake, N. F. The dating of Old English poetry. *In* An English miscellany p14-27
Luecke, J. M. Measuring Old English rhythm: measuring the rhythm of the Five Types. *In* Literary monographs v9 p75-95
Luecke, J. M. Measuring Old English rhythm: surveying the history of Old English prosody. *In* Literary monographs v9 p4-30
Luecke, J. M. Measuring Old English rhythm: the suspect verses and a summary. *In* Literary monographs v9 p96-111

Criticism, Textual
Cross, . E. The poem in transmitted text —editor and critic. *In* English Association. Essays and studies, 1974 p84-97

History and criticism
Diamond, R. E. The diction of the Old English Christ. *In* Anglo-Saxon poetry: essays in appreciation p301-11
Hieatt, C. B. The rhythm of the alliterative long line. *In* Chaucer and Middle English studies in honour of Rossell Hope Robbins p119-30
Hume, K. The concept of the hall in Old English poetry. *In* Anglo-Saxon England 3 p63-74
Mitchell, B. C. Linguistic facts and the interpretation of Old English poetry. *In* Anglo-Saxon England 4 p11-28
Renoir, A. A reading context for The wife's lament. *In* Anglo-Saxon poetry: essays in appreciation p224-41
Schroeder, P. R. Stylistic analogies between Old English art and poetry. *In* Viator: medieval and Renaissance studies v5 p185-97

Anglo-Saxon prose literature
Bibliography
Gatch, M. M. Beginnings continued: a decade of studies of Old English prose. *In* Anglo-Saxon England 5 p225-43

Anglo-Saxons
Loyn, H. R. Kinship in Anglo-Saxon England. *In* Anglo-Saxon England 3 p197-209
Meinhard, H. H. The patrilineal principle in early Teutonic kinship. *In* Studies in social anthropology p 1-29

Genealogy
Dumville, D. N. The Anglian collection of royal genealogies and regnal lists. *In* Anglo-Saxon England 5 p23-50

Anglo-Saxons in Byzantium
Fell, C. E. The Icelandic saga of Edward the Confessor: its version of the Anglo-Saxon emigration to Byzantium. *In* Anglo-Saxon England 3 p179-96

Angola
Valdés, N. P. Revolutionary solidarity in Angola. *In* Cuba in the world p87-117

Historiography
Bender, G. and Isaacman, A. F. The changing historiography of Angola and Mozambique. *In* African studies since 1945 p220-48

History
Marcum, J. Angola: division or unity? *In* Carter, G. M. and O'Meara, P. eds. Southern Africa in crisis p136-62

Politics and government
Marcum, J. Angola: division or unity? *In* Carter, G. M. and O'Meara, P. eds. Southern Africa in crisis p136-62
Marcum, J. A. Angola: perilous transition to independence. *In* Carter, G. M. and O'Meara, P. eds. Southern Africa: the continuing crisis p175-98
Wheeler, D. L. Rebels and rebellions in Angola, 1672-1892. *In* African dimensions p81-93

Angoni
Barnes, J. A. The material culture of the Fort Jameson Ngoni. *In* The Occasional papers of the Rhodes-Livingstone Museum p 1-20

Angress, Werner T.
The takeover that remained in limbo: the German experience, 1918-1923. *In* Hammond, T. T. ed. The anatomy of Communist takeovers p163-91

Animal babies. See Animals, Infancy of

Animal behavior. See Animals, Habits and behavior of

Animal communication
Bronowski, J. Human and animal languages. *In* Bronowski, J. A sense of the future p104-31
Bronowski, J. Language in a biological frame. *In* Bronowski, J. A sense of the future p132-54
Marler, P. Affective and symbolic meaning: some zoosemiotic speculations. *In* Sebeok, T. A. ed. Sight, sound, and sense p113-23

Animal folklore. See Animal lore
Animal heat
Coleman, W. Bergmann's rule: animal heat as a biological phenomenon. *In* Studies in history of biology v 3 p67-88

Animal intelligence. See Animals, Habits and behavior of

Animal language. See Animal communication

Animal lore
Radbill, S. X. The role of animals in infant feeding. *In* American folk medicine p21-30
See also Parapsychology and animals

Animal magnetism
Tatar, M. M. From Mesmer to Freud: animal magnetism, hypnosis, and suggestion. *In* Tatar, M. M. Spellbound p3-44
See also Mesmerism

Animal painting and illustration. See Animals in art

Animals
Mandel'shtam, O. E. Around the naturalists. *In* Mandel'shtam, O. E. Selected essays p196-200

Animals, Habits and behavior of
Beach, F. A. Sociobiology and interspecific comparisons of behavior. *In* Sociobiology and human nature p116-35

Animals, Habits and behavior of—*Continued*

Bischof, N. Comparative ethology of incest avoidance. *In* Biosocial anthropology p37-67

Chance, M. R. A. Social cohesion and the structure of attention. *In* Biosocial anthropology p93-113

Griffin, D. R. Humanistic aspects of ethology. *In* Sociobiology and human nature p240-59

Jones, N. B. Ethology, anthropology, and childhood. *In* Biosocial anthropology p69-92

Kass-Simon, G. Female strategies: animal adaptations and adaptive significance. *In* Roberts, J. I. ed. Beyond intellectual sexism p74-84

MacLean, P. D. The imitative-creative interplay of our three mentalities. *In* Harris, H. A. ed. Astride the two cultures p187-213

Thomas, L. The medusa and the snail. *In* Thomas, L. The medusa and the snail p 1-6

Thomas, L. The Tucson zoo. *In* Thomas, L. The medusa and the snail p7-11

Washburn, S. L. Animal behavior and social anthropology. *In* Sociobiology and human nature p53-74

See also Animals, Infancy of

Animals, Infancy of

Rowell, T. E. Growing up in a monkey group. *In* Schwartz, T. ed. Socialization as cultural communication p21-36

Animals, Legends and stories of. See Animals in literature; Fables

Animals and parapsychology. See Parapsychology and animals

Animals in art

Rice, T. T. Animal combat scenes in Byzantine art. *In* Studies in memory of David Talbot Rice p17-23

Animals in folklore. See Animal lore

Animals in literature

Benson, J. Hog in sloth, fox in stealth: man and beast in moral thinking. *In* Royal Institute of Philosophy. Nature and conduct p265-80

Edwards, M. S. The play of "downward comparisons": animal anthropomorphism in the poems of Robert Frost. *In* Frost: centennial essays II p236-45

Reed, R. The animal world in Robert Frost's poetry. *In* Frost: centennial essays II p159-69

Reed, T. J. Nietzsche's animals: idea, image and influence. *In* Pasley, J. M. S. ed. Nietzsche: imagery and thought p159-219

Rubin, L. D. Uncle Remus and the ubiquitous Rabbit. *In* Rubin, L. D. William Elliott shoots a bear p82-106

Steadman, J. M. Epilogue. *In* Steadman, J. M. Nature into myth p241-48

Animals in poetry. See Animals in literature

Animated cartoons. See Moving-picture cartoons

Animation (Cinematography) See Moving-picture cartoons

Animism. See Idealism; Materialism; Soul; Spiritualism; Transmigration

Ankori, Zvi

From Zudecha to Yahudi Mahallesi: the Jewish quarter of Candia in the seventeenth century. *In* Salo Wittmayer Baron v 1 p63-127

Annales

Hexter, J. H. Fernand Braudel and the monde braudellien. . . . *In* Hexter, J. H. On historians p61-145

Annenskii, Innokentii Fedorovich

The aesthetics of Gogol's Dead souls and its legacy. *In* Erlich, V. ed. Twentieth-century Russian literary criticism p51-60

Annenskij, Innokentij. See Annenskii, Innokentii Fedorovich

Anning, N. J.

Pasternak. *In* Freeborn, R. ed. Russian literary attitudes from Pushkin to Solzhenitsyn p99-119

Solzhenitsyn. *In* Freeborn, R. ed. Russian literary attitudes from Pushkin to Solzhenitsyn p120-40

Anniversaries. See Festivals

Annotations and citations (Law) See Law reports, digests, etc.

Annunzio, Gabriele d'

About

Ledeen, M. A. Italy: war as a style of life. *In* The War generation p104-34

Meyers, J. Gabriele D'Annunzio. *In* Meyers, J. A fever at the core p89-111

Pacifici, S. Gabriele d'Annunzio: the birth of superman. *In* Pacifici, S. The modern Italian novel: from Capuana to Tozzi p32-48

Perella, N. J. Gabriele d'Annunzio. *In* Perella, N. J. Midday in Italian literature p114-44

Anonyms and pseudonyms

Hamburger, M. On anonymity. *In* Hamburger, M. Art as second nature p34-37

Anonymus Ravennas. See Ravennas, Anonymus

Anouilh, Jean

About

Auger, P. P. Post-war drama in France and Belgium. *In* Nicoll, A. World drama p821-37

Anrig, Gregory Richard

Education in China. *In* Wagschal, P. H. ed. Learning tomorrows p63-72

Anscombe, Gertrude Elizabeth Margaret

The first person. *In* Guttenplan, S. D. ed. Mind and language p45-65

About individual works

Hume reconsidered

Weinberg, J. R. Two recent criticisms of Hume. *In* Weinberg, J. R. Ockham, Descartes, and Hume p135-40

Anselm, Saint, Abp. of Canterbury

About

Weinberg, J. R. The argument of Anselm and some medieval critics. *In* Weinberg, J. R. Ockham, Descartes, and Hume p 3-14

Weinberg, J. R. Gregory of Rimini's critique of Anselm. *In* Weinberg, J. R. Ockham, Descartes, and Hume p15-21

Anson, John Seller

The female transvestite in early monasticism: the origin and development of a motif. *In* Viator: medieval and Renaissance studies v5 p 1-32

Antarctic regions. See South Pole

Anthony, Dick, and Robbins, Thomas L.

The effect of detente on the growth of new religions: Reverend Moon and the Unification Church. *In* Needleman, J. and Baker, G. eds. Understanding the new religions p80-100

The Meher Baba movement: its affect [sic!] on post-adolescent social alienation. *In* Zaretsky, I. I. and Leone, M. P. eds. Religious movements in contemporary America p479-511

Anthony, Robert N.

Can nonprofit organizations be well managed? *In* Managing nonprofit organizations p 7-15

Anthropo-geography

See also Geopolitics; Human ecology; Man —Influence of climate; Man—Migrations

Methodology

Kniffen, F. B. American cultural geography and folklife. *In* Yoder, D. ed. American folklife p51-70

Africa, Eastern

Grottanelli, V. L. The peopling of the Horn of Africa. *In* Chittick, H. N. and Rotberg, R. I. eds. East Africa and the Orient p44-75

Trimingham, J. S. The Arab geographers and the East African coast. *In* Chittick, H. N. and Rotberg, R. I. eds. East Africa and the Orient p115-46

Malagasy Republic

Southall, A. W. The problem of Malagasy origins. *In* Chittick, H. N. and Rotberg, R. I. eds. East Africa and the Orient p192-215

United States

Kniffen, F. B. American cultural geography and folklife. *In* Yoder, D. ed. American folklife p51-70

Anthropological ethics

Mead, M. The evolving ethics of applied anthropology. *In* Eddy, E. M. and Partridge, W. L. eds. Applied anthropology in America p425-37

Anthropological research

Colby, B. N. and Knaus, R. Men, grammars, and machines, a new direction for the study of man. *In* On language, culture, and religion: in honor of Eugene A. Nida p187-97

Langness, L. L. Margaret Mead and the study of socialization. *In* Schwartz, T. ed. Socialization as cultural communication p5-20

Van de Castle, R. L. Some possible anthropological contributions to the study of parapsychology. *In* Parapsychology: its relation to physics, biology, psychology, and psychiatry p151-61

Whyte, W. F. Organizational behavior research—where do we go from here? *In* Eddy, E. M. and Partridge, W. L. eds. Applied anthropology in America p129-43

Africa

Colson, E. Changing anthropology in Africa. *In* African dimensions p15-27

Latin America

Hunt, R. C. Social anthropology. *In* Quantitative social science research on Latin America p62-103

Anthropology

Kimball, S. T. Anthropology as a policy science. *In* Eddy, E. M. and Partridge, W. L. eds. Applied anthropology in America p277-91

Washburn, S. L. Animal behavior and social anthropology. *In* Sociobiology and human nature p53-74

See also Acculturation; Anthropogeography; Anthropometry; Applied anthropology; Demographic anthropology; Educational anthropology; Ethnology; Ethnopsychology; Language and languages; Man; Physical anthropology; Social change

Case studies

Hicks, G. L. and Handler, M. J. Ethnicity, public policy, and anthropologists. *In* Eddy, E. M. and Partridge, W. L. eds. Applied anthropology in America p292-325

Partridge, W. L. Uses and nonuses of anthropological data on drug abuse. *In* Eddy, E. M. and Partridge, W. L. eds. Applied anthropology in America p350-72

Data processing

Colby, B. N. and Knaus, R. Men, grammars, and machines, a new direction for the study of man. *In* On language, culture, and religion: in honor of Eugene A. Nida p187-97

Field work

Medicine, B. Learning to be an anthropologist and remaining "native." *In* Eddy, E. M. and Partridge, W. L. eds. Applied anthropology in America p182-96

Peterson, J. H. The changing role of an applied anthropologist. *In* Eddy, E. M. and Partridge, W. L. eds. Applied anthropology in America p165-81

Sayles, M. Behind locked doors. *In* Eddy, E. M. and Partridge, W. L. eds. Applied anthropology in America p210-28

Taylor, C. Anthropologist-in-residence. *In* Eddy, E. M. and Partridge, W. L. eds. Applied anthropology in America p229-44

Research

See Anthropological research

Anthropology, Biblical. See Man (Theology)

Anthropology, Doctrinal. See Man (Theology)

Anthropology, Philosophical. See Philosophical anthropology

Anthropology, Physical. See Physical anthropology

Anthropology, Structural. See Structural anthropology

Anthropology as a profession

Eddy, E. M. and Partridge, W. L. Training for applied anthropology. *In* Eddy, E. M. and Partridge, W. L. eds. Applied anthropology in America p415-24

Anthropometry

Australia

Oettle, T. H. G. and Larnach, S. L. The identification of aboriginal traits in forensic medicine. *In* Grafton Elliot Smith p103-08

Anthropomorphism

Benson, J. Hog in sloth, fox in stealth: man and beast in moral thinking. *In* Royal Institute of Philosophy. Nature and conduct p265-80

Gellner, E. A. The new idealism—cause and meaning in the social sciences. *In* Giddens, A. ed. Positivism and sociology p129-

Anthropomorphism in literature
Edwards, M. S. The play of "downward comparisons": animal anthropomorphism in the poems of Robert Frost. *In* Frost: centennial essays II p236-45

Antiballistic missiles. See Antimissile missiles

Antibody-antigen reactions. See Antigen-antibody reactions

Anti-Catholicism
United States
Bennett, D. H. Women and the Nativist movement. *In* "Remember the ladies": new perspectives on women in American history p71-89
See also Nativism

Antichrist
Stein, S. J. Cotton Mather and Jonathan Edwards on the number of the beast: eighteenth-century speculation about the Antichrist. *In* American Antiquarian Society. Proceedings v84 pt2 p293-315

Antichrist in literature
Miłosz, C. Science fiction and the coming of the Antichrist. *In* Miłosz, C. Emperor of the earth p15-31

Anti-clericalism
Europe
Chadwick, O. The rise of anticlericalism. *In* Chadwick, O. The secularization of the European mind in the nineteenth century p107-39

Anti-colonialism. See Colonies

Anticommunism and American foreign policy. Ørvik, N. *In* [Truth and tragedy]: a tribute to Hans Morgenthau p284-304

Anti-discrimination. See Race discrimination

Anti-discrimination laws. See Race discrimination

Antigen-antibody reactions
Edelman, G. M. The problem of molecular recognition by a selective system. *In* Ayala, F. J. and Dobzhansky, T. G. eds. Studies in the philosophy of biology p45-56

Antigens. See Antigen-antibody reactions

Anti-infective agents. See Chemotherapy

The Anti-Jacobin; or, Weekly examiner (Periodical)
Butler, M. The anti-Jacobins. *In* Butler, M. Jane Austen and the war of ideas p88-123

Antimissile missiles
Schelling, T. C. The importance of agreements. *In* The Dynamics of the arms race p65-77

Anti-Nazi movement
Galbraith, J. K. Germany: July 20, 1944. *In* Galbraith, J. K. Annals of an abiding liberal p211-20

Antinomianism
Adler, N. Ritual, release, and orientation: maintenance of the self in the antinomian personality. *In* Zaretsky, I. I. and Leone, M. P. eds. Religious movements in contemporary America p283-97
Cohen, R. D. Church and state in seventeenth-century Massachusetts: another look at the antinomian controversy. *In* Vaughan, A. T. and Bremer, F. J. eds. Puritan New England p174-86

Schneider, L. Dialectical orientation and the sociology of religion. *In* Johnson, H. M. ed. Religious change and continuity p49-73
Stoever, W. K. B. The dialectic of nature and grace. *In* Stoever, W. K. B. 'A faire and easie way to heaven' p3-20
Stoever, W. K. B. The nature of New England antinomianism. *In* Stoever, W. K. B. 'A faire and easie way to heaven' p161-83
Stoever, W. K. B. The New England controversy. *In* Stoever, W. K. B. 'A faire and easie way to heaven' p21-33
Stoever, W. K. B. The preeminence of the spirit: John Cotton. *In* Stoever, W. K. B. 'A faire and easie way to heaven' p34-57
Stoever, W. K. B. "Preparation for salvation." *In* Stoever, W. K. B. 'A faire and easie way to heaven' p192-99
Stoever, W. K. B. The quest for assurance: radical solutions and Puritan dialectics. *In* Stoever, W. K. B. 'A faire and easie way to heaven' p138-60

Antinomy
Quine, W. V. On a supposed antinomy. *In* Quine, W. V. The ways of paradox, and other essays p19-21
Quine, W. V. The ways of paradox. *In* Quine, W. V. The ways of paradox, and other essays p 1-18

Antinoüs in literature
Schoolfield, G. C. Hadrian, Antinous, and a Rilke poem. *In* Creative encounter p145-70

Antiochus IV, Epiphanes, King of Syria in literature
Schrickx, W. 'Pericles' in a book-list of 1619 from the English Jesuit mission and some of the play's special problems. *In* Shakespeare survey v29 p21-32

Antipathies. See Prejudices and antipathies

Anti-poverty legislation (U.S.) See Economic assistance, Domestic—United States

Antiquities. See Archaeology

Antiquities, Persian. See Persian antiquities

Antiquities, Prehistoric. See Archaeology

Antiquity of man. See Man—Origin

Antisemitism
Dawidowicz, L. S. Smut and anti-Semitism. *In* Dawidowicz, L. S. The Jewish presence p216-24
Hertzberg, A. Anti-Semitism and Jewish uniqueness: ancient and contemporary. *In* Tradition and change in Jewish experience p211-25
Rudin, A. J. Jews and Judaism in Reverend Moon's Divine principle. *In* Horowitz, I. L. ed. Science, sin, and scholarship p74-83
Tanenbaum, M. H. Addendum [to Jews and Judaism in Reverend Moon's Divine principle]. *In* Horowitz, I. L. ed. Science, sin, and scholarship p84-85
Watson, G. Race and the Socialists. *In* Watson, G. Politics and literature in modern Britain p120-34
See also Jews—Persecutions

Book reviews
Dawidowicz, L. S. Can anti-Semitism be measured? *In* Dawidowicz, L. S. The Jewish presence p193-215

History
Talmon, J. L. Mission and testimony: the universal significance of modern anti-Semitism. *In* Sidorsky, D. ed. Essays on human rights p336-59

Antisemitism—*Continued*

Germany

Cassirer, E. Judaism and the modern political myths. *In* Cassirer, E. Symbol, myth, and culture p233-41

Tal, U. Young German intellectuals on romanticism and Judaism—spiritual turbulence in the early 19th century. *In* Salo Wittmayer Baron v2 p919-38

Poland

Duker, A. G. Frankism as a movement of Polish-Jewish synthesis. *In* Király, B. K. ed. Tolerance and movements of religious dissent in Eastern Europe p133-64

Russia

Dinstein, Y. Soviet Jewry and international human rights. *In* Sidorsky, D. ed. Essays on human rights p126-43

Rogger, H. Russian ministers and the Jewish question, 1881-1917. *In* California Slavic studies v8 p15-76

Antisemitism in literature

Doubleday, J. The speech of Stephen and the tone of Elene. *In* Anglo-Saxon poetry: essays in appreciation p116-23

Duker, A. G. Adam Mickiewicz's anti-Jewish period: studies in "The books of the Polish nation and of the Polish pilgrimage." *In* Salo Wittmayer Baron v 1 p311-43

Lewis, B. An anti-Jewish ode: the qasida of Abu Ishaq against Joseph ibn Nagrella. *In* Salo Wittmayer Baron v2 p657-68

Antisemitism in motion pictures

Taylor, R. The Wandering Jew. *In* Taylor, R. Film propaganda p190-206

Anti-State Church Association. See Society for the Liberation of Religion from State Patronage and Control

Anti-submarine warfare

Tsipis, K. M. Anti-submarine warfare and missile submarines. *In* The Dynamics of the arms race p36-46

Antitrust laws. See Trusts, Industrial

Anti-war movements (Vietnamese Conflict, 1961-1975) See Vietnamese Conflict, 1961-1975—Protest movements

Anton, John Peter

Tragic vision and philosophic theoria in classical Greece. *In* Philosophy and the civilizing arts p 1-23

Antonio da Monza, Fra

About individual works
Pentecost

Brown, D. A. The London Madonna of the rocks in light of two Milanese adaptations. *In* Collaboration in Italian Renaissance art p167-86

Antonioni, Michelangelo

About

Nowell-Smith, G. Shape and a black point. *In* Nichols, B. ed. Movies and methods p354-63

About individual works
L'Avventura

Kauffmann, S. L'Avventura. *In* Kauffmann, S. Living images p332-40

Lesser, S. O. L'Avventura: a closer look. *In* Lesser, S. O. The whispered meanings p105-12

Murray, E. L'Avventura. *In* Murray, E. Ten film classics p134-48

Blow-up

Samuels, C. T. The blow-up: sorting things out. *In* Samuels, C. T. Mastering the film, and other essays p119-35

La notte

Kauffmann, S. La notte; excerpt from "A world of film." *In* Denby, D. ed. Awake in the dark p107-12

Antonius Albus. See Albus, L. Antonius

Antoon, A. J.

About

Kauffmann, S. Much ado about nothing. *In* Kauffmann, S. Persons of the drama p99-102

Anttila, Inkeri

The foundation of co-operation in European criminological research: Sir Leon Radzinowicz and the Criminological Scientific Council at the Council of Europe. *In* Crime, criminology and public policy p25-32

Antwerp

Commerce

Dietz, B. Antwerp and London: the structure and balance of trade in the 1560s. *In* Wealth and power in Tudor England p186-203

Anvil (Periodical)

Conroy, J. On Anvil. *In* Anderson, E. and Kinzie, M. eds. The little magazine in America: a modern documentary history p111-29

Anxiety

May, R. Anxiety and values. *In* May, R. Psychology and the human dilemma p72-83

May, R. Historical roots of modern anxiety theories. *In* May, R. Psychology and the human dilemma p55-71

May, R. Personal identity in an anonymous world. *In* May, R. Psychology and the human dilemma p40-52

See also Worry

Anzilotti, Rolando

Foreign scholarship: Italian contributions. *In* American literary scholarship, 1975 p487-94

Foreign scholarship: Italian contributions [another essay] *In* American literary scholarship, 1976 p446-55

Foreign scholarship: Italian contributions [another essay] *In* American literary scholarship, 1977 p493-98

Apache language

Semantics

Basso, K. H. 'Wise words' of the Western Apache: metaphor and semantic theory. *In* Basso, K. H. and Selby, H. A. eds. Meaning in anthropology p93-121

Terms and phrases

Basso, K. H. 'Wise words' of the Western Apache: metaphor and semantic theory. *In* Basso, K. H. and Selby, H. A. eds. Meaning in anthropology p93-121

Apartheid. See South Africa—Race question; Segregation

Apel, Karl-Otto

The conflicts of our time and the problem of political ethics. *In* Dallmayr, F. R. ed. From contract to community p81-101

Apes

Behavior

Lancaster, J. B. Sex and gender in evolutionary perspective. *In* Katchadourian, H. A. ed. Human sexuality p51-80

Aphasia

Whitaker, H. and Whitaker, H. Language disorders. *In* Wardhaugh, R. and Brown, H. D. eds. A survey of applied linguistics p250-74

See also Aphasics

Aphasiacs. See Aphasics

Aphasics

Language

Zurif, E. B. and Blumstein, S. E. Language and the brain. *In* Linguistic theory and psychological reality p229-45

Aphorisms and apothegms

Orr, L. The limit of limits: aphorism in Char's Feuuillets d'Hypnos. *In* Symbolism and modern literature p248-63

See also Maxims; Proverbs

Aphrodite (goddess) See Venus (goddess) in fiction, drama, poetry, etc.

Apius and Virginia

Southern, R. Methods of presentation in pre-Shakespearian theatre. *In* The Elizabethan theatre, V p45-53

Apocalyptic art

Nolan, B. Anagogy, aevum and two later medieval visionary arts. *In* Nolan, B. The Gothic visionary perspective p35-83

Apocalyptic literature

Nolan, B. Anagogy, aevum and two later medieval visionary arts. *In* Nolan, B. The Gothic visionary perspective p35-83

Nolan, B. The later medieval spiritual quest: through time to aevum. *In* Nolan, B. The Gothic visionary perspective p124-55

Nolan, B. New directions in twelfth-century spirituality. *In* Nolan, B. The Gothic visionary perspective p3-34

Nolan, B. Pearl: a fourteenth-century vision in August. *In* Nolan, B. The Gothic visionary perspective p156-204

Nolan, B. The vita nuova: Dante's Book of Revelation. *In* Nolan, B. The Gothic visionary perspective p84-123

Nolan, B. Will's dark visions of Piers the Plowman. *In* Nolan, B. The Gothic visionary perspective p205-58

Rosenthal, B. G. Revolution as apocalypse: the case of Bely. *In* Janecek, G. ed. Andrey Bely p181-92

Scott, N. A. "New heav'ns, new earth"—the landscape of contemporary apocalypse. *In* Philosophy and the civilizing arts p389-432

Summers, J. H. Some apocalyptic strains in Marvell's poetry. *In* Friedenreich, K. ed. Tercentenary essays in honor of Andrew Marvell p180-203

Watson, G. The myth of catastrophe. *In* Watson, G. Politics and literature in modern Britain p98-109

Wittreich, J. A. "A poet amongst poets": Milton and the tradition of prophecy. *In* Wittreich, J. A. ed. Milton and the line of vision p97-142

Apollinaire, Guillaume

About

Berry, D. Apollinaire's solar imagery. *In* Cardinal, R. ed. Sensibility and creation p36-56

Apollo

Art

Harrison, E. B. Apollo's cloak. *In* Studies in classical art and archaeology p91-98

Winternitz, E. The curse of Pallas Athena. *In* Winternitz, E. Musical instruments and their symbolism in Western art p150-65

Apollo in literature

Siemens, W. L. Apollo's metamorphosis in Pantaleón y las visitadoras. *In* Rossman, C. R. and Friedman, A. W. eds. Mario Vargas Llosa p88-100

Apollonius of Tyana

About

Penella, R. J. An unpublished letter of Apollonius of Tyana to the Sardians. *In* Harvard Studies in classical philology v79 p305-11

Apollonius Rhodius

About

Haslam, M. W. Appolonius Rhodius and the papyri. *In* Illinois classical studies v3, 1978 p47-73

About individual works

Argonautica

Heiserman, A. R. Resourceless Jason. *In* Heiserman, A. R. The novel before the novel p11-29

Apologetics

Early church, ca. 30-600

Fiorenza, E. S. Miracles, mission, and apologetics: an introduction. *In* Aspects of religious propaganda in Judaism and early Christianity p 1-25

20th century

Kantzer, K. S. Unity and diversity in evangelical faith. *In* Wells, D. F. and Woodbridge, J. D. eds. The evangelicals p38-67

Apostles

Achtemeier, P. J. Jesus and the disciples as miracle workers in the Apocryphal New Testament. *In* Aspects of religious propaganda in Judaism and early Christianity p149-86

Highet, G. Jesus and his pupils. *In* Highet, G. The immortal profession p199-215

Apostolic Church. See Church history—Primitive and early church

Appadurai, Arjun

Understanding Gandhi. *In* Homans, P. ed. Childhood and selfhood p113-43

Apparitions. See Visions

Appeal to reason (Periodical) See American freeman (Periodical)

Appearance. Arendt, H. *In* Arendt, H. The life of the mind v 1 p17-65

Appel, Alfred

Nabokov's dark cinema: a diptych. *In* The Bitter air of exile p196-273

Tristram in movielove: Lolita at the movies. *In* A Book of things about Vladimir Nabokov p123-70

Appel, Willa

The myth of the jettatura. *In* The Evil eye p16-27

Appelbaum, Richard P.

Marxist method: structural constraints and social praxis. *In* McNall, S. G. ed. Theoretical perspectives in sociology p200-13

Appellate courts

United States

White, G. E. The tradition and the future: a summary. *In* White, G. E. The American judicial tradition p369-75

United States—History

White, G. E. The tradition at the close of the nineteenth century. *In* White, G. E. The American judicial tradition p146-49

Appellate procedure. See Civil procedure

Apperception. See Consciousness; Comprehension; Knowledge, Theory of; Perception

Appetency. See Desire

Apple, Michael W.
Ivan Illich and deschooling society: the politics of slogan systems. *In* Social forces and schooling p337-60

Apple in literature
Littlewood, A. R. The symbolism of the apple in Greek and Roman literature. *In* Harvard Studies in classical philology v72 p147-81

Applied anthropology
Arensberg, C. M. Theoretical contributions of industrial and development studies. *In* Eddy, E. M. and Partridge, W. L. eds. Applied anthropology in America p49-78

Eddy, E. M. and Partridge, W. L. Training for applied anthropology. *In* Eddy, E. M. and Partridge, W. L. eds. Applied anthropology in America p415-24

Eggan, F. R. Applied anthropology in the Mountain Province, Philippines. *In* Social organization and the applications of anthropology p196-209

Goodenough, W. H. Multiculturalism as the normal human experience. *In* Eddy, E. M. and Partridge, W. L. eds. Applied anthropology in America p79-86

Makielski, S. K. Population policy for the United States: the role of applied anthropology. *In* Eddy, E. M. and Partridge, W. L. eds. Applied anthropology in America p373-89

Mead, M. The evolving ethics of applied anthropology. *In* Eddy, E. M. and Partridge, W. L. eds. Applied anthropology in America p425-37

Neville, G. K. Marginal communicant: the anthropologist in religious groups and agencies. *In* Eddy, E. M. and Partridge, W. L. eds. Applied anthropology in America p197-209

Partridge, W. L. and Eddy, E. M. The development of applied anthropology in America. *In* Eddy, E. M. and Partridge, W. L. eds. Applied anthropology in America p3-45

Peterson, J. H. The changing role of an applied anthropologist. *In* Eddy, E. M. and Partridge, W. L. eds. Applied anthropology in America p165-81

Sayles, M. Behind locked doors. *In* Eddy, E. M. and Partridge, W. L. eds. Applied anthropology in America p210-28

Applied linguistics
Brown, H. D. What is applied linguistics? *In* Wardhaugh, R. and Brown, H. D. eds. A survey of applied linguistics p 1-7

Malmstrom, J. First language teaching. *In* Wardhaugh, R. and Brown, H. D. eds. A survey of applied linguistics p44-68

Oller, J. W. Language testing. *In* Wardhaugh, R. and Brown, H. D. eds. A survey of applied linguistics p275-300

Richards, J. C. Second language learning. *In* Wardhaugh, R. and Brown, H. D. eds. A survey of applied linguistics p113-37

Rutherford, W. E. Second language teaching. *In* Wardhaugh, R. and Brown, H. D. eds. A survey of applied linguistics p138-63

Shuy, R. W. Dialectology. *In* Wardhaugh, R. and Brown, H. D. eds. A survey of applied linguistics p182-206

Weber, R. M. Reading. *In* Wardhaugh, R. and Brown, H. D. eds. A survey of applied linguistics p92-112

See also Machine translating; Mathematical linguistics

Applied science. See Technology

Appraisal of books. See Books and reading; Criticism

Appreciation of art. See Art criticism

Apprehension. See Perception

Apprentices. See Interns (Civil service)

Appropriations and expenditures. See subdivision Appropriations and expenditures under names of countries, states, etc. and under names of departments, institutions, etc., e.g. United States. Department of Defense—Appropriations and expenditures

Approval, Social. See Social acceptance

ApRoberts, Ruth
Carlyle and Trollope. *In* Carlyle and his contemporaries p205-26

Emily and Nora and Dorothy and Priscilla and Jemima and Carry. *In* Levine, R. A. The Victorian experience: the novelists p87-120

Apronti, E. O.
The tyranny of time: the theme of time in the artistic consciousness of South African writers. *In* African literature today no. 8: Drama in Africa p106-14

Apter, T. E.
Let's hear what the male chauvinist is saying: The plumed serpent. *In* Smith, A. ed. Lawrence and women p156-77

Romanticism and romantic love in Wuthering Heights. *In* Smith, A. ed. The art of Emily Brontë p205-22

Apuleius, Lucius. See Apuleius Madaurensis

Apuleius Madaurensis

About individual works

The golden ass

Heiserman, A. R. Antonine comedy. *In* Heiserman, A. R. The novel before the novel p117-66

Massey, I. The golden ass: character versus structure. *In* Massey, I. The gaping pig p34-75

Tobin, J. J. M. Apuleius and the Bradleian tragedies. *In* Shakespeare survey v31 p33-43

Characters—Lucius

Torrance, R. M. Bondservant and beast of burden. *In* Torrance, R. M. The comic hero p60-82

Influence—Shakespeare

Tobin, J. J. M. Apuleius and the Bradleian tragedies. *In* Shakespeare survey v31 p33-43

Aquinas, Saint Thomas. See Thomas Aquinas, Saint

Arabs

See also Palestinian Arabs

History

Brett, M. The military interest of the Battle of Haydarān. *In* War, technology and society in the Middle East p78-88

Hill, D. R. The role of the camel and the horse in the early Arab conquests. *In* War, technology and society in the Middle East p32-43

Arabs in Israel

Layish, A. Social and political changes in Arab society in Israel. *In* The Palestinians p81-87

Arabs in Palestine. See Palestinian Arabs

Arabs in Spain

García Gómez, E. Moorish Spain. *In* Lewis, B. ed. Islam and the Arab world p225-44

Monroe, J. T. The Hispanic-Arabic world. *In* Américo Castro and the meaning of Spanish civilization p69-90

See also Mudéjares

Arabs in the United States

Leuchtenburg, W. E. The American perception of the Arab world. *In* Arab and American cultures p15-25

Aradeon, David

Using local resources. *In* Strategies for human settlements: habitat and environment p106-14

Arafat, Yasir

About

Neyer, J. The emergence of Yasser Arafat. *In* The Palestinians p128-32

Parry, A. Arafat and other sacrificers. *In* Parry, A. Terrorism: from Robespierre to Arafat p449-68

Aragon, Louis

About individual works

Anicet; ou, Le panorama

Balakian, A. E. Anicet, or The pursuit of pulchérie. *In* Symbolism and modern literature p237-47

The red front

Spender, S. Louis Aragon's The red front. *In* Spender, S. The thirties and after p30-31

Araki, Kengo

Confucianism and Buddhism in the late Ming. *In* The Unfolding of Neo-Confucianism p39-66

Aranguren, José Luis L.

A new model for Hispanic history. *In* Américo Castro and the meaning of Spanish civilization p309-15

Aranha, José Pereira da Graça. See Graça Aranha, José Pereira da

Arasaratnam, Sinnappah

Dutch commercial policy and interests in the Malay Peninsula, 1750-1795. *In* Kling, B. B. and Pearson, M. N. eds. The age of partnership p159-89

Aratus of Soli. See Aratus Solensis

Aratus Solensis

About

Levitan, W. Plexed artistry: Aratean acrostics. *In* Glyph 5 p55-68

Araya Goubet, Guillermo

The evolution of Castro's theories. *In* Américo Castro and the meaning of Spanish civilization p41-66

Arbatov, Georgi A.

Challenge of the next two decades: dangers and opportunities. *In* World change and world security p88-102

Arbitration, Industrial

Schmertz, E. J. Compulsory arbitration revisited: the relevance of the public sector experience in private sector management. *In* Benton, L. R. ed. Management for the future p257-69

Japan

Clark, R. C. Union-management conflict in a Japanese company. *In* Modern Japan p209-26

Arbitration, International

Davis, C. D. Arbitration, mediation, and conciliation. *In* Encyclopedia of American foreign policy p33-42

See also International courts; Mediation, International

Arblay, Frances (Burney) d'

About

Skilton, D. Sterne, sentiment and its opponents. *In* Skilton, D. The English novel p45-58

Spacks, P. A. M. Dynamics of fear: Fanny Burney. *In* Spacks, P. A. M. Imagining a self p158-92

Arcadia in literature. See Pastoral literature

Arcadian literature. See Pastoral literature

Arce, Juan Bautista Avalle- See Avalle-Arce, Juan Bautista

Archaeology

Coomaraswamy, A. K. Walter Andrae's Die ionische Säule: Bauform oder Symbol?: a review; excerpt from "Figures of thought or figures of speech: collected essays on the traditional or 'normal' view of art." *In* Coomaraswamy, A. K. Selected papers v 1 p341-49

Steward, J. H. The direct historical approach to archeology. *In* Steward, J. H. Evolution and ecology p201-07

Steward, J. H. Function and configuration in archeology. *In* Steward, J. H. Evolution and ecology p208-14

See also Aerial photography in archaeology; Africa—Antiquities; Architecture, Primitive; Excavations (Archaeology); Tombs

Methodology

Adams, R. M. The emerging place of trade in civilizational studies. *In* Ancient civilization and trade p451-65

Cotter, J. L. Archaeology and material history: a personal approach to discovery of the past. *In* Luedtke, L. S. ed. The study of American culture p77-97

Cowgill, G. L. Archaeology. *In* Quantitative social science research on Latin America p103-31

Price, B. J. The burden of the cargo: ethnographical models and archaeological inference. *In* Mesoamerican archaeology p445-65

See also Radiocarbon dating

United States

Cotter, J. L. Archaeology and material history: a personal approach to discovery of the past. *In* Luedtke, L. S. ed. The study of American culture p77-97

Archdeacons

England

Sayers, J. Monastic archdeacons. *In* Church and government in the Middle Ages p177-203

Archenholz, Johann Wilhelm von

About individual works

The history of the Seven Years' War in Germany

Koselleck, R. Chance as motivation for the unexplained in historical writing: notes on Archenholtz's History of the Seven Years' War. *In* Amacher, R. E. and Lange, V. eds. New perspectives in German literary criticism p212-24

Archeology. See Archaeology

Archer, William

About

Baylen, J. O. Edmund Gosse, William Archer, and Ibsen in late Victorian Britain. *In* Tennessee Studies in literature v XX p124-37

Archetypes of C. G. Jung, The intellect in Plotinus and the. Schwyzer, H. R. *In* Kephalaion p214-22

Archidamian War. See Greece—History—Peloponnesian War, 431-404 B.C.

Archilochus

About individual works

[Fragmenta]

Moran, W. L. An Assyriological gloss on the new Archilochus fragment. *In* Harvard Studies in classical philology v82 p17-19

Archipoeta

About

Jackson, W. T. H. The politics of a poet: the Archipoeta as revealed by his imagery. *In* Philosophy and humanism p320-38

Architects

Gropius, W. Programme for the establishment of a company for the provision of housing on aesthetically consistent principles. *In* Sharp, D. ed. The rationalists p50-57

Kostof, S. The architect in the Middle Ages, East and West. *In* Kostof, S. ed. The architect p59-95

Wilkinson, C. The new professionalism in the Renaissance. *In* Kostof, S. ed. The architect p124-60

Egypt

Kostof, S. The practice of architecture in the ancient world: Egypt and Greece. *In* Kostof, S. ed. The architect p3-27

England

Wilton-Ely, J. The rise of the professional architect in England. *In* Kostof, S. ed. The architect p180-208

France

Rosenfeld, M. N. The Royal Building Administration in France from Charles V to Louis XIV. *In* Kostof, S. ed. The architect p161-79

Greece

Kostof, S. The practice of architecture in the ancient world: Egypt and Greece. *In* Kostof, S. ed. The architect p3-27

Ionia (Asia Minor)

Holloway, R. R. Architect and engineer in archaic Greece. *In* Harvard Studies in classical philology v73 p281-90

Italy

Ettlinger, L. D. The emergence of the Italian architect during the fifteenth century. *In* Kostof, S. ed. The architect p96-123

Rome

MacDonald, W. L. Roman architects. *In* Kostof, S. ed. The architect p28-58

United States

Boyle, B. M. Architectural practice in America, 1865-1965—ideal and reality. *In* Kostof, S. ed. The architect p309-44

Draper, J. The Ecole des beaux-arts and the architectural profession in the United States: the case of John Galen Howard. *In* Kostof, S. ed. The architect p209-37

Wright, G. On the fringe of the profession: women in American architecture. *In* Kostof, S. ed. The architect p280-308

Architectural criticism

Buddensieg, T. Criticism of ancient architecture in the sixteenth and seventeenth centuries. *In* Classical influences on European culture A.D. 1500-1700 p335-48

Architectural decoration and ornament. See Decoration and ornament, Architectural

Architectural design

Broadbent, G. The rational and the functional. *In* Sharp, D. ed. The rationalists p142-58

Kahn, L. I. Architecture and human agreement. *In* The Uneasy coalition: design in corporate America p17-30

Richards, J. M. Towards a rational aesthetic. *In* Sharp, D. ed. The rationalists p130-42

Skolimowski, H. Rationality in architecture and in the design process. *In* Sharp, D. ed. The rationalists p160-72

Architectural designs. See Architecture—Designs and plans

Architectural drawing. See Architectural rendering

Architectural perspective. See Perspective

Architectural practice

United States

Boyle, B. M. Architectural practice in America, 1865-1965—ideal and reality. *In* Kostof, S. ed. The architect p309-44

Architectural rendering

Lotz, W. The rendering of the interior in architectural drawings of the Renaissance. *In* Lotz, W. Studies in Italian Renaissance architecture p 1-65

Architectural renderings. See Architectural rendering

Architectural services. See Architectural practice

Architectural symbolism. See Symbolism in architecture

Architectural symbols. See Symbolism in architecture

Architecture

Agrest, D. and Gandelsonas, M. Semiotics and the limits of architecture. *In* Sebeok, T. A. ed. A perfusion of signs p90-120

Bronowski, J. Architecture as a science and architecture as an art. *In* Bronowski, J. The visionary eye p45-56

Architecture—*Continued*

Mukařovský, J. On the problem of functions in architecture. *In* Mukařovský, J. Structure, sign, and function p236-50

See also Decoration and ornament, Architectural; Fascism and architecture; Mannerism (Architecture); Palaces; Public buildings; Structural engineering; Symbolism in architecture; Tombs

Book reviews

Paul, S. Louis Sullivan and organic architecture. *In* Paul, S. Repossessing and renewing p111-30

Conservation and restoration

Fitch, J. M. Uses of the artistic past. *In* Yoder, D. ed. American folklife p27-49

Criticism

See Architectural criticism

Decoration and ornament

See Decoration and ornament, Architectural

Designs and plans

Gowans, A. Towards a humane environment: first principles for architectural design and history. *In* Mann, D. A. ed. The arts in a democratic society p19-42

Details

See Domes; Woodwork

Ecclesiastical

See Church architecture

History

Gowans, A. Towards a humane environment: first principles for architectural design and history. *In* Mann, D. A. ed. The arts in a democratic society p19-42

Human factors

Lasswell, H. D. Building as political communication: the signature of power on environment. *In* Lerner, D. and Nelson, L. M. eds. Communication research—a half-century appraisal p280-94

See also Architecture and society

Philosophy

Jeanneret-Gris, C. É. Twentieth-century living and twentieth-century building. *In* Sharp, D. ed. The rationalists p72-77

Practice

See Architectural practice

Study and teaching

Jeanneret-Gris, C. É. If I had to teach you architecture. *In* Sharp, D. ed. The rationalists p79-83

Study and teaching—England

McCarthy, M. The education in architecture of the man of taste. *In* Studies in eighteenth-century culture v5 p337-53

Study and teaching—United States

Echerick, J. Architectural education in the thirties and seventies: a personal view. *In* Kostof, S. ed. The architect p238-79

Egypt

See Architecture, Egyptian

England—History

McCarthy, M. The education in architecture of the man of taste. *In* Studies in eighteenth-century culture v5 p 337-53

Europe, Western

Watkin, D. Pevsner. *In* Watkin, D. Morality and architecture p71-111

Watkin, D. The theme in the nineteenth century: Pugin. *In* Watkin, D. Morality and architecture p17-23

Watkin, D. The theme in the nineteenth century: Viollet-Le-Duc. *In* Watkin, D. Morality and architecture p23-31

Watkin, D. The theme in the twentieth century: Brave new world. *In* Watkin, D. Morality and architecture p37-61

Watkin, D. The theme in the twentieth century: Furneaux Jordan. *In* Watkin, D. Morality and architecture p61-68

Watkin, D. The theme in the twentieth century: Lethaby. *In* Watkin, D. Morality and architecture p33-37

France

Rosenfeld, M. N. The Royal Building Administration in France from Charles V to Louis XIV. *In* Kostof, S. ed. The architect p161-79

Great Britain—History

Stanton, P. B. Architecture, history, and the spirit of the age. *In* Altholz, J. L. ed. The mind and art of Victorian England p146-58

Greece

See Architecture, Greek

Ireland—History

Stokstad, M. and Gill, L. Antiquarianism and architecture in eighteenth-century Ireland. *In* Orel, H. ed. Irish history and culture p165-87

Italy

See Architecture, Italian

Nigeria

Cole, H. M. The history of Ibo mbari houses—facts and theories. *In* African images p104-32

Rome

See Architecture, Roman

Russia—History

Bowlt, J. E. Art and architecture in Soviet Russia, 1917-1972. *In* Auty, R. and Obolensky, D. eds. An introduction to Russian art and architecture p145-72

Bowlt, J. E. Art and architecture in the age of revolution, 1860-1917. *In* Auty, R. and Obolensky, D. eds. An introduction to Russian art and architecture p112-44

Milner-Gulland, R. R. Art and architecture in the Petersburg age, 1700-1860. *In* Auty, R. and Obolensky, D. ed. An introduction to Russian art and architecture p71-111

Milner-Gulland, R. R. Art and architecture of Old Russia, 988-1700. *In* Auty, R. and Obolensky, D. eds. An introduction to Russian art and architecture p1-70

Scotland

Stell, G. Architecture: the changing needs of society. *In* Brown, J. M. ed. Scottish society in the fifteenth century p153-83

Architecture—*Continued*

United States

Perin, C. The symbolic landscape: authority and the American way. *In* Mann, D. A. ed The arts in a democratic society p43-57

See also Architecture, American

Architecture, American

Banham, R. Mediated environments or: You can't build that here. *In* Bigsby, C. W. E. Superculture p69-82

Draper, J. The Ecole des beaux-arts and the architectural profession in the United States: the case of John Galen Howard. *In* Kostof, S. ed. The architect p209-37

Architecture, Ancient. See Architecture, Greek, and similar headings; Basilicas

Architecture, Anglo-Saxon

Hewett, C. A. Anglo-Saxon carpentry. *In* Anglo-Saxon England 7 p205-29

Architecture, Arab. See Architecture, Islamic

Architecture, Baroque

Blunt, A. Baroque architecture and classical antiquity. *In* Classical influences on European culture A.D. 1500-1700 p349-54

Italy

Scarfe, L. The baroque of Salento. *In* The Saturday book 34 p172-84

Rome (City)

Wittkower, R. Carlo Rainaldi and the architecture of the High Baroque in Rome. *In* Wittkower, R. Studies in the Italian baroque p9-52

Architecture, British. See Architecture, English

Architecture, Carlovingian

Horn, W. W. On the selective use of sacred numbers and the creation in Carolingian architecture of a new aesthetic based on modular concepts. *In* Viator: medieval and Renaissance studies v6 p351-90

Architecture, Church. See Church architecture

Architecture, Domestic

Alcock, N. W. Vernacular architecture: historical evidence and historical problems. *In* Material culture and the study of American life p109-20

Nubia

Walz, T. House decoration in Lower Nubia. *In* African images p190-222

Architecture, Domestic in literature

Henn, T. R. 'The big house.' *In* Henn, T. R. Last essays p207-20

Architecture, Early Christian

Hanfmann, G. M. A. Instinctu divinitatis: the Tetrarchs, Constantine, and Constantinople. *In* Hanfmann, G. M. A. From Croesus to Constantine p75-97

Architecture, Ecclesiastical. See Church architecture

Architecture, Egyptian

Kostof, S. The practice of architecture in the ancient world: Egypt and Greece. *In* Kostof, S. ed. The architect p3-27

Architecture, English

Wilton-Ely, J. The rise of the professional architect in England. *In* Kostof, S. ed. The architect p180-208

Architecture, Gothic

See also Gothic revival (Architecture)

France

Edelman, N. The case against Gothicism. *In* Edelman, N. The eye of the beholder p86-106

Architecture, Greek

Kostof, S. The practice of architecture in the ancient world: Egypt and Greece. *In* Kostof, S. ed. The architect p3-27

McCredie, J. R. The architects of the Parthenon. *In* Studies in classical art and archaeology p69-73

See also Columns, Ionic

Architecture, Hellenistic

Lehmann, P. L. W. Lefkadia and the second style. *In* Studies in classical art and archaeology p225-29

Asia Minor

Hanfmann, G. M. A. Hellenization takes command. *In* Hanfmann, G. M. A. From Croesus to Constantine p22-40

Architecture, Irish. See Architecture—Ireland

Architecture, Islamic

Ettinghausen, R. The man-made setting. *In* Lewis, B. ed. Islam and the Arab world p57-88

Grabar, O. Architecture and art. *In* The Genius of Arab civilization p77-116

Turkey

Bates, U. U. Women as patrons of architecture in Turkey. *In* Beck, L. and Keddie, N. R. eds. Women in the Muslim world p245-60

Architecture, Italian

Ettlinger, L. D. The emergence of the Italian architect during the fifteenth century. *In* Kostof, S. ed. The architect p96-123

Lotz, W. Italian architecture in the later sixteenth century. *In* Lotz, W. Studies in Italian Renaissance architecture p152-80

Wilkinson, C. The new professionalism in the Renaissance. *In* Kostof, S. ed. The architect p124-60

Architecture, Lombard

Lewis, S. Problems of architectural style and the Ambrosian liturgy in late fourth-century Milan. *In* Enggass, R. C. and Stokstad, M. eds. Hortus imaginum p11-19

Architecture, Medieval

Kostof, S. The architect in the Middle Ages, East and West. *In* Kostof, S. ed. The architect p59-95

See also Architecture, Lombard

Architecture, Modern

19th century

See Architecture, Victorian

19th century—Great Britain

Cook, O. The fabric of a dream. *In* The Saturday book 34 p185-201

20th century

Breuer, M. Where do we stand? *In* Sharp, D. ed. The rationalists p85-90

Broadbent, G. The rational and the functional. *In* Sharp, D. ed. The rationalists p142-58

Jeanneret-Gris, C. É Twentieth-century living and twentieth-century building. *In* Sharp, D. ed. The rationalists p72-77

Jencks, C. Irrational rationalism: the Rats since 1960. *In* Sharp, D. ed. The rationalists p208-30

Architecture, Modern—20th century—*Cont.*

Rowe, C. Mannerism and modern architecture. *In* Sharp, D. ed. The rationalists p174-89

Safdie, M. Collective consciousness in making environment. *In* The Frontiers of knowledge p201-34

Skolimowski, H. Rationality in architecture and in the design process. *In* Sharp, D. ed. The rationalists p160-72

See also Constructivism (Architecture); Functionalism (Architecture)

20th century—Europe

Banham, R. Mediated environments or: You can't build that here. *In* Bigsby, C. W. E. Superculture p69-82

20th century—Italy

Zevi, B. The Italian rationalists. *In* Sharp, D. ed. The rationalists p118-29

20th century—Russia

Bowlt, J. E. Art and architecture in Soviet Russia, 1917–1972. *In* Auty, R. and Obolensky, D. eds. An introduction to Russian art and architecture p145-72

20th century—United States

Mann, D. A. Architectural icons: the best surprise is no surprise. *In* Browne, R. B. and Fishwick, M. W. eds. Icons of America p35-56

Architecture, Muslim. See Architecture, Islamic

Architecture, Nigerian. See Architecture—Nigeria

Architecture, Primitive

Fitch, J. M. Uses of the artistic past. *In* Yoder, D. ed. American folklife p27-49

Architecture, Renaissance

Buddensieg, T. Criticism of ancient architecture in the sixteenth and seventeenth centuries. *In* Classical influences on European culture A.D. 1500-1700 p335-48

Hersey, G. L. Marsilio Ficino's cosmic temple. *In* Collaboration in Italian Renaissance art p91-97

Kubler, G. Drawings by G. A. Montorsoli in Madrid. *In* Collaboration in Italian Renaissance art p143-64

Wilkinson, C. The new professionalism in the Renaissance. *In* Kostof, S. ed. The architect p124-60

See also Mannerism (Architecture)

Italy

Lotz, W. Italian architecture in the later sixteenth century. *In* Lotz, W. Studies in Italian Renaissance architecture p152-80

Lotz, W. The rendering of the interior in architectural drawings of the Renaissance. *In* Lotz, W. Studies in Italian Renaissance architecture p 1-65

Architecture, Roman

Buddensieg, T. Criticism of ancient architecture in the sixteenth and seventeenth centuries. *In* Classical influences on European culture A.D. 1500-1700 p335-48

Frazer, A. K. The pyre of Faustina Senior. *In* Studies in classical art and archaeology p271-74

Lehmann, P. L. W. Lefkadia and the second style. *In* Studies in classical art and archaeology p225-29

MacDonald, W. L. Roman architects. *In* Kostof, S. ed. The architect p28-58

Influence

Blunt, A. Baroque architecture and classical antiquity. *In* Classical influences on European culture A.D. 1500-1700 p349-54

Asia Minor

Hanfmann, G. M. A. Ad claras Asiae volemus urbes: Roman governors and urban renewal. *In* Hanfmann, G. M. A. From Croesus to Constantine p41-56

Italy

Ward-Perkins, J. B. Taste, tradition and technology: some aspects of the architecture of late republican and early imperial central Italy. *In* Studies in classical art and archaeology p197-204

Rome (City)

Richardson, L. Basilica Fulvia modo Aemilia. *In* Studies in classical art and archaeology p209-15

Architecture, Rural. See Architecture, Domestic

Architecture, Victorian

Great Britain

Crook, J. M. Sydney Smirke: the architecture of compromise. *In* Seven Victorian architects p50-65

Gradidge, R. Edwin Lutyens: the last High Victorian. *In* Seven Victorian architects p122-36

Hobhouse, H. Philip and Philip Charles Hardwick: an architectural dynasty. *In* Seven Victorian architects p32-49

Lloyd, D. D. John Loughborough Pearson: noble seriousness. *In* Seven Victorian architects p66-83

Smith, S. A. Alfred Waterhouse: civic grandeur. *In* Seven Victorian architects p102-21

Stanton, P. B. Architecture, history, and the spirit of the age. *In* Altholz, J. L. ed. The mind and art of Victorian England p146-58

Verey, D. George Frederick Bodley: climax of the Gothic revival. *In* Seven Victorian architects p84-101

Walker, D. M. William Burn: the country house in transition. *In* Seven Victorian architects p8-31

Architecture and communism. See Communism and architecture

Architecture and fascism. See Fascism and architecture

Architecture and liturgy. See Liturgy and architecture

Architecture and politics. See Architecture and state

Architecture and religion

Watkin, D. The theme in the nineteenth century: Pugin. *In* Watkin, D. Morality and architecture p17-23

See also Church architecture; Liturgy and architecture

Architecture and society

Fitch, J. M. Uses of the artistic past. *In* Yoder, D. ed. American folklife p27-49

Gowans, A. Towards a humane environment: first principles for architectural design and history. *In* Mann, D. A. ed. The arts in a democratic society p19-42

Architecture and society—*Continued*

Mann, D. A. Architectural icons: the best surprise is no surprise. *In* Browne, R. B. and Fishwick, M. W. eds. Icons of America p35-56

Watkin, D. The theme in the nineteenth century: Viollet-Le- Duc. *In* Watkin, D. Morality and architecture p23-31

Watkin, D. The theme in the twentieth century: Brave new world. *In* Watkin, D. Morality and architecture p37-61

Watkin, D. The theme in the twentieth century: Furneaux Jordan. *In* Watkin, D. Morality and architecture p61-68

See also Architecture—Human factors

Architecture and sociology. See Architecture and society

Architecture and state

Italy

Millon, H. A. Some new towns in Italy in the 1930s. *In* Millon, H. A. and Nochlin, L. eds. Art and architecture in the service of politics p326-41

Moos, S. von. The palace as a fortress: Rome and Bologna under Pope Julius II. *In* Millon, H. A. and Nochlin, L. eds. Art and architecture in the service of politics p46-79

Italy—Rome (City)

Kostof, S. K. The Emperor and the Duce: the planning of Piazzale Augusto Imperatore in Rome. *In* Millon, H. A. and Nochlin, L. eds. Art and architecture in the service of politics p270-325

Schroeter, E. Rome's first national state architecture: the Palazzo delle Finanze. *In* Millon, H. A. and Nochlin, L. eds. Art and architecture in the service of politics p128-49

Italy—Urbino

Westfall, C. W. Chivalric declaration: the Palazzo Ducale in Urbino as a political statement. *In* Millon, H. A. and Nochlin, L. eds. Art and architecture in the service of politics p20-45

Netherlands—Amsterdam

Searing, H. With red flags flying: housing in Amsterdam, 1915-1923. *In* Millon, H. A. and Nochlin, L. eds. Art and architecture in the service of politics p230-69

Rome

Stapleford, R. Constantinian politics and the atrium church. *In* Millon, H. A. and Nochlin, L. eds. Art and architecture in the service of politics p2-19

Architecture and the aged

Lindheim, R. Designs for living. *In* Jarvik, L. F. Aging into the 21st century p153-68

Architecture in literature

Tristram, P. Stories in stones. *In* Smith, A. ed. The novels of Thomas Hardy p145-68

Archives

Osborn, J. M. The search for English literary documents. *In* Wimsatt, W. K. ed. Literary criticism: idea and act p15-31

See also Church records and registers; Diplomatics; Manuscripts

Normandy—History—500 to 1500

Chibnall, M. Charter and chronicle: the use of archive sources by Norman historians. *In* Church and government in the Middle Ages p 1-17

United States

Burch, F. W. Archives and the design of transportation research. *In* Pattern and process p215-23

Clark, A. H. First things first. *In* Pattern and process p9-21

Archpriests. See Archdeacons

Arctic expeditions. See Arctic regions

Arctic races. See Eskimos

Arctic regions

Loomis, C. C. The Arctic sublime. *In* Knoepflmacher, U. D. and Tennyson, G. B. eds. Nature and the Victorian imagination p95-112

Discovery and exploration

See Arctic regions

Arcy, François d' and Jobert, Bruno

Urban planning in France. *In* Planning, politics and public policy p295-315

Ardal, Páll Steinthórsson

Convention and value. *In* David Hume p51-68

Some implications of the virtue of reasonableness in Hume's Treatise. *In* Livingston, D. W. and King, J. T. eds. Hume p91-106

Ardant, Gabriel

Financial policy and economic infrastructure of modern states and nations. *In* Tilly, C. ed. The formation of national states in Western Europe p164-242

Arden, John

About

Kennedy, A. K. Arden. *In* Kennedy, A. K. Six dramatists in search of a language p213-29

About individual works

Serjeant Musgrave's dance

Kauffmann, S. Serjeant Musgrave's dance. *In* Kauffmann, S. Persons of the drama p171-73

Arden, John, and D'Arcy, Margaretta

About individual works

The Ballygombeen bequest

Brustein, R. S. Two plays about Ireland: Richard's cork leg and The Ballygombeen bequest. *In* Brustein, R. S. The culture watch p53-56

The island of the mighty

Brustein, R. S. Mr Arden versus Mr Jones. *In* Brustein, R. S. The culture watch p74-79

Ardener, Edwin

Belief and the problem of women. *In* Ardener, S. G. ed. Perceiving women p 1-17

Language, ethnicity, and population. *In* Studies in social anthropology p343-53

The 'problem' revisited. *In* Ardener, S. G. ed. Perceiving women p19-27

Ardener, Shirley G.

Sexual insult and female militancy. *In* Ardener, S. G. ed. Perceiving women p29-53

Area linguistics. See Areal linguistics

Area research. See Area studies

Area studies

Steward, J. H. Concepts and methods of area research; excerpt from "Area research: theory and practice." *In* Steward, J. H. Evolution and ecology p217-39

Areal linguistics

Kaufman, T. S. Areal linguistics and Middle America. *In* Sebeok, T. A. ed. Native languages of the Americas v2 p63-87

Sherzer, J. Areal linguistics in North America. *In* Sebeok, T. A. ed. Native languages of the Americas v 1 p121-73

See also Languages in contact

Arendt, Hannah

Home to roost. *In* Warner, S. B. ed. The American experiment p61-79

The Jew as pariah: Jewish identity and politics in the modern age

Contents

Creating a cultural atmosphere
"The formidable Dr. Robinson": a reply by Hannah Arendt
Herzl and Lazare
The Jew as pariah: a hidden tradition
Jewish history, revised
The Jewish state: fifty years after
The moral of history
Organized guilt and universal responsibility
Peace or armistice in the Near East?
Portrait of a period
To save the Jewish homeland
We refugees
Zionism reconsidered

The life of the mind v 1 Thinking

Contents

Appearance
Mental activities in a world of appearances
What makes us think?
Where are we when we think?

The life of the mind v2 Willing

Contents

Conclusions
The philosophers and the will
Quaestio mihi factus sum: the discovery of the inner man
Will and intellect

Martin Heidegger at eighty. *In* Murray, M. E. ed. Heidegger and modern philosophy p293-303

Public rights and private interests: in response to Charles Frankel. *In* Small comforts for hard times p103-08

About

Bernstein, R. J. Hannah Arendt: the ambiguities of theory and practice. *In* Political theory and praxis p141-58

Denneny, M. The privilege of ourselves: Hannah Arendt on judgment. *In* Hannah Arendt: the recovery of the public world p245-74

Draenos, S. S. Thinking without a ground: Hannah Arendt and the contemporary situation of understanding. *In* Hannah Arendt: the recovery of the public world p209-24

Feldman, R. H. Introduction: the Jew as pariah: the case of Hannah Arendt. *In* Arendt, H. The Jew as pariah: Jewish identity and politics in the modern age p15-52

Nichols, R. L. Rebels, beginners, and buffoons: politics as action. *In* Political theory and praxis p159-99

O'Sullivan, N. Hannah Arendt: Hellenic nostalgia and industrial society. *In* De Crespigny, A. and Minogue, K. R. eds. Contemporary political philosophers p228-52

Young-Bruehl, E. From the pariah's point of view: reflections on Hannah Arendt's life and work. *In* Hannah Arendt: the recovery of the public world p3-26

About individual works

Eichmann in Jerusalem

Bettelheim, B. Eichmann: the system, the victims. *In* Bettelheim, B. Surviving, and other essays p258-73

Laqueur, W. Z. Footnotes to the Holocaust. *In* Arendt, H. The Jew as pariah: Jewish identity and politics in the modern age p252-59

Laqueur, W. Z. A reply to Hannah Arendt. *In* Arendt, H. The Jew as pariah: Jewish identity and politics in the modern age p277-79

"The formidable Dr. Robinson": a reply by Hannah Arendt

Laqueur, W. Z. A reply to Hannah Arendt. *In* Arendt, H. The Jew as pariah: Jewish identity and politics in the modern age p277-79

The human condition

Bakan, M. Hannah Arendt's concepts of labor and work. *In* Hannah Arendt: the recovery of the public world p49-65

Frampton, K. The status of man and the status of his objects: a reading of The human condition. *In* Hannah Arendt: the recovery of the public world p101-30

Fuss, P. L. Hannah Arendt's conception of political community. *In* Hannah Arendt: the recovery of the public world p157-76

Major, R. W. A reading of Hannah Arendt's "unusual" distinction between labor and work. *In* Hannah Arendt: the recovery of the public world p131-55

West, T. R. Nature and artifice: Hannah Arendt, Theodore Roszak, Paul Goodman. *In* West, T. R. Nature, community, & will p97-137

The life of the mind (v2 Willing)

Gray, J. G. The abyss of freedom—and Hannah Arendt. *In* Hannah Arendt: the recovery of the public world p225-44

On revolution

Miller, J. The pathos of novelty: Hannah Arendt's image of freedom in the modern world. *In* Hannah Arendt: the recovery of the public world p177-208

On violence

O'Neill, J. Violence, technology, and the body politic. *In* Stanage, S. M. ed. Reason and violence p5-26

The origins of totalitarianism

Crick, B. R. On rereading The origins of totalitarianism. *In* Hannah Arendt: the recovery of the public world p27-47

Political science

Bakan, M. Hannah Arendt's concepts of labor and work. *In* Hannah Arendt: the recovery of the public world p49-65

Frampton, K. The status of man and the status of his objects: a reading of The human condition. *In* Hannah Arendt: the recovery of the public world p101-30

Fuss, P. L. Hannah Arendt's conception of political community. *In* Hannah Arendt: the recovery of the public world p157-76

Arendt, Hannah—Political science—*Cont.*

Hill, M. A. The fictions of mankind and the stories of men. *In* Hannah Arendt: the recovery of the public world p275-300

Parekh, B. C. Hannah Arendt's critique of Marx. *In* Hannah Arendt: the recovery of the public world p67-100

Arendt, Jermaine D.

Promoting pluralism in the public schools. *In* Minority language and literature p121-29

Arensberg, Conrad Maynadier

Theoretical contributions of industrial and development studies. *In* Eddy, E. M. and Partridge, W. L. eds. Applied anthropology in America p49-78

See also Garrison, V. E. jt. auth.

Arestad, Sverre

The Ibsen hero. *In* The Hero in Scandinavian literature p15-37

Aretino, Pietro

About individual works
Dialogues

Lyons, J. O. Whores and rakes in the gardens of delight. *In* Lyons, J. O. The invention of the self p176-96

Aretinus, Guido. See Guido, Aretinus

Arezzo, Guido d' See Guido, Aretinus

Argentine fiction

20th century—History and criticism

Foster, D. W. Alternatives to progressive narrative in the contemporary Argentine novel: some constants. *In* Foster, D. W. Currents in the contemporary Argentine novel: Arlt, Mallea, Sabato, and Cortázar p128-48

Foster, D. W. Introduction to the Argentine novel. *In* Foster, D. W. Currents in the contemporary Argentine novel: Arlt, Mallea, Sabato, and Cortázar p 1-18

Argentine Republic

Economic conditions

Corradi, J. E. Argentina. *In* Chilcote, R. H. and Edelstein, J. C. eds. Latin America: the struggle with dependency and beyond p305-407

Economic conditions—1918-

Ferns, H. S. Argentina in travail. *In* The Year book of world affairs, 1975 p56-71

Emigration and immigration

Solberg, C. Mass migrations in Argentina, 1870-1970. *In* Human migration p146-70

Foreign relations

Moneta Testa, C. Argentine foreign policy in the Cold war. *In* Siracusa, J. M. and Barclay, G. S. eds. The impact of the Cold war p101-24

History—1810-

Solberg, C. Mass migrations in Argentina, 1870-1970. *In* Human migration p146-70

Politics and government—1910-1943

Smith, P. H. The breakdown of democracy in Argentina, 1916-30. *In* The Breakdown of democratic regimes pt.3 p3-27

Politics and government—1943-

Moneta Testa, C. Argentine foreign policy in the Cold war. *In* Siracusa, J. M. and Barclay, G. S. eds. The impact of the Cold war p101-24

Politics and government—1955-

O'Donnell, G. A. Permanent crisis and the failure to create a democratic regime: Argentina, 1955-66. *In* The Breakdown of democratic regimes pt.3 p138-77

Parry, A. The morbid tango. *In* Parry, A. Terrorism: from Robespierre to Arafat p261-73

Social conditions

Corradi, J. E. Argentina. *In* Chilcote, R. H. and Edelstein, J. C. eds. Latin America: the struggle with dependency and beyond p305-407

Arguedas, José María

About individual works
The fox from above and the fox from below

Brotherston, G. Tupac Amaru dismembered: José María Arguedas. *In* Brotherston, G. The emergence of the Latin American novel p98-109

Argumentation. See Debates and debating; Logic; Reasoning

Argyle, Michael

Non-verbal communication and language. *In* Royal Institute of Philosophy. Communication and understanding p63-78

Argyle, William Johnson

Size and scale as factors in the development of nationalist movements. *In* Smith, A. D. ed. Nationalist movements p31-53

Ariadne

Miller, J. H. Ariadne's thread: repetition and the narrative line. *In* Valdés, M. J. and Miller, O. J. eds. Interpretation of narrative p148-66

Art

Richardson, E. H. The story of Ariadne in Italy. *In* Studies in classical art and archaeology p189-95

Arianism. See Socinianism

Arid regions. See Deserts

Aridjis, Homero

About

Forster, M. H. Four contemporary Mexican poets: Marco Antonio Montes de Oca, Gabriel Zaid, José Emilio Pacheco, Homero Aridjis. *In* Forster, M. H. ed. Tradition and renewal p139-56

Ariés, Philippe

Death inside out. *In* Death inside out p9-24

The family and the city. *In* Rossi, A. S.; Kagan, J. and Hareven, T. K. eds. The family p227-35

Same as The family and the city in the Old World and the New. *In* Tufte, V. and Myerhoff, B. G. eds. Changing images of the family p29-41

A prison of love; excerpt from "Centuries of childhood." *In* Gross, B. and Gross, R. eds. The children's rights movement p135-40

The reversal of death: changes in attitudes toward death in Western societies. *In* Death in America p134-58

About individual works
Western attitudes toward death: from the Middle Ages to the present

Darnton, R. The history of mentalités: recent writings on revolution, criminality, and death in France. *In* Brown, R. H. and Lyman, S. M. eds. Structure, consciousness, and history p106-36

Ariosto, Lodovico

About

Marinelli, P. V. Redemptive laughter: comedy in the Italian romances. *In* Ruggiers, P. G. ed. Versions of medieval comedy p227-48

About individual works
Orlando furioso

Giamatti, A. B. Headlong horses, headless horsemen: an essay on the chivalric epics of Pulci, Boiardo, and Ariosto. *In* Italian literature: roots and branches p265-307

Kennedy, W. J. The epic genre and varieties of form. *In* Kennedy, W. J. Rhetorical norms in Renaissance literature p128-88

Parker, P. A. Ariosto. *In* Parker, P. A. Inescapable romance p16-53

Schmidgall, G. George Frederic Handel. *In* Schmidgall, G. Literature as opera p29-65

Aristocracy

Mencken, H. L. The need for an aristocracy; excerpt from "Prejudices: second series." *In* Crunden, R. M. ed. The superfluous men p73-79

See also Democracy; Nobility; Upper classes; and subdivision Nobility under names of countries, e.g. France—Nobility

Aristocracy in literature

Henn, T. R. 'The big house.' *In* Henn, T. R. Last essays p207-20

Holman, C. H. April in Queenborough: Ellen Glasgow's comedies of manners. *In* Holman, C. H. Windows on the world p98-117

Aristophanes

About

Fornara, C. W. Plutarch and the Megarian decree. *In* Yale classical studies v24 p213-28

Nicoll, A. Aristophanes and the Old Comedy. *In* Nicoll, A. World drama p60-73

Sandbach, F. H. Aristophanes. *In* Sandbach, F. H. The comic theatre of Greece and Rome p26-40

About individual works
The Acharnians

Sandbach, F. H. An Athenian comedy. *In* Sandbach, F. H. The comic theatre of Greece and Rome p15-25

The birds (Lines 593-595)

Gill, D. Birds 593-595: a note. *In* Harvard Studies in classical philology v79 p69-72

The clouds (Lines 723-796)

Haslam, M. W. Attribution and action in Aristophanes Clouds 723-796. *In* Harvard Studies in classical philology v80 p45-47

Frogs

Griffith, J. G. ΑΗΚΥΘΙΟΝ ΑΠΩΛΕΣΕΝ: a postscript. *In* Harvard Studies in classical philology v74 p43-44

Taplin, O. Aeschylean silences and silences in Aeschylus. *In* Harvard Studies in classical philology v76 p57-97

Frogs (Line 862)

Dickerson, G. W. Aristophanes' Ranae 862: a note on the anatomy of Euripidean tragedy. *In* Harvard Studies in classical philology v78 p177-88

Frogs (Lines 1200-1248)

Henderson, J. The lekythos and Frogs 1200-1248. *In* Harvard Studies in classical philology v76 p133-43

Whitman, C. H. ΑΗΚΥΘΙΟΝ ΑΠΩΛΕΣΕΝ. *In* Harvard Studies in classical philology v73 p109-12

Wasps

Long, T. The parodos of Aristophanes' Wasps. *In* Illinois classical studies, v 1 1976 p15-21

Wasps (Lines 1360-1369)

Rusten, J. S. Wasps 1360-1369: Philokleon's ΤΩΘΑΣΜΟΣ. *In* Harvard Studies in classical philology v81 p157-61

Characters

Torrance, R. M. Jackanapes in the highest. *In* Torrance, R. M. The comic hero p37-59

Criticism, Textual

Dover, K. J. Ancient interpolation in Aristophanes. *In* Illinois classical studies v2, 1977 p136-62

Aristoteles

About

Cranz, F. E. Editions of the Latin Aristotle accompanied by the commentaries of Averroes. *In* Philosophy and humanism p116-28

Diamond, M. Ethics and politics: the American way. *In* The Moral foundations of the American Republic p39-72

Downs, R. B. Universal man. *In* Downs, R. B. Books that changed the world p69-92

Funkenstein, A. The dialectical preparation for scientific revolutions. *In* The Copernican achievement p165-203

Furley, D. J. Aristotle and the Atomists on motion in a void. *In* Motion and time, space and matter p83-100

Gordon, G. N. Aristotle as a modern propagandist. *In* Havelock, E. A. and Hershbell, J. P. eds. Communication arts in the ancient world p55-61

Huby, P. M. Greek ethics. *In* New studies in ethics v 1 p 1-78

Jones, T. B. and Nicol, B. de B. Introduction: Aristotle and Horace. *In* Jones, T. B. and Nicol, B. D. Neo-classical dramatic criticism, 1560-1770 p 1-17

Randall, J. H. Paduan Aristotelianism reconsidered. *In* Philosophy and humanism p275-82

Romilly, J. de. Logic versus magic: Aristotle and later writers. *In* Romilly, J. de. Magic and rhetoric in ancient Greece p67-88

Shell, M. The Golden Fleece and the voice of the shuttle: economy in literary theory. *In* Shell, M. The economy of literature p89-112

Tracy, T. J. Perfect friendship in Aristotle's Nicomachean Ethics. *In* Illinois classical studies v4, 1979 p65-75

Turnbull, R. G. The role of the "special sensibles" in the perception theories of Plato and Aristotle. *In* Studies in perception p3-26

Warminski, A. Pre-positional by-play. *In* Glyph 3 p98-117

Wingler, H. Aristotle in the thought of Nietzsche and Thomas Aquinas. *In* O'Flaherty, J. C.; Sellner, T. F. and Helm, R. M. eds. Studies in Nietzsche and the classical tradition p33-54

Aristoteles—*Continued*
About individual works
Athenian Constitution

McCoy, W. J. Aristotle's Athenaion Politeia and the establishment of the Thirty Tyrants. *In* Yale classical studies v24 p131-45

Categories

Hijmans, B. L. Athenodorus on the Categories and a pun on Athenodorus. *In* Kephalaion p105-14

De motu animalium

Nussbaum, M. C. The text of Aristotle's De motu animalium. *In* Harvard Studies in classical philology v80 p111-59

De mundo

Blau, J. L. On the supposedly Aristotelian character of Gabirol's Keter malkut. *In* Salo Wittmayer Baron v 1 p219-28

Ethics

Post, G. Philosophy and citizenship in the thirteenth century—laicisation, the two laws and Aristotle. *In* Order and innovation in the Middle Ages p401-08

Tracy, T. J. Perfect friendship in Aristotle's Nicomachean ethics. *In* Illinois classical studies v4, 1979 p65-75

Verbeke, G. Moral behaviour and time in Aristotle's Nichomachean ethics. *In* Kephalaion p78-90

Metaphysics

Berti, E. Logical and ontological priority among the genera of substance in Aristotle. *In* Kephalaion p55-69

Ivry, A. L. al-Kindi's On first philosophy and Aristotle's Metaphysics. *In* Essays on Islamic philosophy and science p15-24

Meteorological

Otte, J. K. The role of Alfred Sareshel (Alfredus Anglicus) and his commentary on the Metheora in the reacquisition of Aristotle. *In* Viator: medieval and Renaissance studies v7 p197-209

Oeconomica

Soudek, J. A fifteenth-century humanistic bestseller: the manuscript diffusion of Leonardo Bruni's annotated Latin version of the (pseudo-) Aristotelian Economics. *In* Philosophy and humanism p129-43

On the heavens (IV)

Hahm, D. E. Weight and lightness in Aristotle and his predecessors. *In* Motion and time, space and matter p56-82

Physics

Moody, E. A. Ockham and Aegidius of Rome. *In* Moody, E. A. Studies in medieval philosophy, science, and logic p161-88

Owen, G. E. L. Aristotle on time. *In* Motion and time, space and matter p3-27

Turnbull, R. G. "Physics" I: sense universals, principles, multiplicity, and motion. *In* Motion and time, space and matter p28-55

Poetics

Brower, R. A. The heresy of plot. *In* Brower, R. A. Mirror on mirror p123-38

Fergusson, F. The Poetics of Aristotle. *In* Fergusson, F. Literary landmarks p3-36

Howell, W. S. Aristotle and Horace on rhetoric and poetics. *In* Howell, W. S. Poetics, rhetoric, and logic p45-72

Kropf, C. R. Catharsis in eighteenth-century England. *In* Tennessee Studies in literature v22 p63-72

Olson, E. The poetic method of Aristotle: its powers and limitation. *In* Olson, E. On value judgments in the arts, and other essays p186-99

Renna, T. J. Aristotle and the French monarchy, 1260-1303. *In* Viator: medieval and Renaissance studies v9 p309-24

Wheelwright, P. E. Mimesis and katharsis: an archetypal consideration. *In* Wimsatt, W. K. ed. Literary criticism: idea and act p110-27

The problems of Aristotle

Simon, B. Aristotle on melancholy. *In* Simon, B. Mind and madness in ancient Greece p228-37

Rhetoric

Brownstein, O. L. Aristotle and the rhetorical process. *In* Rhetoric: a tradition in transition p19-32

Howell, W. S. Aristotle and Horace on rhetoric and poetics. *In* Howell, W. S. Poetics, rhetoric, and logic p45-72

Ethics

Fisch, M. H. The poliscraft. *In* Philosophy and the civilizing arts p24-48

Influence—Ibn Gabirol

Blau, J. L. On the supposedly Aristotelian character of Gabirol's Keter malkut. *In* Salo Wittmayer Baron v 1 p219-28

Influence—Levi ben Gershon

Feldman, S. N. O. Platonic themes in Gersonides' cosmology. *In* Salo Wittmayer Baron v 1 p383-405

Political science

Ball, T. Plato and Aristotle: the unity versus the autonomy of theory and practice. *In* Political theory and praxis p57-69

Aristotle. See Aristoteles

Ariwara, Narihira, supposed author

About individual works
Ise monogatari

Rimer, J. T. Source books I: Tales of Ise, The tale of Genji. *In* Rimer, J. T. Modern Japanese fiction and its traditions p82-96

Arizona

Antiquities

Longacre, W. A. Population dynamics at the Grasshopper pueblo, Arizona. *In* Zubrow, E. B. W. ed. Demographic anthropology p169-84

Arkes, Hadley Philip

Civility and the restriction of speech: rediscovering the defamation of groups. *In* The Supreme Court review, 1974 p281-335

Arkin, Arthur Malcolm

Notes on anticipatory grief. *In* Anticipatory grief p10-13

Arlt, Roberto

About individual works
The seven madmen

Foster, D. W. Roberto Arlt and the neurotic rationale. *In* Foster, D. W. Currents in the contemporary Argentine novel: Arlt, Mallea, Sabato, and Cortázar p20-45

Armah, Ayi Kwei
About
Izevbaye, D. S. Ayi Kwei Armah and the 'I' of the beholder. *In* King, B. A. and Ogungbesan, K. eds. A celebration of Black and African writing p232-44

About individual works
The beautyful ones are not yet born
Gakwandi, S. A. Freedom as nightmare: Armah's The beautyful ones are not yet born. *In* Gakwandi, S. A. The novel and contemporary experience in Africa p87-99

Ogungbesan, K. Symbol and meaning in The beautyful ones are not yet born. *In* African literature today no. 7: Focus on criticism p93-110

Why are we so blest?
Fraser, R. The American background in Why are we so blest? *In* African literature today no. 9: Africa, America and the Caribbean p39-46

Armaments
Badurina, B. Military force in the Mediterranean. *In* Borgese, E. M. and Krieger, D. eds. The tides of change p197-209

Kaldor, M. The role of arms in capitalist economies: the process of overdevelopment and underdevelopment. *In* Arms control and technological innovation p322-41

Knorr, K. E. Military strength: economic and non-economic bases. *In* Knorr, K. E. and Trager, F. N. eds. Economic issues and national security p183-99

See also Arms control; Disarmament; Munitions; Ordnance

Armato, Philip Michele
Tennessee Williams' meditations on life and death in Suddenly last summer, The night of the iguana and The milk train doesn't stop here anymore. *In* Tennessee Williams: a tribute p558-70

Armayor, O. Kimball
Did Herodotus ever go to the Black Sea? *In* Harvard Studies in classical philology v82 p45-62

Armed Forces
Edmonds, M. Reserve forces: mobilization demands in modern war. *In* Beaumont, R. A. and Edmonds, M. eds. War in the next decade p35-54

Reserves
Edmonds, M. Reserve forces: mobilization demands in modern war. *In* Beaumont, R. A. and Edmonds, M. eds. War in the next decade p35-54

See also subdivision Armed Forces—Reserves under names of countries, e.g. United States—Armed Forces—Reserves

Vocational guidance
Janowitz, M. The emergent military *In* Beaumont, R. A. and Edmonds, M. eds. War in the next decade p21-34

Peru—Political activity
Stepan, A. C. Inclusionary and exclusionary military responses to radicalism: with special attention to Peru; excerpt from "The state and society: Peru in comparative perspective." *In* Radicalism in the contemporary age v3 p221-39

Armed Neutrality, 1780 and 1800. See Neutrality, Armed

Armed Services. See Armed Forces

Armer, Michael J. and Gewirtz, Marian
Sociocultural change in contemporary Africa. *In* Martin, P. M. and O'Meara, P. eds. Africa p280-94

Armerding, Carl Edwin. See Armerding, Hudson T.

Armerding, Hudson T.
Were David's sons really priests? *In* Current issues in Biblical and patristic interpretation p75-86

Armies
See also Disarmament

History
Bosworth, C. E. Recruitment, muster, and review in medieval Islamic armies. *In* War, technology and society in the Middle East p59-77

Vryonis, S. Byzantine and Turkish societies and their sources of manpower. *In* War, technology and society in the Middle East p125-52

Yapp, M. E. The modernization of Middle Eastern armies in the nineteenth century: a comparative view. *In* War, technology and society in the Middle East p330-66

Armitage, Andrew
Canada. *In* Kammerman, S. B. and Kahn, A. J. eds. Family policy p367-99

Armory Show. See New York (City) International Exhibition of Modern Art, 1913

Arms, Profession of. See Military service as a profession

Arms and armor. See Bayonets; Firearms

Arms control
Ignatieff, G. The achievements of arms control. *In* Griffiths, F. and Polanyi, J. C. eds. The dangers of nuclear war p67-82

See also Disarmament; Nuclear nonproliferation

Armstrong, Arthur Hilary
Beauty and the discovery of divinity in the thought of Plotinus. *In* Kephalaion p155-63

Armstrong, Charles Arthur John
Sir John Fastolf and the law of arms. *In* War, literature, and politics in the late Middle Ages p46-56

Armstrong, Christopher J. R.
The dialectical road to truth: the dialogue. *In* French Renaissance studies, 1540-70 p36-51

Armstrong, George M.
An unworn and edged tool: H. L. Davis's last word on the West, "The kettle of fire." *In* Bingham, E. R. and Love, G. A. eds. Northwest perspectives p169-85

Armstrong, Henry Edward
About
Dolby, R. G. A. Debates over the theory of solution: a study of dissent in physical chemistry in the English-speaking world in the late nineteenth and early twentieth centuries. *In* Historical studies in the physical sciences v7 p297-404

Armstrong, Isobel
Browning and Victorian poetry of sexual love. *In* Armstrong, I. ed. Robert Browning p267-98

Armstrong, Rebecca
The Great Chain of Being in Dryden's All for love. *In* A Provision of human nature p133-43

Armstrong, Terry R.
The roots of power. *In* Armstrong, T. R. and Cinnamon, K. M. eds. Power and authority in law enforcement p5-12

Armstrong, W. A.
Synge's communities and dissenters. *In* Drama and society p117-28

Army. See Armies

Arnaut, Daniel

About

Topsfield, L. T. Arnaut Daniel. *In* Topsfield, L. T. Troubadours and love p195-218

Influence

Wilhelm, J. J. Arnaut Daniel's legacy to Dante and to Pound. *In* Italian literature: roots and branches p67-83

Arndt, John Richard. See Part 2 under title: The German contribution to the building of the Americas

Arner, Robert David
The blackness of darkness: satire, romance, and Ebenezer Cooke's The sot-weed factor. *In* Tennessee Studies in literature v 21 p 1-10
The Connecticut wits. *In* Emerson, E. H. ed. American literature, 1764-1789 p233-52
Literature to 1800. *In* American literary scholarship, 1974 p167-91
Literature to 1800 [another essay] *In* American literary scholarship, 1975 p203-29
Literature to 1800 [another essay] *In* American literary scholarship, 1976 p169-94
Literature to 1800 [another essay] *In* American literary scholarship, 1977 p189-206

Arnheim, Rudolf
Space as an image of time. *In* Kroeber, K. and Walling, W. eds. Images of romanticism p 1-12

Arnold, Christopher
Analyses of right. *In* Human rights p74-86

Arnold, Matthew
The last word
Contents
Amiel
Civilisation in the United States
Common schools abroad
Count Leo Tolstoi
Disestablishment in Wales
A 'friend of God'
From Easter to August
General Grant
Milton
The nadir of liberalism
Sainte-Beuve
Schools in the reign of Queen Victoria
Shelley
Special report on certain points connected with elementary education in Germany, Switzerland, and France
Up to Easter
The zenith of conservatism

About

Ball, P. M. 'The fates, it is clear, are against us.' *In* Ball, P. M. The heart's events p32-57
Dawson, C. Dramatic elegists: Arnold, Clough, and Browning at mid-century. *In* Dawson, C. Victorian noon p63-104

DeLaura, D. J. The future of poetry: a context for Carlyle and Arnold. *In* Carlyle and his contemporaries p148-80
Haley, B. Anarchy and physical culture. *In* Haley, B. The healthy body and Victorian culture p161-79
Langbaum, R. W. Arnold: waning energy. *In* Langbaum, R. W. The mysteries of identity p51-82
Lewis, W. Matthew Arnold. *In* Lewis, W. Enemy salvoes p179-83
Marcus, S. Some questions in general education today. *In* Small comforts for hard times p281-302
Neiman, F. A reader's guide to Arnold. *In* Allott, K. ed. Matthew Arnold p 1-38
Prickett, S. Demythologising and mythmaking: Arnold versus MacDonald. *In* Prickett, S. Romanticism and religion p211-48
Simpson, J. Arnold and Goethe. *In* Allott, K. ed. Matthew Arnold, p286-318
Stead, C. K. Eliot, Arnold, and the English poetic tradition. *In* The Literary criticism of T. S. Eliot p184-206
Super, R. H. Arnold and literary criticism: (ii) critical practice. *In* Allott, K. ed. Matthew Arnold p149-77
Super, R. H. The humanist at bay: the Arnold-Huxley debate. *In* Knoepflmacher, U. C. and Tennyson, G. B. eds. Nature and the Victorian imagination p231-45
Watson, G. The social criticism of Matthew Arnold. *In* Watson, G. Politics and literature in modern Britain p135-52

About individual works
Culture and anarchy

Colmer, J. The idealist vision. *In* Colmer J. Coleridge to Catch-22 p18-29
Cooper, B. Culture and anarchy: the politics of Matthew Arnold. *In* Prospects for constitutional democracy p21-35

Dover Beach

Trilling, L. Matthew Arnold: Dover Beach. *In* Trilling, L. Prefaces to The experience of literature p249-53

Empedocles on Etna

McAleer, E. C. Empedocles, Omar Khayyám, and Rabbi Ben Ezra. *In* Tennessee Studies in literature v XX p76-84

Notebooks (ed. by Howard Foster Lowry, Karl Young and Waldo Hilary Dunn)

Frye, N. Long, sequacious notes. *In* Frye, N. Northrop Frye on culture and literature p170-77

Bibliography

Neiman, F. A reader's guide to Arnold. *In* Allott, K. ed. Matthew Arnold p 1-38

Contemporaries

See Arnold, Matthew—Friends and associates

Friends and associates

Bertram, J. M. Arnold and Clough. *In* Allott, K. ed. Matthew Arnold p178-206

Knowledge—Criticism

See Arnold, Matthew—Knowledge—Literature

Arnold, Matthew—*Continued*

Knowledge—Literature

Anderson, W. D. Arnold and the classics. *In* Allott, K. ed. Matthew Arnold p259-85
DeLaura, D. J. Arnold and literary criticism: (i) critical ideas. *In* Allott, K. ed. Matthew Arnold p118-48

Knowledge—Political science

See Arnold, Matthew—Political and social views

Philosophy

Knights, B. The majority and the remnant: Matthew Arnold. *In* Knights, B. The idea of the clerisy in the nineteenth century p100-39
See also Arnold, Matthew—Religion and ethics

Poetic works

Allott, K. and Allott, M. F. Arnold the poet: (ii) narrative and dramatic poems. *In* Allott, K. ed. Matthew Arnold p70-117
Madden, W. A. Arnold the poet: (i) lyric and elegiac poems. *In* Allott, K. ed. Matthew Arnold p39-69

Political and social views

Keating, P. J. Arnold's social and political thought. *In* Allott. K. ed. Matthew Arnold p207-35
Knights, B. The majority and the remnant: Matthew Arnold. *In* Knights, B. The idea of the clerisy in the nineteenth century p100-39

Religion and ethics

DeLaura, D. J. Carlyle and Arnold: the religious issue. *In* Fielding, K. J. and Tarr, R. L. ed. Carlyle past and present p127-54
Willey, B. Arnold and religion. *In* Allott, K. ed. Matthew Arnold p236-58

Social views

See Arnold, Matthew—Political and social views

Sources

Anderson, W. D. Arnold and the classics. *In* Allott, K. ed. Matthew Arnold p259-85

Arnold, Thomas

About

Haley, B. Growing up healthy: images of boyhood. *In* Haley, B. The healthy body and Victorian culture p141-60

Arnow, Harriette Louisa (Simpson)

About individual works

The dollmaker

Oates, J. C. The nightmare of naturalism: Harriette Arnow's "The dollmaker". *In* Oates, J. C. New heaven, new earth: the visionary experience in literature p97-110

Arnstein, Helene S.

The crisis of becoming a father. *In* Gross, L. ed. Sexual issues in marriage p93-100

Aron, Raymond

Allies and rivals. *In* The New Atlantic challenge p37-41
On the proper use of ideologies. *In* Culture and its creators p 1-14
Politics and history

Contents

The dawn of universal history
The evolution of modern strategic thought (1945-1968)
History and politics
The liberal definition of freedom
Machiavelli and Marx
Macht, power, puissance: democratic prose or demoniac poetry?
On the historical condition of the sociologist
The philosophy of history
The social responsibility of the philosopher
Sociology and the philosophy of human rights
Three forms of historical intelligibility
Thucydides and the historical narrative
What is a theory of international relations?

About

Ionescu, G. Raymond Aron: a modern classicist. *In* De Crespigny, A. and Monogue, K. R. eds. Contemporary political philosophers p191-208

Arons, Arnold Boris

Teaching science. *In* Cahn, S. M. ed. Scholars who teach p101-30

Aronson, Sidney H.

Bell's electrical toy: what's the use? The sociology of early telephone usage. *In* The Social impact of the telephone p15-39

Aronstam, Robin Ann

The Blickling homilies: a reflection of popular Anglo-Saxon belief. *In* Law, church, and society p271-80

Arras, Gautier d'. See Gautier d'Arras

Arp, Jean

About

Krauss, R. E. A game plan: the terms of surrealism. *In* Krauss, R. E. Passages in modern sculpture p105-46

Arras, Gautier d'. See Gautier, d'Arras

Arrest

United States

LaFave, W. R. "Case-by-case adjudication" versus "standardized procedures": the Robinson dilemma. *In* The Supreme Court review, 1974 p127-63
White, J. B. The fourth amendment as a way of talking about people: a study of Robinson and Matlock. *In* The Supreme Court review, 1974 p165-232
See also Speedy trial

Arrian (Flavius Arrianus) See Arrianus, Flavius

Arrianus, Flavius

About

Bosworth, A. B. Arrian and the Alani. *In* Harvard Studies in classical philology v81 p217-55

Arrojo, Manuel Lopez-Rey y. See Lopez-Rey y Arrojo, Manuel

Arrow, Kenneth Joseph

The trade-off between growth and equity. *In* Theory for economic efficiency: essays in honor of Abba P. Lerner p 1-11

Arrufat, Antón

About

Dauster, F. N. The theater of Antón Arrufat. *In* Lyday, L. F. and Woodyard, G. W. eds. Dramatists in revolt p3-18

Arson

France

Abbiateci, A. Arsonists in eighteenth-century France: an essay in the typology of crime. *In* Deviants and the abandoned in French society p157-79

Art

Harris, N. Iconography and intellectual history: the half-tone effect. *In* Higham, J. and Conkin, P. K. eds. New directions in American intellectual history p196-211

Steadman, J. M. The iconographical approach. *In* Steadman, J. M. Nature into myth p23-45

Warnock, M. Imagination and creative art: Hume, Kant and Schelling. *In* Warnock, M. Imagination p35-71

See also Action in art; Aesthetics; Artists; Biology in art; Bronzes; Carving (Art industries); Children in art; Clocks and watches in art; Collage; Color in art; Communication in art; Creation (Literary, artistic, etc.); Cubism; Drawing; Erotic art; Fascism and art; Folk art; Forgery of works of art; Futurism (Art); Grotesque in art; Group work in art; Heroes in art; History in art; Illustration of books; Imitation (in art); Old age in art; Painting; Politics in art; Preraphaelitism; Realism in art; Symbolism in art

Analysis, interpretation, appreciation

See Aesthetics; Art—Philosophy; Art—Study and teaching; Art criticism; Painting

Cataloging

See Cataloging of art

Collectors and collecting

See Art as an investment

Criticism

See Art criticism

Education

See Art—Study and teaching

Forgeries

Meyer, L. B. Forgery and the anthropology of art; excerpt from "Music, the arts, and ideas." *In* Aagaard-Mogensen, L. ed. Culture and art p53-66

Historiography

Jauss, H. R. History of art and pragmatic history. *In* Amacher, R. E. and Lange, V. eds. New perspectives in German literary criticism p432-64

Winternitz, E. The knowledge of musical instruments as an aid to the art historian. *In* Winternitz, E. Musical instruments and their symbolism in Western art p43-56

History

See Art criticism

History—17th-18th centuries

See Art, Modern—17th-18th centuries

History—20th century

See Art, Modern—20th century

Philosophy

Beardsley, M. C. Is art essentially institutional? *In* Aagaard-Mogensen, L. ed. Culture and art p194-209

Bettelheim, B. Art and art education: a personal vision. *In* Bettelheim, B. Surviving, and other essays p412-26

Binkley, T. Deciding about art. *In* Aagaard-Mogensen, L. ed. Culture and art p90-109

Binkley, T. Piece: contra aesthetics. *In* Margolis, J. Z. ed. Philosophy looks at the arts p25-44

Cassirer, E. The educational value of art. *In* Cassirer, E. Symbol, myth, and culture p196-215

Cassirer, E. Language and art I. *In* Cassirer, E. Symbol, myth, and culture p145-65

Cassirer, E. Language and art II. *In* Cassirer, E. Symbol, myth, and culture p166-95

Coomaraswamy, A. K. Ars sine scientia nihil; excerpt from "Figures of speech or figures of thought: collected essays on the traditional or 'normal' view of art." *In* Coomaraswamy, A. K. Selected papers v 1 p229-32

Coomaraswamy, A. K. The part of art in Indian life. *In* Coomaraswamy, A. K. Selected papers v 1 p71-100

Coomaraswamy, A. K. Symptom, diagnosis, and regimen; excerpt from "Figures of speech or figures of thought: collected essays on the traditional or 'normal' view of art." *In* Coomaraswamy, A. K. Selected papers v 1 p316-19

Danto, A. C. The artworld. *In* Aagaard-Mogensen, L. ed. Culture and art p9-20

Also in Margolis, J. Z. ed. Philosophy looks at the arts p132-44

Dickie, G. What is art? Excerpt from "Art and the aesthetic: an institutional analysis." *In* Aagaard-Mogensen, L. ed. Culture and art p21-32

Glickman, J. Creativity in the arts. *In* Aagaard-Mogensen, L. ed. Culture and art p130-46

Goodman, N. Reality remade; excerpt from "Languages of art". *In* Margolis, J. Z. ed. Philosophy looks at the arts p225-48

Henrich, D. Art and philosophy of art today: reflections with reference to Hegel. *In* Amacher, R. E. and Lange, V. eds. New perspectives in German literary criticism p108-33

Iseminger, G. Appreciation, the artworld, and the aesthetic. *In* Aagaard-Mogensen, L. ed. Culture and art p118-30

Kjørup, S. Art broadly and wholly conceived. *In* Aagaard-Mogensen, L. ed. Culture and art p45-53

Kouwenhoven, J. A. Art, disorder, and American experience: half a truth is better than none. *In* Mann, D. A. ed. The arts in a democratic society p70-97

Lyas, C. Danto and Dickie on art. *In* Aagaard-Mogensen, L. ed. Culture and art p170-93

Malraux, A. Anti-critique. *In* Courcel, M. H. de, ed. Malraux p223-57

Margolis, J. Z. Works of art are physically embodied and culturally emergent entities. *In* Aagaard-Mogensen, L. ed. Culture and art p32-45

Maynard, P. Depiction, vision, and convention. *In* Margolis, J. Z. ed. Philosophy looks at the arts p273-306

Meyer, L. B. Forgery and the anthropology of art; excerpt from "Music, the arts, and ideas." *In* Aagaard-Mogensen, L. ed. Culture and art p53-66

Miller, J. W. A meditation on a painting. *In* Miller, J. W. The paradox of cause, and other essays p169-73

Miller, J. W. What does art do? *In* Miller, J. W. The paradox of cause, and other essays p161-68

Art—Philosophy—*Continued*

Mukařovský, J. The essence of the visual arts. *In* Matejka, L. and Titunik, I. R. eds. Semiotics of art p229-44

Also in Mukařovský, J. Structure sign and function p220-35

Sclafani, R. J. The theory of art. *In* Aagaard-Mogensen, L. ed. Culture and art p146-70

Truitt, W. H. Art for the people. *In* Mann, D. A. ed. The arts in a democratic society p58-69

Wollheim, R. On drawing an object. *In* Margolis, J. Z. ed. Philosophy looks at the arts p249-72

Prices
See Art as an investment

Private collections—Great Britain
Shone, R. and Grant, D. J. C. The picture collector. *In* Keynes, M. ed. Essays on John Maynard Keynes p280-89

Psychology
Gombrich, Sir E. H. J. Illusion and art. *In* Gregory, R. L. and Gombrich, Sir E. H. J. eds. Illusion in nature and art p193-243

Gombrich, Sir E. H. J. The sky is the limit: the vault of heaven and pictorial vision. *In* Perception p84-94

Howard, V. A. Artistic practice and skills. *In* Perkins, D. and Leondar, B. eds. The arts and cognition p208-40

Kennedy, J. M. and Fox, N. Pictures to see and pictures to touch. *In* Perkins, D. and Leondar, B. eds. The arts and cognition p118-35

Kolers, P. A. Reading pictures and reading text. *In* Perkins, D. and Leondar, B. eds. The arts and cognition p136-64

Reproduction
See Forgery of works of art

Study and teaching
Bettelheim, B. Art and art education: a personal vision. *In* Bettelheim, B. Surviving, and other essays p412-26

Kramer, E. Art and emptiness: new problems in art education and therapy. *In* Ulman, E. and Dachinger, P. eds. Art therapy p33-42

Naumburg, M. Spontaneous art in education and psychotherapy. *In* Ulman, E. and Dachinger, P. eds. Art therapy p221-39

Pine, S. Fostering growth through art education, art therapy, and art in psychotherapy. *In* Ulman, E. and Dachinger, P. eds. Art therapy p60-94

Themal, J. H. Children's work as art. *In* Ulman, E. and Dachinger, P. eds. Art therapy p95-105

Study and teaching—New York (City)
Glannon, E. The WPA experience. *In* Roots of open education in America p91-100

Therapeutic use
See Art therapy

Africa
Willett, F. African arts and the future: decay or development? *In* African themes p213-26

See also Art, African

Africa, Sub-Saharan
Sieber, R. Traditional arts of Black Africa. *In* Martin, P. M. and O'Meara, P. eds. Africa p221-42

China
Sullivan, M. Values through art. *In* Terrill, R. ed. The China difference p305-25

England—History
Landow, G. P. There began to be a great talking about the fine arts. *In* Altholz, J. L. ed. The mind and art of Victorian England p 124-45

Willis, P. The visual arts. *In* Rogers, P. ed. The eighteenth century p208-39

Germany—Exhibitions
Rosenberg, H. On the edge: Documenta 5. *In* Rosenberg, H. Art on th eedge p262-73

India
Coomaraswamy, A. K. The part of art in Indian life. *In* Coomaraswamy, A. K. Selected papers v 1 p71-100

Ireland—History
Stokstad, M. and Nelson, M. J. The arts in twentieth-century Ireland. *In* Orel, H. ed. Irish history and culture p271-89

Italy
See Art, Italian

Netherlands
Jaffe, H. L. C. Introduction to De Stijl. *In* Kaplan, P. and Manso, S. eds. Major European art movements, 1900-1945 p222-49

Russia
Milner-Gulland, R. R. Art and architecture of Old Russia, 988-1700. *In* Auty, R. and Obolensky, D. eds. An introduction to Russian art and architecture p 1-70

See also Art, Russian

United States—Galleries and museums
Rosenberg, H. The old age of modernism. *In* Rosenberg, H. Art on the edge p281-87

Art, Abelam (New Guinea tribe) See Painting, Abelam (New Guinea tribe)

Art, Abstract

Long, R. C. W. Kandinsky and abstraction: the role of the hidden image. *In* Kaplan, P. and Manso, S. eds. Major European art movements, 1900-1945 p275-98

Osborne, H. Epilogue. *In* Osborne, H. Abstraction and artifice in twentieth-century art p181-86

Osborne, H. The new sensibility of the 1960s. *In* Osborne, H. Abstraction and artifice in twentieth-century art p149-62

Osborne, H. Non-iconic abstraction and Kandinsky. *In* Osborne, H. Abstraction and artifice in twentieth-century art p97-110

Osborne, H. Semantic abstraction. *In* Osborne, H. Abstraction and artifice in twentieth-century art p28-41

Schapiro, M. Nature of abstract art. *In* Schapiro, M. Selected papers v2 p185-232

See also Abstract expressionism; Concrete art; Modernism; Neoplasticism

Art, African

Bravmann, R. A. Contemporary dimensions of African art. *In* Martin, P. A. and O'Meara, P. eds. Africa p348-66

Art, African—*Continued*

Sieber, R. Some aspects of religion and art in Africa. *In* African religions: a symposium p141-57

See also Art—Africa

History

Sieber, R. Traditional arts of Black Africa. *In* Martin, P. M. and O'Meara, P. eds. Africa p221-42

Influence

Donne, J. B. African art and Paris studios, 1905-20. *In* Greenhalgh, M. and Megaw, J. V. S. eds. Art in society p105-20

Art, Afro-American. See Afro-American art

Art, Ancient. See Art, Greek, and similar headings; Art, Primitive

Art, Anglo-Saxon

Deshman, R. The Leofric missal and tenth-century English art. *In* Anglo-Saxon England 6 p145-73

Schroeder, P. R. Stylistic analogies between Old English art and poetry. *In* Viator: medieval and Renaissance studies v5 p185-97

Art, Apocalyptic. See Apocalyptic art

Art, Arab. See Art, Islamic

Art, Asian. See Art, Oriental

Art, Aztec. See Aztecs—Art

Art, Baroque

Blunt, A. **Naples as seen by French travellers, 1630-1780.** *In* **The Artist and the writer in France p 1-14**

Art, Benin

Shaw, T. The art of Benin through the eyes of the artist, the art historian, the ethnographer and the archaeologist. *In* Greenhalgh, M. and Megaw, J. V. S. eds. Art in society p207-23

Art, British. See Aesthetic movement (British art); Art, English

Art, Buddhist. See Buddhist art and symbolism

Art, Byzantine

Rice, T. T. Animal combat scenes in Byzantine art. *In* Studies in memory of David Talbot Rice p17-23

Art, Canadian

Hutchings, P. A. E. Some contemporary realisms. *In* Concerning contemporary art p89-132

Art, Carlovingian

Bullough, D. A. 'Imagines regum' and their significance in the early medieval West. *In* Studies in memory of David Talbot Rice p223-76

Art, Christian. See Christian art and symbolism

Art, Classical

See also Art, Roman

Influence

Wittkower, R. The role of classical models in Bernini's and Poussin's preparatory work. *In* Wittkower, R. Studies in the Italian baroque p103-14

Art, Classical. See Art, Roman

Art, Conceptual. See Conceptual art

Art, Concrete. See Concrete art

Art, Decorative

See also Bronzes; Illustration of books

England—History

Willis, P. The visual arts. *In* Rogers, P. ed. The eighteenth century p208-39

Art, Early Renaissance. See Art, Renaissance—Early Renaissance

Art, East Asian. See Art, Far Eastern

Art, Ecclesiastical. See Christian art and symbolism

Art, Effect of. See Art therapy

Art, Egyptian

Influence

Wittkower, R. Piranesi and eighteenth-century Egyptomania. *In* Wittkower, R. Studies in the Italian baroque p259-73

Art, English

History

Jones, D. An aspect of the art of England. *In* Jones, D. The dying Gaul, and other writings p59-62

Art, Erotic. See Erotic art

Art, Eskimo. See Eskimos—Art

Art, Etruscan

Richardson, E. H. The story of Ariadne in Italy. *In* Studies in classical art and archaeology p189-95

Art, European

Sturtevant, W. C. First visual images of native America. *In* First images of America p417-54

Egyptian influences

Wittkower, R. Piranesi and eighteenth-century Egyptomania. *In* Wittkower, R Studies in the Italian baroque p259-73

Mexican influences

Robertson, D. Mexican Indian art and the Atlantic filter: sixteenth to eighteenth centuries. *In* First images of America p483-94

Art, Far Eastern

Coomaraswamy, A. K. Introduction to the art of Eastern Asia. *In* Coomaraswamy, A. K. Selected papers v 1 p101-27

Art, Folk. See Folk art

Art, French

African influences

Donne, J. B. African art and Paris studios, 1905-20. *In* Greenhalgh, M. and Megaw, J. V. S. eds. Art in society p105-20

Art, Gothic

Influence

Easson, R. R. Blake and the Gothic. *In* Essick, R. N. and Pearce, D. R. eds. Blake in his time p145-54

Rose, E. J. The "Gothicized imagination" of "Michaelangelo Blake." *In* Essick, R. N. and Pearce, D. R. eds. Blake in his time p155-69

Art, Graphic. See Graphic arts

Art, Greek

Harrison, E. B. Apollo's cloak. *In* Studies in classical art and archaeology p91-98

Havelock, C. M. Art as communication in ancient Greece. *In* Havelock, E. A. and Hershbell, J. P. eds. Communication arts in the ancient world p95-118

Art, High Renaissance. See Art, Renaissance—High Renaissance

Art, Modern—20th century—*Continued*

Rosenberg, H. What's new: ritual revolution. *In* Rosenberg, H. Art on the edge p251-61

Tilghman, B. R. Artistic puzzlement. *In* Aagaard-Mogensen, L. ed. Culture and art p77-90

See also Art, Abstract; Assemblage (Art); Concrete art; Constructivism (Art); Cubism; Dadaism; Expressionism (Art); Fauvism; Futurism (Art); Happening (Art); Modernism (Art); Pop art; Surrealism

20th century—African influences

Donne, J. B. African art and Paris studios, 1905-20. *In* Greenhalgh, M. and Megaw, J. V. S. eds. Art in society p105-20

20th century—Exhibitions

Rosenberg, H. On the edge: Documenta 5. *In* Rosenberg, H. Art on the edge p262-73

20th century—History

Osborne, H. From impressionism to expressionism. *In* Osborne, H. Abstraction and artifice in twentieth-century art p42-54

Schapiro, M. The introduction of modern art in America: the Armory Show. *In* Schapiro, M. Selected papers v2 p135-77

20th century—Netherlands

Jaffe, H. L. C. Introduction to De Stijl. *In* Kaplan, P. and Manso, S. eds. Major European art movements, 1900-1945 p222-49

20th century—Russia

Bowlt, J. E. Art and architecture in Soviet Russia, 1917-1972. *In* Auty, R. and Obolensky, D. eds. An introduction to Russian art and architecture p145-72

Bowlt, J. E. Art and architecture in the age of revolution, 1860-1917. *In* Auty, R. and Obolensky, D. eds. An introduction to Russian art and architecture p112-44

Bowlt, J. E. Artists of the world, disunite! *In* Kaplan, P. and Manso, S. eds. Major European art movements 1900-1945 p299-309

20th century—United States

Chase, L. Existential vs. humanist realism; excerpt from "Photo realism." *In* Battcock, G. ed. Super realism p81-95

Henry, G. The real thing. *In* Battcock, G. ed. Super realism p3-20

Karp, I. C. Rent is the only reality, or The hotel instead of the hymns. *In* Battcock, G. ed. Super realism p21-35

Levin, K. The ersatz object. *In* Battcock, G. ed. Super realism p96-110

Marandel, J. P. The deductive image. *In* Battcock, G. ed. Super realism p36-48

Nemser, C. The closeup vision. *In* Battcock, G. ed. Super realism p49-63

Nochlin, L. Realism now. *In* Battcock, G. ed. Super realism p111-25

Nochlin, L. Some women realists. *In* Battcock, G. ed. Super realism p64-78

Raymond, H. D. Beyond freedom, dignity, and ridicule. *In* Battcock, G. ed. Super realism p126-34

Rosenberg, H. Place patriotism and the New York mainstream. *In* Rosenberg, H. Art on the edge p206-15

Rosenberg, H. Reality again. *In* Battcock, G. ed. Super realism p135-42

Rosenberg, H. Reality again: the new photorealism. *In* Rosenberg, H. Art on the edge p236-44

Rosenberg, H. Shall these bones live?: art movement ghosts. *In* Rosenberg, H. Art on the edge p227-35

Rosenberg, H. Trials of Eros. *In* Rosenberg, H. Art on the edge p216-26

Tashjian, D. L. Aftermath and conclusion. *In* Tashjian, D. L. Skyscraper primitives p227-30

Art, Modernist. See Modernism (Art)

Art, Moorish. See Art, Islamic

Art, Mozarabic

Schapiro, M. From Mozarabic to Romanesque in Silos. *In* Schapiro, M. Selected papers v 1 p28-101

Art, Muslim. See Art, Islamic

Art, Non-objective. See Art, Abstract

Art, Oriental

Philosophy

Coomaraswamy, A. K. The philosophy of mediaeval and Oriental art. *In* Coomaraswamy, A. K. Selected papers v 1 p43-70

Art, Persian. See Art, Iranian

Art, Popular. See Folk art

Art, Primitive

Cardew, M. Design and meaning in pre-literate art. *In* Greenhalgh, M. and Megaw, J. V. S. eds. Art in society p15-20

Dark, P. J. C. What is art for anthropologists? *In* Greenhalgh, M. and Megaw, J. V. S. eds. Art in society p31-50

Greenhalgh, M. European interest in the non-European: the sixteenth century and pre-Columbian art and architecture. *In* Greenhalgh, M. and Megaw, J. V. S. eds. Art in society p89-103

Korn, S. M. The formal analysis of visual systems as exemplified by a study of Abelam (Papua New Guinea) paintings. *In* Greenhalgh, M. and Megaw, J. V. S. eds. Art in society p161-73

Layton, Art and visual communication. *In* Greenhalgh, M. and Megaw, J. V. S. eds. Art in society p21-30

See also Folk art

Art, Renaissance

Barolsky, P. Love, laughter and revelry. *In* Barolsky, P. Infinite jest: wit and humor in Italian Renaissance art p209-26

Barolsky, P. The place of humor in Renaissance art. *In* Barolsky, P. Infinite jest: wit and humor in Italian Renaissance art p 1-17

Gordon, D. J. Ripa's fate. *In* Gordon, D. J. The Renaissance imagination p51-74

Kemp, M. From "mimesis" to "fantasia": the quattrocento vocabulary of creation, inspiration and genius in the visual arts. *In* Viator: medieval and Renaissance studies v8 p347-98

Middeldorf, U. Some Florentine painted Madonna reliefs. *In* Collaboration in Italian Renaissance art p77-90

Early Renaissance—Italy—History

Barolsky, P. Quattrocento mirth. *In* Barolsky, P. Infinite jest: wit and humor in Italian Renaissance art p18-50

Art, Renaissance—*Continued*

High Renaissance

Trevor-Roper, H. R. Charles V and the failure of humanism. *In* Trevor-Roper, H. R. Princes and artists p11-45

High Renaissance—Florence—History

Barolsky, P. The lighter side of Cosimo de' Medici's court. *In* Barolsky, P. Infinite jest: wit and humor in Italian Renaissance art p139-57

High Renaissance—Italy—History

Barolsky, P. Mannerist bizzarrie. *In* Barolsky, P. Infinite jest: wit and humor in Italian Renaissance art p101-38

Art, Rococo

Brady, P. A sweet disorder: atomistic empiricism and the rococo mode of vision. *In* Studies in eighteenth-century culture v7 p451-61

Art, Roman

Richardson, E. H. The story of Ariadne in Italy. *In* Studies in classical art and archaeology p189-95

History

Harlow, B. Realignment:. Alois Riegl's image of late Roman art industry. *In* Glyph 3 p118-36

Art, Romanesque

Schapiro, M. From Mozarabic to Romanesque in Silos. *In* Schapiro, M. Selected papers v 1 p28-101

Schapiro, M. On geometrical schematism in Romanesque art. *In* Schapiro, M. Selected papers v 1 p265-84

Schapiro, M. On the aesthetic attitude in Romanesque art. *In* Schapiro, M. Selected papers v 1 p 1-27

Schapiro, M. Two Romanesque drawings in Auxerre and some iconographic problems. *In* Schapiro, M. Selected papers v 1 p306-27

Mozarabic influences

Schapiro, M. From Mozarabic to Romanesque in Silos. *In* Schapiro, M. Selected papers v 1 p28-101

Art, Russian

Howlett, J. The origins of Socialist realism in Soviet visual art. *In* Oxford Slavonic papers new ser. v9 p91-101

See also Suprematism in art

History

Bowlt, J. E. Art and architecture in Soviet Russia, 1917-1972. *In* Auty, R. and Obolensky, D. eds. An introduction to Russian art and architecture p145-72

Bowlt, J. E. Art and architecture in the age of revolution, 1860-1917. *In* Auty, R. and Obolensky, D. eds. An introduction to Russian art and architecture p112-44

Bowlt, J. E. Artists of the world, disunite! *In* Kaplan, P. and Manso, S. eds. Major European art movements, 1900-1945 p299-309

Milner-Gulland, R. R. Art and architecture in the Petersburg age, 1700-1860. *In* Auty, R. and Obolensky, D. ed. An introduction to Russian art and architecture p71-111

Milner-Gulland, R. A. Art and architecture of Old Russia, 988-1700. *In* Auty, R. and Obolensky, D. eds. An introduction to Russian art and architecture p1-70

Art, Victorian

Great Britain

Landow, G. P. There began to be a great talking about the fine arts. *In* Altholz, J. L. ed. The mind and art of Victorian England p124-45

Art, Yoruba

Lawal, B. Yoruba-Sango ram symbolism: from ancient Sahara or dynastic Egypt? *In* African images p225-51

Art and communism. See Communism and art

Art and history. See History in art

Art and industry

Williamson, A. Industrial change and the artist. *In* Williamson, A. Artists and writers in revolt p11-15

Art and literature

Gilman, E. B. Introduction: "I have been studying how I might compare." *In* Gilman, E. B. The curious perspective p 1-15

Henn, T. R. Yeats and the picture galleries. *In* Henn, T. R. Last essays p157-72

Herman, J. The painter and literature. *In* English Association. Essays and studies, 1977 p70-72

Hunt, J. D. 'Broken images': T. S. Eliot and modern painting. *In* The Waste land in different voices p163-84

Kunitz, S. J. The sister arts. *In* Kunitz, S. J. A kind of order, a kind of folly p131-34

Lind, I. D. The effect of painting on Faulkner's poetic form. *In* Faulkner, modernism, and film: Faulkner and Yoknapatawpha, 1978 p127-48

Meyers, J. Bellini, Giotto, Mantegna, Botticelli and Swann's way. *In* Meyers, J. Painting and the novel p96-111

Meyers, J. Bronzino, Veronese and The wings of the dove. *In* Meyers, J. Painting and the novel p19-30

Meyers, J. Dürer and Doctor Faustus. *In* Meyers, J. Painting and the novel p157-74

Meyers, J. Fra Angelico and The rainbow. *In* Meyers, J. Painting and the novel p53-64

Meyers, J. Ghirlandaio and Where angels fear to tread; Giotto and A room with a view. *In* Meyers, J. Painting and the novel p31-45

Meyers, J. Greuze and The Leopard. *In* Meyers, J. Painting and the novel p124-34

Meyers, J. Guido Reni and The marble faun. *In* Meyers, J. Painting and the novel p6-18

Meyers, J. Gustave Moreau and Against nature. *In* Meyers, J. Painting and the novel p84-95

Meyers, J. Holbein and The idiot. *In* Meyers, J. Painting and the novel p136-47

Meyers, J. Mark Gertler and Women in love. *In* Meyers, J. Painting and the novel p65-82

Meyers, J. Maurice Greiffenhagen and The white peacock. *In* Meyers, J. Painting and the novel p46-52

Meyers, J. Van Eyck and The Fall. *In* Meyers, J. Painting and the novel p148-56

Meyers, J. Vermeer and The captive. *In* Meyers, J. Painting and the novel p112-23

Nemerov, H. On poetry and painting, with a thought of music. *In* Nemerov, H. Figures of thought p95-99

Art therapy—*Continued*

Denny, J. M. Techniques for individual and group art therapy. *In* Ulman, E. and Dachinger, P. eds. Art therapy p132-49

Dewdney, I. An art therapy program for geriatric patients. *In* Ulman, E. and Dachinger, P. eds. Art therapy p126-31

Kramer, E. Art and craft. *In* Ulman, E. and Dachinger, P. eds. Art therapy p106-09

Kwiatkowska, H. Y. Family art therapy: experiments with a new technique. *In* Ulman, E. and Dachinger, P. eds. Art therapy p113-25

Lehnsen, E. Correlation between clinical course and pictorial expression of a schizophrenic patient. *In* Ulman, E. and Dachinger, P. eds. Art therapy p286-310

Marinow, A. The self-portraits of a schizophrenic patient. *In* Ulman, E. and Dachinger, P. eds. Art therapy p325-27

Ulman, E. Art therapy: problems of definition. *In* Ulman, E. and Dachinger, P. eds. Art therapy p3-13

Ulman, E. Therapy is not enough: the contribution of art to general hospital psychiatry. *In* Ulman, E. and Dachinger, P. eds. Art therapy p14-32

Ulman, E. and Dachinger, P. Therapeutic art programs around the world. *In* Ulman, E. and Dachinger, P. eds. Art therapy p208-12

Wittenberg, D. Art therapy for adolescent drug abusers. *In* Ulman, E. and Dachinger, P. eds. Art therapy p150-58

Cases, clinical reports, statistics

Day, J. and Kwiatkowska, H. Y. The psychiatric patient and his "well" sibling: a comparison through their art productions. *In* Ulman, E. and Dachinger, P. eds. Art therapy p345-60

Dewdney, S. H. Elda's art therapy in the context of a quarter century of psychiatric treatment. *In* Ulman, E. and Dachinger, P. eds. Art therapy p240-75

Garai, J. E. The use of painting to resolve an artist's identity conflicts. *In* Ulman, E. and Dachinger, P. eds. Art therapy p311-24

Kramer, E. The practice of art therapy with children. *In* Ulman, E. and Dachinger, P. eds. Art therapy p159-80

Kramer, E. The problem of quality in art. *In* Ulman, E. and Dachinger, P. eds. Art therapy p43-59

Naumburg, M. Spontaneous art in education and psychotherapy. *In* Ulman, E. and Dachinger, P. eds. Art therapy p221-39

Pine, S. Fostering growth through art education, art therapy, and art in psychotherapy. *In* Ulman, E. and Dachinger, P. eds. Art therapy p60-94

Ulman, E. A new use of art in psychiatric diagnosis. *In* Ulman, E. and Dachinger, P. eds. Art therapy p361-86

Ulman, E. and Levy, B. I. An experimental approach to the judgment of psychopathology from paintings. *In* Ulman, E. and Dachinger, P. eds. Art therapy p393-402

Voegeli, H. T.; Goldberg, M. L. and Schneider, I. A marital crisis precipitated by art therapy. *In* Ulman, E. and Dachinger, P. eds. Art therapy p276-85

Artaud, Antonin

About

Bersani, L. Artaud, defecation and birth. *In* Bersani, L. A future for Astyanax p259-72

Chiaromonte, N. Antonin Artaud and his theater. *In* Chiaromonte, N. The worm of consciousness, and other essays p107-26

Derrida, J. La parole soufflée. *In* Derrida, J. Writing and difference p169-95

Derrida, J. The theater of cruelty and the closure of representation. *In* Derrida, J. Writing and difference p232-50

Glicksberg, C. I. Artaud and metaphysical madness. *In* Glicksberg, C. I. The literature of commitment p131-40

About individual works

Héliogabale

Jacobs, C. Artaud: the assimilating harmony: Héliogabale. *In* Jacobs, C. The dissimulating harmony p51-86

Artaud, Jean Baptiste

About individual works

La centenaire de Molière

Gravit, F. W. The first centenary of Molière's death. *In* Johnson, R. B.; Neumann, E. S. and Trail, G. T. eds. Molière and the commonwealth of letters: patrimony and posterity p547-56

Arthur, David Tallmadge

Millerism. *In* The Rise of Adventism p154-72

Arthur, John

Rights and the duty to bring aid. *In* Aiken, W. and La Follette, H. eds. World hunger and moral obligation p37-48

Arthur, Marylin B.

The curse of civilization: the choral odes of the Phoenissae. *In* Harvard Studies in classical philology v81 p163-85

Arthur of Little Britain. See Artus de Bretagne

Arthurian romances

Coomaraswamy, A. K. On the Loathly Bride. *In* Coomaraswamy, A. K. Selected papers v 1 p353-70

Griffith, R. R. The political bias of Malory's "Morte Darthur". *In* Viator: medieval and Renaissance studies v5 p365-86

Hanning, R. W. Afterword: the evolution of chivalric romance in the early thirteenth century. *In* Hanning, R. W. The individual in twelfth-century romance p234-42

Leviant, C. Jewish influence upon Arthurian legends. *In* Salo Wittmayer Baron v2 p639-56

Segre, C. Deconstruction and reconstruction of a tale: from La mort le roi Artu to the Novellino. *In* Segre, C. Structures and time p58-64

Staines, D. King Arthur in Victorian fiction. *In* The Worlds of Victorian fiction p267-93

Wilson, R. H. Malory and the ballad "King Arthur's death." *In* Medievalia et humanistica no. 6 p139-49

Articles of Confederation. See United States. Articles of Confederation

Artifacts, Functioning objects, facts, and. Miller, J. W. *In* Miller, J. W. The paradox of cause, and other essays

Artificial intelligence

Boden, M. A. Human values in a mechanistic universe. *In* Royal Institute of Philosophy. Human values p135-71

See also Machine translating

Artificial satellites

York, H. F. Reconnaissance satellites and the arms race. *In* Arms control and technological innovation p224-31

Artificial thinking. See Artificial intelligence

Artillery

History

Vale, M. G. A. New techniques and old ideals: the impact of artillery on war and chivalry at the end of the Hundred Years War. *In* War, literature, and politics in the late Middle Ages p57-72

Artisans

Genoa

Hughes, D. O. Domestic ideals and social behavior: evidence from medieval Genoa. *In* Rosenberg, C. E. ed. The family in history p115-43

Tunis

Champault, F. D. Tunisia: the artisans of the medina. *In* United Nations Educational, Scientific and Cultural Organization. The conservation of cities p140-45

Artistic communication. See Communication in art

Artistic photography. See Photography, Artistic

Artists

Herman, J. The modern artist in modern society. *In* Greenhalgh, M. and Megaw, J. V. S. eds. Art in society p121-30

See also Architects; Painters

Psychology

Mukařovský, J. Personality in art. *In* Mukařovský, J. Structure, sign, and function p150-68

Artists, American

Smelstor, M. R. Expatriation and exploration: the exiled artists of the 1920s. *In* Kagle, S. E. ed. America: exploration and travel p136-52

Artists, Indic

Coomaraswamy, A. K. The intellectual operation in Indian art; excerpt from "Figures of speech or figures of thought: collected essays on the traditional or 'normal' view of art." *In* Coomaraswamy, A. K. Selected papers v 1 p131-46

Artists in literature

Daemmrich, H. S. Mann's portrait of the artist: archetypal patterns. *In* Garvin, H. R. ed. Makers of the twentieth-century novel p166-78

Artizans. See Artisans

Arts

Graff, G. The myth of the postmodern breakthrough. *In* Graff, G. Literature against itself p31-62

Imdahl, M. Overstepping esthetic limits in visual art: four aspects of the problem. *In* Amacher, R. E. and Lange, V. eds. New perspectives in German literary criticism p279-92

Pasternak, B. L. From A safe-conduct. *In* Proffer, C. R. ed. Modern Russian poets on poetry p87-95

Sessions, R. Art, freedom, and the individual. *In* Sessions, R. Roger Sessions on music p105-19

Sessions, R. Music and the crisis of the arts. *In* Sessions, R. Roger Sessions on music p175-86

Trilling, L. On not talking. *In* Trilling, L. A gathering of fugitives p153-63

See also Artists

Criticism

See Art criticism

Economic aspects

Shell, M. John Ruskin and the political economy of literature. *In* Shell, M. The economy of literature p129-51

History

Hartman, G. H. History-writing as answerable style. *In* Cohen, R. ed. New directions in literary history p95-105

Also in Hartman, G. H. The fate of reading p101-13

See also Art criticism

Philosophy

Auden, W. H. Mimesis and allegory. *In* Wimsatt, W. K. ed. Literary criticism: idea and act p32-43

Cavell, S. A matter of meaning it. *In* Cavell, S. Must we mean what we say? p213-37

Coomaraswamy, A. K. A figure of speech or a figure of thought? Excerpt from "Figures of speech or figures of thought: collected essays on the traditional or 'normal' view of art." *In* Coomaraswamy, A. K. Selected papers v 1 p13-42

Coomaraswamy, A. K. Imitation, expression, and participation; excerpt from "Figures of speech or figures of thought: collected essays on the traditional or 'normal' view of art." *In* Coomaraswamy, A. K. Selected papers v 1 p276-85

Elliott, R. K. Aesthetic theory and the experience of art. *In* Margolis, J. Z. ed. Philosophy looks at the arts p45-87

Gass, W. H. Carrots, noses, snow, rose, roses. *In* Gass, W. H. The world within the word p280-307

Gass, W. H. Groping for trouts. *In* Gass, W. H. The world within the word p262-79

Glickman, J. Creativity in the arts. *In* Margolis, J. Z. ed. Philosophy looks at the arts p145-60

Goodman, N. When is art? *In* Perkins, D. and Leondar, B. eds. The arts and cognition p11-19

Huxley, A. L. Art. *In* Huxley, A. L. The Human situation p182-97

Koestler, A. The discoveries of art. *In* Koestler, A. Janus p137-61

Koestler, A. Literature and the law of diminishing returns. *In* Koestler, A. The heel of Achilles p119-37

Margolis, J. Z. The ontological peculiarity of works of art. *In* Margolis, J. Z. ed. Philosophy looks at the arts p213-24

Marquard, O. On the importance of the theory of the unconscious for a theory of no longer fine art. *In* Amacher, R. E. and Lange, V. eds. New perspectives in German literary criticism p260-78

Mukařovský, J. The aesthetic norm. *In* Mukařovský, J. Structure, sign, and function p49-56

Mukařovský, J. Art as semiotic fact. *In* Matejka, L. and Titunik, I. R. eds. Semiotics of art p3-9

Same as: Art as a semiotic fact. *In* Mukařovský, J. Structure, sign and function p82-88

Arts—Philosophy—*Continued*

Mukařovský, J. Can there be a universal aesthetic value in art. *In* Mukařovský, J. Structure, sign, and function p57-69

Mukařovský, J. The concept of the whole in the theory of art. *In* Mukařovský, J. Structure, sign, and function p70-81

Mukařovský, J. Intentionality and unintentionality in art. *In* Mukařovský, J. Structure, sign, and function p89-128

Mukařovský, J. On structuralism. *In* Mukařovský, J. Structure, sign, and function p17-30

Mukařovský, J. Personality in art. *In* Mukařovský, J. Structure, sign, and function p150-68

Olson, E. The dialectical foundations of critical pluralism. *In* Olson, E. On value judgments in the arts, and other essays p327-59

Olson, E. A dialogue on the function of art in society. *In* Olson, E. On value judgments in the arts, and other essays p254-67

Olson, E. On value judgments in the arts. *In* Olson, E. On value judgments in the arts, and other essays p307-26

Romilly, J. de. Plato and conjurers. *In* Romilly, J. de. Magic and rhetoric in ancient Greece p23-43

Romilly, J. de. Rhetoric and the classification of arts in the fourth century B.C. *In* Romilly, J. de. Magic and rhetoric in ancient Greece p45-66

Sircello, G. J. Expressive properties of art; excerpt from "Mind & art: an essay on the varieties of expression." *In* Margolis, J. Z. ed. Philosophy looks at the arts p325-45

Sparshott, F. E. Zeno on art: anatomy of a definition. *In* Rist, J. M. ed. The Stoics p273-90

Thomson, B. Some properties of art. *In* Lot's wife and the Venus of Milo p139-54

Tormey, A. Art and expression: a critique; excerpt from "The concept of expression: a study in philosophical psychology and aesthetics." *In* Margolis, J. Z. ed. Philosophy looks at the arts p346-69

Walton, K. L. Categories of art. *In* Margolis, J. Z. ed. Philosophy looks at the arts p88-131

Wollheim, R. Art and its objects; excerpt. *In* Margolis, J. Z. ed. Philosophy looks at the arts p169-88

Wolterstorff, N. Toward an ontology of art works. *In* Margolis, J. Z. ed. Philosophy looks at the arts p189-212

Psychology

Gardner, H. Senses, symbols, operations: an organization of artistry. *In* Perkins, D. and Leondar, B. eds. The arts and cognition p88-117

Richards, I. A. Emotion and art. *In* Richards, I. A. Complementarities p7-11

Social aspects

See Arts and society

Study and teaching

Dent, F. L. Initiating the audience. *In* Perkins, D. and Leondar, B. eds. The arts and cognition p320-32

Maslow, A. H. Education, art, and peak experiences. *In* Fairfield, R. P. ed. Humanistic frontiers in American education p185-93

Peckham, M. Arts for the cultivation of radical sensitivity. *In* Peckham, M. Romanticism and behavior p285-312

England—History

Burrow, J. W. The sense of the past. *In* Lerner, L. ed. The Victorians p120-38

Spain

García Lorca, F. The duende: theory and divertissement; excerpt from "The poet in New York." *In* Gibbons, R. ed. The poet's work: 29 masters of 20th century poetry on the origins and practice of their art p28-41

Spain—History

Ilie, P. Concepts of the grotesque before Goya. *In* Studies in eighteenth-century culture v5 p183-201

United States

Gans, H. J. Democracy and the arts: adversary or ally? *In* Mann, D. A. ed. The arts in a democratic society p98-117

Kouwenhoven, J. A. Art, disorder, and American experience: half a truth is better than none. *In* Mann, D. A. ed. The arts in a democratic society p70-97

Lowry, W. M. The arts in America: evolution and tradition. *In* The American Revolution: a continuing commitment p41-52

Mann, D. A. Conclusions. *In* Mann, D. A. ed. The arts in a democratic society p140-50

Mann, D. A. Introduction: the arts in a democratic society. *In* Mann, D. A. ed. The arts in a democratic society p3-18

Wertheim, A. F. Constance Rourke and the discovery of American culture in the 1930's. *In* Luedtke, L. S. ed. The study of American culture p49-61

Vienna—History

Yates, W. E. Cultural life in early nineteenth-century Vienna. *In* Branscombe, P. ed. Austrian life and literature, 1780-1938 p12-25

Wales

Jones, D. Wales and visual form. *In* Jones, D. The dying Gaul, and other writings p63-93

Arts, Afro-American. See Afro-American arts

Arts, American. See Afro-American arts

Arts, Chinese

Mote, F. W. The arts and the 'theorizing mode' of the civilization. *In* Artists and traditions p3-8

Arts, Decorative. See Art, Decorative; Decoration and ornament

Arts, Fine. See Art

Arts, Graphic. See Graphic arts

Arts, Islamic

Ettinghausen, R. The man-made setting. *In* Lewis, B. ed. Islam and the Arab world p57-88

Arts, Modern

See also Art, Modern

Philosophy

Mukařovský, J. Dialectic contradictions in modern art. *In* Mukařovský, J. Structure, sign, and function p129-49

20th century

Jones, D. Notes on the 1930s. *In* Jones, D. The dying Gaul, and other writings p41-49

Kunitz, S. J. A kind of order. *In* Kunitz, S. J. A kind of order, a kind of folly p3-13

Ashantis

Schildkrout, E. The ideology of regionalism in Ghana. *In* Shack, W. A. and Skinner, E. P. eds. Strangers in African societies p183-207

Wilks, I. Dissidence in Asante politics: two tracts from the late nineteenth century. *In* African themes p47-63

Ashbee, Felicity

Nevill Forbes, 1883-1929: some family letters from Russia. *In* Oxford Slavonic papers, new ser. v9 p79-90

Ashbery, John

About

Bloom, H. John Ashbery: the charity of the hard moments. *In* Boyers, R. ed. Contemporary poetry in America p110-38

Kalstone, D. A final note. *In* Kalstone, D. Five temperaments p200-03

Kalstone, D. John Ashbery: self-portrait in a convex mirror. *In* Kalstone, D. Five temperaments p170-99

About individual works

Self-portrait in a convex mirror

Lieberman, L. John Ashbery: unassigned frequencies: whispers out of time. *In* Lieberman, L. Unassigned frequencies p 3-61

Ashby, Eric

Reconciliation of tradition and modernity in universities. *In* McMurrin, S. M. ed. On the meaning of the university p13-27

Ashe, A. H. See Davidson, E. J. jt. auth.

Asheim, Lester Eugene

About

Berninghausen, D. K. Asheim's liberal approach to intellectual freedom. *In* As much to learn as to teach p38-50

Carnovsky, R. F. Biographical sketch. *In* As much to learn as to teach p16-24

Stevenson, G. T. Lester E. Asheim—an appreciation. *In* As much to learn as to teach p11-15

Asher, Herbert Bernard

The changing status of the freshman Representative. *In* Ornstein, N. J. ed. Congress in change p216-39

Ashley-Montagu, Montague Francis. See Montagu, Ashley

Ashmead, Ann Hardwell. See Phillips, K. M. jt. auth.

Ashmore, Harry Scott

An exercise in demi-diplomacy: the case of Vietnam. *In* Unofficial diplomats p130-41

Ashtarak, Armenia

Mandel'shtam, O. E. Ashtarak. *In* Mandel'-shtam, O. E. Selected essays p201-03

Ashton, Dore

Stripping down to cosmos; excerpt from "A reading of modern art." *In* Kaplan, P. and Manso, S. eds. Major European art movements, 1900-1945 p337-52

Ashtor, Eliyahu

An essay on the diet of the various classes in the medieval Levant. *In* Biology of man in history p125-62

Ashworth, John Edward

About individual works

Olivier, Freud, and Hamlet

Lesser, S. O. Freud and Hamlet again. *In* Lesser, S. O. The whispered meanings p20-31

Asia

Commerce—History

Prakash, O. Asian trade and European impact: a study of the trade from Bengal, 1630-1720. *In* Kling, B. B. and Pearson, M. N. eds. The age of partnership p43-70

Defenses

Pfaltzgraff, R. L. and Davis, J. K. The Asian/Pacific region—implications for U.S. global strategy. *In* Pacific Asia and U.S. policies: a political-economic-strategic assessment p16-27

Economic conditions

Saubolle, L. E. The economic face of communism in Asia. *In* Pacific Asia and U.S. policies: a political-economic-strategic assessment p108-14

Economic conditions—1945-

Perkins, D. H. Asian economic growth: the influence of the United States and Japan. *In* Clapp, P. and Halperin, M. H. eds. United States-Japanese relations, the 1970's. p94-119

Foreign relations—Great Britain

Watt, D. C. Britain and the Cold war in the Far East, 1945-58. *In* The Origins of the Cold war in Asia p89-122

Foreign relations—Russia

Slusser, R. M. Soviet Far Eastern policy, 1945-50: Stalin's goals in Korea. *In* The Origins of the Cold war in Asia p123-46

Foreign relations—United States

Johnson, C. A. A need for priorities. *In* Pacific Asia and U.S. policies: a political-economic-strategic assessment p36-48

Scalapino, R. A. Competitive strategic perceptions underlying U.S. policy in Asia. *In* Pacific Asia and U.S. policies: a political-economic-strategic assessment p 1-15

Politics and government

Boyd, G. Forms of political penetration in China's East Asian statecraft. *In* Pacific Asia and U.S. policies: a political-economic-strategic assessment p115-39

Watt, D. C. Britain and the Cold war in the Far East, 1945-58. *In* The Origins of the Cold war in Asia p89-122

Zagoria, D. S. Stability in Asia—can it last? *In* Pacific Asia and U.S. policies: a political-economic-strategic assessment p63-66

Social conditions

Madge, C. The relevance of family patterns in the process of modernization in East Asia. *In* Social organization and the applications of anthropology p161-95

Asia, Central

Relations (general) with China

Rossabi, M. Muslim and Central Asian revolts. *In* Spence, J. D. and Wills, J. E. eds. From Ming to Ch'ing p167-99

Asia, East. See East Asia

Asia, South. See South Asia

Asia, Southeastern

Commerce—History

Wheatley, P. Satyānṛta in Suvarṇadvīpa: from reciprocity to redistribution in ancient Southeast Asia. *In* Ancient civilization and trade p227-83

Asia, Southeastern—*Continued*
Economic conditions
Golay, F. H. Southeast Asia: the "colonial drain" revisited. *In* Southeast Asian history and historiography p368-87

Emigration and immigration
McGee, T. G. Rural-urban mobility in South and Southeast Asia: different formulations, different answers. *In* Human migration p199-224

Foreign relations
Mahajani, U. Sino-American rapprochement and the new configurations in Southeast Asia. *In* The Year book of world affairs, 1975 p106-20

Mahajani, U. Sino-Soviet conflict and rivalry in South-East Asia in the post-Vietnam phase. *In* The Year book of world affairs, 1978 p153-74

Foreign relations—United States
Kahin, G. M. The United States and the anticolonial revolutions in Southeast Asia, 1945-50. *In* The Origins of the Cold war in Asia p338-61

Weatherbee, D. E. U.S. policy and the two Southeast Asias. *In* Pacific and U.S. policies: a political-economic-strategic assesment p80-94

Historiography
Legge, J. D. Southeast Asian history and the social sciences. *In* Southeast Asian history and historiography p388-404

History
Wheatley, P. Satyānŗta in Suvarṇadvīpa: from reciprocity to redistribution in ancient Southeast Asia. *In* Ancient civilization and trade p227-83

Politics and government
Esman, M. J. Communal conflict in Southeast Asia. *In* Glazer, N. and Moynihan, D. P. eds. Ethnicity p391-419

Kearney, R. N. South and Southeast Asia: a regional survey. *In* Kearney, R. N. ed. Politics and modernization in South and Southeast Asia p 1-38

Mahajani, C. Sino-American rapprochement and the new configurations in Southeast Asia. *In* The Year book of world affairs, 1975 p106-20

Mahajani, U. Sino-Soviet conflict and rivalry in South-East Asia in the post-Vietnam phase. *In* The Year book of world affairs, 1978 p153-74

Melchor, A. Assessing ASEAN's viability in a changing world. *In* Pacific Asia and U.S. policies: a political-economic-strategic assessment p67-79

Tanigawa, Y. The Cominform and Southeast Asia. *In* The Origins of the Cold war in Asia p362-77

Weatherbee, D. E. U.S. policy and the two Southeast Asias. *In* Pacific Asia and U.S. policies: a political-economic-strategic assessment p80-94

Yano, T. Who set the stage for the Cold war in Southeast Asia? *In* The Origins of the Cold war in Asia p321-37

Relations (general) with China
Freedman, M. An epicycle of Cathay; or, The southward expansion of the Sinologists. *In* Social organization and the applications of anthropology p302-32

Religion
Lee, P. K. H. Between the old and the new. *In* The Emergent gospel p124-36

Social conditions
Esman, M. J. Communal conflict in Southeast Asia. *In* Glazer, N. and Moynihan, D. P. eds. Ethnicity p391-419

Kearney, R. N. South and Southeast Asia: a regional survey. *In* Kearney, R. N. ed. Politics and modernization in South and Southeast Asia p 1-38

Asia Minor
City planning
See Cities and towns—Planning—Asia Minor

Asian Americans
Ching, F. The Asian experience in the United States. *In* The Immigrant experience in America p192-214

Social life and customs
Ogawa, D. M. Asian Americans. *In* Gochros, H. L. and Gochros, J. S. eds. The sexually oppressed p192-201

Asians in the United States
See also Asian Americans

Historiography
Daniels, R. American historians and East Asian immigrants. *In* The Asian American: the historical experience p 1-25

Asians in Uganda
Kuper, J. "Goan" and "Asian" in Uganda: an analysis of racial identity and cultural categories. *In* Shack, W. A. and Skinner, E. P. eds. Strangers in African societies p243-59

Mazrui, A. A. Casualties of an underdeveloped class structure: the expulsion of Luo workers and Asian bourgeoisie from Uganda. *In* Shack, W. A. and Skinner, E. P. eds. Strangers in African societies p261-88

Mazrui, A. A. The de-Indianization of Uganda: who is a citizen? *In* Smock, D. R. and Bentsi-Enchill, K. eds. The search for national integration in Africa p77-90

Asimov, Isaac
The moon as threshold. *In* The Frontiers of knowledge p359-99

Social science fiction. *In* Knight, D. F. ed. Turning points p29-61

There's nothing like a good foundation. *In* Knight, D. F. ed. Turning points p273-76

About
Asimov, I. There's nothing like a good foundation. *In* Knight, D. F. ed. Turning points p273-76

Moore, M. Asimov, Calvin, and Moses. *In* Clareson, T. D. ed. Voices for the future: essays on major science fiction writers v 1 p88-103

Asinou. Panagia Phorbiotissa (Church)
Weitzmann, K. A group of early twelfth-century Sinai icons attributed to Cyprus. *In* Studies in memory of David Talbot Rice p47-63

Aslachi, Cunradus. See Aslakssøn, Cort
Aslaksen, Kort. See Aslakssøn, Cort
Aslakssøn, Cort
About
Moesgaard, K. P. Cosmology in the wake of Tycho Brahe's astronomy. *In* Cosmology, history, and theology p293-305

Asmoneans. See Maccabees

Aspen, Colo.

Dubos, R. J. The diversity of human life. *In* Dubos, R. J. Beast or angel? p171-80

Aspin, Les

The defense budget and foreign policy: the role of Congress. *In* Long, F. A. and Rathjens, G. W. eds. Arms, defense policy, and arms control p155-74

Asquith, Herbert Henry. See Oxford and Asquith, Herbert Henry Asquith, 1st Earl of

Assad, Thomas J.

Browning's "Childe Roland to the dark tower came." *In* Tulane Studies in English v21 p67-76

Hopkins' "Spelt from Sibyl's leaves." *In* Tulane Studies in English v22 p103-15

Assassination

See also Terrorism

Japan—History

Shillony, B. A. Myth and reality in Japan of the 1930s. *In* Modern Japan p81-88

Southern States

Grantham, D. W. Three violent scenes in Southern politics. *In* Grantham, D. W. The regional imagination p53-63

The assassination of Trotsky (Motion picture)

Kauffmann, S. The assassination of Trotsky. *In* Kauffmann, S. Living images p140-42

Sarris, A. The assassination of Trotsky. *In* Sarris, A. Politics and cinema p57-58

Assault, Criminal. See Rape

Assault on foreign officials. See Assaulting a foreign official

Assaulting a foreign official

Murphy, J. The role of international law in the prevention of terrorist kidnapping of diplomatic personnel. *In* International terrorism and political crimes p285-313

Asselberg, Willem Jan Marie Anton. See Asselbergs, Willem Jan Marie Anton

Asselbergs, Willem Jan Marie Anton

About individual works

Ballade van de Katholiek

Krispyn, E. Joseph Roth and the art of adaptation. *In* Strelka, J. P.; Bell, R. F. and Dobson, E. eds. Protest—form—tradition p97-109

Translations

Krispyn, E. Joseph Roth and the art of adaptation. *In* Strelka, J. P.; Bell, R. F. and Dobson, E. eds. Protest—form—tradition p97-109

Asselineau, Roger

The French face of William Faulkner. *In* Tulane Studies in English, v23 p157-93

Assemblage (Art)

See also Collage

United States

Tashjian, D. L. The art of assemblage. *In* Tashjian, D. L. Skyscraper primitives p188-203

Assembly, Right of. See Liberty of speech

Assembly-line methods

Clayre, A. Some effects of repetitive work on leisure. *In* Clayre, A. Work and play p171-80

Assiete au beurre

Shikes, R. E. Five artists in the service of politics in the pages of L'Assiette au beurre. *In* Millon, H. A. and Nochlin, L. eds. Art and architecture in the service of politics p162-81

Assimilation (Sociology)

D'Antonio, W. V. Ethnicity and assimilation: a reconsideration. *In* Studies in Italian American social history p10-27

Deloria, V. The new Exodus. *In* Smithsonian Institution. The cultural drama p89-105

Dillon, W. S. E pluribus unum? *In* Smithsonian Institution. The cultural drama p33-67

Piore, M. J. Immigration, work expectations, and labor market structure. *In* The Diverse society: implications for social policy p109-27

See also Acculturation; Americanization; Emigration and immigration; Minorities

Astrology. See Medical astrology; Occult sciences

Assis, Joaquim Maria Machado de. See Machado de Assis, Joaquim Maria Machado de

Association. See Social groups

Association of South East Asian Nations

Melchor, A. Assessing ASEAN's viability in a changing world. *In* Pacific Asia and U.S. policies: a political-economic-strategic assessment p67-79

Weatherbee, D. E. U.S. policy and the two Southeast Asias. *In* Pacific and U.S. policies: a political-economic-strategic assessment p80-94

Assumptio Mariae

Kahrl, S. J. Teaching medieval drama as theatre. *In* The Learned and the lewed p305-18

Assumption. See Hypothesis

Assurance (Theology)

Stoever, W. K. B. The order of redemption and the ground of assurance. *In* Stoever, W. K. B. 'A faire and easie way to heaven' p119-37

Stoever, W. K. B. The quest for assurance: radical solutions and Puritan dialectics. *In* Stoever, W. K. B. 'A faire and easie way to heaven' p138-60

See also Antinomianism

Assyria

History

Tadmor, H. Assyria and the West: the ninth century and its aftermath. *In* Unity and diversity p36-48

Assyro-Babylonian cultus. See Cultus, Assyro-Babylonian

Assyro-Babylonian literature. See Cuneiform inscriptions

Assyro-Babylonian mythology. See Mythology, Assyro-Babylonian

Assyro Babylonian proverbs. See Proverbs, Assyro-Babylonian

Astell, Mary

About

Janes, R. M. Mary, Mary, quite contrary, or, Mary Astell and Mary Wollstonecraft compared. *In* Studies in eighteenth-century culture v5 p121-39

Asteroids. See Planets, Minor

Aston, Margaret E.

Huizinga's harvest: England and The waning of the Middle Ages. *In* Medievalia et humanistica; new ser. no. 9 p 1-24

Lollardy and sedition, 1381-1431. *In* Peasants, knights and heretics p273-318

Aston, Trevor Howard

Robin Hood. *In* Peasants, knights and heretics p270-72

Astor family

Auchincloss, L. Two conversation pieces: the Astors and the Vanderbilts. *In* Auchincloss, L. Life, law and letters p79-89

Astrampsychus

About individual works
Oraculorum decades CIII

Browne, G. M. The origin and date of the Sortes Astrampsychi. *In* Illinois classical studies, v 1 1976 p53-58

Astro, Richard

Phlebas sails the Caribbean: Steinbeck, Hemingway, and the American waste land. *In* French, W. G. ed. The twenties p215-33

Astrodiagnosis. See Medical astrology

Astrology. See Medical astrology Occult sciences

Astrology, Chinese

Hou, Ching-lang. The Chinese belief in baleful stars. *In* Welch, H. and Seidel, A. K. eds. Facets of Taoism p193-228

Astrology, Hindu

Pingree, D. E. The Indian and pseudo-Indian passages in Greek and Latin astronomical and astrological texts. *In* Viator: medieval and Renaissance studies v7 p141-95

Astrology, Persian

Pingree, D. E. Māshā'allāh: some Sasanian and Syriac sources. *In* Essays on Islamic philosophy and science p5-14

Astronautics. See Outer space—Exploration

Astronomical instruments

See also Astronomical models

History

Digby, A. Crossed trapezes: a pre-Columbian astronomical instrument. *In* Mesoamerican archaeology p271-83

Gibbs, S. L. The first scientific instruments. *In* Brecher, K. and Feirtag, M. eds. Astronomy of the ancients p39-59

Astronomical mathematics. See Astronomy—Mathematics

Astronomical models

McCrea, W. H. Models, laws, and the universe. *In* Cosmology, history, and theology p59-73

Astronomical observations. See Astronomy—Observations

Astronomical physics. See Astrophysics

Astronomy

See also Comets; Cosmogony; Indians of Mexico—Astronomy; Mechanics, Celestial; Moon; Parallax; Planets; Quasars; Solar system; Sun

Charts, diagrams, etc.

See Astronomical models

History

Aveni, A. F. Old and New World naked-eye astronomy. *In* Brecher, K. and Feirtag, M. eds. Astronomy of the ancients p62-89

Westman, R. S. The Wittenberg interpretation of the Copernican theory. *In* The Nature of scientific discovery p393-429

Mathematics

Abers, E. S. and Kennel, C. F. Commentary: the role of error in ancient methods for determining the solar distance. *In* The Copernican achievement p130-36

Henderson, J. A. Erasmus Reinhold's determination of the distance of the sun from the earth. *In* The Copernican achievement p108-29

Observations

Gingerich, O. J. Commentary: remarks on Copernicus' observations. *In* The Copernican achievement p99-107

Heelan, P. A. Quantum relativity and the cosmic observer. *In* Cosmology, history, and theology p29-37

Hoskin, M. A. The English background to the cosmology of Wright and Herschel. *In* Cosmology, history, and theology p219-31

Penzias, A. A. An observational view of the cosmos. *In* Cosmology, history, and theology p101-12

See also Moon—Observations

Philosophy

Funkenstein, A. The dialectical preparation for scientific revolutions. *In* The Copernican achievement p165-203

Jaki, S. L. The history of science and the idea of an oscillating universe. *In* Cosmology, history, and theology p233-51

Machamer, P. K. Commentary: fictionalism and realism in 16th century astronomy. *In* The Copernican achievement p346-53

See also Cosmology

Astronomy, Ancient

Aveni, A. F. Old and New World naked-eye astronomy. *In* Brecher, K. and Feirtag, M. eds. Astronomy of the ancients p62-89

Gibbs, S. L. The first scientific instruments. *In* Brecher, K. and Feirtag, M. eds. Astronomy of the ancients p39-59

Gingerich, O. J. The basic astronomy of Stonehenge. *In* Brecher, K. and Feirtag, M. eds. Astronomy of the ancients p117-32

Lettvin, J. Y. The Gorgon's eye. *In* Brecher, K. and Feirtag, M. eds. Astronomy of the ancients p133-51

Pingree, D. E. The Indian and pseudo-Indian passages in Greek and Latin astronomical and astrological texts. *In* Viator: medieval and Renaissance studies v7 p141-95

Reiche, H. A. T. The language of archaic astronomy: a clue to the Atlantis myth? *In* Brecher, K. and Feirtag, M. eds. Astronomy of the ancients p153-89

Astronomy, Arabic

Sabra, A. I. The scientific enterprise. *In* Lewis, B. ed. Islam and the Arab world p181-200

Astronomy, Hindu

Pingree, D. E. The Indian and pseudo-Indian passages in Greek and Latin astronomical and astrological texts. *In* Viator: medieval and Renaissance studies v7 p141-95

Astronomy, Maya. See Indians of Mexico—Astronomy

Astronomy, Medieval

Abrams, J. W. The development of medieval astronomy. *In* Jeffrey, D. L. ed. By things seen: reference and recognition in medieval thought p187-209

Astronomy, Medieval—*Continued*

Pedersen, O. Astronomy. *In* Lindberg, D. C. ed. Science in the Middle Ages p303-37

Pingree, D. E. The Indian and pseudo-Indian passages in Greek and Latin astronomical and astrological texts. *In* Viator: medieval and Renaissance studies v7 p141-95

Astronomy, Mexican Indian. See Indians of Mexico—Astronomy

Astronomy, Spherical and practical

See also Parallax; Precession; Vernal equinox

Early works to 1800

Donahue, W. H. The solid planetary spheres in post-Copernican natural philosophy. *In* The Copernican achievement p244-75

Machamer, P. K. Commentary: fictionalism and realism in 16th century astronomy. *In* The Copernican achievement p346-53

History

Heilbron, J. L. Commentary: Duhem and Donahue. *In* The Copernican achievement p276-84

Astrophysics

Burbidge, G. and Burbidge, M. Modern riddles of cosmology. *In* Neyman, J. ed. The heritage of Copernicus: theories "pleasing to the mind" p116-39

Zonn, W. Explosive events in the universe. *In* Neyman, J. ed. The heritage of Copernicus: theories "pleasing to the mind" p95-115

See also Red shift

Astruc, Alexandre

About individual works
Les mauvaises rencontres

Truffaut, F. Alexandre Astruc: Les mauvaises rencontres. *In* Truffaut, F. The films in my life p305-07

Asturias, Miguel Ángel

About individual works
Men of maize

Brotherston, G. America's magic forest: Miguel Ángel Asturias. *In* Brotherston, G. The emergence of the Latin American novel p25-44

Aswad, Barbara C.

Women, class, and power: examples from the Hatay, Turkey. *In* Beck, L. and Keddie, N. R. eds. Women in the Muslim world p473-81

Aswân High Dam

Terry, J. J. The consequences of economic absention: the Aswan Dam. *In* Higham, R. D. ed. Intervention or abstention: the dilemma of American foreign policy p129-43

Asylum, Right of

Walker, W. O. Asylum. *In* Encyclopedia of American foreign policy p49-57

See also Extradition; Refugees, Political —Legal status, laws, etc.

At the Sign of the Black Manikin. See Black Manikin Press

Atatürk, Kamâl, President Turkey

Szyliowicz, J. S. Elites and modernization in Turkey. *In* Political elites and political development in the Middle East p23-66

Atayal

Weaving

See Weaving—Atayal

Atchity, Kenneth John

Dante's Purgatorio: the poem reveals itself. *In* Italian literature: roots and branches p85-115

Atchley, Martha W.; Cohen, Susan Blecker, and Weinstein, Lois

Anticipatory grief in a cancer hospital. *In* Anticipatory grief p124-34

Athabascan languages. See Athapascan languages

Athapascan Indians. See Kaska Indians

Athapascan languages

Krauss, M. E. Na-Dene. *In* Sebeok, T. A. ed. Native languages of the Americas v 1 p283-358

Atheism. See Deism; Skepticism

Atheling, William, pseud. See Blish, James

Athelstan, King of England

About

Barker, E. E. Two lost documents of King Athelstan. *In* Anglo-Saxon England 6 p137-43

Athelstane, King of England. See Athelstan, King of England

Athena

Art

Winternitz, E. The curse of Pallas Athena. *In* Winternitz, E. Musical instruments and their symbolism in Western art p150-65

Cult

Stoop, M. W. Conjectures on the end of a sanctuary. *In* Studies in classical art and archaeology p179-83

Athenodorus Calvus

Hijmans, B. L. Athenodorus on the Categories and a pun on Athenodorus. *In* Kephalaion p105-14

Athens

History

Forrest, W. G. G. An Athenian generation gap. *In* Yale classical studies v24 p37-52

See also Thirty tyrants

History—Historiography

Momigliano, A. Athens in the third century B.C. and the discovery of Rome in the histories of Timaeus of Tauromenium. *In* Momigliano, A. Essays in ancient and modern historiography p37-66

Politics and government

Forrest, W. G. G. An Athenian generation gap. *In* Yale classical studies v24 p37-52

Athens. Byzantine Museum. See St John's Apocalypse no. 786 (Icons)

Athens. Parthenon

McCredie, J. R. The architects of the Parthenon. *In* Studies in classical art and archaeology p69-73

Robertson, M. Two question-marks on the Parthenon. *In* Studies in classical art and archaeology p75-87

Atherton, Alfred LeRoy

The Nixon administration and the Arab-Israeli conflict. *In* The New world balance and peace in the Middle East: reality or mirage? p196-208

Athletes
Political activity
Rehberg, R. A. and Cohen, M. A. Political attitudes and participation in extracurricular activities. *In* Social problems in athletics p201-11

Spady, W. G. A commentary on sport and the New Left. *In* Social problems in athletics p212-23

Athletes, Afro-American. See Afro-American athletes

Athletics
See also Sports

Social aspects—United States
Ingham, A. G. Sport and the "New Left"; some reflections upon opposition without praxis. *In* Social problems in athletics p238-48

Schafer, W. E. Sport and youth counter-culture; contrasting socialization themes. *In* Social problems in athletics p183-200

Atjeh, Indonesia
History
Siegel, J. T. Awareness of the past in the Hikajat Potjoet Moehamat. *In* Southeast Asian history and historiography p321-31

Atkins, Anselm
Ironic action in "After the storm." *In* Benson, J. J. ed. The short stories of Ernest Hemingway: critical essays p227-30

Atkinson, Dorothy Grace Gillis
August 1914: historical novel or novel history. *In* Dunlop, J. B.; Haugh, R. and Klimoff, A. eds. Aleksander Solzhenitsyn: critical essays and documentary materials 2d ed. p408-29

Society and the sexes in the Russian past. *In* Women in Russia p 3-38

Atlantis
Fears, J. R. Atlantis and the Minoan thalassocracy: a study in modern mythopoeism. *In* Ramage, E. S. ed. Atlantis, fact or fiction? p103-34

Fredericks, S. C. Plato's Atlantis: a mythologist looks at myth. *In* Ramage, E. S. ed. Atlantis, fact or fiction? p81-99

Reiche, H. A. T. The language of archaic astronomy: a clue to the Atlantis myth? *In* Brecher, K. and Feirtag, M. eds. Astronomy of the ancients p153-89

Vitaliano, D. B. Atlantis from the geologic point of view. *In* Ramage, E. S. ed. Atlantis, fact or fiction? p137-60

Wright, H. E. Glacial fluctuations, sea-level changes, and catastrophic floods. *In* Ramage, E. S. ed. Atlantis, fact or fiction? p161-74

Atlantis in literature
Luce, J. V. The sources and literary form of Plato's Atlantis narrative. *In* Ramage, E. S. ed. Atlantis, fact or fiction? p49-78

Ramage, E. S. Perspectives ancient and modern. *In* Ramage, E. S. ed. Atlantis, fact or fiction? p3-45

Ātman
Coomaraswamy, A. K. Bhakta aspects of the Ātman doctrine. *In* Coomaraswamy, A. K. Selected papers v2 p386-97

Coomaraswamy, A. K. The Vedānta and Western tradition. *In* Coomaraswamy, A. K. Selected papers v2 p3-22

Atomic bomb and disarmament. See Atomic weapons and disarmament

Atomic bombs (International law) See Atomic weapons (International law)

Atomic energy
Church, F. Arms, energy, and the atom: the lethal dilemma. *In* World change and world security p159-66

Feld, B. T. Nuclear energy—fact versus myth. *In* International terrorism and world security p131-39

O'Leary, J. F. Nuclear energy and public policy issues. *In* Kalter, R. J. and Vogely, W. A. eds. Energy supply and government policy p235-54

Law and legislation
See Atomic power—Law and legislation

Atomic energy industries

Safety regulations
See Atomic power—Law and legislation

Atomic fuel. See Nuclear fuels

Atomic mass
Siegel, D. M. Classical-electromagnetic and relativistic approaches to the problem of non-integral atomic masses. *In* Historical studies in the physical sciences v9 p323-60

Atomic models. See Atoms—Models

Atomic nuclei. See Nuclear physics

Atomic power
See also Atomic energy

International control
Church, F. Arms, energy, and the atom: the lethal dilemma. *In* World change and world security p159-66

Law and legislation—
United States
O'Leary, J. F. Nuclear energy and public policy issues. *In* Kalter, R. J. and Vogely, W. A. eds. Energy supply and government policy p235-54

Safety regulations
See Atomic power—Law and regulation

Atomic structure
Kragh, H. Niels Bohr's second atomic theory. *In* Historical studies in the physical sciences v10 p123-86

See also Atomic theory

Atomic submarines
Steinbruner, J. D. and Carter, B. Organizational and political dimensions of the strategic posture: the problems of reform. *In* Long, F. A. and Rathjens, G. W. eds. Arms, defense policy, and arms control p131-54

See also Fleet ballistic missile weapons systems

Atomic theory
Kragh, H. Niels Bohr's second atomic theory. *In* Historical studies in the physical sciences v10 p123-86

Laudan, L. The methodological foundations of Mach's anti-atomism and their historical roots. *In* Motion and time, space and matter p390-417

Rocke, A. J. Atoms and equivalents: the early development of the chemical atomic theory. *In* Historical studies in the physical sciences v9 p225-63

See also Atomism; Quantum theory

Atomic warfare

Bundy, M. The avoidance of nuclear war since 1945. *In* Griffiths, F. and Polanyi, J. C. eds. The dangers of nuclear war p27-33

Carlton, D. The doctrine of tactical nuclear warfare and some alternatives. *In* The Dynamics of the arms race p135-42

Epstein, W. Nuclear terrorism and nuclear war. *In* Griffiths, F. and Polanyi, J. C. eds. The dangers of nuclear war p109-24

Freier, S. Local wars and their escalation. *In* Griffiths, F. and Polanyi, J. C. eds. The dangers of nuclear war p125-34

Garwin, R. L. Weapons developments and the threat of nuclear war. *In* Griffiths, F. and Polanyi, J. C. eds. The dangers of nuclear war p93-106

Griffiths, F. A forecast. *In* Griffiths, F. and Polanyi, J. C. eds. The dangers of nuclear war p169-81

Polanyi, J. C. The dangers of nuclear war. *In* Griffiths, F. and Polanyi, J. C. eds. The dangers of nuclear war p182-93

Rathjens, G. W. Nuclear war between the super-powers. *In* Griffiths, F. and Polanyi, J. C. eds. The dangers of nuclear war p135-46

Steinbruner, J. An assessment of nuclear crises. *In* Griffiths, F. and Polanyi, J. C. eds. The dangers of nuclear war p34-49

Winters, F. X. The nuclear arms race: machine versus man. *In* Ethics and nuclear strategy? p144-55

See also Atomic weapons

Environmental aspects

Mark, J. C. Consequences of nuclear war. *In* Griffiths, F. and Polanyi, J. C. eds. The dangers of nuclear war p7-21

Moral and religious aspects

Ford, H. P. What these sobering essays tell us. *In* Ethics and nuclear strategy? p 1-13

Physiological effect

Mark, J. C. Consequences of nuclear war. *In* Griffiths, F. and Polanyi, J. C. eds. The dangers of nuclear war p7-21

Atomic warfare (International law) See Atomic weapons (International law)

Atomic-weapon-free zones

Husbands, J. L. Nuclear proliferation and the inter-American system. *In* Farer, T. J. ed. The future of the inter-American system p204-31

Atomic weapons

Baker, S. J. The international political economy of proliferation. *In* Arms control and technological innovation p70-101

Carlton, D. The Anglo-American nuclear relationship: proliferatory or anti-proliferatory? *In* Arms control and technological innovation p132-45

Carlton, D. The British independent nuclear deterrent and the future of European security. *In* International terrorism and world security p277-94

Church, F. Arms, energy, and the atom: the lethal dilemma. *In* World change and world security p159-66

Freier, S. Local wars and their escalation. *In* Griffiths, F. and Polanyi, J. C. eds. The dangers of nuclear war p125-34

Garwin, R. L. Weapons developments and the threat of nuclear war. *In* Griffiths, F. and Polanyi, J. C. eds. The dangers of nuclear war p93-106

Hagan, K. J. Nuclear weapons and diplomacy. *In* Encyclopedia of American foreign policy p692-702

Lakoff, S. A. Scientists, technologists and political power. *In* Science, technology and society p355-91

Martin, L. W. Limited nuclear war. *In* Howard, M. ed. Restraints on war p103-21

Miller, G. E. Existing systems of command and control. *In* Griffiths, F. and Polanyi, J. C. eds. The dangers of nuclear war p50-66

Morton, L. Who next? The spread of nuclear weapons. *In* Baldwin, D. A. ed. America in an interdependent world p29-60

Pasti, N. The military balance between East and West in Europe. *In* International terrorism and world security p189-233

Schütze, W. A world of many nuclear powers. *In* Griffiths, F. and Polanyi, J. C. eds. The dangers of nuclear war p85-92

White, E. B. Sootfall and fallout. *In* White, E. B. Essays of E. B. White p90-99

See also Atomic weapons and disarmament

History

York, H. F. An outline history of nuclear proliferation. *In* International terrorism and world security p105-17

Testing

Halsted, T. A. Nuclear testing—no end in sight? *In* Arms control and technological innovation p210-23

Atomic weapons (International law)

Blau, T. Plowshare, proliferation, and the N+1 country. *In* International terrorism and world security p118-30

Atomic weapons and disarmament

Allison, G. T. and Morris, F. A. Armaments and arms control: exploring the determinants of military weapons. *In* Long, F. A. and Rathjens, G. W. eds. Arms, defense policy, and arms control p99-129

Blau, T. Plowshare, proliferation, and the N+1 country. *In* International terrorism and world security p118-30

Brooks, H. The military innovation system and the qualitative arms race. *In* Long, F. A. and Rathjens, G. W. eds. Arms, defense policy, and arms control p75-97

Carter, B. E. The strategic debate in the United States. *In* Kirk, G. L. and Wessell, N. H. eds. The Soviet threat p15-29

Chayes, A. Nuclear arms control after the Cold War. *In* Long, F. A. and Rathjens, G. W. eds. Arms, defense policy, and arms control p15-33

Corden, P. S. Ethics and deterrence: moving beyond the just-war tradition. *In* Ethics and nuclear strategy? p156-80

Doty, P. Strategic arms limitation after SALT I. *In* Long, F. A. and Rathjens, G. W. eds. Arms, defense policy, and arms control p63-74

Epstein, W. A new approach to strategic arms limitation and reduction. *In* Arms control and technological innovation p176-97

Falk, R. A. Arms control, foreign policy, and global reform. *In* Long, F. A. and Rathjens, G. W. eds. Arms, defense policy, and arms control p35-52

Ford, H. P. Politics, ethics, and the arms race. *In* Ethics and nuclear strategy? p51-71

Ford, H. P. What these sobering essays tell us. *In* Ethics and nuclear strategy? p 1-13

Atomic weapons and disarmament—*Cont.*

Halsted, T. A. Nuclear testing—no end in sight? *In* Arms control and technological innovation p210-23

Ignatieff, G. The achievements of arms control. *In* Griffiths, F. and Polanyi, J. C. eds. The dangers of nuclear war p67-82

Kashi, J. The role of deterrence in disarmament: some theories and some defects. *In* The Dynamics of the arms race p92-103

Levine, H. M. Summary of proceedings. *In* Arms control and technological innovation p11-35

Luck, E. C. The Soviet Union and conventional arms control. *In* Kirk, G. L. and Wessell, N. H. eds. The Soviet threat p57-65

Milstein, M. A. Strategic arms limitation and military strategic concepts. *In* Arms control and technological innovation p198-209

Morgenthau, H. J. The fallacy of thinking conventionally about nuclear weapons. *In* Arms control and technological innovation p255-64

Mushkat, M. The diffusion of economic and military power and its impact on the Middle East conflict. *In* Arms control and technological innovation p247-54

Myrdal, A. R. An "outsider's" view of the arms race. *In* Ethics and nuclear strategy? p82-91

Nacht, M. L. Arms and politics: old issues, new perceptions. *In* Arms control and technological innovation p161-69

Nalewajek, R. A. The realities of arms control: the cruise missile case. *In* Arms control and technological innovation p232-46

Nitze, P. H. The global military balance. *In* Kirk, G. L. and Wessell, N. H. eds. The Soviet threat p4-14

Rathjens, G. W. Changing perspectives on arms control. *In* Long, F. A. and Rathjens, G. W. eds. Arms, defense policy, and arms control p201-14

Rathjens, G. W. Slowing down the arms race. *In* The Dynamics of the arms race p82-91

Ruina, J. The arms race and SALT. *In* The Dynamics of the arms race p47-56

Russett, B. M. A countercombatant alternative to nuclear MADNESS. *In* Ethics and nuclear strategy? p124-43

Schoettle, E. C. B. Arms limitation and security policies required to minimise the proliferation of nuclear weapons. *In* Arms control and technological innovation p102-31

Scoville, H. A different approach to arms control—reciprocal unilateral restraint. *In* Arms control and technological innovation p170-75

Scoville, H. Flexible MADNESS? The case against counterforce. *In* Ethics and nuclear strategy? p113-23

Tate, D. Disarmament. *In* Encyclopedia of American foreign policy p244-52

Winters, F. X. The nuclear arms race: machine versus man. *In* Ethics and nuclear strategy? p144-55

Wohlstetter, A. Nuclear threats and Allied responses in an era of negotiation. *In* The New Atlantic challenge p235-60

Woolsey, R. J. Chipping away at the bargains. *In* Long, F. A. and Rathjens, G. W. eds. Arms, defense policy, and arms control p175-85

See also Atomic-weapon-free zones

Atomic weights

Siegel, D. M. Classical-electromagnetic and relativistic approaches to the problem of non-integral atomic masses. *In* Historical studies in the physical sciences v9 p323-60

Atomism

Furley, D. J. Aristotle and the Atomists on motion in a void. *In* Motion and time, space and matter p83-100

Atoms

Trenn, T. J. Rutherford and recoil atoms: the metamorphosis and success of a once stillborn theory. *In* Historical studies in the physical sciences v6 p513-47

See also Atomic structure; Electrons; Nuclear physics

Models

Cassidy, D. C. Heisenberg's first core model of the atom: the formation of a professional style. *In* Historical studies in the physical sciences v10 p187-224

MacKinnon, E. M. Heisenberg, models, and the rise of matrix mechanics. *In* Historical studies in the physical sciences v8 p137-88

Atonement

Biblical teaching

Dunn, J. D. G. Paul's understanding of the death of Jesus. *In* Reconciliation and hope p125-41

Gerhardsson, B. Sacrificial service and atonement in the Gospel of Matthew. *In* Reconciliation and hope p25-35

Marshall, I. H. The development of the concept of redemption in the New Testament. *In* Reconciliation and hope p153-69

Ridderbos, H. N. The earliest confession of the atonement in Paul. *In* Reconciliation and hope p76-89

Atriums. See Courtyards

Atrocities in literature

Langer, L. L. Aleksandr Solzhenitsyn and the journey through humiliation. *In* Langer, L. L. The age of atrocity p163-200

Langer, L. L. Charlotte Delbo and a heart of ashes. *In* Langer, L. L. The age of atrocity p201-44

Langer, L. L. Dying voices. *In* Langer, L. L. The age of atrocity p34-68

Attack and defense (Military science) See Deterrence (Strategy)

Attali, Jacques, and Stourdze, Yves

The birth of the telephone and economic crisis: the slow death of monologue in French society. *In* The Social impact of the telephone p97-111

Attan. See Ātman

Attention

Tart, C. T. Putting the pieces together: a conceptual framework for understanding discrete states of consciousness. *In* Alternate states of consciousness p158-219

Attitude (Psychology)

Fishbein, M. Attitudes and behavioral prediction: an overview. *In* Major social issues p377-89

Kelman, H. C. Attitude and behavior: a social-psychological problem. *In* Major social issues p412-20

Pollock, J. C. Early socialization and elite behavior. *In* Schwartz, D. C. and Schwartz, S. K. eds. New directions in political socialization p203-26

Auden, Wystan H.—*Continued*

About individual works
A certain world

Connolly, C. W. H. Auden. *In* Connolly, C. The evening colonnade p331-34

Edel, L. The poetics of biography. *In* Contemporary approaches to English studies p38-58

In memory of Sigmund Freud

Trilling, L. W. H. Auden: In memory of Sigmund Freud (d. Sept. 1939). *In* Trilling, L. Prefaces to The experience of literature p291-97

Nones

Fraser, G. S. Auden's later manner. *In* Fraser, G. S. Essays on twentieth-century poets p146-51

The rake's progress (Libretto)

Josipovici, G. The rake's progress. *In* Josipovici, G. The lessons of modernism p151-66

The shield of Achilles

Fraser, G. S. Auden's later manner. *In* Fraser, G. S. Essays on twentieth-century poets p146-51

Auden, Wystan Hugh, and Isherwood, Christopher

About individual works
The ascent of F6

Spender, S. The poetic dramas of W. H. Auden and Christopher Isherwood. *In* Spender, S. The thirties and after p36-43

The dog beneath the skin

Spender, S. The poetic dramas of W. H. Auden and Christopher Isherwood. *In* Spender, S. The thirties and after p36-43

Auden, Wystan Hugh, and MacNeice, Louis

About individual works
Letters from Iceland

Share, B. 'A fancy turn, you know.' *In* Time was away p39-42

Audi, Robert

Violence, legal sanctions, and law enforcement. *In* Stanage, S. M. ed. Reason and violence p29-50

Audiences, Theater. See Theater audiences

Audio-visual education

Postlethwait, S. N. Students, teachers, and technology. *In* Buxton, T. H. and Prichard, K. W. eds. Excellence in university teaching p220-31

See also Television in education

Auditing, Legislative. See Legislative auditing

Aue, Hartmann von. See Hartmann von Aue

Auen (African people) See !Kung (African people)

Auerbach, Carl A.

Freedom of movement in international law and United States policy. *In* Human migration p317-35

Auerbach, Erich

Frate Alberto; excerpt from "Mimesis." *In* Dombroski, R. S. ed. Critical perspectives on The Decameron p69-81

Auerbach, Jerold S.

The Depression decade. *In* The Pulse of freedom p65-104

Lawyers and social change in the Depression decade. *In* Braeman, J.; Bremner, R. H. and Brody, D. eds. The New Deal v 1 p133-69

Auerbach, Nina

Austen and Alcott on matriarchy: new women or new wives? *In* Spilka, M. ed. Towards a poetics of fiction p266-86

Communities of women

Contents

Beyond the family: idyll and inferno

Beyond the self: the spectacle of history and a new religion

Introduction: the communal eye

Waiting together: two families

A world at war: one big Miss Brodie

Dickens and Dombey: a daughter after all. *In* Dickens Studies Annual v5 p95-114

This changeful life: Emily Brontë's anti-romance. *In* Gilbert, S. M. and Gubar, S. eds. Shakespeare's sisters p49-64

Auger, Pierre Paul

Post-war drama in France and Belgium. *In* Nicoll, A. World drama p821-37

Aughrim, Battle of, 1691

Simms, J. G. The Battle of Aughrim: history and poetry. *In* Harmon, M. ed. Richard Murphy: poet of two traditions p36-51

Augsburg, Germany. Cathedral

Sheppard, C. D. The bronze doors of Augsburg Cathedral. *In* Enggass, R. C. and Stokstad, M. eds. Hortus imaginum p21-27

Augustine, Saint, Bp. of Hippo. See Augustinus, Aurelius, Saint, Bp. of Hippo

Augustinus, Aurelius, Saint, Bp. of Hippo

About

Arendt, H. Quaestio mihi factus sum: the discovery of the inner man. *In* Arendt, H. The life of the mind v2 p53-110

Downs, R. B. Fathers of the Church. *In* Downs, R. B. Books that changed the world p151-62

Helm, R. M. Plato in the thought of Nietzsche and Augustine. *In* O'Flaherty, J. C.; Sellner, T. F. and Helm, R. M. eds. Studies in Nietzsche and the classical tradition p16-32

Hermassi, K. C. "The interim reading of life." *In* Hermassi K. C. Polity and theater in historical perspective p95-101

Koenen, L. Augustine and Manichaeism in light of the Cologne Mani Codex. *In* Illinois classical studies v3, 1978 p154-95

Osborn, E. F. Augustine of Hippo. *In* Osborn, E. F. Ethical patterns in early Christian thought p143-82

Scharfstein, B. A. 'Cogito ergo sum': Descartes, Augustine, and Sankara. *In* Philosophy East/philosophy West p199-217

About individual works
Confessions

Grant, P. Redeeming the time: the Confessions of St. Augustine. *In* Jeffrey, D. L. ed. By things seen: reference and recognition in medieval thought p21-32

Lyons, J. O. Autobiography. *In* Lyons, J. O. The invention of the self p55-74

Zacher, C. K. Curiositas. *In* Zacher, C. K. Curiosity and pilgrimage p18-41

Augustus, Emperor of Rome

About

Rudd, N. History: Ovid and the Augustan myth. *In* Rudd, N. Lines of enquiry p 1-31

Auld, Louis Eugene

Music as dramatic device in the secular theater of Marguerite de Navarre. *In* Renaissance drama [1976] p193-217

Aulus, Cluentius Habitus. See Cluentius, Aulus Habitus

Auma-Osolo, Agola

Rationality and foreign policy process. *In* The Year book of world affairs, 1977 p257-88

Aumann, Moshe

Land ownership in Palestine, 1880-1948. *In* The Palestinians p21-29

Aune, David Edward

The significance of the delay of the Parousia for early Christianity. *In* Current issues in Biblical and patristic interpretation p87-109

Aungerville, Richard, known as Richard de Bury, Bp. of Durham

About individual works

Philobiblon

Gilbert, N. W. Richard de Bury and the "quires of yesterday's sophisms." *In* Philosophy and humanism p229-57

Zacher, C. K. The bibliophile as curious pilgrim: Richard de Bury's Philobiblon. *In* Zacher, C. K. Curiosity and pilgrimage p60-86

Aurelius Antoninus, Marcus, Emperor of Rome

Influence—Walt Whitman

Allen, G. W. Walt Whitman and stoicism. *In* The Stoic strain in American literature p43-60

Aurenche, Jean

About

Truffaut, F. A certain tendency of the French cinema. *In* Nichols, B. ed. Movies and methods p224-37

Aurobindo, Sri. See Ghose, Aurobindo

Austen, Jane

About

Auchincloss, L. Jane Austen and the good life. *In* Auchincloss, L. Life, law and letters p69-78

Brower, R. A. From the Iliad to Jane Austen, via The rape of the lock. *In* Halperin, J. ed. Jane Austen p43-60

Same as: From the Iliad to the novel, via The rape of the lock. *In* Brower, R. A. Mirror on mirror p77-95

Brown, L. W. The business of marrying and mothering. *In* Jane Austen's achievement p27-43

Butler, M. Conclusion. *In* Butler, M. Jane Austen and the war of ideas p292-99

Butler, M. The juvenilia and Northanger Abbey. *In* Butler, M. Jane Austen and the war of ideas p168-81

Butler, M. Seeing a meaning. *In* Butler, M. Jane Austen and the war of ideas p161-67

Cockshut, A. O. J. Jane Austen. *In* Cockshut, A. O. J. Man and woman: a study of love and the novel, 1740-1940 p54-71

Donovan, R. A. The mind of Jane Austen. *In* Weinsheimer, J. ed. Jane Austen today p109-27

Duckworth, A. M. 'Spillikins, paper ships, riddles, conundrums, and cards': games in Jane Austen's life and fiction. *In* Halperin, J. ed. Jane Austen p279-97

Greene, D. J. The myth of limitation. *In* Weinsheimer, J. ed. Jane Austen today p142-75

Hardy, B. N. Properties and possessions in Jane Austen's novels p79-105

Harrison, B. J. Muriel Spark and Jane Austen. *In* Josipovici, G. ed. The modern English novel: the reader, the writer and the work p225-51

Hodge, J. A. Jane Austen and her publishers. *In* Halperin, J. ed. Jane Austen p75-85

Jenkins, E. Jane Austen and the human condition. *In* Royal Society of Literature of the United Kingdom, London. Essays by divers hands v39 p57-75

Kennard, J. E. Jane Austen: the establishment. *In* Kennard, J. E. Victims of convention p21-45

Lascelles, M. Jane Austen and the novel. *In* Halperin, J. ed. Jane Austen p235-46

Lee, H. 'Taste' and 'tenderness' as moral values in the novels of Jane Austen. *In* Davies, R. T. and Beatty, B. G. eds. Literature of the romantic period, 1750-1850 p82-95

McMaster, J. Love and pedagogy. *In* Weinsheimer, J. ed. Jane Austen today p64-91

Mudrick, M. Jane Austen's drawing-room. *In* Halperin, J. ed. Jane Austen p247-61

Page, N. Orders of merit. *In* Weinsheimer, J. ed. Jane Austen today p92-108

Pascal, R. Early accomplishment: Jane Austen. *In* Pascal, R. The dual voice p45-60

Skilton, D. Austen, Scott and the Victorians. *In* Skilton, D. The English novel p80-98

Southam, B. C. Sanditon: the seventh novel. *In* Jane Austen's achievement p 1-26

Tave, S. M. Jane Austen and one of her contemporaries. *In* Halperin, J. ed. Jane Austen p61-74

Tomlinson, T. B. Doubts and reticence: Sense and sensibility to Persuasion. *In* Tomlinson, T. B. The English middle-class novel p36-51

Trowbridge, F. H. Mind, body, and estate: Jane Austen's system of values. *In* Trowbridge, F. H. From Dryden to Jane Austen p275-92

Weinsheimer, J. Jane Austen's anthropocentrism. *In* Weinsheimer, J. ed. Jane Austen today p128-41

Welty, E. The radiance of Jane Austen. *In* Welty, E. The eye of the story p 3-13

Whalley, G. Jane Austen: poet. *In* Jane Austen's achievement p106-33

Wiesenfarth, J. Austen and Apollo. *In* Weinsheimer, J. ed. Jane Austen today p46-63

About individual works

Emma

Butler, M. Emma. *In* Butler, M. Jane Austen and the war of ideas p250-74

Halperin, J. The worlds of Emma: Jane Austen and Cowper. *In* Halperin, J. ed. Jane Austen p197-206

Hough, G. G. Narrative and dialogue in Jane Austen. *In* Hough, G. G. Selected essays p46-82

Austen, Jane—*Continued*

Paraphrases, tales, etc.
See Austen, Jane—Adaptations

Study and teaching
Trilling, L. Why we read Jane Austen. *In* Trilling, L. The last decade p204-25

Style
See Austen, Jane—Technique

Technique
Hough, G. G. Narrative and dialogue in Jane Austen. *In* Hough, G. G. Selected essays p46-82

Translations
Wright, A. H. Jane Austen abroad. *In* Halperin, J. ed. Jane Austen p298-317

Translators
See Austen, Jane—Translations

Auster, Henry
George Eliot and the modern temper. *In* The Worlds of Victorian fiction p75-101

Austin, John Langshaw

About
Cavell, S. Austin at criticism. *In* Cavell, S. Must we mean what we say? p97-114
Derrida, J. Limited Inc. *In* Glyph 2 p162-254
Searle, J. R. Reiterating the differences: a reply to Derrida. *In* Glyph I p198-208

About individual works
How to do things with words
Derrida, J. Signature event context. *In* Glyph I p172-97
Manser, A. R. Austin's 'linguistic phenomenology.' *In* Pivčević, E. ed. Phenomenology and philosophical understanding p109-24

Philosophical papers
Cavell, S. Austin at criticism. *In* Cavell, S. Must we mean what we say? p97-114

Austin, Norman
The function of digressions in the Iliad. *In* Wright, J. H. ed. Essays on the Iliad p70-84

Australia

Civilization
Koestler, A. The faceless continent. *In* Koestler, A. The heel of Achilles p171-81

Emigration and immigration
Koestler, A. The faceless continent. *In* Koestler, A. The heel of Achilles p171-81

Foreign relations
Barclay, G. S. Australia and the Cold war. *In* Siracusa, J. M. and Barclay, G. S. eds. The impact of the Cold war p3-25
Chapman, C. Towards a new Pacific alliance. *In* The Year book of world affairs, 1975 p88-105

History
Jackson, W. T. Australians and the comparative frontier. *In* Essays on Walter Prescott Webb p17-51

Politics and government—1945-
Barclay, G. S. Australia and the Cold war. *In* Siracusa, J. M. and Barclay, G. S. eds. The impact of the Cold war p3-25

Social conditions
Chapman, C. Towards a new Pacific alliance. *In* The Year book of world affairs, 1975 p88-105

Australia in literature
Healy, J. J. The absolute and the image of man in Australia: Judith Wright and Patrick White. *In* Narasimhaiah, C. D. ed. Awakened conscience p3-13

Australian aborigines
Jacobs, W. R. The fatal confrontation: early native-white relations on the frontiers of Australia, New Guinea, and America—a comparative study. *In* The American Indian p27-54
Leavitt, R. Rohrlich-; Sykes, B. and Weatherford, E. Aboriginal woman: male and female anthropological perspectives. *In* Reiter, R. R. ed. Toward an anthropology of women p110-26

Anthropometry
See Australian aborigines—Craniology

Craniology
Larnach, S. L. and Macintosh, N. W. G. A comparative study of Solo and Australian aboriginal crania. *In* Grafton Elliot Smith p95-102

Psychology
Berndt, C. H. In aboriginal Australia. *In* Montague, A. ed. Learning non-aggression p144-60

Social life and customs
McCarthy, F. D. Relationships between Australian aboriginal material culture, and Southeast Asia and Melanesia. *In* Grafton Elliot Smith p210-26

Australian ballads. See Ballads, Australian

Australian drama

20th century—History and criticism
Brisbane, K. Post-war drama in Australia. *In* Nicoll, A. World drama p891-94

Australian fiction

20th century—History and criticism
Hamilton, K. G. A prefatory sketch. *In* Hamilton, K. G. ed. Studies in the recent Australian novel p 1-28

Australian literature

History and criticism
Cantrell, L. A. G. Stephens, the Bulletin, and the 1890s. *In* Bards, bohemians, and bookmen p98-113
Elliott, B. R. Aust. lit. &c.—a chaplet of wattle blossom? *In* Bards,. bohemians, and bookmen p320-27
Kiernan, B. Literature, history, and literary history: perspectives on the nineteenth century in Australia. *In* Bards, bohemians, and bookmen p 1-18
Webby, E. "Parents rather than critics": some early reviews of Australian literature. *In* Bards, bohemians, and bookmen p19-38

Australian poetry

History and criticism
Thompson, L. B. Mosaic and monolith: a comparison of Canadian and Australian poetic responses to the Great Depression. *In* Narasimhaiah, C. D. ed. Awakened conscience p164-84

Australians (Native people) See Australian aborigines

Austria

History
Schoenberg, H. W. The partition of Germany and the neutralization of Austria. *In* Hammond, T. T. ed. The anatomy of Communist takeovers p368-84

Austria—*Continued*

History—1815-1848
Sked, A. Metternich and the federalist myth. *In* Crisis and controversy p 1-22

Politics and government—1918-1938
Simon, W. B. Democracy in the shadow of imposed sovereignty: the First Republic of Austria. *In* The Breakdown of democratic regimes pt 2 p80-121

Austrian drama (German) See German drama—Austrian authors

Austrian literature

History and criticism
Rogers, M. A. "Dies Österreich ist eine kleine welt." *In* Branscombe, P. ed. Austrian life and literature, 1780-1938 p72-80

Austrian scientists. See Scientists, Austrian

Austrians in the United States
Andre, J. and Fröschle, H. The American expedition of Emperor Joseph II and Bernhard Moll's silhouettes. *In* The German contribution to the building of the Americas p135-72

Ausubel, Herman
Robert Owen and his New view of society. *In* Salo Wittmayer Baron v 1 p129-34

Autant-Lara, Claude

About individual works
En cas de malheur
Truffaut, F. En cas de malheur. *In* Truffaut, F. The films in my life p173-76

Authenticity (Philosophy)
Bayley, J. The authentic and the sincere. *In* Bayley, J. The uses of division p17-25

Grene, M. G. Authenticity: an existential virtue. *In* Grene, M. G. Philosophy in and out of Europe p50-60

Van Breda, H. L. A note on reduction and authenticity according to Husserl. *In* Elliston, F. A. and McCormick, P. eds. Husserl p124-25

Author and publisher. See Authors and publishers

Authoritarianism
Collier, R. B. Political change and authoritarian rule. *In* Martin, P. M. and O'Meara, P. eds. Africa p295-310

DeLeon, D. Statist radicalism. *In* DeLeon, D. The American as anarchist p102-14

Flew, A. G. N. Wants, or needs, choices or commands. *In* Fitzgerald, R. ed. Human needs and politics p213-28

See also Authority; Despotism; Fascism; National socialism; Totalitarianism

Authority
De George, R. T. The concept of authority. *In* Armstrong, T. R. and Cinnamon, K. M. eds. Power and authority in law enforcement p39-55

Koestler, A. Ad majorem gloriam. . . . *In* Koestler, A. Janus p77-97

Molnar, T. S. On authority; excerpt from "Authority and its enemies." *In* A Public philosophy reader p219-27

Neff, F. W. and Lubin, B. Observations on power and authority from a training program for police managers. *In* Armstrong, T. R. and Cinnamon, K. M. eds. Power and authority in law enforcement p115-30

Whisenand, P. and Ferguson, R. F. Controlling: the use of authority, power, and influence; excerpt from "The managing of police organizations." *In* Armstrong, T. R. and Cinnamon, K. M. eds. Power and authority in law enforcement p56-74

Wrong, D. H. Competent authority: reality and legitimating model. *In* The Uses of controversy in sociology p262-72

See also Consensus (Social sciences)

Authority (Religion)
See also Popes—Infallibility

History of doctrines
Tierney, B. "Only the truth has authority": the problem of "reception" in the decretists and in Johannes de Turrecremata. *In* Law, church, and society p69-96

Authority in literature
Lane, J. His master's voice? The questioning of authority in literature. *In* Josipovici, G. ed. The modern English novel: the reader, the writer and the work p113-29

Authors
Barthes, R. The death of the author. *In* Barthes, R. Image, music, text p142-48

Eberhart, R. Literary death. *In* Eberhart, R. Of poetry and poets p89-91

Foucault, M. What is an author? *In* Foucault, M. Language, counter-memory, practice p113-38

Sheed, W. The company of writers. *In* Sheed, W. The good word & other words p16-19

Sheed, W. On keeping closets closed. *In* Sheed, W. The good word & other words p73-76

Stegner, W. E. The writer and the concept of adulthood. *In* Erikson, E. H. ed. Adulthood p227-36

See also Anonyms and pseudonyms; Children as authors; Women authors

Biography
Mendelson, E. Authorized biography and its discontents. *In* Studies in biography p9-26

Interviews
Sheed, W. The interview as art. *In* Sheed, W. The good word & other words p206-11

Political and social views
Lessing, D. M. The small personal voice. *In* Lessing, D. M. A small personal voice p3-21

Sheed, W. Writers' politics. *In* Sheed, W. The good word & other words p62-67

Psychology
Cowley, M. Rebels, artists, and scoundrels. *In* Cowley, M.—And I worked at the writer's trade p249-66

Stierlin, H. Liberation and self-destruction in the creative process. *In* Psychiatry and the humanities, v 1 p51-72

Authors, Afro-American. See Afro-American authors

Authors, American
Bellow, S. Writers and literature in American society. *In* Culture and its creators p172-96

Cowley, M. "And Jesse begat. . ." a note on literary generation. *In* Cowley, M.—And I worked at the writer's trade p 1-20

Autobiography—*Continued*

Grosskurth, P. Where was Rousseau? *In* Landow, G. P. ed. Approaches to Victorian autobiography p26-38

Harbert, E. N. Henry Adams's Education and autobiographical tradition. *In* Tulane Studies in English v22 p133-41

Hart, F. R. Notes for an anatomy of modern autobiography. *In* Cohen, R. ed. New directions in literary history p221-47

Helsinger, E. K. Ulysses to Penelope: Victorian experiments in autobiography. *In* Landow, G. P. ed. Approaches to Victorian autobiography p3-25

Helsinger, H. Credence and credibility: the concern for honesty in Victorian autobiography. *In* Landow, G. P. ed. Approaches to Victorian autobiography p39-63

Landow, G. P. Introduction. *In* Landow, G. P. ed. Approaches to Victorian autobiography p xiii-vlvi

Lyons, J. O. Autobiography. *In* Lyons, J. O. The invention of the self p55-74

May, G. C. Autobiography and the eighteenth century. *In* Martz, L. L. and Williams, A. L. eds. The author in his work p319-35

Nevins, A. The autobiography. *In* Nevins, A. Allan Nevins on history p236-46

Perkins, J. A. The ironic mode in autobiography: Franklin and Rousseau. *In* Studies in eighteenth-century culture v6 p215-28

Spacks, P. A. M. Female identities. *In* Spacks, P. A. M. Imagining a self p57-91

Spacks, P. A. M. Identity in fiction and in fact. *In* Spacks, P. A. M. Imagining a self p 1-27

Spacks, P. A. M. Selfhood, given and formed. *In* Spacks, P. A. M. Imagining a self p300-15

Walther, L. The invention of childhood in Victorian autobiography. *In* Landow, G. P. ed. Approaches to Victorian autobiography p64-83

See also Biography (as a literary form); Fiction, Autobiographic

History and criticism

See Autobiography

Technique

See Autobiography

Automated information networks. See Information networks

Automatic translating. See Machine translating

Automation. See Assembly-line methods

Automobiles

Social aspects—United States

Foley, D. L. Accessibility for residents in the metropolitan environment. *In* Hawley, A. H. and Rock, V. P. eds. Metropolitan America in contemporary perspective p157-98

Goist, P. D. Automobility and community: the middle landscape of American automobiles. *In* Goist, P. D. From Main Street to State Street p35-45

Autonomy

Dearden, R. F. Autonomy as an educational ideal I. *In* Philosophers discuss education p3-18

Jacob, P. E. Autonomy and political responsibility: the enigmatic verdict of a cross-national comparative study of community dynamics. *In* Walton, J. and Masotti, L. H. eds. The city in comparative perspective p97-118

Kothari, R. World politics and world order: the issue of autonomy. *In* On the creation of a just world order p39-69

Mansfield, H. C. Independence and accountability for federal contractors and grantees. *In* Smith, B. L. R. ed. The new political economy: the public use of the private sector p319-35

Telfer, E. Autonomy as an educational ideal II. *In* Philosophers discuss education p19-35

Ubbelohde, C. The idea of independence. *In* Suggs, G. G. ed. Perspectives on the American Revolution p37-50

Autonomy (Psychology)

Bettelheim, B. Alienation and autonomy. *In* Bettelheim, B. Surviving, and other essays p333-49

May, R. Freedom and responsibility reexamined. *In* May, R. Psychology and the human dilemma p168-81

See also Free will and determinism

Autonomy, University. See University autonomy

Autrecourt, Nicolaus von. See Nicolaus de Autricuria

Auty, Phyllis

Yugoslavia and the Cold war. *In* Siracusa, J. M. and Barclay, G. S. eds. The impact of the Cold war p125-43

Auty, Robert

B. O. Unbegaun's contributions to Russian and Slavonic philology. *In* Oxford Slavonic papers new ser. v7 p 1-12

The Russian language. *In* Auty, R. and Obolensky, D. eds. An introduction to Russian language and literature p 1-40

Russian writing and printing: writing. *In* Auty, R. and Obolensky, D. eds. An introduction to Russian language and literature p41-47

Sixteenth-century Croatian glagolitic books in the Bodleian library. *In* Oxford Slavonic papers, new ser. v11 p132-35

Auty, Susan G.

The comic spirit of eighteenth-century novels

Contents

Auxerre, France. Saint-Étienne (Cathedral)

Schapiro, M. Two Romanesque drawings in Auxerre and some iconographic problems. *In* Schapiro, M. Selected papers v 1 p306-27

Avalle-Arce, Juan Bautista
Vital and artistic structures in the life of Don Quixote. *In* Medieval and Renaissance studies [1974] p104-21

Avant-garde (Aesthetics)
Brustein, R. S. On the new cultural conservatism. *In* Brustein, R. S. The culture watch p26-31

Forster, M. H. Latin American vanguardismo: chronology and terminology. *In* Forster, M. H. ed. Tradition and renewal p12-50

Goodheart, E. The formalist avant-garde and the autonomy of aesthetic values. *In* Goodheart, E. The failure of criticism p105-18

Greenberg, C. Avant-garde attitudes: new art in the sixties. *In* Concerning contemporary art p5-15

Rosenberg, H. What's new: ritual revolution. *In* Rosenberg, H. Art on the edge p251-61

Simon, J. I. New, newer, newest. *In* Simon, J. I. Singularities p119-25

Avant-garde films. See Experimental films

Avant-garde theater. See Experimental theater

Avanti! (Motion picture)
Kauffman, S. Avanti! *In* Kauffman, S. Living images p169-71

Avellaneda, Gertrudis Gómez de. See Gómez de Avellaneda y Arteaga, Gertrudis

Avempace
About
Moody, E. A. Galileo and Avempace: the dynamics of the Leaning Tower Experiment. *In* Moody, E. A. Studies in medieval philosophy, science, and logic p203-86

Avendaño, Fausto
The Spanish language in the Southwest: past, present, and future. *In* Trejo, A. D. ed. The Chicanos p133-50

Aveni, Anthony F.
Old and New World naked-eye astronomy. *In* Brecher, K. and Feirtag, M. eds. Astronomy of the ancients p62-89

Avenpace. See Avempace

Averitt, Robert T.
Time's structure, man's strategy: the American experience. *In* Evolution of international management structures p13-35

Averroes
About
Cranz, F. E. Editions of the Latin Aristotle accompanied by the Commentaries of Averroes. *In* Philosophy and humanism p116-28

About individual works
Commentary on Aristotle's Nicomachean ethics
Butterworth, C. E. New light on the political philosophy of Averroës. *In* Essays on Islamic philosophy and science p118-27

Commentary on Plato's Republic
Butterworth, C. E. New light on the political philosophy of Averroës. *In* Essays on Islamic philosophy and science p118-27

Avery, Fred. See Avery, Tex

Avery, Gillian Elise
The later years. *In* Drabble, M. ed. The genius of Thomas Hardy p44-54

Avery, Mary Ellen
About
Harvey, A. M. Johns Hopkins—its role in medical education for women. *In* Harvey, A. M. Adventures in medical research p225-47

Avery, Tex
About
Thompson, R. Meep meep. *In* Nichols, B. ed. Movies and methods p126-35

Avianus, Flavius
About individual works
Fabulae
Bailey, D. R. S. Avianiana. *In* Harvard Studies in classical philology v82 p295-301

Avianus Flaccus family
D'Arms, J. H. CIL X, 1792: a municipal notable of the Augustan age. *In* Harvard Studies in classical philology v76 p207-16

Aviation. See Aeronautics

Avicebron. See Ibn Gabirol, Solomon ben Judah

Avicenna
About
Lindberg, D. C. The intromission-extramission controversy in Islamic visual theory: Alkindi versus Avicenna. *In* Studies in perception p137-59

About individual works
Metaphysics
Marmura, M. E. Avicenna's chapter, "On the relative," in the Metaphysics of the Shifā. *In* Essays on Islamic philosophy and science p83-99

Avineri, Shlomo
Political and social aspects of Israeli and Arab nationalism. *In* The Palestinians p97-111

Avison, Margaret
About
Doerksen, D. W. Search and discovery: Margaret Avison's poetry. *In* Woodcock, G. ed. Poets and critics p123-37

Avneri, Uri. See Avnery, Uri

Avnery, Uri
The Palestinian option. *In* The Palestinians p187-93

Avni, Abraham Albert
Molière and writers of the English romantic era, especially Byron. *In* Johnson, R. B.; Neumann, E. S. and Trail, G. T. eds. Molière and the commonwealth of letters: patrimony and posterity p232-44

Avotins, Ivars
The holders of the chairs of rhetoric at Athens. *In* Harvard Studies in classical philology v79 p313-24

Lucretius 2.16-2.33. *In* Harvard Studies in classical philology v82 p167-73

L'Avventura (Motion picture)
Kauffmann, S. L'Avventura. *In* Kauffmann, S. Living images p332-40

Lesser, S. O. L'Avventura: a closer look. *In* Lesser, S. O. The whispered meanings p105-12

Murray, E. L'Avventura. *In* Murray, E. Ten film classics p134-48

Awakening, Great. See Great Awakening

Awami League

Choudhury, G. W. Roles and careers of middle-rank politicians: some cases from East Bengal. *In* The Making of politicians: studies from Africa and Asia p195-206

Awareness

Tart, C. T. Putting the pieces together: a conceptual framework for understanding discrete states of consciousness. *In* Alternate states of consciousness p158-219

Awe, Bolanle

The Iyalode in the traditional Yoruba political system. *In* Schlegel, A. E. ed. Sexual stratification p144-60

Awoonor, Kofi

Tradition and continuity in African literature. *In* Exile and tradition p166-72

Axiology. See Values

Axioms

Quine, M. V. Implicit definition sustained. *In* Quine, W. V. The ways of paradox, and other essays p133-36

Axton, Marie

The Tudor mask and Elizabethan court drama. *In* English drama: forms and development p24-47

Axton, Marie, and Williams, Raymond

About individual works
English drama

Alexander, N. English drama, edited by Marie Axton and Raymond Williams and Judith Weil's Christopher Marlowe. *In* Drama and society p279-89

Axton, Richard

Folk play in Tudor interludes. *In* English drama: forms and development p1-23

Axton, William F.

Dickens now. *In* Levine, R. A. The Victorian experience: the novelists p19-48

Great expectations: yet again. *In* Dickens Studies Annual v2 p278-93

Victorian landscape painting: a change in outlook. *In* Knoepflmacher, U. C. and Tennyson, G. B. eds. Nature and the Victorian imagination p281-308

Ayala, Francisco Jose

The concept of biological progress. *In* Ayala, F. J. and Dobzhansky, T. G. eds. Studies in the philosophy of biology p339-54

Ayala, Ramon Pérez de. See Pérez de Ayala, Ramon

Ayalon, David

Preliminary remarks on the mamlūk military institution in Islam. *In* War, technology and society in the Middle East p44-58

Ayckbourn, Alan

About individual works
Absurd person singular

Kauffmann, S. Absurd person singular. *In* Kauffmann, S. Persons of the drama p245-48

Ayele, Negussay

The foreign policy of Ethiopia. *In* Aluko, O. ed. The foreign policies of African states p47-71

Ayer, Sir Alfred Jules

André Malraux: the early novels. *In* Courcel, M. H. de, ed. Malraux p51-57

Professor Malcolm on dreams. *In* Dunlop, C. E. M. ed. Philosophical essays on dreaming p127-48

Self-evidence. *In* Pivčević, E. ed. Phenomenology and philosophical understanding p79-92

Wittgenstein on certainty. *In* Royal Institute of Philosophy. Understanding Wittgenstein p226-45

Aymard, Maurice

Toward the history of nutrition: some methodological remarks. *In* Food and drink in history p 1-16

el-Ayouty, Yassin

The OAU and the Arab-Israeli conflict: a case of mediation that failed. *In* El-Ayouty, Y. ed. The Organization of African Unity after ten years p189-212

Ayres, Clarence Edwin

About

Breit, W. and Culbertson, W. P. Clarence Edwin Ayres: an intellectual's portrait. *In* Science and ceremony p3-22

Buchanan, J. M. Methods and morals in economics: the Ayres-Knight discussion. *In* Science and ceremony p163-74

Chalk, A. F. Ayres's views on moral relativism. *In* Science and ceremony p147-61

Coats, A. W. Clarence Ayres's place in the history of American economics: an interim assessment. *In* Science and ceremony p23-48

Frankel, S. H. Clarence Ayres and the roots of economic progress. *In* Science and ceremony p63-74

Hartwell, R. M. C. E. Ayres on the Industrial Revolution. *In* Science and ceremony p49-62

Levy, M. J. Clarence E. Ayres as a university teacher. *In* Science and ceremony p181-86

Parsons, T. Clarence Ayres's economics and sociology. *In* Science and ceremony p175-79

Rostow, W. W. Technology and the price system. *In* Science and ceremony p75-113

About individual works
Science: the false messiah

Tullock, G. Science's feet of clay. *In* Science and ceremony p135-45

Ayres, Robert U.

Fortress America or a world of hope? Technology. *In* Isolation or interdependence? p149-65

Azef, Evno Fishelevich

About

Parry, A. Azef: terror chief as double agent. *In* Parry, A. Terrorism: from Robespierre to Arafat p120-30

Azerbaijan

History

Ramazani, R. K. The autonomous Republic of Azerbaijan and the Kurdish People's Republic: their rise and fall. *In* Hammond, T. T. ed. The anatomy of Communist takeovers p448-74

Azerbaijan, Iran (Province)

Social life and customs

Tapper, N. The women's subsociety among the Shahsevan nomads of Iran. *In* Beck, L. and Keddie, N. R. eds. Women in the Muslim world p374-98

Azmon, Yael

Traditional elements in Socialist systems: comparative remarks. *In* Eisenstadt, S. N. and Azmon, Y. eds. Socialism and tradition p228-40

Azorín, pseud. See Martínez Ruiz, José

Azoury, Negib

About

Kedourie, É. The politics of political literature: Kawakibi, Azoury and Jung. *In* Kedourie, É. Arabic political memoirs and other studies p107-23

Aztec art. See Aztecs—Art

Aztec literature

De Gerez, T. A basket of fireflies: Quetzalcoatl and the Nahuatl poetry of Mexico. *In* Egoff, S. A. ed. One ocean touching p138-46

Aztec mythology. See Aztecs—Religion and mythology

Aztecs

Art

Furst, P. T. Morning glory and mother goddess at Tepantitla, Teotihuacan: iconography and analogy in pre-Columbian art. *In* Mesoamerican archaeology p187-215

Religion and mythology

Brotherston, G. Huitzilopochtli and what was made of him. *In* Mesoamerican archaeology p155-66

Furst, P. T. Morning glory and mother goddess at Tepantitla, Teotihuacan: iconography and analogy in pre-Columbian art. *In* Mesoamerican archaeology p187-215

B

Baakpe women (African people) See Women, Bakwiri (African people)

Baar, Carl

Judicial behavior and comparative rights policy. *In* Claude, R. P. ed. Comparative human rights p353-81

Babbidge, Homer D.

Leadership, legitimacy, and academic governance. *In* Murphy, T. P. ed. Universities in the urban crisis p315-24

Babbitt, Irving

Democracy and leadership; excerpt. *In* Crunden, R. M. ed. The superfluous men p212-21

What is humanism? Excerpt from "Literature and the American college." *In* Crunden, R. M. ed. The superfluous men p133-34

About

More, P. E. Irving Babbitt. *In* Crunden, R. M. ed. The superfluous men p136-45

Tate, A. Humanism and naturalism. *In* Tate, A. Memoirs and opinions, 1926-1974 p170-94

About individual works
Democracy and leadership

Eliot, T. S. The humanism of Irving Babbitt. *In* Eliot, T. S. Selected prose of T. S. Eliot p277-84

Babcock, Barbara Allen

Introduction. *In* Babcock, B. A. ed. The reversible world p13-36

"Liberty's a whore": inversions, marginalia, and picaresque narrative. *In* Babcock, B. A. ed. The reversible world p95-116

Voir dire: preserving "its wonderful power." *In* Stanford legal essays p21-41

Babel, Isaac. See Babel' Isaak Émmanuilovich

Babel', Isaak Émmanuilovich

About

Voronskii, A. K. Isaac Babel. *In* Erlich, V. ed. Twentieth-century Russian literary criticism p182-97

About individual works
Collected stories

Farrell, J. T. The collected stories of Isaac Babel. *In* Farrell, J. T. Literary essays, 1954-1974 p99-100

Howe, I. The stories of Isaac Babel. *In* Howe, I. Celebrations and attacks p53-58

Di Grasso: A tale of Odessa

Trilling, L. Isaac Babel: Di Grasso: A tale of Odessa. *In* Trilling, L. Prefaces to The experience of literature p136-40

In Odessa

Berryman, J. The mind of Isaac Babel. *In* Berryman, J. The freedom of the poet p115-28

Red cavalry

Thomson, B. The difference of art: some Soviet writers of the 1920s and 1930s. *In* Thomson, B. Lot's wife and the Venus of Milo p98-122

Sunset

Kauffmann, S. Sunset. *In* Kauffmann, S. Persons of the drama p176-78

Babín, María Teresa

Contemporary Puerto Rican literature in translation. *In* Minority language and literature p115-20

Babington-Smith, Constance

Rose Macaulay in her writings. *In* Royal Society of Literature of the United Kingdom, London. Essays by divers hands v38 p143-58

Babrii. See Babrius

Babrius

About

Vaio, J. A new manuscript of Babrius: fact or fable? *In* Illinois classical studies, v2 1977 p173-83

Babula, William

The avenger and the satirist: John Marston's Malevole. *In* The Elizabethan theatre, VI p48-58

Whatever happened to Prince Hal? An essay on 'Henry V.' *In* Shakespeare survey 30 p47-59

Baby animals. See Animals, Infancy of

Baby Doll (Motion picture)

Truffaut, F. Elia Kazan: Baby Doll. *In* Truffaut, F. The films in my life p110-13

Babylonian proverbs. See Proverbs, Assyro-Babylonian

Bacalski-Martínez, Roberto R.

Aspects of Mexican American cultural heritage. *In* Trejo, A. D. ed. The Chicanos p19-35

Bacchanalia

Henrichs, A. Greek maenadism from Olympias to Messalina. *In* Harvard Studies in classical philology v82 p121-60

Bacchantes

Henrichs, A. Greek maenadism from Olympias to Messalina. *In* Harvard Studies in classical philology v82 p121-60

Bacchus. See Dionysus

Bacchylides

About individual works

Odes (Ode 5)

Lefkowitz, M. R. Bacchylides' Ode 5: imitation and originality. *In* Harvard Studies in classical philology v73 p45-96

Sources

Lefkowitz, M. R. Bacchylides' Ode 5: imitation and originality. *In* Harvard Studies in classical philology v73 p45-96

Bacdayan, Albert Somebang

Mechanistic cooperation and sexual equality among the western Bontoc. *In* Schlegel, A. E. ed. Sexual stratification p270-91

Bachi, Roberto. See Schmelz, O. jt. auth.

Bachofen, Johann Jacob

About individual works

Mother right

Hyman, S. E. Myths and mothers. *In* Hyman, S. E. The critic's credentials p298-304

Bachrach, Bernard S.

A study in feudal politics: relations between Fulk Nerra and William the Great, 995-1030. *In* Viator: medieval and Renaissance studies v7 p111-22

Bachtin, Nicholas. See Bakhtin, Nikolaĭ Mikhailovich

Backman, Jules

Economic growth, standards of living, and quality of life. *In* Tomorrow's American p69-89

Backman, Melvin

Death and birth in Hemingway. *In* The Stoic strain in American literature p115-33

Backscheider, Paula Rice

Defoe's women: snares and prey. *In* Studies in eighteenth-century culture v5 p103-20

Backward areas. See Underdeveloped areas

Bacon, Francis, Viscount St Albans

About

McCanles, M. Myth and method in the scientific philosophy of Francis Bacon. *In* McCanles, M. Dialectical criticism and Renaissance literature p14-53

Ravetz, J. R. '. . . et augebitur scientia.' *In* Harré, R. ed. Problems of scientific revolution p42-57

Wallace, K. R. Bacon, rhetoric, and ornament of words. *In* Rhetoric: a tradition in transition p49-65

Influence—Brecht

Ley, R. J. Francis Bacon, Galileo, and the Brechtian theater. *In* Mews, S. and Knust, H. eds. Essays on Brecht p174-89

Philosophy

Trowbridge, F. H. White of Selborne: the ethos of probabilism. *In* Trowbridge, F. H. From Dryden to Jane Austen p249-72

Bacon, Lloyd

About individual works

Marked woman

Kay, K. Sisters of the night. *In* Nichols, B. ed. Movies and methods p185-94

Bacon, Roger

About individual works

Opus majus

Matthews, G. B. A medieval theory of vision. *In* Studies in perception p186-99

Baconthorpe, John

About

Ullmann, W. John Baconthorpe as a canonist. *In* Church and government in the Middle Ages p223-46

Bacteria, Pathogenic

War use

See Biological warfare

Bacterial warfare. See Biological warfare

Bacteriological warfare. See Biological warfare

Badeau, John Stothoff

The Arab role in Islamic culture. *In* The Genius of Arab civilization p5-13

Bader, Arno Lehman

The structure of the modern short story. *In* May, C. E. ed. Short story theories p107-15

Badian, E.

A king's notebooks. *In* Harvard Studies in classical philology v72 p183-204

Nearchus the Cretan. *In* Yale classical studies v24 p147-70

Badlands (Motion picture)

Kauffmann, S. Badlands. *In* Kauffmann, S. Living images p271-73

Badurina, Berislav

Military force in the Mediterranean. *In* Borgese, E. M. and Krieger, D. eds. The tides of change p197-209

Baeck, Leo

About

Kaufman, W. E. Leo Baeck: the far yet near God. *In* Kaufman, W. E. Contemporary Jewish philosophies p125-41

Baer, Joachim Theodore

Wacław Berent's Ozimina: an analysis. *In* For Wiktor Weintraub p43-57

Baer, Werner, and Coes, Donald V.

Changes in the inter-American economic system. *In* Farer, T. J. ed. The future of the inter-American system p35-53

Baerns, Barbara

International business public relations. *In* Fischer, H. D. and Merrill, J. C. eds. International and intercultural communication p316-28

Baetzhold, Howard G.

Mark Twain on scientific investigation: contemporary allusions in "Some learned fables for good old boys and girls." *In* Literature and ideas in America p128-54

Baeumer, Max L.

Nietzsche and the tradition of the Dionysian. *In* O'Flaherty, J. C.; Sellner, T. F. and Helm, R. M. eds. Studies in Nietzsche and the classical tradition p165-89

Simplicity and grandeur: Winckelmann, French classicism, and Jefferson. *In* Studies in eighteenth-century culture v7 p63-78

Baganda

Nahemow, N. and Adams, B. N. Old age among the Baganda: continuity and change. *In* Gubrium, J. F. ed. Late life p147-66

Obbo, C. Village strangers in Buganda society. *In* Shack, W. A. and Skinner, E. P. eds. Strangers in African societies p227-41

Bage, Robert

About

Kelly, G. Robert Bage. *In* Kelly, G. The English Jacobin novel, 1780-1805 p20-63

About individual works

Hermsprong; or, Man as he is not

Butler, M. The Jacobin novel II: Caleb Williams and Hermsprong. *In* Butler, M. Jane Austen and the war of ideas p57-87

Bagehot, Walter

About

Tener, R. H. Walter Bagehot: some attributions. *In* Virginia. University. Bibliographical Society. Studies in bibliography v29 p346-59

Bagolini, Luigi

The topicality of Adam Smith's notion of sympathy and judicial evaluations. *In* Skinner, A. S. and Wilson, T. eds. Essays on Adam Smith p100-13

Bagpipe

History

Winternitz, E. Bagpipes and hurdy-gurdies in their social setting. *In* Winternitz, E. Musical instruments and their symbolism in Western art p66-85

Bagpipe in art

Winternitz, E. Bagpipes and hurdy-gurdies in their social setting. *In* Winternitz, E. Musical instruments and their symbolism in Western art p66-85

Bagritskiĭ, Eduard Georgievich

About individual works

February

Thomson, B. The secret of art: two Soviet myths. *In* Thomson, B. Lot's wife and the Venus of Milo p77-97

Bagwell, Philip S. and Mingay, G. E.

Britain and America: social progress, 1850-1939; excerpt from "Britain and America." *In* Burton, D. H. ed. American history—British historians p289-318

Bahasa Indonesia. See Indonesian language

Bahaya. See Haya (African tribe)

Bahr, Gisela E.

Roundheads and Peakheads: the truth about evil times. *In* Mews, S. and Knust, H. eds. Essays on Brecht p141-55

Bailey, Cyril, ed. and tr.

About individual works

De rerum natura

Stewart, D. J. The silence of Magna Mater. *In* Harvard Studies in classical philology v74 p75-84

Bailey, David Roy Shackleton

Avianiana. *In* Harvard Studies in classical philology v82 p295-301

Emendations of pseudo-Quintilian's longer declamations. *In* Harvard Studies in classical philology v80 p187-217

On Valerius Flaccus. *In* Harvard Studies in classical philology v81 p199-215

Bailey, David Tixany, and Haulman, Bruce E.

Ethnic differences on the Southwestern United States frontier, 1860. *In* Miller, D. H. and Steffen, J. O. eds. The frontier p243-57

Bailey, Donald M.

Pottery lamps. *In* Strong, D. E. and Brown, D. eds. Roman crafts p93-103

Bailey, L. H.

Ferdinand Kürnberger, Friedrich Schlögl and the feuilleton in Gründerzeit Vienna. *In* Branscombe, P. ed. Austrian life and literature, 1780-1938 p59-71

Bailey, Stephen Kemp

A finer order, a more general happiness. *In* The Third century p153-57

Bailiffs (Baillis) See Baillis

Baillis

Flanders

De Gryse, L. M. Some observations on the origin of the Flemish bailiff (bailli): the reign of Philip of Alsace. *In* Viator: medieval and Renaissance studies v7 p243-94

Bain, David Alexander

Transtemporal communication. *In* Egoff, S. A. ed. One ocean touching p3-17

Bain, Robert Addison

The Federalist. *In* Emerson, E. H. ed. American literature, 1764-1789 p253-73

Baines, Sir Edward, 1800-1890

About

Fraser, D. Edward Baines. *In* Hollis, P. ed. Pressure from without p183-209

Baird, James

Djuna Barnes and surrealism: "backward grief". *In* Baldwin, K. H. and Kirby, D. K. eds. Individual and community p160-81

Baird, John D.

Cowper's concept of truth. *In* Studies in eighteenth-century culture v7 p367-73

Baird, W. David

The quest for a red-faced white man: reservation whites view their Indian wards. *In* Red Men and hat-wearers p113-31

Bakan, Mildred

Hannah Arendt's concepts of labor and work. *In* Hannah Arendt: the recovery of the public world p49-65

Bā Kathīr, 'Alī Ahmad

About

Omotoso, K. Arabic drama and Islamic belief-system in Egypt. *In* African literature today no. 8: Drama in Africa p99-105

Baker, Anthony S.

Fernand Pelloutier and the making of a revolutionary syndicalism. *In* Essays on modern European revolutionary history p39-68

Baker, Carlos Heard

The boy and the lions; excerpt from "The writer as artist. 4th ed." *In* Wagner, L. W. ed. Ernest Hemingway p306-19

Hemingway's empirical imagination. *In* Baldwin, K. H. and Kirby, D. K. eds. Individual and community p94-111

The two African stories. *In* Benson, J. J. ed. The short stories of Ernest Hemingway: critical essays p45-53

Baker, Carlos H.—*Continued*
About individual works
Ernest Hemingway
Connolly, C. Ernest Hemingway: 2. *In* Connolly, C. The evening colonnade p258-61

Ernest Hemingway: a life story
Howe, I. The wounds of all generations. *In* Howe, I. Celebration and attacks p155-60

Baker, David Nathaniel. See Whalum, W. jt. auth.

Baker, Derek
Legend and reality: the case of Waldef of Melrose. *In* Church, society and politics p59-82

Baker, George
Language and mind in the study of new religious movements. *In* Needleman, J. and Baker, G. eds. Understanding the new religions p285-98

Baker, Helen
Growing up unheard. *In* Gross, B. and Gross, R. eds. The children's rights movement p187-99

Baker, John Ross
From imitation to rhetoric: the Chicago Critics, Wayne C. Booth, and Tom Jones. *In* Spilka, M. ed. Towards a poetics of fiction p136-56

Baker, Josephine
About
Reed, I. Remembering Josephine Baker. *In* Reed, I. Shrovetide in old New Orleans p286-89

Baker, Ray Stannard
About individual works
Following the color line
Grantham, D. W. Ray Stannard Baker's report on American Negro citizenship in the Progressive Era. *In* Grantham, D. W. The regional imagination p107-16

Baker, Rilda L.
"Of how to be and what to see while you are being": the reader's performance in The time of the hero. *In* Rossman, C. R. and Friedman, A. W. eds. Mario Vargas Llosa p3-14

Baker, Robert
"Pricks" and "chicks": a plea for "persons." *In* Baker, R. and Elliston, F. A. eds. Philosophy & sex p45-64

Baker, Robert Lewis
The government of Calais in 1363. *In* Order and innovation in the Middle Ages p207-14

Baker, Sheridan Warner
Hemingway's Two-hearted river. *In* Benson, J. J. ed. The short stories of Ernest Hemingway: critical essays p150-59

Baker, Steven J.
The international political economy of proliferation. *In* Arms control and technological innovation p70-101

Baker, William
Leigh Hunt, George Henry Lewes and Henry Hallam's Introduction to the literature of Europe. *In* Virginia. University. Bibliographical Society. Studies in bibliography v32 p252-73

Baker-Smith, Dominic
Juan Vives and the Somnium Scipionis. *In* Classical influences on European culture A.D. 1500-1700 p239-44

Bakers and bakeries
Bronx (Borough)
Parenti, M. J. The blessings of private enterprise: a personal reminiscence. *In* Studies in Italian American social history p81-83

Bakhtin, Nikolai Mikhailovich
About
Christian, R. F. Some unpublished poems of Nicholas Bachtin. *In* Oxford Slavonic papers, new ser. v10 p 107-19

Bakke, John Paul
Edmund Burke and the East Indian reform movement. *In* Rhetoric: a tradition in transition p122-41

Bakker, J. W. M.
Contemporary Buddhism in Indonesia. *In* Dumoulin, H. ed. Buddhism in the modern world p147-53

Bako, Elemer
Louis Kossuth. *In* Abroad in America: Visitors to the new Nation, 1776-1914 p124-33

Bakunin, Mikhail Aleksandrovich
About
Berlin, Sir I. Herzen and Bakunin on individual liberty. *In* Berlin, Sir I. Russian thinkers p82-113

Lehning, A. Bakunin's conceptions of revolutionary organisations and their role: a study of his 'secret societies'. *In* Essays in honour of E. H. Carr p57-81

Parry, A. Anarchists: philosophers with bombs. *In* Parry, A. Terrorism: from Robespierre to Arafat p78-91

Voegelin, E. Bakunin: the anarchist. *In* Voegelin, E. From Enlightenment to revolution p217-39

Voegelin, E. Revolutionary existence: Bakunin. *In* Voegelin, E. From Enlightenment to revolution p195-216

Bakwedi women (African people) See Women, Bakwiri (African people)

Bakweri women (African people) See Women, Bakwiri (African people)

Bakwileh women (African people) See Women, Bakwiri (African people)

Bakwili women (African people) See Women, Bakwiri (African people)

Bakwiri (African people)
Rites and ceremonies
Ardener, E. Belief and the problem of women. *In* Ardener, S. G. ed. Perceiving women p 1-17

Bakwiri women (African people) See Women, Bakwiri (African people)

Balaam and Balak
Mills, D. The two versions of Chester play V: Balaam and Balak. *In* Chaucer and Middle English studies in honour of Rossell Hope Robbins p366-71

Balaban, Lana
Mekong bus ride. *In* Aeolian harps p7-14

Balakian, Anna Elizabeth
Anicet, or The pursuit of pulchérie. *In* Symbolism and modern literature p237-47

Balakian, Nona

Critical encounters

Contents

Affirmation and love in T. S. Eliot

Afterword

Beautiful and undammed: stories by Fitzgerald

Bitches and sad ladies

Black odyssey, white world

Britain's lopsided view

Carson McCullers: love perverse and perfect

The charmed circle: the Irish writers

Crisis—in fiction or in readership?

Criticism par excellence: V. S. Pritchett

Crossing the ethnic barrier

A day of one's own: Eudora Welty

The decline of "mass markets"

Despiritualized Americans: Soviet views of
American literature

The flight from innocence: England's newest literary generation

God bless you, Mr. Vonnegut

Huxley revisited

The lowly state of book reviewing

Memo: to Bernard Shaw

The multiform American imagination

The new transcendentalists: a quasi-religious
mode in American fiction

On the reading of modern fiction

A passion for letters: Scofield Thayer and
The Dial

Poet of the air—and earth: Antoine de Saint-
Exupéry

Poets, printers and pamphleteers

The prophetic vogue of the anti-heroine

Realists of the interior: women poets of today

Reviews by Trilling

Shaw and his Boswell

Spearhead of British modernism

A specialist of the hoax: Max Beerbohm

They gambled on genius

Three post-psychological novels

The tragedy of delusion: criticism by Joyce
Carol Oates

Unwilling ironists

Where the center always holds: stories by
Brendan Gill

The world of William Saroyan

A writer and her vision: Ivy Compton-
Burnett

Balance

Brown, J. E. The science of weights. *In*
Lindberg, D. C. ed. Science in the Middle
Ages p179-205

Balance of nature. See Ecology

Balance of payments

Kelly, J. S. International monetary systems
and national security. *In* Knorr, K. E. and
Trager, F. N. eds. Economic issues and
national security p231-58

See also International liquidity

Mathematical models

Bryant, R. C. Empirical research on financial capital flows. *In* Kenen, P. B. ed. International trade and finance p321-62

Balance of power

Aron, R. Macht, power, puissance: democratic prose or demoniac poetry? *In* Aron, R.
Politics and history p102-21

Campbell, A. E. Balance of power. *In* Encyclopedia of American foreign policy p58-65

Craig, G. A. The United States and the
European balance. *In* Two hundred years of
American foreign policy p67-89

Etzold, T. H. Power politics. *In* Encyclopedia of American foreign policy p784-89

Knorr, K. E. The limits of economic and
military power. *In* Vernon, R. ed. The oil
crisis p229-43

Nitze, P. H. The global military balance. *In*
Kirk, G. L. and Wessell, N. H. eds. The
Soviet threat p4-14

Vernon, R. The distribution of power.
In Vernon, R. ed. The oil crisis p245-57

See also Great powers

Balance of trade. See Mercantile system

Balassa, Bela A.

Project appraisal in developing countries.
In Economic development and planning
p40-60

Balcer, Jack Martin

The date of Herodotus IV.1: Darius' Scythian expedition. *In* Harvard Studies in
classical philology v76 p99-132

Baldeshwiler, Eileen

The lyric short story: the sketch of a history. *In* May, C. E. ed. Short story theories
p202-13

Sherwood Anderson and the lyric story.
In French, W. G. ed. The twenties p65-74

Baldo degli Ubaldi, 1327?-1400

About

Kirshner, J. "Ar imitatur naturam": a
consilium of Baldus on naturalization in
Florence. *In* Viator: medieval and Renaissance studies v5 p289-331

Baldock, Cora Vellekoop. See Lally, J.
jt. auth.

Baldry, Harold C.

Theatre and society in Greek and Roman
antiquity. *In* Drama and society p 1-21

Baldus de Perugia. See Baldo degli Ubaldi,

Baldwin, David Allen

Foreign policy problems. 1975-1980:
framework for analysis. *In* Baldwin, D. A.
ed. America in an interdependent world p3-
27

Baldwin, Fletcher N.

Constitutional limitations on government
in Mexico, the United States, and Uganda.
In Claude, R. P. ed. Comparative human
rights p76-98

Baldwin, Frank

The Korea lobby. *In* Horowitz, I. L. ed.
Science, sin, and scholarship p160-74

Baldwin, Harold W.

Conceptualizations of experimental clairvoyance. *In* Ludwig, J. K. ed. Philosophy and
parapsychology p255-62

Baldwin, James, 1924-

About individual works

The devil finds work

Sheed, W. The twin urges of James Baldwin. *In* Sheed, W. The good word & other
words p194-200

Going to meet the Man

Freese, P. James Baldwin, Going to meet
the Man. *In* Bruck, P. ed. The Black American short story in the 20th century p171-85

Bibliography

Dance, D. C. James Baldwin. *In* Inge,
M. T.; Duke, J. M. and Bryer, J. R. eds.
Black American writers v2 p73-120

Baldwin, Joseph Glover

About

Current-Garcia, E. Joseph Glover Baldwin: humorist or moralist? *In* Inge, M. T. ed. The frontier humorists p170-86

Baldwin, Stanley Baldwin, 1st Earl

Introduction to Precious bane by Mary Webb. *In* Praise from famous men: an anthology of introductions p10-13

Balestri, Charles

The Bacchae. *In* Seidel, M. A. and Mendelson, E. eds. Homer to Brecht p191-213

Balewa, Sir Abubakar Tafawa

About individual works

Shaihu Umar

Taiwo, O. Social criticism. *In* Taiwo, O. Culture and the Nigerian novel p34-73

Balfour Declaration

Weizmann, C. The Jewish people and Palestine; excerpts. *In* The Palestinians p46-50

Bali (Island)

Social life and customs

Bateson, G. Some components of socialization for trance. *In* Schwartz, T. ed. Socialization as cultural communication p51-63

Balkan Peninsula

History

Petrović, D. Fire-arms in the Balkans on the eve of and after the Ottoman conquests of the fourteenth and fifteenth centuries. *In* War, technology and society in the Middle East p164-94

Rogel, C. The wandering monk and the Balkan national awakening. *In* Nationalism in a non-national state p77-101

History—War of 1912-1913

Swanson, G. W. War, technology, and society in the Ottoman Empire from the reign of Abdülhamid II to 1913: Mahmud Savket and the German military mission. *In* War, technology and society in the Middle East p367-85

Ball, Christopher. See Mitchell, B. C. jt. auth.

Ball, George Wildman

America's changing world posture. *In* The National purpose reconsidered p11-28

The problem stated. *In* The New Atlantic challenge p17-25.

Ball, Joseph W.

The rise of the northern Maya chiefdoms: a socioprocessual analysis. *In* The Origins of Maya civilization p101-32

Ball, Patricia M.

The heart's events

Contents

Conclusion: The heart's events
'The difference to me'
'The fates, it is clear, are against us'
'If I be dear to someone else'
'Till all my widowed race be run'
'To marry her and take her home'

Ball, Richard Allen

Qualitative evaluation of criminal justice programs. *In* Riedel, M. and Chappell, D. eds. Issues in criminal justice: planning and evaluation p36-47

Sociology and general systems theory. *In* McNall, S. G. ed. Theoretical perspectives in sociology p115-27

Ball, Terence

Plato and Aristotle: the unity versus the autonomy of theory and practice. *In* Political theory and praxis p57-69

Ball, William

About

Kauffmann, S. The American Conservatory Theater. *In* Kauffmann, S. Persons of the drama p31-35

Ballads

See also Folk songs

History and criticism

Katz, M. R. The influence of folk ballads and the ballad revival on Russian literary ballads. *In* Katz, M. R. The literary ballad in early nineteenth-century Russian literature p3-18

Ballads. See Folk songs

Ballads, American

History and criticism

Gower, H. The Scottish element in traditional ballads collected in America. *In* Ballad studies p117-51

Ballads, Australian

History and criticism

Paniker, K. A. Folk humour: a comparison of the comic ballads of Australia and Kerala (India). *In* Narasimhaiah, C. D. ed. Awakened conscience p236-50

Ballads, English

Reppert, J. D. F. J. Child and the ballad *In* The Learned and the lewed p197-212

Richards, I. A. Reversals in poetry. *In* Richards, I. A. Poetries p59-70

Utley, F. L. Oral genres as a bridge to written literature. *In* Folklore genres p3-15

History and criticism

Holt, J. C. The origins and audience of the ballads of Robin Hood. *In* Peasants, knights and heretics p236-57

Nygard, H. O. Popular ballad and medieval romance. *In* Ballad studies p 1-19

Ballads, Indic

History and criticism

Paniker, K. A. Folk humour: a comparison of the comic ballads of Australia and Kerala (India). *In* Narasimhaiah, C. D. ed. Awakened conscience p236-50

Ballads, Irish

Lloyd, A. L. On an unpublished Irish ballad. *In* Rebels and their causes p177-207

History and criticism

Medwin, A. G. Miss Reburn's ballads: a nineteenth-century repertoire from Ireland. *In* Ballad studies p93-116

Wilgus, D. K. Irish traditional narrative songs in English: 1800-1916. *In* Casey, D. J. and Rhodes, R. E. eds. Views of the Irish peasantry, 1800-1916 p107 28

Ballads, Latin

Momigliano, A. Perizonius, Niebuhr and the character of early Roman tradition. *In* Momigliano, A. Essays in ancient and modern historiography p231-51

Ballads, Russian

History and criticism

Katz, M. R. The influence of folk ballads and the ballad revival on Russian literary ballads. *In* Katz, M. R. The literary ballad in early nineteenth-century Russian literature p3-18

Katz, M. R. Polemics. *In* Katz, M. R. The literary ballad in early nineteenth-century Russian literature p101-20

Katz, M. R. Russian literary ballads of the 1790s. *In* Katz, M. R. The literary ballad in early nineteenth-century Russian literature p19-36

Katz, M. R. Zhukovsky's imitators. *In* Katz, M. R. The literary ballad in early nineteenth-century Russian literature p121-38

Ballads, Scottish

Reppert, J. D. F. J. Child and the ballad *In* The Learned and the lewed p197-212

Ballantine, Lesley Frost

In Aladdin's lamp light. *In* Frost: centennial essays III p313-15

Ballard, J. G.

About

Franklin, H. B. What are we to make of J. G. Ballard's apocalypse? *In* Clareson, T. D. ed. Voices for the future: essays on major science fiction writers v2 p82-105

Ballesteros, David

Bilingual-bicultural education: a must for Chicanos. *In* Trejo, A. D. ed. The Chicanos p151-65

Ballew v. Georgia. *In* The Supreme Court review, 1978 p191-224

Ballinger, William Pitt

About

Bloomfield, N. H. William Pitt Ballinger, Confederate lawyer. *In* Bloomfield, M. H. American lawyers in a changing society, 1776-1876 p271-301

Ballistic missiles. See Fleet ballistic missile weapons systems

Balloons, Dirigible. See Air-ships

The Ballygombeen bequest (criticism) Arden, J. and D'Arcy, M. *In* Brustein, R. S. The culture watch p53-56

Balsac, Robert de

About

Contamine, P. The war literature of the late Middle Ages: The treatises of Robert de Balsac and Béraud Stuart, Lord of Aubigny. *In* War, literature, and politics in the late Middle Ages p102-21

Baltic States

History

Tomson, E. The annexation of the Baltic States. *In* Hammond, T. T. ed. The anatomy of Communist takeovers p214-28

Relations (general) with Russia

Vardys, V. S. The role of the Baltic republics in Soviet society. *In* Szporluk, R. ed. The influence of East Europe and the Soviet West on the USSR p147-79

Baltimore, David

Limiting science: a biologist's perspective. *In* Holton, G. J. and Morison, R. S. eds. Limits of scientific inquiry p37-45

Baltrušaitis, Jurgis

About individual works

La stylistique ornamentale dans la sculpture romane

Schapiro, M. On geometrical schematism in Romanesque art. *In* Schapiro, M. Selected papers v 1 p265-84

Ba-luba. See Baluba

Baluba

Religion

Booth, N. S. The view from Kasongo Niembo. *In* African religions: a symposium p31-67

Balzac, Honoré de

About

Larkin, M. Man and beast: the Balzacian jungle. *In* Larkin, M. Man and society in nineteenth-century realism p31-41

Peyre, H. Stendhal and Balzac as admirers and followers of Molière. *In* Johnson, R. B.; Neumann, E. S. and Trail, G. T. eds. Molière and the commonwealth of letters: patrimony and posterity p133-44

Robinson, C. Science, reason and the material world. *In* Robinson, C. French literature in the nineteenth century p50-107

Snow, C. P. Baron Snow. Balzac. *In* Snow, C. P. Baron Snow. The realists p35-71

Terdiman, R. Balzac: the logic of failure. *In* Terdiman, R. The dialectics of isolation p39-59

About individual works

Cousin Bette

Larkin, M. Une société embourgeoisée? Balzac's France. *In* Larkin, M. Man and society in nineteenth-century realism p42-51

The hidden masterpiece

Lanes, J. Art criticism and the authorship of the Chef-d'oeuvre inconnu: a preliminary study. *In* The Artist and the writer in France p86-99

The human comedy

Tatar, M. M. The metaphysics of the will: voyeurs and visionaries in Balzac's "Comédie humaine." *In* Tatar, M. M. Spellbound p152-88

Lost illusions

Alter, R. The self-conscious novel in eclipse. *In* Alter, R. Partial magic p84-137

Mount, A. J. H. de Balzac: Lost illusions. *In* Williams, D. A. ed. The monster in the mirror p17-39

Bamberger, Jeanne

In search of a tune. *In* Perkins, D. and Leondar, B. eds. The arts and cognition p284-319

Bambrough, Renford

Essay on man. *In* Royal Institute of Philosophy. Nature and conduct p 1-13

How to read Wittgenstein. *In* Royal Institute of Philosophy. Understanding Wittgenstein p117-32

Bambute

Psychology

Turnbull, C. M. The politics of non-aggression. *In* Montagu, A. ed. Learning non-aggression p161-221

Bance, A. F.

Ödön Von Horvath: Kasimir und Karoline. *In* Branscombe, P. ed. Austrian life and literature, 1780-1938 p81-93

Bancroft, George

About

Nevins, A. George Bancroft. *In* Nevins, A. Allan Nevins on history p305-19

Tichi, C. Questioning and chronicling: Thoreau, Cooper, Bancroft. *In* Tichi, C. New World, new earth p151-205

Bandinelli, Orlando. See Alexander III, Pope

Bandinelli, Ranuccio Bianchi. See Bianchi Bandinelli, Ranuccio

Bandman, Bertram, and Bandman, Elsie L.
Rights, justice, and euthanasia. *In* Kohl, M. ed. Beneficent euthanasia p81-99

Bandman, Elsie L. See Bandman, B. jt. auth.

Banerjee, Bibhuti Bhusan

About individual works

Pather panchali: Song of the road: a Bengali novel

Gunawardana, A. J. From the village to the city: The song of the road. *In* Narasimhaiah, C. D. ed. Awakened conscience p206-15

Banerji, Bibhutibhushan. See Banerjee, Bibhuti Bhusan

Banfield, Edward C.
The city and the revolutionary tradition. *In* America's continuing revolution p229-44

Bang the drum slowly (Motion picture)
Kauffmann, S. Bang the drum slowly. *In* Kauffmann, S. Living images p215-17

Bangladesh

Famines

Singer, P. Famine, affluence, and morality. *In* Aiken, W. and La Follette, H. eds. World hunger and moral obligation p22-36

Politics and government

Choudhury, G. W. Roles and careers of middle-rank politicians: some cases from East Bengal. *In* The Making of politicians: studies from Africa and Asia p195-206

LaPorte, R. Pakistan and Bangladesh. *In* Kearney, R. N. ed. Politics and modernization in South and Southeast Asia p109-52

Banham, Martin
Eldred Durosimi Jones: The writing of Wole Soyinka; Gerald Moore: Wole Soyinka. *In* African literature today no. 7: Focus on criticism p153-54

Banham, Reyner
Adolf Loos: ornament and crime. *In* Sharp, D. ed. The rationalists p26-33

Mediated environments or: You can't build that here. *In* Bigsby, C. W. E. Superculture p69-82

Banians in eighteenth-century Calcutta, Masters and. Marshall, P. *In* Kling, B. B. and Pearson, M. N. eds. The age of partnership p191-213

The banished wife's lament. See The wife's lament (Anglo-Saxon poem)

Banister, Judith
International effects of China's population situation. *In* China's changing role in the world economy p83-113

Banjo, Ayo
Language policy in Nigeria. *In* Smock, D. R. and Bentsi-Enchill, K. eds. The search for national integration in Africa p206-19

Bank, Alice. See Bank, Alisa Vladimirovna

Bank, Alisa Vladimirovna
A copper-gilt plaque of the archangel Gabriel. *In* Studies in memory of David Talbot Rice p6-9

Bank loans
Syz, J. Recent North-South relations and multilateral soft loans. *In* The Year book of world affairs, 1975 p196-207

Bank management
Scott, I. O. Thrift institution management: tomorrow and today. *In* Benton, L. R. ed. Management for the future p271-82

Bank of the United States, 1816-1836
Ambacher, B. I. Urban response to Jacksonian democracy: Philadelphia Democrats and the Bank War, 1832-1834. *In* Essays on urban America p55-87

Bank War. See Bank of the United States, 1816-1836

Banker, James R.
The ars dictaminis and rhetorical textbooks at the Bolognese University in the fourteenth century. *In* Medievalia et humanistica no. 5 p153-68

Bankers, Jewish. See Banks and banking—Jews

Banking. See Banks and banking

Banks, Robert
The eschatological role of law in pre- and post-Christian Jewish thought. *In* Reconciliation and hope p173-85

Banks and banking
See also Bills of exchange; Development banks; Interest and usury; Money; Savings-banks

La paix du ménage

Riffaterre, M. The reader's perception of narrative: Balzac's Paix du ménage. *In* Valdés, M. J. and Miller, O. J. eds. Interpretation of narrative p28-37

History

Bergier, J. F. From the fifteenth century in Italy to the sixteenth century in Germany: a new banking concept? *In* The Dawn of modern banking p105-29

Lopez, R. S. The dawn of medieval banking. *In* The Dawn of modern banking p 1-23

Udovitch, A. L. Bankers without banks: commerce, banking, and society in the Islamic world of the Middle Ages. *In* The Dawn of modern banking p255-73

Jews

Landes, D. S. Bleichröders and Rothschilds: the problem of continuity in the family firm. *In* Rosenberg, C. E. ed. The family in history p95-114

Stern, F. R. Capitalism and the cultural historian. *In* From Parnassus p209-24

Management

See Bank management

Taxation—United States

Kane, E. J. A cross-section study of tax avoidance by large commercial banks. *In* Inflation, trade and taxes p218-46

Africa, East

Letiche, J. M. Dependent monetary systems and economic development: the case of sterling East Africa. *In* Economic development and planning p186-236

Banks and banking—*Continued*
Italy—History
Blomquist, T. W. The dawn of banking in an Italian commune: thirteenth century Lucca. *In* The Dawn of modern banking p53-75

Scotland—History
Checkland, S. G. Adam Smith and the bankers. *In* Skinner, A. S. and Wilson, T. eds. Essays on Adam Smith p504-23

Spain—History
Riu, M. Banking and society in late medieval and early modern Aragon. *In* The Dawn of modern banking p131-67

United States
Golembe, C. H. Challenges confronting American banking. *In* Prochnow, H. V. ed. Dilemmas facing the nation p109-24

Banneker, Benjamin
Bibliography
Klinkowitz, J. Early writers: Jupiter Hammon, Phillis Wheatley, and Benjamin Banneker. *In* Inge, M. T.; Duke, J. M. and Bryer, J. R. eds. Black American writers v 1 p 1-20

Banner, Lois W.
Religious benevolence as social control: a critique of an interpretation. *In* Mulder, J. M. and Wilson, J. F. eds. Religion in American history p218-35

Banner, William A.
Compensatory justice and the meaning of equity. *In* Social justice & preferential treatment p199-216

Bannerman, John W. M.
The Lordship of the Isles. *In* Brown, J. M. ed. Scottish society in the fifteenth century p209-40

Banners. See Flags

Banta, Martha
They shall have faces, minds, and (one day) flesh: women in late nineteenth-century and early twentieth-century American literature. *In* Springer, M. A. ed. What manner of woman p235-70

Banton, Michael P.
1960: a turning point in the study of race relations. *In* Mintz, S. W. ed. Slavery, colonialism, and racism p31-44

Bantu marriage customs and rites. See Marriage customs and rites, Bantu

Bantus
Ardener, E. Language, ethnicity, and population. *In* Studies in social anthropology p343-53
White, C. M. N. The material culture of the Lunda-Lovale peoples. *In* The Occasional papers of the Rhodes-Livingstone Museum p53-70
See also Ambo (African tribe); Baganda; Banyoro; Haya (African tribe); Nguni; Nyakyusa (African tribe)

Banyoro
Beattie, J. H. M. Tonya: a lakeside settlement in Bunyoro. *In* Studies in social anthropology p30-40

Barabanov, Evgeny
The schism betwen the Church and the world. *In* From under the rubble p172-93

Baraka, Imamu Amiri. See Jones, LeRoi

Barasch, Frances K.
HEW, the university, and women. *In* Gross, B. R. ed. Reverse discrimination p54-65

Barash, David P.
Evolution as a paradigm for behavior. *In* Sociobiology and human nature p13-32

Barafs, German Markovich
About
Dunlop, D. M. H. M. Baratz and his view of Khazar influence on the earliest Russian literature, juridical and historical. *In* Salo Wittmayer Baron v 1 p345-67

Baratz, H. M. See Barafs, German Markovich

Barbarelli, Giorgio. See Giorgione, Giorgio Barbarelli, known as

Barbarian invasions of Rome
Burns, T. S. The Alpine frontiers and early medieval Italy to the middle of the seventh century. *In* The Frontier v2 p51-68
Ladner, G. B. On Roman attitudes toward barbarians in late antiquity. *In* Viator: medieval and Renaissance studies v7 p 1-26

Barbeau, Anne T.
The wild and the garden: a double focus on reality in Pope's An essay on man. *In* Tennessee Studies in literature v22 p73-84

Barbeau, Charles Marius
The career of a medicine-man; excerpt from "Medicine-men on the North Pacific coast." *In* Tedlock, D. E. ed. Teachings from the American earth p3-12

Barbeau, Marius. See Barbeau, Charles Marius

Barber, Benjamin R.
The compromised Republic: public purposelessness in America. *In* The Moral foundations of the American Republic p19-38

Barber, Bernard
Toward a new view of the sociology of knowledge. *In* The Idea of social structure p103-16

Barber, Cesar Lombardi
A mask presented at Ludlow Castle: the masque as a masque. *In* Wimsatt, W. K. ed. Literary criticism: idea and act p382-401

Barber, Giles
Dr Johnson and cookery. *In* The Dress of words p91-104

Barber, James P.
White rule and the outward policy. *In* Leftwich, A. ed. South Africa: economic growth and political change p319-42

Barber, Patricia
What if Bartleby were a woman? *In* Diamond, A. and Edwards, L. R. eds. The authority of experience p212-23

Barber, Sotirios A.
National League of Cities v. Usery: new meaning for the Tenth Amendment? *In* The Supreme Court review, 1976 p161-82

Barbier, Auguste
About individual works
Iambes
Struve, G. Osip Mandelstam and Auguste Barbier. *In* California Slavic studies v8 p131-66

Barbour, Douglas
Poet as philosopher: Louis Dudek. *In* Woodcock, G. ed. Poets and critics p110-22

Barbu, Zevedei
Popular culture: a sociological approach. *In* Bigsby, C. W. E. ed. Approaches to popular culture p39-68

Barbusse, Henri

About individual works
Under fire
King, J. Henri Barbusse: Le feu and the crisis of social realism. *In* Klein, H. M. ed. The First World War in fiction p43-52

Barcia, José Rubia. See Rubia Barcia, José

Barclay, Glen St John
Anatomy of horror: the masters of occult fiction

Contents
The Devil and Dennis Wheatley
Love after death: Henry Rider Haggard
The lure of the occult
The myth that never was: Howard P. Lovecraft
Orthodox horrors: Charles Williams and William P. Blatty
Sex and horror: Bram Stoker
Vampires and ladies: Sheridan Le Fanu
Australia and the Cold war. *In* Siracusa, J. M. and Barclay, G. S. eds. The impact of the Cold war p3-25

Bardach, Eugene
Reason, responsibility, and the new social regulation. *In* Burnham, W. D. and Weinberg, M. W. eds. American politics and public policy p364-90

Bardi family
Krekić, B. Four Florentine commercial companies in Dubrovnik (Ragusa) in the first half of the fourteenth century. *In* The Medieval city p25-41

Bards and bardism
Creed, R. P. Widsith's journey through Germanic tradition. *In* Anglo-Saxon poetry: essays in appreciation p376-87

The barefoot contessa (Motion picture)
Truffaut, F. Joseph Mankiewicz: The barefoot contessa. *In* Truffaut, F. The films in my life p129-32

Barfield, Arthur Owen. See Barfield, Owen

Barfield, Owen
The rediscovery of meaning, and other essays

Contents
The coming trauma of materialism
Dream, myth, and philosophical double vision
Form in art and in society
The harp and the camera
Imagination and inspiration
Language and discovery
Matter, imagination, and spirit
The meaning of "literal"
Participation and isolation: a fresh light on present discontents
Philology and the Incarnation
Poetic diction and legal fiction
The Psalms of David
The rediscovery of allegory (I)
The rediscovery of allegory (II)
The rediscovery of meaning
Science and quality
Self and reality
The "Son of God" and the "Son of Man"
Where is fancy bred?

About
Harwood, A. C. Owen Barfield. *In* Evolution of consciousness p31-33

Reilly, R. J. A note on Barfield, romanticism, and time. *In* Evolution of consciousness p183-90
Tennyson, G. B. Etymology and meaning. *In* Evolution of consciousness p168-82

About individual works
Saving the appearances
Barfield, A. O. Participation and isolation: a fresh light on present discontents. *In* Barfield, A. O. The rediscovery of meaning, and other essays p201-16

Barfield, R. H.
Darwinism. *In* Evolution of consciousness p69-82

Bargainnier, Earl F.
The plantation: Southern icon. *In* Browne, R. B. and Fishwick, M. W. eds. Icons of America p271-83

Barghoorn, Frederick Charles
The post-Khrushchev campaign to suppress dissent: perspectives, strategies, and techniques of repression. *In* Tokes, R. L. ed. Dissent in the USSR p35-95

Barham, Charles Middleton, 1st Baron

About
Moody, M. E. Religion in the life of Charles Middleton, First Baron Barham. *In* The Dissenting tradition p140-63

Barickman, Richard
The spiritual journey of Amy Dorrit and Arthur Clennam. *In* Dickens Studies Annual v7 p163-89

Barish, Jonas A.
The true and false families of The revenger's tragedy. *In* English Renaissance drama p142-54

Barkan, Leonard
The imperialist arts of Inigo Jones. *In* Renaissance drama [1976] p257-85

Barkentin, Marjorie

About individual works
Ulysses in Nighttown
Kauffmann, S. Ulysses in Nighttown. *In* Kauffmann, S. Persons of the drama p149-52

Barker, Eric E.
Two lost documents of King Athelstan. *In* Anglo-Saxon England 6 p137-43

Barker, Harley Granville Granville- See Granville-Barker, Harley Granville

Barker, Roger Garlock

About individual works
Ecological psychology: concepts and methods for studying the environment of human behavior
Fox, K. A. Combining economic and non-economic objectives in development planning: problems of concept and measurement. *In* Economic development and planning p104-41

Barkley, John Monteith
The Presbyterian Church in Ireland and the Government of Ireland Act (1920) *In* Church, society and politics p393-403

Barley, Nigel F.
Old English colour classification: where do matters stand? *In* Anglo-Saxon England 3 p15-28

Barlingay, Surendra Sheodas
Indian epistemology and logic. *In* Bishop, D. H. ed. Indian thought p148-75

Barlow, Joel
About
Arner, R. D. The Connecticut wits. *In* Emerson, E. H. ed. American literature, 1764-1789 p233-52

About individual works
The Columbiad
Tichi, C. Joel Barlow and the engineered millennium. *In* Tichi, C. New World, new earth p114-50

Barnard, John
The murder of Falstaff, David Jones, and the 'disciplines of war.' *In* Evidence in literary scholarship p13-27

Barnard, Robert
Imagery and theme in Great expectations. *In* Dickens Studies Annual v1 p238-51

Barnds, William J.
China in American foreign policy. *In* China and America p196-248

Barnes, Annette
Female criticism: a prologue. *In* Diamond, A. and Edwards, L. R. eds. The authority of experience p 1-15

Barnes, Barry. See MacKenzie, D. jt. auth.; Shapin, S. jt. auth.

Barnes, Christopher J.
Boris Pasternak's revolutionary year. *In* Barnes, C. J. ed. Studies in twentieth century Russian literature p46-60

Barnes, Djuna
About
Baird, J. Djuna Barnes and surrealism: "backward grief". *In* Baldwin, K. H. and Kirby, D. K. eds. Individual and community p160-81

Barnes, James John
John Miller: first transatlantic publisher's agent. *In* Virginia. University. Bibliographical Society. Studies in bibliography v29 p373-79

Barnes, John
Such is life and the observant reader. *In* Bards, bohemians and bookmen p153-69

Barnes, John Arundel
The material culture of the Fort Jameson Ngoni. *In* The Occasional papers of the Rhodes-Livingstone Museum p 1-20

Barnes, Samuel H.
The dark side of pluralism: Italian democracy and the limits of political engineering. *In* Prospects for constitutional democracy p75-100

Barnes, Timothy David
Constans and Gratian in Rome. *In* Harvard Studies in classical philology v79 p325-33

Origen, Aquila, and Eusebius. *In* Harvard Studies in classical philology v74 p313-16

Sossianus Hierocles and the antecedents of the "Great persecution." *In* Harvard Studies in classical philology v80 p239-52

Barnes, Winston Herbert Frederick
The rational theology of Thomas Hobbes. *In* The Personal universe p54-63

Barnet, Richard J.
The "dirty-tricks" gap. *In* Borosage, R. L. and Marks, J. D. eds. The CIA file p214-28

In search of the national interest. *In* [Truth and tragedy]: a tribute to Hans Morgenthau p153-61

Barnett, Evelyn Brooks
Nannie Burroughs and the education of Black women. *In* Harley, S. and Terborg-Penn, R. eds. The Afro-American woman p97-108

Barney, Stephen A.
Allegories of history, allegories of love
Contents
Adornment: the Romance of the Rose
Blighting words: Hawthorne's "Rappaccini's daughter"
The dream of history: Langland's Piers Plowman
The knight at one: The Faerie Queene, Book one
The natural woman: The Faerie Queene, Books three and four
The siege of paradise: Prudentius's Psychomachia
The sun's a thief: Melville's The confidence-man
Without a counterpart: Kafka's The castle

Barnhart, Joe E. and Barnhart, Mary Ann
The myth of the complete person. *In* Feminism and philosophy p277-90

Barnhart, Joseph E. See Barnhart, Joe E.

Barnhart, Mary Ann. See Barnhart, J. E. jt. auth.

Barnhart, Richard
Li Kung-Lin's use of past styles. *In* Artists and traditions p51-71

Barnouw, Dagmar
Disorderly company: from The golden notebook to The four-gated city. *In* Pratt, A. V. and Dembo, L. S. eds. Doris Lessing p74-97

Barnouw, Erik
The media revolution. *In* The American Revolution: a continuing commitment p27-39

Barnouw, Jeffrey
Materialism and freedom: commentary on papers by Robert E. Schofield and Aram Vartanian. *In* Studies in eighteenth-century culture v7 p193-212

Barnouw, Victor
An interpretation of Wisconsin Ojibwa culture and personality: a review. *In* Spindler, G. D. ed. The making of psychological anthropology p64-86

Baroda (City), India
Politics and government
Pantham, T. The formation of the politically active stratum: evidence from the career origins of party activists in an Indian city. *In* The Making of politicians: studies from Africa and Asia p207-26

Baroja y Nessi, Pío
About
Shaw, D. L. Baroja: anguish, action, and ataraxia. *In* Shaw, D. L. The generation of 1898 in Spain p95-126

Barolsky, Paul
Infinite jest: wit and humor in Italian Renaissance art
Contents
Facetiae by Raphael and his friends
The grotesque and mock-heroic in north Italy
Laughter from the Venetian boudoir
The lighter side of Cosimo de' Medici's court
Love, laughter, and revelry

Barth, John—About individual works—Giles goat-boy—*Continued*

Tilton, J. W. Giles goat-boy: satire given tragic depth. *In* Garvin, H. R. ed. Makers of the twentieth-century novel p290-308

Same as: Tilton, J. W. Giles goat-boy: man's precarious purchase on reality. *In* Tilton, J. W. Cosmic satire in the contemporary novel p43-68

Lost in the funhouse

Hyman, S. E. Fun and love. *In* Hyman, S. E. The critic's credentials p118-23

Scholes, R. E. Metafiction. *In* Scholes, R. E. Fabulation and metafiction p103-38

Trachtenberg, S. Berger and Barth: the comedy of decomposition. *In* Cohen, S. B. ed. Comic relief p45-69

Barth, Karl

Jesus Christ and the movement for social justice. *In* Hunsinger, G. ed. Karl Barth and radical politics p19-45

About

Hunsinger, G. Conclusion: Toward a radical Barth. *In* Hunsinger, G. ed. Karl Barth and radical politics p181-233

Obitts, S. R. Historical explanation and Barth on Christ's Resurrection. *In* Current issues in Biblical and patristic interpretation p365-77

Ethics

Bettis, J. Political theology and social ethics: the Socialist humanism of Karl Barth. *In* Hunsinger, G. ed. Karl Barth and radical politics p159-79

Theology

Bettis, J. Political theology and social ethics: the Socialist humanism of Karl Barth. *In* Hunsinger, G. ed. Karl Barth and radical politics p159-79

Diem, H. Karl Barth as Socialist: controversy over a new attempt to understand him. *In* Hunsinger, G. ed. Karl Barth and radical politics p121-38

Gollwitzer, H. Kingdom of God and socialism in the theology of Karl Barth. *In* Hunsinger, G. ed. Karl Barth and radical politics p77-120

Marquardt, F. W. Socialism in the theology of Karl Barth. *In* Hunsinger, G. ed. Karl Barth and radical politics p47-76

Schellong, D. On reading Karl Barth from the left. *In* Hunsinger, G. ed. Karl Barth and radical politics p139-57

Barthel, Thomas S.

Writing systems. *In* Sebeok, T. A. ed. Native languages of the Americas v2 p27-53

Barthelme, Donald

About

Scholes, R. E. Metafiction. *In* Scholes, R. E. Fabulation and metafiction p103-38

Vidal, G. American plastic: the matter of fiction. *In* Vidal, G. Matters of fact and of fiction p99-126

Barthes, Roland

Image, music, text

Contents

Change the object itself

The death of the author

Diderot, Brecht, Eisenstein

From work to text

The grain of the voice

Introduction to the structural analysis of narratives

Lesson in writing

Musica practica

The photographic message

Rhetoric of the image

The struggle with the Angel

The third meaning

Writers, intellectuals, teachers

Toward a psychosociology of contemporary food consumption. *In* Food and drink in history p166-73

About

Davidson, H. M. Sign, sense, and Roland Barthes. *In* Wimsatt, W. K. ed. Literary criticism: idea and act p228-41

Lodge, D. The novel and the nouvelle critique. *In* Lodge, D. The modes of modern writing p57-71

Vidal, G. American plastic: the matter of fiction. *In* Vidal, G. Matters of fact and of fiction p99-126

Watkins, E. Criticism and method: Hirsch, Frye, Barthes, Derrida. *In* Watkins, E. The critical act p56-94

About individual works

The metaphor of the eye

Fitch, B. T. A critique of Roland Barthes' essay on Bataille's Histoire de l'oeil. *In* Valdés, M. J. and Miller, O. J. eds. Interpretation of narrative p48-57

Bartky, Sandra Lee

Toward a phenomenology of feminist consciousness. *In* Feminism and philosophy p22-34

Bartlett, R. P.

Scottish cannon-founders and the Russian Navy, 1768-85. *In* Oxford Slavonic papers, new ser. v10 p51-72

Bartlett, Ruhl Jacob

Neutrality. *In* Encyclopedia of American foreign policy p679-87

Bartley, Numan V.

The South and sectionalism in American politics. *In* Havard, W. C. and Bernd, J. L. eds. 200 years of the Republic in retrospect p239-57

Bartley, Robert L.

A role for social science? *In* Hook, S.; Kurtz, P. W. and Todorovich, M. eds. The philosophy of the curriculum: the need for general education p169-73

Barton, Anne

He that plays the king: Ford's Perkin Warbeck and the Stuart history play. *In* English drama: forms and development p69-93

'A light to lesson ages': Byron's political plays. *In* Jump, J. D. ed. Byron p138-62

Barton, John H.

Behind the legal explosion. *In* Stanford legal essays p43-60

An educational strategy for arms control. *In* International terrorism and world security p308-13

Barton, Josef J.

Eastern and southern Europeans. *In* Ethnic leadership in America p150-75

Bartram, John

About

Wilson, D. S. John Bartram, a Pennsylvania farmer. *In* Wilson, D. S. In the presence of nature p89-122

Bassiouni, M. Cherif—*Continued*

The political offense exception in extradition law and practice. *In* International terrorism and political crimes p398-447

Unlawful seizures of persons by states as alternatives to extradition. *In* International terrorism and political crimes p343-68

Basso, Keith Hamilton

'Wise words' of the Western Apache: metaphor and semantic theory. *In* Basso, K. H. and Selby, H. A. eds. Meaning in anthropology p93-121

Bastianini, Attilio, and Urbani, Giuliano

Land-use planning in Italy. *In* Planning, politics and public policy p358-77

Bastid, Suzanne (Basdivant)

The special significance of the Helsinki Final Act. *In* Human rights, international law and the Helsinki Accord p11-19

Bastide, Roger

The present status of Afro-American research in Latin America. *In* Mintz, S. W. ed. Slavery, colonialism, and racism p111-23

Bastille, Paris in literature

Brombert, V. H. The myth of the Bastille. *In* Brombert, V. H. The romantic prison p30-45

Basu, Asoke. See Lipset, S. M. jt. auth.

Basuto (African people) See Sotho (Bantu people)

Bat. See Bats

Bataille, Georges

About

Derrida, J. From restricted to general economy: a Hegelianism without reserve. *In* Derrida, J. Writing and difference p251-77

Foucault, M. A preface to transgression. *In* Foucault M. Language, counter-memory, practice p29-52

About individual works
The story of the eye

Fitch, B. T. A critique of Roland Barthes' essay on Bataille's Histoire de l'oeil. *In* Valdés, M. J. and Miller, O. J. eds. Interpretation of narrative p48-57

Bate, Walter Jackson

The second temple; excerpt from "The burden of the past and the English poet." *In* Primeau, R. ed. Influx p100-17

About individual works
Samuel Johnson

Middendorf, J. H. Johnson on the couch. *In* Review, v 1 1979 p 1-12

Bateman, John Jay

Aldus Manutius' Fragmenta grammatica. *In* Illinois classical studies, v 1 1976 p226-61

Bates, Herbert Ernest

The modern short story: retrospect. *In* May, C. E. ed. Short story theories p72-79

About

Cavaliero, G. The enduring land: H. E. Bates. *In* Cavaliero, G. The rural tradition in the English novel, 1900-1939 p196-200

Bates, Ralph

About individual works
The fields of paradise

Walker, R. G. Appendix: The fields of paradise. *In* Walker, R. G. Infernal paradise p322-29

Bates, Ülkü Ülküsal

Women as patrons of architecture in Turkey. *In* Beck, L. and Keddie, N. R. eds. Women in the Muslim world p245-60

Bateson, Frederick Wilse

The application of thought to an eighteenth-century text: The school for scandal. *In* Evidence in literary scholarship p321-35

Contributions to a dictionary of critical terms. *In* Roberts, J. R. ed. Essential articles for the study of John Donne's poetry p58-65

Criticism's lost leader. *In* The Literary criticism of T. S. Eliot p 1-19

How old was Leontes? *In* English Association. Essays and studies, 1978 p65-74

Bateson, Gregory

Afterword. *In* About Bateson p233-47

Some components of socialization for trance. *In* Schwartz, T. ed. Socialization as cultural communication p51-63

About

Bateson, M. C. Daddy, can a scientist be wise? *In* About Bateson p57-73

Birdwhistell, R. L. Some discussion of ethnography, theory, and method. *In* About Bateson p103-41

Lipset, D. Gregory Bateson: early biography. *In* About Bateson p21-54

Influence

Mead, M. End linkage: a tool for cross-cultural analysis. *In* About Bateson p171-231

Knowledge, Theory of

Bateson, G. Afterword. *In* About Bateson p233-47

May, R. Gregory Bateson and humanistic psychology. *In* About Bateson p77-99

Bateson, Mary Catherine

Daddy, can a scientist be wise? *In* About Bateson p57-73

Ritualization: a study in texture and texture change. *In* Zaretsky, I. I. and Leone, M. P. eds. Religious movements in contemporary America p150-65

Bateson, William

About

Lipset, D. Gregory Bateson: early biography. *In* About Bateson p21-54

Bateson family

Lipset, D. Gregory Bateson: early biography. *In* About Bateson p21-54

Bath, Michael Edwin

The legend of Caesar's deer. *In* Medievalia et humanistica; new ser. no. 9 p53-66

Bath and Wells (Diocese)

History

Sims-Williams, P. Continental influence at Bath monastery in the seventh century. *In* Anglo-Saxon England 4 p 1-28

Bathory, Peter Dennis, and McWilliams, Wilson Carey

Political theory and the people's right to know. *In* Galnoor, I. ed. Government secrecy in democracies p3-21

Bathrick, David

Brecht's Marxism and America. *In* Mews, S. and Knust, H. eds. Essays on Brecht p209-25

Bathrick, Serafina Kent

Independent woman, doomed sister. *In* Peary, G. and Shatzkin, R. eds. The modern American novel and the movies p143-55

Batllori, Miguel
The papal division of the world and its consequences. *In* First images of America p211-20

Bats
Nagel, T. What is it like to be a bat? *In* Nagel, T. Mortal questions p165-80

Batson, C. Daniel
Moon madness: greed or creed? *In* Horowitz, I. L. ed. Science, sin, and scholarship p218-25

Battenhouse, Roy Wesley
The relation of Henry V to Tamburlaine. *In* Shakespeare survey 27 p71-79

Batteries. See Artillery

Battestin, Martin C.
The problem of Amelia: Hume, Barrow, and the conversion of Captain Booth. *In* ELH essays for Earl R. Wasserman p320-55

Battistello. See Caracciolo, Giovanni Battista, known as Battistello

Battle of Harlaw (Ballad) See Harlaw (Scottish ballad)

Battle of Maldon (poem) See Maldon (Anglo-Saxon poem)

Baudelaire, Charles Pierre
About
Abrams, M. H. Coleridge, Baudelaire, and modernist poetics. *In* Amacher, R. E. and Lange, V. eds. New perspectives in German literary criticism p150-81

Brombert, V. H. Baudelaire: confinement and infinity. *In* Brombert, V. H. The romantic prison p133-48

Connolly, C. Shades of spleen. *In* Connolly, C. The evening colonnade p143-47

Eliot, T. S. From Baudelaire. *In* Eliot, T. S. Selected prose of T. S. Eliot p231-36

Kelley, D. 'Modernité' in Baudelaire's art criticism. *In* the Artist and the writer in France p138-52

Morse, J. M. Baudelaire, Stephen Dedalus, and Shem the Penman. *In* Garvin, H. R. ed. Makers of the twentieth-century novel p19-27

Nalbantian, S. Baudelaire and his contemporaries: the mortal soul. *In* Nalbantian, S. The symbol of the soul from Hölderlin to Yeats p49-65

Rawson, C. J. The nightmares of Strephon: nymphs of the city in the poems of Swift, Baudelaire, Eliot. *In* English literature in the age of disguise p57-97

Reed, A. Abysmal influence: Baudelaire, Coleridge, De Quincey, Piranesi, Wordsworth. *In* Glyph 4 p189-206

Robinson, C. Subjective reality. *In* Robinson, C. French literature in the nineteenth century p108-70

Sabin, M. Beauty and taste. *In* Sabin, M. English romanticism and the French tradition p181-201

Sabin, M. The language of nature. *In* Sabin, M. English romanticism and the French tradition p21-34

Sabin, M. The lovely behavior of things: Hopkins and Baudelaire. *In* Sabin, M. English romanticism and the French tradition p168-78

Sabin, M. Symbolic light. *In* Sabin, M. English romanticism and the French tradition p202-20

About individual works
De la coleur
Shattuck, R. Vibratory organism: crise de prose. *In* Symbolism and modern literature p193-204

Flowers of evil
Crane, J. St. Clair. Edna St. Vincent Millay's afterthoughts on the translation of Bauderlaire. *In* Virginia. University. Bibliographical Society. Studies in bibliography v29 p382-86

Influence—Eliot
Ward, N. 'Fourmillante cité': Baudelaire and 'The waste land.' *In* The Waste land in different voices p87-104

Baudouin de Courtenay, Jan Ignacy Nieciskaw
About
Rothstein, R. A. The linguist as dissenter: Jan Baudouin de Courtenay. *In* For Wiktor Weintraub p391-405

Baugh, Edward
The poem as autobiographical novel: Derek Walcott's 'Another life' in relation to Wordsworth's 'Prelude' and Joyce's 'Portrait.' *In* Narasimhaiah, C. D. ed. Awakened conscience p226-35

Baughman, Martin L. and Hnyilicza, Esteban
System interdependencies and government policy. *In* Kalter, R. J. and Vogely, W. A. eds. Energy supply and government policy p255-79

Baulant, Micheline
The scattered family:: another aspect of seventeenth-century demography. *In* Family and society p104-16

Baum, Richard
Politics and the citizen. *In* Terrill, R. ed. The China difference p161-81

Bauman, Richard. See Abrahams, R. D. jt. auth.

Bauman, Zygmunt
East European and Soviet social science: a case study in stimulus diffusion. *In* Szporluk, R. ed. The influence of East Europe and the Soviet West on the USSR p91-116
Hermeneutics and social science
Contents
Consensus and truth
Introduction: The challenge of hermeneutics
The rise of hermeneutics
Understanding as expansion of the form of life
Understanding as the work of history: Karl Mannheim
Understanding as the work of history: Karl Marx
Understanding as the work of history: Max Weber
Understanding as the work of life: From Schutz to ethnomethodology
Understanding as the work of life: Martin Heidegger
Understanding as the work of reason: Edmund Husserl
Understanding as the work of reason: Talcott Parsons

Baumann, Fred
Is the university a special case? *In* Hook, S.; Kurtz, P. W. and Todorovich, M. eds. The university and the state: what role for government in higher education? p237-44

Baumann, Fred—*Continued*

Objectivity and indoctrination. *In* Hook, S.; Kurtz, P. and Todorovich, M. eds. The ethics of teaching and scientific research p53-59

Baumbach, Jonathan

Who do they think they are? A personal history of the Fiction Collective. *In* Anderson, E. and Kinzie, M. eds. The little magazine in America: a modern documentary history p625-34

Baumgartner, Tom; Burns, Tom R. and DeVillé, Philippe Raymond

Actors, games, and systems: the dialectics of social action and system structuring. *In* McNall, S. G. ed. Theoretical perspectives in sociology p128-48

Bäuml, Franz H. and Spielmann, Edda

From illiteracy to literacy: prolegomena to a study of the Nibelungenlied. *In* Duggan, J. J. ed. Oral literature p62-73

Baumol, William J.

Acceleration incentives and x-efficiency. *In* Econometrics and economic theory p167-75

Smith versus Marx on business morality and the social interest. *In* Glahe, F. R. ed. Adam Smith and The wealth of nations p111-22

Baumrin, Bernard H.

Sexual immorality delineated. *In* Baker, R. and Elliston, F. A. eds. Philosophy & sex p116-28

Bawcutt, N. W.

The revival of Elizabethan drama and the crisis of romantic drama. *In* Davies, R. T. and Beatty, B. G. eds. Literature of the romantic period, 1750-1850 p96-113

Shakespeare's life, times, and stage. *In* Shakespeare survey 28 p164-73

Shakespeare's life, times, and stage [another essay]. *In* Shakespeare survey v29 p168-77

Shakespeare's life, times, and stage [another essay]. *In* Shakespeare survey 30 p191-203

Bawcutt, Priscilla

Aspects of Dunbar's imagery. *In* Chaucer and Middle English studies in honour of Rossell Hope Robbins p190-200

Douglas and Surrey: translators of Virgil. *In* English Association. Essays and studies, 1974 p52-67

About individual works
Gavin Douglas: a critical study

Ridley, F. H. Gawain Douglas re-catalogued. *In* Review, v 1 1979 p255-63

Bawden, Nina

The imprisoned child. *In* Blishen, E. ed. The thorny paradise p62-64

Baxter, James K.

About

Alcock, P. James K. Baxter and the terror of history: the de-colonisation of a New Zealander. *In* Narasimhaiah, C. D. ed. Awakened conscience p92-110

About individual works
Pig Island letters

Alcock, P. James K. Baxter and the terror of history: the de-colonisation of a New Zealander. *In* Narasimhaiah, C. D. ed. Awakened conscience p92-110

Baxter, John: Member of the "Society of Friends of Liberty"

About individual works
A new and impartial history of England

Walton, C. Hume and Jefferson on the uses of history. *In* Philosophy and the civilizing arts p103-25

Baxter, R. R.

The Geneva Conventions of 1949 and wars of national liberation. *In* International terrorism and political crimes p120-32

Bay, Christian

Access to political knowledge as a human right. *In* Galnoor, I. ed. Government secrecy in democracies p22-39

Education for citizenship. *In* Fairfield, R. P. ed. Humanistic frontiers in American education p148-55

Essay 7. *In* Fitzgerald, R. ed. What it means to be human p128-41

From contract to community: thoughts on liberalism and postindustrial society. *In* Dallmayr, F. R. ed. From contract to community p29-45

Human needs and political education. *In* Fitzgerald, R. ed. Human needs and politics p 1-25

Bay, Edna G.

The heart-shaped face in African art. *In* African images p252-67

Bayat-Philipp, Mangol

Women and revolution in Iran, 1905-1911. *In* Beck, L. and Keddie, N. R. eds. Women in the Muslim world p295-308

Baylen, Joseph O.

Edmund Gosse, William Archer, and Ibsen in late Victorian Britain. *In* Tennessee Studies in literature v XX p124-37

Bayles, Michael D.

Marriage, love, and procreation. *In* Baker, R. and Elliston, F. A. eds. Philosophy & sex p190-206

Bayley, David H.

The police and political development in Europe. *In* Tilly, C. ed. The formation of national states in Western Europe p328-79

Bayley, John

Hardy's poetical metonymy. *In* English Association. Essays and studies, 1978 p115-30

John Berryman: a question of imperial sway. *In* Boyers, R. ed. Contemporary poetry in America p59-77

The uses of division

Contents

Another view of the question

'Antony and Cleopatra' and 'Coriolanus'

'Art speech'

The authentic and the sincere

Cressida as a character

Dickens and his critics

The divisions of rhetoric

Dogma and fantasy

The importance of elsewhere

Keats and sex

Living in the present

The meaning of impression

Measure for measure

Novelist and critic

The puzzles of Kipling

Reality in division

The self as available reality

Send for Macbeth

The 'serious character'

Bayley, John
The uses of division
Contents—Continued
Shestov's law
The Troilus atmosphere
The vulgar and the heroic in 'bad poetry'
'We must live as we can'

Baylis, Charles Augustus

About

Lachs, J. The omnicolored sky: Baylis on perception. *In* Fact, value, and perception p139-50

Baym, Nina Zippin
Hawthorne. *In* American literary scholarship, 1973 p15-31
Hawthorne [another essay]. *In* American literary scholarship 1974 p15-27
Portrayal of women in American literature, 1790-1870. *In* Springer, M. A. ed. What manner of woman p211-34
Woman's fiction

Contents

Ann Stephens, Mary Jane Holmes, and Marion Harland
Augusta Evans and the waning of woman's fiction
Caroline Chesebro'
Catharine Sedgwick and other early novelists
E. D. E. N. Southworth and Caroline Lee Hentz
The form and ideology of woman's fiction
Introduction and conclusions
Maria McIntosh
Other novelists of the fifties
Susan Warner, Anna Warner, and Maria Cummins

Bayonets
Buechler, J. "Give 'em the bayonet"—a note on Civil War mythology. *In* Hubbell, J. T. ed. Battles lost and won p135-39

Bayreuth festival
Craft, R. Taking the Wagner cure. *In* Craft, R. Current convictions p71-81

Bazelon, David Lionel
The role of psychiatry in society: a jurist's viewpoint. *In* American psychiatry: past, present, and future p157-69

Bazerman, Charles
The grant, the scholar and the university community. *In* Hook, S.; Kurtz, P. W. and Todorovich, M. eds. The university and the state: what role for government in higher education? p221-25

Bazin, André
The evolution of the Western. *In* Nichols, B. ed. Movies and methods p 150-57

About

Henderson, B. Two types of film theory. *In* Nichols, B. ed. Movies and methods p388-400
Perkins, V. F. A critical history of early film theory; excerpt from "Film as film." *In* Nichols, B. ed. Movies and methods p401-22

Bazire, Joyce, and Mills, David
Middle English: Chaucer. *In* English Association. The year's work in English studies v53 p106-20
Middle English: Chaucer [another essay]. *In* English Association. The year's work in English studies v54 p109-23
Middle English: Chaucer [another essay]. *In* English Association. The year's work in English studies v55 p148-66

Middle English: Chaucer [another essay]. *In* English Association. The year's work in English studies v56 p118-29
Middle English: Chaucer [another essay]. *In* English Association. The year's work in English studies v57 p89-100

Be bop music. See Jazz music

Beach, Frank Ambrose
Animal models and psychological inference. *In* Katchadourian, H. A. ed. Human sexuality p98-112
Sociobiology and interspecific comparisons of behavior. *In* Sociobiology and human nature p116-35

Beach, Ruth Isabel
A case history of affirmative action. *In* Women in academia p128-38

Beach, Sylvia
Shakespeare and company. *In* Bookselling in America and the world p149-55

About

Ford, H. D. From Princeton to Paris: Sylvia Beach. *In* Ford, H. D. Published in Paris p3-33
Tate, A. Memories of Sylvia Beach. *In* Tate, A. Memoirs and opinions, 1926-1974 p67-68

Beacham, Walton
Technique and the sense of play in the poetry of Robert Frost. *In* Frost: centennial essays II p246-61

Beaconsfield, Benjamin Disraeli, 1st Earl of

About individual works

Sybil

Himmelfarb, G. Social history and the moral imagination. *In* Art, politics, and will p28-58
Tomlinson, T. B. Love and politics in the English novel, 1840s-1860s. *In* Tomlinson, T. B. The English middle-class novel p69-82

Beale, Calvin Lunsford
The Black American in agriculture. *In* The Black American reference book p284-315

Bean, Lowell John
California Indian shamanism and folk curing. *In* American folk medicine p109-23

Bear, Thomas Drew-. See Drew-Bear, Thomas

Beardsley, Aubrey Vincent

About

Lind, I. D. The effect of painting on Faulkner's poetic form. *In* Faulkner, modernism, and film: Faulkner and Yoknapatawpha, 1978 p127-48

Beardsley, Elizabeth Lane
Referential genderization. *In* Gould, C. C. and Wartofsky, M. W. eds. Women and philosophy p285-93
Traits and genderization. *In* Feminism and philosophy p117-23

Beardsley, James
Constitutional review in France. *In* The Supreme Court review, 1975 p189-259

Beardsley, Monroe Curtis
Aesthetic intentions and fictive illocutions. *In* Hernadi, P. ed. What is literature? p161-77

The aesthetic point of view. *In* Margolis, J. Z. ed. Philosophy looks at the arts p6-24

Beardsley, Monroe C.—*Continued*

Is art essentially institutional? *In* Aaga-ard-Mogensen, L. ed. Culture and art p194-209

The testability of an interpretation; excerpt from "The possibility of criticism." *In* Margolis, J. Z. ed. Philosophy looks at the arts p370-86

See also Wimsatt, W. K. jt. auth.

Beardsley, Theodore S.
The Hispanic impact upon the United States. *In* The Immigrant experience in America p9-43

Spanish literature. *In* Jones, W. M. ed. The present state of scholarship in sixteenth-century literature p71-110

Béarn

Social conditions
Bourdieu, P. Marriage strategies as strategies of social reproduction. *In* Family and society p117-44

Bears (in religion, folk-lore, etc.)
Brooks, M. Z. The bear in Slavic and Polish mythology and folklore. *In* For Wiktor Weintraub p107-11

Beasley-Murray, George Raymond
How Christian is the Book of Revelation? *In* Reconciliation and hope p275-84

Beat generation. See Bohemianism

The Beatles
Brauer, R. Iconic modes: The Beatles. *In* Browne, R. B. and Fishwick, M. W. eds. Icons of America p112-23

Beatniks. See Bohemianism

Beaton, James F.
Dickey down the river. *In* Peary, G. and Shatzkin, R. eds. The modern American novel and the movies p293-306

Beats. See Bohemianism

Beattie, Hilary J.
The alternative to resistance: the case of T'ung-ch'eng, Anhwei. *In* Spence, J. D. and Wills, J. E. eds. From Ming to Ch'ing p239-76

Beattie, John Hugh Marshall
Tonya: a lakeside settlement in Bunyoro. *In* Studies in social anthropology p30-40

Beattie, Munro
Henry James: 'the voice of stoicism.' *In* The Stoic strain in American literature p63-75

Beatty, Bernard G.
Lord Byron: poetry and precedent. *In* Davies, R. T. and Beatty, B. G. eds. Literature of the romantic period, 1750-1850 p114-34

Beaty, Jerome
On first looking into George Eliot's Middlemarch. *In* Levine, R. A. The Victorian experience: the novelists p151-75

Beauchamp, Tom L.
The justification of reverse discrimination. *In* Social justice & preferential treatment p84-110

Beaujeau, Renauld de. See Renaud, de Beaujeau

Beaulieu, France. Benedictine Abbey
Beitscher, J. K. Monastic reform at Beaulieu, 1031-1095. *In* Viator: medieval and Renaissance studies v5 p199-210

Beaumarchais, Pierre Augustin Caron de

About
Brereton, G. Beaumarchais. *In* Brereton, G. French comic drama p237-55

About individual works
The marriage of Figaro
Schmidgall, G. Wolfgang Amadeus Mozart. *In* Schmidgall, G. Literature as opera p67-107

Bibliography
Besterman, T. Bibliographical notes on the Beaumarchais-Goezman lawsuit. *In* Literature and history in the age of ideas p311-19

Beaumont, Roger A.
Polemology: promises and a problem. *In* Beaumont, R. A. and Edmonds, M. eds. War in the next decade p203-10

Beaune, Jean-Claude
Technology from an encyclopedic point of view. *In* Bugliarello, G. and Doner, D. B. eds. The history and philosophy of technology p202-26

Beautiful, The. See Aesthetics

Beauty. See Aesthetics; Art

Beauvoir, Simone de

About individual works
The coming of age
Connolly, C. Tears before bedtime. *In* Connolly, C. The evening colonnade p433-36

Beaver, Donald DeB.
Possible relationships between the history and sociology of science. *In* Gaston, J. ed. Sociology of science p140-61

Beaver Indians (Athapascan tribe). See Tsattine Indians

Bebbington, D. W.
Gladstone and the Nonconformists: a religious affinity in politics. *In* Church, society and politics p369-82

Bebop music. See Jazz music

Bechert, Heinz, and Vu Duy-Tu
Buddhism in Vietnam. *In* Dumoulin, H. ed. Buddhism in the modern world p186-93

Beck, Ervin
Terence improved: the paradigm of the Prodigal son in English Renaissance comedy. *In* Renaissance drama [1973] p107-22

Beck, Jacob
Dimensions of an achromatic surface color. *In* Perception p166-84

Beck, Lois
Women among Qashqa'i nomadic pastoralists in Iran. *In* Beck, L. and Keddie, N. R. eds. Women in the Muslim world p351-73

Becker, Carl Lotus

About individual works
Everyman his own historian
Hexter, J. H. Carl Becker and historical relativism. *In* Hexter, J. H. On historians p 13-41

The heavenly city of the eighteenth century philosophers
Guerlac, H. Newton's changing reputation in the eighteenth century. *In* Guerlac, H. Essays and papers in the history of modern science p69-81

Becker, Gary Stanley, and Stigler, George Joseph

Law enforcement, malfeasance, and compensation of enforcers. *In* Capitalism and freedom p230-52

Becker, Harold K.

Historical-philosophical development of administration; excerpt from "Issues in police administration." *In* Armstrong, T. R. and Cinnamon, K. M. eds. Power and authority in law enforcement p77-103

Becker, Howard S. and Horowitz, Irving Louis

The culture of civility. *In* Henslin, J. M. ed. Deviant life-styles p337-48

Becker, Jacques

About individual works

The adventures of Arsène Lupin

Truffaut, F. Jacques Becker: Arsène Lupin. *In* Truffaut, F. The films in my life p180-83

The hole

Truffaut, F. Jacques Becker. Le trou. *In* Truffaut, F. The films in my life p183-86

Becker, Jens Peter

The mean streets of Europe: the influence of the American 'hard-boiled school' on European detective fiction. *In* Bigsby, C. W. E. Superculture p152-59

Beckerman, Bernard

Shakespeare and the life of the scene. *In* English Renaissance drama p36-45

Becket, Thomas à. See Thomas à Becket, Saint, Abp. of Canterbury

Beckett, Samuel

About

Adams, R. M. Samuel Beckett. *In* Adams, R. M. Afterjoyce p90-113

Bronsen, D. Consuming struggle vs. killing time: preludes to dying in the dramas of Ibsen and Beckett. *In* Spicker, S. F.; Woodward, K. M. and Van Tassel, D. D. eds. Aging and the elderly p261-81

Hassan, I. H. Joyce—Beckett: a scenario in 8 scenes and a voice. *In* Hassan, I. H. Paracriticisms p63-73

Kennedy, A. K. Beckett. *In* Kennedy, A. K. Six dramatists in search of a language p130-64

Kennedy, S. The Irishness of Beckett: Spirals of need: Irish prototypes in Samuel Beckett's fiction. *In* Yeats, Joyce, and Beckett p153-66

Langbaum, R. W. Beckett: zero identity. *In* Langbaum, R. W. The mysteries of identity p120-44

Lee, R. The fictional topography of Samuel Beckett. *In* Josipovici, G. ed. The modern English novel: the reader, the writer and the work p206-24

Lodge, D. Postmodernist fiction. *In* Lodge, D. The modes of modern writing p220-45

McMillan, D. Samuel Beckett. *In* McMillan, D. Transition p148-56

Mercier, V. The Irishness of Beckett: Ireland/the world: Beckett's Irishness. *In* Yeats, Joyce, and Beckett p147-52

Rabinovitz, R. The craftsmanship of Beckett: the deterioration of outside reality in Samuel Beckett's fiction. *In* Yeats, Joyce, and Beckett p167-71

Schwarz, A. Condemned to exist. *In* Schwarz, A. From Büchner to Beckett p334-56

Webb, E. The ambiguities of secularization: modern transformations of the Kingdom in Nietzsche, Ibsen, Beckett, and Stevens. *In* Webb, E. The dark dove p34-87

Wicker, B. Beckett and the death of the God-narrator. *In* Wicker, B. The story-shaped world p169-83

Worth, K. J. Beckett. *In* Worth, K. J. The Irish drama of Europe from Yeats to Beckett p241-65

About individual works

Act without words

Segre, C. The function of language in Samuel Beckett's Acte sans paroles. *In* Segre, C. Structures and time p225-44

Endgame

Cavell, S. Ending the waiting game: a reading of Beckett's Endgame. *In* Cavell, S. Must we mean what we say? p115-62

Mendelson, E. The Caucasian chalk circle and Endgame. *In* Seidel, M. A. and Mendelson, E. eds. Homer to Brecht p336-52

Schlueter, J. Beckett's Didi and Gogo, Hamm and Clov. *In* Schlueter, J. Metafictional characters in modern drama p53-69

How it is

Unterecker, J. E. Fiction at the edge of poetry: Durrell, Beckett, Green. *In* Forms of modern British fiction p165-99

Jack MacGowran in the works of Samuel Beckett

Kauffmann, S. MacGowran in Beckett. *In* Kauffmann, S. Persons of the drama p211-13

Molloy, Malone dies, The unnamable: a trilogy

Frye, N. The nightmare life in death. *In* Frye, N. Northrop Frye on culture and literature p219-29

Oates, J. C. Anarchy and order in Beckett's Trilogy. *In* Oates, J. C. New heaven, new earth: the visionary experience in literature p83-95

Waiting for Godot

Mayer, H. Brecht's Drums, a dog, and Beckett's Godot. *In* Mews, S. and Knust, H. eds. Essays on Brecht p71-78

Northam, J. R. Waiting for Prospero. *In* English drama: forms and development p186-202

Schlueter, J. Beckett's Didi and Gogo, Hamm and Clov. *In* Schlueter, J. Metafictional characters in modern drama p53-69

Sherzer, D. De-construction in Waiting for Godot. *In* Babcock, B. A. ed. The reversible world p129-46

Watt

Glicksberg, C. I. Samuel Beckett: the cosmic nihilist. *In* Glicksberg, C. I. The literature of nihilism p234-45

Characters

Schlueter, J. Beckett's Didi and Gogo, Hamm and Clov. *In* Schlueter, J. Metafictional characters in modern drama p53-69

Beckford, James A.

Two contrasting types of sectarian organization. *In* Wallis, R. ed. Sectarianism p70-85

Beckford, William, 1760-1844

About

Fothergill, B. William Beckford, prince of amateurs. *In* Royal Society of Literature of the United Kingdom, London. Essays by divers hands v38 p33-47

About individual works
Vathek

Graham, K. W. Implications of the grotesque: Beckford's Vathek and the boundaries of fictional reality. *In* Tennessee Studies in literature v23 p61-74

Graham, K. W. Vathek in English and French. *In* Virginia. University. Bibliographical Society. Studies in bibliography v28 p153-66

Beckman, William

About

Van Baron, J. The grand style. *In* Battcock, G. ed. Super realism p230-36

Beckner, Morton

Reduction, hierarchies and organicism. *In* Ayala, F. J. and Dobzhansky, T. G. eds. Studies in the philosophy of biology p163-76

Beckstrom, John H.

Handicaps of legal-social engineering in a developing nation. *In* African themes p195-212

Beckwith, John

Some early Byzantine rock crystals. *In* Studies in memory of David Talbot Rice p 1-5

Beckwith, Lillian

About

Hart, F.R. Highlands of the humorists. *In* Hart, F. R. The Scottish novel p374-84

Bed and board (Motion picture)

Kauffmann, S. Bed and board. *In* Kauffmann, S. Living images p38-41

Beda Venerabilis

About individual works
Ecclesiastical history of the English people

Hill, R. M. T. Holy kings—the bane of seventh-century society. *In* Church, society and politics p39-43

Kendall, C. A. Rhetoric in early medieval Latin: Bede's Historia ecclesiasticia: the rhetoric of faith. *In* Murphy, J. J. ed. Medieval eloquence p145-72

Beda Venerabilis, supposed author. See Liber epigrammatum heroico metro

Bedau, Hugo Adam

Compensatory justice and the Black Manifesto. *In* The Abdication of philosophy: philosophy and the public good p175-94

Free speech, the right to listen, and disruptive interference. *In* The Concept of academic freedom p191-211

Reply to Alan Pasch. *In* The Concept of academic freedom p217-25

Social science research in the aftermath of Furman v. Georgia: creating new knowledge about capital punishment in the United States. *In* Riedel, M. and Chappell, D. eds. Issues in criminal justice: planning and evaluation p75-86

About individual works
Free speech, the right to listen, and disruptive interference

Pasch, A. Comments on Bedau's "Free speech, the right to listen, and disruptive interference." *In* The Concept of academic freedom p212-16

Beddoes, Thomas Lovell

About individual works
Death's jest book; or, The fool's tragedy

Coxe, L. O. Thomas Lovell Beddoes: the mask of parody. *In* Coxe, L. O. Enabling acts p27-43

Bede, Cuthbert, pseud. See Bradley, Edward

Bede, The Venerable. See Beda Venerabilis

Bedford, Denton R.

About individual works
Tsali

Larson, C. R. History of the people. *In* Larson, C. R. American Indian fiction p97-132

Bedford, Sybille

About individual works
Aldous Huxley

Craft, R. In search of Aldous Huxley. *In* Craft, R. Current convictions p234-44

Sale, R. H. Huxley & Bennett, Bedford & Drabble. *In* Sale, R. H. On not being good enough p93-105

Bedient, Calvin

Sylvia Plath, romantic. . . . *In* Lane, G. ed. Sylvia Plath p3-18

Bedouins in Lebanon

Chatty, D. Changing sex roles in Bedouin society in Syria and Lebanon. *In* Beck, L. and Keddie, N. R. eds. Women in the Muslim world p399-415

Bedouins in Syria

Chatty, D. Changing sex roles in Bedouin society in Syria and Lebanon. *In* Beck, L. and Keddie, N. R. eds. Women in the Muslim world p399-415

Beebe, Maurice

The masks of Conrad. *In* Garvin, H. R. ed. Makers of the twentieth-century novel p70-83

Beech, George Thomas

Prosopography. *In* Powell, J. M. ed. Medieval studies p151-84

Beecher, Henry Ward

About individual works
Norwood: or, Village life in New England

Smith, H. N. A textbook of the genteel tradition: Henry Ward Beecher's Norwood. *In* Smith, H. N. Democracy and the novel p56-74

Beecher family

Michaelsen, R. The Beecher family: microcosm of a chapter in the evolution of religious sensibility in America. *In* Reynolds, F. E. and Capps, D. eds. The biographical process p253-71

Beek, Gus Willard van

The land of Sheba. *In* Pritchard, J. B. ed. Solomon & Sheba p40-63

Beer, Gillian

'Coming wonders': uses of theatre in the Victorian novel. *In* English drama: forms and development p164-85

Beer, John B.

Influence and independence in Blake. *In* Interpreting Blake p196-261

Beer, Lawrence Ward

Freedom of expression in Japan with comparative reference to the United States. *In* Claude, R. P. ed. Comparative human rights p99-126

Beer, William R.

The social class of ethnic activists in contemporary France. *In* Esman, M. J. ed. Ethnic conflict in the Western world p143-58

Beer-Hofmann, Richard

About

Elstun, E. B. Richard Beer-Hofmann: the poet as exculpator dei. *In* Strelka, J. P.; Bell, R. F. and Dobson, E. eds. Protest—form—tradition p123-32

About individual works

Jacob's dream

Wilder, T. N. Richard Beer-Hofmann's Jaakobs traum. *In* Wilder, T. N. American characteristics, and other essays p127-34

Beerbohm, Sir Max

About

Acton, Sir H. M. M. Max Beerbohm: a dandy among English classics. *In* Royal Society of Literature of the United Kingdom, London. Essays by divers hands v38 p 1-14

Auden, W. H. One of the family; excerpt from "Forewords and afterwords". *In* Riewald, J. G. ed. The surprise of excellence p159-74

Balakian, N. A specialist of the hoax: Max Beerbohm. *In* Balakian, N. Critical encounters p203-06

Behrman, S. N. The silver thread of lunacy; excerpt from "Portrait of Max". *In* Riewald, J. G. ed. The surprise of excellence p123-30

Boas, G. The magic of Max. *In* Riewald, J. G. ed. The surprise of excellence p6-20

Cecil, Lord D. The Max Beerbohm entertainment. *In* Riewald, J. G. ed. The surprise of excellence p229-38

Felstiner, J. Max Beerbohm and the wings of Henry James. *In* Riewald, J. G. ed. The surprise of excellence p192-214

Huss, R. G. The aesthete as realist. *In* Riewald, J. G. ed. The surprise of excellence p113-22

Kronenberger, L. Max Beerbohm; excerpt from "The republic of letters". *In* Riewald, J. G. ed. The surprise of excellence p21-29

McElderry, B. R. Max Beerbohm: essayist, caricaturist, novelist. *In* Riewald, J. G. ed. The surprise of excellence p215-28

Riewald, J. G. Max Beerbohm and Oscar Wilde; excerpt from "Sir Max Beerbohm, man and writer". *In* Riewald, J. G. ed. The surprise of excellence p47-64

Roberts, Sir S. C. Max Beerbohm. *In* Riewald, J. G. ed. The surprise of excellence p96-112

Rothenstein, Sir J. K. M. Introduction to The poets' corner. *In* Riewald, J. G. ed. The surprise of excellence p 1-5

Stanford, D. The writing of Sir Max Beerbohm. *In* Riewald, J. G. ed. The surprise of excellence p77-91

Stevenson, D. H. Irony and deception. *In* Riewald, J. G. ed. The surprise of excellence p65-76

Waugh, E. Max Beerbohm: a lesson in manners. *In* Riewald, J. G. ed. The surprise of excellence p92-95

Wells, S. W. Shakespeare in Max Beerbohm's theatre criticism. *In* Shakespeare survey v29 p133-44

Wilson, E. An analysis of Max Beerbohm; excerpt from "Classics and commercials". *In* Riewald, J. G. ed. The surprise of excellence p38-46

Wilson, E. A miscellany of Max Beerbohm; excerpt from "The bit between my teeth". *In* Riewald, J. G. ed. The surprise of excellence p138-51

About individual works

A Christmas garland

Ledger, M. Ring around A Christmas garland. *In* Aeolian harps p227-46

Max in verse: rhymes and parodies

Updike, J. Rhyming Max; excerpt from "Assorted prose". *In* Riewald, J. G. ed. The surprise of excellence p152-58

Zuleika Dobson

Dupee, F. W. Max Beerbohm and the rigors of fantasy. *In* Riewald, J. G. ed. The surprise of excellence p175-91

Nicolson, Sir H. G. Zuleika Dobson—a revaluation. *In* Riewald, J. G. ed. The surprise of excellence p30-37

Friends and associates

Mix, K. L. Max on Shaw. *In* Riewald, J. G. ed. The surprise of excellence p131-37

Relations with contemporaries

See Beerbohm, Sir Max—Friends and associates

Beers, Burton F.

Protection of American citizens abroad. *In* Encyclopedia of American foreign policy p827-35

Beethoven, Ludwig van

About

Hamburger, M. Music and words: Beethoven. *In* Hamburger, M. Art as second nature p6-11

About individual works

Fidelio

Dent, E. J. Beethoven and Schubert. *In* Dent, E. J. The rise of romantic opera p125-44

Beginning. See Causation

Beh, Siew Hwa

Vivre sa vie. *In* Nichols, B. ed. Movies and methods p180-85

The woman's film. *In* Nichols, B. ed. Movies and methods p201-04

Béhague, Gerard H.

Notes on regional and national trends in Afro-Brazilian cult music. *In* Forster, M. H. ed. Tradition and renewal p68-80

Behan, Brendan

About individual works

Richard's cork leg

Brustein, R. S. Two plays about Ireland: Richard's cork leg and The Ballygombeen bequest. *In* Brustein, R. S. The culture watch p53-56

Behavior. See Conduct of life

Behavior (Psychology) See Animals, Habits and behavior of; Human behavior

Behavior, Child. See Child psychology

Behavior, Operant. See Operant behavior

Behavior, Verbal. See Verbal behavior

Behavior genetics
Fuller, J. L. Genes, brains, and behavior. *In* Sociobiology and human nature p98-115

Behavior in organizations. See Organizational behavior

Behavior modification
Benassi, V. A. and Larson, K. M. Modification of family interaction with the child as the behavior-change agent. *In* Behavior modification and families p331-37

Conway, J. B. and Bucher, B. D. Transfer and maintenance of behavior change in children: a review and suggestions. *In* Behavior modification and families p119-59

Koestler, A. An alternative to despair. *In* Koestler, A. Janus p98-106

Miller, L. K. and others. The positive community: a strategy for applying behavioral engineering to the redesign of family and community. *In* Behavior modification and families p91-112

Peterson, R. F. Power, programming, and punishment: could we be overcontrolling our children? *In* Behavior modification and families p338-52

See also Behavior therapy

Behavior of children. See Children—Management

Behavior problems (Children) See Problem children

Behavior therapy
Birk, L. and Birk, A. B. The learning therapies. *In* Overview of the psychotherapies p51-67

Johnson, S. M.; Bolstad, O. D. and Lobitz, G. K. Generalization and contrast phenomena in behavior modification with children. *In* Behavior modification and families p160-88

Saslow, G. Application of behavior therapy. *In* Overview of the psychotherapies p68-91

Behaviorism (Psychology)
Day, W. F. On the behavioral analysis of self-deception and self-development. *In* Mischel, T. ed. The self p224-49

Fancher, R. E. Psychology as the science of behavior: Ivan Pavlov and John B. Watson. *In* Fancher, R. E. Pioneers of psychology p295-338

Fishbein, M. Attitudes and behavioral prediction: an overview. *In* Major social issues p377-89

Flew, A. G. N. Human psychology and Skinnerian behaviourism. *In* Flew, A. G. N. A rational animal p140-50

Kelman, H. C. Attitude and behavior: a social-psychological problem. *In* Major social issues p412-20

Nott, K. The Trojan horses: Koestler and the behaviourists. *In* Harris, H. A. ed. Astride the two cultures p162-74

Schuman, H. Introduction: ambiguities in the attitude-behavior relation. *In* Major social issues p373-76

Behrens, Peter
About
Shand, P. M. Peter Behrens. *In* Sharp, D. ed. The rationalists p6-15

Behrens, William. See Randers, J. jt. auth.

Behrman, Samuel Nathaniel
The silver thread of lunacy; excerpt from "Portrait of Max". *In* Riewald, J. G. ed. The surprise of excellence p123-30

Being. See Ontology

Beirnaert, Louis
Introduction to the reading of Freud's texts on religion. *In* Wolman, B. B. ed. Psychoanalysis and Catholicism p19-30

Beirut. American University. See American University of Beirut

Beisel, David R.
Toward a psychohistory of Jimmy Carter. *In* DeMause, L. and Ebel, H. eds. Jimmy Carter and American fantasy p59-96

Beispiel (The word)
Warminski, A. Pre-positional by-play. *In* Glyph 3 p98-117

Beitscher, Jane Katherine
Monastic reform at Beaulieu, 1031-1095. *In* Viator: medieval and Renaissance studies v5 p199-210

Bel canto
Schmidgall, G. Gaetano Donizetti. *In* Schmidgall, G. Literature as opera p109-47

Bel Geddes, Joan
The rights of children in world perspective. *In* Gross, B. and Gross, R. eds. The children's rights movement p214-16

Belgion, Montgomery
About
Richards, I. A. Notes on the practice of interpretation. *In* Richards, I. A. Complementarities p189-97

Belgium
Zolberg, A. R. Splitting the difference: federalization without federalization in Belgium. *In* Esman, M. J. ed. Ethnic conflict in the Western world p103-42

Foreign relations
Govaerts, F. Belgium and the Cold war. *In* Siracusa, J. M. and Barclay, C. S. eds. The impact of the Cold war p40-63

Politics and government
Govaerts, F. Belgium and the Cold war. *In* Siracusa, J. M. and Barclay, G. S. eds. The impact of the Cold war p40-63

Petersen, W. On the subnations of Western Europe. *In* Glazer, N. and Moynihan, D. P. eds. Ethnicity p177-208

Population
Lesthaeghe, R. and Van de Walle, E. Economic factors and fertility decline in France and Belgium. *In* Economic factors in population growth p205-28

Belief and doubt
Burrow, J. W. Faith, doubt and unbelief. *In* Lerner, L. ed. The Victorians p153-73

Copleston, F. C. Christianity without belief in God. *In* Copleston, F. C. Philosophers and philosophies p68-78

Curley, E. M. Descartes, Spinoza and the ethics of belief. *In* Freeman, E. and Mandelbaum, M. H. eds. Spinoza p159-89

Belief and doubt—*Continued*

Murphey, M. G. The place of beliefs in modern culture. *In* Higham, J. and Conkin, P. K. eds. New directions in American intellectual history p151-65

Passmore, J. A. Hume and the ethics of belief. *In* David Hume p77-92

Richards, I. A. Belief. *In* Richards, I. A. Complementarities p24-36

Richards, I. A. What is belief? *In* Richards, I. A. Poetries p234-41

Weinberg, J. R. Hume's theory of causal belief. *In* Weinberg, J. R. Ockham, Descartes, and Hume p92-111

Yandell, K. E. Hume on religious belief. *In* Livingston, D. W. and King, J. T. eds. Hume p109-25

See also Evidence; Faith; Irrationalism Philosophy); Rationalism; Skepticism; Truth

Belief and doubt in literature

Kurz, P. K. The fool and doubt: on one aspect of the work of Friedrich Dürrenmatt. *In* Kurz, P. K. On modern German literature v4 p37-58

Belinskiĭ, Vissarion Grigor'evich

About

Berlin, Sir I. A remarkable decade: Vissarion Belinsky. *In* Berlin, Sir I. Russian thinkers p150-85

Dunn, P. P. Fathers and sons revisited: the childhood of Vissarion Belinskii. *In* DeMause, L. ed. The new psychohistory p131-49

Mathewson, R. W. Belinsky: "My heroes are the destroyers." *In* Mathewson, R. W. The positive hero in Russian literature p25-45

Stacy, R. H. Belinsky. *In* Stacy, R. H. Russian literary criticism p38-54

Belinsky, Vissarion. See Belinskiĭ, Vissarion Grigor'evich

Belitt, Ben

Adam's dream

Contents

Imitations: translation as personal mode
The moving finger and the unknown Neruda
Neruda's Joaquín Murieta: a note on the poetics of translation
Neruda's Memoirs: a reading from Homer
Pablo Neruda: A revaluation
Pablo Neruda: Splendor and death
The translator as nobody in particular
Translator's preface: Juan de Mairena
Translator's preface: Poet in New York
Translator's preface: The selected poems of Pablo Neruda
Translator's preface: The selected poems of Rafael Alberti

About

Boyers, R. To confront nullity: the poetry of Ben Belitt. *In* Boyers, R. Excursions p176-92

Landis, J. H. A "wild severity": toward a reading of Ben Belitt. *In* Boyers, R. ed. Contemporary poetry in America p221-39

Belize

Antiquities

Hammond, N. Ex oriente lux: a view from Belize. *In* The Origins of Maya civilization p45-76

Bell, Adrian

About

Cavaliero, G. Farmer novelists: H. W. Freeman, A. G. Street, Adrian Bell. *In* Cavaliero, G. The rural tradition in the English novel, 1900-1939 p101-17

Bell, Barbara Currier, and Ohmann, Carol Burke

Virginia Woolf's criticism: a polemical preface. *In* Donovan, J. C. ed. Feminist literary criticism p48-60

Bell, Bernard W.

African-American writers. *In* Emerson, E. H. ed. American literature, 1764-1789 p171-93

Bell, Coral

Détente and the American national interest. *In* Rosecrance, R. N. ed. America as an ordinary country p38-59

Bell, Daniel

Beyond modernism, beyond self. *In* Art, politics, and will p213-53

Ethnicity and social change. *In* Glazer, N. and Moynihan, D. P. eds. Ethnicity p141-74

The "intelligentsia" in American society. *In* Tomorrow's American p21-46

Technology, nature, and society. *In* The Frontiers of knowledge p27-78

Also in Technology and the frontiers of knowledge p23-71

Bell, Derrick A.

The racial imperative in American law. *In* The Age of segregation: race relations in the South, 1890-1945 p3-28

Bell, Inge Powell

Buddhist sociology: some thoughts on the convergence of sociology and the Eastern paths of liberation. *In* McNall, S. G. ed. Theoretical perspectives in sociology p53-68

Bell, J. Bowyer

Proliferation: sophisticated weapons and revolutionary options—the sub-state perspective. *In* Arms control and technological innovation p146-60

Revolutionary organisations: special cases and imperfect models. *In* International terrorism and world security p78-92

Strategy, tactics, and terror: an Irish perspective. *In* International terrorism p65-89

Bell, Millicent

About individual works

Edith Wharton and Henry James, the story of their friendship

Connolly, C. Edith Wharton and Henry James. *In* Connolly, C. The evening colonnade p179-81

Bell, Wendell

Futuristics and social behavior. *In* Bundy, R. F. ed. Images of the future: the twenty-first century and beyond p57-65

Bell, Whitfield Jenks

The colonial physician & other essays

Contents

Benjamin Franklin and the practice of medicine

Dr James Smith and the public encouragement for vaccination for smallpox

The Fielding H. Garrison lecture: a portrait of the colonial physician

James Hutchinson (1752-1793): a physician in politics

Bell, Whitfield J.
The colonial physician & other essays
Contents—*Continued*
John Morgan, founder of the medical school
John Redman, medical preceptor (1722-1808)
Joseph M. Toner (1825-1896) as a medical historian
Lives in medicine: the biographical dictionaries of Thacher, Williams, and Gross
Philadelphia medical students in Europe, 1750-1800
Thomas Parke, M. D., physician and friend

Bellah, Robert Neely
The new consciousness and the Berkeley New Left. *In* The New religious consciousness p77-92
New religious consciousness and the crisis in modernity. *In* The New religious consciousness p333-52
Religious studies as "new religion." *In* Needleman, J. and Baker, G. eds. Understanding the new religions p106-12
To kill and survive or to die and become: the active life and the contemplative life as ways of being adult. *In* Erikson, E. H. ed. Adulthood p61-80

Bellamy, Edward
About individual works
Looking backward, 2000-1887
Suvin, D. Anticipating the sunburst: dream, vision—or nightmare? *In* Suvin, D. Metamorphoses of science fiction p170-207

Bellany, Ian
The acquisition of arms by poor states. *In* The Year book of world affairs, 1976 p174-89

Bellette, Antony F.
Truth and utterance in 'The winter's tale.' *In* Shakespeare survey v31 p65-75

Belligerency. See Combatants and noncombatants (International law)

Bellini, Gentile
About individual works
Sultan Mahomet II
Meyers, J. Bellini, Giotto, Mantegna, Botticelli and Swann's way. *In* Meyers, J. Painting and the novel p96-111

Bellini, Giovanni. See Orpheus (formerly attributed to Giovanni Bellini)

Bellini, Vincenzo
About
Dent, E. J. Bellini. *In* Dent, E. J. The rise of romantic opera p162-75

Belloni, Luigi
Marcello Malpighi and the founding of anatomical microscopy. *In* Bonelli, M. L. R. and Shea, W. R. eds. Reason, experiment, and mysticism in the scientific revolution p95-110

Bellow, Saul
Literature in the age of technology. *In* The Frontiers of knowledge p3-25
Also in Technology and the frontiers of knowledge p1-22
Writers and literature in American society. *In* Culture and its creators p172-96

About
Guttmann, A. Saul Bellow's humane comedy. *In* Cohen, S. B. ed. Comic relief p127-51

Josipovici, G. Saul Bellow. *In* Josipovici, G. The lessons of modernism p64-84
Roth, P. Imagining Jews. *In* Roth, P. Reading myself and others p215-46

About individual works
The adventures of Augie March
Berry, J. A note on Augie. *In* Berryman, J. The freedom of the poet p22-24

Henderson the rain king
Alter, R. Jewish humor and the domestication of myth. *In* Alter, R. Defenses of the imagination p155-67
Majdiak, D. The romantic self and Henderson the rain king. *In* Garvin, H. R. ed. Makers of the twentieth-century novel p276-89

Herzog
Rahv, P. Saul Bellow's progress. *In* Rahv, P. Essays on literature and politics, 1932-1972 p62-66
Richter, D. H. Bellow's Herzog. *In* Richter, D. H. Fable's end p185-92

Mr. Sammler's planet
Boyers, R. Nature and social reality in Bellow's "Sammler." *In* Boyers, R. Excursions p25-46
Graff, G. Babbitt at the abyss. *In* Graff, G. Literature against itself p207-39
Vernier, J. Mr Sammler's lesson. *In* Johnson, I. D. and Johnson, C. [eds.] Les américanistes p16-36

Belmont, Nicole
Levana; or, How to raise up children. *In* Family and society p 1-15

Beloff, John
Explaining the paranormal, with Epilogue—1977. *In* Ludwig, J. K. ed. Philosophy and parapsychology p353-70
Koestler's philosophy of mind. *In* Harris, H. A. ed. Astride the two cultures p69-83
Parapsychology and its neighbors. *In* Wheatley, J. M. O. and Edge, H. L. eds. Philosphical dimensions of parapsychology p374-87

Beloff, Max
The Whitehall factor: the role of the higher civil service, 1919-39. *In* Peele, G. and Cook, C. eds. The politics of reappraisal, 1918-1939 p209-31

Belsen (Concentration camp)
Dawidowicz, L. S. Belsen remembered. *In* Dawidowicz, L. S. The Jewish presence p289-97

Belsey, Catherine
Senecan vacillation and Elizabethan deliberation: influence or confluence? *In* Renaissance drama [1973] p65-88

Belsley, David A.
United States silver coinage: what remains of an extinct specie. *In* Inflation, trade and taxes p50-72

Beltrán, S. Luis Ramiro
TV etchings in the minds of Latin Americans: conservatism, materiallism and conformism. *In* Fischer, H. D. and Melnik, S. R. eds. Entertainment: a cross-cultural examination p190-95

Bely, Andrei, pseud. See Bugaev, Boris Nikolaevich

Belyj, Andrej, pseud. See Bugaev, Boris Nikolaevich

Bemmelen, Reinout Willem van
The present formulation of the undation theory. *In* The Frontiers of human knowledge p255-74

Ben-Amos, Dan
Analytical categories and ethnic genres. *In* Folklore genres p215-42
Introduction. *In* Folklore genres p ix-xlv

Ben-Amos, Paula
Professionals and amateurs in Benin court carving. *In* African images p170-89

Benamou, Michel
The concept of marginality in ethnopoetics. *In* Minority language and literature p150-60

Benassi, Victor A. and Larson, Kathryn M.
Modification of family interaction with the child as the behavior-change agent. *In* Behavior modification and families p331-37

Ben-David, Joseph
Emergence of national traditions in the sociology of science: the United States and Great Britain. *In* Gaston, J. ed. Sociology of science p197-218
Organization, social control, and cognitive change in science. *In* Culture and its creators p244-65

Bender, Barbara
The first revolution. *In* Goodall, V. M. ed. The quest for man p105-28

Bender, Eileen. See Gross, S. L. jt. auth.

Bender, Gerald, and Isaacman, Allen F.
The changing historiography of Angola and Mozambique. *In* African studies since 1945 p220-48

Bender, Thomas
The cultures of intellectual life: the city and the professions. *In* Higham, J. and Conkin, P. K. eds. New directions in American intellectual history p181-95

Bendix, Reinhard
Province and metropolis: the case of eighteenth-century Germany. *In* Culture and its creators p119-49

Bene Israel. See Beni-Israel

Benecke, Gerhard
The German Reichskirche. *In* Callahan, W. J. and Higgs, D. eds. Church and society in Catholic Europe of the eighteenth century p77-87

Benedict, Michael Les
Preserving Federalism: Reconstruction and the Waite Court. *In* The Supreme Court review, 1978 p39-79
The rout of radicalism: Republicans and the elections of 1867. *In* Swierenga, R. P. ed. Beyond the Civil War synthesis p137-47

Benedictines, Cluniac. See Cluniacs

Benedictus, Saint, Abbot of Monte Cassino
About individual works
The rule of Saint Benedict
Gretsch, M. Æthelwold's translation of the Regula Sancti Benedicti and its Latin exemplar. *In* Anglo-Saxon England 3 p125-51

Benefices, Ecclesiastical
McCurry, C. Utilia metensia: local benefices for the papal Curia, 1212—c.1370. *In* Law, church, and society p311-23
See also Patronage, Ecclesiastical

Benefit societies. See Friendly societies

Benet of Canfield. See Benoit de Canfield, Father

Benet, Juan. See Benet Goitia, Juan

Benét, Stephen Vincent
About
Harris, W. J. Stephen Vincent Benét's "hair-raising defects"? *In* Filler, L. ed. A question of quality: popularity and value in modern creative writing p172-80

Benet Goitia, Juan
About individual works
Volverás a Región
Schwartz, R. Juan Benet and Volverás a Región (You'll probably return to Región) (1967). *In* Schwartz, R. Spain's New Wave novelists, 1950-1974 p233-44

Benevolence
Gaylin, W. In the beginning: helpless and dependent. *In* Doing good p 1-38
Glasser, I. Prisoners of benevolence: power versus liberty in the welfare state. *In* Doing good p97-170
Marcus, S. Their brothers' keepers: an episode from English history. *In* Doing good p39-66
Mott, S. C. The power of giving and receiving: reciprocity in Hellenistic benevolence. *In* Current issues in Biblical and patristic interpretation p60-72
Rothman, D. J. The state as parent: social policy in the Progressive Era. *In* Doing good p67-96

Bengal
Commerce—History
Prakash, O. Asian trade and European impact: a study of the trade from Bengal, 1630-1720. *In* Kling, B. B. and Pearson, M. N. eds. The age of partnership p43-70
Economic conditions
Marshall, P. Masters and banians in eighteenth-century Calcutta. *In* Kling, B. B. and Pearson, M. N. eds. The age of partnership p191-213
Politics and government
Broomfield, J. H. Peasant mobilization in twentieth-century Bengal. *In* Forging nations: a comparative view of rural ferment and revolt p41-60
Rural conditions
Broomfield, J. H. Peasant mobilization in twentieth-century Bengal. *In* Forging nations: a comparative view of rural ferment and revolt p41-60

Bengal, East. See Bangladesh

Ben-Horin, Meir
Scholars' "opinions": documents in the history of the Dropsie University. *In* Salo Wittmayer Baron v 1 p167-208

Beni-Israel
Strizower, S. The Bene Israel and the Jewish people. *In* Salo Wittmayer Baron v2 p859-86

Benin. See Bini (African people)

Benin art. See Art, Benin

Benitez, José Conrado
National planning for human settlements. *In* Strategies for human settlements: habitat and environment p19-27

Benítez, Rubén
An appraisal of the immediate past and present. *In* Américo Castro and the meaning of Spanish civilization p239-66

Bennett, Scott Boyce

John Murray's family library and the cheapening of books in early nineteenth century Britain. *In* Virginia. University. Bibliographical Society. Studies in bibliography v29 p139-66

Bennett, Warren

Character, irony, and resolution in "A clean, well-lighted place." *In* Benson, J. J. ed. The short stories of Ernest Hemingway: critical essays p261-69

Bennigsen, Alexandre A.

The Bolshevik conquest of the Moslem borderlands. *In* Hammond, T. T. ed. The anatomy of Communist takeovers p61-70

Bennigsen, Alexandre A. and Wimbush, S. Enders

Migration and political control: Soviet Europeans in Soviet Central Asia. *In* Human migration p173-87

Benoît de Canfield, Father

About individual works
The rule of perfection

Grant, P. Richard Crashaw and the Capucins: images and the force of belief. *In* Grant, P. Images and ideas in literature of the English Renaissance p89-128

Benoît de Sainte-More

About individual works
Le roman de Troie

Levenson, J. L. Shakespeare's Troilus and Cressida and the monumental tradition in tapestries and literature. *In* Renaissance drama [1976] p43-84

Benoliel, Jeanne Quint

Anticipatory grief in physicians and nurses. *In* Anticipatory grief p218-28

Dying is a family affair. *In* Home care p17-34

Nurses and the human experience of dying. *In* Feifel, H. [ed.] New meanings of death p123-42

Ben Porath, Yoram

Fertility in Israel: a mini-survey and some new findings. *In* Economic factors in population growth p136-72

Bensimon, Marc Joseph

Modes of perception of reality in the Renaissance. *In* The Darker vision of the Renaissance p221-72

Benson, Frederick R.

About individual works
Writers in arms

Connolly, C. The Spanish Civil War: 2. *In* Connolly, C. The evening colonnade p317-19

Benson, Herbert

The relaxation response: techniques and clinical applications. *In* Sobel, D. S. ed. Ways of health p331-51

Benson, Jackson J.

(comp.) A comprehensive checklist of Hemingway short fiction criticism, explication, and commentary. *In* Benson, J. J. ed. The short stories of Ernest Hemingway: critical essays p312-75

Ernest Hemingway as short story writer. *In* Benson, J. J. ed. The short stories of Ernest Hemingway: critical essays p272-310

An introduction: Bernard Malamud and the haunting of America. *In* The Fiction of Bernard Malamud p13-42

Benson, Jerry Kenneth

A power strategy. *In* Lauer, R. H. ed. Social movements and social change p107-20

See also Wardell, M. L. jt. auth.

Benson, John

Hog in sloth, fox in stealth: man and beast in moral thinking. *In* Royal Institute of Philosophy. Nature and conduct p265-80

Benson, Larry Dean

A reader's guide to writings on Chaucer. *In* Brewer, D. S. ed. Geoffrey Chaucer p321-72

Benson, Robert Louis

Medieval canonistic origins of the debate on the lawfulness of the Spanish Conquest. *In* First images of America p327-34

Benstock, Bernard

The Joyce industry: the James Joyce industry: a reassessment. *In* Yeats, Joyce, and Beckett p118-32

A light from some other world: symbolic structure in A portrait of the artist. *In* Staley, T. F. and Benstock, B. eds. Approaches to Joyce's Portrait p185-211

A portrait of the artist in Finnegans wake. *In* Garvin, H. R. ed. Makers of the twentieth-century novel p28-39

Bentham, Jeremy

About

Quinton, A. Utilitarian ethics. *In* New studies in ethics v2 p 1-118

Bentley, Edmund Clerihew

About individual works
Trent's last case

Panek, L. L. E. C. Bentley. *In* Panek, L. M. Wateau's shepherds: the detective novel in Britain, 1914-1940 p29-37

Bentley, Gerald Eades

A jewel in an Ethiop's ear. *In* Essick, R. N. and Pearce, D. R. eds. Blake in his time p213-40

Bentley, William H.

Bible believers in the Black community. *In* Wells, D. F. and Woodbridge, J. D. eds. The evangelicals p108-21

Benton, John F.

The accounts of Cepperello da Prato for the tax on nouveaux acquêts in the bailliage of Troyes. *In* Order and innovation in the Middle Ages p111-35

Benton, John F. and Ercoli, Fiorella Prosperetti

The style of the "Historia calamitatum": a preliminary test of the authenticity of the correspondence attributed to Abelard and Heloise. *In* Viator: medieval and Renaissance studies v6 p59-86

Benton, Robert Milton

The preachers. *In* Emerson, E. H. ed. American literature, 1764-1789 p73-85

Benz, Ernst

Buddhism in the Western world. *In* Dumoulin, H. ed. Buddhism in the modern world p305-22

Benzoni, Girolamo

About individual works
History of the New World

Keen, B. The vision of America in the writings of Urbain Chauveton. *In* First images of America p107-20

Beolco, Angelo, called Ruzzante
About
Fido, F. An introduction to the theater of Angelo Beolco. *In* Renaissance drama [1973] p203-18

Beowulf
Burlin, R. B. Gnomic indirection in Beowulf. *In* Anglo-Saxon poetry: essays in appreciation p41-49

Donahue, C. Potlatch and charity: notes on the heroic in Beowulf. *In* Anglo-Saxon poetry: essays in appreciation p23-40

Eliason, N. E. Beowulf, Wiglaf and the Wægmundings. *In* Anglo-Saxon England 7 p95-105

Eliason, N. E. Healfdene's daughter. *in* Anglo-Saxon poetry: essays in appreciation p3-13

Gardner, J. C. Guilt and the world's complexity: the murder of Ongentheow and the slaying of the dragon. *In* Anglo-Saxon poetry: essays in appreciation p14-22

Greenfield, S. B. The authenticating voice in Beowulf. *In* Anglo-Saxon England 5 p51-62

Hamilton, D. B. Andreas and Beowulf: placing the hero. *In* Anglo-Saxon poetry: essays in appreciation p81-98

Hanning, R. W. Beowulf as heroic history. *In* Medievalia et humanistica no. 5 p77-102

Hanning, R. W. The individual and mimesis, I: time and space in chivalric romance. *In* Hanning, R. W. The individual in twelfth-century romance p139-70

Huppé, B. F. The concept of the hero in the early Middle Ages. *In* Concepts of the hero in the Middle Ages and the Renaissance p 1-26

Luecke, J. M. Measuring Old English rhythm: applying the method to Beowulf. *In* Literary monographs v9 p49-74

Luecke, J. M. Measuring Old English rhythm: the suspect verses and a summary. *In* Literary monographs v9 p96-111

Renoir, A. Beowulf: a contextual introduction to its contents and techniques. *In* Oinas, F. J. ed. Heroic epic and saga p99-119

Renoir, A. The terror of the dark waters: a note on Virgilian and Beowulfian techniques. *In* The Learned and the lewed p147-60

Vickrey, J. F. The narrative structure of Hengest's revenge in Beowulf. *In* Anglo-Saxon England 6 p91-103

Beppu, Keiko
Foreign scholarship: Japanese contributions. *In* American literary scholarship, 1975 p494-97

Foreign scholarship: Japanese contributions [another essay] *In* American literary scholarship, 1976 p455-59

Foreign scholarship: Japanese contributions [another essay] *In* American literary scholarship, 1977 p499-504

Bérard, Christian
About
Wilder, T. N. Christian Bérard, 1902-1949. *In* Wilder, T. N. American characteristics, and other essays p229-33

Berberova, Nina Nikolaevna
A memoir and a comment: the "circle" of Petersburg. *In* Janecek, G. ed. Andrey Bely p115-20

Bercovitch, Sacvan
Emerson the prophet: romanticism, Puritanism, and auto-American-biography. *In* Levin, D. ed. Emerson: prophecy, metamorphosis, and influence p 1-27

The historiography of Johnson's Wonder-working providence. *In* Vaughan, A. T. and Bremer, F. J. eds. Puritan New England p268-86

New England's errand reappraised. *In* Higham, J. and Conkin, P. K. eds. New directions in American intellectual history p85-104

Berdíaev, Nikolaï Aleksandrovich
Philosophic truth and the moral truth of the intelligentsia. *In* Landmarks p3-22

Berdyaev, Nicholas. See Berdíaev, Nikolaï Aleksandrovich

Berdyaev, Nikolai. See Berdíaev, Nikolaï Aleksandrovich

Bereavement
Blank, I. M. Anticipatory grief. *In* Anticipatory grief p343-45

Gerber, I. Anticipatory bereavement. *In* Anticipatory grief p26-30

Weisman, A. D. Is mourning necessary? *In* Anticipatory grief p14-18

See also Grief

Psychological aspects
Benoliel, J. Q. Dying is a family affair. *In* Home care p17-34

Berenbaum, Michael
The additional covenant. *In* Rosenfeld, A. H. and Greenberg, I. eds. Confronting the Holocaust p169-85

Berenda, Carlton Warren. See Shewmaker, K. L. jt. auth.

Bérenger, Jean
The Austrian church. *In* Callahan, W. J. and Higgs, D. eds. Church and society in Catholic Europe of the eighteenth century p88-105

Berent, Venceslas. See Berent, Wacław

Berent, Wacław
About individual works
Ozimina
Baer, J. T. Wacław Berent's Ozimina: an analysis. *In* For Wiktor Weintraub p43-57

Berg, Alban
About individual works
Wozzeck
Schmidgall, G. Alban Berg. *In* Schmidgall, G. Literature as opera p287-319

Berg, Elliot J.
A comparative analysis of industrial relations systems in French West Africa and the Gold Coast. *In* African dimensions p171-96

Berg, Geri, and Gadow, Sally
Toward more human meanings of aging: ideals and images from philosophy and art. *In* Spicker, S. F.; Woodward, K. M. and Van Tassel, D. D. eds. Aging and the elderly p83-92

Berg, Jean de, pseud.
About individual works
The image
Bersani, L. Persons in pieces. *In* Bersani, L. A future for Astyanax p286-315

Berg, Kent T. Van Den. See Van Den Berg, Kent, T.

Berg, Leila

Personal actions; excerpt from "Look at kids." *In* Gross, B. and Gross, R. eds. The children's rights movement p306-15

Berger, Abraham

Ayalta: from the doe in the field to the mother of the messiahs. *In* Salo Wittmayer Baron v 1 p209-17

Berger, Bennett Maurice

American pastoralism, suburbia and the commune movement: an exercise in the microsociology of knowledge. *In* On the making of Americans p235-50

Berger, Carl

The writing of Canadian history

Contents

Arthur Lower and a national community
Conclusion
Donald Creighton and the artistry of history
The founders of critical history: George M. Wrong and Adam Shortt
Frank Underhill: history as political criticism
Harold Innis: the search for limits
A North American nation
Reorientation
Reorientation and tradition
The rise of liberty
William Morton: the delicate balance of region and nation

Berger, John

The look of things

Contents

Alexander Herzen
A belief in uniforms (Lovis Corinth)
The changing view of man in the portrait
'Che' Guevara
Czechoslovakia alone
Drawing
Drawings by Watteau
Fernand Léger
Jack Yeats
Le Corbusier
The moment of cubism
The nature of mass demonstrations
On the edge of a foreign city
Painting a landscape
Past seen from a possible future
Peter Peri
The political uses of photo-montage
Revolutionary undoing
Romantic notebooks
The sight of a man
Thicker than water (Corot)
Through the bars
Understanding a photograph
Victor Serge
Walter Benjamin
Zadkine

Berger, Peter L.

In praise of particularity: the concept of mediating structures. *In* An Almost chosen people p107-18

Modern identity: crisis and continuity. *In* Smithsonian Institution. The cultural drama p159-81

Religion in a revolutionary society. *In* America's continuing revolution p143-58

About

Lemert, C. C. Phenomenological sociology: Schutz, Berger, Luckmann. *In* Lemert, C. C. Sociology and the twilight of man p135-64

Berger, Philip A.; Hamburg, Beatrix, and Hamburg, David A.

Mental health: progress and problems. *In* Knowles, J. H. ed. Doing better and feeling worse p261-76

Berger, Suzanne Doris

Bretons and Jacobins: reflections on French regional ethnicity. *In* Esman, M. J. ed. Ethnic conflict in the Western world p159-78

Berger, Thomas

About individual works

Little Big Man

Bezanson, M. Berger and Penns' West: visions and revisions. *In* Peary, G. and Shatzkin, R. eds. The modern American novel and the movies p272-81

Royot, D. Aspects of the American picaresque in "Little Big Man." *In* Johnson, I. D. and Johnson, C. [eds.] Les américanistes p37-52

Trachtenberg, S. Berger and Barth: the comedy of decomposition. *In* Cohen, S. B. ed. Comic relief p45-69

Vital parts

Trachtenberg, S. Berger and Barth: the comedy of decomposition. *In* Cohen, S. B. ed. Comic relief p45-69

Bergeron, David M.

The play-within-the play in 3 Henry VI. *In* Tennessee Studies in literature v22 p37-45

The restoration of Hermoine [sic] in The winter's tale. *In* Shakespeare's romances reconsidered p125-33

Berghe, Pierre L. van den. See Van den Berghe, Pierre L.

Bergia, Silvio

Einstein and the birth of special relativity. *In* Einstein p65-89

Bergier, Jean-François

From the fifteenth century in Italy to the sixteenth century in Germany: a new banking concept? *In* The Dawn of modern banking p105-29

Bergin, Thomas Goddard. See Part 2 under title: Italian literature: roots and branches

Bergman, Ingmar

About

Steene, B. Bergman's movement toward nihilism: the antiheroic stance in Secrets of women, Brink of life, The seventh seal, and the Chamber Film trilogy. *In* The Hero in Scandinavian literature p87-105

Truffaut, F. Ingmar Bergman: Bergman's opus. *In* Truffaut, F. The films in my life p253-57

Truffaut, F. Ingmar Bergman: Cries and whispers. *In* Truffaut, F. The films in my life p257-60

About individual works

Cries and whispers

Kauffmann, S. Cries and whispers. *In* Kauffmann, S. Living images p164-66

Penley, C. Cries and whispers. *In* Nichols, B. ed. Movies and methods p204-08

Samuels, C. T. Tampering with reality. *In* Samuels, C. T. Mastering the film, and other essays p198-210

The magic flute

Craft, R. Playing with The magic flute. *In* Craft, R. Current convictions p34-48

Bergman, Ingmar—About individual works
—*Continued*

The passion of Anna

Simon, J. I. The passion of Anna; excerpt from "Movies into film." *In* Denby, D. ed. Awake in the dark p128-36

Persona

Boyers, R. Bergman's "Persona": an essay on tragedy. *In* Boyers, R. Excursions p47-70

Kauffmann, S. Persona. *In* Kauffmann, S. Living images p340-50

The touch

Kauffmann, S. The touch. *In* Kauffmann, S. Living images p64-65

Wild strawberries

Erikson, E. H. Reflections on Dr Borg's life cycle. *In* Erikson, E. H. ed. Adulthood p1-31

Murray, E. Wild strawberries. *In* Murray, E. Ten film classics p102-20

Bergmann, Carl Georg Lucas Christian

About

Coleman, W. Bergmann's rule: animal heat as a biological phenomenon. *In* Studies in history of biology v3 p67-88

Bergmann, Peter Gabriel

General relativity and our view of the physical universe. *In* Cosmology, history, and theology p25-28

Bergmann, Sven Arne. See Burnham, D. L. jt. auth.

Bergmann's rule

Coleman, W. Bergmann's rule: animal heat as a biological phenomenon. *In* Studies in history of biology v3 p67-88

Bergson, Abram

Consumer's and producer's surplus and general equilibrium. *In* Theory for economic efficiency: essays in honor of Abba P. Lerner p12-23

Bergson, Henri Louis

About individual works

Two sources of morality and religion

Copleston, F. C. Bergson on morality. *In* Copleston, F. C. Philosophers and philosophies p131-47

Ethics

Copleston, F. C. Bergson on morality. *In* Copleston, F. C. Philosophers and philosophies p131-47

Bergsten, C. Fred

Economic tensions: America versus the Third World. *In* Rosecrance, R. N. ed. America as an ordinary country p199-223

U.S.-Latin American economic relations to 1980: the international framework and some possible new approaches. *In* The Americas in a changing world p173-95

Berheide, Catherine White. See Segal, M. T. jt. auth.

Beringer, Richard E.

The unconscious "spirit of party" in the Confederate Congress. *In* Swierenga, R. P. ed. Beyond the Civil War synthesis p185-201

Berkeley, Anthony, pseud. See Cox, Anthony Berkeley

Berkeley, George, Bp. of Cloyne

About

Donagan, A. Berkeley's theory of the immediate objects of vision. *In* Studies in perception p312-35

Hoffman, Y. 'Dream-world' philosophers: Berkeley and Vasubandhu. *In* Philosophy East/philosophy West p247-68

Sellars, W. S. Berkeley and Descartes: reflections on the theory of ideas. *In* Studies in perception p259-311

Berkeley, Calif. University of California. See California. University

Berkhofer, Robert F.

Native Americans. *In* Ethnic leadership in America p119-49

The political context of a new Indian history. *In* The American Indian p101-26

Berkhout, Carl Theodore and others

Bibliography for 1977. *In* Anglo-Saxon England 7 p267-303

Berki, Robert N.

State and society: an antithesis of modern political thought. *In* Hayward, J. E. S. and Berki, R. N. eds. State and society in contemporary Europe p 1-20

Berki, Robert N. and Hayward, Jack Ernest Shalom

The state of European society. *In* Hayward, J. E. S. and Berki, R. N. eds. State and society in contemporary Europe p253-64

Berkner, Lutz K.

Inheritance, land tenure and peasant family structure: a German regional comparison. *In* Family and inheritance p71-95

Berkowitz, Gerald M.

Williams' "other places"—a theatrical metaphor in the plays. *In* Tennessee Williams: a tribute p712-19

Berlin, Sir Isaiah

Concepts and categories

Contents

The concept of scientific history
Does political theory still exist?
Empirical propositions and hypothetical statements
Equality
'From hope and fear set free'
Logical translation
The purpose of philosophy
Verification

Georges Sorel. *In* Essays in honour of E. H. Carr p3-35

Hume and the sources of German antirationalism. *In* David Hume p93-116

Russian thinkers

Contents

Fathers and children
The hedgehog and the fox
Herzen and Bakunin on individual liberty
A remarkable decade: Alexander Herzen
A remarkable decade: German romanticism in Petersburg and Moscow
A remarkable decade: The birth of the Russian intelligentsia
A remarkable decade: Vissarion Belinsky
Russia and 1848
Russian Populism
Tolstoy and enlightenment

About

Kelly, A. Introduction: a complex vision. *In* Berlin, Sir I. Russian thinkers pxiii-xxiv

Berlin, Normand
Complementarity in A streetcar named Desire. *In* Tennessee Williams: a tribute p97-103

Berlin
Galbraith, J. K. Berlin. *In* Galbraith, J. K. Annals of an abiding liberal p188-210

Description
Benjamin, W. A Berlin chronicle. *In* Benjamin, W. Reflections p3-60

Intellectual life
Benjamin, W. A Berlin chronicle. *In* Benjamin, W. Reflections p3-60

Berlioz, Hector
About
Cairns, D. Spontini's influence on Berlioz. *In* From Parnassus p25-41

About individual works
Benvenuto Cellini
Schmidgall, G. Hector Berlioz. *In* Schmidgall, G. Literature as opera p149-77

Berman, Maureen R. and Johnson, Joseph Esrey
The growing role of unofficial diplomacy. *In* Unofficial diplomats p1-33

Berman, Ronald S.
Intellect and education in revolutionary society. *In* America's continuing revolution p273-91
Justifying the humanities. *In* Hook, S.; Kurtz, P. W. and Todorovich, M. eds. The philosophy of the curriculum: the need for general education p75-79

Bernal, Martha Estella and others
Comparison of boys' behaviors in homes and classrooms. *In* Behavior modification and families p204-27
See also Delfini, L. F. jt. auth.

Bernal, Martin
Liu Shih-p'ei and National Essence. *In* The Limits of change p90-112

Bernanos, Georges
About individual works
The diary of a country priest
Sayre, R. F. Journal d'un curé de campagne: the saint's Gethsemane. *In* Sayre, R. F. Solitude in society p133-54

Bernard de Clairvaux, Saint
About
Jambeck, T. J. Everyman and the implications of Bernardine humanism in the character "Knowledge." *In* Medievalia et humanistica no. 8 p103-23

About individual works
The steps of humility
Zacher, C. K. Curiositas. *In* Zacher, C. K. Curiosity and pilgrimage p18-41

Art
Janke, R. S. The Vision of St. Bernard: a study in Florentine iconography. *In* Enggass, R. C. and Stokstad, M. eds. Hortus imaginum p45-50

Bernard de Ventadour. See Bernart de Ventadorn

Bernard, Jessie Shirley, and others
How to make marital sex more exciting—5 views. *In* Gross, L. ed. Sexual issues in marriage p17-24

Bernardo, Aldo S.
New beginnings in general education. *In* Hook, S.; Kurtz, P. W. and Todorovich, M. eds. The philosophy of the curriculum: The need for general education p257-59

Bernart de Ventadorn
About
Topsfield, L. T. Bernart de Ventadorn. *In* Topsfield, L. T. Troubadours and love p111-36

Berndt, Catherine H.
In aboriginal Australia. *In* Montagu, A. ed. Learning non-aggression p144-60

Berners, John Bourchier, 2d Baron, tr.
About individual works
Artus de Bretagne
Oberembt, K. J. Lord Berners' translation of Artus de la petite Bretagne. *In* Medievalia et humanistica no. 5 p191-99

Bernhard, Leopold Frederik Everhard Julius Coert Karel Godfried Pieter, H.R.H. Prince
The Atlantic nucleus. *In* The New Atlantic challenge p31-35

Bernhard of The Netherlands. See Bernhard, Leopold Frederik Everhard Julius Coert Karel Godfried Pieter, H.R.H. Prince

Berninghausen, David Knipe
Asheim's liberal approach to intellectual freedom. *In* As much to learn as to teach p38-50

Berninghausen, John. See Pai, Chih-ang

Bernini, Giovanni Lorenzo
About
Wittkower, R. The role of classical models in Bernini's and Poussin's preparatory work. *In* Wittkower, R. Studies in the Italian baroque p103-14

About individual works
Louis XIV (Statue)
Wittkower, R. The vicissitudes of a dynastic monument: Bernini's equestrian statue of Louis XIV. *In* Wittkower, R. Studies in the Italian baroque p83-102

Piazzo San Pietro
Wittkower, R. A counter-project to Bernini's Piazza S. Pietro. *In* Wittkower, R. Studies in the Italian baroque p61-82
Wittkower, R. The third arm of Bernini's Piazza S. Pietro. *In* Wittkower, R. Studies in the Italian baroque p53-60

Bernoulli, Jean
About
Brown, H. From London to Lapland: Maupertuis, Johann Bernoulli I, and La Terre applatie, 1728-1738. *In* Literature and history in the age of ideas p69-94

Bernoulli, Johann. See Bernoulli, Jean

Berns, Walter Fred
Religion and the founding principle. *In* The Moral foundations of the American Republic p157-82

Bernstein, Alan E.
Magisterium and license: corporate autonomy against papal authority in the medieval University of Paris. *In* Viator: medieval and Renaissance studies v9 p291-307

Bernstein, Arnold
My own suicide. *In* Wolman, B. B. ed. Between survival and suicide p95-102

Bernstein, Barton J.
Containment. *In* Encyclopedia of American foreign policy p191-203

Bernstein, Basil B.

About individual works
Class, codes and control

Edge, D. On the purity of science. *In* Niblett, W. R. ed. The sciences, the humanities and the technological threat p42-64

Bernstein, Leonard

About individual works
Candide

Kauffmann, S. Candide. *In* Kauffmann, S. Persons of the drama p263-66

Bernstein, Richard Jacob
Hannah Arendt: the ambiguities of theory and practice. *In* Political theory and praxis p141-58

Béroul

About individual works
Le roman de Tristan

York, E. C. Isolt's trial in Béroul and La Folie Tristan d'Oxford. *In* Medievalia et humanistica no. 6 p157-61

Berreman, Gerald Duane
Bazar behavior: social identity and social interaction in urban India. *In* Ethnic identity p71-105

Berri, Claude

About individual works
Le vieil homme et l'enfant

Truffaut, F. Claude Berri: Le vieil homme et l'enfant. *In* Truffaut, F. The films in my life p331-34

Berry, David
Apollinaire's solar imagery. *In* Cardinal, R. ed. Sensibility and creation p36-56

Berry, Francis
The poet of Childe Harold. *In* Jump, J. D. ed. Byron p16-34

About

Hobsbaum, P. The poetry of barbarism. *In* Hobsbaum, P. Tradition and experiment in English poetry p308-30

Berry, Jack
Marking tone in the Krio dictionary. *In* African themes p227-30

Berry, James Junior
Deviant categories and organizational typing of delinquents. *In* Davis, F. J. and Stivers, R. eds. The collective definition of deviance p350-59

Berry, Mary Frances
Repression of Blacks in the South 1890-1945: enforcing the system of segregation. *In* The Age of segregation: race relations in the South, 1890-1945 p29-43

Berry, Ralph
'To say one': an essay on 'Hamlet.' *In* Shakespeare survey 28 p107-15

Berry, Sara Shepherd Sweezy
Economic change in contemporary Africa. *In* Martin, P. M. and O'Meara, P. eds. Africa p261-79

Berry, Wendell
The specialization of poetry. *In* Gibbons, R. ed. The poet's work: 29 masters of 20th century poetry on the origins and practice of their art p139-56

Berryman, John
The freedom of the poet
Contents

Conrad's journey
Despondency and madness: on Lowell's "Skunk hour"
The development of Anne Frank
Dylan Thomas: the loud hill of Wales
Enslavement: Three American cases; Dreiser's "The titan"
Enslavement: Three American cases; F. Scott Fitzgerald
Enslavement: Three American cases; The case of Ring Lardner
Enslavement: Three American cases; Theodore Dreiser
The freedom of the Don
From the middle and senior generations
Hardy and his thrush
Hemingway's "A clean, well-lighted place"
Marlowe's damnations
The mind of Isaac Babel
The monk and its author
A note on Augie
Notes on Macbeth
One answer to a question: changes
Poetry chronicle, 1948: waiting for the end, boys
The poetry of Ezra Pound
Prufrock's dilemma
The ritual of W. B. Yeats
Robert Lowell and others
Shakespeare at thirty
Shakespeare's last word
"Song of myself": intention and substance
The sorrows of Captain Carpenter
Stephen Crane: "The open boat"
Stephen Crane: The red badge of courage
Thomas Nashe and The unfortunate traveller
Thursday out
The world of Henry James

About

Bayley, J. John Berryman: a question of imperial sway. *In* Boyers, R. ed. Contemporary poetry in America p59-77

Bayley, J. The self as available reality. *In* Bayley, J. The uses of division p157-71

Berryman, J. One answer to a question: changes. *In* Berryman, J. The freedom of the poet p323-31

Martz, W. J. John Berryman. *In* Donoghue, D. ed. Seven American poets from MacLeish to Nemerov p171-208

Miller, J. E. Poetic metamorphoses: Lowell and Berryman (a prologue). *In* Miller, J. E. The American quest for a supreme fiction p2-11

Thurley, G. John Berryman: the struggle towards dislocation. *In* Thurley, G. The American moment p51-69

About individual works
Berryman's sonnets

Lieberman, L. John Berryman, William Stafford, and James Dickey: the expansional poet: a return to personality. *In* Lieberman, L. Unassigned frequencies p263-71

Dream songs

Miller, J. E. The American bard/embarrassed Henry heard himself a-being: John Berryman's "Dream songs." *In* Miller, J. E. The American quest for a supreme fiction p234-75

Berryman, John—About individual works
—*Continued*

Homage to Mistress Bradstreet

Kunitz, S. J. No middle flight. *In* Kunitz, S. J. A kind of order, a kind of folly p213-19

Bersani, Leo

Flaubert and Emma Bovary: the hazards of literary fusion. *In* Spilka, M. ed. Towards a poetics of fiction p303-15

A future for Astyanax

Contents

Artaud, defecation and birth
Desire and metamorphosis
Emma Bovary and the sense of sex
The Jamesian lie
Lawrentian stillness
Murderous lovers
The paranoid hero in Stendhal
Persons in pieces
Racine, psychoanalysis and Oedipus
Realism and the fear of desire
Rimbaud's simplicity
Theaters of desire (Joe Chaikin, Robert Wilson and others)

Bershady, Harold Joshua

About individual works

Ideology and social knowledge

Parsons, T. Review of Harold J. Bershady, Ideology and social knowledge. *In* Parsons, T. Social systems and the evolution of action theory p122-41

Berte, Neal R.

New currents in Southern higher education. *In* The Rising South v2 p162-77

Berthoff, Rowland Tappan

Independence and attachment, virtue and interest: from republican citizen to free enterpriser, 1787-1837. *In* Uprooted Americans p97-124

Bertholf, Robert John

Shelley, Stevens and Robert Duncan: the poetry of approximations. *In* Artful thunder p269-99

Berthrong, Donald J.

Changing concepts: the Indians learn about the "Long Knives" and settlers (1849-1890s). *In* Red Men and hat-wearers p47-61

Berti, Enrico

Logical and ontological priority among the genera of substance in Aristotle. *In* Kephalaion p55-69

Bertolini, John A.

Ecphrasis and dramaturgy: Leonardo's Leda in Rucellai's Oreste. *In* Renaissance drama [1976] p151-76

Bertolucci, Bernardo

About individual works

The conformist

Kauffmann, S. The conformist. *In* Kauffmann, S. Living images p51-52

Last tango in Paris

Kauffmann, S. Last tango in Paris. *In* Kauffmann, S. Living images p173-76

Bertram, James M.

Arnold and Clough. *In* Allott, K. ed. Matthew Arnold p178-206

Bertran de Born, seigneur de Hautefort

About

Paden, W. D. Bertran de Born in Italy. *In* Italian literature: roots and branches p39-65

Bérulle, Pierre de Cardinal

About individual works

Bref discours de l'abnegation interieure

Grant, P. John Norris and the Oratorians: belief and the images in God. *In* Grant, P. Images and ideas in literature of the English Renaissance p154-91

Berzelius, Jöns Jakob, Friherre

About

Rocke, A. J. Atoms and equivalents: the early development of the chemical atomic theory. *In* Historical studies in the physical sciences v9 p225-63

Besant, Sir Walter

About individual works

The art of fiction

Spilka, M. Henry James and Walter Besant: "The art of fiction" controversy. *In* Spilka, M. ed. Towards a poetics of fiction p190-208

Bessarabia

History

Fischer-Galati, S. F. The Moldavian Soviet Republic in Soviet domestic and foreign policy. *In* Szporluk, R. ed. The influence of East Europe and the Soviet West on the USSR p229-50

Bessette, Joseph M.

The Presidency. *In* Graham, G. J. and Graham, S. G. eds. Founding principles of American government p197-222

Bessinger, Jess B.

The Gest of Robin Hood revisited. *In* The Learned and the lewed p355-69

Best, Geoffrey

Restraints on war by land before 1945. *In* Howard, M. ed. Restraints on war p17-37

Best sellers

Cawelti, J. G. The best-selling social melodrama. *In* Cawelti, J. G. Adventure, mystery, and romance p260-95

Hackett, A. P. Best sellers in the bookstores, 1900-1975. *In* Bookselling in America and the world p109-37

Street, D. and Street, W. P. Print media in urban society. *In* Handbook of contemporary urban life p428-67

Sutherland, J. A. Mass market and big business: novel publishing at midcentury. *In* Sutherland, J. A. Victorian novelists and publishers p41-71

Vidal, G. The top ten best sellers according to the Sunday New York Times as of January 7, 1973. *In* Vidal, G. Matters of fact and of fiction p3-26

History

Showalter, E. Subverting the feminine novel: sensationalism and feminine protest. *In* Showalter, E. A literature of their own p153-81

The best years of our lives (Motion picture)

Jackson, M. A. The uncertain peace: The best years of our lives. *In* O'Connor, J. E. and Jackson, M. A. eds. American history/American film p147-65

Bester, Alfred

Gourmet dining in outer space. *In* Knight, D. F. ed. Turning points p259-66

Besterman, Theodore

Bibliographical notes on the Beaumarchais-Goezman lawsuit. *In* Literature and history in the age of ideas p311-19

Bestman, Martin T.

Sembène Ousmane: social commitment and the search for an African identity. *In* King, B. A. and Ogungbesan, K. eds. A celebration of Black and African writing p139-49

Beston, John B.

How much was known of the Breton lai in fourteenth-century England? *In* The Learned and the lewed p319-36

Béteille, André

Race, caste and ethnic identity. *In* United Nations Educational, Scientific and Cultural Organization. Race, science and society p211-33

Bethge, Eberhard

Love without limits. *In* The Context of contemporary theology p243-49

Beti, Mongo

About individual works
Mission to Kala

Gakwandi, S. A. The illusion of progress: Beti's Mission to Kala. *In* Gakwandi, S. A. The novel and contemporary experience in Africa p37-42

Betjeman, Sir John

Hardy and architecture. *In* Drabble, M. ed. The genius of Thomas Hardy p150-53

Bettelheim, Bruno

Surviving, and other essays

Contents

About Summerhill
About the sexual revolution
Alienation and autonomy
Art and art education: a personal vision
The decision to fail
Education and the reality principle
Eichmann: the system, the victims
German concentration camps
Growing up female
The Holocaust—one generation later
The ignored lesson of Anne Frank
Individual and mass behavior in extreme situations
Mental health and urban design
Obsolete youth
"Owners of their faces"
Portnoy psychoanalyzed
Remarks on the psychological appeal of totalitarianism
Schizophrenia as a reaction to extreme situations
Some comments on privacy
Surviving
Trauma and reintegration
The ultimate limit
Unconscious contributions to one's undoing
Violence: a neglected mode of behavior

Bettelheim, Judith

Jamaican Jonkonnu and related Caribbean festivals. *In* Crahan, M. E. and Knight, F. W. eds. Africa and the Caribbean p80-100

Betting. See Gambling

Bettis, Joseph

Political theology and social ethics: the Socialist humanism of Karl Barth. *In* Hunsinger, G. ed. Karl Barth and radical politics p159-79

Betz, Hans Dieter

In defense of the spirit: Paul's letter to the Galatians as a document of early Christian apologetics. *In* Aspects of religious propaganda in Judaism and early Christianity p99-114

Beuve, Charles Augustin Sainte- See Sainte-Beuve, Charles Augustin

Bever, Thomas Gordon

The psychology of language and structuralist investigations of nativism. *In* Harman, G. ed. On Noam Chomsky p146-64

Bever, Thomas Gordon; Lackner, James R. and Kirk, R.

The underlying structures of sentences are the primary units of immediate speech processing. *In* Harman, G. ed. On Noam Chomsky p118-45

Beveridge, William Henry Beveridge, Baron

About

Harris, J. Social planning in war-time: some aspects of the Beveridge report. *In* War and economic development p239-56

Beverley, Robert

About individual works
The history and present state of Virginia

Seelye, J. On His Majesty's service: Robert Beverley, William Byrd, and the Palladian version of American pastoral. *In* Seelye, J. Prophetic waters p341-81

Bevington, David M.

"But we are spirits of another sort": the dark side of love and magic in A midsummer night's dream. *In* Medieval and Renaissance studies [1975] p80-92

Discontinuity in medieval acting traditions. *In* The Elizabethan theatre, V p 1-16

Beye, Charles Rowan

The rhythm of Hesiod's Works and days. *In* Harvard Studies in classical philology v76 p23-43

Beye, Holly, and McCleery, William

The most mysterious people in the Village. *In* Morgan, R. G. ed. Kenneth Patchen: a collection of essays p45-51

Beyer, Jürgen

The morality of the amoral. *In* Cooke, T. D. and Honeycutt, B. L. eds. The humor of the fabliaux p15-42

Beyer, Thomas R.

The Bely-Zhirmunsky polemic. *In* Janecek, G. ed. Andrey Bely p205-13

Beyle, Marie Henri

About

Brombert, V. H. Stendhal: the happy prison. *In* Brombert, V. H. The romantic prison p62-87

Brombert, V. H. Stendahl's silken prison. *In* Martz, L. L. and Williams, A. L. eds. The author in his work p365-73

Larkin, M. Determinist thought: Stendhal and the eighteenth-century inheritance. *In* Larkin, M. Man and society in nineteenth-century realism p17-30

Larkin, M. The shaping forces of society: Stendhal's Europe. *In* Larkin, M. Man and society in nineteenth-century realism p9-16

May, G. Molière and Stendahl. *In* Johnson, R. B.; Neumann, E. S. and Trail, G. T. eds. Molière and the commonwealth of letters: patrimony and posterity p 125-32

Beyle, Marie H.—About—*Continued*

May, G. Stendhal and the age of ideas. *In* Literature and history in the age of ideas p343-57

Peyre, H. Stendhal and Balzac as admirers and followers of Molière. *In* Johnson, R. B.; Neumann, E. S. and Trail, G. T. eds. Molière and the commonwealth of letters: patrimony and posterity p133-44

Pritchett, V. S. Stendhal: an early outsider. *In* Pritchett, V. S. The myth makers p136-44

Ragusa, O. Stendhal, Tomasi di Lampedusa, and the novel. *In* Ragusa, O. Narrative and drama p 1-34

Robinson, C. The idealist revolt. *In* Robinson, C. French literature in the nineteenth century p13-49

Snow, C. P. Baron Snow. Stendhal. *In* Snow, C. P. Baron Snow. The realists p 1-34

Wakefield, D. Stendhal and Delécluze at the Salon of 1824. *In* The Artist and the writer in France p76-85

About individual works
The charterhouse of Parma

Brombert, V. H. Stendhal: the happy prison. *In* Brombert, V. H. The romantic prison p62-87

Goodheart, E. Aristocrats and Jacobins: the happy few in The charterhouse of Parma. *In* Goodheart, E. The failure of criticism p119-36

Lamiel

Turnell, M. Stendhal's last novel. *In* Turnell, M. The rise of the French novel p145-68

Characters—Heroes

Terdiman, R. Stendhal: unhappiness in action. *In* Terdiman, R. The dialectics of isolation p16-38

Characters—Julien Sorel

Bersani, L. The paranoid hero in Stendhal. *In* Bersani, L. A future for Astyanax p106-27

Beysterveldt, Antonie Adrianus van
A new perspective of Cervantes' work. *In* Américo Castro and the meaning of Spanish civilization p167-91

Beysterveldt, Antony van. See Beysterveldt, Antonie Adrianus van

Bezanson, Mark
Berger and Penn's West: visions and revisions. *In* Peary, G. and Shatzkin, R. eds. The modern American novel and the movies p272-81

Bhagavadgītā. Mahābhārata. See Mahābhārata. Bhagavadgītā

Bhajan, Yogi. See Singh, Harbhajan

Bhakti
Coomaraswamy, A. K. Bhakta aspects of the Ātman doctrine. *In* Coomaraswamy, A. K. Selected papers v2 p386-97

Bhakti-margi. See Bhakti

Bhatt, G. S.
Social philosophy. *In* Bishop, D. H. ed. Indian thought p197-232

Bhattacharya, Bhabani

About

Singh, R. S. From social criticism to utopianism: Bhabani Bhattacharya. *In* Singh, R. S. Indian novel in English p96-118

Biafran Conflict, 1967-1970. See Nigeria—History—Civil War, 1967-1970

Bialer, Seweryn
On the meanings, sources, and carriers of radicalism in contemporary industrialized societies: introductory remarks. *In* Radicalism in the contemporary age v1 p3-29

The resurgence and changing nature of the Left in industrialized democracies. *In* Radicalism in the contemporary age v3 p3-81

Biallas, Leonard J.
America: the myth of the hunter. *In* America in theological perspective p206-29

Bianchi Bandinelli, Ranuccio, ed.

About individual works
The buried city

Connolly, C. Leptis magna. *In* Connolly, C. The evening colonnade p41-44

Biasin, Gian-Paolo
Literary diseases
Contents

From anatomy to criticism
Moscarda's mirror
Narcisa's poison
The pen, the mother
Zeno's last bomb
Strategies of the anti-hero: Svevo, Pirandello, and Montale. *In* Italian literature: roots and branches p363-81

Bibbiena, Bernardo Dovizi, Cardinal. See Dovizi, Bernardo, da Bibbiena, Cardinal

Bible
Biography
Peterson, L. H. Biblical typology and the self-portrait of the poet in Robert Browning. *In* Landow, G. P. ed. Approaches to Victorian autobiography p235-68

Canon, Catholic vs. Protestant
Geisler, N. L. The extent of the Old Testament canon. *In* Current issues in Biblical and patristic interpretation p31-46

Characters
See Bible—Biography

Cosmology
See Cosmology, Biblical

Criticism, interpretation, etc.
Carter, J. R. Translational theology: an expression of Christian faith in a religiously plural world. *In* Christian faith in a religiously plural world p168-80

Downs, R. B. The Book of Books. *In* Downs, R. B. Books that changed the world p27-35

Lewalski, B. K. The Biblical symbolic mode: typology and the religious lyric. *In* Lewalski, B. K. Protestant poetics and the seventeenth-century religious lyric p111-44

Lewalski, B. K. The poetic texture of scripture: tropes and figures for the religious lyric. *In* Lewalski, B. K. Protestant poetics and the seventeenth-century religious lyric p72-110

Ong, W. J. Maranatha: death and life in the text of the Book. *In* Ong, W. J. Interfaces of the word p230-71

See also Bible as literature

Bible—*Continued*

**Criticism, interpretation, etc.—History
—Middle Ages, 600-1500**

Froehlich, K. "Always to keep the literal sense in Holy Scripture means to kill one's soul": the state of Biblical hermeneutics at the beginning of the fifteenth century. *In* Miner, E. R. ed. Literary uses of typology p20-48

Criticism, interpretation, etc., Jewish

See Bible. Old Testament—Criticism, interpretation, etc., Jewish

Criticism, interpretation, etc.—Theory, methods, etc.

See Bible—Hermeneutics

Criticism, Textual

Dalton, W .J. "So that your faith may also be your hope in God" (I Peter 1:21). *In* Reconciliation and hope p262-74

Martin, R. P. Reconciliation and forgiveness in the letter to the Colossians. *In* Reconciliation and hope p104-24

Drama

See Mysteries and miracle-plays

Ethics

See Sociology, Biblical

Evidences, authority, etc.

See Miracles

Exegesis

See Bible—Hermeneutics

Folk-lore

See Folk-lore—Jews

Food

See Food in the Bible

Hermeneutics

Mazzeo, J. A. Interpretation and its occasions. *In* Mazzeo, J. A. Varieties of interpretation p1-25

Mazzeo, J. A. New wine in old bottles: reflections on historicity and the problems of allegory. *In* Mazzeo, J. A. Varieties of interpretation p47-69

Mazzeo, J. A. Style as interpretation. *In* Mazzeo, J. A. Varieties of interpretation p27-45

Shaffer, E. S. The fall of Jerusalem: Coleridge's unwritten epic. *In* Shaffer, E. S. 'Kubla Khan' and The fall of Jerusalem p17-61

Shaffer, E. S. The oriental idyll. *In* Shaffer, E. S. 'Kubla Khan' and The fall of Jerusalem p96-144

Shaffer, E. S. The visionary character: Revelation and the lyrical ballad. *In* Shaffer, E. S. 'Kubla Khan' and The fall of Jerusalem p62-95

Hermeneutics—History

See Bible—Criticism, interpretation, etc.—History

History of Biblical events

Frye, N. History and myth in the Bible. *In* Fletcher, A. J. S. ed. The literature of fact p 1-19

Sayers, D. L. A vote of thanks to Cyrus; excerpt from "Unpopular opinions." *In* Sayers, D. L. The whimsical Christian p53-59

History of inter-testamental events

See Judaism—History—Post-exilic period, 586 B.C.-210 A.D.

Illustrations

See Bible—Pictures, illustrations, etc.

Influence

Lewalski, B. K. Art and the sacred subject: sermon theory, Biblical personae, and Protestant poetics. *In* Lewalski, B. K. Protestant poetics and the seventeenth century religious lyric p213-50

Lewalski, B. K. The poetic texture of scripture: tropes and figures for the religious lyric. *In* Lewalski, B. K. Protestant poetics and the seventeenth-century religious lyric p72-110

Interpretation

See Bible—Criticism, interpretation, etc.; Bible—Hermeneutics

Language, Style

Wicker, B. Metaphor and 'God.' *In* Wicker, B. The story-shaped world p71-106

See also Greek language, Biblical

Law

See Jewish law

Legends

Pritchard, J. B. Introduction. *In* Pritchard, J. B. ed. Solomon & Sheba p7-15

Literary criticism

See Bible—Criticism, interpretation, etc.

Manuscripts

See Bible. Manuscripts

Miracles

See Miracles

Mythology

See Myth in the Bible

Philology

See Greek language, Biblical

Philosophy

See Philosophy, Jewish

Pictures, illustrations, etc.

Kitzinger, E. The role of miniature painting in mural decoration. *In* The Place of book illumination in Byzantine art p99-142

Weitzmann, K. The study of Byzantine book illumination, past, present, and future. *In* The Place of book illumination in Byzantine art p 1-60

Poetry

See Hebrew poetry

Prophecies

See Apocalyptic literature

Sociology

See Sociology, Biblical

Symbolism

See Symbolism in the Bible

Textual criticism

See Bible—Criticism, Textual

Translating

Leser, P. W. No man, having put his hand to the plow. . . *In* On language, culture, and religion: in honor of Eugene A. Nida p241-58

Bible—Translating—*Continued*

Mundhenk, N. The subjectivity of anachronism. *In* On language, culture, and religion: in honor of Eugene A. Nida p259-73

Smalley, W. A. Restructuring translations of the psalms as poetry. *In* On language, culture, and religion: in honor of Eugene A. Nida p337-71

Thompson, C. R. Scripture for the ploughboy and some others. *In* Studies in the continental background of Renaissance English literature: essays presented to John L. Lievsay p3-28

Waard, J. de. A Greek translation-technical treatment of Amos 1:15. *In* On language, culture, and religion: in honor of Eugene A. Nida p111-18

Typology

See Typology (Theology)

Versions—Theory, methods, etc.

See Bible—Translating

Versions—New English

Hyman, S. E. Illumination for the unchurched. *In* Hyman, S. E. The critic's credentials p305-12

Bible. Manuscripts

Thomson, R. The date of the Bury Bible reexamined. *In* Viator: medieval and Renaissance studies v6 p51-58

Bible. Manuscripts, Coptic

Browne, G. M. The Sahidic version of Kingdoms IV. *In* Illinois classical studies v3, 1978 p196-205

Bible. New Testament

Antiquities

Hyman, S. E. History and sacred history. *In* Hyman, S. E. The critic's credentials p313-25

Criticism, interpretation, etc.

Hyman, S. E. History and sacred history. *In* Hyman, S. E. The critic's credentials p313-25

Jarrott, C. A. L. Erasmus's annotations and Colet's commentaries on Paul: a comparison of some theological themes. *In* Essays on the works of Erasmus p125-44

Kee, H. C. The linguistic background of "shame" in the New Testament. *In* On language, culture, and religion: in honor of Eugene A. Nida p133-47

Little, P. E. Some reflections on evangelism in the New Testament. *In* Current issues in Biblical and patristic interpretation p318-23

Mare, W. H. A study of the New Testament concept of the Parousia. *In* Current issues in Biblical and patristic interpretation p336-45

Criticism, interpretation, etc.—History—20th century

Fiorenza, E. S. Wisdom mythology and the Christological hymns of the New Testament. *In* Aspects of wisdom in Judaism and early Christianity p17-41

Criticism, Textual

Martini, C. M. Eclecticism and Atticism in the textual criticism of the Greek New Testament. *In* On language, culture, and religion: in honor of Eugene A. Nida p149-56

Ethics

Osborn, E. F. New Testament. *In* Osborn, E. F. Ethical patterns in early Christian thought p15-49

Relation to Old Testament

Epp, E. J. Wisdom, Torah, Word: the Johannine Prologue and the purpose of the Fourth Gospel. *In* Current issues in Biblical and patristic interpretation p128-46

Theology

Elwell, W. A. The deity of Christ in the writings of Paul. *In* Current issues in Biblical and patristic interpretation p297-308

Ladd, G. E. Apocalyptic and New Testament theology. *In* Reconciliation and hope p285-96

Versions

Metzger, B. M. Early Arabic versions of the New Testament. *In* On language, culture, and religion: in honor of Eugene A. Nida p157-68

Rabil, A. Erasmus's Paraphrases of the New Testament. *In* Essays on the works of Erasmus p145-61

Bible. New Testament. Acts

Criticism, interpretation, etc.

Black, M. W. Notes on the longer and the shorter text of Acts. *In* On language, culture, and religion: in honor of Eugene A. Nida p119-31

Bruce, F. F. The speeches in Acts—thirty years after. *In* Reconciliation and hope p53-68

Bible. New Testament. Acts XIX

Criticism, interpretation, etc.

Fiorenza, E. S. Miracles, mission and apologetics: an introduction. *In* Aspects of religious propaganda in Judaism and early Christianity p 1-25

Bible. New Testament. Apocryphal books

Criticism, interpretation, etc.

Achtemeier, P. J. Jesus and the disciples as miracle workers in the Apocryphal New Testament. *In* Aspects of religious propaganda in Judaism and early Christianity p149-86

Bible. New Testament. Apocryphal books. Abgar letters

Lutz, C. E. The Apocryphal Abgarus-Jesus Epistles in England in the Middle Ages. *In* Lutz, C. E. Essays on manuscripts and rare books p57-62

Bible. New Testament. Apocryphal books. Epistle of Jesus Christ

Jones, W. R. The heavenly letter in medieval England. *In* Medievalia et humanistica no. 6 p163-78

Bible. New Testament. Colossians

Criticism, interpretation, etc.

Martin, R. P. Reconciliation and forgiveness in the letter to the Colossians. *In* Reconciliation and hope p104-24

Bible. New Testament. Colossians I, 27

Criticism, interpretation, etc.

Bowers, W. P. A note on Colossians 1:27a. *In* Current issues in Biblical and patristic interpretation p110-14

Bible New Testament. Revelation—Criticism, interpretation, etc.—Continued

Nolan, B. New directions in twelfth-century spirituality. *In* Nolan, B. The Gothic visionary perspective p3-34

Shaffer, E. S. The visionary character: Revelation and the lyrical ballad. *In* Shaffer, E. S. 'Kubla Khan' and The fall of Jerusalem p62-95

Influence

Wittreich, J. A. Painted prophecies: the tradition of Blake's illuminated books. *In* Essick, R. N. and Pearce, D. R. eds. Blake in his time p101-15

Pictures, illustrations, etc.

Cutler, A. The Apocalypse icon in the Byzantine Museum, Athens. *In* Studies in memory of David Talbot Rice p94-112

Bible. New Testament. Romans VIII, 19-21

Criticism, interpretation, etc.

Cranfield, C. E. B. Some 'observations on Romans 8:19-21. *In* Reconciliation and hope p224-30

Bible. New Testament. Romans XII, 8

Criticism, interpretation, etc.

Unnik, W. C. van. The interpretation of Romans 12:8: ὁ μεταδιδοὺς ἐν ἁπλότητι. *In* On language, culture, and religion: in honor of Eugene A. Nida p169-83

Bible. Old Testament

Commentaries

Ferrante, J. M. Biblical exegesis. *In* Ferrante, J. M. Woman as image in medieval literature p17-35

Criticism, interpretation, etc.

Brichto, H. C. The Hebrew Bible on human rights. *In* Sidorsky, D. ed. Essays on human rights p215-33

Feldman, L. H. Josephus as an apologist to the Greco-Roman world: his portrait of Solomon. *In* Aspects of religious propaganda in Judaism and early Christianity p69-98

Jacobson, R. Absence, authority, and the text. *In* Glyph 3 p137-47

Laporte, J. Philo in the tradition of Biblical wisdom literature. *In* Aspects of wisdom in Judaism and early Christianity p103-41

Samuel, M. Race, nation, and people in the Jewish Bible. *In* Tradition and change in Jewish experience p26-45

Schoedel, W. R. Jewish wisdom and the formation of the Christian ascetic. *In* Aspects of wisdom in Judaism and early Christianity p169-99

Soler, J. The semiotics of food in the Bible. *In* Food and drink in history p126-38

Walker, L. L. "Love" in the Old Testament: some lexical observations. *In* Current issues in Biblical and patristic interpretation p277-88

Wilken, R. L. Wisdom and philosophy in early Christianity. *In* Aspects of wisdom in Judaism and early Christianity p143-68

Criticism, interpretation, etc., Jewish

Daube, D. The rabbis and Philo on human rights. *In* Sidorsky, D. ed. Essays on human rights p234-46

Goldin, J. "This song." *In* Salo Wittmayer Baron v 1 p539-54

Simon, E. The neighbor (re'a) whom we shall love. *In* Modern Jewish ethics p29-56

Wolfson, H. A. Saadia on the semantic aspect of the problem of attribute. *In* Salo Wittmayer Baron v2 p1009-22

Criticism, Textual

Edelmann, R. מסורת and its historical background. *In* Salo Wittmayer Baron v 1 p369-82

McKane, W. Observations on the tiḳḳûnê sôpᵉrîm. *In* On language, culture, and religion: in honor of Eugene A. Nida p53-77

Ethnology

Samuel, M. Race, nation, and people in the Jewish Bible. *In* Tradition and change in Jewish experience p26-45

Illustrations

See Bible. Old Testament—Pictures, illustrations, etc.

Influence

Laporte, J. Philo in the tradition of Biblical wisdom literature. *In* Aspects of wisdom in Judaism and early Christianity p103-41

Legends

See Legends, Jewish

Manuscripts, Hebrew

Edelmann, R. מסורת and its historical background. *In* Salo Wittmayer Baron v 1 p369-82

Mythology

See Myth in the Old Testament

Pictures, illustrations, etc.

Schapiro, M. Chagall's Illustrations for the Bible. *In* Schapiro, M. Selected papers v2 p121-34

Political science

Konvitz, M. R. Human dignity: from creation to Constitution. *In* Konvitz, M. R. Judaism and the American idea p33-51

Race problems

See Bible. Old Testament—Ethnology

Bible. Old Testament. Amos I,15

Criticism, interpretation, etc.

nical treatment of Amos 1:15. *In* On language, culture, and religion: in honor of Eugene A. Nida p111-18

Bible. Old Testament. Apocrypha

Influence

Mollenkott, V. R. The pervasive influence of the Apocrypha in Milton's thought and art. *In* Patrick, J. M. and Sundell, R. H. eds. Milton and the art of sacred song p23-43

Bible. Old Testament. Apocrypha. 2 Maccabees

Criticism, interpretation, etc.

Habicht, C. Royal documents in Maccabees II. *In* Harvard Studies in classical philology v80 p 1-18

Bible. Old Testament. Apocryphal books. Enoch

Influence

Bentley, G. E. A jewel in an Ethiop's ear. *In* Essick, R. N. and Pearce, D. R. eds. Blake in his time p213-40

Biblical cosmology. See Cosmology, Biblical

Biblical Greek. See Greek language, Biblical

Biblical law. See Jewish law

Bibliography.
Bowers, F. T. The bibliographical way. *In* Bowers, F. T. Essays in bibliography, text, and editing p54-74

Bowers, F. T. Bibliography and Restoration drama. *In* Bowers, F. T. Essays in bibliography, text, and editing p135-50

Bowers, F. T. Bibliography, pure bibliography, and literary studies. *In* Bowers, F. T. Essays in bibliography, text, and editing p37-53

Bowers, F. T. Bibliography revisited. *In* Bowers, F. T. Essays in bibliography, text, and editing p151-95

Bowers, F. T. Four faces of bibliography. *In* Bowers, F. T. Essays in bibliography, text, and editing p94-108

Bowers, F. T. Some relations of bibliography to editorial problems. *In* Bowers, F. T. Essays in bibliography, text, and editing p15-36

Tanselle, G. T. Descriptive bibliography and library cataloguing. *In* Virginia. University. Bibliographical Society. Studies in bibliography v30 p 1-56

See also Errors and blunders, Literary; Manuscripts; Transmission of texts; and subdivision Bibliography under names of persons, places and subjects, e.g. War—Bibliography

Bibliography—America
Adams, T. R. Some bibliographical observations on and questions about the relationship between the discovery of America and the invention of printing. *In* First images of America p529-36

Early printed books
Bowers, F. T. Bibliographical evidence from the printer's measure. *In* Bowers, F. T. Essays in bibliography, text, and editing p258-68

Bowers, F. T. The headline in early books. *In* Bowers, F. T. Essays in bibliography, text, and editing p199-211

Bowers, F. T. Running-title evidence for determining half-sheet imposition. *In* Bowers, F. T. Essays in bibliography, text, and editing p254-57

Hay, D. 1500-1700: the bibliographical problem: a continental S.T.C.? *In* Classical influences on European culture A.D. 1500-1700 p33-39

Early printed books—15th century
See Incunabula

Editions
Bowers, F. T. Established texts and definitive editions. *In* Bowers, F. T. Essays in bibliography, text, and editing p359-74

Bowers, F. T. Practical texts and definitive editions. *In* Bowers, F. T. Essays in bibliography, text, and editing p412-39

See also Transmission of texts

Methodology
See Bibliography—Theory, methods, etc.

Rare books
Bowers, F. T. Bibliography and modern librarianship. *In* Bowers, F. T. Essays in bibliography, text, and editing p75-93

See also Bibliography—Early printed book; Incunabula; Manuscripts

Theory, methods, etc.
Bowers, F. T. Bibliography and the university. *In* Bowers, F. T. Essays in bibliography, text, and editing p3-14

Bowers, F. T. Purposes of descriptive bibliography with some remarks on methods. *In* Bowers, F. T. Essays in bibliography, text, and editing p111-34

Universal catalogs
See Bibliography, International

Bibliography, International
Hay, D. 1500-1700: the bibliographical problem. A continental S.T.C.? *In* Classical influences on European culture A.D. 1500-1700 p33-39

Bibliography, Universal. See Bibliography, International

Bicentennial celebration (U.S.), 1976. See American Revolution Bicentennial, 1776-1976

Bichat, Marie François Xavier

About
Albury, W. R. Experiment and explanation in the physiology of Bichat and Magendie. *In* Studies in history of biology, v1 p47-131

Bichat, Xavier. See Bichat, Marie François Xavier

Bickel, Alexander Mordecai
The aims of education and the proper standards of the university. *In* Universities in the Western world p3-11

About individual works
The morality of consent
Bork, R. H. Alexander M. Bickel, political philosopher. *In* The Supreme Court review, 1975 p419-21

Bickerton, Ian J.
Foreign aid. *In* Encyclopedia of American foreign policy p372-79

Bicknell, John, supposed author

About individual works
Musical travels through England
Lonsdale, R. H. Dr Burney, 'Joel Collier', and Sabrina. *In* Evidence in literary scholarship p281-308

Bickwit, Leonard and Brownlee, Michael B.
Chemical pollution control in the USA. *In* Against pollution and hunger p278-86

Biculturalism
Ballesteros, D. Bilingual-bicultural education: a must for Chicanos. *In* Trejo, A. D. ed. The Chicanos p151-65

Fernando, L. A note from the Third World towards the re-definition of culture. *In* Narasimhaiah, C. D. ed. Awakened conscience p327-38

Guerra, M. H. Bilingualism and biculturalism: assets for Chicanos. *In* Trejo, A. D. ed. The Chicanos p121-32

Canada
Brazeau, J. and Cloutier, E. Interethnic relations and the language issue in contemporary Canada: a general appraisal. *In* Esman, M. J. ed. Ethnic conflict in the Western world p204-27

Porter, J. A. Ethnic pluralism in Canadian perspective. *In* Glazer, N. and Moynihan, D. P. eds. Ethnicity p267-304

The bicycle thief (Motion picture)
Murray, E. The bicycle thief. *In* Murray, E. Ten film classics p33-47

Biddle, Martin, and others
Bibliography for 1973. *In* Anglo-Saxon England 3 p233-70
Bibliography for 1974. *In* Anglo-Saxon England 4 p223-62
Sutton Hoo published: a review. *In* Anglo-Saxon England 6 p249-65

Biddulph, Howard Lowell
Protest strategies of the Soviet intellectual opposition. *In* Tokes, R. L. ed. Dissent in the USSR p96-115

Biderman, Shlomo
Scriptures, revelation, and reason. *In* Philosophy East/philosophy West p128-61

Bidwell, John
The size of the sheet in America: papermoulds manufactured by N & D. Sellers of Philadelphia. *In* American Antiquarian Society. Proceedings v87 pt2 p299-342

Bie, Pierre de
Contemporary sociology in Belgium. *In* Mohan, R. P. and Martindale, D. A. eds. Handbook of contemporary developments in world sociology p31-45

Biebuyck, Daniel P.
The African heroic epic. *In* Oinas, F. J. ed. Heroic epic and saga p336-67

Bieler, Ludwig
Hagiography and romance in medieval Ireland. *In* Medievalia et humanistica no. 6 p13-24

Biemel, Walter
Husserl's Encyclopaedia Britannica article and Heidegger's remarks thereon. *In* Elliston, F. A. and McCormick, P. eds. Husserl p286-303

Bien, Peter
Metaphysics, myth, and politics. *In* Buxton, T. H. and Prichard, K. W. eds. Excellence in university teaching p157-88

Bienfang, Ralph
On being a professor. *In* Buxton, T. H. and Prichard, K. W. eds. Excellence in university teaching p55-61

Bienstock, Beverly Gray
The changing image of the American Jewish mother. *In* Tufte, V. and Myerhoff, B. G. eds. Changing images of the family p173-91

Bierlaire, Franz
Erasmus at school: the De civilitate morum puerilium libellus. *In* Essays on the works of Erasmus p239-51

Bierstedt, Robert S.
Comment on Lenski's evolutionary perspective. *In* Blau, P. M. ed. Approaches to the study of social structure p154-58

Biesheuvel, Simon
An examination of Jensen's theory concerning educability, heritability and population differences. *In* Montagu, A. ed. Race and IQ p59-72

The big parade (Motion picture)
Isenberg, M. T. The Great War viewed from the twenties: The big parade. *In* O'Connor, J. E. and Jackson, M. A. eds. American history/American film p17-37

The big sleep (Motion picture)
Shatzkin, R. Who cares who killed Owen Taylor? *In* Peary, G. and Shatzkin, R. eds. The modern American novel and the movies p80-94

Big Table
Michelson, P. On The Purple Sage, Chicago Review, and Big Table. *In* Anderson. E. and Kinzie, M. eds. The little magazine in America: a modern documentary history p341-75

Big Thicket National Park, Tex. (Proposed)
Gunter, P. A. Y. The Big Thicket: a case study in attitudes toward environment. *In* Philosophy & environmental crisis p117-37

Bigger than life (Motion picture)
Truffaut, F. Nicholas Ray: Bigger than life. *In* Truffaut, F. The films in my life p143-47

Biggins, Dennis
"O Jankyn, be ye there?" *In* Chaucer and Middle English studies in honour of Rossell Hope Robbins p249-54

Bigras, Julien
French psychoanalysis. *In* Roland, A. ed. Psychoanalysis, creativity, and literature p11-21

Bigsby, Christopher W. E.
Europe, America and the cultural debate. *In* Bigsby, C. W. E. Superculture p 1-27
Hemingway: the recoil from history. *In* French, W. G. ed. The twenties p203-13
The politics of popular culture. *In* Bigsby, C. W. E. ed. Approaches to popular culture p3-25

Bilan, R. P.
The basic concepts and criteria of F. R. Leavis's novel criticism. *In* Spilka, M. ed. Towards a poetics of fiction p157-76

Bildungsroman, American style, The. Holman, C. H. *In* Holman, C. H. Windows on the world p168-97

Bildungsroman as a genre, The. Swales, M. *In* Swales, M. The German Bildungsroman from Wieland to Hess p9-37

Bildungsroman tradition, A portrait and the. Mitchell, B. *In* Staley, T. F. and Benstock, B. eds. Approaches to Joyce's Portrait p61-74

Biliary tract. See Gall-bladder

Bilingual education. See Education, Bilingual

Bilingualism
Ballesteros, D. Bilingual-bicultural education: a must for Chicanos. *In* Trejo, A. D. ed. The Chicanos p151-56
Fishman, J. A. The sociology of language: yesterday, today, and tomorrow. *In* Current issues in linguistic theory p51-75
Guerra, M. H. Bilingualism and biculturalism: assets for Chicanos. *In* Trejo, A. D. ed. The Chicanos p121-32
Richards, J. C. Second language learning. *In* Wardhaugh, R. and Brown, H. D. eds. A survey of applied linguistics p113-37
Rutherford, W. E. Second language teaching. *In* Wardhaugh, R. and Brown, H. D. eds. A survey of applied linguistics p138-63
Spolsky, B. Bilingualism. *In* Wardhaugh, R. and Brown, H. D. eds. A survey of applied linguistics p164-81

United States
Cafferty, P. S. Bilingualism in America. *In* The Diverse society: implications for social policy p163-76

Bilinî. See Byliny

Bilinsky, Yaroslav

The incorporation of Western Ukraine and its impact on politics and society in Soviet Ukraine. *In* Szporluk, R. ed. The influence of East Europe and the Soviet West on the USSR p180-228

Bill of Rights (United States) See United States. Constitution. 1st-10th amendments

Biller, Henry B. and Meredith, Dennis L.

The invisible American father. *In* Gross, L. ed. Sexual issues in marriage p277-87

Billet, Leonard

Justice, liberty and economy. *In* Glahe, F. R. ed. Adam Smith and The wealth of nations p83-109

Billings, William

About

Crawford, R. A. and McKay, D. P. Music in manuscript: a Massachusetts tune-book of 1782. *In* American Antiquarian Society. Proceedings v84 pt 1 p43-64

Hamm, C. E. The ecstatic and the didactic: a pattern in American music. *In* Current thought in musicology p41-62

Billington, David Perkins

Technology and the structuring of cities. *In* Small comforts for hard times p182-98

About individual works

Technology and the structuring of cities

Salvadori, M. G. The aesthetics of technology: in response to David P. Billington. *In* Small comforts for hard times p199-203

Billington, Ray Allen

Allan Nevins, historian: a personal reminiscence. *In* Nevins, A. Allan Nevins on history p ix-xxvii

Nelson Manfred Blake: pioneering historian. *In* "Remember the ladies": new perspectives on women in American history p xiii-xvi

Billon, S. Alexander

Soviet management structure: stability and change. *In* Evolution of international management structures p114-43

Bills of exchange

Great Britain—History

Munro, J. H. A. Bullionism and the bill of exchange in England, 1272-1663: a study in monetary management and popular prejudice. *In* The Dawn of modern banking p169-239

Bimetallism. See Currency question

Binding sites (Biochemistry). See Immunospecificity

Bindman, David

Blake's theory and practice of imitation. *In* Essick, R. N. and Pearce, D. R. eds. Blake in his time p91-98

Bindoff, Stanley Thomas. See Part 2 under title: Wealth and power in Tudor England

Binford, Lewis Roberts, and Chasko, W. J.

Nunamiut demographic history: a provocative case. *In* Zubrow, E. B. W. ed. Demographic anthropology p63-143

Bingen, Jean

The third-century B.C. land-leases from Tholthis. *In* Illinois classical studies v3, 1978 p74-80

Binham, Philip

New Finnish drama—the fifties and after. *In* Dauenhauer, R. and Binham, P. eds. Snow in May p48-50

Bini (African people)

Ben-Amos, P. Professionals and amateurs in Benin court carving. *In* African images p170-89

Dark, P. J. C. Benin bronze heads: styles and chronology. *In* African images p25-103

Binion, Rudolph

Hitler looks East. *In* DeMause, L. ed. The new psychohistory p181-98

Binkley, Robert Williams

The ultimate justification of moral rules. *In* Fact, value, and perception p53-65

Binkley, Timothy

Consensus and the justification of force. *In* Stanage, S. M. ed. Reason and violence p123-41

Deciding about art. *In* Aagaard-Mogensen, L. ed. Culture and art p90-109

Piece: contra aesthetics. *In* Margolis, J. Z. ed. Philosophy looks at the arts p25-44

Binyon, Timothy John

Valery Bryusov and the nature of art. *In* Oxford Slavonic papers new ser. v7 p96-111

Biochemistry. See Biological chemistry

Bioclimatology. See Bergmann's rule; Man —Influence of climate

Bioengineering. See Human engineering

Bioethics

Blackstone, W. T. Ethics and ecology. *In* Philosophy & environmental crisis p16-42

Davis, B. D. The scientific versus the adversary approach in bio-medical research. *In* Hook, S.; Kurtz, P. and Todorovich, M. eds. The ethics of teaching and scientific research p165-68

Fletcher, J. F. Our duty to the unborn. *In* Fletcher, J. F. Humanhood: essays in biomedical ethics p106-31

Nagel, T. Ethics without biology. *In* Nagel, T. Mortal questions p142-46

Nash, R. Do rocks have rights? Thoughts on environmental ethics. *In* Small comforts for hard times p120-34

Odum, E. P. Environmental ethic and the attitude revolution. *In* Philosophy & environmental crisis p10-15

Siegel, S. An ethical approach to bio-medical research. *In* Hook, S.; Kurtz, P. and Todorovich, M. eds. The ethics of teaching and scientific research p169-73

Walters, L. Genetics, reproductive biology and bioethics. *In* The Tricentennial people p66-74

See also Biology—Social aspects; Human genetics; Medical ethics

Biofeedback training

Schwartz, G. E. Biofeedback and the treatment of disregulation disorders. *In* Sobel, D. S. ed. Ways of health p353-86

Shapiro, D. A biofeedback strategy in the study of consciousness. *In* Alternate states of consciousness p145-57

Biogeography. See Geographical distribution of animals and plants

Biography

Nevins, A. Is history made by heroes? *In* Nevins, A. Allan Nevins on history p168-80

See also Autobiographies; Genealogy

History and criticism

See Biography (as a literary form)

Biology—*Continued*
Philosophy
Ayala, F. J. The concept of biological progress. *In* Ayala, F. J. and Dobzhansky, T. G. eds. Studies in the philosophy of biology p339-54

Beckner, M. Reduction, hierarchies and organicism. *In* Ayala, F. J. and Dobzhansky, T. G. eds. Studies in the philosophy of biology p163-76

Birch, L. C. Chance, necessity and purpose. *In* Ayala, F. J. and Dobzhansky, T. G. eds. Studies in the philosophy of biology p225-39

Bronowski, J. New concepts in the evolution of complexity. *In* Bronowski, J. A sense of the future p175-95.

Bronowski, J. Toward a philosophy of biology. *In* Bronowski, J. A sense of the future p163-74

Campbell, D. T. 'Downward causation' in hierarchically organised biological systems. *In* Ayala, F. J. and Dobzhanksy, T. G. eds. Studies in the philosophy of biology p179-86

Goodfield, G. J. Changing strategies: a comparison of reductionist attitudes in biological and medical research in the nineteenth and twentieth centuries. *In* Ayala, F. J. and Dobzhansky, T. G. eds. Studies in the philosophy of biology p65-86

Hall, D. L. Biology, sex hormones and sexism in the 1920's. *In* Gould, C. C. and Wartofsky, M. W. eds. Women and philosophy p81-96

Holbrook, D. Conclusions. *In* Holbrook, D. Lost bearings in English poetry p217-44

Holbrook, D. Poetry has lost confidence in itself. *In* Holbrook, D. Lost bearings in English poetry p11-24

Monod, J. On chance and necessity. *In* Ayala, F. J. and Dobzhansky, T. G. eds. Studies in the philosophy of biology p357-61

Montalenti, G. From Aristotle to Democritus via Darwin: a short survey of a long historical and logical journey. *In* Ayala, F. J. and Dobzhanksy, T. G. eds. Studies in the philosophy of biology p3-19

Popper, K. R. Scientific reduction and the essential incompleteness of all science. *In* Ayala, F. J. and Dobzhansky, T. G. eds. Studies in the philosophy of biology p259-83

Rensch, B. Polynomistic determination of biological processes. *In* Ayala, F. J. and Dobzhansky, T. G. eds. Studies in the philosophy of biology p241-55

Skolimowski, H. Problems of rationality in biology. *In* Ayala, F. J. and Dobzhansky, T. G. eds. Studies in the philosophy of biology p205-23

Smith, R. C. The human significance of biology: Carpenter, Darwin, and the vera causa. *In* Knoepflmacher, U. C. and Tennyson, G. B. eds. Nature and the Victorian imagination p216-30

Thorpe, W. H. Arthur Koestler and biological thought. *In* Harris, H. A. ed. Astride the two cultures p50-68

Thorpe, W. H. Reductionism in biology. *In* Ayala, F. J. and Dobzhansky, T. G. eds. Studies in the philosophy of biology p109-36

See also Mechanism (Philosophy); Vitalism

Research
See Biological research

Social aspects
Luria, S. E. What can biologists solve? *In* Montagu, A. ed. Race and IQ p42-51

Statistical methods
See Biometry

Russia—History
Adams, M. B. From "gene fund" to "gene pool": on the evolution of evolutionary language. *In* Studies in history of biology v3 p241-85

Biology, Experimental. See Biology—Methodology; Psychobiology, Experimental

Biology, Molecular. See Molecular biology

Biology in art
Wimsatt, W. K. Organic form: some questions about a metaphor. *In* Wimsatt, W. K. Day of the leopards p205-33

Biomathematics. See Biometry

Biomedical engineering
Research
Gaylin, W. The technology of life and death. *In* Small comforts for hard times p152-69

Social aspects
Callahan, D. J. Biomedical progress and the limits of human health. *In* Small comforts for hard times p170-81

Biomedical ethics. See Bioethics; Medical ethics

Biometry
History
MacKenzie, D. and Barnes, B. Scientific judgment: the biometry-Mendelism controversy. *In* Barnes, B. and Shapin, S. eds. Natural order p191-210

Biostatistics. See Biometry

Biosynthesis. See Amino acid synthesis; Nucleic acid synthesis

Biot, Jean Baptiste
About
Frankel, E. J. B. Biot and the mathematization of experimental physics in Napoleonic France. *In* Historical studies in the physical sciences v8 p33-72

Bioy Casares, Adolfo
About individual works
The invention of Morel, and other stories

MacAdam, A. J. Adolfo Bioy Casares: Satire & self-portrait. *In* MacAdam, A. J. Modern Latin American narratives p29-36

A plan for escape

MacAdam, A. J. Adolfo Bioy Casares: The lying compass. *In* MacAdam, A. J. Modern Latin American narratives p37-43

Bipartisanship. Tompkins, C. D. *In* Encyclopedia of American foreign policy p78-89

Biraben, Jean Noel, and Le Goff, Jacques
The plague in the early Middle Ages. *In* Biology of man in history p48-80

Birch, Brian P.
British evaluation of the forest opening and prairie edges of the North-Central states, 1800-1850. *In* The Frontier v2 p167-92

Birch, Charles. See Birch, Louis Charles

Birch, Cyril
Change and continuity in Chinese fiction. *In* Modern Chinese literature in the May Fourth era p385-404

Some concerns and methods of the Ming Ch'uan-ch'i drama. *In* Birch, C. ed. Studies in Chinese literary genres p220-58

Birch, Louis Charles
Chance, necessity and purpose. *In* Ayala, F. J. and Dobzhansky, T. G. eds. Studies in the philosophy of biology p225-39

Bird, Bill. See Bird, William

Bird, Frederick
Charisma and ritual in new religious movements. *In* Needleman, J. and Baker, G. eds. Understanding the new religions p173-89

Bird, William
About
Ford, H. D. Bill Bird and the Three mountains. *In* Ford, H. D. Published in Paris p95-116

Birds, Protection of
Law and legislation—United States
Lofgren, C. A. Missouri v. Holland in historical perspective. *In* The Supreme Court review, 1975 p77-122

Birds in art
McCall, D. F. The hornbill and analogous forms in West African sculpture. *In* African images p269-324

Birds in literature
Chadbourne, R. M. Chateaubriand's aviary: birds in the Mémoires d'outre-tombe. *In* Symbolism and modern literature p65-80

Birdwhistell, Ray L.
Some discussion of ethnography, theory, and method. *In* About Bateson p103-41

Birk, Lee, and Brinkley-Birk, Ann
The learning therapies. *In* Overview of the psychotherapies p51-67

Birnbaum, Eleazar
Turkey: from cosmopolitan Empire to nation state. *In* Savory, R. M. ed. Introduction to Islamic civilisation p179-88

Turkish literature through the ages. *In* Savory, R. M. ed. Introduction to Islamic civilisation p79-87

Birnbaum, Henrik
Lord Novgorod the Great: its place in medieval culture. *In* Viator: medieval and Renaissance studies v8 p215-54

The New York Croato-Glagolitic missal and its background (preliminary communication). *In* California Slavic studies v10 p225-40

The sublimation of grief: poems by two mourning fathers. *In* For Wiktor Weintraub p85-98

Birnbaum, Norman
On the possibility of a new politics in the West. *In* Beyond the crisis p201-32

Birney, Earle
About
Wilson, M. T. Poet without a muse: Earle Birney. *In* Woodcock, G. ed. Poets and critics p26-32

Birom
Social life and customs
Smedley, A. Women of Udu: survival in a harsh land. *In* Matthiasson, C. J. ed. Many sisters p205-28

Birren, James E.
A gerontologist's overview. *In* Jarvik, L. F. ed. Aging into the 21st century p197-208

Birtchnell, John
An analysis of the art productions of a psychiatric patient who was preoccupied with his nose. *In* Ulman, E. and Dachinger, P. eds. Art therapy p328-41

Birth. See Childbirth

Birth (in religion, folk-lore, etc.)
Belmont, N. Levana; or, How to raise up children. *In* Family and society p 1-15
See also Couvade

Birth control
Burton, R. G. A philosopher looks at the population bomb. *In* Philosophy & environmental crisis p105-16

Ris, H. W. The essential emancipation: the control of reproduction. *In* Roberts, J. I. ed. Beyond intellectual sexism p85-110

Stycos, J. M. Some minority opinions on birth control. *In* Population policy and ethics p169-96
See also Abortion; Contraception

Catholic Church
Cohen, C. Sex, birth control, and human life. *In* Baker, R. and Elliston, F. A. eds. Philosophy & sex p150-65

Le Roy Ladurie, E. From Brantôme to Paul VI. *In* Le Roy Ladurie, E. The territory of the historian p235-38

Paulus VI, Pope. Humanae vitae. *In* Baker, R. and Elliston, F. A. eds. Philosophy & sex p131-49

Religious aspects
Dyck, A. J. Religious views. *In* Population policy and ethics p277-323

Byzantine Empire
Patlagean, E. Birth control in the early Byzantine Empire. *In* Biology of man in history p 1-22

France
Le Roy Ladurie, E. From Brantôme to Paul VI. *In* Le Roy Ladurie, E. The territory of the historian p235-38

France—Languedoc
Le Roy Ladurie, E. Demography and the "sinful secrets": the case of Languedoc in the late eighteenth and early nineteenth centuries. *In* Le Roy Ladurie, E. The territory of the historian p239-54

Korea
Rogers, E. M. Network analysis of the diffusion of innovations: family planning in Korean villages. *In* Lerner, D. and Nelson, L. M. eds. Communication research—a half-century appraisal p117-47

United States
Veatch, R. M. and Draper, T. F. The values of physicians. *In* Population policy and ethics p377-408

Birth defects. See Deformities

Birth order
Renshon, S. A. Birth order and political socialization. *In* Schwartz, D. C. and Schwartz, S. K. eds. New directions in political socialization p69-95

Birthmarks
Fife, A. E. Birthmarks and psychic imprinting of babies in Utah folk medicine. *In* American folk medicine p273-83

Bischof, Norbert
Comparative ethology of incest avoidance. *In* Biosocial anthropology p37-67

Bisected brain. See Split brain

Biser, Eugen
Between Inferno and Purgatorio: thoughts on a structural comparison of Nietzsche with Dante. *In* O'Flaherty, J. C.; Sellner, T. F. and Helm, R. M. eds. Studies in Nietzsche and the classical tradition p55-70

Bisexuality. See Homosexuality

Bishirjian, Richard J.
The nature of public philosophy. *In* A Public philosophy reader p17-70

Bishop, Donald Harold
The Bhagavad Gītā. *In* Bishop, D. H. ed. Indian thought p62-80
Buddhism. *In* Bishop, D. H. ed. Indian thought p115-42
Epilogue. *In* Bishop, D. H. ed. Indian thought p364-83
Introduction. *In* Bishop, D. H. ed. Indian thought p13-22

Bishop, Elizabeth
About
Gordon, J. B. Days and distances: the cartographic imagination of Elizabeth Bishop. *In* Boyers, R. ed. Contemporary poetry in America p348-59
Kalstone, D. Elizabeth Bishop: questions of memory, questions of travel. *In* Kalstone, D. Five temperaments p12-40

Bishop, John Peale
About
Coxe, L. O. Romance of the rose: John Peale Bishop and Phelps Putnam. *In* Coxe, L. O. Enabling acts p150-60
Tate, A. John Peale Bishop. *In* Tate, A. Memoirs and opinions, 1926-1974 p69-75

Bishop, Michael
Eyes and seeing in the poetry of Pierre Reverdy. *In* Cardinal, R. ed. Sensibility and creation p57-71

Bishop, Norman
Aspects of European penal systems. *In* Progress in penal reform p83-100

Bishop, Peter Orlebar
Grafton Elliot Smith's contribution to visual neurology and the influence of Thomas Henry Huxley. *In* Grafton Elliot Smith p50-57

Bishops. See Episcopacy; and subdivision Bishops under names of denominations, e.g. Church of England—Bishops

Bissell, Claude Thomas
The place of learning and the arts in Canadian life. *In* Perspectives on revolution and evolution p180-212

Bissell, R. Ward
Concerning the date of Caravaggio's Amore Vincitore. *In* Enggass, R. C. and Stokstad, M. eds. Hortus imaginum p113-23

Bissell, Richard E.
The ostracism of South Africa. *In* The Year book of world affairs, 1978 p139-52
Southern Africa: testing détente. *In* Kirk, G. L. and Wessell, N. H. eds. The Soviet threat p88-98

Bisson, Thomas N.
Credit, prices and agrarian production in Catalonia: a Templar account (1180-1188) *In* Order and innovation in the Middle Ages p87-102
Ramon de Caldes (c.1135-c.1200): Dean of Barcelona and King's Minister. *In* Law, church, and society p281-92

Bitek, Okot p'
About
Ward, M. R. Okot p'Bitek and the rise of East African writing. *In* King, B. A. and Ogungbesan, K. eds. A celebration of Black and African writing p217-31
The **biter:** a late Hellenistic astragal player. Herrmann, A. *In* Studies in classical art and archaeology p163-73

Bitsilli, Pëtr Mikhaĭlovich
From Chekhonte to Chekhov. *In* Erlich, V. ed. Twentieth-century Russian literary criticism p212-18
V. Nabokov's Invitation to a beheading and The eye. *In* A Book of things about Vladimir Nabokov p65-69

Bittker, Boris I.
Identifying the beneficiaries; excerpt from 'The case for Black reparations." *In* Gross, B. R. ed. Reverse discrimination p279-87

Bitzer, Lloyd F.
Rhetoric and public knowledge. *In* Burks, D. M. ed. Rhetoric, philosophy, and literature: an exploration p67-93
The rhetorical situation. *In* Rhetoric: a tradition in transition p247-60

Bjork, Kenneth O.
The Norwegians in America: "giants in the earth." *In* The Immigrant experience in America p63-94

Bjørnson, Bjørnstjerne
About
Skard, S. Bjørnstjerne Bjørnson and Halvdan Koht. *In* Abroad in America: Visitors to the new Nation, 1776-1914 p195-206

Bjornson, Richard
The picaresque hero in European fiction
Contents
The ambiguous success of the picaresque hero in Defoe's Moll Flanders
The birth of the picaresque: Lazarillo de Tormes and the socializing process
El buscón: Quevedo's annihilation of the picaresque
The dissemination of the picaresque: Guzmán de Alfarache and the converso problem
In the wake of Guzmán: variations on the picaresque-life theme
The picaresque hero arrives: sentiment and success in LeSage's Gil Blas
The picaresque hero as young nobleman: victimization and vindication in Smollett's Roderick Random
Translations & transitions
The universality of the picaresque: visions of truth in Grimmelshausen's Simplicissimus
The waning of the Spanish picaresque: El diablo cojuelo and Estebanillo González

Bjorvand, Einar
Spenser's defence of poetry: some structural aspects of the Fowre Hymnes. *In* Røstvig, M. S. ed. Fair forms p13-53

Blachère, Gérard
Innovative building technology in developed and developing countries. *In* Strategies for human settlements: habitat and environment p142-44

Blachernae Palace, Istanbul. See Istanbul. Blachernae Palace

Black, Cyril Edwin
The Great Society in a little America? Political and social values and institutions. *In* Isolation or interdependence? p81-102

Black, Donald J.
A strategy of pure sociology. *In* McNall, S. G. ed. Theoretical perspectives in sociology p149-68

Black, Hugo LaFayette

About
White, G. E. The mosaic of the Warren Court: Frankfurter, Black, Warren and Harlan. *In* White, G. E. The American judicial tradition p317-68

Black, James
The unfolding of 'Measure for measure'. *In* Shakespeare survey 26 p119-28

Black, John

About
Shackleton, R. John Black and Montesquieu—the search for a correspondence. *In* Evidence in literary scholarship p215-27

Black, Joseph, 1728-1799
Donovan, A. L. Toward a social history of technological ideas: Joseph Black, James Watt, and the separate condenser. *In* Bugliarello, G. and Doner, D. B. eds. The history and philosophy of technology p19-30

About
Guerlac, H. Joseph Black. *In* Guerlac, H. Essays and papers in the history of modern science p285-303

Black, Kenneth, and Wilson, Robert O.
The environment of management in the future. *In* Benton, L. R. ed. Management for the future p9-26

Black, Matthew Wilson
Notes on the longer and the shorter text of Acts. *In* On language, culture, and religion: in honor of Eugene A. Nida p119-31

Black, Max
More about metaphor. *In* Ortony, A. ed. Metaphor and thought p19-43
Some tasks for 'the humanities'. *In* Niblett, W. R. ed. The sciences, the humanities and the technological threat p79-89

Black, Sir Misha
The designer and manager syndrome. *In* The Uneasy coalition: design in corporate America p41-55

Black, R. D. Collison
Smith's contribution in historical perspective. *In* The Market and the state p42-63

Black, Shirley (Temple)

About
Boring, P. Z. Shirley Temple: super child. *In* Browne, R. B. and Fishwick, M. W. eds. Icons of America p100-11

Black, Stephen

About individual works
Mind and body
Koestler, A. Hypnotic horizons. *In* Koestler, A. The heel of Achilles p81-86

Black, Virginia
The erosion of legal principles in the creation of legal policies. *In* Gross, B. R. ed. Reverse discrimination p163-83

Black, William

About
Hart, F. R. Late Victorian Celticisms. *In* Hart, F. R. The Scottish novel p336-47

Black Africa. See Africa, Sub-Saharan

Black Americans. See Afro-Americans

Black art. See Witchcraft

Black comedy (Literature) See Black humor (Literature)

Black death
Dols, M. W. The comparative communal responses to the Black Death in Muslim and Christian societies. *In* Viator: medieval and Renaissance studies v5 p269-87

Black drama (African) See African drama

Black drama (American) See American drama—Afro-American authors

Black Elk, Oglala Indian

About
Brown, J. E. Hanblecheyapi: Crying for a vision; excerpt from "The sacred pipe." *In* Tedlock, D. E. and Tedlock, B. eds. Teachings from the American earth p20-41

Black English
Chennault, S. D. Black dialect: a cultural shock. *In* Minority language and literature p71-79
Gates, H. L. Dis and dat: dialect and the descent. *In* Fisher, D. and Stepto, R. B. eds. Afro-American literature p88-119
Jackson, B. A review of J. L. Dillard's Black English. *In* Jackson, B. The waiting years p146-54
Kochman, T. "Rapping" in the Black ghetto. *In* Henslin, J. M. ed. Deviant lifestyles p39-58

Black fiction (African) See African fiction

Black fiction (American) See American fiction—Afro-American authors

Black folk-lore. See Folk-lore, Black

Black humor (Literature)
Scholes, R. E. Comedy and grotesquerie. *In* Scholes, R. E. Fabulation and metafiction p139-92
Schulz, M. F. Toward a definition of black humor; excerpt from "Black humor fiction of the sixties." *In* Cohen, S. B. ed. Comic relief p14-27

Black literature (African). See African literature

Black literature (American) See American literature—Afro-American authors

Black literature (Ecuadorian) See Ecuadorian literature—Black authors

Black literature (French) See French literature—Black authors

Black literature (Latin American) See Latin American literature—Black authors

Black literature (South African) See South African literature (English)—Black authors

Black Manikin Bookshop. See Black Manikin Press

Black Manikin Press
Ford, H. D. Edward Titus at the Sign of the Black Manikin. *In* Ford, H. D. Published in Paris p117-67

Black Mass. See Satanism

Black militant organizations

United States

Brisbane, R. H. Black protest in America. *In* The Black American reference book p537-79

Smithey, R. A. The new militancy and its impact on the Afro-American middle class. *In* Johnson, H. A. ed. Negotiating the mainstream p196-216

Black Mountain College, Black Mountain, N.C.

Thurley, G. Black Mountain academy: Charles Olson as critic and poet. *In* Thurley, G. The American moment p126-38

The Black Mountain Review

Creeley, R. On Black Mountain Review; excerpt from "Was that a real poem & other essay." *In* Anderson, E. and Kinzie, M. eds. The little magazine in America: a modern documentary history p248-79

Black nationalism

Stuckey, S. David Walker and the ideological origins of Black nationalism. *In* African themes p25-45

South Africa

Carter, G. M. South Africa: battleground of rival nationalisms. *In* Carter, G. M. and O'Meara, P. eds. Southern Africa in crisis p89-135

Black Panther Party

Parry, A. Fanon and the Black Panthers. *In* Parry, A. Terrorism: from Robespierre to Arafat p301-21

Black poetry (African) See African poetry

Black poetry (American) See American poetry—Afro-American authors

Black poetry (Cuban) See Cuban poetry—Black authors

Black poetry (South African) See South African poetry (English)—Black authors

Black poetry (Spanish American) See Spanish American poetry—Black authors

Black power

See also Black nationalism

United States

Benson, J. K. A power strategy. *In* Lauer, R. H. ed. Social movements and social change p107-20

Black race in literature. See Blacks in literature

Black Sea

Holt, S. J. Mediterranean and Black Sea fisheries. *In* Borgese, E. M. and Krieger, D. eds. The tides of change p166-78

Black separatism. See Black nationalism

Black short stories. See Short stories, American—Afro-American authors

Black studies. See Afro-American studies

Black Sun Press

Ford, H. D. Harry and Caresse Crosby and the Black sun. *In* Ford, H. D. Published in Paris p168-230

Black theology

Boesak, A. Coming in out of the wilderness. *In* The Emergent gospel p76-95

Black whale. See Sperm whale

Blackfaced minstrel shows. See Minstrel shows

Blackmore, Richard White

About

Everitt, M. R. W. Blackmore (1791-(1791-1882) an English chaplain in Cronstadt. *In* Oxford Slavonic papers, new ser. v10 p98-106

Blacks

Snowden, F. M. Ethiopians and the Graeco-Roman world. *In* Kilson, M. L. and Rotberg, R. I. eds. The African diaspora p11-36

See also Afro-Americans

Folk-lore

See Folk-lore, Black

Race identity

Case, F. I. Négritude and utopianism *In* African literature today no. 7: Focus on criticism p65-75

Dixon, M. Rivers remembering their source: comparative studies in Black literary history—Langston Hughes, Jacques Roumain, and négritude. *In* Fisher, D. and Stepto, R. B. eds. Afro-American literature p25-43

Dorsinville, M. Senghor or the song of exile. *In* Exile and tradition p62-73

Knight, V. W. Haiti and Martinique. *In* King, B. and Ogungbesan, K. eds. A celebration of Black and African writing p46-59

Religion

See Black theology

America

Szwed, J. F. and Abrahams, R. D. After the myth: studying Afro-American cultural patterns in the plantation literature. *In* Crowley, D. J. ed. African folklore in the New World p65-86

Arab countries—History

Lewis, B. The African diaspora and the civilization of Islam. *In* Kilson, M. L. and Rotberg, R. I. eds. The African diaspora p37-56

Brazil

Béhague, G. H. Notes on regional and national trends in Afro-Brazilian cult music. *In* Forster, M. H. ed. Tradition and renewal p68-80

Conrad, R. Nineteenth-century Brazilian slavery *In* Toplin, R. B. ed. Slavery and race relations in Latin America p146-75

Corwin, A. F. Afro-Brazilians: myths and realities *In* Toplin, R. B. ed. Slavery and race relations in Latin America p385-437

Fernandes, F. Beyond poverty: the Negro and the mulatto in Brazil *In* Toplin, R. B. ed. Slavery and race relations in Latin America p277-97

MacLachlan, C. M. African slave trade and economic development in Amazonia, 1700-1800 *In* Toplin, R. B. ed. Slavery and race relations in Latin America p112-45

Toplin, R. B. Abolition and the issue of the Black freedman's future in Brazil *In* Toplin, R. B. ed. Slavery and race relations in Latin America p253-76

Brazil—Religion

Sturm, F. G. Afro-Brazilian cults. *In* African religions: a symposium p217-39

Caribbean area

Hoetink, H. The cultural links. *In* Crahan, M. E. and Knight, F. W. eds. Africa and the Caribbean p20-40

Blacks in literature—*Continued*

Wynter, S. The eye of the other: images of the Black in Spanish literature. *In* DeCosta, M. ed. Blacks in Hispanic literature p8-19

Young, A. V. The Black woman in Afro-Caribbean poetry. *In* DeCosta, M. ed. Blacks in Hispanic literature p137-42

Blacksmithing

Rome

Manning, W. H. Blacksmithing. *In* Strong, D. E. and Brown, D. eds. Roman crafts p143-53

Blackstone, Sir William

About

Sutherland, L. S. William Blackstone and the legal chairs at Oxford. *In* Evidence in literary scholarship p229-40

About individual works

Commentaries on the laws of England

Raeff, M. The Empress and the Vinerian Professor: Catherine II's projects of government reforms and Blackstone's Commentaries. *In* Oxford Slavonic papers new ser. v7 p18-41

Blackstone, William T.

Ethics and ecology. *In* Philosophy & environmental crisis p16-42

Reverse discrimination and compensatory justice. *In* Social justice & preferential treatment p52-83

Blackwell, James E.

The power basis of ethnic conflict in American society. *In* The Uses of controversy in sociology p179-96

Blackwell, Thomas

About individual works

An enquiry into the life and writings of Homer

Simonsuuri, K. Thomas Blackwell: the problem of Homer's genius. *In* Simonsuuri, K. Homer's original genius p99-107

Blackwell, William L.

Modernization and urbanization in Russia: a comparative view. *In* Hamm, M. F. ed. The city in Russian history p291-330

Blackwood, Algernon

About

Sullivan, J. The visionary ghost story: Algernon Blackwood. *In* Sullivan, J. Elegant nightmares p112-29

Blair, Eric Arthur. See Orwell, George

Blair, Ron

About

Morley. P. A. 'In God's name': ironic forms of religious drama in Canada and Australia. *In* Narasimhaiah, C. D. ed. Awakened conscience p275-83

Blair, Walter

"The big bear of Arkansas": T.B. Thorpe and his masterpiece. *In* Inge, M. T. ed. The frontier humorists p105-17

Humor of the Old Southwest; excerpt from "Native American humor." *In* Inge, M. T. ed. The frontier humorists p45-82

Blaise, Clark

The Commonwealth writer and his material. *In* Narasimhaiah, C. D. ed. Awakened conscience. p118-26

Blake, John B.

Health reform. *In* The Rise of Adventism p30-49

Blake, Nelson Manfred

About

Billington, R. A. Nelson Manfred Blake: pioneering historian. *In* "Remember the ladies": new perspectives on women in American history p xiii-xvi

Blake, Nicholas, pseud. See Day-Lewis, Cecil

Blake, Norman Francis

Coleridge's poetic language. *In* Davies, R. T. and Beatty, B. G. eds. Literature of the romantic period, 1750-1850 p72-81

The dating of Old English poetry. *In* An English miscellany p14-27

The genesis of The Battle of Maldon. *In* Anglo-Saxon England 7 p119-29

Middle English alliterative revivals. *In* Review, v 1 1979 p205-14

The relationship between the Hengwrt and Ellesmere manuscripts of the 'Canterbury tales.' *In* English Association. Essays and studies, 1979 p 1-18

Varieties of Middle English religious prose. *In* Chaucer and Middle English studies in honour of Rossell Hope Robbins p348-56

Blake, William

About

Bindman, D. Blake's theory and practice of imitation. *In* Essick, R. N. and Pearce, D. R. eds. Blake in his time p91-98

Bloom, H. Blake and revisionism. *In* Bloom, H. Poetry and repression p28-51

Brisman, L. Re: generation in Blake. *In* Brisman, L. Romantic origins p224-75

Butlin, M. Cataloguing William Blake. *In* Essick, R. N. and Pearce, D. R. eds. Blake in his time p77-90

Christian, D. Inversion and the erotic: the case of William Blake. *In* Babcock, B. A. ed. The reversible world p117-28

Cooke, M. G. The will to art: Logic, vision, and actuality: the state of art in Blake. *In* Cooke, M. G. The romantic will p187-201

Davie, D. Dissent and the Wesleyans, 1740-1800. *In* Davie, D. A gathered Church p37-54

Easson, K. P. Blake and the art of the book. *In* Essick, R. N. and Pearce, D. R. eds. Blake in his time p35-52

Easson, R. R. Blake and the Gothic. *In* Essick, R. N. and Pearce, D. R. eds. Blake in his time p145-54

Essick, R. N. Preludium: meditations on a fiery Pegasus. *In* Essick, R. N. and Pearce, D. N. eds. Blake in his time p 1-10

Gleckner, R. F. Most holy forms of thought: some observations on Blake and language. *In* ELH essays for Earl R. Wasserman p262-84

Hagstrum, J. H. Blake and British art: the gifts of grace and terror. *In* Kroeber, K. and Walling, W. eds. Images of romanticism p61-80

Hagstrum, J. H. Romney and Blake: gifts of grace and terror. *In* Essick, R. N. and Pearce, D. R. eds. Blake in his time p201-12

James, G. I. Blake's mixed media: a mixed blessing. *In* English Association. Essays and studies, 1977 p 61-69

Blake, William—About—*Continued*

Knights, L. C. Early Blake. *In* Knights, L. C. Explorations 3 p52-63

La Belle, J. Blake's visions and re-visions of Michelangelo. *In* Essick, R. N. and Pearce, D. R. eds. Blake in his time p13-22

Marks, M. Renovation of form: time as hero in Blake's major prophecies. *In* Studies in eighteenth-century culture v5 p55-66

Mellor, A. K. Physiognomy, phrenology, and Blake's visionary heads. *In* Essick, R. N. and Pearce, D. R. eds. Blake in his time p53-74

Paley, M. D. "Wonderful originals"—Blake and ancient sculpture. *In* Essick, R. N. and Pearce, D. R. eds. Blake in his time p170-97

Rose, E. J. The "Gothicized imagination" of "Michelangelo Blake." *In* Essick, R. N. and Pearce, D. R. eds. Blake in his time p155-69

Sherry, P. M. The "predicament" of the autograph: "William Blake." *In* Glyph 4 p131-55

Suvin, D. The shift to anticipation: radical rhapsody and romantic recoil. *In* Suvin, D. Metamorphoses of science fiction p115-44

Tannenbaum, L. Blake and the iconography of Cain. *In* Essick, R. N. and Pearce, D. R. eds. Blake in his time p23-34

Wittreich, J. A. Painted prophecies: the tradition of Blake's illuminated books. *In* Essick, R. N. and Pearce, D. R. eds. Blake in his time p101-15

About individual works
The book of Urizen

Kittel, H. A. The book of Urizen and An essay concerning human understanding. *In* Phillips, M. C. ed. Interpreting Blake p111-44

Designs to a series of ballads

Mulhallen, K. G. 'For friendship's sake': some additions to Blake's sheets for Designs to a series of ballads (1802). *In* Virginia. University. Bibliographical Society. Studies in bibliography v29 p331-41

For children: The gates of paradise

Parisi, F. M. Emblems of melancholy: For children: The gates of paradise. *In* Phillips, M. C. ed. Interpreting Blake p70-110

The four Zoas

DiSalvo, J. Blake encountering Milton: politics and the family in Paradise lost and The four Zoas. *In* Wittreich, J. A. ed. Milton and the line of vision p143-84

[Illustrations of the] Book of Enoch

Bentley, G. E. A jewel in an Ethiop's ear. *In* Essick, R. N. and Pearce, D. R. eds. Blake in his time p213-40

[Illustrations of the] Book of Job

Frye, N. Blake's reading of the Book of Job. *In* Frye, N. Spiritus mundi p228-44

An island in the moon

England, M. W. The satiric Blake: apprenticeship at the Haymarket? *In* Wimsatt, W. K. ed. Literary criticism: idea and act p483-505

Jerusalem

Cooke, M. G. The extremes of self and system: Blake's Jerusalem: a self without selfhood, a system against system. *In* Cooke, M. G. The romantic will p118-44

Ferguson, J. P. Prefaces to Jerusalem. *In* Phillips, M. C. ed. Interpreting Blake p164-95

London (I wander thro' each charter'd street)

Hill, A. A. Imagery and meaning: a passage from Lycidas and a poem by Blake. *In* Hill, A. A. Constituent and pattern in poetry p71-82

Thompson, E. P. 'London.' *In* Phillips, M. C. ed. Interpreting Blake p5-31

Milton

Butter, P. H. Milton: the final plates. *In* Phillips, M. C. ed. Interpreting Blake p145-63

Milton (The Bard's song)

Carothers, Y. M. Space and time in Milton: the "Bard's song." *In* Essick, R. N. and Pearce, D. R. eds. Blake in his time p116-27

Songs of innocence and experience

Dyson, A. E. and Lovelock, J. The road of excess: Blake's Songs of innocence and experience. *In* Dyson, A. E. and Lovelock, J. Masterful images p125-35

Glen, H. Blake's criticism of moral thinking in Songs of innocence and of experience. *In* Phillips, M. C. ed. Interpreting Blake p32-69

Shrimpton, N. Hell's hymnbook: Blake's Songs of innocence and of experience and their models. *In* Davies, R. T. and Beatty, B. G. eds. Literature of the romantic period, 1750-1850 p19-35

The tiger

Epstein, E. L. The self-reflexive artefact: the function of mimesis in an approach to a theory of value for literature. *In* Fowler, R. ed. Style and structure in literature p40-78

Trilling, L. William Blake: Tyger! Tyger! *In* Trilling, L. Prefaces to The experience of literature p215-19

Autographs

Sherry, P. M. The "predicament" of the autograph: "William Blake." *In* Glyph 4 p131-55

Books and reading

Adams, H. Revisiting Reynold's [sic] Discourses and Blake's annotations. *In* Essick, R. N. and Pearce, D. R. eds. Blake in his time p128-44

Influence

Heffernan, J. A. W. Politics and freedom: refractions of Blake in Joyce Cary and Allen Ginsberg. *In* Bornstein, G. ed. Romantic and modern p177-95

Sources

Beer, J. B. Influence and independence in Blake. *In* Interpreting Blake p196-261

Bloom, H. Blake and revisionism. *In* Bloom, H. Poetry and repression p28-51

Blakemore, Colin

The baffled brain. *In* Gregory, R. L. and Gombrich, Sir E. H. J. eds. Illusion in nature and art p9-47

Blakemore, Michael Howell

About

Brustein, R. S. The prevalence of style: The cherry orchard. *In* Brustein, R. S. The culture watch p108-11

Blalock, Hubert M.

About

Lemert, C. C. Theory constructionism: Hubert Blalock. *In* Lemert, C. C. Sociology and the twilight of man p51-79

Blanchard, Lydia

Mothers and daughters in D. H. Lawrence: The rainbow and selected shorter works. *In* Smith, A. ed. Lawrence and women p75-100

Blanchard, Margaret A.

The institutional press and its First Amendment privileges. *In* The Supreme Court review, 1978 p225-96

Blanckenhagen, Peter Heinrich von

About

Winternitz, E. Peter H. Von Blanckenhagen. *In* Studies in classical art and archaeology p xi-xiv

Bland, Edith (Nesbit)

About

Prickett, S. Worlds within worlds: Kipling and Nesbit. *In* Prickett, S. Victorian fantasy p198-239

Blank, H. Robert

Anticipatory grief and mourning. *In* Anticipatory grief p276-80

Blank, Irwin M.

Anticipatory grief. *In* Anticipatory grief p343-45

Blank, Stephen

Britain's economic problems: lies and damn lies. *In* Kramnick, I. ed. Is Britain dying? p66-88

Blanshard, Brand

Democracy and distinction in American education. *In* McMurrin, S. M. ed. On the meaning of the university p29-49

Practical reason: reason and feeling in 20th-century ethics. *In* The Abdication of philosophy: philosophy and the public good p49-65

Blanshard, Paul

Public money and Church schools: two Supreme Court decisions. *In* Fairfield, R. P. ed. Humanistic frontiers in American education p94-101

Blasier, Cole

COMECON in Cuban development. *In* Cuba in the world p225-55

The Soviet Union in the Cuban-American conflict. *In* Cuba in the world p37-51

Blasing, Mutlu Konuk

The art of life

Contents

Coda: new life in a New World

The economies of Walden

Frank O'Hara and the poetics of love

Henry Adams, connoisseur of chaos

Henry James's prefaces, or The story of the stories

Introduction: The form of history and the history of form

Paterson: notes toward an American revolution

"Walt Whitman, a kosmos, of Manhattan the son"

The story of the stories: Henry James's Prefaces as autobiography. *In* Landow, G. P. ed. Approaches to Victorian autobiography p311-32

Blastomycetic dermatitis. See Blastomycosis

Blastomycosis

Harvey, A. M. Two mycoses first described at Johns Hopkins. *In* Harvey, A. M. Adventures in medical research p32-38

Blatty, William Peter

About individual works

The exorcist

Barclay, G. S. Orthodox horrors: Charles Williams and William P. Blatty. *In* Barclay, G. S. Anatomy of horror: the masters of occult fiction p97-110

Blau, Joseph Leon

On the supposedly Aristotelian character of Gabirol's Keter malkut. *In* Salo Wittmayer Baron v 1 p219-28

Science and social progress. *In* Philosophy and the civilizing arts p166-77

Blau, Peter Michael

Parameters of social structure. *In* Blau, P. M. ed. Approaches to the study of social structure p220-53

Structural constraints of status complements. *In* The Idea of social structure p117-38

Blau, Thomas

Consultations in NATO during and after the October War. *In* International terrorism and world security p234-47

Plowshare, proliferation, and the N+1 country. *In* International terrorism and world security p118-30

Blau DuPlessis, Rachel

The critique of consciousness and myth in Levertov, Rich, and Rukeyser. *In* Gilbert, S. M. and Gubar, S. eds. Shakespeare's sisters p280-300

Blaug, Mark

The economics of education in English classical political economy: a re-examination. *In* Skinner, A. S. and Wilson, T. eds. Essays on Adam Smith p568-99

Blavatsky, Helene Petrovna (Hahn-Hahn)

About

Ellwood, R. S. Colonel Olcott and Madame Blavatsky journey to the East. *In* Ellwood, R. S. Alternative altars p104-35

Blaydon, Colin C. and Stack, Carol B.

Income support policies and the family. *In* Rossi, A. S.; Kagan, J. and Hareven, T. K. eds. The family p147-62

Bleandonu, Gérard, and Le Gaufey, Guy

The creation of the insane asylums of Auxerre and Paris. *In* Deviants and the abandoned in French society p180-212

Bleau, N. Arthur

Robert Frost's favorite poem. *In* Frost: centennial essays III p174-77

Blechman, Elaine A. and Manning, Martha

A reward-cost analysis of the single-parent family. *In* Behavior modification and families p61-90

Bleeth, Kenneth Alan

The image of paradise in The merchant's tale. *In* The Learned and the lewed p45-60

Blegvad, Mogens, and Jeppesen, Steen Leth
Danish universities in transition. *In* Universities in the Western world p181-94

Bleichröder family
Landes, D. S. Bleichröders and Rothschilds: the problem of continuity in the family firm. *In* Rosenberg, C. E. ed. The family in history p95-114
Stern, F. R. Capitalism and the cultural historian. *In* From Parnassus p209-24

Bleier, Ruth H.
Brain, body, and behavior. *In* Roberts, J. I. ed. Beyond intellectual sexism p63-73

Bleikasten, André
The heresy of Flannery O'Connor. *In* Johnson, I. D. and Johnson, C. [eds.] Les américanistes p53-70

Blessing, Richard Allen
The shape of the psyche: vision and technique in the late poems of Sylvia Plath. *In* Lane, G. ed. Sylvia Plath p57-73

Blickling homilies
Aronstam, R. A. The Blickling homilies: a reflection of popular Anglo-Saxon belief. *In* Law, church, and society p271-80

Blimps. See Air-ships

Blish, James
Cathedrals in space; excerpt from "The issue at hand." *In* Knight, D. F. ed. Turning points p144-62

Blishen, Edward
Reflections and recollections. *In* Egoff, S. A. ed. One ocean touching p121-30

Bliss, Michael D.
John Warburton as antiquary and collector: evidence from the sale catalogue of his collection. *In* Virginia. University. Bibliographical Society. Studies in bibliography v29 p296-306

Blixen, Karen

About individual works
Last tales
Welty, E. Isak Dinesen's Last tales. *In* Welty, E. The eye of the story p261-63

Out of Africa
Lessing, D. M. A deep darkness: a review of Out of Africa by Karen Blixen. *In* Lessing, D. M. A small personal voice p147-52

The sailor-boy's tale
Trilling, L. Isak Dinesen: The sailor-boy's tale. *In* Trilling, L. Prefaces to The experience of literature p141-44

Bliznakov, Milka
Urban planning in the USSR: integrative theories. *In* Hamm, M. F. ed. The city in Russian history p243-56

Bloch, Adèle
Dom Juan and Don Giovanni. *In* Johnson, R. B.; Neumann, E. S. and Trail, G. T. eds. Molière and the commonwealth of letters: patrimony and posterity p287-98

Bloch, Ernest
About
Sessions, R. Ernest Bloch. *In* Sesssions, R. Roger Sessions on music p329-38

Block, Haskell M.
The concept of influence in comparative literature. *In* Primeau, R. ed. Influx p74-81
Heine and the French symbolists. *In* Creative encounter p25-39

Block, Richard L. and Ross, David J.
A technique for utilizing precoded variables in the review of programs in criminal justice research. *In* Riedel, M. and Chappell, D. eds. Issues in criminal justice: planning and evaluation p24-35

Blockade
Merli, F. J. and Ferrell, R. H. Blockades and quarantines. *In* Encyclopedia of American foreign policy p90-103
See also Continental system of Napoleon; Embargo

Blockage in the literature of the sublime, The notion of. Hertz, N. *In* Hartman, G. H. ed. Psychoanalysis and the question of the text p62-85

Blodgett, Edward Dickinson
The masks of D. G. Jones. *In* Woodcock, G. ed. Poets and critics p159-78

Blodgett, Geoffrey
A new look at the Gilded Age: politics in a cultural context. *In* Howe, D. W. ed. Victorian America p95-108

Blok, Aleksandr Aleksandrovich
On the mission of the poet. *In* Proffer, C. R. ed. Modern Russian poets on poetry p71-80

About
Kostka, E. K. Blok, Schiller, and the Bolshevik revolution. *In* Kostka, E. K. Glimpses of Germanic-Slavic relations from Pushkin to Heinrich Mann p55-68
Mandel'shtam, O. E. Badger's burrow. *In* Mandel'shtam, O. E. Selected essays p89-93
Thomson, B. The necessity of art: the last years of Aleksandr Blok. *In* Thomson, B. Lot's wife and the Venus of Milo p29-52
Weidle, W. The poison of modernism. *In* Gibian, G. and Tjalsma, H. W. eds. Russian modernism p18-30
Zhirmunskiĭ, V. M. The passion of Aleksandr Blok. *In* Erlich, V. ed. Twentieth-century Russian literary criticism p117-37

Blok, Alexander. See Blok, Aleksandr Aleksandrovich

Blom-Cooper, Louis Jacques
The constitutional framework of the English penal system. *In* Progress in penal reform p25-34
Sentencing structure: a paradigm for the future. *In* Progress in penal reform p174-81

Blomquist, Thomas W.
The dawn of banking in an Italian commune: thirteenth century Lucca. *In* The Dawn of modern banking p53-75

Blood
Circulation—Research
See Cardiovascular research

Diseases
Harvey, A. M. Hematological firsts at Hopkins. *In* Harvey, A. M. Adventures in medical research p288-313

Examination
See Blood—Diseases

Groups
See Blood groups

Blood groups
Sunderland, E. Biological components of the races of man. *In* Racial variation in man p9-25

Blood of the condor (Motion picture)
Kauffmann, S. Blood of the condor. *In* Kauffmann, S. Living images p213-15

Bloom, Allan
A response to President McGill. *In* Hook, S.; Kurtz, P. W. and Todorovich, M. eds. The university and the state: what role for government in higher education? p155-61

Bloom, Claire

About

Brustein, R. S. The evolution of a woman: A doll's house. *In* Brustein, R. S. The culture watch p79-81

Bloom, Edward A. and Bloom, Lillian D.
Steele and his answerers: May 1709-February 1714. *In* The Dress of words p167-97

Bloom, Harold
Clinamen, or Poetic misprision; excerpt from "The anxiety of influence." *In* Primeau, R. ed. Influx p82-99

Coleridge: the anxiety of influence. *In* Wimsatt, W. K. ed. Literary criticism: idea and act p506-20

The freshness of transformation: Emerson's dialectics of influence. *In* Levin, D. ed. Emerson: prophecy, metamorphosis, and influence p129-48

John Ashbery: the charity of the hard moments. *In* Boyers, R. ed. Contemporary poetry in America p110-38

Poetry and repression

Contents

Blake and revisionism
Browning: good moments and ruined quests
Emerson and Whitman: the American sublime
Keats: romance revised
Poetry, revisionism, repression
Shelley and his precursors
Tennyson: in the shadow of Keats
Wallace Stevens: the transcendental strain
Wordsworth and the scene of instruction
Yeats, Gnosticism, and the sacred void

About individual works
The anxiety of influence

Hartman, G. H. War in heaven. *In* Hartman, G. H. The fate of reading p41-56

Nemerov, H. Figures of thought. *In* Nemerov, H. Figures of thought p18-29

Watkins, E. Charles Tomlinson: the poetry of experience. *In* Watkins, E. The critical act p95-137

Bloom, Lillian D.
Addison's popular aesthetic: the rhetoric of the Paradise lost papers. *In* Martz, L. L. and Williams, A. L. eds. The author in his work p263-81

See also Bloom, E. A. jt. auth.

Bloom, Lois
Language development. *In* Wardhaugh, R. and Brown, H. D. eds. A survey of applied linguistics p8-43

Bloomfield, Arthur Irving
Adam Smith and the theory of international trade. *In* Skinner, A. S. and Wilson, T. eds. Essays on Adam Smith p455-81

Bloomfield, Lincoln Palmer
BELLEX—the Bellagio "mini-game." *In* Unofficial diplomats p222-40

Bloomfield, Maxwell H.
American lawyers in a changing society, 1776-1876
Contents
Antilawyer sentiment in the early Republic
Conclusion
The family in antebellum law
Frederick Grimké and the dynamics of social change
John Mercer Langston and the training of Black lawyers
Peter Van Schaack and the problem of allegiance
Riot control in Philadelphia
Upgrading the professional image
William Pitt Ballinger, Confederate lawyer
William Sampson and the codification movement

Bloomfield, Morton Wilfred
The merchant's tale: a tragicomedy of the neglect of counsel—the limits of art. *In* Medieval and Renaissance studies [1975] p37-50

The problem of the hero in the later medieval period. *In* Concepts of the hero in the Middle Ages and the Renaissance p27-48

Quoting and alluding: Shakespeare in the English language. *In* Shakespeare: aspects of influence p 1-20

Bloomfield, Richard Joseph
The inter-American system: does it have a future? *In* Farer, T. J. ed. The future of the inter-American system p3-19

The new dialogue with Latin America and the Working Group on Transnational Enterprises: Calvo versus Hickenlooper. *In* Farer, T. J. ed. The future of the inter-American system p73-80

Blotner, Joseph Leo
Raintree County revisited. *In* Filler, L. ed. A question of quality: popularity and value in modern creative writing p204-12

Romantic elements in Faulkner. *In* Bornstein, G. ed. Romantic and modern p207-21

The sole owner and proprietor. *In* Faulkner: fifty years after The marble faun p 1-20

About individual works
Faulkner: a biography

Gass, W. H. Mr. Blotner, Mr. Feaster, and Mr. Faulkner. *In* Gass, W. H. The world within the word p45-62

Blount, Trevor
Dickens and Mr Krook's spontaneous combustion. *In* Dickens Studies Annual v1 p183-211

Blow-job (Motion picture)
Koch, S. Blow-job and pornography. *In* Nichols, B. ed. Movies and methods p305-09

Blow-up (Motion picture)
Samuels, C. T. The blow-up: sorting things out. *In* Samuels, C. T. Mastering the film, and other essays p119-35

Blue Suede Shoes (Periodical)
Abbott, K. Blue Suede Shoes, issue 379 (the Babe Ruth essay). *In* Anderson, E. and Kinzie, M. eds. The little magazine in America: a documentary history p473-81

Bluebond-Langner, Myra Honore
I know, do you? A study of awareness, communication, and coping in terminally ill children. *In* Anticipatory grief p171-81

Meanings of death to children. *In* Feifel, H. [ed.] New meanings of death p47-66

Blues (Songs, etc.)

Harrison, D. D. Black women in the blues tradition. *In* Harley, S. and Terborg-Penn, R. eds. The Afro-American woman p58-73

Hyman, S. E. The blues. *In* Hyman, S. E. The critic's credentials p147-68

Hyman, S. E. Really the blues. *In* Hyman, S. E. The critic's credentials p169-82

Oster, H. The blues as a genre. *In* Folklore genres p59-75

Book reviews

Hyman, S. E. The blues. *In* Hyman, S. E. The critic's credentials p147-68

Hyman, S. E. Really the blues. *In* Hyman, S. E. The critic's credentials p169-82

Influence

Oliver, P. Blue-eyed blues: the impact of blues on European popular culture. *In* Bigsby, C. W. E. ed. Approaches to popular culture p227-39

Williams, S. A. The blues roots of contemporary Afro-American poetry. *In* Fisher, D. and Stepto, R. B. eds. Afro-American literature p72-87

Bluestone, Irving

Work humanization in practice: what can labor do? *In* Heisler, W. J. and Houck, J. W. eds. A matter of dignity p165-78

Bluestone, Naomi

"He's a sick man—he belongs in the hospital." *In* Home care p90-97

Blum, Jerome

Russia. *In* Spring, D. ed. European landed elites in the nineteenth century p68-97

Blum, Larry and others

Altruism and women's oppression. *In* Gould, C. C. and Wartofsky, M. W. eds. Women and philosophy p222-47

Blumberg, Rae Lesser

The erosion of sexual equality in the kibbutz: a structural interpretation. *In* Roberts, J. I. ed. Beyond intellectual sexism p320-39

Blumen, Jean Lipman- See Lipman-Blumen, Jean

Blumenberg, Hans

The concept of reality and the possibility of the novel. *In* Amacher, R. E. and Lange, V. eds. New perspectives in German literary criticism p29-48

Blumenfeld, David, and Blumenfeld, Jean Beer

Can I know that I am not dreaming? *In* Hooker, M. ed. Descartes p234-55

Blumenfeld, Jean Beer. See Blumenfeld, D. jt. auth.

Blumenthal, Arthur L.

Psycholinguistics: some historical issues. *In* Riegel, K. F. and Rosenwald, G. C. eds. Structure and transformation p135-52

Blumenthal, Uta-Renate

Patrimonia and regalia in 1111. *In* Law, church, and society p 9-20

Blumer, Herbert

About

Lemert, C. C. Symbolic interactionism: Herbert Blumer. *In* Lemert, C. C. Sociology and the twilight of man p109-34

Blumler, Jay G. See Gurevitch, M. jt. auth.

Blumstein, Sheila

Structuralism in linguistics: methodological and theoretical perspectives. *In* Riegel, K. F. and Rosenwald, G. C. eds. Structure and transformation p153-65

Blunden, Edmund Charles

Biographical introduction to John Clare: poems chiefly from manuscript. *In* Praise from famous men: an anthology of introductions p19-44

Blunt, Anthony

Baroque architecture and classical antiquity. *In* Classical influences on European culture A.D. 1500-1700 p349-54

Naples as seen by French travellers, 1630-1780. *In* The Artist and the writer in France p 1-14

Blunt, Wilfred Scawen

About

Meyers, J. Wilfred Scawen Blunt. *In* Meyers, J. A fever at the core p13-38

Bly, Robert

About

Altieri, C. F. Varieties of immanentist experience: Robert Bly, Charles Olson, and Frank O'Hara. *In* Altieri, C. F. Enlarging the temple p78-127

Thurley, G. Devices among words: Kinnell, Bly, Simic. *In* Thurley, G. The American moment p210-28

Blyden, Edward Wilmot

About

Wilson, H. S. Edward Wilmot Blyden. *In* Abroad in America: Visitors to the new Nation, 1776-1914 p157-66

Blythe, Ronald

The dangerous idyll: sweet Auburn to Akenfield. *In* Royal Society of Literature of the United Kingdom, London. Essays by divers hands v38 p15-32

The school-leaver. *In* The Saturday book 34 p148-56

Boalt, Gunnar, and Herlin, Helena

Sociology in Sweden, 1965-1973: a description based on a sociometric method. *In* Mohan, R. P. and Martindale, D. A. eds. Handbook of contemporary developments in world sociology p91-105

Board of Education v. Allen. *In* Fairfield, R. P. ed. Humanistic frontiers in American education p194-201

Boarding schools

France

Frijhoff, W. and Julia, D. The diet in boarding schools at the end of the ancien régime. *In* Food and drink in history p73-85

Boardman, Michael Moore

Defoe's political rhetoric and the problem of irony. *In* Tulane studies in English v22 p87-102

Boas, Guy

The magic of Max. *In* Riewald, J. G. ed. The surprise of excellence p6-20

Boats and boating

See also Sailing

Louisiana

Knipmeyer, W. B. Folk boats of eastern French Louisiana. *In* Yoder, D. ed. American folklife p105-49

Boatwright, James

A manifesto (sotto voce). *In* Anderson, E. and Kinzie, M. eds. The little magazine in America: a modern documentary history p185-215

Bobrowski, Johannes

About

Hamburger, M. Johannes Bobrowski: an introduction. *In* Hamburger, M. Art as second nature p131-33

Boccaccio, Giovanni

About

Branca, V. The myth of the hero in Boccaccio. *In* Concepts of the hero in the Middle Ages and the Renaissance p268-93

Cairns, C. The Italian heritage. *In* Cairns, C. Italian literature p13-44

Dombroski, R. S. Introduction. *In* Dombroski, R. S. ed. Critical perspectives on The Decameron p 1-13

Foscolo, U. Boccaccio. *In* Dombroski, R. S. ed. Critical perspectives on The Decameron p15-25

Oliver, R. P. The Second Medicean ms. and the text of Tacitus. *In* Illinois classical studies, v 1 1976 p190-225

About individual works

The Decameron

Branca, V. The epic of the Italian merchant. *In* Dombroski, R. S. ed. Critical perspectives on The Decameron p38-47

Cottino-Jones, M. Comic modalities in The Decameron. *In* Ruggiers, P. G. ed. Versions of medieval comedy p151-71

De'Negri, E. The legendary style of The Decameron. *In* Dombroski, R. S. ed. Critical perspectives on The Decameron p82-98

Dombroski, R. S. Introduction. *In* Dombroski, R. S. ed. Critical perspectives on The Decameron p 1-13

Fido, F. Boccaccio's ars narrandi in the sixth day of the Decameron. *In* Italian literature: roots and branches p225-42

Greene, T. M. Forms of accomodation in The Decameron. *In* Dombroski, R. S. ed. Critical perspectives on The Decameron p113-28

Mazzotta, G. F. The Decameron: the marginality of literature. *In* Dombroski, R. S. ed. Critical perspectives on The Decameron p129-48

Nelson, J. C. Love and sex in The Decameron. *In* Philosophy and humanism p339-51

Petronio, G. The place of The Decameron. *In* Dombroski, R. S. ed. Critical perspectives on The Decameron p48-60

Pincherle, A. Boccaccio; excerpt from "Man as an end, a defence of humanism." *In* Dombroski, R. S. ed. Critical perspectives on The Decameron p99-112

Sanctis, F. de. Boccaccio's human comedy; excerpt from "History of Italian literature." *In* Dombroski, R. S. ed. Critical perspectives on The Decameron p26-37

Shklovskiĭ, V. B. Some reflections on The Decameron. *In* Dombroski, R. S. ed. Critical perspectives on The Decameron p61-68

The Decameron (II⁷)

Segre, C. Comical structure in the tale of Alatiel. *In* Segre, C. Structures and time p122-35

The Decameron (IV, 2)

Auerbach, E. Frate Alberto; excerpt from "Mimesis." *In* Dombroski, R. S. ed. Critical perspectives on The Decameron p69-81

The Decameron (VII)

Segre, C. Functions, oppositions, and symmetries in Day VII of the Decameron. *In* Segre, C. Structures and time p95-120

The Decameron—Fiammetta

Stilling, R. Gismond of Salern: in love. *In* Stilling, R. Love and death in Renaissance tragedy p11-25

Fiammetta

Segre, C. Structures and registers in the Fiammetta. *In* Segre, C. Structures and time p66-92

Il Filostrato

Clogan, P. M. Two verse commentaries on the ending of Boccaccio's Filostrato. *In* Medievalia et humanistica no. 7 p147-52

Teseida

Hollander, R. The validity of Boccaccio's self-exegesis in his Teseida. *In* Medievalia et humanistica no. 8 p163-83

Characters—Frate Alberto

Auerbach, E. Frate Alberto; excerpt from "Mimesis." *In* Dombroski, R. S. ed. Critical perspectives on The Decameron p69-81

Characters—Getto Alatiel

Segre, C. Comical structure in the tale of Alatiel. *In* Segre, C. Structures and time p122-35

Influence—Chaucer

Schless, H. H. Transformations: Chaucer's use of Italian. *In* Brewer, D. S. ed. Geoffrey Chaucer p184-223

Style

De'Negri, E. The legendary style of The Decameron. *In* Dombroski, R. S. ed. Critical perspectives on The Decameron p82-98

Boccioni, Umberto

About

Zevi, B. The Italian rationalists. *In* Sharp, D. ed. The rationalists p118-29

Bochner, Salomon

Commentary [on Rheticus, Ravetz and the "necessity" of Copernicus' innovation]. *In* The Copernican achievement p40-48

Bock, Fritz

The impact of international economic factors on the conduct of foreign policy. *In* The Interaction of economics and foreign policy p130-50

Bockel, Pierre

Malraux and the challenge of faith. *In* Courcel, M. H. de, ed. Malraux p58-67

Bockelman, Wayne L.

Local government in colonial Pennsylvania. *In* Daniels, B. C. ed. Town and county p216-37

Bode, Barbara

Citizen action for children. *In* Gross, B. and Gross, R. eds. The children's rights movement p260-72

Boden, Margaret A.

Human values in a mechanistic universe. *In* Royal Institute of Philosophy. Human values p135-71

Bodenheim, Maxwell

About

Ravitz, A. C Ballyhoo, gargoyles, & firecrackers: Ben Hecht's aesthetic calliope. *In* Filler, L. ed. A question of quality: popularity and value in modern creative writing p229-43

Bodenheimer, Susanne Jonas
Guatemala: land of eternal struggle. *In* Chilcote, R. H. and Edelstein, J. C. eds. Latin America: the struggle with dependency and beyond p89-219

Boderianus, Guido Fabritius. See Le Fevre de la Boderie, Guy

Bodley, George Frederick

About
Verey, D. George Frederick Bodley: climax of the Gothic revival. *In* Seven Victorian architects p84-101

Bodmer, Walter F.
Biomedical advances: a mixed blessing? *In* Harré, R. ed. Problems of scientific revolution p25-41
Race and IQ: the genetic background. *In* Montagu, A. ed. Race and IQ p252-86

Body, Human
See also Body image; Mind and body; Physiology

Psychological aspects
See Mind and body

Body and mind. See Mind and body

Body and soul (Philosophy) See Mind and body

Body care. See Hygiene

Body image
Schwartz, D. C.; Garrison, J., and Alouf, J. Health, body images, and political socialization. *In* Schwartz, D. C. and Schwartz, S. K. eds. New directions in political socialization p96-126

Body size. See Bergmann's rule

Body temperature. See Animal heat

Boer, Pieter Arie Hendrik de
The perfect with waw in 2 Samuel 6:16. *In* On language, culture, and religion: in honor of Eugene A. Nida p43-52

Boer, Willem den
Aspects of religion in classical Greece. *In* Harvard Studies in classical philology v77 p 1-21

Boer War, 1899-1902. See South African War, 1899-1902

Boer War, 1899-1902 in literature. See South African War, 1899-1902 in literature

Boers
Du Toit, A. Ideological change, Afrikaner nationalism and pragmatic racial domination in South Africa. *In* Thompson, L. M. and Butler, J. eds. Change in contemporary South Africa p19-50
Van Zyl Slabbert, F. Afrikaner nationalism, white politics, and political change in South Africa. *In* Thompson, L. M. and Butler, J. eds. Change in contemporary South Africa p3-18
Welsh, D. The political economy of Afrikaner nationalism. *In* Leftwich, A. ed. South Africa: economic growth and political change p249-85
Welsh, D. The politics of white supremacy. *In* Thompson, L. M. and Butler, J. eds. Change in contemporary South Africa p51-78

Boesak, Allan
Coming in out of the wilderness. *In* The Emergent gospel p76-95

Boesiger, Ernest
Evolutionary theories after Lamarck and Darwin. *In* Ayala, F. J. and Dobzhansky, T. G. eds. Studies in the philosophy of biology p21-43

Boesman and Lena (criticism) Fugard, A. *In* Kauffmann, S. Persons of the drama p204-08

Boethius

About individual works
De differentiis topicis
Leff, M. C. The logician's rhetoric: Boethius' De differentiis topicis, Book IV. *In* Murphy, J. J. ed. Medieval eloquence p3-24

Boettinger, Henry M.
Our sixth-and-a-half sense. *In* The Social impact of the telephone p200-07

Bogan, Louise
The pleasures of formal poetry; excerpt from "A poet's alphabet." *In* Gibbons, R. ed. The poet's work: 29 masters of 20th century poetry on the origins and practice of their art p203-14

About individual works
Collected poems, 1923-53
Olson, E. Louise Bogan and Léonie Adams. *In* Olson, E. On value judgments in the arts, and other essays p36-49

Poems and new poems
Kunitz, S. J. Land of dust and flame. *In* Kunitz, S. J. A kind of order, a kind of folly p194-97

Bogart, Humphrey DeForest

About
Truffaut, F. A portrait of Humphrey Bogart. *In* Truffaut, F. The films in my life p292-95

Bogart, Leo
Mass media today and tomorrow. *In* Fischer, H. D. and Merrill, J. C. eds. International and intercultural communication p63-70

Bogatyrev, Petr Grigor'èvich
Costume as a sign. *In* Matejka, L. and Titunik, I. R. eds. Semiotics of art p13-19
Folk song from a functional point of view. *In* Matejka, L. and Titunik, I. R. eds. Semiotics of art p20-32
Forms and functions of folk theater. *In* Matejka, L. and Titunik, I. R. eds. Semiotics of art p51-56
Semiotics in the folk theater. *In* Matejka, L. and Titunik, I. R. ed. Semiotics of art p33-50

Bogdanos, Theodore
"The Shepherd of Hermas" and the development of medieval visionary allegory. *In* Viator: medieval and Renaissance studies v8 p33-46

Bogue, Allan G.
Bloc and party in the United States Senate: 1861-1863. *In* Swierenga, R. P. ed. Beyond the Civil War synthesis p203-23
Recent developments in political history: the case of the United States. *In* The Frontiers of human knowledge p79-109

Bohannan, Paul
Tiv divination. *In* Studies in social anthropology p149-66

Böheim, Hans. See Böhm, Hans

Bohemian Brethren

History

Fousek, M. S. On secular authority and military service among the Bohemian Brethren in the 16th and early 17th centuries. *In* Király, B. K. ed. Tolerance and movements of religious dissent in Eastern Europe p53-64

Bohemian sculpture. See Sculpture, Bohemian

Bohemianism

Kurz, P. K. Beat—Pop—underground. *In* Kurz, P. K. On modern German literature v4 p202-41

See also Hippies

United States

Glicksberg, C. I. The politics of madness. *In* Glicksberg, C. I. The literature of commitment p163-85

Krim, S. A backward glance o'er beatnik roads. *In* Anderson, E. and Kinzie, M. eds. The little magazine in America: a modern documentary history p324-37

Sheed, W. Beat down and beatific. *In* Sheed, W. The good word & other words p110-15

Sheed, W. The Beat movement concluded. *In* Sheed, W. The good word & other words p116-20

Bohm, David

Imagination, fancy, insight, and reason in the process of thought. *In* Evolution of consciousness p51-68

Böhm, Hans

About

Lackner, B. K. Hans Böhm: shepherd, piper, prophet. *In* Essays on medieval civilization p73-107

Böhme, Gernot

Models for the development of science. *In* Science, technology and society p319-51

Bohomolec, Franciszek

About

Durer, C. S. Molière and Polish comedy. *In* Johnson, R. B.; Neumann, E. S. and Trail, G. T. eds. Molière and the commonwealth of letters: patrimony and posterity p365-78

Bohr, Niels Henrik David

About

Kragh, H. Niels Bohr's second atomic theory. *In* Historical studies in the physical sciences v10 p123-86

Miller, A. I. Visualization lost and regained: the genesis of the quantum theory in the period 1913-27. *In* Wechsler, J. ed. On aesthetics in science p73-102

Richards, I. A. Complementarities. *In* Richards, I. A. Complementarities p108-26

Boiardo, Matteo Maria, Conte di Scandiano. See Bojardo, Matteo Maria, Conte di Scandiano

Boigny, Félix Houphouët. See Houphouët-Boigny, Félix, President Ivory Coast

Boileau-Despréaux, Nicolas

About individual works

The art of poetry

Edelman, N. L' art poétique: "longtemps plaire et jamais ne lasser." *In* Edelman, N. The eye of the beholder p142-53

Boine, Giovanni

About individual works

Agonia

Perella, N. J. Some twentieth-century voices. *In* Perella, N. J. Midday in Italian literature p145-200

Bois, Paul

About individual works

Paysans de l'Ouest

Le Roy Ladurie, E. The "event" and the "long term" in social history: the case of the Chouan uprising. *In* Le Roy Ladurie, E. The territory of the historian p111-31

Boissevain, Charles

About individual works

From the North to the South

Hollander, A. N. J. den. Charles Boissevain. *In* Abroad in America: Visitors to the new Nation. 1776-1914 p186-94

Bojardo, Matteo Maria, Conte de Scandiano

About

Marinelli, P. V. Redemptive laughter: comedy in the Italian romances. *In* Ruggiers, P. G. ed. Versions of medieval comedy p227-48

About individual works

Orlando innamorato

Giamatti, A. B. Headlong horses, headless horsemen: an essay on the chivalric epics of Pulci, Boiardo, and Ariosto. *In* Italian literature: roots and branches p265-307

Bok, Bart Jan

Harlow Shapley and the discovery of the center of our galaxy. *In* Neyman, J. ed. The heritage of Copernicus: theories "pleasing to the mind" p26-62

Bok, Sissela

Freedom and risk. *In* Holton, G. J. and Morison, R. S. eds. Limits of scientific inquiry p115-27

Bolgar, R. R.

Hero or anti-hero? *In* Concepts of the hero in the Middle Ages and the Renaissance p120-46

Bolgen, Kaare

There are no hopeless children. *In* Fairfield, R. P. ed. Humanistic frontiers in American education p220-36

Bolingbroke, Henry Saint-John, 1st Viscount

About

Skinner, Q. The principles and practice of opposition: the case of Bolingbroke versus Walpole. *In* Historical perspectives p93-128

Bolívar, Simón

About

Cuevas Cancino, F. Bolivar's commonwealth of nations. *In* [Truth and tragedy]: a tribute to Hans Morgenthau p322-32

Bolivia

Rural conditions

Hess, D. W. Pioneering as ecological process: a model and test case of frontier adaptation. *In* The Frontier v2 p123-51

Bolkhovitinov, Nikolai Nikolaevich

The American Revolution and the Russian Empire. *In* The Impact of the American Revolution abroad p81-97

Böll, Heinrich

The imprisoned world of Solzhenitsyn's The first circle. *In* Dunlop, J. B.; Haugh, R. and Klimoff, A. eds. Aleksandr Solzhenitsyn: critical essays and documentary materials 2d ed. p219-30

Solzhenitsyn and new realism. *In* Dunlop, J. B.; Haugh, R. and Klimoff, A. eds. Aleksandr Solzhenitsyn: critical essays and documentary materials 2d ed. p185-87

About

Kurz, P. K. Heinrich Böll: not reconciled. *In* Kurz, P. K. On modern German literature v4 p3-36

Bollas, Christopher. See Schwartz, M. M. jt. auth.

Bolle, Kees W.

Structures of Renaissance mysticism. *In* The Darker vision of the Renaissance p119-45

Bollier, E. P.

Against the American grain: William Carlos Williams between Whitman and Poe. *In* Tulane Studies in English, v23 p123-42

Bolling, Douglass Townshend

Structure and theme in Briefing for a descent into hell. *In* Pratt, A. V. and Dembo, L. S. eds. Doris Lessing p133-47

Bolling, Landrum Rymer

Quaker work in the Middle East following the June 1967 War. *In* Unofficial diplomats p80-88

Bolling, Richard

The management of Congress. *In* Managing nonprofit organizations p102-08

Bologna. Università

Banker, J. R. The ars dictaminis and rhetorical textbooks at the Bolognese University in the fourteenth century. *In* Medievalia et humanistica no. 5 p153-68

Bölöni, Sándor Farkas

About

Katona, A. Sándor Farkas Bölöni and Ágoston Mokcsai Haraszthy. *In* Abroad in America: Visitors to the new Nation. 1776-1914 p43-51

Bolshevism. See Communism

Bolstad, Orin D. See Johnson, S. M. jt. auth.

Bolsterli, Margaret Jones

Woman's vision: the worlds of women in Delta wedding, Losing battles and The optimist's daughter. *In* Prenshaw, P. W. ed. Eudora Welty p149-56

Bolt, Christine

Red, Black and white in nineteenth-century America. *In* Hepburn, A. C. ed. Minorities in history p116-34

Bolt, Robert

About individual works

A man for all seasons

Schwarz, A. The experience of history as fateful. *In* Schwarz, A. From Büchner to Beckett p61-99

Bolton, Brenda M.

Fulk of Toulouse: the escape that failed. *In* Church, society and politics p83-93

Mulieres sanctae. *In* Stuard, S. M. ed. Women in medieval society p141-58

Bolton, Herbert Eugene

The mission as a frontier institution in the Spanish American colonies. *In* Weber, D. J. ed. New Spain's far northern frontier p49-65

Bólyai, János

About

Lukacs, E. Non-Euclidean geometry. *In* Neyman, J. ed. The heritage of Copernicus: theories "pleasing to the mind" p359-77

Bolzano (Province)

Katzenstein, P. J. Ethnic political conflict in South Tyrol. *In* Esman, M. J. ed. Ethnic conflict in the Western world p287-323

Pinter, F. Changes in the South Tyrol issue. *In* The Year book of world affairs, 1977 p64-74

Bonandrea, Giovanni di. See Giovanni di Bonandrea

Bonati, Félix Martínez

Hermeneutic criticism and the description of form. *In* Valdés, M. J. and Miller, O. J. eds. Interpretation of narrative p78-99

Bonaventura, Saint, Cardinal

About

Seung, T. K. Bonaventure's figural exemplarism in Dante. *In* Italian literature: roots and branches p117-54

Boncompagno da Signa

About

Purkart, J. Rhetoric in later Latin: Boncompagno of Signa and the rhetoric of love. *In* Murphy, J. J. ed. Medieval eloquence p319-31

Bond, Douglas

About

Henry, G. The silk purse of high-style interior decoration. *In* Battcock, G. ed. Super realism p163-69

Bond, George

Minor prophets and Yombe cultural dynamics. *In* Colonialism and change p145-62

Bond, Marjorie (Nix) See Bond, R. P. jt. auth.

Bond, Richmond Pugh

See also Part 2 under title: The Dress of words

About individual works

English burlesque poetry, 1700-1750

England, A. B. Further additions to Bond's Register of burlesque poems. *In* Virginia. University. Bibliographical Society. Studies in bibliography v28 p284-90

Bond, Richmond Pugh, and Bond, Marjorie (Nix)

The minute books of the St James's Chronicle. *In* Virginia. University. Bibliographical Society. Studies in bibliography v28 p17-40

Bondi, Sir Hermann

Relativity theory and gravitation. *In* Einstein p113-29

What is progress in science? *In* Harré, R. ed. Problems of scientific revolution p 1-10

Bone, Robert A.
  Down home
    Contents
  Arna Bontemps
  Charles Chesnutt
  Eric Walrond
  The Harlem Renaissance: a reappraisal
  Jean Toomer
  Langston Hughes
  Literary forebears
  The oral tradition
  Paul Dunbar
  Three versions of pastoral
Le bone Florence de Rome. See Florence
de Rome
Bonebakker, Seger Adrianus
  Religious prejudice against poetry in early
  Islam. *In* Medievalia et humanistica no. 7
  p77-99
Bonet, Honoré
        About individual works
          The tree of battles
  Wright, N. A. R. The tree of battles of
  Honoré Bouvet and the laws of war. *In*
  War, literature, and politics in the late
  Middle Ages p12-31
Bonham, George Wolfgang
  Opening the academic gates. *In* Hook, S.;
  Kurtz, P. W. and Todorovich, M. eds. The
  university and the state: what role for gov-
  ernment in higher education? p163-66
  Who runs the show? *In* The Third century
  p158-65
Bonhoeffer, Dietrich
        About
  Poole, R. Essay 9. *In* Fitzgerald, R. ed.
  What it means to be human p164-85
        About individual works
          Sanctorum communio
  Green, C. A theology of sociality: Bon-
  hoeffer's Sanctorum communio. *In* The Con-
  text of contemporary theology p65-84
Bonifacius VIII, Pope
          Unam sanctam
  Luscombe, D. E. The 'lex divinitas' in
  the bull 'Unam sanctam' of Pope Boniface
  VIII. *In* Church and government in the
  Middle Ages p205-21
Bonjour tristesse (Motion picture)
  Truffaut, F. Otto Preminger: Bonjour
  tristesse. *In* Truffaut, F. The films in my life
  p137-40
Bonnaud, Jean-Jacques
  Planning and industry in France. *In* Plan-
  ning, politics and public policy p93-110
Bonnefoy, Yves
        About
  Price, J D. Yves Bonnefoy: the sense of
  things. *In* Cardinal, R. ed. Sensibility and
  creation p204-19
Bonner, Edmund, Bp. of London
        About
  Alexander, G. Victim or spendthrift? The
  Bishop of London and his income in the six-
  teenth century. *In* Wealth and power in
  Tudor England p128-45
Bonnet, Jean-Claude
  The culinary system in the Encyclopédie.
  In Food and drink in history p139-65

Bonneville, Douglas A.
  Diderot's artist: puppet and poet. *In* Lit-
  erature and history in the age of ideas p245-
  52
Bonnie and Clyde (Motion picture)
  Kael, P. Bonnie and Clyde; excerpt from
  "Kiss kiss bang bang." *In* Denby, D. ed.
  Awake in the dark p77-97
  Murray, E. Bonnie and Clyde. *In* Mur-
  ray, E. Ten film classics p149-66
  Murray, L. L. Hollywood, nihilism, and
  the youth culture of the sixties: Bonnie and
  Clyde. *In* O'Connor, J. E. and Jack-
  son, A. eds. American history/American
  film p237-56
  Samuels, C. T. Bonnie and Clyde. *In* Sam-
  uels, C. T. Mastering the film, and other
  essays p136-43
Bono, Edward de. See De Bono, Edward
Bontemps, Arna Wendell
  The Black contribution to American let-
  ters: Part I. *In* The Black American refer-
  ence book p741-66
        About
  Bone, R. A. Arna Bontemps. *In* Bone,
  R. A. Down home p272-87
Bontoc Igorot (Philippine people). See Bon-
toks (Philippine people)
Bontoks (Philippine people)
          Women
  Bacdayan, A. S. Mechanistic cooperation
  and sexual equality among the western Bon-
  toc. *In* Schlegel, A. E. ed. Sexual stratifica-
  tion p270-91
Bonwick, C. C.
  English Dissenters and the American
  Revolution. *In* Allen, H. C. and Thomp-
  son, R. eds. Contrast and connection p88-112
Booher, Edward E.
  Publishing in the USSR and Yugoslavia.
  In Altbach, P. G. and McVey, S. eds. Per-
  spectives on publishing p173-86
Book awards. See Literary prizes
Book censorship. See Censorship
Book collecting
  Eberhart, R. A haphazard poetry collect-
  ing. *In* Eberhart, R. Of poetry and poets
  p92-107
Book collectors
  Connolly, C. A collector's year. *In* Con-
  nolly, C. The evening colonnade p419-22
          Kent, England—History
  Clark, P. The ownership of books in En-
  gland, 1560-1640: the example of some Ken-
  tish townfolk. *In* Schooling and society
  p95-111
Book illustration. See Illustration of books
Book industries and trade
  See also Booksellers and bookselling;
  Paper making and trade; Publishers and
  publishing
          England
  Rogers, P. Introduction: the writer and
  society. *In* Rogers, P. ed. The eighteenth century p 1-80
          New England
  Hall, D. D. The world of print and col-
  lective mentality in seventeenth-century
  New England. *In* Higham, J. and Conkin,
  P. K. eds. New directions in American in-
  tellectual history p166-80

Books and reading—*Continued*

France

Rosbottom, R. C. A matter of competence: the relationship between reading and novel-making in eighteenth-century France. *In* Studies in eighteenth-century culture v6 p245-63

Germany

Fabian, B. English books and their eighteenth-century German readers. *In* Korshin, P. J. ed. The widening circle p117-96

New England

Hall, D. D. The world of print and collective mentality in seventeenth-century New England. *In* Higham, J. and Conkin, P. K. eds. New directions in American intellectual history p166-80

United States

Garrison, D. Immoral fiction in the late Victorian library. *In* Howe, D. W. ed. Victorian America p141-59

Ohmann, R. M. The social definition of literature. *In* Hernadi, P. ed. What is literature? p89-101

Sale, R. H. Novelists, readers, critics. *In* Sale, R. H. On not being good enough p53-66

Smith, H. N. The issues. *In* Smith, H. N. Democracy and the novel p3-15

Books and reading for children

Aiken, J. A free gift. *In* Blishen, E. ed. The thorny paradise p36-52

Bain, D. A. Transtemporal communication. *In* Egoff, S. A. ed. One ocean touching p3-17

Drury, R. W. "Realism plus fantasy equals magic." *In* Horn Book Magazine. Crosscurrents of criticism p178-84

Elkind, D. Ethnicity and reading: three avoidable dangers. *In* Elkind, D. The child and society p41-47

Stokes, R. B. Envoi. *In* Egoff, S. A. ed. One ocean touching p232-40

See also Children's literature

Japan

Ishii, M. Modern Japanese children's books. *In* Egoff, S. A. ed. One ocean touching p79-92

Russia

Morton, M. Young Soviet readers and their literature. *In* Egoff, S. A. ed. One ocean touching p38-59

Singapore

Perumbulavil, V. Children's books and reading in a plural society—Singapore. *In* Egoff, S. A. ed. One ocean touching p60-78

Books and reading for youth

Cameron, E. McLuhan, youth, and literature. *In* Horn Book Magazine. Crosscurrents of criticism p98-120

Engdahl, S. L. Why write for today's teenagers? *In* Horn Book Magazine. Crosscurrents of criticism p144-49

Holland, I. The walls of childhood. *In* Horn Book Magazine. Crosscurrents of criticism p27-34

United States

Egoff, S. A. Children's books: a Canadian's view of the current American scene. *In* Horn Book Magazine. Crosscurrents of criticism p128-36

Books for children. *See* Children's literature

Booksellers and bookselling

Smith, G. R. The future of bookselling. *In* Bookselling in America and the world p138-40

Toynbee, A. J. Bookselling, a way to international understanding. *In* Bookselling in America and the world p184-86

See also Book industries and trade; Publishers and publishing

Colportage, subscription trade, etc.

Hodgart, M. J. C. The subscription list for Pope's Iliad, 1715. *In* The Dress of words p25-34

History

Shaw, E. P. Censorship and subterfuge in eighteenth-century France. *In* Literature and history in the age of ideas p287-309

Taubert, S. World bookselling: some historical comments. *In* Bookselling in America and the world p26-64

Subscription trade

See Booksellers and bookselling—Colportage, subscription trade, etc.

Boston

Melcher, F. G. Bookselling in Boston. *In* Bookselling in America and the world p156-62

England

Garnett, D. Never be a bookseller. *In* Bookselling in America and the world p171-75

France

Darnton, R. Trade in the taboo: the life of a clandestine book dealer in prerevolutionary France. *In* Korshin, P. J. ed. The widening circle p11-83

Great Britain—History

Barnes, J. J. John Miller: first transatlantic publisher's agent. *In* Virginia. University. Bibliographical Society. Studies in bibliography v29 p373-79

Landon, R. G. Small profits do great things: James Lackington and eighteenth-century bookselling. *In* Studies in eighteenth-century culture v5 p387-99

Philadelphia—History

Harlan, R. D. A colonial printer as bookseller in eighteenth-century Philadelphia: the case of David Hall. *In* Studies in eighteenth-century culture v5 p355-69

United States—History

Kroch, A. Early years in the book business. *In* Bookselling in America and the world p176-80

Mencken, H. L. Lo, the poor bookseller. *In* Bookselling in America and the world p163-70

Tebbel, J. W. A brief history of American bookselling. *In* Bookselling in America and the world p3-25

Boorman, John

About individual works

Deliverance

Samuels, C. T. How not to film a novel. *In* Samuels, C. T. Mastering the film, and other essays p190-97

Boorsch, Suzanne Renee

America in festival presentations. *In* First images of America p503-15

Boorstin, Daniel Joseph

From "naughtiness" to "behavior deviation"; excerpt from "The Americans: the democratic experience". *In* Davis, F. J. and Stivers, R. eds. The collective definition of deviance p147-55

The indivisible community. *In* Libraries and the life of the mind in America p115-30

Political revolutions and revolutions in science and technology. *In* America's continuing revolution p161-80

Statistical morality; excerpt from "The Americans: the democratic experience". *In* Davis, F. J. and Stivers, R. eds. The collective definition of deviance p156-61

About

Metcalf, K. D. Introduction of Daniel J. Boorstin. *In* Libraries and the life of the mind in America p109-13

About individual works

The genius of American politics

Reinitz, R. Niebuhrian irony and historical interpretation: the relationship between consensus and New Left history. *In* Canary, R. H. and Kozicki, H. J. eds. The writing of history p93-128

Booth, Edward Charles

About

Cavaliero, G. Problems of the rural novelist: E. C. Booth. *In* Cavaliero, G. The rural tradition in the English novel, 1900-1939 p14-25

Booth, Graham

The price of being an artist. *In* Egoff, S. A. ed. One ocean touching p155-63

About

Booth, G. The price of being an artist. *In* Egoff, S. A. ed. One ocean touching p155-63

Booth, Jeremy

Rationalization and crisis: a quarter century of British publishing. *In* Altbach, P. G. and McVey, S. eds. Perspectives on publishing p59-69

Booth, Michael R.

Going on stage. *In* Altholz, J. L. ed. The mind and art of Victorian England p107-23

Irish landscape in the Victorian theatre. *In* Place, personality and the Irish writer p159-72

The social value of nieteenth-century English drama. *In* Drama and society p59-74

Booth, Newell S.

An approach to African religion. *In* African religions: a symposium p 1-11

God and the gods in West Africa. *In* African religions: a symposium p159-81

Islam in Africa. *In* African religions: a symposium p297-343

The view from Kasongo Niembo. *In* African religions: a symposium p31-67

Booth, Stephen

On the value of Hamlet. *In* Wimsatt, W. K. ed. Literary criticism: idea and act p284-310

Booth, Wayne Clayson

The pleasure and pitfalls of irony: or, Why don't you say what you mean? *In* Burks, D. M. ed. Rhetoric, philosophy, and literature: an exploration p 1-13

The rhetoric of fiction and the poetics of fictions. *In* Spilka, M. ed. Towards a poetics of fiction p77-89

About individual works

The rhetoric of fiction

Baker, J. R. From imitation to rhetoric: the Chicago Critics, Wayne C. Booth, and Tom Jones. *In* Spilka, M. ed. Towards a poetics of fiction p136-56

Booth, W. C. The rhetoric of fiction and the poetics of fictions. *In* Spilka, M. ed. Towards a poetics of fiction p77-89

Borah, Woodrow Wilson

Latin American history in world perspective. *In* The Future of history p151-72

The mixing of populations. *In* First images of America p707-22

Borchardt, Frank L.

First contacts with Italy. *In* Hoffmeister, G. ed. The Renaissance and Reformation in Germany p 1-16

Medievalism in Renaissance Germany. *In* Creative encounter p73-85

Borcoman, James W.

Notes on the early use of combination printing. *In* One hundred years of photographic history p15-18

Bordeaux

Poor

Forrest, A. The condition of the poor in Revolutionary Bordeaux. *In* French society and the Revolution p217-47

Social conditions

Forrest, A The condition of the poor in Revolutionary Bordeaux. *In* French society and the Revolution p217-47

Border life. See Frontier and pioneer life

Bordwell, David

Citizen Kane. *In* Nichols, B. ed. Movies and methods p273-90

Boredom

Altschule, M. D. Acedia—its evolution from deadly sin to psychiatric syndrome. *In* Altschule, M. D. Origins of concepts in human behavior p75-83

Borel, Petrus

About individual works

Madame Putiphar

Brombert, V. H. Pétrus Borel: prison and the Gothic tradition. *In* Brombert, V. H. The romantic prison p49-61

Boren, James Lewis

The design of the Old English Deor. *In* Anglo-Saxon poetry: essays in appreciation p264-76

Borges, Jorge Luis

About

Barth, J. The literature of exhaustion. *In* Federman, R. ed. Surfiction p19-33

Borinsky, A. Repetition, museums, libraries: Jorge Luis Borges. *In* Glyph 2 p88-102

Grossvogel. D. I. Borges: the dream dreaming the dreamer. *In* Grossvogel, D. I. Mystery and its fictions: from Oedipus to Agatha Christie p127-46

Philmus, R. M. Borges and Wells and the labyrinths of time. *In* H. G. Wells and modern science fiction p159-78

Pritchett, V. S. Jorge Luis Borges: medallions. *In* Pritchett, V. S. The myth makers p174-84

Scholes, R. E. Fabulation and reality. *In* Scholes, R. E. Fabulation and metafiction p5-20

Borges, Jorge L.—*Continued*

About individual works

Death and the compass

Grossvogel, D. I. Borges: the dream dreaming the dreamer. *In* Grossvogel, D. I. Mystery and its fictions: from Oedipus to Agatha Christie p127-46

Borgese, Elisabeth Mann

A constitution for the oceans. *In* Borgese, E. M. and Krieger, D. eds. The tides of change p340-52

A Mediterranean Council to Combat Pollution. *In* Borgese, E. M. and Krieger, D. eds. The tides of change p210-17

(ed.) Recommendations from Pacem in Maribus IV to the United Nations Committee on the Peaceful Uses of the Sea-Bed. *In* Borgese, E. M. and Krieger, D. eds. The tides of change p353-57

Borgese, Giuseppe Antonio

About

Pacifici, S. Giuseppe A. Borgese: the ideological void. *In* Pacifici, S. The modern Italian novel: from Capuana to Tozzi p78-85

Borgmann, Albert

Heidegger and symbolic logic. *In* Murray, M. E. ed. Heidegger and modern philosophy p 3-22

Boring, Phyllis Zatlin

Shirley Temple: super child. *In* Browne, R. B. and Fishwick, M. W. eds. Icons of America p100-11

Borinsky, Alicia

Repetition, museums, libraries: Jorge Luis Borges. *In* Glyph 2 p88-102

Borisov, Vadim

Personality and national awareness. *In* From under the rubble p194-228

Borj Hammoud, Lebanon

Social life and customs

Joseph, S. Women and the neighborhood street in Borj Hammoud, Lebanon. *In* Beck, L. and Keddie, N. R. eds. Women in the Muslim world p541-57

Bork, Robert H.

Alexander M. Bickel, political philosopher. *In* The Supreme Court review, 1975 p419-21

Can democratic government survive? *In* Aspects of American liberty p174-86

The limits of governmental regulation. *In* Hook, S.; Kurtz, P. W. and Todorovich, M. eds. The university and the state: what role for government in higher education? p169-75

Vertical restraints: Schwinn overruled. *In* The Supreme Court review, 1977 p171-92

Borman, Leonard D.

American Indian tribal support systems and economic development. *In* The Diverse society: implications for social policy p149-62

Born, Bertran de, seigneur de Hautefort. See Bertran de Born, seigneur de Hautefort

Bornkamm, Günther

The revelation of Christ to Paul on the Damascus Road and Paul's doctrine of justification and reconciliation. *In* Reconciliation and hope p90-103

Bornkamm, Heinrich

Luther and his father: observations on Erik H. Erikson's Young man Luther: a study in psychoanalysis and history. *In* Homans. P. ed. Childhood and selfhood p59-88

Bornstein, George

The antinomial structure of John Butler Yeat's Early memories: some chapters of autobiography. *In* Landow, G. P. ed. Approaches to Victorian autobiography p200-11

Pound and Eliot. *In* American literary scholarship, 1977 p119-33

Yeats and the greater romantic lyric. *In* Bornstein, G. ed. Romantic and modern p91-110

Bororo Indians

Crocker, J. C. My brother the parrot. *In* The Social use of metaphor p164-92

Borosage, Robert L.

The Central Intelligence Agency: the king's men and the constitutional order. *In* Borosage, R. L. and Marks, J. D. eds. The CIA file p125-41

Borosage, Robert L. and Marks, John D.

Destabilizing Chile. *In* Borosage, R. L. and Marks, J. D. eds. The CIA file p79-89

Borowitz, Albert

Innocence and arsenic

Contents

Dr. Jekyll and Mr. Stevenson

Henri de Latouche and the murder memoirs of Clarisse Manson

The Jackal and I, or How to do research in London

M. Tullius Cicero for the defense

The mystery of Edwin Drood

New gaslight on Jack the Ripper

Psychological kidnapping in Italy: the case of Aldo Braibanti

Salieri and the "murder" of Mozart

The Snows on the Moors: C. P. Snow and Pamela Hansford Johnson on the Moors murder case

Why Thackeray went to see a man hanged

Borowitz, Eugene B.

A Jewish response: the lure and limits of universalizing our faith. *In* Christian faith in a religiously plural world p59-68

About

Kaufman, W. E. Eugene B. Borowitz and Emil L. Fackenheim: from covenant theology to commanding voice. *In* Kaufman, W. E. Contemporary Jewish philosophies p94-121

Borro, Girolamo

About individual works

Multae sunt nostrarum ignorationum causae

Schmitt, C. B. Girolamo Borro's Multae sunt nostrarum ignorationum causae (Ms. Vat. Ross. 1009) *In* Philosophy and humanism p462-76

Borroff, Marie

Robert Frost: "To earthward." *In* Frost: centennial essays II p21-39

Borromini, Francesco

About

Blunt, A. Baroque architecture and classical antiquity. *In* Classical influences on European culture A.D. 1500-1700 p349-54

Wittkower, R. Francesco Borromini, his character and life. *In* Wittkower, R. Studies in the Italian baroque p153-76

Borsalino (Motion picture)
Kauffmann, S. Borsalino. *In* Kauffmann, S. Living images p3-5

Borstal system. See Juvenile detention homes —Great Britain

Borstein, Irving J. and Klein, Annette
Parents of fatally ill children in a parents' group. *In* Anticipatory grief p164-70

Bory, Jean-François
Notes. *In* Federman, R. ed. Surfiction p287-89

Borzage, Frank

About individual works
Disputed passage
Camper, F. Disputed passage. *In* Nichols, B. ed. Movies and methods p339-44

Bosch, Hieronymous van Aken, known as

About individual works
The garden of earthly delights
Morris, W. Unearthly adornments. *In* Morris, W. Earthly delights, unearthly adornments p181-89
Sussman, H. The all-embracing metaphor: reflections of Kafka's "The burrow." *In* Glyph I p100-31

Bosch, Jerome. See Bosch, Hieronymous van Aken, known as

Boshier, Adrian
The religions of Africa. *In* Life after death p54-66

Boshin War, 1868. See Japan—History— Civil War, 1868

Bosk, Charles L.
The routinization of charisma: the case of the zaddik. *In* Johnson, H. M. ed. Religious change and continuity p150-67

Boss, Medard
Flight from death—mere survival; and flight into death—suicide. *In* Wolman, B. B. ed. Between survival and suicide p 1-23

Bossert, Steven T.
Education in urban society. *In* Handbook of contemporary urban life p288-318

Bossuet, Jacques Bénigne, Bp. of Meaux

About
Voegelin, E. The emergence of secularized history: Bossuet and Voltaire. *In* Voegelin, E. From Enlightenment to revolution p3-34

Bost, Pierre

About
Truffaut, F. A certain tendency of the French cinema. *In* Nichols, B. ed. Movies and methods p224-37

Bostert, Russell Henry
Teaching history. *In* Cahn, S. M. ed. Scholars who teach p1-35

Boston

Charities, Medical
Vogel, M. J Patrons, practitioners, and patients: the voluntary hospital in mid-Victorian Boston. *In* Howe, D. W. ed. Victorian America p121-38

Charters
Heymann, P. B. and Weinberg, M. W. The paradox of power: mayoral leadership on charter reform in Boston. *In* Burnham, W. D. and Weinberg, M. W. eds. American politics and public policy p280-303

Hospitals
Vogel, M. J. Patrons, practitioners, and patients: the voluntary hospital in mid-Victorian Boston. *In* Howe, D. W. ed. Victorian America p121-38

Learned institutions and societies—History
Whitehill, W. M. Early learned societies in Boston and vicinity. *In* Oleson, A. and Brown, S. C. eds. The pursuit of knowledge in the early American Republic p151-73

Museum of Fine Arts
Coomaraswamy, A. K. Chinese painting at Boston. *In* Coomaraswamy, A. K. Selected papers v 1 p308-15

Politics and government
Heymann, P. B. and Weinberg, M. W. The paradox of power: mayoral leadership on charter reform in Boston. *In* Burnham, W. D. and Weinberg, M. W. eds. American politics and public policy p280-303

Boston metropolitan area
Moyer, J. A. Urban growth and the development of the telephone: some relationships at the turn of the century. *In* The Social impact of the telephone p342-69

Boston Society of Natural History
Kohlstedt, S. G. From learned society to public museum: the Boston Society of Natural History. *In* Oleson, A. and Voss, J. eds. The organization of knowledge in modern America, 1860-1920 p386-406

Boswell, James

About
Davies, R. T. Samuel Johnson, James Boswell, and the romantic. *In* Davies, R. T. and Beatty, B. G. eds. Literature of the romantic period, 1750-1850 p 1-18
Dowling, W. C. Boswell and the problem of biography. *In* Studies in biography p73-93
Ober, W. B. Boswell's clap. *In* Ober, W. B. Boswell's clap, and other essays p 1-42
Spacks, P. A. M. Young men's fancies: James Boswell, Henry Fielding. *In* Spacks, P. A. M. Imagining a self p227-63

About individual works
Boswell for the defence 1769-1774
Spacks, P. A. M. Laws of time: Fielding and Boswell. *In* Spacks, P. A. M. Imagining a self p264-99

Boswell in extremis, 1776-1778
Connolly, C. Boswell. *In* Connolly, C. The evening colonnade p128-30

London journal, 1762-1763
Bruss, E. W. James Boswell: genius and stenography. *In* Bruss, E. W. Autobiographical acts p61-92
Frye, N. The young Boswell. *In* Frye, N. Northrop Frye on culture and literature p165-69
Lyons, J. O. Confessional high tide. *In* Lyons, J. O. The invention of the self p89-120
Mudrick, M. The entertainer. *In* Mudrick, M. Books are not life but then what is? p39-51
Spacks, P. A. M. Young men's fancies: James Boswell, Henry Fielding. *In* Spacks, P. A. M. Imagining a self p227-63

Boswell, James—*Continued*

Friends and associates

Lustig, I. S. The friendship of Johnson and Boswell: some biographical considerations. *In* Studies in eighteenth-century culture v6 p199-214

Relations with contemporaries

See Boswell, James—Friends and associates

Bosworth, A. B.

Arrian and the Alani. *In* Harvard Studies in classical philology v81 p217-55

Bosworth, Clifford Edmund

Armies of the Prophet. *In* Lewis, B. ed. Islam and the Arab world p201-24

The historical background of Islamic civilisation. *In* Savory, R. M. ed. Introduction to Islamic civilisation p15-31

Recruitment, muster, and review in medieval Islamic armies. *In* War, technology and society in the Middle East p59-77

Bosworth, Edmund. See Bosworth, Clifford Edmund

Boszormenyi-Nagy, Ivan, and Spark, Geraldine M.

About individual works

Invisible loyalties: reciprocity in intergenerational family therapy

Friedman, M. S. Healing through meeting: a dialogical approach to psychotherapy and family therapy. *In* Psychiatry and the humanities v 1 p191-233

Botanical geography. See Phytogeography

Botany

See also Ethnobotany; Fertilization of plants

Classification

Dean, J. Controversy over classification: a case study from the history of botany. *In* Barnes, B. and Shapin, S. eds. Natural order p211-30

Geographical distribution

See Phytogeography

History

Dean, J. Controversy over classification: a case study from the history of botany. *In* Barnes, B. and Shapin, S. eds. Natural order p211-30

Taxonomy

See Botany—Classification

America

Ewan, J. A. The Columbian discoveries and the growth of botanical ideas with special reference to the sixteenth century. *In* First images of America p807-12

Sauer, J. D. Changing perception and exploitation of New World plants in Europe, 1492-1800. *In* First images of America p813-32

United States—Texas

Jordan, T. G. Vegetational perception and choice of settlement site in frontier Texas. *In* Pattern and process p244-57

Botany, Economic. See Ethnobotany; Plant introduction; Plants, Edible

Botany, Medical

Gilges, W. Some African poison plants and medicines of Northern Rhodesia. *In* The Occasional papers of the Rhodes-Livingstone Museum p389-426

See also Materia medica, Vegetable

Bothmer, Dietrich Felix von

A bronze oinochoe in New York. *In* Studies in classical art and archaeology p63-67

Botkin, Vasilii Petrovich

About

Kostka, E. K. A trailblazer of Russian Westernism: V. P. Botkin. *In* Kostka, E. K. Glimpses of Germanic-Slavic relations from Pushkin to Heinrich Mann p69-84

Botkin, Vasily Petrovich. See Botkin, Vasilii Petrovich

Botswana

Politics and government—1966-

Morgan, E. P. Botswana: democratic politics and development. *In* Carter, G. M. and O'Meara, P. eds. Southern Africa in crisis p200-25

Morgan, E. P. Botswana: development, democracy, and vulnerability. *In* Carter, G. M. and O'Meara, P. eds. Southern Africa: the continuing crisis p228-48

Social conditions

Morgan, E. P. Botswana: development, democracy, and vulnerability. *In* Carter, G. M. and O'Meara, P. eds. Southern Africa: the continuing crisis p228-48

Botticelli, Sandro

About individual works

The youth of Moses

Meyers, J. Bellini, Giotto, Mantegna, Botticelli and Swann's way. *In* Meyers, J. Painting and the novel p96-111

Bottomore, Thomas Burton

Structure and history. *In* Blau, P. M. ed. Approaches to the study of social structure p159-71

Bottoms, A. E.

On the decriminalization of English juvenile courts. *In* Crime, criminology and public policy p319-45

Bottoms, A. E. and Wiles, Paul

Race, crime and violence. *In* Racial variation in man p131-49

Boucicault, Dion

About

Booth, M. R. Irish landscape in the Victorian theatre. *In* Place, personality and the Irish writer p159-72

Boudouris, James

The politics of research. *In* Riedel, M. and Chappel, D. eds. Issues in criminal justice: planning and evaluation p59-65

Bouhier, Jean

About

Wade, I. O. Notes on the making of a philosophe: Cuenz and Bouhier. *In* Literature and history in the age of ideas p97-123

Bouissac, Paul

A semiotic approach to nonsense: clowns and limericks. *In* Sebeok, T. A. ed. Sight, sound, and sense p244-63

Semiotics and spectacles: the circus institution and representations. *In* Sebeok, T. A. ed. A perfusion of signs p143-52

Boulay, F. R. H. du. See Du Boulay, F. R. H.

Boulby, Mark

Nietzsche and the finis Latinorum. *In* O'Flaherty, J. C.; Sellner, T. F. and Helm, R. M. eds. Studies in Nietzsche and the classical tradition p214-33

Boulding, Elise
Adolescent culture: reflections of divergence. *In* Social forces and schooling p187-220

Educational structure and community transformation. *In* Wagschal, P. H. ed. Learning tomorrows p97-107

Religion, futurism, and models of social change. *In* Bundy, R. F. ed. Images of the future: the twenty-first century and beyond p169-81

Boulding, Kenneth Ewart
The puzzle of the North-South differential. *In* Lewis, W. D. and Griessman, B. E. eds. The Southern mystique p 1-13

Sociobiology or biosociology? *In* Sociobiology and human nature p260-76

Boulter, Patricia N.
A bronze bull in Cincinnati. *In* Studies in classical art and archaeology p251-54

Boundaries
McNeill, W. H. On national frontiers: ethnic homogeneity and pluralism. *In* Small comforts for hard times p207-19

See also Continental shelf; Ethnic barriers, Geopolitics

Bouquet, Sarah
Voices from the Southwest. *In* Voices from the Southwest p33-44

Bourchier, Sir John. 2nd Baron. See Berners, John Bourchier, 2d Baron

Bourdeaux, Michael
Religion. *In* Brown, A. H. and Kaser, M. eds. The Soviet Union since the fall of Khrushchev p157-80

Bourdeaux, Michèle
Blazing a trail to a history of customary law by means of geographic hematology. *In* Biology of man in history p191-205

Bourdieu, Pierre
Marriage strategies as strategies of social reproduction. *In* Family and society p117-44

See also Reynaud, J. D. jt. auth.

Bourdon, Sébastien

About individual works
Acts of mercy
Fowle, G. E. Sébastien Bourdon's Acts of mercy: their significance as a series. *In* Enggass, R. C. and Stokstad, M. eds. Hortus imaginum p147-54

Bourgeoisie. See Middle classes

Bourguignon, Erika Eichhorn
Cross-cultural perspectives on the religious uses of altered states of consciousness. *In* Zaretsky, I. I. and Leone, M. P. eds. Religious movements in contemporary America p228-43

Spirit possession and altered states of consciousness: the evolution of an inquiry. *In* Spindler, G. D. ed. The making of psychological anthropology p479-515

Bourke, John Gregory

About
Dobie, J. F. Captain John G. Bourke as soldier, writer and man. *In* Dobie, J. F. Prefaces p131-39

Bourne, Randolph Silliman

About
Paul, S. Randolph Bourne. *In* Paul, S. Repossessing and renewing p137-78
Also in Ross, R. G. ed. Makers of American thought p120-56

Bourneuf, Alice. See Part 2 under title: Inflation, trade and taxes

Bourodimos, Efstathios Lampros
Thermopollution in the aquatic environment. *In* Against pollution and hunger p183-209

Bourque, Susan Carolyn
The clash of empires: Peru's enduring paradox. *In* Aftermath of empire p65-81

Bourricaud, François
The French university as a "fixed society" or, the futility of the 1968 "reform." *In* Universities in the Western world p232-45

Indian, mestizo and cholo as symbols in the Peruvian system of stratification. *In* Glazer, N. and Moynihan, D. P. eds. Ethnicity p350-87

Bouthoul, Gaston
Definitions of terrorism. *In* International terrorism and world security p50-59

Boutros-Ghali, Boutros
Arab diplomacy: failures and successes. *In* Arab and American cultures p221-36

The foreign policy of Egypt. *In* Aluko, O. ed. The foreign policies of African states p41-45

The League of Arab States and the Organization of African Unity. *In* El-Ayouty, Y. ed. The Organization of African Unity after ten years p47-61

Bouvet, Honoré. See Bonet, Honoré

Bouwsma, Oets Kolk
Descartes' skepticism of the senses. *In* Dunlop, C. E. M. ed. Philosophical essays on dreaming p52-63

Bouwsma, William James
Changing assumptions in later Renaissance culture. *In* Viator: medieval and Renaissance studies v7 p421-40

Christian adulthood. *In* Erikson, E. H. ed. Adulthood p81-96

Bovet, Honoré. See Bonet, Honoré

Bowden, Betsy
The art of courtly copulation. *In* Medievalia et humanistica; new ser. no. 9 p67-85

Bowden, Gordon T.
A response: planning—yes, but by whom? *In* Planning, politics, and the public interest p161-66

Bowden, Martyn J.
The Great American Desert in the American mind: the historiography of a geographical notion. *In* Geographies of the mind p119-47

Persistence, failure, and mobility in the inner city: preliminary notes. *In* Pattern and process p169-92

Bowen, Elizabeth
The Faber Book of modern short stories. *In* May, C. E. ed. Short story theories p152-58

About
Gindin, J. Ethical structures in John Galsworthy, Elizabeth Bowen, and Iris Murdoch. *In* Forms of modern British fiction p15-41

About individual works
Pictures and conversations
Welty, E. Elizabeth Bowen's Pictures and conversations. *In* Welty, E. The eye of the story p269-76

Bowen, Howard Rothmann
Higher education and human equality *In* The Third century p90-97

Bower, Dallas
MacNeice: sound and vision. *In* Time was away p97-102

Bower, Thomas Gillie Russell
The evolution of sensory systems. *In* Perception p141-52

Bowers, A. Joan
The Tree of Charity in Piers Plowman: its allegorical and structural significance. *In* Literary monographs, v6 p 1-34

Bowers, David G.
Work humanization in practice: what is business doing? *In* Heisler, W. J. and Houck, J. W. eds. A matter of dignity p147-64

Bowers, Fredson Thayer
Essays in bibliography, text, and editing
   Contents
Bibliographical evidence from the printer's measure
The bibliographical way
Bibliography and modern librarianship
Bibliography and Restoration drama
Bibliography and the university
Bibliography, pure bibliography, and literary studies
Bibliography revisited
Current theories of copy-text, with an illustration from Dryden
Elizabethan proofing
Established texts and definitive editions
An examination of the method of proof correction in King Lear Q1
The facsimile of Whitman's blue book
The folio Othello: compositor E
Four faces of bibliography
The headline in early books
Motteux's "Love's a jest" (1696): a running-title and presswork problem
Multiple authority: new problems and concepts of copy-text
Old-spelling editions of dramatic texts
Old wine in new bottles: problems of machine printing
Practical texts and definitive editions
Purposes of descriptive bibliography with some remarks on methods
Remarks on eclectic texts
Running-title evidence for determining half-sheet imposition
Some relations of bibliography to editorial problems
The text of Johnson
Textual criticism and the literary critic

Foul papers, Compositor B, and the speech-prefixes of All's well that ends well. *In* Virginia. University. Bibliographical Society. Studies in bibliography v32 p60-81

Greg's "Rationale of copy-text" revisited. *In* Virginia. University. Bibliographical Society. Studies in bibliography v31 p90-161

Samson Agonistes: justice and reconciliation. *In* The Dress of words p 1-23

Transcription of manuscripts: the record of variants. *In* Virginia. University. Bibliographical Society. Studies in bibliography v29 p212-64

   About
Cook, D. L. Bowers does Fielding. *In* Review, v 1 1979 p13-27

   About individual works
   Essays in bibliography, text, and editing
Tanselle, G. T. Bowers's collected essays. *In* Review, v 1 1979 p195-204

Bowers, John Waite, and Sanders, Robert E.
Paradox as a rhetorical strategy. *In* Rhetoric: a tradition in transition p300-15

Bowers, W. Paul
A note on Collossians 1:27a. *In* Current issues in Biblical and patristic interpretation p110-14

Bowersock, Glen Warren
The addressee of the Eighth Eclogue: a response. *In* Harvard Studies in classical philology v82 p201-02

A date in the Eighth Eclogue. *In* Harvard Studies in classical philology v75 p73-80

Gibbon on civil war and rebellion in The decline of the Roman Empire. *In* Edward Gibbon and The decline and fall of the Roman Empire p27-35

Herodian and Elagabalus. *In* Yale classical studies v24 p229-36

Limes Arabicus. *In* Harvard Studies in classical philology v80 p219-29

The proconsulate of Albus. *In* Harvard Studies in classical philology v72 p289-94

Pseudo-Xenophon. *In* Harvard Studies in classical philology v71 p33-55

Bowes, Sir Jerome
   About
Croskey, R. A further note on Sir Jerome Bowes. *In* Oxford Slavonic papers, new ser. v10 p39-45

Lur'e, I. S. An unpublished epigram on an English ambassador to Russia. *In* Oxford Slavonic papers, new ser. v7 p13-17

Bowie, Malcolm
Paul Eluard. *In* Cardinal, R. ed. Sensibility and creation p149-67

Bowle, John, 1725-1788
   About
Brooks, C. Thomas Percy, Don Quixote, and Don Bowle. *In* Evidence in literary scholarship p247-61

Bowler, Clara Ann. See Kitch, E. W. jt. auth.

Bowler, Peter J.
The early development of scientific societies in Canada. *In* Oleson, A. and Brown, S. C. eds. The pursuit of knowledge in the early American Republic p326-39

Bowles, Samuel. See Gintis, H. M. jt. auth.

Bowley, Marian
Some aspects of the treatment of capital in The wealth of nations. *In* Skinner, A. S. and Wilson, T. eds. Essays on Adam Smith p361-76

Bowling
Steele, P. D. The bowling hustler: a study of deviance in sport. *In* Social problems in athletics p86-92

Bowling games. See Bowling

Bowlt, John E.
Art and architecture in Soviet Russia, 1917-1972. *In* Auty, R. and Obolensky, D. eds. An introduction to Russian art and architecture p145-72

Art and architecture in the age of revolution, 1860-1917. *In* Auty, R. and Obolnesky, D. eds. An introduction to Russian art and architecture p112-44

Artists of the world, disunite! *In* Kaplan, P. and Manso, S. eds. Major European art movements, 1900-1945 p299-309

Bowlt, John E.—*Continued*

Russian sculpture and Lenin's plan of monumental propaganda. *In* Millon, H. A. and Nochlin, L. eds. Art and architecture in the service of politics p182-93

The "Union of Youth." *In* Gibian, G. and Tjalsma, H. W. eds. Russian modernism p165-87

Bowman, Albert Hall

Presidential advisers. *In* Encyclopedia of American foreign policy p790-804

Bowman, Mary Jean. See Anderson, C. A. jt. auth.

Bowman, Peter Muschamp Boyd- See Boyd-Bowman, Peter Muschamp

Bowsky, William M.

Italian diplomatic history: a case for the smaller commune. *In* Order and innovation in the Middle Ages p55-74

Boxer, Charles Ralph

European missionaries and Chinese clergy, 1654-1810. *In* Kling, B. B. and Pearson, M. N. eds. The age of partnership p97-121

Boxes, Ornamental

Sicily

Robertson, E. The Rome casket. *In* Studies in memory of David Talbot Rice p11-15

Boxhill, Bernard

The morality of reparation. *In* Gross, B. R. ed. Reverse discrimination p270-78

Boxing stories

History and criticism

Fenton, C. A. No money for the kingbird: Hemingway's prizefight stories. *In* Benson, J. J. ed. The short stories of Ernest Hemingway: critical essays p53-63

Boyce, Douglas W.

Did a Tuscarora confederacy exist? *In* Hudson, C. M. ed. Four centuries of Southern Indians p28-45

Boycott

New York (City)

Gordon, M. Irish immigrant culture and the labor boycott in New York City, 1880-1886. *In* Immigrants in industrial America, 1850-1920 p111-22

Boyd, Antonio Olliz. See Olliz Boyd, Antonio

Boyd, Gavin

Forms of political penetration in China's East Asian statecraft. *In* Pacific Asia and U.S. policies: a political-economic-strategic assessment p115-39

Boyd, Martin

About individual works

A difficult young man

Hamilton, K. G. Two difficult young men: Martin Boyd's A difficult young man and Christina Stead's The people with the dogs. *In* Hamilton, K. G. ed. Studies in the recent Australian novel p141-67

Boyd, Richard Newell

Metaphor and theory change: What is "metaphor" a metaphor for? *In* Ortony, A. ed. Metaphor and thought p356-408

About individual works

Metaphor and theory change: What is "metaphor" a metaphor for?

Kuhn, T. S. Metaphor in science. *In* Ortony, A. ed. Metaphor and thought p409-19

Pylyshyn, Z. W. Metaphorical imprecision and the "top-down" research strategy. *In* Ortony, A. ed. Metaphor and thought p420-36

Boyd-Barrett, Oliver

The global news wholesalers. *In* Gerbner, G. ed. Mass media policies in changing cultures p13-20

Boyd-Bowman, Peter Muschamp

Spanish emigrants to the Indies, 1595-98: a profile. *In* First images of America p723-35

Boyer, Abel

About

Snyder, H. L. The contribution of Abel Boyer as Whig journalist and writer of The Protestant Post-Boy, 1711-1712. *In* The Dress of words p139-49

About individual works

The history of the reign of Queen Anne digested into annals

Anderson, G. L. Mr. Abel stops the press. *In* Virginia. University. Bibliographical Society. Studies in bibliography v29 p292-95

Boyer, Ernest L.

Toward a new interdependence. *In* The Third century p72-79

Boyers, Robert

Excursions

Contents

Alan Dugan: the poetry of survival

Also in Boyers, R. ed. Contemporary poetry in America p339-47

Attitudes toward sex in American "high culture"

Bergman's "Persona": an essay on tragedy

The family novel

Gombrowicz's "Cosmos": the clinical fiction as novel

Howard Nemerov's true voice of feeling

Language and reality in Kosinski's "Steps"

More on Sylvia Plath

Nature and social reality in Bellow's "Sammler"

On Adrienne Rich: intelligence and will

Also in Boyers, R. ed. Contemporary poetry in America p157-73

On Robert Lowell

The Roethke Letters

Sylvia Plath: the trepanned veteran

To confront nullity: the poetry of Ben Belitt

A very separate peace: on Roethke

The little magazine in its place: literary culture and anarchy. *In* Anderson, E. and Kinzie, M. eds. The little magazine in America: a modern documentary history p50-67

Boyette, Purvis Elton

Shakespeare's Sonnets: homosexuality and the critics. *In* Tulane Studies in English v21 p35-46

Wanton humour and wanton poets: homosexuality in Marlowe's Edward II. *In* Tulane Studies in English v22 p33-50

Boylan, James Richard

Journalists and foreign policy. *In* Encyclopedia of American foreign policy p507-14

Bradley, Thompson

Aleksandr Solzhenitsyn's Cancer ward: the failure of defiant stoicism. *In* Dunlop, J. B.; Haugh, R. and Klimoff, A. eds. Aleksandr Solzhenitsyn: critical essays and documentary materials 2d ed. p295-302

Bradley, William Warren

About individual works
Life on the run

Sale, R. H. Bradley & Maclean. *In* Sale, R. H. On not being good enough p84-93

Bradová, Ludmila

Antonín Dvořák. *In* Abroad in America: Visitors to the new Nation, 1776-1914 p228-37

Bradstreet, Anne (Dudley)

About

Daly, R. J. Anne Bradstreet and the practice of weaned affections. *In* Daly, R. J. God's altar p82-127

Martin, W. Anne Bradstreet's poetry: a study of subversive piety. *In* Gilbert, S. M. and Gubar, S. eds. Shakespeare's sisters p19-31

Rich, A. C. The tensions of Anne Bradstreet. *In* Rich, A. C. On lies, secrets, and silence p21-32

Stanford, A. Anne Bradstreet: dogmatist and rebel. *In* Vaughan, A. T. and Bremer, F. J. eds. Puritan New England p287-98

Brady, Patrick

A sweet disorder: atomistic empiricism and the rococo mode of vision. *In* Studies in eighteenth-century culture v7 p451-61

Bragg, Braxton

About

McWhiney, G. The Confederacy's first shot. *In* Hubbell, J. T. ed. Battles lost and won p73-82

Bragg, Melvyn

Thomas Hardy and Jude the Obscure. *In* Royal Society of Literature of the United Kingdom, London. Essays by divers hands v39 p24-46

Brahe, Tycho de. See Brahe, Tyge

Brahe, Tyge

About

Moesgaard, K. P. Cosmology in the wake of Tycho Brahe's astronomy. *In* Cosmology, history, and theology p293-305

Westman, R. S. Three responses to the Copernican theory: Johannes Praetorius, Tycho Brahe, and Michael Maestlin. *In* The Copernican achievement p285-345

Brahm, John Gerar William de. See De Brahm, John Gerar William

Brahmanism. See Hinduism

Brahmans in literature

Hahn, T. G. The Indian tradition in Western medieval intellectual history. *In* Viator: medieval and Renaissance studies v9 p213-34

Brahmins. See Brahmans in literature

Braibanti, Aldo

About

Borowitz, A. Psychological kidnapping in Italy: the case of Aldo Braibanti. *In* Borowitz, A. Innocence and arsenic p116-31

Braibanti, Ralph J. D.

Context, cause, and change. *In* Prospects for constitutional democracy p165-82

Braibanti, Ralph J. D. and Spengler, Joseph John, eds.

About individual works
Tradition, values, and socio-economic development

Thrupp, S. L. Tradition and development: a choice of views. *In* Thrupp, S. L. Society and history p198-206

Brain, James Lewton

Witchcraft in Africa: a hardy perennial. *In* Colonialism and change p179-201

Brain

Brown, B. B. On the nature of the human mind. *In* Hanna, T. ed. Explorers of humankind p73-86

Eccles, Sir J. C. The brain-mind problem as a frontier of science. *In* The Future of science p73-89

MacLean, P. D. The imitative-creative interplay of our three mentalities. *In* Harris, H. A. ed. Astride the two cultures p187-213

Pribram, K. H. From infinities to nothing: an exploration of brain function. *In* Hanna, T. ed. Explorers of humankind p106-17

Pribram, K. H. Some observations on the organization of studies of mind, brain, and behavior. *In* Alternate states of consciousness p220-29

Thomas, L. The scrambler in the mind. *In* Thomas, L. The medusa and the snail p121-24

See also Memory; Mind and body; Nervous system; Phrenology

Diseases

See Aphasia; Nervous system—Diseases

Growth

Thomas, L. On embryology. *In* Thomas, L. The medusa and the snail p155-57

Localization of functions

See Split brain

Brain, Split. See Split brain

Brain bisection. See Split brain

Brain death

Ad Hoc Committee of the Harvard Medical School to Examine the Definition of Brain Death. A definition of irreversible coma. *In* Weir, R. F. ed. Ethical issues in death and dying p82-89

Braisted, William Reynolds

Naval diplomacy. *In* Encyclopedia of American foreign policy p668-78

Braithwaite, Richard Bevan

Keynes as a philosopher. *In* Keynes, M. ed. Essays on John Maynard Keynes p237-46

Brake, Laurel, and Ogden, James

The later seventeenth century. *In* English Association. The year's work in English studies v54 p252-75

Brake, Laurel; Chapple, J. A. V. and Knowles, Owen

The nineteenth century: Victorian period. *In* English Association. The year's work in English studies v57 p262-314

Brake, Laurel; Chapple, J. A. V. and Watson, John Richard

The nineteenth century. *In* English Association. The year's work in English studies v55 p359-438

The nineteenth century [another essay]. *In* English Association. The year's work in England studies v56 p277-339

Bramante, Donato
About individual works
Piazza Ducale, Vigevano
Lotz, W. The Piazza Ducale in Vigevano: a princely forum of the late fifteenth century. *In* Lotz, W. Studies in Italian Renaissance architecture p117-39

Bramble, John C.
Cui non dictus Hylas puer? Propertius I.20. *In* Woodman, T. and West, D. eds. Quality and pleasure in Latin poetry p81-93

Brameld, Theodore Burghard Hurt
Illusions and disillusions in American education. *In* Fairfield, R. P. ed. Humanistic frontiers in American education p17-27

Branagan, Thomas
About
Leary, L. G. Thomas Branagan: Republican rhetoric and romanticism in America. *In* Leary, L. G. Soundings p229-52

Branca, Patricia
Towards a social history of medicine. *In* Branca, P. ed. The medicine show p89-101

Branca, Vittore
The epic of the Italian merchant. *In* Dombroski, R. S. ed. Critical perspectives on The Decameron p38-47

The myth of the hero in Boccaccio. *In* Concepts of the hero in the Middle Ages and the Renaissance p268-93

Brancati, Vitaliano
About
Pacifici, S. The "southern" novel. *In* Pacifici, S. The modern Italian novel: from Pea to Moravia p47-78

Branch, Edgar Marquess
James T. Farrell. *In* Walcutt, C. C. ed. Seven novelists in the American naturalist tradition p245-89

James T. Farrell: four decades after Studs Lonigan. *In* Filler, L. ed. A question of quality: popularity and value in modern creative writing p80-91

Brancusi, Constantin
About
Krauss, R. E. Forms of readymade: Duchamp and Brancusi. *In* Krauss, R. E. Passages in modern sculpture p69-103

Brand, Christianna. See Lewis, Mary Christianna (Milne)

Brand, Jack
From Scotland with love. *In* Kramnick, I. ed. Is Britain dying? p169-82

Brandeis, Louis Dembitz
About
White, G. E. Holmes, Brandeis, and the origins of judicial liberalism. *In* White, G. E. The American judicial tradition p150-77

Brandenburg
History
Braun, R. Taxation, sociopolitical structure, and state-building: Great Britain and Brandenburg-Prussia. *In* Tilly, C. ed. The formation of national states in Western Europe p243-327

Brandi, Giacinto
About
Dowley, F. H. Giacinto Brandi's paintings at the Palazzo Taverna. *In* Enggass, R. C. and Stokstad, M. eds. Hortus imaginum p165-73

Brando, Marlon
About
Haskell, M. Marlon Brando. *In* Denby, D. ed. Awake in the dark p361-71

Brandon, Elizabeth
Folk medicine in French Louisiana. *In* American folk medicine p215-34

Brandt, George
Twentieth-century comedy. *In* Howarth, W. D. ed. Comic drama p165-86

Brandt, John Conrad
Pictographs and petroglyphs of the Southwest Indians. *In* Brecher, K. and Feirtag, M. eds. Astronomy of the ancients p25-38

Brandt, Reinhard
The beginnings of Hume's philosophy. *In* David Hume p117-27

Brandt, Richard B.
A moral principle about killing. *In* Kohl, M. ed. Beneficent euthanasia p106-14

Brandt, Sebastian. See Brant, Sebastian

Brandt, Willy
Security in a changing world. *In* World change and world security p17-27

Branfman, Fred
The President's secret army: a case study —the CIA in Laos, 1962-1972. *In* Borosage, R. L. and Marks, J. D. eds. The CIA file p46-78

Brannan, William Penn, supposed author.
See The harp of a thousand strings

Branscombe, Peter
The use of leitmotifs in Stifter's Brigitta. *In* Branscombe, P. ed. Austrian life and literature, 1780-1938 p49-58

Brant, Sebastian
About individual works
The ship of fools
Dünnhaupt, P. R. G. Sebastian Brant: The ship of fools. *In* Hoffmeister, G. ed. The Renaissance and Reformation in Germany p69-81

Braque, Georges
About
Fry, E. Introduction, the history of cubism, cubism as a stylistic and historical phenomenon; excerpt from "Cubism." *In* Kaplan, P. and Manso, S. eds. Major European art movements, 1900-1945 p101-46

Greenberg, C. Collage; excerpt from "Art and culture (Revised edition)" *In* Kaplan, P. and Manso, S. eds. Major European art movements, 1900-1945 p147-63

Brashear, William R.
The gorgon's head
Contents
The boundless deep: Tennyson
The empty bench: Arthur Miller and social drama
The mirror of despair: Conrad
Nietzsche and Spengler on Hamlet
The play as will and idea: Shaw and O'Neill
The power of negative thinking
The trouble with Housman
The wisdom of Silenus: O'Neill's spiritual ancestors

Brasted, Robert Crocker
The introductory course in chemistry. *In* Buxton, T. H. and Prichard, K. W. eds. Excellence in university teaching p109-19

Brasz, Hendrikus Aandries
The Netherlands. *In* Galnoor, I. ed. Government secrecy in democracies p201-15

Brasz, Henk A. See Brasz, Hendrikus Aandries

Brathwaite, Edward
The African presence in Caribbean literature. *In* Mintz, S. W. ed. Slavery, colonialism, and racism p73-109
Roger Mais's Brother Man as jazz novel. *In* Baugh, E. ed. Critics on Caribbean literature p103-12

About
Goodwin, K. L. Invective and obliqueness in political poetry: Kasaipwalova, Brathwaite, and Soyinka. *In* Narasimhaiah, C. D. ed. Awakened conscience p251-60

About individual works
The arrivants
New, W. H. New language, new world. *In* Narasimhaiah, C. D. ed. Awakened conscience p360-77

Rights of passage
Rohlehr, G. Blues and rebellion: Edward Brathwaite's Rights of passage. *In* Baugh, E. ed. Critics on Caribbean literature p63-74

Bratton, Jacqueline, and others
The twentieth century. *In* English Association. The year's work in English studies v54 p363-405
The twentieth century [another essay] *In* English Association. The year's work in English studies v55 p439-81

Braude, Stephen Edward
On the meaning of 'paranormal.' *In* Ludwig, J. K. ed. Philosophy and parapsychology p227-44

Braudel, Fernand

About individual works
The Mediterranean and the Mediterranean world in the age of Philip II
Hexter, J. H. Fernand Braudel and the monde braudellien. . . . *In* Hexter, J. H. On historians p61-145

Influence
Hexter, J. H. Fernand Braudel and the monde braudellien. . . . *In* Hexter, J. H. On historians p61-145

Braudy, Leo Beal
Penetration and impenetrability in Clarissa. *In* Harth, J. P. ed. New approaches to eighteenth-century literature p177-206

Brauer, Ralph
Iconic modes: The Beatles. *In* Browne, R. B. and Fishwick, M. W. eds. Icons of America p112-23

Brault, Gerard J.
The French chansons de geste. *In* Oinas, F. J. ed. Heroic epic and saga p193-215

Braun, Rudolf
Taxation, sociopolitical structure, and state-building: Great Britain and Bradenburg-Prussia. *In* Tilly, C. ed. The formation of national states in Western Europe p243-327

Bravmann, René A.
Contemporary dimensions of African art. *In* Martin, P. M. and O'Meara, P. eds. Africa p348-66
Masking tradition and figurative art among the Islamized Mande. *In* African images p144-69

Brawley, Benjamin Griffith

About individual works
A social history of the American Negro
Cruse, H. The creative and performing arts and the struggle for identity and credibility. *In* Johnson, H. A. ed. Negotiating the mainstream p47-102

Bray, Donald William, and Harding, Timothy F.
Cuba. *In* Chilcote, R. H. and Edelstein, J. C. eds. Latin America: the struggle with dependency and beyond p579-734

Bray, René

About individual works
La préciosité et les precieux de Thibaudet de Champagne à Jean Giraudoux
Edelman, N. Book reviews. *In* Edelman, N. The eye of the beholder p166-205

Brazeau, Jacques, and Cloutier, Edouard
Interethnic relations and the language issue in contemporary Canada: a general appraisal. *In* Esman, M. J. ed. Ethnic conflict in the Western world p204-27

Brazil

Economic conditions
Santo, T. dos. Brazil: the origins of a crisis. *In* Chilcote, R. H. and Edelstein, J. C. eds. Latin America: the struggle with dependency and beyond p409-490

Foreign relations
Roett, R. Brazil and the inter-American system. *In* Farer, T. J. ed. The future of the inter-American system p235-55

Foreign relations—United States
Hilton, S. E. The United States and Brazilian independence. *In* From colony to nation p109-29

History
Russell-Wood, A. J. R. Preconditions and precipitants of the independence movement in Portuguese America. *In* From colony to nation p3-40

History—1763-1821
Burns, E. B. The intellectuals as agents of change and the independence of Brazil, 1724-1822. *In* From colony to nation p211-46
Cardozo, M. da S. S. The modernization of Portugal and the independence of Brazil. *In* From colony to nation p185-210
Costa, E. V. da. The political emancipation of Brazil. *In* From colony to nation p43-88
Dias, M. O. S. The establishment of the royal court in Brazil. *In* From colony to nation p89-108

Intellectual life
Burns, E. B. The intellectuals as agents of change and the indepedence of Brazil, 1724-1822. *In* From colony to nation p211-46

Politics and government—1763-1821
Schwartz, S. B. Elite politics and the growth of a peasantry in late colonial Brazil. *In* From colony to nation p133-54

Politics and government—1930-1954
Leeds, A. and Leeds, E. R. Accounting for behavioral differences: three political systems and the responses of squatters in Brazil, Peru, and Chile. *In* Walton, J. and Masotti, L. H. eds. The city in comparative perspective p193-248

Brazil—*Continued*

Politics and government—1954-

Stepan, A. Political leadership and regime breakdown: Brazil. *In* The Breakdown of democratic regimes pt.3 p110-37

Race question

Corwin, A. F. Afro-Brazilians: myths and realities. *In* Toplin, R. B. ed. Slavery and race relations in Latin America p385-437

Fernandes, F. Beyond poverty: the Negro and the mulatto in Brazil. *In* Toplin, R. B. ed. Slavery and race relations in Latin America p277-97

Rout, L. B. The African in colonial Brazil. *In* Kilson, M. L. and Rotberg, R. I. eds. The African diaspora p132-71

Toplin, R. B. Abolition and the issue of the Black freedman's future in Brazil. *In* Toplin, R. B. ed. Slavery and race relations in Latin America p253-76

Religion

Béhague, G. H. Notes on regional and national trends in Afro-Brazilian cult music. *In* Forster, M. H. ed. Tradition and renewal p68-80

Rural conditions

Katzman, M. T. Social relations of production on the Brazilian frontier. *In* Miller, D. H. and Steffen, J. O. eds. The frontier p275-96

Social conditions

Santos, T. dos. Brazil: the origins of a crisis. *In* Chilcote, R. H. and Edelstein, J. C. eds. Latin America: the struggle with dependency and beyond p409-490

Brazilian drama

History and criticism

Cardona, R. Post-war Hispanic and Brazilian drama. *In* Nicoll, A. World drama p872-80

Brazilian literature

20th century—History and criticism

Aiex, A Graça Aranha and Brazilian modernism. *In* Forster, M. H. ed. Tradition and renewal p51-67

Breakfast at Tiffany's (Motion picture)

Clark, L. Brunch on Moon River. *In* Peary, G. and Shatzkin, R. eds. The modern American novel and the movies p236-46

Brecher, Kenneth

Sirius enigmas. *In* Brecher, K. and Feirtag. M. eds. Astronomy of the ancients p91-115

Brecht, Bertolt

About

Bathrick, D. Brecht's Marxism and America. *In* Mews, S. and Knust, H. eds. Essays on Brecht p209-25

Chiaromonte, N. The political theater. *In* Chiaromonte, N. The worm of consciousness, and other essays p127-52

Glicksberg, C. I. Bertolt Brecht: the prophet of commitment. *In* Glicksberg, C. I. The literature of commitment p319-36

Grimm, R. Naturalism and epic drama. *In* Mews, S. and Knust, H. eds. Essays on Brecht p3-27

Hamburger, M. Brecht and his successors. *In* Hamburger, M. Art as second nature p112-30

Hermassi, K. C. Reclaiming the state. *In* Hermassi, K. C. Polity and theater in historical perspective p166-77

Hermassi, K. C. Reconstituting the audience. *In* Hermassi, K. C. Polity and theater in historical perspective p155-65

Hermassi, K. C. Workable pictures of the world. *In* Hermassi, K. C. Polity and theater in historical perspective p178-95

Knust, H. Piscator and Brecht: affinity and alienation. *In* Mews, S. and Knust, H. eds. Essays on Brecht p44-68

Kurz, P. K. Bertolt Brecht: the man and his work. *In* Kurz, P. K. On modern German literature v2 p22-103

Ley, R. J. Francis Bacon, Galileo, and the Brechtian theater. *In* Mews, S. and Knust, H. eds. Essays on Brecht p174-89

Schoeps, K. H. Epic structures in the plays of Bernard Shaw and Bertolt Brecht. *In* Mews, S. and Knust, H. eds. Essays on Brecht p28-43

Schwarz, A. The outmoded individual. *In* Schwarz, A. From Büchner to Beckett p307-33

About individual works

The Caucasian chalk circle

Mendelson, E. The Caucasian chalk circle and Endgame. *In* Seidel, M. A. and Mendelson, E. eds. Homer to Brecht p336-52

Drums in the night

Mayer, H. Brecht's Drums, a dog, and Beckett's Godot. *In* Mews, S. and Knust, H. eds. Essays on Brecht p71-78

Galileo

Ley, R. J. Francis Bacon, Galileo, and the Brechtian theater. *In* Mews, S. and Knust, H. eds. Essays on Brecht p174-89

Trilling, L. Bertolt Brecht: Galileo. *In* Trilling, L. Prefaces to The experience of literature p56-66

The good woman of Setzuan

Fuegi, J. The alienated woman: Brecht's The good person of Setzuan. *In* Mews, S. and Knust, H. eds. Essays on Brecht p190-96

In the jungle of cities

Mews, S. and English, R. The Jungle transcended: Brecht and Zuckmayer. *In* Mews, S. and Knust, H. eds. Essays on Brecht p79-98

A man's a man

Lyon, J. K. Kipling's "Soldiers three" and Brecht's A man's a man. *In* Mews, S. and Knust, H. eds. Essays on Brecht p99-113

Me-ti. Books of twists and turns

Wirth, A. Brecht: writer between ideology and politics. *In* Mews, S. and Knust, H. eds. Essays on Brecht p199-208

Roundheads and Peakheads

Bahr, G. E. Roundheads and Peakheads: the truth about evil times. *In* Mews, S. and Knust, H. eds. Essays on Brecht p141-55

Saint Joan of the stockyards

Suvin, D. Saint Joan of the slaughterhouses: structures of a slaughterhouse world. *In* Mews, S. and Knust, H. eds. Essays on Brecht p114-40

Brereton, Geoffrey
French comic drama
  Contents
Beaumarchais
Bourgeois comedy: sentiment and moralization
The comedies of Pierre Corneille
Conclusion
The cynical generation: Dancourt, Regnard, Dufresny, Lesage
French comedy before 1630
Marivaux
Molière: life and theatrical career
Molière's comedy
Rotrou and romantic comedy
Scarron and burlesque comedy
The shadow of Molière

Breslau
History
Hoffmann, R. C. Wrocław citizens as rural landholders. *In* The Medieval city p293-311

Breslin, James E.
Poetry: the 1930s to the present. *In* American literary scholarship, 1977 p365-87

Breslin, Jimmy
About individual works
The greening of Dermott Davey
Sheed, W. There is no (Irish) Mafia. *In* Sheed, W. The good word & other words p100-04

Bresnan, Joan
A realistic transformational grammar. *In* Linguistic theory and psychological reality p1-59

Bresson, Henri Cartier-. See Cartier-Bresson, Henri

Bresson, Robert
About individual works
Les dames du Bois de Boulogne
Truffaut, F. Robert Bresson: Les dames du Bois de Boulogne. *In* Truffaut, F. The films in my life p188-90

Une femme douce
Kauffmann, S. Une femme douce. *In* Kauffmann, S. Living images p57-59

A man escaped
Truffaut, F. Robert Bresson: Un condamné à mort s'est échappé. *In* Truffaut, F. The films in my life p190-96

Brest, Paul
The conscientious legislator's guide to constitutional interpretation. *In* Stanford legal essays p61-77

Breton, André
About
Sheringham, M. From the labyrinth of language to the language of the senses: the poetry of Andre Breton. *In* Cardinal, R. ed. Sensibility and creation p72-102

Brett, Michael
The military interest of the Battle of Haydarān. *In* War, technology and society in the Middle East p78-88

Brett Young, Francis. See Young, Francis Brett

Bretton Woods, N.H. United Nations Monetary and Financial Conference, 1944. See United Nation Monetary and Financial Conference, Bretton Woods, N.H. 1944

Breuer, Marcel
Where do we stand? *In* Sharp, D. ed. The rationalists p85-90

Breuning, Eleonore
Brockdorff-Rantzau: the 'Wanderer between two worlds'. *In* Essays in honour of E. H. Carr p126-51

Brevoord, Cornelius
Effective management in the future. *In* Benton, L. R. ed. Management for the future p27-46

Brewer, Derek Stanley
Chaucer and Chrétien and Arthurian romance. *In* Chaucer and Middle English studies in honour of Rossell Hope Robbins p255-59

Gothic Chaucer. *In* Brewer, D. S. ed. Geoffrey Chaucer p 1-32

Breyer, Stephen G. and MacAvoy, Paul W.
Regulating natural gas producers. *In* Kalter, R. J. and Vogely, W. A. eds. Energy supply and government policy p161-92

Brichto, Herbert Chanan
The Hebrew Bible on human rights. *In* Sidorsky, D. ed. Essays on human rights p215-33

Bricke, John
Hume on self-identity, memory and causality. *In* David Hume p167-74

Bridge, Susan
Some causes of political change in modern Yugoslavia. *In* Esman, M. J. ed. Ethnic conflict in the Western world p343-68

Bridgeport, Conn.
Politics and government
Stave, B. M. The Great Depression and urban political continuity: Bridgeport chooses socialism. *In* Stave, B. M. ed. Socialism and the cities p157-83

Bridges, Robert Seymour
A letter to a musician on English prosody; excerpt from "Collected essays." *In* Gross, H. S. ed. The structure of verse p53-67

Bridges, Covered. See Covered bridges

Bridgman, Percy Williams
Probability, logic, and ESP. *In* Ludwig, J. K. ed. Philosophy and parapsychology p191-95

Bridgman, Richard
Ernest Hemingway; excerpt from "The colloquial style in America". *In* Wagner, L. W. ed. Ernest Hemingway p160-88

Bridgwater, Patrick
English writers and Nietzsche. *In* Pasley, J. M. S. ed. Nietzsche: imagery and thought p220-58

Bridie, James, pseud. See Mavor, Osborne Henry

Brier, Bob. See Brier, Robert

Brier, Robert
Magicians, alarm clocks, and backward causation. *In* Wheatley, J. M. O. and Edge, H. L. eds. Philosophical dimensions of parapsychology p235-44

The metaphysics of precognition. *In* Thakur, S. C. ed. Philosophy and physical research p46-58

Mundle, Broad, Ducasse and the precognition problem. *In* Ludwig, J. K. ed. Philosophy and parapsychology p341-49

Brigands and robbers. See Klephts

Briggs, Asa
The pleasure telephone: a chapter in the prehistory of the media. *In* The Social impact of the telephone p40-65

Briggs, Harry
Scientific leadership and the price system. *In* Against pollution and hunger p273-77

Briggs, Jean L.
Eskimo women: makers of men. *In* Matthiasson, C. J. ed. Many sisters p261-304
The origins of nonviolence: Inuit management of aggression. *In* Montagu, A. ed. Learning non-aggression p54-93

Briggs, Julia
Night visitors
Contents
Ancestral voices: the ghost story from Lucian to Le Fanu
Diabolism and decadence: the mood of the nineties
Epilogue: Ghosts and poets
Far away and long ago: Stevenson's Scotland and Kipling's India
Ghosts troop home: the Great War and its aftermath
No mere antiquary: M. R. James
Not without but within: the psychological ghost story
On the edge: Walter De La Mare
A scientific spirit: mesmerism, drugs and psychic doctors
A sense of the past: Henry James and Vernon Lee

Briggs, Katharine M.
Symbols in fairy tales. *In* Symbols of power p131-55

Bright, David Forbes
Confectum carmine munus: Catullus 68. *In* Illinois classical studies, v 1 1976 p86-112

Bright, William Oliver
North American Indian language contact. *In* Sebeok, T. A. ed. Native languages of the Americas v 1 p59-72

Brik, Osip Maksimovich, and Shklovskii, Viktor Borisovich
The Lef arena. *In* Nichols, B. ed. Movies and methods p15-22

Brinkley-Birk, Ann. See Birk, L., jt. auth.

Brisbane, Katharine
Post-war drama in Australia. *In* Nicoll, A. World drama p891-94

Brisbane, Robert Hughes
Black protest in America. *In* The Black American reference book p537-79

Brisman, Leslie
Romantic origins
Contents
Byron: troubled stream from a pure source
Coleridge and the ancestral voices
George Darley: buoyant as young time
Keats and a new birth
Re: generation in Blake
Reintroduction: from the seats of power divine
Shelley: from the caverns of dreamy youth
Wordsworth: how shall I seek the origin?

Brissenden, Robert Francis H.
Mansfield Park: freedom and the family. *In* Halperin, J. ed. Jane Austen p156-71

Brissot de Warville, Jacques Pierre
About
Stern, M. B. Brissot de Warville and the Franco-American press. *In* Virginia. University. Bibliographical Society. Studies in bibliography v29 p362-72

British and North American Royal Mail Steam Packet Company. See Cunard Steam Ship Company Ltd.

British Association for the Advancement of Science
Photograph collections
Michaelson, K. The first photographic record of a scientific conference. *In* One hundred years of photographic history p109-16

British Broadcasting Corporation
Wheldon, H. P. Creativity and collaboration in television programs. *In* The Frontiers of knowledge p177-99

About individual works
BBC pronouncing dictionary of British names
Quirk, R. A commodity of good names. *In* Quirk, R. The linguist and the English language p118-27

British Cast Plate Glass Company. See British Plate Glass Company

British Commonwealth of Nations. See Commonwealth of Nations

British-French War, 1294-1298. See Anglo-French War, 1294-1298

British Guiana. See Guyana

British in Africa
Katzenellenbogen, S. E. British businessmen and German Africa, 1885-1919. *In* Great Britain and her world, 1750-1914 p237-62

British in India
Brennig, J. J. Joint-stock companies of Coromandel. *In* Kling, B. B. and Pearson, M. N. eds. The age of partnership p71-96
Marshall, P. Masters and banians in eighteenth-century Calcutta. *In* Kling, B. B. and Pearson, M. N. eds. The age of partnership p191-213

British in Russia
Everitt, M. R. W. Blackmore (1791-1882), an English chaplain in Cronstadt. *In* Oxford Slavonic papers, new ser. v10 p98-106
Robinson, E. The transference of British technology to Russia, 1760-1820: a preliminary enquiry. *In* Great Britain and her world, 1750-1914 p 1-26

British in the United States
Birch, B. P. British evaluations of the forest openings and prairie edges of the North-Central states, 1800-1850. *In* The Frontier v2 p167-92

British literature. See English literature; Scottish literature

British missions. See Missions, British

British newspapers. See English newspapers

British opinion of Ireland. See Ireland—Foreign opinion, British

British painters. See Painters, British

British periodicals. See English periodicals

British Plate Glass Company
Harris, J. R. Saint-Gobain and Ravenhead. *In* Great Britain and her world, 1750-1914 p27-70

Brittan, Samuel

Can democracy manage an economy? *In* Skidelsky, R. J. A. ed. The end of the Keynesian era p41-46

The economic tensions of British democracy. *In* Tyrrell, R. E. ed. The future that doesn't work p126-43

Inflation and democracy. *In* The Political economy of inflation p161-85

Brittany

History

Jones, M. C. E. 'Mon pais et ma nation': Breton identity in the fourteenth century. *In* War, literature, and politics in the late Middle Ages p144-68

Le Goff, T. J. A. and Sutherland, D. M. G. The Revolution and the rural community in eighteenth-century Brittany. *In* French society and the Revolution p29-52

History—Autonomy and independence movements

Berger, S. D. Bretons and Jacobins: reflections on French regional ethnicity. *In* Esman, M. J. ed. Ethnic conflict in the Western world p159-78

Britten, Benjamin

About individual works

Curlew River

Josipovici, G. Two moments in modern music-theatre. *In* Josipovici, G. The lessons of modernism p177-94

Death in Venice

Schmidgall, G. Benjamin Britten. *In* Schmidgall, G. Literature as opera p321-55

Britten, Edward Benjamin. See Britten, Benjamin

Britton, James N.

Teaching writing. *In* Davies, A. ed. Problems of language and learning p113-33

Britton, Karl W.

Hume on some non-natural distinctions. *In* David Hume p205-09

Symbols. *In* Royal Institute of Philosophy. Communication and understanding p208-22

Broad, Charlie Dunbar

Personal identity and survival. *In* Wheatley, J. M. O. and Edge, H. L. eds. Philosophical dimensions of parapsychology p348-65

The philosophical implications of foreknowledge. *In* Ludwig, J. K. ed. Philosophy and parapsychology p287-312

Also in Wheatley J. M. O. and Edge, H. L. eds. Philosophical dimensions of parapsychology p198-226

The relevance of psychical research to philosophy. *In* Ludwig, J. K. ed. Philosophy and parapsychology p43-63

Also in Wheatley, J. M. O. and Edge, H. L. eds. Philosophical dimensions of parapsychology p198-226

Review of Kneale, Robinson, and Mundle Symposium. *In* Ludwig, J. K. ed. Philosophy and parapsychology p110-16

About

Ducasse, C. J. A theory of the relation of causality to precognition; excerpt from "Broad on the relevance of psychical research to philosophy." *In* Wheatley, J. M. O. and Edge, H. L. eds. Philosophical dimensions of parapsychology p227-34

Pappas, G. S. Broad, sensa, and explanation. *In* Studies in perception p402-21

About individual works

The notion of precognition

Brier, R. Mundle, Broad, Ducasse and the precognition problem. *In* Ludwig, J. K. ed. Philosophy and parapsychology p341-49

Broadbent, Geoffrey

The rational and the functional. *In* Sharp, D. ed. The rationalists p142-58

Broadcasting. See Broadcasting policy; Radio broadcasting; Television broadcasting

Broadcasting, International. See International broadcasting

Broadcasting and state. See Broadcasting policy

Broadcasting policy

Malaysia

Guimary, D. L. Broadcasting in Malaysia. *In* Gerbner, G. ed. Mass media policies in changing cultures p159-63

Broadsheets. See Broadsides

Broadsides

15th and 16th centuries

Kunzle, D. World upside down: the iconography of a European broadsheet type. *In* Babcock, B. A. ed. The reversible world p39-94

Broch, Hermann

About

Adams, R. M. Döblin, Broch. *In* Adams, R. M. Afterjoyce p134-45

Alter, R. Defenses of the imagination. *In* Alter, R. Defenses of the imagination p 3-22

Canetti, E. Hermann Broch. *In* Canetti, E. The conscience of words p 1-13

About individual works

The sleepwalkers

Kurz, P. K. Herman Broch's trilogy Die Schlafwandler. *In* Kurz, P. K. On modern German literature v 1 p105-30

Brock, Peter

The Hutterites and war, 1530-1800. *In* Király, B. K. ed. Tolerance and movements of religious dissent in Eastern Europe p43-51

Brock, William Ranulf

The nature of the Reconstruction crisis; excerpt from "An American crisis: Congress and Reconstruction, 1865-67." *In* Burton, D. H. ed. American history—British historians p169-86

Brockbank, John Philip

Hamlet the Bonesetter. *In* Shakespeare survey 30 p103-15

Brockdorff-Rantzau, Ulrich Karl Christian, Graf

About

Breuning, E. Brockdorff-Rantzau: the 'Wanderer between two worlds'. *In* Essays in honour of E. H. Carr p126-51

Brockman, Bennett A.

Cain and Abel in the Chester creation: narrative tradition and dramatic potential. *In* Medievalia et humanistica no. 5 p169-82

Broderick, Carlfred Bartholomew

Adolescence. *In* Sexuality and human values p50-61

Heterosexuality. *In* Sexuality and human values p12-23

Broderick, John Caruthers
Finding (and counting) American literary manuscripts. *In* Review, v 1 1979 p295-300

Brodhead, Richard H.
Mardi: creating the creative. *In* Pullin, F. ed. New perspectives on Melville p29-53

Brody, Baruch. See Brody, Boruch A.

Brody, Boruch A.
Fetal humanity and the theory of essentialism. *In* Baker, R. and Elliston, F. A. eds. Philosophy & sex p338-55

Voluntary euthanasia and the law. *In* Kohl, M. ed. Beneficent euthanasia p218-32

Brody, David
The New Deal and World War II. *In* Braeman, J.; Bremner, R. H. and Brody, D. eds. The New Deal v 1 p267-309

Brody, Howard, and Sobel, David Stuart
A systems view of health and disease. *In* Sobel, D. S. ed. Ways of health p87-115

Brody, Robert
Mario Vargas Llosa and the totalization impulse. *In* Rossman, C. R. and Friedman, A. W. eds. Mario Vargas Llosa p120-27

Brody, Saul Nathaniel
The comic rejection of courtly love. *In* In pursuit of perfection p221-61

Broedel, Max

About
Harvey, A. M. The second professor of gynecology and the Department of Art as applied to medicine. *In* Harvey, A. M. Adventures in medical research p173-87

Brogan, Sir Denis William
The character of American life; excerpt from "America in the modern world." *In* Burton, D. H. ed. American history—British historians p3-23

Brogan, James E.
Teaching gay literature in San Francisco. *In* Crew, L. ed. The gay academic p152-63

Broglie, Louis, Prince de
My meeting with Einstein at the Solvay Conference of 1927. *in* Einstein p14-17

Brognart, Gilbert

About
Miłosz, C. Brognart: a story told over a drink. *In* Miłosz, C. Emperor of the earth p 1-14

Broken symmetry (Physics)
Morrison, P. On broken symmetries. *In* Wechsler, J. ed. On aesthetics in science p55-70

Bromberg, Joan Lisa
The concept of particle creation before and after quantum mechanics. *In* Historical studies in the physical sciences v7 p161-91

Bromberger, Norman
Economic growth and political change in South Africa. *In* Leftwich, A. ed. South Africa: economic growth and political change p61-123

Brombert, Victor H.
Excursus: Sartre and the drama of ensnarement. *In* Wimsatt, W. K. ed. Literary criticism: idea and act p602-15

The romantic prison
Contents

Baudelaire: confinement and infinity
Epilogue: The borderline zone
Huysmans: the prison house of decadence
The myth of the Bastille

Nerval's privileged enclosures
Pascal's dungeon
Pétrus Borel: prison and the Gothic tradition
Sartre and the drama of ensnarement
Servitude and solidarity
Stendhal: the happy prison
Victor Hugo: the spaceless prison

Stendhal's silken prison. *In* Martz, L. L. and Williams, A. L. eds. The author in his work p365-73

About individual works
The novels of Flaubert

Pritchett, V. S. Gustave Flaubert: the quotidian. *In* Pritchett, V. S. The myth makers p128-35

Brome, Richard

About
Winnington-Ingram, R. P. The musical art of Richard Brome's comedies. *In* Renaissance drama [1976] p219-42

Bronfenbrenner, Martin
The consumer. *In* McKie, J. W. ed. Social responsibility and the business predicament p169-90

A harder look at alienation. *In* Capitalism and freedom p197-218

Bronfenbrenner, Urie
Is early intervention effective? Some studies of early education in familial and extra-familial settings. *In* Montagu, A. ed. Race and IQ p287-322

Nature with nurture: a reinterpretation of the evidence. *In* Montagu, A. ed. Race and IQ p114-44

"Our system for making human beings human is breaking down." *In* Gross, B. and Gross, R. eds. The children's rights movement p251-55

Bronowski, Jacob
Copernicus as a humanist. *In* The Nature of scientific discovery p170-88

A sense of the future
Contents

The creative process
The disestablishment of science
The fulfillment of man
Human and animal languages
The human values
Humanism and the growth of knowledge
Language in a biological frame
The logic of experiment
The logic of nature
The logic of the mind
A moral for an age of plenty
New concepts in the evolution of complexity
On art and science
The principle of tolerance
The reach of imagination
A sense of the future
Toward a philosophy of biology
The values of science
Where do we go from here?

The visionary eye
Contents

The act of recognition
Architecture as a science and architecture as an art
Imagination as plan and as experiment
The imaginative mind in art
The imaginative mind in science
Music, metaphor, and meaning

Bronsen, David
Consuming struggle vs. killing time: preludes to dying in the dramas of Ibsen and Beckett. *In* Spicker, S. F.; Woodward, K. M. and Van Tassel, D. D. eds. Aging and the elderly p261-81

Bronté, Charlotte

About

Kennard, J. E. A question of mastery: the novels of Charlotte Brontë. *In* Kennard, J. E. Victims of convention p80-107

Showalter, E. Feminine heroines: Charlotte Bronte and George Eliot. *In* Showalter, E. A literature of their own p100-32

Tillotson, G. Charlotte and Emily Brontë. *In* Tillotson, G. A view of Victorian literature p187-225

About individual works
Jane Eyre

Adams, M. Family disintegration and creative reintegration: the case of Charlotte Brontë and Jane Eyre p148-79

Adams, M. Jane Eyre: woman's estate. *In* Diamond, A. and Edwards, L. R. eds. The authority of experience p137-59

Gilbert, S. M. and Gubar, S. A dialogue of self and soul: plain Jane's progress. *In* Gilbert, S. M. and Gubar, S. The madwoman in the attic p336-71

Griffin, A. Fire and ice in Frankenstein. *In* Levine, G. L. and Knoepflmacher, U. C. eds. The endurance of Frankenstein p49-73

Hardy, B. N. Fantasy and dream. *In* Hardy, B. N. Tellers and listeners p19-55

Howells, C. A. Charlotte Brontë, Jane Eyre. *In* Howells, C. A. Love, mystery, and misery p159-87

Rich, A. C. Jane Eyre: the temptations of a motherless woman. *In* Rich, A. C. On lies, secrets, and silence p89-106

Rigney, B. H. "The frenzied moment": sex and insanity in Jane Eyre. *In* Rigney, B. H. Madness and sexual politics in the feminist novel p13-37

The professor

Gilbert, S. M. and Gubar, S. A secret, inward wound: The professor's pupil. *In* Gilbert, S. M. and Gubar, S. The madwoman in the attic p311-35

Shirley

Gilbert, S. M. and Gubar, S. The genesis of hunger according to Shirley. *In* Gilbert, S. M. and Gubar, S. The madwoman in the attic p372-98

Villette

Auerbach, N. Beyond the family: idyll and inferno. *In* Auerbach, N. Communities of women p75-113

Gilbert, S. M. and Gubar, S. The buried life of Lucy Snowe. *In* Gilbert, S. M. and Gubar, S. The madwoman in the attic p399-440

Characters—Jane Eyre

Adams, M Jane Eyre: woman's estate. *In* Diamond, A. and Edwards, L. R. eds The authority of experience p137-59

Characters—Lucy Snowe

Gilbert, S. M. and Gubar, S. The buried life of Lucy Snowe. *In* Gilbert, S. M. and Gubar, S. The madwoman in the attic p399-440

Brontë, Emily Jane

About

Auerbach, N. This changeful life: Emily Brontë's anti-romance. *In* Gilbert, S. M. and Gubar, S. eds. Shakespeare's sisters p49-64

Tillotson, G. Charlotte and Emily Brontë. *In* Tillotson, G. A view of Victorian literature p187-225

About individual works
Wuthering Heights

Apter, T. E. Romanticism and romantic love in Wuthering Heights. *In* Smith, A. ed. The art of Emily Brontë p205-22

Bersani, L. Desire and metamorphosis. *In* Bersani, L. A future for Astyanax p189-229

Cockshut, A. O. J. The pessimists: Emily Brontë. *In* Cockshut, A. O. J. Man and woman: a study of love and the novel, 1740-1940 p107-11

Gilbert, S. M. and Gubar, S. Looking oppositely: Emily Brontë's Bible of Hell. *In* Gilbert, S. M. and Gubar, S. The madwoman in the attic p248-308

Goodridge, J. F. A new heaven and a new earth. *In* Smith, A. ed. The art of Emily Brontë p160-81

Kennedy, A. The thread in the garment. *In* Kennedy, A. Meaning and signs in fiction p30-57

Sagar, K. M. The originality of Wuthering Heights. *In* Smith, A. ed. The art of Emily Brontë p121-59

Smith, A. Introduction: Towards a new assessment. *In* Smith, A. ed. The art of Emily Brontë p7-29

Tobin, P. D. Subverting the father: some nineteenth-century precursors. *In* Tobin, P. D. Time and the novel p29-53

Tristram, P. "Divided sources." *In* Smith, A. ed. The art of Emily Brontë p182-204

Wilson, C. A personal response to Wuthering Heights. *In* Smith, A. ed. The art of Emily Brontë p223-37

Poetic works

Grove, R. "It would not do": Emily Brontë as poet. *In* Smith, A. ed. The art of Emily Brontë p33-67

Hardy, B. N. The lyricism of Emily Brontë. *In* Smith, A. ed. The art of Emily Brontë p94-118

Miles, R. A baby god: the creative dynamism of Emily Brontë's poetry. *In* Smith, A. ed. The art of Emily Brontë p68-93

Brontë family
Adams, M. Family disintegration and creative reintegration: the case of Charlotte Brontë and Jane Eyre. *In* Wohl, A. S. ed. The Victorian family p148-79

Cunningham, V. The Brontës. *In* Cunningham, V. Everywhere spoken against p113-26

Brontë family—*Continued*

Karl, F. R. The Brontës: the self defined, redefined, and refined. *In* Levine, R. A. The Victorian experience: the novelists p121-50

Skilton, D. Victorian views of the individual: the Brontës, Thackeray, Trollope and George Eliot. *In* Skilton, D. The English novel p136-62

Bronze. See Bronzes

Bronze figurines

Greece—Olympia

Kopcke, G. More about Olympia B 1701 and B 1999. *In* Studies in classical art and archaeology p17-21

Ohio—Cincinnati

Boulter, P. N. A bronze bull in Cincinnati. *In* Studies in classical art and archaeology p251-54

Bronzes

Ohio—Cincinnati

Boulter, P. N. A bronze bull in Cincinnati. *In* Studies in classical art and archaeology p251-54

Bronzes, Greek

Greece—Olympia

Kopcke, G. More about Olympia B 1701 and B 1999. *In* Studies in classical art and archaeology p17-21

New York (City)

Bothmer, D. F. von. A bronze oinochoe in New York. *In* Studies in classical art and archaeology p63-67

Bronzes, Nigerian

Dark, P. J. C. Benin bronze heads: styles and chronology. *In* African images p25-103

Bronzes, Roman

Rome

Brown, D. Bronze and pewter. *In* Strong, D. E. and Brown, D. eds. Roman crafts p25-42

Hill, D. K. Jupiter: variations on the theme of Olympian Zeus. *In* Studies in classical art and archaeology p247-50

Bronzino, Agnolo

About

Barolsky, P. The lighter side of Cosimo de' Medici's court. *In* Barolsky, P. Infinite jest: wit and humor in Italian Renaissance art p139-57

About individual works
Lucrezia Panciatichi

Meyers, J. Bronzino, Veronese and The wings of the dove. *In* Meyers, J. Painting and the novel p19-30

Brook, Donald

Flight from the object. *In* Concerning contemporary art p16-34

Brook, Peter

About

Kauffmann, S. Peter Brook. *In* Kauffmann, S. Persons of the drama p51-62

About individual works
King Lear (Motion picture)

Jorgens, J. J. King Lear: Peter Brook and Grigori Kozintsev. *In* Jorgens, J. J. Shakespeare on film p235-51

Brooke, Christopher Nugent Lawrence

Geoffrey of Monmouth as a historian. *In* Church and government in the Middle Ages p77-91

Brooke, Fulke Greville, 1st Baron

About

Gilman, E. B. The Pauline perspectives in Donne, Herbert, and Greville. *In* Gilman, E. B. The curious perspective p167-203

Ure, P. Fulke Greville's dramatic characters. *In* Ure, P. Elizabethan and Jacobean drama p104-22

Ure, P. A note on 'opinion' in Daniel, Greville and Chapman. *In* Ure, P. Elizabethan and Jacobean drama p209-20

Brooke, John Hedley

Laurent, Gerhardt, and the philosophy of chemistry. *In* Historical studies in the physical sciences v6 p405-30

Brooke, Nicholas

'All's well that ends well.' *In* Shakespeare survey 30 p73-84

Crazy Jane and 'Byzantium.' *In* English Association. Essays and studies, 1974 p68-83

Brookhouse, Christopher. See Brookhouse, John Christopher

Brookhouse, John Christopher

In search of Chaucer: the needed narrative. *In* The Learned and the lewed p67-80

Brooks, Charles Benton

Williams' comedy. *In* Tennessee Williams: a tribute. p720-35

Brooks, Charles Van Wyck. See Selver, C. jt. auth.

Brooks, Cleanth

Eudora Welty and the Southern idiom. *In* Dollarhide, L. and Abadie, A. J. eds. Eudora Welty: a form of thanks p3-24

Literary criticism: Marvell's "Horatian ode". *In* Wimsatt, W. K. ed. Literary criticism: idea and act p423-43

The modern writer and the burden of history. *In* Tulane Studies in English v22 p155-68

Thomas Percy, Don Quixote, and Don Bowle. *In* Evidence in literary scholarship p247-61

William Faulkner and William Butler Yeats: parallels and affinities. *In* Faulkner: fifty years after The marble faun p139-58

About

Heilman, R. B. Cleanth Brooks: some snapshots, mostly from an old album. *In* Simpson, L. P. ed. The possibilities of order: Cleanth Brooks and his work p128-49

Rooney, W. J. "The canonization"—the language of paradox reconsidered. *In* Roberts, J. R. ed. Essential articles for the study of John Donne's poetry p271-78

Spears, M. K. Cleanth Brooks and the responsibilities of criticism. *In* Simpson, L. P. ed. The possibilities of order: Cleanth Brooks and his work p230-52

Tate, A. What I owe to Cleanth Brooks. *In* Simpson, L. P. ed. The possibilities of order: Cleanth Brooks and his work p125-27

Wellek, R. Cleanth Brooks, critic of critics. *In* Simpson, L. P. ed. The possibilities of order: Cleanth Brooks and his work p196-229

Young, T. D. A little divergence: the critical theories of John Crowe Ransom and Cleanth Brooks. *In* Simpson, L. P. ed. The possibilities of order: Cleanth Brooks and his work p168-95

Brooks, Cleanth—*Continued*

About individual works

William Faulkner: toward Yoknapatawpha and beyond

McHaney, T. L. Brooks on Faulkner: the end of the long view. *In* Review, v 1 1979 p29-45

Brooks, Cleanth, and Warren, Robert Penn

"The killers". *In* Benson, J. J. eds. The short stories of Ernest Hemingway: critical essays p187-96

Brooks, George E.

European relations with Africa before 1870. *In* Martin, P. M. and O'Meara, P. eds. Africa p114-31

Goree and the Cape Verde rivers. *In* African dimensions p69-80

Brooks, Gwendolyn

About

Spillers, H. J. Gwendolyn the terrible: propositions on eleven poems. *In* Gilbert, S. M. and Gubar, S. eds. Shakespeare's sisters p233-44

Brooks, Harvey

The military innovation system and the qualitative arms race. *In* Long, F. A. and Rathjens, G. W. eds. Arms, defense policy, and arms control p75-97

Policies for technology transfer and international investment. *In* The New Atlantic challenge p157-79

The problem of research priorities. *In* Holton, G. J. and Morison, R. S. eds. Limits of scientific inquiry p171-90

Brooks, John Bradbury

Thomas Middleton. *In* Logan, T. P. and Smith, D. S. eds. The popular school p51-84

Brooks, John Nixon

The first and only century of telephone literature. *In* The Social impact of the telephone p208-24

Brooks, Maria Zagórska

The bear in Slavic and Polish mythology and folklore. *In* For Wiktor Weintraub p107-11

Brooks, Michael

Love and possession in a Victorian household: the example of the Ruskins. *In* Wohl, A. S. ed. The Victorian family p82-100

Brooks, Nicholas

Anglo-Saxon charters: the work of the last twenty years. *In* Anglo-Saxon England 3 p211-31

Brooks, Peter

"Godlike science/unhallowed arts": language, nature, and monstrosity. *In* Levine, G. L. and Knoepflmacher, U. C. eds. The endurance of Frankenstein p205-20

Brooks, Richard A.

Rousseau's antifeminism in the Lettre à d'Alembert and Emile. *In* Literature and history in the age of ideas p209-27

Brooks, Van Wyck

About

Paul, S. Van Wyck Brooks's ordeal and pilgrimage. *In* Paul, S. Repossessing and renewing p131-36

Wasserstrom, W. Van Wyck Brooks. *In* Ross, R. G. ed. Makers of American thought p157-91

Broom (Periodical)

Tashjian, D. L. Broom and Secession. *In* Tashjian, D. L. Skyscraper primitives p116-42

Broomfield, John Hindle

Peasant mobilization in twentieth-century Bengal. *In* Forging nations: a comparative view of rural ferment and revolt p41-60

Brosnahan, Leger

Now (this), now (that) and BD 646. *In* The Learned and the lewed p11-18

Brosse, Guy de La. See La Brosse, Guy de

Brotherhood. See Brotherliness

Brotherliness

DeMott, B. Equality and fraternity: a note on subjective realities. *In* Small comforts for hard times p72-84

Brotherston, Gordon

The emergence of the Latin American novel

Contents

America's magic forest: Miguel Ángel Asturias

An end to secular solitude: Gabriel García Márquez

The genesis of America: Alejo Carpentier

Intellectual geography: Julio Cortázar

A permanent home?

Province of dead souls: Juan Rulfo

Settings and people

Social structures: Mario Vargas Llosa

Survival in the sullied city: Juan Carlos Onetti

Tupac Amaru dismembered: José María Arguedas

Huitzilopochtli and what was made of him. *In* Mesoamerican archaeology p155-66

Brough, John B.

The emergence of an absolute consciousness in Husserl's early writings on time-consciousness. *In* Elliston, F. A. and McCormick, P. eds. Husserl p83-100

Broughton, Panthea Reid

Faulkner. *In* American literary scholarship, 1976 p119-40

Faulkner [another essay] *In* American literary scholarship, 1977 p135-61

Brower, Alston

Black studies and changing times. *In* Fairfield, R. P. ed. Humanistic frontiers in American education p134-38

Brower, Reuben Arthur

Mirror on mirror

Contents

Dryden's epic manner and Virgil

From the Iliad to the novel, via The rape of the lock

Same as: Brower, R. A. From the Iliad to Jane Austen, via The rape of the lock. *In* Halperin, J. ed. Jane Austen p43-60

The heresy of plot

Introduction: Translation as parody

Poetic and dramatic design in versions and translations of Shakespeare

A poet's Odyssey

Pope's Iliad for twentieth-century readers

Seven Agamemnons

The Theban eagle in English plumage

Visual and verbal translation of myth: Neptune in Virgil, Rubens, Dryden

With Gibbon in Puerto Rico. *In* Edward Gibbon and The decline and fall of the Roman Empire p247-49

Brown, H. Douglas
What is applied linguistics? *In* Wardhaugh, R. and Brown, H. D. eds. A survey of applied linguistics p 1-7

Brown, Harcourt
From London to Lapland: Maupertuis, Johann Bernoulli I, and La Terre applatie, 1728-1738. *In* Literature and history in the age of ideas p69-94

Brown, Harrison Scott
Some quasi-Copernican revolutions in man's utilization of energy. *In* Neyman, J. ed. The heritage of Copernicus: theories "pleasing to the mind" p526-36

Brown, Homer Obed
The displaced self in the novels of Daniel Defoe. *In* Studies in eighteenth-century culture v4 p69-94

Brown, Howard Mayer
Instruments and voices in the fifteenth-century chanson. *In* Current thought in musicology p89-137

Brown, James R.
About
Harvey, A. M. Pioneers in urology: James R. Brown and Howard A. Kelly. *In* Harvey, A. M. Adventures in medical research p8-17

Brown, Janet H.
The narrator's role in David Copperfield. *In* Dickens Studies Annual v2 p197-207

Brown, Jennifer M.
The exercise of power. *In* Brown, J. M. ed. Scottish society in the fifteenth century p33-65

Brown, John, 1800-1859
About
Oates, S. B. John Brown and his judges: a critique of the historical literature. *In* Swierenga, R. P. ed. Beyond the Civil War synthesis p57-76

Brown, Jonathan
Images and ideas in seventeenth-century Spanish painting
Contents
El Arte de la pintura as an academic document
A community of scholars
Hieroglyphs of death and salvation: the decoration of the Church of the Hermandad de la Caridad, Seville
On the meaning of Las meninas
Theory into practice: the arts and the academy
Zurbarán's paintings in the sacristy of the monastery of Guadalupe
Pen drawings by Herrera the Younger. *In* Enggass, R. C. and Stokstad, M. eds. Hortus imaginum p129-38

Brown, Joseph E.
The science of weights. *In* Lindberg, D. C. ed. Science in the Middle Ages p179-205

Brown, Joseph Epes
The roots of renewal. *In* Seeing with a native eye p25-34
About
Brown, J. E. Hanblecheyapi: crying for a vision; excerpt from "The sacred pipe." *In* Tedlock, D. E. and Tedlock, B. eds. Teachings from the American earth p20-41

Brown, Judith K.
Iroquois women: an ethnohistoric note. *In* Reiter, R. R. ed. Toward an anthropology of women p235-51

Brown, Judith M.
'Gandhi's men', 1917-22: the role of the major leader in the careers of middle-rank politicians. *In* The Making of politicians: studies from Africa and Asia p126-39

Brown, Julia M.
Women in physical education: the dribble index of liberation. *In* Roberts, J. I. ed. Beyond intellectual sexism p365-80

Brown, Keith
'Form and cause conjoin'd': 'Hamlet' and Shakespeare's workshop. *In* Shakespeare survey 26 p11-20

Brown, Lawrence D.
Mayors and models: notes on the study of urban politics. *In* Burnham, W. D. and Weinberg, M. W. eds. American politics and public policy p251-79

Brown, Lee Bateman
Animadversions on the autonomy of art. *In* Viva Vivas! p183-223

Brown, Lester Russell
Issues of human welfare. *In* Bundy, R. F. ed. Images of the future: the twenty-first century and beyond p81-95

Brown, Lloyd Wellesley
The African heritage and the Harlem Renaissance: a re-evaluation. *In* African literature today no. 9: Africa, America and the Caribbean p 1-9
The business of marrying and mothering. *In* Jane Austen's achievement p27-43
The revolutionary dream of Walcott's Makak. *In* Baugh, E. ed. Critics on Caribbean literature p58-62

Brown, Malcolm
A pre-Aristotelian mathematician on deductive order. *In* Philosophy and humanism p258-74

Brown, Martha A.
The administration of professors as decision makers. *In* Managing nonprofit organizations p303-12

Brown, Merle Elliott
Kenneth Burke. *In* Ross, R. G. ed. Makers of American thought p192-226

Brown, Michael Eugene
The condemnation and persecution of hippies. *In* Henslin, J. M. ed. Deviant life-styles p349-71
Sociology as critical theory. *In* McNall, S. G. ed. Theoretical perspectives in sociology p251-75

Brown, Neville
Threats to security in Europe. *In* The New Atlantic challenge p219-28

Brown, Norman Oliver
On interpretation. *In* Evolution of consciousness p34-41
About
Bell, D. Beyond modernism, beyond self. *In* Art, politics, and will p213-53
Crews, F. C. Norman O. Brown: the world dissolves. *In* Crews, F. C. Out of my system p19-39

Brown, Peter Douglas
Gibbon's views on culture and society in the fifth and sixth centuries. *In* Edward Gibbon and The decline and fall of the Roman Empire p37-52

Brown, Peter Gilbert
The general welfare. *In* Population policy and ethics p41-46

Brown, Peter Gilbert, and Corfman, Eunice Luccock
Moral-political values: an historical analysis. *In* Population policy and ethics p55-126

Brown, Richard D.
Modernization: a Victorian climax. *In* Howe, D. W. ed. Victorian America p29-44

Brown, Richard Harvey
The emergence of existential thought: philosophical perspectives on positivist and humanist forms of social theory. *In* Douglas, J. D. and Johnson, J. M. [eds.] Existential sociology p77-100

History and hermeneutics: Wilhelm Dilthey and the dialectics of interpretive method. *In* Brown, R. H. and Lyman, S. M. eds. Structure, consciousness, and history p38-52

Symbolic realism and sociological thought: beyond the positivist-romantic debate. *In* Brown, R. H. and Lyman, S. M. eds. Structure, consciousness, and history p13-37

Brown, Richard Harvey, and Lyman, Stanford Morris
Symbolic realism and cognitive aesthetics: an invitation. *In* Brown, R. H. and Lyman, S. M. eds. Structure, consciousness, and history p 1-10

Brown, Rita Mae
The lesbian woman: two points of view: A woman's place is wherever she wants it to be. *In* Gochros, H. L. and Gochros, J. S. eds. The sexually oppressed p152-59

Brown, Robert Carlton

About

Ford, H. D. Four new directions: fourth-dimensional writing: The Roving eye. *In* Ford, H. D. Published in Paris p302-11

Brown, Robert Eldon
Did the American Revolution really happen? *In* Suggs, G. G. ed. Perspectives on the American Revolution p13-35

Brown, Robert Loveridge, and Steinmann, Martin
Native readers of fiction: a speech-act and genre-rule approach to defining literature. *In* Hernadi, P. ed. What is literature? p141-60

Brown, Robert McAfee
Reinhold Niebuhr: a study in humanity and humility. *In* Scott, N. A. ed. The legacy of Reinhold Niebuhr p 1-7

Brown, Robert R.
The new criminology. *In* Law and society p81-107

Brown, Roger William
Development of the first language in the human species. *In* Bloomfield, M. W. and Haugen, E. I. eds. Language as a human problem p121-36

Brown, Roscoe Conkling
A commentary on racial myths and the Black athlete. *In* Social problems in athletics p168-73

Brown, Seyom
A world of multiple relationships. *In* Atlantis lost p103-18

Brown, Sidney DeVere
Shidehara Kijūrō: the diplomacy of the yen. *In* Burns, R. D. and Bennett, E. M. eds. Diplomats in crisis p201-25

Brown, Stuart C.
Academic freedom. *In* Philosophers discuss education p205-20

Religion and the limits of language. *In* Reason and religion p233-55

What is the verifiability criterion a criterion of? *In* Royal Institute of Philosophy. Impressions of empiricism p137-53

About individual works
Academic freedom

Griffiths, A. P. Academic freedom: a reply to Dr Brown. *In* Philosophers discuss education p221-42

Brown, Susan E.
Love unites them and hunger separates them: poor women in the Dominican Republic. *In* Reiter, R. R. ed. Toward an anthropology of women p322-32

Brown, Terence
MacNeice: father and son. *In* Time was away p21-34

Brown, Thomas Richardson

About

Harvey, A. M. Medical students on the march: Brown, MacCallum, and Opie. *In* Harvey, A. M. Adventures in medical research p18-31

Brown, Virginia
The "insular intermediary" in the tradition of Lucretius. *In* Harvard Studies in classical philology v72 p301-08

Brown, William Oscar. See Part 2 under title: African dimensions

Brown v. Board of Education of the City of Topeka. *In* Have we overcome? Race relations since Brown p3-30

Brown v. Board of Education of the City of Topeka. *In* Have we overcome? Race relations since Brown p79-119

Brown v. Board of Education of the City of Topeka. *In* Have we overcome? Race relations since Brown p173-87

Browne, Gerald M.
Harpocration panegyrista. *In* Illinois classical studies, v2 1977 p184-96

Late Roman papyri from the Michigan collection. *In* Harvard Studies in classical philology v75 p177-90

The origin and date of the Sortes Astrampsychi. *In* Illinois classical studies, v 1 1976 p53-58

Ostraca Harvardiana. *In* Harvard Studies in classical philology v76 p245-58

The Sahidic version of Kingdoms IV. *In* Illinois classical studies v3, 1978 p196-205

Three papyri from fourth-century Karanis. *In* Harvard Studies in classical philology v74 p317-31

Browne, Hablot Knight

About

Steig, M. Martin Chuzzlewit's progress by Dickens and Phiz. *In* Dickens Studies Annual v2 p119-48

Browne, John Ross

About individual works
Adventures in the Apache country

Dillon, R. H. J. Ross Browne and Arizona. *In* Voices from the Southwest p92-101

Browne, Ray Broadus

Academicons-sick sacred cows. *In* Browne, R. B. and Fishwick, M. W. eds. Icons of America p292-301

Irving Wallace: independent drummer. *In* Filler, L. ed. A question of quality: popularity and value in modern creative writing p92-107

See also Packard, C. jt. auth.

Brownell, Blaine A.

The urban South comes of age, 1900-1940. *In* Brownell, B. A. and Goldfield, D. R. eds. The city in Southern history p123-58

Brownell, Blaine A. and Goldfield, David R.

Southern urban history. *In* Brownell, B. A. and Goldfield, D. R. eds. The city in Southern history p5-22

Brownell, David Blair

The two worlds of Charlotte Yonge. *In* The Worlds of Victorian fiction p165-78

Browning, Barton W.

Joseph Roth's Legende vom heiligen Trinker: essence and elixir. *in* Strelka, J. P.; Bell, R. F. and Dobson, E. eds. Protest—form—tradition p81-95

Browning, Don S.

Erikson and the search for a normative image of man. *In* Homans, P. ed. Childhood and selfhood p264-92

Browning, Elizabeth (Barrett)

About

Cooper, H. Working into light: Elizabeth Barrett Browning. *In* Gilbert, S. M. and Gubar, S. eds. Shakespeare's sisters p65-81

About individual works
Aurora Leigh

Gilbert, S. M. and Gubar, S. The aesthetics of renunciation. *In* Gilbert, S. M. and Gubar, S. The madwoman in the attic p539-80

Browning, Robert, 1812-1889

About

Armstrong, I. Browning and Victorian poetry of sexual love. *In* Armstrong, I. ed Robert Browning p267-98

Bloom, H. Browning: good moments and ruined quests. *In* Bloom, H. Poetry and repression p175-204

Johnson, W. S. Marriage and divorce in Browning. *In* Johnson, W. S. Sex and marriage in Victorian poetry p185-251

Mason, M. Browning and the dramatic monologue. *In* Armstrong, I. ed. Robert Browning p231-66

Melchiori, B. Browning in Italy. *In* Armstrong, I. ed. Robert Browning p168-83

Peckham, M. Browning and romanticism. *In* Armstrong, I. ed. Robert Browning p47-76

Peterson, L. H. Biblical typology and the self-portrait of the poet in Robert Browning. *In* Landow, G. P. ed. Approaches to Victorian autobiography p235-68

Tillotson, G. Browning. *In* Tillotson, G. A view of Victorian literature p328-82

About individual works
Aristophanes' apology

Ryals, C. de L. "Analyzing humanity back into its elements": Browning's Aristophanes' apology and Carlyle. *In* Carlyle and his contemporaries p280-97

By the fireside

Poston, L. Browning and the altered romantic landscape. *In* Knoepflmacher, U. C. and Tennyson, G. B. eds. Nature and the Victorian imagination p426-40

Childe Roland to the dark tower came

Assad, T. J. Browning's "Childe Roland to the dark tower came." *In* Tulane Studies in English v21 p67-76

Poston, L. Browning and the altered romantic landscape. *In* Knoepflmacher, U. C. and Tennyson, G. B. eds. Nature and the Victorian imagination p426-40

Christmas-eve and Easter-day

Dawson, C. Dramatic elegists: Arnold, Clough, and Browning at mid-century. *In* Dawson, C. Victorian noon p63-104

A death in the desert

Fricke, D. G. "A death in the desert": the Gospel according to Robert Browning. *In* Aeolian harps p167-78

Shaffer, E. S. Browning's St John: the casuistry of the higher criticism. *In* Shaffer, E. S. 'Kubla Khan' and The fall of Jerusalem p191-224

In a year

Cornet, R. J. Irony without positive norms: Robert Browning's "In a year." *In* Aeolian harps p149-66

James Lee's wife

Ball, P. M. 'If I be dear to someone else.' *In* Ball, P. M. The heart's events p105-66

Mr Sludge, "The medium"

Neel, B. B. The rule of reverse in "Mr Sludge, 'The medium.' " *In* Tennessee Studies in literature v XX p60-68

Pauline

Mill, J. S. Browning's Pauline. *In* Mill, J. S. Essays on poetry p23-27

Pippa passes

Hill, A. A. Pippa's song: two attempts at structural criticism. *In* Hill, A. A. Constituent and pattern in poetry p23-27

Rabbi Ben Ezra

McAleer, E. C. Empedocles, Omar Khayyám, and Rabbi Ben Ezra. *In* Tennessee Studies in literature v XX p76-84

The ring and the book

Litzinger, B. The new vision of Judgment: the case of St Guido. *In* Tennessee Studies in literature v XX p69-75

Peckham, M. Historiography and The ring and the book. *In* Peckham, M. Romanticism and behavior p109-25

Bibliography

Keating, P. J. Robert Browning: a reader's guide. *In* Armstrong, I. ed. Robert Browning p299-341

Books and reading

Woolford, J. Sources and resources in Browning's early reading. *In* Armstrong, I. ed. Robert Browning p 1-46

Characters—
Count Guido Franceschini

Litzinger, B. The new vision of Judgment: the case of St Guido. *In* Tennessee Studies in literature v XX p69-75

Browning, Robert, 1812-1889—*Continued*

Knowledge—Art

Ormond, L. Browning and painting. *In* Armstrong, I. ed. Robert Browning p184-210

Knowledge—History

Sharrock, R. Browning and history. *In* Armstrong, I. ed. Robert Browning p77-103

Knowledge—Music

See Browning, Robert—Music

Knowledge—Political science

See Browning, Robert—Political and social views

Music

Gay, P. Browning and music. *In* Armstrong, I. ed. Robert Browning p211-30

Philosophy

Drew, P. Browning and philosophy. *In* Armstrong, I. ed. Robert Browning p104-41

Political and social views

Lloyd, T. Browning and politics. *In* Armstrong, I. ed. Robert Browning p142-67

Sources

Woolford, J. Sources and resources in Browning's early reading. *In* Armstrong, I. ed. Robert Browning p 1-46

Browning, Robert, 1914-
Homer in Byzantium. *In* Viator: medieval and Renaissance studies v6 p15-33

Browning, Robert Willard
The study of Asian philosophy: for history; for comparison; for synthesis? *In* Viva Vivas! p289-330

Brownists
Collinson, P. Towards a broader understanding of the early dissenting tradition. *In* The Dissenting tradition p3-38

Brownlee, Michael B. See Bickwit, L. jt. auth.

Brownley, Martine Watson
Gibbon: the formation of mind and character. *In* Edward Gibbon and The decline and fall of the Roman Empire p13-25

Brownrigg, Linda L.
Manuscripts containing English decoration 871-1066, catalogued and illustrated: a review. *In* Anglo-Saxon England 7 p239-66

Brownstein, Oscar Lee
Aristotle and the rhetorical process. *In* Rhetoric: a tradition in transition p19-32

Bruce, Frederick Fyvie
The speeches in Acts—thirty years after. *In* Reconciliation and hope p53-68

Bruce-Mitford, Rupert Leo Scott

About individual works

The Sutton Hoo ship burial

Biddle, M. and others. Sutton Hoo published: a review. *In* Anglo Saxon England 6 p249-65

Bruck, Peter
Black American short fiction in the 20th century: problems of audience, and the evolution of artistic stances and themes. *In* Bruck, P. ed. The Black American short story in the 20th century p 1-19

Langston Hughes, The blues I'm playing. *In* Bruck, P. ed. The Black American short story in the 20th century p71-83

Bruehl, Elisabeth Young-. See Young-Bruehl, Elisabeth

Bruford, Alan
The grey selkie. *In* Ballad studies p41-65

Bruford, Walter Horace
The German tradition of self-cultivation
Contents
Adalbert Stifter: Der Nachsommer (1857)
Arthur Schopenhauer: Aphorismen zur Lebensweisheit (1851)
The conversion of an unpolitical man
Friedrich Nietzsche: Also sprach Zarathustra (1883-5)
Friedrich Schleiermacher: Monologen (1801)
Friedrich Theodor Vischer: Auch einer (1879)
Goethe: Wilhelm Meisters Lehrjahre (1795-6)
Goethe: Wilhelm Meisters Wanderjahre (1829)
Theodor Fontane: Frau Jenny Treibel (1892)
Thomas Mann: Der Zauberberg (1924)
Wilhelm von Humboldt in his letters

Brumfield, William C.
Sleptsov redivivus. *In* California Slavic studies v9 p27-70

Brumfitt, John Henry
Historical Pyrrhonism and Enlightenment historiography in France. *In* Literature and history in the age of idea p15-28

Brundage, James A.
Holy war and the medieval lawyers. *In* The Holy war p99-140

Brunei, Borneo (State)

Historiography

Tarling, N. Some notes on the historiography of British Borneo. *In* Southeast Asian history and historiography p285-95

Brunelleschi, Filippo

About

Sunderland, E. R. The system of proportion of Filippo Brunelleschi. *In* Enggass, R. C. and Stokstad, M. eds. Hortus imaginum p65-72

Bruner, Jerome Seymour
Language as an instrument of thought. *In* Davies, A. ed. Problems of language and learning p61-88

Learning how to do things with words. *In* Human growth and development p62-84

On knowing
(See note in: List of books indexed)
Contents
The act of discovery
After John Dewey, what?
Art as a mode of knowing
The conditions of creativity
The control of human behavior
Fate and the possible
Freud and the image of man
Identity and the modern novel
Myth and identity
On learning mathematics
Psychology and the image of man

Brunette, Peter
Two Wrights, one wrong. *In* Peary, G. and Shatzkin, R. eds. The modern American novel and the movies p131-42

Bruni, Leonardo Aretino

About

Soudek, J. A fifteenth-century humanistic bestseller: the manuscript diffusion of Leonardo Bruni's annotated Latin version of the (pseudo-) Aristotelian Economics. *In* Philosopy and humanism p129-43

Brunius, Teddy

Theory and ideologies in aesthetics. *In* Aagaard-Mogensen, L. ed. Culture and art p66-77

Brunner, Georg, and Kaschkat, Hannes

Party, state and groups in Eastern Europe. *In* Hayward, J. E. S. and Berki, R. N. eds. State and society in contemporary Europe p95-117

Brunner, John

Science fiction and the larger lunacy. *In* Nicholls, P. ed. Science fiction at large p73-103

About

De Bolt, J. The development of John Brunner. *In* Clareson, T. D. ed. Voices for the future: essays on major science fiction writers v2 p106-35

Bruno, Giordano

About individual works

The heroic frenzies

Røstvig, M. S. In ordine di ruota: circular structure in "The unfortunate lover" and Upon Appleton House. *In* Friedenreich, K. ed. Tercentenary essays in honor of Andrew Marvell p245-67

Influence—Marvell

Røstvig, M. S. In ordine di ruota: circular structure in "The unfortunate lover" and Upon Appleton House. *In* Friedenreich, K. ed. Tercentenary essays in honor of Andrew Marvell p245-67

Bruno, Giordano in fiction, drama, poetry, etc.

Wilder, T. N. Giordano Bruno's last meal in Finnegans wake. *In* American characteristics, and other essays p278-85

Brus, Włodzimierz

Staninism and the "peoples' democracies." *In* Staninism p239-56

Brušák, Karel

Signs in the Chinese theater. *In* Matejka, L. and Titunik, I. R. eds. Semiotics of art p59-73

Bruss, Elizabeth W.

Autobiographical acts

Contents

Conclusion
From act to text
Introduction: Literary acts
James Boswell: genius and stenography
John Bunyan: the patriarch and the way
Thomas De Quincey: sketches and sighs
Vladimir Nabokov: illusions of reality and the reality of illusions

Brustein, Robert Sanford

The crack in the chimney: reflections on contemporary American playwriting. *In* Images and ideas in American culture p141-57

The culture watch

Contents

Acting in England and America
Art in an age of ideology: England's Ireland

Back to the wilderness: the Open Theatre
Broadway and the nonprofit theatre: a misalliance
The contemporary English theatre: mirror or lamp?
Cultural schizophrenia
The curses of Caliban: Kaspar
A Dean's goodbye: a speech to the graduates of the School of Drama
The evolution of a woman: A doll's house
Freedom and constraint in the American theatre
The great American tragedy
In defense of repertory theatre
The limits of English realism
Mr Arden versus Mr Jones
The money crisis and the performing arts
A new conspiracy theory: Lenny
New fads, ancient truths
News theatre
No more masterpieces revisited: a speech to the Shakespeare '74 Convention at Brooklyn College
On the new cultural conservatism
The prevalence of style: The Cherry Orchard
The profession is not supporting the profession!
Reflections on privacy
Repertory in the doldrums
Sam Shepard's America: The unseen hand
Seminal and consumer theatre
A tale of two cities
Theatre and the university
Thebes and Watergate
Two plays about Ireland: Richard's cork leg and The Ballygombeen bequest
Window on the world: the World Theatre Festival
The Yale idea: an address to students at the School of Drama

Bruton, John W.

The text of Colley Cibber's The double gallant: or, The sick lady's cure. *In* Virginia. University. Bibliographical Society. Studies in bibliography v30 p186-96

Brutus, Dennis

About

Egudu, R. N. Pictures of pain: the poetry of Dennis Brutus. *In* Heywood, C. ed. Aspects of South African literature p131-44

Bruyère, Jean de la. See La Bruyère, Jean de

Bruzina, Ronald Charles

Heidegger on the metaphor and philosophy. *In* Murray, M. E. ed. Heidegger and modern philosophy p184-200

Bryant, Coralie, and White, Louise G.

Housing policies and comparative urban politics. *In* Walton, J. and Masotti, L. H. eds. The city in comparative perspective p81-95

Bryant, Donald Cross

Literature and politics. *In* Burks, D. M. ed. Rhetoric, philosophy, and literature: an exploration p95-107

See also Part 2 under title: Rhetoric: a tradition in transition

Bryant, Joseph Allen

Eudora Welty. *In* Howard, M. ed. Seven American women writers of the twentieth century p166-213

The recovery of the confident narrator: A curtain of green to Losing battles. *In* Prenshaw, P. W. ed. Eudora Welty p68-82

Bryant, Keith L.
Oklahoma and the New Deal. *In* Braeman, J.; Bremner, R. H. and Brody, D. eds. The New Deal v2 p166-97

Bryant, Paul T.
The family journey to the West. *In* Kagle, S. E. ed. America: exploration and travel p153-65

Bryant, Ralph C.
Empirical research on financial capital flows. *In* Kenen, P. B. ed. International trade and finance p321-62

Bryant, William Cullen

About

Doubleday, N. F. Redwood and Bryant's review. *In* Doubleday, N. F. Variety of attempt p147-59

Bryce, James Bryce, Viscount

About individual works
The American commonwealth

Ions, E. S. James Bryce. *In* Abroad in America: Visitors to the new Nation, 1776-1914. p207-17

Bryce-Laporte, Roy Simon
On models of multiethnic societies: a commentary. *In* Major social issues p66-77

About individual works
On models of multiethnic societies: a commentary

DeVos, G. A. and Pettigrew, T. F. Comments on the discussion of Roy S. Bryce-Laporte. *In* Major social issues p78-81

Bryer, Jackson R.
Fitzgerald and Hemingway. *In* American literary scholarship, 1973 p150-76
Fitzgerald and Hemingway [another essay]. *In* American literary scholarship 1974 p139-64
Fitzgerald and Hemingway [another essay]. *In* American literary scholarship, 1975 p167-200
Fitzgerald and Hemingway [another essay]. *In* American literary scholarship, 1976 p141-66
Fitzgerald and Hemingway [another essay]. *In* American literary scholarship, 1977 p163-86
William Styron: bibliography. *In* Morris, R. K. and Malin, I. eds. The achievement of William Styron p242-77

Brygos

About

Phillips, K. M. and Ashmead, A. H. Three goddesses and a falcon. *In* Studies in classical art and archaeology p45-52

Bryusov, Valeri Yakovlevich
Burnt to ashes. *In* Maguire, R. A. ed. Gogol from the twentieth century p103-31

About

Binyon, T. J. Valery Bryusov and the nature of art. *In* Oxford Slavonic papers new ser. v7 p96-111

Bryusov, Valery. See Bryusov, Valeri Yakovlevich

Brzezinski, Zbigniew Kazimierz
The European crossroads. *In* Atlantis lost p85-102
The global triangle: the changing power balance in Asia and its consequences for the foreign policy of the Atlantic nations. *In* The New Atlantic challenge p315-28

Soviet politics: from the future to the past? *In* Cocks, P.; Daniels, R. V. and Heer, N. W. eds. The dynamics of Soviet politics p337-51

Brzozowski, Stanisław

About

Miłosz, C. A one-man army: Stanisław Brzozowski. *In* Miłosz, C. Emperor of the earth p186-253
Kaufman, W. E. Martin Buber: can God be encountered? *In* Kaufman, W. E. Contemporary Jewish philosophies p55-77

Buber, Martin

About

Scott, N. A. Martin Buber—guide to the world of Thou. *In* Scott, N. A. Mirrors of man in existentialism p184-217

About individual works
I and Thou

Scott, N. A. Martin Buber—guide to the world of Thou. *In* Scott, N. A. Mirrors of man in existentialism p184-217

Bubonic plague. See Plague

Buchan, Alastair
An expedition to the poles. *In* The Year book of world affairs, 1975 p4-21
Mothers and daughters (or Greeks and Romans) *In* Two hundred years of American foreign policy p20-66
United States foreign policy and the future. *In* Rosecrance, R. N. ed. America as an ordinary country p20-37
The United States in tomorrow's international system. *In* Tomorrow's American p 1-20

Buchan, David D.
History and Harlaw. *In* Ballad studies p29-40

Buchan, John

About

Cawelti, J. G. The joys of Buchaneering. *In* Essays in honor of Russel B. Nye p7-30
Hart, F. R. Stevenson, Munro, and Buchan. *In* Hart, F. R. The Scottish novel p154-81
Lambert, G. The thin protection: John Buchan. *In* Lambert, G. The dangerous edge p79-104

About individual works
Sick Heart River

Tiffin, H. Towards place and placelessness: two journey patterns in Commonwealth literature. *In* Narasimhaiah, C. D. ed. Awakened conscience p146-63

Characters—Richard Hannay

Cawelti, J. G. The joys of Buchaneering. *In* Essays in honor of Russel B. Nye p7-30

Buchanan, Albert Russell
American attitudes toward war. *In* Encyclopedia of American foreign policy p16-24

Buchanan, George

About individual works
The Sphera

McFarlane, I. D. The history of George Buchanan's Sphæra. *In* French Renaissance studies, 1540-70 p194-212

Buchanan, James M.

The justice of natural liberty. *In* Glahe, F. R. ed. Adam Smith and The wealth of nations p61-81

Methods and morals in economics: the Ayres-Knight discussion. *In* Science and ceremony p163-74

The political economy of franchise in the welfare state. *In* Capitalism and freedom p52-77

Public goods and natural liberty. *In* The Market and the state p271-86

Buchanan (Colin) and Partners

About individual works

City of Edinburgh Planning and Transportation Study

Hare, R. Contrasting methods of environmental planning. *In* Royal Institute of Philosophy. Nature and conduct p281-97

Bucher, Bradley D. See Conway, J. B. jt. auth.

Buchler, Justus

About individual works

The main of light

Richards, I. A. The enlightening eye. *In* Richards, I. A. Complementarities p127-35

Büchner, Georg

About

Canetti, E. Georg Büchner. *In* Canetti, E. The conscience of words p192-202

Larkin, M. Pessimism. *In* Larkin, M. Man and society in nineteenth-century realism p55-65

Schwarz, A. Society and human passion as a tragic motive. *In* Schwarz, A. From Büchner to Beckett p100-60

About individual works

Danton's death

Hamburger, M. Büchner's Danton's death. *In* Hamburger, M. Art as second nature p64-67

Schwarz, A. The experience of history as fateful. *In* Schwarz, A. From Büchner to Beckett p61-99

Simon, J. I. Danton's death. *In* Simon, J. I. Singularities p20-31

Lenz

Pascal, R. Early accomplishment: Georg Büchner: Lenz. *In* Pascal, R. The dual voice p60-66

Swales, M. Büchner: Lenz. *In* Swales, M. The German Novelle p99-113

Woyzeck

Schmidgall, G. Alban Berg. *In* Schmidgall, G. Literature as opera p287-319

Buchthal, Hugo

Toward a history of Palaeologan illumination. *In* The Place of book illumination in Byzantine art p143-77

Buchwald, Jed Z.

William Thomson and the mathematization of Faraday's electrostatics. *In* Historical studies in the physical sciences v8 p101-36

Buck, John Dawson Carl

The motives of puffing: John Newbery's advertisements 1742-1767. *In* Virginia. University. Bibliographical Society. Studies in bibliography v30 p196-210

Buckalew, Ronald E.

Leland's transcript of Ælfric's Glossary. *In* Anglo-Saxon England 7 p149-64

Buckingham, Edward Stafford, 3d duke of

About

Harris, B. J. Landlords and tenants in England in the later Middle Ages: the Buckingham estates. *In* Peasants, knights and heretics p216-20

Buckingham, Willis J.

Whitman and Dickinson. *In* American literary scholarship, 1977 p65-97

See also Fisher, M. jt. auth.

Buckle, Richard

On loving Lydia. *In* Keynes, M. ed. Essays on John Maynard Keynes p49-59

Buckley, Irene G.

Fulfillment of life in the presence of death. *In* Home care p199-204

Buckley, Irene G. and Michaels, Ruth

Variations on a theme: case reports from cancer care. *In* Anticipatory grief p135-43

Buckley, Jerome Hamilton

The fear of art; excerpt from "The Victorian temper". *In* Sambrook, J. ed. Pre-Raphaelitism p186-205

Victorian England: the self-conscious society. *In* Altholz, J. L. ed. The mind and art of Victorian England p3-15

A world of literature: Gissing's New Grub Street. *In* The Worlds of Victorian fiction p223-34

Buckley, Thomas Hugh

John Van Antwerp MacMurray: the diplomacy of an American mandarin. *In* Burns, R. D. and Bennett, E. M. eds. Diplomats in crisis p27-48

Buckley, William Frank

The road to serfdom: the intellectuals and socialism. *In* Essays on Hayek p95-106

Buckley v. Valeo. *In* The Supreme Court review, 1976 p 1-43

Buckroyd, Julia

The Resolutioners and the Scottish nobility in the early months of 1660. *In* Church, society and politics p245-52

Bucolic literature. See Pastoral literature

Bucolic poetry. See Pastoral poetry

Budd, Louis J.

Mark Twain. *In* American literary scholarship, 1976 p79-91

Buddensieg, Tilmann

Criticism of ancient architecture in the sixteenth and seventeenth centuries. *In* Classical influences on European culture A.D. 1500-1700 p335-48

Buddhism

Bishop, D. H. Buddhism. *In* Bishop, D. H. ed. Indian thought p115-42

Goleman, D. The Buddha on meditation and states of consciousness. *In* Tart, C. T. ed. Transpersonal psychologies p203-30

Ogibenin, B. L. A semiotic approach to religion. *In* Sebeok, T. A. ed. Sight, sound, and sense p232-43

See also Hinayana Buddhism; Sociology, Buddhist; Zen Buddhism

Bibliography

Reynolds, F. E. Buddhism. *In* Adams, C. J. ed. A reader's guide to the great religions p156-222

Influence

Benz, E. Buddhism in the Western world. *In* Dumoulin, H. ed. Buddhism in the modern world p305-22

Buddhism—_Continued_

Psychology

Coomaraswamy, A. K. On the Indian and traditional psychology, or rather pneumatology. _In_ Coomaraswamy, A. K. Selected papers v2 p333-78

Goleman, D. The Buddha on meditation and states of consciousness. _In_ Tart, C. T. ed. Transpersonal psychologies p203-30

Relations—Confucianism

Araki, K. Confucianism and Buddhism in the late Ming. _In_ The Unfolding of Neo-Confucianism p39-66

Burma

King, W. L. Contemporary Burmese Buddhism. _In_ Dumoulin, H. ed. Buddhism in the modern world p81-98

Cambodia

Zago, M. Contemporary Khmer Buddhism. _In_ Dumoulin, H. ed. Buddhism in the modern world p109-19

China

Welch, H. H. Buddhism in China today. _In_ Dumoulin, H. ed. Buddhism in the modern world p164-78

China—History

Greenblatt, K. Y. Chu-hung and lay Buddhism in the late Ming. _In_ The Unfolding of Neo-Confucianism p3-140

Germany

Benz, E. Buddhism in the Western world. _In_ Dumoulin, H. ed. Buddhism in the modern world p305-22

Great Britain

Benz, E. Buddhism in the Western world. _In_ Dumoulin, H. ed. Buddhism in the modern world p305-22

India

Fiske, A. M. Buddhism in India today. _In_ Dumoulin, H. ed. Buddhism in the modern world p130-46

Indonesia

Bakker, J. W. M. Contemporary Buddhism in Indonesia. _In_ Dumoulin, H. ed. Buddhism in the modern world p147-53

Japan

Dumoulin, H. Buddhism in modern Japan. _In_ Dumoulin, H. ed. Buddhism in the modern world p215-76

Korea

Dumoulin, H. Contemporary Buddhism in Korea. _In_ Dumoulin, H. ed. Buddhism in the modern world p202-14

Laos

Zago, M. Buddhism in contemporary Laos. _In_ Dumoulin, H. ed. Buddhism in the modern world p120-29

Malaysia

Wayman, A. Buddhism in Malaysia. _In_ Dumoulin, H. ed. Buddhism in the modern world p194-201

Nepal

Locke, J. K. Present-day Buddhism in Nepal. _In_ Dumoulin, H. ed. Buddhism in the modern world p294-301

Sri Lanka

Fernando, A. Contemporary Buddhism in Sri Lanka (Ceylon) _In_ Dumoulin, H. ed. Buddhism in the modern world p65-80

Taiwan

Raguin, Y. Buddhism in Taiwan. _In_ Dumoulin, H. ed. Buddhism in the modern world p179-85

Thailand

Kirsch, A. T. Economy, polity, and religion in Thailand. _In_ Change and persistence in Thai society p172-96

Swearer, D. K. Recent developments in Thai Buddhism. _In_ Dumoulin, H. ed. Buddhism in the modern world p99-108

Tibet

Snellgrove, D. L. Tibetan Buddhism today. _In_ Dumoulin, H. ed. Buddhism in the modern world p277-93

United States

Benz, E. Buddhism in the Western world. _In_ Dumoulin, H. ed. Buddhism in the modern world p305-22

Prebish, C. S. Reflections on the transmission of Buddhism to America. _In_ Needleman, J. and Baker, G. eds. Understanding the new religions p153-72

Vietnam

Bechert, H. and Vu Duy-Tu. Buddhism in Vietnam. _In_ Dumoulin, H. ed. Buddhism in the modern world p186-93

Buddhism, Tantric. See Tantric Buddhism

Buddhist art and symbolism

Coomaraswamy, A. K. Introduction to the art of Eastern Asia. _In_ Coomaraswamy, A. K. Selected papers v 1 p101-27

Coomaraswamy, A. K. The inverted tree. _In_ Coomaraswamy, A. K. Selected papers v 1 p376-404

Coomaraswamy, A. K. The nature of Buddhist art; excerpt from "Figures of speech or figures of thought: collected essays on the traditional or 'normal' view of art." _In_ Coomaraswamy, A. K. Selected papers v 1 p147-78

Coomaraswamy, A. K. Svayamātrnnā: Janua coeli. _In_ Coomaraswamy, A. K. Selected papers v 1 p465-520

Coomaraswamy, A. K. The symbolism of the dome. _In_ Coomaraswamy, A. K. Selected papers v 1 p415-64

Buddhist doctrines

Nakamura, H. The basic teachings of Buddhism. _In_ Dumoulin, H. ed. Buddhism in the modern world p3-31

Buddhist ethics

Ingersoll, J. Merit and identity in village Thailand. _In_ Change and persistence in Thai society p219-51

Sharma, I. C. Indian ethics. _In_ Bishop, D. H. ed. Indian thought p233-51

Buddhist literature, Thai

Wyatt, D. K. Chronicle traditions in Thai historiography. _In_ Southeast Asian history and historiography p107-22

Buddhist psychology. See Buddhism—Psychology

Buddhist sects

See also Hinayana Buddhism; Mahayana Buddhism

Japan

Dumoulin, H. Buddhism in modern Japan. _In_ Dumoulin, H. ed. Buddhism in the modern world p215-76

Buddhist sects—*Continued*

Nepal

Locke, J. K. Present-day Buddhism in Nepal. *In* Dumoulin, H. ed. Buddhism in the modern world p294-301

Buddhist sociology. See Sociology, Buddhist

Buddhist symbolism. See Buddhist art and symbolism

Buddhist theology. See Buddhist doctrines

Buddhists in Ceylon. See Buddhists in Sri Lanka

Buddhists in Sri Lanka

Obeyesekere, G. Sinhalese-Buddhist identity in Ceylon. *In* Ethnic identity p231-58

Budget

See also Legislative auditing

United States

Weinberger, C. W. Creativity and collaboration in government—the budget process. *In* The Frontiers of knowledge p235-66

Budner, Stanley

The concept of anticipatory grief from a research perspective. *In* Anticipatory grief p48-52

Shall we look before we leap? *In* Home care p232-36

Buechler, John

"Give 'em the bayonet"—a note on Civil War mythology. *In* Hubbell, J. T. ed. Battles lost and won p135-39

Buell, Lawrence

Emerson, Thoreau, and transcendentalism. *In* American literary scholarship, 1974 p3-14

Emerson, Thoreau, and transcendentalism [another essay] *In* American literary scholarship, 1975 p3-15

Buergenthal, Thomas

International Human Rights Law and the Helsinki Final Act: conclusions. *In* Human rights, international law and the Helsinki Accord p 3-10

Bufford, John Henry

About

Tatham, D. John Henry Bufford: American lithographer. *In* American Antiquarian Society. Proceedings v86 pt 1 p47-73

Bugaev, Boris Nikolaevich

Gogol. *In* Erlich, V. ed. Twentieth-century Russian literary criticism p33-50

About

Beyer, T. R. The Bely-Zhirmunsky polemic. *In* Janecek, G. ed. Andrey Bely p205-13

Elsworth, J. D. Andrei Bely's theory of symbolism. *In* Barnes, C. J. ed. Studies in twentieth century Russian literature p17-45

Elsworth, J. D. Bely's Moscow novels. *In* Janecek, G. ed. Andrey Bely p127-34

Hartmann, H. The time bomb. *In* Janecek, G. ed Andrey Bely p121-26

Janecek, G. Introduction. *In* Janecek, G. ed. Andrey Bely p 1-17

Kalbouss, G. Andrey Bely and the Modernist movement in Russian drama. *In* Janecek, G. ed. Andrey Bely p146-55

Rosenthal, B. G. Revolution as apocalypse: the case of Bely. *In* Janecek, G. ed. Andrey Bely p181-92

Struve, G. Andrey Bely redivivus. *In* Janecek, G. ed. Andrey Bely p21-43

About individual works
Adam

Douglas, C. "Adam" and the modern vision. *In* Janecek, G. ed. Andrey Bely p56-70

Petersburg

Berberova, N. N. A memoir and a comment: the "circle" of Petersburg. *In* Janecek, G. ed. Andrey Bely p115-20

Prishedshy

Yurieff, Z. Prishedshy: A. Bely and A. Chekhov. *In* Janecek, G. ed. Andrey Bely p44-55

Aesthetics

Hughes, R. P. Bely's musical aesthetics. *In* Janecek, G. ed. Andrey Bely p137-45

Appreciation

Struve, G. Andrey Bely redivivus. *In* Janecek, G. ed. Andrey Bely p21-43

Friends and associates

Keys, R. The Bely-Ivanov-Razumnik correspondence. *In* Janecek, G. ed. Andrey Bely p193-204

Levin, A. A. Andrey Bely, M. O. Gershenzon, and Vekhi: a rejoinder to N. Valentinov. *In* Janecek, G. ed. Andrey Bely p169-80

Rabinowitz, S. J. Bely and Sologub: toward the history of a friendship. *In* Janecek, G. ed. Andrey Bely p156-68

Knowledge—Music

See Bugaev, Boris Nikolaevich—Music

Music

Hughes, R. P. Bely's musical aesthetics. *In* Janecek, G. ed. Andrey Bely p137-45

Poetic works

Eagle, H. Typographical devices in the poetry of Andrey Bely. *In* Janecek, G. ed. Andrey Bely p71-85

Relations with contemporaries

See Bugaev, Boris Nikolaevich—Friends and associates

Technique

Cioran, S. D. A prism for the absolute: the symbolic colors of Andrey Bely. *In* Janecek, G. ed. Andrey Bely p103-14

Eagle, H. Typographical devices in the poetry of Andrey Bely. *In* Janecek, G. ed. Andrey Bely p71-85

Janecek, G. Rhythm in prose: the special case of Bely. *In* Janecek, G. ed. Andrey Bely p86-102

Buganda

Politics and government

Rowe, J. A. The pattern of political administration in precolonial Buganda. *In* African themes p65-76

Bugliarello, George

The engineer and the historian. *In* Bugliarello, G. and Doner, D. B. eds. The history and philosophy of technology p50-56

Building

Blachère, G. Innovative building technology in developed and developing countries. *In* Strategies for human settlements: habitat and environment p142-44

Fuller, R. B. Innovative building technologies: the dome. *In* Strategies for human settlements: habitat and environment p148-51

See also Architecture

Technological innovations

Palanco, R. L. Evolution of building technology. *In* Bugliarello, G. and Doner, D. B. eds. The history and philosophy of technology p344-57

Building design. See Architecture

Building industry. See Construction industry

Buildings, Public. See Public buildings

Buildings, School. See School buildings

Buitenhuis, Peter

E. J. Pratt. *In* Staines, D. ed. The Canadian imagination p46-68

The stoic strain in American literature. *In* The Stoic strain in American literature p3-16

Bukharin, Nikolai Ivanovich

About

Nove, A. Some observations on Bukharin and his ideas. *In* Essays in honour of E. H. Carr p181-203

Bulfinch, Charles

Kirker, H. C. The Bulfinch drawings in the American Antiquarian Society. *In* American Antiquarian Society. Proceedings v86 pt 1 p125-28

Bulgakov, Mikhail Afanas'evich

About individual works

The master and Margarita

Lakshin, IA. Mikhail Bulgakov's The master and Margarita. *In* Erlich, V. ed. Twentieth-century Russian literary criticism p247-83

Bulgakov, Sergeĭ Nikolaevich

Heroism and asceticism: reflection on the religious nature of the Russian intelligentsia. *In* Landmarks p23-63

About

Slonim, M. L. Posthumous revivals: Bulgakov, Platonov, Zabolotsky. *In* Slonim, M. L. Soviet Russian literature p352-62

Bulgaria

Antiquities

See Patleina Monastery site, Bulgaria

Politics and government—1944-

Oren, N. A revolution administered: the Sovietization of Bulgaria. *In* Hammond, T. T. ed. The anatomy of Communist takeovers p321-38

Bulgarian Communist Party. See Communist Party of Bulgaria

Bulgarska Komunisticheska partiĭa. See Communist Party of Bulgaria

Bulkeley, Peter

About

Stoever, W. K. B. The objectivity of regenerating grace: Thomas Shepard and Peter Bulkeley. *In* Stoever, W. K. B. 'A faire and easie way to heaven' p58-80

Bull, Hedley

The Third World and international society. *In* The Year book of world affairs, 1979 p15-31

Bull of demarcation. See Demarcation line of Alexander VI

Bulletin (Sydney)

Cantrell, L. A. G. Stephens, the Bulletin, and the 1890s. *In* Bards, bohemians, and bookmen p98-113

Bullough, Donald A.

'Imagines regum' and their significance in the early medieval West. *In* Studies in memory of David Talbot Rice p223-76

See also Rahtz, P. jt. auth.

Bullough, Geoffrey

Another analogue of Measure for measure. *In* English Renaissance drama p108-17

Bulls in art

Boulter, P. N. A bronze bull in Cincinnati. *In* Studies in classical art and archaeology p251-54

Bulman, James C.

The date and production of 'Timon' reconsidered. *In* Shakespeare survey 27 p111-27

Shakespeare's use of the 'Timon' comedy. *In* Shakespeare survey v29 p103-16

Bülow, Nicolaus

About

Miller, D. B. The Lübeckers Bartholomäus Ghotan and Nicolaus Bülow in Novgorod and Moscow and the problem of early Western influences on Russian culture. *In* Viator: medieval and Renaissance studies v9 p395-412

Bultena, Gordon Louis

Structural effects on the morale of the aged: a comparison of age-segregated and age-integrated communities. *In* Gubrium, J. F. ed. Late life p18-31

Bultmann, Rudolf Karl

About

Keylock, L. R. Bultmann's law of increasing distinctness. *In* Current issues in Biblical and patristic interpretation p193-210

Theology

Mazzeo, J. A. Myth and science in the theology of Rudolf Bultmann. *In* Mazzeo, J. A. Varieties of interpretation p129-53

Bunche, Ralph Johnson

About individual works

The political status of the Negro in the age of FDR

Grantham, D. W. Ralph J. Bunche and the making of a documentary classic. *In* Grantham, D. W. The regional imagination p133-52

Bundela genealogy and legends: the past of an indigenous ruling group of Central India. Jain, R. K. *In* Studies in social anthropology p238-72

Bundy, McGeorge

The Americans and the U.S.S.R. *In* World change and world security p28-38

The Americans and the world. *In* A New America? p289-303

The avoidance of nuclear war since 1945. *In* Griffiths, F. and Polanyi, J. C. eds. The dangers of nuclear war p27-33

Bundy, Mary Lee

A nonmale image of the future. *In* Bundy, R. F. ed. Images of the future: the twenty-first century and beyond p152-58

Bundy, Robert Franklin

Up the downward path: the futures movement and the social imagination. *In* Bundy, R. F. ed. Images of the future: the twenty-first century and beyond p66-77

Bundy, W. McGeorge. See Bundy, McGeorge

Bunge, Mario Augusto

Philosophical inputs and outputs of technology. *In* Bugliarello, G. and Doner, D. B. eds. The history and philosophy of technology p262-81

Bunraku. See Puppets and puppet-plays—Japan

Bunting, Basil

About individual works

Briggflats

Connolly, C. Basil Bunting: 1. *In* Connolly, C. The evening colonnade p365-68

Collected poems

Connolly, C. Basil Bunting: 2. *In* Connolly, C. The evening colonnade p369-71

Bunting, Mary Ingraham

Creating opportunities for women in science. *In* Women in academia p115-19

Buñuel, Luis

About

Truffaut, F. Buñuel the builder. *In* Truffaut, F. The films in my life p261-68

About individual works

The discreet charm of the bourgeoisie

Kauffmann, S. The discreet charm of the bourgeoisie. *In* Kauffmann, S. Living images p153-55

Samuels, C. T. Tampering with reality. *In* Samuels, C. T. Mastering the film, and other essays p198-210

Tristana

Kauffmann, S. Tristana. *In* Kauffmann, S. Living images p17-19

Bunyan, John

About individual works

Grace abounding to the chief of sinners

Bruss, E. W. John Bunyan: the patriarch and the way. *In* Bruss, E. W. Autobiographical acts p33-60

Bunyoro. See Banyoro

Bunzel, Joseph H.

Contemporary sociology in Austria. *In* Mohan, R. P. and Martindale, D. A. eds. Handbook of contemporary developments in world sociology p83-89

Buonarroti, Michel Angelo, 1475-1564

About

Barolsky, P. Michelangelo's sense of humor. *In* Barolsky, P. Infinite jest: wit and humor in Italian Renaissance art p51-74

About individual works

Brutus

Gordon, D. J. Giannotti, Michelangelo and the cult of Brutus. *In* Gordon, D. J. The Renaissance imagination p233-45

David

Summers, D. David's scowl. *In* Collaboration in Italian Renaissance art p113-24

Leda and the swan

Watson, P. F. Titan and Michelangelo: the Danae of 1545-1546. *In* Collaboration in Italian Renaissance art p245-50

Pietà

Hinz, E. J. and Teunissen, J. J. The Pietà as icon in The golden notebook. *In* Pratt, A. V. and Dembo, L. S. eds. Doris Lessing p40-53

Influence

La Belle, J. Blake's visions and re-visions of Michelangelo. *In* Essick, R. N. and Pearce, D. R. eds. Blake in his time p13-22

Rose, E. J. The "Gothicized imagination" of "Michelangelo Blake." *In* Essick, R. N. and Pearce, D. R. eds. Blake in his time p155-69

Bura (African people)

Cohen, R. The pull of opposites: incorporation and autonomy in Nigeria. *In* African themes p149-73

Burawoy, Michael

Contemporary currents in Marxist theory. *In* McNall, S. G. ed. Theoretical perspectives in sociology p16-39

Burbank, Garin

Socialism in an Oklahoma boom-town: "Milwaukeeizing" Oklahoma City. *In* Stave, B. M. ed. Socialism and the cities p99-115

Burbidge, Geoffrey, and Burbidge, Margaret

Modern riddles of cosmology. *In* Neyman, J. ed. The heritage of Copernicus: theories "pleasing to the mind" p116-39

Burbidge, Margaret. See Burbidge, G. jt. auth.

Burch, Franklin W.

Archives and the design of transportation research. *In* Pattern and process p215-23

Burchenal, Joseph Holland

The relevance of research in tropical medicine today. *In* Cahill, K. M. ed. Health and development p59-68

Burchfield, Robert W.

Further aspects of short-term historical lexicography. *In* James B. McMillan: essays in linguistics by his friends and colleagues p115-31

Some thoughts on the revision of the O.E.D. *In* An English miscellany p208-18

See also Burnett, L. jt. auth.

Burchfield, Robert W. ed. See The Oxford English dictionary. A supplement to the Oxford English dictionary

Burckhardt, Jakob Christoph

About

Wieruszowski, H. Jacob Burckhardt (1818-1897) and Vespasiano de Bisticci (1422-1498) *In* Philosophy and humanism p387-405

About individual works

The civilization of the Renaissance in Italy

Nisbet, R. A. The myth of the Renaissance. *In* The Idea of social structure p471-96

History of Greek culture

Momigliano, A. Introduction to the Griechische Kulturgeschichte by Jacob Burckhardt. *In* Momigliano, A. Essays in ancient and modern historiography p295-305

Burdick, Daniel

On the nature of cancer: continuing care of the cancer patient. *In* Home care p205-07

Bureaucracy

Fischer, W. and Lundgreen, P. The recruitment and training of administrative and technical personnel. *In* Tilly, C. ed. The formation of national states in Western Europe p456-561

See also Civil service

Burgan, William M.

The refinement of contrast: manuscript revision in Edwin Drood. *In* Dickens Studies Annual v6 p167-82

Burge, Stuart, and Dexter, John

About individual works

Othello

Jorgens, J. J. Stuart Burge and John Dexter's Othello. *In* Jorgens, J. J. Shakespeare on film p191-206

Burger, André

About individual works

Lexique de la langue de Villon

Edelman, N. Book reviews. *In* Edelman, N. The eye of the beholder p166-205

Burger, Laura J. See Monts, E. A. jt. auth.

Burger, Warren Earl

At last—innovation in the Federal judicial system. *In* Managing nonprofit organizations p313-18

Burges, William

About

Cook, O. The fabric of a dream. *In* The Saturday book 34 p185-201

Burgess, Anthony, pseud. See Wilson, John Anthony Burgess

Burgess, M. A. S.

The age of classicism (1700-1820). *In* Auty, R. and Obolensky, D. eds. An introduction to Russian language and literature p111-32

The early theatre. *In* Auty, R. and Obolensky, D. eds. An introduction to Russian language and literature p231-46

The nineteenth- and early twentieth-century theatre. *In* Auty, R. and Obolensky, D. eds. An introduction to Russian language and literature p247-70

Burgh, Hubert de, Earl of Kent

About

Weiss, M. The castellan: the early career of Hubert De Burgh. *In* Viator: medieval and Renaissance studies v5 p235-52

Burgoyne, John

About

Morpurgo, J. E. Richer in esteem: a reappraisal of John Burgoyne. *In* Essays in honor of Russel B. Nye p151-67

Burguière, André

From Malthus to Max Weber: belated marriage and the spirit of enterprise. *In* Family and society p237-50

Burgundy

Rural conditions

Jolas, T. and Zonabend, F. F. Tillers of the fields and woodspeople. *In* Rural society in France p126-51

Burhans, Clinton S.

The complex unity of In our time. *In* Benson, J. J. ed. The short stories of Ernest Hemingway: critical essays p15-29

Jay Gatsby and Dr. Diver: Fitzgerald's Songs of innocence and experience. *In* Garvin, H. R. ed. Makers of the twentieth-century novel p228-44

Burhoe, Ralph Wendell

A cosmic perspective on man's future. *In* Bundy, R. F. ed. Images of the future: the twenty-first century and beyond p182-92

Burial. See Tombs

Burial customs. See Funeral rites and ceremonies

Buridan, Jean

About

Moody, E. A. Buridan and a dilemma of nominalism. *In* Moody, E. A. Studies in medieval philosophy, science, and logic p353-70

Moody, E. A. Jean Buridan. *In* Moody, E. A. Studies in medieval philosophy, science, and logic p441-51

Moody, E. A. John Buridan on the habitability of the earth. *In* Moody, E. A. Studies in medieval philosophy, science, and logic p111-19

Moody, E. A. Ockham, Buridan, and Nicholas of Autrecourt. *In* Moody, E. A. Studies in medieval philosophy, science, and logic p127-60

Buridanus, Joannes. See Buridan, Jean

Burke, Alan R.

The house of Chuzzlewit and the architectural city. *In* Dickens Studies Annual v3 p14-40

Burke, Edmund

About

Bakke, J. P. Edmund Burke and the East Indian reform movement. *In* Rhetoric: a tradition in transition p122-41

Gronbeck, B. E. Edmund Burke and the Regency Crisis of 1788-89. *In* Rhetoric: a tradition in transition p142-71

About individual works

A philosophical enquiry into the origin of our ideas of the sublime and beautiful

Albrecht, W. P. Burke. *In* Albrecht, W. P. The sublime pleasures of tragedy p39-51

Reflections on the French Revolution

Myers, M. Politics from the outside: Mary Wollstonecraft's first Vindication. *In* Studies in eighteenth-century culture v6 p113-32

Burke, John G.

Hermetism as a Renaissance world view. *In* The Darker vision of the Renaissance p95-117

Burke, John J.

History without history: Henry Fielding's theory of fiction. *In* A Provision of human nature p45-63

Hume's History of England: waking the English from a dogmatic slumber. *In* Studies in eighteenth-century culture v7 p235-50

Burke, Kenneth

(Nonsymbolic) motion/(symbolic) action. *In* Roland A. ed. Psychoanalysis, creativity, and literature p117-43

On literary form. *In* Young, T. D. ed. The New Criticism and after p80-90

Rhetoric, poetics, and philosophy. *In* Burks, D. M. ed. Rhetoric, philosophy, and literature: an exploration p15-33

Burke, Kenneth—*Continued*

About

Brown, M. E. Kenneth Burke. *In* Ross, R. G. ed. Makers of American thought p192-226

Crocker, J. C. The social functions of rhetorical forms. *In* The Social use of metaphor p33-66

Hyman, S. E. Kenneth Burke at seventy. *In* Hyman, S. E. The critic's credentials p69-73

Murray, T. C. Kenneth Burke's logology: a mock logomachy. *In* Glyph 2 p144-61

About individual works
Counter-statement

Howell, W. S. Kenneth Burke's "Lexicon rhetoricae": A critical examination. *In* Howell, W. S. Poetics, rhetoric, and logic p234-55

Language as symbolic action

Hyman, S. E. Kenneth Burke at seventy. *In* Hyman, S. E. The critic's credentials p69-73

Burke, Peter

Oblique approaches to the history of popular culture. *In* Bigsby, C. W. E. ed. Approaches to popular culture p69-84

Tradition and experience: the idea of decline from Bruni to Gibbon. *In* Edward Gibbon and The decline and fall of the Roman Empire p87-102

Burkert, Walter

Air-imprints or eidola: Democritus' aetiology of vision. *In* Illinois classical studies, v2 1977 p97-109

Burkhardt, Richard Wellington

Closing the door on Lord Morton's mare: the rise and fall of telegony. *In* Studies in history of biology v3 p 1-21

Burkholder, John Richard

"The law knows no heresy": marginal religious movements and the courts. *In* Zaretsky, I. I. and Leone, M. P. eds. Religious movements in contemporary America p27-50

Burks, Mary

The one-room schoolhouse—South. *In* Roots of open education in America p59-66

Burland, Cottie Arthur

Primitive societies. *In* Life after death p39-53

Burlesque (Literature)

Brereton, G. Scarron and burlesque comedy. *In* Brereton, G. French comic drama p51-84

See also Farce; Grotesque; Parody

History and criticism

England, A. B. Further additions to Bond's Register of burlesque poems. *In* Virginia. University. Bibliographical Society. Studies in bibliography v28 p284-90

Nykrog, P. Courtliness and the townspeople: the fabliaux as a courtly burlesque. *In* Cooke, T. D. and Honeycutt, B. L. eds. The humor of the fabliaux p59-73

Burlesque (Theater) *See* Strip-tease

Burley, Walter

About individual works
De vita et moribus philosophorum

Lutz, C. E. Walter Burley's De vita et moribus philosophorum. *In* Lutz, C. E. Essays on manuscripts and rare books p51-56

Burlin, Katrin Ristkok

The pen of the contriver': the four fictions of Northanger Abbey. *In* Halperin, J. ed. Jane Austen p89-111

Burlin, Robert B.

Gnomic indirection in Beowulf. *In* Anglo-Saxon poetry: essays in appreciation p41-49

Burlington, Richard Boyle, 3d Earl of

About

Wittkower, R. A sketchbook of Filippo Juvarra at Chatsworth. *In* Wittkower, R. Studies in the Italian baroque p187-210

Burma

Antiquities

Luce, G. H. Sources of early Burma history. *In* Southeast Asian history and historiography p31-42

History—1824-1948
See Burmese War, 1852

Politics and government

Rudner, M. Traditionalism and socialism in Burma's political development. *In* Eisenstadt, S. N. and Azmon, Y. eds. Socialism and tradition p105-39

Burman language. See Burmese language

A Burmese-English dictionary

Hla Pe, U. A short history of a Burmese-English dictionary, 1913-1963. *In* Southeast Asian history and historiography p86-99

Burmese language

Phonology

Jones, R. B. Prolegomena to a phonology of Old Burmese. *In* Southeast Asian history and historiography p43-50

Burmese War, 1852

Philips, Sir C. H. Dalhousie and the Burmese War of 1852. *In* Southeast Asian history and historiography p51-58

Burn, William

About

Walker, D. M. William Burn: the country house in transition. *In* Seven Victorian architects p8-31

Burne-Jones, Sir Edward Coley, bart.

About

Williamson, A. Burne-Jones: the stained-glass influence. *In* Williamson, A. Artists and writers in revolt p132-60

Burnett, Anne Pippin

Trojan women and the Ganymede ode. *In* Yale classical studies v25 p291-316

About individual works
Catastrophe survived: Euripides' play of mixed reversal

Sansone, D. The Bacchae as satyr-play? *In* Illinois classical studies v3, 1978 p40-46

Burnett, Ivy Compton- See Compton-Burnett, Ivy

Burnett, Jacquetta Hill-. See Hill-Burnett, Jacquetta

Burnett, Lesley, and Burchfield, Robert W.

The language of Francis Warner. *In* Prentki, T. ed. Francis Warner p 1-12

Burney, Charles

About

Lonsdale, R. H. Dr. Burney, 'Joel Collier', and Sabrina. *In* Evidence in literary scholarship p281-308

Burney, Fanny. See Arblay, Frances (Burney) d'

Burney, Frances. See Arblay, Frances (Burney) d'

Burnham, Donald Love, and Bergmann, Sven Arne
August Strindberg's need-fear dilemma, as seen in his relationship with Harriet Bosse. *In* Psychiatry and the humanities v 1 p73-97

Burnham, Walter Dean
American politics in the 1970's: beyond party? *In* The American party systems p308-57

The 1976 election: has the crisis been adjourned? *In* Burnham, W. D. and Weinberg, M. W. eds. American politics and public policy p 1-25

Revitalization and decay: looking toward the third century of American electoral politics. *In* Havard, W. C. and Bernd, J. L. eds. 200 years of the Republic in retrospect p146-72

Burns, E. Bradford
The intellectuals as agents of change and the independence of Brazil, 1724-1822. *In* From colony to nation p211-46

Burns, Eedson Louis Millard
Peace in the Middle East. *In* The Elusive peace in the Middle East p311-47

Burns, Richard Dean
Stanley K. Hornbeck: the diplomacy of the Open Door. *In* Burns, R. D. and Bennett, E. M. eds. Diplomats in crisis p91-123

Burns, Robert

About individual works
A red, red rose
Wilbur, R. Explaining the obvious. *In* Wilbur, R. Responses p139-45

Burns, Robert Ignatius
Mudejar history today: new directions. *In* Viator: medieval and Renaissance studies v8 p127-43

Burns, Thomas S.
The Alpine frontiers and early medieval Italy to the middle of the seventh century. *In* The Frontier v2 p51-68

Burns, Tom R. See Baumgartner, T. jt. auth.

Burnt offering. See Sacrifice

Burridge, K. O. L. See Burridge Kenelm

Burridge, Kenelm
The Melanesian manager. *In* Studies in social anthropology p86-104

Burroughs, Nannie Helen

About
Barnett, E. B. Nannie Burroughs and the education of Black women. *In* Harley, S. and Terborg-Penn, R. eds. The Afro-American woman p97-108

Burroughs, William S.

About
Oxenhandler, N. Listening to Burroughs' voice. *In* Federman, R. ed. Surfiction p181-201

About individual works
Naked lunch
Lodge, D. William Burroughs: 'The naked lunch.' *In* Lodge, D. The modes of modern writing p35-38

Burrow, John Wyon
Faith, doubt and unbelief. *In* Lerner, L. ed. The Victorians p153-73

The sense of the past. *In* Lerner, L. ed. The Victorians p120-38

'The village community' and the uses of history in late nineteenth-century England. *In* Historical perspectives p255-84

Burstyn, Harold Lewis
What can the history of technology contribute to our understanding? *In* Bugliarello, G. and Doner, D. B. eds. The history and philosophy of technology p57-80

Burton, John Wear

About individual works
Conflict & communication
Kelman, H. C. The problem-solving workship in conflict resolution. *In* Unofficial diplomats p168-200

Burton, Richard, 1925-

About
Kauffman, S. Hamlet. *In* Kauffmann, S. Persons of the drama p91-93

Burton, Sir Richard Francis

About
Foster, S. W. The annotated Burton. *In* Crew, L. ed. The gay academic p92-103

Burton, Robert E.
The New Deal in Oregon. *In* Braeman, J.; Bremner, R. H. and Brody, D. eds. The New Deal v2 p355-75

Burton, Robert G.
A philosopher looks at the population bomb. *In* Philosophy & environmental crisis p105-16

Bury, Richard de. See Aungerville, Richard, known as Richard de Bury, Bp. of Durham

Bury St Edmunds Abbey
Thomson, R. M. The date of the Bury Bible reexamined. *In* Viator: medieval and Renaissance studies v6 p51-58

Burying-grounds. See Cemeteries

Busck, Lars
The Family Guidance Center in Copenhagen. *In* Davis, K. C. Discretionary justice in Europe and America p115-31

Buscombe, Ed

About individual works
The idea of genre in the American cinema
Collins, R. Genre: a reply to Ed Buscombe. *In* Nichols, B. ed. Movies and methods p157-63

El buscón: Quevedo's annihilation of the picaresque. Bjornson, R. *In* Bjornson, R. The picaresque hero in European fiction p106-26

Bush, Douglas
Collected works of Erasmus; volume one. *In* Medievalia et humanistica no. 6 p199-202

Keats and Shakespeare. *In* Shakespeare: aspects of influence p71-89

Stephen Leacock. *In* Staines, D. ed. The Canadian imagination p123-51

Bushido
Miwa, K. In the shadow of leaves and Mishima's death. *In* Postwar trends in Japan p229-49

Bushman, Richard L.
Jonathan Edwards and Puritan consciousness. *In* Vaughan, A. T. and Bremer, F. J. eds. Puritan New England p346-62

Jonathan Edwards as great man. *In* Mulder, J. M. and Wilson, J. F. eds. Religion in American history p105-26

On the uses of psychology: conflict and conciliation in Benjamin Franklin. *In* Kren, G. M. and Rappoport, L. H. eds. Varieties of psychohistory p81-98

"This new man": dependence and independence, 1776. *In* Uprooted Americans p77-96

Bushmen (African tribe) See San (African people)

Bushrui, Suheil. See Bushrvi, Suheil

Bushrvi, Suheil
The poetry. *In* Prentki, T. ed. Francis Warner p110-30

Business
Ekblom, H. E. Managing the future is managing ideas and change. *In* Benton, L. R. ed. Management for the future p87-100

See also Advertising; Business enterprises; Corporations; Entrepreneur; Profit; Wealth

Historiography

Nevins, A. Business and the historian. *In* Nevins, A. Allan Nevins on history p68-81

International cooperation

Vale, V. Trusts and tycoons: British myth and American reality. *In* Allen, H. C. and Thompson, R. eds. Contrast and connection p225-44

Removal

See Business relocation

Social aspects

See Industry—Social aspects

Business and government. See Industry and state

Business and politics

United States

Hawley, E. W. The New Deal and business. *In* Braeman, J.; Bremner, R. H. and Brody, D. eds. The New Deal v 1 p50-82

Business and social problems. See Industry—Social aspects

Business corporations. See Corporations

Business cycles

Mathematical models

Tintner, G.; Kadekodi, G. and Rama Sastry, M. V. A macro model of the economy for the explanation of trend and business cycle with applications to India. *In* Econometrics and economic theory p139-46

Business districts, Central. See Central business districts

Business enterprises
See also Corporations; International business enterprises

United States

Johnson, A. M. The business of America. *In* Alderson, W. T. ed. America issues p81-96

Business enterprises, Foreign
See also Investments, Foreign

Political aspects

Vaitsos, C. V. Foreign investment and productive knowledge. *In* Erb, G. F. and Kallab, V. eds. Beyond dependency p75-94

Business enterprises, Government. See Government business enterprises

Business enterprises, International. See International business enterprises

Business ethics
Baumol, W. J. Smith versus Marx on business morality and the social interest. *In* Glahe, F. R. ed. Adam Smith and The wealth of nations p111-22

History

McKie, J. W. Changing views. *In* McKie, J. W. ed. Social responsibility and the business predicament p17-40

Business forecasting
Davis, K. Some fundamental trends affecting management in the future. *In* Benton, L. R. ed. Management for the future p63-76

Jones, R. H. What is the future of the corporation? *In* Benton, L. R. ed. Management for the future p189-97

Business relocation

United States

Chinitz, B. Regional development. *In* McKie, J. W. ed. Social responsibility and the business predicament p247-73

Businessmen

Africa

Katzenellenbogen, S. E. British businessmen and German Africa, 1885-1919. *In* Great Britain and her world, 1750-1914 p237-62

Busiris
Steadman, J. M. Paradise lost: the Devil and Pharaoh's chivalry. Etymological and typological imagery and Renaissance chronography. *In* Steadman, J. M. Nature into myth p185-212

Busse, Ewald William
Aging research: a review and critique. *In* Aging: the process and the people p129-65

Bustamante, Jorge A.
The "Wetback" as deviant: an application of labeling theory. *In* Davis, F. J. and Stivers, R. eds. The collective definition of deviance p256-67

Buster Keaton Festival
Kauffmann, S. Buster Keaton Festival. *In* Kauffmann, S. Living images p19-22

Bustin, Edouard
Government policy toward African cult movements: the case of Katanga. *In* African dimensions p113-35

The Busy Body papers
Granger, B. I. Early Philadelphia serials. *In* Granger, B. I. American essay serials from Franklin to Irving p41-69

Busza, Andrzej
Rhetoric and ideology in Conrad's Under Western eyes. *In* Joseph Conrad: a commemoration p105-18

Butcher, Sarnia A.
Enamelling. *In* Strong, D. E. and Brown, D. eds. Roman crafts p43-51

Buthelezi, Manas
Toward indigenous theology in South Africa. *In* The Emergent gospel p56-75

Butler, Charles

About individual works

Oratoriae libri duo

Ochs, D. J. Charles Butler on methods of persuasion: a translation. *In* Rhetoric: a tradition in transition p66-98

Butler, Christopher
Tragedy and moral education. *In* Contemporary approaches to English studies p77-93

Butler, Jeffrey
The significance of recent changes within the white ruling caste. *In* Thompson, L. M. and Butler, J. eds. Change in contemporary South Africa p79-103

Butler, Jonathan M.
Adventism and the American experience. *In* The Rise of Adventism p173-206

Butler, Joseph, Bp. of Durham

About individual works

The analogy of religion, natural and revealed, to the constitution and course of nature

Wiggins, D. Locke, Butler and the stream of consciousness: and men as a natural kind. *In* Rorty, A. O. ed. The identities of persons p139-73

Butler, Lance St John
How it is for Thomas Hardy. *In* Butler, L. S. ed. Thomas Hardy after fifty years p116-25

Butler, Lord. See Butler, Richard Austen, Baron

Butler, Marilyn
Jane Austen and the war of ideas

Contents

The anti-Jacobins
Conclusion
Emma
The Jacobin novel I: revolution and reason
The Jacobin novel II: Caleb Williams and Hermsprong
The juvenilia and Northanger Abbey
Mansfield Park
Maria Edgeworth
Persuasion and Sanditon
Pride and prejudice
Seeing a meaning
Sense and sensibility
Sentimentalism: the radical inheritance

Butler, Pierce, 1866-1939

About

White, G. E. The Four Horsemen: the sources of judicial notoriety. *In* White, G. E. The American judicial tradition p178-99

Butler, Richard Austen, Baron
The foundation of the Institute of Criminology in Cambridge. *In* Crime, criminology and public policy p 1-10

Butler, Robert N.
Afterword: humanistic perspectives in gerontology. *In* Spicker, S. F.; Woodward, K. M. and Van Tassel, D. D. eds. Aging and the elderly p389-91

Overview on aging. *In* Aging: the process and the people p1-19

Butler, Ronald Joseph
Hume's impressions. *In* Royal Institute of Philosophy. Impressions of empiricism p122-36

Butler, Ross Erin
Terrorism in Latin America. *In* International terrorism p46-61

Butler, Ruth
Long live the Revolution, the Republic, and especially the Emperor: the political sculpture of Rude. *In* Millon, H. A. and Nochlin, L. eds. Art and architecture in the service of politics p92-107

Butler, Samuel, 1612-1680

About individual works

Hudibras

Farley-Hills, D. Hudibras. *In* Farley-Hills, D. The benevolence of laughter: comic poetry of the Commonwealth and Restoration p46-71

Butler, Samuel, 1835-1902

About

Alcorn, J. Butler: the new spirit. *In* Alcorn, J. The nature novel from Hardy to Lawrence p25-41

Skilton, D. New approaches: Meredith, Hardy and Butler. *In* Skilton, D. The English novel p163-77

About individual works

Erewhon

Colmer, J. Utopian fantasy. *In* Colmer, J. Coleridge to Catch-22 p162-76

The way of all flesh

Fleishman, A. Personal myth: three Victorian autobiographers. *In* Landow, G. P. ed. Approaches to Victorian autobiography p215-34

Tobin, P. D. Subverting the father: some nineteenth-century precursors. *In* Tobin, P. D. Time and the novel p29-53

Butler, Walter Ernest
Methodological innovations in Soviet international legal doctrine. *In* The Year book of world affairs, 1978 p334-41

Butlin, Martin
Cataloguing William Blake. *In* Essick, R. N. and Pearce, D. R. eds. Blake in his time p77-90

Butscher, Edward
In search of Sylvia: an introduction. *In* Butscher, E. ed. Sylvia Plath p 3-29

Butter, Peter H.
Milton: the final plates. *In* Phillips, M. C. ed. Interpreting Blake p145-63

Butterfield, Sir Herbert
Global good and evil: the moderate cupidity of Everyman. *In* [Truth and tragedy]: a tribute to Hans Morgenthau p199-202

Butterworth, Charles E.
New light on the political philosophy of Averroës. *In* Essays on Islamic philosophy and science p118-27

Butterworth, Ruth
The future of South Africa. *In* The Year book of world affairs, 1977 p27-45

Butwin, Joseph
The paradox of the clown in Dickens. *In* Dickens Studies Annual v5 p115-32

Buxton, Dorothy Frances (Jebb)

About

Robbins, K. Church and politics: Dorothy Buxton and the German church struggle. *In* Church, society and politics p419-33

Buxton, Jean Carlile
Initiation and bead-sets in western Mandari. *In* Studies in social anthropology p310-37

Buxton, Thomas H.
A humanistic approach to teaching. *In* Buxton, T. H. and Prichard, K. W. eds. Excellence in university teaching p120-27

Buzzati, Dino

About

Pacifici, S. Dino Buzzati: the Gothic novel. *In* Pacifici, S. The modern Italian novel: from Pea to Moravia p79-89

About individual works
Larger than life

Hyman, S. E. Fable Italian style. *In* Hyman, S. E. The critic's credentials p211-16

A love affair

Hyman, S. E. The oldest story. *In* Hyman, S. E. The critic's credentials p206-10

Byers, John Ray

The geography and framework of Hawthorne's "Roger Malvin's burial." *In* Tennessee Studies in literature v21 p11-20

Byles, Mather

About

Granger, B. I. Early Boston serials. *In* Granger, B. I. American essay serials from Franklin to Irving p13-40

Byliny

Oinas, F. J. Russian byliny. *In* Oinas, F. J. ed. Heroic epic and saga p236-56

Bynum, Caroline Walker

Franciscan spirituality: two approaches. *In* Medievalia et humanistica no. 7 p195-97

Bynum, David E.

The generic nature of oral epic poetry. *In* Folklore genres p35-58

Byrd, William, 1674-1744

About

Downs, R. B. An American Pepys. *In* Downs, R. B. Books that changed the South p15-26

Seelye, J. On His Majesty's service: Robert Beverley, William Byrd, and the Palladian version of American pastoral. *In* Seelye, J. Prophetic waters p341-81

Wolf, E. More books from the library of the Byrds of Westover. *In* American. Antiquarian. Society. Proceedings v88 pt 1 p51-82

About individual works
Histories of the dividing line betwixt Virginia and North Carolina

Downs, R. B. An American Pepys. *In* Downs, R. B. Books that changed the South p15-26

Byron, George Gordon Noël Byron, 6th Baron

About

Ball, P. M. 'The difference to me.' *In* Ball, P. M. The heart's events p9-31

Beatty, B. G. Lord Byron: poetry and precedent. *In* Davies, R. T. and Beatty, B. G. eds. Literature of the romantic period, 1750-1850 p114-34

Brisman, L. Byron: troubled stream from a pure source. *In* Brisman, L. Romantic origins p103-36

Hagstrum, J. H. Byron's songs of innocence: the poems to 'Thyrza.' *In* Evidence in literary scholarship p379-93

Jump, J. D. Byron's prose. *In* Jump, J. D. ed. Byron p16-34

Meisel, M. The material sublime: John Martin, Byron, Turner, and the theater. *In* Kroeber, K. and Walling, W. eds. Images of romanticism p211-32

Phelps, G. The Byronic Byron. *In* Jump, J. D. ed. Byron p52-75

Rowse, A. L. Byron's Cornish ancestry. *In* Jump, J. D. ed. Byron p 1-15

Ruddick, W. Don Juan in search of freedom: Byron's emergence as a satirist. *In* Jump, J. D. ed. Byron p113-37

Stone, D. D. Trollope, Byron, and the conventionalities. *In* The Worlds of Victorian fiction p179-203

Taylor, A. Self-destroying enthrallments: Byron and Keats. *In* Taylor, A. Magic and English romanticism p221-50

Yarker, P. M. Byron and the satiric temper. *In* Jump, J. D. ed. Byron p76-93

About individual works
Childe Harold's pilgrimage

Berry, F. The poet of Childe Harold. *In* Jump, J. D. ed. Byron p35-51

Cooke, M. G. The will to art: Conclusion. *In* Cooke, M. G. The romantic will p216-22

Don Juan

Avni, A. A. Molière and writers of the English romantic era, especially Byron. *In* Johnson, R. B.; Neuman, E. S. and Trail, G. T. eds. Molière and the commonwealth of letters: patrimony and posterity p232-44

England, A. B. The style of Don Juan and Augustan poetry. *In* Jump, J. D. ed. Byron p94-112

Don Juan (Canto II)

Trilling, L. George Gordon, Lord Byron. Don Juan: an episode from Canto II. *In* Trilling, L. Prefaces to The experience of literature p232-37

Go—triumph securely

McGann, J. J. The significance of biographical context: two poems by Lord Byron. *In* Martz, L. L. and Williams, A. L. eds. The author in his work p347-64

The island

Fleck, P. D. Romance in Byron's The island. *In* Jump, J. D. ed. Byron p163-83

Marino Faliero

Barton, A. 'A light to lesson ages': Byron's political plays. *In* Jump, J. D. ed. Byron p138-62

Sardanapalus

Barton, A. 'A light to lesson ages': Byron's political plays. *In* Jump, J. D. ed. Byron p138-62

The two Foscari

Barton, A. 'A light to lesson ages': Byron's political plays. *In* Jump, J. D. ed. Byron p138-62

When we two parted

McGann, J. J. The significance of biographical context: two poems by Lord Byron. *In* Martz, L. I. and Williams, A. L. eds. The author in his work p347-64

Characters—Don Juan

Torrance, R. M. Insouciant lover and insatiable stumblebums. *In* Torrance, R. M. The comic hero p206-39

Criticism and interpretation

Sanders, C. R. The Carlyles and Byron. *In* Sanders, C. R. Carlyle's friendships, and other studies p61-93

Byron, George G. N. B, 6th Baron—*Cont.*

Influence—Nietzsche

Fraser, R. S. Nietzsche, Byron, and the classical tradition. *In* O'Flaherty, J. C.; Sellner, T. F. and Helm, R. M. eds. Studies in Nietzsche and the classical tradition p190-98

Byron family

Rowse, A. L. Byron's Cornish ancestry. *In* Jump, J. D. ed. Byron p 1-15

Byzantine art metal-work. See Art metal-work, Byzantine

Byzantine copper articles. See Copper articles, Byzantine

Byzantine Empire

Hanfmann, G. M. A. Instinctu divinitatis: the Tetrarchs, Constantine, and Constantinople. *In* Hanfmann, G. M. A. From Croesus to Constantine p75-97

Vryonis, S. Byzantine and Turkish societies and their sources of manpower. *In* War, technology and society in the Middle East p125-52

Historiography

Runciman, Sir S. Gibbon and Byzantium. *In* Edward Gibbon and The decline and fall of the Roman Empire p53-60

Intellectual life

Browning, R. Homer in Byzantium. *In* Viator: medieval and Renaissance studies v6 p15-33

Laws, statutes, etc.

Kleimola, A. M. Law and social change in medieval Russia: the Zakon sudnyi lyudem as a case study. *In* Oxford Slavonic papers new ser. v9 p17-27

Social conditions

Patlagean, E. Birth control in the early Byzantine Empire. *In* Biology of man in history p 1-22

Teall, J. L. Byzantine urbanism in the military handbooks. *In* The Medieval city p201-05

Byzantine illumination of books and manuscripts. See Illumination of books and manuscripts, Byzantine

Byzantine medicine. See Medicine, Byzantine

Byzantine miniature paintings. See Miniature paintings, Byzantine

Byzantine mural painting and decoration. See Mural painting and decoration, Byzantine

Byzantine sculpture. See Sculpture, Byzantine

C

CB radio. See Citizens band radio

CBR warfare. See Atomic warfare; Biological warfare; Chemical warfare

CCIA. See Commission of the Churches on International Affairs

CIA. See United States. Central Intelligence Agency

COMECON. See Council for Mutual Economic Assistance

CPI. See Communist Party of India

CPSU. See Communist Party of Russia

CUNY. See New York (City). City University of New York

Čaadaev, P. J. See Chaadaev, Petr IAkolevich

Cabanis, Pierre Jean Georges

About

Staum, M. S. Medical components in Cabanis's science of man. *In* Studies in history of biology, v2 p 1-31

Cabaret (Motion picture)

Kauffmann, S. Cabaret. *In* Kauffmann, S Living images p97-99

Sheed, W. I am a cabaret. *in* Sheed, W. The good word & other words p201-05

Cabell, James Branch

About

Duke, M. The baroque waste land of James Branch Cabell. *In* French, W. G. ed. The twenties p75-86

MacDonald, E. E. Glasgow, Cabell, and Richmond. *In* Ellen Glasgow p25-45

Cabins. See Log cabins

Cable, George Washington

About

Rubin, L. D. Politics and the novel: George W. Cable and the genteel tradition. *In* Rubin, L. D. William Elliott shoot a bear p61-81

About individual works

Old Creole days

Downs, R. B. Romantic New Orleans. *In* Downs, R. B. Books that changed the South p148-55

Cable television. See Community antenna television

Cabrera Infante, Guillermo

About individual works

Three trapped tigers

MacAdam, A. J. Guillermo Cabrera Infante: the vast fragment. *In* MacAdam, A. J. Modern Latin American narratives p61-68

Cachalot. See Sperm whale

Caddoan languages

Chafe, W. L. Siouan, Iroquoian, and Caddoan. *In* Sebeok, T. A. ed. Native languages of the Americas v 1 p527-72

Cadoria, Sherian G.

Women officers in the United States Army: liberated? *In* Henderson, G. ed. Human relations in the military p95-105

Cady, Edwin Harrison

Philip Freneau as archetypal American poet. *In* Literature and ideas in America p 1-19

Caedmon manuscript

Fry, D. K. Caedmon as a formulaic poet. *In* Duggan, J. J. ed. Oral literature p41-61

Raw, B. C. The probable derivation of most of the illustrations in Junius II from an illustrated Old Saxon Genesis. *In* Anglo-Saxon England 5 p133-48

See also Genesis (Anglo-Saxon poem)

Caenegem, Raoul C. van

Public prosecution of crime in twelfth-century England. *In* Church and government in the Middle Ages p41-76

Caesar, Caius Julius

About

Yavetz, Z. Existimatio, fama, and the ides of March. *In* Harvard Studies in classical philology p78 p35-65

Caesarius, Saint, Bp. of Arles

About

Trahern, J. B. Caesarius of Arles and Old English literature: some contributions and a recapitulation. *In* Anglo-Saxon England 5 p105-19

Cafe La Mama. See La Mama, ETC (Experimental theater club) New York (City)

Cafferty, Pastora San Juan

Bilingualism in America. *In* The Diverse society: implications for social policy p163-76

Cagan, Phillip, and Schwartz, Anna Jacobson

How feasible is a flexible monetary policy? *In* Capitalism and freedom p262-93

Cage-birds

Eitner, L. E. A. Cages, prisons, and captives in eighteenth-century art. *In* Kroeber, K. and Walling, W. eds. Images of romanticism p13-38

Cagney, James

About

Ferguson, O. Cagney: great guy; excerpt from "The film criticism of Otis Ferguson." *In* Denby, D. ed. Awake in the dark p338-39

Cagnon, Maurice Arthur, and Smith, Stephen L.

J. M. G. Le Clézio: fiction's double bind. *In* Federman, R. ed. Surfiction p215-26

Cahan, Abraham

About individual works

The rise of David Levinsky

Lyons, B. David Levinsky: modern man as orphan. *In* Tulane Studies in English, v23 p85-93

Cahiers du cinéma

Comolli, J. L. and Narboni, J. Cinema/ideology/criticism. *In* Nichols, B. ed. Movies and methods p22-30

Elsasser, T. Two decades in another country: Hollywood and the cinéphiles. *In* Bigsby, C. W. E. Superculture p199-216

Cahill, James F.

The Orthodox movement in early Ch'ing painting. *In* Artists and traditions p169-81

Style as idea in Ming-Ch'ing painting. *In* Meisner, M. J. and Murphey, R. eds. The Mozartian historian p137-56

Cain (Biblical character) in art

Tannenbaum, L. Blake and the iconography of Cain. *In* Essick, R. N. and Pearce, D. R. eds. Blake in his time p23-34

Cain (Biblical character) in fiction, drama, poetry, etc.

Brockman, B. A. Cain and Abel in the Chester creation: narrative tradition and dramatic potential. *In* Medievalia et humanistica no. 5 p169-82

Cain, Seymour

Medieval and modern Judaism. *In* Adams, C. J. ed. A reader's guide to the great religions p321-44

Cain, Thomas Grant Stevens

"Times trans-shifting": Herrick in meditation. *In* Rollin, R. B. and Patrick, J. M. eds. "Trust to good verses": Herrick tercentenary essays p103-23

Cairncross, Sir Alexander Kirkland

The market and the state. *In* The Market and the state p113-34

Cairns, Christopher

Italian literature

Contents

The Catholic conscience
The dissection of man: the twentieth century
The Italian heritage
The political conscience
Social change

Cairns, David

Spontini's influence on Berlioz. *In* From Parnassus p25-41

Cairns, Francis

Venusta Sirmio: Catullus 31. *In* Woodman, T. and West, D. eds. Quality and pleasure in Latin poetry p 1-17

Cairo

Commerce—History

Udovitch, A. L. A tale of two cities: commercial relations between Cairo and Alexandria during the second half of the eleventh century. *In* The Medieval city p143-62

Social life and customs

el-Messiri, S. Self-images of traditional urban women in Cairo. *In* Beck, L. and Keddie, N. R. eds. Women in the Muslim world p552-40

Synagogues—History

Hirschberg, J. W. The agreement between the Musta'ribs and the Maghribis in Cairo 1527. *In* Salo Wittmayer Baron v2 p577-90

Cairo Genizah

Goitein, S. D. F. A mansion in Fustat: a twelfth-century description of a domestic compound in the ancient capital of Egypt. *In* The Medieval city p163-78

Goitein, S. D. F. New sources on the Palestinian gaonate. *In* Salo Wittmayer Baron v 1 p503-37

Caistor, Nick

The image of night in Rene Char's poetry. *In* Cardinal, R. ed. Sensibility and creation p168-82

Caitanya. See Chaitanya

Cajetan, Thomas de Vio, Cardinal. See Vio, Tommaso de, called Caetano, Cardinal

Cajetan, Tommaso de Vio Gaetani. See Vio, Tommaso de, called Caetano, Cardinal

Cajuns

Brandon, E. Folk medicine in French Louisiana. *In* American folk medicine p215-34

Calais

History

Baker, R. L. The government of Calais in 1363. *In* Order and innovation in the Middle Ages p207-14

el-Calamawy, Sahair

The impact of tradition on the development of modern Arabic literature. *In* Arab and American cultures p47-53

Calculating-machines

Hammersley, J. M. The technology of thought. *In* Neyman, J. ed. The heritage of Copernicus: theories "pleasing to the mind" p394-415

Calculators. See Calculating-machines

Calculus, Predicate. See Predicate calculus

Calculus, Propositional. See Propositional calculus

Calcutta

Politics and government

McGuire, J. Kristo Das Pal: politician as intermediary. *In* The Making of politicians: studies from Africa and Asia p93-102

Calcutta Conference. See Conference of Youth and Students of Southeast Asia Fighting for Freedom and Independence, Calcutta, 1948

Calder, Alexander

About

Krauss, R. E. Mechanical ballets: light, motion, theater. *In* Krauss, R. E. Passages in modern sculpture p201-42

Calder, Angus
Russia discovered
Contents

Fiction and politics: the art of Turgenev
Literature and morality: Leskov, Chekhov, late Tolstoy
Literature and serfdom: Gogol, Lermontov and Goncharov
Man, woman and male woman: Tolstoy's Anna and after
Pushkin's Russia
Revolt and the golden age: Dostoevsky's later fiction
Tolstoy to War and peace: man against history
Underground man: Dostoevsky to Crime and punishment

Calder, Daniel G.
Guthlac A and Guthlac B: some discriminations. *In* Anglo-Saxon poetry: essays in appreciation p65-80

Calder, Peter Ritchie, Baron Ritchie Calder-. See Ritchie-Calder, Peter Ritchie, Baron Ritchie Calder

Calder, William Musgrave
The correspondence of Ulrich Von Wilamowitz-Moellendorff with Werner Jaeger. *In* Harvard Studies in classical philology v82 p303-47
Seventeen letters of Ulrich von Wilamowitz-Moellendorff to Eduard Fraenkel. *In* Harvard Studies in classical philology v81 p275-97
Ulrich von Wilamowitz-Moellendorff to James Loeb: two unpublished letters. *In* Illinois classical studies, v2 1977 p315-32

Calderón, Héctor Neri Castañeda. See Castañeda Calderón, Héctor Neri

Calderon, Pierre
Jean Follain: objects in time. *In* Cardinal, R. ed. Sensibility and creation p136-48

Calderón de la Barca, Pedro

About

Muir, K. The comedies of Calderón. *In* Muir, K. The singularity of Shakespeare, and other essays p149-58
Nicoll, A. The Spanish stage under Lope de Vega and Calderón. *In* Nicoll, A. World drama p161-89

Caldes, Ramon de. See Ramon de Caldes

Caldes de Montbui, Ramon. See Ramon de Caldes

Caldwell, Erskine

About

Cowley, M. Georgia boy. *In* Cowley, M. —And I worked at the writer's trade p113-32
Gray, R. J. The good farmer: some variations on a historical theme. *In* Gray, R. J. The literature of memory p106-49
Holman, C. H. Detached laughter in the South. *In* Holman, C. H. Windows on the world p27-47
Martin, J. H. Erskine Caldwell's singular devotions. *In* Filler, L. ed. A question of quality: popularity and value in modern creative writing p40-56

About individual works
Tobacco Road

Gomery, D. Three roads taken: the novel, the play, and the film. *In* Peary, G. and Shatzkin, R. eds. The modern American novel and the movies p9-18

Caldwell, Lynton Keith
1992: threshold of the postmodern world. *In* A Time to hear and answer: essays for the Bicentennial season p175-218
Responsiveness and responsibility: the anomalous problem of the environment. *In* Rieselbach, L. N. ed. People vs. government: the responsiveness of American institutions p300-27

Caldwell, Robert Lee
Malcolm and the criterion of sleep. *In* Dunlop, C. E. M. ed. Philosophical essays on dreaming p157-73

Calendar
North, J. D. Chronology and the age of the world. *In* Cosmology, history, and theology p307-33
Ware, R. D. Medieval chronology: theory and practice. *In* Powell, J. M. ed. Medieval studies p213-37

Calendar, Ecclesiastical. See Church calendar

Calendar, Indic
Kelley, D. H. Eurasian evidence and the Mayan calendar correlation problem. *In* Mesoamerican archaeology p135-43

Calendar, Maya
Gossen, G. H. A Chamula solar calendar board from Chiapas, Mexico. *In* Mesoamerican archaeology p217-53
Kelley, D. H. Eurasian evidence and the Mayan calendar correlation problem. *In* Mesoamerican archaeology p135-43
Marshack, A. The Chamula calendar board: an internal and comparative analysis. *In* Mesoamerican archaeology p255-70

Calhoun, John Caldwell

About

Downs, R. B. Political philosopher. *In* Downs, R. B. Books that changed the South p103-13

About individual works
A disquisition on government

Downs, R. B. Political philosopher. *In* Downs, R. B. Books that changed the South p103-13

Califano, Joseph A.
The Washington lawyer: when to say no. *In* Nader, R. and Green, M. J. eds. Verdicts on lawyers p187-96

California

Colonization

Hutchinson, C. A. The California frontier. *In* Weber, D. J. ed. New Spain's far northern frontier p171-99

History—To 1846

Hutchinson, C. A. The California frontier. *In* Weber, D. J. ed. New Spain's far northern frontier p171-99

Servín, M. P. California's Hispanic heritage: a view into the Spanish myth. *In* Weber, D. J. ed. New Spain's far northern frontier p117-33

Laws, statutes, etc.

Levy, F. What Ronald Reagan can teach the United States about welfare reform. *In* Burnham, W. D. and Weinberg, M. W. eds. American politics and public policy p336-43

Legislature

Muir, W. K. The state legislature as a school of political capacity. *In* Burnham, W. D. and Weinberg, M. W. eds. American politics and public policy p222-47

Race relations

Servín, M. P. California's Hispanic heritage: a view into the Spanish myth. *In* Weber, D. J. ed. New Spain's far northern frontier p117-33

California Institute of Technology, Pasadena

History

Kargon, R. H. Temple to science: cooperative research and the birth of the California Institute of Technology. *In* Historical studies in the physical sciences v8 p3-31

California Rural Legal Assistance, Inc.

Conyers, J. R. Undermining poverty lawyers. *In* Nader, R. and Green, M. J. eds. Verdicts on lawyers p129-43

California. University

Religion

Bellah, R. N. The new consciousness and the Berkeley New Left. *In* The New religious consciousness p77-92

Students

Bellah, R. N. The new consciousness and the Berkeley New Left. *In* The New religious consciousness p77-92

Callahan, Daniel John

Abortion: a summary of the arguments. *In* Population policy and ethics p431-43

Biomedical progress and the limits of human health. *In* Small comforts for hard times p170-81

Health and society: some ethical imperatives. *In* Knowles, J. H. ed. Doing better and feeling worse p23-33

Callahan, Virginia Noreen (Woods)

The De copia: the bounteous horn. *In* Essays on the works of Erasmus p99-109

Callahan, William James

The Spanish church. *In* Callahan, W. J. and Higgs, D. eds. Church and society in Catholic Europe of the eighteenth century p34-50

Callan, Hilary

The premiss of dedication: notes towards an ethnography of diplomats' wives. *In* Ardener, S. G. ed. Perceiving women p87-104

Calleo, David P.

America, Europe and the oil crisis: hegemony reaffirmed? *In* Atlantis lost p119-47

Keynes and the 'Pax Americana.' *In* Skidelsky, R. J. A. ed. The end of the Keynesian era p95-103

Callicrates

About

McCredie, J. R. The architects of the Parthenon. *In* Studies in classical art and archaeology p69-73

Calligraphy, Chinese

History

Soper, A. C. The relationship of early Chinese painting to its own past. *In* Artists and traditions p21-47

Callimachus

Influence—Catullus

Clausen, W. Catullus and Callimachus. *In* Harvard Studies in classical philology v74 p85-94

Influence—Propertius

Pillinger, H. E. Some Callimachean influences on Propertius, Book 4. *In* Harvard Studies in classical philology v73 p171-99

Ross, D. O. Propertius: from ardoris poeta to Romanus Callimachus. *In* Ross, D. O. Backgrounds to Augustan poetry: Gallus, elegy and Rome p107-30

Manuscripts

Lloyd-Jones, H. and Rea, J. Callimachus, fragments 260-261. *In* Harvard Studies in classical philology v72 p125-45

Callinus, of Ephesus

About

Adkins, A. W. H. Callinus 1 and Tyrtaeus 10 as poetry. *In* Harvard Studies in classical philology v81 p59-97

Calor animalis. See Animal heat

Calotypes

Michaelson, K. The first photographic record of a scientific conference. *In* One hundred years of photographic history p109-16

Calvert, Peter

On attaining sovereignty. *In* Smith, A. D. ed. Nationalist movements p134-49

Calvin, Jean

About

Sellin, P. R. The hidden God: Reformation awe in Renaissance English literature. *In* The Darker vision of the Renaissance p147-96

Willis, E. D. Rhetoric and responsibility in Calvin's theology. *In* The Context of contemporary theology p43-63

Calvin, John. See Calvin, Jean

Calvinism

Hall, D. D. Understanding the Puritans. *In* Mulder, J. M. and Wilson, J. F. eds. Religion in American history p 1-16

See also Antinomianism; New England theology; Puritans

United States

Heimert, A. E. The Great Awakening as watershed; excerpt from "Religion and the American mind, from the Great Awakening to the Revolution." *In* Mulder, J. M. and Wilson, J. F. eds. Religion in American history p127-44

Calvino, Italo

Myth in the narrative. *In* Federman, R. ed. Surfiction p75-81

About

Vidal, G. Calvino's novels. *In* Vidal, G. Matters of fact and of fiction p39-60

Calvos, Andreas. See Kalvos, Andreas

Calvus, C. Licinius Macer

About

Gruen, E. S. Cicero and Licinius Calvus. *In* Harvard Studies in classical philology v71 p215-33

Calvus, Gaius Licinius. See Calvus, C. Licinius Macer

Cambodia

Social life and customs

Ebihara, M. M. Khmer village women in Cambodia: a happy balance. *In* Matthiasson, C. J. ed. Many sisters p305-47

Cambon, Glauco

Ungaretti's "Lindoro di deserto": jongleur of the self. *In* Italian literature: roots and branches p407-19

Cambridge. University

History

McWilliams-Tullberg, R. Women and degrees at Cambridge University, 1862-1897. *In* Vicinus, M. ed. A widening sphere p117-45

Morgan, V. Cambridge University and "the country," 1560-1640. *In* The University in society v 1 p183-245

Cambridge. University. Institute of Criminology

Butler, R. A. Baron. The foundation of the Institute of Criminology in Cambridge. *In* Crime, criminology and public policy p 1-10

The Cambridge songs

Rigg, A. G. and Wieland, G. R. A Canterbury classbook of the mid-eleventh century (The 'Cambridge songs' manuscript) *In* Anglo-Saxon England 4 p113-30

Camels

Hill, D. R. The role of the camel and the horse in the early Arab conquests. *In* War, technology and society in the Middle East p32-43

Camera Work (Periodical)

Tashjian, D. L. Camera Work and the anti-art of photography. *In* Tashjian, D. L. Skyscraper primitives p15-28

Cameras

Barfield, A. O. The harp and the camera. *In* Barfield, A. O. The rediscovery of meaning, and other essays p65-78

Camerini, Ingrid

The ideal and the reality: women in Sweden. *In* Roberts, J. I. ed. Beyond intellectual sexism p277-85

Cameron, Alan

Theodosius the Great and the regency of Stilico. *In* Harvard Studies in classical philology v73 p247-80

Cameron, Alastair Graham Walter

History of the solar system. *In* Man and cosmos p31-35

Cameron, Angus Fraser

Middle English in Old English manuscripts. *In* Chaucer and Middle English studies in honour of Rossell Hope Robbins p218-29

See also Mitchell, B. C. jt. auth.

Cameron, Eleanor

High fantasy: A wizard of Earthsea. *In* Horn Book Magazine. Crosscurrents of criticism p333-41

McLuhan, youth, and literature. *In* Horn Book Magazine. Crosscurrents of criticism p98-120

Cameron, Julia Margaret (Pattle)

About

Gibbs-Smith, C. H. Mrs Julia Margaret Cameron, Victorian photographer. *In* One hundred years of photographic history p69-76

Cameronians, The Kirk and the. Thompson, W. *In* Rebels and their causes p93-106

Cameroon

History

Fonlon, B. The language problem in Cameroon: a historical perspective. *In* Smock, D. R. and Bentsi-Enchill, K. eds. The search for national integration in Africa p189-205

Languages

Fonlon, B. The language problem in Cameroon: a historical perspective. *In* Smock, D. R. and Bentis-Enchill, K. eds. The search for national integration in Africa p189-205

Politics and government

Le Vine, V. T. Political integration and the United Republic of Cameroon. *In* Smock, D. R. and Bentsi-Enchill, K. eds. The search for national integration in Africa p270-84

Politics and government—1960-

Johnson, W. R. The Cameroon Federation: laboratory for Pan-Africanism. *In* Kilson, M. ed. New states in the modern world p89-118

Social conditions

Johnson, W. R. The Cameroon Federation: laboratory for Pan-Africanism? *In* Kilson, M. ed. New states in the modern world p89-118

Cameroon, West. See West Cameroon

Camouflage (Biology). See Protective coloration (Biology)

Camp, cruelty, colloquialism. Cohn, R. *In* Cohen, S. B. ed. Comic relief p281-303

Campaign buttons. See Campaign insignia

Campaign insignia

Mayo, E. Ladies and liberation: icon and iconoclast in the women's movement. *In* Browne, R. B. and Fishwick, M. W. eds. Icons of America p209-27

Campaign paraphernalia. See Campaign insignia

Campaign pins. See Campaign insignia

Campaigns, Presidential. See Presidents—United States—Election

Campanella, Tommaso

About

Kelly-Gadol, J. Tommaso Campanella: the agony of political theory in the counter-Reformation. *In* Philosophy and humanism p164-89

Campbell, A. G. M. See Duff, R. S. jt. auth.

Campbell, Alan K. and Dollenmayer, Judith, A.

Governance in a metropolitan society. *In* Hawley, A. H. and Rock, V. P. eds. Metropolitan America in contemporary perspective p355-96

Camus, Albert—About—*Continued*

Sayre, R. F. La chute: the egocentric individual. *In* Sayre, R. F. Solitude in society p155-75

Schwarz, A. "Condemned to be free": the will in action and paralysis. *In* Schwarz, A. From Büchner to Beckett p261-304

Scott, N. A. Albert Camus—resistance, rebellion. . . . *In* Scott, N. A. Mirrors of the man in existentialism p118-49

About individual works
The fall

Franco, J. Conversations and confessions: self and character in The fall and Conversation in the cathedral. *In* Rossman, C. R. and Friedman, A. W. eds. Mario Vargas Llosa p59-75

Girard, R. The underground critic. *In* Girard, R. "To double business bound" p36-60

Khan, M. R. Suicide: the condition of consciousness. *In* Abbs, P. ed. The black rainbow p63-91

Meyers, J. Van Eyck and The fall. *In* Meyers, J. Painting and the novel p148-56

Sayre, R. F. La chute: the egocentric individual. *In* Sayre, R. F. Solitude in society p155-75

The guest

Trilling, L. Albert Camus: The guest. *In* Trilling, L. Prefaces to The experience of literature p166-69

The myth of Sisyphus

Richter, D. H. Novel forms of thesis: Camus's The stranger. *In* Richter, D. H. Fable's end p83-100

The outsider

Khan, M. R. Suicide: the condition of consciousness. *In* Abbs, P. ed. The black rainbow p63-91

The rebel

Nichols, R. L. Rebels, beginners, and buffoons: politics as action. *In* Political theory and praxis p159-99

The stranger

Girard, R. Camus's stranger retried. *In* Girard, R. "To double business bound" p9-35

Grossvogel, D. I. Camus: a sense of life, the unknowable death. *In* Grossvogel, D. I. Mystery and its fictions: from Oedipus to Agatha Christie p75-91

Richter, D. H. Novel forms of thesis: Camus's The stranger. *In* Richter, D. H. Fable's end p83-100

Characters—Meursault

Grossvogel, D. I. Camus: a sense of life, the unknowable death. *In* Grossvogel, D. I. Mystery and its fictions: from Oedipus to Agatha Christie p75-91

Cana, Marriage in. See Marriage in Cana (Miracle)

Canada

Anecdotes, facetiae, satire, etc.

Howard, V. M. The Canadian crank. *In* Essays in honor of Russel B. Nye p92-104

Civilization

Kuz, L. Children's books and multiculturalism in Canada. *In* Egoff, S. A. ed. One ocean touching p221-31

McLuhan, H. M. Canada: the borderline case. *In* Staines, D. ed. The Canadian imagination p226-48

Preston, R. A. Some conclusions about the revolution-evolution problem. *In* Perspectives on revolution and evolution p268-87

Colonization

Harris, R. C. The extension of France into rural Canada. *In* European settlement and development in North America: essays on geographical change in honour and memory of Andrew Hill Clark p27-45

Economic conditions

Raynauld, A. The implications of an evolutionary tradition for the structure and functioning of Canada's economic development. *In* Perspectives on revolution and evolution p133-51

Emigration and immigration

Porter, J. R. Melting pot or mosaic: revolution or reversion? *In* Perspectives on revolution and evolution p152-79

English-French relations

Brazeau, J. and Cloutier, E. Interethnic relations and the language issue in contemporary Canada: a general appraisal. *In* Esman, M. J. ed. Ethnic conflict in the Western world p204-27

Morf, G. Ethnic groups and developmental models: the case of Quebec. *In* Said, A. A. and Simmons, L. R. eds. Ethnicity in an international context p76-91

Porter, J. A. Ethnic pluralism in Canadian perspective. *In* Glazer, N. and Moynihan, D. P. eds. Ethnicity p267-304

Smiley, D. V. French-English relations in Canada and consociational democracy. *In* Esman, M. J. ed. Ethnic conflict in the Western world p179-203

See also Québec (Province)—Autonomy and independence movements

Foreign relations

Doxey, M. P. Canada's international connections. *In* The Year book of world affairs, 1978 p43-63

French-English relations

See Canada—English-French relations

Historiography

Berger, C. Conclusion. *In* Berger, C. The writing of Canadian history p259-66

Berger, C. A North American nation. *In* Berger, C. The writing of Canadian history p137-59

Berger, C. The rise of liberty. *In* Berger, C. The writing of Canadian history p32-53

Historiography—Congresses

Winks, R. W. Cliché and the Canadian-American relationship. *In* Perspectives on revolution and evolution p12-21

History—1914-1945—Historiography

Berger, C. Reorientation. *In* Berger, C. The writing of Canadian history p160-86

Berger, C. Reorientation and tradition. *In* Berger, C. The writing of Canadian history p187-207

History—1945- —Historiography

Berger, C. Reorientation. *In* Berger, C. The writing of Canadian history p160-86

Berger, C. Reorientation and tradition. *In* Berger, C. The writing of Canadian history p187-207

Canada—*Continued*

Languages

Warburton, T. R. Nationalism and language in Switzerland and Canada. *In* Smith, A. D. ed. Nationalist movements p88-109

Politics and government

Albinski, H. S. Organized politics and political temper: predisposing factors and outcomes. *In* Perspectives on revolution and evolution p66-102

Berger, C. A North American nation. *In* Berger, C. The writing of Canadian history p137-59

Lipset, S. M. Revolution and counter-revolution—some comments at a conference analyzing the Bicentennial of a celebrated North American divorce. *In* Perspectives on revolution and evolution p22-45

Presthus, R. V. Evolution and Canadian political culture: the politics of accommodation. *In* Perspectives on revolution and evolution p103-32

Smiley, D. V. French-English relations in Canada and consociational democracy. *In* Esman, M. J. ed. Ethnic conflict in the Western world p179-203

Social conditions

Presthus, R. V. Evolution and Canadian political culture: the politics of accommodation. *In* Perspectives on revolution and evolution p103-32

Social policy

Briggs, H. Scientific leadership and the price system. *In* Against pollution and hunger p273-77

Canadian children's literature. See Children's literature, Canadian

Canadian Communist Movement (Marxist-Leninist) See Communist Party of Canada (Marxist-Leninist)

Canadian drama

20th Century—History and criticism

Parker, R. B. Is there a Canadian drama? *In* Staines, D. ed. The Canadian imagination p152-87

Canadian fiction

History and criticism

Atwood, M. E. Canadian monsters: some aspects of the supernatural in Canadian fiction. *In* Staines, D. ed. The Canadian imagination p97-122

Woodcock, G. Possessing the land: notes on Canadian fiction. *In* Staines, D. ed. The Canadian imagination p69-96

Canadian literature

See also French-Canadian literature

History and criticism

Bissell, C. T. The place of learning and the arts in Canadian life. *In* Perspectives on revolution and evolution p180-212

Smith, A. J. M. Evolution and revolution as aspects of English-Canadian and American literature. *In* Perspectives on revolution and evolution p213-37

Canadian poetry

History and criticism

Frye, N. Haunted by lack of ghosts: some patterns in the imagery of Canadian poetry. *In* Staines, D. ed. The Canadian imagination p22-45

20th century—History and criticism

Thompson, L. B. Mosaic and monolith: a comparison of Canadian and Australian poetic responses to the Great Depression. *In* Narasimhaiah, C. D. ed. Awakened conscience p164-84

Canadian Student Movement. See Communist Party of Canada (Marxist-Leninist)

Canadians. See French-Canadians

Canals

Mexico—Campeche (State)

Thompson, J. E. S. 'Canals' of the Rio Candelaria basin, Campeche, Mexico. *In* Mesoamerican archaeology p297-302

Canary, Robert H.

Science fiction as fictive history. *In* Clareson, T. D. ed. Many futures, many worlds p164-81

Canavan, Francis P.

The problem of indoctrination. *In* Hook, S.; Kurtz, P. and Todorovich, M. eds. The ethics of teaching and scientific research p29-35

The prospects for a united Ireland. *In* Prospects for constitutional democracy p118-33

Cancer

Biography

Kelly, O. E. Make today count. *In* Feifel, H. [ed.] New meanings of death p181-93

Chemotherapy

Dahlberg, C. C. LSD therapy: a case study. *In* Anticipatory grief p296-310

Personal narratives

See Cancer—Biography

Psychological aspects

Atchley, M. W.; Cohen, S. B. and Weinstein, L. Anticipatory grief in a cancer hospital. *In* Anticipatory grief p124-34

Buckley, I. G. and Michaels, R. Variations on a theme: case reports from cancer care. *In* Anticipatory grief p135-43

Dahlberg, C. C. LSD therapy: a case study. *In* Anticipatory grief p296-310

Gullo, S. V.; Cherico, D. J. and Shadick, R. G. Suggested stages and response styles in life-threatening illness: a focus on the cancer patient. *In* Anticipatory grief p53-78

Kelly, W. D. and Friesen, S. R. Do cancer patients want to be told? *In* Weir, R. F. ed. Ethical issues in death and dying p3-8

Oken, D. What to tell cancer patients: a study of medical attitudes. *In* Weir, R. F. ed. Ethical issues in death and dying p 9-25

Plumb, M. M. and Holland, J. C. B. Cancer in adolescents: the symptom is the thing. *In* Anticipatory grief p193-209

Robbins, G. F. Anticipatory grief and cancer. *In* Anticipatory grief p115-18

Rush, B. F. A surgical oncologist's observations. *In* Anticipatory grief p98-106

Cancer—Psychological aspects—*Continued*

Torpie, R. J. The patient and prolonged terminal malignant disease: experiences from a radiation therapy center. *In* Anticipatory grief p119-23

Vachon, M. L. S.; Lyall, W. A. L. and Pollack, H. How group meetings ease the stress of cancer on patients and their families. *In* Home care p70-76

Surgery

Harvey, A. M. Early contributions to the surgery of cancer: William S. Halsted, Hugh H. Young, and John G. Clark. *In* Harvey, A. M. Adventures in medical research p69-83

Cancer Care, Inc.

Buckley, I. G. Fulfillment of life in the presence of death. *In* Home care p199-204

Cancer patients

Care and treatment

Burdick, D. On the nature of cancer: continuing care of the cancer patient. *In* Home care p205-07

Home care

Buckley, I. G. Fulfillment of life in the presence of death. *In* Home care p199-204

Budner, S. Shall we look before we leap? *In* Home care p232-36

Gaynor, A. The patient's home is his castle. *In* Home care p101-08

Kaylor, C. Evaluation of home care for the terminal cancer patient: a proposed model. *In* Home care p247-59

Lefebvre, K. Problems and considerations for effective home care of the cancer patient. *In* Home care p165-71

Rossman, I. Home care of the cancer patient. *In* Home care p60-69

Sexual behavior

Jaffe, L. Sexual problems of the terminally ill. *In* Home care p109-27

Cancino, Francisco Cuevas. See Cuevas Cancino, Francisco

The candidate (Motion picture)

Kauffmann, S. The candidate. *In* Kauffmann, S. Living images p124-26

Sarris, A. The candidate. *In* Sarris, A. Politics and cinema p16-20

Candide (criticism) Bernstein, L. *In* Kauffmann, S. Persons of the drama p263-66

Canetti, Elias

The conscience of words

Contents

The Arch of Triumph
Confucius in his Conversations
Dialogue with the cruel partner
Dr Hachiya's Diary of Hiroshima
The first book: Auto-da-Fé
Georg Büchner
Hermann Broch
Hitler, according to Speer
Kafka's other trial: the letters to Felice
Karl Kraus: the school of resistance
The new Karl Kraus
Power and survival
Realism and new reality
Tolstoy: the final ancestor
Word attacks
The writer's profession

About

Durzak, M. From dialect-play to philosophical parable: Elias Canetti in exile. *In* Strelka, J. P.; Bell, R. F. and Dobson, E. eds. Protest—form—tradition p35-56

About individual works

Auto-da-Fé

Canetti, E. The first book: Auto-da-Fé. *In* Canetti, E. The conscience of words p203-13

Caneva, Kenneth L.

From galvanism to electrodynamics: the transformation of German physics and its social context. *In* Historical studies in the physical sciences v9 p63-159

Canfield, John V.

Judgements in sleep. *In* Dunlop, C. E. M. ed. Philosophical essays on dreaming p149-56

Canny, Nicholas P.

Dominant minorities: English settlers in Ireland and Virginia, 1550-1650. *In* Hepburn, A. C. ed. Minorities in history p51-69

Canon law

Early church

Lynch, J. H. A Carolingian borrowing from Second Nicaea (787). *In* Medievalia et humanistica no. 5 p127-38

History

Peters, E. M. The Archbishop and the hedgehog. *In* Law, church, and society p167-84

Tierney, B. "Only the truth has authority": the problem of "reception" in the decretists and in Johannes de Turrecremata. *In* Law, church, and society p69-96

Canon law, Eastern

History

Erickson, J. H. Oikonomia in Byzantine canon law. *In* Law, church, and society p225-36

Cantar de mio Cid. See Poema del Cid

Cantelli, Gianfranco

Myth and language in Vico. *In* Giambattista Vico's science of humanity p47-63

Cantor, Geoffrey

The reception of the wave theory of light in Britain: a case study illustrating the role of methodology in scientific debate. *In* Historical studies in the physical sciences v6 p109-32

Cantor, Georg

About

Ulam, S. M. Infinities. *In* Neyman, J. ed. The heritage of Copernicus: theories "pleasing to the mind" p378-93

Cantor, Marjorie H. See Gurian, B. S. jt. auth.

Cantor, Norman L.

A patient's decision to decline lifesaving medical treatment: bodily integrity versus the preservation of life. *In* Weir, R. F. ed. Ethical issues in death and dying p241-70

Cantor, Paul Arthur

"A distorting mirror": Shelley's The Cenci and Shakespearean tragedy. *In* Shakespeare: aspects of influence p91-108

Cantrell, Leon

A. G. Stephens, the Bulletin, and the 1890s. *In* Bards, bohemians, and bookmen p98-113

The new novel: David Ireland's The unknown industrial prisoner, Michael Wilding's The short story embassy, and Frank Moorhouse's The electrical experience. *In* Hamilton, K. G. ed. Studies in the recent Australian novel p225-57

Capacity and disability. See Age (Law)

Capaldi, Nicholas

Hume's theory of the passions. *In* Livingston, D. W. and King, J. T. eds. Hume p172-90

Čapek, Karel

About

Suvin, D. Karel Čapek, or the aliens amongst us. *In* Suvin, D. Metamorphoses of science fiction p270-83

About individual works

The Makropulos case

Williams, B. A. O. The Makropulos case: reflections on the tedium of immortality; excerpt from "Problems of the self." *In* Donnelly, J. P. ed. Language, metaphysics, and death p228-42

Capella, Martianus Minneus Felix. See Martianus Capella

Capellanus, Andreas. See Andre le Chapelain

Capers, Charlotte

Eudora Welty: a friend's view. *In* Dollarhide, L. and Abadie, A. J. eds. Eudora Welty: a form of thanks p129-35

Capey, A. C.

The language of enlightenment. *In* Abbs, P. ed. The black rainbow p92-113

Capgrave, John

About individual works

The life of St. Katharine of Alexandria

Pearsall, D. A. John Capgrave's Life of St. Katharine and popular romance style. *In* Medievalia et humanistica no. 6 p121-37

Capital

Bowley, M. Some aspects of the treatment of capital in The wealth of nations. *In* Skinner, A. S. and Wilson, T. eds. Essays on Adams Smith p361-76

See also Capitalism; Human capital; Interest and usury; Profit; Wealth

Capital and labor. See Industrial relations

Capital exports. See Foreign exchange

Capital imports. See Foreign exchange

Capital investments

See also Replacement of industrial equipment

Mathematical models

See Acceleration principle (Economics)

Capital punishment

See also Hanging

United States

Bedau, H. A. Social science research in the aftermath of Furman v. Georgia: creating new knowledge about capital punishment in the United States. *In* Riedel, M. and Chappell, D. eds. Issues in criminal justice: planning and evaluation p75-86

Zeisel, H. The deterrent effect of the death penalty: facts v. faiths. *In* The Supreme Court review, 1976 p317-43

Capitalism

Agursky, M. Contemporary socioeconomic systems and their future prospects. *In* From under the rubble p67-87

Baumol, W. J. Smith versus Marx on business morality and the social interest. *In* Glahe, F. R. ed. Adam Smith and The wealth of nations p111-22

Birnbaum, N. On the possibility of a new politics in the West. *In* Beyond the crisis p201-32

Crouch, C. The state, capital and liberal democracy. *In* Crouch, C. State and economy in contemporary capitalism p13-54

DeLeon, D. Capitalism and community. *In* DeLeon, D. The American as anarchist p24-36

Galbraith, J. K. Defenders of the faith, II: Irving Kristol. *In* Galbraith, J. K. Annals of an abiding liberal p109-17

Hartwell, R. M. Capitalism and the historians. *In* Essays on Hayek p73-93

McCracken, P. W. Can capitalism survive? *In* Prochnow, H. V. ed. Dilemmas facing the nation p134-52

Macpherson, C. B. Capitalism and the changing concept of property. *In* Kamenka, E. and Neale, R. S. eds. Feudalism, capitalism and beyond p104-24

Neale, R. S. 'The bourgeoisie, historically, has played a most revolutionary part.' *In* Kamenka, E. and Neale, R. S. eds. Feudalism, capitalism and beyond p84-102

Reed, I. Image and money. *In* Reed, I. Shrovetide in old New Orleans p53-59

Stern, F. R. Capitalism and the cultural historian. *In* From Parnassus p209-24

Strinati, D. Capitalism, the state and industrial relations. *In* Crouch, C. ed. State and economy in contemporary capitalism p191-236

Supek, R. The visible hand and the degradation of individuality. *In* Beyond the crisis p49-80

See also Entrepreneur

Psychological aspects

Lane, R. E. Capitalist man, Socialist man. *In* Laslett, P. and Fishkin, J. eds. Philosophy, politics and society p57-77

Capitalism and Protestantism. See Protestantism and capitalism

Capitalists and financiers. See Capitalism

Capitulations, Military

Franklin, W. M. Unconditional surrender. *In* Encyclopedia of American foreign policy p986-93

Caplan, Gerald M.

New directions in criminal justice research. *In* Contemporary issues in criminal justice p47-57

Caplow, Theodore

How many books? *In* From Parnassus p66-74

Caponigri, Aloysius Robert

The timelessness of the Scienza nuova of Giambattista Vico. *In* Italian literature: roots and branches p309-31

Capote, Truman

About individual works

Breakfast at Tiffany's

Clark, L. Brunch on Moon River. *In* Peary, G. and Shatzkin, R. eds. The modern American novel and the movies p236-46

Capouya, Emile
On privacy and community. *In* Small comforts for hard times p109-19

Cappannari, Stephen C. See Moss, L. W. jt. auth.

The Cappers' Company
Winnington-Ingram, R. P. "To find the players and all that longeth therto": notes on the production of medieval drama in Coventry. *In* The Elizabethan theatre, V p17-44

Capps, Donald
Lincoln's martyrdom: a study of exemplary mythic patterns. *In* Reynolds, F. E. and Capps, D. eds. The biographical process p393-412

Newman's illness in Sicily: the reformer as biographer. *In* Reynolds, F. E. and Capps, D. ed. The biographical process p201-18

Psychohistory and historical genres: the plight and promise of Eriksonian biography. *In* Homans, P. ed. Childhood and selfhood p189-228

Capps, Walter H.
The interpenetration of new religion and religious studies. *In* Needleman, J. and Baker, G. eds. Understanding the new religions p101-05

Capra, Frank
About
Richards, J. Frank Capra and the cinema of Populism. *In* Nichols, B. ed. Movies and methods p65-77

About individual works
Mr Deeds goes to town
Rohdie, S. Totems and movies. *In* Nichols, B. ed. Movies and methods p469-81

Capron, Alexander Morgan, and Kass, Leon Richard
A statutory definition of the standards for determining human death: an appraisal and a proposal. *In* Weir, R. F. ed. Ethical issues in death and dying p103-24

Capuana, Luigi
About
Pacifici, S. Luigi Capuana: the theorist as novelist. *In* Pacifici, S. The modern Italian novel: from Capuana to Tozzi p16-31

Caputo, John D.
The question of being and transcendental phenomenology: reflections on Heidegger's relationship to Husserl. *In* Radical phenomenology p84-105

Caracciolo, Giovanni Battista, known as Battistello
About individual works
The judgement of Solomon
Stoughton, M. A late painting by Giovanni Battista Caracciolo: The judgement of Solomon. *In* Enggass, R. C. and Stokstad, M. eds. Hortus imaginum p125-28

Caracciolo, Roberto
Main issues in the disarmament negotiations. *In* The Dynamics of the arms race p123-34

Caradon, Hugh Mackintosh Foot, Baron
Is peace possible? What are the options? *In* The New world balance and peace in the Middle East: reality or mirage? p217-26

About individual works
A start in freedom
Kedourie, E. Sir Hugh Foot's memoirs. *In* Kedourie, E. Arabic political memoirs and other studies p231-35

Caradon, Lord. See Caradon, Hugh Mackintosh Foot, Baron

Carafiol, Peter C.
Puritanism in two dimensions. *In* Review, v 1 1979 p81-89

Caraib Indians. See Carib Indians

Caraley, Demetrios
The Carter Congress and urban programs: first soundings. *In* Burnham, W. D. and Weinberg, M. W. eds. American politics and public policy p188-221

Caravaggio, Michelangelo Merisi da
About individual works
Amor Victorious
Bissell, R. W. Concerning the date of Caravaggio's Amore Vincitore. *In* Enggass, R. C. and Stokstad, M. eds. Hortus imaginum p113-23

Carballido, Emilio
About
Skinner, E. R. The theater of Emilio Carballido: spinning a web. *In* Lyday, L. F. and Woodyard, G. W. eds. Dramatists in revolt p19-36

Carbon
Isotypes
See Radiocarbon dating

Carden, Patricia J.
Ornamentalism and modernism. *In* Gibian, G. and Tjalsma, H. W. eds. Russian modernism p49-64

Cardew, Michael
Design and meaning in preliterate art. *In* Greenhalgh, M. and Megaw, J. V. S. eds. Art in society p15-20

Cardinal, Roger
Introduction. *In* Cardinal, R. ed. Sensibility and creation p 1-15
Jacques Dupin. *In* Cardinal, R. ed. Sensibility and creation p220-50

Cardini, Maria Timpanaro-. See Timpanaro-Cardini, Maria

Cardiovascular research
Harvey, A. M. Cardiovascular research at Johns Hopkins. *In* Harvey, A. M. Adventures in medical research p261-87

Cardiovascular system
Research
See Cardiovascular research

Cardona, Elizabeth de. See De Cardona, Elizabeth

Cardona, Rudolfo
Post-war Hispanic and Brazilian drama. *In* Nicoll, A. World drama p872-80

Cardozo, Benjamin Nathan
About
Auchincloss, L. The styles of Mr. Justice Cardozo. *In* Auchincloss, L. Life, law and letters p47-58

White, G. E. Cardozo, Learned Hand, and Frank: the dialectic of freedom and constraint. *In* White, G. E. The American judicial tradition p251-91

Cardozo, Manoel da Silveira Soares

The modernization of Portugal and the independence of Brazil. *In* From colony to nation p185-210

Cards in literature

Kimball, S. L. Games people play in Congreve's The way of the world. *In* A Provision of human nature p191-207

Quirino, L. The cards indicate a voyage on A streetcar named Desire. *In* Tennessee Williams: a tribute p77-96

Wimsatt, W. K. Belinda ludens. *In* Wimsatt, W. K. Day of the leopards p99-116

Carducci, Giosué

About

Perella, N. J. The nineteenth century. *In* Perella, N. J. Midday in Italian literature p70-113

Cardullo, Bert

Drama of intimacy and tragedy of incomprehension: A streetcar named Desire reconsidered. *In* Tennessee Williams: a tribute p137-53

Cardwell, Donald Stephen Lowell

Problems of the data base. *In* Bugliarello, G. and Doner, D. B. eds. The history and philosophy of technology p3-18

Care of the sick

Jaffe, L. The terminally ill. *In* Gochros, H. L. and Gochros, J. S. eds. The sexually oppressed p277-92

See also Home care services; Nursing; Terminal care

Career education. See Vocational education

Careers. See Professions

Carens, James Francis

Four Revival figures: Lady Gregory, A. E. (George W. Russell), Oliver St. John Gogarty, and James Stephens. *In* Finneran, R. J. ed. Anglo-Irish literature p436-69

Carens, Marilyn M.

Handscóh and Grendel: the motif of the hand in Béowulf. *In* Aeolian harps p39-55

Carew, Jan

The origins of racism in the Americas. *In* African themes p3-23

Carey, George Wescott

The separation of powers. *In* Graham, G. J. and Graham, S. G. eds. Founding principles of American government p98-134

Carey, George Wescott, and McClellan, James Paul

Towards the restoration of the American political tradition. *In* Havard, W. C. and Bernd, J. L. eds. 200 years of the Republic in retrospect p110-27

Carey, Hugh L.

A humane mission for American foreign policy. *In* Cahill, K. M. ed. Health and development p15-22

Carey, James Charles

The consequences of economic intervention: Peru & Chile. *In* Higham, R. D. ed. Intervention or abstention: the dilemma of American foreign policy p144-65

Carey, John L.

Art and reality in The golden notebook. *In* Pratt, A. V. and Dembo, L. S. eds. Doris Lessing p20-39

Carey, Mathew

About

Barnes, J. J. John Miller: first transatlantic publisher's agent. *In* Virginia. University. Bibliographical Society. Studies in bibliography v29 p373-79

Carey, R. See Smith, M. H. jt. auth.

Carey, Susan

The child as word learner. *In* Linguistic theory and psychological reality p264-93

Carib Indians

Carew, J. The origins of racism in the Americas. *In* African themes p3-23

See also Accawai Indians

Caribbean area

Mintz, S. W. The Caribbean region. *In* Mintz, S. W. ed. Slavery, colonialism, and racism p45-71

Civilization

Hoetink, H. The cultural links. *In* Crahan, M. E. and Knight, F. W. eds. Africa and the Caribbean p20-40

Knight, F. W. and Crahan, M. E. The African migration and the origins of an Afro-American society and culture. *In* Crahan, M. E. and Knight, F. W. eds. Africa and the Caribbean p 1-19

Economic integration

Carnegie, A. R. Commonwealth Caribbean regionalism: legal aspects. *In* The Year book of world affairs, 1979 p180-200

Parkinson, F. International economic integration in Latin America and the Caribbean: a survey. *In* The Year book of world affairs, 1977 p236-56

Emigration and immigration

Paterson, H. O. Migration in Caribbean societies: socioeconomic and symbolic resource. *In* Human migration p106-45

Foreign relations—Cuba

Jones, R. E. Cuba and the English-speaking Caribbean. *In* Cuba in the world p131-45

Languages

Lewis, M. W. The African impact on language and literature in the English-speaking Caribbean. *In* Crahan, M. E. and Knight, F. W. eds. Africa and the Caribbean p101-23

Religion

Barrett, L. E. African religion in the Americas: the "islands in between." *In* African religions: a symposium p183-215

Simpson, G. E. Religions of the Caribbean. *In* Kilson, M. L. and Rotberg, R. I. eds. The African diaspora p280-311

Social life and customs

Bettelheim, J. Jamaican Jonkonnu and related Caribbean festivals. *In* Crahan, M. E. and Knight, F. W. eds. Africa and the Caribbean p80-100

Paterson, H. O. Migration in Caribbean societies: socioeconomic and symbolic resource. *In* Human migration p106-45

A **Caribbean** Community for Ocean Development. Krieger, D. *In* Borgese, E. M. and Krieger, D. eds. The tides of change p278-301

Caribbean literature

History and criticism

Brathwaite, E. K. The African presence in Caribbean literature. *In* Mintz, S. W. ed. Slavery, colonialism, and racism p73-109

Caribbean literature (English)

Lewis, M. W. The African impact on language and literature in the English-speaking Caribbean. *In* Crahan, M. E. and Knight, F. W. eds. Africa and the Caribbean p101-23

Caribbean poetry

History and criticism

DeCosta, M. Social lyricism and the Caribbean poet/rebel. *In* DeCosta, M. ed. Blacks in Hispanic literature p114-22

Wilson, L. N. La poesia negra: its background, themes and significance. *In* DeCosta, M. ed. Blacks in Hispanic literature p90-104

Caribbean region

Emery, K. O. and Uchupi, E. The oil potential of the Caribbean. *In* Borgese, E. M. and Krieger, D. eds. The tides of change p239-53

Galindo Pohl, R. Pacem in Maribus in the Caribbean. *In* Borgese, E. M. and Krieger, D. eds. The tides of change p264-77

Krieger, D. A Caribbean Community for Ocean Development. *In* Borgese, E. M. and Krieger, D. eds. The tides of change p278-301

Mathews, T. G. Historical patterns of Caribbean communication. *In* Borgese, E. M. and Krieger, D. eds. The tides of change p222-38

Caricature. See Caricatures and cartoons; Grotesque

Caricatures and cartoons

See also Comic books, strips, etc.; Moving picture cartoons

Great Britain

Hunter, K. M. H. The informing word: verbal strategies in visual satire. *In* Studies in eighteenth-century culture v4 p271-96

The West

Dobie, J. F. Jim Williams and "Out our way." *In* Dobie, J. F. Prefaces p112-18

Carleton, William

About

Harmon, M. Cobwebs before the wind: aspects of the peasantry in Irish literature from 1800 to 1916. *In* Casey, D. J. and Rhodes, R. E. eds. Views of the Irish peasantry, 1800-1916 p129-59

Carli, Enzo

Two stucco reliefs by Neroccio di Bartolomeo. *In* Collaboration in Italian Renaissance art p21-29

Carlisle, Donald Steven

Modernization, generations, and the Uzbek Soviet intelligentsia. *In* Cocks, P.; Daniels, R. V. and Heer, N. W. eds. The dynamics of Soviet politics p239-64

Carlisle, Howard M. See Shetty, Y. K. jt. auth.

Carlo, Antonio

Structural causes of the Soviet coexistence policy. *In* Jahn, E. ed. Soviet foreign policy p57-90

Carlovingian art. See Art, Carlovingian

Carlovingians

Lynch, J. H. A Carolingian borrowing from Second Nicaea (787). *In* Medievalia et humanistica no. 5 p127-38

Carlson, Elof Axel

Genetics and the biological basis of the human condition. *In* The Tricentennial people p3-17

Carlson, Leland Henry

About

Scott, F. D. Leland Henry Carlson: man and career. *In* The Dissenting tradition p xi-xx

Carlton, David

The Anglo-American nuclear relationship: proliferatory or anti-proliferatory? *In* Arms control and technological innovation p132-45

The British independent nuclear deterrent and the future of European security. *In* International terrorism and world security p277-94

The doctrine of tactical nuclear warfare and some alternatives. *In* The Dynamics of the arms race p135-42

Carlyle, Jane Baillie (Welsh)

About

Clubbe, J. Grecian destiny: Froude's portraits of the Carlyles. *In* Carlyle and his contemporaries p317-53

Haight, G. S. The Carlyles and the Leweses. *In* Carlyle and his contemporaries p181-204

Sanders, C. R. The Carlyles and Byron. *In* Sanders, C. R. Carlyle's friendships, and other studies p61-93

Friends and associates

Fielding, K. J. Froude's revenge, or The Carlyles and Erasmus A. Darwin. *In* English Association. Essays and studies, 1978 p75-97

Sanders, C. R. The Carlyles and Thackeray. *In* Sanders, C. R. Carlyle's friendships, and other studies p226-66

Carlyle, Thomas

About

ApRoberts, R. Carlyle and Trollope. *In* Carlyle and his contemporaries p205-26

Clubbe, J. Grecian destiny: Froude's portraits of the Carlyles. *In* Carlyle and his contemporaries p317-53

Dawson, C. Poetics: the hero as poet. *In* Dawson, C. Victorian noon p16-35

DeLaura, D. J. The future of poetry: a context for Carlyle and Arnold. *In* Carlyle and his contemporaries p148-80

Edwards, J. R. Carlyle and the fictions of belief: Sartor resartus to Past and present. *In* Carlyle and his contemporaries p91-111

Fielding, K. J. Carlyle and the Saint-Simonians (1830-1832): new considerations. *In* Carlyle and his contemporaries p35-59

Fielding, K. J. Froude and Carlyle: some new considerations. *In* Fielding, K. J. and Tarr, R. L. eds. Carlyle past and present p239-69

Ford, G. H. Stern Hebrews who laugh: further thoughts on Carlyle and Dickens. *In* Fielding, K. J. and Tarr, R. L. eds. Carlyle past and present p112-26

Haight, G. S. The Carlyles and the Leweses. *In* Carlyle and his contemporaries p181-204

Carlyle, Thomas—*Continued*

Religion and ethics

Campbell, I. Carlyle's religion: the Scottish background. *In* Carlyle and his contemporaries p3-20

DeLaura, D. J. Carlyle and Arnold: the religious issue. *In* Fielding, K. J. and Tarr, R. L. eds. Carlyle past and present p127-54

Social views

See Carlyle, Thomas—Political and social views

Style

Tennyson, G. B. Parody as style: Carlyle and his parodists. *In* Carlyle and his contemporaries p298-316

Technique

Sanders, C. R. The Victorian Rembrandt: Carlyle's portraits of his contemporaries. *In* Sanders, C. R. Carlyle's friendships, and other studies p3-35

Carman, John B.

Religion as a problem for Christian theology. *In* Christian faith in a religiously plural world p83-103

Carman, Robert L.

Lasers—evolution and technological use. *In* Neyman, J. ed. The heritage of Copernicus: theories "pleasing to the mind" p508-25

Carmelite nuns in England

Williams, D. The Brides of Christ. *In* Ardener, S. G. ed. Perceiving women p105-25

Carmichael, Joel

About individual works
The shaping of the Arabs

Kedourie, E. Arabs ancient and modern. *In* Kedourie, E. Arabic political memoirs and other studies p162-69

Carmines, Alvin

About individual works
The faggot

Kauffmann, S. The faggot. *In* Kauffmann, S. Persons of the drama p261-63

Carnal knowledge (Motion picture)

Kauffmann, S. Carnal knowledge. *In* Kauffmann, S. Living images p61-64

Carnap, Rudolf

The overcoming of metaphysics through logical analysis of language. *In* Murray, M. E. ed. Heidegger and modern philosophy p23-34

About

Quine, W. V. Carnap and logical truth. *In* Quine, W. V. The ways of paradox, and other essays p107-32

Quine, W. V. Homage to Rudolf Carnap. *In* Quinn, W. V. The ways of paradox, and other essays p40-43

Salmon, W. C. Russell on scientific inference. *In* Nakhnikian, G. ed. Bertrand Russell's philosophy p183-208

Ontology

Quine, W. V. On Carnap's views on ontology. *In* Quine, W. V. The ways of paradox, and other essays p203-11

Carnegie, A. R.

Commonwealth Caribbean regionalism: legal aspects. *In* The Year book of world affairs, 1979 p180-200

Carnegie Endowment for International Peace

Goormaghtigh, J. How an INGO contributed to broadening the scope and competence of an IGO. *In* Unofficial diplomats p250-58

Carnegie Institution of Washington

Reingold, N. National science policy in a private foundation: the Carnegie Institution of Washington. *In* Oleson, A. and Voss, J. eds. The organization of knowledge in modern America, 1860-1920 p313-41

Carnegie-Mellon University

Beach, R. I. A case history of affirmative action. *In* Women in academia p128-38

Carner, Vern D.; Kubo, Sakae, and Rice, Curt

Bibliographical essay. *In* The Rise of Adventism p207-317

Carnes, Valerie

Icons of popular fashion. *In* Browne, R. B. and Fishwick, M. W. eds. Icons of America p228-40

Carnival. See Mumming; and subdivision Carnival under names of cities, e.g. New Orleans—Carnival

Carnovsky, Ruth French

Biographical sketch. *In* As much to learn as to teach p16-24

Caro, Anthony

About

Krauss, R. E. Tanktotem: welded images. *In* Krauss, R. E. Passages in modern sculpture p147-200

Caro, Robert A.

About individual works
The power broker: Robert Moses and the fall of New York

Vidal, G. What Robert Moses did to New York City. *In* Vidal, G. Matters of fact and of fiction p237-51

Caroff, Phyllis, and Dobrof, Rose

Social work: its institutional role. *In* Anticipatory grief p251-63

Carolingian architecture. See Architecture, Carlovingian

Carolingian art. See Art, Carlovingian

Carolingians. See Carlovingians

Carols, English

History and criticism

Friedman, A. B. A carol in tradition. *In* Chaucer and Middle English studies in honour of Rossell Hope Robbins p298-302

Greene, R. L. Carols in Tudor drama. *In* Chaucer and Middle English studies in honour of Rossell Hope Robbins p357-65

Caron, Louis le. See Le Caron, Louis

Caron, Loys de. See Le Caron, Louis

Carothers, Yvonne M.

Space and time in Milton: the "Bard's song." *In* Essick, R. N. and Pearce, D. R. eds. Blake in his time p116-27

Caroz, Ya'acob

The Palestinians: who they are. *In* The Palestinians p77-80

Carpenter, Andrew

Double vision in Anglo-Irish literature. *In* Place, personality and the Irish writer p173-89

Carpenter, Edward

About

Colmer, J. Continuity and change. *In* Colmer, J. Coleridge to Catch-22 p122-38

Carpenter, Frederic Ives

Hemingway achieves the fifth dimension; excerpt from "American literature and the dream". *In* Wagner, L. W. ed. Ernest Hemingway p279-87

Carpenter, James O. and Hall, Georgia

Anticipatory grief and the disciplined professions. *In* Anticipatory grief p229-36

Carpenter, Nan Cooke

Shakespeare and music: unexplored areas. *In* Renaissance drama [1976] p243-55

Carpenter, William Benjamin

About

Smith, R. C. The human significance of biology: Carpenter, Darwin, and the vera causa. *In* Knoepflmacher, U. C. and Tennyson, G. B. eds. Nature and the Victorian imagination p216-30

Carpentier, Alejo

About individual works

Explosion in a cathedral

Brotherston, G. The genesis of America: Alejo Carpentier. *In* Brotherston, G. The emergence of the Latin American novel p45-59

Carpentry. See Woodwork

Carpetbag rule. See Reconstruction

Carpovich, Vera V.

The Gulag Archipelago, volume one: notes on its lexical peculiarities. *In* Dunlop, J. B.; Haugh, R. and Klimoff, A. eds. Alexandr Solzhenitsyn: critical essays and documentary materials 2d ed. p527-33

Lexical peculiarities of Solzhenitsyn's language. *In* Dunlop, J. B.; Haugh, R. and Klimoff, A. eds. Aleksandr Solzhenitsyn: critical essays and documentary materials 2d ed. p188-94

Carr, Burgess

Africa's moral imperatives: liberation, identity, humanness. *In* World change and world security p103-16

Carr, David

Husserl's problematic concept of the lifeworld. *In* Elliston, F. A. and McCormick, P. eds. Husserl p202-12

Intentionality. *In* Pivčević, E. ed. Phenomenology and philosophical understanding p17-36

Carr, Dickson, pseud. See Carr, John Dickson

Carr, Edward Hallett

About

Abramsky, C. Tribute to E. H. Carr. *In* Essays in honour of E. H. Carr pvii-viii

About individual works

The twenty years' crisis, 1912-1939

Morgan, R. P. E. H. Carr and the study of international relations. *In* Essays in honour of E. H. Carr p171-80

What is history?

Flew, A. G. N. Hume and historical necessity. *In* Flew, A. G. N. A rational animal p49-74

Carr, Emily

About individual works

Klee Wyck

Dilworth, I. Foreword by Ira Dilworth to Klee Wyck by Emily Carr. *In* Praise from famous men: an anthology of introductions p49-59

Carr, John Dickson

About

Panek, L. L. John Dickson Carr. *In* Panek, L. L. Watteau's shepherds: the detective novel in Britain, 1914-1940 p145-84

Carr, Lois Green

The foundations of social order: local government in colonial Maryland. *In* Daniels, B. C. ed. Town and county p72-110

Carr, William

National socialism: foreign policy and Wehrmacht. *In* Laqueur, W. Z. ed. Fascism: a reader's guide p151-78

Carrascal, José María

About individual works

Groovy

Schwartz, R. Jose Maria Carrascal and Groovy. *In* Schwartz, R. Spain's New Wave novelists, 1950-1974 p278-87

Carrefour

Ford, H. Four new directions: the need for anonymity: Carrefour. *In* Ford, H. D. Published in Paris p290-302

Carribean literature (English) See West Indian literature (English)

Carrier, Roch

About

Joyaux, G. J. Roch Carrier's trilogy: a second look at Quebec's dark years. *In* Essays in honor of Russel B. Nye p105-28

Carrier Indians

Steward, J. H. Carrier acculturation: the direct historical approach. *In* Steward, J. H. Evolution and ecology p188-200

Steward, J. H. Determinism in primitive society? *In* Steward, J. H. Evolution and ecology p180-87

Carrington, John F.

About individual works

La voix des tambours: comment comprendre le langage tambouriné d'Afrique

Ong, W. J. African talking drums and oral noetics. *In* Ong, W. J. Interfaces of the word p92-120

Carroll, Berenice A.

Peacemaking. *In* Encyclopedia of American foreign policy p742-51

Carroll, Horace Bailey

About individual works

Texas county histories

Webb, W. P. Foreword to Texas county histories: a bibliography by H. Bailey Carroll. *In* Praise from famous men: an anthology of introductions p147-57

Carroll, Lewis, pseud. See Dodgson, Charles Lutwidge

Carroll, William

Nabokov's signs and symbols. *In* A Book of things about Vladimir Nabokov p203-17

Carron Company, London
Bartlett, R. P. Scottish cannon-founders and the Russian Navy, 1768-85. *In* Oxford Slavonic papers, new ser. v10 p51-72

Carson, Anthony

About individual works
Travels near and far
Hyman, S. E. The bulging pockets of Anthony Carson. *In* Hyman, S. E. The critic's credentials p140-44

Carson, Barbara Harrell
Winning: Katherine Anne Porter's women. *In* Diamond, A. and Edwards, L. R. eds. The authority of experience p239-56

Carson, Cary
Doing history with material culture. *In* Material culture and the study of American life p41-64

Carson, George Barr
National sovereignty at the bar: revolution by law? *In* Essays on modern European revolutionary history p105-32

Carson, Neil
John Webster: the apprentice years. *In* The Elizabethan theatre, VI p76-87

The staircases of the frame: new light on the structure of the Globe? *In* Shakespeare survey 29 p127-32

Carson, Rachel Louise

About individual works
Silent spring
Downs, R. B. Upsetting the balance of nature; excerpt from "Books that changed America." *In* Downs, R. B. Books that changed the world p383-91

Carson, W. G.
Symbolic and instrumental dimensions of early factory legislation: a case study in the social origins of criminal law. *In* Crime, criminology and public policy p107-38

Carsten, Francis Ludwig
Interpretations of fascism. *In* Laqueur, W. Z. ed. Fascism: a reader's guide p415-34

Carstensen, Vernon Roscoe
The Land of Plenty. *In* Alderson, W. T. ed. American issues p17-31

Cartagena agreement. See Acuerdo de Cartagena

Carter, Alan
The Anglo-Saxon origins of Norwich: the problems and approaches. *In* Anglo-Saxon England 7 p175-204

Carter, Barry E.
The strategic debate in the United States. *In* Kirk, G. L. and Wessell, N. H. eds. The Soviet threat p15-29

See also Steinbruner, J. D. jt. auth.

Carter, Charles Howard
The New World as a factor in international relations, 1492-1739. *In* First images of America p231-63

Carter, Dan T.
Southern political style. *In* The Age of segregation: race relations in the South, 1890-1945 p45-66

Carter, Elliott
Music and the time screen. *In* Current thought in musicology p63-88

About
Carter, E. Music and the time screen. *In* Current thought in musicology p63-88

Carter, Gwendolen Margaret
A case study of the Republic of South Africa. *In* Martin, P. M. and O'Meara, P. eds. Africa p378-94

South Africa: battleground of rival nationalism. *In* Carter, G. M. and O'Meara, P. eds. Southern Africa in crisis p89-135

South Africa: growing Black-white confrontation. *In* Carter, G. M. and O'Meara, P. eds. Southern Africa: the continuing crisis p93-140

See also entry in Part 2 under title: African themes

Carter, James Earl. See Carter, Jimmy, President U.S.

Carter, Jimmy, President U.S.

About
Grantham, D. W. Jimmy Carter and the Americanization of Southern politics. *In* Grantham, D. W. The regional imagination p221-31

Wildavsky, A. B. and Knott, J. Jimmy Carter's theory of governing. *In* Burnham, W. D. and Weinberg, M. W. eds. American politics and public policy p55-76

Personality
Beisel, D. R. Toward a psychohistory of Jimmy Carter. *In* DeMause, L. and Ebel, H. eds. Jimmy Carter and American fantasy p59-96

DeMause, L. Jimmy Carter and American fantasy. *In* DeMause, L. and Ebel, H. eds. Jimmy Carter and American fantasy p9-31

Ebel, H. But what kind of baby is Jimmy Carter? *In* DeMause, L. and Ebel, H. eds. Jimmy Carter and American fantasy p117-27

Elovitz, P. H. Three days in Plains. *In* DeMause, L. and Ebel, H. eds. Jimmy Carter and American fantasy p33-57

Hartman, J. J. Carter and the utopian group-fantasy. *In* DeMause, L. and Ebel, H. eds. Jimmy Carter and American fantasy p97-116

Carter, John Ross
Translational theology: an expression of Christian faith in a religiously plural world. *In* Christian faith in a religiously plural world p168-80

Carter, Joseph Coleman
The date of the sculptured coffer lids from the Temple of Athene Polias at Priene. *In* Studies in classical art and archaeology p139-51

Carter, Lillian

About
Beisel, D. R. Toward a psychohistory of Jimmy Carter. *In* DeMause, L. and Ebel, H. eds. Jimmy Carter and American fantasy p59-96

Elovitz, P. H. Three days in Plains. *In* DeMause, L. and Ebel, H. eds. Jimmy Carter and American fantasy p33-57

Carter, Peter
Mies van der Rohe. *In* Sharp, D. ed. The rationalists p59-72

Carter, Vincent O.

About individual works
The Bern book
Balakian, N. Black odyssey, white world. *In* Balakian, N. Critical encounters p206-09

Carter family

Beisel, D. R. Toward a psychohistory of Jimmy Carter. *In* DeMause, L. and Ebel, H. eds. Jimmy Carter and American fantasy p59-96

Cartesian dualism. See Descartes, René; Dualism

Cartesian linguistics. See Universals (Linguistics)

Cartesian philosophy. See Descartes, René

Carthage

History

Sumner, G. V. Roman policy in Spain before the Hannibalic War. *In* Harvard Studies in classical philology v72 p205-46

Carthaginians in Spain

History

Sumner, G. V. Roman policy in Spain before the Hannibalic War. *In* Harvard Studies in classical philology v72 p205-46

Cartier, Jacques

About

Seelye, J. Diverse voyages: Columbus, Cartier, and the Conradian shape of adventure in America. *In* Seelye, J. Prophetic waters p9-22

Cartier-Bresson, Henri

About individual works

Man and machine

Barrow, T. Three photographers and their books. *In* One hundred years of photographic history p7-14

Cartography

History

Robinson, A. H. Mapmaking and map printing: the evolution of a working relationship. *In* Woodward, D. A. ed. Five centuries of map printing p 1-23

Thrower, N. J. W. New geographical horizons: maps. *In* First images of America p659-74

Africa

Lane-Pool, E. H. The discovery of Africa: a history of the exploration of Africa as reflected in the maps in the collection of the Rhodes-Livingstone Museum. *In* The Occasional papers of the Rhodes-Livingstone Museum p215-48

Cartoons. See Caricatures and cartoons

Carvajal, Orlando P.

The context of theology. *In* The Emergent gospel p99-111

Carvallo de Núñez, Carlota

Children's literature in South America. *In* Egoff, S. A. ed. One ocean touching p131-37

Carver, Jonathan

About individual works

Travels through the interior part of North-America, in the years 1766, 1767, 1768

Medeiros, P. M. Three travelers: Carver, Bartram, and Woolman. *In* Emerson, E. H. ed. American literature, 1764-1789 p195-211

Wilson, D. S. Jonathan Carver, a Connecticut Yankee. *In* Wilson, D. S. In the presence of nature p47-87

Carving (Art industries)

Ben-Amos, P. Professionals and amateurs in Benin court carving. *In* African images p170-89

Cary, Joyce

About

Gardner, Dame H. L. The novels of Joyce Cary. *In* English Association. Essays and studies, 1975 p76-93

Goonetilleke, D. C. R. A. Joyce Cary: the clash of cultures in Nigeria. *In* Goonetilleke, D. C. R. A. Developing countries in British fiction p199-244

Kennedy, A. Language, mimesis and the numinous in Joyce Cary's second trilogy. *In* Kennedy, A. The protean self p99-149

Taiwo, O. Historical and cultural influences on the Nigerian novelists. *In* Taiwo, O. Culture and the Nigerian novel p 1-33

About individual works

The horse's mouth

Heffernan, J. A. W. Politics and freedom: refractions of Blake in Joyce Cary and Allen Ginsberg. *In* Bornstein, G. ed. Romantic and modern p177-95

Mister Johnson

Wren, R. M. 'Mister Johnson' and the complexity of 'Arrow of God.' *In* Narasimhaiah, C. D. ed. Awakened conscience p50-62

Cary, Lorin Lee. See Kay, M. L. M. jt auth.

Casa Italiana. See Columbia University. Casa Italiana. Educational Bureau

Casanova, Giovanni Giacomo. See Casanova de Seingalt, Giacomo Girolama

Casanova de Seingalt, Giacomo Girolama

About individual works

Memoirs

Lyons, J. O. Whores and rakes in the gardens of delight. *In* Lyons, J. O. The invention of the self p176-96

Casares, Adolfo Bioy. See Bioy Casares, Adolfo

Case, Frederick Ivor

Négritude and utopianism. *In* African literature today no. 7: Focus on criticism p65-75

The case of the Naves brothers (Motion picture)

Sarris, A. The case of the Naves brothers. *In* Sarris, A. Politics and cinema p61-62

Casement, Sir Roger David

About

Meyers, J. Roger Casement. *In* Meyers, J. A fever at the core p59-88

Caserio, Robert L.

Plot, story, and the novel

Contents

The divine inert: Melville

The family plot: Conrad, Joyce, Lawrence, Woolf, and Faulkner

The featuring of act as "the rescue": story in Dickens and George Eliot

Narrative reason: the sense of plot and historical experience

Plot and the point of reversal: Dickens and Poe

Plot, purpose, and the modern self

The sense of plot

The story in it: James

Casey, Edward S.
Imagination and phenomenological method. *In* Elliston, F. A. and McCormick, P. eds. Husserl p70-82

Casey, Kathleen
Women in Norman and Plantagenet England. *In* Kanner, B. ed. The women of England p83-123

Casey, Michael

About individual works
Obscenities
Kunitz, S. J. Michael Casey. *In* Kunitz, S. J. A kind of order, a kind of folly p276-81

Cash, Joseph H.
The reservation Indian meets the white man (1860-1914). *In* Red Men and hat-wearers p93-111

Cash, Wilbur Joseph

About individual works
The mind of the South
Downs, R. B. Nation within a nation. *In* Downs, R. B. Books that changed the South p248-58

Casini, Paolo
Newton, a sceptical alchemist? *In* Bonelli, M. L. R. and Shea, W. R. eds. Reason, experiment, and mysticism in the scientific revolution p233-38

Caso, Ralph G.
Managing the unmanageable. *In* Benton, L. R. ed. Management for the future p47-62

Casper, Gerhard, and Posner, Richard A.
The caseload of the Supreme Court: 1975 and 1976 terms. *In* The Supreme Court review, 1977 p87-98

Casper, Leonard
Triangles of transaction in Tennessee Williams. *In* Tennessee Williams: a tribute p736-52

Cassa per il Mezzogiorno
Cassese, S. State grants for the south of Italy. *In* Davis, K. C. Discretionary justice in Europe and America p149-60

Cassedy, James H.
Medicine and the learned society in the United States, 1660-1850. *In* Oleson, A. and Brown, S. C. eds. The pursuit of knowledge in the early American Republic p261-78

Cassell, Eric J.
Dying in a technological society. *In* Death inside out p43-48

Cassese, Antonio
The Helsinki Declaration and self-determination. *In* Human rights, international law and the Helsinki Accord p83-110

Cassese, Sabino
State grants for the south of Italy. *In* Davis, K. C. Discretionary justice in Europe and America p149-60

Cassianus, Johannes

About individual works
De institutis coenobiorum et de octo principalium vitiorum remediis libri xii
Altschule, M. D. Acedia—its evolution from deadly sin to psychiatric syndrome. *In* Altschule, M. D. Origins of concepts in human behavior p75-83

Cassidy, David Charles
Heisenberg's first core model of the atom: the formation of a professional style. *In* Historical studies in the physical sciences v10 p187-224

Cassidy, Frederic Gomes
Use of computers in one lexicographical project: DARE. *In* James B. McMillan: essays in linguistics by his friends and colleagues p133-42

Cassirer, Ernst
Symbol, myth, and culture
Contents
The concept of philosophy as a philosophical problem
Critical idealism as a philosophy of culture
Descartes, Leibniz, and Vico
The educational value of art
Hegel's theory of the state
Judaism and the modern political myths
Language and art I
Language and art II
Philosophy and politics
The philosophy of history
Reflections on the concept of group and the theory of perception
The technique of our modern political myths

About
Morris, W. A. The centrality of language. *In* Morris, W. A. Friday's footprint p84-146
Verene, D. P. Introduction. *In* Cassirer, E. Symbol, myth, and culture p 1-45

About individual works
The philosophy of symbolic forms
Verene, D. P. Vico's science of imaginative universals and the philosophy of symbolic forms. *In* Giambattista Vico's science of humanity p295-317

The philosophy of symbolic forms, v 1
Frye, N. Myth as information. *In* Frye, N. Northrop Frye on culture and literature p67-75

Cassius Dio Cocceianus

About individual works
Roman history
Bowersock, G. W. Herodian and Elagabalus. *In* Yale classical studies v24 p229-36

Castan, Nicole
Summary justice. *In* Deviants and the abandoned in French society p111-56

Castañeda, Héctor-Neri. See Castañeda Calderón, Héctor Neri

Castañeda Calderón, Héctor Neri
Goodness, intentions, and propositions. *In* Fact, value, and perception p67-83

Caste
See also Social classes

India
Berreman, G. D. Bazar behavior: social identity and social interaction in urban India. *In* Ethnic identity p71-105
Béteille, A. Race, caste and ethnic identity. *In* United Nations Educational, Scientific and Cultural Organization. Race, science and society p211-33
Ullrich, H. E. Caste differences between Brahmin and non-Brahmin women in a south Indian village. *In* Schlegel, A. E. Sexual stratification p94-108

Castein, H. C. See Castein, Hanne

Castein, Hanne
German social drama in the 1960s. *In* Drama and society p195-207

Castel, Albert E.

The historian and the General: Thomas L. Connelly versus Robert E. Lee. *In* Hubbell, J. T. ed. Battles lost and won p215-28

Quantrill's bushwhackers: a case study in partisan warfare. *In* Hubbell, J. T. ed. Battles lost and won p171-81

Castelli di Melide, Domenico di Bernardo, d. 1657

Varriano, J. L. Domenico Castelli's façade for San Girolamo della Carità in Rome. *In* Enggass, R. C. and Stokstad, M. eds. Hortus imaginum p139-45

Castello, Francesco. See Borromini, Francesco

Castells, Manuel

Urban sociology and urban politics: from a critique to new trends of research. *In* Walton, J. and Masotti, L. H. eds. The city in comparative perspective p291-300

About individual works
The urban question: a Marxist approach

Harloe, M. Marxism, the state and the urban question: critical notes on two recent French theories. *In* Crouch, C. ed. State and economy in contemporary capitalism p122-56

Castiglione, Baldassare, conte

About individual works
The book of the courtier

Altman, J. B. Propaedeutic for drama: questions as fiction. *In* Altman, J. B. The Tudor play of mind p64-106

Hallam, G. W. In praise of being a gentleman: 1528-1976. *In* Renaissance and modern p3-10

Lanham, R. A. The self as middle style: Cortegiano. *In* Lanham, R. A. The motives of eloquence p144-64

Martines, L. The gentleman in Renaissance Italy: strains of isolation in the body politic. *In* The Darker vision of the Renaissance p77-93

Saccone, E. Grazia, sprezzatura, and the affettazione in Castiglione's Book of the courtier. *In* Glyph 5 p34-54

Castile, Philip

Women and myth in Faulkner's first novel. *In* Tulane Studies in English, v23 p175-86

Castillo Puche, José Luis

About individual works
Paralelo 40

Schwartz, R. Jose Luis Castillo-Puche and Paralelo 40 (The fortieth parallel) (1963). *In* Schwartz, R. Spain's New Wave novelists, 1950-1974 p171-86

Castle, Barbara

A Socialist view. *In* Kramnick, I. ed. Is Britain dying? p45-52

Women and equality in Britain. *In* Kramnick, I. ed. Is Britain dying? p126-36

Castle, Robert Leon van de. See Van de Castle, Robert Leon

Castles

France

Cheyette, F. L. The castles of the Trencavels: a preliminary aerial survey. *In* Order and innovation in the Middle Ages p255-72

Castro, Américo

The meaning of Spanish civilization. *In* Américo Castro and the meaning of Spanish civilization p23-40

About

Aranguren, J. L. L. A new model for Hispanic history. *In* Américo Castro and the meaning of Spanish civilization p309-15

Araya Goubet, G. The evolution of Castro's theories. *In* Américo Castro and the meaning of Spanish civilization p41-66

Benítez, R. An appraisal of the immediate past and present. *In* Américo Castro and the meaning of Spanish civilization p239-66

Gilman, S. Literature and historical insight. *In* Américo Castro and the meaning of Spanish civilization p317-24

Johnson, C. B. The classical theater and its reflection of life. *In* Américo Castro and the meaning of Spanish civilization p193-220

Meregalli, F. A parallel observer and innovator: José Ortega y Gasset. *In* Américo Castro and the meaning of Spanish civilization p267-91

Rodríguez Cepeda, E. The Spanishness of the eighteenth century. *In* Américo Castro and the meaning of Spanish civilization p223-38

Rubia Barcia, J. What's in a name: Américo Castro (y Quesada) *In* Américo Castro and the meaning of Spanish civilization p3-22

Silverman, J. H. The Spanish Jews: early references and later effects. *In* Américo Castro and the meaning of Spanish civilization p137-65

About individual works
Iberoamerica, su historia y su cultura

Morínigo, M. A. The Hispanic inheritance of Iberoamerica. *In* Américo Castro and the meaning of Spanish civilization p295-307

La peculiaridad lingüística rioplatense y su sentido histórico

Morínigo, M. A. The Hispanic inheritance of Iberoamerica. *In* Américo Castro and the meaning of Spanish civilization p295-307

El pensamiento de Cervantes

Beysterveldt, A. A. van. A new perspective of Cervantes' work. *In* Américo Castro and the meaning of Spanish civilization p167-91

Casuistry. See Probabilism

Cat on a hot tin roof (criticism) *In* Kauffmann, S. Persons of the drama p152-55

Cataldo, Michael F. See Risley, T. R. jt. auth.

Cataloging

Tanselle, G. T. Descriptive bibliography and library cataloguing. *In* Virginia. University. Bibliographical Society. Studies in bibliography v30 p 1-56

Cataloging, Cooperative. See Bibliography, International

Cataloging of art

Butlin, M. Cataloguing William Blake. *In* Essick, R. N. and Pearce, D. R. eds. Blake in his time p77-90

Catalogs, Universal. See Bibliography, International

Catalonia

History

Riu, M. Banking and society in late medieval and early modern Aragon. *In* The Dawn of modern banking p131-67

Catalonia—*Continued*

History—Autonomy and independence movements

Jones, N. L. The Catalan question since the Civil War. *In* Preston, P. ed. Spain in crisis p234-67

History—Separatist movement

See Catalonia—History—Autonomy and independence movements

Politics and government

Jones, N. L. The Catalan question since the Civil War. *In* Preston, P. ed. Spain in crisis p234-67

Separatist movement

See Catalonia—History—Autonomy and independence movements

Catastrophes (Geology) See Deluge

Catawba Indians

Hudson, C. M. The Catawba Indians of South Carolina: a question of ethnic survival. *In* Williams, W. L. ed. Southeastern Indians since the removal era p110-20

Catawba language. See Siouan languages

Cate, Curtis

About individual works

Antoine de Saint-Exupéry: his life and times

Balakian, N. Poet of the air—and earth: Antoine de Saint-Exupéry. *In* Balakian, N. Critical encounters p142-45

George Sand: a biography

Pritchett, V. S. George Sand: George Sand. *In* Pritchett, V. S. The myth makers p115-27

Cate, George Allen

Ruskin's discipleship to Carlyle: a revaluation. *In* Carlyle and his contemporaries p227-56

Categories (Mathematics) See Functor theory

Categories (Philosophy) See Whole and parts (Philosophy)

Categorization (Psychology)

Percy, W. The loss of the creature. *In* Percy, W. The message in the bottle p46-63

Cater, Douglass

Introduction: Television and thinking people. *In* Television as a social force: new approaches to TV criticism p 1-7

Caterpillar (Periodical)

Eshleman, C. Doing Caterpillar. *In* Anderson, E. and Kinzie, M. eds. The little magazine in America: a documentary history p450-71

Catesby, Mark

About individual works

The natural history of Carolina, Florida, and the Bahama Islands

Wilson, D. S. Mark Catesby, a Georgian reporter. *In* Wilson, D. S. In the presence of nature p123-59

Catharine, Saint of Alexandria

Legend

Pearsall, D. A. John Capgrave's Life of St. Katharine and popular romance style. *In* Medievalia et humanistica no. 6 p121-37

Catharsis

Kropf, C. R. Catharsis in eighteenth-century England. *In* Tennessee Studies in literature v22 p63-72

Rahv, P. Excerpts from "the literary class war." *In* Rahv, P. Essays on literature and politics, 1932-1972 p281-83

Simon, B. Tragedy and therapy. *In* Simon, B. Mind and madness in ancient Greece p122-54

Cathedral, Gurk, Austria. See Gurk, Austria. Dom

Cathedrals

Austria

See Gurk, Austria. Dom

Cather, Willa Sibert

About

Celli, A. Italian perspectives. *In* The Art of Willa Cather p103-20

Cunliffe, M. The two or more worlds of Willa Cather. *In* The Art of Willa Cather p21-42

Edel, L. Homage to Willa Cather. *In* The Art of Willa Cather p185-204

Gervaud, M. Willa Cather and France: elective affinities. *In* The Art of Willa Cather p65-83

Knopf, A. A. Miss Cather. *In* The Art of Willa Cather p205-24

Miller, J. E. Willa Cather and the art of fiction. *In* The Art of Willa Cather p121-55

Morris, W. Willa Cather. *In* Morris, W. Earthly delights, unearthly adornments p59-67

Sato, H. Willa Cather in Japan. *In* The Art of Willa Cather p84-102

Slote, B. An appointment with the future: Willa Cather. *In* French, W. G. ed. The twenties p39-49

Slote, B. A gathering of nations. *In* The Art of Willa Cather p248-53

Sutherland, D. Willa Cather: the classic voice. *In* The Art of Willa Cather p156-82

Van Ghent, D. B. Willa Cather. *In* Howard, M. ed. Seven American women writers of the twentieth century p79-121

Welty, E. The house of Willa Cather. *In* The Art of Willa Cather p3-20

Also in Welty, E. The eye of the story p41-60

Woodress, J. L. Willa Cather: American experience and European tradition. *In* The Art of Willa Cather p43-64

About individual works

Death comes for the Archbishop

Watkins, F. C. Death comes for the Archbishop: worlds old and new. *In* Watkins, F. C. In time and place p105-30

My Ántonia

Watkins, F. C. My Ántonia: "still, all day long, Nebraska." *In* Watkins, F. C. In time and place p73-101

The professor's house

Stineback, D. C. "Roving tribes" and "brutal invaders": Willa Cather's The professor's house. *In* Stineback, D. C. Shifting world p101-14

Aesthetics

Miller, J. E. Willa Cather and the art of fiction. *In* The Art of Willa Cather p121-55

Cather, Willa S.—*Continued*

Knowledge—Nebraska

Watkins, F. C. My Ántonia: "still, all day long, Nebraska." *In* Watkins, F. C. In time and place p73-101

Knowledge—Southwest (New)

Watkins, F. C. Death comes for the Archbishop: worlds old and new. *In* Watkins, F. C. In time and place p105-30

Catherine the Great. See Catherine II, Empress of Russia

Catherine II, Empress of Russia

About

Brown, A. H. S. E. Desnitsky, Adam Smith, and the Nakaz of Catherine II. *In* Oxford Slavonic papers, new ser. v7 p42-59

Griffiths, D. M. Catherine the Great, the British opposition and the American Revolution. *In* The American Revolution and "a candid world" p85-110

Raeff, M. The Empress and the Vinerian Professor: Catherine II's projects of government reforms and Blackstone's Commentaries. *In* Oxford Slavonic papers, new ser. v7 p18-41

Catheterization. See Urinary catheterization

Catholic authors

Kunkel, F. L. The sexy Cross. *In* Kunkel, F. L. Passion and the Passion p157-68

Catholic Church

Hesburgh, T. M. The post-Vatican II Church. *In* Hesburgh, T. M. The Hesburgh papers p177-89

See also Canon law; Oxford movement

Benefices

See Benefices, Ecclesiastical

Ceremonies and practices

Jones, D. A Christmas message, 1960. *In* Jones, D. The dying Gaul, and other writings p167-76

Clergy

Boxer, C. R. European missionaries and Chinese clergy, 1654-1810. *In* Kling, B. B. and Pearson, M. N. eds. The age of partnership p97-121

Curia romana

McCurry, C. Utilia metensia: local benefices for the papal Curia, 1212—c.1370. *In* Law, church, and society p311-23

Doctrinal and controversial works—Protestant authors

See Anti-clericalism

Education

See Catholic universities and colleges

Finance

See Benefices, Ecclesiastical

History

Robinson, I. S. "Periculosus homo": Pope Gregory VII and episcopal authority. *In* Viator: medieval and Renaissance studies v9 p103-31

See also Councils and synods

History—Sources

Wallach, L. Origin and composition of the Libri Carolini. *In* Wallach, L. Diplomatic studies in Latin and Greek documents from the Carolingian age p47-58

History—Middle Ages, 600-1500

See Church history—Middle Ages, 600-1500

History—Modern period, 1500-

O'Malley, J. W. The discovery of America and reform thought at the Papal Court in the early Cinquecento. *In* First images of America p185-200

Infallibility

See Popes—Infallibility

Liturgy and ritual—Coronation service [France]

Sherman, C. R. The Queen in Charles V's "Coronation Book": Jeanne de Bourbon and the "Ordo ad reginam benedicendam." *In* Viator: medieval and Renaissance studies v8 p255-98

Liturgy and ritual—Gradual

See Graduals (Music)

Liturgy and ritual—Sacramentary (Sacramentarium Gregorianum)

Lutz, C. E. A bifolium from a Sacramentarium Gregorianum. *In* Lutz, C. E. Essays on manuscripts and rare books p28-38

Missions

Boxer, C. R. European missionaries and Chinese clergy, 1654-1810. *In* Kling, B. B. and Pearson, M. N. eds. The age of partnership p97-121

Relation to the state

See Church and state—Catholic Church

Relations—Byzantine Empire

Lynch, J. H. A Carolingian borrowing from Second Nicaea (787). *In* Medievalia et humanistica no. 5 p127-38

Relations—Judaism

Grayzel, S. Pope Alexander III and the Jews. *In* Salo Wittmayer Baron v2 p555-72

Sacraments

See Sacraments—Catholic Church

Societies, etc.

McKeown, E. K. Catholic identity in America. *In* America in theological perspective p56-68

See also Confraternities

Catholic Church. Pope, 772-795 (Hadrianus I) See Hadrianus I, Pope

Catholic Church. Pope, 795-816 (Leo III) See Leo III, Saint, Pope

Catholic Church. Pope, 1099-1118 (Paschalis II) See Paschalis II, Pope

Catholic Church. Pope, 1198-1216 (Innocentius III) See Innocentius III, Pope

Catholic Church. Pope, 1294-1303 (Bonifacius VIII) See Bonifacius VIII, Pope

Catholic Church. Pope, 1963-1978 (Paulus VI) See Paulus VI, Pope

Catholic Church and abortion. See Abortion—Religious aspects—Catholic Church

Catholic Church and art

Brown, J. Theory into practice: the arts and the academy. *In* Brown, J. Images and ideas in seventeenth-century Spanish painting p63-83

Catholic Church and birth control. See Birth control—Catholic Church

Catholic societies. See Catholic Church—Societies, etc.

Catholic universities and colleges

Hesburgh, T. M. The Catholic university and freedom. *In* Hesburgh, T. M. The Hesburgh papers p63-67

Hesburgh, T. M. The vision of the Catholic university in the world of today. *In* Hesburgh, T. M. The Hesburgh papers p37-49

United States

Canavan, F. P. The problem of indoctrination. *In* Hook, S.; Kurtz, P. and Todorovich, M. eds. The ethics of teaching and scientific research p29-35

Hesburgh, T. M. The changing face of Catholic higher education. *In* Hesburgh, T. M. The Hesburgh papers p69-80

Hesburgh, T. M. New focus for Catholic higher education in the 1970s. *In* Hesburgh, T. M. The Hesburgh papers p83-88

Catholics

Societies, etc.

See Catholic Church—Societies, etc.

Ireland

O'Connell, M. R. Daniel O'Connell and the Irish eighteenth century. *In* Studies in eighteenth-century culture v5 p475-95

Palmer, S. H. Rebellion, emancipation, starvation: the dilemma of peaceful protest in Ireland, 1798-1848. *In* Essays on modern European revolutionary history p3-38

Northern Ireland

Hepburn, A. C. Catholics in the north of Ireland, 1850-1921: the urbanization of a minority. *In* Hepburn, A. C. ed. Minorities in history p84-102

United States

Hennesey, J. Square peg in a round hole: on being Roman Catholic in America. *In* America in theological perspective p3-12

McKeown, E. K. Catholic identity in America. *In* America in theological perspective p56-68

Maguire, D. C. Catholic ethics with an American accent. *In* America in theological perspective p13-36

United States—History

McAvoy, T. T. The formation of the Catholic minority in the United States, 1820-1860. *In* Mulder, J. M. and Wilson, J. F. eds. Religion in American history p254-69

Wales

Jones, D. Welsh culture. *In* Jones, D. The dying Gaul, and other writings p117-22

Catholics in literature

Kurz, P. K. Heinrich Böll: not reconciled. *In* Kurz, P. K. On modern German literature v4 p3-36

Sayre, R. F. Journal d'un curé de campagne: the saint's Gethsemane. *In* Sayre, R. F. Solitude in society p133-54

Sheed, W. Mary Gordon: Final payments. *In* Sheed, W. The good word & other words p259-65

Sheed, W. Walker Percy redivivus. *In* Sheed, W. The good word & other words p127-31

Catholics, Irish, in the United States

Yetman, N. R. The Irish experience in America. *In* Orel, H. ed. Irish history and culture p347-76

Catholics, Puerto Rican, in the United States

Garrison, V. E. Sectarianism and psychosocial adjustment: a controlled comparison of Puerto Rican Pentecostals and Catholics. *In* Zaretsky, I. I. and Leone, M. P. eds. Religious movements in contemporary America p298-329

Catlin, Stanton L.

Political iconography in the Diego Rivera frescoes at Cuernavaca, Mexico. *In* Millon, H. A. and Nochlin, L. eds. Art and architecture in the service of politics p194-215

Cattell, David Tredwell

Soviet cities and consumer welfare planning. *In* Hamm, M. F. ed. The city in Russian history p257-75

Cattermole, George

About

Cohen, J. R. Strained relations: Charles Dickens and George Cattermole. *In* Dickens Studies Annual v1 p81-92

The cattle raid of Cooley. See Táin bó Cúailnge

Cattle ranches. See Ranches

Cattle trade

United States—History

Hagan, W. T. Kiowas, Comanches, and cattlemen, 1867-1906: a case study of the failure of U.S. reservation policy. *In* The American Indian p77-99

Catton, William R.

Carrying capacity, overshoot, and the quality of life. *In* Major social issues p231-49

Catton, William R. and Dunlap, Riley E.

Environmental sociology: a new paradigm. *In* McNall. S. G. ed. Theoretical perspectives in sociology p465-78

Catullus, C. Valerius

About

Elder, J. P. Catullus I, his poetic creed, and Nepos. *In* Harvard Studies in classical philology v71 p143-49

About individual works

Poem 31

Cairns, F. Venusta Sirmio: Catullus 31. *In* Woodman, T. and West, D. eds. Quality and pleasure in Latin poetry p 1-17

Poem 64

Clausen, W. V. Ariadne's leave-taking: Catullus 64.116-20. *In* Illinois classical studies, v2 1977 p219-23

Poems, 65, 66

Clausen, W. Catullus and Callimachus. *In* Harvard Studies in classical philology v74 p85-94

Poem 68

Bright, D. F. Confectum carmine munus: Catullus 68. *In* Illinois classical studies, v 1 1976 p86-112

Thomas, R. F. An alternative to ceremonial negligence (Catullus 68.73-78) *In* Harvard Studies in classical philology v82 p175-78

Poem 85 (Odi et amo)

Rudd, N. Translation. *In* Rudd, N. Lines of enquiry p182-210

Translations, English

Rudd, N. Translation. *In* Rudd, N. Lines of enquiry p182-210

Catullus, Gaius Valerius. See Catullus, C. Valerius

Caucasus
History
Jones, M. V. The sad and curious story of Karass. *In* Oxford Slavonic papers, new ser. v8 p53-81

Caughey, John Walton
McCarthyism rampant. *In* The Pulse of freedom p154-210

Caulfield, Ernest Joseph. See Slater, J. A. jt. auth.

Causality. See Causality (Physics); Causation

Causality (Physics)
Wilson, M. D. Leibniz's dynamics and contingency in nature. *In* Motion and time, space and matter p264-89

Causation
Bricke, J. Hume on self-identity, memory and causality. *In* David Hume p167-74

Brier, R. Magicians, alarm clocks, and backward causation. *In* Wheatley, J. M. O. and Edge, H. L. eds. Philosophical dimensions of parapsychology p235-44

Ducasse, C. J. A theory of the relation of causality to precognition; excerpt from "Broad on the relevance of psychical research to philosophy." *In* Wheatley, J. M. O. and Edge, H. L. eds. Philosophical dimensions of parapsychology p227-34

Khamara, E. J. and MacNabb, D. G. C. Hume and his predecessors on the causal maxim. *In* David Hume p146-55

Machamer, P. K. Causality and explanation in Descartes' natural philosophy. *In* Motion and time, space and matter p168-99

Miller, J. W. The paradox of cause. *In* Miller, J. W. The paradox of cause, and other essays p11-18

Robison, W. L. Hume's causal scepticism. *In* David Hume p156-66

Wicker, B. Metaphor and 'nature.' *In* Wicker, B. The story-shaped world p50-70

Wilson, M. D. Leibniz's dynamics and contingency in nature. *In* Motion and time, space and matter p264-89

See also Necessity (Philosophy); Teleology

Cause and effect. See Causation

Causley, Charles
About
Scannell, V. Alan Ross and Charles Causley. *In* Scannell, V. Not without glory p113-33

Caute, David
About individual works
Comrade Jacob
George, C. H. Gerrard Winstanley: a critical retrospect. *In* The Dissenting tradition p191-225

Cavaignac, Godefroy
About
Hilles, F. W. The hero as revolutionary: Godefroy Cavaignac. *In* Carlyle and his contemporaries p74-90

Cavaignac, Jacques Eléonor Louis Godefroi. See Cavaignac, Godefroy

Cavaliero, Glen
The rural tradition in the English novel, 1900-1939
Contents
Conclusion: The earth and the land
The enduring land: H. E. Bates
Farmer novelists: H. W. Freeman, A. G. Street, Adrian Bell

The land and the city
The land of lost content: Henry Williamson, Llewelyn Powys
A land of one's own: Constance Holme
Literary regionalism: Hugh Walpole, Sheila Kaye-Smith
Problems of the rural novelist: E. C. Booth
Romantic landscapes: Mary Webb, E. H. Young
Rural fantasies: Kenneth Grahame, T. H. White and others
Rural symbolism: T. F. Powys
Town and country: Francis Brett Young, Winifred Holtby

Cavalletti, Francesco
Contributions of Western Europe to disarmament. *In* The Dynamics of the arms race p143-59

Cavalli-Sforza, Luigi Luca. See Ammerman, A. J. jt. auth.

Cavarozzi, Marcelo J. and Petras, James F.
Chile. *In* Chilcote, R. H. and Edelstein, J. C. eds. Latin America: the struggle with dependency and beyond p491-578

Cave, Terence Christopher
Copia and cornucopia. *In* French Renaissance studies, 1540-70 p52-69

Cave-drawings. See Pectoglyphs

Cavell, Stanley
Must we mean what we say?
Contents
Aesthetic problems of modern philosophy
Austin at criticism
The availability of Wittgenstein's later philosophy
The avoidance of love: a reading of King Lear
Ending the waiting game: a reading of Beckett's Endgame
Kierkegaard's On authority and revelation
Knowing and acknowledging
A matter of meaning it
Music discomposed
Must we mean what we say?

Cavers, Dorothy L.
In support of the use of place-names as an aid to the study of Middle English dialects. *In* An English miscellany p54-71

Caves, Richard E.
Looking at inflation in the open economy. *In* Inflation, trade and taxes p75-95

Caves (in religion, folk-lore, etc.)
Gilbert, S. M. and Gubar, S. The parables of the cave. *In* Gilbert, S. M. and Gubar, S. The madwoman in the attic p93-104

Cawelti, John G.
Adventure, mystery, and romance
Contents
The art of the classical detective story
The best-selling social melodrama
The formula of the classical detective story
Hammett, Chandler, and Spillane
The hard-boiled detective story
The mythology of crime and its formulaic embodiments
Notes toward a typology of literary formulas
The study of literary formulas
The Western: a look at the evolution of a formula

The joys of Buchaneering. *In* Essays in honor of Russel B. Nye p7-30

Literary formulas and their cultural significance. *In* Luedtke, L. S. ed. The study of American culture p177-217

Cawkwell, George

Thucydides' judgment of Periclean strategy. *In* Yale classical studies v24 p53-70

Caws, Peter James

Praxis and techne. *In* Bugliarello, G. and Doner, D. B. eds. The history and philosophy of technology p227-37

Caxton, William

About

Pearsall, D. A. The English romance in the fifteenth century. *In* English Association. Essays and studies, 1976 p56-83

Cazden, Courtney B.

Problems for education: language as curriculum content and learning environment. *In* Bloomfield, M. W. and Haugen, E. I. eds. Language as a human problem p137-50

Cazden, Robert Edgar

Johann Georg Wesselhöft and the German book trade in America. *In* The German contribution to the building of the Americas p217-34

Cazemajou, Jean

Stephen Crane. *In* Walcutt, C. C. ed. Seven novelists in the American naturalist tradition p21-54

Cazes, Bernard

The use of long-term studies in planning. *In* Planning, politics and public policy p424-32

Cebes

About individual works
Tabula

Lutz, C. E. Aesticampianus' edition of the Tabula attributed to Cebes. *In* Lutz, C. E. Essays on manuscripts and rare books p79-86

Cecil, Lord David

Hardy the historian. *In* Drabble, M. ed. The genius of Thomas Hardy p154-61

The Max Beerbohm entertainment. *In* Riewald, J. G. ed. The surprise of excellence p229-38

About individual works
Max

Auden, W. H. One of the family; excerpt from "Forewords and afterwords". *In* Riewald, J. G. ed. The surprise of excellence p159-74

Cela, Camilo José

About individual works
The hive

Schwartz, R. Cela and La colmena (The hive) (1951). *In* Schwartz, R. Spain's New Wave novelists, 1950-1974 p32-49

Celestial mechanics. See Mechanics, Celestial

Celibacy

Anson, J. S. The female transvestite in early monasticism: the origin and development of a motif. *In* Viator: medieval and Renaissance studies v5 p 1-32

Céline, Louis Ferdinand, pseud. See Destouches, Louis Ferdinand

Cell function. See Cell physiology

Cell organelles. See Lysosomes

Cell physiology

De Duve, C. R. Cells age: are lysosomes among the villains? *In* Jarvik, L. F. ed. Aging into the 21st century p25-31

Tomkins, G. M. The "metabolic code"— a key to prolonging life? *In* Jarvik, L. F. ed. Aging into the 21st century p33-40

Celli, Aldo

Italian perspectives. *In* The Art of Willa Cather p103-20

Cellini, Benvenuto

About individual works
Autobiography of Benvenuto Cellini

Schmidgall, G. Hector Berlioz. *In* Schmidgall, G. Literature as opera p149-77

Cells

Cohen, S. S. On the origins of cells: the development of a Copernican revolution. *In* Neyman, J. ed. The heritage of Copernicus: theories "pleasing to the mind" p207-27

See also Embryology; Irritability

Cellulose industry

Great Britain—History

Coleman, D. C. War demand and industrial supply: the 'dope scandal', 1915-19. *In* War and economic development p205-27

Celtic language. See Welsh language

Celtic literature. See Scottish literature

Celts

Jones, D. The dying Gaul. *In* Jones, D. The dying Gaul, and other writings p50-58

Celts in literature

Moynahan, J. Lawrence, woman and the Celtic fringe. *In* Smith, A. ed. Lawrence and women p122-35

Cemeteries

Names

Zelinsky, W. Unearthly delights: cemetery names and the map of the changing American afterworld. *In* Geographies of the mind p171-95

United States

French, S. G. The cemetery as cultural institution: the establishment of Mount Auburn and the "rural cemetery" movement. *In* Death in America p69-91

Zelinsky, W. Unearthly delights: cemetery names and the map of the changing American afterworld. *In* Geographies of the mind p171-95

Censorship

Berninghausen, D. K. Asheim's liberal approach to intellectual freedom. *In* As much to learn as to teach p38-50

Maggs, P. B. Legal controls on American publication of heterodox Soviet writings. *In* Tokes, R. L. ed. Dissent in the USSR p310-25

Pilpel, H. F. Libraries and the First Amendment. *In* Libraries and the life of the mind in America p87-106

Shaw, E. P. Censorship and subterfuge in eighteenth-century France. *In* Literature and history in the age of ideas p287-309

Steloff, F. Censorship and the Gotham Book Mart. *In* Bookselling in America and the world p181-83

See also Liberty of the press

Egypt

Farah, C. E. Censorship and freedom of expression in Ottoman Syria and Egypt. *In* Nationalism in a non-national state p151-94

Great Britain—History

Youngs, F. J. The Tudor governments and dissident religious books. *In* The Dissenting tradition p167-90

Censorship—*Continued*

Russia

Mandel'shtam, O. E. Fourth prose. *In* Mandel'shtam, O. E. Selected essays p157-69

Solzhenitsyn, A. I. Letter to the Fourth Congress of Soviet writers. *In* Dunlop, J. B.; Haugh, R. and Klimoff, A. eds. Aleksandr Solzhenitsyn: critical essays and documentary materials 2d ed. p541-49

South Africa

Gordimer, N. English-language literature and politics in South Africa. *In* Heywood, C. ed. Aspects of South African literature p99-120

Syria

Farah, C. E. Censorship and freedom of expression in Ottoman Syria and Egypt. *In* Nationalism in a non-national state p151-94

Venice—History

Grendler, P. F. Venice, science, and the Index of Prohibited Books. *In* The Nature of scientific discovery p335-47

Censorship in libraries. See Libraries—Censorship

Censorship of the press. See Liberty of the press

Censorship of the stage. See Theater—Censorship

Center for the Study of Democratic Institutions

Ashmore, H. S. An exercise in demi-diplomacy: the case of Vietnam. *In* Unofficial diplomats p130-41

Central African Federation. See Rhodesia and Nyasaland

Central America

Antiquities

Willey, G. R. The rise of Maya civilization: a summary view. *In* The Origins of Maya civilization p383-423

Religion—Bibliography

Vázquez, J. A. The religions of Mexico and of Central and South America. *In* Adams, C. J. ed. A reader's guide to the great religions p78-89

Central business districts

United States

Suttles, G. D. Changing priorities for the urban heartland. *In* Handbook of contemporary urban life p519-47

Central Europe

History

Von Klemperer, K. Empire lost—myth and reality in post-imperial societies: the case of Central Europe since 1918. *In* Aftermath of empire p11-36

Intellectual life

Von Klemperer, K. Empire lost—myth and reality in post-imperial societies: the case of Central Europe since 1918. *In* Aftermath of empire p11-36

Central Intelligence Agency. See United States. Central Intelligence Agency

Central nervous system. See Brain

Centralization in government. See Decentralization in government

Centrifugal force. See Gravitation

Centueri, Guglielmo

About

Gilbert, N. W. A letter of Giovanni Dondi dall'Orologio to Fra'Guglielmo Centueri: a fourteenth-century episode in the Quarrel of the Ancients and the Moderns. *In* Viator: medieval and Renaissance studies v8 p299-346

Cepeda, Enrique Rodríguez. See Rodríguez Cepeda, Enrique

Cepperello da Prato. See Ciappelletto, Ser

Ceramics (Art) See Pottery

Cerebral cortex

Simons, J. R. The brain and evolution of lower mammals. *In* Grafton Elliot Smith p39-49

Cerebral death. See Brain death

Cerebral hemispheres. See Split brain

Ceremonies. See Rites and ceremonies

Cernuda, Luis

Words before a reading. *In* Gibbons, R. ed. The poet's work: 29 masters of 20th century poetry on the origins and practice of their art p42-47

Černyševskij, Nikolaj Gavrilovič. See Chernyshevskii, Nikolaĭ Gavrilovich

Cerri, Giovanni. See Gentili, B. jt. auth.

Certainty

Ayer, Sir A. J. Wittgenstein on certainty. *In* Royal Institute of Philosophy. Understanding Wittgenstein p226-45

Garber, D. Science and certainty in Descartes. *In* Hooker, M. ed. Descartes p114-51

Nelson, B. N. The quest for certitude and the books of Scripture, nature, and conscience. *In* The Nature of scientific discovery p355-72

Tlumak, J. Certainty and Cartesian method. *In* Hooker, M. ed. Descartes p40-73

See also Truth

Certification of death. See Death—Proof and certification

Cervantes, Miguel de. See Cervantes Saavedra, Miguel de

Cervantes Saavedra, Miguel de

About

Beysterveldt, A. A. van. A new perspective of Cervantes' work. *In* Américo Castro and the meaning of Spanish civilization p167-91

About individual works

Don Quixote de la Mancha

Alter, R. The mirror of knighthood and the world of mirrors. *In* Alter, R. Partial magic p 1-29

Avalle-Arce, J. B. Vital and artistic structures in the life of Don Quixote. *In* Medieval and Renaissance studies [1974] p104-21

Berryman, J. The freedom of the Don. *In* Berryman, J. The freedom of the poet p144-58

Brooks, C. Thomas Percy, Don Quixote, and Don Bowle. *In* Evidence in literary scholarship p247-61

Close, A. J. Don Quixote and the 'intentionalist fallacy.' *In* On literary intention p174-93

DiBattista, M. A. Don Quixote. *In* Seidel, M. A. and Mendelson, E. eds. Homer to Brecht p105-22

Cervantes Saavedra, Miguel de—*Continued*

Hardy, B. N. Fantasy and dream. *In* Hardy, B. N. Tellers and listeners p19-55

Karl, F. R. Don Quixote as archetypal artist and Don Quixote as archetypal novel. *In* Karl, F. R. The adversary literature p55-67

Levin, H. Excursus: the example of Cervantes: the novel as parody. *In* Wimsatt, W. K. ed. Literary criticism: idea and act p330-45

Lewis, W. Cervantes; excerpt from "The lion and the fox." *In* Lewis, W. Enemy salvoes p75-76

Poggioli, R. The pastoral of the self. *In* Poggioli, R. The oaten flute p166-81

Segre, C. Rectilinear and spiral constructions in Don Quixote. *In* Segre, C. Structures and time p161-96

Snodgrass, W. D. Glorying in failure: Cervantes and Don Quixote. *In* Snodgrass, W. D. In radical pursuit p241-74

Don Quixote de la Mancha (translated by Samuel Putnam)

Frye, N. The acceptance of innocence. *In* Frye, N. Northrop Frye on culture and literature p159-64

Characters—Don Quixote

Karl, F. R. Don Quixote as archetypal artist and Don Quixote as archetypal novel. *In* Karl, F. R. The adversary literature p55-67

Predmore, R. L. On interpreting Don Quixote's character. *In* Studies in the continental background of Renaissance English literature: essays presented to John L. Lievsay p186-201

Torrance, R. M. Aberrant hidalgo. *In* Torrance, R. M. The comic hero p144-76

Influence

Skilton, D. Quixotic and picaresque fiction. *In* Skilton, D. The English novel p32-44

Cervenka, Zdenek

The OAU and the Nigerian Civil War. *In* El-Ayouty, Y. ed. The Organization of African Unity after ten years p152-73

Césaire, Aimé

About

Case, F. I. Négritude and utopianism. *In* African literature today no. 7: Focus on criticism p65-75

Dash, J. M. The example of Aimé Césaire. *In* King, B. A. and Ogungbesan, K. eds. A celebration of Black and African writing p74-86

Snyder, E. Aimé Césaire: the reclaiming of the land. *In* Exile and tradition p31-43

Ceylon. See Sri Lanka

Cézanne, Paul

About

Berger, J. The sight of a man. *In* Berger, J. The look of things p190-97

Osborne, H. Cubism, Cézanne, and perceptual realism. *In* Osborne, H. Abstraction and artifice in twentieth-century art p63-76

Schapiro, M. The apples of Cézanne: an essay on the meaning of still-life. *In* Schapiro, M. Selected papers v2 p 1-45

Chaadaev, Petr fAkolevich

About

Mandel'shtam, O. E. Peter Chaadaev. *In* Mandel'shtam, O. E. Selected essays p101-07

Chaber, M. E. pseud. See Crossen, Kendell Foster

Chabrol, Claude

About

Monaco, J. Chabrol: films noirs in color. *In* Monaco, J. The New Wave p253-85

Taylor, J. R. Claude Chabrol. *In* Taylor, J. R. Directors and directions p8-43

About individual works

This man must die

Kauffmann, S. This man must die. *In* Kauffmann, S. Living images p24-26

Chace, James

Europe: is there a price to be paid? *In* Atlantis lost p65-83

Chadbourne, Richard McClain

Chateaubriand's aviary: birds in the Mémoires d'outre-tombe. *In* Symbolism and modern literature p65-80

Chadwick, Owen

Gibbon and the church historians. *In* Edward and The decline and fall of the Roman Empire p219-31

The secularization of the European mind in the nineteenth century

Contents

The attitudes of the worker

History and the secular

Karl Marx

The moral nature of man

On a sense of providence

On liberalism

The rise of anticlericalism

Science and religion

Voltaire in the nineteenth century

Chafe, Wallace L.

The recall and verbalization of past experience. *In* Current issues in linguistic theory p215-46

Siouan, Iroquoian, and Caddoan. *In* Sebeok, T. A. ed. Native languages of the Americas v 1 p527-72

Chafee, Zechariah

About

Gunther, G. Learned Hand and the origins of modern first amendment doctrine: some fragments of history. *In* Stanford legal essays p195-249

Chaffee, Steven Henry

Mass media effects: new research perspectives. *In* Lerner, D. and Nelson, L. M. eds. Communication research—a half-century appraisal p210-41

Chagall, Marc

About individual works

Illustrations for the Bible

Schapiro, M. Chagall's Illustrations for the Bible. *In* Schapiro, M. Selected papers v2 p121-34

Chaïkovskiĭ, Petr Il'ich

About individual works

Eugene Onegin

Schmidgall, G. Peter Ilyich Tchaikovsky. *In* Schmidgall, G. Literature as opera p217-46

Chaitanya

About

Dimock, E. C. Religious biography in India: the 'nectar of the acts' of Caitanya. *In* Reynolds, F. E. and Capps, D. eds. The biographical process p109-17

Chandigarh, India—*Continued*

Public buildings

Moos, S. von. The politics of the open hand: notes on Le Corbusier and Nehru at Chandigarh. *In* Walden, R. ed. The open hand p412-57

Chandler, Alfred Dupont

The multi-unit enterprise: a historical and international comparative analysis and summary. *In* Evolution of international management structures p225-54

Chandler, David Lee

Health conditions in the slave trade of colonial New Granada. *In* Toplin, R. B. ed. Slavery and race relations in Latin America p51-88

Chandler, Raymond

About

Cawelti, J. G. Hammett, Chandler, and Spillane. *In* Cawelti, J. G. Adventure, mystery, and romance p162-91

Hartman, G. H. Literature high and low: the case of the mystery story. *In* Hartman, G. H. The fate of reading p203-22

Lambert, G. A private eye. *In* Lambert, G. The dangerous edge p210-34

About individual works
The big sleep

Shatzkin, R. Who cares who killed Owen Taylor? *In* Peary, G. and Shatzkin, R. eds. The modern American novel and the movies p80-94

Chandran, J. Russell

Development of Christian theology in India: a critical survey. *In* The Emergent gospel p157-72

Chaney, David C. and Chaney, Judith H.

The audience for mass leisure. *In* Fischer, H. D. and Melnik, S. R. eds. Entertainment: a cross-cultural examination p129-43

Chaney, Judith H. See Chaney, D. C. jt. auth.

Chang, Chu-po

About individual works
Commentary on the Chin p'ing mei

Roy, D. T. Chang Chu-p'o's Commentary on the Chin p'ing mei. *In* Chinese narrative p115-23

Chang, Fu-mei Chen- See Chen-Chang, Fu-mei

Chang, Hao

New Confucianism and the intellectual crisis of contemporary China. *In* The Limits of change p276-302

Chang, Hui-yen

About individual works
Tz'u hsüan

Yeh, Chia-ying. The Ch'ang-chou School of Tz'u criticism. *In* Chinese approaches to literature from Confucius to Liang Ch'i-ch'ao p151-88

Chang, Joseph S. M. J. and Hammersmith, James P.

Thomas Heywood. *In* Logan, T. P. and Smith, D. S. eds. The popular school p105-21

Chang, Kwang-chih

Ancient trade as economics or as ecology. *In* Ancient civilization and trade p211-24

Chang, Mei Yuan

Malraux and Chinese thinking. *In* Courcel, M. H. de, ed. Malraux p103-11

Chang, Ping-lin

About

Furth, C. The sage as rebel: the inner world of Chang Ping-lin. *In* The Limits of change p113-50

Change, Educational. See Educational innovations

Change, Linguistic. See Linguistic change

Change, Social. See Social change

Change of attitude. See Attitude change

Change of sex

Driscoll, J. P. Transsexuals. *In* Henslin, J. M. ed. Deviant life-styles p167-89

The changing room (criticism) Storey, D. *In* Kauffmann, S. Persons of the drama p329-35

Channing, William Ellery, 1780-1842

About

Meyer, D. H. William Ellery Channing and the inward enlightenment. *In* Meyer, D. H. The democratic Enlightenment p199-209

Chanson, Polyphonic

Brown, H. M. Instruments and voices in the fifteenth-century chanson. *In* Current thought in musicology p89-137

Heartz, D. The chanson in the humanist era. *In* Current thought in musicology p193-230

Chanson de Roland

Brault, G. J. The French chansons de geste. *In* Oinas, F. J. ed. Heroic epic and saga p193-215

Hanning, R. W. The individual and mimesis I: time and space in chivalric romance. *In* Hanning, R. W. The individual in twelfth-century romance p139-70

Huppé, B. F. The concept of the hero in the early Middle Ages. *In* Concepts of the hero in the Middle Ages and the Renaissance p 1-26

Jones, D. The Roland epic and ourselves. *In* Jones, D. The dying Gaul, and other writings p94-104

Niles, J. D. The ideal depiction of Charlemagne in "La Chanson de Roland." *In* Viator: medieval and Renaissance studies v7 p123-39

Thorpe, L. Dorothy L. Sayers as a translator of Le roman de Tristan and La chanson de Roland. *In* Hannay, M. P. ed. As her whimsey took her p109-22

Chansons de geste

History and criticism

Brault, G. J. The French chansons de geste. *In* Oinas, F. J. ed. Heroic epic and saga p193-215

Chantraine, Georges G.

The Ratio verae theologiae (1518) *In* Essays on the works of Erasmus p179-85

Chants (Plain, Gregorian, etc.)

Crocker, R. L. The early Frankish sequence: a new musical form. *In* Viator: medieval and Renaissance studies v6 p341-49

Luecke, J. M. Measuring Old English rhythm: the unequal measures of Gregorian chant. *In* Literary monographs v9 p31-48

Chao, Chia-Ying Yeh. See Yeh, Chia-ying

Chaos (Theology)

Tomita, K. On a chaotic early universe. *In* Cosmology, history, and theology p131-39

Chapaev (Motion picture)

Ferro, M. The fiction film and historical analysis. *In* Smith, P. ed. The historian and film p80-94

Chaplains, University and college

Hargrove, B. W. Church student ministries and the new consciousness. *In* The New religious consciousness p205-26

Chaplin, Sir Charles Spencer

About

Truffaut, F. Charlie Chaplin: Who is Charlie Chaplin? *In* Truffaut, F. The films in my life p60-62

About individual works
City lights

Mukařovský, J. An attempt at a structural analysis of a dramatic figure. *In* Mukařovský, J. Structure, sign, and function p171-77

The gold rush

Kauffmann, S. The gold rush. *In* Kauffmann, S. Living images p298-306

The great dictator

Truffaut, F. Charlie Chaplin: The great dictator. *In* Truffaut, F. The films in my life p54-57

A king in New York

Kauffmann, S. A king in New York. *In* Kauffmann, S. Living images p246-49

Truffaut, F. Charlie Chaplin: A king in New York. *In* Truffaut, F. The films in my life p57-60

Chaplin, Charlie. See Chaplin, Sir Charles Spencer

Chapman, Colin

Towards a new Pacific alliance. *In* The Year book of world affairs, 1975 p88-105

Chapman, George

About

Ure, P. Chapman's tragedies. *In* Ure, P. Elizabethan and Jacobean drama p166-86

Ure, P. A note on 'opinion' in Daniel, Greville, and Chapman. *In* Ure, P. Elizabethan and Jacobean drama p209-20

Ure, P. On some differences between Senecan and Elizabethan tragedy. *In* Ure, P. Elizabethan and Jacobean drama p63-74

About individual works
Bussy D'Ambois

Altman, J. B. Tragic perspectives among the Elizabethans. *In* Altman, J. B. The Tudor play of mind p249-320

The conspiracy and tragedy of Charles, Duke of Byron

Ure, P. The main outline of Chapman's Byron. *In* Ure, P. Elizabethan and Jacobean drama p123-44

Hero and Leander

Gordon, D. J. The Renaissance poet as classicist: Chapman's Hero and Leander. *In* Gordon, D. J. The Renaissance imagination p102-33

The memorable masque of the two honourable houses or inncs of court; the Middle Temple, and Lyncolnes Inne

Gordon, D. J. Chapman's Memorable masque. *In* Gordon, D. J. The Renaissance imagination p194-202

Ovid's banquet of sense

Jahn, J. D. Chapman's enargia and the popular perspective on Ovids banquet of sence. *In* Tennessee Studies in literature v23 p15-30

Bibliography

Logan, T. P. George Chapman. *In* Logan, T. P. and Smith, D. S. eds. The new intellectuals p117-70

Chapman, Janet G.

Equal pay for equal work? *In* Women in Russia p225-39

Chapman, John Jay

About

Paul, S. The identities of John Jay Chapman. *In* Paul, S. Repossessing and renewing p57-70

Chapman, Robert L.

Dictionary reviews and reviewing: 1900-1975. *In* James B. McMillan: essays in linguistics by his friends and colleagues p143-61

Chapman, William

No pink lampshades: wit and humour in the plays. *In* Prentki, T. ed. Francis Warner p67-82

Chappell, Vere Claiborne

The concept of dreaming. *In* Dunlop, C. E. M. ed. Philosophical essays on dreaming p280-308

Chappelle, Yvonne Juanita Reed. See Brown, C. S. jt. auth.

Chapple, J. A. V. See Brake, L. jt. auth.; Watson, J. R. jt. auth.

Char, René

About

Caistor, N. The image of night in Rene Char's poetry. *In* Cardinal, R. ed. Sensibility and creation p168-82

Greene, R. W. René Char. *In* Greene, R. W. Six French poets of our time p99-123

About individual works
Leaves of Hypnos

Orr, L. The limit of limits: aphorism in Char's Feuillets d'Hypnos. *In* Symbolism and modern literature p248-63

Character

Williams, B. A. O. Persons, character and morality. *In* Rorty, A. O. ed. The identities of persons p197-216

See also Conduct of life; Temperament

Character and characteristics

Benjamin, W. The destructive character. *In* Benjamin, W. Reflections p301-03

Benjamin, W. Fate and character. *In* Benjamin, W. Reflections p304-11

O'Hara, J. Characters in search. *In* O'Hara, J. "An artist is his own fault" p126-30

Character education. See Moral education

Characteristics. See Characters and characteristics; National characteristics

Characters and characteristics in literature

Bersani, L. Murderous lovers. *In* Bersani, L. A future for Astyanax p3-14

Bersani, L. Realism and the fear of desire. *In* Bersani, L. A future for Astyanax p51-88

Echeruo, M. J. C. The conditioned imagination. *In* Echeruo, M. J. C. The conditioned imagination from Shakespeare to Conrad p1-23

Characters and characteristics in literature
—*Continued*

Haley, B. The true gentleman and the washed rough in broadcloth. *In* Haley, B. The healthy body and Victorian culture p205-26

Hawkins, H. 'Stay, illusion!': some poetic godgames. *In* Hawkins, H. Poetic freedom and poetic truth p105-35

Schlueter, J. Introduction. *In* Schlueter, J. Metafictional characters in modern drama p1-17

Torrance, R. M. Introduction: comic butt and comic hero. *In* Torrance, R. M. The comic hero p 1-11

See also Detectives in literature; Dissenters in literature; Jews in literature; Old age in literature; Physicians in literature; Plots (Drama, novel, etc.); Widows in literature; Women in literature

Characters and characteristics in moving-pictures

Steene, B. Bergman's movement toward nihilism: the antiheroic stance in Secrets of women, Brink of life, The seventh seal, and the Chamber Film trilogy. *In* The Hero in Scandinavian literature p87-105

See also Frankenstein films

Chardin, Pierre Teilhard de. See Teilhard de Chardin, Pierre

Charibbs. See Carib Indians

Charismatic movement. See Pentecostalism

Charitable uses, trusts, and foundations. See Endowments

Charities

Field, J. A. Philanthropy. *In* Encyclopedia of American foreign policy p763-72

See also Food relief; Friendly societies; Poor

United States

Pifer, A. J. The jeopardy of private institutions. *In* Smith, B. L. R. ed. The new political economy: the public use of the private sector p68-82

Charities, Medical. See subdivision Charities, Medical under names of cities, e.g. Boston —Charities, Medical

Chariton

About individual works

The loves of Chaereas and Callirrhoe

Heiserman, A. R. Aphrodisian chastity. *In* Heiserman, A. R. The novel before the novel p75-93

Charity, Alan Clifford

T. S. Eliot: The Dantean recognitions. *In* The Waste land in different voices p117-62

Charity in literature

Grant, P. The tempest and the magic of charity: believing the images. *In* Grant, P. Images and ideas in literature of the English Renaissance p63-88

Utley, F. L. Chaucer's Troilus and St Paul's charity. *In* Chaucer and Middle English studies in honour of Rossell Hope Robbins p272-87

Charity laws and legislation. See Poor laws

Charlemagne

About

Wallach, L. The genuine and the forged oath of Pope Leo III. *In* Wallach, L. Diplomatic studies in Latin and Greek documents from the Carolingian age p299-327

Wallach, L. The Roman synod of December 800 and the alleged trial of Leo III. *In* Wallach, L. Diplomatic studies in Latin and Greek documents from the Carolingian age p328-52

Romances

Niles, J. D. The ideal depiction of Charlemagne in "La Chanson de Roland." *In* Viator: medieval and Renaissance studies v7 p123-39

Charles I, King of Spain. See Charles V, Emperor of the Holy Roman Empire

Charles IV, Emperor of Germany. See Karl IV, Emperor of Germany

Charles V, Emperor of Germany. See Karl V, Emperor of Germany

Charles V, Emperor of the Holy Roman Empire

Art patronage

Trevor-Roper, H. R. Charles V and the failure of humanism. *In* Trevor-Roper, H. R. Princes and artists p11-45

Charles V, King of France

Coronation

Sherman, C. R. The Queen in Charles V's "Coronation Book": Jeanne de Bourbon and the "Ordo ad reginam benedicendam." *In* Viator: medieval and Renaissance studies v8 p255-98

Charles d'Orléans

Kelly, D. Imagination in the poetry of Charles d'Orléans and René d'Anjou. *In* Kelly, D. Medieval imagination p204-29

Charles, dead or alive (Motion picture)

Kauffmann, S. La salamandre; Charles, dead or alive. *In* Kauffmann, S. Living images p118-21

Charles-Quint. See Karl V, Emperor of Germany

Charlestown, Mass. First Church

Kirker, H. C. The Bulfinch drawings in the American Antiquarian Society. *In* American Antiquarian Society. Proceedings v86 pt 1 p125-28

Charlewood, John

About

Jackson, M. P. The printer of the first quarto of Astrophil and Stella (1591). *In* Virginia. University. Bibliographical Society. Studies in bibliography v31 p201-03

Charley Varrick (Motion picture)

Kauffmann, S. Charley Varrick. *In* Kauffmann, S. Living images p241-42

Charms

Frye, N. Charms and riddles. *In* Frye, N. Spiritus mundi p123-47

Gray, D. Notes on some Middle English charms. *In* Chaucer and Middle English studies in honour of Rossell Hope Robbins p56-71

Hill, T. D. The æcerbot charm and its Christian user. *In* Anglo-Saxon England 6 p213-21

Swiderski, R. From folk to popular: plastic evil eye charms. *In* The Evil eye p28-41

See also Amulets; Evil eye

Charney, Maurice Myron

Webster vs. Middleton, or the Shakespearean yardstick in Jacobean tragedy. *In* English Renaissance drama p118-27

Charnley, Sir John K.

Experiences in the development of a clean air operating room. *In* The Frontiers of human knowledge p45-58

Charny, Israel W. and others

How does marital quarreling affect sexual relations? *In* Gross, L. ed. Sexual issues in marriage p121-28

Charters. See subdivision Charters under names of American colonies, states, and cities, e.g. Boston. Charters, and subdivision: Charters, grants, privileges, under foreign countries, cities, etc., e.g. Normandy —Charters, grants, privileges

Chartism

Wilson, A. The suffrage movement. *In* Hollis, P. ed. Pressure from without p80-104

Chase, Colin Robert

God's presence through grace as the theme of Cynewulf's Christ II and the relationship of this theme to Christ I and Christ III. *In* Anglo-Saxon England 3 p87-101

Chase, Gilbert

Musicology, history, and anthropology: current thoughts. *In* Current thought in musicology p231-46

Chase, Linda

Existential vs. humanist realism; excerpt from "Photo realism." *In* Battcock, G. ed. Super realism p81-95

Chase, Richard Volney

About individual works

The democratic vista

Howe, I. Culture and radicalism. *In* Howe, I. Celebrations and attacks p62-67

Chase, William W.

Technology, ecology, and the learning environment. *In* Fairfield, R. P. ed. Humanistic frontiers in American education p173-80

Chasidism. See Hasidism

Chasko, W. J. See Binford, L. R. jt. auth.

Chassé, Richard

Patient counseling in home care. *In* Home care p172-77

Chasteen, Edgar

Legal change. *In* Lauer, R. H. ed. Social movements and social change p156-73

Chastel, André

Two Roman statues: Saints Peter and Paul. *In* Collaboration in Italian Renaissance art p59-73

Chastellux, François Jean, Marquis de

About

Kors, A. C. François-Jean Marquis de Chastellux. *In* Abroad in America: Visitors to the new Nation, 1776-1914 p3-11

Chateaubriand, François Auguste René, Vicomte de

About individual works

Mémoires d'outre- tombe

Chadbourne, R. M. Chateaubriand's aviary: birds in the Mémoires d'outre-tombe. *In* Symbolism and modern literature p65-80

Travels in America

Amelinckx, F. C. Exploration and creativity: Chateaubriand's Travels in America. *In* Kagle, S. E. ed. America: exploration and travel p40-49

Chatfield, Charles

Pacifism. *In* Encyclopedia of American foreign policy p722-29

Chatman, Seymour

The structure of narrative transmission. *In* Fowler, R. ed. Style and structure in literature p213-57

Chatterji, Pritibhushan

Ramakrishna. *In* Bishop, D. H. ed. Indian thought p346-56

Chattopadhyaya, Debiprasad

Lokāyata materialism. *In* Bishop, D. H. ed. Indian thought p101-14

Chatty, Dawn

Changing sex roles in Bedouin society in Syria and Lebanon. *In* Beck, L. and Keddie, N. R. eds. Women in the Muslim world p399-415

Chaucer, Geoffrey

About

Brewer, D. S. Chaucer and Chrétien and Arthurian romance. *In* Chaucer and Middle English studies in honour of Rossell Hope Robbins p255-59

Brewer, D. S. Gothic Chaucer. *In* Brewer, D. S. ed. Geoffrey Chaucer p 1-32

Brookhouse, J. C. In search of Chaucer: the needed narrative. *In* The Learned and the lewed p67-80

Clogan, P. M. Literary criticism in William Godwin's Life of Chaucer. *In* Medievalia et humanistica no. 6 p189-98

Doyle, A. I. and Pace, G. B. Further texts of Chaucer's minor poems. *In* Virginia. University. Bibliographical Society. Studies in bibliography v28 p41-61

Du Boulay, F. R. H. The historical Chaucer. *In* Brewer, D. S. ed. Geoffrey Chaucer p33-57

Ferris, S. J. Chaucer, Richard II, Henry IV, and 13 October. *In* Chaucer and Middle English studies in honour of Rossell Hope Robbins p210-17

Garbáty, T. J. Chaucer and comedy. *In* Ruggiers, P. G. ed. Versions of medieval comedy p173-90

Howard, D. R. Chaucer's idea of an idea. *In* English Association. Essays and studies, 1976 p39-55

Howard, D. R. Flying through space: Chaucer and Milton. *In* Wittreich, J. A. ed. Milton and the line of vision p3-23

Kelly, D. Verisimilitude and imagination: the crisis in late courtly poetry. *In* Kelly, D. Medieval imagination p177-203

Lanham, R. A. Games and high seriousness: Chaucer. *In* Lanham, R. A. The motives of eloquence p65-81

Lenaghan, R. T. The clerk of Venus: Chaucer and medieval romance. *In* The Learned and the lewed p31-43

Leyerle, J. The heart and the chain. *In* The Learned and the lewed p113-45

Manzalaoui, M. Chaucer and science. *In* Brewer, D. S. ed. Geoffrey Chaucer p224-61

Reinecke, G. F. Speculation, intention, and the teaching of Chaucer. *In* The Learned and the lewed p81-93

Reiss, E. Chaucer's courtly love. *In* The Learned and the lewed p95-111

Shepherd, G. Religion and philosophy in Chaucer. *In* Brewer, D. S. ed. Geoffrey Chaucer p262-89

Windeatt, B. Gesture in Chaucer. *In* Medievalia et humanistica; new ser. no. 9 p143-61

Chaucer, Geoffrey—*Continued*

About individual works

The book of the Duchess (Line 646)

Brosnahan, L. Now (this), now (that) and BD 646. *In* The Learned and lewed p11-18

Canterbury tales

Blake, N. F. The relationship between the Hengwrt and the Ellesmere manuscripts of the 'Canterbury tales.' *In* English Association. Essays and studies, 1979 p 1-18

Hawkins, H. Introduction: Poetic injustice: some winners and losers in medieval and Renaissance literature. *In* Hawkins, H. Poetic freedom and poetic truth p 1-25

Hobsbaum, P. Chaucer: experimentalist extraordinary. *In* Hobsbaum, P. Tradition and experiment in English poetry p30-67

Leyerle, J. Thematic interlace in 'The Canterbury tales.' *In* English Association. Essays and studies, 1976 p107-21

Olson, C. C. The interludes of the Marriage Group in the Canterbury tales. *In* Chaucer and Middle English studies in honour of Rossell Hope Robbins p164-72

Prins, A. A. The dating in the Canterbury tales. *In* Chaucer and Middle English studies in honour of Rossell Hope Robbins p342-47

Robertson, D. W. Chaucer criticism. *In* Medievalia et humanistica no. 8 p252-55

Zacher, C. K. Curiosity and the instability of pilgrimage: Chaucer's Canterbury tales. *In* Zacher, C. K. Curiosity and pilgrimage p87-129

Canterbury tales—Manuscripts

Silvia, D. S. Some fifteenth-century manuscripts of the Canterbury tales. *In* Chaucer and Middle English studies in honour of Rossell Hope Robbins p153-63

Canterbury tales—The clerk's tale

Cunningham, J. V. Ideal fiction: The clerk's tale. *In* Cunningham, J. V. The collected essays of J. V. Cunningham p277-81

Hawkins, H. 'The victim's side': Webster's Duchess of Malfi and Chaucer's Clerk's tale. *In* Hawkins, H. Poetic freedom and poetic truth p26-54

Canterbury tales—The man of law's tale

Clogan, P. M. The narrative style of The man of law's tale. *In* Medievalia et humanistica no. 8 p217-33

Schlauch, M. A Polish analogue of The man of law's tale. *In* Chaucer and Middle English studies in honour of Rossell Hope Robbins p372-80

Canterbury tales—The merchant's tale

Bleeth, K. A. The image of paradise in The merchant's tale. *In* The Learned and the lewed p45-60

Bloomfield, M. W. The merchant's tale: a tragi-comedy of the neglect of counsel— the limits of art. *In* Medieval and Renaissance studies [1975] p37-50

Brown, E. L. Biblical women in The merchant's tale: feminism, antifeminism, and beyond. *In* Viator: medieval and Renaissance studies p387-412

Canterbury tales—The miller's tale

Rowland, B. Chaucer's blasphemous churl: a new interpretation of The miller's tale. *In* Chaucer and Middle English studies in honour of Rossell Hope Robbins p43-55

Canterbury tales—The nun's priest's tale

Steadman, J. M. "The nun's priest's tale": Chauntecleer and medieval natural history. *In* Steadman, J. M. Nature into myth p86-94

Steadman, J. M. "The nun's priest's tale": flattery and the moralitas of the beast. *In* Steadman, J. M. Nature into myth p78-85

Canterbury tales—The pardoner's tale

Patterson, L. W. Chaucerian confession: penitential literature and the pardoner. *In* Medievalia et humanistica no. 7 p153-73

Steadman, J. M. "The pardoner's tale": old age and contemptus mundi. *In* Steadman, J. M. Nature into myth p104-14

Canterbury tales—Prologue

Cunningham, J. V. Convention as structure: the Prologue to the Canterbury tales. *In* Cunningham, J. V. The collected essays of J. V. Cunningham p180-95

Canterbury tales—Prologue to The wife of Bath's tale

Steadman, J. M. The wife of Bath's prologue: book-burning and the Veda of women's wiles. *In* Steadman, J. M. Nature into myth p95-103

Canterbury tales—The reeve's tale

Kirby, T. A. An analogue (?) to The reeve's tale. *In* Chaucer and Middle English studies in honour of Rossell Hope Robbins p381-83

Canterbury tales—The second nun's tale

Glasser, M. D. Marriage and The second nun's tale. *In* Tennessee Studies in literature v23 p 1-14

Canterbury tales—The wife of Bath's tale

Matthews, W. The wife of Bath and all her sect. *In* Viator: medieval and Renaissance studies v5 p413-43

The cock and the fox

Manlove, C. N. Dryden. *In* Manlove, C. N. Literature and reality, 1600-1800 p57-75

The complaint to his lady

Clogan, P. M. The textual reliability of Chaucer's lyrics: A complaint to his lady. *In* Medievalia et humanistica no. 5 p183-89

The complete poetry and prose of Geoffrey Chaucer, edited by John Hurt Fisher

Hanna, R. A new edition of Chaucer. *In* Review, v 1 1979 p61-74

The House of Fame

David, A. How Marcia lost her skin: a note on Chaucer's mythology. *In* The Learned and the lewed p19-29

Steadman, J. M. "The House of Fame:" the eagle as contemplative symbol. *In* Steadman, J. M. Nature into myth p67-77

Troilus and Criseyde

Manlove, C. N. 'Rooteles moot grene soone deye': the helplessness of Chaucer's Troilus and Criseyde. *In* English Association. Essays and studies, 1978 p 1-22

Mehl, D. The audience of Chaucer's Troilus and Criseyde. *In* Chaucer and Middle English studies in honour of Rossell Hope Robbins p173-89

Chaucer, Geoffrey—About individual works
—Troilus and Criseyde—*Continued*

Mudrick, M. Looking for Kellermann. *In* Mudrick, M. The man in the machine p11-36

Ridley, F. H. A plea for the Middle Scots. *In* The Learned and the lewed p175-96

Troilus and Criseyde—Manuscripts

Owen, C. A. Minor changes in Chaucer's Troilus and Criseyde. *In* Chaucer and Middle English studies in honour of Rossell Hope Robbins p303-19

Bibliography

Bazire, J. and Mills, D. Middle English: Chaucer. *In* English Association. The year's work in English studies v53 p106-20

Bazire, J. and Mills, D. Middle English: Chaucer [another essay] *In* English Association. The year's work in English studies v54 p109-23

Bazire, J. and Mills, D. Middle English: Chaucer [another essay] *In* English Association. The year's work in English studies v55 p 148-66

Bazire, J. and Mills, D. Middle English: Chaucer [another essay] *In* English Association. The year's work in English studies v56 p118-29

Bazire, J. and Mills, D. Middle English: Chaucer [another essay] *In* English Association. The year's work in English studies v57 p89-100

Benson, L. D. A reader's guide to writings on Chaucer. *In* Brewer, D. S. ed. Geoffrey Chaucer p321-72

Characters

Hawkins, H. Introduction: Poetic injustice: some winners and losers in medieval and Renaissance literature. *In* Hawkins, H. Poetic freedom and poetic truth p 1-25

Severs, J. B. Chaucer's clerks. *In* Chaucer and Middle English studies in honour of Rossell Hope Robbins p140-52

Characters—Alison

Biggins, D. "O Jankyn, be ye there?". *In* Chaucer and Middle English studies in honour of Rossell Hope Robbins p249-54

Characters—The clerk

Longsworth, R. Chaucer's clerk as teacher. *In* The Learned and the lewed p61-66

Characters—Criseyde

Fries, M. "Slydynge of corage": Chaucer's Criseyde as feminist and victim. *In* Diamond, A. and Edwards, L. R. eds. The authority of experience p45-59

Utley, F. L. Chaucer's Troilus and St Paul's charity. *In* Chaucer and Middle English studies in honour of Rossell Hope Robbins p272-87

Characters—Troilus

Stanley, E. G. About Troilus. *In* English Association. Essays and studies, 1976 p84-106

Utley, F. L. Chaucer's Troilus and St Paul's charity. *In* Chaucer and Middle English studies in honour of Rossell Hope Robbins p272-87

Characters—The wife of Bath

Biggins, D. "O Jankyn, be ye there?" *In* Chaucer and Middle English studies in honour of Rossell Hope Robbins p249-54

Donaldson, E. T. Designing a camel; or, Generalizing the Middle Ages. *In* Tennessee Studies in literature v22 p1-16

Characters—Women

Brown, E. L. Biblical women in The merchant's tale: feminism, antifeminism, and beyond. *In* Viator: medieval and Renaissance studies v5 p387-412

Diamond, A. Chaucer's women and women's Chaucer. *In* Diamond, A. and Edwards, L. R. eds. The authority of experience p60-83

Haskell, A. S. The portrayal of women by Chaucer and his age. *In* Springer, M. A. ed. What manner of woman p1-14

Contemporary England

Du Boulay, F. R. H. The historical Chaucer. *In* Brewer, D. S. ed. Geoffrey Chaucer p33-57

Criticism, Textual

Doyle, A. I. and Pace, G. B. Further texts of Chaucer's minor poems. *In* Virginia. University. Bibliographical Society. Studies in bibliography v28 p41-61

Fletcher, B. Y. Printer's copy for Stow's Chaucer. *In* Virginia. University. Bibliographical Society. Studies in bibliography v31 p184-201

Garbáty, T. J. Wynkyn de Worde's "Sir Thopas" and other tales. *In* Virginia. University. Bibliographical Society. Studies in bibliography v31 p57-67

Mack, M. Pope's copy of Chaucer. *In* Evidence in literary scholarship p105-21

Silvia, D. S. Some fifteenth-century manuscripts of the Canterbury tales. *In* Chaucer and Middle English studies in honour of Rossell Hope Robbins p153-63

Criticism and interpretation

Mudrick, M. The blind men and the elephant. *in* Mudrick, M. Books are not life but then what is? p177-92

Iconography

Kolve, V. A. Chaucer and the visual arts. *In* Brewer, D. S. ed. Geoffrey Chaucer p290-320

Influence—Henryson

Schmitz, G. Cresseid's trial: a revision. Fame and defamation in Henryson's 'Testament of Cresseid." *In* English Association. Essays and studies, 1979 p44-56

Influence—Hunt

Clogan, P. M. Chaucer and Leigh Hunt. *In* Medievalia et humanistica; new ser. no. 9 p163-74

Influence—Milton

Howard, D. R. Flying through space: Chaucer and Milton. *In* Wittreich, J. A. ed. Milton and the line of vision p3-23

Knowledge—Astronomy

Prins, A. A. The dating in the Canterbury tales. *In* Chaucer and Middle English studies in honour of Rossell Hope Robbins p342-47

Knowledge—Science

Manzalaoui, M. Chaucer and science. *In* Brewer, D. S. Geoffrey Chaucer p224-61

Language

Davis, N. Chaucer and fourteenth-century English. *In* Brewer, D. S. ed. Geoffrey Chaucer p58-84

Manuscripts

Donaldson, E. T. The manuscripts of Chaucer's works and their use. *In* Brewer, D. S. ed. Geoffrey Chaucer p85-108

Chaucer, Geoffrey—*Continued*

Sources

Dronke, P. and Mann, J. Chaucer and the medieval Latin poets. *In* Brewer, D. S. ed. Geoffrey Chaucer p154-83

Eisner, S. Chaucer's use of Nicholas of Lynn's Calendar. *In* English Association. Essays and studies, 1976 p 1-22

Harbert, B. Chaucer and the Latin classics. *In* Brewer, D. S. ed. Geoffrey Chaucer p137-53

Schless, H. H. Transformations: Chaucer's use of Italian. *In* Brewer, D. S. ed. Geoffrey Chaucer p184-223

Wimsatt, J. I. Chaucer and French poetry. *In* Brewer, D. S. ed. Geoffrey Chaucer p109-36

Style

Payne, R. O. Rhetoric in Chaucer: Chaucer's realization of himself as rhetor. *In* Murphy, J. J. ed. Medieval eloquence p270-87

Technique

Mustanoja, T. F. Verbal rhyming in Chaucer. *In* Chaucer and Middle English studies in honour of Rossell Hope Robbins p104-10

Chaucer, Geoffrey, supposed author. See The craft of lovers

Chaudhuri, Haridas

Yoga psychology. *In* Tart, C. T. ed. Transpersonal psychologies p231-80

Chaunu, Pierre

About

Le Roy Ladurie, E. Chaunu, Lebrun, Vovelle: the new history of death. *In* Le Roy Ladurie, E. The territory of the historian p273-84

Chaussée, Pierre Claude Nivelle de la. See La Chaussée, Pierre Claude Nivelle de

Chauveton, Urbain

About

Keen, B. The vision of America in the writings of Urbain Chauveton. *In* First images of America p107-20

Chauvin, Rémy

To reconcile PSI and physics. *In* Wheatley, J. M. O. and Edge, H. L. eds. Philosophical dimensions of parapsychology p409-12

Chávez, Ester Gallegos y. See Gallegos y Chávez, Ester

Chayes, Abram

Nuclear arms control after the Cold War. *In* Long, F. A. and Rathjens, G. W. eds. Arms, defense policy, and arms control p15-33

Chazan, Naomi

Myths and realities in African socialism. *In* Eisenstadt, S. N. and Azmon, Y. eds. Socialism and tradition p141-71

Nkrumaism: Ghana's experiment with African socialism. *In* Eisenstadt, S. N. and Azmon, Y. eds. Socialism and tradition p173-92

Chazan, Robert

Emperor Frederick I, the Third Crusade, and the Jews. *In* Viator: medieval and Renaissance studies v8 p83-93

Chazars. See Khazars

Checkland, S. G.

Adam Smith and the bankers. *In* Skinner, A. S. and Wilson, T. eds. Essays on Adam Smith p504-23

Chekhov, Anton Pavlovich

About

Bitsilli, P. M. From Chekhonte to Chekhov. *In* Erlich, V. ed. Twentieth-century Russian literary criticism p212-18

Calder, A. Literature and morality: Leskov, Chekhov, late Tolstoy. *In* Calder, A. Russia discovered p238-75

Eekman, T. A. The narrator and the hero in Chekhov's prose. *In* California Slavic studies v8 p93-129

Larkin, M. The dismal science: economic man. *In* Larkin, M. Man and society in nineteenth-century realism p139-51

Larkin, M. Hope and despair. *In* Larkin, M. Man and society in nineteenth-century realism p163-74

Larkin, M. Society versus the individual. *In* Larkin, M. Man and society in nineteenth-century realism p152-62

Larkin, M. The ubiquitous doctor. *In* Larkin, M. Man and society in nineteenth-century realism p134-38

Mudford, P. Anton Chekhov. *In* Medford, P. The art of celebration p110-22

Mudrick, M. Chekhov. *In* Mudrick, M. The man in the machine p153-77

Nicoll, A. The extension of the realistic. *In* Nicoll, A. World drama p577-607

Ober, W. B. Chekhov among the doctors: the doctor's dilemma. *In* Ober, W. B. Boswell's clap and other essays p193-205

Pritchett, V. S. Anton Chekhov: a doctor. *In* Pritchett, V. S. The myth makers p37-49

Rahv, P. The education of Anton Chekhov. *In* Rahv, P. Essays on literature and politics, 1932-1972 p227-31

Welty, E. Reality in Chekhov's stories. *In* Welty, E. The eye of the story p61-81

About individual works
The cherry orchard

Barricelli, J. P. Counterpoint on the snapping string: Chekhov's The cherry orchard. *In* California Slavic studies v10 p121-36

Reed, W. L. The cherry orchard and Hedda Gabler. *In* Seidel, M. A. and Mendelson, E. eds. Homer to Brecht p317-35

Enemies

Trilling, L. Anton Chekhov: Enemies. *In* Trilling, L. Prefaces to The experience of literature p96-101

The island

Hyman, S. E. Counting the cats. *In* Hyman, S. E. The critic's credentials p235-40

Letters of Anton Chekhov, ed. by Avrahm Yarmolinsky

Mudrick, M. Chekhov. *In* Mudrick, M. The man in the machine p153-77

Letters of Anton Chekhov, ed. by Simon Karlinsky

Mudrick, M. Chekhov. *In* Mudrick, M. The man in the machine p153-77

Selected letters (ed. by Lillian Hellman)

Rahv, P. The education of Anton Chekhov. *In* Rahv, P. Essays on literature and politics, 1932-1972 p227-31

The three sisters

Trilling, L. Anton Chekhov: The three sisters. *In* Trilling, L. Prefaces to The experience of literature p28-36

Chekhov, Anton P.—About individual works
—*Continued*

Uncle Vanya

Kauffmann, S. Uncle Vanya. *In* Kauffmann, S. Persons of the drama p146-48

Criticism and interpretation

Pritchett, V. S. Anton Chekhov: a doctor. *In* Pritchett, V. S. The myth makers p37-49

Influence—Bugaev

Yurieff, Z. Prishedshy: A. Bely and A. Chekhov. *In* Janecek, G. ed. Andrey Bely p44-55

Chemical elements. See Actinide elements; Atomic weights; Valence (Theoretical chemistry)

Chemical genetics. See Molecular biology

Chemical mutagenesis

Gillberg, B. O. Chemically induced genetic damage. *In* Against pollution and hunger p213-14

Lenz, W. Chemicals as a cause of human malformations. *In* Against pollution and hunger p89-96

Strømanæs, Ø. The impact on human genetics. *In* Against pollution and hunger p215-17

Chemical warfare

Davidon, W. C. Chemical and biological warfare: pollution by design. *In* Against pollution and hunger p223-29

Goldblat, J. The main issues in the CW debate. *In* The Dynamics of the arms race p178-84

Reutov, O. A. Some modern problems concerning the prohibition of the development, production and stockpiling of chemical warfare agents. *In* The Dynamics of the arms race p185-91

Chemistry

See also Alchemy; Biological chemistry; Environmental chemistry; Fire; Stereochemistry

History

Guerlac, H. The background to Dalton's atomic theory. *In* Guerlac, H. Essays and papers in the history of modern science p217-42

Levere, T. H. The rich economy of nature: chemistry in the nineteenth century. *In* Knoepflmacher, U. C. and Tennyson, G. B. eds. Nature and the Victorian imagination p189-200

History—China

Needham, J. Alchemy and early chemistry in China. *In* The Frontiers of human knowledge p171-81

History—England

Roberts, G. K. The establishment of the Royal College of Chemistry: an investigation of the social context of early-Victorian chemistry. *In* Historical studies in the physical sciences v7 p437-85

History—France

Guerlac, H. Some French antecedents of the chemical revolution. *In* Guerlac, H. Essays and papers in the history of modern science p340-74

History—United States

Kevles, D. J. The physics, mathematics, and chemistry communities: a comparative analysis. *In* Oleson, A. and Voss, J. eds. The organization of knowledge in modern America, 1860-1920 p139-72

Philosophy—History

Brooke, J. H. Laurent, Gerhardt, and the philosophy of chemistry. *In* Historical studies in the physical sciences v6 p405-30

Debus, A. G. The chemical debates of the seventeenth century: the reaction to Robert Fludd and Jean Baptiste van Helmont. *In* Bonelli, M. L. R. and Shea, W .R. eds. Reason, experiment, and mysticism in the scientific revolution p19-47

Study and teaching (Higher)—
United States

Brasted, R. C. The introductory course in chemistry. *In* Buxton, T. H. and Prichard, K. W. eds. Excellence in university teaching p109-19

Chemistry, Biological. See Biological chemistry

Chemistry, Environmental. See Environmental chemistry

Chemistry, Organic

See also Stereochemistry

Synthesis

Miller, S. L. The first laboratory synthesis of organic compounds under primitive earth conditions. *In* Neyman, J. ed. The heritage of Copernicus: theories "pleasing to the mind" p228-42

Chemistry, Physical and theoretical

Rocke, A. J. Atoms and equivalents: the early development of the chemical atomic theory. *In* Historical studies in the physical sciences v9 p225-63

See also Molecular theory; Quantum theory; Stereochemistry

History

Dolby, R. G. A. Debates over the theory of solution: a study of dissent in physical chemistry in the English-speaking world in the late nineteenth and early twentieth centuries. *In* Historical studies in the physical sciences v7 p297-404

Guerlac, H. Chemistry as a branch of physics: Laplace's collaboration with Lavoisier. *In* Historical studies in the physical sciences v7 p193-276

Kohler, R. E. The Lewis-Langmuir theory of valence and the chemical community, 1920-1928. *In* Historical studies in the physical sciences v6 p431-68

Chemistry, Synthetic. See Chemistry, Organic—Synthesis

Chemistry in warfare. See Chemical warfare

Chemotherapy

Grof, S. and Halifax-Grof, J. Psychedelics and the experience of death. *In* Life after death p182-202

See also Psychopharmacology

History

Harvey, A. M. The story of chemotherapy at Johns Hopkins: Perrin H. Long, Eleanor A. Bliss, and E. Kennerly Marshall, Jr. *In* Harvey, A. M. Adventures in medical research p390-400

Ch'ên, Hung-shou

About

Fong, Wen C. Archaism as a 'primitive' style. *In* Artists and traditions p89-109

Chen, Katy. See Lauer, R. H. jt. auth.

Chen, Shih-hsiang
The Shih-ching: its generic significance in Chinese literary history and poetics. *In* Birch, C. ed. Studies in Chinese literary genres p8-41

Chen, Yü-shih
The literary theory and practice of Ouyang Hsiu. *In* Chinese approaches to literature from Confucius to Liang Ch'i-ch'ao p67-96
Mao Dun and the use of political allegory in fiction: a case study of his "Autumn in Kuling." *In* Modern Chinese literature in the May Fourth era p261-80

Chen-Chang, Fu-mei
Local control of convicted thieves in eighteenth-century China. *In* Conflict and control in late imperial China p121-42

Cheney, Christopher Robert. See Part 2 under title: Church and government in the Middle Ages

Cheney, Mary Hall
William Fitzstephen and his Life of Archbishop Thomas. *In* Church and government in the Middle Ages p139-56

Cheng, Ching-mao
The impact of Japanese literary trends on modern Chinese writers. *In* Modern Chinese literature in the May Fourth era p63-88

Cheng, Chung-ying
Mind and body: aspects of identity. *In* Philosophical aspects of the mind-body problem p78-98
Reason, substance, and human desires in seventeenth-century Neo-Confucianism. *In* The Unfolding of Neo-Confucianism p469-509

Cheng, Philip H.
A comparative value analysis: traditional versus revolutionary opera. *In* Chu, G. C. Popular media in China p104-23
See also Chu, G. C. jt. auth.

Cheng, Ronald Ye-lin
The effect of prerevolutionary values, beliefs, and social structures on revolutionary mobilization and success. *In* Johnson, H. M. ed. Religious change and continuity p168-90

Chénier, André Marie

About
Mandel'shtam, O. E. Notes about Chénier. *In* Mandel'shtam, O. E. Selected essays p108-13
Starobinski, J. André Chénier and the allegory of poetry. *In* Kroeber, K. and Walling, W. eds. Images of romanticism p39-60

Chennault, Stephen D.
Black dialect: a cultural shock. *In* Minority language and literature p71-79

Cheremisses
Sebeok, T. A. The seventeenth century Cheremis: the evidence from Witsen. *In* On language, culture, and religion: in honor of Eugene A. Nida p301-14

Cherico, Daniel J. See Gullo, S. V. jt. auth.

Chernaik, Warren L.
Marvell's Satires: the artist as Puritan. *In* Friedenreich, K. ed. Tercentenary essays in honor of Andrew Marvell p268-96

Cherniavsky, Michael
Russia. *In* National consciousness, history, and political culture in early-modern Europe p118-43

Chernysheva, Tatyana
The folktale, Wells, and modern science fiction. *In* H. G. Wells and modern science fiction p35-47

Chernyshevskiĭ, Nikolaĭ Gavrilovich

About
Mathewson, R. W. Chernyshevsky: "The salt of the salt of the earth." *In* Mathewson, R. W. The positive hero in Russian literature p63-83
Stacy, R. H. The civic critics. *In* Stacy, R. H. Russian literary criticism p55-65

Cherokee Indians
McLoughlin, W. G. Cherokee anomie, 1794-1809: new roles for Red men, Red women, and Black slaves. *In* Uprooted Americans p125-60
Neely, S. Acculturation and persistence among North Carolina's eastern band of Cherokee Indians. *In* Williams, W. L. ed. Southeastern Indians since the removal era p154-73

Culture
McLoughlin, W. G. Cherokee anomie, 1794-1809: new roles for Red men, Red women, and Black slaves. *In* Uprooted Americans p125-60

Magic
Fogelson, R. D. An analysis of Cherokee sorcery and witchcraft. *In* Hudson, C. M. ed. Four centuries of Southern Indians p113-31

Oklahoma—Social conditions
Wahrhaftig, A. L. Institution building among Oklahoma's traditional Cherokees. *In* Hudson, C. M. ed. Four centuries of Southern Indians p132-47

Cherokee Indians as soldiers
O'Donnell, J. H. The Southern Indians in the War for American independence, 1775-1783. *In* Hudson, C. M. ed. Four centuries of Southern Indians p46-64

Cherokee language. See Iroquoian languages

Cherry, Christopher
Agreement, objectivity and the sentiment of humanity in morals. *In* Royal Institute of Philosophy. Nature and conduct p83-98

Cherry, Colin
The telephone system: creator of mobility and social change. *In* The Social impact of the telephone p112-26

The cherry orchard (criticism) Chekhov, A. P. *In* Brustein, R. S. The culture watch p108-11

Cherubini, Luigi

About
Dent, E. J. The school of Paris—I. *In* Dent, E. J. The rise of romantic opera p47-63
Dent, E. J. The school of Paris—III. *In* Dent, E. J. The rise of romantic opera p80-94

Cherubini, Maria Luigi Carlo Zenobio Salvatore. See Cherubini, Luigi

Chesebro', Caroline

About
Baym, N. Z. Caroline Chesebro'. *In* Baym, N. Z. Woman's fiction p208-30

Chesler, S. Alan
Tennessee Williams: reassessment and assessment. *In* Tennessee Williams: a tribute p848-80

Chesnutt, Charles Waddell

About

Bone, R. A. Literary forebears. *In* Bone, R. A. Down home p3-18

About individual works

The conjure woman

Bone, R. A. Charles Chesnutt. *In* Bone, R. A. Down home p74-105

The sheriff's children

Selke, H. K. Charles Waddell Chesnutt, The sheriff's children. *In* Bruck, P. ed. The Black American short story in the 20th century p21-38

The wife of his youth, and other stories of the color line

Bone, R. A. Charles Chesnutt. *In* Bone, R. A. Down home p74-105

Chess

Koestler, A. The glorious and bloody game: Reflections of an addict. *In* Koestler, A. The heel of Achilles p206-14

Tournaments, 1972

Koestler, A. The glorious and bloody game: Requiem for Reykjavik. *In* Koestler, A. The heel of Achilles p214-31

Chestang, Leon

Environmental influences on social functioning: the Black experience. *In* The Diverse society: implications for social policy p59-74

Chester plays

Brockman, B. A. Cain and Abel in the Chester creation: narrative tradition and dramatic potential. *In* Medievalia et humanistica no. 5 p169-82

See also Balaam and Balak; The shepherd's play

The **Chesterfield** House Library portraits. Piper, D. *In* Evidence in literary scholarship p179-95

Chesterton, Gilbert Keith

About

Lambert, G. Final problems: G. K. Chesterton. *In* Lambert, G. The dangerous edge p63-78

Monod, S. Confessions of an unrepentant Chestertonian. *In* Dickens Studies Annual v3 p214-28

Chettwinde, Phillip. See Chetwin, Philip

Chetwin, Philip

About

Williams, W. P. Chetwin, Crooke, and the Jonson folios. *In* Virginia. University. Bibliographical Society. Studies in bibliography v30 p75-95

Chetwyn, Phillip. See Chetwin, Philip

Cheuse, Alan

Mario Vargas Llosa and Conversation in the cathedral: the question of naturalism. *In* Rossman, C. R. and Friedman, A. W. eds. Mario Vargas Llosa p52-58

Chevan, Albert. See O'Rourke, J. F. jt. auth.

Cheyette, Fredric L.

The castles of the Trencavels: a preliminary aerial survey. *In* Order and innovation in the Middle Ages p255-72

The invention of the state. *In* Essays on medieval civilization p143-78

Cheyne, George

About

Altschule, M. D. George Cheyne and his English malady. *In* Altschule, M. D. Origins of concepts in human behavior p50-74

About individual works

The English malady

Altschule, M. D. George Cheyne and his English malady. *In* Altschule, M. D. Origins of concepts in human behavior p50-74

Cheyney-Coker, Syl

About individual works

Concerto for an exile

Salt, M. J. Syl Cheyney-Coker: Concerto for an exile. *In* African literature today no. 7: Focus on criticism p159-62

Chhindwara, India

Jain, R. K. Bundela genealogy and legends: the past of an indigenous ruling group of central India. *In* Studies in social anthropology p238-72

Chi (The word)

Achebe, C. Chi in Igbo cosmology. *In* Achebe, C. Morning yet on creation day p159-75

Ch'i in Chinese literary theory. Pollard, D. E. *In* Chinese approaches to literature from Confucius to Liang Ch'i-ch'ao p43-66

Chiang, Kai-shek

About

Eastman, L. E. The Kuomintang in the 1930s. *In* The Limits of change p191-210

Chiang, Ping-chih

About

Feuerwerker, Y. M. The changing relationship between literature and life: aspects of the writer's role in Ding Ling. *In* Modern Chinese literature in the May Fourth era p281-307

Chiang-yin

History

Wakeman, F. E. Localism and loyalism during the Ch'ing conquest of Kiangnan: the tragedy of Chiang-yin. *In* Conflict and control in late imperial China p43-85

Chiangkhan, Thailand

Commerce—History

Moerman, M. Chiangkham's trade in the "old days." *In* Change and persistence in Thai society p151-71

Chiao, Hung

About

Ch'ien, E. T. Chiao Hung and the revolt against Ch'eng-Chu orthodoxy. *In* The Unfolding of Neo-Confucianism p271-303

Chiapas, Mexico

Antiquities

Lee, T. A. The Middle Grijalva regional chronology and ceramic relations: a preliminary report. *In* Mesoamerican archaeology p 1-20

Lowe, G. W. The Mixe-Zoque as competing neighbors of the early Lowland Maya. *In* The Origins of Maya civilization p197-248

History—Chronology

Lee, T. A. The Middle Grijalva regional chronology and ceramic relations: a preliminary report. *In* Mesoamerican archaeology p 1-20

Chiarenza, Carl

Notes on aesthetic relationships between seventeenth-century Dutch painting and nineteenth-century photography. *In* One hundred years of photographic history p19-34

Chiaromonte, Nicola

The worm of consciousness, and other essays

Contents

Albert Camus
Antonin Artaud and his theater
The ceremonial theater of Jean Genet
The death of Gandhi
The Jesuit
Lost Italians
The mass situation and noble values
Modern tyranny
Paris, 1951
Pirandello and humor
The political theater
Simone Weil's Iliad
Spain: the War
The student revolt
Theater in Utopia
Three lines from Dante
The worm of consciousness

Chibnall, Marjorie

Charter and chronicle: the use of archive sources by Norman historians. *In* Church and government in the Middle Ages p 1-17

Chicago

Politics and government

Rakove, M. L. Power, self-interest, and Chicago politics: a comparison of the theory of Politics among nations and the reality of politics in Chicago. *In* [Truth and tragedy]: a tribute to Hans Morgenthau p112-24

Chicago. John Hancock Tower

Billington, D. P. Technology and the structuring of cities. *In* Small comforts for hard times p182-98

Chicago Literary Times

Ravitz, A. C. Ballyhoo, gargoyles, & firecrackers: Ben Hecht's aesthetic calliope. *In* Filler, L. ed. A question of quality: popularity and value in modern creative writing p229-43

The Chicago Review

Michelson, P. On The Purple Sage, Chicago Review, and Big Table. *In* Anderson, E. and Kinzie, M. eds. The little magazine in America: a modern documentary history p341-75

Chicano literature (English) See American literature—Mexican American authors

Chicano literature (Spanish) See Mexican American literature (Spanish)

Chicanos. See Mexican Americans

Chief Eagle, Dallas

About individual works

Winter count

Larson, C. R. History of the people. *In* Larson, C. R. American Indian fiction p97-132

Ch'ien, Edward T.

Chiao Hung and the revolt against Ch'eng-Chu orthodoxy. *In* The Unfolding of Neo-Confucianism p271-303

Chih-kuai and the birth of fiction, The Six Dynasties. Dewoskin, K. J. *In* Chinese narrative p21-52

The **Chih-yen-chai** Commentary and the Dream of the red chamber. Wang, J. Ching-yu. *In* Chinese approaches to literature from Confucius to Liang Ch'i-ch'ao p189-220

Chihamba

Turner, V. W. African ritual and Western literature: is a comparative symbology possible? *In* Fletcher, A. J. S. ed. The literature of fact p45-81

Chihara, Charles Seiyo

What dreams are made on. *In* Dunlop, C. E. M. ed. Philosophical essays on dreaming p251-64

Chihara, Charles Seiyo, and Fodor, Jerry A.

Operationalism and ordinary language: a critique of Wittgenstein. *In* Dunlop, C. E. M. ed. Philosophical essays on dreaming p174-204

Child, Francis James

About

Reppert, J. D. F. J. Child and the ballad. *In* The Learned and the lewed p197-212

About individual works

English and Scottish ballads

Medwin, A. G. Miss Reburn's ballads: a nineteenth-century repertoire from Ireland. *In* Ballad studies p93-116

Child, Irvin L.

Parapsychology and the rest of psychology: a mutual challenge. *In* Parapsychology: its relation to physics, biology, psychology, and psychiatry p95-121

Child, John

The Inter-American Military System: historical development, current status, and implications for U.S. policy. *In* Farer, T. J. ed. The future of the inter-American system p155-94

Child abuse

Bettelheim, B. Unconscious contributions to one's undoing. *In* Bettelheim, B. Surviving, and other essays p241-45

Case studies

Cottle, T. J. The child is father to the man; excerpt from "The abandoners." *In* Gross, B. and Gross, R. eds. The children's rights movement p58-71

Illinois—Chicago

Greene, B. They tried to help. *In* Gross, B. and Gross, R. eds. The children's rights movement p37-42

United States

Shannon, W. V. Our lost children. *In* Gross, B. and Gross, R. eds. The children's rights movement p148-50

Child and father. See Father and child

Child and mother. See Mother and child

Child and parent. See Parent and child

Child authors. See Children as authors

Child behavior. See Child psychology; Children—Management

Child birth. See Childbirth

Child care centers. See Day care centers

Child custody. See Custody of children

Child development

Bain, D. A. Transtemporal communication. *In* Egoff, S. A. ed. One ocean touching p3-17

Child development—Continued

Bettelheim, B. Alienation and autonomy. *In* Bettelheim, B. Surviving, and other essays p333-49

Elkind, D. The early years: the vital years. *In* Elkind, D. The child and society p101-12

Gaylin, W. In the beginning: helpless and dependent. *In* Doing good p1-38

Horowitz, F. D. Directions for parenting. *In* Behavior modification and families p7-33

Jones, N. B. Ethology, anthropology, and childhood. *In* Biosocial anthropology p69-92

Kagan, J. Resilience in cognitive development. *In* Schwartz, T. ed. Socialization as cultural communication p139-55

Martin, S. and others. The comparability of behavioral data in laboratory and natural settings. *In* Behavior modification and families p189-203

Mead, M. The evocation of psychologically relevant responses in ethnological field work. *In* Spindler, G. D. ed. The making of psychological anthropology p89-139

Newson, E. Unreasonable care: the establishment of selfhood. *In* Royal Institute of Philosophy. Human values p 1-26

Rohter, I. S. A social-learning approach to political socialization. *In* Schwartz, D. C. and Schwartz, S. K. eds. New directions in political socialization p129-62

Rosenau, N. The sources of children's political concepts: an application of Piaget's theory. *In* Schwartz, D. C. and Schwartz, S. K. eds. New directions in political socialization p163-87

Rutter, M. Early sources of security and competence. *In* Human growth and development p33-61

Sears, R. R. Sex-typing, object choice, and child rearing. *In* Katchadourian, H. A. ed. Human sexuality p204-22

See also Child psychology; Children—Growth

Testing
See Psychological tests for children

Tahiti
Levy, R. I. Tahitian gentleness and redundant controls. *In* Montagu, A. ed. Learning non-aggression p222-35

Child health. See Children—Care and hygiene

Child health services

United States
Richmond, J. B. The needs of children. *In* Knowles, J. H. ed. Doing better and feeling worse p247-59

Child labor. See Children—Employment

Child molesting

United States
Schultz, L. G. Sexual victims. *In* Gochros, H. L. and Gochros, J. S. eds. The sexually oppressed p110-25

Child neglect. See Child abuse

Child psychiatry. See Child psychotherapy

Child psychology

Berg, L. Personal actions; excerpt from "Look at kids." *In* Gross, B. and Gross, R. eds. The children's rights movement p306-15

Elkind, D. Cognitive development and psychopathology: observations on egocentrism and ego defense. *In* Elkind, D. The child and society p202-22

Elkind, D. Cognitive frames and family interactions. *In* Elkind, D. The child and society p65-79

Elkind, D. Observing classroom frames. *In* Elkind, D. The child and society p135-42

Kracke, W. H. A psychoanalyst in the field: Erikson's contributions to anthropology. *In* Homans, P. ed. Childhood and selfhood p147-88

Maccoby, E. E. Gender identity and sex-role adoption. *In* Katchadourian, H. A. ed. Human sexuality p194-203

See also Adolescent psychology; Aggressiveness (Child psychology); Cognition in children; Decision-making in children; Learning, Psychology of; Moral development; Psychohistory; Psychological tests for children; Reasoning (Child psychology); Sick children—Psychology

History
Boorstin, D. J. From "naughtiness" to "behavior deviation"; excerpt from "The Americans: the democratic experience". *In* Davis, F. J. and Stivers, R. eds. The collective definition of deviance p147-55

Methodology
Elkind, D. The study of spontaneous religion in the child. *In* Elkind, D. The child and society p255-68

Child psychotherapy

Kramer, E. The practice of art therapy with children. *In* Ulman, E. and Dachinger, P. eds. Art therapy p159-80

Child rearing. See Children—Management

Child study. See Child development; Child psychology

Child welfare. See Child abuse; Juvenile delinquency

Childbirth

Miller, J. H. 'Temple and sewer'; childbirth, prudery, and Victoria Regina. *In* Wohl, A. S. ed. The Victorian family p23-43

See also Birth (in religion, folk-lore, etc.)

Childbirth in literature

Backman, M. Death and birth in Hemingway. *In* The Stoic strain in American literature p115-33

Children

Nemerov, H. The first county of places. *In* Images and ideas in American culture p158-68

See also Child development; Education of children; School children; Youth

Anecdotes and sayings
See Wit and humor, Juvenile

Bibliography
Gross, B. and Gross, R. Best further reading to become more capable of helping children and young people. *In* Gross, B. and Gross, R. eds. The children's rights movement p343-57

Books and reading
See Books and reading for children

Children as artists

Korzenik, D. Saying it with pictures. *In* Perkins, D. and Leondar, B. eds. The arts and cognition p192-207

See also Children's art

Children as authors

Leondar, B. Hatching plots: genesis of storymaking. *In* Perkins, D. and Leondar, B. eds. The arts and cognition p172-91

Children as poets. See Children as authors

Children in art

Kunzle, D. William Hogarth: the ravaged child in the corrupt city. *In* Tufte, V. and Myerhoff, B. G. eds. Changing images of the family p99-140

See also Children as artists

Children in literature

Guillory, D. L. The mystique of childhood in American literature. *In* Tulane Studies in English, v23 p229-47

Knoepflmacher, U. C. Mutations of the Wordsworthian child of nature. *In* Knoepflmacher, U. C. and Tennyson, G. B. eds. Nature and the Victorian imagination p391-425

Walther, L. The invention of childhood in Victorian autobiography. *In* Landow, G. P. ed. Approaches to Victorian autobiography p64-83

Children in motion pictures

Appel, A. Tristram in movielove: Lolita at the movies. *In* A Book of things about Vladimir Nabokov p123-70

Children of Israel. See Bene Israel

Children of migrant laborers

Coles, R. "God save them, those children; and for allowing such a state of affairs to continue, God save us, too"; excerpt from "Uprooted children." *In* Gross, B. and Gross, R. eds. The children's rights movement p118-22

Children's art

Kramer, E. The practice of art therapy with children. *In* Ulman, E. and Dachinger, P. eds. Art therapy p159-80

Site, M. Art and the slow learner. *In* Ulman, E. and Dachinger, P. eds. Art therapy p191-207

Themal, J. H. Children's work as art. *In* Ulman, E. and Dachinger, P. eds. Art therapy p95-105

Ulman, E. and Dachinger, P. Therapeutic art programs around the world. *In* Ulman, E. and Dachinger, P. eds. Art therapy p208-12

See also Children as artists

Children's books. See Children's literature

Children's courts. See Juvenile courts

Children's dreams

Shweder, R. A. and LeVine, R. A. Dream concepts of Hausa children: a critique of the "doctrine of invariant sequence" in cognitive development. *In* Schwartz, T. ed. Socialization as cultural communication p117-38

Children's films

History and criticism

Heins, E. L. Literature bedeviled: a searching look at filmstrips. *In* Horn Book Magazine. Crosscurrents of criticism p88-95

Children's literature

Aiken, J. A free gift. *In* Blishen, E. ed. The thorny paradise p36-52

Carvallo de Núñez, C. Children's literature in South America. *In* Egoff, S. A. ed. One ocean touching p131-37

Lifton, B. J. On children's literature: a runcible symposium. *In* Horn Book Magazine. Crosscurrents of criticism p7-14

See also Books and reading for children; Fairy tales Picture-books for children

Authorship

Aubry, C. The Canadian author for children still lost in the barren lands. *In* Egoff, S. A. ed. One ocean touching p197-201

Engdahl, S. L. Why write for today's teenagers? *In* Horn Book Magazine. Crosscurrents of criticism p144-49

Garfield, L. An evening with Leon Garfield. *In* Egoff, S. A. ed. One ocean touching p110-20

Hill, K. Journeying with Glooscap. *In* Egoff, S. A. ed. One ocean touching p186-88

Karl J. E. Between chaos and creativity: the role of the children's editor. *In* Egoff, S. A. ed. One ocean touching p164-76

Nichols, R. Something of myself. *In* Egoff, S. A. ed. One ocean touching p189-94

Southall, I. One man's Australia. *In* Egoff, S. A. ed. One ocean touching p18-37

Awards

Meltzer, M. Where do all the prizes go? The case for nonfiction. *In* Horn Book Magazine. Crosscurrents of criticism p51-57

Book reviews

Chambers, A. Reviewers' railments: a game for children's book people. *In* Horn Book Magazine. Crosscurrents of criticism p15-19

History and criticism

Cameron, E. McLuhan, youth, and literature. *In* Horn Book Magazine. Crosscurrents of criticism p98-120

Drury, R. W. "Realism plus fantasy equals magic." *In* Horn Book Magazine. Crosscurrents of criticism p178-84

Heins, P. Coming to terms with criticism. *In* Horn Book Magazine. Crosscurrents of criticism p82-87

Heins, P. Out on a limb with the critics: some random thoughts on the present state of the criticism of children's literature. *In* Horn Book Magazine. Crosscurrents of criticism p72-81

Holland, I. The walls of childhood. *In* Horn Book Magazine. Crosscurrents of criticism p27-34

Langton, J. The weak place in the cloth: a study of fantasy for children. *In* Horn Book Magazine. Crosscurrents of criticism p185-96

Lively, P. Children and memory. *In* Horn Book Magazine. Crosscurrents of criticism p226-33

McNeill, J. When the magic has to stop. *In* Horn Book Magazine. Crosscurrents of criticism p35-40

Meltzer, M. Where do all the prizes go? The case for nonfiction. *In* Horn Book Magazine. Crosscurrents of criticism p51-57

Townsend, J. R. An elusive border. *In* Horn Book Magazine. Crosscurrents of criticism p41-50

Children's rights—United States—*Continued*

Farson, R. E. Birthrights. *In* Gross, B. and Gross, R. eds. The children's rights movement p325-28

Holt, J. Why not a Bill of Rights for children? Excerpt from "Escape from childhood." *In* Gross, B. and Gross, R. eds. The children's rights movement p319-25

Kohler, M. To what are children entitled? *In* Gross, B. and Gross, R. eds. The children's rights movement p217-32

U.S. News & World Report. Nationwide drive for children's rights. *In* Gross, B. and Gross, R. eds. The children's rights movement p206-13

Youth Liberation of Ann Arbor. "We do not recognize their right to control us." *In* Gross, B. and Gross, R. eds. The children's rights movement p125-34

Youth Liberation of Ann Arbor. Youth Liberation program. *In* Gross, B. and Gross, R. eds. The children's rights movement p329-33

Children's songs, Chinese. See Folk-songs, Chinese

Children's stories

See also Fairy tales; Story-telling

Authorship

Bawden, N. The imprisoned child. *In* Blishen, E. ed. The thorny paradise p62-64

Fish, N. One thumping lie only. *In* Blishen, E. ed. The thorny paradise p117-22

Gardam, J. Mrs Hookaneye and I. *In* Blishen, E. ed. The thorny paradise p77-80

Gordon, J. On firm ground. *In* Blishen, E. ed. The thorny paradise p34-35

Hodges, C. W. Children? What children? *In* Blishen, E. ed. The thorny paradise p53-57

McIllwraith, M. M. H. (McV) The last lord of Redhouse Castle. *In* Blishen, E. ed. The thorny paradise p128-39

Peyton, K. M. pseud. On not writing a proper book. *In* Blishen, E. ed. The thorny paradise p123-27

Storr, C. Why write? Why write for children? *In* Blishen, E. ed. The thorny paradise p25-33

Walsh, J. P. Seeing green. *In* Blishen, E. ed. The thorny paradise p58-61

Willard, B. The thorny paradise. *In* Blishen, E. ed. The thorny paradise p158-62

Children's wit and humor. See Wit and humor, Juvenile

Childress, Diana T.

Are Shakespeare's late plays really romances? *In* Shakespeare's late plays p44-55

Chile

Armed Forces

Joxe, A. The Chilean Armed Forces and the making of the Coup. *In* O'Brien, P. J. ed. Allende's Chile p244-72

O'Brien, P. J. The military in power and the lessons of Chile. *In* O'Brien, P. J. ed. Allende's Chile p273-94

Economic conditions

Cavarozzi, M. J. and Petras, J. F. Chile. *In* Chilcote, R. H. and Edelstein, J. C. eds. Latin America: the struggle with dependency and beyond p491-578

Economic policy

Nove, A. The political economy of the Allende regime. *In* O'Brien, P. J. ed. Allende's Chile p51-78

Foreign relations—United States

O'Brien, P. J. Was the United States responsible for the Chilean Coup? *In* O'Brien, P. J. ed. Allende's Chile p217-43

History—Coup d'état, 1973

Hutchinson, G. W. The Coup in Chile and its implications. *In* The Year book of world affairs, 1975 p72-87

Joxe, A. The Chilean Armed Forces and the making of the Coup. *In* O'Brien, P. J. ed. Allende's Chile p244-72

O'Brien, P. J. The military in power and the lessons of Chile. *In* O'Brien, P. J. ed. Allende's Chile p273-94

O'Brien, P. J. Was the United States responsible for the Chilean Coup? *In* O'Brien, P. J. ed. Allende's Chile p217-43

Roxborough, I. Reversing the Revolution: the Chilean opposition to Allende. *In* O'Brien, P. J. ed. Allende's Chile p192-216

Politics and government

Cavarozzi, M. J. and Petras, J. F. Chile. *In* Chilcote, R. H. and Edelstein, J. C. eds. Latin America: the struggle with dependency and beyond p491-578

Skidmore, D. The Chilean experience of change: the primacy of the political. *In* Leftwich, A. ed. South Africa: economic growth and political change p213-48

Politics and government—1810-

Joxe, A. The Chilean Armed Forces and the making of the Coup. *In* O'Brien, P. J. ed. Allende's Chile p244-72

Politics and government—1920-

Leeds, A. and Leeds, E. R. Accounting for behavioral differences: three political systems and the responses of squatters in Brazil, Peru, and Chile. *In* Walton, J. and Masotti, L. H. eds. The city in comparative perspective p193-248

Roddick, J. F. Class structure and class politics in Chile. *In* O'Brien, P. J. ed. Allende's Chile p 1-26

Valenzuela, A. A. The breakdown of democratic regimes: Chile. *In* The Breakdown of democratic regimes pt4 p3-81

Politics and government—1970-

Gonzalez, M. Ideology and culture under Popular Unity. *In* O'Brien, P. J. ed. Allende's Chile p106-27

Kay, C. Agrarian reform and the transition to socialism. *In* O'Brien, P. J. ed. Allende's Chile p79-105

Lira, P. pseud. The crisis of hegemony in the Chilean Left. *In* O'Brien, P. J. ed. Allende's Chile p27-50

Nove, A. The political economy of the Allende regime. *In* O'Brien, P. J. ed. Allende's Chile p51-78

O'Brien, P. J. The military in power and the lessons of Chile. *In* O'Brien, P. J. ed. Allende's Chile p273-94

Roxborough, I. Reversing the Revolution: the Chilean opposition to Allende. *In* O'Brien, P. J. ed. Allende's Chile p192-216

Santa Lucia, P. pseud. The industrial working class and the struggle for power in Chile. *In* O'Brien, P. J. ed. Allende's Chile p128-66

Threlfall, M. Shantytown dwellers and people's power. *In* O'Brien, P. J. ed. Allende's Chile p167-91

Chile—*Continued*

Popular culture

Gonzalez, M. Ideology and culture under Popular Unity. *In* O'Brien, P. J. ed. Allende's Chile p106-27

Race question

Sater, W. F. The Black experience in Chile. *In* Toplin, R. B. ed. Slavery and race relations in Latin America p13-50

Social conditions

Skidmore, D. The Chilean experience of change: the primacy of the political. *In* Leftwich, A. ed. South Africa: economic growth and political change p213-48

Valenzuela, A. A. The breakdown of democratic regimes: Chile. *In* The Breakdown of democratic regimes pt4 p3-81

Chiliasm. See Millenium

Chilman, Catherine S.

The poor. *In* Gochros, H. L. and Gochros, J. S. eds. The sexually oppressed p202-12

Chilongo, Lamec

About

Bond, G. Minor prophets and Yombe cultural dynamics. *In* Colonialism and change p145-62

Chimes at midnight (Motion picture) See Falstaff (Motion picture)

Chimpanzees

Behavior

Lawick-Goodall, Barones J. van. The chimpanzee. *In* Goodall, V. M. ed. The quest for man p131-69

Chin, Ai-li S. See Chu, G. C. jt. auth.

Chin, Ai-li S. and Liu, Nien-ling

Short stories in China: theory and practice, 1973-1975. *In* Chu, G. C. Popular media in China p124-83

Chin p'ing mei

Roy, D. T. Chang Chu-p'o's Commentary on the Chin p'ing mei. *In* Chinese narrative p115-23

China

Civilization

Lapidus, I. M. Hierarchies and networks: a comparison of Chinese and Islamic societies. *In* Conflict and control in late imperial China p26-42

Scharfstein, B. A. Three philosophical civilizations: a preliminary comparison. *In* Philosophy East/philosophy West p48-127

Commerce—History

Chang, Kwang-chih. Ancient trade as economics or as ecology. *In* Ancient civilization and trade p211-24

Wills, J. E. Maritime China from Wang Chih to Shih Lang: themes in peripheral history. *In* Spence, J. D. and Wills, J. E. eds. From Ming to Ch'ing p201-38

Commerce—Japan

Haley, P. E. and Rood, H. W. China's major trading partner: Japan dependent. *In* China's changing role in the world economy p187-212

Description and travel—1949-

Schell, O. Private life in a public culture. *In* Terrill, R. ed. The China difference p23-35

Economic conditions—1949-

Lin, P. T. K. Development guided by values: comments on China's road and its implications. *In* On the creation of a just world order p259-94

Saubolle, L. E. The economic face of communism in Asia. *In* Pacific Asia and U.S. policies: a political-economic-strategic assessment p108-14

Economic policy

Denny, D. L. Recent developments in the international financial policies of the People's Republic of China. *In* China's changing role in the world economy p163-86

Howe, C. B. and Walker, K. R. The economist. *In* Wilson, R. G. ed. Mao Tse-tung in the scales of history p174-222

Foreign economic relations

Denny, D. L. Recent developments in the international financial policies of the People's Republic of China. *In* China's changing role in the world economy p163-86

Friedman, E. The international political economy and Chinese politics. *In* China's changing role in the world economy p 1-14

Foreign economic relations—Russia

Ray, D. M. Chinese perceptions of social imperialism and economic dependency: the impact of Soviet aid. *In* China's changing role in the world economy p36-82

Foreign economic relations—United States

Eckstein, A. Sino-American economic relations. *In* China and America p53-108

Luther, D. G. China, lump sum settlements, and executive agreements. *In* China's changing role in the world economy p213-22

Foreign opinion, American

Isaacs, H. R. Some concluding remarks: the turning mirrors. *In* Iriye, A. ed. Mutual images p258-65

Foreign relations

Banister, J. International effects of China's population situation. *In* China's changing role in the world economy p83-113

Chu, Paochin. V. K. Wellington Koo: the diplomacy of nationalism. *In* Burns, R. D. and Bennett, E. M. eds. Diplomats in crisis p125-51

Gittings, J. The statesman. *In* Wilson, R. G. ed. Mao Tse-tung in the scales of history p246-71

Iriye, A. The United States in Chinese foreign policy. *In* China and America p11-52

Okabe, T. The Cold war and China. *In* The Origins of the Cold war in Asia p224-51

Tsou, T. China and the world in the Mao and post-Mao eras. *In* Kaplan, M. A. ed. The many faces of communism p333-52

Warner, G. America, Russia, China and the origins of the Cold war, 1945-1950. *In* Siracusa, J. M. and Barclay, G. S. eds. The impact of the Cold war p144-62

Woodard, K. People's China and the world energy crisis: the Chinese attitude toward global resource. *In* China's changing role in the world economy p114-42

Foreign relations—Japan

Brown, S. D. Shidehara Kijūrō: the diplomacy of the yen. *In* Burns, R. D. and Bennett, E. M. eds. Diplomats in crisis p201-25

China—*Continued*
Religion
Stein, R. A. Religious Taoism and popular religion from the second to seventh centuries. *In* Welch, H. and Seidel, A. K. eds. Facets of Taoism p53-81

Welch, H. The fate of religion. *In* Terrill, R. ed. The China difference p117-37

Religion—Bibliography
Dobson, W. A. C. H. The religions of China (excepting Buddhism) *In* Adams, C. J. ed. A reader's guide to the great religions p90-105

Social conditions
Banister, J. International effects of China's population situation. *In* China's changing role in the world economy p83-113

Elvin, M. Chinese cities since the Sung Dynasty. *In* Towns in societies p79-89

Klein, D. W. Universal values and Chinese politics—a balance sheet. *In* Terrill, R. ed. The China difference p201-18

Lin, P. T. K. Development guided by values: comments on China's road and its implications. *In* On the creation of a just world order p259-94

Munro, D. J. The shape of Chinese values in the eye of an American philosopher. *In* Terrill, R. ed. The China difference p37-56

Ray, D. M. Chinese perceptions of social imperialism and economic dependency: the impact of Soviet aid. *In* China's changing role in the world economy p36-82

Wong, A. K. Women in China: past and present. *In* Matthiasson, C. J. ed. Many sisters p229-59

Social life and customs
Eberhard, W. The upper-class family in traditional China. *In* Rosenberg, C. E. ed. The family in history p59-94

Chinatown, San Francisco. See San Francisco—Chinatown

Chinatown Youth Services and Coordinating Center, San Francisco
Krisberg, B. A. and Takagi, P. Ethical issues in evaluating criminal justice demonstration projects. *In* Riedel, M. and Chappell, D. eds. Issues in criminal justice: planning and evaluation p66-74

Chinese. See Missions to Chinese

Chinese arts. See Arts, Chinese

Chinese astrology. See Astrology, Chinese

Chinese classics. See Chinese literature—to 221 B.C.

Chinese Communist Party. See Communist Party of China

Chinese demonology. See Demonology, Chinese

Chinese drama

History and criticism
Birch, C. Some concerns and methods of the Ming Ch'uan-ch'i drama. *In* Birch, C. ed. Studies in Chinese literary genres p220-58

Crump, J. I. The conventions and craft of Yuan drama. *In* Birch, C. ed. Studies in Chinese literary genres p192-219

Nicoll, A. The drama of China. *In* Nicoll, A. World drama p539-45

Chinese fiction
See also Short stories, Chinese

History and criticism
Eoyang, Eugene Chen. A taste for apricots: approaches to Chinese fiction. *In* Chinese narrative p53-69

Hanan, P. The early Chinese short story: a critical theory in outline. *In* Birch, C. ed. Studies in Chinese literary genres p299-338

Hegel, R. G. Sui T'ang yen-i and the aesthetics of the seventeenth-century Suchou elite. *In* Chinese narrative p124-59

Hsia, Chih-tsing. The military romance: a genre of Chinese fiction. *In* Birch, C. ed. Studies in Chinese literary genres p339-90

Plaks, A. H. Towards a critical theory of Chinese narrative. *In* Chinese narrative p309-52

Průšek, J. Urban centers: the cradle of popular fiction. *In* Birch, C. ed. Studies in Chinese literary genres p259-98

20th century—History and criticism
Birch, C. Change and continuity in Chinese fiction. *In* Modern Chinese literature in the May Fourth era p385-404

Link, P. Traditional-style popular urban fiction in the teens and twenties. *In* Modern Chinese literature in the May Fourth era p327-49

Chinese folk-songs. See Folk-songs, Chinese

Chinese in Asia, Southeastern
Wang, G. The limits of Nanyang Chinese nationalism, 1912-1937. *In* Southeast Asian history and historiography p405-23

Commerce
Go Gien Tjwan. The changing trade position of the Chinese in South-East Asia. *In* United Nations Educational, Scientific and Cultural Organization. Race, science and society p301-16

Chinese in Guyana
Patterson, H. T. O. Context and choice in ethnic allegience: a theoretical framework and Caribbean case study. *In* Glazer, N. and Moynihan, D. P. eds. Ethnicity p305-49

Chinese in Jamaica
Patterson, H. T. O. Context and choice in ethnic allegiance: a theoretical framework and Caribbean case study. *In* Glazer, N. and Moynihan, D. P. eds. Ethnicity p305-49

Chinese in San Francisco
Lyman, S. M. Conflict and the web of group affiliation in San Francisco's Chinatown, 1850-1910. *In* The Asian American: the historical experience p26-52

Chinese in Thailand
Kirsch, A. T. Economy, polity, and religion in Thailand. *In* Change and persistence in Thai society p172-96

Chinese in the United States

Historiography
Ts'ai, S. H. Chinese immigration through Communist Chinese eyes: an introduction to the historiography. *In* The Asian American: the historical experience p53-66

Chinese landscape painting. See Landscape painting, Chinese

Chinese literature

History and criticism
Dewoskin, K. J. The Six Dynasties Chih-kuai and the birth of fiction. *In* Chinese narrative p21-52

Chinese literature—History and criticism —*Continued*

Holzman, D. Confucius and ancient Chinese literary criticism. *In* Chinese approaches to literature from Confucius to Liang Ch'i-ch'ao p21-41

Pollard, D. E. Ch'i in Chinese literary theory. *In* Chinese approaches to literature from Confucius to Liang Ch'i-ch'ao p43-66

To 221 B.C.

Wang, John Ching-yu. Early Chinese narrative: the Tso-Chuan as example. *In* Chinese narrative p3-20

20th century—History and criticism

Cheng, Ching-mao. The impact of Japanese literary trends on modern Chinese writers. *In* Modern Chinese literature in the May Fourth era p63-88

Doleželová-Velingerová, M. The origins of modern Chinese literature. *In* Modern Chinese literature in the May Fourth era p17-35

Eber, I. Images of oppressed peoples and modern Chinese literature. *In* Modern Chinese literature in the May Fourth era p127-41

McDougall, B. S. The impact of Western literary trends. *In* Modern Chinese literature in the May Fourth era p37-61

Mills, H. C. Literature in fetters. *In* Terrill, R. ed. The China difference p285-304

Pickowicz, P. G. Qu Qiubai's critique of the May Fourth generation: early Chinese Marxist literary criticism. *In* Modern Chinese literature in the May Fourth era p351-84

Vogel, E. F. The unlikely heroes: the social role of the May Fourth writers. *In* Chinese literature in the May Fourth era p145-59

Chinese medicine. See Medicine, Chinese

Chinese national characteristics. See National characteristics, Chinese

Chinese Nationalist party. See Chung-kuo kuo min tang

Chinese opera. See Opera, Chinese

Chinese painting. See Painting, Chinese

Chinese philosophy. See Philosophy, Chinese

Chinese poetry

See also Tz'u

History and criticism

Chen, Shih-hsiang. The Shih-ching: its generic significance in Chinese literary history and poetics. *In* Birch, C. ed. Studies in Chinese literary genres p8-41

Frankel, H. H. Yüeh-fŭ poetry. *In* Birch, C. ed. Studies in Chinese literary genres p69-107

Hightower, J. R. Allusion in the poetry of T'ao Ch'ien. *In* Birch, C. ed. Studies in Chinese literary genres p108-32

Liu, Jo-yü. Tradition and creativity in early Ch'ing poetics. *In* Artists and traditions p17-19

Lynn, R. J. Orthodoxy and enlightenment: Wang Shih-chen's theory of poetry and its antecedents. *In* The Unfolding of Neo-Confucianism p217-69

Ching, Frank

The Asian experience in the United States. *In* The Immigrant experience in America p192-214

Ch'ing Shêng-tsu, Emperor of China

About individual works

Emperor of China: self-portrait of K'ang-Hsi

Mudrick, M. The Emperor of China. *In* Mudrick, M. Books are not life but then what is? p3-11

Chinitz, Benjamin

Regional development. *In* McKie, J. W. ed. Social responsibility and the business predicament p247-73

Chinnici, Joseph P.

New religious movements and the structure of religious sensibility. *In* Needleman, J. and Baker, G. eds. Understanding the new religions p26-33

Chipewyan language. See Athapascan language

Chippewa Indians

Psychology

Barnouw, V. An interpretation of Wisconsin Ojibwa culture and personality: a review. *In* Spindler, G. D. ed. The making of psychological anthropology p64-86

Religion and mythology

Hallowell, A. I. Ojibwa ontology, behavior, and world view. *In* Tedlock, D. E. and Tedlock, B. eds. Teachings from the American earth p141-78

Chirelstein, Marvin A.

Corporate law reform. *In* McKie, J. W. ed. Social responsibility and the business predicament p41-77

Chisholm, Roderick Milton

Coming into being and passing away: can the metaphysician help? *In* Donnelly, J. P. ed. Language, metaphysics, and death p 1-24

On the nature of acquaintance: a discussion of Russell's theory of knowledge. *In* Nakhnikian, G. ed. Bertrand Russell's philosophy p47-56

On the observability of the self. *In* Donnelly, J. P. ed. Language, metaphysics, and death p137-49

Chittick, H. Neville

The peopling of the East African coast. *In* Chittick, H. N. and Rotberg, R. I. eds. East Africa and the Orient p16-43

Chittick, Neville. See Chittick, H. Neville

Chitty, Thomas

Accident and coincidence in 'Tess of the d'Urbervilles.' *In* Drabble, M. ed. The genius of Thomas Hardy p74-79

Chivalry

Keen, M. H. Chivalry, nobility, and the man-at-arms. *In* War, literature, and politics in the late Middle Ages p32-45

Keen, M. H. Huizinga, Kilgour and the decline of chivalry. *In* Medievalia et humanistica no. 8 p 1-20

See also Courtly love; Knights and knighthood

Romances

See Romances

Chivalry in literature

Harvey, L. P. Oral composition and the performance of novels of chivalry in Spain. *In* Duggan, J. J. ed. Oral literature p84-100

Chloe in the afternoon (Motion picture)

Kauffmann, S. Chloe in the afternoon. *In* Kauffmann, S. Living images p142-45

Chlorites

Lamberg-Karlovsky, C. C. Third millennium modes of exchange and modes of production. *In* Ancient civilization and trade p341-68

Chlysty. See Khlysty

Chmaj, Betty E.

Some paradox! Some irony! Changing images of American woman, 1930-1974. *In* Luedtke, L. S. ed. The study of American culture p121-76

Choctaw Indians

Peterson, J. H. The changing role of an applied anthropologist. *In* Eddy, E. M. and Partridge, W. L. eds. Applied anthropology in America p165-81

Peterson, J. H. Three efforts at development among the Choctaws of Mississippi. *In* Williams, W. L. ed. Southeastern Indians since the removal era p142-53

Land transfers

DeRosier, A. H. Myths and realities in Indian westward removal: the Choctaw example. *In* Hudson, C. M. ed. Four centuries of Southern Indians p83-100

Social life and customs

Peterson, J. H. Louisiana Choctaw life at the end of the nineteenth century. *In* Hudson, C. M. ed. Four centuries of Southern Indians p101-12

Chodorov, Jerome. See Fields, J. jt. auth.

Chodorow, Stanley Alan

Dishonest litigation in the Church courts, 1140-98. *In* Law, church, and society p187-206

Choice (Psychology)

Dubos, R. J. Adventure and fantasy. *In* Dubos, R. J. Beast or angel? p190-97

Flew, A. G. N. The Darwinian framework. *In* Flew, A. G. N. A rational animal p7-33

Flew, A. G. N. Powers, checks, and choice in Malthus. *In* Flew, A. G. N. A rational animal p34-48

Foot, P. Goodness and choice. *In* Foot, P. Virtues and vices, and other essays in moral philosophy p132-47

Taylor, C. What is human agency? *In* Mischel, T. ed. The self p103-35

See also Decision-making

Choice of books. See Books and reading

Choice of college. See College, Choice of

Choice of school. See School, Choice of

Chojnacki, Stanley John

Dowries and kinsmen in early Renaissance Venice. *In* Stuard, S. M. ed. Women in medieval society p173-98

Choldin, Harvey M.

Social life and the physical environment. *In* Handbook of contemporary urban life p352-84

Cholera, Asiatic

Russia

Frieden, N. M. The Russian cholera epidemic, 1829-93, and medical professionalization. *In* Branca, P. ed. The medicine show p259-80

Chomsky, Noam

Conditions on rules of grammar. *In* Current issues in linguistic theory p3-50

Foreign policy and the intelligentsia. *In* Images and ideas in American culture p15-59

Language and unconscious knowledge. *In* Psychoanalysis and language p3-44

Toward a humanistic conception of education. *In* Feinberg, W. and Rosemont, H. eds. Work, technology, and education p204-20

About

Greene, J. Psycholinguistics: competence and performance. *In* Royal Institute of Philosophy. Communication and understanding p79-90

Hymes, D. H. Review of Noam Chomsky. *In* Harman, G. ed. On Noam Chomsky p316-33

Morris, W. A. The centrality of language. *In* Morris, W. A. Friday's footprint p84-146

Nagel, T. Linguistics and epistemology. *In* Harman, G. ed. On Noam Chomsky p219-28

Quine, W. V. Methodological reflections on current linguistic theory. *In* Harman, G. ed. On Noam Chomsky p104-17

Searle, J. R. Chomsky's revolution in linguistics. *In* Harman, G. ed. On Noam Chomsky p2-33

Pribram, K. H. The linguistic act. *In* Psychoanalysis and language p75-98

Steiner, G. Whorf, Chomsky, and the student of literature. *In* Steiner, G. On difficulty and other essays p137-63

Also in Wimsatt, W. K. ed. Literary criticism: idea and act p242-62

About individual works

Language and mind

Harman, G. Review of Language and mind. *In* Harman, G. ed. On Noam Chomsky p201-18

Syntactic structures

Lees, R. B. Review of Syntactic structures. *In* Harman, G. ed. On Noam Chomsky p34-79

Chong Lim Kim. See Kim, Chong Lim

Chopin, Kate (O'Flaherty)

About individual works

The awakening

Allen, P. Old critics and new: the treatment of Chopin's The awakening. *In* Diamond, A. and Edwards, L. R. eds. The authority of experience p224-38

Characters—Edna Pontellier

Allen, P. Old critics and new: the treatment of Chopin's The awakening. *In* Diamond, A. and Edwards, L. R. eds. The authority of experience p224-38

Fryer, J The new woman: Edna Pontellier: The new woman as woman. *In* Fryer, J. The faces of Eve p243-58

Choron, Jacques

About individual works

Suicide

Gass, W. H. The doomed in their sinking. *In* Gass, W. H. The world within the word p3-15

Chorus (Drama) See Drama—Chorus; Drama—Chorus (Greek drama)

A chorus line (criticism) Hamlisch, M. *In* Kauffmann, S. Persons of the drama p266-70

Chosen people (Jews) See Jews—Election, Doctrine of

Chou, Fo-hai

About

Lin, Han-sheng. Chou Fo-hai: the diplomacy of survival. *In* Burns, R. D. and Bennett, E. M. eds. Diplomats in crisis p171-99

Chou, Tso-jên

About

Pollard, D. E. Chou Tso-jen: a scholar who withdrew. *In* The Limits of change p332-56

Choudhury, Golam Waham

Roles and careers of middle-rank politicians: some cases from East Bengal. *In* The making of politicians: studies from Africa and Asia p195-206

Chow, Shu-jên

About

Fokkema, D. W. Lu Xun: the impact of Russian literature. *In* Modern Chinese literature in the May Fourth era p89-101

Lee, Leo Ou-fan. Genesis of a writer: notes on Lu Xun's educational experience, 1881-1909. *In* Modern Chinese literature in the May Fourth era p161-88

Mills, H. C. Lu Xun: literature and revolution—from Mara to Marx. *In* Modern Chinese literature in the May Fourth era p189-220

About individual works

Medicine

Doleželová-Velingerová, M. Lu Xun's "Medicine." *In* Modern Chinese literature in the May Fourth era p221-31

Chrestien de Troyes

About

Brewer, D. S. Chaucer and Chrétien and Arthurian romance. *In* Chaucer and Middle English studies in honour of Rossell Hope Robbins p255-59

Hanning, R. W. The individual and mimesis, I: time and space in chivalric romance. *In* Hanning, R. W. The individual in twelfth-century romance p139-70

Hanning, R. W. The individual and mimesis, II: multiple perspectives on reality. *In* Hanning, R. W. The individual in twelfth-century romance p171-93

Hanning, R. W. The romance plot and the crisis of inner awareness. *In* Hanning, R. W. The individual in twelfth-century romance p194-233

About individual works

Cligés

Hanning, R. W. "Engin" in twelfth-century courtly texts. *In* Hanning, R. W. The individual in twelfth-century romance p105-38

Erec and Enide

Hanning, R. W. Critical moments: individuality in chivalric romance. *In* Hanning, R. W. The individual in twelfth-century romance p53-104

Lancelot (Le Chevalier de la charrette)

Hays, P. L. Malamud's Yiddish-accented medieval stories. *In* The Fiction of Bernard Malamud p87-96

Yvain (Le Chevalier au lion)

Hanning, R. W. "Engin" in twelfth-century courtly texts. *In* Hanning, R. W. The individual in twelfth-century romance p105-38

Chrétien de Troyes. See Chrestien de Troyes

Christ. See Jesus Christ

Christ, Carol

Victorian masculinity and The angel in the house. *In* Vicinus, M. ed. A widening sphere p146-62

Christ, Ronald J.

Transcriptions with writers. *In* Review, v 1 1979 p321-27

Christ in Gethsemane (Sculpture)

Stokstad, M. Christ in Gethsemane: sculpture in the University of Kansas Museum of Art. *In* Enggass, R. C. and Stokstad, M. eds. Hortus imaginum p95-101

Christensen, Cheryl J.

Food and national security. *In* Knorr, K. E. and Trager, F. N. eds. Economic issues and national security p289-320

Structural power and national security. *In* Knorr, K. E. and Trager, F. N. eds. Economic issues and national security p127-59

Christensen, Francis

A lesson from Hemingway ("The undefeated"). *In* Benson, J. J. ed. The short stories of Ernest Hemingway: critical essays p121-29

Christian, Diane

Inversion and the erotic: the case of William Blake. *In* Babcock, B. A. ed. The reversible world p117-28

Christian, R. F.

Some unpublished poems of Nicholas Bachtin. *In* Oxford Slavonic papers, new ser. v10 p107-19

Christian antiquities. See Christian art and symbolism; Church architecture

Christian art and symbolism

Grigg, R. Constantine the Great and the cult without images. *In* Viator: medieval and Renaissance studies v8 p 1-32

Milner-Gulland, R. A. Art and architecture of Old Russia, 988-1700. *In* Auty, R. and Obolensky, D. eds. An introduction to Russian art and architecture p 1-70

Parsons, T. Religious and economic symbolism in the Western world. *In* Johnson, H. M. ed. Religious change and continuity p 1-48

Schapiro, M. From Mozarabic to Romanesque in Silos. *In* Schapiro, M. Selected papers v 1 p28-101

Schapiro, M. New documents on Saint-Gilles. *In* Schapiro, M. Selected papers v 1 p328-46

Schapiro, M. On geometrical schematism in Romanesque art. *In* Schapiro, M. Selected papers v 1 p265-84

Schapiro, M. On the aesthetic attitude in Romanesque art. *In* Schapiro, M. Selected papers v 1 p 1-27

Schapiro, M. The Romanesque sculpture of Moissae. *In* Schapiro, M. Selected papers v 1 p131-264

Schapiro, M. The sculptures of Souillac. *In* Schapiro, M. Selected papers v 1 p102-30

Schapiro, M. Two Romanesque drawings in Auxerre and some iconographic problems. *In* Schapiro, M. Selected papers v 1 p306-27

Sheppard, C. D. The bronze doors of Augsburg Cathedral. *In* Enggass, R. C. and Stokstad, M. eds. Hortus imaginum p21-27

Stokstad, M. The art of prehistoric and early Christian Ireland. *In* Orel, H. ed. Irish history and culture p43-78

Christian art and symbolism—*Continued*

Stokstad, M. Medieval art. *In* Orel, H. ed. Irish history and culture p79-108

See also Art, Medieval; Bible—Pictures, illustrations, etc.; Catholic Church and art; Emblems; Icons; Illumination of books and manuscripts; Mosaics; Symbolism of numbers

History

Watson, P. F. The Queen of Sheba in Christian tradition. *In* Pritchard, J. B. ed. Solomon & Sheba p115-45

Christian biography. See Hagiography

Christian civilization. See Civilization, Christian

Christian decoration and ornament. See Christian art and symbolism

Christian doctrine. See Theology, Doctrinal

Christian drama, English

History and criticism

Reynolds, W. Dorothy Sayers and the drama of orthodoxy. *In* Hannay, M. P. ed. As her whimsey took her p91-106

Christian education. See Sunday-schools

Christian ethics

Coffey, J. W The Christian realism of Reinhold Niebuhr. *In* Political realism in American thought p79-124

Foot, P. Nietzsche: the revaluation of values. *In* Foot, P. Virtues and vices, and other essays in moral philosophy p81-95

Maguire, D. C. Catholic ethics with an American accent. *In* America in theological perspective p13-36

Ple, A. Christian morality and Freudian morality. *In* Wolman, B. B. ed. Psychoanalysis and Catholicism p97-110

Reist, B. A. Beyond ideological theology. *In* The Context of contemporary theology p171-86

Sayers, D. L. Christian morality; excerpt from "Unpopular opinions." *In* Sayers, D. L. The whimsical Christian p151-56

Sayers, D. L. The other six deadly sins; excerpt from "Creed or chaos?" *In* Sayers, D. L. The whimsical Christian p157-79

See also Sin; Social ethics; Vices

Early church, ca. 30-600

Osborn, E. F. Conclusion. *In* Osborn, E. F. Ethical patterns in early Christian thought p214-20

Osborn, E. F. Four problems. *In* Osborn, E. F. Ethical patterns in early Christian thought p183-213

Ste Croix, G. E. M. de. Early Christian attitudes to property and slavery. *In* Church, society and politics p 1-38

Modern period, 1500-

See Christian ethics

Christian fiction

Percy, W. Notes for a novel about the end of the world. *In* Percy, W. The message in the bottle p101-18

Christian hymns. See Hymns

Christian leadership

Smith, T. L. Lay initiative in the religious life of American immigrants, 1880-1950. *In* Mulder, J. M. and Wilson, J. F. eds. Religion in American history p358-78

Christian life

Arnold, M. A 'friend of God.' *In* Arnold, M. The last word p180-89

Sayers, D. L. Problem picture; excerpt from "The mind of the Maker." *In* Sayers, D. L. The whimsical Christian p122-50

See also Asceticism; Christian ethics; Conduct of life; Faith; Piety; Spiritual life

Christian literature

Nolan, B. The later medieval spiritual quest: through time to aevum. *In* Nolan, B. The Gothic visionary perspective p124-55

Nolan, B. New directions in twelfth-century spirituality. *In* Nolan, B. The Gothic visionary perspective p3-34

See also Christianity and literature; Christianity in literature

History and criticism

Kurz, P. K. Why is Christian literature at an end? *In* Kurz, P. K. On modern German literature v4 p109-28

Christian literature, American

New England—History and criticism

Lowance, M. I. Typology and millenial eschatology in early New England. *In* Miner, E. R. ed. Literary uses of typology p228-73

Christian literature, Early

See also Latin literature, Medieval and modern; Literature, Medieval

History and criticism

Ferrante, J. M. Biblical exegesis. *In* Ferrante, J. M. Woman as image in medieval literature p17-35

Greek authors—Appreciation

Rice, E. F. The humanist idea of Christian antiquity and the impact of Greek patristic work on sixteenth-century thought. *In* Classical influences on European culture A.D. 1500-1700 p199-203

Christian literature, English

History and criticism

Blake, N. F. Varieties of Middle English religious prose. *In* Chaucer and Middle English studies in honour of Rossell Hope Robbins p348-56

Early modern, 1500-1700—History and criticism

Lewalski, B. K. Typological symbolism and the "progress of the soul" in seventeenth-century literature. *In* Miner, E. R. ed. Literary uses of typology p79-114

Christian martyrs

Cult—Milan

Lewis, S. Problems of architectural style and the Ambrosian liturgy in late fourth-century Milan. *In* Enggass, R. C. and Stokstad, M. eds. Hortus imaginum p11-19

Invocation

See Christian martyrs—Cult

Veneration

See Christian martyrs—Cult

Worship

See Christian martyrs—Cult

Christian Observer. See Christian Observer and Advocate (London)

Christian Observer and Advocate (London)

Pickering, S. The Christian Observer and the novel. *In* Pickering, S. The moral tradition in English fiction, 1785-1850 p65-87

Christian pilgrims and pilgrimages

Zacher, C. K. Pilgrimage. *In* Zacher, C. K. Curiosity and pilgrimage p42-59

Christian pilgrims and pilgrimages in literature

Zacher, C. K. Curiosity and the instability of pilgrimage: Chaucer's Canterbury tales. *In* Zacher, C. K. Curiosity and pilgrimage p87-129

Christian poetry, English

History and criticism

Lewalski, B. K. Art and the sacred subject: sermon theory, Biblical personae, and Protestant poetics. *In* Lewalski, B. K. Protestant poetics and the seventeenth century religious lyric p213-50

Lewalski, B. K. Biblical genre theory: precepts and models for the religious lyric. *In* Lewalski. B. K. Protestant poetics and the seventeenth-century religious lyric p31-71

Lewalski, B. K. The Biblical symbolic mode: typology and the religious lyric. *In* Lewalski, B. K. Protestant poetics and the seventeenth-century religious lyric p111-44

Lewalski, B. K. "Is there in truth no beautie?" Protestant poetics and the Protestant paradigm of salvation. *In* Lewalski, B. K. Protestant poetics and the seventeenth-century religious lyric p3-27

Lewalski, B. K. The poetic texture of scripture: tropes and figures for the religious lyric. *In* Lewalski, B. K. Protestant poetics and the seventeenth-century religious lyric p72-110

Lewalski, B. K. Protestant emblematics: sacred emblems and religious lyrics. *In* Lewalski, B. K. Protestant poetics and the seventeenth-century religious lyric p179-212

Lewalski, B. K. Protestant meditation: kinds, structures, and strategies of development for the meditative lyric. *In* Lewalski, B. K. Protestant poetics and the seventeenth century religious lyric p147-78

Christian saints in art. See Santos (Art)

Christian sects

See also Jansenists

United States

See Afro-American churches

Christian socialism. See Socialism, Christian

Christian sociology. See Sociology, Christian

Christian symbolism. See Christian art and symbolism

Christian World Liberation Front

Heinz, D. The Christian World Liberation Front. *In* The New religious consciousness p143-61

Christianity

Coomaraswamy, A. K. The Vedānta and Western tradition. *In* Coomaraswamy, A. K. Selected papers v2 p3-22

Copleston, F. C. Christianity without belief in God. *In* Copleston, F. C. Philosophers and philosophies p68-78

Krass, A. C. Accounting for the hope that is in me. *In* Christian faith in a religiously plural world p155-67

Malone, T. P. The Christian sacred tradition and psychotherapy. *In* Needleman, J. and Lewis, D. eds. On the way to self knowledge p26-45

Parsons, T. Christianity. *In* Parsons, T. Action theory and the human condition p173-212

Patterson, R. L. An analysis of faith. *In* Fact, value, and perception p85-105

See also Civilization, Christian; God; Jesus Christ; Miracles; Missions; Protestantism; Reformation; Sociology, Christian

Early church, ca. 30-600

Georgi, D. Socioeconomic reasons for the "divine man" as a propagandistic pattern. *In* Aspects of religious propaganda in Judaism and early Christianity p27-42

Schoedel, W. R. Jewish wisdom and the formation of the Christian ascetic. *In* Aspects of wisdom in Judaism and early Christianity p169-99

Tarachow, S. St Paul and early Christianity. *In* Wolman, B. B. ed. Psychoanalysis and Catholicism p143-207

Wilken, R. L. Wisdom and philosophy in early Christianity. *In* Aspects of wisdom in Judaism and early Christianity p143-68

Bibliography

Walsh, H. H. Christianity. *In* Adams, C. J. ed. A reader's guide to the great religions p345-406

Philosophy

Frye, N. The rhythm of growth and decay. *In* Frye, N. Northrop Frye on culture and literature p141-46

Africa

Dickson, K. A. The African theological task. *In* The Emergent gospel p46-49

Nyamiti, C. Approaches to African theology. *In* The Emergent gospel p31-45

Reber, C. H. Traditional Christianity as an African religion. *In* African religions: a symposium p255-74

Asia, Southeastern

Lee, P. K. H. Between the old and the new. *In* The Emergent gospel p124-36

India

Amalorpavadass, D. S. The Indian universe of a new theology. *In* The Emergent gospel p137-56

Chandran, J. R. Development of Christian theology in India: a critical survey. *In* The Emergent gospel p157-72

Latin America

Couch, B. M. New visions of the Church in Latin America: a Protestant view. *In* The Emergent gospel p195-226

Dussel, E. D. The political and ecclesial context of liberation theology in Latin America. *In* The Emergent gospel p175-92

Russia

Andreev, G. The Christianity of L. N. Tolstoy and of the contributors to "From under the rubble." *In* Medvedev, R. A. ed. The Samizdat register p267-314

Elagin, S. Repentance: its theory, history and prescription for today. *In* Medvedev, R. A. ed. The Samizdat register p237-66

South Africa

Buthelezi, M. Toward indigenous theology in South Africa. *In* The Emergent gospel p56-75

Christianity—*Continued*

United States

Fiorenza, F. S. American culture and Modernism: Shailer Mathew's interpretation of American Christianity. *In* America in theological perspective p163-86

Mawhinney, J. J. H. Richard Niebuhr and reshaping American Christianity. *In* America in theological perspective p140-62

Moberg, D. O. Fundamentalists and evangelicals in society. *In* Wells, D. F. and Woodbridge, J. D. eds. The evangelicals p143-69

Ransom, J. C. God without thunder; excerpt. *In* Crunden, R. M. ed. The superfluous men p262-68

Christianity and capitalism. See Protestantism and capitalism

Christianity and culture

Eliot, T. S. From Notes towards the definition of culture. *In* Eliot, T. S. Selected prose of T. S. Eliot p292-305

Christianity and democracy

United States

Gower, J. F. Democracy as a theological problem in Isaac Hecker's apologetics. *In* America in theological perspective p37-55

Christianity and economics

Parsons, T. Religious and economic symbolism in the Western world. *In* Johnson, H. M. ed. Religious change and continuity p 1-48

See also Protestantism and capitalism; Sociology, Christian

Christianity and existentialism

Boulding, E. Religion, futurism, and models of social change. *In* Bundy, R. F. ed. Images of the future: the twenty-first century and beyond p169-81

Christianity and international affairs

Rees, E. Exercises in private diplomacy: selected activities of the Commission of the Churches on International Affairs. *In* Unofficial diplomats p111-29

Christianity and literature

Donaldson, E. T. Patristic exegesis in the criticism of medieval literature: the opposition. *In* Wimsatt, W. K. ed. Literary criticism: idea and act p170-88

Goodheart, E. English social criticism and the spirit of Reformation. *In* Goodheart, E. The failure of criticism p28-50

Grabo, N. S. Colonial American theology: holiness and the lyric impulse. *In* Essays in honor of Russel B. Nye p74-91

Hynes, S. L. The trials of a Christian critic. *In* The Literary criticism of T. S. Eliot p64-88

Kurz, P. K. Literature and theology today. *In* Kurz, P. K. On modern German literature v 1 p80-104

Owomoyela, O. Vernacular literatures. *In* Owomoyela, O. African literatures: an introduction p23-35

Wilt, J. Frankenstein as Mystery play. *In* Levine, G. L. and Knoepflmacher, U. C. eds. The endurance of Frankenstein p31-48

Woolf, R. The wanderer, The seafarer, and the genre of planctus. *In* Anglo-Saxon poetry: essays in appreciation p192-207

See also Christian literature; Christianity in literature

Christianity and other religions

Anderson, G. H. Religion as a problem for the Christian mision. *In* Christian faith in a religiously plural world p104-16

Dawe, D. G. Christian faith in a religiously plural world. *In* Christian faith in a religiously plural world p13-33

Palihawadana, M. A Buddhist response: religion beyond ideology and power. *In* Christian faith in a religiously plural world p34-45

Smith, W. C. An historian of faith reflects on what we are doing here. *In* Christian faith in a religiously plural world p139-48

See also Paganism

Hinduism

Rao, K. L. S. A Hindu response: the value of religious pluralism. *In* Christian faith in a religiously plural world p46-58

Islam

Rahman, F. A. Muslim response: Christian particularity and the faith of Islam. *In* Christian faith in a religiously plural world p69-79

Savory, R. M. Christendom vs. Islam: interaction and co-existence. *In* Savory, R. M. ed. Introduction to Islamic civilisation p127-35

Thomson, R. M. William of Malmesbury and some other Western writers on Islam. *In* Medievalia et humanistica no. 6 p179-87

Judaism

Hertzberg, A. Anti-Semitism and Jewish uniqueness: ancient and contemporary. *In* Tradition and change in Jewish experience p211-25

Christianity and philosophy. See Philosophy and religion

Christianity and politics

Coffey, J. W. The Christian realism of Reinhold Niebuhr. *In* Coffey, J. W. Political realism in American thought p79-124

Ricoeur, P. Adventures of the state and the task of Christians. *In* Ricoeur, P. Political and social essays p201-16

Wilhelmsen, F. D. Donoso Cortés and the meaning of political power. *In* Wilhelmsen, F. D. Christianity and political philosophy p139-73

Wilhelmsen, F. D. Jaffa, the school of Strauss, and the Christian tradition. *In* Wilhelmsen, F. D. Christianity and political philosophy p209-25

Wilhelmsen, F. D. The problem of political power and the forces of darkness. *In* Wilhelmsen, F. D. Christianity and political philosophy p60-110

Wilhelmsen, F. D. Professor Voegelin and the Christian tradition. *In* Wilhelmsen, F. D. Christianity and political philosophy p193-208

See also Christianity and democracy; Church and international organization

Christianity and revolution. See Revolution (Theology)

Christianity and science. See Religion and science

Christianity and the world. See Church and the world; Sociology, Christian

Christianity and war. See War and religion

Christianity in literature

Bleikasten, A. The heresy of Flannery O'Connor. *In* Johnson, I. D. and Johnson, C. [eds.] Les américanistes p53-70

Christianity in literature—*Continued*

Curran, T. The word made flesh: the Christian aesthetic in Dorothy L. Sayers's The man born to be king. *In* Hannay, M. P. ed. As her whimsey took her p67-77

Dale, A. S. The man born to be king: Dorothy L. Sayers's best mystery plot. *In* Hannay, M. P. ed. As her whimsey took her p78-90

Donadio, S. L. Emerson, Christian identity, and the dissolution of the social order. *In* Art, politics, and will p99-123

Donahue, C. Potlatch and charity: notes on the heroic in Beowulf. *In* Anglo-Saxon poetry: essays in appreciation p23-40

Duhamel, P. A. The novelist as prophet. *In* Friedman, M. J. and Lawson, L. A. eds. The added dimension p88-107

Gilman, E. B. The Pauline perspectives in Donne, Herbert, and Greville. *In* Gilman, E. B. The curious perspective p167-203

Goldsmith, M. E. The enigma of The husband's message. *In* Anglo-Saxon poetry: essays in appreciation p242-63

Gordon, C. An American girl. *In* Friedman, M. J. and Lawson, L. A. eds. The added dimension p123-37

Harris, J. C. Christian form and Christian meaning in Halldórs þáttr I. *In* The Learned and the lewed p249-64

Hoffman, F. J. The search for redemption: Flannery O'Connor's fiction. *In* Friedman, M. J. and Lawson, L. A. eds. The added dimension p32-48

Howard, D. R. Renaissance world-alienation. *In* The Darker vision of the Renaissance p47-76

Kunkel, F. L. Conclusion. *In* Kunkel, F. L. Passion and the Passion p169-83

Kunkel, F. L. Jean Genet: counterfeit saint. *In* Kunkel, F. L. Passion and the Passion p108-28

Kunkel, F. L. John Updike: between heaven and earth. *In* Kunkel, F. L. Passion and the Passion p75-98

Kunkel, F. L. The sexy Cross. *In* Kunkel, F. L. Passion and the Passion p157-68

Kunkel, F. L. Wrestlers with Christ and Cupid. *In* Kunkel, F. L. Passion and the Passion p129-56

Kurz, P. K. Fences and camps. *In* Kurz, P. K. On modern German literature v3 p95-127

MacMillan, D. J. His 'magnum o': stoic humanism in Faulkner's A fable. *In* The Stoic strain in American literature p136-76

Malin, I. Flannery O'Connor and the grotesque. *In* Friedman, M. J. and Lawson, L. A. eds. The added dimension p108-22

Manlove, C. N. Milton. *In* Manlove, C. N. Literature and reality, 1600-1800 p30-56

Manlove, C. N. Swift. *In* Manlove, C. N. Literature and reality, 1600-1800 p114-24

Morley, P. A. 'In God's name': ironic forms of religious drama in Canada and Australia. *In* Narasimhaiah, C. D. ed. Awakened conscience p275-83

Nolan, B. Pearl: a fourteenth-century vision in August. *In* Nolan, B. The Gothic visionary perspective p156-204

Nolan, B. Will's dark visions of Piers the Plowman. *In* Nolan, B. The Gothic visionary perspective p205-58

Poggioli, R. The Christian pastoral. *In* Poggioli, R. The oaten flute p105-34

Quinn, M. B. Flannery O'Connor, a realist of distances. *In* Friedman, M. J. and Lawson, L. A. eds. The added dimension p157-83

Rahv, P. The legend of the Grand Inquisitor. *In* Rahv, P. Essays on literature and politics, 1932-1972 p129-48

Rahv, P. The other Dostoevsky. *In* Rahv, P. Essays on literature and politics, 1932-1972 p186-207

Rubin, L. D. Flannery O'Connor and the Bible Belt. *In* Friedman, M. J. and Lawson, L. A. eds. The added dimension p49-72

Scott, N. A. Flannery O'Connor's testimony: the pressure of glory. *In* Friedman, M. J. and Lawson, L. A. eds. The added dimension p138-56

Sellin, P. R. The hidden God: Reformation awe in Renaissance English literature. *In* The Darker vision of the Renaissance p147-96

Shaffer, E. S. Hölderlin's 'Patmos' ode and 'Kubla Khan': mythological doubling. *In* Shaffer, E. S. 'Kubla Khan' and The fall of Jerusalem p145-90

Tixier, E. Imagination baptized, or "Holiness" in the chronicles of Narnia. *In* Schakel, P. J. ed. The longing for a form p136-58

Zogby, E. G. Triadic patterns in Lewis's life and thought. *In* Schakel, P. J. ed. The longing for a form p20-39

Christians in Europe, Eastern

History

Fischer-Galati, S. A. Judeo-Christian aspects of Pax Ottomanica. *In* Király, B. K. ed. Tolerance and movements of religious dissent in Eastern Europe p185-97

Christiansen, Drew

Blind prophets and quick-witted kings. *In* Bundy, R. F. ed. Images of the future: the twenty-first century and beyond p45-53

Christiansen, Karl O.

Seriousness of criminality and concordance among Danish twins. *In* Crime, criminology and public policy p63-77

Christie, Dame Agatha (Miller)

About

Cawelti, J. G. The art of the classical detective story. *In* Cawelti, J. G. Adventure, mystery, and romance p106-38

Fremlin, C. The Christie everybody knew. *In* Agatha Christie: first lady of crime p111-20

Gilbert, M. F. A very English lady. *In* Agatha Christie: first lady of crime p49-78

Hughes, D. B. F. The Christie nobody knew. *In* Agatha Christie: first lady of crime p121-30

Lathen, E. pseud. Cornwallis's revenge. *In* Agatha Christie: first lady of crime p79-94

Panek, L. L. Agatha Christie. *In* Panek, L. L. Watteau's shepherds: the detective novel in Britain, 1914-1940 p38-63

Symons, J. The mistress of complication. *In* Agatha Christie: first lady of crime p25-38

Trewin, J. C. A Midas gift to the theatre. *In* Agatha Christie: first lady of crime p131-54

Walter, E. The case of the escalating sales. *In* Agatha Christie: first lady of crime p11-24

Christie, Dame Agatha M.—About—*Cont.*

Watson, C. The message of Mayhem Parva. *In* Agatha Christie: first lady of crime p95-110

Weaver, W. T. Music and mystery. *In* Agatha Christie: first lady of crime p183-92

About individual works
The mysterious affair at Styles

Grossvogel, D. I. Agatha Christie: containment of the unknown. *In* Grossvogel, D. I. Mystery and its fictions: from Oedipus to Agatha Christie p39-52

Characters—Hercule Poirot

Keating, H. R. F. Hercule Poirot—a companion portrait. *In* Agatha Christie: first lady of crime p205-16

Characters—Miss Marple

Lewis, M. C. Miss Marple—a portrait. *In* Agatha Christie: first lady of crime p193-204

Film adaptations

Jenkinson, P. The Agatha Christie films. *In* Agatha Christie: first lady of crime p155-82

Christie, Nils

Utility and social values in court decisions on punishment. *In* Crime, criminology and public policy p281-96

Christine de Pizan. See Pisan, Christine de

Christmas, Peter

Little Dorrit: the end of good and evil. *In* Dickens Studies Annual v6 p134-53

Christmas

Chambers, A. B. Christmas: the liturgy of the Church and English verse of the Renaissance. *In* Literary monographs v6 p109-53

Fiction
See Christmas stories

Poetry

Chambers, A. B. Christmas: the liturgy of the Church and English verse of the Renaissance. *In* Literary monographs v6 p109-53

Florida

White, E. B. What do our hearts treasure? *In* White, E. B. Essays of E. B. White p150-53

Christmas poetry. See Christmas—Poetry

Christmas stories

History and criticism

Prickett, S. Christmas at Scrooge's. *In* Prickett, S. Victorian fantasy p38-74

Christology. See Jesus Christ

Christopher, Saint

Art

Frinta, M. S. A statue of St. Christopher at the M. H. de Young Memorial Museum at San Francisco. *In* Enggass, R. C. and Stokstad, M. eds. Hortus imaginum p57-63

Christopher, Joe R.

Archetypal patterns in Till we have faces. *In* Schakel, P. J. ed. The longing for a form p193-212

Christopher, Thomas W.

The role of leadership. *In* The Rising South v2 p48-69

Christopherson, Lois K. and Gonda, Thomas Andrew

Organ transplantation. *In* Anticipatory grief p107-14

Chromatic aberration (Optics) See Achromatism

Chronology. See Calendar; Clocks and watches

Chronology, Ecclesiastical. See Church calendar

Chronology, Historical

North, J. D. Chronology and the age of the world. *In* Cosmology, history, and theology p307-33

See also Calendar; History Ancient—Chronology

Chronometry, Mental. See Time perception

Chrysippus, the Stoic

About

Long, A. A. Dialectic and the Stoic sage. *In* Rist, J. M. ed. The Stoics p101-24

Reesor, M. E. Necessity and fate in Stoic philosophy. *In* Rist, J. M. ed. The Stoics p187-202

Chrysostom, Saint, Patriarch of Constantinople. See Chrysostomus, Joannes, Saint, Patriarch of Constantinople

Chrysostomus, Joannes, Saint, Patriarch of Constantinople

About

Osborn, E. F. John Chrysostom. *In* Osborn, E. F. Ethical patterns in early Christian thought p114-42

Ch'u, Ch'iu-pai

About

Pickowicz, P. G. Qu Qiubai's critique of the May Fourth generation: early Chinese Marxist literary criticism. *In* Modern Chinese literature in the May Fourth era p351-84

Widmer, E. Qu Qiubai and Russian literature. *In* Modern Chinese literature in the May Fourth era p103-25

Chu, Godwin Chien

Bibliography of the works of Wilbur Schramm. *In* Lerner, D. and Nelson, L. M. eds. Communication research—a half-century appraisal p331-40

Popular media: a glimpse of the new Chinese culture. *In* Chu, G. C. ed. Popular media in China p1-15

Problems of cross-cultural communication research. *In* Fischer, H. D. and Merrill, J. C. eds. International and intercultural communication p435-42

Chu, Godwin Chien, and Cheng, Philip H.

Revolutionary opera: an instrument for cultural change. *In* Chu, G. C. ed. Popular media in China p73-103

Chu, Godwin Chien, and Chin, Ai-li

Cultural processes in China: continuity and change. *In* Chu, G. C. ed. Popular media in China p222-48

Chu, Hsi

About

Araki, K. Confucianism and Buddhism in the late Ming. *In* The Unfolding of Neo-Confucianism p39-66

Ch'u, Jên-huo

About individual works
Sui Tang yen-i

Hegel, R. G. Sui T'ang yen-i and the aesthetics of the seventeenth-century Suchou elite. *In* Chinese narrative p124-59

Chu, Leonard L.
Sabers and swords for the Chinese children, revolutionary children's folk songs. *In* Chu, G. C. ed. Popular media in China p16-50

Chu, Pao-chin
V. K. Wellington Koo: the diplomacy of nationalism. *In* Burns, R. D. and Bennett, E. M. eds. Diplomats in crisis p125-51

Chu-hung, 1535-1615

About

Greenblatt, K. Y. Chu-hung and lay Buddhism in the late Ming. *In* The Unfolding of Neo-Confucianism p93-140

Chuang-tzŭ

About

Rubin, V. A. Nature against civilization *In* Rubin, V. A. Individual and state in ancient China p89-114

Chuangtse. See Chuang-tzŭ

Chudacoff, Howard P.
New branches on the tree.: household structure in early stages of the family cycle in Worcester, Massachusetts, 1860-1880. *In* American Antiquarian Society. Proceedings v86 pt2 p303-20

Chukovskaía, Lidiía Korneevna
Breakthrough. *In* Dunlop, J. B. Haugh, R. and Klimoff, R. eds. Aleksandr Solzhenitsyn: critical essays and documentary materials 2d ed. p456-57

Chukovskiĭ, Korneĭ Ivanovich

About

Ørvig, M. A Russian view of childhood: the contribution of Kornei I. Chukovsky (1882-1969). *In* Horn Book Magazine. Crosscurrents of criticism p261-74

Chukovsky, Kornei Ivanovich. See Chukovskiĭ, Korneĭ Ivanovich

Chün-i T'ang. See Tang, Chün-i

Chung-kuo kung ch'an tang. See Communist Party of China

Chung-kuo kuo min tang
Domes, J. The model for revolutionary people's war: the Communist takeover of China. *In* Hammond, T. T. ed. The anatomy of Communist takeovers p516-33
Eastman, L. E. The Kuomintang in the 1930s. *In* The Limits of change p191-210
Kindermann, G. K. The attempted revolution in China: the first Sino-Soviet alliance, 1924-1927. *In* Hammond, T. T. ed. The anatomy of Communist takeovers p192-213

Church, Benjamin

About individual works

The entertaining history of King Philip's war, which began in the month of June, 1775

Seelye, J. Providential passages: wherein a matron, a minister, a militiaman, and a madam display the cardinal points of the Puritan compass. *In* Seelye, J. Prophetic waters p279-309

Church, Frank
Arms, energy, and the atom: the lethal dilemma. *In* World change and world security p159-66

Church, Margaret
Kafka and Proust: a contrast in time. *In* Garvin, H. R. ed. Makers of the twentieth-century novel p149-53

A portrait and Giambattista Vico: a source study. *In* Staley, T. F. and Benstock, B. eds. Approaches to Joyce's Portrait p77-88

Church, Robert Le Valley
Economists as experts: the rise of an academic profession in the United States, 1870-1920. *In* The University in society v2 p571-609

Church, William Farr
France. *In* National consciousness, history, and political culture in early-modern Europe p43-66

Church
See also Christianity

Infallibility
See Popes—Infallibility

Church administration. See Church management

Church and college

United States

Hesburgh, T. M. The challenges of Christian higher education. *In* Hesburgh, T. M. The Hesburgh papers p51-61
Hesburgh, T. M. New focus for Catholic higher education in the 1970s. *In* Hesburgh, T. M. The Hesburgh papers p83-88

Church and education

France

Mitchell, H. The world between the literate and oral traditions in eighteenth-century France: ecclesiastical instruction and popular mentalities. *In* Studies in eighteenth-century culture v8 p33-67

Church and homosexuality. See Homosexuality and Christianity

Church and international affairs. See Christianity and international affairs

Church and international organization
Ricoeur, P. From nation to humanity: task of Christians. *In* Ricoeur, P. Political and social essays p134-59

Church and labor

United States

Gutman, H. G. Protestantism and the American labor movement: the Christian spirit in the Gilded Age. *In* Mulder, J. M. and Wilson, J. F. eds. Religion in American history p318-41

Church and slavery. See Slavery and the church

Church and social problems
Couch, B. M. New visions of the Church in Latin America: a Protestant view. *In* The Emergent gospel p193-226
See also Abortion—Religious aspects—Catholic Church; Church and international organization; Liberation theology; Population policy—Moral and religious aspects; Sociology, Christian

Catholic Church

Russo, N. J. From Mezzogiorno to metropolis: Brooklyn's new Italian immigrants. *In* Studies in Italian American social history p118-31

New York (City)

Russo, N. J. From Mezzogiorno to metropolis: Brooklyn's new Italian immigrants. *In* Studies in Italian American social history p118-31

Church and social problems—*Continued*

San Francisco Bay Region—
Protestant churches

Wolfe, J. Three congregations. *In* The New religious consciousness p227-44

United States

Bedau, H. A. Compensatory justice and the Black Manifesto. *In* The Abdication of philosophy: philosophy and the public good p175-94

Church and society. See Church and the world

Church and state

Ricoeur, P. Ye are the salt of the earth. *In* Ricoeur, P. Political and social essays p105-24

See also Anti-clericalism; Christianity and politics; Church and international organization; Nationalism and religion; Patronage, Ecclesiastical; Popes—Temporal power; Religion and state; Religious education—Law and legislation; Religious liberty; Secularization

Catholic Church

Chinnici, J. P. New religious movements and the structure of religious sensibility. *In* Needleman, J. and Baker, G. eds. Understanding the new religions p26-33

See also Church and state in Europe; Church and state in France; and similar headings

Church of England

See Church and state in Great Britain

History

McCready, W. D. Papalists and anti-papalists: aspects of the Church/state controversy in the later Middle Ages. *In* Viator: medieval and Renaissance studies v6 p241-73

Church and state in Bohemia

Fousek, M. S. On secular authority and military service among the Bohemian Brethren in the 16th and early 17th centuries. *In* Király, B. K. ed. Tolerance and movements of religious dissent in Eastern Europe p53-64

Heymann, F. G. The role of the Bohemian cities during and after the Hussite revolution. *In* Király, B. K. ed. Tolerance and movements of religious dissent in Eastern Europe p27-41

Church and state in England. See Church and state in Great Britain

Church and state in Europe

Blumenthal, U. R. Patrimonia and regalia in 1111. *In* Law, church, and society p9-20

Church and state in France

McManners, J. Jansenism and politics in the eighteenth century. *In* Church, society and politics p253-73

Church and state in Germany

Benecke, G. The German Reichskirche. *In* Callahan, W. J. and Higgs, D. eds. Church and society in Catholic Europe of the eighteenth century p77-87

1933-1945

Rees, O. G. The Barmen Declaration (May 1934) *In* Church, society and politics p405-17

Robbins, K. Church and politics: Dorothy Buxton and the German church struggle. *In* Church, society and politics p419-33

Church and state in Great Britain

McNab, B. Obligations of the Church in English society: military arrays of the clergy, 1369-1418. *In* Order and innovation in the Middle Ages p293-314

Rack, H. D. 'Christ's Kingdom not of this world:' the case of Benjamin Hoadly versus William Law reconsidered. *In* Church, society and politics p275-91

Zinberg, C. The usable dissenting past: John Strype and Elizabethan Puritanism. *In* The Dissenting tradition p123-39

See also Church of England—Bishops—Temporal power; Church of England—Establishment and disestablishment; Puritans

History

Curtis, M. H. The trials of a Puritan in Jacobean Lancashire. *In* The Dissenting tradition p78-99

Church and state in Hungary

Király, B. K. The Hungarian church. *In* Callahan, W. J. and Higgs, D. eds. Church and society in Catholic Europe of the eighteenth century p106-21

Király, B. K. Protestantism in Hungary between the Revolution and the Ausgleich. *In* Király, B. K. ed. Tolerance and movements of religious dissent in Eastern Europe p65-85

Church and state in Russia

1917-

Barabanov, E. The schism between the Church and the world. *In* From under the rubble p172-93

Church and state in Scotland

Buckroyd, J. The Resolutioners and the Scottish nobility in the early months of 1660. *In* Church, society and politics p245-52

Church and state in the United States

Burkholder, J. R. "The law knows no heresy": marginal religious movements and the courts. *In* Zaretsky, I. I. and Leone, M. P. eds. Religious movements in contemporary America p27-50

Marty, M. E. Of darters and schools and clergymen: the religion clauses worse confounded. *In* The Supreme Court review, 1978 p171-90

Williams, G. H. and Petersen, R. L. Evangelicals: society, the state, the nation. *In* Wells, D. F. and Woodbridge, J. D. eds. The evangelicals p211-48

History

Hanley, T. O. Church/state relations in the American Revolutionary era. *In* America in theological perspective p87-98

Pfeffer, L. The legitimation of marginal religions in the United States. *In* Zaretsky, I. I. and Leone, M. P. eds. Religious movements in contemporary America p9-26

Church and state in Wales. See Church in Wales—Establishment and disestablishment

Church and the world

Barabanov, E. The schism between the Church and the world. *In* From under the rubble p172-93

Boulding, E. Religion, futurism, and models of social change. *In* Bundy, R. F. ed. Images of the future: the twenty-first century and beyond p169-81

Churches
See also Church architecture; names of individual churches, e.g. Seville. La Caridad (Church); and subdivision Churches under names of cities

Administration
See Church management

Fund raising
See Church fund raising

Management
See Church management

Italy—Florence
Sunderland, E. R. The system of proportion of Filippo Brunelleschi. *In* Enggass, R. C. and Stokstad, M. eds. Hortus imaginum p65-72

Turkey—Dăg Pazari
Gough, M. Dăg Pazari. The basilical church 'extra muros.' *In* Studies in memory of David Talbot Rice p147-63

Churches, Afro-American. See Afro-American churches

Churches, City. See City churches

Churches, Town. See City churches
Churches, Urban. See City churches

Churchill, Frederick B.
Sex and the single organism: biological theories of sexuality in mid-nineteenth century. *In* Studies in history of biology v3 p139-77

Churchill, Sir Winston Leonard Spencer

About
Addison, P. Journey to the centre: Churchill and Labour in coalition, 1940-5. *In* Crisis and controversy p165-93

Ch'u tz'ŭ
Hawkes, D. The quest of the goddess. *In* Birch, C. ed. Studies in Chinese literary genres p42-68

Chyzhevs'kyĭ, Dmytro
About Gogol's "Overcoat". *In* Maguire, R. A. ed. Gogol from the twentieth century p293-322

Ciano, Galeazzo, conte

About
Gilbert, F. Ciano and his ambassadors. *In* Gilbert, F. History p351-76

Ciappelletto, Ser
Benton, J. F. The accounts of Cepperello da Prato for the tax on nouveaux acquêts in the bailliage of Troyes. *In* Order and innovation in the Middle Ages p111-35

Ciardi, John
Kenneth Patchen: poetry, and poetry with jazz. *In* Morgan, R. G. ed. Kenneth Patchen: a collection of essays p29-30

Cibber, Colley

About individual works
An apology for his life
Spacks, P. A. M. The sense of audience: Samuel Richardson, Colley Cibber. *In* Spacks, P. A. M. Imagining a self p193-226

The double gallant: or, The sick lady's cure
Bruton, J. W. The text of Colley Cibber's The double gallant: or, The sick lady's cure. *In* Virginia. University. Bibliographical Society. Studies in bibliography v30 p186-96

The refusal
Hayley, R. L. The "swingeing" of Cibber: the suppression of the first edition of The refusal. *In* Virginia. University. Bibliographical Society. Studies in bibliography v28 p290-97

Criticism, Textual
Bruton, J. W. The text of Colley Cibber's The double gallant: or, The sick lady's cure. *In* Virginia. University. Bibliographical Society. Studies in bibliography v30 p186-96

Cibola
Allen, J. L. Lands of myth, waters of wonder: the place of the imagination in the history of geographical exploration. *In* Geographies of the mind p41-61

Cicada (Greek Anacreontic poem)
Dihle, A. The poem on the cicada. *In* Harvard Studies in classical philology v71 p107-13

Cicero, Marcus Tullius

About
Borowitz, A. M. Tullius Cicero for the defense. *In* Borowitz, A. Innocence and arsenic p100-15

Gruen, E. S. Cicero and Licinius Calvus. *In* Harvard Studies in classical philology v71 p215-33

Zetzel, J. E. G. Cicero and the Scipionic Circle. *In* Harvard Studies in classical philology v76 p173-79

About individual works
Ad Herennium
Ward, J. O. The commentator's rhetoric: from antiquity to the Renaissance: glosses and commentaries on Cicero's Rhetorica. *In* Murphy, J. J. ed. Medieval eloquence p25-67

De inventione
Ward, J. O. The commentator's rhetoric, from antiquity to the Renaissance: glosses and commentaries on Cicero's Rhetorica. *In* Murphy, J. J. ed. Medieval eloquence p25-67

De officiis
De Lacy, P. H. The four Stoic personae. *In* Illinois classical studies, v2 1977 p163-72

The dream of Scipio
Baker-Smith, D. Juan Vives and the Somnium Scipionis. *In* Classical influences on European culture A.D. 1500-1700 p239-44

Chronology
Linderski, J. The aedileship of Favonius, Curio the Younger and Cicero's election to the augurate. *In* Harvard Studies in classical philology v76 p181-200

Influence—Vives
Baker-Smith, D. Juan Vives and the Somnium Scipionis. *In* Classical influences on European culture A.D. 1500-1700 p239-44

Political science
Wilhelmsen, F. D. Cicero and the politics of the public orthodoxy. *In* Wilhelmsen, F. D. Christianity and political philosophy p25-59

Wilhelmsen, F. D. and Kendall, W. Cicero and the politics of the public orthodoxy. *In* A Public philosophy reader p112-41

Religion
Wilhelmsen, F. D. Cicero and the politics of the public orthodoxy. *In* Wilhelmsen, F. D. Christianity and political philosophy p25-59

Cicero, Marcus T.—Religion—*Continued*
Wilhelmsen, F. D. and Kendall, W. Cicero and the politics of the public orthodoxy. *In* A Public philosophy reader p112-41

Ciceronianism
Phillips, M. M. From the Ciceronianus to Montaigne. *In* Classical influences on European culture A.D. 1500-1700 p191-97

Cicognani, Bruno
About
Pacifici, S. Three writers in search of the novel. *In* Pacifici, S. The modern Italian novel: from Pea to Moravia p18-46

Cicourel, Aaron Victor
About
Lemert, C. C. Ethnomethodology: Aaron Cicourel. *In* Lemert, C. C. Sociology and the twilight of man p165-93

El Cid Campeador
Simmons, M. E. The Spanish epic. *In* Oinas, F. J. ed. Heroic epic and saga p216-35

Cimon
About
Cole, J. R. The Oresteia and Cimon. *In* Harvard Studies in classical philology v81 p99-111

Cinema. See Moving-pictures

Cinematography
Place, J. A. and Peterson, L. S. Some visual motifs of film noir. *In* Nichols, B. ed. Movies and methods p325-38

Cingalese. See Sinhalese

Cintio, Giovanni Battista Giraldi. See Giraldi Cintio, Giovanni Battista

Cioffi, Frank
Intention and interpretation in criticism. *In* Margolis, J. Z. ed. Philosophy looks at the arts p307-24
Also in On literary intention p55-73

Cioran, Samuel David
A prism for the absolute: the symbolic colors of Andrey Bely. *In* Janecek, G. ed. Andrey Bely p103-14

Cipolla, Carlo M.
A plague doctor. *In* The Medieval city p65-72

Circulation, Pulmonary. See Pulmonary circulation

Circus
Bouissac, P. Semiotics and spectacles: the circus institution and representations. *In* Sebeok, T. A. ed. A perfusion of signs p143-52

Florida
White, E. B. The ring of time. *In* White, E. B. Essays of E. B. White p142-49

Circus performers. See Clowns

Čišinski, Jakub, pseud. See Bart, Jakub

Cismaru, Alfred
Molière's presence in selected plays of Marivaux. *In* Johnson, R. B.; Neumann, E. S. and Trail, G. T. eds. Molière and the commonwealth of letters: patrimony and posterity p68-81

Citara. See Cithara

Cithara
History
Winternitz, E. The survival of the kithara and the evolution of the English cittern: a study in morphology. *In* Winternitz, E. Musical instruments and their symbolism in Western art p57-65

Cithern
History
Winternitz, E. The survival of the kithara and the evolution of the English cittern: a study in morphology. *In* Winternitz, E. Musical instruments and their symbolism in Western art p57-65

Cities, Imaginary. See Geographical myths

Cities and towns
Dubos, R. J. Cities old and new. *In* Dubos, R. J. Beast or angel? p77-82
See also Community; Education, Urban; Sociology, Urban; Urbanization

Civic improvement
See Urban renewal

Economic aspects
See Urban economics

Growth
Ward, D. The early Victorian city in England and America: on the parallel development of an urban image. *In* European settlement and development in North America: essays on geographical change in honour and memory of Andrew Hill Clark p170-89
See also Land subdivision; Metropolitan areas; Residential mobility

History
Thrupp, S. L. The city as the idea of social order. *In* Thrupp, S. L. Society and history p89-100
Thrupp, S. L. The creativity of cities. *In* Thrupp, S. L. Society and history p212-25

Planning
See City planning

Africa
Aradeon, D. Using local resources. *In* Strategies for human settlements: habitat and environment p106-14

Bohemia—History
Heymann, F. G. The role of the Bohemian cities during and after the Hussite revolution. *In* Király, B. K. ed. Tolerance and movements of religious dissent in Eastern Europe p27-41

Brazil—History
Morse, R. M. Brazil's urban development: colony and empire. *In* From colony to nation p155-81

Cairo
Abū-Lughd, J. The legitimacy of comparisons in comparative urban studies: a theoretical position and an application to North African cities. *In* Walton, J. and Masotti, L. H. eds. The city in comparative perspective p17-39

China—History
Elvin, M. Chinese cities since the Sung Dynasty. *In* Towns in societies p79-89

England—History
Phythian-Adams, C. Urban decay in late medieval England. *In* Towns in societies p159-85

Cities and towns, Medieval

Hibbert, A. B. The origins of the medieval town patriciate. *In* Towns in societies p91-104

Kearney, M. E. Regensburg burgher factions and the failure of the Swabian Town League in 1389. *In* Viator: medieval and Renaissance studies v6 p275-94

Langer, L. N. The medieval Russian town. *In* Hamm, M. F. ed. The city in Russian history p11-33

Prawer, J. Crusader cities. *In* The Medieval city p179-99

Thrupp, S. L. Social control in the medieval town. *In* Thrupp, S. L. Society and history p9-24

History

Hammond, M. The emergence of mediaeval towns: independence or continuity? *In* Harvard Studies in classical philology v78 p 1-33

England

Phythian-Adams, C. Urban decay in late medieval England. *In* Towns in societies p159-85

Italy—Genoa

Hughes, D. O. Urban growth and family structure in medieval Genoa. *In* Towns in societies p105-30

Cities and towns, Movement to. See Cities and towns—Growth; Rural urban migration; Urbanization

Cities and town, Muslim. See Cities and towns, Islamic

Cities and towns, Renaissance

Florence

Herlihy, D. The distribution of wealth in a Renaissance community: Florence 1427. *In* Towns in societies p131-57

Cities and towns, Ruined, extinct, etc.

Asia Minor

Hanfmann, G. M. A. Ad claras Asiae volemus urbes: Roman governors and urban renewal. *In* Hanfmann, G. M. A. From Croesus to Constantine p41-56

Hanfmann, G. M. A. Hellenization takes command. *In* Hanfmann, G. M. A. From Croesus to Constantine p22-40

Hanfmann, G. M. A. Sardis, Croesus, and the Persians. *In* Hanfmann, G. M. A. From Croesus to Constantine p1-21

Cities and towns in art

Taylor, W. R. Psyching out the city. *In* Uprooted Americans p245-87

Cities and towns in literature

Alter, R. The modernist revival of self-conscious fiction. *In* Alter, R. Partial magic p138-79

Alter, R. The self-conscious novel in eclipse. *In* Alter, R. Partial magic p84-137

Donaldson, S. and Massa, A. City and country. *In* Donaldson, S. and Massa, A. American literature: nineteenth and early twentieth centuries p47-80

Fisher, P. J. City matters: city minds. *In* The Worlds of Victorian fiction p371-89

Goist, P. D. Afterword. *In* Goist, P. D. From Main Street to State Street p159-64

Goist, P. D. The city and the middle border: Hamlin Garland. *In* Goist, P. D. From Main Street to State Street p59-67

Goist, P. D. The city as noncommunity: Theodore Dreiser and Henry Blake Fuller. *In* Goist, P. D. From Main Street to State Street p68-79

Goist, P. D. The ideal questioned but not abandoned: Sherwood Anderson, Sinclair Lewis, and Floyd Dell. *In* Goist, P. D. From Main Street to State Street p21-34

Goist, P. D. The town as ideal community: Booth Tarkington and Zona Gale. *In* Goist, P. D. From Main Street to State Street p13-20

Holman, C. H. Anodyne for the village virus. *In* Holman, C. H. Windows on the world p48-60

Rawson, C. J. The nightmares of Strephon: nymphs of the city in the poems of Swift, Baudelaire, Eliot. *In* English literature in the age of disguise p57-97

Sarotte, G. M. The circumstances of the homosexual as reflected in the novel and theater: Small town and big city. *In* Sarotte, G. M. Like a brother, like a lover p153-63

Ward, N. 'Fourmillante cité': Baudelaire and 'The waste land.' *In* The Waste land in different voices p87-104

Weitzman, A. J. Dr. Johnson's philurbanism. *In* Aeolian harps p95-109

Citizen Kane (Motion picture)

Bordwell, D. Citizen Kane. *In* Nichols, B. ed. Movies and methods p273-90

Murray, E. Citizen Kane. *In* Murray, E Ten film classics p18-32

Truffaut, F. Orson Wells: Citizen Kane: the fragile giant. *In* Truffaut, F. The films in my life p278-85

Citizen participation. See subdivision Citizen participation under specific subjects, e.g. Environmental policy—Citizen participation; Research—Citizen participation

Citizen suits (Civil procedure)

Halpern, C. R. The public interest bar: an audit. *In* Nader, R. and Green, M. J. eds. Verdicts on lawyers p158-71

See also Class actions (Civil procedure)

Citizens band radio

United States

Pollman, J. CB radio as icon. *In* Browne, R. B. and Fishwick, M. W. eds. Icons of America p161-76

Citizen's defender. See Ombudsman

Citizens radio service. See Citizens band radio

Citizenship

Post, G. Philosophy and citizenship in the thirteenth-century—laicisation, the two laws and Aristotle. *In* Order and innovation in the Middle Ages p401-08

Tassi, A. Communitas and polis. *In* Roth, R. J. ed. Person and community p133-40

See also Civics; Naturalization; Patriotism

Italy

Riesenberg, P. N. Citizenship at law in late medieval Italy. *In* Viator: medieval and Renaissance studies v5 p333-46

City and town life

Dubos, R. J. Life in the city. *In* Dubos, R. J. Beast or angel? p92-102

Foramitti, H. and Piperek, M. Anxieties of city dwellers. *In* United Nations Educational, Scientific and Cultural Organization. The conservation of cities p43-56

Religious aspects

See Cities and towns—United States—Religious life

City planning—Russia—*Continued*

Starr, S. F. The revival and schism of urban planning in twentieth-century Russia. *In* Hamm, M. F. ed. The city in Russian history p222-42

Starr, S. F. Visionary town planning during the cultural revolution. *In* Cultural revolution in Russia, 1928-1931 p207-40

Sardis

Hanfmann, G. M. A. Sardis, Croesus, and the Persians. *In* Hanfmann, G. M. A. From Croesus to Constantine p1-21

Tunisia

Kafi, J. el. Tunisia: hopes for the medina of Tunis. *In* United Nations Educational, Scientific and Cultural Organization. The conservation of cities p125-39

United States

Bowden, M. J. Persistence, failure, and mobility in the inner city: preliminary notes. *In* Pattern and process p169-92

Choldin, H. M. Social life and the physical environment. *In* Handbook of contemporary urban life p352-84

Goist, P. D. Planning the American city: Charles Mulford Robinson and John Nolen. *In* Goist, P. D. From Main Street to State Street p121-42

Goist, P. D Regionalism and community: the urbanism of Lewis Mumford. *In* Goist, P. D. From Main Street to State Street p143-57

Tunnard, C. The United States: federal funds for rescue. *In* United Nations Educational, Scientific and Cultural Organization. The conservation of cities p81-106

United States—History

Reps, J. W. Bonanza towns: urban planning on the Western mining frontier. *In* Pattern and process p271-89

City schools. See Urban schools

City-states, Nationalism and the patriotism of. Minogue, K. R. *In* Smith, A. D. ed. Nationalist movements p54-73

Civic planning. See City planning

Civics

Bay, C. Education for citizenship. *In* Fairfield, R. P. ed. Humanistic frontiers in American education p148-55

Horwitz, R. H. John Locke and the preservation of liberty: a perennial problem of civic education. *In* The Moral foundations of the American Republic p129-56

Niemeyer, G. The commitments of political education. *In* A Public philosophy reader p246-56

See also Civil rights; Patriotism; Political ethics

Civics, American. See Civics

Civil disobedience. See Government, Resistance to

Civil engineering

See also Structural engineering

Study and teaching

See Engineering—Study and teaching

Civil government. See Political science

Civil law

History

Strayer, J. R. The rule of law. *In* Aspects of American liberty p16-36

England—History

Stein, P. Vacarius and the civil law. *In* Church and government in the Middle Ages p119-37

Civil law (Islamic law) See Islamic law

Civil liberty. See Liberty

Civil-military relations. See Civil supremacy over the military

Civil procedure

Scott, K. E. Two models of the civil process. *In* Stanford legal essays p413-26

See also Class actions (Civil procedure); Judgments; Jury

Civil religion. See Religion and culture

Civil rights

Arendt, H. Public rights and private interests: in response to Charles Frankel. *In* Small comforts for hard times p103-08

Aron, R. Sociology and the philosophy of human rights. *In* Aron, R. Politics and history p122-38

Bedau, H. A. Free speech, the right to listen, and disruptive interference. *In* The Concept of academic freedom p191-211

Benn, S. I. Human rights—for whom and for what? *In* Human rights p59-73

Claude, R. P. Comparative rights research: some intersections between law and the social sciences. *In* Claude, R. P. ed. Comparative human rights p382-407

Frankel, C. Private rights and the public good. *In* Small comforts for hard times p87-102

Garment, L. Majoritarianism at the United Nations and human rights. *In* Sidorsky, D. ed. Essays on human rights p30-36

Hauser, R. E. A. A First World view. *In* Kommers, D. P. and Loescher, G. D. eds. Human rights and American foreign policy p85-89

Hauser, R. E. A. International human-rights protection: the dream and the deceptions. *In* Sidorsky, D. ed. Essays on human rights p21-29

Henkin, L. Human rights: reappraisal and readjustment. *In* Sidorsky, D. ed. Essays on human rights p68-87

Jonathan, G. C. and Jacqué, J. P. Obligations assumed by the Helsinki signatories. *In* Human rights, international law and the Helsinki Accord p43-70

Kamenka, E. The anatomy of an idea. *In* Human rights p 1-12

Kleinig, J. Human rights, legal rights and social change. *In* Human rights p36-47

Konvitz, M. R. From Jewish rights to human rights. *In* Konvitz, M. R. Judaism and the American idea p161-80

Konvitz, M. R. Human dignity: from creation to Consitution. *In* Konvitz, M. R. Judaism and the American idea p33-51

Laqueur, W. Z. The issue of human rights. *In* Sidorsky D. ed. Essays on human rights p5-20

Leary, V. The implementation of the human rights provisions of the Helsinki Final Act: a preliminary assessment: 1975-1977. *In* Human rights, international law and the Helsinki Accord p111-60

Liskofsky, S. The United Nations and human rights: "alternative approaches." *In* Sidorsky, D. ed. Essays on human rights p46-67

Civil rights—*Continued*

Robertson, A. H. Human rights: a global assessment. *In* Kommers, D. P. and Loescher, G. D. eds. Human rights and American foreign policy p5-28

Schneider, H. W. Declaration, theory, and existence of human rights. *In* The Abdication of philosophy: philosophy and the public good p89-92

Sidorsky, D. Contemporary reinterpretations of the concept of human rights. *In* Sidorsky, D. ed. Essays on human rights p88-109

Stourzh, G. The American Revolution, modern constitutionalism, and the protection of human rights. *In* [Truth and tragedy]: a tribute to Hans Morgenthau p162-76

Strouse, J. C. and Claude, R. P. Empirical comparative rights research: some preliminary tests of development hypotheses. *In* Claude, R. P. ed. Comparative human rights p51-67

Tay, A. Erh Soon. Marxism, socialism and human rights. *In* Human rights p104-12

Van Dyke, V. The individual, the state, and ethnic communities in political theory. *In* Kommers, D. P. and Loescher, G. D. eds. Human rights and American foreign policy p36-62

Wellman, C. A new conception of human rights. *In* Human rights p48-58

Whitaker, B. C. G. Minority rights and self-determination. *In* Kommers, D. P. and Loescher, G. D. eds. Human rights and American foreign policy p63-76

See also Children's rights; Due process of law; Equality before th law; Freedom of association; Freedom of information; Jews —Legal status, laws, etc; Liberty; Liberty of speech; Natural law; Religious liberty; Right of property; Right to counsel; Searches and seizures; Speedy trial; Teaching, Freedom of

Bibliography

Sigler, J. A. Research resources on comparative rights policies. *In* Claude, R. P. ed. Comparative human rights p286-94

History

Claude, R. P. The classical model of human rights development. *In* Claude, R. P. ed. Comparative human rights p6-50

Public opinion

Devall, W. B. Social science research on support of human rights. *In* Claude, R. P. ed. Comparative human rights p326-52

Gallatin, J. E. The conceptualization of rights: psychological development and cross-national perspectives. *In* Claude, R. P. ed. Comparative human rights p302-25

America

Wood, B. Human rights and the inter-American system. *In* Farer, T. J. ed. The future of the inter-American system p119-52

China

Li, V. M. Human rights in a Chinese context. *In* Terrill, R. ed. The China difference p219-35

Europe

Wenner, M. W. The politics of equality among European linguistic minorities. *In* Claude, R. P. ed. Comparative human rights p184-213

Gaza Strip

Shestack, J. J. Human-rights issues in Israel's rule of the West Bank and Gaza. *In* Sidorsky, D. ed. Essays on human rights p193-209

Jordan (Territory under Israeli occupation, 1967-)

Shestack, J. J. Human-rights issues in Israel's rule of the West Bank and Gaza. *In* Sidorsky, D. ed. Essays on human rights p193-209

Russia

Dinstein, Y. Soviet Jewry and international human rights. *In* Sidorsky, D. ed. Essays on human rights p126-43

Litvinov, P. M. The human-rights movement in the Soviet Union. *In* Sidorsky, D. ed. Essays on human rights p113-25

Reddaway, P. B. Theory and practice of human rights in the Soviet Union. *In* Kommers, D. P. and Loescher, G. D. eds. Human rights and American foreign policy p115-29

Underdeveloped areas

See Underdeveloped areas—Civil rights

United States

Auerbach, J. S. The Depression decade. *In* The Pulse of freedom p65-104

Caughey, J. W. McCarthyism rampant. *In* The Pulse of freedom p154-210

Doar, J. Civil rights and self-government. *In* The National purpose reconsidered p97-118

Fellman, D. The nationalization of American civil liberties. *In* Essays on the Constitution of the United States p49-60

Freund, P. A. Liberty and law in America. *In* The American Revolution: a continuing commitment p3-11

Glasser, I. Prisoners of benevolence: power versus liberty in the welfare state. *In* Doing good p97-170

Glazer, N. Individual rights against group rights. *In* Human rights p87-103

Jackson, M. Broad societal changes. *In* Lauer, R. H. ed. Social movement and social change p190-96

Konvitz, M. R. The flower and the thorn. *In* The Pulse of freedom p211-80

Laue, J. H. Unanticipated change. *In* Lauer, R. H. ed. Social movements and social change p190-96

Murphy, P. L. "Certain unalienable rights." *In* Alderson, W. T. ed. American issues p33-48

Murphy, P. L. Communities in conflict. *In* The Pulse of freedom p23-64

Preston, W. Shadows of war and fear. *In* The Pulse of freedom p105-53

Reitman, A. Past, present, and future. *In* The Pulse of freedom p281-342

Skolnick, J. H. Changing civil rights through law: can it be done? *In* Major social issues p141-48

Wyzanski, C. E. The rights of man. *In* Warner, S. B. ed. The American experiment p39-52

See also Afro-Americans—Civil rights

Civil rights (International law)

Auerbach, C. A. Freedom of movement in international law and United States policy. *In* Human migration p317-35

Buergenthal, T. International Human Rights Law and the Helsinki Final Act: conclusions. *In* Human rights, international law and the Helsinki Accord p 3-10

Civil rights (International law)—*Continued*

Cohen, R. Human rights decision-making in the executive branch: some proposals for a coordinated strategy. *In* Kommers, D. P. and Loescher, G. D. eds. Human rights and American foreign policy p216-46

Fraser, D. M. Congress's role in the making of international human rights policy. *In* Kommers, D. P. and Loescher, G. D. eds. Human rights and American foreign policy p247-54

Henkin, L. Human rights and "domestic jurisdiction." *In* Human rights, international law and the Helsinki Accord p21-40

Lillich, R. B. A United States policy of humanitarian intervention and intercession. *In* Kommers, D. P. and Loescher, G. D. eds. Human rights and American foreign policy p278-98

Robertson, A. H. The Helsinki Agreement and human rights. *In* Kommers, D. P. and Loescher, G. D. eds. Human rights and American foreign policy p130-48

Rodley, N. S. Monitoring human rights by the U.N. system and nongovernmental organizations. *In* Kommers, D. P. and Loescher, G. D. eds. Human rights and American foreign policy p157-78

Starke, J. G. Human rights and international law. *In* Human rights p113-31

Wiseberg, L. S. and Scoble, H. M. Monitoring human rights violations: the role of nongovernmental organizations. *In* Kommers, D. P. and Loescher, G. D. eds. Human rights and American foreign policy p179-208

Bibliography

Sigler, J. A. research resources on comparative rights policies. *In* Claude, R. P. ed. Comparative human rights p286-94

Civil rights (Jewish law)

Brichto, H. C. The Hebrew Bible on human rights. *In* Sidorsky, D. ed. Essays on human rights p215-33

Daube, D. The rabbis and Philo on human rights. *In* Sidorsky, D. ed. Essays on human rights p234-46

Goitein, S. D. Human rights in Jewish thought and life in the Middle Ages. *In* Sidorsky, D. ed. Essays on human rights p247-64

Konvitz, M. R. Human dignity: from creation to Constitution. *In* Konvitz, M. R. Judaism and the American idea p33-51

Civil Rights Act of 1964. See United States. Laws, statutes, etc. Civil Rights Act of 1964

Civil service

See also Bureaucracy

Great Britain—History

Beloff, M. The Whitehall factor: the role of the higher civil service, 1919-39. *In* Peele, G. and Cook, C. eds. The politics of reappraisal, 1918-1939 p209-31

Fischer, W. and Lundgreen, P. The recruitment and training of administrative and technical personnel. *In* Tilly, C. ed. The formation of national states in Western Europe p456-561

Russia—History

Lincoln, W. B. The daily life of St Petersburg officials in the mid nineteenth century. *In* Oxford Slavonic papers new ser v8 p82-100

United States—States

Murphy, T. P. Urban governmental manpower. *In* Murphy, T. P. ed. Universities in the urban crisis p49-70

Civil service interns. See Interns (Civil service)

Civil service reform. See Patronage, Political

Civil supremacy over the military

United States

Sherman, E. F. Accountability and responsiveness of the military establishment. *In* Rieselbach, L. N. ed. People vs. government: the responsiveness of American institutions p226-73

Civil war

Novogrod, J. C. Internal strife, self-determination, and world order. *In* International terrorism and political crimes p98-119

United States

See United States—History—Civil War, 1861-1865

Civilian Conservation Corps. See United States—Civilian Conservation Corps

Civilian control of the military. See Civil supremacy over the military

Civility, The culture of. Becker, H. S. and Horowitz, I. L. *In* Henslin, J. M. ed. Deviant life-styles p337-48

Civilization

See also Culture; Education; Ethics; Ethnology; Humanism; Personality and culture; Popular culture; Progress; Religion and culture; Renaissance; Social evolution; Society, Primitive; Technology and civilization

Historiography

Burke, P. Tradition and experience: the idea of decline from Bruni to Gibbon. *In* Edward Gibbon and The decline and fall of the Roman Empire p87-102

History

Dubos, R. J. The incarnations of humankind. *In* Dubos, R. J. Beast or angel? p150-60

Goodall, V. M. Setting the scene. *In* Goodall, V. M. Setting the scene. *In* Goodall, V. M. Setting the scene. *In* Goodall, V. M.

Highet, G. The class of '64. *In* Highet, G. The immortal profession p133-44

See also Civilization, Modern

Philosophy

Cassirer, E. Critical idealism as a philosophy of culture. *In* Cassirer, E. Symbol, myth, and culture p64-91

Frye, N. Total identification. *In* Frye, N. Northrop Frye on culture and literature p107-10

See also Man (Philosophy); Philosophical anthropology; Regression (Civilization)

Civillization, Aegean. See Minoans

Civilization, African

Chittick, H. N. The peopling of the East African coast. *In* Chittick, H. N. and Rotberg, R. I. eds. East Africa and the Orient p16-43

Grottanelli, V. L. The peopling of the Horn of Africa. *In* Chittick, H. N. and Rotberg, R. I. eds. East Africa and the Orient p44-75

Trimingham, J. S. The Arab geographers and the East African coast. *In* Chittick, H. N. and Rotberg, R. I. eds. East Africa and the Orient p115-46

Civilization, Modern—*Continued*

Glicksberg, C. I. Religion and nihilism. *In* Glicksberg, C. I. The literature of nihilism p39-52

Sennett, R. Destructive Gemeinschaft. *In* Beyond the crisis p171-97

See also Detribalization; Renaissance

17th century

Wilkes, J. W. The transformation of dissent: a review of the change from the seventeenth to the eighteenth centuries. *In* The Dissenting tradition p108-22

18th century

Lyons, J. O. Out of the void. *In* Lyons, J. O. The invention of the self p 1-17

Payne, H. C. Elite versus popular mentality in the eighteenth century. *In* Studies in eighteenth-century culture v8 p3-32

18th century—Study and teaching

Wiles, R. M. The ivory tower, new style. *In* Studies in eighteenth-century culture v4 p3-11

19th century

Brown, R. D. Modernization: a Victorian climax. *In* Howe, D. W. ed. Victorian America p29-44

Mandel'shtam, O E. The nineteenth century. *In* Mandel'shtam, O. E. Selected essays p94-100

20th century

Barfield, A. O. The coming trauma of materialism. *In* Barfield, A. O. The rediscovery of meaning, and other essays p187-200

Caldwell, L. K. 1992: threshold of the postmodern world. *In* A Time to hear and answer: essays for the Bicentennial season p175-218

Canetti, E. Realism and new reality. *In* Canetti, E. The conscience of words p55-59

Chiaromonte, N. Modern tyranny. *In* Chiaromonte, N. The worm of consciousness, and other essays p208-35

Connolly, C. The twenties. *In* Connolly, C. The evening colonnade p5-7

Fackenheim, E. L. The human condition after Auschwitz: a Jewish testimony a generation after. *In* Tradition and change in Jewish experience p226-43

Graff, G. The myth of the postmodern breakthrough. *In* Graff, G. Literature against itself p31-62

Hamburg, D. A. Ancient man in the twentieth century. *In* Goodall, V. M. ed. The quest for man p27-54

Holbrook, D. Poetry has lost confidence in itself. *In* Holbrook, D. Lost bearings in English poetry p11-24

Jaberg, R. L. Search for a center. *In* America in theological perspective p230-46

Jones, D. Notes on the 1930s. *In* Jones, D. The dying Gaul, and other writings p41-49

Kellogg, G. Simultaneity and contemporary cultural history. *In* Kellogg, G. Dark prophets of hope p157-77

Koestler, A. A glance through the keyhole *In* Koestler, A. Janus p274-86

Koestler, A. Prologue: the new calendar. *In* Koestler, A. Janus p 1-20

Koestler, A. Rebellion in a vacuum. *In* Koestler, A. The heel of Achilles p20-32

Koestler, A. The urge to self-destruction. *In* Koestler, A. The heel of Achilles p3-19

Kunitz, S. J. A kind of order. *In* Kunitz, S. J. A kind of order, a kind of folly p3-13

Lidz, V. M. Secularization, ethical life, and religion in modern societies. *In* Johnson, H. M. ed. Religious change and continuity p191-217

McGill, A. C. Structures of inhumanity. *In* Disguises of the demonic p116-33

Mead, M. The transforming power of culture. *In* Hanna, T. ed. Explorers of humankind 140-47

O'Neill, J. Violence, technology, and the body politic. *In* Stanage, S. M. ed. Reason and violence p5-26

Russell, B. R. 3d Earl. The duty of a philosopher in this age. *In* The Abdication of philosophy: philosophy and the public good p15-22

Werkmeister, W. H. Reflections on our times. *In* The Abdication of philosophy: philosophy and the public good p243-49

Wolman, B. B. The anticulture of suicide. *In* Wolman, B. B. ed. Between survival and suicide p77-94

1950-

Agursky, M. Contemporary socioeconomic systems and their future prospects. *In* From under the rubble p67-87

Dreitzel, H. P. On the political meaning of culture. *In* Beyond the crisis p83-129

Hassan, I. H. The new Gnosticism: speculations on an aspect of the postmodern mind. *In* Hassan, I. H. Paracriticisms p121-47

Mihajlov, M. The shoots of hope. *In* Mihajlov, M. Underground notes p13-18

Mihajlov, M. Two convergences. *In* Mihajlov, M. Underground notes p 1-5

Moscivici, S. The reenchantment of the world. *In* Beyond the crisis p133-68

Peckham, M. The cultural crisis of the 1970s. *In* Peckham, M. Romanticism and behavior p362-79

Solzhenifsyn, A. I. As breathing and consciousness return. *In* From under the rubble p3-25

Touraine, A. Crisis or transformation? *In* Beyond the crisis p17-45

Touraine, A. Introduction. *In* Beyond the crisis p 3-13

Civilization, Muslim. See Civilization, Islamic

Civilization, Occidental

Ellul, J. Search for an image. *In* Bundy, R. F. ed. Images of the future: the twenty-first century and beyond p24-34

Hsu, Francis Lang Kwang. Passage to understanding. *In* Spindler, G. D. ed. The making of psychological anthropology p142-73

Scharfstein, B. A. Three philosophical civilizations: a preliminary comparison. *In* Philosophy East/philosophy West p48-127

History

Downs, R. B. Ideas in the flow of civilization. *In* Downs, R. B. Books that changed the world p 1-25

Near Eastern influences

Wickens, G. M. What the West borrowed from the Middle East. *In* Savory, R. M. ed. Introduction to Islamic civilisation p120-25

Civilization, Pre-Columbian. See Indians—Culture

Civilization, Spanish. See Civilization, Hispanic

Civilization, Western. See Civilization, Occidental

Civilization and computers. See Computers and civilization

Civilization and machinery. See Technology and civilization

Civilization and personality. See Personality and culture

Civilization and science. See Science and civilization

Civilization and technology. See Technology and civilization

Čiževskij, Dmitri. See Chyzhevs'kyĭ, Dmytro

Claire's knee (Motion picture)
Kauffmann, S. Claire's knee. In Kauffmann, S. Living images p45-48

Clairmont, Christoph W.
The lekythos of Myrrhine. In Studies in classical art and archaeology p103-10

Clairvoyance
Baldwin, H. W. Conceptualizations of experimental clairvoyance. In Ludwig, J. K. ed. Philosophy and parapsychology p255-62
Price, H. H. Some philosophical questions about telepathy and clairvoyance. In Wheatley, J. M. O. and Edge, H. L. eds. Philosophical dimensions of parapsychology p105-32
See also Extrasensory perception; Second sight; Thought-transference; Trance

Clandestine literature. See Underground literature

Clans and clan system
See also Kinship; Tribes and tribal system

Senegal
Cruise O'Brien, D. B. Clan, community, nation: dimensions of political loyalty in Senegal. In Smock, D. R. and Bentsi-Enchill, K. eds. The search for national integration in Africa p255-69

Somalia
Lewis, I. M. The nation, state, and politics in Somalia. In Smock, D. R. and Bentsi-Enchill, K. eds. The search for national integration in Africa p285-306

Clapp, Priscilla
U.S. domestic politics and relations with Japan. In Clapp, P. and Halperin, M. H. eds. United States-Japanese relations, the 1970's p35-57

Clapp, Priscilla and Halperin, Morton H.
U.S. elite images of Japan: the postwar period. In Iriye, A. ed. Mutual images p202-22

Clare, John

About individual works
Poems, chiefly from manuscript
Blunden, E. C. Biographical introduction to John Clare: poems chiefly from manuscript. In Praise from famous men: an anthology of introductions p19-44

Clarenbach, Kathryn F.
Women in legal perspective. In Roberts, J. I. ed. Beyond intellectual sexism p231-40

Clareson, Thomas D.
Clifford D. Simak: the inhabited universe. In Clareson, T. D. ed. Voices for the future: essays on major science fiction writers v 1 p64-87

The cosmic loneliness of Arthur C. Clarke. In Clareson, T. D. ed. Voices for the future: essays on major science fiction writers v 1 p216-37

The fictions of Robert Silverberg. In Clareson, T. D. ed. Voices for the future: essays on major science fiction writers v2 p 1-33

Lost lands, lost races: a pagan princess of their very own. In Clareson, T. D. ed. Many futures, many worlds p117-39

Many futures, many worlds. In Clareson, T. D. ed. Many futures, many worlds p14-26

Claridge, Amanda. See Strong, D. E. jt. auth.

Clark, Andrew Hill
First things first. In Pattern and process p9-21

About
Meinig, D. W. Prologue: Andrew Hill Clark, historical geographer. In European settlement and development in North America: essays on geographical change in honour and memory of Andrew Hill Clark p3-26

Warkentin, J. Epilogue. In European settlement and development in North America: essays on geographical change in honour and memory of Andrew Hill Clark p208-20

Clark, Christine Philpot
Young Black Americans. In The Black American reference book p378-409

Clark, Eve V.
From gesture to word: on the natural history of deixis in language acquisition. In Human growth and development p85-120

Clark, Harry Hayden. See Part 2 under title: Literature and ideas in America

Clark, Hewitt Blystone. See Risley, T. R. jt. auth.

Clark, John Goodrich

About
Harvey, A. M. Early contributions to the surgery of cancer: William S. Halsted, Hugh H. Young, and John G. Clark. In Harvey, A. M. Adventures in medical research p69-83

Clark, John Pepper

About individual works
Song of a goat
Soyinka, W. Drama and the African worldview. In Exile and tradition p173-90

Clark, John R. See Motto, A. L. jt. auth.

Clark, Katerina
Little heroes and big deeds: literature responds to the First Five-Year Plan. In Cultural revolution in Russia, 1928-1931 p189-206

Utopian anthropology as a context for Stalinist literature. In Stalinism p180-98

Clark, Kenneth Bancroft
The American revolution: democratic politics and popular education. In America's continuing revolution p295-306

Everyday life and social identity. In Smithsonian Institution. The cultural drama p183-95

The impact of a personality. In From Parnassus p337-41

Clark, L. D.
The making of a novel: the search for the definitive text of D. H. Lawrence's "The plumed serpent." In Voices from the Southwest p113-30

Clark, Leslie
Brunch on Moon River. *In* Peary, G. and Shatzkin, R. eds. The modern American novel and the movies p236-46

Clark, Margaret Macdonald
Language and reading: research trends. *In* Davies, A. ed. Problems of language and learning p89-112

Clark, Norman H.
Notes for a tricentennial historian. *In* Bingham, E. R. and Love, G. A. eds. Northwest perspectives p44-58

Clark, Peter
The ownership of books in England, 1560-1640: the example of some Kentish townsfolk. *In* Schooling and society p95-111

Clark, Priscilla Parkhurst, and Clark, Terry Nichols
Patrons, publishers, and prizes: the writer's estate in France. *In* Culture and its creators p197-225

Clark, R. C.
Union-management conflict in a Japanese company. *In* Modern Japan p209-26

Clark, Ramsey
Crisis at Justice. *In* Nader, R. and Green, M. J. eds. Verdicts on lawyers p218-30

Clark, Romane L.
Considerations for a logic for naive realism. *In* Studies in perception p525-56

Facts, fact-correlates, and fact-surrogates. *In* Fact, value, and perception p3-17

Ontology and the philosophy of mind in Sellars' critique of Russell. *In* Nakhnikian, G. ed. Bertrand Russell's philosophy p101-16

Clark, Ronald William

About individual works
The life of Bertrand Russell
Mudrick, M. Agèd eagles and dirty old men. *In* Mudrick, M. Books are not life but then what is? p132-42

Clark, Ted
The oppression of youth; excerpt. *In* Gross, B. and Gross, R. eds. The children's rights movement p158-65

Clark, Terry Nichols. See Clark, P. P. jt. auth.

Clarke, Arthur Charles
Son of Dr Strangelove; or, How I learned to stop worrying and love Stanley Kubrick; excerpt from "Report on Planet Three and other speculations." *In* Knight, D. F. ed. Turning points p277-84

Technology and the limits of knowledge. *In* The Frontiers of knowledge p117-40
Also in Technology and the frontiers of knowledge p111-34

About
Clareson, T. D. The cosmic loneliness of Arthur C. Clarke. *In* Clareson, T. D. ed. Voices for the future: essays on major science fiction writers v 1 p216-37

Clarke, A. C. Son of Dr Strangelove; or, How I learned to stop worrying and love Stanley Kubrick; excerpt from "Report on Planet Three and other speculations." *In* Knight, D. F. ed. Turning points p277-84

Clarke, Austin
Reminiscences of Yeats: glimpses of W. B. Yeats. *In* Yeats, Joyce, and Beckett p46-51

Clarke, John Clem

About
Marandel, J. P. The deductive image. *In* Battcock, G. ed. Super realism p36-48

Clarke, John Henrik
Black Americans: immigrants against their will. *In* The Immigrant experience in America p172-91

Clarke, John Henrik, ed.

About individual works
William Styron's Nat Turner: ten Black writers respond
Gross, S. L. and Bender, E. History, politics, and literature: the myth of Nat Turner. *In* Morris, R. K. and Malin, I. eds. The achievement of William Styron p168-207

Clarke, John J.
Mysticism and the paradox of survival. *In* Donnelly, J. P. ed. Language, metaphysics, and death p216-27

Clarke, Kenneth W.
Jesse Stuart's use of folklore. *In* LeMaster, J. R. and Clarke, M. W. eds. Jesse Stuart p117-29

Clarke, Marcus Andrew Hislop

About
Wilding, M. The short stories of Marcus Clarke. *In* Bards, bohemians, and bookmen p72-97

About individual works
For the term of his natural life
Hergenhan, L. T. English publication of Australian novels in the nineteenth century: the case of His natural life. *In* Bards, bohemians, and bookmen p56-71

Holiday peak and other tales
Wilding, M. The short stories of Marcus Clarke. *In* Bards, bohemians, and bookmen p72-97

Clarke, Mary Washington
Jesse Stuart's educational saga as humanistic affirmation. *In* LeMaster, J. R. and Clarke, M. W. eds. Jesse Stuart p130-48

Clarke, Robert L.
Some sources in the National Archives for studies of Afro-American population: growth and movement. *In* Pattern and process p73-80

Clarke, William Norris
Interpersonal dialogue: key to realism. *In* Roth, R. J. ed. Person and community p141-53

Class actions (Civil procedure)
Moore, B. C. and Harris, F. R. Class actions: let the people in. *In* Nader, R. and Green, M. J. eds. Verdicts on lawyers p172-84

United States
Dam, K. W. Class action notice: who needs it? *In* The Supreme Court review, 1974 p97-126

Class conflict. See Social conflict

Class distinction. See Social classes

Classes (Mathematics) See Set theory

Classes, Social. See Social classes

Classical antiquities. See Art, Greek; Numismatics, Greek; Numismatics, Roman; Pottery, Greek; Pottery Roman

Classical art. See Art, Classical

Classical drama. See Greek drama

Classical drama (Comedy)
History and criticism
Sandbach, F. H. Drama at Rome. *In* Sandbach, F. H. The comic theatre of Greece and Rome p103-17

Classical education
Voegelin, E. On classical studies. *In* A Public philosophy reader p257-65

See also Education, Humanistic; Humanism; Humanities

Classical epic poetry. See Epic poetry, Classical

Classical field theory. See Field theory (Physics)

Classical geography
Mathew, G. The dating and the significance of the Periplus of the Erythrean Sea. *In* Chittick, H. N. and Rotberg, R. I. eds. East Africa and the Orient p147-63

Classical letters. See Latin letters

Classical literature
Eliot, T. S. What is a classic? *In* Eliot, T. S. Selected prose of T. S. Eliot p115-31
See also Latin literature

Appreciation
Levi, A. H. T. Erasmus, the early Jesuits and the classics. *In* Classical influences on European culture A.D. 1500-1700 p223-38

Appreciation—Great Britain
Anderson, W. D. Arnold and the classics. *In* Allott, K. ed. Matthew Arnold p259-85

History and criticism
Littlewood, A. R. The symbolism of the apple in Greek and Roman literature. *In* Harvard Studies in classical philology v72 p147-81

Romilly, J. de. Logic versus magic: Aristotle and later writers. *In* Romilly, J. de. Magic and rhetoric in ancient Greece p67-88

Sayre, R. F. Antiquity and the Middle Ages. *In* Sayre, R. F. Solitude in society p13-33

Influence
Braden, G. Herrick's classical quotations. *In* Rollin, R. B. and Patrick, J. M. eds. "Trust to good verses": Herrick tercentenary essays p127-47

Classical marble sculpture. See Marble sculpture, Classical

Classical world, Structure, inversion, and game in Shakespeare's. Erlich, B. S. *In* Shakespeare survey v31 p53-63

Classicism
Baeumer, M. L. Simplicity and grandeur: Winckelmann, French classicism, and Jefferson. *In* Studies in eighteenth-century culture v7 p63-78

Edelman, N. The eye of the beholder: reflections on classical order. *In* Edelman, N. The eye of the beholder p154-58

Nicoll, A. French romanticism and classicism. *In* Nicoll, A. World drama p154-60
See also Neoclassicism (Literature)

Classicism in art. See Neoclassicism (Art)

Classification
See also Classification of sciences
Botany
See Botany—Classification

Classification (Psychology) See Categorization (Psychology)

Classification of sciences
Medawar, Sir P. B. A geometric model of reduction and emergence. *In* Ayala, F. J. and Dobzhansky, T. G. eds. Studies in the philosophy of biology p57-63

Weisheipl, J. A. The nature, scope, and classification of the sciences. *In* Lindberg, D. C. ed. Science in the Middle Ages p461-82

Classroom management
O'Dwyer, J. P. Classroom collage: one perspective. *In* Parents, teachers, and children: prospects for choice in American education p37-58

Claude, Inis Lothair
Domestic jurisdiction and colonialism. *In* Kilson, M. ed. New states in the modern world p121-35

International organization. *In* Encyclopedia of American foreign policy p473-81

The problem of evaluating war. *In* New dimensions of world politics p109-26

Claude, Richard P.
The classical model of human rights development. *In* Claude, R. P. ed. Comparative human rights p6-50

Comparative rights research: some intersections between law and the social sciences. *In* Claude, R. P. ed. Comparative human rights p382-407

The Supreme Court Nine: judicial responsibility and responsiveness. *In* Rieselbach, L. N. ed. People vs. government: the responsiveness of American institutions p119-50

See also Strouse, J. C. jt. auth.

Claudel, Paul
About
Peyre, H. Claudel and the French literary tradition. *In* Peyre, H. French literary imagination and Dostoevsky, and other essays p115-37

Robinson, C. Collective values. *In* Robinson, C. French literature in the nineteenth century p171-206

Schwarz, A. The purgation of the will: tragic theater in the Christian tradition. *In* Schwarz, A. From Büchner to Beckett p223-60

Claudianus, Claudius
Criticism, Textual
Luck, G. Disiecta membra: on the arrangement of Claudian's Carmina minora. *In* Illinois classical studies v4, 1979 p200-13

Claudius Pulcher, Publius. See Clodius Pulcher, Publius

Clausen, Alden Winship
The future of our freedom-based economy. *In* Prochnow, H. V. ed. Dilemmas facing the nation p32-40

Clausen, Wendell
Catullus and Callimachus. *In* Harvard Studies in classical philology v74 p85-94

Duellum. *In* Harvard Studies in classical philology v75 p69-72

On the date of the First Eclogue. *In* Harvard Studies in classical philology v76 p201-05

Clausen, Wendell Vernon
Ariadne's leave-taking: Catullus 64:116-20. *In* Illinois classical studies, v2 1977 p219-23

Juvenal and Virgil. *In* Harvard Studies in classical philology v80 p181-86

Clemens, Samuel L.—About individual works
—*Continued*

*Some learned fables for good
old boys and girls*

Baetzhold, H. G. Mark Twain on scientific investigation: contemporary allusions in "Some learned fables for good old boys and girls." *In* Literature and ideas in America p128-54

Bibliography

Budd, L. J. Mark Twain. *In* American literary scholarship, 1976 p79-91
Hill, H. L. Mark Twain. *In* American literary scholarship, 1973 p99-115
Hill, H. L. Mark Twain [another essay] *In* American literary scholarship, 1974 p75-85
Hill, H. L. Mark Twain [another essay] *In* American literary scholarship, 1975 p103-14

Books and reading

Gribben, A. "I detest novels, poetry & theology": origin of a fiction concerning Mark Twain's reading. *In* Tennessee Studies in literature v22 p154-61

Characters—Huckleberry Finn

Towers, T. H. Love and power in Huckleberry Finn. *In* Tulane Studies in English, v23 p17-37

Clemens, Titus Flavius Alexandrinus

About

Osborn, E. F. Clement of Alexandria. *In* Osborn, E. F. Ethical patterns in early Christian thought p50-83

Clément, René

About individual works
Knave of hearts

Truffaut, F. René Clément: Monsieur Ripois. *In* Truffaut, F. The films in my life p197-200

Clement of Alexandria. See Clemens, Titus Flavius Alexandrinus

Clergy

See also Benefices, Ecclesiastical; Catholic Church—Clergy; Patronage, Ecclesiastical and subdivision Clergy under church denominations, e.g. Catholic Church in France —Clergy

France—Dauphiné—Political activity

Tackett, T. N. The citizen priest: politics and ideology among the parish clergy of eighteenth century Dauphiné. *In* Studies in eighteenth century culture v7 p307-28

Clergy in literature

Howe, I. Treacheries of faith. *In* Howe, I. Celebrations and attacks p102-08
Kurz, P. K. The priest in the modern novel. *In* Kurz, P. K. On modern German literature v4 p129-50
Sayre, R. F. Journal d'un curé de campagne: the saint's Gethsemane. *In* Sayre, R. F. Solitude in society p133-54
Steadman, J. M. The Faerie Queene: Una and the clergy. *In* Steadman, J. M. Nature into myth p131-37
Vargo, E. P. Struggling with a bugaboo: the priest-character in Achebe and Greene and Keneally. *In* Narasimhaiah, C. D. ed. Awakened conscience p284-93

Cleveland, Harlan

America's not-so-manifest destiny. *In* The American Revolution: a continuing commitment p67-88

Words and meanings. *In* The Abdication of philosophy: philosophy and the public good p237-42

Clézio, Jean Marie Gustave, Le. See Le Clézio, Jean Marie Gustave

Clienetela. See Patron and client

Clifford, Clark McAdams

Has America lost her way? A retrospect on Mr. Truman. *In* The Korean War p237-43

Clifford, Isabelle M.

Comprehensive planning for care and the home health agency. *In* Home care p223-31

Clifford, James Lowry

"Hanging up looking glasses at odd corners": ethnobiographical prospects. *In* Studies in biography p41-56
Johnson's first club. *In* Evidence in literary scholarship p197-213

Clignet, Remi

The impact of educational structures and processes on national integration in Cameroon. *In* Smock, D. R. and Bentsi-Enchill, K. eds. The search for national integration in Africa p139-58

Clignet, Remi, and Sween, Joyce A.

Some prerequisites for the planning of modernization processes. *In* African themes p113-47

Climacus, Joannes, Saint. See Joannes Climacus, Saint

Climate. See Climatology

Climate, Influence of. See Man—Influence of climate

Climatology

Historiography

Le Roy Ladurie, E. The history of rain and fine weather. *In* Le Roy Ladurie, E. The territory of the historian p293-319
Le Roy Ladurie, E. Writing the history of the climate. *In* Le Roy Ladurie, E. The territory of the historian p287-91

Clinard, Marshall Barron, and Abbott, Daniel J.

Community organization and property crime: a comparative study of social control in the slums of an African city. *In* Delinquency, crime, and society p186-206

Cline, Ray S.

The two-China dilemma. *In* Pacific Asia and U.S. policies: a political-economic-strategic assessment p49-57

Clinical medicine. See Medicine, Clinical

Clinton, Richard L.

Population dynamics and future prospects for development. *In* Orr, D. W. and Soroos, M. S. eds. The global predicament p56-74

Clive, John

English "Cliographers": a preliminary inquiry. *In* Studies in biography p27-39
Gibbon's humor. *In* Edward Gibbon and The decline and fall of the Roman Empire p183-91

Clô, Alberto. See Prodi, R. jt. auth.

Clock paradox. See Time dilatation

A clockwork orange (Motion picture)
Kauffmann, S. Living images p88-90

Clocks and watches

Salmon, W. C. Clocks and simultaneity in special relativity or, which twin has the Timex? *In* Motion and time, space and matter p508-45

See also Time clocks

Clocks and watches in art

Macey, S. L. Hogarth and the iconography of time. *In* Studies in eighteenth-century culture v5 p41-53

A clockwork orange (Motion picture)

Elsaesser, T. Screen violence: emotional structure and ideological function in 'A clockwork orange.' *In* Bigsby, C. W. E. ed. Approaches to popular culture p171-200

Kauffmann, S. A clockwork orange. *In* Samuels, C. T. The context of A clockwork orange. *In* Samuels, C. T. Mastering the film, and other essays p171-78

Clodius Pulcher, Publius

About

Wiseman, T. P. Pulcher Claudius. *In* Harvard Studies in classical philology v74 p207-21

Clogan, Paul Maurice

Chaucer and Leigh Hunt. *In* Medievalia et humanistica; new ser. no. 9 p163-74

Literary criticism in William Godwin's Life of Chaucer. *In* Medievalia et humanistica no. 6 p189-98

The narrative style of The man of law's tale. *In* Medievalia et humanistica no. 8 p217-33

The textual reliability of Chaucer's lyrics: A complaint to his lady. *In* Medievalia et humanistica no. 5 p183-89

Two verse commentaries on the ending of Boccaccio's Filostrato. *In* Medievalia et humanistica no. 7 p147-52

Clonal selection theory

Edelman, G. M. The problem of molecular recognition by a selective system. *In* Ayala, F. J. and Dobzhansky, T. G. eds. Studies in the philosophy of biology p45-56

Cloning

Thomas, L. On cloning a human being. *In* Thomas, L. The medusa and the snail p51-56

Clopinel de Meun, Jean. See Jean de Meun

Clopper, Lawrence M.

Langland's Trinitarian analogies as key to meaning and structure. *In* Medievalia et humanistica; new ser. no. 9 p87-110

Close, Anthony J.

Don Quixote and the 'intentionalist fallacy.' *In* On literary intention p174-93

Close, Charles. See Close, Chuck

Close, Chuck

About

Dyckes, W. The photo as subject: the painting and drawings of Chuck Close. *In* Battcock, G. ed. Super realism p145-62

Closed-circuit television. See Television in education

Cloth. See Textile industry and fabrics

Clothing and dress. See Costume; Fashion

Clough, Arthur Hugh

About

Dawson, C. Dramatic elegists: Arnold, Clough, and Browning at mid-century. *In* Dawson, C. Victorian noon p63-104

Hardy, B. N. Clough's self-consciousness. *In* Hardy, B. N. The advantage of lyric p33-53

About individual works

Amours de voyage

Ball, P. M. 'The fates, it is clear, are against us.' *In* Ball, P. M. The heart's events p32-57

The bothie of Tober-na-Vuolich

Ball, P. M. 'To marry her and take her home.' *In* Ball, P. M. The heart's events p167-221

Contemporaries

See Clough, Arthur Hugh—Friends and associates

Friends and associates

Bertram, J. M. Arnold and Clough. *In* Allott, K. ed. Matthew Arnold p178-206

Clough, Ralph Nelson

The Taiwan issue in Sino-American relations. *In* China and America p149-95

Cloutier, Edouard. See Brazeau, J. jt. auth.

Clouzot, Henri-Georges

About individual works

The mystery of Picasso

Truffaut, F. Henri-Georges Clouzot: Le mystère Picasso. *In* Truffaut, F. The films in my life p201-03

Clowning. See Clowns

Clowns

Bouissac, P. A semiotic approach to nonsense: clowns and limericks. *In* Sebeok, T. A. ed. Sight, sound, and sense p244-63

Peacock, J. L. Symbolic reversal and social history: transvestites and clowns of Java. *In* Babcock, B. A. ed. The reversible world p209-24

Clowns (in religion, folk-lore, etc.)

Steward, J. H. The ceremonial buffoon of the American Indian. *In* Steward, J. H. Evolution and ecology p347-65

Tedlock, B. The clown's way. *In* Tedlock, D. E. and Tedlock, B. eds. Teachings from the American earth p105-18

The clowns (Motion picture)

Kauffmann, S. The clowns. *In* Kauffmann, S. Living images p59-61

Clowns in literature

Butwin, J. The paradox of the clown in Dickens. *In* Dickens Studies Annual v5 p115-32

Clubb, Louise George

Italian Renaissance comedy. *In* Ruggiers, P. G. ed. Versions of medieval comedy p191-210

Woman as wonder: a generic figure in Italian and Shakespearean comedy. *In* Studies in the continental background of Renaissance English literature: essays presented to John L. Lievsay p109-32

Clubbe, John

Carlyle on Sartor resartus. *In* Fielding, K. J. and Tarr, R. L. eds. Carlyle past and present p51-60

Charles Richard Sanders. *In* Carlyle and his contemporaries pxiii-xxiii

Grecian destiny: Froude's portraits of the Carlyles. *In* Carlyle and his contemporaries p317-53

Cluentius, Aulus Habitus

About

Borowitz, A. M. Tullius Cicero for the defense. *In* Borowitz, A. Innocence and arsenic p100-15

Clune, William H.

The Supreme Court's treatment of wealth discriminations under the Fourteeenth Amendment. *In* The Supreme Court review, 1975 p289-354

Cluniacs

Constable, G. Cluniac administration and administrators in the twelfth century. *In* Order and innovation in the Middle Ages p17-30

Cluny, Order of. See Cluniacs

Coady, Robert J.

About

Tashjian, D. L. The Soil and Contact. *In* Tashjian, D. L. Skyscraper primitives p71-90

Coakley, James Francis

Time and tide on the Camino Real. *In* Tennessee Williams: a tribute p232-36

Coal

United States

Gordon, R. L. Coal—the swing fuel. *In* Kalter, R. J. and Vogely, W. A. eds. Energy supply and government policy p193-215

Coal-miners

United States

Corbin, D. A. Mine mules and coal tipples: icons of the coalfields. *In* Browne, R. B. and Fishwick, M. W. eds. Icons of America p253-62

Coal mines and mining

United States

Corbin, D. A. Mine mules and coal tipples: icons of the coalfields. *In* Browne, R. B. and Fishwick, M. W. eds. Icons of America p253-62

Coasts. See Territorial waters

Coates, John

'The choice of Hercules' in 'Antony and Cleopatra'. *In* Shakespeare survey v31 p45-52

Coates, Robert Myron

About

Cowley, M. Figure in a crowd. *In* Cowley, M.—And I worked at the writer's trade p81-94

About individual works
Yesterday's burdens

Cowley, M. Figure in a crowd. *In* Cowley, M.—And I worked at the writer's trade 94

Coates, Wells

About

Richards, J. M. Wells Coates, 1893-1958. *In* Sharp, D. ed. The rationalists p93-99

Coats, Alfred William

Adam Smith and the mercantile system. *In* Skinner, A. S. and Wilson, T. eds. Essays on Adam Smith p218-36

Clarence Ayres's place in the history of American economics: an interim assessment. *In* Science and ceremony p23-48

Cobb, Martha K.

Afro-Arabs, Blackamoors and Blacks: an inquiry into race concepts through Spanish literature. *In* DeCosta, M. ed. Blacks in Hispanic literature p20-28

Cobb, Richard Charles

About

Darnton, R. The history of mentalités: recent writings on revolution, criminality, and death in France. *In* Brown, R. H. and Lyman, S. M. eds. Structure, consciousness, and history p106-36

Cobbett, William

About

Rickword, E. William Cobbett's Two-penny trash. *In* Rebels and their causes p141-49

Cobbett's Political Register

Rickword, E. William Cobbett's Two-penny trash. *In* Rebels and their causes p141-49

Cobden, Richard

About

Yakobson, S. Richard Cobden's sojourn in Russia, 1847. *In* Oxford Slavonic papers new ser. v 7 p60-74

Coben, Stanley

The assault on Victorianism in the twentieth century. *In* Howe, D. W. ed. Victorian America p160-81

Cocchiarella, Nino Barnabas

Formal ontology and the foundations of mathematics. *In* Nakhnikian, G. ed. Bertrand Russell's philosophy p29-46

Cochran, William G.

The vital role of randomization in experiments and surveys. *In* Neyman, J. ed. The heritage of Copernicus: theories "pleasing to the mind" p445-63

Cockcroft, James D.

Mexico. *In* Chilcote, R. H. and Edelstein, J. C. eds. Latin America: the struggle with dependency and beyond p222-303

Cockpit Theatre (Drury Lane), London

Orrell, J. Inigo Jones at the Cockpit. *In* Shakespeare survey 30 p157-68

Cocks, Paul

The policy process and bureaucratic politics. *In* Cocks, P.; Daniels, R. V. and Heer, N. W. eds. The dynamics of Soviet politics p156-78

Cockshut, A. O. J.

Hardy's philosophy. *In* Drabble, M. ed. The genius of Thomas Hardy p139-49

Man and woman: a study of love and the novel, 1740-1940

Contents

Jane Austen
The lesbian theme
Love and the novel
The male homosexual
The male homosexual: Forster
The male homosexual: Satire
The optimists
The optimists: Lawrence
The pessimists: Emily Brontë
The pessimists: George Gissing
The pessimists: J. A. Froude
The pessimists: Swinburne
The pessimists: Thomas Hardy
The realists: Mrs. Gaskell
The realists: Thackeray
Richardson and Fielding
Sterne

Cocteau, Jean

About individual works
The infernal machine

Fergusson, F. Excursus: poetry in the theatre and poetry of the theatre: Cocteau's Infernal machine. *In* Wimsatt, W. K. ed. Literary criticism: idea and act p590-601

Fergusson, F. Oedipus according to Freud, Sophocles, and Cocteau. *In* Fergusson, F. Literary landmarks p101-13

Cocteau, Jean—About individual works
—*Continued*

Testament of Orpheus

Truffaut, F. Jean Cocteau: Le testament d'Orphée. *In* Truffaut, F. The films in my life p204-08

Codex rossanensis

Loerke, W. C. The monumental miniature. *In* The Place of book illumination in Byzantine art p61-97

Coe, Michael D.

Olmec and Maya: a study in relationships. *In* The Origins of Maya civilization p183-95

Coe, Richard N.

About individual works
The vision of Jean Genet

Connolly, C. Jean Genet. *In* Connolly, C. The evening colonnade p354-57

Pritchett, V. S. Jean Genet: a modern nihilist. *In* Pritchett, V. S. The myth makers p102-07

Coes, Donald V. See Baer, W. jt. auth.

Coexistence. See World politics—1945-

Coffee

Paris

Leclant, J. Coffee and cafés in Paris, 1644-1693. *In* Food and drink in history p86-108

Coffee-houses

Paris

Leclant, J. Coffee and cafés in Paris, 1644-1693. *In* Food and drink in history p86-108

Coffey, Brian

Denis Devlin: poet of distance. *In* Place, personality and the Irish writer p137-57

Coffey, John W.

Political realism in American thought

Contents

The Christian realism of Reinhold Niebuhr
Epilogue: faith, reason, and the scientific method
Hans Morgenthau and the Western political tradition
The mind of the realist
Realism and foreign policy

Cognition

Cole, M. and Scribner, S. Theorizing about socialization of cognition. *In* Schwartz, T. ed. Socialization as cultural communication p157-76

Kagan, J. Resilience in cognitive development. *In* Schwartz, T. ed. Socialization as cultural communication p139-55

Meissner, W. W. Cognitive aspects of the paranoia process—prospectus. *In* Thought, consciousness, and reality p159-216

Watanabe, S. Can the cognitive process be totally mechanized? *In* Philosophical aspects of the mind-body problem p182-99

Weinberg, J. R. The problem of sensory cognition. *In* Weinberg, J. R. Ockham, Descartes, and Hume p33-49

See also Awareness; Cognition and culture; Knowledge, Theory of; Perception; Thought and thinking

Psychology

Gardner, H. Senses, symbols, operations: an organization of artistry. *In* Perkins, D. and Leondar, B. eds. The arts and cognition p88-117

Cognition (Child psychology). See Cognition in children

Cognition and culture

Cole, M. Ethnographic psychology of cognition—so far. *In* Spindler, G. D. ed. The making of psychological anthropology p614-31

Darnton, R. The history of mentalités: recent writings on revolution, criminality, and death in France. *In* Brown, R. H. and Lyman, S. M. eds. Structure, consciousness, and history p106-36

Price-Williams, D. Cognition: anthropological and psychological nexus. *In* Spindler, G. D. ed. The making of psychological anthropology p586-611

Cognition in children

Elkind, D. Cognitive development and psychopathology: observations on egocentrism and ego defense. *In* Elkind, D. The child and society p202-22

Elkind, D. Cognitive frames and family interactions. *In* Elkind, D. The child and society p65-79

Elkind, D. Life and death: concepts and feelings of children. *In* Elkind, D. The child and society p281-93

Elkind, D. The origins of religion in the child. *In* Elkind, D. The child and society p269-80

Elkind, D. Piaget and Montessori in the classroom. *In* Elkind, D. The child and society p143-55

Elkind, D. We can teach reading better. *In* Elkind, D. The child and society p156-64

Inhelder, B. New currents in genetic epistemology and developmental psychology. *In* Human growth and development p121-38

Lewis, M. and Lee-Painter, S. The origin of interactions: methodological issues. *In* Riegel, K. F. and Rosenwald, G. C. eds. Structures and transformation p119-31

Looft, W. R. and Svoboda, C. P. Structuralism in cognitive developmental psychology: past, contemporary and future perspectives. *In* Riegel, K. F. and Rosenwald, G. C. eds. Structure and transformation p49-60

Mora, G. Vico, Piaget and genetic epistemology. *In* Giambattista Vico's science of humanity p365-92

Wozniak, R. H. Dialecticism and structuralism: the philosophical foundation of Soviet psychology and Piagetian cognitive developmental theory. *In* Riegel, K. F. and Rosenwald, G. C. eds. Structure and transformation p25-45

Cognitive dissonance. See Dissonance (Psychology)

Cohen, Aharon

Israel and Jewish-Arab peace: governmental and nongovernmental approaches. *In* The Elusive peace in the Middle East p102-65

Cohen, Albert Kircidel

Introduction: the study of crime, items for an agenda. *In* Major social issues p151-55

Local control of community services. *In* The Uses of controversy in sociology p292-97

Cohen, Amnon

West Bank sentiments, 1967-1973. *In* The Palestinians p88-93

Cohen, Arthur A.
About
Kaufman, W. E. Arthur A. Cohen and Jacob B. Agus: the supernatural and the absolute· self. *In* Kaufman, W. E. Contemporary Jewish philosophies p217-50

Cohen, Arthur M.
On the road to a learning society. *In* The Third century p52-57

Cohen, Benjamin J.
International reserves and liquidity. *In* Kenen, P. B. ed. International trade and finance p411-51

Cohen, Carl
Revolutions and Copernican revolutions. *In* Science and society: past, present, and future p86-103
Sex, birth control, and human life. *In* Baker, R. and Elliston, F. A. eds. Philosophy & sex p150-65

Cohen, G. A.
Being, consciousness and roles: on the foundations of historical materialism. *In* Essays in honour of E. H. Carr p82-97

Cohen, Hermann
About
Rosenthal, E. I. J. Hermann Cohen and Heinrich Graetz. *In* Salo Wittmayer Baron v2 p725-43

Cohen, Howard
Abortion and the quality of life. *In* Feminism and philosophy p429-40

Cohen, Huguette
Rhetoric versus truth: Diderot's writings as an illustration of stability and innovation in eighteenth-century literature. *In* Studies in eighteenth-century culture v7 p433-50.

Cohen, I. Bernard
Einstein and Newton. *In* Einstein p40-42
The many faces of the history of science. *In* The Future of history p65-110
Science and the growth of the American Republic. *In* An Almost chosen people p67-106

Cohen, Jane Rabb
Strained relations: Charles Dickens and George Cattermole. *In* Dickens Studies Annual v 1 p81-92

Cohen, Jerome Alan
Due process? *In* Terrill, R. ed. The China difference p237-59

Cohen, Jon Sheldon, and Weitzman, Martin L.
Enclosures and depopulation: a Marxian analysis. *In* Parker, W. N. and Jones, E. L. eds. European peasants and their markets p161-76

Cohen, Laurence Jonathan
The semantics of metaphor. *In* Ortony, A. ed. Metaphor and thought p64-77
Why should the science of nature be empirical? *In* Royal Institute of Philosophy. Impressions of empiricism p168-83

Cohen, Leonard
About
Djwa, S. A. Leonard Cohen: black romantic. *In* Woodcock, G. ed. Poets and critics p179-90

Cohen, Louis
The shule. *In* Roots of open education in America p42-48

Cohen, Martin A.
The Hasmonean revolution politically considered. *In* Salo Wittmayer Baron v 1 p263-85

Cohen, Mary
"Out of the chaos, a new kind of strength": Doris Lessing's The golden notebook. *In* Diamond, A. and Edwards, L. R. eds. The authority of experience p178-93

Cohen, Michael A. See Rehberg, R. A. jt. auth.

Cohen, Murray
Sensible words: linguistic theory in late seventeenth-century England. *In* Studies in eighteenth-century culture v5 p229-52

Cohen, Peter M.
The future of gold. *In* The Year book of world affairs, 1977 p176-89

Cohen, Ralph
Innovation and variation: a problem of literary history. *In* Studies in eighteenth-century culture v4 p297-315
On a shift in the concept of interpretation. *In* Young, T. D. ed. The New Criticism and after p61-79
On the interrelations of eighteenth-century literary forms. *In* Harth, J. P. ed. New approaches to eighteenth-century literature p33-78
Pope's meanings and the strategies of interrelation. *In* English literature in the age of disguise p101-30

Cohen, Robert Sonne
Cosmic order and human disorder. *In* Cosmology, history, and theology p335-45

Cohen, Roberta
Human rights decision-making in the executive branch: some proposals for a coordinated strategy. *In* Kommers, D. P. and Loescher, G. D. eds. Human rights and American foreign policy p216-46

Cohen, Ronald
The pull of opposites: incorporation and autonomy in Nigeria. *In* African themes p149-73

Cohen, Ronald Dennis
Church and state in seventeenth-century Massachusetts: another look at the antinomian controversy. *In* Vaughan, A. T. and Bremer, F. J. eds. Puritan New England p174-86

Cohen, Sarah Blacher
Introduction: the variety of humors. *In* Cohen, S. B. ed. Comic relief p 1-13
The Jewish literary comediennes. *In* Cohen, S. B. ed. Comic relief p172-86

Cohen, Seymour Stanley
On the origins of cells: the development of a Copernican revolution. *In* Neyman, J. ed. The heritage of Copernicus: theories "pleasing to the mind" p207-27

Cohen, Sidney L.
The earliest Scandinavian towns. *In* The Medieval city p313-25

Cohen, Stephen F.
Bolshevism and Stalinism. *In* Stalinism p3-29

Cohen, Susan Blecker. See Atchley, M. W. jt. auth.

Cohen, Warren I
The China lobby. *In* Encyclopedia of American foreign policy p104-10
Consortia. *In* Encyclopedia of American foreign policy p167-76

Cohen, William
Congressional power to interpret due process and equal protection. *In* Stanford legal essays p79-96

Cohen, Yehudi A.
The state system, schooling, and cognitive and motivational patterns. *In* Social forces and schooling p103-40

Cohn, Ruby
Camp, cruelty, colloquialism. *In* Cohen, S. B. ed. Comic relief p281-303

Coin operated machines. See Pinball machines; Slot machines

Coinage
See also Currency question; Mints; Money

History
Shell, M. The language of character: an introduction to a poetics of monetary inscriptions. *In* Shell, M. The economy of literature p63-88

Europe—History
Wolff, P. The significance of the "feudal period" in the monetary history of Europe. *In* Order and innovation in the Middle Ages p77-85

Great Britain
Munro, J. H. A. Bullionism and the bill of exchange in England, 1272-1663: a study in monetary management and popular prejudice. *In* The Dawn of modern banking p169-239

United States
Belsley, D. A. United States silver coinage: what remains of an extinct specie. *In* Inflation, trade and taxes p50-72

Coinage of words. See Words, New

Coins
Smart, V. Corrections to Hildebrand's corpus of Anglo-Saxon moneyers: from Cnut to Edward the Confessor. *In* Anglo-Saxon England 4 p155-70

Coins, Anglo-Saxon
Keynes, S. An interpretation of the pacx, pax and paxs pennies. *In* Anglo-Saxon England 7 p165-73
Lyon, S. Some problems in interpreting Anglo-Saxon coinage. *In* Anglo-Saxon England 5 p173-224

Coins, Roman
Sellwood, D. Minting. *In* Strong, D. E. and Brown, D. eds. Roman crafts p63-73

Coke, F. Van Deren
The cubist photographs of Paul Strand and Morton Schamberg. *In* One hundred years of photographic history p35-42
Introduction: Beaumont Newhall. *In* One hundred years of photographic history p viii-x

Coke, Van Deren. See Coke, F. Van Deren

Coke industry

United States
Gordon, R. L. Coal—the swing fuel. *In* Kalter, R. J. and Vogely, W. A. eds. Energy supply and government policy p193-215

Colaclides, Peter
On the verb vero in Ennius. *In* Harvard Studies in classical philology v71 p121-23

Colby, Benjamin N. and Knaus, Rodger
Men, grammars, and machines, a new direction for the study of man. *In* On language, culture, and religion: in honor of Eugene A. Nida p187-97

Colby, William Egan
The view from Langley. *In* Borosage, R. L. and Marks, J. D. eds. The CIA file p181-87

About individual works
Honorable men: my life in the CIA
Galbraith, J. K. The global strategic mind. *In* Galbraith, J. K. Annals of an abiding liberal p331-40

Cold. See Heat

Cold War. See World politics—1945-

Cole, C. Robert
"Hope without illusion": A. J. P. Taylor's dissent, 1955-1961. *In* The Dissenting tradition p226-61

Cole, Edward A.
Paris 1848: a Russian ideological spectrum. *In* California Slavic studies v8 p 1-13

Cole, Herbert M.
The history of Ibo mbari houses—facts and theories. *In* African images p104-32

Cole, John Richard
The Oresteia and Cimon. *In* Harvard Studies in classical philology v81 p99-111

Cole, John Young
Storehouses and workshops: American libraries and the uses of knowledge. *In* Oleson, A. and Voss, J. eds. The organization of knowledge in modern America, 1860-1920 p364-85

Cole, Jonathan Richard, and Zuckerman, Harriet Anne
The emergence of a scientific specialty: the self-exemplifying case of the sociology of science. *In* The Idea of social structure p139-74

Cole, Larry
Kill each other, be killed, kill yourself; excerpt from "Street kids." *In* Gross, B. and Gross, R. eds. The children's rights movement p74-78

Cole, Michael
Ethnographic psychology of cognition—so far. *In* Spindler, G. D. ed. The making of psychological anthropology p614-31

Cole, Michael, and Scribner, Sylvia
Theorizing about socialization of cognition. *In* Schwartz, T. ed. Socialization as cultural communication p157-76

Cole, Phyllis B.
Emerson, England, and fate. *In* Levin, D. ed. Emerson: prophecy, metamorphosis, and influence p83-105

Cole, Robert Taylor. See Cole, Taylor

Cole, Stephen
The growth of scientific knowledge: theories of deviance as a case study. *In* The Idea of social structure p175-220

Cole, Taylor. See Part 2 under title: Prospects for constitutional democracy

Coleman, Donald Cuthbert
War demand and industrial supply: the 'dope scandal', 1915-19. *In* War and economic development p205-27

Coleman, Dorothy Gabe
Montaigne's 'Sur des vers de Virgile': taboo subject, taboo author. *In* Classical influences on European culture A.D. 1500-1700 p135-40

Coleman, Elizabeth
Values in the arts and sciences: a course. *In* Aeolian harps p15-36

Coleman, Emily R.

Infanticide in the early Middle Ages. *In* Stuard, S. M. ed. Women in medieval society p47-70

Coleman, James Samuel

The emergence of sociology as a policy science. *In* The Uses of controversy in sociology p253-61

Introduction: choice in American education. *In* Parents, teachers, and children: prospects for choice in American education p 1-12

Needed: new routes to adulthood. *In* Gross, B. and Gross, R. eds. The children's rights movement p244-50

Social structure and a theory of action. *In* Blau, P. M. ed. Approaches to the study of social structure p76-93

About individual works
Social structure and a theory of action

Wallace, W. L. Structure and action in the theories of Coleman and Parsons. *In* Blau, P. M. ed. Approaches to the study of social structure p121-34

Coleman, James Smoot

Legitimate and illegitimate use of power. *In* The Idea of social structure p221-36

Tradition and nationalism in tropical Africa. *In* Kilson, M. ed. New states in the modern world p3-36

Coleman, Terry

The early years. *In* Drabble, M. ed. The genius of Thomas Hardy p12-18

Coleman, William

Bergmann's rule: animal heat as a biological phenomenon. *In* Studies in history of biology v3 p67-88

Coleridge, Samuel Taylor

About

Abrams, M. H. Coleridge, Baudelaire, and modernist poetics. *In* Amacher, R. E. and Lange, V. eds. New perspectives in German literary criticism p150-81

Bloom, H. Coleridge: the anxiety of influence. *In* Wimsatt, W. K. ed. Literary criticism: idea and act p506-20

Brisman, L. Coleridge and the ancestral voices. *In* Brisman, L. Romantic origins p21-54

Colmer, J. The idealist vision. *In* Colmer, J. Coleridge to Catch-22 p18-29

Cooke, M. G. The will in English romanticism: The question of the will. *In* Cooke, M. G. The romantic will p5-29

Donoghue, D. The eye and the mind's eye. *In* Donoghue, D. The sovereign ghost p128-82

Peckham, M. Poet and critic: or, The damage Coleridge has done. *In* Peckham, M. Romanticism and behavior p196-205

Prickett, S. 'A liberty of speculation which no Christian can tolerate'—the later Coleridge. *In* Prickett, S. Romanticism and religion p34-69

Prickett, S. 'The living educts of the imagination': Coleridge on religious language. *In* Prickett, S. Romanticism and religion p9-33

Rand, R. A. Geraldine. *In* Glyph 3 p74-97

Reed, A. Abysmal influence: Baudelaire, Coleridge, De Quincey, Piranesi, Wordsworth. *In* Glyph 4 p189-206

Richards, I. A. Coleridge's other poems. *In* Richards, I. A. Poetries p112-27

Sabin, M. Beauty and taste. *In* Sabin, M. English romanticism and the French tradition p181-201

Sabin, M. The language of nature. *In* Sabin, M. English romanticism and the French tradition p221-34

Sabin, M. Symbolic light. *In* Sabin, M. English romanticism and the French tradition p202-20

Shaffer, E. S. The fall of Jerusalem: Coleridge's unwritten epic. *In* Shaffer, E. S. 'Kubla Khan' and The fall of Jerusalem p17-61

Shaffer, E. S. The visionary character: Revelation and the lyrical ballad. *In* Shaffer, E. S. 'Kubla Khan' and The fall of Jerusalem p62-95

Taylor, A. Coleridge and the magical power of the imagination. *In* Taylor, A. Magic and English romanticism p64-98

Taylor, A. Coleridge and the potent voice. *In* Taylor, A. Magic and English romanticism p99-133

Taylor, A. Wordsworth's arguments against magical words. *In* Taylor, A. Magic and English romanticism p134-83

Warnock, M. Coleridge and Wordsworth, theory and practice: imagination and the mental image. *In* Warnock, M. Imagination p72-130

About individual works
Biographia literaria

Fogel, D. M. A compositional history of the Biographia literaria. *In* Virginia. University. Bibliographical Society. Studies in bibliography v30 p219-34

Hocks, R. A. "Novelty" in polarity to "the most admitted truths": tradition and the individual talent in S. T. Coleridge and T. S. Eliot. *In* Evolution of consciousness p83-97

Knights, L. C. Two notes on Coleridge: Coleridge as critic. *In* Explorations 3 p38-44

Sugerman, S. G. An "essay" on Coleridge on imagination. *In* Evolution of consciousness p191-201

Christabel

Rand, R. A. Geraldine. *In* Glyph 3 p74-97

The friend

Knights, L. C. Two notes on Coleridge: A tract for the times: Coleridge and The friend. *In* Knights, L. C. Explorations 3 p44-51

Richards, I. A. The vulnerable poet and the friend. *In* Richards, I. A. Poetries p128-45

Inquiring spirit: a new presentation of Coleridge from his published and unpublished prose writings

Frye, N. Long, sequacious notes. *In* Frye, N. Northrop Frye on culture and literature p170-77

Kubla Khan

Shaffer, E. S. Hölderlin's 'Patmos' ode and 'Kubla Khan': mythological doubling. *In* Shaffer, E. S. 'Kubla Khan' and The fall of Jerusalem p145-90

Shaffer, E. S. The oriental idyll. *In* Shaffer, E. S. 'Kubla Khan' and The fall of Jerusalem p96-144

Trilling, L. Coleridge, Samuel Taylor: Kubla Khan or a vision in a dream: a fragment. *In* Trilling, L. Prefaces to The experience of literature p226-31

Coleridge, Samuel T.—About individual works—*Continued*

The rime of the ancient mariner

Cooke, M. G. The will in English romanticism: The will in romantic poetry. *In* Cooke, M. G. The romantic will p29-51

Dyson, A. E. and Lovelock, J. Uncertain hour: the ancient mariner's destiny. *In* Dyson, A. E. and Lovelock, J. Masterful images p175-92

Jones, D. An introduction to The rime of the ancient mariner. *In* Jones, D. The dying Gaul, and other writings p186-225

Sanders, C. R. The ancient mariner and Coleridge's theory of poetic art. *In* Sanders, C. R. Carlyle's friendships, and other studies p312-30

Aesthetics

Sanders, C. R. The ancient mariner and Coleridge's theory of poetic art. In Sanders, C. R. Carlyle's friendships, and other studies p312-30

Criticism, Textual

Fogel, D. M. A compositional history of the Biographia literaria. *In* Virginia. University. Bibliographical Society. Studies in bibliography v30 p219-34

Criticism and interpretation

Sanders, C. R. The background of Carlyle's portrait of Coleridge in The life of John Sterling. *In* Sanders, C. R. Carlyle's friendships, and other studies p36-60

Influence

Hough, G. G. Coleridge and the Victorians. *In* Hough, G. G. Selected essays p92-109

Knowledge—Art

Woodring, C. R. What Coleridge thought of pictures. *In* Kroeber, K. and Walling, W. eds Images of romanticism p83-91

Language

Blake, N. F. Coleridge's poetic language. *In* Davies, R. T. and Beatty, B. G. eds. Literature of the romantic period, 1750-1850 p72-81

Poetic works

Blake, N. F. Coleridge's poetic language. *In* Davies, R. T. and Beatty, B. G. eds. Literature of the romantic period, 1750-1850 p72-81

Hough, G. G. The poetry of Coleridge. *In* Hough, G. G. Selected essays p83-91

Philosophy

Knights, B. The idea of the clerisy: Samuel Taylor Coleridge. *In* Knights, B. The idea of the clerisy in the nineteenth century p37-71

Political and social views

Knights, B. The idea of the clerisy: Samuel Taylor Coleridge. *In* Knights, B. The idea of the clerisy in the nineteenth century p37-71

Social views

See Coleridge, Samuel Taylor—Political and social views

Style

See Coleridge, Samuel Taylor—Language

Coles, Robert

"God save them, those children; and for allowing such a state of affairs to continue, God save us, too"; excerpt from "Uprooted children." *In* Gross, B. and Gross, R. eds. The children's rights movement p118-22

The method; excerpt from "Migrants, sharecroppers, mountaineers". *In* Explorations in psychohistory p165-81

The South revisited. *In* Lewis, W. D. and Griessman, B. E. eds. The Southern mystique p93-108

Work and self-respect. *In* Erikson, E. H. ed. Adulthood p217-26

About

Coles, R. The South revisited. *In* Lewis, W. D. and Griessman, B. E. eds. The Southern mystique p93-108

About individual works

Migrants, sharecroppers, mountaineers (Children of crisis, v2)

Coles, R. The method; excerpt from "Migrants, sharecroppers, mountaineers". *In* Coles, R. Explorations in psychohistory p165-81

The mind's fate: ways of selling psychiatry and psychoanalysis

Mudrick, M. Mad dogs and Anglo shrinks. *In* Mudrick, M. Books are not life but then what is? p227-33

Colet, John

About

Jarrott, C. A. L. Erasmus's annotations and Colet's commentaries on Paul: a comparison of some theological themes. *In* Essays on the works of Erasmus p125-44

Bibliography

Trapp, J. B. John Colet, his manuscripts and the ps.-Dionysius. *In* Classical influences on European culture A.D. 1500-1700 p205-21

Coletta, Paolo Enrico

Recognition policy. *In* Encyclopedia of American foreign policy p882-92

Colette, Gabrielle Claudine. See Colette, Sidonie Gabrielle

Colette, Sidonie Gabrielle

About

Gass, W. H. Three photos of Colette. *In* Gass, W. H. The world within the word p124-46

About individual works

The complete Claudine

Gass, W. H. Three photos of Colette. *In* Gass, W. H. The world within the word p124-46

Coletti, Theresa

Music and The tempest. *In* Shakespeare's late plays p185-99

Theology and politics in the Towneley Play of the talents. *In* Medievalia et humanistica; new ser. no. 9 p111-26

Colie, Rosalie Littell

The rhetoric of transcendence. *In* Roberts, J. R. ed. Essential articles for the study of John Donne's poetry p199-219

Colker, Marvin L.

Recent books about medieval manuscripts. *In* Medievalia et humanistica no. 5 p229-32

Some recent works for palaeographers. *In* Medievalia et humanistica no. 8 p235-42

Collaboration in literature. See Authorship —Collaboration

Collage

Greenberg, C. Collage; excerpt from "Art and culture (Revised edition)." *In* Kaplan, P. and Manso, S. eds. Major European art movements, 1900-1945 p147-63

Collage—*Continued*

Keim, J. A. Photomontage after World War I. *In* One hundred years of photographic history p83-90

Rosenberg, H. Collage: philosophy of put-togethers. *In* Rosenberg, H. Art on the edge p173-80

Collages, American

Tashjian, D. L. The art of assemblage. *In* Tashjian, D. L. Skyscraper primitives p188-203

La collectionneuse (Motion picture)

Kauffmann, S. La collectionneuse. *In* Kauffmann, S. Living images p55-57

Collective bargaining. See Arbitration, Industrial; Trade-unions

Collective behavior. See Violence

Collective farms

Russia

Davies, R. W. The Soviet rural economy in 1929-1930: the size of the kolkhoz. *In* Essays in honour of E. H. Carr p255-80

Collective psychotherapy. See Group psychotherapy

Collective security. See Security, International

Collective settlements

Bennett, J. W. Cultural integrity and personal identity: the communitarian response. *In* Smithsonian Institution. The cultural drama p197-235

Heller, A. and Vajda, M. Communism and the family. *In* The Humanisation of socialism p7-26

Hudson, W. S. A time of religious ferment. *In* The Rise of Adventism p 1-17

Whitworth, J. M. Communitarian groups and the world. *In* Wallis, R. ed. Sectarianism p117-37

See also Collective farms

History

Hine, R. V. Communitarianism. *In* The Rise of Adventism p70-78

Israel

Bettelheim, B. Alienation and autonomy. *In* Bettelheim, B. Surviving, and other essays p333-49

Blumberg, R. L. The erosion of sexual equality in the kibbutz: a structural interpretation. *In* Roberts, J. I. ed. Beyond intellectual sexism p320-39

Kansas—Case studies

Miller, L. K. and others. The positive community: a strategy for applying behavioral engineering to the redesign of family and community. *In* Behavior modification and families p91-112

United States

Berger, B. M. American pastoralism, suburbia and the commune movement: an exercise in the microsociology of knowledge. *In* On the making of Americans p235-50

Collectivism

Markus, M. and Hegedüs, A. Community and individuality. *In* The Humanisation of socialism p91-105

Oakeshott, M. J. The political economy of freedom. *In* Oakeshott, M. J. Rationalism in politics p37-58

See also Communism; Individualism; Socialism; Totalitarianism

Collectors and collecting. See Book collectors

College, Choice of

Rever, P. R. The dynamics of admission to the less-selective public and private sector colleges. *In* Hurdles p111-44

Tilley, D. C. Opening admissions and the postselective era: a view from the public sector. *In* Hurdles p76-110

College administrators. See College presidents

College admissions. See Universities and colleges—Admission

College and church. See Church and college

College and community. See Community and college

College autonomy. See University autonomy

College chaplains. See Chaplains, University and college

College cooperation. See University cooperation

College costs

Willingham, W. W. Free-access colleges: where they are and whom they serve. *In* Murphy, T. P. ed. Universities in the urban crisis p197-213

See also Student aid

College education costs. See College costs

College faculty. See College teachers; Universities and colleges—Faculty; Women college teachers

College faculty. See Universities and colleges—United States—Faculty

College graduates

Employment

McConnell, T. R. Surfeit or dearth of highly educated people? *In* McMurrin, S. M. ed. On the meaning of the university p63-80

College humor. See College wit and humor

College libraries. See Libraries, University and college

College presidents

Hesburgh, T. M. The university president. *In* Hesburgh, T. M. The Hesburgh papers p3-16

College sports. See Football

College students

Shneidman, E. S. The college student and death. *In* Feifel, H. [ed.] New meanings of death p67-86

Attitudes

Bien, P. Metaphysics, myth, and politics. *In* Buxton, T. H. and Prichard, K. W. eds. Excellence in university teaching p157-88

Conduct of life

Rothblatt, S. The student sub-culture and the examination system in early 19th century Oxbridge. *In* The University in society v 1 p247-303

Sexual behavior

Sarrel, L. J. and Sarrel, P. M. The college subculture. *In* Sexuality and human values p71-84

Berkeley, Calif.

Piazza, T. Jewish identity and the counterculture. *In* The New religious consciousness p245-64

China

Jen, E. An experience with Peking youth. *In* Terrill, R. ed. The China difference p141-60

College students—*Continued*

Japan—Political activity

Tsurumi, K. Student movements in 1960 and 1969: continuity and change. *In* Postwar trends in Japan p195-227

San Francisco Bay Region—
Religious life

Hargrove, B. W. Church student ministries and the new consciousness. *In* The New religious consciousness p205-26

United States

Hesburgh, T. M. The generation gap. *In* Hesburgh, T. M. The Hesburgh papers p141-48

Hesburgh, T. M. In defense of the younger generation. *In* Hesburgh, T. M. The Hesburgh papers p129-38

United States—Political activity

Crews, F. C. Offing culture: literary study and the Movement. *In* Crews, F. C. Out of my system p121-44

Dixon, J. P. Permanent campus revolution? *In* Fairfield, R. P. ed. Humanistic frontiers in American education p261-68

College students, Afro-American. See Afro-American college students

College students, Jewish

Piazza, T. Jewish identity and the counterculture. *In* The New religious consciousness p245-64

College teachers

Brown, M. A. The administration of professors as decision makers. *In* Managing nonprofit organizations p303-12

See also Universities and colleges—Faculty; Women college teachers

United States

Browne, R. B. Academicons-sick sacred cows. *In* Browne, R. B. and Fishwick, M. W. eds. Icons of America p292-301

United States—Selection and
appointment

Hook, S. The bias in anti-bias regulations. *In* Gross, B. R. ed. Reverse discrimination p88-96

Seabury, P. HEW and the universities. *In* Gross, B. R. ed. Reverse discrimination p97-112

College teachers, Professional ethics for

Miller, A. H. The ethics of teaching political science: another perspective. *In* Hook, S.; Kurtz, P. and Todorovich, M. eds. The ethics of teaching and scientific research p43-48

Rosenzweig, R. M. Faculty and standards of ethical conduct. *In* Hook, S.; Kurtz, P. and Todorovich, M. eds. The ethics of teaching and scientific research p73-82

Van Alstyne, W. W. Faculty codes and professional responsibility. *In* Hook, S.; Kurtz, P. and Todorovich, M. eds. The ethics of teaching and scientific research p83-86

College teaching

Allen, J. Personal observations of effective teaching. *In* Buxton, T. H. and Prichard, K. W. eds. Excellence in university teaching p132-39

Bienfang, R. On being a professor. *In* Buxton, T. H. and Prichard, K. W. eds. Excellence in university teaching p55-61

Buxton, T. H. A humanistic approach to teaching. *In* Buxton, T. H. and Prichard, K. W. eds. Excellence in university teaching p120-27

Cooper, K. S. Did you ever think of Aristotle as a college freshman? *In* Buxton, T. H. and Prichard, K. W. eds. Excellence in university teaching p86-93

Fairfield, R. P. A teacher as radical humanist. *In* Fairfield, R. P. ed. Humanistic frontiers in American education p237-47

Frank, G. W. "On my honor I will. . ." *In* Buxton, T. H. and Prichard, K. W. eds. Excellence in university teaching p140-46

Goldwin, R. A. Teaching and the shaping of souls. *In* Hook, S.; Kurtz, P. and Todorovich, M. eds. The ethics of teaching and scientific research p37-41

Hart, F. R. Toward the discipline of humane teaching. *In* Buxton, T. H. and Prichard, K. W. eds. Excellence in university teaching p189-206

Highet, G. Teaching college teachers how to teach. *In* Highet, G. The immortal profession p91-116

Keller, W. D. On teaching and learning. *In* Buxton, T. H. and Prichard, K. W. eds. Excellence in university teaching p62-66

Langford, T. A. The conveyance of personal knowledge. *In* Buxton, T. H. and Prichard, K. W. eds. Excellence in university teaching p147-53

Mann, R. D. The multiple goals of teaching. *In* Buxton, T. H. and Prichard, K. W. eds. Excellence in university teaching p39-47

Manning, D. In search of substantive change. *In* Buxton, T. H. and Prichard, K. W. eds. Excellence in university teaching p239-45

Marcus, I. M. Observations on teaching. *In* Buxton, T. H. and Prichard, K. W. eds. Excellence in university teaching p67-69

Oviatt, A. B. Reflections on effective teaching. *In* Buxton, T. H. and Prichard, K. W. eds. Excellence in university teaching p48-54

Panuska, J. A. Open-endedness as an educational goal. *In* Buxton, T. H. and Prichard, K. W. eds. Excellence in university teaching p94-102

Peckham, M. Arts for the cultivation of radical sensitivity. *In* Peckham, M. Romanticism and behavior p285-312

Phenix, P. H. Teaching as celebration. *In* Buxton, T. H. and Prichard, K. W. eds. Excellence in university teaching p22-29

Reckford, K. J. Teaching the heroic journey. *In* Buxton, T. H. and Prichard, K. W. eds. Excellence in university teaching p11-21

Sherwin, R. C. The presentation of educational self in the classroom. *In* Buxton, T. H. and Prichard, K. W. eds. Excellence in university teaching p30-38

Smith, H. Two kinds of teaching. *In* Buxton, T. H. and Prichard, K. W. eds. Excellence in university teaching p207-19

Strickland, C. G. Students' rights and the teacher's obligations in the classroom. *In* Buxton, T. H. and Prichard, K. W. eds. Excellence in university teaching p80-85

Zimmerman, M. Objectivity in education. *In* Hook, S.; Kurtz, P. and Todorovich, M. eds. The ethics of teaching and scientific research p49-51

See also Teaching

College teaching—*Continued*

United States

Baumann, F. Objectivity and indoctrination. *In* Hook, S.; Kurtz, P. and Todorovich, M. eds. The ethics of teaching and scientific research p53-59

Canavan, F. P. The problem of indoctrination. *In* Hook, S.; Kurtz, P. and Todorovich, M. eds. The ethics of teaching and scientific research p29-35

Diamond, M. Teaching about politics as a vocation. *In* Hook, S.; Kurtz, P. and Todorovich, M. eds. The ethics of teaching and scientific research p3-22

Eurich, N. Learning in America. *In* From Parnassus p75-83

Frankel, C. Facts, values, and responsible choice. *In* Hook, S.; Kurtz, P. and Todorovich, M. eds. The ethics of teaching and scientific research p23-28

Novotny, H. R. F. Objectivity and biased skepticism in higher education. *In* Hook, S.; Kurtz, P. and Todorovich, M. eds. The ethics of teaching and scientific research p61-69

College theater

Brustein, R. S. Theatre and the university. *In* Brustein, R. S. The culture watch p166-73

College theatricals. See College theater

College wit and humor

Rovit, E. H. College humor and the modern audience. *In* Cohen, S. B. ed. Comic relief p238-48

Colleges. See Universities and colleges

Colleges, Afro-American. See Afro-American universities and colleges

Colleges for women. See Women's colleges

Collegiality of bishops. See Episcopacy

Collier, Abram T.

On celebrating American independence. *In* Warner, S. B. ed. The American experiment p 1-10

Collier, Christopher

Johnny and Sam: old and new approaches to the American Revolution. *In* Horn Book Magazine. Crosscurrents of criticism p234-40

See also Collier, J. L. jt. auth.

Collier, James Lincoln, and Collier, Christopher

About individual works

My brother Sam is dead

Collier, C. Johnny and Sam: old and new approaches to the American Revolution. *In* Horn Book Magazine. Crosscurrents of criticism p234-40

Collier, Joel, pseud.

About individual works

Musical travels through England

Lonsdale, R. H. Dr. Burney, 'Joel Collier', and Sabrina. *In* Evidence in literary scholarship p281-308

Collier, Ruth Berins

Political change and authoritarian rule. *In* Martin, P. M. and O'Meara, P. eds. Africa p295-310

Collin d'Harleville, Jean François

About individual works

Le vieux célibataire

Koch, P. Regnard and Collin d'Harleville on legacies by bachelor uncles. *In* Studies in eighteenth-century culture v8 p291-309

Collingwood, Robin George

About individual works

The new Leviathan

Stanage, S. M. Violatives: modes and themes of violence. *In* Stanage, S. M. ed. Reason and violence p207-38

The principles of art

Sclafani, R. J. The theory of art. *In* Aagaard-Mogensen, L. ed. Culture and art p146-70

Collins, Anthony

About

Luehrs, R. B. The problematical compromise: the early deism of Anthony Collins. *In* Studies in eighteenth-century culture v6 p59-77

Collins, Carvell Emerson

Faulkner and certain earlier Southern fiction. *In* Inge, M. T. ed. The frontier humorists p259-65

Collins, L. J. D.

The military organization and tactics of the Crimean Tatars, 16th-17th centuries. *In* War, technology and society in the Middle East p257-76

Collins, Leslie E.

Death-profit, "evil," and the Chinese feminist movement. *In* Kren, G. M. and Rapoport, L. H. eds. Varieties of psychohistory p264-81

Collins, Margery L. and Pierce, Christine

Holes and slime: sexism in Sartre's psychoanalysis. *In* Gould, C. C. and Wartofsky, M. W. eds. Women and philosophy p112-27

Collins, Peter

Auguste Perret. *In* Sharp, D. ed. The rationalists p16-25

Collins, Philip Arthur William

Charles Dickens. *In* Abroad in America: Visitors to the new Nation, 1776-1914 p82-91

Dickens' public readings: texts and performances. *In* Dickens Studies Annual v3 p182-97

A tale of two novels: A tale of two cities and Great expectations in Dickens' career. *In* Dickens Studies Annual v2 p336-51

Collins, Richard

Genre: a reply to Ed Buscombe. *In* Nichols, B. ed. Movies and methods p157-63

Collins, Wilkie

About

Lambert, G. Enemy country. *In* Lambert, G. The dangerous edge p 1-30

About individual works

The moonstone

Ousby, I. Wilkie Collins and other sensation novelists. *In* Ousby, I. Bloodhounds in heaven p111-36

The woman in white

Kennard, J. E. Aristocrat versus commoner. *In* Kennard, J. E. Victims of convention p46-79

Knoepflmacher, U. C. The counterworld of Victorian fiction and The woman in white. *In* The Worlds of Victorian fiction p351-69

Influence—Sayers

Gregory, E. R. Wilkie Collins and Dorothy L. Sayers. *In* Hannay, M. P. ed. As her whimsey took her p51-64

Collins, William

About

Ober, W. B. Madness and poetry: a note on Collins, Cowper, and Smart. *In* Ober, W. B. Boswell's clap and other essays p137-92

Collins, William Wilkie. See Collins, Wilkie

Collinson, Patrick

Toward a broader understanding of the early dissenting tradition. *In* The Dissenting tradition p3-38

Collison Black, R. D. See Black, R. D. Collison

Collotti· Pischel, Enrica

The teacher. *In* Wilson, R. G. ed. Mao Tse-tung in the scales of history p144-73

Colman, Hila

About individual works
Mixed-marriage daughter

Kimmel, E. A. Jewish identity in juvenile fiction: a look at three recommended books. *In* Horn Book Magazine. Crosscurrents of criticism p150-58

Colmer, John

Coleridge to Catch-22

Contents

The comic spirit
The 'condition of England' question
Continuity and change
The cult of power and the power of culture
The idealist vision
The modern 'condition of England' novel
Political action and the crisis of conscience
Protest and anti-war literature
Science fiction
Sex, the family and the new woman
The utilitarian approach
Utopian fantasy
The Victorian 'condition of England' novel
The writer as critic of society

Colombia

Politics and government

Wilde, A. W. Conversations among gentlemen: oligarchical democracy in Colombia. *In* The Breakdown of democratic regimes pt 3 p28-81

Race question

Sharp, W. F. Manumission, libres, and Black resistance: the Colombian Chocó, 1680-1810. *In* Toplin, R. B. ed. Slavery and race relations in Latin America p89-111

Colombo, Cristoforo

About

Carew, J. The origins of racism in the Americas. *In* African themes p3-23

Seelye, J. Diverse voyages: Columbus, Cartier, and the Conradian shape of adventure in America. *In* Seelye, J. Prophetic waters p9-22

Spengemann, W. C. The poetics of adventure. *In* Spengemann, W. C. The adventurous muse p6-67

Colonial wars. See United States—History—Colonial period, ca. 1600-1775

Colonialism. See Colonies; Imperialism; World politics

Colonies

Bennett, E. M. Colonialism. *In* Encyclopedia of American foreign policy p134-40

Letman, S. T. Some sociological aspects of terror-violence in a colonial setting. *In* International terrorism and political crimes p33-42

See also Colonies in Africa, Land settlement

Economic conditions

Golay, F. H. Southeast Asia: the "colonial drain" revisited. *In* Southeast Asian history and historiography p368-87

International law

See Colonies (International law)

Colonies (International law)

Grisel, É. The beginnings of international law and general public law doctrine: Francisco de Vitoria's De Indiis prior. *In* First images of America p305-25

Colonies in Africa

Geller, S. The colonial era. *In* Martin, P. M. and O'Meara, P. eds. Africa p132-49

Colonies in Asia, Southeastern

Kahin, G. M. The United States and the anticolonial revolutions in Southeast Asia, 1945-50. *In* The Origins of the Cold war in Asia p338-61

Colonization

See also Subdivision Colonization under names of countries, regions, etc. e.g. Canada —Colonization

History

Parry, J. H. A secular sense of responsibility. *In* First images of America p287-304

Colonna, Egidio, Abp.

About individual works
Commentarii in octo libros Physicorum Aristotelis

Moody, E. A. Ockham and Aegidius of Rome. *In* Moody, E. A. Studies in medieval philosophy, science, and logic p161-88

Color

Smart, J. J. C. On some criticisms of a physicalist theory of colors. *In* Philosophical aspects of the mind-body problem p54-63

Psychological aspects

See Color vision

Terminology

See Colors, Words for

Color cinematography. See Color moving-pictures

Color discrimination. See Color vision

Color in art

Hefferman, J. A. W. The English romantic perception of color. *In* Kroeber, K. and Walling, W. eds. Images of romanticism p133-48

Heron, P. The shape of colour. *In* Concerning contemporary art p154-80

Color in literature

Hefferman, J. A. W. The English romantic perception of color. *In* Kroeber, K. and Walling, W. eds. Images of romanticism p133-48

Shattuck, R. Vibratory organism: crise de prose. *In* Symbolism and modern literature p193-204

Color in sculpture. See Polychromy

Color moving-pictures

Eisenstein, S. M. Colour film; excerpt from "Notes of a film director." *In* Nichols, B. ed. Movies and methods p381-88

Color of animals. See Protective coloration (Biology)

Color perception. See Color-sense

Color perception. See Color vision

Color sense. See Color vision

Color vision

Beck, J. Dimensions of an achromatic surface color. *In* Perception p166-84

Hahm, D. E. Early Hellenistic theories of vision and the perception of color. *In* Studies in perception p60-95

Lloyd, B. B. L. Culture and colour coding. *In* Royal Institute of philosophy. Communication and understanding p140-61

Metelli, F. Achromatic color conditions in the perception of transparency. *In* Perception p95-116

Smart, J. J. C. On some criticisms of a physicalist theory of colors. *In* Philosophical aspects of the mind-body problem p54-63

Colorado

Politics and government—1876-1950

Wickens, J. F. Depression and the New Deal in Colorado. *In* Braeman, J.; Bremner, R. H. and Brody, D. eds. The New Deal v2 p269-310

Coloration, Protective (Biology) See Protective coloration (Biology)

Colored people (U.S.) See Afro-Americans

Colors

See also Color; Symbolism of colors in literature

Terminology

See Colors, Words for

Colors, Words for

Barley, N. F. Old English colour classification: where do matters stand? *In* Anglo-Saxon England 3 p15-28

Hacker, P. M. S. Locke and the meaning of colour words. *In* Royal Institute of Philosophy. Impressions of empiricism p23-46

Lloyd, B. B. L. Culture and colour coding. *In* Royal Institute of Philosophy. Communication and understanding p140-61

Colson, Audrey Butt

Birth customs of the Akawaio. *In* Studies in social anthropology p285-309

Colson, Elizabeth

Changing anthropology in Africa. *In* African dimensions p15-27

Life among the cattle-owning plateau Tonga. *In* The Occasional papers of the Rhodes-Livingstone Museum p167-213

Colum, Mary (Maguire)

About individual works

From these roots

Kunitz, S. J. The single conscience. *In* Kunitz, S. J. A kind of order, a kind of folly p187-93

Columbia University

Strike

Trilling, D. On the steps of Low Library. *In* Trilling, D. We must march my darlings p77-153

Columbia University. Casa Italiana. Educational Bureau

Cordasco, F. Leonard Covello and the Casa Italiana Educational Bureau: a note on the beginnings of systematic Italian-American studies. *In* Studies in Italian American social history p 1-9

Columbus, Christopher. See Colombo, Cristoforo

Columbus, Claudette Kemper

Ruskin's Praeterita as thanatography. *In* Landow, G. P. ed. Approaches to Victorian autobiography p109-27

Columns, Ionic

Coomarswamy, A. K. Walter Andrae's die ionische Säule: Bauform oder Symbol?: a review; excerpt from "Figures of thought or figures of speech: collected essays on the traditional or 'normal' view of art." *In* Coomaraswamy, A. K. Selected papers v 1 p341-49

Columns of Hercules (Heraldic device)

Rosenthal, E. S. Plus Oultre: the idea imperial of Charles V in his columnar device on the Alhambra. *In* Enggass, R. C. and Stokstad, M. eds. Hortus imaginum p85-93

Colville, Alex

About

Hutchings, P. A. E. Some contemporary realisms. *In* Concerning contemporary art p89-132

Coma. See Brain death

Comanche Indians

Reservations

Hagan, W. T. Kiowas, Comanches, and cattlemen, 1867-1906: a case study of the failure of U.S. reservation policy. *In* The American Indian p77-99

Combatants and noncombatants (International law)

Lahey, K. A. and Sang, L. M. Control of terrorism through a broader interpretation of Article 3 of the four Geneva Conventions of 1949. *In* International terrorism and political crimes p191-200

Veuthey, M. A survey of international humanitarian law in noninternational armed conflicts: 1949-1974. *In* International terrorism and political crimes p86-97

Combs, Jerald A.

Embargoes. *In* Encyclopedia of American foreign policy p310-21

Combustion. See Fire

Combustion, Theory of

Guerlac, H. The origin of Lavoisier's work on combustion. *In* Guerlac, H. Essays and papers in the history of modern science p375-92

Comédie-Française. See Paris. Comédie-Française

Comedy

Brandt, G. Twentieth-century comedy. *In* Howarth, W. D. ed. Comic drama p165-86

Frye, N. Romance as masque. *In* Frye, N. Spiritus mundi p148-78

Also in Shakespeare's romances reconsidered p11-39

Goodlad, S. On the social significance of television comedy. *In* Bigsby, C. W. E. ed. Approaches to popular culture p213-25

Howarth, W. D. Introduction: theoretical considerations. *In* Howarth, W. D. ed. Comic drama p 1-21

Ruggiers, P. G. Introduction: some theoretical considerations of comedy in the Middle Ages. *In* Ruggiers, P. G. ed. Versions of medieval comedy p 1-17

Waith, E. M. "Give me your hands": reflections on the author's agents in comedy. *In* Martz, L. L. and Williams, A. L. eds. The author in his work p197-211

See also Comic, The; Commedia dell'arte; Farce; Greek drama (Comedy); Grotesque; Tragicomedy

Comedy—*Continued*

History and criticism
Farley-Hills, D. Comic poetry of the Commonwealth. *In* Farley-Hills, D. The benevolence of laughter: comic poetry of the Commonwealth and Restoration p21-45

Nicoll, A. The comic spirit and social unrest. *In* Nicoll, A. World drama p711-26

Nicoll, A. The growth of bourgeois comedy. *In* Nicoll, A. World drama p307-29

Comedy films

History and criticism
Agee, J. Comedy's greatest era; excerpt from "Agee on film v 1." *In* Denby, D. ed. Awake in the dark p230-48

Seldes, G. The Keystone the builders rejected; excerpt from "The seven lively arts." *In* Denby, D. ed. Awake in the dark p18-30

Comedy programs
Taylor, P. A. The studio audience for television situation comedies. *In* Fischer, H. D. and Melnik, S. R. eds. Entertainment: a cross-cultural examination p22-33

Comenius, Johann Amos

About individual works
The visible world
Margolin, J. C. The method of "words and things" in Erasmus's De pueris instituendis (1529) and Comenius's Orbis sensualium pictus (1658) *In* Essays on the works of Erasmus p221-38

Comenius, John Amos. See Comenius, Johann Amos

Comerford, Brenda
Parental anticipatory grief and guidelines for caregivers. *In* Anticipatory grief p147-57

Comets
Marsden, B. G. The comets. *In* Man and cosmos p152-64

Comfort, Alexander
A biologist laments and exhorts. *In* Jarvik, L. F. ed. Aging into the 21st century p41-60

Comic, The
Auty, S. G. Fresh streams of mirth in society and literature. *In* Auty, S. G. The comic spirit of eighteenth-century novels p6-33

Auty, S. G. Perpetual mirth. *In* Auty, S. G. The comic spirit of eighteenth-century novels p180-83

Girard, R. Perilous balance: A comic hypothesis. *In* Girard, R. "To double business bound" p121-35

Torrance, R. M. Afterword: in lieu of conclusion. *In* Torrance, R. M. The comic hero p274-77

Torrance, R. M. Introduction: comic butt and comic hero. *In* Torrance, R. M. The comic hero p 1-11

Wallace, R. H. Never mind that the nag's a pile of bones: the contemporary American comic novel and the comic tradition. *In* Wallace, R. H. The last laugh p 1-25

Wallace, R. H. No more happy endings. *In* Wallace, R. H. The last laugh p136-43

Comic books, strips, etc.
Schechter, H. Comicons. *In* Browne, R. B. and Fishwick, M. W. eds. Icons of America p263-70

Chile—Political aspects
Kunzle, D. Art of the new Chile: mural, poster, and comic book in a "revolutionary process." *In* Millon, H. A. and Nochlin, L. eds. Art and architecture in the service of politics p356-81

Great Britain
Lewis, R. Captain America meets the Bash Street Kids: the comic form in Britain and the United States. *In* Bigsby, C. W. E. Superculture p175-89

United States
Lewis, R. Captain America meets the Bash Street Kids: the comic form in Britain and the United States. *In* Bigsby, C. W. E. Superculture p175-89

Comic literature. See Burlesque (Literature); Comedy; Commedia dell' arte; Farce; Parody; Satire

Comic strips. See Comic books, strips, etc.

Comics. See Comic books, strips, etc.

Cominform. See Communist Information Bureau

Command of troops
Higginbotham, D. Military leadership in the American Revolution. *In* Library of Congress Symposia on the American Revolution, 3d, 1974. Leadership in the American Revolution p91-111

Commedia dell'arte
Nicoll, A. The popular play: the commedia dell'arte. *In* Nicoll, A. World drama p147-53

Commerce
Bloomfield, A. I. Adam Smith and the theory of international trade. *In* Skinner, A. S. and Wilson, T. eds. Essays on Adam Smith p455-81

Caves, R. E. Looking at inflation in the open economy. *In* Inflation, trade and taxes p75-95

Meltzer, R. I. Contemporary security dimensions of international trade relations. *In* Knorr, K. E. and Trager, F. N. eds. Economic issues and national security p200-30

Mundell, R. A. Abba Lerner and the theory of foreign trade. *In* Theory for economic efficiency: essays in honor of Abba P. Lerner p 144-50

Winberg, A. R. Resource politics: the future of international markets for raw materials. *In* Orr, D. W. and Soroos, M. S. eds. The global predicament p178-94

See also Central business districts; Comparative advantage (Commerce); Competition, International; Exchange; International business enterprises; Money; Prices; subdivision Commerce under names of countries, cities, etc. e.g. Africa, East—Commerce; subdivision Finance, Commerce, under names of wars; also names of articles of commerce, e.g. Cotton, Leather, Lumber; and headings beginning with the world Commercial

History
Lopez, R. S. Proxy in medieval trade. *In* Order and innovation in the Middle Ages p187-94

Polanyi, K. Traders and trade. *In* Ancient civilization and trade p133-54

Renfrew, C. Trade as action at a distance: questions of integration and communication. *In* Ancient civilization and trade p3-59

Commerce—*Continued*

History—Sources

Fishbein, M. H. Selected materials in the National Archives relating to commerce and industry. *In* Pattern and process p224-28

Mathematical models

Stern, R. M. Testing trade theories. *In* Kenen, P. B. ed. International trade and finance p3-49

Commercial ethics. See Business ethics

Commercial law

See also Trusts, Industrial—Law

United States

Danzig, R. A comment on the jurisprudence of the Uniform Commercial Code. *In* Stanford legal essays p97-111

Commercial policy

Smith, A. J. R. Future problems of trade policy: a question of political leadership. *In* The New Atlantic challenge p79-95

See also Tariff

Commercial products. See Raw materials

Commercial treaties. See Reciprocity; and subdivision Commercial treaties, under names of countries, e.g. France—Commercial treaties

Commission of the Churches on International Affairs

Rees, E. Exercises in private diplomacy: selected activities of the Commission of the Churches on International Affairs. *In* Unofficial diplomats p111-29

Commission of the European Communities

Meessen, K. M. The application of the antitrust rules of the EEC Treaty by the Commission of the European Communities. *In* Davis, K. C. Discretionary justice in Europe and America p75-99

Commissions, Independent regulatory. See Independent regulatory commissions

Commissura magna cerebri. See Corpus callosum

Committee on Children and Young Persons. See Great Britain—Committee on Children and Young Persons

Committee on Government Operations. Subcommittee on Intergovernmental Relations. See United States. Congress. Senate. Committee on Government Operations. Subcommittee on Intergovernmental Relations

Committee on the Peaceful Uses of the Sea-Bed and the Ocean Floor Beyond the Limits of National Jurisdiction. See United Nations. General Assembly. Committee on the Peaceful Uses of the Sea-Bed and the Ocean Floor Beyond the Limits of National Jurisddiction

Committees

Thomas, L. On committees. *In* Thomas, L. The medusa and the snail p115-20

Common lands. See Commons

Common law

Great Britain

Greenberg, J. The legal status of the English woman in early eighteenth-century common law and equity. *In* Studies in eighteenth-century culture v4 p171-81

United States—History

Ely, J. W. Law in a republican society: continuity and change in the legal system of postrevolutionary America. *In* Perspectives on revolution and evolution p46-65

Common market countries. See European Economic Community countries

Common schools. See Public schools

Common sense

O'Neill, J. The mutuality of accounts: an essay on trust. *In* McNall, S. G. ed. Theoretical perspectives in sociology p369-80

Commoner, Barry

Energy, environment, and economics. *In* Eppen, G. D. ed. Energy: the policy issues p25-40

A new historic passage: energy, the era of constraints. *In* The National purpose reconsidered p53-72

Commonplace-books

Ong, W. J. Commonplace rhapsody: Ravisius Textor, Zwinger and Shakespeare. *In* Classical influences on European culture A.D. 1500-1700 p91-126

Same as: Typographic rhapsody: Ravisius Texton, Zwinger, and Shakespeare. *In* Ong, W. J. Interfaces of the word p 147-88

Commonplaces. See Terms and phrases

Commons

See also Village Communities

Europe

Hoffmann, R. C. Medieval origins of the common fields. *In* Parker, W. N. and Jones, E. L. eds. European peasants and their markets p23-71

Great Britain

McCloskey, D. N. The persistence of English common fields. *In* Parker, W. N. and Jones, E. L. eds. European peasants and their markets p73-119

Thirsk, J. The common fields. *In* Peasants, knights and heretics p10-32

Thirsk, J. The origin of the common fields. *In* Peasants, knights and heretics p51-56

Titow, J. Z. Medieval England and the open-field system. *In* Peasants, knights and heretics p33-50

Commonwealth, The. See Political science; State, The

Commonwealth of Nations

Doxey, M. P. The Commonwealth Secretariat. *In* The Year book of world affairs, 1976 p69-96

Doxey, M. P. Continuity and change in the Commonwealth. *In* The Year book of world affaris, 1979 p76-101

Yardley, D. C. M. The effectiveness of the Westminster model of constitution. *In* The Year book of world affairs, 1977 p342-51

Study and teaching

Jones, J. Method or madness: how may we expect Commonwealth studies to affect the teaching of English? *In* Narasimhaiah, C. D. ed. Awakened conscience p408-12

Commonwealth of Nations fiction (English) See English fiction—Commonwealth of Nations authors

Commonwealth of Nations literature (English) See English literature—Commonwealth of Nations authors

Commonwealth of Nations poetry (English) See English poetry—Commonwealth of Nations authors

Communism—Europe—*Continued*

Ferrarotti, F. The Italian Communist Party and Eurocommunism. *In* Kaplan, M. A. ed. The many faces of communism p30-71

Hermens, F. A. Return to democratic government. *In* The Year book of world affairs, 1978 p191-207

Europe, Eastern

Machala, P. Eastern Europe, Eurocommunism, and the problems of détente. *In* Kaplan, M. A. ed. The many faces of communism p228-65

Rakowska-Harmstone, T. Eastern European communism in the seventies. *In* Kaplan, M. A. ed. The many faces of communism p194-227

Finland

Smith, C. J. Soviet Russia and the Red revolution of 1918 in Finland. *In* Hammond, T. T. ed. The anatomy of Communist takeovers p71-93

Germany

Angress, W. T. The takeover that remained in limbo: the German experience, 1918-1923. *In* Hammond, T. T. ed. The anatomy of Communist takeovers p163-91

Hungary

Ignotus, P. The first two Communist takeovers of Hungary: 1919 and 1948. *In* Hammond, T. T. ed. The anatomy of Communist takeovers p385-98

Schöpflin, G. Hungary: an uneasy stability. *In* Brown, A. H. and Gray, J. eds. Political culture and political change in Communist states p131-58

India—Kerala

May, C. J. Some lesser leaders of the Communist movement in Kerala. *In* The Making of politicians: studies from Africa and Asia p166-82

Mongolia

Hammond, T. T. The Communist takeover of Outer Mongolia: model for Eastern Europe? *In* Hammond, T. T. ed. The anatomy of Communist takeovers p107-44

Poland

Kolankiewicz, G. and Taras, R. Poland: socialism for Everyman? *In* Brown, A. H. and Gray, J. eds. Political culture and political change in Communist states p101-30

Lotarski, S. S. The Communist takeover in Poland. *In* Hammond, T. T. ed. The anatomy of Communist takeovers p339-67

Romania

Fischer-Galati, S. A. The Communist takeover of Rumania: a function of Soviet power. *In* Hammond, T. T. ed. The anatomy of Communist takeovers p310-20

Russia

Agursky, M. The Soviet legitimacy crisis and its international implications. *In* Kaplan, M. A. ed. The many faces of communism p146-93

Bialer, S. The resurgence and changing nature of the Left in industrialized democracies. *In* Radicalism in the contemporary age v3 p 3-81

Cohen, S. F. Bolshevism and Stalinism. *In* Stalinism p3-29

Golan, G. Elements of Russian traditions in Soviet socialism. *In* Eisenstadt, S. N. and Azmon, Y. eds. Socialism and tradition p19-39

Kołakowski, L. Marxist roots of Stalinism. *In* Stalinism p283-98

Lewin, M. The social background of Stalinism. *In* Stalinism p111-36

McNeal, R. H. Trotskyist interpretations of Stalinism. *In* Stalinism p30-52

Medvedev, R. A. New pages from the political biography of Stalin. *In* Stalinism p199-235

Mihajlov, M. The phenomenology of the Kingdom of Lies. *In* Mihajlov, M. Underground notes p32-36

Rigby, T. H. Stalinism and the mono-organizational society. *In* Stalinism p53-76

Thomson, B. The problem of art. *In* Thomson, B. Lot's wife and the Venus of Milo p 5-28

Tucker, R. C. Stalinism and comparative communism. *In* Stalinism pxi-xx

Tucker, R. C. Stalinism as revolution from above. *In* Stalinism p77-108

White, S. The USSR: patterns of autocracy and industrialism. *In* Brown, A. H. and Gray, J. eds. Political culture and political change in Communist states p25-65

Yugoslavia

Dyker, D. A. Yugoslavia: unity out of diversity? *In* Brown, A. H. and Gray, J. eds. Political culture and political change in Communist states p66-100

Furtak, R. K. Yugoslavia: a special case. *In* Hayward, J. E. S. and Berki, R. N. eds. State and society in contemporary Europe p158-78

Golan, G. National traditions and socialism in Eastern Europe: the cases of Czechoslovakia and Yugoslavia. *In* Eisenstadt, S. N. and Azmon, Y. eds. Socialism and tradition p41-76

Reinhartz, D. Milovan Djilas: the transcendence of a revolutionary. *In* Essays on modern European revolutionary history p69-88

Wilson, Sir D. Yugoslavia and Soviet policy. *In* Kirk, G. L. and Wessell, N. H. eds. The Soviet threat p77-87

Communism and architecture

Starr, S. F. Visionary town planning during the cultural revolution. *In* Cultural revolution in Russia, 1928-1931 p207-40

Communism and art

Howlett, J. The origins of Socialist realism in Soviet visual art. *In* Oxford Slavonic papers new ser. v9 p91-101

Middleton, J. C. 'Bolshevism in art': dada and politics. *In* Middleton, J. C. Bolshevism in art p38-61

Mihajlov, M. The artist as the enemy. *In* Mihajlov, M. Underground notes p6-8

Thomson, B. Some properties of art. *In* Thomson, B. Lot's wife and the Venus of Milo p139-54

See also **Communist aesthetics**

Chile

Kunzle, D. Art of the new Chile: mural, poster, and comic book in a "revolutionary process." *In* Millon, H. A. and Nochlin, L. eds. Art and architecture in the service of politics p356-81

Communism and literature—*Continued*

Mathewson, R. W. Marxism, realism, and the hero. *In* Mathewson, R. W. The positive hero in Russian literature p115-35

Mathewson, R. W. Two bureaucracies. *In* Mathewson, R. W. The positive hero in Russian literature p211-32

Mills, H. C. Literature in fetters. *In* Terrill, R. ed. The China difference p285-304

Pickowicz, P. G. Qu Qiubai's critique of the May Fourth generation: early Chinese Marxist literary criticism. *In* Modern Chinese literature in the May Fourth era p351-84

Rahv, P. Excerpts from "the literary class war." *In* Rahv, P. Essays on literature and politics, 1932-1972 p281-83

Rahv, P. Proletarian literature: a political autopsy. *In* Rahv, P. Essays on literature and politics, 1932-1972 p293-304

Spender, S. Background to the thirties. *In* Spender, S. The thirties and after p3-20

Spender, S. Notes on revolutionaries and reactionaries: Revolutionaries. *In* Spender, S. The thirties and after p146-54

Stacy, R. H. Marxist and Soviet criticism. *In* Stacy, R. H. Russian literary criticism p185-230

Watson, G. Did Stalin dupe the intellectuals? *In* Watson, G. Politics and literature in modern Britain p46-70

See also Communism in literature

Communism and mass media

Craig, D. Marxism and popular culture. *In* Bigsby, C. W. E. ed. Approaches to popular culture p129-49

China

Chu, G. C. Popular media: a glimpse of the new Chinese culture. *In* Chu, G. C. ed. Popular media in China p 1-15

Communism and religion

Bourdeaux, M. Religion. *In* Brown, A. H. and Kaser, M. eds. The Soviet Union since the fall of Khrushchev p157-80

Welch, H. The fate of religion. *In* Terrill, R. ed. The China difference p117-37

Communism and science

Haraway, D. J. Reinterpretation or rehabilitation: an exercise in contemporary Marxist history of science. *In* Studies in history of biology v2 p193-209

Communism and social sciences

Bauman, Z. East European and Soviet social science: a case study in stimulus diffusion. *In* Szporluk, R. ed. The influence of East Europe and the Soviet West on the USSR p91-116

Solomon, S. G. Rural scholars and the cultural revolution. *In* Cultural revolution in Russia, 1928-1931 p129-53

Communism and society

Heller, A. Marx's theory of revolution and the revolution in everyday life. *In* The Humanisation of socialism p52-57

See also Marxian school of sociology

Communism in literature

Chin, Ai-li S. and Liu, Nien-ling. Short stories in China: theory and practice, 1973-1975. *In* Chu, G. C. ed. Popular media in China p124-83

Chu, L. L. Sabers and swords for the Chinese children: revolutionary children's folk songs. *In* Chu, G. C. ed. Popular media in China p16-50

Frye, N. Orwell and Marxism. *In* Frye, N. Northrop Frye on culture and literature p204-06

Glicksberg, C. I. Arthur Koestler and the Revolution betrayed. *In* Glicksberg, C. I. The literature of commitment p277-88

Glicksberg, C. I. Bertolt Brecht: the prophet of commitment. *In* Glicksberg, C. I. The literature of commitment p319-36

Glicksberg, C. I. George Orwell and the morality of politics. *In* Glicksberg, C. I. The literature of commitment p289-318

Glicksberg, C. I. The moral protest of Solzhenitsyn. *In* Glicksberg, C. I. The literature of commitment p381-401

Kurz, P. K. Bertolt Brecht: the man and his work. *In* Kurz, P. K. On modern German literature v2 p22-103

Communist aesthetics

Eagleton, T. Marxist literary criticism. *In* Contemporary approaches to English studies p94-103

Halley, J. A. Beyond the sociology of art: recent interdisciplinary developments in the critical analysis of culture. *In* McNall, S. G. ed. Theoretical perspectives in sociology p276-91

Watkins, E. Dialectic and form. *In* Watkins, E. The critical act p158-87

Watkins, E. Raymond Williams and Marxist criticism. *In* Watkins, E. The critical act p141-57

Communist countries

Brus, W. Stalinism and "peoples' democracies." *In* Stalinism p239-56

McNeill, T. State and nationality under communism. *In* Hayward, J. E. S. and Berki, R. N. eds. State and society in contemporary Europe p118-40

Tucker, R. C. The perils of success—deradicalization. *In* Lauer, R. H. ed. Social movements and social change p227-55

Economic policy

Nussbaumer, A. The economic systems of Socialist Eastern Europe: principles, development, and operation. *In* The Year book of world affairs, 1975 p222-41

Portes, R. Inflation under central planning. *In* The Political economy of inflation p73-87

Foreign relations—European Economic Community countries

Pinder, J. The Community and the state trading countries. *In* Twitchett, K. J. ed. Europe and the world p57-76

Foreign relations—United States

Ørvik, N. Anticommunism and American foreign policy. *In* [Truth and tragedy]: a tribute to Hans Morgenthau p284-304

Politics and government

Brown, A. H. Introduction. *In* Brown, A. H. and Gray, J. eds. Political culture and political change in Communist states p 1-24

Gray, J. Conclusions. *In* Brown, A. H. and Gray, J. eds. Political culture and political change in Communist states p253-72

Communist education

China

Anrig, G. R. Education in China. *In* Wagschal, P. H. ed. Learning tomorrows p63-72

Communist Party of Russia

Daniels, R. V. Office holding and elite status: the Central Committee of the CPSU. *In* Cocks, P.; Daniels, R. V. and Heer, N. W. eds The dynamics of Soviet politics p77-95

Frank, P. J. The changing composition of the Communist Party. *In* Brown, A. H. and Kaser, M. eds. The Soviet Union since the fall of Khrushchev p96-120

Hodgson, J H. The problem of succession. *In* Cocks, P.; Daniels, R. V. and Herr, N. W. eds. The dynamics of Soviet politics p96-116

Hough, J. F. Party "saturation" in the Soviet Union. *In* Cocks, P.; Daniels, R. V. and Heer, N. W. eds. The dynamics of Soviet politics p117-33

Lewin, M. The social background of Stalinism. *In* Stalinism p111-36

Rakowska-Harmstone, T. Toward a theory of Soviet leadership maintenance. *In* Cocks, P.; Daniels, R. V. and Herr, N. W. eds. The dynamics of Soviet politics p51-76

Rigby, T. H. Stalinism and the mono-organizational society. *In* Stalinism p53-76

Schapiro, L. B. The structure of the Soviet state: government and politics. *In* Auty, R. and Obolensky, D. eds. An introduction to Russian history p331-49

Purges

Connor, W. D. The manufacture of deviance: the case of the Soviet purge, 1936-1938. *In* Davis, F. J. and Stivers, R. eds. The collective definition of deviance p241-55

Communist Party of Spain

Mujal-León, E. M. Portuguese and Spanish communism in comparative perspective. *In* Kaplan, M. A. ed. The many faces of communism p122-45

Communist Party of the Czechoslovak Republic

Tigrid, P. The Prague Coup of 1948: the elegant takeover. *In* Hammond, T. T. ed. The anatomy of Communist takeovers p399-432

Communist Party of the United States of America

Rahv, P. Proletarian literature: a political autopsy. *In* Rahv, P. Essays on literature and politics, 1932-1972 p293-304

Communist Party of Uzbek

Carlisle, D. S. Modernization, generations, and the Uzbek Soviet intelligentsia. *In* Cocks, P.; Daniels, R. V. and Heer, N. W. eds. The dynamics of Soviet politics p239-64

Communist Party of Vietnam

Duncanson, D. J. Vietnam: from bolshevism to people's war. *In* Hammond, T. T. ed. The anatomy of Communist takeovers p490-515

Communist propaganda. See Propaganda, Communist

Communist self-criticism

Hegedüs, A. The self-criticism of Socialist society: a reality and a necessity. *In* The Humanisation of socialism p161-75

Communist state

Brown, A. H. Introduction. *In* Brown, A. H. and Gray, J. eds. Political culture and political change in Communist states p 1-24

Brunner, G. and Kaschkat, H. Party, state and groups in Eastern Europe. *In* Hayward, J. E. S. and Berki, R. N. eds. State and society in contemporary Europe p95-117

Gray, J. Conclusions. *In* Brown, A. H. and Gray, J. eds. Political culture and political change in Communist states p253-72

Harloe, M. Marxism, the state and the urban question: critical notes on two recent French theories. *In* Crouch, C. ed. State and economy in contemporary capitalism p122-56

Communistic settlements. See Collective settlements

Communitas (The word)

Tassi, A. Communitas and polis. *In* Roth, R. J. ed. Person and community p133-40

Community

Ariès, P. The family and the city in the Old World and the New. *In* Tufte, V. and Myerhoff, B. G. eds. Changing images of the family p29-41

Bay, C. From contract to community: thoughts on liberalism and postindustrial society. *In* Dallmayr, F. R. ed. From contract to community p29-45

Cohen, A. K. Local control of community services. *In* The Uses of controversy in sociology p292-97

Goist, P. D. Afterword. *In* Goist, P. D. From Main Street to State Street p159-64

Goist, P. D. Alternative perspective: the "radical" journalism of Hutchins Hapgood and Ernest Poole. *In* Goist, P. D. From Main Street to State Street p94-109

Goist, P. D. Automobility and community: the middle landscape of American automobiles. *In* Goist, P. D. From Main Street to State Street p35-45

Goist, P. D. The city as noncommunity: Theodore Dreiser and Henry Blake Fuller. *In* Goist, P. D. From Main Street to State Street p68-79

Goist, P. D. The ideal questioned but not abandoned: Sherwood Anderson, Sinclair Lewis, and Floyd Dell. *In* Goist, P. D. From Main Street to State Street p21-34

Goist, P. D. Middletown and the "eclipse of community": Robert and Helen Lynd. *In* Goist, P. D. From Main Street to State Street p46-56

Goist, P. D. Regionalism and community: the urbanism of Lewis Mumford. *In* Goist, P. D. From Main Street to State Street p143-57

Goist, P. D. Social workers, reformers, and the city: Jane Addams and Jacob Riis. *In* Goist, P. D. From Main Street to State Street p80-93

Goist, P. D. A sociologist and the city: the experience of Robert Park. *In* Goist, P. D. From Main Street to State Street p110-20

Goist, P. D. The town as ideal community: Booth Tarkington and Zona Gale. *In* Goist, P. D. From Main Street to State Street p13-20

Hunter, A. Persistence of local sentiments in mass society. *In* Handbook of contemporary urban life p133-62

Keller, S. I. The planning of communities: anticipations and hindsights. *In* The Idea of social structure p283-99

Keller, S. I. The telephone in new (and old) communities. *In* The Social impact of the telephone p281-99

Compagnia dei Frescobaldi
Prestwich, M. Italian merchants in late thirteenth and early fourteenth century England. *In* The Dawn of modern banking p77-104

Compagnie De Saint-Gobain. See Saint-Gobain, s.a.

Compagnie royale des glaces. See Saint-Gobain, s.a.

Compania dei Bardi
Krekić, B. Four Florentine commercial companies in Dubrovnik (Ragusa) in the first half of the fourteenth century. *In* The Medieval city p25-41

Compania dei Peruzzi
Krekić, B. Four Florentine commercial companies in Dubrovnik (Ragusa) in the first half of the fourteenth century. *In* The Medieval city p25-41

Companies. See Corporations

Companion spirits in literature. See Genius (Companion spirit) in literature

Company law. See Corporation law

Comparative advantage (Commerce)
Samuelson, P. A. Illogic of neo-Marxian doctrine of unequal exchange. *In* Inflation, trade and taxes p96-107

Comparative costs. See Comparative advantage (Commerce)

Comparative economic systems. See Comparative economics

Comparative economics
Agursky, M. Contemporary socioeconomic systems and their future prospects. *In* From under the rubble p67-87
Chandler, A. D. The multi-unit enterprise: a historical and international comparative analysis and summary. *In* Evolution of in-

Comparative jurisprudence. See Comparative law

Comparative law
Claude, R. P. Comparative rights research: some intersections between law and the social sciences. *In* Claude, R. P. ed. Comparative human rights p382-407
ternational management structures p225-54

Comparative linguistics
Said, E. W. Renan's philological laboratory. *In* Art, politics, and will p59-98
See also Language and languages

Comparative literature. See Literature, Comparative

Comparative philosophy. See Philosophy, Comparative

Comparative religion. See Religions

Comparative Studies in Society and History (Periodical)
Thrupp, S. L. Comparative Studies in Society and History: a working alliance among specialists. *In* Thrupp, S. L. Society and history p332-45

Comparetti, Marco Milani- See Milani-Comparetti, Marco

Comparison (Psychology) See Identity

Comparison of cultures. See Cross-cultural studies

Compassion (Ethics) See Sympathy

Compensation. See Wages

Compensation (Law)

United States
Bittker, B. I. Identifying the beneficiaries; excerpt from "The case for Black reparations." *In* Gross, B. R. ed. Reverse discrimination p279-87
Boxhill, B. The morality of reparation. *In* Gross, B. R. ed. Reverse discrimination p270-78

Compensation for victims of crime. See Reparation

Compensatory education
Weaver, W. T. Growth, distribution, and the professional frame of reference. *In* Bundy, R. F. ed. Images of the future: the twenty-first century and beyond p195-200

Compensatory motion. See Irritability

Competition
Richardson, G. B. Adam Smith on competition and increasing returns. *In* Skinner, A. S. and Wilson, T. eds. Essays on Adam Smith p350-60
Sylos Labini, P. Competition: the product markets. *In* The Market and the state p200-32
See also Oligopolies; Social Darwinism

Competition (Psychology)
Devereux, E. C. Backyard versus Little League baseball: the impoverishment of children's games. *In* Social problems in athletics p37-56
Martens, R. Competition: in need of a theory. *In* Social problems in athletics p9-17
Sherif, C. W. The social context of competition. *In* Social problems in athletics p18-36

Competition, International
Iriye, A. Japan as a competitor, 1895-1917. *In* Iriye, A. ed. Mutual images p73-99

Competitive behavior. See Competition (Psychology)

Complaints (Military law)

United States
Ford, B. L. Justice is more than a word. *In* Henderson, G. ed. Human relations in the military p127-44

Complancha. See Laments

Complementarities. Richards, I. A. *In* Richards, I. A. Complementarities p108-26

Complementarity (Physics)
Richards, I. A. Complementarities. *In* Richards, I. A. Complementarities p108-26

Complexes (Psychology). See Oedipus complex

Compliance of patients. See Patient compliance

Composite photography. See Photography, Composite

Composition. See Rhetoric

Composition (Music)
Bamberger, J. In search of a tune. *In* Perkins, D. and Leondar, B. eds. The arts and cognition p284-319
Cavell, S. Music discomposed. *In* Cavell, S. Must we mean what we say? p180-212
Sessions, R. The composer and his message. *In* Sessions, R. Roger Sessions on music p3-26
Sessions, R. The composer in the university. *In* Sessions, R. Roger Sessions on music p193-203

Composition (Music)—*Continued*

Sessions, R. Problems and issues facing the composer today. *In* Sessions, R. Roger Sessions on music p71-87

Sessions, R. Song and pattern in music today. *In* Sessions, R. Roger Sessions on music p53-70

Composition (Photography)

Borcoman, J. W. Notes on the early use of combination printing. *In* One hundred years of photographic history p15-18

Composition (Rhetoric) See Rhetoric

Compostela, Spain. See Santiago de Compostela, Spain

Comprehension

Bauman, Z. Consensus and truth. *In* Bauman, Z. Hermeneutics and social science p225-46

Bauman, Z. The rise of hermeneutics. *In* Bauman, Z. Hermeneutics and social science p23-47

Bauman, Z. Understanding as expansion of the form of life. *In* Bauman, Z. Hermeneutics and social science p194-224

Bauman, Z. Understanding as the work of history: Karl Mannheim. *In* Bauman, Z. Hermeneutics and social science p89-110

Bauman, Z. Understanding as the work of history: Karl Marx. *In* Bauman, Z. Hermeneutics and social science p48-68

Bauman, Z. Understanding as the work of history: Max Weber. *In* Bauman, Z. Hermeneutics and social science p69-88

Bauman, Z. Understanding as the work of life: From Schutz to ethnomethodology. *In* Bauman, Z. Hermeneutics and social science p172-93

Bauman, Z. Understanding as the work of life: Martin Heidegger. *In* Bauman, Z. Hermeneutics and social science p148-71

Bauman, Z. Understanding as the work of reason: Edmund Husserl. *In* Bauman, Z. Hermeneutics and social science p111-30

Bauman, Z. Understanding as the work of reason: Talcott Parsons. *In* Bauman, Z. Hermeneutics and social science p131-47

Harrison, B. J. On understanding a general name. *In* Royal Institute of Philosophy. Communication and understanding p116-39

Parkinson, G. H. R. The translation theory of understanding. *In* Royal Institute of Philosophy. Communication and understanding p 1-19

Stewart, M. A. Locke, Steiner and understanding. *In* Royal Institute of Philosophy. Communication and understanding p20-45

Compton-Burnett, Ivy

About

Gillie, C. Diversification of the novel, 1920-1930. *In* Gillie, C. Movements in English literature, 1900-1940 p90-121

About individual works
A father and his fate

Balakian, N. Three post-psychological novels. *In* Balakian, N. Critical encounters p95-104

The last and the first

Balakian, N. A writer and her vision: Ivy Compton-Burnett. *In* Balakian, N. Critical encounters p105-08

Compulsory military service. See Military service, Compulsory

Compulsory non-military service. See Service, Compulsory non-military

Computer composition. See Computer music

Computer music

Bamberger, J. In search of a tune. *In* Perkins, D. and Leondar, B. eds. The arts and cognition p284-319

Computer reliabilty. See Computers—Reliability

Computer translating. See Machine translating

Computers

Le Roy Ladurie, E. The historian and the computer. *In* Le Roy Ladurie, E. The territory of the historian p3-6

See also Electronic data processing

Reliability

Thomas, L. To err is human. *In* Thomas, L. The medusa and the snail p36-40

Computers and civilization

Lowi, T. J. The information revolution, politics, and the prospects for an open society. *In* Galnoor, I. ed. Government secrecy in democracies p40-61

Computers in literature

Rhodes, C. H. Tyranny by computer: automated data processing and oppressive government in science fiction. *In* Clareson, T. D. ed. Many futures, many worlds p66-93

Computing machines. See Calculating-machines

Comstock, W. Richard

On seeing with the eye of the native European. *In* Seeing with a native eye p58-78

Comte, Auguste

About

Chadwick, O. The moral nature of man. *In* Chadwick, O. The secularization of the European mind in the nineteenth century p229-49

Voegelin, E. The apocalypse of man: Comte. *In* Voegelin, E. From Enlightenment to revolution p136-59

Voegelin, E. The religion of humanity and the French Revolution. *In* Voegelin, E. From Enlightenment to revolution p160-94

Conceit (The English word)

Greene, D. J. The term 'conceit' in Johnson's literary criticism. *In* Evidence in literary scholarship p337-51

Concentration. See Attention

Concentration camps

See also Political prisoners

Psychological aspects

Eitinger, L. On being a psychiatrist and a survivor. *In* Rosenfeld, A. H. and Greenberg, I. eds. Confronting the Holocaust p186-99

Germany

Bettelheim, B. German concentration camps. *In* Bettelheim, B. Surviving, and other essays p38-47

Germany—Psychological aspects

Bettelheim, B. Individual and mass behavior in extreme situations. *In* Bettelheim, B. Surviving and other essays p48-83

Bettelheim, B. "Owners of their faces." *In* Bettelheim, B. Surviving, and other essays p105-11

Concentration camps—Germany—Psychological aspects—*Continued*

Bettelheim, B. Surviving. *In* Bettelheim, B. Surviving and other essays p274-314

Bettelheim, B. Trauma and reintegration. *In* Bettelheim, B. Surviving, and other essays p19-37

Bettelheim, B. The ultimate limit. *In* Bettelheim, B. Surviving, and other essays p3-18

Concentration camps in literature

Brombert, V. H. Servitude and solidarity. *In* Brombert, V. H. The romantic prison p173-84

Conception

Gaylin, W. The technology of life and death. *In* Small comforts for hard times p152-69

Prevention

See Contraceptives

Concepts

Pivčević, E. Concepts, phenomenology and philosophical understanding. *In* Pivčević, E. ed. Phenomenology and philosophical understanding p271-86

Conceptual art

Osborne, H. Concrete art and the repudiation of artifice. *In* Osborne, H. Abstraction and artifice in twentieth-century art p163-80

Concert of Europe

Vincent, R. J. The idea of concert and international order. *In* The Year book of world affairs, 1975 p34-55

Concerts. See Music—Performance

Conciliation, International. See Mediation, International

Concrete art

Osborne, H. Concrete art and the repudiation of artifice. *In* Osborne, H. Abstraction and artifice in twentieth-century art p163-80

See also Concrete poetry; Constructivism (Art)

Concrete poetry

Morgan, E. Into the constellation: some thoughts on the origin and nature of concrete poetry. *In* Morgan, E. Essays p20-34

Condemned books. See Censorship; Index librorum prohibitorum

Condensers (Steam)

Donovan, A. L. Toward a social history of technological ideas: Joseph Black, James Watt, and the separate condenser. *In* Bugliarello, G. and Doner, D. B. eds. The history and philosophy of technology p19-30

Conditional reflexes. See Conditioned response

Conditioned response

Fancher, R. E. Psychology as the science of behavior: Ivan Pavlov and John B. Watson. *In* Fancher, R. E. Pioneers of psychology p295-338

See also Operant behaviour; Reinforcement (Psychology)

Condominas, Georges

Phībān cults in rural Laos. *In* Change and persistence in Thai society p252-73

Condon, John C. See Neher, W. W. jt. auth.

Condorcet, Marie Jean Antoine Nicolas Caritat, marquis de

About

Voegelin, E. The conflict between progress and political existence after Turgot. *In* Voegelin, E. From Enlightenment to revolution p110-35

Williams, D. Condorcet, feminism, and the egalitarian principle. *In* Studies in eighteenth-century culture v5 p151-63

Condottieri

Keen, M. H. Chivalry, nobility, and the man-at-arms. *In* War, literature, and politics in the late Middle Ages p32-45

Condren, Conal

The quest for a concept of needs. *In* Fitzgerald, R. ed. Human needs and politics p244-60

Conduct of life

Bellah, R. N. To kill and survive or to die and become: the active life and the contemplative life as ways of being adult. *In* Erikson, E. H. ed. Adulthood p61-80

Israel, M. The nature of eternal life: a mystical consideration. *In* Life after death p154-65

Nock, A. J. Pantagruelism. *In* Crunden, R. M. ed. The superfluous men p98-106

See also Character; Characters and characteristics; Christian life; Culture; Duty; Ethics; Gratitude; Justice; Spiritual life; Sportsmanship; Vices; Virtue; Virtues

Cone, Carl B.

George III—America's unknown king. *In* The American Revolution and "a candid world" p 1-16

Confederate States of America

See also United States—History—Civil War 1861-1865

Army

Connelly, T. L. Robert E. Lee and the western Confederacy: a criticism of Lee's strategic ability. *In* Hubbell, J. T. ed. Battles lost and won p197-213

Army—Pay, allowances, etc.

Scheiber, H. N. The pay of Confederate troops and problems of demoralization: a case of administrative failure. *In* Hubbell, J. T. ed. Battles lost and won p229-39

Politics and government

Beringer, R. E. The unconscious "spirit of party" in the Confederate Congress. *In* Swierenga, R. P. ed. Beyond the Civil War synthesis p185-201

Secret service

See United States—History—Civil War, 1861-1865 — Secret service — Confederate States

Conference of Red Cross Experts on the Reaffirmation and Development of International Law Applicable in Armed Conflicts

Veuthey, M. A survey of international humanitarian law in noninternational armed conflicts: 1949-1974. *In* International terrorism and political crimes p86-97

Conference of Youth and Students of Southeast Asia Fighting for Freedom and Independence, Calcutta, 1948

Tanigawa, Y. The Cominform and Southeast Asia. *In* The Origins of the Cold war in Asia p362-77

Conference on Security and Cooperation in Europe, Helsinki, 1975
Bastid, S. B. The special significance of the Helsinki Final Act. *In* Human rights, international law and the Helsinki Accord p11-19
Buergenthal, T. International Human Rights Law and the Helsinki Final Act: conclusions. *In* Human rights, international law and the Helsinki Accord p 3-10
Cassese, A. The Helsinki Declaration and self-determination. *In* Human rights, international law and the Helsinki Accord p83-110
Frowein, J. A. The interrelationship between the Helsinki Final Act, the International Covenants on Human Rights, and the European Convention on Human Rights. *In* Human rights, international law and the Helsinki Accord p71-82
Jonathan, G. C. and Jacqué, J. P. Obligations assumed by the Helsinki signatories. *In* Human rights, international law and the Helsinki Accord p43-70
Leary, V. The implementation of the human rights provisions of the Helsinki Final Act: a preliminary assessment: 1975-1977. *In* Human rights, international law and the Helsinki Accord p111-60
Robertson, A. H. The Helsinki Agreement and human rights. *In* Kommers, D. P. and Loescher, G. D. eds. Human rights and American foreign policy p130-48

Conference on the Limitation of Armament, Washington, D.C., 1921-1922
Nish, I. H. Japan and naval aspects of the Washington Conference. *In* Modern Japan p67-80

Confession (Law) See Self-incrimination

The confession (Motion picture)
Kauffmann, S. The confession. *In* Kauffmann, S. Living images p27-31

Confession in literature
Lyons, J. O. Confessional high tide. *In* Lyons, J. O. The invention of the self p89-120

Configuration (Psychology) See Gestalt psychology

Confirmation (Logic) See Verification (Logic)

Conflict, Social. See Social conflict

Conflict of criminal jurisdiction. See Criminal jurisdiction

Conflict of cultures. See Culture conflict

Conflict of generations
Elkind, D. Exploitation and the generational conflict. *In* Elkind, D. The child and society p80-89
Herlihy, D. The generations in medieval history. *In* Viator: medieval and Renaissance studies v5 p347-64
Hesburgh, T. M. The generation gap. *In* Hesburgh, T. M. The Hesburgh papers p141-48

Conflict of laws

Criminal law
See Criminal jurisdiction

Criminal procedure
See Criminal jurisdiction

United States
Hancock, M. Some choice-of-law problems posed by antiguest statutes: realism in Wisconsin and rule-fetishism in New York. *In* Stanford legal essays p251-65

The conformist (Motion picture)
Kauffmann, S. The conformist. *In* Kauffmann, S. Living images p51-52

Conformity. See Deviant behavior; Individuality

Confraternities
McCrank, L. J. The foundation of the confraternity of Tarragona by Archbishop Oleguer Bonestruga, 1126-1129. *In* Viator: medieval and Renaissance studies v9 p157-77

Confucian philosophy. See Philosophy, Confucian

Confucianism
Biderman, S. Scriptures, revelation, and reason. *In* Philosophy East/philosophy West p128-61
Tu, Wei-ming. The Confucian perception of adulthood. *In* Erikson, E. H. ed. Adulthood p113-27
See also Neo-Confucianism; Philosophy, Confucian

Relations—Buddhism
Araki, K. Confucianism and Buddhism in the late Ming. *In* The Unfolding of Neo-Confucianism p39-66

China—20th century
Chang, Hao. New Confucianism and the intellectual crisis of contemporary China. *In* The Limits of change p276-302
Tu, Wei-ming. Hsiung Shih-li's quest for authentic existence. *In* The Limits of change p242-75

Confucius

About
Holzman, D. Confucius and ancient Chinese literary criticism. *In* Chinese approaches to literature from Confucius to Liang Ch'i-ch' ao p21-41
Rubin, V. A. Tradition and human personality. *In* Rubin, V. A. Individual and state in ancient China p 1-31

About individual works
The analects; or, The conversations of Confucius
Canetti, E. Confucius in his Conversations. *In* Canetti, E. The conscience of words p171-76

Congenital diseases. See Medical genetics

Congo, Belgian. See Zaire

Congregation. See Antinomianism

Congregationalism. See; Puritans Brownists; Covenants (Church polity); Dissenters, Religious; Puritans

Congress. See United States. Congress

Congress Party (India) See Indian National Congress

Congressional reform. See United States. Congress—Reform

Congressmen. See Legislators

Congreve, William

About individual works
Incognita
Kennedy, A. From Shakespeare to Congreve: between drama and novel. *In* Kennedy, A. Meaning and signs in fiction p17-29

Love for love
Hoffman, A. W. Allusions and the definition of themes in Congreve's Love for love. *In* Martz, A. L. and Williams, A. L. eds. The author in his work p283-96

Consensus (Social sciences)—*Continued*

Thomas, L. On committees. *In* Thomas, L. The medusa and the snail p115-20

See also Authority; Power (Social sciences)

Consent (Law)

Humphreys, L. G. The fallout of the legal mind in research. *In* Hook, S.; Kurtz, P. and Todorovich, M. eds. The ethics of teaching and scientific research p161-64

Conservation of energy. See Force and energy

Conservation of natural resources

Shaw, C. A. Dilemmas of supergrowth: depleting irreplaceable raw materials. *In* The Year book of world affairs, 1976 p273-91

See also Human ecology

Study and teaching

Emmelin, L. An environmental studies program. *In* Against pollution and hunger p256-59

Conservation of waste products. See Recycling (Waste, etc.)

Conservatism

Oakeshott, M. J. On being conservative. *In* Oakeshott, M. J. Rationalism in politics p168-96

Schwartz, B. I. Notes on conservatism in general and in China in particular. *In* The Limits of change p3-21

Wolin, S. S. Hume and conservatism. *In* Livingston, D. W. and King, J. T. eds. Hume p239-56

China

Bernal, M. Liu Shih-p'ei and National Essence. *In* The Limits of change p90-112

Furth, C. Culture and politics in modern Chinese conservatism. *In* The Limits of change p22-53

Schwartz, B. I. Notes on conservatism in general and in China in particular. *In* The Limits of change p3-21

United States

Galbraith, J. K. The conservative majority syndrome. *In* Galbraith, J. K. Annals of an abiding liberal p47-53

Conservative Party (Great Britain)

Arnold, M. The zenith of conservatism. *In* Arnold, M. The last word p122-43

Cosgrave, P. The failure of the Conservative Party, 1945-75. *In* Tyrrell, R. E. ed. The future that doesn't work p95-125

Stubbs, J. The impact of the Great War on the Conservative Party. *In* Peele, G. and Cook, C. eds. The politics of reappraisal, 1918-1939 p14-38

Conservators. See Conservatorships

Conservatorships

Law and legislation

Marson, C. C.; Crosby, M. C. and Schlosser, A. L. On the civil liberties of sect members: Part 1. *In* Horowitz, I. L. ed. Science, sin, and scholarship p192-97

Vavuris, S. L. On the civil liberties of sect members: Part 2. *In* Horowitz, I. L. ed. Science, sin, and scholarship p198-207

Consolation in literature

Douglas, A. Heaven our home: consolation literature in the northern United States, 1830-1880. *In* Death in America p49-68

Consolidation of local governments. See Metropolitan government

Consortium (Finance) See Syndicates (Finance)

Constable, Giles

Cluniac administration and administrators in the twelfth century. *In* Order and innovation in the Middle Ages p17-30

The structure of medieval society according to the dictatores of the twelfth century. *In* Law, church, and society p253-67

Constans I, Roman Emperor

About

Barnes, T. D. Constans and Gratian in Rome. *In* Harvard Studies in classical philology v79 p325-33

Constant, Benjamin. See Constant de Rebecque, Henri Benjamin

Constant de Rebecque, Henri Benjamin

About individual works

Adolphe

Robinson, C. Subjective reality. *In* Robinson, C. French literature in the nineteenth century p108-70

Constantia, pseud. See Murray, Judith (Sargent)

Constantine I, the Great, Emperor Of Rome. See Constantinus I the Great. Emperor of Rome

Constantine, Donation of. See Donation of Constantine

Constantinople. See Istanbul

Constantinople. Blachernae Palace. See Istanbul. Blachernae Palace

Constantinus I, the Great, Emperor of Rome

About

Hanfmann, G. M. A. Instinctu divinitatis: the Tetrarchs, Constantine, and Constantinople. *In* Hanfmann, G. M. A. From Croesus to Constantine p75-97

Grigg, R. Constantine the Great and the cult without images. *In* Viator: medieval and Renaissance studies v8 p 1-32

Stapleford, R. Constantinian politics and the atrium church. *In* Millon, H. A. and Nochlin, L. eds. Art and architecture in the service of politics p2-19

The constitution of Athens

Bowersock, G. W. Pseudo-Xenophon. *In* Harvard Studies in classical philology v71 p33-55

Constitutional history

Keodurie, É. The fate of constitutionalism in the Middle East. *In* Kedourie, É. Arabic political memoirs and other studies p 1-27

Stourzh, G. The American Revolution, modern constitutionalism, and the protection of human rights. *In* [Truth and tragedy]: a tribute to Hans Morgenthau p162-76

See also Political science and subdivision Constitutional history under names of countries, states, etc. e.g. United States—Constitutional history

Constitutional history. See United States—Constitutional history

Constitutional law

See also Civil rights; Due process of law; Equality before the law; Executive power; Federal government; Judicial review; Natural law; Rule of law; Treaty-making power; War and emergency powers; and subdivision Constitutional law under name of countries, e.g. United States—Constitutional law

Continuing education centers

United States

Spear, G. E. The university and adult education. *In* Murphy, T. P. ed. Universities in the urban crisis p181-96

Continuing legal education. See Law—Study and teaching (Continuing education)

Continuity

Lewis, D. K. Survival and identity. *In* Rorty, A. O. ed. The identities of persons p17-40

Parfit, D. Lewis, Perry, and what matters. *In* Rorty, A. O. ed. The identities of persons p91-107

Perry, J. R. The importance of being identical. *In* Rorty, A. O. ed. The identities of persons p67-90

Rey, G. Survival. *In* Rorty, A. O. ed. The identities of persons p41-66

Wise, M. N. Wlliam Thomson's mathematical route to energy conservation: a case study of the role of mathematics in concept formation. *in* Historical studies in the physical sciences v10 p49-83

Continuum. See Continuity

Continuum mechanics. See Field theory (Physics)

Continuum physics. See Field theory (Physics)

Contraception

See also Birth control

Europe

Flandin, J. L. Contraception, marriage, and sexual relations in the Christian West. *In* Biology of man in history p23-47

France

Burguière, A. From Malthus to Max Weber: belated marriage and the spirit of enterprise. *In* Family and society p237-50

Contraceptives

Ris, H. W. The essential emancipation: the control of reproduction. *In* Roberts, J. I. ed. Beyond intellectual sexism p85-110

Contracting Parties to the General Agreement on Tariffs and Trade

Goldsmith, P. and Sonderkötter, F. Equality and discrimination in international economic law (V): The European communities and the wider world. *In* The Year book of world affairs, 1975 p265-82

Sutton, A. Equality and discrimination in international economic law (VI): trends in the regulation of international trade in textiles. *In* The Year book of world affairs, 1977 p190-216

The **contractor** (criticism) Storey, D. *In* Kauffmann, S. Persons of the drama p329-35

Contractors

Mansfield, H. C. Independence and accountability for federal contractors and grantees. *In* Smith, B. L. R. ed. The new political economy: the public use of the private sector p319-35

Contracts, Government. See Public contracts

Contracts, Public. See Public contracts

Contrafactum. See Mass (Music)

Contrition. See Repentance

Control (Psychology)

Canetti, E. Power and survival. *In* Canetti, E. The conscience of words p14-28

Selzer, M. Narcissism and the quest for power. *In* [Truth and tragedy]: a tribute to Hans Morgenthau p130-41

Controlled fusion reactors. See Fusion reactors

Controlled thermonuclear reactors. See Fusion reactors

Conundrums. See Riddles

Conurbations. See Metropolitan areas

Convention (Philosophy)

Árdal, P. S. Convention and value. *In* David Hume p51-68

Convention on the prohibition of the development, production and stockpiling of bacteriological (biological) and toxin weapons and on their destruction

Goldblat, J. The Biological Disarmament Convention. *In* The Dynamics of the arms race p170-77

Conventions, Political. See Political conventions

Conversation

Oakeshott, M. J. The voice of poetry in the conversation of mankind. *In* Oakeshott, M. J. Rationalism in politics p197-247

Kauffmann, S. The conversation. *In* Kauffmann, S. Living images p276-77

The conversation (Motion picture)

Sarris, A. The conversation. *In* Sarris, A. Politics and cinema p37-48

Conversations with writers

Christ, R. J. Transcriptions with writers. *In* Review, v 1 1979 p321-27

Conversion

Psychology

Batson, C. D. Moon madness: greed or creed? *In* Horowitz, I. L. ed. Science, sin, and scholarship p218-25

Converts from Judaism

Duker, A. G. Frankism as a movement of Polish-Jewish synthesis. *In* Király, B. K. ed. Tolerance and movements of religious dissent in Eastern Europe p133-64

Converts to Christianity from Judaism. See Converts from Judaism

Convict labor

France

Zysberg, A. Galley rowers in the mid-eighteenth century. *In* Deviants and the abandoned in French society p83-110

Conviction. See Belief and doubt; Truth

Conway, John B. and Bucher, Bradley D.

Transfer and maintenance of behavior change in children: a review and suggestions. *In* Behavior modification and families p119-59

Conyers, John R.

Undermining poverty lawyers. *In* Nader, R. and Green, M. J. eds. Verdicts on lawyers p129-43

Cook, Alice Hanson

Sex discrimination at universities: an ombudsman's view. *In* Women in academia p120-27

Cook, Bruce

About individual works

The beat generation

Sheed, W. Beat down and beatific. *In* Sheed, W. The good word & other words p110-15

Cook, Bruce—About individual works—The beat generation—*Continued*

Sheed, W. The beat movement concluded. *In* Sheed, W. The good word & other words p116-20

Cook, Chris

Labour and the downfall of the Liberal Party, 1906-14. *In* Crisis and controversy p38-65

Liberals, Labour and local elections. *In* Peele, G. and Cook, C. eds. The politics of reappraisal, 1918-1939 p166-88

Cook, Don Lewis

Bowers does Fielding. *In* Review, v 1 1979 p13-27

Cook, Ebenezer

About individual works

The sot-weed factor; or, A voyage to Maryland

Arner, R. D. The blackness of darkness: satire, romance, and Ebenezer Cooke's The sot-weed factor. *In* Tennessee Studies in literature v21 p 1-10

Cook, James Henry

About

Dawson, R. F. Rudolf Erich Raspe: the geologist Captain Cook refused. *In* Studies in eighteenth-century culture v8 p269-90

Dobie, J. F. Captain Cook's place among reminiscencers of the West. *In* Dobie, J. F. Prefaces p119-23

Cook, Marjorie

Acceptance in Frost's poetry: conflict as play. *In* Frost: centennial essays II p223-35

Cook, Olive

The fabric of a dream. *In* The Saturday book 34 p185-201

Cook, Reginald Lansing

Robert Frost in context. *In* Frost: centennial essays III p123-73

Cook, Sakakohe

Akwesasne education. *In* Roots of open education in America p 7-12

Cook, Samuel Dubois

Democracy and tyranny in America: the radical paradox of the Bicentennial and Blacks in the American political system. *In* Havard, W. C. and Bernd, J. L. eds. 200 years of the Republic in retrospect p276-94

Southern politics since 1954: a note on change and continuity. *In* Two decades of change p5-19

Cooke, Michael G.

The romantic will

Contents

The extremes of self and system

The extremes of self and system: Blake's Jerusalem: a self without selfhood, a system against system

The extremes of self and system: Fruitful failure and incidental cause: the will in The prelude

The extremes of self and system: The symbiosis of self and system in the neoclassical regimen

The extremes of self and system: Volatile self and system in the romantic complex

The will in English romanticism: Introduction: consciousness and conduct

The will in English romanticism: The question of the will

The will in English romanticism: The will in romantic poetry

The will to art

The will to art: Conclusion

The will to art: Excursus: the will to art in romanticism

The will to art: Keats and the aesthetics of redemption

The will to art: Logic, vision, and actuality: the state of art in Blake

The will to art: Wordsworth and the stoical resolution of art

Cooke, Thomas D.

Pornography, the comic spirit, and the fabliaux. *In* Cooke, T. D. and Honeycutt, B. L. eds. The humor of the fabliaux p137-62

Cookery

History

Bonnet, J. C. The culinary system in the Encyclopédie. *In* Food and drink in history p139-65

Cookery, British

Barber, G. Dr Johnson and cookery. *In* The Dress of words p91-104

Cooley, Rita Weber

Teaching social science. *In* Cahn, S. M. ed. Scholars who teach p131-61

Cooley, Thomas

Educated lives: the rise of modern autobiography in America

Contents

The dissolving man: Henry Adams

The next generation; Future perfect: Lincoln Steffens

The next generation; The continuous present: Gertrude Stein

The next generation; Then as now: Sherwood Anderson

Origins of the self: autobiography in America before 1865

A sporting life: Henry James

This pathetic drift: Mark Twain

The wilderness within: W. D. Howells

Cooley, Thomas McIntyre

About

White, G. E. Political ideologies, professional norms, and the state judiciary in the late nineteenth century: Cooley and Doe. *In* White, G. E. The American judicial tradition p109-28

Coolidge, Calvin, President U.S.

About individual works

The autobiography of Calvin Coolidge

Graff, H. F. Presidents as penmen. *In* From Parnassus p3-15

Coolidge, Ellen Wayles (Randolph)

About

Malone, D. Mr Jefferson's private life. *In* American Antiquarian Society. Proceedings v84 pt 1 p65-72

Coolidge, Olivia E.

Writing about Abraham Lincoln. *In* Horn Book Magazine. Crosscurrents of criticism p241-45

About individual works

The apprenticeship of Abraham Lincoln

Coolidge, O. E. Writing about Abraham Lincoln. *In* Horn Book Magazine. Crosscurrents of criticism p241-45

The statesmanship of Abraham Lincoln

Coolidge, O. E. Writing about Abraham Lincoln. *In* Horn Book Magazine. Crosscurrents of criticism p241-45

Coomaraswamy, Ananda Kentish
Selected papers v 1

Contents

Ars sine scientia nihil
Chinese painting at Boston
Le Corps parsemé d'yeux
A figure of speech or a figure of thought?
Imitation, expression, and participation
An Indian temple: the Kandarya Mahadeo
The intellectual operation in Indian art
Intention
Introduction to the art of Eastern Asia
The inverted tree
Literary symbolism
The mediaeval theory of beauty
The meeting of eyes
The nature of Buddhist art
Note on the philosophy of Persian art
On the Loathly Bride
Ornament
The part of art in Indian life
The philosophy of mediaeval and Oriental art
Primitive mentality
The rape of a Nāgī: an Indian Gupta seal
Samvega: aesthetic shock
The sea
Shaker furniture
Svayamātrnnā: Janua coeli
The symbolism of the dome
Symplegades
Symptom, diagnosis, and regimen
Walter Andrae's Die ionische Säule: Bauform oder Symbol: a review

Selected papers v2
Contents

Ākimcañña: self-naughting
Ātmayajña: self-sacrifice
Bhakta aspects of the Ātman doctrine
Does "Socrates is old" imply that "Socrates is"?
The "E" at Delphi
The flood in Hindu tradition
Kha and other words denoting "zero," in connection with the Indian metaphysics of space
Līlā
Mahā purusa: "Supreme Identity"
Manas
The meaning of death
Measures of fire
Nirukta = hermeneia
On the Indian and traditional psychology, or rather pneumatology
On the one and only transmigrant
Play and seriousness
Recollection, Indian and platonic
The seventieth birthday address
Some Pāli words
Sri Ramakrishna and religious tolerance
The Tantric doctrine of divine biunity
Two passages in Dante's Paradiso
The Vedānta and Western tradition
The Vedic doctrine of "silence"
Vedic exemplarism
Vedic "monotheism"
Also in Disguises of the demonic p57-68

About

Coomaraswamy, A. K. The seventieth birthday address. *In* Coomaraswamy, A. K. Selected papers v2 p433-35

Lipsey, R. Introduction. *In* Coomaraswamy, A. K. Selected papers v 1 pxxix-xxxviii

Coombs, Frank Alan
The impact of the New Deal on Wyoming politics. *In* Braeman, J.; Bremner, R. H. and Brody, D. eds. The New Deal v2 p198-239

Coons, John E. and Sugarman, Stephen D.
A case for choice; excerpt from "Education by choice: the case for family control." *In* Parents, teachers, and children: prospects for choice in American education p129-48

Coope, Christopher
Wittgenstein's theory of knowledge. *In* Royal Institute of Philosophy. Understanding Wittgenstein p246-67

Cooper, Anna Julia

About

Harley, S. Anna J. Cooper: a voice for Black women. *In* Harley, S. and Terborg-Penn, R. eds. The Afro-American woman p87-96

Cooper, Barry
Culture and anarchy: the politics of Matthew Arnold. *In* Prospects for constitutional democracy p21-35

Cooper, David E.
ESP and the materialist theory of mind. *In* Thakur, S. C. ed. Philosophy and psychical research p59-80

Essay 5. *In* Fitzgerald, R. ed. What it means to be human p83-101

Quality and equality in education. *In* Philosophers discuss education p113-29

About individual works
Quality and equality in education

O'Hagan, T. Quality and equality in education: a critique of David Cooper. *In* Philosophers discuss education p130-43

Cooper, Helen
Magic that does not work. *In* Medievalia et humanistica no. 7 p131-46

Working into light: Elizabeth Barrett Browning. *In* Gilbert, S. M. and Gubar, S. eds. Shakespeare's sisters p65-81

Cooper, James Fenimore

About

Cawelti, J. G. The Western: a look at the evolution of a formula. *In* Cawelti, J. G. Adventure, mystery, and romance p192-259

Donaldson, S. and Massa, A. The New World and the Old World. *In* Donaldson, S. and Massa, A. American literature: nineteenth and early twentieth centuries p9-46

Leary, L. G. James Fenimore Cooper's lover's quarrel with America. *In* Leary, L. G. Soundings p271-91

Milne, G. The beginnings. *In* Milne, G. The sense of society p19-42

Steeves, E. L. "No time for fainting" the frontier woman in some early American novels. *In* Kagle, S. E. ed. America: exploration and travel p191-205

Tichi, C. Questioning and chronicling: Thoreau, Cooper, Bancroft. *In* Tichi, C. New World, new earth p151-205

About individual works
The deerslayer

Spengemann, W. C. The poetics of domesticity. *In* Spengemann, W. C. The adventurous muse p68-118

Cooper, James F.—About individual works
—*Continued*

The leather-stocking tales

Pilkington, J. Nature's legacy to William Faulkner. *In* The South and Faulkner's Yoknapatawpha p104-27

The pioneers

Doubleday, N. F. Templeton, late December, 1793—October, 1794. *In* Doubleday, N. F. Variety of attempt p128-46

Schachterle, L. E. American bibliographical notes. *In* American Antiquarian Society. Proceedings v84 pt 1 p219-32

Stineback, D. C. "This comes of settling a country!": James Fenimore Cooper's The pioneers. *In* Stineback, D. C. Shifting world p23-42

Characters

Gelpi, A. Emily Dickinson and the Deerslayer: the dilemma of the women poet in America. *In* Gilbert, S. M. and Gubar, S. eds. Shakespeare's sisters p122-34

Criticism, Textual

Schachterle, L. E. American bibliographical notes. *In* American Antiquarian Society. Proceedings v84 pt 1 p219-32

Cooper, Jilly
The perfect gentleman. *In* The Saturday book 34 p114-25

Cooper, John Phillips
Patterns of inheritance and settlement by great landowners from the fifteenth to the eighteenth centuries. *In* Family and inheritance p192-327

Cooper, Kenneth Schaff
Did you ever think of Aristotle as a college freshman? *In* Buxton, T. H. and Prichard, K. W. eds. Excellence in university teaching p86-93

Cooper, Lee R.
"Publish" or perish: Negro Jehovah's Witness adaptation in the ghetto. *In* Zaretsky, I. I. and Leone, M. P. eds. Religious movements in contemporary America p700-21

Cooper, Louis Jacques Blom- See Blom-Cooper, Louis Jacques

Cooper, Norman B.
The Church: from crusade to Christianity. *In* Preston, P. ed. Spain in crisis p48-81

Cooperation
Nevins, A. The limits of individualism. *In* Nevins, A. Allan Nevins on history p203-14
See also Collective settlements; International cooperation

Cooperation, International. See International cooperation

Cooperation of patients. See Patient compliance

Cooperative fisheries. See Fisheries, Cooperative

Cooperative housing. See Housing, Cooperative

Cooperative production. See Cooperative societies

Cooperative societies

Africa

Traoré, S. An African experiment in grass roots development. *In* Erb, G. F. and Kallab, V. eds. Beyond dependency p111-19

Cooperman, Stanley
John Dos Passos' Three soldiers: aesthetics and the doom of individualism. *In* Klein, H. M. ed. The First World War in fiction p23-31

Coopland, George William

About

Myers, A. R. George William Coopland: a biographical appreciation. *In* War, literature, and politics in the late Middle Ages p 1-11

Coote, Mary Putney
Serbocroatian heroic songs. *In* Oinas, F. J. ed. Heroic epic and saga p257-85

Cooter, Roger
The power of the body: the early nineteenth century. *In* Barnes, B. and Shapin, S. eds. Natural order p73-92

Cooter, William S.
Preindustrial frontiers and interaction spheres: prolegomenon to a study of Roman frontier regions. *In* Miller, D. H. and Steffen, J. O. eds. The frontier p81-107

Coover, Robert

About

Durand, R. The exemplary fictions of Robert Coover. *In* Johnson, I. D. and Johnson, C. [eds.] Les américanistes p130-37

Watkins, E. Criticism and community: on literary value. *In* Watkins, E. The critical act p213-51

About individual works
Pricksongs & descants

Scholes, R. E. Metafiction. *In* Scholes, R. E. Fabulation and metafiction p103-38

The Universal Baseball Association, inc., J. Henry Waugh, prop.

Wallace, R. H. The great American game: Robert Coover's The Universal Baseball Association, inc., J. Henry Waugh, prop. *In* Wallace, R H. The last laugh p115-36

Coox, Alvin D.
Shigemitsu Mamoru: the diplomacy of crisis. *In* Burns, R. D. and Bennett, E. M. eds. Diplomats in crisis p251-73

Cope, Jackson Irving
The constant couple: Farquhar's four plays-in-one. *In* ELH essays for Earl R. Wasserman p184-200

Copeland, Miles

About individual works
The game of nations: the amorality of power politics

Kedourie, E. The apprentice sorcerers. *In* Kedourie, E. Arabic political memoirs and other studies p170-76

Copenhagen Family Guidance Center
Busck, L. The Family Guidance Center in Copenhagen. *In* Davis, K. C. Discretionary justice in Europe and America p115-31

Copernicus, Nicholas. See Copernicus, Nicolaus

Copernicus, Nicolaus

About

Bronowski, J. Copernicus as a humanist. *In* The Nature of scientific discovery p170-88

Cohen, C. Revolutions and Copernican revolutions. *In* Science and society: past, present, and future p86-103

Copyright—*Continued*

United States

Abrams, H. B. and Abrams, R. H. Goldstein v. California: sound, fury, and significance. *In* The Supreme Court review, 1975 p147-87

Perlman, H. S. and Rhinelander, L. H. Williams & Wilkins Co. v. United States: photo-copying, copyright, and the judicial process. *In* The Supreme Court review, 1975 p355-417

Copyright, International

Maggs, P. B. Legal controls on American publication of heterodox Soviet writings. *In* Tokes, R. L. ed. Dissent in the USSR p310-25

Coquery-Vidrovitch, Catherine

Changes in African historical studies in France. *In* African studies since 1945 p200-08

Corbin, David A.

Mine mules and coal tipples: icons of the coalfields. *In* Browne, R. B. and Fishwick, M. W. eds. Icons of America p253-62

Corbin, Peter, and Sedge, Douglas

Shakespeare. *In* English Association. The year's work in English studies v53 p147-92

Cordasco, Francesco

Leonard Covello and the Casa Italiana Educational Bureau: a note on the beginnings of systematic Italian-American studies. *In* Studies in Italian American social history p 1-9

Cordell, Helen, comp.

Publications of D. G. E. Hall. *In* Southeast Asian history and historiography p25-27

Corden, Pierce S.

Ethics and deterrence: moving beyond the just-war tradition. *In* Ethics and nuclear strategy? p156-80

Corden, Warner Max

The costs and consequences of protection: a survey of empirical work. *In* Kenen, P. B. ed. International trade and finance p51-91

Cordesse, Gérard

The impact of American science fiction on Europe. *In* Bigsby, C. W. E. Superculture p161-74

Cordle, Thomas H.

Malraux and Nietzsche's Birth of tragedy. *In* Garvin, H. R. ed. Makers of the twentieth-century novel p133-43

Core, George

The confessions of Nat Turner and the burden of the past. *In* Morris, R. K. and Malin, I. eds. The achievement of William Styron p150-67

Corfman, Eunice Luccock. See Brown, P. G. jt. auth.

Corina, John

Planning and the British labour market: incomes and manpower policy, 1965-70. *In* Planning, politics and public policy p177-201

Corinth, Louis

About

Berger, J. A belief in uniforms (Lovis Corinth). *In* Berger, J. The look of things p122-24

Corinth, Lovis. See Corinth, Louis

Corinth Books

Wilentz, T. and Zavatsky, B. Behind the writer, ahead of the reader: a short history of Corinth Books. *In* Anderson, E. and Kinzie, M. eds. The little magazine in America: a modern documentary history p595-613

Corliss, Richard

Introduction: notes on a screenwriter's theory, 1973—introduction to Talking pictures. *In* Denby, D. ed. Awake in the dark p215-26

Corman, Brian

Toward a generic theory of Restoration comedy: some preliminary considerations. *In* Studies in eighteenth-century culture v7 p423-32

Corman, Cid

Origin. *In* Anderson, E. and Kinzie, M. eds. The little magazine in America: a modern documentary history p239-47

Corn crake. See Corncrake

Corncrake

Whilde, A. A note on the storm petrel and corncrake. *In* Harmon, M. ed. Richard Murphy: poet of two traditions p70-72

Corneille, Pierre

About

Auchincloss, L. The Roman Empire of Pierre Corneille. *In* Auchincloss, L. Life, law and letters p59-67

Brereton, G. The comedies of Pierre Corneille. *In* Brereton, G. French comic drama p12-43

Nicoll, A. Racine and the tragedy of sentiment. *In* Nicoll, A. World drama p243-57

Cornelius, Wayne A.

The impact of cityward migration on urban land and housing markets: problems and policy alternatives in Mexico City. *In* Walton, J. and Masotti, L. H. eds. The city in comparative perspective p249-70

Cornell, Brenda G.

Ambiguous necessity: a study of The ponder heart. *In* Prenshaw, P. W. ed. Eudora Welty p208-19

Cornell, Julien D.

About individual works

The trial of Ezra Pound

Connolly, C. Ezra Pound: 1. *In* Connolly, C. The evening colonnade p217-21

Cornell University. New York State College of Human Ecology

Vallance, T. R. Home economics and the development of new forms of human service education. *In* Land-grant universities and their continuing challenge p79-103

Cornet, Robert James

Irony without positive norms: Robert Browning's "In a year." *In* Aeolian harps p149-66

Cornfeld, Bernie

About

Galbraith, J. K. Bernard Cornfeld: benefactor. *In* Galbraith, J. K. Annals of an abiding liberal p311-16

Cornford, Francis Macdonald

About individual works

Thucydides Mythistoricus

Egan, K. Thucydides, tragedian. *In* Canary, R. H. and Kozicki, H. J. eds. The writing of history p63-92

Cornforth, Maurice Campbell
A. L. Morton—portrait of a Marxist historian. *In* Rebels and their causes p7-19

El corno emplumado
Randall, M. El corno emplumado, 1961-1969: some notes in retrospect, 1975. *In* Anderson, E. and Kinzie, M. eds. The little magazine in America: a modern documentary history p405-22

Cornog, William Hafner
The options market in education. *In* Parents, teachers, and children: prospects for choice in American education p149-64

Cornwall in literature
Rowse, A. L. Hardy and Cornwall. *In* Drabble, M. ed. The genius of Thomas Hardy p119-38

Cornwell, David John Moore

About individual works
The spy who came in from the cold
Rutherford, A. The spy as hero: Le Carré and the Cold War. *In* Rutherford, A. The literature of war p135-56

Cornwell, Regina
Paul Sharits: illusion and object. *In* Nichols, B. ed. Movies and methods p363-73

Coromandel, Joint-stock companies of. Brennig, J. J. *In* Kling, B. B. and Pearson, M. N. eds. The age of partnership p71-96

Coronation Book of Charles V of France
Sherman, C. R. The Queen in Charles V's "Coronation Book": Jeanne de Bourbon and the "Ordo ad reginam benedicendam." *In* Viator: medieval and Renaissance studies v8 p255-98

Coronations. See subdivision Coronation under names of rulers, e.g. Charles V, King of France—Coronation

Corot, Jean Baptiste Camille

About
Berger, J. Thicker than water (Corot). *In* Berger, J. The look of things p125-29

Corporate legal departments
Smyser, J. M. In-house corporate counsel: the erosion of independence. *In* Nader, R. and Green, M. J. eds. Verdicts on lawyers p208-16

Corporate state
Winkler, J. T. The coming corporatism. *In* Skidelsky, R. J. A. ed. The end of the Keynesian era p78-87

Corporation for Public Broadcasting
Lyle, J. Public television: too much ambition and overcommitment? *In* Lerner, D. and Nelson, L. M. eds. Communication research—a half-century appraisal p193-209

Corporation law
Chirelstein, M. A. Corporate law reform. *In* McKie, J. W. ed. Social responsibility and the business predicament p41-77
See also Corporate legal departments; Corporations, International

Corporations
Manne, H. G. Corporate altruism and individualistic methodolgy. *In* Capitalism and freedom p128-42

Peckham, M. The corporation's role in today's crisis of cultural incoherence. *In* Peckham, M. Romanticism and behavior p263-84
See also Corporation law; International business enterprises

Laws and legislation
See Corporation law

France—Taxation
Merlin, C. Tax relief contracts in France. *In* Davis, K. C. Discretionary justice in Europe and America p161-78

United States
Galbraith, J. K. The valid image of the modern economy. *In* Galbraith, J. K. Annals of an abiding liberal p3-19
Galbraith, J. K. What comes after General Motors. *In* Galbraith, J. K. Annals of an abiding liberal p73-85
Jones, R. H. What is the future of the corporation? *In* Benton, L. R. ed. Management for the future p189-97
Wardell, N. N. The corporation. *In* A New America? p97-110

Corporations (Corporate state) See Corporate state

Corporations, Business. See Corporations

Corporations, Foreign

Underdeveloped areas
See Underdeveloped countries—Corporations, Foreign

Corporations, Government. See Government business enterprises

Corporations, Nonprofit

Management
Anthony, R. N. Can nonprofit organizations be well managed? *In* Managing nonprofit organizations p 7-15
Drucker, P. F. Managing the public service institution. *In* Managing nonprofit organizations p16-31
Dubin, R. J. Determining results in the generosity business. *In* Managing nonprofit organizations p270-79
Fallon, K. P. Participatory management: an alternative in human service delivery systems. *In* Managing nonprofit organizations p244-51
McConkey, D. D. Applying management by objectives to nonprofit organizations. *In* Managing nonprofit organizations p141-54
McConkey, D. D. The future: its challenge and its promise; excerpt from "MBO for nonprofit organizations." *In* Managing nonprofit organizations p199-206

United States
Pifer, A. J. The jeopardy of private institutions. *In* Smith, B. L. R. ed. The new political economy: the public use of the private sector p68-82

Corporatism. See Corporate state

Corpus callosum
Simons, J. R. The brain and evolution of lower mammals. *In* Grafton Elliot Smith p39-49

Corpus inscriptionum Latinarum IV, 10566
Lebek, W. D. Heminarium: Quintilian Institutio oratoria 6.3.52 and CIL IV 10566. *In* Harvard Studies in classical philology v82 p271-75

Corpus inscriptionum Latinarum X, 1792
D'Arms, J. H. CIL X, 1792: a municipal notable of the Augustan age. *In* Harvard Studies in classical philology v76 p207-16

Corradi, Juan Eugenio
Argentina. *In* Chilcote, R. H. and Edelstein, J. C. eds. Latin America: the struggle with dependency and beyond p305-407

Correctional institutions. See Juvenile detention homes; Prisons

Correctional law. See Sentences (Criminal procedure)

Correctional services. See Corrections

Corrections
See also Community-based corrections; Imprisonment; Juvenile corrections; Probation; Punishment; Rehabilitation of criminals

Research—United States
Adams, S. N. Evaluative research in corrections: status and prospects. *In* Riedel, M. and Chappell, D. eds. Issues in criminal justice: planning and evaluation p9-23

Connecticut
Hollander, B. L. A private ombudsman or a public agency: planning and development of the Connecticut correctional system ombudsman. *In* Riedel, M. and Chappell, D. eds. Issues in criminal justice: planning and evaluation p87-98

Great Britain
Blom-Cooper, L. J. The constitutional framework of the English penal system. *In* Progress in penal reform p25-34

Illinois
Lieberman, L. M. An attempt to decentralize adult correctional services. *In* Riedel, M. and Chappell, D. eds. Issues in criminal justice: planning and evaluation p114-25

United States—Administration
Luger, M. and Lobenthal, J. S. Cushioning future shock in corrections. *In* Riedel, M. and Chappell, D. eds. Issues in criminal justice: planning and evaluation p126-33

Corrections in the community. See Community-based corrections

Corrigan, Beatrice
Sir Thomas More: personage and symbol on the Italian stage. *In* Studies in the continental background of Renaissance English literature: essays presented to John L. Lievsay p91-108

Corrigan, Beatrice, and Mitchell, Bonner
Italian literature. *In* Jones, W. M. ed. The present state of scholarship in sixteenth-century literature p 1-43

Corrigan, Mary Ann
Beyond verisimilitude: echoes of expressionism in Williams' plays. *In* Tennessee Williams: a tribute p375-412

Corruption (in politics)

Great Britain
Hurstfield, J. The politics of corruption in Shakespeare's England. *In* Shakespeare survey 28 p15-28

Corruption (in politics) in literature
Hurstfield, J. The politics of corruption in Shakespeare's England. *In* Shakespeare survey 28 p15-28

Corry, James Alexander
The prospects for constitutional democracy. *In* Prospects for constitutional democracy p53-74

Corsairs. See Pirates; Privateering

Corso, Gregory

About
Thurley, G. The development of the new language: Wieners, Jones, McClure, Whalen, Corso. *In* Thurley, G. The American moment p187-209

Corson, John A.
Families as mutual control systems: optimization by systematization of reinforcement. *In* Behavior modification and families p317-30

Cortázar, Julio

About individual works
Hopscotch
Brotherston, G. Intellectual geography: Julio Cortázar. *In* Brotherston, G. The emergence of the Latin American novel p81-97
Foster, D. W. Julio Cortázar and the intellectual as Everyman. *In* Foster, D. W. Currents in the contemporary Argentine novel: Arlt, Mallea, Sabato, and Cortázar p98-127
MacAdam, A. J. Julio Cortázar: self-explanation & self-destruction. *In* MacAdam, A. J. Modern Latin American narratives p51-60

Cortés, Donoso. See Donoso Cortés, Juan Marques de Valdegamas

Cortina, Juan Nepomuceno

About
Evans, J. L. Ethnic tensions in the Lower Rio Grande Valley to 1860. *In* Yoder, D. ed. American folklife p239-55

Cortona, Pietro Berrettini da

About
Wittkower, R. Pietro da Cortona's project for reconstructing the Temple of Palestrina. *In* Wittkower, R. Studies in the Italian baroque p115-24

Corwin, Arthur F.
Afro-Brazilians: myths and realities. *In* Toplin, R. B. ed. Slavery and race relations in Latin America p385-437

Corwin, Edward Samuel
Presidential power and the Constitution
Contents
The dissolving structure of our constitutional law
The natural law and constitutional law
Our constitutional revolution and how to round it out
President and Court: a crucial issue
The President as administrative chief
The President's power
Some probable repercussions of "Nira" on our constitutional system
The steel seizure case: a judicial brick without straw
The war and the Constitution: President and Congress
War, the Constitution moulder
Wilson and the Senate
Woodrow Wilson and the Presidency

Cory, William Johnson

About
Blythe, R. The school-leaver. *In* The Saturday book 34 p148-56

Coşar, Fatma Mansur
Women in Turkish society. *In* Beck, L. and Keddie, N. R. eds. Women in the Muslim world p124-40

Coser, Lewis Alfred
Merton's uses of the European sociological tradition. *In* The Idea of social structure p85-100
Publishers as gatekeepers of ideas. *In* Altbach, P. G. and McVey, S. eds. Perspectives on publishing p17-25
Structure and conflict. *In* Blau, P. M. ed. Approaches to the study of social structure p210-19
Two methods in search of a substance. *In* The Uses of controversy in sociology p329-41

Coser, Rose Laub
The complexity of roles as a seedbed of individual autonomy. *In* The Idea of social structure p237-63

Cosgrave, Patrick
The failure of the Conservative Party, 1945-75. *In* Tyrrell, R. E. ed. The future that doesn't work p95-125

Cosgrove, Carol Ann. See Cosgrove-Twitchett, Carol

Cosgrove-Twitchett, Carol
From association to partnership. *In* Twitchett, K. J. ed. Europe and the world p121-50
Towards a Community development policy. *In* Twitchett, K. J. ed. Europe and the world p151-74

Cosimo I, de' Medici, il Grande, grand-duke of Tuscany

Art patronage
Barolsky, P. The lighter side of Cosimo de' Medici's court. *In* Barolsky, P. Infinite jest: wit and humor in Italian Renaissance art p139-57

Cosmic physics. See Astrophysics

Cosminsky, Sheila
The evil eye in a Quiché community. *In* The Evil eye p163-74

Cosmogony
Porter, R. Creation and credence: the career of theories of the earth in Britain, 1660-1820. *In* Barnes, B. and Shapin, S. eds. Natural order p97-123
Schmidt, M. Quasars and the universe. *In* The Nature of scientific discovery p246-60
Wheeler, J. A. The universe as home for man. *In* The Nature of scientific discovery p261-96

History
Wheeler, J. A. Man's view of the cosmos in America, 1776-1976. *In* A Time to hear and answer: essays for the Bicentennial season p59-101

Cosmogony, Biblical. See Creation

Cosmography

History
Lamb, U. S. Cosmographers of Seville: nautical science and social experience. *In* First images of America p675-86

Cosmological argument. See God—Proof, Cosmological

Cosmology
Alfvén, H. Cosmology; myth or science? *In* Cosmology, history, and theology p 1-14
Burbidge, G. and Burbidge, M. Modern riddles of cosmology. *In* Neyman, J. ed. The heritage of Copernicus: theories "pleasing to the mind" p116-39

Feldman, S. N. O. Platonic themes in Gersonides' cosmology. *In* Salo Wittmayer Baron v 1 p383-405
Frye, N. The times of the signs. *In* Frye, N. Spiritus mundi p66-96
Heidmann, J. The expansion of the universe in the frame of conventional general relativity. *In* Cosmology, history, and theology p39-57
Hoyle, Sir F. On the origin of the universe. *In* The Frontiers of knowledge p295-323
Lapidge, M. Stoic cosmology. *In* Rist, J. M. ed. The Stoics p161-85
Merleau-Ponty, J. Laplace as a cosmologist. *In* Cosmology, history, and theology p283-91
Meynell, H. A. The intelligibility of the universe. *In* Reason and religion p23-43
Misner, C. W. Cosmology and theology. *In* Cosmology, history, and theology p75-100
Penzias, A. A. An observational view of the cosmos. *In* Cosmology, history, and theology p101-12
Stopes-Roe, H. V. The intelligibility of the universe. *In* Reason and religion p44-71
Tomita, K. On a chaotic early universe. *In* Cosmology, history, and theology p131-39
Yourgrau, W. On some cosmological theories and constants. *In* Cosmology, history, and theology p179-210
Wightman, W. P. D. Cosmological and technological trends in the French Renaissance. *In* French Renaissance studies, 1540-70 p70-80
See also Astronomy—Philosophy; Creation; God—Proof, Cosmological; Philosophy of nature; Red shift; Teleology; Theosophy

Early works to 1800
Grant, E. Cosmology. *In* Lindberg, D. C. ed. Science in the Middle Ages p265-302

History
Wheeler, J. A. Man's view of the cosmos in America, 1776-1976. *In* A Time to hear and answer: essays for the Bicentennial season p59-101

Cosmology, Biblical
Hefner, P. J. Basic Christian assumptions about the cosmos. *In* Cosmology, history, and theology p347-64
Peacocke, A. R. Cosmos and creation. *In* Cosmology, history, and theology p365-81
Peat, D. W. Creation and redemption. *In* Cosmology, history, and theology p383-86
See also Creation

Cosmology in literature
Frye, N. The times of the signs. *In* Frye, N. Spiritus mundi p66-96

Cost and standard of living
See also Purchasing power

United States
Backman, J. Economic growth, standards of living, and quality of life. *In* Tomorrow's American p69-89

Cost benefit analysis. See Cost effectiveness

Cost effectiveness
Self, P. Techniques and values in policy decisions. *In* Royal Institute of Philosophy. Nature and conduct p298-312

Cost of Living Council. See United States. Cost of Living Council

Cost of medical care. See Medical care, Cost of

Costa, Emília Viotti da
The political emancipation of Brazil. *In* From colony to nation p43-88

Costa, Uriel da. See Acosta, Uriel

Costa-Gavras

About individual works
State of siege
Sarris, A. State of siege. *In* Denby, D. ed. Awake in the dark p200-14
Sarris, A. State of siege. *In* Sarris, A. Politics and cinema p63-77

Costabel, Pierre
Mathematics and Galileo's inclined plane experiments. *In* Bonelli, M. L. R. and Shea, W. R. eds. Reason, experiment, and mysticism in the scientific revolution p177-87

Costanzo, Gesu Aldo
Economics and health. *In* Cahill, K. M. ed. Health and development p69-82

Costs, Industrial. See Cost effectiveness; Prices

Costume
Bogatyrev, P. G. Costume as a sign. *In* Matejka, L. and Titunik, I. R. eds. Semiotics of art p13-19

History—20th century
Carnes, V. Icons of popular fashion. *In* Browne, R. B. and Fishwick, M. W. eds. Icons of America p228-40

Cotler, Julio
A structural-historical approach to the breakdown of democratic institutions: Peru. *In* The Breakdown of democratic regimes pt3 p178-206

Cottages in literature
Ford, G. H. Felicitous space: the cottage controversy. *In* Knoepflmacher, U. C. and Tennyson, G. B. eds. Nature and the Victorian imagination p29-48

Cotter, John L.
Archaeology and material history: a personal approach to discovery of the past. *In* Luedtke, L. S. ed. The study of American culture p63-75

Cottino-Jones, Marga
Comic modalities in The Decameron. *In* Ruggiers, P. G. ed. Versions of medieval comedy p151-71

Cottle, Thomas J.
The child is father to the man; excerpt from "The abandoners." *In* Gross, B. and Gross, R. eds. The children's rights movement p58-71
"Show me a scientist who's helped poor folks and I'll kiss her hand." *In* Science and society: past, present, and future p216-27
An unemployed family. *In* On the making of Americans p143-72

Cotton, John, 1585-1652

About
Stoever, W. K. B. The nature of New England antinomianism. *In* Stoever, W. K. B. 'A faire and easie way to heaven' p161-83
Stoever, W. K. B. The objectivity of regenerating grace: Thomas Shepard and Peter Bulkeley. *In* Stoever, W. K. B. 'A faire and easie way to heaven' p58-80
Stoever, W. K. B. The preeminence of the spirit: John Cotton. *In* Stoever, W. K. B. 'A faire and easie way to heaven' p34-57

Cotton, Sir Robert Bruce, bart.

About
Grant, R. J. S. Laurence Nowell's transcript of BM Cotton Otho B. xi. *In* Anglo-Saxon England 3 p111-24

Cotton fabrics
Marrison, A. J. Great Britain and her rivals in the Latin American cotton piece-goods market, 1880-1914. *In* Great Britain and her world, 1750-1914 p309-48

Cotton famine, 1861-1864
Farnie, D. A. The Cotton famine in Great Britain. *In* Great Britain and her world, 1750-1914 p153-78

Cotton trade

Great Britain—History
Farnie, D. A. The Cotton famine in Great Britain. *In* Great Britain and her world, 1750-1914 p153-78

United States
Warren, G. H. The King Cotton theory. *In* Encyclopedia of American foreign policy p515-20

Cottrell, Robert D.
Ulcerated hearts: love in Voltaire's La mort de César. *In* Literature and history in the age of ideas p169-77

Couch, Beatriz Melano
New visions of the Church in Latin America; a Protestant view. *In* The Emergent gospel p193-226

Couch, William Terry
The sacred and golden cord. *In* Viva Vivas! p87-137

Couloumbis, Theodore A, See Kitromilides, P. M. jt. auth.

Couloumbis, Theodore A. and Tredway, M'Kean M.
U.S. intervention & abstention in Greece, 1944-1970. *In* Higham, R. D. ed. Intervention or abstention: the dilemma of American foreign policy p95-113

Coulson, Noel James, and Hinchcliffe, Doreen
Women and law reform in contemporary Islam. *In* Beck, L. and Keddie, N. R. eds. Women in the Muslim world p37-51

Coultass, Clive
Film preservation: the archives. *In* Smith, P. ed. The historian and film p32-47

Coulter, Harris L.
Homeopathic medicine. *In* Sobel, D. S. ed. Ways of health p289-317

Council for Mutual Economic Assistance
Blasier, C. COMECON in Cuban development. *In* Cuba in the world p225-55
Nussbaumer, A. The economic systems of Socialist Eastern Europe: principles, development, and operation. *In* The Year book of world affairs, 1975 p222-41
Uschakow, A. COMECON: inter-state economic co-operation in Eastern Europe. *In* Hayward, J. E. S. and Berki, R. N. eds. State and society in contemporary Europe p218-36

Council for the Encouragement of Music and the Arts. See Arts Council of Great Britain

Council of Europe. European Committee on Crime Problems
Anttila, I. The foundation of co-operation in European criminological research: Sir Leon Radzinowicz and the Criminological Scientific Council at the Council of Europe. *In* Crime, criminology and public policy p25-32

Council of Nicaea, 2d, 787. See Nicaea, Council of, 2d, 787

Councils, Press. See Press councils

Councils and synods

History

Somerville, R. E. Cardinal Stephan of St Grisogono: some remarks on legates and legatine councils in the eleventh century. *In* Law, church, and society p157-66

Rome

Wallach, L. The Roman synod of December 800 and the alleged trial of Leo III. *In* Wallach, L. Diplomatic studies in Latin and Greek documents from the Carolingian age p328-52

Rouen

Foreville, R. The synod of the province of Rouen in the eleventh and twelfth centuries. *In* Church and government in the Middle Ages p19-39

Counseling

Chassé, R. Patient counseling in home care. *In* Home care p172-77

See also Genetic counseling; Hotlines (Counseling); Marriage counseling

Counter culture. See Collective settlements; College students; Drugs and youth; Hippies; Radicalism; Subculture

Counter-Reformation. See Reformation

Countercultures and social change. Yinger, J. M. *In* Major social issues p476-97

Counterintelligence. See Intelligence service

Counterrevolutions

Weber, E. J. Revolution? Counterrevolution? What revolution? *In* Laqueur, W. Z. ed. Fascism: a reader's guide p435-67

The country girl (criticism) Odets, C. Simon, J. I. Singularities p195-209

The country girl (Motion picture)

French, B. A night without a star. *In* French, B. On the verge of revolt p61-72

Country life

See also Country life in literature; Pastoral poetry; Rural conditions; Sociology, Rural

Maine

White, E. B. Home-coming. *In* White, E. B. Essays of E. B. White p7-13

White, E. B. A report in January. *In* White, E. B. Essays of E B White p46-52

White, E. B. A report in spring. *In* White, E. B. Essays of E. B. White p14-16

White, E. B. The winter of the great snows. *In* White, E. B. Essays of E. B. White p53-59

Country life in literature

Blythe, R. The dangerous idyll: sweet Auburn to Akenfield. *In* Royal Society of Literature of the United Kingdom, London. Essays by divers hands v38 p15-32

Brown, D. B. The village writers. *In* Brown, D. B. Soviet Russian literature since Stalin p218-52

Cavaliero, G. Conclusion: The earth and the land. *In* Cavaliero, G. The rural tradition in the English novel, 1900-1939 p201-09

Cavaliero, G. The cult of the primitive: Eden Phillpotts, John Trevena. *In* Cavaliero, G. The rural tradition in the English novel, 1900-1939 p46-65

Cavaliero, G. Farmer novelists: H. W. Freeman, A. G. Street, Adrian Bell. *In* Cavaliero, G. The rural tradition in the English novel, 1900-1939 p101-17

Cavaliero, G. The land and the city. *In* Cavaliero, G. The rural tradition in the English novel, 1900-1939 p 1-13

Cavaliero, G. The land of lost content: Henry Williamson, Llewelyn Powys. *In* Cavaliero, G. The rural tradition in the English novel, 1900-1939 p118-32

Cavaliero, G. Literary regionalism: Hugh Walpole, Sheila Kaye-Smith. *In* Cavaliero, G. The rural tradition in the English novel, 1900-1939 p66-80

Cavaliero, G. Problems of the rural novelist: E. C. Booth. *In* Cavaliero, G. The rural tradition in the English novel, 1900-1939 p14-25

Cavaliero, G. Romantic landscapes: Mary Webb, E. H. Young. *In* Cavaliero, G. The rural tradition in the English novel, 1900-1939 p133-56

Cavaliero, G. Rural fantasies: Kenneth Grahame, T. H. White and others. *In* Cavaliero, G. The rural tradition in the English novel, 1900-1939 p26-45

Cavaliero, G. Town and country: Francis Brett Young, Winifred Holtby. *In* Cavaliero, G. The rural tradition in the English novel, 1900-1939 p81-100

Donaldson, S. and Massa, A. City and country. *In* Donaldson, S. and Massa, A. American literature: nineteenth and early twentieth centuries p47-80

Manlove, C. N. Goldsmith and Crabbe. *In* Manlove, C. N. Literature and reality, 1600-1800 p177-92

See also Farm life in literature; Pastoral literature

Country schools. See Rural schools

Courage

Bulgakov, S. N. Heroism and asceticism: reflections on the religious nature of the Russian intelligentsia. *In* Landmarks p23-63

Courbet, Gustav

About

Schapiro, M. Courbet and popular imagery. *In* Schapiro, M. Selected papers v2 p47-85

Self-portraits

Fried, M. The beholder in Courbet: his early self-portraits and their place in his art. *In* Glyph 4 p85-129

Courcel, Martine Hallade de

Introduction. *In* Courcel, M. H. de, ed. Malraux p 1-15

Courlander, Harold

About individual works

A treasury of Afro-American folklore

Reed, I. A treasury of Afro-American folklore. *In* Reed, I. Shrovetide in old New Orleans p126-28

Courses of study. See Education—Curricula

Court administration

United States

Burger, W. E. At last—innovation in the Federal judicial system. *In* Managing nonprofit organizations p313-18

Court drama, The Tudor mask and Elizabethan. Axton, M. *In* English drama: forms and development p24-47

Court management. See Court administration

Court of Justice of the European Communities

Bredima, A. Comparative law in the Court of Justice of the European Communities. *In* The Year book of world affairs, 1978 p320-33

Carson, G. B. National sovereignty at the bar: revolution by law? *In* Essays on modern European revolutionary history p105-32

Court reports. See Law reports, digests, etc.

Courtly love

Brody, S. N. The comic rejection of courtly love. *In* In pursuit of perfection p221-61

Economou, G. D. The two Venuses and courtly love. *In* In pursuit of perfection p17-50

Ferrante, J. M. The conflict of lyric conventions and romance form. *In* In pursuit of perfection p135-78

Ferrante, J. M. Courtly literature. *In* Ferrante, J. M. Woman as image in medieval literature p65-97

Karlin, R. The challenge to courtly love. *In* In pursuit of perfection p101-33

Kelly, D. Allegory of love. *In* Kelly, D. Medieval imagination p13-25

Kelly, D. Guillaume de Machaut and the sublimation of courtly love in imagination. *In* Kelly, D. Medieval imagination p121-54

Kelly, D. Imagination and the Second Rhetoric. *In* Kelly, D. Medieval imagination p96-120

Kelly, D. Verisimilitude and imagination: the crisis in late courtly poetry. *In* Kelly, D. Medieval imagination p177-203

Reiss, E. Fin'amors: its history and meaning in medieval literature. *In* Medieval and Renaissance studies 1976 p74-99

Topsfield, L. T. Arnaut Daniel. *In* Topsfield, L. T. Troubadours and love p195-218

Topsfield, L. T. Bernart de Ventadorn. *In* Topsfield, L. T. Troubadours and love p111-36

Topsfield, L. T. Guilhem de Montanhagol, Peire Cardenal and Guiraut Riquier. *In* Topsfield, L. T. Troubadours and love p241-52

Topsfield, L. T. Guilhem IX of Aquitaine and the quest for joy. *In* Topsfield, L. T. Troubadours and love p11-41

Topsfield, L. T. Jaufre Rudel and love from afar. *In* Topsfield, L. T. Troubadours and love p42-69

Topsfield, L. T. Marcabru and Fin'amors. *In* Topsfield, L. T. Troubadours and love p70-107

Topsfield, L. T. Peire d'Alvernhe. *In* Topsfield, L. T. Troubadours and love p159-91

Topsfield, L. T. Raimbaut d'Aurenga. *In* Topsfield, L. T. Troubadours and love p137-58

Topsfield, L. T. Raimon de Miraval and the joy of the court. *In* Topsfield, L. T. Troubadours and love p219-37

See also Minnesingers; Troubadours

Courts

See also Civil procedure; Criminal procedure; Judicial review; Jury; Juvenile courts

Administration

See Court administration

France

Castan, N. Summary justice. *In* Deviants and the abandoned in French society p111-56

Courts, Church. See Ecclesiastical courts

Courts, Ecclesiastical. See Ecclesiastical courts

Courts, International. See International courts

Courtship. See Dating (Social customs)

Courtship in literature. See Love in literature

Courtyards

Stapleford, R. Constantinian politics and the atrium church. *In* Millon, H. A. and Nochlin, L. eds. Art and architecture in the service of politics p2-19

Couser, G. Thomas

American autobiography

Contents

Deism and prophecy: Benjamin Franklin's Autobiography

Frederick Douglass: abolitionism and prophecy

Gertrude Stein: the making of a prophet

Henry Adams: heretic and prophet

Henry David Thoreau: retreat and pilgrimage

John Woolman: a prophet among prophets

Piety and prophecy in Puritan spiritual autobiography

Three contemporaries: Malcolm X, Norman Mailer, and Robert Pirsig

Two prophetic architects: Louis Sullivan and Frank Lloyd Wright

Walt Whitman: vision and revision

Cousin, Victor

Influence

Spitzer, A. B. Victor Cousin and the French generation of 1820. *In* From Parnassus p177-94

Cousins, Ewert H.

The many-leveled psyche: correlation between psychotherapy and the spiritual life. *In* Wolman, B. B. ed. Psychoanalysis and Catholicism p31-64

Couturier, Maurice

Foreign scholarship: French contributions. *In* American literary scholarship, 1977 p467-74

Nabokov's performative writing. *In* Johnson, I. D. and Johnson, C. [eds.] Les américanistes p156-81

Couvade

Colson, A. B. Birth customs of the Akawaio. *In* Studies in social anthropology p285-309

Couzens, Tim J.

Early South African Black writing. *In* King, B. A. and Ogungbesan, K. eds. A celebration of Black and African writing p 1-14

The social ethos of Black writing in South Africa, 1920-50. *In* Heywood, C. ed. Aspects of South African literature p66-81

Sol Plaatje's Mhudi. *In* Parker, K. ed. The South African novel in English p57-76

Covello, Leonard

About

Cordasco, F. Leonard Covello and the Casa Italiana Educational Bureau: a note on the beginnings of systematic Italian-American studies. *In* Studies in Italian American social history p 1-9

Covenant of grace. See Covenants (Theology)

Covenant of works. See Covenants (Theology)

Covenants (Church polity)

Hall, M. G. and Joyce, W. L. The Halfway covenant of 1662: some new evidence. *In* American Antiquarian Society. Proceedings v87 pt 1 p97-110

Morgan, E. S. The Halfway covenant; excerpt from "Visible saints." *In* Mulder, J. M. and Wilson, J. F. eds. Religion in American history p29-44

Covenants (Jewish theology)

Eckhardt, A. R. The recantation of the covenant? *In* Rosenfeld, A. H. and Greenberg, I. eds. Confronting the Holocaust p159-68

Covenants (Theology)

Miller, P. The marrow of Puritan divinity. *In* Vaughan, A. T. and Bremer, F. J. eds. Puritan New England p44-65

Stoever, W. K. B. The dialectic of nature and grace. *In* Stoever, W. K. B. 'A faire and easie way to heaven' p3-20

Stoever, W. K. B. The doctrine of the two covenants: I. *In* Stoever, W. K. B. 'A faire and easie way to heaven' p 81-96

Stoever, W. K. B. The doctrine of the two covenants: II. *In* Stoever, W. K. B. 'A faire and easie way to heaven' p97-118

Stoever, W. K. B. The New England controversy. *In* Stoever, W. K. B. 'A faire and easie way to heaven' p21-33

Stoever, W. K. B. The objectivity of regenerating grace: Thomas Shepard and Peter Bulkeley. *In* Stoever, W. K. B. 'A faire and easie way to heaven' p58-80

Coventry, Francis

About individual works

The history of Pompey the Little; or, The life and adventures of a lap-dog

Auty, S. G. Fielding's followers: Pompey the Little. *In* Auty, S. G. The comic spirit of eighteenth-century novels p55-65

Coventry Corpus Christi plays

Bevington, D. M. Discontinuity in medieval acting traditions. *In* The Elizabethan theatre, V p 1-16

Winnington-Ingram, R. P. "To find the players and all that longeth therto": notes on the production of medieval drama in Coventry. *In* The Elizabethan theatre, V p17-44

Coventry plays. See names of individual plays, e.g. Assumptio Mariae

Covered bridges

Jakle, J. A. and Janiskee, R. L. Why covered bridges? Toward the management of historic landscapes—the case of Parke County, Indiana. *In* Pattern and process p193-201

Covici, Pascal

Mark Twain and the humor of the Old Southwest; excerpt from "Mark Twain's humor: the image of a world." *In* Inge, M. T. ed. The frontier humorists p233-58

Covington, James Warren

Relations between the eastern Timucuan Indians and the French and Spanish, 1564-1567. *In* Hudson, C. M. ed. Four centuries of Southern Indians p11-27

Cowan, Charles Donald

D. G. E. Hall: a biographical sketch. *In* Southeast Asian history and historiography p11-23

Cowan, Donald A.

Science, history and the evidence of things not seen. *In* From Parnassus p313-23

Cowan, Ian Borthwick

Church and society. *In* Brown, J. M. ed. Scottish society in the fifteenth century p112-35

Cowan, James C.

D. H. Lawrence's dualism: the Apollonian-Dionysian polarity and The Ladybird. *In* Forms of modern British fiction p73-99

Cowan, Ruth Schwartz

Nature and nurture: the interplay of biology and politics in the work of Francis Galton. *In* Studies in history of biology v 1 p133-208

Cowasjee, Saros

The problems of teaching Indian fiction in Commonwealth countries. *In* Narasimhaiah, C. D. ed. Awakened conscience p413-19

Cowboys. See Gauchos

Cowdrey, Herbert Edward John

The genesis of the Crusades: the springs of Western ideas of holy war. *In* The Holy war p9-32

Cowen, Zelman

The governance of the universities. *In* Universities in the Western world p58-74

The way we live now. *In* Prospects for constitutional democracy p3-20

Cowgill, Donald Olen

Aging and modernization: a revision of the theory. *In* Gubrium, J. F. ed. Late life p123-46

Cowgill, George Lewis

Archaeology. *In* Quantitative social science research on Latin America p104-31

Quantitive studies of urbanization at Teotihuacan. *In* Mesoamerican archaeology p363-96

Cowley, Malcolm

—And I worked at the writer's trade

Contents

—And I worked at the writer's trade
"And Jesse begat. . ." a note on literary generations
Conrad Aiken: from Savannah to Emerson
A defense of storytelling
Faulkner: the etiology of his art
Figure in a crowd
Georgia boy
How writers write
Laforgue in America: a testimony
Mr Papa and the parricides
The New England voice
The 1930s: faith and works
A personal record
Rebels, artists, and scoundrels
The sense of guilt
"Sir: I have the honor"

Magic in Faulkner. *In* Faulkner, modernism, and film: Faulkner and Yoknapatawpha, 1978 p3-19

About

Cowley, M. —And I worked at the writer's trade. *In* Cowley, M. —And I worked at the writer's trade p51-68

Cowley, M. The New England voice. *In* Cowley, M. —And I worked at the writer's trade p35-50

Cowley, M. A personal record. *In* Cowley, M. —And I worked at the writer's trade p153-60

Smelstor, M. R. Expatriation and exploration: the exile artists of the 1920s. *In* Kagle, S. E. ed. America: exploration and travel p136-52

Cowper, William

About

Baird, J. D. Cowper's concept of truth. *In* Studies in eighteenth-century culture p367-73

Hartley, L. Harlequin intrudes: William Cowper's venture into the satiric mode. *In* The Dress of words p127-37

Ober, W. B. Madness and poetry: a note on Collins, Cowper, and Smart. *In* Ober, W. B. Boswell's clap and other essays p137-92

About individual works

Memoir of the early life of William Cowper, esq.

Spacks, P. A. M. The soul's imaginings: Daniel Defoe, William Cowper. *In* Spacks, P. A. M. Imagining a self p28-56

The task

Feingold, R. Art divorced from nature: The task and bucolic tradition. *In* Feingold, R. Nature and society p155-92

Feingold, R. William Cowper: state, society, and countryside. *In* Feingold, R. Nature and society p121-53

Halperin, J. The worlds of Emma: Jane Austen and Cowper. *In* Halperin, J. ed. Jane Austen p197-206

Manlove, C. N. Cowper. *In* Manlove, C. N. Literature and reality, 1600-1800 p193-208

Yardley oak

Manlove, C. N. Cowper. *In* Manlove, C. N. Literature and reality, 1600-1800 p193-208

Influence—Austen

Halperin, J. The worlds of Emma: Jane Austen and Cowper. *In* Halperin, J. ed. Jane Austen p197-206

Political and social views

Feingold, R. William Cowper: state, society, and countryside. *In* Feingold, R. Nature and society p121-53

Social views

See Cowper, William—Political and social views

Cox, Anthony Berkeley

About

Panek, L. L. Anthony Berkeley Cox. *In* Panek, L. L. Watteau's shepherds: the detective novel in Britain, 1914-1940 p111-25

Cox, Archibald

Harvard College amicus curiae, DeFunis v. Odegaard. *In* Gross, B. R. ed. Reverse discrimination p184-97

Cox, Charles Brian

The editing of Critical Quarterly. *In* From Parnassus p135-46

Cox, Gregory Stevens- See Stevens-Cox, Gregory

Cox, Harvey Gallagher

Deep structures in the study of new religions. *In* Needleman, J. and Baker, G. eds. Understanding the new religions p122-30

About individual works

The secular city

Hesburgh, T. M. The challenges of Christian higher education. *In* Hesburgh, T. M. The Hesburgh papers p51-61

Ricoeur, P. Urbanization and secularization. *In* Ricoeur, P. Political and social essays p176-97

Cox, James, 1851-1901

About

Dobie, J. F. James Cox and his "Cattle industry." *In* Dobie, J. F. Prefaces p146-58

About individual works

Historical and biographical record of the cattle industry and the cattlemen of Texas and adjacent territory

Dobie, J. F. James Cox and his "Cattle industry." *In* Dobie, J. F. Prefaces p146-58

Cox, James Melville

R. W. Emerson: the circles of the eye. *In* Levin, D. ed. Emerson: prophecy, metamorphosis, and influence p57-81

Cox, John D.

Epistemological release in The silver chair. *In* Schakel, P. J. ed. The longing for a form p159-68

Cox, Robert Gene

Choices for partnership or bloodshed in Panama. *In* The Americas in a changing world p132-55

Coxe, Antony D. Hippisley

La Vie parisienne. *In* The Saturday book 34 p24-44

Coxe, Louis Osborne

Enabling acts

Contents

After words
The complex world of James Gould Cozzens
Edward Thomas and the real world
Edwin Arlington Robinson: the lost tradition
Herman Melville's The Encantadas
History and imagination
The narrative poem: novel of the future?
Poetry and—religion?
Romance of the rose: John Peale Bishop and Phelps Putnam
Thomas Lovell Beddoes: the mask of parody
What Edith Wharton saw in Innocence
You never can tell: George Bernard Shaw reviewed

Coyotes (in religion, folk-lore, etc.)

Toelken, J. B. The "pretty languages" of Yellowman: genre, mode, and texture in Navaho coyote narratives. *In* Folklore genres p145-70

Cozumel Island

Sabloff, J. A. and others. Trade and power in postclassic Yucatan. initial observations. *In* Mesoamerican archaeology p397-416

Antiquities

Sabloff, J. A. and Freidel, D. A. A model of a pre-Columbian trading center. *In* Ancient civilization and trade p369-408

Cozzens, James Gould

About

Coxe, L. O. The complex world of James Gould Cozzens. *In* Coxe, L. O. Enabling acts p44-61

Lora, R. By love possessed: the Cozzens-Macdonald affair. *In* Filler, L. ed. A question of quality: popularity and value in modern creative writing p57-79

Milne, G. Practitioners, 1920-1960. *In* Milne, G. The sense of society p205-35

Cozzens, James G.—About—*Continued*

About individual works

By love possessed

Lora, R. By love possessed: the Cozzens-Macdonald affair. *In* Filler, L. ed. A question of quality: popularity and value in modern creative writing p57-79

Crab Nebula

Brandt, J. C. Pictographs and petroglyphs of the Southwest Indians. *In* Brecher, K. and Feirtag, M. eds. Astronomy of the ancients p25-38

Crabbe, George, 1754-1832

About

Ober, W. B. Drowsed with the fume of poppies: opium and John Keats. *In* Ober, W. B. Boswell's clap and other essays p118-36

About individual works

Poetical works with his letters and journals and his life, by his son

Faulkner, T. C. George Crabbe: Murray's 1834 edition of the life and poems. *In* Virginia. University. Bibliographical Society. Studies in bibliography v32 p246-52

The village

Manlove, C. N. Goldsmith and Crabbe. *In* Manlove, C. N. Literature and reality, 1600-1800 p177-92

Crabbe, George, 1785-1857

About individual works

Life of George Crabbe by his son

Faulkner, T. C. George Crabbe: Murray's 1834 edition of the life and poems. *In* Virginia. University. Bibliographical Society. Studies in bibliography v32 p246-52

Crabbe, John K.

The harmony of her mind: Peacock's emancipated women. *In* Tennessee Studies in literature v23 p75-86

Crackanthorpe, David

About individual works

Hubert Crackanthorpe and English realism in the 1890's

Weintraub, S. Three views of the nineties. *In* Review, v 1 1979 p301-08

Cracow. Uniwersytet Jagielloński. See Krakow. Uniwersytet Jagielloński

Cracraft, James

Feofan Prokopovich: a bibliography of his works. *In* Oxford Slavonic papers new ser v8 p 1-36

Craft, Robert

Current convictions

Contents

A "beautiful coloured, musical thing"
The discreet charm of the bourgeoisie
The Doctor Faustus case
Edvard Munch: self-portraitist
Elegy for Mary Hartman, Mary Hartman
Elektra and Richard Strauss
Figaro at the Met: a marriage on the rocks
The giant of Busseto
In search of Aldous Huxley
In the mouse trap
Ives's world
Lisztomania
Mozart's "opera of all operas"
Musical B for a political season

A new interpretation of Hegel?
The nostalgic kingdom of Maurice Ravel
The Paris Opéra in New York
Parsifal: the worship of Wagnerism
Playing with The magic flute
"A prodigy of nature"
Der Rosenkavalier: "something Mozartian"?
Salzburg, Mozart, and Così
Taking the Wagner cure
Telling time
Towards Schoenberg
Verdi, Shakespeare, and Falstaff
"Winnie" and "Uncle Wolf"

The Craft of lovers

Edwards, A. S. G. and Hedley, J. H. John Stowe. The Craft of lovers and T.C.C. R.3.19. *In* Virginia. University. Bibliographical Society. Studies in bibliography v28 p265-68

Crafts (Handicraft) See Handicraft

Crahan, Margaret Ellen. See Knight, F. W. jt. auth.

Craig, David

Marxism and popular culture. *In* Bigsby, C. W. E. ed. Approaches to popular culture p129-49

Craig, Edward Gordon

About

Worth, K. J. The syntax achieved. *In* Worth, K. J. The Irish drama of Europe from Yeats to Beckett p48-71

Craig, George

Reading: who is doing what to whom? *In* Josipovici, G. ed. The modern English novel: the reader, the writer and the work p15-36

Craig, Gordon. See Craig, Edward Gordon

Craig, Gordon Alexander

The United States and the European balance. *In* Two hundred years of American foreign policy p67-89

Craik, Thomas Wallace

The reconstruction of stage action from early dramatic texts. *In* The Elizabethan theatre, V p76-91

Cram, Ralph Adams

My life in architecture; excerpt. *In* Crunden, R. M. ed. The superfluous men p20-26

Why we do not behave like human beings; excerpt from "Convictions and controversies." *In* Crunden, R. M. ed. The superfluous men p86-94

About

Cram, R. A. My life in architecture; excerpt. *In* Crunden, R. M. ed. The superfluous men p20-26

Cramer, Maurice Browning. See Part 2 under title: Aeolian harps

Crandall, Ralph J.

Family types, social structure, and mobility in early America: Charlestown, Massachusetts, a case study. *In* Tufte, V. and Myerhoff, B. G. eds. Changing images of the family p61-81

Crane, Hart

General aims and theories; excerpt from "The complete poetry and selected letters and prose of Hart Crane." *In* Gibbons, R. ed. The poet's work: 29 masters of 20th century poetry on the origins and practice of their art p179-82

Crane, Hart—*Continued*

About

Crane, H. General aims and theories; excerpt from "The complete poetry and selected letters and prose of Hart Crane." *In* Gibbons, R. ed. The poet's work: 29 masters of 20th century poetry on the origins and practice of their art p179-82

McMillan, D. Hart Crane. *In* McMillan, D. Transition p125-47

Pemberton, V. H. Hart Crane's heritage. *In* Artful thunder p221-40

About individual works
The bridge

Miller, J. E. An epic of the modern consciousness: Hart Crane's "Bridge." *In* Miller, J. E. The American quest for a supreme fiction p162-99

Morgan, E. Three views of Brooklyn Bridge. *In* Morgan, E. Essays p43-57

Pease, D. The bridge: emotional dynamics of an epic of consciousness. *In* French, W. G. ed. The twenties p387-403

Tashjian, D. L. Hart Crane and the machine. *In* Tashjian, D. L. Skyscraper primitives p143-64

The bridge (Ave Maria)

Voelcker, H. The case for casque. *In* Crew, L. ed. The gay academic p193-99

White buildings

Tate, A. Introduction to White buildings by Hart Crane. *In* Tate, A. Memoirs and opinions, 1926-1974 p110-14

Crane, Joan St. Clair

Edna St. Vincent Millay's afterthoughts on the translation of Baudelaire. *In* Virginia. University. Bibliographical Society. Studies in bibliography v29 p382-86

Robert Frost's "Kitty Hawk." *In* Virginia. University. Bibliographical Society. Studies in bibliography v30 p241-48

Crane, Ronald Salmon

About

Baker, J. R. From imitation to rhetoric: the Chicago Critics, Wayne C. Booth, and Tom Jones. *In* Spilka, M. ed. Towards a poetics of fiction p136-56

Crane, Stephen

About

Cazemajou, J. Stephen Crane. *In* Walcutt, C. C. ed. Seven novelists in the American naturalist tradition p21-54

Morris, W. Stephen Crane. *In* Morris, W. Earthly delights, unearthly adornments p51-57

About individual works
Men, women and boats

Starrett, V. "Stephen Crane: an estimate." Introduction to Men, women and boats by Stephen Crane. *In* Praise from famous men: an anthology of introductions p136-46

The open boat

Berryman, J. Stephen Crane: "The open boat." *In* Berryman, J. The freedom of the poet p176-84

The red badge of courage

Berryman, J. Stephen Crane: The red badge of courage. *In* Berryman, J. The freedom of the poet p168-76

Crane family

Pemberton, V. H. Hart Crane's heritage. *In* Artful thunder p221-40

Cranfield, C. E. B.

Some observations on Romans 8:19-21. *In* Reconciliation and hope p224-30

Craniology. See Phrenology

Crankshaw, Edward

Conrad and Russia. *In* Joseph Conrad: a commemoration p91-104

Cranston, Maurice William

Jean-Paul Sartre: solitary man in a hostile universe. *In* De Crespigny, A. and Minogue, K. R. eds. Contemporary political philosophers p209-27

Cranz, Ferdinand Edward

Editions of the Latin Aristotle accompanied by the commentaries of Averroes. *In* Philosophy and humanism p116-28

Crashaw, Richard

About

Grant, P. Richard Crashaw and the Capucins: images and the force of belief. *In* Grant, P. Images and ideas in literature of the English Renaissance p89-128

McCanles, M. The rhetoric of the sublime in Crashaw's poetry. *In* Sloan, T. O. and Waddington, R. B. eds. The rhetoric of Renaissance poetry p189-211

About individual works
Epithalamium

LeClercq, R. V. Crashaw's Epithalamium: pattern and vision. *In* Literary monographs v6 p71-108

Craven, Alan Elliott

The reliability of Simmes's Compositor A. *In* Virginia. University. Bibliographical Society. Studies in bibliography v32 p186-97

Craven, John Pinna

A legal regime for arms control and pollution control in the oceans. *In* Borgese, E. M. and Krieger, D. eds. The tides of change p100-09

Crawford, Barbara Elizabeth

Scotland's foreign relations: Scandinavia. *In* Brown, J. M. ed. Scottish society in the fifteenth century p85-100

Crawford, Charles

About

Leary, L. G. Charles Crawford: a forgotten poet of early Philadelphia. *In* Leary, L. G. Soundings p97-111

Crawford, James Walter

Art for the mentally retarded: directed or creative? *In* Ulman, E. and Dachinger, P. eds. Art therapy p387-92

Crawford, Richard Arthur, and McKay, David P.

Music in manuscript: a Massachusetts tune-book of 1782. *In* American Antiquarian Society. Proceedings v84 pt 1 p43-64

Craytor, Josephine K.

Working with dying patients and their families. *In* Home care p37-48

Creation

McCrea, W. H. Models, laws, and the universe. *In* Cosmology, history, and theology p59-73

Peacocke, A. R. Cosmos and creation. *In* Cosmology, history, and theology p365-81

Creation—*Continued*

Peat, D. W. Creation and redemption. *In* Cosmology, history, and theology p383-86

Philberth, K. The generation of matter and the conservation of energy. *In* Cosmology, history, and theology p113-29

Porter, R. Creation and credence: the career of theories of the earth in Britain, 1660-1820. *In* Barnes, B. and Shapin, S. eds. Natural order p97-123

Rosen, E. The impact of Copernicus on man's conception of his place in the world. *In* Science and society: past, present, and future p52-67

See also Chaos (Theology); Cosmology; Deluge

Creation (Islam)

Marmura, M. E. God and his creation: two medieval Islamic views. *In* Savory, R. M. ed. Introduction to Islamic civilisation p46-53

Creation (Literary, artistic, etc.)

Bronowski, J. On art and science. *In* Bronowski, J. A sense of the future p16-21

Derrida, J. Edmond Jabès and the question of the book. *In* Derrida, J. Writing and difference p64-78

Derrida, J. Ellipsis. *In* Derrida, J. Writing and difference p294-300

Gilbert, S. M. and Gubar, S. The queen's looking glass: female creativity, male images of women, and the metaphor of literary paternity. *In* Gilbert, S. M. and Gubar, S. The madwoman in the attic p3-44

Glickman, J. Creativity in the arts. *In* Aagaard-Mogensen, L. ed. Culture and art p130-46

Also in Margolis, J. Z. ed. Philosophy looks at the arts p145-68

Hope, A. D. The three faces of love; excerpt. *In* Gibbons, R. ed. The poet's work: 29 masters of 20th century poetry on the origins and practice of their art p110-20

Howard, V. A. Artistic practice and skills. *In* Perkins, D. and Leondar, B. eds. The arts and cognition p208-40

Koestler, A. The discoveries of art. *In* Koestler, A. Janus p137-61

Menaker, E. Creativity as the central concept in the psychology of Otto Rank. *In* Roland, A. ed. Psychoanalysis, creativity, and literature p162-77

Mukařovský, J. Intentionality and unintentionality in art. *In* Mukařovský, J. Structure, sign, and function p89-128

Nettleship, M. A. Weaving in its social context among the Atayal of Taiwan. *In* Greenhalgh, M. and Megaw, J. V. S. eds. Art in society p175-91

Peckham, M. The deplorable consequences of the idea of creativity. *In* Peckham, M. Romanticism and behavior p206-21

Rothenberg, A. The unconscious and creativity. *In* Roland, A. ed. Psychoanalysis, creativity, and literature p144-61

Zwicky, F. Essay 11. *In* Fitzgerald, R. ed. What it means to be human p209-20

See also Creative ability; Creative thinking (Education); Inspiration; Originality

The **creation** of the world and other business (criticism) Miller, A. *In* Kauffmann, S. Persons of the drama p230-33

Creative ability

Barron, F. X. Bisociates: artist and scientist in the act of creation. *In* Harris, H. A. ed. Astride the two cultures p37-49

Gelwick, R. Essay 8. *In* Fitzgerald, R. ed. What it means to be human p142-63

Sayers, D. L. Creative mind; excerpt from "Unpopular opinions." *In* Sayers, D. L. The whimsical Christian p92-112

Sayers, D. L. The image of God; excerpt from "The mind of the Maker." *In* Sayers, D. L. The whimsical Christian p113-21

Sayers, D. L. Problem picture; excerpt from "The mind of the Maker." *In* Sayers, D. L. The whimsical Christian p122-50

Tu, Wei-ming. 'Inner experience': the basis of creativity in Neo-Confucian thinking. *In* Artists and traditions p 9-15

See also Creation (Literary, artistic, etc.); Creative thinking (Education); Originality

Psychological aspects

Stierlin, H. Liberation and self-destruction in the creative process. *In* Psychiatry and the humanities v 1 p51-72

Creative ability in art. See Creation (Literary, artistic, etc.)

Creative ability in science

Bronowski, J. The creative process. *In* Bronowski, J. A sense of the future p 6-15

Fisch, R. Psychology of science. *In* Science, technology and society p277-318

Gelwick, R. Essay 8. *In* Fitzgerald, R. ed. What it means to be human p142-63

Koestler, A. The art of discovery. *In* Koestler, A. Janus p131-36

Creative thinking (Education)

Hope, A. D. The three faces of love; excerpt. *In* Gibbons, R. ed. The poet's work: 29 masters of 20th century poetry on the origins and practice of their art p110-20

Warnock, M. Educating the imagination. *In* Royal Institute of Philosophy. Human values p44-60

Creativeness. See Creation (Literary, artistic etc.); Creative ability

Creativity

MacLean, P. D. The imitative-creative interplay of our three mentalities. *In* Harris, H. A. ed. Astride the two cultures p187-213

See also Creation (Literary, artistic, etc.); Creative ability

Creativity (Education) See Creative thinking (Education)

Creativity as a theme in literature. See Creativity in literature

Creativity in literature

Adelman, J. Creation and the place of the poet in Paradise lost. *In* Martz, L. L. and Williams, A. L. eds. The author in his work p51-69

Crébillon, Claude Prosper Jolyot de

About

Turnell, M. Crébillon fils. *In* Turnell, M. The rise of the French novel p71-106

About individual works
The wayward head and heart

Turnell, M. Crébillon fils. *In* Turnell, M. The rise of the French novel p71-106

Credit. See Debts, Public

Cree Indians

Art

Graburn, N. H. H. 'I like things to look more different than that stuff did': an experiment in cross-cultural art appreciation. *In* Greenhalgh, M. and Megaw, J. V. S. eds. Art in society p51-70

Legends

Anderson, A. The home of We-sake-cha. *In* Egoff, S. A. ed. One ocean touching p181-85

Cree language

Anderson, A. The home of We-sake-cha. *In* Egoff, S. A. ed. One ocean touching p181-85

Creed, Robert P.

Widsith's journey through Germanic tradition. *In* Anglo-Saxon poetry: essays in appreciation p376-87

Creeds. See Covenants (Church polity); Nicene Creed

Creek Indians

Paredes, J. A. Back from disappearance: the Alabama Creek Indian community. *In* Williams, W. L. ed. Southeastern Indians since the removal era p123-41

Creek Indians as soldiers

O'Donnell, J. H. The Southern Indians in the War for American Independence, 1775-1783. *In* Hudson, C. M. ed. Four centuries of Southern Indians p46-64

Creelan, Paul G.

Social theory as confession: Parsonsian sociology and the symbolism of evil. *In* Brown, R. H. and Lyman, S. M. eds. Structure, consciousness, and history p173-96

Creeley, Robert

On Black Mountain Review; excerpt from "Was that a real poem & other essays." *In* Anderson, E. and Kinzie, M. eds. The little magazine in America: a modern documentary history p248-79

About

Altieri, C. F. The struggle with absence: Robert Creeley and W. S. Merwin. *In* Altieri, C. F. Enlarging the temple p170-224

Creese, Walter L.

Imagination in the suburb. *In* Knoepflmacher, U. C. and Tennyson, G. B. eds. Nature and the Victorian imagination p49-67

Crehan, Joseph

Near Eastern societies. *In* Life after death p97-122

Creighton, Donald Grant

About

Berger, C. Donald Creighton and the artistry of history. *In* Berger, C. The writing of Canadian history p208-37

Creighton, Roger L.

About individual works
Urban transportation planning

Hare, R. Contrasting methods of environmental planning. *In* Royal Institute of Philosophy. Nature and conduct p281-97

Creighton, Thomas Richmond Mandell

Some thoughts on Hardy and religion. *In* Butler, L. S. ed. Thomas Hardy after fifty years p64-77

Cremation. See Funeral rites and ceremonies

Creole dialects

Sierra Leone

Berry, J. Marking tone in the Krio dictionary. *In* African themes p227-30

Creoles

Simmons, A. Class or communalism? A study of the politics of Creoles in Mauritius. *In* Kilson, M. L. and Rotberg, R. I. eds. The African diaspora p366-90

Sundiata, I. K. Creolization on Fernando Po: the nature of society. *In* Kilson, M. L. and Rotberg, R. I. eds. The African diaspora p391-413

Cressey, Donald Ray

Law, order and the motorist. *In* Crime, criminology and public policy p213-34

Restraint of trade, recidivism, and delinquent neighborhoods. *In* Delinquency, crime, and society p209-38

Cresswell, Helen

Ancient and modern and incorrigibly plural. *In* Blishes, E. ed. The thorny paradise p108-16

Crestien de Troyes. See Chrestien de Troyes

Cretans. See Minoans

Crete

History

Ankori, Z. From Zudecha to Yahudi Mahallesi: the Jewish quarter of Candia in the seventeenth century. *In* Salo Wittmayer Baron v 1 p63-127

Vitaliano, D. B. Atlantis from the geologic point of view. *In* Ramage, E. S. ed. Atlantis, fact or fiction? p137-60

Crèvecoeur, Jean Hector St John de. See Crèvecoeur, Michel Guillaume St Jean de, called Saint John de Crèvecoeur

Crèvecoeur, Michel Guillaume St Jean de, called Saint John de Crèvecoeur

About

Plumstead, A. W. Hector St John de Crèvecoeur. *In* Emerson, E. H. ed. American literature, 1764-1789 p213-31

Crew, Louie

Before emancipation: gay persons as viewed by chairpersons in English. *In* Crew, L. ed. The gay academic p3-48

Crews, Frederick C.

Out of my system

Contents

Anaesthetic criticism
Anxious energetics
Can literature be psychoanalyzed?
Conrad's uneasiness—and ours
Do literary studies have an ideology?
Norman O. Brown: the world dissolves
Offing culture: literary study and the Movement
Reductionism and its discontents
Student protest and academic distance

Crichton Smith, Iain

About

Morgan, E. The raging and the grace: some notes on the poetry of Iain Crichton Smith. *In* Morgan, E. Essays p222-31

About individual works
Consider the lilies

Hart, F. R. The tragedy of the Clearances. *In* Hart, F. R. The Scottish novel p325-35

Crick, Bernard R.

On rereading The origins of totalitarianism. *In* Hannah Arendt: the recovery of the public world p27-47

The political in Britain's two national theatres. *In* Drama and society p169-94

Cries and whispers (Motion picture)

Kauffmann, S. Cries and whispers. *In* Kauffmann, S. Living images p164-66

Penley, C. Cries and whispers. *In* Nichols, B. ed. Movies and methods p204-08

Samuels, C. T. Tampering with reality. *In* Samuels, C. T. Mastering the film, and other essays p198-210

Crime and age. See Juvenile delinquency

Crime and criminals

Ancel, M. The relationship between criminology and 'politique criminelle.' *In* Crime, criminology and public policy p269-80

Bottoms, A. E. and Wiles, P. Race, crime and violence. *In* Racial variation in man p131-49

Brown, R. R. The new criminology. *In* Law and society p81-107

Christiansen, K. O. Seriousness of criminality and concordance among Danish twins. *In* Crime, criminology and public policy p63-77

Cohen, A. K. Introduction: the study of crime, items for an agenda. *In* Major social issues p151-55

López-Rey y Arrojo, M. United Nations social defence policy and the problem of crime. *In* Crime, criminology and public policy p489-508

McClintock, F. H. Facts and myths about the state of crime. *In* Crime, criminology and public policy p33-46

Nettler, G. Description, prescription, and science: on differences between knowing something and knowing enough, promising and predicting. *In* Major social issues p156-71

Reed, I. The world needs more guys like Pee Wee. *In* Reed, I. Shrovetide in old New Orleans p290-92

Tittle, C. R. Labelling and crime: an empirical evaluation. *In* Gove, W. R. ed. The labelling of deviance p157-79

Walker, N. D. Lost causes in criminology. *In* Crime, criminology and public policy p47-62

See also Crime prevention; Female offenders; Juvenile delinquency; Thieves; White collar crimes

Research—Europe

Anttila, I. The foundation of co-operation in European criminological research: Sir Leon Radzinowicz and the Criminological Scientific Council at the Council of Europe. *In* Crime, criminology and public policy p25-32

Research—Great Britain

Butler, R. A. Baron. The foundation of the Institute of Criminology in Cambridge. *In* Crime, criminology and public policy p1-10

Lodge, T. S. The founding of the Home Office Research Unit. *In* Crime, criminology and public policy p11-24

Research—London

Borowitz, A. The Jackal and I, or How to do research in London. *In* Borowitz, A. Innocence and arsenic p163-70

Social aspects

Finestone, H. The delinquent and society: the Shaw and McKay tradition. *In* Delinquency, crime, and society p23-49

Social aspects—United States

Reiss, A. J. Settling the frontiers of a pioneer in American criminology: Henry McKay. *In* Delinquency, crime, and society 64-88

France

Castan, N. Summary justice. *In* Deviants and the abandoned in French society p111-56

Perrot, M. Delinquency and the penitentiary system in nineteenth-century France. *In* Deviants and the abandoned in French society p213-45

Zysberg, A. Galley rowers in the mid-eighteenth century. *In* Deviants and the abandoned in French society p83-110

Germany, East

Jescheck, H. H. Modern criminal policy in the Federal Republic of Germany and the German Democratic Republic. *In* Crime, criminology and public policy p509-25

Germany, West

Jescheck, H. H. Modern criminal policy in the Federal Republic of Germany and the German Democratic Republic. *In* Crime, criminology and public policy p509-25

Great Britain

Walker, N. D. Caution: some thoughts on the penal involvement rate. *In* Progress in penal reform p221-37

Wilson, J. Q. Crime and punishment in England. *In* Tyrrell, R. E. ed. The future that doesn't work p64-94

Great Britain—History

McLachlan, N. Penal reform and penal history: some reflections. *In* Progress in penal reform p1-24

Ousby, I. Thief-taking and thief-making. *In* Ousby, I. Bloodhounds of heaven p3-18

Russia

Solomon, P. H. Soviet criminology—its demise and rebirth, 1928-1963. *In* Crime, criminology and public policy p571-93

Sicily

Vassalli, G. An Italian enquiry concerning the Mafia. *In* Crime, criminology and public policy p595-622

United States

Mattick, H. W. Reflections of a former prison warden. *In* Delinquency, crime, and society p287-315

Miller, W. B. Youth gangs in the urban crisis era. *In* Delinquency, crime, and society p91-128

Wolfgang, M. E. Real and perceived changes of crime and punishment. *In* A New America? p143-57

United States—History

Rothman, D. J. The challenge of crime; excerpt from "The discovery of the asylum". *In* Davis, F. J. and Stivers, R. eds. The collective definition of deviance p130-46

Crime and criminals, Sexual. See Sex crimes

Crime deterrence, Punishment in. See Punishment in crime deterrence

Crime films. See Gangster films

Criminal justice, Administration of—*Cont.*

United States

Ball, R. A. Qualitative evaluation of criminal justice: planning and evaluation. *In* Riedel, M. and Chappell, D. eds. Issues in criminal justice: planning and evaluation p36-47

Laycock, D. Federal interference with state prosecutions: the need for prospective relief. *In* The Supreme Court review, 1977 p193-238

Mattick, H. W. Reflections of a former prison warden. *In* Delinquency, crime, and society p287-315

Motley, C. B. Criminal law: "law and order" and the criminal justice system. *In* Perspectives on justice p39-72

Criminal Justice Act, 1972. See Great Britain. Laws, statutes, etc. Criminal Justice Act, 1972

Criminal law

Ancel, M. The relationship between criminology and 'politique criminelle.' *In* Crime, criminology and public policy p269-80

Hughes, G. Morals and the criminal law. *In* Summers, R. S. ed. Essays in legal philosophy p183-207

Quinney, R. A sociological theory of criminal law. *In* Davis, F. J. and Stivers, R. eds. The collective definition of deviance p40-49

See also Abduction; Criminal justice, Administration of; Criminal procedure; Gambling; Infanticide; International offenses; Kidnapping; Obscenity (Law); Political crimes and offenses; Punishment; Rape; Recidivists; Reparation; Sex crimes; Suicide; Vagrancy

Conflict of laws

See Criminal jurisdiction

Pleading and practice

See Criminal procedure

Great Britain

Drewry, G. Parliament and penal policy. *In* Progress in penal reform p35-53

United States

Motley, C. B. Criminal law: "law and order" and the criminal justice system. *In* Perspectives on justice p39-72

Wechsler, H. The model penal code and the codification of American criminal law. *In* Crime, criminology and public policy p419-68

Criminal law, International. See Criminal jurisdiction; International offenses

Criminal procedure

Amsterdam, A. G. Speedy criminal trial: rights and remedies. *In* Stanford legal essays p 1-19

See also Double jeopardy; Jury; Prosecution; Searches and seizures; Sentences (Criminal procedure)

Conflict of laws

See Criminal jurisdiction

Great Britain

Walker, N. D. Caution: some thoughts on the penal involvement rate. *In* Progress in penal reform p221-37

Great Britain—History

Caenegem, R. C. van. Public prosecution of crime in twelfth-century England. *In* Church and government in the Middle Ages p41-76

Criminal procedure (International law)

Bassiouni, M. C. Unlawful seizures of persons by states as alternatives to extradition. *In* International terrorism and political crimes p343-68

O'Higgins, P. Unlawful seizure of persons by states. *In* International terrorism and political crimes p336-42

Criminal psychiatry. See Prisoners—Psychiatric care

Criminal psychology. See Prison psychology

Criminal statistics

McClintock, F. H. Facts and myths about the state of crime. *In* Crime, criminology and public policy p33-46

United States

Zeisel, H. The deterrent effect of the death penalty: facts v. faiths. *In* The Supreme Court review, 1976 p317-43

Criminals. See Crime and criminals

Criminals, Rehabilitation of. See Rehabilitation of criminals

Criminological Scientific Council at the Council of Europe. See Council of Europe. European Committee on Crime Problems

Criminology. See Crime and criminals

Cripps, Thomas Robert

"Race movies" as voices of the Black bourgeoisie: The scar of shame. *In* O'Connor, J. E. and Jackson, M. A. eds. American history/American film p39-55

Crisafulli, Alessandro S.

The Journal des Sçavans and The Lettres persanes. *In* Literature and history in the age of ideas p59-66

Crisis intervention (Psychiatry) See Hotlines (Counseling)

Crisis management and prediction. Freymond, J. *In* [Truth and tragedy]: a tribute to Hans Morgenthau p272-83

Crisp, Tobias

About

Stoever, W. K. B. The quest for assurance: radical solutions and Puritan dialectics. *In* Stoever, W. K. B. 'A faire and easie way to heaven' p138-60

Criterion (London)

Donoghue, D. Eliot and the Criterion. *In* The Literary criticism of T. S. Eliot p20-41

Critical care medicine. See Terminal care

Critical Quarterly (Manchester)

Cox, C. B. The editing of Critical Quarterly. *In* From Parnassus p135-46

Critical Review (China). See Hsüeh hêng

Critical theory (Sociology) See Frankfurt school of sociology

Criticism

Abrams, M. H. Belief and the suspension of disbelief. *In* Wimsatt, W. K. ed. Literary criticism: idea and act p149-69

Abrams, M. H. Coleridge, Baudelaire, and modernist poetics. *In* Amacher, R. E. and Lange, V. eds. New perspectives in German literary criticism p150-81

Abrams, M. H. A note on Wittgenstein and literary criticism. *In* ELH essays for Earl R Wasserman p248-61

Adams, T. Contemporary ideas of literature: terrible beauty or rough beast? *In* Krieger, M. and Dembo, L. S. eds. Directions for criticism p55-83

Criticism—*Continued*

Kennedy, W. J. Conclusion. *In* Kennedy, W. J. Rhetorical norms in Renaissance literature p189-91

Kennedy, W. J. Introduction: rhetorical criticism and literary theory. *In* Kennedy, W. J. Rhetorical norms in Renaissance literature p 1-19

Kermode, J. F. Can we say absolutely anything we like? *In* Art, politics, and will p159-72

Lodge, D. Criticism and realism. *In* Lodge, D. The modes of modern writing p53-56

Lodge, D. What is literature? *In* Lodge, D. The modes of modern writing p 1-9

McCanles, M. Dialectical criticism and beyond. *In* McCanles, M. Dialectical criticism and Renaissance literature p214-73

Margolis, J. Z. Robust relativism. *In* Margolis, J. Z. ed. Philosophy looks at the arts p387-437

Miller, J. H. Ariadne's thread: repetition and the narrative line. *In* Valdés, M. J. and Miller, O. J. eds. Interpretation of narrative p148-66

Miller, O. J. Reading as a process of reconstruction: a critique of recent structuralist formulations. *In* Valdés, M. J. and Miller, O. J. eds. Interpretation of narrative p19-27

Morris, W. A. Stylistics. *In* Morris, W. A. Friday's footprint p147-87

Murray, T. C. Kenneth Burke's logology: a mock logomachy. *In* Glyph 2 p144-61

Olson, E. The dialectical foundations of critical pluralism. *In* Olson, E. On value judgments in the arts, and other essays p327-59

Olson, E. William Empson, contemporary criticism, and poetic diction. *In* Olson, E. On value judgments in the arts, and other essays p118-56

Ong, W. J. From rhetorical culture to new criticism: the poem as a closed field. *In* Simpson, L. P. ed. The possibilities of order: Cleanth Brooks and his work p150-67

Peckham, M. The intentional? Fallacy? *In* On literary intention p139-57

Plantinga, A. Possible but unactual objects on what there isn't; excerpt from "The nature of necessity." *In* Margolis, J. Z. ed. Philosophy looks at the arts p438-81

Redpath, T. The meaning of a poem. *In* On literary intention p14-25

Reed, I. You can't be a literary magazine and hate writers. *In* Reed, I. Shrovetide in old New Orleans p246-48

Reiss, T. J. Discursive criticism and epistemology. *In* Valdés, M. J. and Miller, O. J. eds. Interpretation of narrative p38-47

Richards, I. A. The instruments of criticism: expression. *In* Richards, I. A. Complementarities p12-15

Roland, A. Toward a reorientation of psycho-analytic literary criticism. *In* Roland, A. ed. Psychoanalysis, creativity, and literature p248-70

Said, E. W. Roads taken and not taken in contemporary criticism. *In* Krieger, M. and Dembo, L. S. eds. Directions for criticism p33-54

Schumacher, D. Subjectivities: a theory of the critical process. *In* Donovan, J. C. ed. Feminist literary criticism p29-37

Scott, N. A. Criticism and the religious prospect. *In* English Association. Essays and studies, 1977 p98-108

Shapiro, K. J. What is not poetry? Excerpt from "In defense of ignorance." *In* Gibbons, R. ed. The poet's work: 29 masters of 20th century poetry on the origins and practice of their art p92-109

Silhol, R. Portrait of an ideal critic. *In* Johnson, I. D. and Johnson, C. [eds.] Les américanistes p202-15

Sparshott, F. E. Criticism and performance; excerpt from "The concept of criticism." *In* On literary intention p104-15

Stacy, R. H. Marxist and Soviet criticism. *In* Stacy, R. H. Russian literary criticism p185-230

Steiner, G. Whorf, Chomsky and the student of literature. *In* Wimsatt, W. K. ed. Literary criticism: idea and act p242-62

Stockinger, J. Homotextuality: a proposal. *In* Crew, L. ed. The gay academic p135-51

Sukenick, L. On women and fiction. *In* Diamond, A. and Edwards, L. R. eds. The authority of experience p28-44

Thurley, G. The intellectualist position. *In* Thurley, G. The ironic harvest p 1-22

Trilling, L. Criticism and aesthetics. *In* Trilling, L. A gathering of fugitives p143-52

Trilling, L. What is criticism? *In* Trilling, L. The last decade p57-99

Trilling, L. Why we read Jane Austen. *In* Trilling, L. The last decade p204-25

Wasiolek, E. The future of psychoanalytic criticism. *In* The Frontiers of literary criticism p149-68

Watkins, E. Criticism and community: on literary value. *In* Watkins, E. The critical act p213-51

Watkins, E. Criticism and method: Hirsch, Frye, Barthes, Derrida. *In* Watkins, E. The critical act p56-94

Watkins, E. Introduction: Poetics, poetry, and the practice of criticism. *In* Watkins, E. The critical act p3-23

Watkins, E. Poetic autonomy. *In* Watkins, E. The critical act p24-55

Watson, G. The literary past; excerpt from "The story of literature." *In* On literary intention p158-73

Wellek, R. Cleanth Brooks, critic of critics. *In* Simpson, L. P. ed. The possibilities of order: Cleanth Brooks and his work p196-229

Wellek, R. The parallelism between literature and the arts. *In* Wimsatt, W. K. ed. Literary criticism: idea and act p44-65

White, H. V. The Absurdist moment in contemporary literary theory. *In* Krieger, M. and Dembo, L. S. eds. Directions for criticism p85-110

Also in White, H. V. Tropics of discourse p261-82

Williamson, E. Guiding principles in Fielding's criticism of the critics. *In* A Provision of human nature p 1-24

Wimsatt, W. K. Battering the object. *In* Wimsatt, W. K. Day of the leopards p183-204

Wimsatt, W. K. Genesis: a fallacy revisited. *In* On literary intention p116-38

Same as: Wimsatt, W. K. Genesis: an argument resumed. *In* Wimsatt, W. K. Day of the leopards p11-39

Criticism—Great Britain—History—*Cont.*

Howell, W. S. Poetics, rhetoric, and logic in Renaissance criticism. *In* Classical influences on European culture A.D. 1500-1700 p155-62

Kropf, C. R. Catharsis in eighteenth-century England. *In* Tennessee Studies in literature v22 p63-72

Great Britain—History—19th century

Haley, B. The thoroughly healthy mind: Victorian criticism. *In* Haley, B. The healthy body and Victorian culture p46-68

Italy—Bibliography

Anzilotti, R. Foreign scholarship: Italian contributions. *In* American literary scholarship, 1975 p487-94

Anzilotti, R. Foreign scholarship: Italian contributions [another essay] *In* American literary scholarship, 1976 p446-55

Anzilotti, R. Foreign scholarship: Italian contributions [another essay] *In* American literary scholarship, 1977 p493-98

Japan—Bibliography

Beppu, K. Foreign scholarship: Japanese contributions. *In* American literary scholarship, 1975 p494-97

Beppu, K. Foreign scholarship: Japanese contributions [another essay]. *In* American literary scholarship, 1976 p455-59

Beppu, K. Foreign scholarship: Japanese contributions [another essay] *In* American literary scholarship, 1977 p499-504

Revière, J. and others. Foreign scholarship. *In* American literary scholarship, 1974 p433-58

Russia

Balakian, N. Despiritualized Americans: Soviet views of American literature. *In* Balakian, N. Critical encounters p215-18

Russia—History

Brown, E. J. Some new directions in Russian literary criticism. *In* The Frontiers of literary criticism p169-89

Erlich, V. Modern Russian criticism from Andrej Belyj to Andrej Sinjavskij: trends, issues, personalities. *In* Erlich, V. ed. Twentieth-century Russian literary criticism p3-30

Stacy, R. H. The aesthetic critics. *In* Stacy, R. H. Russian literary criticism p66-79

Stacy, R. H. The age of Pushkin. *In* Stacy, R. H. Russian literary criticism p25-37

Stacy, R. H. The Formalists. *In* Stacy, R. H. Russian literary criticism p163-84

Stacy, R. H. The modernists. *In* Stacy, R. H. Russian literary criticism p105-62

Stacy, R. H. Tolstoy and Dostoevsky. *In* Stacy, R. H. Russian literary criticism p80-104

Scandinavia—Bibliography

Lundén, R. Foreign scholarship: Scandinavian contributions. *In* American literary scholarship, 1975 p498-501

Lundén, R. Foreign scholarship: Scandinavian contributions [another essay]. *In* American literary scholarship, 1976 p459-62

Lundén, R. Foreign scholarship: Scandinavian contributions [another essay]. *In* American literary scholarship, 1977 p505-15

Scotland

Simonsuuri, K. The primitivists and the primitive bard. *In* Simonsuuri, K. Homer's original genius p119-32

United States

Baker, J. R. From imitation to rhetoric: the Chicago Critics, Wayne C. Booth, and Tom Jones. *In* Spilka, M. ed. Towards a poetics of fiction p136-56

Cohen, R. On a shift in the concept of interpretation. *In* Young, T. D. ed. The New Criticism and after p61-79

Nelson, C. The psychology of criticism, or what can be said. *In* Hartman, G. H. ed. Psychoanalysis and the question of the text p45-61

Register, C. American feminist literary criticism: a bibliographical introduction. *In* Donovan, J. C. ed. Feminist literary criticism p 1-28

United States—Bibliography

Hoffman, M. J. Themes, topics, and criticism. *In* American literary scholarship, 1973 p411-38

Hoffman, M. J. Themes, topics, criticism [another essay] *In* American literary scholarship, 1974 p411-32

Hoffman, M. J. Themes, topics, criticism [another essay] *In* American literary scholarship, 1975 p447-72

Hoffman, M. J. Themes, topics, criticism [another essay] *In* American literary scholarship, 1976 p401-29

Hoffman, M. J. Themes, topics, criticism [another essay] *In* American literary scholarship, 1977 p433-62

Criticism (Philosophy)

Agger, B. On happiness and the damaged life. *In* O'Neill, J. ed. On critical theory p12-33

Davies, J. Time, aesthetics, and critical theory. *In* O'Neill, J. ed. On critical theory p58-77

Misgeld, D. Critical theory and hermeneutics: the debate between Habermas and Gadamer. *In* O'Neill, J. ed. On critical theory p164-83

O'Neill, J. Critique and remembrance. *In* O'Neill, J. ed. On critical theory p 1-11

Piccone, P. Beyond identity theory. *In* O'Neill, J. ed. On critical theory p129-44

Shapiro, J. J. The slime of history: embeddedness in nature and critical theory. *In* O'Neill, J. ed. On critical theory p145-63

Weber, S. M. Aesthetic experience and self-reflection as emancipatory processes: two complementary aspects of critical theory. *In* O'Neill, J. ed. On critical theory p78-103

Wellmer, A. Communications and emancipation: reflections on the linguistic turn in critical theory. *In* O'Neill, J. ed. On critical theory p231-63

Wilson, H. T. Science, critique, and criticism: the "open society" revisited. *In* O'Neill, J. ed. On critical theory p205-30

Criticism, Communist. See Communist self-criticism

Criticism, Textual

Barthes, R. From work to text. *In* Barthes, R. Image, music, text p155-64

Bowers, F. T. Current theories of copy-text, with an illustration from Dryden. *In* Bowers, F. T. Essays in bibliography, text, and editing p277-88

Crook, Richard
Political centralization and local politics in Ghana: the careers of Nana Wiafe Akenten II and E. K. Duncan-Williams of Offinso (Ashanti) *In* The Making of politicians: studies from Africa and Asia p28-48

Crooke, Andrew

About

Williams, W. P. Chetwin, Crooke, and the Jonson folios. *In* Virginia. University. Bibliographical Society. Studies in bibliography v30 p75-95

Crookshank, Anne
The new culture: painting and sculpture. *In* De Breffny, B. ed. The Irish world p164-70

Crops. See Agriculture

Cropsey, Joseph
Adam Smith and political philosophy. *In* Skinner, A. S. and Wilson, T. eds. Essays on Adam Smith p132-53

The United States as regime and the sources of the American way of life. *In* The Moral foundations of the American Republic p86-101

Crosby, Caresse

About

Ford, H. D. Harry and Caresse Crosby and the Black sun. *In* Ford, H. D. Published in Paris p168-230

Crosby, Harry

About

Ford, H. D. Harry and Caresse Crosby and the Black sun. *In* Ford, H. D. Published in Paris p168-230

Crosby, Margaret C. See Marson, C. C. jt. auth.

Croskey, Robert
A further note on Sir Jerome Bowes. *In* Oxford Slavonic papers, new ser. v10 p39-45

Crosland, Margaret

About individual works

Jean Cocteau

Connolly, C. Jean Cocteau: 1. *In* Connolly, C. The evening colonnade p306-08

Crosland, Maurice P. and Smith, Crosbie
The transmission of physics from France to Britain: 1800-1840. *In* Historical studies in the physical sciences v9 p 1-61

Cross, A. G.
Yakov Smirnov: a Russian priest of many parts. *In* Oxford Slavonic papers new ser. v8 p37-52

Cross, James E.
The poem in transmitted text—editor and critic. *In* English Association. Essays and studies, 1974 p84-97

Cross, Kathryn Patricia
For all and for each. *In* The Third century p109-13

Cross, Mary Ann (Evans) See Eliot, George, pseud.

Cross, Robert Dougherty
The Irish. *In* Ethnic leadership in America p176-97

Cross. See Holy Cross; Holy Cross in literature

Cross-cultural studies
Kracke, W. H. A psychoanalyst in the field: Erikson's contributions to anthropology. *In* Homans, P. ed. Childhood and selfhood p147-88

Mead, M. End linkage: a tool for cross-cultural analysis. *In* About Bateson p171-231

Crossen, Kendell Foster

About individual works

Year of consent

Rhodes, C. H. Tyranny by computer: automated data processing and oppressive government in science fiction. *In* Clareson, T. D. ed. Many futures, many worlds p66-93

Crosses. See Christian art and symbolism

Crouch, Colin
Inflation and the political organization of economic interests. *In* The Political economy of inflation p217-39

The state, capital and liberal democracy. *In* Crouch, C. ed. State and economy in contemporary capitalism p13-54

Crout, John Richard
Drug regulation by government: the nature of regulatory choices. *In* The Frontiers of human knowledge p59-68

Crouzet, François
Trade and empire: the British experience from the establishment of free trade until the First World War. *In* Great Britain and her world, 1750-1914 p209-35

Croves, Hal. See Traven, B. pseud.

Crow, Charles R. See Part 2 under title: Shakespeare's late plays

Crow, Christine M.
Valery and the image of the tree-top. *In* Cardinal, R. ed. Sensibility and creation p16-35

Crow, James F.

About individual works

Some possibilities for measuring selection intensities in man

Spuhler, J. N. The maximum opportunity for natural selection in some human populations. *In* Zubrow, E. B. W. ed. Demographic anthropology 185-226

Crowder, Richard H.
Poetry: 1900 to the 1930s. *In* American literary scholarship, 1973 p304-28

Poetry: 1900 to the 1930s [another essay] *In* American literary scholarship, 1974 p321-44

Poetry: 1900 to the 1930s [another essay] *In* American literary scholarship, 1975 p363-78

Poetry: 1900 to the 1930s [another essay] *In* American literary scholarship, 1976 p319-37

Poetry: 1900 to the 1930s [another essay] *In* American literary scholarship, 1977 p343-64

Crowding stress
Dubos, R. J. Crowds and machines. *In* Dubos, R. J. Beast or angel? p103-06

Crowds. See Demonstrations

Crowe, Charles Robert
Indians and Blacks in white America. *In* Hudson, C. M. ed. Four centuries of Southern Indians p148-69

Crowley, Joseph Donald
Hawthorne. *In* American literary scholarship, 1975 p17-34

Hawthorne [another essay] *In* American literary scholarship, 1976 p15-32

Hawthorne [another essay] *In* American literary scholarship, 1977 p17-33

Crowley, Richard C.
Coriolanus and the epic genre. *In* Shakespeare's late plays p114-30

Crown lands

Essex, England
McIntosh, M. K. The privileged villeins of the English ancient demesne. *In* Viator: medieval and Renaissance studies v7 p295-328

Crowne, John

Criticism, Textual
McMullin, B. J. The direction line as bibliographical evidence: Sheet K in Crowne's City politiques, 1683. *In* Virginia. University. Bibliographical Society. Studies in bibliography v31 p178-84

Crozier, Michel
The problem of power. *In* Armstrong, T. R. and Cinnamon, K. M. eds. Power and authority in law enforcement p23-38

The crucible (criticism) Miller, A. *In* Kauffmann, S. Persons of the drama p139-42

Crucifixion of Christ. See Jesus Christ—Crucifixion

Crucifixion with Saints Nicholas Of Bari and Gregory (attributed to Duccio di Buoninsegna)
Stubblebine, J. H. The Boston Ducciesque tabernacle, a collaboration. *In* Collaboration in Italian Renaissance art p 1-19

Cruelty, Theater of. See Drama—20th century

Cruelty in literature
Cohn, R. Camp, cruelty, colloquialism. *In* Cohen, S. B. ed. Comic relief p281-303

Cruelty to children. See Child abuse

Cruikshank, George

About
Vogler, R. A. Oliver Twist: Cruikshank's pictorial prototypes. *In* Dickens Studies Annual v2 p98-116

Cruise missiles
Nalewajek, R. A. The realities of arms control: the cruise missile case. *In* Arms control and technological innovation p232-46

Cruise O'Brien, Conor
Actors, roles, and stages. *In* Smithsonian Institution. The cultural drama p71-85

Cruise O'Brien, Donal Brian
Clan, community, nation: dimensions of political loyalty in Senegal. *In* Smock, D. R. and Bentsi-Enchill, K. eds. The search for national integration in Africa p255-69

Crump, James Irving
The conventions and craft of Yuan drama. *In* Birch, C. ed. Studies in Chinese literary genres p192-219

Crusades
Cowdrey, H. E. J. The genesis of the Crusades: the springs of Western ideas of holy war. *In* The Holy war p9-32

Prawer, J. Crusader cities. *In* The Medieval city p179-99

Savory, R. M. Christendom vs. Islam: interaction and co-existence. *In* Savory, R. M. ed. Introduction to Islamic civilisation p127-35

White, L. T. The Crusades and the technological thrust of the West. *In* War, technology and society in the Middle East p97-112

Songs and music
Crocker, R. L. Early Crusade songs. *In* The Holy war p78-98

First, 1096-1099
McGinn, B. Iter sancti Sepulchri: the piety of the first Crusaders. *In* Essays on medieval civilization p33-71

Third, 1189-1192
Chazan, R. Emperor Frederick I, the Third Crusade, and the Jews. *In* Viator: medieval and Renaissance studies v8 p83-93

Seventh, 1248-1250
Jordan, W. C. Supplying Aigues-Mortes for the Crusade of 1248: the problem of restructuring trade. *In* Order and innovation in the Middle Ages p165-72

Cruse, Harold
The creative and performing arts and the struggle for identity and credibility. *In* Johnson, H. A. ed. Negotiating the mainstream p47-102

Cruz, Juana Inés de la, Sister. See Juana Inés de la Cruz, Sister

Crystal, David
American English in Europe. *In* Bigsby, C. W. E. Superculture p57-68
The problem of language variety: an example from religious language. *In* Royal Institute of Philosophy. Communication and understanding p195-207

Crystal City, Tex.

Politics and government
Shockley, J. S. Landless laborers and the Chicano movement in south Texas. *In* Forging nations: a comparative view of rural ferment and revolt p128-49

Crystallography, Mathematical
Kottler, D. B. Louis Pasteur and molecular dissymmetry, 1844-1857. *In* Studies in history of biology, v2 p57-98

Crystallometry. See Crystallography, Mathematical

Crystals

Mathematical models
See Crystallography, Mathematical

Cuba

Armed Forces
Domínguez, J. I. The armed forces and foreign relations. *In* Cuba in the world p53-86

Civilization
Bray, D. W. and Harding, T. F. Cuba. *In* Chilcote, R. H. and Edelstein, J. C. eds. Latin America: the struggle with dependency and beyond p579-734

Economic conditions—1959-
Mesa-Lago, C. The economy and international economic relations. *In* Cuba in the world p169-98

Ritter, A. R. M. The transferability of Cuba's revolutionary development models. *In* Cuba in the world p313-34

Economic policy
MacEwan, A. Incentives, equality, and power in revolutionary Cuba. *In* Radosh, R. ed. The new Cuba: paradoxes and potentials p74-101

Cuba—*Continued*

Foreign economic relations

Mesa-Lago, C. The economy and international economic relations. *In* Cuba in the world p169-98

Foreign economic relations— Latin America

Reed, S. L. Participation in multinational organizations and programs in the hemisphere. *In* Cuba in the world p297-312

Foreign economic relations—Russia

Pérez-López, J. F. Sugar and petroleum in Cuban-Soviet terms of trade. *In* Cuba in the world p273-96

Foreign economic relations— United States

Mesa-Lago, C. The economics of U.S.-Cuban rapprochement. *In* Cuba in the world p199-224

Foreign opinion, American

Radosh, R. The Cuban Revolution and Western intellectuals. *In* Radosh, R. ed. The new Cuba: paradoxes and potentials p37-55

Foreign relations

Levi, R. Cuba and the nonaligned movement. *In* Cuba in the world p147-51

Foreign relations—1959-

Gonzalez, E. Institutionalization, political elites, and foreign policy. *In* Cuba in the world p3-36

Foreign relations—Arab countries

Shapira, Y. D. Cuba and the Arab-Israeli conflict. *In* Cuba in the world p153-66

Foreign relations—Caribbean area

Jones, R. E. Cuba and the English-speaking Caribbean. *In* Cuba in the world p131-45

Foreign relations—Israel

Shapira, Y. D. Cuba and the Arab-Israeli conflict. *In* Cuba in the world p153-66

Foreign relations—Russia

Blasier, C. The Soviet Union in the Cuban-American conflict. *In* Cuba in the world p37-51

Foreign relations—United States

Blasier, C. The Soviet Union in the Cuban-American conflict. *In* Cuba in the world p37-51

Dominguez, J. I. U.S. policy toward Cuba: a discussion of options. *In* The Americas in a changing world p112-31

Duberman, M. B. The questions raised by Cuba. *In* Radosh, R. ed. The new Cuba: paradoxes and potentials p19-34

Linsley, A. U.S.-Cuban relations: the role of Puerto Rico. *In* Cuba in the world p119-30

Petras, J. F. The U.S.-Cuban policy debate. *In* Radosh, R. ed. The new Cuba: paradoxes and potentials p173-89

History

Duberman, M. B. The questions raised by Cuba. *In* Radosh, R. ed. The new Cuba: paradoxes and potentials p19-34

History—1959-

Lyons, P. The New Left and the Cuban Revolution. *In* Radosh, R. ed. The new Cuba: paradoxes and potentials p211-46

See also Cuban Missile Crisis, Oct. 1962

Intellectual life

Halperin, M. Culture and the Revolution; excerpt from "The rise and decline of Fidel Castro." *In* Radosh, R. ed. The new Cuba: paradoxes and potentials p190-210

Military policy

Domínguez, J. I. The armed forces and foreign relations. *In* Cuba in the world p53-86

Politics and government—1933-1959

Goldenberg, B. Radicalization of a Latin-American state: the establishment of communism in Cuba. *In* Hammond, T. T. ed. The anatomy of Communist takeovers p583-95

Politics and government—1959-

Enzensberger, H. M. Portrait of a party: prehistory, structure, and ideology of the PCC; excerpt from "Politics and crime." *In* Radosh, R. ed. The new Cuba: paradoxes and potentials p102-37

Goldenberg, B. Radicalization of a Latin-American state: the establishment of communism in Cuba. *In* Hammond, T. T. ed. The anatomy of Communist takeovers p583-95

Lambert, F. Cuba: Communist state or personal dictatorship? *In* Brown, A. H. and Gray, J. eds. Political culture and political change in Communist state p231-52

Radosh, R. Cuba: a personal report. *In* Radosh, R. ed. The new Cuba: paradoxes and potentials p56-73

Race question

Knight, F. W. Slavery, race, and social structure in Cuba during the nineteenth century. *In* Toplin, R. B. ed. Slavery and race relations in Latin America p204-27

Masferrer, M. and Mesa Lago, C. The gradual integration of the Black in Cuba: under the Colony, the Republic, and the Revolution. *In* Toplin, R. B. ed. Slavery and race relations in Latin America p348-84

Social conditions

Duberman, M. B. The questions raised by Cuba. *In* Radosh, R. ed. The new Cuba: paradoxes and potentials p19-34

FitzGerald, F. A reporter at large: slightly exaggerated enthusiasms. *In* Radosh, R. ed. The new Cuba: paradoxes and potentials p138-72

Cuban literature

History and criticism

Ojo-Ade, F. De origen Africano, soy cubano: African elements in the literature of Cuba. *In* African literature today no. 9: Africa, America and the Caribbean p47-57

African influences

Ojo-Ade, F. De origen Africano, soy cubano: African elements in the literature of Cuba. *In* African literature today no. 9: Africa, America and the Caribbean p47-57

Cuban military assistance. See Military assistance, Cuban

Cuban Missile Crisis, Oct. 1962

Steinbruner, J. An assessment of nuclear crises. *In* Griffiths, F. and Polanyi, J. C. eds. The dangers of nuclear war p34-49

Cuban poetry

Black authors—History and criticism

DeCosta, M. Social lyricism and the Caribbean poet/rebel. *In* DeCosta, M. ed. Blacks in Hispanic literature p114-22

Cuber, John Frank

Age-discrepant marriages. *In* Gross, L. ed. Sexual issues in marriage p245-58

Sex in five types of marriage. *In* Gross L. ed. Sexual issues in marriage p3-10

Cubism

Berger, J. The moment of cubism. *In* Berger, J. The look of things p133-62

Fry, E. Introduction, the history of cubism, cubism as a stylistic and historical phenomenon; excerpt from "Cubism." *In* Kaplan, P. and Manso, S. eds. Major European art movements, 1900-1945 p101-46

Greenberg, C. Collage; excerpt from "Art and culture (Revised edition)" *In* Kaplan, P. and Manso, S. eds. Major European art movements, 1900-1945 p147-63

Greene, R. W. Pierre Reverdy. *In* Greene, R. W. Six French poets of our time p23-58

Osborne, H. Cubism, Cézanne, and perceptual realism. *In* Osborne, H. Abstraction and artifice in twentieth-century art p63-76

Rosenberg, H. The cubist epoch. *In* Rosenberg, H. Art on the edge p162-72

See also Purism (Art)

Cubitt, Thomas

About

Connolly, C. Thomas Cubitt, master builder. *In* Connolly, C. The evening colonnade p412-14

Cubo-futurism. See Futurism

Cuchulain

Melia, D. F. Parallel versions of "The boyhood deeds of Cuchulainn." *In* Duggan, J. J. ed. Oral literature p25-40

Cuentz, Gaspar. See Cuenz, Gaspar

Cuenz, Gaspar

About

Wade, I. O. Notes on the making of a philosophe: Cuenz and Bouhier. *In* Literature and history in the age of ideas p97-123

Cuernavaca, Mexico. Palacio de Cortés

Catlin, S. L. Political iconography in the Diego Rivera frescoes at Cuernavaca, Mexico. *In* Millon, H. A. and Nochlin, L. eds. Art and architecture in the service of politics p194-215

Cuervo, Robert F.

The definition of public philosophy: Lippmann and Murray. *In* A Public philosophy reader p97-102

Cuevas Cancino, Francisco

Bolivar's commonwealth of nations. *In* [Truth and tragedy]: a tribute to Hans Morgenthau p322-32

Cuff, John, supposed author. See Verses, occasion'd by the sight of a chamera obscura

Cuisenier, Jean

Kinship and social organization in the Turko-Mongolian cultural area. *In* Family and society p204-36

Cukor, George Dewey

About individual works
It should happen to you

Truffaut, F. George Cukor: It should happen to you. *In* Truffaut, F. The films in my life p104-06

Culao—a Vietnamese fishing cooperative and its problems. Kaufman, H. K. *In* Social organization and the applications of anthropology p235-72

Culbert, David Holbrook

Our awkward ally: Mission to Moscow. *In* O'Connor, J. E. and Jackson, M. A. eds. American history/American film p121-45

Culbert, T. Patrick

Early Maya development at Tikal, Guatemala. *In* The Origins of Maya civilization p27-43

See also Adams, R. E. W. jt. auth.

Culbertson, William Patton. See Breit, W. jt. auth.

Cullen, Countee

About

Jackson, B. Largo for Adonais. *In* Jackson, B. The waiting years p42-62

Cullen, Thomas Stephen

About

Harvey, A. M. The second professor of gynecology and the Department of Art as applied to medicine. *In* Harvey, A. M. Adventures in medical research p173-87

Culler, Arthur Dwight

About individual works
The poetry of Tennyson

Joseph, G. Imperial criticism. *In* Review, v 1 1979 p75-80

Culler, Jonathan D.

Defining narrative units. *In* Fowler, R. ed. Style and structure in literature p123-42

Structuralism and literature. *In* Contemporary approaches to English studies p59-76

Towards a theory of non-genre literature. *In* Federman, R. ed. Surfiction p255-62

About individual works
Structural poetics: structuralism, linguistics, and the study of literature

Graff, G. How not to talk about fictions. *In* Graff, G. Literature against itself p151-80

Culliton, Barbara J.

Science's restive public. *In* Holton, G. J. and Morison, R. S. eds. Limits of scientific inquiry p147-56

Culpepper, Emily

The spiritual movement of radical feminist consciousness. *In* Needleman, J. and Baker, G. eds. Understanding the new religions p220-34

Cult

Eister, A. W. Culture crises and new religious movements: a paradigmatic statement of a theory of cults. *In* Zaretsky, I. I. and Leone, M. P. eds. Religious movements in contemporary America p612-27

Wallis, R. The cult and its transformation. *In* Wallis, R. ed. Sectarianism p35-49

See also Ritual

Cults

Ellwood, R. S. Inner worlds: the psychology of excursus religion. *In* Ellwood, R. S. Alternative altars p42-61

China

Miyakawa, H. Local cults around Mount Lu at the time of Sun En's rebellion. *In* Welch, H. and Seidel, A. K. eds. Facets of Taoism p83-101

Stein, R. A. Religious Taoism and popular religion from the second to seventh centuries. *In* Welch, H. and Seidel, A. K. eds. Facets of Taoism p53-81

United States

Ellwood, R. S. Epilogue. *In* Ellwood, R. S. Alternative altars p167-73

Ellwood, R. S. Excursus religion. *In* Ellwood, R. S. Alternative altars p20-41

Ellwood, R. S. Temple and cave in America. *In* Ellwood, R. S. Alternative altars p 1-19

Foss, D. A. and Larkin, R. W. The roar of the lemming: youth, postmovement groups, and the life construction crisis. *In* Johnson, H. M. ed. Religious change and continuity p264-85

Shepherd, W. C. Conversion and adhesion. *In* Johnson, H. M. ed. Religious change and continuity p251-63

Tipton, S. M. New religious movements and the problem of a modern ethic. *In* Johnson, H. M. ed. Religious change and continuity p286-312

Cultural anthropology. See Ethnology

Cultural assimilation. See Assimilation (Sociology)

Cultural change. See Social change

Cultural diffusion. See Culture diffusion

Cultural evolution. See Social change; Social evolution

Cultural relations

Iriye, A. Intercultural relations. *In* Encyclopedia of American foreign policy p428-42

Preiswerk, A. R. The place of intercultural relations in the study of international relations. *In* The Year book of world affairs, 1978 p251-67

Cultural relativism

Deregowski, J. B. Illusion and culture. *In* Gregory, R. L. and Gombrich, Sir E. H. J. eds. Illusion in nature and art p161-91

Skorupski, J. The meaning of another culture's beliefs. *In* Hookway, C. and Pettit, P. eds. Action and interpretation p83-106

Culturally deprived children. See Socially handicapped children

Culturally handicapped children. See Socially handicapped children

Culture

Alcock, A. E.; Taylor, B. K. and Welton, J. M. Conclusions. *In* Alcock, A. E.; Taylor, B. K. and Welton, J. M. eds. The future of cultural minorities p177-99

Barbu, Z. Popular culture: a sociological approach. *In* Bigsby, C. W. E. ed. Approaches to popular culture p39-68

Barzun, J. The imagination of the real, or ideas and their environment. *In* Art, politics, and will p 3-27

Bigsby, C. W. E. The politics of popular culture. *In* Bigsby, C. W. E. ed. Approaches to popular culture p3-25

Brustein, R. S. Cultural schizophrenia. *In* Brustein, R. S. The culture watch p17-25

Brustein, R. S. On the new cultural conservatism. *In* Brustein, R. S. The culture watch p26-31

Dreitzel, H. P. On the political meaning of culture. *In* Beyond the crisis p83-129

Dubos, R. J. Adventure and fantasy. *In* Dubos, R. J. Beast or angel? p190-97

Eliot, T. S. From Notes towards the definition of culture. *In* Eliot, T. S. Selected prose of T. S. Eliot p292-305

Goodenough, W. H. Multiculturalism as the normal human experience. *In* Eddy, E. M. and Partridge, W. L. eds. Applied anthropology in America p79-86

Goody, J. R. Literacy, criticism, and the growth of knowledge. *In* Culture and its creators p226-43

Halley, J. A. Beyond the sociology of art: recent interdisciplinary developments in the critical analysis of culture. *In* McNall, S. G. ed. Theoretical perspectives in sociology p276-91

Hindle, B. How much is a piece of the true cross worth? *In* Material culture and the study of American life p5-20

Hoggart, R. Culture and its ministers. *In* Art, politics, and will p191-212

Josipovici, G. English studies and European culture. *In* Josipovici, G. The lessons of modernism p87-108

Knights, B. Epilogue: Cultural studies without a clerisy. *In* Knights, B. The idea of the clerisy in the nineteenth century p214-32

Kuznetsov, B. G. Einstein, science and culture. *In* Einstein p167-83

Lechtman, H. and Steinberg, A. The history of technology: an anthropological point of view. *In* Bugliarello, G. and Doner, D. B. eds. The history and philosophy of technology p135-60

Leiris, M. Race and culture. *In* United Nations Educational, Scientific and Cultural Organization. Race, science and society p135-72

Luedtke, L. S. Not so common ground: controversies in contemporary American studies. *In* Luedtke, L. S. ed. The study of American culture p323-67

McMurrin, S. M. Ideas and the processes of history. *In* The Abdication of philosophy: philosophy and the public good p109-28

Mazrui, A. A. World culture and the search for human consensus. *In* On the creation of a just world order p 1-37

Ong, W. J. "I see what you say": sense analogues for intellect. *In* Ong, W. J. Interfaces of the word p121-44

Ong, W. J. Transformations of the word and alienation. *In* Ong, W. J. Interfaces of the word p17-49

Ong, W. J. Voice and the opening of closed systems. *In* Ong, W. J. Interfaces of the word p305-41

Peckham, M. The arts and the centers of power. *In* Peckham, M. Romanticism and behavior p328-50

Peckham, M. The corporation's role in today's crisis of cultural incoherence. *In* Peckham, M. Romanticism and behavior p263-84

Peckham, M. The cultural crisis of the 1970s. *In* Peckham, M. Romanticism and behavior p362-79

Culture—*Continued*

Reyburn, W. D. Secular culture, missions, and spiritual values. *In* On language, culture, and religion: in honor of Eugene A. Nida p287-99

Ricoeur, P. Ethics and culture: Habermas and Gadamer in dialogue. *In* Ricoeur, P. Political and social essays p243-70

Ricoeur, P. Faith and culture. *In* Ricoeur, P. Political and social essays p125-33

Schneider, D. M. Notes toward a theory of culture. *In* Basso, K. H. and Selby, H. A. eds. Meaning in anthropology p197-220

Schwimmer, E. Semiotics and culture. *In* Sebeok, T. A. ed. A perfusion of signs p153-79

Shoemaker, F. New dimensions for world cultures. *In* Fairfield, R. P. ed. Humanistic frontiers in American education p289-301

Singer, M. For a semiotic anthropology. *In* Sebeok, T. A. ed. Sight, sound, and sense p202-31

Taylor, B. K. Culture: whence, whither and why? *In* Alcock, A. E.; Taylor, B. K. and Welton, J. M. eds. The future of cultural minorities p9-29

Tuttle, H. N. The epistemological status of the cultural world in Vico and Dilthey. *In* Giambattista Vico's science of humanity p241-50

Wilder, T. N. Culture in a democracy. *In* Wilder, T. N. American characteristics, and other essays p67-73

See also Acculturation; Biculturalism; Civilization; Cognition and culture; Cross-cultural studies; Culture diffusion; Education; Educational anthropology; Humanism; Learning and scholarship; Personality and culture; Popular culture; Social evolution

Culture, Evolution of. See Social evolution

Culture, Popular. See Popular culture

Culture and Christianity. See Christianity and culture

Culture and cognition. See Cognition and culture

Culture and communism. See Communism and culture

Culture and education. See Educational anthropology

Culture and personality. See Personality and culture

Culture and religion. See Religion and culture

Culture conflict

Goonetilleke, D. C. R. A. Joyce Cary: the clash of cultures in Nigeria. *In* Goonetilleke, D. C. R. A. Developing countries in British fiction p199-244

See also Marginality, Social

Culture conflict in literature

Fernando, L. A note from the Third World towards the re-definition of culture. *In* Narasimhaiah, C. D. ed. Awakened conscience p327-38

Culture contact. See Acculturation

Culture diffusion

Bauman, Z. East European and Soviet social science: a case study in stimulus diffusion. *In* Szporluk, R. ed. The influence of East Europe and the Soviet West on the USSR p91-116

Dart, R. A. Cultural diffusion from, in and to Africa. *In* Grafton Elliot Smith p160-74

Elkin, A. P. Elliot Smith and the diffusion of culture. *In* Grafton Elliot Smith p139-59

Lindberg, D. C. The transmission of Greek and Arabic learning to the West. *In* Lindberg, D. C. ed. Science in the Middle Ages p52-90

Lopez, R. S. The practical transmission of medieval culture. *In* Jeffrey, D. L. ed. By things seen: reference and recognition in medieval thought p125-42

McCarthy, F. D. Relationships between Australian aboriginal material culture, and Southeast Asia and Melanesia. *In* Grafton Elliot Smith p210-26

MacLaurin, E. C. B. Cultural diffusion in the Middle East during the second millennium BC. *In* Grafton Elliot Smith p175-96

Mitchell, R. D. The formation of early American cultural regions: an interpretation. *In* European settlement and development in North America: essays on geographical change in honour and memory of Andrew Hill Clark p66-90

Wang, Gungwu. Chinese civilization and the diffusion of culture. *In* Grafton Elliot Smith p197-209

Culture of tissues. See Tissue culture

Cultures (Biology) See Tissue culture

Cultus

See also Christian martyrs—Cult; Cult; Liturgics; Ritual

Brazil

Sturm, F. G. Afro-Brazilian cults. *In* African religions: a symposium p217-39

Katanga, Zaire

Bustin, E. Government policy toward African cult movements: the case of Katanga. *In* African dimensions p113-34

Cultus, Assyro-Babylonian

Roberts, J. J. M. Divine freedom and cultic manipulation in Israel and Mesopotamia. *In* Unity and diversity p181-90

Cultus, Greek. See Bacchantes

Cultus, Jewish. See Worship (Judaism)

Cultus, Roman. See Bacchanalia

Cummings, Edward Estlin

About

Dumas, B. K. E. E. Cummings in the twenties. *In* French, W. G. ed. The twenties p365-75

Kunitz, S. J. E. E. Cummings: a personal note. *In* Kunitz, S. J. A kind of order, a kind of folly p244-46

Paz, O. E. E. Cummings. *In* Paz, O. The siren & the seashell p131-36

Tashjian, D. L. E. E. Cummings and dada formalism. *In* Tashjian, D. L. Skyscraper primitives p165-87

About individual works

The enormous room

Walsh, J. The painful process of unthinking: E. E. Cummings' social vision in The enormous room. *In* Klein, H. M. ed. The First World War in fiction p32-42

My father moved through dooms of love

Trilling, L. E. E. Cummings: My father moved through dooms of love. *In* Trilling, L. Prefaces to The experience of literature p288-90

Cummins, Maria Susanna

About

Baym, N. Z. Susan Warner, Anna Warner, and Maria Cummins. *In* Baym, N. Z. Woman's fiction p140-74

Cuna Indians

Howe, J. Carrying the village: Cuna political metaphors. *In* The Social use of metaphor p132-63

Cuna language

Howe, J. Carrying the village: Cuna political metaphors. *In* The Social use of metaphor p132-63

Cunard, Nancy

About

Ford, H. D. Nancy Cunard's twenty-four Hours. *In* Ford, H. D. Published in Paris p253-89

Cunard Steam Ship Company, Ltd.

Hyde, F. E. Cunard and North Atlantic steamship agreements, 1850-1914. *In* Great Britain and her world, 1750-1914 p263-86

Cuneiform inscriptions

Lambert, W. G. The problem of the love lyrics. *In* Unity and diversity p98-135

See also Tell-el-Amarna tablets

Cunliffe, Marcus

Congressional leadership in the American Revolution. *In* Library of Congress Symposia on the American Revolution, 3d, 1974. Leadership in the American Revolution p41-61

Frances Trollope. *In* Abroad in America: Visitors to the new Nation, 1776-1914 p32-42

The two or more worlds of Willa Cather. *In* The Art of Willa Cather p21-42

Cunningham, Agnes, and others

Critique of the theology of the Unification Church as set forth in Divine principle. *In* Horowitz, I. L. ed. Science, sin, and scholarship p102-18

Cunningham, James Vincent

The collected essays of J. V. Cunningham

Contents

The ancient quarrel between history and poetry
Aught of woe or wonder
Classical and medieval: Statius on sleep
Convention as structure: the Prologue to the Canterbury tales
The Donatan tradition
Edwin Arlington Robinson: a brief biography
Graduate training in English
The heart of his mystery
How shall the poem be written?
Idea as structure: The phoenix and turtle
Ideal fiction: The Clerk's tale
In Shakespeare's day
The journal of John Cardan
Logic and lyric: Marvell, Dunbar, and Nashe
Lyric style in the 1590s
Plots and errors: Hamlet and King Lear
Poetry, structure, and tradition
The problem of form
The problem of style
The quest of the opal: a commentary on The helmsman
Reason panders will
The Renaissance in England
Ripeness is all
Several kinds of short poem
Sorting out: the case of Dickinson
The styles and procedures of Wallace Stevens

T. S. Eliot on poetry and poets
Technology and poetry
Tradition and modernity: Wallace Stevens
Tragedy as essence
With that facility: false starts and revisions in Love's labour's lost
Wonder

About

Cunningham, J. V. The quest of the opal: a commentary on The helmsman. *In* Cunningham, J. V. The collected essays of J. V. Cunningham p405-24

Cunningham, J. V. Several kinds of short poem. *In* Cunningham, J. V. The collected essays of J. V. Cunningham p431-38

About individual works

The helmsman

Cunningham, J. V. The quest of the opal: a commentary on The helmsman. *In* Cunningham, J. V. The collected essays of J. V. Cunningham p405-24

Cunningham, Joseph Sandy

Pope, Eliot, and 'The mind of Europe.' *In* The Waste land in different voices p67-85

Cunningham, Valentine

Everywhere spoken against

Contents

All sorts and conditions
The Brontës
Charles Dickens
George Eliot
Mrs Gaskell
Mrs Oliphant and the tradition
Openness
Places and politics
The presence of dissent
The sense of an ending
Was there a revolution in Tanner's Lane?

Cunninghame-Graham, Robert Bontine

About

Dobie, J. F. The gauchos and horses of Hudson and Graham. *In* Dobie, J. F. Prefaces p187-200

Meyers, J. Robert Bontine Cunninghame Graham. *In* Meyers, J. A fever at the core p39-58

Cupid

Wlosok, A. Amor and Cupid. *In* Harvard Studies in classical philology v79 p165-79

Cupolas. See Domes

Cups and saucers. See Drinking cups

Curators. See Museum directors

Curievici, Ion

Besieging the fortress. *In* Bugliarello, G. and Doner, D. B. eds. The history and philosophy of technology p339-43

Curio, C. Scribonius

About

Linderski, J. The aedileship of Favonius, Curio the Younger and Cicero's election to the augurate. *In* Harvard Studies in classical philology v76 p181-200

Curiosity in literature

Zacher, C. K. Curiositas. *In* Zacher, C. K. Curiosity and pilgrimage p18-41

Zacher, C. K. A new sense of the world. *In* Zacher, C. K. Curiosity and pilgrimage p3-17

Curle, Adam

Peace studies. *In* The Year book of world affairs, 1976 p5-13

Curley, Edwin M.
(comp.) Bibliography. *In* Freeman, E. and Mandelbaum, M. H. eds. Spinoza p263-316

Descartes, Spinoza and the ethics of belief. *In* Freeman, E. and Mandelbaum, M. H. eds. Spinoza p159-89

Dreaming and conceptual revision. *In* Dunlop, C. E. M. ed. Philosophical essays on dreaming p317-46

Spinoza and recent philosophy of religion. *In* Shahan, R. W. and Biro, J. I. eds. Spinoza: new perspectives p161-75

Curran, Stuart
The siege of hateful contraries: Shelley, Mary Shelley, Byron, and Paradise lost. *In* Wittreich, J. A. ed. Milton and the line of vision p209-30

Curran, Terrie
The word made flesh: the Christian aesthetic in Dorothy L. Sayers's The man born to be king. *In* Hannay, M. P. ed. As her whimsey took her p67-77

Curran, Thomas J.
From "Paddy" to the Presidency: the Irish in America. *In* The Immigrant experience in America p95-114

See also Coppa, F. J. jt. auth.

Currency. See Money

Currency devaluation. See Currency question

Currency question
Hinshaw, R. W. Devaluation and absorption: an alternative analysis. *In* Inflation, trade and taxes p108-18

See also Gold; Inflation (Finance); Monetary policy; Money; Silver

Venice

Lane, F. C. The first infidelities of the Venetian lire. *In* The Medieval city p43-63

Current-Garcia, Eugene
Joseph Glover Baldwin: humorist or moralist? *In* Inge, M. T. ed. The frontier humorists p170-86

Curricula (Courses of study) See Education —Curricula

Curriculum planning. See Interdisciplinary approach in education

Currie, David P.
Congress, the Court, and water pollution. *In* The Supreme Court review, 1977 p39-62

The Supreme Court and Federal jurisdiction: 1975 term. *In* The Supreme Court review, 1976 p183-219

Currie, Elliott P.
Crimes without criminals: witchcraft and its control in Renaissance Europe. *In* Davis, F. J. and Stivers, R. eds. The collective definition of deviance p296-316

Curry, Martha Mulroy
Anderson's theories on writing fiction. *In* Anderson, D. D. ed. Sherwood Anderson: dimensions of his literary art p90-109

Curry, Richard Orr
The Civil War and Reconstruction, 1861-1877: a critical overview of recent trends and interpretations. *In* Swierenga, R. P. ed. Beyond the Civil War synthesis p33-56

Curschmann, Michael
The concept of the oral formula as an impediment to our understanding of medieval oral poetry. *In* Medievalia et humanistica no. 8 p63-76

Curtin, Philip D.
The Black experience of colonialism and imperialism. *In* Mintz. S. W. ed. Slavery, colonialism, and racism p17-29

Postwar migrations in sub-Saharan Africa. *In* Human migration p188-98

Curtis, James C.
Clio's dilemma: to be a muse or to be amusing. *In* Material culture and the study of American life p201-18

Curtis, Mark H.
The trials of a Puritan in Jacobean Lancashire. *In* The Dissenting tradition p78-99

Curzon, David
The generic secrets of government decision making. *In* Galnoor, I. ed. Government secrecy in democracies p93-109

Cushner, Arnold W.
Some observations on Marlowe's Edward II. *In* Renaissance and modern p11-20

Custody of children

England

Walker, S. S. Widow and ward: the feudal law of child custody in medieval England. *In* Stuard, S. M. ed. Women in medieval society p159-72

New York (State)

Katz, S. N. Who looks after Laura? *In* Gross, B. and Gross, R. eds. The children's rights movement p48-54

United States

Rich, A. C. Husband-right and father-right. *In* Rich, A. C. On lies, secrets, and silence p215-22

Customary law

France

Bordeaux, M. Blazing a trail to a history of customary law by means of geographic hematology. *In* Biology of man in history p191-205

Customs administration

United States

Tabachnik, L. Political patronage and ethnic groups: foreign-born in the United States Customhouse Service, 1821-1861. *In* Swierenga, R. P. ed. Beyond the Civil War synthesis p245-54

Cuthswith, abbess of Worcester

About

Sims-Williams, P. Cuthswith, seventh-century abbess of Inkberrow, near Worcester, and the Würzburg manuscript of Jerome on Ecclesiastes. *In* Anglo-Saxon England 5 p 1-21

Cutler, Anthony
The Apocalypse icon in the Byzantine Museum, Athens. *In* Studies in memory of David Talbot Rice p94-112

Cutler, M. Ebbitt
Ah, publishing! *In* Egoff, S. A. ed. One ocean touching p212-20

Cutler, May. See Cutler, M. Ebbitt

Cutler, Neal E.
Toward a generational conception of political socialization. *In* Schwartz, D. C. and Schwartz, S. K. eds. New directions in political socialization p254-88

Cutter, Donald C.
Spanish scientific exploration along the Pacific Coast. *In* Weber, D. J. ed. New Spain's far northern frontier p35-47

Cuzzani, Agustín

About

Kuehne, A. de The spectacular in the theater of Agustín Cuzzani. *In* Lyday, L. F. and Woodyard, G. W. eds. Dramatists in revolt p37-58

Cybernetics

Beaune, J. C. Technology from an encyclopedic point of view. *In* Bugliarello, G. and Doner, D. B. eds. The history and philosophy of technology p202-26

Schlossberg, E. For my father. *In* About Bateson p145-67

Cycles

Said, E. W. On repetition. *In* Fletcher, A. J. S. ed. The literature of fact p134-58

See also Biology—Periodicity

Cyclic theory. See Cycles

Cyclopean remains. See Megalithic monuments

Cymric language. See Welsh language

Cynewulf

About

Frese, D. W. The art of Cynewulf's runic signatures. *In* Anglo-Saxon poetry: essays in appreciation p312-34

About individual works

The Christ of Cynewulf

Chase, C. R. God's presence through grace as the theme of Cynewulf's Christ II and the relationship of this theme to Christ I and Christ III. *In* Anglo-Saxon England 3 p87-101

Diamond, R. E. The diction of the Old English Christ. *In* Anglo-Saxon poetry: essays in appreciation p301-11

Isaacs, N. D. Up a tree: to see The fates of men. *In* Anglo-Saxon poetry: essays in appreciation p363-75

Elene

Doubleday, J. The speech of Stephen and the tone of Elene. *In* Anglo-Saxon poetry: essays in appreciation p116-23

Fates of the Apostles

Rice, R. C. The penitential motif in Cynewulf's Fates of the Apostles and in his epilogues. *In* Anglo-Saxon England 6 p105-19

Juliana

Schneider, C. Cynewulf's devaluation of heroic tradition in Juliana. *In* Anglo-Saxon England 7 p107-18

Wittig, J. S. Figural narrative in Cynewulf's Juliana. *In* Anglo-Saxon England 4 p37-55

Authorship

Diamond, R. E. The diction of the Old English Christ. *In* Anglo-Saxon poetry: essays in appreciation p301-11

Characters

Doubleday, J. The speech of Stephen and the tone of Elene. *In* Anglo-Saxon poetry: essays in appreciation p116-23

Cynicism

Schwartz, S. K. Patterns of cynicism: differential political socialization among adolescents. *In* Schwartz, D. C. and Schwartz, S. K. eds. New directions in political socialization p188-202

Cypess, Sandra Messinger

The plays of Griselda Gambaro. *In* Lyday, L. F. and Woodyard, G. W. eds. Dramatists in revolt p95-109

Cypriote vases. See Vases, Cypriote

Cyprus

Antiquities

See Vases, Cypriote

History—Cyprus Crisis, 1963

Kitromilides, P. M. and Couloumbis, T. A. Ethnic conflict in a strategic area: the case of Cyprus. *In* Said, A. A. and Simmons, L. R. eds. Ethnicity in an international context p167-202

History—Cyprus Crisis, 1974-

Talbot, P. The Cyprus seminar. *In* Unofficial diplomats p159-67

Cyprus Crisis, 1963. See Cyprus—History—Cyprus Crisis, 1963

Cyranides. See Virtutes aquile

Cyril. See Cyrillus, glossator

Cyrillus, glossator

Criticism, Textual

Naoumides. M. The v-recension of St. Cyril's Lexicon. *In* Illinois classical studies v4, 1979 p94-135

Cyrus, Earland

A historical perspective on home health care. *In* Home care p12-16

Cystic fibrosis

Psychological aspects

Lorin, M. I. Implications for therapy in the pediatric patient. *In* Anticipatory grief p182-86

Cytology. See Cell physiology

Czech aesthetics. See Aesthetics, Czech

Czech literature

20th century—History and criticism

Brown, D. B. Czechoslovak and Polish influences on Soviet literature. *In* Szporluk, R. ed. The influence of East Europe and the Soviet West on the USSR p117-46

Czech poetry

History and criticism

Jakobson, R. Signum et signatum. *In* Matejka, L. and Titunik, I. R. eds. Semiotics of art p176-87

Jakobson, R. What is poetry? *In* Matejka, L. and Titunik, I. R. eds. Semiotics of art p164-75

Czechoslovak Communist Party. See Communist Party in Czechoslovakia

Czechoslovakia

History—Coup d'état, 1948

Tigrid, P. The Prague Coup of 1948: the elegant takeover. *In* Hammond, T. T. ed. The anatomy of Communist takeovers p399-432

History—Intervention, 1968-

Griffith, W. E. The Prague spring and the Soviet intervention in Czechoslovakia. *In* Hammond, T. T. ed. The anatomy of Communist takeovers p606-19

Politics and government—1945-

Brown, A. H. and Wightman, G. Czechoslovakia: revival and retreat. *In* Brown, A. H. and Gray, J. eds. Political culture and political change in Communist states p159-96

Skilling, H. G. Stalinism and Czechoslovak political culture. *In* Stalinism p257-80

Politics and government—1968-

Berger, J. Czechoslovakia alone. *In* Berger, J. The look of things p225-44

Czudnowski, Moshe M.
Aspiring and established politicians: the structure of value systems and role profiles. *In* Eulau, H. and Czudnowski, M. M. eds. Elite recruitment in democratic polities p45-78

D

DARE. See Dictionary of American regional English (proposed)

DDT (Insecticide)
Laird, M. Osiris, Asklepios, and the Harpies: the development of an African river basin. *In* A Time to hear and answer: essays for the Bicentennial season p103-40

DNA (Nucleic acid) See Deoxyribonucleic acid

Daalder, Hans
The Dutch universities between the "new democracy" and "new management." *In* Universities in the Western world p195-231

Dace, Letitia
Amiri Baraka (LeRoi Jones). *In* Inge, M. T.; Duke, J. M. and Bryer, J. R. eds. Black American writers v2 p121-87

Dachinger, Penny. See Ulman, E. jt. auth.

Dacier, Mme. Anne (Lefèvre)

About
Simonsuuri, K. The interpretation of early Greek epic: Mme Dacier and the Homeric war. *In* Simonsuuri, K. Homer's original genius p46-56

Da Cortona, Pietro Berrettini. See Cortona, Pietro Berrettini da

Da Costa, Emília Viotti. See Costa, Emília Viotti da

Da Costa, Uriel. See Acosta, Uriel

Dada, Idi Amin. See Amin, Idi

Dadaũân, Vladislav Surenovich
A long-term macroeconomic forecasting model of the Soviet economy. *In* Economic development and planning p61-74

Dadaism
Elderfield, J. "Dada": a code for saints? *In* Kaplan, P. and Manso, S. eds. Major European art movements, 1900-1945 p310-24

Gascoyne, D. Introducing Kenneth Patchen. *In* Morgan, R. G. ed. Kenneth Patchen: a collection of essays p144-51

Glicksberg, C. I. Dada: to hell with culture and art. *In* Glicksberg, C. I. The literature of commitment p141-49

McMillan, D. Dadaism. *In* McMillan, D. Transition p102-09

Middleton, J. C. The art of unreason. *In* Middleton, J. C. Bolshevism in art p78-86

Tashjian, D. L. Camera Work and the anti-art of photography. *In* Tashjian, D. L. Skyscraper primitives p15-28

Tashjian, D. L. 291 and Francis Picabia. *In* Tashjian, D. L. Skyscraper primitives p29-48

See also Assemblage (Art)

History
Middleton, J. C. 'Bolshevism in art': dada and politics. *In* Middleton, J. C. Bolshevism in art p38-61

Middleton, J. C. Dada versus expressionism, or The red king's dream. *In* Middleton, J. C. Bolshevism in art p62-77

Middleton, J. C. The rise of primitivism and its relevance to the poetry of expressionism and dada. *In* Middleton, J. C. Bolshevism in art p23-37

Influence
Tashjian, D. L. Aftermath and conclusion. *In* Tashjian, D. L. Skyscraper primitives p227-30

Tashjian, D. L. Broom and Secession. *In* Tashjian, D. L. Skyscraper primitives p116-42

Tashjian, D. L. E. E. Cummings and dada formalism. *In* Tashjian, D. L. Skyscraper primitives p165-87

Tashjian, D. L. Hart Crane and the machine. *In* Tashjian, D. L. Skyscraper primitives p143-64

Tashjian, D. L. Painting the machine. *In* Tashjian, D. L. Skyscraper primitives p204-26

Tashjian, D. L. The Soil and Contact. *In* Tashjian, D. L. Skyscraper primitives p71-90

Tashjian, D. L. William Carlos Williams. *In* Tashjian, D. L. Skyscraper primitives p91-115

Dadajan, V. S. See Dadaũân, Vladislav Surenovich

Dadian, Levan

About
Allen, W. E. D. A Russian embassy to Mingrelia (1639-40). *In* Studies in memory of David Talbot Rice p294-316

Daedalus

Art
Robertson, M. Two question-marks on the Parthenon. *In* Studies in classical art and archaeology p75-87

Daemmrich, Horst S.
Mann's portrait of the artist: archetypal patterns. *In* Garvin, H. R. ed. Makers of the twentieth-century novel p166-78

Dağ Pazarī site. Turkey
Gough, M. Dag Pazarī. The basilical church 'extra muros.' *In* Studies in memory of David Talbot Rice p147-63

D'Agincourt, Jean Baptiste Louis George Seroux. See Seroux d'Agincourt, Jean Baptiste Louis George

D'Agostino, Salvo
Hertz's research on electromagnetic waves. *In* Historical studies in the physical sciences v6 p261-324

Dağpazarī site. Turkey. See Dağ Pazarī site, Turkey

Dahl, Roald

About individual works
Charlie and the chocolate factory
Cameron, E. McLuhan, youth, and literature. *In* Horn Book Magazine. Crosscurrents of criticism p98-120

Dahl, Robert Alan
Procedural democracy. *In* Laslett, P. and Fishkin, J. eds. Philosophy, politics and society p97-133

Dahlberg, Charles Clay
LSD therapy: a case study. *In* Anticipatory grief p296-310

Dahomey (African people) See Fon (African people)

Dahomeyans in Nigeria
Challenor, H. S. Strangers as colonial intermediaries: the Dahomeyans in Francophone Africa. *In* Shack, W. A. and Skinner, E. P. eds. Strangers in African societies p67-83

Dahomeyans in the Ivory Coast
Challenor, H. S. Strangers in colonial intermediaries: the Dahomeyans in Francophone Africa. *In* Shack, W. A. and Skinner, E. P. eds. Strangers in African societies p67-83

Dahrendorf, Ralf
The educational class. *In* Universities in the Western world p47-57

Daiches, David
Jim Osborn: some personal notes. *In* Evidence in literary scholarship pxvi-xxii

Daidalos. See Daedalus

Daifuku, Hiroshi
Introduction: Urban retrieval too. *In* United Nations Educational, Scientific and Cultural Organization. The conservation of cities p9-23

Dain, Norman
American psychiatry in the 18th century. *In* American psychiatry: past, present, and future p15-27

Dainton, Sir Frederick Sydney
A note on science in higher education. *In* Niblett, W. R. ed. The sciences, the humanities and the technological threat p36-41

Dakota Indians
Medicine, B. Learning to be an anthropologist and remaining "native." *In* Eddy, E. M. and Partridge, W. L. eds. Applied anthropology in America p182-96
See also Oglala Indians

History

Seymour, F. W. A look back at Wounded Knee. *In* American Antiquarian Society. Proceedings v84 pt 1 p33-42

Dakota language. See Siouan languages

Dale, Alzina Stone
The man born to be king: Dorothy L. Sayers's best mystery plot. *In* Hannay, M. P. ed. As her whimsey took her p78-90

Dale, Jonathan
Drieu La Rochelle: the war as 'comedy.' *In* Klein, H. M. ed. The First World War in fiction p63-72

Daléchamps, Jacques

About

Schmitt, C. B. The correspondence of Jacques Daléchamps. *In* Viator: medieval and Renaissance studies v8 p399-434

D'Alembert, Jean Le Rond. See Alembert, Jean Lerond d'

Dales, Richard C.
A twelfth-century concept of the natural order. *In* Viator: medieval and Renaissance studies v9 p179-92

Dalhousie, James Andrew Broun Ramsay, 1st marquess of

About

Philips, Sir C. H. Dalhousie and the Burmese War of 1852. *In* Southeast Asian history and historiography p51-58

Dallin, Alexander
Conclusion. *In* Women in Russia p385-98

Retreat from optimism: on Marxian models of revolution. *In* Radicalism in the contemporary age v3 p117-57

Dallmayr, Fred R.
Introduction: political theory at the crossroads. *In* Dallmayr, F. R. ed. From contract to community p 1-16

Dalton, George
Karl Polanyi's analysis of long-distance trade and his wider paradigm. *In* Ancient civilization and trade p63-132

D'Alton, Ian
A contrast in crises: southern Irish Protestantism, 1820-43 and 1885-1910. *In* Hepburn, A. C. ed. Minorities in history p70-83

Dalton, John

About

Rocke, A. J. Atoms and equivalents: the early development of the chemical atomic theory. *In* Historical studies in the physical sciences v9 p225-63

Dalton, William Joseph
"So that your faith may also be your hope in God" (I Peter 1:21). *In* Reconciliation and hope p262-74

Daly, Robert James
God's altar

Contents

Anne Bradstreet and the practice of weaned affections
Ars poetica
Edward Taylor: Christ's creation and the dissatisfactions of metaphor
Gnostics and naturalists
In critic's hands: a bibliographical essay
Introduction: Puritanism and poetry
The world's body

Dam, Kenneth W.
Class action notice: who needs it? *In* The Supreme Court review, 1974 p97-126

Damas, Léon Gontran

About

Jones, B. Léon Damas. *In* King, B. A. and Ogungbesan, K. eds. A celebration of Black and African writing p60-73

Dameron, Charles
Arthur Nortje: craftsman for his muse. *In* Heywood, C. ed. Aspects of South African literature p155-62

Les dames du Bois de Boulogne (Motion picture)
Truffaut, F. Robert Bresson: Les dames du Bois de Boulogne. *In* Truffaut, F. The films in my life p188-90

Damian, Peter. See Pietro Damiani, Saint

Damon, Samuel Foster

About

Cowley, M. The New England voice. *In* Cowley, M. —And I worked at the writer's trade p35-50

Dampierre, Jean

About

Phillips, M. M. From the Ciceronianus to Montaigne. *In* Classical influences on European culture A.D. 1500-1700 p191-97

Dams. See Fishways

Dana, Richard Henry, 1815-1822

About individual works

Two years before the mast

Spengemann, W. C. The poetics of adventure. *In* Spengemann, W. C. The adventurous muse p6-67

Dance, Daryl C.
James Baldwin. *In* Inge, M. T.; Duke, J.M. and Bryer, J. R. eds. Black American writers v2 p73-120

Dance, Sir Nathaniel

About

Goodreau, D. Pictorial sources of the neoclassical style: London or Rome? *In* Studies in eighteenth-century culture v4 p247-70

Dance, S. Peter

About individual works
Shell collecting

Connolly, C. Shell collecting. *In* Connolly, C. The evening colonnade p423-25

Dancing

Zambia

Brelsford, W. V. African dances of Northern Rhodesia. *In* The Occasional papers of the Rhodes-Livingstone Museum p21-51

Dancing (in religion, folk-lore, etc.)
Brelsford, W. V. African dances of Northern Rhodesia. *In* The Occasional papers of the Rhodes-Livingstone Museum p21-51

See also Indians of North America—Dances

Dancing in literature
Silver, I. Ronsard on the marriage of poetry, music, and the dance. *In* Studies in the continental background of Renaissance English literature: essays presented to John L. Lievsay p155-69

Dancourt, Florent Carton, sieur d'Ancourt, called

About

Brereton, G. The cynical generation: Dancourt, Regnard, Dufresny, Lesage *In* Brereton, G. French comic drama p163-93

Dandies
Connolly, C. The dandy: 2. *In* Connolly, C. The evening colonnade p133-35

D'Andrade, Roy G.
A propositional analysis of U.S. American beliefs about illness. *In* Basso, K. H. and Selby, H. A. eds. Meaning in anthropology p155-80

D'Andrea, Paul Philip
"Thou starre of poets": Shakespeare as DNA. *In* Shakespeare: aspects of influence p163-91

Dandy, Walter Edward

About

Harvey, A. M. Neurosurgical genius: Walter Edward Dandy. *In* Harvey, A. M. Adventures in medical research p60-68

Daner, Francine J.
Conversion to Krishna Consciousness: the transformation from hippie to religious ascetic. *In* Wallis, R. ed. Sectarianism p53-69

Danforth, Samuel

About individual works
A brief recognition of New England's errand into the wilderness

Bercovitch, S. New England's errand reappraised. *In* Higham, J. and Conkin, P. K. eds. New directions in American intellectual history p85-104

Daniel, Arnaut. See Arnaut Daniel

Daniel, Samuel

About

LaBranche, A. Samuel Daniel: a voice of thoughtfulness. *In* Sloan, T. O. and Waddington, R. B. eds. The rhetoric of Renaissance poetry p123-39

Ure, P. A note on 'opinion' in Daniel, Greville, and Chapman. *In* Ure, P. Elizabethan and Jacobean drama p209-20

Bibliography

Godshalk, W. L. Samuel Daniel. *In* Logan, T. P. and Smith, D. S. eds. The new intellectuals p281-301

Daniell, David J.
Opening up the text: Shakespeare's Henry VI plays in performance. *In* Drama and society p247-77

Daniell, David J. and Easson, Angus
Shakespeare. *In* English Association. The year's work in English studies v57 p108-45

Daniell, David J.; Easson, Angus, and Sanders, Andrew
Shakespeare. *In* English Association. The year's work in English studies v56 p136-76

Daniell, David J. and others
Shakespeare. *In* English Association. The year's work in English studies v54 p153-84

Shakespeare [another essay] *In* English Association. The year's work in English studies v55 p193-230

Daniels, Bruce Colin
The political structure of local government in colonial Connecticut. *In* Daniels, B. C. ed. Town and county p44-71

Daniels, Gordon
The great Tokyo Air Raid, 9-10 March 1945. *In* Modern Japan p113-34

Daniels, Robert Vincent
Office holding and elite status: the Central Committee of the CPSU. *In* Cocks, P.; Daniels, R. V. and Heer, N. W. eds. The dynamics of Soviet politics p77-95

Daniels, Roger
American historians and East Asian immigrants. *In* The Asian American: the historical experience p 1-25

The Japanese. *In* Ethnic leadership in America p36-63

Daniels, Steven V.
Pickwick and Dickens: stages of development. *In* Dickens Studies Annual v4 p56-77

Danish drama

20th century—History and criticism

Kistrup, J. Post-war drama in Scandinavia. *In* Nicoll, A. World drama p854-60

D'Annunzio, Gabriele. See Annunzio, Gabriele d'

Dansby, Jesse L.
Race relations at Base X. *In* Henderson, G. ed. Human relations in the military p59-75

Dante Alighieri

About

Cairns, C. The Italian heritage. *In* Cairns, C. Italian literature p13-44

Dawson, C. In memoriam: the uses of Dante and Wordsworth. *In* Dawson, C. Victorian noon p36-51

Della Terza, D. An unbridgeable gap? Medieval poetics and the contemporary Dante reader. *In* Medievalia et humanistica no. 7 p65-76

Dante Alighieri—About—*Continued*

Ferrante, J. M. Dante. *In* Ferrante, J. M. Women as image in medieval literature p129-52

Peters, E. M. Pars, parte: Dante and an urban contribution to political thought. *In* The Medieval city p113-40

Sayers, D. L. Dante and Charles Williams; excerpt from "The poetry of search and the poetry of statement and other posthumous essays on literature, religion, and language." *In* Sayers, D. L. The whimsical Christian p180-204

Wilhelm, J. J. Arnaut Daniel's legacy to Dante and to Pound. *In* Italian literature: roots and branches p67-83

About individual works
The Divine comedy

Biser, E. Between Inferno and Purgatorio: thoughts on a structural comparison of Nietzsche with Dante. *In* O'Flaherty, J. C.; Sellner, T. F. and Helm, R. M. eds. Studies in Nietzsche and the classical tradition p55-70

Eliot, T. S. Dante. *In* Eliot, T. S. Selected prose of T. S. Eliot p205-30

Fergusson, F. The Divine comedy as a bridge across time. *In* Fergusson, F. Literary landmarks p62-75

Girard, R. The mimetic desire of Paolo and Francesca. *In* Girard, R. "To double business bound" p 1-8

Hollander, R. Typology and secular literature: some medieval problems and examples. *In* Miner, E. R. ed. Literary uses of typology p3-19

Liapunov, V. Limbo and the sharashka. *In* Dunlop, J. B.; Haugh, R. and Klimoff, A. eds. Aleksandr Solzhenitsyn: critical essays and documentary materials 2d ed. p231-40

Mandel'shtam, O. E. Conversation about Dante. *In* Mandel'shtam, O. E. Selected essays p3-44

Nemerov, H. The dream of Dante. *In* Nemerov, H. Figures of thought p71-84

O'Malley, G. Dante, Shelley, and T. S. Eliot. *In* Bornstein, G. ed. Romantic and modern p165-76

Schless, H. H. Dante: comedy and conversion. *In* Ruggiers, P. G. ed. Versions of medieval comedy p135-49

Seung, T. K. Bonaventure's figural exemplarism in Dante. *In* Italian literature: roots and branches p117-54

Steadman, J. M. "The House of Fame:" the eagle as contemplative symbol. *In* Steadman, J. M. Nature into myth p67-77

Steiner, G. Dante now: the gossip of eternity. *In* Steiner, G. On difficulty and other essays p164-85

The Divine comedy—Inferno

Freccero, J. Dante's Ulysses: from epic to novel. *In* Concepts of the hero in the Middle Ages and the Renaissance p101-19

Nohrnberg, J. C. The Inferno. *In* Seidel, M. A. and Mendelson, E. eds. Homer to Brecht p76-104

Snodgrass, W. D. Analysis of depths: the Inferno. *In* Snodgrass, W. D. In radical pursuit p275-319

The Divine comedy—Inferno (Canto V)

Reynolds, M. T. Dante's Francesca and James Joyce's "Sirens." *In* Italian literature: roots and branches p155-200

The Divine comedy—Inferno (Canto V, lines 127-38)

Smith, A. J. Sense and innocence: two love episodes in Dante and Milton. *In* An English miscellany p119-30

The Divine comedy—Inferno (Canto IX)

Freccero, J. Dante's Medusa: allegory and autobiography. *In* Jeffrey, D. L. ed. By things seen: reference and recognition in medieval thought p33-46

The Divine comedy—Paradise

Barney, S. A. Conclusion. *In* Barney, S. A. Allegories of history, allegories of love p310-15

Coomaraswamy, A. K. Two passages in Dante's Paradiso. *In* Coomaraswamy, A. K. Selected papers v2 p241-55

The Divine comedy—Paradise (Canto XXXIII, lines 64-66)

Chiaromonte, N. Three lines from Dante. *In* Chiaromonte, N. The worm of consciousness, and other essays. p72-79

The Divine comedy—Purgatory

Atchity, K. J. Dante's Purgatorio: the poem reveals itself. *In* Italian literature: roots and branches p85-115

Poggioli, R. Dante "poco tempo silvano": a pastoral oasis in the Commedia. *In* Poggioli, R. The oaten flute p135-52

Turner, V. W. African ritual and Western literature: is a comparative symbology possible? *In* Fletcher, A J. S. ed. The literature of fact p45-81

The new life

Mazzaro, J. The fact of Beatrice in The vita nuova. *In* Fletcher, A. J. S. ed. The literature of fact p83-108

Nolan, B. The vita nuova: Dante's Book of Revelation. *In* Nolan, B. The Gothic visionary perspective p84-123

Characters—Beatrice

Mazzaro, J. The fact of Beatrice in The vita nuova. *In* Fletcher, A. J. S. ed. The literature of fact p83-108

Characters—Bertran de Born

Paden, W. D. Bertran de Born in Italy. *In* Italian literature: roots and branches p39-65

Characters—Francesca

Reynolds, M. T. Dante's Francesca and James Joyce's "Sirens." *In* Italian literature: roots and branches p155-200

Criticism and interpretation

Reynolds, B. Dorothy L. Sayers, interpreter of Dante. *In* Hannay, M. P. ed. As her whimsey took her p123-32

Seung, T. K. Bonaventure's figural exemplarism in Dante. *In* Italian literature: roots and branches p117-54

Influence

O'Malley, G. Dante, Shelley, and T. S. Eliot. *In* Bornstein, G. ed. Romantic and modern p165-76

Influence—Chaucer

Schless, H. H. Transformations: Chaucer's use of Italian. *In* Brewer, D. S. ed. Geoffrey Chaucer p184-223

Dante Alighieri—*Continued*

Influence—Eliot

Charity, A. C. T. S. Eliot: The Dantean recognitions. *In* The Waste land in different voices p117-62

Hough, G. G. Dante and Eliot. *In* Hough, G. G. Selected essays p200-16

Influence—Joyce

Reynolds, M. T. Dante's Francesca and James Joyce's "Sirens." *In* Italian literature: roots and branches p155-200

Influence—Shelley

Milne, F. L. Shelley's The Cenci: the ice motif and the ninth circle of Dante's Hell. *In* Tennessee Studies in literature v22 p117-32

Style

Scaglione, A. D. Rhetoric in Italian literature: Dante and the rhetorical theory of sentence structure. *In* Murphy, J. J. ed. Medieval eloquence p252-69

Translations, English

Dunlap, B. J. Through a dark wood of criticism: the rationale and reception of Dorothy L. Sayers's translation of Dante. *In* Hannay, M. P. ed. As her whimsey took her p133-49

Dante, Nicholas. See Kirkwood, J. jt. auth.

Danto, Arthur Coleman

The artworld. *In* Aagaard-Mogensen, L. ed. Culture and art p9-20

Also in Margolis, J. Z. ed. Philosophy looks at the arts p132-44

Freudian explanations and the language of the unconscious. *In* Psychoanalysis and language p325-53

The representational character of ideas and the problem of the external world. *In* Hooker, M. ed. Descartes p287-97

About

Sclafani, R. J. The theory of art. *In* Aagaard-Mogensen, L. ed. Culture and art p146-70

About individual works
Artworks and real things

Lyas, C. Danto and Dickie on art. *In* Aagaard-Mogensen, L. ed. Culture and art p170-93

The artworld

Lyas, C. Danto and Dickie on art. *In* Aagaard-Mogensen, L. ed. Culture and art p170-93

Danto, Bruce L.

Drug ingestion and suicide during anticipatory grief. *In* Anticipatory grief p311-14

D'Antonio, William V.

Ethnicity and assimilation: a reconsideration. *In* Studies in Italian American social history p10-27

About

D'Antonio, W. V. Ethnicity and assimilation: a reconsideration. *In* Studies in Italian American social history p10-27

Danzig, Richard

A comment on the jurisprudence of the Uniform Commercial Code. *In* Stanford legal essays p97-111

How questions begot answers in Felix Frankfurter's first flag salute opinion. *In* The Supreme Court review, 1977 p257-74

Daor, Dan

Modes of argument. *In* Philosophy East/philosophy West p162-95

Two metaphysical concepts: Li and idea. *In* Philosophy East/philosophy West p235-46

Da Ponte, Lorenzo

About individual works
Don Giovanni

Bloch, A. Dom Juan and Don Giovanni. *In* Johnson, R. B.; Neumann, E. S. and Trail, G. T. eds. Molière and the commonwealth of letters: patrimony and posterity p287-98

D'Arcy, François. See Arcy, François d'

D'Arcy, Margaretta. See Arden, J. jt. auth

Darcy, Robert L.

Economic education, human values, and the quality of life. *In* Fairfield, R. P. ed. Humanistic frontiers in American education p102-11

Darío, Rubén

About

Paz, O. The siren and the seashell. *In* Paz, O. The siren & the seashell p17-56

Darius I, King of Persia

Chronology

Balcer, J. M. The date of Herodotus IV.1: Darius' Scythian expedition. In Harvard Studies in classical philology v76 p99-132

Dark, Philip John Crosskey

Benin bronze heads: styles and chronology. *In* African images p25-103

What is art for anthropologists? *In* Greenhalgh, M. and Megaw, J. V. S. eds. Art in society p31-50

Dark humor (Literature) See Black humor (Literature)

Darley, George

About

Brisman, L. George Darley: buoyant as young time. *In* Brisman, L. Romantic origins p183-223

D'Arms, John H.

CIL X, 1792: a municipal notable of the Augustan age. *In* Harvard Studies in classical philology v76 p207-16

Darmstadter, Joel, and Landsberg, Hans Herman

The economic background. *In* Vernon, R. ed. The oil crisis p15-37

Darnton, Robert

The Encyclopédie wars of prerevolutionary France. *In* Studies in eighteenth-century culture v6 p3-33

The High Enlightenment and the low-life of literature in pre-revolutionary France. *In* French society and the Revolution p53-87

The history of mentalités: recent writings on revolution, criminality, and death in France. *In* Brown, R. H. and Lyman, S. M. eds. Structure, consciousness, and history p106-36

Trade in the taboo: the life of a clandestine book dealer in prerevolutionary France. *In* Korshin, P. J. ed. The widening circle p11-83

Darrah, William Culp

Stereographs: a neglected source of history of photography. *In* One hundred years of photographic history p43-46

Dart, Raymond Arthur

Cultural diffusion from, in and to Africa. *In* Grafton Elliot Smith p160-74

Sir Grafton Elliot Smith and the evolution of man. *In* Grafton Elliot Smith p25-38

Darwin, Charles Robert

About

Boesiger, E. Evolutionary theories after Lamarck and Darwin. *In* Ayala, F. J. and Dobzhansky, T. G. eds. Studies in the philosophy of biology p21-43

Gruber, H. E. Darwin's "tree of nature" and other images of wide scope. *In* Wechsler, J. ed. On aesthetics in science p121-40

Hyman, S. E. A Darwin sidelight: the shape of the young man's nose. *In* Hyman, S. E. The critic's credentials p261-78

Larkin, M. La bête humaine. *In* Larkin, M. Man and society in nineteenth-century realism p123-33

Shapin, S. and Barnes, B. Darwin and social Darwinism: purity and history. *In* Barnes, B. and Shapin, S. eds. Natural order p125-42

Sulloway, F. J. Geographic isolation in Darwin's thinking: the vicissitudes of a crucial idea. *In* Studies in history of biology v3 p23-65

Todes, D. P. V. O. Kovalevskii: the genesis, content, and reception of his paleontological work. *In* Studies in history of biology, v2 p99-165

About individual works

The origin of species

Downs, R. B. Survival of the fittest. *In* Downs, R. B. Books that changed the world p349-61

Flew, A. G. N. The Darwinian framework. *In* Flew, A. G. N. A rational animal p7-33

Flew, A. G. N. Evolutionary ethics. *In* New studies in ethics v2 p217-86

Lewontin, R. C. Darwin and Mendel—the materialist revolution. *In* Neyman, J. ed. The heritage of Copernicus: theories "pleasing to the mind" p166-83

White, H. V. The fictions of factual representation. *In* Fletcher, A. J. S. ed. The literature of fact p21-44

Influence

Mudford, P. The backcloth changes. . . *In* Mudford, P. The art of celebration p21-33

Darwin, Erasmus Alvey

About

Fielding, K. J. Froude's revenge, or The Carlyles and Erasmus A. Darwin. *In* English Association. Essays and studies, 1978 p75-97

Darwinism. See Evolution

Darwinism, Social. See Social Darwinism

Dasent, Sir George Webbe

About

Quirk, R. Dasent, Morris, and aspects of translation. *In* Quirk, R. The linguist and the English language p97-109

Das Gupta, Ashin

Gujarati merchants and the Red Sea trade, 1700-1725. *In* Kling, B. B. and Pearson, M. N. eds. The age of partnership p123-58

Dasgupta, Jyotirindra

Ethnicity, language demands, and national development in India. *In* Glazer, N. and Moynihan, D. P. eds. Ethnicity p466-88

Dash, Irene G.

A penchant for Perdita on the eighteenth-century English stage. *In* Studies in eighteenth-century culture v6 p331-46

Dash, J. Michael

The example of Aimé Césaire. *In* King, B. A. and Ogungbesan, K. eds. A celebration of Black and African writing p74-86

The peasant novel in Haiti. *In* African literature today no. 9: Africa, America and the Caribbean p77-90

Dashwood, Julie R.

The Italian futurist theatre. *In* Drama and society p129-46

Da Silveira Soares Cardozo, Manoel. See Cardozo, Manoel da Silveira Soares

Das Pal, Kristo. See Pal, Kristo Das

Dassin, Jules

About individual works

He who must die

Truffaut, F. Jules Dassin: Celui qui doit mourir. *In* Truffaut, F. The films in my life p210-13

Datan, Nancy

Ecological antecedents and sex-role consequences in traditional and modern Israeli subcultures. *In* Schlegel, A. E. ed. Sexual stratification p326-43

Date line, International. See International date line

Dating (Social customs)

White, E. B. Afternoon of an American boy. *In* White, E. B. Essays of E. B. White p157-61

Dating, Radiocarbon. See Radiocarbon dating

Daube, David

The rabbis and Philo on human rights. *In* Sidorsky, D. ed. Essays on human rights p234-46

D'Aubigné, Théodore Agrippa. See Aubigné, Théodore Agrippa d'

Daudel, Raymond

Structure of molecular physics and its relations with other sciences. *In* The Frontiers of human knowledge p243-53

Dauenhauer, Richard

Footnote on Finnish drama. *In* Dauenhauer, R. and Binham, P. eds. Snow in May p51-52

Some notes on Zen Buddhist tendencies in modern Finnish poetry. *In* Dauenhauer, R. and Binham, P. eds. Snow in May p60-66

The view from the Aspen Grove: Paavo Haavikko in national and international context. *In* Dauenhauer, R. and Binham, P. eds. Snow in May p67-97

Dauer, Manning Julian

The impact of the American independence and the American Constitution: 1776-1848; with a brief epilogue. *In* Havard, W. C. and Bernd, J. L. eds. 200 years of the Republic in retrospect p37-55

Daugherty, Mary Lee

Serpent handling as sacrament. *In* Browne, R. B. and Fishwick, M. W. eds. Icons of America p124-38

Daughters and fathers in literature. See Fathers and daughters in literature

Daughters and mothers in literature. See Mothers and daughters in literature

Daughters in literature
Auerbach, N. Dickens and Dombey: a daughter after all. *In* Dickens Studies Annual v5 p95-114

Daunton, M. J.
Towns and economic growth in eighteenth-century England. *In* Towns in societies p245-77

Dauphiné

Church history
Tackett, T. N. The citizen priest: politics and ideology among the parish clergy of eighteenth-century Dauphiné. *In* Studies in eighteenth-century culture v7 p307-28

Dauster, Frank N.
The game of chance: the theater of José Triana. *In* Lyday, L. F. and Woodyard, G. W. eds. Dramatists in revolt p167-89

The theater of Antón Arrufat. *In* Lyday, L. F. and Woodyard, G. W. eds. Dramatists in revolt p3-18

D'Avenant, Sir William

About individual works
Salmacida spolia
Gordon, D. J. Roles and mysteries. *In* The Renaissance imagination p3-23

Davenport, Edward
Why theorize about literature? *In* Hernadi, P. ed. What is literature? p35-46

Davenport, Francis Garvin
Renewal and historical consciousness in The wide net. *In* Prenshaw, P. W. ed. Eudora Welty p189-200

Davenport, Nicholas Ernest Harold
Keynes in the City. *In* Keynes, M. ed. Essays on John Maynard Keynes p224-29

Davenport, William Anthony, and Williams, D. J.
Middle English: excluding Chaucer. *In* English Association. The year's work in English studies v53 p85-105

Davey, Frank. See Davey, Thomas Frank

Davey, Thomas Frank
E. J. Pratt: apostle of corporate man. *In* Woodcock, G. ed. Poets and critics p 1-13

David, King of Israel
Armerding, H. T. Were David's sons really priests? *In* Current issues in Biblical and patristic interpretation p75-86

David, Alfred
How Marcia lost her skin: a note on Chaucer's mythology. *In* The Learned and the lewed p19-29

Davidon, William C.
Chemical and biological warfare: pollution by design. *In* Against pollution and hunger p223-29

Davids, Jules
Extraterritoriality. *In* Encyclopedia of American foreign policy p359-71

Davidson, Basil. See Part 2 under title: African studies since 1945

Davidson, Donald
H. L. Mencken. *In* Crunden, R. M. ed. The superfluous men p232-35

I'll take my stand: a history. *In* Crunden, R. M. ed. The superfluous men p196-207

The world as Ford factory. *In* Crunden, R. M. ed. The superfluous men p81-84

About
Gray, R. J. The Nashville Agrarians. *In* Gray, R. J. The literature of memory p40-105

O'Brien, M. Donald Davidson: "the creed of memory." *In* O'Brien, M. The idea of the American South, 1920-1941 p185-209

Davidson, Donald Herbert
Reply to Foster [on Meaning and truth theory]. *In* Evans, G. L. and McDowell, J. H. eds. Truth and meaning p33-41

Semantics for natural languages. *In* Harman, G. ed. On Noam Chomsky p242-52

Thought and talk. *In* Guttenplan, S. D. ed. Mind and language p7-23

About
Føllesdal, D. Meaning and experience. *In* Guttenplan, S. D. ed. Mind and language p25-44

About individual works
Truth and meaning
Foster, J. A. Meaning and truth theory. *In* Evans, G. L. and McDowell, J. H. eds. Truth and meaning p 1-32

Loar, B. Two theories of meaning. *In* Evans, G. L. and McDowell, J. H. eds. Truth and meaning p138-61

Davidson, E. J.; Ashe, A. H. and Redmond, James
The twentieth century. *In* English Association. The year's work in English studies v53 p361-409

Davidson, Hugh McCullough
Fontenelle, Perrault, and the realignment of the arts. *In* Literature and history in the age of ideas p3-13

Sign, sense, and Roland Barthes. *In* Wimsatt, W. K. ed. Literary criticism: idea and act p228-41

Davidson, Jeffrey L. See Street, D. jt. auth.

Davidson, Julian M.
Biological determinants of sex: their scope and limitations. *In* Katchadourian, H. A. ed. Human sexuality p134-49

Davidson, Sara

About individual works
Loose change: three women of the sixties
Mickelson, A. Z. Piecemeal liberation: Marge Piercy, Sara Davidson, Marilyn French, Grace Paley. *In* Mickelson, A. Z. Reaching out: sensitivity and order in recent American fiction by women p175-234

Davidson, Virginia Spencer
Johnson's Life of Savage: the transformation of a genre. *In* Studies in biography p57-72

Davie, Donald
British criticism: the necessity for humility. *In* The Frontiers of literary criticism p25-34

Eliot in one poet's life. *In* The Waste land in different voices p221-37

A gathered Church
Contents
Dissent and the agnostics, 1850-1900
Dissent and the Evangelicals, 1800-1850
Dissent and the Wesleyans, 1740-1800
Dissent in the present century
The Nonconformist contribution to English culture
Old dissent, 1700-1740

Davie, Donald—*Continued*

About individual works
Articulate energy

Epstein, E. L. The self-reflexive artefact: the function of mimesis in an approach to a theory of value for literature. *In* Fowler, R. ed. Style and structure in literature p40-78

Davie, George Elder

Edmund Husserl and 'the as yet, in its most important respect, unrecognised greatness of Hume.' *In* David Hume p69-76

Davies, H. Neville

Dryden's Rahmenerzählung: the form of 'An essay of dramatick poesie.' *In* Røstvig, M. S. ed. Fair forms p119-46

Laid artfully together: stanzaic design in Milton's 'On the morning of Christ's Nativity.' *In* Røstvig, M. S. ed. Fair forms p85-117

Davies, James Arthur

Striving for honesty: an approach to Forster's Life. *In* Dickens Studies Annual v7 p34-48

Davies, James Chowning

The development of individuals and the development of politics. *In* Fitzgerald, R. ed. Human needs and politics p74-95

Essay 4. *In* Fitzgerald, R. ed. What it means to be human p64-82

Davies, Joan

Time, aesthetics, and critical theory. *In* O'Neill, J. ed. On critical theory p58-77

Davies, John Paton

America and East Asia. *In* Two hundred years of American foreign policy p90-141

Davies, Maxwell. See Davies, Peter Maxwell

Davies, Peter Maxwell

About individual works
Eight songs for a mad king

Josipovici, G. Two moments in modern music-theatre. *In* Josipovici, G. The lessons of modernism p177-94

Taverner

Josipovici, G. Maxwell Davie's Taverner: thoughts on the libretto. *In* Josipovici, G. The lessons of modernism p167-76

Davies, Reginald Thorne

Samuel Johnson, James Boswell, and the romantic. *In* Davies, R. T. and Beatty, B. G. eds. Literature of the romantic period, 1750-1850 p 1-18

Davies, Robert William

The Soviet rural economy in 1929-1930: the size of the kolkhoz. *In* Essays in honour of E. H. Carr p255-80

Da Vinci, Leonardo. See Leonardo da Vinci

Davis, Bernard David

The scientific versus the adversary approach in bio-medical research. *In* Hook, S.; Kurtz, P. and Todorovich, M. eds. The ethics of teaching and scientific research p165-68

Davis, Bertram Hylton

Academic freedom, academic neutrality, and the social system. *In* The Concept of academic freedom p27-36

Davis, Calvin DeArmond

Arbitration, mediation, and conciliation. *In* Encyclopedia of American foreign policy p33-42

Davis, Charles E. and Hudson, Martha B.

Humor of the Old Southwest: a checklist of criticism. *In* Inge, M. T. ed. The frontier humorists p303-23

Davis, David Brion

Cultural history and the American identity. *In* Smithsonian Institution. The cultural drama p139-56

The emergence of immediatism in British and American antislavery thought. *In* Mulder, J. M. and Wilson, J. F. eds. Religion in American history p236-53

Slavery and the post-World War II historians. *In* Mintz, S. W. ed. Slavery, colonialism, and racism p 1-16

Davis, Earle Rosco

Dickens and significant tradition. *In* Dickens Studies Annual v7 p49-67

Davis, Elmer Holmes

Introduction to This is London by Edward R. Murrow. *In* Praise from famous men: an anthology of introductions p45-48

Davis, Floyd James

Beliefs, values, power, and public definitions of deviance. *In* Davis, F. J. and Stivers, R. eds. The collective definition of deviance p50-59

Davis, Gerald L.

Afro-American coil basketry in Charleston County, South Carolina. *In* Yoder, D. ed. American folklife p151-84

Davis, Glenn

Theodore Roosevelt and the Progressive Era: a study in individual and group psychohistory. *In* DeMause, L. ed. The new psychohistory p245-305

Davis, Harold Lenoir

About individual works
The kettle of fire

Armstrong, G. M. An unworn and edged tool: H. L. Davis's last word on the West, "The kettle of fire." *In* Bingham, E. R. and Love, G. A. eds. Northwest perspectives p169-85

Davis, Jacquelyn K. See Pfaltzgraff, R. L. jt. auth.

Davis, Jo Ann

Henry IV: from satirist to satiric butt. *In* Aeolian harps p81-93

Davis, John Whitney

Hume on qualitative content. *In* David Hume p175-80

Davis, Joseph Kimbrell

Landscapes of the dislocated mind in Williams' The glass menagerie. *In* Tennessee Williams: a tribute p192-206

Davis, Keith

Some fundamental trends affecting management in the future. *In* Benton, L. R. ed. Management for the future p63-76

Davis, Kenneth Culp

The inquiry—the subject, objectives, background, and method. *In* Davis, K. C. Discretionary justice in Europe and America p 1-15

Davis, Kenneth Waldron; Higdon, David Leon, and Rude, Donald W.

On editing Conrad. *In* Joseph Conrad: a commemoration p143-55

Davis, Kingsley

Mental hygiene and the class structure. *In* Davis, F. J. and Stivers, R. eds. The collective definition of deviance p99-113

Davis, Lillian J.
Tolerance of ambiguity in interpersonal bargaining. *In* International terrorism and world security p314-24

Davis, Mary E.
Mario Vargas Llosa: the necessary scapegoat. *In* Rossman, C. R. and Friedman, A. W. eds. Mario Vargas Llosa p136-50

Davis, Michael I. See Landis, E. S. jt. auth.

Davis, Moshe
The Jewish people in metamorphosis. *In* Tradition and change in Jewish experience p 1-25

Davis, Natalie Ann (Zemon)
Ghosts, kin, and progeny: some features of family life in early modern France. *In* Rossi, A. S; Kagan, J. and Hareven, T. K. eds. The family p87-114

Women on top: symbolic sexual inversion and political disorder in early modern Europe. *In* Babcock, B. A. ed. The reversible world p147-90

Davis, Norman
Chaucer and fourteenth-century English. *In* Brewer, D. S. ed. Geoffrey Chaucer p58-84

Davis, Robert Gorham
C. P. Snow. *In* Stade, G. ed. Six contemporary British novelists p57-114

Davis, Sara DeSaussure
The Bostonians reconsidered. *In* Tulane Studies in English, v23 p39-60

Davis, Susan Schaefer
Working women in a Moroccan village. *In* Beck, L. and Keddie, N. R. eds. Women in the Muslim world p416-33

Davis, Thomas Marion
Emily Dickinson and the right of way to Tripoli. *In* Artful thunder p209-19

Davis, Thomas Marion, and Jeske, Jeff
(eds.) Solomon Stoddard's 'Arguments' concerning admission to the Lord's Supper. *In* American Antiquarian Society. Proceedings v86 pt 1 p75-111

Davis, Tom, and Hamlyn, Susan
What do we do when two texts differ? She stoops to conquer and textual criticism. *In* Evidence in literary scholarship p263-79

Davison, Frank Dalby

About individual works
The white thorntree

Hadgraft, C. Indulgence: David Martin's The hero of Too, Frank Dalby Davidson's [sic] The white thorntree, Dal Stivens's A horse of air, David Malouf's Johnno, and Frank Hardy's But the dead are many. *In* Hamilton, K. G. ed. Studies in the recent Australian novel p194-224

Davison, Richard Allan
Frank Norris' The octopus: some observations on Vanamee, Shelgrim and St Paul. *In* Literature and ideas in America p182-203

A reading of Frank Norris's The pit. *In* The Stoic strain in American literature p77-94

Davison, Roderic H.
Nationalism as an Ottoman problem and the Ottoman response. *In* Nationalism in a non-national state p25-56

Davison, Walter Phillips
The role of communication in democracies; excerpt from "International political communication." *In* Fischer, H. D. and Merrill, J. C. eds. International and intercultural communication p29-36

Dawe, Donald G.
Christian faith in a religiously plural world. *In* Christian faith in a religiously plural world p13-33

Dawe, Roger David
Some reflections on ate and hamartia. *In* Harvard Studies in classical philology v72 p89-123

Dawidowicz, Lucy S.
The Jewish presence
Contents
Arnold Schoenberg: a search for Jewish identity
Belsen remembered
Blaming the Jews: the charge of perfidy
Bleaching the black lie: the case of Theresienstadt
Can anti-Semitism be measured?
Explaining American Jews
From past to past: Jewish East Europe to Jewish East Side
In Hitler's service: Albert Speer
Jewish identity: a matter of fate, a matter of choice
The Jewishness of the American Jewish labor movement
Max Weinreich: scholarship of Yiddish
Middle-class Judaism
An obedient killer: Franz Stangl, Commandant of Treblinka
On being a woman in shul
Picturing the past
Resistance: a doomed struggle
Smut and anti-Semitism
When Reform was young
Yiddish and its translation
Yiddish: past, present, and perfected

About individual works
The war against the Jews

Howe, I. The Holocaust and moral judgment. *In* Howe, I. Celebrations and attacks p234-38

Dawson, Carl
Victorian noon
Contents
Dramatic elegists: Arnold, Clough, and Browning at mid-century
The germ: aesthetic manifesto
In memoriam: the uses of Dante and Wordsworth
"The lamp of memory": Wordsworth and Dickens
Men of letters as hacks and heroes
Phases of the soul: the Newman brothers
Poetics: the hero as poet
Polemics: Charles Kingsley and Alton Locke
Postscripts: on the eve of the Great Exhibition

Dawson, Giles Edwin
Problems in editing sixteenth- and seventeenth-century letters. *In* Medieval and Renaissance studies [1974] p87-103

Dawson, Ruth P.
Rudolf Erich Raspe: the geologist Captain Cook refused. *In* Studies in eighteenth-century culture v8 p269-90

Dawson, S. W.
Precarious complacenecy. *In* Abbs, P. ed. The black rainbow p55-62

Day, Donald
The humorous works of George W. Harris. *In* Inge, M. T. ed. The frontier humorists p118-34

Day, Douglas

About individual works
Malcolm Lowry

Gass, W. H. Malcolm Lowry. *In* Gass, W. H. The world within the word p16-38

Day, Juliana, and Kwiatkowska, Hanna Yaxa
The psychiatric patient and his "well" sibling: a comparison through their art productions. *In* Ulman, E. and Dachinger, P. eds. Art therapy p345-60

Day, Michael H.
The evolution of man. *In* Racial variation in man p3-8

Day, Thomas

About

Lonsdale, R. H. Dr. Burney, 'Joel Collier', and Sabrina. *In* Evidence in literary scholarship p281-308

Day, Virginia
The influence of the catechetical narratio on Old English and some other medieval literature. *In* Anglo-Saxon England 3 p51-61

Day, Willard F.
On the behavioral analysis of self-deception and self-development. *In* Mischel, T. ed. The self p224-49

Day-Lewis, Cecil

About

Smith, E. E. C. Day-Lewis: the iron lyricist. *In* Smith, E. E. The angry young men of the thirties p 1-34

Day care centers

Great Britain

Tizard, J. Nursery needs and choices. *In* Human growth and development p139-67

United States

Elkind, D. Day care in America. *In* Elkind, D. The child and society p17-32

Woolsey, S. H. Pied Piper politics and the child-care debate. *In* Rossi, A. S.; Kagan, J. and Hareven, T. K. eds. The family p127-46

Day for night (Motion picture)
Kauffmann, S. Day for night. *In* Kauffmann, S. Living images p226-28

A day in the death of Joe Egg (Motion picture)
Kauffmann, S. A day in the death of Joe Egg. *In* Kauffmann, S. Living images p114-15

Day nurseries. See Day care centers

The day of the Jackal (Motion picture)
Kauffmann, S. The day of the Jackal. *In* Kauffmann, S. Living images p200-01

The day of the locust (Motion picture)
Gottlieb, S. The madding crowd in the movies. *In* Peary, G. and Shatzkin, R. eds. The modern American novel and the movies p95-106

Dayan, Daniel
The tutor-code of classical cinema. *In* Nichols, B. ed. Movies and methods p438-51

About individual works
The tutor-code of classical cinema

Rothman, W. Against "the system of the suture." *In* Nichols, B. ed. Movies and methods p451-59

Days. See Festivals

Dazai, Osamu, pseud.

About

Ueda, M. Dazai Osamu. *In* Ueda, M. Modern Japanese writers p145-72

About individual works
The setting sun

Rimer, J. T. Dazai Osamu: the death of the past. *In* Rimer, J. T. Modern Japanese fiction and its traditions p182-99

Deacon, Lois
Hardy's secret love. *In* Drabble, M. ed. The genius of Thomas Hardy p19-31

Dead
May, W. F. Attitudes toward the newly dead. *In* Death inside out p139-49
See also Cemeteries

Dead (in religion, folk-lore, etc.)
Kelly, P. F. Death in Mexican folk culture. *In* Death in America p92-111

Laroche, M. The myth of the zombi. *In* Exile and tradition p44-61

Dead, Communication with the. See Spiritualism

Dead Sea scrolls
Sanders, J. A. The Qumran Psalms scroll (11QPs^a) reviewed. *In* On language, culture, and religion: in honor of Eugene A. Nida p79-99

Deadly sins
Sayers, D. L. The other six deadly sins; excerpt from "Creed or chaos?" *In* Sayers, D. L. The whimsical Christian p157-79
See also Laziness

Deaf

Sexual behavior

Smith, M. S. The deaf. *In* Gochros, H. L. and Gochros, J. S. eds The sexually oppressed p268-76

Deakin, Motley Freemont
The real and fictive quest of Henry James. *In* Garvin, H. R. ed. Makers of the twentieth-century novel p179-91

Deal, Borden

About

Emerson, O. B. Some contemporary literary views of the newest South. *In* The Rising South v2 p117-25

Dean, Althea, and Lurie, Abraham
Family involvement with the dying patient. *In* Home care p84-89

Dean, James

About

Truffaut, F. James Dean is dead. *In* Truffaut, F. The films in my life p296-99

Dean, John
Controversy over classification: a case study from the history of botany. *In* Barnes, B. and Shapin, S. eds. Natural order p211-30

Death—Proof and certification—*Continued*

Task Force on Death and Dying of the Institute of Society, Ethics, and the Life Sciences. Refinements in criteria for the determination of death: an appraisal. *In* Weir, R. F. ed. Ethical issues in death and dying p90-102

Psychological aspects

Aldrich, C. K. Some dynamics of anticipatory grief. *In* Anticipatory grief p3-9

Ariès, P. Death inside out. *In* Death inside out p9-24

Arkin, A. M. Notes on anticipatory grief. *In* Anticipatory grief p10-13

Benoliel, J. Q. Dying is a family affair. *In* Home care p17-34

Bettelheim, B. The ultimate limit. *In* Bettelheim, B. Surviving, and other essays p3-18

Blank, H. R. Anticipatory grief and mourning. *In* Anticipatory grief p267-80

Buckley, I. G. and Michaels, R. Variations on a theme: case reports from cancer care. *In* Anticipatory grief p135-43

Budner, S. The concept of anticipatory grief from a research perspective. *In* Anticipatory grief p48-52

Caroff, P. and Dobrof, R. Social work: its institutional role. *In* Anticipatory grief p251-63

Carpenter, J. O. and Hall, G. Anticipatory grief and the disciplined professions. *In* Anticipatory grief p229-36

Cassell, E. J. Dying in a technological society. *In* Death inside out p43-48

Craytor, J. K. Working with dying patients and their families. *In* Home care p37-48

Dean, A. and Lurie, A. Family involvement with the dying patient. *In* Home care p84-89

Gaynor, A. The patient's home is his castle. *In* Home care p101-08

Goldstein, E. G. and Malitz, S. Psychotherapy and pharmacotherapy as enablers in the anticipatory grief of a dying patient: a case study. *In* Anticipatory grief p285-95

Grof, S. and Halifax-Grof, J. Psychedelics and the experience of death. *In* Life after death p182-202

Gullo, S. V.; Cherico, D. J. and Shadick, R. G. Suggested stages and response styles in life-threatening illness: a focus on the cancer patient. *In* Anticipatory grief p53-78

Gutmann, D. L. Dying to power: death and the search for self-esteem. *In* Feifel, H. [ed.] New meanings of death p335-47

Hildebrandt, H. The community center in the life of a dying person with no family involvement. *In* Home care p215-22

Kalish, R. A. Dying and preparing for death: a view of families. *In* Feifel, H. [ed.] New meanings of death p215-32

Kastenbaum, R. Death and development through the lifespan. *In* Feifel, H. [ed.] New meaning of death p17-45

Kaufmann, W. A. On death and lying. *In* Psychiatry and the humanities v 1 p235-40

Kutscher, A. H. 1923- and Kutscher, A. H. Medical school curriculum and anticipatory grief: faculty attitudes. *In* Anticipatory grief p213-17

Lifton, R. J. The sense of immortality: on death and the continuity of life. *In* Explorations in psychohistory p271-87

Also in Feifel, H. [ed] New meaning of death p273-90

Same as Lifton, R. J. On death and the continuity of life: a "new" paradigm. *In* Wolman, B. B. ed. Between survival and suicide p55-76

Lockwood, J. A. From life to death. *In* Home care p263-67

May, W. F. The metaphysical plight of the family. *In* Death inside out p49-60

Meyerowitz, J. H. Dying: dromenon versus drama. *In* Anticipatory grief p79-93

Moss, S. A. Home is not necessarily "home." *In* Home care p77-83

Neale, R. E. Initiatory grief. *In* Anticipatory grief p331-42

Nighswonger, C. A. The vectors and vital signs in grief synchronization. *In* Anticipatory grief p267-75

Nolan, T. Ritual and therapy. *In* Anticipatory grief p358-64

Nowitz, L. Dying and the aged person: process and implications for social work practice. *In* Home care p185-95

Pritchard, E. R. The social worker's responsibility. *In* Anticipatory grief p237-45

Ramsey, P. The indignity of 'death with dignity.' *In* Death inside out p81-96

Ramshorn, M. T. Selected tasks for the dying patient and family members. *In* Anticipatory grief p246-50

Reed, A. W. Anticipatory grief work. *In* Anticipatory grief p346-57

Reeves, R. B. Reflections on two false expectations. *In* Anticipatory grief p281-84

Tallmer, M. A societal response. *In* Anticipatory grief p19-25

Torpie, R. J. The patient and prolonged terminal malignant disease: experiences from a radiation therapy center. *In* Anticipatory grief p119-23

Weisman, A. D. The psychiatrist and the inexorable. *In* Feifel, H. [ed.] New meanings of death p107-22

See also Children and death; Death instinct; Youth and death

Social aspects

Gutmann, D. L. Dying to power: death and the search for self-esteem. *In* Feifel, H. [ed.] New meanings of death p335-47

Study and teaching

Leviton, D. Death education. *In* Feifel, H. [ed.] New meanings of death p253-72

Death (Biology)

Gaylin, W. The technology of life and death. *In* Small comforts for hard times p152-69

Jonas, D. F. Life, death, awareness, and concern: a progression. *In* Life after death p169-81

Morison, R. S. Death: process or event? *In* Death inside out p63-70

Thomas, L. The Deacon's masterpiece. *In* Thomas, L. The medusa and the snail p130-36

Thomas, L. On natural death. *In* Thomas, L. The medusa and the snail p102-05

See also Brain death; Death—Proof and certification

Death (Hinduism)

Coomaraswamy, A. K. The meaning of death. *In* Coomaraswamy, A. K. Selected papers v2 p426-29

Death, Mercy. See Euthanasia

Death and children. See Children and death

Death and youth. See Youth and death

Death in art. See Death—Art

Death in literature

Armato, P. M. Tennessee Williams' meditations on life and death in Suddenly last summer, The night of the iguana and The milk train doesn't stop here anymore. *In* Tennessee Williams: a tribute p558-70

Backman, M. Death and birth in Hemingway. *In* The Stoic strain in America literature p115-33

Bronsen, D. Consuming struggle vs. killing time: preludes to dying in the dramas of Ibsen and Beckett. *In* Spicker, S. F.; Woodward, K. M. and Van Tassel, D. D. eds. Aging and the elderly p261-81

Cunningham, J. V. Ripeness is all. *In* Cunningham, J. V. The collected essays of J. V. Cunningham p 1-8

Douglas, A. Heaven our home: consolation literature in the northern United States, 1830-1880. *In* Death in America p49-68

Friedenreich, K. The mower mown: Marvell's Dances of death. *In* Friedenreich, K. ed. Tercentenary essays in honor of Andrew Marvell p153-79

Glicksberg, C. I. Ionesco and the comedy of the Absurd. *In* Glicksberg, C. I. The literature of nihilism p222-33

Henn, T. R. 'The property of the dead.' *In* Henn, T. R. Last essays p221-39

Hermassi, K. C. Theatron, polis, and Thanatos. *In* Hermassi, K. C. Polity and theater in historical perspective p25-42

Hruby, A. The plowman from Bohemia. *In* Hoffmeister, G. ed. The Renaissance and Reformation in Germany p17-32

Langer, L. L. Albert Camus and the limits of the possible. *In* Langer, L. L. The age of atrocity p113-62

Langer, L. L. Dying voices. *In* Langer, L. L. The age of atrocity p34-68

Langer, L. L. The examined death. *In* Langer, L. L. The age of atrocity p 1-33

Langer, L. L. Thomas Mann and death on the mountain. *In* Langer, L. L. The age of atrocity p69-112

Lougy, R. E. Remembrances of death past and future: a reading of David Copperfield. *In* Dickens Studies Annual v6 p72-101

May, W. F. The metaphysical plight of the family. *In* Death inside out p49-60

Moss, W. G. Why the anxious fear? Aging and death in the works of Turgenev. *In* Spicker, S. F.; Woodward, K. M. and Van Tassel, D. D. eds. Aging and the elderly p241-60

Simpson, M. A. Death and modern poetry. *In* Feifel, H. [ed.] New meanings of death p313-33

Smith, S. R. Death, dying, and the elderly in seventeenth-century England. *In* Spicker, S. F.; Woodward, K. M. and Van Tassel, D. D. eds. Aging and the elderly p205-19

Steadman, J. M. "The pardoner's tale": old age and contemptus mundi. *In* Steadman, J. M. Nature into myth p104-14

Yu, B. The still center of Hemingway's world. *In* Wagner, L. W. ed. Ernest Hemingway p109-31

Death instinct

Pontalis, J. B. On death-work in Freud, in the self, in culture. *In* Roland A. ed. Psychoanalysis, creativity, and literature p85-95

Death of a salesman (criticism) Miller, A. *In* Kauffmann, S. Persons of the drama p142-45

Death penalty. See Capital punishment

Death rate. See Mortality

"Deb", pseud.

Do you want to get beat up at home or in prison? *In* Gross, B. and Gross, R. eds. The children's rights movement p43-47

De Balsac, Robert. See Balsac, Robert de

De Balzac, Honoré. See Balzac, Honoré de

De Barros, Plínio Marcos. See Marcos, Plínio

DeBary, William Theodore

General education and the university crisis. *In* Hook, S.; Kurtz, P. W. and Todorovich, M. eds. The philosophy of the curriculum: the need for general education p3-25

Neo-Confucian cultivation and the seventeenth-century "enlightenment." *In* The Unfolding of Neo-Confucianism p141-216

The university, society, and the critical temper: in response to George W. Pierson. *In* Small comforts for hard times p277-80

About individual works
Education and the university crisis

Schwab, J. J. On reviving liberal education—in the seventies. *In* Hook, S.; Kurtz, P. W. and Todorovich, M. eds. The philosophy of the curriculum: the need for general education p37-48

Debates and debating

Voegelin, E. On debate and existence. *In* A Public philosophy reader p152-67

De Beauvoir, Simone. See Beauvoir, Simone de

DeBell, Diane

Strategies of survival: David Jones, In parenthesis, and Robert Graves, Goodbye to all that. *In* Klein, H. M. ed. The First World War in fiction p160-73

De Bie, Pierre. See Bie, Pierre de

De Boer, Pieter Arie Hendrik. See Boer, Pieter Arie Hendrik de

De Bolt, Joe

The development of John Brunner. *In* Clareson, T. D. ed. Voices for the future: essays on major science fiction writers v2 p106-35

De Bono, Edward

Lateral thinking and science fiction. *In* Nicholls, P. ed. Science fiction at large p35-55

De Brahm, John Gerar William

About individual works
Report of the general survey in the southern district of North America

De Vorsey, L. La Florida revealed: the De Brahm surveys of British East Florida, 1765-1771. *In* Pattern and process p87-102

De Brahm, John William Gerar. See De Brahm, John Gerar William

De Brahm, William Gerard. See De Brahm, John Gerar William

Debray, Régis
About
Parry, A. Wanton romantics: Guevara, Debray, Marighella. *In* Parry, A. Terrorism: from Robespierre to Arafat p244-60

De Breffny, Brian
The end of the old order: from the Reformation to the Jacobite defeat. *In* De Breffny, B. ed. The Irish world p99-126

Debt. See Debts, External

Debts, External
Van Alstyne, R. W. Debt collection. *In* Encyclopedia of American foreign policy p212-18

Debts, International. See Debts, External

Debts, Public
United States
Lerner, A. P. Money, debt and wealth. *In* Econometrics and economic theory p247-59

DeBurger, James Edward
Sex in troubled marriages. *In* Gross, L. ed. Sexual issues in marriage p65-72

De Burgh, Hubert. See Burgh, Hubert de, Earl of Kent

Debus, Allen G.
The chemical debates of the seventeenth century: the reaction to Robert Fludd and Jean Baptiste van Helmont. *In* Bonelli, M. L. R. and Shea, W. R. eds. Reason, experiment, and mysticism in the scientific revolution p19-47

Debutts, John Delany
The management of complexity. *In* Benton, L. R. ed. Management for the future p77-86

Decadence (Literary movement)
Briggs, J. Diabolism and decadence: the mood of the nineties. *In* Briggs, J. Night visitors p76-97
Glicksberg, C. I. The unpolitical writer. *In* Glicksberg, C. I. The literature of commitment p113-30

Decadence as a theme in literature. See Decadence in literature

Decadence in literature
Briggs, J. Diabolism and decadence: the mood of the nineties. *In* Briggs, J. Night visitors p76-97
Brombert, V. H. Huysmans: the prison house of decadence. *In* Brombert, V. H. The romantic prison p149-70
Oberg, A. K. Sylvia Plath and the new decadence. *In* Butscher, E. ed. Sylvia Plath p177-85
Peckham, M. Edgar Saltus and the heroic decadence. *In* Tulane Studies in English, v23 p61-69

De Caldes, Ramon. See Ramon de Caldes

De Cardona, Elizabeth
American television in Latin America. *In* Gerbner, G. ed. Mass media policies in changing cultures p57-62

De Castle, Robert Leon van. See Van de Castle, Robert Leon

De Cecco, John P. and Shively, Michael G.
Conflicts over rights and needs in homosexual relationships. *In* Crew, L. ed. The gay academic p305-14

De Cecco, Marcello
The last of the Romans. *In* Skidelsky, R.J.A. ed. The end of the Keynesian era p18-24

Deceit in literature. See Deception in literature

Decentralization in government
United States
Fitch, L. C. Fiscal and productive efficiency in urban government systems. *In* Hawley, A. H. and Rock, V. P. eds. Metropolitan America in contemporary perspective p397-429

Deception in literature
Edwards, P. Shakespeare and the healing power of deceit. *In* Shakespeare survey v31 p115-25

De Cervantes Saavedra, Miguel. See Cervantes Saavedra, Miguel de

De Chardin, Pierre Teilhard. See Teilhard de Chardin, Pierre

Decision (Ethics) See Decision-making (Ethics)

Decision (Psychology). See Decision-making

Decision-making
Lloyd, A. C. Emotion and decision in Stoic psychology. *In* Rist, J. M. ed. The Stoics p233-46
See also Choice (Psychology); Consensus (Social sciences)

Decision-making (Ethics)
Hampshire, S. On having a reason. *In* Royal Institute of Philosophy. Human values p86-98
McKean, R. N. Collective choice. *In* McKie, J. W. ed. Social responsibility and the business predicament p109-34
Nagel, T. The fragmentation of value. *In* Nagel, T. Mortal questions p128-41
Warwick, D. P. Freedom. *In* Population policy and ethics p17-29

Decision-making, Group
Janis, I. L. Groupthink among policy makers. *In* Kren, G. M. and Rappoport, L. H. eds. Varieties of psychohistory p315-29

Decision-making in children
Nicholson, S. Children as planners. *In* Gross, B. and Gross, R. eds. The children's rights movement p287-95

Decision-making in political science
Auma-Osolo, A. Rationality and foreign policy process. *In* The Year book of world affairs, 1977 p257-88
Curzon, D. The generic secrets of government decision making. *In* Galnoor, I. ed. Government secrecy in democracies p93-109
Mills, R. M. The virgin lands since Krushchev: choices and decisions in Soviet policy making. *In* Cocks, P.; Daniels, R. V. and Heer, N. W. eds. The dynamics of Soviet politics p178-92
Rosenau, J. N. Decision-making approaches and theories. *In* Encyclopedia of American foreign policy p219-28

Decision-making in school management
Brown, M. A. The administration of professors as decision makers. *In* Managing nonprofit organizations p303-12

Declaration of Independence. See United States. Declaration of Independence

Declaration of Paris, 1856. See Paris, Declaration of, 1856

Decline of civilization. See Regression (Civilization)

Decoration and ornament

Coomaraswamy, A. K. Ornament; excerpt from "Figures of speech or figures of thought: collected essays on the traditional or 'normal' view of art." *In* Coomaraswamy, A. K. Selected papers v 1 p241-53

See also Art, Decorative; Carving (Art industries); Graffito decoration; Stucco

Victorian style

Frank, E. E. The domestication of nature: five houses in the Lake District. *In* Knoepflmacher, U. C. and Tennyson, G. B. eds. Nature and the Victorian imagination p68-92

Decoration and ornament, Architectural

Izmir (City), Turkey

Dwyer, E. J. On the meaning of the griffin pelta. *In* Studies in classical art and archaeology p235-38

Nigeria

Cole, H. M. The history of Ibo mbari houses—facts and theories. *In* African images p104-32

Nubia

Walz, T. House decoration in Lower Nubia. *In* African images p190-222

Preslav, Bulgaria

Akrabova-Zhandova, I. Preslav inlaid ceramics. *In* Studies in memory of David Talbot Rice p25-33

Priene, Asia Minor

Carter, J. C. The date of the sculptured coffer lids from the Temple of Athene Polias at Priene. *In* Studies in classical art and archaeology p139-51

Rome

Dwyer, E. J. On the meaning of the griffin pelta. *In* Studies in classical art and archaeology p235-38

Decoration and ornament, Hindu

Coomaraswamy, A. K. Ornament; excerpt from "Figures of speech or figures of thought: collected essays on the traditional or 'normal' view of art." *In* Coomaraswamy, A. K. Selected papers v 1 p241-53

Decorative art. See Art, Decorative

Decorative arts. See Art, Decorative

DeCosta, Miriam

Social lyricism and the Caribbean poet/rebel. *In* DeCosta, M. ed. Blacks in Hispanic literature p114-22

De Courcel, Martine Hallade. See Courcel, Martine Hallade de

De Crespigny, Anthony

F. A. Hayek: freedom for progress. *In* De Crespigny, A. and Minogue, K. R. eds. Contemporary political philosophers p49-66

Decter, Midge

About individual works

The new chastity, and other arguments against women's liberation

Rich, A. C. The antifeminist woman. *In* Rich, A. C. On lies, secrets, and silence p69-84

Dedham, Mass.

Church history

Lockridge, K. A. The history of a Puritan church, 1637-1736. *In* Vaughan, A. T. and Bremer, F. J. eds. Puritan New England p92-108

Deduction (Logic) See Logic

Deductive logic. See Logic

De Duve, Christian Rene

Cells age: are lysosomes among the villains? *In* Jarvik, L. F. ed. Aging into the 21st century p25-31

Deely, John N.

Toward the origin of semiotic. *In* Sebeok, T. A. ed. Sight, sound, and sense p 1-30

Deep throat (Motion picture)

Sarris, A. Cock-tale parties on the East Side. *In* Sarris, A. Politics and cinema p135-37

Deer (in religion, folk-lore, etc.)

Bath, M. E. The legend of Caesar's deer. *In* Medievalia et humanistica; new ser. no. 9 p53-66

Berger, A. Ayalta: from the doe in the field to the mother of the messiahs. *In* Salo Wittmayer Baron v 1 p209-17

De facto doctrine. See Recognition (International law)

De facto doctrine (International law) See Recognition (International law)

DeFalco, Joseph M.

Hemingway and revolution: mankinde not Marx. *In* Renaissance and modern p143-59

Initiation ("Indian camp" and "The doctor and the doctor's wife.") *In* Benson, J. J. ed. The short stories of Ernest Hemingway: critical essays p159-67

The defeat of the Yuan. See Yuan Pâi

Defectives. See Handicapped

Defense (Criminal procedure). See Right to counsel

Defense contracts

United States

Edmonds, M. Accountability and the military-industrial complex. *In* Smith, B. L. R. ed. The new political economy: the public use of the private sector p149-80

Defense mechanisms (Psychology) See Repression (Psychology)

Defense research. See Military research

Defensiveness (Psychology) See Aggressiveness (Psychology)

Deficit financing

Mathematical models

Tobin, J. Deficit spending and crowding out in shorter and longer runs. *In* Theory for economic efficiency: essays in honor of Abba P. Lerner p217-36

Deficit spending. See Deficit financing

Definability. See Definition (Logic)

Definition (Logic)

Quine, W. V. Truth by convention. *In* Quine, W. V. The ways of paradox, and other essays p77-106

Quine, W. V. Vagaries of definition. *In* Quine, W. V. The ways of paradox, and other essays p50-55

Richards, I. A. Multiple definition. *In* Richards, I. A. Complementarities p56-72

See also Semantics (Philosophy)

Defoe, Daniel

About

Brown, H. O. The displaced self in the novels of Daniel Defoe. *In* Studies in eighteenth-century culture v4 p69-94

Defoe, Daniel—About—*Continued*

McEwen, G. D. "A turn of thinking": Benjamin Franklin, Cotton Mather, and Daniel Defoe on "doing good." *In* The Dress of words p53-65

Manlove, C. N. Defoe. *In* Manlove, C. N. Literature and reality, 1600-1800 p99-113

Schonhorn, M. Defoe: the literature of politics and the politics of some fictions. *In* English literature in the age of disguise p15-56

Skilton, D. Defoe and the Augustan age. *In* Skilton, D. The English novel p7-18

About individual works

Moll Flanders

Bjornson, R. The ambiguous success of the picaresque hero in Defoe's Moll Flanders. *In* Bjornson, R. The picaresque hero in European fiction p188-206

Karl, F. R. Daniel Defoe: the politics of necessity. *In* Karl, F. R. The adversary literature p68-98

Lerenbaum, M. Moll Flanders: "a woman on her own account." *In* Diamond, A. and Edwards, L. R. eds. The authority of experience p101-17

McCoy, K. The femininity of Moll Flanders. *In* Studies in eighteenth-century culture v7 p413-22

Robinson Crusoe

Karl, F. R. Daniel Defoe: the politics of necessity. *In* Karl, F. R. The adversary literature p68-98

Spacks, P. A. M. The soul's imaginings: Daniel Defoe, William Cowper. *In* Spacks, P. A. M. Imagining a self p28-56

The shortest way with the Dissenters

Boardman, M. M. Defoe's political rhetoric and the problem of irony. *In* Tulane studies in English v22 p87-102

A tour thro' the whole island of Great Britain, divided into circuits or journies

Rogers, P. Samuel Richardson and Defoe's Tour (1738): the evidence of bibliography. *In* Virginia. University. Bibliographical Society. Studies in bibliography v28 p305-07

Characters

Backscheider, P. R. Defoe's women: snares and prey. *In* Studies in eighteenth-century culture v5 p103-20

Language—Style

See Defoe, Daniel—Style

Style

Boardman, M. M. Defoe's political rhetoric and the problem of irony. *In* Tulane studies in English v22 p87-102

Technique

See also Defoe, Daniel—Style

Deforestation. See Clear-cutting

Deformities. See Abnormalities, Human

DeFunis v. Odegaard. *In* Gross, B. R. ed. Reverse discrimination p184-97

DeFunis v. Odegaard [another essay] *In* Gross, B. R. ed. Reverse discrimination p198-207

DeFunis v. Odegaard. *In* The Supreme Court review, 1974 p 1-32

De Gálvez, José, Marqués de Sonora. See Gálvez, José de, Marqués de Sonora

De García-Barrio, Constance Sparrow. See García-Barrio, Constance Sparrow de

De Gaulle, Charles, President France. See Gaulle, Charles de, President France

Degenfelder, E. Pauline

Rites of passage: novel to film. *In* Peary, G. and Shatzkin, R. eds. The modern American novel and the movies p178-86

De George, Richard T.

The concept of authority. *In* Armstrong, T. R. and Cinnamon, K. M. eds. Power and authority in law enforcement p39-55

De Gerez, Toni

A basket of fireflies: Quetzalcoatl and the Nahuatl poetry of Mexico. *In* Egoff, S. A. ed. One ocean touching p138-46

Dégh, Linda, and Vázsonyï, Andrew

Legend and belief. *In* Folklore genres p93-123

De Gracia, Juan José Linz Storch. See Linz Storch de Gracia, Juan José

De Graft, J. C. See De Graft-Johnson, John Coleman

De Graft-Johnson, John Coleman

Roots in African drama and theatre. *In* African literature today no. 8: Drama in Africa p 1-25

De Gryse, Louis M

Some observations on the origin of the Flemish bailiff (bailli): the reign of Philip of Alsace. *In* Viator: medieval and Renaissance studies v7 p243-94

Dei-Anang, Michael

Foreign policy of the independent African states. *In* African studies since 1945 p66-76

Deighton, H. S.

Multiracial societies—an historical perspective. *In* Racial variation in man p179-90

Deikman, Arthur J.

The missing center. *In* Alternate states of consciousness p230-41

Deininger, Whitaker Thompson

Promise and peril in pragmatic historical thought: a contemporary dialogue. *In* Philosophy and the civilizing arts p264-82

Deir el Bahari. Michałowski, K. *In* The Frontiers of human knowledge p163-69

De Iriarte y Oropesa, Tomàs. See Iriarte y Oropesa, Tomàs de

Deism

French, R. S. Elihu Palmer, radical deist, radical republican: a reconsideration of American free thought. *In* Studies in eighteenth-century culture v8 p87-108

Gawlick, G. Hume and the deists: a reconsideration. *In* David Hume p128-38

Luehrs, R. B. The problematical compromise: the early deism of Anthony Collins. *In* Studies in eighteenth-century culture v6 p59-77

See also Cosmology; God; Positivism; Theism

Dejection. See Depression, Mental

De Jouvenel, Bertrand. See Jouvenel, Bertrand de

Dekker, Thomas

Bibliography

Wine, M. L. Thomas Dekker. *In* Logan, T. P. and Smith, D. S. eds. The popular school p3-50

Dekker, Thomas, and Middleton, Thomas

About individual works

The honest whore; parts 1-2

Ure, P. Patient madman and honest whore: the Middleton-Dekker oxymoron. *In* Ure, P. Elizabethan and Jacobean drama p187-208

Characters—Bellafront

Ure, P. Patient madman and honest whore: the Middleton-Dekker oxymoron. *In* Ure, P. Elizabethan and Jacobean drama p187-208

Characters—Candido

Ure, P. Patient madman and honest whore: the Middleton-Dekker oxymoron. *In* Ure, P. Elizabethan and Jacobean drama p187-208

DeKosky, Robert K.

The role of classical humanism in the Copernican achievement. *In* Hoffmeister, G. ed. The Renaissance and Reformation in Germany p203-21

De Kuehne, Alyce. See Kuehne, Alyce de

De la Bruyère, Jean. See La Bruyère, Jean de

Delacroix, Eugène

About individual works

Journal

Trilling, L. On not talking. *In* Trilling, L. A gathering of fugitives p153-63

De Lacy, Phillip H.

The four Stoic personae. *In* Illinois classical studies, v2 1977 p163-72

De La Fontaine, Jean. See La Fontaine, Jean de

De la Garza, Rudolph O.

The politics of Mexican Americans. *In* Trejo, A. D. ed. The Chicanos p101-20

De la Garza, Rudolph O. and Rivera, Rowena

The socio-political world of the Chicano: a comparative analysis of social scientific and literary perspectives. *In* Minority language and literature p42-64

De La Mare, Walter John

About

Briggs, J. On the edge: Walter De La Mare. *In* Briggs, J. Night visitors p182-95

De la Motte, Antoine Houdar. See La Motte, Antoine Houdar de

Delany, Samuel R.

Critical methods: speculative fiction. *In* Clareson, T. D. ed. Many futures, many worlds p278-91

De la Peyrère, Isaac. See La Peyrère, Isaac de

De la Ramée, Pierre. See La Ramée, Pierre de

Delasselle, Claude

Abandoned children in eighteenth-century Paris. *In* Deviants and the abandoned in French society p47-82

De Latouche, Henri. See Latouche, Henri de

DeLaura, David Joseph

The allegory of life: the autobiographical impulse in Victorian prose. *In* Landow, G. P. ed. Approaches to Victorian autobiography p333-54

Arnold and literary criticism: (i) critical ideas. *In* Allott, K. ed. Matthew Arnold p118-48

Carlyle and Arnold: the religious issue. *In* Fielding, K. J. and Tarr, R. L. eds. Carlyle past and present p127-54

The future of poetry: a context for Carlyle and Arnold. *In* Carlyle and his contemporaries p148-80

The poetry of thought. *In* Altholz, J. L. ed. The mind and art of Victorian England p35-57

Delbanco, Andrew

Thomas Shepard's America: the biography of an idea. *In* Studies in biography p159-82

Delbo, Charlotte

About

Langer, L. L. Charlotte Delbo and a heart of ashes. *In* Langer, L. L. The age of atrocity p201-44

Delécluze, Étienne Jean

About

Wakefield, D. Stendhal and Delécluze at the Salon of 1824. *In* The Artist and the writer in France p76-85

Deledda, Grazia

About

Pacifici, S. Voices from the provinces: Grazia Deledda and Marino Morietti. *In* Pacifici, S. The modern Italian novel: from Capuana to Tozzi p86-107

DeLeon, David

The American as anarchist

Contents

Capitalism and community

Conscience and community

The future of the radical past

Left libertarianism

Liberalism

Old visions of the New World

Overview

Right libertarianism

Space and community

Statist radicalism

Deleuze, Gilles

About

Foucault, M. Theatrum philosophicum. *In* Foucault, M. Language, counter-memory, practice p165-96

Deleuze, Gilles, and Guattari, Felix

About individual works

Anti-Oedipus

Girard, R. Delirium as system. *In* Girard, R. "To double business bound" p84-120

Delfini, Leo F.; Bernal, Martha Estella, and Rosen, Paul M.

Comparison of deviant and normal boys in home settings. *In* Behavior modification and families p228-48

Delibes, Miguel

About individual works

Parable of the drowning man

Schwartz, R. Miguel Delibes and Parábola del náufrago (Parable of the drowning man) (1969). *In* Schwartz, R. Spain's New Wave novelists, 1950-1974 p245-64

Delinquency, Juvenile. See Juvenile delinquency

Delinquent women. See Female offenders

Delinquents

Finestone, H. The delinquent and society: the Shaw and McKay tradition. *In* Delinquency, crime, and society p23-49

See also Crime and criminals; Juvenile delinquency; Social work with delinquents and criminals

Deliverance (Motion picture)

Beaton, J. F. Dickey down the river. *In* Peary, G. and Shatzkin, R. eds. The modern American novel and the movies p293-306

Samuels, C. T. How not to film a novel. *In* Samuels, C. T. Mastering the film, and other essays p190-97

Dell, Floyd

About individual works
Moon-calf

Goist, P. D. The ideal questioned but not abandoned: Sherwood Anderson, Sinclair Lewis, and Floyd Dell. *In* Goist, P. D. From Main Street to State Street p21-34

Dell, François C. and Selkirk, Elisabeth O.

On a morphologically governed vowel alternation in French. *In* Keyser, S. J. ed. Recent transformational studies in European languages p 1-51

Della Terza, Dante

An unbridgeable gap? Medieval poetics and the contemporary Dante reader. *In* Medievalia et humanistica no.7 p65-76

Deloria, Vine

The future of racial minorities in American society. *In* Bundy, R. F. ed. Images of the future: the twenty-first century and beyond p159-65

The new Exodus. *In* Smithsonian Institution. The cultural drama p89-105

The twentieth century. *In* Red Men and hat-wearers. p155-66

Delorme, Nicole

The foreign policy of the Ivory Coast. *In* Aluko, O. ed. The foreign policies of African states p118-35

Delors, Jacques

The attitudes of adolescents to education and work. *In* Adolescence and youth in prospect p201-12

De Loyola, Ignacio, Saint. See Loyola, Ignacio de, Saint

Del Paso, Fernando. See Paso, Fernando del

Delphi. Temple of Apollo

Coomaraswamy, A. K. The "E" at Delphi. *In* Coomaraswamy, A. K. Selected papers v2 p43-45

Deluge

Coomaraswamy, A. K. The flood in Hindu tradition. *In* Coomaraswamy, A. K. Selected papers v2 p398-407

Fredericks, S. C. Plato's Atlantis: a mythologist looks at myth. *In* Atlantis, fact or fiction? p81-99

Deluge (Hinduism)

Coomaraswamy, A. K. The flood in Hindu tradition. *In* Coomaraswamy, A. K. Selected papers v2 p398-407

De Lully, Jean Baptiste. See Lully, Jean Baptiste de

Delusional insanity. See Paranoia

De Maeztu, Ramiro. See Maeztu, Ramiro de

De Mallac, Guy. See Mallac, Guy de

De Man, Paul

The purloined ribbon. *In* Glyph I p28-49

About individual works
Blindness and insight

Hartman, G. H. Signs of the times. *In* Hartman, G. H. The fate of reading p303-14

Demarcation line of Alexander VI

Batllori, M. The papal division of the world and its consequences. *In* First images of America p211-20

Weckmann-Muñoz, L. The Alexandrine bulls of 1493: pseudo-Asiatic documents. *In* First images of America p201-09

De Marivaux, Pierre Carlet de Chamblain. See Marivaux, Pierre Carlet de Chamblain de

De Maupassant, Guy. See Maupassant, Guy de

DeMause, Lloyd

The evolution of childhood. *In* Kren, G. M. and Rappoport, L. H. eds. Varieties of psychohistory p123-79

The independence of psychohistory. *In* DeMause, L. ed. The new psychohistory p7-27

Jimmy Carter and American fantasy. *In* DeMause, L. and Ebel, H. eds. Jimmy Carter and American fantasy p 9-31

The nightmare of childhood. *In* Gross, B. and Gross, R. The children's rights movement p17-36

Psychohistory and psychotherapy. *In* DeMause, L. ed. The new psychohistory p307-13

De Mauvelain, Bruzard. See Mauvelain, Bruzard de

Dembowski, Peter Florian

Literary problems of hagiography in Old French. *In* Medievalia et humanistica no.7 p117-30

Dementia praecox. See Schizophrenia

De Méré, Antoine Gombaud, chevalier. See Méré, Antoine Gombaud, chevalier de

Demesne, Royal. See Crown lands

Demeter, Anna

About individual works
Legal kidnapping

Rich, A. C. Husband-right and father-right. *In* Rich, A. C. On lies, secrets, and silence p215-22

Demetz, Peter

Transformations of recent Marxist criticism: Hans Mayer, Ernst Fischer, Lucien Goldman. *In* The Frontiers of literary criticism p75-92

De Meyer, Victoria Junco. See Meyer, Victoria Junco

Demmin, Julia, and Curley, Daniel

Golden apples and silver apples. *In* Prenshaw, P. W. ed. Eudora Welty p242-57

Democracy

Babbitt, I. Democracy and leadership; excerpt. *In* Crunden, R. M. ed. The superfluous men p212-21

Barry, B. M. Is democracy special? *In* Laslett, P. and Fishkin, J. eds. Philosophy, politics and society p155-96

Bathory, P. D. and McWilliams, W. C. Political theory and the people's right to know. *In* Galnoor, I. ed. Government secrecy in democracies p3-21

Bay, C. Access to political knowledge as a human right. *In* Galnoor, I. ed. Government secrecy in democracies p22-39

Democracy—*Continued*

Bialer, S. The resurgence and changing nature of the Left in industrialized democracies. *In* Radicalism in the contemporary age v3 p 3-81

Bork, R. H. Can democratic government survive? *In* Aspects of American liberty p174-86

Brittan, S. Can democracy manage an economy? *In* Skidelsky, R. J. A. ed. The end of the Keynesian era p41-46

Brittan, S. Inflation and democracy. *In* The Political economy of inflation p161-85

Corry, J. A. The prospects for constitutional democracy. *In* Prospects for constitutional democracy p53-74

Crouch, C. The state, capital and liberal democracy. *In* Crouch, C. State and economy in contemporary capitalism p13-54

Dahl, R. A. Procedural democracy. *In* Laslett, P. and Fishkin, J. eds. Philosophy, politics and society p97-133

Eulau, H. Elite analysis and democratic theory: the contribution of Harold D. Lasswell. *In* Eulau, H. and Czudnowski, M. M. eds. Elite recruitment in democratic polities p7-28

Fishkin, J. Tyranny and democratic theory. *In* Laslett, P. and Fishkin, J. eds. Philosophy, politics and society p197-226

Gans, H. J. Democracy and the arts: adversary or ally? *In* Mann, D. A. ed. The arts in a democratic society p98-117

Graham, S. G. and Graham, G. J. The future of American democracy. *In* Graham, G. J. and Graham, S. G. eds. Founding principles of American government p347-53

Lovink, J. A. A. Prospects for democratic control. *In* Prospects for constitutional democracy p36-52

Macpherson, C. B. The false roots of Western democracy. *In* Dallmayr, F. R. ed. From contract to community p17-27

Mencken, H L. Notes on democracy; excerpt. *In* Crunden, R. M. ed. The superfluous men p223-30

Miller, J. W. Freedom as a characteristic of man in a democratic society. *In* Miller, J. W. The paradox of cause, and other essays p97-105

Owsley, F. L. The foundations of democracy. *In* Crunden, R. M. ed. The superfluous men p118-27

Sacksteder, W. Spinoza on democracy. *In* Freeman, E. and Mandelbaum, M. H. eds. Spinoza p117-38

Sennett, R. What Tocqueville feared. *In* On the making of Americans p105-25

Wilder, T. N. Culture in a democracy. *In* Wilder, T. N. American characteristics, and other essays p67-73

Wood, G. S. The democratization of mind in the American Revolution. *In* The Moral foundations of the American Republic p102-28

See also Aristocracy; Equality; Federal government; Liberty; Representative government and representation; Socialism

Democracy and Christianity. See Christianity and democracy

Democracy and Judaism. See Judaism and democracy

Democratic Party

Ambacher, B. I. Urban response to Jacksonian democracy: Philadelphia Democrats and the Bank War, 1832-1834. *In* Essays on urban America p55-87

Meerse, D. E. The northern Democratic Party and the Congressional election of 1858. *In* Swierenga, R. P. ed. Beyond the Civil War synthesis p79-97

Nakamura, R. T. and Sullivan, D. G. Party democracy and democratic control. *In* Burnham, W. D. and Weinberg, M. W. eds. American politics and public policy p26-40

Democratic Party. National Convention, Chicago, 1968

Sheed, W. Chicago on my mind. *In* Sheed, W. The good word & other words p266-74

Democratic. Party. National Convention, Miami, Florida, 1972

Sheed, W. Miami: 1972. *In* Sheed, W. The good word & other words p279-88

Democratic Party. National Convention, New York, 1976

Hartman, J. J. Carter and the utopian group-fantasy. *In* DeMause, L. and Ebel, H. eds. Jimmy Carter and American fantasy p97-116

Democritus

About

Burkert, W. Air-imprints or eidola: Democritus' aetiology of vision. *In* Illinois classical studies, v2 1977 p97-109

Henrichs, A. Two doxographical notes: Democritus and Prodicus on religion. *In* Harvard Studies in classical philology v79 p93-123

Demographic anthropology

Zubrow, E. B. W. Demographic anthropology: an introductory analysis. *In* Zubrow, E. B. W. ed. Demographic anthropology p 1-25

Zubrow, E. B. W. Stability and instability: a problem in long-term regional growth. *In* Zubrow, E. B. W. ed. Demographic anthropology p245-74

See also subdivision Population under names of specific ethnic groups, e.g. Indians of North America—Population; Nunamiut (Eskimo tribe)—Population

Demography

Jones, G. W. The influence of demographic variables on development via their impact on education. *In* Economic factors in population growth p553-80

Lefferts, H. L. Frontier demography: an introduction. *In* Miller, D. H. and Steffen, J. O. eds. The frontier p33-55

Lockridge, K. A. Historical demography. *In* The Future of history p53-64

Nassef, A. F. Problems of maintaining employment in developing countries in the face of rapid population growth. *In* Economic factors in population growth p394-410

Roy, K. Population policy from the southern perspective. *In* Erb, G. F. and Kallab, V. eds. Beyond dependency p95-110

Thrupp, S. L. Plague effects in medieval Europe. *In* Thrupp, S. L. Society and history 150-62

Thrupp, S. L. The problem of replacement-rates in late medieval English population. *In* Thrupp, S. L. Society and history p163-89

Todaro, M. P. Rural-urban migration, unemployment and job probabilities: recent theoretical and empirical research. *In* Economic factors in population growth p367-85

See also Demographic anthropology; Population; Population forecasting; Population policy; and subdivision Population under names of countries, e.g. Russia—Population

DeMolen, Richard L.
Introduction: Opera omnia Desiderii Erasmi: rungs on the ladder to the philosophia Christi. *In* Essays on the works of Erasmus p 1-50

Demonet, Michel. See Klapisch, C. jt. auth.

Demoniac possession. See Spirit possession

Demonology
Olson, A. M. The mythic language of the demonic: an introduction. *In* Disguises of the demonic p9-16
Ulanov, A. B. The psychological reality of the demonic. *In* Disguises of the demonic p135-49
Walter, E. V. Demons and disenchantment. *In* Disguises of the demonic p17-30
See also Charms; Devil; Witchcraft

Demonology, Chinese
Hou, Ching-lang. The Chinese belief in baleful stars. *In* Welch, H. and Seidel, A. K. eds. Facets of Taoism p193-228

Demonology, Christian. See Demonology

Demonology in literature. See Devil in literature

Demonomania. See Exorcism

Demonstrations
Berger, J. The nature of mass demonstrations. *In* Berger, J. The look of things p245-50

De Montaigne, Michel Eyquem. See Montaigne, Michel Eyquem de

De Montherlant, Henry. See Montherlant, Henry de

Demos, John
Developmental perspectives on the history of childhood. *In* Kren, G. M. and Rappoport, L. H. eds. Varieties of psychohistory p180-92
Images of the American family, then and now. *In* Tufte, V. and Myerhoff, B. G. eds. Changing images of the family p43-60
Underlying themes in the witchcraft of seventeenth century New England. *In* Mulder, J. M. and Wilson, J. F. eds. Religion in American history p86-104
Also in Vaughan, A. T. and Bremer, F. J. eds. Puritan New England p250-66
Witchcraft and local culture in Hampton, New Hampshire. *In* Uprooted Americans p9-42

DeMott, Benjamin
Equality and fraternity: a note on subjective realities. *In* Small comforts for hard times p72-84
Gentlemen of principle, priests of presumption. *In* Bigsby, C. W. E. ed. Approaches to popular culture p264-74
The viewer's experience: notes on TV criticism and public health. *In* Television as a social force: new approaches to TV criticism p49-60

DeMott, Robert J.
Robinson Jeffers' "Tamar." *In* French, W. G. ed. The twenties p405-25

Dempsey, Peter J. R.
A note on the phenomenon of Pharisaism. *In* Wolman, B. B. ed. Psychoanalysis and Catholicism p111-14

Demus, Otto
Elijah and Alexander. *In* Studies in memory of David Talbot Rice p64-67

Den Berg. Kent T. Van. See Van Den Berg, Kent T.

Den Berghe, Pierre L. van. See Van den Berghe, Pierre L.

Den Boer, Willem. See Boer, Willem den

De'Negri, Enrico
The legendary style of The Decameron. *In* Dombroski, R. S. ed. Critical perspectives on The Decameron p82-98

Denfeld, Duane
Swinging: the search for an alternative. *In* Gross, L. ed. Sexual issues in marriage p217-30

Dengler, Ian C.
Turkish women in the Ottoman Empire: the classical age. *In* Beck, L. and Keddie, N. R. eds. Women in the Muslim world p229-44

Denham, Sir James Steuart, bart. See Steuart Denham, Sir James, bart.

Denham, Sir John

About individual works
Coopers Hill
Cohen, R. Innovation and variation: a problem of literary history. *In* Studies in eighteenth-century culture v4 p297-315
Wallace, J. M. Coopers Hill: the manifesto of parliamentary royalism, 1641. *In* ELH essays for Earl R. Wasserman p201-47

Denham, Robert D.
Introduction. *In* Frye, N. Northrop Frye on culture and literature p 1-64

Den Hollander, Arie Nicholaas Jan. See Hollander, Arie Nicholaas Jan den

Denich, Bette
Women, work, and power in modern Yugoslavia. *In* Schlegel, A. E. ed. Sexual stratification p215-44

Denis l'Areopagite. See Dionysius Areopagita, Pseudo-

Denitch, Bogdan Denis
Eurocommunism: a threat to Soviet hegemony? *In* Kirk, G. L. and Wessell, N. H. eds. The Soviet threat p148-57

Denneny, Michael
The privilege of ourselves: Hannah Arendt on judgment. *In* Hannah Arendt: the recovery of the public world p245-74

Dennerline, Jerry
Fiscal reform and local control: the gentrybureaucratic alliance survives the conquest. *In* Conflict and control in late imperial China p86-120
Hsü Tu and the lesson of Nanking: political integration and the local defense in Chiang-nan, 1634-1645. *In* Spence, J. D. and Wills, J. E. eds. From Ming to Ch'ing p89-132

Dennett, Daniel Clement
Are dreams experiences? *In* Dunlop, C. E. M. ed. Philsophical essays on dreaming p227-50
Conditions of personhood. *In* Rorty, A. O. ed. The identities of persons p175-96

Denney, Reuel Nicholas
Feast of strangers: varieties of sociable experience in America. *In* On the making of Americans p251-69

Dennie, Joseph
About
Leary, L. G. The literary opinions of Joseph Dennie. *In* Leary, L. G. Soundings p253-70

Dennie, Joseph—*Continued*

About individual works

The farrago (Essays)

Granger, B. I. Joseph Dennie. *In* Granger, B. I. American essay serials from Franklin to Irving p145-63

The lay preacher

Granger, B. I. Joseph Dennie. *In* Granger, B. I. American essay serials from Franklin to Irving p145-63

Dennis, John

About

Albrecht, W. P. Dennis. *In* Albrecht, W. P. The sublime pleasures of tragedy p13-24

Dennis, Nigel Forbes

About individual works

Jonathan Swift

Connolly, C. Swift. *In* Connolly, C. The evening colonnade p109-11

Dennison, Walter Traill

About

Bruford, A. The grey selkie. *In* Ballad studies p41-65

Denny, David L.

Recent developments in the international financial policies of the People's Republic of China. *In* China's changing role in the world economy p163-86

Denny, James M.

Techniques for individual and group art therapy. *In* Ulman, E. and Dachinger, P. eds. Art therapy p132-49

Denominations, Religious. See Sects

Denommé, Robert T.

French theater reform and Vigny's translation of Othello in 1829. *In* Symbolism and modern literature p81-102

De Novo, John A.

The Eisenhower doctrine. *In* Encyclopedia of American foreign policy p292-301

Densen, Paul M.

Public accountability and reporting systems in Medicare and other health programs. *In* Smith, B. L. R. ed. The new political economy: the public use of the private sector p229-44

Den Steinen, Karl von. See Von den Steinen, Karl

Dent, Edward Joseph

The rise of romantic opera

Contents

Beethoven and Schubert
Bellini
Conclusion
The conventions of opera
The heritage of Gluck
Introduction
Rossini
The school of Paris—I
The school of Paris—II
The school of Paris—III
Spontini
Weber and his contemporaries

Dent, Frank Lloyd

Initiating the audience. *In* Perkins, D. and Leondar, B. eds. The arts and cognition p320-32

Dent, Warren T. See Hildreth, C. jt. auth.

Dentan, Robert Knox

Notes on childhood in a nonviolent context: the Semai case. *In* Montagu, A. ed. Learning non-aggression p94-143

Denton, Jeffrey

Walter Reynolds and ecclesiastical politics, 1313-1316: a postscript to 'Councils & synods, II.' *In* Church and government in the Middle Ages p247-74

De Núñez, Carlota Carvallo. See Carvallo de Núñez, Carlota

De Onis, José

José Marti. *In* Abroad in America: Visitors to the new Nation, 1776-1914 p218-27

Deontic logic

Binkley, R. W. The ultimate justification of moral rules. *In* Fact, value, and perception p53-65

Castañeda Calderón, H. N. Goodness, intentions, and propositions. *In* Fact, value, and perception p67-83

Simpson, E. Discrimination as an example of moral irrationality. *In* Fact, value, and perception p107-22

Deontology. See Ethics

Deor

Boren, J. L. The design of the Old English Deor. *In* Anglo-Saxon poetry: essays in appreciation p264-76

Deoxyribonucleic acid

Dupree, A. H. Biological and social theories—a new opportunity for a union of system. *In* Science and society: past, present, and future p136-74

Fletcher, J. F. Recombining DNA. *In* Fletcher, J. F. Humanhood: essays in biomedical ethics p190-99

Sinsheimer, R. L. The molecular basis of life. *In* Neyman, J. ed. The heritage of Copernicus: theories "pleasing to the mind" p143-65

Thomas, L. The wonderful mistake. *In* Thomas, L. The medusa and the snail p27-30

See also Recombinant DNA

De Panizza Lorch, Maristella

Voluptas, molle quoddam et non invidiosum nomen: Lorenzo Valla's defense of voluptas in the preface to his De voluptate. *In* Philosophy and humanism p214-28

Department of Health, Education, and Welfare. See United States. Department of Health, Education, and Welfare

Department of State. See United States. Department of State

Department stores

United States

Harris, N. Museums, merchandising, and popular taste: the struggle for influence. *In* Material culture and the study of American life p140-74

DePauw, Jacques

Illicit sexual activity and society in eighteenth-century Nantes. *In* Family and society p145-91

Dependencies. See Colonies

Dependency (Psychology)

Gaylin, W. In the beginning: helpless and dependent. *In* Doing good p 1-38

De Pinedo, Baltasar. See Pinedo, Baltasar de

Deportation. See Extradition

Depreciation

Jorgenson, D. W. The economic theory of replacement and depreciation. *In* Econometrics and economic theory p190-221

Depression, Mental

Altschule, M. D. George Cheyne and his English malady. *In* Altschule, M. D. Origins of concepts in human behavior p50-74

Altschule, M. D. St Isidore of Seville and his depressing ideas about depression. *In* Altschule, M. D. Origins of concepts in human behavior p35-50

Lipton, M. A. and Nemeroff, C. B. The biology of aging and its role in depression. *In* Aging: the process and the people p47-95

Simon, B. Aristotle on melancholy. *In* Simon, B. Mind and madness in ancient Greece p228-37

Depressions

1929—United States—Historiography

Romasco, A. U. Hoover-Roosevelt and the Great Depression: a historiographic inquiry into a perennial comparison. *In* Braeman, J.; Bremner, R. H. and Brody, D. eds. The New Deal v 1 p3-26

Depressions in poetry

Thompson, L. B. Mosaic and monolith: a comparison of Canadian and Australian poetic responses to the Great Depression. *In* Narasimhaiah, C. D. ed. Awakened conscience p164-84

Depressive psychoses. See Depression, Mental

Deprivation (Psychology)

Williams, R. M. Relative deprivation. *In* The Idea of social structure p355-78

Deprivation, Paternal. See Paternal deprivation

DEPTHnews: A model for a Third World feature agency. Matlub Ali, S. *In* Horton, P, C. ed. The Third World and press freedom p187-96

The **Deputy** (criticism) Hochhuth, R. *In* Kauffmann, S. Persons of the drama p160-62

De Quincey, Thomas

About

Howell, W. S. De Quincey on science, rhetoric, and poetry. *In* Howell, W. S. Poetics, rhetoric, and logic p191-214

Maniquis, R. M. Lonely empires: personal and public visions of Thomas De Quincey. *In* Literary monographs v8 p47-127

About individual works

Autobiographic sketches

Bruss, E. W. Thomas De Quincey: sketches and sighs. *In* Bruss, E. W. Autobiographical acts p93-126

Confessions of an opium eater

Reed, A. Abysmal influence: Baudelaire, Coleridge, De Quincey, Piranesi, Wordsworth. *In* Glyph 4 p189-206

Suspiria de profundis

Bruss, E. W. Thomas De Quincey: sketches and sighs. *In* Bruss, E. W. Autobiographical acts p93-126

Derber, Milton

The New Deal and labor. *In* Braeman, J.; Bremner, R. H. and Brody, D. eds. The New Deal v 1 p110-32

Derby (Motion picture)

Kauffmann, S. Derby. *In* Kauffmann, S. Living images p53-54

Deregowski, Jan B.

Illusion and culture. *In* Gregory, R. L. and Gombrich, Sir E. H. J. eds. Illusion in nature and art p161-91

Derian, Patricia Murphy

Mayflies no more: a fresh look at the Southern woman. *In* The Rising South v 1 p59-71

De Rijk, Lambertus Marie. See Rijk, Lambertus Marie de

Der Kroef, Justus Maria van. See Van Der Kroef, Justus Maria

De Robespierre, Maximilien Marie Isadore. See Robespierre, Maximilien Marie Isadore de

Derolez, René Lodewijk Maurit

Cross-Channel language ties. *In* Anglo-Saxon England 3 p 1-14

De Ronsard, Pierre. See Ronsard, Pierre de

De Roover, Raymond Adrien

Cardinal Cajetan on "cambium" or exchange dealings. *In* Philosophy and humanism p423-33

De Ropp, Robert S.

Drugs, yoga and psychotransformism. *In* Needleman, J. and Lewis, D. eds. On the way to self knowledge p148-69

DeRosier, Arthur H.

Myths and realities in Indian westward removal: the Choctaw example. *In* Hudson, C. M. ed. Four centuries of Southern Indians p83-100

Derrida, Jacques

Coming into one's own. *In* Hartman, G. H. ed. Psychoanalysis and the question of the text p114-48

Limited Inc. *In* Glyph 2 p162-254

Signature event context. *In* Glyph I p172-97

Writing and difference

Contents

Cogito and the history of madness
Edmond Jabès and the question of the book
Ellipsis
Force and signification
Freud and the scene of writing
From restricted to general economy: a Hegelianism without reserve
"Genesis and structure" and phenomenology
La parole soufflée
Structure, sign and play in the discourse of the human sciences
The Theater of Cruelty and the closure of representation
Violence and metaphysics: an essay on the thought of Emmanuel Levinas

About

Grene, M. G. Life, death, and language: some thoughts on Wittgenstein and Derrida. *In* Grene, M. G. Philosophy in and out of Europe p142-54

Watkins, E. Criticism and method: Hirsch, Frye, Barthes, Derrida. *In* Watkins, E. The critical act p56-94

Weber, S. It. *In* Glyph 4 p 1-31

About individual works

Glas

Hartman, G. H. Psychoanalysis: the French connection. *In* Hartman, G. H. ed. Psychoanalysis and the question of the text p86-113

Derrida, Jacques—About individual works
—*Continued*

The purveyor of truth

Johnson, B. The frame of reference: Poe, Lacan, Derrida. *In* Hartman, G. H. ed. Psychoanalysis and the question of the text p149-71

Signature event context

Derrida, J. Limited Inc. *In* Glyph 2 p162-254

Searle, J. R. Reiterating the differences: a reply to Derrida. *In* Glyph I p198-208

Der Weele, Steve J. van. See Van Der Weele, Steve J.

De Sade, Donatien Alphonse François, comte, called marquis. See Sade, Donatien Alphonse François, comte, called marquis de

De Sagasti Perrett, Heli E. See Perrett, Heli E. de Sagasti

Desai, Anita

About

Singh, R. S. Aloneness alone: Anita Desai and Arun Joshi. *In* Singh, R. S. Indian novel in English p164-78

De Saint-Évremond, Charles. See Saint-Évremond, Charles de Marguetel de Saint Denis, seigneur de

De Saint-Exupéry, Antoine. See Saint-Exupéry, Antoine de

De Saint-Simon, Louis de Rouvroy, duc. See Saint-Simon, Louis de Rouvroy, duc de

De Salzmann, Michel

Man's ever new and eternal challenge. *In* Needleman, J. and Lewis, D. eds. On the way to self knowledge p54-75

De Sanctis, Francesco. See Sanctis, Francesco de

Desani, Govindas Vishnoodas

Difficulties of communicating an Oriental to a Western audience. *In* Narasimhaiah, C. D. ed. Awakened conscience p401-07

About

Desani, G. V. Difficulties of communicating an Oriental to a Western audience. *In* Narasimhaiah, C. D. ed. Awakened conscience p401-07

About individual works

All about Hatterr

Harrex, S. C. The novel as gesture. *In* Narasimhaiah, C. D. ed. Awakened conscience p73-85

DeSantis, Vincent P.

Italy and the Cold war. *In* Siracusa, J. M. and Barclay, G. S. eds. The impact of the Cold war p26-39

Descartes, René

About

Anderson, W. E. Cartesian motion. *In* Motion and time, space and matter p200-23

Arendt, H. Appearance. *In* Arendt, H. The life of the mind v 1 p17-65

Blumenfeld, D. and Blumenfeld, J. B. Can I know that I am not dreaming? *In* Hooker, M. ed. Descartes p234-55

Bouwsma, O. K. Descartes' skepticism of the senses. *In* Dunlop, C. E. M. ed. Philosophical essays on dreaming p52-63

Cassirer, E. Descartes, Leibniz, and Vico. *In* Cassirer, E. Symbol, myth, and culture p95-107

Curley, E. M. Descartes, Spinoza and the ethics of belief. *In* Freeman, E. and Mandelbaum, M. H. eds. Spinoza p159-89

Doney, W. Spinoza on philosophical skepticism. *In* Freeman, E. and Mandelbaum, M. H. eds. Spinoza p139-57

Duchesneau, F. Malpighi, Descartes, and the epistemological problems of iatromechanism. *In* Bonelli, M. L. R. and Shea, W. R. eds. Reason, experiment, and mysticism in the scientific revolution p111-30

Edelman, N. The mixed metaphor in Descartes. *In* Edelman, N. The eye of the beholder p107-20

Fancher, R. E. René Descartes and the foundations of modern psychology. *In* Fancher, R. E. Pioneers of psychology p3-42

Flew, A. G. N. Lenin and the Cartesian inheritance. *In* Flew, A. G. N. A rational animal p196-221

Flew, A. G. N. Mind/brain identity and the Cartesian framework. *In* Flew, A. G. N. A rational animal p123-50

Frankfurt, H. C. Descartes on the consistency of reason. *In* Hooker, M. ed. Descartes p26-39

Hausman, A. M. Innate ideas. *In* Studies in perception p200-30

Hooker, M. Descartes's denial of mind-body identity. *In* Hooker, M. ed. Descartes p171-85

Kern, I. The three ways to the transcendental phenomenological reduction in the philosophy of Edmund Husserl. *In* Elliston, F. A. and McCormick, P. eds. Husserl p126-49

Mattern, R. Descartes's correspondence with Elizabeth: concerning both the union and distinction of mind and body. *In* Hooker, M. ed. Descartes p212-22

Nancy, J. L. Larvatus pro deo. *In* Glyph 2 p14-36

Scharfstein, B. A. 'Cogito ergo sum': Descartes, Augustine, and Śankara. *In* Philosophy East/philosophy West p199-217

Sellars, W. S. Berkeley and Descartes: reflections on the theory of ideas. *In* Studies in perception p259-311

Verene, D. P. Vico's science of imaginative universals and the philosophy of symbolic forms. *In* Giambattista Vico's science of humanity p295-317

Weinberg, J. R. Descartes on the distinction of mind and body. *In* Weinberg, J. R. Ockham, Descartes, and Hume p71-82

Wightman, W. P. D. Adam Smith and the history of ideas. *In* Skinner, A. S. and Wilson, T. eds. Essays on Adam Smith p44-67

About individual works

A discourse on method

Nancy, J. L. Larvatus pro deo. *In* Glyph 2 p14-36

Meditations

Malcolm, N. Dreaming and skepticism. *In* Dunlop, C. E. M. ed. Philosophical essays on dreaming p103-26

Yost, R. M. and Kalish, D. Miss MacDonald on sleeping and waking. *In* Dunlop, C. E. M. ed. Philosophical essays on dreaming p81-102

Meditations on first philosophy

Derrida, J. Cogito and the history of madness. *In* Derrida, J. Writing and difference p31-63

Descartes, René—About individual works—
Meditations on first philosophy—*Cont.*

Donagan, A. Descartes's "synthetic" treatment of the real distinction between mind and body. *In* Hooker, M. ed. Descartes p186-96

Marlies, M. Doubt, reason and Cartesian therapy. *In* Hooker, M. ed. Descartes p89-113

Tlumak, J. Certainty and Cartesian method. *In* Hooker, M. ed. Descartes p40-73

Bibliography

Doney, W. Some recent work on Descartes: a bibliography. *In* Hooker, M. ed. Descartes p299-312

Knowledge, Theory of

Danto, A. C. The representational character of ideas and the problem of the external world. *In* Hooker, M. ed Descartes p287-97

Weinberg, J. R. The sources and nature of Descartes' cogito. *In* Weinberg, J. R. Ockham, Descartes, and Hume p83-91

Logic

Doney, W The geometrical presentation of Descartes's a priori proof. *In* Hooker, M. ed. Descartes p 1-25

Garber, D. Science and certainty in Descartes. *In* Hooker, M. ed. Descartes p114-51

Metaphysics

Nakhnikian, G. Descartes's dream argument. *In* Hooker, M. ed. Descartes p256-86

Methodology

Garber, D. Science and certainty in Descartes. *In* Hooker, M. ed. Descartes p114-51

Hintikka, K. J. J. A discourse on Descartes's method. *In* Hooker, M. ed. Descartes p74-88

Marlies, M. Doubt, reason, and Cartesian therapy. *In* Hooker, M. ed. Descartes p89-113

Rodis-Lewis, G. Limitations of the mechanical model in the Cartesian conception of the organism. *In* Hooker, M. ed. Descartes p152-70

Tlumak, J. Certainty and Cartesian method. *In* Hooker, M. ed. Descartes p40-73

Ontology

Sommers, F. Dualism in Descartes: the logical ground. *In* Hooker, M. ed. Descartes p223-33

Wilson, M. D. Cartesian dualism. *In* Hooker, M. ed. Descartes p197-211

Psychology

Fancher, R. E. René Descartes and the foundations of modern psychology. *In* Fancher, R. E. Pioneers of psychology p3-42

Teleology

Machamer, P. K. Causality and explanation in Descartes' natural philosophy. *In* Motion and time, space and matter p168-99

Descent. See Heredity

Descents. See Inheritance and succession

De Schosne, Augustin Théodore Vincent Lebeau. See Lebeau de Schosne, Augustin Théodore Vincent

DeSchutter, Bart
Problems of jurisdiction in the international control and repression of terrorism. *In* International terrorism and political crimes p377-90

Desegregation in education. See School integration

Deserts

United States

Bowden, M. J. The Great American Desert in the American mind: the historiography of a geographical notion. *In* Geographies of the mind p119-47

De Sévigné, Marie (de Rabutin Chantal) marquise. See Sevigné, Marie (de Rabutin Chantal) marquise de

Deshman, Robert
The Leofric missal and tenth-century English art. *In* Anglo-Saxon England 6 p145-73

De Sica, Vittorio

About individual works

The bicycle thief

Murray, E. The bicycle thief. *In* Murray, E. Ten film classics p33-47

The garden of the Finzi-Continis

Kauffmann, S. The garden of the Finzi-Continis. *In* Kauffmann, S. Living images p95-96

Design
Bronowski, J. The shape of things. *In* Bronowski, J. The visionary eye p33-44

See also Architectural design

Design (Philosophy) See Teleology

Design, Architectural. See Architectural design

Design, Industrial
Black, Sir M. The designer and manager syndrome. *In* The Uneasy coalition: design in corporate America p41-55

Kaufmann, E. A profitable art. *In* The Uneasy coalition: design in corporate America p31-39

Richards, J. M. Towards a rational aesthetic. *In* Sharp, D. ed. The rationalists p130-42

Truex, V. D. The environment for creating good design. *In* The Uneasy coalition: design in corporate America p81-89

Watson, T. J. Good design is good business. *In* The Uneasy coalition: design in corporate America p57-79

Management

Black, Sir M. The designer and manager syndrome. *In* The Uneasy coalition: design in corporate America p41-55

Hoving, W. and O'Brien, G. The crisis of design and aesthetics in American management. *In* The Uneasy coalition: design in corporate America p 1-16

United States

Hanks, N. Design for America's third century. *In* The Uneasy coalition: design in corporate America p91-105

Hoving, W. and O'Brien, G. The crisis of design and aesthetics in American management. *In* The Uneasy coalition: design in corporate America p 1-16

Design, Theatrical. See Theaters—Stage-setting and scenery

Designing genetic change. See Genetic engineering

Designs, Architectural. See Architecture—Designs and plans

Desinit (The word)
Kretzmann, N. Incipit/desinit. *In* Motion and time, space and matter p101-36

Desire

Flew, A. G. N. Wants or needs, choices or commands. *In* Fitzgerald, R. ed. Human needs and politics p213-28

Foot, P. Reasons for action and desires. *In* Foot, P. Virtues and vices, and other essays in moral philosophy p148-56

Macpherson, C. B. Needs and wants: an ontological or historical problem? *In* Fitzgerald, R. ed. Human needs and politics p26-35

Wollheim, R. Needs, desires and moral turpitude. *In* Royal Institute of Philosophy. Nature and conduct p162-79

Desire in literature

Bersani, L. Desire and metamorphosis. *In* Bersani, L. A future for Astyanax p189-229

Bersani, L. Realism and the fear of desire. *In* Bersani, L. A future for Astyanax p51-88

Bersani, L. Theaters of desire (Joe Chaikin, Robert Wilson and others) *In* Bersani, L. A future for Astyanax p273-85

Deslandes, Delaunay. See Deslandes, Pierre de Launay

Deslandes, Pierre de Launay

Harris, J. R. Saint-Gobain and Ravenhead. *In* Great Britain and her world, 1750-1914 p27-70

Desnifskiĭ, Semen Efimovich

About

Brown, A. H. Adam Smith's first Russian followers. *In* Skinner, A. S. and Wilson, T. eds. Essays on Adam Smith p247-73

Brown, A. H. S. E. Desnitsky, Adam Smith, and the Nakaz of Catherine II. *In* Oxford Slavonic papers new ser v7 p42-59

Desnitsky, Semyon Efimovich. See Desnifskiĭ, Semen Efimovich

DeSoignie, Raphael R.

The fairs of Nimes: evidence on their function, importance, and demise. *In* Order and innovation in the Middle Ages p195-205

De Sola Pool, Ithiel. See Pool, Ithiel de Sola

De Sousa, Ronald B.

Rational homunculi. *In* Rorty, A. O. ed. The identities of persons p217-38

De Souza, Eunice. See Souza, Eunice de

De Soverosa, Vataça Anes. See Soverosa, Vataça Anes de

Desoxyribonucleic acid. See Deoxyribonucleic acid

Desperate characters (Motion picture)

Kauffmann, S. Desperate characters. *In* Kauffmann, S. Living images p73-76

Despicht, Nigel Stanley. See Thoenig, J. C. jt. auth.

De Spinoza, Benedictus. See Spinoza, Benedictus de

Desportes, Philippe

Appreciation—England

Prescott, A. L. Desportes. *In* Prescott, A. L. French poets and the English Renaissance p132-66

Influence

Prescott, A. L. Desportes. *In* Prescott, A. L. French poets and the English Renaissance p132-66

Despotism

Chiaromonte, N. Modern tyranny. *In* Chiaromonte, N. The worm of consciousness, and other essays p208-35

Despréaux, Nicolas Boileau- See Boileau-Despréaux, Nicolas

Des Pres, Terrence

The authority of silence in Elie Wiesel's art. *In* Rosenfeld, A. H. and Greenberg, I. eds. Confronting the Holocaust p49-57

The heroism of survival. *In* Dunlop, J. B.; Haugh, R. and Klimoff, A. eds. Aleksandr Solzhenitsyn: critical essays and documentary materials 2d ed. p45-62

About individual works

The survivor

Bettelheim, B. Surviving. *In* Bettelheim, B. Surviving, and other essays p274-314

Dessauer, John P.

Pity poor Pascal: some sobering reflections on the American book scene. *In* Altbach, P. G. and McVey, S. eds. Perspectives on publishing p205-16

Dessner, Lawrence Jay

The case of Raintree County. *In* Filler, L. ed. A question of quality: popularity and value in modern creative writing p213-18

De Staël-Holstein, Anne Louise Germaine (Necker) baronne. See Staël-Holstein, Anne Louise Germaine (Necker) baronne de

De Ste Croix, Geoffrey E. M. See Ste Croix, Geoffrey E. M. de

De Stendhal. See Beyle, Marie Henri

De Stijl, Introduction to. Jaffe, H. L. C. *In* Kaplan, P. and Manso, S. eds. Major European art movements, 1900-1945 p222-49

Destiny. See Fate and fatalism

Destouches, Louis Ferdinand

About

Glicksberg, C. I. The countercommitment in Céline. *In* Glicksberg, C. I. The literature of commitment p69-83

Howe, I. Anti-Semite and Jew. *In* Howe, I. Celebrations and attacks p68-71

Destouches, Philippe Néricault

About

Brereton, G. Bourgeois comedy: sentiment and moralization. *In* Brereton, G. French comic drama p214-36

Destruction of the Jews (1939-1945) See Holocaust, Jewish (1939-1945)

De Strycker, Emile. See Strycker, Emile de

Detective and mystery stories

History and criticism

Becker, J. P. The mean streets of Europe: the influence of the American 'hard-boiled school' on European detective fiction. *In* Bigsby, C. W. E. Superculture p152-59

Cawelti, J. G. The art of the classical detective story. *In* Cawelti, J. G. Adventure, mystery, and romance p106-38

Cawelti, J. G. The formula of the classical detective story. *In* Cawelti, J. G. Adventure, mystery, and romance p80-105

Cawelti, J. G. The mythology of crime and its formulaic embodiments. *In* Cawelti, J. G. Adventure, mystery, and romance p51-79

Hartman, G. H. Literature high and low: the case of the mystery story. *In* Hartman, G. H. The fate of reading p203-22

Snow, C. P. Baron Snow. The classical detective story. *In* From Parnassus p16-22

Detective and mystery stories, American

Donald, M. Popular fiction. *In* Donald, M. The American novel in the twentieth century p176-95

History and criticism

Becker, J. P. The mean streets of Europe: the influence of the American 'hard-boiled school' on European detective fiction. *In* Bigsby, C. W. E. Superculture p152-59

Cawelti, J. G. Hammett, Chandler, and Spillane. *In* Cawelti, J. G. Adventure, mystery, and romance p162-91

Cawelti, J. G. The hard-boiled detective story. *In* Cawelti, J. G. Adventure, mystery, and romance p139-61

Detective and mystery stories, English

Panek, L. L. The end. *In* Panek, L. L. Watteau's shepherds: the detective novel in Britain, 1914-1940 p198-99

History and criticism

Panek, L. L. Backgrounds and approaches. *In* Panek, L. L. Watteau's shepherds: the detective novel in Britain, 1914-1940 p5-28

Detectives

Fiction

See Detective and mystery stories

Detectives in literature

Cawelti, J. G. Hammett, Chandler, and Spillane. *In* Cawelti, J. G. Adventure, mystery, and romance p162-91

Cawelti, J. G. The hard-boiled detective story. *In* Cawelti, J. G. Adventure, mystery, and romance p139-61

Ousby, I. Arthur Conan Doyle. *In* Ousby, I. Bloodhounds of heaven p139-75

Ousby, I. Caleb Williams. *In* Ousby, I. Bloodhounds of heaven p19-42

Ousby, I. Charles Dickens. *In* Ousby, I. Bloodhounds of heaven p79-110

Ousby, I. Vidocq translated. *In* Ousby, I. Bloodhounds of heaven p43-75

Ousby, I. Wilkie Collins and other sensation novelists. *In* Ousby, I. Bloodhounds in heaven p111-36

Detente

Alting von Geusau, F. A. M. Détente after Helsinki. *In* The Year book of world affairs, 1978 p8-22

Bell, C. Détente and the American national interest. *In* Rosecrance, R. N. ed. America as an ordinary country p38-59

Bissell, R. E. Southern Africa: testing détente. *In* Kirk, G. L. and Wessell, N. H. eds. The Soviet threat p88-98

Ekirch, A. A. Détente. *In* Encyclopedia of American foreign policy. p239-43

Juviler, P. H. and Zawadzka, H. J. Détente and Soviet domestic politics. *In* Kirk, G. L. and Wessell, N. H. eds. The Soviet threat p158-67

Machala, P. Eastern Europe, Eurocommunism, and the problems of détente. *In* Kaplan, M. A. ed. The many faces of communism p228-65

Popovic, N. D. Yugoslavia's crucial place in world politics. *In* Kaplan, M. A. ed. The many faces of communism p266-78

Rotermundt, R. and Schmiederer, U. Social structure and foreign policy in the Soviet Union. *In* Jahn, E. ed. Soviet foreign policy p91-113

Simes, D. K. Human rights and détente. *In* Kirk, G. L. and Wessell, N. H. eds. The Soviet threat p135-47

Ticktin, H. The relation between détente and Soviet economic reforms. *In* Jahn, E. ed. Soviet foreign policy p41-56

Detention homes, Juvenile. See Juvenile detention homes

Detention of persons. See Juvenile detention homes

Determinism and indeterminism. See Free will and determinism

Deterrence (Strategy)

Corden, P. S. Ethics and deterrence: moving beyond the just-war tradition. *In* Ethics and nuclear strategy? p156-80

Gessert, R. A. Deterrence and the defense of Europe. *In* Ethics and nuclear strategy? p92-112

Kashi, J. The role of deterrence in disarmament: some theories and some defects. *In* The Dynamics of the arms race p92-103

Deterrence of crime through punishment. See Punishment in crime deterrence

De Tjarks, Alicia Vidaurreta. See Tjarks, Alicia Vidaurreta de

De Tocqueville, Alexis Charles Henri Maurice Clérel. See Tocqueville, Alexis Charles Henri Maurice Clérel de

De Torquemada, Juan, Cardinal. See Torquemada, Juan de, Cardinal

Detribalization

Uchendu, V. C. The dilemma of ethnicity and polity primacy in Black Africa. *In* Ethnic identity p265-75

Detroit. Institute of Arts

Kozloff, M. The Rivera frescoes of modern industry at the Detroit Institute of Arts: proletarian art under capitalist patronage. *In* Millon, H. A. and Nochlin, L. eds. Art and architecture in the service of politics p216-29

Detroit. University. Center for Black Studies. See Detroit. University. Institute for Afro-American Studies

Detroit. University. Institute for Afro-American Studies

Washington, M. H. Politics of the outsider: Black studies in the university, 1976. *In* Minority language and literature p130-33

De Unamuno y Jugo, Miguel. See Unamuno y Jugo, Miguel de

Deutsch, Babette

A poet of the steel works. *In* Morgan, R. G. ed. Kenneth Patchen: a collection of essays p10-12

Deutsch, Dennis

The Palestine question: domestic pressures on the President for intervention, 1944-1948. *In* Higham, R. D. ed. Intervention or abstention: the dilemma of American foreign policy p79-94

Deutsch, Karl Wolfgang, and Senghaas, Dieter

The fragile sanity of states: a theoretical analysis. *In* Kilson, M. ed. New states in the modern world p200-44

Deutscher, Isaac

About individual works

The prophet outcast: Trotsky, 1929-1940

Rahv, P. The great outsider. *In* Rahv, P. Essays on literature and politics, 1932-1972 p335-40

De Valk, Jacobus Mattheus Maria. See Valk, Jacobus Mattheus Maria de

Devall, William B.
Social science research on support of human rights. *In* Claude, R. P. ed. Comparative human rights p326-52

Devaluation of currency. See Currency question

Developing countries. See Underdeveloped areas

Development. See Evolution

Development, Child. See Child development

Development banks
Syz, J. Recent North-South relations and multilateral soft loans. *In* The Year book of world affairs, 1975 p196-207

Developmental biology. See Child development; Human growth; Developmental psychobiology; Ontogeny

Developmental psychobiology
Hinde, R. A. Social development: a biological approach. *In* Human growth and development p 1-32

See also Child development; Developmental psychology

Developmental psychology
Davies, J. C. The development of individuals and the development of politics. *In* Fitzgerald, R. ed. Human needs and politics p74-95
Erikson, E. H. Reflections on Dr Borg's life cycle. *In* Erikson, E. H. ed. Adulthood p 1-31
Keniston, K. Psychological development and historical change. *In* Explorations in psychohistory p149-64
McCall, G. J. The social looking-glass: a sociological perspective of self-development. *In* Mischel, T. ed. The self p274-87
Sagan, E. Religion and magic: a developmental view. *In* Johnson, H. M. ed. Religious change and continuity p87-116

See also Child study; Maturation (Psychology)

Devereux, Edward Clifton
Backyard versus Little League baseball: the improvement of children's games. *In* Social problems in athletics p37-56

Devereux, George
Ethnic identity: its logical foundations and its dysfunctions. *In* Ethnic identity p42-70
Time: history versus chronicle; socialization as cultural preexperience. *In* Schwartz, T. ed. Socialization as cultural communication p189-200
The works of George Devereux. *In* Spindler, G. D. ed. The making of psychological anthropology p364-406

Deviancy. See Deviant behavior

Deviant behavior
Becker, H. S. and Horowitz, I. L. The culture of civility. *In* Henslin, J. M. ed. Deviant life-style p337-48
Cole, S. The growth of scientific knowledge: theories of deviance as a case study. *In* The Idea of social structure p175-220
Conover, P. W. A reassessment of labeling theory: a constructive response to criticism. *In* The Uses of controversy in sociology p228-43
Davis, F. J. and Stivers, R. eds. Beliefs, values, power, and public definitions of deviance. *In* Davis, F. J. and Stivers, R. eds. The collective definition of deviance p50-59

Edgerton, R. B. The study of deviance—marginal man or Everyman? *In* Spindler, G. D. ed. The making of psychological anthropology p444-76
Erikson, K. T. On the sociology of deviance. *In* Davis, F. J. and Stivers, R. eds. The collective definition of deviance p11-21
Gove, W. R. Deviant behavior, social intervention, and labeling theory. *In* The Uses of controversy in sociology p219-27
Gove, W. R. Labelling perspective: an overview. *In* Gove, W. R. ed. The labelling of deviance p3-20
Gusfield, J. R. Moral passage: the symbolic process in public designation of deviance. *In* Davis, F. J. and Stivers, R. eds. The collective definition of deviance p85-98
Jackson, B. Deviance as success: the double inversion of stigmatized roles. *In* Babcock, B. A. ed. The reversible world p258-75
Kobrin, S. The labeling approach: problems and limits. *In* Delinquency, crime, and society p239-53
Lemert, E. M. Response to critics: feedback and choice. *In* The Uses of controversy in sociology p244-49
Smith, R. T. Societal reaction and physical disability: contrasting perspectives. *In* Gove, W. R. ed. The labelling of deviance p147-56

See also Crime and criminals

Social aspects
Wallis, R. Societal reaction to scientology: a study in the sociology of deviant religion. *In* Wallis, R. ed. Sectarianism p86-116

Deviation, Sexual. See Sexual deviation

Devices. See Mottoes

De Vigny, Alfred Victor, comte. See Vigny, Alfred Victor, comte de

Devil
Coomaraswamy, A. K. Who is "Satan" and where is "Hell"? *In* Coomaraswamy, A. K. Selected papers v2 p23-33
Also in Disguises of the demonic p57-68
Hallie, P. P. Satan, evil, and good in history. *In* Stanage, S. M. ed. Reason and violence p53-69
Karefa-Smart, J. A. M. Doctors, development, and demons in Africa. *In* Disguises of the demonic p150-56
Kohak, E. V. Speaking of the Devil: a modest methodological proposal. *In* Disguises of the demonic p48-56
Olson, A. M. The mythic language of the demonic: an introduction. *In* Disguises of the demonic p9-16
Rubinoff, L. Violence and the retreat from reason. *In* Stanage, S. M. ed. Reason and violence p73-118
Sayers, D. L. The Faust legend and the idea of the Devil; excerpt from "The poetry of search and the poetry of statement and other posthumous essays on literature, religion, and language." *In* Sayers, D. L. The whimsical Christian p257-75

History of doctrines
Lindberg, C. H. Mask of God and Prince of Lies: Luther's theology of the demonic. *In* Disguises of the demonic p87-103

Devil in literature
Curran, S. The siege of hateful contraries: Shelley, Mary Shelley, Byron, and Paradise lost. *In* Wittreich, J. A. ed. Milton and the line of vision p209-30

Devil in literature—*Continued*

Florescu, R. R. The Devil in Romanian literature and folklore. *In* Disguises of the demonic p69-86

May, J. R. American literary variations on the demonic. *In* Disguises of the demonic p31-47

Merezhkovskiĭ, D. Gogol and the Devil. *In* Maguire, R. A. ed. Gogol from the twentieth century p55-102

Sayers, D. L. The Faust legend and the idea of the Devil; excerpt from "The poetry of search and the poetry of statement and other posthumous essays on literature, religion, and language." *In* Sayers, D. L. The whimsical Christian p257-75

DeVillé, Philippe Raymond. See Baumgartner, T. jt. auth.

The **devils** (criticism) Whiting, J. *In* Kauffmann, S. Persons of the drama p163-65

The devils (Motion picture)

Kauffmann, S. The devils. *In* Kauffmann, S. Living images p72-73

Devlin, Albert J.

Eudora Welty's Mississippi. *In* Prenshaw, P. W. ed. Eudora Welty p157-78

Devlin, Denis

About

Coffey, B. Denis Devlin: poet of distance. *In* Place, personality and the Irish writer p137-57

Devlin, Kevin

Finland in 1948: the lesson of a crisis. *In* Hammond, T. T. ed. The anatomy of Communist takeovers p433-47

De Vogel, Cornelia J. See Part 2 under title: Kephalaion

De Voltaire, François Marie Arouet. See Voltaire, François Marie Arouet de

De Vorsey, Louis

La Florida revealed: the De Brahm surveys of British East Florida, 1765-1771. *In* Pattern and process p87-102

De Vos, George A.

Affective dissonance and primary socialization: implications for a theory of incest avoidance. *In* Schwartz, T. ed. Socialization as cultural communication p73-90

Ethnic pluralism: conflict and accommodation. *In* Ethnic identity p5-41

The Japanese adapt to change. *In* Spindler, G. D. ed. The making of psychological anthropology p219-57

Selective permeability and reference group sanctioning: psychocultural continuities in role degradation. *In* Major social issues p7-24

DeVos, George A. and Pettigrew, Thomas Fraser

Comments on the discussion of Roy S. Bryce-Laporte. *In* Major social issues p78-81

De Vos, George A. and Romanucci-Ross, Lola

Ethnicity: vessel of meaning and emblem of contrast. *In* Ethnic identity p363-90

DeVries, Carl E.

Paul's "cutting" remarks about a race: Galatians 5:1-12. *In* Current issues in Biblical and patristic interpretation p115-20

DeVries, Duane

Two glimpses of Dickens' early development as a writer of fiction. *In* Dickens Studies Annual v 1 p55-64

De Vries, Gerrit Jacob. See Vries, Gerrit Jacob de

De Vries, Jan

Peasant demand patterns and economic development: Friesland, 1550-1750. *In* Parker, W. N. and Jones, E. L. eds. European peasants and their markets p205-66

Dew, Marjorie C.

Black-hearted Melville: "geniality" reconsidered. *In* Artful thunder p177-94

De Waard, Jan. See Waard, Jan de

De Walle, Etienne van. See Van de Walle, Etienne

DeWater, Richard van. See Van de Water, Richard

Dewdney, Irene

An art therapy program for geriatric patients. *In* Ulman, E. and Dachinger, P. eds. Art therapy p126-31

Dewdney, Selwyn H.

Elda's art therapy in the context of a quarter century of psychiatric treatment. *In* Ulman, E. and Dachinger, P. eds. Art therapy p240-75

Dewey, John

The motivation of Hobbes's political philosophy. *In* Ross, R.; Schneider, H. W. and Waldman, T. eds. Thomas Hobbes in his time p8-30

About

Featherstone, J. L. Dewey's synthesis: science and feeling. *In* Roots of open education in America p118-25

Featherstone, J. L. John Dewey and David Riesman: from the lost individual to the lonely crowd. *In* On the making of Americans p3-39

Krash, O. Several humanisms and John Dewey. *In* Fairfield, R. P. ed. Humanistic frontiers in American education p116-22

Olafson, F. A. The school and society: reflections on John Dewey's philosophy of education. *In* Cahn, S. M. ed. New studies in the philosophy of John Dewey p172-203

Rorty, R. Overcoming the tradition: Heidegger and Dewey. *In* Murray, M. E. ed. Heidegger and modern philosophy p239-58

Roth, R. J. Person and technology: a Deweyan perspective. *In* Roth, R. J. ed. Person and community p87-102

Aesthetics

Kadish, M. R. John Dewey and the theory of the aesthetic practice. *In* Cahn, S. M. ed. New studies in the philosophy of John Dewey p75-116

Ethics

Rachels, J. John Dewey and the truth about ethics. *In* Cahn, S. M. ed. New studies in the philosophy of John Dewey p149-71

Knowledge, Theory of

Margolis, J. Z. The relevance of Dewey's epistemology. *In* Cahn, S. M. ed. New studies in the philosophy of John Dewey p117-48

Metaphysics

Rorty, R. Dewey's metaphysics. *In* Cahn, S. M. ed. New studies in the philosophy of John Dewey p45-74

Political science

Frankel, C. John Dewey's social philosophy. *In* Cahn, S. M. ed. New studies in the philosophy of John Dewey p 3-44

Sociology

Frankel, C. John Dewey's social philosophy. *In* Cahn, S. M. ed. New studies in the philosophy of John Dewey p 3-44

Dewhirst, Martin
Soviet Russian literature and literary policy. *In* Brown, A. H. and Kaser, M. eds. The Soviet Union since the fall of Khrushchev p181-95

De Worde, Wynkyn. See Worde, Wynkyn de

Dewoskin, Kenneth J.
The Six Dynasties Chih-kuai and the birth of fiction. *In* Chinese narrative p21-52

Dexter, John. See Burge, S. jt. auth.

De Zayas, Marius. See Zayas, Marius de

D'Harleville, Jean François Collin. See Collin d'Harleville, Jean François

Dharma-palā, Anagārika. See Dharmapala, Anagarika

Dharmapala, Anagarika

About

Obeyesekere, G. Personal identity and cultural crisis: the case of Anagārika Dharmapala of Sri Lanka. *In* Reynolds, F. E. and Capps, D. eds. The biographical process p221-52

Obeyesekere, G. Sinhalese-Buddhist identity in Ceylon. *In* Ethnic identity p231-58

Dharmapāla, Dēvamitra. See Dharmapala, Anagarika

Dharmapala, Devamitta. See Dharmapala, Anagarika

Dharmapalá, H. See Dharmapala, Anagarika

Dharmapala, Hevaritárana. See Dharmapala, Anagarika

Dharmapala, Hevavitárana. See Dharmapala, Anagarika

Dhegiha language. See Siouan languages

Dhlomo, Herbert I. E.

About

Couzens, T. J. Early South African Black writing. *In* King, B. A. and Ogungbesan, K. eds. A celebration of Black and African writing p 1-14

Dhondy, Farrukh

About

Souza, E. de. The expatriate experience. *In* Narasimhaiah, C. D. ed. Awakened conscience p339-45

Diabolism and decadence: The mood of the nineties. Briggs, J. *In* Briggs, J. Night visitors p76-97

Diaconus, Paulus. See Paulus Diaconus

Diagnosis
Goffman, E. The insanity of place; excerpt from "Relations in public". *In* Davis, F. J. and Stivers, R. eds. The collective definition of deviance p325-33

See also Medicine, Clinical

The Dial
Balakian, N. A passion for letters: Scofield Thayer and The Dial. *In* Balakian, N. Critical encounters p198-202

Dialectic
Lacoue-Labarthe, P. The caesura of the speculative. *In* Glpyh 4 p57-84

Long, A. A. Dialectic and the Stoic sage. *In* Rist, J. M. ed. The Stoics p101-24

Olson, E. The dialectical foundations of critical pluralism. *In* Olson, E. On value judgments in the arts, and other essays p327-59

Schneider, L. Dialectical orientation and the sociology of religion. *In* Johnson, H. M. ed. Religious change and continuity p49-73

Walls, D. S. Dialectical social science. *In* McNall, S. G. ed. Theoretical perspectives in sociology p214-31

Wardell, M. L. and Benson, J. K. A dialectical view: foundation for an alternative sociological method. *In* McNall, S. G. ed. Theoretical perspectives in sociology p232-48

Watkins, E. Dialectic and form. *In* Watkins, E. The critical act p159-87

Dialectic (Logic) See Logic

Dialectic in literature
Preyer, R. O. The burden of culture and the dialectic of literature. *In* Evolution of consciousness p98-105

Dialectical materialism
Cohen, G. A. Being, consciousness and roles: on the foundations of historical materialism. *In* Essays in honour of E. H. Carr p82-97

Medvedev, R. A. The October Revolution and the problem of history as a law-governed process. *In* Medvedev, R. A. ed. The Samizdat register p 1-71

Voegelin, E. Marx: inverted dialectics. *In* Voegelin, E. From Enlightenment to revolution p240-72

Wozniak, R. H. Dialecticism and structuralism: the philosophical foundation of Soviet psychology and Piagetian cognitive developmental theory. *In* Riegel, K. F. and Rosenwald, G. C. eds. Structure and transformation p25-45

See also Historical materialism

Dialectology. See subdivision Dialectology under names of languages and groups of languages, e.g. English language—Dialectology

Dialects. See names of particular dialects, and subdivisions Dialects, Idioms, corrections, errors, and Provincialisms under names of languages or groups of languages, e.g. English language—Dialects

Dialexeis
Robinson, T. M. A Sophist on omniscience, polymathy, and omnicompetence: Δ. Λ. 8.1—13[1] *In* Illinois clasical studies, v2 1977 p125-35

Dialogue
Armstrong, C. J. R. The dialectical road to truth: the dialogue. *In* French Renaissance studies, 1540-70 p36-51

O'Hara, J. Dialog, detail, and type. *In* O'Hara, J. "An artist is his own fault" p3-20

Veltruský, J. Basic features of dramatic dialogue. *In* Matejka, L. and Titunik, I. R. eds. Semiotics of art p128-33

Veltruský, J. Construction of semantic contexts. *In* Matejka, L. and Titunik, I. R. eds. Semiotics of art p134-44

See also Drama; Monologue

Diamond, Arlyn
Chaucer's women and women's Chaucer. *In* Diamond, A. and Edwards, L. R. eds. The authority of experience p60-83

Diamond, Martin
Ethics and politics: the American way. *In* The Moral foundations of the American Republic p39-72

The idea of equality: the view from the founding. *In* An Almost chosen people p19-37

Dickens, Charles—About individual works
—*Continued*

Dombey and son

Auerbach, N. Dickens and Dombey: a daughter after all. *In* Dickens Studies Annual v5 p95-114

Jackson, A. M. Reward, punishment, and the conclusion of Dombey and son. *In* Dickens Studies Annual v7 p103-27

Kennedy, A. Agents and patients in Dickens. *In* Kennedy, A. Meaning and signs in fiction p70-104

Lerner, L. An essay on Dombey and son. *In* Lerner, L. ed. The Victorians p195-208

Marcus, D. D. Symbolism and mental process in Dombey and son. *In* Dickens Studies Annual v6 p57-71

Pearson, G. Towards a reading of Dombey and son. *In* Josipovici, G. ed. The modern English novel: the reader, the writer and the work p54-76

Pickering, S. Dombey and son and Unitarianism. *In* Pickering, S. The moral tradition in English fiction, 1785-1850 p149-68

Steig, M. Iconography of sexual conflict in Dombey and son. *In* Dickens Studies Annual v 1 p161-67

Talon, H. A. Dombey and son: a closer look at the text. *In* Dickens Studies Annual v 1 p147-60

Tomlinson, T. B. Dickens: Dombey and sons, Bleak House. *In* Tomlinson, T. B. The English middle-class novel p52-68

George Silverman's explanation

Thomas, D. A. The equivocal explanation of Dickens' George Silverman. *In* Dickens Studies Annual v3 p134-43

Gone astray

Greaves, J. Going astray. *In* Dickens Studies Annual v3 p144-61

Great expectations

Axton, W. F. Great expectations: yet again. *In* Dickens Studies Annual v2 p278-93

Barnard, R. Imagery and theme in Great expectations. *In* Dickens Studies Annual v 1 p238-51

Collins, P. A. W. A tale of two novels: A tale of two cities and Great expectations in Dickens' career. *In* Dickens Studies Annual v2 p336-51

McWilliams, J. P. Great expectations: the beacon, the gibbet, and the ship. *In* Dickens Studies Annual v2 p255-66

Millhauser, M. Great expectations: the three endings. *In* Dickens Studies Annual v2 p267-77

Pearlman, E. Inversion in Great expectations. *In* Dickens Studies Annual v7 p190-202

Rosenberg, E. A preface to Great expectations: the Pale Usher dusts his lexicons. *In* Dickens Studies Annual v2 p294-335

Talon, H. A. Space, time, and memory in Great expectations. *In* Dickens Studies Annual v3 p122-33

Tick, S. Toward Jaggers. *In* Dickens Studies Annual v5 p133-49

Winner, A. Character and knowledge in Dickens: the enigma of Jaggers. *In* Dickens Studies Annual v3 p100-21

Young, M. Distorted expectations: Pip and the problems of language. *In* Dickens Studies Annual v7 p203-20

Hard times

Benn, J. M. A landscape with figures: characterization and expression in Hard times. *In* Dickens Studies Annual v 1 p168-82

Butwin, J. The paradox of the clown in Dickens. *In* Dickens Studies Annual v5 p115-32

Haberman, M. The courtship of the void: the world of Hard times. *In* The Worlds of Victorian fiction p37-55

Lougy, R. E. Dickens' Hard times: the romance as radical literature. *In* Dickens Studies Annual v2 p237-54

Sadock, G. J. Dickens and Dr Leavis: a critical commentary on Hard times. *In* Dickens Studies Annual v2 p208-16

Smith, F. E. Perverted balance: expressive form in Hard times. *In* Dickens Studies Annual v6 p102-18

Winters, W. W. Dickens' Hard times: the lost childhood. *In* Dickens Studies Annual v2 p217-36

Little Dorrit

Barickman, R. The spiritual journey of Amy Dorrit and Arthur Clennam. *In* Dickens Studies Annual v7 p163-89

Christmas, P. Little Dorrit: the end of good and evil. *In* Dickens Studies Annual v6 p134-53

Heatley, E. The redeemed feminine of Little Dorrit. *In* Dickens Studies Annual v4 p153-64

Kennedy, A. Agents and patients in Dickens. *In* Kennedy, A. Meaning and signs in fiction p70-104

Roopnaraine, R. R. Time and the circle in Little Dorrit. *In* Dickens Studies Annual v3 p54-76

Splitter, R. Guilt and the trappings of melodrama in Little Dorrit. *In* Dickens Studies Annual v6 p119-33

Tick, S. The sad end of Mr Meagles. *In* Dickens Studies Annual v3 p87-99

Martin Chuzzlewit

Burke, A. R. The house of Chuzzlewit and the architectural city. *In* Dickens Studies Annual v3 p14-40

Evans, E. J. The established self: the American episodes of Martin Chuzzlewit. *In* Dickens Studies Annual v5 p59-73

Gold, J. "Living in a wale": Martin Chuzzlewit. *In* Dickens Studies Annual v2 p150-62

Mudrick, M. Mrs. Harris and the hend of all things. *In* Mudrick, M. Books are not life but then what is? p337-48

Steig, M. Martin Chuzzlewit's progress by Dickens and Phiz. *In* Dickens Studies Annual v2 p119-48

The mystery of Edwin Drood

Borowitz, A. The mystery of Edwin Drood. *In* Borowitz, A. Innocence and arsenic p53-62

Burgan, W. M. The refinement of contrast: manuscript revision in Edwin Drood. *In* Dickens Studies Annual v6 p167-82

Frank, L. D. The intelligibility of madness in Our mutual friend and The mystery of Edwin Drood. *In* Dickens Studies Annual v5 p150-95

Gottschalk, P. A. Time in Edwin Drood. *In* Dickens Studies Annual v 1 p265-72

Dickens, Charles—*Continued*
Technique
Davis, E. R. Dickens and significant tradition. *In* Dickens Studies Annual v7 p49-67

Dunn, R. J. Far, far better things: Dickens' later endings. *In* Dickens Studies Annual v7 p221-36

Paroissien, D. H. Dickens and the cinema. *In* Dickens Studies Annual v7 p68-80

Dickens, David R.
Phenomenology. *In* McNall, S. G. ed. Theoretical perspectives in sociology p325-47

Dickerson, Gregory W.
Aristophanes' Ranae 862: a note on the anatomy of Euripidean tragedy. *In* Harvard Studies in classical philology v78 p177-88

Dickey, James
About
Oates, J. C. Out of stone, into flesh: the imagination of James Dickey. *In* Oates, J. C. New heaven, new earth: the visionary experience in literature p205-63

Silverstein, N. James Dickey's muscular eschatology. *In* Boyers, R. ed. Contemporary poetry in America p303-13

About individual works
Deliverance
Beaton, J. F. Dickey down the river. *In* Peary, G. and Shatzkin, R. eds. The modern American novel and the movies p293-306

Poems, 1957-1967
Lieberman, L. James Dickey: The deepening of being. *In* Lieberman, L. Unassigned frequencies p83-106

Lieberman, L. James Dickey: The worldly mystic. *In* Lieberman, L. Unassigned frequencies p74-82

Lieberman, L. John Berryman, William Stafford, and James Dickey: the expansional poet: a return to personality. *In* Lieberman, L. Unassigned frequencies p263-71

Dickie, George
What is art? Excerpt from "Art and the aesthetic: an institutional analysis." *In* Aagaard-Mogensen, L. ed. Culture and art p21-32

About individual works
Aesthetics
Alexander, H. G. On defining in aesthetics. *In* Aagaard-Mogensen, L. ed. Culture and art p110-18

Lyas, C. Danto and Dickie on art. *In* Aagaard-Mogensen, L. ed. Cuture and art p170-93

Art and the aesthetic: an institutional analysis
Iseminger, G. Appreciation, the artworld, and the aesthetic. *In* Aagaard-Morgensen, L. ed. Culture and art p118-30

What is art?
Binkley, T. Deciding about art. *In* Aagaard-Mogensen, L. ed. Cuture and art p90-109

Dickie, Matthew W.
The argument and form of Simonides 542 PMG. *In* Harvard Studies in classical philology v82 p21-33

On the meaning of ἐφήμερος. *In* Illinois classical studies, v 1 1976 p7-14

Dickinson, Emily
About
Auchincloss, L. Emily Dickinson: the private publication. *In* Auchincloss, L. Life, law and letters p31-37

Cunningham, J. V. Sorting out: the case of Dickinson. *In* Cunningham, J. V. The collected essays of J. V. Cunningham p353-74

Davis, T. M. Emily Dickinson and the right of way to Tripoli. *In* Artful thunder p209-19

Diggory, T. Armored women, naked men: Dickinson, Whitman, and their successors. *In* Gilbert, S. M. and Gubar, S. eds. Shakespeare's sisters p135-50

Gelpi, A. Emily Dickinson and the Deerslayer: the dilemma of the woman poet in America. *In* Gilbert, S. M. and Gubar, S. eds. Shakespeare's sisters p122-34

Gilbert, S. M. and Gubar, S. The aesthetics of renunciation. *In* Gilbert, S. M. and Gubar, S. The madwoman in the attic p539-80

Gilbert, S. M. and Gubar, S. A woman-white: Emily Dickinson's yarn of pearl. *In* Gilbert, S. M. and Gubar, S. The madwoman in the attic p581-650

Hill, A. A. Figurative structure and meaning: two poems by Emily Dickinson. *In* Hill, A. A. Constituent and pattern in poetry p123-35

Kammer, J. The art of silence and the forms of women's poetry. *In* Gilbert, S. M. and Gubar, S. eds. Shakespeare's sisters p153-64

Kaufman, J. S. Emily Dickinson and the involvement of retreat. *In* Tulane Studies in English v21 p77-90

Rich, A. C. Vesuvius at home: the power of Emily Dickinson. *In* Gilbert, S. M. and Gubar, S. eds. Shakespeare's sister p99-121

Also in Rich, A. C. On lies, secrets, and silence p157-83

Wain, J. Homage to Emily Dickinson. *In* Wain, J. Professing poetry p76-90

Wilbur, R. "Sumptuous destitution." *In* Wilbur, R. Responses p3-15

Wilder, T. N. Emily Dickinson. *In* Wilder, T. N. American characteristics, and other essays p48-63

About individual works
"Go tell it"—what a message
Trilling, L. Emily Dickinson: "Go tell it" —what a message—. *In* Trilling, L. Prefaces to The experience of literature p265-68

Bibliography
Buckingham, W. J. Whitman and Dickinson. *In* American literary scholarship, 1977 p65-97

Fisher, M. and Buckingham, W. J. Whitman and Dickinson. *In* American literary scholarship, 1975 p83-102

Fisher, M. and Buckingham, W. J. Whitman and Dickinson [another essay] *In* American literary scholarship, 1976 p61-78

Slote, B. Whitman and Dickinson. *In* American literary scholarship, 1973 p85-98

Slote, B. Whitman and Dickinson [another essay] *In* American literary scholarship, 1974 p61-74

Dickinson, Samuel Nelson

About

Silver, R. G. Flash of the comet: the typographical career of Samuel N. Dickinson. *In* Virginia, University. Bibliographical Society. Studies in bibliography v31 p68-89

Dickler, Robert A.

Organization and change in productivity in Eastern Prussia. *In* Parker, W. N. and Jones, E. L. eds. European peasants and their markets p269-92

Dickson, Carter, pseud. See Carr, John Dickson

Dickson, Donald T.

Bureaucracy and morality: an organizational perspective on a moral crusade. *In* Davis, F. J. and Stivers, R. eds. The collective definition of deviance p334-49

Dickson, Kwamina Busumafi

Development planning and national integration in Ghana. *In* Smock, D. R. and Bentsi-Enchill, K. eds. The search for national integration in Africa p100-16

Dickson, Kwesi A.

The African theological task. *In* The Emergent gospel p46-49

Dickson, Vivienne

A streetcar named Desire: its development through the manuscripts. *In* Tennessee Williams: a tribute p154-71

Dictators. See Despotism

Diction

Olson, E. William Empson, contemporary criticism, and poetic diction. *In* Olson, E. On value judgments in the arts, and other essays p118-56

Wimsatt, W. K. In search of verbal mimesis (supplement to "Laokoon: an oracle reconsulted"). *In* Wimsatt, W. K. Day of the leopards p57-73

See also Style, Literary

Dictionary of American regional English (proposed)

Cassidy, F. G. Use of computer in one lexicographical project: DARE. *In* James B. McMillan: essays in linguistics by his friends and colleagues p133-42

Didactic fiction, African

Achebe, C. The novelist as teacher. *In* Achebe, C. Morning yet on creation day p67-73

Didactic literature. See Exempla

Didactic poetry, English

Farnham, A. E. The art of high prosaic seriousness: John Gower as didactic raconteur. *In* The Learned and the lewed p161-73

Didactics. See Teaching

Diderot, Denis

About

Cohen, H. Rhetoric versus truth: Diderot's writings as an illustration of stability and innovation in eighteenth-century literature. *In* Studies in eighteenth-century culture v7 p433-50

Jones, T. B. and Nicol, B. de B. Diderot and Mercier. *In* James, T. B. and Nicol, B. de B. Neo-classical dramatic criticism, 1560-1770 p145-76

Mehlman, J. Cataract: Diderot's discursive politics, 1749-1751. *In* Glyph 2 p37-63

Watson, F. Diderot and Houdon: a little-known bust. *In* The Artist and the writer in France p15-20

About individual works

Jacques, the fatalist, and his master

Alter, R. Diderot's Jacques: this is and is not a story. *In* Alter, R. Partial magic p57-83

Memoirs of a nun

Fellows, O. E. Diderot's Supplément as pendant for La religieuse. *In* Literature and history in the age of ideas p229-43

The paradox of acting

Bonneville, D. A. Diderot's artist: puppet and poet. *In* Literature and history in the age of ideas p245-52

Supplement to Bougainville's voyages

Fellows, O. E. Diderot's Supplément as pendant for La religieuse. *In* Literature and history in the age of ideas p229-43

Aesthetics

Barthes, R. Diderot, Brecht, Eisenstein. *In* Barthes, R. Image, music, text p69-78

Characters—Jacques

Torrance, R. M. Moral rake and masterful lackey. *In* Torrance, R. M. The comic hero p177-205

Diderot, Denis, and Alembert, Jean Lerond d'

About individual works

Encyclopedia

Bonnet, J. C. The culinary system in the Encyclopédie. *In* Food and drink in history p139-65

Darnton, R. The Encyclopédie wars of prerevolutionary France. *In* Studies in eighteenth-century culture v6 p3-33

Kafker, F. A. The fortunes and misfortunes of a leading French bookseller-printer: André François Le Breton, chief publisher of the Encyclopédie. *In* Studies in eighteenth-century culture v5 p371-85

Monty, J. R. Voltaire's debt to the Encyclopédie in the Opinion en alphabet. *In* Literature and history in the age of ideas p153-67

Rex, W. E. The philosophical articles by Abbé Pestré in Diderot's Encyclopédie. *In* Studies in eighteenth-century culture v7 p251-62

Didion, Joan

About individual works

A book of common prayer

Mickelson, A. Z. Joan Didion: the hurting woman. *In* Mickelson, A. Z. Reaching out: sensitivity and order in recent American fiction by women p87-111

Play it as it lays

Mickelson, A. Joan Didion: the hurting woman. *In* Mickelson, A. Reaching out: sensitivity and order in recent American fiction by women p87-111

Diebold, William

U.S. trade policy: the new political dimensions. *In* Bundy, W. P. ed. The world economic crisis p140-64

Dieckmann, Herbert

The transformation of the concept of imitation in eighteenth-century French esthetics. *In* Amacher, R. E. and Lange, V. eds. New perspectives in German literary criticism p49-85

Diehl, James M.

Germany: veterans' politics under three flags. *In* The War generation p135-86

Diem, Hermann
Karl Barth as Socialist: controversy over a new attempt to understand him. *In* Hunsinger, G. ed. Karl Barth and radical politics p121-38

Dienstag, Jacob Israel
Christian translators of Maimonides' Mishneh Torah into Latin. *In* Salo Wittmayer Baron v 1 p287-309

Diet

Economic aspects
Zabinski, Z. The biological index of the buying power of money. *In* Biology of man in history p179-90

France
Frijhoff, W. and Julia, D. The diet in boarding schools at the end of the ancien régime. *In* Food and drink in history p73-85

Hémardinquer, J. J. The family pig of the ancien régime: myth or fact? *In* Food and drink in history p50-72

Near East
Ashtor, E. An essay on the diet of the various classes in the medieval Levant. *In* Biology of man in history p125-62

Dietary laws, Jewish. See Jews—Dietary laws

Dieter Stempel, Wolf- See Stempel, Wolf-Dieter

Dieterle, William. See Reinhardt, M. jt. auth.

Dietrich, Sheila Claire
An introduction to women in Anglo-Saxon society. *In* Kanner, B. ed. The women of England p32-56

Dietz, Brian
Antwerp and London: the structure and balance of trade in the 1560s. *In* Wealth and power in Tudor England p186-203

Dietz, Jean
Foster homes that are not "too loving." *In* Gross, B. and Gross, R. eds. The children's rights movement p55-57

Dietze, Gottfried
Hayek on the rule of law. *In* Essays on Hayek p107-46

Dieuzeide, Henri
Education and development. *In* Wagschal, P. H. ed. Learning tomorrows p89-96

Díez, Luis A.
The sources of The green house: the mythical background of a fabulous novel. *In* Rossman, C. R. and Friedman, A. W. eds. Mario Vargas Llosa p36-51

Díez, Luys A. See Díez, Luis A.

Difference (Philosophy)
Foucault, M. Theatrum philosophicum. *In* Foucault, M. Language, counter-memory, practice p165-96

Diffusion of innovations
Rogers, E. M. Network analysis of the diffusion of innovations: family planning in Korean villages. *In* Lerner, D. and Nelson, L. M. eds. Communication research—a half-century appraisal p117-47
See also Technology transfer

Digby, Adrian
Crossed trapezes: a pre-Columbian astronomical instrument. *In* Mesoamerican archaeology p271-83

Digests of cases. See Law reports, digests, etc.

Diggers. See Levellers

Diggle, James
Notes on the Electra of Euripides. *In* Illinois classical studies, v2 1977 p110-24

Diggory, Terence
Armored women, naked men; Dickinson, Whitman, and their successors. *In* Gilbert, S. M. and Gubar, S. eds. Shakespeare's sisters p135-50

Digital computer simulation. See Artificial intelligence

Dignity
Stanley, M. Dignity versus survival? Reflections on the moral philosophy of social order. *In* Brown, R. H. and Lyman, S. M. eds. Structure, consciousness, and history p197-234

Stern-Mitscherlich, A. L. On value and human dignity. *In* The Personal universe p74-90

Dihle, Albrecht
The poem on the cicada. *In* Harvard Studies in classical philology v71 p107-13

Di Lampedusa, Giuseppe Tomasi. See Tomasi di Lampedusa, Giuseppe

Dilatation of time. See Time dilatation

Dillard, Heath
Women in reconquest Castile: the fueros of Sepúlveda and Cuenca. *In* Stuard, S. M. ed. Women in medieval society p71-94

Dillard, Joey Lee

About individual works
Black English
Jackson, B. A review of J. L. Dillard's Black English. *In* Jackson, B. The waiting years p146-54

Diller, Aubrey
The manuscript tradition of Aeschines' orations. *In* Illinois classical studies v4, 1979 p34-64

Dillingham, William B.

About individual works
Melville's short fiction, 1853-1856
Parker, H. Tromping through fairyland: two books on Melville's tales. *In* Review, v 1 1979 p183-93

Dillon, George, and Millay, Edna St. Vincent, trs.

About individual works
Flowers of evil
Crane, J. St C. Edna St Vincent Millay's afterthoughts on the translation of Baudelaire. *In* Virginia. University. Bibliographical Society. Studies in bibliography v29 p382-86

Dillon, Richard H.
J. Ross Browne and Arizona. *In* Voices from the Southwest p92-101

Dillon, Wilton S.
E pluribus unum? *In* Smithsonian Institution. The cultural drama p33-67

Dilman, Ilham
Wittgenstein on the soul. *In* Royal Institute of Philosophy. Understanding Wittgenstein p162-92

Dilthey, Wilhelm

About
Bauman, Z. The rise of hermeneutics. *In* Bauman, Z. Hermeneutics and social science p23-47

Dilthey Wilhelm—About—*Continued*

Brown, R. H. History and hermeneutics: Wilhelm Dilthey and the dialectics of interpretive method. *In* Brown, R. H. and Lyman, S. M. eds. Structure, consciousness, and history p38-52

Ricoeur, P. The task of hermeneutics. *In* Murray, M. E. ed. Heidegger and modern philosophy p141-60

Tuttle, H. N. The epistemological status of the cultural world in Vico and Dilthey. *In* Giambattista Vico's science of humanity p241-50

Dilworth, Ira

Foreword by Ira Dilworth to Klee Wyck by Emily Carr. *In* Praise from famous men: an anthology of introductions p49-59

Dime novels

Cawelti, J. G. The Western: a look at the evolution of a formula. *In* Cawelti, J. G. Adventure, mystery, and romance p192-259

Dimeo, R. Steven. See DiMeo, Stephen

DiMeo, Stephen

Novel into film: so it goes. *In* Peary, G. and Shatzkin, R. eds. The modern American novel and the movies p282-92

Dimock, Edward C.

Religious biography in India: the 'nectar of the acts' of Caitanya. *In* Reynolds, F. E. and Capps, D. eds. The biographical process p109-17

Dimock, George Edward

Euripides' Hippolytus, or Virtue rewarded. *In* Yale classical studies v25 p239-58

Dimsdale, N. H.

Keynes and the finance of the First World War. *In* Keynes, M. ed. Essays on John Maynard Keynes p142-61

Dinesen, Isak, pseud. See Blixen, Karen

Dingoes

Macintosh, N. W. G. Early man and the dog in Australia. *In* Grafton Elliot Smith p83-94

Dinstein, Yoram

The new Geneva protocols: a step forward or backward? *In* The Year book of world affairs, 1979 p265-83

Soviet Jewry and international human rights. *In* Sidorsky, D. ed. Essays on human rights p126-43

Terrorism and war of liberation: an Israeli perspective of the Arab-Israeli conflict. *In* International terrorism and political crimes p155-72

Dio Cassius Cocceianus. See Cassius Dio Cocceianus

Dioceses. See Archdeacons

Dio Cocceianus Cassius. See Cassius Dio Cocceianus

Diodorus Siculus

About

Rice, D. G. Xenophon, Diodorus and the year 379/378 B.C. Reconstruction and reappraisal. *In* Yale classical studies v24 p95-130

Diola (African people)

Sapir, J. D. The fabricated child. *In* The Social use of metaphor p193-223

Diola-Fogny. See Diola (African people)

Dionisopoulos-Mass, Regina

The evil eye and bewitchment in a peasant village. *In* The Evil eye p42-62

Dionysia. See Bacchantes; Greek drama (Satyr play)

Dionysius, Saint, called the Areopagite. See Dionysius Areopagita, Pseudo-

Dionysius Areopagita, Pseudo-

About

Luscombe, D. E. The 'lex divinitatis' in the bull 'Unam sanctam' of Pope Boniface VIII. *In* Church and government in the Middle Ages p205-21

Dionysos. See Dionysus

Dionysus

Baeumer, M. L. Nietzsche and the tradition of the Dionysian. *In* O'Flaherty, J. C.; Sellner, T. F. and Helm, R. M. eds. Studies in Nietzsche and the classical tradition p165-89

Smith, M. On the Wine God in Palestine (Gen. 18, Jn. 2, and Achilles Tatius) *In* Salo Wittmayer Baron v2 p815-29

Steadman, J. M. A mask at Ludlow: Comus and Dionysiac revel. *In* Steadman, J. M. Nature into myth p213-40

Art

Richardson, E. H. The story of Ariadne in Italy. *In* Studies in classical art and archaeology p189-95

Dioptrics. See Refraction

Di Pietro, Robert J.

Humanism in linguistic theory: a lesson from Vico. *In* Giambattista Vico's science of humanity p341-50

Diplomacy

Berman, M. R. and Johnson, J. E. The growing role of unofficial diplomacy. *In* Unofficial diplomats p 1-33

Gilbert, F. The "new diplomacy" of the eighteenth century. *In* Gilbert, F. History p323-49

Hambro, E. I. Permanent representatives to international organisations. *In* The Year book of world affairs, 1976 p30-41

See also Diplomats

Diplomatic and consular service. See Diplomatic protection; Diplomats; Diplomats' wives

Diplomatic Conference for the Establishment of International Conventions for the Protection of Victims of War, Geneva, 1949

Dinstein, Y. The new Geneva protocols: a step forward or backward? *In* The Year book of world affairs, 1979 p265-83

Draper, G. I. A. D. Wars of national liberation and war criminality. *In* Howard, M. ed. Restraints on war p135-62

Diplomatic negotiations in international disputes

Hassner, P. The political aspects of European security. *In* International terrorism and world security p173-88

Psychological aspects

Davis, L. J. Tolerance of ambiguity in interpersonal bargaining. *In* International terrorism and world security p314-24

Diplomatic protection

Beers, B. F. Protection of American citizens abroad. *In* Encyclopedia of American foreign policy p827-35

Murphy, J. The role of international law in the prevention of terrorist kidnapping of diplomatic personnel. *In* International terrorism and political crimes p285-313

See also Intervention (International law)

Discourse analysis

Brown, R. L. and Steinmann, M. Native readers of fiction: a speech-act and genre-rule approach to defining literature. *In* Hernadi, P. ed. What is literature? p141-60

McCanles, M. "All discourse aspires to the analytic proposition." *In* Hernadi, P. ed. What is literature? p190-205

Discoverers. See Discoveries (in geography)

Discoveries (in geography)

Allen, J. L. Lands of myth, waters of wonder: the place of the imagination in the history of geographical exploration. *In* Geographies of the mind p41-61

See also Geography—15th-16th centuries; Northwest Passage

Discoveries in science. See Science

The discreet charm of the bourgeoisie (Motion picture)

Kauffmann, S. The discreet charm of the bourgeoisie. *In* Kauffmann, S. Living images p153-55

Samuels, C. T. Tampering with reality. *In* Samuels, C. T. Mastering the film, and other essays p198-210

Discretion (Law) See Judicial discretion

Discretion, Judicial. See Judicial discretion

Discrimination

Simpson, E. Discrimination as an example of moral irrationality. *In* Fact, value, and perception p107-22

See also Civil rights; Discrimination in education; Discrimination in employment; Discrimination in public accommodations; Minorities; Race discrimination; Sex discrimination

United States

Beauchamp, T. L. The justification of reverse discrimination. *In* Social justice & preferential treatment p84-110

Black, V. The erosion of legal principles in the creation of legal policies. *In* Gross, B. R. ed. Reverse discrimination p163-83

Blackstone, W. T. Reverse discrimination and compensatory justice. *In* Social justice & preferential treatment p52-83

Glazer, N. The emergence of an American ethnic pattern; excerpt from "Affirmative discrimination: ethnic inequality and public policy." *In* Gross, B. R. ed. Reverse discrimination p132-55

Glazer, N. Individual rights against group rights. *In* Human rights p87-103

Gross, B. R. Is turn about fair play? *In* Gross, B. R. ed. Reverse discrimination p379-87

Hoffman, R. Justice, merit, and the good. *In* Gross, B. R. ed. Reverse discrimination p358-72

Lerner, B. Washington v. Davis: quantity, quality and equality in employment testing. *In* The Supreme Court review, 1976 p263-316

Newton, L. H. Reverse discrimination as unjustified. *In* Gross, B. R. ed. Reverse discrimination p373-78

Nickel, J. W. Discrimination and morally relevant characteristics. *In* Gross, B. R. ed. Reverse discrimination p288-90

Nickel, J. W. Should reparations be to individuals or to groups? *In* Gross, B. R. ed. Reverse discrimination p314-20

Rusk, D. Preferential treatment: some reflections. *In* Social justice & preferential treatment p154-60

Shiner, R. A. Individuals, groups, and inverse discrimination. *In* Gross, B. R. ed. Reverse discrimination p310-13

Discrimination, Racial. See Race discrimination

Discrimination, Sexual. See Sex discrimination

Discrimination against women. See Sex discrimination against women

Discrimination in education

Posner, R. A. The DeFunis case and the constitutionality of preferential treatment of racial minorities. *In* The Supreme Court review, 1974 p 1-32

See also Segregation in education; Sex discrimination in education

Case studies

Miner, A. S. Affirmative action at Stanford University; introductory notes. *In* Women in academia p139-62

Law and legislation—United States

Cox, A. Harvard College amicus curiae, DeFunis v. Odegaard. *In* Gross, B. R. ed. Reverse discrimination p184-97

Douglas, W. O. DeFunis v. Odegaard, dissenting opinion (April 23, 1974). *In* Gross, B. R. ed. Reverse discrimination p198-207

Greenawalt, R. K. Judicial scrutiny of "benign" racial preference in law school admissions. *In* Gross, B. R. ed. Reverse discrimination p217-38

United States

Crocker, L. Preferential treatment. *In* inism and philosophy p190-209

Goldman, A. H. Limits to the justification of reverse discrimination. *In* Feminism and philosophy p225-41

Heslep, R. D. Preferential treatment in admitting racial minority students. *In* Social justice & preferential treatment p33-51

Hook, S. Discrimination, color blindness, and the quota system. *In* Gross, B. R. ed. Reverse discrimination p84-87

Nell, O. O. How do we know when opportunities are equal? *In* Feminism and philosophy p177-89

Also in Gould, C. C. and Wartofsky, M. W. ed. Women and philosophy p334-41

O'Neil, R. M. The case for preferential admissions; excerpt from "Discriminating against discrimination: preferential admissions in the DeFunis case." *In* Gross, B. R. ed. Reverse discrimination p66-83

Todorovich, M. and Glickstein, H. A. Discrimination in higher education: a debate on faculty employment. *In* Gross, B. R. ed. Reverse discrimination p12-40

Wasserstrom, R. A. The university and the case for preferential treatment. *In* Social justice & preferential treatment p16-32

Wilson, P. E. Discrimination against Blacks in education: an historical perspective. *In* Social justice & preferential treatment p161-75

Discrimination in employment

See also Affirmative action programs; Equal pay for equal work

Case studies

Miner, A. S. Affirmative action at Stanford University; introductory notes. *In* Women in academia p139-62

Discrimination in employment—*Continued*

Law and legislation—United States

Sandler, B. Sex discrimination, educational institutions, and the law: a new issue on campus. *In* Women in academia p20-36

Weitzman, L. J. Legal requirements, structures, and strategies for eliminating sex discrimination in academe. *In* Women in academia p45-81

United States

Cook, A. H. Sex discrimination at universities: an ombudsman's view. *In* Women in academia p120-27

Crocker, L. Preferential treatment. *In* Feminism and philosophy p190-209

Fried, M. G. In defense of preferential hiring. *In* Gould, C. C. and Wartofsky, M. W. eds. Women and philosophy p309-19

Fullinwider, R. K. On preferential hiring. *In* Feminism and philosophy p210-24

Goldman, A. H. Limits to the justification of reverse discrimination. *In* Feminism and philosophy p225-41

Hook, S. Discrimination, color blindness, and the quota system. *In* Gross, B. R. ed. Reverse discrimination p84-87

Jones, H. E. On the justifiability of reverse discrimination. *In* Gross, B. R. ed. Reverse discrimination p348-57

Lee, G. R. A federal equal-employment-opportunity program. *In* Henderson, G. ed. Human relations in the military p237-48

Nell, O. O. How do we know when opportunities are equal? *In* Feminism and philosophy p177-89

Also in Gould, C. C. and Wartofsky, M. W. eds. Women and philosophy p334-46

Pottinger, J. S. The drive toward equality. *In* Gross, B. R. ed. Reverse discrimination p41-49

Pottinger, J. S. Race, sex, and jobs: the drive toward equality. *In* Women in academia p37-44

Scott, E. L. Developing criteria and measures of equal opportunities for women. *In* Women in academia p82-114

Seidman, A. W. Women who work for wages. *In* Roberts, J. I. ed. Beyond intellectual sexism p265-73

Thalberg, I. Reverse discrimination and the future. *In* Gould, C. C. and Wartofsky, M. W. eds. Women and philosophy p294-308

Todorovich, M. and Glickstein, H. A. Discrimination in higher education: a debate on faculty employment. *In* Gross, B. R. ed. Reverse discrimination p12-40

Vetterling, M. K. Some common sense notes on preferential hiring. *In* Gould, C. C. and Wartofsky, M. W. eds. Women and philosophy p320-24

Discrimination in housing

New York (City)

Kantrowitz, N. New York segregation: implications for social policy. *In* The Diverse society: implications for social policy p27-40

United States

See Afro-Americans—Housing

Discrimination in public accommodations

United States

Chasteen, E. Legal change. *In* Lauer, R. H. ed. Social movements and social change p156-73

Discrimination in sports. See Segregation in sports

Discussion. See Debates and debating

Disease (Pathology) See Pathology

Diseases

Causes and theories of causation

Temkin, O. Health and disease. *In* Temkin, O. The double face of Janus p419-40

Temkin, O. The scientific approach to disease: specific entity and individual sickness. *In* Temkin, O. The double face of Janus p441-55

See also Infection

Psychological aspects

See Sick—Psychology

Public opinion

D'Andrade, R. G. A propositional analysis of U.S. American beliefs about illness. *In* Basso, K. H. and Selby, H. A. eds. Meaning in anthropology p155-80

Diseases, Mental. See Mental illness; Psychoses

Diseases in literature

Biasin, G. P. From anatomy to criticism. *In* Biasin, G. P. Literary diseases p3-35

Disneyland Park, Anaheim, Calif.

Marin, L. Disneyland: a degenerate utopia. *In* Glyph I p50-66

Disorders of speech. See Speech, Disorders of

Dispersion. See Achromatism

Dispersion of the Jews. See Jews—Diaspora

Display techniques. See Museum techniques

Disposal of refuse. See Refuse and refuse disposal

Disputed passage (Motion picture)

Camper, F. Disputed passage. *In* Nichols, B. ed. Movies and methods p339-44

Disputing. See Quarreling

Disraeli, Benjamin. See Beaconsfield, Benjamin Disraeli, 1st Earl of

Dissei Logi. See Dialexeis

Dissent in literature

Robbins, R. H. Dissent in Middle English literature: the spirit of (thirteen) seventy-six. *In* Medievalia et humanistica; new ser. no. 9 p25-51

Dissenters

See also Dissenters, Religious

England

Cunningham, V. The sense of an ending. *In* Cunningham, V. Everywhere spoken against p278-86

Great Britain

Hill, J. E. C. From Lollard to Levellers. *In* Rebels and their causes p49-67

Russia

Barghoorn, F. C. The post-Khrushchev campaign to suppress dissent: perspectives, strategies, and techniques of repression. *In* Tokes, R. L. ed. Dissent in the USSR p35-95

Dissenters—Russia—*Continued*

Connor, W. D. Differentiation, integration, and political dissent in the USSR. *In* Tokes, R. L. ed. Dissent in the USSR p139-57

Friedgut, T. H. The democratic movement: dimensions and perspectives. *In* Tokes, R. L. ed. Dissent in the USSR p116-36

Hollander, G. D. Political communication and dissent in the Soviet Union. *In* Tokes, R. L. ed. Dissent in the USSR p233-75

Maggs, P. B. Legal controls on American publication of heterodox Soviet writings. *In* Tokes, R. L. ed. Dissent in the USSR p310-25

Reddaway, P. The development of dissent and opposition. *In* Brown, A. H. and Kaser, M. eds. The Soviet Union since the fall of Khrushchev p121-56

Reddaway, P. B. Theory and practice of human rights in the Soviet Union. *In* Kommers, D. P. and Loescher, G. D. eds. Human rights and American foreign policy p115-29

Simes, D. H. Human rights and détente. *In* Kirk, G. L. and Wessell, N. H. eds. The Soviet threat p135-47

Slusser, R. M. History and the democratic opposition. *In* Tokes, R. L. ed. Dissent in the USSR p329-53

Solzhenitsyn, A. I. The smatterers. *In* From under the rubble p229-78

Sosin, G. Magnitizdat: uncensored songs of dissent. *In* Tokes, R. L. ed. Dissent in the USSR p276-309

Spechler, D. Permitted dissent in the decade after Stalin: criticism and protest in Novy Mir, 1953-1964. *In* Cocks, P.; Daniels, R. V. and Heer, N. W. eds. The dynamics of Soviet politics p28-50

United States

Weigley, R. F. Dissent in wars. *In* Encyclopedia of American foreign policy p253-67

Dissenters, Religious

History

Collinson, P. Toward a broader understanding of the early dissenting tradition. *In* The Dissenting tradition p3-38

England

Cunningham, V. Places and politics. *In* Cunningham, V. Everywhere spoken against p67-105

Davie, D. Dissent in the present century. *In* Davie, D. A gathered Church p91-108

Davie, D. The Nonconformist contribution to English culture. *In* Davie, D. A gathered Church p 1-18

England—History

Bebbington, D. W. Gladstone and the Nonconformists: a religious affinity in politics. *In* Church, society and politics p369-82

Bonwick, C. C. English Dissenters and the American Revolution. *In* Allen, H. C. and Thompson, R. eds. Contrast and connection p88-112

Davie, D. Old dissent, 1700-1740. *In* Davie, D. A gathered Church p19-36

Wilkes, J. W. The transformation of dissent: a review of the change from the seventeenth to the eighteenth centuries. *In* The Dissenting tradition p108-22

Europe, Eastern—History

Hillerbrand, H. J. Religious dissent and toleration: introductory reflections. *In* Király, B. K. ed. Tolerance and movements of religious dissent in Eastern Europe p 1-8

Great Britain

Cunningham, V. All sorts and conditions. *In* Cunningham, V. Everywhere spoken against p25-66

Hill, J. E. C. From Lollards to Levellers. *In* Rebels and their causes p49-67

Russia

Jancar, B. W. Religious dissent in the Soviet Union. *In* Tokes, R. L. eds. Dissent in the USSR p191-230

Dissenters in literature

Cunningham, V. All sorts and conditions. *In* Cunningham, V. Everywhere spoken against p25-66

Cunningham, V. The Brontës. *In* Cunningham, V. Everywhere spoken against p113-26

Cunningham, V. Charles Dickens. *In* Cunningham, V. Everywhere spoken against p190-230

Cunningham, V. George Eliot. *In* Cunningham, V. Everywhere spoken against p143-89

Cunningham, V. Mrs. Gaskell. *In* Cunningham, V. Everywhere spoken against p127-42

Cunningham, V. Mrs Oliphant and the tradition. *In* Cunningham, V. Everywhere spoken against p231-48

Cunningham, V. Openness. *In* Cunningham, V. Everywhere spoken against p8-24

Cunningham, V. The presence of dissent. *In* Cunningham, V. Everywhere spoken against p106-12

Cunningham, V. The sense of an ending. *In* Cunningham, V. Everywhere spoken against p278-86

Cunningham, V. Was there a revolution in Tanner's Lane? *In* Cunningham, V. Everywhere spoken against p249-77

Cunningham, V. Places and politics. *In* Cunningham. V. Everywhere spoken against p67-105

Davie, D. Dissent in the present century. *In* Davie, D. A. gathered Church p91-108

Davie, D. The Nonconformist contribution to English culture. *In* Davie, D. A gathered Church p 1-18

Thompson, D. Dissent and protest. *In* Thompson, D. The uses of protest p137-72

Dissidents. See Dissenters

Dissonance (Psychology)

De Vos, G. A. Affective dissonance and primary socialization: implications for a theory of incest avoidance. *In* Schwartz, T. ed. Socialization as cultural communication p73-90

Distribution (Economic theory)

Musgrave, R. A. Adam Smith on public finance and distribution. *In* The Market and the state p296-319

See also Income distribution; Profit

Distribution of income. See Income distribution

Distribution of wealth. See Wealth

Divination. See Clairvoyance; Second sight

Divine Light Mission
Messer, J. Guru Maharaj Ji and the Divine Light Mission. *In* The New religious consciousness p52-72

Divine principle. See Holy Spirit association for the unification of world Christianity. Divine principle

Divinity of Christ. See Jesus Christ—Divinity

Division of labor
Markus, M. and Hegedüs, A. Free time and the division of labour. *In* The Humanisation of socialism p106-23

Division of powers. See Federal government; Separation of powers

Divorce
Barnhart, J. E. and Barnhart, M. A. The myth of the complete person. *In* Feminism and philosophy p277-90

Germany
McNamara, J. A. and Wemple, S. F. Marriage and divorce in the Frankish kingdom. *In* Stuard, S. M. ed. Women in medieval society p95-124

United States
Weiss, R. S. A new marital form: the marriage of uncertain duration. *In* On the making of Americans p221-33

United States—History
O'Neill, W. L. Divorce as a moral issue: a hundred years of controversy. *In* "Remember the ladies": new perspectives on women in American history p127-43

Diwakar, Ranganath Ramachandra
Aurobindo. *In* Bishop, D. H. ed. Indian thought p324-36

Dixon, James Payson
Permanent campus revolution? *In* Fairfield, R. P. ed. Humanistic frontiers in American education p261-68

Dixon, Melvin
Rivers remembering their source: comparative studies in Black literary history—Langston Hughes, Jacques Roumain, and négritude. *In* Fisher, D. and Stepto, R. B. eds. Afro-American literature p25-43

Dixon, Thomas
About
Downs, R. B. Hymn of hate. *In* Downs, R. B. Books that changed the South p208-17

About individual works
The clansman: an historical romance of the Ku Klux Klan
Downs, R. B. Hymn of hate. *In* Downs, R. B. Books that changed the South p208-17

The leopard's spots
Riggio, T. P. Uncle Tom reconstructed: a neglected chapter in the history of a book. *In* Zenderland, L. ed. Recycling the past p66-80

Dizard, Wilson P.
Television's global networks. *In* Fischer, H. D. and Merrill, J. C. eds. International and intercultural communication p83-89

Toward a wired world. *In* Fischer, H. D. and Merrill, J. C. eds. International and intercultural communication p333-49

Djilas, Milovan
The Gulag Archipelago. *In* Dunlop, J. B.; Haugh, R. and Klimoff, A. eds. Aleksandr Solzhenitsyn: critical essays and documentary materials 2d ed. p512-14

Indomitable faith. *In* Dunlop, J. B.; Haugh, R. and Klimoff, A. eds. Aleksandr Solzhenitsyn: critical essays and documentary materials 2d ed. p328-31

About
Reinhartz, D. Milovan Djilas: the transcendence of a revolutionary. *In* Essays on modern European revolutionary history p69-88

About individual works
On alienation
Mihajlov, M. Djilas versus Marx: the theory of alienation. *In* Mihajlov, M. Underground notes p105-24

The unperfect society: beyond the new class
Mihajlov, M. Comments on The unperfect society. *In* Mihajlov, M. Underground notes p125-52

Djwa, Sandra Ann
Leonard Cohen: black romantic. *In* Woodcock, G. ed. Poets and critics p179-90

Doane, Alger Nicolaus
Legend, history and artifice in "The Battle of Maldon." *In* Viator: medieval and Renaissance studies v9 p39-66

Doar, John
Civil rights and self-government. *In* The National purpose reconsidered p97-118

Dobb, Leonard William, ed.

About individual works
Resolving conflict in Africa
Kelman, H. C. The problem-solving workshop in conflict resolution. *In* Unofficial diplomats p168-200

Dobb, Maurice Herbert
Ricardo and Adam Smith. *In* Skinner, A. S. and Wilson, T. eds. Essays on Adam Smith p324-35

Some historical reflections on planning and the market. *In* Essays in honor of E. H. Carr p324-38

Dobie, James Frank
Prefaces
Contents
Andy Adams, cowboy chronicler
Also in Praise from famous men: an anthology of introductions p60-68
Belling the lead steer
Captain Cook's place among reminiscencers of the West
Captain John G. Bourke as soldier, writer and man
Charlie Siringo, writer and man
The conservatism of Charles M. Russell
Foreword to "A Texas ranger," by Napoleon Augustus Jennings
Foreword to "Recollections of early Texas," by John Holland Jenkins
Foreword to "Sheep, life on the South Dakota range," by Archer B. Gilfillan
The gauchos and horses of Hudson and Graham

Dobie, James F.
Prefaces
Contents—Continued
Helen Hunt Jackson and "Ramona"
Introduction to "Home on the Double Bayou," by Ralph Semmes Jackson
James Cox and his "Cattle industry"
Jim Williams and "Out our way"
A preface on authentic liars
Preface to "A treasury of Western folklore," ed. by B. A. Botkin
A salute to Gene Rhodes
A summary introduction to Frederic Remington

Döblin, Alfred

About individual works
Alexanderplatz, Berlin
Adams, R. M. Döblin, Broch. *In* Adams, R. M. Afterjoyce p134-45

Dobratz, Betty A. See Kourvetaris, G. A. jt. auth.

Dobrée, Bonamy

About individual works
English literature in the early eighteenth century, 1700-1740
Frye, N. Nature methodized. *In* Frye, N. Northrop Frye on culture and literature p147-55

Dobrianov, Velichko, and Stavrov, Boris
Contemporary sociology in Bulgaria. *In* Mohan, R. P. and Martindale, D. A. eds. Handbook of contemporary developments in world sociology p227-45

Dobrof, Rose. See Caroff, P. jt. auth.

Dobroliūbov, Nikolaï Aleksandrovich

About
Mathewson, R. W. Dobrolyubov: beyond the superfluous man. *In* Mathewson, R. W. The positive hero in Russian literature p46-62
Stacy, R. H. The civic critics. *In* Stacy, R. H. Russian literary critics p55-65

Dobrolyubov, Nikolay. See Dobroliūbov, Nikolaï Aleksandrovich

Dobson, Richard B.
Educational policies and attainment. *In* Women in Russia p267-92

Dobson, William Arthur Charles Harvey
The religions of China (excepting Buddhism) *In* Adams, C. J. ed. A reader's guide to the great religions p90-105

Dobyns, Henry F.
Taking the witness stand. *In* Eddy, E. M. and Partridge, W. L. eds. Applied anthropology in American p261-76

Dobzhansky, Theodosius Grigorievich
Chance and creativity in evolution. *In* Ayala, F. J. and Dobzhansky, T. G. eds. Studies in the philosophy of biology p307-37
Evolution and man's self-image. *In* Goodall, V. M. ed. The quest for man p189-220

About
Adams, M. B. From "gene fund" to "gene pool": on the evolution of evolutionary language. *In* Studies in history of biology v3 p241-85

Dobzhansky, Theodosius Grigorievich, and Montagu, Ashley
Natural selection and the mental capacities of mankind. *In* Montagu, A. ed. Race and IQ p104-13

Doctor-patient relationship. See Physician and patient

Dr Strangelove; or, How I learned to stop worrying and love the bomb (Motion picture)
Suid, L. The Pentagon and Hollywood: Dr Strangelove, or: How I learned to stop worrying and love the bomb. *In* O'Connor, J. E. and Jackson, M. A. eds. American history/American film p219-35

Doctors, See Physicians

Doctrinal theology. See Theology, Doctrinal

Documenta 5, Kassel. See Art—Germany—Exhibitions

Documentary films. See Moving-pictures, Documentary

Documentary moving-pictures. See Moving-pictures, Documentary

Documentary photography. See Photography, Documentary

Documents. See Diplomatics

Documents, Conservation of. See Archives

Documents, Legal. See Legal documents

Dodd, Philip; Lincoln, Andrew, and Watson, John Richard
The nineteenth century: romantic period. *In* English Association. The year's work in English studies v57 p236-61

Dodds, Eric Robertson
Louis MacNeice at Birmingham. *In* Time was away p35-38

About individual works
Why I do not believe in survival
Ducasse, C. J. How stands the case for the reality of survival; excerpt from "A critical examination of the belief in a life after death." *In* Wheatley, J. M. O. and Edge, H. L. eds. Philosophical dimensions of parapsychology p282-94

Dodge, Norton T.
Women in the professions. *In* Women in Russia p205-24

Dodgson, Charles Lutwidge

About
Praz, M. Two masters of the absurd: Grandville and Carroll. *In* The Artist and the writer in France p134-37
Prickett, S. Consensus and nonsense: Lear and Carroll. *In* Prickett, S. Victorian fantasy p114-49

About individual works
Alice's adventures in Wonderland
Hardy, B. N. Fantasy and dream. *In* Hardy, B. N. Tellers and listeners p19-55
Massey, I. Aspects of metamorphosis in Alice. *In* Massey, I. The gaping pig p76-97

Dodsley, Robert

About
Wendorf, R. Robert Dodsley as editor. *In* Virginia. University. Biblographical Society. Studies in bibliography v31 p235-48

Dodsley, Robert, ed.

About individual works
Selected fables of Esop and other fabulists
Noel, T. Dodsley and England at mid-century. *In* Noel, T. Theories of the fable in the eighteenth century p114-21

Dodson, Daniel B.
Malcolm Lowry. *In* Stade, G. ed. Six contemporary British novelists p115-64

Doe, Charles

About

White, G. E. Political ideologies, professional norms, and the state judiciary in the late nineteenth century: Cooley and Doe. *In* White, G. E. The American judicial tradition p109-28

Doebler, John Willard
Orlando: athlete of virtue. *In* Shakespeare survey 26 p111-17

Doenecke, Justus Drew
The most-favored-nation principle. *In* Encyclopedia of American foreign policy p603-09

Doerksen, Daniel W.
Search and discovery: Margaret Avison's poetry. *In* Woodcock, G. ed. Poets and critics p123-37

Doern, G. Bruce
Canada. *In* Galnoor, I. ed. Government secrecy in democracies p143-56

Dog. See Dogs

Dog day afternoon (Motion picture)
Sarris, A. Dog day afternoon. *In* Sarris, A. Politics and cinema p32-36

Dogmatic theology. See Theology, Doctrinal

Dogood, Silence, pseud. See Franklin, Benjamin

Dogs
White, E. B. Bedfellows. *In* White, E. B. Essays of E. B. White p80-89

Dogs, Fossil
Macintosh, N. W. G. Early man and the dog in Australia. *In* Grafton Elliot Smith p83-94

Dogs in literature
Rowe, W. W. Nabokov: the hounds of fate. *In* Rowe, W. W. Nabokov & others: patterns in Russian literature p85-123

Dohm, Christian Wilhelm von

About

Altmann, A. Letters from Dohm to Mendelssohn. *In* Salo Wittmayer Baron v 1 p39-62

Dohm, Peter Meyer-. See Meyer-Dohm, Peter

Doillon, Jacques

About individual works

Fingers in the head

Truffaut, F. Jacques Doillon: Les doigts dans la tête. *In* Truffaut, F. The films in my life p343-45

Dolan, Paul J.
Of war and war's alarms

Contents

Conrad: the price of politics
Dostoyevsky: the political gospel
Hawthorne: the politics of puberty
James: the aesthetics of politics
Kafka: the political machine
The lamps of Europe
Mann: art, politics, and the apocalypse

Dolan, T. P.; Mitchell, L. E. and McTurk, R. W.
Middle English: excluding Chaucer. *In* English Association. The year's work in English studies v57 p60-88

Dolby, R. G. A.
Debates over the theory of solution: a study of dissent in physical chemistry in the English-speaking world in the late nineteenth and early twentieth centuries. *In* Historical studies in the physical sciences v7 p297-404

Dolce, Philip C.
The McCarran-Walter Act and the conflict over immigration policy during the Truman administration. *In* The Immigrant experience in America p215-32

La dolce vita (Motion picture)
Halperin, M. Culture and the Revolution; excerpt from "The rise and decline of Fidel Castro." *In* Radosh, R. ed. The new Cuba: paradoxes and potentials p190-210

Dole, Gertrude E.
The marriages of Pacho: a woman's life among the Amahuaca. *In* Matthiasson, C. J. ed. Many sisters p3-35

Doležel, Lubomír
A scheme of narrative time. *In* Matejka, L. and Titunik, I. R. eds. Semiotics of art p209-17

Doleželová-Velingerová, Milena
The origins of modern Chinese literature. *In* Modern Chinese literature in the May Fourth era p17-35

Lu Xun's "Medicine." *In* Modern Chinese literature in the May Fourth era p221-31

Dolgin, Janet L.
Latter-Day sense and substance. *In* Zaretsky, I. I. and Leone, M. P. eds. Religious movements in contemporary America p519-46

Dollar diplomacy. Trani, E. P. *In* Encyclopedia of American foreign policy p268-74

Dollenmayer, Judith A. See Campbell, A. K. jt. auth.

Dolley, Michael. See Dolley, Reginald Hugh Michael

Dolley, Reginald Hugh Michael
Towards a revision of the internal chronology of the coinages of Edward the Elder and Plegmund. *In* Anglo-Saxon England 3 p175-77

A **doll's** house (criticism) Ibsen, H. *In* Brustein, R. S. The culture watch p79-81

A **doll's** house (criticism) Ibsen, H. *In* Kauffmann, S. Persons of the drama p120-23

A **doll's** house (criticism) (another essay) Ibsen, H. *In* Kauffmann, S. Persons of the drama p125-29

Dolmatoff, Gerardo Reichel- See Reichel-Dolmatoff, Gerardo

Dols, Michael W.
The comparative communal responses to the Black Death in Muslim and Christian societies. *In* Viator: medieval and Renaissance studies v5 p269-87

Dom, Gurk, Austria. See Gurk, Austria. Dom

Domain, Public. See Public domain

Dombroski, Robert Stanley
Introduction. *In* Dombroski, R. S. ed. Critical perspectives on The Decameron p 1-13

Domes, Jürgen
The model for revolutionary people's war: the Communist takeover of China. *In* Hammond, T. T. ed. The anatomy of Communist takeovers p516-33

Domes

Coomaraswamy, A. K. The symbolism of the dome. *In* Coomaraswamy, A. K. Selected papers v 1 p415-64

Italy

Wittkower, R. Vittone's domes. *In* Wittkower, R. Studies in the Italian baroque p211-22

Domesday book

Kreisler, F. F. Domesday book and the Anglo-Norman synthesis. *In* Order and innovation in the Middle Ages p3-16

Domestic animals. See Camels; Horses

Domestic architecture. See Architecture, Domestic

Domestic education. See Children—Management

Domestic jurisdiction. See Jurisdiction (International law)

Domestic relations

Heller, A. The future of relations between the sexes. *In* The Humanisation of socialism p27-41

Morse, S. J. Family law in transition: from traditional families to individual liberty. *In* Tufte, V. and Myerhoff, B. G. eds. Changing images of the family p319-60

Whiting, J. W. M. and Whiting, B. B. Aloofness and intimacy of husbands and wives: a cross-cultural study. *In* Schwartz, T. ed. Socialization as cultural communication p91-115

See also Family; Husband and wife; Marriage law

Syria

Sweet, L. E. In reality: some Middle Eastern women. *In* Matthiasson, C. J. ed. Many sisters p379-97

United States

Bloomfield, M. H. The family in antebellum law. *In* Bloomfield, M. H. American lawyers in a changing society, 1776-1876 p91-135

Domestic service. See Servants

Domínguez, Jorge Ignacio

The armed forces and foreign relations. *In* Cuba in the world p53-86

U.S. policy toward Cuba: a discussion of options. *In* The Americas in a changing world p112-31

Dominic, R. B. See Lathen, Emma, pseud.

Dominican Republic

Foreign relations—United States

Haley, P. E. Comparative intervention: Mexico in 1914 & Dominica in 1965. *In* Higham, R. D. ed. Intervention or abstention: the dilemma of American foreign policy p40-59

The **domino** theory. Gregory, R. *In* Encyclopedia of American foreign policy p275-80

Don Juan

Bloch, A. Dom Juan and Don Giovanni. *In* Johnson, R. B.; Neumann, E. S. and Trail, G. T. eds. Molière and the commonwealth of letters: patrimony and posterity p287-98

Donadio, Stephen Louis

Emerson, Christian identity, and the dissolution of the social order. *In* Art, politics, and will p99-123

Donagan, Alan

Berkeley's theory of the immediate objects of vision. *In* Studies in perception p312-35

Descartes's "synthetic" treatment of the real distinction between mind and body. *In* Hooker, M. ed. Descartes p186-96

Donahue, Charles

Potlatch and charity: notes on the heroic in Beowulf. *In* Anglo-Saxon poetry: essays in appreciation p23-40

Donahue, William H.

The solid planetary spheres in post-Copernican natural philosophy. *In* The Copernican achievement p244-75

About individual works

The solid planetary spheres in post-Copernican natural philosophy

Heilbron, J. L. Commentary: Duhem and Donahue. *In* The Copernican achievement p276-84

Donald, Miles

The American novel in the twentieth century

Contents

Fantasy
The fate of the traditional novel
The minorities
Popular fiction
The traditional novel

Donaldson, Ethelbert Talbot

Designing a camel; or, Generalizing the Middle Ages. *In* Tennessee Studies in literature v22 p 1-16

The manuscripts of Chaucer's works and their use. *In* Brewer, D. S. ed. Geoffrey Chaucer p85-108

Patristic exegesis in the criticism of medieval literature: the opposition. *In* Wimsatt, W. K. ed. Literary criticism: idea and act p170-88

Donaldson, Ian

Jonson and the moralists. *In* Kernan, A. B. ed. Two Renaissance mythmakers p146-64

Donaldson, Robert H.

Global power relationships in the seventies: the view from the Kremlin. *In* Cocks, P.; Daniels, R. V. and Heer, N. W. eds. The dynamics of Soviet politics p309-33

Donaldson, Scott, and Massa, Ann

American literature: nineteenth and early twentieth centuries

Contents

City and country
Dreams and nightmares
Freedom and repression
Individual and society
The New World and the Old World
Religion and irreligion: Doubts and certainties
Religion and irreligion: God and Mammon

Donatello

About individual works

David

Paoletti, J. T. The Bargello David and public sculpture in fifteenth-century Florence. *In* Collaboration in Italian Renaissance art 99-111

Donation of Constantine

Pascoe, L. B. Gerson and the Donation of Constantine: growth and development within the Church. *In* Viator: medieval and Renaissance studies v5 p469-85

Wallach, L. Actus Silvestri, Libri Carolini, and the Constantine Donation: the solution of a pseudo-problem. *In* Wallach, L. Diplomatic studies in Latin and Greek documents from the Carolingian age p152-59

Donations. See Endowments

Donato, Eugenio

The idioms of the text: notes on the language of philosophy and the fictions of literature. *In* Glyph 2 p 1-13

Donatus, Aelius

About individual works
Terentius

Cunningham, J. V. The Donatan tradition. *In* Cunningham, J. V. The collected essays of J. V. Cunningham p30-52

Manuscripts

Reeve, M. D. and Rouse, R. H. New light on the transmission of Donatus's "commentum Terentii." *In* Viator: medieval and Renaissance studies v9 p235-49

Donchin, Georgette

Gorky, *In* Freeborn, R. ed. Russian literary attitudes from Pushkin to Solzhenitsyn p79-98

Pushkin. *In* Freeborn, R. ed. Russian literary attitudes from Pushkin to Solzhenitsyn p19-38

Dondi dall'Orologio Giovanni. See Dondi, Giovanni de

Dondi, Giovanni de

About

Gilbert, N. W. A letter of Giovanni Dondi dall'Orologio to Fra'Guglielmo Centueri: a fourteenth-century episode in the Quarrel of the Ancients and the Moderns. *In* Viator: medieval and Renaissance studies v8 p299-346

Donegan, Jane Bauer

Man-midwifery and the delicacy of the sexes. *In* "Remember the ladies": new perspectives on women in American history p90-109

Doney, Willis

The geometrical presentation of Descartes's a priori proof. *In* Hooker, M. ed. Descartes p1-25

Some recent work on Descartes: a bibliography. *In* Hooker, M. ed. Descartes p299-312

Spinoza on philosophical skepticism. *In* Freeman, E. and Mandelbaum, M. H. eds. Spinoza p139-57

Donizetti, Gaetano

About

Schmidgall, G. Gaetano Donizetti. *In* Schmidgall, G. Literature as opera p109-47

Donkey in literature

Steadman, J. M. The Faerie Queene: Una and the clergy. *In* Steadman, J. M. Nature into myth p131-37

Donne, J. B.

African art and Paris studios, 1905-20. *In* Greenhalgh, M. and Megaw, J. V. S. eds. Art in society p105-20

Donne, John, 1573-1631

About

Allen, D. C. John Donne's knowledge of Renaissance medicine. *In* Roberts, J. R. ed. Essential articles for the study of John Donne's poetry p93-106

Gilman, E. B. The Pauline perspectives in Donne, Herbert, and Greville. *In* Gilman, E. B. The curious perspective p167-203

Hardy, B. N. Thinking and feeling in the songs and sonnets of John Donne. *In* Hardy, B. N. The advantage of lyric p18-32

Hughes, M. Y. Kidnapping Donne. *In* Roberts, J. R. ed. Essential articles for the study of John Donne's poetry p37-57

Hughes, M. Y. Some of Donne's 'Ecstasies.' *In* Roberts, J. R. ed. Essential articles for the study of John Donne's poetry p259-70

Knights, L. C. All or nothing: a theme in John Donne. *In* Knights, L. C. Explorations 3 p95-100

Le Comte, E. S. Jack Donne: from rake to husband. *In* Le Comte, E. S. Poets' riddles p44-66

Lewalski, B. K. John Donne: writing after the copy of a metaphorical God. *In* Lewalski, B. K. Protestant poetics and the seventeenth-century religious lyric p253-82

McCanles, M. The dialectical structure of the metaphysical lyric: Donne, Herbert, Marvell. *In* McCanles, M. Dialectical criticism and Renaissance literature p54-119

McCanles, M. Paradox in Donne. *In* Roberts, J. R. ed. Essential articles for the study of John Donne's poetry p220-35

Manlove, C. N. Donne and Marvell. *In* Manlove, C. N. Literature and reality, 1600-1800 p3-15

Martz, L. L. Donne and the meditative tradition. *In* Roberts, J. R. ed. Essential articles for the study of John Donne's poetry p142-49

Ornstein, R. Donne, Montaigne, and natural law. *In* Roberts, J. R. ed. Essential articles for the study of John Donn'e poetry p129-41

Richards, I. A. The interinanimations of words. *In* Richards, I. A. Poetries p71-84

Tillotson, K. M. Donne's poetry in the nineteenth century (1800-1872). *In* Roberts, J. R. ed. Essential articles for the study of John Donne's poetry p20-33

About individual works
The anniversaries

Colie, R. L. The rhetoric of transcendence. *In* Roberts, J. R. ed. Essential articles for the study of John Donne's poetry p199-219

Mahony, P. J. The anniversaries: Donne's rhetorical approach to evil. *In* Roberts, J. R. ed. Essential articles for the study of John Donne's poetry p363-67

Quinn, D. B. Donne's Anniversaries as celebration. *In* Roberts, J. R. ed. Essential articles for the study of John Donne's poetry p368-73

Sicherman, C. M. Donne's timeless Anniversaries. *In* Roberts, J. R. ed. Essential articles for the study of John Donne's poetry p374-86

Stanwood, P. G. "Essentiall joye" in Donne's Anniversaries. *In* Roberts, J. R. ed. Essential articles for the study of John Donne's poetry p387-96

Donne, John, 1573-1631—About individual works—*Continued*

Biathanatos

Sullivan, E. W. Authoritative manuscript corrections in Donne's Biathanatos. *In* Virginia. University. Bibliographical Society. Studies in bibliography v28 p268-76

Sullivan, E. W. Manuscript materials in the first edition of Donne's Biathanatos. *In* Virginia University Bibliographical Society. Studies in bibliography v31 p210-21

Sullivan, E. W. Marginal rules as evidence. *In* Virginia. University. Bibliographical Society. Studies in bibliography v30 p171-80

The canonization

Rooney, W. J. "The canonization"—the language of paradox reconsidered. *In* Roberts, J. R. ed. Essential articles for the study of John Donne's poetry p271-78

La Corona

Chambers, A. B. The meaning of the "temple" in Donne's La Corona. *In* Roberts, J. R. ed. Essential articles for the study of John Donne's poetry p349-52

The ecstasy

Gardner, Dame H. L. The argument about 'The ectasy.' *In* Roberts, J. R. ed. Essential articles for the study of John Donne's poetry p239-58

Hughes, M. Y. Some of Donne's 'Ecstasies.' *In* Roberts, J. R. ed. Essential articles for the study of John Donne's poetry p259-70

Marotti, A. F. Donne and "The extasie". *In* Sloan, T. O. and Waddington, R. B. eds. The rhetoric of Renaissance poetry p140-73

Richards, I. A. "The exstasie." *In* Richards, I. A. Poetries p85-94

Elegies

LaBranche, A. 'Blanda elegeia': the background to Donne's 'Elegies.' *In* Roberts, J. R. ed. Essential articles for the study of John Donne's poetry p399-410

Epithalamion made at Lincoln's Inn

Novarr, D. Donne's 'Epithalamion made at Lincoln's Inn': context and date. *In* Roberts, J. R. ed. Essential articles for the study of John Donne's poetry p439-50

First anniversary

Love, H. The argument of Donne's First anniversary. *In* Roberts, J. R. ed. Essential articles for the study of John Donne's poetry p355-62

Good Friday, 1613. Riding Westward

Chambers, A. B. Goodfriday, 1613. Riding Westward: the poem and the tradition. *In* Roberts, J. R. ed. Essential articles for the study of John Donne's poetry p333-48

Holy sonnets

Peterson, D. L. John Donne's Holy sonnets and the Anglican doctrine of contrition. *In* Roberts, J. R. ed. Essential articles for the study of John Donne's poetry p313-23

Holy sonnets (VIII and XVII)

Grenander, M. E. Holy sonnets VIII and XVII: John Donne. *In* Roberts, J. R. ed. Essential articles for the study of John Donne's poetry p324-32

Letters to severall persons of honour

Stapleton, L. The theme of virtue in Donne's verse epistles. *In* Roberts, J. R. ed. Essential articles for the study of John Donne's poetry p451-61

The metempsychosis

Murray, W. A. What was the soul of the apple? *In* Roberts, J. R. ed. Essential articles for the study of John Donne's poetry p462-74

A nocturnall upon S. Lucies day

Miller, C. H. Donne's "A nocturnall upon S. Lucies day" and the nocturns of matins. *In* Roberts, J. R. ed. Essential articles for the study of John Donne's poetry p305-10

The relique

Morillo, M. G. Donne's "The relique" as satire. *In* Tulane Studies in English v21 p47-55

Satires

Andreasen, N. J. C. Theme and structure in Donne's Satyres. *In* Roberts, J. R. ed. Essential articles for the study of John Donne's poetry p411-23

Williams, A. L. What Pope did to Donne. *In* A Provision of human nature p111-19

Satires (III)

Sloan, T. O. The persona as rhetor: an interpretation of Donne's Satyre III. *In* Roberts, J. R. ed. Essential articles for the study of John Donne's poetry p424-38

The sunne rising

Dyson, A. E. and Lovelock, J. Contracted thus: Donne's 'The sunne rising.' *In* Dyson, A. E. and Lovelock, J. Masterful images p21-28

A valediction forbidding mourning

Freccero, J. Donne's "Valediction: forbidding mourning." *In* Roberts, J. R. ed. Essential articles for the study of John Donne's poetry p279-304

Trilling, L. John Donne: A valediction: forbidding mourning. *In* Trilling, L. Prefaces to The experience of literature p188-93

Allusions

Johnson, B. H. Classical allusions in the poetry of Donne. *In* Roberts, J. R. ed. Essential articles for the study of John Donne's poetry p85-92

Criticism, Textual

Redpath, T. Some textual problems in Donne's 'Songs and sonets.' *In* English Association. Essays and studies, 1979 p57-79

Sullivan, E. W. Marginal rules as evidence. *In* Virginia. University. Bibliographical Society. Studies in bibliography v30 p171-80

Knowledge—Medicine

Allen, D. C. John Donne's knowledge of Renaissance medicine. *In* Roberts, J. R. ed. Essential articles for the study of John Donne's poetry p93-106

Language—Style

See Donne, John, 1573-1631—Style

Monuments, etc.

Gardner, Dame H. L. Dean Donne's monument in St. Paul's. *In* Evidence in literary scholarship p29-44

Donne, John, 1573-1631—*Continued*

Sources

Guss, D. L. Donne's Petrarchism. *In* Roberts, J. R. ed. Essential articles for the study of John Donne's poetry p150-58

Murray, W. A. Donne and Paracelsus: an essay in interpretation. *In* Roberts, J. R. ed. Essential articles for the study of John Donne's poetry p122-28

Style

Lederer, J. John Donne and the emblematic practice. *In* Roberts, J. R. ed. Essential articles for the study of John Donne's poetry p107-21

Sloan, T. O. The rhetoric in the poetry of John Donne. *In* Roberts, J. R. ed. Essential articles for the study of John Donne's poetry p189-98

Technique

See Donne, John, 1573-1631—Style

Versification

Moloney, M. F. Donne's metrical practice. *In* Roberts, J. R. ed. Essential articles for the study of John Donne's poetry p171-77

Stein, A. S. Meter and meaning in Donne's verse. *In* Roberts, J. R. ed. Essential articles for the study of John Donne's poetry p161-70

Donne, John, 1604-1662

About individual works
The epistle dedicatory

Sullivan, E. W. Authoritative manuscript corrections in Donne's Biathanatos. *In* Virginia. University. Bibliographical Society. Studies in bibliography v28 p268-76

Sullivan, E. W. Manuscript materials in the first edition of Donne's Biathanatos. *In* Virginia. University. Bibliographical Society. Studies in bibliography v31 p210-21

Donnelly, John

The metaphysics of peace. *In* Roth, R. J. ed. Person and community p25-41

Donnelly, John Patrick

Calvinist Thomism. *In* Viator: medieval and Renaissance studies v7 p441-55

Death and Ivan Ilych. *In* Donnelly, J. P. ed. Language, metaphysics, and death p116-30

Suicide and rationality. *In* Donnelly, J. P. ed. Language, metaphysics, and death p88-105

Donnini, Rosita. See Selan, V. jt. auth.

Donno, Elizabeth Story

The unhoopable Marvell. *In* Friedenreich, K. ed. Tercentenary essays in honor of Andrew Marvell p21-46

Donoghue, Denis

Eliot and the Criterion. *In* The Literary criticism of T. S. Eliot p20-41

John Butler Yeats. *In* Abroad in America: Visitors to the new Nation, 1776-1914 p260-69

The sovereign ghost
Contents

The American style of failure
The essential power
The eye and the mind's eye
Nuances of a theme by Allen Tate
The sovereign ghost
"The word within a word"
Also in The Wasteland in different voices p185-201
Writing against time

About individual works
Thieves of fire

Nemerov, H. Figures of thought. *In* Nemerov, H. Figures of thought p18-29

Richards, I. A. The enlightening eye. *In* Richards, I. A. Complementarities p127-35

Donoso, José

About

Nigro, K. F. From criollismo to the grotesque: approaches to José Donoso. *In* Forster, M. H. ed. Tradition and renewal p208-32

About individual works
The obscene bird of night

MacAdam, A. J. José Donoso: endgame. *In* MacAdam, A. J. Modern Latin American narratives p110-20

Donoso Cortés, Juan, Marques de Valdegamas

About

Wilhelmsen, F. D. Donoso Cortés and the meaning of political power. *In* Wilhelmsen, F. D. Christianity and political philosophy p139-73

Donovan, Arthur L.

Toward a social history of technological ideas: Joseph Black, James Watt, and the separate condenser. *In* Bugliarello, G. and Doner, D. B. eds. The history and philosophy of technology p19-30

Donovan, Bruce Elliot

Prometheus bound 114-117 reconsidered. *In* Harvard Studies in classical philology v77 p125-27

Donovan, Joseph Campbell

Afterword: critical re-vision. *In* Donovan, J. C. ed. Feminist literary criticism p74-81

Donovan, Mortimer J.

Middle English Emare and the cloth worthily wrought. *In* The Learned and the lewed p337-42

Donovan, Robert Alan

The mind of Jane Austen. *In* Weinsheimer, J. ed. Jane Austen today p109-27

Doolittle, Hilda

About

Kammer, J. The art of silence and the forms of women's poetry. *In* Gilbert, S. M. and Gubar, S. eds. Shakespeare's sisters p153-64

Thurley, G. Phenomenalist idioms: Doolittle, Moore, Levertov. *In* Thurley, G. The American moment p109-25

About individual works

Trilogy: The walls do not fall, Tribute to the angels, The flowering of the rod

Gubar, S. The echoing spell of H. D's Trilogy. *In* Gilbert, S. M. and Gubar, S. eds. Shakespeare's sisters p200-18

Kunitz, S. J. H. D.'s War trilogy. *In* Kunitz, S. J. A kind of order, a kind of folly p204-09

Doomsday book. See Domesday book

Doors. See Church doors

Doors (in religion, folk-lore, etc.)

Coomaraswamy, A. K. Symplegades. *In* Coomaraswamy, A. K. Selected papers v 1 p521-44

Doppler effect

Burbidge, G. and Burbidge, M. Modern riddles of cosmology. *In* Neyman, J. ed. The heritage of Copernicus: theories "pleasing to the mind" p116-39

See also Red shift

Doppler shift. See Doppler effect

Doran, Barbara Giusti

Origins and consolidation of field theory in nineteenth-century Britain: from the mechanical to the electromagnetic view of nature. *In* Historical studies in the physical sciences v6 p133-260

Doran, Charles F.

Oil politics and the rise of codependence. *In* Orr, D. W. and Soroos, M. S. eds. The global predicament p195-208

Doran, Madeleine. See entry in Part 2 under title: English Renaissance drama

Dorenlot, Françoise

Unity of purpose through art and action. *In* Courcel, M. H. de, ed. Malraux p129-40

Dorfer, Ingemar N. H.

Science and technology policy in Sweden. *In* Science policies of industrial nations p169-90

Dorfman, Gerald Allen

The Heath years: some further thoughts about union influence. *In* Kramnick, I. ed. Is Britain dying? p55-65

Dorgelès, Roland

About individual works
Wooden crosses

Flower, J. E. The soldier's stage: Roland Dorgelès, Les croix de bois. *In* Klein, H. M. ed. The First World War in fiction p53-62

Doric columns. See Columns, Ionic

Dorling, Geoffrey

Approaches to the teaching of special relativity. *in* Einstein p245-60

Dornan, Peter

Andrei Sakharov: the conscience of a liberal scientist. *In* Tokes, R. L. ed. Dissent in the USSR p354-417

Dorsch, Eduard

About

Albrecht, E. A. Eduard Dorsch and the Civil War. *In* The German contribution to the building of the Americas p275-87

Dorsch, T. S.

Literary history and criticism: general works. *In* English Association. The year's work in English studies v53 p17-36

Literary history and criticism: general works [another essay] *In* English Association. The year's work in English studies v54 p17-36

Literary history and criticism: general works [another essay] *In* English Association. The year's work in English studies, v55 p17-33

Literary history and criticism: general works [another essay] *In* English Association. The year's work in English studies, v56 p17-34

Literary history and criticism: general works [another essay] *In* English Association. The year's work in English studies, v57 p1-10

Dorsett, Lyle W.

Kansas City and the New Deal. *In* Braeman, J.; Bremner, R. H. and Brody, D. eds. The New Deal v2 p407-19

Dorsey, David

Minority literature in the service of cultural pluralism. In Minority language and literature p16-19

Dorsey, Gray L.

Legal ethics and the adversary system. *In* Hook, S.; Kurtz, P. and Todorovich, M. eds. The ethics of teaching and scientific research p99-115

A proposal for a new division of the curriculum. *In* Hook, S.; Kurtz, P. W. and Todorovich, M. eds. The philosophy of the curriculum: the need for general education p247-52

Dorsinville, Max

Senghor or the song of exile. *In* Exile and tradition p62-73

Dorson, Richard Mercer

The African connection: comments on African folklore in the New World. *In* Crowley, D. J. ed. African folklore in the New World p87-91

About

Dundes, A. African and Afro-American tales. *In* Crowley, D. J. ed. African folklore in the New World p35-53

Dos. See Dowry

Dos Passos, John

About

Knowles, A. S. Dos Passos in the twenties. *In* French, W. G. ed. The twenties p123-37

Morris, W. John Dos Passos. *In* Morris, W. Earthly delights, unearthly adornments p123-29

Sanders, D. A. John Dos Passos as conservative. *In* Filler, L. ed. A question of quality: popularity and value in modern creative writing p115-23

Wagner, L. W. John Dos Passos: reaching past poetry. *In* Essays in honor of Russel B. Nye p226-46

About individual works
The great days

Farrell, J. T. How should we rate Dos Passos? *In* Farrell, J. T. Literary essays, 1954-1974 p118-21

A pushcart at the curb

Wagner, L. W. John Dos Passos: reaching past poetry. *In* Essays in honor of Russel B. Nye p226-46

Three soldiers

Cooperman, S. John Dos Passos' Three soldiers: aesthetics and the doom of individualism. *In* Klein, H. M. ed. The First World War in fiction p23-31

U.S.A.

Bradbury, M. The denuded place: war and form in Parade's end and U.S.A. *In* Klein, H. M. ed. The First World War in fiction p193-209

Donald, M. The traditional novel. *In* Donald, M. The American novel in the twentieth century p13-72

Dos Santos, Theotonio. See Santos, Theotonio dos

Douglass, Frederick—About individual works
—Narrative of the life of Frederick Douglass, an American slave, written by himself—*Continued*

O'Meally, R. G. Frederick Douglass' 1845 Narrative: the text was meant to be preached. *In* Fisher, D. and Stepto, R. B. eds. Afro-American literature p192-211

Stepto, R. B. Narration, authentication, and authorial control in Frederick Douglass' Narrative of 1845. *In* Fisher, D. and Stepto, R. B. eds. Afro-American literature p178-91

Bibliography

Turner, W. B. The polemicists: David Walker, Frederick Douglass, Booker T. Washington, and W. E. B. Du Bois. *In* Inge, M. T.; Duke, J. M. and Bryer, J. R. eds. Black American writers v 1 p47-132

Douglass, Joseph Henry, and Smythe, Mabel Murphy
The Black family. *In* The Black American reference book p316-40

Dover, Kenneth James
Ancient interpolation in Aristophanes. *In* Illinois classical studies, v2 1977 p136-62

Dovizi, Bernardo, da Bibbiena, Cardinal

About individual works
La Calandria

Clubb, L. G. Italian Renaissance comedy. *In* Ruggiers, P. G. ed. Versions of medieval comedy p191-210

Dowden, Edward

About individual works
The life of Percy Bysshe Shelley

Arnold, M. Shelley. *In* Arnold, M. The last word p305-27

Dowley, Francis Hotham
Giacinto Brandi's paintings at the Palazzo Taverna. *In* Enggass, R. C. and Stokstad, M. eds. Hortus imaginum p165-73

The moment in eighteenth-century art criticism. *In* Studies in eighteenth-century culture v5 p317-36

Dowling, John Clarkson
Moratín's circle of friends: intellectual ferment in Spain, 1780-1800. *In* Studies in eighteenth-century culture v5 p165-83

Dowling, William C.
Boswell and the problem of biography. *In* Studies in biography p73-93

Downs, Anthony
The impact of housing policies on family life in the United States since World War II. *In* Rossi, A. S.; Kagan, J. and Hareven, T. K. eds. The family p163-80

Downs, Ernest C.
The struggle of the Louisiana Tunica Indians for recognition. *In* Williams, W. L. ed. Southeastern Indians since the removal era p72-89

Downs, Robert Bingham
Books that changed the South
Contents

An American Pepys
American statesman
Antebellum South
Black folktales
Black protestant
Father of Waters
The first American
Folk hero
From slavery to freedom
The great compromiser
Hated Helper
History versus legend
Hymn of hate
Moonlight and magnolia
Nation within a nation
Nostalgia for never-never land
Political philosopher
Reconstruction to the new freedom
Regional inventory
Romantic New Orleans
Slave plantation
Southern panorama
Southern traveler
Terrestrial paradise
Yarns of frontier life

Books that changed the world
Contents

American firebrand
Anatomy of power politics
The Book of Books
Celestial revolution
Crusader for the lowly
Dawn of scientific medicine
Discoverer of vaccination
Epic poet
Famed fabulist
Father of scientific anatomy
Fathers of the Church
First of a new genus
Greek and Roman scientists
Harbinger of the atomic age
Heartland and world-island
Ideas in the flow of civilization
Individual versus state
Judge of nature and mankind
Leviathan against elephant
Masters of dramatic art
Patron saint of free enterprise
Prophet of the proletariat
Psychologist of the unconscious
Sense of the past
Study in megalomania
Survival of the fittest
System of the world
Too many mouths
Universal man
Upsetting the balance of nature

Changing trends in academic libraries. *In* As much to learn as to teach p203-16

Down's syndrome. See Mongolism

Dowry

Venice

Chojnacki, S. J. Dowries and kinsmen in early Renaissance Venice. *In* Stuard, S. M. ed. Women in medieval society p173-98

Dowson, Ernest Christopher

About

Connolly, C. Ernest Dowson. *In* Connolly, C. The evening colonnade p159-62

Dowty, Alan
A comparative approach to the study of international conflict. *In* The Dynamics of the arms race p193-201

International guarantees with special reference to the Middle East. *In* The Dynamics of the arms race p215-30

Doxey, Margaret P.
Canada's international connections. *In* The Year book of world affairs, 1978 p43-63

The Commonwealth Secretariat. *In* The Year book of world affairs, 1976 p69-96

Continuity and change in the Commonwealth. *In* The Year book of worll affairs, 1979 p76-101

Doxey, Margaret P.—*Continued*

International organization in foreign policy perspective. *In* The Year book of world affairs, 1975 p173-95

Doyle, Anthony Ian

The shaping of the Vernon and Simeon manuscripts. *In* Chaucer and Middle English studies in honour of Rossell Hope Robbins p328-41

Doyle, Anthony Ian, and Pace, George B.

Further texts of Chaucer's minor poems. *In* Virginia. University. Bibliographical Society. Studies in bibliography v28 p41-61

Doyle, Sir Arthur Conan

About

Lambert, G. Final problems: Sir Arthur Conan Doyle. *In* Lambert, G. The dangerous edge p31-63

Ousby, I. Arthur Conan Doyle. *In* Ousby, I. Bloodhounds of heaven p139-75

About individual works

The adventure of the Sussex vampire

O'Toole, L. M. Analytic and synthetic approaches to narrative structure: Sherlock Holmes and 'The Sussex vampire'. *In* Fowler, R. ed. Style and structure in literature p143-76

The Red-Headed League

Sayers, D. L. The dates in The Red-Headed League; excerpt from "Unpopular opinions." *In* Sayers, D. L. The whimsical Christian p60-72

Characters—Sherlock Holmes

Ousby, I. Arthur Conan Doyle. *In* Ousby, I. Bloodhounds of heaven p139-75

Doyle, Denis P.

The politics of choice: a view from the bridge. *In* Parents, teachers, and children: prospects for choice in American education p227-55

Doyle, Mike, 1928-

Proteus at Roblin Lake: Al Purdy's transformations. *In* Woodcock, G. ed. Poets and critics p92-109

Doyle, William

Was there an aristocratic reaction in pre-revolutionary France? *In* French society and the Revolution p3-28

Drabble, Margaret

Hardy and the natural world. *In* Drabble, M. ed. The genius of Thomas Hardy p162-69

About

Showalter, E. Beyond the female aesthetic: contemporary women novelists. *In* Showalter, E. A literature of their own p298-319

About individual works

Arnold Bennett: a biography

Sale, R. H. Huxley & Bennett, Bedford & Drabble. *In* Sale, R. H. On not being good enough p93-105

The needle's eye

Sale, R. H. Williams, Weesner, Drabble. *In* Sale, R. H. On not being good enough p42-53

Draenos, Stan Spyros

Thinking without a ground: Hannah Arendt and the contemporary situation of understanding. *In* Hannah Arendt: the recovery of the public world p209-24

Dragonflies

Africa, Central

Pinhey, E. C. G. Dragonflies (Odonata) of Central Africa. *In* The Occasional papers of the Rhodes-Livingstone Museum p539-648

Dragún, Osvaldo

About

Schmidt, D. L. The theater of Osvaldo Dragún. *In* Lyday, L. F. and Woodyard. G. W. eds. Dramatists in revolt p77-94

Drain, Richard

'The waste land': the prison and the key. *In* The Waste land in different voices p29-45

Drake, Daniel

About

Shapiro, H. D. The Western Academy of Natural Sciences of Cincinnati and the structure of science in the Ohio Valley, 1810-1850. *In* Oleson, A. and Brown, S. C. eds. The pursuit of knowledge in the early American Republic p219-47

Drake, Stillman

Galileo's new science of motion. *In* Bonelli, M. L. R. and Shea, W. R. eds. Reason, experiment, and mysticism in the scientific revolution p131-56

Drama

Fergusson, F. Poetry and drama. *In* Symbolism and modern literature p13-25

Hermassi, K. C. What theatre means. *In* Hermassi, K. C. Polity and theater in historical perspective p3-24

Miller, A. On social plays. *In* Miller, A. The theater essays of Arthur Miller p51-68

Veltruský, J. Dramatic text as a component of theater. *In* Matejka, L. and Titunik, I. R. eds. Semiotics of art p94-117

See also Acting; Comedy; Dialogue; Dramatic criticism; Dramatists; Farce; Historical drama; Interludes; Masques; Melodrama; One-act plays; Religion in drama; Stage adaptations; Television plays; Theater; Tragedy; Tragicomedy; Verse drama

Authorship

See Playwriting

Bibliography—Catalogs

Stoddard, R. E. A catalogue of the dramatic imprints of David and Thomas Longworth, 1802-1821. *In* American Antiquarian Society. Proceedings v84 pt2 p317-98

Chorus

Jones, G. P. 'Henry V': the chorus and the audience. *In* Shakespeare survey v31 p93-104

Lenson, D. R. Choric equivalents in modern drama. *In* Lenson, D. R. Achilles' choice p117-36

Chorus (Greek drama)

Lenson, D. R. Choric equivalents in modern drama. *In* Lenson, D. R. Achilles' choice p117-36

History and criticism

Chiaromonte, N. The political theater. *In* Chiaromonte, N. The worm of consciousness, and other essays p127-52

Goldman, M. The ghost of joy: reflections on romanticism and the forms of modern drama. *In* Bornstein, G. ed. Romantic and modern p53-68

Grimm, R. Naturalism and epic drama. *In* Mews, S. and Knust, H. eds. Essays on Brecht p3-27

Dramatic criticism—*Continued*

Simon, J. I. What is taste? *In* Simon, J. I. Singularities p92-98

Simon, J. I. When you write that, smile! *In* Simon, J. I. Singularities p81-83

See also Moving picture criticism

History

Jones, T. B. and Nicol, B. de B. Conclusion. *In* Jones, T. B. and Nicol, B. de B. Neo-classical dramatic criticism, 1560-1770 p177-81

Jones, T. B. and Nicol, B. de B. From Robortello to Ben Jonson. *In* Jones, T. B. and Nicol, B. de B. Neo-classical dramatic criticism, 1560-1770 p18-48

Jones, T. B. and Nicol, B. de B. Introduction: Aristotle and Horace. *In* Jones, T. B. and Nicol, B. de B. Neoclassical dramatic criticism, 1560-1770 p 1-17

England—History

Jones, T. B. and Nicol, B. de B. The English scene—Restoration and early eighteenth-century criticism. *In* Jones, T. B. and Nicol, B. de B. Neo-classical dramatic criticism, 1560-1770 p95-123

France—History

Jones, T. B. and Nicol, B. de B. French neo-classicism. *In* Jones, T. B. and Nicol, B. de B. Neo-classical dramatic criticism, 1560-1770 p49-94

United States

Brustein, R. S. Freedom and constraint in the American theatre. *In* Brustein, R. S. The culture watch p31-46

Dramatic monologue. See Monologue

Dramatic music. See Music in theaters

Dramatic plots. See Plots (Drama, novel, etc.)

Dramatists

Kauffmann, S. Homosexual drama and its disguises. *In* Kauffmann, S. Persons of the drama p291-94

Kauffmann, S. On the acceptability of the homosexual. *In* Kauffmann, S. Persons of the drama p295-98

Dramaturgy. See Drama—Technique

Draper, Gerald Irving A. Dare

Wars of national liberation and war criminality. *In* Howard, M. ed. Restraints on war p135-62

Draper, Joan

The Ecole des beaux-arts and the architectural profession in the United States: the case of John Galen Howard. *In* Kostof, S. ed. The architect p209-37

Draper, Patricia

!Kung women: contrasts in sexual egalitarianism in foraging and sedentary contexts. *In* Reiter, R. R. ed. Toward an anthropology of women p77-109

The learning environment for aggression and anti-social behavior among the !Kung. *In* Montagu, A. ed. Learning non-aggression p31-53

Draper, Ronald P.

Hardy and respectability. *In* An English miscellany p179-207

Draper, Thomas F. See Veatch, R. M. jt. auth.

Drawing

Berger, J. Drawing. *In* Berger, J. The look of things p165-71

Wollheim, R. On drawing an object. *In* Margolis, J. Z. ed. Philosophy looks at the arts p249-72

See also Drawing, Psychology of; Perspective

Scientific applications

See Scientific illustration

Drawing, Psychology of

Kennedy, J. M. Perception, pictures, and the etcetera principle. *In* Perception p209-26

Korzenik, D. Saying it with pictures. *In* Perkins, D. and Leondar, B. eds. The arts and cognition p192-207

Draya, Ren

The fiction of Tennessee Williams. *In* Tennessee Williams: a tribute p647-62

Drayton, Michael

Bibliography

Hardin, R. F. Michael Drayton. *In* Logan, T. P. and Smith, D. S. eds. The popular school p137-47

The dream of the rood

Lee, A. A. Toward a critique of The dream of the rood. *In* Anglo-Saxon poetry: essays in appreciation p163-91

Smith, J. The garments that honour the Cross in The dream of the rood. *In* Anglo-Saxon England 4 p29-35

Dreams

Ayer, Sir A. J. Professor Malcolm on dreams. *In* Dunlop, C. E. M. ed. Philosophical essays on dreaming p127-48

Barfield, O. Dream, myth, and philosophical double vision. *In* Barfield, O. The rediscovery of meaning, and other essays p22-31

Blumenfeld, D. and Blumenfeld, J. B. Can I know that I am not dreaming? *In* Hooker, M. ed. Descartes p234-55

Bouwsma, O. K. Descartes' skepticism of the senses. *In* Dunlop, C. E. M. ed. Philosophical essays on dreaming p52-63

Caldwell, R. L. Malcolm and the criterion of sleep. *In* Dunlop, C. E. M. ed. Philosophical essays on dreaming p157-73

Canfield, J. V. Judgments in sleep. *In* Dunlop, C. E. M. ed. Philosophical essays on dreaming p149-56

Chappell, V. C. The concept of dreaming. *In* Dunlop, C. E. M. ed. Philosophical essays on dreaming p280-308

Chihara, C. S. What dreams are made on. *In* Dunlop, C. E. M. ed. Philosophical essays on dreaming p251-64

Curley, E. M. Dreaming and conceptual revision. *In* Dunlop, C. E. M. ed. Philosophical essays on dreaming p317-46

Dennett, D. C. Are dreams experiences? *In* Dunlop, C. E. M. ed. Philosophical essays on dreaming p227-50

Landesman, C. Dreams: two types of explanations. *In* Dunlop, C. E. M. ed. Philosophical essays on dreaming p309-16

MacDonald, M. Sleeping and waking. *In* Dunlop, C. E. M. ed. Philosophical essays on dreaming p64-80

Malcolm, N. Dreaming and skepticism. *In* Dunlop, C. E. M. ed. Philosophical essays on dreaming p103-26

Dreams—*Continued*

Morris, W. Unearthly adornments. *In* Morris, W. Earthly delights, unearthly adornments p181-89

Nakhnikian, G. Descartes's dream argument. *In* Hooker, M. ed. Descartes p256-86

Palombo, S. R. Dreams, memory, and the origin of thought. *In* Thought, consciousness, and reality p49-83

Pears, D. F. Dreaming. *In* Dunlop, C. E. M. ed. Philosophical essays on dreaming p205-26

Siegler, F. A. Remembering dreams. *In* Dunlop, C. E. M. ed. Philosophical essays on dreaming p265-79

Ullman, M. Psychiatry and parapsychology: the consummation of an uncertain romance. *In* Parapsychology: its relation to physics, biology, psychology, and psychiatry p171-207

Wood, P. H. Television as dream. *In* Television as a cultural force p17-35

Yost, R. M. and Kalish, D. Miss MacDonald on sleeping and waking. *In* Dunlop, C. E. M. ed. Philosophical essays on dreaming p81-102

See also Children's dreams; Nightmares; Psychoanalysis

Dreams in literature

Hanna, R. Cresseid's dream and Henryson's Testament. *In* Chaucer and Middle English studies in honour of Rossell Hope Robbins p288-97

Hardy, B. N. Fantasy and dream. *In* Hardy, B. N. Tellers and listeners p19-55

Lee, A. A. Toward a critique of The dream of the rood. *In* Anglo-Saxon poetry: essays in appreciation p163-91

Lesser, S. O. Macbeth: drama and dream. *In* Lesser, S. O. The whispered meanings p212-34

Dreiser, Theodore

About

Auchincloss, L. Dreiser's love of America. *In* Auchincloss, L. Life, law and letters p111-19

Berryman, J. Enslavement: Three American cases; Theodore Dreiser. *In* Berryman, J. The Freedom of the poet p185-89

Farrell, J. T. A Dreiser revival: introduction to the Laurel Dreiser. *In* Farrell, J. T. Literary essays, 1954-1974 p26-33

Frohock, W. M. Theodore Dreiser. *In* Walcutt, C. C. ed. Seven novelists in the American naturalist tradition p92-130

About individual works

An American tragedy

Frohock, W. M. Theodore Dreiser. *In* Walcutt, C. C. ed. Seven novelists in the American naturalist tradition p92-130

Harter, C. C. Strange bedfellows: The waste land and An American tragedy. *In* French, W. G. ed. The twenties p51-64

Sister Carrie

Goist, P. D. The city as noncommunity: Theodore Dreiser and Henry Blake Fuller. *In* Goist, P. D. From Main Street to State Street p68-79

The stoic

Gerber, P. L. Dreiser's Stoic: a study in literary frustration. *In* Literary monographs v7 p85-144

The titan

Berryman, J. Enslavement: Three American cases; Dreiser's "The titan." *In* Berryman, J. The freedom of the poet p190-97

Dreitzel, Hans Peter

On the political meaning of culture. *In* Beyond the crisis p83-129

Drew, Jane Beverly. See Fry, Jane Beverly (Drew)

Drew, Philip

Browning and philosophy. *In* Armstrong, I. ed. Robert Browning p104-41

Drew-Bear, Thomas

A fourth-century Latin soldier's epitaph at Nakolea. *In* Harvard Studies in classical philology v81 p257-74

Two ghost-words and a consul: inscriptions of Pergamum and Tarsus. *In* Harvard Studies in classical philology v79 p301-03

Drewry, Gavin

Parliament and penal policy. *In* Progress in penal reform p35-53

Dreyer, Carl Theodor

About

Truffaut, F. The whiteness of Carl Dreyer. *In* Truffaut, F. The films in my life p48-49

About individual works

The passion of Joan of Arc

Potamkin, H. A. The passion of Jeanne D'Arc. *In* Denby, D. ed. Awake in the dark p102-05

Dreyfus, Alfred

About

Robinson, C. Collective values. *In* Robinson, C. French literature in the nineteenth century p171-206

Dreyfus, Hubert L. and Haugeland, John

Husserl and Heidegger: philosophy's last stand. *In* Murray, M. E. ed. Heidegger and modern philosophy p222-38

Driesch, Hans Adolf Edward

About

Haraway, D. J. Reinterpretation or rehabilitation: an exercise in contemporary Marxist history of science. *In* Studies in history of biology, v2 p193-209

Drieu La Rochelle, Pierre

About individual works

The comedy of Charleroi

Dale, J. Drieu La Rochelle: the war as 'comedy.' *In* Klein, H. M. ed. The First World War in fiction p63-72

Drift

Wright, H. E. Glacial fluctuations, sea-level changes, and catastrophic floods. *In* Ramage, E. S. ed. Atlantis, fact or fiction? p161-74

Drinan, Robert F.

Should there be a legal right to die? *In* Weir, R. F. ed. Ethical issues in death and dying p297-307

Drinker, Elizabeth (Sandwith)

About

Scott, A. F. Self-portraits: three women. *In* Uprooted Americans p43-76

Drinking cups

Mertens, J. R. A white-ground cup by Euphronios. *In* Harvard Studies in classical philology v76 p271-81

Drinking vessels. See Drinking cups

Driscoll, James P.

Transsexuals. *In* Henslin, J. M. ed. Deviant life-styles p167-89

Driscoll, William J.

Independent study: a new emphasis for the 1970s. *In* Buxton, T. H. and Prichard, K. W. eds. Excellence in university teaching p232-38

Driver, C. J.

About

Smith, R. The plot beneath the skin: the novels of C. J. Driver. *In* Heywood, C. ed. Aspects of South African literature p145-54

Dromedaries. See Camels

Dronke, Peter

Two thirteenth-century religious lyrics. *In* Chaucer and Middle English studies in honour of Rossell Hope Robbins p392-406

Dronke, Peter, and Mann, Jill

Chaucer and the medieval Latin poets. *In* Brewer, D. S. ed. Geoffrey Chaucer p154-83

Drop-outs. See Dropouts

Dropouts

United States

Edelman, M. W. We are failing the children. *In* Gross, B. and Gross, R. eds. The children's rights movement p109-14

Dropsie College for Hebrew and Cognate Learning, Philadelphia

History—Sources

Ben-Horin, M. Scholars' "opinions": documents in the history of the Dropsie University. *In* Salo Wittmayer Baron v 1 p167-208

Dropsie University. See Dropsie College for Hebrew and Cognate Learning, Philadelphia

Droysen, Johann Gustav

About

Gilbert, F. Johann Gustav Droysen. *In* Gilbert, F. History p17-37

Momigliano, A. J. G. Droysen between Greeks and Jews. *In* Momigliano, A. Essays in ancient and modern historiography p307-23

Drubel, Richard. See Western, P. jt. auth.

Drucker, Peter Ferdinand

How to make the Presidency manageable. *In* Managing nonprofit organizations p280-88

Managing the public service institution. *In* Managing nonprofit organizations p16-31

Drug abuse

See also Drugs and youth

Physiological effect

See Drugs—Physiological effect

Research

Partridge, W. L. Uses and nonuses of anthropological data on drug abuse. *In* Eddy, E. M. and Partridge, W. L. eds. Applied anthropology in America p350-72

Treatment

Wittenberg, D. Art therapy for adolescent drug abusers. *In* Ulman, E. and Dachinger, P. ed. Art therapy p150-58

Drug abuse and military personnel. See Drugs and military personnel

Drug addicts. See Narcotic addicts

Drug research. See Pharmaceutical research

Drug therapy. See Chemotherapy

Drug trade

Law and legislation

See Drugs—Laws and legislation

Europe—History

Talbot, C. H. America and the European drug trade. *In* First images of America p833-44

Drugs

De Ropp, R. S. Drugs, yoga, and psychotransformism. *In* Needleman, J. and Lewis, D. eds. On the way to self knowledge p148-69

Laws and legislation—United States

Crout, J. R. Drug regulation by government: the nature of regulatory choices. *In* The Frontiers of human knowledge p59-68

Physiological effect

Huxley, A. L. Chemical persuasion; excerpt from "Brave new world revisited." *In* Knight, D. F. ed. Turning points p231-37

Research

See Pharmaceutical research

Drugs and military personnel

United States

Eisenhart, T. S. Rehabilitation: one man's opinion. *In* Henderson, G. ed. Human relations in the military p177-86

Thornton, O. D. The Vietnam connection. *In* Henderson, G. ed. Human relations in the military p163-75

Drugs and youth

United States

Lauer, R. H. Movement ideology, program, recruitment. *In* Lauer, R. H. ed. Social movements and social change p46-60

Drum language

Ong, W. J. African talking drums and oral noetics. *In* Ong, W. J. Interfaces of the word p92-120

Drums along the Mohawk (Motion picture)

O'Connor, J. E. A reaffirmation of American ideals: Drums along the Mohawk. *In* O'Connor, J. E. and Jackson, M. A. eds. American history/American film p97-119

Drury, Roger Wolcott

"Realism plus fantasy equals magic." *In* Horn Book Magazine. Crosscurrents of criticism p178-84

Drusus, M. Livius

About

Weinrib, E. J. The family connections of M. Livius Drusus Libo. *In* Harvard Studies in classical philology v72 p247-78

Dry, Murray

Congress. *In* Graham, G. J. and Graham, S. G. eds. Founding principles of American government p223-57

Dryden, Edgar A.

The limits of romance: a reading of The marble faun. *In* Baldwin, K. H. and Kirby, D. K. eds. Individual and community p17-48

Dryden, John

About

Adams, P. G. John Dryden's heavenly harmony. *In* Adams, P. G. Graces of harmony p57-86

Dryden, John—About—*Continued*

Brower, R. A. Dryden's epic manner and Virgil. *In* Brower, R. A. Mirror on mirror p103-22

Farley-Hills, D. John Dryden. *In* Farley-Hills, D. The benevolence of laughter: comic poetry of the Commonwealth and Restoration p99-131

Jones, T. B. and Nicol, B. de B. The English scene—Restoration and early eighteenth-century criticism. *In* Jones, T. B. and Nicol, B. de B. Neo-classical dramatic criticism, 1560-1770 p95-123

Manlove, C. N. Dryden. *In* Manlove, C. N. Literature and reality, 1600-1800 p57-75

Miner, E. R. Time, sequence, and plot in Restoration literature. *In* Studies in eighteenth-century culture v5 p67-85

Morgan, E. Dryden's drudging. *In* Morgan, E. Essays p100-17

Ormsby-Lennon, H. Radical physicians and conservative poets in Restoration England: Dryden among the doctors. *In* Studies in eighteenth-century culture v7 p389-411

Partridge, A. C. Form and language in English neo-classical poetry. *In* An English miscellany p131-48

Roper, A. Characteristics of Dryden's prose. *In* ELH essays for Earl R. Wasserman p375-99

Sigworth, O. F. A way of looking at some baroque poems. *In* Studies in eighteenth-century culture v4 p31-41

Trowbridge, F. H. Dryden on the Elizabethans. *In* Trowbridge, F. H. From Dryden to Jane Austen p3-12

Trowbridge, F. H. Perception, imagination, and feeling in Dryden's criticism. *In* Trowbridge, F. H. From Dryden to Jane Austen p32-77

Trowbridge, F. H. The place of rules in Dryden's criticism. *In* Trowbridge, F. H. From Dryden to Jane Austen p13-31

Zwicker, S. N. Politics and panegyric: the figural mode from Marvell to Pope. *In* Miner, E. R. ed. Literary uses of typology p115-46

About individual works
Absalom and Achitophel

Dyson, A. E. and Lovelock, J. Beyond the polemics: the opening of Dryden's Absalom and Achitophel. *In* Dyson, A. E. and Lovelock, J. Masterful images p71-96

Farley-Hills, D. John Dryden. *In* Farley-Hills, D. The benevolence of laughter: comic poetry of the Commonwealth and Restoration p99-131

Harth, J. P. Legends no histories: the case of Absalom and Achitophel. *In* Studies in eighteenth-century culture v4 p13-29

Maresca, T. E. The context of Dryden's Absalom and Achitophel. *In* ELH essays for Earl R. Wasserman p50-68

Maresca, T. E. Dryden. *In* Maresca, T. E. Epic to novel p3-75

Saslow, E. L. Shaftesbury cursed: Dryden's revision of the Achitophel lines. *In* Virginia. University. Bibliographical Society. Studies in bibliography v28 p276-83

All for love

Armstrong, R. The Great Chain of Being in Dryden's All for love. *In* A Provision of human nature p133-43

Novak, M. E. Criticism, adaptation, politics, and the Shakespearean model of Dryden's All for love. *In* Studies in eighteenth-century culture v7 p375-87

Defence of an Essay of dramatic poesy

Trowbridge, F. H. The place of rules in Dryden's criticism. *In* Trowbridge, F. H. From Dryden to Jane Austen p13-31

An essay of dramatic poesy

Davies, H. N. Dryden's Rahmenerzählung: the form of 'An essay of dramatick poesie.' *In* Røstvig, M. S. ed. Fair forms p119-46

The Indian emperor

Bowers, F. T. Current theories of copy-text, with an illustration from Dryden. *In* Bowers, F. T. Essays in bibliography, text, and editing p277-88

Mac Flecknoe

Maresca, T. E. Dryden. *In* Maresca, T. E. Epic to novel p3-75

Vieth, D. M. The discovery of the date of Mac Flecknoe. *In* Evidence in literary scholarship p63-87

Contemporaries

Miner, E. R. The poetics of the critical act: Dryden's dealings with rivals and predecessors. *In* Evidence in literary scholarship p45-62

Criticism, Textual

Bowers, F. T. Current theories of copy-text, with an illustration from Dryden. *In* Bowers, F. T. Essays in bibliography, text, and editing p277-88

Language

Sherbo, A. Dryden. *In* Sherbo, A. English poetic diction from Chaucer to Wordsworth p105-31

Style

Sherbo, A. Dryden. *In* Sherbo, A. English poetic diction from Chaucer to Wordsworth p105-31

Dryden, John, tr.

About individual works
The Aeneid

Brower, R. A. Visual and verbal translation of myth: Neptune in Virgil, Rubens, Dryden. *In* Brower, R. A. Mirror on mirror p17-45

Dualism

Lewis, H. D. Immortality and dualism. *In* Reason and religion p282-300

Shoemaker, S. Immortality and dualism. *In* Reason and religion p259-81

Sommers, F. Dualism in Descartes: the logical ground. *In* Hooker, M. ed. Descartes p223-33

Thakur, S. C. Telepathy, evolution and dualism. *In* Thakur, S. C. ed. Philosophy and psychical research p195-210

Wilson, M. D. Cartesian dualism. *In* Hooker, M. ed. Descartes p197-211

See also Idealism; Materialism; Mind and body; Monism; Soul

Du Bartas, Guillaume de Salluste, seigneur

Appreciation—England

Prescott, A. L. Du Bartas. *In* Prescott, A. L. French poets and the English Renaissance p167-234

Du Bartas, Guillaume de Salluste, seigneur
—*Continued*

Influence

Prescott, A. L. Du Bartas. *In* Prescott, A. L. French poets and the English Renaissance p167-234

Du Bellay, Joachim

Appreciation—England

Prescott, A. L. Du Bellay. *In* Prescott, A. L. French poets and the English Renaissance p37-75

Influence

Prescott, A. L. Du Bellay. *In* Prescott, A. L. French poets and the English Renaissance p 37-75

Duberman, Martin B.
The questions raised by Cuba. *In* Radosh, R. ed. The new Cuba: paradoxes and potentials p19-34

Dubin, Robert J.
Determining results in the generosity business. *In* Managing nonprofit organizations p270-79

Dubinin, Nikolaï Petrovich
Race and contemporary genetics. *In* United Nations Educational, Scientific and Cultural Organization. Race, science and society p68-94

Dublin in literature
Kain, R. M. Epiphanies of Dublin. *In* Staley, T. F. and Benstock, B. eds. Approaches to Joyce's Portrait p91-110

Dubnow, Semen Markovich

About

Kochan, L. Graetz and Dubnow: two Jewish historians in an alien world. *In* Essays in honour of E. H. Carr p352-66

Dubnow, Simon. See Dubnow, Semen Markovich

Du Bois, William Edward Burghardt

About

Downs, R. B. Black protestant. *In* Downs, R. B. Books that changed the South p197-207

Williamson, J. W. E. B. Du Bois as a Hegelian. *In* What was freedom's price? p21-49

About individual works
The autobiography of W. E. B. Du Bois

Howe, I. W. E. B. DuBois: glory and shame. *In* Howe, I. Celebrations and attacks p170-79

The souls of Black folk

Downs, R. B. Black protestant. *In* Downs, R. B. Books that changed the South p197-207

Bibliography

Turner, W. B. The polemicists: David Walker, Frederick Douglass, Booker T. Washington, and W. E. B. Du Bois. *In* Inge, M. T.; Duke, J. M. and Bryer, J. R. eds. Black American writers v 1 p47-132

Dubos, René Jules
Beast or angel?

Contents

Adventure and fantasy
The bestiality of the human species
Biological Freudianism
The camp and the open road
The cave and the horizon
Cities old and new
The clan and the stranger
Crowds and machines
The diversity of human life
Hauts lieux and monuments
Humanity and the beast
The humanness of the human species
The incarnations of humankind
Individualism and collectivity
Joie de vivre and happiness
Life in the city
Old World and New World
Pluralism and world order
The races of man
Revolutions and resurrection
The saga of the human species
Social adaptations
Technologic utopia
Ulysses and the American frontier
Yesterday's future shock

Creative adaptations to the future. *In* Aspects of American liberty p162-73

Hippocrates in modern dress. *In* Sobel, D. S. ed. Ways of health p205-30

Human ecology. *In* Sobel, D. S. ed. Ways of health p387-96

Medicine evolving; excerpts from "Man adapting." *In* Sobel, D. S. ed. Ways of health p21-44

Du Bouchet, André

About

Greene, R. W. André du Bouchet. *In* Greene, R. W. Six French poets of our time p124-39

Du Boulay, F. R. H.
The historical Chaucer. *In* Brewer, D. S. ed. Geoffrey Chaucer p33-57

Dubravius, Jan, Bp. of Olomouc

About

Lutz, C. E. A diamond and a Dürer in Dubravius' commentary on Martianus Capella. *In* Lutz, C. E. Essays on manuscripts and rare books p105-13

About individual works
A new book of good husbandry

Lutz, C. E. Bishop Dubravius on fishponds. *In* Lutz, C. E. Essays on manuscripts and rare books p99-104

Theriobulia

Lutz, C. E. The Theriobulia of Jan Dubravius. *In* Lutz, C. E. Essays on manuscripts and rare books p114-26

Dubravius, Johannes. See Dubravius, Jan, Bp. of Olomouc

Dubraw, Jan. See Dubravius, Jan, Bp. of Olomouc

Dubrovnik, Yugoslavia

Commerce—History

Krekić, B. Contributions of foreigners to Dubrovnik's economic growth in the late Middle Ages. *In* Viator: medieval and Renaissance studies v9 p375-94

Krekić, B. Four Florentine commercial companies in Dubrovnik (Ragusa) in the first half of the fourteenth century. *In* The Medieval City p25-41

Krekić, B. Italian creditors in Dubrovnik (Ragusa) and the Balkan trade, thirteenth through fifteenth centuries. *In* The Dawn of modern banking p241-54

Dubrovnik, Yugoslavia—*Continued*

Gentry

Stuard, S. M. Women in charter and statute law: medieval Ragusa/Dubrovnik. *In* Stuard, S. M. ed. Women in medieval society p199-208

Social conditions

Stuard, S. M. Women in charter and statute law: medieval Ragusa/Dubrovnik. *In* Stuard, S. M. ed. Women in medieval society p199-208

Dubuffet, Jean

About

Rosenberg, H. Dubuffet: shockers and fairy tales. *In* Rosenberg, H. Art on the edge p87-97

Duby, Georges

Lineage, nobility, and chivalry in the region of Mâcon during the twelfth century. *In* Family and society p16-40

Ducasse, Curt John

How stands the case for the reality of survival; excerpt from "A critical examination of the belief in a life after death." *In* Wheatley, J. M. O. and Edge, H. L. eds. Philosophical dimensions of parapsychology p282-94

Knowing the future. *In* Wheatley, J. M. O. and Edge, H. L. eds. Philosophical dimensions of parapsychology p193-97

The philosophical importance of "psychic phenomena." *In* Ludwig, J. K. ed. Philosophy and parapsychology p128-41

Also in Wheatley, J. M. O. and Edge, H. L. eds. Philosophical dimensions of parapsychology p30-45

A theory of the relation of causality to precognition; excerpt from "Broad on the relevance of psychical research to philosophy." *In* Wheatley, J. M. O. and Edge, H. L. eds. Philosophical dimensions of parapsychology p227-34

About individual works

Causation and the types of necessity

Brier, R. Mundle, Broad, Ducasse and the precognition problem. *In* Ludwig, J. K. ed. Philosophy and parapsychology p341-49

Ducasse, Isidore Lucien

About individual works

The lay of Maldoror

Bersani, L. Desire and metamorphosis. *In* Bersani, L. A future for Astyanax p189-229

Duccio di Buoninsegna. See Crucifixion with Saints Nicholas of Bari and Gregory (attributed to Duccio di Buoninsegna)

Ducey, Cathryn A.

Travel narratives of D. F. Sarmiento: a seminal frontier thesis. *In* Kagle, S. E. ed. America: exploration and travel p50-66

Duchamp, Marcel

About

Binkley, T. Piece: contra aesthetics. *In* Margolis, J. Z. ed. Philosophy looks at the arts p25-44

Krauss, R. E. Forms of readymade: Duchamp and Brancusi. *In* Krauss, R. E. Passages in modern sculpture p69-103

Paz, O. Marcel Duchamp, or, The castle of purity; excerpt. *In* Kaplan, P. and Manso, S. eds. Major European art movements, 1900-1945 p353-96

Rosenberg, H. Duchamp: private and public. *In* Rosenberg, H. Art on the edge p3-21

Tashjian, D. L. Marcel Duchamp and Man Ray. *In* Tashjian, D. L. Skyscraper primitives p49-70

Duchêne, François

The United States and European Community. *In* Rosecrance, R. N. ed. America as an ordinary country p87-109

Duchesneau, François

Malpighi, Descartes, and the epistemological problems of iatromechanism. *In* Bonelli, M. L. R. and Shea, W. R. eds. Reason, experiment, and mysticism in the scientific revolution p111-30

Duckert, Audrey R.

The winds of change. *In* James B. McMillan: essays in linguistics by his friends and colleagues p21-28

Duckles, Vincent Harris

The library of the mind: observations on the relationship between musical scholarship and bibliography. *In* Current thought in musicology p277-96

Duckworth, Alistair M.

Prospects and retrospects. *In* Weinsheimer, J. ed. Jane Austen today p 1-32

'Spillikins, paper ships, riddles, conundrums, and cards': games in Jane Austen's life and fiction. *In* Halperin, J. ed. Jane Austen p279-97

Dudek, Louis

About

Barbour, D. Poet as philosopher: Louis Dudek. *In* Woodcock, G. ed. Poets and critics p110-22

Dudevant, Amantine Lucile Aurore (Dupin)

See Sand, George, pseud of Mme Dudevant

Dudley, Billy J.

Military government and national integration in Nigeria. *In* Smock, D. R. and Bentsi-Enchill, K. eds. The search for national integration in Africa p28-46

Due process of law

Cohen, W. Congressional power to interpret due process and equal protection. *In* Stanford legal essays p79-96

Tushnet, M. V. The newer property: suggestion for the revival of substantive due process. *In* The Supreme Court review, 1975 p261-88

Wilkinson, J. H. Goss v. Lopez: the Supreme Court as school superintendent. *In* The Supreme Court review, 1975 p25-75

See also Double jeopardy; Right to counsel

China

Cohen, J. A. Due process? *In* Terrill, R. ed. The China difference p237-59

United States

Porter, M. C. That commerce shall be free: a new look at the old laissez-faire Court. *In* The Supreme Court review, 1976 p135-59

Duellum (The word)

Clausen, W. Duellum. *In* Harvard Studies in classical philology v75 p69-72

Duff, Raymond S. and Campbell, A. G. M.

Moral and ethical dilemmas in the special-care nursery. *In* Weir, R. F. ed. Ethical issues in death and dying p133-44

Dufresny, Charles, sieur de la Rivière

About

Brereton, G. The cynical generation: Dancourt, Regnard, Dufresny, Lesage. *In* Brereton, G. French comic drama p163-93

Dugan, Alan

About

Boyers, R. Alan Dugan: the poetry of survival. *In* Boyers, R. ed. Contemporary poetry in America p339-47

Also *in* Boyers, R. Excursions p193-200

Duggan, Hoyt N.

The role of formulas in the dissemination of a Middle English alliterative romance. *In* Virginia. University. Bibliographical Society. Studies in bibliography v29 p265-88

Duggan, Joseph J.

Formulaic diction in the Cantar de mio Cid and the old French epic. *In* Duggan, J. J. ed. Oral literature p74-83

Duhamel, Pierre Albert

Medieval intuition and seventeenth-century dialectic. *In* Medievalia et humanistica no. 5 p243-46

The novelist as prophet. *In* Friedman, M. J. and Lawson, L. A. eds. The added dimension p88-107

Duhem, Pierre Maurice Marie

About individual works

To save the phenomena, an essay on the idea of physical theory from Plato to Galileo

Donahue, W. H. The solid planetary spheres in post-Copernican natural philosophy. *In* The Copernican achievement p244-75

Heilbron, J. L. Commentary: Duhem and Donahue. *In* The Copernican achievement p276-84

Duke, Jean Maurice. See Duke, Maurice

Duke, Maurice

The baroque waste land of James Branch Cabell. *In* French, W. G. ed. The twenties p75-86

Duker, Abraham Gordon

Adam Mickiewicz's anti-Jewish period: studies in "The books of the Polish nation and of the Polish pilgrimage." *In* Salo Wittmayer Baron v 1 p311-43

Frankism as a movement of Polish-Jewish synthesis. *In* Király, B. K. ed. Tolerance and movements of religious dissent in Eastern Europe p133-64

Dumas, Bethany K.

E. E. Cummings in the twenties. *In* French, W. G. ed. The twenties p365-75

Dumas, Lloyd J.

National security and the arms race. *In* International terrorism and world security p158-64

Dummett, Michael A. E.

What is a theory of meaning? *In* Guttenplan, S. D. ed. Mind and language p97-138

What is a theory of meaning? (II). *In* Evans, G. L. and McDowell, J. H. eds. Truth and meaning p66-137

About

McDowell, J. H. Truth conditions, bivalence, and verificationism. *In* Evans, G. L. and McDowell, J. H. eds. Truth and meaning p42-66

About individual works

Can an effect precede its cause?

Brier, R. Magicians, alarm clocks, and backward causation. *In* Wheatley, J. M. O. and Edge, H. L. eds. Philosophical dimensions of parapsychology p235-44

Frege

Geach, P. T. Names and identity. *In* Guttenplan, S. D. ed. Mind and language p139-58

The reality of the past

McDowell, J. H. On 'The reality of the past.' *In* Hookway, C. and Pettit, P. eds. Action and interpretation p127-44

Dumont, Louis

Preface by Louis Dumont to the French edition of The Nuer. *In* Studies in social anthropology p328-42

Dumoulin, Heinrich

Buddhism in modern Japan. *In* Dumoulin, H. ed. Buddhism in the modern world p215-76

Contemporary Buddhism in Korea. *In* Dumoulin, H. ed. Buddhism in the modern world p202-14

Dumville, David N.

The Anglian collection of royal genealogies and regnal lists. *In* Anglo-Saxon England 5 p23-50

Dunbar, Paul Laurence

About

Bone, R. A. Literary forebears. *In* Bone, R. A. Down home p3-18

Bone, R. A. Paul Dunbar. *In* Bone, R. A. Down home p42-73

About individual works

The scapegoat

Wakefield, J. Paul Laurence Dunbar, The scapegoat. *In* Bruck, P. ed. The Black American short story in the 20th century p39-51

Dunbar, William

About

Bawcutt, P. Aspects of Dunbar's imagery. *In* Chaucer and Middle English studies in honour of Rossell Hope Robbins p190-200

Kinneavy, G. B. Metaphors of the poet and his craft in William Dunbar. *In* Aeolian harps p57-64

Morgan, E. Dunbar and the language of poetry. *In* Morgan, E. Essays p81-99

Swart, J. On re-reading William Dunbar. *In* Chaucer and Middle English studies in honour of Rossell Hope Robbins p201-09

About individual works

Lament for the Makaris

Cunningham, J. V. Logic and lyric: Marvell, Dunbar, and Nashe. *In* Cunningham, J. V. The collected essays of J. V. Cunningham p162-79

Duncan, Alistair Robert Campbell

No man is an island . . . *In* The Personal universe p40-53

Duncan, Carol

Ingres's Vow of Louis XIII and the politics of the Restoration. *In* Millon, H. A. and Nochlin, L. eds. Art and architecture in the service of politics p80-91

Duncan, Jane

About

Hart, F. R. Jane Duncan and George Mackay Brown. *In* Hart, F. R. The Scottish novel p385-97

Duncan, Richard Ray

Marylanders and the invasion of 1862. *In* Hubbell, J. T. ed. Battles lost and won p183-96

Duncan, Robert Edward

Notes on poetic form. *In* Gibbons, R. ed. The poet's work: 29 masters of 20th century poetry on the origins and practice of their art p260-62

About

Altieri, C. F. Process as plenitude: the poetry of Gary Snyder and Robert Duncan. *In* Altieri, C. F. Enlarging the temple p128-69

Bertholf, R. J. Shelley, Stevens and Robert Duncan: the poetry of approximations. *In* Artful thunder p269-99

Thurley, G. Robert Duncan: the myth of open form. *In* Thurley, G. The American moment p139-55

About individual works
The fire, Passages 13

Haven, R. Some perspectives in three poems by Gray, Wordsworth, and Duncan. *In* Bornstein, G. ed. Romantic and modern p69-88

Duncan-Williams, E. K.

About

Crook, R. Political centralization and local politics in Ghana: the careers of Nana Wiafe Akenten II and E. K. Duncan-Williams of Offinso (Ashanti) *In* The Making of politicians: studies from Africa and Asia p28-48

Duncanson, Dennis J.

Vietnam: from bolshevism to people's war. *In* Hammond, T. T. ed. The anatomy of Communist takeovers p490-515

Dundes, Alan

African and Afro-American tales. *In* Crowley, D. J. ed. African folklore in the New World p35-53

Dunlap, Barbara J.

Through a dark wood of criticism: the rationale and reception of Dorothy L. Sayers's translation of Dante. *In* Hannay, M. P. ed. As her whimsey took her p133-49

Dunlap, Riley E. See Catton, W. R. jt. auth.

Dunlap, William

About

Leary, L. G. The education of William Dunlap. *In* Leary, L. G. Soundings p208-28

Dunlop, Douglas M.

H. M. Baratz and his view of Khazar influence on the earliest Russian literature, juridical and historical. *In* Salo Wittmayer Baron v 1 p345-67

Dunlop, Frank

About individual works
Scapino

Kauffmann, S. Scapino. *In* Kauffmann, S. Persons of the drama p130-33

Dunlop, Ian

About individual works
The shock of the new

Rosenberg, H. Art and the crowd. *In* Rosenberg, H. Art on the edge p155-61

Dunlop, John B.

The odyssey of a skeptic: Gleb Nerzhin. *In* Dunlop, J. B.; Haugh, R. and Klimoff, A. eds. Aleksandr Solzhenitsyn: critical essays and documentary materials 2d ed. p241-59

A select Solzhenitsyn bibliography. *In* Dunlop, J. B.; Haugh, R. and Klimoff, A. eds. Aleksandr Solzhenitsyn: critical essays and documentary materials 2d ed. p650-64

Solzhenitsyn's "sketches." *In* Dunlop, J. B.; Haugh, R. and Klimoff, A. eds. Aleksandr Solzhenitsyn: critical essays and documentary materials 2d ed. p317-25

Dunlop, John Thomas

Past and future tendencies in American labor organizations. *In* A New America? p79-96

Dunn, Catherine M.

The changing image of woman in Renaissance society and literature. *In* Springer, M. A. ed. What manner of woman p15-38

Dunn, Ellen Catherine

French medievalists and the saint's play: a problem for American scholarship. *In* Medievalia et humanistica no. 6 p51-62

Dunn, Ethel

Russian rural women. *In* Women in Russia p167-87

Dunn, James D. G.

Paul's understanding of the death of Jesus. *In* Reconciliation and hope p125-41

Dunn, John M.

The eligible and the elect: Arminian thoughts on the social predestination of Ahafo leaders. *In* The Making of politicians: studies from Africa and Asia p49-65

Practising history and social science on 'realist' assumptions. *In* Hookway, C. and Pettit, P. eds. Action and interpretation p145-75

The success and failure of modern revolutions. *In* Radicalism in the contemporary age v3 p83-114

Dunn, Leslie Clarence

Race and biology. *In* United Nations Educational, Scientific and Cultural Organization. Race, science and society p31-67

Dunn, Lewis A.

Fortress America and the promise of American life: the contours of American responsibility. *In* Isolation or interdependence? p103-13

Dunn, Mary Kaye

Hospice-based home care services. *In* Home care p153-58

Dunn, Patrick P.

Fathers and sons revisited: the childhood of Vissarion Belinskii. *In* DeMause, L. ed. The new psychohistory p131-49

Dunn, Richard John

Far, far better things: Dickens' later endings. *In* Dickens Studies Annual v7 p221-36

"Illuminating distortions" and the Dickens critics. *In* Review, v 1 1979 p91-104

Dunn, Robert Paul

"The laughter of the universe": Dorothy L. Sayers and the whimsical vision. *In* Hannay, M. P. ed. As her whimsey took her p200-12

Dunn, Samuel Watson

The international language of advertising. *In* Fischer, H. D. and Merrill, J. C. eds. International and intercultural communication p308-15

Dunne, John William

About individual works
An experiment with time

Flew, A. G. The sources of serialism. *In* Thakur, S. C. ed. Philosophy and psychical research p81-96

Dunner, Joseph
On the condition of political science. *In* Hook, S.; Kurtz, P. W. and Todorovich, M. eds. The philosophy of the curriculum: the need for general education p253-55

Dunnett, Dorothy

About

Hart, F. R. Mitchison and later romancers. *In* Hart, F. R. The Scottish novel p182-97

Dünnhaupt, Gerhard. See Dünnhaupt, P. R. Gerhard

Dünnhaupt, P. R. Gerhard
Sebastian Brant: The ship of fools. *In* Hoffmeister, G. ed. The Renaissance and Reformation in Germany p69-81

Duns, Joannes Scotus

About

Arendt, H. Will and intellect. *in* Arendt, H. The life of the mind v2 p111-46

Duns Scotus, Joannes. See Duns, Joannes Scotus

Dunston, Arthur John
Venetian 'woodcut' capitals. *In* Virginia. University. Bibliographical Society. Studies in bibliography v30 p136-44

Dunton, John

About

Jenkins, A. Dunton's Post-Angel: messenger of remarkable providences. *In* The Dress of words p151-65

Duodu, Cameron

About individual works
The gab boys

Gakwandi, S. A. Freedom as nightmare: Duodu's The gab boys. *In* Gakwandi, S. A. The novel and contemporary experience in Africa p99-107

Dupee, Frederick Wilcox
Max Beerbohm and the rigors of fantasy. *In* Riewald, J. G. ed. The surprise of excellence p175-91

Dupin, Jacques

About

Cardinal, R. Jacques Dupin. *In* Cardinal, R. ed. Sensibility and creation p220-50
Greene, R. W. Jacques Dupin. *In* Greene, R. W. Six French poets of our time p140-58

DuPlessis, Rachel Blau. See Blau DuPlessis, Rachel

Dupré, Louis K.
The mystical experience of the self and its philosophical significance. *In* Psychiatry and the humanities v 1 p101-25

Dupree, A. Hunter
Biological and social theories—a new opportunity for a union of systems. *In* Science and society: past, present, and future p136-74

The National Academy of Sciences and the American definition of science. *In* Oleson, A. and Voss, J. eds. The organization of knowledge in modern America, 1860-1920 p342-63

The national pattern of American learned societies, 1769-1863. *In* Oleson, A. and Brown, S. C. eds. The pursuit of knowledge in the early American Republic p21-32

Durand, Régis
The exemplary fictions of Robert Coover. *In* Johnson, I. D. and Johnson, C. [eds.] Les américanistes p130-37

Durant, Jack Davis
The "art of thriving" in Fielding's comedies. *In* A Provision of human nature p25-35

Duration, Intuition of. See Time perception

Dürer, Albrecht

About

Meyers, J. Dürer and Doctor Faustus. *In* Meyers, J. Painting and the novel p157-74

Durer, Christopher S.
Molière and Polish comedy. *In* Johnson, R. B.; Neumann, E. S. and Trail, G. T. eds. Molière and the commonwealth of letters: patrimony and posterity p365-78

Durfee, Harold Allen
Analytic philosophy, phenomenology, and the concept of consciousness. *In* Thought, consciousness, and reality p111-30

Durgnat, Raymond
Six films of Josef Von Sternberg. *In* Nicols, B. ed. Movies and methods p262-73

Durkheim, Émile

About

Houck, J. W. Early historical traces of the contemporary debate about work alienation. *In* Heisler, W. J. and Houck, J. W. eds. A matter of dignity p49-63

About individual works
The elementary forms of the religious life

Parsons, T. Durkheim on religion revisited: another look at The elementary forms of the religious life. *In* Parsons, T. Action theory and the human condition p213-32

Suicide

Krauss, H. H. Suicide—a psychosocial phenomenon. *In* Wolman, B. B. ed. Between survival and suicide p26-54

Duroselle, Jean Baptiste
Georges Clemenceau. *In* Abroad in America: Visitors to the new Nation, 1776-1914 p167-75
Treaties. *In* Encyclopedia of American foreign policy p961-79

Durrant, Geoffrey
The new barbarians. *In* Gold, J. ed. In the name of language! p97-130

Durrant, Michael
Some comments on "Meaning and religious language." *In* Reason and religion p222-32

About individual works
Some comments on "Meaning and religious language"

Brown, S. C. Religions and the limits of language. *In* Reason and religion p233-55

Durrell, Lawrence

About

Fraser, G. S. Lawrence Durrell. *In* Fraser, G. S. Essays on twentieth-century poets p175-81
Unterecker, J. E. Fiction at the edge of poetry: Durrell, Beckett, Green. *In* Forms of modern British fiction p165-99
Unterecker, J. E. Lawrence Durrell. *In* Stade, G. ed. Six contemporary British novelists p219-69

About individual works
The Alexandria quartet

Scholes, R. E. The nature of romance. *In* Scholes, R. E. Fabulation and metafiction p21-45

Dürrenmatt, Friedrich

About

Kurz, P. K. The fool and doubt: on one aspect of the work of Friedrich Dürrenmatt. *In* Kurz, P. K. On modern German literature v4 p37-58

Kurz, P. K. Wolves and lambs: Friedrich Dürrenmatt's dramaturgy of politics. *In* Kurz, P. K. On modern German literature v4 p59-72

Durzak, Manfred

From dialect-play to philosophical parable: Elias Canetti in exile. *In* Strelka, J. P.; Bell, R. F. and Dobson, E. eds. Protest—form—tradition p35-56

Dussel, Enrique D.

The political and ecclesial context of liberation theology in Latin America. *In* The Emergent gospel p175-92

Dust (Periodical)

Fulton, L. Dust: a tribal seed. *In* Anderson, E. and Kinzie, M. eds. The little magazine in America: a modern documentary history p423-37

Dutch East India Company. See Nederlandsche Oost-Indische Compagnie

Dutch in Bengal

Prakash, O. Asian trade and European impact: a study of the trade from Bengal, 1630-1720. *In* Kling, B. B. and Pearson, M. N. eds. The age of partnership p43-70

Dutch in Malay Peninsula

Arasaratnam, S. Dutch commercial policy and interests in the Malay Peninsula, 1750-1795. *In* Kling, B. B. and Pearson, M. N. eds. The age of partnership p159-89

Dutch language

Grammar, Comparative—English

Riemsdijk, H. van. On the diagnosis of Wh movement. *In* Keyser, S. J. ed. Recent transformational studies in European languages p189-206

Dutch painting. See Painting, Dutch

Du Toit, André

Ideological change, Afrikaner nationalism and pragmatic racial domination in South Africa. *In* Thompson, L. M. and Butler, J. eds. Change in contemporary South Africa p19-50

Duty

Arnold, C. Analyses of right. *In* Human rights p74-86

Foot, P. Are moral considerations overriding? *In* Foot, P. Virtues and vices, and other essays in moral philosophy p181-88

Foot, P. Morality as a system of hypothetical imperatives. *In* Foot, P. Virtues and vices, and other essays in moral philosophy p157-73

See also Conscience; Deontic logic; Ethics

Duval, Merlin Kearfott

The provider, the government, and the consumer. *In* Knowles, J. H. ed. Doing better and feeling worse p185-92

Duvalier, François, President Haiti

About

Reed, I. I hear you, Doc. *In* Reed, I. Shrovetide in old New Orleans p259-85

Duvall, Raymond D. See Gurr, T. R. jt. auth.

Duy-Tu, Vu. See Vu Duy-Tu

Dvořák, Antonín

About

Bradová, L. Antonín Dvořák. *In* Abroad in America: Visitors to the new Nation, 1776-1914 p228-37

Dwellings

See also Architecture, Domestic; Log cabins

Psychological aspects

Bettelheim, B. Mental health and urban design. *In* Bettelheim, B. Surviving, and other essays p201-20

Dubos, R. J. The cave and the horizon. *In* Dubos, R. J. Beast or angel? p69-76

Egypt—History

Goitein, S. D. F. A mansion in Fustat: a twelfth-century description of a domestic compound in the ancient capital of Egypt. *In* The Medieval city p163-78

Great Britain

Connolly, C. Confessions of a house-hunter. *In* Connolly, C. The evening colonnade p426-32

Dwight, Timothy, 1752-1817

About

Arner, R. D. The Connecticut wits. *In* Emerson, E. H. ed. American literature, 1764-1789 p233-52

Dworkin, Gerald

Paternalism. *In* The abdication of philosophy: philosophy and the public good p209-27

Also in Laslett, P. and Fishkin, J. eds. Philosophy, politics and society p78-96

Dworkin, Ronald Myles

Is law a system of rules? *In* Summers, R. S. ed. Essays in legal philosophy p25-60

Liberalism. *In* Hampshire, S. ed. Public and private morality p113-43

Dwyer, Daisy Hilse

Bridging the gap between the sexes in Moroccan legal practice. *In* Schlegel, A. E. ed. Sexual stratification p41-66

Women, Sufism, and decision-making in Moroccan Islam. *In* Beck, L. and Keddie, N. R. eds. Women in the Muslim world p585-98

Dwyer, Eugene J.

On the meaning of the griffin pelta. *In* Studies in classical art and archaeology p235-38

Dyck, Arthur J.

An alternative to the ethic of euthanasia. *In* Weir, R. F. ed. Ethical issues in death and dying p281-96

Beneficent euthanasia and benemortasia: alternative views of mercy. *In* Kohl, M. ed. Beneficent euthanasia p117-29

Religious views. *In* Population policy and ethics p277-323

Dyckes, William

The photo as subject: the paintings and drawings of Chuck Close. *In* Battcock, G. ed. Super realism p145-62

Dyer, Chrisopher
A redistribution of incomes in fifteenth-century England? *In* Peasants, knights and heretics p192-215

Dyer, Denis

About individual works
The stories of Kleist
Mudrick, M. I don't care what mama don't allow. *In* Mudrick, M. Books are not life but then what is? p52-64

Dyer, John, 1700-1758

About individual works
The fleece
Feingold, R. Two worlds of work: John Dyer's The fleece. *In* Feingold, R. Nature and society p83-119

Dyhouse, Carol
The condition of England 1860-1900. *In* Lerner, L. ed. The Victorians p70-89

The role of women: from self-sacrifice to self-awareness. *In* Lerner, L. ed. The Victorians p174-92

Dying children. See Terminally ill children

The dying Gaul (Sculpture)
Jones, D. The dying Gaul. *In* Jones, D. The dying Gaul, and other writings p50-58

Dying patient. See Terminal care

Dyker, David A.
Yugoslavia: unity out of diversity? *In* Brown, A. H. and Gray, J. eds. Political culture and political change in Communist states p66-100

Dynamic linguistics. See Historical linguistics

Dynamics. See Electrodynamics; Force and energy; Mechanics; Motion; Physics; Statics

Dynamics and statics (Social sciences) See Statics and dynamics (Social sciences)

Dynes, Wayne
Tradition and innovation in medieval art. *In* Powell, J. M. ed. Medieval studies p313-42

Dyson, Anthony Edward, and Lovelock, Julian
Masterful images
Contents
Beyond the polemics: the opening of Dryden's Absalom and Achitophel
Contracted thus: Donne's 'The sunne rising'
The epic of selfhood: Wordsworth's The prelude
Event perverse: Milton's epic of exile
'Ever', 'Never': the world of Keats's Grecian urn
Herbert's 'Redemption'
In spite of all her art: Pope's The rape of the lock
Mighty harmonies: Shelley's Ode to the West Wind
The road of excess: Blake's Songs of innocence and experience
Serpent in Eden: Marvell's 'The picture of little T.C. in a prospect of flowers'
Uncertain hour: the ancient mariner's destiny

E

EAM. See National Liberation Front (Greece)

EBU. See European Broadcasting Union

ECAFE. See United Nations. Economic Commission for Asia and the Far East. Population Division

ECCP. See Council of Europe. European Committee on Crime Problems

ECOWAS. See Economic Community of West African States

EEC. See European Economic Community

EOKA-B. See EOKA-Beta

EOKA-Beta
Bell, J. B. Revolutionary organisations: special cases and imperfect models. *In* International terrorism and world security p78-92

ESP. See Extrasensory perception

ETA. See Basque Nation and Liberty

Eades, Jeremy S.
Kinship and entrepreneurship among Yoruba in northern Ghana. *In* Shack, W. A. and Skinner, E. P. eds. Strangers in African societies p169-82

Eadie, John William
Civitates and clients: Roman frontier policies in Pannonia and Mauretania Tingitana. *In* Miller, D. H. and Steffen, J. O. eds. The frontier p57-80

Eagle, Herbert
Typographical devices in the poetry of Andrey Bely. *In* Janecek, G. ed. Andrey Bely p71-85

Eagle (in religion, folklore, etc.)
Sheldon, S. E. The eagle: bird of magic and medicine in a Middle English translation of the Kyraniddes. *In* Tulane studies in English v22 p 1-31

Eagle in literature
Steadman, J. M. "The House of Fame:" the eagle as contemplative symbol. *In* Steadman, J. M. Nature into myth p67-77

Eagleton, Terence
Marxist literary criticism. *In* Contemporary approaches to English studies p94-103

Eakin, Paul John
The New England girl
Contents
Henry James and the New England consciousness: Roderick Hudson, The Europeans, Hawthorne
The Howells heroine: from The lady of the Aroostook to April hopes
New England in extremis: The Bostonians
Renunciation in New England: Harriet Beecher Stowe and The minister's wooing
Self-culture: Margaret Fuller and Hawthorne's heroines
The tragedy of self-culture: The portrait of a lady

Eakins, Rosemary L.
Tess: the pagan and Christian traditions. *In* Smith, A. ed. The novels of Thomas Hardy p107-25

Earle, Carville, and Hoffman, Ronald
The urban South: the first two centuries. *In* Brownell, B. A. and Goldfield, D. R. eds. The city in Southern history p23-51

Earle, Valerie A.
The Federal structure. *In* Graham, G. J. and Graham, S. G. eds. Founding principles of American government p135-67

Earle, William A.
Styled thought: an open letter to Eliseo Vivas. *In* Viva Vivas! p23-35

Early Christian architecture. See Architecture, Early Christian

Early Christian literature. See Christian literature, Early

Early Christian mosaics. See Mosaics, Early Christian

Early man. See Fossil man

Early man in the Americas. See Paleo-Indians

Early printed books. See Bibliography—Early printed books; Incunabula

Early Renaissance art. See Art, Renaissance—Early Renaissance

Earth. See Cosmogony, Cosmography; Cosmology

Earth, Effect of man on. See Man—Influence on nature

Earth satellites. See Artificial satellites

Earthenware. See Pottery

Easson, Angus
Marshalsea prisoners: Mr Dorrit and Mr Hemens. *In* Dickens Studies Annual v3 p77-86

The Old Curiosity Shop: from manuscript to print. *In* Dickens Studies Annual v1 p93-128

See also Daniell, D. jt. auth.

Easson, Kay Parkhurst
Blake and the art of the book. *In* Essick, R. N. and Pearce, D. R. eds. Blake in his time p35-52

Easson, Roger R.
Blake and the Gothic. *In* Essick, R. N. and Pearce, D. R. eds. Blake in his time p145-54

East (Far East) See East Asia

East (Far East) in literature. See East Asia in literature

East (Near East) See Near East

East Africa. See Africa, East

East Anglia
Virgoe, R. The recovery of the Howards in East Anglia, 1485-1529. *In* Wealth and power in Tudor England p 1-20

East Asia

Foreign relations—United States
Hunt, K. America in the Far East: political & military dimensions. *In* Rosecrance, R. N. ed. America as an ordinary country p136-57

Relations (general))with China
Boyd, G. Forms of political penetration in China's East Asian statecraft. *In* Pacific Asia and U.S. policies: a political-economic-strategic assessment p115-39

Relations (military) with the United States
Hunt, K. America in the Far East: political & military dimensions. *In* Rosecrance, R. N. ed. America as an ordinary country p136-57

East Asia in literature
Goonetilleke, D. C. R. A. Challenges and problems of the Far East: Conrad's tales. *In* Goonetilleke, D. C. R. A. Developing countries in British fiction p33-51

East Bengal. See Bangladesh

East Germany. See Germany, East

East India Company (English)
Bakke, J. P. Edmund Burke and the East Indian reform movement. *In* Rhetoric: a tradition in transition p122-41

East Indian orations (English). See Indic orations (English)

East Indians in Canada
Fraser, T. G. Imperial policy and Indian minorities overseas, 1905-23. *In* Hepburn, A. C. ed. Minorities in history p154-69

East Indians in Kenya
Fraser, T. G. Imperial policy and Indian minorities overseas, 1905-23. *In* Hepburn, A. C. ed. Minorities in history p154-69

East Indians in literature
Nandan, S. The immigrant Indian experience in literature: Trinidad and Fiji. *In* Narasimhaiah, C. D. ed. Awakened conscience p346-59

Souza, E. de. The expatriate experience. *In* Narasimhaiah, C. D. ed. Awakened conscience p339-45

East Indians in South Africa
Fraser, T. G. Imperial policy and Indian minorities overseas, 1905-23. *In* Hepburn, A. C. ed. Minorities in history p154-69

Moodley, K. A. South African Indians: the wavering minority. *In* Thompson, L. M. and Butler, J. eds. Change in contemporary South Africa p250-79

East Indians in the United States
Hess, G. R. The forgotten Asian Americans: the East Indian community in the United States. *In* The Asian American: the historical experience p157-77

East Indians in Uganda
Kuper, J. "Goan" and "Asian" in Uganda: an analysis of racial identity and cultural categories. *In* Shack, W. A. and Skinner, E. P. eds. Strangers in African societies p243-59

Eastburn, David Plumb
Our vanishing golden age? *In* Prochnow, H. V. ed. Dilemmas facing the nation p41-54

Easter

Drama
See Drama, Medieval

Easter Rebellion, 1916. See Ireland—History—Sinn Fein Rebellion, 1916

Easterlin, Richard Ainley
New directions for the economics of fertility. *In* Major social issues p310-17

Easterling, P. E.
The infanticide in Euripides' Medea. *In* Yale classical studies v25 p177-91

Philoctetes and modern criticism. *In* Illinois classical studies v3, 1978 p27-39

Eastern Empire. See Byzantine Empire

Eastern Europe. See Europe, Eastern

Eastern Germany. See Germany, East

Eastern Orthodox Church. See Orthodox Eastern Church

Eastern question (Far East)
Van Alstyne, R. W. The Open Door policy. *In* Encyclopedia of American foreign policy p711-21

Williams, W. A. Open Door interpretation. *In* Encyclopedia of American foreign policy p703-10

See also Pan Pacific relations

Eastern Schism. See Schism—Eastern and Western Church

Eastern State Hospital, Williamsburg, Va. See Virginia. Eastern State Hospital, Williamsburg

Eastman, Lloyd E.
The Kuomintang in the 1930s. *In* The Limits of change p191-210

Eastman, Max

About individual works
The literary mind
Richards, I. A. Max Eastman's The literary mind: its place in an age of science. *In* Richards, I. A. Complementarities p49-55

Easy rider (Motion picture)
Trilling, D. Easy rider and its critics. *In* Trilling, D. We must march my darlings p175-86

Eaton, John, 1575-1641

About
Stoever, W. K. B. The quest for assurance: radical solutions and Puritan dialectics. *In* Stoever, W. K. B. 'A faire and easie way to heaven' p138-60

Eatwell, John; Llewellyn, John, and Tarling, Roger
An ocean development tax. *In* Borgese, E. M. and Krieger, D. eds. The tides of change p33-47

Eaves, Thomas Cary Duncan
Amelia and Clarissa. *In* A Provision of human nature p95-110

Ebbo

About individual works
The life of Otto, Apostle of Pomerania
Morrison, K. F. The structure of holiness in Othloh's Vita Bonifatti and Ebo's Vita Ottonis. *In* Law, church, and society p131-56

Ebel, Henry, 1938-
But what kind of baby is Jimmy Carter? *In* DeMause, L. and Ebel, H. eds. Jimmy Carter and American fantasy p117-27

Eber, Irene
Images of oppressed peoples and modern Chinese literature. *In* Modern Chinese literature in the May Fourth era p127-41

Eberhard, Wolfram
The upper-class family in traditional China. *In* Rosenberg, C. E. ed. The family in history p59-94

Eberhart, Richard
Of poetry and poets
Contents
Emerson and Wallace Stevens
Empson's poetry
A haphazard poetry collecting
Literary death
Memory of meeting Yeats, AE, Gogarty, James Stephens
Notes on poetry
On Theodore Roethke's poetry
Poetry and politics

Poetry as a creative principle
The poet as teacher
Pound's new cantos
Pure poetry
Reflections on Wallace Stevens in 1976
Remarks on Auden
Robert Frost: his personality
Robert Frost in the clearing
Some memories of Dylan Thomas
The theory of poetry
West coast rhythms
Why I write poetry
Will and psyche in poetry

About
Eberhart, R. The theory of poetry. *In* Eberhart, R. Of poetry and poets p76-85

Mills, R. J. Richard Eberhart. *In* Donoghue, D. ed. Seven American poets from MacLeish to Nemerov p55-91

Library
Eberhart, R. A haphazard poetry collecting. *In* Eberhart, R. Of poetry and poets p92-107

Ebert, Robert Higgins
Medical education in the United States. *In* Knowles, J. H. ed. Doing better and feeling worse p171-84

Ebihara, May Mayko
Khmer village women in Cambodia: a happy balance. *In* Matthiasson, C. J. ed. Many sisters p305-47

Ebner, Michael H.
Socialism and progressive political reform: the 1911 change-of-government in Passaic. *In* Stave, B. M. ed. Socialism and the cities p116-40

Ebon, Martin, ed.

About individual works
Psychic discoveries by the Russians
Koestler, A. Telepathy and dialectics. *In* Koestler, A. The heel of Achilles p102-06

Eça de Queiroz, José Maria de

About
Pritchett, V. S. Eça de Queiroz: a Portuguese diplomat. *In* Pritchett, V. S. The myth makers p145-51

Eccles, Sir John Carew
The brain-mind problem as a frontier of science. *In* The Future of science p73-89

Cerebral activity and consciousness. *In* Ayala, F. J. and Dobzhansky, T. G. eds. Studies in the philosophy of biology p87-105

Eccles, Mark. See entry in Part 2 under title: English Renaissance drama

Ecclesiastical architecture. See Church architecture

Ecclesiastical benefices. See Benefices, Ecclesiastical

Ecclesiastical calendar. See Church calendar

Ecclesiastical courts

History
Chodorow, S. A. Dishonest litigation in the Church courts, 1140-98. *In* Law, church, and society p187-206

Ecclesiastical law. See Canon law

Ecclesiastical patronage. See Patronage, Ecclesiastical

Ecclesiastical records and registers. See Church records and registers

Echeruo, Michael J. C.
Chinua Achebe. *In* King, B. A. and Ogung-besan, K. eds. A celebration of Black and African writing p150-63

The conditioned imagination from Shake-speare to Conrad
Contents
The conditioned imagination
Conrad's Nigger
The context of Othello's tragedy
The exo-cultural hero of the Enlightenment
Shylock and the conditioned imagination

Echo (Mythological figure) in literature
Ragussis, M. Epilogue: the echo. *In* Ragussis, M. The subterfuge of art p230-33

Eckardt, Arthur Roy
The recantation of the covenant? *In* Rosenfeld, A. H. and Greenberg, I eds. Confronting the Holocaust p159-68

Eckart, Dennis Ray, and Ries, John C.
The American Presidency. *In* Rieselbach, L. N. ed. People vs. government: the responsiveness of American institutions p15-65

Eckman, Frederick
Edna St Vincent Millay: notes toward a reappraisal. *In* Filler, L. ed. A question of quality: popularity and value in modern creative writing p193-203

Eckstein, Alexander
Sino-American economic relations. *In* China and America p53-108

Eclipses, Solar
Weil, A. T. The marriage of the sun and moon. *In* Alternate states of consciousness p37-52

Eclogues. See Pastoral poetry

Eco, Umberto
Articulations of the cinematic code. *In* Nichols, B. cd. Movies and methods p590-607

Semiotics: a discipline or an interdisciplinary method? *In* Sebeok, T. A. ed. Sight, sound, and sense p73-83

École des beaux-arts. See Paris. École nationale supérieure des beaux-arts

École nationale supérieure des beaux-arts. See Paris. École nationale supérieure des beaux-arts

Ecology
Blackstone, W. T. Ethics and ecology. *In* Philosophy & environmental crisis p16-42

London, B. and Flanagan, W. G. Comparative urban ecology: a summary of the field. *In* Walton, J. and Masotti, L. H. eds. The city in comparative perspective p41-66

Wojciechowski, J. A. The ecology of knowledge. *In* Science and society: past, present, and future p258-302

See also Conservation of natural resources; Environmental chemistry; Human ecology

Social aspects
See Human ecology

Study and teaching
Schein, R. D. The land-grant university and environmental affairs. *In* Land-grant universities and their continuing challenge p178-89

Southwest, New—Historiography
Kessell, J. L. Spaniards, environment, and the Pepsi generation. *In* Weber, D. J. ed. New Spain's far northern frontier p285-91

Ecology, Human. See Human ecology

Ecology, Social. See Human ecology

Econometrics
Adelman, I. and Morris, C. T. The derivation of cardinal scales from ordinal data: an application of multidimensional scaling to measure levels of national development. *In* Economic development and planning p 1-39

Hildreth, C. and Dent, W. T. An adjusted maximum likelihood estimator of autocorrelation in disturbances. *In* Econometrics and economic theory p3-25

Johnston, H. N.; Klein, L. R. and Shinjo, K. Estimation and prediction in dynamic econometric models. *In* Econometrics and economic theory p27-56

Kuh, E. An essay on aggregation theory and practice. *In* Econometrics and economic theory p57-99

Sengupta, J. K. Economic policy simulation in dynamic control models under econometric estimation. *In* Econometrics and economic theory p114-37

Economic assistance, American
Bickerton, I. J. Foreign aid. *In* Encyclopedia of American foreign policy p372-79

Smith, G. The Marshall plan. *In* Encyclopedia of American foreign policy p535-44

Norway
Erichsen, E. Norway: twenty years after the Marshall plan. *In* Inflation, trade and taxes p163-77

Economic assistance, Domestic
See also Grants-in-aid

United States
Benson, J. K. A power strategy. *In* Lauer, R. H. ed. Social movements and social change p107-20

Economic assistance, Russian
Cuba
Blasier, C. COMECON in Cuban development. *In* Cuba in the world p225-55

Near East
Ofer, G. Economic aspects of Soviet involvement in the Middle East. *In* Ro'i, Y. ed. The limits to power p67-93

Economic Community of West African States
Elias, T. O. The economic community of West Africa. *In* The Year book of world affairs, 1978 p93-116

Economic development
Backman, J. Economic growth, standards of living, and quality of life. *In* Tomorrow's American p69-89

Boulding, K. E. The puzzle of the North-South differential. *In* Lewis, W. D. and Griessman, B. E. eds. The Southern mystique p 1-13

Eltis, W. A. Adam Smith's theory of economic growth. *In* Skinner, A. S. and Wilson, T. eds. Essays on Adam Smith p426-54

Fei, J. C. H. and Ranis, G. Technological transfer, employment and development. *In* Economic development and planning p75-103

Frankel, S. H. Clarence Ayres and the roots of economic progress. *In* Science and ceremony p63-74

Economic development—*Continued*

Freeman, C. Economics of research and development. *In* Science, technology and society p223-75

Johnson, H. G. An informal classical model of the current economic development problem. *In* Economic development and planning p157-67

Johnson, H. G. Keynes and the developing world. *In* Skidelsky, R. J. A. ed. The end of the Keynesian era p88-94

Lewis, Sir W. A. The diffusion of development. *In* The Market and the state p135-56

Spengler, J. J. Limits to growth: biospheric or institutional? *In* Science and ceremony p115-33

See also Development banks; Underdeveloped areas

Environmental aspects

Hilton, A. M. Against pollution and hunger: environment and development. *In* Against pollution and hunger p27-59

Mathematical models

Adelman, I. and Morris, C. T. The derivation of cardinal scales from ordinal data: an application of multidimensional scaling to measure levels of national development. *In* Economic development and planning p 1-39

Social aspects

Adams, R. N. Rural collective action and the state: a discussion. *In* Forging nations: a comparative view of rural ferment and revolt p150-67

Anderson, C. A. and Bowman, M. J. Education and economic modernization in historical perspective. *In* Schooling and society p3-19

Caldwell, L. K. 1992: threshold of the post-modern world. *In* A Time to hear and answer: essays for the Bicentennial season p175-218

Markus, M. and Hegedüs, A. The role of values in the long-range planning of distribution and consumption. *In* The Humanisation of socialism p140-60

Economic equilibrium. See Equilibrium (Economics)

Economic forecasting

See also Business forecasting

Mathematical models

Hildreth, C. and Dent, W. T. An adjusted maximum likelihood estimator of autocorrelation in disturbances. *In* Econometrics and economic theory p3-25

Johnston, H. N.; Klein, L. R. and Shinjo, K. Estimation and prediction in dynamic econometric models. *In* Econometrics and economic theory p27-56

India

Tintner, G.; Kadekodi, G. and Rama Sastry, M. V. A macro model of the economy for the explanation of trend and business cycle with applications to India. *In* Econometrics and economic theory p139-46

Russia—Mathematical models

Dadaîan, V. S. A long-term macroeconomic forecasting model of the Soviet economy. *In* Economic development and planning p61-74

Economic growth. See Economic development

Economic history

Gilpin, R. G. Economic interdependence and national security in historical perspective. *in* Knorr, K. E. and Trager, F. N. eds. Economic issues and national security p19-66

Nussbaumer, A. The market economies of the West. *In* The Year book of world affairs, 1976 p223-42

Skidelsky, R. J. A. The decline of Keynesian politics. *In* Crouch, C. ed. State and economy in contemporary capitalism p55-87

Thrupp, S. L. The role of comparison in the development of economic history. *In* Thrupp, S. L. Society and history p274-92

See also Industry—History; and subdivision Economic conditions under names of countries, regions, cities, etc. e.g. Great Britain—Economic conditions

Historiography

Hartwell, R. M. Capitalism and the historians. *In* Essays on Hayek p73-93

Medieval, 500-1500

Hallam, H. E. The medieval social picture. *In* Kamenka, E. and Neale, R. S. eds. Feudalism, capitalism and beyond p28-49

Kaeuper, R. W. The Societas Riccardorum and economic change. *In* Jeffrey, D. L. ed. By things seen: reference and recognition in medieval thought p161-72

Lopez, R. S. The dawn of medieval banking. *In* The Dawn of modern banking p 1-23

Osheim, D. J. Rural population and the Tuscan economy in the late Middle Ages. *In* Viator: medieval and Renaissance studies v7 p329-46

20th century

Maier, C. S. The politics of inflation in the twentieth century. *In* The Political economy of inflation p37-72

1945-

Watson, M. A comparative evaluation of planning practice in the liberal democratic state. *In* Planning, politics and public policy p445-83

Economic integration, International. See International economic integration

Economic life (of economic goods) See Depreciation; Replacement of industrial equipment

Economic planning. See Economic policy

Economic policy

Klein, L. R. Political aspects of economic control. *In* Theory for economic efficiency: essays in honor of Abba P. Lerner p76-91

Nizard, L. Planning as the regulatory reproduction of the status quo. *In* Planning, politics and public policy p433-44

Oakeshott, M. J. The political economy of freedom. *In* Oakeshott, M. J. Rationalism in politics p37-58

Skidelsky, R. J. A. The political meaning of the Keynesian revolution. *In* Skidelsky, R. J. A. ed. The end of the Keynesian era p33-40

Vickrey, W. S. Justice, equality, and the economic system. *In* Small comforts for hard times p59-71

Economic policy—*Continued*

Watson, M. A comparative evaluation of planning practice in the liberal democratic state. *In* Planning, politics and public policy p445-83

See also Agriculture and state; Commercial development; Fiscal policy; Industry and state; Inflation (Finance); International economic relations; Labor policy; Labor supply; Laissez-faire; Manpower policy; Mercantile system; Monetary policy; National security; Physiocrats; Social policy; Underdeveloped areas—Economic policy; Welfare economics; also subdivision Economic policy under names of countries, e.g. France—Economic policy

Mathematical models

Sengupta, J. K. Economic policy simulation in dynamic control models under econometric estimation. *In* Econometrics and economic theory p114-37

Zellner, A. The quality of quantitative economic policy-making when targets and costs of change are mis-specified. *In* Econometrics and economic theory p147-64

Economic policy, Foreign. See International economic relations

Economic relations, Foreign. See International economic relations

Economic sanctions. See Sanctions (International law)

Economic statistics. See Econometrics

Economic theory. See Economics

Economics

Adams, W. The contribution of economics to public policy formulation. *In* Major social issues p358-69

Arrow, K. J. The trade-off between growth and equity. *In* Theory for economic efficiency: essays in honor of Abba P. Lerner p 1-11

Brittan, S. Can democracy manage an economy? *In* Skidelsky, R. J. A. ed. The end of the Keynesian era p41-46

Buchanan, J. M. Methods and morals in economics: the Ayres-Knight discussion. *In* Science and ceremony p163-74

Cairncross, Sir A. K. The market and the state. *In* The Market and the state p113-34

Flew, A. G. N. Wants or needs, choices or commands. *In* Fitzgerald, R. ed. Human needs and politics p213-28

Gilpin, R. G. Economic interdependence and national security in historical perspective. *In* Knorr, K. E. and Trager, F. N. eds. Economic issues and national security p19-66

Graham, A. G. Impartiality and bias in economics. *In* Montefiore, A. ed. Neutrality and impartiality p49-71

Machlup, F. Hayek's contribution to economics. *In* Essays on Hayek p13-59

See also Capital; Capitalism; Commerce; Competition; Debts, Public; Demography; Economic development; Economic history; Economic policy; Equilibrium (Economics); Exchange; Entrepreneur; Finance, Public; Free trade and protection; Individualism; Keynesian economics; Labor and laboring classes; Labor economics; Land; Macroeconomics; Marginal productivity; Marxian

economics; Mercantile system; Microeconomics; Money; Monopolies; Physiocrats; Prices; Profit; Property; Self-interest; Socialism; Statics and dynamics (Social sciences); Urban economics; Value; Wealth; Welfare economics; and subdivision Economic aspects under special subjects, e.g. Agriculture—Economic aspects

History—20th century

Galbraith, J. K. The valid image of the modern economy. *In* Galbraith, J. K. Annals of an abiding liberal p3-19

History—Great Britain

Johnson, H. G. Keynes and British economics. *In* Keynes, M. ed. Essays on John Maynard Keynes p108-22

History—United States

Church, R. L. Economists as experts: the rise of an academic profession in the United States, 1870-1920. *In* The University in society v2 p571-609

Methodology

Graham, A. G. Impartiality and bias in economics. *In* Montefiore, A. ed. Neutrality and impartiality p49-71

Lowe, A. Adam Smith's system of equilibrium growth. *In* Skinner, A. S. and Wilson, T. eds. Essays on Adam Smith p415-25

Political aspects

Crouch, C. Inflation and the political organization of economic interests. *In* The Political economy of inflation p217-39

Maier, C. S. The politics of inflation in the twentieth century. *In* The Political economy of inflation p37-72

Psychological aspects

Maynes, E. S. Attitudes, behavior, and economics. *In* Major social issues p390-411

Social aspects

Goldthorpe, J. H. The current inflation: towards a sociological account. *In* The Political economy of inflation p186-216

Study and teaching

Darcy, R. L. Economic education, human values, and the quality of life. *In* Fairfield, R. P. ed. Humanistic frontiers in American education p102-11

United States

Johnson, H. G. Economics and the radical challenge: the hard social science and the soft social reality. *In* Culture and its creators p97-118

Economics, Comparative. See Comparative economics

Economics, International. See International economic relations

Economics, Mathematical. See Econometrics

Economics, Primitive

Adams, R. M. The emerging place of trade in civilizational studies. *In* Ancient civilization and trade p451-65

Chang, Kwang-chih. Ancient trade as economics or as ecology. *In* Ancient civilization and trade p211-24

Dalton, G. Karl Polanyi's analysis of long-distance trade and his wider paradigm. *In* Ancient civilization and trade p63-132

Economics, Primitive—*Continued*

Polanyi, K. Traders and trade. *In* Ancient civilization and trade p133-54

Renfrew, C. Trade as action at a distance: questions of integration and communication. *In* Ancient civilization and trade p3-59

Webb, M. C. The flag follows trade: an essay on the necessary interaction of military and commercial factors in state formation. *In* Ancient civilization and trade p155-209

Economics and Christianity. See Christianity and economics

Economics and Islam. See Islam and economics

Economics in literature

Shell, M. Conclusion. *In* Shell, M. The economy of literature p152-56

Shell, M. The Golden Fleece and the voice of the shuttle: economy in literary theory. *In* Shell, M. The economy of literature p89-112

Shell, M. Introduction. *In* Shell, M. The economy of literature p 1-10

Shell, M. John Ruskin and the political economy of literature. *In* Shell, M. The economy of literature p129-51

See also Money in literature

Economists

United States

Church, R. L. Economists as experts: the rise of an academic profession in the United States, 1870-1920. *In* The University in society v2 p571-609

Galbraith, J. K. Economists and the economics of professional contentment. *In* Galbraith, J. K. Annals of an abiding liberal p20-35

Economos, Judith J.

Identity and "the difference." *In* Philosophical aspects of the mind-body problem p154-61

Economou, George D.

The two Venuses and courtly love. *In* In pursuit of perfection p17-50

Ecstasy. See Trance

Ecuadorian literature

Black authors—History and criticism

Ortiz, A. Negritude in Latin American culture. *In* DeCosta, M. ed. Blacks in Hispanic literature p74-82

Edari, Ronald S.

Social change in Mombasa, Kenya. *In* Walton, J. and Masotti, L. H. eds. The city in comparative perspective p179-92

Eddy, Elizabeth M.

The reorganization of schooling: an anthropological challenge. *In* Eddy, E. M. and Partridge, W. L. eds. Applied anthropology in America p326-49

See also Partridge, W. L. jt. auth.

Eddy, Elizabeth M. and Partridge, William L.

Training for applied anthropology. *In* Eddy, E. M. and Partridge, W. L. eds. Applied anthropology in America p415-24

Eddy, John Allen

Medicine wheels and Plains Indian astronomy. *In* Brecher, K. and Feirtag, M. eds. Astronomy of the ancients p 1-24

Edel, Abraham

A philosophic perspective. *In* Small comforts for hard times p335-84

Preferential consideration and justice. *In* Social justice & preferential treatment p111-34

Edel, Leon

Homage to Willa Cather. *In* The Art of Willa Cather p185-204

The poetics of biography. *In* Contemporary approaches to English studies p38-58

About individual works
Henry James, the master: 1901-1916

Rahv, P. Henry James and his cult. *In* Rahv, P. Essays on literature and politics, 1932-1972 p93-104

Henry James: The treacherous years, 1895-1900

Connolly, C. Henry James. *In* Connolly, C. The evening colonnade p175-78

Edel, Matthew; Harris, John Rees, and Rothenberg, Jerome

Urban concentration and deconcentration. *In* Hawley, A. H. and Rock, V. P. eds. Metropolitan America in contemporary perspective p123-56

Edelheit, Henry

On the biology of language: Darwinian/Lamarckian homology in human inheritance (with some thoughts about the Lamarckism of Freud.) *In* Psychoanalysis and language p45-74

Edelman, Gerald Maurice

The problem of molecular recognition by a selective system. *In* Ayala, F. J. and Dobzhansky, T. G. eds. Studies in the philosophy of biology p45-56

Edelman, Johann Christian

About

Grossmann, W. Edelmann and the silent Reimarus. *In* Studies in eighteenth-century culture v4 p195-203

Edelman, Marian Wright

We are failing the children. *In* Gross, B. and Gross, R. eds. The children's rights movement p109-14

Edelman, Nathan

The eye of the beholder

Contents

L'art poétique: "longtemps plaire, et jamais ne lasser"

Book reviews

The case against Gothicism

The central image in Phèdre

Criticism, in a thousand hard lessons

The early uses of medium aevum, moyen age, Middle Ages

The eye of the beholder: reflections on classical order

The mixed metaphor in Descartes

The motion of Phèdre from Act III into Act IV: an alternative reading

Other early uses of moyen age and moyen temps

A scriptural key to Villon's Testament

The unity of Villon's Testament

Villon's Epitaphe: a reading

The vogue of François Villon in France from 1828 to 1873

Edelman, Peter

The children's rights movement. *In* Gross, B. and Gross, R. eds. The children's rights movement p203-06

Edelmann, Rafael

מסורת and its historical background. *In* Salo Wittmayer Baron v 1 p369-82

Edelson, Marshall

What is the psychoanalyst talking about? *In* Psychoanalysis and language p99-170

Edelstein, Alex

New variables for cross-cultural study. *In* Gerbner, G. ed. Mass media policies in changing cultures p207-21

Eden. See Tree of life

Edgar, Harold S. and Greenawalt, R. Kent

The legal tradition. *In* Population policy and ethics p127-66

Edge, David

On the purity of science. *In* Niblett, W. R. ed. The sciences, the humanities and the technological threat p42-64

Technological metaphor and social control. *In* Bugliarello, G. and Doner, D. B. eds. The history and philosophy of technology p309-24

Edgerton, Robert B.

The study of deviance—marginal man or Everyman? *In* Spindler, G. D. ed. The making of psychological anthropology p444-76

Edgeworth, Maria

About

Butler, M. Maria Edgeworth. *In* Butler, M. Jane Austen and the war of ideas p124-57

Gilbert, S. M. and Gubar, S. Jane Austen's cover story (and its secret agents). *In* Gilbert, S. M. and Gubar, S. The madwoman in the attic p146-83

About individual works

Castle Rackrent

Doubleday, N. F. Honest Thady's tale. *In* Doubleday, N. F. Variety of attempt p7-18

Edible plants. See Plants, Edible

Edinburgh

Intellectual life

Shapin, S. Homo phrenologicus: anthropological perspectives on an historical problem. *In* Barnes, B. and Shapin, S. eds. Natural order p41-71

Edinburgh. University

History

Phillipson, N. T. Culture and society in the 18th century province: the case of Edinburgh and the Scottish Enlightenment. *In* The University in society v2 p407-48

Edinburgh Review

Jones, L. M. Hazlitt, Reynolds, and the Edinburgh Review. *In* Virginia. University. Bibliographical Society. Studies in bibliography v29 p342-46

Editing

Bowers, F. T. Greg's "Rationale of copy-text" revisited. *In* Virginia. University. Bibliographical Society. Studies in bibliography v31 p90-161

Bowers, F. T. Some relations of bibliography to editorial problems. *In* Bowers, F. T. Essays in bibliography, text, and editing p15-36

Cook, D. L. Bowers does Fielding. *In* Review, v 1 1979 p13-27

Davis, K. W.; Higdon, D. L. and Rude, D. W. On editing Conrad. *In* Joseph Conrad: a commemoration p143-55

Dawson, G. E. Problems in editing sixteenth- and seventeenth-century letters. *In* Medieval and Renaissance studies [1974] p87-103

Lane, M. Shapers of culture: the editor in book publishing. *In* Altbach, P. G. and McVey, S. eds. Perspectives on publishing p27-35

Tanselle, G. T. The editing of historical documents. *In* Virginia. University. Bibliographical Society. Studies in bibliography v31 p 1-56

Tanselle, G. T. External fact as an editorial problem. *In* Virginia. University. Bibliographical Society. Studies in bibliography v32 p 1-47

Tanselle, G. T. Greg's theory of copy-text and the editing of American literature. *In* Virginia. University. Bibliographical Society. Studies in bibliography v28 p167-229

See also Criticism, Textual; Editors

Editions. See Bibliography—Editions

Editors

Karl, J. E. Between chaos and creativity: the role of the children's editor. *In* Egoff, S. A. ed. One ocean touching p164-76

Editors (Literature) See Editors

Edmands, Ursula

Olive Schreiner. *In* Parker, K. ed. The South African novel in English p27-45

Edmonds, Martin

Accountability and the military-industrial complex. *In* Smith, B. L. R. ed. The new political economy: the public use of the private sector p149-80

The horizons of war: problems of projection. *In* Beaumont, R. A. and Edmonds, M. eds. War in the next decade p 1-20

Reserve forces: mobilization demands in modern war. *In* Beaumont, R. A. and Edmonds, M. eds. War in the next decade p35-54

Edmunds, Lowell

Sophocles Oedipus Tyrannus 80-81. *In* Harvard Studies in classical philology v80 p41-44

Thucydides' ethics as reflected in the description of stasis (3.82-83). *In* Harvard Studies in classical philology v79 p73-92

Edmunds, Lowell, and Martin, Richard

Thucydides 2.65.8: ΕΛΕΥΘΕΡΩΣ. *In* Harvard Studies in classical philology v81 p187-93

Edmunds, R. David

Indian humor: can the Red Man laugh? *In* Red men and hat-wearers p141-53

Education

Anderson, C. A. and Bowman, M. J. Education and economic modernization in historical perspective. *In* Schooling and society p3-19

Blaug, M. The economics of education in English classical political economy: a re-examination. *In* Skinner, A. S. and Wilson, T. eds. Essays on Adam Smith p568-99

Boulding, E. Educational structure and community transformation. *In* Wagschal, P. H. ed. Learning tomorrows p97-107

Dieuzeide, H. Education and development. *In* Wagschel, P. H. ed. Learning tomorrows p89-96

Fuller, R. B. Learning tomorrows: education for a changing world. *In* Wagschal, P. H. ed. Learning tomorrows p 1-26

Illich, I. Radical alternatives to schools. *In* Smithsonian Institution. The cultural drama p305-17

Education—*Continued*

Thompson, K. W. Values and education: a worldwide review. *In* The Year book of world affairs, 1977 p327-41

See also Adult education; Child study; Culture; Education of children; Education of women; Illiteracy; International education; Learning, Psychology of; Learning and scholarship; Moral education; Moving-pictures in education; Professional education; Public schools; Rural schools; Socialization; Teachers; Teaching; Telephone in education; Television in education; Vocational education; Youth; and subdivision Study and teaching under special subjects, e.g. Literature—Study and teaching; and headings beginning with the word Educational

Aims and objectives

Apple, M. W. Ivan Illich and deschooling society: the politics of slogan systems. *In* Social forces and schooling p337-60

Barrow, R. A. S. Neill (1883-1973). *In* Barrow, R. Radical education p64-91

Barrow, R. A critical look at certain themes in Rousseau. *In* Barrow, R. Radical education p39-63

Barrow, R. Jean-Jacques Rousseau (1712-88). *In* Barrow, R. Radical education p12-38

Barrow, R. Paul Goodman (1911-73) [sic]. *In* Barrow, R. Radical education p92-126

Bay, C. Education for citizenship. *In* Fairfield, R. P. ed. Humanistic frontiers in American education p148-55

Cornog, W. H. The options market in education. *In* Parents, teachers, and children: prospects for choice in American education p149-64

Dearden, R. F. Autonomy as an educational ideal I. *In* Philosophers discuss education p3-18

Hawkins, D. Developing a new educational agenda. *In* Roots of open education in America p49-58

Morris, B. On discovering what it means to be human. *In* Niblett, W. R. ed. The sciences, the humanities and the technological threat p90-105

O'Neill, O. Some inconsistent educational aims. *In* Small comforts for hard times p303-07

Scrupski, A. The social system of the school. *In* Social forces and schooling p141-86

Telfer, E. Autonomy as an educational ideal II. *In* Philosophers discuss education p19-35

Weaver, R. M. Education and the individual. *In* A Public philosophy reader p229-45

See also Educational equalization; Educational sociology

Curricula

Greene, M. The artistic-aesthetic and curriculum. *In* Greene, M. Landscapes of learning p168-84

Langford, G. Education and human being II. *In* Philosophers discuss education p73-84

Shoemaker, F. New dimensions for world cultures. *In* Fairfield, R. P. ed. Humanistic frontiers in American education p289-301

Economic aspects

Nash, P. Some economic questions. *In* Roots of open education in America p126-30

Stone, J. R. N. Demographic variables in the economics of education. *In* Economic factors in population growth p521-52

Experimental methods

Barrow, R. Everett Reimer (b. 1922) and Ivan Illich (b. 1926). *In* Barrow, R. Radical education p127-53

Barrow, R. Last words. *In* Barrow, R. Radical education p177-202

Barrow, R. Neil Postman and Charles Weingartner. *In* Barrow, R. Radical education p154-76

London, H. I. Questions of viability in nontraditional education. *In* Hook, S.; Kurtz, P. W. and Todorovich, M. eds. The philosophy of the curriculum: the need for general education p221-26

Perrone, V. A view of school reform. *In* Roots of open education in America p173-90

Scrupski, A. Educational horizon: promise, challenge, vulnerability. *In* Social forces and schooling p361-368

Winsor, C. B. Early Progressive schools —II. *In* Roots of open education in America p135-47

See also Educational innovations; Open plan schools

Federal aid

See Federal aid to education

Finance

Wagner, R. E. American education and the economics of caring. *In* Parents, teachers, and children: prospects for choice in American education p111-25

History

Coleman, J. S. Introduction: choice in American education. *In* Parents, teachers and children: prospects for choice in American education p 1-12

Strauss, G. The state of pedagogical theory c. 1530: what Protestant reformers knew about education. *In* Schooling and society p69-94

History—Medieval, 500-1500

See Education, Medieval

Integration

See School integration

Philosophy

Barrow, R. A. S. Neill (1883-1973). *In* Barrow, R. Radical education p64-91

Barrow, R. A critical look at certain themes in Rousseau. *In* Barrow, R. Radical education p39-63

Barrow, R. Everett Reimer (b.1922) and Ivan Illich (b.1926). *In* Barrow, R. Radical education p127-53

Barrow, R. Introduction. *In* Barrow, R. Radical education p 1-11

Barrow, R. Jean-Jacques Rousseau (1712-88). *In* Barrow, R. Radical education p12-38

Barrow, R. Last words. *In* Barrow, R. Radical education p177-202

Barrow, R. Neil Postman and Charles Weingartner. *In* Barrow, R. Radical education p154-76

Barrow, R. Paul Goodman (1911-73) [sic]. *In* Barrow, R. Radical education p92-126

Benne, K. D. Technology and community: conflicting bases of educational authority. *In* Feinberg, W. and Rosemont, H. eds. Work, technology, and education p142-65

Education, Elementary—*Continued*

Germany
Arnold, M. Special report on certain points connected with elementary education in Germany, Switzerland, and France. *In* Arnold, M. The last word p 1-53

Great Britain
Arnold, M. Schools in the reign of Queen Victoria. *In* Arnold, M. The last word p210-45

Switzerland
Arnold, M. Special report on certain points connected with elementary education in Germany, Switzerland, and France. *In* Arnold, M. The last word p 1-53

United States—History
Zilversmit, A. The failure of progressive education, 1920-1940. *In* Schooling and society p252-63

Education, Ethical. See Moral education

Education, Higher
Huxley, A. L. Integrate education. *In* Huxley, A. L. The Human situation p 1-11

Kerr, C. Higher education: paradise lost? *In* The Frontiers of human knowledge p183-99

Miller, P. A. Administrative orientations from anthropology: thoughts of a college president. *In* Eddy, E. M. and Partridge, W. L. eds. Applied anthropology in America p147-64

Niblett, W. R. The individual and the social future. *In* Niblett, W. R. ed. The sciences, the humanities and the technological threat p157-65

Sowell, T. Social science and general education. *In* Hook, S.; Kurtz, P. W. and Todorovich, M. eds. The philosophy of the curriculum: the need for general education p165-68

See also Church and college; Federal aid to higher education; Higher education and state; Higher education of women; Minorities —Education (Higher); Moving-pictures in higher education; Professional education; Unversities and colleges; University extension; Women's colleges

Aims and objectives
Bickel, A. M. The aims of education and the proper standards of the university. *In* Universities in the Western world p3-11

Jackson, S. C. Is the university superfluous in the urban crisis? *In* Murphy, T. P. ed. Universities in the urban crisis p3-13

Lowenthal, R. The university's autonomy versus social priorities. *In* Universities in the Western world p75-84

Murphy, T. P. Free universities and urban higher education. *In* Murphy, T. P. ed. Universities in the urban crisis p113-35

Murphy, T. P. and Seyffert, M. G. The future urban university. *In* Murphy, T. P. ed. Universities in the urban crisis p381-400

Osgood, C. E. How should a university be? *In* Lerner, D. and Nelson, L. M. eds. Communication research—a half-century appraisal p104-14

Panuska, J. A. Open-endedness as an educational goal. *In* Buxton, T. H. and Prichard, K. W. eds. Excellence in university teaching p94-102

Peckham, M. Arts for the cultivation of radical sensitivity. *In* Peckham, M. Romanticism and behavior p285-312

Peckham, M. Cultural stagnation in American universities and colleges. *In* Peckham, M. Romanticism and behavior p313-27

Spear, G. E. The university public service mission. *In* Murphy, T. P. ed. Universities in the urban crisis p95-111

Economic aspects—United States
Millett, J. D. Money and other trifles. *In* The Third century p64-71

Research
Osgood, C. E. How should a university be? *In* Lerner, D. and Nelson, L. M. eds. Communication research—a half-century appraisal p104-14

Standards
Bickel, A. M. The aims of education and the proper standards of the university. *In* Universities in the Western world p3-11

State aid
See State aid to higher education

Canada
Bissell, C. T. The place of learning and the arts in Canadian life. *In* Perspectives on revolution and evolution p180-212

Japan—History
Kato, H. Development nineteenth-century style: some historical parallels between the United States and Japan. *In* On the making of Americans p173-90

Underdeveloped areas
See Underdeveloped areas — Education (Higher)

United States
Bailey, S. K. A finer order, a more general happiness. *In* The Third century p153-57

Berman, R. S. Intellect and education in a revolutionary society. *In* America's continuing revolution p273-91

Blanshard, B. Democracy and distinction in American education. *In* McMurrin, S. M. ed. On the meaning of the university p29-49

Bonham, G. W. Who runs the shows? *In* The Third century p158-65

Bowen, H. R. Higher education and human equality. *In* The Third century p90-97

Cohen, A. M. On the road to a learning society. *In* The Third Century p52-57

Cross, K. P. For all and for each. *In* The Third century p109-13

DeBary, W. T. General education and the university crisis. *In* Hook, S.; Kurtz, P. W. and Todorovich, M. eds. The philosophy of the curriculum: the need for general education p3-25

Eurich, N. Learning in America. *In* From Parnassus p75-83

Frankel, C. Epilogue: Reflections on a worn-out model. *In* Universities in the Western world p279-89

Gardner, D. P. Forces for change in American higher education. *In* McMurrin, S. M. ed. On the meaning of the university p103-23

Glazer, N. Introduction: The business of the future. *In* The Third century p7-21

Gleazer, E. J. The promise of lifelong learning. *In* The Third century p127-34

Educaton, Higher—United States—*Cont.*

Gould, S. B. A disease with a patient. *In* The Third century p33-38

Hesburgh, T. M. Education in the year 2000. *In* Hesburgh, T. M. The Hesburgh papers p190-95

Hesburgh, T. M. Making prophecies of our goals. *In* The Third century p188-91

Hesburgh, T. M. The past and present of American higher education. *In* Hesburgh, T. M. The Hesburgh papers p19-33

Howe, H. The interplay of mass and class. *In* The Third century p101-08

Huitt, R. K. Autonomy on the line. *In* The Third century p80-82

Keeton, M. T. Beyond the cloister. *In* The Third century p175-80

Kerr, C. En attendant 2000. *In* The Third century p39-42

Marcus, S. Some questions in general education today. *In* From Parnassus p84-104

Mayhew, L. B. Lessening influence and the search for purpose. *In* The Third century p44-51

Merrit, K. Women and higher education: voices from the sexual Siberia. In Roberts, J. I. ed. Beyond intellectual sexism p353-64

Ness, F. W. Consensus and preservation. *In* The Third century p135-40

Newman, F. Taking the helm. *In* The Third century p116-26

Norton, J. A. Notes from a diary. *In* The Third century p181-87

Novotny, H. R. F. Objectivity and biased skepticism in higher education. *In* Hook, S.; Kurtz, P. and Todorovich, M. eds. The ethics of teaching and scientific research p61-69

Ostar, A. W. A confederacy of concerns. *In* The Third century p168-74

Parsons, T. The future of the university. *In* Parsons, T. Action theory and the human condition p96-114

Parsons, T. Some considerations on the growth of the American system of higher education and research. *In* Culture and its creators p266-84

Pell, C. The question of access—and to what. *In* The Third century p98-100

Pifer, A. J. A clash of tangled forces. *In* The Third century p58-63

Rees, M. S. The ivory tower and the marketplace. *In* McMurrin, S. M. ed. On the meaning of the university p81-101

Reinert, P. C. Three reforms. *In* The Third century p141-46

Riesman, D. Small steps to a larger vision. *In* The Third century p24-32

Silber, J. R. The rest was history. *In* The Third century p194-96

Also in Parsons, T. Action theory and the human condition p115-32

Trilling, L. The uncertain future of the humanistic educational ideal. *In* Trilling, L. The last decade p160-76

United States—Aims and objectives

Anderson, G. L. Land-grant universities and their continuing challenge. *In* Land-grant universities and their continuing challenge p 1-10

Boyer, E. L. Toward a new interdependence. *In* The Third century p72-79

Browne, R. B. Academicons-sick sacred cows. *In* Browne, R. B. and Fishwick, M. W. eds. Icons of America p292-301

Hook, S. General education: the minimum indispensables. *In* Hook, S.; Kurtz, P. W. and Todorovich, M. eds. The philosophy of the curriculum: the need for general education p27-36

Hook, S. On sharpening the horns. *In* Hook, S.; Kurtz, P. W. and Todorovich, M. eds. The philosophy of the curriculum: the need for general education p211-15

Huitt, R. K. What's ahead for the land-grant colleges? *In* Land-grant universities and their continuing challenge p11-22

Kadish, M. R. The desirability of pulling in one's horns. *In* Hook, S.; Kurtz, P. W. and Todorovich, M. eds. The philosophy of the curriculum: the need for general education p205-09

Kampf, L. The radical faculty: What are its goals? *In* Fairfield, R. P. ed. Humanistic frontiers in American education p61-68

Madsen, D. L. The land-grant university: myth and reality. *In* Land-grant universities and their continuing challenge p23-48

Masson, M. W. Pessimism surpassed: new colleges as bastions against barbarism in colonial America. *In* Studies in eighteenth-century culture v8 p69-86

Quie, A. H. The tyranny of the urgent. *In* The Third century p147-52

United States—History

Trow, M. Aspects of diversity in American higher education. *In* On the making of Americans p271-90

United States—Research

Scanlon, T. M. Academic freedom and the control of research. *In* The Concept of academic freedom p237-54

Thomson, J. J. Academic freedom and research. *In* The Concept of academic freedom p255-62

Education, Humanistic

Bernardo, A. S. New beginnings in general education. *In* Hook, S.; Kurtz, P. W. and Todorovich, M. eds. The philosophy of the curriculum: the need for general education p257-59

Black, M. Some tasks for 'the humanities.' *In* Niblett, W. R. ed. The sciences, the humanities and the technological threat p79-89

DeBary, W. T. General education and the university crisis. *In* Hook, S.; Kurtz, P. W. and Todorovich, M. eds. The philosophy of the curriculum: the need for general education p3-25

Edel, A. A philosophic perspective. *In* Small comforts for hard times p335-84

Grant, G. P. The university curriculum and the technological threat. *In* Niblett, W. R. ed. The sciences, the humanities and the technological threat p21-35

Greene, M. Significant landscapes: an approach to the arts in interrelationship. *In* Greene, M. Landscapes of learning p198-210

Greene, M. Towards wide-awakeness: an argument for the arts and humanities in education. *In* Greene, M. Landscapes of learning p161-67

Education vouchers. See Educational vouchers

Educational administration. See School management and organization; Universities and colleges—Administration

Educational anthropology

Arvizu, S. F. Education for constructive marginality. *In* Smithsonian Institution. The cultural drama p123-35

Cohen, Y. A. The state system, schooling, and cognitive and motivational patterns. *In* Social forces and schooling p103-40

Eddy, E. M. The reorganization of schooling: an anthropological challenge. *In* Eddy, E. N. and Partridge, W. L. eds. Applied anthropology in America p326-49

Greene, M. The predicaments of American selfhood: a response to the new irrationalism. *In* Greene, M. Landscapes of learning p7-21

Greene, M. Steamboats and critiques. *In* Greene, M. Landscapes of learning p111-25

Miller, P. A. Administrative orientations from anthropology: thoughts of a college president. *In* Eddy, E. M. and Partridge, W. L. eds. Applied anthropology in America p147-64

Case studies

Hill-Burnett, J. Developing anthropological knowledge through application. *In* Eddy, E. M. and Partridge, W. L. eds. Applied anthropology in America p112-28

Educational change. See Educational innovations

Educational cooperation. See University cooperation

Educational discrimination. See Discrimination in education

Educational endowments. See Endowment of research; Endowments

Educational equalization

Cooper, D. E. Quality and equality in education. *In* Philosophers discuss education p113-29

O'Hagan, T. Quality and equality in education: a critique of David Cooper. *In* Philosophers discuss education p130-43

Weaver, W. T. Growth, distribution, and the professional frame of reference. *In* Bundy, R. F. ed. Images of the future: the twenty-first century and beyond p195-200

United States

Lazerson, M. Consensus and conflict in American education: historical perspectives. *In* Parents, teachers, and children: prospects for choice in American education p15-36

Lipset, S. M. Opportunity and welfare in the first new nation. *In* America's continuing revolution p333-59

Educational innovations

Cornog, W. H. The options market in education. *In* Parents, teachers, and children: prospects for choice in American education p149-64

Doyle, D. P. The politics of choice: a view from the bridge. *In* Parents, teachers, and children: prospects for choice in American education p227-55

Fairfield, R. P. Learning: rivers and nets! *In* Bundy, R. F. ed. Images of the future: the twenty-first century and beyond p207-17

Oliver, D. W. Utilitarian perfectionism and education: a critique of underlying forces of innovative education. *In* Social forces and schooling p250-81

See also Education—Experimental methods

United States

Chase, W. W. Technology, ecology, and the learning environment. *In* Fairfield, R. P. ed. Humanistic frontiers in American education p173-80

Feinberg, W. and Rosemont, H. Training for the welfare state: the progressive education movement. *In* Feinberg, W. and Rosemont, H. eds. Work, technology, and education p60-91

Jerome, J. Toward an ideal college. *In* Fairfield, R. P. ed. Humanistic frontiers in American education p207-15

Murphy, T. P. Free universities and urban higher education. *In* Murphy, T. P. ed. Universities in the urban crisis p113-35

Taylor, H. The teacher in the world. *In* Fairfield, R. P. ed. Humanistic frontiers in American education p302-10

Theobald, R. and McInnis, N. F. A certain education for an uncertain time. *In* Fairfield, R. P. ed. Humanistic frontiers in American education p194-201

United States—Evaluation

Gintis, H. M. and Bowles, S. The contradictions of liberal educational reform. *In* Feinberg, W. and Rosemont, H. eds. Work, technology, and education p92-141

Educational law and legislation

See also Religious education—Law and legislation; State aid to private schools; Students—Legal status, laws, etc.; Universities and colleges—Law and legislation

United States—California

Singleton, R. California: the Self-Determination in Education Act, 1968. *In* Parents, teachers, and children: prospects for choice in American education p77-83

Educational measurements. See Educational tests and measurements

Educational policy. See Education and state

Educational psychology

Levy, R. I. A conjunctive pattern in middle class informal and formal education. *In* Schwartz, T. ed. Socialization as cultural communication p177-87

Nicholson, S. Children as planners. *In* Gross, B. and Gross, R. eds. The children's rights movement p287-95

See also Intelligence levels; Learning, Psychology of; Memory; Mental tests; Thought and thinking

Educational research

See also Education, Higher—Research

United States

Horn, J. L. The ethics of research: a case history and its lessons. *In* Hook, S.; Kurtz, P. and Todorovich, M. eds. The ethics of teaching and scientific research p135-59

Educational sociology

Apple, M. W. Ivan Illich and deschooling society: the politics of slogan systems. *In* Social forces and schooling p337-60

Ashby, E. Reconciliation of tradition and modernity in universities. *In* McMurrin, S. M. ed. On the meaning of the university p13-27

Educational sociology—*Continued*

Blanshard, B. Democracy and distinction in American education. *In* McMurrin, S. M. ed. On the meaning of the university p29-49

Bowen, H. R. Higher education and human equality. *In* The Third century p90-97

Boyer, E. L. Toward a new interdependence. *In* The Third century p72-79

Cohen, Y. A. The state system, schooling, and cognitive and motivational patterns. *In* Social forces and schooling p103-40

Cross, K. P. For all and for each. *In* The Third century p109-13

Dahrendorf, R. The educational class. *In* Universities in the Western world p47-57

Gardner, D. P. Forces for change in American higher education. *In* McMurrin, S. M. ed. On the meaning of the university p103-23

Gardner, J. W. The individual and society. *In* McMurrin, S. M. ed. On the meaning of the university p51-62

Greene, M. The agon of "basics": backward looks and future possibilities. *In* Greene, M. Landscapes of learning p74-86

Greene, M. The new freedom and the moral life. *In* Greene, M. Landscapes of learning p147-57

Greene, M. Paul Goodman and anarchistic education. *In* Social forces and schooling p313-36

Greene, M. Pedagogy and praxis: the problem of malefic generosity. *In* Greene, M. Landscapes of learning p95-110

Greene, M. The rational and the emancipatory: towards a role for imaginative literature. *In* Greene, M. Landscapes of learning p22-41

Greene, M. Steamboats and critiques. *In* Greene, M. Landscapes of learning p111-25

Greene, M. Wide-awakeness and the moral life. *In* Greene, M. Landscapes of learning p42-52

Howe, H. The interplay of mass and class. *In* The Third century p101-08

Lowenthal, R. The university's autonomy versus social priorities. *In* Universities in the Western world p75-84

McMurrin, S. M. The philosophy of education. *In* McMurrin, S. M. ed. On the meaning of the university p 1-12

Martin, B. The mining of the ivory tower. *In* Universities in the Western world p98-115

Mayhew, L. B. Lessening influence and the search for purpose. *In* The Third century p44-51

Niblett, W. R. The individual and the social future. *In* Niblett, W. R. ed. The sciences, the humanities and the technological threat p157-65

Novak, M. Conclusion: social trust. *In* Parents, teachers, and children: prospects for choice in American education p257-78

Olafson, F. A. The school and society: reflections on John Dewey's philosophy of education. *In* Cahn, S. M. ed. New studies in the philosophy of John Dewey p172-203

Parsons, T. The future of the university. *In* Parsons, T. Action theory and the human condition p96-114

Parsons, T. Some considerations on the growth of the American system of higher education and research. *In* Culture and its creators p266-84

Also in Parsons, T. Action theory and its human condition p115-32

Parsons, T. Stability and change in the American university. *In* Parsons, T. Action theory and the human condition p154-64

Parsons, T. The university "bundle": a study of the balance between differentiation and integration. *In* Parsons, T. Action theory and the human condition p133-53

Rees, M. S. The ivory tower and the marketplace. McMurrin, S. M. ed. On the meaning of the university p81-101

Scrupski, A. The social system of the school. *In* Social forces and schooling p141-86

Shils, E. A. The academic ethos under strain. *In* Universities in the Western world p16-46

Shils, E. A. Governments and universities. *In* Hook, S.; Kurtz, P. W., and Todorovich, M. eds. The university and the state: what role for government in higher education? p177-204

Weaver, W. T. Growth, distribution, and the professional frame of reference. *In* Bundy, R. F. ed. Images of the future: the twenty-first century and beyond p195-200

See also Afro-Americans—Education; Education—Aims and objectives; Students socioeconomic status

United States

Brameld, T. B. H. Illusions and disillusions in American education. *In* Fairfield, R. P. ed. Humanistic frontiers in American education p17-27

Brower, A. Black studies and changing times. *In* Fairfield, R. P. ed. Humanistic frontiers in American education p134-38

Dixon, J. P. Permanent campus revolution? *In* Fairfield, R. P. ed. Humanistic frontiers in American education p261-68

Edel, A. A philosophic perspective. *In* Small comforts for hard times p335-84

Fantini, M. D. Relevance=humanistic education. *In* Fairfield, R. P. ed. Humanistic frontiers in American education p28-36

Friedenberg, E. Z. Status and role in education. *In* Fairfield, R. P. ed. Humanistic frontiers in American education p37-47

Gordon, E. W. and Green, D. An affluent society's excuses for inequality: developmental, economic, and educational. *In* Montagu, A. ed. Race and IQ p73-103

Gross, F. Thoughts on a social-science curriculum. *In* Hook, S.; Kurtz, P. W. and Todorovich, M. eds. The philosophy of the curriculum: the need for general education p261-73

Marcus, S. Some questions in general education today. *In* Small comforts for hard times p281-302

Park, R. The disestablished humanities. *In* Small comforts for hard times p308-20

Pierson, G. W. The university and American society. *In* Small comforts for hard times p263-76

Riesman, D. Small steps to a larger vision. *In* The Third century p24-32

Taylor, H. The teacher in the world. *In* Fairfield, R. P. ed. Humanistic frontiers in American education p302-10

Educational technology

See also Audio-visual education; Programmed instruction

United States

Chase, W. W. Technology, ecology, and the learning environment. *In* Fairfield, R. P. ed. Humanistic frontiers in American education p173-80

Educational television. See Television in education

Educational television stations

United States

Lyle, J. Public television: too much ambition and overcommitment? *In* Lerner, D. and Nelson, L. M. eds. Communication research —a half-century appraisal p193-209

Educational tests and measurements

Hoffmann, B. Magic, science and evaluation. *In* From Parnassus p324-33
See also Mental tests

Educational vouchers

Doyle, D. P. The politics of choice: a view from the bridge. *In* Parents, teachers, and children: prospects for choice in American education p227-55

Greenawalt, R. K. Voucher plans and sectarian schools: the constitutional problem. *In* Parents, teachers, and children: prospects for choice in American education p207-25

Greeley, A. M. Freedom of choice: "our commitment to integration." *In* Parents, teachers, and children: prospects for choice in American education p183-205

Edward

Trilling, L. Edward: Anonymous. *In* Trilling, L. Prefaces to The experience of literature p177-81

Edward the Confessor, Saint, King of England

About

Fell, C. E. English history and Norman legend in the Icelandic saga of Edward the Confessor. *In* Anglo-Saxon England 6 p223-36

Fell, C. E. The Icelandic saga of Edward the Confessor: its version of the Anglo-Saxon emigration to Byzantium. *In* Anglo-Saxon England 3 p179-96

Edward I, King of England

Kaeuper, R. W. Royal finance and the crisis of 1297. *In* Order and innovation in the Middle Ages p103-10

About

Prestwich, M. Italian merchants in late thirteenth and early fourteenth century England. *In* The Dawn of modern banking p77-104

Edward VI, King of England

About

Miller, H. Henry VIII's unwritten will: grants of lands and honours in 1547. *In* Wealth and power in Tudor England p87-105

Edwards, Anthony S. G.

New texts of Marvell's Satires: II. *In* Virginia. University. Bibliographical Society. Studies in bibliography v31 p221-26

Edwards, Anthony S. G. and Hedley, J. Henry

John Stowe, The craft of lovers and T.C.C. R.3.19. *In* Virginia. University. Bibliographical Society. Studies in bibliography v28 p265-68

Edwards, Anthony S. G. and Schuler, Robert M.

New texts of Marvell's Satires. *In* Virginia. University. Bibliographical Society. Studies in bibliography v30 p180-85

Edwards, E. Babette

Why a Harlem Parents Union? *In* Parents, teachers, and children: prospects for choice in American education p59-65

Edwards, Janet Ray

Carlyle and the fictions of belief: Sartor resartus to Past and present. *In* Carlyle and his contemporaries p91-111

Edwards, Jonathan

About

Bushman, R. L. Jonathan Edwards and Puritan consciousness. *In* Vaughan, A. T. and Bremer, F. J. eds. Puritan New England p346-62

Bushman, R. L. Jonathan Edwards as great man. *In* Mulder, J. M. and Wilson, J. F. eds. Religion in American history p105-26

Heimert, A. E. The Great Awakening as watershed: excerpt from "Religion and the American mind, from the Great Awakening to the Revolution." *In* Mulder, J. M. and Wilson, J. F. eds. Religion in American history p127-44

Lowance, M. I. Typology and millennial eschatology in early New England. *In* Miner, E. R. ed. Literary uses of typology p228-73

Meyer, D. H. Jonathan Edwards and the reality of the unseen. *In* Meyer, D. H. The democratic Enlightenment p18-34

Stein, S. J. Cotton Mather and Jonathan Edwards on the number of the beast; eighteenth-century speculation about the Antichrist. *In* American Antiquarian Society. Proceedings v84 pt2 293-315

About individual works

Personal narrative

Couser, G. T. Piety and prophecy in Puritan spiritual autobiography. *In* Couser, G. T. American autobiography p10-27

Shea, D. B. The art and instruction of Jonathan Edwards's Personal narrative. *In* Vaughan, A. T. and Bremer, F. J. eds. Puritan New England p299-311

Edwards, Lee R.

War and roses: the politics of Mrs Dalloway. *In* Diamond, A. and Edwards, L. R. eds. The authority of experience p160-77

Edwards, Margaret Sellars

The play of "downward comparisons": animal anthropomorphism in the poems of Robert Frost. *In* Frost: centennial essays II p236-45

Edwards, Mark U.

Erikson, experimental psychology, and Luther's identity. *In* Homans, P. ed. Childhood and selfhood p89-112

Edwards, Mark W.

Homeric speech introductions. *In* Harvard Studies in classical philology v74 p 1-36

Edwards, Owen Dudley

The impact of the American Revolution on Ireland. *In* The Impact of the American Revolution abroad p127-58

Edwards, Paul

Existentialism and death: a survey of some confusions and absurdities. *In* Donnelly, J. P. ed. Language, metaphysics, and death p32-61

Edwards, Paul Geoffrey

West African literature and English studies. *In* African studies since 1945 p91-95

Edwards, Paul Geoffrey, and Walvin, James
Africans in Britain, 1500-1800. *In* Kilson, M. L. and Rotberg, R. I. eds. The African diaspora p172-204

Edwards, Peter David
The daunting doubts of William Hay. *In* Bards, bohemians, and bookmen p218-35

Edwards, Philip
The royal pretenders in Massinger and Ford. *In* English Association. Essays and studies, 1974 p18-36
Shakespeare and the healing power of deceit. *In* Shakespeare survey v31 p115-25

Edwards, Richard
The orthodoxy of the unorthodox. *In* Artists and traditions p185-99

Edwards, Samuel, pseud. See Gerson, Noel B.

Edwards, William F.
Niccolò Leoniceno and the origins of humanist discussion of methods. *In* Philosophy and humanism p283-305

Eekman, Thomas Adam
The narrator and the hero in Chekhov's prose. *In* California Slavic studies v8 p93-129

Effect and cause. See Causation

Efficiency, Industrial
Baumol, W. J. Acceleration incentives and x-efficiency. *In* Econometrics and economic theory p167-75
Leibenstein, H. Efficiency wages, X-efficiency, and urban unemployment. *In* Economic development and planning p168-85

Mathematical models
Marschak, J. Efficient organizational design. *In* Theory for economic efficiency: essays in honor of Abba P. Lerner p110-19

Efficiency rating. See Teachers, Rating of

Efrat, Edgar S.
Terrorism in South Africa. *In* International terrorism p194-208

Efremov, Ivan Antonovich

About
Versins, P. Contact. *In* Knight, D. F. ed. Turning points p163-67

Egan, Kieran
Thucydides, tragedian. *In* Canary, R. H. and Kozicki, H. J. eds. The writing of history p63-92

Egan, Michael
Yu Dafu and the transition to modern Chinese literature. *In* Modern Chinese literature in the May Fourth era p309-24

Egbuna, Obi B.

About individual works
Wind versus polygamy
Taiwo, O. Social criticism. *In* Taiwo, O. Culture and the Nigerian novel p34-73

Egerod, Søren
Freedom and equality in the universities. *In* Universities in the Western world p12-15

Eggan, Frederick Russell
Applied anthropology in the Mountain Province, Philippines. *In* Social organization and the applications of anthropology p196-209

Egge, Bjørn
An international multipurpose surveillance system. *In* Borgese, E. M. and Krieger, D. eds. The tides of change p121-39

Eggs as food
White, E. B. Riposte. *In* White, E. B. Essays of E. B. White p60-61

Egil Skallagrimsson

About
Birnbaum, H. The sublimation of grief: poems by two mourning fathers. *In* For Wiktor Weintraub p85-98

Egils saga Skallagrímssonar
Birnbaum, H. The sublimation of grief: poems by two mourning fathers. *In* For Wiktor Weintraub p85-98

Église de Jésus-Christ sur la terre par le Prophète Simon Kimbangu
Thomas, G. B. Kimbanguism: authentically African, authentically Christian. *In* African religions: a symposium p275-96

Ego (Psychology)
Coomaraswamy, A. K. Ākimcañña: self-naughting. *In* Coomaraswamy, A. K. Selected papers v2 p88-106
De Salzmann, M. Man's ever new and eternal challenge. *In* Needleman, J. and Lewis, D. eds. On the way to self knowledge p54-75
Hughes, H. S. The advent of ego psychology. *In* Hughes, H. S. The sea change p189-239
Huxley, A. L. The ego. *In* Huxley, A. L. The Human situation p137-51
Kockelmans, J. J. Husserl and Kant on the pure ego. *In* Elliston, F. A. and McCormick, P. eds. Husserl p269-85
See also Identity (Psychology)

Egoff, Sheila A.
Children's books: a Canadian's view of the current American scene. *In* Horn Book Magazine. Crosscurrents of criticism p128-36

Egoism. See Altruism

Egudu, Romanus Nnagbo
Pictures of pain: the poetry of Dennis Brutus. *In* Heywood, C. ed. Aspects of South African literature p131-44

Egudu, Romanus Nnagbo, and Nwoga, Donatus Ibe

About individual works
Igbo traditional verse
Salt, M. J. Romanus Egudu and Donatus Nwoga: Igbo traditional verse. *In* African literature today no. 7: Focus on criticism p156-58

Egypt

Antiquities
Michałowski, K. Deir el Bahari. *In* The Frontiers of human knowledge p163-69

Antiquities, Roman
Gilliam, J. F. Some Roman elements in Roman Egypt. *In* Illinois classical studies v3, 1978 p115-31

Army—History
Ayalon, D. Preliminary remarks on the mamlūk military institution in Islam. *In* War, technology and society in the Middle East p44-48

Army—Military life—History
Rabie, H. The training of the mamlūk fāris. *In* War, technology and society in the Middle East p153-63

Egypt—*Continued*
Charters, grants, privileges
Safran, N. Egypt's search for ideology: the Nasser era. *In* Kilson, M. ed. New states in the modern world p37-56

Civilization—Arabian influences
el-Hamamsy, L. S. The assertion of Egyptian identity. *In* Ethnic identity p276-306

Foreign relations
Boutros-Ghali, B. The foreign policy of Egypt. *In* Aluko, O. ed. The foreign policies of African states p41-45

Foreign relations—Israel
Dowty, A. International guarantees with special reference to the Middle East. *In* The Dynamics of the arms race p215-30

Foreign relations—Russia
Ro'i, Y. The Soviet Union and Egypt: the constraints of a power-client relationship. *In* Ro'i, Y. ed. The limits to power p181-212

Foreign relations—United States
Terry, J. J. The consequences of economic abstention: the Aswan Dam. *In* Higham, R. D. ed. Intervention or abstention: the dilemma of American foreign policy p129-43

History
Farah, C. E. Censorship and freedom of expression in Ottoman Syria and Egypt. *In* Nationalism in a non-national state p151-94
el-Hamamsy, L. S. The assertion of Egyptian identity. *In* Ethnic identity p276-306

History—Greco-Roman period, 332 B.C.-640 A.D.
Bingen, J. The third-century B.C. land-leases from Tholthis. *In* Illinois classical studies v3, 1978 p74-80
Browne, G. M. Harpocration panegyrista. *In* Illinois classical studies, v2 1977 p184-96
Gilliam, J. F. Some Roman elements in Roman Egypt. *In* Illinois classical studies v3, 1978 p115-31
Turner, E. G. Oxyrhynchus and Rome. *In* Harvard Studies in classical philology v79 p 1-24
Youtie, H. C. ΑΓΡΑΜΜΑΤΟΣ: an aspect of Greek society in Egypt. *In* Harvard Studies in classical philology v75 p161-76

History—1250-1517
See Mamelukes

History—British occupation, 1882-1936
Smith, R. Y. The British and Sa'd Zaghlul, 1906-1912. *In* Nationalism in a non-national state p195-206

Intellectual life
Mahmoud, Z. N. The intellectual life in contemporary Egypt. *In* Arab and American cultures p201-08

Politics and government
Akhavi, S. Egypt: neo-patrimonial elite. *In* Political elites and political development in the Middle East p69-113
Kedourie, E. Anti-Marxism in Egypt. *In* Kedourie, E. Arabic political memoirs and other studies p206-17

Politics and government—1952-
Safran, N. Egypt's search for ideology: the Nasser era. *In* Kilson, M. ed. New states in the modern world p37-56

Religion
Goedicke, H. Unity and diversity in the oldest religion of ancient Egypt. *In* Unity and diversity p201-17

Egypt, Deir el Bahri. Temple of Hatshepsut
Michałowski, K. Deir el Bahari. *In* The Frontiers of human knowledge p163-69

Egyptian architecture. See Architecture, Egyptian

Egyptian literature
History and criticism
Mahmoud, Z. N. The intellectual life in contemporary Egypt. *In* Arab and American cultures p201-08

Egyptian mythology. See Mythology, Egyptian

Egyptians
Psychology
el-Hamamsy, L. S. The assertion of Egyptian identity. *In* Ethnic identity p276-306

Ehre, Milton
On August 1914. *In* Dunlop, J. B.; Haugh, R. and Klimoff, A. eds. Aleksandr Solzhenitsyn: critical essays and documentary materials 2d ed. p365-71

About individual works
Oblomov and his creator
Pritchett, V. S. Ivan Goncharov: the dream of a censor. *In* Pritchett, V. S. The myth makers p57-62

Ehrenhaft, Felix
About
Holton, G. J. Subelectrons, presuppositions, and the Millikan-Ehrenhaft dispute. *In* Historical studies in the physical sciences v9, p161-224

Ehrenpreis, Irvin
Meaning: implicit and explicit. *In* Harth, J. P. ed. New approaches to eighteenth-century literature p117-55

Ehrenwald, Jan
Parapsychology and the seven dragons: a neuropsychiatric model of psi phenomena. *In* Parapsychology: its relation to physics, biology, psychology, and psychiatry p246-63

Ehrhardt, Anke A.
The interactional model of sex hormones and behavior. *In* Katchadourian, H. A. ed. Human sexuality p150-60

Ehrlich, Alan
A steercar named Desire under the elms: a study of dramatic space in A streetcar named Desire and Desire under the elms. *In* Tennessee Williams: a tribute p126-36

Ehrlich, Isaac, and Mark, Randall
Deterrence and economics: a perspective on theory and evidence. *In* Major social issues p172-88

Ehrlich, Paul
About
Temkin, O. The era of Paul Ehrlich. *In* Temkin, O. The double face of Janus p261-68

Ehrlich, Thomas

The legal process in foreign affairs: military intervention—a testing case. *In* Stanford legal essays p113-28

Ehrmann, Jacques

The death of literature. *In* Federman, R. ed. Surfiction p229-53

Eibesfeldt, Irenäus, Eibl. See Eibl-Eibesfeldt, Irenäus

Eibl-Eibesfeldt, Irenäus

The Bushmen. *In* Goodall, V. M. ed. The quest for man p171-86

About individual works
Love and hate

Koestler, A. Not by hate alone. *In* Koestler, A. The heel of Achilles p77-80

Eichwald, Hanna

An organized home care program. *In* Home care p148-52

Eickenbaum, Boris. See Eikhenbaum, Boris Mikhaïlovich

Eidetic imagery

Patočka, J. The Husserlian doctrine of eidetic intuition and its recent critics. *In* Elliston, F. A. and McCormick, P. eds. Husserl p150-59

8 ½ (Motion picture)

Macdonald, D. 8 ½: Fellini's obvious masterpiece; excerpt from "Dwight Macdonald on movies." *In* Denby, D. ed. Awake in the dark p113-27

Eighteenth century

Brumfitt, J. H. Historical Pyrrhonism and Enlightenment historiography in France. *In* Literature and history in the age of ideas p15-28

Gilbert, F. The "new diplomacy" of the eighteenth century. *In* Gilbert, F. History p323-49

Mathias, P. Swords and ploughshares: the armed forces, medicine and public health in the late eighteenth century. *In* War and economic development p73-90

May, G. C. Probability and improbability in eighteenth-century research. *In* Studies in eighteenth-century culture v5 p3-10

See also Civilization, Modern—18th century; Enlightenment

Eigner, Edwin M.

British television drama and society in the 1970s. *In* Drama and society p209-25

Eikhenbaum, Boris Mikhaïlovich

How Gogol's "Overcoat" is made. *In* Maguire, R. A. ed. Gogol from the twentieth century p267-91

On Tolstoy's crises. *In* Erlich, V. ed. Twentieth-century Russian literary criticism p97-101

Pushkin's path to prose. *In* Erlich, V. ed. Twentieth-century Russian literary criticism p86-96

Eikons. See Icons

Eingedenken (The word)

Wohlfarth, I. On the messianic structure of Walter Benjamin's last reflections. *In* Glyph 3 p148-212

Einhorn, Eric S.

Denmark, Norway, and Sweden. *In* Galnoor, I. ed. Government secrecy in democracies p255-72

Einstein, Albert

About

Bergia, S. Einstein and the birth of special relativity. *In* Einstein p65-89

Bondi, H. Relativity theory and gravitation. *In* Einstein p113-29

Broglie, L. Prince de. My meeting with Einstein at the Solvay Conference of 1927. *In* Einstein p14-17

Cohen, I. B. Einstein and Newton. *In* Einstein p40-42

Dorling, G. Approaches to the teaching of special relativity. *In* Einstein p245-60

French, A. P. Einstein—a condensed biography. *In* Einstein p53-64

French, A. P. Einstein and world affairs. *In* Einstein p185-97

French, A. P. The story of general relativity. *In* Einstein p91-111

Gamow, G. Reminiscence; excerpt from "My world line." *In* Einstein p29-30

Halsman, P. Einstein; excerpt from "Halsman: sight and insight." *In* Einstein p27-28

Hirosige, T. The ether problem, the mechanistic worldview, and the origins of the theory of relativity. *In* Historical studies in the physical sciences v7 p3-82

Holton, G. J. 'What, precisely, is "thinking"?' *In* Einstein p153-64

Hörz, H. Philosophical concepts of space and time. *In* Einstein p229-41

Klein, M. J. Einstein and the academic establishment. *In* Einstein p209-13

Klein, M. J. Einstein and the development of quantum physics. *In* Einstein p133-51

Kuznetsov, B. G. Einstein, science and culture. *In* Einstein p167-83

Loria, A. Einstein and education. *In* Einstein p215-27

Oppenheimer, J. R. On Albert Einstein. *In* Einstein p44-49

Pais, A. Einstein, Newton, and success. *In* Einstein p35-37

Pyenson, L. Einstein's early scientific collaboration. *In* Historical studies in the physical sciences v7 p83-123

Schaffner, K. F. Space and time in Lorentz, Poincaré, and Einstein: divergent approaches to the discovery and development of the special theory of relativity. *In* Motion and time, space and matter p465-507

Shankland, R. S. Conversations with Albert Einstein. *In* Einstein p38-39

Snow, C. P. Baron Snow. Albert Einstein 1879-1955; excerpt from "Variety of men." *In* Einstein p3-8

Solovine, M. Excerpts from a memoir. *In* Einstein p9-13

Straus, E. G. Memoir. *In* Einstein p31-32

Tauber, G. E. Einstein and Zionism. *In* Einstein p199-207

Wheeler, J. A. Memoir. *In* Einstein p21-22

Whyte, L. L. Reminiscences of Einstein; excerpt from "Focus and diversions." *In* Einstein p18-20

Wigner, E. P. Memoir. *In* Einstein p33

About individual works
Relativity

Downs, R. B. Harbinger of the atomic age. *In* Downs, R. B. Books that changed the world p374-82

Eisdorfer, Carl

Psychophysiologic and cognitive studies in the aged. *In* Aging: the process and the people p96-128

Societal response to aging: some possible consequences. *In* Jarvik, L. F. ed. Aging into the 21st century p123-35

Eisenberg, Leon

The search for care. *In* Knowles, J. H. ed. Doing better and feeling worse p235-46

Eisenberg, Marvin

An antiphonal page of the Sienese Quattrocento. *In* Enggass, R. C. and Stokstad, M. eds. Hortus imaginum p51-55

Eisenhart, Thomas S.

Rehabilitation: one man's opinion. *In* Henderson, G. ed. Human relations in the military p177-86

The **Eisenhower** Doctrine. DeNovo, J. A. *In* Encyclopedia of American foreign policy p292-301

Eisenstadt, Samuel Noah

Cultural settings and adolescence and youth around the year 2000. *In* Adolescence and youth in prospect p114-24

The patterns of incorporation of different dimensions of Socialist tradition. *In* Eisenstadt, S. N. and Azmon, Y. eds. Socialism and tradition p221-27

Socialism and tradition. *In* Eisenstadt, S. N. and Azmon, Y. eds. Socialism and tradition p 1-18

The sociological tradition: origins, boundaries, patterns of innovation, and crises. *In* Culture and its creators p43-71

Eisenstein, Sergeĭ Mikhaĭlovich

Colour film; excerpt from "Notes of a film director." *In* Nichols, B. ed. Movies and methods p381-88

About

Barthes, R. Diderot, Brecht, Eisenstein. *In* Barthes, R. Image, music, text p69-78

Henderson, B. Two types of film theory. *In* Nichols, B. ed. Movies and methods p388-400

About individual works

Alexander Nevsky

Taylor, R. Alexander Nevsky. *In* Taylor, R. Film propaganda p116-30

Dickens, Griffith and the film today

Paroissien, D. H. Dickens and the cinema. *In* Dickens Studies Annual v7 p68-80

Ivan the Terrible

Barthes, R. The third meaning. *In* Barthes, R. Image, music, text p52-68

October

Brik, O. M. and Shklovskiĭ, V. B. The Lef arena. *In* Nichols, B. ed. Movies and methods p15-22

Taylor, R. October. *In* Taylor, R. Film propaganda p92-102

Potemkin

Kauffmann, S. Potemkin. *In* Kauffmann, S. Living images p290-98

Murray, E. Potemkin. *In* Murray, E. Ten film classics p 1-17

Eisenstein-Barzilay, Isaac

Finalizing an issue: Modena's authorship of the Qol sakhal. *In* Salo Wittmayer Baron v 1 p135-66

Eisinger, Chester E.

Traditionalism and modernism in Eudora Welty. *In* Prenshaw, P. W. ed. Eudora Welty p3-25

Eisner, Sigmund

Chaucer's use of Nicholas of Lynn's Calendar. *In* English Association. Essays and studies, 1976 p 1-22

Eister, Allan W.

Culture crises and new religious movements: a paradigmatic statement of a theory of cults. *In* Zaretsky, I. I. and Leone, M. P. eds. Religious movements in contemporary America p612-27

Eitinger, Leo

On being a psychiatrist and a survivor. *In* Rosenfeld, A. H. and Greenberg, I. eds. Confronting the Holocaust p186-99

Eitner, Lorenz Edwin Alfred

Cages, prisons, and captives in eighteenth-century art. *In* Kroeber, K. and Walling, W. eds. Images of romanticism p13-38

Ejection (Psychology) See Anthropomorphism

Ek, Grete

Mistaken conduct and proper 'feeling': a study of Jane Austen's Pride and prejudice. *In* Røstvig, M. S. ed. Fair forms p178-202

Ekblom, Harry Edward

Managing the future is managing ideas and change. *In* Benton, L. R. ed. Management for the future p87-100

Ekirch, Arthur Alphonse

Détente. *In* Encyclopedia of American foreign policy p239-43

Eklund, Sigvard

Critical decisions in relation to energy. *In* World change and world security p61-72

Ekman, Paul

Facial signs: facts, fantasies, and possibilities. *In* Sebeok, T. A. ed. Sight, sound, and sense p124-56

See also Harrison, R. P. jt. auth.

Ekwensi, Cyprian

About

Lindfors, B. The blind men and the elephant. *In* African literature today no. 7: Focus on criticism p53-64

Elagabalus. See Heliogabalus, Emperor of Rome

Elagin, Sergei

Repentance: its theory, history and prescription for today. *In* Medvedev, R. A. ed. The Samizdat register p237-66

El-Ayouty, Yassin

The OAU and the Arab-Israeli conflict: a case of mediation that failed. *In* El-Ayouty, Y. ed. The Organization of African Unity after ten years p189-212

El-Calamawy, Sahair

The impact of tradition on the development of modern Arabic literature. *In* Arab and American cultures p47-53

El Cid, Díaz de Vivar, Rodrigo, called El Cid. See El Cid Campeador

Elcock, Howard J.

J. M. Keynes at the Paris Peace Conference. *In* Keynes, M. ed. Essays on John Maynard Keynes p162-76

Elder, Donald
About individual works
Ring Lardner
Berryman, J. Enslavement: Three American cases; the case of Ring Lardner. *In* Berryman, J. The freedom of the poet p204-16

Elder, Jacob D.
Morality in a Yoruba ritual in Trinidad. *In* Yoder, D. ed. American folklife p281-91

Elder, John Petersen
Catullus I, his poetic creed, and Nepos. *In* Harvard Studies in classical philology v71 p143-49

Elder, Neil C.
The functions of the modern state. *In* Hayward, J. E. S. and Berki, R. N. eds. State and society in contemporary Europe p58-74

Elderfield, John
"Dada": a code for saints? *In* Kaplan, P. and Manso, S. eds. Major European art movements, 1900-1945 p310-24

Eldest child. See Children, First-born

Eldredge, Laurence Milton
The concept of God's absolute power at Oxford in the later fourteenth century. *In* Jeffrey, D. L. ed. By things seen: reference and recognition in medieval thought p211-26

The state of "Pearl" studies since 1933. *In* Viator: medieval and Renaisance studies v6 p171-94

Elections
See also Local elections; Presidents—United States—Election; Representative government and representation; Voting; and subdivision Elections under names of legislative bodies of countries, states, etc., e.g., United States. Congress—Elections

Akita, Japan—History
Sims, R. L. National elections and electioneering in Akita Ken, 1930-1942. *In* Modern Japan p89-112

United States
King, M. R. and Seligman, L. G. Critical elections, Congressional recruitment and public policy. *In* Eulau, H. and Czudnowski, M. M. eds. Elite recruitment in democratic politics p263-99

Polsby, D. D. Buckley v. Valeo: the special nature of political speech. *In* The Supreme Court review, 1976 p 1-43

See also Afro-Americans—Politics and suffrage
United States—History
Benedict, M. L. The rout of radicalism: Republicans and the elections of 1867. *In* Swierenga, R. P. ed. Beyond the Civil War synthesis p137-47

Elections, Municipal. See Local elections

Electra in literature
Falk, E. H. Some concepts of the tragic in versions of Electra. *In* Creative encounter p3-16

Electric utilities
United States—Costs
Kaufman, A. Electric power: regulation of a natural monopoly. *In* Kalter, R. J. and Vogely, W. A. eds. Energy supply and government policy p216-34

Electric waves. See Electrodynamics

Electricity
Caneva, K. L. From galvanism to electrodynamics: the transformation of German physics and its social context. *In* Historical studies in the physical sciences v9 p63-159

Tatar, M. M. Salvation by electricity: science, poetry, and "Naturphilosophie." *In* Tatar, M. M. Spellbound p45-81

Electricity, Static. See Electrostatics

Electrodynamics
Caneva, K. L. From galvanism to electrodynamics: the transformation of German physics and its social context. *In* Historical studies in the physical sciences v9 p63-159

D'Agostino, S. Hertz's researches on electromagnetic waves. *In* Historical studies in the physical science v6 p261-324

Electromagnetic theory
Doran, B. G. Origins and consolidation of field theory in nineteenth-century Britain: from the mechanical to the electromagnetic view of nature. *In* Historical studies in the physical sciences v6 p133-260

See also Electrodynamics; Electrons

Electromagnetism
Siegel, D. M. Classical-electromagnetic and relativistic approaches to the problem of nonintegral atomic masses. *In* Historical studies in the physical sciences v9 p323-60

Electronic brains. See Artificial intelligence

Electronic data processing. See Artificial intelligence; and subdivision Data processing under subjects; e.g. Anthropology—Data processing

Electronic music. See Computer music

Electronic translating. See Machine translating

Electrons
Holton, G. J. Subelectrons, presuppositions, and the Millikan-Ehrenhaft dispute. *In* Historical studies in the physical sciences v9 p161-224

See also Photoelectricity

Emission
See Photoelectricity

Electrostatics
Buchwald, J. Z. William Thomson and the mathematization of Faraday's electrostatics. *In* Historical studies in the physical sciences v8 p101-36

Elegiac poetry
See also Laments

History and criticism
Ludwig, W. Petrus Lotichius Secundus and the Roman elegists: prolegomena to a study of Neo-Latin elegy. *In* Classical influences on European culture A.D. 1500-1700 p171-90

Poggioli, R. The funeral elegy. *In* Poggioli, R. The oaten flute p64-82

Elegiac poetry, Latin
LaBranche, A. 'Blanda elegeia': the background to Donne's 'Elegies.' *In* Roberts, J. R. ed. Essential articles for the study of John Donne's poetry p399-410

History and criticism
Ludwig, W. Petrus Lotichius Secundus and the Roman elegists: prologomena to a study of Neo-Latin elegy. *In* Classical influences on European culture A.D. 1500-1700 p171-90

Eliot, George—About individual works
—Continued
Middlemarch

Beaty, J. On first looking into George Eliot's Middlemarch. In Levine, R. A. The Victorian experience: the novelists p151-75

Gilbert, S. M. and Gubar, S. George Eliot as the Angel of Destruction. In Gilbert, S. M. and Gubar, S. The madwoman in the attic p478-535

Johnson, E. D. H. "The truer measure": setting in Emma, Middlemarch, and Howards End. In Bornstein, G. ed. Romantic and modern p197-205

Jones, P. Imagination and egoism in Middlemarch. In Jones, P. Philosophy and the novel p7-50

Kiely, R. The limits of dialogue in Middlemarch. In The Worlds of Victorian fiction p103-23

Lerner, L. Literature and money. In English Association. Essays and studies, 1975 p106-22

Miller, J. H. Narrative and history. In ELH essays for Earl R. Wasserman p165-83

Miller, J. H. Optic and semiotic in Middlemarch. In The Worlds of Victorian fiction p125-45

Sabin, M. Middlemarch: beyond the voyage to Cythera. In Sabin, M. English romanticism and the French tradition p237-57

Stoneman, P. G. Eliot: Middlemarch. In Williams, D. A. ed. The monster in the mirror p102-30

Sutherland, J. A. Marketing 'Middlemarch.' In Sutherland, J. A. Victorian novelists and publishers p188-205

Tomlinson, T. B. Middlemarch and modern society. In Tomlinson, T. B. The English middle-class novel p102-13

Trickett, R. Vitality of language in nineteenth-century fiction. In Josipovici, G. ed. The modern English novel: the reader, the writer and the work p37-53

The mill on the Floss

Haley, B. Two staunch walkers: Tom Thurnall and Tom Tulliver. In Haley, B. The healthy body and Victorian culture p180-204

Romola

Sanders, A. 'Romola's waking': George Eliot's historical novel. In Sanders, A. The Victorian historical novel, 1840-1880 p168-96

Scenes of clerical life

Gilbert, S. M. and Gubar, S. George Eliot as the Angel of Destruction. In Gilbert, S. M. and Gubar, S. The madwoman in the attic p478-535

Characters

Gilbert, S. M. and Gubar, S. Made keen by loss: George Eliot's veiled vision. In Gilbert, S. M. and Gubar, S. The madwoman in the attic p443-77

Sabin, M. Middlemarch: beyond the voyage to Cythera. In Sabin, M. English romanticism and the French tradition p237-57

Philosophy

Jones, P. George Eliot and philosophy. In Jones, P. Philosophy and the novel p50-69

Plots

Caserio, R. L. The featuring of act as "the rescue": story in Dickens and George Eliot. In Caserio, R. L. Plot, story, and the novel p91-132

Eliot, Thomas Lamb
About

Singer, B. Oregon's nineteenth-century notables: Simeon Gannett Reed and Thomas Lamb Eliot. In Bingham, E. R. and Love, G. A. eds. Northwest perspectives p61-76

Eliot, Thomas Stearns

Reflections on vers libre; excerpt from "To criticize the critics." In Gross, H. S. ed. The structure of verse p227-33

Selected prose of T. S. Eliot
Contents

Andrew Marvell
Dante
Francis Herbert Bradley
From Baudelaire
From Ezra Pound: his metric and poetry
From The idea of a Christian society
From Milton II
From The music of poetry
From Notes towards the definition of culture
From Philip Massinger
From Thomas Middleton
From The use of poetry and the use of criticism
The function of criticism
Hamlet
The humanism of Irving Babbitt
In memoriam
Lancelot Andrewes
Marie Lloyd
The metaphysical poets
Milton I
The perfect critic
Poetry and drama
Reflections on vers libre
Religion and literature
Tradition and the individual talent
Also in Primeau, R. ed. Influx p15-24
Ulysses, order, and myth
What is a classic?
Yeats

About

Bateson, F. W. Criticism's lost leader. In The Literary criticism of T. S. Eliot p 1-19

Charity, A. C. T. S. Eliot: The Dantean recognitions. In The Waste land in different voices p117-62

Colmer, J. The idealist vision. In Colmer, J. Coleridge to Catch-22 p18-29

Connolly, C. T. S. Eliot: 1. In Connolly, C. The evening colonnade p207-11

Davie, D. Eliot in one poet's life. In The Waste land in different voices p221-37

Donoghue, D. Eliot and the Criterion. In The Literary criticism of T. S. Eliot p20-41

Eliot, T. S. Poetry and drama. In Eliot, T. S. Selected prose of T. S. Eliot p132-47

Fraser, G. S. T. S. Eliot: a reappraisal. In Fraser, G. S. Essays on twentieth-century poets p108-24

French, W. G. The age of Eliot: the twenties as waste land. In French, W. G. ed. The twenties p 1-26

Gillie, C. Drama 1900-1940. In Gillie, C. Movements in English literature, 1900-1940 p164-82

Gillie, C. The recovery of poetry, 1900-1920. In Gillie, C. Movements in English literature, 1900-1940 p65-89

Gillie, C. Yeats and Eliot: the climax. In Gillie, C. Movements in English literature, 1900-1940 p150-63

Eliot, Thomas S.—About individual works —*Continued*

The use of poetry and the use of criticism

Robson, W. W. A poet's notebook: The use of poetry and the use of criticism. *In* The Literary criticism of T. S. Eliot p139-59

The waste land

Adams, R. P. Sunrise out of The waste land. *In* Wagner, L. W. ed. Ernest Hemingway p241-51

Cunningham, J. S. Pope, Eliot, and 'The mind of Europe.' *In* The Waste land in different voices p67-85

DeMott, R. J. Robinson Jeffers' "Tamar." *In* French, W. G. ed. The twenties p405-25

Donoghue, D. "The word within a word." *In* Donoghue, D. The sovereign ghost p183-206

Also in The Waste land in different voices p185-201

Drain, R. 'The waste land': the prison and the key. *In* The Waste land in different voices p29-45

Fraser, G. S. 'The wasteland' revisited. *In* Fraser, G. S. Essays on twentieth-century poets p89-98

French, W. G. The age of Eliot: the twenties as waste land. *In* French, W. G. ed. The twenties p 1-26

Gordon, L. G. Meaning and myth in The sound and the fury and The waste land. *In* French, W. G. ed. The twenties p269-302

Harding, D. C. W. What the thunder said. *In* The Waste land in different voices p15-28

Harris, B. 'This music crept by me': Shakespeare and Wagner. *In* The Waste land in different voices p105-16

Harter, C. C. Strange bedfellows: The waste land and An American tragedy. *In* French, W. G. ed. The twenties p51-64

Hunt, J. D. 'Broken images': T. S. Eliot and modern painting. *In* The Waste land in different voices p163-84

Jackson, B. Jean Toomer's Cane: an issue of genre. *In* French, W. G. ed. The twenties p317-33

Johnson, K. Eliot as enemy: William Carlos Williams and The waste land. *In* French, W. G. ed. The twenties p377-86

Langbaum, R. W. Eliot: the walking dead. *In* Langbaum, R. W. The mysteries of identity p83-119

Miller, J. E. Fitzgerald's Gatsby: the world as ash heap. *In* French, W. G. ed. The twenties p181-202

Miller, J. E. Personal mood transmuted into epic: T. S. Eliot's "Waste land." *In* Miller, J. E. The American quest for a supreme fiction p100-25

Moody, A. D. 'To fill all the desert with inviolable voice.' *In* The Waste land in different voices p47-66

Morris, W. T. S. Eliot. *In* Morris, W. Earthly delights, unearthly adornments p95-103

Owen, G. Robert Frost and The waste land. *In* French, W. G. ed. The twenties p351-63

Rajan, B. The dialect of the tribe. *In* The Waste land in different voices p 1-14

Slote, B. An appointment with the future: Willa Cather. *In* French, W. G. ed. The twenties p39-49

Trilling, L. Thomas Stearns Eliot: The waste land. *In* Trilling, L. Prefaces to The experience of literature p274-83

Ward, N. 'Fourmillante cité': Baudelaire and 'The waste land.' *In* The Waste land in different voices p87-104

Widmer, K. The waste land and the American breakdown. *In* French, W. G. ed. The twenties p475-96

The waste land: a facsimile and transcript of the original draft including the annotations of Ezra Pound

Connolly, C. T. S. Eliot: 2 *In* Connolly, C. The evening colonnade p212-16

The waste land—Manuscripts

Kenner, H. The urban apocalypse. *In* Wimsatt, W. K. ed. Literary criticism: idea and act p616-35

Bibliography

Bornstein, G. Pound and Eliot. *In* American literary scholarship, 1977 p119-33

Ludwig, R. M. Pound and Eliot. *In* American literary scholarship, 1974 p101-21

McDougal, S. Y. Pound and Eliot. *In* American literary scholarship, 1975 p131-42

McDougal, S. Y. Pound and Eliot [another essay] *In* American literary scholarship, 1976 p109-18

Influence—Davie

Davie, D. Eliot in one poet's life. *In* The Waste land in different voices p221-37

Knowledge—Art

Hunt, J. D. 'Broken images': T. S. Eliot and modern painting. *In* The Waste land in different voices p163-84

Language

Fraser, G. S. A language by itself. *In* Fraser, G. S. Essays on twentieth-century poets p99-107

Philosophy

Righter, W. The 'philosophical critic.' *In* The Literary criticism of T. S. Eliot p111-38

Religion and ethics

Nott, K. Ideology and poetry. *In* The Waste land in different voices p203-20

Sources

Harris, B. 'This music crept by me': Shakespeare and Wagner. *In* The Waste land in different voices p105-16

Elite (Social sciences)

Blum, J. Russia. *In* Spring, D. ed. European landed elites in the nineteenth century p68-97

Cohen, Y. A. The state system, schooling and cognitive and motivational patterns. *In* Social forces and schooling p103-40

Crook, R. Political centralization and local politics in Ghana: the careers of Nana Wiafe Akenten II and E. K. Duncan-Williams of Offinso (Ashanti) *In* The Making of politicians: studies from Africa and Asia p28-48

Daniels, R. V. Office holding and elite status: the Central Committee of the CPSU. *In* Cocks, P.; Daniels, R. V. and Heer N. W. eds. The dynamics of Soviet politics p77-95

Elite (Social sciences)—*Continued*

Eulau, H. Elite analysis and democratic theory: the contribution of Harold D. Lasswell. *In* Eulau, H. and Czudnowski, M. M. eds. Elite recruitment in democratic polities p7-28

Gonzalez, E. Institutionalization, political elites, and foreign policies. *In* Cuba in the world p3-36

Herr, R. Spain. *In* Spring, D. ed. European landed elites in the nineteenth century p98-126

Kaltefleiter, W. The recruitment market of the German political elite. *In* Eulau, H. and Czudnowski, M. M. eds. Elite recruitment in democratic polities p239-62

Kirkendall, R. S. Elitism and foreign policy. *In* Encyclopedia of American foreign policy p302-09

Payne, H. C. Elite versus popular mentality in the eighteenth century. *In* Studies in eighteenth-century culture v8 p3-32

Pollock, J. C. Early socialization and elite behavior. *In* Schwartz, D. C. and Schwartz, S. K. eds. New directions in political socialization p203-26

Prewitt, K. and McAllister, W. Changes in the American executive elite, 1930-1970. *In* Eulau, H. and Czudnowski, M. M. eds. Elite recruitment in democratic polities p105-32

Spring, D. Landed elites compared. *In* Spring, D. ed. European landed elites in the nineteenth century p 1-21

Stern, F. R. Prussia. *In* Spring, D. ed. European landed elites in the nineteenth century p45-67

Thompson, F. M. L. Britain. *In* Spring, D. ed. European landed elites in the nineteenth century p22-44

Zeldin, T. France. *In* Spring, D. ed. European landed elites in the nineteenth century p127-39

Algeria

Zartman, I. W. Algeria: a post-revolutionary elite. *In* Political elites and political development in the Middle East p255-92

Egypt

Akhavi, S. Egypt: neo-patrimonial elite. *In* Political elites and political development in the Middle East p69-113

Iran

Zonis, M. The political elite of Iran: a second stratum? *In* Political elites and political development in the Middle East p193-216

Israel

Torgovnik, E. Israel: the persistent elite. *In* Political elites and political development in the Middle East p219-53

Near East

Tachau, F. Conclusion. *In* Political elites and political development in the Middle East p293-305

Tachau, F. Introduction: Political elites and political development in the Middle East. *In* Political elites and political development in the Middle East p 1-21

Saudi Arabia

Wenner, M. W. Saudi Arabia: survival of traditional elites. *In* Political elites and political development in the Middle East p157-91

Syria

Van Dusen, M. H. Syria: downfall of a traditional elite. *In* Political elites and political development in the Middle East p115-55

Turkey

Szyliowicz, J. S. Elites and modernization in Turkey. *In* Political elites and political development in the Middle East p23-66

Elites (Social sciences). See Elite (Social sciences)

Elixir of life

Talbot, C. H. The elixir of youth. *In* Chaucer and Middle English studies in honour of Rossell Hope Robbins p31-42

See also Alchemy

El Kafi

Tunisia: hopes for the medina of Tunis. *In* United Nations Educational, Scientific and Cultural Organization. The conservation of cities p125-39

Elkes, Joel

Subjective and objective observation in psychiatry: a note toward discussion. *In* Alternate states of consciousness p242-63

Elkin, Adolphus Peter

Elliot Smith and the diffusion of culture. *In* Grafton Elliot Smith p139-59

Elkin, Robert

A systems approach to planning and managing programs for the handicapped. *In* Managing nonprofit organizations p71-77

Elkind, David

The child and society

Contents

The active classroom and children with special needs: affective and social dimensions

Borderline retardation in low-and middle-income adolescents

Choosing to be gay: the roots of homosexuality

Cognitive development and psychopathology: observations on egocentrism and ego defense

Cognitive frames and family interactions

Conclusion

Culture, change, and children

The curriculum-disabled child

Day care in America

The early years: the vital years

Ethnicity and reading: three avoidable dangers

Exploitation and the generational conflict

From ghetto school to college campus

Humanizing the curriculum

Life and death: concepts and feelings of children

Middle-class delinquency

Observing classroom frames

The origins of religion in the child

Piaget and Montessori in the classroom

The study of spontaneous religion in the child

Teacher-child contracts

Understanding the young adolescent

We can teach reading better

Elliott, Brian Robinson

Aust. lit. &c.—a chaplet of wattle blossom? *In* Bards, bohemians, and bookmen p320-27

Elliott, Emory

From father to son: the evolution of typology in Puritan New England. *In* Miner, E. R. ed. Literary uses of typology p204-27

Elliott, John Huxtable

Renaissance Europe and America: a blunted impact? *In* First images of America p11-23

Elliott, Maurice Slater

Respecting our organs. *In* Gold, J. ed. In the name of language! p161-204

Elliott, R. K.

Aesthetic theory and the experience of art. *In* Margolis, J. Z. ed. Philosophy looks at the arts p45-87

Education and human being I. *In* Philosophers discuss education p45-72

About individual works
Education and human being I

Langford, G. Education and human being II. *In* Philosophers discuss education p73-84

Elliott, Richard Smith

About individual works
Notes taken in sixty years

Joost, N. T. The traveller as antihero: Richard Smith Elliott in the Mexican War. *In* Kagle, S. E. ed. America: exploration and travel p83-91

Elliott, Robert C.

Swift's satire: rules of the game. *In* ELH essays for Earl R. Wasserman p123-38

Elliott, S. James

Homosexuality in the crucial decade: three novelists' views. *In* Crew, L. ed. The gay academic p164-77

Elliott, William

About

Rubin, L. D. William Elliott shoots a bear. *In* Rubin, L. D. William Elliott shoots a bear p 1-27

About individual works
Carolina sports by land and water

Rubin, L. D. William Elliott shoots a bear. *In* Rubin, L. D. William Elliott shoots a bear p 1-27

Ellis, Brian David

Physicalism and the contents of sense experience. *In* Philosophical aspects of the mind-body problem p64-77

Ellis, Edward Earle

"Christ crucified". *In* Reconciliation and hope p69-75

The composition of Luke 9 and the sources of its Christology. *In* Current issues in Biblical and patristic interpretation p121-27

Ellis, Frank Hale

Johnson and Savage: two failed tragedies and a failed tragic hero. *In* Martz, L. L. and Williams, A. L. eds. The author in his work p337-46

Ellis, Havelock

About

Cockshut, A. O. J. The optimists. *In* Cockshut, A. O. J. Man and woman: a study of love and the novel, 1740-1940 p136-52

About individual works
The new spirit

Alcorn, J. Butler: the new spirit. *In* Alcorn, J. The nature novel from Hardy to Lawrence p25-41

Ellis, Henry

About

Shy, J. W. The spectrum of imperial possibilities: Henry Ellis and Thomas Pownall, 1763-1775. *In* Shy, J. W. A people numerous and armed p35-72

Ellis, John Rogers

Medical education—a personal view. *In* The Frontiers of human knowledge p69-78

Ellis, Kate

Monsters in the garden: Mary Shelley and the bourgeois family. *In* Levine, G. L. and Knoepflmacher, U. C. eds. The endurance of Frankenstein p123-42

Ellison, Ralph

About

Feuser, W. F. The men who lived underground: Richard Wright and Ralph Ellison. *In* King, B. A. and Ogungbesan, K. eds. A celebration of Black and African writing p87-101

Nichols, C. H. Comic modes in Black America (a ramble through Afro-American humor). *In* Cohen, S. B. ed. Comic relief p105-26

O'Meally, R. G. Riffs and rituals: folklore in the work of Ralph Ellison. *In* Fisher, D. and Stepto, R. B. eds. Afro-American literature p153-69

About individual works
Invisible man

Howe, I. A Negro in America. *In* Howe, I. Celebrations and attacks p29-31

Pryse, M. Invisible man: the world in a man-of-war. *In* Pryse, M. The mark and the knowledge p143-67

King of the bingo game

Real, W. Ralph Ellison, King of the bingo game. *In* Bruck, P. ed. The Black American short story in the 20th century p111-27

Bibliography

Giza, J. Ralph Ellison. *In* Inge, M. T.; Duke, J. M. and Bryer, J. R. eds. Black American writers v2 p47-71

Characters

Pryse, M. Invisible man: the world in a man-of-war. *In* Pryse, M. The mark and the knowledge p143-67

Elliston, Frederick A.

Husserl's phenomenology of empathy. *In* Elliston, F. A. and McCormick, P. eds. Husserl p213-46

In defense of promiscuity. *In* Baker, R. and Elliston, F. A. eds. Philosophy & sex p222-43

Ellmann, Richard

Two faces of Edward. *In* Wimsatt, W. K. ed. Literary criticism: idea and act p560-75

About individual works
Golden codgers

Mudrick, M. Ellmann on Joyce, etc. *In* Mudrick, M. The man in the machine p145-51

Ellrodt, Robert

Self-consciousness in Montaigne and Shakespeare. *In* Shakespeare survey 28 p37-50

Ellsworth, Oliver Bryant

A fourteenth-century proposal for equal temperament. *In* Viator: medieval and Renaissance studies v5 p445-53

Ellul, Jacques

International propaganda and myths. *In* Fischer, H. D. and Merrill, J. C. eds. International and intercultural communication p273-79

Search for an image. *In* Bundy, R. F. ed. Images of the future: the twenty-first century and beyond p24-34

Technological morality; excerpt from "To will & to do". *In* Davis, F. J. and Stivers, R. eds. The collective definition of deviance p162-76

About

Sale, R. H. Toynbee, Ellul, Safdie, Negroponte. *In* Sale, R. H. On not being good enough p188-202

About individual works

The technological society

Stivers, R. Social control in the technological society. *In* Davis, J. J. and Stivers, R. eds. The collective definition of deviance p376-91

Ellwood, Robert Scott

Alternative altars

Contents

Colonel Olcott and Madame Blavatsky journey to the East

Epilogue

Excursus religion

Inner worlds: the psychology of excursus religion

Shakers and spiritualists

Temple and cave in America

Zen journeys to the West

Emergent religion in America: an historical perspective. *In* Needleman, J. and Baker, G. eds. Understanding the new religions p267-84

Ellwood, Sheelagh

The working class under the Franco régime. *In* Preston, P. ed. Spain in crisis p157-82

El Mallakh, Dorothea. See Mallakh, Dorothea

El Mallakh, Ragaei. See Mallakh, Raja'i

Elmendorf, Mary Lindsay

Mexico: the many worlds of women. *In* Giele, J. Z. and Smock, A. C. eds. Women: roles and status in eight countries p127-72

El-Messiri, Sawsan

Self-images of traditional urban women in Cairo. *In* Beck, L. and Keddie, N. R. eds. Women in the Muslim world p522-40

Elmore, Albert E.

Herrick and the poetry of song. *In* Rollin, R. B. and Patrick, J. M. eds. "Trust to good verses": Herrick tercentenary essays p65-75

Elovitz, Paul H.

Three days in Plains. *In* DeMause, L. and Ebel, H. eds. Jimmy Carter and American fantasy p33-57

Elsaesser, Thomas

Screen violence: emotional structure and ideological function in 'A clockwork orange.' *In* Bigsby, C. W. E. ed. Approaches to popular culture p171-200

Shock corridor by Sam Fuller. *In* Nichols, B. ed. Movies and methods p290-97

Two decades in another country: Hollywood and the cinéphiles. *In* Bigsby, C. W. E. Superculture p199-216

Else, Gerald Frank

Ritual and drama in Aischyleian tragedy. *In* Illinois classical studies, v2 1977 p70-87

El-Shamy, Hasan

African world view and religion. *In* Martin, P. M. and O'Meara, P. eds. Africa p208-20

Elstun, Esther Nies

Richard Beer-Hofmann: the poet as exculpator dei. *In* Strelka, J. P.; Bell, R. F. and Dobson, E. eds. Protest—form—tradition p123-32

Elsworth, John David

Andrei Bely's theory of symbolism. *In* Barnes, C. J. ed. Studies in twentieth century Russian literature p17-45

Bely's Moscow novels. *In* Janecek, G. ed. Andrey Bely p127-34

Eltis, Walter Alfred

Adam Smith's theory of economic growth. *In* Skinner, A. S. and Wilson, T. eds. Essays on Adam Smith p426-54

Elton, Geoffrey Rudolph

The sessional printing of statutes, 1484-1547. *In* Wealth and power in Tudor England p68-86

Taxation for war and peace in early-Tudor England. *In* War and economic development p33-48

Éluard, Paul

About

Bowie, M. Paul Eluard. *In* Cardinal, R. ed. Sensibility and creation p149-67

Elvin, Mark

Chinese cities since the Sung Dynasty. *In* Towns in societies p79-89

Elwell, Walter A.

The deity of Christ in the writings of Paul. *In* Current issues in Biblical and patristic interpretation p297-308

Ely, James W.

Law in a republican society: continuity and change in the legal system of postrevolutionary America. *In* Perspectives on revolution and evolution p46-65

Ely, John Hart

The constitutionality of reverse racial discrimination. *In* Gross, B. R. ed. Reverse discrimination p208-16

Ely, John Wilton- See Wilton-Ely, John

Ely, England (Diocese)

Charters, grants, privileges

Owen, D. The muniments of Ely Cathedral priory. *In* Church and government in the Middle Ages p157-76

Ely Monastery

Owen, D. The muniments of Ely Cathedral priory. *In* Church and government in the Middle Ages p157-76

Emad, Parvis

Heidegger's value-criticism and its bearing on the phenomenology of values. *In* Radical phenomenology p190-208

Emancipation of slaves. See Slavery in the United States—Emancipation

Emancipation of women. See Women's rights

Emare

Donovan, M. J. Middle English Emare and the cloth worthily wrought. *In* The Learned and the lewed p337-42

Embargo

Combs, J. A. Embargoes. *In* Encyclopedia of American foreign policy p310-21

See also Blockade

Emblem books

Lewalski, B. K. Protestant emblematics: sacred emblems and religious lyrics. *In* Lewalski, B. K. Protestant poetics and the seventeenth-century religious lyric p179-212

Emblems

Lewalski, B. K. Protestant emblematics: sacred emblems and religious lyrics. *In* Lewalski, B. K. Protestant poetics and the seventeenth-century religious lyric p179-212

Tung, M. Whitney's A choice of emblemes revisited: a comparative study of the manuscript and the printed versions. *In* Virginia. University. Bibliographical Socety. Studies in bibliography v29 p32-101

See also Mottoes

Emblems, National. See Flags

Emboden, William Allen

Plant hypnotics among the North American Indians. *In* American folk medicine p159-67

Embodiment and behavior. Shoemaker, S. *In* Rorty, A. O. ed. The identities of persons p109-37

Embrey, Glenn

The subterranean world of The night of the iguana. *In* Tennessee Williams: a tribute p325-40

Embryology

Thomas, L. On embryology. *In* Thomas, L. The medusa and the snail p155-57

See also Ontogeny; Reproduction

Emden, Cecil Stuart

Shakespeare and the eye. *In* Shakespeare survey 26 p129-37

Emenyonu, Ernest N.

Who does Flora Nwapa write for? *In* African literature today no. 7: Focus on criticism p28-33

About individual works

African literature: what does it take to be its critic?

Lindfors, B. The blind men and the elephant. *In* African literature today no. 7: Focus on criticism p53-64

Emergency food supply. See Food relief

Emergency medical care. See Emergency medical services

Emergency medical services

Hinds, S. W. On the relations of medical triage to world famine: an historical survey. *In* Lucas, G. R. and Ogletree, T. W. eds. Lifeboat ethics p29-51

Emergency powers. See Executive power; War and emergency powers

Emerson, Everett H.

The cultural context of the American Revolution. *In* Emerson, E. H. ed. American literature, 1764-1789 p3-17

Emerson, O. B.

Sóme contemporary literary views of the newest South. *In* The Rising South v2 p117-25

Emerson, Ralph Waldo

About

Allen, G. W. A new look at Emerson and science. *In* Literature and ideas in America p58-78

Bercovitch, S. Emerson the prophet: romanticism, Puritanism, and auto-American-biography. *In* Levin, D. ed. Emerson: prophecy, metamorphosis, and influence p 1-27

Bloom, H. Emerson and Whitman: the American sublime. *In* Bloom, H. Poetry and repression. p235-66

Bloom, H. The freshness of transformation: Emerson's dialectics of influence. *In* Levin, D. ed. Emerson: prophecy, metamorphosis, and influence p129-48

Cole, P. B. Emerson, England, and fate. *In* Levin, D. ed. Emerson: prophecy, metamorphosis, and influence p83-105

Cox, J. M. R. W. Emerson: the circles of the eye. *In* Levin, D. ed. Emerson: prophecy, metamorphosis, and influence p57-81

Eberhart, R. Emerson and Wallace Stevens. *In* Eberhart, R. Of poetry and poets p153-71

Gelpi, A. Emerson: the paradox of organic form. *In* Levin, D. ed. Emerson: prophecy, metamorphosis, and influence p149-70

Gonnaud, M. Emerson and the imperial self: a European critique. *In* Levin, D. ed. Emerson: prophecy, metamorphosis, and influence p107-28

Hedges, W. L. From Franklin to Emerson. *In* Lemay, J. A. L. ed. The oldest revolutionary p139-56

Hutch, R. A. Ralph Waldo Emerson: the birth of a seer. *In* Reynolds, F. E. and Capps, D. eds. The biographical process p187-200

La Rosa, R. C. Necessary truths: the poetics of Emerson's proverbs. *In* Literary monographs v8 p129-92

Porte, J. Emerson in 1838: essaying to be. *In* Studies in biography p183-99

Richardson, R. D. Emerson. *In* Richardson, R. D. Myth and literature in the American renaissance p65-89

Shea, D. B. Emerson and the American metamorphosis. *In* Levin, D. ed. Emerson: prophecy, metamorphosis, and influence p29-56

Tanner, T. Emerson: the unconquered eye and the enchanted circle. *In* Tanner, T. The reign of wonder p26-45

Young, G. L. "The fountainhead of all forms": poetry and the unconscious in Emerson and Howard Nemerov. *In* Artful thunder p241-67

About individual works

Essays

Paul, S. Emerson's Essays. *In* Paul, S. Repossessing and renewing p 1-13

Peckham, M. An introduction to Emerson's Essays. *In* Peckham, M. Romanticism and behavior p126-38

Literary ethics

Sealts, M. M. Emerson on the scholar, 1838: a study of "Literary ethics." *In* Literature and ideas in America p40-57

Representative men

Harris, K. M. Transcendental biography: Carlyle and Emerson. *In* Studies in biography p95-112

Emerson, Ralph W.—*Continued*

Bibliography

Buell, L. I. Emerson, Thoreau, and transcendentalism. *In* American literary scholarship, 1974 p3-14

Buell, L. Emerson, Thoreau, and transcendentalism. [another essay] *In* American literary scholarship, 1975 p31-5

Glick, W. Emerson, Thoreau, and transcendentalism. *In* American literary scholarship, 1976 p5-14

Glick, W. Emerson, Thoreau, and transcendentalism. [another essay] *In* American literary scholarship, 1977 p3-16

Harding, W. R. Emerson, Thoreau, and transcendentalism. *In* American literary scholarship, 1973 p3-14

Mysticism

See Emerson, Ralph Waldo—Religion and ethics

Religion

See Emerson, Ralph Waldo—Religion and ethics

Religion and ethics

Donadio, S. L. Emerson, Christian identity, and the dissolution of the social order. *In* Art, politics, and will p99-123

Mulqueen, J. E. Emersonian transcendentalism: over-soul or over-self? *In* Tennessee Studies in literature v21 p21-27

Emerson, Rupert. See Part 2 under Kilson, M. ed. New states in the modern world

Emery, Kenneth Orris, and Uchupi, Elazar
The oil potential of the Caribbean. *In* Borgese, E. M. and Krieger, D. eds. The tides of change p239-53

The emigrants (Motion picture)
Kauffmann, S. The emigrants. *In* Kauffmann, S. Living images p137-40

Samuels, C. T. Tampering with reality. *In* Samuels, C. T. Mastering the film, and other essays p198-210

Emigrants, Church work with. See Church work with emigrants

Emigration and immigration
See also Anthropo-geography; Assimilation (Sociology); Church work with emigrants; Man—Migrations; and subdivision Emigration and immigration under names of countries, cities, etc. e.g. Canada—Emigration and immigration; and names of special nationalities, e.g. Mexicans in California

Economic aspects

Schultz, T. W. Migration: an economist's view. *In* Human migration p377-86

Stolnitz, G. J. International migration policies: some demographic and economic contexts. *In* Human migration p307-16

Economic aspects—Buffalo, N.Y.

Glasco, L. Ethnicity and occupation in the mid-nineteenth century: Irish, Germans, and native-born whites in Buffalo, New York. *In* Immigrants in industrial America, 1850-1920 p151-75

Economic aspects—Manchester, N.H.

Hareven, T. K. Family and work patterns of immigrant laborers in a planned industrial town, 1900-1930. *In* Immigrants in industrial America, 1850-1920 p47-66

Economic aspects—New York (City)

Gordon, M. Irish immigrant culture and the labor boycott in New York City, 1880-1886. *In* Immigrants in industrial America, 1850-1920 p111-22

Groneman, C. "She earns as a child—she pays as a man": women workers in a mid-nineteenth-century New York City community. *In* Immigrants in industrial America, 1850--1920 p33-46

Economic aspects—Philadelphia

Laurie, B.; Hershberg, T. and Alter, G. Immigrants and industry: the Philadelphia experience, 1850-1880. *In* Immigrants in industrial America, 1850-1920 p123-50

Economic aspects—Poughkeepsie, N.Y.

Griffen, C. The "old" immigration and industrialization: a case study. *In* Immigrants in industrial America, 1850-1920 p176-210

Economic aspects—United States

Golab, C. The impact of the industrial experience on the immigrant family: the huddled masses reconsidered. *In* Immigrants in industrial America, 1850-1920 p 1-32

Montgomery, D. Immigrant workers and managerial reform. *In* Immigrants in industrial America, 1850-1920 p96-110

Moral and religious aspects

Marty, M. E. Migration: the moral framework. *In* Human migration p387-403

Psychological aspects

Akerman, S. Towards an understanding of emigrational processes. *In* Human migration p287-306

Rin, H. The synthesizing mind in Chinese ethnocultural adjustment. *In* Ethnic identity p137-55

Shils, E. A. Roots—the sense of place and past: the cultural gains and losses of migration. *In* Human migration p404-26

Emigration and immigration law

Auerbach, C. A. Freedom of movement in international law and United States policy. *In* Human migration p317-35

Zolberg, A. R. International migration policies in a changing world system. *In* Human migration p241-86

See also Refuges, Political—Legal status, laws, etc.

United States

Dolce, P. C. The McCarran-Walter Act and the conflict over immigration policy during the Truman administration. *In* The Immigrant experience in America p215-32

Rosberg, G. M. Legal regulation of the migration process: the "crisis" of illegal immigration. *In* Human migration p336-76

Sadler, B. L. Legal and ethical implications of reducing immigration. *In* Population policy and ethics p411-29

Emigrés. See Refugees, Political

Eminent domain (International law)

Cases

Seidl-Hohenveldern, I. Counter-nationalisation. *In* The Year book of world affairs, 1979 p257-64

Emmelin, Lars
An environmental studies program. *In* Against pollution and hunger p256-59

Emmitt, Robert J.
Love, death, and resurrection in The great Gatsby. *In* Aeolian harps p273-89

Emmons, Terence

Russia's banquet campaign. *In* California Slavic studies v10 p45-86

Emotions

Franck, I. Spinoza, Freud, and Hampshire on psychic freedom. *In* Thought, consciousness, and reality p257-309

Frankfurt, H. G. Identification and externality. *In* Rorty, A. O. ed. The identities of persons p239-51

Kemper, T. D. A sociology of emotions: some problems and some solutions. *In* McNall, S. G. ed. Theoretical perspectives in sociology p431-49

Koestler, A. The three dimensions of emotion. *In* Koestler, A. Janus p70-76

Lloyd, A. C. Emotion and decision in Stoic psychology. *In* Rist, J. M. ed. The Stoics p233-46

Penelhum, T. Self-identity and self-regard. *In* Rorty, A. O. ed. The identities of persons p253-80

Richards, I. A. Emotion and art. *In* Richards, I. A. Complementarities p7-11

Shott, S. The sociology of emotion: some starting points. *In* McNall, S. G. ed. Theoretical perspectives in sociology p450-62

See also Belief and doubt; Catharsis; Desire; Facial expression; Impulse; Jealousy; Laughter; Love; Melancholy; Pleasure; Temperament; Worry

Empathy

Elliston, F. A. Husserl's phenomenology of empathy. *In* Elliston, F. A. and McCormick, P. eds. Husserl p213-46

Empey, LaMar Taylor

Juvenile lawbreaking: its character and social location. *In* Empey, L. T. ed. Juvenile justice p71-104

The Progressive legacy and the concept of childhood. *In* Empey, L. T. ed. Juvenile justice p3-33

Empire, Islamic. See Islamic Empire

Empiricism

Berlin, Sir I. Empirical propositions and hypothetical statements. *In* Berlin, Sir I. Concepts and categories p32-55

Brady, P. A sweet disorder: atomistic empiricism and the rococo mode of vision. *In* Studies in eighteenth-century culture v7 p451-61

Cohen, L. J. Why should the science of nature be empirical? *In* Royal Institute of Philosophy. Impressions of empiricism p168-83

Copleston, F. C. The logical empiricism of Nicholas of Autrecourt. *In* Copleston, F. C. Philosophers and philosophies p79-89

Føllesdal, D. Meaning and experience. *In* Guttenplan, S. D. ed. Mind and language p25-44

Grene, M. G. Philosophy in and out of Europe: The European sources of recent Anglo-American philosophy. *In* Grene, M. C. Philosophy in and out of Europe p11-23

Harris, E. E. Empiricism in science and philosophy. *In* Royal Institute of Philosophy. Impressions of empiricism p154-67

Körner, S. Empiricism in ethics. *In* Royal Institute of Philosophy. Impressions of empiricism p216-30

Moody, E. A. Empiricism and metaphysics in medieval philosophy. *In* Moody, E. A. Studies in medieval philosophy, science and logic p287-304

Percy, W. Symbol as hermeneutic in existentialism. *In* Percy, W. The message in the bottle p277-87

Taylor, D. M. An empirical account of mind. *In* Royal Institute of Philosophy. Impressions of empiricism p66-78

Wheatley, J. M. O. Knowledge, empiricism and ESP. *In* Wheatley, J. M. O. and Edge, H. L. eds. Philosophical dimensions of parapsychology p142-53

Woolhouse, R. S. The empiricist account of dispositions. *In* Royal Institute of Philosophy. Impressions of empiricism p184-99

See also Realism

Employee-employer relations. See Industrial relations

Employee incentives. See Incentives in industry

Employees, dismissal of. See Teachers—Tenure

Employer-employee relations. See Industrial relations

Employment (Economic theory)

Singer, H. W. International policies and their effect on employment. *In* Economic development and planning p237-49

See also Labor supply; Manpower policy

Mathematical models

Fei, J. C. H. and Ranis, G. Technological transfer, employment and development. *In* Economic development and planning p75-103

Employment and homosexuality. See Homosexuality and employment

Employment discrimination. See Discrimination in employment

Employment forecasting

Resnick, I. N. Manpower requirements and allocation of educational resources in underdeveloped countries. *In* African dimensions p155-69

Employment of children. See Children—Employment

Employment of women. See Women—Employment

Employment tests

United States

Lerner, B. Washington v. Davis: quantity, quality and equality in employment testing. *In* The Supreme Court review, 1976 p263-316

Empson, William

Natural magic and populism in Marvell's poetry. *In* Andrew Marvell p36-61

About

Eberhart, R. Empson's poetry. *In* Eberhart, R. Of poetry and poets p111-25

Fraser, G. S. 'Not wrongly moved . . . (William Empson). *In* Fraser, G. S. Essays on twentieth-century poets p162-68

Thurley, G. 'Partial fires': Empson's poetry. *In* Thurley, G. The ironic harvest p38-53

Wain, J. The poetry of William Empson. *In* Wain, J. Professing poetry p177-223

Empson, William—About—*Continued*

About individual works

Seven types of ambiguity

Hough, G. G. An eighth type of ambiguity. *In* On literary intention p222-41

Olson, E. William Empson, contemporary criticism and poetic diction. *In* Olson, E. On value judgments in the arts, and other essays p118-56

En cas de malheur (Motion picture)

Truffaut, F. En cas de malheur. *In* Truffaut, F. The films in my life p173-76

Enamel and enameling, Roman

Butcher, S. A. Enamelling. *In* Strong, D. E. and Brown, D. eds. Roman crafts p43-51

Encina, Juan del

About

Sullivan, H. W. Towards a new chronology for the dramatic eclogues of Juan del Encina. *In* Virginia. University. Bibliographical Society. Studies in bibliography v30 p257-75

Enclosures. See Inclosures

Encounter (Periodical)

Spender, S. Background to the fifties. *In* Spender, S. The thirties and after p121-30

Encounter groups. See Group relations training

Enculturation. See Socialization

Encyclopedists

Beaune, J. C. Technology from an encyclopedic point of view. *In* Bugliarello, G. and Donner, D. B. eds. The history and philosophy of technology p202-26

Levi, A. H. T. Ethics and the encyclopedia in the sixteenth century. *In* French Renaissance studies, 1540-70 p170-84

McGhee, D. M. Encyclopedism and its conscience: evolution and revolution. *In* Literature and history in the age of ideas p377-86

Perkins, J. A. The Physiocrats and the Encyclopedists. *In* Studies in eighteenth-century culture v8 p323-36

End linkage: a tool for cross-cultural analysis. Mead, M. *In* About Bateson p171-231

End of the world. See Antichrist

End of the world in literature

Percy, W. Notes for a novel about the end of the world. *In* Percy, W. The message in the bottle p101-18

Endō, Shūsaku

About

Mathy, F. Shusaku Endo: the second period. *In* Postwar trends in Japan p3-14

Rimer, J. T. Tradition and contemporary consciousness: Ibuse, Endō, Kaiko, Abe. *In* Rimer, J. T. Modern Japanese fiction and its traditions p245-70

Endocrinology. See Hormones, Sex

Endowment of research

See also Education and state; Federal aid to research; Science and state; Technology and state

United States

Horn, J. L. The ethics of research: a case history and its lessons. *In* Hook, S.; Kurtz, P. and Todorovich, M. eds. The ethics of teaching and scientific research p135-59

Endowments

Wiggins, J. R. Charting cultural priorities. *In* American Antiquarian Society. Proceedings v87 pt2 p291-97

See also Charities; Endowment of research

United States

Jordan, V. E. Blacks and American foundations: Attitudes and outlook. *In* The Black American reference book p485-91

Kaiser, E. Blacks and American foundations: A historical survey. *In* The Black American reference book p480-85

Ends and means

Goretti, M. The heterogenesis of ends in Vico's thought: premises for a comparison of ideas. *In* Giambattista Vico's science of humanity p213-19

Eneas (Romance)

Hanning, R. W. "Engin" in twelfth-century courtly texts. *In* Hanning, R. W. The individual in twelfth-century romance p105-38

The Enemy (Periodical)

Lewis, W. The solitary outlaw. *In* Lewis, W. Enemy salvoes p23-30

Energy. See Force and energy; Power resources

Energy and state. See Energy policy

Energy conservation. See Energy policy; Recycling (Waste, etc.)

Energy policy

Brown, H. S. Some quasi-Copernican revolutions in man's utilization of energy. *In* Neyman, J. ed. The heritage of Copernicus: theories "pleasing to the mind" p526-36

Levy, W. J. An Atlantic-Japanese energy policy. *In* The New Atlantic challenge p119-49

Environmental aspects—United States

Krutilla, J. V. and Page, R. T. Energy policy from an environmental perspective. *In* Kalter, R. J. and Vogely, W. A. eds. Energy supply and government policy p76-98

International cooperation

Morgenthau, H. J. World politics and the politics of oil. *In* Eppen, G. D. ed. Energy: the policy issues p43-51

Woodard, K. People's China and the world energy crisis: the Chinese attitude toward global resource. *In* China's changing role in the world economy p114-42

Social aspects

Eklund, S. Critical decisions in relation to energy. *In* World change and world security p61-72

China

Woodard, K. People's China and the world energy crisis: the Chinese attitude toward global resource. *In* China's changing role in the world economy p114-42

Connecticut

Grasso, E. T. The role of energy management. *In* Benton, L. R. ed. Management for the future p139-47

United States

Adelman, M. A. The hinge of energy policy: relations between energy markets in the United States and abroad. *In* Eppen, G. D. ed. Energy: the policy issues p71-81

Energy policy—United States—*Continued*

Baughman, M. L. and Hnyilicza, E. System interdependencies and government policy. *In* Kalter, R. J. and Vogely, W. A. eds. Energy supply and government policy p255-79

Johnson, W. A. The impact of price controls on the oil industry: how to worsen an energy crisis. *In* Eppen, G. D. ed. Energy: the policy issues p99-121

Johnson, W. A. Why U.S. energy policy has failed. *In* Kalter, R. J. and Vogely, W. A. eds. Energy supply and government policy p280-305

Kalter, R. J. and Tyner, W. E. Disposal policy of energy resources in the public domain. *In* Kalter, R. J. and Vogely, W. A. eds. Energy supply and government policy p51-75

Ronall, J. O. The energy crisis and its potential effects upon American policy. *In* The New world balance and peace in the Middle East: reality or mirage? p119-24

Sachs, R. G. Our energy options—so what else is new? *In* Eppen, G. D. ed. Energy: the policy issues p3-24

Smith, W. D. The energy crisis and the Middle East. *In* The New world balance and peace in the Middle East: reality or mirage? p105-17

Swearingen, J. E. What price dependence? *In* Prochnow, H. V. ed. Dilemmas facing the nation p96-108

Vogely, W. A. Federal government energy organization. *In* Kalter, R. J. and Vogely, W. A. eds. Energy supply and government policy p306-25

Weeks, R. R. The energy crisis and the capital shortage. *In* Benton, L. R. ed. Management for the future p307-15

Energy research. See Power resources—Research

Energy resources. See Power resources

Enforcement of law. See Law enforcement

Engdahl, Sylvia Louise
Why write for today's teenagers? *In* Horn Book Magazine. Crosscurrents of criticism **p144-49**

Engel, Arthur
Emerging concepts of the academic profession at Oxford, 1800-1854. *In* The University in society v 1 p305-52

Engelhardt, Hugo Tristram
The counsels of finitude. *In* Death inside out p115-25

Ethical issues in aiding the death of young children. *In* Kohl, M. ed. Beneficent euthanasia p180-92

Individuals and communities, present and future: towards a morality in a time of famine. *In* Lucas, G. R. and Ogletree, T. W. eds. Lifeboat ethics p70-83

Engels, Friedrich

About

Chadwick, O. Karl Marx. *In* Chadwick, O. The secularization of the European mind in the nineteenth century p48-87

Gallie, W. B. Marx and Engels on revolution and war. *In* Gallie, W. B. Philosophers of peace and war p66-69

Mathewson, R. W. Complete and incomplete men. *In* Mathewson, R. W. The positive hero in Russian literature p136-55

Mathewson, R. W. Marxism, realism and the hero. *In* Mathewson, R. W. The positive hero in Russian literature p115-35

Wellmer, A. Communications and emancipation: reflections on the linguistic turn in critical theory. *In* O'Neill, J. ed. On critical theory p231-63

About individual works
The condition of the working class in England in 1844

Lucas, W. J. Engels, Mrs Gaskell and Manchester. *In* Lucas, W. J. The literature of change p34-56

The origin of the family, private property and the state

Sacks, K. Engels revisited: women, the organization of production, and private property. *In* Reiter, R. R. ed. Toward an anthropology of women p211-34

Enggass, Robert Clarence
Paolo Campi: an introduction. *In* Enggass, R. C. and Stokstad, M. eds. Hortus imaginum p185-92

Engin (The word)
Hanning, R. W. "Engin" in twelfth-century courtly texts. *In* Hanning, R. W. The individual in twelfth-century romance p105-38

Engineering
See also Mechanics

Study and teaching—United States

Lancaster, O. E. The future of engineering education in land-grant universities. *In* Land-grant universities and their continuing challenge p104-31

Engineering, Structural. See Structural engineering

Engineering schools

United States

Lancaster, O. W. The future of engineering education in land-grant universities. *In* Land-grant universities and their continuing challenge p104-31

England, A. B.
Further additions to Bond's Register of burlesque poems. *In* Virginia. University. Bibliographical Society. Studies in bibliography v28 p284-90

The style of Don Juan and Augustan poetry. *In* Jump, J. D. ed. Byron p94-112

England, Martha Winburn
The satiric Blake: apprenticeship at the Haymarket? *In* Wimsatt, W. K. ed. Literary criticism: idea and act p483-505

England

Biography

Dowling, W. C. Boswell and the problem of biography. *In* Studies in biography p73-93

Civilization—18th century

Hexter, J. H. The historical method of Christopher Hill. *In* Hexter, J. H. On historians p227-51

Rogers, P. Introduction: the writer and society. *In* Rogers, P. ed. The eighteenth century p 1-80

Civilization—19th century

Burrow, J. W. The sense of the past. *In* Lerner, L. ed. The Victorians p120-38

England—*Continued*
Foreign relations—Scotland
Macdougall, N. A. T. Foreign relations: England and France. *In* Brown, J. M. ed. Scottish society in the fifteenth century p101-11

Intellectual life
Burrow, J. W. The sense of the past. *In* Lerner, L. ed. The Victorians p120-38

Politics and government
See Great Britain—Politics and government

Religion—18th century
Price, J. V. Religion and ideas. *In* Rogers, P. ed. The eighteenth century p120-52

Religion—19th century
Burrow, J. W. Faith, doubt and unbelief. *In* Lerner, L. ed. The Victorians p153-73

Social conditions
Casey, K. Women in Norman and Plantagenet England. *In* Kanner, B. ed. The women of England p83-123

Ferguson, N. A. Women in twentieth-century England. *In* Kanner, B. ed. The women of England p345-87

Masek, R. Women in an age of transition, 1485-1714. *In* Kanner, B. ed. The women of England p138-82

Meyer, M. A. Land charters and the legal position of Anglo-Saxon women. *In* Kanner, B. ed. The women of England p57-82

Schnorrenberg, B. B. The eighteenth-century Englishwoman. *In* Kanner, B. ed. The women of England p183-228

Stone, L. The rise of the nuclear family in early modern England: the patriarchal stage. *In* Rosenberg, C. E. ed. The family in history p13-57

Social conditions—Historiography
Le Roy Ladurie, E. From Waterloo to Colyton. *In* Le Roy Ladurie, E. The territory of the historian p223-34

Social conditions—Medieval period, 1066-1485
Hanawalt, B. A. The female felon in fourteenth-century England. *In* Stuard, S. M. ed. Women in medieval society p125-40

Kittel, M. R. Women under the law in medieval England, 1066-1485. *In* Kanner, B. ed. The women of England p124-37

Walker, S. S. Widow and ward: the feudal law of child custody in medieval England. *In* Stuard, S. M. ed. Women in medieval society p159-72

Weimann, R. The folk play and social custom. *In* Weimann, R. Shakespeare and the popular tradition in the theater: studies in the social dimension of dramatic form and function p15-48

Social conditions—19th century
Dyhouse, C. The condition of England 1860-1900. *In* Lerner, L. ed. The Victorians p70-89

Supple, B. E. Material development: the condition of England 1830-1860. *In* Lerner, L. ed. The Victorians p49-69

Social life and customs—Medieval period, 1066-1485
Weimann, R. The folk play and social custom. *In* Weimann, R. Shakespeare and the popular tradition in the theater: studies in the social dimension of dramatic form and function p15-48

Social life and customs—16th century
Weimann, R. The folk play and social custom. *In* Weimann, R. Shakespeare and the popular tradition in the theater: studies in the social dimenson of dramatic form and function p15-48

Social life and customs—17th century
Hibbard, G. R. Love, marriage and money in Shakespeare's theatre and Shakespeare's England. *In* the Elizabethan theatre, VI p134-55

Statistics, Vital
Johansson, S. R. Sex and death in Victorian England: an examination of age- and sex-specific death rates, 1840-1910. *In* Vicinus, M. ed. A widening sphere p163-81

England, Church of. See Church of England

England in literature
Cole, P. B. Emerson, England, and fate. *In* Levin, D. ed. Emerson: prophecy, metamorphosis, and influence p83-105

Goldman, A. Melville's England. *In* Pullin, F. ed. New perspectives on Melville p68-85

Skilton, D. Industrialisation and the condition of England. *In* Skilton, D. The English novel p120-35

England's Ireland (criticism) *In* Brustein, R. S. The culture watch p56-59

English, Jane
Abortion and the concept of a person. *In* Feminism and philosophy p417-28

English, Raymond. See Mews, S. jt. auth.

English actors. See Actors, English

English architecture. See Architecture, English

English art. See Art, English

English ballads. See Ballads, English

English carols. See Carols, English

English children's literature. See Children's literature, English

English Christian drama. See Christian drama, English

English detective stories. See Detective and mystery stories, English

English drama
See also Moralities, English; Verse drama, English

History and criticism
Williams, R. Social environment and theatrical environment: the case of English naturalism. *In* English drama: forms and development p203-23

Irish authors—Bibliography
Hogan, R. G.; Scott, B. K. and Henderson, G. The modern drama. *In* Finneran, R. J. ed. Anglo-Irish literature p518-61

Irish authors—History and criticism
Booth, M. R. Irish landscape in the Victorian theatre. *In* Place, personality and the Irish writer p159-72

English drama—Irish authors—History and criticism—*Continued*

Evans, G. L. Post-war drama in England and Ireland. *In* Nicoll, A. World drama p806-20

Nicoll, A. The extension of the realistic. *In* Nicoll, A. World drama p577-607

Orel, H. A drama for the nation. *In* Orel, H. ed. Irish history and culture p251-69

Worth, K. J. Beckett. *In* Worth, K. J. The Irish drama of Europe from Yeats to Beckett p241-65

To 1500—History and criticism

Brockman, B. A. Cain and Abel in the Chester creation: narrative tradition and dramatic potential. *In* Medievalia et humanistica no. 5 p169-82

Kahrl, S. J. The civic religious drama of medieval England: a review of recent scholarship. *In* Renaissance drama [1973] p237-48

Weimann, R. The mystery cycles. *In* Weimann, R. Shakespeare and the popular tradition in the theater: studies in the social dimension of dramatic form and function p49-97

Early modern and Elizabethan, 1500-1600—Bibliography

Axton, M. The Tudor mask and Elizabethan court drama. *In* English drama: forms and development p24-47

Bawcutt, N. W. The revival of Elizabethan drama and the crisis of romantic drama. *In* Davies, R. T. and Beatty, B. G. eds. Literature of the romantic period, 1750-1850 p96-113

Bawcutt, N. W. Shakespeare's life, times, and stage. *In* Shakespeare survey v29 p168-77

Gibbons, B. and Harris, B. English drama 1550-1660, excluding Shakespeare. *In* English Association. The year's work in English studies v53 p193-206

Gibbons, B. and Harris, B. English drama 1550-1660, excluding Shakespeare [another essay] *In* English Association. The year's work in English studies v54 p185-99

Gibbons, B. and Harris, B. English drama, 1550-1660, excluding Shakespeare [another essay] *In* English Association. The year's work in English studies v55 p231-47

Harris, B. and Gibbons, B. English drama 1550-1660, excluding Shakespeare [another essay] *In* English Association. The year's work in English studies v56 p176-81

Harris, B. and Gibbons, B. English drama, 1550-1660, excluding Shakespeare [another essay] *In* English Association. The year's work in English studies v57 p146-53

Leech, C. Studies in Shakespearian and other Jacobean tragedy, 1918-1972: a retrospect. *In* Shakespeare survey 26 p 1-9

Early modern and Elizabethan, 1500-1666—History and criticism

Altman, J. B. Conclusion. *In* Altman, J. B. The Tudor play of mind p389-95

Altman, J. B. Inventing answers in English comedy. *In* Altman, J. B. The Tudor play of mind p148-95

Altman, J. B. Seneca and the declamatory structure of tragedy. *In* Altman, J. B. The Tudor play of mind p229-48

Belsey, C. Senecan vacillation and Elizabethan deliberation: influence or confluence? *In* Renaissance drama [1973] p65-88

Bowers, F. T. Old-spelling editions of dramatic texts. *In* Bowers, F. T. Essays in bibliography, text, and editing p289-95

Greene, R. L. Carols in Tudor drama. *In* Chaucer and Middle English studies in honour of Rossell Hope Robbins p357-65

Harbage, A. Copper into gold. *In* English Renaissance drama p 1-14

Honigmann, E. A. J. Re-enter the stage direction: Shakespeare and some contemporaries. *In* Shakespeare survey v29 p117-25

Hoy, C. H. Jacobean tragedy and the mannerist style. *In* Shakespeare survey 26 p49-67

Hunter, G. K. Henry IV and the Elizabethan two-part play. *In* Hunter, G. K. Dramatic identities and cultural tradition p303-18

Hunter, G. K. Seneca and English tragedy. *In* Hunter, G. K. Dramatic identities and cultural tradition p174-213

Nicoll, A. The popular beginnings. *In* Nicoll, A. World drama p197-205

Riggs, D. "Plot" and "episode" in early neoclassical criticism. *In* Renaissance drama [1973] p149-75

Ure, P. Marriage and the domestic drama in Heywood and Ford. *In* Ure, P. Elizabethan and Jacobean drama p145-65

Ure, P. On some differences between Senecan and Elizabethan tragedy. *In* Ure, P. Elizabethan and Jacobean drama p63-74

Weimann, R. The Elizabethan drama. *In* Weimann, R. Shakespeare and the popular tradition in the theater: studies in the social dimension of dramatic form and function p161-207

Early modern and Elizabethan, 1500-1600—History and criticism—Bibliography

Lancashire, A. B. and Levenson, J. L. Anonymous plays. *In* Logan, T. P. and Smith, D. S. eds. The popular school p148-249

Logan, T. P. and Smith, D. S. Other dramatists. *In* Logan, T. P. and Smith, D. S. eds. The new intellectuals p323-40

Logan, T. P. and Smith, D. S. Other dramatists. *In* Logan, T. P. and Smith, D. S. eds. The popular school p250-74

Early modern and Elizabethan, 1500-1600—Italian influences

Hunter, G. K. Italian tragicomedy on the English stage. *In* Hunter, G. K. Dramatic identities and cultural tradition p133-56

Early modern and Elizabethan, 1500-1600—Roman influences

Hunter, G. K. Seneca and the Elizabethans: a case-study in 'influence.' *In* Hunter, G. K. Dramatic identities and cultural tradition p159-73

17th century—Bibliography

Gibbons, B. and Harris, B. English drama, 1550-1660, excluding Shakespeare. *In* English Association. The year's work in English studies v54 p185-99

Gibbons, B. and Harris, B. English drama [another essay] *In* English Association. The year's work in English studies v57 p146-53

English drama—17th century—Bibliography
—*Continued*

Harris, B. and Gibbons, B. English drama, 1550-1660: excluding Shakespeare. *In* English Association. The year's work in English studies v55 p231-47

Harris, B. and Gibbons, B. English drama, 1550-1660, excluding Shakespeare [another essay] *In* English Association. The year's work in English studies v56 p176-81

17th century—History and criticism

Barton, A. He that plays the king: Ford's Perkin Warbeck and the Stuart history play. *In* English drama: forms and development p69-93

Champion, L. S. Epilogue. *In* Champion, L. S. Tragic patterns in Jacobean and Caroline drama p210-13

Champion, L. S. Prologue. *In* Champion, L. S. Tragic patterns in Jacobean and Caroline drama p3-18

Heinemann, M. Popular drama and Leveller style—Richard Overton and John Harris. *In* Rebels and their causes p69-92

Hoy, C. H. Shakespeare and the drama of his time. *In* Shakespeare: aspects of influence p21-41

Leech, C. Masking and unmasking in the last plays. *In* Shakespeare's romances reconsidered p40-59

Luckett, R. Exotick but rational entertainments: the English dramatick operas. *In* English drama: forms and development p123-41

Nicoll, A. Early seventeenth-century tragedy and comedy. *In* Nicoll, A. World drama p224-40

Stilling, R. John Ford and the Jacobeans. *In* Stilling, R. Love and death in Renaissance tragedy p266-76

**17th century—History and criticism
—Bibliography**

Lancashire, A. B. and Levenson, J. L. Anonymous plays. *In* Logan, T. P. and Smith, D. S. eds. The new intellectuals p302-22

Logan, T. P. and Smith, D. S. Other dramatists. *In* Logan, T. P. and Smith, D. S. eds. The new intellectuals p323-40

**Restoration, 1660-1700—History
and criticism**

Bowers, F. T. Bibliography and Restoration drama. *In* Bowers, F. T. Essays in bibliography, text, and editing p135-50

Mudrick, M. Restoration comedy and later. *In* Wimsatt, W. K. ed. Literary criticism: idea and act p444-62

Nicoll, A. The Restoration comedy of manners. *In* Nicoll, A. World drama p275-87

**Restoration, 1600-1700—History and
criticism—Bibliography**

Lancashire, A. B. and Levenson, J. L. Anonymous plays. *In* Logan, T. P. and Smith, D. S. eds. The popular school p148-249

Logan, T. P. and Smith, D. S. Other dramatists. *In* Logan, T. P. and Smith, D. S. eds. The popular school p250-74

18th century—History and criticism

Matlack, C. S. "Spectatress of the mischief which she made": tragic woman perceived and perceiver. *In* Studies in eighteenth-century culture v6 p317-30

19th century—History and criticism

Bawcutt, N. W. The revival of Elizabethan drama and the crisis of romantic drama. *In* Davies, R. T. and Beatty, B. G. eds. Literature of the romantic period, 1750-1850 p96-113

Booth, M. R. The social value of nineteenth-century English drama. *In* Drama and society p59-74

Rosador, K. T. von. Myth and Victorian melodrama. *In* English Association. Essays and studies, 1979 p97-114

20th century—History and criticism

Brustein, R. S. The limits of English realism. *In* Brustein, R. S. The culture watch p89-93

Evans, G. L. Post-war drama in England and Ireland. *In* Nicoll, A. World drama p806-20

Kennedy, A. K. Conclusion. *In* Kennedy, A. K. Six dramatists in search of a language p230-43

Kennedy, A. K. Introduction. *In* Kennedy, A. K. Six dramatists in search of a language p 1-37

Worth, K. J. The vitality of the Yeatsian theatre. *In* Worth, K. J. The Irish drama of Europe from Yeats to Beckett p194-219

English drama (Comedy)

History and criticism

Altman, J. B. Inventing answers in English comedy. *In* Altman, J. B. The Tudor play of mind p148-95

Beck, E. Terence improved: the paradigm of the Prodigal son in English Renaissance comedy. *In* Renaissance drama [1973] p107-22

Hare, A. English comedy. *In* Howarth, W. D. ed. Comic drama p122-43

Mudrick, M. Restoration comedy and later. *In* Wimsatt, W. K. ed. Literary criticism: idea and act p444-62

Nicoll, A. The Restoration comedy of manners. *In* Nicoll, A. World drama p275-87

Waith, E. M. "Give me your hands": reflections on the author's agents in comedy. *In* Martz, L. L. and Williams, A. L. eds. The author in his work p197-211

Wickham, G. W. G. Medieval comic traditions and the beginnings of English comedy. *In* Howarth, W. D. ed. Comic drama p40-62

**Restoration, 1660-1700—History
and criticism**

Corman, B. Toward a generic theory of Restoration comedy: some preliminary considerations. *In* Studies in eighteenth-century culture v7 p423-32

Kearful, F. J. Molière among the English, 1660-1737. *In* Johnson, R. B.; Neumann, E. S. and Trail, G. T. eds. Molière and the commonwealth of letters: patrimony and posterity p199-217

English drama (Tragedy)

Cunningham, J. V. The Donatan tradition. *In* Cunningham, J. V. The collected essays of J. V. Cunningham p30-52

Bibliography

Leech, C. Studies in Shakespearian and other Jacobean tragedy, 1918-1972: a retrospect. *In* Shakespeare survey 26 p 1-9

English drama (Tragedy)—*Continued*

History and criticism

Altman, J. B. Seneca and the declamatory structure of tragedy. *In* Altman, J. B. The Tudor play of mind p229-48

Altman, J. B. Tragic perspectives among the Elizabethans. *In* Altman, J. B. The Tudor play of mind p249-320

Belsey, C. Senecan vacillation and Elizabethan deliberation: influence or confluence? In Renaissance drama [1973] p65-88

Champion, L. S. Epilogue. *In* Champion, L. S. Tragic patterns in Jacobean and Caroline drama p210-13

Champion, L. S. Prologue. *In* Champion, L. S. Tragic patterns in Jacobean and Caroline drama p3-18

Hoy, C. H. Jacobean tragedy and the mannerist style. *In* Shakespeare survey 26 p49-67

Ure, P. On some differences between Senecan and Elizabethan tragedy. *In* Ure, P. Elizabethan and Jacobean drama p63-74

Woolf, R. The influence of the mystery plays upon the popular tragedies of the 1560's. *In* Renaissance drama [1973] p89-105

English epigrams. See Epigrams, English

English essays

History and criticism

Granger, B. I. Introduction. *In* Granger, B. I. American essay serials from Franklin to Irving p3-12

English fiction

See also Detective and mystery stories, English; Historical fiction, English

History and criticism

Bayley, J. The authentic and the sincere. *In* Bayley, J. The uses of division p17-25

Cockshut, A. O. J. The lesbian theme. *In* Cockshut, A. O. J. Man and woman: a study of love and the novel, 1740-1940 p186-208

Cockshut, A. O. J. Love and the novel. *In* Cockshut, A. O. J. Man and woman: a study of love and the novel, 1740-1940 p9-31

Cockshut, A. O. J. The male homosexual. *In* Cockshut, A. O. J. Man and woman: a study of love and the novel, 1740-1940 p161-69

Cockshut, A. O. J. The optimists. *In* Cockshut, A. O. J. Man and woman: a study of love and the novel, 1740-1940 p136-52

Hardy, B. N. Good stories, good listeners. *In* Hardy, B. N. Tellers and listeners p131-62

Hardy, B. N. Memory and memories. *In* Hardy, B. N. Tellers and listeners p56-101

Kennedy, A. Significant action and cannibal clothes. *In* Kennedy, A. Meaning and signs in fiction p 1-16

Kennedy, A. The thread in the garment. *In* Kennedy, A. Meaning and signs in fiction p30-57

Mudrick, M. Looking for Kellermann. *In* Mudrick, M. The man in the machine p11-36

Steiner, G. Eros and idiom. *In* Steiner, G. On difficulty and other essays p95-136

Tomlinson, T. B. Conclusion. *In* Tomlinson, T. B. The English middle-class novel p198-202

Tomlinson, T. B. 'Fits of spiritual dread': George Eliot and later novelists. *In* Tomlinson, T. B. The English middle-class novel p114-30

Tomlinson, T. B. The novel and middle-class England. *In* Tomlinson, T. B. The English middle-class novel p7-20

Indic authors

See Indic fiction (English)

Irish authors—Bibliography

Kilroy, J. F. Nineteenth-century writers. *In* Finneran, R. J. ed. Anglo-Irish literature p24-47

Nigerian authors

See Nigerian fiction (English)

Scottish authors—History and criticism

Hart, F. R. Kennaway, Spark and after. *In* Hart, F. R. The Scottish novel p287-321

Hart, F. R. Novelists of the modern renaissance. *In* Hart, F. R. The Scottish novel p207-45

Hart, F. R. Retrospect: notes for a theory of Scottish fiction. *In* Hart, F. R. The Scottish novel p398-408

South African authors

See South African fiction (English)

West Indian authors

See West Indian fiction (English)

Women authors—History and criticism

Rigney, B. H. Introduction. *In* Rigney, B. H. Madness and sexual politics in the feminist novel p 1-12

Rigney, B. H. The self-created other: integration and survival. *In* Rigney, B. H. Madness and sexual politics in the feminist novel p117-27

Showalter, E. Beyond the female aesthetic: contemporary women novelists. *In* Showalter, E. A literature of their own p298-319

Showalter, E. The double critical standard and the feminine novel. *In* Showalter, E. A literature of their own p73-99

Showalter, E. The female tradition. *In* Showalter, E. A literature of their own p3-36

Showalter, E. Feminine heroes: the woman's man. *In* Showalter, E. A literature of their own p133-52

Showalter, E. The feminine novelists and the will to write. *In* Showalter, E. A literature of their own p37-72

Showalter, E. The feminist novelists. *In* Showalter, E. A literature of their own p182-215

Showalter, E. Subverting the feminine novel: sensationalism and feminine protest. *In* Showalter, E. A literature of their own p153-81

Showalter, E. Women writers and the suffrage movement. *In* Showalter, E. A literature of their own p216-39

18th century—History and criticism

Auty, S. G. Perpetual mirth. *In* Auty, S. G. The comic spirit of eighteenth-century novels p180-83

Butler, M. The anti-Jacobins. *In* Butler, M. Jane Austen and the war of ideas p88-123

Butler, M. The Jacobin novel I: revolution and reason. *In* Butler, M. Jane Austen and the war of ideas p29-56

English fiction—18th century—History and criticism—*Continued*

Howells, C. A. Gothic themes, values, techniques. *In* Howells, C. A. Love, mystery, and misery p5-27

Karl, F. R. The development of technique in the eighteenth-century novel. *In* Karl, F. R. The adversary literature p290-336

Karl, F. R. Gothic, Gothicism, and Gothicists. *In* Karl, F. R. The adversary literature p235-74

Karl, F. R. Introduction: the novel as subversion. *In* Karl, F. R. The adversary literature p3-54

Karl, F. R. Near-novels. *In* Karl, F. R. The adversary literature p275-89

Kelly, G. Conclusion. *In* Kelly, G. The English Jacobin novel, 1780-1805 p261-69

Kelly, G. Introduction. *In* Kelly, G. The English Jacobin novel, 1780-1805 p 1-19

Palmer, W. J. Dickens and the eighteenth century. *In* Dickens Studies Annual v6 p15-39

Skilton, D. Gothic, romantic and heroic. *In* Skilton, D. The English novel p59-79

Skilton, D. Quixotic and picaresque fiction. *In* Skilton, D. The English novel p32-44

Spacks, P. A. M. Female identities. *In* Spacks, P. A. M. Imagining a self p57-91

Spacks, P. A. M. Identity in fiction and in fact. *In* Spacks, P. A. M. Imagining a self p 1-27

Spacks, P. A. M. Selfhood, given and formed. *In* Spacks, P. A. M. Imagining a self p300-15

Watt, I. P. Serious reflections on The rise of the novel. *In* Spilka, M. ed. Towards a poetics of fiction p90-103

19th century—History and criticism

Auerbach, N. Introduction: the communal eye. *In* Auerbach, N. Communities of women p 1-32

Beer, G. 'Coming wonders': uses of theatre in the Victorian novel. *In* English drama: forms and development p164-85

Briggs, J. Diabolism and decadence: the mood of the nineties. *In* Briggs, J. Night visitors p76-97

Cavaliero, G. The land and the city. *In* Cavaliero, G. The rural tradition in the English novel, 1900-1939 p 1-13

Colmer, J. The 'condition of England' question. *In* Colmer, J. Coleridge to Catch-22 p57-68

Colmer, J. The Victorian 'condition of England' novel. *In* Colmer, J. Coleridge to Catch-22 p69-90

Cunningham, V. All sorts and conditions. *In* Cunningham, V. Everywhere spoken against p25-66

Cunningham, V. Charles Dickens. *In* Cunningham, V. Everywhere spoken against p190-230

Cunningham, V. Openness. *In* Cunningham, V. Everywhere spoken against p8-24

Cunningham, V. Places and politics. *In* Cunningham, V. Everywhere spoken against p67-105

Cunningham, V. The presence of dissent. *In* Cunningham, V. Everywhere spoken against p106-12

Cunningham, V. The sense of an ending. *In* Cunningham, V. Everywhere spoken against p278-86

Dawson, C. Men of letters as hacks and heroes. *In* Dawson, C. Victorian noon p153-78

Doubleday, N. F. Roads out of the land of fiction. *In* Doubleday, N. F. Variety of attempt p203-12

Doubleday, N. F. Variety of attempt. *In* Doubleday, N. F. Variety of attempt p 1-6

Hemstedt, G. The novel. *In* Lerner, L. ed. The Victorians p3-24

Hillegas, M. R. Victorian "extraterrestrials." *In* The Worlds of Victorian fiction p391-414

Howells, C. A. Gothic themes, values, techniques. *In* Howells, C. A. Love, mystery, and misery p5-27

Kennard, J. E. Capital punishment. *In* Kennard, J. E. Victims of convention p63-79

Kennard, J. E. Introduction. *In* Kennard, J. E. Victims of convention p9-20

Knoepflmacher, U. C. The counterworld of Victorian fiction and The woman in white. *In* The Worlds of Victorian fiction p351-69

Levine, G. L. High and low: Ruskin and the novelists. *In* Knoepflmacher, U. C. and Tennyson, G. B. eds. Nature and the Victorian imagination p137-52

Lucas, W. J. A note on the treatment of love and marriage in later Victorian fiction. *In* Lucas, W. J. The literature of change p192-207

Maynard, J. R. Broad canvas, narrow perspective: the problem of the English historical novel in the nineteenth century. *In* The Worlds of Victorian fiction p237-65

Moers, E. Performing heroinism: the myth of Corinne. *In* The Worlds of Victorian fiction p319-50

Moynahan, J. Pastoralism as culture and counter-culture in English fiction, 1800-1928: from a view to a death. *In* Spilka, M. ed. Towards a poetics of fiction p239-54

Otto, P. C. Women in the mirror: using novels to study Victorian women. *In* Kanner, B. ed. The women of England p296-344

Ousby, I. Wilkie Collins and other sensation novelists. *In* Ousby, I. Bloodhounds in heaven p111-36

Pickering, S. Afterword. *In* Pickering, S. The moral tradition in English fiction, 1785-1850 p169-73

Pickering, S. The Christian Observer and the novel. *In* Pickering, S. The moral tradition in English fiction, 1785-1850 p65-87

Pickering, S. The Sunday school movement: new readers and the novel. *In* Pickering, S. The moral tradition in English fiction, 1785-1850 p11-64

Sanders, A. Introduction. *In* Sanders, A. The Victorian historical novel, 1840-1880 p 1-31

Showalter, E. The double critical standard and the feminine novel. *In* Showalter, E. A literature of their own p73-99

Showalter, E. Family secrets and domestic subversion: rebellion in the novels of the 1860s. *In* Wohl, A. S. ed. The Victorian family p101-16

Showalter, E. The female tradition. *In* Showalter, E. A literature of their own p3-36

Showalter, E. Feminine heroes: the woman's man. *In* Showalter, E. A literature of their own p133-52

English fiction—19th century—History and criticism—*Continued*

Showalter, E. The feminine novelists and the will to write. *In* Showalter, E. A literature of their own p37-72

Showalter, E. The feminist novelists. *In* Showalter, E. A literature of their own p182-215

Showalter, E. Subverting the feminine novel: sensationalism and feminine protest. *In* Showalter, E. A literature of their own p153-81

Showalter, E. Women writers and the suffrage movement. *In* Showalter, E. A literature of their own p216-39

Skilton, D. Industrialisation and the condition of England. *In* Skilton, D. The English novel p120-35

Staines, D. King Arthur in Victorian fiction. *In* The Worlds of Victorian fiction p267-93

Sutherland, J. A. Craft versus trade: novelists and publishers. *In* Sutherland, J. A. Victorian novelists and publishers p72-98

Sutherland, J. A. Dickens as publisher. *In* Sutherland, J. A. Victorian novelists and publishers p166-87

Sutherland, J. A. Mass market and big business: novel publishing at midcentury. *In* Sutherland, J. A. Victorian novelists and publishers p41-71

Sutherland, J. A. Novel publishing, 1830-1870. *In* Sutherland, J. A. Victorian novelists and publishers p9-40

Trickett, R. Vitality of language in nineteenth-century fiction. *In* Josipovici, G. ed. The modern English novel: the reader, the writer and the work p37-53

20th century—History and criticism

Adams, R. M. Counterparts. *In* Adams, R. M. Afterjoyce p162-93

Alcorn, J. Spirit of place: The novel. *In* Alcorn, J. The nature novel from Hardy to Lawrence p60-77

Alcorn, J. Toward Freud. *In* Alcorn, J. Lawrence: a version of pastoral. *In* Alcorn, J. The nature novel from Hardy to Lawrence p107-12

Cavaliero, G. Conclusion: The earth and the land. *In* Cavaliero, G. The rural tradition in the English novel, 1900-1939 p201-09

Cavaliero, G. The land and the city. *In* Cavaliero, G. The rural tradition in the English novel, 1900-1939 p 1-13

Cavaliero, G. Rural fantasies: Kenneth Grahame, T. H. White and others. *In* Cavaliero, G. The rural tradition in the English novel, 1900-1939 p26-45

Dawson, S. W. Precarious complacency. *In* Abbs, P. ed. The black rainbow p55-62

Friedman, A. W. The once and future age of modernism: an introduction. *In* Forms of modern British fiction p3-14

Kennard, J. E. Afterthoughts. *In* Kennard, J. E. Number and nightmare p203-06

Kennedy, A. Conclusion: A quick look around. *In* Kennedy, A. The protean self p261-85

Kennedy, A. The novel as a social fiction. *In* Kennedy, A. The protean self p63-98

Lodge, D. Two kinds of modern fiction. *In* Lodge, D. The modes of modern writing p41-52

Mudrick, M. Fiction and truth. *In* Mudrick, M. Books are not life but then what is? p276-99

Rutherford, A. The common man as hero: literature of the Western Front. *In* Rutherford, A. The literature of war p64-112

Showalter, E. Beyond the female aesthetic: contemporary women novelists. *In* Showalter, E. A literature of their own p298-319

Commonwealth of Nations authors— History and criticism

Fernando, L. A note from the Third World towards the re-definition of culture. *In* Narasimhaiah, C. D. ed. Awakened conscience p327-38

English folk-drama. See Folk-drama, English

English ghost stories. See Ghost stories, English

English historical fiction. See Historical fiction, English

English in India. See British in India

English interludes. See Interludes, English

English language

Capey, A. C. The language of enlightenment. *In* Abbs, P. ed. The black rainbow p92-113

Quirk, R. Thinking of words. *In* Quirk, R. The linguist and the English language p128-43

Steiner, G. Why English? *In* Contemporary approaches to English studies p8-23

Americanisms

See Americanisms

Analysis and parsing

See English language—Grammar

Bibliography

Strang, B. M. H. and Brennan, M. English language. *In* English Association. The year's work in English studies v57 p11-42

Dialectology

Allen, H. B. The Linguistic atlas of the Upper Midwest as a source of sociolinguistic information. *In* James B. McMillan: essays in linguistics by his friends and colleagues p3-19

Duckert, A. R. The winds of change. *In* James B. McMillan: essays in linguistics by his friends and colleagues p21-28

McDavid, R. I. and O'Cain, R. K. "Existential" there and it: an essay on method and interpretation of data. *In* James B. McMillan: essays in linguistics by his friends and colleagues p29-40

McDavid, V. The social distribution of selected verb forms in the Linguistic atlas of the North Central States. *In* James B. McMillan: essays in linguistics by his friends and colleagues p41-50

Shuy, R. W. Dialectology. *In* Wardhaugh, R. and Brown, H. D. eds. A survey of applied linguistics p182-206

Dialects

Cavers, D. L. In support of the use of place-names as an aid to the study of Middle English dialects. *In* An English miscellany p54-71

English language—*Continued*

Remedial teaching

Skurnick, B. J. A basic writing program at an urban university. *In* Minority language and literature p80-85

Rhetoric—Study and teaching (Higher)—New York (City)

Skurnick, B. J. A basic writing program at an urban university. *In* Minority language and literature p80-85

Semantics

Langendoen, D. T. Speak and talk: a vindication of syntactic deep structure. *In* On language, culture, and religion: in honor of Eugene A. Nida p237-40

Sentences

Gass, W. H. The ontology of the sentence, or How to make a world of words. *In* Gass, W. H. The world within the word p308-38

Slang

See Words, Obscene—English

Spelling

See English language—Orthography and spelling

Standardization

Sledd, J. H. We have met the enemy—and he is us. *In* Minority language and literature p65-70

Study and teaching

Malmstrom, J. First language teaching. *In* Wardhaugh, R. and Brown, H. D. eds. A survey of applied linguistics p44-68

Quirk, R. The study of the mother-tongue. *In* Quirk, R. The linguist and the English language p77-96

Shuy, R. W. Dialectology. *In* Wardhaugh, R. and Brown, H. D. eds. A survey of applied linguistics p182-206

Sledd, J. H. We have met the enemy—and he is us. *In* Minority language and literature p65-70

Study and teaching—Canada

Durrant, G. The new barbarians. *In* Gold, J. ed. In the name of language! p97-130

Style

Morris, W. An image sampler. *In* Morris, W. Earthly delights, unearthly adornments p13-17

Syntax

Epstein, E. L. The self-reflexive artefact: the function of mimesis in an approach to a theory of value for literature. *In* Fowler, R. ed. Style and structure in literature p40-78

Tense

Woods, M. J. Existence and tense. *In* Evans, G. L. and McDowell, J. H. eds. Truth and meaning p248-62

Usage

Algeo, J. Grammatical usage: modern shibboleths. *In* James B. McMillan: essays in linguistics by his friends and colleagues p53-71

Quirk, R. Our knowledge of English. *In* Quirk, R. The linguist and the English language p164-76

Verb

McDavid, V. The social distribution of selected verb forms in the Linguistic atlas of the North Central States. *In* James B. McMillan: essays in linguistics by his friends and colleagues p41-50

Marino, M. Toward a modal paradigm. *In* James B. McMillan: essays in linguistics by his friends and colleagues p73-89

Versification

Bridges, R. S. A letter to a musician on English prosody; excerpt from "Collected essays." *In* Gross, H. S. ed. The structure of verse p53-67

Gross, H. S. ed. Introduction: toward a phenomenology of rhythm. *In* Gross, H. S. ed. The structure of verse p5-17

Halle, M. and Keyser, S. J. The iambic pentameter; excerpt from "Versification: major language types." *In* Gross, H. S. ed. The structure of verse p173-93

Hamburger, M. On 'metrical' verse, 'free' verse and prose. *In* Hamburger, M. Art as second nature p12-23

Hollander, J. The metrical frame; excerpt from "Vision and resonance: two senses of poetic form." *In* Gross, H. S. ed. The structure of verse p77-101

Jespersen, O. Notes on metre; excerpt from "Linguistica." *In* Gross, H. S. ed. The structure of verse p105-28

Justice, D. Meters and memory. *In* Gross, H. S. ed. The structure of verse p269-76

Pound, E. L. Treatise on metre; excerpt from "ABC of reading." *In* Gross, H. S. ed. The structure of verse p234-40

Richards, I. A. Rhythm and metre; excerpt from "Principles of literary criticism." *In* Gross, H. S. ed. The structure of verse p68-76

Stevenson, C. L. The rhythm of English verse. *In* Gross, H. S. ed. The structure of verse p194-224

Wimsatt, W. K. and Beardsley, M. C. The concept of meter: an exercise in abstraction; excerpt from "Hateful contraries, studies in literature and criticism." *In* Gross, H. S. ed. The structure of verse p147-72

See also Free verse

Versification—History

Fussell, P. The historical dimension; excerpt from "Poetic meter and poetic form." *In* Gross, H. S. ed. The structure of verse p40-52

To 1100

See Anglo-Saxon language

Middle English, 1100-1500

Cavers, D. L. In support of the use of place-names as an aid to the study of Middle English dialects. *In* An English miscellany p54-71

Davis, N. Chaucer and fourteenth-century English. *In* Brewer, D. S. ed. Geoffrey Chaucer p58-84

English language in Africa

Mazrui, A. A. The Afro-Saxons. *In* Said, A. A. and Simmons, L. R. eds. Ethnicity in an international context p203-17

English language in Canada

Hornyansky, M. Is your English destroying your image? *In* Gold, J. ed. In the name of language! p71-96

English language in India

Rao, R. The caste of English. *In* Narasimhaiah, C. D. ed. Awakened conscience p420-22

English language in Scotland

Morgan, E. Registering the reality of Scotland. *In* Morgan, E. Essays p153-57

English language in the United States

Algeo, J. Grammatical usage: modern shibboleths. *In* James B. McMillan: essays in linguistics by his friends and colleagues p53-71

Allen, H. C. The cultural tie; excerpt from "Conflict and concord, the Anglo-American relationship since 1783." *In* Burton, D. H. ed. American history—British historians p75-91

Duckert, A. R. The winds of change. *In* James B. McMillan: essays in linguistics by his friends and colleagues p21-28

Steiner, G. Why English? *In* Contemporary approaches to English studies p8-23

See also Americanisms; Black English

English letters

Dawson, G. E. Problems in editing sixteenth- and seventeenth-century letters. *In* Medieval and Renaissance studies [1974] p87-103

History and criticism

Wilder, T. N. On reading the great letter writers. *In* Wilder, T. N. American characteristics, and other essays p151-64

English literature

See also Christian literature, English

History and criticism

Bate, W. J. The second temple; excerpt from "The burden of the past and the English poet." *In* Primeau, R. ed. Influx p100-17

Blythe, R. The dangerous idyll: sweet Auburn to Akenfield. *In* Royal Society of Literature of the United Kingdom, London. Essays by divers hands v38 p15-32

Bridgwater, P. English writers and Nietzsche. *In* Pasley, J. M. S. ed. Nietzsche: imagery and thought p220-58

Briggs, J. Ancestral voices: the ghost story from Lucian to Le Fanu. *In* Briggs, J. Night visitors p 25-51

Cooke, M. G. The extremes of self and system. *In* Cooke, M. G. The romantic will p52-56

Cunningham, J. V. *In* Cunningham, J. V. The collected essays of J. V. Cunningham p53-96

Echeruo, M. J. C. The conditioned imagination. *In* Echeruo, M. J. C. The conditioned imagination from Shakespeare to Conrad p 1-23

Echeruo, M. J. C. The exo-cultural hero of the Enlightenment. *In* Echeruo, M. J. C. The conditioned imagination from Shakespeare to Conrad p71-92

Fabian, B. English books and their eighteenth-century German readers. *In* Korshin, P. J. ed. The widening circle p117-96

Gilman, E. B. Conclusion: the witness as rational amphibian. *In* Gilman, E. B. The curious perspective p232-38

Goonetilleke, D. C. R. A. Antecedents. *In* Goonetilleke, D. C. R. A. Developing countries in British fiction p13-32

Hardy, B. N. Abuses of narrative. *In* Hardy, B. N. Tellers and listeners p102-30

Hawkins, H. 'Stay, illusion!': some poetic godgames. *In* Hawkins, H. Poetic freedom and poetic truth p105-35

Johnson, W. S. Victorian and modern. *In* Johnson, W. S. Sex and marriage in Victorian poetry p252-62

Knoepflmacher, U. C. and Tennyson, G. B. Afterglow and aftermath. *In* Knoepflmacher, U. C. and Tennyson, G. B. eds. Nature and the Victorian imagination p489-99

Korshin, P. J. The development of abstracted typology in England, 1650-1820. *In* Miner, E. R. ed. Literary uses of typology p147-203

Lodge, D. Metaphor and metonymy. *In* Lodge, D. The modes of modern writing p73-124

Ragussis, M. The subterfuge of art: Literature and regression. *In* Ragussis, M. The subterfuge of art p5-16

Schneider, D. J. The Manichean vision and the reading of symbolist works. *In* Schneider, D. J. Symbolism: the Manichean vision p 1-39

Steadman, J. M. The iconographical approach. *In* Steadman, J. M. Nature into myth p23-45

Steadman, J. M. Introduction. *In* Steadman, J. M. Nature into myth p 1-19

Steadman, J. M. The lexicographical approach. *In* Steadman, J. M. Nature into myth p46-63

Taiwo, O. Historical and cultural influences on the Nigerian novelists. *In* Taiwo, O. Culture and the Nigerian novel 1-33

Taylor, A. Magical language and poetic analogy. *In* Taylor, A. Magic and English romanticism p38-63

History and criticism—Bibliography

Dorsch, T. S. Literary history and criticism: general works. *In* English Association. The year's work in English studies v53 p17-36

Dorsch, T. S. Literary history and criticism: general works [another essay] *In* English Association. The year's work in English studies v54 p17-36

Dorsch, T. S. Literary history and criticism: general works [another essay] *In* English Association. The year's work in English studies v55 p17-33

Dorsch, T. S. Literary history and criticism: general works [another essay] *In* English Association. The year's work in English studies v56 p17-34

Dorsch, T. S. Literary history and criticism: general works [another essay] *In* English Association. The year's work in English studies v57 p 1-10

Study and teaching

Jones, J. Method or madness: how may we expect Commonwealth studies to affect the teaching of English? *In* Narasimhaiah, C. D. ed. Awakened conscience p408-12

Josipovici, G. English studies and European culture. *In* Josipovici, G. The lessons of modernism p87-108

English literature—Study and teaching
—Continued

Knights, L. C. Literature and the teaching of literature. In Niblett, W. R. ed. The sciences, the humanities and the technological threat p127-38

Whalley, G. Picking up the thread. In Gold, J. ed. In the name of language! p46-70

Study and teaching—Africa

Edwards, P. G. West African literature and English studies. In African studies since 1945 p91-95

Study and teaching—Canada

Durrant, G. The new barbarians. In Gold, J. ed. In the name of language! p97-130

Elliott, M. S. Respecting our organs. In Gold, J. ed. In the name of language! p161-204

Gold, J. A word to the wise. In Gold, J. ed. In the name of language! p 1-17

Priestley, F. E. L. English: an obsolete industry? In Gold, J. ed. In the name of language! p18-45

Whalley, G. Where are English studies going? In Gold, J. ed. In the name of language! p131-60

Study and teaching—United States

Fiedler, L. Elite literature and mass society. In Mann, D. A. ed. The arts in a democratic society p118-39

Study and teaching (Higher)

Cunningham, J. V. Graduate training in English. In Cunningham, J. V. The collected essays of J. V. Cunningham p272-73

Study and teaching (Higher)— United States

Graff, G. English in America. In Graff, G. Literature against itself p103-27

Partridge, E. B. Teaching English. In Cahn, S. M. ed. Scholars who teach p37-73

Shapiro, K. J. The poetry wreck. In Shapiro, K. J. The poetry wreck p353-65

Translations from Russian

Polushkin, M. A few words on translation. In Horn Book Magazine. Crosscurrents of criticism p283-86

African authors

See African literature (English)

Fijian authors

See Fijian literature (English)

Indic authors

See Indic literature (English)

Irish authors—Bibliography

Kain, R. M. General works. In Finneran, R. J. ed. Anglo-Irish literature p1-23

Irish authors—History and criticism

Balakian, N. The charmed circle: the Irish writers. In Balakian, N. Critical encounters p219-22

Carpenter, A. Double vision in Anglo-Irish literature. In Place, personality and the Irish writer p173-89

Harmon, M. Cobwebs before the wind: aspects of the peasantry in Irish literature from 1800 to 1916. In Casey, D. J. and Rhodes, R. E. eds. Views of the Irish peasantry, 1800-1916 p129-59

Henn, T. R. The lighter side of the Irish Literary Revival. In Henn, T. R. Last essays p119-36

Henn, T. R. The weasel's tooth. In Henn, T. R. Last essays p26-50

Innes, C. L. Through the looking glass: African and Irish nationalist writing. In African literature no. 9: Africa, America and the Caribbean p10-24

Jeffares, A. N. Place, space and personality and the Irish writer. In Place, personality and the Irish writer p11-40

Lyons, F. S. L. The Parnell theme in literature. In Place, personality and the Irish writer p69-95

Marcus, P. L. The Celtic revival: literature and the theatre. In De Breffny, B. ed. The Irish world p199-226

O'Brien, D. In Ireland after A portrait. In Staley, T. F. and Benstock, B. eds. Approaches to Joyce's Portrait p213-35

O'Driscoll, R. Return to the hearthstone: ideals of the Celtic Literary Revival. In Place, personality and the Irish writer p41-68

Welsh authors

Jones, D. On the difficulties of one writer of Welsh affinity whose language is English. In Jones, D. The dying Gaul, and other writings p30-34

West Indian authors

See West Indian literature (English)

To 1100

See Anglo Saxon literature

Middle English, 1100-1500—Bibliography

Allen, R. and Williams, D. J. Middle English: excluding Chaucer. In English Association. The year's work in English studies v54 p83-108

Davenport, W. A. and Williams, D. J. Middle English: excluding Chaucer. In English Association. The year's work in English studies v53 p85-105

Dolan, T. P.; Mitchell, L. E. and McTurk, R. W. Middle English: excluding Chaucer. In English Association. The year's work in English studies v57 p60-88

McTurk, R. W. and Williams, D. J. Middle English: excluding Chaucer. In English Association. The year's work in English studies v55 p92-147

McTurk, R. W. and Williams, D. J. Middle English: excluding Chaucer [another essay] In English Association. The year's work in English studies v56 p81-117

Middle English, 1100-1500— History and criticism

Campbell, J. J. Rhetoric in Old English literature: adaptation of classical rhetoric in Old English literature. In Murphy, J. J. ed. Medieval eloquence p173-97

Donaldson, E. T. Patristic exegesis in the criticism of medieval literature: the opposition. In Wimsatt, W. K. ed. Literary criticism: idea and act p170-88

Robbins, R. H. Dissent in Middle English literature: the spirit of (thirteen) seventy-six. In Medievalia et humanistica; new ser. no. 9 p25-51

Zacher, C. K. A new sense of the world. In Zacher, C. K. Curiosity and pilgrimage p3-17

English literature—*Continued*

Middle English, 1100-1500—History and criticism—Bibliography

Theiner, P. F. Medieval English literature. *In* Powell, J. M. ed. Medieval studies p239-75

Middle English, 1100-1500—Study and teaching

Quirk, R. The 'language' of language and literature. *In* Quirk, R. The linguist and the English language p65-76

Early modern, 1500-1700—Bibliography

Brake, L. and Ogden, J. The later seventeenth century. *In* English Association. The year's work in English studies v54 p252-75

Malekin, P. and Crane, D. E. L. The later seventeenth century. *In* English Association. The year's work in English studies v53 p250-72

Ogden, J. The later seventeenth century. *In* English Association. The year's work in English studies v55 p297-321

Ogden, J. The later seventeenth century [another essay] *In* English Association. The year's work in English studies v56 p221-41

Ogden, J. The later seventeenth century [another essay] *In* English Association. The year's work in English studies v57 p130-204

Rathmell, J. C. A. The later sixteenth century, excluding drama. *In* English Association. The year's work in English studies v53 p207-21

Rhodes, M. The earlier sixteenth century. *In* English Association. The year's work in English studies v56 p130-35

Rhodes, M. The earlier sixteenth century [another essay] *In* English Association. The year's work in English studies v57 p101-07

Robbins, R. The earlier seventeenth century, excluding drama. *In* English Association. The year's work in English studies v53 p222-38

Robbins, R. The earlier seventeenth century, excluding drama [another essay] *In* English Association. The year's work in English studies v54 p218-41

Robbins, R. The earlier seventeenth century, excluding drama [another essay] *In* English Association. The year's work in English studies v55 p263-81

Robbins, R. The earlier seventeenth century, excluding drama [another essay] *In* English Association. The year's work in English studies v56 p195-209

Robbins, R. The earlier seventeenth century, excluding drama [another essay] *In* English Association. The year's work in English studies v57 p164-77

Roe, J. The later sixteenth century: excluding drama. *In* English Association. The year's work in English studies v54 p200-17

Roe, J. The later sixteenth century: excluding drama [another essay] *In* English Association. The year's work in English studies v55 p248-62

Roe, J. The later sixteenth century: excluding drama [another essay] *In* English Association. The year's work in English studies v56 p182-94

Roe, J. The later sixteenth century: excluding drama [another essay] *In* English Association. The year's work in English studies v57 p154-63

Tydeman, W. The earlier sixteenth century. *In* English Association. The year's work in English studies v53 p121-46

Tydeman, W. The earlier sixteenth century [another essay] *In* English Association. The year's work in English studies v54 p124-52

Tydeman, W. The earlier sixteenth century [another essay]. *In* English Association. The year's work in English studies v55 p167-92

Early modern, 1500-1700—History and criticism

Adams, R. P. Opposed Tudor myths of power: Machiavellian tyrants and Christian kings. *In* Studies in the continental background of Renaissance English literature: essays presented to John L. Lievsay p67-90

Bowers, F. T. Elizabethan proofing. *In* Bowers, F. T. Essays in bibliography, text, and editing p240-53

Cunningham, J. V. The Renaissance in England. *In* Cunningham, J. V. The collected essays of J. V. Cunningham p282-310

Dunn, C. M. The changing image of woman in Renaissance society and literature. *In* Springer, M. A. ed. What manner of woman p15-38

Gill, R. B. The Renaissance conventions of envy. *In* Medievalia et humanistica; new ser. no. 9 p215-30

Gilman, E. B. The curious perspective in England. *In* Gilman, E. B. The curious perspective p50-66

Hamilton, A. C. On the concept of the English literary renaissance. *In* Medieval and Renaissance studies 1976 p119-37

Harrier, R. C. Invention in Tudor literature: historical perspectives. *In* Philosophy and humanism p370-86

Helgerson, R. The mirror of duty. *In* Helgerson, R. The Elizabethan prodigals p16-43

Helgerson, R. Patterns of prodigality. *In* Helgerson, R. The Elizabethan prodigals p 1-15

Howard, D. R. Renaissance world-alienation. *In* The Darker vision of the Renaissance p47-76

Hunter, G. K. Elizabethans and foreigners. *In* Hunter, G. K. Dramatic identities and cultural tradition p3-30

Latt, D. J. Praising virtuous ladies: the literary image and historical reality of women in seventeenth-century England. *In* Springer, M. A. ed. What manner of woman p39-64

McCanles, M. Dialectical criticism and beyond. *In* McCanles, M. Dialectical criticism and Renaissance literature p114-73

Manlove, C. N. Conclusion. *In* Manlove, C. N. Literature and reality, 1600-1800 p209-11

Miner, E. R. Time, sequence, and plot in Restoration literature. *In* Studies in eighteenth-century culture v5 p67-85

Richetti, J. J. The portrayal of women in Restoration and eighteenth-century English literature. *In* Springer, M. A. ed. What manner of woman p65-97

English literature—19th century—History and criticism—*Continued*

Haley, B. Conclusion. *In* Haley, B. The healthy body and Victorian culture p252-61

Haley, B. The true gentleman and the washed rough in broadcloth. *In* Haley, B. The healthy body and Victorian culture p205-26

Heilbrun, C. G. Marriage perceived: English literature, 1873-1941. *In* Springer, M. A. ed. What manner of woman p160-83

Knoepflmacher, U. C. Mutations of the Wordsworthian child of nature. *In* Knoepflmacher, U. C. and Tennyson, G. B. eds. Nature and the Victorian imagination p391-425

Langbaum, R. W. The art of Victorian literature. *In* Altholz, J. L. ed. The mind and art of Victorian England p16-34

Masson, D. Pre-Raphaelitism in art and literature. *In* Sambrook, J. ed. Pre-Raphaelitism p71-91

Miller, J. H. Nature and the linguistic moment. *In* Knoepflmacher, U. C. and Tennyson, G. B. eds. Nature and the Victorian imagination p440-51

Prickett, S. Christmas at Scrooge's. *In* Prickett, S. Victorian fantasy p38-74

Prickett, S. Dreams and nightmares: monsters under the hill. *In* Prickett, S. Victorian fantasy p75-113

Prickett, S. The evolution of a word. *In* Prickett, S. Victorian fantasy p 1-37

Springer, M. A. Angels and other women in Victorian literature. *In* Springer, M. A. ed. What manner of woman p124-59

Supple, B. E. Material development: the condition of England 1830-1860. *In* Lerner, L. ed. The Victorians p49-69

Tayler, I. B. S. and Luria, G. Gender and genre: women in British romantic literature. *In* Springer, M. A. ed. What manner of woman p98-123

Tillotson, G. 'Earnestness.' *In* Tillotson, G. A view of Victorian literature p23-54

Tillotson, G. Introduction. *In* Tillotson, G. A view of Victorian literature p 1-22

20th century—Bibliography

Bratton, J. and others. The twentieth century. *In* English Association. The year's work in English studies v54 p363-405

Bratton, J. and others. The twentieth century [another essay] *In* English Association. The year's work in English studies v55 p439-81

Davidson, E. J.; Ashe, A. H. and Redmond, J. The twentieth century. *In* English Association. The year's work in English studies v53 p361-409

Moran, M.; Painter, S. and Redmond, J. The twentieth century. *In* English Association. The year's work in English studies v56 p340-92

Moran, M.; Painter, S. and Redmond, J. The twentieth century [another essay] *In* English Association. The year's work in English studies v57 p315-81

20th century—History and criticism

Alcorn, J. Butler: the new spirit. *In* Alcorn, J. The nature novel from Hardy to Lawrence p25-41

Alcorn, J. Epilogue: Is Great Pan dead? *In* Alcorn, J. The nature novel from Hardy to Lawrence p113-23

Alcorn, J. Spirit of space: The travel book. *In* Alcorn, J. The nature novel from Hardy to Lawrence p42-59

Balakian, N. The flight from innocence: England's newest literary generation. *In* Balakian, N. Critical encounters p56-72

Briggs, J. Ghosts troop home: the Great War and its aftermath. *In* Briggs, J. Night visitors p165-81

Colmer, J. Continuity and change. *In* Colmer, J. Coleridge to Catch-22 p122-38

Davie, D. Dissent in the present century. *In* Davie, D. A gathered Church p91-108

Ellmann, R. Two faces of Edward. *In* Wimsatt, W. K. ed. Literary criticism: idea and act p560-75

Gillie, C. Introduction: The world of art and art in the world: twentieth-century differences. *In* Gillie, C. Movements of English literature, 1900-1940 p 1-23

Heilbrun, C. G. Marriage perceived: English literature, 1873-1941. *In* Springer, M. A. ed. What manner of woman p160-83

Lodge, D. In the thirties. *In* Lodge, D. The modes of modern writing p188-212

Pritchard, W. H. England seen through. *In* Pritchard, W. H. Seeing through everything p23-50

Richards, I. A. Nineteen hundred and now. *In* Richards, I. A. Complementarities p167-77

Ries, L. R. Literature and violence. *In* Ries, L. R. Wolf masks p3-32

Spender, S. Background to the thirties. *In* Spender, S. The thirties and after p3-20

Spender, S. Notes on revolutionaries and reactionaries: Reactionaries. *In* Spender, S. The thirties and after p154-65

Spender, S. Notes on revolutionaries and reactionaries: Revolutionaries. *In* Spender, S. The thirties and after p146-54

Watson, G. Did Stalin dupe the intellectuals? *In* Watson, G. Politics and literature in modern Britain p46-70

Watson, G. Left and Right. *In* Watson, G. Politics and literature in modern Britain p85-97

Watson, G. The literature of fascism. *In* Watson, G. Politics and literature in modern Britain p71-84

Watson, G. The myth of catastrophe. *In* Watson, G. Politics and literature in modern Britain p98-109

Watson, G. The New Left. *In* Watson, G. Politics and literature in modern Britain p15-37

Commonwealth of Nations authors—
History and criticism

Anand, M. R. Variety of ways: is there a shared tradition in Commonwealth literature? *In* Narasimhaiah, C. D. ed. Awakened conscience p441-46

Blaise, C. The Commonwealth writer and his material. *In* Narasimhaiah, C. D. ed. Awakened conscience p118-26

New, W. H. New language, new world. *In* Narasimhaiah, C. D. ed. Awakened conscience p360-77

Niven, A. The Scottish element in Commonwealth literature. *In* Narasimhaiah, C. D. ed. Awakened conscience p29-41

South Africa
See South African literature (English)

English love poetry. See Love poetry, English

English moralities. See Moralities, English

English mystery and miracle-plays. See Mystery and miracle-plays, English

English mystery stories. See Detective and mystery stories, English

English newspapers
Seymour-Ure, C. The press and the party system between the Wars. *In* Peele, G. and Cook, C. eds. The politics of reappraisal, 1918-1939 p232-57

English nonsense literature. See Nonsense literature, English

English nonsense-verses. See Nonsense-verses, English

English novelists. See Novelists, English

English opera. See Opera, English

English parodies. See Parodies, English

English pastoral poetry. See Pastoral poetry, English

English periodicals
Mitchell, S. The forgotten woman of the period: penny weekly family magazines of the 1840's and 1850's. *In* Vicinus, M. ed. A widening sphere p29-51

History
Granger, B. I. Introduction. *In* Granger, B. I. American essay serials from Franklin to Irving p3-12

English philology

Bibliography
Strang, B. M. H. and Pellowe, J. English language. *In* English Association. The year's work in English studies v53 p37-66

Strang, B. M. H. and Pellowe, J. English language [another essay] *In* English Association. The year's work in English studies v54 p37-68

Strang, B. M. H. and Pellowe, J. English language [another essay] *In* English Association. The year's work in English studies v55 p34-75

Strang, B. M. H. and Pellowe, J. English language [another essay] *In* English Association. The year's work in English studies v56 p35-62

English philosophy. See Philosophy, English

English poetry
See also Epigrams, English; Political poetry, English; Revolutionary poetry, English

History and criticism
Adams, P. G. The continuing echo. *In* Adams, P. G. Graces of harmony p164-89

Adams, P. G. Definitions and the tradition. *In* Adams, P. G. Graces of harmony p 1-56

Bloom, H. Clinamen, or Poetic misprision; excerpt from "The anxiety of influence." *In* Primeau, R. ed. Influx p82-99

Clemen, W. H. The pursuit of influence. *In* English Association. Essays and studies, 1975 p94-105

Donoghue, D. The eye and the mind's eye. *In* Donoghue, D. The sovereign ghost p128-82

Epstein, E. L. The self-reflexive artefact: the function of mimesis in an approach to a theory of value for literature. *In* Fowler, R. ed. Style and structure in literature p40-78

Fussell, P. The historical dimension; excerpt from "Poetic meter and poetic form." *In* Gross, H. S. ed. The structure of verse p40-52

Gross, H. S. ed. Introduction: toward a phenomenology of rhythm. *In* Gross, H. S. ed. The structure of verse p5-17

Hamburger, M. On 'metrical' verse, 'free' verse and prose. *In* Hamburger, M. Art as second nature p12-23

Hardy, B. N. The advantage of lyric. *In* Hardy, B. N. The advantage of lyric p 1-17

Hartman, G. H. Evening star and evening land. *In* Hartman, G. H. The fate of reading p147-78

Hobsbaum, P. The poetry of debate. *In* Hobsbaum, P. Tradition and experiment in English poetry p157-79

Hobsbaum, P. The rise of the dramatic monologue. *In* Hobsbaum, P. Tradition and experiment in English poetry p233-54

Hollander, J. The metrical frame; excerpt from "Vision and resonance: two senses of poetic form." *In* Gross, H. S. ed. The structure of verse p77-101

Preyer, R. O. The burden of culture and the dialectic of literature. *In* Evolution of consciousness p98-105

Ragussis, M. Epilogue: the echo. *In* Ragussis, M. The subterfuge of art p230-33

Richards, I. A. Beauty and truth. *In* Richards, I. A Complementarities p215-25

Richards, I. A. The interinanimations of words. *In* Richards, I. A. Poetries p71-84

Sherbo, A. Prolegomena. *In* Sherbo, A. English poetic diction from Chaucer to Wordsworth p 1-20

Sherbo, A. Some origins of poetic diction. *In* Sherbo, A. English poetic diction from Chaucer to Wordsworth p21-43

Stead, C. K. Eliot, Arnold, and the English poetic tradition. *In* The Literary criticism of T. S. Eliot p184-206

Thurley, G. American poetry: sketch of a theory. *In* Thurley, G. The American moment p3-32

Thurley, G. F. R. Leavis and the English existential tradition. *In* Thurley, G. The ironic harvest p23-37

Thurley, G. The intellectualist position. *In* Thurley, G. The ironic harvest p 1-22

Wain, J. On the breaking of forms. *In* Wain, J. Professing poetry p91-112

Wilbur, R. Poetry and happiness. *In* Wilbur, R. Responses p91-114

Wimsatt, W. K. Genesis: an argument resumed. *In* Wimsatt. W. K. Day of the leopards p11-39

Study and teaching
Nemerov, H. Speaking silence. *In* Nemerov, H. Figures of thought p100-14

Irish authors—Bibliography
Kilroy, J. F. Nineteenth-century writers. *In* Finneran, R. J. ed Anglo-Irish literature p24-47

West Indian authors
See West Indian poetry (English)

Women authors—History and criticism
Gilbert, S. M. and Gubar, S. Introduction: gender, creativity, and the woman poet. *In* Gilbert, S. M. and Gubar, S. eds. Shakespeare's sisters pxv-xxvi

English poetry—*Continued*

To 1100

See Anglo-Saxon poetry

Middle English, 1100-1500—
History and criticism

Mustanoja, T. F. Verbal rhyming in Chaucer. *In* Chaucer and Middle English studies in honour of Rossell Hope Robbins p104-10

Pearsall, D. A. The English romance in the fifteenth century. *In* English Association. Essays and studies, 1976 p56-83

Sherbo, A. Chaucer to Spenser. *In* Sherbo, A. English poetic diction from Chaucer to Wordsworth p44-68

Early modern, 1500-1700—
History and criticism

Bateson, F. W. Contributions to a dictionary of critical terms. *In* Roberts, J. R. ed. Essential articles for the study of John Donne's poetry p58-65

Colie, R. L. The rhetoric of transcendence. *In* Roberts, J. R. ed. Essential articles for the study of John Donne's poetry p199-219

Cunningham, J. V. Lyric style in the 1590s. *In* Cunningham, J. V. The collected essays of J. V. Cunningham p311-24

Eliot, T. S. The metaphysical poets. *In* Eliot, T. S. Selected prose of T. S. Eliot p59-67

Farley-Hills, D. Comic poetry of the Commonwealth. *In* Farley-Hills, D. The benevolence of laughter: comic poetry of the Commonwealth and Restoration p21-45

Hobsbaum, P. Ben Jonson in the seventeenth century. *In* Hobsbaum, P. Tradition and experiment in English poetry p126-56

Hobsbaum, P. Elizabethan poetry. *In* Hobsbaum, P. Tradition and experiment in English poetry p68-88

Kermode, J. F. Dissociation of sensibility. *In* Roberts, J. R. ed. Essential articles for the study of John Donne's poetry p66-82

Lewalski, B. K. Art and the sacred subject: sermon theory, Biblical personae, and Protestant poetics. *In* Lewalski, B. K. Protestant poetics and the seventeenth-century religious lyric p213-50

Lewalski, B. K. Biblical genre theory: precepts and models for the religious lyric. *In* Lewalski, B. K. Protestant poetics and the seventeenth-century religious lyric p31-71

Lewalski, B. K. The Biblical symbolic mode: typology and the religious lyric. *In* Lewalski, B. K. Protestant poetics and the seventeenth-century religious lyric p111-44

Lewalski, B. K. "Is there in truth no beautie?" Protestant poetics and the Protestant paradigm of salvation. *In* Lewalski, B. K. Protestant poetics and the seventeenth-century religious lyric p3-27

Lewalski, B. K. The poetic texture of scripture: tropes and figures for the religious lyric. *In* Lewalski, B. K. Protestant poetics and the seventeenth-century religious lyric p72-110

Lewalski, B. K. Protestant emblematics: sacred emblems and religious lyrics. *In* Lewalski, B. K. Protestant poetics and the seventeenth-century religious lyric p179-212

Lewalski, B. K. Protestant meditation: kinds, structures, and strategies of development for the meditative lyric. *In* Lewalski, B. K. Protestant poetics and the seventeenth-century religious lyric p147-78

Ormsby-Lennon, H. Poetic standards on the early Augustan battleground. *In* Studies in eighteenth-century culture v5 p253-80

Praz, M. The critical importance of the revived interest in seventeenth-century metaphysical poetry. *In* Roberts, J. R. ed. Essential articles for the study of John Donne's poetry p3-10

Shawcross, T. T. The poet as orator: one phase of his judicial pose. *In* Sloan, T. O. and Waddington, R. B. eds. The rhetoric of Renaissance poetry p5-36

Sherbo, A. Chaucer to Spenser. *In* Sherbo, A. English poetic diction from Chaucer to Wordsworth p44-68

Sloan, T. O. The crossing of rhetoric and poetry in the English Renaissance. *In* Sloan, T. O. and Waddington, R. B. eds. The rhetoric of Renaissance poetry p212-42

Williams, K. The moralized song: some Renaissance themes in Pope. *In* ELH essays for Earl R. Wasserman p285-308

18th century—History and criticism

Adams, P. G. Graces of harmony in varied verse. *In* Adams, P. G. Graces of harmony p136-63

Davie, D. Dissent and the Wesleyans, 1740-1800. *In* Davie, D. A gathered Church p37-54

Davie, D. Old dissent, 1700-1740. *In* Davie, D. A gathered Church p19-36

Ehrenpreis, I. Meaning: implicit and explicit. *In* Harth, J. P. ed. New approaches to eighteenth-century literature p117-55

Nelson, J. W. War and peace and the British poets of sensibility. *In* Studies in eighteenth-century culture v7 p345-66

Wimsatt, W. K. Imitation as freedom—1717-1798. *In* Wimsatt, W. K. Day of the leopards p117-39

Also in Wimsatt, W. K. Literary criticism: idea and act p463-82

19th century—History and criticism

Albrecht, W. P. The sublime of vision. *In* Albrecht, W. P. The sublime pleasures of tragedy p97-114

Allott, K. Victorian poetry and the legacy of romanticism. *In* Davies, R. T. and Beatty, B. G. eds. Literature of the romantic period, 1750-1850 p189-206

Altieri, C. F. Modern and post modern: symbolist and immanentist modes of poetic thought. *In* Altieri, C. F. Enlarging the temple p29-52

Armstrong, I. Browning and Victorian poetry of sexual love. *In* Armstrong, I. ed. Robert Browning p267-98

Ball, P. M. Conclusion: The heart's events. *In* Ball, P. M. The heart's events p222-23

Bayley, J. The vulgar and the heroic in 'bad poetry.' *In* Bayley, J. The uses of division p115-30

Bornstein, G. Yeats and the greater romantic lyric. *In* Bornstein, G. Romantic and modern p91-110

Brisman, L. Introduction. *In* Brisman, L. Romantic origins p11-20

Brisman, L. Reintroduction: from the seats of power divine. *In* Brisman, L. Romantic origins p362-405

English poetry—19th century—History and criticism—*Continued*

Cooke, M. G. The extremes of self and system: Volatile self and system in the romantic complex. *In* Cooke, M. G. The romantic will p76-84

Cooke, M. G. The will in English romanticism: The question of the will. *In* Cooke, M. G. The romantic will p5-29

Cooke, M. G. The will in English romanticism: The will in romantic poetry. *In* Cooke, M. G The romantic will p29-51

Cooke, M. G. The will to art. *In* Cooke, M. G. The romantic will p145-50

Cooke, M. G. The will to art: Conclusion. *In* Cooke, M. G. The romantic will p216-22

Cooke, M. G. The will to art: Excursus: The will to art in romanticism. *In* Cooke, M. G. The romantic will p182-87

Dawson, C. Poetics: the hero as poet. *In* Dawson, C. Victorian noon p16-35

DeLaura, D. J. The future of poetry: a context for Carlyle and Arnold. *In* Carlyle and his contemporaries p148-80

DeLaura, D. J. The poetry of thought. *In* Altholz, J. L. ed. The mind and art of Victorian England p35-57

Eliot, T. S. From the use of poetry and the use of criticism. *In* Eliot, T. S. Selected prose of T. S. Eliot p79-96

Evert, W. H. Coadjutors of oppression: a romantic and modern theory of evil. *In* Bornstein, G. ed. **Romantic and modern** p29-52

Heffernan, J. A. W. The English romantic perception of color. *In* Kroeber, K. and Walling, W. eds. Images of romanticism p133-48

Hobsbaum, P. The romantic dichotomy. *In* Hobsbaum, P. Tradition and experiment in English poetry p206-32

House, H. Pre-Raphaelite poetry; excerpt from "All in due time". *In* Sambrook, J. ed. Pre-Raphaelitism p126-32

Hunt, J. D. A moment's monument: reflections on pre-Raphaelite vision in poetry and painting. *In* Sambrook, J. ed. Pre-Raphaelitism p243-64

Johnson, W. S. Sexual attitudes: secular, sacramental, and ideal. *In* Johnson, W. S. **Sex and marriage in Victorian poetry** p34-109

Landow, G. P. Moses striking the rock: typological symbolism in Victorian poetry. *In* Miner, E. R. ed. Literary uses of typology p315-44

Lerner, L. Poetry. *In* Lerner, L. ed. The Victorians p25-45

Sabin, M. Victor Hugo: from spectacle to symbol. *In* Sabin, M. English romanticism and the French tradition p142-67

Sanders, C. R. Two kinds of poetry. *In* Sanders, C. R. Carlyle's friendships, and other studies p305-11

Sperry, S. M. Toward a definition of romantic irony in English literature. *In* Bornstein, G. ed. Romantic and modern p3-28

Storch, R. F. Abstract idealism in English romantic poetry and painting. *In* Kroeber, K. and Walling, W. eds. Images of romanticism p189-209

Taylor, A. Conclusion. *In* Taylor, A. Magic and English romanticism p251-55

Wimsatt, W. K. Imitation as freedom—1717-1798. *In* Wimsatt, W. K. Day of the leopards p117-39

Also in Wimsatt, W. K. ed. Literary criticism idea and act p463-82

20th century—History and criticism

Berryman, J. Poetry chronicle, 1948: waiting for the end, boys. *In* Berryman, J. The freedom of the poets p297-309

Briggs, J. Epilogue: Ghosts and poets. *In* Briggs, J. Night visitors p196-212

Gillie, C. The recovery of poetry, 1900-1920. *In* Gillie, C. Movements in English literature, 1900-1940 p65-89

Glicksberg, C. I. Poetry and radicalism in England. *In* Glicksberg, C. I. The literature of commitment p250-76

Hobsbaum, P. The growth of English modernism. *In* Hobsbaum, P. Tradition and experiment in English poetry p289-307

Holbrook, D. Modern poetry and the death of sympathy. *In* Holbrook, D. Lost bearings in English poetry p164-93

Lewis, W. The machine poets. *In* Lewis, W. Enemy salvoes p173-76

Robinson, I. Paper tygers or, The circus animals' desertion in the new pop poetry. *In* Abbs, P. ed. The black rainbow p19-31

Scannell, V. Henry Reed and others. *In* Scannell, V. Not without glory p134-71

Scannell, V. Setting the scene. *In* Scannell, V. Not without glory p7-22

Smith, E. E. From romantic revolution to welfare state. *In* Smith, E. E. The angry young men of the thirties p134-53

Thurley, G. The new poetry in England. *In* Thurley, G. The ironic harvest p190-212

Commonwealth of Nations authors—
History and criticism

Amanuddin, S. Toward a view of Commonwealth poetic tradition. *In* Narasimhaiah, C. D. ed. Awakened conscience p423-32

English political poetry. See Political poetry, English

English political satire. See Political satire, English

English prose literature

19th century—History and criticism

DeLaura, D. J. The allegory of life: the autobiographical impulse in Victorian prose. *In* Landow, G. P. ed. Approaches to Victorian autobiography p333-54

Gelpi, B. C. The innocent I: Dickens' influence on Victorian autobiography. *In* The Worlds of Victorian fiction p57-71

Grosskurth, P. Where was Rousseau? *In* Landow, G. P. ed. Approaches to Victorian autobiography p26-38

Helsinger, E. K. Ulysses to Penelope: Victorian experiments in autobiography. *In* Landow, G. P. ed. Approaches to Victorian autobiography p3-25

Helsinger, H. Credence and credibility: the concern for honesty in Victorian autobiography. *In* Landow, G. P. ed. Approaches to Victorian autobiography p39-63

Johnson, W. S. Sexual attitudes: "Victorian" and Victorian. *In* Johnson, W. S. Sex and marriage in Victorian poetry p13-33

English prose literature—19th century—History and criticism—_Continued_

Landow, G. P. Introduction. _In_ Landow, G. P. ed. Approaches to Victorian autobiography pxiii-xlvi

Walther, L. The invention of childhood in Victorian autobiography. _In_ Landow, G. P. ed. Approaches to Victorian autobiography p64-83

English religious poetry. See Religious poetry, English

English satire. See Satire, English

English science fiction. See Science fiction, English

English wit and humor, Pictorial

Gilman, E. B. The curious perspective in England. _In_ Gilman, E. B. The curious perspective p50-66

Engraving

Printing—History

Verner, C. Copperplate printing. _In_ Woodward, D. A. ed. Five centuries of map printing p51-75

Enigmas. See Riddles

Enlightenment

Darnton, R. The High Enlightenment and the low-life of literature in pre-revolutionary France. _In_ French society and the Revolution p53-87

Davidson, H. M. Fontenelle, Perrault, and the realignment of the arts. _In_ Literature and history in the age of ideas p3-13

Echeruo, M. J. C. The exo-cultural hero of the Enlightenment. _In_ Echeruo, M. J. C. The conditioned imagination from Shakespeare to Conrad p71-92

Meyer, D. H. The civilized Americans. _In_ Meyer, D. H. The democratic Enlightenment p49-60

Meyer, D. H. The critical period in American intellectual history. _In_ Meyer, D. H. The democratic Enlightenment p171-81

Meyer, D. H. The ethics of belief and the conduct of the mind. _In_ Meyer. D. H. The democratic Enlightenment p82-93

Meyer, D. H. From piety to moralism. _In_ Meyer, D. H. The democratic Enlightenment p35-45

Meyer, D. H. John Witherspoon and the education of the public conscience. _In_ Meyer, D. H. The democratic Enlightenment p182-98

Meyer, D. H. Religion and the experimental method of reasoning. _In_ Meyer, D. H. The democratic Enlightenment p3-17

Meyer, D. H. Science, rhetoric, and revolution. _In_ Meyer, D. H. The democratic Enlightenment p97-108

Meyer, D. H. William Ellery Channing and the inward enlightenment. _In_ Meyer, D. H. The democratic Enlightenment p199-209

Palmer, R. R. The European Enlightenment in its American setting. _In_ Aspects of American liberty p47-55

Schneider, H. W. "Reasonable rationalism: the heritage of the Enlightenment." _In_ Philosophy and the civilizing arts p474-86

Shklar, J. N. Politics and the intellect. _In_ Studies in eighteenth-century culture v7 p139-51

Tichi, C. The revolution begins the world anew. _In_ Tichi, C. New World, new earth p67-113

Vartanian, A. Necessity or freedom? The politics of an eighteenth-century metaphysical debate. _In_ Studies in eighteenth-century culture v7 p153-74

White, H. V. The irrational and the problem of historical knowledge in the Enlightenment. _In_ White, H. V. Tropics of discourse p135-39

Ennius, Quintus

About

Knoche, U. The satires of Quintus Ennius. _In_ Knoche, U. Roman satire p17-30

About individual works
The annals of Quintus Ennius

Colaclides, P. On the verb vero in Ennius. _In_ Harvard Studies in classical philology v71 p121-23

Satires

Knoche, U. The satires of Quintus Ennius. _In_ Knoche, U. Roman satire p17-30

Ramage, E. S. Ennius and the origins of Roman satire. _In_ Roman satirists and their satire p8-26

Criticism, Textual

Skutsch, O. Notes on Ennian tragedy. _In_ Harvard Studies in classical philology v71 p125-42

Language—Grammar

Mikalson, J. D. Ennius' usage of is ea id. _In_ Harvard Studies in classical philology v80 p171-77

Enownment, Consciousness, thought, and.

Hofstadter, A. _In_ Thought, consciousness, and reality p85-109

Ensembles (Mathematics) See Set theory

Enstice, Andrew

The fruit of the Tree of knowledge. _In_ Smith, A. ed. The novels of Thomas Hardy p9-22

Enteen, George M.

Marxist historians during the cultural revolution: a case study of professional infighting. _In_ Cultural revolution in Russia, 1928-1931 p154-68

Entertainers

United States

See Afro-Americans in the performing arts

Entertaining

Lewis, W. S. A house-party at Stowe. _In_ The Dress of words p117-25

Enthoven, Alain C.

1963 nuclear strategy revisited. _In_ Ethics and nuclear strategy? p72-81

Enthusiasm

McCarthy, J. A. Shaftesbury and Wieland: the question of enthusiasm. _In_ Studies in eighteenth-century culture v6 p79-95

Entrenchments. See Intrenchments

Entrepreneur

Schmitt, H. A. Landed and moneyed princes: the harvest of tradition and conflict in German business and politics. _In_ Evolution of international management structures p67-88

Entrepreneur—*Continued*

Spengler, J. J. Adam Smith and society's decision -makers. *In* Skinner, A. S. and Wilson, T. eds. Essays on Adam Smith p390-414

See also Profit

Entwisle, Doris R.

Socialization and the young family. *In* Major social issues p208-16

Environment. See Adaptation (Biology); Ecology; Human ecology; Man—Influence on nature; Nature and nurture

Environment, Human. See Human ecology

Environment and state. See Environmental policy

Environmental chemistry

Bickwit, L. and Brownlee, M. B. Chemical pollution control in the USA. *In* Against pollution and hunger p278-86

Thring, M. W. Physical and chemical aspects of pollution. *In* Against pollution and hunger p63-88

Environmental control. See Environmental law; Environmental policy

Environmental education. See Conservation of natural resources—Study and teaching; Ecology—Study and teaching

Environmental engineering (Buildings). See Architecture—Human factors

Environmental impact analysis

Singer, H. W. Environmental factors in project analysis: a conceptual note. *In* Theory for economic efficiency: essays in honor of Abba P. Lerner p186-94

Environmental law

Feinberg, J. The rights of animals and unborn generations. *In* Philosophy & environmental crisis p43-68

Piper, D. C. Unilateral acts of states with regard to environmental protection. *In* Orr, D. W. and Soroos, M. S. eds. The global predicament p264-81

See also Water—Pollution—Law and legislation

United States

Bickwit, L. and Brownlee, M. B. Chemical pollution control in the USA. *In* Against pollution and hunger p278-86

Environmental management. See Environmental law; Environmental policy

Environmental policy

Catton, W. R. and Dunlap, R. E. Environmental sociology: a new paradigm. *In* McNall, S. G. ed. Theoretical perspectives in sociology p465-78

Dubos, R. J. Creative adaptations to the future. *In* Aspects of American liberty p162-73

Juda, L. International environmental concern: perspectives of and implications for developing states. *In* Orr, D. W. and Soroos, M. S. eds. The global predicament p90-107

Odum, E. P. Environmental ethic and the attitude revolution. *In* Philosophy & environmental crisis p10-15

Orr, D. W. and Hill, S. Leviathan, the open society, and the crisis of ecology. *In* Orr, D. W. and Soroos, M. S. eds. The global predicament p308-26

Soroos, M. S. Ecology and the time dimension in human relationships. *In* Orr, D. W. and Soroos, M. S. eds. The global predicament p327-43

Strong, M. F. "Where are we growing?" *In* The Frontiers of human knowledge p229-42

Taulbee, J. L. Law, organization, and environmental concerns. *In* Orr, D. W. and Soroos, M. S. eds. The global predicament p249-63

See also Conservation of natural resources; Environmental law; Human ecology; Man—Influence on nature

Citizen participation

Hare, R. Contrasting methods of environmental planning. *In* Royal Institute of Philosophy. Nature and conduct p281-97

Rothenberg, J. The physical environment. *In* McKie, J. W. ed. Social responsibility and the business predicament p191-215

Canada

Briggs, H. Scientific leadership and the price system. *In* Against pollution and hunger p273-77

United States

Briggs, H. Scientific leadership and the price system. *In* Against pollution and hunger p273-77

Caldwell, L. K. Responsiveness and responsibility: the anomalous problem of the environment. *In* Rieselbach, L. N. ed. People vs. government: the responsiveness of the American institutions p300-27

Humpstone, C. C. The rich man's burden: an examination of environmental consequences of isolation for the United States. *In* Isolation or interdependence? p193-204

Nash, R. Do rocks have rights? Thoughts on environmental ethics. *In* Small comforts for hard times p120-34

Environmental pollution. See Pollution

Environmental protection. See Environmental law; Environmental policy; Landscape protection

Environmental studies. See Conservation of natural resources—Study and teaching

Envy

Stein, H. F. Envy and the evil eye: an essay in the psychological ontogeny of belief and ritual. *In* The Evil eye p193-222

Envy in literature

Gill, R. B. The Renaissance conventions of envy. *In* Medievalia et humanistica; new ser. no. 9 p215-30

Enzensberger, Hans Magnus

Portrait of a party: prehistory, structure, and ideology of the PCC; excerpt from "Politics and crime." *In* Radosh, R. ed. The new Cuba: paradoxes and potentials p102-37

Eolian harp. See Aeolian harp

Eörsi, Istvan

Illusion and conflict: drama in Eastern European societies. *In* Drama and society p241-43

Eoyang, Eugene Chen

A taste for apricots: approaches to Chinese fiction. *In* Chinese narrative p53-69

Ephemeros (The word)

Dickie, M. W. On the meaning of ἐφήμερος. *In* Illinois classical studies, v 1 1976 p7-14

Epic literature

Ferguson, M. A. Losing battles as a comic epic in prose. *In* Prenshaw, P. W. ed. Eudora Welty p305-24

Havelock, E. A. The function of epic in preliterate societies. *In* Havelock, E. A. The Greek concept of justice p15-37

History and criticism

Grimm, R. Naturalism and epic drama. *In* Mews, S. and Knust, H. eds. Essays on Brecht p3-27

Epic literature, Mesopotamian

History and criticism

Renger, J. M. Mesopotamian epic literature. *In* Oinas, F. J. ed. Heroic epic and saga p27-48

Epic literature, Turkish

History and criticism

Başöz, I. The epic tradition among Turkic peoples. *In* Oinas, F. J. ed. Heroic epic and saga p310-35

Epic poetry

Bynum, D. E. The generic nature of oral epic poetry. *In* Folklore genres p35-58

Russo, J. and Simon, B. Homeric psychology and the oral epic tradition. *In* Wright, J. H. ed. Essays on the Iliad p41-57

See also Romances

History and criticism

Simonsuuri, K. Epic genius: the departure from the neoclassical model. *In* Simonsuuri, K. Homer's original genius p77-89

Steadman, J. M. The arming of an archetype. *In* Concepts of the hero in the Middle Ages and the Renaissance p147-96

Therapeutic use

Simon, B. Epic as therapy. *In* Simon, B. Mind and madness in ancient Greece p78-88

Epic poetry, African

History and criticism

Biebuyck, D. P. The African heroic epic. *In* Oinas, F. J. ed. Heroic epic and saga p336-67

Epic poetry, American

History and criticism

Miller, J. E. Bards of the great idea: seekers of the supreme fiction. *In* Miller, J. E. The American quest for a supreme fiction p318-32

Miller, J. E. The care & feeding of long poems: the American epic from Barlow to Berryman. *In* Miller, J. E. The American quest for a supreme fiction p12-29

Epic poetry, Classical

History and criticism

Hansen, W. F. The Homeric epics and oral poetry. *In* Oinas, F. J. ed. Heroic epic and saga p7-26

Epic poetry, Estonian

History and criticism

Oinas, F. J. The Balto-Finnic epics. *In* Oinas, F. J. ed. Heroic epic and saga p286-309

Epic poetry, French

See also Chansons de geste

History and criticism

Duggan, J. J. Formulaic diction in the Cantar de mio Cid and the old French epic. *In* Duggan, J. J. ed. Oral literature p74-83

Epic poetry, Greek

History and criticism

Nagy, G. J. Phaethon, Sappho's Phaon, and the White Rock of Leukas. *In* Harvard Studies in classical philology v77 p137-77

Simon, B. Epic as therapy. *In* Simon, B. Mind and madness in ancient Greece p78-88

Epic poetry, Iranian

History and criticism

Hanaway, W. L. The Iranian epics. *In* Oinas, F. J. ed. Heroic epic and saga p76-98

Epic poetry, Russian. See Byliny

Epic poetry, Serbo-Croatian

History and criticism

Coote, M. P. Serbocroatian heroic songs. *In* Oinas, F. J. ed. Heroic epic and saga p257-85

Epic poetry, Spanish

History and criticism

Simmons, M. E. The Spanish epic. *In* Oinas, F. J. ed. Heroic epic and saga p216-35

Epictetus

About

Arendt, H. Quaestio mihi factus sum: the discovery of the inner man. *In* Arendt, H. The life of the mind v2 p53-110

Influence—Whitman

Allen, G. W. Walt Whitman and stoicism. *In* The Stoic strain in American literature p43-60

Epicurus

About individual works

Letter to Herodotus

Lee, E. N. The sense of an object: Epicurus on seeing and hearing. *In* Studies in perception p27-59

Epidemics. See Black death

Epigrams

Marlborough, H. Herrick's epigrams of praise. *In* Rollin, R. B. and Patrick, J. M. eds. "Trust to good verses": Herrick tercentenary essays p159-69

See also Aphorisms and apothegms; Proverbs

Episcopacy

Thompson, W. D. J. C. Sir Francis Knollys' campaign against the jure divino theory of episcopacy. *In* The Dissenting tradition p39-77

Episcopal Church. See Church of England

Epistemology. See Knowledge, Theory of

Epistolary poetry, German

History and criticism

Motsch, M. F. The forgotten genre: the poetic epistle in eighteenth-century German literature. *In* Studies in eighteenth-century culture v4 p119-24

Epitaphs

Zográfos, Greece

Clairmont, C. W. The lekythos of Myrrhine. *In* Studies in classical art and archaeology p103-10

Epithets

Ong, W. J. From epithet to logic: Miltonic epic and the closure of existence. *In* Ong, W. J. Interfaces of the word p189-212

See also Names

Epithets in literature

Katz, M. R. The epithet in Zhukovsky's literary ballads. *In* Katz, M. R. The literary ballad in early nineteenth-century Russian literature p76-100

Epp, Eldon Jay

Wisdom, Torah, Word: the Johannine Prologue and the purpose of the Fourth Gospel. *In* Current issues in Biblical and patristic interpretation p128-46

Epstein, Beryl (Williams)

The Revolution of 1905 and Russian foreign policy. *In* Essays in honour of E. H. Carr p98-125

Epstein, Edmund L.

"Notes on Lord of the flies"; epilogue to Lord of the flies by William Golding. *In* Praise from famous men: an anthology of introductions p69-74

The self-reflexive artefact: the function of mimesis in an approach to a theory of value for literature. *In* Fowler, R. ed. Style and structure in literature p40-78

Epstein, William

A new approach to strategic arms limitation and reduction. *In* Arms control and technological innovation p176-97

Nuclear terrorism and nuclear war. *In* Griffiths, F. and Polanyi, J. C. eds. The dangers of nuclear war p109-24

The outlook for disarmament. *In* The Dynamics of the arms race p104-15

Equal educational opportunity. See Educational equalization

Equal employment opportunity. See Affirmative action programs; Discrimination in employment

Equal pay for equal work

See also Women—Employment

Russia

Chapman, J. G. Equal pay for equal work? *In* Women in Russia p225-39

Equal protection of the law. See Equality before the law

Equality

Berlin, Sir I. Equality. *In* Berlin, Sir I. Concepts and categories p81-102

Bork, R. H. Can democratic government survive? *In* Aspects of American liberty p174-86

Bowen, H. R. Higher education and human equality. *In* The Third century p90-97

Bradford, M. E. The heresy of equality. *In* A Public philosophy reader p309-36

DeMott, B. Equality and fraternity: a note on subjective realities. *In* Small comforts for hard times p72-84

Diamond, M. The idea of equality: the view from the founding. *In* An Almost chosen people p19-37

Freund, P. A. Equality, race, and preferential treatment. *In* Small comforts for hard times p26-33

Gans, H. J. The costs of inequality: in response to Robert A. Nisbet. *In* Small comforts for hard times p50-58

Glazer, N. Individualism and equality in the United States. *In* On the making of Americans p127-42

Honderich, T. On inequality and violence, and the differences we make between them. *In* Royal Institute of Philosophy. Nature and conduct p46-82

McWilliams, W. C. On equality as the moral foundation for community. *In* The Moral foundations of the American Republic p183-213

Nagel, T. Equality. *In* Nagel, T. Mortal questions p106-27

Nisbet, R. A. The costs of equality. *In* Small comforts for hard times p34-49

Parsons, T. Equality and inequality in modern society, or social stratification revisited. *In* Parsons, T. Social systems and the evolution of action theory p321-80

Racevskis, K. The French Academy as a proponent of egalitarianism. *In* Studies in eighteenth-century culture v7 p105-16

Rawls, J. A well-ordered society. *In* Laslett, P. and Fishkin, J. eds. Philosophy, politics and society p6-20

Sennett, R. What Tocqueville feared. *In* On the making of Americans p105-25

Vickrey, W. S. Justice, equality, and the economic system. *In* Small comforts for hard times p59-71

Wililams, D. Condorcet, feminism, and the egalitarian principle. *In* Studies in eighteenth-century culture v5 p151-63

See also Democracy; Social classes; Social justice; Socialism

Equality before the law

See also Race discrimination—Law and legislation

Canada

Stephens, O. H. Equal justice and counsel rights in the United States and Canada. *In* Claude, R. P. ed. Comparative human rights p161-83

United States

Clune, W. H. The Supreme Court's treatment of wealth discriminations under the Fourteenth Amendment. *In* The Supreme Court review, 1975 p289-354

Cohen, W. Congressional power to interpret due process and equal protection. *In* Stanford legal essays p79-96

Hoffman, R. Justice, merit, and the good. *In* Gross, B. R. ed. Reverse discrimination p358-72

Newton, L. H. Reverse discrimination as unjustified. *In* Gross, B. R. ed. Reverse discrimination p373-78

Nickel, J. W. Preferential policies in hiring and admissions: a jurisprudential approach. *In* Gross, B. R. ed. Reverse discrimination p324-47

Rosberg, G. M. The protection of aliens from discriminatory treatment by the national government. *In* The Supreme Court review, 1977 p275-339

Sandalow, T. Racial preferences in higher education: political responsibility and the judicial role. *In* Gross, B. R. ed. Reverse discrimination p239-64

Stephens, O. H. Equal justice and counsel rights in the United States and Canada. *In* Claude, R. P. ed. Comparative human rights p161-83

Equality of states. See Great powers

Equalization, Educational. See Educational equalization

Equatorial Guinea. Macías Nguema Byogo. See Macías Nguema Byogo

Equestrian statues. See Statues

Equiano, Olaudah (Gustavus Vassa)

About

Bell, B. W. African-American writers. *In* Emerson, E. H. ed. American literature, 1764-1789 p171-93

Equilibrium

Stuewer, R. H. G. N. Lewis on detailed balancing, the symmetry of time, and the nature of light. *In* Historical studies in the physical sciences v6 p469-511

See also Statics

Equilibrium (Economics)

Bergson, A. Consumer's and producer's surplus and general equilibrium. *In* Theory for economic efficiency: essays in honor of Abba P. Lerner p12-23

Mathematical models

Harberger, A. C. The case of the three numeraires. *In* Economic development and planning p142-56

Equilibrium (Social sciences) See Statics and dynamics (Social sciences)

Equinox, Vernal. See Vernal equinox

Equity

Banner, W. A. Compensatory justice and the meaning of equity. *In* Social justice & preferential treatment p199-216

Equus (criticism) Shaffer, P. *In* Kauffmann, S. Persons of the drama p249-51

Eran, Oded. See Eran Feinberg, Oded

Eran Feinberg, Oded

The Soviet perception of influence: the case of the Middle East 1973-1976. *In* Ro'i, Y. ed. The limits to power p127-48

Erasmus, Desiderius

About

DeMolen, R. L. Introduction: Opera omnia Desiderii Erasmi: rungs on the ladder to the philosophia Christi. *in* Essays on the works of Erasmus p 1-50

Gilmore, M. P. Apologiae: Erasmus's defenses of Folly. *In* Essays on the works of Erasmus p111-23

Jarrott, C. A. L. Erasmus's annotations and Colet's commentaries on Paul: a comparison of some theological themes. *In* Essays on the works of Erasmus p125-44

Levi, A. H. T. Erasmus, the early Jesuits and the classics. *In* Classical influences on European culture A.D. 1500-1700 p223-38

Rabil, A. Erasmus's Paraphrases of the New Testament. *In* Essays on the works of Erasmus p145-61

Rebhorn, W. H. Desiderius Erasmus: cosmopolitan Christian humanism. *In* Hoffmeister, G. ed. The Renaissance and Reformation in Germany p83-97

About individual works

The Christian's manual, being a translation of the Enchiridion militis Christiani

Kohls, E. W. The principal theological thoughts in the Enchiridion militis Christiani. *In* Essays on the works of Erasmus p61-82

Ciceronianus, or a dialogue on the best style of speaking

Phillips, M. M. From the Ciceronianus to Montaigne. *In* Classical influences on European culture A.D. 1500-1700 p191-97

Telle, E. V. Erasmus's Ciceronianus: a comical colloquy. *In* Essays on the works of Erasmus p211-20

Collected works of Erasmus

Bush, D. Collected works of Erasmus: volume one. *In* Medievalia et humanistica no. 6 p199-202

The colloquies of Erasmus

Thompson, G. As bones to the body: the scope of inventio in the Colloquies of Erasmus. *In* Essays on the works of Erasmus p163-78

De civilitate morum puerilium libellus

Bierlaire, F. Erasmus at school: the De civilitate morum puerilium libellus. *In* Essays on the works of Erasmus p239-51

De copia

Callahan, V. N. W. The De copia: the bounteous horn. *In* Essays on the works of Erasmus p99-109

De duplici copia verborum

Cave, T. C. Copia and cornucopia. *In* French Renaissance studies, 1540-70 p52-69

De libero arbitrio

Gerrish, B. A. De libero arbitrio (1524): Erasmus on piety, theology, and the Lutheran dogma. *In* Essays on the works of Erasmus p187-209

De pueris instituendis

Margolin, J. C. The method of "words and things" in Erasmus's De pueris instituendis (1529) and Comenius's Orbis sensualium pictus (1658) *In* Essays on the works of Erasmus p221-38

Ecclesiastes sive de ratione concionandi

Kleinhans, R. G. Ecclesiastes sive de ratione concionandi. *In* Essays on the works of Erasmus p253-66

Paraclesis

Thompson, C. R. Scripture for the ploughboy and some others. *In* Studies in the continental background of Renaissance English literature: essays presented to John L. Lievsay p 3-28

The praise of Folly

Altman, J. B. The moral cultivation of ambivalence. *In* Altman, J. B. The Tudor play of mind p31-63

Gilmore, M. P. Apologiae: Erasmus's defenses of Folly. *In* Essays on the works of Erasmus p111-23

Hardin, J. Erasmus: The praise of Folly. *In* Hoffmeister, G. ed. The Renaissance and Reformation in Germany p99-110

Kennedy, W. J. The style of ironic discourse. *In* Kennedy, W. J. Rhetorical norms in Renaissance literature p79-127

McCombie, F. 'Hamlet' and the 'Moriae encomium'. *In* Shakespeare survey 27 p59-69

Miller, C. H. The logic and rhetoric of proverbs in Erasmus's Praise of Folly. *In* Essays on the works of Erasmus p83-98

Erasmus, Desiderius—About individual works
—*Continued*

Proverbs and adages

Phillips, M. M. Ways with adages. *In* Essays on the works of Erasmus p51-60

Ratio verae theologiae

Chantraine, G. G. The Ratio verae theologiae (1518) *In* Essays on the works of Erasmus p179-85

Influence—Shakespeare

McCombie, F. 'Hamlet' and the 'Moriae encomium'. *In* Shakespeare survey 27 p59-69

Erb, Guy F.
The developing world's "challenge" in perspective. *In* Erb, G. F. and Kallab, V. eds. Beyond dependency p135-56

Ercoli, Fiorella Prosperetti. See Benton, J. F. jt. auth.

Erdman, Howard L.
The United States, India, and India's neighbors. *In* Baldwin, D. A. ed. America in an interdependent world p245-72

Erech, Babylonia. See Warka, Mesopotamia

Erichsen, Eivind
Norway: twenty years after the Marshall plan. *In* Inflation, trade and taxes p163-77

Erickson, John
The European military balance. *In* Kirk, G. L. and Wessell, N. H. eds. The Soviet threat p110-21
Some military and political aspects of the 'militia army' controversy, 1919-1920. *In* Essays in honour of E. H. Carr p204-28

Erickson, John Hilding
Oikonomia in Byzantine canon law. *In* Law, church, and society p225-36

Erikson, Erik Homburger
The legend of Hitler's childhood; excerpt from "Childhood and society." *In* Kren, G. N. and Rappoport, L. H. eds. Varieties of psychohistory p99-110
On the nature of psychohistorical evidence: in search of Gandhi; excerpt from "Life history and the historical moment". *In* Explorations in psychohistory p42-77
Play and actuality. *In* Explorations in psychohistory p109-35
Reflections on Dr Borg's life cycle. *In* Adulthood p 1-31

About

Browning, D. S. Erikson and the search for a normative image of man. *In* Homans, P. ed. Childhood and selfhood p264-92
Capps, D. Psychohistory and historical genres: the plight and promise of Eriksonian biography. *In* Homans, P. ed. Childhood and selfhood p189-228
Homans, P. Introduction. *In* Homans, P. ed. Childhood and selfhood p13-54
Homans, P. The significance of Erikson's psychology for modern understandings of religion. *In* Homans, P. ed. Childhood and selfhood p231-63
Hughes, H. S. The advent of ego psychology. *In* Hughes, H. S. The sea change p189-239

About individual works

Childhood and society

Kracke, W. H. A psychoanalyst in the field: Erikson's contributions to anthropology. *In* Homans, P. ed. Childhood and selfhood p147-88

Gandhi's truth

Appadurai, A. Understanding Gandhi. *In* Homans, P. ed. Childhood and selfhood p113-43

Young man Luther

Bornkamm, H. Luther and his father: observations on Erik H. Erikson's Young man Luther: a study in psychoanalysis and history. *In* Homans, P. ed. Childhood and selfhood p59-88
Edwards, M. U. Erikson, experimental psychology, and Luther's identity. *In* Homans, P. ed. Childhood and selfhood p89-112

Erikson, Erik Homburger, and Erikson, Joan M.
Introduction: reflections on aging. *In* Spicker, S. F.; Woodward, K. M. and Van Tassel, D. D. eds. Aging and the elderly p 1-8

Erikson, Joan M. See Erikson, E. H. jt. auth.

Erikson, Kai T.
On the sociology of deviance. *In* Davis, F. J. and Stivers, R. eds. The collective definition of deviance p11-21

Eritrean Liberation Front
Bell, J. B. Revolutionary organisations: special cases and imperfect models. *In* International terrorism and world security p78-92

Erlich, Alexander
Stalinism and Marxian growth models. *In* Stalinism p137-54

Erlich, Bruce Sewell
Structure, inversion, and game in Shakespeare's classical world. *In* Shakespeare survey v31 p53-63

Erlich, Victor
Modern Russian criticism from Andrej Belyj to Andrej Sinjavskij: trends, issues, personalities. *In* Erlich, V. ed. Twentieth-century Russian literary criticism p3-30
Solzhenitsyn's quest. *In* Dunlop, J. B.; Haugh, R. and Klimoff, A. eds. Aleksandr Solzhenitsyn: critical essays and documentary materials 2d ed. p351-55
The writer as witness: the achievement of Aleksandr Solzhenitsyn. *In* Dunlop, J. B.; Haugh, R. and Klimoff, A. eds. Aleksandr Solzhenitsyn: critical essays and documentary materials 2d ed. p16-27

Ermakov, Ivan Dmitrievich
"The nose"; excerpt from "Sketches for an analysis of the art of N. V. Gogol." *In* Maguire, R. A. ed. Gogol from the twentieth century p155-98

Ernst, Eldon Gilbert
Dimensions of new religion in American history. *In* Needleman, J. and Baker, G. eds. Understanding the new religions p34-45

Ernst, Max

About

Scharf, A. Max Ernst, Étienne-Jules Marey, and the poetry of scientific illustration. *In* One hundred years of photographic history p117-26

Ernst, Morris Leopold
Foreword to Ulysses by James Joyce. *In* Praise from famous men: an anthology of introductions p75-78

Eros. See Cupid

Erotic art
Rosenberg, H. Trials of Eros. *In* Rosenberg, H. Art on the edge p216-26

Esman, Milton J.—*Continued*

Perspectives on ethnic conflict in industrialized societies. *In* Esman, M. J. ed. Ethnic conflict in the Western world p343-68

Scottish nationalism, North Sea oil, and the British response. *In* Esman, M. J. ed. Ethnic conflict in the Western world p251-86

Esoteric Buddhism. See Tantric Buddhism

Espionage

Falk, R. A. CIA covert operations and international law. *In* Borosage, R. L. and Marks, J. D. eds. The CIA file p142-58

See also Spies

Espionage, American

Equipment and supplies

Scoville, H. The role of technology in covert intelligence collection. *In* Borosage, R. L. and Marks, J. D. eds. The CIA file p109-22

Political aspects

Halperin, M. H. Covert operations: effects of secrecy on decision-making. *In* Borosage, R. L. and Marks, J. D. eds. The CIA file p159-77

Laos

Branfman, F. The President's secret army: a case study—the CIA in Laos, 1962-1972. *In* Borosage, R. L. and Marks, J. D. eds. The CIA file p46-78

Esposito, Frances Ferguson, and Esposito, Louis

Industry price changes, market structure and inflation. *In* Inflation, trade and taxes p29-49

Esposito, Louis. See Esposito, F. F. jt. auth.

Esprit, Jacques

About individual works

The falsehood of human virtues

Horowitz, L. K. Jacques Esprit. *In* Horowitz, L. K. Love and language p113-23

Esquimaux. See Eskimos

Essay

Hamburger, M. An essay on the essay. *In* Hamburger, M. Art as second nature p3-5

Essence (Philosophy)

Patočka, J. The Husserlian doctrine of eidetic intuition and its recent critics. *In* Elliston, F. A. and McCormick, P. eds. Husserl p150-59

Wiggins, D. The De re 'must': a note on the logical form of essentialist claims. *In* Evans, G. L. and McDowell, J. H. eds. Truth and meaning p285-312

Essenin, Serghei. See Esenin, Sergeĭ Aleksandrovich

Essick, Robert N.

Preludium: meditations on a fiery Pegasus. *In* Essick, R. N. and Pearce, D. R. eds. Blake in his time p 1-10

Essien-Udom, Essien Udosen

Tribalism and racism. *In* United Nations Educational, Scientific and Cultural Organization. Race, science and society p234-61

Esslin, Martin

The television series as folk epic. *In* Superculture p190-98

Estates (Law)

United States

Shaffer, T. L. and Rodes, R. E. Law for those who are to die. *In* Feifel, H. [ed.] New meanings of death p291-311

Estates (Social order) See Ministerials; Social classes

Esteban, Joan

The economic policy of Francoism: an interpretation. *In* Preston, P. ed. Spain in crisis p82-100

Esthetics. See Aesthetics

Esthus, Raymond A.

Protectorates and spheres of influence. *In* Encyclopedia of American foreign policy p836-43

Estonian epic poetry. See Epic poetry, Estonian

Estrangement (Social psychology) See Alienation (Social psychology)

Étaples, Jacques le Fèvre d'. See Le Fèvre, Jacques, d'Étaples

Eternal life. See Future life

Ether (of space)

Doran, B. G. Origins and consolidation of field theory in nineteenth-century Britain: from the mechanical to the electromagnetic view of nature. *In* Historical studies in the physical science v6 p133-260

Hirosige, T. The ether problem, the mechanistic worldview, and the origins of the theory of relativity. *In* Historical studies in the physical sciences v7 p3-82

Etherton, Michael

The dilemma of the popular playwright: the work of Kabwe Kasoma and V. E. Musinga. *In* African literature today no. 8: Drama in Africa p26-41

Ethical development. See Moral development

Ethical education. See Moral education

Ethical relativism

Harrison, G. A. Relativism and tolerance. *In* Laslett, P. and Fishkin, J. eds. Philosophy, politics and society p273-90

Leys, W. A. R. Political and moral pluralism. *In* The Abdication of philosophy: philosophy and the public good p93-107

See also Ethics, Evolutionary

Ethical theology. See Christian ethics

Ethics

Aiken, W. The right to be saved from starvation. *In* Aiken, W. and La Follette, H. eds. World hunger and moral obligation p85-102

Binkley, R. W. The ultimate justification of moral rules. *In* Fact, value, and perception p53-65

Boden, M. A. Human values in a mechanical universe. *In* Royal Institute of Philosophy. Human values p135-71

Bronowski, J. The fulfillment of man. *In* Bronowski, J. A sense of the future p249-62

Bronowski, J. The human values. *In* Bronowski, J. A sense of the future p206-10

Campbell, T. D. Scientific explanation and ethical justification in the Moral sentiments. *In* Skinner, A. S. and Wilson, T. eds. Essays on Adam Smith p68-82

Ethics—*Continued*

Castañeda Calderón, H. N. Goodness, intentions, and propositions. *In* Fact, value, and propositions. *In* Fact, value, and perception p67-83

Chadwick, O. The moral nature of man. *In* Chadwick, O. The secularization of the European mind in the nineteenth century p229-49

Cherry, C. Agreement, objectivity and the sentiment of humanity in morals. *In* Royal Institute of Philosophy. Nature and conduct p83-98

Couch, W. T. The sacred and golden cord. *In* Viva Vivas! p87-137

Fisch, H. H. The poliscraft. *In* Philosophy and the civilizing arts p24-48

Fletcher, J. F. Goodness. *In* Fletcher, J. F. Humanhood: essays in biomedical ethics p27-40

Foot, P. Are moral considerations overriding? *In* Foot, P. Virtues and vices, and other essays in moral philosophy p181-88

Foot, P. Moral arguments. *In* Foot, P. Virtues and vices, and other essays in moral philosophy p96-109

Foot, P. Moral beliefs. *In* Foot, P. Virtues and vices, and other essays in moral philosophy p110-31

Foot, P. Morality as a system of hypothetical imperatives. *In* Foot, P. Virtues and vices, and other essays in moral philosophy p157-73

Foot, P. A reply to Professor Frankena. *In* Foot, P. Virtues and vices, and other essays in moral philosophy p174-80

Harrison, G. A. Relativism and tolerance. *In* Laslett, P. and Fishkin, J. eds. Philosophy, politics and society p273-90

Heath, P. L. The idea of a phenomenological ethics. *In* Pivčević, E. ed. Phenomenology and philosophical understanding p159-72

Holland, R. F. Absolute ethics, mathematics and the impossibility of politics. *In* Royal Institute of Philosophy. Human values p172-88

Hudson, W. D. Ethical intuitionism. *In* New studies in ethics v 1 p229-303

Johann, R. O. Person, community and moral commitment. *In* Roth, R. J. ed. Person and community p155-75

Kidd, I. G. Moral actions and rules in Stoic ethics. *In* Rist, J. M. ed. The Stoics p247-58

Körner, S. Empiricism in ethics. *In* Royal Institute of Philosophy. Impressions of empiricism p216-30

Lea, F. R. What's the good? *In* Abbs, P. ed. The black rainbow p189-210

Letwin, S. R. Nature, history and morality. *In* Royal Institute of Philosophy. Nature and conduct p229-50

Levy, D. The ethical life and the political life. *In* Viva Vivas! p65-86

Lidz, T. The family, myth, and ethics. *In* Psychiatry and the humanities v 1 p173-90

Mayo, B. Moral integrity. *In* Royal Institute of Philosophy. Human values p27-43

Mihajlov, M. Three paradoxes. *In* Mihajlov, M. Underground notes p19-22

Mizuta, H. Moral philosophy and civil society. *In* Skinner, A. S. and Wilson, T. eds. Essays on Adam Smith p114-31

Nagel, T. Ethics without biology. *In* Nagel, T. Mortal questions p142-46

Nagel, T. Moral luck. *In* Nagel, T. Mortal questions p24-38

Narveson, J. Morality and starvation. *In* Aiken, W. and La Follette, H. eds. World hunger and moral obligation p49-65

Oakeshott, M. J. The Tower of Babel. *In* Oakeshott, M. J. Rationalism in politics p59-79

O'Neill, O. O. Lifeboat earth. *In* Aiken, W. and La Follette, H. eds. World hunger and moral obligation p148-64

Raphael, D. D. The impartial spectator. *In* Skinner, A. S. and Wilson, T. eds. Essays on Adam Smith p83-99

Ricoeur, P. Ethics and culture: Habermas and Gadamer in dialogue. *In* Ricoeur, P. Political and social essays p243-70

Rosenhan, D. L. Moral character. *In* Stanford legal essays p401-11

Schneewind, J. B. Sociobiology, social policy, and Nirvana. *In* Sociobiology and human nature p225-39

Sidorsky, D. The autonomy of moral objectivity. *In* Modern Jewish ethics p153-73

Williams, B. A. O. Persons, character and morality. *In* Rorty, A. O. ed. The identities of persons p197-216

See also Asceticism; Altruism; Benevolence; Bioethics; Christian ethics; Communist ethics; Conduct of life; Conscience; Courage; Decision-making (Ethics); Duty; Ends and means; Ethical relativism; Existential ethics; Free will and determinism; Good and evil; Happiness; Humanistic ethics; Judgment (Ethics); Justice; Language and ethics; Legal ethics; Literature and morals; Medical ethics; Moral education; Natural law; Obedience; Pleasure; Poiltical ethics; Probabilism; Responsibility Science and ethics; Self-sacrifice; Sexual ethics; Social ethics; Suicide; Sympathy; Teachers, Professional ethics for; Truthfulness and falsehood; Utilitarianism; Values; Virtue; Wealth, Ethics of; and subdivision Moral and religious aspects under specific subjects, e.g. Food relief—Moral and religious aspects

History

Findlay, J. N. Axiological ethics. *In* New studies in ethics v2 p119-213

Ethics, Anthropological. See Anthropological ethics

Ethics, Buddhist. See Buddhist ethics

Ethics, Christian. See Christian ethics

Ethics, Commercial. See Business ethics

Ethics, Communist. See Communist ethics

Ethics, Evolutionary

Flew, A. G. N. Evolutionary ethics. *In* New studies in ethics v2 p217-86

Sidorsky, D. The autonomy of moral objectivity. *In* Modern Jewish ethics p153-73

See also Ethical relativism

Ethics, Existential. See Existential ethics

Ethics, Greek

Huby, P. M. Greek ethics. *In* New studies in ethics v 1 p 1-78

Ethics, Humanistic. See Humanistic ethics

Ethics, Indian. See Indians of North America—Ethics

Ethics, Islamic. See Islamic ethics

Ethics, Japanese. See Bushido

Ethnic literature (American) See American literature—Minority authors

Ethnic psychology. See Ethnopsychology

Ethnic studies

Minneapolis

Arendt, J. D. Promoting pluralism in the public schools. *In* Minority language and literature p121-29

Ethnicity

Bell, D. Ethnicity and social change. *In* Glazer, N. and Moynihan, D. P. eds. Ethnicity p141-74

Béteille, A. Race, caste and ethnic identity. *In* United Nations Educational, Scientific and Cultural Organization. Race, science and society p211-33

Blackwell, J. E. The power basis of ethnic conflict in American society. *In* The Uses of controversy in sociology p179-96

Connor, W. F. The political significance of ethnonationalism within Western Europe. *In* Said, A. A. and Simmons, L. R. eds. Ethnicity in an international context p110-33

D'Antonio, W. V. Ethnicity and assimilation: a reconsideration. *In* Studies in Italian American social history p10-27

Dasgupta, J. Ethnicity, language demands, and national development in India. *In* Glazer, N. and Moynihan, D. P. eds. Ethnicity p466-88

Gans. H. J. Symbolic ethnicity: the future of ethnic groups and cultures in America. *In* On the making of Americans p193-220

Gerson, L. L. Ethnics in American politics. *In* Havard, W. C. and Bernd, J. L. eds. 200 years of the Republic in retrospect p336-46

Greeley, A M. Why study ethnicity? *In* The Diverse society: implications for social policy p3-12

Grossman, L. Ethnicity and health delivery systems. *In* The Diverse society: implications for social policy p129-48

Horowitz, D. L. Ethnic identity. *In* Glazer, N. and Moynihan, D. P. eds. Ethnicity p111-40

Kronus, S. Race, ethnicity, and community. *In* Handbook of contemporary urban life p202-32

McNeill, W. H. On national frontiers: ethnic homogeneity and pluralism. *In* Small comforts for hard times p207-19

May, J. G. Personality development and ethnic identity. *In* The Diverse society: implications for social policy p43-58

Mintz, S. W. Ethnicity and leadership: an afterword. *In* Ethnic leadership in America p198-205

Mowlana, H. and Robinson, A. E. Ethnic mobilization and communication theory. *In* Said, A. A. and Simmons, L. R. eds. Ethnicity in an international context p48-63

Parsons, T. Some theoretical considerations on the nature and trends of change of ethnicity. *In* Parsons, T. Social systems and the evolution of action theory p381-404

Same as: Parsons. T. The theoretical considerations on the nature and trends of change of ethnicity. *In* Glazer, N. and Moynihan, D. P. eds. Ethnicity p53-83

Rakowska-Harmstone, T. Ethnic autonomy in the Soviet Union. *In* Said, A. A. and Simmons, L. R. eds. Ethnicity in an international context p150-66

Reed, I. Before the War, poems as they happened. *In* Reed, I. Shrovetide in old New Orleans p115-17

Said, A. A. and Simmons, L. R. The ethnic factor in world politics. *In* Said, A. A. and Simmons, L. R. eds. Ethnicity in an international context p15-47

Simić, A. White ethnic and Chicano families: continuity and adaptation in the New World. *In* Tufte, V. and Myerhoff, B. K. eds. Changing images of the family p251-69

Snetsinger, J. G. Ethnicity and foreign policy. *In* Encyclopedia of American foreign policy p322-29

Stavrou, N. A. Ethnicity in Yugoslavia: roots and impact. *In* Said, A. A. and Simmons, L. R. eds. Ethnicity in an international context p134-49

Yinger, J. M. Ethnicity in complex societies: structural, cultural, and characterological factors. *In* The Uses of controversy in sociology p197-216

See also Pluralism (Social sciences); and subdivision Race identity under names of individual races or ethnic groups, e.g. Afro-Americans—Race identity

Ethnikon Apeleftherotikon Metopon. See National Liberation Front (Greece)

Ethnobotany

Emboden, W. A. Plant hypnotics among the North American Indians. *In* American folk medicine p159-67

Vogel, V. J. American Indian foods used as medicine. *In* American folk medicine p125-41

Ethnocentrism

Africa

Paden, J. N. Dimensions of national integration in Africa. *In* African themes p175-93

Ethnography. See Ethnology

Ethnology

Bauman, Z. Understanding as expansion of the form of life. *In* Bauman, Z. Hermeneutics and social science p194-224

Bogatyrev, P. G. Costume as a sign. *In* Matejka, L. and Titunik, I. R. eds. Semiotics of art p13-19

Clifford, J. L. "Hanging up looking glasses at odd corners": ethnobiographical prospects. *In* Studies in biography p41-56

De Vos, G. Ethnic pluralism: conflict and accommodation. *In* Ethnic identity p5-41

Kracke, W. H. A psychoanalyst in the field: Erikson's contributions to anthropology. *In* Homans, P. ed. Childhood and selfhood p147-88

Leach, E. R. Cultural components in the concept of race. *In* Racial variation in man p27-54

LeVine, R. A. Anthropology and sex: developmental aspects. *in* Katchadourian, H. A. ed. Human sexuality p309-19

Schwimmer, E. Semiotics and culture. *In* Sebeok, T. A. ed. A perfusion of signs p153-79

Ethnology—*Continued*

Whiting, B. B. Contributions of anthropology to the study of gender identity, gender role, and sexual behavior. *In* Katchadourian, H. A. ed. Human sexuality p320-31

See also Acculturation; Anthropo-geography; Archaeology; Art, Primitive; Costume; Couvade; Cultural relativism; Ethnic groups; Ethnicity; Ethnobotany; Ethnopsychology; Kinship; Man, Primitive; Nativistic movements; Religion, Primitive; Society, Primitive; Structural anthropology; Totemism; and names of ethnic groups and peoples, e.g. Ndembu (African tribe); and subdivision Social life and customs under names of countries

Methodology

Birdwhistell, R. L. Some discussion of ethnography, theory, and method. *In* About Bateson p103-41

Geertz, C. "From the native's point of view": on the nature of anthropological understanding. *In* Basso, K. H. and Selby, H. A. eds. Meaning in anthropology p221-37

Graves, T. D. and Graves, N. B. Evolving strategies in the study of culture change. *In* Spindler, G. D. ed. The making of psychological anthropology p516-55

Honigmann, J. J. The personal approach in culture and personality research. *In* Spindler, G. D. ed. The making of psychological anthropology p302-29

La Barre, W. The clinic and the field. *In* Spindler, G. D. ed. The making of psychological anthropology p259-99

Mead, M. The evocation of psychologically relevant responses in ethnological field work. *In* Spindler, G. D. ed. The making of psychological anthropology p89-139

Price, B. J. The burden of the cargo: ethnographical models and archaeological inference. *In* Mesoamerican archaeology p445-65

Schneider, D. M. Notes toward a theory of culture. *In* Basso, K. H. and Selby, H. A. eds. Meaning in anthropology p197-220

Schwartz, T. Where is the culture? Personality as the distributive locus of culture. *In* Spindler, G. D. ed. The making of psychological anthropology p419-41

Spindler, L. S. Researching the psychology of culture change and urbanization. *In* Spindler, G. D. ed. The making of psychological anthropology p176-200

Spiro, M. E. Culture and human nature. *In* Spindler, G. D. ed. The making of psychological anthropology p331-60

Whiting, J. and Whiting, B. A strategy for psychocultural research. *In* Spindler, G. D. ed. The making of psychological anthropology p41-61

See also Cross-cultural studies; Interviewing in ethnology

Moving-pictures

MacDougall, D. Prospects of the ethnographic film. *In* Nichols, B. ed. Movies and methods p135-50

Philosophy

Birdwhistell, R. L. Some discussion of ethnography, theory, and method. *In* About Bateson p103-41

See also Noble savage

Africa

Dart, R. A. Cultural diffusion from, in and to Africa. *In* Grafton Elliot Smith p160-74

Lienhardt, G. Social anthropology of Africa. *In* African studies since 1945 p179-85

Africa, East

Posnansky, M. Connections between the Lacustrine peoples and the coast. *In* Chittick, H. N. and Rotberg, R. I. eds. East Africa and the Orient p216-25

See also Luo (Nilotic tribe)

Africa, Eastern

Chittick, H. N. The peopling of the East African coast. *In* Chittick, H. N. and Rotberg, R. I. eds. East Africa and the Orient p16-43

Africa, Southern

See !Kung (African people); Nguni

Asia, Southeastern

Hanks, J. R. Recitation of patrilineages among the Akha. *In* Social organization and the applications of anthropology p114-27

Australia

See Australian aborigines

Bali (Island)

Geertz, C. "From the native's point of view": on the nature of anthropological understanding. *In* Basso, K. H. and Selby, H. A. eds. Meaning in anthropology p221-37

Botswana

Draper, P. !Kung women: contrasts in sexual egalitarianism in foraging and sedentary contexts. *In* Reiter, R. R. ed. Toward an anthropology of women p77-109

Cameroons

Ardener, E. Language, ethnicity, and population. *In* Studies in social anthropology p343-53

Ardener, S. G. Sexual insult and female militancy. *In* Ardener, S. G. ed. Perceiving women p29-53

Clignet, R. The impact of educational structures and processes on national integration in Cameroon. *In* Smock, D. R. and Bentsi-Enchill, K. eds. The search for national integration in Africa p139-58

Caroline Islands—Yap

Schneider, D. M. Depopulation and the Yap tabinau. *In* Social organization and the applications of anthropology p94-113

China

Wang, G. Chinese civilization and the diffusion of culture. *In* Grafton Elliot Smith p197-209

Congo

See Lunda (Bantu tribe)

Ghana

Smock, A. C. Education and national integration in Ghana. *In* Smock, D. R. and Bentsi-Enchill, K. eds. The search for national integration in Africa p117-38

Ethnology—Ghana—*Continued*

Smock, D. R. Language policy in Ghana. *In* Smock, D. R. and Bentsi-Enchill, K. eds. The search for national integration in Africa p169-88

See also Talansi (African tribe)

India

Dasgupta, J. Ethnicity, language demands, and national development in India. *In* Glazer, N. and Moynihan, D. P. eds. Ethnicity p466-88

Jain, R. K. Bundela genealogy and legends: the past of an indigenous ruling group of central India. *In* Studies in social anthropology p238-72

See also Caste—India

Iran

See Kashkai tribe

Italy—Ascoli Piceno

Romanucci-Ross, L. Italian ethnic identity and its transformations. *In* Ethnic identity p198-226

Java

Geertz, C. "From the native's point of view": on the nature of anthropological understanding. *In* Basso, K. H. and Selby, H. A. eds. Meaning in anthropology p221-37

Kansas

McQuillan, D. A. Territory and ethnic identity: some new measures of an old theme in the cultural geography of the United States. *In* European settlement and development in North America: essays on geographical change in honour and memory of Andrew Hill Clark p136-69

Kenya

See Kikuyu tribe; Sapiny (African tribe)

Lithuania—Vilna

Miłosz, C. Vilnius, Lithuania: an ethnic agglomerate. *In* Ethnic identity p339-52

Louisiana

Knipmeyer, W. B. Folk boats of eastern French Louisiana. *In* Yoder, D. ed. American folklife p105-49

See also Cajuns

Malagasy Republic

Southall, A. W. The problem of Malagasy origins. *In* Chittick, H. N. and Rotberg, R. I. eds. East Africa and the Orient p192-215

Vérin, P. Austronesian contributions to the culture of Madagascar: some archaeological problems. *In* Chittick, H. N. and Rotberg, R. I. eds. East Africa and the Orient p164-91

Malawi

See Angoni

Malaya

See Sakai

Malaysia

See Melanau (Malaysian people)

Melanesia

Burridge, K. The Melanesian manager. *In* Studies in social anthropology p86-104

Schwartz, T. Cultural totemism: ethnic identity primitive and modern. *In* Ethnic identity p106-31

Morocco

Geertz, C. "From the native's point of view": on the nature of anthropological understanding. *In* Basso, K. H. and Selby, H. A. eds. Meaning in anthropology p221-37

Near East

See Sea Peoples

Nigeria

Ojo, A. Law and government in Nigeria. *In* Smock, D. R. and Bentsi-Enchill, K. eds. The search for national integration in Africa p47-67

North America

Berkhofer, R. F. The political context of a new Indian history. *In* The American Indian p101-26

Philippine Islands

Eggan, F. R. Applied anthropology in the Mountain Province, Philippines. *In* Social organization and the applications of anthropology p196-209

South Africa

See Bushmen

Sudan

See Nilotic tribes

Tahiti

Levy, R. I. Tahitian gentleness and redundant controls. *In* Montagu, A. ed. Learning non-aggression p222-35

Trinidad—Gasparillo

Elder, J. D. Morality in Yoruba ritual in Trinidad. *In* Yoder, D. ed. American folklife p281-91

Truk Islands

Goodenough, W. H. Changing social organization on Romónum, Truk, 1947-1965. *In* Social organization and the applications of anthropology p62-93

Uganda

Mazrui, A. A. The de-Indianization of Uganda: who is a citizen? *In* Smock, D. R. and Bentsi-Enchill, K. eds. The search for national integration in Africa p77-90

Mazuri, A. A. Ethnic stratification and the military-agrarian complex: the Uganda case. *In* Glazer, N. and Moynihan, D. P. eds. Ethnicity p420-49

Southall, A. W. The current state of national integration in Uganda. *In* Smock, D. R. and Bentsi-Enchill, K. eds. The search for national integration in Africa p307-31

United States

Kniffen, F. B. American cultural geography and folklife. *In* Yoder, D. ed. American folklife p51-70

Mead, M. Ethnicity and anthropology in America. *In* Ethnic identity p173-97

Mechling, J. E. In search of an American ethnophysics. *In* Luedtke, L. S. ed. The study of American culture p241-77

See also Afro-Americans; German-Americans; Irish-Americans; Japanese Americans

United States—Study and teaching

Goodenough, W. H. Folklife study and social change. *In* Yoder, D. ed. American folklife p19-26

Yoder, D. Folklife studies in American scholarship. *In* Yoder, D. ed. American folklife p3-18

Ethnology—*Continued*

Zaire

See Bambute

Zambia

See Ambo (African tribe); Ndembu (African tribe)

Ethnomethodology

Bauman, Z. Understanding as the work of life: From Schutz to ethnomethodology. *In* Bauman, Z. Hermeneutics and social science p172-93

Johnson, J. M. Ethnomethodology and existential sociology. *In* Douglas, J. D. and Johnson, J. M. [eds.] Existential sociology p153-73

Lemert, C. C. Ethnomethodology: Aaron Cicourel. *In* Lemert, C. C. Sociology and the twilight of man p165-93

Zimmerman, D. H. Ethnomethodology. *In* McNall, S. G. ed. Theoretical perspectives in sociology p381-96

Ethnomusicology

Chase, G. Musicology, history, and anthropology: current thoughts. *In* Current thought in musicology p231-46

Ethnophysics, In search of an American. Mechling, J. E. *In* Luedtke, L. S. ed. The study of American culture p241-77

Ethnopsychology

Berreman, G. D. Bazar behavior: social identity and social interaction in urban India. *In* Ethnic identity p71-105

Bourguignon, E. E. Spirit possession and altered states of consciousness: the evolution of an inquiry. *In* Spindler, G. D. ed. The making of psychological anthropology p479-515

Devereux, G. Ethnic identity: its logical foundations and its dysfunctions. *In* Ethnic identity p42-70

Devereux, G. The works of George Devereux. *In* Spindler, G. D. ed. The making of psychological anthropology p364-406

De Vos, G. Ethnic pluralism: conflict and accommodation. *In* De Vos, G. Ethnic identity p5-41

De Vos, G. and Romanucci-Ross, L. Ethnicity: vessel of meaning and emblem of contrast. *In* Ethnic identity p363-90

Edgerton, R. B. The study of deviance—marginal man or Everyman? *In* Spindler, G. D. ed. The making of psychological anthropology p444-76

Graves, T. D. and Graves, N. B. Evolving strategies in the study of culture change. *In* Spindler, G. D. ed. The making of psychological anthropology p516-55

Honigmann, J. J. The personal approach in culture and personality research. *In* Spindler, G. D. ed. The making of psychological anthropology p302-20

Hsu, Francis Lang Kwang. Passage to understanding. *In* Spindler, G. D. ed. The making of psychological anthropology p142-73

La Barre, W. The clinic and the field. *In* Spindler, G. D. ed. The making of psychological anthropology p259-99

Mead, M. The evocation of psychologically relevant responses in ethnological field work. *In* Spindler, G. D. ed. The making of psychological anthropology p89-139

Montagu, A. Introduction. *In* Montagu, A. ed. Learning non-aggression p3-11

Pinderhughes, C. A. Black personality in American society. *In* The Black American reference book p128-58

Schwartz, T. Where is the culture? Personality as the distributive locus of culture. *In* Spindler, G. D. ed. The making of psychological anthropology p419-41

Spiro, M. E. Culture and human nature. *In* Spindler, G. D. ed. The making of psychological anthropology p331-60

Wallace, A. F. C. Basic studies, applied projects, and eventual implementation: a case history of biological and cultural research in mental health. *In* Spindler, G. D. ed. The making of psychological anthropology p203-16

Whiting, J. and Whiting, B. A strategy for psychocultural research. *In* Spindler, G. D. ed. The making of psychological anthropology p41-61

See also Afro-Americans—Race identity; Cognition and culture; Cultural relativism; National characteristics; Personality and culture; Race awareness; Social psychology

Ethology. See Animals, Habits and behavior of; Character; Ethics; Human behavior

Etienne, Cardinal

About

Somerville, R. E. Cardinal Stephan of St Grisogono: some remarks on legates and legatine councils in the eleventh century. *In* Law, church, and society p157-66

Etiology. See Diseases—Causes and theories of causation

Etiquette

See also Etiquette for men; Etiquette for women; Salutations

Handbooks, manuals, etc.

Sheed, W. The novel of manners. *In* Sheed, W. The good word & other words p28-32

Etiquette for men

Cooper, J. The perfect gentleman. *In* The Saturday book 34 p114-25

Etiquette for women

Marshall, A. The perfect lady. *In* The Saturday book 34 p127-33

Etruscan art. See Art, Etruscan

Etruscan masks. See Masks, Etruscan

Etruscan terra cottas. See Terra-cottas, Etruscan

Ettinghausen, Richard

The man-made setting. *In* Lewis, B. ed. Islam and the Arab world p57-88

Ettlinger, Leopold D.

The emergence of the Italian architect during the fifteenth century. *In* Kostof, S. ed. The architect p96-123

Etulain, Richard W.

Ernest Haycox: popular novelist of the Pacific Northwest. *In* Bingham, E. R. and Love, G. A. eds. Northwest perspectives p136-50

Etymology. See Language and languages—Etymology

Etymology (The word)

Tennyson, G. B. Etymology and meaning. *In* Evolution of consciousness p168-82

Etzold, Thomas H.

The Nixon doctrine. *In* Encyclopedia of American foreign policy p688-91

Power politics. *In* Encyclopedia of American foreign policy p784-89

Euben, J. Peter

Creatures of a day: thought and action in Thucydides. *In* Political theory and praxis p28-56

Eucharist. See Lord's supper

Euclides

About individual works
Elements of geometry

Hausman, A. M. Non-Euclidean geometry and relative consistency proofs. *In* Motion and time, space and matter p418-35

Murdoch, J. E. Euclides Graeco-Latinus: a hitherto unknown medieval Latin translation of the Elements made directly from the Greek. *In* Harvard Studies in classical philology v71 p249-302

Timpanaro-Cardini, M. Two questions of Greek geometrical terminology. *In* Kephalaion p183-88

Translations, Latin

Murdoch, J. E. Euclides Graeco-Latinus: a hitherto unknown medieval Latin translation of the Elements made directly from the Greek. *In* Harvard Studies in classical philology v71 p249-302

Eugenics

Bodmer, W. F. Biomedical advances: a mixed blessing? *In* Harré, R. ed. Problems of scientific revolution p25-41

See also Genetics; Heredity; Malthusianism

Eulau, Heinz

Elite analysis and democratic theory: the contribution of Harold D. Lasswell. *In* Eulau, H. and Czudnowski, M. M. eds. Elite recruitment in democratic polities p7-28

Eulogies

Gilmore, M. T. Eulogy as symbolic biography: the iconography of revolutionary leadership, 1776-1826. *In* Studies in biography p131-57

Euphronios

About

Mertens, J. R. A white-ground cup by Euphronios. *In* Harvard Studies in classical philology v76 p271-81

Euphronius. See Euphronios

Eurich, Nell

Learning in America. *In* From Parnassus p75-83

Euripides

About

Nicoll, A. The dawn of realism: Euripides *In* Nicoll, A. World drama p42-59

Stahl, H. P. On 'extra-dramatic' communication of characters in Euripides. *In* Yale classical studies v25 p159-76

About individual works
Alcestis

Griffith, M. Euripides Alkestis 636-641. *In* Harvard Studies in classical philology v82 p83-86

Alcestis (Lines 1092-1098)

Whitfield, M. A. Euripides, Alcestis 1092-1098. *In* Harvard Studies in classical philology v73 p105-08

Andromache

Kovačs, D. Three passages from the Andromache. *In* Harvard Studies in classical philology v81 p123-56

The Bacchae

Balestri, C. The Bacchae. *In* Seidel, M. A. and Mendelson, E. eds. Homer to Brecht p191-213

Kepple, L. R. The broken victim: Euripides Bacchae 969-970. *In* Harvard Studies in classical philology v80 p107-09

Sansone, D. The Bacchae as satyr-play? *In* Illinois classical studies v3, 1978 p40-46

Simon, B. Mental life in Greek tragedy. *In* Simon, B. Mind and madness in ancient Greece p89-121

Electra

Diggle, J. Notes on the Electra of Euripides. *In* Illinois classical studies, v2 1977 p110-24

Kubo, M. The norm of myth: Euripides' Electra. *In* Harvard Studies in classical philology v71 p15-31

Walsh, G. B. The first stasimon of Euripides' Electra. *In* Yale classical studies v25 p277-89

Helen

Wolff, C. On Euripides' Helen. *In* Harvard Studies in classical philology v77 p61-84

Heracles

Gregory, J. Euripides' Heracles. *In* Yale classical studies v25 p259-75

Lesky, A. On the Heraclidae of Euripides. *In* Yale classical studies v25 p227-38

Simon, B. Tragedy and therapy. *In* Simon, B. Mind and madness in ancient Greece p122-54

Hippolytus

Dimock, G. E. Euripides' Hippolytus, or Virtue rewarded. *In* Yale classical studies v25 p239-58

Medea

Easterling, P. E. The infanticide in Euripides' Medea. *In* Yale classical studies v25 p177-91

Knox, B. M. W. The Medea of Euripides. *In* Yale classical studies v25 p193-225

Orestes

Simon, B. Mental life in Greek tragedy. *In* Simon, B. Mind and madness in ancient Greece p89-121

The Phoenician women

Arthur, M. B. The curse of civilization: the choral odes of the Phoenissae. *In* Harvard Studies in classical philology v81 p163-85

Rhesus

Kitto, H. D. F. The Rhesus and related matters. *In* Yale classical studies v25 p317-50

The suppliants

Smith, W. D. Expressive form in Euripides' Suppliants. *In* Harvard Studies in classical philology v71 p151-70

The Trojan women

Burnett, A. P. Trojan women and the Ganymede ode. *In* Yale classical studies v25 p291-316

Criticism, Textual

Lesky, A. On the Heraclidae of Euripides. *In* Yale classical studies v25 p227-38

Tragedies

Koniaris, G. L. Alexander, Palamedes, Troades, Sisyphus—a connected tetralogy? A connected trilogy? *In* Harvard Studies in classical philology v77 p85-124

Euripides—*Continued*

Translations, English

McDonald, M. Does Euripides call the gods μακάριοι? *In* Illinois classical studies v4, 1979 p27-33

Europe

Civilization

Le Roy Ladurie, E. Rural civilization. *In* Le Roy Ladurie, E. The territory of the historian p79-110

Civilization—Foreign influences

Bigsby, C. W. E. Europe, America and the cultural debate. *In* Bigsby, C. W. E. Superculture p 1-27

Civilization—History

Hexter, J. H. Wallace K. Ferguson and Hiram Hayden [sic]: the Renaissance again —and again. *In* Hexter, J. H. On historians p45-59

Commerce—History

Symcox, G. W. The battle of the Atlantic, 1500-1700. *In* First images of America p265-77

Defenses

Brown, N. Threats to security in Europe. *In* The New Atlantic challenge p219-28

Carlton, D. The British independent nuclear deterrent and the future of European security. *In* International terrorism and world security p277-94

Erickson, J. The European military balance. *In* Kirk, G. L. and Wessell, N. H. eds. The Soviet threat p110-21

Gessert, R. A. Deterrence and the defense of Europe. *In* Ethics and nuclear strategy? p92-112

Hassner, P. The political aspects of European security. *In* International terrorism and world security p173-88

Holst, J. W. NATO, the European Community, and the transatlantic order. *In* The New Atlantic challenge p265-77

Packard, D. Perceptions of the military balance. *In* The New Atlantic challenge p203-16

Strausz-Hupé, R. America and the defense of the West. *In* Prochnow, H. V. ed. Dilemmas facing the nation p271-93

Zoppo, C. E. Arms control in the Mediterranean and European security. *In* International terrorism and world security p248-76

Economic conditions

Ardant, G. Financial policy and economic infrastructure of modern states and nations. *In* Tilly, C. ed. The formation of national states in Western Europe p164-242

Jones, E. L. Afterword. *In* Parker, W. N. and Jones, E. L. eds. European peasants and their markets p327-60

Larkin, M. The dismal science: economic man. *In* Larkin, M. Man and society in nineteenth-century realism p139-51

Parker, W. N. Introduction. *In* Parker, W. N. and Jones, E. L. eds. European peasants and their markets p3-22

Economic conditions—History

Hamilton, E. J. What the New World gave the economy of the Old. *In* First images of America p853-84

Hoffmann, R. C. Medieval origins of the common fields. *In* Parker, W. N. and Jones, E. L. eds. European peasants and their markets p23-71

Economic integration

Wohlfarht, J. The European Economic Community: expectations and realities of integration. *In* Hayward, J. E. S. and Berki, R. N. eds. State and society in contemporary Europe p203-17

Emigration and immigration

Hoffmann-Nowotny, H. J. European migration after World War II. *In* Human migration p85-105

Hughes, H. S. The great migration. *In* Hughes, H. S. The sea change p 1-34

Tilly, C. Migration in modern European history. *In* Human migration p48-72

Foreign relations

Morse, E. L. The Atlantic economy in crisis. *In* Atlantis lost p149-82

Foreign relations—Japan

Mushakoji, K. A note on trilateral crisis diplomacy: the irritants in the Japan-U.S.-E.C. relations. *In* Postwar trends in Japan p15-36

Foreign relations—Near East

Javits, J. K. Western Europe and the tensions in the Middle East. *In* The New world balance and peace in the Middle East: reality or mirage? p74-78

Foreign relations—United States

Aron, R. Allies and rivals. *In* The New Atlantic challenge p37-41

Ball, G. W. The problem stated. *In* The New Atlantic challenge p17-25

Bernhard, L. F. E. J. C. K. G. P., H.R.H. Prince. The Atlantic nucleus. *In* The New Atlantic challenge p31-35

Brown, S. A world of multiple relationships. *In* Atlantis lost p103-18

Brzezinski, Z. K. The European crossroads. *In* Atlantis lost p85-102

Calleo, D. P. America, Europe and the oil crisis: hegemony reaffirmed? *In* Atlantis lost p119-47

Chace, J. Europe: is there a price to be paid? *In* Atlantis lost p65-83

Craig, G. A. The United States and the European balance. *In* Two hundred years of American foreign policy p67-89

Duchêne, F. The United States and European Community. *In* Rosecrance, R. N. ed. America as an ordinary country p87-109

Hallstein, W. The need for vision. *In* The New Atlantic challenge p27-30

Hassner, P. Europe and the contradictions in American policy. *In* Rosecrance, R. N. ed. America as an ordinary country p60-86

Hoffmann, S. No trumps, no luck, no will: gloomy thoughts on Europe's plight. *In* Atlantis lost p 1-46

Jenkins, R. H. The United States and a united Europe: are we now uncertain partners? *In* World change and world security p 1-16

Kirby, S. Great-Power involvement in European systems. *In* Hayward, J. E. S. and Berki, R. N. eds. State and society in contemporary Europe p181-202

Kohnstamm, M. Institutions for interdependence. *In* The New Atlantic challenge p355-64

European literature—*Continued*

Medieval, 500-1510
See Literature, Medieval

18th century
See Rococo literature
European War, 1914-1918

Economic aspects
See also European War, 1914-1918—Finance

Economic aspects—Great Britain
Coleman, D. C. War demand and industrial supply: the 'dope scandal', 1915-19. *In* War and economic development p205-27
MacLeod, R. M. and MacLeod, K. War and economic development: government and the optical industry in Britain, 1914-18. *In* War and economic development p165-203
Trebilcock, C. War and the failure of industrial mobilisation: 1899 and 1914. *In* War and economic development p139-64

Fiction
Bradbury, M. The denuded place: war and form in Parade's end and U.S.A. *In* Klein, H. M. ed. The First World War in fiction p193-209
Cooperman, S. John Dos Passos' Three soldiers: Aesthetics and the doom of individualism. *In* Klein, H. M. ed. The First World War in fiction p23-31
Dale, J. Drieu La Rochelle: the war as 'comedy.' *In* Klein, H. M. ed. The First World War in fiction p63-72
Flower, J. E. The soldier's stage: Roland Dorgelès, Les croix de bois. *In* Klein, H. M. ed. The First World War in fiction p53-62
Garrety, M. Love and war: R. H. Mottram, The Spanish farm trilogy and Ernest Hemingway, A farewell to arms. *In* Klein, H. M. ed. The First World War in fiction p10-22
King, J. Henri Barbusse: Le feu and the crisis of social realism. *In* Klein, H. M. ed. The First World War in fiction p43-52
Klein, H. M. Introduction. *In* Klein, H. M. ed. The First World War in fiction p 1-9
Klein, H. M. Projections of Everyman: the common soldier in Franconi, Wiechert and Williamson. *In* Klein, H. M. ed. The First World War in fiction p84-100
Morris, J. Richard Aldington and Death of a hero—or life of an anti-hero? *In* Klein, H. M. ed. The First World War in fiction p183-92
Pynsent, R. B. The last days of Austria: Hasek and Kraus. *In* Klein, H. M. ed. The First World War in fiction p136-48
Redfern, W. D. Against nature: Jean Giono and Le grand troupeau. *In* Klein, H. M. ed. The First World War in fiction p73-83
Rowley, B. A. Journalism into fiction: Im Westen nichts Neues. *In* Klein, H. M. ed. The First World War in fiction p101-11
Sebald, W. G. Humanitarianism and law: Arnold Zweig. Der Streit um den Sergeanten Grischa. *In* Klein, H. M. ed. The First World War in fiction p126-35
Smith, C. N. The very plain song of it: Frederic Manning, Her privates we. *In* Klein, H. M. ed. The First World War in fiction p174-82

Stern, J. P. The embattled style: Ernst Jünger, In Stahlgewittern. *In* Klein, H. M. ed. The First World War in fiction p121-25
Wagstaff, C. Dead man erect: F. T. Marinetti, L'alcova d'acciaio. *In* Klein, H. M. ed. The First World War in fiction p149-59
Walsh, J. The painful process of unthinking: E. E. Cummings' social vision in The enormous room. *In* Klein, H. M. ed. The First World War in fiction p32-42

Finance—Great Britain
Dimsdale, N. H. Keynes and the finance of the First World War. *In* Keynes, M. ed. Essays on John Maynard Keynes p142-61

Food question—Germany
Lee, J. Administrators and agriculture: aspects of German agricultural policy in the First World War. *In* War and economic development p229-38

Literature and the war
Briggs, J. Ghosts troop home: the Great War and its aftermath. *In* Briggs, J. Night visitors p165-81
DeBell, D. Strategies of survival: David Jones, In parenthesis, and Robert Graves, Goodbye to all that. *In* Klein, H. M. ed. The First World War in fiction p160-73
Lewis, W. The war writers; excerpt from "The old gang and the new gang." *In* Lewis, W. Enemy salvoes p212-16

Peace
Smith, D. M. The Fourteen Points. *In* Encyclopedia of American foreign policy p380-86

Poetry
Scannell, V. Setting the scene. *In* Scannell, V. Not without glory p7-22

Reconstruction
See Reconstruction (1914-1939)

War-songs
See European War, 1914-1918—Poetry

Great Britain
Stubbs, J. The impact of the Great War on the Conservative Party. *In* Peele, G. and Cook, C. eds. The politics of reappraisal, 1918-1939 p14-38

Italy—Foreign public opinion, American
Nelli, H. S. Chicago's Italian-language press and World War I. *In* Studies in Italian American social history p66-80

United States
Thompson, J. A. American Progressive publicists and the First World War, 1914-1917. *In* Burton, D. H. ed. American history —British historians p187-217

Europeans in India
Marshall, P. Masters and banians in eighteenth-century Calcutta. *In* Kling, B. B. and Pearson, M. N. eds. The age of partnership p191-213

Eurovision. See European Broadcasting Union

Eusebius Pamphili, Bp. of Caesarea

About individual works

Contra Hieroclem

Barnes, T. D. Sossianus Hierocles and the antecedents of the "Great persecution." *In* Harvard Studies in classical philology v80 p239-52

The ecclesiastical history of Eusebius Pamphilus

Barnes, T. D. Origen, Aquila, and Eusebius. *In* Harvard Studies in classical philoloy v74 p313-16

Euskadi Ta Askatasuna. See Basque Nation and Liberty

Eustace, Saint. See Eustachius, Saint

Eustachius, Saint

Legends

Heffernan, T. J. An analysis of the narrative motifs in the legend of St. Eustace. *In* Medievalia et humanistica no. 6 p63-89

Euthanasia

Bandman, B. and Bandman, E. L. Rights, justice, and euthanasia. *In* Kohl, M. ed. Beneficent euthanasia p81-99

Barrington, M. R. Voluntary Euthanasia Act, 198—? *In* Kohl, M. ed. Beneficent euthanasia p209-17

Brandt, R. B. A moral principle about killing. *In* Kohl, M. ed. Beneficent euthanasia p106-14

Brody, B. Voluntary euthanasia and the law. *In* Kohl, M. ed. Beneficent euthanasia p218-32

Drinan, R. F. Should there be a legal right to die? *In* Weir, R. F. ed. Ethical issues in death and dying p297-307

Dyck, A. J. An alternative to the ethic of euthanasia. *In* Weir, R. F. ed. Ethical issues in death and dying p281-96

Dyck, A. J. Beneficent euthanasia and benemortasia: alternative views of mercy. *In* Kohl, M. ed. Beneficent euthanasia p117-29

Engelhardt, H. T. Ethical issues in aiding the death of young children. *In* Kohl, M. ed. Beneficent euthanasia p180-92

Fletcher, J. F. Ethics and euthanasia. *In* Weir, R. F. ed. Ethical issues in death and dying p348-59

Fletcher, J. F. Euthanasia. *In* Fletcher, J. F. Humanhood: essays in biomedical ethics p149-58

Fletcher, J. F. The "right" to live and the "right" to die. *In* Kohl, M. ed. Beneficent euthanasia p44-53

Foot, P. Euthanasia. *In* Foot, P. Virtues and vices, and other essays in moral philosophy p33-61

Furlow, T. W. Euthanasia and the tyranny of technology. *In* Kohl, M. ed. Beneficent euthanasia p169-79

Kohl, M. Voluntary beneficent euthanasia. *In* Kohl, M. ed. Beneficent euthanasia p130-41

Kohl, M. and Kurtz, P. W. A plea for beneficent euthanasia. *In* Kohl, M. ed. Beneficent euthanasia p233-38

Maguire, D. C. A Catholic view of mercy killing. *In* Kohl, M. ed. Beneficent euthanasia p12-33

Morison, R. S. Death: process or event? *In* Death inside out p63-70

Ramsey, P. On (only) caring for the dying. *In* Weir, R. F. ed. Ethical issues in death and dying p189-225

Sherwin, B. L. Jewish views of euthanasia. *In* Kohl, M. ed. Beneficent euthanasia p3-11

Smith, D. H. On letting some babies die. *In* Death inside out p129-38

Sullivan, J. V. Bp. The immorality of euthanasia. *In* Kohl, M. ed. Beneficent euthanasia p12-33

Summerskill, E. On the Voluntary Euthanasia Bill of 1969. *In* Kohl, M. ed. Beneficent euthanasia p204-08

Tupin, J. P. Some psychiatric issues of euthanasia. *In* Kohl, M. ed. Beneficent euthanasia p193-203

Williams, G. L. Euthanasia and the physician. *In* Kohl, M. ed. Beneficent euthanasia p145-68

Social aspects

Maguire, D. C. Deciding for yourself: the objections. *In* Weir, R. F. ed. Ethical issues in death and dying p320-47

Euthenics. See Eugenics

Evaluation of literature. See Books and reading; Criticism

Evangelical religion. See Evangelicalism

Evangelical Revival

See also Evangelicalism; Great Awakening

Influence

Marsden, G. M. From fundamentalism to evangelicalism: a historical analysis. *In* Wells, D. F. and Woodbridge, J. D. eds. The evangelicals p122-42

Evangelical work. See Missions

Evangelicalism

Beckford, J. A. Two contrasting types of sectarian organization. *In* Wallis, R. ed. Sectarianism p70-85

Holmer, P. L. Contemporary evangelical faith: an assesment and critique. *In* Wells, D. F. and Woodbridge, J. D. eds. The evangelicals p68-95

See also Fundamentalism; Pietism

Church of England

Moody, M. E. Religion in the life of Charles Middleton, First Baron Barham. *In* The Dissenting tradition p140-63

History

Gerstner, J. H. The theological boundaries of evangelical faith. *In* Wells, D. F. and Woodbridge, J. D. eds. The evangelicals p21-37

Great Britain

Davie, D. Dissent and the Evangelicals, 1800-1850. *In* Davie, D. A gathered Church p55-72

United States

Bentley, W. H. Bible believers in the Black community. *In* Wells, D. F. and Woodbridge, J. D. eds. The evangelicals p108-21

Kantzer, K. S. Unity and diversity in evangelical faith. *In* Wells, D. F. and Woodbridge, J. D. eds. The evangelicals p38-67

Marty, M. E. Tensions within contemporary evangelicalism: a critical appraisal. *In* Wells, D. F. and Woodbridge, J. D. eds. The evangelicals p170-88

Moberg, D. O. Fundamentalists and evangelicals in society. *In* Wells, D. F. and Woodbridge, J. D. eds. The evangelicals p143-69

Evangelicalism—United States—_Continued_

Pannell, W. E. The religious heritage of Blacks. _In_ Wells, D. F. and Woodbridge, J. D. eds. The evangelicals p96-107

United States—History

Ahlstrom, S. E. From Puritanism to evangelicalism: a critical perspective. _In_ Wells, D. F. and Woodbridge, J. D. eds. The evangelicals p269-89

Linder, R. D. The resurgence of evangelical social concern (1925-75). _In_ Wells, D. F. and Woodbridge, J. D. eds. The evangelicals p189-210

Marsden, G. M. From fundamentalism to evangelicalism: a historical analysis. _In_ Wells, D. F. and Woodbridge, J. D. eds. The evangelicals p122-42

Meyer, D. H. From piety to moralism. _In_ Meyer, D. H. The democratic Enlightenment p35-45

Williams, G. H. and Petersen, R. L. Evangelicals: society, the state, the nation. _In_ Wells, D. F. and Woodbridge, J. D. eds. The evangelicals p211-48

Evangelists

Moberg, D. O. Fundamentalists and evangelicals in society. _In_ Wells, D. F. and Woodbridge, J. D. eds. The evangelicals p143-69

Evangelists (Bible)

Art

Buchthal, H. Toward a history of Palaeologan illumination. _In_ The Place of book illumination in Byzantine art p143-77

Evans, Alona Elizabeth

Aircraft hijacking: what is being done. _In_ International terrorism and political crimes p219-47

Evans, Sir Arthur John

About individual works

Through Bosnia and the Herzegóvina on foot during the insurrection, August and September, 1875

Bynum, D. E. The generic nature of oral epic poetry. _In_ Folklore genres p35-58

Evans, Arthur R.

Ernst Jünger's Auf den Marmorklippen: a sketch toward an interpretation. _In_ Symbolism and modern literature p26-62

Evans, Augusta. See Wilson, Augusta Jane

Evans, Edward J.

The established self: the American episodes of Martin Chuzzlewit. _In_ Dickens Studies Annual v5 p59-73

Evans, Emyr Estyn

Introduction: The Irish—fact and fiction. _In_ De Breffny, B. ed. The Irish world p 7-18

Peasant beliefs in nineteenth-century Ireland. _In_ Casey, D. J. and Rhodes, R. E. eds. Views of the Irish peasantry, 1800-1916 p37-56

Prehistoric Ireland: from the earliest migrations to about AD 500. _In_ De Breffny, B. ed. The Irish world p20-46

Evans, Gareth Lloyd

Post-war drama in England and Ireland. _In_ Nicoll, A. World drama p806-20

Semantic structure and logical form. _In_ Evans, G. L. and McDowell, J. H. eds. Truth and meaning p199-222

Evans, James Leroy

Ethnic tensions in the Lower Rio Grande Valley to 1860. _In_ Yoder, D. ed. American folklife p239-55

Evans, Mary Ann. See Eliot, George, pseud.

Evans, Rowland, and Novak, Robert D.

Lyndon B. Johnson: the ascent to leadership; excerpt from "Lyndon B. Johnson: the exercise of power." _In_ Ornstein, N. J. ed. Congress in change p117-41

Evans, William McKee

The North Carolina Lumbees: from assimilation to revitalization. _In_ Williams, W. L. ed. Southeastern Indians since the removal era p49-71

Evans-Pritchard, Edward Evan

About individual works

The Nuer

Dumont, L. Preface by Louis Dumont to the French edition of The Nuer. _In_ Studies in social anthropology p328-42

Everett, Barbara

'Hamlet': a time to die. _In_ Shakespeare survey 30 p117-23

The shooting of the bears: poetry and politics in Andrew Marvell. _In_ Andrew Marvell p62-103

Everett, Peter

About individual works

Negatives

Hyman, S. E. Playing doctor, playing war. _In_ Hyman, S. E. The critic's credentials p135-39

Evergates, Theodore

Historiography and sociology in early feudal society: the case of Hariulf and the "milites" of Saint-Riquier. _In_ Viator: medieval and Renaissance studies v6 p35-49

Everitt, Mark

R. W. Blackmore (1791-1882), an English chaplain in Cronstadt. _In_ Oxford Slavonic papers, new ser. v10 p98-106

Evers, Hans-Dieter

Urban expansion and landownership in underdeveloped societies. _In_ Walton, J. and Masotti, L. H. eds. The city in comparative persepective p67-79

Everson, William K.

Thoughts on a great adaptation. _In_ Peary, G. and Shatzkin, R. eds. The modern American novel and the movies p63-69

Evert, Richard. See Greenfield, S. B. jt. auth.

Evert, Walter H.

Coadjutors of oppression: a romantic and modern theory of evil. _In_ Bornstein, G. ed. Romantic and modern p29-52

Everyman

Jambeck, T. J. Everyman and the implications of Bernardine humanism in the character "Knowledge." _In_ Medievalia et humanistica no. 8 p103-23

Sellin, P. R. The hidden God: Reformation awe in Renaissance English literature. _In_ The Darker vision of the Renaissance p147-96

Evidence

Ayer, A. J. Self-evidence. _In_ Pivčević, E. ed. Phenomenology and philosophical understanding p79-92

Evidence—*Continued*

Pietersma, H. Husserl's views on the evident and the true. *In* Elliston, F. A. and McCormick, P. eds. Husserl p38-53

See also Prediction (Logic)

Evidence (Criminal) See Self-incrimination

Evidence (Law)

United States

Friedenthal, J. H. The rulemaking power of the Supreme Court: a contemporary crisis. *In* Stanford legal essays p149-62

Evidence, Expert

Dobyns, H. F. Taking the witness stand. *In* Eddy, E. M. and Partridge, W. L. eds. Applied anthropology in America p261-76

Evil. See Good and evil

Evil, Non-resistance to. See Government, Resistance to

Evil eye

Appel, W. The myth of the jettatura. *In* The Evil eye p16-27

Cosminsky, S. The evil eye in a Quiché community. *In* The Evil eye p163-74

Garrison, V. E. and Arensberg, C. M. The evil eye: envy or risk of seizure? Paranoia or patronal dependency? *In* The Evil eye p286-328

Kearney, M. A world-view explanation of the evil eye. *In* The Evil eye p175-92

Maloney, C. Don't say "pretty baby" lest you zap it with your eye—the evil eye in South Asia. *In* The Evil eye p102-48

Meiser, E. P. Flores-. The hot mouth and evil eye. *In* The Evil eye p149-62

Moss, L. W. and Cappanari, S. C. Mal'occhio, ayin ha ra, oculus fascinus, Judenblick: the evil eye hovers above. *In* The Evil eye p 1-15

Reminick, R. A. The evil eye belief among the Amhara. *In* The Evil eye p85-101

Roberts, J. M. Belief in the evil eye in world perspective. *In* The Evil eye p223-78

Spooner, B. Anthropology and the evil eye. *In* The Evil eye p279-85

Spooner, B. The evil eye in the Middle East. *In* The Evil eye p76-84

Stein, H. F. Envy and the evil eye: an essay in the psychological ontogeny of belief and ritual. *In* The Evil eye p193-222

Teitelbaum, J. M. The leer and the loom—social controls on handloom weavers. *In* The Evil eye p63-75

See also Charms; Superstition; Witchcraft

Evil in literature

Evert, W. H. Coadjutors of oppression: a romantic and modern theory of evil. *In* Bornstein, G. ed. Romantic and modern p29-52

Kazin, A. The drama of good and evil in American writing. *In* An Almost chosen people p51-66

Ragussis, M. E. M. Forster: the vision of evil in fiction: the narrative structure of A passage to India. *In* Ragussis, M. The subterfuge of art p133-71

Ragussis, M. W. B. Yeats: the vision of evil and poetic objectivity in "Nineteen hundred and nineteen." *In* Ragussis, M. The subterfuge of art p85-108

Stock, R. D. and Stock, B. The agents of evil and justice in the novels of Dorothy L. Sayers. *In* Hannay, M. P. ed. As her whimsey took her p14-22

Evil spirits. See Demonology

Evolution

Allen, G. E. Naturalists and experimentalists: the genotype and the phenotype. *In* Studies in history of biology v 3 p179-209

Ayala, F. J. The concept of biological progress. *In* Ayala, F. J. and Dobzhansky, T. G. eds. Studies in the philosophy of biology p339-54

Barfield, R. H. Darwinism. *In* Evolution of consciousness p69-82

Birch, L. C. Chance, necessity and purpose. *In* Ayala, F. J. and Dobzhansky, T. G. eds. Studies in the philosophy of biology p225-39

Boesiger, E. Evolutionary theories after Lamarck and Darwin. *In* Ayala, F. J. and Dobzhansky, T. G. eds. Studies in the philosophy of biology p21-43

Bronowski, J. New concepts in the evolution of complexity. *In* Bronowski, J. A sense of the future p175-95

Bronowski, J. Toward a philosophy of biology. *In* Bronowski, J. A sense of the future p163-74

Chadwick, O. Science and religion. *In* Chadwick, O. The secularization of the European mind in the nineteenth century p161-88

Dobzhansky, T. G. Chance and creativity in evolution. *In* Ayala, F. J. and Dobzhansky, T. G. eds. Studies in the philosophy of biology p307-37

Dobzhansky, T. G. Evolution and man's self-image. *In* Goodall, V. M. ed. The quest for man p189-220

Flew, A. G. N. The Darwinian framework. *In* Flew, A. G. N. A rational animal p7-33

Hull, D. L. Scientific bandwagon or traveling medicine show? *In* Sociobiology and human nature p136-63

Hyman, S. E. A Darwin sidelight: the shape of the young man's nose. *In* Hyman, S. E. The critic's credentials p261-78

Koestler, A. Crumbling citadels. *In* Koestler, A. Janus p165-92

Koestler, A. Lamarck revisited. *In* Koestler, A. Janus p193-204

Koestler, A. Strategies and purpose in evolution. *In* Koestler, A. Janus p205-26

Larkin, M. La bête humaine. *In* Larkin, M. Man and society in nineteenth-century realism p123-33

Margoliash, E. Informational macromolecules and biological evolution. *In* Neyman, J. ed. The heritage of Copernicus: theories "pleasing to the mind" p184-206

Medawar, Sir P. B. Technology and evolution. *In* The Frontiers of knowledge p105-15

Also in Technology and the frontiers of knowledge p99-110

Monod, J. L. On the molecular theory of evolution. *In* Harré, R. ed. Problems of scientific revolution p11-24

Napier, J. R. The tree of evolution. *In* Goodall, V. M. ed. The quest for man p57-78

Provine, W. B. Francis B. Sumner and the evolutionary synthesis. *In* Studies in history of biology v 3 p211-40

Shapere, D. On the relations between compositional and evolutionary theories. *In* Ayala, F. J. and Dobzhansky, T. G. eds. Studies in the philosophy of biology p187-201

Evolution—*Continued*

Stebbins, G. L. Adaptive shifts and evolutionary novelty: a compositionist approach. *In* Ayala, F. J. and Dobzhansky, T. G. eds. Studies in the philosophy of biology p285-306

Temkin, O. The idea of descent in postromantic German biology: 1848-1858. *In* Temkin, O. The double face of Janus p390-415

Thakur, S. C. Telepathy, evolution and dualism. *In* Thakur, S. C. ed. Philosophy and psychical research p195-210

Thorpe, W. H. Arthur Koestler and biological thought. *In* Harris, H. A. ed. Astride the two cultures p50-68

See also Adaptation (Biology); Bergman's rule; Ethics, Evolutionary; Holism; Human evolution; Modernist-fundamentalist controversy; Natural selection; Ontogeny; Social evolution; Teleology

History

Ospovat, D. Perfect adaptation and teleological explanation: approaches to the problem of the history of life in the mid-nineteenth century. *In* Studies in history of biology, v2 p33-56

Provine, W. B. The role of mathematical population geneticists in the evolutionary synthesis of the 1930s and 1940s. *In* Studies in history of biology, v2 p167-92

Todes, D. P. V. O. Kovalevskii: the genesis, content, and reception of his paleontological work. *In* Studies in history of biology v2 p99-165

Evolution and Christianity

Anderson, V. E. Evangelicals and science: fifty years after the Scopes trial (1925-75). *In* Wells, D. F. and Woodbridge, J. D. eds. The evangelicals p249-68

Evolution and religion

Mudford, P. The backcloth changes. . . *In* Mudford, P. The art of celebration p21-33

See also Evolution and Christianity

Evolution in literature

Vernier, J. P. Evolution as a literary theme in H. G. Wells's science fiction. *In* H. G. Wells and modern science fiction p70-89

Evolutionary ethics. See Ethics, Evolutionary

Evolutionary linguistics. See Historical linguistics

Evra, James van. See Van Evra, James

Evreinov, Nikolaĭ Nikolaevich

About

Nicoll, A. The theatre symbolic and theatrical. *In* Nicoll, A. World drama p608-15

Ewan, Joseph Andorfer

The Columbian discoveries and the growth of botanical ideas with special reference to the sixteenth century *In* First images of America p807-12

The growth of learned and scientific societies in the southeastern United States to 1860. *In* Oleson, A. and Brown, S. C. eds. The pursuit of knowledge in the early American Republic p208-18

Ewbank, Inga-Stina

Drama and society in Ibsen's Pillars of the community. *In* Drama and society p75-97

'Hamlet' and the power of words. *In* Shakespeare survey 30 p85-102

"What words, what looks, what wonders?": language and spectacle in the theatre of George Peele. *In* The Elizabethan theatre, V p124-54

Ewe (African people) See Fon (African people)

Ewell, Barbara C.

Parodic echoes of The portrait of a lady in Howells's Indian summer. *In* Tulane studies in English v22 p117-31

Ewers, John Canfield

Indian views of the white man prior to 1850: an interpretation. *In* Red Men and hat-wearers p7-23

Excavations (Archaeology)

See also Cities and towns, Ruined, extinct, etc.

Bulgaria

See Patleina Monastery site, Bulgaria

Kenya

Kirkman, J. S. Some conclusions from archaeological excavations on the coast of Kenya, 1948-1966. *In* Chittick, H. N. and Rotberg, R. I. eds. East Africa and the Orient p226-47

Turkey

Mitten, D. G. and Yŭğrüm, G. The Gygean Lake, 1969: Eski Balikhane, preliminary report. *In* Harvard Studies in classical philology v75 p191-95

See also Dag Pazarī site, Turkey

Exceptions & rules. Nemerov, H. *In* Evolution of consciousness p42-47

Also in Nemerov, H. Figures of thought p42-48

Exchange

Kindleberger, C. P. Is symmetry possible in international money? *In* Theory for economic efficiency: essays in honor of Abba P. Lerner p62-75

See also Commerce; Money

Exchange, Bills of. See Bills of exchange

Exchange, Foreign. See Foreign exchange

Exchange theory (Sociology)

Hingers, R. H. and Willer, D. Prevailing postulates of social exchange. *In* McNall, S. G. ed. Theoretical perspectives in sociology p169-86

Exchanges, Literary and scientific. See Information networks

Executions and executioners. See Hanging

Executions and executioners in literature

Lodge, D. Arnold Bennett: 'The old wives' tale.' *In* Lodge, D. The modes of modern writing p27-35

Lodge, D. George Orwell's 'A hanging', and Michael Lake describes. . .'. *In* Lodge, D. The modes of modern writing p9-17

Lodge, D. Metaphor and metonymy. *In* Lodge, D. The modes of modern writing p73-124

Executive ability. See Leadership

Executive agencies. See Administrative agencies

Executive agreements. See subdivision Foreign relations—Executive agreements under names of countries, e.g. United States—Foreign relations—Executive agreements

Executive power

See also Executive privilege (Government information); Judicial review; Presidents; Separation of powers; Treating-making power

United States

Bessette, J. M. The Presidency. *In* Graham, G. J. and Graham, S. G. eds. Founding principles of American government p197-222

Bowman, A. H. Presidential advisers. *In* Encyclopedia of American foreign policy p790-804

Corwin, E. S. Our constitutional revolution and how to round it out. *In* Corwin, E. S. Presidential power and the Constitution p157-76

Corwin, E. S. The President as administrative chief. *In* Corwin, E. S. Presidential power and the Constitution p72-112

Corwin, E. S. The President's power. *In* Corwin, E. S. Presidential power and the Constitution p137-40

Corwin, E. S. The steel seizure case: a judicial brick without straw. *In* Corwin, E. S. Presidential power and the Constitution p121-37

Corwin, E. S. The war and the Constitution: President and Congress. *In* Corwin, E. S. Presidential power and the Constitution p112-20

Corwin, E. S. War, the Constitution moulder. *In* Corwin, E. S. Presidential power and the Constitution p23-27

Corwin, E. S. Woodrow Wilson and the Presidency. *In* Corwin, E. S. Presidential power and the Constitution p32-53

Dry, M. Congress. *In* Graham, G. J. and Graham, S. G. eds. Founding principles of American government p223-57

Eckart, D. R. and Ries, J. C. The American Presidency. *In* Rieselbach, L. N. ed. People vs. government: the responsiveness of American institutions p15-65

Karl, B. D. Executive reorganization and Presidential power. *In* The Supreme Court review, 1977 p 1-37

Pletcher, D. M. Presidential power in foreign affairs. *In* Encyclopedia of American foreign policy p805-26

Prewitt, K. and McAllister, W. Changes in the American executive elite, 1930-1970. *In* Eulau, H. and Czudnowski, M. M. eds. Elite recruitment in democratic polities p105-32

Executive privilege (Government information)

Schwartz, B. The United States: the doctrine of executive privilege. *In* Galnoor, I. ed. Government secrecy in democracies p129-42

Exempla

Olsson, K. O. Rhetoric, John Gower, and the late medieval exemplum. *In* Medievalia et humanistica no. 8 p185-200

Stierle, K. H. Story as exemplum—exemplum as story: on the pragmatics and poetics of narrative texts. *In* Amacher, R. E. and Lange, V. eds. New perspectives in German literary criticism p389-417

See also Fables

Exemplarism, Vedic. Coomaraswamy, A. K. *In* Coomaraswamy, A. K. Selected papers v2 p177-97

Exercise

Haskell, W. L. Physical activity in health maintenance. *In* Sobel, D. S. ed. Ways of health p435-57

The Exeter book (Maxims II)

Greenfield, S. B. and Evert, R. Maxims II: gnome and poem. *In* Anglo-Saxon poetry: essays in appreciation p337-54

The Exeter book (Riddles)

Robinson, F. C. Artful ambiguities in the Old English "book-moth" Riddle. *In* Anglo-Saxon poetry: essays in appreciation p355-62

Exhibitions

Harris, N. All the world a melting pot? Japan at American fairs, 1876-1904. *In* Iriye, A. ed. Mutual images p24-54

Harris, N. Museums, merchandising, and popular taste: the struggle for influence. *In* Material culture and the study of American life p140-74

See also Museum techniques

Exhibits. See Exhibitions

Exiles. See Refugees, Political

Existential ethics

Warnock, M. Existentialist ethics. *In* New studies in ethics v2 p361-420

Existential psychology

May, K. M. A new synthesis. *In* May, K. M. Out of the maelstrom p98-121

May, R. Dangers in the relation of existentialism to psychotherapy. *In* May, R. Psychology and the human dilemma p147-57

May, R. Existential therapy and the American scene. *In* May, R. Psychology and the human dilemma p128-37

May, R. Jean-Paul Sartre and psychoanalysis. *In* May, R. Psychology and the human dilemma p138-46

Straus, E. W. The existential approach to psychiatry. *In* Psychiatry and the humanities v 1 p127-43

See also Phenomenological psychology

Existentialism

Brown, R. H. The emergence of existential thought: philosophical perspectives on positivist and humanist forms of social theory. *In* Douglas, J. D. and Johnson, J. M. [eds.] Existential sociology p77-100

Copleston, F. C. The existentialist concept of man. *In* Copleston, F. C. Philosophers and philosophies p160-71

Douglas, J. D. Existential sociology. *In* Douglas, J. D. and Johnson, J. M. [eds.] Existential sociology p 3-73

Edwards, P. Existentialism and death: a survey of some confusions and absurdities. *In* Donnelly, J. P. ed. Language, metaphysics, and death p32-61

Grene, M. G. Authenticity: an existential virtue. *In* Grene, M. G. Philosophy in and out of Europe p50-60

Kotarba, J. A. Existential sociology. *In* McNall, S. G. ed. Theoretical perspectives in sociology p348-68

Madison, G. B. Phenomenology and existentialism: Husserl and the end of idealism. *In* Elliston, F. A. and McCormick, P. eds. Husserl p247-68

Mays, W. Phenomenology and Marxism. *In* Pivčević, E. ed. Phenomenology and philosophical understanding p231-50

Percy, W. Symbol as hermeneutic in existentialism. *In* Percy, W. The message in the bottle p277-87

Existentialism—*Continued*

Scott, N. A. The achievement of existentialism. *In* Scott, N. A. Mirrors of man in existentialism p218-28

Slote, M. A. Existentialism and the fear of dying. *In* Donnelly, J. P. ed. Language, metaphysics, and death p69-87

See also Existential ethics; Existential psychology

History

Scott, N. A. Existentialism and the tragic sense of reality. *In* Scott, N. A. Mirrors of man in existentialism p 1-24

Existentialism and Christianity. See Christianity and existentialism

Existentialism in literature

Glicksberg, C. I. Jean-Paul Sartre: from existentialism to communism. *In* Glicksberg, C. I. The literature of commitment p222-35

Greene, R. W. Pierre Reverdy. *In* Greene, R. W. Six French poets of our time p23-58

Kellogg, G. Existentialism, violence, and communism. *In* Kellogg, G. Dark prophets of hope p74-88

Lamont, R. C. Elie Wiesel: in search of a tongue. *In* Rosenfeld, A. H. and Greenberg, I. eds. Confronting the Holocaust p80-98

Slabey, R. M. As I lay dying as an existential novel. *In* Garvin, H. R. ed. Makers of the twentieth-century novel p208-17

Existenzphilosophie. See Existentalism

Existimatio (The word)

Yavetz, Z. Existimatio, fama, and the ides of March. *In* Harvard Studies in classical philology v78 p35-65

Exner, Franz

About

Hanle, P. A. Indeterminacy before Heisenberg: the case of Franz Exner and Erwin Schrödinger. *In* Historical studies in the physical sciences v10 p225-69

Exodus (Anglo-Saxon poem)

Trahern, J. B. More scriptural echoes in the Old English Exodus. *In* Anglo-Saxon poetry: essays in appreciation p291-98

Exorcism

Walter, E. V. Demons and disenchantment. *In* Disguises of the demonic p17-30

The exorcist (Motion picture)

Kauffmann, S. The exorcist. *In* Kauffmann, S. Living images p254-56

Exoticism in art

Sturtevant, W. C. First visual images of native America. *In* First images of America p417-54

Exoticism in literature. See Utopias in literature

Expansion (U.S. politics) See Imperialism; United States—Territorial expansion

Expatriate literature. See Literature—Exiled authors

Expeditions, Arctic. See Arctic regions

Expeditions, Scientific. See Scientific expeditions

Expenditures, Public. See Budget; Inflation (Finance) and public expenditures

Experience

Chafe, W. L. The recall and verbalization of past experience. *In* Current issues in linguistic theory p215-46

Harrison, R. The concept of prepredicative experience. *In* Pivčević, E. ed. Phenomenology and philosophical understanding p93-107

Miller, J. W. Accidents will happen. *In* Miller, J. W. The paradox of cause, and other essays p42-55

Nagel, T. What is it like to be a bat? *In* Nagel, T. Mortal questions p165-80

Owen, D. H. The psychophysics of prior experience. *In* Studies in perception p467-524

Ross, R. G. The experience of value. *In* Philosophy and the civilizing arts p316-44

See also Empiricism; Facts (Philosophy); Immanence (Philosophy); Wisdom

Experience in literature

Rahv, P. The cult of experience in American writing. *In* Rahv P. Essays on literature and politics, 1932-1972 p8-22

Experimental farms. See Agricultural experiment stations

Experimental films

Sarris, A. Avant-garde films are more boring than ever. *In* Sarris, A. Politics and cinema p196-206

Experimental living project. See Kansas. University. Experimental living project

Experimental methods in education. See Education—Experimental methods

Experimental physiology. See Physiology, Experimental

Experimental psychobiology. See Psychobiology, Experimental

Experimental theater

Brustein, R. S. New fads, ancient truths. *In* Brustein, R. S. The culture watch p3-7

Brustein, R. S. Seminal and consumer theatre. *In* Brustein, R. S. The culture watch p150-58

Experimentation on man, Medical. See Human experimentation in medicine

Expert evidence. See Evidence, Expert

Exploitation, oppression and self-sacrifice. Tormey, J. F. *In* Gould, C. C. and Wartofsky, M. W. eds. Women and philosophy p206-21

Exploration of space. See Outer space—Exploration

Explorers. See Discoveries (in geography)

Explorers, Spanish

Cutter, D. C. Spanish scientific exploration along the Pacific Coast. *In* Weber, D. J. ed. New Spain's far northern frontier p35-47

Hammond, G. P. The search for the fabulous in the settlement of the Southwest. *In* Weber, D. J. ed. New Spain's far northern frontier p17-33

Exports. See Commerce

Expositions. See Exhibitions

Expression

Sircello, G. J. Expressive properties of art; excerpt from "Mind & art: an essay on the varieties of expression." *In* Margolis, J. Z. ed. Philosophy looks at the arts p325-45

See also Facial expression; Nonverbal communication; Rhetoric

Expression (Philosophy)

Elliott, R. K. Aesthetic theory and the experience of art. *In* Margolis, J. Z. ed. Philosophy looks at the arts p45-87

Expression (Philosophy)—*Continued*

Tormey, A. Art and expression: a critique; excerpt from "The concept of expression: a study in philosophical psychology and aesthetics." *In* Margolis, J. Z. ed. Philosophy looks at the arts p346-69

Expressionism

Corrigan, M. A. Beyond verisimilitude: echoes of expressionism in Williams' plays. *In* Tennessee Williams: a tribute p375-412

McMillan, D. Expressionism. *In* McMillan, D. Transition p90-101

Miller, J. Y. Expressionism: The waste land enacted. *In* French, W. G. ed. The twenties p439-54

Nicoll, A. The expressionistic movement. *In* Nicoll, A. World drama p674-88

See also Dadaism; Surrealism

Influence

Douglas, D. Influence and individuality: the indebtedness of Patrick White's The ham funeral and The season at Sarsaparilla to Strindberg and the German expressionist movement. *In* Bards, bohemians, and bookmen p266-80

Expressionism (Art)

Osborne, H. From impressionism to expressionism. *In* Osborne, H. Abstraction and artifice in twentieth-century art p42-54

See also Abstract expressionism

History

Middleton, J. C. Dada versus expressionism, or The red king's dream. *In* Middleton, J. C. Bolshevism in art p62-77

Middleton, J. C. The rise of primitivism and its relevance to the poetry of expressionism and dada. *In* Middleton, J. C. Bolshevism in art p23-37

Germany

Osborne, H. Expressionism in Germany. *In* Osborne, H. Abstraction and artifice in twentieth-century art p55-62

Expulsion of students. See Student expulsion

Expurgated books. See Censorship

Extemporaneous preaching. See Preaching, Extemporaneous

Extended care facilities. See Nursing homes

Extension work, Agricultural. See Agricultural extension work

Extermination, Jewish (1939-1945) See Holocaust, Jewish (1939-1945)

Exterritorial crime. See Criminal jurisdiction

Exterritoriality

Davids, J. Extraterritoriality. *In* Encyclopedia of American foreign policy p359-71

Extinction (Psychology) See Reinforcement (Psychology)

Extradition

Bassiouni, M. C. The political offense exception in extradition law and practice. *In* International terrorism and political crimes p398-447

Bassiouni, M. C. Unlawful seizures of persons by states as alternatives to extradition. *In* International terrorism and political crimes p343-68

Vogler, T. Perspectives on extradition and terrorism. *In* International terrorism and political crimes p391-97

Extrasensory perception

Bridgman, P. W. Probability, logic, and ESP. *In* Ludwig, J. K. ed. Philosophy and parapsychology p191-95

Brier, R. Mundle, Broad, Ducasse and the precognition problem. *In* Ludwig, J. K. ed. Philosophy and parapsychology p341-49

Cooper, D. E. ESP and the materialist theory of mind. *In* Thakur, S. C. ed. Philosophy and psychical research p59-80

Gauld, A. ESP and attempts to explain it. *In* Thakur, S. C. ed. Philosophy and psychical research p17-45

Heywood, R. Illusion—or what? *In* Life after death p203-37

Meehl, P. E. and Scriven, M. Compatibility of science and ESP. *In* Wheatley, J. M. O. and Edge, H. L. eds. Philosophical dimensions of parapsychology p405-08

Mundle, C. W. K. Strange facts in search of a theory. *In* Wheatley, J. M. O. and Edge, H. L. eds. Philosophical dimensions of parapsychology p76-97

Price, G. R. Science and the supernatural. *In* Ludwig, J. K. ed. Philosophy and parapsychology p145-71

Price, G. R. Where is the definitive experiment? *In* Ludwig, J. K. ed. Philosophy and parapsychology p196-202

Rhine, J. B. The experiment should fit the hypothesis. *In* Ludwig, J. K. ed. Philosophy and parapsychology p202-04

Rhine, J. B. The science of nonphysical nature. *In* Ludwig, J. K. ed. Philosophy and parapsychology p117-27

Roll, W. G. ESP and memory. *In* Wheatley, J. M. O. and Edge, H. L. eds. Philosophical dimensions of parapsychology p154-84

Wheatley, J. M. O. Knowledge, empiricism and ESP. *In* Wheatley, J. M. O. and Edge, H. L. eds. Philosophical dimensions of parapsychology p142-53

Wheatley, J. M. O. Notes on guessing. *In* Ludwig, J. K. ed. Philosophy and parapsychology p245-54

Extraterritoriality. See Exterritoriality

Eyck, Jan van

About individual works
The adoration of the Lamb

Meyers, J. Van Eyck and The Fall. *In* Meyers, J. Painting and the novel p148-56

Eye

See also Eye (in religion, folklore, etc.)

Movements

Gippenrieter, Y. B. and Romanov, V. Y. A method of investigation of the internal form of visual activity. *In* Perception p227-49

Kolers, P. A. Reading pictures and reading text. *In* Perkins, D. and Leondar, B. eds. The arts and cognition p136-64

Eye (in religion, folklore, etc.)

Coomaraswamy, A. K. Le Corps parsemé d'yeux. *In* Coomaraswamy, A. K. Selected papers v 1 p371-75

See also Evil eye

Eye in art

Coomaraswamy, A. K. The meeting of eyes; excerpt from "Figures of speech or figures of thought: collected essays on the traditional or 'normal' view of art." *In* Coomaraswamy, A. K. Selected papers v 1 p233-37

Eye in literature
 Bishop, M. Eyes and seeing in the poetry of Pierre Reverdy. In Cardinal, R. ed. Sensibility and creation p57-71
 Emden, C. S. Shakespeare and the eye. In Shakespeare survey 26 p129-37

Eyre, James

About
 Quirk, R. A glimpse of eighteenth-century prescriptivism. In Quirk, R. The linguist and the English language p37-45

Ezrahi, Sidra
 The Holocaust writer and the lamentation tradition: responses to catastrophe in Jewish literature. In Rosenfeld, A. H. and Greenberg, I. eds. Confronting the Holocaust p133-49

F

F 111 (Fighter planes)
 Steinbruner, J. D. and Carter, B. Organizational and political dimensions of the strategic posture: the problems of reform. In Long, F. A. and Rathjens, G. W. eds. Arms, defense policy, and arms control p131-54

FBI. See United States. Federal Bureau of Investigation

FCC v. National Citizens Committee for Broadcasting. In The Supreme Court review, 1978 p 1-38

FDA. See United States. Food and Drug Administration

FDES. See Fonds de développement économique et social

FLQ. See Front de Libération du Quebec

Faba, Guido. See Fava, Guido

Faber, Eunice
 Overcoming obstacles to curriculum change in foreign languages. In Minority language and literature p107-14

Fabian, Bernhard
 English books and their eighteenth-century German readers. In Korshin, P. J. ed. The widening circle p117-96

Fabius Pictor, Quintus

About
 Momigliano, A. Did Fabius Pictor lie? In Momigliano, A. Essays in ancient and modern historiography p99-105

Fables
 Henderson, A. C. "Of heigh or lough estat": medieval fabulists as social critics. In Viator: medival and Renaissance studies v9 p265-90
 Richter, D. H. Open form and the fable. In Richter, D. H. Fable's end p 1-21
 Steadman, J. M. "The nun's priest's tale:" flattery and the moralitas of the beast. In Steadman, J. M. Nature into myth p78-85

History and criticism
 Noel, T. Dissolution of a functioning literary genre. In Noel, T. Theories of the fable in the eighteenth century p145-56
 Noel, T. Herder and the romantic turn. In Noel, T. Theories of the fable in the eighteenth century p122-39

Noel, T. The popularity of the fable and the rationale. In Noel, T. Theories of the fable in the eighteenth century p 1-13
 Noel, T. Rousseau and the fable in education. In Noel, T. Theories of the fable in the eighteenth century p102-13
 West, M. L. Near Eastern material in Hellenistic and Roman literature. In Harvard Studies in classical philology v73 p113-34

Fables, English

History and criticism
 Noel, T. Aesop as a popular figure and the fable in England. In Noel, T. Theories of the fable in the eighteenth century p25-37
 Noel, T. Dodsley and England at mid-century. In Noel, T. Theories of the fable in the eighteenth century p114-21

Fables, French

History and criticism
 Noel, T. French ideas at mid-century. In Noel, T. Theories of the fable in the eighteenth century p74-84
 Noel, T. La Fontaine and the seventeenth-century forerunners. In Noel, T. Theories of the fable in the eighteenth century p14-24

Fables, German

History and criticism
 Noel, T. The fable in Germany during the first half-century. In Noel, T. Theories of the fable in the eighteenth century p47-73
 Noel, T. Lessing's Aesopian fables and the anti-Lessing. In Noel, T. Theories of the fable in the eighteenth century p85-101

Fabliaux. See Tales, French

Fabricant, Carole
 Binding and dressing nature's loose tresses: the ideology of Augustan landscape design. In Studies in eighteenth-century culture v8 p109-35

Faccio, Rina

About
 Pacifici, S. Women writers: Neera and Aleramo. In Pacifici, S. The modern Italian novel: from Capuana to Tozzi p49-67

Face
 Ekman, P. Facial signs: facts, fantasies, and possibilities. In Sebeok, T. A. ed. Sight, sound, and sense p124-56
 See also Physiognomy

Expression
See Facial expression

Face in art
 Bay, E. G. The heart-shaped face in African art. In African images p252-67

A face in the crowd (Motion picture)
 Truffaut, F. Elia Kazan: A face in the crowd. In Truffaut, F. The films in my life p113-15

Facial expression
 Ekman, P. Facial signs: facts, fantasies, and possibilities. In Sebeok, T. A. ed. Sight, sound, and sense p124-56

Fackenheim, Emil L.
 The human condition after Auschwitz: a Jewish testimony a generation after. In Tradition and change in Jewish experience p226-43

Fackenheim, Emil L.—*Continued*

Midrashic existence after the Holocaust: re-flections occasioned by the work of Elie Wiesel. *In* Rosenfeld, A. H. and Greenberg, I. eds. Confronting the Holocaust p99-116

About

Kaufman, W. E. Eugene B. Borowitz and Emil L. Fackenheim: from covenant theology to commanding voice. *In* Kaufman, W. E. Contemporary Jewish philosophies p94-121

Factories

Law and legislation

See Factory laws and legislation

Factory laws and legislation

Great Britain

Carson, W. G. Symbolic and instrumental dimensions of early factory legislation: a case study in the social origins of criminal law. *In* Crime, criminology and public policy p107-38

Factory management

United States

Montgomery, D. Immigrant workers and managerial reform. *In* Immigrants in industrial America, 1850-1920 p96-110

Factory system

China

Parish, W. L. The view from the factory. *In* Terrill, R. ed. The China difference p183-98

Facts (Philosophy)

Miller, J. W. Functioning objects, facts, and artifacts. *In* Miller, J. W. The paradox of cause, and other essays p124-29

Faculty (Education) See Teachers; Universities and colleges—Faculty; and subdivision Faculty under names of specific universities, e.g. Oxford. University—Faculty

Faculty integration

United States

Hook, S. The bias in anti-bias regulations. *In* Gross, B. R. ed. Reverse discrimination p88-96

Pottinger, J. S. The drive toward equality. *In* Gross, B. R. ed. Reverse discrimination p41-49

Todorovich, M. and Glickstein, H. A. Discrimination in higher education: a debate on faculty employment. *In* Gross, B. R. ed. Reverse discrimination p12-40

Fadeev, Aleksandr Aleksandrovich

About individual works

The rout

Mathewson, R. W. Leather men. *In* Mathewson, R. W. The positive hero in Russian literature p179-210

Fadiman, Clifton

A second look: a centennial for Tom. *In* Horn Book Magazine. Crosscurrents of criticism p320-25

Fægri, Knut

Pollination ecology: trends and problems. *In* The Frontiers of human knowledge p275-88

Faessler, Marc

Youth in the year 2000: the problem of values. *In* Adolescence and youth in prospect p125-36

The **faggot** (criticism) Carmines, A. *In* Kauffmann, S. Persons of the drama p261-63

Faience

Egypt—Alexandria

Thompson, D. B. A faience fellah. *In* Studies in classical art and archaeology p175-78

Fair employment practice. See Discrimination in employment

Fair trade (Tariff) See Free trade and protection; Reciprocity

Fairbank, John King

J.R.L.—getting started. *In* Meisner, M. J. and Murphey, R. eds. The Mozartian historian p27-42

Self-expression in China. *In* Terrill, R. ed. The China difference p81-98

Fairbanks, Douglas, 1883-1939

About

Sarris, A. His picture in the papers: a speculation on celebrity in America, based on the life of Douglas Fairbanks, Sr. *In* Sarris, A. Politics and cinema p168-71

Fairer, David

The writing and printing of Joseph Warton's Essay on Pope. *In* Virginia. University. Bibliographical Society. Studies in bibliography v30 p211-19

Fairfield, Roy P.

Learning: rivers and nets! *In* Bundy, R. F. ed. Images of the future: the twenty-first century and beyond p207-17

The paradox of power. *In* Armstrong, T. R. and Cinnamon, K. M. eds. Power and authority in law enforcement p13-22

A teacher as radical humanist. *In* Fairfield, R. P. ed. Humanistic frontiers in American education p237-47

Teacher education: a new immersion! *In* Fairfield, R. P. ed. Humanistic frontiers in American education p75-83

Fairies

Drama

See Fairy plays

Fairlie, Alison

Flaubert and some painters of his time. *In* The Artist and the writer in France p111-25

Fairness. See Justice

Fairs. See Exhibitions; and subdivision Fairs under names of countries, cities, e.g. Nimes—Fairs

Fairy plays

Nicoll, A. Comedy and extravaganza. *In* Nicoll, A. World drama p370-80

Fairy tales

Briggs, K. M. Symbols in fairy tales. *In* Symbols of power p131-55

Lüthi, M. Aspects of the Märchen and the legend. *In* Folklore genres p17-33

Wicker, B. Metaphor and 'fiction.' *In* Wicker, B. The story-shaped world p33-49

Faith

Glicksberg, C. I. Religion and nihilism. *In* Glicksberg, C. I. The literature of nihilism p39-52

Glicksberg, C. I. Unamuno and the quest for faith. *In* Glicksberg, C. I. The literature of nihilism p53-70

Lyas, C. The groundlessness of religious belief. *In* Reason and religion p158-80

Faith—*Continued*

Malcolm, N. The groundlessness of belief. *In* Reason and religion p143-57

Meyer, D. H. American intellectuals and the Victorian crisis of faith. *In* Howe, D. W. ed. Victorian America p59-77

More, P. E. Rationalism and faith; excerpt from "The skeptical approach to religion." *In* Crunden, R. M. ed. The superfluous men p252-60

Parsons, T. Belief, unbelief, and disbelief. *In* Parsons, T. Action theory and the human condition p233-63

Patterson, R. L. An analysis of faith. *In* Fact, value, and perception p85-105

Ricoeur, P. Faith and culture. *In* Ricoeur, P. Political and social essays p125-33

See also Evidence; Faith and reason; Hope; Skepticism

Biblical teaching

Painter, J. Eschatological faith in the Gospel of John. *In* Reconciliation and hope p36-52

Faith and justification. See Justification

Faith and reason

Meyer, D. H. Religion and the experimental method of reasoning. *In* Meyer, D. H. The democratic Enlightenment p3-17

Faith-cure

Barrett, L. E. Healing in a balmyard: the practice of folk healing in Jamaica, W.I. *In* American folk medicine p285-300

Faith healing. See Faith-cure

Faithfulness, Conjugal. Hutchings, P. Æ. *In* Royal Institute of Philosophy. Human values p61-85

Faithorn, Elizabeth

The concept of pollution among the Kâfe of the Papua New Guinea Highlands. *In* Reiter, R. R. ed. Toward an anthropology of women p127-40

Fáj, Attila

Vico as philosopher of metabasis. *In* Giambattista Vico's science of humanity p87-109

el Fakharani, Fawzi

The "Lighthouse" of Abusir in Egypt. *In* Harvard Studies in classical philology v78 p257-72

Fakhry, Majid

Philosophy and history. *In* The Genius of Arab civilization p55-73

Falange Española Tradicionalista y de las Juntas Ofensivas Nacional-Sindicalistas

Southworth, H. R. The Falange: an analysis of Spain's Fascist heritage. *In* Preston, P. ed. Spain in crisis p 1-22

Falangist Movement and Syndicalist Juntas of the National Offensive. See Falange Española Tradicionalista y de las Juntas Ofensivas Nacional-Sindicalistas

Falashas

Leslau, W. Taamrat Emmanuel's notes of Falasha monks and holy places. *In* Salo Wittmayer Baron v2 p623-37

Falk, Eugene H.

Some concepts of the tragic in versions of Electra. *In* Creative encounter p3-16

Falk, Richard Anderson

Arms control, foreign policy, and global reform. *In* Long, F. A. and Rathjens, G. W. eds. Arms, defense policy, and arms control p35-52

CIA covert operations and international law. *In* Borosage, R. L. and Marks, J. D. eds. The CIA file p142-58

Normative constraints on statecraft: some comments on Morgenthau's perspective. *In* [Truth and tragedy]: a tribute to Hans Morgenthau p77-84

Toward a new world order: modest methods and drastic visions. *In* On the creation of a just world order p211-58

Falk, Robert

Henry James's The American as a centennial novel. *In* Essays in honor of Russel B. Nye p31-41

Fall of man

McKelway, A. J. Eden revisited: hope beyond tragedy. *In* The Context of contemporary theology p25-42

Fall of man in literature

Hill, T. D. The fall of angels and man in the Old English Genesis B. *In* Anglo-Saxon poetry: essays in appreciation p279-90

The fall of the House of Usher (Moving-picture by James Sibley Watson, Jr.)

Weaver, M. Edgar Allan Poe and the early avant-garde film. *In* English Association. Essays and studies, 1977 p73-85

The fall of the House of Usher (Moving-picture by Jean Epstein)

Weaver, M. Edgar Allan Poe and the early avant-garde film. *In* English Association. Essays and studies, 1977 p73-85

Fallibility. See Errors

Fallico, Arturo B.

Philosophy and human commitment. *In* The Abdication of philosophy: philosophy and the public good p81-87

Fallis, Guadalupe Valdés

Spanish language programs for Hispanic minorities: current needs and priorities. *In* Minority language and literature p86-98

Fallon, Kenneth P.

Participatory management: an alternative in human service delivery systems. *In* Managing nonprofit organizations p244-51

Fallon, Robert Thomas

Miltonic documents in the Public Record Office, London. *In* Virginia. University. Bibliographical Society. Studies in bibliography v32 p82-100

Fallout, Radioactive. See Radioactive fallout

Falsehood. See Truthfulness and falsehood

Falstaff (Motion picture)

Jorgens, J. J. Orson Welles's Chimes at midnight (Falstaff) *In* Jorgens, J. J. Shakespeare on film p106-21

Fama (The word)

Yavetz, Z. Existimatio, fama, and the ides of March. *In* Harvard Studies in classical philology v78 p35-65

Families, Afro-American. See Afro-American families

Family

Aberlee, K. G. The origin of the family. *In* Reiter, R. R. ed. Toward an anthropology of women p51-76

Ariès, P. The family and the city. *In* Rossi, A. S.; Kagan, J. and Hareven, T. K. eds. The family p227-35

Same as: Ariès, P. The family and the city in the Old World and the New. *In* Tufte, V. and Meyerhoff, B. G. eds. Changing images of the family p29-41

Family—*Continued*

Ariès, P. A prison of love; excerpt from "Centuries of childhood." *In* Gross, B. and Gross, R. eds. The children's rights movement p135-40

Corson, J. A. Families as mutual control systems: optimization by systematization of reinforcement. *In* Behavior modification and families p317-30

Cottle, T. J. An unemployed family. *In* On the making of Americans p143-72

Entwisle, D. R. Socialization and the young family. *In* Major social issues p208-16

Kalish, R. A. Dying and preparing for death: a view of families. *In* Feifel, H. [ed.] New meanings of death p215-32

Lautman, F. Differences or changes in family organization. *In* Family and society p251-61

Lidz, T. The family, myth, and ethics. *In* Psychiatry and the humanities v1 p173-90

Maccoby, E. E. Current changes in the family and their impact upon the socialization of children. *In* Major social issues p195-207

Margolis, J. Z. and Margolis, C. The separation of marriage and family. *In* Feminism and philosophy p291-307

Patterson, G. R. The aggressive child: victim and architect of a coercive system. *In* Behavior modification and families p267-316

Piotrowski, J. Family and adolescents in the near future. *In* Adolescence and youth in prospect p159-70

Risley, T. R.; Clark, H. B. and Cataldo, M. F. Behavioral technology for the normal middle-class family. *In* Behavior modification and families p34-60

Rosenberg, C. E. Introduction: History and experience. *In* Rosenberg, C. E. ed. The family in history p 1-11

Rossi, A. S. A biosocial perspective on parenting. *In* Rossi, A. S.; Kagan, J. and Hareven, T. K. eds. The family p1-32

Sennett, R. Destructive Gemeinschaft. *In* Beyond the crisis p171-97

Whiting, B. B. The dependency hang-up and experiments in alternative life styles. *In* Major social issues p217-26

See also Divorce; Domestic relations; Fathers; Kinship; Matriarchy; Parent and child; Single-parent family; Tribes and tribal system

Economic aspects

Sawhill, I. V. Economic perspectives on the family. *In* Rossi, A. S.; Kagan, J. and Hareven, T. K. eds. The family p115-26

History

Kern, S. Explosive intimacy: psychodynamics of the Victorian family. *In* DeMause, L. ed. The new psychohistory p29-53

Rich, A. C. The antifeminist woman. *In* Rich, A. C. On lies, secrets, and silence p69-84

Wrigley, E. A. Reflections on the history of the family. *In* Rossi, A. S.; Kagan, J. and Hareven, T. K. eds. The family p71-86

Law

See Domestic relations

Research

See Family research

Asia

Madge, C. The relevance of family patterns in the process of modernization in East Asia. *In* Social organization and the applications of anthropology p161-95

Austria

Krebs, E. and Schwarz, M. Austria. *In* Kamerman, S. B. and Kahn, A. J. eds. Family policy p183-216

Canada

Armitage, A. Canada. *In* Kamerman, S. B and Kahn, A. J. eds. Family policy p367-99

China—History

Eberhard, W. The upper-class family in traditional China. *In* Rosenberg, C. E. ed. The family in history p59-94

Czechoslovakia

Vergeiner, W. Czechoslovakia. *In* Kamerman, S. B. and Kahn, A. J. eds. Family policy p91-116

Denmark

Vedel-Petersen, J. Denmark. *In* Kamerman, S. B. and Kahn, A. J. eds. Family policy p295-327

England—History

Stone, L. The rise of the nuclear family in early modern England: the patriarchal stage. *In* Rosenberg, C. E. ed. The family in history p13-57

Europe

Coleman, E. R. Infanticide in the early Middle Ages. *In* Stuard, S. M. ed. Women in medieval society p47-70

Europe—History

Sabean, D. W. Aspects of kinship behaviour and property in rural Western Europe before 1800. *In* Family and inheritance p96-111

Scott, J. W. and Tilly, L. A. Women's work and the family in nineteenth century Europe. *In* Rosenberg, C. E. ed. The family in history p145-78

Finland

Lindgren, J. Finland. *In* Kamerman, S. B. and Kahn, A. J. eds. Family policy p270-94

France

Baulant, M. The scattered family: another aspect of seventeenth-century demography. *In* Family and society p104-16

Questiaux, N. and Fournier, J. France. *In* Kamerman, S. B. and Kahn, A. J. eds. Family policy p117-82

France—History

Le Roy Ladurie, E. Family structures and inheritance customs in sixteenth-century France. *In* Family and inheritance p37-70

Le Roy Ladurie, E. A system of customary law: family structures and inheritance customs in sixteenth-century France. *In* Family and society p75-103

Same as Le Roy Ladurie, E. Family structures and inheritance customs in sixteenth-century France. *In* Family and inheritance p37-70

France—Mâcon

Duby, G. Lineage. nobility, and chivalry in the region of Mâcon during the twelfth century. *In* Family and society p16-40

Family—*Continued*

Genoa—History

Hughes, D. O. Domestic ideals and social behavior: evidence from medieval Genoa. *In* Rosenberg, C. E. ed. The family in history p115-43

Hughes, D. O. Urban growth and family structure in medieval Genoa. *In* Towns in societies p105-30

Germany—History

Berkner, L. K. Inheritance, land tenure and peasant family structure: a German regional comparison. *In* Family and inheritance p71-95

Germany, West

Neidhardt, F. The Federal Republic of Germany. *In* Kamerman, S. B. and Kahn, A. J. eds. Family policy p217-38

Ghana

Nukunya, G. K. The family and social change. *In* Colonialism and change p163-77

Great Britain

Land, H. and Parker, R. United Kingdom. *In* Kamerman, S. B. and Kahn, A. J. eds. Family policy p331-66

Great Britain—History

Roberts, D. The paterfamilias of the Victorian governing classes. *In* Wohl, A. S. ed. The Victorian family p59-81

Hungary

Ferge, Z. Hungary. *In* Kamerman, S. B. and Kahn, A. J. eds. Family policy p68-90

Israel

Honig, M. H. and Shamai, N. Israel. *In* Kamerman, S. B. and Kahn, A. J. eds. Family policy p400-27

Japan

Wagatsuma, H. Some aspects of the contemporary Japanese family: once Confucian, now fatherless? *In* Rossi, A. S.; Kagan, J. and Hareven, T. K. eds. The family p181-210

Kenya

Whiting, B. B. Changing life styles in Kenya. *In* Rossi, A. S.; Kagan, J. and Hareven, T. K. eds. The family p211-26

Massachusetts—Charlestown

Crandall, R. J. Family types, social structure, and mobility in early America: Charlestown, Massachusetts, a case study. *In* Tufte, V. and Myerhoff, B. G. eds. Changing images of the family p61-81

New Hampshire—Manchester

Hareven, T. K. Family and work patterns of immigrant laborers in a planned industrial town, 1900-1930. *In* Immigrants in industrial America, 1850-1920 p47-66

New York (State)—Buffalo

Yans-McLaughlin, V. A flexible tradition: South Italian immigrants confront a new work experience. *In* Immigrants in industrial America, 1850-1920 p67-84

Norway

Henriksen, H. V. and Holter, H. Norway. *In* Kamerman, S. B. and Kahn, A. J. eds. Family policy p49-67

Poland

Kula, W. The seigneury and the peasant family in eighteenth-century Poland. *In* Family and society p192-203

Sokołowska, M. Poland. *In* Kamerman, S. B. and Kahn, A. J. eds. Family policy p239-69

Sweden

Liljeström, R. Sweden. *In* Kamerman, S. B. and Kahn, A. J. eds. Family policy p19-48

Turkey

Cuisenier, J. Kinship and social organization in the Turko-Mongolian cultural area. *In* Family and society p204-36

Tuscany

Klapisch, C. and Demonet, M. "A uno pane e uno vino": the rural Tuscan family at the beginning of the fifteenth century. *In* Family and society p41-74

United States

Bronfenbrenner, U. "Our system for making human beings human is breaking down." *In* Gross, B. and Gross, R. eds. The children's rights movement p251-55

Downs, A. The impact of housing policies on family life in the United States since World War II. *In* Rossi, A. S.; Kagan, J. and Hareven, T. K. eds. The family p163-80

Golab, C. The impact of the industrial experience on the immigrant family: the huddled masses reconsidered. *In* Immigrants in industrial America, 1850-1920 p 1-32

Hareven, T. K. Historical changes in the life course and the family: policy implications. *In* Major social issues p338-45

Harkess, S. Family and sex roles in urban society. *In* Handbook of contemporary urban life p163-201

Kamerman, S. B. and Kahn, A. J. The United States. *In* Kamerman, S. B. and Kahn, A. J. eds. Family policy p428-75

Kuznets, S. S. Demographic aspects of the distribution of income among families: recent trends in the United States. *In* Econometrics and economic theory p223-45

Laslett, B. The significance of family membership. *In* Tufte, V. and Myerhoff, B. G. eds. Changing images of the family p231-50

Orr, J. B. The changing family: a social ethical perspective. *In* Tufte, V. and Myerhoff, B. G. eds. Changing images of the family p377-88

Shannon, W. V. Our lost children. *In* Gross, B, and Gross, R. eds. The children's rights movement p148-50

Simić, A. White ethnic and Chicano families: continuity and adaptation in the New World. *In* Tufte, V. and Myerhoff, B. G. eds. Changing images of the family p251-69

Skolnick, A. Public images, private realities: the American family in popular culture and social science. *In* Tufte, V. and Myerhoff, B. G. eds. Changing images of the family p297-315

Stannard, D. E. Changes in the American family: fiction and reality. *In* Tufte, V. and Myerhoff, B. G. eds. Changing images of the family p83-96

Veysey, L. R. Growing up in America. *In* Alderson, W. T. ed. American issues p113-28

Family—United States—Continued

Weiss, R. S. A new marital form: the marriage of uncertain duration. *In* On the making of Americans p221-33

See also Afro-American families

United States—History

Demos, J. Images of the American family, then and now. *In* Tufte, V. and Myerhoff, B. G. eds. Changing images of the family p43-60

Family allowances

Blaydon, C. C. and Stack, C. B. Income support policies and the family. *In* Rossi, A. S.; Kagan, J. and Hareven, T. K. eds. The family p147-62

Family and communism. See Communism and family

Family and state. See Family policy

Family courts. See Juvenile courts

Family group therapy. See Family psychotherapy

Family Herald

Michell, S. The forgotten woman of the period: penny weekly family magazines of the 1840's and 1850's. *In* Vicinus, M. ed. A widening sphere p29-51

Family in art

Kunzle, D. William Hogarth: the ravaged child in the corrupt city. *In* Tufte, V. and Myerhoff, B. G. eds. Changing images of the family p99-140

Family in literature

Auerbach, N. Austen and Alcott on matriarchy: new women or new wives? *In* Spilka, M. ed. Towards a poetics of fiction p266-86

Auerbach, N. Waiting together: two families. *In* Auerbach, N. Communities of women p33-73

Boyers, R. The family novel. *In* Boyers, R. Excursions p5-24

Bradford, M. E. Fairchild as composite protagonist in Delta wedding. *In* Prenshaw, P. W. ed. Eudora Welty p201-07

Brownell, D. B. The two worlds of Charlotte Yonge. *In* The Worlds of Victorian fiction p165-78

Caserio, R. L. The family plot: Conrad, Joyce, Lawrence, Woolf, and Faulkner. *In* Caserio, R. L. Plot, story, and the novel p232-79

DiSalvo, J. Blake encountering Milton: politics and the family in Paradise lost and The four Zoas. *In* Wittreich, J. A. ed. Milton and the line of vision p143-84

Ellis, K. Monsters in the garden: Mary Shelley and the bourgeois family. *In* Levine, G. L. and Knoepflmacher, U. C. eds. The endurance of Frankenstein p123-42

Ferguson, M. A. Losing battles as a comic epic in prose. *In* Prenshaw, P. W. ed. Eudora Welty p305-24

Gossett, L. Y. Losing battles: festival and celebration. *In* Prenshaw, P. W. ed. Eudora Welty p341-50

Gross, S. L. A long day's living: the angelic ingenuities of Losing battles. *In* Prenshaw, P. W. ed. Eudora Welty p325-40

Hardy, J. E. Marrying down in Eudora Welty's novels. *In* Prenshaw, P. W. ed. Eudora Welty p93-119

Hinton, J. L. The role of family in Delta wedding, Losing battles and The optimist's daughter. *In* Prenshaw, P. W. ed. Eudora Welty p120-31

Kern, S. Explosive intimacy: psychodynamics of the Victorian family. *In* DeMause, L. ed. The new psychohistory p29-53

Kerr, E. M. The world of Eudora Welty's women. *In* Prenshaw, P. W. ed. Eudora Welty p132-48

Manning, S. Families in Dickens. *In* Tufte, V. and Myerhoff. B. G. eds. Changing images of the family p141-53

Miller, A. The family in modern drama. *In* Miller, A. The theater essays of Arthur Miller p69-85

Palamari, D. The shark who swallowed his epoch: family, nature, and society in the novels of Emile Zola. *In* Tufte, V. and Myerhoff. B. G. eds. Changing images of the family p155-72

Rice, T. J. Barnaby Rudge: a vade mecum for the theme of domestic government in Dickens. *In* Dickens Studies Annual v7 p81-102

Tobin, P. D. "A colored spiral in a ball of glass": Vladimir Nabokov, Ada, or Ardor: a family chronicle. *In* Tobin, P. D. Time and the novel p133-63

Tobin, P. D. Conclusion: whither the novel: the wager on surface. *In* Tobin, P. D. Time and the novel p192-213

Tobin, P. D. "Everything is known": Gabriel García Márquez, One hundred years of solitude. *In* Tobin, P. D. Time and the novel p164-91

Tobin, P. D. Introduction: whence the novel: the genealogical imperative. *In* Tobin, P. D. Time and the novel p3-28

Tobin, P. D. "Links in a chain": Thomas Mann, Buddenbrooks. *In* Tobin, P. D. Time and the novel p54-80

Tobin, P. D. "The shadowy attenuation of time": William Faulkner, Absalom, Absalom! *In* Tobin, P. D. Time and the novel p107-32

Tobin, P. D. Subverting the father: some nineteenth-century precursors. *In* Tobin, P. D. Time and the novel p29-53

Family in mass media

Wahlstrom, B. J. Images of the family in the mass media: an American iconography? *In* Tufte, V. and Myerhoff, B. G. eds. Changing images of the family p193-227

Family law. See Domestic relations

Family life education. See Sex instruction

Family planning. See Birth control

Family policy

Kamerman, S. B. and Kahn, A. J. Family policy as field and perspective. *In* Kamerman, S. B. and Kahn, A. J. eds. Family policy p476-503

Austria

Krebs, E. and Schwarz, M. Austria. *In* Kamerman, S. B. and Kahn, A. J. eds. Family policy p183-216

Canada

Armitage, A. Canada. *In* Kamerman, S. B. and Kahn, A. J. eds. Family policy p367-99

Czechoslovakia

Vergeiner, W. Czechoslovakia. *In* Kamerman, S. B. and Kahn, A. J. eds. Family policy p91-116

Fanon, Frantz

About

Parry, A. Fanon and the Black Panthers. *In* Parry, A. Terrorism, from Robespierre to Arafat p301-21

About individual works

The wretched of the earth

Letman, S. T. Some sociological aspects of terror-violence in a colonial setting. *In* International terrorism and political crimes p33-42

Fantastic fiction

Manlove, C. N. Conclusion. *In* Manlove, C. N. Modern fantasy p258-93

Manlove, C. P. Introduction. *In* Manlove, C. P. Modern fantasy p 1-12

See also Science fiction

History and criticism

Alexander, L. High fantasy and heroic romance. *In* Horn Book Magazine. Crosscurrents of criticism p170-77

Drury, R. W. "Realism plus fantasy equals magic." *In* Horn Book Magazine. Crosscurrents of criticism p178-84

Fredericks, S. C. Revivals of ancient mythologies in current science fiction and fantasy. *In* Clareson, T. D. ed. Many futures, many worlds p50-65

Langton, J. The weak place in the cloth: a study of fantasy for children. *In* Horn Book Magazine. Crosscurrents of criticism p185-96

Fantastic literature, English

History and criticism

Prickett, S. The evolution of a word. *In* Prickett, S. Victorian fantasy p 1-37

19th century—

History and criticism

Prickett, S. Christmas at Scrooge's. *In* Prickett, S. Victorian fantasy p38-74

Prickett, S. Dreams and nightmares: monsters under the hill. *In* Prickett, S. Victorian fantasy p75-113

Fantasy

Barfield, O. Where is fancy bred? *In* Barfield, O. The rediscovery of meaning, and other essays p79-92

Fantasy (The word)

Prickett, S. The evolution of a word. *In* Prickett, S. Victorian fantasy p 1-37

Fantasy in literature

Barfield, O. Where is fancy bred? *In* Barfield, O. The rediscovery of meaning, and other essays p79-92

Hardy, B. N. Fantasy and dream. *In* Hardy, B. N. Tellers and listeners p19-55

Sheckley, R. The search for the marvellous. *In* Nicholls, P. ed. Science fiction at large p185-98

Fantham, Elaine

Adaptation and survival: a genre study of Roman comedy in relation to its Greek sources. *In* Ruggiers, P. G. ed. Versions of medieval comedy p19-49

Fantini, Mario D.

From school system to educational system. *In* Wagschal, P. H. ed. Learning tomorrows p109-17

Relevance=humanistic education. *In* Fairfield, R. P. ed. Humanistic frontiers in American education p28-36

Far Eastern question. See Eastern question (Far East)

al-Fārābī

About individual works

The attainment of happiness

Mahdi, M. Remarks on Alfarabi's Attainment of happiness. *In* Essays on Islamic philosophy and science p47-66

Faraday, Michael

About

Buchwald, J. Z. William Thomson and the mathematization of Faraday's electrostatics. *In* Historical studies in the physical sciences v8 p101-36

Davie, D. Dissent and the Evangelicals, 1800-1850. *In* Davie, D. A gathered Church p55-72

Doran, B. G. Origins and consolidation of field theory in nineteenth-century Britain: from the mechanical to the electromagnetic view of nature. *In* Historical studies in the physical sciences v6 p133-260

Farah, Caesar E.

Censorship and freedom of expression in Ottoman Syria and Egypt. *In* Nationalism in a non-national state p151-94

Farber, Leslie H.

About individual works

The ways of the will

Friedman, M. S. Healing through meeting: a dialogical approach to psychotherapy and family therapy. *In* Psychiatry and the humanities v 1 p191-233

Farber, Manny

The decline of the actor. *In* Denby, D. ed. Awake in the dark p340-49

Preston Sturges: success in the movies. *In* Denby, D. ed. Awake in the dark p305-19

Underground films; excerpt from "Negative space." *In* Denby, D. ed. Awake in the dark p65-77

Farce

Sumberg, L. A. M. From farce in the âge bourgeois (1440-1500) to farce Molièresque: the structure of generic change. *In* Johnson, R. B.; Neumann, E. S. and Trail, G. T. eds. Molière and the commonwealth of letters: patrimony and posterity p430-42

History and criticism

Wilder, T. N. Noting the nature of farce. *In* Wilder, T. N. American characteristics, and other essays p112-14

Farer, Tom J.

The changing context of inter-American relations. *In* Farer, T. J. ed. The future of the inter-American system p xv-xxiii

Limiting intraregional violence: the costs of regional peacekeeping. *In* Farer, T. J. ed. The future of the inter-American system p195-203

On a collision course: the American campaign for human rights and the antiradical bias in the Third World. *In* Kommers, D. P. and Loescher, G. D. eds. Human rights and American foreign policy p263-77

Farer, Tom J.—*Continued*

Policy implications of the possible conflict between capitalist development and human rights in developing countries. *In* Farer, T. J. ed. The future of the inter-American system p115-18

Toward regional accommodation: is there anything to negotiate? *In* Farer, T. J. ed. The future of the inter-American system p66-72

Faris, James C.

The productive basis of aesthetic traditions: some African examples. *In* Greenhalgh, M. and Megaw, J. V. S. eds. Art in society p317-39

Farley-Hills, David

The benevolence of laughter: comic poetry of the Commonwealth and Restoration

Contents

Comic poetry of the Commonwealth
Hudibras
John Dryden
John Wilmot, Earl of Rochester
Last instructions to a painter
Rochester: the major satires

Farm laborers. See Agricultural laborers

Farm life. See Country life; Rural conditions

Farm life in literature

Gray, R. J. The good farmer: some variations on a historical theme. *In* Gray, R. J. The literature of memory p106-49

Farm tenancy

Economic aspects—United States

See Share-cropping

Farm workers. See Agricultural laborers

Farmer, Norman K.

Herrick's Hesperidean garden: ut pictura poesis applied. *In* Rollin, R. B. and Patrick, J. M. eds. "Trust to good verses": Herrick tercentenary essays p15-51

Farmer, Penelope

Discovering the pattern. *In* Blishen, E. ed. The thorny paradise p103-07

Farmer, Philip José

About

Wymer, T. L. Philip José Farmer: the trickster as artist. *In* Clareson, T. D. ed. Voices for the future: essays on major science fiction writers v2 p 34-55

Farmers. See Peasantry

Farmers, Afro-Americans. See Afro-American farmers

Farming. See Agriculture

Farms. See Ranches

Farms, Experimental. See Agricultural experiment stations

Farneti, Paolo

Social conflict, parliamentary fragmentation, institutional shift, and the rise of fascism: Italy. *In* The Breakdown of democratic regimes pt2 p3-33

Farnham, Anthony E.

The art of high prosaic seriousness: John Gower as didactic raconteur. *In* The Learned and the lewed p161-73

Farnie, D. A.

The Cotton famine in Great Britain. *In* Great Britain and her world, 1750-1914 p153-78

Farnol, Jeffery

About

Turner, E. S. The world of Jeffery Farnol. *In* The Saturday book 34 p45-52

Farnsworth, Beatrice Brodsky

Bolshevik alternatives and the Soviet family: the 1926 marriage law debate. *In* Women in Russia p139-65

Farnsworth, Lee Winfield

Hirota Kōki: the diplomacy of expansionism. *In* Burns, R. D. and Bennett, E. M. eds. Diplomats in crisis p227-49

Farquhar, George

About individual works

The beaux' stratagem

Kenny, S. S. Piracies of two plays by Farquhar. *In* Virginia. University. Bibliographical Society. Studies in bibliography v28 p297-305

The constant couple; or, A trip to the Jubilee

Cope, J. I. The constant couple: Farquhar's four-plays-in-one. *In* ELH essays for Earl R. Wasserman p184-200

The recruiting officer

Kenny, S. S. Piracies of two plays by Farquhar. *In* Virginia. University. Bibliographical Society. Studies in bibliography v28 p297-305

The stage-coach

Kenny, S. S. The mystery of Farquhar's Stage-coach reconsidered. *In* Virginia. University. Bibliographical Society. Studies in bibliography v32 p219-36

Farrell, James Thomas

Literary essays, 1954-1974

Contents

A chance meeting with Mencken and Masters
The collected stories of Isaac Babel
The development of the American novel
A Dreiser revival: introduction to the Laurel Dreiser
Ernest Hemingway
The eternal question of John O'Hara
F. Scott Fitzgerald and his romanticism
From bunk to buncombe
Harold Frederic's The damnation of Theron Ware
Harvey Swados: a Veblen of the novel
How should we rate Dos Passos?
The Irish cultural renaissance in the last century
Journalism or creative writing course?
A Mencken revival: introduction to Prejudices
The mind of Ben Hecht
Nelson Algren's A walk on the wild side
On being an American writer
On Oscar Wilde's De profundis
On Zola
Sinclair Lewis
The value of literature in modern society
Writers of the thirties
Writers with few readers

About

Branch, E. M. James T. Farrell. *In* Walcutt, C. C. ed. Seven novelists in the American naturalist tradition p245-89

Branch, E. M. James T. Farrell: four decades after Studs Lonigan. *In* Filler, L. ed. A question of quality: popularity and value in modern creative writing p80-91

Farson, Richard Evans

Birthrights. *In* Gross, B. and Gross, R. eds. The children's rights movement p325-28

Fasciculus morum

Wenzel, S. The English verses in the Fasciculus morum. *In* Chaucer and Middle English studies in honour of Rossell Hope Robbins p230-48

Fascism

Carsten, F. L. Interpretations of fascism. *In* Laqueur, W. Z. ed. Fascism: a reader's guide p415-34

Hughes, H. S. Conclusion: The sea change. *In* Hughes, H. S. The sea change p240-72

Hughes, H. S. The critique of fascism. *In* Hughes, H. S. The sea change p70-133

Sternhell, Z. Fascist ideology. *In* Laqueur, W. Z. ed. Fascism: a reader's guide p315-76

Weber, E. J. Revolution? Counterrevolution? What revolution? *In* Laqueur, W. Z. ed. Fascism: a reader's guide p435-67

See also National socialism

Economic aspects

Milward, A. S. Fascism and the economy *In* Laqueur, W. Z. ed. Fascism: a reader's guide p379-412

Moving-pictures

Sarris, A. Fascinating fascism meets leering leftism. *In* Sarris, A. Politics and cinema p107-15

Europe

Linz Storch de Gracia, J. J. Some notes toward a comparative study of fascism in sociological historical perspective. *In* Laqueur, W. Z. ed. Fascism: a reader's guide p3-121

Europe, Eastern

Vago, B. Fascism in Eastern Europe. *In* Laqueur, W. Z. ed. Fascism: a reader's guide p229-53

Europe, Western

Payne, S. G. Fascism in Western Europe. *In* Laqueur, W. Z. ed. Fascism: a reader's guide p295-311

Italy

Farneti, P. Social conflict, parliamentary fragmentation, institutional shift, and the rise of fascism: Italy. *In* The Breakdown of democratic regimes pt2 p3-33

Lyttelton, A. Italian fascism. *In* Laqueur, W. Z. ed. Fascism: a reader's guide p125-50

Italy—Public opinion

Nazzaro, P. Fascist and anti-Fascist reaction in the United States to the Matteotti murder. *In* Studies in Italian American social history p50-65

Latin America

Hennessy, C. A. M. Fascism and Populism in Latin America. *In* Laqueur, W. Z. ed. Fascism: a reader's guide p255-94

Spain

Southworth, H. R. The Falange: an analysis of Spain's Fascist heritage. *In* Preston, P. ed. Spain in crisis p 1-22

Fascism and architecture

Italy

Millon, H. A. Some new towns in Italy in the 1930s. *In* Millon, H. A. and Nochlin, L. eds. Art and architecture in the service of politics p326-41

Italy—Rome (City)

Kostof, S. K. The Emperor and the Duce: the planning of Piazzale Augusto Imperatore in Rome. *In* Millon, H. A. and Nochlin, L. eds. Art and architecture in the service of politics p270-325

Fascism and art

Sontag, S. Fascinating fascism. *In* Nichols, B. ed. Movies and methods p31-43

Fascism and literature

Cairns, C. The political conscience. *In* Cairns, C. Italian literature p45-90

Glicksberg, C. I. Ezra Pound and the commitment to fascism. *In* Glicksberg, C. I. The literature of commitment p100-10

Glicksberg, C. I. Wyndham Lewis: the reactionary artist and his commitment. *In* Glicksberg, C. I. The literature of commitment p84-99

Pacifici, S. Background of the modern Italian novel. *In* Pacifici, S. The modern Italian novel: from Pea to Moravia p 1-17

Spender, S. Notes on revolutionaries and reactionaries: Reactionaries. *In* Spender, S. The thirties and after p154-65

Fashion

Carnes, V. Icons of popular fashion. *In* Browne, R. B. and Fishwick, M. W. eds. Icons of America p228-40

See also Costume

Fass, Paula S.

Television as cultural document: promises and problems. *In* Television as a cultural force p37-57

Fassò, Guido

The problem of law and the historical origin of The new science. *In* Giambattista Vico's science of humanity p3-14

Fastolf, Sir John

About

Armstrong, C. A. J. Sir John Fastolf and the law of arms. *In* War, literature, and politics in the late Middle Ages p46-56

Fasts and feasts. See Church calendar; Festivals; Holidays

Fat city (Motion picture)

Samuels, C. T. How not to film a novel. *In* Samuels, C. T. Mastering the film, and other essays p190-97

Fatalism. See Fate and fatalism

Fatally ill children. See Terminally ill children

Fate and fatalism

Benjamin, W. Fate and character. *In* Benjamin, W. Reflections p304-11

Pine, M. Pietro Pomponazzi and the medieval tradition of God's foreknowledge. *In* Philosophy and humanism p100-15

Reesor, M. E. Necessity and fate in Stoic philosophy. *In* Rist, J. M. ed. The Stoics p187-202

See also Free will and determinism

Fate and fatalism in literature

Cole, P. B. Emerson, England, and fate. *In* Levin, D. ed. Emerson: prophecy, metamorphosis, and influence p83-105

The fates of men

Isaacs, N. D. Up a tree: to see The fates of men. *In* Anglo-Saxon poetry: essays in appreciation p363-75

Fath

Weisband, E. and Roguly, D. Palestinian terrorism: violence, verbal strategy, and legitimacy. *In* International terrorism p258-319

Father and child

Roberts, D. The paterfamilias of the Victorian governing classes. *In* Wohl, A. S. ed. The Victorian family p59-81

See also Fathers and sons; Paternal deprivation

Father-child relationship. See Father and child

Father-separated children. See Paternal deprivation

Fathers

Arnstein, H. S. The crisis of becoming a father. *In* Gross, L. ed. Sexual issues in marriage p93-100

See also Parent and child

Fathers and daughters in literature

Hoy, C. H. Fathers and daughters in Shakespeare's romances. *In* Shakespeare's romances reconsidered p77-90

Fathers and sons

Cottle, T. J. The child is father to the man; excerpt from "The abandoners." *In* Gross, B. and Gross, R. eds. The children's rights movement p58-71

Fathers and sons in literature

Tobin, P. D. Conclusion: whither the novel: the wager on surface. *in* Tobin, P. D. Time and the novel p192-213

Tobin, P. D. "Links in a chain": Thomas Mann, Buddenbrooks. *In* Tobin, P. D. Time and the novel p54-80

Tobin, P. D. "The shadowy attenuation of time": William Faulkner, Absalom, Absalom! *In* Tobin, P. D. Time and the novel p107-32

Tobin, P. D. Subverting the father: some nineteenth-century precursors. *In* Tobin, P. D. Time and the novel p29-53

Fathers in literature

Knoepflmacher, U. C. Thoughts on the aggression of daughters. *In* Levine, G. L. and Knopflmacher, U. C. eds. The endurance of Frankenstein p88-119

Fathers of the Church

Rice, E. F. The humanist idea of Christian antiquity and the impact of Greek patristic work on sixteenth-century thought. *In* Classical influences on European culture A.D. 1500-1700 p199-203

Wallach, L. The Libri Carolini and patristics, Latin and Greek. *In* Wallach, L. Diplomatic studies in Latin and Greek documents from the Carolingian age p59-122

See also Church history—Primitive and early church, ca. 30-600

Fatigue, Mental. See Boredom

Faulhaber, Charles Bailey

The letter-writer's rhetoric: the Summa dictaminis of Guido Faba. *In* Murphy, J. J. ed. Medieval eloquence p85-111

Faulk, Odie B.

The presidio: fortress or farce? *In* Weber, D. J. ed. New Spain's far northern frontier p67-76

Faulkner, Robert R.

Making violence by doing work: selves, situations, and the world of professional hockey. *In* Social problems in athletics p93-112

Faulkner, Thomas C.

George Crabbe: Murray's 1834 edition of the life and poems. *In* Virginia. University. Bibliographical Society. Studies in bibliography v32 p246-52

Faulkner, William

About

Aaron, D. The South in American history. *In* The South and Faulkner's Yoknapatawpha p3-21

Adams, R. M. Woolf and Faulkner: streams of consciousness. *In* Adams, R. M. Afterjoyce p65-89

Adams, R. P. Faulkner: the European roots. *In* Faulkner: fifty years after The marble faun p21-41

Alexander, M. A. W. Faulkner & race. *In* The Maker and the myth: Faulkner and Yoknapatawpha, 1977 p105-21

Blotner, J. L. Romantic elements in Faulkner. *In* Bornstein, G. ed. Romantic and modern p207-21

Blotner, J. L. The sole owner and proprietor. *In* Faulkner: fifty years after The marble faun p 1-20

Brooks, C. William Faulkner and William Butler Yeats: parallels and affinities. *In* Faulkner: fifty years after The marble faun p139-58

Brown, C. S. Faulkner's localism. *In* The Maker and the myth: Faulkner and Yoknapatawpha, 1977 p3-24

Brown, C. S. Faulkner's universality. *In* The Maker and the myth: Faulkner and Yoknapatawpha, 1977 p146-69

Collins, C. E. Faulkner and certain earlier Southern fiction. *In* Inge, M. T. ed. The frontier humorists p259-65

Cowley, M. Faulkner: the etiology of his art. *In* Cowley, M. —And I worked at the writer's trade p214-30

Donald, M. The fate of the traditional novel. *In* Donald, M. The American novel in the twentieth century p73-107

Gass, W. H. Mr. Blotner, Mr. Feaster, and Mr. Faulkner. *In* Gass, W. H. The world within the word p45-62

Gray, R. J. The individual talent: William Faulkner and the Yoknapatawpha novels. *In* Gray, R. J. The literature of memory p197-256

Guerard, A. J. The Faulknerian voice. *In* The Maker and the myth: Faulkner and Yoknapatawpha, 1977 p25-42

Holman, C. H. Detached laughter in the South. *In* Holman, C. H. Windows on the world p27-47

Inge, M. T. William Faulkner and George Washington Harris: in the tradition of Southwestern humor *In* Inge, M. T. ed. The frontier humorist p266-80

Kawin, B. F. Faulkner's film career: the years with Hawks. *In* Faulkner, modernism, and film: Faulkner and Yoknapatawpha, 1978 p163-81

Kenner, H. Faulkner and the avant-garde. *In* Faulkner, modernism, and film: Faulkner and Yoknapatawpha, 1978 p182-96

Kenner, H. The last novelist. *In* Kenner, H. A homemade world p194-221

Kerr, E. M. The world of Eudora Welty's women. *In* Prenshaw, P. W. ed. Eudora Welty p132-48

Lewis, W. William Faulkner; excerpt from "Men without art." *In* Lewis, W. Enemy salvoes p146-58

Faulkner, William—About—*Continued*

Meriwether, J. B. Faulkner's essays on Anderson. *In* Faulkner: fifty years after The marble faun p159-81

Millgate, M. Faulkner and history. *In* The South and Faulkner's Yoknapatawpha p22-39

Millgate, M. Faulkner and the South: some reflections. *In* The South and Faulkner's Yoknapatawpha p195-210

Momberger, P. Faulkner's "country" as ideal community. *In* Baldwin, K. H. and Kirby, D. K. eds. Individual and community p112-36

Noyes, C. E. Welcome to Faulkner and Yoknapatawpha, 1977. *In* The Maker and the myth: Faulkner and Yoknapatawpha, 1977 pxi-xiv

Page, S. R. Faulkner's sense of the sacred. *In* Faulkner: fifty years after The marble faun p101-21

Peckham, M. The place of sex in the work of William Faulkner. *In* Peckham, M. Romanticism and behavior p159-76

Rose, A. H. The limits of humanity in the fiction of William Faulkner. *In* Rose, A. H. Demonic vision p101-18

Rubin, L. D. William Faulkner: the discovery of a man's vocation. *In* Faulkner: fifty years after The marble faun p43-68

Ruoff, G. W. Faulkner: the way out of the waste land. *In* French, W. G. ed. The twenties p235-48

Simpson, L. P. Faulkner and the legend of the artist. *In* Faulkner: fifty years after The marble faun p69-100

Simpson, L. P. Sex & history: origins of Faulkner's apocrypha. *In* The Maker and the myth: Faulkner and Yoknapatawpha, 1977 p43-70

Simpson, L. P. Yoknapatawpha & Faulkner's fable of civilization. *In* The Maker and the myth: Faulkner and Yoknapatawpha, 1977 p122-45

Tate, A. William Faulkner, 1897-1962. *In* Tate, A. Memoirs and opinions, 1926-1974 p82-86

Turner, D. T. Faulkner and slavery. *In* The South and Faulkner's Yoknapatawpha p62-85

Wagner, L. W. Faulkner and (Southern) women. *In* The South and Faulkner's Yoknapatawpha p128-46

Watkins, F. C. Habet: Faulkner and the ownership of property. *In* Faulkner: fifty years after The marble faun p123-37

West, R. B. Hemingway and Faulkner: Two masters of the modern short story. *In* Benson, J. J. The short stories of Ernest Hemingway: critical essays p2-14

About individual works
Absalom, Absalom!

Hagan, J. Déjà vu and the effect of timelessness in Faulkner's Absalom, Absalom! *In* Garvin, H. R. ed. Makers of the twentieth-century novel p192-207

Lenson, D. R. Classical analogy: Giraudoux versus Faulkner. *In* Lenson, D. R. Achilles' choice p98-116

Rubin, L. D. Scarlett O'Hara and the two Quentin Compsons. *In* The South and Faulkner's Yoknapatawpha p168-94

Tobin, P. D. "The shadowy attenuation of time": William Faulkner, Absalom, Absalom! *In* Tobin, P. D. Time and the novel p107-32

Watkins, E. The fiction of interpretation: Faulkner's Absalom, Absalom! *In* Watkins, E. The critical act p188-212

Young, T. D. Narration as creative act: the role of Quentin Compson in Absalom, Absalom! *In* Faulkner, modernism, and film: Faulkner and Yoknapatawpha, 1978 p82-101

As I lay dying

Richmond, L. J. The education of Vardaman Bundren in Faulkner's As I lay dying. *In* Renaissance and modern p133-42

Slabey, R. M. As I lay dying as an existential novel. *In* Garvin, H. R. ed. Makers of the twentieth-century novel p208-17

Watkins, F. C. As I lay dying: the dignity of earth. *In* Watkins, F. C. In time and place p175-89

Barn burning

Trilling, L. William Faulkner: Barn burning. *In* Trilling, L. Prefaces to The experience of literature p150-55

The bear

Cowley. M. Magic in Faulkner. *In* Faulkner, modernism, and film: Faulkner and Yoknapatawpha, 1978 p3-19

Morris, W. A. The pilgrimage of being. *In* Morris, W. A. Friday's footprint p 1-83

Dry September

Pryse, M. Faulkner's "Dry September" and "Red leaves": caste and outcast. *In* Pryse, M. The mark and the knowledge p92-107

A fable

MacMillan, D. J. His 'magnum o': stoic humanism in Faulkner's A fable. *In* The Stoic strain in American literature p136-76

Go down, Moses

Cleman, J. L. "Pantaloon in black": its place in Go down, Moses. *In* Tennessee Studies in literature v22 p170-81

Hochberg, M. R. The unity of Go down, Moses. *In* Tennessee Studies in literature v21 p58-65

Morris, W. A. The pilgrimage of being. *In* Morris, W. A. Friday's footprint p 1-83

Pilkington, J. Nature's legacy to William Faulkner. *In* The South and Faulkner's Yoknapatawpha p104-27

The hamlet

Stineback, D. C. "The price had been necessity": William Faulkner's The hamlet. *In* Stineback, D. C. Shifting world p142-55

Intruder in the dust

Degenfelder, E. P. Rites of passage: novel to film. *In* Peary, G. and Shatzkin, R. eds. The modern American novel and the movies p178-86

Welty, E. William Faulkner's Intruder in the dust. *In* Welty, E. The eye of the story p207-11

Light in August

Fowler, D. F. Faith as a unifying principle in Faulkner's Light in August. *In* Tennessee Studies in literature v21 p49-57

Holman, C. H. Faulkner's August avatars. *In* Holman, C. H. Windows on the world p129-43

Kellogg, G. Alienated man and the faculty of categorization. *In* Kellogg, G. Dark prophets of hope p136-56

Faulkner, William—Continued

Plots

Caserio, R. L. The family plot: Conrad, Joyce, Lawrence, Woolf, and Faulkner. In Caserio, R. L. Plot, story, and the novel p232-79

Sources

Krefft, J. H. A possible source for Faulkner's Indians: Oliver La Farge's Laughing boy. In Tulane Studies in English, v23 p187-92

Lind I. D. Faulkner's uses of poetic drama. In Faulkner, modernism, and film: Faulkner and Yoknapatawpha, 1978 p66-81
Millgate, M. Faulkner's masters. in Tulane Studies in English, v23 p143-55

Style

Guerard, A. J. The Faulknerian voice. In The Maker and the myth: Faulkner and Yoknapatawpha, 1977 p25-42

Morris, W. William Faulkner. In Morris, W. Earthly delights, unearthly adornments p131-40

See also Faulkner, William—Technique

Technique

Guerard, A. J. Faulkner the innovator. In The Maker and the myth: Faulkner and Yoknapatawpha, 1977 p71-88

Kawin, B. The montage element in Faulkner's fiction. In Faulkner, modernism, and film: Faulkner and Yoknapatawpha, 1978 p103-25

Lind, I. D. The effect of painting on Faulkner's poetic form. In Faulkner, modernism, and film: Faulkner and Yoknapatawpha, 1978 p127-48

See also Faulkner, William—Style

Will

Hamblin, R. W. Lucas Beauchamp, Ned Barnett, and William Faulkner's 1940 will. In Virginia. University. Bibliographical Society. Studies in bibliography v32 p281-83

Faulquemont, France

Social conditions

Forster, R. The "world" between seigneur and peasant. In Studies in eighteenth-century culture v5 p401-21

Faure, Olivier

Physicians in Lyon during the nineteenth century: an extraordinary social success. In Branca, P. ed. The medicine show p243-58

Faust

Schindler, M. S. The history of Dr Johann Faustus. In Hoffmeister, G. ed. The Renaissance and Reformation in Germany p189-202

Faustina, Anna Galeria, The Elder

Monuments, etc.

Frazer, A. K. The pyre of Faustina Senior. In Studies in classical art and archaeology p271-74

Faustina, Senior. See Faustina, Anna Galeria, The Elder

Fauves (School of art). See Fauvism

Fauvism

Goldwater, R. The primitivism of the Fauves, the Brücke, the primitivism of the Blaue Reiter; excerpt from "Primitivism in modern art." In Kaplan, P. and Manso, S. eds. Major European art movements, 1900-1945 p42-90

Fava, Guido

About

Faulhaber, C. B. The letter-writer's rhetoric: the Summa dictaminis of Guido Faba. In Murphy, J. J. ed. Medieval eloquence p85-111

Favier, Jacques

Space and settor in short science fiction. In Johnson, I. D. and Johnson, C. [eds.] Les américanistes p182-201

Favonius, Marcus

About

Linderski, J. The aedileship of Favonius, Curio the Younger and Cicero's election to the augurate. In Harvard Studies in classical philology v76 p181-200

Favre, Maurice

Le Corbusier in an unpublished dossier and a little-known novel. In Walden, R. ed. The open hand p96-113

Fay, Brian C.

How people change themselves: the relationship between critical theory and its audience. In Political theory and praxis p200-33

Fay, Charles Ryle

The undergraduate. In Keynes, M. ed. Essays on John Maynard Keynes p36-38

Fayence. See Faience

Fearing, Kenneth

About individual works
New and selected poems

Kunitz, S. J. Private eye. In Kunitz, S. J. A kind of order, a kind of folly p210-12

Fears, Jesse Rufus

Atlantis and the Minoan thalassocracy: a study in modern mythopoeism. In Ramage, E. S. ed. Atlantis, fact or fiction? p103-34

Featherstone, Joseph Luke

Dewey's synthesis: science and feeling. In Roots of open education in America p118-25

John Dewey and David Riesman: from the lost individual to the lonely crowd. In On the making of Americans p3-39

Feature films. See Science fiction films

Febvre, Lucien Paul Victor

Man or productivity. In Rural society in France p 1-5

Febvre, Lucien Paul Victor, and Martin, Henri Jean

About individual works
The coming of the book: the impact of printing 1450-1800

Wells, J. M. Imprint on history. In Review, v 1 1979 p309-19

Fechner, Gustav Theodor

About individual works
Elements of psychophysics

Townsend, J. T. The mind-body equation revisited. In Philosophical aspects of the mind-body problem p200-18

Fedayeen

Caroz, Y. The Palestinians: who they are. In The Palestinians p77-80

Fedayeen—*Continued*

Harkabi, Y. The debate at the 12th Palestinian National Council. *In* The Palestinians p159-65

Harkabi, Y. A Palestinian democratic state as the political goal of the Palestinians. *In* The Palestinians p154-58

Harkabi, Y. The Palestinian National Covenant. *In* The Palestinians p143-53

Neyer, J. The emergence of Yasser Arafat. *In* The Palestinians p128-32

Norton, A. R. Moscow and the Palestinians: a new tool of Soviet policy in the Middle East. *In* The Palestinians p228-48

Prittie, T. C. F. Israel and the Palestinian question. *In* The Palestinians p213-27

Rouleau, E. Peace without the Palestinians? *In* The New world balance and peace in the Middle East: reality or mirage? p155-64

Watad, M. Insufferable silence. *In* The Palestinians p133-35

Waxman, C. I. Varieties of Palestinian nationalism. *In* The Palestinians p112-20

Weisband, E. and Roguly, D. Palestinian terrorism: violence, verbal strategy, and legitimacy. *In* International terrorism p258-319

Fedder, Norman Joseph

Tennessee Williams' dramatic technique. *In* Tennessee Williams: a tribute p795-812

Federal aid to education

Greenawalt, R. K. Voucher plans and sectarian schools: the constitutional problem. *In* Parents, teachers, and children: prospects for choice in American education p207-25

See also Federal aid to libraries

Federal aid to higher education

United States

Andringa, R. C. A view from Capitol Hill. *In* Hook, S.; Kurtz, P. W. and Todorovich, M. eds. The university and the state: what role for government in higher education? p133-36

Bonham, G. W. Opening the academic gates. *In* Hook, S.; Kurtz, P. W. and Todorovich, M. eds. The university and the state: what role for government in higher education? p163-66

Finn, C. E. Federal patronage of the universities: a rose by many other names? *In* Hook, S.; Kurtz, P. W. and Todorovich, M. eds. The university and the state: what role for government in higher education? p7-49

Goldwin, R. A. How "different" are universities? *In* Hook, S.; Kurtz, P. W. and Todorovich, M. eds. The university and the state: what role for government in higher education? p215-20

Howe, H. The interplay of mass and class. *In* The Third century p101-08

Kramer, M. The Frankenstein fallacy. *In* Hook, S.; Kurtz, P. W. and Todorovich, M. eds. The university and the state: what role for government in higher education? p95-96

Murphy, T. P. and Knipe, E. A. The federal government and urban higher education. *In* Murphy, T. P. Universities in the urban crisis p353-79

Norton, J. A. The interaction of state and Federal policy. *In* Hook, S.; Kurtz, P. W. and Todorovich, M. eds. The university and the state: what role for government in higher education? p73-76

Pell, C. The question of access—and to what. *In* The Third century p98-100

Perkins, C. D. The view from the Hill. *In* The Third century p83-88

Powell, A. G. Harvard's School of Education and the Federal government: institutional effects of interaction in the 1960s. *In* Hook, S.; Kurtz, P. W. and Todorovich, M. eds. The university and the state: what role for government in higher education? p51-72

Sasseen, R. F. Patronage and the academy. *In* Hook, S.; Kurtz, P. W. and Todorovich, M. eds. The university and the state: what role for government in higher education? p87-93

Searle, J. R. A more balanced view. *In* Hook, S.; Kurtz, P. W. and Todorovich, M. eds. The university and the state: what role for government in higher education? p205-13

Tollett, K. S. What is all the shouting about? *In* Hook, S.; Kurtz, P. W. and Todorovich, M. eds. The university and the state: what role for government in higher education? p77-85

Van Alstyne, C. The costs to colleges and universities of implementing federally mandated social programs. *In* Hook, S.; Kurtz, P. W. and Todorovich, M. eds. The university and the state: what role for government in higher education? p115-22

Federal aid to hospitals

United States

Warner, D. C. Government initiatives and controls in American medical care. *In* Smith, B. L. R. ed. The new political economy: the public use of the private sector p214-28

Federal aid to libraries

United States

Molz, R. K. Libraries and the development and future of tax support. *In* Libraries and the life of the mind in America p41-63

Federal aid to research

See also Research grants

United States

Brooks, H. The problem of research priorities. *In* Holton, G. J. and Morison, R. S. eds. Limits of scientific inquiry p171-90

Price, D. K. Endless frontier or bureaucratic morass? *In* Holton, G. J. and Morison. R. S. eds. Limits of scientific inquiry p74-92

Federal Art Project

Rosenberg, H. The profession of art: the W.P.A. Art Project. *In* Rosenberg, H. Art on the edge p195-205

Federal City College

Nichols, D. C. Federal City College: a model for new urban universities? *In* Land-grant universities and their continuing challenge p205-22

Federal-city relations

United States

Campbell, A. K. and Dollenmayer, J. A. Governance in a metropolitan society. *In* Hawley, A. H. and Rock, V. P. eds. Metropolitan America in contemporary perspective p355-96

Federal Communications Commission. See United States. Federal Communications Commission

Federal government

See also Decentralization in government, Federal-city relations; Grants-in-aid; State government

Federal government—*Continued*

United States

Cohen, W. Congressional power to interpret due process and equal protection. *In* Stanford legal essays p79-96

Earle, V. A. The Federal structure. *In* Graham, G. J. and Graham, S. G. eds. Founding principles of American government p135-67

Jones, H. W. The Articles of Confederation and the creation of a federal system. *In* Aspects of American liberty p126-45

Hamilton, E. K. On nonconstitutional management of a constitutional problem. *In* A New America? p111-28

Weinberg, L. A new judicial Federalism? *In* A New America? p129-41

Federal Party

Horwitz, R. H. John Locke and the preservation of liberty: a perennial problem of civic education. *In* The Moral foundations of the American Republic p129-56

Federal revenue sharing. See Intergovernmental fiscal relations

Federal-state fiscal relations. See Intergovernmental fiscal relations

Federal-state relations. See Federal government

Federal theology. See Covenants (Theology)

Federalism. See Federal government

The Federalist

Adair, D. G. "That politics may be reduced to a science": David Hume, James Madison, and the tenth Federalist. *In* Livingston, D. W. and King, J. T. eds. Hume p404-17

Bain, R. A. The Federalist. *In* Emerson, E. H. ed. American literature, 1764-1789 p253-73

Diamond, M. Ethics and politics: the American way. *In* The Moral foundations of the American Republic p39-72

Meyer, D. H. Political mechanics and the new consciousness. *In* Meyer, D. H. The democratic Enlightenment p149-68

Nisbet, R. A. Public opinion versus popular opinion. *In* A Public philosophy reader p169-97

Federalists (United States) See Federal Party

Federigo, Count of Montefeltro, Duke of Urbino

About

Westfall, C. W. Chivalric declaration: the Palazzo Ducale in Urbino as a political statement. *In* Millon, H. A. and Nochlin, L. eds. Art and architecture in the service of politics p20-45

Federman, Raymond

Surfiction—four propositions in form of an introduction. *In* Federman, R. ed. Surfiction p5-15

Feedback (Psychology) See Biofeedback training

Feeling. See Perception; Touch

Feelings. See Emotions

Feest, Christian F.

Charles Sealsfield (Karl Postl). *In* Abroad in America: Visitors to the new Nation, 1776-1914 p22-31

Fei, John C. H. and Ranis, Gustav

Technological transfer, employment and development. *In* Economic development and planning p75-103

Feibleman, James Kern

Philosophical perspectives on justice. *In* Perspectives on justice p75-117

Feifel, Herman

Death in contemporary America. *In* Feifel, H. [ed.] New meanings of death p3-12

Epilogue. *In* Feifel, H. [ed.] New meanings of death p351-55

Feifer, George

No protest: the case of the passive minority. *In* Tokes, R. L. ed. Dissent in the USSR p418-37

Feigl, Herbert

The outlook of scientific humanism. *In* The Abdication of philosophy: philosophy and the public good p73-79

Some crucial issues of mind-body monism. *In* Philosophical aspects of the mind-body problem p20-34

Feijoo, Benito Gerónimo

About

Aldridge, A. O. Feijoo, Voltaire, and the mathematics of procreation. *In* Studies in eighteenth-century culture v4 p131-38

Feinberg, Joel

The rights of animals and unborn generations. *In* Philosophy & environmental crisis p43-68

Feinberg, Oded Eran. See Eran Feinberg, Oded

Feinberg, Walter, and Rosemont, Henry

Training for the welfare state: the progressive education movement. *In* Feinberg, W. and Rosemont, H. eds. Work, technology, and education p60-91

Feingold, Richard

Nature and society

Contents

Art divorced from nature: The task and bucolic tradition

Bucolic tradition and virtuous work: Arthur Young and Adam Smith

Epilogue: eighteenth-century endings, romantic beginnings

The good society and the bucolic mode: Virgil and Pope

Two worlds of work: John Dyer's The fleece

William Cowper: state, society, and countryside

Feinman, Saul

Biosociological approaches to social behavior. *In* McNall, S. G. ed. Theoretical perspectives in sociology p399-413

Feiwel, Raphael Joseph

Arthur Koestler and George Orwell. *In* Harris, H. A. ed. Astride the two cultures p149-61

Felashas. See Falashas

Feld, Bernard Taub

Nuclear energy—fact versus myth. *In* International terrorism and world security p131-39

Feldenkrais, Moshé

Man and the world. *In* Hanna, T. ed. Explorers of mankind p19-29

Feldman, Lawrence H.
Shells from afar: 'Panamic' molluscs in Mayan sites. *In* Mesoamerican archaeology p129-33

Feldman, Louis H.
Josephus as an apologist to the Greco-Roman world: his portrait of Solomon. *In* Aspects of religious propaganda in Judaism and early Christianity p69-98

Feldman, Ron H.
Introduction: the Jew as pariah: the case of Hannah Arendt. *In* Arendt, H. The Jew as pariah: Jewish identity and politics in the modern age p15-52

Feldman, Seymour Nat Oscar
Platonic themes in Gersonides' cosmology. *In* Salo Wittmayer Baron v 1 p383-405

Feldstein, Leonard Charles
Bifurcated psyche and social self: implications of Freud's theory of the unconscious. *In* Roth, R. J. ed. Person and community p43-62

Félix-Tchicaya, Gerald

About
Wake, C. Tchicaya U Tam'si. *In* King, B. A. and Ogungbesan, K. eds. A celebration of Black and African writing p124-38

Fell, Christine E.
English history and Norman legend in the Icelandic saga of Edward the Confessor. *In* Anglo-Saxon England 6 p223-36
The Icelandic saga of Edward the Confessor: its version of the Anglo-Saxon emigration to Byzantium. *In* Anglo-Saxon England 3 p179-96

Fellatio. See Oral intercourse

Fellini, Federico

About
Samuels, C. T. Federico Fellini: juxtaposition. *In* Samuels, C. T. Mastering the film, and other essays p85-115

About individual works
The clowns
Kauffmann, S. The clowns. *In* Kauffmann, S. Living images p59-61

8 ½
Macdonald, D. 8 ½: Fellini's obvious masterpiece; excerpt from "Dwight Macdonald on movies." *In* Denby, D. ed. Awake in the dark p113-27

Roma
Kauffmann, S. Fellini's Roma. *In* Kauffmann, S. Living images p148-50

La strada
Murray, E. La strada. *In* Murray, E. Ten film classics p62-85

Fellman, David
The nationalization of American civil liberties. *In* Essays on the Constitution of the United States p49-60

Fellner, William John
Neo-Keynesianism, monetarism and the short and the long run. *In* Theory for economic efficiency: essays in honor of Abba P. Lerner p24-45

Fellows, Otis Edward
Diderot's Supplément as pendant for La religieuse. *In* Literature and history in the age of ideas p229-43

Fellows Jensen, Gillian
The Vikings in England: a review. *In* Anglo-Saxon England 4 p181-206

Felony. See Criminal law

Felperin, Howard Michael
Romance and romanticism: some reflections on The tempest and Heart of darkness, or When is romance no longer romance? *In* Shakespeare's romances reconsidered p60-76

Felstiner, John
Max Beerbohm and the wings of Henry James. *In* Riewald, J. G. ed. The surprise of excellence p192-214

About individual works
The lies of art
Balakian, N. A specialist of the hoax: Max Beerbohm. *in* Balakian, N. Critical encounters p203-06

Female. See Women

Female Middle Class Emigration Society
Hammerton, A. J. Feminism and female emigration, 1861-1886. *In* Vicinus, M. ed. A widening sphere p52-71

Female offenders

England
Hanawalt, B. A. The female felon in fourteenth-century England. *In* Stuard, S. M. ed. Women in medieval society p125-40
Also in Viator; medieval and Renaissance studies v5 p253-68
See also Women prisoners

Female sex hormone. See Hormones, Sex

Femininity (Psychology)
Bettelheim, B. Growing up female. *In* Bettelheim, B. Surviving, and other essays p221-38
Dickason, A. The feminine as a universal. *In* Feminism and philosophy p79-100
Rigney, B. H. Introduction. *In* Rigney, B. H. Madness and sexual politics in the feminist novel p 1-12

Feminism
Bartky, S. L. Toward a phenomenology of feminist consciousness. *In* Feminism and philosophy p22-34
Culpepper, E. The spiritual movement of radical feminist consciousness. *In* Needleman, J. and Baker, G. eds. Understanding the new religions p220-34
Donovan, J. C. Afterword: critical revision. *In* Donovan, J. C. ed. Feminist literary criticism p74-81
Harding, S. G. Feminism: reform or revolution? *In* Gould, C. C. and Wartofsky, M. W. eds. Women and philosophy p271-84
Hein, H. On reaction and the women's movement. *In* Gould, C. C. and Wartofsky, M. W. eds. Women and philosophy p248-70
Holly, M. Consciousness and authenticity: toward a feminist aesthetic. *In* Donovan, J. C. ed. Feminist literary criticism p38-47
Howe, F. Women and the power to change. *In* Women and the power to change p127-71
Marković, M. Women's liberation and human emancipation. *In* Gould, C. C. and Wartofsky, M. W. eds. Women and philosophy p145-67
Rapaport, E. On the future of love: Rousseau and the radical feminists. *In* Gould, C. C. and Wartofsky, M. W. eds. Women and philosophy p185-205

Feminism—*Continued*

Register, C. American feminist literary criticism: a bibliographical introduction. *In* Donovan, J. C. ed. Feminist literary criticism p 1-28

Rich, A. C. The antifeminist woman. *In* Rich, A. C. On lies, secrets, and silence p69-84

Rich, A. C. Disloyal to civilization: feminism, racism, gynephobia. *In* Rich, A. C. On lies, secrets, and silence p275-310

Schumacher, D. Subjectivities: a theory of the critical process. *In* Donovan, J. C. ed. Feminist literary criticism p29-37

Segal, M. T. and Berheide, C. W. Towards a women's perspective in sociology: directions and prospects. *In* McNall, S. G. ed. Theoretical perspectives in sociology p69-82

Sheed, W. Now that men can cry. . . . *In* Sheed, W. The good word & other words p289-300

Valian, V. Linguistics and feminism. *In* Feminism and philosophy p154-66

See also Sex discrimination against women; Women—Social conditions; Women's rights

History

Jaggar, A. M. Political philosophies of women's liberation. *In* Feminism and philosophy p 5-21

Cameroon

Ardener, S. G. Sexual insult and female militancy. *In* Ardener, S. G. ed. Perceiving women p29-53

China

Collins, L. E. Death-profit, "evil," and the Chinese feminist movement. *In* Kren, G. M. and Rappoport, L. H. eds. Varieties of psychohistory p264-81

Egypt

Philipp, T. Feminism and nationalist politics in Egypt. *In* Beck, L. and Keddie, N. R. eds. Women in the Muslim world p277-94

Europe—History

Fisher, M. J. Eighteenth-century theorists of women's liberation. *In* "Remember the ladies": new perspectives on women in American history p39-47

Great Britain

Hammerton, A. J. Feminism and female emigration, 1861-1886. *In* Vicinus, M. ed. A widening sphere p52-71

Japan—History

Shimada, N. and others. Ume Tsuda and Motoko Hani: echoes of American cultural feminism in Japan. *In* "Remember the ladies": new perspectives on women in American history p161-78

Nigeria—History

Ifeka-Moller, C. Female militancy and colonial revolt: the women's war of 1929, Eastern Nigeria. *In* Ardener, S. G. ed. Perceiving women p127-57

Russia—History

Meyer, A. G. Marxism and the women's movement. *In* Women in Russia p84-112

Sudan

Fluehr-Lobban, C. Agitation for change in the Sudan. *In* Schlegel, A. E. ed. Sexual stratification p127-43

United States

Mayo, E. Ladies and liberation: icon and iconoclast in the women's movement. *In* Browne, R. B. and Fishwick, M. W. eds. Icons of America p209-27

Trilling, D. Women's liberation: Female biology in a male culture. *In* Trilling, D. We must march my darlings p189-98

Trilling, D. Women's liberation: The prisoner of sex. *In* Trilling, D. We must march my darlings p199-210

United States—History

Bennett, D. H. Women and the Nativist movement. *In* "Remember the ladies": new perspectives on women in American history p71-89

Terborg-Penn, R. Discrimination against Afro-American women in the woman's movement, 1830-1920. *In* Harley, S. and Terborg-Penn, R. eds. The Afro-American woman p17-27

Feminism and literature

Gilbert, S. M. and Guber, S. The aesthetics of renunciation. *In* Gilbert, S. M. and Gubar, S. The madwoman in the attic p539-80

Gilbert, S. M. and Gubar, S. The buried life of Lucy Snowe. *In* Gilbert, S. M. and Gubar, S. The madwoman in the attic p399-440

Gilbert, S. M. and Gubar, S. A dialogue of self and soul: plain Jane's progress. *In* Gilbert, S. M. and Gubar, S. The madwoman in the attic p336-71

Gilbert, S. M. and Gubar, S. The genesis of hunger according to Shirley. *In* Gilbert, S. M. and Gubar, S. The madwoman in the attic p372-98

Gilbert, S. M. and Gubar, S. Introduction: gender, creativity, and the woman poet. *In* Gilbert, S. M. and Gubar, S. eds. Shakespeare's sisters pxv-xxvi

Feminism in literature

Davis, S. D. The Bostonians reconsidered. *In* Tulane Studies in English, v23 p39-60

Fetterley, J. The Bostonians: Henry James's eternal triangle. *In* Fetterley, J. The resisting reader p101-53

Janes, R. M. Mary, Mary, quite contrary, or, Mary Astell and Mary Wollstonecraft compared. *In* Studies in eighteenth-century culture v5 p121-39

Rigney, B. H. "After the failure of logic": descent and return in Surfacing. *In* Rigney, B. H. Madness and sexual politics in the feminist novel p91-115

Showalter, E. Beyond the female aesthetic: contemporary women novelists. *In* Showalter, E. A literature of their own p298-319

Showalter, E. The feminist novelists. *In* Showalter, E. A literature of their own p182-215

Williams, D. Condorcet, feminism, and the egalitarian principle. *In* Studies in eighteenth-century culture v5 p151-63

Feminist studies. See Women's studies

Feminists

Great Britain

Halsband, R. "Condemned to petticoats": Lady Mary Wortley Montague as feminist and writer. *In* The Dress of words p35-52

Une femme douce (Motion picture)

Kauffmann, S. Une femme douce. *In* Kauffmann, S. Living images p57-59

Fénelon, François De Salignac de La Mothe-, Abp.

About individual works

Dialogues concerning eloquence in general

Howell, W. S. Oratory and poetry in Fénelon's literary theory. *In* Howell, W. S. Poetics, rhetoric, and logic p123-40

Letter to the Academy

Howell, W. S. Oratory and poetry in Fénelon's literary theory. *In* Howell, W. S. Poetics, rhetoric, and logic p123-40

Fenians. See Irish question

Fenjas. See Falashas

Fennell, John Lister Illingworth
The struggle for power in north-east Russia, 1246-9: an investigation of the sources. *In* Oxford Slavonic papers new ser. v7 p112-21

Fennelly, Laurence W.
W. B. Yeats and S. L. MacGregor Mathers. *In* Yeats and the occult p285-306

Fennema, Elizabeth
Women and girls in the public schools: defeat or liberation? *In* Roberts, J. I. ed. Beyond intellectual sexism p343-52

Fenno, Richard F.
If, as Ralph Nader says, Congress is "the broken branch," how come we love our Congressmen so much? *In* Ornstein, N. J. ed. Congress in change p277-87

Fenton, Charles A.
No money for the kingbird: Hemingway's prizefight stories. *In* Benson, J. J. ed. The short stories of Ernest Hemingway: critical essays p53-63
The revision of "chapter III" from In our time. *In* Benson, J. J. ed. The short stories of Ernest Hemingway: critical essays p80-84

Fenton, Edward
Blind idiot: the problems of translation. *In* Horn Book Magazine. Crosscurrents of criticism p290-305

Feofan, Abp. of Novgorod

About

Cracraft, J. Feofan Prokopovich: a bibliography of his works. *In* Oxford Slavonic papers new ser. v8 p 1-36

Ferdowsī. See Firdawsī

Ferge, Zsuzsa
Hungary. *In* Kamerman, S. B. and Kahn, A. J. eds. Family policy p68-90

Ferguson, Ann
Androgyny as an ideal for human development. *In* Feminism and philosophy p45-69

Ferguson, Charles Albert
Language problems of variation and repertoire. *In* Bloomfield, M. W. and Haugen, E. I. eds. Language as a human problem p23-32
New directions in phonological theory: language acquisition and universals research. *In* Current issues in linguistic theory p247-99

Ferguson, Clarence Clyde
Free men and revolution: a Black perspective. *In* The American Revolution: a continuing commitment p13-25

Ferguson, Clyde R.
Carolina and Georgia patriot and loyalist militia in action, 1778-1783. *In* The Southern experience in the American Revolution p174-99

Ferguson, F. S. See Jackson, W. A. jt. auth.

Ferguson, James P.
Prefaces to Jerusalem. *In* Phillips, M. C. ed. Interpreting Blake p164-95

Ferguson, Mary Anne
Losing battles as a comic epic in prose. *In* Prenshaw, P. W. ed. Eudora Welty p305-24

Ferguson, Neal Allen
Women in twentieth-century England. *In* Kanner, B. ed. The women of England p345-87

Ferguson, Oliver Watkins
Antisentimentalism in Goldsmith's The good natur'd man: the limits of parody. *In* The Dress of words p105-16

Ferguson, Otis
Artists among the flickers; excerpt from "The film criticism of Otis Ferguson." *In* Denby, D. ed. Awake in the dark p375-77
Cagney: great guy; excerpt from "The film criticism of Otis Ferguson." *In* Denby, D. ed. Awake in the dark p338-39
Life goes to the pictures; excerpt from "The film criticism of Otis Ferguson." *In* Denby, D. ed. Awake in the dark p49-59

Ferguson, R. Fred. See Whisenand, P. jt. auth.

Ferguson, Wallace Klippert

About individual works

The Renaissance in historical thought

Hexter, J. H. Wallace K. Ferguson and Hiram Hayden [sic]: The Renaissance again —and again. *In* Hexter, J. H. On historians p45-59

Fergusson, Francis
Excursus: poetry in the theatre and poetry of the theatre: Cocteau's Infernal machine. *In* Wimsatt, W. K. ed. Literary criticism: idea and act p590-601
Literary landmarks

Contents

Auden in mid-career
The Divine comedy as a bridge across time
Ibsen's The lady from the sea
James in the theater
James's dramatic form
Maritain's Creative intuition
Molière
Oedipus according to Freud, Sophocles, and Cocteau
On F. R. Leavis
The Poetics of Aristotle
Sartre as playwright
The theater of Paul Valéry

Poetry and drama. *In* Symbolism and modern literature p13-25

About individual works

Dante's drama of the mind: a modern reading of the Purgatorio

Frye, N. Ministry of angels. *in* Frye, N. Northrop Frye on culture and literature p130-40

Ferlosio, Rafael Sánchez. See Sánchez Ferlosio, Rafael

Fern, Alan Maxwell
Remarks toward an ideal museum of photography. *In* One hundred years of photographic history p47-52

Fernandes, Florestan
Beyond poverty: the Negro and the mulatto in Brazil. *In* Toplin, R. B. ed. Slavery and race relations in Latin America p277-97

Fernandez, Guido
ACACAN [sic]: a solution to the problem of news flow in the Third World. *In* Horton, P. C. ed. The Third World and press freedom p151-55

Fernandez, James W.
The performance of ritual metaphors. *In* The Social use of metaphor p100-31

Fernández Santos, Jesús

About individual works
Los bravos
Schwartz, R. Jesus Fernandez Santos and Los bravos (The savage ones) (1954). *In* Schwartz, R. Spain's New Wave novelists, 1950-1974 p74-86

Fernando, Anthony
Contemporary Buddhism in Sri Lanka (Ceylon) *In* Dumoulin, H. ed. Buddhism in the modern world p65-80

Fernando, Lloyd
A note from the Third World towards the redefinition of culture. *In* Narasimhaiah. C. D. ed. Awakened conscience p327-38

Fernando Póo, See Macías Nguema Byogo

Ferns, Henry Stanley
Argentinia in travail. *In* The Year book of world affairs, 1975 p56-71

Ferrante, Joan M.
The conflict of lyric conventions and romance form. *In* In pursuit of perfection p135-78

Woman as image in medieval literature

Contents
Allegory
Biblical exegesis
Courtly literature
Dante
In the thirteenth century

Ferrari, Gaudenzio

About
Winternitz, E. Early violins in paintings by Gaudenzio Ferrari and his school. *In* Winternitz, E. Musical instruments and their symbolism in Western art p99-109

Ferrarotti, Franco
The Italian Communist Party and Eurocommunism. *In* Kaplan, M. A. ed. The many faces of communism p30-71

Ferrell, Robert Hugh
Peace movements. *In* Encyclopedia of American foreign policy p752-62
See also Merli, F. J. jt. auth.

Ferrier, Carole
The beekeeper's apprentice. *In* Lane, G. ed. Sylvia Plath p203-17

Ferrier, Susan Edmondstone

About
Hart, F. R. The other Blackwoodians. *In* Hart, F. R. The Scottish novel p53-84

About individual works
Marriage
Doubleday, N. F. A very lively work. *In* Doubleday, N. F. Variety of attempt p61-77

Ferris, Norman Bernard
Transatlantic misunderstanding: William Henry Seward and the Declaration of Paris negotiation of 1861. *In* Rank and file p55-78

Ferris, Sumner J.
Chaucer, Richard II, Henry IV, and 13 October. *In* Chaucer and Middle English studies in honour of Rossell Hope Robbins p210-17

Ferro, Marc
The fiction film and historical analysis. *In* Smith, P. ed. The historian and film p80-94

Fertility, Human
Easterlin, R. A. New directions for the economics of fertility. *In* Major social issues p310-17
Namboodiri, N. K. On fertility analysis: where sociologists, economists, and biologists meet. *In* Major social issues p295-309
Schultz, T. P. Determinants of fertility: a micro-economic model of choice. *In* Economic factors in population growth p89-124

Belgium
Lesthaeghe, R. and Van de Walle, E. Economic factors and fertility decline in France and Belgium. *In* Economic factors in population growth p205-28

France
Lesthaeghe, R. and Van de Walle, E. Economic factors and fertility decline in France and Belgium. *In* Economic factors in population growth p205-28

Hungary
Szabady, E. Economic factors in the decline of fertility in Hungary in the nineteenth and early twentieth century. *In* Economic factors in population growth p238-40

Islamic countries
Youssef, N. H. The status and fertility patterns of Muslim women. *In* Beck, L. and Keddie, N. R. eds. Women in the Muslim world p69-99

Israel
Ben Porath, Y. Fertility in Israel: a minisurvey and some new findings. *In* Economic factors in population growth p136-72

Taiwan
Hermalin, A. I. Empirical research in Taiwan on factors underlying differences in fertility. *In* Economic factors in population growth p243-66

Fertilization of plants
Fægri, K. Pollination ecology: trends and problems. *In* The Frontiers of human knowledge p275-88

Festa, Conrad
Vonnegut's satire. *In* Klinkowitz, J. and Lawler, D. L. eds. Vonnegut in America p133-49

Festivals
Abrahams, R. D. and Bauman, R. Ranges of festival behavior. *In* Babcock, B. A. ed. The reversible world p193-208

Caribbean area
Bettelheim, J. Jamaican Jonkonnu and related Caribbean festivals. *In* Crahan, M. E. and Knight, F. W. eds. Africa and the Caribbean p80-100

Festivals—*Continued*

Europe

Boorsch, S. R. America in festival presentations. *In* First images of America p503-15

Ireland

Smith, R. J. Festivals and calendar customs. *In* Orel, H. ed. Irish history and culture p129-45

Feticide. See Abortion

Fetishism

White, H. V. The Noble Savage theme as fetish. *In* First images of America p121-35

Fetterley, Judith

The resisting reader

Contents

An American dream: "Hula, hula," said the witches

The Bostonians: Henry James's eternal triangle

A farewell to arms: Hemingway's "resentful cryptogram"

Also in Diamond, A. and Edwards, L. R. eds. The authority of experience p257-73

The Great Gatsby: Fitzgerald's droit de seigneur

Palpable designs: four American short stories: A rose for "A rose for Emily"

Palpable designs: four American short stories: An American dream: "Rip Van Winkle"

Palpable designs: four American short stories: Growing up male in America: "I want to know why"

Palpable designs: four American short stories: Women beware science: "The birthmark"

Fetus

Brody, B. A. Fetal humanity and the theory of essentialism. *In* Baker, R. and Elliston, F. A. eds. Philosophy & sex p338-55

Research—Moral and religious aspects

Fletcher, J. F. Fetal research. *In* Fletcher, J. F. Humanhood: essays in biomedical ethics p93-105

Fetus, Death of the. See Abortion

Feudal tenure. See Feudalism

Feudalism

Evergates, T. Historiography and sociology in early feudal society: the case of Hariulf and the "milites" of Saint-Riquier. *In* Viator: medieval and Renaissance studies v6 p35-49

Hibbert, A. B. The origins of the medieval town patriciate. *In* Towns in societies p91-104

Soboul, A. Persistence of "feudalism" in the rural society of nineteenth-century France. *In* Rural society in France p50-71

West, F. J. On the ruins of feudalism—capitalism? *In* Kamenka, E. and Neale, R. S. eds. Feudalism, capitalism and beyond p50-61

See also Middle Ages; Ministerials; Peasantry

Feuer, Kathryn Beliveau

August 1914: Solzhenitsyn and Tolstoy. *In* Dunlop, J. B.; Haugh, R. and Klimoff, A. eds. Aleksandr Solzhenitsyn: critical essays and documentary materials 2d ed. p372-81

Solzhenitsyn and the legacy of Tolstoy. *In* Dunlop, J. B.; Haugh, R. and Klimoff, A. eds. Aleksandr Solzhenitsyn: critical essays and documentary materials 2d ed. p129-46

Feuer, Lewis Samuel

About individual works

The conflict of generations

Crews, F. C. Student protest and academic distance. *In* Crews, F. C. Out of my system p89-103

Feuerwerker, Yi-tsi M.

The changing relationship between literature and life: aspects of the writer's role in Ding Ling. *In* Modern Chinese literature in the May Fourth era p281-307

Feuilletons

History and criticism

Bailey, L. H. Ferdinand Kürnberger, Friedrich Schlögl and the feuilleton in Gründerzeit Vienna. *In* Branscombe, P. ed. Austrian life and literature, 1780-1938 p59-71

Feuser, Willfried F.

The men who lived underground: Richard Wright and Ralph Ellison. *In* King, B. A. and Ogungbesan, K. eds. A celebration of Black and African writing p87-101

Prophet of violence: Chester Himes. *In* African literature today no. 9: Africa, America and the Caribbean p58-76

Feustle, Joseph A.

Mario Vargas Llosa: a labyrinth of solitude. *In* Rossman, C. R. and Friedman, A. W. eds. Mario Vargas Llosa p128-35

Fèvre, Jacques le. See Le Fèvre, Jacques, d'Étaples

Ffolliott, Rosemary

The new culture: domestic life and the arts, 1680-1830. *In* De Breffny, B. ed. The Irish world p127-64

Ficino, Marsilio

About

Hersey, G. L. Marsilio Ficino's cosmic temple. *In* Collaboration in Italian Renaissance art p91-97

Ficken, Carl Frederick Wilhelm

Point of view in the Nick Adams stories. *In* Benson, J. J. ed. The short stories of Ernest Hemingway: critical essays p93-112

Ficks, Robert Snowden

The burgeoning arsenal: developments and projections. *In* Beaumont, R. A. and Edmonds, M. eds. War in the next decade p135-56

Fiction

Alter, R. Mimesis and the motive for fiction. *In* Images and ideas in American culture p99-123

Blumenberg, H. The concept of reality and the possibility of the novel. *In* Amacher, R. E. and Lange, V. eds. New perspectives in German literary criticism p29-48

Brown, R. L. and Steinmann, M. Native readers of fiction: a speech-act and genre-rule approach to defining literature. *In* Hernadi, P. ed. What is literature? p141-60

Federman, R. Surfiction—four propositions in form of an introduction. *In* Federman, R. ed. Surfiction p5-15

Gass, W. H. Carrots, noses, snow, rose, roses. *In* Gass, W. H. The world within the word p280-307

Graff, G. How not to talk about fictions. *In* Graff, G. Literature against itself p151-80

Fiction—History and criticism—*Continued*

Steiner, G. Eros and idiom. *In* Steiner, G. On difficulty and other essays p95-136

Sukenick, L. On women and fiction. *In* Diamond, A. and Edwards, L. R. eds. The authority of experience p28-44

Tobin, P. D. Introduction: whence the novel: the genealogical imperative. *In* Tobin, P. D. Time and the novel p3-28

Welty, E. Place in fiction. *In* Welty, E. The eye of the story p116-33

Welty, E. Some notes on time in fiction. *In* Welty, E. The eye of the story p163-73

Williams, D. A.The practice of realism. *In* Williams, D. A. ed. The monster in the mirror p257-79

Moral and religious aspects

Garrison, D. Immoral fiction in the late Victorian library. *In* Howe, D. W. ed. Victorian America p141-59

Martin, A. From Marmontel to Berquin: the dynamic concept of morality in eighteenth-century French fiction. *In* Studies in eighteenth-century culture v6 p285-302

Plot

See Plots (Drama, novel, etc.)

Technique

Chatman, S. The structure of narrative transmission. *In* Fowler, R. ed. Style and structure in literature p213-57

Cowley, M. A defense of storytelling. *In* Cowley, M. —And I worked at the writer's trade p194-213

O'Hara, J. Dialog, detail, and type. *In* O'Hara, J. "An artist is his own fault" p3-20

O'Hara, J. Logistics of the novel. *In* O'Hara, J. "An artist is his own fault" p20-37

O'Hara, J. Method and technique of the novel. *In* O'Hara, J. "An artist is his own fault" p37-52

Pascal, R. Conclusions. *In* Pascal, R. The dual voice p135-41

Pascal, R. The narrator problem. *In* Pascal, R. The dual voice p 1-36

Pearce, R. Enter the frame. *In* Federman, R. ed. Surfiction p47-57

Richter, D. H. Conclusions. *In* Richter, D. H. Fable's end p166-84

Welty, E. Words into fiction. *In* Welty, E. The eye of the story p134-45

See also Setting (Literature)

18th century—History and criticism

Lyons, J. O. The circumference of the self. *In* Lyons, J. O. The invention of the self p197-218

Lyons, J. O. Into our age. *In* Lyons, J. O. The invention of the self p219-29

19th century—History and criticism

Alter, R. The self-conscious novel in eclipse. *In* Alter, R. Partial magic p84-137

Bersani, L. Realism and the fear of desire. *In* Bersani, L. A future for Astyanax p51-88

Dolan, P. J. The lamps of Europe. *In* Dolan, P. J. Of war and war's alarms p 1-15

Peckham, M. Reflections on historical modes in the nineteenth century. *In* Peckham, M. Romanticism and behavior p40-66

Tobin, P. D. Subverting the father: some nineteenth-century precursors. *In* Tobin, P. D. Time and the novel p29-53

20th century—History and criticism

Adams, R. M. The Joyce era? *In* Adams, R. M. Afterjoyce p194-201

Alter, R. The inexhaustible genre. *In* Alter, R. Partial magic p218-45

Alter, R. The modernist revival of self-conscious fiction. *In* Alter, R. Partial magic p138-79

Balakian, N. On the reading of modern fiction. *in* Balakian, N. Critical encounters p29-36

Boyers, R. The family novel. *In* Boyers, R. Excursions p5-24

Cowley, M. A. defense of storytelling. *In* Cowley, M. —And I worked at the writers' trade p194-213

Dolan, P. J. The lamps of Europe. *In* Dolan, P. J. Of war and war's alarms p 1-15

Evert, W. H. Coadjutors of oppression: a romantic and modern theory of evil. *In* Bornstein, G. ed. Romantic and modern p29-52

Frye, N. Novels on several occasions. *In* Frye, N. Northrop Frye on culture and literature p207-18

Garvin, H. R. American and European makers of the twentieth-century novel. *In* Garvin, H. R. ed. Makers of the twentieth-century novel p11-18

Glicksberg, C. I. Various aspects of modern nihilism. *In* Glicksberg, C. I. The literature of nihilism p246-71

Graff, G. Babbitt at the abyss. *In* Graff, G. Literature against itself p207-39

Hyman, S. E. The critic's credentials. *In* Hyman, S. E. The critic's credentials p3-20

Kennard, J. E. Conclusion. *In* Kennard, J. E. Victims of convention p158-67

Kennedy, A. Conclusion. *In* Kennedy, A. Meaning and signs in fiction p128-38

Kennedy, A. Conclusion: A quick look around. *In* Kennedy, A. The protean self p261-85

Kennedy, A. The novel as a social fiction. *In* Kennedy, A. The protean self p63-98

Kunkel, F. L. Conclusion. *In* Kunkel, F. L. Passion and the Passion p169-83

Kunkel, F. L. The sexy Cross. *In* Kunkel, F. L. Passion and the Passion p157-68

Kurz, P. K. The priest in the modern novel. *In* Kurz, P. K. On modern German literature v4 p129-50

Kurz, P. K. Vicissitudes of the modern novel. *In* Kurz, P. K. On modern German literature v 1 p3-29

May, K. M. A new synthesis. *In* May, K. M. Out of the maelstrom p98-121

Morris, W. An image sampler. *In* Morris, W. Earthly delights, unearthly adornments p13-17

Mudrick, M. Old pros with news from nowhere. *In* Mudrick, M. Books are not life but then what is? p245-75

Sarotte, G. M. Conclusion: another country. *In* Sarotte, G. M. Like a brother, like a lover p293-305

Schulz, M. F. Toward a definition of black humor; excerpt from "Black humor fiction of the sixties." *In* Cohen, S. B. ed. Comic relief p14-27

Sheed, W. Genre writers. *In* Sheed, W. The good word & other words p33-37

Sukenick, R. The new tradition in fiction. *In* Federman, R. ed. Surfiction p35-45

Swales, M. Excursus: the Bildungsroman as a taxonomic genre. *In* Swales, M. The German Bildungsroman from Wieland to Hesse p161-66

Fiction—20th century—History and criticism
—*Continued*

Tilton, J. W. On learning by going where the critic has to go. *In* Tilton, J. W. Cosmic satire in the contemporary novel p13-20

Tobin, P. D. Conclusion: whither the novel: the wager on surface. *In* Tobin, P. D. Time and the novel p192-213

See also Black humor (Literature)

Fiction (Periodical)

Mirsky, M. J. On Fiction. *In* Anderson, E. and Kinzie, M. eds. The little magazine in America: a modern documentary history p515-23

Fiction, Autobiographic

History and criticism

Benstock, B. A portrait of the artist in Finnegans wake. *In* Garvin, H. R. ed. Makers of the twentieth-century novel p28-39

Lyons, J. O. The circumference of the self. *In* Lyons, J. O. The invention of the self p197-218

Lyons, J. O. Into our age. *In* Lyons, J. O. The invention of the self p219-29

Patten, R. L. Autobiography into autobiography: the evolution of David Copperfield. *In* Landow, G. P. ed. Approaches to Victorian autobiography p269-91

Fiction, Gothic. See Gothic revival (Literature)

Fiction, Historical. See Historical fiction

Fiction Collective

Baumbach, J. Who do they think they are? A personal history of the Fiction Collective. *In* Anderson, E. and Kinzie, M. eds. The little magazine in America: a modern documentary history p625-34

Lyons, G. Report on the Fiction Collective. *In* Anderson, E. and Kinzie, M. eds. The little magazine in America: a modern documentary history p635-47

Fictions (Law)

Barfield, O. Poetic diction and legal fiction. *In* Barfield, O. The rediscovery of meaning, and other essays p44-64

Fictitious places. See Geographical myths

Fidā'iyun. See Fedayeen

Fiddler on the roof (Motion picture)

Kauffmann, S. Fiddler on the roof. *In* Kauffmann, S. Living images p86-87

Fido, Franco

Boccaccio's ars narrandi in the sixth day of the Decameron. *In* Italian literature: roots and branches p225-42

An introduction to the theater of Angelo Beolco. *In* Renaissance drama [1973] p203-18

Fieandt, Kai von

Some psychological constituents and aspects of object perception. *In* Perception p72-83

Fiedler, Leonhard M.

Molière on Max Reinhardt's stage. *In* Johnson, R. B.; Neumann, E. S. and Trail, G. T. eds. Molière and the commonwealth of letters: patrimony and posterity p591-602

Fiedler, Leslie Aaron

The defense of the illusion and the creation of myth; device and symbol in the plays of Shakespeare. *In* Wimsatt, W. K. ed. Literary criticism: idea and act p97-109

Elite literature and mass society. *In* Mann, D. A. ed. The arts in a democratic society p118-39

The many names of S. Levin: an essay in genre criticism. *In* The Fiction of Bernard Malamud p149-61

Towards a definition of popular literature. *In* Bigsby, C. W. E. Superculture p28-42

About

Sale, R. H. Leslie Fiedler. *In* Sale, R. H. On not being good enough p144-48

About individual works
The death and rebirth of the novel

Vidal, G. The hacks of academe. *In* Vidal, G. Matters of fact and of fiction p89-98

Love and death in the American novel

Howe, I. Literature on the couch. *In* Howe, I. Celebrations and attacks p150-54

The return of the vanishing American

Lander, D. Eve among the Indians. *In* Diamond, A. and Edwards, L. R. eds. The authority of experience p194-211

Fiefs. See Feudalism; Land tenure

Field, James A.

Philanthropy. *In* Encyclopedia of American foreign policy p763-72

Field, Leslie A.

Bernard Malamud and the marginal Jew. *In* The Fiction of Bernard Malamud p97-116

Field, Phyllis Frances

Republicans and Black suffrage in New York State: the grass roots response. *In* Swierenga, R. P. ed. Beyond the Civil War synthesis p149-62

Field, Stephen Johnson

About

White, G. E. Miller, Bradley, Field and the reconstructed Constitution. *In* White, G. E. The American judicial tradition p84-108

Field theory (Physics)

See also Gravitation

History

Doran, B. G. Origins and consolidation of field theory in nineteenth-century Britain: from the mechanical to the electromagnetic view of nature. *In* Historical studies in the physical sciences v6 p133-260

Field work (Educational method)

Stephenson, J. B. and Sexton, R. F. Experiential education and revitalization of the liberal arts. *In* Hook, S.; Kurtz, P. W. and Todorovich, M. eds. The philosophy of the curriculum: the need for general education p177-96

Field work (Social sciences) See Social sciences—Field work

Fielding, Henry

About

Auty, S. G. "The new species of writing founded by Mr Fielding." *In* Auty, S. G. The comic spirit of eighteenth-century novels p34-54

Burke, J. J. History without history: Henry Fielding's theory of fiction. *In* A Provision of human nature p45-63

Durant, J. D. The "art of thriving" in Fielding's comedies. *In* A Provision of human nature p25-35

Fielding, Henry—About—*Continued*

Lyons, J. O. The circumference of the self. *In* Lyons, J. O. The invention of the self p197-218

Skilton, D. Richardson and Fielding. *In* Skilton, D. The English novel p19-31

Williamson, E. Guiding principles in Fielding's criticism of the critics. *In* A Provision of human nature p 1-24

About individual works
Amelia

Battestin, M. C. The problem of Amelia: Hume, Barrow, and the conversion of Captain Booth. *In* ELH essays for Earl R. Wasserman p320-55

Eaves, T. C. D. Amelia and Clarissa. *In* A Provision of human nature p95-110

Maresca, T. E. Fielding. *In* Maresca, T. E. Epic to novel p181-233

Rothstein, E. Amelia. *In* Rothstein, E. Systems of order and inquiry in later eighteenth-century fiction p154-207

Spacks, P. A. M. Laws of time: Fielding and Boswell. *In* Spacks, P. A. M. Imagining a self p264-99

An apology for the life of Mrs Shamela Andrews

Manlove, C. N. Fielding. *In* Manlove, C. N. Literature and reality, 1600-1800 p136-48

Joseph Andrews

Karl, F. R. Henry Fielding: the novel, the epic, and the comic sense of life. *In* Karl, F. R. The adversary literature p146-82

Maresca, T. E. Fielding. *In* Maresca, T. E. Epic to novel p181-233

Joseph Andrews (Chapters V and VIII)

Cockshut, A. O. J. Richardson and Fielding. *In* Cockshut, A. O. J. Man and woman: a study of love and the novel, 1740-1940 p32-45

Tom Jones

Baker, J. R. From imitation to rhetoric: the Chicago Critics, Wayne C. Booth, and Tom Jones. *In* Spilka, M. ed. Towards a poetics of fiction p136-56

Hutchens, E. N. O Attic shape! The cornering of square. *In* A Provision of human nature p37-44

Karl, F. R. Henry Fielding: the novel, the epic, and the comic sense of life. *In* Karl, F. R. The adversary literature p146-82

Manlove, C. N. Fielding. *In* Manlove, C. N. Literature and reality, 1600-1800 p136-48

Maresca, T. E. Fielding. *In* Maresca, T. E. Epic to novel p181-233

Miller, S. Eighteenth-century play and the game of Tom Jones. *In* A Provision of human nature p83-93

Park, W. Ironist and moralist: the two readers of Tom Jones. *In* Studies in eighteenth-century culture v8 p233-42

Røstvig, M. S. Tom Jones and the choice of Hercules. *In* Røstvig, M. S. ed. Fair forms p147-77

Spacks, P. A. M. Young men's fancies: James Boswell, Henry Fielding. *In* Spacks, P. A. M. Imagining a self p227-63

Characters—Tom Jones

Torrance, R. M. Moral rake and masterful lackey. *In* Torrance, R. M. The comic hero p177-205

Characters—William Booth

Battestin, M. C. The problem of Amelia: Hume, Barrow, and the conversion of Captain Booth. *In* ELH essays for Earl R. Wasserman p320-55

Characters—Women

Rogers, K. Richardson's empathy with women. *In* Diamond, A. and Edwards, L. R. eds. The authority of experience p118-36

Editors

Cook, D. L. Bowers does Fielding. *In* Review v 1 1979 p13-27

Ethics

See Fielding, Henry—Religion and ethics

Knowledge—Folklore, mythology

Røstvig, M. S. Tom Jones and the choice of Hercules. *In* Røstvig, M. S. ed. Fair forms p147-77

Religion and ethics

Wolfe, G. H. Lessons in evil: Fielding's ethics in The Champion essays. *In* A Provision of human nature p65-81

Fielding, Henry, supposed author
About individual works
An address to the electors of Great Britain, wherein the power of the people is traced from its original, and confirmed by undoubted authorities

Cleary, T. R. The case for Fielding's authorship of An address to the electors of Great Britain (1740) reopened. *In* Virginia. University. Bibliographical Society. Studies in bibliography v28 p308-18

Fielding, K. J.

Carlyle and the Saint-Simonians (1830-1832): new considerations. *In* Carlyle and his contemporaries p35-59

Froude and Carlyle: some new considerations. *In* Fielding, K. J. and Tarr, R. L. eds. Carlyle past and present p239-69

Froude's revenge, or The Carlyles and Erasmus A. Darwin. *In* English Association. Essays and studies, 1978 p75-97

Fields, Joseph, and Chodorov, Jerome
About individual works
The ponder heart

Cornell, B. G. Ambiguous necessity: a study of The ponder heart. *In* Prenshaw, P. W. ed. Eudora Welty p208-19

Fields, William Claude
About

Sheed, W. Toward the Black Pussy Cafe. *In* Sheed, W. The good word & other words p184-93

Fiene, Donald M.

Kurt Vonnegut as an American dissident: his popularity in the Soviet Union and his affinities with Russian literature. *In* Klinkowitz, J. and Lawler, D. L. eds. Vonnegut in America p258-93

Fiesole, Giovanni da, called Fra Angelico
About individual works
The Last Judgement

Meyers, J. Fra Angelico and The rainbow. *In* Meyers, J. Painting and the novel p53-64

Fife, Austin E.
Birthmarks and psychic imprinting of babies in Utah folk medicine. *In* American folk medicine p273-83

Fifteenth century
Kemp, M. From "mimesis" to "fantasia": the quattrocento vocabulary of creation, inspiration and genius in the visual arts. *In* Viator: medieval and Renaissance studies v8 p347-98

Rotz, R. A. Investigating urban uprisings with examples from Hanseatic towns, 1374-1416. *In* Order and innovation in the Middle Ages p215-33

Fighter planes. See F 111 (Fighter planes)

Fighting. See War

Fighting (Psychology) See Aggressiveness (Psychology)

Figueroa, John J.
Derek Walcott's 'Poopa, da' was a fête! and Evan Jones's 'Lament of the Banana Man.' *In* Baugh, E. ed. Critics on Caribbean literature p149-52

Figures of speech
Arendt, H. Mental activities in a world of appearance. *In* Arendt, H. The life of the mind v 1 p67-125

Barfield, O. Poetic diction and legal fiction. *In* Barfield, O. The rediscovery of meaning, and other essays p44-64

Burke, K. Rhetoric, poetics, and philosophy. *In* Burks, D. M. ed. Rhetoric, philosophy, and literature: an exploration p15-33

Hill, A. A. Analogies, icons, and images. *In* Hill, A. A. Constituent and pattern in poetry p53-70

Miller, J. H. Nature and the linguistic moment. *In* Knoepflmacher, U. C. and Tennyson, G. B. eds. Nature and the Victorian imagination p440-51

Morris, W. Closing the gap. *In* Morris, W. Earthly delights, unearthly adornments p7-12

Morris, W. An image sampler. *In* Morris, W. Earthly delights, unearthly adornments p13-17

Morris, W. Origins: the self-imaged imagemaker. *in* Morris, W. Earthly delights, unearthly adornments p169-79

Morris, W. Unearthly adornments. *In* Morris, W. Earthly delights, unearthly adornments p181-89

Natanson, M. A. The arts of indirection. *In* Burks, D. M. ed. Rhetoric, philosophy, and literature: an exploration p35-47

Sadock, J. M. Figurative speech and linguistics. *In* Ortony, A. ed. Metaphor and thought p46-63

Sapir, J. D. The anatomy of metaphor. *In* The Social use of metaphor p3-32

White, H. V. Historicism, history, and the figurative imagination. *In* White, H. V. Tropics of discourse p101-20

See also particular figures of speech, e.g. Metonymy

Figurines. See Bronze figurines; Terracottas

Figurines, Bronze. See Bronze figurines

Fijian literature (English)
Nandan, S. The immigrant Indian experience in literature: Trinidad and Fiji. *In* Narasimhaiah, C. D. ed. Awakened conscience p346-59

Filarete, Antonio di Pietro Averlino, called

About individual works

St Peter's, Vatican, Doors

Spencer, J. R. Filarete's bronze doors at St Peter's. *In* Collaboration in Italian Renaissance art p33-57

Filer, Malva Esther
Vargas Llosa, the novelist as a critic. *In* Rossman, C. R. and Friedman, A. W. eds. Mario Vargas Llosa p109-19

Filipinos

Ethnology

See Ethnology—Philippine Islands

Filipinos in the United States
Melendy, H. B. Filipinos in the United States. *In* The Asian American: the historical experience p101-28

Filler, Louis
Consensus: how academics keep from murdering each other at professional meetings. *In* Essays in honor of Russel B. Nye p42-64

Introduction: a question of quality. *In* Filler, L. ed. A question of quality: popularity and value in modern creative writing p 1-7

Meyer Levin's Compulsion. *In* Filler, L. ed. A question of quality: popularity and value in modern creative writing p148-59

Fillmore, Charles J.
Topics in lexical semantics. *In* Current issues in linguistic theory p76-138

Film acting. See Moving-picture acting

Film adaptations
Heins, E. L. Literature bedeviled: a searching look at filmstrips. *In* Horn Book Magazine. Crosscurrents of criticism p88-95

Powell, E. D. The film of the book. *In* Royal Society of Literature of the United Kingdom, London. Essays by divers hands v38 p93-111

Truffaut, F. A certain tendency of the French cinema. *In* Nichols, B. ed. Movies and methods p224-37

Film authorship. See Moving-picture authorship

Film collections. See Moving-picture film collections

Film kinesics. See Nonverbal communication in motion pictures

Film noir, Notes on. Schrader, P. *In* Denby, D. ed. Awake in the dark p278-90

Filmed books. See Film adaptations

Films. See Moving-pictures

Films from books. See Film adaptations

Final cause. See Causation; Teleology

Finance
See also Foreign exchange; Inflation (Finance); International finance; Money; Profit

Underdeveloped areas
See Underdeveloped areas—Finance

Finance, International. See International finance

Finance, Public
Musgrave, R. A. Adam Smith on public finance and distribution. *In* The Market and the state p296-319

Finance, Public—*Continued*

Peacock, A. T. The treatment of the principles of public finance in The wealth of nations. *In* Skinner, A. S. and Wilson, T. eds. Essays on Adam Smith p553-67

See also Budget; Debts, Public; Deficit financing; Metropolitan finance; Money; Taxation

Accounting

See Legislative auditing

Genoa—History

Kirshner, J. Conscience and public finance: a Questio disputata of John of Legano on the public debt of Genoa. *In* Philosophy and humanism p434-53

Great Britain—History

Kaeuper, R. W. Royal finance and the crisis of 1297. *In* Order and innovation in the Middle Ages p103-10

Prestwich, M. Italian merchants in late thirteenth and early fourteenth century England. *In* The Dawn of modern banking p77-104

United States

Smith, B. L. R. The public use of the private sector. *In* Smith, B. L. R. ed. The new political economy: the public use of the private sector p 1-45

Finch, Anne (Kingsmill) Countess of Winchilsea. See Winchilsea, Anne (Kingsmill) Finch, Countess of

Finch, Chauncey Edgar

Three textual notes. *In* Illinois classical studies v3, 1978 p262-72

Finch, Christopher

About individual works

The art of Walt Disney

Craft, R. In the mouse trap. *In* Craft, R. Current convictions p285-98

Findlay, John Niemayer

Axiological ethics. *In* New studies in ethics v2 p119-213

The constitution of human values. *In* Royal Institute of Philosophy. Human values p189-207

Phenomenology and the meaning of realism. *In* Pivčević, E. ed. Phenomenology and philosophical understanding p143-58

Finé, Oronce

About

Heninger, S. K. Oronce Finé and English textbooks for the mathematical sciences. *In* Studies in the continental background of Renaissance English literature: essays presented to John L. Lievsay p170-85

Fine arts. See Art; Arts

Finegan, Jack

About individual works

The archeology of the New Testament

Hyman, S. E. History and sacred history. *In* Hyman, S. E. The critic's credentials p313-25

Finer, Samuel Edward

State- and nation-building in Europe: the role of the military. *In* Tilly, C. ed. The formation of national states in Western Europe p84-163

Finestone, Harold

The delinquent and society: the Shaw and McKay tradition. *In* Delinquency, crime, and society p23-49

Finger, Seymour Maxwell

International terrorism and the United Nations. *In* International terrorism p323-48

The Nixon Doctrine and the Middle East. *In* The New world balance and peace in the Middle East: reality or mirage? p209-16

Fingers in the head (Motion picture)

Truffaut, F. Jacques Doillon: Les doigts dans le tête. *In* Truffaut, F. The films in my life p343-45

Fink, Howard

The shadow of Men like gods: Orwell's Coming up for air as parody. *In* H. G. Wells and modern science fiction p144-58

Finland

History—Revolution, 1917-1918

Smith, C. J. Soviet Russia and the Red revolution of 1918 in Finland. *In* Hammond, T. T. ed. The anatomy of Communist takeovers p71-93

History—1939-

Devlin, K. Finland in 1948: the lesson of a crisis. *In* Hammond, T. T. ed. The anatomy of Communist takeovers p433-47

Politics and government—1917-

Alapuro, R. and Allardt, E. The Lapua movement: the threat of rightist takeover in Finland, 1930-32. *In* The Breakdown of democratic regimes pt2 p122-41

Finlayson, Geoffrey Beauchamp Alistair Mowbray

Shaftesbury. *In* Hollis, P. ed. Pressure from without p159-82

Finley, John Huston, 1904-

Politics and early Attic tragedy. *In* Harvard Studies in classical philology v71 p 1-13

Finn, Chester E.

Federal patronage of the universities: a rose by many other names? *In* Hook, S.; Kurtz, P. W. and Todorovich, M. eds. The university and the state: what role for government in higher education? p7-49

Finn MacCool. See Finn Mac Cumaill

Finn Mac Cumaill

MacKillop, J. J. Finn MacCool: the hero and the anti-hero in Irish folk tradition. *In* Casey, D. J. and Rhodes, R. E. eds. Views of the Irish peasantry, 1800-1916 p86-106

About

Wain, J. Alternative poetry. *In* Wain, J. Alternative poetry. *In* Wain, J. Professing poetry p13-44

Finneran, Richard J.

A preliminary note on the text of A vision (1937). *In* Yeats and the occult p317-20

The sources of James Stephen's Reincarnations: "alone I did it, barring for the noble assistance of the gods." *In* Tulane studies in English v22 p143-53

W. B. Yeats. *In* Finneran, R. J. ed. Anglo-Irish literature p216-314

W. B. Yeats: some recent bibliographical and editorial work. *In* Review, v 1 1979 p233-48

Finneran, Richard J. and Harper, George Mills

"He loved strange thought": W. B. Yeats and William Thomas Horton. *In* Yeats and the occult p190-203

Finney, Brian H.

D. H. Lawrence's progress to maturity: from holograph manuscript to final publication of The Prussian officer and other stories. *In* Virginia. University. Bibliographical Society. Studies in bibliography v28 p321-32

Finney, Charles Grandison

About

McLoughlin, W. G. Revivalism. *In* The Rise of Adventism p119-53

Finnish Communist Party. See Communist Party of Finland

Finnish drama

History and criticism

Binham, P. New Finnish drama—the fifties and after. *In* Dauenhauer, R. and Binham, P. eds. Snow in May p48-50

Dauenhauer, R. Footnote on Finnish drama. *In* Dauenhauer, R. and Binham, P. eds. Snow in May p51-52

Finnish fiction

History and criticism

Laitinen, K. From the forest to the city: the great tradition in Finnish prose. *In* Dauenhauer, R. and Binham, P. eds. Snow in May p21-28

Finnish literature

History and criticism

Dauenhauer, R. The view from the Aspen Grove: Paavo Haavikko in national and international context. *In* Dauenhauer, R. and Binham, P. eds. Snow in May p67-97

Knight, W. Some general notes on what contemporary Finnish writing is like (it's like blueberries) and what it's not like. *In* Dauenhauer, R. and Binham, P. eds. Snow in May p41-47

Finnish poetry

History and criticism

Dauenhauer, R. Some notes on Zen Buddhist tendencies in modern Finnish poetry. *In* Dauenhauer, R. and Binham, P. eds. Snow in May p60-66

Svedberg, I. Political poetry in modern Finnish literature. *In* Dauenhauer, R. and Binham, P. eds. Snow in May p53-57

Finnish political poetry. See Political poetry, Finnish

Finocchiaro, Maurice A.

Commentary: dialectical aspects of the Copernican revolution: conceptual elucidations and historiographical problems. *In* The Copernican achievement p204-12

Fionn Mac Cumhail. See Finn Mac Cumaill

Fiorenza, Elisabeth Schüssler

Miracles, mission, and apologetics: an introduction. *In* Aspects of religious propaganda in Judaism and early Christianity p 1-25

Wisdom mythology and the Christological hymns of the New Testament. *In* Aspects of wisdom in Judaism and early Christianity p17-41

Fiorenza, Francis Schüssler

American culture and Modernism: Shailer Mathews's interpretation of American Christianity. *In* America in theological perspective p163-86

Work and critical theology. *In* Heisler, W. J. and Houck, J. W. eds. A matter of dignity p23-44

Fiorina, Morris P.; Rohde, David W. and Wissel, Peter

Historical change in House turnover. *In* Ornstein, N. J. ed. Congress in change p24-57

Firdausi. See Firdawsī

Firdawsī

About individual works

Shāhnāma

Hanaway, W. L. The Iranian epics. *In* Oinas, F. J. ed. Heroic epic and saga p76-98

Firdousi. See Firdawsī

Firdūsī. See Firdawsī

Fire

Verdenius, W. J. Heraclitus' conception of fire. *In* Kephalaion p 1-8

Fire (in religion, folklore, etc.)

Coomaraswamy, A. K. Measures of fire. *In* Coomaraswamy, A. K. Selected papers v2 p159-65

Nagy, G. J. Six studies of sacral vocabulary relating to the fireplace. *In* Harvard Studies in classical philology v78 p71-106

Fire in literature

Griffin, A. Fire and ice in Frankenstein. *In* Levine, G. L. and Knoepflmacher, U. C. eds. The endurance of Frankenstein p49-73

Firearms

Ficks, R. S. The burgeoning arsenal: developments and projections. *In* Beaumont, R. A. and Edmonds, M. eds. War in the next decade p135-56

Williams, R. Science, technology, and the future of warfare. *In* Beaumont, R. A. and Edmonds, M. eds. War in the next decade p157-79

History

Inalcik, H. The socio-political effects of the diffusion of fire-arms in the Middle East. *In* War, technology and society in the Middle East p195-217

Petrović, D. Fire-arms in the Balkans on the eve of and after the Ottoman conquests of the fourteenth and fifteenth centuries. *In* War, technology and society in the Middle East p164-94

First-born children. See Children, First-born

First-order logic

Peacocke, C. An appendix to David Wiggins' 'note.' *In* Evans, G. L. and McDowell, J. H. eds. Truth and meaning p313-24

First printings of American authors: contributions toward descriptive checklists

Matheson, W. American literary bibliography—FPAA style. *In* Review, v 1 1979 p173-81

Firth, Felicity M.

Comedy in Italy. *In* Howarth, W. D. ed. Comic drama p63-80

Firth, Raymond William

Relations between personal kin (waris) among Kelantan Malays. *In* Social organization and the applications of anthropology p23-61

Fiscal policy

Machlup, F. The effects of fiscal policy and the choice of definitions. *In* Theory for economic efficiency: essays in honor of Abba P. Lerner p92-109

See also Monetary policy

Fiscal relations, Intergovernmental. See Intergovernmental fiscal relations

Fisch, Harold
A response to Ernst Simon. *In* Modern Jewish ethics p57-61

Shakespeare and the Puritan dynamic. *In* Shakespeare survey 27 p81-92

Fisch, Max Harold
Peirce's general theory of signs. *In* Sebeok, T. A. ed. Sight, sound, and sense p31-70

The poliscraft. *In* Philosophy and the civilizing arts p24-48

Vico's Pratica. *In* Giambattista Vico's science of humanity p423-30

Fisch, Rudolf
Psychology of science. *In* Science, technology and society p277-318

Fischel, Henry Albert
The transformation of wisdom in the world of Midrash. *In* Aspects of wisdom in Judaism and early Christianity p67-101

Fischel, Walter Joseph
Garcia de Orta—a militant Marrano in Portuguese-India in the 16th century. *In* Salo Wittmayer Baron v 1 p407-32

Fischer, Claude S.
The metropolitan experience. *In* Hawley, A. H. and Rock, V. P. eds. Metropolitan America in contemporary perspective p201-34

Fischer, David Hackett
The braided narrative: substance and form in social history. *In* Fletcher, A. J. S. ed. The literature of fact p109-33

Fischer, Ernst
About
Demetz, P. Transformations of recent Marxist criticism: Hans Mayer, Ernst Fischer, Lucien Goldmann. *In* The Frontiers of literary criticism p75-92

Fischer, Heinz Dietrich
The contribution of Eurovision and Intervision to global television. *In* Fischer, H. D. and Merrill, J. C. eds. International and intercultural communication p350-71

Entertainment—an underestimated central function of communication. *In* Fischer, H. D. and Melnik, S. R. eds. Entertainment: a cross-cultural examination p2-19

Forms and functions of supranational communication. *In* Fischer, H. D. and Merrill, J. C. eds. International and intercultural communication p5-17

From cooperation to quasi-congruency—interdependencies between the Olympic games and television. *In* Fischer, H. D. and Melnik, S. R. eds. Entertainment: a cross-cultural examination p208-33

Periodicals and the international communication system. *In* Fischer, H. D. and Merrill, J. C. eds. International and intercultural communication p99-114

Press councils throughout the world: an empirical approach. *In* Fischer, H. D. and Merrill, J. C. eds. International and intercultural communication p161-74

Fischer, Michael M. J.
On changing the concept and position of Persian women. *In* Beck, L. and Keddie, N. R. eds. Women in the Muslim world p189-215

Fischer, Robert
About
Koestler, A. The glorious and bloody game: Requiem for Reykjavik. *In* Koestler, A. The heel of Achilles p214-31

Fischer, Wolfram, and Lundgreen, Peter
The recruitment and training of administrative and technical personnel. *In* Tilly, C. ed. The formation of national states in Western Europe p456-561

Fischer-Galati, Stephen A.
The Communist takeover of Rumania: a function of Soviet power. *In* Hammond, T. T. ed. The anatomy of Communist takeovers p310-20

Judeo-Christian aspects of Pax Ottomanica. *In* Király, B. K. ed. Tolerance and movements of religious dissent in Eastern Europe p185-97

The Moldavian Soviet Republic in Soviet domestic and foreign policy. *In* Szporluk, R. ed. The influence of East Europe and the Soviet West on the USSR p229-50

Fish, Peter G.
William Howard Taft and Charles Evans Hughes: conservative politicians as chief judicial reformers. *In* The Supreme Court review, 1975 p123-45

Fish, Stanley Eugene
Catechizing the reader: Herbert's Socratean rhetoric. *In* Sloan, T. O. and Waddington, R. B. eds. The rhetoric of Renaissance poetry p174-88

Literature in the reader: affective stylistics. *In* Primeau, R. ed. Influx p154-79

Problem solving in Comus. *In* Illustrious evidence p115-31

About individual works
Self-consuming artifacts: the experience of seventeenth-century literature
Duhamel, P. A. Medieval intuition and seventeenth-century dialectic. *In* Medievalia et humanistica no. 5 p243-46

Fish as food. See Sea food

Fish law. See Fishery law and legislation

Fishbein, Martin
Attitudes and behavioral prediction: an overview. *In* Major social issues p377-89

Fishbein, Meyer Harry
Selected materials in the National Archives relating to commerce and industry. *In* Pattern and process p224-28

Fishel, Edwin C.
The mythology of Civil War intelligence. *In* Hubbell, J. T. ed. Battles lost and won p83-106

Fisher, Alan W.
Crimean separatism in the Ottoman Empire. *In* Nationalism in a non-national state p57-76

Fisher, Bud. See Fisher, Rudolph

Fisher, Elizabeth Ann
Two notes on the Heroides. *In* Harvard Studies in classical philology v74 p193-205

Fisher, John Hurt, ed.
About individual works
The complete poetry and prose of Geoffrey Chaucer
Hanna, R. A new edition of Chaucer. *In* Review, v 1 1979 p61-74

Fisher, Marguerite J.
Eighteenth-century theorists of women's liberation. *In* "Remember the ladies": new perspectives on women in American history p39-47

Fisher, Marvin

About individual works
Going under: Melville's short fiction and the American 1850s
Parker, H. Tromping through fairyland: two books on Melville's tales. *In* Review, v 1 1979 p183-93

Fisher, Marvin, and Buckingham, Willis J.
Whitman and Dickinson. *In* American literary scholarship, 1975 p83-102
Whitman and Dickinson [another essay] *In* American literary scholarship, 1976 p61-78

Fisher, Mary Frances (Kennedy)

About individual works
The art of eating
Auden, W. H. Introduction to The art of eating by M. F. K. Fisher. *In* Praise from famous men: an anthology of introductions p 1-9

Fisher, Philip James
City matters: city minds. *In* The Worlds of Victorian fiction p371-89

Fisher, Rudolph

About
Bone, R. A. Three versions of pastoral. *In* Bone, R. A. Down home p139-70

Fisher, Susan M.
The smell of waste. *In* Gross, B. and Gross, R. eds. The children's rights movement p100-09

Fisher, Sydney Nettleton. See Part 2 under title: Nationalism in a non-national state

Fisher, Vardis

About
Meldrum, B. Vardis Fisher's Antelope people: pursuing an elusive dream. *In* Bingham, E. R. and Love, G. A. eds. Northwest perspectives p152-66

Fisher King
Hays, P. L. Hemingway and the Fisher King ("God rest you merry, gentlemen.") *In* Benson, J. J. ed. The short stories of Ernest Hemingway: critical essays p223-27

Fisheries
Holt, S. J. Mediterranean and Black Sea fisheries. *In* Borgese, E. M. and Krieger, D. eds. The tides of change p166-78
Kent, G. Ocean fisheries management. *In* Orr, D. W. and Soroos, M. S. eds. The global predicament p232-48
See also Fishways; Herring-fisheries

Law
See Fishery law and legislation

Africa
Maclaren, P. I. R. The fishing devices of Central and Southern Africa. *In* The Occasional papers of the Rhodes-Livingstone Museum p427-88

Fisheries, Cooperative

Vietnam—Case studies
Kaufman, H. K. Culao—a Vietnamese fishing cooperative and its problems. *In* Social organization and the applications of anthropology p235-72

Fishery cooperatives. See Fisheries, Cooperative

Fishery law and legislation

United States
Morrison, F. L. The right to fish for seacoast products: Gibbons v. Ogden resurrected. *In* The Supreme Court review, 1977 p239-56

Fishes. See Fisheries

Fishing

Implements and appliances
Maclaren, P. I. R. The fishing devices of Central and Southern Africa. *In* The Occasional papers of the Rhodes-Livingstone Museum p427-88

Fishing regulations. See Fishery law and legislation

Fishkin, James
Tyranny and democratic theory. *In* Laslett, P. and Fishkin, J. eds. Philosophy, politics and society p197-226

Fishman, Joshua A.
The sociology of language: yesterday, today, and tomorrow. *In* Current issues in linguistic theory p51-75

Fishman, Robert
From the radiant city to Vichy: Le Corbusier's plans and politics, 1928-1942. *In* Walden, R. ed. The open hand p244-83

Fishways

Mexico—Campeche (State)
Thompson, J. E. S. 'Canals' of the Rio Candelaria basin, Campeche, Mexico. *In* Mesoamerican archaeology p297-302

Fishwick, Duncan
Flamen Augustorum. *In* Harvard Studies in classical philology v74 p299-312

Fishwick, Marshall William
Icons of America. *In* Browne, R. B. and Fishwick, M. W. eds. Icons of America p 3-12
The thingness of things. *In* Essays in honor of Russel B. Nye p65-73

Fisk, Milton
Academic freedom in class society. *In* The Concept of academic freedom p5-26
Comments on Hardy Jones and Bertram Davis. *In* The Concept of academic freedom p52-55

About individual works
Academic freedom in class society
Davis, B. H. Academic freedom, academic neutrality, and the social system. *In* The Concept of academic freedom p27-36
Jones, H. E. Academic freedom as a moral right. *In* The Concept of academic freedom p37-51

Fisk, Nicholas
One thumping lie only. *In* Blishen, E. ed. The thorny paradise p117-22

Fiske, Adele M.
Buddhism in India today. *In* Dumoulin, H. ed. Buddhism in the modern world p130-46

Fiske, Marjorie
The reality of psychological change. *In* Jarvik, L. F. ed. Aging into the 21st century p97-111

Fitch, Brian T.

A critique of Roland Barthes' essay on Bataille's Histoire de l'oeil. *in* Valdés, M. J. and Miller, O. J. eds. Interpretation of narrative p48-57

Fitch, Frederic Brenton

Towards proving the consistency of Principia mathematica. *In* Nakhnikian, G. ed. Bertrand Russell's philosophy p 1-17

Fitch, James Marston

Uses of the artistic past. *In* Yoder, D. ed. American folklife p27-49

Fitch, Lyle Craig

Fiscal and productive efficiency in urban government systems. *In* Hawley, A. H. and Rock, V. P. eds. Metropolitan America in contemporary perspective p397-429

Fitch, William. See Benoit de Canfield, Father

Fitzgerald, Charles Patrick

About individual works

The southern expansion of the Chinese people: southern fields and southern ocean

Freedman, M. An epicycle of Cathay; or, The southward expansion of the Sinologists. *In* Social organization and the applications of anthropology p302-32

FitzGerald, Edward, tr.

About individual works

The Rubaiyat of Omar Khayyam

McAleer, E. C. Empedocles, Omar Khayyám, and Rabbi Ben Ezra. *In* Tennessee Studies in literature v20 p76-84

FitzGerald, Frances

A reporter at large: slightly exaggerated enthusiasms. *In* Radosh, R. ed. The new Cuba: paradoxes and potentials p138-72

Fitzgerald, Francis Scott Key

About

Berryman, J. Enslavement: Three American cases; F. Scott Fitzgerald. *In* Berryman, J. The freedom of the poet p197-204

Farrell, J. T. F. Scott Fitzgerald and his romanticism. *In* Farrell, J. T. Literary essays, 1954-1974 p54-57

Kenner, H. The Promised Land. *In* Kenner, H. A homemade world p20-49

Milne, G. Practitioners, 1920-1960. *In* Milne, G. The sense of society p205-35

O'Hara, J. An artist is his own fault. *In* O'Hara, J. "An artist is his own fault" p142-54

O'Hara, J. In memory of Scott Fitzgerald: certain aspects. *In* O'Hara, J. "An artist is his own fault" p135-37

O'Hara, J. Scott Fitzgerald—odds and ends. *In* O'Hara, J. "An artist is his own fault" p138-42

Sheed, W. F. Scott Fitzgerald. *In* Sheed, W. The good word & other words p243-47

About individual works

The Basil and Josephine stories

Balakian, N. Beautiful and undammed: stories by Fitzgerald. *In* Balakian, N. Critical encounters p146-48

The great Gatsby

Burhans, C. S. Jay Gatsby and Dr. Diver; Fitzgerald's Songs of innocence and experience. *In* Garvin, H. R. ed. Makers of the twentieth-century novel p228-44

Donald, M. The traditional novel. *In* Donald, M. The American novel in the twentieth century p13-72

Emmitt, R. J. Love, death, and resurrection in The great Gatsby. *In* Aeolian harps p273-89

Fetterley, J. The great Gatsby: Fitzgerald's droit de seigneur. *In* Fetterley, J. The resisting reader p72-100

Marx, L. The American Revolution and the American landscape. *In* America's continuing revolution p247-69

Miller, J. E. Fitzgerald's Gatsby: the world as ash heap. *In* French, W. G. ed. The twenties p181-202

Letters

Connolly, C. F. Scott Fitzgerald. *In* Connolly, C. The evening colonnade p269-72

Tender is the night

Burhans, C. S. Jay Gatsby and Dr. Diver: Fitzgerald's Songs of innocence and experience. *In* Garvin, H. R. ed. Makers of the twentieth-century novel p228-44

Rahv, P. F. Scott Fitzgerald on the Riviera. *In* Rahv, P. Essays on literature and politics, 1932-1972 p23-24

Bibliography

Bryer, J. R. Fitzgerald and Hemingway. *In* American literary scholarship, 1973 p150-76

Bryer, J. R. Fitzgerald and Hemingway [another essay] *In* American literary scholarship, 1974 p139-64

Bryer, J. R. Fitzgerald and Hemingway [another essay] *In* American literary scholarship, 1975 p167-200

Bryer, J. R. Fitzgerald and Hemingway [another essay] *In* American literary scholarship, 1976 p141-66

Bryer, J. R. Fitzgerald and Hemingway [another essay] *In* American literary scholarship, 1977 p163-86

Biography—Character

Sarotte, G. M. Latent homosexuality: short of and beyond true heterosexuality: Francis Scott Fitzgerald: self-virilization and its failure. *In* Sarotte, G. M. Like a brother, like a lover p212-28

Psychology

See Fitzgerald, Francis Scott Key—Biography—Character

Style

Morris, W. Scott Fitzgerald. *In* Morris, W. Earthly delights, unearthly adornments p117-22

Fitz Gerald, Gregory

The satiric short story: a definition. *In* May, C. E. ed. Short story theories p128-88

FitzGerald, Mary M.

A Richard Murphy bibliography. *In* Harmon, M. ed. Richard Murphy: poet of two traditions p104-17

Fitzgerald, Robert, tr.

About individual works

The Odyssey

Brower, R. A. A poet's Odyssey. *In* Brower, R. A. Mirror on mirror p96-102

Fitzgerald, Ross

Abraham Maslow's hierarchy of needs—an exposition and evaluation. *In* Fitzgerald, R. ed. Human needs and politics p36-51

The ambiguity and rhetoric of 'need.' *In* Fitzgerald, R. ed. Human needs and politics p195-212

Essay 3. *In* Fitzgerald, R. ed. What it means to be human p44-63

Fitzgerald, Zelda (Sayre)

About

Going, W. T. Zelda Sayre Fitzgerald and Sara Haardt Mencken. *In* Going, W. T. Essays on Alabama literature p114-41

Fitz Gibbon, Constantine

About individual works

The life of Dylan Thomas

Kunitz, S. J. Sea son of the wave. *In* Kunitz, S. J. A kind of order, a kind of folly p228-32

Fitzhugh, George

About

West, T. R. The devices of nature: George Fitzhugh and Thomas Carlyle. *In* West, T. R. Nature, community & will p15-39

Fitzpatrick, Joseph P.

Transitional values of Puerto Ricans. *In* The Diverse society: implications for social policy p93-107

Fitzpatrick, Marjorie Ann

Molière and the early years of French-Canadian theater. *In* Johnson, R. B.; Neumann, E. S. and Trail, G. T. eds. Molière and the commonwealth of letters: patrimony and posterity p385-99

Fitzpatrick, Sheila

Cultural revolution as class war. *In* Cultural revolution in Russia, 1928-1931 p 8-40

Fitzroy, Robert

About

Hyman, S. E. A Darwin sidelight: the shape of the young man's nose. *In* Hyman, S. E. The critic's credentials p261-78

Fitzstephen, William

About individual works

Vita Sancti Thomae

Cheney, M. H. William Fitzstephen and his Life of Archbishop Thomas. *In* Church and government in the Middle Ages p139-56

Five Civilized Tribes. See Cherokee Indians; Choctaw Indians; Creek Indians; Seminole Indians

Five easy pieces (Motion picture)

Kauffmann, S. Five easy pieces. *In* Kauffmann, S. Living images p11-15

Flaccus, Avianus family. See Avianus Flaccus family

Flagellants and flagellation in literature

Ober, W. B. Swinburne's masochism: neuropathology and psychopathology. *In* Ober, W. B. Boswell's clap and other essays p43-88

Flags

Wales

Jones, D. The Welsh dragon. *In* Jones, D. The dying Gaul, and other writings p108-16

Flaherty, Joe

About individual works

Fogarty & Co

Sheed, W. There is no (Irish) Mafia. *In* Sheed, W. The good word & other words p100-04

Flanagan, Dorothy Belle. See Hughes, Dorothy Belle (Flanagan)

Flanagan, John Theodore

Folklore. *In* American literary scholarship, 1973 p382-410

Folklore [another essay] *In* American literary scholarship, 1974 p387-410

Jesse Stuart, regional novelist. *In* LeMaster J. R. and Clarke, M. W. eds. Jesse Stuart p70-88

Flanagan, William G. See London, B. jt. auth.

Flanders

Commerce—Great Britain

Munro, J. H. A. Industrial protectionism in medieval Flanders: urban or national? *In* The Medieval city p229-67

History

De Gryse, L. M. Some observations on the origin of the Flemish bailiff (bailli): the reign of Philip of Alsace. *In* Viator: medieval and Renaissance studies v7 p243-94

Industries

Mendels, F. F. Agriculture and peasant industry in eighteenth-century Flanders. *In* Parker, W. N. and Jones, E. L. eds. European peasants and their markets p179-204

Flandino, Ambrogio

About

Lemay, R. J. The fly against the elephant: Flandinus against Pomponazzi on fate. *In* Philosophy and humanism p70-99

Flandinus, Ambrosius. See Flandino, Ambrogio

Flandrin, Jean-Louis

Contraception, marriage, and sexual relations in the Christian West. *In* Biology of man in history p23-47

Flap (Motion picture)

Kauffmann, S. Flap. *In* Kauffmann, S. Living images p34-35

The flapper and her critics. Critoph, G. E. *In* "Remember the ladies": new perspectives on women in American history p145-60

Flast v. Cohen

In Fairfield, R. P. ed. Humanistic frontiers in American education p94-101

Flaubert, Gustave

About

Fairlie, A. Flaubert and some painters of his time. *In* The Artist and the writer in France p111-25

Goodheart, E. Flaubert and the powerlessness of art. *In* Goodheart, E. The failure of criticism p137-57

Larkin, M. More pessimism: Flaubert. *In* Larkin, M. Man and society in nineteenth-century realism p66-73

Lesser, S. O. The role of unconscious understanding in Flaubert and Dostoevsky. *In* Lesser, S. O. The whispered meanings p86-104

Flaubert, Gustave—About—*Continued*

Lewis, W. Gustave Flaubert; excerpt from "Men without art." *In* Lewis, W. Enemy salvoes p203-07

Pritchett, V. S. Gustave Flaubert: the quotidian. *In* Pritchett, V. S. The myth makers p128-35

Robinson, C. The idealist revolt. *In* Robinson, C. French literature in the nineteenth century p13-49

Terdiman, R. Flaubert and after: failure formalized. *In* Terdiman, R. The dialectics of isolation p60-95

About individual works
Flaubert in Egypt: a sensibility on tour

Connolly, C. Flaubert: 1. *In* Connolly, C. The evening colonnade p148-50

The legend of Saint Julien, hospitalier

Massey, I. Flaubert and "La légende de Saint-Julien l'hospitalier." *In* Massey, I. The gaping pig p156-84

Madame Bovary

Bersani, L. Flaubert and Emma Bovary: the hazards of literary fusion. *In* Spilka, M. ed. Towards a poetics of fiction p303-15

Lesser, S. O. The role of unconscious understanding in Flaubert and Dostoevsky. *In* Lesser, S. O. The whispered meanings p86-104

Pascal, R. The French masters: Gustave Flaubert: Madame Bovary. *In* Pascal, R. The dual voice p98-112

Sabin, M. The poverty of nature in Madame Bovary. *In* Sabin, M. English romanticism and the French tradition p258-76

Turnell, M. Flaubert. *In* Turnell, M. The rise of the French novel p169-218

Sentimental education

Williams, D. A. G. Flaubert: Sentimental education. *In* Williams, D. A. ed. The monster in the mirror p75-101

The temptation of Saint Anthony

Foucault, M. Fantasia of the library. *In* Foucault, M. Language, counter-memory, practice p87-109

Reff, T. Images of Flaubert's Queen of Sheba in later nineteenth-century art. *In* The Artist and the writer in France p126-33

Three tales

Raitt, A. W. Flaubert and the art of the short story. *In* Royal Society of Literature of the United Kingdom, London. Essays by divers hands v38 p112-26

Characters—Bouvard

Torrance, R. M. Insouciant lover and insatiable stumblebums. *In* Torrance, R. M. The comic hero p206-39

Characters—Emma Bovary

Bersani, L. Emma Bovary and the sense of sex. *In* Bersani, L. A future for Astyanax p89-105

Bersani, L. Flaubert and Emma Bovary: the hazards of literary fusion. *In* Spilka, M. ed. Towards a poetics of fiction p303-15

Characters—Pécuchet

Torrance, R. M. Insouciant lover and insatiable stumblebums. *In* Torrance, R. M. The comic hero p206-39

Influence—Vargas Llosa

Filer, M. E. Vargas Llosa, the novelist as a critic. *In* Rossman, C. R. and Friedman, A. W. eds. Mario Vargas Llosa p109-19

Flaxman, John

About

Bentley, G. E. A jewel in an Ethiop's ear. *In* Essick, R. N. and Pearce, D. R. eds. Blake in his time p213-40

Fleck, P. D.

Romance in Byron's The island. *In* Jump, J. D. ed. Byron p163-83

Fleet ballistic missile weapons systems

Tsipis, K. M. Anti-submarine warfare and missle submarines. *In* The Dynamics of the arms race p36-46

Fleischer, Robert

About individual works
Marsyas und Achaios

Hanfmann, G. M. A. The crucified donkey man: Achaios and Jesus. *In* Studies in classical art and archaeology p205-07

Fleischman, Albert Sidney

Laughter and children's literature. *In* Horn Book Magazine. Crosscurrents of criticism p199-204

About

Fleischman, A. S. Laughter and children's literature. *In* Horn Book Magazine. Crosscurrents of criticism p199-204

Fleischman, Sid. See Fleischman, Albert Sidney

Fleishman, Avrom

Personal myth: three Victorian autobiographers. *In* Landow, G. P. ed. Approaches to Victorian autobiography p215-34

The socialization of Catherine Morland. *In* ELH essays for Earl R. Wasserman p356-74

Speech and writing in Under Western eyes. *In* Joseph Conrad: a commemoration p119-28

Virginia Woolf: tradition and modernity. *In* Forms of modern British fiction p133-63

Fleissner, Robert F.

'Love's labour's won' and the occasion of 'Much ado'. *In* Shakespeare survey 27 p105-10

Fleming, George James

The Black role in American politics: Part II, The past. *In* The Black American reference book p622-37

Fleming, John Marcus

Mercantilism and free trade today. *In* The Market and the state p164-85

Flemings

Zolberg, A. R. Splitting the difference: federalization without federalization in Belgium. *In* Esman, M. J. ed. Ethnic conflict in the Western world p103-42

Flemming, J. Stanton

The economic explanation of inflation. *In* The Political economy of inflation p13-36

Fletcher, Bradford Y.

Printer's copy for Stow's Chaucer. *In* Virginia. University. Bibliographical Society. Studies in bibliography v31 p184-201

Fletcher, George P.

Prolonging life. *In* Weir, R. F. ed. Ethical issues in death and dying p226-40

Fletcher, I. M.

David Livingstone: a short portrait of the great missionary-explorer. *In* The Occasional papers of the Rhodes-Livingstone Museum p297-333

Fletcher, Ian, and Stokes, John

Oscar Wilde. *In* Finneran, R. J. ed. Anglo-Irish literature p48-137

Fletcher, Joseph Francis

Ethics and euthanasia. *In* Weir, R. F. ed. Ethical issues in death and dying p348-59

Feeding the hungry: an ethical appraisal. *In* Lucas, G. R. and Ogletree, T. W. eds. Lifeboat ethics p52-69

Give if it helps but not if it hurts. *In* Aiken, W. and La Follette, H. eds. World hunger and moral obligation p103-14

Humanhood: essays in biomedical ethics

Contents

Abortion
Cerebration
Distributive justice
Euthanasia
Experiments on humans
Fetal research
Genetic engineering
Goodness
Happiness
Humanness
Infanticide
Our duty to the unborn
Recombining DNA
Sharing with others
Suicide
Wasting human bodies

Medical diagnosis: our right to know the truth. *In* Weir, R. F. ed. Ethical issues in death and dying p26-41

The "right" to live and the "right" to die. *In* Kohl, M. ed. Beneficent euthanasia p44-53

Flew, Antony Garrard Newton

Describing and explaining; excerpt from "A new approach to psychical research." *In* Ludwig, J. K. ed. Philosophy and parapsychology p207-26

Evolutionary ethics. *In* New studies in ethics v2 p217-86

Infinite divisibility in Hume's Treatise. *In* Livingston, D. W. and King, J. T. eds. Hume p257-69

Is there a case for disembodied survival? *In* Wheatley, J. M. O. and Edge, H. L. eds. Philosophical dimensions of parapsychology p330-47

Is there a 'problem of freedom'? *In* Pivčević, E. ed. Phenomenology and philosophical understanding p195-209

Parapsychology revisited: laws, miracles, and repeatability. *In* Ludwig, J. K. ed. Philosophy and parapsychology p263-69

A rational animal

Contents

The Darwinian framework
Epilogue
Human psychology and Skinnerian behaviorism
Hume and historical necessity
Lenin and the Cartesian inheritance
Mind/brain identity and the Cartesian framework
Motives and Freud's unconscious
Powers, checks, and choice in Malthus
Psychoanalysis and freewill
A rational animal
Sartre and unconditional responsibility

The sources of serialism. *In* Thakur, S. C. ed. Philosophy and psychical research p81-96

Wants or needs, choices or commands. *In* Fitzgerald, R. ed. Human needs and politics p213-28

About

Brier, R. Magicians, alarm clocks, and backward causation. *In* Wheatley, J. M. O. and Edge, H. L. eds. Philosophical dimensions of parapsychology p235-44

Flock, Howard Raymond

Stimulus structure in lightness and brightness experiments. *In* Perception p185-208

Flood (Hinduism) See Deluge (Hinduism)

Flood, Biblical. See Deluge

Floors. See Pavements, Mosaic

Florence

Commerce—History

Krekić, B. Four Florentine commercial companies in Dubrovnik (Ragusa) in the first half of the fourteenth century. *In* The Medieval city p25-41

History

Bowsky, W. M. Italian diplomatic history: a case for the smaller commune. *In* Order and innovation in the Middle Ages p55-74

Gilbert, F. Bernardo Rucellai and the Orti Oricellari: a study of the origin of modern political thought. *In* Gilbert, F. History p215-46

Gilbert, F. The Venetian constitution in Florentine political thought. *In* Gilbert, F. History p179-214

Herlihy, D. The distribution of wealth in a Renaissance community: Florence 1427. *In* Towns in societies p131-57

Herlihy, D. Family and property in Renaissance Florence. *In* The Medieval city p 3-24

Trexler, R. C. Measures against water pollution in fifteenth-century Florence. *In* Viator: medieval and Renaissance studies v5 p455-67

Intellectual life

Gilbert, F. Bernardo Rucellai and the Orti Oricellari: a study of the origin of modern political thought. *In* Gilbert, F. History p215-46

Florence. Palazzo Vecchio (Staircase)

Pillsbury, E. P. Vasari's staircase in the Palazzo Vecchio. *In* Collaboration in Italian Renaissance art p125-41

Florence. Santa Maria Novella (Church). Strozzi Chapel

Winternitz, E. Muses and music in a burial chapel: an interpretation of Filippino Lippi's window wall in the Cappella Strozzi. *In* Winternitz, E. Musical instruments and their symbolism in Western art p166-84

Florence de Rome

Lee, A. T. Le bone Florence of Rome: a Middle English adaptation of a French romance. *In* The Learned and the lewed p343-54

Flores-Meiser, Enya P.

The hot mouth and the evil eye. *In* The Evil eye p149-62

Florescu, Radu R.

The Devil in Romanian literature and folklore. *In* Disguises of the demonic p69-86

Florida
Description and travel
White, E. B. On a Florida key. *In* White, E. B. Essays of E. B. White p137-41
Economic conditions
Lewis, C. B. Agricultural evolution on secondary frontiers: a Florida model. *In* The Frontier v2 p205-33

Florida Keys
Maps
De Vorsey, L. La Florida revealed: the De Brahm surveys of British East Florida, 1765-1771. *In* Pattern and process p87-102

Flourens, Pierre
About
Fancher, R. E. The physiology of mind: conceptions of the brain from Gall to Penfield. *In* Fancher, R. E. Pioneers of psychology p43-86

Flower, John Ernest
The soldier's stage: Roland Dorgelès, Les croix de bois. *In* Klein, H. M. ed. The First World War in fiction p53-62

Flud, Robert. See Fludd, Robert

Fludd, Robert
About
Debus, A. G. The chemical debates of the seventeenth century: the reaction to Robert Fludd and Jean Baptiste van Helmont. *In* Bonelli, M. L. R. and Shea, W. R. eds. Reason, experiment, and mysticism in the scientific revolution p19-47

Fluehr-Lobban, Carolyn
Agitation for change in the Sudan. *In* Schlegel, A. E. ed. Sexual stratification p127-43

Flyer, Helene Hartmann-. See Hartmann, Helene

Flying Dutchman
Doubleday, N. F. Fiction in a new nation: the naturalization of legend. *In* Doubleday, N. F. Variety of attempt p113-27

Flying saucers (in religion)
Wallis, R. The Aetherius Society: a case study in the formation of a mystagogic congregation. *In* Wallis, R. ed. Sectarianism p17-34

Foa, Pamela
What's wrong with rape. *In* Feminism and philosophy p347-59

Foakes, R. A.
The art of cruelty: Hamlet and Vindice. *In* Shakespeare survey 26 p21-31

On Marston, The malcontent, and The revenger's tragedy. *In* The Elizabethan theatre, VI p59-75

"The power of prospect": Wordsworth's visionary poetry. *In* Martz, L. L. and Williams, A. L. eds. The author in his work p103-21

Foard, James H.
The loneliness of Matsuo Bashō. *In* Reynolds, F. E. and Capps, D. eds. The biographical process p363-91

Fodor, Jerry A. See Chihara, C. S. jt. auth.

Foerster, Heinz von. See Von Foerster, Heinz

Foerster, Norman
About individual works
American criticism
Tate, A. Humanism and naturalism. *In* Tate, A. Memoirs and opinions, 1926-1974 p170-94

Foetus. See Fetus

Fogel, Daniel Mark
A compositional history of the Biographia literaria. *In* Virginia. University. Bibliographical Society. Studies in bibliography v30 p219-34

Fogel, David
Prison: the fortress model vs. the justice model. *In* Contemporary issues in criminal justice p119-28

Fogelmark, Staffan
Two cases of ΑΔΥΝΑΤΟΝ: AG. 612 and Theodoridas AP XIII.21. *In* Harvard Studies in classical philology v79 p149-63

Fogelson, Raymond D.
An analysis of Cherokee sorcery and witchcraft. *In* Hudson, C. M. ed. Four centuries of Southern Indians p113-31

Foggara. See Falashas

Fogle, French Rowe
Marvell's "tough reasonableness" and the Coy mistress. *In* Friedenreich, K. ed. Tercentenary essays in honor of Andrew Marvell p121-39

Fohlen, Claude
The impact of the American Revolution on France. *In* The Impact of the American Revolution abroad p21-38

Fokkema, Douwe W.
Lu Xun: the impact of Russian literature. *In* Modern Chinese literature in the May Fourth era p89-101

Foley, Donald L.
Accessibility for residents in the metropolitan environment. *In* Hawley, A. H. and Rock, V. P. eds. Metropolitan America in contemporary perspective p157-98

La Folie Tristan d'Oxford, Isolt's trial in Béroul and. York, C. C. *In* Medievalia et humanistica no. 6 p157-61

Foliot, Gilbert, Bp. of London
About individual works
Multiplicem nobis
Peters, E. M. The Archbishop and the hedgehog. *In* Law, church, and society p167-84

Folk art
Fitch, J. M. Uses of the artistic past. *In* Yoder, D. ed. American folklife p27-49
See also Children as artists; Santos (Art)
India
Parmer, S. Traditional folk forms in India and their use in national development; excerpt from "Traditional folk media in India." *In* Fischer, H. D. and Melnik, S. R. eds. Entertainment: a cross-cultural examination p74-82
United States
Rosenberg, H. The peaceable kingdom: American folk art. *In* Rosenberg, H. Art on the edge p288-95

Folk costume. See Costume

Folk-lore, Germanic
Robbins, W. L. Wishing in and shooting in the New Year among the Germans in the Carolinas. *In* Yoder, D. ed. American folklife p257-79

Folk-lore, Indian
Ramsey, J. The Indian literature of Oregon. *In* Bingham, E. R. and Love, G. A. eds. Northwest perspectives p2-19
See also Totems

Folk-lore, Irish
MacKillop, J. J. Finn MacCool: the hero and the anti-hero in Irish folk tradition. *In* Casey, D. J. and Rhodes, R. E. eds. Views of the Irish peasantry, 1800-1916 p86-106

Folk-lore, Jewish. See Folk-lore—Jews

Folk-lore, Medical. See Folk medicine

Folk-lore, Mexican
Kelly, P. F. Death in Mexican folk culture. *In* Death in America p92-111

Folk-lore, Persian
Friedl, E. Women in contemporary Persian folktales. *In* Beck, L. and Keddie, N. R. eds. Women in the Muslim world p629-50

Folk-lore, Romanian
Florescu, R. R. The Devil in Romanian literature and folklore. *In* Disguises of the demonic p69-86

Folk-lore and children
Schwartz, A. Children, humor, and folklore. *In* Horn Book Magazine. Crosscurrents of criticism p205-16
See also Folk-lore of children

Folk-lore and literature. See Literature and folk-lore

Folk-lore and youth. See Folk-lore and children

Folk-lore in literature
Chernysheva, T. The folktale, Wells, and modern science fiction. *In* H. G. Wells and modern science fiction p35-47
Clarke, K. W. Jesse Stuart's use of folklore. *In* LeMaster, J. R. and Clarke, M. W. eds. Jesse Stuart p117-29

Folk-lore of birth. See Birth (in religion, folk-lore, etc.)

Folk-lore of children
Sapir, J. D. The fabricated child. *In* The Social use of metaphor p 193-223
See also Folk-lore and children

Folk-lore of clowns. See Clowns (in religion, folk-lore, etc.)

Folk-lore of coyotes. See Coyotes (in religion, folk-lore, etc.)

Folk-lore of fire. See Fire (in religion, folklore, etc.)

Folk-lore of initiations. See Initiations (in religion, folk-lore, etc.)

Folk-lore of Jews. See Folk-lore—Jews

Folk-lore of mistletoe. See Mistletoe (in religion, folk-lore, etc.)

Folk-lore of moles (Animals) See Moles (Animals) (in religion, folk-lore, etc.)

Folk-lore of mules. See Mules (in religion, folk lore, etc.)

Folk-lore of stars. See Stars (in religion, folk-lore, etc.)

Folk-lore of the dead. See Dead (in religion, folk-lore, etc.)

Folk-lore of the sky. See Stars (in religion, folk-lore, etc.)

Folk-lore of the sun. See Sun (in religion, folk-lore, etc.)

Folk-lore of trees
Coomaraswamy, A. K. The inverted tree. *In* Coomaraswamy, A. K. Selected papers v 1 p376-404
Isaacs, N. D. Up a tree: to see The fates of men. *In* Anglo-Saxon poetry: essays in appreciation p363-75

Folk-lore of women. See Women (in religion, folklore, etc.)

Folk medicine
Gebhard, B. The interrelationship of scientific and folk medicine in the United States of America since 1850. *In* American folk medicine p87-98
Hand, W. D. The mole in folk medicine: a survey from Indic antiquity to modern America II. *In* American folk medicine p37-48
Hostetler, J. A. Folk medicine and sympathy healing among the Amish. *In* American folk medicine p249-58
Jackson, B. The other kind of doctor: conjure and magic in Black American folk medicine. *In* American folk medicine p259-72
Jones, M. O. Doing what, with which, and to whom? The relationship of case history accounts to curing. *In* American folk medicine p301-14
Talbot, C. H. Folk medicine and history. *In* American folk medicine p7-10

Arizona
Granger, B. H. Some aspects of folk medicine among Spanish-speaking people in southern Arizona. *In* American folk medicine p191-202

Canada
Lacourcière, L. A survey of folk medicine in French Canada from early times to the present. *In* American folk medicine p203-14

Egypt—Fateha
Morsy, S. A. Sex differences and folk illness in an Egyptian village. *In* Beck, L. and Keddie, N. R. eds. Women in the Muslim world p599-616

England
Gray, D. Notes on some Middle English charms. *In* Chaucer and Middle English studies in honour of Rossell Hope Robbins p56-71

Jamaica
Barrett, L. E. Healing in a balmyard: the practice of folk healing in Jamaica, W.I. *In* American folk medicine p285-300

Latin America
Guerra, F. Medical folklore in Spanish America. *In* American folk medicine p169-74

Louisiana
Brandon, E. Folk medicine in French Louisiana. *In* American folk medicine p215-34

New Mexico
Ford, R. I. Communication networks and information hierarchies in native American folk medicine: Tewa Pueblos, New Mexico. *In* American folk medicine p143-57

Folk medicine—*Continued*

Texas

Anderson, J. Q. Texas and Southwest medical lore in the Anderson Collection, University of Houston. *In* American folk medicine p315-19

Graham, J. S. The role of the curandero in the Mexican American folk medicine system in west Texas. *In* American folk medicine p175-89

Zambia

Turner, V. W. Lunda medicine and the treatment of disease. *In* The Occasional papers of the Rhodes-Livingstone Museum p649-719

Folk music. See Folk-songs

Folk-plays. See Folk-drama

Folk poetry

See also Folk-songs

History and criticism

Hansen, W. F. The Homeric epics and oral poetry. *In* Oinas, F. J. ed. Heroic epic and saga p7-26

Folk-psychology. See Ethnopsychology

Folk-songs

Bogatyrev, P. G. Folk song from a functional point of view. *In* Matejka, L. and Titunik, I. R. eds. Semiotics of art p20-32

Chu, L. L. Sabers and swords for the Chinese children: revolutionary children's folk songs. *In* Chu, G. C. ed. Popular media in China p16-50

See also Folk-lore

Folk-songs, Afro-American. See Afro-American songs

Folk-songs, Chinese

Chu, L. L. Sabers and swords for the Chinese children: revolutionary children's folk songs. *in* Chu, G. C. ed. Popular media in China p16-50

Folk-songs, Russian. See Byliny

Folk-tales. See Folk-lore; Legends

Folkert, Kendall W.

The Jainas. *In* Adams, C. J. ed. A reader's guide to the great religions p231-46

Folklore. See Folk-lore

Folklore, American. See Folk-lore, American

Follain, Jean

About

Calderon, P. Jean Follain: objects in time. *In* Cardinal, R. ed. Sensibility and creation p136-48

Follath, Erich

An international comparison of broadcasting systems. *In* Fischer, H. D. and Merrill, J. C. eds. International and intercultural communication p71-82

Føllesdal, Dagfinn

Meaning and experience. *In* Guttenplan, S. D. ed. Mind and language p25-44

Folly in literature

Kinsman, R. S. Folly, melancholy, and madness: a study in shifting styles of medical analysis and treatment, 1450-1675. *In* The Darker vision of the Renaissance p273-320

Folque of Nerra. See Fulk Nerra, Count of Anjou

Folquet de Marseille, Bp. of Toulouse

About

Bolton, B. M. Fulk of Toulouse: the escape that failed. *In* Church, society and politics p83-93

Foltz, William Jay

Two forms of unofficial conflict intervention: the problem-solving and the process-promoting workshops. *In* Unofficial diplomats p201-21

Fon (African people)

Religion

Booth, N. S. God and the gods in West Africa. *In* African religions: a symposium p159-81

Fon gods. See Gods, Fon

Fonds développement économique et social

Merlin, C. Tax relief contracts in France. *In* Davis, K. C. Discretionary justice in Europe and America p161-78

Fone, Byrne R. S.

Sons and lovers: three English portraits. *In* Crew, L. ed. The gay academic p200-15

Foner, Eric

The causes of the American Civil War: recent interpretations and new directions. *In* Swierenga, R. P. ed. Beyond the Civil War synthesis p15-32

Fong, Wen C.

Archaism as a 'primitive' style. *In* Artists and traditions p89-109

Fonlon, Bernard

The language problem in Cameroon: a historical perspective. *In* Smock, D. R. and Bentsi-Enchill, K. eds. The search for national integration in Africa p189-205

Fontana, Andrea, and Van de Water, Richard

The existential thought of Jean-Paul Sartre and Maurice Merleau-Ponty. *In* Douglas, J. D. and Johnson, J. M. [eds.] Existential sociology p101-29

Fontana, Bernard L.

Artifacts of the Indians of the Southwest. *In* Material culture and the study of American life p75-108

The faces and forces of Pimeria Alta. *In* Voices from the Southwest p45-54

Fontane, Theodor

About

Larkin, M. Society versus the individual. *In* Larkin, M. Man and society in nineteenth-century realism p152-62

About individual works

Effi Briest

Turner, D. Theodor Fontane: Effi Briest. *In* Williams, D. A. ed. The monster in the mirror p234-56

Frau Jenny Treibel

Bruford, W. H. Theodor Fontane: Frau Jenny Treibel (1892). *In* Bruford, W. H. The German tradition of self-cultivation p190-205

Fontenelle, Bernard Le Bovier de

About

Davidson, H. M. Fontenelle, Perrault, and the realignment of the arts. *In* Literature and history in the age of ideas p3-13

Food

See also Diet; Nutrition; Sea food

Food—*Continued*
Prices
See Food prices

Social aspects—France
Barthes, R. Toward a psychosociology of contemporary food consumption. *In* Food and drink in history p166-73

Food aid programs. See Food relief

Food control. See Food supply

Food in literature
Mann, J. Eating and drinking in 'Piers Plowman.' *In* English Association. Essays and studies, 1979 p26-43

Tanner, T. 'Gnawed bones' and 'artless tales'—eating and narrative in Conrad. *In* Joseph Conrad: a commemoration p17-36

Food in the Bible
Soler, J. The semiotics of food in the Bible. *In* Food and drink in history p126-38

See also Food prices; Food supply

Europe
Pyke, M. The influence of American foods and food technology in Europe. *In* Bigsby, C. W. E. Superculture p83-95

United States—Technological innovations
Pyke, M. The influence of American foods and food technology in Europe. *In* Bigsby, C. W. E. Superculture p83-95

Food plants. See Plants, Edible

Food prices
Schertz, L. P. World food: prices and the poor. *In* Bundy, W. P. ed. The world economic crisis p179-205

Food processing. See Food industry and trade

Food relief
Hinds, S. W. On the relations of medical triage to world famine: an historical survey. *In* Lucas, G. R. and Ogletree, T. W. eds. Lifeboat ethics p29-51

Lucas, G. R. Political and economic dimensions of hunger: strategies to combat famine in the 1970's. *In* Lucas, G. R. and Ogletree, T. W. eds. Lifeboat ethics p 1-28

Moral and religious aspects
Aiken, W. The right to be saved from starvation. *In* Aiken, W. and La Follette, H. eds. World hunger and moral obligation p85-102

Arthur, J. Rights and the duty to bring aid. *In* Aiken, W. and La Follette, H. eds. World hunger and moral obligation p37-48

Engelhardt, H. T. Individuals and communities, present and future: towards a morality in a time of famine. *In* Lucas, G. R. and Ogletree, T. W. eds. Lifeboat ethics p70-83

Fletcher, J. F. Feeding the hungry: an ethical appraisal. *In* Lucas, G. R. and Ogletree, T. W. eds. Lifeboat ethics p52-69

Fletcher, J. F. Give if it helps but not if it hurts. *In* Aiken, W. and La Follette, H. eds. World hunger and moral obligation p103-14

Fletcher, J. F. Sharing with others. *In* Fletcher, J. F. Humanhood: essays in biomedical ethics p54-64

Frankena, W. K. Moral philosophy and world hunger. *In* Aiken, W. and La Follette, H. eds. World hunger and moral obligation p66-84

Hardin, G. J. Carrying capacity as an ethical concept. *In* Lucas, G. R. and Ogletree, T. W. eds. Lifeboat ethics p120-37

Hardin, G. J. Lifeboat ethics: the case against helping the poor. *In* Aiken, W. and La Follette, H. eds. World hunger and moral obligation p11-21

Narveson, J. Morality and starvation. *In* Aiken, W. and La Follette, H. eds. World hunger and moral obligation p49-65

O'Neill, O. Lifeboat earth. *In* Aiken, W. and La Follette, H. eds. World hunger and moral obligation p148-64

Richards, H. Productive justice. *In* Aiken, W. and La Follette, H. eds. World hunger and moral obligation p165-79

Sellers, J. E. Famine and interdependence: toward a new identity for America and the West. *In* Lucas, G. R. and Ogletree, T. W. eds. Lifeboat ethics p100-19

Shriver, D. W. Lifeboaters and mainlanders: a response. *In* Lucas, G. R. and Ogletree, T. W. eds. Lifeboat ethics p141-50

Singer, P. Famine, affluence, and morality. *In* Aiken, W. and La Follette, H. eds. World hunger and moral obligation p22-36
Also in Laslett, P. and Fishkin, J. eds. Philosophy, politics and society p21-35

Watson, R. A. Reason and morality in a world of limited food. *In* Aiken, W. and La Follette, H. eds. World hunger and moral obligation p115-23

Food relief, American

India
Hardin, G. J. Carrying capacity as an ethical concept. *In* Lucas, G. R. and Ogletree, T. W. eds. Lifeboat ethics p120-37

Food supply
Christensen, C. J. Food and national security. *In* Knorr, K. E. and Trager, F. N. eds. Economic issues and national security p289-320

Hardin, G. J. Lifeboat ethics: the case against helping the poor. *In* Aiken, W. and La Follette, H. eds. World hunger and moral obligation p11-21

Hilton, A. M. Against pollution and hunger: environment and development. *In* Against pollution and hunger p27-59

Holsti, O. R. Global food problems and Soviet agriculture. *In* Orr, D. W. and Soroos, M. S. eds. The global predicament p150-75

Lucas, G. R. Political and economic dimensions of hunger: strategies to combat famine in the 1970's. *In* Lucas, G. R. and Ogletree, T. W. eds. Lifeboat ethics p 1-28

Meadows, D. H. Food and population: policies for the United States. *In* Baldwin, D. A. ed. America in an interdependent world p163-220

Rachels, J. Vegetarianism and "the other weight problem." *In* Aiken, W. and La Follette, H. eds. World hunger and moral obligation p180-93

Richards, H. Productive justice. *In* Aiken, W. and La Follette, H. eds. World hunger and moral obligation p165-79

Schertz, L. P. World food: prices and the poor. *In* Bundy, W. P. ed. The world economic crisis p179-205

Food supply—*Continued*

Sellers, J. E. Famine and interdependence: toward a new identity for America and the West. *In* Lucas, G. R. and Ogletree, T. W. eds. Lifeboat ethics p100-19

Sloan, T. J. A look at America's potential roles in a global food crisis. *In* Orr, D. W. and Soroos, M. S. eds. The global predicament p110-30

Soroos, M. S. Lifeboat ethics versus one-worldism in international food and resource policy. *In* Orr, D. W. and Soroos, M. S. eds. The global predicament p131-49

See also Agriculture; Famines; Food industry and trade

Europe—History

Tilly, C. Food supply and public order in modern Europe. *In* Tilly, C. ed. The formation of national states in Western Europe p380-455

Rome (City)

Revel, J. A capital city's privileges: food supplies in early-modern Rome. *In* Food and drink in history p37-49

Food trade. See Food industry and trade

Fools and jesters in literature

McCarron, R. M. Folly and wisdom: three Dickensian wise fools. *In* Dickens Studies Annual v6 p40-56

Weimann, R. The mimus. *In* Weimann, R. Shakespeare and the popular tradition in the theater: studies in the social dimension of dramatic form and function p 1-14

Foot, Sir Hugh. See Caradon, Hugh Mackintosh Foot, Baron

Foot, Hugh Mackintosh, Baron Caradon. See Caradon, Hugh Mackintosh Foot, Baron

Foot, Michael Richard Daniel

Resistance, war and revolution. *In* The Year book of world affairs, 1977 p158-75

Foot, Philippia

Virtues and vices, and other essays in moral philosophy

Contents

Approval and disapproval
Are moral considerations overriding?
Euthanasia
Free will as involving determinism
Goodness and choice
Hume on moral judgement
Moral arguments
Moral beliefs
Morality as a system of hypothetical imperatives
Nietzsche: the revaluation of values
The problem of abortion and the doctrine of the double effect
Reasons for action and desires
A reply to Professor Frankena
Virtues and vices

Foot-ball. See Football

Football

MacLeish, A. Moonlighting on Yale Field. *In* MacLeish, A. Riders on the earth p94-102

Madison, D. R. and Landers, D. M. Racial discrimination in football: a test of the "stacking" of playing positions hypothesis. *In* Social problems in athletics p151-56

Sheed, W. Unnecessary roughness. *In* Sheed, W. The good word & other words p148-53

Foote, Horton

On first dramatizing Faulkner. *In* Faulkner, modernism, and film: Faulkner and Yoknapatawpha, 1978 p49-65

Tomorrow: the genesis of a screenplay. *In* Faulkner, modernism, and film: Faulkner and Yoknapatawpha, 1978 p149-62

Foote, Samuel

About

England, M. W. The satiric Blake: apprenticeship at the Haymarket? *In* Wimsatt, W. K. ed. Literary criticism: idea and act p483-505

For whom the bell tolls (Motion picture)

Pohl, C. The "unmaking" of a political film. *In* Peary, G. and Shatzkin, R. eds. The modern American novel and the movies p317-24

Foramitti, Hans, and Piperek, Maximilian

Anxieties of city dwellers. *In* United Nations Educational, Scientific and Cultural Organization. The conservation of cities p43-56

Forbes, Duncan

Hume's science of politics. *In* David Hume p39-50

Sceptical Whiggism, commerce, and liberty. *In* Skinner, A. S. and Wilson, T. eds. Essays on Adam Smith p179-201

Forbes, Esther

About individual works
Johnny Tremain

Collier, C. Johnny and Sam: old and new approaches to the American Revolution. *In* Horn Book Magazine. Crosscurrents of criticism p234-40

Forbes, Nevill

About

Ashbee, F. Nevill Forbes, 1883-1929: some family letters from Russia. *In* Oxford Slavonic papers new ser. v9 p79-90

Forbes, Thomas Rogers

The madstone. *In* American folk medicine p11-19

Forbes, William Cameron

About

Ross, G. M. W. Cameron Forbes: the diplomacy of a Darwinist. *In* Burns, R. D. and Bennett, E. M. eds. Diplomats in crisis p49-64

Forbes family

Ashbee, F. Nevill Forbes, 1883-1929: some family letters from Russia. *In* Oxford Slavonic papers new ser. v9 p79-90

Forbush, Edward Howe

About individual works
Birds of Massachusetts and other New England states

White, E. B. Mr Forbush's friends. *In* White, E. B. Essays of E. B. White p262-77

Force (Law) See Violence (Law)

Force and energy

Heimann, P. M. Mayer's concept of "force": the "axis" of a new science of physics. *In* Historical studies in the physical sciences v7 p277-96

Philberth, K. The generation of matter and the conservation of energy. *In* Cosmology, history, and theology p113-29

Force and energy—*Continued*

Weisskopf, V. F. The impact of quantum theory on modern physics. *In* Neyman, J. ed. The heritage of Copernicus: theories "pleasing to the mind" p311-31

Wise, M. N. William Thomson's mathematical route to energy conservation: a case study of the role of mathematics in concept formation. *In* Historical studies in the physical sciences v10 p49-83

See also Mechanics; Motion

Forced labor. See Service, Compulsory nonmilitary

Ford, Brian L.

Justice is more than a word. *In* Henderson, G. ed. Human relations in the military p127-44

Ford, Ford Madox

About

Colmer, J. The modern 'condition of England' novel. *In* Colmer, J. Coleridge to Catch-22 p139-61

Pritchard, W. H. Some 1920s fiction: Ford, Forster, Woolf. *In* Pritchard, W. H. Seeing through everything p90-113

Smith, G. C. Ford Madox Ford. *In* Stade, G. ed. Six modern British novelists p87-129

About individual works
The good soldier

Jacobs, C. The (too) good soldier: "a real story." *In* Glyph 3 p32-51

Moser, T. C. Conrad and The good soldier. *In* Joseph Conrad: a commemoration p174-82

Parade's end

Bradbury, M. The denuded place: war and form in Parade's end and U.S.A. *In* Klein, H. M. ed. The First World War in fiction p193-209

Characters—John Dowell

Jacobs, C. The (too) good soldier: "a real story." *In* Glyph 3 p32-51

Technique

Vidan, I. Ford's interpretation of Conrad's technique. *In* Joseph Conrad: a commemoration p183-93

Ford, George Harry

Felicitous space: the cottage controversy. *In* Knoepflmacher, U. C. and Tennyson, G. B. eds. Nature and the Victorian imagination p29-48

Stern Hebrews who laugh: further thoughts on Carlyle and Dickens. *In* Fielding, K. J. and Tarr, R. L. eds. Carlyle past and present p112-26

Ford, Greg

Mostly on Rio Lobo. *In* Nichols, B. ed. Movies and methods p344-54

Ford, Harold P.

The new power politics of counterforce. *In* [Truth and tragedy]: a tribute to Hans Morgenthau p259-71

Politics, ethics, and the arms race. *In* Ethics and nuclear strategy? p51-71

What these sobering essays tell us. *In* Ethics and nuclear strategy? p 1-13

Ford, Henry, 1863-1947

About individual works
Moving forward

Davidson, D. The world as Ford factory. *In* Crunden, R. M. ed. The superfluous men p81-84

Ford, Henry, 1917-

Two developments which challenge management for the future. *In* Benton, L. R. ed. Management for the future p101-07

Ford, Hugh D.

Published in Paris

Contents

Bill Bird and the Three mountains
Edward Titus at the Sign of the Black Manikin
Four new directions: content over form: New review
Four new directions: fourth-dimensional writing: The Roving eye
Four new directions: the need for anonymity: Carrefour
Four new directions: the revolution of the word: Servire
From Princeton to Paris: Sylvia Beach
Gertrude Stein's Plain editions
Harrison of Paris
Harry and Caresse Crosby and the Black sun
Jack Kahane and the guardian Obelisk
Nancy Cunard's twenty-four Hours
Robert McAlmon's Contact publishing company

About individual works
Published in Paris

Balakian, N. They gambled on genius. *In* Balakian, N. Critical encounters p242-45

Ford, John, 1586-1640?

About individual works
The broken heart

Champion, L. S. Ford: 'Tis pity she's a whore, The broken heart. *In* Champion, L. S. Tragic patterns in Jacobean and Caroline drama p180-209

Stilling, R. John Ford and the Jacobeans. *In* Stilling, R. Love and death in Renaissance tragedy p266-76

Ure, P. Marriage and the domestic drama in Heywood and Ford. *In* Ure, P. Elizabethan and Jacobean drama p145-65

Waith, E. M. Struggle for calm: the dramatic structure of The broken heart. *In* English Renaissance drama p155-66

Love's sacrifice

Ure, P. Cult and initiates in Ford's Love's sacrifice. *In* Ure, P. Elizabethan and Jacobean drama p93-103

The chronicle history of Perkin Warbeck: a strange truth

Barton, A. He that plays the king: Ford's Perkin Warbeck and the Stuart history play. *In* English drama: forms and development p69-93

Edwards, P. The royal pretenders in Massinger and Ford. *In* English Association. Essays and studies, 1974 p18-36

Neill, M. "Anticke pageantrie": the mannerist art of Perkin Warbeck. *In* Renaissance drama [1976] p117-50

Ford, John, 1586-1640?—About individual works—*Continued*

'Tis pity she's a whore

Champion, L. S. Ford: 'Tis pity she's a whore, The broken heart. *In* Champion, L. S. Tragic patterns in Jacobean and Caroline drama p180-209

Stilling, R. John Ford and the Jacobeans. *In* Stilling, R. Love and death in Renaissance tragedy p266-76

Ford, John, 1895-1973

About

Wollen, P. The auteur theory; excerpt from "Signs and meanings in the cinema." *In* Nichols, B. ed. Movies and methods p529-42

About individual works

The grapes of wrath

Sarris, A. John Ford: The grapes of wrath. *In* Denby, D. ed. Awake in the dark p320-25

My darling Clementine

Nichols, B. Style, grammar, and the movies. *In* Nichols, B. ed. Movies and methods p607-28

Young Mr Lincoln

John Ford's Young Mr Lincoln. *In* Nichols, B. ed. Movies and methods p493-529

Nichols, B. Style, grammar, and the movies. *In* Nichols, B. ed. Movies and methods p607-28

Ford, Patrick Kildea

The death of Merlin in the Chronicle of Elis Gruffydd. *In* Viator: medieval and Renaissance studies v7 p379-90

Ford, Richard I.

Communication networks and information hierarchies in native American folk medicine: Tewa Pueblos, New Mexico. *In* American folk medicine p143-57

Evolutionary ecology and the evolution of human ecosystems: a case study from the Midwestern U.S.A. *In* Explanation of prehistoric change p153-84

Ford automobile

White, E. B. Farewell, my lovely! *In* White, E. B. Essays of E. B. White p162-68

Forecasting

Eisenstadt, S. N. Cultural settings and adolescence and youth around the year 2000. *In* Adolescence and youth in prospect p114-24

Faessler, M. Youth in the year 2000: the problem of values. *In* Adolescence and youth in prospect p125-36

Hartup, W. W. Adolescent peer relations: a look to the future. *In* Adolescence and youth in prospect p171-85

Heinlein, R. A. Pandora's box; excerpt from "The worlds of Robert A. Heinlein." *In* Knight, D. F. ed. Turning points p238-58

Hesburgh, T. M. Education in the year 2000. *In* Hesburgh, T. M. The Hesburgh papers p190-95

Hill, J. P. and others. Summary record and conclusions. *In* Adolescence and youth in prospect p13-27

Koestler, A. Life in 1980—the rule of mediocracy. *In* Koestler, A. The heel of Achilles p41-46

Mahler, F. Adolescents' ethics and morals in the year 2000. *In* Adolescence and youth in prospect p79-94

Piotrowski, J. Family and adolescents in the near future. *In* Adolescence and youth in prospect p159-70

Polak, F. L. Responsibility for the future. *In* Bundy, R. F. ed. Images of the future: the twenty-first century and beyond p9-15

Raskin, M. G. Futurology and its radical critique. *In* Radicalism in the contemporary age v2 p155-73

Soroos, M. S. Exploring global ecological futures. *In* Orr, D. W. and Soroos, M. S. eds. The global predicament p39-53

See also Social prediction; also subdivision Forecasts under specific century, e.g. Twenty-first century—Forecasts

Forecasting, Business. See Business forecasting

Forecasting, Employment. See Employment forecasting

Forecasting, Population. See Population forecasting

Foreign affairs. See International relations, and subdivision Foreign relations under names of countries

Foreign aid program. See Economic assistance; Technical assistance

Foreign economic policy. See International economic relations

Foreign economic relations. See International economic relations

Foreign exchange

Mazur, M. P. Interdependence, flexible exchange rates, and capital controls: the international monetary order in transition. *In* Baldwin, D. A. ed. America in an interdependent world p63-89

Ross, L. W. Flexible exchange rates. *In* The Year book of world affairs, 1976 p258-72

Samuelson, P. A. Illogic of neo-Marxian doctrine of unequal exchange. *In* Inflation, trade and taxes p96-107

Mathematical models

Helliwell, J. Adjustment under fixed and flexible exchange rates. *In* Kenen, P. B. ed. International trade and finance p379-410

Foreign exchange problem

Kelly, J. S. International monetary systems and national security. *In* Knorr, K. E. and Trager, F. N. eds. Economic issues and national security p231-58

Foreign investments. See Investments, Foreign

Foreign news

Boyd-Barrett, O. The global news wholesalers. *In* Gerbner, G. ed. Mass media policies in changing cultures p13-20

Rosengren, K. E. International news: time and type of report. *In* Fischer, H. D. and Merrill, J. C. eds. International and intercultural communication p251-56

Foreign opinion of the United States. See United States—Foreign opinion

Foreign policy. See International relations, and subdivision Foreign relations under names of countries

Foreign population. See Emigration and immigration; and subdivisions Emigration and immigration under names of countries, e.g. Canada—Emigration and immigration, and Foreign population under countries, etc. e.g. Ghana—Foreign population; London—Foreign population

Foreign propagandists in the United States
Baldwin, F. The Korea lobby. *In* Horowitz, I. L. ed. Science, sin, and scholarship p160-74

Foreign relations. See International relations, and subdivision Foreign relations under names of countries

Foreign trade. See Commerce

Foreign trade promotion

Underdeveloped areas
See Underdeveloped areas—Foreign trade promotion

Foreigners. See Aliens

Foreigners in literature. See Aliens in literature

Foreknowledge, The philosophical implications of. Broad, C. D. *In* Ludwig, J. K. ed. Philosophy and parapsychology p287-312
Also in Wheatley, J. M. O. and Edge, H. L. eds. Philosophical dimensions of parapsychology p198-226

Foreman, Richard

About
Kauffmann, S. Ontological-Hysteric Theater. *In* Kauffmann, S. Persons of the drama p35-39

Forensic medicine. See Medical jurisprudence

Forer, Lois Goldstein
"No one will lissen"; excerpt. *In* Gross, B. and Gross, R. eds. The children's rights movement p82-100

Forests in literature. See Trees in literature

Foreville, Raymonde
The synod of the Province of Rouen in the eleventh and twelfth centuries. *In* Church and government in the Middle Ages p19-39

Forgery of works of art. See Art—Forgeries

Forging. See Blacksmithing

Forker, Charles R.
Cyril Tourneur. *In* Logan, T. P. and Smith, D. S. eds. The new intellectuals p248-80
Immediacy and remoteness in The taming of the shrew and The winter's tale. *In* Shakespeare's romances reconsidered p134-48

Form, William Humbert
Conflict within the working class: the skilled as a special-interest group. *In* The Uses of controversy in sociology p51-73

Form (Aesthetics)
Barfield, O. Form in art and in society. *In* Barfield, O. The rediscovery of meaning, and other essays p217-27
Wimsatt, W. K. Organic form: some questions about a metaphor. *In* Wimsatt, W. K. Day of the leopards p205-33

Form (Philosophy) See Structuralism

Form, Literary. See Literary form

Form psychology. See Gestalt psychology

Formalism (Russian literature)
Beyer, T. R. The Bely-Zhirmunsky polemic. *In* Janecek, G. ed. Andrey Bely p205-13

Scholes, R. E. The contributions of formalism and structuralism to the theory of fiction. *In* Spilka, M. ed. Towards a poetics of fiction p107-24
Stacy, R. H. The Formalists. *In* Stacy, R. H. Russian literary criticism p163-84
Wellek, R. Russian formalism. *In* Gibian, G. and Tjalsma, H. W. eds. Russian modernism p31-48

Formalism, French. Riffaterre, M. *In* The Frontiers of literary criticism p93-119

Forman, Simon

About individual works
Book of plays, or notes in 1611 on Shakespeare's Richard II, Winter's tale, Cymbeline, and Macbeth . . .
Scragg, L. Macbeth on horseback. *In* Shakespeare survey 26 p81-88

Formosa. See Taiwan

Formosans. See Taiwanese

Fornara, Charles W.
Plutarch and the Megarian decree. *In* Yale classical studies v24 p213-28

Forrest, Alan
The condition of the poor in Revolutionary Bordeaux. *In* French society and the Revolution p217-47

Forrest, William George Grieve
An Athenian generation gap. *In* Yale classical studies v24 p37-52

Forrester, Randal G. See Huggins, J. jt. auth.

Forster, Edward Morgan
Introductory note to Twenty years a-growing by Maurice O'Sullivan. *In* Praise from famous men: an anthology of introductions p79-81

About
Bayley, J. Dogma and fantasy. *In* Bayley, J. The uses of division p42-50
Cockshut, A. O. J. The male homosexual: Foster. *In* Cockshut, A. O. J. Man and woman: a study of love and the novel, 1740-1940 p169-81
Gillie, C. Diversification of the novel, 1920-1930. *In* Gillie, C. Movements in English literature, 1900-1940 p90-121
Goonetilleke, D. C. R. A. Difficulties of connection in India: Kipling and Forster. *In* Goonetilleke, D. C. R. A. Developing countries in British fiction p134-69
Meyers, J. Forster: A room with a view, Maurice, The life to come. *In* Meyers, J. Homosexuality and literature, 1890-1930 p90-113
Moore, H. T. E. M. Forster. In Stade, G. ed. Six modern British novelists p219-68
Mudford, P. E. M. Forster. *In* Mudford, P. The art of celebration p123-37
Richards, I. A. A passage to Forster. *In* Richards, I. A. Complementarities p159-66

About individual works
Howards End
Bayley, J. 'Art speech.' *In* Bayley, J. The uses of division p25-42
Colmer, J. The modern 'condition of England' novel. *In* Colmer, J. Coleridge to Catch-22 p139-61
Johnson, E. D. H. "The truer measure": setting in Emma, Middlemarch, and Howards End. *In* Bornstein, G. ed. Romantic and modern p197-205

Foster, Charles Howell
Robert Frost at Bread Loaf. *In* Frost: centennial essays III p70-82

Foster, David William
Currents in the contemporary Argentine novel: Arlt, Mallea, Sabato, and Cortázar
Contents
Alternatives to progressive narrative in the contemporary Argentine novel: some constants
Eduardo Mallea and the dilemma of the prophetic observer
Ernesto Sabato and the anatomy of a national unconscious
Introduction to the Argentine novel
Julio Cortázar and the intellectual as Everyman
Roberto Arlt and the neurotic rationale

Foster, J. A.
Meaning and truth theory. *In* Evans, G. L. and McDowell, J. H. eds. Truth and meaning p 1-32

About individual works
Meaning and truth theory

Davidson, D. H. Reply to Foster [on Meaning and truth theory]. *In* Evans, G. L. and McDowell, J. H. eds. Truth and meaning p33-41

Foster, Lewis Allen
The causal objection to precognition. *In* Ludwig, J. K. ed. Philosophy and parapsychology p313-26

Foster, Ludmila A.
Nabokov in Russian emigre criticism. *In* A Book of things about Vladimir Nabokov p42-53

Foster, Richard Jackson
The two Frosts and the poetics of confession. *In* Frost: centennial essays III p350-67

Foster, Ruel E.
The short stories of Jesse Stuart. *In* LeMaster, J. R. and Clarke, M. W. eds. Jesse Stuart p40-53

Foster, S.
W. D. Howells: The rise of Silas Lapham. *In* Williams, D. A. ed. The monster in the mirror p149-78

Foster, Stephen. See Breen, T. H. jt. auth.

Foster, Stephen Wayne
The annotated Burton. *In* Crew, L. ed. The gay academic p92-103

Foster care, Home. See Foster home care

Foster family care. See Foster home care

Foster home care

Massachusetts
Dietz, J. Foster homes that are not "too loving." *In* Gross, B. and Gross, R. eds. The children's rights movement p55-57

New York (State)
Katz, S. N. Who looks after Laura? *In* Gross, B. and Gross, R. eds. The children's rights movement p48-54

Fothergill, Brian
William Beckford, prince of amateurs. *In* Royal Society of Literature of the United Kingdom, London. Essays by divers hands v38 p33-47

Foucault, Michel
Language, counter-memory, practice
Contents
Fantasia of the library
The father's "no"
History of systems of thought
Language to infinity
Nietzsche, genealogy, history
A preface to transgression
Theatrum philosophicum
What is an author?

About
White, H. V. Foucault decoded: notes from underground. *In* White, H. V. Tropics of discourse p230-60

About individual works
Madness and civilization

Derrida, J. Cogito and the history of madness. *In* Derrida, J. Writing and difference p31-63
Marcus, S. Madness, literature, and society. *In* Marcus, S. Representations p137-60

The order of things: an archaeology of the human sciences

White, H. V. Foucault decoded: notes from underground. *In* White, H. V. Tropics of discourse p230-60

Fougeret de Monbron, Louis Charles

About individual works
La capitale des Gaules

Lafarge, C. Paris and myth: one vision of horror. *In* Studies in eighteenth-century culture v5 p281-91

Foulque III Nerra, comte d'Anjou. See Fulk Nerra, Count of Anjou

Foulques of Marseilles. See Folquet de Marseille, Bp. of Toulouse

Found objects (Art) See Assemblage (Art); Collage

Foundations (Endowments) See Endowments

The fountainhead (Motion picture)
McGann, K. Ayn Rand in the stockyard of the spirit. *In* Peary, G. and Shatzkin, R. eds. The modern American novel and the movies p325-35

The 400 blows (Motion picture)
Murray, E. The 400 blows. *In* Murray, E. Ten films classics p121-33

Fourcroy, Antoine François, comte de

About
Guerlac, H. The chemical revolution: a word from Monsieur Fourcroy. *In* Guerlac, H. Essays and papers in the history of modern science p405-10

Fourier, Jean Baptiste Joseph, Baron

About individual works
The analytical theory of heat

Friedman, R. M. The creation of a new science: Joseph Fourier's analytical theory of heat. *In* Historical studies in the physical sciences v8 p73-99

Fournier, Alain

About individual works
The lost domain

Turnell, M. Alain-Fournier. *In* Turnell, M. The rise of the French novel p219-56

Fournier, Henri Alban. See Fournier, Alain

Fournier, Jacques. See Questiaux, N. jt. auth.

Fourteenth century

Rotz, R. A. Investigating urban uprisings with examples from Hanseatic towns, 1374-1416. *In* Order and innovation in the Middle Ages p215-33

Fourth dimension. See Space and time

Fourth world. See Underdeveloped areas

Fousek, Marianka Sasha

On secular authority and military service among the Bohemian Brethren in the 16th and early 17th centuries. *In* Király, B. K. ed. Tolerance and movements of religious dissent in Eastern Europe p53-64

Fowle, Geraldine E.

Sebastien Bourdon's Acts of mercy: their significance as a series. *In* Enggass, R. C. and Stokstad, M. ed. Hortus imaginum p147-54

Fowler, Alastair

Intention floreat. *In* On Literary intention p242-55

Leontes' contrition and the repair of nature. *In* English Association. Essays and studies, 1978 p36-64

The life and death of literary forms. *In* Cohen, R. ed. New directions in literary history p77-94

Fowler, Doreen F.

Faith as a unifying principle in Faulkner's Light in August. *In* Tennessee Studies in literature v21 p49-57

Fowler, Henry H.

International economic policy as a system. *In* The New Atlantic challenge p61-75

Fowler, John M.

Science education and the new heretics. *In* Science and society: past, present, and future p200-11

Fowler, Roger

Language and the reader: Shakespeare's Sonnet 73. *In* Fowler, R. ed. Style and structure in literature p79-122

Literature as discourse. *In* Royal Institute of Philosophy. Communication and understanding p174-94

Fowles, John

Hardy and the hag. *In* Butler, L. S. ed. Thomas Hardy after fifty years p28-42

About

Kennedy, A. John Fowles's sense of an ending. *In* Kennedy, A. The protean self p251-60

Lodge, D. Postmodernist fiction. *In* Lodge, D. The modes of modern writing p220-45

About individual works
The magus

Scholes, R. E. The nature of romance. *In* Scholes, R. E. Fabulation and metafiction p21-45

Fowlie, Wallace

About

Warren, A. A Boston friendship. *In* Symbolism and modern literature p3-10

About individual works
A reading of Proust

Connolly, C. Marcel Proust: 3. *In* Connolly, C. The evening colonnade p189-92

Fox, Karl August

Combining economic and noneconomic objectives in development planning: problems of concept and measurement. *In* Economic development and planning p104-41

Fox, Marvin

Judaism, secularism and textual interpretation. *In* Modern Jewish ethics p3-26

On the rational commandments in Saadia's philosophy: a reexamination. *In* Modern Jewish ethics p174-87

Fox, Nathan. See Kennedy, J. M. jt. auth.

Fox, Renée C.

The medicalization and demedicalization of American society. *In* Knowles, J. H. ed. Doing better and feeling worse p9-22

See also Parsons, T. jt. auth. The "gift of life" and its reciprocation. *In* Parsons, T. Action theory and the human condition p264-99

Fox, Robin

Primate kin and human kinship. *In* Biosocial anthropology p9-35

Foxholes. See Intrenchments

Fraenkel, Eduard

About

Calder, W. M. Seventeen letters of Ulrich von Wilamowitz-Moellendorff to Eduard Fraenkel. *In* Harvard Studies in classical philology v81 p275-97

Fraenkel, Gioachino

Italian industrial policy in the framework of economic planning. *In* Planning, politics and public policy p128-40

Frame, Donald Murdoch

About individual works
Montaigne

Edelman, N. Book reviews. *In* Edelman, N. The eye of the beholder p166-205

Framo, James L. and others

How does an affair affect a marriage? *In* Gross, L. ed. Sexual issues in marriage p187-98

Frampton, Kenneth

The status of man and the status of his objects: a reading of The human condition. *In* Hannah Arendt: the recovery of the public world p101-30

France

Administration des bâtiments
royaux

Rosenfeld, M. N. The Royal Building Administration in France from Charles V to Louis XIV. *In* Kostof, S. ed. The architect p161-79

Church history

Beitscher, J. K. Monastic reform at Beaulieu, 1031-1095. *In* Viator: medieval and Renaissance studies v5 p199-210

Patterson, W. B. Jean de Serres and the politics of religious pacification, 1594-8. *In* Church, society and politics p223-44

Church history—18th century

Mitchell, H. The world between the literate and oral traditions in eighteenth-century France: ecclesiastical instruction and popular mentalities. *In* Studies in eighteenth-century culture v8 p33-67

City planning

See City planning—France

France—*Continued*

Colonies—Africa

Challenor, H. S. Strangers as colonial intermediaries: the Dahomeyans in Francophone Africa. *In* Shack, W. A. and Skinner, E. P. eds. Strangers in African societies p67-83

Colonies—America

Covington, J. W. Relations between the eastern Timucuan Indians and the French and Spanish, 1564-1567. *In* Hudson, C. M. ed. Four centuries of Southern Indians p11-27

Commerce—History

Jordan, W. C. Supplying Aigues-Mortes for the Crusade of 1248: the problem of restructuring trade. *In* Order and innovation in the Middle Ages p165-72

Commerce—Great Britain

Ratcliffe, B. M. The origins of the Anglo-French commercial treaty of 1860: a reassessment. *In* Great Britain and her world, 1750-1914 p125-51

Commercial policy—History

Brooks, G. E. Goree and the Cape Verde rivers. *In* African dimensions p69-80

Commercial treaties

Ratcliffe, B. M. The origins of the Anglo-French commercial treaty of 1860: a reassessment. *In* Great Britain and her world, 1750-1914 p125-51

Constitutional law

Beardsley, J. Constitutional review in France. *In* The Supreme Court review, 1975 p189-259

Economic conditions

Attali, J. and Stourdze, Y. The birth of the telephone and economic crisis: the slow death of monologue in French society. *In* The Social impact of the telephone p97-111

Economic conditions—Historiography

Le Roy Ladurie, E. The chief defects of Gregory King. *In* Le Roy Ladurie, E. The territory of the historian p173-91

Le Roy Ladurie, E. The quantitative revolution and French historians: record of a generation (1932-1968) *In* Le Roy Ladurie, E. The territory of the historian p7-15

Le Roy Ladurie, E. Tithes and net agricultural output (fifteenth to eighteenth century) *In* Le Roy Ladurie, E. The territory of the historian p193-202

Economic conditions—1945-

Hayward, J. E. S. and Corina, J. Comparative preliminaries. *In* Planning, politics and public policy p155-58

Economic policy

Merlin, C. Tax relief contracts in France. *In* Davis, K. C. Discretionary justice in Europe and America p161-78

Economic policy—1945-

Bonnaud, J. J. Planning and industry in France. *In* Planning, politics and public policy p93-110

Cazes, B. The use of long-term studies in planning. *In* Planning, politics and public policy p424-32

Hayward, J. E. S. Planning and the French labour market: incomes and industrial training. *In* Planning, politics and public policy p159-76

Ullmo, Y. France. *In* Planning, politics and public policy p22-51

Young, S. A comparison of the industrial experiences. *In* Planning, politics and public policy p141-54

Foreign relations—Ethiopia

Marcus, H. G. The British and the Ethiopian railway. *In* African dimensions p29-51

Foreign relations—Scotland

Macdougall, N. A. T. Foreign relations: England and France. *In* Brown, J. M. ed. Scottish society in the fifteenth century p101-11

Foreign relations—United States

Kaplan, L. S. Toward isolationism: the rise and fall of the Franco-American alliance, 1775-1801. *In* The American Revolution and "a candid world" p134-60

Gentry

Le Roy Ladurie, E. In Normandy's woods and fields. *In* Le Roy Ladurie, E. The territory of the historian p133-71

Brumfitt, J. H. Historical Pyrrhonism and Enlightenment historiography in France. *In* Literature and history in the age of ideas p15-28

Historiography

Church, W. F. France. *In* National consciousness, history, and political culture in early-modern Europe p43-66

Le Roy Ladurie, E. The "event" and the "long term" in social history: the case of the Chouan uprising. *In* Le Roy Ladurie, E. The territory of the historian p111-31

Le Roy Ladurie, E. Quantitative history: the 6th section of the École Pratique des Hautes Études. *In* Le Roy Ladurie, E. The territory of the historian p17-31

History—To 987

Evergates, T. Historiography and sociology in early feudal society: the case of Hariulf and the "milites" of Saint-Riquier. *In* Viator: medieval and Renaissance studies v6 p35-49

History—Capetians, 987-1328

Brown, E. A. R. Royal salvation and needs of state in late Capetian France. *In* Order and innovation in the Middle Ages p365-83

Wood, C. T. Queens, queans, and kingship: an inquiry into theories of royal legitimacy in late medieval England and France. *In* Order and innovation in the Middle Ages p385-400

History—Francis I, 1515-1547

Knecht, R. J. Francis I, 'Defender of the Faith'? *In* Wealth and power in Tudor England p106-27

History—Bourbons, 1589-1789

Le Roy Ladurie, E. Rural revolts and protest movements in France from 1675-1788. *In* Studies in eighteenth-century culture v5 p423-51

History—18th century

Lefebvre, G. The place of the Revolution in the agrarian history of France. *In* Rural society in France p31-49

France—*Continued*

History—Revolution—1789-

Voegelin, E. The religion of humanity and the French Revolution. *In* Voegelin, E. From Enlightenment to revolution p160-94

History—Revolution—1789-1796

Hufton, O. H. Women in revolution 1789-1796. *In* French society and the Revolution p148-66

History—Revolution, 1789-1799

Doyle, W. Was there an aristocratic reaction in pre-revolutionary France? *In* French society and the Revolution p3-28

Forster, R. The survival of the nobility during the French Revolution. *In* French society and the Revolution p132-47

Le Goff, T. J. A. and Sutherland, D. M. G. The Revolution and the rural community in eighteenth-century Brittany. *In* French society and the Revolution p29-52

Lucas, C. R. Nobles, bourgeois and the origins of the French Revolution. *In* French society and the Revolution p88-131

Mitchell, H. Resistance to the Revolution in western France. *In* French society and the Revolution p248-85

Parry, A. The guillotine athirst. *In* Parry, A. Terrorism: from Robespierre to Arafat p55-66

Parry, A. Robespierre's bloody virtue. *In* Parry, A. Terrorism: from Robespierre to Arafat p39-54

History—Revolution, 1789-1799—
Influence on literature

Terdiman, R. The coherence of the tradition. *In* Terdiman, R. The dialectics of isolation p3-15

History—Revolution, 1789-1799—Literature and the revolution

Sterrenburg, L. W. Mary Shelley's monster: politics and psyche in Frankenstein. *In* Levine, G. L. and Knoepflmacher, U. C. eds. The endurance of Frankenstein p143-71

History—Revolution, 1789-1815

Lewis, G. The White Terror of 1815 in the department of the Gard: counter-revolution, continuity and the individual. *In* French society and the Revolution p286-313

History—Revolution, 1792-1794

Andrews, R. M. The justices of the peace of Revolutionary Paris, September 1792-November 1794 (Frimaire Year III). *In* French society and the Revolution p167-216

History—Revolution, 1795-1799

Rosenfield, L. D. C. The rights of women in the French Revolution. *In* Studies in eighteenth-century culture v7 p117-37

History—Restoration, 1814-1830

Duncan, C. Ingres's Vow of Louis XIII and the politics of the Restoration. *In* Millon, H. A. and Nochlin, L. eds. Art and architecture in the service of politics p80-91

History—February Revolution, 1848

Gilbert, F. From political to social history: Lorenz von Stein and the Revolution of 1848. *In* Gilbert, F. History p411-21

History—February Revolution, 1848—Influence

Cole, E. A. Paris 1848: A Russian ideological spectrum. *In* California Slavic studies v8 p 1-13

Industries

Bonnaud, J. J. Planning and industry in France. *In* Planning, politics and public policy p93-110

Intellectual life

Darnton, R. The High Enlightenment and the low-life of literature in pre-revolutionary France. *In* French society and the Revolution p53-87

Davidson, H. M. Fontenelle, Perrault, and the realignment of the arts. *In* Literature and history in the age of ideas p3-13

McGhee, D. M. Encyclopedism and its conscience: evolution and revolution. *In* Literature and history in the age of ideas p377-86

Starobinski, J. From the decline of erudition to the decline of nations: Gibbon's response to French thought. *In* Edward Gibbon and The decline and fall of the Roman Empire p139-57

Intellectual life—American influences

Fohlen, C. The impact of the American Revolution on France. *In* The Impact of the American Revolution abroad p21-38

Kings and rulers—Succession

Wood, C. T. Queens, queans, and kingship: an inquiry into theories of royal legitimacy in late medieval England and France. *In* Order and innovation in the Middle Ages p385-400

Ministère d'Etat chargé des affaires culturelles

Holleaux, A. P. The administration of culture. *In* Courcel, M. H. de, ed. Malraux p79-94

Moral conditions

Burguière, A. From Malthus to Max Weber: belated marriage and the spirit of enterprise. *In* Family and society p237-50

Rossiaud, J. Prostitution, youth, and society in the towns of southeastern France in the fifteenth century. *In* Deviants and the abandoned in French society p 1-46

Nobility—History

Doyle, W. Was there an aristocratic reaction in pre-revolutionary France? *In* French society and the Revolution p3-28

Duby, G. Lineage, nobility, and chivalry in the region of Mâcon during the twelfth century. *In* Family and society p16-40

Forster, R. The survival of the nobility during the French Revolution. *In* French society and the Revolution p132-47

Lewis, P. S. Of Breton alliances and other matters. *In* War, literature, and politics in the late Middle Ages p122-43

Lucas, C. R. Nobles, bourgeois and the origins of the French Revolution. *In* French society and the Revolution p88-131

Rogozinski, J. Ennoblement by the Crown and social stratification in France, 1285-1322: a prosopographical survey. *In* Order and innovation in the Middle Ages p273-91

Zeldin, T. France. *In* Spring, D. ed. European landed elites in the nineteenth century p127-39

France—*Continued*

Politics and government—1589-1789

Marvick, E. W. Childhood history and decisions of state: the case of Louis XIII. *In* DeMause, L. ed. The new psychohistory p199-244

Politics and government—18th century

Fohlen, C. The impact of the American Revolution on France. *In* The Impact of the American Revolution abroad p21-38

Vartanian, A. Necessity or freedom? The politics of an eighteenth-century metaphysical debate. *In* Studies in eighteenth-century culture v7 p153-74

Politics and government—1914-1940

Soucy, R. J. France: veterans' politics between the Wars. *In* The War generation p59-103

Politics and government—1969-

Poulard, J. V. The French Communist Party and the popular union. *In* Kaplan, M. A. ed. The many faces of communism p72-121

Population

Lesthaeghe, R. and Van de Walle, E. Economic factors and fertility decline in France and Belgium. *In* Economic factors in population growth p205-28

Religion

Mitchell, H. The world between the literate and oral traditions in eighteenth-century France: ecclesiastical instruction and popular mentalities. *In* Studies in eighteenth-century culture v8 p33-67

Rural conditions—History

Pesez, J. M. and Le Roy Ladurie, E. The deserted villages of France: an overview. *In* Rural society in France p72-106

Soboul, A. Persistence of "feudalism" in the rural society of nineteenth-century France. *In* Rural society in France p50-71

Social conditions

Abbiateci, A. Arsonists in eighteenth-century France: an essay in the typology of crime. *In* Deviants and the abandoned in French society p157-79

Baulant, M. The scattered family: another aspect of seventeenth-century demography. *In* Family and society p104-16

Bleandonu, G. and Le Gaufey, G. The creation of the insane asylums of Auxerre and Paris. *In* Deviants and the abandoned in French society p180-212

Castan, N. Summary justice. *In* Deviants and the abandoned in French society p111-56

Delasselle, C. Abandoned children in eighteenth-century Paris. *In* Deviants and the abandoned in French society p47-82

Frijhoff, W. and Julia, D. The diet in boarding schools at the end of the ancien régime. *In* Food and drink in history p73-85

Hémardinquer, J. J. The family pig of the ancien régime: myth or fact? *In* Food and drink in history p50-72

Larkin, M. Une société embourgeoisée? Balzac's France. *In* Larkin, M. Man and society in nineteenth-century realism p42-51

Le Roy Ladurie, E. The conscripts of 1868: a study of the correlation between geographical mobility, delinquency and physical stature, and other aspects of the situation of the young Frenchmen called to do military service in that year. *In* Le Roy Ladurie, E. The territory of the historian p33-60

Le Roy Ladurie, E. A system of customary law: family structures and inheritance customs in sixeteenth-century France. *In* Family and society p75-103

Perrot, M. Delinquency and the penitentiary system in nineteenth-century France. *In* Deviants and the abandoned in French society p213-45

Peter, J. P. Disease and the sick at the end of the eighteenth century. *In* Biology of man in history p81-124

Zysberg, A. Galley rowers in the mid-eighteenth century.. *In* Deviants and the abandoned in French society p83-110

Social conditions—Historiography

Le Roy Ladurie, E. From Waterloo to Colyton. *In* Le Roy Ladurie, E. The territory of the historian p223-34

Social policy

Cazes, B. The use of long-term studies in planning. *In* Planning, politics and public policy p424-32

Franchise. See Suffrage

Francis I, King of France

About

Knecht, R. J. Francis I, 'Defender of the Faith'? *In* Wealth and power in Tudor England p106-27

Francis, R. A.

The first-person narrator in the Abbé Prévost's Memoires d'un homme de qualité. *In* Studies in eighteenth-century culture v6

Francis, Robert, 1901-

About individual works

The trouble with Francis

Hamburger, M. The trouble with Francis. *In* Hamburger, M. Art as second nature p150-52

Franciscans

Spiritual life

Jeffrey, D. L. Franciscan spirituality and the growth of vernacular culture. *In* Jeffrey, D. L. ed. By things seen: reference and recognition in medieval thought p143-60

Spiritual life—Book reviews

Bynum, C. W. Franciscan spirituality: two approaches. *In* Medievalia et humanistica no. 7 p195-97

Francisco de Vitoria

About individual works

The first relectio on the Indians lately discovered

Grisel, É. The beginnings of international law and general public law doctrine: Francisco de Vitoria's De Indiis prior. *In* First images of America p305-25

Franck, Isaac

Spinoza, Freud, and Hampshire on psychic freedom. *In* Thought, consciousness, and reality p257-309

Franco, Jean

Conversations and confessions: self and character in The fall and Conversation in the cathedral. *In* Rossman. C. R. and Friedman, A. W. eds. Mario Vargas Llosa p59-75

Franco-American press, Brissot de Warville and the. Stern, M. B. *In* Virginia, University. Bibliographical Society. Studies in bibliography v29 p362-72

Franco-English War, 1294-1298. See Anglo-French War, 1294-1298.

Francoeur, Robert Thomas

Human nature and human relations. *In* Bundy, R. F. ed. Images of the future: the twenty-first century and beyond p125-34

Franconi, Gabriel Tristan

About individual works

Un Tel de L'Armée française

Klein, H. M. Projections of Everyman: the common soldier in Franconi, Wiechert and Williamson. *In* Klein, H. M. ed. The First World War in fiction p84-100

Frank, Anne

About individual works

The diary of a young girl

Berryman, J. The development of Anne Frank. *In* Berryman, J. The freedom of the poet p91-106

Bettelheim, B. The ignored lesson of Anne Frank. *In* Bettelheim, B. Surviving, and other essays p246-57

Frank, Bernhard

Homosexual love in four poems by Rilke. *In* Crew, L. ed. The gay academic p244-51

Frank, Ellen E.

The domestication of nature: five houses in the Lake District. *In* Knoepflmacher, U. C. and Tennyson, G. B. eds. Nature and the Victorian imagination p68-92

Frank, Glenn W.

"On my honor I will . . ." *In* Buxton, T. H. and Prichard, K. W. eds. Excellence in university teaching p140-46

Frank, Jakób Józef

About

Duker, A. G. Frankism as a movement of Polish-Jewish synthesis. *In* Király, B. K. ed. Tolerance and movements of religious dissent in Eastern Europe p133-64

Frank, Jane Lakes. See Tunney, J. V. jt. auth.

Frank, Jerome

About

White, G. E. Cardozo, Learned Hand, and Frank: the dialectic of freedom and constraint. *In* White, G. E. The American judicial tradition p251-91

Frank, Jerome David

Nonmedical healing: religious and secular; excerpt from "Persuasion and healing." *In* Sobel, D. S. ed. Ways of health p231-66

An overview of psychotherapy. *In* Overview of the psychotherapies p3-21

Frank, Lawrence Dyer

The intelligibility of madness in Our mutual friend and The mystery of Edwin Drood. *In* Dickens Studies Annual v5 p150-95

"Through a glass darkly": Esther Summerson and Bleak House. *In* Dickens Studies Annual v4 p91-112

Frank, Mike

Shakespeare's existential comedy. *In* Shakespeare's late plays p142-65

Frank, Mortimer H.

Milton's knowledge of music: some speculations. *In* Patrick, J. M. and Sundell, R. H. eds. Milton and the art of sacred song p83-98

Frank, Peter John

The changing composition of the Communist Party. *In* Brown, A. H. and Kaser, M. eds. The Soviet Union since the fall of Khrushchev p96-120

Frank, Robert. See Rosen, S. J. jt. auth.

Frank, Semen Lîûdvigovich

The ethics of nihilism: a characterization of the Russian intelligentsia's moral outlook. *In* Landmarks p155-84

Frank, Waldo David

Influence—Toomer

Bone, R. A. Jean Toomer. *In* Bone, R. A. Down home p204-38

Frankel, Charles

Epilogue: reflections on a worn-out model. *In* Universities in the Western world p279-89

Facts, values, and responsible choice. *In* Hook, S.; Kurtz, P. and Todorovich, M. eds. The ethics of teaching and scientific research p23-28

John Dewey's social philosophy. *In* Cahn, S. M. ed. New studies in the philosophy of John Dewey p 3-44

Private rights and the public good. *In* Small comforts for hard times p87-102

About individual works

Facts, values, and responsible choice

Baumann, F. Objectivity and indoctrination. *In* Hook, S.; Kurtz, P. and Todorovich, M. eds. The ethics of teaching and scientific research p53-59

Private rights and the public good

Arendt, H. Public rights and private interests: in response to Charles Frankel. *In* Small comforts for hard times p103-08

Frankel, David

Pottery decoration as an indicator of social relationships: a prehistoric Cypriot example. *In* Greenhalgh, M. and Megaw, J. V. S. eds. Art in society p147-60

Frankel, Eugene

J. B. Biot and the mathematization of experimental physics in Napoleonic France. *In* Historical studies in the physical sciences v8 p33-72

Frankel, Hans Hermann

Yüeh-fu poetry. *In* Birch, C. ed. Studies in Chinese literary genres p69-107

Frankel, Hermann Ferdinand

About individual works

Man's 'ephemeros' nature according to Pindar and others

Dickie, M. W. On the meaning of ἐφήμερος. *In* Illinois classical studies, v 1 1976 p7-14

Frankel, Marvin E.

Legal ethics and the ethics of law teaching. *In* Hook, S.; Kurtz, P. and Todorovich, M. eds. The ethics of teaching and scientific research p87-91

Frankel, Sally Herbert

Clarence Ayres and the roots of economic progress. *In* Science and ceremony p63-74

Frankena, William Klaas

Moral philosophy and world hunger. *In* Aiken, W. and La Follette, H. eds. World hunger and moral obligation p66-84

Spinoza's "new morality": notes on book IV. *In* Freeman, E. and Mandelbaum, M. H. ed. Spinoza p85-100

About individual works
The philosopher's attack on morality

Foot, P. A reply to Professor Frankena. *In* Foot, P. Virtues and vices, and other essays in moral philosophy p174-80

Frankenstein films

LaValley, A. J. The stage and film children of Frankenstein: a survey. *In* Levine, G. L. and Knoepflmacher, U. C. eds. The endurance of Frankenstein p243-89

Nestrick, W. V. Coming to life: Frankenstein and the nature of film narrative. *In* Levine, G. L. and Knoepflmacher, U. C. eds. The endurance of Frankenstein p290-315

Frankfort, Enriqueta Harris

El Greco's Holy Family with the sleeping Christ Child and the infant Baptist: an image of silence and mystery. *In* Enggass, R. C. and Stokstad, M. eds. Hortus imaginum p103-11

Frankfurt, Harry G.

Descartes on the consistency of reason. *In* Hooker, M. ed. Descartes p26-39

Identification and externality. *In* Rorty, A. O. ed. The identities of persons p239-51

Frankfurt am Main. Institut für Zocialforschung

Piccone, P. Beyond identity theory. *In* O'Neill, J. ed. On critical theory p129-44

Frankfurt school of sociology

Appelbaum, R. P. Marxist method: structural constraints and social praxis. *In* McNall, S. G. ed. Theoretical perspectives in sociology p200-13

Brown, M. E. Sociology as critical theory. *In* McNall, S. G. ed. Theoretical perspectives in sociology p251-75

Sewart, J. J. Critical theory and the critique of conservative method. *In* McNall, S. G. ed. Theoretical perspectives in sociology p310-22

Frankfurt sociologists. See Frankfurt school of sociology

Frankfurter, Felix

About

Danzig, R. How questions begot answers in Felix Frankfurter's first flag salute opinion. *In* The Supreme Court review, 1977 p257-74

White, G. E. The mosaic of the Warren Court: Frankfurter, Black, Warren and Harlan. *In* White, G. E. The American judicial tradition p317-68

Frankists

Duker, A. G. Frankism as a movement of Polish-Jewish synthesis. *In* Király B. K. ed. Tolerance and movements of religious dissent in Eastern Europe p133-64

Frankl, Paul

About individual works
The Gothic

Edelman, N. Book reviews. *In* Edelman, N. The eye of the beholder p166-205

Frankl, Viktor Emil

Man's search for ultimate meaning. *In* Needleman, J. and Lewis, D. eds. On the way to self knowledge p182-203

Franklin, Benjamin

About

Adams, P. G. Benjamin Franklin and the travel-writing tradition. *In* Lemay, J. A. L. ed. The oldest revolutionary p33-50

Bell, W. J. Benjamin Franklin and the practice of medicine. *In* Bell, W. J. The colonial physician & other essays p119-35

Bushman, R. L. On the uses of psychology: conflict and conciliation in Benjamin Franklin. *In* Kren, G. M. and Rappoport, L. H. eds. Varieties of psychohistory p81-98

Granger, B. I. Early Philadelphia serials. *In* Granger, B. I. American essay serials from Franklin to Irving p41-69

Granger, B. I. Franklin as press agent in England. *In* Lemay, J. A. L. ed. The oldest revolutionary p21-32

Griffith, J. Franklin's sanity and the man behind the masks. *In* Lemay, J. A. L. ed. The oldest revolutionary p123-38

Hedges, W. L. From Franklin to Emerson. *In* Lemay, J. A. L. ed. The oldest revolutionary p139-56

Leary, L. G. Benjamin Franklin and the requirements of literature. *In* Leary, L. G. Soundings p8-43

McEwen, G. D. "A turn of thinking": Benjamin Franklin, Cotton Mather, and Daniel Defoe on "doing good." *In* The Dress of words p53-65

Meyer, D. H. Benjamin Franklin and the art of virtue. *In* Meyer, D. H. The democratic Enlightenment p61-81

Rucker, M. E. Benjamin Franklin. *In* Emerson, E. H. ed. American literature, 1764-1789 p105-25

Simpson, L. P. The printer as a man of letters: Franklin and the symbolism of the third realm. *In* Lemay, J. A. L. ed. The oldest revolutionary p3-20

Wetherell, C. 'For these or such like reasons': John Holt's attack on Benjamin Franklin. *In* American Antiquarian Society. Proceedings v88 pt2 p251-75

About individual works
Autobiography

Couser, G. T. Deism and prophecy: Benjamin Franklin's Autobiography. *In* Couser, G. T. American autobiography p41-50

Parker, D. L. From sound believer to practical preparationist: some Puritan harmonics in Franklin's Autobiography. *In* Lemay, J. A. L. ed. The oldest revolutionary p67-75

Perkins, J. A. The ironic mode in autobiography: Franklin and Rousseau. *In* Studies in eighteenth-century culture v6 p215-28

Zall, P. M. A portrait of the autobiographer as an old artificer. *In* Lemay, J. A. L. ed. The oldest revolutionary p53-65

Dogood papers

Granger, B. I. Early Boston serials. *In* Granger, B. I. American essay serials from Franklin to Irving p13-40

Poor Richard's almanack

Nickels, C. C. Franklin's Poor Richard almanacs: "the humblest of his labors." *In* Lemay, J. A. L. ed. The oldest revolutionary p77-89

Franklin, Benjamin, supposed author. See
The speech of Miss Polly Baker, before a
court of judicature, at Connecticut near
Boston in New England

Franklin, Howard Bruce
Science fiction before Gernsback; excerpt
from "Future perfect." *In* Knight, D. F. ed.
Turning points p96-99
What are we to make of J. G. Ballard's
apocalypse? *In* Clareson, T. D. ed. Voices
for the future: essays on major science fiction writers v2 p82-105

Franklin, John Hope
A brief history. *In* The Black American
reference book p 1-89
Libraries in a pluralistic society. *In* Libraries and the life of the mind in America
p3-15

Franklin, Marc A.
Personal injury accidents in New Zealand
and the United States: some striking similarities. *In* Stanford legal essays p129-48

Franklin, Stephen L.
Dickens and time: the clock without hands.
In Dickens Studies Annual v4 p 1-35

Franklin, Wayne
Speaking and touching: the problem of inexpressibility in American travel books. *In*
Kagle, S. E. ed. America: exploration and
travel p18-38

Franklin, William McHenry
Unconditional surrender. *In* Encyclopedia
of American foreign policy p986-93

Franklin Institute, Philadelphia
Sinclair, B. Science, technology, and the
Franklin Institute. *In* Oleson, A. and Brown,
S. C. eds. The pursuit of knowledge in the
early American Republic p194-207

Frantz, Joe Bertram
Walter Prescott Webb and the South. *In*
Essays on Walter Prescott Webb p3-15

Fraser, Bruce
The interpretation of novel metaphors. *In*
Ortony, A. ed. Metaphor and thought p172-
85

Fraser, Derek
Edward Baines. *In* Hollis, P. ed. Pressure from without p183-209

Fraser, Donald MacKay
Congress's role in the making of international human rights policy. *In* Kommers,
D. P. and Loescher, G. D. eds. Human
rights and American foreign policy p247-54

**Fraser, Donald MacKay, and Nathanson,
Iric**
Rebuilding the House of Representatives.
In Ornstein, N. J. ed. Congress in change
p288-94

Fraser, George Sutherland
Essays on twentieth-century poets
Contents
Auden in midstream
Auden's later manner
Dylan Thomas
Evasive honesty: the poetry of Louise Mac-
Neice
Keith Douglas: a poet of the Second World
War
A language by itself
Lawrence Durrell
Norman MacCaig: four poems examined
'Not wrongly moved . . .' (William Empson)
Philip Larkin: the lyric note and the grand
style

The poetry of Robert Graves
A poetry of search (Stephen Spender)
The poetry of Thom Gunn
Pound: masks, myth, man
Seven poems by Yeats
T. S. Eliot: a reappraisal
W. B. Yeats
'The wasteland' revisited
Yeats and the ballad style
Yeats: two dream poems

Fraser, Ralph Sidney
Nietzsche, Byron, and the classical tradition. *In* O'Flaherty, J. G.; Sellner, T. F. and
Helm, R. M. eds. Studies in Nietzsche and
the classical tradition p190-98

Fraser, Robert
The American background in Why are we
so blest? *In* African literature today no. 9,
Africa, America and the Caribbean p39-46

Fraser, Russell A.

About individual works
The Dark Ages and the Age of Gold
Duhamel, P. A. Medieval intuition and
seventeenth-century dialectic. *In* Medievalia
et humanistica no. 5 p243-46

Fraser, Thomas G.
Imperial policy and Indian minorities
overseas, 1905-23. *In* Hepburn, A. C. ed. Minorities in history p154-69

Fraternal benefit societies. See Friendly societies

Fraternity. See Brotherliness

Frazee, Monique Parent
Ellen Glasgow as feminist. *In* Ellen Glasgow p167-87

Frazer, Alfred K.
The pyre of Faustina Senior. *In* Studies in
classical art and archaeology p271-74

Frazer, Sir James George

About individual works
The golden bough
Frye, N. Symbolism of the unconscious.
In Frye, N. Northrop Frye on culture and
literature p84-94

Frazer, Winifred L.
Drama. *In* American literary scholarship,
1976 p355-68
Drama. [another essay]. *In* American literary scholarship, 1977 p389-403

Frazier, Edward Franklin
The Negro church: a nation within a nation; excerpt from "The Negro church in
America." *In* Mulder, J. M. and Wilson, J. F.
eds. Religion in American history p288-301

Frazier, Shervert H.
Psychopharmacology in a psychotherapeutic setting. *In* Overview of the psychotherapies p118-24

Freccero, John
Dante's Medusa: allegory and autobiography. *In* Jeffrey, D. L. ed. By things seen:
reference and recognition in medieval thought
p33-46
Dante's Ulysses: from epic to novel. *In*
Concepts of the hero in the Middle Ages
and the Renaissance p101-19
Donne's "Valediction: forbidding mourning." *In* Roberts, J. R. ed. Essential articles
for the study of John Donne's poetry p279-
304

Frede, Michael
Principles of Stoic grammar. *In* Rist, J. M.
ed. The Stoics p27-75

Frederic, Harold

About individual works

The damnation of Theron Ware

Farrell, J. T. Harold Frederic's The damnation of Theron Ware. *In* Farrell, J. T. Literary essays, 1954-1974 p126-29

Characters—Celia Madden

Fryer, J. The temptress: Celia Madden: The temptress as "Greek." *In* Fryer, J. The faces of Eve p54-62

Frederick I, Barbarossa, Emperor of the Holy Roman Empire. See Friedrich I, Barbarossa, Emperor of Germany

Fredericks, Sigmund Casey

Irony of overstatement in the satires of Juvenal. *In* Illinois classical studies v4, 1979 p178-91

Juvenal: a return to invective. *In* Roman satirists and their satire p136-69

Juvenal's Fifteenth Satire. *In* Illinois classical studies, v 1 1976 p174-89

Plato's Atlantis: a mythologist looks at myth. *In* Ramage, E. S. ed. Atlantis, fact or fiction? p81-99

Revivals of ancient mythologies in current science fiction and fantasy. *In* Clareson, T. D. ed. Many futures, many worlds p50-65

Seneca and Petronius: Menippean satire under Nero. *In* Roman satirists and their satire p89-113

Frederickson, Donald Sharp

Health and the search for new knowledge. *In* Knowles, J. H. ed. Doing better and feeling worse p159-70

Fredrickson, George M.

After emancipation: a comparative study of white responses to the new order of race relations in the American South, Jamaica & the Cape Colony of South Africa. *In* What was freedom's price? p71-92

Fredro, Aleksander, Count

About

Durer, C. S. Molière and Polish comedy. *In* Johnson, R. B.; Neumann, E. S. and Trail, G. T. eds. Molière and the commonwealth of letters: patrimony and posterity p365-78

Free, William J.

Williams in the seventies: directions and discontents. *In* Tennessee Williams: a tribute p815-28

Free agency. See Free will and determinism

Free enterprise. See Laissez-faire

Free schools

Keyes, R. Freeing the university. *In* Fairfield, R. P. ed. Humanistic frontiers in American education p202-06

Scrupski, A. Educational horizon: promise, challenge, vulnerability. *In* Social forces and schooling p361-68

See also Open plan schools

Free speech. See Liberty of speech

Free thought. See Rationalism; Skepticism

Free trade and protection

Fleming, J. M. Mercantilism and free trade today. *In* The Market and the state p164-85

Munro, J. H. A. Industrial protectionism in medieval Flanders: urban or national? *In* The Medieval city p229-67

See also Laissez-faire; Mercantile system; Tariff

Free verse

Eliot, T. S. Reflections on vers libre. *In* Eliot, T. S. Selected prose of T. S. Eliot p31-36

Also in Gross, H. S. ed. The structure of verse p227-33

See also Imagist poetry

Free will and determinism

Barnouw, J. Materialism and freedom: commentary on papers by Robert E. Schofield and Aram Vartanian. *In* Studies in eighteenth-century culture v7 p193-212

Berlin, Sir I. 'From hope and fear set free.' *In* Berlin, I. Concepts and categories p173-98

Dearden, R. F. Autonomy as an education ideal I. *In* Philosophers discuss education p3-18

Ducasse, C. J. Knowing the future. *In* Wheatley, J. M. O. and Edge, H. L. eds. Philosophical dimensions of parapsychology p193-97

Fitzgerald, R. Essay 3. *In* Fitzgerald, R. ed. What it means to be human p44-63

Flew, A. G. N. Is there a 'problem of freedom'? *In* Pivčević, E. ed. Phenomenology and philosophical understanding p195-209

Flew, A. G. N. Psychoanalysis and freewill. *In* Flew, A. G. N. A rational animal p172-95

Flew, A. G. N. A rational animal. *In* Flew, A. G. N. A rational animal p89-122

Foot, P. Free will as involving determinism. *In* Foot, P. Virtues and vices, and other essays in moral philosophy p62-73

Franck, I. Spinoza, Freud, and Hampshire on psychic freedom. *In* Thought, consciousness, and reality p257-309

Gray, J. G. The abyss of freedom—and Hannah Arendt. *In* Hannah Arendt: the recovery of the public world p225-44

Hampshire, S. Spinoza's theory of human freedom. *In* Freeman, E. and Mandelbaum, M. H. eds. Spinoza p35-47

Haskell, T. L. Deterministic implications of intellectual history. *In* Higham, J. and Conkin, P. K. eds. New directions in American intellectual history p132-48

Koenen, L. Augustine and Manichaeism in light of the Cologne Mani Codex. *In* Illinois classical studies v3, 1978 p154-95

Koestler, A. Free will in a hierarchic context. *In* Koestler, A. Janus p229-41

Larkin, M. Determinist thought: Stendhal and the eighteenth-century inheritance. *In* Larkin, M. Man and society in nineteenth-century realism p17-30

Parkinson, G. H. R. Spinoza on the power and freedom of man. *In* Freeman, E. and Mandelbaum, M. H. eds. Spinoza p7-33

Pine, M. Pietro Pompanazzi and the medieval tradition of God's foreknowledge. *In* Philosophy and humanism p100-15

Ricoeur, P. Nature and freedom. *In* Ricoeur, P. Political and social essays p23-45

Ricoeur, P. Phenomenology of freedom. *In* Pivčević, E. ed. Phenomenology and philosophical understanding p173-94

Stough, C. L. Stoic determinism and moral responsibility. *In* Rist, J. M. ed. The Stoics p203-31

Telfer, E. Autonomy as an educational ideal II. *In* Philosophers discuss education p19-35

Free will and determinism—*Continued*

Vartanian, A. Necessity or freedom? The politics of an eighteenth-century metaphysical debate. *In* Studies in eighteenth-century culture v7 p153-74

Watkins, J. W. N. Three views concerning human freedom. *In* Royal Institute of Philosophy. Nature and conduct p200-28

Weber, M. Subjectivity and determinism. *In* Giddens, A. ed. Positivism and sociology p23-31

See also Decision-making (Ethics); Freedom (Theology); necessity (Philosophy); Responsibility

Freeborn, Richard

Dostoevsky, *In* Freeborn, R. ed. Russian literary attitudes from Pushkin to Solzhenitsyn p39-59

Russian literary attitudes from Pushkin to Solzhenitsyn. *In* Freeborn, R. ed. Russian literary attitudes from Pushkin to Solzhenitsyn p 1-18

Tolstoy. *In* Freeborn, R. ed. Russian literary attitudes from Pushkin to Solzhenitsyn p60-78

Freed, John B.

The formation of the Salzburg ministerial-age in the tenth and eleventh centuries: an example of upward social mobility in the early Middle Ages. *In* Viator: medieval and Renaissance studies v9 p67-102

The friars and the delineation of state boundaries in the thirteenth century. *In* Order and innovation in the Middle Ages p31-40

The origins of the European nobility: the problems of the ministerials. *In* Viator: medieval and Renaissance studies v1 p211-41

Freedman, David Noel

Early Israelite history in the light of early Israelite poetry. *In* Unity and diversity p3-35

Freedman, Lawrence

Whose crisis?: Britain as an international problem. *In* Kramnick, I. ed. Is Britain dying? p203-14

Freedman, Mark

Toward a gay psychology. *In* Crew, L. ed. The gay academic p315-26

Freedman, Maurice

An epicycle of Cathay; or, The southward expansion of the Sinologists. *In* Social organization and the applications of anthropology p302-32

Freedman, Monroe H.

Advertising and soliciting: the case for ambulance chasing. *In* Nader, R. and Green, M. J. eds. Verdicts on lawyers p94-104

Freedman, Ralph

Intentionality and the literary object. *In* Krieger, M. and Dembo, L. S. eds. Directions for criticism p137-59

Freedman, Richard

Sufficiently decayed: gerontophobia in English literature. *In* Spicker, S. F.; Woodward, K. M. and Van Tassel, D. D. eds. Aging and the elderly p49-61

Freedman, Robert Owen

The Soviet conception of a Middle East peace settlement. *In* Ro'i, Y. ed. The limits to power p282-327

Soviet policy toward international terrorism. *In* International terrorism p115-47

Freedmen

McPherson, J. M. The new Puritanism: values and goals of freedmen's education in America. *In* The University in society v2 p611-42

Freedom. See Liberty

Freedom (Psychology) See Autonomy (Psychology)

Freedom (Theology)

Gollwitzer, H. The gospel and the struggle for freedom. *In* The Context of contemporary theology p87-97

Herzog, F. Reorientation in theology: listening to Black theology. *In* The Context of contemporary theology p225-41

Moltmann, J. Liberation in the light of hope. *In* The Context of contemporary theology p127-46

Patrick, J. M. The idea of liberty in the theological writings of Sir Henry Vane the Younger. *In* The Dissenting tradition p100-07

Freedom of association

Marson, C. C.; Crosby, M. C. and Schlosser, A. L. On the civil liberties of sect members: Part 1. *In* Horowitz, I. L. ed. Science, sin, and scholarship p192-97

Freedom of decision (Ethics) See Decision-making (Ethics)

Freedom of information

Bathory, P. D. and McWilliams, W. C. Political theory and the people's right to know. *In* Galnoor, I. ed. Government secrecy in democracies p3-21

Bay, C. Access to political knowledge as a human right. *In* Galnoor, I. ed. Government secrecy in democracies p22-39

Gross, L. International law aspects of the freedom of information and the right to communicate. *In* Horton, P. C. ed. The Third World and press freedom p55-73

Lacy, D. M. Libraries and the freedom of access to information. *In* Libraries and the life of the mind in America p19-37

See also Government and the press; Government information Liberty of speech; Liberty of the press

Freedom of religion. See Religious liberty

Freedom of speech. See Liberty of speech

Freedom of teaching. See Teaching, Freedom of

Freedom of the press. See Liberty of the press

Freedom of the seas

Rappaport, A. Freedom of the seas. *In* Encyclopedia of American foreign policy 387-97

Freedom of the will. See Free will and determinism

Freedom of worship. See Religious liberty

Freehold. See Land tenure

Freeman, Bonnie Cook

Power patriarchy, and "political primitives." *In* Roberts, J. I. ed. Beyond intellectual sexism p241-64

Freeman, Christopher

Economics of research and development. *In* Science, technology and society p223-75

Freeman, Donald C.

Literature. *In* Wardhaugh, R. and Brown, H. D. eds. A survey of applied linguistics p229-49

Freeman, Donald C.—*Continued*

The strategy of fusion: Dylan Thomas's syntax. *In* Fowler, R. ed. Style and structure in literature p19-39

Freeman, Harold Webber

About

Cavaliero, G. Farmer novelists: H. W. Freeman, A. G. Street, Adrian Bell. *In* Cavaliero, G. The rural tradition in the English novel, 1900-1939 p101-17

Freese, Peter

James Baldwin, Going to meet the Man. *In* Bruck, P. ed. The Black American short story in the 20th century p171-85

John A. Williams, Son in the afternoon. *In* Bruck, P. ed. The Black American short story in the 20th century p141-55

Frege, Friedrich Ludwig Gottlob. See Frege, Gottlob

Frege, Gottlob

Review of Dr E. Husserl's Philosophy of arithmetic. *In* Elliston, F. A. and McCormick, P. eds. Husserl p314-24

About

Geach, P. T. Names and identity. *In* Guttenplan, S. D. ed. Mind and language p139-58

Influence

Grene, M. G. Philosophy in and out of Europe: The European sources of recent Anglo-American philosophy. *In* Grene, M. G. Philosophy in and out of Europe p11-23

About individual works
Dialog mit Punjer über Existenz

Rosen, S. Thinking about nothing. *In* Murray, M. E. ed. Heidegger and modern philosophy p116-37

Frei, Eduardo. See Frei Montalva, Eduardo, President Chile

Frei Montalva, Eduardo, President Chile

The political realities of health in a developing nation. *In* Cahill, K. M. ed. Health and development p4-14

Freidel, David A. See Sabloff, J. A. jt. auth.

Freier, Shalheveth

Local wars and their escalation. *In* Griffiths, F. and Polanyi, J. C. eds. The dangers of nuclear war p125-34

Frelimo. See Mozambique Liberation Front

Fremlin, Celia

The Christie everybody knew. *In* Agatha Christie: first lady of crime p111-20

French, Anthony Philip

Einstein—a condensed biography. *In* Einstein p53-64

Einstein and world affairs. *In* Einstein p185-97

The story of general relativity. *In* Einstein p91-111

French, Brandon

The celluloid Lolita: a not-so-crazy quilt. *In* Peary, G. and Shatzkin, R. eds. The modern American novel and the movies p224-35

On the verge of revolt
Contents

The amiable spouse
Androgyny, anyone?
Brides of Christ
Dogs like us

The eleven-year itch
The hard and the soft
The joys of marriage
A minimal feast
A night without a star
Oppression in sheep's clothing
The scarlet "A"
Some pretty natural noises

French, Marilyn

About individual works
The women's room

Mickelson, A. Z. Piecemeal liberation: Marge Piercy, Sara Davidson, Marilyn French, Grace Paley. *In* Mickelson, A. Z. Reaching out: sensitivity and order in recent American fiction by women p175-234

French, Paul, pseud. See Asimov, Isaac

French, Roderick Stuart

Elihu Palmer, radical deist, radical republican: a reconsideration of American free thought. *In* Studies in eighteenth-century culture v8 p87-108

French, Stanley Goodwin

The cemetery as cultural institution: the establishment of Mount Auburn and the "rural cemetery" movement. *In* Death in America p69-91

French, Thomas R. See Williams, W. L. jt. auth.

French, Warren G.

The age of Eliot: the twenties as waste land. *In* French, W. G. ed. The twenties p1-26

"All things are double": Eudora Welty as a civilized writer. *In* Prenshaw, P. W. ed. Eudora Welty p179-88

"The death of the hired man": modernism and transcendence. *In* Frost: centennial essays III p382-401

Fiction: 1900 to the 1930s. *In* American literary scholarship, 1973 p224-57

Frost country. *In* Frost: centennial essays II p5-20

19th-century literature. *In* American literary scholarship, 1974 p193-225

19th-century literature [another essay]. *In* American literary scholarship, 1975 p231-66

19th-century literature [another essay]. *In* American literary scholarship, 1976 p195-225

French Academy. See Academie française, Paris

French aesthetics. See Aesthetics, French

French-Canadian children's literature. See Children's literature, French-Canadian

French-Canadian literature

History and criticism

Leland, M. E. Quebec literature in its American context. *In* Staines, D. ed. The Canadian imagination p188-225

French-Canadians

Lacourcière, L. A survey of folk medicine in French Canada from early times to the present. *In* American folk medicine p203-14

Rocher, G. The quiet revolution and revolutionary movements among Quebec French Canadians. *In* Perspectives on revolution and evolution p238-67

See also Canada—English-French relations

French-Canadians in Quebec

Alcock, A. E. Three case-studies in minority protection: South Tyrol, Cyprus, Quebec. *In* Hepburn, A. C. ed. Minorities in history p189-225

French children's literature. See Children's literature, French

French Communist Party. See Communist Party of France

The French connection (Motion picture)
Kauffmann, S. The French connection. *In* Kauffmann, S. Living images p84-86

French drama

16th century—History and criticism
Nicoll, A. French romanticism and classicism. *In* Nicoll, A. World drama p154-60

17th century—History and criticism
Nicoll, A. French romanticism and classicism. *In* Nicoll, A. World drama p154-60

18th century—History and criticism
Koch, P. Regnard and Collin d'Harleville on legacies by bachelor uncles. *In* Studies in eighteenth-century culture v8 p291-309

19th century—History and crticism
Denommé, R. T. French theater reform and Vigny's translation of Othello in 1829. *In* Symbolism and modern literature p81-102
Nicoll, A. The play of ideas in France. *In* Nicoll, A. World drama p493-502
Nicoll, A. The realm of fancy. *In* Nicoll, A. World drama p387-405
Robinson, C. Science, reason and the material world. *In* Robinson, C. French literature in the nineteenth century p50-107

20th century—History and criticism
Auger, P. P. Post-war drama in France and Belgium. *In* Nicoll, A. World drama p821-37

French drama (Comedy)

History and criticism
Brereton, G. Bourgeois comedy: sentiment and moralization. *In* Brereton, G. French comic drama p214-36
Brereton, G. Conclusion. *In* Brereton, G. French comic drama p256-71
Brereton, G. The cynical generation: Dancourt, Regnard, Dufresny, Lesage. *In* Brereton, G. French comic drama p163-93
Brereton, G. French comedy before 1630. *In* Brereton, G. French comic drama p 1-11
Brereton, G. The shadow of Molière. *In* Brereton, G. French comic drama p150-62
Howarth, W. D. Comedy in France. *In* Howarth, W. D. ed. Comic drama p102-21
Koch, P. Regnard and Collin d'Harleville on legacies by bachelor uncles. *In* Studies in eighteenth-century culture v8 p291-309
Lawrence, F. L. Le misanthrope reprised: four versions of Molière's theme. *In* Johnson, R. B.; Neumann, E. S. and Trail, G. T. eds. Molière and the commonwealth of letters: patrimony and posterity p82-89
Sumberg, L. A. M. From farce in the âge bourgeois (1440-1500) to farce Moliéresque: the structure of generic change. *In* Johnson, R. B.; Neumann, E. S. and Trail, G. T. eds. Molière and the commonwealth of letters: patrimony and posterity p430-42

French-English War, 1294-1298. See Anglo-French War, 1294-1298

French epic poetry. See Epic poetry, French

French fiction

History and criticism
Terdiman, R. The coherence of the tradition. *In* Terdiman, R. The dialectics of isolation p3-15

Terdiman, R. Conclusion. *In* Terdiman, R. The dialectics of isolation p227-48
Turnell, M. From Marivaux to Raymond Radiguet. *In* Turnell, M. The rise of the French novel p 1-28

Haitian authors
See Haitian fiction

North African authors
See North African fiction (French)

18th century—History and criticism
Martin, A. From Marmontel to Berquin: the dynamic concept of morality in eighteenth-century French fiction. *In* Studies in eighteenth-century culture v6 p285-302
Mylne, V. Social realism in the dialogue of eighteenth-century French fiction. *In* Studies in eighteenth-century culture v6 p265-84
Rosbottom, R. C. A matter of competence: the relationship between reading and novel-making in eighteenth-century France. *In* Studies in eighteenth-century culture v6 p245-63

19th century—History and criticism
Robinson, C. Subjective reality. *In* Robinson, C. French literature in the nineteenth century p108-70
Terdiman, R. Balzac: the logic of failure. *In* Terdiman, R. The dialectics of isolation p39-59
Terdiman, R. Flaubert and after: failure formalized. *In* Terdiman, R. The dialectics of isolation p60-95

20th century—History and criticism
Alter, R. The inexhaustible genre. *In* Alter, R. Partial magic p218-45
Brombert, V. H. Epilogue: The borderline zone. *In* Brombert, V. H. The romantic prison p200-09
Ricardou, J. Nouveau roman, Tel Quel. *In* Federman, R. ed. Surfiction p101-33
Vidal, G. French letters: theories of the new novel. *In* Vidal, G. Matters of fact and of fiction p65-88

French in Canada
Harris, R. C. The extension of France into rural Canada. *In* European settlement and development in North America: essays on geographical change in honour and memory of Andrew Hill Clark p27-45

French in Italy
Blunt, A. Naples as seen by French travellers, 1630-1780. *In* The Artist and the writer in France p 1-14

French language

Etymology
Edelman, N. Other early uses of moyen age and moyen temps. *In* Edelman, N. The eye of the beholder p82-85

History
See French language—Etymology

Obscene words
See Words, Obscene—French

Slang
See Words, Obscene—French

Syntax
Pollock, J. Y. Trace theory and French syntax. *In* Keyser, S. J. ed. Recent transformational studies in European languages p65-112

French language—*Continued*
Vowels
Dell, F. C. and Selkirk, E. O. On a morphologically governed vowel alternation in French. *In* Keyser, S. J. ed. Recent transformational studies in European languages p 1-51

Word formation
Dell, F. C. and Selkirk, E. O. On a morphologically governed vowel alternation in French. *In* Keyser, S. J. ed. Recent transformatonal studies in European languages p 1-51

Word history
See French language—Etymology

French literature
See also Encyclopedists

History and criticism
Brombert, V. H. Introduction: The prison dream. *In* Brombert, V. H. The romantic prison p3-17

Brombert, V. H. The myth of the Bastille. *In* Brombert, V. H. The romantic prison p30-45

Malraux, A. Anti-critique. *In* Courcel, M. H. de, ed. Malraux p223-57

Peyre, H. French literary imagination and Dostoevsky. *In* Peyre, H. French literary imagination and Dostoevsky, and other essays p 1-56

Peyre, H. The notion of the Absurd in contemporary French literature. *In* Peyre, H. French literary imagination and Dostoevsky, and other essays p57-73

Peyre, H. Poets against music in the age of symbolism. *In* Symbolism and modern literature p179-92

Sayre, R. F. Afterword. *In* Sayre, R. F. Solitude in society p195-201

Sayre, R. F. L'Ancien régime; agreeable wilderness, pleasant solitude. *In* Sayre, R. F. Solitude in society p34-55

Influence
Shackleton, R. The impact of French literature on Gibbon. *In* Edward Gibbon and The decline and fall of the Roman Empire p207-18

African authors
See African literature (French)

Black authors
Knight, V. W. Haiti and Martinique. *In* King, B. A. and Ogungbesan, K. eds. A celebration of Black and African writing p46-59

Catholic authors
Robinson, C. Collective values. *In* Robinson, C. French literature in the nineteenth century p171-206

To 1500—History and criticism
Dembowski, P. F. Literary problems of hagiography in Old French. *In* Medievalia et humanistica no. 7 p117-30

Kelly, D. Rhetoric in French literature: topical invention in medieval French literature. *In* Murphy, J. J. ed. Medieval eloquence p231-51

Mermier, G. R. The grotesque in French medieval literature: a study in forms and meanings. *In* Ruggiers, P. G. ed. Versions of medieval comedy p101-34

16th century—History and criticism
Bensimon, M. J. Modes of perception of reality in the Renaissance. *In* The Darker vision of the Renaissance p221-72

16th century—History and criticism— Bibliography
Stone, D. A. French literature. *In* Jones, W. M. ed. The present state of scholarship in sixteenth-century literature p45-69

17th century
Simonsuuri, K. Ancients and moderns: the problem of cultural progress. *In* Simonsuuri, K. Homer's original genius p19-36

18th century—History and criticism
Cooke, M. G. The extremes of self and system: The symbiosis of self and system in the neoclassical regimen. *In* Cooke, M. G. The romantic will p57-76

Darnton, R. The High Enlightenment and the low-life of literature in pre-revolutionary France. *In* French society and the Revolution p53-87

Runte, R. The Matron of Ephesus in eighteenth-century France: the lady and the legend. *In* Studies in eighteenth-century culture v6 p361-75

19th century—History and criticism
Robinson, C. Conclusion. *In* Robinson, C. French literature in the nineteenth century p207-10

Robinson, C. The idealist revolt. *In* Robinson, C. French literature in the nineteenth century p13-49

Sayre, R. F. Modern times. *In* Sayre, R. F. Solitude in society p56-87

20th century—History and criticism
Brombert, V. H. Servitude and solidarity. *In* Brombert, V. H. The romantic prison p173-84

Culler, J. D. Towards a theory of non-genre literature. *In* Federman, R. ed. Surfiction p255-62

Canada
See French-Canadian literature

French love poetry. See Love poetry, French

French monarchy. See Monarchy, French

French moving-pictures. See Moving-pictures, French

French opera. See Opera, French

French part-songs. See Part-songs, French

French philosophy. See Philosophy, French

French poetry
See also Chansons de geste; Lays; Prose poems, French; Romances; Troubadors

Appreciation—England
Prescott, A. L. Afterword. *In* Prescott, A. L. French poets and the English Renaissance p235-39

To 1500—Book reviews
Nichols, S. G. Old French narrative poetry: some recent studies. *In* Medievalia et humanistica no. 5 p233-37

To 1500—History and criticism
Kelly, D. Imagination and the Second Rhetoric. *In* Kelly, D. Medieval imagination p96-120

Kelly, D. Rhetoric and poetry. *In* Kelly, D. Medieval imagination p3-12

French poetry—To 1500—History and criticism—*Continued*

Kelly, D. Verisimilitude and imagination: the crisis in late courtly poetry. *In* Kelly, D. Medieval imagination p177-203

Pearcy, R. J. Investigations into the principles of fabliau structure. *In* Ruggiers, P. G. ed. Versions of medieval comedy p67-100

Silver, I. The marriage of poetry and music in France: Ronsard's predecessors and contemporaries. *In* Poetry and poetics from ancient Greece to the Renaissance p152-84

Togeby, K. The nature of the fabliaux. *In* Cooke, T. D. and Honeycutt, B. L. eds. The humor of the fabliaux p7-13

Wimsatt, J. I. Chaucer and French poetry. *In* Brewer, D. S. ed. Geoffrey Chaucer p109-36

16th century—History and criticism

Prescott, A. L. Afterword. *In* Prescott, A. L. French poets and the English Renaissance p235-39

Silver, I. The marriage of poetry and music in France: Ronsard's predecessors and contemporaries. *In* Poetry and poetics from ancient Greece to the Renaissance p152-84

Wiley, W. L. Mary, Queen of Scots, in France. *In* Studies in the continental background of Renaissance English literature: essays presented to John L. Lievsay p133-54

19th century—History and criticism

Block, H. M. Heine and the French symbolists. *In* Creative encounter p25-39

Nalbantian, S. The Symbolists: the failing soul. *In* Nalbantian, S. The symbol of the soul from Hölderlin to Yeats p66-85

Robinson, C. Subjective reality. *In* Robinson, C. French literature in the nineteenth century p108-70

20th century—History and criticism

Cardinal, R. Introduction. *In* Cardinal, R. ed. Sensibility and creation p 1-15

Greene, R. W. Afterword. *In* Greene, R. W. Six French poets of our time p177-79

Greene, R. W. Introduction. *In* Greene, R. W. Six French poets of our time p3-22

French prose poems. See Prose poems, French

French Revolution. See France—History—Revolution

French salons. See Salons

French sculpture. See Sculpture, French

French West Africa. See Africa, French speaking West

French West Indies. See West Indies, French

Freneau, Philip Morin

About

Andrews, W. D. Philip Freneau and Francis Hopkinson. *In* Emerson, E. H. ed. American literature, 1764-1789 p127-44

Cady, E. H. Philip Freneau as archetypal American poet. *In* Literature and ideas in America p 1-19

Granger, B. I. Philip Freneau. *In* Granger, B. I. American essay serials from Franklin to Irving p116-44

Leary, L. G. Philip Freneau: a reassessment. *In* Leary, L. G. Soundings p131-60

Frenzy (Motion picture)

Kauffmann, S. Frenzy. *In* Kauffmann, S. Living images p121-24

Samuels, C. T. Hyphens of the self. *In* Samuels, C. T. Mastering the film, and other essays p179-89

Frequencies of oscillating systems. See Doppler effect

Frerichs, Sarah Cutts

Elizabeth Missing Sewell: concealment and revelation in a Victorian everywoman. *In* Landow, G. P. ed. Approaches to Victorian autobiography p175-99

Fresco painting. See Mural painting and decoration

Frescobaldi. See Compagnia dei Frescobaldi

Frese, Dolores Warwick

The art of Cynewulf's runic signatures. *In* Anglo-Saxon poetry: essays in appreciation p312-34

Fresh-water ecology. See Thermal pollution of rivers, lakes, etc.

Freud, Sigmund

Preface to Ritual: psycho-analytic studies by Theodor Reik. *In* Praise from famous men: an anthology of introductions p82-88

About

Alcorn, J. Toward Freud. *In* Alcorn, J. The nature novel from Hardy to Lawrence p107-12

Bartemeier, L. H. Psychoanalysis and religion. *In* Wolman, B. B. ed. Psychoanalysis and Catholicism p7-18

Beirnaert, L. Introduction to the reading of Freud's texts on religion. *In* Wolman, B. B. ed. Psychoanalysis and Catholicism p19-30

Connolly, C. Freud. *In* Connolly, C. The evening colonnade p402-04

Danto, A. C. Freudian explanations and the language of the unconscious. *In* Psychoanalysis and language p325-53

Derrida, J. Freud and the scene of writing. *In* Derrida, J. Writing and difference p196-231

Deutsch, K. W. and Senghaas, D. The fragile sanity of states: a theoretical analysis. *In* Kilson, M. ed. New states in the modern world p200-44

Edelheit, R. On the biology of language: Darwinian/Lamarckian homology in human inheritance (with some thoughts about the Lamarckism of Freud) *In* Psychoanalysis and language p45-74

Fancher, R. E. Man in conflict: the psychoanalytic psychology of Sigmund Freud. *In* Fancher, R. E. Pioneers of psychology p205-49

Feldstein, L. C. Bifurcated psyche and social self: implications of Freud's theory of the unconscious. *In* Roth, R. J. ed. Person and community p43-62

Fergusson, F. Oedipus according to Freud, Sophocles, and Cocteau. *In* Fergusson, F. Literary landmarks p101-13

Flew, A. G. N. Motives and Freud's unconscious. *In* Flew, A. G. N. A rational animal p151-71

Franck, I. Spinoza, Freud, and Hampshire on psychic freedom. *In* Thought, consciousness, and reality p257-309

Gaylin, W. In the beginning: helpless and dependent. *In* Doing good p 1-38

Girard, R. The underground critic. *In* Girard, R. "To double business bound" p36-60

Freud, Sigmund—About—*Continued*

Homans, P. Introduction. *In* Homans, P. ed. Childhood and selfhood p13-54

Hyman, S. E. Images of Sigmund Freud. *In* Hyman, S. E. The critic's credentials p279-83

Krauss, H. H. Suicide—a psychosocial phenomenon. *In* Wolman, B. B. ed. Between survival and suicide p26-54

Lesser, S. O. Freud and Hamlet again. *In* Lesser, S. O. The whispered meanings p20-31

Litowitz, B. E. On overdetermination. *In* Psychoanalysis and language p355-94

Loewald, H. W. Primary process, secondary process, and language. *In* Psychoanalysis and language p235-70

Marquard, O. On the importance of the theory of the unconscious for a theory of no longer fine art. *In* Amacher, R. E. and Lange, V. eds. New perspectives in German literary criticism p260-78

May, K. M. The burden of consciousness. *In* May, K. M. Out of the maelstrom p 1-23

May, K. M. The nature of the unconscious. *In* May, K. M. Out of the maelstrom p24-42

Muir, K. Some Freudian interpretations of Shakespeare. *In* Muir, K. The singularity of Shakespeare, and other essays p110-23

Ple, A. Christian morality and Freudian morality. *In* Wolman, B. B. ed. Psychoanalysis and Catholicism p97-110

Pontalis, J. B. On death-work in Freud, in the self, in culture. *In* Roland A. ed. Psychoanalysis, creativity, and literature p85-95

Pribram, K. H. The linguistic act. *In* Psychoanalysis and language p75-98

Ragussis, M. The subterfuge of art: Lawrence, Freud, and "verbal consciousness." *In* Ragussis, M. The subterfuge of art p 1-5

Ricoeur, P. Image and language in psychoanalysis. *In* Psychoanalysis and language p293-324

Ricoeur, P. Psychoanalysis and the work of art. *In* Psychiatry and the humanities v 1 p3-33

Rieff, P. Freud and the authority of the past; excerpt from "Freud: the mind of the moralist". *In* Explorations in psychohistory p78-108

Schwartz, M. M. Critic, define thyself. *In* Hartman, G. H. ed. Psychoanalysis and the question of the text p 1-17

Simon, B. On the babel of tongues in contemporary psychiatry. *In* Simon, B. Mind and madness in ancient Greece p 1-30

Simon, B. Plato and Freud. *In* Simon, B. Mind and madness in ancient Greece p200-12

Steiner, G. A remark on language and psychoanalysis. *In* Steiner, G. On difficulty and other essays p48-60

Tatar, M. M. From Mesmer to Freud: animal magnetism, hypnosis, and suggestion. *In* Tatar, M. M. Spellbound p3-44

Turner, V. W. Encounter with Freud: the making of a comparative symbologist. *In* Spindler, G. D. ed. The making of psychological anthropology p558-83

Weber, S. The divaricator: remarks on Freud's Witz. *In* Glyph I p 1-27

Weber, S. It. *In* Glyph 4 p 1-31

About individual works
Beyond the pleasure principle (Chapter 2)

Derrida, J. Coming into one's own. *In* Hartman, G. H. ed. Psychoanalysis and the question of the text p114-48

Fragment of an analysis of a case of hysteria (The case of Dora)

Marcus, S. Freud and Dora: story, history, case history. *In* Marcus, S. Representations p247-310

The interpretation of dreams

Downs, R. B. Psychologist of the unconscious. *In* Downs, R. B. Books that changed the world p362-73

Palombo, S. R. Dreams, memory, and the origins of thought. *In* Thought, consciousness, and reality p49-83

Parsons, T. The interpretation of dreams by Sigmund Freud. *In* Parsons, T. Action theory and the human condition p82-88

Jokes and their relation to the unconscious

Weber, S. The divaricator: remarks on Freud's Witz. *In* Glyph I p 1-27

On narcissism: an introduction

Girard, R. Narcissism: the Freudian myth demythified by Proust. *In* Roland, A. ed. Psychoanalysis, creativity, and literature p293-311

An outline of psychoanalysis

Trilling, L. Freud's last book. *In* Trilling, L. A gathering of fugitives

Psychopathic characters on the stage

Lacoue-Labarthe, P. Theatrum analyticum. *In* Glyph 2 p122-43

Freud, Sigmund, and Jung, Carl Gustav

About individual works
The Freud/Jung letters

Trilling, L. The Freud/Jung letters. *In* Trilling, L. The last decade p177-84

Freund, Paul Abraham

Equality, race, and preferential treatment. *In* Small comforts for hard times p26-33

Liberty and law in America. *In* The American Revolution: a continuing commitment p3-11

Frey, Charles

Tragic structure in The winter's tale: the affective dimension. *In* Shakespeare's romances reconsidered p113-24

Freymond, Jacques

Crisis management and prediction. *In* [Truth and tragedy]: a tribute to Hans Morgenthau p272-83

The International Committee of the Red Cross as a neutral intermediary. *In* Unofficial diplomats p142-51

Freystadt, Germany. Mariahilf (church)

Heisner, B. F. Viscardi's Mariahilfkirche at Freystadt and the development of the central plan church in eighteenth century Germany. *In* Enggass, R. C. and Stokstad, M. eds. Hortus imaginum p175-83

Friars

Freed, J. B. The friars and the delineation of state boundaries in the thirteenth century. *In* Order and innovation in the Middle Ages p31-40

Frick, George F.
The Royal Society in America. *In* Oleson, A. and Brown, S. C. eds. The pursuit of knowledge in the early American Republic p70-83

Fricke, Donna G.
"A death in the desert": the Gospel according to Robert Browning. *In* Aeolian harps p167-78

Fricke, Douglas Charles
The Proserpine figure in Swinburne's Poems and ballads I. *In* Aeolian harps p192-205

Fried, Marlene Gerber
In defense of preferential hiring. *In* Gould, C. C. and Wartofsky, M. W. eds. Women and philosophy p309-19

Fried, Michael
The beholder in Courbet: his early self-portraits and their place in his art. *In* Glyph 4 p85-129

Friedel, Johann

About individual works
Eleonore

Horwath, P. Richardsonian characters and motifs in Johann Friedel's novel Eleonore. *In* Branscombe, P. ed. Austrian life and literature, 1780-1938 p 1-11

Friedelbaum, Stanley Herman
The 1971 wage-price freeze: unchallenged presidential power. *In* The Supreme Court review, 1974 p 1-32

Frieden, Nancy M.
The Russian cholera epidemic, 1829-93, and medical professionalization. *In* Branca, P. ed. The medicine show p259-80

Friedenberg, Edgar Zodiag
Gaiety and the laity: avoiding the excesses of professionalism. *In* Crew, L. ed. The gay academic p49-56
How schools subjugate youth. *In* Gross, B. and Gross, R. eds. The children's rights movement p166-74
Status and role in education. *In* Fairfield, R. P. ed. Humanistic frontiers in American education p37-47

Friedenreich, Kenneth
Introduction: the first Marvell tercentenary 1921. *In* Friedenreich, K. ed. Tercentenary essays in honor of Andrew Marvell p11-20
The mower mown: Marvell's Dances of death. *In* Friedenreich, K. ed. Tercentenary essays in honor of Andrew Marvell p153-79

Friedenthal, Jack H.
The rulemaking power of the Supreme Court: a contemporary crisis. *In* Stanford legal essays p149-62

Friedenthal, Richard

About individual works
Goethe, his life and times

Hamburger, M. Art as second nature: Goethe. *In* Hamburger, M. Art as second nature p24-33

Friedenwald, Jonas Stein

About

Harvey, A. M. More bright stars in the Johns Hopkins galaxy. *In* Harvey, A. M. Adventures in medical research p333-63

Friedgut, Theodore H.
The democratic movement: dimensions and perspectives. *In* Tokes, R. L. ed. Dissent in the USSR p116-36
The domestic image of Soviet involvement in the Arab-Israeli conflict. *In* Ro'i, Y. ed. The limits to power p149-77

Friedl, Erika
Women in contemporary Persian folktales. *In* Beck, L. and Keddie, N. R. eds. Women in the Muslim world p629-50

Friedlaender, Ann Fetter
Absolute poverty and macroeconomic activity. *In* Inflation, trade and taxes p194-217

Friedlander, Robert A.
Problems of the Mediterranean: a geopolitical perspective. *In* The Year book of world affairs, 1978 p175-80

Friedman, Alan Warren
The once and future age of modernism: an introduction. *In* Forms of modern British fiction p3-14

Friedman, Albert Barron
A carol in tradition. *In* Chaucer and Middle English studies in honour of Rossell Hope Robbins p298-302
"When Adam delved. . .": contexts of an historic proverb. *In* The Learned and the lewed p213-30

Friedman, Edward
The innovator. *In* Wilson, R. G. ed. Mao Tse-tung in the scales of history p300-20
The international political economy and Chinese politics. *In* China's changing role in the world economy p 1-14

Friedman, Irving Sigmund
Democracy and persistent inflation. *In* Prochnow, H. V. ed. Dilemmas facing the nation p55-81

Friedman, Lawrence Meir
San Benito 1890: legal snapshot of a county. *In* Stanford legal essays p163-77

Friedman, Maurice S.
Healing through meeting: a dialogical approach to psychotherapy and family therapy. *In* Psychiatry and the humanities v 1 p191-233

Friedman, Melvin J.
Introduction. *In* Friedman, M. J. and Lawson. L. A. eds. The added dimension p 1-31
"The perplex business": Flannery O'Connor and her critics enter the 1970s. *In* Friedman, M. J. and Lawson, L. A. eds. The added dimension p207-34

Friedman, Milton
Adam Smith's relevance for 1976. *In* Glahe, F. R. ed. Adam Smith and The wealth of nations p7-20
See also Part 2 under title: Capitalism and freedom

About

Gordon, R. A. A skeptical look at the "natural rate" hypothesis. *In* Theory for economic efficiency: essays in honor of Abba P. Lerner p46-61
Lilley, P. Two critics of Keynes: Friedman and Hayek. *In* Skidelsky, R. J. A. ed. The end of the Keynesian era p25-32

Friedman, Norman
What makes a short story short? *In* May, C. E. ed. Short story theories p131-46

Friedman, Renee C. and Friedman, Robert S.
Social and behavioral sciences in the 1970s. *In* Land-grant universities and their continuing challenge p160-77

Friedman, Robert Marc

The creation of a new science: Joseph Fourier's analytical theory of heat. *In* Historical studies in the physical sciences v8 p73-99

Friedman, Robert S. See Friedman, R. C. jt. auth.

Friedman, Ruth. See Alfin-Slater, R. B. jt. auth.

Friedman, Stanley

Dickens' mid-Victorian theodicy: David Copperfield. *In* Dickens Studies Annual v7 p128-50

Friedrich I, Barbarossa, Emperor of Germany

About

Chazan, R. Emperor Frederick I, the Third Crusade, and the Jews. *In* Viator: medieval and Renaissance studies v8 p83-93

Friedrich, Carl Joachim

Some reflexions on the politics of the public good. *In* The Abdication of philosophy: philosophy and the public good p67-72

Friedrichs, Christopher R.

Capitalism, mobility and class formation in the early modern German city. *In* Towns in societies p187-213

Frieling, Kenneth

The becoming of Gertrude Stein's The making of Americans. *In* French, W. G. ed. The twenties p157-70

Friend, Beverly

The Sturgeon connection. *In* Clareson, T. D. eds. Voices for the future: essays in major science fiction writers v 1 p153-66

Virgin territory: the bonds and boundaries of women in science fiction. *In* Clareson, T. D. ed. Many futures, many worlds p140-63

Friendly societies

Great Britain

Supple, B. E. Legislation and virtue: an essay on working class self-help and the state in the early nineteenth century. *In* Historical perspectives p211-54

Friends, Society of

Bolling, L. R. Quaker work in the Middle East following the June 1967 War. *In* Unofficial diplomats p80-88

Yarrow, C. H. Quaker efforts toward conciliation in the India-Pakistan War of 1965. *In* Unofficial diplomats p89-110

Friendship in literature

Griffith, A. J. Henny Penny, Eudora Welty, and the aggregation of friends. *In* Prenshaw, P. W. ed. Eudora Welty p83-92

LaFleur, R. A. Amicitia and the unity of Juvenal's first book. *In* Illinois classical studies v4, 1979 p158-77

Tracy, T. J. Perfect friendship in Aristotle's Nicomachean Ethics. *In* Illinois classical studies v4, 1979 p65-75

Fries, Maureen

"Slydynge of corage": Chaucer's Criseyde as feminist and victim. *In* Diamond, A. and Edwards, L. R. eds. The authority of experience p45-59

Friesen, Gerhard Kurt

Forgotten scion of a famous family: Carlos von Gagern, nineteenth-century cosmopolitan and Mexican patriot. *In* The German contribution to the building of the Americas p235-73

Friesen, Stanley Richard. See Kelly, W. D. jt. auth.

Friesland

Antiquities

TeBrake, W. H. Ecology and economy in early medieval Frisia. *In* Viator: medieval and Renaissance studies v9 p 1-29

Economic conditions

De Vries, J. Peasant demand patterns and economic development: Friesland, 1550-1750. *In* Parker, W. N. and Jones, E. L. eds. European peasants and their markets p205-66

Friezes

Turkey

See Pergamum. Altar of Zeus. Frieze

Friis, Herman Ralph

Original and published sources in research in historical geography: a comparison. *In* Pattern and process p139-59

Frijhoff, Willem, and Julia, Dominique

The diet in boarding schools at the end of the ancien régime. *In* Food and drink in history p73-85

Frings, Manfred S.

Nothingness and being: a Schelerian comment. *In* Radical phenomenology p182-89

Frinta, Mojmír Svatoplur

A statue of St. Christopher at the M. H. de Young Memorial Museum at San Francisco. *In* Enggass, R. C. and Stokstad, M. eds. Hortus imaginum p57-63

Frisch, Max

About

Kurz, P. K. Identity and society: the world of Max Frisch. *In* Kurz, P. K. On modern German literature v2 p104-54

Frisia. See Friesland

Froehlich, Karlfried

"Always to keep the literal sense in Holy Scripture means to kill one's soul": the state of Biblical hermeneutics at the beginning of the fifteenth century. *In* Miner, E. R. ed. Literary uses of typology p20-48

Froeschle, Hartmut. See Fröschle, Hartmut

Frohock, Wilbur Merrill

Frank Norris. *In* Walcutt, C. C. ed. Seven novelists in the American naturalist tradition p55-91

Theodore Dreiser. *In* Walcutt, C. C. ed. Seven novelists in the American naturalist tradition p92-130

Froissart, Jean

About

Kelly, D. Imagination in the writings of Jean Froissart. *In* Kelly, D. Medieval imagination p155-76

Frolic, Bennie Michael

The new Moscow city plan. *In* Hamm, M. F. ed. The city in Russian history p276-88

From here to eternity (Motion picture)

French, B. The hard and the soft. *In* French, B. On the verge of revolt p48-60

Fromm, Erich

About

O'Brien, K. Death and revolution: a reappraisal of identity theory. *In* O'Neill, J. ed. On critical theory p104-28

Frondizi, Risieri

The problem of freedom: from philosophical theory to human reality. *In* The Abdication of philosophy and the public good p229-35

The front (Motion picture)

Sarris, A. The front. *In* Sarris, A. Politics and cinema p49-51

Front de Libération du Quebec

Parry, A. Canada's white niggers. *In* Parry, A. Terrorism: from Robespierre to Arafat p364-75

Rocher, G. The quiet revolution and revolutionary movements among Quebec French Canadians. *In* Perspectives on revolution and evolution p238-67

Front for the Liberation of Quebec (RGPL)

See Front de Libération du Quebec

Frontier and pioneer life

LeMay, J. A. L. The frontiersman from lout to hero: notes on the significance of the comparative method and the stage theory in early American literature and culture. *In* American Antiquarian Society. Proceedings v88 pt2 p187-223

See also Pioneers

Historiography

Savage, W. W. and Thompson, S. I. The comparative study of the frontier: an introduction. *In* The Frontier v2 p3-24

Research

Hudson, J. C. Theory and methodology in comparative frontier studies. *In* Miller, D. H. and Steffen, J. O. eds. The frontier p11-31

Lefferts, H. L. Frontier demography: an introduction. *In* Miller, D. H. and Steffen, J. O. eds. The frontier p31-55

Australia

Jackson, W. T. Australians and the comparative frontier. *In* Essays on Walter Prescott Webb p17-51

Australia—Victoria

Wills, M. W. The California-Victoria irrigation frontiers, 1880-1900. *In* The Frontier v2 p235-49

Bolivia

Hess, D. W. Pioneering as ecological process: a model and test case of frontier adaptation. *In* The Frontier v2 p123-51

Brazil

Katzman, M T. Social relations of production on the Brazilian frontier. *In* Miller, D. H. and Steffen, J. O. eds. The frontier p275-96

California

Wills, M. W. The California-Victoria irrigation frontiers, 1880-1900. *In* The Frontier v2 p235-49

Florida

Lewis, C. B. Agricultural evolution on secondary frontiers: a Florida model. *In* The Frontier v2 p205-33

Latin America

Willems, E. Social change on the Latin American frontier. *In* Miller, D. H. and Steffen, J. O. eds. The frontier p259-73

Zavala, S. A. The frontiers of Hispanic America. *In* Weber, D. J. ed. New Spain's far northern frontier p179-99

Ontario

Osborne, B. S. Frontier settlement in eastern Ontario in the nineteenth century: a study in changing perceptions of land and opportunity. *In* Miller, D. H. and Steffen, J. O. eds. The frontier p201-25

Wall, G. Nineteenth-century land use and settlement on the Canadian Shield frontier. *In* Miller, D. H. and Steffen, J. O. eds. The frontier p227-41

San Antonio

Bailey, D. T. and Haulman, B. E. Ethnic differences on the Southwestern United States frontier, 1860. *In* Miller, D. H. and Steffen, J. O. eds. The frontier p243-57

Santa Fe

Bailey, D. T. and Haulman, B. E. Ethnic differences on the Southwestern United States frontier, 1860. *In* Miller, D. H. and Steffen, J. O. eds. The frontier p243-57

Southwest, New

Bouquet, S. Voices from the Southwest. *In* Voices from the Southwest p33-44

United States

Birch, B. P. British evaluations of the forest openings and prairie edges of the North-Central states, 1800-1850. *In* The Frontier v2 p167-92

Virginia

Lewis, K. E. An archaeological perspective on social change—the Virginia frontier. *In* Miller, D. H. and Steffen, J. O. eds. The frontier p139-59

LeMay, J. A. L. The frontiersman from lout to hero: notes on the significance of the comparative method and the stage theory in early American literature and culture. *In* American Antiquarian Society. Proceedings v88 pt2 p187-223

Frontier hypothesis. See Frontier thesis

Frontier thesis

Hudson, J. C. Theory and methodology in comparative frontier studies. *In* Miller, D. H. and Steffen, J. O. eds. The frontier p11-31

Hutchinson, C. A. The California frontier. *In* Weber, D. J. ed. New Spain's far northern frontier p171-99

Jackson, W. T. Australians and the comparative frontier. *In* Essays on Walter Prescott Webb p17-51

Potter, J. Some British reflections on Turner and the frontier. *In* Burton, D. H. ed. American history—British historians p127-48

Savage, W. W. and Thompson, S. I. The comparative study of the frontier: an introduction. *In* The Frontier v2 p3-24

Case studies

Aldrich, D. M. Frontier militias: militia laws on the North American and South African frontiers. *In* The Frontier v2 p153-66

Sullivan, R. E. The medieval monk as frontiersman. *In* The Frontier v2 p25-49

Frontiers. See Boundaries

The frontiersman from lout to hero: notes on the significance of the comparative method and the stage theory in early American literature and culture. LeMay, J. A. L. *In* American Antiquarian Society. Proceedings v88 pt2 p187-223

Frost, Robert—*Continued*

Philosophy

Cook, M. Acceptance in Frost's poetry: conflict as play. *In* Frost: centennial essays II p223-35

Montgomery, M. Robert Frost: one who shrewdly pretends. *In* Frost: centennial essays II p213-22

See also Frost, Robert—Political and social views; Frost, Robert—Religion and ethics

Political and social views

Stanlis, P. J. Robert Frost: politics in theory and practice. *In* Frost: centennial essays II p48-82

Religion and ethics

Ballantine, L. F. In Aladdin's lamp light. *In* Frost: centennial essays III p313-15

Hall, D. J. An Old Testament Christian. *In* Frost: centennial essays III p316-49

Kau, J. L. C. "Trust . . . to go by contraries": incarnation and the paradox of belief in the poetry of Frost. *In* Frost: centennial essays II p99-111

McClanahan, T. Frost's theodicy: "word I had no one left but God." *In* Frost: centennial essays II p112-26

Perrine, L. Robert Frost and the idea of immortality. *In* Frost: centennial essays II p85-98

Social views

See Frost, Robert—Political and social views

Style

See Frost, Robert—Language

Technique

See Frost, Robert—Versification

Tomb

Tyler, D. The strong are saying nothing *In* Frost: centennial essays II p305-16

Versification

Beacham, W. Technique and the sense of play in the poetry of Robert Frost. *In* Frost: centennial essays II p246-61

Rood, K. L. Robert Frost's "sentence sounds": wildness opposing the sonnet form. *In* Frost: centennial essays II p196-210

Froude, James Anthony

About

Cockshut, A. O. J. The pessimists: J. A. Froude. *In* Cockshut, A. O. J. Man and woman: a study of love and the novel, 1740-1940 p100-07

Fielding, K. J. Froude and Carlyle: some new considerations. *In* Fielding, K. J. and Tarr, R. L. eds. Carlyle past and present p239-69

About individual works

Thomas Carlyle

Clubbe, J. Grecian destiny: Froude's portraits of the Carlyles. *In* Carlyle and his contemporaries p317-53

Froude, James Anthony, ed.

About individual works

Reminiscences, by Thomas Carlyle

Fielding, K. J. Froude's revenge, or The Carlyles and Erasmus A. Darwin. *In* English Association. Essays and studies, 1978 p75-97

Frowein, Jochen Abraham

The interrelationship between the Helsinki Final Act, the International Covenants on Human Rights, and the European Convention on Human Rights. *In* Human rights, international law and the Helsinki Accord p71-82

Frumkin, Robert Martin

Contemporary sociology in the United States. *In* Mohan, R. P. and Martindale, D. A. eds. Handbook of contemporary developments in world sociology p131-57

Fry, Christopher

Theatre and history. *In* English Association. Essays and studies, 1977 p86-87

Fry, Donald K.

Caedmon as a formulaic poet. *In* Duggan, J. J. ed. Oral literature p41-61

Fry, Edward

Introduction, the history of cubism, cubism as a stylistic and historical phenomenon; excerpt from "Cubism." *In* Kaplan, P. and Manso, S. eds. Major European art movements, 1900-1945 p101-46

Fry, Edwin Maxwell

Le Corbusier at Chandigarh. *In* Walden, R. ed. The open hand p350-63

Fry, Jane Beverly (Drew)

Le Corbusier as I knew him. *In* Walden, R. ed. The open hand p364-73

Fry, Maxwell. See Fry, Edwin Maxwell

Fry, Norman. See New, M. jt. auth.

Fry, Paul H.

Oedipus the King. *In* Seidel, M. A. and Mendelson, E. eds. Homer to Brecht p171-90

Phaedra. *In* Seidel, M. A. and Mendelson, E. eds. Homer to Brecht p273-91

Fry, Roger Eliot

About

Richards, I. A. Art and science. *In* Richards, I. A. Complementarities p3-6

Frye, Herman Northrop. See Frye, Northrop

Frye, Marilyn

Male chauvinism: a conceptual analysis. *In* Baker, R. and Elliston, F. A. eds. Philosophy & sex p65-79

See also Shafer, C. M. jt. auth.

Frye, Northrop

Dickens and the comedy of humors. *In* Wimsatt, W. K. ed. Literary criticism: idea and act p537-59

Haunted by lack of ghosts; some patterns in the imagery of Canadian poetry. *In* Staines, D. ed. The Canadian imagination p22-45

History and myth in the Bible. *In* Fletcher, A. J. S. ed. The literature of fact p 1-19

Northrop Frye on culture and literature

Contents

The acceptance of innocence
Art in a new modulation
Forming fours
Graves, gods, and scholars
Interior monologue of M. Teste
Long, sequacious notes
Ministry of angels
Myth as information
Nature methodized
Neoclassical agony
The nightmare life in death

Frye, Northrop
Northrop on culture and literature
Contents—Continued
Novels on several occasions
Orwell and Marxism
Phalanx of particulars
The rhythm of growth and decay
The shapes of history
Symbolism of the unconscious
Total identification
World enough without time
The young Boswell
Romance as masque. *In* Shakespeare's romances reconsidered p11-39
Spiritus mundi
Contents
Agon and logos
Blake's reading of the Book of Job
Charms and riddles
Expanding eyes
The renaissance of books
The rising of the moon
Romance as masque
The search for acceptable words
Spengler revisited
The times of the signs
The university and personal life
Wallace Stevens and the variation form

About

Denham, R. D. Introduction. *In* Frye, N. Northrop Frye on culture and literature p 1-64
Hartman, G. H. Ghostlier demarcations. *In* Wimsatt, W. K. ed. Literary criticism: idea and act p212-27
Watkins, E. Criticism and method: Hirsch, Frye, Barthes, Derrida. *In* Watkins, E. The critical act p56-94
Wimsatt, W. K. Northrop Frye: criticism as myth. *In* Wimsatt, W. K. Day of the leopards p74-96

About individual works
Anatomy of criticism
Crews, F. C. Anaesthetic criticism. *In* Crews, F. C. Out of my system p63-87
Frye, N. Expanding eyes. *In* Frye, N. Spiritus mundi p99-122

Frye, Roland Mushat

About individual works
Milton's imagery and The visual arts: iconographic tradition in the epic poems
Wittreich, J. A. The new Milton criticism. *In* Review, v 1 1979 p123-64

Fryer, Judith
The faces of Eve
Contents
The American princess: Daisy Miller
The American princess: Isabel Archer
The American princess: Maggie Verver
The American princess: Milly Theale
The American princess: The Pale Maiden
The Great Mother: The archetype: Olive Chancellor
The Great Mother: The mother-surrogates
The Great Mother: The neglecters
The Great Mother: The real witch-bitches
The myth of America as New World Garden of Eden: The American Adam
The myth of America as New World Garden of Eden: The American Eve
The myth of America as New World Garden of Eden: The Garden

The new woman: Edna Pontellier: The new woman as woman
The new woman: The new myth of Atalanta
The new woman: The unnatural lady reformers of Boston
The new woman: Through the eye of the needle
The new woman: Zenobia: The new woman as tragedy-queen
The temptress: Beatrice Rappaccini: The literary convention as allegory
The temptress: Celia Madden: The temptress as "Greek"
The temptress: Elsie Venner: The literary convention with psychological trappings
The temptress: Hawthorne's Miriam: The temptress as Jew
The temptress: Hester Prynne: The Dark Lady as "deviant"
The temptress: In which the ambiguities of the Dark Lady are compounded by the appearance of the Pale Maiden: Melville's Isabel

Fuchs, Daniel
Ernest Hemingway, literary critic. *In* Wagner, L. W. ed. Ernest Hemingway p39-56

Fuegi, John
The alienated woman: Brecht's The good person of Setzuan. *In* Mews, S. and Knust, H. eds. Essays on Brecht p190-96

Fuel. See Coal; Petroleum as fuel

Fuel oil. See Petroleum as fuel

Fugard, Athol

About

Green, R. J. Politics and literature in Africa: the drama of Athol Fugard. *In* Heywood, C. ed. Aspects of South African literature p163-73

About individual works
Boesman and Lena
Kauffmann, S. Boesman and Lena. *In* Kauffmann, S. Persons of the drama p204-08

Fugard, Athol; Kani, John, and Ntshona, Winston

About individual works
The island
Kauffmann, S. Sizwe Banzi is dead/The island. *In* Kauffmann, S. Persons of the drama p208-11

Sizwe Banzi is dead
Kauffmann, S. Sizwe Banzi is dead/The island. *In* Kauffmann, S. Persons of the drama p208-11

The Fugitive (Periodical)
Rubin, L. D. Fugitives as agrarians: the impulse behind I'll take my stand. *In* Rubin, L. D. William Elliott shoots a bear p145-63
Tate, A. The Fugitive, 1922-1925: a personal recollection twenty years after. *In* Tate, A. Memoirs and opinions, 1926-1974 p24-38

Fuhrmann, Manfred
Myth as a recurrent theme in Greek tragedy and twentieth-century drama. *In* Amacher, R. E. and Lange, V. eds. New perspectives in German literary criticism p295-319

Fuks, Lajk, and Fuks, Rena
Jewish historiography in the Netherlands in the 17th and 18th centuries. *In* Salo Wittmayer Baron v 1 p433-66

Fuks, Leo. See Fuks, Lajk

Fuks, Rena. See Fuks, L. jt. auth.

Fukui, Haruhiro
The Japanese Communist Party: the Miyamoto line and its problems. *In* Kaplan, M. A. ed. The many faces of communism p279-332

Fulc Nerra. See Fulk Nerra, Count of Anjou

Fulk Nerra, Count of Anjou
Bachrach, B. S. A study in feudal politics: relations between Fulk Nerra and William the Great, 995-1030. *In* Viator: medieval and Renaissance studies v7 p111-22

Fulk of Toulouse. See Folquet de Marseille, Bp. of Toulouse

Fulk III (Nerra of Anjou). See Fulk Nerra, Count of Anjou

Full employment policies. See Deficit financing

Fuller, Buckminster. See Fuller, Richard Buckminster

Fuller, Henry Blake

About individual works
With the procession
Goist, P. D. The city as noncommunity: Theodore Dreiser and Henry Blake Fuller. *In* Goist, P. D. From Main Street to State Street p68-79

Fuller, John L.
Genes, brains, and behavior. *In* Sociobiology and human nature p98-115

Fuller, Margaret. See Ossoli, Sarah Margaret (Fuller)

Fuller, Richard Buckminster
Innovative building technologies: the dome. *In* Strategies for human settlements: habitat and environment p148-51
Learning tomorrows: education for a changing world. *In* Wagschal, P. H. ed. Learning tomorrows p 1-26
Preparing for a small town world. *In* Strategies for human settlements: habitat and environment p5-14

About
Sale, R. H. Mumford & Fuller. *In* Sale, R. H. On not being good enough p202-18

Fuller, Roy Broadbent

About
Scannell, V. Roy Fuller. *In* Scannell, V. Not without glory p95-112
Thurley, G. The legacy of Auden: the poetry of Roy Fuller, Philip Larkin and Peter Porter. *In* Thurley, G. The ironic harvest p137-62

Fuller, Samuel

About individual works
Shock corridor
Elsaesser, T. Shock corridor by Sam Fuller. *In* Nichols, B. ed. Movies and methods p290-97
Verboten
Truffaut, F. Samuel Fuller: Verboten. *In* Truffaut, F. The films in my life p107-09

Fullinwider, Robert K.
On preferential hiring. *In* Feminism and philosophy p210-24

Fulton, Len
Dust: a tribal seed. *In* Anderson, E. and Kinzie, M. eds. The little magazine in America: a modern documentary history p423-37

Function in architecture. See Functionalism (Architecture)

Functional analysis. See Functor theory

Functional representation. See Functor theory

Functional sentence perspective (Grammar) See Grammar, Comparative and general

Functionalism (Architecture)
Broadbent, G. The rational and the functional. *In* Sharp, D. ed. The rationalists p142-58
Jencks, C. Le Corbusier on the tightrope of functionalism. *In* Walden, R. ed. The open hand p186-214

Functionalism in architecture. See Functionalism (Architecture)

Functor theory
Quine, W. V. Algebraic logic and predicate functors. *In* Quine, W. V. The ways of paradox, and other essays p283-307
Quine, W. V. Truth and disquotation. *In* Quine, W. V. The ways of paradox, and other essays p308-21

Fund raising. See Church fund raising

Fundamentalism
Marty, M. E. Tensions within contemporary evangelicalism: a critical appraisal. *In* Wells, D. F. and Woodbridge, J. D. eds. The evangelicals p170-88
Pattison, E. M. Ideological support for the marginal middle class: faith healing and glossolalia. *In* Zaretsky, I. I. and Leone, M. P. eds. Religious movements in contemporary America p418-55
See also Evangelicalism; Modernist-fundamentalist controversy

History
Marsden, G. M. From fundamentalism to evangelicalism: a historical analysis. *In* Wells, D. F. and Woodbridge, J. D. eds. The evangelicals p122-42
Sandeen, E. R. The origins of Fundamentalism. *In* Mulder, J. M. and Wilson, J. F. eds. Religion in American history p415-30

Funeral rites and ceremonies
Ariès, P. Death inside out. *In* Death inside out p9-24
May, W. F. Attitudes toward the newly dead. *In* Death inside out p139-49
See also Mourning customs

United States
Raether, H. C. and Slater, R. C. Immediate postdeath activities in the United States. *In* Feifel, H. [ed.] New meanings of death p233-48

Funkenstein, Amos
The dialectical preparation for scientific revolutions. *In* The Copernican achievement p165-203
Natural science and social theory: Hobbes, Spinoza, and Vico. *In* Giambattista Vico's science of humanity p187-212
Periodization and self-understanding in the Middle Ages and early modern times. *In* Medievalia et humanistica no. 5 p3-23

Funkenstein, Amos—*Continued*

About individual works

The dialectical preparation for scientific revolutions

Finocchiaro, M. A. Commentary: dialectical aspects of the Copernican revolution: conceptual elucidations and historiographical problems. *In* The Copernican achievement p204-12

Funnies. See Comic books, strips, etc.

Fur trade

Canada

Ray, A. J. The Hudson's Bay Company fur trade in the eighteenth century: a comparative economic study. *In* European settlement and development in North America: essays on geographical change in honour and memory of Andrew Hill Clark p116-35

The West—History

Wishart, D. J. The fur trade of the West, 1807-1840: a geographic synthesis. *In* Miller, D. H. and Steffen, J. O. eds. The frontier p161-200

Furber, Holden

About

Kling, B. B. Holden Furber at work. *In* Kling, B. B. and Pearson, M. N. eds. The age of partnership p237-47

Furet, François

Civilization and barbarism in Gibbon's history. *In* Edward Gibbon and The decline and fall of the Roman Empire p159-66

Furibundi

Dronke, P. Two thirteenth-century religious lyrics. *In* Chaucer and Middle English studies in honour of Rossell Hope Robbins p392-406

Furioso

Whittemore, R. On editing Furioso. *In* Anderson, E. and Kinzie, M. eds. The little magazine in America: a modern documentary history p100-10

Furley, David J.

Aristotle and the Atomists on motion in a void. *In* Motion and time, space and matter p83-100

Furlow, Thomas W.

Euthanasia and the tyranny of technology. *In* Kohl, M. ed. Beneficent euthanasia p169-79

Furman v Georgia. *In* Riedel, M. and Chappell, D. eds. Issues in criminal justice: planning and evaluation p75-86

Furmanov, Dmitrii Andreevich

About individual works

Chapayev

Mathewson, R. W. Leather men. *In* Mathewson, R. W. The positive hero in Russian literature p179-210

Furneaux Jordan, Robert. See Jordan, Robert Furneaux

Furniture, Shaker

Coomaraswamy, A. K. Shaker furniture; excerpt from "Figures of speech or figures of thought: collected essays on the traditional or 'normal' view of art." *In* Coomaraswamy, A. K. Selected papers v 1 p255-59

Furnivall, John Sydenham

About

Fortes, M. The plural society in Africa. *In* Leftwich, A. ed. South Africa: economic growth and political change p 1-27

Furphy, Joseph

About individual works

Such is life

Barnes, J. Such is life and the observant reader. *In* Bards, bohemians, and bookmen p153-69

Furst, Peter T.

"High states" in culture-historical perspective. *In* Alternate states of consciousness p53-88

Morning glory and mother goddess at Tepantitla, Teotihuacan: iconography and analogy in pre-Columbian art. *In* Mesoamerican archaeology p187-215

Furtak, Robert K.

Yugoslavia: a special case. *In* Hayward, J. E. S. and Berki, R. N. eds. State and society in contemporary Europe p158-78

Furth, Charlotte

Culture and politics in modern Chinese conservation. *In* The Limits of change p22-53

The sage as rebel: the inner world of Chang Ping-lin. *In* The Limits of change p113-50

Furuhashi, Yusaku

Evolving Japanese policy toward inward foreign direct investment in the postwar period. *In* Postwar trends in Japan p61-118

Fusion reactors

Kaplan, I. Mater omnium: automated energy and material wealth from the sea. *In* Borgese, E. M. and Krieger, D. eds. The tides of change p48-75

Fuss, Peter L.

Hannah Arendt's conception of political community. *In* Hannah Arendt: the recovery of the public world p157-76

Theory and practice in Hegel and Marx: an unfinished dialogue. *In* Political theory and praxis p97-116

Fussell, Paul

The historical dimension; excerpt from "Poetic meter and poetic form." *In* Gross, H. S. ed. The structure of verse p40-52

Fustel de Coulanges, Numa Denis

About individual works

The ancient city

Momigliano, A. The ancient city of Fustel de Coulanges. *In* Momigliano, A. Essays in ancient and modern historiography p325-43

Futabatei, Shimei, pseud.

About

Yamanouchi, H. Two precursors: Tsubouchi Shōyō and Futabatei Shimei. *In* Yamanouchi, H. The search for authenticity in modern Japanese literature p6-19

Future. See Chance

Future generations, Obligations to. Golding, M. P. *In* The Abdication of philosophy: philosophy and the public good p195-207

Future in literature. See Science fiction

Future life

Boshier, A. The religions of Africa. *In* Life after death p54-66

G

GATT. See Contracting Parties to the General Agreement on Tariffs and Trade

Gabba, Emilio
The Perusine War and triumviral Italy. *In* Harvard Studies in classical philology v75 p139-60

Gabirol, Solomon. See Ibn Gabirol, Solomon ben Judah

Gabler, Hans Walter
The seven lost years of A portrait of the artist as a young man. *In* Staley, T. F. and Benstock, B. eds. Approaches to Joyce's Portrait p25-56

Gabo, Naum
About
Krauss, R. E. Analytic space: futurism and constructivism. *In* Krauss, R. E. Passages in modern sculpture p39-67

Gabriel (Archangel)
Goldin, J. A short note on the archangel Gabriel. *In* Law, church, and society p 1-4

Gabriel (Archangel) in art
Bank, A. V. A copper-gilt plaque of the archangel Gabriel. *In* Studies in memory of David Talbot Rice p6-9

Gadamer, Hans-Georg
The historicity of understanding as hermeneutic principle; excerpt from "Truth and method." *In* Murray, M. E. ed. Heidegger and modern philosophy p161-83
About individual works
Hegel's dialectic: five hermeneutical studies
Craft, R. A new interpretation of Hegel? *In* Craft, R. Current convictions p244-55

Truth and method
Misgeld, D. Critical theory and hermeneutics: the debate between Habermas and Gadamer. *In* O'Neill, J. ed. On critical theory p164-83
Ricoeur, P. The task of hermeneutics. *In* Murray, M. E. ed. Heidegger and modern philosophy p141-60

Gadda, Carlo Emilio
About
Adams, R. M. Carlo Emilio Gadda. *In* Adams, R. M. Afterjoyce p114-33
Biasin, G. P. The pen, the mother. *In* Biasin, G. P. Literary diseases p127-55
Pacifici, S. Carlo Emilio Gadda: the experimental novel. *In* Pacifici, S. The modern Italian novel: from Pea to Moravia p99-117
Ragusa, O. Gadda, Pasolini, and experimentalism: form or ideology? *In* Ragusa, O. Narrative and drama p134-54

Gaddis, John Lewis
Korea in American politics, strategy, and diplomacy, 1945-50. *In* The Origins of the Cold war in Asia p277-98
Mr. "X" is consistent and right. *In* Decline of the West? George Kennan and his critics p135-56
About individual works
Mr. "X" is consistent and right
Mark, E. Mr. "X" is inconsistent and wrong. *In* Decline of the West? George Kennan and his critics p157-72

Gadol, Joan Kelly- See Kelly-Gadol, Joan

Gaelic League
Waters, M. J. Peasants and emigrants: considerations of the Gaelic League as a social movement. *In* Casey, D. J. and Rhodes, R. E. eds. Views of the Irish peasantry p160-77

Gaeng, Paul A.
Interpreting second declension singular forms in -u. *In* Illinois classical studies v4, 1979 p214-19

Gage, Thomas
About
Shy, J. W. The Empire militant: Thomas Gage and the coming of war. *In* Shy, J. W. A people numerous and armed p73-107

Gagern, Carlos de
About
Friesen, G. K. Forgotten scion of a famous family: Carlos von Gagern, nineteenth-century cosmopolitan and Mexican patriot. *In* The German contribution to the building of the Americas p235-73

Gagnon, John H.
The interaction of gender roles and sexual conduct. *In* Katchadourian, H. A. ed. Human sexuality p225-45

Gaines, Ernest J.
About individual works
A long day in November
Puschmann-Nalenz, B. Ernest J. Gaines, A long day in November. *In* Bruck, P. ed. The Black American short story in the 20th century p157-69

Gair, Reavley. See Gair, W. Reavley

Gair, W. Reavley
The presentation of plays at Second Paul's: the early phase (1559-1602) *In* The Elizabethan theatre, VI p21-47

Gaisser, Julia Haig
A structural analysis of the digressions in The Iliad and The Odyssey. *In* Harvard Studies in classical philology v73 p 1-43

Gaither, Edmund B.
Afro-American art. *In* The Black American reference book p827-45

Gaitz, Charles Milton
Aged patients, their families and physicians. *In* Aging: the process and the people p206-39

Gakwandi, Shatto Arthur
The novel and contemporary experience in Africa
Contents
Colonial injustice: La Guma's A walk in the night
Colonial injustice: Oyono's Houseboy
Commitment: Ngugi's A grain of wheat
Commitment: Ousmane's God's bits of wood
Conclusion: Realism and the African novel
Disenchantment: Soyinka's The interpreters and Achebe's A man of the people
Freedom as nightmare: Armah's The beautyful ones are not yet born
Freedom as nightmare: Duodu's The gab boys
The illusion of progress: Achebe's No longer at ease
The illusion of progress: Beti's Mission to Kala
Nationalism: Abrahams' A wreath for Udomo
Nationalism: Aluko's One man one matchet

Galambos, Louis

The American economy and the reorganization of the sources of knowledge. *In* Oleson, A. and Voss, J. eds. The organization of knowledge in modern America, 1860-1920 p269-82

Galati, Stephen A. Fischer-. See Fischer-Galati, Stephen A.

Galaxies

Goldsmith, D. W. Edwin Hubble and the universe outside our galaxy. *In* Neyman, J. ed. The heritage of Copernicus: theories "pleasing to the mind" p63-94

Zonn, W. Explosive events in the universe. *In* Neyman, J. ed. The heritage of Copernicus: theories "pleasing to the mind" p95-115

See also Milky Way

Galbraith, John Kenneth

Annals of an abiding liberal

Contents

Anthony Trollope

Berlin

Bernard Cornfeld: benefactor

The conservative majority syndrome

Defenders of the faith, I: William Simon

Defenders of the faith, II: Irving Kristol

Defenders of the faith, III: Wright and Slick

Economists and the economics of professional contentment

Evelyn Waugh

The founding faith: Adam Smith's Wealth of nations

Germany: July 20, 1944

The global strategic mind

The higher economic purpose of women

The Indian-Pacific train

John Bartlow Martin and Adlai Stevenson

John Dean, ambition and the White House

Last word on the Hiss case ?

The multinational corporation: how to put your worst foot forward or in your mouth

My forty years with the FBI

The North Dakota plan

A note on the psychopathology of the very affluent

RN: the memoirs of Richard Nixon

Robert Vesco: swindler

Seven wonders

Should stealing from the rich be punished?

The valid image of the modern economy

What comes after General Motors

Who was Thorstein Veblen?

Writing and typing

How Keynes came to America. *In* Keynes, M. ed. Essays on John Maynard Keynes p132-41

The structure of the firm and the structure of the industry: a study in industrial development. *In* Evolution of international management structures p3-12

About

Galbraith, J. K. My forty years with the FBI. *In* Galbraith, J. K. Annals of an abiding liberal p155-81

Galdós, Benito Pérez. See Pérez Galdós, Benito

Gale, Robert L.

Henry James. *In* American literary scholarship, 1977 p99-118

Gale, Zona

About

Goist, P. D. The town as ideal community: Booth Tarkington and Zona Gale. *In* Goist, P. D. From Main Street to State Street p13-20

Galen, Claudius. See Galenus

Galenus

About

Temkin, O. The classical roots of Glisson's doctrine of irritation. *In* Temkin, O. The double face of Janus p290-316

Temkin, O. A Galenic model for quantitative physiological reasoning? *In* Temkin, O. The double face of Janus p162-66

Temkin, O. On Galen's pneumatology. *In* Temkin, O. The double face of Janus p154-61

Tracy, T. J. Plato, Galen, and the center of consciousness. *In* Illinois classical studies, v 1 1976 p43-52

About individual works

Ars medica

Edwards, W. F. Niccolò Leoniceno and the origins of humanist discussion of method. *In* Philosophy and humanism p283-305

De sectis ad introducendos

Temkin, O. Studies on late Alexandrian medicine. *In* Temkin, O. The double face of Janus p178-97

Galilei, Galileo

About

Costabel, P. Mathematics and Galileo's inclined plane experiments. *In* Bonelli, M. L. R. and Shea, W. R. eds. Reason, experiment, and mysticism in the scientific revolution p177-87

Crombie, A. C. Sources of Galileo's early natural philosophy. *In* Bonelli, M. L. R. and Shea, W. R. eds. Reason, experiment, and mysticism in the scientific revolution p157-75

Drake, S. Galileo's new science of motion. *In* Bonelli, M. L. R. and Shea, W. R. eds. Reason, experiment, and mysticism in the scientific revolution p131-56

Finocchiaro, M. A. Commentary: dialectical aspects of the Copernican revolution: conceptual elucidations and historiographical problems. *In* The Copernican achievement p204-12

Funkenstein, A. The dialectical preparation for scientific revolutions. *In* The Copernican achievement p165-203

Moody, E. A. Galileo and Avempace: the dynamics of the Leaning Tower Experiment. *In* Moody, E. A. Studies in medieval philosophy, science, and logic p203-86

Moody, E. A. Galileo and his precursors. *In* Moody, E. A. Studies in medieval philosophy, science, and logic p393-408

About individual works

The sidereal messenger

Gingerich, O. Dissertatio cum Professore Righini et Sidereo nuncio. *In* Bonelli, M. L. R. and Shea, W. R. eds. Reason, experiment, and mysticism in the scientific revolution p77-88

Righini, G. New light on Galileo's lunar observations. *In* Bonelli, M. L. R. and Shea, W. R. eds. Reason, experiment, and mysticism in the scientific revolution p59-68

Galileo. See Galilei, Galileo

Galindo Pohl, Reynaldo

Pacem in Maribus in the Caribbean. *In* Borgese, E. M. and Krieger, D. eds. The tides of change p264-77

Galinsky, Gotthard Karl

Ovid's metamorphosis of myth. *In* Perspectives of Roman poetry p105-27

Galinsky, Hans

Foreign scholarship: German contributions. *In* American literary scholarship, 1975 p476-87

Foreign scholarship: German contributions [another essay]. *In* American literary scholarship, 1976 p435-46

Foreign scholarship: German contributions [another essay] *In* American literary scholarship, 1977 p474-92

Galison, Peter Louis

Minkowski's space-time: from visual thinking to the absolute world. *In* Historical studies in the physical sciences v10 p85-121

Gall, Franz Joseph

About

Fancher, R. E. The physiology of mind: conceptions of the brain from Gall to Penfield. *In* Fancher, R. E. Pioneers of psychology p43-86

Gall-bladder

Temkin, O. The classical roots of Glisson's doctrine of irritation. *In* Temkin, O. The double face of Janus p290-316

Gallafent, Edward, and Jarrett, David

American literature: the twentieth century. *In* English Association. The year's work in English studies v56 p413-56

Gallatin, Judith E.

The conceptualization of rights: psychological development and cross-national perspectives. *In* Claude, R. P. ed. Comparative human rights p302-25

Gallegos y Chávez, Ester

The northern New Mexican woman: a changing silhouette. *In* Trejo, A. D. ed. The Chicanos p67-79

Gallie, W. B.

Philosophers of peace and war

Contents

Clausewitz on the nature of war
Concluding remarks
Kant on perpetual peace
Marx and Engels on revolution and war
Tolstoy: from 'War and peace' to 'The kingdom of God is within you'

Galliner, Peter

Improving news flow in the Third World. *In* Horton, P. C. ed. The Third World and press freedom p93-103

Gallivan, Patricia

Science and art in Jude the obscure. *In* Smith, A. ed. The novels of Thomas Hardy p126-44

Gallo, Ernest

The grammarian's rhetoric: the Poetria nova of Geoffrey of Vinsauf. *In* Murphy, J. J. ed. Medieval eloquence p68-84

Gallo-roman terra-cottas. See Terra-cottas, Gallo-roman

Galloway, David

William Melvin Kelley, The poker party. *In* Bruck, P. ed. The Black American short story in the 20th century p129-40

Galloway, K. Bruce, and Johnson, Robert Bowie

About individual works

West Point

Vidal, G. West Point. *In* Vidal, G. Matters of fact and of fiction p191-205

Gallus, Caius Cornelius

About

Ross, D. O. Gallus the elegist. *In* Ross, D. O. Backgrounds to Augustan poetry: Gallus, elegy and Rome p39-50

Influence—Vergilius Maro

Ross, D. O. Gallus and the Tenth Eclogue. *In* Ross, D. O. Backgrounds to Augustan poetry. Gallus, elegy and Rome p85-106

Ross, D. O. The Sixth Eclogue: Virgil's poetic genealogy. *In* Ross, D. O. Backgrounds to Augustan poetry: Gallus, elegy and Rome p18-38

Gallus, Gaius Cornelis. See Gallus, Caius Cornelius

Galnoor, Itzhak

The information marketplace. *In* Galnoor, I. ed. Government secrecy in democracies p77-92

Israel. *In* Galnoor, I. ed. Government secrecy in democracies p176-200

What do we know about government secrecy? *In* Galnoor, I. ed. Government secrecy in democracies p275-313

Galsworthy, John

About

Gindin, J. Ethical structures in John Galsworthy, Elizabeth Bowen, and Iris Murdoch. *In* Forms of modern British fiction p15-41

Galt, John

About

Hart, F. R. John Galt. *In* Hart, F. R. The Scottish novel p31-52

About individual works

Annals of the parish

Doubleday, N. F. Mr Balwhidder's half-century. *In* Doubleday, N. F. Variety of attempt p78-94

Galton, Sir Francis

About

Cowan, R. S. Nature and nurture: the interplay of biology and politics in the work of Francis Galton. *In* Studies in history of biology v 1 p133-208

Fancher, R. E. The measurement of mind: Francis Galton and the psychology of individual differences. *In* Fancher, R. E. Pioneers of psychology p250-94

Galtung, Johan

Nonterritorial actors and the problem of peace. *In* On the creation of a just world order p151-88

Galuth. See Jews—Diaspora

Galvanism. See Electricity

Gálvez, José de, Marqués de Sonora

About

García Navarro, L. The North of New Spain as a political problem in the eighteenth century. *In* Weber, D. J. ed. New Spain's far northern frontier p201-15

Gambaro, Griselda

About

Cypess, S. M. The plays of Griselda Gambaro. *In* Lyday, L. F. and Woodyard, G. W. eds. Dramatists in revolt p95-109

Gambill, Edward Lee

Who were the Senate radicals? *In* Swierenga, R. P. ed. Beyond the Civil War synthesis p225-32

Gambling

See also Slot machines

United States

Shagan, M. D. Is gambling worth enforcement gamble? *In* Contemporary issues in criminal justice p16-39

Game theory

Bloomfield, L. P. BELLEX—the Bellagio "mini-game." *In* Unofficial diplomats p222-40

Games. See Pinball machines; Play

Games in literature

Duckworth, A. M. 'Spillikins, paper ships, riddles, conundrums, and cards': games in Jane Austen's life and fiction. *In* Halperin, J. ed. Jane Austen p279-97

Games of chance. See Gambling

Gaming. See Gambling

Gamow, George

Reminiscence; excerpt from "My world line." *In* Einstein p29-30

Gamwell, Franklin I.

Reinhold Niebuhr's theistic ethic. *In* Scott, N. A. ed. The legacy of Reinhold Niebuhr p63-84

Gance, Abel

About individual works

Napoléon

Truffaut, F. Abel Gance: Napoléon. *In* Truffaut, F. The films in my life p29-32

La tour de Nesle

Truffaut, F. La tour de Nesle. *In* Truffaut, F. The films in my life p33-35

Ganda. See Baganda

Gandelsonas, Mario. See Agrest, D. jt auth.

Gandhi, Indira (Nehru)

About

Tinker, H. Indira Gandhi. *In* The Year book of world affairs, 1979 p102-25

Gandhi, Mahatma. See Gandhi, Mohandas Karamchand

Gandhi, Mohandas Karamchand

About

Appadurai, A. Understanding Gandhi. *In* Homans, P. ed. Childhood and selfhood p113-43

Brown, J. M. 'Ghandhi's men', 1917-22: the role of the major leader in the careers of middle-rank politicians. *In* The Making of politicians: studies from Africa and Asia p126-39

Chiaromonte, N. The death of Gandhi. *In* Chiaromonte, N. The worm of consciousness, and other essays p66-70

Erikson, E. H. On the nature of psychohistorical evidence: in search of Gandhi; excerpt from "Life history and the historical moment". *In* Explorations in psychohistory p42-77

Koestler, A. A re-evaluation. *In* Koestler, A. The heel of Achilles p235-73

Mahadevan, T. K. Gandhi—a modernist heresy. *In* Bishop, D. H. ed. Indian thought p357-63

About individual works

Autobiography or the story of my experiments with truth, translated by Mahadev Desai

Ravenscroft, A. African, Boer, and Indian attitudes to an imperialist war. *In* Narasimhaiah, C D. ed. Awakened conscience p315-26

Gangs

New York (City)

Hentoff, N. Turning kids into waste. *In* Gross, B. and Gross, R. eds. The children's rights movement p78-81

United States

Chambliss, W. J. The Saints and the Roughnecks. *In* Henslin, J. M. ed. Deviant life-styles p289-304

Krisberg, B. A. The gang and the community: the case of the urban leadership training program. *In* Riedel, M. and Chappeli, D. eds. Issues in criminal justice; planning and evaluation p99-113

Miller, W. B. White gangs. *In* Henslin, J. M. ed. Deviant life-styles p261-88

Miller, W. B. Youth gangs in the urban crisis era. *In* Delinquency, crime, and society p91-128

Short, J. F. Gangs, politics, and the social order. *In* Delinquency, crime, and society p129-63

Gangster films

Hess, J. D. Godfather II: a deal Coppola couldn't refuse. *In* Nichols, B. ed. Movies and methods p81-90

History and criticism

Cawelti, J. G. The mythology of crime and its formulaic embodiments. *In* Cawelti, J. G. Adventure, mystery, and romance p51-79

Gangsters. See Criminals

Ganivet, Angel

About

Shaw, D. L. Ganivet and the emergence of the generation. *In* Shaw, D. L. The generation of 1898 in Spain p17-40

Gans, Herbert J.

The costs of inequality: in response to Robert A. Nisbet. *In* Small comforts for hard times p50-58

Democracy and the arts: adversary or ally? *In* Mann, D. A. ed. The arts in a democratic society p98-117

Symbolic ethnicity: the future of ethnic groups and cultures in America. *In* On the making of Americans p193-220

Ganschow, Thomas W.

The aged in a revolutionary milieu: China. *In* Spicker, S. F.; Woodward, K. M. and Van Tassel, D. D. eds. Aging and the elderly p303-20

Gansevoort, Guert

About

Homberger, E. Melville, Lt Guert Gansevoort and authority: an essay in biography. *In* Pullin, F. ed. New perspectives on Melville p255-74

The Ganymede ode. Trojan women and.

Burnett, A. P. *In* Yale classical studies v25 p291-316

Ganz, Margaret

Pickwick papers: humor and the refashioning of reality. *In* Dickens Studies Annual v4 p36-55

The vulnerable ego: Dickens' humor in decline. *In* Dickens Studies Annual v 1 p23-40

Ganzheit (Psychology) See Whole and parts (Psychology)

Gara, Larry

Slavery and the slave power: a critical distinction. *In* Swierenga, R. P. ed. Beyond the Civil War synthesis p295-308

Garai, Josef E.
The use of a painting to resolve an artist's identity conflicts. *In* Ulman, E. and Dachinger, P. eds. Art therapy p311-24

Garai, Joseph E. See Garai, Josef E.

Garbáty, Thomas Jay
Chaucer and comedy. *In* Ruggiers, P. G. ed. Versions of medieval comedy p173-90
Wynkyn de Worde's "Sir Thopas" and other tales. *In* Virginia. University. Bibliographical Society. Studies in bibliography v31 p57-67

Garber, Daniel
Science and certainty in Descartes. *In* Hooker, M. ed. Descartes p114-51

Garber, Elizabeth
Molecular science in late-nineteenth-century Britain. *In* Historical studies in the physical sciences v9 p265-97

Garber, Marjorie B.
"Infinite riches in a little room": closure and enclosure in Marlowe. *In* Kernan, A. B. ed. Two Renaissance mythmakers p 3-21

Garbus, Martin, and Seligman, Joel
Sanctions and disbarment: they sit in judgment. *In* Nader, R. and Green, M. J. eds. Verdicts on lawyers p33-46

Garcia, Eugene Current- See Current-Garcia, Eugene

Garcia, M. G.
The Armed Forces: poor relation of the Franco régime. *In* Preston, P. ed. Spain in crisis p23-47

García-Barrio, Constance Sparrow de
The image of the Black man in the poetry of Nicolás Guillén. *In* DeCosta, M. ed. Blacks in Hispanic literature p105-13

Garcia de Orta. See Orta, Garcia de

García Gómez, Emilio
Moorish Spain. *In* Lewis, B. ed. Islam and the Arab world p225-44

Garcia Hortelano, Juan

About individual works
Summer storm
Schwartz, R. Juan Garcia Hortelano and Tormenta de verano (Summer storm) (1962). *In* Schwartz, R. Spain's New Wave novelists, 1950-1974 p143-52

García Lorca, Federico
The duende: theory and divertissement; excerpt from "The poet in New York." *In* Gibbons, R. ed. The poet's work: 29 masters of 20th century poetry on the origins and practice of their art p28-41

About individual works
The poet in New York
Morgan, E. Three views of Brooklyn Bridge. *In* Morgan, E. Essays p43-57

Poet in New York (Translated by Ben Belitt)
Belitt, B. Translator's preface: Poet in New York. *In* Belitt, B. Adam's dream p79-83

García Márquez, Gabriel

About
Pritchett, V. S. Gabriel Garcia Marquez: the myth makers. *In* Pritchett, V. S. The myth makers p164-73

About individual works
One hundred years of solitude
Brotherston, G. An end to secular solitude: Gabriel García Márquez. *In* The emergence of the Latin American novel p122-35
MacAdam, A. J. Gabriel García Márquez: a commodius vicus of recirculation. *In* MacAdam, A. J. Modern Latin American narratives p78-87
Nazareth, P. Time in the Third World: a fictional exploration. *In* Narasimhaiah, C. D. ed. Awakened conscience p195-205
Tobin, P. D. "Everything is known": Gabriel García Márquez. One hundred years of solitude. *In* Tobin, P. D. Time and the novel p164-91

García Navarro, Luis
The North of New Spain as a political problem in the eighteenth century. *In* Weber, D. J. ed. New Spain's far northern frontier p201-15

Garcilaso de la Vega, 1503-1536

About individual works
First eclogue
Segre, C. A conceptual analysis of the First eclogue of Garcilaso. *In* Segre, C. Structures and time p137-59

Garcilaso de la Vega, el Inca

About
Marichal, J. A. The New World from within: the Inca Garcilaso. *In* First images of America p57-61

Gard, France (Dept.)

History
Lewis, G. The White Terror of 1815 in the department of the Gard: counter-revolution, continuity and the individual. *In* French society and the Revolution p286-313

Gardam, Jane
Mrs Hookaneye and I. *In* Blishen, E. ed. The thorny paradise p77-80

The garden of the Finzi-Continis (Motion picture)
Kauffmann, S. The garden of the Finzi-Continis. *In* Kauffmann, S. Living images p95-96

Gardening. See Landscape gardening

Gardens

Symbolic aspects
See Gardens in literature

Gardens in literature
Barbeau, A. T. The wild and the garden: a double focus on reality in Pope's An essay on man. *In* Tennessee Studies in literature v22 p73-84
Farmer, N. K. Herrick's Hesperidean garden: ut pictura poesis applied. *In* Rollin, R. B. and Patrick, J. M. eds. "Trust to good verses": Herrick tercentenary essays p15-51
Hughes, D. Y. The garden in Wells's early science fiction. *In* H. G. Wells and modern science fiction p48-69

Gardezi, Hassan Nawaz
Contemporary sociology in Pakistan and Bangladesh. *In* Mohan, R. P. and Martindale, D. A. eds. Handbook of contemporary developments in world sociology p413-22

Gardiner, Harold Charles

Flannery O'Connor's clarity of vision. *In* Friedman, M. J. and Lawson, L. A. eds. The added dimension p184-206

Gardner, Adrienne

The craftsmanship of Yeats: Deirdre: Yeats's other Greek tragedy. *In* Yeats, Joyce, and Beckett p35-38

Gardner, Burleigh Bradford

Doing business with management. *In* Eddy, E. M. and Partridge, W. L. eds. Applied anthropology in America p245-60

Gardner, David Pierpont

Forces for change in American higher education. *In* McMurrin, S. M. ed. On the meaning of the university p103-23

Gardner, Dame Helen Louise

The argument about 'The ecstasy.' *In* Roberts, J. R. ed. Essential articles for the study of John Donne's poetry p239-58

Dean Donne's monument in St. Paul's. *In* Evidence in literary scholarship p29-44

The novels of Joyce Cary. *In* English Association. Essays and studies, 1975 p76-93

Gardner, Howard

Senses, symbols, operations: an organization of artistry. *In* Perkins, D. and Leondar, B. eds. The arts and cognition p88-117

Vico's theories of knowledge in the light of contemporary social science. *In* Giambattista Vico's science of humanity p351-64

Gardner, John Champlin

Guilt and the world's complexity: the murder of Ongentheow and the slaying of the dragon. *In* Anglo-Saxon poetry: essays in appreciation p14-22

Gardner, John William

The individual and society. *In* McMurrin, S. M. ed. On the meaning of the university p51-62

Gardner, Lloyd C.

Consensus history and foreign policy. *In* Encyclopedia of American foreign policy p158-66

Gardner, Mary A.

The evolution of the Inter American Press Association. *In* Fischer, H. D. and Merril, J. C. eds. International and intercultural communication p392-404

Gardner, Richard N.

Bretton Woods. *In* Keynes, M. ed. Essays on John Maynard Keynes p202-15

Gardner, Robert D.

The bicentennial of Eastern State Hospital. *In* American psychiatry: past, present, and future p3-7

Gardner-Medwin, Alisoun

Miss Reburn's ballads: a nineteenth-century repertoire from Ireland. *In* Ballad studies p93-116

Garfield, Charles A.

Impact of death on the health-care professional. *In* Feifel, H. [ed.] New meanings of death p143-51

Garfield, Leon

Bookmaker and punter. *In* Blishen, E. ed. The thorny paradise p81-86

An evening with Leon Garfield. *In* Egoff, S. A. ed. One ocean touching p110-20

About

Garfield, L. An evening with Leon Garfield. *In* Egoff, S. A. ed. One ocean touching p110-20

Garfinkel, Harold

The rational properties of scientific and common-sense activities. *In* Giddens, A. ed. Positivism and sociology p53-73

Garland, Hamlin

About

Goist, P. D. The city and the middle border: Hamlin Garland. *In* Goist, P. D. From Main Street to State Street p59-67

Garment, Leonard

Majoritarianism at the United Nations and human rights. *In* Sidorsky, D. ed. Essays on human rights p30-36

Garner, Alan

Inner time. *In* Nicholls, P. ed. Science fiction at large p119-38

About

Garner, A. Inner time. *In* Nicholls, P. ed. Science fiction at large p119-38

About individual works

Red shift

Chambers, A. Letter from England: Literary crossword puzzle . . . or masterpiece? *In* Horn Book Magazine. Crosscurrents of criticism p315-18

Garner, Ann M. See Terdal, L. G. jt. auth.

Garnett, David

Maynard Keynes as a biographer. *In* Keynes, M. ed. Essays on John Maynard Keynes p254-59

Never be a bookseller. *In* Bookselling in America and the world p171-75

Garnett, John C.

The concept of war .*In* The Year book of world affairs, 1976 p133-49

Limited conventional war in the nuclear age. *in* Howard, M. ed. Restraints on war p79-102

Garratt, Evie

Working with Warner. *In* Prentki, T. ed. Francis Warner p83-87

Garrett, George Palmer

Dreaming with Adam: notes on imaginary history. *In* Cohen, R. ed. New directions in literary history p249-63

Ladies in Boston have their hats: notes on WASP humor. *In* Cohen, S. B. ed. Comic relief p207-37

About individual works

Death of the fox

Garrett, G. P. Dreaming with Adam notes on imaginary history. *In* Cohen, R. ed. New directions in literary history p249-63

Garrety, Michael

Love and war: R. H. Mottram. The Spanish farm trilogy and Ernest Hemingway, A farewell to arms. *In* Klein, H. M. ed. The First World War in fiction p10-22

Garrigue, Jean

About

Lieberman, L. Jean Garrigue: the body of the dream. *In* Lieberman, L. Unassigned frequencies p107-15

Garrison, Dee

Immoral fiction in the late Victorian library. *In* Howe, D. W. ed. Victorian America p141-59

Garrison, Joseph. See Schwartz, D. C. jt. auth.

Garrison, Vivian Eva
Sectarianism and psychosocial adjustment: a controlled comparison of Puerto Rican Pentecostals and Catholics. *In* Zaretsky, I. I. and Leone, M. P. eds. Religious movements in contemporay America p298-329

Garrison, Vivian Eva, and Arensberg, Conrad Maynadier
The evil eye: envy or risk of seizure? Paranoia or patronal dependency? *In* The Evil eye p286-328

Garrison, William Lloyd
About
Stewart, J. B. The aim and impact of Garrisonian abolitionism, 1840-1860. *In* Swierenga, R. P. ed. Beyond the Civil War synthesis p329-41
Wyatt-Brown, B. William Lloyd Garrison and antislavery unity: a reappraisal. *In* Swierenga, R. P. ed. Beyond the Civil War synthesis p309-28

Garson, Barbara
About individual works
Macbird!
Kauffmann, S. Macbird. *In* Kauffmann, S. Persons of the drama p178-81

Garson, Robert
The Atlantic alliance, Eastern Europe and the origins of the Cold war: from Pearl Harbor to Yalta. *In* Allen, H. C. and Thompson, R. eds. Contrast and connection p296-320

Gartner, Lloyd P.
Documents on Roumanian Jewry, Consul Peixotto, and Jewish diplomacy, 1870-1875. *In* Salo Wittmayer Baron v 1 p467-90

Garvin, Harry Raphael
American and European makers of the twentieth-century novel. *In* Garvin, H. R. ed. Makers of the twentieth-century novel p11-18

Garwin, Richard Lawrence
Weapons developments and the threat of nuclear war. *In* Griffiths, F. and Polanyi, J. C. eds. The dangers of nuclear war p93-106

Garza, Rudolph O. de la. See De la Garza, Rudolph O.

Garzoni, Giovanni
About
Matsen, H. S. Giovanni Garzoni (1419-1505) to Alessandro Achillini (1463-1512): an unpublished letter and defense. *In* Philosophy and humanism p518-30

Gas
Law and legislation—United States
Breyer, S. G. and MacAvoy, P. W. Regulating natural gas producers. *In* Kalter, R. J. and Vogely, W. A. eds. Energy supply and government policy p161-92

Gas, Natural. See Gas industry

Gas industry
Law and legislation
See Gas—Law and legislation
United States
Breyer, S. G. and MacAvoy, P. W. Regulating natural gas producers. *In* Kalter, R. J. and Vogely, W. A. eds. Energy supply and government policy p161-92

Gas manufacture and works. See Gas industry

Gasché, Rodolphe
The scene of writing: a deferred outset. *In* Glyph I p150-71

Gascoigne, George
About
Helgerson, R. Gascoigne. *In* Helgerson, R. The Elizabethan prodigals p44-57
About individual works
The lullaby of a lover
Nathan, L. E. Gascoigne's "Lullabie" and structures in the Tudor lyric. *In* Sloan, T. O. and Waddington, R. S. eds. The rhetoric of Renaissance poetry p58-72

Gascoyne, David
Introducing Kenneth Patchen. *In* Morgan, R. G. ed. Kenneth Patchen: a collection of essays p144-51
About
Thurley, G. David Gascoyne: phenomena of zero. *In* Thurley, G. The ironic harvest p98-120

Gases
Guerlac, H. Joseph Priestley's first papers on gases and their reception in France. *In* Guerlac, H. Essays and papers in the history of modern science p304-13

Gases, Asphyxiating and poisonous
War use
See Chemical warfare

Gasiorowska, Xenia
Solzhenitsyn's women. *In* Dunlop, J. B.; Haugh, R. and Klimoff, A. eds. Aleksandr Solzhenitsyn: critical essays and documentary materials 2d ed. p117-28

Gaskell, Elizabeth Cleghorn (Stevenson)
About
Cunningham, V. Mrs Gaskell. *In* Cunningham, V. Everywhere spoken against p127-42
Davie, D. Dissent and the Evangelicals, 1800-1850. *In* Davie, D. A gathered Church p55-72
Larkin, M. The Industrial Revolution. *In* Larkin, M. Man and society in nineteenth-century realism p74-88
Lucas, W. J. Mrs Gaskell and the nature of social change. *In* Lucas, W. J. The literature of change p 1-33
Tillotson, G. Mrs Gaskell. *In* Tillotson, G. A view of Victorian literature p226-54
Tomlinson, T. B. Love and politics in the English novel, 1840s-1860s. *In* Tomlinson, T. B. The English middle-class novel p69-82
About individual works
Cranford
Auerbach, N. Beyond the family: idyll and inferno. *In* Auerbach, N. Communities of women p75-113
Mary Barton
Kennard, J. E. Aristocrat versus commoner. *In* Kennard, J. E. Victims of convention p46-79
Lucas, W. J. Engels, Mrs Gaskell and Manchester. *In* Lucas, W. J. The literature of change p34-56
Ruth
Cockshut, A. O. J. The realists: Mrs Gaskell. *In* Cockshut, A. O. J. Man and woman: a study of love and the novel, 1740-1940 p86-99

Gaskell, Elizabeth Cleghorn (Stevenson)—
About individual works—*Continued*

Sylvia's lovers

Rance, N. Elizabeth Gaskell: Sylvia's lovers (1863). *In* Rance, N. The historical novel and popular politics in nineteenth-century England p137-54

Sanders, A. Suffering a sea-change: Mrs Gaskell's Sylvia's lovers. *In* Sanders, A. The Victorian historical novel, 1840-1880 p197-228

Wives and daughters

Cockshut, A. O. J. The realists: Mrs Gaskell. *In* Cockshut, A. O. J. Man and woman: a study of love and the novel, 1740-1940 p86-99

Gass, William H.
The world within the word

Contents

The anatomy of mind
Carrots, noses, snow, rose, roses
The doomed in their sinking
Food and beast language
Gertrude Stein and the geography of the sentence
Groping for trouts
Malcolm Lowry
Mr. Blotner, Mr. Feaster, and Mr. Faulkner
The ontology of the sentence, or How to make a world of words
Paul Valéry
Proust at 100
Sartre on theater
Three photos of Colette
Upright among staring fish
Wisconsin death trip

About

Scholes, R. E. Metafiction. *In* Scholes, R. E. Fabulation and metafiction p103-38

Gasset, José Ortega. See Ortega y Gasset, José

Gaston, Paul M.
Sutpen's door: the South since the Brown decision. *In* Two decades of change p95-114

Gatch, Milton McCormick
Beginnings continued: a decade of studies of Old English prose. *In* Anglo-Saxon England 5 p225-43 ·

Old English literature and the liturgy: problems and potential. *In* Anglo-Saxon England 6 p237-47

Gates, Henry-Louis
Binary oppositions in chapter one of Narrative of the life of Frederick Douglass an American slave written by himself. *In* Fisher, D. and Stepto, R. B. eds. Afro-American literature p212-32

Dis and dat: dialect and the descent. *In* Fisher, D. and Stepto, R. B. eds. Afro-American literature p88-119

Preface to Blackness: text and pretext. *In* Fisher, D. and Stepto, R. B. eds. Afro-American literature p44-69

They think you're an airplane, but you're really a bird: the education of an Afro-American. *In* Hurdles p193-211

About

Gates, H. L. They think you're an airplane, but you're really a bird: the education of an Afro-American. *In* Hurdles p193-211

Gathercole, Peter W.
Obstacles to the study of Maori carving: the collector, the connoisseur, and the faker. *In* Greenhalgh, M. and Megaw, J. V. S. eds. Art in society p275-88

Gatrell, Simon
Hardy, house-style, and the aesthetics of punctuation. *In* Smith, A. ed. The novels of Thomas Hardy p169-92

Gatt-Rutter, John
G. Verga: Mastro-Don Gesualdo. *In* Williams, D. A. ed. The monster in the mirror p204-33

Gattey, Charles Neilson
Hellgate, Cripplegate, and Newgate. *In* The Saturday book 34 p157-66

Gauchos
Dobie, J. F. The gauchos and horses of Hudson and Graham. *In* Dobie, J. F. Prefaces p187-200

Gauld, Alan
ESP and attempts to explain it. *In* Thakur, S. C. ed. Philosophy and psychical research p17-45

Gaulle, Charles de, President France

Friends and associates

Palewski, G. A surprising friendship: Malraux and De Gaulle. *In* Courcel, M. H. de, ed. Malraux p68-78

Gault, Pierre
Genesis and functions of Hencher in "The lime twig." *In* Johnson, I. D. and Johnson, C. [eds.] Les américanistes p138-55

Gautama Buddha

About

Reynolds, F. E. The many lives of Buddha: a study of sacred biography and Theravāda tradition. *In* Reynolds, F. E. and Capps, D. eds. The biographical process p37-61

Gauthier, Howard L.
Geography. *In* Quantitative social science research on Latin America p132-61

Gautier d'Arras

About individual works
Eracle

Hanning, R. W. The individual and mimesis, II: multiple perspectives on reality. *In* Hanning, R. W. The individual in twelfth-century romance p171-93

Gavazzi, Alessandro

About

Hall, B. Alessandro Gavazzi: a Barnabite friar and the Risorgimento (Presidential address) *In* Church, society and politics p303-56

Gawad, Mohamed Abdel
Attempts of the Arab world to participate in balancing the flow of information. *In* Horton, P. C. ed. The Third World and press freedom p173-86

Gawain and the Grene Knight
Eldredge, L. M. The state of "Pearl" studies since 1933. *In* Viator: medieval and Renaissance studies v6 p171-94

Kane, G. Some reflections on critical method. *In* English Association. Essays and studies, 1976 p23-38

Käsmann, H. Numerical structure in Fitt III of Sir Gawain and the Green Knight. *In* Chaucer and Middle English studies in honour of Rossell Hope Robbins p131-39

Leyerle, J. The game and play of hero. *In* Concepts of the hero in the Middle Ages and the Renaissance p49-82

Gawlick, Günter
Hume and the deists: a reconsideration. *In* David Hume p128-38

Gay, Ebenezer
About
Smith, D. S. Old age and the 'great transformation': a New England case study. *In* Spicker, S. F.; Woodward, K. M. and Van Tassel, D. D. eds. Aging and the elderly p285-302

Gay, John
About
Erskine-Hill, H. H. The significance of Gay's drama. *In* English drama: forms and development p142-63

About individual works
The shepherd's week
Trowbridge, F. H. Pope, Gay, and The shepherd's week. *In* Trowbridge, F. H. From Dryden to Jane Austen p124-34

Gay, Leslie Newton
About
Harvey, A. M. Contributions of the part-time staff of the Johns Hopkins Hospital: Moore, King, and Gay. *In* Harvey, A. M. Adventures in medical research p248-60

Gay, Penelope
Browning and music. *In* Armstrong, I. ed. Robert Browning p211-30

Gay, Peter
For Beckmesser. *In* From Parnassus p42-54

Gay lib. See Gay liberation movement

Gay liberation movement
Kyper, J. Coming out: toward a social analysis. *In* Crew, L. ed. The gay academic p387-414

Lehman, J. L. Gay students. *In* Crew, L. ed. The gay academic p57-63

Rich, A. C. The meaning of our love for women is what we have constantly to expand. *In* Rich, A. C. On lies, secrets, and silence p223-30

Risch, S. J. Towards a gay analysis of science and education. *In* Crew, L. ed. The gay academic p369-83

Gaylin, Willard
In the beginning: helpless and dependent. *In* Doing good p 1-38

The technology of life and death. *In* Small comforts for hard times p152-69

Gaynor, Anne
The patient's home is his castle. *In* Home care p101-08

Gaza Strip
Civil rights
See Civil rights—Gaza Strip

Gazzola, Piero
Back to the agora! *In* United Nations Educational, Scientific and Cultural Organization. The conservation of cities p57-65

Geach, Peter Thomas
Immortality. *In* Donnelly, J. P. ed. Language, metaphysics, and death p208-15

Names and identity. *In* Guttenplan, S. D. ed. Mind and language p139-58

Geary, Susan E.
Mrs. Stowe's income from the serial version of Uncle Tom's cabin. *In* Virginia. University. Bibliographical Society. Studies in bibliography v29 p380-82

Gebhard, Bruno
The interrelationship of scientific and folk medicine in the United States of America since 1850. *In* American folk medicine p87-98

Geddes, Joan Bel. See Bel Geddes, Joan

Geertgen tot Sint Jans
About individual works
Virgin and Child
Winternitz, E. On angel concerts in the 15th century: a critical approach to realism and symbolism in sacred painting. *In* Winternitz, E. Musical instruments and their symbolism in Western art p137-49

Geertz, Clifford
Centers, kings, and charisma: reflections on the symbolics of power. *In* Culture and its creators p150-71

"From the native's point of view": on the nature of anthropological understanding. *In* Basso, K. H. and Selby, H. A. eds. Meaning in anthropology p221-37

About individual works
From the native's point of view: on the nature of anthropological understanding
Trilling, L. Why we read Jane Austen. *In* Trilling, L. The last decade p204-25

Geese
Behavior
White, E. B. The geese. *In* White, E. B. Essays of E. B. White p62-68

Geis, Gilbert
Compensation to victims of violent crime. *In* Contemporary issues in criminal justice p94-115

Geisler, Norman L.
The extent of the Old Testament canon. *In* Current issues in Biblical and patristic interpretation p31-46

Geismar, Maxwell David
About individual works
American moderns, from rebellion to conformity
Marcus, S. Three obsessed critics. *In* Marcus, S. Representations p102-17

Geiss, Imanuel
The study of African history in Germany. *In* African studies since 1945 p209-19

Geist, Christopher D.
Historic sites and monuments as icons. *In* Browne, R. B. and Fishwick, M. W. eds. Icons of America p57-66

Gella, Aleksander
Current developments in Polish sociology. *In* Mohan, R. P. and Martindale, D. A. eds. Handbook of contemporary developments in world sociology p203-26

Gellar, Sheldon
The colonial era. *In* Martin, P. M. and O'Meara, P. eds. Africa p132-49

Gelling, Margaret
Latin loan-words in Old English place-names. *In* Anglo-Saxon England 6 p 1-13

Gellner, Ernest André
The new idealism—cause and meaning in the social sciences. *In* Giddens, A. ed. Positivism and sociology p129-56

Gelpi, Albert
Emerson: the paradox of organic form. *In* Levin, D. ed. Emerson: prophecy, metamorphosis, and influence p149-70

Emily Dickinson and the Deerslayer: the dilemma of the woman poet in America. *In* Gilbert, S. M. and Gubar, S. eds. Shakespeare's sisters p122-34

Gelpi, Barbara Charlesworth

A common language: the American woman poet. *In* Gilbert, S. M. and Gubar, S. eds. Shakespeare's sisters p269-79

The innocent I: Dickens' influence on Victorian autobiography. *In* The Worlds of Victorian fiction p57-71

Gelwick, Richard

Essay 8. *In* Fitzgerald, R. ed. What it means to be human p142-63

Gelzer, Matthias

About individual works
Die Nobilität der römischen Republik

Oliver, R. P. Tacitean nobilitas. *In* Illinois classical studies v3, 1978 p238-61

Gemmill, Gary R.

Postscript: toward the person-centered organization. *In* Heisler, W. J. and Houck, J. W. eds. A matter of dignity p197-205

Gems. See Intaglios

Gems in literature

Kitson, P. Lapidary traditions in Anglo-Saxon England: part I, the background; the Old English lapidary. *In* Anglo-Saxon England 7 p9-60

Gender. See Grammar, Comparative and general—Gender

Genealogical research. See Genealogy

Genealogy

Foucault, M. Nietzsche, genealogy, history. *In* Foucault, M. Language, counter-memory, practice p139-64

See also Anglo-Saxons—Genealogy; and subdivision Genealogy under names of places, e.g. Worcester, Mass—Genealogy

Research
See Genealogy

General Accounting Office. See United States. General Accounting Office

General Agreement on Tariffs and Trade. See Contracting Parties to the General Agreement on Tariffs and Trade

General relativity (Physics)

Bergmann, P. G. General relativity and our view of the physical universe. *In* Cosmology, history, and theology p25-28

French, A. P. The story of general relativity. *In* Einstein p91-111

Heelan, P. A. Quantum relativity and the cosmic observer. *In* Cosmology, history, and theology p29-37

Heidmann, J. The expansion of the universe in the frame of conventional general relativity. *In* Cosmology, history, and theology p39-57

General semantics. See Pragmatics

General stores

Jackson—Mississippi
Welty, E. The little store. *In* Welty, E. The eye of the story p326-35

General Strike, Great Britain, 1926

McDonald, G. The defeat of the General Strike. *In* Peele, G. and Cook, C. eds. The politics of reappraisal, 1918-1939 p64-87

General will. See Consensus (Social sciences)

Generation. See Reproduction

Generation gap. See Conflict of generations

Generative grammar

Bever, T. G. The psychology of language and structuralist investigations of nativism. *In* Harman, G. ed. On Noam Chomsky p146-64

Bresnan, J. A realistic transformational grammar. *In* Linguistic theory and psychological reality p 1-59

Chomsky, N. Conditions on rules of grammar. *In* Current issues in linguistic theory p3-50

Jackendoff, R. S. Grammar as evidence for conceptual structure. *In* Linguistic theory and psychological reality p201-28

Partee, B. H. Linguistic metatheory. *In* Harman, G. ed. On Noam Chomsky p303-15

Steiner, G. Whorf, Chomsky, and the student of literature. *In* Steiner, G. On difficulty and other essays p137-63

Genes. See Heredity

Genesis (Anglo-Saxon poem)

Hill, T. D. The fall of angels and man in the Old English Genesis B. *In* Anglo-Saxon poetry: essays in appreciation p279-90

Raw, B. C. The probable derivation of most of the illustrations in Junius 11 from an illustrated Old Saxon Genesis. *In* Anglo-Saxon England 5 p133-48

Illustrations

Henderson, G. The programme of illustrations in Bodleian M S Junius XI. *In* Studies in memory of David Talbot Rice p113-45

Genêt, Jean

About

Chiaromonte, N. The ceremonial theater of Jean Genet. *In* Chiaromonte, N. The worm of consciousness, and other essays p160-82

Kunkel, F. L. Jean Genet: counterfeit saint. *In* Kunkel, F. L. Passion and the Passion p108-28

Pritchett, V. S. Jean Genet: a modern nihilist. *In* Pritchett, V. S. The myth makers p102-07

Schlueter, J. Genet's maids, brothel patrons, and Blacks. *In* Schlueter, J. Metafictional characters in modern drama p35-52

About individual works
Funeral rites

Bersani, L. Persons in pieces. *In* Bersani, L. A future for Astyanax p286-315

Characters

Schlueter, J. Genet's maids, brothel patrons, and Blacks. *In* Schlueter, J. Metafictional characters in modern drama p35-52

Criticism and interpretation

Hartman, G. H. Psychoanalysis: the French connection. *In* Hartman, G. H. ed. Psychoanalysis and the question of the text p86-113

Genetic code

Margoliash, E. Informational macromolecules and biological evolution. *In* Neyman, J. ed. The heritage of Copernicus: theories "pleasing to the mind" p184-206

Genetic counseling

Murray, R. F. Genetic counseling: boon or bane? *In* The Tricentennial people p29-46

Shaw, M. W. S. Genetics and the law. *In* The Tricentennial people p48-57

Genetic engineering

See also Cloning; Recombinant DNA

Moral and religious aspects

Fletcher, J. F. Genetic engineering. *In* Fletcher, J. F. Humanhood: essays in biomedical ethics p79-92

Fletcher, J. F. Recombining DNA. *In* Fletcher, J. F. Humanhood: essays in biomedical ethics p190-99

Genetic load

Carlson, E. A. Genetics and the biological basis of the human condition. *In* The Tricentennial people p3-17

Genetic psychology. See Adulthood; Intelligence levels; Sociobiology

Geneticists

History

Provine, W. B. The role of mathematical population geneticists in the evolutionary synthesis of the 1930s and 1940s. *In* Studies in history of biology v2 p167-92

Genetics

Milani-Comparetti, M. Genetics and adolescent development: perspectives for the future. *In* Adolescence and youth in prospect p137-47

See also Adaptation (Biology); Behavior genetics; Evolution; Heredity; Human genetics; Molecular genetics; Natural selection; Nature and nurture; Population genetics; Variation (Biology)

History

Adams, M. B. From "gene fund" to "gene pool": on the evolution of evolutionary language. *In* Studies in history of biology v3 p241-85

MacKenzie, D. and Barnes, B. Scientific judgment: the biometry-Mendelism controversy. *In* Barnes, B. and Shapin, S. eds. Natural order p191-210

Ravin, A. W. The gene as catalyst; the gene as organism. *In* Studies in history of biology v 1 p 1-45

Genetics and environment. See Nature and nurture

Geneva

History

Kingdon, R. M. Was the Protestant Reformation a revolution? The case of Geneva. *In* Church, society and politics p203-22

Genius. See Creation (Literary, artistic etc.); Creative ability; Originality

Geneval conventions. See Diplomatic Conference for the Establishment of International Conventions for the Protection of Victims of War, Geneva, 1949

Genius (Companion spirit) in literature

Oram, W. A. Nature, poetry, and Milton's genii. *In* Patrick, J. M. and Sundell, R. H. eds. Milton and the art of sacred song p47-64

Genoa

Gilds

Kedar, B. Z. The Genoese notaries of 1382: the anatomy of an urban occupational group. *In* The Medieval city p73-94

History

Hughes, D. O. Kinsmen and neighbors in medieval Genoa. *In* The Medieval city p75-111

Kedar, B. Z. The Genoese notaries of 1382: the anatomy of an urban occupational group. *In* The Medieval city p73-94

Social conditions

Hughes, D. O. Urban growth and family structure in medieval Genoa. *In* Towns in societies p105-30

Social life and customs

Hughes, D. O. Domestic ideals and social behavior: evidence from medieval Genoa. *In* Rosenberg, C. E. ed. The family in history p115-43

Genocide

Mansson, H. H. Justifying the Final Solution. *In* Weir, R. F. ed. Ethical issues in death and dying p308-19

See also Holocaust, Jewish (1939-1945)

Genre (Literature) See Literary form

Genre painting. See Narrative painting

Gentile, Giovanni

About

Watkins, E. Poetic autonomy. *In* Watkins, E. The critical act p24-55

Gentili, Bruno, and Cerri, Giovanni

Written and oral communication in Greek historiographical thought. *In* Havelock, E. A. and Hershbell, J. P. eds. Communication arts in the ancient world p137-55

The Gentleman's Magazine, London

Kuist, J. M. The Gentleman's magazine in the Folger Library: the history and significance of the Nichols family collection. *In* Virginia. University. Bibliographical Society. Studies in bibliography v29 p307-22

Gentlemen prefer blondes (Motion picture)

Truffaut, F. Howard Hawks: Gentlemen prefer blondes. *In* Truffaut, F. The films in my life p71-72

Gentry. See subdivision Gentry under names of countries, regions, etc., e.g. Dubrovnik, Yugoslavia—Gentry

Geodynamics

Bemmelen, R. W. van. The present formulation of the undation theory. *In* The Frontiers of human knowledge p255-74

Geoffrey of Monmouth, Bp. of St Asaph

About

Brooke, C. N. L. Geoffrey of Monmouth as a historian. *In* Church and government in the Middle Ages p77-91

Geoffrey of Vinsauf. See Vinsauf, Geoffrey de

Geographers

United States

Bowden, M. J. The Great American Desert in the American mind: the historiography of a geographical notion. *In* Geographies of the mind p119-47

Mikesell, M. W. The rise and decline of "sequent occupance": a chapter in the history of American geography. *In* Geographies of the mind p149-69

Geographical boundaries. See Boundaries

Geographical distribution of animals and plants

Sulloway, F. J. Geographical isolation in Darwin's thinking: the vicissitudes of a crucial idea. *In* Studies in history of biology v3 p23-65

See also Phytogeography

Geographical distribution of man. See Anthropogeography; Ethnology, Man —Migrations

Geographical distribution of plants and animals. See Geographical distribution of animals and plants

Geographical myths

Hammond, G. P. The search for the fabulous in the settlement of the Southwest. *In* Weber, D. J. ed. New Spain's far northern frontier p17-33

Hand, W. D. The effect of the discovery on ethnological and folklife studies in Europe. *In* First images of America p45-55

Geographical names. See Names, Geographical

Geographical research

Latin America
Gauthier, H. L. Geography. *In* Quantitative social science research on Latin America p132-61

Geography
See also Anthropo-geography; Classical geography; Discoveries (in geography); Geographers

Early works
See Classical geography; Geography—15th-16th centuries; Geography, Medieval

History
See Discoveries (in geography); Geographical myths

Research
See Geographical research

Study and teaching (Higher)—
United States
Koelsch, W. A. Terrae incognitae and arcana Siwash: toward a richer history of academic geography. *In* Geographies of the mind p63-87

Terminology
See Names, Geographical

400-1400
See Geography, Medieval

15th-16th centuries
Gilmore, M. P. The New World in French and English historians of the sixteenth century. *In* First images of America p519-27
Johnson, H. B. New geographical horizons: concepts. *In* First images of America p615-33

15th-16th centuries—Bibliography
Quinn, D. B. New geographical horizons: literature. *In* First images of America p635-58

Geography, Ancient
Staab, F. Ostrogothic geographers at the court of Theodoric the Great: a study of some sources of the anonymous cosmographer of Ravenna. *In* Viator: medieval and Renaissance studies v7 p27-64
See also Cities and towns, Ancient

Geography, Classical. See Classical geography

Geography, Historical
Clark, A. H. First things first. *In* Pattern and process p9-21
Warkentin, J. Epilogue. *In* European settlement and development in North America: essays on geographical change in honour and memory of Andrew Hill Clark p208-20

Sources
Friis, H. R. Original and published sources in research in historical geography: a comparison. *In* Pattern and process p139-59

Geography, Mathematical. See Cosmography

Geography, Medieval
Stabb, F. Ostrogothic geographers at the court of Theodoric the Great: a study of some sources of the anonymous cosmographer of Ravenna. *In* Viator: medieval and Renaissance studies v7 p27-64

Trimingham, J. S. The Arab geographers and the East African coast. *In* Chittick, H. N. and Rotberg, R. I. eds. East Africa and the Orient p115-46

Geography, Political. See Geopolitics

Geography, Social. See Anthropo-geography

Geology
Lawrence, P. Heaven and earth—the relation of the nebular hypothesis to geology. *In* Cosmology, history, and theology p253-81
See also Drift

History
Gould, S. J. Agassiz's marginalia in Lyell's Principles, or the perils of uniformity and the ambiguity of heroes. *In* Studies in history of biology v3 p119-38

Great Britain—History
Porter, R. Creation and credence: the career of the theories of the earth in Britain, 1660-1820. *In* Barnes, B. and Shapin, S. eds. Natural order p97-123

Geometrical drawing. See Perspective

Geometry
Medawar, Sir P. B. A geometric model of reduction and emergence. *In* Ayala, F. J. and Dobzhansky, T. G. eds. Studies in the philosophy of biology p57-63
See also Transformations (Mathematics)

Foundations
See Geometry, Non-Euclidean

Early works to 1800
Timpanaro-Cardini, M. Two questions of Greek geometrical terminology. *In* Kephalaion p183-88

Geometry, Non-Euclidean
Hausman, A. M. Non-Euclidean geometry and relative consistency proofs. *In* Motion and time, space and matter p418-35
Richards, J. L. The reception of a mathematical theory: non-Euclidean geometry in England, 1868-1883. *In* Barnes, B. and Shapin, S. eds. Natural order p143-66
See also Parallels (Geometry)

Geonic literature. See Rabbinical literature

Geonim
Goitein, S. D. F. New sources on the Palestinian gaonate. *In* Salo Wittmayer Baron v 1 p503-37

Geophysics. See Geodynamics

Geopiety: a theme in man's attachment to nature and to place. Tuan, Yi-Fu. *In* Geographies of the mind p11-39

Geopolitics
See also Boundaries; Demography; World politics

Latin America
Roett, R. The changing nature of Latin American international relations: geopolitical realities. *In* The Americas in a changing world p95-111

Nigeria
Akinyemi, A. B. National unity within the context of regional relations: the Nigerian experience. *In* Smock, D. R. and Bentsi-Enchill, K. eds. The search for national integration in Africa p68-76

George III, King of Great Britain

About
Cone, C. B. George III—America's unknown king. *In* The American Revolution and "a candid world" p 1-16

George III—King of Great Britain—Cont.

Gronbeck, B. E. Edmund Burke and the Regency Crisis of 1788-89. *In* Rhetoric: a tradition in transition p142-77

George, Alexander Lawrence, and George, Juliette Lombard

Woodrow Wilson and Colonel House: research note; excerpt from "Woodrow Wilson and Colonel House, a personality study." *In* Kren, G. M. and Rappoport, L. H. eds. Varieties of psychohistory p111-19

George, Carol V. R.

Anne Hutchinson and the "revolution which never happened." *In* "Remember the ladies": new perspectives on women in American history p13-37

George, Charles H.

Gerrard Winstanley: a critical retrospect. *In* The Dissenting tradition p191-225

George, Stefan Anton

About individual works

Das Jahr der Seele

Nalbantian, S. The post-Symbolists: the winter of the soul. *In* Nalbantian, S. The symbol of the soul from Hölderlin to Yeats p86-99

Georgi, Dieter

Socioeconomic reasons for the "divine man" as a propagandistic pattern. *In* Aspects of religious propaganda in Judaism and early Christianity p27-42

Geralton, James, pseud. See Holton, Gerald James

Gerard of Haarlem. See Geertgen tot Sint Jans

Gérard de Nerval, Gérard Labrunie, known as

About

Brombert, V. H. Nerval's privileged enclosures. *In* Brombert, V. H. The romantic prison p120-32

Gerard, Alexander

About individual works

An essay on taste

Albrecht, W. P. Gerard. *In* Albrecht, W. P. The sublime pleasures of tragedy p53-68

Gérard, Jean Ignace Isidore, called Grandville. See Grandville, Jean Ignace Isidore Gérard, called

Gerber, Douglas E.

Herodas 5.1. *In* Harvard Studies in classical philology v28 p161-65

Gerber, Helmut E.

George Moore. *In* Finneran, R. J. ed. Anglo-Irish literature p138-66

Gerber, Irwin

Anticipatory bereavement. *In* Anticipatory grief p26-30

Gerber, Philip L.

Dreiser's Stoic: a study in literary frustration. *In* Literary monographs v7 p85-144

Gerber, Rudolph J.

Obscenity-lust's labors lost and won. *In* Contemporary issues in criminal justice p40-56

Gerbi, Antonello

The earliest accounts on the New World. *In* First images of America p37-43

Gerbner, George

Comparative cultural indicators. *In* Gerbner, G. ed. Mass media policies in changing cultures p199-205

Gerbrands, Adrian A. See Gerbrands, Adrianus Alexander

Gerbrands, Adrianus Alexander

Talania and Nake, master carver and apprentice: two woodcarvers from the Kilenge (western New Britain). *In* Greenhalgh, M. and Megaw, J. V. S. eds. Art in society p193-205

Gergen, Kenneth J.

The social construction of self-knowledge. *In* Mischel, T. ed. The self p139-69

Gerhardsson, Birger

Sacrificial service and atonement in the Gospel of Matthew. *In* Reconciliation and hope p25-35

Gerhardt, Charles Frédéric

About

Brooke, J. H. Laurent, Gerhardt, and the philosophy of chemistry. *In* Historical studies in the physical sciences v6 p405-30

Geriatric psychiatry

Dewdney, I. An art therapy program for geriatric patients. *In* Ulman, E. and Dachinger, P. eds. Art therapy p126-31

Gaitz, C. M. Aged patients, their families and physicians. *In* Aging: the process and the people p206-39

Gerlach, Luther P.

Pentecostalism: revolution or counter-revolution? *In* Zaretsky, I. I. and Leone, M. P. eds. Religious movements in contemporary America p669-99

Germ theory of disease. See Diseases—Causes and theories of causation

The Germ: thoughts toward nature in poetry, literature and art

Dawson, C. The Germ: aesthetic manifesto. *In* Dawson, C. Victorian noon p203-23

Germ warfare. See Biological warfare

German-American leadership

Luebke, F. C. The Germans. *In* Ethnic leadership in America p64-90

German-American literature

Ward, R. E. The case for German-American literature. *In* The German contribution to the building of the Americas p373-91

German-American newspapers

History

Waldenrath, A. The Pennsylvania-Germans: development of their printing and their newspress in the War for American Independence. *In* The German contribution to the building of the Americas p47-74

German Americans

Coppa, F. J. and Curran, T. J. From the Rhine to the Mississippi: the German emigration to the United States. *In* The Immigrant experience in America p44-62

Luebke, F. C. The Germans. *In* Ethnic leadership in America p64-90

German Communist Party. See Communist Party of Germany

German drama

Austrian authors—History and criticism

Haider-Pregler, H. German-language postwar drama. *In* Nicoll, A. World drama p838-53

German drama—*Continued*

19th century—History and criticism

Nicoll, A. From tragedy to melodrama. *In* Nicoll, A. World drama p342-69

Nicoll, A. The independent theatre in Germany. *In* Nicoll, A. World drama p475-92

20th century—History and criticism

Castein, H. German social drama in the 1960s. *In* Drama and society p195-207

Haider-Pregler, H. German-language postwar drama. *In* Nicoll, A. World drama p838-53

Nicoll, A. The expressionistic movement. *In* Nicoll, A. World drama p674-88

German epistolary poetry. See Epistolary poetry, German

German fiction

History and criticism

Swales, M. Excursus: the Bildungsroman as a taxonomic genre. *In* Swales, M. The German Bildungsroman from Wieland to Hesse p161-66

19th century—History and criticism

Swales, M. The Bildungsroman as a genre. *In* Swales, M. The German Bildungsroman from Wieland to Hesse p9-37

Swales, M. Conclusion. *In* Swales, M. The German Bildungsroman from Wieland to Hesse p146-60

Swales, M. Conclusion. *In* Swales, M. The German Novelle p202-14

Swales, M. The Novelle as historical genre. *In* Swales, M. The German Novelle p8-18

Swales, M. The theory of the Novelle. *In* Swales, M. The German Novelle p19-58

20th century—History and criticism

Kurz, P. K. The contemporary novel about Jesus. *In* Kurz, P. K. On modern German literature v4 p151-75

Pynsent, R. B. Contemporary German fiction: the dimensions of experimentation. *In* Federman, R. ed. Surfiction p135-61

German historians. See Historians, German

German idealism. See Idealism, German

German Jews in the United States. See Jews, German in the United States

German language

Canetti, E. Word attacks. *In* Canetti, E. The conscience of words p140-44

Etymology

See Raspelbrot (The word)

German literature

See also Austrian literature; German-American literature

Criticism, Textual

Zeller, H. A new approach to the critical constitution of literary texts. *In* Virginia. University. Bibliographical Society. Studies in bibliography v28 p231-64

History and criticism

Kurz, P. K. Literature and theology today. *In* Kurz, P. K. On modern German literature v 1 p80-104

Middle High German, 1050-1500— History and criticism

Borchardt, F. L. Medievalism in Renaissance Germany. *In* Creative encounter p73-85

Early modern, 1500-1700—History and criticism—Bibliography

Sobel, E. German literature. *In* Jones, W. M. ed. The present state of scholarship in sixteenth-century literature p169-96

18th century—History and criticism

Lange, V. Reflections on the "classical age" of German literature. *In* Studies in eighteenth-century culture v7 p 1-21

20th century—History and criticism

Kurz, P. K. Beat—Pop—underground. *In* Kurz, P. K. On modern German literature v4 p202-41

Kurz, P. K. Fences and camps. *In* Kurz, P. K. On modern German literature v3 p95-127

Kurz, P. K. Group 47. *In* Kurz, P. K. On modern German literature v3 p74-94

Kurz, P. K. Tendencies observable in the most recent literature. *In* Kurz, P. K. On modern German literature v4 p177-201

Kurz, P. K. Why is Christian literature at an end? *In* Kurz, P. K. On modern German literature v4 p109-28

Middleton, J. C. Paragraphs on translation. *In* Middleton, J. C. Bolshevism in art p123-50

Strelka, J. P. Material collectors, political rhetoricians, and amateurs: current methodological problems in German exile literature studies. *In* Strelka, J. P.; Bell, R. F. and Dobson, E. eds. Protest—form—tradition p 1-14

German literature in foreign countries

Kostka, E. K. A trailblazer of Russian Westernism: V. P. Botkin. *In* Kostka, E. K. Glimpses of Germanic-Slavic relations from Pushkin to Heinrich Mann p69-84

Strelka, J. P. Material collectors, political rhetoricians, and amateurs: current methodological problems in German exile literature studies. *In* Strelka, J. P.; Bell, R. F. and Dobson, E. eds. Protest—form—tradition p 1-14

Bibliography

Kostka, E. K. comp. Bibliography. *In* Kostka, E. K. Glimpses of Germanic-Slavic relations from Pushkin to Heinrich Mann p144-54

German opera. See Opera, German

German philosophy. See Philosophy, German

German physicists. See Physicists—Germany

German poetry

18th century—History and criticism

Greenway, J. L. The gateway to innocence: Ossian and the Nordic bard as myth. *In* Studies in eighteenth-century culture v4 p161-70

Motsch, M. F. The forgotten genre: the poetic epistle in eighteenth-century German literature. *In* Studies in eighteenth-century culture v4 p119-24

20th century—History and criticism

Hamburger, M. Brecht and his successors. *In* Hamburger, M. Art as second nature p112-30

Kurz, P. K. The individual's awareness of self and world as manifested in German lyric poetry since 1945. *In* Kurz, P. K. On modern German literature v3 p3-38

Kurz, P. K. Lyric poetry today? *In* Kurz, P. K. On modern German literature v3 p65-73

German poetry in foreign countries

History and criticism

Weissenberger, K. Poetic rhythm and the exile situation. *In* Strelka, J. P.; Bell, R. F. and Dobson, E. eds. Protest—form—tradition p133-44

German propaganda. See Propaganda, German

German refugees. See Refugees, German

German-Soviet pact. See Russo-German treaty, 1939

Germanic languages. See Anglo-Saxon language

Germanic tales. See Tales, Germanic

Germanic tribes

Relations (general) with Rome

Miller, D. H. and Savage, W. W. Ethnic stereotypes and the frontier: a comparative study of Roman and American experience. *In* Miller, D. H. and Steffen, J. O. eds. The frontier p109-37

Germanic tribes in the Balkan Peninsula. See Barbarian invasions of Rome

Germans in Africa

Katzenellenbogen, S. E. British businessmen and German Africa, 1885-1919. *In* Great Britain and her world, 1750-1914 p237-62

Germans in Missouri

Schroeder, A. E. The survival of German traditions in Missouri. *In* The German contribution to the building of the Americas p289-313

Germans in New York (City)

History

Ward, D. Some locational implications of the ethnic division of labor in mid-nineteenth-century American cities. *In* Pattern and process p258-70

Germans in North Carolina

Robbins, W. L. Wishing in and shooting in the New Year among the Germans in the Carolinas. *In* Yoder, D. ed. American folklife p257-79

Germans in the United States

Cazden, R. E. Johann Georg Wesselhöft and the German book trade in America. *In* The German contribution to the building of the Americas p217-34

Jantz, H. E. S. German men of letters in the early United States. *In* The German contribution to the building of the Americas p75-95

Meyer, H. Some remarks about German-American relations. *In* The German contribution to the building of the Americas p359-72

See also German Americans

Germans in Venezuela

Smith, D. ". . . beschreibung eyner Landtschafft der Wilden Nacketen/Grimmigen Menschfresser Leuthen": the German image of America in the sixteenth century. *In* The German contribution to the building of the Americas p 1-19

Germany

See also Germany, East; Germany, West

Civilization—French influences

Bendix, R. Province and metropolis: the case of eighteenth-century Germany. *In* Culture and its creators p119-49

Colonies—Africa

Katzenellenbogen, S. E. British businessmen and German Africa, 1885-1919. *In* Great Britain and her world, 1750-1914 p237-62

Description and travel

Spender, S. Rhineland journey; excerpt from "European witness." *In* Spender, S. The thirties and after p102-18

Economic conditions

Lee, J. J. Aspects of urbanization and economic development in Germany, 1815-1914. *In* Towns in societies p279-93

Lundgreen, P. Educational expansion and economic growth in nineteenth-century Germany: a quantitative study. *In* Schooling and society p20-66

Emigration and immigration

Szajkowski, Z. East European Jewish workers in Germany during World War I. *In* Salo Wittmayer Baron v2 p887-918

Foreign relations—1918-1933

Binion, R. Hitler looks East. *In* DeMause, L. ed. The new psychohistory p181-98

Foreign relations—1933-1945—Historiography

Carr, W. National socialism: foreign policy and Wehrmacht. *In* Laqueur, W. Z. ed. Fascism: a reader's guide p151-78

Historiography

Krieger, L. Germany. *In* National consciousness, history, and political culture in early-modern Europe p67-97

Moses, J. A. Germany and the Cold war: historiographical consequences. *In* Siracusa, J. M. and Barclay, G. S. eds. The impact of the Cold war p64-83

History

Schoenberg, H. W. The partition of Germany and the neutralization of Austria. *In* Hammond, T. T. ed. The anatomy of Communist takeovers p368-84

History—Revolution, 1918

Angress, W. T. The takeover that remained in limbo: the German experience, 1918-1923. *In* Hammond, T. T. ed. The anatomy of Communist takeovers p163-91

Intellectual life—History

Bendix, R. Province and metropolis: the case of eighteenth-century Germany. *In* Culture and its creators p119-49

Berlin, Sir I. Hume and the sources of German anti-rationalism. *In* David Hume p93-116

Overfield, J. H. Scholastic opposition to humanism in pre-Reformation Germany. *In* Viator: medieval and Renaissance studies v7 p391-420

Ringer, F. K. The German academic community. *In* Oleson, A. and Voss, J. eds. The organization of knowledge in modern America, 1860-1920 p409-29

Tal, U. Young German intellectuals on romanticism and Judaism—spiritual turbulence in the early 19th century. *In* Salo Wittmayer Baron v2 p919-38

Intellectual life—19th century

Knights, B. Introduction. *In* Knights, B. The idea of the clerisy in the nineteenth century p 1-36

Germany—*Continued*

Nobility

McClelland, C. E. The aristocracy and university reform in eighteenth-century Germany. *In* Schooling and society p146-73

Stern, F. R. Prussia. *In* Spring, D. ed. European landed elites in the nineteenth century p45-67

Politics and government

Angermann, E. The impact of the American Revolution on Germany—a comment. *In* The Impact of the American Revolution abroad p160-63

Politics and government—1871-1918

Diehl, J. M. Germany: veterans' politics under three flags. *In* The War generation p135-86

Politics and government—1918-1933

Diehl, J. M. Germany: veterans' politics under three flags. *In* The War generation p135-86

Lepsius, M. R. From fragmented party democracy to government by emergency decree and National Socialist takeover: Germany. *In* The Breakdown of democratic regimes pt2 p34-79

Politics and government—1933-1945

Parry, A. Hitler's Holocaust. *In* Parry, A. Terrorism: from Robespierre to Arafat p203-10

Social conditions

Friedrichs, C. R. Capitalism, mobility and class formation in the early modern German city. *In* Towns in societies p187-213

Social conditions—To 1517

McNamara, J. A. and Wemple, S. F. Marriage and divorce in the Frankish kingdom. *In* Stuard, S. M. ed. Women in medieval society p95-124

Wehrmacht

Carr, W. National socialism: foreign policy and Wehrmacht. *In* Laqueur, W. Z. ed. Fascism: a reader's guide p151-78

Germany, Democratic Republic of. See Germany, East

Germany, East

Historiography

Moses, J. A. Germany and the Cold war: historiographical consequences. *In* Siracusa, J. M. and Barclay, G. S. eds. The impact of the Cold war p64-83

Germany, Eastern. See Germany, East

Germany, Federal Republic of. See Germany, West

Germany, West

Foreign relations—United States

Katzenstein, P. West Germany's place in American foreign policy: pivot, anchor, or broker? *In* Rosecrance, R. N. ed. America as an ordinary country p110-35

Historiography

Moses, J. A. Germany and the Cold war: historiographical consequences. *In* Siracusa, J. M. and Barclay, G. S. eds. The impact of the Cold war p64-83

Politics and government

Kuhn, H. Germany—divided once more. *In* Prospects for constitutional democracy p101-17

Germany, Western. See Germany, West

Germino, Dante L.

Eric Voegelin: the in-between of human life. *In* De Crespigny, A. and Minogue, K. R. eds. Contemporary political philosophers p100-19

Gernsheim, Helmut

Cuthbert Bede (The Rev. Edward Bradley, 1827-1889), Robert Hunt F.R.S. (1807-1887), and Thomas Sutton (1819-1875). *In* One hundred years of photographic history p59-67

Gerontology. See Aged; Aging; Old age

Gerrard, Nathan L.

The serpent-handling religions of West Virginia. *In* Henslin, J. M. ed. Deviant lifestyles p79-86

Gerrish, Brian Albert

De libero arbitrio (1524): Erasmus on piety, theology, and the Lutheran dogma. *In* Essays on the works of Erasmus p187-209

Gershenson, Mikhail Osipovich. See Gershenzon, Mikhail Osipovich

Gershenzon, Mikhail Osipovich

Creative self-cognition. *In* Landmarks p64-87

Influence—Bugaev

Levin, A. A. Andrey Bely, M. O. Gershenzon, and Vekhi: a rejoinder to N. Valentinov. *In* Janecek, G. ed. Andrey Bely p169-80

Gershenzon Mikhail Osipovich, and Ivanov, Viâcheslav Ivanovich

About individual works

Correspondence from two corners

Thomson, B. The problem of art. *In* Thomson, B. Lot's wife and the Venus of Milo p 5-28

Gershwin, George

About

Sheed, W. Rhapsodist in blue. *In* Sheed, W. The good word & other words p154-58

Gerson, Jean Charlier de. See Gerson, Joannes

Gerson, Joannes

About

Froehlich, K. "Always to keep the literal sense in Holy Scripture means to kill one's soul": the state of Biblical hermeneutics at the beginning of the fifteenth century. *In* Miner, E. R. ed. Literary uses of typology p20-48

Pascoe, L. B. Gerson and the Donation of Constantine: growth and development within the Church. *In* Viator: medieval and Renaissance studies v5 p469-85

Gerson, Louis L.

Ethnics in American politics. *In* Havard, W. C. and Bernd, J. L. eds. 200 years of the Republic in retrospect p336-46

Gerson, Noel B.

About individual works

Trelawny's world: a biography of Edward John Trelawny

Reiman, D. H. Trelawny and the decay of lying. *In* Review, v 1 1979 p275-94

Gersonides. See Levi ben Gershon

Gerstner, John H.

The theological boundaries of evangelical faith. *In* Wells, D. F. and Woodbridge, J. D. eds. The evangelicals p21-37

Gerstner, Patsy A.

The Academy of Natural Sciences of Philadelphia 1812-1850. *In* Oleson, A. and Brown, S. C. eds. The pursuit of knowledge in the early American Republic p174-93

Gertler, Mark

About individual works

Merry-go-round

Meyers, J. Mark Gertler and Women in love. *In* Meyers, J. Painting and the novel p65-82

Gervasi, Sean

The politics of "accelerated economic growth." *In* Thompson, L. M. and Butler, J. eds. Change in contemporary South Africa p349-68

Gervaud, Michel

Willa Cather and France: elective affinities. *In* The Art of Willa Cather p65-83

Gerz, Jochen

Towards a language of doing. *In* Federman, R. ed. Surfiction p279-81

Geschwender, James Arthur

On power and powerlessness: or with a little help from our friends. *In* Major social issues p439-54

Gessert, Robert A.

Deterrence and the defense of Europe. *In* Ethics and nuclear strategy? p92-112

A Gest of Robyn Hode

Bessinger, J. B. The Gest of Robin Hood revisited. *In* The Learned and the lewed p355-69

Gestalt psychology

Fancher, R. E. The sensing and perceiving mind: Kant, Helmholtz, and the Gestalt psychologists. *In* Fancher, R. E. Pioneers of psychology p87-125

Henle, M. On naive realism. *In* Perception p40-56

See also Whole and parts (Psychology)

Gesture. See Sign language

The getaway (Motion picture)

Kauffmann, S. The getaway. *In* Kauffmann, S. Living images p167-69

Gettino, Octavio. See Solanas, F. jt. auth.

Geusau, Frans A. M. Alting von. See Alting von Geusau, Frans A. M.

Gewirtz, Marian. See Armer, M. J. jt. auth.

Gey, George O.

About

Harvey, A. M. Johns Hopkins—the birthplace of tissue culture: the story of Ross G. Harrison, Warren H. Lewis, and George O. Gey. *In* Harvey, A. M. Adventures in medical research p114-23

Ghali, Boutros Boutros- See Boutros-Ghali, Boutros

Ghana

Economic policy

Dickson, K. B. Development planning and national integration in Ghana. *In* Smock, D. R. and Bentsi-Enchill, K. eds. The search for national integration in Africa p100-16

Foreign population

Peil, M. Host reactions: aliens in Ghana. *In* Shack, W. A. and Skinner, E. P. eds. Strangers in African societies p123-40

Sudarkasa, N. From stranger to alien: the sociopolitical history of the Nigerian Yoruba in Ghana, 1900-1970. *In* Shack, W. A. and Skinner, E. P. eds. Strangers in African societies p141-67

Foreign relations

Aluko, O. Ghana's foreign policy. *In* Aluko, O. ed. The foreign policies of African states p72-97

Industrial relations

See Industrial relations—Ghana

Languages

Smock, D. R. Language policy in Ghana. *In* Smock, D. R. and Bentsi-Enchill, K. eds. The search for national integration in Africa p169-88

Politics and government

Chazan, N. Nkrumaism: Ghana's experiment with African socialism. *In* Eisenstadt, S. N. and Azmon, Y. eds. Socialism and tradition p173-92

Crook, R. Political centralization and local politics in Ghana: the careers of Nana Wiafe Akenten II and E. K. Duncan-Williams of Offinso (Ashanti) *In* The Making of politicians: studies from Africa and Asia p28-48

Dunn, J. M. The eligible and the elect: Arminian thoughts on the social predestination of Ahafo leaders. *In* The Making of politicians: studies from Africa and Asia p49-65

Kilson, M. Cleavage management in African politics: the Ghana case. *In* Kilson, M. ed. New states in the modern world p75-88

Social conditions

Dickson, K. B. Development planning and national integration in Ghana. *In* Smock, D. R. and Bentsi-Enchill, K. eds. The search for national integration in Africa p100-16

Nukunya, G. K. The family and social change. *In* Colonialism and change p163-77

Schildkrout, E. The ideology of regionalism in Ghana. *In* Shack, W. A. and Skinner, E. P. eds. Strangers in African societies p183-207

Ghazali. See al-Ghazzālī

Gheorghiu, Constantin Virgil

About individual works

The twenty-fifth hour

Trilling, L. A novel in passing. *In* Trilling, L. A gathering of fugitives p85-90

Ghettos. See Afro-Americans—Segregation

Ghibellines. See Guelfs and Ghibellines

Ghirlandaio, Domenico

About

Meyers, J. Ghirlandaio and Where angels fear to tread; Giotto and A room with a view. *In* Meyers, J. Painting and the novel p31-45

Ghose, Aurobindo

About

Diwakar, R. R. Aurobindo. *In* Bishop, D. H. ed. Indian thought p324-36

Ghost dance

Mooney, J. The doctrine of the Ghost dance; excerpt from "The ghost-dance religion and the Sioux outbreak of 1890." *In* Tedlock, D. E. and Tedlock, B. eds. Teachings from the American earth p75-95

Ghost stories, English
History and criticism
Briggs, J. Ancestral voices: the ghost story from Lucian to Le Fanu. *In* Briggs, J. Night visitors p25-51

Briggs, J. Diabolism and decadence: the mood of the nineties. *In* Briggs, J. Night visitors p76-97

Briggs, J. Ghosts troop home: the Great War and its aftermath. *In* Briggs, J. Night visitors p165-81

Briggs, J. Introduction. *In* Briggs, J. Night visitors p11-24

Briggs, J. Not without but within: the psychological ghost story. *In* Briggs, J. Night visitors p142-64

Sullivan, J. The antiquarian ghost story: Montague Rhodes James. *In* Sullivan, J. Elegant nightmares p69-90

Sullivan, J. Beginnings: Sheridan Le Fanu. *In* Sullivan, J. Elegant nightmares p32-68

Sullivan, J. Conclusion: ghost stories as enigmas. *In* Sullivan, J. Elegant nightmares p130-35

Sullivan, J. Ghost stories of other antiquaries. *In* Sullivan, J. Elegant nightmares p91-111

Sullivan, J. "Green tea": the archetypal ghost story. *In* Sullivan, J. Elegant nightmares p11-31

Sullivan, J. Introduction. *In* Sullivan, J. Elegant nightmares p 1-10

Sullivan, J. The visionary ghost story: Algernon Blackwood. *In* Sullivan, J. Elegant nightmares p112-29

Ghosts. See Mediums

Ghosts in literature
Briggs, J. Epilogue: Ghosts and poets. *In* Briggs, J. Night visitors p196-212

Ghotan, Bartholomäus
About
Miller, D. B. The Lübeckers Bartholomäus Ghotan and Nicolaus Bülow in Novgorod and Moscow and the problem of early Western influences on Russian culture. *In* Viator: medieval and Renaissance studies v9 p395-412

Ghothan, Bartholomäus. See Ghotan, Bartholomäus

Giacometti, Alberto
About
Rosenberg, H. Giacometti: reality at cockcrow. *In* Rosenberg, H. Art on the edge p120-31

Giacosa, Giuseppe
About
Lawton, B. Giuseppe Giacosa and Giacomo Puccini. *In* Abroad in America: Visitors to the new Nation, 1776-1914 p247-59

Giamatti, A. Bartlett
Headlong horses, headless horsemen: an essay on the chivalric epics of Pulci, Boiardo, and Ariosto. *In* Italian literature: roots and branches p265-307

Primitivism and the process of civility in Spenser's Faerie Queene. *In* First images of America p71-82

Giampietrino. See Pedrini, Giovanni

Giannotti, Donato
About
Gordon, D. J. Giannotti, Michelangelo and the cult of Brutus. *In* Gordon, D. J. The Renaissance imagination p233-45

Giarrizzo, Giuseppe
Toward the Decline and fall: Gibbon's other historical interests. *In* Edward Gibbon and The decline and fall of the Roman Empire p233-46

Gibbon, Constantine Fitz. See Fitz Gibbon, Constantine

Gibbon, Edward
About
Brownley, M. W. Gibbon: the formation of mind and character. *In* Edward Gibbon and The decline and fall of the Roman Empire p13-25

Giarrizzo, G. Toward the Decline and fall: Gibbon's other historical interests. *In* Edward Gibbon and The decline and fall of the Roman Empire p233-46

Jordan, D. P. Edward Gibbon: the historian of the Roman Empire. *In* Edward Gibbon and The decline and fall of the Roman Empire p 1-12

Manuel, F. E. Edward Gibbon: historien-philosophe. *In* Edward Gibbon and The decline and fall of the Roman Empire p167-81

About individual works
The autobiographies of Edward Gibbon
Spacks, P. A. M. The defenses of form: Edward Gibbon. *In* Spacks, P. A. M. Imagining a self p92-126

The decline and fall of the Roman Empire
Bowersock, G. W. Gibbon on civil war and rebellion in The decline of the Roman Empire. *In* Edward Gibbon and The decline and fall of the Roman Empire p27-35

Brower, R. A. With Gibbon in Puerto Rico. *In* Edward Gibbon and The decline and fall of the Roman Empire p247-49

Brown, P. D. Gibbon's views on culture and society in the fifth and sixth centuries. *In* Edward Gibbon and The decline and fall of the Roman Empire p37-52

Burke, P. Tradition and experience: the idea of decline from Bruni to Gibbon. *In* Edward Gibbon and The decline and fall of the Roman Empire p87-102

Chadwick, O. Gibbon and the church historians. *In* Edward Gibbon and The decline and fall of the Roman Empire p219-31

Clive, J. Gibbon's humor. *In* Edward Gibbon and The decline and fall of the Roman Empire p183-91

Furet, F. Civilization and barbarism in Gibbon's history. *In* Edward Gibbon and The decline and fall of the Roman Empire p159-66

Graubard, S. R. Edward Gibbon: contraria sunt complementa. *In* Edward Gibbon and The decline and fall of the Roman Empire p121-37

Jordan, D. P. Edward Gibbon: the historian of the Roman Empire. *In* Edward Gibbon and The decline and fall of the Roman Empire p 1-12

Lewis, B. Gibbon on Muhammad. *In* Edward Gibbon and The decline and fall of the Roman Empire p61-73

Manuel, F. E. Edward Gibbon: historien-philosophe. *In* Edward Gibbon and The decline and fall of the Roman Empire p167-81

Momigliano, A. Gibbon from an Italian point of view. *In* Edward Gibbon and The decline and fall of the Roman Empire p75-85

Gibbon, Edward—About—Continued

Pocock, J. G. A. Between Machiavelli and Hume: Gibbon as civic humanist and philosophical historian. *In* Edward Gibbon and The decline and fall of the Roman Empire p103-19

Shackleton, R. The impact of French literature on Gibbon. *In* Edward Gibbon and The decline and fall of the Roman Empire p207-18

The decline and fall of the Roman Empire (chapter 48)

Runciman, Sir S. Gibbon and Byzantium. *In* Edward Gibbon and The decline and fall of the Roman Empire p53-60

An essay on the study of literature

Starobinski, J. From the decline of erudition to the decline of nations: Gibbon's response to French thought. *In* Edward Gibbon and The decline and fall of the Roman Empire p139-57

Extrait raisenné on Hurd's Commentaries on Horace's Epistles

Trowbridge, F. H. Edward Gibbon, literary critic. *In* Trowbridge, F. H. From Dryden to Jane Austen p185-99

Appreciation—Italy

Momigliano, A. Gibbon from an Italian point of view. *In* Edward Gibbon and The decline and fall of the Roman Empire p75-85

Influence

Haskell, F. Gibbon and the history of art. *In* Edward Gibbon and The decline and fall of the Roman Empire p193-205

Gibbon, Lewis Grassic, pseud. See Mitchell, James Leslie

Gibbons, Brian, and Harris, Bernard
English drama 1550-1660, excluding Shakespeare. *In* English Association. The year's work in English studies v53 p193-206

English drama, 1500-1660, excluding Shakespeare [another essay]. *In* English Association. The year's work in English studies v54 p185-99

English drama 1550-1600: excluding Shakespeare [another essay]. English Association. The year's work in English studies v57 p146-53

See also Harris, B. jt. auth.

Gibbs, James
The origins of A dance of the forests. *In* African literature today no. 8: Drama in Africa p66-71

Gibbs, Sharon L.
The first scientific instruments. *In* Brecher, K. and Feirtag, M. eds. Astronomy of the ancients p39-50

Gibbs-Smith, Charles Harvard
Mrs Julia Margaret Cameron, Victorian photographer. *In* One hundred years of photographic history p69-76

Gibraltar

Description and travel

Spender, S. Tangiers and Gibraltar now. *In* Spender, S. The thirties and after p43-46

History

Lewis, A. R. Northern European sea power and the Straits of Gibraltar, 1031-1350 A.D. *In* Order and innovation in the Middle Ages p139-64

Gibson, Ian

About individual works
The death of Lorca

Connolly, C. Lorca. *In* Connolly, C. The evening colonnade p320-23

Gibson, James Jerome
The perceiving of hidden surfaces. *In* Studies in perception p422-34
See also Part 2 under title: Perception

About

Machamer, P. K. Gibson and the conditions for perception. *In* Studies in perception p435-66

About individual works
A theory of visual perception

Roupas, T. G. Information and pictorial representation. *In* Perkins, D. and Leonder, B. eds. The arts and cognition p48-79

Gibson, James R.
Old Russia in the New World: adversaries and adversities in Russian America. *In* European settlement and development in North America: essays on geographical change in honour and memory of Andrew Hill Clark p46-65

Gibson, Margaret
The continuity of learning, circa 850-circa 1050. *In* Viator: medieval and Renaissance studies v6 p 1-13

Gibson, Margaret Brenman-. See Brenman-Gibson, Margaret

Giddens, Anthony
Hermeneutics, ethnomethodology, and problems of interpretative analysis. *In* The Uses of controversy in sociology p315-28

Giddis, Diane
The divided woman: Bree Daniels in Klute. *In* Nichols, B. ed. Movies and methods p194-201

Gide, André Paul Guillaume

About

Connolly, C. Memories of Gide. *In* Connolly, C. The evening colonnade p304-05

Glicksberg, C. I. Gide and the rationale of commitment. *In* Glicksberg, C. I. The literature of commitment p197-207

Jay, K. Male homosexuality and lesbianism in the works of Proust and Gide. *In* Crew, L. ed. The gay academic p216-43

Peyre, H. French literary imagination and Dostoevsky. *In* Peyre, H. French literary imagination and Dostoevsky, and other essays p 1-56

Shepard, L. A. The development of Gide's concept of personality. *In* Garvin, H. R. ed. Makers of the twentieth-century novel p118-32

About individual works
The immoralist

Meyers, J. Gide: The immoralist. *In* Meyers, J. Homosexuality and literature, 1890-1930 p32-41

Lafcadio's adventures

Alter, R. The modernist revival of self-conscious fiction. *In* Alter, R. Partial magic p138-79

Self-portraits, the Gide/Valéry letters, 1890-1942

Connolly, C. The Gide-Valéry letters. *In* Connolly, C. The evening colonnade p300-03

Gide, André P. G.—*Continued*

Characters

Shepard, L. A. The development of Gide's concept of personality. *In* Garvin, H. R. ed. Makers of the twentieth-century novel p118-32

Sources

Peyre, H. Gide and literary influences. *In* Peyre, H. French literary imagination and Dostoevsky, and other essays p93-114

Giele, Janet Zollinger
Introduction: The status of women in comparative perspective. *In* Giele, J. Z. and Smock, A. C. eds. Women: roles and status in eight countries p 1-31

United States: a prolonged search for equal rights. *In* Giele, J. Z. and Smock, A. C. eds. Women: roles and status in eight countries p301-45

Giergielewicz, Mieczysław
Priests and exorcists in Mickiewicz's Forefathers. *In* For Wiktor Weintraub p135-50

Gieryn, Thomas F.
Problem retention and problem change in science. *In* Gaston, J. ed. Sociology of science p96-115

Gifford, James C.
Recent thought concerning the interpretation of Maya prehistory. *In* Mesoamerican archaeology p77-98

Gifted children. See Children as artists

Gigantomachy, Poseidon in the. Moore, M. B. *In* Studies in classical art and archaeology p23-27

Gilbert, Felix
Bicentennial reflections. *In* Two hundred years of American foreign policy p 1-19

History

Contents

Bernardo Rucellai and the Orti Oricellari: a study on the origin of modern political thought
Ciano and his ambassadors
The composition and structure of Machiavelli's Discorsi
Friedrich Meinecke
From art history to the history of civilization: Aby Warburg
From political to social history: Lorenz von Stein and the Revolution of 1848
The historian as guardian of national consciousness: Italy between Guicciardini and Muratori
Same as: Gilbert, F. Italy. *In* National consciousness, history and political culture in early modern Europe p21-42
History and philology: Politian
The humanist concept of the prince and The prince of Machiavelli
Johann Gustav Droysen
Machiavelli's Istorie Fiorentine: an essay in interpretation
Machiavellism
The "new dipomacy" of the eighteenth century
Otto Hintze
Reflections on the history of the professor of history
Religion and politics in the thought of Gasparo Contarini

The Venetian constitution in Florentine political thought
Venetian diplomacy before Pavia: from reality to myth
Venice in the crisis of the League of Cambrai

Italy. *In* National consciousness, history, and political culture in early modern Europe p21-42
Same as: Gilbert, F. The historian as guardian of national consciousness: Italy between **Guicciardini and Muratori.** *In* Gilbert, F. History

The last will of a Venetian Grand Chancellor. *In* Philosophy and humanism p502-17

Gilbert, Michael Francis
A very English lady. *In* Agatha Christie: first lady of crime p49-78

Gilbert, Neal Ward
A letter of Giovanni Dondi dall'Orologio to Fra'Guglielmo Centueri: a fourteenth-century episode in the Quarrel of the Ancients and the Moderns. *In* Viator: medieval and Renaissance studies v8 p299-346
Richard de Bury and the "quires of yesterday's sophisms." *In* Philosophy and humanism p229-57

Gilbert, Sandra M.
A fine, white flying myth: the life/work of Sylvia Plath. *In* Gilbert, S. M. and Gubar, S. eds. Shakespeare's sisters p245-60

Gilbert, Sandra M. and Gubar, Susan
Introduction: gender, creativity, and the woman poet. *In* Gilbert, S. M. and Gubar, S. eds. Shakespeare's sisters pxv-xxvi

The madwoman in the attic

Contents

The aesthetics of renunciation
The buried life of Lucy Snowe
A dialogue of self and soul: plain Jane's progress
The genesis of hunger according to Shirley
George Eliot as the Angel of Destruction
Horror's twin: Mary Shelley's monstrous Eve
Infection in the sentence: the woman writer and the anxiety of authorship
Jane Austen's cover story (and its secret agents)
Looking oppositely: Emily Brontë's Bible of Hell
Made keen by loss: George Eliot's veiled vision
Milton's bogey: patriarchal poetry and women readers
The parables of the cave
The queen's looking glass: female creativity, male images of women, and the metaphor of literary paternity
A secret, inward wound: The professor's pupil
Shut up in prose: gender and genre in Austen's juvenilia
A woman—white: Emily Dickinson's yarn of pearl

Gilbert, called the Universal, Bp. of London. See Foliot, Gilbert, Bp. of London

Gilbert Foliot, Bp. of London. See Foliot, Gilbert, Bp. of London

Gilchrist, T. Caspar

About

Harvey, A. M. Two mycoses first described at Johns Hopkins. *In* Harvey, A. M. Adventures in medical research p32-38

Gild socialism. See Corporate state

Gilds

Great Britain
Thrupp, S. L. Medieval gilds reconsidered. *In* Thrupp, S. L. Society and history p226-36

See also subdivision Gilds under names of cities, e.g. Genoa—Gilds

Gildzen, Alex
A celebration of Howard Vincent. *In* Artful thunder p9-10

Gilfillan, Archer Butler

About
Dobie, J. F. Foreword to "Sheep, life on the South Dakota range," by Archer B. Gilfillan. *In* Dobie, J. F. Prefaces p124-30

Gilges, W.
Some African poison plants and medicines of Northern Rhodesia. *In* The Occasional papers of the Rhodes-Livingstone Museum p389-426

Gilinsky, Victor
Fuelling the Western world's reactors: problems and issues. *In* International terrorism and world security p140-57

Gilkey, Langdon Brown
The future of science. *In* The Future of science p105-28

Reinhold Niebuhr's theology of history. *In* Scott, N. A. ed. The legacy of Reinhold Niebuhr p36-62

The structure of academic revolutions. *In* The Nature of scientific discovery p462-67

Toward a religious criterion of religion. *In* Needleman, J. and Baker, G. eds. Understanding the new religions p131-37

Gill, Brendan

About individual works
Ways of loving
Balakian, N. Where the center always holds: stories by Brendan Gill. *In* Balakian, N. Critical encounters p149-52

Gill, David
Birds 593-595: a note. *In* Harvard Studies in classical philology v79 p69-72

Gill, Gerald R.
"Win or lose—we win": the 1952 Vice Presidential campaign of Charlotta A. Bass. *In* Harley, S. and Terborg-Penn, R. eds. The Afro-American woman p109-18

Gill, James E.
Discovery and alienation, nature and reason in Gulliver's Travels, Parts I-III. *In* Tennessee Studies in literature v22 p85-104

Man and Yahoo: dialectic and symbolism in Gulliver's "Voyage to the country of the Houyhnhnms." *In* The Dress of words p67-90

Gill, Linda. See Stokstad, M. jt. auth.

Gill, R. B.
The Renaissance conventions of envy. *In* Medievalia et humanistica; new ser. no. 9 p215-30

Gill, Sam D.
The shadow of a vision yonder. *In* Seeing with a native eye p44-57

Gillberg, Björn O.
Chemically induced genetic damage. *In* Against pollution and hunger p213-14

Gilles, Herbert Michael
The ecology of disease in the tropics. *In* Cahill, K. M. ed. Health and development p49-58

Gilliam, J. F.
Some Roman elements in Roman Egypt. *In* Illinois classical studies v3, 1978 p115-31

Gilliatt, Penelope
Langdon; excerpt from "Unholy fools." *In* Denby, D. ed. Awake in the dark p356-61

Gillie, Christopher
Movements in English literature, 1900-1940

Contents
The critical decade, 1930-1940
D. H. Lawrence (1885-1930)
Diversification of the novel, 1920-1930
Drama, 1900-1940
The early twentieth-century novel: James, Wells and Conrad
Introduction: The world of art and art in the world: twentieth-century differences
The recovery of poetry, 1900-1920
Yeats and Eliot: the climax

Gilligan, Carol Friedman
Sexual dilemmas at the high-school level. *In* Sexuality and human values p98-110

Gillis, Donald C.
The Persephone myth in Mandelstam's Tristia. *In* California Slavic studies v9 p139-59

Gillispie, Charles Coulston
The liberating influence of science in history. *In* Aspects of American liberty p37-46

Gilliver, Lawton

About
McLaverty, J. Lawton Gilliver: Pope's bookseller. *In* Virginia. University. Bibliographical Society. Studies in bibliography v32 p101-24

Gillon, Adam
Conrad's reception in Poland for the last sixty years. *In* Joseph Conrad: a commemoration p206-18

Gilman, Ernest B.
The curious perspective

Contents
The Albertian perspective and the curious perspective
Conclusion: the witness as rational amphibian
The curious perspective in England
Marvell's perspectives of the mind
The "natural perspective" of Shakespearean comedy: Twelfth night and A midsummer night's dream
The Pauline perspectives in Donne, Herbert, and Greville
Richard II and the perspectives of history
Also in Renaissance drama [1976] p85-115
Tesauro on visual and verbal wit

Gilman, Sander L.
Parody and parallel: Heine, Nietzsche, and the classical world. *In* O'Flaherty, J. C.; Sellner, T. F. and Helm, R. M. eds. Studies in Nietzsche and the classical tradition p199-213

Gilman, Stephen
Literature and historical insight. *In* Américo Castro and the meaning of Spanish civilization p317-24

Gilmore, Al-Tony
The Black Southerner's response to the Southern system of race relations: 1900 to post—World War II. *In* The Age of segregation: race relations in the South, 1890-1945 p67-88

Gilmore, Michael T.
Eulogy as symbolic biography: the iconography of revolutionary leadership, 1776-1826. *In* Studies in biography p131-57

Gilmore, Myron Piper
Apologiae: Erasmus's defenses of Folly. *In* Essays on the works of Erasmus p111-23
The New World in French and English historians of the sixteenth century. *In* First images of America p519-27

Gilmore, Tom
The South is rising again—in living colors. *In* The Rising South v 1 p50-58

Gilpin, Robert G.
Economic interdependence and national security in historical perspective. *In* Knorr, K. E. and Trager, F. N. eds. Economic issues and national security p19-66
The multinational corporation and American foreign policy. *In* Rosecrance, R. N. ed. America as an ordinary country p174-98
Science, technology, and French independence. *In* Science policies of industrial nations p110-32

Gindin, James
Ethical structures in John Galsworthy, Elizabeth Bowen, and Iris Murdoch. *In* Forms of modern British fiction p15-41

Giner, Salvador
Power, freedom and social change in the Spanish university, 1939-75. *In* Preston, P. ed. Spain in crisis p183-211

The **gingerbread** lady (criticism) Simon, N. *In* Kauffmann, S. Persons of the drama p190-93

Gingerich, Owen J.
The basic astronomy of Stonehenge. *In* Brecher, K. and Feirtag, M. eds. Astronomy of the ancients p117-32
Commentary: remarks on Copernicus' observations. *In* The Copernican achievement p99-107
Dissertatio cum Professore Righini et Sidereo nuncio. *In* Bonelli, M. L. R. and Shea, W. R. eds. Reason, experiment, and mysticism in the scientific revolution p77-88
Introduction: Does science have a future? *In* The Nature of scientific discovery p237-45
The sun. *In* Man and cosmos p37-47

Ginsberg, Allen
About
Heffernan, J. A. W. Politics and freedom: refractions of Blake in Joyce Cary and Allen Ginsberg. *In* Bornstein, G. ed. Romantic and modern p177-95
Simpson, L. "The eye altering alters all." *In* Simpson, L. A revolution in taste p43-82
Thurley, G. Allen Ginsberg: the whole man in. *In* Thurley, G. The American moment p172-86

About individual works
The fall of America
Miller, J. E. Dreaming of the lost America of love: Allen Ginsberg's "Fall of America." *In* Miller, J. E. The American quest for a supreme fiction p276-316

Ginsberg, Elaine K.
The patriot pamphleteers. *In* Emerson, E. H. ed. American literature, 1764-1789 p19-38

Ginsberg, Leon H.
The institutionalized mentally disabled, *In* Gochros, H. L. and Gochros, J. S. eds. The sexually oppressed p215-24

Ginsburg, Ruth Bader
Gender in the Supreme Court: the 1973 and 1974 terms. *In* The Supreme Court review, 1975 p 1-24
Realizing the equality principle. *In* Social justice & preferential treatment p135-53

Ginsburg, Sigmund G.
Management for the future: a prognosis and prescription with specific concern for university and governmental management. *In* Benton, L. R. ed. Management for the future p109-24

Gintis, Herbert M. and Bowles, Samuel
The contradictions of liberal educational reform. *In* Feinberg, W. and Rosemont, H. eds. Work, technology, and education p92-141

Ginzberg, Eli
Health services, power centers, and decision-making mechanisms. *In* Knowles, J. H. ed. Doing better and feeling worse p203-13
Jew and Negro: notes on the mobility of two minority groups in the United States. *In* Salo Wittmayer Baron v 1 p491-501
Manpower planning in a pluralist economy. *In* Planning, politics, and the public interest p28-37

Ginzburg, Lidiíâ Sakovlevich
The poetics of Osip Mandelstam. *In* Er-lich, V. ed. Twentieth-century Russian literary criticism p284-312

Ginzburg, Lidija. See Ginzburg, Lidiíâ Sakovlevich

Giono, Jean
About individual works
To the slaughterhouse
Redfern, W. D. Against nature: Jean Giono and Le grand troupeau. *In* Klein, H. M. ed. The First World War in fiction p73-83

Giorgione, Giorgio Barbarelli, known as
About
Sheard, W. S. The Widener Orpheus: attribution, type, invention. *In* Collaboration in Italian Renaissance art p189-231

Giotto di Bondone
About
Miller, J. W. A meditation on a painting. *In* Miller, J. W. The paradox of cause, and other essays p169-73
About individual works
The ascension of St John the Evangelist
Meyers, J. Ghirlandaio and Where angels fear to tread; Giotto and A room with a view. *In* Meyers, J. Painting and the novel p31-45
Charity
Meyers, J. Bellini, Giotto, Mantegna, Botticelli and Swann's way. *In* Meyers, J. Painting and the novel p96-111

Giovanni di Bonandrea
About
Banker, J. R. The ars dictaminis and rhetorical textbooks at the Bolognese University in the fourteenth century. *In* Medievalia et humanistica no. 5 p153-68
Giovanni of Fiesole. See Fiesole, Giovanni da, called Fra Angelico

Gippenreiter, Yu. B. and Romanov, V. Ya.
A method of investigation of the internal form of visual activity. *In* Perception p227-49

Gippius, Vasiliĭ Vasil'evich
The Inspector General: structure and problems. *In* Maguire, R. A. ed. Gogol from the twentieth century p215-65

Gippius, Vasily. See Gippius, Vasiliĭ Vasil'evich

Gipson, Lawrence Henry

About

Shy, J. W. The Empire remembered: Lawrence Gipson, historian. *In* Shy, J. W. A people numerous and armed p109-31

Giraldi Cintio, Giovanni Battista

About individual works
Hecatommithi (Dec. V, Nov. VI)

Bullough, G. Another analogue of Measure for measure. *In* English Renaissance drama p108-17

Giraldus Cambrensis

About

Hunt, R. W. The preface to the "Speculum ecclesiae" of Giraldus Cambrensis. *In* Viator: medieval and Renaissance studies v8 p189-213

Girard, René
Differentiation and undifferentiation in Lévi-Strauss and current critical theory. *In* Krieger, M. and Dembo, L. S. eds. Directions for criticism p111-36
Same as: Girard, R. Differentiation and reciprocity in Lévi-Strauss and contemporary theory. *In* Girard, R. "To double business bound"
Myth and identity crisis in A midsummer night's dream. *In* The Frontiers of literary criticism p121-48
Narcissism: the Freudian myth demythified by Proust. *In* Roland, A. ed. Psychoanalysis, creativity, and literature p293-311

"To double business bound"

Contents

Camus's Stranger retried
Delirium as system
Differentiation and reciprocity in Lévi-Strauss and contemporary theory
Same as: Girard, R. Differentiation and undifferentiation in Lévi-Strauss and current critical theory. *In* Krieger, M. and Dumbo, L. S. eds. Directions for criticism p 11-36
The mimetic desire of Paolo and Francesca
Perilous balance: A comic hypothesis
The plague in literature and myth
Strategies of madness—Nietzsche, Wagner, and Dostoevski
The underground critic
Violence and representation in the mythical text

Giraudoux, Jean

About individual works
Electra

Falk, E. H. Some concepts of the tragic in versions of Electra. *In* Creative encounter p3-16
Lenson, D. R. Classical analogy: Giraudoux versus Faulkner. *In* Lenson, D. R. Achilles' choice p98-116

Girls

Education
See Education of women

Societies and clubs
See Gangs

Girod, Roger
Contemporary sociology in Switzerland. *In* Mohan, R. P. and Martindale, D. A. eds. Handbook of contemporary developments in world sociology p59-68

Gironella, José María

About individual works
The cypresses believe in God

Schwartz, R. Gironella and Los cipreses creen en Dios (The cypresses believe in God) (1953). *In* Schwartz, R. Spain's New Wave novelists, 1950-1954 p50-65

Girvan, Norman
Economic nationalism. *In* Vernon, R. ed. The oil crisis p145-58

Girvetz, Harry K.
An anatomy of violence. *In* Stanage, S. M. ed. Reason and violence p183-204

Gismond of Salern in love
Stilling, R. Gismond of Salern: in love. *In* Stilling, R. Love and death in Renaissance tragedy p11-25

Gissing, George Robert

About

Cockshut, A. O. J. The pessimists: George Gissing. *In* Cockshut, A. O. J. Man and woman: a study of love and the novel, 1740-1940 p131-35
Korg, J. George Gissing: humanist in exile. *In* Levine, R. A. The Victorian experience: the novelists p239-73
Skilton, D. Late-Victorian choices: James, Wilde, Gissing and Moore. *In* Skilton, D. The English novel p178-91

About individual works
New Grub Street

Buckley, J. H. A world of literature: Gissing's New Grub Street. *In* The Worlds of Victorian fiction p223-34
Colmer, J. Continuity and change. *In* Colmer, J. Coleridge to Catch-22 p122-38

The odd women

Auerbach, N. Beyond the self: the spectacle of history and a new religion. *In* Auerbach, N. Communities of women p115-57
Colmer, J. Sex, the family and the new women. *In* Colmer, J. Coleridge to Catch-22 p105-21
Kennard, J. E. Her transitory self. *In* Kennard, J. E. Victims of convention p136-57

The private papers of Henry Ryecroft

Fleishman, A. Personal myth: three Victorian autobiographers. *In* Landow, G. P. ed. Approaches to Victorian autobiography p215-34

Gitelman, Zvi Y.
The diffusion of political innovation: from East Europe to the Soviet Union. *In* Szporluk, R. ed. The influence of East Europe and the Soviet West on the USSR p11-67

Gitksan Indians. See Kitgsan Indians

Gitter, Lena L.
Montessori and the compulsive cleanliness of severely retarded children. *In* Ulman, E. and Dachinger, P. eds. Art therapy p181-90

Gittings, Barbara
Combatting the lies in the libraries. *In* Crew, L. ed. The gay academic p107-18

Glasser, Marc D.

Marriage and The second nun's tale. *In* Tennessee Studies in literature v23 p 1-14

Glassow, Michael Arthur

Population aggregation and systemic change: examples from the American Southwest. *In* Explanation of pre-historic change p185-214

Glassware

United States

Palmer, A. M. Through the glass case: the curator and the object. *In* Material culture and the study of American life p219-44

Glazer, Nathan

The emergence of an American ethnic pattern; excerpt from "Affirmative discrimination: ethnic inequality and public policy." *In* Gross, B. R. ed. Reverse discrimination p132-55

From Ruth Benedict to Herman Kahn: the post-war Japanese image in the American mind. *In* Iriye, A. ed. Mutual images p138-68

Individual rights against group rights. *In* Human rights p87-103

Individualism and equality in the United States. *In* On the making of Americans p127-42

Introduction: The business of the future. *In* The Third century p7-21

The Jews. *In* Ethnic leadership in America p19-35

Public education and American pluralism. *In* Parents, teachers, and children: prospects for choice in American education p85-109

The social sciences in liberal education. *In* Hook, S.; Kurtz, P. W. and Todorovich, M. eds. The philosophy of the curriculum: the need for general education p145-58

Glazes

Megaw, A. H. S. An early thirteenth-century Aegean glazed ware. *In* Studies in memory of David Talbot Rice p34-45

Glazing (Ceramics) See Glazes

Gleason, Abbott

Pavel Svin'in. *In* Abroad in America: Visitors to the new Nation, 1776-1914 p12-21

Gleason, Henry Allan

Linguistics and philology. *In* On language, culture, and religion: in honor of Eugene A. Nida p199-212

Gleazer, Edmund John

The promise of lifelong learning. *In* The Third century p127-34

Gleckner, Robert Francis

Most holy forms of thought: some observations on Blake and language. *In* ELH essays for Earl R. Wasserman p262-84

Glen, Heather

Blake's criticism of moral thinking in Songs of innocence and of experience. *In* Phillips, M. C. ed. Interpreting Blake p32-69

Glennon, Robert J. and Nowak, John E.

A functional analysis of the Fourteenth Amendment "state action" requirement. *In* The Supreme Court review, 1976 p221-61

Glenny, Michael

The Soviet theatre. *In* Auty, R. and Obolensky, D. eds. An introduction to Russian language and literature p271-85

Glick, Wendell

Emerson, Thoreau, and transcendantalism. *In* American literary scholarship, 1976 p5-14

Emerson, Thoreau, and transcendentalism [another essay]. *In* American literary scholarship, 1977 p3-16

Glickman, Jack

Creativity in the arts. *In* Aagaard-Mogensen, L. ed. Culture and art p130-46

Also in Margolis, J. Z. ed. Philosophy looks at the arts p145-68

Glickman, Rose L.

The Russian factory woman, 1880-1914. *In* Women in Russia p63-83

Glicksberg, Charles Irving

The literature of commitment

Contents

Albert Camus: art versus politics
André Malraux: tragic humanism and the political imperative
Artaud and metaphysical madness
Arthur Koestler and the Revolution betrayed
Bertolt Brecht: the prophet of commitment
Commitment, coercion, and conformity
Conclusion
The countercommitment in Céline
Dada: to hell with culture and art
Ezra Pound and the commitment of fascism
From surrealism to communism
George Orwell and the morality of politics
Gide and the rationale of commitment
Jean-Paul Sartre: from existentialism to communism
Literature and social responsibility
Mayakovsky: the suicide of a committed poet
The moral protest of Solzhenitsyn
The mystique of commitment
Poetry and radicalism in England
The politics of madness
The politics of the Absurd
The unpolitical writer
Wyndham Lewis: the reactionary artist and his commitment

The literature of nihilism

Contents

Albert Camus: from nihilism to revolt
The battle against the Absurd in France
Conclusion
Franz Kafka: the prophet of the Absurd
Henry de Montherlant: hedonism and the Absurd
Ionesco and the comedy of the Absurd
Kazantzakis: Dionysian nihilism
Malraux: the riposte of conscience
Nihilism and suicide
Nihilism in the Russian soul
Religion and nihilism
Samuel Beckett: the cosmic nihilist
Sartre: from Nausea to communism
Unamuno and the quest for faith
The universe of the Absurd
Various aspects of modern nihilism

The world of Kenneth Patchen. *In* Morgan, R. G. ed. Kenneth Patchen: a collection of essays p181-92

Glickstein, Howard Alan. See Todorovich, M. jt. auth.

Glide Memorial Church

Wolfe, J. Three congregations. *In* The New religious consciousness p227-44

Glisson, Francis

About

Temkin, O. The classical roots of Glisson's doctrine of irritation. *In* Temkin, O. The double face of Janus p290-316

Globe Theatre, Southwark, England
Carson, N. The staircases of the frame: new light on the structure of the Globe? *In* Shakespeare survey v29 p127-32

Glock, Charles Y.
Consciousness among contemporary youth: an interpretation. *In* The New religious consciousness p353-66

Glossolalia. See Pentecostalism

Glossop, Ronald John
Hume, Stevenson, and Hare on moral language. *In* Livingston, D. W. and King, J. T. eds. Hume p362-85

Glover, Jonathan
Assessing the value of saving lives. *In* Royal Institute of Philosophy. Human values p208-27

Gluck, Christoph Willibald, Ritter von
Isherwood, R. M. The third war of the musical Enlightenment. *In* Studies in eighteenth-century culture v4 p223-45

Gluckman, Max
New dimensions of change, conflict and settlement. *In* United Nations Educational, Scientific and Cultural Organization. Race, science and society p319-40

Glyptics. See Intaglios; Plaques, plaquettes; Seals (Numismatics)

Gneuss, Helmut
Latin hymns in medieval England: future research. *In* Chaucer and Middle English studies in honour of Rossell Hope Robbins p407-24

Gnomes (Maxims) See Proverbs

Gnomic poetry, Anglo-Saxon

History and criticism
Burlin, R. B. Gnomic indirection in Beowulf. *In* Anglo-Saxon poetry: essays in appreciation p41-49
Greenfield, S. B. and Evert, R. Maxims II: gnome and poem. *In* Anglo-Saxon poetry: essays in appreciation p337-54

Gnosticism
Bloom, H. Yeats, Gnosticism, and the sacred void. *In* Bloom, H. Poetry and repression p205-34
Hassan, I. H. The new Gnosticism: speculations on an aspect of the postmodern mind. *In* Hassan, I. H. Paracriticisms p121-47

Gnosticism in literature
Bloom, H. Yeats, Gnosticism, and the sacred void. *In* Bloom, H. Poetry and repression p205-34

The go-between (Motion picture)
Kauffmann, S. The go-between. *In* Kauffmann, S. Living images p69-71

Go Gien Tjwan
The changing trade position of the Chinese in South-East Asia. *In* United Nations Educational, Scientific and Cultural Organization. Race, science and society p301-16

Goats (in religion, folklore, etc.)
Berger, A. Ayalta: from the doe in the field to the mother of the messiahs. *In* Salo Wittmayer Baron v 1 p209-17

Gobetz, Giles Edward; Goricar, Jože, and Jambrek, Peter
Yugoslav sociology. *In* Mohan, R. P. and Martindale, D. A. eds. Handbook of contemporary developments in world sociology p273-86

Goble, Ross Lawrence
Leadership for a society in transition. *In* Benton, L. R. ed. Management for the future p125-38

Gochros, Harvey L. and Gochros, Jean S.
Introduction: Who are the sexually oppressed? *In* Gochros, H. L. and Gochros, J. S. eds. The sexually oppressed p xix-xxiii

Gochros, Jean S.
Women—minority in transition. *In* Gochros,, H. L. and Gochros, J. S. eds. The sexually oppressed p71-83
See also Gochros, H. L. jt. auth.

God
Coomaraswamy, A. K. On the one and only transmigrant. *In* Coomaraswamy, A. K. Selected papers v2 p66-87
Coomaraswamy, A. K. The Tantric doctrine of divine biunity. *In* Coomaraswamy, A. K. Selected papers v2 p231-40
Copleston, F. C. Christianity without belief in God. *In* Copleston, F. C. Philosophers and philosophies p68-78
Copleston, F. C. Man, transcendence and the absence of God. *In* Copleston, F. C. Philosophers and philosophies p57-67
Nathan, G. J. The existence and nature of God in Hume's theism. *In* Livingston, D. W. and King, J. T. eds. Hume p126-49
Wicker, B. Metaphor and 'God.' *In* Wicker, B. The story-shaped world p71-106
See also Causation; Christianity; Deism; Jesus Christ; Metaphysics; Monotheism; Ontology; Polytheism; Providence and government of God; Religion; Son of God

Image
See Image of God

Name
See God (Judaism)—Name

Omnipotence
Eldridge, L. M. The concept of God's absolute power at Oxford in the later fourteenth century. *In* Jeffrey, D. L. ed. By things seen: reference and recognition in medieval thought p211-26

Permissive will
See Theodicy

Proof
Frankfurt, H. C. Descartes on the consistency of reason. *In* Hooker, M. ed. Descartes p26-39
Tlumak, J. Certainty and Cartesian methods. *In* Hooker, M. ed. Descartes p40-73

Proof, Cosmological
Cohen, R. S. Cosmic order and human disorder. *In* Cosmology, history, and theology p335-45
Meynell, H. A. The intelligibility of the universe. *In* Reason and religion p23-43
Stopes-Roe, H. V. The intelligibility of the universe. *In* Reason and religion p44-71

Proof, Ontological
Doney, W. The geometrical presentation of Descartes's a priori proof. *In* Hooker, M. ed. Descartes p 1-25

Providence and government
See Providence and government of God

Sovereignty
See Providence and government of God

God—*Continued*

Throne

See Throne of God

Worship and love

See Bhakti

God (Brahmanism) See God (Hinduism)

God (Fon religion) See Gods, Fon

God (Hinduism)

Coomaraswamy, A. K. Mahā purusa: "Supreme Identity." *In* Coomaraswamy, A. K. Selected papers v2 p379-86

Coomaraswamy, A. K. Manas. *In* Coomaraswamy, A. K. Selected papers v2 p209-19

Coomaraswamy, A. K. The Vedic doctrine of "silence." *In* Coomaraswamy, A. K. Selected papers v2 p198-208

Coomaraswamy, A. K. Vedic "monotheism." *In* Coomaraswamy, A. K. Selected papers v2 p166-76

God (Islam)

Marmura, M. E. God and his creation: two medieval Islamic views. *In* Savory, R. M. ed. Introduction to Islamic civilisation p46-53

God (Judaism)

Roberts, J. J. M. Divine freedom and cultic manipulation in Israel and Mesopotamia. *In* Unity and diversity p181-90

Attributes

Neher, A. Shaddai: the God of the broken arch (a theological approach to the Holocaust) *In* Rosenfeld, A. H. and Greenberg, I. eds. Confronting the Holocaust p150-58

Wicker, B. Metaphor and 'God.' *In* Wicker, B. The story-shaped world p71-106

Wolfson, H. A. Saadia on the semantic aspect of the problem of attribute. *In* Salo Wittmayer Baron v2 p1009-22

Name

Neher, A. Shaddai: the god of the broken arch (a theological approach to the Holocaust) *In* Rosenfeld, A. H. and Greenberg, I. eds. Confronting the Holocaust p150-58

Petersen, D. L. Max Weber and the sociological study of ancient Israel. *In* Johnson, H. M. ed. Religious change and continuity p117-49

God (Yoruba religion) See Gods, Yoruba

God, Providence and government of. See Providence and government of God

Godard, Jean-Luc

About

Henderson, B. Toward a non-bourgeois camera style. *In* Nichols, B. ed. Movies and methods p422-38

Monaco, J. Godard: A season in hell: icy poetry. *In* Monaco, J. The New Wave p153-86

Monaco, J. Godard: Modes of discourse. *In* Monaco, J. The New Wave p126-52

Monaco, J. Godard: Returning to zero (picture and act). *In* Monaco, J. The New Wave p187-212

Monaco, J. Godard: Theory and practice: the Dziga-Vertov period. *In* Monaco, J. The New Wave p213-52

Monaco, J. Godard: Women and the outsider. *In* Monaco, J. The New Wave p98-125

About individual works

My life to live

Beh, S. H. Vivre sa vie. *In* Nichols, B. ed. Movies and methods p180-85

Tout va bien

Kauffmann, S. Tout va bien. *In* Kauffmann, S. Living images p179-81

Wind from the East

MacBean, J. R. Vent d'Est or Godard and Rocha at the crossroads. *In* Nichols, B. ed. Movies and methods p91-106

Godbey, John W.

Central-state materialism and parapsychology. *In* Ludwig, J. K. ed. Philosophy and parapsychology p401-04

Goddard, Ives

Philological approaches to the study of North American Indian languages: documents and documentation. *In* Sebeok, T. A. ed. Native languages of the Americas v 1 p73-91

Goddard, Susanna Heath, comp.

About individual works

Collection from sundry authors

Crawford, R. A. and McKay, D. P. Music in manuscript: a Massachusetts tune-book of 1782. *In* American Antiquarian Society. Proceedings v84 pt 1 p43-64

Goddard, William

About

Wetherell, C. 'For these or such like reasons': John Holt's attack on Benjamin Franklin. *In* American Antiquarian Society. Proceedings v88 pt2 p251-75

Godden, M. R.

Old English composite homilies from Winchester. *In* Anglo-Saxon England 4 p57-65

Goddesses

Asia Minor

Merkelbach, R. The girl in the rosebush: a Turkish tale and its roots in ancient ritual. *In* Harvard Studies in classical philology v82 p 1-15

The Godfather (Motion picture)

Kauffmann, S. The Godfather. *In* Kauffmann, S. Living images p104-05

Sarris, A. The Godfather. *In* Sarris, A. Politics and cinema p24-31

The Godfather, part II (Motion picture)

Hess, J. D. Godfather II: a deal Coppola couldn't refuse. *In* Nichols, B. ed. Movies and methods p81-90

Gods. See Myth; Religions; Sacred marriage (Mythology); also names of deities, e.g. Marduk

Gods, Fon

Booth, N. S. God and the gods in West Africa. *In* African religions: a symposium p159-81

Gods, Hindu

Raghavachar, S. S. Saiva-Siddhānta, Viśiṣṭadvaita, Dvaita. *In* Bishop, D. H. ed. Indian thought p301-15

Gods, Yoruba

Booth, N. S. God and the gods in West Africa. *In* African religions: a symposium p159-81

Gods in art

Hiesinger, U. W. Three images of the god Mên. *In* Harvard Studies in classical philology v71 p303-10

Godshalk, William Leigh

Ben Jonson. *In* Logan, T. P. and Smith, D. S. eds. The new intellectuals p3-116

Samuel Daniel. *In* Logan, T. P. and Smith, D. S. eds. The new intellectuals p281-301

Godspell (Motion picture)
Kauffmann, S. Godspell. *In* Kauffmann, S. Living images p197-98

Godwin, Gail

About individual works
The odd woman

Mickelson, A. Z. Gail Godwin: order and accommodation. *In* Mickelson, A. Z. Reaching out: sensitivity and order in recent American fiction by women p68-86

Godwin, Mary (Wollstonecraft)

About

Janes, R. M. Mary, Mary, quite contrary, or, Mary Astell and Mary Wollstonecraft compared. *In* Studies in eighteenth-century culture v5 p121-39

About individual works
Letters written during a short residence in Sweden, Norway, and Denmark

Myers, M. Mary Wollstonecraft's Letters written . . . in Sweden: toward romantic autobiography. *In* Studies in eighteenth-century culture v8 p165-85

A vindication of the rights of men

Myers, M. Politics from the outside: Mary Wollstonecraft's first Vindication. *In* Studies in eighteenth-century culture v6 p113-32

A vindication of the rights of women

Downs, R. B. First of a new genus; excerpt from "Molders of the modern mind." *In* Downs, R. B. Books that changed the world p202-05

Korsmeyer, C. W. Reason and morals in the early feminist movement: Mary Wollstonecraft. *In* Gould, C. C. and Wartofsky, M. W. eds. Women and philosophy p97-111

Godwin, William

About individual works
Caleb Williams

Butler, M. The Jacobin novel II: Caleb Williams and Hermsprong. *In* Butler, M. Jane Austen and the war of ideas p57-87

Kelly, G. William Godwin: Caleb Williams. *In* Kelly, G. The English Jacobin novel, 1780-1805 p179-208

Palmer, W. J. Dickens and the eighteenth century. *In* Dickens Studies Annual v6 p15-39

Rothstein, E. Caleb Williams. *In* Rothstein, E. Systems of order and inquiry in later eighteenth-century fiction p208-42

Fleetwood

Kelly, G. William Godwin: Fleetwood. *In* Kelly, G. The English Jacobin novel, 1780-1805 p237-60

Life of Geoffrey Chaucer

Clogan, P. M. Literary criticism in William Godwin's Life of Chaucer. *In* Medievalia et humanistica no. 6 p189-98

St Leon

Kelly, G. William Godwin: St Leon. *In* Kelly, G. The English Jacobin novel, 1780-1805 p209-36

Characters—Caleb Williams
Ousby, I. Caleb Williams. *In* Ousby, I. Bloodhounds of heaven p19-42

Goedicke, Hans
Unity and diversity in the oldest religion of ancient Egypt. *In* Unity and diversity p201-17

Goering, John M.
The Marxist perspective and urban sociology. *In* McNall, S. G. ed. Theoretical perspectives in sociology p479-93

Goertzel, Ted George
Domestic pressures for abstention: Vietnam. *In* Higham, R. D. ed. Intervention or abstention: the dilemma of American foreign policy p166-83

Goethals, Gregor
Sacred-secular icons. *In* Browne, R. B. and Fishwick, M. W. eds. Icons of America p24-34

Goethe, Johann Wolfgang von

About

Hamburger, M. Art as second nature: Goethe. *In* Hamburger, M. Art as second nature p24-33

Hammer, C. Intimations of Molière in Goethe's Leipzig comedies. *In* Johnson, R. B.; Neumann, E. S. and Trail, G. T. eds. Molière and the commonwealth of letters: patrimony and posterity p276-86

Heller, E. Goethe in Marienbad. *In* Heller, E. The poet's self and the poem p 1-27

Lange, V. Reflections on the "classical age" of German literature. *In* Studies in eighteenth-century culture v7 p 1-21

Nicoll, A. From tragedy to melodrama. *In* Nicoll, A. World drama p342-69

Schlechta, K. The German "classicist" Goethe as reflected in Nietzsche's works. *In* O'Flaherty, J. C.; Sellner, T. F. and Helm, R. M. eds. Studies in Nietzsche and the classical tradition p144-55

Wilder, T. N. Goethe and world literature. *In* Wilder, T. N. American characteristics, and other essays p137-48

About individual works
Elective affinities

Pascal, R. Early accomplishment: Goethe: The elective affinities. *In* Pascal, R. The dual voice p37-45

The Erl-King

Hartman, G. H. Wordsworth and Goethe in literary history. *In* Hartman, G. H. The fate of reading p179-97

Faust

Lenson, D. R. A case of migration through genres. *In* Lenson, D. R. Achilles' choice p24-39

Nichols, F. J. Faust. *In* Seidel, M. A. and Mendelson, E. eds. Homer to Brecht p292-316

Stahl, E. L. The 'Faust' translation: a personal account. *In* Time was away p67-71

Novella

Swales, M. Goethe: Novelle. *In* Swales, M. The German Novelle p59-76

Poetry and truth

Lyons, J. O. Confessional high tide. *In* Lyons, J. O. The invention of the self p89-120

Romeo and Juliet

Phelps, L. R. Goethe's adaptation of Romeo and Juliet. *In* Creative encounter p17-24

Goethe, Johann W. von—About individual works—*Continued*

Torquato Tasso

Poggioli, R. "Arkadisch frei sei unser Glück!" Goethe and the pastoral. *In* Poggioli, R. The oaten flute p220-40

Wandrers Sturmlied

Weigand, H. J. "Wandrers Sturmlied": once more with obiter dicta. *In* Creative encounter p105-16

Wilhelm Meister

Lyons, J. O. The circumference of the self. *In* Lyons, J. O. The invention of the self p197-218

Wilhelm Meister's apprenticeship

Bruford, W. H. Goethe: Wilhelm Meisters Lehrjahre (1795-6). *In* Bruford, W. H. The German tradition of self-cultivation p29-57

Swales, M. Goethe: Wilhelm Meister's apprenticeship (1795-1796). *In* Swales, M. The German Bildungsroman from Wieland to Hesse p57-73

Wilhelm Meister's travels

Bruford, W. H. Goethe: Wilhelm Meisters Wanderjahre (1829). *In* Bruford, W. H. The German tradition of self-cultivation p88-112

World literature and the modern mind

Wilder, T. N. Goethe and world literature. *In* Wilder, T. N. American characteristics, and other essays p137-48

Influence—Arnold

Simpson, J. Arnold and Goethe. *In* Allott, K. ed. Matthew Arnold p286-318

Influence—Carlyle

Moore, C. Carlyle and Goethe as scientist. *In* Carlyle and his contemporaries p21-34

Goff, Regina M.

Educating Black Americans. *In* The Black American reference book p410-52

Goffman, Erving

The insanity of place; excerpt from "Relations in public". *In* Davis, F. J. and Stivers, R. eds. The collective definition of deviance p325-33

Gogarty, Oliver St John

Bibliography

Carens, J. F. Four Revival figures: Lady Gregory, A. E. (George W. Russell), Oliver St. John Gogarty, and James Stephens. *In* Finneran, R. J. ed. Anglo-Irish literature p436-69

Gogh, Vincent van

About individual works
Crows over the wheat field

Schapiro, M. On a painting of Van Gogh. *In* Schapiro, M. Selected papers v2 p87-99

Gogol', Nikolaĭ Vasil'evich

About

Bryusov, V. Y. Burnt to ashes. *In* Maguire, R. A. ed. Gogol from the twentieth century p103-31

Bugaev, B. N. Gogol. *In* Erlich, V. ed. Twentieth-century Russian literary criticism p33-50

Calder, A. Literature and serfdom: Gogol, Lermontov and Goncharov. *In* Calder, A. Russia discovered p37-72

Nicoll, A. Comedy and extravaganza. *In* Nicoll, A. World drama p370-80

Pereverzev, V. F. The evolution of Gogol's art; excerpt from "The art of Gogol". *In* Maguire, R. A. ed. Gogol from the twentieth century p133-54

Rahv, P. Gogol as a modern instance. *In* Rahv, P. Essays on literature and politics, 1932-1972 p222-26

Slonimskiĭ, A. L. The technique of the comic in Gogol. *In* Maguire, R. A. ed. Gogol from the twentieth century p323-73

Stilman, L. The "all-seeing eye" in Gogol. *In* Maguire, R. A. ed. Gogol from the twentieth century p375-89

Stilman, L. Men, women, and matchmakers: notes on a recurrent motif in Gogol. *In* Maguire, R. A. ed. Gogol from the twentieth century p390-403

About individual works
Dead souls

Annenskiĭ, I. F. The aesthetics of Gogol's Dead souls and its legacy. *In* Erlich, V. ed. Twentieth-century Russian literary criticism p51-60

Rowe, W. W. Gogol's descriptive double image and its use in Dead souls; excerpt from "Through Gogol's looking glass." *In* Rowe, W. W. Nabokov & others: patterns in Russian literature p37-46

Diary of a madman

Peace, R. A. The logic of madness: Gogol"s Zapiski sumasshedshego. *In* Oxford Slavonic papers new serv. v9 p28-45

The Inspector General

Gippius, V. V. The Inspector General: structure and problems. *In* Maguire, R. A. ed. Gogol from the twentieth century p215-65

Ivanov, V. I. Gogol's Inspector General and the comedy of Aristophanes. *In* Maguire, R. A. ed. Gogol from the twentieth century p199-214

The Nevsky Prospect

Hughes, O. R. The apparent and the real in Gogol's "Nevskij Prospekt." *In* California Slavic studies v8 p77-91

The nose

Ermakov, I. D. "The nose"; excerpt from "Sketches for an analysis of the art of N. V. Gogol". *In* Maguire, R. A. ed. Gogol from the twentieth century p155-98

Massey, I. Metamorphosis in Gogol: "The nose." *In* Massey, I. The gaping pig p59-75

Old-world landowners

Poggioli, R. Gogol's Old-fashioned landowners: an inverted eclogue. *In* Poggioli, R. The oaten flute p241-64

The overcoat

Chyzhevs'kyĭ, D. About Gogol's "Overcoat". *In* Maguire, R. A. ed. Gogol from the twentieth century p293-322

Eikhenbaum, B. M. How Gogol's "Overcoat" is made. *In* Maguire, R. A. ed. Gogol from the twentieth century p267-91

Selected passages from correspondence with friends

Tynĩaov, I. N. Dostoevsky and Gogol. *In* Erlich, V. ed. Twentieth-century Russian literary criticism p102-16

Gogol', Nïkolaĭ V.—*Continued*

Characters

Merezhkovskiĭ, D. Gogol and the Devil. *In* Maguire, R. A. ed. Gogol from the twentieth century p55-102

Influence—Dostoevskiĭ

Tynīanov, I. N. Dostoevsky and Gogol. *In* Erlich, V. ed. Twentieth-century Russian literary criticism p102-16

Gohstand, Robert

The shaping of Moscow by nineteenth-century trade. *In* Hamm, M. F. ed. The city in Russian history p160-81

Goicoechea Omar, Alejandro

Innovative transport technologies: the vertebrate train. *In* Strategies for human settlements: habitat and environment p157-63

Going, William Thornbury

Essays on Alabama literature

Contents

Alabama geography in Shirley Ann Grau's The keepers of the house

Alabama in the short story: notes for an anthology

Philip Henry Gosse on the Old Southwest frontier

The Prestons of Talladega and the Hubbards of Bowen: a dramatic note

Samuel Minturn Peck, gentleman of letters

Some in addition: the uncollected stories of William March

Store and Mockingbird: two Pulitzer novels about Alabama

William March's Alabama

Zelda Sayre Fitzgerald and Sara Haardt Mencken

Goist, Park Dixon

From Main Street to State Street

Contents

Afterword

Alternative perspective: the "radical" journalism of Hutchins Hapgood and Ernest Poole

Automobility and community: the middle landscape of American automobiles

The city and the middle border: Hamlin Garland

The city as noncommunity: Theodore Dreiser and and Henry Blake Fuller

The ideal questioned but not abandoned: Sherwood Anderson, Sinclair Lewis, and Floyd Dell

Middletown and the "eclipse of community": Robert and Helen Lynd

Planning the American city: Charles Mulford Robinson and John Nolen

Regionalism and community: the urbanism of Lewis Mumford

Social workers, reformers, and the city: Jane Addams and Jacob Riis

A sociologist and the city: the experience of Robert Park

The town as ideal community: Booth Tarkington and Zona Gale

Goitein, Shelomo Dov. See Goitein, Solomon Dob Fritz

Goitein, Solomon Dob Fritz

Human rights in Jewish thought and life in the Middle Ages. *In* Sidorsky, D. ed. Essays on human rights p247-64

A mansion in Fustat: a twelfth-century description of a domestic compound in the ancient capital of Egypt. *In* The Medieval city p163-78

New sources on the Palestinian gaonate. *In* Salo Wittmayer Baron v 1 p503-37

Golab, Caroline

The impact of the industrial experience on the immigrant family: the huddled masses reconsidered. *In* Immigrants in industrial America, 1850-1920 p 1-32

Gołab, Zbigniew

Linguistic traces of primitive religious dualism in Slavic. *In* For Wiktor Weintraub p151-59

Golan, Galia

The Arab-Israeli conflict in Soviet-US relations. *In* Ro'i, Y. ed. The limits to power p7-31

Elements of Russian traditions in Soviet socialism. *In* Eisenstadt, S. N. and Azmon, Y. eds. Socialism and tradition p19-39

National traditions and socialism in Eastern Europe: the cases of Czechoslovakia and Yugoslavia. *In* Eisenstadt, S. N. and Azmon, Y. eds. Socialism and tradition p41-76

Golan, Galia, and Rabinovich, Itamar

The Soviet Union and Syria: the limits of co-operation. *In* Ro'i, Y. ed. The limits to power p213-31

Golay, Frank H.

Southeast Asia: the "colonial drain" revisited. *In* Southeast Asian history and historiography p368-87

Gold, Frank. See Pollock, J. C. jt. auth.

Gold, Joseph, 1933-

"Living in a wale": Martin Chuzzlewit. *In* Dickens Studies Annual v2 p150-62

A word to the wise. *In* Gold, J. ed. In the name of language! p 1-17

Gold

Cohen, P. M. The future of gold. *In* The Year book of world affairs, 1977 p176-89

See also Coinage

Gold Coast. See Ghana

Gold mines and mining

United States—The West—History

Reps, J. W. Bonanza towns: urban planning on the Western mining frontier. *In* Pattern and process p271-89

The gold rush (Motion picture)

Kauffmann, S. The gold rush. *In* Kauffmann, S. Living images p298-306

Goldberg, Leah

About

Alter, R. Lea Goldberg: poetry in dark times. *In* Alter, R. Defenses of the imagination p91-101

Goldberg, Maxwell Henry

Liberal learning and the land-grant system: futures and optatives. *In* Land-grant universities and their continuing challenge p132-59

Goldberg, Michael

A universal "howl of execration": Carlyle's Latter-Day pamphlets and their critical reception. *In* Carlyle and his contemporaries p129-47

Goldberg, Miriam L. See Voegeli, H. T. jt. auth.

Goldberg, Stanley

Max Planck's philosophy of nature and his elaboration of the special theory of relativity. *In* Historical studies in the physical sciences v7 p125-60

Goldblat, Jozef
The Biological Disarmament Convention. *In* The Dynamics of the arms race p170-77
The main issues in the CW debate. *In* The Dynamics of the arms race p178-84

Goldenberg, Boris
Radicalization of a Latin-American state: the establishment of communism in Cuba. *In* Hammond, T. T. ed. The anatomy of Communist takeovers p538-95

Goldfarb, Alvin
Period of adjustment and the new Tennessee Williams. *In* Tennessee Williams: a tribute p310-17

Goldfield, David R.
Pursuing the American urban dream: cities in the Old South. *In* Brownell, B. A. and Goldfield, D. R. eds. The city in Southern history p52-91
See also Brownell, B. A. jt. auth.

Goldfish
Thomas, L. Ponds. *In* Thomas, L. The medusa and the snail p31-35

Goldin, Frederick
The array of perspectives in the early courtly love lyric. *In* In pursuit of perfection p51-100

Goldin, Judah
Early and classical Judaism. *In* Adams, C. J. ed. A reader's guide to the great religions p283-320
The magic of magic and superstition. *In* Aspects of religious propaganda in Judaism and early Christianity p115-47
A short note on the archangel Gabriel. *In* Law, church, and society p 1-4
"This song." *In* Salo Wittmayer Baron v 1 p539-54

Golding, Martin Phillip
Obligations to future generations. *In* The Abdication of philosophy: philosophy and the public good p195-207
Principled decision-making and the Supreme Court. *In* Summers, R. S. ed. Essays in legal philosophy p208-36
Security/survival. *In* Population policy and ethics p47-52

Golding, William Gerald
About
Hynes, S. L. William Golding. *In* Stade, G. ed. Six contemporary British novelists p165-218
Kennard, J. E. William Golding: islands. *In* Kennard, J. E. Number and nightmare p176-202
About individual works
Lord of the flies
Epstein, E. L. "Notes on Lord of the flies"; epilogue to Lord of the flies by William Golding. *In* Praise from famous men: an anthology of introductions p69-74
Richter, D. H. Allegory versus fable: Golding's Lord of the flies. *In* Richter, D. H. Fable's end p61-82
The spire
Kunkel, F. L. Golding's The spire: the prayer and the phallus. *In* Kunkel, F. L. Passion and the Passion p58-74

Goldman, Alan Harris
Limits to the justification of reverse discrimination. *In* Feminism and philosophy p225-41

Goldman, Arnold
Melville's England. *In* Pullin, F. ed. New perspectives on Melville p68-85
Yeats, spiritualism, and psychical research. *In* Yeats and the occult p108-29

Goldman, Marshall Irwin
The Soviet Union. *In* Vernon, R. ed. The oil crisis p129-43

Goldman, Michael
The ghost of joy: reflections on romanticism and the forms of modern drama. *In* Bornstein, G. ed. Romantic and modern p53-68
Marlowe and the histrionics of ravishment. *In* Kernan, A. B. ed. Two Renaissance mythmakers p22-40

Goldmann, Lucien
About
Demetz, P. Transformations of recent Marxist criticism: Hans Mayer, Ernst Fischer, Lucien Goldmann. *In* The Frontiers of literary criticism p75-92

Goldoni, Carlo
About
Nicoll, A. The growth of bourgeois comedy. *In* Nicoll, A. World drama p307-29

Goldschmidt, Walter Rochs
Absent eyes and idle hands: socialization for low affect among the Sebei. *In* Schwartz, T. ed. Socialization as cultural communication p65-71

Goldsmith, Cornelia
The first day care program. *In* Roots of open education in America p148-60

Goldsmith, Donald
The Copernicus satellite in the new era of space astronomy. *In* Neyman, J. ed. The heritage of Copernicus: theories "pleasing to the mind" p487-507
Edwin Hubble and the universe outside our galaxy. *In* Neyman, J. ed. The heritage of Copernicus: theories "pleasing to the mind" p63-94
Introduction. *In* Goldsmith, D. ed. Scientists confront Velikovsky p19-28

Goldsmith, Margaret E.
The enigma of The husband's message. *In* Anglo-Saxon poetry: essays in appreciation p242-63

Goldsmith, Oliver
About individual works
The deserted village
Manlove, C. N. Goldsmith and Crabbe. *In* Manlove, C. N. Literature and reality, 1600-1800 p177-92
The good natured man
Ferguson, O. W. Antisentimentalism in Goldsmith's The good natur'd man: the limits of parody. *In* The Dress of words p105-16
She stoops to conquer
Davis, T. and Hamlyn, S. What do we do when two texts differ? She stoops to conquer and textual criticism. *In* Evidence in literary scholarship p263-79
The Vicar of Wakefield
Auty, S. G. Fielding's followers: The Vicar of Wakefield. *In* Auty, S. G. The comic spirit of eighteenth-century novels p78-87

Goldsmith, Oliver—Continued

Criticism, Textual

Davis, T. and Hamlyn, S. What do we do when two texts differ? She stoops to conquer and textual criticism. *In* Evidence in literary scholarship p263-79

Poetic works

Lonsdale, R. "A garden, and a grave": the poetry of Oliver Goldsmith. *In* Martz, L. L. and Williams, A. L. eds. The author in his work p3-30

Goldsmith, Peter, and Sonderkötter, Friedrich

Equality and discrimination in international economic law (V): The European communities and the wider world. *In* The Year book of world affairs, 1975 p265-82

Goldstein, Eda G. and Malitz, Sidney

Psychotherapy and pharmacotherapy as enablers in the anticipatory grief of a dying patient: a case study. *In* Anticipatory grief p285-95

Goldstein, Joseph

On being adult and being an adult in secular law. *In* Erikson, E. H. ed. Adulthood p249-67

Goldstein, Paul

Kewanee Oil Co. v. Bicron Corp.: notes on a closing circle. *In* The Supreme Court review, 1974 p81-85

Goldstein, Sidney Merril

An Etruscan helmet in the McDaniel collection. *In* Harvard Studies in classical philology v72 p383-90

A terracotta lamp in the McDaniel collection. *In* Harvard Studies in classical philology v73 p291-303

Goldstein, Thomas Eugene

Impulses of Italian Renaissance culture behind the age of discoveries. *In* First images of America p27-35

Goldstein, Walter, 1930-

The politics of planning for the public interest: the role of liberal ideology in a conservative society. *In* Planning, politics, and the public interest p181-200

Goldstein v. California. *In* The Supreme Court review, 1975 p147-87

Goldthorpe, John H.

The current inflation: towards a sociological account. *In* The Political economy of inflation p186-216

Goldwater, Robert

The primitivism of the Fauves, the Brücke, the primitivism of the Blaue Reiter; excerpt from "Primitivism in modern art." *In* Kaplan, P. and Manso, S. eds. Major European art movements, 1900-1945 p42-90

Goldweights, Ashanti

McLeod, M. D. Aspects of Asante images. *In* Greenhalgh, M. and Megaw, J. V. S. eds. Art in society p305-16

Goldwin, Robert Allen

How "different" are universities? *In* Hook, S.; Kurtz, P. W. and Todorovich, M. eds. The university and the state: what role for government in higher education? p215-20

Of men and angels: a search for morality in the Constitution. *In* The Moral foundations of the American Republic p 1-18

Teaching and the shaping of souls. *In* Hook, S.; Kurtz, P. and Todorovich, M. eds. The ethics of teaching and scientific research p37-41

Goleman, Daniel

The Buddha on meditation and states of consciousness. *In* Tart, C. T. ed. Transpersonal psychologies p203-30

The impact of the new religions on psychology. *In* Needleman, J. and Baker, G. eds. Understanding the new religions p113-21

Golembe, Carter H.

Challenges confronting American banking. *In* Prochnow, H. V. ed. Dilemmas facing the nation p109-24

Goliards

Wailes, S. L. Vagantes and the fabliaux. *In* Cooke, T. D. and Honeycutt, B. L. eds. The humor of the fabliaux p43-58

Gollancz, Israel, ed.

About individual works

The Caedmon manuscript of Anglo-Saxon Biblical poetry, Junius XI in the Bodleian library, with introduction by Sir Israel Gollancz

Henderson, G. The programme of illustrations in Bodleian M S Junius XI. *In* Studies in memory of David Talbot Rice p113-45

Gollwitzer, Helmut

The gospel and the struggle for freedom. *In* The Context of contemporary theology p87-97

Kingdom of God and socialism in the theology of Karl Barth. *In* Hunsinger, G. ed. Karl Barth and radical politics p77-120

Goltz, Colmar, Freiherr von der

About

Swanson, G. W. War, technology, and society in the Ottoman Empire from the reign of Abdülhamid II to 1913: Mahmud Şevket and the German military mission. *In* War, technology and society in the Middle East p367-85

Gombrich, Sir Ernst Hans Josef

Illusion and art. *In* Gregory, R. L. and Gombrich, Sir E. H. J. eds. Illusion in nature and art p193-243

Malraux's philosophy of art in historical perspective. *In* Courcel, M. H. de, ed. Malraux p169-83

The Renaissance—period or movement? *In* Background to the English Renaissance p9-30

The sky is the limit: the vault of heaven and pictorial vision. *In* Perception p84-94

About individual works

Symbolic images

Barfield, O. The rediscovery of allegory (II) *In* Barfield, O. The rediscovery of meaning, and other essays p101-10

Gombrowicz, Witold

About individual works

Cosmos

Boyers, R. Gombrowicz's "Cosmos": the clinical fiction as novel. *In* Boyers, R. Excursions p87-108

Gomery, Douglas

Three roads taken: the novel, the play, and the film. *In* Peary, G. and Shatzkin, R. eds. The modern American novel and the movies p9-18

Gomes, Alfredo Dias

About

Lyday, L. F. The theater of Alfredo Dias Gomes. *In* Lyday, L. F. and Woodyard, G. W. eds. Dramatists in revolt p221-42

Gomes, Dias. See Gomes, Alfredo Dias

Gómez, Emilio García. See García Gómez, Emilio

Gómez de Avellaneda y Arteaga, Gertrudis

About individual works

Sab

Jackson, S. M. Fact from fiction: another look at slavery in three Spanish-American novels. *In* DeCosta, M. ed. Blacks in Hispanic literature p83-89

Goncharov, Ivan Aleksandrovich

About

Pritchett, V. S. Ivan Goncharov: the dream of a censor. *In* Prichett, V. S. The myth makers p57-62

About individual works

Oblomov

Calder, A. Literature and serfdom: Gogol, Lermontov and Goncharov. *In* Calder, A. Russia discovered p37-72

Gonda, Thomas Andrew. See Christopherson, L. K. jt. auth.

Gonen, Amiram

Mediterranean tourism: some geographic perspectives. *In* Borgese, E. M. and Krieger, D. eds. The tides of change p179-96

Gonnaud, Maurice

Emerson and the imperial self: a European critique. *In* Levin, D. ed. Emerson: prophecy, metamorphosis, and influence p107-28

Gonorrhea

Cases, clinical reports, statistics

Ober, W. B. Boswell's clap. *In* Ober, W. B. Boswell's clap and other essays p 1-42

Gonzales, Sylvia Alicia

The Chicana perspective: a design for self-awareness. *In* Trejo, A. D. ed. The Chicanos p81-99

Gonzalez, Edward

Institutionalization, political elites, and foreign policy. *In* Cuba in the world p3-36

González, Esteban, supposed author. See Vida y hechos de Estevanillo González

Gonzalez, Mike

Ideology and culture under Popular Unity *In* O'Brien, P. J. ed. Allende's Chile p106-27

González López, Emilio

The myth of Saint James and its functional reality. *In* Américo Castro and the meaning of Spanish civilization p91-111

Good, Graham

Lukacs' Theory of the novel. *In* Spilka, M. ed. Towards a poetics of fiction p125-35

Good, Mary-Jo DelVecchio

A comparative perspective on women in provincial Iran and Turkey. *In* Beck, L. and Keddie, N. R. eds. Women in the Muslim world p482-500

Good and evil

Hallie, P. P. Satan, evil, and good in history. *In* Stanage, S. M. ed. Reason and violence p53-69

Kilby, C. S. The ugly and the evil. *In* Evolution of consciousness p202-10

Kohak, E. V. Speaking of the Devil: a modest methodological proposal. *In* Disguises of the demonic p48-56

McGill, A. C. Structures of inhumanity. *In* Disguises of the demonic p116-33

Phillips, D. Z. The problem of evil. *In* Reason and religion p103-21

Pittenger, W. N. Evils and God—from a 'process' perspective. *In* Crew, L. ed. The gay academic p361-66

Rubinoff, L. Violence and the retreat from reason. *In* Stanage, S. M. ed. Reason and violence p73-118

Swinburne, R. The problem of evil. *In* Reason and religion p81-102

See also Evil in literature; Good in literature

Good as a theme in literature. See Good in literature

Good in literature

Kazin, A. The drama of good and evil in American writing. *In* An Almost chosen people p51-66

McEwen, G. D. "A turn of thinking": Benjamin Franklin, Cotton Mather, and Daniel Defoe on "doing good." *In* The Dress of words p53-65

Goodall, Barones Jane van Lawick-. See Lawick-Goodall, Barones Jane van

Goodall, Vanne Morris

Setting the scene. *In* Goodall, V. M. ed. The quest for man p11-25

Goode, William Josiah

Homans' and Merton's structural approach. *In* Blau, P. M. ed. Approaches to the study of social structure p66-75

Goodenough, Ward Hunt

Changing social organization on Romónum, Truk, 1947-1965. *In* Social organization and the applications of anthropology p62-93

Folklife study and social change. *In* Yoder, D. ed. American folklife p19-26

Multiculturalism as the normal human experience. *In* Eddy, E. M. and Partridge, W. L. eds. Applied anthropology in America p79-86

Goodfield, Gwyneth June

Changing strategies: a comparison of reductionist attitudes in biological and medical research in the nineteenth and twentieth centuries. *In* Ayala, F. J. and Dobzhansky, T. G. eds. Studies in the philosophy of biology p65-86

Goodfield, June. See Goodfield, Gwyneth June

Goodheart, Eugene

The failure of criticism

Contents

Aristocrats and Jacobins: the happy few in The charterhouse of Parma

The blasphemy of Joycean art

English social criticism and the spirit of Reformation

Flaubert and the powerlessness of art

The formalist avant-garde and the autonomy of aesthetic values

Modernism and the critical spirit

The organic society of F. R. Leavis

A postscript to the higher criticism: the case of Philip Rieff

The reality of disillusion in T.S. Eliot

Goodich, Michael
Childhood and adolescence among the thirteenth-century saints. *In* Kren, G. M. and Rappoport, L. H. eds. Varieties of psychohistory p193-218

Goodlad, Sinclair
Mass entertainment in perspective: the need for a theory of the middle range. *In* Fischer, H. D. and Melnik, S. R. eds. Entertainment: a cross-cultural examination p120-28
On the social significance of television comedy. *In* Bigsby, C. W. E. ed. Approaches to popular culture p213-25

Goodman, Bernice
The lesbian woman: two points of view: The problems of lesbians. *In* Gochros, H. L. and Gochros, J. S. eds. The sexually oppressed p145-51

Goodman, Eric K.
Medical school, law school, and beyond. *In* Hurdles p268-87

About
Goodman, E. K. Medical school, law school, and beyond. *In* Hurdles p268-87

Goodman, Felicitas D.
Prognosis: a new religion? *In* Zaretsky, I. I. and Leone, M. P. eds. Religious movements in contemporary America p244-54

Goodman, Lenn Evan
Rāzī's myth of the fall of soul: its function in his philosophy. *In* Essays on Islamic philosophy and science p25-40

Goodman, Louis J. and others
Low-cost housing technology: problems, issues, and a proposed solution. *In* Strategies for human settlements: habitat and environment p126-41

Goodman, Nelson
Reality remade; excerpt from "Languages of art." *In* Margolis, J. Z. ed. Philosophy looks at the arts p225-48
When is art? *In* Perkins, D. and Leondar, B. eds. The arts and cognition p11-19

About individual works
Languages of art
Roupas, T. G. Information and pictorial representation. *In* Perkins, D. and Leondar, B. eds. The arts and cognition p48-79

Goodman, Paul, 1911-1972
Reflections on children's rights. *In* Gross, B. and Gross, R. eds. The children's rights movement p140-47
The sweet style of Ernest Hemingway. *In* Wagner, L. W. ed. Ernest Hemingway p153-60

About
Greene, M. Paul Goodman and anarchistic education. *In* Social forces and schooling p313-36
West, T. R. Nature and artifice: Hannah Arendt, Theodore Roszak, Paul Goodman. *In* West, T. R. Nature, community, & will p97-137

About individual works
Compulsory miseducation
Barrow, R. Paul Goodman (1911-73) [sic]. *In* Barrow, R. Radical education p92-126

Growing up absurd
Barrow, R. Paul Goodman (1911-73) [sic]. *In* Barrow, R. Radical education p92-126

Speaking and language: defence of poetry
Langendoen, D. T. The problem of linguistic theory in relation to language behavior: a tribute and reply to Paul Goodman. *In* Bloomfield, M. W. and Haugen, E. I. eds. Language as a human problem p197-203

Goodman, Paul, 1934-
The politics of industrialism: Massachusetts, 1830-1870. *in* Uprooted Americans p161-207

Goodreau, David
Pictorial sources of the neo-classical style: London or Rome? *In* Studies in eighteenth-century culture v4 p247-70

Goodrich, Peter Spang
Manchester's urban univer-city. *In* Murphy, T. P. ed. Universities in the urban crisis p161-78

Goodridge, Jonathan Francis
A new heaven and a new earth. *In* Smith, A. ed. The art of Emily Brontë p160-81

Goodwin, K. L.
Invective and obliqueness in political poetry: Kasaipwalova, Brathwaite, and Soyinka. *In* Narasimhaiah, C. D. ed. Awakened conscience p251-60

Goody, Jack. See Goody, John Rankine

Goody, John Rankine
Death and the interpretation of culture: a bibliographic overview. *In* Death in America p 1-8
Inheritance, property and women: some comparative considerations. *In* Family and inheritance p10-36
Literacy, criticism, and the growth of knowledge. *In* Culture and its creators p226-43

Goold, G. P.
The nature of Homeric composition. *In* Illinois classical studies, v2 1977 p 1-34
Noctes-Propertianae. *In* Harvard Studies in classical philology v71 p59-106
Servius and the Helen episode. *In* Harvard Studies in classical philology v74 p101-68
Walton Brooks McDaniel: a biographical note. *In* Harvard Studies in classical philology v76 p xi-xvii

Goonetilleke, D. C. R. A.
Developing countries in British fiction
Contents
Antecedents
Between cultures
Challenges and problems of the Far East: Conrad's Malayan novels
Challenges and problems of the Far East: Conrad's tales
Conrad's African tales: ironies of progress
Conrad's Malayan novels: problems of authenticity
Conrad's Nostromo: the morality of 'material interests'
D. H. Lawrence: primitivism?
Difficulties of connection in India: Kipling and Forster
Joyce Cary: the clash of cultures in Nigeria

Goormaghtigh, John
How an INGO contributed to broadening the scope and competence of an IGO. *In* Unofficial diplomats p250-58

Gopinathan, Saravanan

Publishing in a plural society: the case of Singapore. *In* Altbach, P. G. and McVey, S. eds. Perspectives in publishing p157-71

Gorbanevsaiâ, Natal'iâ

About individual works
Selected poems; with a transcript of her trial and papers relating to her detention in a prison and psychiatric hospital

Rich, A. C. Caryatid: Two columns: Natalya Gorbanevskaya. *In* Rich, A. C. On lies, secrets, and silence p116-19

Gordimer, Nadine

English-language literature and politics in South Africa. *In* Heywood, C. ed. Aspects of South African literature p99-120

"The flash of fireflies." *In* May, C. E. ed. Short story theories p178-81

Writers in South Africa: the new Black poets. *In* Exile and tradition p132-51

About
Parker, K. Nadine Gordimer and the pitfalls of liberalism. *In* Parker, K. ed. The South African novel in English p114-30

About individual works
A guest of honour

Wade, M. Nadine Gordimer and Europe-in-Africa. *In* Parker, K. ed. The South African novel in English p131-63

Gordis, Robert

Jewish tradition in the modern world: conservation and renewal. *In* Tradition and change in Jewish experience p141-68

Gordon, Adam Lindsay

About
Perkins, E. Towards seeing minor poets steadily and whole. *In* Bards, bohemians, and bookmen p39-55

Gordon, Caroline

An American girl. *In* Friedman, M. J. and Lawson, L. A. eds. The added dimension p123-37

About individual works
None shall look back

Gray, R. J. Back to the old plantation: the recovery and reexamination of a dream. *In* Gray, R. J. The literature of memory p150-96

Gordon, Donald James

The Renaissance imagination

Contents

Academicians build a theatre and give a play: the Accademia Olimpica

Ben Jonson's Haddington masque: the story and the fable

Chapman's Memorable masque

Giannotti, Michelangelo and the cult of Brutus

Hymenæi: Ben Jonson's masque of union

The imagery of Ben Jonson's Masques of blacknesse and beautie

Name and fame: Shakespeare's Coriolanus

Poet and architect: the intellectual setting of the quarrel between Ben Jonson and Inigo Jones

The Renaissance poet as classicist: Chapman's Hero and Leander

Ripa's fate

Roles and mysteries

Rubens and the Whitehall ceiling

Veritas filia temporis: Hadrianus Junius and Geoffrey Whitney

Gordon, Edmund W. and Green, Derek

An affluent society's excuses for inequality: developmental, economic, and educational. *In* Montagu, A. ed. Race and IQ p73-103

Gordon, George N.

Aristotle as a modern propagandist. *In* Havelock, E. A. and Hershbell, J. P. eds. Communication arts in the ancient world p55-61

Gordon, Jan B.

Days and distances: the cartographic imagination of Elizabeth Bishop. *In* Boyers, R. ed. Contemporary poetry in America p348-59

Permutations of death: a reading of Lie down in darkness. *In* Morris, R. K. and Malin, I. eds. The achievement of William Styron p88-99

Gordon, John, 1925-

On firm ground. *In* Blishen, E. ed. The thorny paradise p34-35

Gordon, Lois G.

Meaning and myth in The sound and the fury and The waste land. *In* French, W. G. ed. The twenties p269-302

Gordon, Mary

About individual works
Final payments

Sheed, W. Mary Gordon: Final payments. *In* Sheed, W. The good word & other words p259-65

Gordon, Michael

Irish immigrant culture and the labor boycott in New York City, 1880-1886. *In* Immigrants in industrial America, 1850-1920 p111-22

Gordon, Milton Myron

Toward a general theory of racial and ethnic group relations. *In* Glazer, N. and Moynihan, D. P. eds. Ethnicity p84-110

Gordon, Richard L.

Coal—the swing fuel. *In* Kalter, R. J. and Vogely, W. A. eds. Energy supply and government policy p193-215

Gordon, Robert Aaron

Examining labelling theory: the case of mental retardation. *In* Gove, W. R. ed. The labelling of deviance p83-146

A skeptical look at the "natural rate" hypothesis. *In* Theory for economic efficiency: essays in honor of Abba P. Lerner p46-61

Gordon, Robert Morris

The abortion issue. *In* The Abdication of philosophy: philosophy and the public good p267-77

Gordon, Walter M.

The monastic achievement and More's utopian dream. *In* Medievalia et humanistica; new ser. no. 9 p199-214

Gorée, Senegal

History
Brooks, G. E. Goree and the Cape Verde rivers. *In* African dimensions p69-80

Gorer, Geoffrey

English identity over time and Empire. *In* Ethnic identity p156-72

Goretti, Maria

The heterogenesis of ends in Vico's thought: premises for a comparison of ideas. *In* Giambattista Vico's science of humanity p213-19

Gorfain, Phyllis

Puzzle and artifice: the riddle as metapoetry in 'Pericles.' *In* Shakespeare survey v29 p11-20

Gorgias, of Leontini

About

Romilly, J. de. Gorgias and magic. *In* Romilly, J. de. Magic and rhetoric in ancient Greece p 1-22

Gorgons

Lettvin, J. Y. The Gorgon's eye. *in* Brecher, K. and Feirtag, M. eds. Astronomy of the ancients p133-51

Gorham, Deborah

Victorian reform as a family business: the Hill family. *In* Wohl, A. S. ed. The Victorian family p119-47

Goricar, Jože. See Gobetz, G. E. jt. auth.

Gorin, Jean-Pierre

About

Monaco, J. Godard: Theory and practice: the Dziga-Vertov period. *In* Monaco, J. The New Wave p213-52

Goring, John Jeremy

Wealden ironmasters in the age of Elizabeth. *In* Wealth and power in Tudor England p204-27

Goring, Marius

The sound of poetry. *In* Royal Society of Literature of the United Kingdom, London. Essays by divers hands v39 p 1-23

Gor'kiĭ, Maksim

About

Donchin, G. Gorky. *In* Freeborn, R. ed. Russian literary attitudes from Pushkin to Solzhenitsyn p79-98

Glicksberg, C. I. Conclusion. *In* Glicksberg, C. I. The literature of commitment p405-24

Kostka, E. K. Maksim Gorky: Russian writer with a Western bent. *In* Kostka, E. K. Glimpses of Germanic-Slavic relations from Pushkin to Heinrich Mann p38-54

Mathewson, R. W. Lenin and Gorky: the turning point. *In* Mathewson, R. W. The positive hero in Russian literature p156-76

Gorky, Arshile

About

Schapiro, M. Arshile Gorky. *In* Schapiro, M. Selected papers v2 p179-83

Gorky, Maxim. See Gor'kiĭ, Maksim

Gorostiza, Carlos

About

Forster, M. H. The theater of Carlos Gorostiza. *In* Lyday, L. F. and Woodyard, G. W. eds. Dramatists in revolt p110-19

Gorovitz, Samuel

John Rawls: a theory of justice. *In* De Crespigny, A. and Minogue, K. R. eds. Contemporary political philosophers p272-89

Gorvine, Harold

The New Deal in Massachusetts. *In* Braeman, J.; Bremner, R. H. and Brody, D. eds. The New Deal v2 p3-44

Gosebrink, Jean E. Meeh

Sources for contemporary Southern Africa. *In* Carter, G. M. and O'Meara, P. eds. Southern Africa: the continuing crisis p363-81

Gosling, Justice Cyril Bertrand

The natural supremacy of conscience. *In* Royal Institute of Philosophy. Nature and conduct p121-38

Gospel music. See Spirituals (Songs)

Goss v. Lopez. *In* The Supreme Court review, 1975 p25-75

Gosse, Sir Edmund William

About

Baylen, J. O. Edmund Gosse, William Archer, and Ibsen in late Victorian Britain. *In* Tennessee Studies in literature v20 p124-37

About individual works

Father and son

Caserio, R. L. Plot, purpose, and the modern self. *In* Caserio, R. L. Plot, story, and the novel p167-97

Gosse, Philip Henry

About

Going, W. T. Philip Henry Gosse on the Old Southwest frontier. *In* Going, W. T. Essays on Alabama literature p156-72

Gossen, Gary Hamilton

A Chamula solar calendar board from Chiapas, Mexico. *In* Mesoamerican archaeology p217-53

Gossett, Louise Young

Losing battles: festival and celebration. *In* Prenshaw, P. W. ed. Eudora Welty p341-50

Gossett, Ruth R.

Black widows. *In* Gochros, H. L. and Gochros, J. S. eds. The sexually oppressed p84-95

Gossip in literature

Hardy, B. N. Abuses of narrative. *In* Hardy, B. N. Tellers and listeners p102-30

Gossman, Lionel

History and literature: reproduction or signification. *In* Canary, R. H. and Kozicki, H. J. eds. The writing of history p3-40

Gostand, Reba

Quest or quesion? Perilous journey to the chapel. *In* Bards, bohemians, and bookmen· p289-304

Gotama Buddha. See Gautama Buddha

Gotesky, Rubin

Social force, social power, and social violence. *In* Stanage, S. M. ed. Reason and violence p145-79

Gotham Book Mart, New York

Steloff, F. Censorship and the Gotham Book Mart. *In* Bookselling in America and the world p181-83

Gothic architecture. See Architecture, Gothic

Gothic art. See Art, Gothic

Gothic literature

Howells, C. A. Gothic themes, values, techniques. *In* Howells, C. A. Love, mystery, and misery p5-27

History and criticism

Brombert, V. H. Pétrus Borel: prison and the Gothic tradition. *In* Brombert, V. H. The romantic prison p49-61

Gothic literature—*Continued*

United States

Bone, R. A. Eric Walrond. *In* Bone, R. A. Down home p171-203

Gothic novel. See Gothic revival (Literature)

Gothic revival (Architecture)
See also Architecture, Victorian

England

Madoff, M. The useful myth of Gothic ancestry. *In* Studies in eighteenth-century culture v8 p337-50

Rowan, A. J. Batty Langley's Gothic. *In* Studies in memory of David Talbot Rice p197-215

See also Strawberry Hill, England (Villa)

Gothic revival (Art) See Gothic revival (Architecture)

Gothic revival (Literature)

England

Madoff, M. The useful myth of Gothic ancestry. *In* Studies in eighteenth-century culture v8 p337-50

Skilton, D. Gothic, romantic and heroic. *In* Skilton, D. The English novel p59-79

Wilt, J. Frankenstein as Mystery play. *In* Levine, G. L. and Knoepflmacher, U. C. eds. The endurance of Frankenstein p31-48

Scotland

Hart, F. R. Scottish variations of the Gothic novel. *In* Hart, F. R. The Scottish novel p13-30

Goths

Italy

Ladner, G. B. On Roman attitudes toward barbarians in late antiquity. *In* Viator: medieval and Renaissance studies v7 p 1-26

See also Barbarian invasions of Rome

Gotoff, Harold C.
The concept of periodicity in the Ad Herennium. *In* Harvard Studies in classical philology v77 p217-23

Tibullus: nunc levis est tractanda Venus. *In* Harvard Studies in classical philology v78 p231-51

Gottdiener, Mark D.
Social planning and metropolitan growth. *In* Handbook of contemporary urban life p494-518

Gottfried von Strassburg

About individual works

The story of Tristan & Iseult

Green, D. H. On damning with faint praise in medieval literature. *In* Viator: medieval and Renaissance studies v6 p117-69

Jaffe, S. P. Rhetoric in German literature: Gottfried von Strassburg and the rhetoric of history. *In* Murphy, J. J. ed. Medieval eloquence p288-318

Quinn, E. C. Beyond courtly love: religious elements in Tristan and La queste del Saint Graal. *In* In pursuit of perfection p179-219

Gottheil, Fred M.
Arab immigration into pre-state Israel: 1922-1931. *In* The Palestinians p30-40

Göttingen. Universität

History

McClelland, C. E. The aristocracy and university reform in eighteenth-century Germany. *In* Schooling and society p146-73

Gottlieb, David
Children as victims; excerpt from "Children's liberation." *In* Gross, B. and Gross, R. eds. The children's rights movement p174-86

Gottlieb, Gideon
China and Japan and the Arab-Israeli conflict. *In* The New world balance and peace in the Middle East: reality or mirage? p126-36

Gottlieb, Lois C. and Keitner, Wendy
Colonialism as metaphor and experience in 'The grass is singing' and 'Surfacing.' *In* Narasimhaiah, C. D. ed. Awakened conscience p307-14

Gottlieb, Sidney
The madding crowd in the movies. *In* Peary, G. and Shatzkin, R. eds. The modern American novel and the movies p95-106

Gottmann, Jean
Megalopolis and antipolis: the telephone and the structure of the city. *In* The Social impact of the telephone p303-17

Gottschalk, Paul A.
Time in Edwin Drood. *In* Dickens Studies Annual v 1 p265-72

Goubert, Jean-Pierre
The extent of medical practice in France around 1780. *In* Branca, P. ed. The medicine show p211-28

Goubet, Guillermo Araya. See Araya Goubet, Guillermo

Gough, Kathleen. See Aberlee, Kathleen Gough

Gough, Michael
Daǧ Pazari. The basilical church 'extra muros.' *In* Studies in memory of David Talbot Rice p147-63

Goulart, João Belchior Marques, President Brazil

About

Stepan, A. Political leadership and regime breakdown: Brazil. *In* The Breakdown of democratic regimes pt3 p110-37

Gould, Carol C.
The woman question: philosophy of liberation and the liberation of philosophy. *In* Gould, C. C. and Wartofsky, M. M. eds. Women and philosophy p5-44

Gould, Keith Alan
Panentheism in The prelude. *In* Aeolian harps p110-31

Gould, Lois

About individual works

A sea-change

Mickelson, A. Z. Lois Gould: the musical chairs of power. *In* Mickelson, A. Z. Reaching out: sensitivity and order in recent American fiction by women p49-67

Such good friends

Mickelson, A. Z. Lois Gould: the musical chairs of power. *In* Mickelson, A. Z. Reaching out: sensitivity and order in recent American fiction by women p49-67

Gould, Samuel B.
A disease with a patient. *In* The Third century p33-38

Gould, Stephen Jay
Agassiz's marginalia in Lyell's Principles, or the perils of uniformity and the ambiguity of heroes. *In* Studies in history of biology v3 p119-38

Racist arguments and IQ. *In* Montagu, A. ed. Race and IQ p145-50

Gould, Warwick
"Lionel Johnson comes the first to mind": sources for Owen Aherne. *In* Yeats and the occult p255-84

Gouldner, Alvin Ward
Sociology and the everyday life. *In* The Idea of social structure p417-32

Goulet, Denis
World health and world hunger: putting development ethics to the test. *In* Cahill, K. M. ed. Health and development p83-101

Govaerts, France. See Govaerts, Frans

Govaerts, Frans
Belgium and the Cold war. *In* Siracusa, J. M. and Barclay, G. S. eds. The impact of the Cold war p40-63

Gove, Walter R.
Deviant behavior, social intervention, and labeling theory. *In* The Uses of controversy in sociology p219-27

Labelling and mental illness: a critique. *In* Gove, W. R. ed. The labelling of deviance p35-81

The labelling perspective: an overview. *In* Gove, W. R. ed. The labelling of deviance p3-20

Government. See Political science

Government, Primitive
Owusu, M. Comparative politics, history, and political anthropology. *In* Colonialism and change p25-65

Government, Resistance to
Konvitz, M. R. Conscience: the movement from duty to right—from the Bible to the Bill of Rights. *In* Konvitz, M. R. Judaism and the American idea p91-137
See also Civil war; Insurgency; Revolutions

Moral and religious aspects
Thompson, W. D. J. C. Luther and the right of resistance to the Emperor. *In* Church, society and politics p159-202

Government agencies. See Administrative agencies

Government and business. See Industry and state

Government and the press
Davison, W. P. The role of communication in democracies; excerpt from "International political communication." *In* Fischer, H. D. and Merrill, J. C. eds. International and intercutural communication p29-36

India
Verghese, G. Press censorship under Indira Gandhi. *In* Horton, P. C. ed. The Third World and press freedom p220-30

South Africa
Qoboza, P. Press censorship in South Africa. *In* Horton, P. C. ed. The Third World and press freedom p231-37

United States
Boylan, J. R. Journalists and foreign policy. *In* Encyclopedia of American foreign policy p507-14

Government attorneys. See Public prosecutors

Government business enterprises

United States
Seidman, H. Government-sponsored enterprise in the United States. *In* Smith, B. L. R. ed. The new political economy: the public use of the private sector p83-108

Government centralization. See Decentralization in government

Government contracts. See Public contracts

Government decentralization. See Decentralization in government

Government departments. See Administrative agencies

Government employees. See Civil service

Government information
Galnoor, I. The information marketplace. *In* Galnoor, I. ed. Government secrecy in democracies p77-92
Galnoor, I. What do we know about government secrecy? *In* Galnoor, I. ed. Government secrecy in democracies p275-313
See also Government and the press

Canada
Doern, G. B. Canada. *In* Galnoor, I. ed. Government secrecy in democracies p143-56

France
Manor, Y. France. *In* Galnoor, I. ed. Government secrecy in democracies p234-54

Germany, West
Reese, J. The Federal Republic of Germany. *In* Galnoor, I. ed. Government secrecy in democracies p216-33

Great Britain
Seymour-Ure, C. Great Britain. *In* Galnoor, I. ed. Government secrecy in democracies p157-75

Israel
Galnoor, I. Israel. *In* Galnoor, I. ed. Government secrecy in democracies p176-200

Netherlands
Brasz, H. A. The Netherlands. *In* Galnoor, I. ed. Government secrecy in democracies p201-15

Scandinavia
Einhorn, E. S. Denmark, Norway, and Sweden. *In* Galnoor, I. ed. Government secrecy in democracies p255-72

United States
Curzon, D. The generic secrets of government decision making. *In* Galnoor, I. ed. Government secrecy in democracies p93-109
Rothman, R. C. The symbolic uses of public information. *In* Galnoor, I. ed. Government secrecy in democracies p62-76
Rourke, F. E. The United States. *In* Galnoor, I. ed. Government secrecy in democracies p113-28

Government liability
Edmonds, M. Accountability and the military-industrial complex. *In* Smith, B. L. R. ed. The new political economy: the public use of the private sector p149-80
Mansfield, H. C. Independence and accountability for federal contractors and grantees. *In* Smith, B. L. R. ed. The new political economy: the public use of the private sector p319-35

Government liability—*Continued*

Reagan, M. D. Accountability and independence in federal grants-in-aid. *In* Smith, B. L. R. ed. The new political economy: the public use of the private sector p181-213

Staats, E. B. New problems of accountability for federal programs. *In* Smith, B. L. R. ed. The new political economy: the public use of the private sector p46-67

Government office practice. See Office practice in government

Government publications. See subdivision Government publications under names of countries, states, counties, cities, etc. e.g. Great Britain—Government publications

Government regulation of commerce. See Industrial laws and legislation; Trade regulation

Government responsibility. See Government liability

Government secrecy. See Executive privilege (Government information); Government information

Government support of science, literature, and art. See State encouragement of science, literature and art

Gowans, Alan

Towards a humane environment: first principles for architectural design and history. *In* Mann, D. A. ed. The arts in a democratic society p19-42

Gower, Herschel

The Scottish element in traditional ballads collected in America. *In* Ballad studies p117-51

Gower, John

About

Olsson, K. O. Rhetoric, John Gower, and the late medieval exemplum. *In* Medievalia et humanistica no. 8 p185-200

About individual works

Confessio amantis

Farnham, A. E. The art of high prosaic seriousness: John Gower as didactic raconteur. *In* The Learned and the lewed p161-73

Kelly, D. Verisimilitude and imagination: the crisis in late courtly poetry. *In* Kelly, D. Medieval imagination p177-203

Gower, Joseph F.

Democracy as a theological problem in Isaac Hecker's apologetics. *In* America in theological perspective p37-55

Gowing, Lawrence

Matisse: the harmony of light. *In* Kaplan, P. and Manso, S. eds. Major European art movements, 1900-1945 p5-41

Goytisolo, Juan

About individual works

Marks of identity

Schwartz, R. Juan Goytisolo and Señas de identidad (Marks of identity) (1966). *In* Schwartz, R. Spain's New Wave novelists, 1950-1974 p187-204

Goytisolo, Luis. See Goytisolo-Gay, Luis

Goytisolo-Gay, Luis

About individual works

Las afueras

Schwartz, R. Luis Goytisolo-Gay and Las afueras (The outskirts) (1958). *In* Schwartz, R. Spain's New Wave novelists, 1950-1974 p100-12

Gozzi, Carlo, conte

About

Nicoll, A. The growth of bourgeois comedy. *In* Nicoll, A. World drama p307-29

Grabar, Oleg

Architecture and art. *In* The Genius of Arab civilization p77-116

Cities and citizens. *In* Lewis, B. ed. Islam and the Arab world p89-116

Graber, Doris Appel

Intervention and nonintervention. *In* Encyclopedia of American foreign policy p482-95

Grabo, Norman S.

Colonial American theology: holiness and the lyric impulse. *In* Essays in honor of Russel B. Nye p74-91

Grabowicz, George

Samuel Twardowski's Wojna domowa: literary context and aspects of genre. *In* For Wiktor Weintraub p169-87

Graburn, Nelson H. H.

'I like things to look more different than that stuff did': an experiment in cross-cultural art appreciation. *In* Greenhalgh, M. and Megaw, J. V. S. eds. Art in society p51-70

Graça Aranha, José Pereira da

About

Aiex, A. Graça Aranha and Brazilian modernism. *In* Forster, M. H. ed. Tradition and renewal p51-67

Grace, Virginia R.

Exceptional amphora stamps. *In* Studies in classical art and archaeology p115-27

Grace (Theology) See Covenants (Theology)

Gracia, Juan José Linz Storch de. See Linz Storch de Gracia, Juan José

Grad, Bernard R.

The biological effects of the "laying on of hands" on animals and plants: implications for biology. *In* Parapsychology: its relation to physics, biology, psychology, and psychiatry p76-89

Healing by the laying on of hands: a review of experiments. *In* Sobel, D. S. ed. Ways of health p267-87

Gradidge, Roderick

Edwin Lutyens: the last High Victorian. *In* Seven Victorian architects p122-36

Grading and marking (Students)

Hoffmann, B. Magic, science and evaluation. *In* From Parnassus p324-33

Graduals (Music)

Hartzell, K. D. An unknown English Benedictine gradual of the eleventh century. *In* Anglo-Saxon England 4 p131-44

Graduate medical education. See Interns (Medicine)

Graduate students. See Women graduate students

Graebner, Norman Arthur

America in the world. *In* Alderson, W. T. ed. American issues p97-112

The Manchurian crisis, 1931-1932. *In* Higham, R. D. ed. Intervention or abstention: the dilemma of American foreign policy p60-78

Morgenthau as historian. *In* [Truth and tragedy]: a tribute to Hans Morgenthau p66-76

Graeser, Andreas
The Stoic theory of meaning. *In* Rist, J. M. ed. The Stoics p77-100

Graetz, Heinrich Hirsch
About
Kochan, L. Graetz and Dubnow: two Jewish historians in an alien world. *In* Essays in honour of E. H. Carr p352-66
Rosenthal, E. I. J. Hermann Cohen and Heinrich Graetz. *In* Salo Wittmayer Baron v2 p725-43

Graff, Gerald
Literature against itself
Contents
Babbitt at the abyss
Culture, criticism and unreality
English in America
How not to save the humanities
How not to talk about fictions
The myth of the postmodern breakthrough
The politics of anti-realism
What was New Criticism?

Graff, Henry Franklin
Presidents as penmen. *In* From Parnassus p3-15

Graffigny, Françoise d'Issembourg d'Happoncourt de
About
Showalter, E. Madame de Graffigny and her salon. *In* Studies in eighteenth-century culture v6 p377-91

Graffito decoration
Paphos
Megaw, A. H. S. An early thirteenth-century Aegean glazed ware. *In* Studies in memory of David Talbot Rice p34-45

Graham, Andrew Guillemard
Impartiality and bias in economics. *In* Montefiore, A. ed. Neutrality and impartiality p49-71

Graham, Billy. See Graham, William Franklin

Graham, George J.
The Supreme Court. *In* Graham, G. J. and Graham, S. G. eds. Founding principles of American government p258-79
See also Graham, S. G. jt. auth.

Graham, Joe S.
The role of the curandero in the Mexican American folk medicine system in west Texas. *In* American folk medicine p175-89

Graham, Kenneth W.
Implications of the grotesque: Beckford's Vathek and the boundaries of fictional reality. *In* Tennessee Studies in literature v23 p61-74
Vathek in English and French. *In* Virginia. University. Bibliographical Society. Studies in bibliography v28 p153-66

Graham, Loren R.
Concerns about science and attempts to regulate inquiry. *In* Holton, G. J. and Morison, R. S. eds. Limits of scientific inquiry p 1-21
The development of science policy in the Soviet Union. *In* Science policies of industrial nations p12-58

Graham, Robert Bontine Cunninghame- See Cunninghame-Graham, Robert Bontine

Graham, Scarlett G.
Government and the economy. *In* Graham, G. J. and Graham, S. G. eds. Founding principles of American government p305-30

Graham, Scarlett G. and Graham, George J.
The future of American democracy. *In* Graham, G. J. and Graham, S. G. eds. Founding principles of American government p347-53

Graham, Sylvester
About
Blake, J. B. Health reform. *In* The Rise of Adventism p30-49

Graham, William Franklin
About
Williams, G. H. and Petersen, R. L. Evangelicals: society, the state, the nation. *In* Wells, D. F. and Woodbridge, J. D. eds. The evangelicals p211-48

Graham, Winston
The novelist as a human being. *In* Royal Society of Literature of the United Kingdom, London. Essays by divers hands v39 p47-56

Grahn, Judy
About individual works
The work of a common woman
Rich, A.C. Power and danger: works of a common woman. *In* Rich, A.C. On lies, secrets, and silence p247-58

Grail
Hyman, S. E. Jessie Weston and the Forest of Broceliande. *In* Hyman, S. E. The critic's credentials p284-97

Legends
Lagorio, V. M. The Joseph of Arimathie: English hagiography in transition. *In* Medievalia et humanistica no. 6 p91-101
Tax, P. W. The Grail kingdom and Parzival's first visit: intrigue, Minne, despair. *In* Medieval and Renaissance studies [1975] p20-36

Grain elevators
United States—Law and legislation
Kitch, E. M. and Bowler, C. A. The facts of Munn v. Illinois. *In* The Supreme Court review, 1978 p313-43

Grain handling. See Grain elevators

Grammar. See Grammar, Comparative and general

Grammar, Comparative and general
Frede, M. Principles of Stoic grammar. *In* Rist, J. M. ed. The Stoics p27-75
Rouveret, A. Result clauses and conditions on rules. *In* Keyser, S. J. ed. Recent transformational studies in European languages p159-87
See also Anaphora (Linguistics); Generative grammar; Linguistic analysis (Linguistics); Systemic grammar

Gender
Beardsley, E. L. Traits and genderization. *In* Feminism and philosophy p117-23
Korsmeyer, C. W. The hidden joke: generic uses of masculine terminology. *In* Feminism and philosophy p138-53
Moulton, J. M. The myth of the neutral "man." *In* Feminism and philosophy p124-37

Grammar, Comparative and general—*Cont.*

Person

Harré, R. The self in monodrama. *In* Mischel, T. ed. The self p318-48

Phonology

Ferguson, C. A. New directions in phonological theory: language acquisition and universals research. *In* Current issues in linguistic theory p247-99

Pronoun

Harré, R. The self in monodrama. *In* Mischel, T. ed. The self p318-48

Sentences

Koster, J. Why subject sentences don't exist. *In* Keyser, S. J. ed. Recent transformational studies in European languages p53-64

Potts, T. C. The place of structure in communication. *In* Royal Institute of Philosophy. Communication and understanding p91-115

Subject and predicate

See Grammar, Comparative and general —Topic and comment

Syntax

Bever, T. G.; Lackner, J. R. and Kirk, R. The underlying structures of sentences are the primary units of immediate speech processing. *In* Harman, G. ed. On Noam Chomsky p118-45

Davidson, D. H. Semantics for natural languages. *In* Harman, G. ed. On Noam Chomsky p242-52

Fillmore, C. J. Topics in lexical semantics. *In* Current issues in linguistic theory p76-138

Katz, J. J. The relevance of linguistics to philosophy. *In* Harman, G. ed. On Noam Chomsky p229-41

Lees, R. B. Review of Syntactic structures. *In* Harman, G. ed. On Noam Chomsky p34-79

Lewis, D. B. Languages, language, and grammar. *In* Harman, G. ed. On Noam Chomsky p253-66

Partee, B. H. Linguistic metatheory. *In* Harman, G. ed. On Noam Chomsky p303-15

Putnam, H. W. Some issues in the theory of grammar. *In* Harman, G. ed. On Noam Chomsky p80-103

Quine, W. V. Logic as a source of syntactical insights. *In* Quine, W. V. The ways of paradox, and other essays p44-49

Ross, J. R. Excerpts from Constraints on variables in syntax. *In* Harman, G. ed. On Noam Chomsky p165-200

Searle, J. R. Chomsky's revolution in linguistics. *In* Harman, G. ed. On Noam Chomsky p2-33

Stampe, D. W. Toward a grammar of meaning. *In* Harman, G. ed. On Noam Chomsky p267-302

See also Grammar, Comparative and general—Topic and comment

Tense

Kretzmann, N. Incipit/desinit. *In* Motion and time, space and matter p101-36

Woods, M. J. Existence and tense. *In* Evans, G. L. and McDowell, J. H. eds. Truth and meaning p248-62

Topic and comment

Clark, R. L. Facts, fact-correlates, and fact-surrogates. *In* Fact, value, and perception p3-17

Geach, P. T. Names and identity. *In* Guttenplan, S. D. ed. Mind and language p139-58

Heintz, J. W. The real subject-predicate asymmetry. *In* Fact, value, and perception p19-29

Wilson, N. L. Notes on the form of certain elementary facts. *In* Fact, value, and perception p43-51

Woods, M. J. Existence and tense. *In* Evans, G. L. and McDowell, J. H. eds. Truth and meaning p248-62

Wright, C. Language-mastery and the Sorites paradox. *In* Evans, G. L. and McDowell, J. H. eds. Truth and meaning p223-47

Grammar, Generative. See Generative grammar

Grammar, Philosophical. See Grammar, Comparative and general

Grammar, Transformational. See Generative grammar

Grammar schools. See Public schools

Grams, Paul

Pnin: the biographer as meddler. *In* A Book of things about Vladimir Nabokov p193-202

Granada (City) Alhambra. See Alhambra

La grande illusion (Motion picture)

Kauffmann, S. La grande illusion. *In* Kauffmann, S. Living images p307-16

Grandville, Jean Ignace Isidore Gérard, called

About

Praz, M. Two masters of the absurd: Grandville and Carroll. *In* The Artist and writer in France p134-37

Graney, Marshall John

The aged and their environment: the study of intervening variables. *In* Gubrium, J. F. ed. Late life p5-17

Granger, Bruce Ingham

American essay serials from Franklin to Irving

Contents

Conclusion
Early Boston serials
Early Philadelphia serials
Early Southern serials
John Trumbull
Joseph Dennie
Judith Sargent Murray
Philip Freneau
Washington Irving
William Wirt

Franklin as press agent in England. *In* Lemay, J. A. L. ed. The oldest revolutionary p21-32

Granger, Byrd Howell

Some aspects of folk medicine among Spanish-speaking people in southern Arizona. *In* American folk medicine p191-202

Grannis, Chandler B.

More than merchants: seventy-five years of the ABA. *In* Bookselling in America and the world p65-108

Granovskiĭ, Timofeĭ Nikolaevich

About

Kostka, E. K. T. N. Granovsky and the ideological lure of the West. *In* Kostka, E. K. Glimpses of Germanic-Slavic relations from Pushkin to Heinrich Mann p85-100

Granovsky, T. N. See Granovskiĭ, Timofeĭ Nikolaevich

Grant, Duncan James Corrowr. See Shone, R. jt. auth.

Grant, Edward
Cosmology. *In* Lindberg, D. C. ed. Science in the Middle Ages p265-302

Place and space in medieval physical thought. *In* Motion and time, space and matter p137-67

Grant, George Parkin
The university curriculum and the technological threat. *In* Niblett, W. R. ed. The sciences, the humanities and the technological threat p21-35

Grant, Gerald
Journalism and social science: continuities and discontinuities. *In* On the making of Americans p291-313

Grant, James

About individual works
The Scottish cavalier

Hart, F. R. Romance after the Enlightenment. *In* Hart, F. R. The Scottish novel p143-53

Grant, Julia Dent

About individual works
The personal memoirs of Julia Dent Grant

Vidal, G. President and Mrs U.S. Grant. *In* Vidal, G. Matters of fact and of fiction p175-90

Grant, Patrick
Images and ideas in literature of the English Renaissance

Contents

The arms of the Red Cross: believing in the images
Conclusion. John Norris and Mr Locke: bodies and the uses of imagination
John Norris and the Oratorians: belief and the images in God
The matter of roots: belief, images, and bodies
Richard Crashaw and the Capucins: images and the force of belief
The tempest and the magic of charity: believing the images
Time and temptation in Paradise regained: belief and the single image

Redeeming the time: the Confessions of St. Augustine. *In* Jeffrey, D. L. ed. By things seen: reference and recognition in medieval thought p21-32

Grant, Raymond J. S.
Laurence Norwell's transcript of BM Cotton Otho B. xi. *In* Anglo-Saxon England 3 p111-24

Grant, Ulysses Simpson, President U.S.

About individual works
Personal memoirs

Arnold, M. General Grant. *In* Arnold, M. The last word p144-79

Graff, H. F. Presidents as penmen. *In* From Parnassus p3-15

Vidal, G. President and Mrs U.S. Grant. *In* Vidal, G. Matters of fact and of fiction p175-90

Grantham, Dewey W.
The regional imagination

Contents

Black Patch War: the Kentucky and Tennessee night riders, 1905-1909
Contemporary American history
Dinner at the White House: Theodore Roosevelt, Booker T. Washington, and the South
Hoke Smith and the New Freedom, 1913-1917
Jimmy Carter and the Americanization of Southern politics
The Little Rock school crisis: Negro rights and the struggle for an integrated America
Ralph J. Bunche and the making of a documentary classic
Ray Stannard Baker's report on American Negro citizenship in the Progressive Era
The regional imagination: social scientists and the American South
The South and the politics of sectionalism
The South and the reconstruction of American politics
The Southern Bourbons revisited
Southern progressives and the racial imperative
Three violent scenes in Southern politics

Grantham, George W.
Scale and organization in French farming, 1840-1880. *In* Parker, W. N. and Jones, E. L. eds. European peasants and their markets p293-326

Grants-in-aid
See also Federal aid to hospitals; Research grants

Italy
Cassese, S. State grants for the south of Italy. *In* Davis, K. C. Discretionary justice in Europe and America p149-60

United States
Reagan, M. D. Accountability and independence in federal grants-in-aid. *In* Smith, B. L. R. ed. The new political economy: the public use of the private sector p181-213

Granville-Barker, Harley Granville

About
Kauffmann, S. The lives of Granville Barker. *In* Kauffmann, S. Persons of the drama p317-28

The grapes of wrath (Motion picture)
Campbell, R. Trampling out the vintage: sour grapes. *In* Peary, G. and Shatzkin, R. eds. The modern American novel and the movies p107-18

Sarris, A. John Ford: The grapes of wrath. *In* Denby, D. ed. Awake in the dark p320-25

Graphic arts

France
Shikes, R. E. Five artists in the service of politics in the pages of L'Assiette au beurre. *In* Millon, H. A. and Nochlin, L. eds. Art and architecture in the service of politics p162-81

Graphology. See Drawing, Psychology of

Grass, Günter

About
Hamburger, M. Moralist and jester: the poetry of Günter Grass. *In* Hamburger, M. Art as second nature p134-49

Grass, Günter—About—*Continued*

Kurz, P. K. The insecure heraldic animal: on Gunter Grass's Uptight and Local anaesthetic. *In* Kurz, P. K. On modern German literature v4 p73-95

About individual works
Dog years

Kurz, P. K. Hundejahre. *In* Kurz, P. K. On modern German literature v 1 p131-48

Poetical works

Kurz, P. K. Wind hens interrogated. *In* Kurz, P. K. On modern German literature v3 p39-64

Grasshopper pueblo, Arizona, Population dynamics at the. Longacre, W. A. *In* Zubrow, E. B. W. ed. Demographic anthropology p169-84

Grassi, Ernesto

Marxism, humanism, and the problem of imagination in Vico's works. *In* Giambattista Vico's science of humanity p275-94

Grasso, Ella Tambussi

The role of energy management. *In* Benton L. R. ed. Management for the future p139-47

Gratian, Roman Emperor

About

Barnes, T. D. Constans and Gratian in Rome. *In* Harvard Studies in classical philology v79 p325-33

Gratian, the Canonist. See Gratianus, the Canonist

Gratianus, the Canonist

About individual works
Decretum

Kuttner, S. G. Gratian and Plato. *In* Church and government in the Middle Ages p93-118

Gratitude

Mott, S. C. The power of giving and receiving: reciprocity in Hellenistic benevolence. *In* Current issues in Biblical and patristic interpretation p60-72

Grau, Shirley Ann

About individual works
The keepers of the house

Going, W. T. Alabama geography in Shirley Ann Grau's The keepers of the house. *In* Going, W. T. Essays on Alabama literature p32-38

Graub, Milton

The thoughts of a bereaved father. *In* Anticipatory grief p158-60

Graubard, Mark Aaron

The sleepwalkers: its contribution and impact. *In* Harris, H. A. ed. Astride the two cultures p20-36

Graubard, Stephen Richards

Edward Gibbon: contraria sunt complementa. *In* Edward Gibbon and The decline and fall of the Roman Empire p121-37

Graver, Lawrence Stanley

Carson McCullers. *In* Howard, M. ed. Seven American women writers of the twentieth century p265-310

Graves, Nancy Beatrice. See Graves, T. D. jt. auth.

Graves, Richard

About individual works
The spiritual Quixote; or, The summer's ramble of Mr Geoffrey Wildgoose

Auty, S. G. Fielding's followers: The spiritual Quixote. *In* Auty, S. G. The comic spirit of eighteenth-century novels p87-102

Graves, Robert

Harp, anvil, oar; excerpt from "The crowning privilege." *In* Gross, H. S. ed. The structure of verse p21-39

About individual works
Collected poems, 1955

Frye, N. Graves, gods, and scholars. *In* Frye, N. Northrop Frye on culture and literature p230-36

Trilling, L. A ramble on Graves. *In* Trilling, L. A gathering of fugitives p23-33

Goodbye to all that

DeBell, D. Strategies of survival: David Jones, In parenthesis, and Robert Graves, Goodbye to all that. *In* Klein, H. M. ed. The First World War in fiction p160-73

Poetic works

Fraser, G. S. The poetry of Robert Graves. *In* Fraser, G. S. Essays on twentieth-century poets p125-35

Pritchard, W. H. English poetry in the 1920s: Graves and Lawrence. *In* Pritchard, W. H. Seeing through everything p114-33

Graves, Theodore Dumaine, and Graves, Nancy Beatrice

Evolving strategies in the study of culture change. *In* Spindler, G. D. ed. The making of psychological anthropology p516-55

Graves. See Cemeteries

Gravestones. See Sepulchral monuments

Graveyards. See Cemeteries

Gravit, Francis West

The first centenary of Molière's death. *In* Johnson, R. B.; Neumann, E. S. and Trail, G. T. eds. Molière and the commonwealth of letters: patrimony and posterity p547-56

Gravitation

Bondi, H. Relativity theory and gravitation. *In* Einstein p113-29

See also Ether (of space); Relativity (Physics)

Gravity. See Weight (Physics)

Gray, Colin S.

Strategic ideas and defense policy: the organizational nexus. *In* Beaumont, R. A. and Edmonds, M. eds. War in the next decade p89-109

Gray, Douglas

Notes on some Middle English charms. *In* Chaucer and Middle English studies in honour of Rossell Hope Robbins p56-71

Gray, Hugh, 1916-

Konda Lakshman Bapuji: a backward classes leader of the Telengana (Andhra Pradesh) *In* The Making of politicians: studies from Africa and Asia p156-65

Gray, Jack

China: communism and Confucianism. *In* Brown, A. H. and Gray, J. eds. Political culture and political change in Communist states p197-230

Conclusions. *In* Brown, A. H. and Gray, J. eds. Political culture and political change in Communist states p253-72

**Great Britain—Church history—16th century
—**Continued

Vander Molen, R. J. Anglican against Puritan: ideological origins during the Marian exile. *In* Vaughan, A. T. and Bremer, F. J. eds. Puritan New England p2-18

Civilization—American influences

Allen, H. C. The cultural tie; excerpt from "Conflict and concord, the Anglo-American relationship since 1783." *In* Burton, D. H. ed. American history—British historians p75-91

Katznelson, I. The Americanization of British politics. *In* Kramnick, I. ed. Is Britain dying? p137-51

Civilization—Medieval period,
1066-1485

Thrupp, S. L. Economy and society in medieval England. *In* Thrupp, S. L. Society and history p29-43

Civilization—17th century

Vieth, D. M. Divided consciousness: the trauma and triumph of Restoration culture. *In* Tennessee Studies in literature v22 p46-62

Civilization—20th century

Stansky, P. Toward 1984: George Orwell and today's Britain. *In* Kramnick, I. ed. Is Britain dying? p269-76

Civilization—1945-

Koestler, A. Life in 1980—the rule of mediocracy. *In* Koestler, A. The heel of Achilles p41-46

Colonies

Aldrich, D. M. Frontier militias: militia laws on the North American and South African frontiers. *in* The Frontier v2 p153-66

Colonies—America

Brown, A. S. The impossible dream: the North ministry, the structure of politics, and conciliation. *In* The American Revolution and "a candid world" p17-39

Cone, C. B. George III—America's unknown king. *In* The American Revolution and "a candid world" p 1-16

Griffiths, D. M. Catherine the Great, the British opposition and the American Revolution. *In* The American Revolution and "a candid world" p85-110

Stevens, D. Adam Smith and the colonial disturbances. *In* Skinner, A. S. and Wilson, T. eds. Essays on Adam Smith p202-17

Colonies—India

Peele, G. Revolt over India. *In* Peele, G. and Cook, C. eds. The politics of reappraisal, 1918-1939 p114-45

Colonies—West Indies

Carnegie, A. R. Commonwealth Caribbean regionalism: legal aspects. *In* The Year book of world affairs, 1979 p180-200

Commerce—History

Crouzet, F. Trade and empire: the British experience from the establishment of free trade until the First World War. *In* Great Britain and her world, 1750-1914 p209-35

Dietz, B. Antwerp and London: the structure and balance of trade in the 1560s. *In* Wealth and power in Tudor England p186-203

Munro, J. H. A. Bullionism and the bill of exchange in England, 1272-1663: a study in monetary management and popular prejudice. *In* The Dawn of modern banking p169-239

Commerce—Flanders

Munro, J. H. A. Industrial protectionism in medieval Flanders: urban or national? *In* The Medieval city p229-67

Commerce—France

Ratcliffe, B. M. The origins of the Anglo-French commercial treaty of 1860: a reassessment. *In* Great Britain and her world, 1750-1914 p125-51

Commerce—Russia

Baron, S. H. Osip Nepea and the opening of Anglo-Russian commercial relations. *In* Oxford Slavonic papers, new ser. v11 p42-63

Commerce—Spain

Ruiz, T. F. Castilian merchants in England, 1248-1350. *In* Order and innovation in the Middle Ages p173-85

Commercial treaties

Ratcliffe, B. M. The origins of the Anglo-French commercial treaty of 1860: a reassessment. *In* Great Britain and her world, 1750-1914 p125-51

Committee on Children and Young Persons

About individual works
Report

Morris, A. Scottish juvenile justice: a critique. *In* Crime, criminology and public policy p347-74

Currency question

Chaloner, W. H. Currency problems of the British empire, 1814-1914. *In* Great Britain and her world, 1750-1914 p179-207

Defenses

Carlton, D. The Anglo-American nuclear relationship: proliferatory or anti-proliferatory? *In* Arms control and technological innovation p132-45

Economic conditions

Braun, R. Taxation, sociopolitical structure, and state-building: Great Britain and Brandenburg-Prussia. *In* Tilly, C. ed. The formation of national states in Western Europe p243-327

Cohen, J. S. and Weitzman, M. L. Enclosures and depopulation: a Marxian analysis. *In* Parker, W. N. and Jones, E. L. eds. European peasants and their markets p161-76

Harvey, P. D. A. The English inflation of 1180-1220. *In* Peasants, knights and heretics p57-84

Kershaw, I. The great famine and agrarian crisis in England, 1315-1322. *In* Peasants, knights and heretics p85-132

Economic conditions—18th century

McCloskey, D. N. The economics of enclosure: a market analysis. *In* Parker, W. N. and Jones, E. L. eds. European peasants and their markets p123-60

Economic conditions—1760-1860

Feingold, R. Bucolic tradition and virtuous work: Arthur Young and Adam Smith. *In* Feingold, R. Nature and society p51-82

Great Britain—*Continued*

Relations (general) with Russia

Robinson, E. The transference of British technology to Russia, 1760-1820: a preliminary enquiry. *In* Great Britain and her world, 1750-1914 p 1-26

Relations (general) with the United States

Campbell, C. S. Edward J. Phelps and Anglo-American relations. *In* Allen, H. C. and Thompson, R. eds. Contrast and connection p210-24

Hall, D. D. The Victorian connection. *In* Howe, D. W. ed. Victorian America p81-94

Morgan, K. O. The future at work: Anglo-American progressivism, 1890-1917. *In* Allen, H. C. and Thompson, R. eds. Contrast and connection p245-71

Religion—19th century

Altholz, J. L. The warfare of conscience with theology. *In* Altholz, J. L. ed. The mind and art of Victorian England p58-77

Hough, G. G. Coleridge and the Victorians. *In* Hough, G. G. Selected essays p92-109

Social conditions

Bagwell, P. S. and Mingay, G. E. Britain and America: social progress, 1850-1939; excerpt from "Britain and America." *In* Burton, D. H. ed. American history—British historians p289-318

Thrupp, S. L. The problem of conservatism in fifteenth-century England. *In* Thrupp, S. L. Society and history p237-44

Social conditions—19th century

Cooter, R. The power of the body: the early nineteenth century. *In* Barnes, B. and Shapin, S. eds. Natural order p73-92

Gorham, D. Victorian reform as a family business: the Hill family. *In* Wohl, A. S. ed. The Victorian family p119-47

Kiernan, E. V. G. Working class and nation in nineteenth-century Britain. *In* Rebels and their causes p122-39

Robson, J. M. Thoughts on social change and political accommodation in Victorian Britain. *In* Altholz, J. L. ed. The mind and art of Victorian England p78-93

Social conditions—1945-

Heath, E. R. G. A Tory view. *In* Kramnick, I. ed. Is Britain dying? p31-44

Jay, P. Englanditis. *In* Tyrrell, R. E. ed. The future that doesn't work p167-85

Social life and customs—18th century

Lewis, W. S. A house-party at Stowe. *In* The Dress of words p117-25

Social life and customs—19th century

Buckley, J. H. Victorian England: the self-conscious society. *In* Altholz, J. L. ed. The mind and art of Victorian England p3-15

Cooper, J. The perfect gentleman. *In* The Saturday book 34 p114-25

McBride, T. M. 'As the twig is bent': the Victorian nanny. *In* Wohl, A. S. ed. The Victorian family p44-58

Marshall, A. The perfect lady. *In* The Saturday book 34 p127-33

Miller, J. H. 'Temple and sewer': childbirth, prudery, and Victoria Regina. *In* Wohl, A. S. ed. The Victorian family p23-43

Tamke, S. S. Human values and aging: the perspective of the Victorian nursery. *In* Spicker, S. F.; Woodward, K. M. and Van Tassel, D. D. eds. Aging and the elderly p63-81

The **Great** Chain of Being in Dryden's All for love. Armstrong, R. *In* A Provision of human nature p133-43

The great dictator (Motion picture)

Truffaut, F. Charlie Chaplin: The great dictator. *In* Truffaut, F. The films in my life p54-57

The great Gatsby (Motion picture)

Kauffmann, S. The great Gatsby. *In* Kauffmann, S. Living images p273-74

Great powers

Buchan, A. An expedition to the poles. *In* The Year book of world affairs, 1975 p4-21

Morgenthau, H. J. Big power confrontations in the Middle East. *In* The New world balance and peace in the Middle East: reality or mirage? p69-73

Sudjatmoko. Reflections on nonalignment in the 1970s. *In* Erb, G. F. and Kallab, V. eds. Beyond dependency p28-37

Vincent, R. J. The idea of concert and international order. *In* The Year book of world affairs, 1975 p34-55

Foreign economic relations

Peña, F. Mulitnational enterprises and North-South relations. *In* Erb, G. F. and Kallab, V. eds. Beyond dependency p57-74

Great silkie of Sule Skerry (Scottish ballad)
Bruford, A. The grey selkie. *In* Ballad studies p41-65

Greater vehicle. See Mahayana Buddhism

The greatest story ever told (Motion picture)

Macdonald, D. The greatest story ever told; excerpt from "Dwight Macdonald on movies." *In* Denby, D. ed. Awake in the dark p382-88

Greaves, John
Going astray. *In* Dickens Studies Annual v3 p144-61

Grebstein, Sheldon Norman
The comic anatomy of Portnoy's complaint. *In* Cohen, S. B. ed. Comic relief p152-71

The reliable and unreliable narrator in Hemingway's stories. *In* Benson, J. J. ed. The short stories of Ernest Hemingway: critical essays p113-21

Greco-Roman civilization. See Civilization, Greco-Roman

Greece

Antiquities
See Vases, Greek

Civilization

Simon, B. The Greeks and the irrational. *In* Simon, B. Mind and madness in ancient Greece p43-49

Historiography

Downs, R. B. Sense of the past. *In* Downs, R. B. Books that changed the world p121-50

History—to 146 B.C.

Rice, D. G. Xenophon, Diodorus and the year 379/378 B.C. Reconstruction and reappraisal. *In* Yale classical studies v24 p95-130

Greece—*Continued*

History—Persian Wars, 500-449 B.C.
—Historiography

Momigliano, A. Eastern elements in Post-exilic Jewish, and Greek, historiography. *In* Momigliano, A. Essays in ancient and modern historiography p25-35

History—Peloponnesian War, 431-404 B.C.

Cawkwell, G. Thucydides' judgment of Periclean strategy. *In* Yale classical studies v24 p53-70

History—Peloponnesian War, 431-404 B.C.—Historiography

Fornara, C. W. Plutarch and the Megarian decree. *In* Yale classical studies v24 p213-28

Intellectual life—History

Simon, B. Hysteria and social issues. *In* Simon, B. Mind and madness in ancient Greece p238-68

Politics and government

Syme, Sir R. Liberty in classical antiquity. *In* Aspects of American liberty p8-15

Religion

Boer, W. den. Aspects of religion in classical Greece. *In* Harvard Studies in classical philology v77 p 1-21

Georgi, D. Socioeconomic reasons for the "divine man" as a propagandistic pattern. *In* Aspects of religious propaganda in Judaism and early Christianity p27-42

Henrichs, A. Two doxographical notes: Democritus and Prodicus on religion. *In* Harvard Studies in classical philology v79 p93-123

Greece, Modern

Foreign relations—Sweden

Sundberg, J. W. F. Thinking the unthinkable or the case of Dr Tsironis. *In* International terrorism and political crimes p448-59

Foreign relations—United States

Couloumbis, T. A. and Tredway, M. M. U.S. intervention & abstention in Greece, 1944-1970. *In* Higham, R. D. ed. Intervention or abstention: the dilemma of American foreign policy p95-113

LaFeber, W. The Truman doctrine. *In* Encyclopedia of American foreign policy p980-85

History—War of Independence, 1821-1829

Skiotis, D. N. Mountain warriors and the Greek Revolution. *In* War, technology and society in the Middle East p308-29

Politics and government—1917-1944

Kousoulas, D. G. The Greek Communists tried three times—and failed. *In* Hammond, T. T. ed. The anatomy of Communist takeovers p293-309

Politics and government—1944-1949

Kousoulas, D. G. The Greek Communists tried three times—and failed. *In* Hammond, T. T. ed. The anatomy of Communist takeovers p293-309

Greece in literature

Velz, J. W. The ancient world in Shakespeare: authenticity or anachronism? A retrospect. *In* Shakespeare survey v31 p 1-12

Greek architecture. See Architecture, Greek

Greek art. See Art, Greek

Greek bronzes. See Bronzes, Greek

Greek Church. See Orthodox Eastern Church

Greek civilization. See Civilization, Greek; Hellenism

Greek Communist Party. See Communist Party of Greece

Greek drama

Chorus

See Drama—Chorus (Greek drama)

History and criticism

Downs, R. B. Masters of dramatic art. *In* Downs, R. B. Books that changed the world p93-120

Presentation, Ancient

See Theater—Greece

Greek drama (Comedy)

History and criticism

Anderson, M. J. The comedy of Greece and Rome. *In* Howarth, W. D. ed. Comic drama p22-39

Fantham, E. Adaptation and survival: a genre study of Roman comedy in relation to its Greek sources. *In* Ruggiers, P. G. ed. Versions of medieval comedy p19-49

Ivanov, V. I. Gogol's Inspector General and the comedy of Aristophanes. *In* Maguire, R. A. ed. Gogol from the twentieth century p199-214

Sandbach, F. H. New Comedy. *In* Sandbach, F. H. The comic theatre of Greece and Rome p55-75

Sandbach, F. H. Old Comedy. *In* Sandbach, F. H. The comic theatre of Greece and Rome p41-54

Segal, E. W. The φύσις of comedy. *In* Harvard Studies in classical philology v77 p129-36

Weimann, R. The mimus. *In* Weimann, R. Shakespeare and the popular tradition in the theater: studies in the social dimension of dramatic form and function p 1-14

Greek drama (Satyr play)

Sansone, D. The Bacchae as satyr-play? *In* Illinois classical studies v3, 1978 p40-46

Sutton, D. F. A handlist of satyr plays. *In* Harvard Studies in classical philology v8 p107-43

Bibliography

Sutton, D. F. A handlist of satyr plays. *In* Harvard Studies in classical philology v78 p107-43

Greek drama (Tragedy)

Kauffmann, S. Trilogy. *In* Kauffmann, S. Persons of the drama p108-11

History and criticism

Else, G. F. Ritual and drama in Aischyleian tragedy. *In* Illinois classical studies, v2 1977 p70-87

Finley, J. H. Politics and early Attic tragedy. *In* Harvard Studies in classical philology v71 p 1-13

Fuhrmann, M. Myth as a recurrent theme in Greek tragedy and twentieth-century drama. *In* Amacher, R. E. and Lange, V. eds. New perspectives in German literary criticism p295-319

Greek poetry—*Continued*
History and criticism
Adkins, A. W. H. Callinus 1 and Tyrtaeus 10 as poetry. *In* Harvard studies in classical philology v81 p59-97

Greek pottery. See Pottery, Greek

Greek rhetoric. See Rhetoric, Ancient

Greek sculpture. See Sculpture, Greek

Greek vase-painting. See Vase-painting, Greek

Greek vases. See Vases, Greek

Greeks in Cyprus
Alcock, A. E. Three case-studies in minority protection: South Tyrol, Cyprus, Quebec. *In* Hepburn, A. C. ed. Minorities in history p189-225

Greeks in Egypt
Bingen, J. The third-century B.C. land-leases from Tholthis. *In* Illinois classical studies v3, 1978 p74-80

Youtie, H. C. ΑΓΡΑΜΜΑΤΟΣ: an aspect of Greek society in Egypt. *In* Harvard Studies in classical philology v75 p161-76

Greeley, Andrew M.
Freedom of choice: "our commitment to integration." *In* Parents, teachers, and children: prospect for choice in American education p183-205

Why study ethnicity? *In* The Diverse society: implications for social policy p3-12

Greeley, Andrew M. and McCready, William C.
The transmission of cultural heritages: the case of the Irish and Italians. *In* Glazer, N. and Moynihan, D. P. eds. Ethnicity p209-35

Green, André
The double and the absent. *In* Roland, A. ed. Psychoanalysis, creativity, and literature p271-92

Green, Brian K.
Spes viva: structure and meaning in The Seafarer. *In* An English miscellany p28-45

Green, Clifford
A theology of sociality: Bonhoeffer's Sanctorum communio. *In* The Context of contemporary theology p65-84

Green, Dan S. See Michaels, J. W. jt. auth.

Green, Dennis Howard
On damning with faint praise in medieval literature. *In* Viator: medieval and Renaissance studies v6 p117-69

The pathway to adventure. *In* Viator: medieval and Renaissance studies v8 p145-88

Green, Derek. See Gordon, E. W. jt. auth.

Green, Henry, 1801-1873, ed.
About individual works
Whitney's choice of emblemes
Tung, M. Whitney's A choice of emblemes revisited: a comparative study of the manuscript and the printed versions. *In* Virginia. University. Bibliographical Society. Studies in bibliography v29 p32-101

Green, Henry, 1905-1974
About
Welty, E. Henry Green: novelist of the imagination. *In* Welty, E. The eye of the story p14-29

About individual works
Back
Russell, J. D. Henry Green: Back, Concluding. *In* Russell, J. D. Style in modern British fiction p158-88

Concluding
Russell, J. D. Henry Green: Back, Concluding. *In* Russell, J. D. Style in modern British fiction p158-88

Loving
Unterecker, J. E. Fiction at the edge of poetry: Durrell, Beckett, Green. *In* Forms of modern British fiction p165-99

Green, James R.
The "salesmen-soldiers" of the "appeal army": a profile of rank-and-file Socialist agitators. *In* Stave, B. M. ed. Socialism and the cities p13-40

Green, John Colton
Science, learning, and utility: patterns of organization in the early American Republic. *In* Oleson, A. and Brown, S. C. eds. The pursuit of knowledge in the early American Republic p 1-20

Green, Justin Jay. See Kim, Chong Lim, jt. auth.

Green, Leslie C.
Jewish issues on the human-rights agenda in the first half of the twentieth century. *In* Sidorsky, D. ed. Essays on human rights p297-308

Terrorism—the Canadian perspective. *In* International terrorism p3-29

Green, Mark J.
The ABA as trade association. *In* Nader, R. and Green, M. J. eds. Verdicts on lawyers p 3-19

The gross legal product: "How much justice can you afford?" *In* Nader, R. and Green, M. J. eds. Verdicts on lawyers p63-79

Green, Matthew
About
Davie, D. Dissent and the Wesleyans, 1740-1800. *In* Davie, D. A gathered Church p37-54

Green, Michael A.
Kheraskov and the Christian tragedy. *In* California Slavic studies v9 p 1-25

Green, Richard
Biological influences on sexual identity. *In* Katchadourian, H. A. ed. Human sexuality p115-33

Green, Robert J.
Politics and literature in Africa: the drama of Athol Fugard. *In* Heywood, C. ed. Aspects of South African literature p163-73

Green, Stanton W.
The agricultural colonization of temperate forest habitats: an ecological model. *In* The Frontier v2 p69-103

Green, Thomas F.
Learning without metaphor. *In* Ortony, A. ed. Metaphor and thought p462-73

Stories and images of the future. *In* Bundy, R. F. ed. Images of the future: the twenty-first century and beyond p35-44

Greenawalt, Kent. See Greenawalt, R. Kent

Greenawalt, R. Kent
Judicial scrutiny of "benign" racial preference in law school admissions. *In* Gross, B. R. ed. Reverse discrimination p217-38

Greenawalt, R. Kent—*Continued*

Perspectives on the right to silence. *In* Crime, criminology and public policy p235-68

Voucher plans and sectarian schools: the constitutional problem. *In* Parents, teachers, and children: prospects for choice in American education p207-25

See also Edgar, H. S. jt. auth.

Greenberg, Clement

Avant-garde attitudes: new art in the sixties. *In* Concerning contemporary art p5-15

Collage; excerpt from "Art and culture (Revised edition)" *In* Kaplan, P. and Manso, S. eds. Major European art movements, 1900-1945 p147-63

About

Goodheart, E. The formalist avant-garde and the autonomy of aesthetic values. *In* Goodheart, E. The failure of criticism p105-18

Greenberg, Janelle

The legal status of the English woman in early eighteenth-century common law and equity. *In* Studies in eighteenth-century culture v4 p171-81

Greenberg, Uri Zevi

About

Alter, R. Uri Zvi Greenberg: a poet of the Holocaust. *In* Alter, R. Defenses of the imagination p103-18

Greenblatt, Kristin Yü

Chu-hung and lay Buddhism in the late Ming. *In* The Unfolding of Neo-Confucianism p93-140

Greenblatt, Stephen Jay

Learning to curse: aspects of linguistic colonialism in the sixteenth century. *In* First images of America p561-80

Marlowe and Renaissance self-fashioning. *In* Kernan, A. B. ed. Two Renaissance myth makers p41-69

Greene, Anthony Hamilton Millard Kirk-. See Kirk-Greene, Anthony Hamilton Millard

Greene, Bob

They tried to help. *In* Gross, B. and Gross, R. eds. The children's rights movement p37-42

Greene, Donald Johnson

From accidie to neurosis: The castle of indolence revisited. *In* English literature in the age of disguise p131-56

Jane Austen's monsters. *In* Halperin, J. ed. Jane Austen p262-78

The myth of limitation. *In* Weinsheimer, J. ed. Jane Austen today p142-75

The study of eighteenth-century literature: past, present, and future. *In* Harth, J. P. ed. New approaches to eighteenth-century literature p 1-32

The term 'conceit' in Johnson's literary criticism. *In* Evidence in literary scholarship p337-51

Greene, Graham

About

Gillie, C. The critical decade, 1930-1940. *In* Gillie, C. Movements in English literature, 1900-1940 p122-49

Kennedy, A. Inconsistencies of narration in Graham Greene. *In* Kennedy, A. The protean self p231-49

Lambert, G. The double agent. *In* Lambert, G. The dangerous edge p132-70

Lodge, D. Graham Greene. *In* Stade, G. ed. Six contemporary British novelists p 1-56

Walker, R. G. Graham Greene and "life on a border." *In* Walker, R. G. Infernal paradise p160-204

About individual works
The heart of the matter

Higdon, D. L. Graham Greene's second thoughts: the text of The heart of the matter. *In* Virginia. University. Bibliographical Society. Studies in bibliography v30 p249-56

Stratford, P. Second thoughts on "Graham Greene's second thoughts": the five texts of The heart of the matter. *In* Virginia. University. Bibliographical Society. Studies in bibliography v31 p263-66

The honorary Consul

Vargo, E. P. Struggling with a bugaboo: the priest-character in Achebe and Greene and Keneally. *In* Narasimhaiah, C. D. ed. Awakened conscience p284-93

The power and the glory

Walker, R. G. A Mexico of the mind: The power and the glory. *In* Walker, R. G. Infernal paradise p205-36

A sort of life

Sheed, W. Graham Greene: A sort of life. *In* Sheed, W. The good word & other words p212-14

Criticism, Textual

Higdon, D. L. Graham Greene's second thoughts: the text of The heart of the matter. *In* Virginia. University. Bibliographical Society. Studies in bibliography v30 p249-56

Stratford, P. Second thoughts on "Graham Greene's second thoughts": the five texts of The heart of the matter. *In* Virginia. University. Bibliographical Society. Studies in bibliography v31 p263-66

Greene, J. Lee

Black literature and the American literary mainstream. *In* Minority language and literature p20-28

Greene, Jack P.

The American Revolution: an explanation. *In* Suggs, G. G. ed. Perspectives on the American Revolution p51-73

'A posture of hostility': a reconsideration of some aspects of the origins of the American Revolution. *In* American Antiquarian Society. Proceedings v87 pt 1 p27-68

"Virtus et Libertas": political culture, social change, and the origins of the American Revolution in Virginia, 1763-1766. *In* The Southern experience in the American Revolution p55-108

Greene, John Colton

Science and religion. *In* The Rise of Adventism p50-69

Greene, Judith

Psycholinguistics: competence and performance. *In* Royal Institute of Philosophy. Communication and understanding p79-90

Greene, Maxine

Landscapes of learning

Contents

The agon of "basics": backward looks and future possibilities

The artistic-aesthetic and curriculum

Equality and inviolability: an approach to compensatory justice

Also in Social justice and preferential treatment p 176-98

Imagination and aesthetic literacy

The impacts of irrelevance: women in the history of American education

The lived world

The matter of mystification: teacher education in unquiet times

The new freedom and the moral life

Pedagogy and praxis: the problem of malefic generosity

The predicaments of American selfhood: a response to the new irrationalism

The rational and the emancipatory: towards a role for imaginative literature

Sexism in the schools

Significant landscapes: an approach to the arts in interrelationship

Steamboats and critiques

Thoughts on educational policy

Towards wide-awakeness: an argument for the arts and humanities in education

Wide-awakeness and the moral life

Paul Goodman and anarchistic education. *In* Social forces and schooling p313-36

Greene, Michael Edward

Rossetti's "absurd trash": "Sir Hugh the Heron" reconsidered. *In* Tennessee Studies in literature v20 p85-91

Greene, Penelope J.; Morgan, Charles J. and Barash, David P.

Sociobiology. *In* McNall, S. G. ed. Theoretical perspectives in sociology p414-30

Greene, Richard Leighton

Carols in Tudor drama. *In* Chaucer and Middle English studies in honour of Rossell Hope Robbins p357-65

Hamlet's skimmington. *In* Evidence in literary scholarship p 1-11

About individual works
The early English carols

Robbins, R. H. Greene's revised carols. *In* Review, v 1 1979 p265-73

Greene, Robert, 1558-1592

About

Helgerson, R. Greene. *In* Helgerson, R. The Elizabethan prodigals p79-104

Muir, K. Robert Greene as dramatist. *In* Muir, K. The singularity of Shakespeare, and other essays p138-48

About individual works
Euphues his censure to Philautus

Whitaker, V. K. Still another source for Troilus and Cressida. *In* English Renaissance drama p100-07

Influence—Shakespeare

Whitaker, V. K. Still another source for Troilus and Cressida. *In* English Renaissance drama p100-07

Greene, Robert W.

Six French poets of our time

Contents

Afterword

André du Bouchet

Francis Ponge

Jacques Dupin

Marcelin Pleynet

Pierre Reverdy

René Char

perspectives on The Decameron p113-28

Greene, Thomas McLernon

Forms of accommodation in The Decameron. *In* Dombroski, R. S. ed. Critical Petrarch and the humanist hermeneutic. *In* Italian literature: roots and branches p201-24

Renaissance warfare: a metaphor in conflict. *In* The Holy war p157-80

Greene County, Ala.

Politics and government

Murphy, S. The meaning of Greene County. *In* The Rising South v2 p78-94

Social conditions

Gilmore, T. The South is rising again—in living colors. *In* The Rising South v 1 p50-58

Greenfield, Stanley B.

The authenticating voice in Beowulf. *In* Anglo-Saxon England 5 p51-62

Greenfield, Stanley B. and Evert, Richard

Maxims II: gnome and poem. *In* Anglo-Saxon poetry: essays in appreciation p337-54

Greenhalgh, Michael

European interest in the non-European: the sixteenth century and pre-Columbian art and architecture. *In* Greenhalgh, M. and Megaw, J. V. S. eds. Art in society p89-103

Greenhill, Leslie P.

Film documentation of folklife. *In* Yoder, D. ed. American folklife p71-104

Greenlandic language. See Eskimo language

Greenway, John Langford

The gateway to innocence: Ossian and the Nordic bard as myth. *In* Studies in eighteenth-century culture v4 p161-70

Greenwood, Davydd James

Continuity in change: Spanish Basque ethnicity as a historical process. *In* Esman, M. J. ed. Ethnic conflict in the Western world p81-102

Greetings. See Salutations

Greg, Sir Walter Wilson

About individual works
The rationale of copy-text

Bowers, F. T. Greg's "Rationale of copy-text" revisited. *In* Virginia. University. Bibliographical Society. Studies in bibliography v31 p90-161

Tanselle, G. T. Greg's theory of copy-text and the editing of American literature. *In* Virginia. University. Bibliographical Society. Studies in bibliography v28 p167-229

Gregg, Larry

Slava snabokovu. *In* A Book of things about Vladimir Nabokov p11-27

Grégoire, Henri, constitutional Bp. of Blois

About individual works

An essay on the physical, moral, and political reformation of the Jews

Popkin, R. H. La Peyrère, the Abbé Grégoire, and the Jewish question in the eighteenth century. *In* Studies in eighteenth-century culture v4 p209-22

Gregor, Ian

Spaces: To the lighthouse. *In* Martz, L. L. and Williams, A. L. eds. The author in his work p375-89

See also Irwin, M. jt. auth.

Gregorian chant. See Chants (Plain, Gregorian, etc.)

Gregorius, Saint, Bp of Nyssa

Aesthetics

Mathew, G. The aesthetic theories of Gregory of Nyssa. *In* Studies in memory of David Talbot Rice p217-22

Gregorius I, the Great, Saint, Pope

About individual works

Dialogues

Yerkes, D. The text of the Canterbury fragment of Werferth's translation of Gregory's Dialogues and its relation to the other manuscripts. *In* Anglo-Saxon England 6 p121-35

Homiliae super Evangelia

Chase, C. R. God's presence through grace as the theme of Cynewulf's Christ II and the relationship of this theme to Christ I and Christ III. *In* Anglo-Saxon England 3 p87-101

Moralia in Job

Lutz, C. E. A manuscript fragment from Bede's monastery. *In* Lutz, C. E. Essays on manuscripts and rare books p19-23

Influence—Cynewulf

Chase, C. R. God's presence through grace as the theme of Cynewulf's Christ II and the relationship of this theme to Christ I and Christ III. *In* Anglo-Saxon England 3 p87-101

Gregorius VII, Saint, Pope

About

Robinson, I. S. "Periculosus homo": Pope Gregory VII and episcopal authority. *In* Viator: medieval and Renaissance studies v9 p103-31

Gregorius de Arimino

About

Weinberg, J. R. Gregory of Rimini's critique of Anselm. *In* Weinberg, J. R. Ockham, Descartes, and Hume p15-21

Gregory I, the Great, Saint, Pope. See Gregorius I, the Great Saint, Pope

Gregory VII, Saint, Pope. See Gregorius VII, Saint, Pope

Gregory of Nyssa. See Gregorius, Saint, Bp of Nyssa

Gregory of Rimini. See Gregorius de Arimino

Gregory, E. R.

Wilkie Collins and Dorothy L. Sayers. *In* Hannay, M. P. ed. As her whimsey took her p51-64

Gregory, Ian

Psycho-analysis, human nature and human conduct. *In* Royal Institute of Philosophy. Nature and conduct p99-120

Gregory, Lady Isabella Augusta Persse

Bibliography

Carens, J. F. Four Revival figures: Lady Gregory, A. E. (George W. Russell), Oliver St. John Gogarty, and James Stephens. *In* Finneran, R. J. ed. Anglo-Irish literature p436-69

Gregory, Justina

Euripides' Heracles. *In* Yale classical studies v25 p259-75

Gregory, Michael S.

Epilogue. *In* Sociobiology and human nature p283-94

Gregory, Richard Langton

The confounded eye. *In* Gregory, R. L. and Gombrich, Sir E. H. J. eds. Illusion in nature and art p49-95

Gregory, Ross

The domino theory. *In* Encyclopedia of American foreign policy p275-80

Greiffenhagen, Maurice

About individual works

An idyll

Meyers, J. Maurice Greiffenhagen and The white peacock. *In* Meyers, J. Painting and the novel p46-52

Greimas, Algirdas Julien

About individual works

Sémantique structurale, recherche de méthode

Laden, R. A. "Les relais du verbe": Perse's reticular rhetoric. *In* Glyph 4 p156-88

Greiser verterbuch fun der Yiddisher shprach

Dawidowicz, L. S. Yiddish: past, present, and perfected. *In* Dawidowicz, L. S. The Jewish presence p133-53

Grella, George

The wings of the falcon and The Maltese dove. *In* Filler, L. ed. A question of quality: popularity and value in modern creative writing p108-14

Grémion, Pierre, and Worms, Jean-Pierre

The French regional planning experiments. *In* Planning, politics and public policy p217-36

Grenander, Mary Elizabeth

Holy sonnets VIII and XVII: John Donne. *In* Roberts, J. R. ed. Essential articles for the study of John Donne's poetry p324-32

Grendler, Paul F.

Venice, science, and the Index of Prohibited Books. *In* The Nature of scientific discovery p335-47

Grene, Marjorie (Glicksman)

Philosophy in and out of Europe

Contents

The aesthetic dialogue of Sartre and Merleau-Ponty

Authenticity: an existential virtue

The career of action and passion in Sartre's philosophical work

The German existentialists

Heidegger: philosopher and prophet

Karl Jaspers: a philosopher of humanity

Grief—*Continued*

Pritchard, E. R. The social worker's responsibility. *In* Anticipatory grief p237-45

Ramshorn, M. T. Selected tasks for the dying patient and family members. *In* Anticipatory grief p246-50

Reed, A. Anticipatory grief work. *In* Anticipatory grief p346-57

Reeves, R. B. Reflections on two false expectations. *In* Anticipatory grief p281-84

Rush, B. F. A surgical oncologist's observations. *In* Anticipatory grief p98-106

Schowalter, J. E. Anticipatory grief and going on the "danger list". *In* Anticipatory grief p187-92

Silverman, P. R. Anticipatory grief from the perspective of widowhood. *In* Anticipatory grief p 320-30

Weisman, A. D. Is mourning necessary? *In* Anticipatory grief p14-18

Grierson, Herbert John Clifford, ed.

About individual works
Metaphysical lyrics & poems of the seventeenth century, Donne to Butler

Eliot, T. S. The metaphysical poets. *In* Eliot, T. S. Selected prose of T. S. Eliot p59-67

Grierson, Philip

Numismatics. *In* Powell, J. M. ed. Medieval studies p103-50

Griessman, Benjamin Eugene

Introduction: The South as a state of mind. *In* Lewis, W. D. and Griessman, B. E. eds. The Southern mystique p xvii-xxi

Will the South rise again or just roll over? *In* Lewis, W. D. and Griessman, B. E. eds. The Southern mystique p125-31

Grievance procedures (Military law) See Complaints (Military law)

Grieve, Christopher Murray

Poetry and science; excerpt from "Selected essays of Hugh MacDiarmid." *In* Gibbons, R. ed. The poet's work: 29 masters of 20th century poetry on the origins and practice of their art p121-35

About

Grieve, C. M. Poetry and science; excerpt from "Selected essays of Hugh MacDiarmid." *In* Gibbons, R. ed. The poet's work: 29 masters of 20th century poetry on the origins and practice of their art p121-35

Morgan, E. MacDiarmid at seventy-five. *In* Morgan, E. Essays p214-21

Morgan, E. Poetry and knowledge in MacDiarmid's later work. *In* Morgan, E. Essays p203-13

About individual works
The battle continues

Morgan, E. MacDiarmid embattled. *In* Morgan, E. Essays p194-202

Griffel, L. Michael

Teaching music. *In* Cahn, S. M. ed. Scholars who teach p193-216

Griffen, Clyde

The "old" immigration and industrialization: a case study. *In* Immigrants in industrial America, 1850-1920 p176-210

Griffin, Andrew

Fire and ice in Frankenstein. *In* Levine, G. L. and Knoepflmacher, U. C. eds. The endurance of Frankenstein p49-73

The interior garden and John Stuart Mill. *In* Knoepflmacher, U. C. and Tennyson, G. B. eds. Nature and the Victorian imagination p171-86

Griffin, Donald Redfield

Humanistic aspects of ethology. *In* Sociobiology and human nature p240-59

Griffin, Susan

Rape: the all-American crime. *In* Feminism and philosophy p313-32

Griffin, William D.

The Irish on the Continent in the eighteenth century. *In* Studies in eighteenth-century culture v5 p453-73

Griffith, Albert Joseph

Henny Penny, Eudora Welty, and the aggregation of friends. *In* Prenshaw, P. W. ed. Eudora Welty p83-92

Griffith, David Mark

Catherine the Great, the British opposition and the American Revolution. *In* The American Revolution and "a candid world" p85-110

Griffith, David Wark

About

Agee, J. David Wark Griffith; excerpt from "Agee on film v 1." *In* Denby, D. ed. Awake in the dark p60-65

About individual works
Way down East

Kauffmann, S. Way down East. *In* Kauffmann, S. Living images p281-89

Griffith, John

Franklin's sanity and the man behind the masks. *In* Lemay, J. A. L. ed. The oldest revolutionary p123-38

Griffith, John Godfrey

ΑΗΚΥΘΙΟΝ ΑΠΩΛΕΣΕΝ. *In* Harvard Studies in classical philology v74 p43-44

Griffith, Mark

Euripides Alkestis 636-641. *In* Harvard Studies in classical philology v82 p83-86

Griffith, Philip Mahone

"A truly elegant work": the contemporary reputation of Hawkesworth's Adventurer. *In* The Dress of words p199-208

Griffith, Richard

Cycles and genres. *In* Nichols, B. ed. Movies and methods p111-18

Griffith, Richard R.

The political bias of Malory's "Morte Darthur". *In* Viator: medieval and Renaissance studies v5 p365-86

Griffith, William E.

The Prague spring and the Soviet intervention in Czechoslovakia. *In* Hammond, T. T. ed. The anatomy of Communist takeovers p596-605

Griffiths, A. Phillips

Academic freedom: a reply to Dr Brown. *In* Philosophers discuss education p221-42

Wittgenstein, Schopenhauer, and ethics. *In* Royal Institute of Philosophy. Understanding Wittgenstein p96-116

Griffiths, Franklyn

A forecast. *In* Griffiths, F. and Polanyi, J. C. eds. The dangers of nuclear war p169-81

Griffiths, Gareth

About individual works

Language and action in the novels of Chinua Achebe

Lindfors, B. The blind men and the elephant. *In* African literature today no. 7: Focus on criticism p53-64

Grigg, John

The do-gooder from Seville gaol. *In* Harris, H. A. ed. Astride the two cultures p123-35

Liberals on trial. *In* Crisis and controversy p23-37

Grigg, Robert

Constantine the Great and the cult without images. *In* Viator: medieval and Renaissance studies v8 p 1-32

Grigor'ev, Apollon Aleksandrovich

About

Stacy, R. H. The aesthetic critics. *In* Stacy, R. H. Russian literary criticism p66-79

Grigoriev, Apollon. See Grigor'ev, Apollon Aleksandrovich

Grigson, Geoffrey

The poems. *In* Drabble, M. ed. The genius of Thomas Hardy p80-93

Grillet, Alain Robbe- See Robbe-Grillet, Alain

Grillparzer, Franz

About

Mullan, W. N. B. Grillparzer and the realist tradition. *In* Branscombe, P. ed. Austrian life and literature, 1780-1938 p26-39

About individual works

The poor minstrel

Swales, M. Grillparzer: Der arme Spielmann. *In* Swales, M. The German Novelle p114-32

Grim, Patrick

Sexism and semantics. *In* Feminism and philosophy p109-16

Grimes, Alan Pendelton

Conservative Revolution and liberal rhetoric: the Declaration of Independence. *In* Havard, W. C. and Bernd, J. L. eds. 200 years of the Republic in retrospect p 1-19

Grimes, José. See Grimes, Joseph Evans

Grimes, Joseph Evans

Descriptive linguistics. *In* Sebeok, T. A. ed. Native languages of the Americas v2 p55-62

Grimké, Frederick

About

Bloomfield, M. H. Frederick Grimké and the dynamics of social change. *In* Bloomfield, M. H. American lawyers in a changing society, 1776-1876 p235-70

About individual works

Considerations upon the nature and tendency of free institutions

Bloomfield, M. H. Frederick Grimké and the dynamics of social change. *In* Bloomfield, M. H. American lawyers in a changing society, 1776-1876 p235-70

Grimm, Jakob Ludwig Karl

Translations, English

Shub, E. An adventure in translation. *In* Horn Book Magazine. Crosscurrents of criticism p287-89

Grimm, Reinhold

Naturalism and epic drama. *In* Mews, S. and Knust, H. eds. Essays on Brecht p3-27

Grimm, Wilhelm Karl

Translations, English

Shub, E. An adventure in translation. *In* Horn Book Magazine. Crosscurrents of criticism p287-89

Grimmelshausen, Hans Jakob Christoffel von

About individual works

The adventurous Simplicissimus

Bjornson, R. The universality of the picaresque: visions of truth in Grimmelshausen's Simplicissimus. *In* Bjornson, R. The picaresque hero in European fiction p166-87

Grin, Henry Louis

About

Hillier, B. The Victorian Crusoe. *In* The Saturday book 34 p135-47

Grindle, Juliet M.

Compulsion and choice in The Mayor of Casterbridge. *in* Smith, A. ed. The novels of Thomas Hardy p91-106

Grinker, Roy Richard

The role of psychiatry in society. *In* American psychiatry: past, present, and future p170-82

Gris, Charles Édouard Jeanneret- See Jeanneret-Gris, Charles Édouard

Griselda Master. See Master of the Griselda legend

Grisel, Étienne

The beginnings of international law and general public law doctrine: Francisco de Vitoria's De Indiis prior. *In* First images of America p305-25

Griswold, Alexander B. and Prasert Na Nagara

A fifteenth-century Siamese historical poem. *In* Southeast Asian history and historiography p123-63

On kingship and society at Sukhodaya. *In* Change and persistence in Thai society p29-92

Grob, Gerald N.

The social history of medicine and disease in America: problems and possibilities. *In* Branca, P. ed. The medicine show p 1-19

Grof, Joan Halifax- See Halifax-Grof, Joan

Grof, Stanislav, and Halifax-Grof, Joan

Psychedelics and the experience of death. *In* Life after death p182-202

Gronbeck, Bruce Elliot

Edmund Burke and the Regency Crisis of 1788-89. *In* Rhetoric: a tradition in transition p142-77

Groneman, Carol

"She earns as a child—she pays as a man": women workers in a mid-nineteenth-century New York City community. *In* Immigrants in industrial America, 1850-1920 p33-46

Gronow, Rees Howell

About individual works

The reminiscences and recollections of Captain Gronow, being anecdotes of the camp, court, clubs & society, 1810-1860

Connolly, C. The dandy: 3. *In* Connolly, C. The evening colonnade p136-38

Gropius, Walter

Programme for the establishment of a company for the provision of housing on aesthetically consistent principles. *In* Sharp, D. ed. The rationalists p50-57

About

Scheffauer, H. G. Walter Gropius. *In* Sharp, D. ed. The rationalists p42-49

Gros, Antoine Jean, Baron

About individual works

Napoleon on the battlefield of Eylau

Herbert, R. L. Baron Gros's Napoleon and Voltaire's Henri IV. *In* The Artist and the writer in France p52-75

Gross, Barry R.

Is turn about fair play? *In* Gross, B. R. ed. Reverse discrimination p379-87

Gross, Beatrice, and Gross, Ronald

Best further reading to become more capable of helping children and young people. *In* Gross, B. and Gross, R. eds. The children's rights movement p343-57

Gross, Feliks

Thoughts on a social-science curriculum. *In* Hook, S.; Kurtz, P. W. and Todorovich, M. eds. The philosophy of the curriculum: the need for general education p261-73

Gross, Harvey Seymour

Introduction: toward a phenomenology of rhythm. *In* Gross, H. S. ed. The structure of verse p5-17

Gross, Leo

International law aspects of the freedom of information and the right to communicate. *In* Horton, P. C. ed. The Third World and press freedom p55-73

On the justiciability of international disputes. *In* [Truth and tragedy]: a tribute to Hans Morgenthau p203-19

The right of self-determination in international law. *In* Kilson, M. ed. New states in the modern world p136-57

Gross, Ronald. See Gross, B. jt. auth.

Gross, Samuel David, ed.

About individual works

Lives of eminent American physicians and surgeons of the nineteenth century

Bell, W. J. Lives in medicine: the biographical dictionaries of Thacher, Williams, and Gross. *In* Bell, W. J. The colonial physician & other essays p149-68

Gross, Seymour Lee

A long day's living: the angelic ingenuities of Losing battles. *In* Prenshaw, P. W. ed. Eudora Welty p325-40

Gross, Seymour Lee, and Bender, Eileen

History, politics, and literature: the myth of Nat Turner. *In* Morris, R. K. and Malin, I. eds. The achievement of William Styron p168-207

Grosseteste, Robert, Bp. of Lincoln

About

Boyle, L. E. Robert Grosseteste and the pastoral care. *In* Medieval and Renaissance studies 1976 p3-51

Grossinger, Richard

A history of Io, 1964-1976. *In* Anderson, E. and Kinzie, M. eds. The little magazine in America: a modern documentary history p482-513

Grosskurth, Phyllis

Where was Rousseau? *In* Landow, G. P. ed. Approaches to Victorian autobiography p26-38

Grossman, Leona

Ethnicity and health delivery systems. *In* The Diverse society: implications for social policy p129-48

Grossmann, Walter

Edelmann and the silent Reimarus. *In* Studies in eighteenth-century culture v4 p195-203

Grosso, Alfonso

About individual works

Guarnicion de silla

Schwartz, R. Alfonso Grosso and Guarnicion de silla (Troop of cavalry) (1971). *In* Schwartz, R. Spain's New Wave novelists, 1950-1974 p265-77

Grossvogel, David I.

Mystery and its fictions: from Oedipus to Agatha Christie

Contents

Agatha Christie: containment of the unknown

Borges: the dream dreaming the dreamer

Camus: a sense of life, the unknowable death

Conclusion: Job and the unendurable mystery

Dostoevsky: divine mystery and literary salvation

Kafka: structure as mystery (I)

Oedipus the King: dis-covering only the dis-coverer

Pirandello: the mask as evidence and limit

"The purloined letter": the mystery of the text

Robbe-Grillet: structure as mystery (II)

Grotesque

Ilie, P. Concepts of the grotesque before Goya. *In* Studies in eighteenth-century culture v5 p185-201

Kern, E. G. Molière and the tradition of the grotesque. *In* Johnson, R. B.; Neumann, E. S. and Trail, G. T. eds. Molière and the commonwealth of letters: patrimony and posterity p507-20

Nicoll, A. The comic spirit and social unrest. *In* Nicoll, A. World drama p711-26

Grotesque in art

Ilie, P. Concepts of the grotesque before Goya. *In* Studies in eighteenth-century culture v5 p185-201

Grotesque in literature

Graham, K. W. Implications of the grotesque: Beckford's Vathek and the boundaries of fictional reality. *In* Tennessee Studies in literature v23 p61-74

Holman, C. H. Detached laughter in the South. *In* Cohen, S. B. ed. Comic relief p87-104

Grotesque in literature—*Continued*

Ilie, P. Concepts of the grotesque before Goya. *In* Studies in eighteenth-century culture v5 p185-201

Malin, I. Flannery O'Connor and the grotesque. *In* Friedman, M. J. and Lawson, L. A. eds. The added dimension p108-22

Mermier, G. R. The grotesque in French medieval literature: a study in forms and meanings. *In* Ruggiers, P. G. ed. Versions of medieval comedy p101-34

Grotjahn, Martin

Group communication and group therapy with the aged: a promising project. *In* Jarvik, L. F. ed. Aging into the 21st century p113-21

Grotowski, Jerzy

About

Kauffmann, S. Grotowski's theater. *In* Kauffmann, S. Persons of the drama p63-72

Simon, J. I. Grotowski's grotesqueries. *In* Simon, J. I. Singularities p148-63

Grottanelli, Vinigi L.

The Lugard Lecture of 1961. *In* African images p3-22

The peopling of the Horn of Africa. *In* Chittick, H. N. and Rotberg, R. I. eds. East Africa and the Orient p44-75

Group counseling

Vachon, M. L. S.; Lyall, W. A. L. and Pollack, H. How group meetings ease the stress of cancer on patients and their families. *In* Home care p70-76

See also Group psychotherapy

Group decision-making. See Decision-making, Group

Group-dieting rituals. Allon, N. *In* Henslin, J. M. ed. Deviant life-styles p101-14

Group 47. Kurz, P. K. *In* Kurz, P. K. On modern German literature v3 p74-94

Group identity, Ethnic. See Ethnicity

Group legal services. See Prepaid legal services

Group prayer. See Prayer groups

Group psychotherapy

Denny, J. M. Techniques for individual and group art therapy. *In* Ulman, E. and Dachinger, P. eds. Art therapy p132-49

Grotjahn, M. Group communication and group therapy with the aged: a promising project. *In* Jarvik, L. F. ed. Aging into the 21st century p113-21

Jones, R. K. Some sectarian characteristics of therapeutic groups with special reference to Recovery, inc. and Neurotics Nomine. *In* Wallis, R. ed. Sectarianism p190-210

Lieberman, M. A. Group therapies. *In* Overview of the psychotherapies p92-117

See also Family psychotherapy; Group counseling

Group relations training

Foltz, W. J. Two forms of unofficial conflict intervention: the problem-solving and the process-promoting workshops. *In* Unofficial diplomats p201-21

Kelman, H. C. The problem-solving workshop in conflict resolution. *In* Unofficial diplomats p168-200

Rogers, C. R. Some new directions: a personal view. *In* Hanna, T. ed. Explorers of humankind p123-35

Stone, D. The Human Potential movement. *In* The New religious consciousness p93-115

Group sex

United States

Denfeld, D. Swinging: the search for an alternative. *In* Gross, L. ed. Sexual issues in marriage p217-30

Kilgo, R. D. Can group marriage work? *In* Gross, L. ed. Sexual issues in marriage p231-36

Palson, C. and Palson, R. Swinging in wedlock. *In* Henslin, J. M. ed. Deviant life-styles p231-54

Group work in art

Italy—Rome

Spencer, J. R. Filarete's bronze doors at St Peter's. *In* Collaboration in Italian Renaissance art p33-57

Italy—Siena

Carli, E. Two stucco reliefs by Neroccio di Bartolomeo. *In* Collaboration in Italian Renaissance art p21-29

Stubblebine, J. H. The Boston Ducciesque tabernacle, a collaboration. *In* Collaboration in Italian Renaissance art p 1-19

Groups, Age. See Age groups

Groups, Ethnic. See Ethnic groups

Groups, Social. See Social groups

Groups, Theory of

Cassirer, E. Reflections on the concept of group and the theory of perception. *In* Cassirer, E. Symbol, myth, and culture p271-91

Grove, David C.

The highland Olmec manifestation: a consideration of what it is and isn't. *In* Mesoamerican archaeology p109-28

Grove, Robin

"It would not do": Emily Brontë as poet. *In* Smith, A. ed. The art of Emily Brontë p33-67

Growth. See Human growth; Maturation (Psychology)

Growth, Personal. See Self-actualization (Psychology)

Grubb, Davis

About individual works

The night of the hunter

Wood, R. Charles Laughton on Grubb Street. *In* Peary, G. and Shatzkin, R. eds. The modern American novel and the movies p204-14

Gruber, Howard Ernest

Darwin's "tree of nature" and other images of wide scope. *In* Wechsler, J. ed. On aesthetics in science p121-40

Gruen, Erich S.

Cicero and Licinius Calvus. *In* Harvard Studies in classical philology v71 p215-33

Gruenewald, Max

"It is enough for the servant to be like his master." *In* Salo Wittmayer Baron v2 p573-76

Gruffydd, Elis

About individual works

Chronicle of the history of the world

Ford, P. K. The death of Merlin in the Chronicle of Elis Gruffydd. *In* Viator: medieval and Renaissance studies v7 p379-90

Gruman, Gerald Joseph

Cultural origins of present-day "age-ism": the modernization of the life cycle. *In* Spicker, S. F.; Woodward, K. M. and Van Tassel, D. D. eds. Aging and the elderly p359-87

Grundy, Isobel

Verses address'd to the imitator of Horace: a skirmish between Pope and some persons of rank and fortune. *In* Virginia. University. Bibliographical Society. Studies in bibliography v30 p96-119

Grundy, Kenneth W.

Economic patterns in the new Southern African balance. *In* Carter, G. M. and O'Meara, P. eds. Southern Africa: the continuing crisis p291-312

Grunebaum, Gustav Edmund von

The hero in medieval Arabic prose. *In* Concepts of the hero in the Middle Ages and the Renaissance p83-100

Relations of philosophy and science: a general view. *In* Essays on Islamic philosophy and science p 1-4

Guadelupe, Spain. Santa Maria (Hieronymite monastery)

Brown J. Zurbarán's paintings in the sacristy of the monastery of Guadalupe. *In* Brown, J. Images and ideas in seventeenth-century Spanish painting p111-27

Gualterus, Rudolphus. See Walther, Rudolf

Guaranty, Treaties of

Dowty, A. International guarantees with special reference to the Middle East. *In* The Dynamics of the arms race p215-30

Guardi, Francesco

About

Knox, G. Francesco Guardi as an apprentice in the studio of Giambattista Tiepolo. *In* Studies in eighteenth-century culture v5 p29-39

Guardian and ward. See Conservatorships; Custody of children

Guarini, Giambattista. See Guarini, Giovanni Battista

Guarini, Giovanni Battista

About individual works

The faithful shepherd

Hunter, G. K. Italian tragicomedy on the English stage. *In* Renaissance drama [1973] p123-48

Guarini, Guarino

About

Wittkower, R. Guarini the man. *In* Wittkower, R. Studies in the Italian baroque p177-86

Guatemala

Antiquities

Puleston, D. E. Intersite areas in the vicinity of Tikal and Uaxactun. *In* Mesoamerican archaeology p303-11

Economic conditions

Bodenheimer, S. J. Guatemala: land of eternal struggle. *In* Chilcote, R. H. and Edelstein, J. C. eds. Latin America: the struggle with dependency and beyond p89-219

Politics and government—1945-

Schneider, R. M. Guatemala: an aborted Communist takeover. *In* Hammond, T. T. ed. The anatomy of Communist takeovers p563-82

Social conditions

Bodenheimer, S. J. Guatemala: land of eternal struggle. *In* Chilcote, R. H. and Edelstein, J. C. eds. Latin America: the struggle with dependency and beyond p89-219

Social life and customs

Cosminsky, S. The evil eye in a Quiché community. *In* The Evil eye p163-74

Guatemalan Communist Party. See Communist Party of Guatemala

Guattari, Felix. See Deleuze, G. jt. auth.

Gubach, Thomas H.

The international film industry. *In* Gerbner, G. ed. Mass media policies in changing cultures p21-40

Gubar, Susan

The echoing spell of H. D.'s Trilogy. *In* Gilbert, S. M. and Gubar, S. eds. Shakespeare's sisters p200-18

See also Gilbert, S. M. jt. auth.

Gubbio, Italy. Palazzo Ducale. Studiolo of Federigo, Count of Montefeltro, Duke of Urbino

Winternitz, E. Quattrocento science in the Gubbio study. *In* Winternitz, E. Musical instruments and their symbolism in Western art p120-28

Gubrium, Jaber F.

On multiple realities in a nursing home. *In* Gubrium, J. F. ed. Late life p61-98

Guelfs and Ghibellines

Headley, J. M. The Habsburg world empire and the revival of Ghibellinism. *In* Medieval and Renaissance studies [1975] p93-127

Peters, E. M. Pars, parte: Dante and an urban contribution to political thought. *In* The Medieval city p113-40

Guelphs. See Guelfs and Ghibellines

Guérard, Albert Joseph

The Conradian voice. *In* Joseph Conrad: a commemoration p 1-16

Faulkner the innovator. *In* The Maker and the myth: Faulkner and Yoknapatawpha, 1977 p71-88

The Faulknerian voice. *In* The Maker and the myth: Faulkner and Yoknapatawpha, 1977 p25-42

About individual works

The triumph of the novel: Dickens, Dostoevsky, Faulkner

Dunn, R. J. "Illuminating distortions" and the Dickens critics. *In* Review, v 1 1979 p91-104

Guerlac, Henry

Chemistry as a branch of physics: Laplace's collaboration with Lavoisier. *In* Historical studies in the physical sciences v7 p193-276

Guilhem de Montanhagol

About

Topsfield, L. T. Guilhem de Montanhagol, Peire Cardenal and Guiraut Riquier. *In* Topsfield, L. T. Troubadours and love p241-52

Guillaume IX, Duke of Aquitaine

About

Topsfield, L. T. Guilhem IX and the quest for joy. *In* Topsfield, L. T. Troubadours and love p11-41

About individual works

Farai un vers de dreyt nien

Nichols, S. G. Toward an aesthetic of the Provençal lyric II: Marcabru's Dire vos vuoill ses doptansa (BdT 293, 18). *In* Italian literature: roots and branches p15-37

Guillaume, comte de Poitiers. See Guillaume V le Grand, comte de Poitiers et duc d'Aquitaine

Guillaume d'Auvergne. See Guilelmus Arvernus, Bp. of Paris

Guillaume de Lorris

Influence—Chaucer

Wimsatt, J. I. Chaucer and French poetry. *In* Brewer, D. S. ed. Geoffrey Chaucer p109-36

Guillaume de Lorris, and Jean de Meun

About individual works

Roman de la Rose

Barney, S. A. Adornment: the Romance of the Rose. *In* Barney, S. A. Allegories of history, allegories of love p179-215

David, A. How Marcia lost her skin: a note on Chaucer's mythology. *In* The Learned and the lewed p19-29

Kelly, D. Guillaume de Lorris and imagination in the Roman de la Rose. *In* Kelly, D. Medieval imagination p57-95

Guillaume de Machaut

About

Kelly, D. Guillaume de Machaut and the sublimation of courtly love in imagination. *In* Kelly, D. Medieval imagination p121-54

Influence—Chaucer

Wimsatt, J. I. Chaucer and French poetry. *In* Brewer, D. S. ed. Geoffrey Chaucer p109-36

Performances

Craft, R. Musical B for a political season. *In* Craft, R. Current convictions p159-68

Guillaume V le Grand, comte de Poitiers et duc d'Aquitaine

Bachrach, B. S. A study in feudal politics: relations between Fulk Nerra and William the Great, 995-1030. *In* Viator: medieval and Renaissance studies v7 p111-22

Guillaume (Chanson de geste)

Niles, J. D. Narrative anomalies in "La Chançun de Willame." *In* Viator: medieval and Renaissance studies v9 p251-64

Guillaumont, Patrick

The optimum rate of population growth. *In* Economic factors in population growth p29-62

Guillelmus de Arvernia. See Guilelmus Arvernus, Bp. of Paris

Guillem de Torrella. See Torrella, Guillem de

Guillén, Claudio

The aesthetics of literary influence; excerpt from "Literature as system." *In* Primeau, R. ed. Influx p49-73

Guillén, Jorge

About

Paz, O. Jorge Guillén. *In* Paz, O. The siren & the seashell p153-60

Guillén, Nicolás

About

García-Barrio, C. S. de. The image of the Black man in the poetry of Nicolás Guillén. *In* DeCosta, M. ed. Blacks in Hispanic literature p105-13

King, L. Nicolás Guillén and Afrocubanismo. *In* King, B. A. and Ogungbesan, K. eds. A celebration of Black and African writing p30-45

Williams, L. V. The African presence in the poetry of Nicolás Guillén. *In* Crahan, M. E. and Knight, F. W. eds. Africa and the Caribbean p124-45

Guilleragues, Gabriel Joseph de Lavergne, vicomte de

About individual works

Lettres portugaises

Horowitz, L. K. The Lettres portugaises. *In* Horowitz, L. K. Love and laughter p125-43

Guillermaz, Jacques

The soldier. *In* Wilson, R. G. ed. Mao Tse-tung in the scales of history p117-43

Guillory, Daniel L.

The mystique of childhood in American literature. *In* Tulane Studies in English, v23 p229-47

Guilt

Mitscherlich, A. and Mitscherlich, M. The inability to mourn. *In* Explorations in psychohistory p257-70

Guilt in literature

Lesser, S. O. The source of guilt and the sense of guilt: Kafka's The trial. *In* Lesser, S. O. The whispered meanings p68-85

Smith, H. N. Guilt and innocence in Mark Twain's later fiction. *In* Smith, H. N. Democracy and the novel p104-27

See also Deception in literature

Guimary, Donald L.

Broadcasting in Malaysia. *In* Gerbner, G. ed. Mass media policies in changing cultures p159-63

Guinagh, Kevin

A preface on prefaces. *In* Praise from famous men: an anthology of introductions p ix-xiv

el Guindi, Fadwa, and Selby, Henry A.

Dialectics in Zapotec thinking. *In* Basso, K. H. and Selby, H. A. eds. Meaning in anthropology p181-96

Guinea

Foreign relations

Adamolekun, 'L. The foreign policy of Guinea. *In* Aluko, O. ed. The foreign policies of African states p98-117

Guitar. See Cithern

Guitry, Sacha

About

Truffaut, F. Sacha Guitry the villain. *In* Truffaut, F. The films in my life p216-19

Guitry, Sacha—*Continued*

About individual works
Lovers and thieves

Truffaut, F. Sacha Guitry: Assassins et voleurs. *In* Truffaut, F. The films in my life p214-16

Gujarat

Commerce—History

Das Gupta, A. Gujarati merchants and the Red Sea trade, 1700-1725. *In* Kling, B. B. and Pearson, M. N. eds. The age of partnership p123-58

Gulick, John, and Gulick, Margaret E.

The domestic social environment of women and girls in Isfahan, Iran. *In* Beck, L. and Keddie, N. R. eds. Women in the Muslim world p501-21

Gulick, Margaret E. See Gulick, J. jt. auth.

Gulland, Robin R. Milner- See Milner-Gulland, Robin R.

Gullason, Thomas A.

The short story: an underrated art. *In* May, C. E. ed. Short story theories p13-31

Gulliver, Philip Hugh

A land dispute in Arusha, Tanzania. *In* African dimensions p 1-14

Gullo, Stephen V.; Cherico, Daniel J. and Shadick, Robert G.

Suggested stages and response styles in life-threatening illness: a focus on the cancer patient. *In* Anticipatory grief p53-78

Guma, Alex La. See La Guma, Alex

Gumilev, Nikolaï Stepanovich

The life of verse. *In* Proffer, C. R. ed. Modern Russian poets on poetry p23-32

Gunawardana, A. J.

From the village to the city: The song of the road. *In* Narasimhaiah, C. D. ed. Awakened conscience p206-15

Gunderson, Keith

Asymmetries and mind-body perplexities. *In* Philosophical aspects of the mind-body problem p99-130

Gungwu Wang. See Wang, Gungwu

Gunn, David M.

Thematic composition and Homeric authorship. *In* Harvard Studies in classical philology v75 p 1-31

Gunn, James Edward

Henry Kuttner, C. L. Moore, Lewis Padgett et al. *In* Clareson, T. D. ed. Voices for the future: essays on major science fiction writers v 1 p185-215

Gunn, Neil Miller

About

Hart, F. R. Neil Gunn. *In* Hart, F. R. The Scottish novel p348-73

Hart, F. R. Late Victorian Celticisms. *In* Hart, F. R. The Scottish novel p336-47

About individual works
Butcher's broom

Hart, F. R. The tragedy of the Clearances. *In* Hart, F. R. The Scottish novel p325-35

Gunn, Thom

About

Fraser, G. S. The poetry of Thom Gunn. *In* Fraser, G. S. Essays on twentieth-century poets p234-42

Ries, L. R. Thom Gunn: the retreat from violence. *In* Ries, L. R. Wolf masks p59-91

Gunnery. See Artillery

Gunter, Pete Addison Y.

The Big Thicket: a case study in attitudes toward environment. *In* Philosophy & environmental crisis p117-37

Gunther, Gerald

Learned Hand and the origins of modern first amendment doctrine: some fragments of history. *In* Stanford Legal essays p195-249

Toward "a more perfect Union": framing and implementing the distinctive nation-building elements of the Constitution. *In* Aspects of American liberty p146-61

Gupta, Ashin Das. See Das Gupta, Ashin

Gurdjieff, Georges Ivanovich

About

Riordan, K. T. Gurdjieff. *In* Tart, C. T. ed. Transpersonal psychologies p281-328

Influence—Toomer

Bone, R. A. Jean Toomer. *In* Bone, R. A. Down home p204-38

Gurevitch, Michael, and Blumler, Jay G.

Mass media and political institutions: the systems approach. *In* Gerbner, G. ed. Mass media policies in changing cultures p251-68

Gurevitz, Baruch

The Soviet Union and the Palestinian organisations. *In* Ro'i, Y. ed. The limits to power p254-81

Gurian, Bennett S. and Cantor, Marjorie H.

Mental health and community support systems for the elderly. *In* Aging: the process and the people p184-205

Gurk, Austria

Churches

See Gurk, Austria. Dom

Dom

Demus, O. Elijah and Alexander. *In* Studies in memory of David Talbot Rice p64-67

Gurland, Robert H.

Teaching mathematics. *In* Cahn, S. M. ed. Scholars who teach p75-100

Gurr, Andrew J.

'Coriolanus' and the body politic. *In* Shakespeare survey 28 p63-69

'Henry V' and the bees' commonwealth. *In* Shakespeare survey 30 p61-72

Gurr, Ted Robert, and Duvall, Raymond D.

Introduction to a formal theory of political conflict. *In* The Uses of controversy in sociology p139-54

Gusfield, Joseph R.

A dramatistic theory of status politics; excerpt from "Symbolic crusade". *In* Davis, F. J. and Stivers, R. eds. The collective definition of deviance p22-39

Moral passage: the symbolic process in public designation of deviance. *In* Davis, F. J. and Stivers, R. eds. The collective definition of deviance p85-98

Movement ideology and composition. *In* Lauer, R. H. ed. Social movements and social change p61-77

The sociological reality of America: an essay on mass culture. *In* On the making of Americans p41-62

Gusfield, Joseph R.—*Continued*
Status conflicts and the changing ideologies of the American temperance movement. *In* Davis, F. J. and Stivers, R. eds. The collective definition of deviance p222-40

Guss, Donald L.
Donne's Pétrarchism. *In* Roberts, J. R. ed. Essential articles for the study of John Donne's poetry p150-58

Gustafson, James M.
Mongolism, parental desires, and the right to life. *In* Weir, R. F. ed. Ethical issues in death and dying p145-72

Gustafsson, Lars
Strindberg as a forerunner of Scandinavian modernism. *In* The Hero in Scandinavian literature p125-41

Guston, Philip

About

O'Connor, F. V. Philip Guston and political humanism. *In* Millon, H. A. and Nochlin, L. eds. Art and architecture in the service of politics p342-55

Gutenberg, Carl Goettlieb. See Guttenberg, Carl

Güterbock, Hans Gustav
Some aspects of Hittite prayers. *In* The Frontiers of human knowledge p125-39

Gutheim, Frederick Albert
The value of community self-help. *In* Strategies for human settlements: habitat and environment p28-29

Guthlac A (Anglo-Saxon poem)
Calder, D. G. Guthlac A and Guthlac B: some discriminations. *In* Anglo-Saxon poetry: essays in appreciation p65-80

Guthlac B (Anglo-Saxon poem)
Calder, D. G. Guthlac A and Guthlac B; some discriminations. *In* Anglo-Saxon poetry: essays in appreciation p65-80

Guthrie, Alfred Bertram

About individual works
These thousand hills
Stineback, D. C. "The lost and impossible miles": A. B. Guthrie, Jr.'s These thousand hills. *In* Stineback, D. C. Shifting world p156-70

Guthrie, Vera Grinstead
Books for children by Jesse Stuart. *In* LeMaster, J. R. and Clarke, M. W. eds. Jesse Stuart p149-61

Gutiérrez, Gustavo
Two theological perspectives: liberation theology and progressivist theology. *In* The Emergent gospel p227-55

Gutkind, Peter Claus Wolfgang
Are the poor politically dangerous? Some thoughts on urbanism, urbanites, and political consciousness. *In* Colonialism and change p85-113

Gutman, Herbert George
Protestantism and the American labor movement: the Christian spirit in the Gilded Age. *In* Mulder, J. M. and Wilson, J. F. eds. Religion in American history p318-41

Gutmann, David Leo
Dying to power: death and the search for self-esteem. *In* Feifel, H. [ed.] New meanings of death p335-47

Guttenberg, Barnett
Plath's cosmology and the house of Yeats. *In* Lane, G. ed. Sylvia Plath p138-52

Guttenberg, Carl

About individual works
The tea tax tempest
Marin, L. An American event on the French stage: notes on an eighteenth-century engraving. *In* Glyph 3 p 1-17

Guttenberger, Carl Gottfried. See Guttenberg, Carl

Gutteridge, William Frank
Arms control and developing countries. *In* The Dynamics of the arms race p212-14
Southern Africa: a study in conflict. *In* The Dynamics of the arms race p231-39

Guttmann, Allen
Saul Bellow's humane comedy. *In* Cohen, S. B. ed. Comic relief p127-51

Guy of Warwick (Romance)
Klausner, D. N. Didacticism and drama in Guy of Warwick. *In* Medievalia et humanistica no. 6 p103-19

Guyana

Religion
Smith, R. T. Religion in the formation of West Indian society: Guyana and Jamaica. *In* Kilson, M. L. and Rotberg, R. I. eds. The African diaspora p312-41

Guyard of Cressonessart. See Guiard of Cressonessart

Guzman, Eduardo Sevilla-. See Sevilla-Guzman, Eduardo

Gwalter, Rudolf. See Walther, Rudolf

Gwynne, Michael Douglas
The origin and spread of some domestic food plants of Eastern Africa. *In* Chittick, H. N. and Rotberg, R. I. eds. East Africa and the Orient p248-71

Gyges in literature
Shell, M. The Ring of Gyges. *In* Shell, M. The economy of literature p11-62

Gyitkshan Indians. See Kitksan Indians

Gynecocracy. See Matriarchy

Gyorgy, Andrew
The Hungarian Revolution of 1956. *In* Hammond, T. T. ed. The anatomy of Communist takeovers p596-605

Gypsies

Women
See Women, Gypsy

H

H. D. pseud. See Doolittle, Hilda

HEW. See United States. Department of Health, Education, and Welfare

Haac, Oscar A.
Faith in the Enlightenment: Voltaire and Rousseau seen by Michelet. *In* Studies in eighteenth-century culture v7 p475-90
Toward a definition of utopia. *In* Studies in eighteenth-century culture v6 p407-16

Haacke, Wilmont
Mass media—the playground for grown-ups. *In* Fischer, H. D. and Melnik, S. R. eds. Entertainment: a cross-cultural examination p94-98

Haaker, Ann
Anthony Munday. *In* Logan, T. P. and Smith, D. S. eds. The popular school p122-36

Haardt, Sara

About

Going, W. T. Zelda Sayre Fitzgerald and Sara Haardt Mencken. *In* Going, W. T. Essays on Alabama literature p114-41

Haas, Edward F.
The Southern metropolis, 1940-1976. *In* Brownell, B. A. and Goldfield, D. R. eds. The city in Southern history p159-91

Haas, Ernest B.
An international 'scientific society'? *In* New dimensions of world politics p73-85

Haas, Mary Rosamond
American Indian linguistic prehistory. *In* Sebeok, T. A. ed. Native languages of the Americas v 1 p23-58

The Southeast. *In* Sebeok, T. A. ed. Native languages of the Americas v 1 p573-612

Haavikko, Paavo

About

Dauenhauer, R. The view from the Aspen Grove: Paavo Haavikko in national and international context. *In* Dauenhauer, R. and Binham, P. eds. Snow in May p67-97

About individual works
Fourteen rulers

Nummi, L. At the sea gate of the palace. *In* Dauenhauer, R. and Binham, P. eds. Snow in May p98-101

Haberman, Melvyn
The courtship of the void: the world of Hard times. *In* The Worlds of Victorian fiction p37-55

Habermas, Jürgen
Rationalism divided in two: a reply to Albert. *In* Giddens, A. ed. Positivism and sociology p195-223

Toward a reconstruction of historical materialism. *In* Dallmayr, F. R. ed. From contract to community p47-63

About

Brown, M. E. Sociology as critical theory. *In* McNall, S. G. ed. Theoretical perspectives in sociology p251-75

Lemert, C. C. Critical theory: Juergen Habermas. *In* Lemmert, C. C. Sociology and the twilight of man p194-225

Misgeld, D. Critical theory and hermeneutics: the debate between Habermas and Gadamer. *In* O'Neill, J. ed. On critical theory p164-83

Sewart, J. J. Critical theory and the critique of conservative method. *In* McNall, S. G. ed. Theoretical perspectives in sociology p310-22

Wellmer, A. Communications and emancipation: reflections on the linguistic turn in critical theory. *In* O'Neill, J. ed. On critical theory p231-63

Wilson, H. T. Science, critique, and criticism: the "open society" revisited. *In* O'Neill, J. ed. On critical theory p205-30

About individual works
The analytical theory of science and dialectics

Albert, H. The myth of total reason: dialectical claims in the light of undialectical criticism. *In* Giddens, A. ed. Positivism and sociology p157-94

Habermas, Jürgen, and Luhmann, Niklas

About individual works
Theorie der Gesellschaft oder Sozialtechnologie

Sixel, F. W. The problem of sense: Habermas v. Luhmann. *In* O'Neill, J. ed. On critical theory p184-204

Habicht, Christian
Royal documents in Maccabees II. *In* Harvard Studies in classical philology v80 p 1-18

Habits of animals. See Animals, Habits and behavior of

Habitual criminals. See Recidivists

Habsburg, House of
Headley, J. M. The Habsburg world empire and the revival of Ghibellinism. *In* Medieval and Renaissance studies [1975] p93-127

Art patronage

Trevor-Roper, H. R. The Archdukes and Rubens. *In* Trevor-Roper, H. R. Princes and artists p127-63

Trevor-Roper, H. R. Rudolf II in Prague. *In* Trevor-Roper, H. R. Princes and artists p85-125

Hachey, Thomas E.
Political terrorism: the British experience. *In* International terrorism p90-114

Hachiya, Michihiko

About individual works
Hiroshima diary

Canetti, E. Dr Hachiya's Diary of Hiroshima. *In* Canetti, E. The conscience of words p184-91

Hack, Richard
Memorial poetry reading for Kenneth Patchen. *In* Morgan, R. G. ed. Kenneth Patchen: a collection of essays p81-97

Hack writers
Sheed, W. Four hacks. *In* Sheed, W. The good word & other words p24-27

Sheed, W. Genre writers. *In* Sheed, W. The good word & other words p33-37

Hacker, Andrew
The new rationality: the clash between the corporate and the public sector conceptions of the national interest. *In* Planning, politics, and the public interest p10-19

Hacker, Peter Michael Stephan
Locke and the meaning of colour words. *In* Royal Institute of Philosophy. Impressions of empiricism p23-46

Hacker, Thorne
Management by objectives for schools. *In* Managing nonprofit organizations p155-63

Hackett, Alice Payne
Best sellers in the bookstores, 1900-1975. *In* Bookselling in America and the world p109-37

Hackett, John
Logic and rhetoric in Marvell's "Coy mistress." *In* Friedenreich, K. ed. Tercentenary essays in honor of Andrew Marvell p140-52

Haddad, George Meri
Arab peace efforts and the solution of the Arab-Israeli problem. *In* The Elusive peace in the Middle East p166-248

Haddad, Robert M.
The Ottoman Empire in the contemporary Middle East. *In* Aftermath of empire p39-61

Haddad, William Woodrow
Nationalism in the Ottoman Empire. *In* Nationalism in a non-national state p3-24

Hadfield, John
The moonlighters. *In* The Saturday book 34 p216-21

Hadgraft, Cecil
Indulgence: David Martin's The hero of Too, Frank Dalby Davidson's [sic] The white thorntree, Dal Stivens's A horse of air, David Malouf's Johnno, and Frank Hardy's But the dead are many *In* Hamilton, K. G. ed. Studies in the recent Australian novel p194-224
See also Part 2 under title: Bards, bohemians, and bookmen

Hadrian I, Pope. See Hadrianus I, Pope

Hadrianus I, Pope

About
Wallach, L. The Greek and Latin versions of II Nicaea, 787, and the Synodica of Hadrian I (JE 2448). *In* Wallach, L. Diplomatic studies in Latin and Greek documents from the Carolingian age p 3-26
Wallach, L. The testimonia of image-worship in Hadrian I's Synodica of 785 (JE 2448). *In* Wallach, L. Diplomatic studies in Latin and Greek documents from the Carolingian age p27-42

Hadrianus, Emperor of Rome, in literature
Schoolfield, G. C. Hadrian, Antinous, and a Rilke poem. *In* Creative encounter p145-70

Haeberle, Erwin J.
Historical roots of sexual oppression. *In* Gochros, H. L. and Gochros, J. S. eds. The sexually oppressed p3-27

Hafley, James
Abstraction and order in the language of Tennessee Williams. *In* Tennessee Williams: a tribute p753-62

Hafnium
Kragh, H. Niels Bohr's second atomic theory. *In* Historical studies in the physical sciences v10 p123-86

Hagan, John
Déjà vu and the effect of timelessness in Faulkner's Absalom, Absalom! *In* Garvin, H. R. ed. Makers of the twentieth-century novel p192-207

Hagan, Kenneth J.
The historical significance of American naval intervention. *In* Higham, R. D. ed. Intervention or abstention: the dilemma of American foreign policy p21-39
Nuclear weapons and diplomacy. *In* Encyclopedia of American foreign policy p692-702

Hagan, William T.
Kiowas, Comanches, and cattlemen, 1867-1906: a case study of the failure of U.S. reservation policy. *In* The American Indian p77-99

Hagerman, Edward Hayes
From Jomini to Dennis Hart Mahan: the evolution of trench warfare and the American Civil War. *In* Hubbell, J. T. ed. Battles lost and won p31-54

Haggard, Sir Henry Rider

About
Barclay, G. S. Love after death: Henry Rider Haggard. *In* Barclay, G. S. Anatomy of horror: the masters of occult fiction p58-80

Haggerty, Robert John
The boundaries of health care. *In* Sobel, D. S. ed. Ways of health p45-60

Hagiography
Altman, C. F. Two types of opposition and the structure of Latin saints' lives. *In* Medievalia et humanistica no. 6 p 1-11
Bieler, L. Hagiography and romance in medieval Ireland. *In* Medievalia et humanistica no. 6 p13-24
Dembrowski, P. F. Literary problems of hagiography in Old French. *In* Medievalia et humanistica no. 7 p117-30
Heist, W. W. Irish saints' lives, romance, and cultural history. *In* Medievalia et humanistica no. 6 p25-40
Legge, M. D. Anglo-Norman hagiography and the romances. *In* Medievalia et humanistica no. 6 p41-49

Hagopian, John V.
Symmetry in "Cat in the rain." *In* Benson, J. J. ed. The short stories of Ernest Hemingway: critical essays p230-32

Hagstrum, Jean H.
Blake and British art: the gifts of grace and terror. *In* Kroeber, K. and Walling, W. eds. Images of romanticism p61-80
Byron's songs of innocence: the poems of 'Thyrza.' *In* Evidence in literary scholarship p379-93
Romney and Blake: gifts of grace and terror. *In* Essick, R. N. and Pearce, D. R. eds. Blake in his time p201-12

Hague

Permanent International Court of Justice
Gross, L. On the justiciability of international disputes. *In* [Truth and tragedy]: a tribute to Hans Morgenthau p203-19
Prott, L. V. The future of the International Court of Justice. *In* The Year book of world affairs, 1979 p284-303
Schwarzenberger, G. The principles of the United Nations. *In* The Year book of world affairs, 1976 p307-37

Hahm, David Edgar
Early Hellenistic theories of vision and the perception of color. *In* Studies in perception p60-95
Weight and lightness in Aristotle and his predecessors. *In* Motion and time, space and matter 56-82

Hahn, Lewis Edwin
Advice to the new philosophy teacher. *In* Philosophy and the civilizing arts p356-69

Hahn, Thomas G.
The Indian tradition in Western medieval intellectual history. *In* Viator: medieval and Renaissance studies v9 p213-34

Hahnemann, Samuel

About
Coulter, H. L. Homoeopathic medicine. *In* Sobel, D. S. ed. Ways of health p289-317

Haider-Pregler, Hilde
German-language post-war drama. *In* Nicoll, A. World drama p838-53

Haight, Gordon S.
The Carlyles and the Leweses. *In* Carlyle and his contemporaries p181-204

Haile, Harry Gerald
Luther as Renaissance writer. *In* Hoff-meister, G. ed. The Renaissance and Reformation in Germany p141-56

Hailperin, Celia Moss
Twenty-five years of home care services. *In* Home care p137-47

Haines, Roy Martin
Church, society and politics in the early fifteenth century as viewed from an English pulpit. *In* Church, society and politics p143-57

Hainsworth, John Bryan
The criticism of an oral Homer. *In* Wright, J. H. ed. Essays on the Iliad p28-40

Haiti
Reed, I. I hear you, Doc. *In* Reed, I. Shrovetide in old New Orleans p259-85

Rotberg, R. I. Vodun and the politics of Haiti. *In* Kilson, M. L. and Rotberg, R. I. eds. The African diaspora p342-65

Haitian fiction

History and criticism
Dash, J. M. The peasant novel in Haiti. *In* African literature today no. 9: Africa, America and the Caribbean p77-90

Haitian literature

History and criticism
Knight, V. W. W. Haiti and Martinique. *In* King, B. and Ogungbesan, K. eds. A celebration of Black and African writing p46-59

Haitian mythology. See Mythology, Haitian

Hakluyt, Richard, 1552?-1616

About
Seelye, J. Divine tobacco: Hakluyt and the Virginia business. *In* Seelye, J. Prophetic waters p23-56

Halacha. See Jewish law

Halakha. See Jewish law

Halberstam, David

About individual works
The best and the brightest
Sheed, W. A fun-house mirror. *In* Sheed, W. The good word & other words p105-09

Hale, George Ellery, 1868-1938

About
Kargon, R. H. Temple to science: cooperative research and the birth of the California Institute of Technology. *In* Historical studies in the physical sciences v8 p3-31

Hale, John Rigby
Printing and military culture of Renaissance Venice. *In* Medievalia et humanistica no. 8 p21-62

The Renaissance label. *In* Background to the English Renaissance p31-42

Hale, Walter Morris-. See Morris-Hale, Walter

Hales, Stephen

About
Guerlac, H. The continental reputation of Stephen Hales. *In* Guerlac, H. Essays and papers in the history of modern science p275-84

Guerlac, H. Stephen Hales: a Newtonian physiologist. *In* Guerlac, H. Essays and papers in the history of modern science p170-92

Haley, Bruce
The healthy body and Victorian culture

Contents

Anarchy and physical culture
The athlete as barbarian: Richard Feverel and Willoughby Patterne
Conclusion
Growing up healthy: images of boyhood
Mens sana in corpore sano: Victorian psychophysiology
The new era: Victorian sport and training
Obeying the laws of life: Carlyle and Spencer
The thoroughly healthy mind: Victorian criticism
The true gentleman and the washed rough in broadcloth
Two staunch walkers: Tom Thurnall and Tom Tulliver
Types of healthy Christianity: Newman and Kingsley

Haley, P. Edward
Comparative intervention: Mexico in 1914 & Dominica in 1965. *In* Higham, R. D. ed. Intervention or abstention: the dilemma of American foreign policy p40-59

Haley, P. Edward, and Rood, Harold William
China's major trading partner: Japan dependent. *In* China's changing role in the world economy p187-212

Half-way covenant. See Covenants (Church polity)

Halhed, Nathaniel Brassey

About
Rocher, R. Alien and empathic: the Indian poems of N. B. Halhed. *In* Kling, B. B. and Pearson, M. N. eds. The age of partnership p215-35

Halifax-Grof, Joan. See Grof, S. jt. auth.

Hall, Alfred Rupert
Introduction: The nature of scientific discovery in the sixteenth century. *In* The Nature of scientific discovery p91-105

Magic, metaphysics and mysticism in the scientific revolution. *In* Bonelli, M. L. R. and Shea, W. R. eds. Reason, experiment, and mysticism in the scientific revolution p275-82

What did the Industrial Revolution in Britain owe to science? *In* Historical perspectives p129-51

Hall, Basil

Alessandro Gavazzi: a Barnabite friar and the Risorgimento (Presidential address) *In* Church, society and politics p303-56

Hall, Daniel George Edward

About

Cowan, C. D. D. G. E. Hall: a biographical sketch. *In* Southeast Asian history and historiography p11-23

Bibliography

Cordell, H. comp. Publications of D. G. E. Hall. *In* Southeast Asian history and historiography p25-27

Hall, David

About

Harlan, R. D. A colonial printer as bookseller in eighteenth-century Philadelphia: the case of David Hall. *In* Studies in eighteenth-century culture v5 p355-69

Hall, David D.

Understanding the Puritans. *In* Mulder, J. F. and Wilson, J. F. eds. Religion in American history p 1-16

The Victorian connection. *In* Howe, D. W. ed. Victorian America p81-94

The world of print and collective mentality in seventeenth-century New England. *In* Higham, J. and Conkin, P. K. eds. New directions in American intellectual history p166-80

Hall, Diana Long

Biology, sex hormones and sexism in the 1920's. *In* Gould, C. C. and Wartofsky, M. W. eds. Women and philosophy p81-96

Hall, Donald Andrew

About

Mills, R. J. Donald Hall's poetry. *In* Mills, R. J. Cry of the human p192-250

Hall, Dorothy Judd

An Old Testament Christian. *In* Frost: centennial essays III p316-49

Hall, Douglas Rowland

Molière: critic and victim of the social institution of marriage. *In* Johnson, R. B.; Neumann, E. S. and Trail, G. T. eds. Molière and the commonwealth of letters: patrimony and posterity p49-53

Hall, Georgia. See Carpenter, J. O. jt. auth.

Hall, Granville Stanley

About

Boorstin, D. J. From "naughtiness" to "behavior deviation"; excerpt from "The Americans: the democratic experience". *In* Davis, F. J. and Stivers, R. eds. The collective definition of deviance p147-55

Hall, Hugh Gaston

The present state of Molière studies. *In* Johnson, R. B.; Neumann, E. S. and Trail, G. T. eds. Molière and the commonwealth of letters: patrimony and posterity p728-46

Hall, James T.

Patchen's angry shoes. *In* Morgan, R. G. ed. Kenneth Patchen: a collection of essays p17-19

Hall, John Whitney

Japanese history in world perspective. *In* The Future of history p173-88

Hall, Joseph, Bp. of Norwich, supposed author. See The return from Parnassus

Hall, Kathleen Mary

Pontus de Tyard: a reply to a recent article. *In* French Renaissance studies, 1540-70 p185-93

Hall, Marie Boas

Newton's voyage in the strange seas of alchemy. *In* Bonelli, M. L. R. and Shea, W. R. eds. Reason, experiment, and mysticism in the scientific revolution p239-46

The spirit of innovation in the sixteenth century. *In* The Nature of scientific discovery p309-21

Hall, Michael Garibaldi, and Joyce, William L.

The Half-way covenant of 1662: some new evidence. *In* American Antiquarian Society. Proceedings v87 pt 1 p97-110

See also Joyce, W. L. jt. auth.

Hall, Peter

About individual works

A midsummer night's dream

Jorgens, J. J. Peter Hall's A midsummer night's dream. *In* Jorgens, J. J. Shakespeare on film p51-65

Hall, Radclyffe

About individual works

The well of loneliness

Cockshut, A. O. J. The lesbian theme. *In* Cockshut, A. O. J. Man and woman: a study of love and the novel, 1740-1940 p186-208

Hall, Robert, 1764-1831

About

Davie, D. Dissent and the evangelicals, 1800-1850. *In* Davie, D. A gathered Church p55-72

Hall, Sallie J.

Henry James and the bluestockings: satire and morality in The Bostonians. *In* Aeolian harps p207-25

Hall, Wade

Humor in Jesse Stuart's fiction. *In* LeMaster, J. R. and Clarke, M. W. eds. Jesse Stuart p89-102

Hallam, George Walter

In praise of being a gentleman: 1528-1976. *In* Renaissance and modern p3-10

Hallam, Henry

About individual works

Introduction to the literature of Europe in the fifteenth, sixteenth, and seventeenth centuries

Baker, W. Leigh Hunt, George Henry Lewes and Henry Hallam's Introduction to the literature of Europe. *In* Virginia. University. Bibliographical Society. Studies in bibliography v32 p252-73

Hallam, Herbert Enoch

The medieval social picture. *In* Kamenka, E. and Neale, R. S. eds. Feudalism, capitalism and beyond p28-49

Halldórs, Tháttr Snorrasonar. I

Harris, J. C. Christian form and Christian meaning in Halldórs páttr I. *In* The Learned and the lewed p249-64

Halle, Louis Joseph

General education and the understanding of politics: the case of Hans J. Morgenthau. *In* [Truth and tragedy]: a tribute to Hans Morgenthau p55-65

Halle, Morris
Knowledge unlearned and untaught: what speakers know about the sounds of their language. *In* Linguistic theory and psychological reality p294-303

Halle, Morris, and Keyser, Samuel Jay
The iambic pentameter; excerpt from "Versification: major language types." *In* Gross, H. S. ed. The structure of verse p173-93

Halle. Universität
See also Wittenberg. Universität

History

McClelland, C. E. The aristocracy and university reform in eighteenth-century Germany. *In* Schooling and society p146-73

Halley, Jeffrey A.
Beyond the sociology of art: recent interdisciplinary developments in the critical analysis of culture. *In* McNall, S. G. ed. Theoretical perspectives in sociology p276-91

Halli, Robert W.
"This torrent of domestic misery": George Lillo's The London merchant. *In* A Provision of human nature p155-68

Halliday, Frank Ernest
Thomas Hardy: the man in his work. *In* Butler, L. S. ed. Thomas Hardy after fifty years p126-34

Halliday, Michael Alexander Kirkwood
Talking one's way in. *In* Davies, A. ed. Problems of language and learning p8-33

Hallie, Philip Paul
Satan, evil, and good in history. *In* Stanage, S. M. ed. Reason and violence p53-69

Hallmundsson, May Newman
The community of law and letters: some notes on Thomas Usk's audience. *In* Viator: medieval and Renaissance studies v9 p357-65

Halloran, James Dermont. See Murdoch, G. jt. auth.

Hallowell, Alfred Irving
Ojibwa ontology, behavior, and world view. *In* Tedlock, D. E. and Tedlock, B. eds. Teachings from the American earth p141-78

Hallstein, Walter
The need for vision. *In* The New Atlantic challenge p27-30

Hallucinations and illusions. See Optical illusions

Hallucinogenic drugs
Furst, P. T. "High states" in culture-historical perspective. *In* Alternate states of consciousness p53-88

Furst, P. T. Morning glory and mother goddess at Tepantitla, Teotihuacan: iconography and analogy in pre-Columbian art. *In* Mesoamerican archaeology p187-215

Grof, S. and Halifax-Grof, J. Psychedelics and the experience of death p182-202

Reichel-Dolmatoff, G. Drug-induced optical sensations and their relationship to applied art among some Colombian Indians. *In* Greenhalgh, M. and Megaw, J. V. S. eds. Art in society p289-304

Hallucinogenic drugs and religious experience
Furst, P. T. "High states" in culture-historical perspective. *In* Alternate states of consciousness p53-88

Halper, Nathan
The craftsmanship of Joyce: The aesthetics of Joyce: James Joyce and his fingernails. *In* Yeats, Joyce, and Beckett p105-17

Halper, Thomas
Paternalism and the elderly. *In* Spicker, S. F.; Woodward, K. M. and Van Tassel, D. D. eds. Aging and the elderly p321-39

Halperen, Max
How to read a canto. *In* French, W. G. ed. The twenties p335-50

Halperin, David M.
The role of the lie in The first circle. *In* Dunlop, J. B.; Haugh, R. and Klimoff, A. eds. Aleksandr Solzhenitsyn: critical essays and documentary materials 2d ed. p260-76

Halperin, John
Introduction: Jane Austen's nineteenth-century critics: Walter Scott to Henry James. *In* Halperin, J. ed. Jane Austen p3-42

The worlds of Emma: Jane Austen and Cowper. *In* Halperin, J. ed. Jane Austen p197-206

About individual works
The theory of the novel
Vidal, G. The hacks of academe. *In* Vidal, G. Matters of fact and of fiction p89-98

Trollope and politics: a study of the Pallisers and others
Hart, F. R. New approaches to the Trollope problem. *In* Review, v 1 1979 p165-72

Halperin, John, comp.
A select bibliography. *In* Halperin, J. ed. Jane Austen p197-206

Halperin, Maurice
Culture and the Revolution; excerpt from "The rise and decline of Fidel Castro." *In* Radosh, R. ed. The new Cuba: paradoxes and potentials p190-210

Halperin, Morton H.
Covert operations: effects of secrecy on decision-making. *In* Borosage, R. L. and Marks, J. D. eds. The CIA file p159-77

U.S.-Japanese security relations. *In* Clapp, P. and Halperin, M. H. eds. United States—Japanese relations, the 1970's p203-22

See also Clapp, P. A. jt. auth.

Halpern, Ben
Jewish nationalism: self-determination as a human right. *In* Sidorsky, D. ed. Essays on human rights p307-35

Halpern, Charles R.
The public interest bar: an audit. *In* Nader, R. and Green, M. J. eds. Verdicts on lawyers p158-71

Halsband, Robert
"Condemned to petticoats": Lady Mary Wortley Montagu as feminist and writer. *In* The Dress of words p35-52

New anecdotes of Lady Mary Wortley Montagu. *In* Evidence in literary scholarship p241-46

Halsman, Philippe
Einstein; excerpt from "Halsman: sight and insight." *In* Einstein p27-28

Halsted, Thomas A.
Nuclear testing—no end in sight? *In* Arms control and technological innovation p210-23

Halsted, William Stewart

About

Harvey, A. M. Early contributions to the surgery of cancer: William S. Halsted, Hugh H. Young, and John G. Clark. *In* Harvey, A. M. Adventures in medical research p69-83

el-Hamamsy, Laila Shukry

The assertion of Egyptian identity. *In* Ethnic identity p276-306

Hamann, Johann Georg

About

Berlin, Sir I. Hume and the sources of German anti-rationalism. *In* David Hume p93-116

Nebel, S. S. Hamann's views on human reason. *In* Studies in eighteenth-century culture v4 p125-30

O'Flaherty, J. C. Language and reason in the thought of Hamann. *In* Creative encounter p86-104

About individual works

Sokratische Denkwürdigkeiten

O'Flaherty, J. C. Socrates in Hamann's Socratic memorabilia and Nietzsche's Birth of tragedy. *In* O'Flaherty, J. C.; Sellner, T. F. and Helm, R. M. eds. Studies in Nietzsche and the classical tradition p134-43

Hamarneh, Sami Khalaf

The life sciences. *In* The Genius of Arab civilization p145-72

Hamblin, Robert W.

Lucas Beauchamp, Ned Barnett, and William Faulkner's 1940 will. *In* Virginia. University. Bibliographical Society. Studies in bibliography v32 p281-83

Hambro, Edvard Isak

Permanent representatives to international organisations. *In* The Year book of world affairs, 1976 p30-41

Hamburg, Beatrix. See Berger, P. A. jt. auth.

Hamburg, David A.

Ancient man in the twentieth century. *In* Goodall, V. M. ed. The quest for man p27-54

Human aggressiveness and conflict resolution. *In* World change and world security p39-60

See also Berger, P. A. jt. auth.

Hamburger, Michael

Art as second nature

Contents

Art as second nature: Goethe
Brecht and his successors
Büchner's Danton's death
Edwin Muir
Edwin Muir's Letters
Egon Schiele: the background
An essay on the essay
Existential psycho-analysis
George Oppen's Collected poems
Hölderlin
Johannes Bobrowski: an introduction
Moralist and jester: the poetry of Günter Grass
Music and words: Beethoven
On anonymity
On 'metrical' verse, 'free' verse and prose

Psycho-analysis and art
A refusal to review Kierkegaard
Returning to Rilke—a note
The trouble with Francis
The unity of T. S. Eliot's poetry
A writer on his work: 'At fifty-five'
Yeats's memoirs

About individual works

At fifty-five

Hamburger, M. A writer on his work: 'At fifty-five.' *In* Hamburger, M. Art as second nature p49-53

Hamilton, A. C.

On the concept of the English literary renaissance. *In* Medieval and Renaissance studies 1976 p119-37

Hamilton, David Bailey

Andreas and Beowulf: placing the hero. *In* Anglo-Saxon poetry: essays in appreciation p81-98

Hamilton, Earl Jefferson

What the New World gave the economy of the Old. *In* First images of America p853-84

Hamilton, Edward K.

On nonconstitutional management of a constitutional problem. *In* A New America? p111-28

Hamilton, Iain

Wonderfully living: Koestler the novelist. *In* Harris, H. A. ed. Astride the two cultures p84-101

Hamilton, James F.

Literature and the "natural man" in Rousseau's Emile. *In* Literature and history in the age of ideas p195-206

Molière and Rousseau: the confrontation of art and politics. *In* Johnson, R. B.; Neumann, E. S. and Trail, G. T. eds. Molière and the commonwealth of letters: patrimony and posterity p100-08

Hamilton, Kenneth Gordon

A prefatory sketch. *In* Hamilton, K. G. ed. Studies in the recent Australian novel p 1-28

Two difficult young men: Martin Boyd's A difficult young man and Christina Stead's The people with the dogs. *In* Hamilton, K. G. ed. Studies in the recent Australian novel p141-67

Hamilton, Richard

Announced entrances in Greek tragedy. *In* Harvard Studies in classical philology v82 p63-82

About

Rosenberg, H. Olitski, Kelly, Hamilton: dogma and talent. *In* Rosenberg, H. Art on the edge p60-70

Hamilton, Richard F.

Old isues and new directions for research. *In* The Uses of controversy in sociology p95-99

Hamilton, Virginia

High John is risen again. *In* Horn Book Magazine. Crosscurrents of criticism p159-67

Hamilton, William Donald

Innate social aptitudes of man: an approach from evolutionary genetics. *In* Biosocial anthropology p133-55

Hamilton, Sir William Rowan

About

Hankins, T. L. Algebra as pure time: William Rowan Hamilton and the foundations of algebra. *In* Motion and time, space and matter p327-59

Hamlet (criticism) Shakespeare, W. *In* Kauffmann, S. Persons of the drama p91-93

Hamlet (Motion picture by Grigorii Mikhaïlovich Kozinfsev)

Jorgens, J. J. Grigori Kozintsev's Hamlet. *In* Jorgens, J. J. Shakespeare on film p218-34

Hamlet (Motion picture by Sir Laurence Olivier)

Jorgens, J. J. Laurence Olivier's Hamlet. *In* Jorgens, J. J. Shakespeare on film p207-17

Hamlin, Cyrus

Strategies of reversal in literary narrative. *In* Valdés, M. J. and Miller, O. J. eds. Interpretation of narrative p61-77

Hamlisch, Marvin

About individual works

A chorus line

Kauffmann, S. A chorus line. *In* Kauffmann, S. Persons of the drama p266-70

Hamlyn, David W.

Self-knowledge. *In* Mischel, T. ed. The self p170-200

Hamlyn, Susan. See Davis, T. jt. auth.

Hamm, Charles E.

The ecstatic and the didactic: a pattern in American music. *In* Current thought in musicology p41-62

Hamm, Michael Franklin

The breakdown of urban modernization: a prelude to the revolutions of 1917. *In* Hamm, M. F. ed. The city in Russian history p182-200

Hamman, Louis

About

Harvey, A. M. Compleat clinician and Renaissance pathologist: Louis Hamman and Arnold R. Rich. *In* Harvey, A. M. Adventures in medical research p139-51

Hammel, Eugene A.

The matrilateral implications of structural cross-cousin marriage. *In* Zubrow, E. B. W. ed. Demographic anthropology p145-68

Hammer, Carl

Intimations of Molière in Goethe's Leipzig comedies. *In* Johnson, R. B.; Neumann, E. S. and Trail, G. T. eds. Molière and the commonwealth of letters: patrimony and posterity p276-86

Hammersley, John M.

The technology of thought. *In* Neyman, J. ed. The heritage of Copernicus: theories "pleasing to the mind" p394-415

Hammersmith, James P. See Chang, J. S. M. J. jt. auth.

Hammerton, A. James

Feminism and female emigration, 1861-1886. *In* Vicinus, M. ed. A widening sphere p52-71

Hammett, Dashiell

About

Cawelti, J. G. Hammett, Chandler, and Spillane. *In* Cawelti, J. G. Adventure, mystery, and romance p162-91

Marcus, S. Dashiell Hammett and the Continental Op. *In* Marcus, S. Representations p311-31

About individual works

The Continental Op, edited by Steven Marcus

Sale, R. H. Dashiell Hammett. *In* Sale, R. H. On not being good enough p73-80

The Maltese falcon

Grella, G. The wings of the falcon and The Maltese dove. *In* Filler, L. ed. *In* A question of quality: popularity and value in modern creative writing p108-14

Hammon, Jupiter

About

Bell, B. W. African-American writers. *In* Emerson, E. H. ed. American literature, 1764-1789 p711-93

Bibliography

Klinkowitz, J. Early writers: Jupiter Hammon, Phillis Wheatley, and Benjamin Banneker. *In* Inge, M. T.; Duke, J. M. and Bryer, J. R. eds. Black American writers v 1 p 1-20

Hammond, George P.

The search for the fabulous in the settlement of the Southwest. *In* Weber, D. J. ed. New Spain's far northern frontier p17-33

Hammond, Mason

The emergence of mediaeval towns: independence or continuity? *In* Harvard Studies in classical philology v78 p 1-33
See also Hirschland, N. L. jt auth.

Hammond, Norman

The distribution of late classic Maya major ceremonial centres in the central area. *In* Mesoamerican archaeology p313-34

Ex oriente lux: a view from Belize. *In* The Origins of Maya civilization p45-76

Hammond, Thomas Taylor

The Communist takeover of Outer Mongolia: model for Eastern Europe? *In* Hammond, T. T. ed. The anatomy of Communist takeovers p107-44

The history of Communist takeovers. *In* Hammond, T. T. ed. The anatomy of Communist takeovers p 1-45

A summing up. *In* Hammond, T. T. ed. The anatomy of Communist takeovers p638-43

Hampshire, Stuart

The explanation of thought. *In* Thought, consciousness, and reality p 3-23

Joyce and Vico: the middle way. *In* Giambattista Vico's science of humanity p321-32

Morality and pessimism. *In* Hampshire, S. ed. Public and private morality p 1-22

On having a reason. *In* Royal Institute of Philosophy. Human values p86-98

Public and private morality. *In* Hampshire, S. ed. Public and private morality p23-53

Spinoza's theory of human freedom. *In* Freeman, E. and Mandelbaum, M. H. eds Spinoza p35-47

Hampshire, Stuart—_Continued_

About

Franck, I. Spinoza, Freud, and Hampshire on psychic freedom. _In_ Thought, consciousess, and reality p257-309

Hampshire, Stuart Newton. See Hampshire, Stuart

Hampton v. Mow Sun Wong. _In_ The Supreme Court review, 1977 p275-339

Hamsun, Knut

About

Naess, H. S. Who was Hamsun's hero? _In_ The Hero in Scandinavian litrature p63-86

Han, Sang Jin

Ideology—critique and social science: the use of discursive method. _In_ McNall, S. G. ed. Theoretical perspectives in sociology p292-309

Hanak, Miroslav John

Molière's dialectics of the grotesque and the struggle for natural order. _In_ Johnson, R. B.; Neumann, E. S. and Trail, G. T. eds. Molière and the commonwealth of letters: patrimony and posterity p499-506

Hanan, Patrick

The early Chinese short story: a critical theory in outline. _In_ Birch, C. ed. Studies in Chinese literary genres p299-338

The nature of Ling Meng-sh'u's fiction. _In_ Chinese narrative p85-114

Hanawalt, Barbara A.

The female felon in fourteenth-century England. _In_ Stuard, S. M. ed. Women in medieval society p125-40

Also in Viator: medieval and Renaissance studies v5 p253-68

Hanaway, William L.

The Iranian epics. _In_ Oinas, F. J. ed. Heroic epic and saga p76-98

Hanchett, Walter S.

Tsarist statutory regulation of municipal government in the nineteenth century. _In_ Hamm, M. F. ed. The city in Russian history p91-114

Hancock, Moffatt

Some choice-of-law problems posed by antiguest statutes: realism in Wisconsin and rule-fetishism in New York. _In_ Stanford legal essays p251-65

Hancock Tower, Chicago. See Chicago. John Hancock Tower

Hand, Herbert H. and Hollingsworth, A. Thomas

Tailoring MBO to hospitals. _In_ Managing nonprofit organizations p176-86

Hand, Learned

About

Gunther, G. Learned Hand and the origins of modern first amendment doctrine: some fragments of history. _In_ Stanford legal essays p195-249

White, G. E. Cardozo, Learned Hand, and Frank: the dialectic of freedom and constraint. _In_ White, G. E. The American judicial tradition p251-91

Hand, Wayland Debs

The effect of the discovery on ethnological and folklore studies in Europe. _In_ First images of America p45-55

The mole in folk medicine: a survey from Indic antiquity to modern America II. _In_ American folk medicine p37-48

Hand in literature

Sanders, C. R. Tennyson and the human hand. _In_ Sanders, C. R. Carlyle's friendships, and other studies p287-304

Hand weaving

Tunisia

Teitelbaum, J. M. The leer and the loom—social controls on handloom weavers. _In_ The Evil eye p63-75

Händel, Georg Friedrich

About

Schmidgall, G. George Frederic Handel. _In_ Schmidgall, G. Literature as opera p29-65

Handicapped

Smith, R. T. Societal reaction and physical disability: contrasting perspectives. _In_ Gove, W. R. ed. The labelling of deviance p147-56

Care and treatment

Elkin, R. A systems approach to planning and managing programs for the handicapped. _In_ Managing nonprofit organizations p71-77

France

Weiner, D. B. Three champions of the handicapped in Revolutionary France. _In_ From Parnassus p161-76

Handicapped children

See also Mentally handicaped children

Education (Elementary)

Elkind, D. The active classroom and children with special needs: affective and social dimensions. _In_ Elkind, D. The child and society p237-51

Handicraft

Kramer, E. Art and craft. _In_ Ulman, E. and Dachinger, P. eds. Art therapy p106-09

See also Artisans; Collage; Glass craft; Jewelry making; Pottery craft

Handke, Peter

About individual works

Kaspar

Brustein, R. S. The curses of Caliban: Kaspar. _In_ Brustein, R. S. The culture watch p72-74

Kaspar, and other plays

Kauffmann, S. Kaspar, and other plays. _In_ Kauffmann, S. Persons of the drama p195-98

The ride across Lake Constance

Kauffmann, S. The ride across Lake Constance. _In_ Kauffmann, S. Persons of the drama p198-201

Schlueter, J. Metafictional theater: Handke's The ride across Lake Constance. _In_ Schlueter, J. Metafictional characters in modern drama p105-19

Characters

Schlueter, J. Metafictional theater: Handke's The ride across Lake Constance. _In_ Schlueter, J. Metafictional characters in modern drama p105-19

Handler, Mark J. See Hicks, G. L. jt. auth.

Handlin, Oscar

About

Solomon, B. M. A portrait of Oscar Handlin. *In* Uprooted Americans p 1-8

Bibliography

Mirak, R. Selected bibliography of the published works of Oscar Handlin. *In* Uprooted Americans p349-65

Handling of snakes (Holiness churches) See Snake cults (Holiness churches)

Hands, Imposition of. See Imposition of hands

Hands, Laying on of. See Imposition of hands

Handy, Robert T.

The American religious depression, 1925-1935. *In* Mulder, J. M. and Wilson, J. F. eds. Religion in American history p431-44

Handy, William J.

The Malamud hero: a quest for existence. *In* The Fiction of Bernard Malamud p65-86

Hanfling, Oswald

Hume and Wittgenstein. *In* Royal Institute of Philosophy. Impressions of empiricism p47-65

Hanfmann, George Maxim Anossov

The crucified donkey man: Achaios and Jesus. *in* Studies in classical art and archaeology p205-07

From Croesus to Constantine

Contents

Ad claras Asiae volemus urbes: Roman governors and urban renewal
Hellenization takes command
Instinctu divinitatis: the Tetrarchs, Constantine and Constantinople
Sardis, Croesus, and the Persians
The social role of sculpture in Roman cities of western Asia Minor

Hanging

Borowitz, A. Why Thackeray went to see a man hanged. *In* Borowitz, A. Innocence and arsenic p33-52

Hanging in literature

Lodge, D. Oscar Wilde: 'The ballad of Reading Gaol.' *In* Lodge, D. The modes of modern writing p17-22

Hani, Motoko

About

Shimada, N. and others. Ume Tsuda and Motoko Hani: echoes of American cultural feminism in Japan. *In* "Remember the ladies": new perspectives on women in American history p161-78

Hanke, Lewis Ulysses

The theological significance of the discovery of America. *In* First images of America p363-89

Hankins, Thomas LeRoy

Algebra as pure time: William Rowan Hamilton and the foundations of algebra. *In* Motion and time, space and matter p327-59

Hanks, Jane Richardson

Recitation of patrilineages among the Akha. *In* Social organization and the applications of anthropology p114-27

Hanks, Lucien Mason

The Thai social order as entourage and circle. *In* Change and persistence in Thai society p197-218

Hanks, Nancy

Design for America's third century. *In* The Uneasy coalition: design in corporate America p91-105

Hanle, Paul Arthur

Indeterminacy before Heisenberg: the case of Franz Exner and Erwin Schrödinger. *In* Historical studies in the physical sciences v10 p225-69

Hanley, James

About individual works

A dream journey

Howe, I. The plebeian realism of James Hanley. *In* Howe, I. Celebrations and attacks p192-94

Hanley, Thomas O'Brien

Church/state relations in the American Revolutionary era. *In* America in theological perspective p87-98

Hanly, Charles

Problems of academic freedom in Canada. *In* Universities in the Western world p157-75

Hanna, Ralph

Cresseid's dream and Henryson's Testament. *In* Chaucer and Middle English studies in honour of Rossell Hope Robbins p288-97

A new edition of Chaucer. *In* Review, v 1 1979 p61-74

Hannay, Margaret Patterson

Harriet's influence on the characterization of Lord Peter Wimsey. *In* Hannay, M. P. ed. As her whimsey took her p36-50

Introduction. *In* Hannay, M. P. ed. As her whimsey took her p xi-xvi

A preface to Perelandra. *In* Schakel, P. J. ed. The longing for a form p73-90

Hannen, Thomas A.

The humanism of Sir Thomas Wyatt. *In* Sloan, T. O. and Waddington, R. S. eds. The rhetoric of Renaissance poetry p37-57

Hanning, Robert W.

Beowulf as heroic history. *In* Medievalia et humanistica no. 5 p77-102

The individual in twelfth-century romance

Contents

Afterword: the evolution of chivalric romance in the early thirteenth century
Critical moments: individuality in chivalric romance
"Engin" in twelfth-century courtly texts
The individual and mimesis, I: Time and space in chivalric romance
The individual and mimesis, II: Multiple perspectives on reality
Individuality in two twelfth-century personal histories
The romance plot and the crisis of inner awareness

A view from the Ivory Tower: in response to Rosemary Park. *In* Small comforts for hard times p321-31

Hansa towns

Rotz, R. A. Investigating urban uprisings with examples from Hanseatic towns, 1374-1416. *In* Order and innovation in the Middle Ages p215-33

Hansen, Bent
Introduction. *In* Economic development and planning p ix-xxiv

Hansen, Bert
Science and magic. *In* Lindberg, D. C. ed. Science in the Middle Ages p483-506

Hansen, Marcus Lee
Immigration and Puritanism. *In* Mulder, J. M. and Wilson, J. F. eds. Religion in American history p342-57

About
Rischin, M. Marcus Lee Hansen: America's first transethnic historian. *In* Uprooted Americans p319-47

Hansen, Roger D.
U.S.-Latin American economic relationships: bilateral, regional or global? *In* The Americas in a changing world p196-238

Hansen, William F.
The Homeric epics and oral poetry. *In* Oinas, F. J. ed. Heroic epic and saga p7-26

Han-shan, 1546-1623

About
Wu, Pei-yi. The spiritual autobiography of Te ch'ing. *In* The Unfolding of Neo-Confucianism p67-92

Hanslick, Eduard

About individual works
The beautiful in music
Gay, P. For Beckmesser. *In* From Parnassus p42-54

Hanson, Duane

About
Masheck, J. D. C. Verist sculpture: Hanson and De Andrea. *In* Battcock, G. ed. Super realism p187-211

Hanson, Philip
The import of Western technology. *In* Brown, A. H. and Kaser, M. eds. The Soviet Union since the fall of Khrushchev p16-48

Hansot, Elisabeth
Reflections on war, utopias, and temporary systems. *In* Small comforts for hard times p246-59

Hapgood, Hutchins

About
Goist, P. D. Alternative perspective: the "radical" journalism of Hutchins Hapgood and Ernest Poole. *In* Goist, P. D. From Main Street to State Street p94-109

About individual works
The smell of mortality
Mudrick, M. The smell of mortality. *In* Mudrick, M. Books are not life but then what is? p157-73

Happening (Art)

United States
Krauss, R. E. Mechanical ballets: light, motion, theater. *In* Krauss, R. E. Passages in modern sculpture p201-42

Happiness
Dubos, R. J. Joie de vivre and happiness. *In* Dubos, R. J. Beast or angel? p198-207

Fletcher, J. F. Happiness. *In* Fletcher, J. F. Humanhood: essays in biomedical ethics p20-26

O'Neill, O. Some inconsistent educational aims. *In* Small comforts for hard times p303-07

Robbins, C. The pursuit of happiness. *In* America's continuing revolution p119-39

Scruton, R. Reason and happiness. *In* Royal Institute of Philosophy. Nature and conduct p139-61

See also Joy

Happy-Healthy-Holy Organization
Tobey, A. The Summer Solstice of the Healthy-Happy-Holy Organization. *In* The New religious consciousness p5-30

Haq, Mahbub ul
Negotiating a new bargain with the rich countries. *In* Erb, G. F. and Kallab, V. eds. Beyond dependency p157-62

Haraszthy, Agostin

About
Katona, A. Sándor Farkas Bölöni and Ágoston Mokcsai Haraszthy. *In* Abroad in America: Visitors to the new Nation, 1776-1914 p43-51

Haraszthy, Ágoston Mokcsai. See Haraszthy, Agostin

Haraway, Donna Jeanne
Reinterpretation or rehabilitation: an exercise in contemporary Marxist history of science. *In* Studies in history of biology v2 p193-209

Harbach, Otto Abels, and Mandel, Frank

About individual works
No, no, Nanette
Simon, J. I. Should Shubert Alley be renamed Memory Lane? *In* Simon, J. I. Singularities p126-32

Harbage, Alfred
Copper into gold. *In* English Renaissance drama p 1-14

Shakespeare and the early Dickens. *In* Shakespeare: aspects of influence p109-34

Harberger, Arnold C.
The case of the three numeraires. *In* Economic development and planning p142-56

Harbert, Bruce
Chaucer and the Latin classics. *In* Brewer, D. S. ed. Geoffrey Chaucer p137-53

King Alfred's 'æstel'. *In* Anglo-Saxon England 3 p103-10

Harbert, Earl Norman
Henry Adams and the critics of his time. *In* Tulane Studies in English, v23 p71-84

Henry Adams's Education and autobiographical tradition. *In* Tulane Studies in English v22 p133-41

Harbottle, Michael
Simulating peace-making in the Middle East: an exercise in reality. *In* Unofficial diplomats p241-49

Harden, Evelyn Jasiulko
The dependence of Apollo Korzeniowski's Komedia upon Griboedov's Gore ot uma. *In* For Wiktor Weintraub p209-26

Hardenberg, Friedrich Leopold, Freiherr von

About individual works
Heinrich von Ofterdingen
Middleton, J. C. Two mountain scenes in Novalis and the question of symbolic style. *In* Middleton, J. C. Bolshevism in art p258-73

Hardie, Colin Graham

Two descents into the underworld. *In* Evolution of consciousness p136-48

Hardin, Charles Mayer

The problem of political power in the United States. *In* [Truth and tragedy]: a tribute to Hans Morgenthau p142-52

Hardin, Clyde Laurence

Spinoza on immortality and time. *In* Shahan, R. W. and Biro, J. I. eds. Spinoza: new perspectives p129-38

Hardin, Garrett James

Carrying capacity as an ethical concept. *In* Lucas, G. R. and Ogletree, T. W. eds. Lifeboat ethics p120-37

Lifeboat ethics: the case against helping the poor. *In* Aiken, W. and La Follette, H. eds. World hunger and moral obligation p11-21

Nice guys finish last. *In* Sociobiology and human nature p183-94

About

Fletcher, J. F. Feeding the hungry: an ethical appraisal. *In* Lucas, G. R. and Ogletree, T. W. eds Lifeboat ethics p52-69

Soroos, M. S. Lifeboat ethics versus oneworldism in international food and resource policy. *In* Orr, D. W. and Soroos, M. S. eds. The global predicament p131-49

Verghese, T. P. Muddled metaphors: an Asian response to Garrett Hardin. *In* Lucas, G. R. and Ogletree, T. W. eds. Lifeboat ethics p151-56

Hardin, James

Erasmus: The praise of folly. *In* Hoffmeister, G. ed. The Renaissance and Reformation in Germany p99-110

Hardin, Nancy Shields

Doris Lessing and the Sufi way. *In* Pratt, A. V. and Dembo, L. S. eds. Doris Lessing p148-64

Hardin, Richard Francis

Michael Drayton. *In* Logan, T. P. and Smith, D. S. eds. The popular school p137-47

Harding, D. W. See Harding, Denys Clement Wyatt

Harding, Denys Clement Wyatt

What the thunder said. *In* The Waste land in different voices p15-28

Harding, Sandra G.

Feminism: reform or revolution? *In* Gould, C. C. and Wartofsky, M. W. eds. Women and philosophy p271-84

Harding, Susan

Women and words in a Spanish village. *In* Reiter, R. R. ed. Toward an anthropology of women p283-308

Harding, Timothy F. See Bray, D. W. jt. auth.

Harding, Vincent

Is America in any sense chosen? A Black response. *In* An Almost chosen people p119-30

Religion and resistance among antebellum Negroes, 1800-1860. *In* Mulder, J. M. and Wilson, J. F. eds. Religion in American history p270-87

So much history, so much future: Martin Luther King, Jr., and the Second Coming of America. *In* Have we overcome? Race relations since Brown p31-78

Harding, Walter Roy

Emerson, Thoreau, and transcendentalism. *In* American literary scholarship, 1973 p3-14

Hardison, Osborne Bennett

Attempting the impossible and accomplishing the unbelievable: thoughts on two American revolutions. *In* A Time to hear and answer: essays for the Bicentennial season p37-58

Petrarch and modern lyric poetry. *In* Studies in the continental background of Renaissance English literature: essays presented to John L. Livesay p29-41

Toward a history of medieval literary criticism. *In* Medievalia et humanistica no. 7 p 1-12

Hardt, John Pearce

Soviet commercial relations and political change. *In* The Interaction of economics and foreign policy p48-83

Soviet economic capabilities and defense resources. *In* Kirk, G. L. and Wessell, N. H. eds. The Soviet threat p122-34

Hardwick, Elizabeth

Domestic manners. *In* A New America? p 1-11

Sue and Arabella. *In* Drabble, M. ed. The genius of Thomas Hardy p67-73

Hardwick, Philip

About

Hobhouse, H. Philip and Philip Charles Hardwick: an architectural dynasty. *In* Seven Victorian architects p32-49

Hardwick, Philip Charles

About

Hobhouse, H. Philip and Philip Charles Hardwick: an architectural dynasty. *In* Seven Victorian architects p32-49

Hardy, Barbara (Nathan)

The advantage of lyric

Contents

The advantage of lyric

Clough's self-consciousness

Forms and feelings in the sonnets of Gerard Manley Hopkins

Passion and contemplation in Yeats's love poetry

The personal and the impersonal in some of Dylan Thomas's lyrics

The poetry of Sylvia Plath

The reticence of W. H. Auden

Thinking and feeling in the songs and sonnets of John Donne

W. H. Auden, thirties to sixties: a face and a map

An approach through narrative. *In* Spilka, M. ed. Towards a poetics of fiction p31-40

The lyricism of Emily Brontë. *In* Smith, A. ed. The art of Emily Brontë p94-118

The objects in Mansfield Park. *In* Halperin, J. ed. Jane Austen p180-96

Properties and possessions in Jane Austen's novels. *In* Jane Austen's achievement p79-105

Tellers and listeners

Contents

Abuses of narrative

Charles Dickens

Fantasy and dream

Good stories, good listeners

James Joyce

Memory and memories

Narrative imagination

Thomas Hardy

Hardy, Barbara (Nathan)—*Continued*

Under the greenwood tree: a novel about the imagination. *In* Smith, A. ed. The novels of Thomas Hardy p45-57

Hardy, Frank J.

About individual works
But the dead are many

Hadgraft, C. Indulgence: David Martin's The hero of Too, Frank Dalby Davidson's [sic] The white thorntree, Dal Stivens's A horse of air, David Malouf's Johnno, and Frank Hardy's But the dead are many. *In* Hamilton, K. G. ed. Studies in the recent Australian novel p194-224

Hardy, John Edward

Marrying down in Eudora Welty's novels. *In* Prenshaw, P. W. ed. Eudora Welty p93-119

Hardy, Owen B.

Systematic processes applied to health care planning. *In* Managing nonprofit organizations p78-94

Hardy, Thomas

About

Alcorn, J. Hardy: a better world. *In* Alcorn, J. The nature novel from Hardy to Lawrence p 1-24

Bragg, M. Thomas Hardy and Jude the Obscure. *In* Royal Society of Literature of the United Kingdom, London. Essays by divers hands v39 p24-46

Butler, L. S. How it is for Thomas Hardy. *In* Butler, L. S. ed. Thomas Hardy after fifty years p116-25

Drabble, M. Hardy and the natural world. *In* Drabble, M. ed. The genius of Thomas Hardy p162-69

Draper, R. P. Hardy and respectability. *In* An English miscellany p179-207

Enstice, A. The fruit of the Tree of knowledge. *In* Smith, A. ed. The novels of Thomas Hardy p9-22

Halliday, F. E. Thomas Hardy: the man in his work. *In* Butler, L. S. ed. Thomas Hardy after fifty years p126-34

Hardy, B. N. Thomas Hardy. *In* Hardy, B. N. Tellers and listeners p175-205

Irwin, M. and Gregor, I. Either side of Wessex. *In* Butler, L. S. ed. Thomas Hardy after fifty years p104-15

Kay-Robinson, D. Hardy's Wessex. *In* Drabble, M. ed. The genius of Thomas Hardy p110-18

Kennard, J. E. Capital punishment. *In* Kennard, J. E. Victims of convention p63-79

Morgan, W. W. The partial vision: Hardy's idea of dramatic poetry. *In* Tenness Studies in literature v20 p100-08

Mudford, P. Thomas Hardy. *In* Mudford, P. The art of celebration p47-60

Palmer, L. H. The ironic word in Hardy's novels. *In* Tennessee Studies in literature v20 p109-23

Paris, B. J. Experiences of Thomas Hardy. *In* Levine, R. A. The Victorian experience: the novelists p203-37

Pinion, F. B. The ranging vision. *In* Butler, L. S. ed. Thomas Hardy after fifty years p 1-12

Rowse, A. L. Hardy and Cornwall. *In* Drabble, M. ed. The genius of Thomas Hardy p119-38

Skilton, D. New approaches: Meredith, Hardy and Butler. *In* Skilton, D. The English novel p163-77

Stewart, J. I. M. The major novels. *In* Drabble, M. ed. The genius of Thomas Hardy p56-66

Sutherland, J. A. Hardy: breaking into fiction. *In* Sutherland, J. A. Victorian novelists and publishers p206-25

About individual works
After a journey

Holbrook, D. Thomas Hardy and the meaning of existence: After a journey. *In* Holbrook, D. Lost bearings in English poetry p204-16

The complete poems of Thomas Hardy (New Wessex edition)

Gittings, R. The improving hand: the New Wessex edition of The complete poems. *In* Butler, L. S. ed. Thomas Hardy after fifty years p43-48

The darkling thrush

Berryman, J. Hardy and his thrust. *In* Berryman, J. The freedom of the poet p242-44

Desperate remedies

Irwin, M. and Gregor, I. Either side of Wessex. *In* Butler, L. S. ed. Thomas Hardy after fifty years p104-15

The dynasts

Orel, H. Hardy and the theatre. *In* Drabble, M. ed. The genius of Thomas Hardy p94-108

Far from the madding crowd

Cockshut, A. O. J. The pessimists: Thomas Hardy. *In* Cockshut, A. O. J. Man and woman: a study of love and the novel, 1740-1940 p116-30

Jude the obscure

Bragg, M. Thomas Hardy and Jude the obscure. *In* Royal Society of Literature of the United Kingdom, London. Essays by divers hands v39 p24-46

Cockshut, A. O. J. The pessimists: Thomas Hardy. *In* Cockshut, A. O. J. Man and woman: a study of love and the novel, 1740-1940 p116-30

Gallivan, P. Science and art in Jude the obscure. *In* Smith, A. ed. The novels of Thomas Hardy p126-44

Hardwick, E. Sue and Arabella. *In* Drabble, M. ed. The genius of Thomas Hardy p67-73

The Mayor of Casterbridge

Grindle, J. M. Compulsion and choice in The Mayor of Casterbridge. *In* Smith, A. ed. The novels of Thomas Hardy p91-106

The new Wessex edition of the stories of Thomas Hardy

Hynes, S. L. Old Wessex, new Wessex. *In* Review, v 1 1979 p215-22

The return of the native

Heilman, R. B. The return: centennial observations. *In* Smith, A. ed. The novels of Thomas Hardy p58-90

Tess of the d'Urbervilles

Chitty, T. Accident and coincidence in 'Tess of the d'Urbervilles.' *In* Drabble, M. ed. The genius of Thomas Hardy p74-79

Hardy, Thomas—About individual works—
Tess of the d'Urbervilles—*Continued*

Eakins, R. L. Tess: the pagan and Christian traditions. *In* Smith, A. ed. The novels of Thomas Hardy p107-25

Holbrook, D. Criticism has lost confidence in itself. *In* Holbrook, D. Lost bearings in English poetry p25-47

Johnson, B. "The perfection of species" and Hardy's Tess. *In* Knoepflmacher, U. C. and Tennyson, G. B. eds. Nature and the Victorian imagination p259-77

Miller, J. H. Fiction and repetition: Tess of the d'Urbervilles. *In* Forms of modern British fiction p43-71

Tomlinson, T. B. Hardy's universe: Tess of the d'Urbervilles. *In* Tomlinson, T. B. The English middle-class novel p131-47

The trumpet-major

Sanders, A. Marching into the night: Thomas Hardy's The trumpet-major. *In* Sanders, A. The Victorian historical novel, 1840-1880 p229-48

Under the greenwood tree

Hardy, B. N. Under the greenwood tree. *In* Smith, A. ed. The novels of Thomas Hardy p45-57

The well beloved

Fowles, J. Hardy and the hag. *In* Butler, L. S. ed. Thomas Hardy after fifty years p28-42

Appreciation

Stevens-Cox, G. The Hardy industry. *In* Drabble, M. ed. The genius of Thomas Hardy p170-81

Biography

Avery, G. E. The later years. *In* Drabble, M. ed. The genius of Thomas Hardy p44-54

Coleman, T. The early years. *In* Drabble, M. ed. The genius of Thomas Hardy p12-18

Deacon, L. Hardy's secret love. *In* Drabble, M. ed. The genius of Thomas Hardy p19-31

Characters—Arabella Donn

Hardwick, E. Sue and Arabella. *In* Drabble, M. ed. The genius of Thomas Hardy p67-73

Characters—Sue Bridehead

Hardwick, E. Sue and Arabella. *In* Drabble, M. ed. The genius of Thomas Hardy p67-73

Characters—Tess Durbeyfield

Johnson, B. "The perfection of species" and Hardy's Tess. *In* Knoepflmacher, U. C. and Tennyson, G. B. eds. Nature and the Victorian imagination p259-77

Paris, B. J. Experiences of Thomas Hardy. *In* Levine, R. A. The Victorian experience: the novelists p203-37

Characters—Women

Fowles, J. Hardy and the hag. *In* Butler, L. S. ed. Thomas Hardy after fifty years p28-42

Lucas, W. J. Hardy's women. *In* Lucas, W. J. The literature of change p119-91

Miles, R. The women of Wessex. *In* Smith, A. ed. The novels of Thomas Hardy p23-44

Commentaries

See Hardy, Thomas—Criticism and interpretation

Contemporaries

See Hardy, Thomas—Friends and associates

Criticism, Textual

Schweik, R. C. Thomas Hardy: fifty years of textual scholarship. *In* Butler, L. S. ed. Thomas Hardy after fifty years p135-48

Criticism and interpretation

Kinkead-Weekes, M. Lawrence on Hardy. *In* Butler, L. S. ed. Thomas Hardy after fifty years p90-103

Sullivan, S. Friends and critics, 1840-1928. *In* Drabble, M. ed. The genius of Thomas Hardy p32-43

Editors

Hynes, S. L. Old Wessex, new Wessex. *In* Review, v 1 1979 p215-22

Friends and associates

Sullivan, S. Friends and critics, 1840-1928. *In* Drabble, M. ed. The genius of Thomas Hardy p32-43

Influence—Lawrence

Alcorn, J. Hardy and Lawrence. *In* Alcorn, J. The nature novel from Hardy to Lawrence p78-89

Paterson, J. Lawrence's vital source: nature and character in Thomas Hardy. *In* Knoepflmacher, U. C. and Tennyson, G. B. eds. Nature and the Victorian imagination p455-69

Knowledge—Architecture

Betjeman, Sir J. Hardy and architecture. *In* Drabble, M. ed. The genius of Thomas Hardy p150-53

Tristam, P. Stories in stones. *In* Smith, A. ed. The novels of Thomas Hardy p145-68

Knowledge—History

Cecil, Lord D. Hardy the historian. *In* Drabble, M. ed. The genius of Thomas Hardy p154-61

Philosophy

Butler, L. S. How it is for Thomas Hardy. *In* Butler, L. S. ed. Thomas Hardy after fifty years p116-25

Cockshut, A. O. J. Hardy's philosophy. *In* Drabble, M. ed. The genius of Thomas Hardy p139-49

Poetic works

Alexander, M. J. Hardy among the poets. *In* Butler, L. S. ed. Thomas Hardy after fifty years p49-63

Bayley, J. Hardy's poetical metonymy. *In* English Association. Essays and studies, 1978 p115-30

Grigson, G. The poems. *In* Drabble, M. ed. The genius of Thomas Hardy p80-93

Religion and ethics

Creighton, T. R. M. Some thoughts on Hardy and religion. *In* Butler, L. S. ed. Thomas Hardy after fifty years p64-77

Style

Gatrell, S. Hardy, house-style, and the aesthetics of punctuation. *In* Smith, A. ed. The novels of Thomas Hardy p169-92

See also Hardy, Thomas—Technique

Hardy, Thomas—_Continued_

Technique

Lodge, D. Thomas Hardy as a cinematic novelist. _In_ Butler, L. S. ed. Thomas Hardy after fifty years p78-89

Rehder, R. M. The form of Hardy's novels. _In_ Butler, L. S. ed. Thomas Hardy after fifty years p13-27

Hare, Arnold

English comedy. _In_ Howarth, W. D. ed. Comic drama p122-43

Hare, Richard Mervyn

Abortion and the Golden Rule. _In_ Baker, R. and Elliston, F. A. eds. Philosophy & sex p356-75

Contrasting methods of environmental planning. _In_ Royal Institute of Philosophy. Nature and conduct p281-97

About individual works
The language of morals

Glossop, R. J. Hume, Stevenson, and Hare on moral language. _In_ Livingston, D. W. and King, J. T. eds. Hume p362-85

Hare Krishna movement. See International Society for Krishna Consciousness

Hareven, Tamara K.

Family and work patterns of immigrant laborers in a planned industrial town, 1900-1930. _In_ Immigrants in industrial America, 1850-1920 p47-66

Historical changes in the life course and the family: policy implications. _In_ Major social issues p338-45

The last stage: historical adulthood and old age. _In_ Erikson, E. H. ed. Adulthood p201-15

Hargens, Lowell L.

Theory and method in the sociology of science. _In_ Gaston, J. Sociology of science p121-39

Hargrove, Barbara W.

Church student ministeries and the new consciousness. _In_ The New religious consciousness p205-26

Integrative and transformative religions. _In_ Needleman, J. and Baker, G. eds. Understanding the new religions p257-66

Some thoughts about the Unification movement and the churches. _In_ Horowitz, I. L. ed. Science, sin, and scholarship p86-100

Harington, Sir John

About

Miller, R. H. Sir John Harington's Irish journals. _In_ Virginia. University. Bibliographical Society. Studies in bibliography v32 p179-86

About individual works
A supplie or addicion to the catalogue of bishops, to the year 1608

Miller, R. H. Sir John Harington's A supplie or addicion to the catalogue of bishops, to the yeare 1608: composition and text. _In_ Virginia. University. Bibliographical Society. Studies in bibliography v30 p145-61

Criticism, Textual

Miller, R. H. Sir John Harington's A supplie or addicion to the catalogue of bishops, to the yeare 1608: composition and text. _In_ Virginia. University. Bibliographical Society. Studies in bibliography v30 p145-61

Hariulf. See Hariulphe, abbé de Saint Pierre d'Oudenbourg

Hariulphe, abbé de Saint Pierre d'Oudenbourg

About individual works
Gesta ecclessiae Centulensis

Evergates, T. Historiography and sociology in early feudal society: the case of Hariulf and the "milites" of Saint-Riquier. _In_ Viator: medieval and Renaissance studies v6 p35-49

Harkabi, Yehoshefat

The debate at the 12th Palestinian National Council. _In_ The Palestinians p154-58

A Palestinian democratic state as the political goal of the Palestinians. _In_ The Palestinians p154-58

The Palestinian National Covenant. _In_ The Palestinians p143-53

Harkess, Shirley

Family and sex roles in urban society. _In_ Handbook of contemporary urban life p163-201

Harkie, Cyrus B.

About

Wight, W. E. Colonel Cyrus B. Harkie: a troubled military career. _In_ Rank and file p79-91

Harkness, David

England's Irish question. _In_ Peele, G. and Cook, C. eds. The politics of reappraisal, 1918-1939 p39-63

Harlan, John Marshall, 1833-1911

About

White, G. E. John Marshall Harlan I: the precursor. _In_ White, G. E. The American judicial tradition p129-45

Harlan, John Marshall, 1899-1971

About

White, G. E. The mosaic of the Warren Court: Frankfurter, Black, Warren and Harlan. _In_ White, G. E. The American judicial tradition p317-68

Harlan, Robert Dale

A colonial printer as bookseller in eighteenth-century Philadelphia: the case of David Hall. _In_ Studies in eighteenth-century culture v5 p355-69

Harlan, Veit

About individual works
Kolberg

Taylor, R. Kolberg. _In_ Taylor, R. Film propaganda p216-29

Harland, Marion, pseud. See Terhune, Mary Virginia (Hawes)

Harlaw (Scottish ballad)

Buchan, D. D. History and Harlaw. _In_ Ballad studies p29-40

Harlem, New York (City)

Jackson, B. Harlem Renaissance in the twenties. _In_ Jackson, B. The waiting years p165-78

Intellectual life

Bone, R. A. The Harlem Renaissance: a reappraisal. _In_ Bone, R. A. Down home p109-38

Reed, I. Harlem Renaissance day. _In_ Reed, I. Shrovetide in old New Orleans p255-58

Harlem Parents Union
Edwards, E. B. Why a Harlem Parents Union? *In* Parents, teachers, and children: prospects for choice in American education p59-65

Harlem Renaissance in the twenties. Jackson, B. *In* Jackson, B. The waiting years p165-78

Harleville, Jean François Collin d'. See Collin d'Harleville, Jean François

Harley, Sharon
Anna J. Cooper: a voice for Black women. *In* Harley, S. and Terborg-Penn, R. eds. The Afro-American woman p87-96

Northern Black female workers: Jacksonian era. *In* Harley, S. and Terborg-Penn, R. eds. The Afro-American woman p5-16

Harloe, Michael
Marxism, the state and the urban question: critical notes on two recent French theories. *In* Crouch, C. ed. State and economy in contemporary capitalism p122-56

Harlow, Barbara
Realignment: Alois Riegl's image of late Roman art industry. *In* Glyph 3 p118-36

Harman, Gilbert
Review of Language and mind. *In* Harman, G. ed. On Noam Chomsky p201-18

Harmer, Ruth Mulvey
Selling death. *In* Against pollution and hunger p97-117

Harmon, Maurice
Beginning with words. *In* Harmon, M. ed. Richard Murphy: poet of two traditions p118-28

Cobwebs before the wind: aspects of the peasantry in Irish literature from 1800 to 1916. *In* Casey, D. J. and Rhodes, R. E. eds. Views of the Irish peasantry, 1800-1916 p129-59

Introduction: the poet and his background. *In* Harmon, M. ed. Richard Murphy: poet of two traditions p7-9

Harmstone, Teresa Rakowska- See Rakowska-Harmstone, Teresa

Harned, Arthur R.
Molière and Lully. *In* Johnson, R. B.; Neumann, E. S. and Trail, G. T. eds. Molière and the commonwealth of letters: patrimony and posterity p31-48

Harold, King of England
Jones, D. The death of Harold. *In* Jones, D. The dying Gaul, and other writings p105-07

Harp, Richard L.
The mind of the Maker: the theological aesthetic of Dorothy Sayers and its application to poetry. *In* Hannay, M. P. ed. As her whimsey took her p176-99

Harp. See Aeolian harp

The harp of a thousand strings
Kummer, G. N. Who wrote "The harp of a thousand strings?" *In* Inge, W. T. ed. The frontier humorists p219-29

Harper, George Mills
"A subject of investigation": miracle at Mirebeau. *In* Yeats and the occult p172-89
Yeats's occult papers. *In* Yeats and the occult p 1-10
See also Finneran, R. J. jt. auth.

Harper, George Mills, and Kelly, John S.
Preliminary examination of the script of E[lizabeth] R[adcliffe]. *In* Yeats and the occult p130-71

Harper, Michael S.

About individual works
Debridement
Lieberman, L. Derek Walcott and Michael S. Harper: the muse of history. *In* Lieberman, L. Unassigned frequencies p284-96

Harper, Paula Hays
Votes for women? A graphic episode in the battle of the sexes. *In* Millon, H. A. and Nochlin, L. eds. Art and architecture in the service of politics p150-61

Harpocration panegyrista. Browne, G. M. *In* Illinois classical studies, v2 1977 p184-96

Harpsichord
Winternitz, E. The golden harpsichord and Todini's Galleria Armonica. *In* Winternitz, E. Musical instruments and their symbolism in Western art p110-15

Harpsichord in art
Winternitz, E. The golden harpsichord and Todini's Galleria Armonica. *In* Winternitz, E. Musical instruments and their symbolism in Western art p110-15

Harpur, Charles

About
Perkins, E. Towards seeing minor poets steadily and whole. *In* Bards, bohemians, and bookmen p39-55

Harré, Rom. See Harré, Romano

Harré, Romano
Architectonic man: on the structuring of lived experience. *In* Brown, R. H. and Lyman, S. M. eds. Structure, consciousness, and history p139-72
The self in monodrama. *In* Mischel, T. ed. The self p318-48

Harrelson, Walter J.
Famine in the perspective of Biblical judgments and promises. *In* Lucas, G. R. and Ogletree, T. W. eds. Lifeboat ethics p84-99

Harrex, Syd C.
The novel as gesture. *In* Narasimhaiah, C. D. ed. Awakened conscience p73-85

Harrier, Richard C.
Invention in Tudor literature: historical perspectives. *In* Philosophy and humanism p370-86

Harries, Karsten
Death and utopia: towards a critique of the ethics of satisfaction. *in* Radical phenomenology p138-52

Fundamental ontology and the search for man's place. *In* Murray, M. E. ed. Heidegger and modern philosophy p65-79

Heidegger as a political thinker. *In* Murray, M. E. ed. Heidegger and modern philosophy p304-28

Harrigan, Patrick Joseph
The social origins, ambitions, and occupations of secondary students in France during the Second Empire. *In* Schooling and society p206-35

Harriman, Averell. See Harriman, W. Averell

Harriman, W. Averell
Mr Truman's way with crises. *In* The Korean War p230-36

Harrington, Fred Harvey
Politics and foreign policy. *In* Encyclopedia of American foreign policy p773-83

Harris, Barbara J.
Landlords and tenants in England in the later Middle Ages: the Buckingham estates. *In* Peasants, knights and heretics p216-20

Harris, Bernard
'This music crept by me': Shakespeare and Wagner. *In* The Waste land in different voices p105-16
See also Gibbons, B. jt. auth.

Harris, Bernard, and Gibbons, Brian
English drama, 1550-1600: excluding Shakespeare. *In* English Association. The year's work in English studies v55 p231-47
English drama 1550-1660, excluding Shakespeare [another essay]. *In* English Asociation. The year's work in English studies v56 p176-81

Harris, Elizabeth M.
Miscellaneous map printing processes in the nineteenth century. *In* Woodward, D. A. ed. Five centures of map printing p113-36

Harris, Errol Eustace
Empiricism in science and philosophy. *In* Royal Institute of Philosophy. Impressions of empiricism p154-67
Science, metaphysics, and teleology. *In* The Personal universe p24-39
Spinoza's theory of human immortality. *In* Freeman, E. and Mandelbaum, M. H. eds. Spinoza p245-62

Harris, Fred R. See Moore, B. C. jt. auth.

Harris, George Washington
About
Rickels, M. The imagery of George Washington Harris. *In* Inge, M. T. ed. The frontier humorists p155-69

About individual works
Sut Lovingood's yarns
Day, D. The humorous works of George W. Harris. *In* Inge, M. T. ed. The frontier humorists p118-34
Rose, A. H. "A plan to wake the devil": race and aesthetics in the tales of George Washington Harris. *In* Rose, A. H. Demonic vision p63-71
Weber, B. Sut Lovingood. *In* Inge, M. T. ed. The frontier humorists p135-45

Influence—Faulkner
Inge, M. T. William Faulkner and George Washington Harris: in the tradition of Southwestern humor. *In* Inge, M. T. ed. The frontier humorists p266-80

Harris, Jocelyn
The reviser observed: the last volume of Sir Charles Grandison. *In* Virginia. University. Bibliographical Society. Studies in bibliography v29 p 1-31

Harris, Joel Chandler
About
Downs, R. B. Black folktales. *In* Downs, R. B. Books that changed the South p156-64
Rubin, L. D. Uncle Remus and the ubiquitous Rabbit. *In* Rubin, L. D. William Elliott shoots a bear p82-106

About individual works
Uncle Remus: his songs and his sayings
Bone, R. A. The oral tradition. *In* Bone, R. A. Down home p19-41
Downs, R. B. Black folktales. *In* Downs, R. B. Books that changed the South p156-64

Characters
Rubin, L. D. Uncle Remus and the ubiquitous Rabbit. *In* Rubin, L. D. William Elliott shoots a bear p82-106

Characters—Brer Rabbit
Bone, R. A. The oral tradition. *In* Bone, R. A. Down home p19-41

Harris, John, fl 1648
About
Heinemann, M. Popular drama and Leveller style—Richard Overton and John Harris. *In* Rebels and their causes p69-92

Harris, John Rees
Saint-Gobain and Ravenhead. *In* Great Britain and her world, 1750-1914 p27-70
See also Edel, M. jt. auth.

Harris, José
Social planning in war-time: some aspects of the Beveridge report. *In* War and economic development p239-56

Harris, Joseph C.
Christian form and Christian meaning in Halldórs páttr I. *In* The Learned and the lewed p249-64

Harris, Kenneth Lee
Organizing to overhaul a mess. *In* Managing nonprofit organizations p229-43

Harris, Kenneth Marc
Transcendental biography: Carlyle and Emerson. *In* Studies in biography p95-112

Harris, Neil
All the world a melting pot? Japan at American fairs, 1876-1904. *In* Iriye, A. ed. Mutual images p24-54
Iconography and intellectual history: the half-tone effect. *In* Higham, J. and Conkin, P. K. eds. New directions in American intellectual history p196-211
The lamp of learning: popular lights and shadows. *In* Oleson, A. and Voss, J. eds. The organization of knowledge in modern America, 1860-1920 p430-39
Museums, merchandising, and popular taste: the struggle for influence. *In* Material culture and the study of American life p140-74
Utopian fiction and its discontents. *In* Uprooted Americans p209-44

Harris, R. Cole. See Harris, Richard Colebrook

Harris, Richard Colebrook
The extension of France into rural Canada. *In* European settlement and development in North America: essays on geographical change in honour and memory of Andrew Hill Clark p27-45

Harris, Robert Jennings
Judicial review: vagaries and varieties. *In* Havard, W. C. and Bernd, J. L. eds. 200 years of the Republic in retrospect p173-208

Harris, Victoria
The incorporative consciousness: Levertov's journey from discretion to unity. *In* Kagle, S. E. ed. America: exploration and travel p166-90

Harris, William James

Stephen Vincent Benét's "hair-raising defects"? *In* Filler, L. ed. A question of quality: popularity and value in modern creative writing p172-80

Harris, Wilson

Tradition and the West Indian novel. *In* Baugh, E. ed. Critics on Caribbean literature p31-37

About

James, L. Wilson Harris and the 'Guyanese quartet.' *In* King, B. A. and Ogungbesan, K. eds. A celebration of Black and African writing p164-74

About individual works
Palace of the peacock

Tiffin, H. Towards place and placelessness: two journey patterns in Commonwealth literature. *In* Narasimhaiah, C. D. ed. Awakened conscience p146-63

Wilkinson, N. The novel and a vision of the land. *In* Narasimhaiah, C. D. ed. Awakened conscience p185-94

Tumatumari

Adler, J. Wilson Harris's Tumatumari and the family of man. *In* Baugh, E. ed. Critics on Caribbean literature p113-20

Harrison, Antony H.

The aesthetics of androgyny in Swinburne's early poetry. *In* Tennessee Studies in literature v23 p87-99

Harrison, Bernard Joseph

Muriel Spark and Jane Austen. *In* Josipovici, G. ed. The modern English novel: the reader, the writer and the work p225-51

On understanding a general name. *In* Royal Institute of Philosophy. Communication and understanding p116-39

Harrison, Brian

The Anglo-Chinese College at Malacca, 1818-1843. *In* Southeast Asian history and historiography p246-61

State intervention and moral reform in nineteenth-century England. *In* Hollis, P. ed. Pressure from without p289-322

Harrison, Daphne Duval

Black women in the blues tradition. *In* Harley, S. and Terborg-Penn, R. eds. The Afro-American woman p58-73

Harrison, Evelyn Byrd

Apollo's cloak. *In* Studies in classical art and archaeology p91-98

Harrison, Geoffrey Ainsworth

Relativism and tolerance. *In* Laslett, P. and Fishkin, J. eds. Philosophy, politics and society p273-90

Harrison, Harry

Worlds beside worlds. *In* Nicholls, P. ed. Science fiction at large p105-14

Harrison, Jonathan

Religion and psychical research. *In* Thakur, S. C. ed. Philosophy and psychical research p97-121

Harrison, Kenneth

Easter cycles and the equinox in the British Isles. *In* Anglo-Saxon England 7 p 1-8

Harrison, Randall Paul, and Ekman, Paul

TV's last frontier: South Africa. *In* Gerbner, G. ed. Mass media policies in changing cultures p189-96

Harrison, Ross

The concept of prepredicative experience. *In* Pivčević, E. ed. Phenomenology and philosophical understanding p93-107

Harrison, Ross Granville

About

Harvey, A. M. Johns Hopkins—the birthplace of tissue culture: the story of Ross G. Harrison, Warren H. Lewis, and George O. Gey. *In* Harvey, A. M. Adventures in medical research p114-23

Harrison, Tony, tr.

About individual works
The misanthrope

Simon, J. I. Translation or adaptation? *In* From Parnassus p147-57

Harrison, William

The British press and the Russian Revolution of 1905-1907. *In* Oxford Slavonic papers new ser. v7 p75-95

Harrison of Paris (Press)

Ford, H. D. Harrison of Paris. *In* Ford, H. D. Published in Paris p323-44

Harrod, Jeffrey

International relations, perceptions and neo-realism. *In* The Year book of world affairs, 1977 p289-305

Transnational power. *In* The Year book of world affairs, 1976 p97-115

Harsh, Joseph L.

On the McClellan-go-round. *In* Hubbell, J. T. ed. Battles lost and won p55-72

Harss, Luis

A city boy. *In* Rossman, C. R. and Friedman, A. W. eds. Mario Vargas Llosa p101-08

Hart, Francis Russell

New approaches to the Trollope problem. *In* Review, v 1 1979 p165-72

Notes for an anatomy of modern autobiography. *In* Cohen, R. ed. New directions in literary history p221-47

The Scottish novel

Contents

The anti-Kailyard as theological furor
Contemporary Scotland in fact and myth
Highlands of the humorists
Jane Duncan and George Mackay Brown
John Galt
Kennaway, Spark and after
Late Victorian Celticisms
The liberals in the Kailyard
Mid-Victorians
Mitchison and later romancers
Neil Gunn
Novelists of survival
Novelists of the modern renaissance
The other Blackwoodians
Retrospect: notes for a theory of Scottish fiction
Romance after the Enlightenment
Scottish variations of the Gothic novel
Stevenson, Munro, and Buchan
The tragedy of the Clearances
Victorian modes and models

Toward the discipline of humane teaching. *In* Buxton, T. H. and Prichard, K. W. eds. Excellence in university teaching p189-206

Hart, Joseph E. See Lilly, J. C. jt. auth.

Harter, Carol Clancy

Strange bedfellows: The waste land and An American tragedy. *In* French, W. G. ed. The twenties p51-64

Harth, John Phillip
Legends no histories: the case of Absalom and Achitophel. *In* Studies in eighteenth-century culture v4 p13-29

Harth, Phillip. See Harth, John Phillip

Hartley, David

About individual works
Observations on man, his frame, his duty, and his expectations

Schofield, R. E. Joseph Priestley on sensation and perception. *In* Studies in perception p336-54

Hartley, Leslie Poles

About

Sullivan, J. Ghost stories of other antiquaries. *In* Sullivan, J. Elegant nightmares p91-111

Hartley, Lodwick
Harlequin intrudes: William Cowper's venture into the satiric mode. *In* The Dress of words p127-37

Hartman, Geoffrey H.
The fate of reading
Contents

Christopher Smart's "Magnificat": toward a theory of representation
Also in E. L. H. essays for Earl R. Wasserman p 139-64
Evening star and evening land
The fate of reading
From the sublime to the hermeneutic
History writing as answerable style
Also in Cohen, R. ed. New directions in literary history p95-105
I. A. Richards and the dream of communication
The interpreter: a self-analysis
Lionel Trilling as man in the middle
Literature high and low: the case of the mystery story
Poem and ideology: a study of Keats's "To autumn"
Signs of the times
Spectral symbolism and authorial self in Keats's "Hyperion"
Valéry's fable of the bee
War in heaven
Wordsworth and Goethe in literary history
Ghostlier demarcations. *In* Wimsatt, W. K. ed. Literary criticism: idea and act p212-27
Psychoanalysis: the French connection. *In* Hartman, G. H. ed. Psychoanalysis and the question of the text p86-113

Hartman, John J.
Carter and the utopian group-fantasy. *In* DeMause, L. and Ebel, H. eds. Jimmy Carter and American fantasy p97-116

Hartman, Robert S.
The value structure of justice. *In* The Abdication of philosophy: philosophy and the public good p129-56

Hartmann, Heinz

About

Hughes, H. S. The advent of ego psychology. *In* Hughes, H. S. The sea change p189-239

Hartmann, Helene
The time bomb. *In* Janecek, G. ed. Andrey Bely p121-26

Hartmann von Aue

About individual works
Erec

Green, D. H. On damning with faint praise in medieval literature. *In* Viator: medieval and Renaissance studies v6 p117-69

Hartner, Willy
Terrestrial interpretations of lunar spots. *In* Bonelli, M. L. R. and Shea, W. R. eds. Reason, experiment, and mysticism in the scientific revolution p89-94

Hartshorne, Charles
The environmental results of technology. *In* Philosophy & environmental crisis p69-78

Hartup, Willard W.
Adolescent peer relations: a look to the future. *In* Adolescence and youth in prospect p171-85

Hartwell, Ronald Maxwell
Adam Smith and the Industrial Revolution. *In* Glahe, F. R. ed. Adam Smith and The wealth of nations p123-47
C. E. Ayres on the Industrial Revolution. *In* Science and ceremony p49-62
Capitalism and the historians. *In* Essays on Hayek p73-93

Hartwig, Joan
Cloten, Autolycus, and Caliban: bearers of parodic burdens. *In* Shakespeare's romances reconsidered p91-103

Hartz, Louis

About

Reinitz, R. Niebuhrian irony and historical interpretation: the relationship between consensus and New Left history. *In* Canary, R. H. and Kozicki, H. J. eds. The writing of history p93-128

About individual works
The liberal tradition in America

Ross, D. The liberal tradition revisited and the republican tradition addressed. *In* Higham, J. and Conkin, P. K. eds. New directions in American intellectual history p116-31

Hartzell, Karl Drew
An unknown English Benedictine gradual of the eleventh century. *In* Anglo-Saxon England 4 p131-44

Haruki. See Shimazaki, Tōson

Harvard University

Curricula

Koelsch, W. A. Terrae incognitae and arcana Siwash: toward a richer history of academic geography. *In* Geographies of the mind p63-87

Harvard University. Graduate School of Education
Powell, A. G. Harvard's School of Education and the Federal government: institutional effects of interaction in the 1960s. *In* Hook, S.; Kurtz, P. W., and Todorovich, M. eds. The university and the state: what role for government in higher education? p51-72

Harvard University. Medical School. Ad Hoc Committee to Examine the Definition of Brain Death. See Ad Hoc Committee of the Harvard Medical School to Examine the Definition of Brain Death

Harvey, Abner McGehee
Adventures in medical research
Contents
Cardiovascular research at John Hopkins
A century of clinical science at Johns Hopkins: contributions to medicine by students, house officers, and faculty
Classical descriptions of disease
Compleat clinician and Renaissance pathologist: Louis Hamman and Arnold R. Rich
Contributions of the part-time staff of the Johns Hopkins Hospital: Moore, King, and Gay
Creators of clinical medicine's scientific base: Franklin Paine Mall, Lewellys Franklin Barker, and Rufus Cole
Discoveries at Johns Hopkins related to the nervous system and its diseases
Early contributions to the surgery of cancer: William S. Halsted, Hugh H. Young, and John G. Clark
The first full-time academic Department of Pediatrics: the story of the Harriet Lane Home
Fountainhead of American physiology: H. Newell Martin and his pupil William Henry Howell
Hematological firsts at Hopkins
John Whitridge Williams—his contributions to obstetrics
Johns Hopkins and biomedical communication
Johns Hopkins—its role in medical education for women
Johns Hopkins—the birthplace of tissue culture: the story of Ross G. Harrison, Warren H. Lewis, and George O. Gey
Medical students on the march: Brown, MacCallum, and Opie
More bright stars in the Johns Hopkins galaxy
Neurosurgical genius: Walter Edward Dandy
A new school of anatomy: the story of Franklin P. Mall, Florence R. Sabin, and John B. MacCallum
Pharmacology's giant: John Jacob Abel
Pioneers in urology: James R. Brown and Howard A. Kelly
Research at John Hopkins on the thyroid gland and its diseases
The second professor of gynecology and the Department of Art as applied to medicine
The story of chemotherapy at Johns Hopkins: Perrin H. Long, Eleanor A. Bliss, and E. Kennerly Marshall, Jr.
Teacher and distinguished pupil: William Henry Welch and George Hoyt Whipple
Two mycoses first described at Johns Hopkins

Harvey, David. See Harvey, F. David

Harvey, F. David
Greeks and Romans learn to write. *In* Havelock, E. A. and Hershbell, J. P. eds. Communication arts in the ancient world p63-78

Harvey, Gabriel

About

Jardine, L. Humanism and dialectic in sixteenth-century Cambridge: a preliminary investigation. *In* Classical influences on European culture A.D. 1500-1700 p141-54

Harvey, Lawrence E.

About individual works

The aesthetics of the Renaissance love sonnet
Edelman, N. Book reviews. *In* Edelman, N. The eye of the beholder p166-205

Harvey, Leonard Patrick
Oral composition and the performance of novels of chivalry in Spain. *In* Duggan, J. J. ed. Oral literature p84-100

Harvey, P. D. A.
The English inflation of 1180-1220. *In* Peasants, knights and heretics p57-84

Harvey, Sally
The knight and the knight's fee in England. *In* Peasants, knights and heretics p133-73

Harvey, William

About individual works

On the motion of the heart and blood in animals
Downs, R. B. Dawn of scientific medicine. *In* Downs, R. B. Books that changed the world p324-33

Harwood, A. C.
Owen Barfield. *In* Evolution of consciousness p31-33

Harwood, Britton J.
Tragedy as habit: A streetcar named Desire. *In* Tennessee Williams: a tribute p104-15

Harwood, Cecil. See Harwood, A. C.

Harwood, Jonathan
Heredity, environment, and the legitimation of social policy. *In* Barnes, B. and Shapin, S. eds. Natural order p231-51

Hasbany, Richard
The shock of vision: an imagist reading of In our time. *In* Wagner, L. W. ed. Ernest Hemingway p224-40

Hasegawa, Tatsunosuke. See Futabatei, Shimei, pseud.

Hašek, Jaroslav

About individual works

The good soldier Schweik
Pynsent, R. B. The last days of Austria: Hašek and Kraus. *In* Klein, H. M. ed. The First World War in fiction p136-48

Hashish

Psychological aspects

Benjamin, W. Hashish in Marseilles. *In* Benjamin, W. Reflections p137-45

Hasidism
Bosk, C. L. The routinization of charisma: the case of the zaddik. *In* Johnson, H. M. ed. Religious change and continuity p150-67

Poland—History

Lamm, N. The phase of dialogue and reconciliation. *In* Király, B. K. ed. Tolerance and movements of religious dissent in Eastern Europe p115-29
Wilensky, M. L. The hostile phase. *In* Király, B. K. ed. Tolerance and movements of religious dissent in Eastern Europe p89-113

Haskell, Ann Sullivan
The portrayal of women by Chaucer and his age. *In* Springer, M. A. ed. What manner of woman p 1-14

Haskell, Francis

Gibbon and the history of art. *In* Edward Gibbon and The decline and fall of the Roman Empire p193-205

Haskell, Molly

Kesey cured: Forman's sweet insanity. *In* Peary, G. and Shatzkin, R. eds. The modern American novel and the movies p266-71

Marlon Brando. *In* Denby, D. ed. Awake in the dark p361-71

Haskell, Thomas L.

Deterministic implications of intellectual history. *In* Higham, J. and Conkin, P. K. eds. New directions in American intellectual history p132-48

Haskell, William Leas

Physical activity in health maintenance. *In* Sobel, D. S. ed. Ways of health p435-57

Haslam, John

Illustrations of madness. *In* Altschule, M. D. Origins of concepts in human behavior p88-121

About individual works

Illustrations of madness: exhibiting a singular case of insanity, and a no less remarkable difference in medical opinion

Altschule, M. D. The singular case of James Tilly Matthews, a clear paranoid. *In* Altschule, M. D. Origins of concepts in human behavior p85-87

Haslam, Michael W.

Appolonius Rhodius and the papyri. *In* Illinois classical studies v3, 1978 p47-73

Attribution and action in Aristophanes Clouds 723-796. *In* Harvard Studies in classical philology v80 p45-47

Hasmonaeans. See Maccabees

Hass, Robert

About individual works
Field guide

Kunitz, S. J. Robert Hass. *In* Kunitz, S. J. A kind of order, a kind of folly p282-88

Hass, Wilbur Adolph

Pragmatic structures of language: historical, formal and developmental issues. *In* Riegel, K. F. and Rosenwald, G. C. eds. Structure and transformation p193-213

Hassan, Ihab Habib

Bernard Malamud: 1976 fictions within our fictions. *In* The Fiction of Bernard Malamud p43-64

Frontiers of criticism: metaphors of silence. *In* The Frontiers of literary criticism p35-52

Paracriticisms

Contents

Fiction and future: an extravaganza for voice and tape

(   ): Finnegans wake and the postmodern imagination

Frontiers of criticism: 1963, 1969, 1972

Joyce—Beckett: a scenario in 8 scenes and a voice

Models of transformation: ideology, utopia, and fantasy in America

The new Gnosticism: speculations on an aspect of the postmodern mind

POSTmodernISM: a paracritical bibliography

The problem of influence in literary history: notes towards a definition. *In* Primeau, R. ed. Influx p34-46

About individual works
The dismemberment of Orpheus

Hassan, I. H. Frontiers of criticism. 1963, 1969, 1972. *In* Hassan, I. H. Paracriticisms p3-36

Radical innocence: studies in the contemporary novel

Balakian, N. Unwilling ironists. *In* Balakian, N. Critical encounter p87-92

Hassner, Pierre

Europe and the contradictions in American policy. *In* Rosecrance, R. N. ed. America as an ordinary country p60-86

The political aspects of European security. *In* International terrorism and world security p173-88

Hastie, James

About

Southall, A. W. White strangers and their religion in East Africa and Madagascar. *In* Shack, W. A. and Skinner, E. P. eds. Strangers in African societies p211-26

Hastings, Warren

About

Rocher, R. Alien and empathic: the Indian poems of N. B. Halhed. *In* Kling, B. B. and Pearson, M. N. eds. The age of partnership p215-35

Hatay, Turkey

Social conditions

Aswad, B. C. Women, class, and power: examples from the Hatay, Turkey. *In* Beck, L. and Keddie, N. R. eds. Women in the Muslim world p473-81

Hatshepsut Temple. See Egypt, Deir el Bahri. Temple of Hatshepsut

Hatteras Indians. See Lumbee Indians

Haugaard, Erik Christian

Random thoughts by a translator of Andersen. *In* Horn Book Magazine. Crosscurrents of criticism p277-82

Haugeland, John. See Dreyfus, H. L. jt. auth.

Haugen, Einar Ingvald

The curse of Babel. *In* Bloomfield, M. W. and Haugen, E. I. eds. Language as a human problem p33-43

Haugh, Richard

The philosophical foundations of Solzhenitsyn's vision of art. *In* Dunlop, J. B.; Haugh, R. and Klimoff, A. eds. Aleksandr Solzhenitsyn: critical essays and documentary materials 2d ed. p168-84

Haulman, Bruce E. See Bailey, D. T. jt. auth.

Hauptmann, Gerhart Johann Robert

About

Nicoll, A. The independent theatre in Germany. *In* Nicoll, A. World drama p475-92

Hausas

Shweder, R. A. and LeVine, R. A. Dream concepts of Hausa children: a critique of the "doctrine of invariant sequence" in cognitive development. *In* Schwartz, T. ed. Socialization as cultural communication p117-38

Hauser, Rita Eleanor Abrams

A First World view. *In* Kommers, D. P. and Loescher, G. D. eds. Human rights and American foreign policy p85-89

International human-rights protection: the dream and the deceptions. *In* Sidorsky, D. ed. Essays on human rights p21-29

Hausman, Alan Michael

Innate ideas. *In* Studies in perception p200-30

Non-Euclidean geometry and relative consistency proofs. *In* Motion and time, space and matter p418-35

Haussas. See Hausas

Haüy, Valentin

About

Weiner, D. B. Three champions of the handicapped in Revolutionary France. *In* From Parnassus p161-76

Havelock, Christine Mitchell

Art as communication in ancient Greece. *In* Havelock, E. A. and Hershbell, J. P. eds. Communication arts in the ancient world p95-118

Havelock, Eric Alfred

The alphabetization of Homer. *In* Havelock, E. A. and Hershbell, J. P. eds. Communication arts in the ancient world p3-21

The Greek concept of justice

Contents

From Homer to Plato: the contours of the problem
The function of epic in preliterate societies
The justice of Aeschylus
The justice of Herodotus
The justice of Hesiod: an essay in detection
The justice of Plato
The justice of Solon
The justice of the Iliad
The justice of the Odyssey
The justice of the pre-Socratics
The legalities of the Odyssey
The method and manner of Homeric storage
The moralities of the Odyssey
A philosophy of the written word
The psychology of rhythmic memorization
The society reported by Homer
Some elements of the Homeric fantasy
The spoken and the written word

In memoriam Adam and Anne Parry. *In* Yale classical studies v24 p ix-xv

Haven, Richard

Some perspectives in three poems by Gray, Wordsworth and Duncan. *In* Bornstein, G. ed. Romantic and modern p69-88

Havens, George Remington

Bibliography

Williams, C. G. S. comp. A bibliography of the writings of George R. Havens. *In* Literature and history in the age of ideas p387-98

Hawaii

Social conditions

Saxe, A. A. On the origin of evolutionary processes: state formation in the Sandwich Islands, a systemic approach. *In* Explanation of prehistoric change p105-51

Hawes, Donald

Marryat and Dickens: a personal and literary relationship. *In* Dickens Studies Annual v2 p39-68

Hawkes, David

The quest of the goddess. *In* Birch, C. ed. Studies in Chinese literary genres p42-68

Hawkes, John

About

Klein, M. John Hawkes' experimental compositions. *In* Federman, R. ed. Surfiction p203-14

Scholes, R. E. Comedy and grotesquerie. *In* Scholes, R. E. Fabulation and metafiction p139-92

About individual works
The blood oranges

Sale, R. H. Hawkes, Malamud, Richler, Oates. *In* Sale, R. H. On not being good enough p30-42

The lime twig

Gault, P. Genesis and functions of Hencher in "The lime twig." *In* Johnson, I. D. and Johnson, C. [eds.] Les américanistes p138-55

Scholes, R. E. Comedy and grotesquerie. *In* Scholes, R. E. Fabulation and metafiction p139-92

Second skin

Wall, C. Solid ground in John Hawkes's Second skin. *In* Garvin, H. R. ed. Makers of the twentieth-century novel p309-19

Wallace, R. H. The rarer action: John Hawkes' Second skin. *In* Wallace, R. H. The last laugh p45-64

Characters—William Hencher

Gault, P. Genesis and functions of Hencher in "The lime twig." *In* Johnson, I. D. and Johnson, C. [eds.] Les américanistes p138-55

Hawkes, Terence

'That Shakespeherian rag.' *In* English Association. Essays and studies, 1977 p22-38

Hawkins, David

Developing a new educational agenda. *In* Roots of open education in America p49-58

Hawkins, Gordon

The ideology of imprisonment. *In* Progress in penal reform p101-15

The new penology. *In* Law and society p108-27

Hawkins, Harriett

'The devil's party': virtues and vices in 'Measure for measure.' *In* Shakespeare survey v31 p105-13

Poetic freedom and poetic truth
Contents

'If this be error': imagination and truth in Shakespeare and Marlowe
Introduction: Poetic injustice: some winners and losers in medieval and Renaissance literature
'Of their vain contest': poetic and critical deadlocks in Paradise lost and Spenser's bower of bliss
'Stay, illusion!': some poetic godgames
'The victim's side': Webster's Duchess of Malfi and Chaucer's Clerk's tale

Hawkins, Hugh

University identity: the teaching and research functions. *In* Oleson, A. and Voss, J. eds. The organization of knowledge in modern America, 1860-1920 p285-312

Hawkins, Sir John, 1719-1789

About

Clifford, J. L. Johnson's first club. *In* Evidence in literary scholarship p197-213

Hawkins, Keith O.

An annotated bibliography of the writings of Leon Radzinowicz. *In* Crime, criminology and public policy p623-35

Hawkridge, David Graham

Communication and education in open learning systems. *In* Lerner, D. and Nelson, L. M. eds. Communication research—a half-century appraisal p70-103

Hawks, Howard

About

Ford, G. Mostly on Rio Lobo. *In* Nichols, B. ed. Movies and methods p344-54

Kawin, B. F. Faulkner's film career: the years with Hawks. *In* Faulkner, modernism, and film: Faulkner and Yoknapatawpha, 1978 p163-81

Wollen, P. The auteur theory; excerpt from "Signs and meanings in the cinema." *In* Nichols, B. ed. Movies and methods p529-42

About individual works

Gentlemen prefer blondes

Truffaut, F. Howard Hawks: Gentlemen prefer blondes. *In* Truffaut, F. The films in my life p71-72

Rio Lobo

Ford, G. Mostly on Rio Lobo. *In* Nichols, B. ed. Movies and methods p344-54

To have and have not

Rothman, W. To have and have not adapted a novel. *In* Peary, G. and Shatzkin, R. eds. The modern American novel and the movies p70-79

Wood, R. To have (written) and have not (directed) *In* Nichols, B. ed. Movies and methods p297-305

Hawley, Amos Henry

Urbanization as process. *In* Handbook of contemporary urban life p3-26

Hawley, Ellis Wayne

The New Deal and business. *In* Braeman, J.; Bremner, R. H. and Brody, D. eds. The New Deal v 1 p50-82

Haworth, Bryan

Film in the classroom. *In* Smith, P. ed. The historian and film p157-68

Hawthorne, Gerald F.

A new English translation of Melito's paschal homily. *In* Current issues in Biblical and patristic interpretation p147-75

Hawthorne, Nathaniel

About

Doubleday, N. F. Hawthorne and the immunities of romance. *In* Doubleday, N. F. Variety of attempt p189-202

Moss, S. P. Hawthorne and Melville: an inquiry into their art and the mystery of their friendship. *In* Literary monographs v7 p45-84

Rahv, P. The Dark Lady of Salem. *In* Rahv, P. Essays on literature and politics, 1932-1972 p25-42

Richardson, R. D. Hawthorne. *In* Richardson, R. D. Myth and literature in the American renaissance p165-94

Smith, H. N. Hawthorne: the politics of romance. *In* Smith, H. N. Democracy and the novel p16-34

Spengemann, W. C. Nathaniel Hawthorne. *In* Spengemann, W. C. The adventurous muse p151-77

Stern, M. R. Nathaniel Hawthorne: "conservative after heaven's own fashion." *In* Essays in honor of Russel B. Nye p195-225

Tatar, M. M. Masters and slaves: the creative process in Hawthorne's fiction. *In* Tatar, M. M. Spellbound p189-229

About individual works

The birthmark

Fetterley, J. Palpable designs: four American short stories: Women beware science: "The birthmark." *In* Fetterley, J. The resisting reader p22-33

Webb, J. C. The implications of control for the human personality: Hawthorne's point of view. *In* Tulane Studies in English v21 p57-66

The Blithedale romance

Eakin, P. J Self-culture: Margaret Fuller and Hawthorne's heroines *In* Eakin, P. J. The New England girl p49-79

Pearce, R. H. Day-dream and fact: the import of The Blithedale romance. *In* Baldwin, K. H. and Kirby, D. K. eds. Individual and community p49-63

Rust, R. D. Coverdale's confession, a key to meaning in The Blithedale romance. *In* Literature and ideas in America p96-110

Footprints on the seashore

Weldon, R. F. Hawthorne's "Foot-prints on the sea-shore" and the literature of walking. *In* Kagle, S. E. ed. America: exploration and travel p127-35

The House of the Seven Gables

Stineback, D. C. "The fluctuating waves of our social life": Nataniel Hawthorne's The House of the Seven Gables. *In* Stineback, D. C. Shifting world p43-60

Stone, E. Hawthorne's House of Pyncheon: a theory of American drama. *In* Artful thunder p69-84

Main street

Doubleday, N. F. Hawthorne's showman and his audience. *In* Doubleday, N. F. Variety of attempt p176-88

The marble faun

Dryden, E. A. The limits of romance: a reading of The marble faun. *In* Baldwin, K. H. and Kirby, D. K. eds. Individual and community p17-48

Meyers, J. Guido Reni and The marble faun. *In* Meyers, J. Painting and the novel p6-18

My kinsman, Major Molineux

Dolan, P. J. Hawthorne: the politics of puberty. *In* Dolan, P. J. Of war and war's alarms p16-35

Lesser, S. O. Hawthorne's "My kinsman, Major Molineux"; excerpt from "Fiction and the unconscious." *In* Lesser, S. O. The whispered meanings p44-53

Trilling, L. Nathaniel Hawthorne: My kinsman, Major Molineux. *In* Trilling, L. Prefaces to The experience of literature p69-73

Hawks, Howard—About individual works
—*Continued*

Rappaccini's daughter

Barney, S. A. Blighting words: Hawthorne's "Rappaccini's daughter." *In* Barney, S. A. Allegories of history, allegories of love p257-82

Webb, J. C. The implications of control for the human personality: Hawthorne's point of view. *In* Tulane Studies in English v21 p57-66

Roger Malvin's burial

Byers, J. R. The geography and framework of Hawthorne's "Roger Malvin's burial." *In* Tennessee Studies in literature v21 p11-20

The scarlet letter

McPherson, H. How hot is The scarlet letter? *In* Essays in honor of Russel B. Nye p141-50

Pryse, M. The scarlet letter: social stigma and art. *in* Pryse, M. The mark and the knowledge p15-48

Spengemann, W. C. Nathaniel Hawthorne. *In* Spengemann, W. C. The adventurous muse p151-77

Twice-told tales

Poe, E. A. Review of Twice-old tales. *In* May, C. E. ed. Short story theories p45-51

Bibliography

Baym, N. Z. Hawthorne. *In* American literary scholarship. 1973 p15-31

Baym, N. Z. Hawthorne [another essay]. *In* American literary scholarship, 1974 p15-27

Crowley, J. D. Hawthorne. *In* American literary scholarship, 1975 p17-34

Crowley, J. D. Hawthorne [another essay]. *In* American literary scholarship, 1976 p15-32

Crowley, J. D. Hawthorne [another essay]. *In* American literary scholarship, 1977 p17-33

Characters

Pryse, M. The scarlet letter: social stigma and art. *In* Pryse, M. The mark and the knowledge p15-48

Webb, J. C. The implications of control for the human personality: Hawthorne's point of view. *In* Tulane Studies in English v21 p57-66

Characters—Beatrice Rappaccini

Fryer, J. The temptress: Beatrice Rappaccini: The literary convention as allegory. *In* Fryer, J. The faces of Eve p40-47

Characters—Hester Prynne

Fryer, J. The temptress: Hester Prynne: The Dark Lady as "deviant." *In* Fryer, J The faces of Eve p72-84

Characters—Hilda

Fryer, J. The American princess: The Pale Maiden. *In* Fryer, J. The faces of Eve p87-97

Characters—Miles Coverdale

Rust, R. D. Coverdale's confession, a key to meaning in The Blithedale romance. *In* Literature and ideas in America p96-110

Characters—Miriam Schaefer

Fryer, J. The temptress: Hawthorne's Miriam: The temptress as Jew. *In* Fryer, J. The faces of Eve p62-71

Characters—Priscilla Moodie

Fryer, J. The American princess: The Pale Maiden. *In* Fryer, J. The faces of Eve p87-97

Characters—Women

Eakin, P. J. Self-culture: Margaret Fuller and Hawthorne's heroines. *In* Eakin, P. J. The New England girl p49-79

Rahv, P. The Dark Lady of Salem. *In* Rahv, P. Essays on literature and politics, 1932-1972 p25-42

Characters—Zenobia Fauntleroy

Fryer, J. The new woman: Zenobia: The new woman as tragedy-queen. *In* Fryer, J. The faces of Eve p208-20

Criticism, Textual

Bowers, F. T. Old wine in new bottles: problems of machine printing. *In* Bowers, F. T. Essays in bibliography, text, and editing p392-411

Hawthorne Middle School, Yonkers, N.Y.

Stauf, R. Young meet old. *In* Gross, B. and Gross, R. eds. The children's rights movement p300-06

Hay, Denys

1500-1700: the bibliographical problem. A continental S.T.C.? *In* Classical influences on European culture A.D. 1500-1700 p33-39

Hay, Eloise Knapp

Impressionism limited. *In* Joseph Conrad: a commemoration p54-64

Hay, John C.

The ghost image: a tool for the analysis of the visual stimulus. *In* Perception p268-75

Hay, John Macdougall

About individual works

Gillespie

Hart, F. R. The anti-Kailyard as theological furor. *In* Hart, F. R. The Scottish novel p131-39

Hay, William, 1875-1945

About individual works

The escape of the notorious Sir William Heans (and the mystery of Mr Daunt) a romance of Tasmania

Edwards, P. D. The daunting doubts of William Hay. *In* Bards, bohemians, and bookmen p218-35

Haya (African tribe)

Seitel, P. Saying Haya sayings: two categories of proverb use. *In* The Social use of metaphor p75-99

Hayakawa, Samuel Ichiye

Youth today: problems in achieving adulthood. *In* A Time to hear and answer: essays for the Bicentennial season p157-74

Haycox, Ernest

About

Etulain, R. W. Ernest Haycox: popular novelist of the Pacific Northwest. *In* Bingham, E. R. and Love, G. A. eds. Northwest perspectives p136-50

Haydarān, The military interest of the Battle of. Brett, M. *In* War, technology and society in the Middle East p78-88

Haydn, Hiram Collins

About individual works
The counter-Renaissance

Hexter, J. H. Wallace K. Ferguson and Hiram Hayden [sic]: the Renaissance again —and again. *in* Hexter, J. H. On historians p45-59

Hayek, Friedrich August von

About

De Crespigny, A. F. A. Hayek: freedom for progress. *In* De Crespigny, A. and Minogue, K. R. eds. Contemporary political philosophers p49-66

Dietze, G. Hayek on the rule of law. *In* Essays on Hayek p107-46

Letwin, S. R. The achievement of Friedrich A. Hayek. *In* Essays on Hayek p147-67

Lilley, P. Two critics of Keynes; Friedman and Hayek. *In* Skidelsky, R. J. A. ed. The end of the Keynesian era p25-32

Machlup, F. Hayek's contribution to economics. *In* Essays on Hayek p13-59

Roche, G. C. The relevance of Friedrich A. Hayek. *In* Essays on Hayek p 1-11

Shenfield, A. A. Friedrich A. Hayek: Nobel prizewinner. *In* Essays on Hayek p171-76

About individual works
Capitalism and the historians

Hartwell, R. M. Capitalism and the historians. *In* Essays on Hayek p73-93

The road to serfdom

Buckley, W. F. The road to serfdom: the intellectuals and socialism. *In* Essays on Hayek p95-106

Scientism and the study of society

Shenfield, A. A. Scientism and the study of society. *In* Essays on Hayek p61-72

Hayford, Harrison
"Loomings": yarns and figures in the fabric. *In* Artful thunder p119-37

Unnecessary duplicates: a key to the writing of Moby-Dick. *In* Pullin, F. ed. New perspectives on Melville p128-61

Hayley, Rodney L.
The "swingeing" of Cibber: the suppression of the first edition of The refusal. *In* Virginia. University. Bibliographical Society. Studies in bibliography v28 p290-97

Haynes, Renée
Some Christian imagery. *In* Life after death p132-43

Wrestling Jacob: Koestler and the paranormal. *In* Harris, H. A. ed. Astride the two cultures p175-86

Hays, David G.
Language and interpersonal relationships. *In* Bloomfield, M. W. and Haugen, E. I. eds. Language as a human problem p205-18

Hays, Peter L.
Hemingway and the Fisher King ("God rest you merry, gentlemen.") *In* Benson, J. J. ed. The short stories of Ernest Hemingway: critical essays p223-27

Malamud's Yiddish-accented medieval stories. *In* The Fiction of Bernard Malamud p87-96

Hayter, Alethea

About individual works
Opium and the romantic imagination

Connolly, C. Opium. *In* Connolly, C. The evening colonnade p139-42

Hayward, Jack Ernest Shalom
Interest groups and the demand for state action. *in* Hayward, J. E. S. and Berki, R. N. eds. State and society in contemporary Europe p23-41

Planning and the French labour market: incomes and industrial training. *In* Planning, politics and public policy p159-76

See also Berki, R. N. jt. auth.

Hayward, Jack Ernest Shalom, and Corina, John
Comparative preliminaries. *In* Planning, politics and public policy p155-58

Hayward, Max
Literature in the Soviet period (1917-1975). *In* Auty, R. and Obolensky, D. eds. An introduction to Russian language and literature p185-230

Hazaz, Haim

About individual works
Gates of bronze

Alter, R. Shtetl and revolution. *In* Alter, R. Defenses of the imagination p199-212

Hazlitt, William

About

Albrecht, W. P. Hazlitt. *In* Albrecht, W. P. The sublime pleasures of tragedy p115-31

Jones, L. M. Hazlitt, Reynolds, and the Edinburgh Review. *In* Virginia. University. Bibliographical Society. Studies in bibliography v29 p342-46

Hazzard, Shirley
A jaded muse. *In* From Parnassus p121-34

About individual works
People in glass houses

Colmer, J. The cult of power and the power of culture. *In* Colmer, J. Coleridge to Catch-22 p177-96

He who must die (Motion picture)
Truffaut, F. Jules Dassin: Celui qui doit mourir. *In* Truffaut, F. The films in my life p210-13

Head, Bessie

About individual works
Maru

Ravenscroft, A. The novels of Bessie Head. *In* Heywood, C. ed. Aspects of South African literature p174-86

A question of power

Ravenscroft, A. The novels of Bessie Head. *In* Heywood, C. ed. Aspects of South African literature 174-86

When rain clouds gather

Ravenscroft, A. The novels of Bessie Head. *In* Heywood, C. ed. Aspects of South African literature 174-86

Head, Sydney W.
Trends in tropical African societies. *In* Gerbner, G. ed. Mass media policies in changing cultures p83-103

Head. See Phrenology

Head in art

Mellor, A. K. Physiognomy, phrenology, and Blake's visionary heads. *In* Essick, R. N. and Pearce, D. R. eds. Blake in his time p53-74

Headley, John M.

The Habsburg world empire and the revival of Ghibellinism. *In* Medieval and Renaissance studies [1975] p93-127

Headley, Neith Elizabeth

Early and Progressive schools—I. *In* Roots of open education in America p131-34

Heads of state

Wilson, T. A. Summit conferences. *In* Encyclopedia of American foreign policy p936-44

See also Kings and rulers

Healing (in religion, folklore, etc.)

Frank, J. D. Nonmedical healing: religious and secular; excerpt from "Persuasion and healing." *In* Sobel, D. S. ed. Ways of health p231-66

Grad, B. R. Healing by the laying on of hands: a review of experiments. *In* Sobel, D. S. ed. Ways of health p267-87

Health

Knowles, J. H. The responsibility of the individual. *In* Knowles, J. H. ed. Doing better and feeling worse p57-80

See also Hygiene

Economic aspects

See Medical economics

Research

Hutt, P. B. Public criticism of health science policy. *In* Holton, G. J. and Morison, R. S. eds. Limits of scientific inquiry p157-69

Health, Public. See Public health

Health attitudes

D'Andrade, R. G. A propositional analysis of U.S. American beliefs about illness. *In* Basso, K. H. and Selby, H. A. eds. Meaning in anthropology p155-80

Illich, I. The political uses of natural death. *In* Death inside out p25-42

Health care. See Medical care

Health care administration. See Health services administration

Health care costs. See Medical care, Cost of

Health care planning. See Health planning

Health facilities. See Nursing homes

Health in literature

Haley, B. The athlete as barbarian: Richard Feverel and Willoughby Patterne. *In* Haley, B. The healthy body and Victorian culture p227-51

Haley, B. Conclusion. *In* Haley, B. The healthy body and Victorian culture p252-61

Haley, B. Introduction: Victorian health. *In* Haley, B. The healthy body and Victorian culture p3-22

Haley, B. Mens sana in corpore sano: Victorian psychophysiology. *In* Haley, B. The healthy body and Victorian culture p23-45

Haley, B. Obeying the laws of life: Carlyle and Spencer. *In* Haley, B. The healthy body and Victorian culture p69-94

Haley, B. The thoroughly healthy mind: Victorian criticism. *In* Haley, B. The healthy body and Victorian culture p46-68

Haley, B. Two staunch walkers: Tom Thurnall and Tom Tulliver. *In* Haley, B. The healthy body and Victorian culture p180-204

Haley, B. Types of healthy Christianity: Newman and Kingsley. *In* Haley, B. The healthy body and Victorian culture p95-119

Health insurance. See Medical care

Health manpower. See Medical personnel

Health misconceptions. See Medical delusions

Health of women. See Women—Health and hygiene

Health personnel. See Medical personnel

Health planning

Hardy, O. B. Systematic processes applied to health care planning. *In* Managing nonprofit organizations p78-94

Health policy. See Medical policy

Health services. See Medical care

Health services administration

Hardy, O. B. Systematic processes applied to health care planning. *In* Managing nonprofit organizations p78-94

Pellegrino, E. D. The academic role of the vice president for health sciences. *In* Managing nonprofit organizations p38-47

See also Hospitals—Administration; Public health administration

Healy, David F.

Imperialism. *In* Encyclopedia of American foreign policy p409-16

Healy, J. J.

The absolute and the image of man in Australia: Judith Wright and Patrick White. *In* Narasimhaiah, C. D. ed. Awakened conscience p3-13

Heaney, Michael

The implications of Richard James's maimanto. *In* Oxford Slavonic papers new ser. v9 p102-09

The sources of early Križanica. *In* Oxford Slavonic papers new ser. v8 p101-36

Heaney, Seamus

Feelings into words. *In* Gibbons, R. ed. The poet's work: 29 masters of 20th century poetry on the origins and practice of their art p263-82

The poetry of Richard Murphy. *In* Harmon, M. ed. Richard Murphy: poet of two traditions p18-30

About

Heaney, S. Feelings into words. *In* Gibbons, R. ed. The poet's work: 29 masters of 20th century poetry on the origins and practice of their art p263-82

Hearing

Lee, E. N. The sense of an object: Epicurus on seeing and hearing. *In* Studies in perception p27-59

Hearn, Lafcadio

About

Bone, R. A. Eric Walrond. *In* Bone, R. A. Down home p171-203

Hearst, Patricia

About

Parry, A. The Symbionese and Patty Hearst. *In* Parry, A. Terrorism: from Robespierre to Arafat p342-64

The heart is a lonely hunter (Motion picture)
Aldridge, R. Two planetary systems. *In* Peary, G. and Shatzkin, R. eds. The modern American novel and the movies p119-30

The heartbreak kid (Motion picture)
Kauffmann, S. The heartbreak kid. *In* Kauffmann, S. Living images p161-62

Heartfield, John

About
Berger, J. The political uses of photomontage. *In* Berger, J. The look of things p183-89

Hearts and minds (Motion picture)
Sarris, A. Hearts and minds. *In* Sarris, A. Politics and cinema p102-06

Heartz, Daniel
The chanson in the humanist era. *In* Current thought in musicology p193-230

Heat
Friedman, R. M. The creation of a new science: Joseph Fourier's analytical theory of heat. *In* Historical studies in the physical sciences v8 p73-99

Guerlac, H. Chemistry as a branch of physics: Laplace's collaboration with Lavoisier. *In* Historical studies in the physical sciences v7 p193-276

See also Animal heat; Fire

Heat pollution of rivers, lakes, etc. See Thermal pollution of rivers, lakes, etc.

Heath, Edward Richard George
A Tory view. *In* Kramnick, I. ed. Is Britain dying? p31-44

Heath, Peter Lauchlan
The idea of a phenomenological ethics. *In* Pivčević, E. ed. Phenomenology and philosophical understanding p159-72

Heath, Sukey. See Goddard, Susanna Heath

Heath, Susanna. See Goddard, Susanna Heath

Heath-Stubbs, John Francis Alexander
Pre-Raphaelitism and the aesthetic withdrawal; excerpt from "The darkling plain". *In* Sambrook, J. ed. Pre-Raphaelitism p166-85

Heathenism. See Paganism

Heating. See Stoves

Heatley, Edward
The redeemed feminine of Little Dorrit. *In* Dickens Studies Annual v4 p153-64

Heaven knows, Mr. Allison (Motion picture)
French, B. Brides of Christ. *In* French, B. On the verge of revolt p121-36

Hebbelinck, Marcel
Biological aspects of development at adolescence. *In* Adolescence and youth in prospect p148-58

Hebebrand, Roger C.
Human relations in practice. *In* Henderson, G. ed. Human relations in the military p19-32

The Hebrew Home for the Aged at Riverdale, New York (City)
Stauf, R. Young meet old. *In* Gross, B. and Gross, R. eds. The children's rights movement p300-06

Hebrew language

Revival
Simonsohn, S. The Hebrew revival among early medieval European Jews. *In* Salo Wittmayer Baron v2 p831-58

Hebrew language in Israel
Schmelz, O. and Bachi, R. Hebrew as everyday language of the Jews in Israel—statistical appraisal. *In* Salo Wittmayer Baron v2 p745-85

Hebrew literature. See Jewish literature; Rabbinical literature

Hebrew poetry

History and criticism
Freedman, D. N. Early Israelite history in the light of early Israelite poetry. *In* Unity and diversity p3-35

Hecht, Anthony

About individual works
The hard hours
Lieberman, L. W. S. Merwin and Anthony Hecht: risks and faiths. *In* Lieberman, L. Unassigned frequencies p257-62

Hecht, Ben

About
Farrell, J. T. The mind of Ben Hecht. *In* Farrell, J. T. Literary essays, 1954-1974 p70-76

Ravitz, A. C. Ballyhoo, gargoyles, & firecrackers: Ben Hecht's aesthetic calliope. *In* Filler, L. ed. A question of quality: popularity and value in modern creative writing p229-43

About individual works
Perfidy
Dawidowicz, L. S. Blaming the Jews: the charge of perfidy. *In* Dawidowicz, L. S. The Jewish presence p269-79

Hecker, Isaac Thomas

About
Gower, J. F. Democracy as a theological problem in Isaac Hecker's apologetics. *In* America in theological perspective p37-55

Hedda Gabler (criticism) Ibsen, H. *In* Kauffmann, S. Persons of the drama p120-23

Hedges, William Leonard
From Franklin to Emerson. *In* Lemay, J. A. L. ed. The oldest revolutionary p139-56

Hedley, J. Henry. See Edwards, A. S. G. jt. auth.

Hedonism. See Pleasure

Hedqvist, Karl-Johan
Some remarks on the behaviour of the parasitic hymenoptera. *In* The Frontiers of human knowledge p289-96

Heeger, Gerald A.
The sources of Communist political power in Kerala. *In* Hammond, T. T. ed. The anatomy of Communist takeovers p620-37

Heelan, Patrick A.
Quantum relativity and the cosmic observer. *In* Cosmology, history, and theology p29-37

Heer, Nancy Whittier
Political leadership in Soviet historiography: cult or collective? *In* Cocks, P.; Daniels, R. V. and Heer, N. W. eds. The dynamics of Soviet politics p11-27

Heffernan, James A. W.
The English romantic perception of color. *In* Kroeber, K. and Walling, W. eds. Images of romanticism p133-48

Hefferman, James A. W.—*Continued*

Politics and freedom: refractions of Blake in Joyce Cary and Allen Ginsberg. *In* Bornstein, G. ed. Romantic and modern p177-95

Heffernan, Thomas J.

An analysis of the narrative motifs in the legend of St. Eustace. *In* Medievalia et humanistica no. 6 p63-89

Heffner, Ray L.

Unifying symbols in the comedy of Ben Jonson. *In* Wimsatt, W. K. ed. Literary criticism: idea and act p346-61

Heflin, Wilson Lumpkin

Sources from the whale-fishery and "The Town-ho's story." *In* Artful thunder p163-76

Hefner, Philip J.

Basic Christian assumptions about the cosmos. *In* Cosmology, history, and theology p347-64

Hegazy, Ezzat

Contemporary sociology in Egypt. *In* Mohan, R. P. and Martindale, D. A. eds. Handbook of contemporary developments in world sociology p379-90

Hegedüs, András

The self-criticism of Socialist society: a reality and a necessity. *In* The Humanisation of socialism p161-75

See also Markus, M. jt. auth.

About

Eörsi, I. Illusion and conflict: drama in Eastern European societies. *In* Drama and society p241-43

Hegel, Georg Wilhelm Friedrich

About

Arendt, H. The philosophers and the will. *in* Arendt, H. The life of the mind v2 p11-51

Clayre, A. Attractive work and struggle to the death. *In* Clayre, A. Work and play p22-29

Craft, R. A new interpretation of Hegel? *In* Craft, R. Current convictions p244-55

Hartman, G. From the sublime to the hermeneutic. *In* Hartman, G. The fate of reading p114-23

Silverman, H. J. Heidegger and Merleau-Ponty: interpreting Hegel. *In* Radical phenomenology p209-24

About individual works

The phenomenology of mind

Derrida, J. From restricted to general economy: a Hegelianism without reserve. *In* Derrida, J. Writing and difference p251-77

Fuss, P. L. Theory and practice in Hegel and Marx: an unfinished dialogue. *In* Political theory and praxis p97-116

Phenomenology of spirit

Kaufmann, W. A. Hegel's conception of phenomenology. *In* Pivčević, E. ed. Phenomenology and philosophical understanding p211-30

The philosophy of history

Warminski, A. Pre-positional by-play. *In* Glyph 3 p98-117

Philosophy of nature

Engelhardt, H. T. The counsels of finitude. *In* Death inside out p115-25

Aesthetics

Henrich, D. Art and philosophy of art today: reflections with reference to Hegel. *In* Amacher, R. E. and Lange, V. eds. New perspectives in German literary criticism p107-33

Ethics

Walsh, W. H. Hegelian ethics. *In* New studies in ethics v 1 p379-464

Influence

Williamson, J. W. E. B. Du Bois as a Hegelian. *In* What was freedom's price? p21-49

Mysticism

Copleston, F. C. Hegel and the rationalization of mysticism. *In* Copleston, F. C. Philosophers and philosophies p-06-16

Political science

Cassirer, E. Hegel's theory of the state. *In* Cassirer, E. Symbol, myth, and culture p108-20

Hegel, Robert G.

Sui T'ang yen-i and the aesthetics of the seventeenth-century Suchou elite. *In* Chinese narrative p124-59

Heiberg, Johanne Luise (Pätges)

About

Krabbe, H. A Danish actress and her conception of the part of Lady Macbeth. *In* Shakespeare survey v29 p145-49

Heide, Wilma Scott

The quest for humanity via higher education. *In* Wagschal, P. H. ed. Learning tomorrows p27-40

Heidegger, Martin

About

Alderman, H. G. Heidegger's critique of science and technology. *In* Murray, M. E. ed. Heidegger and modern philosophy p35-50

Arendt, H. Conclusions. *In* Arendt, H. The life of the mind v2 p147-217

Arendt, H. Martin Heidegger at eighty. *In* Murray, M. E. ed. Heidegger and modern philosophy p293-303

Biemel, W. Husserl's Encyclopaedia Britannica article and Heidegger's remarks thereon. *In* Elliston, F. A. and McCormick, P. eds. Husserl p286-303

Borgmann, A. Heidegger and symbolic logic. *In* Murray, M. E. ed. Heidegger and modern philosophy p 3-22

Caputo, J. D. The question of being and transcendental phenomenology: reflections on Heidegger's relationship to Husserl. *In* Radical phenomenology p84-105

Derrida, J. Violence and metaphysics: an essay on the thought of Emmanuel Levinas. *In* Derrida, J. Writing and difference p79-153

Dreyfus, H. L. and Haugeland, J. Husserl and Heidegger: philosophy's last stand. *In* Murray, M. E. ed. Heidegger and modern philosophy p222-38

Emad, P. Heidegger's value-criticism and its bearing on the phenomenology of values. *In* Radical phenomenology p190-208

Grene, M. G. The German existentialists. *In* Grene, M. G. Philosophy in and out of Europe p71-78

Grene, M. G. Heidegger: philosopher and prophet. *In* Grene, M. G. Philosophy in and out of Europe p61-70

Heidegger, Martin—About—*Continued*

Harries, K. Heidegger as a political thinker. *In* Murray, M. E. ed. Heidegger and modern philosophy p304-28

Kisiel, T. J. Heidegger and the new images of science. *In* Radical phenomenology p163-81

Krell, D. F. Schlag der Lieb, Schlag des Todes: on a theme in Heidegger and Trakl. *In* Radical phenomenology p238-58

Marx, W. Thought and issue in Heidegger. *In* Radical phenomenology p12-30

Mehta, J. L. Finding Heidegger. *In* Radical phenomenology p5-11

Pöggeler, O. Being as appropriation. *In* Murray, M. E. ed. Heidegger and modern philosophy p84-115

Rorty, R. Overcoming the tradition: Heidegger and Dewey. *In* Murray, M. E. ed. Heidegger and modern philosophy p239-58

Rosen, S. Thinking about nothing. *In* Murray, M. E. ed. Heidegger and modern philosophy p116-37

Sallis, J. The origins of Heidegger's thought. *In* Radical phenomenology p43-57

Scott, N. A. Heidegger's path—towards the recovery of being. *In* Scott, N. A. Mirrors of man in existentialism p88-117

Silverman, H. J. Heidegger and Merleau-Ponty: interpreting Hegel. *In* Radical phenomenology p209-24

Taminiaux, J. Heidegger and Husserl's Logical investigations. *In* Radical phenomenology p58-83

Vick, G. R. Heidegger's linguistic rehabilitation of Parmenides' "Being." *In* Murray, M. E. ed. Heidegger and modern philosophy p203-21

Zimmerman, M. E. Some important themes in current Heidegger research. *In* Radical phenomenology p259-81

About individual works
Being and time

Gadamer, H. G. The historicity of understanding as hermeneutic principle; excerpt from "Truth and method." *In* Murray, M. E. ed. Heidegger and modern philosophy p161-83

Grene, M. G. A note on the philosophy of Heidegger: confessions of a young positivist. *In* Grene, M. G. Philosophy in and out of Europe p38-49

Harries, K. Death and utopia: towards a critique of the ethics of satisfaction. *In* Radical phenomenolgy p138-52

Harries, K. Fundamental ontology and the search for man's place. *In* Murray, M. E. ed. Heidegger and modern philosophy p65-79

Hoy, D. C. History, historicity, and historiography in Being and time. *In* Murray, M. E. ed. Heidegger and modern philosophy p329-53

Kockelmans, J. J. Destructive retrieve and hermeneutic phenomenology in 'Being and time.' *In* Radical phenomenology p106-37

Mandel, R. Heidegger and Wittgenstein: a second Kantian revolution. *In* Murray, M. E. ed. Heidegger and modern philosophy p259-70

Murray, M. E. Heidegger and Ryle: two versions of phenomenology. *In* Murray, M. E. ed. Heidegger and modern philosophy p271-90

Pöggeler, O. Being as appropriation. *In* Murray, M. E. ed. Heidegger and modern philosophy p84-115

Ricoeur, P. The task of hermeneutics. *In* Murray, M. E. ed. Heidegger and modern philosophy p141-60

Ryle, G. Heidegger's Sein and Zeit. *In* Murray, M. E. ed. Heidegger and modern philosophy p53-64

Stambaugh, J. An inquiry into authenticity and inauthenticity in Being and time. *In* Radical phenomenology p153-61

Being and time (German ed. pub. 1977)

Maly, K. To re-awaken the matter of being. *In* Radical phenomenology p282-98

Erläuterungen zu Hölderlins Dichtung

Schuwer, A. L. Nature and the holy: on Heidegger's interpretation of Holderlins's hymn "Wie wenn am Feiertage." *In* Radical phenomenology p225-37

The German university's self-affirmation

Harries, K. Heidegger as a political thinker. *In* Murray, M. E. ed. Heidegger and modern philosophy p304-28

On the way to language

Bruzina, R. C. Heidegger on the metaphor and philosophy. *In* Murray, M. E. ed. Heidegger and modern philosophy p184-200

The principle of reason

Bruzina, R. C. Heidegger on the metaphor and philosophy. *In* Murray, M. E. ed. Heidegger and modern philosophy p184-200

Wegmarken (1976 edition)

Sheehan, T. Getting to the topic: the new edition of Wegmarken. *In* Radical phenomenology p299-313

What is metaphysics?

Carnap, R. The overcoming of metaphysics through logical analysis of language. *In* Murray, M. E. ed. Heidegger and modern philosophy p23-34

Ethics

Warnock, M. Existentialist ethics. *In* New studies in ethics v2 p361-420

Knowledge, Theory of

Bauman, Z. Understanding as the work of life: Martin Heidegger. *In* Bauman, Z. Hermeneutics and social science p148-71

Heidmann, Jean

The expansion of the universe in the frame of conventional general relativity. *In* Cosmology, history, and theology p39-57

Heighton, Christy. See Heighton, R. H. jt. auth.

Heighton, Robert H. and Heighton, Christy

Applying the anthropological perspective to social policy. *In* Eddy, E. M. and Partridge, W. L. eds. Applied anthropology in America p390-411

Heikamp, Detlef

American objects in Italian collections of the Renaissance and baroque: a survey. *In* First images of America p455-82

Heike monogatari

Rimer, J. T. Source books II: The tale of the Heike and the nō drama. *In* Rimer, J. T. Modern Japanese fiction and its traditions p97-122

Heilbron, John L.
Commentary: Duhem and Donahue. *In* The Copernican achievement p276-84

Heilbroner, Robert Louis
The paradox of progress: decline and decay in The wealth of nations. *In* Skinner, A. S. and Wilson, T. eds. Essays on Adam Smith p524-39

Heilbrun, Carolyn G.
Axiothea's grief: the disability of the female imagination. *In* From Parnassus p227-36
Marriage perceived: English literature, 1873-1941. *In* Springer, M. A. ed. What manner of woman p160-83

Heilman, Robert Bechtold
Cleanth Brooks: some snapshots, mostly from an old album. *In* Simpson, L. P. ed. The possibilities of order: Cleanth Brooks and his work p128-49
E pluribus unum: parts and whole in Pride and prejudice. *In* Halperin, J. ed. Jane Austen p123-43
Losing battles and winning the war. *In* Prenshaw, P. W. ed. Eudora Welty p269-304
The return: centennial observations. *In* Smith, A. ed. The novels of Thomas Hardy p58-90

Heim, Kathleen M.
Professional education: some comparisons. *In* As much to learn as to teach p128-76

Heimann, P. M.
Mayer's concept of "force": the "axis" of a new science of physics. *In* Historical studies in the physical sciences v7 p277-96

Heimburg, Gregor von

About
Watanabe, M. Gregor Heimburg and early humanism in Germany. *In* Philosophy and humanism p406-22

Heimert, Alan E.
The Great Awakening as watershed; excerpt from "Religion and the American mind, from the Great Awakening to the Revolution." *In* Mulder, J. M. and Wilson, J. F. eds. Religion in American history p127-44

Hein, Hilde
On reaction and the women's movement. *In* Gould, C. C. and Wartofsky, M. W. eds. Women and philosophy p248-70

Hein, Norvin J.
Hinduism. *In* Adams, C. J. ed. A reader's guide to the great religions p106-55

Heine, Heinrich

About
Arendt, H. The Jew as pariah: a hidden tradition. *In* Arendt, H. The Jew as pariah: Jewish identity and politics in the modern age p67-90
Gilman, S. L. Parody and parallel: Heine, Nietzsche, and the classical world. *In* O'Flaherty, J. C.; Sellner, T. F. and Helm, R. M. eds. Studies in Nietzsche and the classical tradition p199-213
Preisendanz, W. Bridging the gap between Heine the poet and Heine the journalist. *In* Amacher, R. E. and Lange, V. eds. New perspectives in German literary criticism p225-59

Influence
Block, H. M. Heine and the French symbolists. *In* Creative encounter p25-39

Heinemann, Margot
Popular drama and Leveller style—Richard Overton and John Harris. *In* Rebels and their causes p69-92

Heinlein, Robert Anson
On the writing of speculative fiction. *In* Knight, D. F. ed. Turning points p199-204
Pandora's box; excerpt from "The worlds of Robert A. Heinlein." *In* Knight, D. F. ed. Turning points p238-58
Science fiction: its nature, faults and virtues. *In* Knight, D. F. ed. Turning points p3-28

About
Samuelson, D. N. The frontier worlds of Robert A. Heinlein. *In* Clareson, T. D. ed. Voices for the future: essays on major science fiction writers v 1 p104-52

Heinrich V, Emperor of Germany

About
Blumenthal, U. R. Patrimonia and regalia in 1111. *In* Law, church, and society p 9-20

Heins, Ethel L.
Literature bedeviled: a searching look at filmstrips. *In* Horn Book Magazine. Crosscurrents of criticism p88-95

Heins, Paul
Coming to terms with criticism. *In* Horn Book Magazine. Crosscurrents of criticism p82-87
Out on a limb with the critics: some random thoughts on the present state of the criticism of children's literature. *In* Horn Book Magazine. Crosscurrents of criticism p72-81

Heintz, John William
The real subject-predicate asymmetry. *In* Fact, value, and perception p19-29

Heinz, Donald
The Christian World Liberation Front. *In* The New religious consciousness p143-61

Heiremans, Luis Alberto

About
Peden, M. S. The theater of Luis Alberto Heiremans: 1928-1964. *In* Lyday, L. F. and Woodyard, G. W. eds. Dramatists in revolt p120-32

Heirs. See Inheritance and succession

Heisenberg, Werner
Tradition in science. *In* The Nature of scientific discovery p219-36

About
Cassidy, D. C. Heisenberg's first core model of the atom: the formation of a professional style. *In* Historical studies in the physical sciences v10 p187-224
MacKinnon, E. M. Heisenberg, models, and the rise of matrix mechanics. *In* Historical studies in the physical sciences v8 p137-88
Miller, A. I. Visualization lost and regained: the genesis of the quantum theory in the period 1913-27. *In* Wechsler, J. ed. On aesthetics in science p73-102
Serwer, D. Unmechanischer Zwang: Pauli, Heisenberg, and the rejection of the mechanical atom, 1923-1925. *In* Historical studies in the physical sciences v8 p189-256

Heisenberg uncertainty principle
Bronowski, J. The principle of tolerance. *In* Bronowski, J. A sense of the future p221-34

Heisenberg uncertainty principle—*Continued*

Hanle, P. A. Indeterminacy before Heisenberg: the case of Franz Exner and Erwin Schrödinger. *In* Historical studies in the physical sciences v10 p225-69

Heiserman, Arthur Ray

The novel before the novel

Contents

Antonine comedy
Aphrodisian chastity
Bits and epitomes
Divine romance
Erotic suffering
Resourceless Jason

Heisler, William J.

Worker alienation: 1900-1975. *In* Heisler, W. J. and Houck, J. W. eds. A matter of dignity p65-84

Heisner, Beverly F.

Viscardi's Mariahilfkirche at Freystadt and the development of the central plan church in eighteenth century Germany. *In* Enggass, R. C. and Stokstadt, M. eds. Hortus imaginum p175-83

Heissenbüttel, Helmut

About

Kurz, P. K. Skeletons of the sayable—demonstrations of a world. *In* Kurz, P. K. On modern German literature v 1 p173-93

Heist, William W.

Irish saints' lives, romance, and cultural history. *In* Medievalia et humanistica no. 6 p25-40

Hejaz, Arabia

History

Ochsenwald, W. L. The financial basis of Ottoman rule in the Hijaz, 1840-1877. *In* Nationalism in a non-national state p129-49

Held, Virginia

Marx, sex, and the transformation of society. *In* Gould, C. C. and Wartofsky, M. W. eds. Women and philosophy p168-84

Helgerson, Richard

The Elizabethan prodigals

Contents

Gascoigne
Greene
Lodge
Lyly
The mirror of duty
Patterns of prodigality
Sidney

Heliogabalus, Emperor of Rome

About

Bowersock, G. W. Herodian and Elagabalus. *In* Yale classical studies v24 p229-36

Hell

Coomaraswamy, A. K. Who is "Satan" and where is "Hell"? *In* Coomaraswamy, A. K. Selected papers v2 p23-33

Hell (Hinduism)

Coomaraswamy, A. K. Who is "Satan" and where is "Hell"? *In* Coomaraswamy, A. K. Selected papers v2 p23-33

Hellenism

Georgi, D. Socioeconomic reasons for the "divine man" as a propagandistic pattern. *In* Aspects of religious propaganda in Judaism and early Christianity p27-42

Momigliano, A. The fault of the Greeks. *In* Momigliano, A. Essays in ancient and modern historiography p9-23

Historiography

Momigliano, A. J. G. Droysen between Greeks and Jews. *In* Momigliano, A. Essays in ancient and modern historiography p307-23

Influence

Schoedel, W. R. Jewish wisdom and the formation of the Christian ascetic. *In* Aspects of wisdom in Judaism and early Christianity p169-99

Hellenistic architecture. See Architecture, Hellenistic

Hellenistic marble sculpture. See Marble sculpture, Hellenistic

Hellenistic sculpture. See Sculpture, Hellenistic

Heller, Agnes

The future of relations between the sexes. *In* The Humanisation of socialism p27-41

Marx's theory of revolution and the revolution in everyday life. *In* The Humanisation of socialism p52-57

Theory and practice from the point of view of human needs. *In* The Humanisation of socialism p58-75

Heller, Agnes, and Vajda, Mihaly

Communism and the family. *In* The Humanisation of socialism p7-26

Heller, Erich

Arthur Schopenhauer. *In* Viva Vivas! p273-87

Observations on psychoanalysis and modern literature. *In* Psychiatry and the humanities v 1 p35-50

The poet's self and the poem

Contents

Goethe in Marienbad
Nietzsche in the waste land
Rilke in Paris
Thomas Mann in Venice

Heller, Joseph

About individual works
Catch-22

Colmer, J. Protest and anti-war literature. *In* Colmer, J. Coleridge to Catch-22 p210-21

Kennard, J. E. Joseph Heller: at war with absurdity. *In* Kennard, J. E. Number and nightmare p41-56

Richter, D. H. The achievement of shape in the twentieth-century fable: Joseph Heller's Catch-22. *In* Richter, D. H. Fable's end p136-65

Heller, Peter

Nietzsche in his relation to Voltaire and Rousseau. *In* O'Flaherty, J. C.; Sellner, T. F. and Helm, R. M. eds. Studies in Nietzsche and the classical tradition p109-33

Hellerstein, Walter

Michelin Tire Corp. v. Wages: enhanced state power to tax imports. *In* The Supreme Court review, 1976 p99-133

Helliwell, John

Adjustment under fixed and flexible exchange rates. *In* Kenen, P. B. ed. International trade and finance p379-410

Hellman, Clarisse Doris

A poem on the occasion of the nova of 1572. *In* Philosophy and humanism p306-09

Hellman, Lillian

About

Going, W. T. The Prestons of Talladega and the Hubbards of Bowen: a dramatic note. *In* Going, W. T. Essays on Alabama literature p142-55

About individual works
Scoundrel time

Howe, I. Lillian Hellman and the Mc-Carthy years. *in* Celebrations and attacks p206-12

Hellmann, Donald C.

Japan and China: competitors in a multi-polar world? *In* Clapp, P. and Halperin, M. H. eds. United States-Japanese relations, the 1970's p164-82

Helm, Robert Meredith

Plato in the thought of Nietzsche and Augustine. *In* O'Flaherty, J. C.; Sellner, T. F. and Helm, R. M. eds. Studies in Nietzsche and the classical tradition p16-32

Helmets

Goldstein, S. M. An Etruscan helmet in the McDaniel collection. *In* Harvard Studies in classical philology v72 p383-90

Helmholtz, Hermann Ludwig Ferdinand von

About

Fancher, R. E. The sensing and perceiving mind: Kant, Helmholtz, and the Gestalt psychologists. *In* Fancher, R. E. Pioneers of psychology p87-125

Pastore, N. Helmholtz on the projection or transfer of sensation. *In* Studies in perception p355-76

Helmont, Jean Baptiste van

About

. Debus, A. G. The chemical debates of the seventeenth century: the reaction to Robert Fludd and Jean Baptiste van Helmont. *In* Bonelli, M. L. R. and Shea, W. R. eds. Reason, experiment, and mysticism in the scientific revolution p19-47

Héloise

About

Benton, J. F. and Ercoli, F. P. The style of the "Historia calamitatum": a preliminary test of the authenticity of the correspondence attributed to Abelard and Heloise. *In* Viator: medieval and Renaissance studies v6 p59-86

Helper, Hinton Rowan

About

Downs, R. B. Hated Helper. *In* Downs, R. B. Books that changed the South p114-24

About individual works
The impending crisis of the South: how to meet it

Downs, R. B. Hated Helper. *In* Downs, R. B. Books that changed the South p114-24

Helsinger, Elizabeth Kramer

The structure of Ruskin's Praeterita. *In* Landow, G. P. ed. Approaches to Victorian autobiography p87-108

Ulysses to Penelope: Victorian experiments in autobiography. *In* Landow, G. P. ed. Approaches to Victorian autobiography p3-25

Helsinger, Howard

Credence and credibility: the concern for honesty in Victorian autobiography. *In* Landow, G. P. ed. Approaches to Victorian autobiography p39-63

Pearls in the swill: comic allegory in the French fabliaux. *In* Cooke, T. D. and Honeycutt, B. L. eds. The humor of the fabliaux p93-105

Helsinki Accords. See Conference on Security and Cooperation in Europe, Helsinki, 1975

Helsinki Agreement. See Conference on Security and Cooperation in Europe, Helsinki, 1975

Helsinki Declaration. See Conference on Security and Cooperation in Europe, Helsinki, 1975

Helsinki Final Act. See Conference on Security and Cooperation in Europe, Helsinki, 1975

Helvétius, Claude Adrien

About

Voegelin, E. Helvétius and the genealogy of passions. *In* Voegelin, E. From Enlightenment to revolution p35-52

Voegelin, E. Helvétius and the heritage of Pascal. *In* Voegelin, E. From Enlightenment to Revolution p53-73

Hémardinquer, Jean-Jacques

The family pig of the ancien régime: myth or fact? *In* Food and drink in history p50-72

Hematologic diseases. See Blood—Diseases

Hematology

Bordeaux, M. Blazing a trail to a history of customary law by means of geographic hematology. *In* Biology of man in history p191-205

Hembry, Phyllis

Episcopal palaces, 1535 to 1660. *In* Wealth and power in Tudor England p146-66

Hemenway, Robert

Are you a flying lark or a setting dove? *In* Fisher, D. and Stepto, R. B. eds. Afro-American literature p122-52

Heminarium (The Latin word)

Lebek, W. D. Heminarium: Quintilian Institutio oratoria 6.3.52 and CIL IV 10566. *In* Harvard Studies in classical philology v82 p271-75

Hemingway, Ernest

About

Astro, R. Phlebas sails the Caribbean: Steinbeck, Hemingway, and the American waste land. *In* French, W. G. ed. The twenties p215-33

Backman, M. Death and birth in Hemingway. *In* The Stoic strain in American literature p115-33

Baker, C. H. Hemingway's empirical imagination. *In* Baldwin, K. H. and Kirby, D. K. eds. Individual and community p94-111

Benson, J. J. Ernest Hemingway as short story writer. *In* Benson, J. J. ed. The short stories of Ernest Hemingway: critical essays p272-310

Bigsby, C. W. E. Hemingway: the recoil from history. *In* French, W. G. ed. The twenties p203-13

Hemingway, Ernest—About—*Continued*

Donald, M. The traditional novel. *In* Donald, M. The American novel in the twentieth century p13-72

Farrell, J. T. Ernest Hemingway. *In* Farrell, J. T. Literary essays, 1954-1974 p23-25

Fuchs, D. Ernest Hemingway, literary critic. *In* Wagner, L. W. ed. Ernest Hemingway p39-56

Howe, I. The wounds of all generations. *In* Howe, I. Celebrations and attacks p155-60

Hurwitz, H. M. Hemingway's tutor, Ezra Pound. *In* Wagner, L. W. ed. Ernest Hemingway p8-21

Kenner, H. Small ritual truths. *In* Kenner, H. A homemade world p119-57

Lewis, W. Ernest Hemingway; excerpt from "Men without art." *In* Lewis, W. Enemy salvoes p132-45

Lodge, D. Ernest Hemingway. *In* Lodge, D. The modes of modern writing p155-59

Peckham, M. Ernest Hemingway: sexual themes in his writing. *In* Peckham, M. Romanticism and behavior p139-58

Sarotte, G. M. Latent homosexuality: short of and beyond true heterosexuality: Ernest Hemingway: the (almost) total sublimation of the homosexual instinct. *In* Sarotte, G. M. Like a brother, like a lover p262-78

Sheed, W. Ernest Hemingway. *In* Sheed, W. The good word & other words p234-42

Tanner, T. Ernest Hemingway's unhurried sensations. *In* Tanner, T. The reign of wonder p228-57

West, R. B. Hemingway and Faulkner: two masters of the modern short story. *In* Benson, J. J. ed. The short stories of Ernest Hemingway: critical essays p2-14

About individual works
Across the river and into the trees

Lisca, P. The structure of Hemingway's Across the river and into the trees. *In* Wagner, L. W. ed. Ernest Hemingway p288-306

O'Hara, J. The author's name is Hemingway. *In* O'Hara, J. "An artist is his own fault" p165-73

After the storm

Atkins, A. Ironic action in "After the storm." *In* Benson, J. J. ed. The short stories of Ernest Hemingway: critical essays p227-30

Big two-hearted river

Baker, S. W. Hemingway's Two-hearted river. *In* Benson, J. J. ed. The short stories of Ernest Hemingway: critical essays p150-59

Wells, E. J. A statistical analysis of the prose style of Ernest Hemingway: Big two-hearted river. *In* Benson, J. J. ed. The short stories of Ernest Hemingway: critical essays p129-35

A canary for one

Smith, J. "A canary for one": Hemingway in the wasteland. *In* Benson, J. J. ed. The short stories of Ernest Hemingway: critical essays p233-38

Cat in the rain

Hagopian, J. V. Symmetry in "Cat in the rain." *In* Benson, J. J. ed. The short stories of Ernest Hemingway: critical essays p230-32

A clean, well-lighted place

Bennett, W. Character, irony, and resolution in "A clean, well-lighted place." *In* Benson, J. J. ed. The short stories of Ernest Hemingway: critical essays p261-69

Berryman, J. Hemingway's "A clean, well-lighted place." *In* Berryman, J. The freedom of the poet p217-21

O'Donovan, M. A clean well-lighted place. *In* Benson, J. J. ed. The short stories of Ernest Hemingway: critical essays p85-92

The doctor and the doctor's wife

DeFalco, J. M. Initiation ("Indian camp" and "The doctor and the doctor's wife.") *In* Benson, J. J. ed. The short stories of Ernest Hemingway: critical essays p159-67

The end of something

Kruse, H. H. Ernest Hemingway's "The end of something": its independence as a short story and its place in the "education of Nick Adams." *In* Benson, J. J. ed. The short stories of Ernest Hemingway: critical essays p210-22

A farewell to arms

Fetterley, J. A farewell to arms: Ernest Hemingway's "resentful cryptogram." *In* Diamond, A. and Edwards, L. R. eds. The authority of experience p257-73

Also in Fetterley, J. The resisting reader p46-71

Garrety, M. Love and war: R. H. Mottram, The Spanish farm trilogy and Ernest Hemingway, A farewell to arms. *In* Klein, H. M. ed. The First World War in fiction p10-22

Schneider, D. J. Hemingway's A farewell to arms: the novel as pure poetry. *In* Wagner, L. W. ed. Ernest Hemingway p252-66

Warren, R. P. Ernest Hemingway; excerpt from "Selected essays". *In* Wagner, L. W. ed. Ernest Hemingway p75-102

Fifty grand

Martine, J. J. Hemingway's "Fifty grand": the other fight(s). *In* Benson, J. J. ed. The short stories of Ernest Hemingway: critical essays p198-203

For whom the bell tolls

Carpenter, F. I. Hemingway achieves the fifth dimension; excerpt from "American literature and the dream". *In* Wagner, L. W. ed. Ernest Hemingway p279-87

DeFalco, J. M. Hemingway and revolution: mankinde not Marx. *In* Renaissance and modern p143-59

Pohl, C. The "unmaking" of a political film. *In* Peary, G. and Shatzkin, R. eds. The modern American novel and the movies p317-24

Stephens, R. O. Language magic and reality in For whom the bell tolls. *In* Wagner, L. W. ed. Ernest Hemingway p266-79

Wagner, L. W. The marinating of For whom the bell tolls. *In* Wagner, L. W. ed. Ernest Hemingway p200-12

The gambler, the nun and the radio

Montgomery, M. Hemingway's "The gambler, the nun, and the radio": a reading and a problem. *In* Benson, J. J. ed. The short stories of Ernest Hemingway: critical essays p203-10

Hemingway, Ernest—About individual works
—*Continued*

God rest you merry, gentlemen

Hays, P. L. Hemingway and the Fisher King ("God rest you merry, gentlemen.") *In* Benson, J. J. ed. The short stories of Ernest Hemingway: critical essays p223-27

Hills like white elephants

Trilling, L. Ernest Hemingway: Hills like white elephants. *In* Trilling, L. Prefaces to The experience of literature p145-49

In another country

Rovit, E. H. Of human dignity: "In another country." *In* Benson, J. J. ed. The short stories of Ernest Hemingway: critical essays p167-70

In our time

Burhans, C. S. The complex unity of In our time. *In* Benson, J. J. ed. The short stories of Ernest Hemingway: critical essays p15-29

Hasbany, R. The shock of vision: an imagist reading of In our time. *In* Wagner, L. W. ed. Ernest Hemingway p224-40

Wilson, E. Introduction to In our time: stories by Ernest Hemingway. *In* Praise from famous men: an anthology of introductions p169-74

Wilson, E. Mr Hemingway's dry-points. *In* Wagner, L. W. ed. Ernest Hemingway p222-23

In our time, (Chapter III)

Fenton, C. A. The revision of "chapter III" from In our time. *In* Benson, J. J. ed. The short stories of Ernest Hemingway: critical essays p80-84

Indian camp

DeFalco, J. M. Initiation ("Indian camp" and "The doctor and the doctor's wife.") *In* Benson, J. J. ed. The short stories of Ernest Hemingway: critical essays p159-67

The killers

Brooks, C. and Warren, R. P. "The killers." *In* Benson, J. J. ed. The short stories of Ernest Hemingway: critical essays p187-96

The light of the world

Martine, J. J. A little light on Hemingway's "The light of the world." *In* Benson, J. J. ed. The short stories of Ernest Hemingway: critical essays p196-98

A moveable feast

Connolly, C. Ernest Hemingway: 1. *In* Connolly, C. The evening colonnade p255-57

The Nick Adams stories

Young, P. "Big world out there": The Nick Adams stories. *In* Benson, J. J. ed. The short stories of Ernest Hemingway: critical essays p29-45

Now I lay me

Hovey, R. B. Hemingway's "Now I lay me": a psychological interpretation. *In* Benson, J. J. ed. The short stories of Ernest Hemingway: critical essays p180-87

The old man and the sea

Baker, C. H. The boy and the lions; excerpt from "The writer as artist. 4th ed." *In* Wagner, L. W. ed. Ernest Hemingway p306-19

Nadeau, R. L. Film and mythic heroism: Sturges's Old man. *In* Peary, G. and Shatzkin, R. eds. The modern American novel and the movies p199-203

Waldmeir, J. J. Confiteor hominem: Ernest Hemingway's religion of man. *In* Wagner, L. W. ed. Ernest Hemingway p144-52

The short happy life of Francis Macomber

Baker, C. The two African stories. *In* Benson, J. J. ed. The short stories of Ernest Hemingway: critical essays p45-53

Hutton, V. R. The short happy life of Macomber. *In* Benson, J. J. ed. The short stories of Ernest Hemingway: critical essays p239-50

The snows of Kilimanjaro

Baker, C. The two African stories. *In* Benson, J. J. ed. The short stories of Ernest Hemingway: critical essays p45-53

Santangelo, G. The dark snows of Kilimanjaro. *In* Benson, J. J. ed. The short stories of Ernest Hemingway: critical essays p251-61

Soldier's home

Lewis, R. W. Hemingway's concept of sport and "Soldier's home." *In* Benson, J. J. ed. The short stories of Ernest Hemingway: critical essays p170-80

The sun also rises

Adams, R. P. Sunrise out of The waste land. *In* Wagner, L. W. ed. Ernest Hemingway p241-51

Goodman, P. The sweet style of Ernest Hemingway. *In* Wagner, L. W. ed. Ernest Hemingway p153-60

To have and have not

Rothman, W. To have and have not adapted a novel. *In* Peary, G. and Shatzkin, R. eds. The modern American novel and the movies p70-79

The undefeated

Christensen, F. A lesson from Hemingway ("The undefeated"). *In* Benson, J. J. ed. The short stories of Ernest Hemingway: critical essays p121-29

Bibliography

Benson, J. J. comp. A comprehensive checklist of Hemingway short fiction criticism, explication, and commentary. *In* Benson, J. J. ed. The short stories of Ernest Hemingway: critical essays p312-75

Bryer, J. R. Fitzgerald and Hemingway. *In* American literary scholarship, 1973 p150-76

Bryer, J. R. Fitzgerald and Hemingway [another essay]. *In* American literary scholarship, 1974 p139-64

Bryer, J. R. Fitzgerald and Hemingway [another essay]. *In* American literary scholarship, 1975 p167-200

Bryer, J. R. Fitzgerald and Hemingway [another essay]. *In* American literary scholarship, 1976 p141-66

Bryer, J. R. Fitzgerald and Hemingway [another essay]. *In* American literary scholarship, 1977 p163-86

Hemingway, Ernest—*Continued*

Characters

Backman, M. Death and birth in Hemingway. *In* The Stoic strain in American literature p115-33

Fenton, C. A. No money for the kingbird: Hemingway's prizefight stories. *In* Benson, J. J. ed. The short stories of Ernest Hemingway: critical essays p53-63

Characters—Catherine Barkley

Fetterley, J. A farewell to arms: Ernest Hemingway's "resentful cryptogram." *In* Diamond, A. and Edwards, L. R. eds. The authority of experience p257-73

Also in Fetterley, J. The resisting reader p46-71

Characters—Lieutenant Frederic Henry

Fetterley, J. A farewell to arms: Ernest Hemingway's "resentful cryptogram." *In* Diamond, A. and Edwards, L. R. eds. The authority of experience p257-73

Also in Fetterley, J. The resisting reader p46-71

Characters—Nick Adams

Ficken, C. F. W. Point of view in the Nick Adams stories. *In* Benson, J. J. ed. The short stories of Ernest Hemingway: critical essays p93-112

Kruse, H. H. Ernest Hemingway's "The end of something": its independence as a short story and its place in the "education of Nick Adams." *In* Benson, J. J. ed. The short stories of Ernest Hemingway: critical essays p210-22

Characters—Women

Holder, A. The other Hemingway. *In* Wagner, L. W. ed. Ernest Hemingway p103-09

Criticism and interpretation

Cowley, M. Mr Papa and the parricides. *In* Cowley, M.—And I worked at the writer's trade p21-34

Ethical ideas

See Hemingway, Ernest—Religion and ethics

Knowledge—Spain

Kinnamon, K. Hemingway, the corrida, and Spain. *In* Wagner, L. W. ed. Ernest Hemingway p57-74

Light, M. Of wasteful deaths: Hemingway's stories about the Spanish War. *In* Benson, J. J. ed. The short stories of Ernest Hemingway: critical essays p64-77

Knowledge—Sports

See Hemingway, Ernest—Knowledge—Sports and recreation

Knowledge—Sports and recreation

Lewis, R. W. Hemingway's concept of sport and "Soldier's home." *In* Benson, J. J. ed. The short stories of Ernest Hemingway: critical essays p170-80

Reardon, J. Hemingway's esthetic and ethical sportsmen. *In* Wagner, L. W. ed. Ernest Hemingway p131-44

Yu, B. The still center of Hemingway's world. *In* Wagner, L. W. ed. Ernest Hemingway p109-31

Knowledge—Writing

Reardon, J. Hemingway's esthetic and ethical sportsmen. *In* Wagner, L. W. ed. Ernest Hemingway p131-44

Language

Stephens, R. O. Language magic and reality in For whom the bell tolls. *In* Wagner, L. W. ed. Ernest Hemingway p266-79

Religion and ethics

Reardon, J. Hemingway's esthetic and ethical sportsmen. *In* Wagner, L. W. ed. Ernest Hemingway p131-44

Scott, N. A. Ernest Hemingway, a critical essay; excerpt. *In* Wagner, L. W. ed. Ernest Hemingway p212-21

Waldmeir, J. J. Confiteor hominem: Ernest Hemingway's religion of man. *In* Wagner, L. W. ed. Ernest Hemingway p144-52

Warren, R. P. Ernest Hemingway; excerpt from "Selected essays". *In* Wagner, L. W. ed. Ernest Hemingway p75-102

Yu, B. The still center of Hemingway's world. *In* Wagner, L. W. ed. Ernest Hemingway p109-31

Style

Bridgman, R. Ernest Hemingway; excerpt from "The colloquial style in America". *In* Wagner, L. W. ed. Ernest Hemingway p160-88

Ficken, C. F. W. Point of view in the Nick Adams stories. *In* Benson, J. J. ed. The short stories of Ernest Hemingway: critical essays p93-112

Goodman, P. The sweet style of Ernest Hemingway. *In* Wagner, L. W. ed. Ernest Hemingway p153-60

Grebstein, S. N. The reliable and unreliable narrator in Hemingway's stories. *In* Benson, J. J. ed. The short stories of Ernest Hemingway: critical essays p113-21

Morris, W. Ernest Hemingway. *In* Morris, W. Earthly delights, unearthly adornments p141-46

Scott, N. A. Ernest Hemingway, a critical essay; excerpt. *In* Wagner, L. W. ed. Ernest Hemingway p212-21

Smith, J. Hemingway and the thing left out. *In* Benson, J. J. ed. The short stories of Ernest Hemingway: critical essays p135-47

Also in Wagner, L. W. ed. Ernest Hemingway p188-200

Wells, E. J. A statistical analysis of the prose style of Ernest Hemingway: Big two-hearted river. *In* Benson, J. J. ed. The short stories of Ernest Hemingway. critical essays p129-35

Technique

Christensen, F. A lesson from Hemingway ("The undefeated"). *In* Benson, J. J. ed. The short stories of Ernest Hemingway: critical essays p121-29

Schneider, D. J. Hemingway's A farewell to arms: the novel as pure poetry. *In* Wagner, L. W. ed. Ernest Hemingway p252-66

Wagner, L. W. The marinating of For whom the bell tolls. *In* Wagner, L. W. ed. Ernest Hemingway p200-12

Hemmings, Frederick William John

About individual works

The life and times of Emile Zola

Pritchett, V. S. Emile Zola: Zola's life. *In* Pritchett, V. S. The myth makers p108-14

Hémon, Louis

About individual works

Monsieur Ripois et la Némésis

Truffaut, F. René Clément: Monsieur Ripois. *In* Truffaut, F. The films in my life p197-200

Film adaptations

Truffaut, F. René Clément: Monsieur Ripois. *in* Truffaut, F. The films in my life p197-200

Hemstedt, Geoffrey

The novel. *In* Lerner, L. ed. The Victorians p3-24

Painting and illustration. *In* Lerner, L. ed. The Victorians p139-52

Henderson, Archibald

About individual works

George Bernard Shaw: man of the century

Balakian, N. Shaw and his Boswell. *In* Balakian, N. Critical encounters p124-28

Henderson, Arnold Clayton

"Of heigh or lough estat": medieval fabulists as social critics. *In* Viator: medieval and Renaissance studies v9 p265-90

Henderson, Bill

Independent publishing: today and yesterday. *In* Altbach, P. G. and McVey, S. eds. Perspectives on publishing p217-29

On Pushcart press. *In* Anderson, E. and Kinzie, M. eds. The little magazine in America: a modern documentary history p614-23

Henderson, Brian

The long take. *In* Nichols, B. ed. Movies and methods p314-24

Toward a non-bourgeois camera style. *In* Nichols, B. ed. Movies and methods p422-38

Two types of film theory. *In* Nichols, B. ed. Movies and methods p388-400

Henderson, David

About individual works

De mayor of Harlem

Reed, I. De mayor of Harlem. *In* Reed, I. Shrovetide in old New Orleans p72-76

Henderson, Edwin Bancroft

The Black American in sports. *In* The Black American reference book p927-63

Henderson, Elmer W.

The Federal government and the fight for basic human rights. *In* Johnson, H. A. ed. Negotiating the mainstream p141-63

Henderson, George

The programme of illustrations in Bodleian MS Junius XI. *In* Studies in memory of David Talbot Rice p113-45

Henderson, Gordon. See Hogan, R. G. jt. auth.

Henderson, Hazel

The politics of reconceptualization. *In* Wagschal, P. H. ed. Learning tomorrows p119-29

Henderson, Janice A.

Erasmus Reinhold's determination of the distance of the sun from the earth. *In* The Copernican achievement p108-29

About individual works

Erasmus Reinhold's determination of the distance of the sun from the earth

Abers, E. S. and Kennel, C. F. Commentary: the role of error in ancient methods for determining the solar distance. *In* The Copernican achievement p130-36

Henderson, Jeffrey

The lekythos and Frogs 1200-1248. *In* Harvard Studies in classical philology v76 p133-43

Henderson, Michael

About individual works

The log of a superfluous son: a novel

Nazareth, P. Time in the Third World: a fictional exploration. *In* Narasimhaiah, C. D. ed. Awakened conscience p195-205

Henderson, Vivian W.

Educational change and the Southern future. *In* Lewis, W. D. and Griessman, B. E. eds. The Southern mystique p63-72

Henderson, William Otto. See Part 2 under title: Great Britain and her world, 1750-1914

Hendrickson, Kenneth Elton

Tribune of the people: George R. Lunn and the rise and fall of Christian Socialism in Schenectady. *In* Stave, B. M. ed. Socialism and the cities p72-98

Hendrix, Scott H.

In quest of the vera ecclesia: the crises of late medieval ecclesiology. *In* Viator: medieval and Renaissance studies v7 p347-78

Heninger, S. K.

Oronce Finé and English textbooks for the mathematical sciences. *In* Studies in the continental background of Renaissance English literature: essays presented to John L. Lievsay p170-85

Sidney and Milton: the poet as maker. *In* Wittreich, J. A. ed. Milton and the line of vision p57-95

Henkin, Louis

The Constitution and foreign affairs. *In* Essays on the Constitution of the United States p113-29

Human rights and "domestic jurisdiction." *In* Human rights, international law and the Helsinki Accord p21-40

Human rights: reappraisal and readjustment. *In* Sidorsky, D. ed. Essays on human rights p68-87

Henle, Mary

On naive realism. *In* Perception p40-56

Henn, Thomas Rice

Last essays

Contents

'The big house'

The centenary Yeats

Choice and chance

George Moore

J. M. Synge: a reconsideration

The lighter side of the Irish Literary Revival

'The place of shells'

'The property of the dead'

The rhetoric of Yeats

The sainthood of A.E.

Towards the values

The weasel's tooth

Yeats and the picture galleries

Yeats and the poetry of war

Henn, Thomas R.—*Continued*

About individual works

The lonely tower

Connolly, C. W. B. Yeats. *In* Connolly, C. The evening colonnade p202-06

Hennesey, James

Square peg in a round hole: on being Roman Catholic in America. *In* America in theological perspective p3-12

Hennessy, Alistair. See Hennessy, Charles Alistair Michael

Hennessy, Charles Alistair Michael

Fascism and Populism in Latin America. *In* Laqueur, W. Z. ed. Fascism: a reader's guide p255-94

Hennessy, James Pope- See Pope-Hennessy, James

Henninger, Peter

On literature and condensation: Robert Musil's early novellas. *In* Glyph 5 p114-32

Henrich, Dieter

Art and philosophy of art today: reflections with reference to Hegel. *In* Amacher, R. E. and Lange, V. eds. New perspectives in German literary criticism p107-33

Henrichs, Albert

Greek maenadism from Olympias to Messalina. *In* Harvard Studies in classical philology v82 p121-60

Mani and the Babylonian Baptists: a historical confrontation. *In* Harvard Studies in classical philology v77 p23-59

Two doxographical notes: Democritus and Prodicus on religion. *In* Harvard Studies in classical philology v79 p93-123

Henriksen, Hildur Ve, and Holter, Harriet

Norway. *In* Kamerman, S. B. and Kahn, A. J. eds. Family policy p49-67

Henriques, Fernando

Contemporary racial problems. *In* Racial variation in man p211-32

Henry V, Emperor of Germany. See Heinrich V, Emperor of Germany

Henry VI, King of England

McKenna, J. W. Piety and propaganda: the cult of King Henry VI. *In* Chaucer and Middle English studies in honour of Rossell Hope Robbins p72-88

Henry VII, King of England

About

Ives, E. W. 'Agaynst taking awaye of women': the inception and operation of the Abduction Act of 1487. *In* Wealth and power in Tudor England p21-44

Henry VIII, King of England

About

Miller, H. Henry VIII's unwritten will: grants of lands and honours in 1547. *In* Wealth and power in Tudor England p87-105

Henry, Gerrit

The real thing. *In* Battcock, G. ed. Super realism p3-20

The silk purse of high-style interior decoration. *In* Battcock, G. ed. Super realism p163-69

Henry, Patrick

Images of the Church in the Second Nicene Council and in the Libri Carolini. *In* Law, church, and society p237-52

Henry, Peter

I. S. Turgenev: Fathers and sons. *In* Williams, D. A. ed. The monster in the mirror p40-74

Henry V (criticism) Shakespeare, W. *In* Kauffmann, S. Persons of the drama p93-96

Henry V (Motion picture)

Jorgens, J. J. Laurence Oliver's Henry V. *In* Jorgens, J. J. Shakespeare on film p122-35

Henry VI (criticism) Shakespeare, W. *In* Kauffmann, S. Persons of the drama p93-96

Henryson, Robert

About individual works

The testament of Cresseid

Ridley, F. H. A plea for the Middle Scots. *In* The Learned and the lewed p175-96

Schmitz, G. Cresseid's trial: a revision. Fame and defamation in Henryson's 'Testament of Cresseid.' *In* English Association. Essays and studies, 1979 p44-56

Characters—Cresseid

Hanna, R. Cresseid's dream and Henryson's Testament. *In* Chaucer and Middle English studies in honour of Rossell Hope Robbins p288-97

Henshaw, Ruth. See Bascom, Ruth (Henshaw) Miles

Hentoff, Nat

Turning kids into waste. *In* Gross, B. and Gross, R. eds. The children's rights movement p78-81

Hentz, Caroline Lee (Whiting)

About

Baym, N. Z. E. D. E. N. Southworth and Caroline Lee Hentz. *In* Baym, N. Z. Woman's fiction p110-39

Hepburn, Anthony C.

Catholics in the north of Ireland, 1850-1921: the urbanization of a minority. *In* Hepburn, A. C. ed. Minorities in history p84-102

Minorities in history. *In* Hepburn, A. C. ed. Minorities in history p 1-10

Hephaestion Thebanus. See Hyphaistion Thevaios

Hera (Greek goddess)

Whitman, C. H. Hera's anvils. *In* Harvard Studies in classical philology v74 p37-42

Heracles

See also Hercules

Art

Robertson, M. Two question-marks on the Parthenon. *In* Studies in classical art and archaeology p75-87

Heraclitus of Ephesus

About

Coomaraswamy, A. K. Measures of fire. *In* Coomaraswamy, A. K. Selected papers v2 p159-65

Shell, M. The Ring of Gyges. *In* Shell, M. The economy of literature p11-62

Verdenius, W. J. Heraclitus' conception of fire. *In* Kephalaion p 1-8

Heradstveit, Daniel
The role of international terrorism in the Middle East conflict and its implication for conflict resolution. *In* International terrorism and world security p93-103

Herakles. See Heracles

Heraldry. See Columns of Hercules (Heraldic device); Emblems

Herbals. See Botany, Medical

Herberg, Will
Judaism in America; excerpt from "Protestant, Catholic, Jew." *In* Mulder, J. M. and Wilson, J. F. eds. Religion in American history p379-96

Herbert, Edward Herbert, Baron

About individual works
Poems
McFarland, R. E. The rhetoric of optics in Lord Herbert's poems to Diana Cecil. *In* Medievalia et humanistica no. 5 p215-28

Herbert, George

About
Fish, S. E. Catechizing the reader: Herbert's Socratean rhetoric. *In* Sloan, T. O. and Waddington, R. B. eds. The rhetoric of Renaissance poetry p174-88
Gilman, E. B. The Pauline perspectives in Donne, Herbert, and Greville. *In* Gilman, E. B. The curious perspective p167-203
Knights, L. C. George Herbert. *In* Knights, L. C. Explorations 3 p64-80
Lewalski, B. K. George Herbert: artful psalms from the temple in the heart. *In* Lewalski, B. K. Protestant poetics and the seventeenth-century religious lyric p283-316
McCanles, M. The dialectical structure of the metaphysical lyric: Donne, Herbert, Marvell. *In* McCanles, M. Dialectical criticism and Renaissance literature p54-119
Thorpe, J. E. Reflections and self-reflections: Outlandish proverbs as a context for George Herbert's other writings. *In* Illustrious evidence p23-37
Vendler, H. H. The re-invented poem: George Herbert's alternatives. *In* Wimsatt, W. K. ed. Literary criticism: idea and act p362-81

About individual works
Outlandish proverbs
Thorpe, J. E. Reflections and self-reflections: Outlandish proverbs as a context for George Herbert's other writings. *In* Illustrious evidence p23-37

Redemption
Dyson, A. E. and Lovelock, J. Herbert's 'Redemption.' *In* Dyson, A. E. and Lovelock, J. Masterful images p29-35

The temple
Lewalski, B. K. Typology and poetry: a consideration of Herbert, Vaughan, and Marvell. *In* Illustrious evidence p41-69

Criticism and interpretation
Richards, I. A. The conduct of verse. *In* Richards, I. A. Complementarities p226-32

Herbert, Robert L.
Baron Gros's Napoleon and Voltaire's Henri IV. *In* The Artist and the writer in France p52-75

Herbert, Xavier
Essay 13. *In* Fitzgerald, R. ed. What it means to be human p241-46

About individual works
Poor fellow my country
Hergenhan, L. T. An Australian tragedy: Xavier Herbert's Poor fellow my country. *In* Hamilton, K. G. ed. Studies in the recent Australian novel p29-60

Herbert, Zbigniew

About individual works
Selected poems
Morgan, E. Zbigniew Herbert. *In* Morgan, E. Essays p67-70

Herbicides

Law and legislation
See Pesticides—Law and legislation

Herbiet, Jean

About
Morley, P. A. 'In God's name': ironic forms of religious drama in Canada and Australia. *In* Narasimhaiah, C. D. ed. Awakened conscience p275-83

Herbs

Therapeutic use
See Materia medica, Vegetable

Hercules
Røstvig, M. S. Tom Jones and the choice of Hercules. *In* Røstvig, M. S. ed. Fair forms p147-77
See also Heracles

Hercules in literature
Coates, J. 'The choice of Hercules' in 'Antony and Cleopatra.' *In* Shakespeare survey v31 p45-52
Pavese, C. The new Heracles poem of Pindar. *In* Harvard Studies in classical philology v72 p47-88

Herder, Johann Gottfried von

About
Noel, T. Herder and the romantic turn. *In* Noel, T. Theories of the fable in the eighteenth century p122-39

Herders. See Gauchos

Hereditary diseases. See Medical genetics

Hereditary succession. See Inheritance and succession

Heredity
Blau, J. L. Science and social progress. *In* Philosophy and the civilizing arts p166-77
Burkhardt, R. W. Closing the door on Lord Morton's mare: the rise and fall of telegony. *In* Studies in history of biology v3 p 1-21
MacKenzie, D. and Barnes, B. Scientific judgment: the biometry-Mendelism controversy. *In* Barnes, B. and Shapin, S. eds. Natural order p191-210
Ravin, A. W. The gene as catalyst; the gene as organism. *In* Studies in history of biology v 1 p 1-45
See also Consanguinity; Eugenics; Evolution; Mendel's law; Natural selection; Nature and nurture; Population genetics

Heredity, Human. See Human genetics

Heredity and environment. See Nature and nurture

Heredity of acquired characters. See Inheritance of acquired characters

Heredity of disease. See Medical genetics

Hereferth, Bp. of Worcester. See Werferth, Bp. of Worcester

Heresies and heretics

Early church, ca. 30-600
See Manichaeism

Middle Ages, 600-1500
Lerner, R. E. An "Angel of Philadelphia" in the reign of Philip the Fair: the case of Guiard of Cressonessart. *In* Order and innovation in the Middle Ages p343-64

Hergenhan, Laurie T.
An Australian tragedy: Xavier Herbert's Poor fellow my country. *In* Hamilton, K. G. ed. Studies in the recent Australian novel p29-60

English publication of Australian novels in the nineteenth century: the case of His natural life. *In* Bards, bohemians, and bookmen p56-71

Hergesheimer, Joseph

About individual works
Java Head
McCallum, J D. Introduction to Java Head by Joseph Hergesheimer. *In* Praise from famous men: an anthology of introductions p94-103

Hérier, Thomas

About
Lemay, E. H. Thomas Hérier, a country surgeon outside Angoulême at the end of the XVIIIth century: a contribution to social history. *In* Branca, P. ed. The medicine show p229-42

Herity, Michael
The High Island hermitage. *In* Harmon, M. ed. Richard Murphy: poet of two traditions p52-69

Herlihy, David
Computer-assisted analysis of the statistical documents of medieval society. *In* Powell, J. M. ed. Medieval studies p185-211

The distribution of wealth in a Renaissance community: Florence 1427. *In* Towns in societies p131-57

Family and property in Renaissance Florence. *In* The Medieval city p 3-24

The generation in medieval history. *In* Viator: medieval and Renaissance studies v5 p347-64

Land, family, and women in continental Europe, 701-1200. *In* Stuard, S. M. ed. Women in medieval society p13-45

Medieval children. *In* Essays on medieval civilization p109-41

The medieval marriage market. *In* Medieval and Renaissance studies [1974] p3-27

Herlin, Helena. See Boalt, G. jt. auth.

Hermalin, Albert I.
Empirical research in Taiwan on factors underlying differences in fertility. *In* Economic factors in population growth p243-66

Herman, Josef
The modern artist in modern society. *In* Greenhalgh, M. and Megaw, J. V. S. eds. Art in society p121-30

The painter and literature. *In* English Association. Essays and studies, 1977 p70-72

Herman, Simon N.
A response to Zvi Yaron. *In* Modern Jewish ethics p243-47

Hermandad de la Caridad, Seville. See Seville. La Caridad (Church)

Hermann, Hanus
A prisoner's perspective. *In* Progress in penal reform p209-20

Hermas (Apostolic Father)
Bogdanos, T. "The Shepherd of Hermas" and the development of medieval visionary allegory. *In* Viator: medieval and Renaissance studies v8 p33-46

Hermassi, Karen Chagi
Polity and theater in historical perspective
Contents
"The interim reading of life"
The play within the play
Political education through tragedy
The political vocation of theatre
Power without love
Reclaiming the state
Reconstituting the audience
Theatre as the city of man
Theatre of political memory
Theatron, polis, and Thanatos
What theatre means
Workable pictures of the world

Hermeneutics
Bauman, Z. Introduction: The challenge of hermeneutics. *In* Bauman, Z. Hermeneutics and social science p7-22

Bauman, Z. Understanding as expansion of the form of life. *In* Bauman, Z. Hermeneutics and social science p194-224

Beardsley, M. C. The testability of an interpretation; excerpt from "The possibility of criticism." *In* Margolis, J. Z. ed. Philosophy looks at the arts p370-86

Bonati, F. M. Hermeneutic criticism and the description of form. *In* Valdés, M. J. and Miller, O. J. eds. Interpretation of narrative p78-99

Brown, N. O. On interpretation. *In* Evolution of consciousness p34-41

Cioffi, F. Intention and interpretation in criticism. *In* Margolis, J. Z. ed. Philosophy looks at the arts p307-24

Also in On literary intention p55-73

Cohen, R. On a shift in the concept of interpretation. *In* Young, T. D. ed. The New Criticism and after p61-79

Coomaraswamy, A. K. Nirukta=hermeneia. *In* Coomaraswamy, A. K. Selected papers v2 p256-63

Gadamer, H. G. The historicity of understanding as hermeneutic principle; excerpt from "Truth and method." *In* Murray, M. E. ed. Heidegger and modern philosophy p161-83

Hernadi, P. So what? How so? and the form that matters. *in* Valdés, M. J. and Miller, O. J. eds. Interpretation of narrative p167-73

Hirsch, E. D. In defense of the author; excerpt from "Validity in interpretation." *In* On literary intention p87-103

Hirsch, E. D. Objective interpretation. *In* On literary intention p26-54

Hirsch, E. D. Three dimensions of hermeneutics. *In* On literary intention p194-209

Holland, N. N. How can Dr. Johnson's remarks on Cordelia's death add to my own response? *In* Hartman, G. H. ed. Psychoanalysis and the question of the text p18-44

Hermeneutics—*Continued*

Hough, G. G. An eighth type of ambiguity. *In* Hough, G. G. Selected essays p23-45

Also in On literary intention p222-41

Margolin, U. Conclusion: literary structuralism and hermeneutics in significant convergence, 1976. *In* Valdés, M. J. and Miller, I. J. eds. Interpretation of narrative p177-85

Mazzeo, J. A. Interpretation and its occasions. *in* Mazzeo, J. A. Varieties of interpretation p 1-25

Mazzeo, J. A. Interpretation, humanistic culture, and cultural change. *In* Mazzeo, J. A. Varieties of interpretation p95-128

Mazzeo, J. A. New wine in old bottles: reflections on historicity and the problem of allegory. *In* Mazzeo, J. A. Varieties of interpretation p47-69

Mazzeo, J. A. The Platonic debate over myth, truth, and virtue. *In* Mazzeo, J. A. Varieties of interpretation p71-94

Mazzeo, J. A. Style as interpretation. *In* Mazzeo, J. A. Varieties of interpretation p27-45

Misgeld, D. Critical theory and hermeneutics: the debate between Habermas and Gadamer. *In* O'Neill, J. ed. On critical theory p164-83

Morris, W. A. Toward a literary hermeneutics. *In* Morris, W. A. Friday's footprint p188-225

Ricoeur, P. The task of hermeneutics. *In* Murray, M. E. ed. Heidegger and modern philosophy p141-60

Roma, E. The scope of the intentional fallacy. *In* On literary intention p74-86

Schwartz, M. M. Critic, define thyself. *In* Hartman, G. H. ed. Psychoanalysis and the question of the text p 1-17

Skinner, Q. Motives, intentions and the interpretation of texts. *In* On literary intention p210-21

Vance, E. Pas de trois: narrative, herneneutics, and structure in medieval poetics. *In* Valdés, M. J. and Miller, O. J. eds. Interpretation of narrative p118-34

Wimsattt, W. K. Genesis: an argument resumed. *In* Wimsatt, W. K. Day of the leopards p11-39

History

Bauman, Z. The rise of hermeneutics. *In* Bauman, Z. Hermeneutics and social science p23-47

Hermeneutics, Biblical. See Bible—Hermeneutics

Hermens, Ferdinand A.

Return to democratic government. *In* The Year book of world affairs, 1978 p191-207

Hermes. See Mercurius

Hermetic art and philosophy. See Alchemy; Occult sciences

Hermitages

Ireland—High Island

Herity, M. The High Island hermitage. *In* Harmon, M. ed. Richard Murphy: poet of two traditions p52-69

Hernadi, Paul

So what? How so? and the form that matters. *In* Valdés, M. J. and Miller, O. J. eds. Interpretation of narrative p167-73

Hernández, Luisa Josefina

About

Knowles, J. K. Louisa Josefina Hernández: the labyrinth of form. *In* Lyday, L. F. and Woodyard, G. W. eds. Dramatists in revolt p133-45

Herod in literature

Weimann, R. The mystery cycles. *In* Weimann, R. Shakespeare and the popular tradition in the theater: studies in the social dimension of dramatic form and function p49-97

Herodas. See Herondas

Herodianus

About individual works

History of the Roman Empire from the death of Marcus Aurelius to the accession of Gordian III

Bowersock, G. W. Herodian and Elagabalus. *In* Yale classical studies v24 p229-36

Herodotus

About

Havelock, E. A. The justice of Herodotus. *In* Havelock, E. A. The Greek concept of justice p296-307

About individual works

The histories of Herodotus (Book I)

Shell, M. The Ring of Gyges. *In* Shell, M. The economy of literature p11-62

The histories of Herodotus (Book IV)

Armayor, O. K. Did Herodotus ever go to the Black Sea? *In* Harvard Studies in classical philology v82 p45-62

History of the Persian wars

Balcer, J. M. The date of Herodotus IV.1: Darius' Scythian expedition. *In* Harvard Studies in classical philology v76 p99-132

Stahl, H. P. Learning through suffering? Croesus' conversations in the history of Herodotus. *In* Yale classical studies v24 p 1-36

Heroes

Knights, B. The hero as man of letters: Thomas Carlyle. *In* Knights, B. The idea of the clerisy in the nineteenth century p72-99

Swanton, M. Heroes, heroism and heroic literature. *In* English Association. Essays and studies, 1977 p 1-21

Heroes in art

Zupnick, I. L. Saint Sebastian. *In* Concepts of the hero in the Middle Ages and the Renaissance p239-67

Heroes in literature

Arestad, S. The Ibsen hero. *In* The Hero in Scandinavian literature p15-37

Bersani, L. The paranoid hero in Stendhal. *In* Bersani, L. A future for Astyanax p106-27

Bloomfield, M. W. The problem of the hero in the later medieval period. *In* Concepts of the hero in the Middle Ages and the Renaissance p27-48

Bolgar, R. R. Hero or anti-hero? *In* Concepts of the hero in the Middle Ages and the Renaissance p120-46

Donahue, C. Potlatch and charity: notes on the heroic in Beowulf. *In* Anglo-Saxon poetry: essays in appreciation p23-40

Heroes in literature—*Continued*

Eekman, T. A. The narrator and the hero in Chekhov's prose. *In* California Slavic studies v8 p93-129

Grunebaum, G. E. von. The hero in medieval Arabic prose. *In* Concepts of the hero in the Middle Ages and the Renaissance p83-100

Handy, W. J. The Malamud hero: a quest for existence. *In* The Fiction of Bernard Malamud p65-86

Hays, P. L. Malamud's Yiddish accented medieval stories. *In* The Fiction of Bernard Malamud p87-96

Hunter, G. K. The heroism of Hamlet. *In* Hunter, G. K. Dramatic identities and cultural tradition p230-50

Huppé, B. F. The concept of the hero in the early Middle Ages. *In* Concepts of the hero in the Middle Ages and the Renaissance p 1-26

Leyerle, J. The game and play of hero. *In* Concepts of the hero in the Middle Ages and the Renaissance p49-82

Linnér, S. The hero in Swedish fiction after World War II. *In* The Hero in Scandinavian literature p107-23

MacKillop, J. J. Finn MacCool: the hero and the anti-hero in Irish folk tradition. *In* Casey, D. J. and Rhodes, R. E. eds. Views of the Irish peasantry, 1800-1916 p86-106

Manheim, L. F. Dickens' heroes, heroes, and heroids. *In* Dickens Studies Annual v5 p 1-22

Mathewson, R. W. The hero and the heritage. *In* **Mathewson, R. W. The positive hero in Russian literature p13-24**

Mathewson, R. W. Rebuttal II: Hamlet and Don Quixote. *In* Mathewson, R. W. The positive hero in Russian literature p97-112

Messina, J. The heroic image in the Last instructions to a painter. *In* Friedenreich, K. ed. Tercentenary essays in honor of Andrew Marvell p297-310

Rutherford, A. The Christian as hero: Waugh's Sword of honour. *In* Rutherford, A. The literature of war p113-34

Rutherford, A. The intellectual as hero: Lawrence of Arabia. *In* Rutherford, A. The literature of war p38-63

Rutherford, A. Introduction. *In* Rutherford, A. The literature of war p 1-10

Rutherford, A. The spy as hero: Le Carré and the Cold War. *In* Rutherford, A. The literature of war p135-56

Rutherford, A. The subaltern as hero: Kipling and frontier war. *In* Rutherford, A. The literature of war p11-37

Showalter, E. Feminine heroes: the woman's man. *In* Showalter, E. A literature of their own p133-52

Spacks, P. A. M. Early fiction and the frightened male. *In* Spilka, M. ed. Towards a poetics of fiction p255-65

Steadman, J. M. The arming of an archetype. *In* Concepts of the hero in the Middle Ages and the Renaissance p147-96

Swanton, M. Heroes, heroism and heroic literature. *In* English Association. Essays and studies, 1977 p 1-21

Torrance, R. M. Aberrant hidalgo. *In* Torrance, R. M. The comic hero p144-76

Torrance, R. M. Afterword: in lieu of conclusion. *In* Torrance, R. M. The comic hero p274-77

Torrance, R. M. Beggar man, king. *In* Torrance, R. M. The comic hero p12-36

Torrance, R. M. Bondservant and beast of burden. *In* Torrance, R. M. The comic hero p60-82

Torrance, R. M. Insouciant lover and unsatiable stumblebums. *In* Torrance, R. M. The comic hero p206-39

Torrance, R. M. Introduction: comic butt and comic hero. *In* Torrance, R. M. The comic hero p 1-11

Torrance, R. M. Jackanapes in the highest. *In* Torrance, R. M. The comic hero p37-59

Torrance, R. M. Monarch of make-believe. *In* Torrance, R. M. The comic hero p111-43

Torrance, R. M. Moral rake and masterful lackey. *In* Torrance, R. M. The comic hero p177-205

Torrance, R. M. Ulysses and Hermes in modern times. *In* Torrance, R. M. The comic hero p240-73

Wardropper, B. W. The epic hero superseded. *In* Concepts of the hero in the Middle Ages and the Renaissance p197-221

Heroic fantasy. See Fantastic fiction

Heroic poetry. See Epic poetry

Heroin

Kaplan, J. A primer on heroin. *In* Stanford legal essays p277-302

Heroines. See Women in literature

Heroism. See Courage; Heroes

Heron, Patrick

The shape of colour. *In* Concerning contemporary art p154-80

About

Heron, P. The shape of colour. *In* Concerning contemporary art p154-80

Herondas

About individual works

Mime V (The jealous woman)

Gerber, D. E. Herodas 5.1. *In* Harvard Studies in classical philology v82 p161-65

Herr, Richard

Spain. *In* Spring, D. ed. European landed elites in the nineteenth century p98-126

Herrera, Francisco, the Younger

About

Brown, J. Pendrawings by Herrera the Younger. *In* Enggass, R. C. and Stokstad, M. eds. Hortus imaginum p129-38

Herrick, Robert, 1591-1674

About

Guibbory, A. "No lust theres like to poetry": Herrick's passion for poetry. *In* Rollin, R. B. and Patrick, J. M. eds. "Trust to good verses": Herrick tercentenary essays p79-87

Ishii, S. Herrick and Japanese classical poetry: a comparison. *In* Rollin, R. B. and Patrick, J. M. eds. "Trust to good verses": Herrick tercentenary essays p187-96

Manlove, C. N. Jonson and Herrick. *In* Manlove, C. N. Literature and reality, 1600-1800 p16-29

Herrick, Robert, 1591-1674—*Continued*

Tillman, J. S. Herrick's Georgic encomia. *In* Rollin, R. B. and Patrick, J. M. eds. "Trust to good verses": Herrick tercentenary essays p149-57

About individual works
Hesperides

Cain, T. G. S. "Times trans-shifting": Herrick in meditation. *In* Rollin, R. B. and Patrick, J. M. eds. "Trust to good verses": Herrick tercentenary essays p103-23

Farmer, N. K. Herrick's Hesperidean garden: ut pictura poesis applied. *In* Rollin, R. B. and Patrick, J. M. eds. "Trust to good verses": Herrick tercentenary essays p15-51

Marlborough, H. Herrick's epigrams of praise. *In* Rollin, R. B. and Patrick, J. M. eds. "Trust to good verses": Herrick tercentenary essays p159-69

Murphy, A. J. Robert Herrick: the self-conscious critic in Hesperides. *In* Rollin, R. B. and Patrick, J. M. eds. "Trust to good verses": Herrick tercentenary essays p53-63

Shawcross, J. T. The names of Herrick's mistresses in Hesperides. *In* Rollin, R. B. and Patrick, J. M. eds. "Trust to good verses": Herrick tercentenary essays p89-102

Summers, C. J. Herrick's political poetry: the strategies of his art. *In* Rollin, R. B. and Patrick, J. M. eds. "Trust to good verses": Herrick tercentenary essays p171-83

Aesthetics

Murphy, A. J. Robert Herrick: the self-conscious critic in Hesperides. *In* Rollin, R. B. and Patrick, J. M. eds. "Trust to good verses": Herrick tercentenary essays p53-63

Appreciation

Patrick, J. M. "Poetry perpetuates the poet": Richard James and the growth of Herrick's reputation. *In* Rollin, R. B. and Patrick, J. M. eds. "Trust to good verses": Herrick tercentenary essays p221-34

Bibliography

Pebworth, T. L. Selected and annotated bibliography. *In* Rollin, R. B. and Patrick, J. M. eds. "Trust to good verses": Herrick tercentenary essays p237-39

Criticism and interpretation

Rollin, R. B. Sweet numbers and sour readers: trends and perspectives in Herrick criticism. *In* Rollin, R. B. and Patrick, J. M. eds. "Trust to good verses": Herrick tercentenary essays p3-11

Religion and ethics

Mollenkott, V. R. Herrick and the cleansing of perception. *In* Rollin, R. B. and Patrick, J. M. eds. "Trust to good verses": Herrick tercentenary essays p197-209

Oram, W. A. Herrick's use of sacred materials. *In* Rollin, R. B. and Patrick, J. M. eds. "Trust to good verses": Herrick tercentenary essays p211-18

Songs and music

Elmore, A. E. Herrick and the poetry of song. *In* Rollin, R. B. and Patrick, J. M. eds. "Trust to good verses": Herrick tercentenary essays p65-75

Sources

Braden, G. Herrick's classical quotations. *In* Rollin, R. B. and Patrick, J. M. eds. "Trust to good verses": Herrick tercentenary essays p127-47

Oram, W. A. Herrick's use of sacred materials *In* Rollin, R. B. and Patrick, J. M. eds. "Trust to good verses": Herrick tercentenary essays p211-18

Style
See Herrick, Robert—Technique

Technique

Elmore, A. E. Herrick and the poetry of song. *In* Rollin, R. B. and Patrick, J. M. eds. "Trust to good verses": Herrick tercentenary essays p65-75

Farmer, N. K. Herrick's Hesperidean garden: ut pictura poesis applied. *In* Rollin, R. B. and Patrick, J. M. eds. "Trust to good verses": Herrick tercentenary essays p15-51

Herrick, Robert, in fiction, drama, poetry, etc.

Patrick, J. M. "Poetry perpetuates the poet": Richard James and the growth of Herrick's reputation. *In* Rollin, R. B. and Patrick, J. M. eds. "Trust to good verses": Herrick tercentenary essays p221-34

Herring, George Cyril

The Cold War. *in* Encyclopedia of American foreign policy p111-23

Herring-fisheries

History

Unger, R. W. The Netherlands herring fishery in the late Middle Ages: the false legend of Willem Beukels of Biervliet. *In* Viator: medieval and Renaissance studies v9 p335-56

Herrmann, Ariel

The biter: a late Hellenistic astragal player. *In* Studies in classical art and archaeology p163-73

Herrmann, Joachim

The German prosecutor. *In* Davis, K. C. Discretionary justice in Europe and America p16-74

Herrnhuter. See Bohemian Brethren

Herschel, John Frederick William

About individual works
A preliminary discourse on the study of natural philosophy

Wilson, D. B. Concepts of physical nature: John Herschel to Karl Pearson. *In* Knoepflmacher, U. C. and Tennyson, G. B. eds. Nature and the Victorian imagination p201-15

Herschel, Sir William

About

Hoskin, M. A. The English background to the cosmology of Wright and Herschel. *In* Cosmology, history, and theology p219-31

Hersey, George L.

Marsilio Ficino's cosmic temple. *In* Collaboration in Italian Renaissance art p91-97

Hershbell, Jackson P.

The ancient telegraph: war and literacy. *In* Havelock, E. A. and Hershbell, J. P. eds. Communication arts in the ancient world p81-92

Hershberg, Theodore. See Laurie, B. jt. auth.

Hershel, Parker. See Higgins, B. jt. auth.

Herter, Hans
The problematic mention of Hippocrates in Plato's Phaedrus. *In* Illinois classical studies, v 1 1976 p22-42

Hertz, Heinrich Rudolph

About
D'Agostino, S. Hertz's researches on electromagnetic waves. *In* Historical studies in the physical science v6 p261-324

Hertz, Neil
The notion of blockage in the literature of the sublime. *In* Hartman, G. H. ed. Psychoanalysis and the question of the text p62-85

Hertzberg, Arthur
Anti-semitism and Jewish uniqueness: ancient and contemporary. *In* Tradition and change in Jewish experience p211-25

Hertzen, Aleksandr Ivanovich

About
Berlin, Sir I. Herzen and Bakunin on individual liberty. *In* Berlin, Sir I. Russian thinkers p82-113

Berlin, Sir I. A remarkable decade: Alexander Herzen. *In* Berlin, Sir I. Russian thinkers p186-209

Partridge, M. Alexander Herzen: his last phase. *In* Essays in honour of E. H. Carr p36-56

About individual works
My past and thoughts
Berger, J. Alexander Herzen. *In* Berger, J. The look of things p80-86

Hervey, John Hervey, Baron. See Montagu, Lady M. P. W., jt. auth.

Herzen, Alexander. See Hertzen, Aleksandr Ivanovich

Herzfelde, Helmut. See Heartfield, John

Herzl, Theodor

About
Arendt, H. Herzl and Lazare. *In* Arendt, H. The Jew as pariah: Jewish identity and politics in the modern age p125-30

Arendt, H. The Jewish state: fifty years after. *In* Arendt, H. The Jew as pariah: Jewish identity and politics in the modern age p164-77

Herzog, Frederick
Reorientation in theology: listening to Black theology. *In* The Context of contemporary theology p225-41

Hesburgh, Theodore Martin
American aspirations and the grounds of hope. *In* An Almost chosen people p131-46

The Hesburgh papers
Contents
A case study: universities and government interact in crisis
The Catholic university and freedom
The challenges of Christian higher education
The changing face of Catholic higher education
The civil rights revolution: from confrontation to education
Education in the year 2000
The generation gap
In defense of the younger generation
The lessons of the student revolution
The moral purpose of higher education
New focus for Catholic higher education in the 1970s
The past and present of American higher education
The post-Vatican II Church
Problems and opportunities on a very interdependent planet
Science and technology in modern perspective
Social science in an age of social revolution
The university president
The vision of the Catholic university in the world of today

Making prophecies of our goals. *In* The Third century p188-91

Heschel, Abraham Joshua

About
Kaufman, W. E. Abraham J. Heschel: the meaning beyond mystery. *In* Kaufman, W. E. Contemporary Jewish philosophies p142-74

Heseltine, Harry P.
"Cyrus Brown of Sydney Town": Christopher Brennan and Dowell O'Reilly. *In* Bards, bohemians, and bookmen p136-52

Hesiod. See Hesiodus

Hesiodus

About
Havelock, E. A. The justice of Hesiod: an essay in detection. *In* Havelock, E. A. The Greek concept of justice p193-217

About individual works
Erga
Pucci, P. True and false discourse in Hesiod. *In* Poetry and poetics from ancient Greece to the Renaissance p29-55

Theogony
Minton, W. W. The frequency and structuring of traditional formulas in Hesiod's Theogony. *In* Harvard Studies in classical philology v79 p25-54

Pucci, P. True and false discourse in Hesiod. *In* Poetry and poetics from ancient Greece to the Renaissance p29-55

Works and days
Beye, C. R. The rhythm of Hesiod's Works and days. *In* Harvard Studies in classical philology p23-43

Heslep, Robert D.
Preferential treatment in admitting racial minority students. *In* Social justice & preferential treatment p33-51

Hess, David W.
Pioneering as ecological process: a model and test case of frontier adaptation. *In* The Frontier v2 p123-51

Hess, Gary R.
The forgotten Asian Americans: the East Indian community in the United States. *In* The Asian American: the historical experience p157-77

Hess, John D.
Godfather II: a deal Coppola couldn't refuse. *In* Nichols, B. ed. Movies and methods p81-90

Hesse, Hermann

About individual works
The journey to the East

Middleton, J. C. Hermann Hesse's Morgenlandfahrt. *In* Middleton, J. C. Bolshevism in art p239-51

Magister Ludi

Middleton, J. C. An enigma transfigured in Hermann Hesse's Glasperlenspiel. *In* Middleton, J. C. Bolshevism in art p233-38

Swales, M. Hesse: The glass bead game (1943). *In* Swales, M. The German Bildungsroman from Wieland to Hesse p129-45

Hesse, Mary B.
Theory and value in the social sciences. *In* Hookway, C. and Pettit, P. eds. Action and interpretation p 1-16

Hester, Al
International information flow. *In* Fischer, H. D. and Merrill, J. C. eds. International and intercultural communication p242-50

Hester, Marcus
The structure of tragedy and the art of painting. *In* O'Flaherty, J. C.; Sellner, T. F. and Helm, R. M. eds. Studies in Nietzsche and the classical tradition p71-88

Hewavitarana, Don David. See Dharmapala, Anagarika

Hewett, Cecil Alec
Anglo-Saxon carpentry. *In* Anglo-Saxon England 7 p205-29

Hewett, Dorothy

About individual works
The chapel perilous (or The perilous adventures of Sally Banner), a play

Gostand, R. Quest or question? Perilous journey to the chapel. *In* Bards, bohemians, and bookmen p289-304

Hewison, Paul
Theology in the plays. *In* Prentki, T. ed. Francis Warner p53-66

Hewlett, Sylvia Ann
Human rights and economic realities in developing nations. *In* Farer, T. J. ed. The future of the inter-American system p83-114

Hexter, Jack H.
On historians

Contents

Carl Becker and historical relativism
Fernand Braudel and the monde braudellien . . .
The historical method of Christopher Hill
Lawrence Stone and the English aristocracy
Republic, virtue, liberty, and the political universe of J. G. A. Pocock
Wallace K. Ferguson and Hiram Hayden [sic]: The Renaissance again—and again

Heymann, Frederick Gotthold
The role of the Bohemian cities during and after the Hussite revolution. *In* Király, B. K. ed. Tolerance and movements of religious dissent in Eastern Europe p27-41

Heymann, Hans
'Self-reliance' revisited: China's technology dilemma. *In* China's changing role in the world economy p15-35

Heymann, Philip B. and Weinberg, Martha Wagner
The paradox of power: mayoral leadership on charter reform in Boston. *In* Burnham, W. D. and Weinberg, M. W. eds. American politics and public policy p280-303

Heywood, Annemarie
The fox's dance: the staging of Soyinka's plays. *In* African literature today no. 8: Drama in Africa p42-51

Heywood, Christopher
Introduction: The quest for identity. *In* Heywood, C. ed. Aspects of South African literature p vii-xv

Olive Schreiner's influence on George Moore and D. H. Lawrence. *In* Heywood, C. ed. Aspects of South African literature p42-53

Heywood, John

About

Altman, J. B. The method staged: debate plays by Heywood and Rastell. *In* Altman, J. B. The Tudor play of mind p107-29

Heywood, Oliver

About

Love, H. Preacher and publisher: Oliver Heywood and Thomas Parkhurst. *In* Virginia. University. Bibliographical Society. Studies in bibliography v31 p227-35

Heywood, Rosalind
Illusion—or what? *In* Life after death p203-37

Heywood, Thomas

About individual works
The English traveller

Stilling, R. Thomas Heywood. *In* Stilling, R. Love and death in Renaissance tragedy p173-96

The exemplary lives and memorable acts of nine of the most worthy women of the world

Waith, E. M. Heywood's women worthies. *In* Concepts of the hero in the Middle Ages and the Renaissance p222-38

A woman killed with kindness

Ornstein, R. Bourgeois morality and dramatic convention in A woman killed with kindness. *In* English Renaissance drama p128-41

Stilling, R. Thomas Heywood. *In* Stilling, R. Love and death in Renaissance tragedy p173-96

Ure, P. Marriage and the domestic drama in Heywood and Ford. *In* Ure, P. Elizabethan and Jacobean drama p145-65

Bibliography

Chang, J. S. M. J. and Hammersmith, J. P. Thomas Heywood. *In* Logan, T. P. and Smith, D. S. eds. The popular school p105-21

Hibbard, Don J. See Whetmore, E. jt. auth.
Hibbard, George Richard
Adumbrations of 'The tempest' in 'A midsummer night's dream.' *In* Shakespeare survey v31 p77-83

'Henry IV' and 'Hamlet.' *In* Shakespeare survey 30 p 1-12

Love, marriage and money in Shakespeare's theatre and Shakespeare's England. *In* The Elizabethan theatre, VI p134-55

Hibberd, Jack

About

Sykes, A. Jack Hibberd and the New Wave drama. *In* Bards, bohemians, and bookmen p305-19

Hibbert, A. B.
The origins of the medieval town patriciate. *In* Towns in societies p91-104

Hibbs, Albert Roach
An engineer's approach to the ethics of research. *In* Hook, S.; Kurtz, P. and Todorovich, M. eds. The ethics of teaching and scientific research p179-86

About individual works
An engineer's approach to the ethics of research

Hook, S. Rejoinder: Dr Hibbs and the ethics of discussion. *In* Hook, S.; Kurtz, P. and Todorovich, M. eds. The ethics of teaching and scientific research p187-90

Hick, John H.
Biology and the soul; excerpt from "Biology and the soul." *In* Donnelly, J. P. ed. Language, metaphysics, and death p150-62

Christian theology and inter-religious dialogue. *In* The Frontiers of human knowledge p 1-14

Hickey, Tom, and Hodgson, James W.
Contextual and developmental issues in the evaluation of adult learning: training in applied gerontology as an example. *In* Gubrium, J. F. ed. Late life p235-55

Hicks, George L. and Handler, Mark J.
Ethnicity, public policy, and anthropologists. *in* Eddy, E. M. and Partridge, W. L. eds. Applied anthropology in America p292-325

Hieatt, Constance B.
The rhythm of the alliterative long line. *In* Chaucer and Middle English studies in honour of Rossell Hope Robbins p119-30

Hiebert, Erwin N.
An appraisal of the work of Ernst Mach: scientist-historian-philosopher. *In* Motion and time, space and matter p360-89

Hierocles, Sossianus, proconsul of Bithynia

About

Barnes, T. D. Sossianus Hierocles and the antecedents of the "Great persecution." *In* Harvard Studies in classical philology v80 p239-52

Hieroglyphics, Maya. See Mayas—Writing

Hieroglyphics, Mexican. See Indians of Mexico—Writing

Hieronymus, Saint

About

Abbott, K. M. Satira and satiricus in late Latin. *In* Illinois classical studies v4, 1979 p192-99

Hiesinger, Ulrich W.
Three images of the god Mên. *In* Harvard Studies in classical philology v71 p303-10

Higden, Ralph. See Higden, Ranulf

Higden, Ranulf

About individual works
The Ars componendi sermones of Ranulph Higden

Jennings, M. The preacher's rhetoric: The Ars componendi sermones of Ranulph Higden. *In* Murphy, J. J. ed. Medieval eloquence p112-26

Higdon, David Leon
Graham Greene's second thoughts: the text of The heart of the matter. *In* Virginia. University. Bibliographical Society. Studies in bibliography v30 p249-56

See also Davis, K. W. jt. auth.

About individual works
Graham Greene's second thoughts: the text of The heart of the matter

Stratford, P. Second thoughts on "Graham Greene's second thoughts": the five texts of The heart of the matter. *In* Virginia. University. Bibliographical Society. Studies in bibliography v31 p263-66

Higginbotham, Don
James Iredell and the origins of American Federalism. *In* Suggs, G. G. ed. Perspectives on the American Revolution p99-115

Military leadership in the American Revolution. *In* Library of Congress Symposia on the American Revolution, 3d, 1974. Leadership in the American Revolution p91-111

Higgins, Brian, and Parker, Hershel
The flawed grandeur of Melville's Pierre. *In* Pullin, F. ed. New perspectives on Melville p162-96

Higgins, Ian
Francis Ponge. *In* Cardinal, R. ed. Sensibility and creation p183-203

Higgins, Norman
The Cambridge Arts Theatre. *In* Keynes, M. ed. Essays on John Maynard Keynes p272-79

Higgins, Reynold Alleyne
Jewellery. *In* Strong, D. E. and Brown, D. eds. Roman crafts p53-62

Terracottas. *In* Strong, D. E. and Brown, D. eds. Roman crafts p105-09

Higgins, William Robert
Charleston: terminus and entrepôt of the colonial slave trade. *In* Kilson, M. L. and Rotberg, R. I. eds. The African diaspora p114-31

Higgs, David
The Portuguese church. *In* Callahan, W. J. and Higgs, D. eds. Church and society in Catholic Europe of the eighteenth century p51-65

Higgs, Elton D.
The path to involvement: the centrality of the Dreamer in Piers Plowman. *In* Tulane Studies in English v21 p 1-34

Post-creation freedom in The tempest. *In* Shakespeare's late plays p200-12

Higgs, Robert
Race and economy in the South, 1890-1950. *In* The Age of segregation: race relations in the South, 1890-1945 p89-116

High Renaissance art. See Art, Renaissance —High Renaissance

High school education. See Education. Secondary

High school seniors

Sacks, H. S. "Bloody Monday": the crisis of the high school seniors. *In* Hurdles p10-47

High school students. See High school seniors

High school teaching

United States

Merideth, R. "It's a small world": high school, American culture studies, and cultural revolution. *In* Luedtke, L. S. ed. The study of American culture p279-322

High seas, Jurisdiction over. See War, Maritime (International law)

High society. See Upper classes

Higham, John

Introduction: the forms of ethnic leadership. *In* Ethnic leadership in America p 1-18

The matrix of specialization. *In* Oleson, A. and Voss, J. eds. The organization of knowledge in modern America, 1860-1920 p3-18

Higher education. See Education, Higher

Higher education and state

Murphy, T. P. and Knipe, E. A. The federal government and urban higher education. *In* Murphy, T. P. ed. Universities in the urban crisis p353-79

Shils, E. A. Governments and universities. *In* Hook, S.; Kurtz, P. W. and Todorovitch, M. eds. The university and the state: what role for government in higher education? p177-204

See also Federal aid to higher education

United States

Anderson, G. L. and Mortimer, K. P. Governance and control of tomorrow's university: whose values? *In* Land-grant universities and their continuing challenge p326-49

Baumann, F. Is the university a special case? *In* Hook, S.; Kurtz, P. W. and Todorovich, M. eds. The university and the state: what role for government in higher education? p237-44

Bork, R. H. The limits of governmental regulation. *In* Hook, S.; Kurtz, P. W. and Todorovich, M. eds. The university and the state: what role for government in higher education? p169-75

Chambers, C. M. An institutional view of the costs of government regulation. *In* Hook, S.; Kurtz, P. W. and Todorovich, M. eds. The university and the state: what role for government in higher education? p123-32

Goldwin, R. A. How "different" are universities? *In* Hook, S.; Kurtz, P. W. and Todorovich, M. eds. The university and the state: what role for government in higher education? p215-20

Hook, S. The state and higher education. *In* Hook, S.; Kurtz, P. W. and Todorovich, M. eds. The university and the state: what role for government in higher education? p227-36

Hornig, D. F. The costs of government regulation. *In* Hook, S.; Kurtz, P. W. and Todorovich, M. eds. The university and the state: what role for government in higher education? p103-13

Ikenberry, S. O. The public interest and institutional autonomy. *In* Land-grant universities and their continuing challenge p309-25

Lichtenstein, D. S. The alienated intellectual and government bureaucracy. *In* Hook, S.; Kurtz, P. W. and Todorovich, M. eds. The university and the state: what role for government in higher education? p249-64

McGill, W. J. Government regulation and academic freedom. *In* Hook, S.; Kurtz, P. W. and Todorovich, M. eds. The university and the state: what role for government in higher education? p139-54

Novotny, H. R. F. The New Class, and "Professor Bill." *In* Hook, S.; Kurtz, P. W. and Todorovich, M. eds. The university and the state: what role for government in higher education? p277-85

Searle, J. R. A more balanced view. *In* Hook, S.; Kurtz, P. W. and Todorovich, M. eds. The university and the state: what role for government in higher education? p205-13

Todorovich, M. Would a reorganized Federal Department of Education mean better higher education? *In* Hook, S.; Kurtz, P. W. and Todorovich, M. eds. The university and the state: what role for government in higher education? p265-75

Higher education of women

See also Professional education of women

United States

Hochschild, A. R. Inside the clockwork of male careers. *In* Women and the power to change p47-80

Howe, F. Women and the power to change. *In* Women and the power to change p127-71

Rich, A. C. Toward a woman-centered university. *In* Women and the power to change p 1-46

Highet, Gilbert

The immortal profession

Contents

Albert Schweitzer
The class of '64
Communication
Gilbert Murray
The illusion of progress
Jesus and his pupils
The liberal teacher
The need for renewal
The pleasure of learning
The scholarly life
Teaching college teachers how to teach

Speech and narrative in The Aeneid. *In* Harvard Studies in classical philology v78 p189-229

Highlands of Scotland in literature

Hart, F. R. Highlands of the humorists. *In* Hart, F. R. The Scottish novel p374-84

Hart, F. R. Jane Duncan and George Mackay Brown. *In* Hart, F. R. The Scottish novel p385-97

Hart, F. R. Late Victorian Celticisms. *In* Hart, F. R. The Scottish novel p336-47

Hart, F. R. Neil Gunn. *In* Hart, F. R. The Scottish novel p348-73

Hart, F. R. The tragedy of the Clearances. *In* Hart, F. R. The Scottish novel p325-35

Hightower, James Robert

Allusion in the poetry of T'ao Ch'ien. *In* Birch, C. ed. Studies in Chinese literary genres p108-32

Higman, Barry W.
African and Creole slave family patterns in Trinidad. *In* Crahan, M. E. and Knight, F. W. eds. Africa and the Caribbean p41-64

Higonnet, Patrice L. R.
Alexis de Tocqueville. *In* Abroad in America: Visitors to the new Nation, 1776-1914 p52-61

Hijacking of aircraft
Evans, A. E. Aircraft hijacking: what is being done. *In* International terrorism and political crimes p219-47

Hubbard, D. G. A glimmer of hope: a psychiatric perspective. *In* International terrorism and political crimes p27-32

Lee, A. International suppression of hijacking. *In* International terrorism and political crimes p248-56

Sundberg, J. W. F. Thinking the unthinkable or the case of Dr Tsironis. *In* International terrorism and political crimes p448-59

Hijaz. See Hejaz, Arabia

Hijmans, Benjamin Lodewijk
Athenodorus on the Categories and a pun on Athenodorus. *In* Kephalaion p105-14

Hikajat Potjoet Moehamat, Awareness of the past in the. Siegel, J. T. *In* Southeast Asian history and historiography p321-31

Hiking. See Mountaineering

Hildebrand, Bror Emil

About individual works
Anglosaxon coins in the Royal Swedish Cabinet of medals

Smart, V. Corrections to Hildebrand's corpus of Anglo-Saxon moneyers: from Cnut to Edward the Confessor. *In* Anglo-Saxon England 4 p155-70

Hildebrandt, Herbert
The community center in the life of a dying person with no family involvement. *In* Home care p215-22

Hildreth, Clifford, and Dent, Warren T.
An adjusted maximum likelihood estimator of autocorrelation in disturbances. *In* Econometrics and economic theory p3-25

Hill, Archibald A.
Constituent and pattern in poetry
Contents
Analogies, icons, and images
An analysis of The windhover: an experiment in method
Figurative structure and meaning: two poems by Emily Dickinson
Imagery and meaning: a passage from Lycidas and a poem by Blake
The locus of the literary work
Pippa's song: two attempts at structural criticism
Poetry and stylistics
Principles governing semantic parallels
A program for the definition of literature
Some points in the analysis of Keats's Ode on a Grecian urn
Toward a literary analysis
Two views of poetic language and meaning: the poem as cryptogram and as example of deviant grammar

Hill, Bennett D.
The Counts of Mortain and the origins of the Norman congregation of Savigny. *In* Order and innovation in the Middle Ages p237-

Hill, Christopher. See Hill, John Edward Christopher

Hill, Christopher R.
South Africa: the future of the liberal spirit. *In* Leftwich, A. ed. South Africa: economic growth and political change p343-57

Hill, Donald Routledge
Mechanical technology. *In* The Genius of Arab civilization p175-88

The role of the camel and the horse in the early Arab conquests. *In* War, technology and society in the Middle East p32-43

Hill, Dorothy Kent
Jupiter: variations on the theme of Olympian Zeus. *In* Studies in classical art and archaeology p247-50

Hill, Hamlin Lewis
Mark Twain. *In* American literary scholarship, 1973 p99-115

Mark Twain [another essay] *In* American literary scholarship, 1974 p75-85

Mark Twain [another essay] *In* American literary scholarship, 1975 p103-134

Hill, Howard H. Erskin-. See Erskin-Hill, Howard H.

Hill, James Newlin
Systems theory and the explanation of change. *In* Explanation of prehistoric change p59-103

Hill, John Edward Christopher
From Lollards to Levellers. *In* Rebels and their causes p49-67

About individual works
Change and continuity in seventeenth-century England

Hexter, J. H. The historical method of Christopher Hill. *In* Hexter, J. H. On historian p227-51

Milton and the English revolution
Wittreich, J. A. The new Milton criticism. *In* Review, v 1 1979 p123-64

Hill, John P. and Mönks, Franz J.
Overview and outcomes. *In* Adolescence and youth in prospect p 1-12

Some perspectives on adolescence in modern societies. *In* Adolescence and youth in prospect p28-78

Hill, John P. and others
Summary record and conclusions. *In* Adolescence and youth in prospect p13-27

Hill, Kathleen
Journeying with Glooscap. *In* Egoff, S. A. ed. One ocean touching p186-88

About
Hill, K. Journeying with Glooscap. *In* Egoff, S. A. ed. One ocean touching p186-88

Hill, Melvyn A.
The fictions of mankind and the stories of men. *In* Hannah Arendt: the recovery of the public world p275-300

Hill, R. F.
Critical studies. *In* Shakespeare survey 30 p181-90

Critical studies [another essay] *In* Shakespeare survey v31 p163-77

'The merchant of Venice' and the pattern of romantic comedy. *In* Shakespeare survey 28 p75-87

Hill, Robert C.
The United States and Latin America: looking ahead. *In* Prochnow, H. V. ed. Dilemmas facing the nation p238-47

Hill, Rosalind M. T.
Holy kings—the bane of seventh-century society. *In* Church, society and politics p39-43

Hill, Stuart. See Orr, D. W. jt. auth.

Hill, Thomas Dana
The æcerbot charm and its Christian user. *In* Anglo-Saxon England 6 p213-21

The fall of angels and man in the Old English Genesis B. *In* Anglo-Saxon poetry: essays in appreciation p279-90

Hill, Thomas Wright

About
Gorham, D. Victorian reform as a family business: the Hill family. *In* Wohl, A. S. ed. The Victorian family p119-47

Hill-Burnett, Jacquetta
Developing anthropological knowledge through application. *In* Eddy, E. M. and Partridge, W. L. eds. Applied anthropology in America p112-28

Hill family
Gorham, D. Victorian reform as a family business: the Hill family. *In* Wohl, A. S. ed. The Victorian family p119-47

Hillary, Sir Edmund
South Pole—continent of adventure. *In* The Frontiers of knowledge p269-94

Hillegas, Mark Robert
Victorian "extraterrestrials." *In* The Worlds of Victorian fiction p391-414

Hillerbrand, Hans Joachim
The popular dimension of the Reformation: an essay in methodology and historiography. *In* Medieval and Renaissance studies [1974] p55-86

Religious dissent and toleration: introductory reflections. *In* Király, B. K. ed. Tolerance and movements of religious dissent in Eastern Europe p 1-8

Hillers, Delbert Roy, and McCall, Marsh Howard
Homeric dictated texts: a reexamination of some Near Eastern evidence. *In* Harvard Studies in classical philology v80 p19-23

Hilles, Frederick Whiley
The hero as revolutionary: Godefroy Cavaignac. *In* Carlyle and his contemporaries p74-90

Hill-forts. See Fortification, Primitive

Hilliard, Sam Bowers
Antebellum interregional trade: the Mississippi River as an example. *In* Pattern and process p202-14

Antebellum tidewater rice culture in South Carolina and Georgia. *In* European settlement and development in North America: essays on geographical change in honour and memory of Andrew Hill Clark p91-115

Hillier, Bevis
The Victorian Crusoe. *In* The Saturday book 34 p135-47

Hillman, James
Peaks and vales. *In* Needleman, J. and Lewis, D. eds. On the way to self knowledge p114-41

Hills, David Farley- See Farley-Hills, David

Hilton, Alice Mary
Against pollution and hunger: environment and development. *In* Against pollution and hunger p27-59

Hilton, Alison
The revolutionary theme in Russian realism. *In* Millon, H. A. and Nochlin, L. eds. Art and architecture in the service of politics p108-27

Hilton, James

About individual works
Goodbye, Mr Chips
Weeks, E. Foreword to Good-bye, Mr Chips by James Hilton. *In* Praise from famous men: an anthology of introductions p158-61

Hilton, Rodney Howard
Freedom and villeinage in England. *In* Peasants, knights and heretics p174-91

The origins of Robin Hood. *In* Peasants, knights and heretics p221-35

Hilton, Stanley E.
The United States and Brazilian independence. *In* From colony to nation p109-29

Himes, Chester B.

About
Feuser, W. Prophet of violence: Chester Himes. *In* African literature today no. 9: Africa, America and the Caribbean p58-76

Reed, I. Chester Himes: writer. *In* Reed, I. Shrovetide in old New Orleans p77-99

About individual works
A Nigger
Liston, M. Chester Himes, A Nigger. *In* Bruck, P. ed. The Black American short story in the 20th century p85-97

Himmelfarb, Gertrude
Observations on humanism and history. *In* Hook, S.; Kurtz, P. W. and Todorovich, M. eds. The philosophy of the curriculum: the need for general education p81-87

Social history and the moral imagination. *In* Art, politics, and will p28-58

Himmelweit, Hilde T.
Yesterday's and tomorrow's television research on children. *In* Lerner, D. and Nelson, L. M. eds. Communication research—a half-century appraisal p 9-36

Hinayana Buddhism
Condominas, G. Phĩbãn cults in rural Laos. *In* Change and persistence in Thai society p252-73

Fernando, A. Contemporary Buddhism in Sri Lanka (Ceylon) *In* Dumoulin, H. ed. Buddhism in the modern world p65-80

Fiske, A. M. Buddhism in India today. *In* Dumoulin, H. ed. Buddhism in the modern world p130-46

King, W. L. Contemporary Burmese Buddhism. *In* Dumoulin, H. ed. Buddhism in the modern world p81-98

Kitagawa, J. M. and Reynolds, F. Theravāda Buddhism in the twentieth century. *In* Dumoulin, H. ed. Buddhism in the modern world p43-64

Palihawadana, M. Is there a Theravada Buddhist idea of grace? *In* Christian faith in a religiously plural world p181-95

Hinayana Buddhism—*Continued*

Reynolds, F. E. The many lives of Buddha : a study of sacred biography and Theravāda tradition. *In* Reynolds, F. E. and Capps, D. eds. The biographical process p37-61

Swearer, D. K. Recent developments in Thai Buddhism. *In* Dumoulin, H. ed. Buddhism in the modern world p99-108

Zago, M. Buddhism in contemporary Laos. *In* Dumoulin, H. ed. Buddhism in the modern world p120-29

Zago, M. Contemporary Khmer Buddhism. *In* Dumoulin, H. ed. Buddhism in the modern world p109-19

Hinchcliffe, Doreen. See Coulson, N. J. jt. auth.

Hinde, Robert A.
Social development: a biological approach. *In* Human growth and development p1-32

Hinde, Thomas, pseud. See Chitty, Thomas

Hindemith, Paul

About individual works
The craft of musical composition
Sessions, R. Hindemith on theory. *In* Sessions, R. Roger Sessions on music p241-48

Mathis der Maler
Sessions, R. Hindemith's Mathis der Maler. *In* Sessions, R. Roger Sessions on music p347-52

Hindle, Brooke
How much is a piece of the True Cross worth? *In* Material culture and the study of American life p 5-20

The underside of the learned society in New York, 1754-1854. *In* Oleson, A. and Brown, S. C. eds. The pursuit of knowledge in the early American republic p84-116

Hindman, Thomas Carmichael
About
Dougan, M. B. Thomas C. Hindman: Arkansas politician and general. *In* Rank and file p21-28

Hinds, Stuart W.
On the relations of medical triage to world famine: an historical survey. *In* Lucas, G. R. and Ogletree, T. W. eds. Lifeboat ethics p29-51

Hindu art. See Art, Hindu

Hindu asceticism. See Asceticism—Hinduism

Hindu astrology. See Astrology, Hindu

Hindu astronomy. See Astronomy, Hindu

Hindu decoration and ornament. See Decoration and ornament, Hindu

Hindu epistemology. See Knowledge, Theory of (Hinduism)

Hindu literature. See Hinduism—Sacred books

Hindu logic
Daor, D. Modes of argument. *In* Philosophy East/philosophy West p162-95

Hindu philosophy. See Philosophy, Hindu

Hindu psychology. See Hinduism—Psychology

Hindu sects
Daner, F. J. Conversion to Krishna Consciousness: the transformation from hippie to religious ascetic. *In* Wallis, R. ed. Sectarianism p53-69
See also Radhasoami Satsong

Hindu symbolism
Allchin, F. R. Religious symbols and Indian thought. *In* Symbols of power p 1-34

Hindu temples. See Temples, Hindu

Hindu theological anthropology. See Man (Hinduism)
Hindu; Vedanta; Yoga

Hinduism
Coomaraswamy, A. K. Vedic exemplarism. *In* Coomaraswamy A. K. Selected papers v2 p177-97
See also Asceticism—Hinduism; Bhakti; Deluge; (Hinduism); God (Hinduism); Gods (Hindu); Hell (Hinduism); Temples, Hindu; Vedanta; Yoga

Bibliography
Hein, N. J. Hinduism. *In* Adams, C. J. ed. A reader's guide to the great religions p106-55

Influence
Mookerjee, G. Malraux and the Hindu vision. *In* Courcel, M. H. de, ed. Malraux p112-19

Psychology
Coomaraswamy, A. K. On the Indian and traditional psychology, or rather pneumatology. *In* Coomaraswamy, A. K. Selected papers v2 p333-78

Relations—Christianity
Rao, K. L. S. A Hindu response: the value of religious pluralism. *In* Christian faith in a religiously plural world p46-58

Rituals
Coomaraswamy, A. K. Atmayajña: self-sacrifice. *In* Coomaraswamy, A. K. Selected papers v2 p107-47

Sacred books
Biderman, S. Scriptures, revelation, and reason. *In* Philosophy East/philosophy West p128-61
Bishop, D. H. Introduction. *In* Bishop, D. H. ed. Indian thought p13-22

Sects
See Hindu sects

India
Allchin, F. R. Religious symbols and Indian thought. *In* Symbols of power p 1-34

Hindus, Milton
Philip Rahv. *In* Images and ideas in American culture p171-203

About individual works
The crippled giant
Howe, I. Anti-Semite and Jew. *In* Howe, I. Celebrations and attacks p68-71

Hindus in Asia, Southeastern
History
Wheatley, P. Satyānrta in Suvarnadvīpa: from reciprocity to redistribution in ancient Southeast Asia. *In* Ancient civilization and trade p227-83

Hindus in literature. See Brahmans in literature

Hine, Robert V.
Communitarianism. *In* The Rise of Adventism p70-78

Hine, Virginia H.
The deprivation and disorganization theories of social movements. *In* Zaretsky, I. I. and Leone, M. P. eds. Religious movements in contemporary America p646-61

Hingers, R. H. and Willer, David
Prevailing postulates of social exchange theory. *In* McNall, S. G. ed. Theoretical perspectives in sociology p169-86

Hingham, Mass.
History
Smith, D. S. Old age and the 'great transformation': a New England case study. *In* Spicker, S. F.; Woodward, K. M. and Van Tassel, D. D. eds. Aging and the elderly p285-302
Social life and customs
Allen, D. G. A tale of two towns: persistent English localism in seventeenth-century Massachusetts. *In* Allen, H. C. and Thompson, R. eds. Contrast and connection p 1-35

Hinkel, Howard H.
Growth without toil: generative indolence in Keats. *In* Tennessee Studies in literature v20 p26-36

Hinnant, Charles Haskell
Sir William Temple's views on science, poetry, and the imagination. *In* Studies in eighteenth-century culture v8 p187-203

Hinshaw, Randall Weston
Devaluation and absorption: an alternative analysis. *In* Inflation, trade and taxes p108-18

Hintikka, Jaakko. See Hintikka, Kaarlo Jaakko Juhani

Hintikka, Kaarlo Jaakko Juhani
A discourse on Descarte's method. *In* Hooker, M. ed. Descartes p74-88

Hinton, David Alban
Late Anglo-Saxon metal-work: an assessment. *In* Anglo-Saxon England 4 p171-80

Hinton, Harwood Perry
Richard J. Hinton and the American Southwest. *In* Voices from the Southwest p82-91

Hinton, Howard Everest
Natural deception. *In* Gregory, R. L. and Gombrich. Sir E. H. T. eds. Illusion in nature and art p97-159

Hinton, Jane L.
The role of family in Delta wedding, Losing battles and The optimist's daughter. *In* Prenshaw, P. W. ed. Eudora Welty p120-31

Hinton, Nicholas
Intermediate treatment. *In* Progress in penal reform p238-44

Hinton, Richard Josiah
About
Hinton, H. P. Richard J. Hinton and the American Southwest. *In* Voices from the Southwest p82-91

Hintze, Otto
About
Gilbert, F. Otto Hintze. *In* Gilbert, F. History p39-65

Hinz, Evelyn J.
Thomas Paine. *In* Emerson, E. H. ed. American literature, 1764-1789 p39-57

Hinz, Evelyn J. and Teunissen, John James
The Pietà as icon in The golden notebook. *In* Pratt, A. V. and Dembo, L. S. eds. Doris Lessing p40-53

Hippies
United States
Brown, M. E. The condemnation and persecution of hippies. *In* Henslin, J. M. ed. Deviant life-styles p349-71

Hippler, Fritz
About individual works
The Wandering Jew
Taylor, R. The Wandering Jew. *In* Taylor, R. Film propaganda p190-206

Hippocrates
From The works of Hippocrates. *In* Sobel, D. S. ed. Ways of health p189-203
About
Herter, H. The problematic mention of Hippocrates in Plato's Phaedrus. *In* Illinois classical studies, v 1 1976 p22-42
Simon, B. The Hippocratic corpus. *In* Simon, B. Mind and madness in ancient Greece p215-27

Hippolytus, Saint, fl. 217-235
About individual works
The apostolic tradition of Hippolytus
Stam, J. E. Charismatic theology in the apostolic tradition of Hippolytus. *In* Current issues in Biblical and patristic interpretation p267-76

Hiram, pseud. See Langley, Batty

Hiraoka, Kimitake. See Mishima, Yukio, pseud.

Hirdman, Sven
Prospects for arms control in the ocean. *In* Borgese, E. M. and Krieger, D. eds. The tides of change p80-99

The hired hand (Motion picture)
Kauffmann, S. The hired hand. *In* Kauffmann, S. Living images p66-68

The hireling (Motion picture)
Kauffmann, S. The hireling. *In* Kauffmann, S. Living images p209-12

Hirosige, Tetu
The ether problem, the mechanistic worldview, and the origins of the theory of relativity. *In* Historical studies in the physical sciences v7 p3-82

Hirota, Jotaro. See Hirota, Kōki

Hirota, Kōki
About
Farnsworth, L. W. Hirota Kōki: the diplomacy of expansionism. *In* Burns, R. D. and Bennett, E. M. eds. Diplomats in crisis p227-49

Hirsch, David Harry
Hamlet, Moby-Dick, and passional thinking. *In* Shakespeare: aspects of influence p135-62

Hirsch, Eric Donald
In defense of the author; excerpt from "Validity in interpretation." *In* On literary intention p87-103

Hirsch, Eric D.—*Continued*

Objective interpretation. *In* On literary intention p26-54

Three dimensions of hermeneutics. *In* On literary intention p194-209

What isn't literature? *In* Hernadi, P. ed. What is literature? p24-34

About

Watkins, E. Criticism and method: Hirsch, Frye, Barthes, Derrida. *In* Watkins, E. The critical act p56-94

Hirsch, Fred

The ideological underlay of inflation. *In* The Political economy of inflation p263-84

Hirsch, Gordon D.

The mysteries in Bleak House: a psychoanalytic study. *In* Dickens Studies Annual v4 p132-52

Hirsch, Paul M.

Television as a national medium. *In* Handbook of contemporary urban life p389-427

Hirsch, Rudolf

Printed reports on the early discoveries and their reception. *In* First images of America p537-59

Hirschberg, Haim Zeev. See Hirschberg, Joachem Wilhelm

Hirschberg, Joachem Wilhelm

The agreement between the Musta'ribs and the Maghribis in Cairo 1527. *In* Salo Wittmayer Baron v2 p577-90

Hirschberg, Stuart

An encounter with the supernatural in Yeats's "The spirit medium." *In* Yeats and the occult p311-16

Hirschi, Travis

Labelling theory and juvenile delinquency: an assessment of the evidence. *In* Gove, W. R. ed. The labelling of deviance p181-203

Reconstructing delinquency: evolution and implications of twentieth-century theory. *In* Empey, L. T. ed. Juvenile justice p180-212

Hirschland, Nancy L. and Hammond, Mason

Stamped potters' marks and other stamped pottery in the McDaniel collection. *In* Harvard Studies in classical philology v72 p369-82

Hirst, Paul Heywood

About individual works

Liberal education and the nature of knowledge

Elliott, R. K. Education and human being I. *In* Philosophers discuss education p45-72

Hirst, Rodney Julian

Science and anti-science in the philosophy of perception. *In* Studies in perception p377-401

Hispanic American literature. See Spanish American literature

Hispanic civilization. See Civilization, Hispanic

Hispanos. See Mexican Americans

Hiss, Alger

About

Galbraith, J. K. Last word on the Hiss case? *In* Galbraith, J. K. Annals of an abiding liberal p303-10

Histochemistry. See Biological chemistry

Histology

Belloni, L. Marcello Malpighi and the founding of anatomical microscopy. *In* Bonelli, M. L. R. and Shea, W. R. eds. Reason, experiment, and mysticism in the scientific revolution p95-110

Historia o Cesarzu Otone

Schlauch, M. A Polish analogue of The man of law's tale. *In* Chaucer and Middle English studies in honour of Rossell Hope Robbins p372-80

Historians

Oakeshott, M. J. The activity of being an historian. *In* Oakeshott, M. J. Rationalism in politics p137-67

See also Church historians

Canada

Berger, C. Conclusion. *In* Berger, C. The writing of Canadian history p259-66

Berger, C. A North American nation. *In* Berger, C. The writing of Canadian history p137-59

Berger, C. Reorientation. *In* Berger, C. The writing of Canadian history p160-86

Berger, C. Reorientation and tradition. *In* Berger, C. The writing of Canadian history p187-207

Berger, C. The rise of liberty. *In* Berger, C. The writing of Canadian history p32-53

Europe

Chadwick, O. History and the secular. *In* Chadwick, O. The secularization of the European mind in the nineteenth century p189-228

France

Church, W. F. France. *In* National consciousness, history, and political culture in early-modern Europe p43-66

Germany

Krieger, L. Germany. *In* National consciousness, history, and political culture in early-modern Europe p67-97

Greece

Downs, R. B. Sense of the past. *In* Downs, R. B. Books that changed the world p121-50

Normandy

Chibnall, M. Charter and chronicle: the use of archive sources by Norman historians. *In* Church and government in the Middle Ages p 1-17

Rome

Downs, R. B. Sense of the past. *In* Downs, R. B. Books that changed the world p121-50

Southwest, New

Simmons, M. Authors and books in colonial New Mexico. *In* Voices from the Southwest p13-32

United States

Bowden, M. J. The Great American Desert in the American mind: the historiography of a geographical notion. *In* Geographies of the mind p119-47

Davis, D. B. Slavery and the post-World War II historians. *In* Mintz, S. W. ed. Slavery, colonialism, and racism p 1-16

Filler, L. Consensus: how academics keep from murdering each other at professional meetings. *In* Essays in honor of Russel B. Nye p42-64

Historical materialism

Enteen, G. M. Marxist historians during the cultural revolution: a case study of professional in-fighting. *In* Cultural revolution in Russia, 1928-1931 p154-68

Habermas, J. Toward a reconstruction of historical materialism. *In* Dallmayr, F. R. ed. From contract to community p47-63

Wellmer, A. Communications and emancipation: reflections on the linguistic turn in critical theory. *In* O'Neill, J. ed. On critical theory p231-63

See also Dialectical materialism

Historical monuments. See Monuments

Historical museums

Hindle, B. How much is a piece of the **True Cross** worth? *In* **Material culture and** the study of American life p 5-20

Historical research

Carson, C. **Doing history with material** culture. *In* Material culture and the study of American life p41-64

See also Historiography

Historical sites. See Historic sites

Historical sociology

Thrupp, S. L. History and sociology: new opportunities for cooperation. *In* Thrupp, S. L. Society and history p293-302

Thrupp, S. L. What history and sociology can learn from each other. *In* Thrupp, S. L. Society and history p303-08

See also Culture; Society, Primitive

Historicism

Flew, A. G. N. Hume and historical necessity. *In* Flew, A. G. N. A rational animal p49-74

Hexter, J. H. Carl Becker and historical relativism. *In* Hexter, J. H. On historians p13-41

Momigliano, A. Historicism revisited. *In* Momigliano, A. Essays in ancient and modern historiography p365-73

Peckham, M. The function of history in nineteenth-century European culture. *In* Peckham, M. Romanticism and behavior p32-39

Peckham, M. Reflections on historical modes in the nineteenth century. *In* Peckham, M. Romanticism and behavior p40-66

White, H. V. Historicism, history and the figurative imagination. *in* White, H. V. Tropics of discourse p101-20

Historiography

Berlin, Sir I. The concept of scientific history. *In* Berlin, Sir I. Concepts and categories p103-42

Darnton, R. The history of mentalités: recent writings on revolution, criminality, and death in France. *In* Brown, R. H. and Lyman, S. M. eds. Structure, consciousness, and history p106-36

Deininger, W. T. Promise and peril in pragmatic historical thought: a contemporary dialogue. *In* Philosophy and the civilizing arts p264-82

Fischer, D. H. The braided narrative: substance and form in social history. *In* Fletcher, A. J. S. ed. The literature of fact p109-33

Gilbert, F. Reflections on the history of the professor of history. *In* Gilbert, F. History p441-53

Gossman, L. History and literature: reproduction or signification. *In* Canary, R. H. and Kozicki, H. J. eds. The writing of history p3-40

Hartman, G. H. History-writing as answerable style. *In* Cohen, R. ed. New directions in literary history p95-105.

Also in Hartman, G. N. The fate of reading p101-13

Jauss, H. R. History of art and pragmatic history. *In* Amacher, R. E. and Lange, V. eds. New perspectives in German literary criticism p432-64

Keylor, W. R. Clio on trial: Charles Péguy as historical critic. *In* From Parnassus p195-208

Koselleck, R. Chance as motivation for the unexplained in historical writing: notes on Archenholtz's History of the Seven Years' War. *In* Amacher, R. E. and Lange, V. eds. New perspectives in German literary criticism p212-24

Mink, L. O. Narrative form as a cognitive instrument. *In* Canary, R. H. and Kozicki, H. J. eds. The writing of history p129-49

Momigliano, A. Historicism revisited. *In* Momigliano, A. Essays in ancient and modern historiography p365-73

Momigliano, A. A Piedmontese view of the history of ideas. *In* Momigliano, A. Essays in ancient and modern historiography p 1-7

Momigliano, A. Polybius' reappearance in Western Europe. *In* Momigliano, A. Essays in ancient and modern historiography p79-98

Momigliano, A. Time in ancient historiography. *In* Momigliano, A. Essays in ancient and modern historiography p179-204

Nevins, A. Advances in the social sciences. *In* Nevins, A. Allan Nevins on history p151-57

Nevins, A. The explosive excitement of history. *In* Nevins, A. Allan Nevins on history p158-67

Nevins, A. New lamps for old in history. *In* Nevins, A. Allan Nevins on history p55-67

Nevins, A. Not Capulets, not Montagus. *In* Nevins, A. Allan Nevins on history p13-35

Nevins, A. The old history and the new. *In* Nevins, A. Allan Nevins on history p181-202

Nevins, A. What's the matter with history? *In* Nevins, A. Allan Nevins on history p3-12

Singer, J. D. The behavioral approach to diplomatic history. *In* Encyclopedia of American foreign policy p66-77

Thrupp, S. L. Some historians on generalization. *In* Thrupp, S. L. Society and history p269-73

White, H. V. The burden of history. *In* White, H. V. Tropics of discourse p27-50

White, H. V. The fictions of factual representation. *In* Fletcher, A. J. S. ed. The literature of fact p21-44

Also in White, H. V. Tropics of discourse p121-34

White, H. V. The historical text as literary artifact. *In* Canary, R. H. and Kozicki, H. J. eds. The writing of history p41-62

Also in White, H. V. Tropics of discourse p81-100

Historiography—*Continued*

White, H. V. Historicism, history, and the figurative imagination. White, H. V. Tropics of discourse p101-20

White, H. V. Interpretation in history. *In* White, H. V. Tropics of discourse p51-80

White, H. V. The irrational and the problem of historical knowledge in the Enlightenment. *In* White, H. V. Tropics of discourse p135-49

See also Diplomatics; Historians; History—Methodology; Local history; Moving-pictures in historiography; Psychohistory; and subdivision Historiography under subjects, e.g. World War, 1939-1945—Historiography

History

Lyons, J. O. Once upon a time. *In* Lyons, J. O. The invention of the self p28-39

Manuel, F. E. The use and abuse of psychology in history. *In* Kren, G. M. and Rappoport, L. H. eds. Varieties of psychohistory p38-62

Momigliano, A. Tradition and the classical historian. *In* Momigliano, A. Essays in ancient and modern historiography p161-77

Stone, L. History and the social sciences in the twentieth century. *In* The Future of history p3-42

England

Kroeber, K. Romantic historicism: the temporal sublime. *In* Kroeber, K. and Walling, W. eds. Images of romanticism p149-65

Netherlands

Fuks, L. and Fuks, R. Jewish historiography in the Netherlands in the 17th and 18th centuries. *In* Salo Wittmayer Baron v 1 p433-66

Russia

Dunlop, D. M. H. M. Baratz and his view of Khazar influence on the earliest Russian literature, juridicial and historical. *In* Salo Wittmayer Baron v 1 p345-67

United States

Whitfield, S. J. "Totalitarianism" in eclipse: the recent fate of an idea. *In* Images and ideas in American culture p60-95

History

Aron, R. Three forms of historical intelligibility. *In* Aron, R. Politics and history p47-61

Himmelfarb, G. Observations on humanism and history. *In* Hook, S.; Kurtz, P. W. and Todorovich, M. eds. The philosophy of the curriculum: the need for general education p81-87

Jauss, H. R. History of art and pragmatic history. *In* Amacher, R. E. and Lange, V. eds. New perspectives in German literary criticism p432-64

Thrupp, S. L. Editorial from the first issue of Comparative Studies in Society and History. *In* Thrupp, S. L. Society and history p328-31

See also Biography; Discoveries (in geography); Heroes; Historians; Historical fiction; Historical sociology; Man—Migrations; Military history; Naval history; Political science; Revolutions; Social history; also subdivision History under specific subjects and under names of countries, states, cities, etc., e.g. France—History

Biography

See Biography

Chronology

See Chronology, Historical

Criticism

See Historiography

Historiography

See Historiography

Methodology

Chadwick, O. History and the secular. *In* Chadwick, O. The secularization of the European mind in the nineteenth century p189-228

Le Roy Ladurie, E. The historian and the computer. *In* Le Roy Ladurie, E. The territory of the historian p3-6

Nevins, A. What the scientist and historian can teach each other. *In* Nevins, A. Allan Nevins on history p133-50

See also Oral history

Museums

See Historical museums

Philosophy

Aron, R. The dawn of universal history. *In* Politics and history p212-33

Aron, R. History and politics. *In* Aron, R. Politics and history p237-48

Aron, R. The philosophy of history. *In* Aron, R. Politics and history p5-19

Bauman, Z. Understanding as the work of history: Karl Mannheim. *In* Bauman, Z. Hermeneutics and social science p89-110

Bauman, Z. Understanding as the work of history: Karl Marx. *In* Bauman, Z. Hermeneutics and social science p48-68

Bauman, Z. Understanding as the work of life: Martin Heidegger. *In* Bauman, Z. Hermeneutics and social science p148-71

Bauman, Z. Understanding as the work of history: Max Weber. *In* Bauman, Z. Hermeneutics and social science p69-88

Berlin, Sir I. The concept of scientific history. *In* Berlin, Sir I. Concepts and categories p103-42

Bottomore, T. B. Structure and history. *In* Blau, P. M. ed. Approaches to the study of social structure p159-71

Cassirer, E. The philosophy of history. *In* Cassirer, E. Symbol, myth, and culture p121-41

Chase, G. Musicology, history, and anthropology: current thoughts. *In* Current thought in musicology p231-46

Cowan, D. A. Science, history and the evidence of things not seen. *In* From Parnassus p313-23

Coxe, L. O. History and imagination. *In* Coxe, L. O. Enabling acts p114-24

Cunningham, J. V. The ancient quarrel between history and poetry. *In* Cunningham, J. V. The collected essays of J. V. Cunningham p120-27

History—Philosophy—*Continued*

Dunn, J. Practising history and social science on 'realist' assumptions. *In* Hookway, C. and Pettit, P. eds. Action and interpretation p145-75

Foucault, M. Nietzsche, genealogy, history. *In* Foucault, M. Language, counter-memory, practice p139-64

Frye, N. The rhythm of growth and decay. *in* Frye, N. Northrop Frye on culture and literature p141-46

Frye, N. The shapes of history. *In* Frye, N. Northrop Frye on culture and literature p76-83

Goretti, M. The heterogenesis of ends in Vico's thought: premises for a comparison of ideas. *In* Giambattista Vico's science of humanity p213-19

Graebner, N. A. Morgenthau as historian. *In* [Truth and tragedy]: a tribute to Hans Morgenthau p66-76

Hexter, J. H. Fernand Braudel and the monde Braudellien. . . . *In* Hexter, J. H. On historians p61-145

Hollinger, D. A. Historians and the discourse of intellectuals. *In* Higham, J. and Conkin, P. K. eds New directions in American intellectual history p42-63

Jordan, R. W. Vico and Husserl: history and historical science. *In* Giambattsta Vico's science of humanity p251-61

Keylor, W. R. Clio on trial: Charles Péguy as historical critic. *In* From Parnassus p195-208

Landgrebe, L. Phenomenology as transcendental theory of history. *In* Elliston, F. A. and McCormick, P. eds. Husserl p101-17

Letwin, S. R. Nature, history and morality. *In* Royal Institute of Philosophy. Nature and conduct p229-50

McMurrin, S. M. Ideas and the processes of history. *In* The Abdication of philosophy: philosophy and the public good p109-28

Mathieu, V. Truth as the mother of history. *In* Giambattista Vico's science of humanity p113-24

Mazzeo, J. A. New wine in old bottles: reflections on historicity and the problem of allegory. *In* Mazzeo, J. A. Varieties of interpretation p47-69

Miller, J. W. The ahistoric ideal. *In* Miller, J. W. The paradox of cause, and other essays p130-60

Miller, J. W. History and humanism. *In* Miller, J. W. The paradox of cause, and other essays p75-96

Miller, J. W. The midworld. *In* Miller, J. W. The paradox of cause, and other essays p106-23

Mink, L. O. History and fiction as modes of comprehension. *In* Cohen, R. ed. New directions in literary history p107-24

Niemeyer, G. The loss and recovery of history. *In* A Public philosophy reader p203-17

Noxon, J. H. Remembering and imagining the past. *In* Livingston, D. W. and King, J. T. eds. Hume p270-95

Pompa, L. Vico and the presuppositions of historical knowledge. *In* Giambattista Vico's science of humanity p125-40

Pons, A. Prudence and providence: the Pratica della scienza nuova and the problem of theory and practice in Vico. *In* Giambattista Vico's science of humanity p431-48

Raleigh, J. H. Tolstoy and the ways of history. *In* Spilka, M. ed. Towards a poetics of fiction p211-24

Runciman, Sir S. History and legend. *In* Royal Society of Literature of the United Kingdom, London. Essays by divers hands v39 p112-25

Said, E. W. On repetition. *In* Fletcher, A. J. S. ed. The literature of fact p134-58

Spitz, L. W. Periodization in history: Renaissance and Reformation. *In* The Future of history p189-217

Walsh, W. H. The logical status of Vico's ideal eternal history. *In* Giambattista Vico's science of humanity p141-53

Walton, C. Hume and Jefferson on the uses of history. *In* Livingston, D. W. and King, J. T. eds. Hume p389-403

Also in Philosophy and the civilizing arts p103-25

Warren, R. P. The use of the past. *In* A time to hear and answer: essays for the Bicentennial season p 1-35

White, H. V. The burden of history. *In* White, H. V. Tropics of discourse p27-50

White, H. V. Interpretation in history. *In* White, H. V. Tropics of discourse p51-80

White, H. V. The irrational and the problem of historical knowledge in the Enlightenment. *In* White, H. V. Tropics of discourse p135-49

White, H. V. The tropics of history: the deep structure of The new science. *In* Giambattista Vico's science of humanity p65-85

See also Historical materialism; Historicism; History (Theology)

Psychological aspects

Kren, G. M. and Rappoport, L. H. Clio and psyche. *In* Kren, G. M. and Rappoport, L. H. eds. Varieties of psychohistory p63-77

Manuel, F. E. The use and abuse of psychology in history. *In* Kren, G. M. and Rappoport, L. H. eds. Varieties of psychohistory p38-62

See also Psychohistory

Research
See Historical research

Sources

Nevins, A. The autobiography. *In* Nevins, A. Allan Nevins on history p236-46

Nevins, A. History and the newspaper. *In* Nevins, A. Allan Nevins on history p263-74

Nevins, A. History this side the horizon. *In* Nevins, A. Allan Nevins on history p275-87

Nevins, A. The role of the manuscript collector. *In* Nevins, A. Allan Nevins on history p254-62

Nevins, A. Why public men keep diaries. *In* Nevins, A. Allan Nevins on history p247-53

See also Diplomatics

Study and teaching

Reeves, M. Why history? *In* Niblett, W. R. ed. The sciences, the humanities and the technological threat p116-26

Study and teaching (Higher)
—United States

Bostert, R. H. Teaching history. *In* Cahn, S. M. ed. Scholars who teach p 1-35

History—Continued

Theology
See History (Theology)

History (Theology)

Gilkey, L. B. Reinhold Niebuhr's theology of history. *In* Scott, N. A. ed. The legacy of Reinhold Niebuhr p36-62

Reeves, M. History and prophecy in medieval thought. *In* Medievalia et humanistica no. 5 p51-75

See also Time (Theology)

History, Ancient

See also Civilization, Ancient; Hittites

Chronology

Balcer, J. M. The date of Herodotus IV.1: Darius' Scythian expedition. *In* Harvard Studies in classical philology v76 p99-132

Historiography

Lyons, J. O. Once upon a time. *In* Lyons, J. O. The invention of the self p28-39

History, Biblical. See Bible—History of Biblical events

History, Constitutional. See Constitutional history

History, Economic. See Economic history

History, Local. See Local history

History, Military. See Military history

History, Modern

Philosophy
See History—Philosophy

18th century
See Eighteenth century

20th century

Wright, G. Contemporary history in the contemporary age. *In* The Future of history p219-30

History, Philosophy of. See History—Philosophy

History, Universal. See World history

History and literature. See Literature and history

History and poetry. See Literature and history

History and science. See Science and civilization

History and social sciences. See Social sciences and history

History in art

Kroeber, K. Romantic historicism: the temporal sublime. *In* Kroeber, K. and Walling, W. eds. Images of romanticism p149-65

History in literature

Cecil, Lord D. Hardy the historian. *In* Drabbie, M. ed. The genius of Thomas Hardy p154-61

Gilman, E. B. Richard II and the perspectives of history. *In* Renaissance drama [1976] p85-115

Harrison, H. Worlds beside worlds. *In* Nicholls, P. ed. Science fiction at large p105-14

Raleigh, J. H. Tolstoy and the ways of history. *In* Spilka, M. ed. Towards a poetics of fiction p211-24

Sharrock, R. Browning and history. *In* Armstrong, I. ed. Robert Browning p77-103

Simpson, L. P. Sex & history: origins of Faulkner's apocrypha. *In* The Maker and the myth: Faulkner and Yoknapatawpha, 1977 p43-70

Simpson, L. P. Yoknapatawpha & Faulkner's fable of civilization. *In* The Maker and the myth: Faulkner and Yoknapatawpha, 1977 p122-45

See also Historical drama; Historical fiction

Histrionics. See Acting; Theater

Hitchcock, Alfred Joseph

About

Lambert, G. The benefits of shock. *In* Lambert, G. The dangerous edge p235-63

Samuels, C. T. Hitchcock. *In* Samuels, C. T. Mastering the film, and other essays p69-84

About individual works
Frenzy

Kauffmann, S. Frenzy. *In* Kauffmann, S. Living images p121-24

Samuels, C. T. Hyphens of the self. *In* Samuels, C. T. Mastering the film, and other essays p179-89

Rear window

Truffaut, F. Alfred Hitchcock: Rear window. *In* Truffaut, F. The films in my life p77-79

To catch a thief

Truffaut, F. Alfred Hitchcock: To catch a thief. *In* Truffaut, F. The films in my life p80-82

The wrong man

Truffaut, F. Alfred Hitchcock: The wrong man. *In* Truffaut, F. The films in my life p83-86

Hitchcock, George

On Kayak. *In* Anderson, E. and Kinzie, M. eds. The little magazine in America: a modern documentary history p438-49

Hitler, Adolf

About

Binion, R. Hitler looks East. *In* DeMause, L. ed. The new psychohistory p181-98

Bracher, K. D. The role of Hitler: perspectives of interpretation. *In* Laqueur, W. Z. ed. Fascism: a reader's guide p211-25

Canetti, E. The Arch of Triumph. *In* Canetti, E. The conscience of words p153-70

Canetti, E. Hitler, according to Speer. *In* Canetti, E. The conscience of words p145-52

Erikson, E. H. The legend of Hitler's childhood; excerpt from "Childhood and society." *In* Kren, G. M. and Rappoport, L. H. eds. Varieties of psychohistory p99-110

Parry, A. Hitler's Holocaust. *In* Parry, A. Terrorism: from Robespierre to Arafat p203-10

About individual works
Mein Kampf

Downs, R. B. Study in megalomania. *In* Downs, R. B. Books that changed the world p274-85

Hittite language

Etymology

Watkins, C. On the family of *arceō*, ἀρκέω, and Hittite *hark-*. *In* Harvard Studies in classical philology v74 p67-74

Hittite language—*Continued*

Terms and phrases

Watkins, C. An Indo-European agricultural term: Latin ador, Hittite hat-. *In* Harvard Studies in classical philology v77 p187-93

Watkins, C. Latin ador, Hittite hat-again: addenda to HSCP 77 (1973) 187-193. *In* Harvard Studies in classical philology v79 p181-87

Hittite mythology. See Mythology, Hittite

Hittites

Güterbock, H. G. Some aspects of Hittite prayers. *In* The Frontiers of human knowledge p125-39

Hoffner, H. A. Propaganda and political justification in Hittite historiography. *In* Unity and diversity p49-62

Hittle, James Michael

The service city in the eighteenth century. *In* Hamm, M. F. ed. The city in Russian history p53-68

Hiz, Henry

Logical basis of semiotics. *In* Sebeok, T. A. ed. A perfusion of signs p40-53

Hka-kaw. See Kaw people

Hla Pe, U.

A short history of a Burmese-English dictionary, 1913-1963. *In* Southeast Asian history and historiography p86-99

Hnyilicza, Esteban. See Baughman, M. L. jt. auth.

Ho, Wai-kam

Tung Ch'i-ch'ang's new orthodoxy and the Southern School theory. *In* Artists and traditions p113-29

Hoadly, Benjamin, Bp. of Winchester, 1676-1761

About

Rack, H. D. 'Christ's Kingdom not of this world:' the case of Benjamin Hoadly versus William Law reconsidered. *In* Church, society and politics p275-91

Hoban, Russell C.

Thoughts on being and writing. *In* Blishen, E. ed. The thorny paradise p65-76

About individual works
The mouse and his child

Townsend, J. R. A second look: "The mouse and his child." *In* Horn Book Magazine. Crosscurrents of criticism p330-32

Hobart and William Smith Colleges, Geneva, N.Y.

Curricula

Kavanaugh, J. V. The artifact in American culture: the development of an undergraduate program in American studies. *In* Material culture and the study of American life p65-74

Hobbes, Thomas

About

Dewey, J. The motivation of Hobbes's political philosophy. *In* Ross, R. G.; Schneider, H. W. and Waldman, T. eds. Thomas Hobbes in his time p8-30

Funkenstein, A. Natural science and social theory: Hobbes, Spinoza, and Vico. *In* Giambattista Vico's science of humanity p187-212

Johnson, P. J. Hobbes's Anglican doctrine of salvation. *In* Ross, R. G.; Schneider, H. W. and Waldman, T. eds. Thomas Hobbes in his time p102-25

Morris, B. On Hobbes' humanism. *In* Philosophy and the civilizing arts p89-102

Oakeshott, M. J. The moral life in the writings of Thomas Hobbes. *In* Oakeshott, M. J. Rationalism in politics p248-300

Ross, R. G. Some puzzles in Hobbes. *In* Ross, R. G.; Schneider, H. W. and Waldman, T. eds. Thomas Hobbes in his time p43-60

Schneider, H. W. The piety of Hobbes. *In* Ross, R. G.; Schneider, H. W. and Waldman, T. eds. Thomas Hobbes in his time p84-101

Waldman, T. Hobbes on the generation of a public person. *In* Ross, R. G.; Schneider, H. W. and Waldman, T. eds. Thomas Hobbes in his time p61-83

Walton, C. The philosophia prima of Thomas Hobbes. *In* Ross, R. G.; Schneider, H. W. and Waldman, T. eds. Thomas Hobbes in his time p31-41

About individual works
Leviathan

Kemp, J. Ethical naturalism. *In* New studies in ethics v 1 p173-228

Ostrom, V. The American contribution to a theory of constitutional choice. *In* Havard, W. C. and Bernd, J. L. eds. 200 years of the Republic in retrospect p56-78

Slavin, A. J. The American principle from More to Locke. *In* First images of America p139-64

Spengler, J. J. Smith versus Hobbes: economy versus polity. *In* Glahe, F. R. ed. Adam Smith and The wealth of nations p35-59

Theology

Barnes, W. H. F. The rational theology of Thomas Hobbes. *In* The Personal universe p54-63

Hobbins, James Minahan

Shaping a provincial learned society: the early history of the Albany Institute. *In* Oleson, A. and Brown, S. C. eds. The pursuit of knowledge in the early American Republic p117-50

Hobbs, Alan Charles

New phenomenalism as an account of perceptual knowledge. *In* Royal Institute of Philosophy. Impressions of empiricism p109-21

Hobday, C. H.

Shakespeare's Venus and Adonis sonnets. *In* Shakespeare survey 26 p103-09

Hobhouse, Hermione

Philip and Philip Charles Hardwick: an architectural dynasty. *In* Seven Victorian architects p32-49

About individual works
Thomas Cubitt, master builder

Connolly, C. Thomas Cubitt, master builder. *In* Connolly, C. The evening colonnade p412-14

Hobhouse, Leonard Trelawney

About individual works
Sociology and philosophy

Parsons, T. Review of L. T. Hobhouse, Sociology and philosophy: a centenary collection of essays and articles. *In* Parsons, T. Social systems and the evolution of action theory p77-81

Hoboes. See Tramps

Hobsbaum, Philip
Tradition and experiment in English poetry

Contents

Ben Jonson in the seventeenth century
Chaucer: experimentalist extraordinary
Eliot, Whitman and American tradition
Elizabethan poetry
The essential Wordsworth
The growth of English modernism
Piers Plowman through modern eyes
The poetry of barbarism
The poetry of debate
The rise of the dramatic monologue
The romantic dichotomy
Shakespeare's handling of his sources

Hobsbawm, Eric John
The Historians' Group of the Communist Party. *In* Rebels and their causes p21-47

Hobson, Anthony Robert Alwyn

About individual works
Great libraries

Connolly, C. Great libraries. *In* Connolly, C. The evening colonnade p415-18

Hobson, Harold
The Warner Requiem. *In* Prentki, T. ed. Francis Warner p13-24

Hobson, R. H.
Rubber: a footnote to Northern Rhodesian history. *In* The Occasional papers of the Rhodes-Livingstone Museum p489-538

Hoccleve, Thomas

About

Reeves, A. C. Thomas Hoccleve, bureaucrat. *In* Medievalia et humanistica no. 5 p201-14

Hoch, David G.
Walden: yoga and creation. *In* Artful thunder p85-102

Hochberg, Jerome A.
The drive to specialization. *In* Nader, R. and Green, M. J. eds. Verdicts on lawyers p118-26

Hochberg, Julian E.
Higher-order stimuli and inter-response coupling in the perception of the visual world. *In* Perception p17-39

Hochberg, Mark Robert
The unity of Go down, Moses. *In* Tennessee Studies in literature v21 p58-65

Hochhuth, Rolf

About individual works
The Deputy

Kauffmann, S. The Deputy. *In* Kauffmann, S. Persons of the drama p160-62

Simon, J. I. The Deputy and its metamorphoses. *In* Simon, J. I. Singularities p167-75

Hochschild, Arlie Russell
Inside the clockwork of male careers. *In* Women and the power to change p47-80

Hockey
Faulkner, R. R. Making violence by doing work: selves, situations, and the world of professional hockey. *In* Social problems in athletics p93-112

Hocks, Richard Allen
"Novelty" in polarity to "the most admitted truths": tradition and the individual talent in S. T. Coleridge and T. S. Eliot. *In* Evolution of consciousness p83-97

Hodgart, Matthew John Caldwell
The subscription list for Pope's Iliad, 1715. *In* The Dress of words p25-34

Hodge, Jane (Aiken)
Jane Austen and her publishers. *In* Halperin, J. ed. Jane Austen p75-85

Hodge, Robert W.
Linguistics and popular culture. *In* Bigsby, C. W. E. ed. Approaches to popular culture p107-28

Hodges, Cyril Walter
Children? What children? *In* Blishen, E. ed. The thorny paradise p53-57

Hodges, Tony
Mozambique: the politics of liberation. *In* Carter, G. M. and O'Meara, P. eds. Southern Africa in crisis p48-88

Also in Carter, G. M. and O'Meara. P. eds. Southern Africa: the continuing crisis p57-92

Hodgkin, Thomas Lionel
Where the paths began. *In* African studies since 1945 p6-16

Hodgson, Godfrey. See Raw, C. jt. auth.

Hodgson, James Day
What lies ahead for U.S.—Japan relations? *In* Prochnow, H. V. ed. Dilemmas facing the nation p248-70

Hodgson, James W. See Hickey, T. jt. auth.

Hodgson, John H.
The problem of succession. *In* Cocks, P.; Daniels, R. V. and Heer, N. W. eds. The dynamics of Soviet politics p96-116

Hoehmann, Hans-Hermann
The state and the economy in Eastern Europe. *In* Hayward, J. E. S. and Berki, R. N. eds. State and society in contemporary Europe p141-57

Hoeniger, F. David
Shakespeare's romances since 1958: a retrospect. *In* Shakespeare survey v29 p 1-10

Hoenigswald, Henry M.
Intentions, assumptions, and contradictions in historical linguistics. *In* Current issues in linguistic theory p168-94

Hoetink, Harry
The cultural links. *In* Crahan, M. E. and Knight, F. W. eds. Africa and the Caribbean p20-40

Hoffacker, Lewis
The U.S. Government response to terrorism: a global approach. *In* International terrorism and political crimes p537-45

Hoffman, Arthur W.
Allusions and the definition of themes in Congreve's Love for love. *In* Martz, L. L. and Williams, A. L. eds. The author in his work p283-96

Hoffman, Frederick John
Kafka's The trial: the assailant as landscape. *In* Garvin, H. R. ed. Makers of the twentieth-century novel p154-65

The search for redemption: Flannery O'Connor's fiction. *In* Friedman, M. J. and Lawson, L. A. eds. The added dimension p32-48

Hoffman, Michael J.

Themes, topics, and criticism. *In* American literary scholarship, 1973 p411-38

Themes, topics, criticism [another essay]. *In* American literary scholarship, 1974 p411-32

Themes, topics, criticism [another essay]. *In* American literary scholarship, 1975 p447-72

Themes, topics, criticism [another essay]. *In* American literary scholarship, 1976 p401-29

Themes, topics, criticism [another essay]. *In* American literary scholarship, 1977 p433-62

Hoffman, Robert

Death and dignity. *In* Kohl, M. ed. Beneficent euthanasia p70-80

Justice, merit, and the good. *In* Gross, B. R. ed. Reverse discrimination p358-72

Hoffman, Ronald. See Earle, C. jt. auth.

Hoffman, Stanton de Voren

Conrad's menagerie: animal imagery and theme. *In* Garvin, H. R. ed. Makers of the twentieth-century novel p84-92

Hoffman, Yoel

'Dream-world' philosophers: Berkeley and Vasubandhu. *In* Philosophy East/philosophy West p247-68

The possibility of knowledge: Kant and Nagarjuna. *In* Philosophy East/philosophy West p269-90

Hoffmann, Banesh

Magic, science and evaluation. *In* From Parnassus p324-33

Hoffmann, Ernst Theodor Amadeus

About

Tatar, M. M. Blindness and insight: visionary experience in the tales of E. T. A. Hoffmann. *In* Tatar, M. M. Spellbound p121-51

About individual works

The sandman

Massey, I. Singles and doubles: narcissism in Hoffmann's "The sandman." *In* Massey, I. The gaping pig p115-23

Hoffmann, Peter

About individual works

The history of the German resistance, 1933-1945

Galbraith, J. K. Germany: July 20, 1944. *In* Galbraith, J. K. Annals of an abiding liberal p211-20

Hoffmann, Richard C.

Medieval origins of the common fields. *In* Parker, W. N. and Jones, E. L. eds. European peasants and their markets p23-71

Wrocław citizens as rural landholders. *In* The Medieval city p293-311

Hoffmann, Stanley

The international system and U.S. policy toward Latin America. *In* The Americas in a changing world p78-94

No trumps, no luck, no will: gloomy thoughts on Europe's plight. *In* Atlantis lost p 1-46

Regulating the new international system. *In* Kilson, M. ed. New states in the modern world p171-99

Hoffmann-Nowotny, Hans-Joachim

European migration after World War II. *In* Human migration p85-105

Hoffmeister, Gerhart

The pagan influence of the Italian Renaissance on German life and letters, 1450-1520. *In* Hoffmeister, G. ed. The Renaissance and Reformation in Germany p51-67

Hoffner, Harry Angier

Hittite mythological texts: a survey. *In* Unity and diversity p136-45

Propaganda and political justification in Hittite historiography. *In* Unity and diversity p49-62

Hofmann, Richard Beer- See Beer-Hofmann, Richard

Hofmannsthal, Hugo Hofmann, Edler von

About

Craft, R. Der Rosenkavalier: "something Mozartian"? *In* Craft, R. Current convictions p136-45

Fiedler, L. M. Molière on Max Reinhardt's stage. *In* Johnson, R. B.; Neumann, E. S. and Trail, G. T. eds. Molière and the commonwealth of letters: patrimony and posterity p591-602

Lewis, H. B. Molière and Hofmannsthal. *In* Johnson, R. B.; Neumann, E. S. and Trail, G. T. eds. Molière and the commonwealth of letters: patrimony and posterity p345-51

Schwarz, A. The purgation of the will: tragic theater in the Christian tradition. *In* Schwarz, A. From Büchner to Beckett p223-60

About individual works

Electra

Falk, E. H. Some concepts of the tragic in versions of Electra. *In* Creative encounter p3-16

Hofstadter, Albert

Consciousness, thought, and enownment. *In* Thought, consciousness, and reality p85-109

Hofstadter, Richard

The Founding Fathers: an age of realism; excerpt from "The American political tradition and the men who made it." *In* The Moral foundations of the American Republic p73-85

Hogan, Jeremiah J.

Lear: a tragedy with a difference; and Shakespeare's tragicomedies or romances. *In* The Frontiers of human knowledge p153-57

Hogan, Patrick G.

The philosophical limitations of science fiction. *In* Clareson, T. D. ed. Many futures, many worlds p260-77

Hogan, Robert Goode; Scott, Bonnie K. and Henderson, Gordon

The modern drama. *In* Finneran, R. J. ed. Anglo-Irish literature p518-61

Hogarth, William

About

Hunter, K. M. H. The informing word: verbal strategies in visual satire. *In* Studies in eighteenth-century culture v4 p271-96

Klinger, M. F. William Hogarth and London theatrical life. *In* Studies in eighteenth-century culture v5 p11-27

Kunzle, D. William Hogarth: the ravaged child in the corrupt city. *In* Tufte, V. and Myerhoff, B. G. eds. Changing images of the family p99-140

Macey, S. L. Hogarth and the iconography of time. *In* Studies in eighteenth-century culture v5 p41-53

Hogarth, William—*Continued*

About individual works

Industry and idleness

Paulson, R. The simplicity of Hogarth's Industry and idleness. *In* ELH essays for Earl R. Wasserman p 1-30

Hogg, James

About

Hart, F. R. Scottish variations of the Gothic novel. *In* Hart, F. R. The Scottish novel p13-30

Hoggart, Richard

Culture and its ministers. *In* Art, politics, and will p191-212

About individual works

Auden

Fergusson, F. Auden in mid-career. *In* Fergusson, F. Literary landmarks p137-42

Hogs. See Swine

Hohenheim, Theophrastus von, called Paracelsus. See Paracelsus

Hohenveldern, Ignaz Seidl- See Seidl-Hohenveldern, Ignaz

Hohman, Johan Georg

About individual works

The long lost friend

Yoder, D. Hohman and Romanus: origins and diffusion of the Pennsylvania German powwow manual. *In* American folk medicine p235-48

Hohman, John George. See Hohman, Johan Georg

Höhmann, Hans-Hermann. See Hoehmann, Hans-Hermann

Hoijer, Harry

History of American Indian linguistics. *In* Sebeok, T. A. ed. Native languages of the Americas v 1 p3-22

Hokan languages

Shipley, W. F. California. *In* Sebeok, T. A. ed. Native languages of the Americas v 1 p427-59

Holahan, Michael Norris

The Oresteia. *In* Seidel, M. A. and Mendelson, E. eds. Homer to Brecht p143-70

The holarchy. Koestler, A. *In* Koestler, A. Janus p23-56

Holbach, Paul Henri Thiry, baron d'

About individual works

The system of nature

Guerlac, H. Three eighteenth-century social philosophers: scientific influences on their thought. *In* Guerlac, H. Essays and papers in the history of modern science p451-64

Holbein, Hans, the younger

About individual works

The ambassadors

Gilman, E. B. Richard II and the perspectives of history. *In* Gilman, E. B. The curious perspective p88-128

Also in Renaissance drama [1976] p85-115

Christ in the tomb

Meyers, J. Holbein and The idiot. *In* Meyers, J. Painting and the novel p136-47

Holberg, Ludvig, Baron

About

Lundquist, A. S. Ludvig Holberg and Molière: imitation or constructive emulation? *In* Johnson, R. B.; Neumann, E. S. and Trail, G. T. eds. Molière and the commonwealth of letters: patrimony and posterity p245-51

Holbo, Paul Sothe

Trade and commerce. *In* Encyclopedia of American foreign policy p945-60

Holborow, Les

The 'prejudice in favour of psychophysical parallelism'. *In* Royal Institute of Philosophy. Understanding Wittgenstein p193-207

Holbraad, Carsten

Middle-power roles in Great-Power triangles. *In* The Year book of world affairs, 1976 p116-32

Holbrook, David

Essay 10. *In* Fitzgerald, R. ed. What it means to be human p186-208

Lost bearings in English poetry

Contents

Conclusions

Criticism has lost confidence in itself

From "vitalism" to a dead Crow: Ted Hughes's failure of confidence

The lack of a creative theme: Erza Pound's stone mouths biting empty air and Eliot's Hollow men

Modern poetry and the death of sympathy

Paralysis as "space is nearer": Robert Lowell's For the Union dead

Poetry has lost confidence in itself

Thomas Hardy and the meaning of existence: After a journey

What can creativity do? W. B. Yeats's Among school children

Politics and the need for meaning. *In* Fitzgerald, R. ed. Human needs and politics p174-94

Ted Hughes' 'Crow' and the longing for non-being. *In* Abbs, P. ed. The black rainbow p32-54

Holcombe, Lee

Victorian wives and property: reform of the Married Women's Property Law, 1857-1882. *In* Vicinus, M. ed. A widening sphere p3-28

Holcroft, Thomas

About individual works

The adventures of Hugh Trevor

Kelly, G. Thomas Holcroft: Hugh Trevor. *In* Kelly, G. The English Jacobin novel, 1780-1805 p145-67

Anna St Ives

Kelly, G. Thomas Holcroft: Anna St Ives. *In* Kelly, G. The English Jacobin novel, 1780-1805 p114-45

The memoirs of Bryan Perdue

Kelly, G. Thomas Holcroft: Bryan Perdue. *In* Kelly, G. The English Jacobin novel, 1780-1805 p167-78

Holder, Alan

The other Hemingway. *In* Wagner, L. W. ed. Ernest Hemingway p103-09

Hölderlin, Friedrich

About

Foucault, M. The father's "no." *In* Foucault, M. Language, counter-memory, practice p68-86

Hamburger, M. Hölderlin. *In* Hamburger, M. Art as second nature p57-63

About individual works
Antigone

Lacoue-Labarthe, P. The caesura of the speculative. *In* Glyph 4 p57-84

Hyperion

Nalbantian, S. Wordsworth, Hölderlin and their contemporaries: the imperial soul. *In* Nalbantian, S. The symbol of the soul from Hölderlin to Yeats p13-37

Patmos

Shaffer, E. S. Hölderlin's 'Patmos' ode and 'Kubla Khan': mythological doubling. *In* Shaffer, E. S. 'Kuba Khan' and The fall of Jerusalem p145-90

Stimme des Volks

Nägele, R. The discourse of the other: Hölderlin's ode "Stimme des Volks" and the dialectic of the Enlightment. *In* Glyph 5 p 1-33

Wie wenn am Feiertage

Schuwer, A. L. Nature and the holy: on Heidegger's interpretation of Holderlins hymn "Wie wenn am Feiertage." *In* Radical phenomenology p225-37

Aesthetics

Lacoue-Labarthe, P. The caesura of the speculative. *In* Glyph 4 p57-84

Holdsworth, Mary

Lenin's Imperialism in retrospect. *In* Essays in honour of E. H. Carr p341-51

Hole, Christina

Protective symbols in the home. *In* Symbols of power p121-30

The hole (Motion picture)

Truffaut, F. Jacques Beck: Le trou. *In* Truffaut, F. The films in my life p183-86

Holidays

See also Christmas

Ireland

Smith, R. J. Festivals and calendar customs. *In* Orel, H. ed. Irish history and culture p129-45

Holiness

Morrison, K. F. The structure of holiness in Othloh's Vita Bonifatii and Ebo's Vita Ottonis. *In* Law, church, and society p131-56

Holiness churches. See Snake cults (Holiness churches)

Holinshed, Raphael

About individual works
Chronicles of England, Scotland, and Ireland

Rossi, J. W. Cymbeline's debt to Holinshed: the richness of III.1. *In* Shakespeare's romances reconsidered p104-12

Holism

Koestler, A. Beyond Eros and Thanatos. *In* Janus p57-69

Koestler, A. The holarchy. *In* Koestler, A Janus p23-56

Holkot, Robertus

About

Moody, E. A. A quodlibetal question of Robert Holkot, O.P. on the problem of the objects of knowledge and of belief. *In* Moody, E. A. Studies in medieval philosophy. science, and logic p321-52

Holland, Isabelle

Tilting at taboos. *In* Horn Book Magazine. Crosscurrents of criticism p137-43

The walls of childhood. *In* Horn Book Magazine. Crosscurrents of criticism p27-34

About individual works
The man without a face

Holland, I. Tilting at taboos. *In* Horn Book Magazine. Crosscurrents of criticism p137-43

Holland, Jimmie C. B. See Plumb, M. M. jt. auth.

Holland, Laurence B.

A "raft of trouble": word and deed in Huckleberry Finn. *In* Glyph 5 p69-87

Holland, Sir Nathaniel Dance- 1st bart. See Dance, Sir Nathaniel

Holland, Norman Norwood

How can Dr. Johnson's remarks on Cordelia's death add to my own response- *In* Hartman, G. H. ed. Psychoanalysis and the question of the text p18-44

Literary interpretation and three phases of psychoanalysis. *In* Roland, A. ed. Psychoanalysis, creativity, and literature p232-47

Literature as transaction. *In* Hernadi, P. ed. What is literature? p206-18

Literature as transformation; excerpt from "The dynamics of literary response." *In* Primeau, R. ed. Influx p137-53

What can a concept of identity add to psycholinguistics? *In* Psychoanalysis and language p171-234

About individual works
The dynamics of literary response

Crews, F. C. Reductionism and its discontents. *In* Crews, F. C. Out of my system p165-85

Holland, R. F.

Absolute ethics, mathematics and the impossibility of politics. *In* Royal Institute of Philosophy. Human values p172-88

Holland, Stuart

Keynes and the Socialists. *In* Skidelsky, R. J. A. ed. The end of the Keynesian era p67-77

Holland. See Netherlands

Hollander, Arie Nicholas Jan den

Charles Boissevain. *In* Abroad in America: Visitors to the new Nation, 1776-1914 p186-94

Hollander, Brian L.

A private ombudsman for a public agency: planning and development of the Connecticut correctional system ombudsman. *In* Riedel, M. and Chappell, D. eds. Issues in criminal justice: planning and evaluation p87-98

Hollander, Gayle Durham

Political communication and dissent in the Soviet Union. *In* Tokes, R .L. ed. Dissent in the USSR p233-75

Hollander, John

The metrical frame; excerpt from "Vision and resonance: two senses of poetic form." *In* Gross, H. S. ed. The structure of verse p77-101

Musica mundana and Twelfth night. *In* Wimsatt, W. K. ed. Literary criticism: idea and act p265-83

Hollander, Robert

Typology and secular literature: some medieval problems and examples. *In* Miner, E. R. ed. Literary uses of typology p3-19

The validity of Boccaccio's self-exegesis in his Teseida. *In* Medievalia et humanistica no. 8 p163-83

Hollander, Samuel

On the role of utility and demand in The wealth of nations. *In* Skinner, A. S. and Wilson, T. eds. Essays on Adam Smith p313-23

Holleaux, André Pierre

The administration of culture. *In* Courcel, M. H. de, ed. Malraux p79-94

Holley, Edward Gailon

Library issues in the seventies. *In* As much to learn as to teach p25-37

Hollinger, David A.

Historians and the discourse of intellectuals. *In* Higham, J. and Conkin, P. K. eds. New directions in American intellectual history p42-63

Hollingsworth, A. Thomas. See Hand, H. H. jt. auth.

Hollis, Martin

My role and its duties. *In* Royal Institute of Philosophy. Nature and conduct p180-99

Hollis, Patricia

Pressure from without: an introduction. *In* Hollis, P. ed. Pressure from without p 1-26

Hollis, Stephanie

The thematic structure of the Sermo Lupi. *In* Anglo-Saxon England 6 p175-95

Hollister, Charles Warren

Magnates and "curiales" in early Norman England. *In* Viator: medieval and Renaissance studies v8 p63-81

Hollon, William Eugene

Walter Prescott Webb's arid West: four decades later. *In* Essays on Walter Prescott Webb p53-72

Holloway, Bruce Kenner

United States grand strategy for the next ten years. *In* Grand strategy for the 1980s p19-36

Holloway, David

Foreign and defence policy. *In* Brown, A. H. and Kaser, M. eds. The Soviet Union since the fall of Khrushchev p49-76

Holloway, R. Ross

Architect and engineer in archaic Greece. *In* Harvard Studies in classical philology v73 p281-90

Holly, Marcia

Consciousness and authenticity: toward a feminist aesthetic. *In* Donovan, J. C. ed. Feminist literary criticism p38-47

Hollyman, John Llewelyn

Basque revolutionary separation: ETA. *In* Preston, P. ed. Spain in crisis p212-33

Holm, Ingvar

Strindberg and the theater. *In* The Hero in Scandinavian literature p143-55

Holman, Clarence Hugh

The comedies of manners. *In* Ellen Glasgow p108-28

Her rue with a difference: Flannery O'Connor and the Southern literary tradition. *In* Friedman, M. J. and Lawson, L. A. eds. The added dimension p73-87

Windows on the world

Contents

Anodyne for the village virus
April in Queenborough: Ellen Glasgow's comedies of manners
Barren ground and the shape of history
The Bildungsroman, American style
Detached laughter in the South

Also in Cohen, S. B. ed. Comic relief p87-104

The dwarf on Wolfe's shoulder
Faulkner's August avatars
Literary realism: an American mode
Marquand, novelist of manners
"Of everything the unexplained and irresponsible specimen": notes on how to read American realism
The Southern provincial in metropolis

Holman, Hugh. See Holman, Clarence Hugh

Holme, Constance

About

Cavaliero, G. A land of one's own: Constance Holme. *In* Cavaliero, G. The rural tradition in the English novel, 1900-1939 p157-72

Holme, Timothy

About individual works

Gondola, gondolier

Connolly, C. Venice: 2 *In* Connolly, C. The evening colonnade p34-36

Holmer, Paul L.

Contemporary evangelical faith: an assessment and critique. *In* Wells, D. F. and Woodbridge, J. D. eds. The evangelicals p68-95

Holmes, Brian

Education in Japan. *In* The Year book of world affairs, 1979 p126-47

Holmes, Charles Shiveley

Ring Lardner: reluctant artist. *In* Filler, L. ed. A question of quality: popularity and value in modern creative writing p26-39

Holmes, Frederic Lawrence

Conceptual history. *In* Studies in history of biology v 1 p209-18

Holmes, Jack David Lazarus

Spanish policy toward the Southern Indians in the 1790s. *In* Hudson, C. M. ed. Four centuries of Southern Indians p65-82

Holmes, Mary Jane (Hawkes)

About

Baym, N. Z. Ann Stephens, Mary Jane Holmes, and Marion Harland. *In* Baym, N. Z. Woman's fiction p175-207

Holmes, Oliver Wendell, 1809-1894

About

Martin, J. S. The novels of Oliver Wendell Holmes: a re-interpretation. *In* Literature and ideas in America p111-27

Holsti, Ole Rudolf
Global food problems and Soviet agriculture. *In* Orr, D. W. and Soroos, M. S. eds. The global predicament p150-75

Holt, J. C.
The origins and audience of the ballads of Robin Hood. *In* Peasants, knights and heretics p236-57

Robin Hood: some comments. *In* Peasants, knights and heretics p267-69

About individual works
The origins and audience of the ballads of Robin Hood

Keen, M. H. Robin Hood—peasant or gentleman? *In* Peasants, knights and heretics p258-66

Holt, James: See Holt, Laurence James

Holt, John, 1721-1784

About
Wetherell, C. 'For these or such like reasons': John Holt's attack on Benjamin Franklin. *In* American Antiquarian Society. Proceedings v88 pt2 p251-75

Holt, John Caldwell
Why not a Bill of Rights for children?; excerpt from "Escape from childhood." *In* Gross, B. and Gross, R. eds. The children's rights movement p319-25

Holt, Laurence James
The New Deal and the American anti-statist tradition. *In* Braeman, J.; Bremner, R. H. and Brody, D. eds. The New Deal v 1 p27-49

Holt, Marion P.
Contemporary translations and stagings of Molière's plays in Spain. *In* Johnson, R. B.; Neumann, E. S. and Trail, G. T. eds. Molière and the commonwealth of letters: patrimony and posterity p190-95

Holt, S. H. See Holt, Sidney Joseph

Holt, Sidney Joseph
Mediterranean and Black Sea fisheries. *In* Borgese, E. M. and Krieger, D. eds. The tides of change p166-78

Holtby, Winifred

About individual works
South Riding

Cavaliero, G. Town and country: Francis Brett Young, Winifred Holtby. *In* Cavaliero, G. The rural tradition in the English novel, 1900-1939 p81-100

Holter, Harriet. See Henriksen, H. V. jt. auth.

Holton, Gerald James
From the endless frontier to the ideology of limits. *In* Holton, G. J. and Morison, R. S. eds. Limits of scientific inquiry p227-41

Mainsprings of scientific discovery. *In* The Nature of scientific discovery p199-217

The new synthesis? *In* Sociobiology and human nature, p75-97

Science, science teaching, and rationality. *In* Hook, S.; Kurtz, P. W. and Todorovich, M. eds. The philosophy of the curriculum: the need for general education p101-18

Subelectrons, presuppositions, and the Millikan-Ehrenhaft dispute. *In* Historical studies in the physical sciences v9 p161-224

'What, precisely, is "thinking"?' Einstein's answer. *In* Einstein p153-64

About individual works
Science, science teaching, and rationality

Nagel, E. In defense of scientific knowledge. *In* Hook, S.; Kurtz, P. W. and Todorovich, M. eds. The philosophy of the curriculum: the need for general education p119-26

Holy, The, in literature
Scott, N. A. Flannery O'Connor's testimony: the pressure of glory. *In* Friedman, M. J. and Lawson, L. A. eds. The added dimension p138-56

Webb, E. The paradox of the sacred. *In* Webb, E. The dark dove p3-11

Webb, E. The tradition of the sacred in the West. *In* Webb, E. The dark dove p12-33

Holy Cross
Smith, J. The garments that honour the Cross in The dream of the rood. *In* Anglo-Saxon England 4 p29-35

Holy Cross in literature
Grant, P. The arms of the Red Cross: believing in the images. *In* Grant, P. Images and ideas in literature of the English Renaissance p27-62

Lee, A. A. Toward a critique of The dream of the rood. *In* Anglo-Saxon poetry: essays in appreciation p163-91

Holy Grail. See Grail

Holy Orthodox Eastern Catholic and Apostolic Church. See Orthodox Eastern Church

Holy Roman Empire

History—Henry V, 1106-1125
Blumenthal, U. R. Patrimonia and regalia in 1111. *In* Law, church, and society p 9-20

History—Charles IV, 1347-1378
Borchardt, F. L. First contacts with Italy. *In* Hoffmeister, G. ed. The Renaissance and Reformation in Germany p 1-16

Holy Spirit. See Pentecostalism

Holy Spirit Association for the Unification of World Christianity
Anthony, D. and Robbins, T. L. The effect of detente on the growth of new religions: Reverend Moon and the Unification Church. *In* Needleman, J. and Baker, G. eds. Understanding the new religions p80-100

Batson, C. D. Moon madness: greed or creed? *In* Horowitz, I. L. ed. Science, sin, and scholarship p218-25

Beckford, J. A. Two contrasting types of sectarian organization. *In* Wallis, R. ed. Sectarianism p70-85

Crittenden, A. Moon's sect pushes pro-Seoul activities. *In* Horowitz, I. L. ed. Science, sin, and scholarship p176-91

Hargrove, B. W. Some thoughts about the Unification movement and the churches. *In* Horowitz, I. L. ed. Science, sin, and scholarship p86-100

Lester, M. Profits, politics, power: the heart of the controversy. *In* Horowitz, I. L. ed. Science, sin, and scholarship p148-59

Holy Spirit Association for the Unification of World Christianity—*Continued*

Rice, B. The pull of Sun Moon. *In* Horowitz, I. L. ed. Science, sin, and scholarship p226-41

Robbins, T. and others. The last civil religion: Reverend Moon and the Unification Church. *In* Horowitz, I. L. ed. Science, sin, and scholarship p46-73

Sontag, F. E. Sun Myung Moon and the Unification Church: charges and responses. *In* Horowitz, I. L. ed. Science, sin, and scholarship p20-43

Welles, C. The eclipse of Sun Myung Moon. *In* Horowitz, I. L. ed. Science, sin, and scholarship p242-58

About individual works
Divine principle

Rudin, A. J. Jews and Judaism in Reverend Moon's Divine principle. *In* Horowitz, I. L. ed. Science, sin, and scholarship p74-83

Theology

Cunningham, A. and others. Critique of the theology of the Unification Church as set forth in Divine principle. *In* Horowitz, I. L. ed. Science, sin, and scholarship p102-18

Holy war (Islam) See Jihad

Holzapfel, Tamara

The theater of René Marqués: in search of identity and form. *In* Lyday, L. F. and Woodyard, G. W. eds. Dramatists in revolt p146-66

Holzman, Donald

Confucius and ancient Chinese literary criticism. *In* Chinese approaches to literature from Confucius to Liang Ch'i-ch'ao p21-41

Homans, George Caspar

What do we mean by social "structure"? *In* Blau, P. M. ed. Approaches to the study of social structure p53-65

About

Goode, W. J. Homans' and Merton's structural approach. *In* Blau, P. M. ed. Approaches to the study of social structure p66-75

Lemert, C. C. Axiomatic explanation: George Homans. *In* Lemert, C. C. Sociology and the twilight of man p23-50

Homans, Peter

Introduction. *In* Homans, P. ed. Childhood and selfhood p13-54

The significance of Erikson's psychology for modern understandings of religion. *In* Homans, P. ed. Childhood and selfhood p231-63

The uses and limits of psychobiography as an approach to popular culture: the case of 'the Western.' *In* Reynolds, F. E. and Capps, D. eds. The biographical process p297-316

Homberger, Eric

Melville, Lt Guert Gansevoort and authority: an essay in biography. *In* Pullin, F. ed. New perspectives on Melville p255-74

Home. See Family

Home and school

Coons, J. E. and Sugarman, S. D. A case for choice; excerpt from "Education by choice: the case for family control." *In* Parents, teachers, and children: prospects for choice in American education p129-48

Sowell, T. Choice in education and parental responsibility. *In* Parents, teachers, and children: prospects for choice in American education p165-82

Home care services

Chassé, R. Patient counseling in home care. *In* Home care p172-77

See also Aged—Home care

Case studies

Lockwood, J. A. Case reports. *In* Home care p128-33

New York (City)

Eichwald, H. An organized home care program. *In* Home care p148-52

Pennsylvania

Hailperin, C. M. Twenty-five years of home care services. *In* Home care p137-47

United States

Adsit, C. In favor of house calls. *In* Home care p98-100

Clifford, I. M. Comprehensive planning for care and the home health agency. *In* Home care p223-31

Cyrus, E. A historical perspective on home health care. *In* Home care p12-16

Dunn, M. K. Hospice-based home care services. *In* Home care p153-58

Jivoff, L. [and others] Home health care and the quality of life. *in* Home care p3-11

Moore, F. M. Homemaker-home health aides—essential thanatologists. *In* Home care p208-14

Morris, R. Long-term severe disability. *In* Home care p237-44

Moss, S. A. Home is not necessarily "home." *In* Home care p77-83

Wessells, V. G. The nurse and home care of the terminally ill. *In* Home care p49-59

Home design. See Architecture, Domestic

Home economics

Study and teaching—United States

Monts, E. A. and Burger, L. J. The status of home economics and the status of women. *In* Roberts, J. I. ed. Beyond intellectual sexism p381-86

Vallance, T. R. Home economics and the development of new forms of human service education. *In* Land-grant universities and their continuing challenge p79-103

Home health agencies. See Home care services

Home Office Research Unit. See Great Britain. Home Department. Research Unit

Home rule (Ireland)

Arnold. M. From Easter to August. *In* Arnold, M. The last word p246-64

Arnold, M. Up to Easter. *In* Arnold, M. The last word p190-209

See also Irish question

Home-stake Production Company

Galbraith, J. K. Should stealing from the rich be punished? *In* Galbraith, J. K. Annals of an abiding liberal p323-30

The homecoming (Motion picture)

Kauffmann, S. The homecoming. *In* Kauffmann, S. Living images p242-46

Homeopathy

Coulter, H. L. Homeopathic medicine. *In* Sobel, D. S. ed. Ways of health p289-317

Homer. See Homerus

Homerus—About individual works—*Cont.*

The wrath of Achilles

Richards, I. A. Sources of our common aim. *In* Richards, I. A. Poetries p165-214

Appreciation

Simonsuuri, K. Introduction. *In* Simonsuuri, K. Homer's original genius p3-16

Authorship

Goold, G. P. The nature of Homeric composition. *In* Illinois classical studies, v2 1977 p 1-34

Gunn, D. M. Thematic composition and Homeric authorship. *In* Harvard Studies in classical philology v75 p 1-31

Characters—Achilles

Mueller, M. Knowledge and delusion in the Iliad. *In* Wright, J. H. ed. Essays on the Iliad p105-27

Redfield, J. M. The wrath of Achilles as tragic error; excerpt from "Nature and culture in the Iliad: the tragedy of Hector." *In* Wright, J. H. ed. Essays on the Iliad p85-92

Characters—Andromache

Owen, E. T. The farewell of Hector and Andromache; excerpt from "The story of the Iliad." *In* Wright, J. H. ed. Essays on the Iliad p93-104

Characters—Hector

Mueller, M. Knowledge and delusion in the Iliad. *In* Wright, J. H. ed. Essays on the Iliad p105-27

Owen, E. T. The farewell of Hector and Andromache; excerpt from "The story of the Iliad." *In* Wright, J. H. ed. Essays on the Iliad p93-104

Characters—Odysseus

Torrance, R. M. Beggar man, king. *In* Torrance, R. M. The comic hero p12-36

Criticism, Textual

Hillers, D. R. and McCall, M. H. Homeric dictated texts: a reexamination of some Near Eastern evidence. *In* Harvard Studies in classical philology v80 p19-23

Criticism and interpretation

Hainsworth, J. B. The criticism of an oral Homer. *In* Wright, J. H. ed. Essays on the Iliad p28-40

Russo, J. and Simon, B. Homeric psychology and the oral tradition. *In* Wright, J. H. ed. Essays on the Iliad p41-57

Simonsuuri, K. The originality of Homer: some conclusions. *In* Simonsuuri, K. Homer's original genius p143-55

Simonsuuri, K. The primitivists and the primitive bard. *In* Simonsuuri, K. Homer's original genius p119-32

Simonsuuri, K. Vico's discovery of the true Homer. *In* Simonsuuri, K. Homer's original genius p90-98

Simonsuuri, K. Voltaire and the poetry of the primitive age. *In* Simonsuuri, K. Homer's original genius p65-73

Influence

Wilson, J. R. ΚΑΙ ΚΕ ΤΙΣ ΩΔ' ΕΡΕΕΙ: an Homeric device in Greek literature. *In* Illinois classical studies v4, 1979 p 1-15

Influence—Bacchylides

Lefkowitz, M. R. Bacchylides' Ode 5: imitation and originality. *In* Harvard Studies in classical philology v73 p45-96

Language—Grammar

Roth, C. P. Thematic s-aorists in Homer. *In* Harvard Studies in classical philology v77 p181-86

Style

Austin, N. The function of digressions in the Iliad. *In* Wright, J. H. ed. Essays on the Iliad p70-84

Technique

See Homerus—Style

Translations, English

Brower, R. A. From the Iliad to Jane Austen, via The rape of the lock. *In* Halperin, J. ed. Jane Austen p43-60

Same as Brower, R. A. From the Iliad to the novel, via The rape of the lock. *In* Brower, R. A. Mirror on mirror p77-95

Brower, R. A. A poet's Odyssey. *In* Brower, R. A. Mirror on mirror p96-102

Brower, R. A. Pope's Iliad for twentieth-century readers. *In* Brower, R. A. Mirror on mirror p55-76

Hodgart, M. J. C. The subscription list for Pope's Iliad, 1715. *in* The Dress of words p25-34

Simonsuuri, K. Pope's view of Homer: 'fire' and invention. *In* Simonsuuri, K. Homer's original genius p57-64

Translations, French

Simonsuuri, K. The interpretation of early Greek epic: Mme Dacier and the Homeric war. *In* Simonsuuri, K. Homer's original genius p46-56

Homesteading. See Frontier and pioneer life

Homicide

Brandt, R. B. A moral principle about killing. *In* Kohl, M. ed. Beneficent euthanasia p106-14

See also Euthanasia; Infanticide; Suicide

Homiletical illustrations. See Exempla

Homiliarius

Lutz, C. E. A manuscript of Charlemagne's Homiliarium. *In* Lutz, C. E. Essays on manuscripts and rare books p24-27

Homma, Nagayo

The impact of the American Revolution on Japan. *In* The Impact of the American Revolution abroad p164-66

Homoeopathy. See Homeopathy

Homophile Movement. See Gay liberation movement

Homosexual liberation movement. See Gay liberation movement

Homosexuality

De Cecco, J. P. and Shively, M. G. Conflicts over rights and needs in homosexual relationships. *In* Crew, L. ed. The gay academic p305-14

Elkind, D. Choosing to be gay: the roots of homosexuality. *In* Elkind, D. The child and society p48-61

Jones, C. R. Christopher Isherwood and the religious quest. *In* Crew, L. ed. The gay academic p350-60

Homosexuality—Continued

Kyper, J. Coming out: toward a social analysis. *In* Crew, L. ed. The gay academic p387-414

Margolis, J. Z. The question of homosexuality. *In* Baker, R. and Elliston, F. A. eds. Philosophy & sex p288-302

Marmor, J. Homosexuality. *In* Sexuality and human values p24-33

Rosán, L. J. Philosophies of homophobia and homophilia. *In* Crew, L. ed. The gay academic p255-81

Sheed, W. On keeping closets closed. *In* Sheed, W. The good word & other words p73-76

Somerville, J. W. F. Aesthetic and sexual relativity. *In* Crew, L. ed. The gay academic p282-302

See also Gay liberation movement; Homosexuals; Lesbianism

History

Crompton, L. W. Gay genocide: from Leviticus to Hitler. *In* Crew, L. ed. The gay academic p67-91

Law and legislation

Crompton, L. W. Gay genocide: from Leviticus to Hitler. *In* Crew, L. ed. The gay academic p67-91

Psychological aspects

Freedman, M. Towards a gay psychology *In* Crew, L. ed. The gay academic p315-26

United States

Huggins, J. and Forrester, R. G. The gay male. *In* Gochros, H. L. and Gochros, J. S. eds. The sexually oppressed p130-44

Kelly, J The aging male homosexual. *In* Gochros, H. L. and Gochros, J. S. eds. The sexually oppressed p160-69

Homosexuality, Female. See Lesbianism

Homosexuality, Male

Bibliography

Sarotte, G. M. The evolution of the American sexual "establishment." *In* Sarotte, G. M. Like a brother, like a lover p3-11

United States

Sarotte, G. M. The evolution of the American sexual "establishment." *In* Sarotte, G. M. Like a brother, like a lover p3-11

Homosexuality, Male in literature

Sarotte, G. M. The circumstances of the homosexual as reflected in the novel and theatre: Small town and big city. *In* Sarotte, G. M. Like a brother, like a lover p153-63

Sarotte, G. M. The circumstances of the homosexual as reflected in the novel and theater: Three categories of homosexuals. *In* Sarotte, G. M. Like a brother, like a lover p164-84

Sarotte, G. M. Conclusion: another country. *In* Sarotte, G. M. Like a brother, like a lover p293-305

Sarotte, G. M. The evolution of the homosexual in the American novel—Melville to Baldwin. *In* Sarotte, G. M. Like a brother, like a lover p12-29

Sarotte, G. M. Four archetypes of the homosexual couple: Adolescents. *In* Sarotte, G. M. Like a brother, like a lover p37-60

Sarotte, G. M. Four archetypes of the homosexual couple: The captain and the soldier. *In* Sarotte, G. M. Like a brother, like a lover p70-91

Sarotte, G. M. Four archetypes of the homosexual couple: Teacher and pupil. *In* Sarotte, G. M. Like a brother, like a lover p61-69

Sarotte, G. M. Four archetypes of the homosexual couple: The white and the Black. *In* Sarotte, G. M. Like a brother, like a lover p92-104

Sarotte, G. M. The homosexual character on the stage. *In* Sarotte, G. M. Like a brother, like a lover p30-33

Sarotte, G. M. Homosexuality and the theatre: Edward Albee: homosexual playwright in spite of himself. *In* Sarotte, G. M. Like a brother, like a lover p134-49

Sarotte, G. M. Homosexuality and the theatre: Tennessee Williams: theater as psychotherapy. *In* Sarotte, G. M. Like a brother, like a lover p107-20

Sarotte, G. M. Homosexuality and the theatre: William Inge: "Homosexual spite" in action. *In* Sarotte, G. M. Like a brother, like a lover p121-33

Sarotte, G. M. Latent homosexuality: short of and beyond true heterosexuality: Ernest Hemingway: the (almost) total sublimation of the homosexual instinct. *In* Sarotte, G. M. Like a brother, like a lover p262-78

Sarotte, G. M. Latent homosexuality: short of and beyond true heterosexuality: Francis Scott Fitzgerald: self-virilization and its failure. *In* Sarotte, G. M. Like a brother, like a lover p212-28

Sarotte, G. M. Latent homosexuality: short of and beyond true heterosexuality: Jack London: the hypervirile syndrome. *In* Sarotte, G. M. Like a brother, like a lover p240-61

Sarotte, G. M. Latent homosexuality: short of and beyond true heterosexuality: Norman Mailer: the overt latent homosexual .*In* Sarotte, G. W. Like a brother, like a lover p279-92

Homosexuality and Christianity

Barrett, E. M. Gay people and moral theology. *In* Crew, L. ed. The gay academic p329-34

Dostourian, A. Gayness: a radical Christian approach. *In* Crew, L. ed. The gay academic p335-49

Homosexuality and employment

Crew, L. Before emancipation: gay persons as viewed by chairpersons in English. *In* Crew, L. ed. The gay academic p3-48

Homosexuality and literature

Kauffmann, S. Homosexual drama and its disguises. *In* Kauffmann, S. Persons of the drama p291-94

Kauffmann, S. On the acceptability of the homosexual. *In* Kauffmann, S. Persons of the drama p295-98

Sarotte, G. M. The circumstances of the homosexual as reflected in the novel and theater: Between the American woman and the American virile ideal. *In* Sarotte, G. M. Like a brother, like a lover p185-92

Sarotte, G. M. Conclusion: another country. *In* Sarotte, G. M. Like a brother, like a lover p293-305

Homosexuality and literature—Continued

Sarotte, G. M. Latent homosexuality: short of and beyond true heterosexuality: Francis Scott Fitzgerald: self-virilization and its failure. *In* Sarotte, G. M. Like a brother, like a lover p212-28

Sarotte, G. M. Latent homosexuality: short of and beyond true heterosexuality: Jack London: the hypervirile syndrome. *In* Sarotte, G. M. Like a brother, like a lover p240-61

Sarotte, G. M. Latent homosexuality: short of and beyond true heterosexuailty: Norman Mailer: the overt latent homosexual. *In* Sarotte, G. W. Like a brother, like a lover p279-92

Homosexuality in literature

Boyette, P. E. Shakespeare's Sonnets: homosexuality and the critics. *In* Tulane Studies in English v21 p35-46

Boyette, P. E. Wanton humor and wanton poets: homosexuality in Marlowe's Edward II. *In* Tulane Studies in English v22 p33-50

Cockshut, A. O. J. The male homosexual. *In* Cockshut, A. O. J. Man and woman: a study of love and the novel, 1740-1940 p161-69

Cockshut, A. O. J. The male homosexual: Forster. *In* Cockshut, A. O. J. Man and woman: a study of love and the novel, 1740-1940 p169-81

Cockshut, A. O. J. The male homosexual: Satire. *In* Cockshut, A. O. J. Man and woman: a study of love and the novel, 1740-1940 p181-85

Elliott, S. J. Homosexuality in the crucial decade: three novelists' views. *In* Crew, L. ed. The gay academic p164-77

Frank, B. Homosexual love in four poems by Rilke. *In* Crew, L. ed. The gay academic p244-51

Holland, I. Tilting at taboos. *In* Horn Book Magazine. Crosscurrents of criticism p137-43

Jay, K. Male homosexuality and lesbianism in the works of Proust and Gide. *In* Crew, L. ed. The gay academic p216-43

Meyers, J. Conrad: Victory. *In* Meyers, J. Homosexuality and literature, 1890-1930 p76-89

Meyers, J. D. H. Lawrence: The white peacock, Women in love, Aaron's rod, The plumed serpent. *In* Meyers, J. Homosexuality and literature, 1890-1930 p131-61

Meyers, J. Forster: A room with a view, Maurice, The life to come. *In* Meyers, J. Homosexuality and literature, 1890-1930 p90-113

Meyers, J. Gide: The immoralist. *In* Meyers, J. Homosexuality and literature, 1890-1930 p32-41

Meyers, J. Introduction. *In* Meyers, J. Homosexuality and literature, 1890-1930 p 1-19

Meyers, J. Mann and Musil: Death in Venice and Young Törless. *In* Meyers, J. Homosexuality and literature, 1890-1930 p42-57

Meyers, J. T. E. Lawrence: Seven pillars of wisdom. *In* Meyers, J. Homosexuality and literature, 1890-1930 p114-30

Meyers, J. Proust: Cities of the plain. *In* Meyers, J. Homosexuality and literature, 1890-1930 p58-75

Meyers, J. Wilde: The picture of Dorian Gray. *In* Meyers, J. Homosexuality and literature, 1890-1930 p20-31

Sklepowich, E. A. In pursuit of the lyric quarry: the image of the homosexual in Tennessee Williams' prose fiction. *In* Tennessee Williams: a tribute p525-44

Steiner, G. Eros and idiom. *In* Steiner, G. On difficulty and other essays p95-136

Stockinger, J. Homotextuality: a proposal. *In* Crew, L. ed. The gay academic p135-51

Trilling, D. Our uncomplaining homosexuals. *In* Trilling, D. We must march my darlings p157-71

Study and teaching

Brogan, J. E. Teaching gay literature in San Francisco. *In* Crew, L. ed. The gay academic p152-63

Homosexuals

Friedenberg, E. Z. Gaiety and the laity: avoiding the excesses of professionalism. *In* Crew, L. ed. The gay academic p49-56

Lehman, J. L. Gay students. *In* Crew, L. ed. The gay academic p57-63

Warren, C. A. B. and Ponse, B. The existential self in the gay world. *In* Douglas, J. D. and Johnson, J. M. [eds.] Existential sociology p273-89

Attitudes

Crew, L. Before emancipation: gay persons as viewed by chairpersons in English. *In* Crew, L. ed. The gay academic p3-48

Homosexuals, Male

Jackson, B. Deviance as success: the double inversion of stigmatized roles. *In* Babcock, B. A. ed. The reversible world p258-75

Lee, J. A. Meeting males by mail. *In* Crew, L. ed. The gay academic p415-27

Rich, A. C. The meaning of our love for women is what we have constantly to expand. *In* Rich, A. C. On lies, secrets, and silence p223-30

Homosexuals, Male in literature

Sarotte, G. M. The circumstances of the homosexual as reflected in the novel and theater: Small town and big city. *In* Sarotte, G. M. Like a brother, like a lover p153-63

Sarotte, G. M. The circumstances of the homosexual as reflected in the novel and theatre: Three categories of homosexuals. *In* Sarotte, G. M. Like a brother, like a lover p164-84

Sarotte, G. M. The evolution of the homosexual in the American novel—Melville to Baldwin. *In* Sarotte, G. M. Like a brother, like a lover p12-29

Sarotte, G. M. Four archetypes of the homosexual couple: Adolescents. *In* Sarotte, G. M. Like a brother, like a lover p37-60

Sarotte, G. M. Four archetypes of the homosexual couple: Teacher and pupil. *In* Sarotte, G. M. Like a brother, like a lover p61-69

Sarotte, G. M. Four archetypes of the homosexual couple: The captain and the soldier. *In* Sarotte, G. M. Like a brother, like a lover p70-91

Sarotte, G. M. Four archetypes of the homosexual couple: The white and Black. *In* Sarotte, G. M. Like a brother, like a lover p92-104

Homosexuals, Male in literature—*Continued*

Sarotte, G. M. The homosexual character on the stage. *In* Sarotte, G. M. Like a brother, like a lover p30-33

Sarotte, G. M. Homosexuality and the theater: Edward Albee: homosexual playwright in spite of himself. *In* Sarotte, G. M. Like a brother, like a lover p134-49

Sarotte, G. M. Homosexuality and the theater: Tennessee Williams: theater as psychotherapy. *In* Sarotte, G. M. Like a brother, like a lover p107-20

Sarotte, G. M. Homosexuality and the theater: William Inge: "Homosexual spite" in action. *In* Sarotte, G. M. Like a brother, like a lover p121-33

Honderich, Ted
On inequality and violence, and the differences we make between them. *In* Royal Institute of Philosophy. Nature and conduct p46-82

Honesty. See Truthfulness and falsehood

Honeycutt, Benjamin L.
The knight and his world as instruments of humor in the fabliaux. *In* Cooke, T. D. and Honeycutt, B. L. eds. The humor of the fabliaux p75-92

Hongkong

Social conditions

Mäding, K. Popular literature in dependent society: the case of colonial Hong Kong. *In* Fischer, H. D. and Melnik, S. R. eds. Entertainment: a cross-cultural examination p180-89

Honig, Marjorie Hanson, and Shamai, Nira
Israel. *In* Kamerman, S. B. and Kahn, A. J. eds. Family policy p400-27

Honigmann, Ernest Anselm Joachim
Re-enter the stage direction: Shakespeare and some contemporaries. *In* Shakespeare survey v29 p117-25

Honigmann, John Joseph
The personal approach in culture and personality research. *In* Spindler, G. D. ed. The making of psychological anthropology p302-29

Honoré, Antony Maurice
Social justice. *In* Summers, R. S. ed. Essays in legal philosophy p61-94

Honwana, Luis Bernardo

About

Moser, G. M. Luís Bernardo Honwana's place among the writers in Mozambique. *In* King, B. A. and Ogungbesan, K. eds. A celebration of Black and African writing p189-203

Honzl, Jindřich
Dynamics of the sign in the theater. *In* Matejka, L. and Titunik, I. R. eds. Semiotics of art p74-93

The hierarchy of dramatic devices. *In* Matejka, L. and Titunik, I. R. eds. Semiotics of art p118-27

Hood, John Bell

About

McMurry, R. M. Rise to glory: a speculative essay on the early career of John Bell Hood. *In* Rank and file p39-54

Hood, Roger G.
Criminology and penal change: a case study of the nature and impact of some recent advice to governments. *In* Crime, criminology and public policy p375-417

Hood, Stuart Clink
The dilemma of the communicators. *In* Bigsby, C. W. E. ed. Approaches to popular culture p201-12

Hood, Walter Kelly
Michael Robartes: two occult manuscripts. *In* Yeats and the occult p204-24

Hook, Sidney
Academic freedom and professional responsibilities. *In* Hook, S.; Kurtz, P. and Todorovich, M. eds. The ethics of teaching and scientific research p117-23

The bias in anti-bias regulations. *In* Gross, B. R. ed. Reverse discrimination p88-96

Discrimination, color blindness, and the quota system. *In* Gross, B. R. ed. Reverse discrimination p84-87

The ethics of suicide. *In* Kohl, M. ed. Beneficent euthanasia p57-69

General education: the minimum indispensables. *In* Hook, S.; Kurtz, P. W. and Todorovich, M. eds. The philosophy of the curriculum: the need for general education p27-36

On sharpening the horns. *In* Hook, S.; Kurtz, P. W. and Todorovich, M. eds. The philosophy of the curriculum: the need for general education p211-15

Prospects for the academic future. *In* Fairfield, R. P. ed. Humanistic frontiers in American education p253-60

Rejoinder: Dr Hibbs and the ethics of discussion. *In* Hook, S.; Kurtz, P. and Todorovich, M. eds. The ethics of teaching and scientific research p187-90

The state and higher education. *In* Hook, S.; Kurtz, P. W. and Todorovich, M. eds. The university and the state: what role for government in higher education? p227-36

Hooker, C. A.
Has the scientist any future in the brave new world? *In* Science and society: past, present, and future p306-56

Hooker, Michael
Descartes's denial of mind-body identity. *In* Hooker, M. ed. Descartes p171-85

Hooker, Thomas

About

Seelye, J. By way of Newtown: how Thomas Hooker crossed his Rubicon and started the Pequot War: a Hudibrastic interlude. *In* Seelye, J. Prophetic waters p187-216

Hookway, Christopher
Indeterminacy and interpretation. *In* Hookway, C. and Pettit, P. eds. Action and interpretation p17-42

Hooper, Walter
Narnia: the author, the critics, and the tale. *In* Schakel, P. J. ed. The longing for a form p105-18

Hooson, David J. M.
The geographical setting. *In* Auty, R. and Obolensky, D. eds. An introduction to Russian history p 1-48

Hooter, Mike

About

Anderson, J. Q. Mike Hooter—the making of a myth. *In* Inge, M. T. ed. The frontier humorists p197-207

Hoover, Herbert Clark, President U.S.

About

Romasco, A. U. Hoover-Roosevelt and the Great Depression: a historiographic inquiry into a perennial comparison. *In* Braeman. J.; Bremner, R. H. and Brody, D. eds. The New Deal v 1 p3-26

Hope, Alec Derwent

The three faces of love; excerpt. *In* Gibbons, R. ed. The poet's work: 29 masters of 20th century poetry on the origins and practice of their art p110-20

Hope

Green, T. F. Stories and images of the future. *In* Bundy, R. F. ed. Images of the future: the twenty-first century and beyond p35-44

Hopi Indians

Sekaquaptewa, E. Hopi Indian ceremonies. *In* Seeing with a native eye p35-43

Women

Schlegel, A. E. Male and female in Hopi thought and action. *In* Schlegel, A. E. ed. Sexual stratification p245-69

Hopi language

Whorf, B. L. An American Indian model of the universe. *In* Tedlock, D. E. and Tedlock, B. eds. Teachings from the American earth p121-29

Hopkins, Arthur George

Clio-antics: a horoscope for African economic history. *In* African studies since 1945 p31-48

Hopkins, Gerard Manley

About

Hardy, B. N. Forms and feelings in the sonnets of Gerard Manley Hopkins. *In* Hardy, B. N. The advantage of lyric p54-66

Richards, I. A. Gerard Hopkins. *In* Richards, I. A. Complementarities p139-47

Sabin, M. The lovely behavior of things: Hopkins and Baudelaire. *In* Sabin, M. English romanticism and the French tradition p168-78

About individual works

The Leaden Echo and the Golden Echo

Trilling, L. Gerard Manley Hopkins: The Leaden Echo and the Golden Echo: Maidens' Song from St. Winefred's Well. *In* Trilling, L. Prefaces to The experience of literature p261-64

Spelt from Sibyl's leaves

Assad, T. J. Hopkins' "Spelt from Sibyl's leaves." *In* Tulane studies in English v22 p103-15

The windhover

Hill, A. A. An analysis of The windhover: an experiment in method. *In* Hill, A. A. Constituent and pattern in poetry p28-38

The wreck of the Deutschland

Miller, J. H. The linguistic moment in "The wreck of the Deutschland." *In* Young, T. D. ed. The New Criticism and after p47-60

Hopkins, Keith

Economic growth and towns in classical antiquity. *In* Towns in societies p35-77

Hopkinson, Francis

About

Andrews, W. D. Philip Freneau and Francis Hopkinson. *In* Emerson, E. H. ed. American literature, 1764-1789 p127-44

Granger, B. I. Early Philadelphia serials. *In* Granger, B. I. American essay serials from Franklin to Irving p41-69

Horace. See Horatius Flaccus, Quintus

Horatius Flaccus, Quintus

About

Anderson, W. C. Autobiography and art in Horace. *In* Perspectives of Roman poetry p33-56

About individual works

Art of poetry

Howell, W. S. Aristotle and Horace on rhetoric and poetics. *In* Howell, W. S. Poetics, rhetoric, and logic p45-72

Epistles

Knoche, U. Horace's Satires and Epistles. *In* Knoche, U. Roman satire p73-98

Epistles (1.14, 6-9)

Kenney, E. J. A question of taste: Horace, Epistles 1.14.6-9. *In* Illinois classical studies, v2 1977 p229-39

Epodes (Eleventh Epode)

Luck, G. An interpretation of Horace's Eleventh Epode. *In* Illinois classical studies, v 1 1976 p122-26

Exegi monumentum aere perennius

Woodman, T. Exegi monumentum: Horace, Odes 3.30. *In* Woodman, T. and West, D. eds. Quality and pleasure in Latin poetry p115-28

Odes

Jones, C. P. Tange Chloen semel arrogantem. *In* Harvard Studies in classical philology v75 p81-83

Odes (I-III)

Ross, D. O. The Roman poetry of Horace and Tibullus. *In* Ross, D. O. Backgrounds to Augustan poetry: Gallus, elegy and Rome p131-62

Odes (Book IV)

Porter, D. H. The recurrent motifs of Horace, Carmina IV. *In* Harvard Studies in classical philology v79 p189-228

Odes IV.7 (Diffugere nives)

Rudd, N. Translation. *In* Rudd, N. Lines of enquiry p182-210

Satires

Knoche, U. Horace's Satires and Epistles. *In* Knoche, U. Roman satire p73-98

Sigsbee, D. L. The disciplined satire of Horace. *In* Roman satirists and their satire p64-88

Satires (Book II, Chapter 6, Lines 77-117)

West, D. A. Of mice and men: Horace, Satires 2.6.77-117. *In* Woodman, T. and West, D. eds. Quality and pleasure in Latin poetry p67-80

Influence—Persius Flaccus

Rudd, N. Imitation: association of ideas in Persius. *In* Rudd, N. Lines of enquiry p54-83

Horatius Flaccus, Quintus—Continued

Translations, English

Rudd, N. Translation. *In* Rudd, N. Lines of enquiry p182-210

Horgan, Paul

An amateur librarian. *In* Voices from the Southwest p65-75

Horie-Webber, A.

Modernisation of the Japanese theatre: the Shingeki movement. *In* Modern Japan p147-65

Horin, Meir Ben- See Ben-Horin, Meir

Horizon (Periodical)

Spender, S. Background to the forties. *In* Spender, S. The thirties and after p63-76

Horkheimer, Max

About

Hughes, H. S. The critique of mass society. *In* Hughes, H. S. The sea change p134-88

Horkheimer, Max, and Adorno, Theodor W.

About individual works

Dialectic of enlightenment

Lenhardt, C. K. The wanderings of enlightenment. *In* O'Neill, J. ed. On critical theory p34-57

Hormones. See Hormones, Sex

Hormones, Sex

Bleier, R. H. Brain, body, and behavior. *In* Roberts, J. I. ed. Beyond intellectual sexism p63-73

Hall, D. L. Biology, sex hormones and sexism in the 1920's. *In* Gould, C. C. and Wartofsky, M. W. eds. Women and philosophy p81-96

Horn, John Leonard

The ethics of research: a case history and its lessons. *In* Hook, S.; Kurtz, P. and Todorovich, M. eds. The ethics of teaching and scientific research p135-59

Horn, Walter William

On the selective use of sacred numbers and the creation in Carolingian architecture of a new aesthetic based on modular concepts. *In* Viator: medieval and Renaissance studies v6 p351-90

Hornback, Bert G.

The hero self. *In* Dickens Studies Annual v7 p151-62

Hornbeck, Stanley Kuhl

About

Burns, R. D. Stanley K. Hornbeck: the diplomacy of the Open Door. *In* Burns, R. D. and Bennett, E. M. eds. Diplomats in crisis p91-123

Horne, Josiah

About

Curtis, M. H. The trials of a Puritan in Jacobean Lancashire. *In* The Dissenting tradition p78-99

Horne, Verda

The fragile, threatened landscapes of the South. *In* The Rising South v 1 p35-49

Hornick, Lita

Kulchur: a memoir. *In* Anderson, E. and Kinzie, M. eds. The little magazine in America: a modern documentary history p281-97

Hornig, Donald Frederick

The costs of government regulation. *In* Hook, S.; Kurtz, P. W. and Todorovich, M. eds. The university and the state: what role for government in higher education? p103-13

Hornig, Lilli Schwenk

Affirmative action through affirmative attitudes. *In* Women in academia p8-19

Hornstein, Lillian Herlands

Medieval romance. *In* Medievalia et humanistica no. 7 p189-94

Hornyansky, Michael

Is your English destroying your image? *In* Gold, J. ed. In the name of language! p71-96

Horology

Craft, R. Telling time. *In* Craft, R. Current convictions p217-22

See also Clocks and watches

Horovitz, Michael, comp.

About individual works

Children of Albion: poetry of the 'Underground' in Britain

Robinson, I. Paper tygers or, The circus animals' desertion in the new pop poetry. *In* Abbs, P. ed. The black rainbow p19-31

Horowitz, Donald Leonard

Ethnic identity. *In* Glazer, N. and Moynihan, D. P. eds. Ethnicity p111-40

Horowitz, Frances Degen

Directions for parenting. *In* Behavior modification and families p7-33

Horowitz, Irving Louis

Jewish ethnicity and Latin American nationalism. *In* Said, A. A. and Simmons, L. R. eds. Ethnicity in an international context p92-109

Science, sin, and sponsorship. *In* Horowitz, I. L. ed. Science, sin, and scholarship p260-81

See also Becker, H. S. jt. auth.

Horowitz, Louise K.

Love and language

Contents

The chevalier de Méré

Jacques Esprit

La Bruyère

La Rochefoucauld

The Lettres portugaises

Madame de Lafayette

Madame de Sévigné

Saint-Evremond

Horror films. See Frankenstein films

Horse sense. See Common sense

Horses

Hill, D. R. The role of the camel and the horse in the early Arab conquests. *In* War, technology and society in the Middle East p32-43

Horsey, Sir Jerome

About

Lur'e, I. S. An unpublished epigram on an English ambassador to Russia. *In* Oxford Slavonic papers new ser. v7 p13-17

Hortelano, Juan Garcia. See Garcia Hortelano, Juan

Horton, John Edwin

Time and cool people. *In* Henslin, J. M. ed. Deviant life-styles p59-72

Horton, Robin

About individual works

African traditional thought and Western science

Goody, J. R. Literacy, criticism, and the growth of knowledge. *In* Culture and its creators p226-43

Horton, Thomas R.

Leadership of the spirit: a present and future need. *In* Benton, L. R. ed. Management for the future p148-63

Horton, William Thomas

About

Finneran, R. J. and Harper, G. M. "He loved strange thought": W. B. Yeats and William Thomas Horton. *In* Yeats and the occult p190-203

Horváth, Ödöm

About individual works

Kasimir und Karoline

Bance, A. F. Ödön Von Horváth: Kasimir und Karoline. *In* Branscombe, P. ed. Austrian life and literature, 1780-1938 p81-93

Horwath, Peter

Hermann J. Oberth. The father of space travel: American perspectives. *In* The German contribution to the building of the Americas p343-58

Richardsonian characters and motifs in Johann Friedel's novel Eleonore. *In* Branscombe, P. ed. Austrian life and literature, 1780-1938 p 1-11

Horwitz, Morton J.

The jurisprudence of Brown and the dilemmas of liberalism. *In* Have we overcome? Race relations since Brown p173-87

Horwitz, Robert Henry

John Locke and the preservation of liberty: a perennial problem of civic education. *In* The Moral foundations of the American Republic p129-56

Horwitz, Steven

Reshaping a decretal chapter: Tua nobis and the canonists. *In* Law, church, and society p207-21

Hörz, Herbert

Philosophical concepts of space and time. *In* Einstein p229-41

Hoskin, Michael A.

The English background to the cosmology of Wright and Herschel. *In* Cosmology, history, and theology p219-31

Hosking, Geoffrey

The search for an image of man in contemporary Soviet fiction. *In* Barnes, C. J. ed. Studies in twentieth century Russian literature p61-77

Hosley, Richard

A reconstruction of the Fortune playhouse: Part I. *In* The Elizabethan theatre, VI p 1-20

Hosmer, Charles Bridgham

The broadening view of the historical preservation movement. *In* Material culture and the study of American life p121-39

Hospice, Inc., New Haven

Dunn, M. K. Hospice-based home care services. *In* Home care p153-58

Hospices (Terminal care). See Terminal care facilities

Hospital care

History

Imhof, A. E. The hospital in the 18th century: for whom? *In* Branca, P. ed. The medicine show p141-63

United States—History

Rosenberg, C. E. And heal the sick: hospital and patient in 19th century America. *In* Branca, P. ed. The medicine show p121-40

Hospital house staff. See Interns (Medicine)

Hospital management. See Hospitals—Administration

Hospital patients

Psychology

Mellette, S. J. Connotations of hospitalization. *In* Home care p268-72

Hospital social work. See Medical social work

Hospitals

See also Operating rooms; Terminal care facilities

Administration

Akula, W. G. and Vora, J. A. Systems planning tomorrow's hospitals today. *In* Managing nonprofit organizations p118-23

Hand, H. H. and Hollingsworth, A. T. Tailoring MBO to hospitals. *In* Managing nonprofit organizations p176-86

Warner, D. C. Government initatives and controls in American medical care. *In* Smith, B. L. R. ed. The new political economy: the public use of the private sector p214-28

Federal aid

See Federal aid to hospitals

House staff

See Interns (Medicine)

Management and regulation

See Hospitals—Administration

Medical staff

See Interns (Medicine)

Hostetler, John Andrew

Folk medicine and sympathy healing among the Amish. *In* American folk medicine p249-58

Hostilities. See War; War (Interntional law)

Hotlines (Counseling)

Lester, D. The use of the telephone in counseling and crisis intervention. *In* The Social impact of the telephone p454-72

Hottentots. See Bushmen

Hotz, Alfred Julius

Morgenthau's influence on the study of international relations. *In* [Truth and tragedy]: a tribute to Hans Morgenthau p316-21

Hou, Ching-lang

The Chinese belief in baleful stars. *In* Welch, H. and Seidel, A. K. eds. Facets of Taoism p193-228

Houchins, Lee

John Manjirō. *In* Abroad in America: Visitors to the new Nation, 1776-1914 p92-103

Houchins, Lee, and Houchins, Chang-su

The Korean experience in America, 1903-1924. *In* The Asian American: the historical experience p129-56

Houck, John W.
Early historical traces of the contemporary debate about work alienation. *In* Heisler, W. J. and Houck, J. W. eds. A matter of dignity p49-63

Houdar de La Motte, Antoine. See La Motte, Antoine Houdar de

Houdon, Jean Antoine

About
Watson, F. Diderot and Houdon: a little-known bust. *In* The Artist and the writer in France p15-20

Hough, Graham Goulden
The aesthetic of pre-Raphaelitism; excerpt from "The last romantics." *In* Sambrook, J. ed. Pre-Raphaelitism p133-52

The poet as critic. *In* The Literary criticism of T. S. Eliot p42-63

Selected essays
Contents
Coleridge and the Victorians
Criticism as a humanist discipline
Dante and Eliot
Edgar Allan Poe
An eighth type of ambiguity
Also in On literary intention p222-41
John Crowe Ransom: the poet and the critic
The modernist lyric
Narrative and dialogue in Jane Austen
The natural theology of In memoriam
The poetry of Coleridge
Vision and doctrine in Four quartets
W. B. Yeats: a study in poetic integration

Hough, Jerry F.
The cultural revolution and Western understanding of the Soviet system. *In* Cultural revolution in Russia, 1928-1931 p241-53

Party "saturation" in the Soviet Union. *In* Cocks, P.; Daniels, R. V. and Heer, N. W. eds. The dynamics of Soviet politics p117-33

Women and women's issues in Soviet policy debates. *In* Women in Russia p355-73

Houghton, Richard Monckton Milnes, Baron

About
Trilling, L. Profession: man of the world. *In* Trilling, L. A gathering of fugitives p115-25

Houle, Cyril Orvin
Seven adult educational roles of the public library. *In* As much to learn as to teach p94-116

Hoult, Thomas Ford
The humanist perspective. *In* McNall, S. G. ed. Theoretical perspectives in sociology p83-95

Houma Indians
Stanton, M. E. Southern Louisiana survivors: the Houma Indians. *In* Williams, W. L. ed. Southeastern Indians since the removal era p90-109

Houphouët-Boigny, Félix, President Ivory Coast

About
Delorme, N. The foreign policy of the Ivory Coast. *In* Aluko, O. ed. The foreign policies of African states p118-35

The hour of the furnaces (Motion picture)
Kauffmann, S. The hour of the furnaces. *In* Kauffmann, S. Living images p41-44

Hourani, George Fadlo
Ethics in medieval Islam: a conspectus. *In* Essays on Islamic philosophy and science p128-35

Hours (Time) See Horology; Time

The Hours press
Ford, H. D. Nancy Cunard's twenty-four Hours. *In* Ford, H. D. Published in Paris p253-89

House, Humphry
Pre-Raphaelite poetry; excerpt from "All in due time." *In* Sambrook, J. ed. Pre-Raphaelitism p126-32

Household moving. See Moving, Household

Housemaids. See Servants

Houses. See Architecture, Domestic; Dwellings

Housing
Goodman, L. J. and others. Low-cost housing technology: problems, issues, and a proposed solution. *In* Strategies for human settlements: habitat and environment p126-41

Gropius, W. Programme for the establishment of a company for the provision of housing on aesthetically consistent principles. *in* Sharp, D. ed. The rationalist p50-57

See also Aged—Dwellings; Public housing

Research
See Housing research

France
Pickvance, C. G. Housing: reproduction of capital and reproduction of labour power: some recent French work. *In* Walton, J. and Masotti, L. H. eds. The city in comparative perspective p271-89

Great Britain
Bryant, C. and White, L. G. Housing policies and comparative urban politics. *In* Walton, J. and Masotti, L. H. eds. The city in comparative perspective p81-95

United States
Bryant, C. and White, L. G. Housing policies and comparative urban politics. *In* Walton, J. and Masotti, L. H. eds. The city in comparative perspective p81-95

Muth, R. F. Economic policy and urban problems. *In* Capitalism and freedom p158-82

Housing, Cooperative

Netherlands—Amsterdam
Searing, H. With red flags flying: housing in Amsterdam, 1915-1923. *In* Millon, H. A. and Nochlin, L. eds. Art and architecture in the service of politics p230-69

Housing and state. See Housing policy

Housing for the aged. See Aged—Dwellings

Housing policy

Philippine Islands
Benitez, J. C. National planning for human settlements. *In* Strategies for human settlements: habitat and environment p19-27

United States
Downs, A. The impact of housing policy on family life in the United States since World War II. *In* Rossi, A. S.; Kagan, J. and Hareven, T. K. eds. The family p163-80

Housing research

Goodman, L. J. and others. Low-cost housing technology: problems, issues, and a proposed solution. *In* Strategies for human settlements: habitat and environment p126-41

France

Pickvance, C. G. Housing: reproduction of capital and reproduction of labour power: some recent French work. *In* Walton, J. and Masotti, L. H. eds. The city in comparative perspective p271-89

Housman, Alfred Edward

About

Brashear, W. R. The trouble with Housman. *In* Brashear, W. R. The gorgon's head p49-58

About individual works

Epitaph on an army of mercenaries

Wilbur, R. Round about a poem of Housman's. *In* Wilbur, R. Responses p16-38

Houston, Tex. University. John Q. Anderson Folklore Archives

Anderson, J. Q. Texas and Southwest medical lore in the Anderson Collection, University of Houston. *In* American folk medicine p315-19

Houthakker, H. S.

The size distribution of labour incomes derived from the distribution of aptitudes. *In* Econometrics and economic theory p177-87

Hovey, Richard Bennett

Hemingway's "Now I lay me": a psychological interpretation. *In* Benson, J. J. ed. The short stories of Ernest Hemingway: critical essays p180-87

Hoving, Walter, and O'Brien, George

The crisis of design and aesthetics in American management. *In* The Uneasy coalition: design in corporate America p 1-16

Howard, David M.

Some reflections on the mission of the Church. *In* Current issues in Biblical and patristic interpretation p309-17

Howard, Dick

The future as present: political and theoretical implications. *In* Radicalism in the contemporary age v2 p129-52

Howard, Donald Roy

Chaucer's idea of an idea. *In* English Association. Essays and studies, 1976 p39-55

Flying through space: Chaucer and Milton. *In* Wittreich, J. A. ed. Milton and the line of vision p3-23

Renaissance world-alienation. *In* The Darker vision of the Renaissance p47-76

About individual works

The idea of the Canterbury tales

Robertson, D. W. Chaucer criticism. *In* Medievalia et humanistica no. 8 p252-55

Howard, Henry, Earl of Surrey. See Surrey, Henry Howard, Earl of

Howard, John Addison

The plight of private enterprise and a possible way out. *In* Prochnow, H. V. ed. Dilemmas facing the nation p82-95

Howard, John Eager

About

Harvey, A. M. More bright stars in the Johns Hopkins galaxy. *In* Harvey, A. M. Adventures in medical research p333-63

Howard, John Galen

About

Draper, J. The Ecole des beaux-arts and the architectural profession in the United States: the case of John Galen Howard. *In* Kostof, S. ed. The architect p209-37

Howard, Maureen

Editor's note on Edith Wharton and Gertrude Stein. *In* Howard, M. ed. Seven American women writers of the twentieth century p28-34

Introduction. *In* Howard, M. ed. Seven American women writers of the twentieth century p3-27

Howard, Michael

Temperamenta belli: can war be controlled? *In* Howard, M. ed. Restraints on war p 1-15

Howard, Richard

About

Lieberman, L. Richard Howard: the archeologist poet. *In* Lieberman, L. Unassigned frequencies p116-21

Lynch, M. The life below the life. *In* Crew, L. ed. The gay academic p178-92

Howard, Vernon A.

Artistic practice and skills. *In* Perkins, D. and Leondar, B. eds. The arts and congnition p208-40

Howard, Victor M.

The Canadian crank. *In* Essays in honor of Russel B. Nye p92-104

Howard family

Virgoe, R. The recovery of the Howards in East Anglia, 1485-1529. *In* Wealth and power in Tudor England p 1-20

Howard University. School of Law

Bloomfield, M. H. John Mercer Langston and the training of Black lawyers. *In* Bloomfield, M. H. American lawyers in a changing society, 1776-1876 p302-39

Howarth, William Driver

Comedy in France. *In* Howarth, W. D. ed. Comic drama p102-21

Introduction: theoretical considerations. *In* Howarth, W. D. ed. Comic drama p 1-21

The playwright as hero: biographical plays with Molière as protagonist: 1673-1972. *In* Johnson, R. B.; Neuman, E. S. and Trail, G. T. eds. Molière and the commonwealth of letters: patrimony and posterity p557-72

Howe, Christopher B.

Japan's policy toward foreign trade: the strategic options. *In* Modern Japan p244-64

Howe, Christopher B. and Walker, Kenneth Richard

The economist. *In* Wilson, R. G. ed. Mao Tse-tung in the scales of history p174-222

Howe, Daniel Walker

Victorian culture in America. *In* Howe, D. W. ed. Victorian America p3-28

Howe, Florence

Women and the power to change. *In* Women and the power to change p127-71

About

Howe, F. Women and the power to change. *In* Women and the power to change p127-71

Howe, Harold

The interplay of mass and class. *In* The Third century p101-08

Howe, Irving
Celebrations and attacks
Contents
Anti-Semite and Jew
The country of the pointed firs
Culture and radicalism
Delmore Schwartz: an appreciation
Doris Lessing: no compromise, no happiness
Endgame: the fate of modernism
A fine novel of academic life
Flannery O'Connor's stories
George Eliot in her letters
George Konrad: the traffic of suffering
God, man and Stalin
Henry James as latter-day saint
The Holocaust and moral judgment
In the day of a false messiah
Lillian Hellman and the McCarthy years
Lionel Trilling: Sincerity and authenticity
Literature and liberalism
Literature on the couch
Mailer's political novel
A man of letters
A neglected American poet
A Negro in America
Octavio Paz: Mexican modernist
The plebeian realism of James Hanley
The poetry of Isaac Rosenberg
Privacy for Joyce?
Richard Wright: a word of farewell
Robert Frost: a momentary stay
The Salinger cult
The Snopes saga
Southern agrarians and American culture
The stories of Bernard Malamud
The stories of Isaac Babel
The stories of Pirandello
Strangers
The suburbs of Babylon
Tomato or cucumber?
Treacheries of faith
Tribune of socialism
W. E. B. DuBois: glory and shame
The wounds of all generations
　Lukacs and Solzhenitsyn. *In* Dunlop, J. B.; Haugh, R. and Klimoff, A. eds. Aleksandr Solzhenitsyn: critical essays and documentary materials 2d ed. p147-55
　The Plath celebration: a partial dissent; excerpt from "The critical point." *In* Butscher, E. ed. Sylvia Plath p225-35
　The pleasures of Kim. *In* Art, politics, and will p145-58

About individual works
The critical point
Sale, R. H. Irving Howe. *In* Sale, R. H. On not being good enough p163-66

Philip Roth reconsidered
Sheed, W. Howe's complaint. *In* Sheed, W. The good word & other words p12-15

Howe, James
Carrying the village: Cuna political metaphors. *In* The Social use of metaphor p132-63

Howell, Cicely
Peasant inheritance customs in the Midlands, 1280-1700. *In* Family and inheritance p112-55

Howell, Wilbur Samuel
Adam Smith' lectures on rhetoric: an historical assessment; excerpt from "Eighteenth-century British logic and rhetoric." *In* Skinner, A. S. and Wilson, T. eds. Essays on Adam Smith p11-43

Poetics, rhetoric, and logic
Contents
Aristotle and Horace on rhetoric and poetics
The arts of literary criticism in Renaissance Britain: a comprehensive view
The Declaration of Independence and eighteenth-century logic
De Quincey on science, rhetoric, and poetry
Kenneth Burke's "Lexicon rhetoricae": A critical examination
Literature as an enterprise in communication
Oratory and poetry in Fénelon's literary theory
Renaissance rhetoric and modern rhetoric: a study in change
Poetics, rhetoric, and logic in Renaissance criticism. *In* Classical influences on European culture A.D. 1500-1700 p155-62

Howell, William Henry
About
Harvey, A. M. Fountainhead of American physiology: H. Newell Martin and his pupil William Henry Powell. *In* Harvey, A. M. Adventures in medical research p84-96

Howells, Coral Ann
Love, mystery, and misery
Contents
Ann Radcliffe, The mysteries of Udolpho
C. R. Maturin, Melmoth the wanderer
Charlotte Brontë, Jane Eyre
Gothic themes, values, techniques
Jane Austen, Northanger Abbey
M. G. Lewis, The monk
Minerva Press fiction, 1796-1819: Regina Maria Roche, The children of the abbey and Mary-Anne Radcliffe, Manfroné; or, The one-handed monk

Howells, William Dean
About
Cooley, T. The wilderness within: W. D. Howells. *In* Cooley, T. Educated lives: the rise of modern autobiography in America p73-99
Holman, C. H. "Of everything the unexplained and irresponsible specimen": notes on how to read American realism. *In* Holman, C. H. Windows on the world p17-26
Milne, G. William Dean Howells. *In* Milne, G. The sense of society p71-99
Smith, H. N. William Dean Howells: the theology of realism. *In* Smith, H. N. Democracy and the novel p75-103

About individual works
A boy's town
Cooley, T. The wilderness within: W. D. Howells. *In* Cooley, T. Educated lives: the rise of modern autobiography in America p73-99

A hazard of new fortunes
Kime, W. R. Critical discrimination and editorial judgment. *In* Review, v 1 1979 p105-22

Indian summer
Ewell, B. C. Parodic echoes of The portrait of a lady in Howells's Indian summer. *In* Tulane studies in English v22 p117-31

The leatherwood god
Kime, W. R. Critical discrimination and editorial judgment. *In* Review, v 1 1979 p105-22

Howells, William D.—About individual works—*Continued*

A modern instance

Smith, H. N. William Dean Howells: the theology of realism. *In* Smith, H. N. Democracy and the novel p75-103

The rise of Silas Lapham

Forster, S. W. D. Howells: The rise of Silas Lapham. *In* Williams, D. A. ed. The monster in the mirror p149-78

Characters—Elsie Venner

Fryer, J. The temptress: Elsie Venner: The literary convention with psychological trappings. *In* Fryer, J. The faces of Eve p29-40

Characters—Eveleth Strange

Fryer, J. The new woman: Through the eye of the needle. *In* Fryer, J. The faces of Eve p234-42

Characters—Grace Breen

Fryer, J. The new woman: Through the eye of the needle. *In* Fryer, J. The faces of Eve p234-42

Characters—Women

Eakin, P. J. The Howells heroine: from The lady of the Aroostook to April hopes. *In* Eakin, P. J. The New England girl p83-130

Editors

Kime, W. R. Critical discrimination and editorial judgment. *In* Review, v 1 1979 p105-22

Howlett, Jana
The origins of Socialist realism in Soviet visual art. *In* Oxford Slavonic papers new ser. v9 p91-101

Howlett, Michael J.
Strategic planning in state government. *In* Managing nonprofit organizations p124-37

Howrigan, Neva Larocque
The one-room schoolhouse—North. *In* Roots of open education in America p67-72

Hoy, Cyrus Henry
Fathers and daughters in Shakespeare's romances. *In* Shakespeare's romances reconsidered p77-90

Jacobean tragedy and the mannerist style. *In* Shakespeare survey 26 p49-67

Shakespeare and the drama of his time. *In* Shakespeare: aspects of influence p21-41

Hoy, David Couzens
History, historicity, and historiography in Being and time. *In* Murray, M. E. ed. Heidegger and modern philosophy p329-53

Hoyle, Sir Fred
On the origin of the universe. *In* The Frontiers of knowledge p295-323

Hrdličková, Venčeslava
Japanese professional storytellers. *In* Folklore genres p171-90

Hrubý, Antonín
The plowman from Bohemia. *In* Hoffmeister, G. ed. The Renaissance and Reformation in Germany p17-32

Hsia, C. T. See Hsia, Chih-tsing

Hsia, Chih-tsing
The military romance: a genre of Chinese fiction. *In* Birch, C. ed. Studies in Chinese literary genres p339-90

The scholar-novelist and Chinese culture: a reappraisal of Ching-hua yuan. *In* Chinese narrative p266-305

Yen Fu and Liang Ch'i-ch'ao as advocates of new fiction. *In* Chinese approaches to literature from Confucius to Liang Ch'i-ch'ao p221-57

The **Hsing-li** ching-i and the Ch'eng-Chu school of the seventeenth century. Chan, Wing-tsit. *In* The Unfolding of Neo-Confucianism p543-79

Hsiung, Shih-li

About

Tu, Wei-ming. Hsiung Shih-li's quest for authentic existence. *In* The Limits of change p242-75

Hsu, Francis Lang-Kwang
Passage to understanding. *In* Spindler, G. D. ed. The making of psychological anthropology p142-73

Hsü, Tu

About

Dennerline, J. Hsü Tu and the lesson of Nanking: political integration and the local defense in Chiang-nan, 1634-1645. *In* Spence, J. D. and Wills, J. E. eds. From Ming to Ch'ing p89-132

Hsüeh hêng
Schneider. L. A. National Essence and the new intelligentsia. *In* The Limits of change p57-89

Hu, Shi

About

Grieder, J. B. Liang, Ch'i-ch'ao and Hu Shih. *In* Abroad in America: Visitors to the new Nation, 1776-1914 p279-92

Hu, Shih

About

Hyer, P. V. Hu Shih: the diplomacy of gentle persuasion. *In* Burns, R. D. and Bennett, E. M. eds. Diplomats in crisis p153-70

Huang, T'ing-chien

About

Rickett, A. A. Method and intuition: the poetic theories of Huang T'ing-chien. *In* Chinese approaches to literature from Confucius to Liang Ch'i-ch'ao p97-119

Huang-ti nei ching su wên
From The Yellow Emperor's classic of internal medicine. *In* Sobel, D. S. ed. Ways of health p173-87

Hubbard, David G.
A glimmer of hope: a psychiatric perspective. *In* International terrorism and political crimes p27-32

Hubbard, Frank McKinney

About

McCann, W. Kin Hubbard and journalistic humor in the Midwest. *In* Essays in honor of Russel B. Nye p129-40

Hubbard, Kin, pseud. See Hubbard, Frank McKinney

Hubbard, La Fayette Ronald
Wallis, R. Societal reaction to scientology: a study in the sociology of deviant religion. *In* Wallis, R. ed. Sectarianism p86-116

Hubbard, William

About individual works

A general history of New England, from the discovery to MDCLXXX

Seelye, J. Ecclesiastic drums: Puritan theocrats, despairing of the present generation, reform the past. *In* Seelye, J. Prophetic waters p217-52

Hubble, Edwin Howell

About

Goldsmith, D. W. Edwin Hubble and the universe outside our galaxy. *In* Neyman, J. ed. The heritage of Copernicus: theories "pleasing to the mind" p63-94

Hubel, David

Neurobiology: a science in need of a Copernicus. *In* Neyman, J. ed. The heritage of Copernicus: theories "pleasing to the mind" p243-60

Huber, Joan

The politics of public assistance: Western Europe and the United States. *In* Major social issues p109-25

Huber, Peter J.

Early cuneiform evidence for the existence of the planet Venus. *In* Goldsmith, D. ed. Scientists confront Velikovsky p117-44

Hubmann, Franz

About individual works

The Jewish family album: the life of a people in photographs

Dawidowicz, L. S. Picturing the past. *In* Dawidowicz, L. S. The Jewish presence p177-90

Hubris (The Greek word)

Michelini, A. ΥΒΡΙΣ and plants. *In* Harvard Studies in classical philology v82 p35-44

Huby, Pamela M.

Greek ethics. *In* New studies in ethics v 1 p 1-78

Some aspects of the problem of survival. *In* Thakur, S. C. ed. Philosophy and psychical research p122-41

Hudson, Charles M.

The Catawba Indians of South Carolina: a question of ethnic survival. *In* Williams, W. L. ed. Southeastern Indians since the removal area p110-20

Hudson, Darril

The World Council of Churches and racism. *In* The Year book of world affairs, 1975 p155-72

Hudson, John C.

Theory and methodology in comparative frontier studies. *In* Miller, D. H. and Steffen, J. O. eds. The frontier p11-31

Hudson, Martha B. See Davis, C. E. jt. auth.

Hudson, Robert Bowman

The Illinois years. *In* Lerner, D. and Nelson, L. M. eds. Communication research—a half-century appraisal p311-16

Hudson, William Donald

Ethical intuitionism. *In* New studies in ethics v 1 p229-303

Hudson, William Henry, 1841-1922

About

Dobie, J. F. The gauchos and horses of Hudson and Graham. *In* Dobie, J. F. Prefaces p187-200

Hudson, Winthrop Still

A time of religious ferment. *In* The Rise of Adventism p 1-17

Hudson's Bay Company

Ray, A. J. The Hudson's Bay Company fur trade in the eighteenth cenutry: a comparative economic study. *In* European settlement and development in North America: essays on geographical change in honour and memory of Andrew Hill Clark p116-35

Hue de Rotelande

About individual works

Ipomedon

Hanning, R. W. "Engin" in twelfth-century courtly texts. *In* Hanning, R. W. The individual in twelfth-century romance p105-38

Hufbauer, G. C.

The multinational corporation and direct investment. *In* Kenen, P. B. ed. International trade and finance p253-319

Hufford, David J.

A new approach to the "old hag": the nightmare tradition reexamined. *In* American folk medicine p73-85

Hufton, Olwen H.

The French church. *In* Callahan, W. J. and Higgs, D. eds. Church and society in Catholic Europe of the eighteenth century p13-33

Women in revolution, 1789-1796. *In* French society and the Revolution p148-66

Huggins, James, and Forrester, Randal G.

The gay male. *In* Gochros, H. L. and Gochros, J. S. eds. The sexually oppressed p130-44

Huggins, Nathan Irvin

Afro-Americans. *In* Ethnic leadership in America p91-118

About individual works

Harlem renaissance

Cruse, H. The creative and performing arts and the struggle for identity and credibility. *In* Johnson, H. A. ed. Negotiating the mainstream p47-102

Hugh of Saint Victor. See Hugo of Saint-Victor

Hughes, Charles Evans

About

Fish, P. G. William Howard Taft and Charles Evans Hughes: conservative politicians as chief judicial reformers. *In* The Supreme Court review, 1975 p123-45

White, G. E. Hughes and Stone: ironies of the Chief Justiceship. *In* White, G. E. The American judicial tradition p200-29

Hughes, David G.

Music and meter in liturgical poetry. *In* Medievalia et humanistica no. 7 p29-43

Hughes, David Yerkes

The garden in Wells's early science fiction. *In* H. G. Wells and modern science fiction p48-69

Hughes, Diane Owen

Domestic ideals and social behavior: evidence from medieval Genoa. *In* Rosenberg, C. E. ed. The family in history p115-43

Kinsmen and neighbors in medieval Genoa. *In* The Medieval city p75-111

Urban growth and family structure in medieval Genoa. *In* Towns in societies p105-30

Human capital—*Continued*

Accounting
Milani, K. It doesn't add up: the role of human resource accounting in effecting work humanization. *In* Heisler, W. J. and Houck, J. W. eds. A matter of dignity p179-95

The human comedy (Motion picture)
McGilligan, P. Mr. Saroyan's thoroughly American movie. *In* Peary, G. and Shatzkin, R. eds. The modern American novel and the movies p156-67

Human ecology
Catton, W. R. Carrying capacity, overshoot, and the quality of life. *In* Major social issues p231-49

Catton, W. R. and Dunlap, R. E. Environmental sociology: a new paradigm. *In* McNall, S. G. ed. Theoretical perspectives in sociology p465-78

Dubos, R. J. The cave and the horizon. *In* Dubos, R .J. Beast or angel? p69-76

Dubos, R. J. Creative adaptations to the future. *In* Aspects of American liberty p162-73

London, B. Ecology as macrosociology: a new look at an old perspective. *In* McNall, S. G. ed. Theoretical perspectives in sociology p494-513

Potter, R. B. The simple structure of the population debate: the logic of the ecology movement. *In* Population policy and ethics p347-63

Rappaport, R. A. Biology, meaning, and the quality of life. *In* Major social issues p265-76

Slobodkin, L. B. Sociology and ecology: the need for mutual concern. *In* Major social issues p250-64

Stanford, G. Recycling in human settlements. *In* Strategies for human settlements: habitat and environment p40-44

Verghese, T. P. Muddled metaphors: an Asian response to Garrett Hardin. *In* Lucas, G. R. and Ogletree, T. W. eds. Lifeboat ethics p151-56

See also Anthropo-geography; Community life; Environmental policy; Man—Influence of environment; Man—Influence on nature; Population; Social psychology

Moral and religious aspects
Shriver, D. W. Lifeboaters and mainlanders: a response. *In* Lucas, G. R. and Ogletree, T. W. eds. Lifeboat ethics p141-50

Amazon Valley
Thompson, S. I. The cultural ecology of pioneer agriculture in contemporary South America. *In* Miller, D. H. and Steffen, J. O. eds. The frontier p297-316

Nissan Island
Chan, G. and Saini, B. S. Integrated farming system and settlement plan for Nissan Island, Papua New Guinea. *In* Strategies for human settlements: habitat and environment p45-66

Human engineering
Koestler, A. An alternative to despair. *In* Koestler, A. Janus p98-106

See also Architecture—Human factors

Human environment. See Human ecology

Human evolution
Barash, D. P. Evolution as a paradigm for behavior. *In* Sociobiology and human nature p13-32

Dart, R. A. Sir Grafton Elliot Smith and the evolution of man. *In* Grafton Elliot Smith p25-38

Edelheit, H. On the biology of language: Darwinian/Lamarckian homology in human inheritance (with some thoughts about the Lamarckism of Freud) *In* Psychoanalysis and language p45-74

See also Evolution; Fossil man; Sociobiology

Human experimentation in medicine
Morris, N. and Mills, M. Prisoners as laboratory animals. *In* Contemporary issues in criminal justice p129-43

Human factors in architecture. See Architecture—Human factors

Human fertility. See Fertility, Human

Human genetics
Biesheuvel, S. An examination of Jensen's theory concerning educability, heritability and population differences. *In* Montagu, A. ed. Race and IQ p59-72

Bodmer, W. F. Race and IQ: the genetic background. *In* Montagu, A. ed. Race and IQ p252-86

Brace, C. L. and Livingstone, F. B. On creeping Jensenism. *In* Montagu, A. ed. Race and IQ p151-73

Bronfenbrenner, U. Nature with nurture: a reinterpretation of the evidence. *In* Montagu, A. ed. Race and IQ p114-44

Carlson, E. A. Genetics and the biological basis of the human condition. *In* The Tricentennial people p3-17

Dubinin, N. P. Race and contemporary genetics. *In* United Nations Educational, Scientific and Cultural Organization. Race, science and society p68-94

Dunn, L. C. Race and biology. *In* United Nations Educational, Scientific and Cultural Organization. Race, science and society p31-67

Gordon, E. W. and Green, D. An affluent society's excuses for inequality: developmental, economic, and educational. *In* Montagu, A. ed. Race and IQ p73-103

Jensen, A. R. Race and mental ability. *In* Racial variation in man p71-108

Layzer, D. Heritability analyses of IQ scores: Science or numerology? *In* Montagu, A. ed. Race and IQ p193-219

Lewontin, R. C. Race and intelligence. *In* Montagu, A. ed. Race and IQ p175-91

Morton, N. E. Interracial crosses and group differences. *In* Racial variation in man p151-69

Sanday, P. R. On the causes of IQ differences between groups and implications for social policy. *In* Montagu, A. ed. Race and IQ p220-51

Strømnæs, Ø. The impact on human genetics. *In* Against pollution and hunger p215-17

Sunderland, E. Biological components of the races of man. *In* Racial variation in man p9-25

Walters, L. Genetics, reproductive biology and bioethics. *In* The Tricentennial people p66-74

See also Genetic counseling

Human genetics—*Continued*

Law and legislation

Shaw, M. W. S. Genetics and the law. *In* The Tricentennial people p48-57

Moral and religious aspects

Nygaard, A. P. The ethical problem of human genetics. *In* Against pollution and hunger p218-19

Social aspects

Bodmer, W. F. Biomedical advances: a mixed blessing? *In* Harré, R. ed. Problems of scientific revolution p25-41

Human geography. See Anthropo-geography

Human growth

Katchadourian, H. A. Medical perspectives on adulthood. *In* Erikson, E. H. ed. Adulthood p33-60

Montagu, A. My conception of the nature of human nature. *In* Hanna, T. ed. Explorers of humankind p90-102

Human interaction. See Social interaction

Human magnetism. See Animal magnetism

Human nature. Hanna, T. *In* Hanna, T. ed. Explorers of humankind p33-47

Human nature, My conception of the nature of. Montagu, A. *In* Hanna, T. ed. Explorers of humankind p90-102

Human paleontology. See Fossil man

Human relations. See Interpersonal relations

Human reproduction

Aldridge, A. O. Feijoo, Voltaire, and the mathematics of procreation. *In* Studies in eighteenth-century culture v4 p131-38

See also Fertility, Human

Human resource development. See Manpower planning; Manpower policy

Human resources. See Human capital

Human rights. See Civil rights

Humanism

Abrams, M. H. The language and methods of humanism. *In* Hook, S.; Kurtz, P. W. and Todorovich, M. eds. The philosophy of the curriculum: the need for general education p89-97

Babbitt, I. What is humanism? Excerpt from "Literature and the American college." *In* Crunden, R. M. ed. The superfluous men p133-34

Borchardt, F. L. First contacts with Italy. *In* Hoffmeister, G. ed. The Renaissance and Reformation in Germany p 1-16

Gilbert, F. The humanist concept of the prince and The prince of Machiavelli. *In* Gilbert, F. History p91-114

Grassi, E. Marxism, humanism, and the problem of imagination in Vico's works. *In* Giambattista Vico's science of humanity p275-94

Himmelfarb, G. Observations on humanism and history. *In* Hook, S.; Kurtz, P. W. and Todorovich, M. eds. The philosophy of the curriculum: the need for general education p81-87

Hoult, T. F. The humanist perspective. *In* McNall, S. G. ed. Theoretical perspectives in sociology p83-95

Krash, O. Several humanisms and John Dewey. *In* Fairfield, R. P. ed. Humanistic frontiers in American education p116-22

Levi, A. H. T. Ethics and the encyclopedia in the sixteenth century. *In* French Renaissance studies, 1540-70 p170-84

Luedtke, L. S. Not so common ground: controversies in contemporary American studies. *In* Luedtke, L. S. ed. The study of American culture p323-67

Mandel'shtam, O. E. Humanism & modern life. *In* Mandel'shtam, O. E. Selected essays p154-56

Martin, D. A. Mutations: religio-political crisis and the collapse of Puritanism and humanism. *In* Universities in the Western world p85-97

Mazzeo, J. A. Interpretation, humanistic culture, and cultural change. *In* Mazzeo, J. A. Varieties of interpretation p95-128

Miller, J. W. History and humanism. *In* Miller, J. W. The paradox of cause, and other essays p75-96

Olafson, F. A. Humanism and the humanities. *In* Hook, S.; Kurtz, P. W. and Todorovich, M. eds. The philosophy of the curriculum: the need for general education p51-74

Overfield, J. H. Scholastic opposition to humanism in pre-Reformation Germany. *In* Viator: medieval and Renaissance studies v7 p391-420

Peckham, M. Humanism, politics, and government in the nineteenth century. *In* Peckham, M. Romanticism and behavior p351-61

Rice, E. F. The humanist idea of Christian antiquity and the impact of Greek patristic work on sixteenth-century thought. *In* Classical influences on European culture A.D. 1500-1700 p199-203

Roszak, T. Ethics, ecstasy, and the study of new religions. *In* Needleman, J. and Baker, G. eds. Understanding the new religions p49-62

Scaglione, A. D. A note on Montaigne's Des cannibales and the humanist tradition. *In* First images of America p63-70

Schmidt, J. Humanism and popular culture. *In* Hoffmeister, G. ed. The Renaissance and Reformation in Germany p177-88

Struever, N. S. Vico, Valla, and the logic of humanist inquiry. *In* Giambattista Vico's science of humanity p173-85

Tate, A. The fallacy of humanism. *In* Crunden, R. M. ed. The superfluous men p150-59

Trevor-Roper, H. R. Charles V and the failure of humanism. *In* Trevor-Roper, H. R. Princes and artists p11-45

Watanabe, M. Gregor Heimburg and early humanism in Germany. *In* Philosophy and humanism p406-22

See also Classical education; Culture; Humanistic ethics; Humanities; Learning and scholarship; Philosophical anthropology; Renaissance

History

Knoll, P. W. The world of the young Copernicus: society, science, and the university. *In* Science and society: past, present, and future p19-44

20th century

Feigl, H. The outlook of scientific humanism. *In* The Abdication of philosophy: philosophy and the public good p73-79

Ricoeur, P. What does humanism mean? *In* Ricoeur, P. Political and social essays p68-87

Humanism in art. See Ut pictura poesis (Aesthetics)

Humanist ethics. See Humanistic ethics

Humanistic education. See Education, Humanistic

Humanistic ethics

Greene, M. The new freedom and the moral life. *In* Greene, M. Landscapes of learning p147-57

Peters, R. S. Subjectivity and standards. *In* Niblett, W. R. ed. The sciences, the humanities and the technological threat p139-56

Humanistic psychology

May, R. Gregory Bateson and humanistic psychology. *In* About Bateson p77-99

Humanists

Hoffmeister, G. The pagan influence of the Italian Renaissance on German life and letters, 1450-1520. *In* Hoffmeister, G. ed. The Renaissance and Reformation in Germany p51-67

Germany

Overfield, J. H. Scholastic opposition to humanism in pre-Reformation Germany. *In* Viator: medieval and Renaissance studies v7 p391-420

Humanitarianism (Religion). See Positivism; Socinianism

Humanities

Berman, R. S. Justifying the humanities. *In* Hook, S.; Kurtz, P. W. and Todorovich, M. eds. The philosophy of the curriculum: the need for general education p75-79

Black, M. Some tasks for 'the humanities.' *In* Niblett, W. R. The sciences, the humanities and the technological threat p79-89

Edel, A. A philosophic perspective. *In* Small comforts for hard times p335-84

Graff, G. How not to save the humanities. *In* Graff, G. Literature against itself p181-205

Kristeller, P. O. The humanities as scholarship and a branch of knowledge. *In* Hook, S.; Kurtz, P. W. and Todorovich, M. eds. The philosophy of the curriculum: the need for general education p217-20

Nichols, M. H. Rhetoric and the humane tradition. *In* Rhetoric: a tradition in transition p178-91

Olafson, F. A. Humanism and the humanities. *In* Hook, S.; Kurtz, P. W. and Todorovich, M. eds. The philosophy of the curriculum: the need for general education p51-74

Peters, R. S. Subjectivity and standards. *In* Niblett, W. R. ed. The sciences, the humanities and the technological threat p139-56

Veysey, L. R. The plural organized worlds of the humanities. *In* Oleson, A. and Voss, J. eds. The organization of knowledge in modern America, 1860-1920 p51-106

See also Classical education; Education, Humanistic; Science and the humanities

Research

Frye, N. The search for acceptable words. *In* Frye, N. Spiritus mundi p3-26

Humanities and science. See Science and the humanities

Humanity. See Benevolence

Humanity, Religion of. See Positivism

Humboldt, Wilhelm, Freiherr von

About individual works

Letters to a female friend

Bruford, W. H. Wilhelm von Humboldt in his letters. *In* Bruford, W. H. The German tradition of self-cultivation p 1-28

Hume, David

About

Brandt, R. The beginnings of Hume's philosophy. *In* David Hume p117-27

Davis, J. W. Hume on qualitative content. *In* David Hume p175-80

Flew, A. G. N. Hume and historical necessity. *In* Flew, A. G. N. A rational animal p49-74

Forbes, D. Sceptical Whiggism, commerce, and liberty. *In* Skinner, A. S. and Wilson, T. eds. Essays on Adam Smith p179-201

Gawlick, G. Hume and the deists: a reconsideration. *In* David Hume p128-38

Hanfling, O. Hume and Wittgenstein. *In* Royal Institute of Philosophy. Impressions of empiricism p47-65

Jones, P. Strains in Hume and Wittgenstein. *In* Livingston, D. W. and King, J. T. eds. Hume p191-209

Livingston, D. W. Hume's conservatism. *In* Studies in eighteenth-century culture v7 p213-33

Livingston, D. W Hume's historical theory of meaning. *In* Livingston, D. W. and King, J. T. eds. Hume p213-38

Robison, W. L. David Hume: naturalist and meta-sceptic. *In* Livingston, D. W. and King, J. T. eds. Hume p23-49

Robison, W. L. Hume's causal scepticism *In* David Hume p156-66

Sapadin, E. Hume's Law, Hume's way. *In* David Hume p210-17

Weinberg, J. R. Hume's theory of causal belief. *In* Weinberg, J. R. Ockham, Descartes, and Hume p92-111

About individual works

Dialogues concerning natural religion

Mossner, E. C. Hume and the legacy of the Dialogues. *In* David Hume p 1-22

Enquiry concerning the principles of morals

Britton, K. Hume on some non-natural distinctions. *In* David Hume p205-09

Essays on national characters

Chamley, P. E. The conflict between Montesquieu and Hume: a study of the origins of Adam Smith's universalism. *In* Skinner, A. S. and Wilson, T. eds. Essays on Adam Smith p274-305

The history of England

Burke, J. J. Hume's History of England: waking the English from a dogmatic slumber. *In* Studies in eighteenth-century culture v7 p235-50

Stockton, C. N. Economics and the mechanism of historical progress in Hume's History. *In* Livingston, D. W. and King, J. T. eds. Hume p296-320

Walton, C. Hume and Jefferson on the uses of history. *In* Livingston, D. W. and King, J. T. eds. Hume p389-403

Also in Philosophy and the civilizing arts p103-25

Hume, David—About individual works
—*Continued*

An inquiry concerning the principles of morals

King, J. T. The place of the language of morals in Hume's second Enquiry. *In* Livingston, D. W. and King, J. T. eds. Hume p343-61

A treatise of human nature

Ardal, P. S. Convention and value. *In* David Hume p51-68

Ardal, P. S. Some implications of the virtue of reasonableness in Hume's Treatise. *In* Livingston, D. W. and King, J. T. eds. Hume p91-106

Bricke, J. Hume on self-identity, memory and causality. *In* David Hume p167-74

Flew, A. G. N. Infinite divisibility in Hume's Treatise. *In* Livingston, D. W. and King, J. T. eds. Hume p257-69

Khamara, E. J. and Macnabb, D. G. C. Hume and his predecessors on the causal maxim. *In* David Hume p146-55

Livingston, D. W. Hume's historical theory of meaning. *In* Livingston, D. W. and King, J. T. eds. Hume p213-38

Lyons, J. O. Dancing on the head of a pin. *In* Lyons, J. O. The invention of the self p18-27

Noxon, J. H. Remembering and imagining the past. *In* Livingston, D. W. and King, J. T. eds. Hume p270-95

Sutherland, S. R. Hume and the concept of pleasure. *In* David Hume p218-24

Van Steenburgh, E. W. Durationless moments in Hume's Treatise. *In* David Hume p181-85

Warnock, M. Imagination and creative art: Hume, Kant and Schelling. *In* Warnock, M. Imagination p35-71

Warnock, M. Imagination and perception: Hume and Kant. *In* Warnock, M. Imagination p13-34

Weinberg, J. R. Kenny, Hume, and causal necessity. *In* Weinberg, J. R. Ockham, Descartes, and Hume p141-44

Weinberg, J. R. Two recent criticisms of Hume. *In* Weinberg, J. R. Ockham, Descartes, and Hume p135-40

A treatise of human nature (Volume 3)

Connon, R. W. The textual and philosophical significance of Hume's MS alterations to Treatise III. *In* David Hume p186-204

A treatise of human nature (Book I, Part IV, Section VI)

Penelhum, T. Self-identity and self-regard. *In* Rorty, A. O. ed. The identities of persons p253-80

Aesthetics

Jones, P. Cause, reason, and objectivity in Hume's aesthetics. *In* Livingston, D. W. and King, J. T. eds. Hume p323-42

Economics

Stockton, C. N. Economics and the mechanism of historical progress in Hume's History. *In* Livingston, D. W. and King, J. T. eds. Hume p296-320

Ethics

Foot, P. Hume on moral judgement. *In* Foot, P. Virtues and vices, and other essays in moral philosophy p74-80

Glossop, R. J. Hume, Stevenson, and Hare on moral language. *In* Livingston, D. W. and King, J. T. eds. Hume p362-85

Kemp, J. Ethical naturalism. *In* New studies in ethics v 1 p173-228

Influence

Berlin, Sir I. Hume and the sources of German anti-rationalism. *In* David Hume p93-116

Influence—Fielding

Battestin, M. C. The problem of Amelia: Hume, Barrow, and the conversion of Captain Booth. *In* ELH essays for Earl R. Wasserman p320-55

Influence—Husserl

Davie, G. E. Edmund Husserl and 'the as yet, in its most important respect, unrecognised greatness of Hume.' *In* David Hume p69-76

Influence—Smith

Raphael, D. D. 'The true old Humean philosophy' and its influence on Adam Smith. *In* David Hume p23-38

Knowledge, Theory of

Anderson, R. F. The location, extension, shape, and size of Hume's perceptions. *In* Livingston, D. W. and King, J. T. eds. Hume p153-71

Butler, R. J. Hume's impressions. *In* Royal Institute of Philosophy. Impressions of empiricism p122-36

Passmore, J. A. Hume and the ethics of belief. *In* David Hume p77-92

Logic

Stove, D. C. Why should probability be the guide of life? *In* Livingston, D. W. and King, J. T. eds. Hume p50-68

Zabeeh, F. Hume's problem of induction: an appraisal. *In* Livingston, D. W. and King, J. T. eds. Hume p69-90

Ontology

Nathan, G. J. The existence and nature of God in Hume's theism. *In* Livingston, D. W. and King, J. T. eds. Hume p126-49

Yandell, K. E. Hume on religious belief. *In* Livingston, D. W. and King, J. T. eds. Hume p109-25

Philosophy

Weinberg, J. R. The novelty of Hume's philosophy. *In* Weinberg, J. R. Ockham, Descartes, and Hume p112-34

Political science

Adair, D. G. "That politics may be reduced to a science": David Hume, James Madison, and the tenth Federalist. *In* Livingston, D. W. and King, J. T. eds. Hume p404-17

Forbes, D. Hume's science of politics. *In* David Hume p39-50

Stockton, C. N. Economics and the mechanism of historical progress in Hume's History. *In* Livingston, D. W. and King, J. T. eds. Hume p296-320

Wolin, S. S. Hume and conservatism. *In* Livingston, D. W. and King, J. T. eds Hume p239-56

Psychology

Capaldi, N. Hume's theory of the passions *In* Livingston, D. W. and King, J. T. eds. Hume p172-90

Hume, Ian M.
Some economic aspects of labour migration in Europe since the Second World War. *In* Economic factors in population growth p491-509

Hume, Ivor Noel. See Noël Hume, Ivor

Hume, Kathryn
The concept of the hall in Old English poetry. *In* Anglo-Saxon England 3 p63-74

Hum-ishu-ma. See Mourning Dove

Humor. See Wit and humor

The humorist
Granger, B. I. Early Southern serials. *In* Granger, B. I. American essay serials from Franklin to Irving p70-96

Humorous poetry. See Nonsense-verses

Humorous poetry, American

History and criticism

Vernon, J. E. Fresh air; humor in contemporary American poetry. *In* Cohen, S. B. ed. Comic relief p304-23

Humpherys, Anne
Dickens and Mayhew on the London poor. *In* Dickens Studies Annual v4 p78-90

Humphreys, Laud
Tearoom trade: impersonal sex in public places. *In* Henslin, J. M. ed. Deviant lifestyles p123-50

Humphreys, Lloyd Girton
The fallout of the legal mind in research. *In* Hook, S.; Kurtz, P. and Todorovich, M. eds. The ethics of teaching and scientific research p161-64

Humpstone, Charles Cheney
The rich man's burden: an examination of environmental consequences of isolation for the United States. *In* Isolation or interdependence? p193-204

Hundred Years' War, 1339-1453
Alban, J. R. and Allmand, C. T. Spies and spying in the fourteenth century. *In* War, literature, and politics in the late Middle Ages p73-101

Palmer, J. J. N. and Wells, A. P. Ecclesiastical reform and the politics of the Hundred Years War during the pontificate of Urban V (1362-70). *In* War, literature, and politics in the late Middle Ages p169-89

Vale, M. G. A. New techniques and old ideals: the impact of artillery on war and chivalry at the end of the Hundred Years War. *In* War, literature, and politics in the late Middle Ages p57-72

Huneker, James Gibbons

About

Mencken, H. L. James Huneker; excerpt from "A book of prefaces." *In* Crunden, R. M. ed. The superfluous men p108-16

Hungary

Economic conditions

Szabady, E. Economic factors in the decline of fertility in Hungary in the nineteenth and early twentieth century. *In* Economic factors in population growth p238-40

History—20th century

Ignotus, P. The first two Communist takeovers of Hungary: 1919 and 1948. *In* Hammond, T. T. ed. The anatomy of Communist takeovers p385-98

History—Revolution, 1956

Gyorgy, A. The Hungarian Revolution of 1956. *In* Hammond, T. T. ed. The anatomy of Communist takeovers p596-605

Politics and government—1945-

Schöpflin, G. Hungary: an uneasy stability. *In* Brown, A. H. and Gray, J. eds. Political culture and political change in Communist states p131-58

Relations (general) with Transylvania

Király, B. K. The Sublime Porte, Vienna, Transylvania and the dissemination of Protestant Reformation in royal Hungary. *In* Király, B. K. ed. Tolerance and movements of religious dissent in Eastern Europe p199-221

Hungiville, Maurice
Epithets and epitaphs: Rudyard Kipling's reputation as a poet. *In* Tennessee Studies in literature v20 p138-50

Hunnis, William

About

May, S. W. William Hunnis and the 1577 Paradise of dainty devices. *In* Virginia. University. Bibliographical Society. Studies in bibliography v28 p63-80

Hunsinger, George
Conclusion: Toward a radical Barth. *In* Hunsinger, G. ed. Karl Barth and radical politics p181-233

Hunt, E. Howard. See Hunt, Howard

Hunt, Howard

About

Vidal, G. The art and arts of E. Howard Hunt. *In* Vidal, G. Matters of fact and of fiction p207-35

Hunt, Sir John

About individual works
The conquest of Everest

Marcus, S. Mt Everest and the British national spirit. *In* Marcus, S. Representations p76-87

Hunt, John Dixon
'Broken images': T. S. Eliot and modern painting. *In* The Waste land in different voices p163-84

A moment's monument: reflections on pre-Raphaelite vision in poetry and painting. *In* Sambrook, J. ed. Pre-Raphaelitism p243-64

Hunt, Kenneth
America in the Far East: political & military dimensions. *In* Rosecrance, R. N. ed. America as an ordinary country p136-57

Hunt, Leigh

About

Baker, W. Leigh Hunt, George Henry Lewes and Henry Hallam's Introduction to the literature of Europe. *In* Virginia. University. Bibliographical Society. Studies in bibliography v32 p252-73

Clogan, P. M. Chaucer and Leigh Hunt. *In* Medievalia et humanistica; new ser. no. 9 p163-74

Contemporaries

See Hunt, Leigh—Friends and associates

Huron language. See Iroquoian languages

Hurricanes
White, E. B. The eye of Edna. *In* White, E. B. Essays of E. B. White p25-33

Hurstfield, Joel
The politics of corruption in Shakespeare's England. *In* Shakespeare survey 28 p15-28

Hurston, Zora Neale

About
Bone, R. A. Three versions of pastoral. *In* Bone, R. A. Down home p139-70

About individual works
Jonah's gourd vine
Hemenway, R. Are you a flying lark or a setting dove? *In* Fisher, D. and Stepto, R. B. eds. Afro-American literature p122-52

Hurwitz, Harold Marvin
Hemingway's tutor, Ezra Pound. *In* Wagner, L. W. ed. Ernest Hemingway p8-21

Husband, Charles
Some aspects of the interaction of the British entertainment media with contemporary race relations. *In* Fischer, H. D. and Melnik, S. R. eds. Entertainment: a cross-cultural examination p196-207

Husband and wife
See also Dowry

Arctic regions
Briggs, J. L. Eskimo women: makers of men. *In* Matthiasson, C. J. ed. Many sisters p261-304

Nigeria
Smedley, A. Women of Udu: survival in a harsh land. *In* Matthiasson, C. J. ed. Many sisters p205-28

Husbands, Jo L.
Nuclear proliferation and the inter-American system. *In* Farer, T. J. ed. The future of the inter-American system p204-31

Husbands
Whitehurst, R. N. Violently jealous husbands. *In* Gross, L. ed. Sexual issues in marriage p75-84

The husband's message (Anglo-Saxon poem)
Goldsmith, M. E. The enigma of The husband's message. *In* Anglo-Saxon poetry: essays in appreciation p242-63

Husén, Torsten
The adolescent and the school in Europe. *In* Adolescence and youth in prospect p186-200

Huss, Roy Gerard
The aesthete as realist. *In* Riewald, J. G. ed. The surprise of excellence p113-22

Hussein, Ebrahim N.

About individual works
Kinjeketile
Mbughuni, L. A. Old and new drama from East Africa. *In* African literature today no. 8: Drama in Africa p85-98

Husserl, Edmund

About
Brough, J. B. The emergence of an absolute consciousness in Husserl's early writings on time-consciousness. *In* Elliston, F. A. and McCormick, P. eds. Husserl p83-100

Caputo, J. D. The question of being and transcendental phenomenology: reflections on Heidegger's relationship to Husserl. *In* Radical phenomenology p84-105

Carr, D. Husserl's problematic concept of the life-world. *In* Elliston, F. A. and McCormick, P. eds. Husserl p202-12

Casey, E. S. Imagination and phenomenological method. *In* Elliston, F. A. and McCormick, P. eds. Husserl p70-82

Davie, G. E. Edmund Husserl and 'the as yet, in its most important respect, unrecognised greatness of Hume.' *In* David Hume p69-76

Derrida, J. "Genesis and structure" and phenomenology. *In* Derrida, J. Writing and difference p154-68

Derrida, J. Violence and metaphysics: an essay on the thought of Emmanuel Levinas. *In* Derrida, J. Writing and difference p79-153

Dickens, D. R. Phenomenology. *In* McNall, S. G. ed. Theoretical perspectives in sociology p325-47

Dreyfus, H. L. and Haugeland, J. Husserl and Heidegger: philosophy's last stand. *In* Murray, M. E. ed. Heidegger and modern philosophy p222-38

Findlay, J. N. Phenomenology and the meaning of realism. *In* Pivčević, E. ed. Phenomenology and philosophical understanding p143-58

Jordan, R. W. Vico and Husserl: history and historical science. *In* Giambattista Vico's science of humanity p251-61

Kern, I. The three ways to the transcendental phenomenological reduction in the philosophy of Edmund Husserl. *In* Elliston, F. A. and McCormick, P. eds.. Husserl p126-49

Kockelmans, J. J. Husserl and Kant on the pure ego. *In* Elliston, F. A. and McCormick, P. eds. Husserl p269-85

Landgrebe, L. Phenomenology as transcendental theory of history. *In* Elliston, F. A. and McCormick, P. eds. Husserl p101-17

Levin, D. M. Husserl's notion of self-evidence. *In* Pivčević, E. ed. Phenomenology and philosophical understanding p53-77

Madison, G. B. Phenomenology and existentialism: Husserl and the end of idealism. *In* Elliston, F. A. and McCormick, P. eds. Husserl p247-68

Olafson, F. A. Husserl's theory of intentionality in contemporary perspective. *In* Elliston, F. A. and McCormick, P. eds. Husserl p160-67

Patočka, J. The Husserlian doctrine of eidetic intuition and its recent critics. *In* Elliston, F. A. and McCormick, P. eds. Husserl p150-59

Van Breda, H. L. A note on reduction and authenticity according to Husserl. *In* Elliston, F. A. and McCormick, P. eds. Husserl p124-25

Welton, D. C. Structure and genesis in Husserl's phenomenology. *In* Elliston, F. A. and McCormick, P. eds. Husserl p54-69

Willard, D. A. The paradox of logical psychologism: Husserl's way out. *In* Elliston, F. A. and McCormick, P. eds. Husserl p10-17

Husserl, Edmund—*Continued*

About individual works

Cartesian meditations: an introduction to phenomenology (5th chapter)

Elliston, F. A. Husserl's phenomenology of empathy. *In* Elliston, F. A. and McCormick, P. eds. Husserl p213-46

The crisis of European science and transcendental phenomenology

Marcuse, H. On science and phenomenology. *In* Giddens, A. ed. Positivism and sociology p225-36

Experience and judgement

Harrison, R. The concept of prepredicative experience. *In* Pivčević, E. ed. Phenomenology and philosophical understanding p93-107

Logical investigations

Mohanty, J. N. Husserl's theory of meaning. *In* Elliston, F. A. and McCormick, P. eds. Husserl p18-34

Taminiaux, J. Heidegger and Husserl's Logical investigations. *In* Radical phenomenology p58-83

Phenomenology (Encyclopaedia Britannica article)

Biemel, W. Husserl's Encyclopaedia Britannica article and Heidegger's remarks thereon. *In* Elliston, F. A. and McCormick, P. eds. Husserl p286-303

Philosophy of arithmetic

Frege, G. Review of Dr E. Husserl's Philosophy of arithmetic. *In* Elliston, F. A. and McCormick, P. eds. Husserl p314-24

Knowledge. Theory of

Bauman, Z. Understanding as the work of reason: Edmund Husserl. *In* Bauman, Z. Hermeneutics and social science p111-30

Pietersma, H. Husserl's views on the evident and the true. *In* Elliston, F. A. and McCormick, P. eds. Husserl p38-53

Hussites

Heymann, F. G. The role of the Bohemian cities during and after the Hussite revolution. *In* Király, B. K. ed. Tolerance and movements of religious dissent in Eastern Europe p27-41

Jakobson, R. Signum et signatum. *In* Matejka, L. and Titunik, I. R. eds. Semiotics of art p176-87

Hustling as a career. Mahigel, E. L. and Stone, G. P. *In* Social problems in athletics p78-85

Huston, John

About

Agee, J. Undirectable director: John Huston; excerpt from "Agee on film v 1." *In* Denby, D. ed. Awake in the dark p293-305

About individual works

Fat city

Samuels, C. T. How not to film a novel. *In* Samuels, C. T. Mastering the film, and other essays p190-97

The treasure of Sierra Madre

Kaminsky, S. M. Gold hat, gold fever, silver screen. *In* Peary, G. and Shatzkin, R. eds. The modern American novel and the movies p53-62

Hutch, Richard A.

Ralph Waldo Emerson: the birth of a seer. *In* Reynolds, F. E. and Capps, D. eds. The biographical process p187-200

Hutchens, Eleanor Newman

An approach through time. *In* Spilka, M. ed. Towards a poetics of fiction p52-61

O Attic shape! The cornering of square. *In* A Provision of human nature p37-44

Hutchings, Patrick Æ

Conjugal faithfulness. *In* Royal Institute of Philosophy. Human value p61-85

Hutchings, Patrick A. E.

Some contemporary realisms. *In* Concerning contemporary art p89-132

Hutchinson, Anne (Marbury)

About

George, C. V. R. Anne Hutchinson and the "revolution which never happened." *In* "Remember the ladies": new perspectives on women in American history p13-37

Stoever, W. K. B. The nature of New England antinomianism. *In* Stoever, W. K. B. 'A faire and easie way to heaven' p161-83

Hutchinson, Cecil Alan

The California frontier. *In* Weber, D. J. ed. New Spain's far northern frontier p171-99

Hutchinson, G. W.

The Coup in Chile and its implications. *In* The Year book of world affairs, 1975 p72-87

Hutchinson, James, 1752-1793

About

Bell, W. J. James Hutchinson (1752-1793) a physician in politics. *In* Bell, W. J. The colonial physician & other essays p99-117

Hutchison, John Alexander

Religion among the liberal arts. *In* Philosophy and the civilizing arts p378-88

Hutchison, Robert A.

About individual works

Vesco

Galbraith, J. K. Robert Vesco: swindler. *In* Galbraith, J. K. Annals of an abiding liberal p317-22

Hüther, Jürgen

Comments on the functional change of television viewing as a leisure pursuit. *In* Fischer, H. D. and Melnik, S. R. eds. Entertainment: a cross-cultural examination p83-91

Hutman, Norma Louise

Célimène as anti-ingenue: Molière and the transformation of comic types. *In* Johnson, R. B.; Neumann, E. S. and Trail, G. T. eds. Molière and the commonwealth of letters: patrimony and posterity p457-61

Hutson, James H.

Early American diplomacy: a reappraisal. *In* The American Revolution and "a candid world" p40-68

Tentative moves toward intercolonial union. *In* Aspects of American liberty p81-94

Hutt, Peter Barton

Public criticism of health science policy. *In* Holton, G. J. and Morison, R. S. eds. Limits of scientific inquiry p157-69

Huttar, Charles Adolph
C. S. Lewis's Narnia and the "grand design." *In* Schakel, P. J. ed. The longing for a form p119-35

Hutten, Ulrich von

About

Wheelis, S. M. Ulrich von Hutten: representative of patriotic humanism. *In* Hoffmeister, G. ed. The Renaissance and Reformation in Germany p111-27

Hutter, Albert D
Reconstructing autobiography: the experience at Warren's Blacking. *In* Dickens Studies Annual v6 p 1-14

Hutterite Brethren
Brock, P. The Hutterites and war, 1530-1800. *In* Király, B. K. ed. Tolerance and movements of religious dissent in Eastern Europe p43-51

Hutton, E. Jeremy; Nehra, Krishan S. and Sastri, Durvasula S.
The right of privacy in the United States, Great Britain, and India. *In* Claude, R. F. ed. Comparative human rights p127-60

Hutton, James. See Part 2 under title: Poetry and poetics from ancient Greece to the Renaissance

Hutton, Virgil Ralph
The short happy life of Macomber. *In* Benson, J. J. ed. The short stories of Ernest Hemingway: critical essays p239-50

Huxley, Aldous Leonard
Chemical persuasion; excerpt from "Brave new world revisited." *In* Knight, D. F. ed. Turning points p231-37
The human situation
Contents
Art
The ego
How original is original sin?
The individual life of man
Integrate education
Language
Latent human potentialities
Man and his planet
Man and religion
More nature in art
Natural history of visions
The population explosion
The problem of human nature
The unconscious
War and nationalism
The world's future

About

Balakian, N. Huxley revisited. *In* Balakian, N. Critical encounters p121-23
Craft, R. In search of Aldoux Huxley. *In* Craft, R. Current convictions p234-44
Pritchard, W. H. England seen through. *In* Pritchard, W. H. Seeing through everything p23-50

About individual works
Beyond the Mexique bay
Walker, R. G. Mexico as scapegoat: Huxley, Lawrence and Beyond the Mexique bay. *In* Walker, R. G. Infernal paradise p105-38

Brave new world
Colmer, J. Utopian fantasy. *In* Colmer, J. Coleridge to Catch-22 p162-76

Eyeless in Gaza
Walker, R. G. Time and the healing of wounds in Huxley's Eyeless in Gaza. *In* Walker, R. G. Infernal paradise p139-59

Letters of Aldous Huxley
Connolly, C. Aldous Huxley: 2. *In* Connolly, C. The evening colonnade p247-50

Literature and science
Kurz, P. K. Literature and science. *In* Kurz, P. K. On modern German literature v 1 p56-79

Huxley, Laura Archera

About individual works
This timeless moment
Balakian, N. Huxley revisited. *In* Balakian, N. Critical encounters p121-23
Connolly, C. Aldous Huxley: 1. *In* Connolly, C. The evening colonnade p244-46

Huxley, Thomas Henry

About

Super, R. H. The humanist at bay: the Arnold-Huxley debate. *In* Knoepflmacher, U. C. and Tennyson, G. B. eds. Nature and the Victorian imagination p231-45

Influence—Smith
Bishop, P. O. Grafton Elliot Smith's contribution to visual neurology and the influence of Thomas Henry Huxley. *In* Grafton Elliot Smith p50-57

Huysmans, Joris Karl

About

Brombert, V. H. Huysmans: the prison house of decadence. *In* Brombert, V. H. The romantic prison p149-70
Glicksberg, C. I. The unpolitical writer. *In* Glicksberg, C. I. The literature of commitment p113-30

About individual works
Against nature
Meyers, J. Gustave Moreau and Against nature. *In* Meyers, J. Painting and the novel p84-95

Hwang, John C.
Lien-huan-hua: revolutionary serial pictures. *In* Chu, G. C. ed. Popular media in China p51-72

Hybrid (The Latin word)
Thomas, L. On etymons and hybrids. *In* Thomas, L. The medusa and the snail 557-64

Hybridity of races. See Miscegenation

Hybridization. See Telegony

Hybris. See Hubris (The Greek word)

Hyde, Francis Edwin
Cunard and North Atlantic steamship agreements, 1850-1914. *In* Great Britain and her world, 1750-1914 p263-86

Hyde, Harford Montgomery
Henry James at home. *In* Royal Society of Literature of the United Kingdom, London. Essays by divers hands v38 p58-77

About individual works
Henry James at home
Connolly, C. Oscar Wilde and Henry James: an imaginary transmogrification. *In* Connolly, C. The evening colonnade p171-74

Hydriae

Pedley, J. G. The Friedlaender hydria. *In* Harvard Studies in classical philology v74 p45-53

Hydrographic surveying

De Vorsey, L. La Florida revealed: the De Brahm surveys of British East Florida, 1765-1771. *In* Pattern and process p87-102

Hyer, Paul V.

Hu Shih: the diplomacy of gentle persuasion. *In* Burns, R. D. and Bennett, E. M. eds. Diplomats in crisis p153-70

Hygiene

Brody, H. and Sobel, D. S. A systems view of health and disease. *In* Sobel, D. S. ed. Ways of health p87-115

Knowles, J. H. The responsibility of the individual. *In* Knowles, J. H. ed. Doing better and feeling worse p57-80

Hygiene, Public. See Medical care; Public health

See also Exercise; Relaxation

Hygiene, Sexual. See Sex instruction

Hygiene, Tropical. See Tropical medicine

Hylomorphism

Multhauf, R. P. The science of matter. *In* Lindberg, D. C. ed. Science in the Middle Ages p369-90

Hyman, Herbert Hiram

Reference individuals and reference idols. *In* The Idea of social structure p265-82

Hyman, Stanley Edgar

The critic's credentials

Contents

Anthropologist of Gopher Prairie
The art of Joseph Mitchell
A blow with a maize stalk
The blues
The book of the year?
The bulging pockets of Anthony Carson
Conscious of the seasons
Counting the cats
Couplings
The critic's credentials
A Darwin sidelight: the shape of the young man's nose
Eight propositions about literature and society
Fable Italian style
Fun and love
Germ's choice, shame's voice
The handle: Invitation to a beheading and Bend sinister
History and sacred history
Ideas in fiction
Illumination for the unchurched
Images of Sigmund Freud
Jessie Weston and the Forest of Broceliande
Kenneth Burke at seventy
The Lawrence mob
Mark Twain, half Twain
A multitude of Lieblings
Myths and mothers
Nabokov's distorting mirrors
The oldest story
Playing doctor, playing war
Prince Myshkin in Hollywood
Really the blues
Richard Wright reappraised
Sad encounters
Salad days, green and cold
A Scythian humanist
A trap named Hope
Truths from the grave
Varangian times
Waiting for Bakayoko

Flannery O'Connor. *In* Howard, M. ed. Seven American women writers of the twentieth century p311-55

Hymenoptera

Hedqvist, K. J. Some remarks on the behaviour of the parasitic hymenoptera. *In* The Frontiers of human knowledge p289-96

Hymes, Dell H.

Review of Noam Chomsky. *In* Harman, G. ed. On Noam Chomsky p316-33

Speech and language: on the origins and foundations of inequality among speakers. *In* Bloomfield, M. W. and Haugen, E. I. eds. Language as a human problem p45-71

Hymns

Owens, W. A. From Isaac Watts to "heaven's radio." *In* From Parnassus p295-310

Hymns, English

Influence

Shrimpton, N. Hell's hymnbook: Blake's Songs of innocence and of experience and their models. *In* Davis, R. T. and Beatty, B. G. eds. Literature of the romantic period, 1750-1850 p19-35

Hymns, Latin

History and criticism

Gneuss, H. Latin hymns in medieval England: future research. *In* Chaucer and Middle English studies in honour of Rossell Hope Robbins p407-24

Hyneman, Charles Shang

A call for political theory. *In* Graham, G. J. and Graham, S. G. eds. Founding principles of American government p331-46

Republican government in America: the idea and its realization. *In* Graham, G. J. and Graham, S. G. eds. Founding principles of American government p3-28

Hynes, Samuel Lynn

Old Wessex, new Wessex. *In* Review, v 1 1979 p215-22

The trials of a Christian critic. *In* The Literary criticism of T. S. Eliot p64-88

The whole contention between Mr Bennett and Mrs Woolf. *In* Spilka, M. ed. Towards a poetics of fiction p179-89

William Golding. *In* Stade, G. ed. Six contemporary British novelists p165-218

Hyperborean languages. See Eskimo language

Hyperspace. See Space and time

Hyphaistion Thevaios

About individual works

Apotelesmaticorum (Book 1)

Markovic, M. Hephaestion, Apotelesmatica, Book 1. *In* Illinois classical studies, v 1 1976 p59-64

Criticism, Textual

Markovic, M. Hephaestion, Apotelesmatica, Book 1. *In* Illinois classical studies, v 1 1976 p59-64

Hypnosis. See Hypnotism

Hypnotics

Emboden, W. A. Plant hypnotics among the North American Indians. *In* American folk medicine p159-67

Hypnotism

Fancher, R. E. Early hypnotists and the psychology of social influence. *In* Fancher, R. E. Pioneers of psychology p170-204

Hypnotism—*Continued*

Therapeutic use

Tatar, M. M. From Mesmer to Freud: animal magnetism, hypnosis, and suggestion. *In* Tatar, M. M. Spellbound p3-44

Hypocrisy in literature

Koppisch, M. S. The faux dévot from Molière to Marivaux. *In* Johnson, R. B.; Neumann, E. S. and Trail, G. T. eds. Molière and the commonwealth of letters: patrimony and posterity p57-67

Hypothesis

Berlin, Sir I. Empirical propositions and hypothetical statements. *In* Berlin, Sir I. Concepts and categories p32-55

Brown, S. C. What is the verifiability criterion a criterion of? *In* Royal Institute of Philosophy. Impressions of empiricism p137-53

Quine, W. V. On simple theories of a complex world. *In* Quine, W. V. The ways of paradox, and other essays p255-58

Hysteria

Simon, B. Hysteria and social issues. *In* Simon, B. Mind and madness in ancient Greece p238-68

See also Trance

I

IACHR. See Inter-American Commission on Human Rights

IAPA. See Inter American Press Association

IBM. See International Business Machines Corporation

ICJ. See Hague. International Court of Justice

ICRC. See Red Cross. International Committee, Geneva

IEA. See International Energy Agency

I. F. Stone's Weekly (Motion picture)

Kauffmann, S. I. F. Stone's Weekly. *In* Kauffmann, S. Living images p233-36

IPI. See International Press Institute

IRA. See Irish Republican Army

ISKCON. See International Society for Krishna Consciousness

Iambic pentameter

Halle, M. and Keyser, S. J. The Iambic pentameter. *In* Gross, H. S. ed. The structure of verse p173-93

Ianni, Francis A. J.

Organized crime and the Italo-American family. *In* Studies in Italian American social history p28-39

Ianno, Octavio

Sociology in Latin America. *In* Mohan, R. P. and Martindale, D. A. eds. Handbook of contemporary developments in world sociology p173-88

Iatmuls

Métraux, R. B. Eidos and change: continuity in process, discontinuity in product. *In* Schwartz, T. ed. Socialization as cultural communication p201-16

Iatromechanism, Malpighi, Descartes, and the epistemological problems of.

Duchesneau, F. *In* Righini Bonelli, M. L. and Shea, W. R. eds. Reason, experiment, and mysticism p111-30

Ibn al-Nafīs, 'Alī ibn Abī al-Ḥazm

About

Temkin, O. Was Servetus influenced by Ibn an-Nafīs? *In* Temkin, O. The double face of Janus p284-86

Ibn an-Nafīs. See Ibn al-Nafīs, 'Alī ibn Abī al-Hazm

Ibn Bag'ah. See Avempace

Ibn-Bajjah. See Avempace

Ibn Ezra, Moses ben Jacob

About individual works

Kitab al-muhadarah

Scheindlin, R. P. Rabbi Moshe Ibn Ezra on the legitimacy of poetry. *In* Medievalia et humanistica no. 7 p101-15

Ibn Ezra, Moses ben Jacob ha-Salah. See Ibn Ezra, Moses ben Jacob

Ibn Gabirol, Solomon ben Judah

About individual works

Keter malkut

Blau, J. L. On the supposedly Aristotelian character of Gabirol's Keter malkut. *In* Salo Wittmayer Baron v 1 p219-28

Ibn Sīnā. See Avicenna

Ibo language

Words—History

See Chi (The Ibo word)

Ibo tribe

Achebe, C. Chi in Igbo cosmology. *In* Achebe, C. Morning yet on creation day p159-75

Cole, H. M. The history of Ibo mbari houses—facts and theories. *In* African images p104-32

Netting, R. M. Maya subsistence: mythologies, analogies, possibilities. *In* The Origins of Maya civilization p299-333

Southall, A. W. From segmentary lineage to ethnic association—Luo, Luhya, Ibo, and others. *In* Colonialism and change p203-29

Ibo tribe in literature

Emenyonu, E. N. Who does Flora Nwapa write for? *In* African literature today no. 7: Focus on criticism p28-33

Ibrāhīm ibn Masʿūd, Abū Ishak, al-Ilbīrī

About individual works

Dīwān

Lewis, B. An anti-Jewish ode: the qasida of Abu Ishaq against Joseph ibn Nagrella. *In* Salo Wittmayer Baron v2 p657-68

Ibsen, Henrik

About

Arestad, S. The Ibsen hero. *In* The Hero in Scandinavian literature p15-37

Baylen, J. O. Edmund Gosse, William Archer, and Ibsen in late Victorian Britain. *In* Tennessee Studies in literature v20 p124-37

Ibsen, Henrik—About—Continued

Bronsen, D. Consuming struggle vs. killing time: preludes to dying in the dramas of Ibsen and Beckett. *In* Spicker, S. F.; Woodward, K. M. and Van Tassel, D. D. eds. Aging and the elderly p261-81

Larkin, M. Hope and despair. *In* Larkin, M. Man and society in nineteenth-century realism p163-74

Larkin, M. Society versus the individual. *In* Larkin, M. Man and society in nineteenth-century realism p152-62

Mudford, P. Henrik Ibsen. *In* Mudford, P. The art of celebration p91-109

Nicoll, A. The triumph of realism: Ibsen. *In* Nicoll, A. World drama p440-59

Schwarz, A. The demonic will in a bourgeois setting. *In* Schwarz, A. From Büchner to Beckett p185-222

About individual works
A doll's house

Brustein, R. S. The evolution of a woman: A doll's house. *In* Brustein, R. S. The culture watch p79-81

Kauffmann, S. A doll's house. *In* Kauffmann, S. Persons of the drama p125-29

Kauffmann, S. A doll's house/Hedda Gabler. *In* Kauffmann, S. Persons of the drama p120-23

An enemy of the people

Miller, A. Preface to an adaptation of Ibsen's An enemy of the people. *In* Miller, A. The theater essays of Arthur Miller p16-21

Hedda Gabler

Kauffmann, S. A doll's house/Hedda Gabler. *In* Kauffmann, S. Persons of the drama p120-23

Reed, W. L. The cherry orchard and Hedda Gabler. *In* Seidel, M. A. and Mendelson, E. eds. Homer to Brecht p317-35

Webb, E. The ambiguities of secularization: modern transformations of the Kingdom in Nietzsche, Ibsen, Beckett, and Stevens. *In* Webb, E. The dark dove p34-87

The lady from the sea

Fergusson, F. Ibsen's The lady from the sea. *In* Fergusson, F. Literary landmarks p114-23

The master builder

Kunkel, F. L. Golding's The spire: the prayer and the phallus. *In* Kunkel, F. L. Passion and the Passion p58-74

Peer Gynt

Simon, J. I. Peer Gynt. *In* Simon, J. I. Singularities p3-16

The pillars of society

Ewbank, I. S. Drama and society in Ibsen's Pillars of the community. *In* Drama and society p75-97

The wild duck

Simon, J. I. The wild duck. *In* Simon, J. I. Singularities p35-51

Trilling, L. Henrik Ibsen: The wild duck. *In* Trilling, L. Prefaces to The experience of literature p22-27

Adaptations

Miller, A. Preface to an adaptation of Ibsen's An enemy of the people. *In* Miller, A. The theater essays of Arthur Miller p16-21

Ibuse, Masuji

About

Rimer, J. T. Tradition and contemporary consciousness: Ibuse, Endō, Kaiko, Abe. *In* Rimer, J. T. Modern Japanese fiction and its traditions p245-70

Ice hockey. See Hockey

Ice in literature

Griffin, A. Fire and ice in Frankenstein. *In* Levine, G. L. and Knoepflmacher, U. C. eds. The endurance of Frankenstein p49-73

Icelandic and Old Norse literature

History and criticism

Andersson, T. M. The Icelandic sagas. *In* Oinas, F. J. ed. Heroic epic and saga p144-71

Translations into English

Quirk, R. Dasent, Morris, and aspects of translation. *In* Quirk, R. The linguist and the English language p97-109

Icelandic literature. See Icelandic and Old Norse literature

The iceman cometh (Motion picture)

Kauffmann, S. The iceman cometh. *In* Kauffmann, S. Living images p237-41

Ichazo, Oscar

About

Lilly, J. C. and Hart, J. E. The Arica training. *In* Tart, C. T. ed. Transpersonal psychologies p329-51

Iconography. See Art; Christian art and symbolism; Idols and images; Portraits

Icons

Goethals, G. Sacred-secular icons. *In* Browne, R. B. and Fishwick, M. W. eds. Icons of America p24-34

Newall, V. Icons as symbols of power. *In* Symbols of power p61-99

Cyprus

Weitzmann, K. A group of early twelfth-century Sinai icons attributed to Cyprus. *In* Studies in memory of David Talbot Rice p47-63

Greece

See St John's Apocalypse no. 786 (Icons)

Russia

See Sophia church calendar (Icons)

Sinai

Weitzmann, K. A group of early twelfth-century Sinai icons attributed to Cyprus. *In* Studies in memory of David Talbot Rice p47-63

Ictinus

About

McCredie, J. R. The architects of the Parthenon. *In* Studies in classical art and archaeology p69-73

Idaho in literature

Meldrum, B. Vardis Fisher's Antelope people: pursuing an elusive dream. *In* Bingham, E. R. and Love, G. A. eds. Northwest perspectives p152-66

Idea (Philosophy)

Danto, A. C. The representational character of ideas and the problem of the external world. *In* Hooker, M. ed. Descartes p287-97

Daor, D. Two metaphysical concepts: Li and idea. *In* Philosophy East/philosophy West p235-46

Identity (Psychology)—Continued

Luria, Z. Psychosocial determinants of gender identity, role, and orientation. *In* Katchadourian, H. A. ed. Human sexuality p163-93

McCall, G J. The social looking-glass: a sociological perspective on self-development. *In* Mischel, T. ed. The self p274-87

Maccoby, E. E. Gender identity and sex-role adoption. *In* Katchadourian, H. A. ed. Human sexuality p194-203

May, J. G. Personality development and ethnic identity. *In* The Diverse society: implications for social policy p43-58

May, K. M. The living self. *In* May, K. M. Out of the maelstrom p43-61

May, K. M. The search for identity. *In* May, K. M. Out of the maelstrom p62-77

May, R. Modern man's loss of significance. *In* May, R. Psychology and the human dilemma p25-39

O'Brien, K. Death and revolution: a reappraisal of identity theory. *In* O'Neill, J. ed. On critical theory p104-28

See also Ego (Psychology)

Identity in literature

Yamanouchi, H. Abe Kōbō and Oe Kenzaburō: the search for identity in contemporary Japanese literature. *In* Modern Japan p166-86

Yamanouchi, H. In search of identity: Abé Kōbō and Ōe Kenzaburō. *In* Yamanouchi H. The search for authenticity in modern Japanese literature p153-74

Identity (Psychology) in literature

Kurz, P. K. Identity and society: the world of Max Frisch. *In* Kurz, P. K. On modern German literature v2 p104-54

Langbaum, R. W. Arnold: waning energy. *In* Langbaum, R. W. The mysteries of identity p51-82

Langbaum, R. W. Beckett: zero identity. *In* Langbaum, R. W. The mysteries of identity p120-44

Langbaum, R. W. Eliot: the walking dead. *In* Langbaum, R. W. The mysteries of identity p83-119

Langbaum, R. W. Exteriority of self. *In* Langbaum, R. W. The mysteries of identity p147-74

Langbaum, R. W. Identity and sexuality. *In* Langbaum, R. W. The mysteries of identity p251-97

Langbaum, R. W. Introduction. *In* Langbaum, R. W. The mysteries of identity p3-21

Langbaum, R. W. The rainbow: the way through hope. *In* Langbaum, R. W. The mysteries of identity p298-327

Langbaum, R W. The self as a work of art. *In* Langbaum, R. W. The mysteries of identity p175-219

Langbaum, R. W. The self as God. *In* Langbaum, R. W. The mysteries of identity p220-47

Langbaum, R. W. Women in love: the way through doom. *In* Langbaum, R. W. The mysteries of identity p328-53

Langbaum, R. W. Wordsworth: the self as process. *In* Langbaum, R. W. The mysteries of identity p25-47

Spacks, P. A. M. Identity in fiction and in fact. *In* Spacks, P. A. M. Imagining a self p 1-27

Spacks, P. A. M. Selfhood, given and formed. *In* Spacks, P. A. M. Imagining a self p300-15

Ideology

Aron, R. On the proper use of ideologies. *In* Culture and its creators p 1-14

Han, Sang Jin. Ideology—critique and social science: the use of discursive method. *In* McNall, S. G. ed. Theoretical perspectives in sociology p292-309

Levinas, E. Ideology and idealism. *In* Modern Jewish ethics p121-38

Lipset, S. M. The end of ideology and the ideology of the intellectuals. *In* Culture and its creators p15-42

Mihajlov, M. The absurdity of non-ideology. *In* Mihajlov, M. Underground notes p78-82

Seabury, P. Ideology and foreign policy. *In* Encyclopedia of American foreign policy p398-408

Voegelin, E. On debate and existence. *In* A Public philosophy reader p152-67

Idolatry. See Idols and images—Worship

Idols and images

Fishwick, M. W. Icons of America. *In* Browne, R. B. and Fishwick, M. W. eds. Icons of America p 3-12

Goethals, G. Sacred-secular icons. *In* Browne, R. B. and Fishwick, M. W. eds. Icons of America p24-34

Orr, D. G. The icon in the time tunnel. *In* Browne, R. B. and Fishwick, M. W. eds. Icons of America p13-23

Worship

Wallach, L. The testimonia of image-worship in Hadrian I's Synodica of 785 (JE 2448). *In* Wallach, L. Diplomatic studies in Latin and Greek documents from the Carolingian age p27-42

Idyllic poetry. See Pastoral poetry

Ifeka-Moller, Caroline

Female militancy and colonial revolt: the women's war of 1929, Eastern Nigeria. *In* Ardener, S. G. ed. Perceiving women p127-57

Iga, Mamoru

Personal situation as a factor in suicide, with reference to Yashunari Kawabata and Yukio Mishima. *In* Wolman, B. B. ed. Between survival and suicide p103-28

Igbo tribe. See Ibo tribe

Igloolikmiut. See Iglulirmiut (Eskimo tribe)

Igluligmiut. See Iglulirmiut (Eskimo tribe)

Iglulirmiut (Eskimo tribe)

Rasmussen, K. J. V. A shaman's journey to the sea spirit Takánakapsâluk; excerpt from "Report of the fifth Thule expedition, 1921-24." *In* Tedlock, D. E. and Tedlock, B. eds. Teachings from the American earth p13-19

Ignatieff, George

The achievements of arms control. *In* Griffiths, F. and Polanyi, J. C. eds. The dangers of nuclear war p67-82

Ignatius, Mary Ann

Christine de Pizan's Epistre Othea: an experiment in literary form. *In* Medievalia et humanistica; new ser. no. 9 p127-42

Ignatow, David

About

Mills, R. J. Earth hard: David Ignatow's poetry. *In* Mills, R. J. Cry of the human p67-133

Ignotus, Paul

The first two Communist takeovers of Hungary: 1919 and 1948. *In* Hammond, T. T. ed. The anatomy of Communist takeovers p385-98

Ihde, Don

A phenomenology of man-machine relations. *In* Feinberg, W. and Rosemont, H. eds. Work, technology, and education p186-203

Ihimaera, Witi

About individual works
Tangi

Tiffin, C. Mates, mum, and Maui: the theme of maturity in three antipodean novels. *In* Narasimhaiah, C. D. ed. Awakened conscience p127-45

Ihrig, Alice Bennett

Librarians and the political process. *In* As much to learn as to teach p83-93

Ijsewijn, Jozef

Neo-Latin satire: Sermo and Satyra Menippea. *In* Classical influences on European culture A.D. 1500-1700 p41-55

Ikenberry, Stanley Oliver

The public interest and institutional autonomy. *In* Land-grant universities and their continuing challenge p309-25

Ikiddeh, Ime

Ngugi wa Thiong'o: the novelist as historian. *In* King, B. A. and Ogungbesan, K. eds. A celebration of Black and African writing p204-16

Ikiru (Motion picture)

Murray, E. Ikiru. *In* Murray, E. Ten film classics p48-61

Ikonne, Chidi

Purpose versus plot: the double vision of Thomas Mofolo's narrator. *In* Heywood, C. ed. Aspects of South African literature p54-65

Ikons. See Icons

Iktinos. See Ictinus

Ilie, Paul

Concepts of the grotesque before Goya. *In* Studies in eighteenth-century culture v5 p185-201

I'll take my stand: the South and agrarian tradition

Davidson, D. I'll take my stand: a history. *In* Crunden, R. M. ed. The superfluous men p196-207

Downs, R. B. Nostalgia for never-never land. *In* Downs, R. B. Books that changed the South p229-36

Duhamel, P. A. The novelist as prophet. *In* Friedman, M. J. and Lawson, L. A. eds. The added dimension p88-107

Gr   R. J. The Nashville Agrarians. *In* Gray,   J. The literature of memory p40-105

Rubin, L. D. Fugitives as agrarians: the impulse behind I'll take my stand. *In* Rubin, L. D. William Elliott shoots a bear p145-63

Illegal literature. See Underground literature

Illegitimacy. See Legitimation of children

Illich, Ivan

Language as a commodity. *In* Wagschal, P. H. ed. Learning tomorrows p41-61

The political uses of natural death. *In* Death inside out p25-42

Radical alternatives to schools. *In* Smithsonian Institution. The cultural drama p305-17

About

Apple, M. W. Ivan Illich and deschooling society: the politics of slogan systems. *In* Social forces and schooling p337-60

Barrow, R. Everett Reimer (b. 1922) and Ivan Illich (b. 1926). *In* Barrow, R. Radical education p127-53

Illinois

Politics and government

Howlett, M. J. Strategic planning in state government. *In* Managing nonprofit organizations p124-37

Illiteracy

Goody, J. R. Literacy, criticism, and the growth of knowledge. *In* Culture and its creators p226-43

Whalley, G. Picking up the thread. *In* Gold, J. ed. In the name of language! p46-70

Egypt—History

Youtie, H. C. ΑΓΡΑΜΜΑΤΟΣ: an aspect of Greek society in Egypt. *In* Harvard Studies in classical philology v75 p161-76

Illumination of books and manuscripts

Deshman, R. The Leofric missal and tenth-century English art. *In* Anglo-Saxon England 6 p145-73

Nolan, B. Anagogy, aevum and two later medieval visionary arts. *In* Nolan, B. The Gothic visionary perspective p35-83

Russia

Waugh, D. C. Azbuka znakami lits: Egyptian hieroglyphs in the Privy Chancellery Archive. *In* Oxford Slavonic papers, new ser. v10 p46-50

Tuscany

Eisenberg, M. An antiphonal page of the Sienese Quattrocento. *In* Enggass, R. C. and Stokstad, M. eds. Hortus imaginum p51-55

Illumination of books and manuscripts, Anglo-Saxon

Brownrigg, L. L. Manuscripts containing English decoration 871-1066, catalogued and illustrated: a review. *In* Anglo-Saxon England 7 p239-66

Illumination of books and manuscripts, Byzantine

Weitzmann, K. The study of Byzantine book illumination, past, present, and future. *In* The Place of book illumination in Byzantine art p 1-60

Illumination of books and manuscripts, Medieval

Raw, B. C. The probable derivation of most of the illustrations in Junius II from an illustrated Old Saxon Genesis. *In* Anglo-Saxon England 5 p133-48

England

Alexander, J. J. G. Some aesthetic principles in the use of colour in Anglo-Saxon art. *In* Anglo-Saxon England 4 p145-54

Illumination of books and manuscripts, Romanesque

Thomson, R. M. The date of the Bury Bible reexamined. *In* Viator: medieval and Renaissance studies v6 p51-58

Illusions, Optical. See Optical illusions

Illustrated books, Children's. See Picture-books for children; Toy and movable books

Illustration, Medical. See Medical illustration

Illustration, Scientific. See Scientific illustration

Illustration of books

Booth, G. The price of being an artist. *In* Egoff, S. A. ed. One ocean touching p155-63

Cleaver, E. Picture books as an art form. *In* Egoff, S. A. ed. One ocean touching p195-96

19th century—England

Easson, K. P. Blake and the art of the book. *In* Essick, R. N. and Pearce, D. R. eds. Blake in his time p35-52

Hemstedt, G. Painting and illustration. *In* Lerner, L. ed. The Victorians p139-52

Ilongot (Philippine tribe)

Rosaldo, R. I. The rhetoric of control: Ilongots viewed as natural bandits and wild Indians. *In* Babcock, B. A. ed. The reversible world p240-57

Biography

Rosaldo, R. I. The story of Tukbaw: 'they listen as he orates.' *In* Reynolds, F. E. and Capps, D. eds. The biographical process p121-51

Image (Theology) See Image of God

Image, Body. See Body image

Image of God

Sayers, D. L. The image of God; excerpt from "The mind of the Maker." *In* Sayers, D. L. The whimsical Christian p113-21

Imagery. See Figures of speech

Imagery (Psychology)

Barthes, R. Rhetoric of the image. *In* Barthes, R. Image, music, text p32-51

Ricoeur, P. Image and language in psychoanalysis. *In* Psychoanalysis and language p293-324

See also Eidetic imagery

Images, Mental. See Imagery (Psychology)

Images and idols. See Idols and images

Imaginary cities. See Geographical myths

Imaginary voyages. See Voyages, Imaginary

Imagination

Barfield, O. The harp and the camera. *In* Barfield, O. The rediscovery of meaning, and other essays p65-78

Barfield, O. Imagination and inspiration. *In* Barfield, O. The rediscovery of meaning, and other essays p111-29

Barfield, O. Matter, imagintaion, and spirit. *In* Barfield, O. The rediscovery of meaning, and other essays p143-54

Bohm, D. Imagination, fancy, insight, and reason in the process of thought. *In* Evolution of consciousness p51-68

Bronowski, J. The imaginative mind in art; excerpt from "Imagination and the university." *In* Bronowski, J. The visionary eye p6-19

Bronowski, J. The imaginative mind in science; excerpt from "Imagination and the university." *In* Bronowski, J. The visionary eye p20-32

Bronowski, J. The reach of imagination. *In* Bronowski, J. A sense of the future p22-31

Bronowski, J. The speaking eye, the visionary ear. *In* Bronowski, J. The visionary eye p75-87

Casey, E. S. Imagination and phenomenological method. *In* Elliston, F. A. and McCormick, P. eds. Husserl p70-82

Donoghue, D. The essential power. *In* Donoghue, D. The sovereign ghost p 1-34

Donoghue, D. Nuances of a theme by Allen Tate. *In* Donoghue, D. The sovereign ghost p84-102

Donoghue, D. The sovereign ghost. *In* Donoghue, D. The sovereign ghost p35-83

Kelly, D. Imagination. *In* Kelly, D. Medieval imagination p26-56

Kelly, D. Imagination and the Second Rhetoric. *In* Kelly, D. Medieval imagination p96-120

Le Guin, U. K. This fear of dragons. *In* Blishen, E. ed. The thorny paradise p87-92

Morris, W. Of memory, emotion and imagination. *In* Morris, W. Earthly delights, unearthly adornments p 1-6

Morris, W. Origins: the self-imaged image-maker. *In* Morris, W. Earthly delights, unearthly adornments p169-79

Noxon, J. H. Remembering and imagining the past. *In* Livingston, D. W. and King, J. T. eds. Hume p270-95

Sabin, M. The sources of imagination. *In* Sabin, M. English romanticism and the French tradition p51-77

Stevens, W. Imagination as value. *In* Wimsatt, W. K. ed. Literary criticism: idea and act p83-96

Sugerman, S. G. An "essay" on Coleridge on imagination. *In* Evolution of consciousness p191-201

Taylor, A. Coleridge and the magical power of the imagination. *In* Taylor, A. Magic and English romanticism p64-98

Warnock, M. Coleridge and Wordsworth, theory and practice: imagination and the mental image. *In* Warnock, M. Imagination p72-130

Warnock, M. Conclusion: imagination and education. *In* Warnock, M. Imagination p196-209

Warnock, M. Educating the imagination. *In* Royal Institute of Philosophy. Human values p44-60

Warnock, M. Imagination and creative art: Hume, Kant and Schelling. *In* Warnock, M. Imagination p35-71

Imagination—Continued

Warnock, M. Imagination and perception: Hume and Kant. In Warnock, M. Imagination p13-34

Warnock, M. The nature of the mental image: phenomenology, Sartre and Wittgenstein. In Warnock, M. Imagination p131-95

Wetherbee, W The theme of imagination in medieval poetry and the allegorical figure "Genius." In Medievalia et humanistica no. 7 p45-64

See also Creation (Literary, artistic, etc.); Creative ability; Fantasy; Imagery (Psychology)

Imagism. See Imagist poetry

Imagist poetry

Hasbany, R. The shock of vision: an imagist reading of In our time. In Wagner, L. W. ed. Ernest Hemingway p224-40

Schneider, D. J. Hemingway's A farewell to arms: the novel as pure poetry. In Wagner, L. W. ed. Ernest Hemingway p252-66

Tanner, T. Transcendentalism and imagism. In Tanner, T. The reign of wonder p87-93

See also Free verse

Imdahl, Max

Overstepping esthetic limits in visual art: four aspects of the problem. In Amacher, R. E. and Lange, V. eds. New perspectives in German literary criticism p279-92

Imhof, Arthur Erwin

The hospital in the 18th century: for whom? In Branca, P. ed. The medicine show p141-63

Imitation

MacLean, P. D. The imitative-creative interplay of our three mentalities. In Harris, H. A. ed. Astride the two cultures p187-213

Imitation (in art)

Bindman, D. Blake's theory and practice of imitation. in Essick, R. N. and Pearce, D. R. eds. Blake in his time p91-98

Dieckmann, H. The transformation of the concept of imitation in eighteenth-century French esthetics. In Amacher, R. E. and Lange, V. eds. New perspectives in German literary criticism p49-85

Imitation (in literature) See Mimesis in literature

Immanence (Philosophy)

Todd, R. B. Monism and immanence: the foundations of Stoic physics. In Rist, J. M. ed. The Stoics p137-60

Immanence of God. See Mysticism

Immigration and Nationality Act (1952; revised 1965)

Dolce, P. C. The McCarran-Walter Act and the conflict over immigration policy during the Truman administration. In The Immigrant experience in America p215-32

Immoral literature. See Literature, Immoral

Immortality

Donnelly, J. The metaphysics of peace. In Roth, R. J. ed. Person and community p25-41

Geach, P. T. Immortality. In Donnelly, J. P. ed. Language, metaphysics, and death p208-15

Harris, E. E. Spinoza's theory of human immortality. In Freeman, E. and Mandelbaum, M. H. eds. Spinoza p245-62

Lewis, H. D. Immortality and dualism. In Reason and religion p282-300

Lifton, R. J. On death and the continuity of life: a "new" paradigm. In Wolman, B. B. ed. Between survival and suicide p55-76

Lifton, R. J. The sense of immortality: on death and the continuity of life. In Explorations in psychohistory p271-87

Also in Feifel, H. [ed.] New meanings of death p273-90

Mahoney, E. P. Nicoletto Vernia on the soul and immortality. In Philosophy and humanism p144-63

Shoemaker, S. Immortality and dualism. In Reason and religion p259-81

Sutherland, S. R. Immortality and resurrection. In Donnelly, J. P. ed. Language, metaphysics, and death p196-207

Williams, B. A. O. The Makropulos case: reflections on the tedium of immortality; excerpt from "Problems of the self." In Donnelly, J. P. ed. Language, metaphysics, and death p228-42

See also Future life

Immortality (Philosophy)

Hardin, C. L. Spinoza and immortality and time. In Shahan, R. W. and Biro, J. I. eds. Spinoza: new perspectives p129-38

Immortality in literature

Perrine, L. Robert Frost and the idea of immortality. In Frost: centennial essays II p85-98

Immune response. See Antigen-antibody reactions

Immunity. See Clonal selection theory

Immunity from self-incrimination. See Self-incrimination

Immunological specifics. See Immunospecificity

Immunology. See Antigen-antibody reactions

Immunospecificity

Edelman, G. M. The problem of molecular recognition by a selective system. In Ayala, F. J. and Dobzhansky, T. G. eds. Studies in the philosophy of biology p45-56

Impeachments

United States

Rodino, P. W. The compact with the people. In Warner, S. B. ed. The American experiment p89-100

Imperial Chemical Industries, ltd.

Wilson, C. H. Multinationals, management, and world markets: a historical view. In Evolution of international management structures p193-216

Imperialism

Andreski, S. Imperialism: past and future. In The Year book of world affairs, 1975 p313-19

Bennett, E. M. Colonialism. In Encyclopedia of American foreign policy p134-40

Curtin, P. D. The Black experience of colonialism and imperialism. In Mintz, S. W. ed. Slavery, colonialism, and racism p17-29

Gellar, S. The colonial era. In Martin, P. M. and O'Meara, P. eds. Africa p132-49

Healy, D. F. Imperialism. In Encyclopedia of American foreign policy p409-16

Imperialism—*Continued*

Tompkins, E. B. Anti-imperialism. *In* Encyclopedia of American foreign policy p25-32

See also Militarism; and subdivision Foreign relations under names of countries, e.g. Italy—Foreign relations

History

Salvadori, M. Aftermath of empire. *In* Aftermath of empire p105-52

Impersonation. See Transvestism

Imports. See Commerce; Tariff

Imposition of hands

Grad, B. R. The biological effects of the "laying on of hands" on animals and plants: implications for biology. *In* Parapsychology: its relation to physics, biology, psychology, and psychiatry p76-89

Impotence in literature

Ober, W. B. The Earl of Rochester and ejaculatio praecox. *In* Ober, W. B. Boswell's clap and other essays p233-52

Impressionism

Hay, E. K. Impressionism limited. *In* Joseph Conrad: a commemoration p54-64

Watt, I. P. Impressionism and symbolism in Heart of darkness. *In* Joseph Conrad: a commemoration p37-53

Imprisonment

Hawkins, G. The ideology of imprisonment. *In* Progress in penal reform p101-15

See also Juvenile detention homes; Prisons

Psychological aspects

May, R. The man who was put in a cage. *In* May, R. Psychology and the human dilemma p161-67

United States

Mattick, H. W. Reflections of a former prison warden. *In* Delinquency, crime, and society p287-315

Impulse

Zaw, S. K. 'Irresistible impulse' and moral responsibility. *In* Royal Institute of Philosophy. Human values p99-134

In the name of the Father (Motion picture)

Kauffmann, S. In the name of the Father. *In* Kauffmann, S. Living images p268-71

In this our life (Motion picture)

Bathrick, S. K. Independent woman, doomed sister. *In* Peary, G. and Shatzkin, R. eds. The modern American novel and the movies p143-55

Inada, Lawson Fusao

About individual works

Before the War

Reed, I. Before the War, poems as they happened. *In* Reed, I. Shrovetide in old New Orleans p115-17

Inalcik, Halil

The socio-political effects of the diffusion of fire-arms in the Middle East. *In* War, technology and society in the Middle East p195-217

Incarnation

Barfield, O. Philology and the Incarnation. *In* Barfield, O. The rediscovery of meaning, and other essays p228-36

Incas. See Peru—History to 1548

Incentive (Psychology) See Reinforcement (Psychology)

Incentives in industry

Cuba

MacEwan, A. Incentives, equality, and power in revolutionary Cuba. *In* Radosh, R. ed. The new Cuba: paradoxes and potentials p74-101

Incest

Bischof, N. Comparative ethology of incest avoidance. *In* Biosocial anthropology p37-67

De Vos, G. A. Affective dissonance and primary socialization: implications for a theory of incest avoidance. *In* Schwartz, T. ed. Socialization as cultural communication p73-90

Wohl, A. S. Sex and the single room: incest among the Victorian working classes. *In* Wohl, A. S. ed. The Victorian family p197-216

Incest in literature

Cockshut, A. O. J. The pessimists: Swinburne. *In* Cockshut, A. O. J. Man and woman: a study of love and the novel, 1740-1940 p111-16

Inchbald, Elizabeth (Simpson)

About individual works

Nature and art

Kelly, G. Elizabeth Inchbald: Nature and art. *In* Kelly, G. The English Jacobin novel, 1780-1805 p93-113

A simple story

Kelly, G. Eizabeth Inchbald: A simple story. *In* Kelly, G. The English Jacobin novel, 1780-1805 p64-93

Incipit (The Latin word)

Kretzmann, N. Incipit/desinit. *In* Motion and time, space and matter p101-36

Inclosures

McCloskey, D. N. The economics of enclosure: a market analysis. *In* Parker, W. N. and Jones, E. L. eds. European peasants and their markets p123-60

Scarisbrick, J. J. Cardinal Wolsey and the common weal. *In* Wealth and power in Tudor England p45-67

Economic aspects

Cohen, J. S. and Weitzman, M. L. Enclosures and depopulation: a Marxian analysis. *In* Parker, W. N. and Jones, E. L. eds. European peasants and their markets p161-76

Income. See Consumption (Economics); Income distribution; Income maintenance program; Profit; Wages

Income distribution

Houthakker, H. S. The size distribution of labour incomes derived from the distribution of aptitudes. *In* Econometrics and economic theory p177-87

Piachaud, D. Inflation and income distribution. *In* The Political economy of inflation p88-116

Watts, H. W. Why, and how well, do we analyze inequality? *In* Major social issues p126-40

Wilensky, H. L. The political economy of income distribution: issues in the analysis of government approaches to the reduction of inequality. *In* Major social issues p87-108

Income distribution—*Continued*
United States
Kuznets, S. S. Demographic aspects of the distribution of income among families: recent trends in the United States. *In* Econometrics and economic theory p223-45

Income maintenance programs
Blaydon, C. C. and Stack, C. B. Income support policies and the family. *In* Rossi, A. S.; Kagan, J. and Hareven, T. K. eds. The family p147-62

Incunabula
Auty, R. Sixteenth-century Croatian glagolitic books in the Bodleian library. *In* Oxford Slavonic papers, new ser. v11 p132-35

Dunston, A. J. Venetian 'woodcut' capitals. *In* Virginia. University. Bibliographical Society. Studies in bibliography v30 p136-44

Lutz, C. E. Manuscripts copied from printed books. *In* Lutz, C. E. Essays on manuscripts and rare books p129-38

Temperley, N. Middleburg Psalms. *In* Virginia. University. Bibliographical Society. Studies in bibliography v30 p162-70

See also Bibliography—Rare books; Printing—History

Indemnity. See Reparations

Independence. See Autonomy

Independent administrative agencies. See Independent regulatory commissions

Independent agencies. See Independent regulatory commissions

Independent regulatory commissions
Bardach, E. Reason, responsibility, and the new social regulation. *In* Burnham, W. D. and Weinberg, M. W. eds. American politics and public policy p364-90
United States
Salamon, L. M. and Wamsley, G. L. The Federal bureaucracy: responsive to whom? *In* Rieselbach, L. N. ed. People vs. government: the responsiveness of American institutions p151-88

Independent study
Driscoll, W. J. Independent study: a new emphasis for the 1970s. *In* Buxton, T. H. and Prichard, K. W. eds. Excellence in university teaching p232-38

Zarnowiecki, J. and Murphy, T. P. University without walls. *In* Murphy, T. P. ed. Universities in the urban crisis p241-58

Indeterminacy principle. See Heisenberg uncertainty principle

Indeterminate sentence. See Probation

Indeterminism. See Free will and determinism

Index expurgatorius. See Index librorum prohibitorum

Index librorum prohibitorum
Grendler, P. F. Venice, science, and the Index of Prohibited Books. *In* The Nature of scientific discovery p335-47

India
Civilization
Parmar, S. Traditional folk forms in India and their use in national development; excerpt from "Traditional folk media in India." *In* Fischer, H. D. and Melnik, S. R. eds. Entertainment: a cross-cultural examination p74-82

Rizvi, S. A. A. Muslim India. *In* Lewis, B. ed. Islam and the Arab world p301-20

Scharfstein, B. A. Three philosophical civilizations: a preliminary comparison. *In* Philosophy East/philosophy West p48-127

Commerce—History
Brennig, J. J. Joint-stock companies of Coromandel. *In* Kling, B. B. and Pearson, M. N. eds. The age of partnership p71-96

Description and travel
Berryman, J. Thursday out. *In* Berryman, J. The freedom of the poet p335-43

Economic conditions
Tintner, G.; Kadekodi, G. and Rama Sastry, M. V. A macro model of the economy for the explanation of trend and business cycle with applications to India. *In* Econometrics and economic theory p139-46

Foreign relations—United States
Erdman, H. L. The United States, India, and India's neighbors. *In* Baldwin, D. A. ed. America in an interdependent world p245-72

Richter, W. L. Relative abstention: India & Pakistan. *In* Higham, R. D. ed. Intervention or abstention: the dilemma of American foreign policy p202-17

History
Rizvi, S. A. A. Muslim India. *In* Lewis, B. ed. Islam and the Arab world p301-20

History—British occupation, 1765-1947
Peele, G. Revolt over India. *In* Peele, G. and Cook, C. eds. The politics of reappraisal, 1918-1939 p114-45

History—Burmese Wars, 1824-1852
See Burmese War, 1852

History—1947-
See India-Pakistan Conflict, 1971-

Languages
Dasgupta, J. Ethicity, language demands, and national development in India. *In* Glazer, N. and Moynihan, D. P. eds. Ethnicity p466-88

Rao, R. The caste of English. *In* Narasimhaiah, C. D. ed. Awakened conscience p420-22

Sharma, A. K. Linguistic nationalism and India's national development. *In* Said, A. A. and Simmons, L. R. eds. Ethnicity in an international context p218-34

Military policy
Bellany, I. The acquisition of arms by poor states. *In* The Year book of world affairs, 1976 p174-89

Politics and government
Brown, J. M. 'Gandhi's men', 1917-22: the role of the major leader in the careers of middle-rank politicians. *In* The Making of politicians: studies from Africa and Asia p126-39

Kochanek, S. A. The Indian political system. *In* Kearney, R. N. ed. Politics and modernization in South and Southeast Asia p39-107

Indians—*Continued*

Medicine
See Medicine-man

Missions
Bolton, H. E. The mission as a frontier institution in the Spanish American colonies. *In* Weber, D. J. ed. New Spain's far northern frontier p49-65

Indians (criticism) Kopit, A. L. *In* Kauffmann, S. Persons of the drama p183-86

Indians, East in literature. See East Indians in literature

Indians, Treatment of

United States
Miller, D. H. and Savage, W. W. Ethnic stereotypes and the frontier: a comparative study of Roman and American experience. *In* Miller, D. H. and Steffen, J. O. eds. The frontier p109-37

See also Indians of North America—Government relations

Indians in literature
Hahn, T. G. The Indian tradition in Western medieval intellectual history. *In* Viator: medieval and Renaissance studies v9 p213-34

Krefft, J. H. A possible source for Faulkner's Indians: Oliver La Farge's Laughing boy. *In* Tulane Studies in English, v23 p187-92

Larson, C. R. The children of Pocahontas. *In* Larson, C. R. American Indian fiction p17-33

Pryse, M. Faulkner's "Dry September" and "Red leaves": caste and outcast. *In* Pryse, M. The mark and the knowledge p92-107

Rose, A. H. Demonic vision and the conventions of antebellum Southern fiction. *In* Rose, A. H. Demonic vision p39-62

Seelye, J. Captain courageous: Captain John Smith, father of us all. *In* Seelye, J. Prophetic waters p57-95

Indians of Central America
See also Carib Indians; Mayas; Quichés

Art
Quirarte, J. Early art styles of Mesoamerica and Early Classic Maya art. *In* The Origins of Maya civilization p249-83

Indic influences
Kelley, D. H. Eurasian evidence and the Mayan calendar correlation problem. *In* Mesoamerican archaeology p135-43

Languages
Landar, H. J. Historiography of native Ibero-American linguistics. *In* Sebeok, T. A. ed. Native languages of the Americas v2 p185-203

Longacre, R. E. Comparative reconstruction of indigenous languages. *In* Sebeok, T. A. ed. Native languages of the Americas v2 p99-139

Suárez S, J. A. Classical languages. *In* Sebeok, T. A. ed. Native languages of the Americas v2 p3-25

Languages—Dialectology
Mayers, M. K. Indigenous dialectology. *In* Sebeok, T. A. ed Native languages of the Americas v2 p89-98

Writing
See Mayas—Writing

Guatemala—Antiquities
Lowe, G. W. The Mixe-Zoque as competing neighbors of the early Lowland Maya. *In* The Origins of Maya civilization p197-248

Guatemala—Languages
Grimes, J. E. Descriptive linguistics. *In* Sebeok, T. A. ed. Native languages of the Americas v2 p55-62

Kaufman, T. S. Areal linguistics and Middle America. *In* Sebeok, T. A. ed. Native languages of the Americas v2 p63-87

Guatemala—Women
Maynard, E. Guatemalan women: life under two types of patriarchy. *In* Matthiasson, C. J. ed. Many sisters p77-98

Indians of Mexico
See also Basket-Maker Indians; Huichol Indians; Mayas; Olmecs; Tzotzil Indians; Zapotec Indians

Antiquities
Heikamp, D. American objects in Italian collections of the Renaissance and baroque: a survey. *In* First images of America p455-82

Pailes, R. A. and Whitecotton, J. W. The greater Southwest and the Mesoamerican "world" system: an exploratory model of frontier relationships. *In* The Frontier v2 p105-21

Sabloff, J. A. and others. Trade and power in postclassic Yucatan: initial observations. *In* Mesoamerican archaeology p397-416

Williams, G. External influences and the upper RioVerde drainage basin at Los Altos, West Mexico. *In* Mesoamerican archaeology p21-50

Art
Quirarte, J. Early art styles of Mesoamerica and Early Classic Maya art. *In* The Origins of Maya civilization p249-83

Robertson, D. Mexican Indian art and the Atlantic filter: sixteenth to eighteenth centuries. *In* First images of America p483-94

Astronomy
Digby, A. Crossed trapezes: a pre-Columbian astronomical instrument. *In* Mesoamerican archaeology p271-83

Languages
Grimes, J. E. Descriptive linguistics. *In* Sebeok, T. A. ed. Native languages of the Americas v2 p55-62

Kaufman, T. S. Areal linguistics and Middle America. *In* Sebeok, T. A. ed. Native languages of the Americas v2 p63-87

Landar, H. J. Historiography of native Ibero-American linguistics. *In* Sebeok, T. A. ed. Native languages of the Americas v2 p185-203

Longacre, R. E. Comparative reconstruction of indigenous languages. *In* Sebeok, T. A. ed. Native languages of the Americas v2 p99-139

McClaran, M. Mexico. *In* Sebeok, T. A. ed. Native languages of the Americas v2 p141-61

Suárez S , J. A. Classical languages. *In* Sebeok, T. A. ed. Native languages of the Americas v2 p3-25

See also Otomian languages

Indians of Mexico—*Continued*

Languages—Bibliography

McClaran, M. Mexico. *In* Sebeok, T. A. ed. Native languages of the Americas v2 p141-61

Languages—Dialectology

Mayers, M. K. Indigenous dialectology. *In* Sebeok, T. A. ed. Native languages of the Americas v2 p89-98

Marriage customs and rites

Noonan, J. T. Marriage in Michoacán. *In* First images of America p351-62

Missions

Hanke, L. U. The theological significance of the discovery of America. *In* First images of America p363-89

Pottery

Lee, T. A. The middle Grijalva regional chronology and ceramic relations: a preliminary report. *In* Mesoamerican archaeology p 1-20

Rands, R. L. The ceramic sequence at Palenque, Chiapas. *In* Mesoamerican archaeology p51-75

Religion and mythology

Tickell, C. C. C. The civilization of pre-Columbian America. *In* Life after death p67-79

See also Aztecs—Religion and mythology; Mayas—Religion and mythology; Nahuas—Religion and mythology

Sculpture

Williams, G. External influences and the upper RioVerde drainage basin at Los Altos, West Mexico. *In* Mesoamerican archaeology p21-50

Social life and customs

See Indians of Mexico—Marriage customs and rites

Women

Molloy, J. P. and Rathje, W. L. Sex-ploitation among the late classic Maya. *In* Mesoamerican archaeology p431-44

Writing

Barthel, T. S. Writing systems. *In* Sebeok, T. A. ed. Native languages of the Americas v2 p27-53

Indians of North America

Berkhofer, R. F. Native Americans. *In* Ethnic leadership in America p119-49

Comstock, W. R. On seeing with the eye of the native European. *In* Seeing with a native eye p58-78

Dubos, R. J. Old World and New World. *In* Dubos, R. J. Beast or angel? p11-15

Momaday, N. S. Native American attitudes to the environment. *In* Seeing with a native eye p79-85

Tyler, D. The Indian Weltanschaung: a summary of views expressed by Indians at the "Viewpoints in Indian History" Conference, August 1974, Colorado State University. *In* Red Men and hat-wearers p135-39

Wax, M. L. Cultural pluralism, political power, and ethnic studies. *In* Smithsonian Institution. The cultural drama p107-20

See also Algonquian Indians; Basket-Maker Indians; Carrier Indians; Catawba Indians; Cherokee Indians; Chippewa Indians; Choctaw Indians; Dakota Indians;

Hopi Indians; Huichol Indians; Huron Indians; Kaska Indians; Lumbee Indians; Mohawk Indians; Navaho Indians; Oglala Indians; Papago Indians; Piman Indians; Seminole Indians; Shoshonean Indians; Tewa Indians; Tsattine Indians; Tunica Indians

Bibliography

Washburn, W. E. The writing of American Indian history: a status report. *In* The American Indian p3-25

Civil rights

Crowe, C. R. Indians and Blacks in white America. *In* Hudson, C. M. ed. Four centuries of Southern Indians p148-69

Civilization

Brown, J. E. The roots of renewal. *In* Seeing with a native eye p25-34

Hallowell, A. I. Ojibwa ontology, behavior, and world view. *In* Tedlock, D. E. and Tedlock, B. eds. Teachings from the American earth p141-78

Cultural assimilation

Jacobs, W. R. The fatal confrontation: early native-white relations on the frontiers of Australia, New Guinea, and America—a comparative study. *In* The American Indian p27-54

Dances

Tedlock, B. The clown's way. *In* Tedlock, D. E. and Tedlock, B. eds. Teachings from the American earth p105-18

See also Ghost dance

Economic conditions

Borman, L. D. American Indian tribal support systems and economic development. *In* The Diverse society: implications for social policy p149-62

Ethics

Moore, E. C. Native American Indian values. *In* Population policy and ethics p237-75

Ethnology

See Ethnology—North America

Folk-lore

See Folk-Lore, Indian

Food

Vogel, V. J. American Indian foods used as medicine. *In* American folk medicine p125-41

Government relations

Hicks, G. L. and Handler, M. J. Ethnicity, public policy, and anthropologists. *In* Eddy, E. M. and Partridge, W. L. eds. Applied anthropology in America p292-325

Parman, D. L. The Indian and the Civilian Conservation Corps. *In* The American Indian p127-45

Steward, J. H. Limitations of applied anthropology: the case of the Indian New Deal. *In* Steward, J. H. Evolution and ecology p333-46

See also Indians, Treatment of—United States

Government relations—1789-1869

Munkres, R. L. The arrival of emigrants & soldiers: curiosity, contempt, confusion & conflict. *In* Red Men and hat-wearers p63-91

Indians of North America—*Continued*

Government relations—1869-1934

Cash, J. H. The reservation Indian meets the white man (1860-1914). *In* Red Men and hat-wearers p93-111

Deloria, V. The twentieth century. *In* Red Men and hat-wearers p155-66

Government relations—1934-

Deloria, V. The twentieth century. *In* Red Men and hat-wearers p155-66

History

Ewers, J. C. Indian views of the white man prior to 1850: an interpretation. *In* Red Men and hat-wearers p7-23

Miller, D. H. The fur men and explorers meet the Indians. *In* Red Men and hat-wearers p25-45

Languages

Bright, W. O. North American Indian language contact. *In* Sebeok, T. A. ed. Native languages of the Americas v 1 p59-72

Goddard, I. Philological approaches to the study of North American Indian languages: documents and documentation. *In* Sebeok, T. A. ed. Native languages of the Americas v 1 p73-91

Haas, M. R. American Indian linguistic prehistory *In* Seboek, T. A. ed. Native languages of the Americas v 1 p23-58

Hoijer, H. History of the American Indian linguistics. *In* Sebeok, T. A. ed. Native languages of the Americas v 1 p3-22

Lee, D. D. Linguistic reflection of Wintu thought; excerpt from "Freedom and culture." *In* Tedlock, D. E. and Tedlock, B. eds. Teachings from the American earth p130-40

Sherzer, J. Areal linguistics in North America. *In* Sebeok, T. A. ed. Native languages of the Americas v 1 p121-73

See also names of Indian languages, e.g. Hopi language

Languages—Bibliography

Bright, W. O. North American Indian language contact. *In* Sebeok, T. A. ed. Native languages of the Americas v1 p 59-72

Landar, H. J. Native North America. *In* Sebeok, T. A. ed. Native languages of the Americas v 1 p93-118

Liquor problem

Lurie, N. O. The world's oldest on-going protest demonstration: North American Indian drinking patterns. *In* The American Indian p55-76

Medicine

Emboden, W. A. Plant hypnotics among the North American Indians. *In* American folk medicine p159-67

Sandner, D. F. Navaho Indian medicine and medicine men. *In* Sobel, D. S. ed. Ways of health p117-46

Vogel, V. J. American Indian foods used as medicine. *In* American folk medicine p125-41

See also Medicine-man

Mines and mining

Kay, J. Indian responses to a mining frontier. *In* The Frontier v2 p193-203

Mythology

See Folk-lore, Indian; Indians of North America—Religion and mythology

Philosophy

Whorf, B. L. An American Indian model of the universe. *In* Tedlock, D. E. and Tedlock, B. eds. Teachings from the American earth p121-29

Picture-writing

See Picture-writing, Indian

Population

Longacre, W. A. Population dynamics at the Grasshopper pueblo, Arizona. *In* Zubrow, E. B. W. ed. Demographic anthropology p169-84

Psychology

Hallowell, A. I. Ojibwa ontology, behavior, and world view. *In* Tedlock, D. E. and Tedlock, B. eds. Teachings from the American earth p141-78

Spindler, L. S. Researching the psychology of culture change and urbanization. *In* Spindler, G. D. ed. The making of psychological anthropology p176-200

Religion and mythology

Hultkrantz, Å. The contribution of the study of North American Indian religions to the history of religions. *In* Seeing with a native eye p86-106

Mooney, J. The doctrine of the Ghost dance; excerpt from "The ghost-dance religion and the Sioux outbreak of 1890." *In* Tedlock, D. E. and Tedlock, B. eds. Teachings from the American earth p75-95

Radin, P. Monotheism among American Indians. *In* Tedlock, D. E. and Tedlock, B. eds. Teachings from the American earth p219-47

Tedlock, D. E. An American Indian view of death. *In* Tedlock, D. E. and Tedlock, B. eds. Teachings from the American earth p248-71

Waters, F. The fifth world—the ninth planet. *In* Voices from the Southwest p55-62

See also Indians of North America—Dances; Peyotism; also subdivision Religion and mythology under names of tribes, e.g. Chippewa Indians—Religion and mythology

Reservations

Baird, W. D. The quest for a red-faced white man: reservation whites view their Indian wards. *In* Red Men and hat-wearers p113-31

Cash, J. H. The reservation Indian meets the white man (1860-1914). *In* Red Men and hat-wearers p93-111

Rites and ceremonies

Furst, P. T. "High states" in culture-historical perspective. *In* Alternate states of consciousness p53-88

Gill, S. D. The shadow of a vision yonder. *In* Seeing with a native eye p44-57

Steward, J. H. The ceremonial buffoon of the American Indian. *In* Steward, J. H. Evolution and ecology p347-65

Weil, A. T. The marriage of the sun and moon. *In* Alternate states of consciousness p37-52

See also Peyotism; and subdivision Rites and ceremonies under names of tribes, e.g. Oglala Indians—Rites and ceremonies

Indians of North America—Southwest, New —Antiquities—*Continued*

Pailes, R. A. and Whitecotton, J. W. The greater Southwest and the Mesoamerican "world" system: an exploratory model of frontier relationships. *In* The Frontier v2 p105-21

Southwest, New—Astronomy

Brandt, J. C. Pictographs and petroglyphs of the Southwest Indians. *In* Brecher, K. and Feirtag, M. eds. Astronomy of the ancients p25-38

Southwest, New— Government relations

Park, J. F. Spanish Indian policy in northern Mexico, 1765-1810. *In* Weber, D. J ed. New Spain's far northern frontier p217-34

Southwest, New—Languages

Voegelin, C. F. and Voegelin, F. M. R. Southwestern and Great Basin languages. *In* Sebeok, T. A. ed. Native languages of the Americas v 1 p461-503

Virginia

Rountree, H. C. The Indians of Virginia: a third race in a biracial state. *In* Williams, W. L. ed. Southeastern Indians since the removal era p27-48

Indians of North America, Civilization of. See Indians of North America—Cultural assimilation.

Indians of South America

See also Accawai Indians; Amahuaca Indians; Carib Indians; Mundurucu Indians

Antiquities

Steward, J. H. Cultural evolution in South America. *In* Steward, J. H. Evolution and ecology p128-50

Art

See Tucano Indians—Art

Languages

Grimes, J. E. Descriptive linguistics. *In* Sebeok, T. A. ed. Native languages of the Americas v2 p55-62

Landar, H. J. Historiography of native Ibero-American linguistics. *In* Sebeok, T. A. ed. Native languages of the Americas v2 p185-203

Longacre, R. E. Comparative reconstruction of indigenous languages. *In* Sebeok, T. A. ed. Native languages of the Americas v2 p99-139

Suárez S , J. A. Classical languages. *In* Sebeok, T. A. ed. Native languages of the Americas v2 p3-25

Languages—Dialectology

Mayers, M. K. Indigenous dialectology. *In* Sebeok, T. A. ed. Native languages of the Americas v2 p89-98

Writing

Barthel, T. S. Writing systems. *In* Sebeok, T. A. ed. Native languages of the Americas v2 p27-53

Peru—Religion and mythology

Tickell, C. C. C. The civilization of pre-Columbian America. *In* Life after death p67-79

Indians of the West Indies. See Carib Indians

Indic art. See Art, Indic

Indic authors. See Authors, Indic

Indic ballads. See Ballads, Indic

Indic calendar. See Calendar, Indic

Indic fiction (English)

History and criticism

Cowasjee, S. The problems of teaching Indian fiction in Commonwealth countries. *In* Narasimhaiah, C. D. ed. Awakened conscience p413-19

Mukherjee, M. Inside the outsider. *In* Narasimhaiah, C. D. ed. Awakened conscience p86-91

Singh, R. S. Fictional technique. *In* Singh, R. S. Indian novel in English p179-203

Singh, R. S. Indo-English fiction: a retrospective introduction. *In* Singh, R. S. Indian novel in English p7-37

Study and teaching

Cowasjee, S. The problems of teaching Indian fiction in Commonwealth countries. *In* Narasimhaiah, C. D. ed. Awakened conscience p413-19

Indic literature (English)

History and criticism

Walsh, W. The Indian sensibility in English. *In* Narasimhaiah, C. D. ed. Awakened conscience p63-72

Indic national characteristics. See National characteristics, Indic

Indic orations (English)

McLeod, A. L. The creation of national images in Indian and Pakistani speeches to the United States Congress. *In* Narasimhaiah, C. D. ed. Awakened conscience p378-88

Indic philosophy. See Philosophy, Indic

Individualism

Buchanan, J. M. The justice of natural liberty. *In* Glahe, F. R. ed. Adam Smith and The wealth of nations p61-81

Dubos, R. J. Individualism and collectivity. *In* Dubos, R. J. Beast or angel? p51-60

Gardner, J. W. The individual and society. *In* McMurrin, S. M. ed. On the meaning of the university p51-62

Glazer, N. Individualism and equality in the United States. *In* On the making of Americans p127-42

Heller, A. Marx's theory of revolution and the revolution in everyday life. *In* The Humanisation of socialism p42-57

Johnson, H. G. The individual and the state: some contemporary problems. *In* Glahe, F. R. ed. Adam Smith and The wealth of nations p21-34

Kamenka, E. and Tay, A. Erh-Soon. Beyond bourgeois individualism: the contemporary crisis in law and legal ideology. *In* Kamenka, E. and Neale, R. S. eds. Feudalism, capitalism and beyond p126-44

Nevins, A. The limits of individualism. *In* Nevins, A. Allan Nevins on history p203-14

Tay, A. Erh Soon. Law, the citizen and the state. *In* Law and society p 1-17

See also Collectivism; Communism; Laissez-faire; Libertarianism; Persons

Individuality

McMurrin, S. M. Ideas and the processes of history. *In* The Abdication of philosophy: philosophy and the public good p109-28

Individuality—*Continued*

Sandler, R. The changing concept of the individual. *In* Savory, R. M. ed. Introduction to Islamic civilisation p137-45

Trilling, L. Two notes on David Riesman. *In* Trilling, L. A gathering of fugitives p91-107

See also Identity; Personality; Self

Individuality in literature

Hanning, R. W. Afterword: the evolution of chivalric romance in the early thirteenth century. *In* Hanning, R. W. The individual in twelfth-century romance p234-42

Hanning, R. W. Critical moments: individuality in chivalric romance. *In* Hanning, R. W. The individual in twelfth-century romance p53-104

Hanning, R. W. The individual and mimesis, I: time and space in chivalric romance. *In* Hanning, R. W. The individual in twelfth-cenutry romance p139-70

Hanning, R. W. The individual and mimesis, II: multiple perspectives on reality. *In* Hanning, R. W. The individual in twelfth-century romance p171-93

Hanning, R. W. Individuality in two twelfth-century personal histories. *In* Hanning, R. W. The individual in twelfth-century romance p17-52

Hanning, R. W. Introduction. *In* Hanning, R. W. The individual in twelfth-century romance p 1-16

Hanning, R. W. The romance plot and the crisis of inner awareness. *In* Hanning, R. W. The individual in twelfth-century romance p194-233

Individualized instruction. See Open plan schools

Individuals (Philosophy) See Individuation

Individuation. See Self (Philosophy)

Indo-English fiction. See Indic fiction (English)

Indo-European languages

Etymology

Nagy, G. J. Six studies of sacral vocabulary relating to the fireplace. *In* Harvard Studies in classical philology v78 p71-106

Watkins, C. On the family of *arceö, ἁρκεω,* and Hittite *hark-. In* Harvard Studies in classical philology v74 p67-74

Syntax

Watkins, C. An Indo-European construction in Greek and Latin. *In* Harvard Studies in classical philology v71 p115-19

Indo-Pakistan Conflict, 1971. See India-Pakistan Conflict, 1971

Indochina

Foreign relations—United States

Siracusa, J. M. FDR, Truman, and Indochina, 1941-1952: the forgotten years. *In* Siracusa, J. M. and Barclay, G. S. eds. The impact of the Cold war p163-83

Indochinese Communist Party. See Communist Party of Vietnam

Indonesia

Foreign relations

Angel, J. R. Indonesian foreign policy since independence: changing preoccupations in pursuit of progress. *In* The Year book of world affairs, 1977 p46-63

Languages

Jones, R. Indonesia: language and nation-building. *In* The Year book of world affairs, 1976 p190-204

Politics and government

Angel, J. R. Indonesian foreign policy since independence: changing preoccupations in pursuit of progress. *In* The Year book of world affairs, 1977 p46-63

Samson, A. A. Indonesia. *In* Kearney, R. N. ed. Politics and modernization in South and Southeast Asia p253-77

Politics and government— 1950-1966

Van der Kroef, J. M. The wages of ambiguity: the 1965 coup in Indonesia, its origins and meaning. *In* Hammond, T. T. ed. The anatomy of Communist takeovers p534-62

Indonesian Communist Party. See Communist Party of Indonesia

Indonesian language

Jones, R. Indonesia: language and nation-building. The Year book of world affairs, 1976 p190-204

See also Malay language

Induction (Logic)

Sternberg, R. J.; Tourangeau, R. and Nigro, G. Metaphor, induction, and social policy: the convergence of macroscopic and microscopic views. *In* Ortony, A. ed. Metaphor and thought p325-53

Zabeeh, F. Hume's problem of induction: an appraisal. *In* Livingston, D. W. and King, J. T. eds. Hume p69-90

Inductive logic. See Induction (Logic)

Industrial arbitration. See Arbitration, Industrial

Industrial arts. See Artisans; Technology

Industrial co-operation and East-West trade. Nussbaumer, A. *In* The Year book of world affairs, 1978 p64-75

Industrial design. See Design, Industrial

Industrial design departments. See Design, Industrial—Management

Industrial efficiency. See Efficiency, Industrial

Industrial laws and legislation

Wilson, J. Q. The politics of regulation. *In* McKie, J. W. ed. Social responsibility and the business predicament p135-68

Industrial management

Chandler, A. D. The multi-unit enterprise: a historical and international comparative analysis and summary. *In* Evolution of international management structures p225-54

See also Efficiency, Industrial; Industrial organization; Industrial relations; Technological innovations

France

Laux, J. M. Managerial structures in France. *In* Evolution of international management structures p95-113

Japan

Yamamura, K. A compromise with culture: the historical evolution of the managerial structure of large Japanese firms. *In* Evolution of international management structures p159-85

Industrial management—*Continued*

Russia

Billon, S. A. Soviet management structure: stability and change. *In* Evolution of international management structures p114-43

Industrial mobilization

Trebilcock, C. War and the failure of industrial mobilisation: 1899 and 1914. *In* War and economic development p139-64

Industrial organization

Great Britain

Mathias, P. Conflicts of function in the rise of big business: the British experience. *In* Evolution of international management structures p40-58

United States

Galbraith, J. K. The structure of the firm and the structure of the industry: a study in industrial development. *In* Evolution of international management structures p3-12

Industrial production. See Industry

Industrial productivity. See Technological innovations

Industrial project management

Evaluation

Balassa, B. A. Project appraisal in developing countries. *In* Economic development and planning p40-60

Industrial relations

Gemmill, G. R. Postscript: toward the person-centered organization. *In* Heisler, W. J. and Houck, J. W. eds. A matter of dignity p197-205

Strinati, D. Capitalism, the state and industrial relations. *In* Crouch, C. ed. State and economy in contemporary capitalism p191-236

See also Arbitration, Industrial

Africa, French West—History

Berg, E. J. A comparative analysis of industrial relations systems in French West Africa and the Gold Coast. *In* African dimensions p171-96

Europe

Mills, T. Leadership from abroad: European developments in industrial democracy. *In* Heisler, W. J. and Houck, J. W. eds. A matter of dignity p115-29

Ghana—History

Berg, E. J. A comparative analysis of industrial relations systems in French West Africa and the Gold Coast. *In* African dimensions p171-96

United States

Bluestone, I. Work humanization in practice: what can labor do? *In* Heisler, W. J. and Houck, J. W. eds. A matter of dignity p165-78

Myers, C. A. Management and the employee. *In* McKie, J. W. ed. Social responsibility and the business predicament p311-49

Industrial research. See Research, Industrial

Industrial revolution. See Industry—History; and subdivisions Economic conditions and Industries under names of countries

Industrial sociology

Clayre, A. Early criticisms of modern society. *In* Clayre, A. Work and play p30-44

Clayre, A. Idealization and reality. *In* Clayre, A. Work and play p79-86

Industrial unions. See Trade-unions

Industrialization. See Underdeveloped areas

Industrialization in literature

Skilton, D. Industrialisation and the condition of England. *In* Skilton, D. The English novel p120-35

Industries. See Industry; and subdivision Industries under names of countries, cities, etc., e.g. France—Industries

Industries, Location of. See Business relocation

Industries, Primitive. See Agriculture, Primitive

Industry

Morita, A. Creativity in modern industry. *In* The Frontiers of knowledge p143-56

See also Efficiency, Industrial; Technology; subdivision Industries under names of countries, regions, cities, etc.

History

Hartwell, R. M. Adam Smith and the Industrial Revolution. *In* Glahe, F. R. ed. Adam Smith and The wealth of nations p123-47

Kindleberger, C. P. The historical background: Adam Smith and the Industrial Revolution. *In* The Market and the state p 1-25

Larkin, M. The Industrial Revolution. *In* Larkin, M. Man and society in nineteenth-century realism p74-88

Williamson, A. Industrial change and the artist. *In* Williamson, A. Artists and writers in revolt p11-15

See also Machinery in industry

History—Sources

Fishbein, M. H. Selected materials in the National Archives relating to commerce and industry. *In* Pattern and process p224-28

Organization

See Industrial organization

Social aspects

Black, K. and Wilson, R. O. The environment of management in the future. *In* Benton, L. R. ed. Management for the future p9-26

Brevoord, C. Effective management in the future. *In* Benton, L. R. ed. Management for the future p27-46

Houck, J. W. Early historical traces of the contemporary debate about work alienation. *In* Heisler, W. J. and Houck, J. W. eds. A matter of dignity p49-63

McKie, J. W. Changing views. *In* McKie, J. W. ed. Social responsibility and the business predicament p17-40

Reynolds, D. P. Business management in an age of change. *In* Benton, L. R. ed. Management for the future p239-45

See also Industrial sociology

Social aspects—New Hampshire—Manchester

Hareven, T. K. Family and work patterns of immigrant laborers in a planned industrial town, 1900-1930. *In* Immigrants in industrial America, 1850-1920 p47-66

Industry—*Continued*

Social aspects—New York (City)

Groneman, C. "She earns as a child—she pays as a man": women workers in a mid-nineteenth-century New York City community. *In* Immigrants in industrial America, 1850-1920 p33-46

Social aspects—New York (State)—Buffalo

Yans-McLaughlin, V. A flexible tradition: South Italian immigrants confront a new work experience. *In* Immigrants in industrial America, 1850-1920 p67-84

Social aspects—United States

Bronfenbrenner, U. "Our system for making human beings human is breaking down." *In* Gross, B. and Gross, R. eds. The children's rights movement p251-55

Golab, C. The impact of the industrial experience on the immigrant family: the huddled masses reconsidered. *In* Immigrants in industrial America, 1850-1920 p 1-32

Industry (Psychology) See Work

Industry and art. See Art and industry

Industry and state

Billet, L. Justice, liberty and economy. *In* Glahe, F. R. ed. Adam Smith and The wealth of nations p83-109

Hawley, E. W. The New Deal and business. *In* Braeman, J.; Bremner, R. H. and Brody, D. eds. The New Deal v 1 p50-82

Javits, J. K. Government's role in economic management. *In* Benton, L. R. ed. Management for the future p165-73

Johnson, H. G. The individual and the state: some contemporary problems. *In* Glahe, F. R. ed. Adam Smith and The wealth of nations p21-34

McKean, R. N. Collective choice. *In* McKie, J. W. ed. Social responsibility and the business predicament p109-34

Markus, M. and Hegedüs, A. Free time and the division of labour. *In* The Humanisation of socialism p106-23

Spengler, J. J. Smith versus Hobbes: economy versus polity. *In* Glahe, F. R. ed. Adam Smith and The wealth of nations p35-59

Strinati, D. Capitalism, the state and industrial relations. *In* Crouch, C. ed. State and economy in contemporary capitalism p191-236

Weidenbaum, M. L. The second managerial revolution: the shift of economic decision-making from business to government. *In* Planning, politics, and the public interest p45-69

See also Corporate state; Economic policy; Government business enterprises; Industrial laws and legislation; Labor policy; Laissez-faire; Public interest; Subsides

Germany

Schmitt, H. A. Landed and moneyed princes: the harvest of tradition and conflict in German business and politics. *In* Evolution of international management structures p67-88

Great Britain

Longstreath, F. H. The city, industry and the state. *In* Crouch, C. ed. State and economy in contemporary capitalism p157-90

United States

Edmonds, M. Accountability and the military-industrial complex. *In* Smith, B. L. R. ed. The new political economy: the public use of the private sector p149-80

Galbraith, J. K. The structure of the firm and the structure of the industry: a study in industrial development. *In* Evolution of international management structures p3-12

Galbraith, J. K. The valid image of the modern economy. *In* Galbraith, J. K. Annals of an abiding liberal p3-19

Industry and war. See War—Economic aspects

Inefficiency, Intellectual. See Mentally handicapped children

Inequality. See Equality

Inequality of income. See Income distribution

Inertia (Mechanics)

Finocchiaro, M. A. Commentary: dialectical aspects of the Copernican revolution: conceptual elucidations and historiographical problems. *In* The Copernican achievement p204-12

Infallibility of the Pope. See Popes—Infallibility

Infancy of animals. See Animals, Infancy of

Infant mortality. See Infants—Mortality

Infante, Guillermo Cabrera. See Cabrera Infante, Guillermo

Infanticide

Fletcher, J. F. Infanticide. *In* Fletcher, J. F. Humanhood: essays in biomedical ethics p140-48

History

Langer, W. L. Infanticide: a historical survey. *In* DeMause, L. ed. The new psychohistory p55-67

Europe

Coleman, E. R. Infanticide in the early Middle Ages. *In* Stuard, S. M. ed. Women in medieval society p47-70

Infants

Mortality

Shorter, E. Maternal sentiment and death in childbirth: a new agenda for psycho-medical history. *In* Branca, P. ed. The medicine show p67-88

Sternglass, E. J. Nuclear radiation and human health. *In* Against pollution and hunger p121-79

Nutrition

See Wet-nurses

Infection

Temkin, O. An historical analysis of the concept of infection. *In* Temkin, O. The double face of Janus p456-71

Infectious diseases. See Infection

Inference (Logic) See Induction (Logic); Prediction (Logic); Probabilities

Infinite

Ulam, S. M. Infinities. *In* Neyman, J. ed. The heritage of Copernicus: theories "pleasing to the mind" p378-93

Infinity. See Infinite

Inflation (Finance)

Anderson, M. Power and inflation. *In* The Political economy of inflation p240-62

Brittan, S. Inflation and democracy. *In* The Political economy of inflation p161-85

Inglis, Tony
Reading late James. *In* Josipovici, G. ed. The modern English novel: the reader, the writer and the work p77-94

Ingram, Forrest L.
Fun at the incinerating plant: Lardner's wry waste land. *In* French, W. G. ed. The twenties p111-22

Ingram, R. W. See Winnington-Ingram, Reginald Pepys

Ingram, Reginald Pepys Winnington- See Winnington-Ingram, Reginald Pepys

Ingratitude. See Gratitude

Ingres, Jean Auguste Dominique

About individual works
Vow of Louis XIII
Duncan, C. Ingres's Vow of Louis XIII and the politics of the Restoration. *In* Millon, H. A. and Nochlin, L. eds. Art and architecture in the service of politics p80-91

Ingwersen, Niels
Problematic protagonists: Marie Grubbe and Niels Lyhne. *In* The Hero in Scandinavian literature p39-61

Inhelder, Bärbel
New currents in genetic epistemology and developmental psychology. *In* Human growth and development p121-38

Inheritance (Biology) See Heredity

Inheritance and succession
Thompson, E. P. The grid of inheritance: a comment. *In* Family and inheritance p328-60
See also Estates (Law); Land tenure

History
Cooper, J. P. Patterns of inheritance and settlement by great landowners from the fifteenth to the eighteenth centuries. *In* Family and inheritance p192-327

Goody, J. R. Inheritance, property and women: some comparative considerations. *In* Family and inheritance p10-36

Thirsk, J. The European debate on customs of inheritance, 1500-1700. *In* Family and inheritance p177-91

Béarn
Bourdieu, P. Marriage strategies as strategies of social reproduction. *In* Family and society p117-44

France
Le Roy Ladurie, E. A system of customary law: family structures and inheritance customs in sixteenth-century France. *In* Family and society p75-103

France—History
Le Roy Ladurie, E. Family structures and inheritance customs in sixteenth-century France. *In* Family and inheritance p37-70

Germany—History
Berkner, L. K. Inheritance, land tenure and peasant family structure: a German regional comparison. *In* Family and inheritance p71-95

Great Britain—History
Howell, C. Peasant inheritance customs in the Midlands, 1280-1700. *In* Family and inheritance p112-55

Spufford, M. Peasant inheritance customs and land distribution in Cambridgeshire from the sixteenth to the eighteenth centuries. *In* Family and inheritance p156-76

Inheritance of acquired characters
Koestler, A. Lamarck revisited. *In* Koestler, A. Janus p193-204

Initiations (in religion, folklore, etc.)
Buxton, J. C. Initiation and bead-sets in western Mandari. *In* Studies in social anthropology p310-27

Coomaraswamy, A. K. The "E" at Delphi. *In* Coomaraswamy, A. K. Selected papers v2 p43-45

Inkeles, Alex
Becoming modern: individual change in six developing countries. *In* Schwartz, T. ed. Socialization as cultural communication p231-50

The future of individual modernity. *In* Major social issues p459-75

Understanding and misunderstanding individual modernity. *In* The Uses of controversy in sociology p103-30

Inlaying in wood. See Marquetry

Innes, Catherine Lynette
Through the looking glass: African and Irish nationalist writing. *In* African literature no. 9: Africa, America and the Caribbean p10-24

Innes, Michael. See Stewart, John Innes Mackintosh

Innis, Harold Adams

About
Berger, C. Harold Innis: the search for limits. *In* Berger, C. The writing of Canadian history p85-111

Innocent III, Pope. See Innocentius III, Pope

Innocentius III, Pope

About individual works
Per venerabilem
Pennington, K. J. Pope Innocent III's views on church and state: a gloss to Per venerabilem. *In* Law, church, and society p49-67
Tua nobis
Horwitz, S. Reshaping a decretal chapter: Tua nobis and the canonists. *In* Law, church, and society p207-21

Innovations, Agricultural. See Agricultural innovations

Innovations, Diffusion of. See Diffusion of innovations

Innovations, Educational. See Educational innovations

Innovations, Technological. See Technological innovations

Innuit. See Eskimos

Input-output analysis. See Production functions (Economic theory)

Inquisition
France
Lerner, R. E. An "Angel of Philadelphia" in the reign of Philip the Fair: the case of Guiard of Cressonessart. *In* Order and innovation in the Middle Ages p343-64

Inquisition—*Continued*

Toulouse

Mundy, J. H. The origins of the College of Saint-Raymond at the University of Toulouse. *In* Philosophy and humanism p454-61

Insane

Care and treatment

See Mentally ill—Care and treatment

Legal status, laws, etc.

See Insanity—Jurisprudence

Insanity

Derrida, J. Cogito and the history of madness. *In* Derrida, J. Writing and difference p31-63

See also Hysteria; Psychiatry; Psychology, Pathological

Jurisprudence—United States

Scheff, T. J. Social conditions for rationality: how urban and rural courts deal with the mentally ill. *In* Davis, F. J. and deviance p317-24

Insanity, Delusional. See Paranoia

Insanity, Hysterical. See Hysteria

Insanity in literature. See Mental illness in literature

Inscriptions. See Epitaphs; Pectoglyphs; Seals (Numismatics)

Inscriptions, Greek

Drew-Bear, T. Two ghost-words and a consul: inscriptions of Pergamum and Tarsus. *In* Harvard Studies in classical philology v79 p301-03

Robb, K. W. Poetic sources of the Greek alphabet: rhythm and abecedarium from Phoenician to Greek. *In* Havelock, E. A. and Hershbell, J. P. eds. Communication arts in the ancient world p23-36

Watkins, C. Observations on the "Nestor's cup" inscription. *In* Harvard Studies in classical philology v80 p25-40

Inscriptions, Latin

Asia Minor

Drew-Bear, T. A fourth-century Latin soldier's epitaph at Nekolea. *In* Harvard Studies in classical philology v81 p257-74

Egypt

Gilliam, J. F. Some elements in Roman Egypt. *In* Illinois classical studies v3, 1978 p115-31

Pozzuoli

D'Arms, J. H. CIL X, 1792: a municipal notable of the Augustan age. *In* Harvard Studies in classical philology v76 p207-16

Inscriptions, Runic. See Runes

Insecticides

Law and legislation

See Pesticides—Law and legislation

Insects. See Hymenoptera

Insignia. See Columns of Hercules (Heraldic device)

Inspiration

Barfield, O. Imagination and inspiration *In* Barfield, O. The rediscovery of meaning, and other essays p111-29

García Lorca, F. The duende: theory and divertissement; excerpt from "The poet in New York." *In* Gibbons, R. ed. The poet's work: 29 masters of 20th century poetry on the origins and practice of their art p28-41

See also Creation (Literary, artistic, etc.); Enthusiasm

Instinct. See Impulse; Orientation (Psychology)

Institute of Criminology. See Cambridge. University. Institute of Criminology

Institute of Society, Ethics, and Life Sciences. Task Force on Death and Dying. See Task Force on Death and Dying of the Institute of Society, Ethics, and the Life Sciences

Institutional care. See Nursing homes

Institutional church. See Church work

Institutional research (Education). See Education, Higher—Research

Institutions, Charitable and philanthropic. See Charities

Institutions, International. See International cooperation

Institutions, Social. See Social institutions

Instruction. See Education; Teaching

Instructional objectives. See Education—Aims and objectives

Instrumental behavior. See Operant behavior

Instrumentation and orchestration. See Musical instruments

Instruments, Astronomical. See Astronomical instruments

Instruments, Musical. See Musical instruments

Insurance, Health

See also Medical care

United States

Densen, P. M. Public accountability and reporting systems in Medicare and other health programs. *In* Smith, B. L. R. ed. The new political economy: the public use of the private sector p229-44

Insurance, Social. See Social security

Insurance, State and compulsory. See Social security

Insurance legal services. See Prepaid legal services

Insurgency

Bell, J. B. Proliferation: sophisticated weapons and revolutionary options—the substate perspective. *In* Arms control and technological innovation p146-60

See also Guerrilla warfare; Internal security; Peasant uprisings; Terrorism

Insurrections. See Revolutions

Intaglios

Beckwith, J. Some early Byzantine rock crystals. *In* Studies in memory of David Talbot Rice p 1-5

Intarsia. See Marquetry

Integrated curriculum. See Interdisciplinary approach in education

Integration, Social. See Social integration

Integration in education. See School integration

Integrity

Mayo, B. Moral integrity. *In* Royal Institute of Philosophy. Human values p27-43

Intellect

Arendt, H. Will and intellect. *In* Arendt, H. The life of the mind v2 p111-46

Coomaraswamy, A. K. Manas. *In* Coomaraswamy, A. K. Selected papers v2 p209-19

Coomaraswamy, A. K. Primitive mentality; excerpt from "Figures of speech or figures of thought: collected essays on the traditional or 'normal' view of art." *In* Coomaraswamy, A. K. Selected papers v 1 p286-307

Eccles, Sir J. C. The brain-mind problem as a frontier of science. *In* The Future of science p73-89

Grene, M. G. Sociobiology and the human mind. *In* Sociobiology and human nature p213-24

Matson, W. I. Spinoza's theory of mind. *In* Freeman, E. and Mandelbaum, M. H. eds. Spinoza p49-60

Odegard, D. A. The body identical with the human mind: a problem in Spinoza's philosophy. *In* Freeman, E. and Mandelbaum, M. H. eds. Spinoza p61-83

Quine, W. V. Mind and verbal dispositions. *In* Guttenplan, S. D. ed. Mind and language p83-95

Schwyzer, H. R. The intellect in Plotinus and the archetypes of C. G. Jung. *In* Kephalaion p214-22

Simon, B. Plato's concept of mind and its disorders. *In* Simon, B. Mind and madness in ancient Greece p157-79

Taylor, D. M. An empirical account of mind. *In* Royal Institute of Philosophy. Impressions of empiricism p66-78

See also Creation (Literary, artistic, etc.); Imagination; Knowledge, Theory of; Logic; Memory; Perception; Reason; Senses and sensation; Thought and thinking; Wisdom

Genetic aspects

Harwood, J. Heredity, environment, and the legitimation of social policy. *In* Barnes, B. and Shapin, S. eds. Natural order p231-51

Intellect and age. See Age and intelligence

Intellectual activity. See Mental work

Intellectual cooperation. See Information networks; International education

Intellectual freedom. See Censorship; Freedom of information; Liberty of speech, Teaching. Freedom of

Intellectual history. See Intellectual life—History

Intellectual life

Ahlstrom, S. E. Thought and social change: reflections on cultural studies. *In* Luedtke, L. S. ed. The study of American culture p63-75

See also Learning and scholarship; Popular culture; also subdivision Intellectual life under particular classes of people and names of countries, cities, etc., e.g. Jews—Intellectual life; Thailand—Intellectual life

Historiography

Conkin, P. K. Intellectual history: past, present, and future. *In* The Future of history p111-33

Haskell, T. L. Deterministic implications of intellectual history. *In* Higham, J. and Conkin, P. K. eds. New directions in American intellectual history p132-48

Hollinger, D. A. Historians and the discourse of intellectuals. *In* Higham, J. and Conkin, P. K. eds. New directions in American intellectual history p42-63

Wood, G. S. Intellectual history and the social sciences. *In* Higham, J. and Conkin, P. K. eds. New directions in American intellectual history p27-41

History

Shklar, J. N. Politics and the intellect. *In* Studies in eighteenth-century culture v7 p139-51

Trilling, L. Mind in the modern world. *In* Trilling, L. The last decade p100-28

Intellectual property. See Copyright

Intellectuals

Buckley, W. F. The road to serfdom: the intellectuals and socialism. *In* Essays on Hayek p95-106

Hollinger, D. A. Historians and the discourse of intellectuals. *In* Higham, J. and Conkin, P. K. eds. New directions in American intellectual history p42-63

Jacobelli, I. A. M. The role of the intellectual in Giambattista Vico. *In* Giambattista Vico's science of humanity p409-21

Knights, B. Epilogue: Cultural studies without a clerisy. *In* Knights, B. The idea of the clerisy in the nineteenth century p214-32

Lipset, S. M. and Basu, A. Intellectual types and political roles. *In* The Idea of social structure p433-70

Rahv, P. Religion and the intellectuals. *In* Rahv, P. Essays on literature and politics, 1932-1972 p310-16

Rahv, P. Twilight of the thirties: passage from an editorial. *In* Rahv, P. Essays on literature and politics, 1932-1972 p305-09

See also Professions

Psychology

Bulgakov, S. N. Heroism and asceticism: reflections on the religious nature of the Russian intelligentsia. *In* Landmarks p23-63

Frank, S. L. The ethic of nihilism: a characterization of the Russian intelligentsia's moral outlook. *In* Landmarks p155-84

Gershenzon, M. O. Creative self-cognition. *In* Landmarks p64-87

Africa

Achebe, C. What do African intellectuals read? *In* Achebe, C. Morning yet on creation day p61-66

Brazil

Burns, E. B. The intellectuals as agents of change and the independence of Brazil, 1724-1822. *In* From colony to nation p211-46

Europe

Hughes, H. S. Conclusion: The sea change. *In* Hughes, H. S. The sea change p240-72

Hughes, H. S. The great migration. *In* Hughes, H. S. The sea change p 1-34

France

Nora, P. America and the French intellectuals. *In* A New America? p325-37

Intellectuals—*Continued*

Great Britain

Watson, G. Did Stalin dupe the intellectuals? *In* Watson, G. Politics and literature in modern Britain p46-70

Welch, C. Intellectuals have consequences. *In* Tyrrell, R. E. ed. The future that doesn't work p42-63

Russia

Berdíaev, N. A. Philosophic truth and the moral truth of the intelligentsia. *In* Landmarks p3-22

Berlin, Sir I. A remarkable decade: The birth of the Russian intelligentsia. *In* Berlin, Sir I. Russian thinkers p114-35

Biddulph, H. L. Protest strategies of the Soviet intellectual opposition. *In* Tokes, R. L. ed. Dissent in the USSR p96-115

Bulgakov, S. N. Heroism and asceticism: reflection on the religious nature of the Russian intelligentsia. *In* Landmarks p23-63

Feifer, G. No protest: the case of the passive minority. *In* Tokes, R. L. ed. Dissent in the USSR p418-37

Frank, S. L. The ethics of nihilism: a characterization of the Russian intelligentsia's moral outlook. *In* Landmarks p155-84

Gershenzon, M. M. Creative self-cognition. *In* Landmarks p64-87

Izgoev, A. On educated youth: notes on its life and sentiments. *In* Landmarks p88-111

Kistyakovsky, B. In the defense of law: the intelligentsia and legal consciousness. *In* Landmarks p112-37

Solzhenifsyn, A. I. The smatterers. *In* From under the rubble p229-78

Struve, P. B. The intelligentsia and revolution. *In* Landmarks p138-54

United States

Bell, D. The "intelligentsia" in American society. *In* Tomorrow's American p21-46

Chomsky, N. Foreign policy and the intelligentsia. *In* Images and ideas in American culture p15-59

Rahv, P. American intellectuals in the postwar situation. *In* Rahv, P. Essays on literature and politics, 1932-1972 p328-34

Trilling, L. The situation of the American intellectual at the present time. *In* Trilling, L. A gathering of fugitives p65-84

Whitfield, S. J. "Totaliarianism" in eclipse: the recent fate of an idea. *In* Images and ideas in American culture p60-95

Intelligence. See Intellect

Intelligence, Artificial. See Artificial intelligence

Intelligence and age. See Age and intelligence

Intelligence levels

Bodmer, W. F. Race and IQ: the genetic background. *In* Montagu, A. ed. Race and IQ p252-86

Brace, C. L. and Livingstone, F. B. On creeping Jensenism. *In* Montagu, A. ed. Race and IQ p151-73

Bronfenbrenner, U. Nature with nurture: a reinterpretation of the evidence. *In* Montagu, A. ed. Race and IQ p114-44

Dobzhansky, T. G. and Montagu, A. Natural selection and the mental capacities of mankind. *In* Montagu, A. ed. Race and IQ p104-13

Gordon, E. W. and Green, D. An affluent society's excuses for inequality: developmental, economic, and educational. *In* Montagu, A. ed. Race and IQ p73-103

Lewontin, R. C. Race and intelligence. *In* Montagu, A. ed. Race and IQ p175-91

Rose, S. P. R. Scientific racism and ideology. *In* Racial variation in man p191-210

Sanday, P. R. On the causes of IQ differences between groups and implications for social policy. *In* Montagu, A. ed. Race and IQ p220-51

Tizard, B. The environment and intellectual functions. *In* Racial variation in man p109-20

Testing

See Intelligence tests

Black race

Biesheuvel, S. An examination of Jensen's theory concerning educability, heritability and population differences. *In* Montagu, A. ed. Race and IQ p59-72

Gould, S. J. Racist arguments and IQ. *In* Montagu, A. ed. Race and IQ p145-50

Jensen, A. R. Race and mental ability. *In* Racial variation in man p71-108

Lewontin, R. C. Race and intelligence. *In* Montagu, A. ed. Race and IQ p175-91

Sanday, P. R. On the causes of IQ differences between groups and implications for social policy. *In* Montagu, A. ed. Race and IQ p220-51

Intelligence service

United States

Kirkpatrick, L. B. Intelligence and counterintelligence. *In* Encyclopedia of American foreign policy p417-27

Ross, T. B. Surreptitious entry: the CIA's operations in the United States. *In* Borosage, R. L. and Marks, J. D. eds. The CIA file p93-108

United States—Political aspects

Barnet, R. J. The "dirty-tricks" gap. *In* Borosage, R. L. and Marks, J. D. eds. The CIA file p214-28

Intelligence tests

Biesheuvel, S. An examination of Jensen's theory concerning educability, heritability and population differences. *In* Montagu, A. ed. Race and IQ p59-72

Gould, S. J. Racist arguments and IQ. *In* Montagu, A. ed. Race and IQ p145-50

Jensen, A. R. Race and mental ability. *In* Racial variation in man p71-108

Kagan, J. The magical aura of the IQ. *In* Montagu, A. ed. Race and IQ p52-58

Klineberg, O. Race and psychology. *In* United Nations Educational, Scientific and Cultural Organization. Race, science and society p173-207

Layzer, D. Heritability analyses of IQ scores: science or numerology? *In* Montagu, A. ed. Race and IQ p193-219

Rose, S. P. R. Scientific racism and ideology. *In* Racial variation in man p191-210

Tizard, B. The environment and intellectual functions. *In* Racial variation in man p109-20

Intelligentsia. See Intellectuals

Intemperance. See Temperance

Intension (Philosophy) See Semantics (Philosophy)

Intention (Logic)

Carr, D. Intentionality. *In* Pivčević, E. ed. Phenomenology and philosophical understanding p17-36

Cavell, S. Must we mean what we say? *In* Cavell, S. Must we mean what we say? p 1-43

Close, A. J. Don Quixote and the 'intentionalist fallacy.' *In* On literary intention p174-93

Coomaraswamy, A. K. Intention; excerpt from "Figures of speech or figures of thought: collected essays on the traditional or 'normal' view of art." *In* Coomaraswamy, A. K. Selected papers v 1 p266-75

Derrida, J. Limited Inc. *In* Glyph 2 p162-254

Freedman, R. Intentionality and the literary object. *In* Krieger, M. and Dembo, L. S. eds. Directions for criticism p137-59

Mackie, J. L. Problems of intentionality. *In* Pivčević, E. ed. Phenomenology and philosophical understanding p37-52

Olafson, F. A. Husserl's theory of intentionality in contemporary perspective. *In* Elliston, F. A. and McCormick, P. eds. Husserl p160-67

Searle, J. R. Reiterating the differences: a reply to Derrida. *In* Glyph I p198-208

Solomon, R. C. Husserl's concept of the noema. *In* Elliston, F. A. and McCormick, P. eds. Husserl p168-81

Intentionalism

Cioffi, F. Intention and interpretation in criticism. *In* Margolis, J. Z. ed. Philosophy looks at the arts p307-24

Kenny, A. Intention and purpose in law. *In* Summers, R. S. ed. Essays in legal philosophy p146-63

Olafson, F. A. Husserl's theory of intentionality in contemporary perspective. *In* Elliston, F. A. and McCormick, P. eds. Husserl p160-67

Solomon, R. C. Husserl's concept of the noema. *In* Elliston, F. A. and McCormick, P. eds. Husserl p168-81

Interaction, Social. See Social interaction

Inter-American Commission on Human Rights

Wood, B. Human rights and the inter-American system. *In* Farer, T. J. ed. The future of the inter-American system p119-52

Inter-American conferences

Bloomfield, R. J. The new dialogue with Latin America and the Working Group on Transnational Enterprises: Calvo versus Hickenlooper. *In* Farer, T. J. ed. The future of the inter-American system p73-80

Inter-American cooperation. See Pan-Americanism

Inter American Press Association

Gardner, M. A. The evolution of the Inter American Press Association. *In* Fischer, H. D. and Merrill, J. C. eds. International and intercultural communication p392-404

Inter-college cooperation. See University cooperation

Intercourse, Oral. See Oral intercourse

Intercultural communication

Fischer, H. D. Forms and functions of supranational communication. *In* Fischer, H. D. and Merrill, J. C. eds. International and intercultural communication p 5-17

Fischer, H. D. Periodicals and the international communication system. *In* Fischer, H. D. and Merrill, J. C. eds. International and intercultural communication p99-114

Maletzke, G. Intercultural and international communication. *In* Fischer, H. D. and Merrill, J. C. eds. International and intercultural communication p409-16

Martin, L. J. The contradiction of cross-cultural communication. *In* Fischer, H. D. and Merrill, J. C. eds. International and intercultural communication p424-34

Martin, L. J. Prospects for international communication. *In* Fischer, H. D. and Merrill, J. C. eds. International and intercultural communication p447-56

Prosser, M. H. The cultural communicator. *In* Fischer, H. D. and Merrill, J. C. eds. International and intercultural communication p417-23

Intercultural education

Glazer, N. Public education and American pluralism. *In* Parents, teachers, and children: prospects for choice in American education p85-109

Intercultural relations. See Cultural relations

Inter-cultural studies. See Cross-cultural studies

Interdependence of nations. See International cooperation; International economic relations; International organization; International relations

Interdisciplinary approach in education

Marx, L. Technology and the study of man. *In* Niblett, W. R. ed. The sciences, the humanities and the technological threat p3-20

Radest, H. B. On interdisciplinary education. *In* Hook, S.; Kurtz, P. W. and Todorovich, M. eds. The philosophy of the curriculum: the need for general education p227-33

Interdisciplinary studies. See Interdisciplinary approach in education

Interest and usury

Le Goff, J. The usurer and Purgatory. *In* The Dawn of modern banking p25-52

Mathematical models

Samuelson, P. A. Land and the rate of interest. *In* Theory for economic efficiency: essays in honor of Abba P. Lerner p167-85

Interest centers approach to teaching. See Open plan schools

Interest groups. See Pressure groups

Intergovernmental fiscal relations

Caraley, D. The Carter Congress and urban programs: first soundings. *In* Burnham, W. D. and Weinberg, M. W. eds. American politics and public policy p188-221

United States

Murphy, T. P. Urban governmental manpower. *In* Murphy, T. P. ed. Universities in the urban crisis p49-70

Interludes

History and criticism

Nicoll, A. Religious drama and profane during the Middle Ages. *In* Nicoll, A. World drama p103-31

Interludes, English

See also Apius and Virginia

Interludes, English—*Continued*

History and criticism

Axton, R. Folk play in Tudor interludes. *In* English drama: forms and development p 1-23

Jones, R. C. Dangerous sport: the audience's engagement with vice in the moral interludes. *In* Renaissance drama [1973] p45-64

Weimann, R. Moralities and interludes. *In* Weimann, R. Shakespeare and the popular tradition in the theater: studies in the social dimension of dramatic form and function p98-160

Intermarriage. See Consanguinity

Intermediate state. See Eschatology

Internal migration. See Migration, Internal

Internal security

China

Pye, L. W. China: ethnic minorities and national security. *In* Glazer, N. and Moynihan, D. P. eds. Ethnicity p489-512

International affairs and Christianity. See Christianity and international affairs

International affairs and religion. See Religion and international affairs

International agencies

Rodley, N. S. Monitoring human rights by the U.N. system and nongovernmental organizations. *In* Kommers, D. P. and Loescher, G. D. eds. Human rights and American foreign policy p157-78

Taulbee, J. L. Law, organization, and environmental concerns. *In* Orr, D. W. and Soroos, M. S. eds. The global predicament p249-63

Wiseberg, L. S. and Scoble, H. M. Monitoring human rights violations: the role of nongovernmental organizations. *In* Kommers, D. P. and Loescher, G. D. eds. Human rights and American foreign policy p179-208

See also International organization

International bibliography. See Bibliography, International

International boundaries. See Boundaries

International broadcasting

Head, S. W. Trends in tropical African societies. *In* Gerbner, G. ed. Mass media policies in changing cultures p83-103

Riegel, O. W. Satellite communication and national power. *In* Gerbner, G. ed. Mass media policies in changing cultures p63-72

Shayon, R. L. Television international. *In* Gerbner, G. ed. Mass media policies in changing cultures p41-55

International business enterprises

Bloomfield, R. J. The new dialogue with Latin America and the Working Group on Transnational Enterprises: Calvo versus Hickenlooper. *In* Farer, T. J. ed. The future of the inter-American system p73-80

Galbraith, J. K. The multinational corporation: how to put your worst foot forward or in your mouth. *In* Galbraith, J. K. Annals of an abiding liberal p54-72

Gilpin, R. G. The multinational corporation and American foreign policy. *In* Rosecrance, R. N. ed. America as an ordinary country p174-98

Hufbauer, G. C. The multinational corporation and direct investment. *In* Kenen, P. B. ed. International trade and finance p253-319

Mazur, M. P. The developing countries in the world economy: a question of bargaining power? *In* Baldwin, D. A. ed. America in an interdependent world p137-61

Morgenthau, R. S. Strangers, nationals, and multinationals in contemporary Africa. *In* Shack, W. A. and Skinner, E. P. eds. Strangers in African societies p105-20

Ringbakk, K. A. Multinational corporations and foreign policy. *In* Baldwin, D. A. ed. America in an interdependent world p91-135

Seidl-Hohenveldern, I. Multinational enterprises and the international law of the future. *In* The Year book of world affairs, 1975 p301-12

Stoiber, C. Equality and discrimination in international economic law (VII): the multinational enterprise. *In* The Year book of world affairs, 1977 p217-35

Vernon, R. National planning and the multinational enterprise: the U.S. case. *In* Planning, politics, and the public interest p77-94

Waldheim, K. Global economic problems and transnational corporations. *In* Benton, L. R. ed. Management for the future p299-305

Williams, R. The multinational enterprise: a 1977 perspective. *In* Hayward, J. E. S. and Berki, R. N. eds. State and society in contemporary Europe p237-52

Wilson, C. H. Multinationals, management, and world markets: a historical view. *In* Evolution of international management structures p193-216

See also Investments, Foreign

Law and legislation

Seidl-Hohenveldern, I. Multinational enterprises and the international law of the future. *In* The Year book of world affairs, 1975 p301-12

Management

Ford, H. Two developments which challenge management for the future. *In* Benton, L. R. ed. Management for the future p101-07

Political aspects

Peña, F. Multinational enterprises and North-South relations. *In* Erb, G. F. and Kallab, V. eds. Beyond dependency p57-74

International Business Machines Corporation

Watson, T. J. Good design is good business. *In* The Uneasy coalition: design in corporate America p57-79

International Committee of the Red Cross. See Red Cross. International Committee, Geneva.

International competition. See Competition, International

International Conference on the Unity of the Sciences, 5th, Washington, D.C. 1976

Horowitz, I. L. Science sin, and sponsorship. *In* Horowitz, I. L. ed. Science, sin, and scholarship p260-81

International Congress of the P.E.N. clubs, Barcelona

Spender, S. Spain invites the world's writers. *In* Spender, S. The thirties and after p50-57

International cooperation

Borgese, E. M. A constitution for the oceans. *In* Borgese, E. M. and Krieger, D. eds. The tides of change p340-52

Haq, M. ul. Negotiating a new bargain with the rich countries. *In* Erb, G. F. and Kallab, V. eds. Beyond dependency p157-62

Kissinger, H. A. Expanding cooperation for global economic development. *In* Benton, L. R. ed. Management for the future p199-218

Levy, W. J. An Atlantic-Japanese energy policy. *In* The New Atlantic challenge p119-49

Nussbaumer, A. Industrial co-operation and East-West trade. *In* The Year book of world affairs, 1978 p64-75

Pardo, A. New institutions for ocean space. *In* Borgese, E. M. and Krieger, D. eds. The tides of change p324-27

Verghese, T. P. Muddled metaphors: an Asian response to Garrett Hardin. *In* Lucas, G. R. and Ogletree, T. W. eds. Lifeboat ethics p151-56

See also European cooperation; International agencies; International police; Libraries, International

Economic aspects

Erb, G. F. The developing world's "challenge" in perspective. *In* Erb, G. F. and Kallab, V. eds. Beyond dependency p135-56

Political aspects

Erb, G. F. The developing world's "challenge" in perspective. *In* Erb, G. F. and Kallab, V. eds. Beyond dependency p135-56

Social aspects

Parmar, S. L. Self-reliant development in an "interdependent" world. *In* Erb, G. F. and Kallab, V. eds. Beyond dependency p3-27

International cooperation in telecommunication. See Telecommunication—International cooperation

International copyright. See Copyright, International

International corporations. See Corporations, International

International Court of Justice. See Hague. International Court of Justice

International courts

Kos-Rabcewicz-Zubkowski, L. The creation of an international criminal court. *In* International terrorism and political crimes p519-36

International Covenants on Human Rights. See United Nations. General Assembly. International Covenants on Human Rights

International criminal law. See Criminal jurisdiction; International offenses

International date line

Lutz, C. E. A fourteenth-century argument for an international date line. *In* Lutz, C. E. Essays on manuscripts and rare books p63-70

International debts. See Debts, External

International disputes, Pacific settlement of. See Pacific settlement of international disputes

International economic integration

Mondale, W. F. Beyond detente: toward international economic security. *In* Bundy, W. P. ed. The world economic crisis p230-52

See also subdivision Economic integration under continents and regions, e.g. Caribbean area—Economic integration

International economic policy. See International economic relations

International economic relations

Aliber, R. Z. Oil and the money crunch. *In* Eppen, G. D. ed. Energy: the policy issues p82-95

Bergsten, C. F. Economic tensions: America versus the Third World. *In* Rosecrance, R. N. ed. America as an ordinary country p199-223

Bergsten, C. F. U.S.-Latin American economic relations to 1980: the international framework and some possible new approaches. *In* The Americas in a changing world p173-95

Bock, F. The impact of international economic factors on the conduct of foreign policy. *In* The Interaction of economics and foreign policy p130-50

Calleo, D. P. Keynes and the 'Pax Americana.' *In* Skidelsky, R. J. A. ed. The end of the Keynesian era p95-103

Campos, R. D. The new international economic order: aspirations and realities. *In* World change and world security p73-87

Caves, R. E. Looking at inflation in the open economy. *In* Inflation, trade and taxes p75-95

Christensen, C. J. Structural power and national security. *In* Knorr, K. E. and Trager, F. N. eds. Economic issues and national security p127-59

Denny, D. L. Recent developments in the international financial policies of the People's Republic of China. *In* China's changing role in the world economy p163-86

Fowler, H. H. International economic policy as a system. *In* The New Atlantic challenge p61-75

Friedman, E. The international political economy and Chinese politics. *In* China's changing role in the world economy p 1-14

Goldsmith, P. and Sonderkötter, F. Equality and discrimination in international economic law (V): The European communities and the wider world. *In* The Year book of world affairs, 1975 p265-82

Hansen, R. D. U.S.-Latin American economic relationships: bilateral, regional or global? *In* The Americas in a changing world p196-238

Kissinger, H. A. Expanding cooperation for global economic development. *In* Benton, L. R. ed. Management for the future p199-218

Knorr, K. E. Economic interdependence and national security. *In* Knorr, K. E. and Trager, F. N. eds. Economic issues and national security p 1-18

Knorr, K. E. International economic leverage and its uses. *In* Knorr, K. E. and Trager, F. N. eds. Economic issues and national security p99-126

Krasner, S. D. Domestic constraints on international economic leverage. *In* Knorr, K. E. and Trager, F. N. eds. Economic issues and national security p127-59

International economic relations—*Continued*

Mazrui, A. A. The new interdependence. *In* Erb, G. F. and Kallab, V. eds. Beyond dependency p38-54

Mazur, M. P. The developing countries in the world economy: a question of bargaining power? *In* Baldwin, D. A. ed. America in an interdependent world p137-61

Meltzer, R. I. Contemporary security dimentions of international trade relations. *In* Knorr, K. E. and Trager, F. N. eds. Economic issues and national security p200-30

Morse, E. L. The Atlantic economy in crisis. *In* Atlantis lost p149-82

Morse, E. L. The new Europe: a unified bloc or blocked unity? *In* **The Interaction of economics and foreign policy p102-29**

Murdock, C. A. Economic factors as objects of security: economics, security and vulnerability. *In* Knorr, K. E. and Trager, F. N. eds. Economic issues and national security p67-98

Nussbaumer, A. Industrial co-operation and East-West trade. *In* The Year book of world affairs, 1978 p64-75

Silk, L. S. America in the world economy. *In* Rosecrance, R. N. ed. America as an ordinary country p158-73

Singer, H. W. International policies and their effect on employment. *In* Economic development and planning p237-49

Smart, I. Uniqueness and generality. *In* Vernon, R. ed. The oil crisis p259-81

Trethewey, R. J. International economics and politics: a theoretical framework. *In* The Interaction of economics and foreign policy p 1-24

Vernon, R. The distribution of power. *In* Vernon, R. ed. The oil crisis p245-57

Waldheim, K. Global economic problems and transnational corporations. *In* Benton, L. R. ed. Management for the future p299-305

Yergin, D. Order and survival. *In* A New America? p263-87

See also Balance of payments; Commercial policy; International business enterprises; International economic integration; International finance; Investments, Foreign; also subdivision Foreign economic relations under names of countries, e.g. United States—Foreign economic relations

Mathematical models

Klein, L. R.; Moriguchi, C. and Van Peeterssen, A. The LINK model of world trade, with applications to 1972-73. *In* Kenen, P. B. ed. International trade and finance p453-83

Magee, S. P. Prices, incomes, and foreign trade. *In* Kenen, P. B. ed. International trade and finance p175-252

International economics. See International economic relations

International education

Nicholson, M. Peace education: a sceptic's view. *In* International terrorism and world security p296-307

Shoemaker, F. New dimensions for world cultures. *In* Fairfield, R. P. ed. Humanistic frontiers in American education p289-301

International Energy Agency

Lantzke, U. The OECD and its International Energy Agency. *In* Vernon, R. ed. The oil crisis p217-27

International exchange. See Foreign exchange

International finance

Mazur, M. P. Interdependence, flexible exchange rates, and capital controls: the international monetary order in transition. *In* Baldwin, D. A. ed. America in an interdependent world p63-89

Triffin, R. Basic considerations on international monetary reform. *In* Inflation, trade and taxes p119-36

See also Balance of payments; Debts, External; Foreign exchange; International liquidity

International institutions. See International cooperation

International jurisdiction. See Jurisdiction (International law)

International law

Bozeman, A. B. International law. *In* Encyclopedia of American foreign policy p455-72

Butler, W. E. Methodological innovation in Soviet international legal doctrine. *In* The Year book of world affairs, 1978 p334-41

Falk, R. A. CIA covert operations and international law. *In* Borosage, R. L. and Marks. J. D. eds. The CIA file p142-58

Gross, L. International law aspects of the freedom of information and the right to communicate. *In* Horton, P. C. ed. The Third World and press freedom p55-73

Gross, L. On the justiciability of international disputes. *In* [Truth and tragedy]: a tribute to Hans Morgenthau p203-19

Gross, L. The right of self-determination in international law. *In* Kilson, M. ed. New states in the modern world p136-57

Lint, G. L. The law of nations and the American Revolution. *In* The American Revolution and "a candid world" p111-33

Midgley, E. B. F. Natural law and the renewal of the philosophy of international relations. *In* The Year book of world affairs, 1975 p121-36

Schwarzenberger, G. Civitas maxima? *In* The Year book of world affairs, 1975 p337-63

Seidl-Hohenveldern, I. Multinational enterprises and the international law of the future. *In* The Year book of world affairs, 1975 p301-12

Vincent, R. J. The idea of concert and international order. *In* The Year book of world affairs, 1975 p34-55

Wolfskill, G. The Webb "Great Frontier" hypothesis and international law. *In* Essays on Walter Prescott Webb p73-93

Yakemtchouk, R. The OAU and international law. *In* El-Ayouty, Y. ed. The Organization of African Unity after ten years p79-102

See also Arbitration, International; Asylum, Right of; Atomic weapons (International law); Boundaries; Children (International law); Civil rights (International law); Colonies (International law); Criminal procedure (International law); Diplomatic

International law—*Continued*
protection; Eminent domain (International law); Freedom of the seas; Great powers; International courts; International offenses; International organization; Intervention (International law); Jurisdiction (International law); Maritime law; Natural law; Political crimes and offenses; Refugees, Political—Legal status, laws, etc.; War (International law)

History

Connelly, A. M. The history of international law: a comparative approach. *In* The Year book of world affairs, 1978 p303-19

History—Russia

Lapenna, I. The Soviet concept of "Socialist" international law. *In* The Year book of world affairs, 1975 p242-64

Interpretation and construction

Sliwowski, G. Legal aspects of terrorism. *In* International terrorism and world security p69-77

International Law Commission. See United Nations. International Law Commission

International liquidity
Cohen, B. J. International reserves and liquidity. *In* Kenen, P. B. ed. International trade and finance p411-51

International mediation. See Mediation, International

International Monetary Fund
Gardner, R. N. Bretton Woods. *In* Keynes, M. ed. Essays on John Maynard Keynes p202-15
Triffin, R. Basic considerations on international monetary reform. *In* Inflation, trade and taxes p119-36

International news. See Foreign news

International offenses
Bassiouni, M. C. Methodological options for international legal control of terrorism. *In* International terrorism and political crimes p485-92
Bassiouni, M. C. Unlawful seizures of persons by states as alternatives to extradition. *In* International terrorism and political crimes p343-68
DeSchutter, B. Problems of jurisdiction in the international control and repression of terrorism. *In* International terrorism and political crimes p377-90
Evans, A. E. Aircraft hijacking: what is being done. *In* International terrorism and political crimes p219-47
Finger, S. M. International terrorism and the United Nations. *In* International terrorism p323-48
Hoffacker, L. The U.S. Government response to terrorism: a global approach. *In* International terrorism and political crimes p537-45
Kos-Rabcewicz-Zubkowski, L. The creation of an international criminal court. *In* International terrorism and political crimes p519-36
Lee, A. International suppression of hijacking. *In* International terrorism and political crimes p248-56
Mallison, W. T. and Mallison, S. V. The concept of public purpose terror in international law: doctrines and sanctions to reduce the destruction of human and material values. *In* International terrorism and political crimes p67-85

Murphy, J. F. United Nations proposals on the control and repression of terrorism. *In* International terrorism and political crimes p493-506
O'Higgins, P. Unlawful seizure of persons by states. *In* International terrorism and political crimes p336-42
Palmer, B. Codification of terrorism as an international crime. *In* International terrorism and political crimes p507-18
Sewell, A. F. Political crime: a psychologist's perspective. *In* International terrorism and political crimes p11-26
Vogler, T. Perspectives on extradition and terrorism. *In* International terrorism and political crimes p391-97
Zlataric, B. History of international terrorism and its legal control. *In* International terrorism and political crimes p474-84
See also Assaulting a foreign official; Terrorism

International organization
Claude, I. L. International organization. *In* Encyclopedia of American foreign policy p473-81
Doxey, M. P. International organization in foreign policy perspective. *In* The Year book of world affairs, 1975 p173-95
Falk, R. A. Toward a new world order: modest methods and drastic visions. *In* On the creation of a just world order p211-58
Kothari, R. World politics and world order: the issue of autonomy. *In* On the creation of a just world order p39-69
Lagos Matus, G. The revolution of being. *In* On the creation of a just world order p71-109
Mazrui, A. A. World culture and the search for human consensus. *In* On the creation of a just world order p1-37
Sakamoto, Y. Toward global identity. *In* On the creation of a just world order p189-210
Sibley, M. Q. Political theory, peace, and the problem of world order. *In* Dallmayr, F. R. ed. From contract to community p127-65
See also Church and international organization; Concert of Europe; International agencies; International cooperation; International law; Regionalism (International organization); Security, International; World politics

International organization and the church. See Church and international organization

International police
Mitchell, C. R. Peace keeping: the police function. *In* The Year book of world affairs, 1976 p150-73
See also United Nations—Armed Forces; International politics. See World politics

International Press Institute
Koszyk, K. The development of the International Press Institute. *In* Fischer, H. D. and Merrill, J. C. eds. International and intercultural communication p372-76
Meyer, E. The bilateral and multilateral meetings of the International Press Institute. *In* Unofficial diplomats p56-65

International propaganda. See Propaganda, International

International relations
Aron, R. What is a theory of international relations? *In* Aron, R. Politics and history p166-85

International relations—*Continued*

Aumo-Osolo, A. Rationality and foreign policy process. *In* The Year book of world affairs, 1977 p257-88

Berman, M. R. and Johnson, J. E. The growing role of unofficial diplomacy. *In* Unofficial diplomats p 1-33

Bock, F. The impact of international economic factors on the conduct of foreign policy. *In* The Interaction of economics and foreign policy p130-50

Brzezinski, Z. K. The global triangle: the changing power balance in Asia and its consequences for the foreign policy of the Atlantic nations. *In* The New Atlantic challenge p315-28

Buchan, A. An expedition to the poles. *In* The Year book of world affairs, 1975 p4-21

Buchan, A. The United States in tomorrow's international system. *In* Tomorrow's American p 1-20

Butterfield, Sir H. Global good and evil: the moderate cupidity of Everyman. *In* [Truth and tragedy]: a tribute to Hans Morgenthau p199-202

Chayes, A. Nuclear arms control after the Cold War. *In* Long, F. A. and Rathjens, G. W. eds. Arms, defense policy, and arms control p15-33

Chomsky, N. Foreign policy and the intelligentsia. *In* Images and ideas in American culture p15-59

Coffey, J. W. The Christian realism of Reinhold Niebuhr. *In* Political realism in American thought p79-124

Coffey, J. W. Realism and foreign policy. *In* Coffey, J. W. Political realism in American thought p48-78

Dowty, A. A comparative approach to the study of international conflict. *In* The Dynamics of the arms race p193-201

Doxey, M. P. International organization in foreign policy perspective. *In* The Year book of world affairs, 1975 p173-95

Freymond, J. Crisis management and prediction. *In* [Truth and tragedy]: a tribute to Hans Morgenthau p272-83

Friedman, E. The international political economy and Chinese politics. *In* China's changing role in the world economy p 1-14

Garment, L. Majoritarianism at the United Nations and human rights. *In* Sidorsky, D. ed. Essays on human right p30-36

Harrod, J. International relations, perceptions and neo-realism. *In* The Year book of world affairs, 1977 p289-305

Harrod, J. Transnational power. *In* The Year book of world affairs, 1976 p97-115

Henkin, L. Human rights: reappraisal and readjustment. *In* Sidorsky, D. ed. Essays on human rights p68-87

Hoffmann, S. Regulating the new international system. *In* Kilson, M. ed. New states in the modern world p171-99

Holbraad, C. Middle-power roles in Great-Power triangles. *In* The Year book of world affairs, 1976 p116-32

Jankowitsch, P. Neutrality and nonalignment: foreign policies of independence in the twentieth century. *In* [Truth and tragedy]: a tribute to Hans Morgenthau p237-58

Joynt, C. B. Behavioural sciences in international relations. *In* The Year book of world affairs, 1979 p224-42

Laqueur, W. Z. The issue of human rights. *In* Sidorsky, D. ed. Essays on human rights p5-20

Liska, G. Morgenthau vs. Machiavelli: political realism and power politics. *In* [Truth and tragedy]: a tribute to Hans Morgenthau p104-11

Liskofsky, S. The United Nations and human rights: "alternative approaches." *In* Sidorsky, D. ed. Essays on human rights p46-67

Midgley, E. B. F. Natural law and the renewal of the philosophy of international relations p121-36

Modelski, G. A. World order-keeping: some alternative structures. *In* New dimensions of world politics p54-72

Nye, J. S. Transnational and transgovernmental relations. *In* New dimensions of world politics p36-53

Preiswerk, A. R. The place of intercultural relations in the study of international relations. *In* The Year book of world affairs, 1978 p251-67

Rosecrance, R. N. International interdependence. *In* New dimensions of world politics p20-35

Russett, B. M. Elite perceptions and theories of world politics. *In* New dimensions of world politics p86-108

Schmidt, H. H. W. New tasks for the Atlantic Alliance. *In* The Year book of world affairs, 1975 p22-33

Schröder, B. Science, technology and foreign policy. *In* Science, technology and society p473-506

Schwarzenberger, G. Civitas maxima? *In* The Year book of world affairs, 1975 p337-63

Scott, A. M. The logic of international interaction. *In* Orr, D. W. and Soroos, M. S. eds. The global predicament p284-307

Shinn, R. L. Realism and ethics in political philosophy. *In* [Truth and tragedy]: a tribute to Hans Morgenthau p95-103

Singer, J. D. The behavioral approach to diplomatic history. *In* Encyclopedia of American foreign policy p66-77

Skolnikoff, E. B. Science, technology and the international system. *In* Science, technology and society p507-33

Trethewey, R. J. International economics and politics: a theoretical framework. *In* The Interaction of economics and foreign policy p 1-24

Vincent, R. J. The idea of concert and international order. *In* The Year book of world affairs, 1975 p34-55

Williams, P. and Smith, M. H. The conduct of foreign policy in democratic and authoritarian states. *In* The Year book of world affairs, 1976 p205-22

Yalem, R. J. The concept of world order. *In* The Year book of world affairs, 1975 p320-36

Yalem, R. J. The decline of international relations theory. *In* The Year book of world affairs, 1976 p292-306

Yalem, R. J. The level-of-analysis problem reconsidered. *In* The Year book of world affairs, 1977 p306-26

International relations—*Continued*

Yalem, R. J. Transnational politics versus international politics. *In* The Year book of world affairs, 1978 p237-50

See also Alliance; Arbitration, International; Balance of power; Cultural relations; Detente; Diplomatic negotiations in international disputes; Diplomatic protection; Diplomats; Disarmament; Geopolitics; Great powers; International cooperation; International courts; International economic relations; International law; International police; Mediation, International; Monroe doctrine; National security; Nationalism; Neutrality, Armed; Pacific settlement of international disputes; Pan-Pacific relations; Peace; Peaceful change (International relations); Security, International; World politics

Anecdotes, facetiae, satire, etc.

Galbraith, J. K. The North Dakota plan. *In* Galbraith, J. K. Annals of an abiding liberal p182-87

Psychological aspects

Deutsch, K. W. and Senghaas, D. The fragile sanity of states: a theoretical analysis. *In* Kilson, M. ed. New states in the modern world p200-44

Study and teaching—United States

Hotz, A. J. Morgenthau's influence on the study of international relations. *In* [Truth and tragedy]: a tribute to Hans Morgenthau p316-21

International relief. See Disaster relief

International security. See Security, International

International Society for Krishna Consciousness

Daner, F. J. Conversion to Krishna Consciousness: the transformation from hippie to religious ascetic. *In* Wallis, R. ed. Sectarianism p53-69

Johnson, G. The Hare Krishna in San Francisco. *In* The New religious consciousness p31-51

Judah, J. S. The Hare Krishna movement. *In* Zaretsky, I. I. and Leone, M. P. eds. Religious movements in contemporary America p463-78

Leahy, J. J. On the civil liberties of sect members: Part 3. *In* Horowitz, I. L. ed. Science, sin, and scholarship p208-16

International style (Architecture) See Functionalism (Architecture)

International Telephone and Telegraph corporation

Vidal, G. Conglomerates. *In* Vidal, G. Matters of fact and of fiction p253-58

International trade. See Commerce

International travel regulations. See Emigration and immigration law

International tribunals. See International courts

International trusteeships

Bennett, E. M. Mandates and trusteeships. *In* Encyclopedia of American foreign policy p521-25

International words. See Language and languages—Foreign words and phrases

Internationalism

Kuehl, W. F. Internationalism. *In* Encyclopedia of American foreign policy p443-54

See also Nationalism

The Internationalists. See Communist Party of Canada (Marxist-Leninist)

Interns (Civil service)

United States

Murphy, T. P. Internships in urban government. *In* Murphy, T. P. ed. Universities in the urban crisis p71-92

Interns (Medicine)

Political activity

Resnick, J. L. The emerging physician: from political activist to professional vanguard. *In* Gerstl, J. E. and Jacobs, G. eds. Professions for the people p175-213

Interpersonal relations

Morris, W. Closing the gap. *In* Morris, W. Earthly delights, unearthly adornments p7-12

Simpson, E. Discrimination as an example of moral irrationality. *In* Fact, value, and perception p107-22

See also Communication—Psychological aspects; Competition (Psychology); Group relations training

Interplanetary voyages. See Outer space—Exploration; Space flight in literature

Interpretation. See Hermeneutics

Interpreting and translating. See Translating and interpreting

Interscholastic athletics. See School sports

Intervention (International law)

Cleveland, H. Words and meanings. *In* The Abdication of philosophy: philosophy and the public good p237-42

Ehrlich, T. The legal process in foreign affairs: military intervention—a testing case. *In* Stanford legal essays p113-28

Graber, D. A. Intervention and nonintervention. *In* Encyclopedia of American foreign policy p482-95

Lillich, R. B. A United States policy of humanitarian intervention and intercession. *In* Kommers, D. P. and Loescher, G. D. eds. Human rights and American foreign policy p278-98

Novogrod, J. C. Internal strife, self-determination, and world order. *In* International terrorism and political crimes p98-119

Intervention (Psychology) See Operant behavior

Interviewing

Anderson, J. P. Practical reasoning in action. *In* Douglas, J. D. and Johnson, J. M. [eds.] Existential sociology p174-98

Interviewing in ethnology

Ardener, E. Belief and the problem of women. *In* Ardener, S. G. ed. Perceiving women p 1-17

Ardener, E. The 'problem' revisited. *In* Ardener, S. G. ed. Perceiving women p19-27

Intolerance. See Religious liberty

Intrenchments

Hagerman, E. H. From Jomini to Dennis Hart Mahan: the evolution of trench warfare and the American Civil War. *In* Hubbell, J. T. ed. Battles lost and won p31-54

Introduction of plants. See Plant introduction

Introspection

Weber, S. M. Aesthetic experience and self-reflection as emancipatory processes: two complementary aspects of critical theory. *In* O'Neill, J. ed. On critical theory p78-103

Introspection (Theory of knowledge) See Self-knowledge, Theory of

Intruder in the dust (Motion picture)

Degenfelder, E. P. Rites of passage: novel to film. *In* Peary, G. and Shatzkin, R. eds. The modern American novel and the movies p178-86

Intuition

Hudson, W. D. Ethical intuitionism. *In* New studies in ethics v 1 p229-303

McDowell, J. H. Truth conditions, bivalence, and verificationism. *In* Evans, G. L. and McDowell, J. H. eds. Truth and meaning p42-66

Patočka, J. The Husserlian doctrine of eidetic intuition and its recent critics. *In* Elliston, F. A. and McCormick, P. eds. Husserl p150-59

Intuition (Psychology). See Perception

Inuit. See Eskimos

Invalids. See Handicapped

Invasion of privacy. See Privacy, Right of

Invasion of the body snatchers (Motion picture)

Samuels, S. The age of conspiracy and conformity: Invasion of the body snatchers. *In* O'Connor, J. E. and Jackson, M. A. eds. American history/American film p203-17

Invasions of Rome, Barbarian. See Barbarian invasions of Rome

Inventions

Cardwell, D. S. L. Problems of the data base. *In* Bugliarello, G. and Doner, D. B. eds. The history and philosophy of technology p3-18

See also Research Industrial; Technological innovations; Technology transfer

Investment banking. See Development banks

Investments, American

Canada

Montgomery, S. S. United States direct investment in Europe and Canada, 1955-1970: a regression study. *In* Inflation, trade and taxes p137-62

Europe

Montgomery, S. S. United States direct investment in Europe and Canada, 1955-1970: a regression study. *In* Inflation, trade and taxes p137-62

Investments, Foreign

Hufbauer, G. C. The multinational corporation and direct investment. *In* Kenen, P. B. ed. International trade and finance p253-319

Vernon, R. Foreign operations. *In* McKie, J. W. ed. Social responsibility and the business predicament p275-310

Japan

Furuhashi, Y. Evolving Japanese policy toward inward foreign direct investment in the postwar period. *In* Postwar trends in Japan p61-118

Underdeveloped areas

See Underdeveloped areas—Investments, Foreign

Investors Overseas Services

Galbraith, J. K. Bernard Cornfeld: benefactor. *In* Galbraith, J. K. Annals of an abiding liberal p311-16

Invocation of Christian martyrs. See Christian martyrs—Cult

Io (Periodical)

Grossinger, R. A history of Io, 1964-1976. *In* Anderson, E. and Kinzie, M. eds. The little magazine in America: a modern documentary history p482-513

Ionesco, Eugène

About

Glicksberg, C. I. Ionesco and the comedy of the Absurd. *In* Glicksberg, C. I. The literature of nihilism p222-33

Glicksberg, C. I. The politics of the Absurd. *In* Glicksberg, C. I. The literature of commitment p186-93

Pellissier, S. L. Ionesco and Molière. *In* Johnson, R. B.; Neumann, E. S. and Trail, G. T. eds. Molière and the commonwealth of letters: patrimony and posterity p145-59

Schwarz, A. Condemned to exist. *In* Schwarz, A. From Büchner to Beckett p334-56

White, K. S. Hypnotic language and its apotheoses: Molière and Ionesco. *In* Johnson, R. B.; Neumann, E. S. and Trail, G. T. eds. Molière and the commonwealth of letters: patrimony and posterity p160-68

About individual works

Fragments of a journal

Simon, J. I. Grope, grapple, fulminate, lament—don't just sit there! *In* Simon, J. I. Singularities p185-87

Ionescu, Ghita

Raymond Aron: a modern classicist. *In* De Crespigny, A. and Minogue, K. R. eds. Contemporary political philosophers p191-208

Ionized air. See Air, Ionized

Ions, Edmund S.

James Bryce. *In* Abroad in America: Visitors to the new Nations, 1776-1914 p207-17

Ions. See Electrons

Ioor, William

About

Watson, C. S. Wiliam Ioor. *In* Watson, C. S. Antebellum Charleston dramatists p52-79

About individual works

The battle of Eutaw Springs and evacuation of Charleston; or, The glorious 14th of December, 1782

Watson, C. S. William Ioor. *In* Watson, C. S. Antebellum Charleston dramatists p52-79

Independence, or Which do you like best, the peer, or the farmer?

Watson, C. S. William Ioor. *In* Watson, C. S. Antebellum Charleston dramatists p52-79

Iowa language. See Siouan languages

Ipitinere Indians. See Amahuaca Indians

Iran

Millward, W. G. Iran. *In* Savory, R. M. ed. Introduction to Islamic civilisation p169-77

Iran—*Continued*

Civilization

Nejad, K. M. The story-teller and mass media in Iran. *In* Fischer, H. D. and Melnik, S. R. eds. Entertainment: a cross-cultural examination p43-62

Savory, R. M. Land of the lion and the sun. *In* Lewis, B. ed. Islam and the Arab world p245-72

History

Bayat-Philipp, M. Women and revolution in Iran, 1905-1911. *In* Beck, L. and Keddie, N. R. eds. Women in the Muslim world p295-308

Savory, R. M. Land of the lion and the sun. *In* Lewis, B. ed. Islam and the Arab world p245-72

History—To 640 A.D.— Historiography

Balcer, J. M. The date of Herodotus IV.1: Darius' Scythian expedition. *In* Harvard Studies in classical philology v76 p99-132

Politics and government

Zonis, M. The political elite of Iran: a second stratum? *In* Political elites and political development in the Middle East p193-216

Iranian epic poetry. See Epic poetry, Iranian

Iraq

Antiquities

Johnson, G. A. Locational analysis and the investigation of Uruk local exchange systems. *In* Ancient civilization and trade p285-339

Lamberg-Karlovsky, C. C. Third millennium modes of exchange and modes of production. *In* Ancient civilization and trade p341-68

Wright, H. T. Toward an explanation of the origin of the state. *In* Explanation of prehistoric change p215-30

Foreign relations—Great Britain

Kedourie, É. The sack of Basra and the farhud in Baghdad. *In* Kedourie, É. Arabic political memoirs and other studies p283-314

History

Kedourie, É. The sack of Basra and the farhud in Baghdad. *In* Kedourie, É. Arabic political memoirs and other studies p283-314

Kedourie, É. Wavell and Iraq. April-May 1941. *In* Kedourie, É. Arabic political memoirs and other studies p273-82

Politics and government

Jwaideh, A. Tribalism and modern society: Iraq, a case study. *In* Savory, R. M. ed. Introduction to Islamic civilisation p160-67

Religion

Jacobsen, T. Religious drama in ancient Mesopotamia. *In* Unity and diversity p65-97

Roberts, J. J. M. Divine freedom and cultic manipulation in Israel and Mesopotamia. *In* Unity and diversity p181-90

Social conditions

Jwaideh, A. Tribalism and modern society: Iraq, a case study. *In* Savory, R. M. ed. Introduction to Islamic civilisation p160-67

Iredell, James

About

Higginbotham, D. James Iredell and the origins of American Federalism. *In* Suggs, G. G. ed. Perspectives on the American Revolution p99-115

Ireland, David

About individual works

The unknown industrial prisoner

Cantrell, L. The new novel: David Ireland's The unknown industrial prisoner, Michael Wilding's The short story embassy, and Frank Moorhouse's The electrical experience. *In* Hamilton, K. G. ed. Studies in the recent Australian novel p225-57

Ireland

Bibliography

Messenger, J. C. Bibliography. *In* Casey, D. J. and Rhodes, R. E. eds. Views of the Irish peasantry, 1800-1916 p203-17

Church history

Hughes, K. The early Irish Church: from the coming of Christianity to the end of the Viking era. *In* De Breffny, B. ed. The Irish world p47-70

Civilization

MacLochlainn, A. Gael and peasant—a case of mistaken identity? *In* Casey, D. J. and Rhodes, R. E. eds. Views of the Irish peasantry, 1800-1916 p17-36

Sheed, W. A great place for bad writers. *In* Sheed, W. The good word & other words p96-99

Economic conditions

Lebow, R. N. British images of poverty in pre-famine Ireland. *In* Casey, D. J. and Rhodes, R. E. eds. Views of the Irish peasantry, 1800-1916 p57-83

Foreign opinion, British

Lebow, R. N. British images of poverty in pre-famine Ireland. *In* Casey, D. J. and Rhodes, R. E. eds. Views of the Irish peasantry, 1800-1916 p57-83

History

Edwards, O. D. The impact of the American Revolution on Ireland. *In* The Impact of the American Revolution abroad p127-58

Evans, E. E. Introduction: The Irish—fact and fiction. *In* De Breffny, B. ed. The Irish world p 7-18

History—To 1172

Evans, E. E. Prehistoric Ireland: from the earliest migrations to about AD 500. *In* De Breffny, B. ed. The Irish world p20-46

History—To 1603

Snyder, H. L. From the accession of the Tudors to the Treaty of Limerick. *In* Orel, H. ed. Irish history and culture p109-27

Snyder, H. L. From the beginnings to the end of the Middle Ages. *In* Orel, H. ed. Irish history and culture p25-41

Stalley, R. The long Middle Ages: from the twelfth century to the Reformation. *In* De Breffny, B. ed. The Irish world p71-98

History—16th century

De Breffny, B. The end of the old order: from the Reformation to the Jacobite defeat. *In* De Breffny, B. ed. The Irish world p99-126

Ireland—*Continued*

History—17th century

De Breffny, B. The end of the old order: from the Reformation to the Jacobite defeat. *In* De Breffny, B. ed. The Irish world p99-126

Ffolliott, R. The new culture: domestic life and the arts, 1680-1830. *In* De Breffny, B. ed. The Irish world p127-64

Snyder, H. L. From the Treaty of Limerick to the union with Great Britain. *In* Orel, H. ed. Irish history and culture p147-64

History—18th century

Ffolliott, R. The new culture: domestic life and the arts, 1680-1830. *In* De Breffny, B. ed. The Irish world p127-64

O'Connell, M. R. Daniel O'Connell and the Irish eighteenth century. *In* Studies in eighteenth-century culture v5 p475-95

Snyder, H. L. From the Treaty of Limerick to the union with Great Britain. *In* Orel, H. ed. Irish history and culture p147-64

History—Rebellion of 1798

Palmer, S. H. Rebellion, emancipation, starvation: the dilemma of peaceful protest in Ireland, 1798-1848. *In* Essays on modern European revolutionary history p 3-38

History—19th century

Ó Tuathaigh, G. The distressed society: the struggle for emancipation and independence, 1801-1918. *In* De Breffny, B. ed. The Irish world p171-98

Palmer, S. H. Rebellion, emancipation, starvation: the dilemma of peaceful protest in Ireland, 1798-1848. *In* Essays on modern European revolutionary history p 3-38

Sidman, C. F. From the Act of Union to the fall of Parnell. *In* Orel, H. ed. Irish history and culture p225-50

Sidman, C. F. From the fall of Parnell to modern Ireland. *In* Orel, H. ed. Irish history and culture p329-46

History—20th century

Barkley, J. M. The Presbyterian Church in Ireland and the Government of Ireland Act (1920) *In* Church, society and politics p393-403

Nowlan, K. B. Modern Ireland: the birth and growth of the new state. *In* De Breffny, B. ed. The Irish world p255-80

Ó Tuathaigh, G. The distressed society: the struggle for emancipation and independence, 1801-1918. *In* De Breffny, B. ed. The Irish world p171-98

Sidman, C. F. From the fall of Parnell to modern Ireland. *In* Orel, H. ed. Irish history and culture p329-46

History—Sinn Fein Rebellion, 1916
—Poetry

Henn, T. R. Yeats and the poetry of war. *In* Henn, T. R. Last essays p81-97

Intellectual life

Farrell, J. T. The Irish cultural renaissance in the last century. *In* Farrell, J. T. Literary essays, 1954-1974 p58-62

Ffolliott, R. The new culture: domestic life and the arts, 1680-1830. *In* De Breffny, B. ed. The Irish world p127-64

Population

Kammeyer, K. C. W. The dynamics of population. *In* Orel, H. ed. Irish history and culture p189-223

Social conditions

De Breffny, B. The end of the old order: from the Reformation to the Jacobite defeat. *In* De Breffny, B. ed. The Irish world p99-126

Ffolliott, R. The new culture: domestic life and the arts, 1680-1830. *In* De Breffny, B. ed. The Irish world p127-64

Kammeyer, K. C. W. The dynamics of population. *In* Orel, H. ed. Irish history and culture p189-223

Ó Tuathaigh, G. The distressed society: the struggle for emancipation and independence, 1801-1918. *In* De Breffny, B. ed. The Irish world p171-98

Unification

See Irish unification question

Ireland in art

Rose, M. G. Jack B. Yeats's picture of the peasant. *In* Casey, D. J. and Rhodes, R. E. eds. Views of the Irish peasantry, 1800-1916 p192-202

Ireland in literature

Booth, M. R. Irish landscape in the Victorian theatre. *In* Place, personality and the Irish writer p159-72

Henn, T. R. 'The place of shells.' *In* Henn, T. R. Last essays p13-25

Jeffares, A. N. Place, space and personality and the Irish writer. *In* Place, personality and the Irish writer p11-40

Kennedy, S. The Irishness of Beckett: Spirals of needs: Irish prototypes in Samuel Beckett's fiction. *In* Yeats, Joyce, and Beckett p153-66

Mercier, V. The Irishness of Beckett: Ireland/the world: Beckett's Irishness. *In* Yeats, Joyce, and Beckett p147-52

O'Driscoll, R. Return to the hearthstone: ideals of the Celtic Literary Revival. *In* Place, personality and the Irish writer p41-68

Orel, H. The Irishry of William Butler Yeats. *In* Orel, H. ed. Irish history and culture p291-307

Orel, H. The two attitudes of James Joyce. *In* Orel, H. ed. Irish history and culture p309-27

Porter, R. J. The Irishness of Joyce: the cracked lookingglass. *In* Yeats, Joyce, and Beckett p87-91

Iriarte y Oropesa, Tomàs de

About individual works
Fables on subjects connected with literature

Noel, T. Samaniego, Iriarte, and the fable in Spain. *In* Noel, T. Theories of the fable in the eighteenth century p140-44

Irish-American leadership

Cross, R. D. The Irish. *In* Ethnic leadership in America p176-97

Irish Americans

Cross, R. D. The Irish. *In* Ethnic leadership in America p176-97

Curran, T. J. From "Paddy" to the Presidency: the Irish in America. *In* The Immigrant experience in America p95-114

Irish ballads. See Ballads, Irish

Irish drama (English) See English drama—Irish authors

Irish fiction (English) See English fiction—Irish authors

Irish folk-lore. See Folk-lore, Irish

Irish in Europe

History

Griffin, W. D. The Irish on the Continent in the eighteenth century. *In* Studies in eighteenth-century culture v5 p453-73

Irish in Jersey City

Political activity

Shaw, D. V. Political leadership in the industrial city: Irish development and nativist response in Jersey City. *In* Immigrants in industrial America, 1850-1920 p85-95

Irish in literature

Sheed, W. There is no (Irish) Mafia. *In* Sheed, W. The good word & other words p100-04

Irish in New York (City)

Groneman, C. "She earns as a child—she pays as a man": women workers in a mid-nineteenth-century New York City community. *In* Immigrants in industrial America, 1850-1920 p33-46

History

Ward, D. Some locational implications of the ethnic division of labor in mid-nineteenth-century American cities. *In* Pattern and process p258-70

Irish in the United States

Greeley, A. M. and McCready, W. C. The transmission of cultural heritages: the case of the Irish and Italians. *In* Glazer, N. and Moynihan, D. P. eds. Ethnicity p209-35

Shannon, W. V. The Irish in America: starvation, struggle and success. *In* De Breffny, B. ed. The Irish world p235-54

Yetman, N. R. The Irish experience in America. *In* Orel, H. ed. Irish history and culture p347-76

See also Irish Americans

Irish literature

To 1100—History and criticism

Ó Coileáin, S. Irish saga literature. *In* Oinas, F. J. ed. Heroic epic and saga p172-92

Irish literature (English) See English literature—Irish authors

Irish mythology. See Mythology, Irish

Irish poetry (English) See English poetry—Irish authors

Irish poets. See Poets, Irish

Irish question

Harkness, D. England's Irish question. *In* Peele, G. and Cook, C. eds. The politics of reappraisal, 1918-1939 p39-63

Henn, T. R. The weasel's tooth. *In* Henn, T. R. Last essays p26-50

See also Home rule (Ireland)

Irish Republican Army

Bell, J. B. Revolutionary organisations: special cases and imperfect models. *In* International terrorism and world security p78-92

Bell, J. B. Strategy, tactics, and terror: an Irish perspective. *In* International terrorism p65-89

Nowlan, K. B. Modern Ireland: the birth and growth of the new state. *In* De Breffny, B. ed. The Irish world p255-80

Parry, A. Crimson in the Irish Green and Orange. *In* Parry, A. Terrorism: from Robespierre to Arafat p376-94

Irish Saints. See Saints, Irish

Irish unification question

Canavan, F. P. The prospects for a united Ireland. *In* Prospects for constitutional democracy p118-33

Irish wit and humor

Henn, T. R. The lighter side of the Irish Literary Revival. *In* Henn, T. R. Last essays p119-36

Iriye, Akira

Continuities in U.S.-Japanese relations, 1941-49. *In* The Origins of the Cold war in Asia p378-407

Intercultural relations. *In* Encyclopedia of American foreign policy p428-42

Japan as a competitor, 1895-1917. *In* Iriye, A. ed. Mutual images p73-99

The United States in Chinese foreign policy. *In* China and America p11-52

Irminon, abbot, fl. 812

About individual works

Polyptyque de l'abbe Irminon

Coleman, E. R. Infanticide in the early Middle Ages. *In* Stuard, S. M. ed. Women in medieval society p47-70

Iron curtain countries. See Communist countries

Iron curtain lands. See Communist countries

Iron industry and trade

Great Britain

Goring, J. J. Wealden ironmasters in the age of Elizabeth. *In* Wealth and power in Tudor England p204-27

Rome

Cleere, H. Ironmaking. *In* Strong, D. E. and Brown, D. eds. Roman crafts p127-41

Ironwork. See Blacksmithing

Irony

Booth, W. C. The pleasures and pitfalls of irony: or, Why don't you say what you mean? *In* Burks, D. M. ed. Rhetoric, philosophy, and literature: an exploration p 1-13

Ong, W. J. From mimesis to irony: writing and print as integuments of voice. *In* Ong, W. J. Interfaces of the word p272-302

Irony in literature

Boardman, M. M. Defoe's political rhetoric and the problem of irony. *In* Tulane studies in English v22 p87-102

Green, D. H. On damning with faint praise in medieval literature. *In* Viator: medieval and Renaissance studies v6 p117-69

Ketterer, D. Take-off to cosmic irony: science-fiction humor and the Absurd. *In* Cohen, S. B. ed. Comic relief p70-86

Kurz, P. K. Thomas Mann and irony. *In* Kurz, P. K. On modern German literature v2 p3-21

Palmer, L. H. The ironic word in Hardy's novels. *In* Tennessee Studies in literature v20 p109-23

Sperry, S. M. Toward a definition of romantic irony in English literature. *In* Bornstein, G. ed. Romantic and modern p3-28

Iroquoian Indians. See Huron Indians

Iroquoian languages

Chafe, W. L. Siouan, Iroquoian, and Caddoan. *In* Sebeok, T. A. ed. Native languages of the America v 1 p527-72

Iroquois Indians

Women

Brown, J. K. Iroquois women: an ethnohistoric note. *In* Reiter, R. R. ed. Toward an anthropology of women p235-51

Iroquois language. See Iroquoian languages

Irrationalism (Philosophy)

Berlin, Sir I. Hume and the sources of German anti-rationalism. *In* David Hume p93-116

Kinsman, R. S. Introduction. *In* The Darker vision of the Renaissance p 1-23

Popper, Sir K. R. The myth of the framework. *In* The Abdication of philosophy: philosophy and the public good p23-48

White, H. V. The irrational and the problem of historical knowledge in the Enlightenment. *In* White, H. V. Tropics of discourse p135-49

See also Absurd (Philosophy)

Irreligion. See Secularism

Irreversible coma. See Brain death

Irrigation

Steward, J. H. Wittfogel's irrigation hypothesis. *In* Steward, J. H. Evolution and ecology p87-99

Zur, B. Controlled irrigation. *In* Strategies for human settlements: habitat and environment p84-90

Australia—Victoria

Wills, M. W. The California-Victoria irrigation frontiers, 1880-1900. *In* The Frontier v2 p235-49

California

Wills, M. W. The California-Victoria irrigation frontiers, 1880-1900. *In* The Frontier v2 p235-49

Irritability

Temkin, O. The classical roots of Glisson's doctrine of irritation. *In* Temkin, O. The double face of Janus p290-316

Temkin, O. Vesalius on an immanent biological motor force. *In* Temkin, O. The double face of Janus p287-89

Irving, Washington

About

Leary, L. G. Washington Irving: an end and a new beginning. *In* Leary, L. G. Soundings p292-329

About individual works

Letters of Jonathan Oldstyle, Gent.

Granger, B. I. Washington Irving. *In* Granger, B. I. American essay serials from Franklin to Irving p203-27

Rip Van Winkle

Fetterley, J. Palpable designs: four American short stories: An American dream: "Rip Van Winkle." *In* Fetterley, J. The resisting reader p 1-11

Salmagundi

Granger, B. I. Washington Irving. *In* Granger, B. I. American essay serials from Franklin to Irving p203-27

Tales of a traveller

Doubleday, N. F. Washington Irving and the mysterious portrait. *In* Doubleday, N. F. Variety of attempt p36-48

The Western journals of Washington Irving (ed. and annotated by John Francis McDermott)

Welty, E. The Western journals of Washington Irving. *In* Welty, E. The eye of the story p177-81

Irwin, Galen Arnold

Party, accountability and the recruitment of municipal councilmen in the Netherlands. *In* Eulau, H. and Czudnowski, M. M. eds. Elite recruitment in democratic polities p163-204

Irwin, John T.

About individual works

Doubling and incest/repetition and revenge: A speculative reading of Faulkner

Cowley, M. Faulkner: the etiology of his art. *In* Cowley, M. —And I worked at the writer's trade p214-30

Irwin, Michael, and Gregor, Ian

Either side of Wessex. *In* Butler, L. S. ed. Thomas Hardy after fifty years p104-15

Isaacman, Allen F. See Bender, G. jt. auth.

Isaacs, Harold Robert

Basic group identity: the idols of the tribe. *In* Glazer, N. and Moynihan, D. P. eds. Ethnicity p29-52

Some concluding remarks: the turning mirrors. *In* Iriye, A. ed. Mutual images p258-65

Isaacs, Jorge

About individual works

Maria

Jackson, S. M. Fact from fiction: another look at slavery in three Spanish-American novels. *In* DeCosta, M. ed. Blacks in Hispanic literature p83-89

Isaacs, Neil D.

Up a tree: to see The fates of men. *In* Anglo-Saxon poetry: essays in appreciation p363-75

Ise monogatari

Rimer, J. T. Source books I: Tales of Ise, The tale of Genji. *In* Rimer, J. T. Modern Japanese fiction and its traditions p82-96

Iseminger, Gary

Appreciation, the artworld, and the aesthetic. *In* Aagaard-Mogensen, L. ed. Culture and art p118-30

Isenberg, Michael Thomas

The Great War viewed from the twenties: The big parade. *In* O'Connor, J. E. and Jackson, M. A. eds. American history/American film p17-37

Iser, Wolfgang

Fiction—the filter of history: a study of Sir Walter Scott's Waverley. *In* Amacher, R. E. and Lange, V. eds. New perspectives in German literary criticism p86-104

Narrative strategies as a means of communication. *In* Valdés, M. J. and Miller, O. J. eds. Interpretation of narrative p100-17

Patterns of communication in Joyce's Ulysses. *In* Amacher, R. E. and Lange, V. eds. New perspectives in German literary criticism p320-56

The reading process: a phenomenological approach. *In* Cohen, R. ed. New directions in literary history p125-45

Isfahan, Iran

City planning

Siroux, M. F. Iran: the vitality of Isfahan. *In* United Nations Educational, Scientific and Cultural Organization. The conservation of cities p146-58

Social life and customs

Gulick, J. and Gulick, M. E. The domestic social environment of women and girls in Isfahan, Iran. *In* Beck, L. and Keddie, N. R. eds. Women in the Muslim world p501-21

Ishāq, Adīb

About

Kedourie, É. The death of Adib Ishaq. *In* Kedourie, É. Arabic political memoirs and other studies p81-100

Isherwood, Christopher

See also Auden, W. H. jt. auth.

About

Fone, B. R. S. Sons and lovers: three English portraits. *In* Crew, L. ed. The gay academic p200-15

Jones, C. R. Christopher Isherwood and the religious quest. *In* Crew, L. ed. The gay academic p350-60

Lodge, D. In the thirties. *In* Lodge, D. The modes of modern writing p188-212

About individual works

A single man

Kennedy, A. Christopher Isherwood's psychological makeup. *In* Kennedy, A. The protean self p213-29

Isherwood, Robert M.

The third war of the musical Enlightenment. *In* Studies in eighteenth-century culture v4 p223-45

Ishida, Tsuyoshi

Contemporary sociology in Japan. *In* Mohan, R. P. and Martindale, D. A. eds. Handbook of contemporary developments in world sociology p439-52

Ishii, Momoko

Modern Japanese children's books. *In* Egoff, S. A. ed. One ocean touching p79-92

Ishii, Shōnosuke

Herrick and Japanese classical poetry: a comparison. *In* Rollin, R. B. and Patrick, J. M. eds. "Trust to good verses": Herrick tercentenary essays p187-96

Ishikawa, Tadao

The normalization of Sino-Japanese relations. *In* Clapp, P. and Halperin, M. H. eds. United States-Japanese relations, the 1970's p147-63

Isidore, Bp. of Seville. See Isidorus, Saint, Bp. of Seville

Isidore, Pseudo-. See Isidorus, Pseudo-

Isidore of Seville. See Isidorus, Saint, Bp. of Seville

Isidorus, Saint, Bp. of Seville

About individual works

Synonyma de homine et ratione

Altschule, M. D. St Isidore of Seville and his depressing ideas about depression. *In* Altschule, M. D. Origins of concepts in human behavior p35-50

Isidorus, Pseudo-

About individual works

Decretales pseudo-Isidorianae

Kuttner, S. G. Gratian and Plato. *In* Church and government in the Middle Ages p93-118

Isike, Unyanyembe chief

About

Bennett, N. R. Isike, ntemi of Unyanyembe. *In* African dimensions p53-67

Iskandar, Albert Z.

The medical bibliography of al-Rāzī. *In* Essays on Islamic philosophy and science p41-46

Islam

Adams, C. J. Islamic faith. *In* Savory, R. M. ed. Introduction to Islamic civilisation. p33-45

Lapidus, I. M. Adulthood in Islam: religious maturity in the Islamic tradition. *In* Erikson. E. H. ed. Adulthood p97-112

Lewis, B. The faith and the faithful. *In* Lewis, B. ed. Islam and the Arab world p25-56

Lichtenstadter, I. Religion as a cultural and political factor in the Middle East— past and present. *In* The New world balance and peace in the Middle East: reality or mirage? p137-42

Thomson, R. M. William of Malmesbury and some other Western writers on Islam. *In* Medievalia et humanistica no. 6 p179-87

See also Sex and Islam

Bibliography

Adams, C. J. Islām. *In* Adams, C. J. ed. A reader's guide to the great religions p407-66

Historiography

Lewis, B. Gibbon on Muhammad. *In* Edward Gibbon and The decline and fall of the Roman Empire p61-73

Psychology

Sandler, R. The changing concept of the individual. *In* Savory, R. M. ed. Introduction to Islamic civilisation p137-45

Relations—Christianity

Rahman, F. A Muslim response: Christian particularity and the faith of Islam. *In* Christian faith in a religiously plural world p69-79

Savory, R. M. ed. Christendom vs. Islam: interaction and co-existence. *In* Savory, R. M. ed. Introduction to Islamic civilisation p127-35

Africa

Booth, N. S. Islam in Africa. *In* African religions: a symposium p297-343

Martin, B. G. The spread of Islam. *In* Martin, P. M. and O'Meara, P. eds. Africa p98-113

Africa, West

Bravmann, R. A. Masking tradition and figurative art among the Islamized Mande. *In* African images p144-69

Palestine

Sharon, M. Palestine in the Islamic and Ottoman period. *In* The Palestinians p9-20

Islam and economics

Udovitch, A. L. Bankers without banks: commerce, banking, and society in the Islamic world of the Middle Ages. *In* The Dawn of modern banking p255-73

Islam and medicine. See Medicine and Islam

Islam and poetry

Bonebakker, S. A. Religious prejudice against poetry in early Islam. *In* Medievalia et humanistica no. 7 p77-99

Islam and science

Grunebaum, G. E. von. Relations of philosophy and science: a general view. *In* Essays on Islamic philosophy and science p 1-4

Wickens, G. M. The Middle East as a world centre of science and medicine. *In* Savory, R. M. ed. Introduction to Islamic civilisation p111-19

Islam and socialism. See Socialism and Islam

Islam and state. See Jihad

Islamic architecture. See Architecture, Islamic

Islamic art. See Art, Islamic

Islamic arts. See Arts, Islamic

Islamic cities and towns. See Cities and towns, Islamic

Islamic civilization. See Civilization, Islamic

Islamic countries

Lewis, B. Epilogue. *In* Lewis, B. ed. Islam and the Arab world p345-47

See also Arab countries

Civilization

Kedourie, E. Islam today. *In* Lewis, B. ed. Islam and the Arab world p321-44

Lewis, B. The faith and the faithful. *In* Lewis, B. ed. Islam and the Arab world p25-56

History

Bosworth, C. E. The historical background of Islamic civilisation. *In* Savory, R. M. ed. Introduction to Islamic civilisation p15-31

Rustow, D. A. Political ends and military means in the late Ottoman and post-Ottoman Middle East. *In* War, technology and society in the Middle East p386-99

History, Military

Bosworth, C. E. Armies of the Prophet. *In* Lewis, B. ed. Islam and the Arab world p201-24

Bosworth, C. E. Recruitment, muster, and review in medieval Islamic armies. *In* War, technology and society in the Middle East p59-77

Relations (general) with Europe

Savory, R. M. Christendom vs. Islam: interaction and co-existence. *In* Savory, R. M. ed. Introduction to Islamic civilisation p127-35

Social conditions

White, E. H. Legal reform as an indicator of women's status in Muslim nations. *In* Beck, L. and Keddie, N. R. eds. Women in the Muslim world p52-68

Islamic Empire

Haddad, R. M. The Ottoman Empire in the contemporary Middle East. *In* Aftermath of empire p39-61

History

Bosworth, C. E. The historical background of Islamic civilisation. *In* Savory, R. M. ed. Introduction to Islamic civilisation p15-31

History—750-1258

See Crusades

History, Military

Ayalon, D. Preliminary remarks on the mamlūk military institution in Islam. *In* War, technology and society in the Middle East p44-58

Islamic ethics

Hourani, G. F. Ethics in medieval Islam: a conspectus. *In* Essays on Islamic philosophy and science p128-35

Islamic holy war. See Jihad

Islamic law

Savory, R. M. Law and traditional society. *In* Savory, R. M. ed. Introduction to Islamic civilisation p54-60

See also Woman—Legal status, laws, etc. (Islamic law)

Egypt

Mohsen, S. K. The Egyptian woman: between modernity and tradition. *In* Matthiasson, C. J. ed. Many sisters p37-58

Islamic legends. See Legends, Islamic

Islamic literature

History and criticism

Pellat, C. Jewellers with words. *In* Lewis, B. ed. Islam and the Arab world p141-60

Islamic philosophy. See Philosophy, Islamic

Islamic psychology. See Islam—Psychology

Islamic sects. See Sunnites

Islamic theology

Early works to 1800

Marmura, M. E. God and his creation: two medieval Islamic views. *In* Savory, R. M. ed. Introduction to Islamic civilisation p46-53

Islamic women. See Women, Muslim

Islamism. See Islam

The **island** (criticism) Fugard, A.; Kani, J. and Ntshona, W. *In* Kauffmann, S. Persons of the drama p208-11

The **island** of the mighty (criticism) Arden, J. and D'Arcy, M. *In* Brustein, R. S. The culture watch p74-79

Islands of the Pacific

Koestler, A. Farewell to Gauguin. *In* Koestler, A. The heel of Achilles p182-91

Isolating mechanisms

Sulloway, F. J. Geographic isolation in Darwin's thinking: the vicissitudes of a crucial idea. *In* Studies in history of biology v3 p23-65

Isolation, Biotic. See Isolating mechanisms

Isolation, Social. See Social isolation

Isolationism. Jonas, M. *In* Encyclopedia of Amercan foreign policy p496-506

Isotopes

Kohler, R. E. Rudolf Schoenheimer, isotopic tracers, and biochemistry in the 1930's. *In* Historical studies in the physical sciences v8 p257-98

Istanbul. Blachernae Palace

Runciman, S. Blachernae Palace and its decoration. *In* Studies in memory of David Talbot Rice p277-83

It should happen to you (Motion picture)

Truffaut, F. George Cukor: It should happen to you. *In* Truffaut, F. The films in my life p104-06

Italian-American newspapers

History

Nelli, H. S. Chicago's Italian-language press and World War I. *In* Studies in Italian American social history p66-80

Italian Americans

Coppa, F. J. Those who followed Columbus: the Italian migration to the United States of America. *In* The Immigrant experience in America p115-46

Kinship

Ianni, F. A. J. Organized crime and the Italo-American family. *In* Studies in Italian American social history p28-39

Valletta, C. L. Family life: the question of independence. *In* Studies in Italian American social history p153-63

Social life and customs

D'Antonio, W. V. Ethnicity and assimilation: a reconsideration. *In* Studies in American social history p10-27

Mangione, J. G. On being a Sicilian American. *In* Studies in Italian American social history p40-49

Swiderski, R. From folk to popular: plastic evil eye charms. *In* The Evil eye p28-41

See also Italian Americans—Kinship

Italian architecture. See Architecture, Italian

Italian art. See Art, Italian

Italian Communist Party. See Communist Party of Italy

Italian drama

History and criticism

Corrigan, B. Sir Thomas More: personage and symbol on the Italian stage. *In* Studies in the continental background of Renaissance English literature: essays presented to John L. Lievsay p91-108

Early to 1700—History and criticism

Hunter, G. K. Italian tragicomedy on the English stage. *In* Renaissance drama [1973] p123-48

Nicoll, A. Comedy, tragedy, and melodrama in Italy. *In* Nicoll, A. World drama p135-46

20th century—History and criticism

Nicoll, A. The extension of the realistic. *In* Nicoll, A. World drama p577-607

Nicoll, A. Post-war drama in Italy. *In* Nicoll, A. World drama p881-90

Italian drama (Comedy)

See also Commedia dell'arte

History and criticism

Clubb, L. G. Italian Renaissance comedy. *In* Ruggiers, P. G. ed. Versions of medieval comedy p191-210

Clubb, L. G. Woman as wonder: a generic figure in Italian and Shakespearean comedy. *In* Studies in the continental background of Renaissance English literature: essays presented to John L. Lievsay p109-32

Firth, F. M. Comedy in Italy. *In* Howarth, W. D. ed. Comic drama p63-80

Wadsworth, P. A. From the commedia erudita to Molière. *In* Johnson, R. B.; Neumann, E. S. and Trail, G. T. eds. Molière and the commonwealth of letters: patrimony and posterity p443-53

Italian fiction

Women authors

Pacifici, S. Women writers: Neera and Aleramo. *In* Pacifici, S. The modern Italian novel: from Capuana to Tozzi p49-67

20th century—History and criticism

Pacifici, S. Background of the modern Italian novel. *In* Pacifici, S. The modern Italian novel: from Pea to Moravia p 1-17

Italian language

Syntax

Rizzi, L. A restructuring rule in Italian syntax. *In* Keyser, S. J. ed. Recent transformational studies in European languages p113-58

Italian literature

History and criticism

Cairns, C. The political conscience. *In* Cairns, C. Italian literature p45-90

Cairns, C. Social change. *In* Cairns, C. Italian literature p91-128

Pacifici, S. Background of the modern Italian novel. *In* Pacifici, S. The modern Italian novel: from Capuana to Tozzi p 1-15

Perella, N. J. Conclusion. *In* Perella, N. J. Midday in Italian literature p263-65

Catholic authors

Cairns, C. The Catholic conscience. *In* Cairns, C. Italian literature p129-51

16th century—History and criticism

Parks, G. B. Italian tributes to Cardinal Pole. *In* Studies in the continental background of Renaissance English literature: essays presented to John L. Lievsay p43-66

16th century—History and criticism—Bibliography

Corrigan, B. and Mitchell, B. Italian literature. *In* Jones, W. M. ed. The present state of scholarship in sixteenth-century literature p 1-43

19th century—History and criticism

Perella, N. J. The nineteenth century. *In* Perella, N. J. Midday in Italian literature p70-113

20th century—History and criticism

Cairns, C. The dissection of man: the twentieth century. *In* Cairns, C. Italian literature p152-74

Italian opera. See Opera, Italian

Italian Parliamentary Commission of Enquiry on the Mafia in Sicily. See Italy. Parliament. Commission of Enquiry on the Mafia in Sicily

Italian poetry

History and criticism

Perella, N. J. From Dante to Pindemonte. *In* Perella, N. J. Midday in Italian literature p33-69

20th century—History and criticism

Perella, N. J. Some twentieth-century voices. *In* Perella, N. J. Midday in Italian literature p145-200

Italian question, 1849-1870. See Italy—History—1849-1870

Italian refugees See Refugees, Italian

Italian romances. See Romances, Italian

Italian wit and humor, Pictorial

Barolsky, P. Facetiae by Raphael and his friends. *In* Barolsky, P. Infinite jest: wit and humor in Italian Renaissance art p75-100

Barolsky, P. The grotesque and mock-heroic in north Italy. *In* Barolsky, P. Infinite jest: wit and humor in Italian Renaissance art p183-208

Barolsky, P. Laughter from the Venetian boudoir. *In* Barolsky, P. Infinite jest: wit and humor in Italian Renaissance art p158-82

Barolsky, P. The lighter side of Cosimo de' Medici's court. *In* Barolsky, P. Infiite jest: wit and humor in Italian Renaissance art p139-57

Barolsky, P. Love, laughter, and revelry. *In* Barolsky, P. Infinite jest: wit and humor in Italian Renaissance art p209-26

Barolsky, P. Mannerist bizzarrie. *In* Barolsky, P. Infinite jest: wit and humor in Italian Renaissance art p101-38

Barolsky, P. The place of humor in Renaissance art. *In* Barolsky, P. Infinite jest: wit and humor in Italian Renaissance art p 1-17

Barolsky, P. Quattrocento mirth. *In* Barolsky, P. Infinite jest: wit and humor in Italian Renaissance art p18-50

Italians in Buffalo

Yans-McLaughlin, V. A flexible tradition: South Italian immigrants confront a new work experience. *In* Immigrants in industrial America, 1850-1920 p67-84

Italians in Great Britain

Prestwich, M. Italian merchants in late thirteenth and early fourteenth century England. *In* The Dawn of modern banking p77-104

Italians in literature

Hunter, G. K. English folly and Italian vice. *In* Hunter, G. K. Dramatic identities and cultural tradition p103-32

Italians in Louisiana

History

Scarpaci, J. A. Immigrants in the new South: Italians in Louisiana's sugar parishes, 1880-1910. *In* Studies in Italian American social history p132-52

Italians in New York (City)

Russo, N. J. From Mezzogiorno to metropolis: Brooklyn's new Italian immigrants. *In* Studies in Italian American social history p118-31

Italians in Philadelphia

Political activity—History

Varbero, R. A. The politics of ethnicity: Philadelphia's Italians in the 1920's. *In* Studies in Italian American social history p164-81

Italians in the United States

Greeley, A. M. and McCready, W. C. The transmission of cultural heritages: the case of the Irish and Italians. *In* Glazer, N. and Moynihan, D. P. eds. Ethnicity p209-35

Pellegrino, J. An effective school of patriotism. *In* Studies in Italian American social history p84-104

See also Italian Americans

Psychology

Rolle, A. F. The American Italians: psychologcial and social adjustments. *In* Studies in Italian American social history p105-17

Social conditions

Velikonja, J. The identity and functional chological and social adjustments. *In* Studies in Italian American social history p182-98

Women

Winsey, V. R. The Italian immigrant women who arrived in the United States before World War I. *In* Studies in Italian American social history p199-210

Italy

Army. Arditi

Ledeen, M. A. Italy: war as a style of life. *In* The War generation p104-34

City planning

See City planning—Italy

Civilization

Altschul, M. Culture and community in the Italian Renaissance: four recent studies. *In* Medievalia et humanistica no. 5 p247-52

Gilbert, F. The historian as guardian of national consciousness: Italy between Guicciardini and Muratori. *In* Gilbert, F. History p387-409

Same as: Gilbert, F. Italy. *In* National consciousness, history, and political culture in early-modern Europe p21-42

Economic conditions—1945-

Hayward, J. E. S. and Corina, J. Comparative preliminaries. *In* Planning, politics and public policy p155-58

Economic policy

Fraenkel, G. Italian industrial policy in the framework of economic planning. *In* Planning, politics and public policy p128-40

Mariani, I. F. Incomes and employment policies in Italian economic planning. *In* Planning, politics and public policy p202-13

Pasquino, G. and Pecchini, U. Italy. *In* Planning, politics and public policy p70-92

Young, S. A comparison of the industrial experiences. *In* Planning, politics and public policy p141-54

Emigration and immigration

Pellegrino, J. An effective school of patriotism. *In* Studies in Italian American social history p84-104

Foreign relations

DeSantis, V. P. Italy and the Cold war. *In* Siracusa, J. M. and Barclay, G. S. eds. The impact of the Cold war p26-39

Italy—*Continued*

Foreign relations—1922-1945
Gilbert, F. Ciano and his ambassadors. *In* Gilbert, F. History p351-76

Historiography
Momigliano, A. Mabillon's Italian disciples. *In* Momigliano, A. Essays in ancient and modern historiography p277-93

History
Gilbert, F. The historian as guardian of national consciousness: Italy between Guicciardini and Muratori. *In* Gilbert, F. History p387-409
Same as: Gilbert, F. Italy. *In* National consciousness, history, and political culture in early-modern Europe p21-42

History—To 476—Historiography
Pearson, L. I. C. Myth and archaeologia in Italy and Sicily—Timaeus and his predecessors. *In* Yale classical studies v24 p171-95

History—19th century
Pacifici, S. Background of the modern Italian novel. *In* Pacifici, S. The modern Italian novel: from Capuana to Tozzi p 1-15

History—1849-1870
Hall, B. Alessandro Gavazzi: a Barnabite friar and the Risorgimento (Presidential address) *In* Church, society and politics p303-56

Industries
Fraenkel, G. Italian industrial policy in the framework of economic planning. *In* Planning, politics and public policy p128-40

Intellectual life
Pacifici, S. Background of the modern Italian novel. *In* Pacifici, S. The modern Italian novel: from Pea to Moravia p 1-17

Parliament—Commission of Enquiry on the Mafia in Italy
Vassalli, G. An Italian enquiry concerning the Mafia. *In* Crime, criminology and public policy p595-622

Politics and government—20th century
Chiaromonte, N. The Jesuit. *In* Chiaromonte, N. The worm of consciousness, and other essays p2-19

Politics and government—1914-1945
Ledeen, M. A. Italy: war as a style of life. *In* The War generation p104-34

Politics and government—1915-1922
Farneti, P. Social conflict, parliamentary fragmentation, institutional shift, and the rise of fascism: Italy. *In* The Breakdown of democratic regimes pt2 p3-33

Politics and government—1945-
Barnes, S. H. The dark side of pluralism: Italian democracy and the limits of political engineering. *In* Prospects for constitutional democracy p75-100
DeSantis, V. P. Italy and the Cold war. *In* Siracusa, J. M. and Barclay, G. S. eds. The impact of the Cold war p26-39

Social conditions
Riesenberg, P. N. Citizenship at law in late medieval Italy. *In* Viator: medieval and Renaissance studies v5 p333-46

Social life and customs
Appel, W. The myth of the jettatura. *In* The Evil eye p16-27

Italy, Southern

Economic policy
Cassese, S. State grants for the south of Italy. *In* Davis, K. C. Discretionary justice in Europe and America p149-60

Italy in literature
Melchiori, B. Browning in Italy. *In* Armstrong, I. ed. Robert Browning p168-83

Itō, Takayuki
The genesis of the Cold war: confrontation over Poland, 1941-44. *In* The Origins of the Cold war in Asia p147-202

Itō, Teiji, and Nishikawa, Kōji
Japan: two ancient capitals and the menace to them. *In* United Nations Educational, Scientific and Cultutral Organization. The conservation of cities p107-24

Itoh, Teiji. See Itō, Teiji

Itui Forest pygmies. See Bambute

Itzkowitz, Norman
The Ottoman Empire. *In* Lewis, B. ed. Islam and the Arab world p273-300

Ivacic, Pero
Toward a freer and multidimensional flow of information. *In* Horton, P. C. ed. The Third World and press freedom p135-50

Ivan the Terrible (Motion picture)
Barthes, R. The third meaning. *In* Barthes, R. Image, music, text p52-68

Ivanov, Georgiĭ Vladimirovich
Esenin's fate. *In* The Bitter air of exile p169-87

About
Markov, V. Georgy Ivanov: nihilist as light-bearer. *In* The Bitter air of exile p139-63

Ivanov, Georgy. See Ivanov, Georgiĭ Vladimirovich

Ivanov, Razumnik Vasil'evich

Friends and associates
Keys, R. The Bely-Ivanov-Rasumnik correspondence. *In* Janecek, G. ed. Andrey Bely p193-204

Relations with contemporaries
See Ivanov, Razumnik Vasil'evich—Friends and associates

Ivanov, Vĭacheslav Ivanovich
Gogol's Inspector General and the comedy of Aristophanes. *In* Maguire, R. A. ed. Gogol from the twentieth century p199-214
See also Gershenzon, M. O. jt. auth.

Ivanov, Vyacheslav. See Ivanov, Vĭacheslav Ivanovich

Ivara, Filippo. See Juvara, Filippo

Ivask, George
Russian modernist poets and the mystic sectarians. *In* Gibian, G. and Tjalsma, H. W. eds. Russian modernism p85-106

Ives, Charles Edward

About
Craft, R. Ives's world. *In* Craft, R. Current convictions p211-14

Ives, Eric William

'Agaynst taking awaye of women': the inception and operation of the Abduction Act of 1487. *In* Wealth and power in Tudor England p21-44

Ivories, Italian

Sicily

Robertson, E. The Rome casket. *In* Studies in memory of David Talbot Rice p11-15

Ivories, Medieval

Spain

Proske, B. I. G. Two ivory Madonnas. *In* Enggass, R. C. and Stokstad, M. eds. Hortus imaginum p37-44

Ivory Coast

Foreign relations

Delorme, N. The foreign policy of the Ivory Coast. *In* Aluko, O. ed. The foreign policies of African states p118-35

Ivre, Ivar

Conflict and resolution in Sweden. *In* Gerbner, G. ed. Mass media policies in changing cultures p119-30

Ivry, Alfred Lyon

al-Kindi's On first philosophy and Aristotle's Metaphysics. *In* Essays on Islamic philosophy and science p15-24

Iwanowska, Wilhelmina

The assimilation of science into our ways of thinking and living. *In* Science and society: past, present, and future p73-81

Iyasere, Solomon Ogbede

African critics on African literature: a study in misplaced hostility. *In* African literature today no. 7: Focus on criticism p20-27

Charles R. Larson: The emergence of African literature. *In* African literature today no. 7: Focus on criticism p143-46

Izbicki, Thomas M.

Infallibility and the erring pope: Guido Terreni and Johannes de Turrecremata. *In* Law, church, and society p97-111

Izevbaye, Daniel S.

Ayi Kwei Armah and the 'I' of the beholder. *In* King, B. A. and Ogungbesan, K. eds. A celebration of Black and African writing p232-44

Language and meaning in Soyinka's The road. *In* African literature today no. 8: Drama in Africa p52-65

The state of criticism in African literature. *In* African literature today no. 7: Focus on criticism p 1-19

Izgoev, Aleksandr

On educated youth: notes on its life and sentiments. *In* Landmarks p88-111

J

JCP. See Communist Party of Japan

Jaberg, Russell L.

Search for a center. *In* America in theological perspective p230-46

Jabès, Edmond

About

Derrida, J. Edmond Jabès and the question of the book. *In* Derrida, J. Writing and difference p64-78

About individual works

The book of questions

Derrida, J. Ellipsis. *In* Derrida, J. Writing and difference p294-300

Jack, Ian Robert James

About individual works

English literature, 1815-1832

Marcus, S. The limits of literary history. *In* Marcus, S. Representations p129-36

Jack MacGowram in the works of Samuel Beckett (criticism) Beckett, S. *In* Kauffmann, S. Persons of the drama p211-13

Jack the Ripper

About

Borowitz, A. New gaslight on Jack the Ripper. *In* Borowitz, A. Innocence and arsenic p87-99

Jackendoff, Ray S.

Grammar as evidence for conceptual structure. *In* Linguistic theory and psychological reality p201-28

Jackson, Andrew, President U.S.

Ambacher, B. I. Urban response to Jacksonian democracy: Philadelphia Democrats and the Bank War, 1832-1834. *In* Essays on urban America p55-87

Jackson, Arlene Marjorie

Reward, punishment, and the conclusion of Dombey and son. *In* Dickens Studies Annual v7 p103-27

Jackson, Blyden

Langston Hughes. *In* Inge, M. T.; Duke, J. M. and Bryer, J. R. eds. Black American writers v 1 p187-206

Renaissance in the twenties. *In* French, W. G. ed. The twenties p303-16

The waiting years

Contents

The case for American Negro literature
An essay in criticism
The ghetto of the Negro novel: a theme with variations
Harlem Renaissance in the twenties
Jean Toomer's Cane: an issue of genre
Also in French, W. G. ed. The twenties p317-33
Largo for Adonais
The minstrel mode
The Negro's image of his universe as reflected in his fiction
A review of J. L. Dillard's Black English
Richard Wright: Black boy from America's Black belt and urban ghettos
Richard Wright in a moment of truth
The ring and the book
A survey course in Negro literature
A word about Simple

Jackson, Bruce

Deviance as success: the double inversion of stigmatized roles. *In* Babcock, B. A. ed. The reversible world p258-75

The other kind of doctor: conjure and magic in Black American folk medicine. *In* American folk medicine p259-72

Jackson, Elender E.

Effective communication in nurse-patient relationships. *In* Henderson, G. ed. Human relations in the military p203-17

Jackson, Esther Merle
Tennessee Williams: poetic consciousness in crisis. *In* Tennessee Williams: a tribute p53-72

Jackson, Gabriele Bernhard
Structural interplay in Ben Jonson's drama. *In* Kernan, A. B. ed. Two Renaissance mythmakers p113-45

Jackson, Helen Maria (Fiske) Hunt

About

Dobie, J. F. Helen Hunt Jackson and "Ramona." *In* Dobie, J. F. Prefaces p159-69

About individual works
Ramona

Dobie, J. F. Helen Hunt Jackson and "Ramona." *In* Dobie, J. F. Prefaces p159-69

Jackson, John Archer
Sociology in contemporary Britain. *In* Mohan, R. P. and Martindale, D. A. eds. Handbook of contemporary developments in world sociology p19-30

Jackson, Luther P.
The popular media: Part I, The mission of Black newsmen. *In* The Black American reference book p846-74

Jackson, MacDonald Pairman
Compositorial practices in Tourneur's The atheist's tragedy. *In* Virginia. University. Bibliographical Society. Studies in bibliography v32 p210-15

The printer of the first quarto of Astrophil and Stella (1591). *In* Virginia. University. Bibliographical Society. Studies in bibliography v31 p201-03

Jackson, Martin A.
The uncertain peace: The best years of our lives. *In* O'Connor, J. E. and Jackson, M. A. eds. American history/American film p147-65

Jackson, Maurice
Broad societal changes. *In* Lauer, R. H. ed. Social movements and social change p174-89

Jackson, Ralph Semmes

About individual works
Home on the Double Bayou, memories of an east Texas ranch

Dobie, J. F. Introduction to "Home on the Double Bayou," by Ralph Semmes Jackson. *In* Dobie, J. F. Prefaces p170-74

Jackson, Robert Houghwout

About

White, G. E. Personal versus impersonal judging: the dilemmas of Robert Jackson. *In* White, G. E. The American judicial tradition p230-50

Jackson, Russell H. See Terdal, L. G. jt. auth.

Jackson, Samuel C.
Is the university superfluous in the urban crisis? *In* Murphy, T. P. ed. Universities in the urban crisis p3-13

Jackson, Shirley M.
Fact from fiction: another look at slavery in three Spanish-American novels. *In* DeCosta, M. ed. Blacks in Hispanic literature p83-89

Jackson, William Alexander; Ferguson, F. S. and Pantzer, Katherine F.

About individual works
A short-title catalogue of books printed in England, Scotland, and Ireland and of English books printed abroad, 1475-1640

Williams, W. P. The revised STC. *In* Review, v 1 1979 p249-54

Jackson, William Thomas Hobdell
The politics of a poet: the Archipoeta as revealed by his imagery. *In* Philosophy and humanism p320-38

Jackson, William Turrentine
Australians and the comparative frontier. *In* Essays on Walter Prescott Webb p17-51

Jackson, Miss.

Description

Welty, E. The flavor of Jackson. *In* Welty, E. The eye of the story p321-25

Jacob, François

About individual works
The logic of living systems: a history of heredity

Holmes, F. L. Conceptual history. *In* Studies in history of biology v 1 p209-18

Jacob, Philip Ernest
Autonomy and political responsibility: the enigmatic verdict of a cross-national comparative study of community dynamics. *In* Walton, J. and Masotti, L. H. eds. The city in comparative perspective p97-118

Jacobelli, Angela Maria. See Jacobelli, Isoldi Angela Maria

Jacobelli, Isoldi Angela Maria
The role of the intellectual in Giambattista Vico. *In* Giambattista Vico's science of humanity p409-21

Jacobi, Friedrich Heinrich

About

Berlin, Sir I. Hume and the sources of German anti-rationalism. *In* David Hume p93-116

Jacobites
Bennett, G. V. Jacobitism and the rise of Walpole. *In* Historical perspectives p70-92

Jacobs, Carol
The dissimulating harmony
Contents
Afterword: "I, the juggler"
Artaud: the assimilating harmony: Héliogabale
Benjamin: Walter Benjamin: image of Proust
Nietzsche: the stammering text: the fragmentary studies preliminary to The birth of tragedy
Rilke: the Tenth Duino elegy, or; The parable of the beheaded reader
The (too) good soldier: "a real story". *In* Glyph 3 p32-51

Jacobs, Henry E. See Kay, C. M. jt. comp.

Jacobs, Jane

About individual works
Death and life of great American cities

Sale, R. H. Jane Jacobs. *In* Sale, R. H. On not being good enough p177-88

Jacobs, Jane—About individual works—*Cont.*

The economy of cities

Sale, R. H. Jane Jacobs. *In* Sale, R. H. On not being good enough p177-88

Jacobs, Wilbur R.

The fatal confrontation: early native-white relations on the frontiers of Australia, New Guinea, and America—a comparative study. *In* The American Indian p27-54

Jacobsen, Jens Peter

About individual works

Marie Grubbe

Ingwersen, N. Problematic protagonists: Marie Grubbe and Niels Lyhne. *In* The Hero in Scandinavian literature p39-61

Niels Lyhne

Ingwersen, N. Problematic protagonists: Marie Grubbe and Niels Lyhne. *In* The Hero in Scandinavian literature p39-61

Jacobsen, Thorkild

Religious drama in ancient Mesopotamia. *In* Unity and diversity p65-97

Jacobson, Doranne

The women of north and central India: goddesses and wives. *In* Matthiasson, C. J. ed. Many sisters p99-175

Jacobson, Helga Eileen

Women in Philippine society: more equal than many. *In* Matthiasson, C. J. ed. Many sisters p349-77

Jacobson, Howard

Structure and meaning in Propertius Book 3. *In* Illinois classical studies, v 1 1976 p160-73

Jacobson, Richard

Absence, authority, and the text. *In* Glyph 3 p137-47

Jacobstein, J. Myron

Some reflections on the control of the publication of Appellate Court opinions. *In* Stanford legal essays p267-75

Jacoby, Russell

About individual works

Social amnesia

Gass, W. H. The anatomy of mind. *In* Gass, W. H. The world within the word p208-52

Jacqué, Jean-Paul. See Jonathan, G. C. jt. auth.

Jaeger, Werner Wilhelm

About

Calder, W. M. The correspondence of Ulrich Von Wilamowitz-Moellendorff with Werner Jaeger. *In* Harvard Studies in classical philology v82 p303-47

About individual works

Paideia

Richards, I. A. Poetry as paideia. *In* Richards, I. A. Poetries p146-48

Jaffa, Harry V.

About

Wilhelmsen, F. D. Jaffa, the school of Strauss, and the Christian tradition. *In* Wilhelmsen, F. D. Christianity and political philosophy p209-25

About individual works

Equality as a conservative principle

Bradford, M. E. The heresy of equality. *In* A Public philosophy reader p309-36

Jaffe, Hans Ludwig C.

Introduction to De Stijl. *In* Kaplan, P. and Manso, S. eds. Major European art movements, 1900-1945 p222-49

Jaffe, Arthur. See Jaffe, L. jt. auth.

Jaffe, Lois

Sexual problems of the terminally ill. *In* Home care p109-27

The terminally ill. *In* Gochros, H. L. and Gochros, J. S. eds. The sexually oppressed p277-92

Jaffe, Lois, and Jaffe, Arthur

Terminal candor and the coda syndrome: A tandem view of fatal illness. *In* Feifel, H. [ed.] New meanings of death p195-211

Jaffe, Samuel Peter

Rhetoric in German literature: Gottfried von Strassburg and the rhetoric of history. *In* Murphy, J. J. ed. Medieval eloquence p288-318

Jaggar, Alison Mary

Abortion and a woman's right to decide. *In* Baker, R. and Elliston, F. A. eds. Philosophy & sex p324-37

Also in Gould, C. C. and Wartofsky, M. W. eds. Women and philosophy p347-60

Political philosophies of women's liberation. *In* Feminism and philosophy p5-21

Jahn, Egbert

Four approaches to the analysis of Soviet foreign policy. *In* Jahn, E. ed. Soviet foreign policy p8-25

Jahn, Jerald D.

Chapman's enargia and the popular perspective on Ovids banquet of sence. *In* Tennessee Studies in literature v23 p15-30

Jain, Ravindra K.

Bundela genealogy and legends: the past of an indigenous ruling group of central India. *In* Studies in social anthropology p238-72

Jainism

Ramakrishna Rao, K. B. Jainism. *In* Bishop, D. H. ed. Indian thought p85-100

Bibliography

Folkert, K. W. The Jainas. *In* Adams, C. J. ed. A reader's guide to the great religions p231-46

Jaki, Stanley L.

The history of science and the idea of an oscillating universe. *In* Cosmology, history, and theology p233-51

Jakle, John A. and Janiskee, Robert L.

Why covered bridges? Toward the management of historic landscapes—the case of Parke County, Indiana. *In* Pattern and process p193-201

Jakobson, Roman

The contours of The safe conduct. *In* Matejka, L. and Titunik, I. R. eds. Semiotics of art p188-96

Is the cinema in decline? *In* Matejka, L. and Titunik, I. R. eds. Semiotics of art p145-52

Jakobson, Roman—*Continued*

Note on August 1914. *In* Dunlop, J. B.; Haugh, R. and Klimoff, A. eds. Aleksandr Solzhenitsyn: critical essays and documentary materials 2d ed. p326-27

On a generation that squandered its poets. *In* Erlich, V. ed. Twentieth-century Russian literary criticism p138-66

Signum et signatum. *In* Matejka, L. and Titunik, I. R. eds. Semiotics of art p176-87

What is poetry? *In* Matejka, L. and Titunik, I. R. eds. Semiotics of art p164-75

About individual works

Child language aphasia and phonological universals

Ferguson, C. A. New directions in phonological theory: language acquisition and universals research. *In* Current issues in linguistic theory p247-99

Linguistics and poetics

Richards, I. A. Factors and functions in linguistics. *In* Richards, I. A. Poetries p 1-16

On lingustic aspects of translation

Richards, I. A. Powers and limits of signs. *In* Richards, I. A. Poetries p17-38

Shakespeare's verbal art in Th' expence of spirit

Richards, I. A. Linguistics into poetics. *In* Richards, I. A. Poetries p39-49

Two aspects of language and two types of aphasic disturbances

Lodge, D. Metaphor and metonymy. *In* Lodge, D. The modes of modern writing p73-124

Schneidau, H. N. Pound and Wordsworth on poetry and prose. *In* Bornstein, G. ed. Romantic and modern p133-45

Jakubowicz, Malgorzata Semil- See Semil-Jakubowicz, Malgorzata

Jamaica

Religion

Smith, R. T. Religion in the formation of West Indian society: Guyana and Jamaica. *In* Kilson, M. L. and Rotberg, R. I. eds. The African diaspora p312-41

Religious life and customs

Schuler, M. Myalism and the African religious tradition in Jamaica. *In* Crahan, M. E. and Knight, F. W. eds. Africa and the Caribbean p65-79

Jambeck, Thomas John

Everyman and the implications of Bernardine humanism in the character "Knowledge." *In* Medievalia et humanistica no. 8 p103-23

Jambrek, Peter. See Gobetz, G. E. jt. auth.

James, Saint, apostle

About

González López, E. The myth of Saint James and its functional reality. *In* Américo Castro and the meaning of Spanish civilization p91-111

James I, King of Great Britain

About individual works

Daemonologie, in form of a dialogue, divided into three books

Latham, J. E. M. 'The tempest' and King James's 'Daemonologie.' *In* Shakespeare survey 28 p117-23

James, Adeola A.

Eustace Palmer: An introduction to the African novel. *In* African literature today no. 7: Focus on criticism p147-52

James, Alan

Recent developments in United Nations peace-keeping. *In* The Year book of world affairs, 1977 p75-97

James, Alice

About

Strouse, J. Semiprivate lives. *In* Studies in biography p113--29

James, Sir Arthur Evan

A judicial note on the control of discretion in the administration of criminal justice. *In* Crime, criminology and public policy p157-59

The sentencing process: present practice and future policy. *In* Progress in penal reform p165-73

James, G. Ingli

Blake's mixed media: a mixed blessing. *In* English Association. Essays and studies, 1977 p61-69

James, Henry, 1843-1916

About

Beattie, M. Henry James: 'the voice of stoicism.' *In* The Stoic strain in American literature p63-75

Berryman, J. The world of Henry James. *In* Berryman, J. The freedom of the poet p161-67

Blasing, M. K. Henry James's prefaces, or The story of the stories. *In* Blasing, M. K. The art of life p55-76

Briggs, J. A sense of the past: Henry James and Vernon Lee. *In* Briggs, J. Night visitors p111-23

Cooley, T. A sporting life: Henry James. *In* Cooley, T. Educated lives: the rise of modern autobiography in America p101-24

Deakin, M. F. The real and fictive quest of Henry James. *In* Garvin, H. R. ed. Makers of the twentieth-century novel p179-91

Donaldson, S. and Massa, A. The New World and the Old World. *In* Donaldson, S. and Massa, A. American literature: nineteenth and early twentieth centuries p9-46

Donoghue, D. The American style of failure. *In* Donoghue, D. The sovereign ghost p103-27

Felstiner, J. Max Beerbohm and the wings of Henry James. *In* Riewald, J. G. ed. The surprise of excellence p192-214

Fergusson, F. James's dramatic form. *In* Fergusson, F. Literary landmarks p48-61

Gillie, C. The early twentieth-century novel: James, Wells and Conrad. *In* Gillie, C. Movements in English literature, 1900-1940 p24-46

Gordon, C. An American girl. *In* Friedman, M. J. and Lawson, L. A. eds. The added dimension p123-37

Holman, C. H. "Of everything the unexplained and irresponsible specimen": notes on how to read American realism. *In* Holman, C. H. Windows on the world p17-26

Howe, I. Henry James as latter-day saint. *In* Howe, I. Celebrations and attacks p72-79

Hyde, H. M. Henry James at home. *In* Royal Society of Literature of the United Kingdom, London. Essays by divers hands v38 p58-77

James, Henry, 1843-1916—About—*Continued*

Inglis, T. Reading late James. *In* Josipovici, G. ed. The modern English novel: the reader, the writer and the work p77-94

Knights, L. C. Henry James and human liberty. *In* Knights, L. C. Explorations 3 p24-37

Lewis, W. Henry James; excerpt from "Men without art." *In* Lewis, W. Enemy salvoes p88-92

Miller, J. E. Willa Cather and the art of fiction. *In* The Art of Willa Cather p121-55

Milne, G. Henry James. *In* Milne ·G. The sense of society p43-70

Oates, J. C. The art of relationships: Henry James and Virginia Woolf. *In* Oates, J. C. New heaven, new earth: the visionary experience in literature p9-35

Page, N. The great tradition revisited. *In* Jane Austen's achievement p44-63

Rahv, P. The heiress of all the ages. *In* Rahv, P. Essays on literature and politics, 1932-1972 p43-61

Rahv, P. Henry James and his cult. *In* Rahv, P. Essays on literature and politics, 1932-1972 p93-104

Schneider, D. J. "A terrible mixture in things": the symbolism of Henry James. *In* Schneider, D. J. Symbolism: the Manichean vision p62-117

Skilton, D. Late-Victorian choices; James, Wilde, Gissing and Moore. *In* Skilton, D. The English novel p178-91

Smith, H. N. Henry James I: sows' ears and silk purses. *In* Smith, H. N. Democracy and the novel p128-42

Smith, H. N. Henry James II: the problem of an audience. *In* Smith, H. N. Democracy and the novel p143-65

Snow, C. P. Baron Snow. Henry James. *In* Snow, C. P. Baron Snow. The realists p256-96

Spilka, M. Henry James and Walter Besant: "The art of fiction" controversy. *In* Spilka, M. ed. Towards a poetics of fiction p190-208

About individual works
The ambassadors

Hardy, B. N. Memory and memories. *In* Hardy, B. N. Tellers and listeners p56-101

Spengemann, W. C. Henry James. *In* Spengemann, W. C. The adventurous muse p241-63

Tomlinson, T. B. Henry James: The ambassadors. *In* Tomlinson, T. B. English middle-class novel p148-65

The American

Auchincloss, L. The late Jamesing of early James. *In* Auchincloss, L. Life, law and letters p91-96

Falk, R. Henry James's The American as a centennial novel. *In* Essays in honor of Russel B. Nye p31-41

Spengemann, W. C. Henry James. *In* Spengemann, W. C. The adventurous muse p241-63

The American scene

Morris, W. Henry James. *In* Morris, W. Earthly delights, unearthly adornments p43-50

The art of the novel

Blasing, M. K. The story of the stories: Henry James's Prefaces as autobiography. *In* Landow, G. P. ed. Approaches to Victorian autobiography p311-32

The awkward age

Tanner, T. Henry James: The range of wonderment. *In* Tanner, T. The reign of wonder p278-308

Tomlinson, T. B. 'Fits of spiritual dread': George Eliot and later novelists. *In* Tomlinson, T. B. The English middle-class novel p114-30

The beast in the jungle

Tate, A. Three commentaries: Poe, James, and Joyce. *In* Tate, A. Memoirs and opinions, 1926-1974 p155-69

The Bostonians

Auerbach, N. Beyond the self: the spectacle of history and a new religion. *In* Auerbach, N. Communities of women p115-57

Cockshut, A. O. J. The lesbian theme. *In* Cockshut, A. O. J. Man and woman: a study of love and the novel, 1740-1940 p186-208

Colmer, J. Sex, the family and the new women. *In* Colmer, J. Coleridge to Catch-22 p105-21

Davis, S. D. The Bostonians reconsidered. *In* Tulane Studies in English, v23 p39-60

Eakin, P. J. New England in extremis: The Bostonians. *In* Eakin, P. J. The New England girl p195-217

Fetterley, J. The Bostonians: Henry James's eternal triangle. *In* Fetterley, J. The resisting reader p101-53

Freyer, J. The new woman: The unnatural lady reformers of Boston. *In* Fryer, J. The faces of Eve p20-34

Hall, S. J. Henry James and the bluestockings: satire and morality in The Bostonians. *In* Aeolian harps p207-25

Stineback, D. C. "Hurried particles in the stream": Henry James's The Bostonians. *In* Stineback, D. C. Shifting world p75-86

Tatar, M. M. From science fiction to psychoanalysis: Henry James's "Bostonians," D. H. Lawrence's "Women in love," and Thomas Mann's "Mario and the magician." *In* Tatar, M. M. Spellbound p230-71

The complete plays of Henry James, ed. by Leon Edel

Fergusson, F. James in the theater. *In* Fergusson, F. Literary landmarks p125-30

The golden bowl

Bersani, L. The Jamesian lie. *In* Bersani, L. A future for Astyanax p128-55

Hawthorne

Eakin, P. J. Henry James and the New England consciousness: Robert Hudson, The Europeans, Hawthorne. *In* Eakin, P. J. The New England girl p131-67

In the cage

Tanner, T. Henry James: The subjective adventure. *In* Tanner, T. The reign of wonder p309-35

A London life

Tanner, T. Henry James: The candid outsider. *In* Tanner, T. The reign of wonder p261-77

James, Henry, 1843-1916—About individual works—*Continued*

The portrait of a lady

Eakin, P. J. The tragedy of self-culture: The portrait of a lady. *In* Eakin, P. J. The New England girl p168-94

Ewell, B. C. Parodic echoes of The portrait of a lady in Howells's Indian summer. *In* Tulane studies in English v22 p117-31

Parrill, A. S. Portraits of ladies. *In* Tennessee Studies in literature v20 p92-99

Rahv, P. The heiress of all the ages. *In* Rahv, P. Essays on literature and politics, 1932-1972 p43-61

The Princess Casamassima

Colmer, J. Political action and the crisis of conscience. *In* Colmer, J. Coleridge to Catch-22 p91-104

Dolan, P. J. James: the aesthetics of politics. *In* Dolan, P. J. Of war and war's alarms p70-95

Page, P. The Princess Casamassima: suicide and "The penetrating imagination." *In* Tennessee Studies in literature v22 p162-69

The pupil

Trilling, L. Henry James: The pupil. *In* Trilling, L. Prefaces to The experience of literature p102-06

The sacred fount

Macnaughton, W. R. The narrator in Henry James's The sacred fount. *In* Literature and ideas in America p155-81

Tanner, T. Henry James: The subjective adventure. *In* Tanner, T. The reign of wonder p309-35

The turn of the screw

Briggs, J. Not without but within: the psychological ghost story. *In* Briggs, J. Night visitors p142-64

What Maisie knew

Tanner, T. Henry James: The range of wonderment. *In* Tanner, T. The reign of wonder p278-308

The wings of the dove

Bersani, L. The Jamesian lie. *In* Bersani, L. A future for Astyanax p128-55

Grella, G. The wings of the falcon and The Maltese dove. *In* Filler, L. ed. A question of quality: popularity and value in modern creative writing p108-14

Meyers, J. Bronzino, Veronese and The wings of the dove. *In* Meyers, J. Painting and the novel p19-30

Aesthetics

Maynard, R. N. Autotelism in Henry James's aesthetic. *In* Tennessee Studies in literature v21 p35-42

Bibliography

Gale, R. L. Henry James. *In* American literary scholarship, 1977 p99-118

Stafford, W. T. Henry James. *In* American literary scholarship, 1973 p116-34

Stafford, W. T. Henry James [another essay]. *In* American literary scholarship, 1974 p87-100

Stafford, W. T. Henry James [another essay]. *In* American literary scholarship, 1975 p115-30

Stafford, W. T. Henry James [another essay]. *In* American literary scholarship, 1976 p93-107

Biography—Character

Sarotte, G. M. Latent homosexuality: short of and beyond true heterosexuality: Henry James: the feminine masochist syndrome. *In* Sarotte, G. M. Like a brother, like a lover p197-211

Characters

Bersani, L. The Jamesian lie. *In* Bersani, L. A future for Astyanax p128-55

Characters—Daisy Miller

Fryer, J. The American princess: Daisy Miller. *In* Fryer, J. The faces of Eve p97-101

Characters—Isabel Archer

Eakin, P. J. The tragedy of self-culture: The portrait of a lady. *In* Eakin, P. J. The New England girl p168-94

Fryer, J. The American princess: Isabel Archer. *In* Fryer, J. The faces of Eve p126-42

Characters—Lambert Strether

Sarotte, G. M. Latent homosexuality: short of and beyond true heterosexuality: Henry James: the feminine masochist syndrome. *In* Sarotte, G. M. Like a brother, like a lover p197-211

Characters—Maggie Verver

Fryer, J. The American princess: Maggie Verver. *In* Fryer, J. The faces of Eve p112-26

Characters—Mildred Theale

Fryer, J. The American princess: Milly Theale. *In* Fryer, J. The faces of Eve p101-12

Characters—Olive Chancellor

Fryer, J. The Great Mother: The archetype: Olive Chancellor. *In* Fryer, J. The faces of Eve p143-52

Characters—Women

Eakin, P. J. Henry James and the New England consciousness: Roderick Hudson, The Europeans, Hawthorne. *In* Eakin, P. J. The New England girl p131-67

Eakin, P. J. New England in extremis: The Bostonians. *In* Eakin, P. J. The New England girl p195-217

Fryer, J. The Great Mother: The mother-surrogates. *In* Fryer, J. The faces of Eve p153-73

Fryer, J. The Great Mother: The neglecters. *In* Fryer, J. The faces of Eve p173-82

Fryer, J. The Great Mother: The real witchbitches. *In* Fryer, J. The faces of Eve p182-202

Fryer, J. The new woman: The unnatural lady reformers of Boston. *In* Fryer, J. The faces of Eve p220-34

Rahv, P. The heiress of all the ages. *In* Rahv, P. Essays on literature and politics, 1932-1972 p43-61

Criticism and interpretation

Smith, H. N. Henry James II: the problem of an audience. *In* Smith, H. N. Democracy and the novel p143-65

Influence—Howells

Ewell, B. C. Parodic echoes of The portrait of a lady in Howells's Indian summer. *In* Tulane studies in English v22 p117-31

James, Henry, 1843-1916—*Continued*

Plots

Caserio, R. L. The story in it: James. *In* Caserio, R. L. Plot, story, and the novel p198-231

Psychology

See James, Henry, 1843-1916—Biography —Character

James, Louis

Pickwick in America! *In* Dickens Studies Annual v 1 p65-80

Wilson Harris and the 'Guyanese quartet.' *In* King, B. A. and Ogungbesan, K. eds. A celebration of Black and African writing p164-74

About

Wynter, S. 'The necessary background.' *In* Baugh, E. ed. Critics on Caribbean literature p19-23

James, Montague Rhodes

About

Briggs, J. No mere antiquary: M. R. James. *In* Briggs, J. Night visitors p124-41

Sullivan, J. The antiquarian ghost story: Montague Rhodes James. *In* Sullivan, J. Elegant nightmares p69-90

James, Richard

About individual works

The muses dirge, consecrated to the remembrance of the high and mighty monarch James

Patrick, J. M. "Poetry perpetuates the poet": Richard James and the growth of Herrick's reputation. *In* Rollin, R. B. and Patrick, J. M. eds. "Trust to good verses": Herrick tercentenary essays p221-34

Russko-angliĭskiĭ slovar'—dnevnik Richarda Dzhemsa

Heaney, M. The implications of Richard James's maimanto. *In* Oxford Slavonic papers new ser. v9 p102-09

James, Theodore E.

A fragment of An exposition of the first letter of Seneca to Lucilius attributed to Peter of Mantua. *In* Philosophy and humanism p531-41

James, William

Final impressions of a psychical researcher; excerpt from "Memories and studies." *In* Ludwig, J. K. ed. Philosophy and parapsychology p407-20

About

Allen, G. W. William James. *In* Ross, R. G. ed. Makers of American thought p49-84

Fancher, R. E. Psychology in the university: Wilhelm Wundt and William James. *In* Fancher, R. E. Pioneers of psychology p126-69

Schneider, H. W. Radical empiricism and religion. *In* Philosophy and the civilizing arts p446-66

Influence—Frost

McClanahan, T. Frost's theodicy: "word I had no one left but God." *In* Frost: centennial essays II p112-26

Miller, L. H. William James, Robert Frost, and "The black cottage." *In* Frost: centennial essays III p368-81

James family

Strouse, J. Semiprivate lives. *In* Studies in biography p113-29

Jameson, Fredric

About

Watkins, E. Dialectic and form. *In* Watkins, E. The critical act p158-87

Jammes, André

Victor Regnault, calotypist. *In* One hundred years of photographic history p77-82

Jancar, Barbara Wolfe

Religious dissent in the Soviet Union. *In* Tokes, R. L. ed. Dissent in the USSR p191-230

Jancsó, Miklós

About

Taylor, J. R. Miklós Jancsó. *In* Taylor, J. R. Directors and directions p204-27

Jandova, Ivanka Akrabova- See Akrabova-Zhandova, Ivanka

Janecek, Gerald

Introduction. *In* Janecek, G. ed. Andrey Bely p 1-17

Rhythm in prose: the special case of Bely. *In* Janecek, G. ed. Andrey Bely p86-102

Janes, Regina M.

Mary, Mary, quite contrary, or, Mary Astell and Mary Wollstonecraft compared. *In* Studies in eighteenth-century culture v5 p121-39

Janik, Allan, and Toulmin, Stephen Edelston

About individual works

Wittgenstein's Vienna

Koestler, A. Wittgensteinomania. *In* Koestler, A. The heel of Achilles p107-11

Janis, Irving Lester

Groupthink among policy makers. *In* Kren, G. M. and Rappoport, L. H. eds. Varieties of psychohistory p315-29

Janiskee, Robert L. See Jakle, J. A. jt. auth.

Janissaries. See Janizaries

Janizaries

Rafeq, A. K. The local forces in Syria in the seventeenth and eighteenth centuries. *In* War, technology and society in the Middle East p277-307

Janke, R. Steven

The Vision of St. Bernard: a study in Florentine iconography. *In* Enggass, R. C. and Stokstad, M. eds. Hortus imaginum p45-50

Jankowitsch, Peter

Neutrality and nonalignment: foreign policies of independence in the twentieth century. *In* [Truth and tragedy]: a tribute to Hans Morgenthau p237-58

Janowitz, Morris

The emergent military. *In* Beaumont, R. A. and Edmonds, M. eds. War in the next decade p21-34

The journalistic profession and the mass media. *In* Culture and its creators p72-96

Some observations on the comparative analysis of Middle Eastern military institutions. *In* War, technology and society in the Middle East p412-40

Janowitz, Morris, and Street, David

Changing social order of the metropolitan area. *In* Handbook of contemporary urban life p90-128

Jansenists

Williams, W. H. The significance of Jansenism in the history of the French Catholic clergy in the pre-Revolutionary era. *In* Studies in eighteenth-century culture v7 p289-306

History

McManners, J. Jansenism and politics in the eighteenth century. *In* Church, society and politics p253-73

Jantz, Harold Edward Stein

German men of letters in the early United States. *In* The German contribution to the building of the Americas p75-95

Images of America in the German Renaissance. *In* First images of America p91-106

Janzen, John Marvin

The tradition of renewal in Kongo religion. *In* African religions: a symposium p69-115

Japan

Bibliography

Kitagawa, J. M. The religions of Japan. *In* Adams, C. J. ed. A reader's guide to the great religions p247-82

Civilization

Harris, N. All the world a melting pot? Japan at American fairs, 1876-1904. *In* Iriye, A. ed. Mutual images p24-54

Makita, T. Television drama and Japanese culture with special emphasis on historical drama. *In* Fischer, H. D. and Melnik, S. R. eds. Entertainment: a cross-cultural examination p63-73

Takemoto, T. Malraux and Japan: an encounter under a cascade. *In* Courcel, M. H. de, ed. Malraux p120-26

Civilization—American influences

Kamei, S. The sacred land of liberty: images of America in nineteenth century Japan. *In* Iriye, A. ed. Mutual images p55-72

Nagai, M. and Nishijima, T. Postwar Japanese education and the United States. *In* Iriye, A. ed. Mutual images p169-87

Civilization—Occidental influences

Wagatsuma, H. Problems of cultural identity in modern Japan. *In* Ethnic identity p307-34

Commerce—China

Haley, P. E. and Rood, H. W. China's major trading partner: Japan dependent. *In* China's changing role in the world economy p187-212

Commerce—United States

Iriye, A. Japan as a competitor, 1895-1917. *In* Iriye, A. ed. Mutual images p73-99

Commercial policy

Howe, C. B. Japan's policy towards foreign trade: the strategic options. *In* Modern Japan p244-64

Constitutional history

Homma, N. The impact of the American Revolution on Japan. *In* The Impact of the American Revolution abroad p164-66

Defenses

Saeki, K. Japan's security in a multipolar world. *In* Clapp, P. and Halperin, M. H. eds. United States—Japanese relations, the 1970's p183-202

Economic conditions—1945-

Rosovsky, H. Japan and the United States: notes from the devil's advocate. *In* Clapp, P. and Halperin, M. H. eds. United States-Japanese relations, the 1970's p79-93

Economic policy—1945-

Furuhashi, Y. Evolving Japanese policy toward inward foreign direct investment in the postwar period. *In* Postwar trends in Japan p61-118

Foreign economic relations

Kim, Y. C. The interaction of economics and Japanese foreign policy. *In* The Interaction of economics and foreign policy p84-101

Foreign economic relations—United States

Kanamori, H. Future U.S.—Japanese economic relations. *In* Clapp, P. and Halperin, M. H. eds. United States-Japanese relations, the 1970's p58-78

Yamamoto, M. The Cold war and U.S.-Japan economic cooperation. *In* The Origins of the Cold war in Asia p408-25

Foreign opinion, American

Clapp, P. and Halperin, M. H. U.S. elite images of Japan: the postwar period. *In* Iriye, A. ed. Mutual images p202-22

Glazer, N. From Ruth Benedict to Herman Kahn: the postwar Japanese image in the American mind. *In* Iriye, A. ed. Mutual images p138-68

Isaacs, H. R. Some concluding remarks: the turning mirrors. *In* Iriye, A. ed. Mutual images p258-65

Foreign relations

Kim, Y. C. The interaction of economics and Japanese foreign policy. *In* The Interaction of economics and foreign policy p84-101

Nish, I. H. Japan and the outbreak of war in 1941. *In* Crisis and controversy p130-47

Teters, B. Matsuoka Yōsuke: the diplomacy of bluff and gesture. *In* Burns, R. D. and Bennett, E. M. eds. Diplomats in crisis p275-96

Foreign relations—China

Brown, S. D. Shidehara Kijūrō: the diplomacy of the yen. *In* Burns, R. D. and Bennett, E. M. eds. Diplomats in crisis p201-25

Farnsworth, L. W. Hirota Kōki: the diplomacy of expansionism. *In* Burns, R. D. and Bennett, E. M. eds. Diplomats in crisis p227-49

Hellmann, D. C. Japan and China: competitors in a multipolar world? *In* Clapp, P. and Halperin, M. H. eds. United States-Japanese relations, the 1970's p164-82

Ishikawa, T. The normalization of Sino-Japanese relations. *In* Clapp, P. and Halperin, M. H. eds. United States-Japanese relations, the 1970's p147-63

Lin, Han-sheng. Chou Fo-hai: the diplomacy of survival. *In* Burns, R. D. and Bennett, E. M. eds. Diplomats in crisis p171-99

Ori, K. Japanese public opinion and Sino-Japanese relations, 1969-1972. *In* Postwar trends in Japan p37-60

Japan—*Continued*

Foreign relations—Europe

Mushakoji, K. A note on trilateral crisis diplomacy: the irritants in the Japan-U.S.-E.C. relations. *In* Postwar trends in Japan p15-36

Foreign relations—Great Britain

Nish, I. H. Japan and naval aspects of the Washington Conference. *In* Modern Japan p67-80

Foreign relations—Near East

Gottlieb, G. China and Japan and the Arab-Israeli conflict. *In* The New world balance and peace in the Middle East: reality or mirage? p126-36

Foreign relations—Russia

Kim, Y. C. The interaction of economics and Japanese foreign policy. *In* The Interaction of economics and foreign policy p84-101

Foreign relations—United States

Aruga, T. The first Japanese mission to the United States 1860. *In* Abroad in America: Visitors to the new Nation, 1776-1914 p134-44

Bennett, E. M. Joseph C. Grew: the diplomacy of pacification. *In* Burns, R. D. and Bennett, E. M. eds. Diplomats in crisis p65-89

Burns, R. D. Stanley K. Hornbeck: the diplomacy of the Open Door. *In* Burns, R. D. and Bennett, E. M. eds. Diplomats in crisis p91-123

Clapp, P. U.S. domestic politics and relations with Japan. *In* Clapp, P. and Halperin, M. H. eds. United States-Japanese relations, the 1970's p35-57

Conroy, H. F. Nomura Kichisaburō: the diplomacy of drama and desperation. *In* Burns, R. D. and Bennett, E. M. eds. Diplomats in crisis p297-316

Davies, J. P. America and East Asia. *In* Two hundred years of American foreign policy p90-141

Hodgson, J. D. What lies ahead for U.S.—Japan relations? *In* Prochnow, H. V. ed. Dilemmas facing the nation p248-70

Iriye, A. Continuities in U.S.-Japanese relations, 1941-49. *In* The Origins of the Cold war in Asia p378-407

Kamiya, F. Summit talks in retrospect. *In* Clapp, P. and Halperin, M. H. eds. United States-Japanese relations, the 1970's p120-46

Mushakoji, K. A note on trilateral crisis diplomacy: the irritants in the Japan-U.S.-E.C. relations. *In* Postwar trends in Japan p15-36

Nish, I. H. Japan and naval aspects of the Washington Conference. *In* Modern Japan p67-80

Ross, G. M. W. Cameron Forbes: the diplomacy of a Darwinist. *In* Burns, R. D. and Bennett, E. M. eds. Diplomats in crisis p49-64

Historiography

Hall, J. W. Japanese history in world perspective. *In* The Future of history p173-88

History—Restoration, 1853-1870

Cheng, R. Ye-lin. The effect of prerevolutionary values, beliefs, and social structures on revolutionary mobilization and success. *In* Johnson, H. M. ed. Religious change and continuity p168-90

History—Civil War, 1868

Sheldon, C. D. The politics of the Civil War of 1868. *In* Modern Japan p27-51

History—Meiji period, 1868-1912

Sheldon, C. D. The politics of the Civil War of 1868. *In* Modern Japan p27-51

History—1912-1945

Shillony, B. A. Myth and reality in Japan of the 1930s. *In* Modern Japan p81-88

History, Naval

Nish, I. H. Japan and naval aspects of the Washington Conference. *In* Modern Japan p67-80

Industries—1945-

Rosovsky, H. Japan and the United States: notes from the devil's advocate. *In* Clapp, P. and Halperin, M. H. eds. United States-Japanese relations, the 1970's p79-93

Politics and government—1912-1945

Sims, R. L. National elections and electioneering in Akita Ken, 1930-1942. *In* Modern Japan p89-112

Politics and government—1945-

Kosaka, M. Political immobility and the uncertain future. *In* Clapp, P. and Halperin, M. H. eds. United States-Japanese relations, the 1970's p19-34

Population

Sovani, N. V. A comparative study of population and agricultural change in some countries of the ECAFE region. *In* Economic factors in population growth p273-92

Relations (general) with China

Li, V. H. China and off-shore oil: the Tiao-yü Tai dispute. *In* China's changing role in the world economy p143-62

Relations (general) with the United States

Harris, N. All the world a melting pot? Japan at American fairs, 1876-1904. *In* Iriye, A. ed. Mutual images p24-54

Nagai, M. and Nishijima, T. Post war Japanese education and the United States. *In* Iriye, A. ed. Mutual images p169-87

Reischauer, E. O. Introduction: An overview. *In* Clapp, P. and Halperin, M. H. eds. United States-Japanese relations, the 1970's p 1-18

Relations (military) with the United States

Halperin, M. H. U.S.-Japanese security relations. *In* Clapp, P. and Halperin, M. H. eds. United States-Japanese relations, the 1970's p203-22

Miwa, K. Japanese images of war with the United States. *In* Iriye, A. ed. Mutual images p115-37

Religion

Rajana, E. W. New religions in Japan: an appraisal of two theories. *In* Modern Japan p187-97

Japan—Religion—*Continued*

Rohlen, T. P. The promise of adulthood in Japanese spiritualism. *In* Erikson, E. H. ed. Adulthood p129-47

Religion—Bibliography

Kitagawa, J. M. The religions of Japan. *In* Adams, C. J. ed. A reader's guide to the great religions p247-82

Social conditions

Devos, G. A. The Japanese adapt to change. *In* Spindler, G. D. ed. The making of psychological anthropology p219-57

Social conditions—19th century

Kato, H. Development nineteenth-century style: some historical parellels between the United States and Japan. *In* On the making of Americans p173-90

Social life and customs

Rohlen, T. P. The promise of adulthood in Japanese spiritualism. *In* Erikson, E. H. ed. Adulthood p129-47

Japanese American leadership

Daniels, R. The Japanese. *In* Ethnic leadership in America p36-63

Japanese Americans

Daniels, R. The Japanese. *In* Ethnic leadership in America p36-63

Nakanishi, D. T. The visual panacea: Japanese-Americans in the city of smog. *In* Iriye, A. ed. Mutual images p223-57

Ethnic identity

Lyman, S. M. Japanese-American generation gap. *In* Henslin, J. M. ed Deviant lifestyles p25-38

Psychology

DeVos, G. A. The Japanese adapt to change. *In* Spindler, G. D. ed. The making of psychological anthropology p219-57

Social life and customs

Lyman, S M. Japanese-American generation gap. *In* Henslin, J. M. ed. Deviant lifestyles p25-38

California

Kitano, H. H. L. Japanese Americans: the development of a middleman minority. *In* The Asian American: the historical experience p81-100

Hawaii

Kitano, H. H. L. Japanese Americans: the development of a middleman minority. *In* The Asian American: the historical experience p81-100

Los Angeles

Modell, J. Class or ethnic solidarity: the Japanese American company union. *In* the Asian American: the historical experience p67-80

Japanese children's literature. See Children's literature, Japanese

Japanese Communist Party. See Communist Party of Japan

Japanese drama. See Kabuki plays; Nō plays

Japanese fiction

History and criticism

Rimer, J. T. Introduction. *In* Rimer, J. T. Modern Japanese fiction and its traditions p3-21

Japanese in Los Angeles

Nakanishi, D. T. The visual panacea: Japanese-Americans in the city of smog. *In* Iriye, A. ed. Mutual images p223-57

Japanese in the United States

Katō, H. America as seen by Japanese travelers. *In* Iriye, A. ed. Mutual images p188-201

Kiefer, C. W. Lessons from the issei. *In* Gubrium, J. F. ed. Late life p167-97

See also Japanese Americans

Japanese literature

History and criticism

Rimer, J. T. Antecedents: the tale, the diary, the monogatari, the essay. *In* Rimer, J. T. Modern Japanese fiction and its traditions p62-81

20th century—History and criticism

Saeki, S. Images of the United States as a hypothetical enemy. *In* Iriye, A. ed. Mutual images p100-14

Japanese national characteristics. See National characteristics, Japanese

Japanese newspapers

Kawanaka, Y. The canons of journalism and trends in Japanese dailies. *In* Postwar trends in Japan p251-72

History

Altman, A. A. Shinbunshi: the early Meiji adaptation of the Western-style newspaper. *In* Modern Japan p52-66

Japanese opinion of the United States. See United States—Foreign opinion, Japanese

Japanese physicists. See Physicists—Japan

Japanese poetry

History and criticism

Ishii, S. Herrick and Japanese classical poetry: a comparison. *In* Rollin, R. B. and Patrick, J. M. eds. "Trust to good verses": Herrick tercentenary essays p187-96

Japanese-Russian Border Conflicts, 1932-1941. See Russo-Japanese Border Conflicts, 1932-1941

Japanese science fiction. See Science fiction, Japanese

Japanese theologians. See Theologians, Japanese

Jarausch, Konrad H.

The sources of German student unrest, 1815-1848. *In* The University in society v2 p533-69

Jarchas. See Muwashshah

Jardine, Lisa

Humanism and dialectic in sixteenth-century Cambridge: a preliminary investigation. *In* Classical influences on European culture A.D. 1500-1700 p141-54

Jardine, Nick

'Realistic' realism and the progress of science. *In* Hookway, C. and Pettit, P. eds. Action and interpretation p107-25

Jarrell, Randall

Stories. *In* May, C. E. ed. Short story theories p32-44

The woman at the Washington Zoo. *In* Gibbons, R. ed. The poet's work: 29 masters of 20th century poetry on the origins and practice of their art p230-39

Jarrell, Randall—*Continued*

About

Kunitz, S. J. Out of the cage. *In* Kunitz, S. J. A kind of order, a kind of folly p241-43

Mazzaro, J. Between two worlds: the post-modernism of Randall Jarrell. *In* Boyers, R. ed. Contemporary poetry in America p78-98

Rosenthal, M. L. Randall Jarrell. *In* Donoghue, D. ed. Seven American poets from MacLeish to Nemerov p132-70

Scannell, V. American poets of the Second World War. *In* Scannell, V. Not without glory p172-237

Shapiro, K. J. The death of Randall Jarrell. *In* Shapiro, K. J. The poetry wreck p268-99

About individual works

The woman at the Washington Zoo

Jarrell, R. The woman at the Washington Zoo. *In* Gibbons, R. ed. The poet's work: 29 masters of 20th century poetry on the origins and practice of their art p230-39

Jarrett, David. See Gallafent, E. jt. auth.

Jarrett, David, and Jarrett, Mary

American literature: the twentieth century. *in* English Association. The year's work in English studies v57 p398-429

American literature to 1900. *In* English Association. The year's work in English studies v55 p482-504

Jarrett, James L.

Educating the person. *In* Philosophy and the civilizing arts p345-55

Jarrett, Mary

American literature to 1900. *In* English Association. The year's work in English studies v56 p393-412

American literature to 1900 [another essay]. *In* English Association. The year's work in English studies v57 p382-97

See also Jarrett, D. jt. auth.

Jarrott, Catherine Anna Louise

Erasmus's annotations and Colet's commentaries on Paul: a comparison of some theological themes. *In* Essays on the works of Erasmus p125-44

Jarvik, Lissy F. See LaRue, A. jt. auth.

Jaryas. See Muwashshah

Jason, Howard McLean

The Negro in Spanish literature to the end of the Siglo de Oro. *In* DeCosta, M. ed. Blacks in Hispanic literature p29-35

Jaspers, Karl

About

Grene, M. G. The German existentialists. *In* Grene, M. G. Philosophy in and out of Europe p71-78

Grene, M. G. Karl Jaspers: a philosopher of humanity. *In* Grene, M. G. Philosophy in and out of Europe p79-86

Játvarðar saga Helga

Fell, C. E. English history and Norman legend in the Icelandic saga of Edward the Confessor. *In* Anglo-Saxon England 6 p223-36

Fell, C. E. The Icelandic saga of Edward the Confessor: its version of the Anglo-Saxon emigration to Byzantium. *In* Anglo-Saxon England 3 p179-96

Jaucourt, Louis, chevalier de

About individual works

Encyclopaedia

Bonnet, J. C. The culinary system in the Encylopédie. *In* Food and drink in history p139-65

Jaufré Rudel

About

Topsfield, L. T. Jaufre Rudel and love from afar. *In* Topsfield, L. T. Troubadours and love p42-69

Jauss, Hans Robert

History of art and pragmatic history. *In* Amacher, R. E. and Lange, V. eds. New perspectives in German literary criticism p432-64

Literary history as a challenge to literary theory. *In* Cohen, R. ed. New directions in literary history p11-41

Theses on the transition from the aesthetics of literary works to a theory of aesthetic experience. *In* Valdés, M. J. and Miller, O. J. eds. Interpretation of narrative p137-47

Java

Historiography

Ricklefs, M. C. Javanese sources in the writing of modern Javanese history. *In* Southeast Asian history and historiography p332-44

History

Naerssen, F. H. van. Tribute to the god and tribute to the king. *In* Southeast Asian history and historiography p296-303

Social life and customs

Peacock, J. L. Symbolic reversal and social history: transvestites and clowns of Java. *In* Babcock, B. A. ed. The reversible world p209-24

Javits, Jacob Koppel

Government's role in economic management. *In* Benton, L. R. ed. Management for the future p165-73

Western Europe and the tensions in the Middle East. *In* The New world balance and peace in the Middle East: reality or mirage? p74-78

Jay, Karla

Male homosexuality and lesbianism in the works of Proust and Gide. *In* Crew, L. ed. The gay academic p216-43

Jay, Peter

Englanditis. *In* Tyrell, R. E. ed. The future that doesn't work p167-85

Jazz music

Whalum, W.; Baker, D. N. and Long, R. A. Afro-American music. *In* The Black American reference book p791-826

See also Blues (Songs, etc.); Ragtime music

Europe

Oliver, P. Jazz is where you find it: the European experience of jazz. *In* Bigsby, C. W. E. Superculture p140-51

Jealousy

Whitehurst, R. N. Violently jealous husbands. *In* Gross, L. ed. Sexual issues in marriage p75-84

See also Envy

Jealousy in literature
Steadman, J. M. The Faerie Queene: The House of Care. *In* Steadman, J. M. Nature into myth p138-58

Jean de Meun. See Guillaume de Lorris, jt. auth.

Jean de Paris

About individual works
De modo existendi corporis Christi, in sacramento altaris
Martin, J. H. The Eucharistic treatise of John Quidort of Paris. *In* Viator: medieval and Renaissance studies v6 p195-240

Jeanne de Bourbon, Queen consort of Charles V, King of France

Coronation
Sherman, C. R. The Queen in Charles V's "Coronation Book": Jeanne de Bourbon and the "Ordo ad reginam benedicendam." *In* Viator: medieval and Renaissance studies v8 p255-98

Jeanneret-Gris, Charles Édouard
If I had to teach you architecture. *In* Sharp, D. ed. The rationalists p79-83
Twentieth-century living and twentieth-century building. *In* Sharp, D. ed. The rationalists p72-77

About
Berger, J. Le Corbusier. *In* Berger, J. The look of things p70-73
Favre, M. Le Corbusier in an unpublished dossier and a little-known novel. *In* Walden, R. ed. The open hand p96-113
Fishman, R. From the radiant city to Vichy: Le Corbusier's plans and politics, 1928-1942. *In* Walden, R. ed. The open hand p244-83
Fry, E. M. Le Corbusier at Chandigarh. *In* Walden, R. ed. The open hand p350-63
Fry, J. B. D. Le Corbusier as I knew him. *In* Walden, R. ed. The open hand p364-73
Jencks, C. Le Corbusier on the tightrope of functionalism. *In* Walden, R. ed. The open hand p186-214
Moos, S. von. The politics of the open hand: notes on Le Corbusier and Nehru at Chandigarh. *In* Walden, R. ed. The open hand p412-57
Purdy, M. Le Corbusier and the theological program. *In* Walden, R. ed. The open hand p286-321
Sarin, M. Chandigarh as a place to live in. *In* Walden, R. ed. The open hand p374-410
Sekler, M. P. M. Le Corbusier, Ruskin, the tree and the open hand. *In* Walden, R. ed. The open hand p42-95
Sutcliffe, A. A vision of utopia: optimistic foundations of Le Corbusier's doctrine d'urbanisme. *In* Walden, R. ed. The open hand p216-43
Taylor, B. B. Le Corbusier at Pessac: professional and client responsibilities. *In* Walden, R. ed. The open hand p162-85
Turner, P. Romanticism, rationalism, and the domino system. *In* Walden, R. ed. The open hand p14-41
Walden, R. New light on Le Corbusier's early years in Paris: the La Roche-Jeanneret houses. *In* Walden, R. ed. The open hand p116-61
Winter, J. A. Le Corbusier's technological dilemma. *In* Walden, R. ed. The open hand p322-47

Jeffares, Alexander Norman
Lever's 'Lord Kilgobbin.' *In* English Association. Essays and studies, 1975 p47-57
Place, space and personality and the Irish writer. *In* Place, personality and the Irish writer p11-40

About individual works
In excited reverie
Connolly, C. W. B. Yeats. *In* Connolly, C. The evening colonnade p202-06

Jeffares, Alexander Norman, ed.

About individual works
W. B. Yeats: the critical heritage
Finneran, R. J. W. B. Yeats: some recent bibliographical and editorial work. *In* Review, v 1 1979 p233-48

Jeffers, Robinson

About individual works
Be angry at the sun
Kunitz, S. J. Barbaric omens. *In* Kunitz, S. J. A kind of order, a kind of folly p198-203

Tamar
DeMott, R. J. Robinson Jeffers' "Tamar." *In* French, W. G. ed. The twenties p405-25

Jefferson, Douglas William
The artistry of 'Bleak House.' *In* English Association. Essays and studies, 1974 p37-51

Jefferson, Joseph

About individual works
The autobiography of Joseph Jefferson
Kauffmann, S. An actor's life. *In* Kauffmann, S. Persons of the drama p301-05

Jefferson, Thomas, President U.S.

About
Allen, J. L. Thomas Jefferson and the passage to India: a pre-exploratory image. *In* Pattern and process p103-13
Baeumer, M. L. Simplicity and grandeur: Winckelmann, French classicism, and Jefferson. *In* Studies in eighteenth-century culture v7 p63-78
Berns, W. F. Religion and the founding principle. *In* The Moral foundations of the American Republic p157-82
Howell, W. S. The Declaration of Independence and eighteenth-century logic. *In* Howell, W. S. Poetics, rhetoric, and logic p163-90
MacLeish, A. The ghost of Thomas Jefferson. *In* MacLeish, A. Riders on the earth p57-65
Malone, D. Mr Jefferson's private life. *In* American Antiquarian Society. Proceedings v84 pt 1 p65-72
Meyer, D. H. Thomas Jefferson and the rhetoric of republicanism. *In* Meyer, D. H. The democratic Enlightenment p109-28
Morgan, R. J. "Time hath found us": the Jeffersonian revolutionary vision. *In* Havard, W. C. and Bernd, J. L. eds. 200 years of the Republic in retrospect p20-36
Philbrick, T. Thomas Jefferson. *In* Emerson, E. H. ed. American literature, 1764-1789 p145-69
Robbins, C. The pursuit of happiness. *In* America's continuing revolution p119-39

Jefferson, Thomas, President U.S.—*Continued*

Walton, C. Hume and Jefferson on the uses of history. *In* Livingston, D. W. and King, J. T. eds. Hume p389-403

Also in Philosophy and the civilizing arts p103-25

About individual works
Declaration of Independence

See United States. Declaration of Independence

Notes on the state of Virginia

Downs, R. B. American statesman. *In* Downs, R. B. Books that changed the South p27-40

Peterson, M. D. Thomas Jefferson's Notes on the state of Virginia. *In* Studies in eighteenth-century culture v7 49-62

Friends and associates

Ketcham, R. L. The Puritan ethic in the Revolutionary era: Abigail Adams and Thomas Jefferson. *In* "Remember the ladies": new perspectives on women in American history p49-65

Jeffrey, David K.

"Ductility and dissimulation": the unity of Ferdinand Count Fathom. *In* Tennessee Studies in literature v23 p47-60

The epistolary format of Pamela and Humphry Clinker. *In* A Provision of human nature p145-54

Jeffrey, David L.

Breaking up the synthesis: from Plato's academy to the "school of Athens." *In* Jeffrey, D. L. ed. By things seen: reference and recognition in medieval thought p227-52

Franciscan spirituality and the growth of vernacular culture. *In* Jeffrey, D. L. ed. By things seen: reference and recognition in medieval thought p143-60

Jehovah. See God (Judaism)—Name

Jehovah's Witnesses

Beckford, J. A. Two contrasting types of sectarian organization. *In* Wallis, R. ed. Sectarianism p70-85

Jehovah's Witnesses, Afro-American

Cooper, L. R. "Publish" or perish: Negro Jehovah's Witness adaptation in the ghetto. *In* Zaretsky, I. I. and Leone, M. P. eds. Religious movements in contemporary America p700-21

Jen, Erica

An experience with Peking youth. *In* Terrill, R. ed. The China difference p141-60

Jencks, Charles

Irrational rationalism: the Rats since 1960. *In* Sharp, D. ed. The rationalists p208-30

Le Corbusier on the tightrope of functionalism. *In* Walden, R. ed. The open hand p186-214

Jencks, Christopher S.

The social basis of unselfishness. *In* On the making of Americans p63-86

Jenkins, Annibel

Dunton's Post-Angel: messenger of remarkable providences. *In* The Dress of words p151-65

Jenkins, Brian M.

International terrorism: a new mode of conflict. *In* International terrorism and world security p13-49

Jenkins, Cecil

Realism and the novel form. *In* Williams, D. A. ed. The monster in the mirror p 1-16

Jenkins, Elizabeth

Jane Austen and the human condition. *In* Royal Society of Literature of the United Kingdom, London. Essays by divers hands v39 p57-75

Jenkins, John Holland

About individual works
Recollections of early Texas

Dobie, J. F. Foreword to "Recollections of early Texas," by John Holland Jenkins. *In* Dobie, J. F. Prefaces p140-45

Jenkins, Ray

Mass media changes in the South since World War II. *In* The Rising South v2 p126-40

Jenkins, Robin

About

Hart, F. R. Novelists of survival. *In* Hart, F. R. The Scottish novel p246-86

Morgan, E. The novels of Robin Jenkins. *In* Morgan, E. Essays p242-45

Jenkins, Roy Harris

The United States and a united Europe: are we now uncertain partners? *In* World change and world security p1-16

Jenkins, Thomas Miller

A rejoinder: the Black experience. *In* Lewis, W. D. and Griessman, B. E. eds. The Southern mystique p89-91

Jenkins, William Fitzgerald

About

Versins, P. Contact. *In* Knight, D. F. ed. Turning points p163-67

Jenkinson, Philip

The Agatha Christie films. *In* Agatha Christie: first lady of crime p155-82

Jenks, James M.

Industrial democracy: a new challenge for management. *In* Benton, L. R. ed. Management for the future p175-88

Jenner, Edward

About individual works
An inquiry into the causes and effects of the variolae vaccinae, a disease discovered in some of the western countries of England, particularly Gloucestershire, and known by the name of the cow pox

Downs, R. B. Discoverer of vaccination; excerpt from "Molders of the modern mind." *In* Downs, R. B. Books that changed the world p345-48

Jennings, Margaret

The art of the Pseudo-Origen homily De Maria Magdalena. *In* Medievalia et humanistica no. 5 p139-52

Piers Plowman and Holychurch. *In* Viator: medieval and Renaissance studies v9 p367-74

The preacher's rhetoric: The Ars componendi sermones of Ranulph Higden. *In* Murphy, J. J. ed. Medieval eloquence p112-26

Jennings, Napoleon Augustus

About individual works
A Texas ranger

Dobie, J. F. Foreword to "A Texas ranger," by Napoleon Augustus Jennings. *In* Dobie, J. F. Prefaces p14-22

Jensen, Anne E.
Molière in Denmark in the 18th century. *In* Johnson, R. B.; Neumann, E. S. and Trail, G. T. eds. Molière and the commonwealth of letters: patrimony and posterity p252-58

Jensen, Arthur Robert
Race and mental ability. *In* Racial variation in man p71-108

About

Biesheuvel, S. An examination of Jensen's theory concerning educability, heritability and population differences. *In* Montagu, A. ed. Race and IQ p59-72

Brace, C. L. and Livingstone, F. B. On creeping Jensenism. *In* Montagu, A. ed. Race and IQ p151-73

Bronfenbrenner, U. Nature with nurture: a reinterpretation of the evidence. *In* Montagu, A. ed. Race and IQ p114-44

Gordon, E. W. and Green, D. An affluent society's excuses for inequality: developmental, economic, and educational. *In* Montagu, A. ed. Race and IQ p73-103

Sanday, P. R. On the causes of IQ differences between groups and implications for social policy. *In* Montagu, A. ed. Race and IQ p220-51

About individual works
How much can we boost I.Q. and scholastic achievement?

Gould, S. J. Racist arguments and IQ. *In* Montagu, A. ed. Race and IQ p145-50

Lewontin, R. C. Race and intelligence. *In* Montagu, A. ed. Race and IQ p175-91

Jensen, Gillian Fellows. See Fellows Jensen, Gillian

Jensen, Richard J.
The religious and occupational roots of party identification: Illinois and Indiana in the 1870's. *In* Swierenga, R. P. ed. Beyond the Civil War synthesis p255-73

Jeopardy, Double. See Double jeopardy

Jeppesen, Steen Leth. See Blegvad, M. jt. auth.

Jeremiah Johnson (Motion picture)
Kauffmann, S. Jeremiah Johnson. *In* Kauffmann, S. Living images p158-60

Jerome, Saint. See Hieronymus, Saint

Jerome, Judson
Toward an ideal college. *In* Fairfield, R. P. ed. Humanistic frontiers in American education p207-15

Jescheck, Hans Heinrich
Modern criminal policy in the Federal Republic of Germany and the German Democratic Republic. *In* Crime, criminology and public policy p509-25

Jeske, Jeff. See Davis, T. M. jt. ed.

Jespersen, Otto
Notes on metre; excerpt from "Linguistica." *In* Gross, H. S. ed. The structure of verse p105-28

Jesuit drama

History and criticism

Nicoll, A. The international theatre of the Jesuits. *In* Nicoll, A. World drama p190-94

Jesuit relations. See Jesuits. Letters from missions (North America)

Jesuits

History

Levi, A. H. T. Erasmus, the early Jesuits and the classics. *In* Classical influences on European culture A.D. 1500-1700 p223-38

Letters from missions (North America)

Altschule, M. D. The ideas of the Huron Indians about the unconscious mind. *In* Altschule, M. D. Origins of concepts in human behavior p19-34

Missions

Romeo, R. The Jesuit sources and the Italian political Utopia in the second half of the sixteenth century. *In* First images of America p165-84

China

Boxer, C. R. European missionaries and Chinese clergy, 1654-1810. *In* Kling, B. B. and Pearson, M. N. eds. The age of partnership p97-121

Italy

Chiaromonte, N. The Jesuit. *In* Chiaromonte, N. The worm of consciousness, and other essays p2-19

Mexico

Romeo, R. The Jesuit sources and the Italian political Utopia in the second half of the sixteenth century. *In* First images of America p165-84

Jesus, Society of. See Jesuits

Jesus Christ
Barth, K. Jesus Christ and the movement for social justice. *In* Hunsinger, G. ed. Karl Barth and radical politics p19-45

Hanfmann, G. M. A. The crucified donkey man: Achaios and Jesus. *In* Studies in classical art and archaeology p205-07

MacDonald, W. G. Christology and "The angel of the Lord." *In* Current issues in Biblical and patristic interpretation p324-35

Sayers, D. L. The greatest drama ever staged; excerpt from "Creed or chaos?" *In* Sayers, D. L. The whimsical Christian p11-16

Takayanagi, S. Christology and postwar theologians in Japan. *In* Postwar trends in Japan p119-67

Wicker, B. Metaphor and 'nature.' *In* Wicker, B. The story-shaped world p50-70

See also Christianity; Lord's Supper

Art

Proske, B. I. G. Two ivory Madonnas. *In* Enggass, R. C. and Stokstad, M. eds. Hortus imaginum p37-44

Schapiro, M. A relief in Rodez and the beginnings of Romanesque sculpture in southern France. *In* Schapiro, M. Selected papers v 1 p285-305

See also Christian art and symbolism; Icons

Biography—Sources
See Jesus Christ—Historicity

Cross
See Holy Cross; Jesus Christ—Crucifixion

Crucifixion

Ellis, E. E. "Christ crucified'". *In* Reconciliation and hope p69-75

Wolman, B. B. Why did Jesus die on the Cross? *In* Wolman, B. B. ed. Psychoanalysis and Catholicism p115-42

Jesus Christ—*Continued*

Divinity

Meeks, W. A. The divine agent and his counterfeit in Philo and the Fourth Gospel. *In* Aspects of religious propaganda in Judaism and early Christianity p43-67

Friends and associates

Highet, G. Jesus and his pupils. *In* Highet, G. The immortal profession p199-215

Historicity

Longenecker, R. N. Literary criteria in life of Jesus research: an evaluation and proposal. *In* Current issues in Biblical and patristic interpretation p217-29

Osborn, E. F. Four problems. *In* Osborn, E. F. Ethical patterns in early Christian thought p183-213

History of doctrines

Lochman, J. M. Toward a theology of Christological concentration. *In* The Context of contemporary theology p209-23

History of doctrines— Early church, ca. 30-600

Longenecker, R. N. The obedience of Christ in the theology of the early Church. *In* Reconciliation and hope p142-52

Humanity

Dunn, J. D. G. Paul's understanding of the death of Jesus. *In* Reconciliation and hope p125-41

Incarnation

See Incarnation

Interpretations, Jewish

See Jesus Christ—Jewish interpretations

Interpretations, New Testament

See Jesus Christ—History of doctrines— Early church, ca. 30-600

Jewish interpretations

Nemoy, L. The attitude of the early Karaites towards Christianity. *In* Salo Wittmayer Baron v2 p697-715

Last Supper

See Last Supper

Lord's prayer

See Lord's prayer

Miracles

Achtemeier, P. J. Jesus and the disciples as miracle workers in the Apocryphal New Testament. *In* Aspects of religious propaganda in Judaism and early Christianity p149-86

Harper, G. M. "A subject of investigation": miracle at Mirebeau. *In* Yeats and the occult p172-89

Miscellanea

Jones, W. R. The heavenly letter in medieval England. *In* Medievalia et humanistica no. 6 p163-78

Name

See Son of God; Son of Man

Nativity

See Christmas

Natures

See Jesus Christ—Divinity; Jesus Christ —Humanity

New Testament interpretations

See Jesus Christ—History of doctrines— Early church, ca. 30-600

Person and offices

Fiorenza, E. S. Wisdom mythology and the Christological hymns of the New Testament. *In* Aspects of wisdom in Judaism and early Christianity p17-41

Poetry

Twitchell, J. B. "Hart-leap well": Wordsworth's Crucifixion poem. *In* Tennessee Studies in literature v20 p11-16

Relation to Judaism

See Jesus Christ—Jewish interpretations

Resurrection

Obitts, S. R. Historical explanation and Barth on Christ's Resurrection. *In* Current issues in Biblical and patristic interpretation p365-77

Palmer, D. W. The Resurrection of Jesus and the mission of the Church. *In* Reconciliation and hope p205-23

Sayings

See Jesus Christ—Words

Second Advent

See Second Advent

Typology

See Typology (Theology)

Words

Robinson, J. M. Jesus as Sophos and Sophia: wisdom tradition and the Gospels. *In* Aspects of wisdom in Judaism and early Christianity p 1-16

Jesus Christ in art. See Jesus Christ—Art

Jesus Christ in fiction, drama, poetry, etc.

Curran, T. The word made flesh: the Christian aesthetic in Dorothy L. Sayers's The man born to be king. *In* Hannay, M. P. ed. As her whimsey took her p67-77

Dale, A. S. The man born to be king: Dorothy L. Sayers's best mystery plot. *In* Hannay, M. P. ed. As her whimsey took her p78-90

Kunkel, F. L. Lawrence's The man who died: the heavenly cock. *In* Kunkel, F. L. Passion and the Passion p37-57

Kurz, P. K. The contemporary novel about Jesus. *In* Kurz, P. K. On modern German literature v4 p151-75

Lee, A. A. Toward a critique of The dream of the rood. *In* Anglo-Saxon poetry: essays in appreciation p163-91

Reynolds, W. Dorothy Sayers and the drama of orthodoxy. *In* Hannay, M. P. ed. As her whimsey took her p91-106

Richards, I. A. Jesus' other life. *In* Richards, I. A. Complementarities p209-14

Striedter, J. The "new myth" of revolution—a study of Mayakovsky's early poetry. *In* Amacher, R. E. and Lange, V. eds. New perspectives in German literary criticism p357-85

Jesus Christ in literature. See Jesus Christ in fiction, drama, poetry, etc.

Jesus Freaks. See Jesus People

Jesus Movement. See Jesus People

Jesus People

Adams, R. L. and Fox, R. J. Mainlining Jesus: the new trip. *In* Henslin, J. M. ed. Deviant life-styles p87-100

Richardson, J. T.; Stewart, M. W. and Simmonds, R. B. Researching a fundamentalist commune. *In* Needleman, J. and Baker, G. eds. Understanding the new religions p235-51

Jet pilot (Motion picture)

Truffaut, F. Josef Von Sternberg: Jet pilot. *In* Truffaut, F. The films in my life p74-76

Jettatura. See Evil eye

Jewelry, Roman

Higgins, R. A. Jewellery. *In* Strong, D. E. and Brown, D. eds. Roman crafts p53-62

Jewelry making

Higgins, R. A. Jewellery. *In* Strong, D. E. and Brown, D. eds. Roman crafts p53-62

Jewett, Sarah Orne

About individual works
The country of the pointed firs

Howe, I. The country of the pointed firs. *In* Howe, I. Celebrations and attacks p132-34

Jewish-Arab relations

Aumann, M. Land ownership in Palestine, 1880-1948. *In* The Palestinians p21-29

El-Ayouty, Y. The OAU and the Arab-Israeli conflict: a case of mediation that failed. *In* El-Ayouty, Y. ed. The Organization of African Unity after ten years p189-212

Heradstveit, D. The role of international terrorism in the Middle East conflict and its implication for conflict resolution. *In* International terrorism and world security p93-103

Kedourie, É. The Arab-Israeli conflict. *In* Kedourie, É. Arabic political memoirs and other studies p218-30

Moral and religious aspects

Pa'il, M. The dynamics of power: morality in armed conflict after the Six Day War. *In* Modern Jewish ethics p191-220

1917-

Avnery, U. The Palestinian option. *In* The Palestinians p187-93

Burns, E. L. M. Peace in the Middle East. *In* The Elusive peace in the Middle East p311-47

Campbell, J. C. American efforts for peace. *In* The Elusive peace in the Middle East p249-310

Cohen, A. Israel and Jewish-Arab peace: governmental and nongovernmental approaches. *In* The Elusive peace in the Middle East p102-65

Dinstein, Y. Terrorism and war of liberation: an Israeli perspective of the Arab-Israeli conflict. *In* International terrorism and political crimes p155-72

Haddad, G. M. Arab peace efforts and the solution of the Arab-Israeli problem. *In* The Elusive peace in the Middle East p166-248

Khouri, F. J. United Nations peace efforts. *In* The Elusive peace in the Middle East p19-101

Mallison, W. T. and Mallison, S. V. An international law appraisal of the juridical characteristics of the resistance of the people of Palestine: the struggle for human rights. *In* International terrorism and political crimes p173-90

Ma'oz, M. A Palestinian state—where? *In* The Palestinians p194-96

Porat, Y. The Palestinian-Arab nationalist movement. *In* The Palestinians p121-27

Prittie, T. C. F. Israel and the Palestinian question. *In* The Palestinians p213-27

Pryce-Jones, D. On Israel's East. *In* The Palestinians p209-12

Rubinstein, A. Palestinian nationalism: an established fact. *In* The Palestinians p183-86

Syrkin, M. Palestinian nationalism: its development and goal. *In* The Palestinians p199-208

Waxman, C. I. Varieties of Palestinian nationalism. *In* The Palestinians p112-20

1917-1949

Arendt, H. Peace or armistice in the Near East? *In* Arendt, H. The Jew as pariah: Jewish identity and politics in the modern age p193-222

Arendt, H. To save the Jewish homeland. *In* Arendt, H. The Jew as pariah: Jewish identity and politics in the modern age p178-92

1967-1973

Caradon, H. M. F. Baron. Is peace possible? What are the options? *In* The New world balance and peace in the Middle East: reality or mirage? p217-26

Cohen, A. West Bank sentiments, 1967-1973. *In* The Palestinians p88-93

Kerr, M. H. The respective positions of the Arabs and Israel on a peace settlement. *In* The New world balance and peace in the Middle East: reality or mirage? p36-42

Lerner, A. P. Demography, economics, and technology and the Middle East conflict. *In* The New world balance and peace in the Middle East: reality or mirage? p98-104

Merlin, S. Summation and projections. *In* The New world balance and peace in the Middle East: reality or mirage? p227-40

Rouleau, E. Peace without the Palestinians? *In* The New world balance and peace in the Middle East: reality or mirage? p155-64

See also Israel-Arab War, 1973

Jewish bankers. See Banks and banking—Jews

Jewish Biblical criticism. See Bible. Old Testament—Criticism, interpretation, etc., Jewish

Jewish civilization. See Jews—Civilization

Jewish converts to Christianity. See Converts from Judaism

Jewish day schools

New York (City)

Cohen, L. The shule. *In* Roots of open education in America p42-48

Jewish ethics. See Ethics, Jewish

Jewish fiction (American) See American fiction—Jewish authors

Jewish folk-lore. See Folk-lore—Jews

Jewish historians. See Historians, Jewish

Jews, German in the United States
Korn, B. W. German-Jewish intellectual influences on American Jewish life, 1824-1972. *In* Tradition and change in Jewish experience p106-40

Jews, Oriental in Israel
Prittie, T. C. F. Middle East refugees. *In* The Palestinians p51-73

Jews in Austria

History

Zuckerman, A. J. Unpublished materials on the relationship of early fifteenth century Jewry to the central government. *In* Salo Wittmayer Baron v2 p1059-95

Jews in Babylonia

History

Neusner, J. Politics and theology in Talmudic Babylonia. *In* Tradition and change in Jewish experience p46-74

Jews in Baghdad
Kedourie, É. The Jews of Baghdad in 1910. *In* Kedourie, É. Arabic political memoirs and other studies p263-72

Jews in Cairo

History

Hirschberg, J. W. The agreement between the Musta'ribs and the Maghribis in Cairo 1527. *In* Salo Wittmayer Baron v2 p577-90

Jews in Candia, Crete

History

Ankori, Z. From Zudecha to Yahudi Mahallesi: the Jewish quarter of Candia in the seventeenth century. *In* Salo Wittmayer Baron v 1 p63-127

Jews in Europe
Dawidowicz, L. S. Jewish identity: a matter of fate, a matter of choice. *In* Dawidowicz, L. S. The Jewish presence p3-31

History

Simonsohn, S. The Hebrew revival among early medieval European Jews. *In* Salo Wittmayer Baron v2 p831-58

Jews in Europe, Eastern

History

Fischer-Galati, S. A. Judeo-Christian aspects of Pax Ottomanica. *In* Király, B. K. ed. Tolerance and movements of religious dissent in Eastern Europe p185-97

Pictorial works

Dawidowicz, L. S. Picturing the past. *In* Dawidowicz, L. S. The Jewish presence p177-90

Jews in France

History

Popkin, R. H. La Peyrère, the Abbé Grégoire, and the Jewish question in the eighteenth century. *In* Studies in eighteenth-century culture v4 p209-22

Jews in Germany
Rosenthal, E. I. J. Hermann Cohen and Heinrich Graetz. *In* Salo Wittmayer Baron v2 p725-43
Stern, F. R. The burden of success: reflections on German Jewry. *In* Art, politics, and will p124-44

History

Chazan, R. Emperor Frederick I, the Third Crusade, and the Jews. *In* Viator: medieval and Renaissance studies v8 p83-93
Kisch, G. An unpublished consilium of Johannes Sichardus. *In* Philosophy and humanism p477-82
Zuckerman, A. J. Unpublished materials on the relationship of early fifteenth century Jewry to the central government. *In* Salo Wittmayer Baron v2 p1059-95

Jews in India

History

Strizower, S. The Bene Israel and the Jewish people. *In* Salo Wittmayer Baron v2 p859-86

Jews in Iraq
Knisbacher, M. The Jews of Iraq and the international protection of the rights of minorities (1856-1976). *In* Sidorsky, D. ed. Essays on human rights p156-78

Jews in Latin America
Horowitz, I. L. Jewish ethnicity and Latin American nationalism. *In* Said, A. A. and Simmons, L. R. eds. Ethnicity in an international context p92-109

Jews in literature
Alter, R. Eliot, Lawrence, and the Jews: two versions of Europe. *In* Alter, R. Defenses of the imagination p137-51
Alter, R. Shtetl and revolution. *In* Alter, R. Defenses of the imagination p199-212
Arendt, H. The Jew as pariah: a hidden tradition. *In* Arendt, H. The Jew as pariah: Jewish identity and politics in the modern age p67-90
Benson, J. J. An introduction: Bernard Malamud and the haunting of America. *In* The Fiction of Bernard Malamud p13-42
Bienstock, B. G. The changing image of the American Jewish mother. *In* Tufte, V. and Myerhoff, B. G. eds. Changing images of the family p173-91
Cohen, S. B. The Jewish literary comediennes. *In* Cohen, S. B. ed. Comic relief p172-86
Echeruo, M. J. C. Shylock and the conditioned imagination. *In* Echeruo, M. J. C. The conditioned imagination from Shakespeare to Conrad p24-43
Elstun, E. B. Richard Beer-Hofmann: the poet as exculpator dei. *In* Strelka, J. P.; Bell, R. F. and Dobson, E. eds. Protest—form—tradition p123-32
Ezrahi, S. The Holocaust writer and the lamentation tradition: responses to catastrophe in Jewish literature. *In* Rosenfeld, A. H. and Greenberg, I. eds. Confronting the Holocaust p133-49
Field, L. A. Bernard Malamud and the marginal Jew. *In* The Fiction of Bernard Malamud p97-116
Goist, P. D. Alternative perspective: the "radical" journalism of Hutchins Hapgood and Ernest Poole. *In* Goist, P. D. From Main Street to State Street p94-109
Grebstein, S. N. The comic anatomy of Portnoy's complaint. *In* Cohen, S. B. ed. Comic relief p152-71
Howe, I. In the day of a false messiah. *In* Celebrations and attacks p49-52
Howe, I. The stories of Bernard Malamud. *In* Howe, I. Celebrations and attacks p32-34
Howe, I. The stories of Isaac Babel. *In* Howe, I. Celebrations and attacks p53-58

Jivoff, Leo and others
Home health care and the quality of life. *In* Home care p3-11

Joannes Climacus, Saint

About individual works
The ladder of divine ascent
Lutz, C. E. Joannes Climacus' Ladder of divine ascent. *In* Lutz, C. E. Essays on manuscripts and rare books p46-49

Johannes de Tepla

About individual works
The plowman from Bohemia
Hruby, A. The plowman from Bohemia. *In* Hoffmeister, G. ed. The Renaissance and Reformation in Germany p17-32

Joannes Garson. See Garzoni, Giovanni

Joannes Parisiensis. See Jean de Paris

Joannes Scholasticus, Saint. See Joannes Climacus, Saint

Johannes von Saaz. See Johannes de Tepla

João VI, King of Portugal

About
Dias, M. O. S. The establishment of the royal court in Brazil. *In* From colony to nation p89-108

João de Santo Thomaz

About individual works
Treatise on signs
Deely, J. N. Toward the origin of semiotic. *In* Sebeok, T. A. ed. Sight, sound, and sense p 1-30

Job discrimination. See Discrimination in employment

Job enlargement. See Job enrichment

Job enrichment
Bluestone, I. Work humanization in practice: what can labor do? *In* Heisler, W. J. and Houck, J. W. eds. A matter of dignity p165-78

Bowers, D. G. Work humanization in practice: what is business doing? *In* Heisler, W. J. and Houck, J. W. eds. A matter of dignity p147-64

Sexton, W. P. Work humanization in practice: what should business do? *In* Heisler, W. J. and Houck, J. W. eds. A matter of dignity p131-45

Job restructuring. See Job enrichment

Job satisfaction
Gemmill, G. R. Postscript: toward the person-centered organization. *In* Heisler, W. J. and Houck, J. W. eds. A matter of dignity p197-205

Heisler, W. J. and Houck, J. W. eds. Humanistic work: its philosophical and cultural implications. *In* Heisler, W. J. and Houck, J. W. eds. A matter of dignity p11-22

Kasl, S. V. Work and mental health: contemporary research evidence. *In* Heisler, W. J. and Houck, J. W. eds. A matter of dignity p85-110

Jobert, Bruno
Urban planning and political institutions: an essay in comparison. *In* Planning, politics and public policy p378-89
See also Arcy, F. d' jt. auth.

Jobs. See Professions

Jocelyn, H. D.
Chrysalus and the Fall of Troy (Plautus, Bacchides 925-978). *In* Harvard Studies in classical philology v73 p135-52

Jocham, K. P. S.

About individual works
W. B. Yeats: a classified bibliography of criticism: including additions to Allan Wade's Bibliography of the writings of W. B. Yeats and a section of the Irish literary and dramatic revival
Finneran, R. J. W. B. Yeats: some recent bibliographical and editorial work. *In* Review, v 1 1979 p233-48

Joda, Robert
Nicholas of Cusa: precursor of humanism. *In* Hoffmeister, G. ed. The Renaissance and Reformation in Germany p33-49

Johann, Robert O.
Person, community, and moral commitment. *In* Roth, R. J. ed. Person and community p155-75

Johannes Climacus, Saint. See Joannes Climacus, Saint

Johannes Climax. See Joannes Climacus, Saint

Johannes de Lignano. See Legnano, Giovanni da

Johannes de Tepla

About individual works
Death and the plowman
Hrubý, A. The plowman from Bohemia. *In* Hoffmeister, G. ed. The Renaissance and Reformation in Germany p17-32

Johannes Scholasticus, Saint. See Joannes Climacus, Saint

Johannes von Saaz. See Johannes de Tepla

Johannesburg, South Africa

Race question
Mayer, P. Class, status, and ethnicity as perceived by Johannesburg Africans. *In* Thompson, L. M. and Butler, J. eds. Change in contemporary South Africa p138-67

Johannsen, Wilhelm Ludvig

About
Allen, G. E. Naturalists and experimentalists: the genotype and the phenotype. *In* Studies in history of biology v3 p179-209

Johansson, Gunnar
Projective transformations as determining visual space perception. *In* Perception p117-38

Johansson, Sheila Ryan
Demographic contributions in the history of Victorian women. *In* Kanner, B. ed. The women of England p259-95

Sex and death in Victorian England: an examination of age- and sex-specific death rates, 1840-1910. *In* Vicinus, M. ed. A widening sphere p163-81

John, Saint, apostle

Art
See St John's Apocalypse no. 786 (Icons)

John, Saint, apostle in literature
Shaffer, E. S. Browning's St John: the casuistry of the higher criticism. *In* Shaffer, E. S. 'Kubla Khan' and The fall of Jerusalem p191-224

Johnson, Harry Alleyn
Public education: the battle and its aftermath. *In* Johnson, H. A. ed. Negotiating the mainstream p 1-46

Johnson, Harry Gordon
Economics and the radical challenge: the hard social science and the soft social reality. *In* Culture and its creators p97-118

The individual and the state: some contemporary problems. *In* Glahe, F. R. ed. Adam Smith and The wealth of nations p21-34

An informal classical model of the current economic development problem. *In* Economic development and planning p157-67

Keynes and British economics. *In* Keynes, M. ed. Essays on John Maynard Keynes p108-22

Keynes and the developing world. *In* Skidelsky, R. J. A. ed. The end of the Keynesian era p88-94

Johnson, Harry Morton
Religion in social change and social evolution. *In* Johnson, H. M. ed. Religious change and continuity p313-39

Religion in urban society. *In* Handbook of contemporary urban life p233-57

Johnson, Helen Armstead
Black influences in the American theater: Part II, 1960 and after. *In* The Black American reference book p705-40

Johnson, Hildegard Binder
New geographical horizons: concepts. *In* First images of America p615-33

The United States land survey as a principle of order. *In* Pattern and process p114-30

About individual works
The United States land survey as a principle of order

Pattison, W. D. Reflections on the American rectangular land survey system. *In* Pattern and process p131-38

Johnson, Ira D. See Johnson, C. jt. auth.

Johnson, James E.
The role of women in the founding of the United States Children's Bureau. *In* "Remember the ladies": new perspectives on women in American history p179-96

Johnson, James Turner
Just war, the Nixon Doctrine and the future shape of American military policy. *In* The Year book of world affairs, 1975 p137-54

Johnson, John Coleman De Graft- See De Graft-Johnson, John Coleman

Johnson, John M.
Behind the rational appearances: fusion of thinking and feeling in sociological research. *In* Douglas, J. D. and Johnson, J. M. [eds.] Existential sociology p201-28

Ethnomethodology and existential sociology. *In* Douglas, J. D. and Johnson, J. M. [eds.] Existential sociology p153-73

Occasioned transcendence. *In* Douglas, J. D. and Johnson, J. M. [eds.] Existential sociology p229-53

Johnson, Joseph

About

Tyson, G. P. Joseph Johnson, an eighteenth-century bookseller. *In* Virginia. University. Bibliographical Society. Studies in bibliography v28 p 1-16

Johnson, Joseph Esrey. See Berman, M. R. jt. auth.

Johnson, Kay Ann
Women in China: problems of sex inequality and socioeconomic change. *In* Roberts, J. I. ed. Beyond intellectual sexism p286-319

Johnson, Kenneth
Eliot as enemy: William Carlos Williams and The waste land. *In* French, W. G. ed. The twenties p377-86

Johnson, Leanor Boulin
Blacks. *In* Gochros, H. L. and Gochros, J. S. eds. The sexually oppressed p173-91

Johnson, Lemuel A.
El tema negro: the nature of primitivism in the poetry of Luis Palés Matos. *In* DeCosta, M. ed. Blacks in Hispanic literature p123-36

Johnson, Lester F.

About

Rosenberg, H. Lester Johnson's abstract men. *In* Rosenberg, H. Art on the edge p71-78

Johnson, Lionel Pigot

About

Gould, W. "Lionel Johnson comes the first to mind": sources for Owen Aherne. *In* Yeats and the occult p255-84

Johnson, Ludwell H.
Civil War military history: a few revisions in need of revising. *In* Hubbell, J. T. ed. Battles lost and won p3-18

Johnson, Lyndon Baines, President U.S.

About

Evans, R. and Novak, R. D. Lyndon B. Johnson: the ascent to leadership; excerpt from "Lyndon B. Johnson: the exercise of power". *In* Ornstein, N. J. ed. Congress in change p117-41

Johnson, Mark D. See Mortimer, K. P. jt. auth.

Johnson, Myra T.
Asexual and autoerotic women: two invisible groups. *In* Gochros, H. L. and Gochros, J. S. eds. The sexually oppressed p96-109

Johnson, Nelson Trusler

About

Wood, H. J. Nelson Trusler Johnson: the diplomacy of benevolent pragmatism. *In* Burns, R. D. and Bennett, E. M. eds. Diplomats in crisis p7-26

Johnson, Pamela Hansford
About individual works
On iniquity

Borowitz, A. The Snows on the Moors: C. P. Snow and Pamela Hansford Johnson on the Moors murder case. *In* Borowitz, A. Innocence and arsenic p 1-25

Johnson, Paul J.
Hobbes's Anglican doctrine of salvation. *In* Ross, R. G.; Schneider, H. W. and Waldman, T. eds. Thomas Hobbes in his time p102-25

Johnson, Robert Bowie. See Galloway, K. B. jt. auth.

Johnson, William, afterwards Cory. See Cory, William Johnson

Johnson, William Arthur

The impact of price controls on the oil industry: how to worsen an energy crisis. *In* Eppen, G. D. ed. Energy: the policy issues p99-121

Why U.S. energy policy has failed. *In* Kalter, R. J. and Vogely, W. A. eds. Energy supply and government policy p280-305

Johnston, Claire

Women's cinema as counter-cinema. *In* Nichols, B. ed. Movies and methods p208-17

Johnston, George

About

Jones, L. W. The cruising auk and the world below. *In* Woodcock, G. ed. Poets and critics p71-79

Johnston, George Henry

About individual works

Clean straw for nothing

Lawson, A. "Where a man belongs": Hal Porter's The paper chase and George Johnston's Clean straw for nothing. *In* Hamilton, K. G. ed. Studies in the recent Australian novel p168-93

Johnston, H. N.; Klein, Lawrence Robert, and Shinjo, K.

Estimation and prediction in dynamic econometric models. *In* Econometrics and economic theory p27-56

Johnston, Margaret Elaine

Surprised by joy: the world of picturebooks. *In* Egoff, S. A. ed. One ocean touching p147-54

Johnstone, Henry Webb

From philosophy to rhetoric and back. *In* Burks, D. M. ed. Rhetoric, philosophy, and literature: an exploration p49-66

Johnstone, John Keith

About individual works

The Bloomsbury group

Balakian, N. Spearhead of British modernism. *In* Balakian, N. Critical encounters p194-97

Joint authors. See Authorship—Collaboration

Joint-stock companies. See Stock companies

Jokes. See Wit and humor

Jolas, Eugène

About

McMillan, D. Getting into print. *In* McMillan, D. Transition p9-26

McMillan, D. Revolution and synthesis: the growth of a theory. *In* McMillan, D. Transition p40-61

McMillan, D. Subversion and quest: the first year. *In* McMillan, D. Transition p27-39

Jolas, Tina, and Zonabend, Françoise Flis

Tillers of the fields and woodspeople. *In* Rural society in France p126-51

Jomini, Antoine Henri, Baron. See Jomini, Henri, Baron

Jomini, Henri, Baron

About

Hagerman, E. H. From Jomini to Dennis Hart Mahan: the evolution of trench warfare and the American Civil War. *In* Hubbell, J. T. ed. Battles lost and won p31-54

Jonas, Doris F.

Life, death, awareness, and concern: a progression. *In* Life after death p169-81

Jonas, Manfred

Isolationism. *In* Encyclopedia of American foreign policy p496-506

Jonas, Susanne (Bodenheimer) See Bodenheimer, Susanne Jonas

Jonathan, Gérard Cohen, and Jacqué, Jean-Paul

Obligations assumed by the Helsinki signatories. *In* Human rights, international law and the Helsinki Accord p43-70

Jones, A. M.

African music in Northern Rhodesia and some other places. *In* The Occasional papers of the Rhodes-Livingstone Museum p71-144

Jones, Aubrey

Inflation as an industrial problem. In Skidelsky, R. J. A. ed. The end of the Keynesian era p50-58

Jones, Bridget

Léon Damas. *In* King, B. A. and Ogungbesan, K. eds. A celebration of Black and African writing p60-73

Jones, Charles Oscar

Somebody must be trusted: an essay on leadership of the U.S. Congress. *In* Ornstein, N. J. ed. Congress in change p265-76

Jones, Charles William

Carolingian aesthetics: why modular verse, *In* Viator: medieval and Renaissance studies v6 p309-40

Jones, Christopher Prestige

Julius Naso and Julius Secundus. *In* Harvard Studies in classical philology v72 p279-88

A leading family of Roman Thespiae. *In* Harvard Studies in classical philology v74 p223-55

The Plancii of Perge and Diana Planciana. *In* Harvard Studies in classical philology v80 p231-37

Tange Chloen semel arrogantem. *In* Harvard Studies in classical philology v75 p81-83

The teacher of Plutarch. *In* Harvard Studies in classical philology v71 p205-13

Jones, Chuck

About

Thompson, R. Meep meep. *In* Nichols, B. ed. Movies and methods p126-35

Jones, Clinton R.

Christopher Isherwood and the religious quest. *In* Crew, L. ed. The gay academic p350-60

Jones, David, 1895-1974

The dying Gaul, and other writings

Contents

Art in relation to war

An aspect of the art of England

A Christmas message, 1960

The death of Harold

The dying Gaul

In illo tempore

An introduction to The rime of the ancient mariner

A London artist looks at contemporary Wales

Notes on the 1930s

Jonson, Ben—*Continued*

About individual works

The alchemist

Young, D. P. Where the bee sucks: A triangular study of Doctor Faustus, The alchemist, and The tempest. *In* Shakespeare's romances reconsidered p149-66

Bartholomew Fair

Heffner, R. L. Unifying symbols in the comedy of Ben Jonson. *In* Wimsatt, W. K. ed. Literary criticism: idea and act p346-61

Catiline

Champion, L. S. Jonson: Sejanus, Catiline. *In* Champion, L. S. Tragic patterns in Jacobean and Caroline drama p62-88

Epicoene; or, The silent woman

Heffner, R. L. Unifying symbols in the comedy of Ben Jonson. *In* Wimsatt, W. K. ed. Literary criticism: idea and act p346-61

Every man in his humor

Altman, J. B. Inventing answers in English comedy. *In* Altman, J. B. The Tudor play of mind p148-95

Hymenaei

Gordon, D. J. Hymenæi: Ben Jonson's masque of union. *In* Gordon, D. J. The Renaissance imagination p157-84

Lord Haddington's masque [The hue and cry after Cupid]

Gordon, D. J. Ben Jonson's Haddington masque: the story and the fable. *In* Gordon, D. J. The Renaissance imagination p185-93

Masque of beauty

Gordon, D. J. The imagery of Ben Jonson's Masques of blacknesse and beautie. *In* Gordon, D. J. The Renaissance imagination p134-56

Masque of blackness

Gordon, D. J. The imagery of Ben Jonson's Masques of blacknesse and beautie. *In* Gordon, D. J. The Renaissance imagination p134-56

Sejanus

Champion, L. S. Jonson: Sejanus, Catiline. *In* Champion, L. S. Tragic patterns in Jacobean and Caroline drama p62-88

Hunter, G. K. A Roman thought: Renaissance attitudes to history exemplified in Shakespeare and Jonson. *In* An English miscellany p93-118

To Penshurst

Manlove, C. N. Jonson and Herrick. *In* Manlove, C. N. Literature and reality, 1600-1800 p16-29

Volpone

Parker, R. B. Volpone and Reynard the Fox. *In* Renaissance drama [1976] p3-42

Salinger, L. Comic form in Ben Jonson: Volpone and the philosopher's stone. *In* English drama: forms and development p48-68

Bibliography

Godshalk, W. L. Ben Jonson. *In* Logan, T. P. and Smith, D. S. eds. The new intellectuals p3-116

Bibliography—Folios

Williams, W. P. Chetwin, Crooke, and the Jonson folios. *In* Virginia. University. Bibliographical Society. Studies in bibliography v30 p75-95

Characters—Volpone

Salinger, L. Comic form in Ben Jonson: Volpone and the philosopher's stone. *In* English drama: forms and development p48-68

Criticism and interpretation

Donaldson, I. Jonson and the moralists. *In* Kernan, A. B. ed. Two Renaissance mythmakers p146-64

Poetic works

Newton, R. C. "Ben./Jonson": the poet in the poems. *In* Kernan, A. B. ed. Two Renaissance mythmakers p165-95

Joost, Nicholas

About individual works

Scofield Thayer and The Dial

Balakian, N. A passion for letters: Scofield Thayer and The Dial. *In* Balakian, N. Critical encounters p198-202

Joost, Nicholas T.

The traveller as antihero: Richard Smith Elliott in the Mexican War. *In* Kagle, S. E. ed. America: exploration and travel p83-91

Joravsky, David

The construction of the Stalinist psyche. *In* Cultural revolution in Russia, 1928-1931 p105-28

What do we ask of the history of technology? *In* Bugliarello, G. and Doner, D. B. eds. The history and philosophy of technology p128-34

Jordan, David P.

Edward Gibbon: the historian of the Roman Empire. *In* Edward Gibbon and The decline and fall of the Roman Empire p 1-12

Jordan, Elijah

About

Rucker, E. D. Institutions and the alienated man. *In* Philosophy and the civilizing arts p283-315

Jordan, Furneaux. See Jordan, Robert Furneaux

Jordan, Robert

Berthold Lubetkin. *In* Sharp, D. ed. The rationalists p101-17

Jordan, Robert Furneaux

About individual works

Victorian architecture

Watkin, D. The theme in the twentieth century: Furneaux Jordan. *In* Watkin, D. Morality and architecture p61-68

Jordan, Robert Welsh

Vico and Husserl: history and historical science. *In* Giambattista Vico's science of humanity p251-61

Jordan, Terry G.

Vegetational perception and choice of settlement site in frontier Texas. *In* Pattern and process p244-57

Jordan, Vernon Eulion

Blacks and American foundations: Attitudes and outlook. *In* The Black American reference book p485-91

Jordan, William C.
Supplying Aigues-Mortes for the Crusade of 1248: the problem of restructuring trade. *In* Order and innovation in the Middle Ages p165-72

Jordan, Winthrop Donaldson
Searching for adulthood in America. *In* Erikson, E. H. ed. Adulthood p189-99

Jordan

History

Mousa, S. The rise of Arab nationalism and the emergence of Transjordan. *In* Nationalism in a non-national state p239-63

Jordan (Territory under Israeli occupation, 1967-) See Civil rights—Jordan (Territory under Israeli occupation, 1967-)

Jordy, William H.
Four approaches to regionalism in the visual arts of the 1930s. *In* Luedtke, L. S. ed. The study of American culture p19-48

Jorgens, Jack J.
Shakespeare on film

Contents

Defining Macbeth: Schaefer, Welles, and Kurosawa
Franco Zeffirelli's Romeo and Juliet
Franco Zeffirelli's Taming of the shrew
Grigori Kozintsev's Hamlet
Joseph Mankiewicz's Julius Caesar
King Lear: Peter Brook and Grigori Kozintsev
Laurence Oliver's Hamlet
Laurence Olivier's Henry V
Laurence Olivier's Richard III
Max Reinhardt and William Dieterle's A midsummer night's dream
Orson Welles's Chimes at midnight (Falstaff)
Orson Welles's Othello
Peter Hall's A midsummer night's dream
Realizing Shakespeare on film
Roman Polanski's Macbeth
Stuart Burge and John Dexter's Othello

Jorgensen, Paul Alfred
Shakespeare's brave new world. *In* First images of America p83-89

Jorgenson, Dale W.
The economic theory of replacement and depreciation. *In* Econometrics and economic theory p190-221

Joseph II, Emperor of Germany

About

Andre, J. and Fröschle, H. The American expedition of Emperor Joseph II and Bernhard Moll's silhouettes. *In* The German contribution to the building of the Americas p135-72

Joseph, Gerhard
Imperial criticism. *In* Review, v 1 1979 p75-80

Joseph, M. S.
Trade unions in Western Europe politics. *in* Hayward, J. E. S. and Berki, R. N. eds. State and society in contemporary Europe p75-91

Joseph, Suad
Women and the neighborhood street in Borj Hammoud, Lebanon. *In* Beck, L. and Keddie, N. R. eds. Women in the Muslim world p541-57

Joseph of Arimathea

Legends

Lagorio, V. M. The Joseph of Arimathie: English hagiography in transition. *In* Medievalia et humanistica no. 6 p91-101

Josephson, Matthew

About

Smelstor, M. R. Expatriation and exploration: the exiled artists of the 1920s. *In* Kagle, S. E. ed. America: exploration and travel p136-52

Tashjian, D. L. Broom and Secession. *In* Tashjian, D. L. Skyscraper primitives p116-42

Josephus, Flavius

About

Feldman, L. H. Josephus as an apologist to the Greco-Roman world: his portrait of Solomon. *In* Aspects of religious propaganda in Judaism and early Christianity p69-98

Joshi, Gajanan Narayan
Metaphysics. *In* Bishop, D. H. ed. Indian thought p176-96

Josipovici, Gabriel
'But time will not relent': modern literature and the experience of time. *In* Josipovici, G. ed. The modern English novel: the reader, the writer and the work p252-72

The lessons of modernism

Contents

An art for the wilderness: Franz Kafka, 1883-1924
English studies and European culture
Fernando Pessoa, 1888-1935
The importance of Stockhausen's Inori
The lessons of modernism
Linearity and fragmentation
Maxwell Davies's Taverner: thoughts on the libretto
The rake's progress
Saul Bellow
Two moments in modern music-theatre
Walter Benjamin, 1892-1940
Words and music today

Joslin, David. See Part 2 under title: War and economic development

Journal des Sçavans
Crisafulli, A. S. The Journal des Sçavans and The Lettres persanes. *In* Literature and history in the age of ideas p59-66

Journal encyclopédique ou universel
Wilkins, K. Attitudes toward women in two eighteenth-century French periodicals. *In* Studies in eighteenth-century culture v6 p393-406

Journalism
Farrell, J. T. Journalism or creative writing course? *In* Farrell, J. T. Literary essays, 1954-1974 p136-38

Janowitz, M. The journalistic profession and the mass media. *In* Culture and its creators p72-96

See also Government and the press; Liberty of the press; Newspapers; Press; Press councils; Television broadcasting of news

Political aspects

Lowenstein, R. L. Press freedom as a barometer of political democracy. *In* Fischer, H. D. and Merrill, J. C. eds. International and intercultural communication p136-47

Journalism—Political aspects—*Continued*

Merrıll, J. C. A conceptual overview of world journalism; excerpts from "Imperative of freedom." *In* Fischer, H. D. and Merrill, J. C. eds. International and intercultural communication p18-28

Meyer, E. The bilateral and multilateral meetings of the International Press Institute. *In* Unofficial diplomats p56-65

Sussman, L. R. Developmental journalism: the ideological factor. *In* Horton, P. C. ed. The Third World and press freedom p74-92

See also Press and politics

Societies, etc.

Gardner, M. A. The evolution of the Inter American Press Association. *In* Fischer, H. D. and Merrill, J. C. eds. International and intercultural communication p392-404

Koszyk, K. The development of the International Press Institute. *In* Fischer, H. D. and Merrill, J. C. eds. International and intercultural communication p372-76

Sarkar, C. Journalists' organizations in Socialist society. *In* Fischer, H. D. and Merrill, J. C. eds. International and intercultural communication p37-50

Arab countries

Gawad, M. A. Attempts of the Arab world to participate in balancing the flow of information. *In* Horton, P. C. ed. The Third World and press freedom p173-86

Argentine Republic

Kraiselburd, R. Establishing and maintaining a free press: a Latin American viewpoint. *In* Horton, P. C. ed. The Third World and press freedom p156-61

Asia

Matlub Ali, S. DEPTHnews: a model for a Third World feature agency. *In* Horton, P. C. ed. The Third World and press freedom p187-96

India

Verghese, G. Press censorship under Indira Gandhi. *In* Horton, P. C. ed. The Third World and press freedom p220-30

Underdeveloped areas

See Underdeveloped areas—Journalism

United States

Grant, G. Journalism and social science: continuities and discontinuities. *In* On the making of Americans p291-313

United States—Historiography

Nevins, A. American journalism and its historical treatment. *In* Nevins, A. Allan Nevins on history p82-102

Vienna

Bailey, L. H. Ferdinand Kürnberger, Friedrich Schlögl and the feuilleton in Gründerzeit Vienna. *In* Branscombe, P. ed. Austrian life and literature, 1780-1938 p59-71

Yugoslavia

Ivacic, P. Toward a freer and multidimensional flow of information. *In* Horton, P. C. ed. The Third World and press freedom p135-50

Journalism, Communist

Prokhorov, Y. The Marxist press concept. *In* Fischer, H. D. and Merrill, J. C. eds. International and intercultural communication p51-58

Journalism, Pictorial. See Photography, Journalistic

Journalistic ethics

Reed, I. An American romance. *In* Reed, I. Shrovetide in old New Orleans p50-52

Journalistic photography. See Photography, Journalistic

Journalists

Communist countries

Sarkar, C. Journalists' organizations in Socialist society. *In* Fischer, H. D. and Merrill, J. C. eds. International and intercultural communication p37-50

Journalists, Afro-American. See Afro-American journalists

The journey of the fifth horse (criticism) Ribman, R. *In* Kauffmann, S. Persons of the drama p173-75

Jouvenel, Bertrand de

An economic view of marine problems. *In* Borgese, E. M. and Krieger, D. eds. The tides of change p4-32

About

Slevin, C. Bertrand de Jouvenel: efficiency and amenity. *In* De Crespigny, A. and Minogue, K. R. eds. Contemporary political philosophers p168-90

Jowett, Garth

Bullets, beer and the Hays Office: Public enemy. *In* O'Connor, J. E. and Jackson, M. A. eds. American history/American film p57-75

Joxe, Alain

The Chilean Armed Forces and the making of the Coup. *In* O'Brien, P. J. ed. Allende's Chile p244-72

Joy

Ness, A. The place of joy in a world of fact. *In* Against pollution and hunger p297-307

See also Happiness

Joyaux, Georges J.

Roch Carrier's trilogy: a second look at Quebec's dark years. *In* Essays in honor of Russel B. Nye p105-28

Joyce, James

About

Adams, R. M. Joyce. *In* Adams, R. M. Afterjoyce p3-35

Adams, R. M. Three thematic interludes. *In* Adams, R. M. Afterjoyce p36-64

Anderson, C. G. Baby Tuckoo: Joyce's "features of infancy." *In* Staley, T. F. and Benstock, B. eds. Approaches to Joyce's Portrait p135-68

Gillie, C. Diversification of the novel, 1920-1930. *In* Gillie, C. Movements in English literature, 1900-1940 p90-121

Goodheart, E. The blasphemy of Joycean art. *In* Goodheart, E. The failure of criticism p158-74

Hampshire, S. Joyce and Vico: the middle way. *In* Giambattista Vico's science of humanity p321-32

Hardy, B. N. James Joyce. *In* Hardy, B. N. Tellers and listeners p206-76

Joyce, William L. and Hall, Michael Gari-baldi

Three manuscripts of Increase Mather. *In* American Antiquarian Society. Proceedings v86 pt 1 p113-23

Joynt, Carey Bonthron

Behavioural sciences in international relations. *In* The Year book of world affairs, 1979 p224-42

Ju/wāsi (African people) *See* !Kung (African people)

Juan, Don. *See* Don Juan

Juana Inés de la Cruz, Sister

About

Paz, O. Sor Juana Inés de la Cruz. *In* Paz, O. The siren & the seashell p3-15

Juda, Lawrence

International environmental concern: perspectives of and implications for developing states. *In* Orr, D. W. and Soroos, M. S. eds. The global predicament p90-107

Judah, J. Stillson

The Hare Krishna movement. *In* Zaretsky, I. I. and Leone, M. P. eds. Religious movements in contemporary America p463-78

New religions and religious liberty. *In* Needleman, J. and Baker, G. eds. Understanding the new religions p201-08

Judaism

Borowitz, E. B. A Jewish response: the lure and limits of universalizing our faith. *In* Christian faith in a religiously plural world p59-68

Davis, M. The Jewish people in metamorphosis. *In* Tradition and change in Jewish experience p 1-25

Fox, M. Judaism, secularism and textual interpretation. *In* Modern Jewish ethics p3-26

Kaufman, W. E. Toward a return to clarity. *In* Kaufman, W. E. Contemporary Jewish philosophies p12-24

Konvitz, M. R. Individual conscience or group consciousness: religious liberty in the United States and Israel. *In* Konvitz, M. R. Judaism and the American idea p139-59

Konvitz, M. R. Life and liberty for the pursuit of happiness. *In* Konvitz, M. R. Judaism and the American idea p181-201

See also Mysticism—Judaism; Sabbath

History

Silberman, L. H. American impact: Judaism in the United States in the early nineteenth century. *In* Tradition and change in Jewish experience p89-105

History—To 70 A.D.

Petersen, D. L. Max Weber and the sociological study of ancient Israel. *In* Johnson, H. M. ed. Religious change and continuity p117-49

History—Pre-Talmudic period, 586 B.C.-10 A.D.

See Judaism—History—Post-exilic period, 586 B.C.-210 A.D.

History—Post-exilic period, 586 B.C.-210 A.D.—Bibliography

Goldin, J. Early and classical Judaism. *In* Adams, C. J. ed. A reader's guide to the great religions p283-320

Momigliano, A. Eastern elements in Post-exilic Jewish, and Greek, historiography. *In* Momigliano, A. Essays in ancient and modern historiography p25-35

Momigliano, A. The fault of the Greeks. *In* Momigliano, A. Essays in ancient and modern historiography p9-23

History—Greco-Roman period, 332 B.C.-210 A.D.

See Judaism—History—Post-exilic period, 586 B.C.-210 A.D.

History—Inter-testamental period, 140 B.C.-30 A.D.

See Judaism—History—Post-exilic period, 586 B.C.-210 A.D.

History—Talmudic period, 10-425

Neusner, J. Politics and theology in Talmudic Babylonia. *In* Tradition and change in Jewish experience p46-74

History—Talmudic period, 10-425—Bibliography

Cain, S. Medieval and modern Judaism. *In* Adams, C. J. ed. A reader's guide to the great religions p321-44

History—Medieval and early modern period, 425-1789—Bibliography

Cain, S Medieval and modern Judaism. *In* Adams, C. J. ed A reader's guide to the great religions p321-44

History—Modern period, 1750-

Gordis, R. Jewish tradition in the modern world: conservation and renewal. *In* Tradition and change in Jewish experience p141-68

History—Modern period, 1750-Bibliography

Cain, S. Medieval and modern Judaism. *In* Adams, C. J. ed. A reader's guide to the great religions p321-44

Liturgy and ritual

See Jews. Liturgy and ritual

Reform movement

See Reform Judaism

Relations—Christianity

Grayzel, S. Pope Alexander III and the Jews. *In* Salo Wittmayer Baron v2 p555-72

20th century

Kaufman, W. E. Introduction: The crisis of meaning. *In* Kaufman, W. E. Contemporary Jewish philosophies p3-11

Levenson, J. R. The choice of Jewish identity. *In* Meisner, M. J. and Murphey, R. eds. The Mozartian historian p180-93

Yaron, Z. Religion and morality in Israel and in the Dispersion. *In* Modern Jewish ethics p228-42

Europe

Dawidowicz, L. S. Jewish identity: a matter of fate, a matter of choice. *In* Dawidowicz, L. S. The Jewish presence p3-31

Israel

Yaron, Z. Religion and morality in Israel and in the Dispersion. *In* Modern Jewish ethics p228-42

Judaism—*Continued*

Portugal—History

Yerushalmi, Y. H. Professing Jews in post-expulsion Spain and Portugal. *In* Salo Wittmayer Baron v2 p1009-22

Spain—History

Yerushalmi, Y. H. Professing Jews in post-expulsion Spain and Portugal. *In* Salo Wittmayer Baron v2 p1009-22

United States

Dawidowicz, L. S. Middle-class Judaism. *In* Dawidowicz, L. S. The Jewish presence p67-91

United States—History

Herberg, W. Judaism in America; excerpt from "Protestant, Catholic, Jew." *In* Mulder, J. M. and Wilson, J. F. eds. Religion in American history p379-96

Judaism, Reform. See Reform Judaism

Judaism and democracy

Konvitz, M. R. Judaism and the democratic ideal. *In* Konvitz, M. R. Judaism and the American idea p69-90

Judaism and philosophy

Copleston, F. C. Philosophy and religion in Judaism and Christianity. *In* Copleston, F. C. Philosophers and philosophies p29-42

Fox, M. Judaism, secularism and textual interpretation. *In* Modern Jewish ethics p3-26

Judaism and science

Fox, M. Judaism, secularism and textual interpretation. *In* Modern Jewish ethics p3-26

Judaism and state. See Zionism

Judaism in literature

Derrida, J. Edmond Jabès and the question of the book. *In* Derrida, J. Writing and difference p64-78

Judas Maccabeus in literature

Schrickx, W. 'Pericles' in a book-list of 1619 from the English Jesuit mission and some of the play's special problems. *In* Shakespeare survey v29 p21-32

Judd, Laurence C.

Social change in Commune Baw, Thailand, 1958-1967. *In* Social organization and the applications of anthropology p210-34

Judges

See also Judicial discretion; Judicial process

Appointment, qualifications, tenure, etc.

MacKenzie, J. P. Of judges and the ABA. *In* Nader, R. and Green, M. J. eds. Verdicts on lawyers p33-46

Schmidt, J. R. Lawyers on judges: competence and selection. *In* Nader, R. and Green, M. J. eds. Verdicts on lawyers p285-94

Correspondence

Ravitz, J. C. Reflections of a radical judge: beyond the courtroom. *In* Nader, R. and Green, M. J. eds. Verdicts on lawyers p255-68

Chicago

Schmidt, J. R. Lawyers on judges: competence and selection. *In* Nader, R. and Green, M. J. eds. Verdicts on lawyers p285-94

New York (City)

Newfield, J. The ten worst judges. *In* Nader, R. and Green, M. J. eds. Verdicts on lawyers p269-84

Judgment

Denneny, M. The privilege of ourselves: Hannah Arendt on judgment. *In* Hannah Arendt: the recovery of the public world p245-74

See also Attitude change; Common sense

Judgment (Ethics)

Foot, P. Goodness and choice. *In* Foot, P. Virtues and vices, and other essays in moral philosophy p132-47

Foot, P. Hume on moral judgement. *In* Foot, P. Virtues and vices, and other essays in moral philosophy p74-80

Hampshire, S. On having a reason. *In* Royal Institute of Philosophy. Human values p86-98

Hampshire, S. Public and private morality. *In* Hampshire, S. ed. Public and private morality p23-53

Kohlberg, L. Justice as reversibility. *In* Laslett, P. and Fishkin, J. eds. Philosophy, politics and society p257-72

Scruton, R. Reason and happiness. *In* Royal Institute of Philosophy. Nature and conduct p139-61

Zaw, S. K. 'Irresistible impulse' and moral responsibility. *In* Royal Institute of Philosophy. Human values p99-134

Judgment (Logic)

Harrison, R. The concept of prepredicative experience. *In* Pivčević, E. ed. Phenomenology and philosophical understanding p93-107

Stock, G. Wittgenstein on Russell's theory of judgment. *In* Royal Institute of Philosophy. Understanding Wittgenstein p62-75

See also Prediction (Logic); Reasoning

Judgment Day. See Second Advent

Judgment Day in literature

Lascelles, M. 'King Lear' and doomsday. *In* Shakespeare survey 26 p69-79

Judgments

Vavuris, S. L. On the civil liberties of sect members: Part 2. *In* Horowitz, I. L. ed. Science, sin, and scholarship p198-207

See also Judicial opinions

Judgments, Criminal. See Sentences (Criminal procedure)

Judicial behavior. See Judicial process

Judicial decision-making. See Judicial process

Judicial discretion

Davis, K. C. The inquiry—the subject, objectives, background, and method. *In* Davis, K. C. Discretionary justice in Europe and America p 1-15

Germany

Herrmann, J. The German prosecutor. *In* Davis, K. C. Discretionary justice in Europe and America p16-74

Great Britain

James, Sir A. E. A judicial note on the control of discretion in the administration of criminal justice. *In* Crime, criminology and public policy p157-59

Judicial discretion—Great Britain—_Continued_

Thomas, D. A. The control of discretion in the administration of criminal justice. _In_ Crime, criminology and public policy p139-55

Judicial ethics

Newfield, J. The ten worst judges. _In_ Nader, R. and Green, M. J. eds. Verdicts on lawyers p269-84

Judicial opinions

United States

Jacobstein, J. M. Some reflections on the control of the publication of Appellate Court opinions. _In_ Stanford legal essays p267-75

Judicial power

See also Separation of powers

United States

Graham, G. J. The Supreme Court. _In_ Graham, G. J. and Graham, S. G. eds. Founding principles of American government p258-79

Judicial process

See also Evidence (Law)

United States

Baar, C. Judicial behavior and comparative rights policy. _In_ Claude, R. P. ed. Comparative human rights p353-81

Judicial review

United States

Graham, G J. The Supreme Court. _In_ Graham, G. J. and Graham, S. G. eds. Founding principles of American government p258-79

Grey, T. C. Do we have an unwritten Constitution? _In_ Stanford legal essays p179-94

Harris, R. J. Judicial review: vagaries and varieties. _In_ Havard, W. C. and Bernd, J. L. eds. 200 years of the Republic in restrospect p173-208

Rabin, R. L. Preclusion of judicial review in the processing of claims for veterans' benefits: a preliminary analysis. _In_ Stanford legal essays p381-99

Judith (Anglo-Saxon poem)

Chamberlain, D. S. Judith: a fragmentary and political poem. _In_ Anglo-Saxon poetry: essays in appreciation p135-59

Raffel, B. Judith: hypermetricity and rhetoric. _In_ Anglo-Saxon poetry: essays in appreciation p124-34

Judson, Jay Richard

Rubens and Moretus. _In_ Medieval and Renaissance studies 1976 p141-59

Juergensmeyer, Mark

Radhasoami as a trans-national movement. _In_ Needleman, J. and Baker, G. eds. Understanding the new religions p190-200

Jugo, Miguel de Unamuno y. See Unamuno y Jugo, Miguel de

Juhasz, Suzanne

Seeking the exit or the home: poetry and salvation in the career of Anne Sexton. _In_ Gilbert, S. M. and Gubar, S. eds. Shakespeare's sisters p261-68

Julia, Dominique. See Frijhoff, W. jt. auth.

Juliana, Saint, of Nicomedia

Legend

Wittig, J. S. Figural narrative in Cynewulf's Juliana. _In_ Anglo-Saxon England 4 p37-55

Juliani, Richard N.

Social change and the athlete. _In_ Gerstl, J. E. and Jacobs, G. eds. Professions for the people p61-94

Julius II, Pope

About

Moos, S. von. The palace as a fortress: Rome and Bologna under Pope Julius II. _In_ Millon, H. A. and Nochlin, L. eds. Art and architecture in the service of politics p46-79

Julius Naso

About

Jones, C. P. Julius Naso and Julius Secundus. _In_ Harvard Studies in classical philology v72 p279-88

Julius Secundus

About

Jones, C. P. Julius Naso and Julius Secundus. _In_ Harvard Studies in classical philology v72 p279-88

Julius Caesar (Motion picture)

Jorgens, J. J. Joseph Mankiewicz's Julius Caesar. _In_ Jorgens, J. J. Shakespeare on film p92-105

Jullian, Philippe

About individual works

Oscar Wilde

Connolly, C. Oscar Wilde and Henry James: an imaginary transmogrification. _In_ Connolly, C. The evening colonnade p171-74

Jump, John Davies

Byron's prose. _In_ Jump, J. D. ed. Byron p16-34

Jumpers (criticism) Stoppard, T. _In_ Kauffmann, S. Persons of the drama p239-42

Junco Meyer, Victoria. See Meyer, Victoria Junco

Jung, Carl Gustav

See also Freud, S. jt. auth.

About

Karier, C. J. The ethics of a therapeutic man. _In_ Kren, G. M. and Rappoport, L. H. eds. Varieties of psychohistory p333-63

May, K. M. The living self. _In_ May, K. M. Out of the maelstrom p43-61

Olney, J. L. The esoteric flower: Yeats and Jung. _In_ Yeats and the occult p27-54

Schwyzer, H. R. The intellect in Plotinus and the archetypes of C. G. Jung. _In_ Kephalaion p214-22

About individual works

Memories, dreams, reflections

Connolly, C. Carl Jung. _In_ Connolly, C. The evening colonnade p405-07

Psychology and alchemy

Frye, N. Forming fours. _In_ Frye, N. Northrop Frye on culture and literature p117-29

Two essays on analytical psychology

Frye, N. Forming fours. _In_ Frye, N. Northrop Frye on culture and literature p117-29

Jung, Eugène

About

Kedourie, É. The politics of political literature: Kawakibi, Azoury and Jung. *In* Kedourie, É. Arabic political memoirs and other studies p107-23

Jung, Franz

About individual works

Der Weg nach unten

Middleton, J. C. The alienated self. *In* Middleton, J. C. Bolshevism in art p87-91

Jung, Udo O. H.

Jean Toomer, Fern. *In* Bruck, P. ed. The Black American short story in the 20th century p53-69

Jünger, Ernst

About individual works

On the marble cliffs

Evans, A. R. Ernst Jünger's Auf de Marmorklippen: a sketch toward an interpretation. *In* Symbolism and modern literature p26-62

The storm of steel

Stern, J. P. The embattled style: Ernst Jünger, In Stahlgewittern. *In* Klein, H. M. ed. The First World War in fiction p112-25

Jungk, Robert

Toward an experimental society. *In* Bundy, R. F. ed. Images of the future: the twenty-first century and beyond p135-40

Jungnickel, Christa

Teaching and research in the physical sciences and mathematics in Saxony, 1820-1850. *In* Historical studies in the physical sciences v10 p3-47

Junior Bonner (Motion picture)

Kauffmann, S. Junior Bonner. *In* Kauffmann, S. Living images p129-32

Junior college students

United States

London, H. B. The perils of opportunity: the working-class community college student in sociological perspective *In* Hurdles p145-92

Junior colleges. See Community colleges

Junius, Hadrianus

About

Gordon, D. J. Veritas filia temporis: Hadrianus Junius and Geoffrey Whitney. *In* Gordon, D. J. The Renaissance imagination p220-32

Junius XI (Manuscript) See Genesis (Anglo-Saxon poem)

Jupiter

Art

Hill, D. K. Jupiter: variations on the theme of Olympian Zeus. *In* Studies in classical art and archaeology p247-50

Jupiter (Planet)

Lewis, J. S. The outer planets. *In* Man and cosmos p117-30

Jupp, James

Five Sinhalese nationalist politicians. *In* The Making of politicians: studies from Africa and Asia p183-94

Modernization and pluralism: Ceylon and Malaysia. *In* Leftwich, A. ed. South Africa: economic growth and political change p187-211

Jurisdiction. See Criminal jurisdiction

Jurisdiction (International law)

Claude, I. L. Domestic jurisdiction and colonialism. *In* Kilson, M. ed. New states in the modern world p121-35

Henkin, L. Human rights and "domestic jurisdiction." *In* Human rights, international law and the Helsinki Accord p21-40

See also International courts

Jurisdiction, Domestic. See Jurisdiction (International law)

Jurisdiction, International.. See Jurisdiction (International law)

Jurisdiction, Territorial. See Territorial waters

Jurisdiction over ships at sea. See Blockade

Jurisprudence

Barton, J. H. Behind the legal explosion. *In* Stanford legal essays p43-60

Danzig, R. A comment on the jurisprudence of the Uniform Commercial Code. *In* Stanford legal essays p97-111

Golding, M. P. Principled decision-making and the Supreme Court. *In* Summers, R. S. ed. Essays in legal philosophy p208-36

Honoré, A. M. Social justice. *In* Summers, R. S. ed. Essays in legal philosophy p61-94

Lucas, J. R. On processes for resolving disputes; excerpt from "The principles of politics." *In* Summers, R. S. ed. Essays in legal philosophy p167-82

Podgorecki, A. Jurisprudence empirically tested. *In* Crime, criminology and public policy p297-317

Scott, K. E. Two models of the civil process. *In* Stanford legal essays p413-26

Williams, G. L. The concept of legal liberty. *In* Summers, R. S. ed. Essays in legal philosophy p121-45

See also Law—Philosophy

History—United States

Horwitz, M. J. The jurisprudence of Brown and the dilemmas of liberalism. *In* Have we overcome? Race relations since

Jury

Babcock, B. A. Voir dire: preserving "its Brown p173-87

wonderful power." *In* Stanford legal essays p21-41

United States

Shuman, I. G. and Mowen, J. The jury system: old problems and a new alternative. *In* Contemporary issues in criminal justice p59-75

Sperlich, P. W. Trial by jury: it may have a future. *In* The Supreme Court review, 1978 p191-224

Just war doctrine

Brundage, J. A. Holy war and the medieval lawyers. *In* The Holy war p99-140

Johnson, J. T. Just war, the Nixon Doctrine and the future shape of American military policy. *In* The Year book of world affairs, 1975 p137-54

Justice, Donald

Meters and memory. *In* Gross, H. S. ed. The structure of verse p269-76

Justice

Billet, L. Justice, liberty and economy. *In* Glahe, F. R. ed. Adam Smith and The wealth of nations p83-109

Justice—*Continued*

Buchanan, J. M. The justice of natural liberty. *In* Glahe, F. R. ed. Adam Smith and The wealth of nations p61-81

Feibleman, J. K. Philosophical perspectives on justice. *In* Perspectives on justice p75-117

Hartman, R. S. The value structure of justice. *In* The Abdication of philosophy: philosophy and the public good p129-56

Hoffman, R. Justice, merit, and the good. *In* Gross, B. R. ed. Reverse discrimination p358-72

Kohlberg, L. Justice as reversibility. *In* Laslett, P. and Fishkin, J. eds. Philosophy, politics and society p257-72

Myers, R. J. An approximation of justice. *In* [Truth and tragedy]: a tribute to Hans Morgenthau p125-29

Newton, L. H. Reverse discrimination as unjustified. *In* Gross, B. R. ed. Reverse discrimination p373-78

Rae, D. W. A principle of simple justice. *In* Laslett, P. and Fishkin J. eds. Philosophy, politics and society p134-54

Rawls, J. A well-ordered society. *In* Laslett, P. and Fishkin, J. eds. Philosophy, politics and society p6-20

Reiman, J. H. Doing justice to criminology: reflections on the implications for criminology of recent developments in the philosophy of justice. *In* Riedel, M. and Chappell, D. eds. Issues in criminal justice: planning and evaluation p134-43

Richards, H. Productive justice. *In* Aiken, W. and La Follette, H. eds. World hunger and moral obligation p165-79

Rist, J. M. The Stoic concept of detachment. *In* Rist, J. M. ed. The Stoics p259-72

Taylor, T. The concept of justice and the laws of war. *In* Perspectives on justice p3-35

Veatch, R. M. Justice. *In* Population policy and ethics p31-39

See also Social justice

Justice, Administration of. See Criminal justice, Administration of; Due process of law; Speedy trial

Justice in literature

Bowers, F. T. Samson Agonistes: justice and reconciliation. *In* The Dress of words p 1-23

Havelock, E. A. The justice of Aeschylus. *In* Havelock, E. A. The Greek concept of justice p272-95

Havelock, E. A. The justice of Herodotus. *In* Havelock, E. A. The Greek concept of justice p296-307

Havelock, E. A. The justice of Hesiod: an essay in detection. *In* Havelock, E. A. The Greek concept of justice p193-217

Havelock, E. A. The justice of Plato. *In* Havelock, .E. A. The Greek concept of justice p308-23

Havelock, E. A. The justice of Solon. *In* Havelock, E. A. The Greek concept of justice p249-62

Havelock, E A. The justice of The Odyssey. *In* Havelock, E. A. The Greek concept of justice p179-92

Havelock, E. A. The justice of the pre-Socratics. *In* Havelock, E. A. The Greek concept of justice p263-71

Havelock, E. A. The spoken and the written word. *In* Havelock, E. A. The Greek concept of justice p218-32

Hunter, G. K. Ironies of justice in The Spanish tragedy. *In* Hunter, G. K. Dramatic identities and cultural tradition p214-29

Stock, R. D. and Stock, B. The agents of evil and justice in the novels of Dorothy L. Sayers. *In* Hannay, M. P. ed. As her whimsey took her p14-22

Justification

Bornkamm, G. The revelation of Christ to Paul on the Damascus Road and Paul's doctrine of justification and reconciliation. *In* Reconciliation and hope p90-103

See also Assurance (Theology)

Justin, Saint, the martyr. See Justinus, Martyr, Saint

Justinus, Martyr, Saint

About

Williams, G. H. Justin glimpsed as martyr among his Roman contemporaries. *In* The Context of contemporary theology p99-126

Justus, James Huff

Fiction: the 1930s to the present. *In* American literary scholarship. 1973 p258-303

Fiction: the 1950s to the present. *In* American literary scholarship, 1974 p279-319

Fiction: the 1950s to the present [another essay] *In* American literary scholarship, 1975 p327-61

Fiction: the 1950s to the present [another essay] *In* American literary scholarship, 1976 p287-318

Fiction: the 1950s to the present [another essay] *In* American literary scholarship, 1977 p303-42

About individual works

Views designed by Cavaliere Don Filippo Juvarra and dedicated to his Excellency Richard Lord Burlington MDCCXXX

Wittkower, R. A sketchbook of Filippo Juvarra at Chatsworth. *In* Wittkower, R. Studies in the Italian baroque p187-210

Juvarra, Filippo. See Juvara, Filippo

Juvenal. See Juvenalis, Decimus Junius

Juvenalis, Decimus Junius

About

Clausen, W. V. Juvenal and Virgil. *In* Harvard Studies in classical philology v80 p181-86

Fredericks, S. C. Irony of overstatement in the satires of Juvenal. *In* Illinois classical studies v4, 1979 p178-91

Knoche, U. Decimus Junius Juvenalis. *In* Knoche, U. Roman satire p143-57

LaFleur, R. A. Amicitia and the unity of Juvenal's first book. *In* Illinois classical studies v4, 1979 p158-77

About individual works
Satires

Fredericks, S. C. Juvenal: a return to invective. *In* Roman satirists and their satire p136-69

Juvenalis, Decimus J.—About individual works—Satires—*Continued*

Knoche, U. Decimus Junius Juvenalis. *In* Knoche, U. Roman satire p143-57

Luck, G. The textual history of Juvenal and the Oxford lines. *In* Harvard Studies in classical philology v76 p217-31

Satires (Satire 7)

Rudd, N. Tone: poets and patrons in Juvenal's Seventh Satire. *In* Rudd, N. Lines of enquiry p84-118

Satires (Satire 10)

Dick, B. F. Seneca and Juvenal 10. *In* Harvard Studies in classical philology v73 p237-46

Satires (Satire 12)

Ramage, E. S. Juvenal, Satire 12: on friendship true and false. *In* Illinois classical studies v3, 1978 p221-37

Satires (Satire 15)

Fredericks, S. C. Juvenal's Fifteenth Satire. *In* Illinois classical studies, v 1 1976 p174-89

Criticism, Textual

Luck, G. The textual history of Juvenal and the Oxford lines. *In* Harvard Studies in classical philology v76 p217-31

Manuscripts

Luck, G. The textual history of Juvenal and the Oxford lines. *In* Harvard Studies in classical philology v76 p217-31

Juvenile corrections

See also Juvenile delinquency; Juvenile detention homes; Social work with delinquents and criminals

United States

Lerman, P. American concerns: keeping order versus fighting crime. *In* Empey, L. T. ed. Juvenile justice p150-79

Schwendinger, H. and Schwendinger, J. Delinquency and social reform: a radical perspective. *In* Empey, L. T. ed. Juvenile justice p245-87

Juvenile courts

Great Britain

Bottoms, A. E. On the decriminalization of English juvenile courts. *In* Crime, criminology and public policy p319-45

Scotland

Morris, A. Scottish juvenile justice: a critique. *In* Crime, criminology and public policy p347-74

United States

Forer, L. G. "No one will lissen"; excerpt. *In* Gross, B. and Gross, R. eds. The children's rights movement p82-100

Juvenile delinquency

Berry, J. J. Deviant categories and organizational typing of delinquents. *In* Davis, F. J. and Stivers, R. eds. The collective definition of deviance p350-59

Elkind, D. Middle-class delinquency. *In* Elkind, D. The child and society p167-74

Hirschi, T. Labelling theory and juvenile delinquency: an assessment of the evidence. *In* Gove, W. R. ed. The labelling of deviance p181-203

Kobrin, S. The labeling approach: problems and limits. *In* Delinquency, crime, and society p239-53

Toby, J. Delinquency in cross-cultural perspective. *In* Empey, L. T. ed. Juvenile justice p105-49

Wolfgang, M. E. Crime in a birth cohort. *In* Crime, criminology and public policy p88-92

See also Gangs; Juvenile courts; Juvenile detention homes; Rehabilitation of juvenile delinquents; Social work with delinquents and criminals

Prevention—San Francisco

Krisberg, B. A. and Takagi, P. Ethical issues in evaluating criminal justice demonstration projects. *In* Riedel, M. and Chappell, D. eds. Issues in criminal justice: planning and evaluation p66-74

Research—United States

Block, R. L. and Ross, D. J. A technique for utilizing precoded variables in the review of programs in criminal justice research. *In* Riedel, M. and Chappell, D. eds. Issues in criminal justice: planning and evaluation p24-35

Accra

Weinberg, S. K. Shaw-McKay theories of delinquency in cross-cultural context. *In* Delinquency, crime, and society p167-85

Chicago

Weinberg, S. K. Shaw-McKay theories of delinquency in cross-cultural context. *In* Delinquency, crime, and society p167-85

Scotland

Morris, A. Scottish juvenile justice: a critique. *In* Crime, criminology and public policy p347-74

United States

Empey, L. T. Juvenile lawbreaking: its character and social location. *In* Empey, L. T. ed. Juvenile justice p71-104

Hirschi, T. Reconstructing delinquency: evolution and implications of twentieth-century theory. *In* Empey, L. T. ed. Juvenile justice p180-212

Lerman, P. American concerns: keeping order versus fighting crime. *In* Empey, L. T. ed. Juvenile justice p150-79

Rothman, D. J. The Progressive legacy: development of American attitudes toward juvenile delinquency. *In* Empey, L. T. ed. Juvenile justice p34-68

Schwendinger, H. and Schwendinger, J. Delinquency and social reform: a radical perspective. *In* Empey, L. T. ed. Juvenile justice p245-87

Simon, W.; Puntil, J. E. and Peluso, E. Continuities in delinquency research. *In* Delinquency, crime, and society p50-63

Wolfgang, M. E. Seriousness of crime and a policy of juvenile justice. *In* Delinquency, crime, and society p267-86

Juvenile detention homes

Great Britain

Stirling, W. R. The role of education in the penal system. *In* Progress in penal reform p142-54

United States

Fisher, S. M. The smell of waste. *In* Gross, B. and Gross, R. eds. The children's rights movement p100-09

Juvenile detention homes—United States
—Continued

Forer, L. G. "No one will lissen"; excerpt. *In* Gross, B. and Gross, R. eds. The children's rights movement p82-100

Juvenile films. See Children's films

Juvenile justice, Administration of

United States

Empey, L. T. The Progressive legacy and the concept of childhood. *In* Empey. L. T. ed. Juvenile justice p3-33

Polier, J. W. Prescriptions for reform: doing what we set out to do? *In* Empey, L. T. ed. Juvenile justice p213-44

Rothman, D. J. The Progressive legacy: development of American attitudes toward juvenile delinquency. *In* Empey, L. T. ed. Juvenile justice p34-68

Juvenile literature. See Children's literature

Juvenile passion (Motion picture)

Truffaut, F. Yasushi Nakahira: Juvenile passion. *In* Truffaut, F. The films in my life p244-47

Juvenile wit and humor. See Wit and humor, Juvenile

Juviler, Peter H.

Women and sex in Soviet law. *In* Women in Russia p243-65

Juviler, Peter H. and Zawadzka, Hannah J.

Détente and Soviet domestic politics. *In* Kirk, G. L. and Wessell, N. H. eds. The Soviet threat p158-67

Jwaideh, Albertine

Tribalism and modern society: Iraq, a case study. *In* Savory, R. M. ed. Introduction to Islamic civilisation p160-67

K

KCIA. See Korea (Republic). Chungang Chŏngbobu

KKE. See Communist Party of Greece

KPD. See Communist Party of Germany

Kabuki

Powell, B. Communist kabuki: a contradiction in terms? *In* Drama and society p147-67

Kabuki plays

History and criticism

Nicoll, A. The Japanese drama. *In* Nicoll, A. World drama p546-61

Kac, Mark

The emergence of statistical thought in exact sciences. *In* Neyman, J. ed. The heritage of Copernicus: theories "pleasing to the mind" p433-44

Kadekodi, Gopal. See Tintner, G. jt. auth.

Kadish, Emilie P. Kostoroski- See Kostoroski, Emilie P.

Kadish, Mortimer Raymond

The desirability of pulling in one's horns. *In* Hook, S.; Kurtz, P. W. and Todorovich, M. eds. The philosophy of the curriculum: the need for general education p205-09

John Dewey and the theory of the aesthetic practice. *In* Cahn, S. M. ed. New studies in the philosophy of John Dewey p75-116

About individual works

The desirability of pulling in one's horns

Hook, S. On sharpening the horns. *In* Hook, S.; Kurtz, P. W. and Todorovich, M. eds. The philosophy of the curriculum: the need for general education p211-15

Kael, Pauline

Bonnie and Clyde; excerpt from "Kiss kiss bang bang." *In* Denby, D. ed. Awake in the dark p77-97

Circles and squares: joys and Sarris; excerpt from "I lost it at the movies." *In* Denby, D. ed. Awake in the dark p146-68

Notes on the nihilist poetry of Sam Peckinpah. *In* Denby, D. ed. Awake in the dark p326-33

Three program notes; excerpt from "Kiss kiss bang bang." *In* Denby, D. ed. Awake in the dark p388-91

About

Murray, E. Pauline Kael and pluralistic, nonaesthetic criticism. *In* Murray, E. Nine American film critics p110-40

Kaemmer, John E.

Changing music in contemporary Africa. *In* Martin, P. M. and O'Meara, P. eds. Africa p367-77

Kaeppler, Adrienne L.

Melody, drone and decoration: underlying structures and surface manifestations in Tongan art and society. *In* Greenhalgh, M. and Megaw, J. V. S. eds. Art in society p261-74

Kaestle, Carl F.

"Between the Scylla of brutal ignorance and the Charybdis of a literary education": elite attitudes toward mass schooling in early industrial England and America. *In* Schooling and society p177-91

Kaeuper, Richard W.

Royal finance and the crisis of 1297. *In* Order and innovation in the Middle Ages p103-10

The Societas Riccardorum and economic change. *In* Jeffrey, D. L. ed. By things seen: reference and recognition in medieval thought p161-72

Kafi, Jellal el

Tunisia: hopes for the medina of Tunis. *In* United Nations Educational, Scientific and Cultural Organization. The conservation of cities p125-39

Kafirs (African people). See Zulus

Kafka, Franz

About

Arendt, H. The Jew as pariah: a hidden tradition. *In* Arendt, H. The Jew as pariah: Jewish identity and politics in the modern age p67-90

Canetti, E. Kafka's other trial: the letters to Felice. *In* Canetti, E. The conscience of words p60-139

Church, M. Kafka and Proust: a contrast in time. *In* Garvin, H. R. ed. Makers of the twentieth-century novel p149-53

Glicksberg, C. I. Franz Kafka: the prophet of the Absurd. *In* Glicksberg, C. I. The literature of nihilism p124-41

Grossvogel, D. I. Kafka: structure as mystery (I). *In* Grossvogel, D. I. Mystery and its fictions: from Oedipus to Agatha Christie p147-64

Kafka, Franz—About—*Continued*

Josipovici, G. An art for the wilderness: Franz Kafka, 1883-1924. *In* Josipovici, G. The lessons of modernism p3-25

Mudrick, M. Portnoy's bachelor uncle. *In* Mudrick, M. Books are not life but then what is? p118-31

Oates, J. C. Kafka's paradise. *In* Oates, J. C. New heaven, new earth: the visionary experience in literature p265-98

Pritchett, V. S. Franz Kafka: estranged. *In* Pritchett, V. S. The myth makers p95-101

Rahv, P. An introduction to Kafka. *In* Rahv, P. Essays on literature and politics, 1932-1972 p251-62

Roth, P. "I always wanted you to admire my fasting"; or, Looking at Kafka. *In* Roth, P. Reading myself and others p247-[70]

About individual works
The burrow
Sussman, H. The all-embracing metaphor: reflections of Kafka's "The burrow." *In* Glyph I p100-31

The castle
Barney, S. A. Without a counterpart: Kafka's The castle. *In* Barney, S. A. Allegories of history, allegories of love p283-309

A country doctor
Kurz, P. K. Doomed existence. *In* Kurz, P. K. On modern German literature v 1 p149-72

He
Arendt, H. Where are we when we think? *In* Arendt, H. The life of the mind v 1 p195-216

A hunger artist
Reed, T. J. Nietzsche's animals: idea, image and influence. *In* Pasley, J. M. S. ed. Nietzsche: imagery and thought p159-219

The hunter Gracchus
Trilling, L. Franz Kafka: The hunter Gracchus. *In* Trilling, L. Prefaces to The experience of literature p118-22

In the penal colony
Dolan, P. J. Kafka: the political machine. *In* Dolan, P. J. Of war and war's alarms p125-44

Letters to Felice
Canetti, E. Kafka's other trial: the letters to Felice. *In* Canetti, E. The conscience of words p60-139

Letters to friends, family, and editors
Mudrick, M. Portnoy's bachelor uncle. *In* Mudrick, M. Books are not life but then what is? p118-31

Pritchett, V. S. Franz Kafka: estranged. *In* Pritchett, V. S. The myth makers p95-101

The metamorphoses
Mudrick, M. Looking for Kellermann. *In* Mudrick, M. The man in the machine p11-36

Selected short stories (Modern library edition)
Rahv, P. An introduction to Kafka. *In* Rahv, P. Essays on literature and politics, 1932-1972 p251-62

The trial
Grossvogel, D. I. Kafka: structure as mystery (I). *In* Grossvogel, D. I. Mystery and its fictions: from Oedipus to Agatha Christie p147-64

Hoffman, F. J. Kafka's The trial: the assailant as landscape. *In* Garvin, H. R. ed. Makers of the twentieth-century novel p154-65

Lesser, S. O. The source of guilt and the sense of guilt: Kafka's The trial. *In* Lesser, S. O. The whispered meanings p68-85

Criticism and interpretation
Kurz, P. K. Perspectives in Kafka interpretation. *In* Kurz, P. K. On modern German literature v 1 p30-55

Lesser, S. O. The source of guilt and the sense of guilt: Kafkas' The trial. *In* Lesser, S. O. The whispered meanings p68-85

Influence—Pinter
Lesser, S. O. Reflections on Pinter's The birthday party. *In* Lesser, S. O. The whispered meanings p203-11

Kafka, John S.
On reality: an examination of object constancy, ambiguity, paradox, and time. *In* Thought, consciousness, and reality p133-58

Kafker, Frank Arthur
The fortunes and misfortunes of a leading French bookseller-printer: André-François Le Breton, chief publisher of the Encyclopédie. *In* Studies in eighteenth-century culture v5 p371-85

Kafū Nagai. See Nagai, Kafū

Kagan, Donald
The speeches in Thucydides and the Mytilene debate. *In* Yale classical studies v24 p71-94

Kagan, Jerome
The child in the family. *In* Rossi, A. S.; Kagan, J. and Hareven, T. K. eds. The family p33-56

The magical aura of the IQ. *In* Montagu, A. ed. Race and IQ p52-58

Resilience in cognitive development. *In* Schwartz, T. ed. Socialization as cultural communication p139-55

Kagan, Richard L.
Universities in Castile, 1500-1810. *In* The University in society v2 p355-405

Kagle, Steven Earl
Science fiction as simulation game. *In* Clareson, T. D. ed. Many futures, many worlds p224-36

Unaccustomed earth: the movement of Americans from travel to exploration. *In* Kagle, S. E. ed. America: exploration and travel p3-7

Kahana, Eva
Matching environments to needs of the aged: a conceptual scheme. *In* Gubrium, J. F. ed. Late life p201-14

Kahane, Henry Romanos, and Kahane, Renée
The role of the papyri in etymological reconstruction. *In* Illinois classical studies v3, 1978 p207-20

Kahane, Jack
About
Ford, H. D. Jack Kahane and the guardian Obelisk. *In* Ford, H. D. Published in Paris p345-84

Kahane, Renée. See Kahane, H. R. jt. auth.

Kahin, George McTurnan
The United States and the anticolonial revolutions in Southeast Asia, 1945-50. *In* The Origins of the Cold war in Asia p338-61

Kahlenberg, Louis

About

Dolby, R. G. A. Debates over the theory of solution: a study of dissent in physical chemistry in the English-speaking world in the late nineteenth and early twentieth centuries. *In* Historical studies in the physical sciences v7 p297-404

Kahmen, Volker

About individual works
Erotic art today
Rosenberg, H. Trials of Eros. *In* Rosenberg, H. Art on the edge p216-26

Kahn, Alfred J. See Kamerman, S. B. jt. auth.

Kahn, Coppélia
The taming of the shrew: Shakespeare's mirror of marriage. *In* Diamond, A. and Edwards, L. R. eds. The authority of experience p84-100

Kahn, Harold L.
An unreconstructed review of Levenson's trilogy. *In* Meisner, M. J. and Murphey, R. eds. The Mozartian historian p50-57

Kahn, Joan, comp.

About individual works
Hanging by a thread
Welty, E. Introduction to Hanging by a thread, ed. by Joan Kahn. *In* Praise from famous men: an anthology of introductions p162-68

Kahn, Louis I.
Architecture and human agreement, *In* The Uneasy coalition: design in corporate America p17-30

Kahn, S. David
"Myers' problem" revisited. *In* Parapsychology: its relation to physics, biology, psychology, and psychiatry p208-34

Kahn, Sy Myron
Baby Doll: a comic fable. *In* Tennessee Williams: a tribute p292-309

Glenway Wescott's variations on the waste land image. *In* French, W. G. ed. The twenties p171-79

The Red Devil battery sign: Williams' Gotterdämmerung in Vienna. *In* Tennessee Williams: a tribute p362-71

Kahrl, Stanley J.
The civic religious drama of medieval England: a review of recent scholarship. *In* Renaissance drama [1973] p237-48

Teaching medieval drama as theatre. *In* The Learned and the lewed p305-18

Kaiko, Takeshi

About

Rimer, J. T. Tradition and contemporary consciousness: Ibuse, Endō, Kaiko, Abe. *In* Rimer, J. T. Modern Japanese fiction and its traditions p245-70

Kaila. See Falashas

Kain, John F.
Urban problems. *In* McKie, J. W. ed. Social responsibility and the business predicament p217-45

Kain, Richard Morgan
Epiphanies of Dublin. *In* Staley, T. F. and Benstock, B. eds. Approaches to Joyce's Portrait p91-110

General works. *In* Finneran, R. J. ed. Anglo-Irish literature p 1-23

Kaiser, Ernest
Blacks and American foundations: A historical survey. *In* The Black American reference book p480-85

Kaiser, Walter C.
The weightier and lighter matters of the law: Moses, Jesus and Paul. *In* Current issues in Biblical and patristic interpretation p176-92

Kalam. See Islamic theology

Kalba, Kas. See Kalba, Konrad K.

Kalba, Konrad K.
The electronic community: a new environment for television viewers and critics. *In* Television as a social force: new approaches to TV criticism p141-63

Kalbouss, George
Andrey Bely and the Modernist movement in Russian drama. *In* Janecek, G. ed. Andrey Bely p146-55

Kaldor, Mary
The role of arms in capitalist economies: the process of overdevelopment and underdevelopment. *In* Arms control and technological innovation p322-41

Kalevala
Oinas, F. J. The Balto-Finnic epics. *In* Oinas, F. J. ed. Heroic epic and saga p286-309

Kālidāsa

About

Nicoll, A. The Sanskrit drama. *In* Nicoll, A. World drama p531-38

Kalilombe, Patrick A.
The presence of the Church in Africa. *In* The Emergent gospel p22-30

Kalish, Donald. See Yost, R. M. jt. auth.

Kalish, Richard A.
Dying and preparing for death: a view of families. *In* Feifel, H. [ed.] New meanings of death p215-32

The one-armed bandit: a lasting icon. *In* Browne, R. B. and Fishwick, M. W. eds. Icons of America p190-97

Kallich, Martin
Swift and the archetypes of hate: A tale of a tub. *In* Studies in eighteenth-century culture v4 p43-67

Kallikrates. See Callicrates

Kalson, Albert E.
Tennessee Williams at the Delta Brilliant. *In* Tennessee Williams: a tribute p774-94

Kalstone, David
Five temperaments

Contents

Adrienne Rich: face to face
Elizabeth Bishop: questions of memory, questions of travel
A final note
James Merrill: transparent things
John Ashbery: self-portrait in a convex mirror
Robert Lowell: the uses of history

Kaltefleiter, Werner
The recuitment market of the German political elite. *In* Eulau, H. and Czudnowski, M. M. eds. Elite recruitment in democratic polities p239-62

Kaltenmark, Max
The ideology of the T'ai-p'ing ching. *In* Welch, H. and Seidel, A. K. eds. Facets of Taoism p19-52

Kalter, Robert John, and Tyner, Wallace E.
Disposal policy for energy resources in the public domain. *In* Kalter, R. J. and Vogely, W. A. eds. Energy supply and government policy p51-75

Kalter, Robert John, and Vogely, William A.
Introduction. *In* Kalter, R. J. and Vogely, W. A. eds. Energy supply and government policy p11-25

Kalvos, Andreas

About

Sherrard, P. Andreas Kalvos and the eighteenth-century ethos. *In* Sherrard, P. The wound of Greece p17-50

Kambonsenga (African tribe) See Ambo (African tribe)

Kamei, Shunsuke
The sacred land of liberty: images of America in nineteenth century Japan. *In* Iriye, A. ed. Mutual images p55-72

Kamenka, Eugene
The anatomy of an idea. *In* Human rights p 1-12

Marxism and ethics. *In* New studies in ethics v2 p287-360

Kamenka, Eugene, and Tay, Alice Erh-Soon
Beyond bourgeois individualism: the contemporary crisis in law and legal ideology. *In* Kamenka, E. and Neale, R. S. eds. Feudalism, capitalism and beyond p126-44

Socialism, anarchism and law. *In* Law and society p48-80

Kamerman, Sheila B. and Kahn, Alfred J.
Family policy as field and perspective. *In* Kamerman, S. B. and Kahn, A. J. eds. Family policy p476-503

The United States. *In* Kamerman, S. B. and Kahn, A. J. eds. Family policy p428-75

Kames, Henry Home, Lord

About individual works
Elements of criticism
Ostrander, G. M. Lord Kames and American Revolutionary culture. *In* Essays in honor of Russel B. Nye p168-79

Essays on the principles of natural morality and religion
Ostrander, G. M. Lord Kames and American Revolutionary culture. *In* Essays in honor of Russel B. Nye p168-79

Influence
Ostrander, G. M. Lord Kames and American Revolutionary culture. *In* Essays in honor of Russel B. Nye p168-79

Kaminsky, Stuart M.
Gold hat, gold fever, silver screen. *In* Peary, G. and Shatzkin, R. eds. The modern American novel and the movies p53-62

Kamiya, Fuji
Summit talks in retrospect. *In* Clapp, P. and Halperin, M. H. eds. United States-Japanese relations, the 1970's p120-46

Kamman, William
Militarism. *In* Encyclopedia of American foreign policy p545-56

Kammen, Michael G.
From liberty to prosperity: reflections upon the role of revolutionary iconography in national tradition. *In* American Antiquarian Society. Proceedings v86 pt2 p237-72

A nation of nations. *In* Alderson, W. T. ed. American issues p 1-15

Kammer, Jeanne
The art of silence and the forms of women's poetry. *In* Gilbert, S. M. and Gubar, S. eds. Shakespeare's sisters p153-64

Kammeyer, Kenneth C. W.
The dynamics of population. *In* Orel, H. ed. Irish history and culture p189-223

Kampf, Louis
The radical faculty: what are its goals? *In* Fairfield, R. P. ed. Humanistic frontiers in American education p61-68

Kamphoevener, Else Sophia von

About individual works
The Bey of Roses
Merkelbach, R. The girl in the rosebush: a Turkish tale and its roots in ancient ritual. *In* Harvard Studies in classical philology v82 p 1-15

Kanamori, Hisao
Future U.S.-Japanese economic relations. *In* Clapp, P. and Halperin, M. H. eds. United States-Japanese relations, the 1970's p58-78

Kandinskiĭ, Vasiliĭ Vasil'evich

About
Long, R. C. W. Kandinsky and abstraction: the role of the hidden image. *In* Kaplan, P. and Manso, S. eds. Major European art movements, 1900-1945 p275-98

Osborne, H. Non-iconic abstraction and Kandinsky. *In* Osborne, H. Abstraction and artifice in twentieth-century art p97-110

Kandinsky, Vassily. See Kandinskiĭ, Vasiliĭ Vasil'evich

Kandinsky, Wassily. See Kandinskiĭ, Vasiliĭ Vasil'evich

Kane, Edward J.
A cross-section study of tax avoidance by large commercial banks. *In* Inflation, trade and taxes p218-46

Kane, George
Some reflections on critical method. *In* English Association. Essays and studies, 1976 p23-38

Kani, John. See Fugard, A. jt. auth.

Kann, Robert A.
Protestantism and German nationialism in the Austro-German Alpine lands (1). *In* Király, B. K. ed. Tolerance and movements of religious dissent in Eastern Europe p11-25

Kanner, Barbara
The women of England in a century of social change, 1815-1914: a select bibliography Part II. *In* Vicinus, M. ed. A widening sphere p199-270

Kansas. University. Experimental Living Project
Miller, L. K. and others. The positive community: a strategy for applying behavioral engineering to the redesign of family and community. *In* Behavior modification and families p91-112

Kansas City, Mo.

Politics and government

Dorsett, L. W. Kansas City and the New Deal. *In* Braeman, J.; Bremner, R. H. and Brody, D. eds. The New Deal v2 p407-19

Kansas-Nebraska bill

Wolff, G. W. Party and section: the Senate and the Kansas-Nebraska bill. *In* Swierenga, R. P. ed. Beyond the Civil War synthesis p165-83

Kant, Immanuel

About

Arendt, H. Appearance. *In* Arendt, H. The life of the mind v 1 p17-65

Hoffmann, Y. The possibility of knowledge: Kant and Nagarjuna. *In* Philosophy East/philosophy West p269-90

Moser, W. Kant: origin and utopia. *In* Studies in eighteenth-century culture v8 p253-68

Rotenstreich, N. Vico and Kant. *In* Giambattista Vico's science of humanity p221-40

Warnock, M. Imagination and perception: Hume and Kant. *In* Warnock, M. Imagination p13-34

Weber, S. M. Aesthetic experience and self-reflection as emancipatory processes: two complementary aspects of critical theory. *In* O'Neill, J. ed. On critical theory p78-103

About individual works

Analytic of the sublime

Hertz, N. The notion of blockage in the literature of the sublime. *In* Hartman, G. H. ed. Psychoanalysis and the question of the text p62-85

The critique of judgment

Warnock, M. Imagination and creative art: Hume, Kant and Schelling. *In* Warnock, M. Imagination p35-71

The critique of pure reason

Hankins, T. L. Algebra as pure time: William Rowan Hamilton and the foundations of algebra. *In* Motion and time, space and matter p327-59

Dreams of a spirit-seer

Tonelli, G. Kant's ethics as a part of metaphysics: a possible Newtonian suggestion? *In* Philosophy and the civilizing arts p236-63

Foundations of the metaphysics of morals

Foot, P. Morality as a system of hypothetical imperatives. *In* Foot, P. Virtues and vices, and other essays in moral philosophy p157-73

Perpetual peace

Gallie, W. B. Kant on perpetual peace. *In* Gallie, W. B. Philosophers of peace and war p 8-36

Ethics

Acton, H. B. Kant's moral philosophy. *In* New studies in ethics v 1 p305-77

Raschke, C. Kant on theory and practice. *In* Political theory and praxis p73-96

Tonelli, G. Kant's ethics as a part of metaphysics: a possible Newtonian suggestion? *In* Philosophy and the civilizing arts p236-63

Warnock, G. J. Kant and anthropology. *In* Royal Institute of Philosophy. Nature and conduct p36-45

Williams, B. A. O. Persons, character and morality. *In* Rorty, A. O. ed. The identities of persons p197-216

Influence—Husserl

Kockelmans, J. J. Husserl and Kant on the pure ego. *In* Elliston, F. A. and McCormick, P. eds. Husserl p269-85

Knowledge, Theory of

Clarke, W. N. Interpersonal dialogue: key to realism. *In* Roth, R. J. ed. Person and community p141-53

Political science

Raschke, C. Kant on theory and practice. *In* Political theory and praxis p73-96

Psychology

Fancher, R. E. The sensing and perceiving mind: Kant, Helmholtz, and the Gestalt psychologists. *In* Fancher, R. E. Pioneers of psychology p87-125

Kanter, Rosabeth Moss

Work in a new America. *In* A New America? p47-78

Kantor-Berg, Friedrich

About individual works

Mein ist die Rache

Moore, E. M. Friedrich Torberg's Mein ist die Rache as a literary work of art. *In* Strelka, J. P.; Bell, R. F. and Dobson, E. eds. Protest—form—tradition p111-21

Kantrowitz, Nathan

New York segregation: implications for social policy. *In* The Diverse society: implications for social policy p27-40

Kantzer, Kenneth Sealer

Unity and diversity in evangelical faith. *In* Wells, D. F. and Woodbridge, J. D. eds. The evangelicals p38-67

Kanza, Thomas R.

Zaire's foreign policy. *In* Aluko, O. ed. The foreign policies of African states p235-43

Kao, Yu-kung

Lyric vision in Chinese narrative tradition: a reading of Hung-lou meng and Ju-lin wai-shih. *In* Chinese narrative p227-43

Kao, Yu-kung, and Mei, Tsu-lin

Ending lines in Wang Shih-chen's 'ch'i-chüeh': convention and creativity in the Ch'ing. *In* Artists and traditions p131-44

Kaplan, Irving

Mater omnium: automated energy and material wealth from the sea. *In* Borgese, E. M. and Krieger, D. eds. The tides of change p48-75

Kaplan, John

A primer on heroin. *In* Stanford legal essays p277-302

Kaplan, Justin

The "real life". *In* Studies in biography p 1-8

Kaplan, Lawrence Samuel

The Korean War and U.S. foreign relations: the case of NATO. *In* The Korean War p36-75

Nationalism. *In* Encyclopedia of American foreign policy p610-22

Toward isolationism: the rise and fall of the Franco-American alliance, 1775-1801. *In* The American Revolution and "a candid world" p134-60

Kaplan, M. A. See Kaplan, Morton A.

Kaplan, Mordecai Menahem

About

Kaufman, W. E. Mordecai M. Kaplan: the natural and the transnatural. *In* Kaufman, W. E. Contemporary Jewish philosophies p175-216

Kaplan, Morton A.

The international political system and the U.S. system of alliances. *In* Isolation or interdependence   p13-23

Introduction: what is communism? *In* Kaplan, M. A. ed. The many faces of communism p 1-29

Uncertainty and security policy. *In* Isolation or interdependence? p25-44

Kaplan, Sydney Janet

Feminine consciousness in the modern British novel

Contents

Doris Lessing
Dorothy M. Richardson
May Sinclair
Rosamond Lehmann
Virginia Woolf

The limits of consciousness in the novels of Doris Lessing. *In* Pratt, A. V. and Dembo, L. S. eds. Doris Lessing p119-32

Kappel, Andrew J. and Patten, Robert L.

Dickens' second American tour and his "utterly worthless and profitless" American "rights". *In* Dickens Studies Annual v7 p 1-33

Kapungu, Leonard T.

The OAU's support for the liberation of Southern Africa. *In* El-Ayouty, Y. ed. The Organization of African Unity after ten years p135-51

Karaites

Nemoy, L. The attitude of the early Karaites towards Christianity. *In* Salo Wittmayer Baron v2 p697-715

Karamazin, Nikolaĭ Mikhailovich

About

Stacy, R. H. The age of Pushkin. *In* Stacy, R. H. Russian literary criticism p25-37

Karass, The sad and curious story of. Jones, M. V. *In* Oxford Slavonic papers new ser. v8 p.53-81

Karber, Philip A. and Mengel, R. William

In defense of Fortress America: autarky as an alternative to isolation and interdependence. *In* Isolation or interdependence? p59-80

Karefa-Smart, John A. M.

Doctors, development, and demons in Africa. *In* Disguises of the demonic p150-56

Kargon, Robert Hugh

Temple to science: cooperative research and the birth of the California Institute of Technology. *In* Historical studies in the physical sciences v8 p3-31

Karier, Clarence J.

The ethics of a therapeutic man. *In* Kren, G. M. and Rappoport, L. H. eds. Varieties of psychohistory p333-63

Karinya Indians. See Carib Indians

Karis, Thomas

United States policy toward South Africa. *In* Carter, G. M. and O'Meara, P. eds. Southern Africa: the continuing crisis p313-62

Karl IV, Emperor of Germany

About

Borchardt, F. L. First contacts with Italy. *In* Hoffmeister, G. ed. The Renaissance and Reformation in Germany p 1-16

Karl V, Emperor of Germany

Rosenthal, E. S. Plus Oultre: the idea imperial of Charles V in his columnar device on the Alhambra. *In* Enggass, R. C. and Stokstad, M. eds. Hortus imaginum p85-93

Karl, Barry Dean

Executive reorganization and Presidential power. *In* The Supreme Court review, 1977 p 1-37

Karl, Frederick Robert

The adversary literature

Contents

Daniel Defoe: the politics of necessity
The development of technique in the eighteenth-century novel
Don Quixote as archetypal artist and Don Quixote as archetypal novel
Gothic, Gothicism, and Gothicists
Henry Fielding: the novel, the epic, and the comic sense of life
Introduction: the novel as subversion
Near-novels
Samuel Richardson and Clarissa
Smollett's Humphry Clinker: the choleric temper
Tristram Shandy, the sentimental novel, and sentimentalists

The Brontës: the self defined, redefined, and refined. *In* Levine, R. A. The Victorian experience: the novelists p121-50

Conrad and Pinker. *In* Joseph Conrad: a commemoration p156-73

Karl, Jean E.

Between chaos and creativity: the role of the children's editor. *In* Egoff, S. A. ed. One ocean touching p164-76

Karlik, John R.

Economic factors influencing American foreign policy. *In* The Interaction of economics and foreign policy p25-47

Karlin, Renata

The challenge to courtly love. *In* In pursuit of perfection p101-33

Karlinsky, Simon

In search of Poplavsky: a collage. *In* The Bitter air of exile p311-33

Karlovsky, C. C. Lamberg-. See Lamberg-Karlovsky, C. C.

Karnataka, India

Politics and government

Manor, J. The lesser leader amid political transformation: the Congress Party in Mysore state in 1941 and 1951. *In* The Making of politicians: studies from Africa and Asia p140-55

Karnes, Thomas L.

Pan-Americanism. *In* Encyclopedia of American foreign policy p730-41

Karp, Abraham J.
Jewish perceptions of America: from melting pot to mosaic. *In* Tradition and change in Jewish experience p244-56

Karp, Ivan C.
Rent is the only reality, or The hotel instead of the hymns. *In* Battcock, G. ed. Super realism p21-35

Karp, Mark
The "Protestant ethic" of the Mourids of Senegal. *In* African dimensions p197-213

Karp, Theodore C.
Medieval music in perspective. *In* Powell, J. M. ed. Medieval studies p343-72

Karrer, Wolfgang
Richard Wright. Fire and cloud. *In* Bruck, P. ed. The Black American short story in the 20th century p99-110

Kasaipwalova, John

About

Goodwin, K. L. Invective and obliqueness in political poetry: Kasaipwalova, Brathwaite, and Soyinka. *In* Narasimhaiah, C. D. ed. Awakened conscience p251-60

Kasarda, John D.
Urbanization, community, and the metropolitan problem. *In* Handbook of contemporary urban life p27-57

Kaschkat, Hannes. See Brunner, G. jt. auth.

Kaser, Michael
The economy: a general assessment. *In* Brown, A. H. and Kaser, M. eds. The Soviet Union since the fall of Khrushchev p196-217
Education in Tsarist and Soviet development. *In* Essays in honour of E. H. Carr p229-54

Kasfir, Nelson M.
Interdependence and American commitment to promote development in the Third World: Africa—the hardest case. *In* Baldwin, D. A. ed. America in an interdependent world p223-43
Seizing half a loaf: Isaya Mukirane and self-recruitment for secession. *In* The Making of politicians: studies from Africa and Asia p66-77

Kashap, S. Paul
Spinoza's use of "idea." *In* Shahan, R. W. and Biro, J. I. eds. Spinoza: new perspectives p57-70

Kashi, Joseph
The role of deterrence in disarmament: some theories and some defects. *In* The Dynamics of the arms race p92-103

Kashi Vidyapith
Pandy, G. The Shastris of Kashi and Lahore: the making of Congress leaders. *In* The Making of politicians: studies from Africa and Asia p116-25

Kashkai tribe
Beck, L. Women among Qashqa'i nomadic pastoralists in Iran. *In* Beck, L. and Keddie, N. R. eds. Women in the Muslim world p351-73

Kaska Indians

Psychology

Honigmann, J. J. The personal approach in culture and personality research. *In* Spindler, G. D. ed. The making of psychological anthropology p302-29

Kaske, Robert E.
Holy Church's speech and the structure of Piers Plowman. *In* Chaucer and Middle English studies in honour of Rossell Hope Robbins p320-27

Kasl, Stanislav Vojtech
Work and mental health: contemporary research evidence. *In* Heisler, W. J. and Houck, J. W. eds. A matter of dignity p85-110

Käsmann, Hans
Numerical structure in Fitt III of Sir Gawain and the Green Knight. *In* Chaucer and Middle English studies in honour of Rossell Hope Robbins p131-39

Kasoma, Godfrey Kabwe

About

Etherton, M. The dilemma of the popular playwright: the work of Kabwe Kasoma and V. E. Musinga. *In* African literature today no. 8: Drama in Africa p26-41

Kasoma, Kabwe. See Kasoma, Godfrey Kabwe

Kaspar (criticism) Handke, P. *In* Brustein, R. S. The culture watch p72-74

Kass, Leon Richard
Death as an event: a commentary on Robert Morison. *In* Weir, R. F. ed. Ethical issues in death and dying p70-81
See also Capron, A. M. jt. auth.

Kass-Simon, G.
Female strategies: animal adaptations and adaptive significance. *In* Roberts, J. I. ed. Beyond intellectual sexism p74-84

Kastenbaum, Robert
Death and development through the life-span. *In* Feifel, H. [ed.] New meanings of death p17-45

Kastner, Israel Rudolf

About

Dawidowicz, L. S. Blaming the Jews: the charge of perfidy. *In* Dawidowicz, L. S. The Jewish presence p269-79

Kataba Indians. See Catawba Indians

Kataev, Valentin Petrovich

About

Russell, R. The problem of self-expression in the later works of Valentin Kataev. *In* Barnes, C. J. ed. Studies in twentieth century Russian literature p78-91

Katayev, Valentin Petrovich. See Kataev, Valentin Petrovich

Katchadourian, Herant A.
Medical perspectives on adulthood. *In* Erikson, E. H. ed. Adulthood p33-60
The terminology of sex and gender. *In* Katchadourian, H. A. ed. Human sexuality p8-34

Katchadourian, Herant A. and Martin, John A.
Analyses of human sexual behavior. *In* Katchadourian, H. A. ed. Human sexuality p35-48

Katharine, Saint of Alexandria. See Catharine, Saint of Alexandria

Kathīr, 'Alī Ahmad Bā. See Bā Kathīr, 'Alī Ahmad

al-Kātibī, 'Ali ibn 'Umar

About individual works

Sun epistle

Rescher, N. and Vander Nat, A. The Arabic theory of temporal modal syllogistic. *In* Essays on Islamic philosophy and science p189-221

Kato, Hidetoshi
America as seen by Japanese travelers. *In* Iriye, A. ed. Mutual images p188-201

Development nineteenth-century style: some historical parallels between the United States and Japan. *In* On the making of Americans p173-90

Popular culture. *In* Lerner, D. and Nelson, L. M. eds. Communication research—a half-century appraisal p242-53

Kato, Ichiro
Japanese universities: student revolt and reform plans. *In* Universities in the Western world p257-63

Katona, Anna
Molière in Hungary: his reputation. *In* Johnson, R. B.; Neumann, E. S. and Trail, G. T. eds. Molière and the commonwealth of letters: patrimony and posterity p355-64

Sándor Farkas Bölöni and Ágoston Mokcsai Haraszthy. *In* Abroad in America: Visitors to the new Nation, 1776-1914 p43-51

Katopes, Peter J. See Miller, R. jt. auth.

Katz, Eve
The problem of the environment in Les rêveries du promeneur solitaire. *In* Studies in eighteenth-century culture v4 p95-107

Katz, Friedrich
Peasants in the Mexican Revolution of 1910. *In* Forging nations: a comparative view of rural ferment and revolt p61-85

Katz, Jacob
Post-emancipation development of rights: liberalism and universalism. *In* Sidorsky, D. ed. Essays on human rights p282-96

Katz, Jerrold J.
The relevance of linguistics to philosophy. *In* Harman, G. ed. On Noam Chomsky p229-41

Katz, Joseph
Epilogue: the admissions process—society's stake and the individual's interest. *In* Hurdles p318-47

Katz, Michael R.
The literary ballad in early nineteenth-century Russian literature

Contents

The epithet in Zhukovsky's literary ballads
The influence of folk ballads and the ballad revival on Russian literary ballads
Lermontov's literary ballads
Polemics
Pushkin's literary ballads
Russian literary ballads of the 1790s
Zhukovsky's imitators
Zhukovsky's literary ballads

Katz, Sanford N.
Who looks after Laura? *In* Gross, B. and Gross, R. eds. The children's rights movement p48-54

Katzenbach v. Morgan. *In* Stanford legal essays p79-96

Katzenellenbogen, Simon E.
British businessmen and German Africa, 1885-1919. *In* Great Britain and her world, 1750-1914 p237-62

Katzenstein, Peter J.
Ethnic political conflict in South Tyrol. *In* Esman, M. J. ed. Ethnic conflict in the Western world p287-323

West Germany's place in American foreign policy: pivot, anchor, or broker? *In* Rosecrance, R. N. ed. America as an ordinary country p110-35

Katzman, Martin T.
Social relations of production on the Brazilian frontier. *In* Miller, D. H. and Steffen, J. O. eds. The frontier p275-96

Katznelson, Ira
The Americanization of British politics. *In* Kramnick, I. ed. Is Britain dying? p137-51

Kau, Joseph L. C.
"Trust . . . to go by contraries": incarnation and the paradox of belief in the poetry of Frost. *In* Frost: centennial essays II p99-111

Kauffmann, Stanley
Living images

Contents

American graffiti
The assassination of Trotsky
Avanti!
L'Avventura
Badlands
Bang the drum slowly
Bed and board
Blood of the condor
Borsalino
Buster Keaton Festival
Cabaret
The candidate
Carnal knowledge
Charley Varrick
Chloe in the afternoon
Claire's knee
A clockwork orange
The clowns
La collectionneuse
The confession
The conformist
Conrack
The conversation
Cops and robbers
Cries and whispers
Day for night
A day in the death of Joe Egg
The day of the Jackal
Derby
Desperate characters
The devils
Diary of a mad housewife
The discreet charm of the bourgeoisie
The emigrants
The exorcist
Fellini's Roma
Une femme douce
Fiddler on the roof
Five easy pieces
Flap
Foreign and domestic: exchanges through film history
The French connection
Frenzy
The garden of the Finzi-Continis
The getaway
The go-between
The Godfather

Kauffmann, Stanley

Persons of the drama

Contents—Continued

Ulysses in Nighttown

Uncle Vanya

Why do critics persist?

About

Murray, E. Stanley Kauffmann and pluralistic, aesthetic criticism. *In* Murray, E. Nine American film critics p141-71

Kaufman, Alvin

Electric power: regulation of a natural monopoly. *In* Kalter, R. J. and Vogely, W. A. eds. Energy supply and government policy p216-34

Kaufman, Bel

Sholom Aleichem. *In* Abroad in America: Visitors to the new Nation, 1776-1914 p270-78

Kaufman, Clifford Lee

Political science. *In* Quantitative social science research on Latin America p162-207

Kaufman, Denis. See Vertov, Dziga

Kaufman, George Simon

About

Sheed, W. The wit of George S. Kaufman and Dorothy Parker. *In* Sheed, W. The good word & other words p159-63

Kaufman, Howard Keva

Culao—a Vietnamese fishing cooperative and its problems. *In* Social organization and the applications of anthropology p235-72

Kaufman, Irving Charles

Learning what comes naturally: the role of life experience in the establishment of species typical behavior. *In* Schwartz, T. ed. Socialization as cultural communication p37-50

Kaufman, Jule Suzanne

Emily Dickinson and the involvement of retreat. *In* Tulane Studies in English v21 p77-90

Kaufman, Terrence Scott

Areal linguistics and Middle America. *In* Sebeok, T. A. ed. Native languages of the Americas v2 p63-87

Kaufman, William E.

Contemporary Jewish philosophies

Contents

Abraham J. Heschel: the meaning beyond mystery

Arthur A. Cohen and Jacob B. Agus: the supernatural and the absolute self

Conclusion: existence, essence, and transcendence

Eugene B. Borowitz and Emil L. Fackenheim: from covenant theology to commanding voice

Franz Rosenzweig: toward an existential Jewish theology

Introduction: The crisis of meaning

Leo Baeck: the far yet near God

Martin Buber: can God be encountered?

Mordecai M. Kaplan: the natural and the transnatural

Richard L. Rubenstein: the encounter with nothingness

Toward a return to clarity

Kaufmann, Edgar

A profitable art. *In* The Uneasy coalition: design in corporate America p31-39

Kaufmann, Walter Arnold

Hegel's conception of phenomenology. *In* Pivčević, E. ed. Phenomenology and philosophical understanding p211-30

Nietzsche and the death of tragedy: a critique. *In* O'Flaherty, J. C.; Sellner, T. F. and Helm, R. M. eds. Studies in Nietzsche and the classical tradition p234-54

On death and lying. *In* Psychiatry and the humanities v 1 p235-40

Kauper, Paul Gerhardt

The higher law and the rights of man in a revolutionary society. *In* America's continuing revolution p45-69

Kaupp, Peter

The misunderstood best-seller: the social function of entertainment literature. *In* Fischer, H. D. and Melnik, S. R. eds. Entertainment: a cross-cultural examination p234-46

Kavanaugh, James V.

The artifact in American culture: the development of an undergraduate program in American studies. *In* Material culture and the study of American life p65-74

Kavanagh, Patrick Joseph Gregory

About

Hobsbaum, P. The poetry of barbarism. *In* Hobsbaum. P. Tradition and experiment in English poetry p308-30

Kaw people

Hanks, J. R. Recitation of patrilineages among the Akha. *In* Social organization and the applications of anthropology p114-27

Kawabata, Yasunari

About

Iga, M. Personal situation as a factor in suicide, with reference to Yasunari Kawabata and Yukio Mishima. *In* Wolman, B. B. ed. Between survival and suicide p103-28

Ueda, M. Kawabata Yasunari. *In* Ueda, M. Modern Japanese writers p173-218

Yamanouchi, H. The eternal womanhood: Tanizaki Jun'ichirō and Kawabata Yasunari. *In* Yamanouchi, H. The search for authenticity in modern Japanese literature p107-36

About individual works

Snow country

Hyman, S. E. Conscious of the seasons. *In* Hyman, S. E. The critic's credentials p227-34

Rimer, J. T. Kawabata Yasunari: Eastern approaches. *In* Rimer, J. T. Modern Japanese fiction and its traditions p162-81

Ueda, M. Kawabata Yasunari. *In* Ueda, M. Modern Japanese writers p173-218

Thousand cranes

Hyman, S. E. Conscious of the seasons. *In* Hyman, S. E. The critic's credentials p227-34

al-Kawākibi, 'Abd-al-Raḥman

About

Kedourie, É. The politics of political literature: Kawakibi, Azoury and Jung. *In* Kedourie, É. Arabic political memoirs and other studies p107-23

Kawanaka, Yasuhiro

The canons of journalism and trends in Japanese dailies. *In* Postwar trends in Japan p251-72

Kawin, Bruce F.
Faulkner's film career: the years with Hawks. *In* Faulkner, modernism, and film: Faulkner and Yoknapatawpha, 1978 p163-81

The montage element in Faulkner's fiction. *In* Faulkner, modernism, and film: Faulkner and Yoknapatawpha, 1978 p103-25

Kay, Carol McGinnis, and Jacobs, Henry E. (comps.)
A selected bibliography on Shakespeare's romances. *In* Shakespeare's romances reconsidered p181-215

Kay, Cristobal
Agrarian reform and the transition to socialism. *In* O'Brien, P. J. ed. Allende's Chile p79-105

Kay, Jeanne
Indian responses to a mining frontier. *In* The Frontier v2 p193-203

Kay, Karyn
Sisters of the night. *In* Nichols, B. ed. Movies and methods p185-94

Kay, Martin
Automatic translation of natural languages. *In* Bloomfield, M. W. and Haugen, E. I. eds. Language as a human problem p219-32

Kay, Marvin Lawrence Michael, and Cary, Lorin Lee
Class, mobility, and conflict in North Carolina on the eve of the Revolution. *In* The Southern experience in the American Revolution. p109-51

Kay-Robinson, Denys
Hardy's Wessex. *In* Drabble, M. ed. The genius of Thomas Hardy p110-18

Kayak (Periodical)
Hitchcock, G. On Kayak. *In* Anderson, E. and Kinzie, M. eds. The little magazine in America: a documentary history p438-49

Kaye-Smith, Sheila

About
Cavaliero, G. Literary regionalism: Hugh Walpole, Sheila Kaye-Smith. *In* Cavaliero, G. The rural tradition in the English novel, 1900-1939 p66-80

Kaylor, Catherine
Evaluation of home care for the terminal cancer patient: a proposed model. *In* Home care p247-59

Kazakhstan
Mills, R. M. The virgin lands since Khrushchev: choices and decisions in Soviet policy making. *In* Cocks, P.; Daniels, R. V. and Heer, N. W. eds. The dynamics of Soviet politics p178-92

Kazan, Elia

About individual works
Baby Doll
Truffaut, F. Elia Kazan: Baby Doll. In Truffaut, F. The films in my life p110-13

A face in the crowd
Truffaut, F. Elia Kazan: A face in the crowd. *In* Truffaut, F. The films in my life p113-15

On the waterfront
Murray, E. On the waterfront. *In* Murray, E. Ten film classics p86-101

Kazantzakēs, Nikos

About
Glicksberg, C. I. Kazantzakis: Dionysian nihilism. *In* Glicksberg, C. I. The literature of nihilism p275-99

Kazantzakis, Nikos. See Kazantzakēs, Nikos

Kazin, Alfred
The drama of good and evil in American writing. *In* An Almost chosen people p51-66

About
Paul, S. Alfred Kazin. *In* Paul, S. Repossessing and renewing p236-94

About individual works
Bright book of life
Sale, R. H. Alfred Kazin. *In* Sale, R. H. On not being good enough p157-62

A walker in the city
Paul, S. Alfred Kazin. *In* Paul, S. Repossessing and renewing p236-94

Kearful, Frank J.
Molière among the English, 1660-1737. *In* Johnson, R. B.; Neumann, E. S. and Trail, G. T. eds. Molière and the commonwealth of letters: patrimony and posterity p199-217

Kearney, Michael
A world-view explanation of the evil eye. *In* The Evil eye p175-92

Kearney, Milo Edward
Regensburg burgher factions and the failure of the Swabian Town League in 1389. *In* Viator: medieval and Renaissance studies v6 p275-94

Kearney, Robert N.
South and Southeast Asia: a regional survey. *In* Kearney, R. N. ed. Politics and modernization in South and Southeast Asia p 1-38

Keast, William Rea
Johnson's criticism of the metaphysical poets. *In* Roberts, J. R. ed. Essential articles for the study of John Donne's poetry p11-19

Keating, Henry Raymond Fitzwalter
Hercule Poirot—a companion portrait. *In* Agatha Christie: first lady of crime p205-16

Keating, Louis Clark
Molière in New York. *In* Johnson, R. B.; Neumann, E. S. and Trail, G. T. eds. Molière and the commonwealth of letters: patrimony and posterity p400-06

Keating, Peter John
Arnold's social and political thought. *In* Allott, K. ed. Matthew Arnold p207-35

Robert Browning: a reader's guide. *In* Armstrong, I. ed. Robert Browning p299-341

Keaton, Buster

About
Kauffmann, S. Buster Keaton Festival. *In* Kauffmann, S. Living images p19-22

Keats, John, 1795-1821

About
Albrecht, W. P. Keats. *In* Albrecht, W. P. The sublime pleasures of tragedy p133-58

Bayley, J. Keats and sex. *In* Bayley, J. The uses of division p130-45

Bayley, J. Reality in division. *In* Bayley, J. The uses of division p107-14

Keats, John, 1795-1821—About—*Continued*

Bayley, J. The vulgar and the heroic in 'bad poetry.' *In* Bayley, J. The uses of division p115-30

Brisman, L. Keats and a new birth. *In* Brisman, L. Romantic origins p55-102

Bush, D. Keats and Shakespeare. *In* Shakespeare: aspects of influence p71-89

Cooke, M. G. The will to art: Excursus: the will to art in romanticism. *In* Cooke, M. G. The romantic will p182-87

Cooke, M. G. The will to art: Keats and the aesthetics of redemption. *In* Cooke, M. G. The romantic will p150-82

Hinkel, H. H. Growth without toil: generative indolence in Keats. *In* Tennessee Studies in literature v20 p26-36

Krause, F. P. Negative capability and objective correlative in Shakespeare's Sonnets. *In* Tennessee Studies in literature v20 p17-25

Kunitz, S. J. The modernity of Keats. *In* Kunitz, S. J. A kind of order, a kind of folly p59-73

Ober, W. B. Drowsed with the fume of poppies: opium and John Keats. *In* Ober, W. B. Boswell's clap and other essays p118-36

Parker, P. A. Keats. *In* Parker, P. A. Inescapable romance p158-218

Taylor, A. Self-destroying enthrallments: Byron and Keats. *In* Taylor, A. Magic and English romanticism p221-50

Trilling, L. The fate of pleasure: Wordsworth to Dostoevski; excerpt from "Beyond culture". *In* Wimsatt, W. K. ed. Literary criticism: idea and act p189-211

About individual works
Endymion

Allott, M. F. Keats's Endymion and Shelley's 'Alastor.' *In* Davies, R. T. and Beatty, B. G. eds. Literature of the romantic period, 1750-1850 p151-70

Nalbantian, S. Shelley and Keats: the battling soul. *In* Nalbantian, S. The symbol of the soul from Hölderlin to Yeats p38-48

The eve of St. Agnes

Ragussis, M. Keats: "Awake sweet dreamer!": narrator and reader in "The eve of St. Agnes." *In* Ragussis, M. The subterfuge of art p70-84

The fall of Hyperion

Bloom, H. Keats: romance revised. *In* Bloom, H. Poetry and repression p112-42

Hartman, G. Spectral symbolism and authorial self. *In* Keats's "Hyperion". *In* Hartman, G. The fate of reading p57-73

Jones, L. M. The dating of the two Hyperions. *In* Virginia. University. Bibliographical Society. Studies in bibliography v30 p120-35

Ragussis, M. Keats: The language of gods and men: the fragmented world of the Hyperion poems. *In* Ragussis, M. The subterfuge of art p35-69

Hyperion

Bloom, H. Keats: romance revised. *In* Bloom, H. Poetry and repression p112-42

Hartman, G. Spectral symbolism and authorial self in Keats's "Hyperion". *In* Hartman, G. The fate of reading p57-73

Jones, L. M. The dating of the two Hyperions. *In* Virginia. University. Bibliographical Society. Studies in bibliography v30 p120-35

Ragussis, M. Keats: the language of gods and men: the fragmented world of the Hyperion poems. *In* Ragussis, M. The subterfuge of art p35-69

Ode on a Grecian urn

Dyson, A. E. and Lovelock, J. 'Ever', 'Never': the world of Keats's Grecian urn. *In* Dyson, A. E. and Lovelock, J. Masterful images p205-17

Hill, A. A. Some points in the analysis of Keats's Ode on a Grecian urn. *In* Hill, A. A. Constituent and pattern in poetry p104-14

Richards, I. A. Beauty and truth. *In* Richards, I. A. Complementarities p215-25

Richards, I. A. Between truth and truth. *In* Richards, I. A. Complementarities p37-48

Ode to a nightingale

Trilling, L. John Keats: Ode to a nightingale. *In* Trilling, L. Prefaces to The experience of literature p243-48

To autumn

Hartman, G. H. Poem and ideology: a study of Keats's "To autumn". *In* Hartman, G. H. The fate of reading p124-46

Criticism and interpretation

Bayley, J. Another view of the question. *In* Bayley, J. The uses of division p145-56

Influence—Tennyson

Bloom, H. Tennyson: in the shadow of Keats. *In* Bloom, H. Poetry and repression p143-74

Keats, John, 1920-

About individual works
You might as well live: the life and times of Dorothy Parker

Sheed, W. The wit of George S. Kaufman and Dorothy Parker. *In* Sheed, W. The good word & other words p159-63

Keble, John

About

Prickett, S. Keble's 'two worlds.' *In* Prickett, S. Romanticism and religion p91-119

Tennyson, G. B. The sacramental imagination. *In* Knoepflmacher, U. C. and Tennyson, G. B. eds. Nature and the Victorian imagination p370-90

Kebra nagast

Ullendorff, E. The Queen of Sheba in Ethiopian tradition. *In* Pritchard, J. B. ed. Solomon & Sheba p104-14

Kedar, Benjamin Z.

The Genoese notaries of 1382: the anatomy of an urban occupational group. *In* the Medieval city p73-94

Keddie, Henrietta

About

Hart, F. R. Mid-Victorians. *In* Hart, F. R. The Scottish novel p93-113

Kedourie, Élie

Arabic political memoirs and other studies

Contents

The Alliance Israélite Universelle, 1860-1960

The American University of Beirut

Anti-Marxism in Egypt

Kelley, Donald R.—*Continued*
Louis Le Caron philosophe. *In* Philosophy and humanism p30-49

Vico's road: from philology to jurisprudence and back. *In* Giambattista Vico's science of humanity p15-29

Kelley, William Melvin

About individual works
The poker party
Galloway, D. William Melvin Kelley, The poker party. *In* Bruck, P. ed. The Black American short story in the 20th century p129-40

Kellogg, Gene
Dark prophets of hope
Contents
Absurd reasoning and the saints without God
Albert Camus and the world of the Absurd
Alienation and solidarity: interlocking opposites
Alienated man and the faculty of categorization
Existentialism, violence, and communism
The opposite predictions: Ivan and Zossima
Simultaneity and contemporary cultural history
Simultaneity of opposites: Jean-Paul Sartre
Suffering and psychic blackmail: Dostoevsky and sadomasochism
William Faulkner and the tyranny of linear consciousness

Kellogg, Jean Defrees. See Kellogg, Gene

Kelly, Aileen
Introduction: a complex vision. *In* Berlin, Sir I. Russian thinkers pxiii-xxiv

Kelly, Alfred Hinsey
American political leadership: the optimistic ethical world view and the Jeffersonian synthesis. *In* Library of Congress Symposia on the American Revolution, 3d, 1974. Leadership in the American Revolution p7-39

The Constitution and foreign policy. *In* Encyclopedia of American foreign policy p177-90

Kelly, Douglas
Medieval imagination
Contents
Allegory of love
Guillaume de Lorris and imagination in the Roman de la Rose
Guillaume de Machaut and the sublimation of courtly love in imagination
Imagination
Imagination and the Second Rhetoric
Imagination in the poetry of Charles d'Orléans and René d'Anjou
Imagination in the writings of Jean Froissart
Rhetoric and poetry
Verisimilitude and imagination: the crisis in late courtly poetry
Rhetoric in French literature: topical invention in medieval French literature. *In* Murphy, J. J. ed. Medieval eloquence p231-51

Kelly, Ellsworth

About
Rosenberg, H. Olitski, Kelly, Hamilton: dogma and talent. *In* Rosenberg, H. Art on the edge p60-70

Kelly, Gary
The English Jacobin novel, 1780-1805
Contents
Conclusion
Elizabeth Inchbald: A simple story
Elizabeth Inchbald: Nature and art
Robert Bage
Thomas Holcroft: Anna St Ives
Thomas Holcroft: Bryan Perdue
Thomas Holcroft: Hugh Trevor
William Godwin: Caleb Williams
William Godwin: Fleetwood
William Godwin: St Leon

Kelly, Howard Atwood

About
Harvey, A. M. Pioneers in urology: James R. Brown and Howard A. Kelly. *In* Harvey, A. M. Adventures in medical research p8-17

Kelly, James
The aging male homosexual. *In* Gochros, H. L. and Gochros, J. S. eds. The sexually oppressed p160-69

Kelly, Janet S.
International monetary systems and national security. *In* Knorr, K. E. and Trager, F. N. eds. Economic issues and national security p231-58

Kelly, John S. See Harper, G. M. jt. auth.

Kelly, Orville E.
Make today count. *In* Feifel, H. [ed.] New meanings of death p181-93

Kelly, Patricia Fernández
Death in Mexican folk culture. *In* Death in America p92-111

Kelly, Robert J. See Sagarin, E. jt. auth.

Kelly, William Daniel, and Friesen, Stanley Richard
Do cancer patients want to be told? *In* Weir, R. F. ed. Ethical issues in death and dying p 3-8

Kelly-Gadol, Joan
Tommaso Campanella: the agony of political theory in the counter-Reformation. *In* Philosophy and humanism p164-89

Kelman, Herbert C.
Attitude and behavior: a social-psychological problem. *In* Major social issues p412-20

The problem-solving workshop in conflict resolution. *In* Unofficial diplomats p168-200

Violence without moral restraint: reflections on the dehumanization of victims and victimizers. *In* Kren, G. M. and Rappoport, L. H. eds. Varieties of psychohistory p282-314

Kelvin, Norman
The divided self: William Styron's fiction from Lie down in darkness to The confessions of Nat Turner. *In* Morris, R. K. and Malin, I. eds. The achievement of William Styron p208-26

Kelvin, William Thomson, 1st Baron

About
Buchwald, J. Z. William Thomson and the mathematization of Faraday's electrostatics. *In* Historical studies in the physical sciences v8 p101-36

Doran, B. G. Origins and consolidation of field theory in nineteenth-century Britain: from the mechanical to the electromagnetic view of nature. *In* Historical studies in the physical sciences v6 p133-260

Kelvin, William T., 1st Baron—About—*Cont.*

Wise, M. N. William Thomson's mathematical route to energy conservation: a case study of the role of mathematics in concept formation. *In* Historical studies in the physical sciences v10 p49-83

Kemble, Fanny. See Kemble, Frances Anne

Kemble, Frances Anne

About

MacLeod, D. J. Fanny Kemble. *In* Abroad in America: Visitors to the new Nation, 1776-1914 p72-81

About individual works
Journal of a residence on a Georgian plantation in 1838-1839

Downs, R. B. Slave plantation. *In* Downs, R. B. Books that changed the South p82-91

Kemp, John

Ethical naturalism. *In* New studies in ethics v 1 p173-228

Kemp, Martin

From "mimesis" to "fantasia": the quattrocento vocabulary of creation, inspiration and genius in the visual arts. *In* Viator: medieval and Renaissance studies v8 p347-98

Kempe, Fritz

A historical sketch of photography in Hamburg. *In* One hundred years of photographic history p91-102

Kemper, Theodore D.

A sociology of emotions: some problems and some solutions. *In* McNall, S. G. ed. Theoretical perspectives in sociology p431-49

Kempton, Winifred

The mentally retarded person. *In* Gochros, H. L. and Gochros, J. S. eds. The sexually oppressed p239-56

Kendall, Calvin B.

Rhetoric in early medieval Latin: Bede's Historia ecclesiastica: the rhetoric of faith. *In* Murphy, J. J. ed. Medieval eloquence p145-72

Kendall, Henry

About

Perkins, E. Towards seeing minor poets steadily and whole. *In* Bards, bohemians, and bookmen p39-55

Kendall, Patricia L.

Theory and research: the case of studies in medical education. *In* The Idea of social structure p301-21

Kendall, Willmore. See Wilhelmsen, F. D. jt. auth.

Kendel, István

116 wars in 30 years. *In* Arms control and technological innovation p303-21

Keneally, Thomas

About individual works
The chant of Jimmie Blacksmith

Tiffin, C. Victims Black and white: Thomas Keneally's The chant of Jimmie Blacksmith. *In* Hamilton, K. G. ed. Studies in the recent Australian novel p121-48

Three cheers for the Paraclete

Vargo, E. P. Struggling with a bugaboo: the priest-character in Achebe and Greene and Keneally. *In* Narasimhaiah, C. D. ed. Awakened conscience p284-93

Keniston, Kenneth

Change the victims—or the society? *In* Gross, B. and Gross, R. eds. The children's rights movement p232-43

Psychological development and historical change. *In* Explorations in psychohistory p149-64

Revolution or counterrevolution; excerpt from "Youth and dissent". *In* Explorations in psychohistory p288-323

Stranded in the present. *In* Kren, G. M. and Rappoport, L. H. eds. Varieties of psychohistory p251-56

Kennan, George Frost

Between earth and hell. *In* Dunlop, J. B.; Haugh, R. and Klimoff, A. eds. Aleksandr Solzhenitsyn: critical essays and documentary materials 2d ed. p501-11

The cloud of danger; excerpts. *In* Decline of the West? George Kennan and his critics p81-95

Soviet doves and American hawks. *In* Decline of the West? George Kennan and his critics p49-60

The United States and the Soviet Union, 1917-1976. *In* Two hundred years of American foreign policy p142-80

Western decadence and Soviet moderation. *In* Decline of the West? George Kennan and his critics p3-9

About

Bernstein, B. J. Containment. *In* Encyclopedia of American foreign policy p191-203

Coffey, J. W. The mind of the realist. *In* Coffey, J. W. Political realism in American thought p25-47

Coffey, J. W. Realism and foreign policy. *In* Coffey, J. W. Political realism in American thought p48-78

Gaddis, J. L. Mr. "X" is consistent and right. *In* Decline of the West? George Kennan and his critics p135-56

Luttwak, E. N. The failure to understand strategy. *In* Decline of the West? George Kennan and his critics p97-111

Mark, E. Mr. "X" is inconsistent and wrong. *In* Decline of the West? George Kennan and his critics p157-72

Novak, M. The banality of evil. *In* Decline of the West? George Kennan and his critics p71-74

Rostow, E. V. Kennan's grand design. *In* Decline of the West? George Kennan and his critics p113-31

Weiss, S. Is Brezhnev a man of peace? *In* Decline of the West? George Kennan and his critics p75-78

About individual works
From containment to . . . self-containment: a conversation between George F. Kennan and George Urban

Seton-Watson, H. How right the old Kennan was! *In* Decline of the West? George Kennan and his critics p39-48

Soviet doves and American hawks

Pipes, R. Basic Soviet institutions have not changed. *In* Decline of the West? George Kennan and his critics p61-69

Kennard, Jean E.
Number and nightmare
Contents
Afterthoughts
Anthony Burgess: double vision
Iris Murdoch: the revelation of reality
James Purdy: fidelity to failure
John Barth: imitations of imitations
Joseph Heller: at war with absurdity
Kurt Vonnegut, Jr.: the sirens of satire
William Golding: islands
Victims of convention
Contents
Aristocrat versus commoner
Capital punishment
Conclusion
Her transitory self
Jane Austen: the establishment
A question of mastery: the novels of Charlotte Brontë
A wife who waddles: the novels of George Eliot

Kennaway, James
About
Hart, F. R. Kennaway, Spark and after. *In* Hart, F. R. The Scottish novel p287-321

Kennedy, Alan
Meaning and signs in fiction
Contents
Agency and scene in Jane Austen
Agents and patients in Dickens
From Shakespeare to Congreve: between drama and novel.
George Eliot: the invisible fabrick and the clothes of time
Significant action and cannibal clothes
The thread in the garment
The protean self
Contents
Cannibals, okapis and self-slaughter in the novels of Muriel Spark
Christopher Isherwood's psychological makeup
Conclusion: A quick look around
Dramatic action, the modern and the postmodern
Inconsistencies of narration in Graham Greene
John Fowles's sense of an ending
Language, mimesis and the numinous in Joyce Cary's second trilogy
The novel as a social fiction

Kennedy, Andrew K.
Six dramatists in search of a language
Contents
Arden
Beckett
Conclusion
Eliot
Osborne
Pinter
Shaw

Kennedy, John Fitzgerald, President U.S.
Preface to Looking outward: years of crisis at the United Nations by Adlai Stevenson. *In* Praise from famous men: an anthology of introductions p89-93
About
Nunnerley, D. JFK: assassination, martyrdom, impact; excerpt from "President Kennedy and Britain." *In* Burton, D. H. ed. American history—British historians p239-54

Peretz, D. The Kennedy and Johnson administrations and the Six-Day War. *In* The New world balance and peace in the Middle East: reality or mirage? p190-95
About individual works
Profiles in courage
Nevins, A. Foreword to Profiles in courage by John F. Kennedy. *In* Praise from famous men: an anthology of introductions p124-30
Assassination
Trilling, D. The assassination of President Kennedy. *In* Trilling, D. We must march my darlings p3-12

Kennedy, John Miller
Perception, pictures, and the etcetera principle. *In* Perception p209-26

Kennedy, John Miller, and Fox, Nathan
Pictures to see and pictures to touch. *In* Perkins, D. and Leondar, B. eds. The arts and cognition p118-35

Kennedy, Sighle
The Irishness of Beckett: Spirals of need: Irish prototypes in Samuel Beckett's fiction. *In* Yeats, Joyce, and Beckett p153-66

Kennedy, Thomas Crawford
Conscription. *In* Encyclopedia of American foreign policy p151-57

Kennedy, William John
Rhetorical norms in Renaissance literature
Contents
The epic genre and varieties of form
The Petrarchan mode in lyric poetry
The style of ironic discourse

Kennel, Charles Frederick. See Abers, E. S. jt. auth.

Kenner, Hugh
Approaches to the artist as a young language teacher. *In* Viva Vivas! p331-53
The Cubist portrait. *In* Staley, T. F. and Benstock, B. eds. Approaches to Joyce's Portrait p171-84
Faulkner and Joyce. *In* Faulkner, modernism, and film: Faulkner and Yoknapatawpha, 1978 p20-33
Faulkner and the avant-garde. *In* Faulkner, modernism, and film: Faulkner and Yoknapatawpha, 1978 p182-96
A homemade world
Contents
Classroom accuracies
Disliking it
The last novelist
The Promised Land
Small ritual truths
So here it is at last
Something to say
The pedagogue as critic. *In* Young, T. D. ed. The New Criticism and after p36-46
Sincerity kills. *In* Lane, G. ed. Sylvia Plath p33-44
The urban apocalypse. *In* Wimsatt, W. K. ed. Literary criticism: idea and act p616-35
About individual works
The counterfeiters
Sale, R. H. Hugh Kenner. *In* Sale, R. H. On not being good enough p136-44
Gnomon
Marcus, S. Three obsessed critics. *In* Marcus, S. Representations p102-17

Kenner, Hugh—About individual works
—*Continued*

The poetry of Ezra Pound

Frye, N. Phalanx of particulars. *In* Frye, N. Northrop Frye on culture and literature p197-203

Kenner, William Hugh. See Kenner, Hugh

Kenney, Edwin James

Notes on Ovid: III. *In* Harvard Studies in classical philology v74 p169-85

A question of taste: Horace, Epistles 1.14.6-9. *In* Illinois classical studies, v2 1977 p229-39

Vivida vis: Polemic and pathos in Lucretius 1.62-101. *In* Woodman, T. and West, D. eds. Quality and pleasure in Latin poetry p18-30

Kenney, William

Parodies and imitations of Johnson in the eighteenth century. *In* Studies in eighteenth-century culture v7 p463-73

Kenny, Anthony

The ghost of the Tractatus. *In* Royal Institute of Philosophy. Understanding Wittgenstein p 1-13

Intention and purpose in law. *In* Summers, R. S. ed. Essays in legal philosophy p146-63

About individual works

The five ways: Saint Thomas Aquinas' proof of God's existence

Weinberg, J. R. Kenny, Hume, and causal necessity. *In* Weinberg, J. R. Ockham, Descartes, and Hume p141-44

Weinberg, J. R. Two recent criticisms of Hume. *In* Weinberg, J. R. Ockham, Descartes, and Hume p135-40

Kenny, L. M.

The modern Arab world. *In* Savory, R. M. ed. Introduction to Islamic civilisation p147-59

Kenny, Shirley Strum

The mystery of Farquhar's Stage-coach reconsidered. *In* Virginia. University. Bibliographical Society. Studies in bibliography v32 p219-36

Piracies of two plays by Farquhar. *In* Virginia. University. Bibliographical Society. Studies in bibliography v28 p297-305

Kent, Charles Willie

About

Young, J. H. Euclid + Lincoln = Kent. *In* From Parnassus p271-82

Kent, Christopher

Image and reality: the actress and society. *In* Vicinus, M. ed. A widening sphere p94-116

Kent, George

Ocean fisheries management. *In* Orr, D. W. and Soroos, M. S. eds. The global predicament p232-48

Kent, James

About

White, G. E. Kent, Story, and Shaw: the judicial function and property rights. *In* White, G. E. The American judicial tradition p35-63

Kentucky

History—1865-1950

Grantham, D. W. Black Patch War: the Kentucky and Tennessee night riders, 1905-1909. *In* Grantham, D. W. The regional imagination p65-75

Kentucky in literature

Flanagan, J. T. Jesse Stuart, regional novelist. *In* LeMaster, J. R. and Clarke, M. W. eds. Jesse Stuart p70-88

Miller, J. W. The gift outright: W-Hollow. *In* LeMaster, J. R. and Clarke, M. W. eds. Jesse Stuart p103-16

Kenya

Antiquities

Kirkman, J. S. Some conclusions from archaeological excavations on the coast of Kenya, 1948-1966. *In* Chittick, H. N. and Rotberg, R. I. eds. East Africa and the Orient p226-47

Foreign relations

Okumu, J. Kenya's foreign policy. *In* Aluko, O. ed. The foreign policies of African states p136-62

Social life and customs

Whiting, B. B. Changing life styles in Kenya. *In* Rossi, A. S.; Kagan, J. and Hareven, T. K. eds. The family p211-26

Kenyon, Cecilia M.

The Declaration of Independence: philosophy of government in a free society. *In* Aspects of American liberty p114-25

Kenyon, John Philipps

Andrew Marvell: life and times. *In* Andrew Marvell p 1-35

The Revolution of 1688: resistance and contract. *In* Historical perspectives p43-69

The Kenyon Review

Macauley, R. The Kenyon Review, 1939-1970. *In* Anderson, E. and Kinzie, M. eds. The little magazine in America: a modern documentary history p71-77

Kepler, Johann

About

Rosen, E. Kepler's mastery of Greek. *In* Philosophy and humanism p310-19

Kepple, Laurence R.

The broken victim: Euripides Bacchae 969-970. *In* Harvard Studies in classical philology v80 p107-09

Ker, Neil Ripley

A supplement to Catalogue of manuscripts containing Anglo-Saxon. *In* Anglo-Saxon England 5 p121-31

About individual works

Medieval manuscripts in British libraries

Preston, J. F. Books before printing: a codicological catalogue. *In* Review, v 1 1979 p223-31

Kerala, India

Politics and government

Heeger, G. A. The sources of Communist political power in Kerala. *In* Hammond, T. T. ed. The anatomy of Communist takeovers p620-37

May, C. J. Some lesser leaders of the Communist movement in Kerala. *In* The Making of politicians: studies from Africa and Asia p166-82

Kerferd, G. B.

What does the wise man know? *In* Rist, J. M. ed. The Stoics p125-36

Kermode, Frank. See Kermode, John Frank

Kermode, John Frank

An approach through history. *In* Spilka, M. ed. Towards a poetics of fiction p23-30

Can we say absolutely anything we like? *In* Art, politics, and will p159-72

Dissociation of sensibility. *In* Roberts, J. R. ed. Essential articles for the study of John Donne's poetry p66-82

Kern, Alexander Carl

Church, Scripture, nature and ethics in Henry Thoreau's religious thought. *In* Literature and ideas in America p79-95

Kern, Edith G.

Molière and the tradition of the grotesque. *In* Johnson, R. B.; Neumann, E. S. and Trail, G. T. eds. Molière and the commonwealth of letters: patrimony and posterity p507-20

Kern, Iso

The three ways to the transcendental phenomenological reduction in the philosophy of Edmund Husserl. *In* Elliston, F. A. and McCormick, P. eds. Husserl p126-49

Kern, Stephen

Explosive intimacy: psychodynamics of the Victorian family. *In* DeMause, L. ed. The new psychohistory p29-53

Kernan, Alvin Bernard

Shakespeare's essays on dramatic poesy: the nature and function of theater within the sonnets and the plays. *In* Martz, L. L. and Williams, A. L. eds. The author in his work p175-96

Kerney, LeRoy G.

The ministry and a parents' sharing group: preliminary report. *In* Anticipatory grief p315-19

Kerouac, John

About

Ellwood, R. S. Zen journeys to the West. *In* Ellwood, R. S. Alternative altars p136-63

Sheed, W. Beat down and beatific. *In* Sheed, W. The good word & other words p110-15

Kerr, Clark

En attendant 2000. *In* The Third century p39-42

Higher education: paradise lost? *In* The Frontiers of human knowledge p183-99

Kerr, Elizabeth Margaret

The world of Eudora Welty's women. *In* Prenshaw, P. W. ed. Eudora Welty p132-48

Kerr, Malcolm H

The respective positions of the Arabs and Israel on a peace settlement. *In* The New world balance and peace in the Middle East: reality or mirage? p36-42

Kersey, Harry A.

Those left behind: the Seminole Indians of Florida. *In* Williams, W. L. ed. Southeastern Indians since the removal era p174-90

Kershaw, Ian

The great famine and agrarian crisis in England, 1315-1322. *In* Peasants, knights and heretics p85-132

Kesey, Ken

About individual works

One flew over the cuckoo's nest

Allen, M. Women of the fabulators: Barth, Pynchon, Purdy, Kesey. *In* Allen, M. The necessary blankness p14-69

Haskell, M. Kesey cured: Forman's sweet insanity. *In* Peary, G. and Shatzkin, R. eds. The modern American novel and the movies p266-71

Wallace, R. H. What laughter can do: Ken Kesey's One flew over the cuckoo's nest. *In* Wallace, R. H. The last laugh p90-115

Kessell, John L.

Spaniards, environment, and the Pepsi generation. *In* Weber, D. J. ed. New Spain's far northern frontier p285-91

Kessler, Warren L.

A note on Spinoza's concept of attribute. *In* Freeman, E. and Mandelbaum, M. H. eds. Spinoza p191-94

Ketcham, Ralph L.

The Puritan ethic in the Revolutionary era: Abigail Adams and Thomas Jefferson. *In* "Remember the ladies": new perspectives on women in American history p49-65

Ketchum, Sara Ann

Liberalism and marriage law. *In* Feminism and philosophy p264-76

Ketterer, David

Take-off to cosmic irony: science-fiction humor and the Absurd. *In* Cohen, S. B. ed. Comic relief p70-86

Kettle, Arnold

Bernard Shaw and the new spirit. *In* Rebels and their causes p209-20

Kettler, David

Herbert Marcuse: alienation and negativity. *In* De Crespigny, A. and Minogue, K. R. eds. Contemporary political philosophers p 1-48

Kety, Seymour Solomon

Biological approaches to treatment and understanding of the major psychoses. *In* American psychiatry: past, present, and future p64-77

Keuls, Eva

Rhetoric and visual aids in Greece and Rome. *In* Havelock, E. A. and Hershbell, J. P. eds. Communication arts in the ancient world p121-34

Kevles, Daniel J.

The physics, mathematics, and chemistry communities: a comparative analysis. *In* Oleson, A. and Voss, J. eds. The organization of knowledge in modern America, 1860-1920 p139-72

Kewanee Oil Co. v. Bicron Corp. *In* The Supreme Court review, 1974 p81-95

Keyes, Charles F.

Kin groups in a Thai-Lao community. *In* Change and persistence in Thai society p274-97

Keyes, Ralph

Freeing the university. *In* Fairfield, R. P. ed. Humanistic frontiers in American education p202-06

Keyes, Sidney Arthur Kilworth

About

Scannell, V. Sidney Keyes. *In* Scannell, V. Not without glory p74-94

Keylock, Leslie R.

Bultmann's law of increasing distinctness. *In* Current issues in Biblical and patristic interpretation p193-210

Keylor, William R.
Clio on trial: Charles Péguy as historical critic. *In* From Parnassus p195-208

Keynes, Sir Geoffrey Langdon
The early years. *In* Keynes, M. ed. Essays on John Maynard Keynes p26-35

Keynes, John Maynard

About

Davenport, N. E. H. Keynes in the City. *In* Keynes, M. ed. Essays on John Maynard Keynes p224-29

De Cecco, M. The last of the Romans. *In* Skidelsky, R. J. A. ed. The end of the Keynesian era p18-24

Dimsdale, N. H. Keynes and the finance of the First World War. *In* Keynes, M. ed. Essays on John Maynard Keynes p142-61

Elcock, H. J. J. M. Keynes at the Paris Peace Conference. *In* Keynes, M. ed. Essays on John Maynard Keynes p162-76

Fay, C. R. The undergraduate. *In* Keynes, M. ed. Essays on John Maynard Keynes p36-38

Garnett, D. Maynard Keynes as a biographer. *In* Keynes, M. ed. Essays on John Maynard Keynes p254-59

Glasgow, M. The concept of the Arts council. *In* Keynes, M. ed. Essays on John Maynard Keynes p260-71

Higgins, N. The Cambridge Arts Theatre. *In* Keynes, M. ed. Essays on John Maynard Keynes p272-79

Keynes, Sir G. L. The early years. *In* Keynes, M. ed. Essays on John Maynard Keynes p26-35

Keynes, M. Maynard and Lydia Keynes. *In* Keynes, M. ed. Essays on John Maynard Keynes p 1-8

Levy, P. The Bloomsbury group. *In* Keynes, M. ed. Essays on John Maynard Keynes p60-72

Moggridge, D. E. Economic policy in the Second World War. *In* Keynes, M. ed. Essays on John Maynard Keynes p177-201

Moggridge, D. E. The influence of Keynes on the economics of his time. *In* Keynes, M. ed. Essays on John Maynard Keynes p73-81

Patinkin, D. The development of Keynes's policy thinking. *In* Theory for economic efficiency: essays in honor of Abba P. Lerner p150-66

Plumptre, A. F. W. Maynard Keynes as a teacher. *In* Keynes, M. ed. Essays on John Maynard Keynes p247-53

Robinson, E. A. G. A personal view. *In* Keynes, M. ed. Essays on John Maynard Keynes p9-23

Rylands, G. H. W. The Kingsman. *In* Keynes, M. ed. Essays on John Maynard Keynes p39-48

Shone, R. and Grant, D. J. C. The picture collector. *In* Keynes, M. ed. Essays on John Maynard Keynes p280-89

Skidelsky, R. J. A. The revolt against the Victorians. *In* Skidelsky, R. J. A. ed. The end of the Keynesian era p 1-9

Vaizey, J. E. Keynes and Cambridge. *In* Skidelsky, R. J. A. ed. The end of the Keynesian era p10-17

Wilson, C. H. Keynes and economic history. *In* Keynes, M. ed. Essays on John Maynard Keynes p230-36

About individual works

The general theory of employment, interest and money

Galbraith, J. K. How Keynes came to America. *In* Keynes, M. ed. Essays on John Maynard Keynes p132-41

Lekachman, R. The radical Keynes. *In* Skidelsky, R. J. A. ed. The end of the Keynesian era p59-66

A treatise on probability

Braithwaite, R. B. Keynes as a philosopher. *In* Keynes, M. ed. Essays on John Maynard Keynes p237-46

Influence

Barraclough, G. The Keynesian era in perspective. *In* Skidelsky, R. J. A. ed. The end of the Keynesian era p104-11

Library

Munby, A. N. L. The book collector. *In* Keynes, M. ed. Essays on John Maynard Keynes p290-98

Keynes, Lydia (Lopokova) Lady

About

Buckle, R. On loving Lydia. *In* Keynes, M. ed. Essays on John Maynard Keynes p49-59

Keynes, M. Maynard and Lydia Keynes. *In* Keynes, M. ed. Essays on John Maynard Keynes p 1-8

Keynes, Milo
Maynard and Lydia Keynes. *In* Keynes, M. ed. Essays on John Maynard Keynes p 1-8

Keynes, Simon
An interpretation of the pacx, pax and paxs pennies. *In* Anglo-Saxon England 7 p165-73

Keynesian economics
Barraclough, G. The Keynesian era in perspective. *In* Skidelsky, R. J. A. ed. The end of the Keynesian era p104-11

Brittan, S. Can democracy manage an economy? *In* Skidelsky, R. J. A. ed. The end of the Keynesian era p41-46

Fellner, W. J. Neo-Keynesianism, monetarism and the short and the long run. *In* Theory for economic efficiency: essays in honor of Abba P. Lerner p24-45

Galbraith, J. K. How Keynes came to America. *In* Keynes, M. ed. Essays on John Maynard Keynes p132-41

Holland. S. Keynes and the Socialists. *In* Skidelsky, R. J. A. ed. The end of the Keynesian era p67-77

Johnson, H. G. Keynes and British economics. *In* Keynes, M. ed. Essays on John Maynard Keynes p108-22

Johnson, H. G. Keynes and the developing world. *In* Skidelsky, R. J. A. ed. The end of the Keynesian era p88-94

Jones, A. Inflation as an industrial problem. *In* Skidelsky, R. J. A. ed. The end of the Keynesian era p50-58

Lilley, P. Two critics of Keynes: Friedman and Hayek. *In* Skidelsky, R. J. A. ed. The end of the Keynesian era p25-32

Martin, A. The dynamics of change in a Keynesian political economy: the Swedish case and its implications. *In* Crouch, C. ed. State and economy in contemporary capitalism p88-121

Meade, J. E. The Keynesian revolution. *In* Keynes, M. ed. Essays on John Maynard Keynes p82-88

Keynesian economics—*Continued*

Moggridge, D. E. The influence of Keynes on the economics of his time. *In* Keynes, M. ed. Essays on John Maynard Keynes p73-81

Patinkin, D. The development of Keynes's policy thinking. *In* Theory for economic efficiency: essays in honor of Abba P. Lerner p150-66

Robinson, J. What has become of the Keynesian revolution? *In* Keynes, M. ed. Essays on John Maynard Keynes p123-31

Skidelsky, R. J. A. The decline of Keynesian politics. *In* Crouch, C. State and economy in contemporary capitalism p55-87

Skidelsky, R. J. A. The reception of the Keynesian revolution. *In* Keynes, M. ed. Essays on John Maynard Keynes p89-107

Winkler, J. T. The coming corporatism. *In* Skidelsky, R. J. A. ed. The end of the Keynesian era p78-87

Political aspects

Skidelsky, R. J. A. The political meaning of the Keynesian revolution. *In* Skidelsky, R. J. A. ed. The end of the Keynesian era p33-40

Keys, Roger

The Bely-Ivanov-Razumnik correspondence. *In* Janecek, G. ed. Andrey Bely p193-204

Keyser, Samuel Jay. See Halle, M. jt. auth.

Kha (The Indic word)

Coomaraswamy, A. K. Kha and other words denoting "zero," in connection with the Indian metaphysics of space. *In* Coomaraswamy, A. K. Selected papers v2 p220-30

Khalid, Mansour

The sociocultural determinants of Arab diplomacy. *In* Arab and American cultures p123-42

The southern Sudan settlement and its African implications. *In* El-Ayouty, Y. ed. The Organization of African Unity after ten years p174-88

Khalidi, Rashid

Arab nationalism in Syria: the formative years, 1908-1914. *In* Nationalism in a non-national state p207-37

Khamara, E. J. and Macnabb, D. G. C.

Hume and his predecessors on the causal maxim. *In* David Hume p146-55

Khan, Masud R.

Suicide: the condition of consciousness. *In* Abbs, P. ed. The black rainbow p63-91

Kharjas. See Muwashshah

Khazars

Dunlop, D .M. H. M. Baratz and his view of Khazar influence on the earliest Russian literature, juridical and historical. *In* Salo Wittmayer Baron v 1 p345-67

Khazirs. See Khazars

Kheraskov, Mikhail Matveevich

About

Green, M. A. Kheraskov and the Christian tragedy. *In* California Slavic studies v9 p 1-25

Khlebnikov, Velemir

About individual works
Night search

Thomson, B. The secret of art: two Soviet myths. *In* Thomson, B. Lot's wife and the Venus of Milo p77-97

Khlebnikov, Viktor (Velemir) Vladimirovich. See Khlebnikov, Velemir

Khlysty

Ivask, G. Russian modernist poets and the mystic sectarians. *In* Gibian, G. and Tjalsma, H. W. eds. Russian modernism p85-106

Khmers

Ebihara, M. M. Khmer village women in Cambodia: a happy balance. *In* Matthiasson, C. J. ed. Many sisters p305-47

Griswold, A. B. and Prasert Na Nagara. On kingship and society at Sukhodaya. *In* Change and persistence in Thai society p29-92

Kirsch, A. T. Kinship, genealogical claims, and societal integration in ancient Khmer society: an interpretation. *In* Southeast Asian history and historiography p190-202

Khodasevich, Vladislav Felitsianovich

The shaken tripod. *In* Proffer, C. R. ed. Modern Russian poets on poetry p61-70

About

Hughes, R. P. Khodasevich: irony and dislocation: a poet in exile. *In* The Bitter air of exile p52-66

Nabokov, V. V. On Khodasevich. *In* The Bitter air of exile p83-87

Khouri, Fred John

United Nations peace efforts. *In* The Elusive peace in the Middle East p19-101

Khouri, Mounah Abdallah

Literature. *In* The Genius of Arab civilization p17-52

!Khung (African people) See !Kung (African people)

Kibbutzim. See Collective settlements—Israel

Kibre, Pearl, and Siraisi, Nancy G.

The institutional setting: the universities. *In* Lindberg, D. C. ed. Science in the Middle Ages p120-44

Kidd, I. G.

Moral actions and rules in Stoic ethics. *In* Rist, J. M. ed. The Stoics p247-58

Kidder, Robert L.

Lawyers for the people: dilemmas of legal activists. *In* Gerstl, J. E. and Jacobs, G. eds. Professions for the people p153-74

Kidnapping

Murphy, J. The role of international law in the prevention of terrorist kidnapping of diplomatic personnel. *In* International terrorism and political crimes p285-313

See also Abduction

Kidneys

Temkin, O. A Galenic model for quantitative physiological reasoning? *In* Temkin, O. The double face of Janus p162-66

Kiefer, Christie Weber

Lessons from the issei. *In* Gubrium, J. F. ed. Late life p167-97

Kiehl, James M.

Love sublimated: Upon Appleton House. *In* Renaissance and modern p56-106

The poems of Howard Nemerov: where loveliness adorns intelligible things. *In* Boyers, R. ed. Contemporary poetry in America p279-302

Kiely, Robert

The limits of dialogue in Middlemarch. *In* The Worlds of Victorian fiction p103-23

Kienzle, Raymond Nicholas. See Ray, Nicholas

Kierkegaard, Søren Aabye

About

Fitzgerald, R. Essay 3. In Fitzgerald, R. ed. What it means to be human p44-63

Scott, N. A. Kierkegaard's strait gate. In Scott, N. A. Mirrors of man in existentialism p25-59

About individual works
Either/or

Hutchings, P. Æ. Conjugal faithfulness. In Royal Institute of Philosophy. Human values p61-85

The last years

Hamburger, M. A refusal to review Kierkegaard. In Hamburger, M. Art as second nature p45-48

On authority and revelation: The book of Adler

Cavell, S. Kierkegaard's On authority and revelation. In Cavell, S. Must we mean what we say? p163-80

Ethics

Warnock, M. Existentialist ethics. In New studies in ethics v2 p361-420

Kiernan, Brian
Literature, history, and literary history: perspectives on the nineteenth century in Australia. In Bards, bohemians, and bookmen p 1-18

Kiernan, E. Victor Gordon
Nationalist movements and social classes. In Smith, A. D. ed. Nationalist movements p110-33

Private property in history. In Family and inheritance p361-98

Working class and nation in nineteenth-century Britain. In Rebels and their causes p122-39

Kiernan, V. G. See Kiernan, E. Victor Gordon

Kiernan, Victor Gordon. See Kiernan, E. Victor Gordon

Kievan Russia. See Russia—History—Kievan period, 862-1237

Kihm, Jean Jacques. See Sprigge, E. jt. auth.

Kikuyu tribe
Whiting, B. B. The dependency hang-up and experiments in alternative life styles. In Major social issues p217-26

Kilby, Clyde S.
Till we have faces: an interpretation. In Schakel, P. J. ed. The longing for a form p171-81

The ugly and the evil. In Evolution of consciousness p202-10

Kilenge (Melanesian people)

Wood-carving

Gerbrands, A. A. Talania and Nake, master carver and apprentice: two woodcarvers from the Kilenge (western New Britain) In Greenhalgh, M. and Megaw, J. V. S. eds. Art in society p193-205

Kilgo, Reese Danley
Can group marriage work? In Gross, L. ed. Sexual issues in marriage p231-36

Kilgour, Raymond Lincoln

About individual works
The decline of chivalry as shown in the French literature of the late Middle Ages

Keen, M. H. Huizinga, Kilgour and the decline of chivalry. In Medievalia et humanistica no. 8 p 1-20

Killam, Douglas
Notions of religion, alienation and archetype in Arrow of God. In Exile and tradition p152-65

Killam, G. D. See Killam, Douglas

The killer elite (Motion picture)
Kael, P. Notes on the nihilist poetry of Sam Peckinpah. In Denby, D. ed. Awake in the dark p326-33

Killham, John

About individual works
The 'second self' in novel criticism

Booth, W. C. The rhetoric of fiction and the poetics of fictions. In Spilka, M. ed. Towards a poetics of fiction p77-89

Killing, Mercy. See Euthanasia

Kilroy, James Francis
Nineteenth-century writers. In Finneran, R. J. ed. Anglo-Irish literature p24-47

Kilson, Marion D. de B.
Afro-American social structure, 1790-1970. In Kilson, M. L. and Rotberg, R. I. eds. The African diaspora p414-58

Kilson, Martin L.
Blacks and neo-ethnicity in American political life. In Glazer, N. and Moynihan, D. P. eds. Ethnicity p236-66

Cleavage management in African politics: the Ghana case. In Kilson, M. ed. New states in the modern world p75-88

The political status of American Negroes in the twentieth century. In Kilson, M. L. and Rotberg, R. I. eds. The African diaspora p459-84

Kilvert, Robert Francis

About individual works
Kilvert's diary

Plomer, W. C. F. Francis Kilvert and his Diary. In Royal Society of Literature of the United Kingdom, London. Essays by divers hands v38 p78-92

Kim, Chong Lim; Green, Justin Jay, and Patterson, Samuel Charles
Partisanship in the recruitment and performance of American state legislature. In Eulau, H. and Czudnowski, M. M. eds. Elite recruitment in democratic polities p79-103

Kim, Young Chin
The interaction of economics and Japanese foreign policy. In The Interaction of economics and foreign policy p84-101

Kimball, Robert

About individual works
Cole

Sheed, W. Rhapsodist in blue. In Sheed, W. The good word & other words p154-58

Kimball, Robert, and Simon, Alfred E.

About individual works
The Gershwins

Sheed, W. Rhapsodist in blue. In Sheed, W. The good word & other words p154-58

Kimball, Solon Toothaker
Anthropology as a policy science. *In* Eddy, E. M. and Partridge, W. L. eds. Applied anthropology in America p277-91

Kimball, Sue L.
Games people play in Congreve's The way of the world. *In* A Provision of human nature p191-207

Kimball, Warren F.
Alliances, coalitions, and ententes. *In* Encyclopedia of American foreign policy p 1-15
The Morgenthau plan. *In* Encyclopedia of American foreign policy p597-602

Kimbangu, Simon

About

Thomas, G. B. Kimbanguism: authentically African, authentically Christian. *In* African religions: a symposium p275-96

Kimbanguist Church of Zaire. See Église de Jésus-Christ zur la terre par le Prophète Simon Kimbangu

Kime, Wayne Raymond
Critical discrimination and editorial judgment. *In* Review, v 1 1979 p105-22

Kimmel, Eric A.
Jewish identity in juvenile fiction: a look at three recommended books. *In* Horn Book Magazine. Crosscurrents of criticism p150-58

Kincaid, James R.

About individual works
The novels of Anthony Trollope

Hart, F. R. New approaches to the Trollope problem. *In* Review, v 1 1979 p165-72

Kindergarten. See Education, Preschool

Kindergarten teachers
Headley, N. E. Early Progressive schools —I. *In* Roots of open education in America p131-34

Kindermann, Gottfried-Karl
The attempted revolution in China: the first Sino-Soviet alliance, 1924-1927. *In* Hammond, T. T. ed. The anatomy of Communist takeovers p192-213

al-Kīndī

About individual works
De aspectibus

Lindberg, D. C. The intromission-extramission controversy in Islamic visual theory: Alkindi versus Avicenna. *In* Studies in perception p137-59

On first philosophy

Ivry, A. L. al-Kīndī's On first philosophy and Aristotle's Metaphysics. *In* Essays on Islamic philosophy and science p15-24

Kindleberger, Charles Poor
The historical background: Adam Smith and the Industrial Revolution. *In* The Market and the state p 1-25
Is symmetry possible in international money? *In* Theory for economic efficiency: essays in honor of Abba P. Lerner p62-75
U.S. foreign economic policy, 1776-1976. *In* Two hundred years of American foreign policy p209-51

Kindness. See Benevolence

Kinetic art
Osborne, H. Concrete art and the repudiation of artifice. *In* Osborne, H. Abstraction and artifice in twentieth-century art p163-80

Kinetics. See Motion

King, Adele
Camara Laye. *In* King, B. A. and Ogungbesan, K. eds. A celebration of Black and African writing p112-23

King, Edward, 1848-1896

About individual works
The great South

Downs, R. B. Southern panorama. *In* Downs, R. B. Books that changed the South p138-47

King, George
Wallis, R. The Aetherius Society: a case study in the formation of a mystagogic congregation. *In* Wallis, R. ed. Sectarianism p17-34

King, Gregory

About individual works
Natural and political observations and conclusions upon the state and condition of England, 1696

Le Roy Ladurie, E. The chief defects of Gregory King. *In* Le Roy Ladurie, E. The territory of the historian p173-91

King, J. Norman
Theology, science fiction, and man's future orientation. *In* Clareson, T. D. ed. Many futures, many worlds p237-59

King, James T.
The place of the language of morals in Hume's second Enquiry. *In* Livingston, D. W. and King, J. T. eds. Hume p343-61

King, John Theodore

About

Harvey, A. M. Contributions of the part-time staff of the Johns Hopkins Hospital: Moore, King, and Gay. *In* Harvey, A. M. Adventures in medical research p248-60

King, Jonathan
Henri Barbusse: Le feu and the crisis of social realism. *In* Klein, H. M. ed. The First World War in fiction p43-52

King, Kenneth James
Educational perspectives on Africa. *In* African studies since 1945 p77-90

King, Lloyd
Nicolás Guillén and Afrocubanismo. *In* King, B. A. and Ogungbesan, K. eds. A celebration of Black and African writing p30-45

King, Martin Luther

About

Harding, V. So much history, so much future: Martin Luther King, Jr., and the Second Coming of America. *In* Have we overcome? Race relations since Brown p31-78

King, Michael Robert, and Seligman, Lester G.
Critical elections, Congressional recruitment and public policy. *In* Eulau, H. and Czudnowski, M. M. eds. Elite recruitment in democratic polities p263-99

King, Peter
All at sea? A critique of the American strategic force structure. *In* Arms control and technological innovation p265-87

King, Thomas B. See Fortmann, H. R. jt. auth.

King, Winston L.

Contemporary Burmese Buddhism. *In* Dumoulin, H. ed. Buddhism in the modern world p81-98

A king in New York (Motion picture)

Kauffmann, S. A king in New York. *In* Kauffmann, S. Living images p246-49

Truffaut, F. Charlie Chaplin: A king in New York. *In* Truffaut, F. The films in my life p57-60

King Lear (Motion picture by Grigorii Mikhaïlovich Kozintsev)

Jorgens, J. J. King Lear: Peter Brook and Grigori Kozintsev. *In* Jorgens, J. J. Shakespeare on film p235-51

King Lear (Motion picture by Peter Brook)

Jorgens, J. J. King Lear: Peter Brook and Grigori Kozintsev. *In* Jorgens, J. J. Shakespeare on film p235-51

The king of Marvin Gardens (Motion picture)

Kauffmann, S. The king of Marvin Garddens. *In* Kauffmann, S. Living images p146-48

Kingdon, Robert McCune

Was the Protestant Reformation a revolution? The case of Geneva. *In* Church, society and politics p203-22

Kings and rulers

Geertz, C. Centers, kings, and charisma: reflections on the symbolics of power. *In* Culture and its creators p150-71

Kings and rulers in art

Bullough, D. A. 'Imagines regum' and their significance in the early medieval West. *In* Studies in memory of David Talbot Rice p223-76

Kings and rulers in literature

Adams, R. P. Opposed Tudor myths of power: Machiavellian tyrants and Christian kings. *In* Studies in the continental background of Renaissance English literature: essays presented to John L. Lievsay p67-90

Akrigg, G. P. V. Shakespeare the kingmaker. *In* English Renaissance drama p46-58

Barton, A. He that plays the king: Ford's Perkin Warbeck and the Stuart history play. *In* English drama: forms and development p69-93

Edwards, P. The royal pretenders in Massinger and Ford. *In* English Association. Essays and studies, 1974 p18-36

Gurr, A. 'Henry V' and the bees' commonwealth. *In* Shakespeare survey 30 p61-72

Kings in art. See Kings and rulers in art

Kingsley, Charles

About

Dawson, C. Polemics: Charles Kingsley and Alton Locke. *In* Dawson, C. Victorian noon p179-202

Haley, B. Types of healthy Christianity: Newman and Kingsley. *In* Haley, B. The healthy body and Victorian culture p95-119

Prickett, S. Adults in allegory land: Kingsley and Macdonald. *In* Prickett, S. Victorian fantasy p150-97

About individual works

Alton Locke, tailor and poet

Dawson, C. Polemics: Charles Kingsley and Alton Locke. *In* Dawson, C. Victorian noon p179-202

Hereward the Wake

Sanders, A. Last of the English: Charles Kingsley's Hereward the Wake. *In* Sanders, A. The Victorian historical novel, 1840-1880 p149-67

Hypatia

Sanders, A. The argument from tradition: Hypatia, Fabiola and Callista. *In* Sanders, A. The Victorian historical novel, 1840-1880 p120-48

Two years ago

Haley, B. Two staunch walkers: Tom Thurnall and Tom Tulliver. *In* Haley, B. The healthy body and Victorian culture p180-204

The water-babies

Manlove, C. N. Charles Kingsley (1819-75) and The water-babies. *In* Manlove, C. N. Modern fantasy p13-54

Westward ho!

Sutherland, J. A. 'Westward ho!': 'a popularly successful book.' *In* Sutherland, J. A. Victorian novelists and publishers p117-32

Kinkead, Duncan T.

An important Vanitas by Juan de Valdès Leal. *In* Enggass, R. C. and Stokstad, M. eds. Hortus imaginum p155-63

Kinkead-Weekes, Mark

Eros and methaphor: sexual relationship in the fiction of Lawrence. *In* Smith, A. ed. Lawrence and women p101-21

Lawrence on Hardy. *In* Butler, L. S. ed. Thomas Hardy after fifty years p90-103

Walt Whitman passes the full-stop by . . . *In* An English miscellany p163-78

Kinnamon, Keneth

Hemingway, the corrida, and Spain. *In* Wagner, L. W ed. Ernest Hemingway p57-74

Kinneavy, Gerald B.

Metaphors of the poet and his craft in William Dunbar. *In* Aeolian harps p57-64

Kinnell, Galway

About

Mills, R. J. A reading of Galway Kinnell. *In* Mills, R. J. Cry of the human p134-91

Thurley, G. Devices among words: Kinnell, Bly, Simic. *In* Thurley, G. The American moment p210-28

Kinship

Diamond, N. Collectivization, kinship, and the status of women in rural China. *In* Reiter, R. R. ed. Toward an anthropology of women p372-95

Eades, J. S. Kinship and entrepreneurship among Yoruba in northern Ghana. *In* Shack, W. A. and Skinner, E. P. eds. Strangers in African societies p169-82

Firth, R. W. Relations between personal kin (waris) among Kelantan Malays. *In* Social organization and the applications of anthropology p23-61

Fox, R. Primate kin and human kinship. *In* Biosocial anthropology p9-35

Hanks, J. R. Recitation of patrilineages among the Akha. *In* Social organization and the applications of anthropology p114-27

Meinhard, H. H. The patrilineal principle in early Teutonic kinship. *In* Studies in social anthropology p 1-29

Nukunya, G. K. The family and social change. *In* Colonialism and change p163-77

Kinship—*Continued*

Reiter, R. R. Men and women in the south of France: public and private domains. *In* Reiter, R. R. ed. Toward an anthropology of women p252-82

Wolf, A. P. Marriage and adoption in northern Taiwan. *In* Social organization and the applications of anthropology p128-60

See also Consanguinity; Family; Tribes and tribal system

Cambodia

Kirsch, A. T. Kinship, genealogical claims, and societal integration in ancient Khmer society: an interpretation. *In* Southeast Asian history and historiography p190-202

Great Britain

Loyn, H. R. Kinship in Anglo-Saxon England. *In* Anglo-Saxon England 3 p197-209

Thailand

Griswold, A. B. and Prasert Na Nagara. On kingship and society at Sukhodaya. *In* Change and persistence in Thai society p29-92

Keyes, C. F. Kin groups in Thai-Lao community. *In* Change and persistence in Thai society p274-97

United States—Terminology

Scheffler, H. W. The "meaning" of kinship in American culture: another view. *In* Basso, K. H. and Selby, H. A. eds. Meaning in anthropology p57-91

Kinsman, Robert S.

Folly, melancholy, and madness: a study in shifting styles of medical analysis and treatment, 1450-1675. *In* The Darker vision of the Renaissance p273-320

Introduction. *In* The Darker vision of the Renaissance p 1-23

Kiowa Apache Indians

Reservations

Hagan, W. T. Kiowas, Comanches, and cattlemen, 1867-1906: a case study of the failure of U.S. reservation policy. *In* The American Indian p77-99

Kiowa Indians

See also Kiowa Apache Indians

Reservations

Hagan, W. T. Kiowas, Comanches, and cattlemen, 1867-1906: a case study of the failure of U.S. reservation policy. *In* The American Indian p77-99

Kiparsky, Paul. See Kiparsky, Rene Paul Viktor

Kiparsky, Rene Paul Viktor

The role of linguistics in a theory of poetry. *In* Bloomfield, M. W. and Haugen, E. I. eds. Language as a human problem p233-49

Kiple, Kenneth Franklin, and Kiple, Virginia H.

Slave child mortality: some nutritional answers to a perennial puzzle. *In* Branca, P. ed. The medicine show p21-46

Kiple, Virginia H. See Kiple, K. F. jt. auth.

Kipling, Rudyard

About

Bayley, J. The puzzles of Kipling. *In* Bayley, J. The uses of division p51-81

Briggs, J. Far away and long ago: Stevenson's Scotland and Kipling's India. *In* Briggs, J. Night visitors p98-110

Goonetilleke, D. C. R. A. Difficulties of connection in India: Kipling and Forster. *In* Goonetilleke, D. C. R. A. Developing countries in British fiction p134-69

Hungiville, M. Epithets and epitaphs: Rudyard Kipling's reputation as a poet. *In* Tennessee Studies in literature v 20 p138-50

Prickett, S. Worlds within worlds: Kipling and Nesbit. *In* Prickett, S. Victorian fantasy p198-239

Rutherford, A. The subaltern as hero: Kipling and frontier war. *In* Rutherford, A. The literature of war p11-37

Stokes, E. 'The Voice of the Hooligan': Kipling and the Commonwealth experience. *In* Historical perspectives p285-301

About individual works
Kim

Howe, I. The pleasures of Kim. *In* Art, politics, and will p145-58

Stalky & Co.

Marcus, S. Stalky & Co. *In* Marcus, S. Representations p61-75

Influence—Brecht

Lyon, L. K. Kipling's "Soldiers three" and Brecht's A man's a man. *In* Mews, S. and Knust, H. eds. Essays on Brecht p99-113

Király, Béla K.

The Hungarian church. *In* Callahan, W. J. and Higgs, D. eds. Church and society in Catholic Europe of the eighteenth century p106-21

Protestantism in Hungary between the Revolution and the Ausgleich. *In* Király, B. K. ed. Tolerance and movements of religious dissent in Eastern Europe p65-85

The Sublime Porte, Vienna, Transylvania and the dissemination of Protestant Reformation in royal Hungary. *In* Király, B. K. ed. Tolerance and movements of religious dissent in Eastern Europe p199-221

Kirby, Stephen

Great-Power involvement in European systems. *In* Hayward, J. E. S. and Berki, R. N. eds. State and society in contemporary Europe p181-202

Kirby, Thomas Austin

An analogue (?) to The reeve's tale. *In* Chaucer and Middle English studies in honour of Rossell Hope Robbins p381-83

Kirchhoff, Frederick

A science against sciences: Ruskin's floral mythology. *In* Knoepflmacher, U. C. and Tennyson, G. B. eds. Nature and the Victorian imagination p246-58

Travel as anti-autobiography: William Morris's Icelandic Journals. *In* Landow, G. P. ed. Approaches to Victorian autobiography p292-310

Kirk, Elizabeth D.

"I would rather have written in Elvish": language, fiction and The Lord of the Rings. *In* Spilka, M. ed. Towards a poetics of fiction p289-302

Kirk, Geoffrey Stephen

About

Parry, A. M. Have we Homer's Iliad? *In* Wright, J. H. ed. Essays on the Iliad p 1-27

Kirk, Jerome Richard. See Eschen, D. von jt. auth.

Kirk, R. See Bever, T. G. jt. auth.

Kirk, Russell

Vivas, Lawrence, Eliot, and the demon. *In* Viva Vivas! p225-49

Kirk, Stuart A.

Society and sexual deviance. *In* Gochros, H. L. and Gochros, J. S. eds. The sexually oppressed p28-37

Kirk-Greene, Anthony Hamilton Millard

Public administration and African studies. *In* African studies since 1945 p125-35

Kirkendall, Richard Stewart

Elitism and foreign policy. *In* Encyclopedia of American foreign policy p302-09

The New Deal and agriculture. *In* Braeman, J.; Bremmer, R. H. and Brody, D. eds. The New Deal v 1 p83-109

Kirker, Harold Clark

The Bulfinch drawings in the American Antiquarian Society. *In* American Antiquarian Society. Proceedings v86 pt 1 p125-28

Kirkman, James Spedding

Some conclusions from archaeological excavations on the coast of Kenya, 1948-1966. *In* Chittick, H. N. and Rotberg, R. I. eds. East Africa and the Orient p226-47

Kirkpatrick, Lyman B.

Intelligence and counterintelligence. *In* Encyclopedia of American foreign policy p417-27

Kirkwood, Gordon MacDonald

Nemean 7 and the theme of vicissitude in Pindar. *In* Poetry and poetics from ancient Greece to the Renaissance p56-90

Kirkwood, James, and Dante, Nicholas

About individual works
A chorus line

Kauffmann, S. A chorus line. *In* Kauffmann, S. Persons of the drama p266-70

Kirsch, Anthony Thomas

Economy, polity, and religion in Thailand. *In* Change and persistence in Thai society p172-96

Kinship, genealogical claims, and societal integration in ancient Khmer society: an interpretation. *In* Southeast Asian history and historiography p190-202

Kirsch, Arthur Clifford

The integrity of 'Measure for measure.' *In* Shakespeare survey 28 p89-105

Kirshner, Julius

"Ars imitatur naturam": a consilium of Baldus on naturalization in Florence. *In* Viator: medieval and Renaissance studies v5 p289-331

Conscience and public finance: a Questio disputata of John of Legnano on the public debt of Genoa. *In* Philosophy and humanism p434-53

Kirstein, Lincoln

About individual works
Rhymes of a Pfc.

Scannell, V. American poets of the Second World War. *In* Scannell, V. Not without glory p172-237

Kisch, Guido

An unpublished consilium of Johannes Sichardus. *In* Philosophy and humanism p477-82

Kisiel, Theodore J.

Heidegger and the new images of science. *In* Radical phenomenology p163-81

Kiss me deadly (Motion picture)

Truffaut, F. Robert Aldrich: Kiss me deadly. *In* Truffaut, F. The films in my life p93-94

Kissinger, Henry Alfred

Expanding cooperation for global economic development. *In* Benton, L. R. ed. Management for the future p199-218

About

Stoessinger, J. G. The stateman and the critic; Kissinger and Morgenthau. *In* [Truth and tragedy]: a tribute to Hans Morgenthau p220-36

Vincent, R. J. Kissinger's system of foreign policy. *In* The Year book of world affairs, 1977 p8-26

Ward, D. Kissinger: a psychohistory. *In* DeMause, L. ed. The new psychohistory p69-130

Kistner, Arthur L. and Kistner, M. K.

The themes and structures of A fair quarrel. *In* Tennessee Studies in literature v23 p31-46

Kistner, M. K. See Kistner, A. L. jt. auth.

Kistrup, Jens

Post-war drama in Scandinavia. *In* Nicoll, A. World drama p854-60

Kistyakovsky, Bogdan

In the defense of law: the intelligentsia and legal consciousness. *In* Landmarks p112-37

Kitagawa, Joseph Mitsuo

Kūkai as master and savior. *In* Reynolds, F. E. and Capps, D. eds. The biographical process p319-41

The religions of Japan. *In* Adams, C. J. ed. A reader's guide to the great religions p247-82

Kitagawa, Joseph Mitsuo and Reynolds, Frank

Theravāda Buddhism in the twentieth century. *In* Dumoulin, H. ed. Buddhism in the modern world p43-64

Kitamura, Tōkoku

About

Yamanouchi, H. From romanticism to naturalism: Kitamura Tōkoku and Shimazaki Tōson. *In* Yamanouchi, H. The search for authenticity in modern Japanese literature p20-39

Kitano, Harry H. L.

Japanese Americans: the development of a middleman minority. *In* The Asian American: the historical experience p81-100

Kitch, Edmund W. and Bowler, Clara Ann

The facts of Munn v. Illinois. *In* The Supreme Court review, 1978 p313-43

Kithara. See Cithara

Kitksan Indians

Religion and mythology

Barbeau, M. The career of a medicineman; excerpt from "Medicine-men on the North Pacific coast." *In* Tedlock, D. E. and Tedlock, B. eds. Teachings from the American earth p3-12

Kitromilides, Paschalis M. and Couloumbis, Theodore A.
Ethnic conflict in a strategic area: the case of Cyprus. *In* Said, A. A. and Simmons, L. R. eds. Ethnicity in an international context p167-202

Kitson, Peter
Lapidary traditions in Anglo-Saxon England: part I, the background; the Old English lapidary. *In* Anglo-Saxon England 7 p9-60

Kittel, Harald A.
The book of Urizen and An essay concerning human understanding. *In* Phillips, M. C. ed. Interpreting Blake p111-44

Kittel, Margaret Ruth
Women under the law in medieval England, 1066-1485. *In* Kanner, B. ed. The women of England p124-37

Kittel, Ruth. See Kittel, Margaret Ruth

Kitto, Humphrey Davy Findley
The Rhesus and related matters. *In* Yale classical studies v25 p317-50

Kittrie, Nicholas N.
Reconciling the irreconcilable: the quest for international agreement over political crime and terrorism. *In* The Year book of world affairs, 1978 p203-86

Kitzinger, Ernst
The role of miniature painting in mural decoration. *In* The Place of book illumination in Byzantine art p99-142

Kivi Aleksis, pseud. See Stenvall, Aleksis

Kjørup, Søren
Art broadly and wholly conceived. *In* Aagaard-Mogensen, L. ed. Culture and art p45-53

Film as a meetingplace of multiple codes. *In* Perkins, D. and Leondar, B. eds. The arts and cognition p20-47

Klapisch, Christiane, and Demonet, Michel
"A uno pane e uno vino": the rural Tuscan family at the beginning of the fifteenth century. *In* Family and society p41-74

Klappert, Peter

About individual works

Lugging vegetables to Nantucket

Kunitz, S. J. Peter Klappert. *In* Kunitz, S. J. A kind of order, a kind of folly p271-75

Klarman, Herbert Elias
The financing of health care. *In* Knowles, J. H. ed. Doing better and feeling worse p215-34

Klass, Dennis
Psychohistory and communal patterns: John Humphrey Noyes and the Oneida Community. *In* Reynolds, F. E. and Capps, D. eds. The biographical process p273-96

Klaus, Patricia Otto. See Otto, Patricia Courtney

Klausner, David Neal
Didacticism and drama in Guy of Warwick. *In* Medievalia et humanistica no. 6 p103-19

Kleban, Edward

About individual works

A chorus line

Kauffmann, S. A chorus line. *In* Kauffmann, S. Persons of the drama p266-70

Klee, Paul

About

Rosenblum, R. Other romantic currents: Klee to Ernst; excerpt from "Modern painting and the northern romantic tradition, Friedrich to Rothko." *In* Kaplan, P. and Manso, S. eds. Major European art movements, 1900-1945 p91-100

Kleimola, Ann Marie
Law and social change in medieval Russia: the Zakon sudnyi lyudem as a case study. *In* Oxford Slavonic papers, new ser v9 p17-27

Klein, Annette. See Borstein, I. J. jt. auth.

Klein, Donald W.
Universal values and Chinese politics—a balance sheet. *In* Terrill, R. ed. The China difference p201-18

Klein, Holger Michael
Introduction. *In* Klein, H. M. ed. The First World War in fiction p 1-9

Molière in English critical thought on comedy to 1800. *In* Johnson, R. B.; Neumann, E. S. and Trail, G. T. eds. Molière and the commonwealth of letters: patrimony and posterity p218-31

Projections of Everyman: the common soldier in Franconi, Wiechert and Williamson. *In* Klein, H. M. ed. The First World War in fiction p84-100

Klein, Lawrence Robert
Political aspects of economic control. *In* Theory for economic efficiency: essays in honor of Abba P. Lerner p76-91

See also Johnston, H. N. jt. auth.

Klein, Lawrence Robert; Moriguchi, Chikashi, and Van Peeterssen, A.
The LINK model of world trade, with applications to 1972-73. *In* Kenen, P. B. ed. International trade and finance p453-83

Klein, Marcus
John Hawkes' experimental compositions. *In* Federman, R. ed. Surfiction p203-14

Klein, Martin J.
Einstein and the academic establishment. *In* Einstein p209-13

Einstein and the development of quantum physics. *In* Einstein p133-51

Klein, Maury
The boys who stayed behind: Northern industrialists and the Civil War. *In* Rank and file p137-56

Klein, Michael
Miss L. gets married. *In* Peary, G. and Shatzkin, R. eds. The modern American novel and the movies p19-28

Klein, Milton Martin
New York lawyers and the coming of the American Revolution. *In* Studies in eighteenth-century culture v7 p23-47

Klein, Thomas

Minorities in central Europe in the sixteenth and early seventeenth centuries. *In* Hepburn, A. C. ed. Minorities in history p31-50

Klein, William F.

Purpose and the "poetics" of The wanderer and The seafarer. *In* Anglo-Saxon poetry: essays in appreciation p208-23

Kleinhans, Robert G.

Ecclesiastes sive de ratione concionandi. *In* Essays on the works of Erasmus p253-66

Kleinig, John

Human rights, legal rights and social change. *In* Human rights p36-47

Kleinjans, Everett

The Hawaii years. *In* Lerner, D. and Nelson, L. M. eds. Communication research—a half-century appraisal p325-30

Kleist, Heinrich von

About

Krumpelmann, J. T. Molière as a source of German comedy. *In* Johnson, R. B.; Neumann, E. S. and Trail, G. T. eds. Molière and the commonwealth of letters: patrimony and posterity p319-26

Mudrick, M. I don't care what mama don't allow. *In* Mudrick, M. Books are not life but then what is? p52-64

Tatar, M. M. Thunder, lightning, and electricity: moments of recognition in Heinrich von Kleist's dramas. *In* Tatar, M. M. Spellbound p82-120

About individual works
Amphitryon

McGlathery, J. M. Kleist's version of Molière's Amphitryon: Olympian cuckolding and unio mystica. *In* Johnson, R. B.; Neuman, E. S. and Trail, G. T. eds. Molière and the commonwealth of letters: patrimony and posterity p327-33

Michael Kohlhaas

Lenson, D. R. A case of migration through genres. *In* Lenson, D. R. Achilles' choice p24-39

Klemperer, Klemens von. See Von Klemperer, Klemens

Klephts

Skiotis, D. N. Mountain warriors and the Greek Revolution. *In* War, technology and society in the Middle East p308-29

Klimoff, Alexis

Solzhenitsyn in English: an evaluation. *In* Dunlop, J. B.; Haugh, R. and Klimoff, A. eds. Aleksandr Solzhenitsyn: critical essays and documentary materials 2d ed. p611-35

Translating Solzhenitsyn (cont'd): The Gulag Archipelago. *In* Dunlop, J. B.; Haugh, R. and Klimoff, A. eds. Aleksandr Solzhenitsyn: critical essays and documentary materials 2d ed. p636-49

Kline, George Louis

Philosophical puns. *In* Philosophy and the civilizing arts p213-35

Recent uncensored Soviet philosophical writings. *In* Tokes, R. L. ed. Dissent in the USSR p158-90

Klineberg, Otto

Race and psychology. *In* United Nations Educational, Scientific and Cultural Organization. Race, science and society p173-207

Kling, Blair B.

Holden Furber at work. *In* Kling, B. B. and Pearson, M. N. eds. The age of partnership p237-47

Klinger, Mary Frances

William Hogarth and London theatrical life. *In* Studies in eighteenth-century culture v5 p11-27

Klinkowitz, Jerome

A do-it-yourself story collection by Kurt Vonnegut. *In* Klinkowitz, J. and Lawler, D. L. eds. Vonnegut in America p53-60

Early writers: Jupiter Hammon, Phillis Wheatley, and Benjamin Banneker. *In* Inge, M. T.; Duke, J. M. and Bryer, J. R. eds. Black American writers v 1 p 1-20

Literary disruptions; or, What's become of American fiction? *In* Federman, R. ed. Surfiction p165-79

A note on Vonnegut in Europe. *In* Klinkowitz, J. and Lawler, D. L. eds. Vonnegut in America p255-57

The Vonnegut bibliography. *In* Klinkowitz, J. and Lawler, D. L. eds. Vonnegut in America p217-52

Vonnegut in America. *In* Klinkowitz, J. and Lawler, D. L. eds. Vonnegut in America p7-36

Klocowski, Jerzy

The Polish church. *In* Callahan, W. J. and Higgs, D. eds. Church and society in Catholic Europe of the eighteenth century p122-37

Kłoczowski, Jerzy. See Klocowski, Jerzy

Klute (Motion picture)

Giddis, D. The divided woman: Bree Daniels in Klute. *In* Nichols, B. ed. Movies and methods p194-201

Klutznick, Philip M.

Problems of the major cities: what can be done? *In* Prochnow, H. V. ed. Dilemmas facing the nation p202-21

Knapp, Bettina Liebowitz

Jean Racine's Esther and two Hebrew translations of this drama. *In* Salo Wittmayer Baron v2 p591-621

Knaus, Rodger. See Colby, Benjamin N. jt. auth.

Knave of hearts (Motion picture)

Truffaut, F. René Clément: Monsieur Ripois. *In* Truffaut, F. The films in my life p197-200

Kneale, Martha Hurst; Robinson, Richard George Frederick, and Mundle, Clement W. K.

Symposium: Is psychical research relevant to philosophy? *In* Ludwig, J. K. ed. Philosophy and parapsychology p64-109

About individual works
Symposium: Is psychical research relevant to philosophy?

Broad, C. D. Review of Kneale, Robinson, and Mundle Symposium. *In* Ludwig, J. K. ed. Philosophy and parapsychology p110-16

Knecht, Robert Jean

Francis I, 'Defender of the Faith'? *In* Wealth and power in Tudor England p106-27

Knickerbocker, Kenneth Leslie

About

Litzinger, B. Kenneth Leslie Knickerbocker. *In* Tennessee Studies in literature v20 p xi-xvii

Kniffen, Fred Bowerman
American cultural geography and folklife. *In* Yoder, D. ed. American folklife p51-70

Knight, Damon Francis
What is science fiction? *In* Knight, D. F. ed. Turning points p62-69

Writing and selling science fiction. *In* Knight, D. F. ed. Turning points p218-28

Knight, Frank Hyneman

About
Buchanan, J. M. Methods and morals in economics: the Ayres-Knight discussion. *In* Science and ceremony p163-74

Knight, Franklin W.
Slavery, race, and social structure in Cuba during the nineteenth century. *In* Toplin, R. B. ed. Slavery and race relations in Latin America p204-27

Knight, Franklin W. and Crahan, Margaret Ellen
The African migration and the origins of an Afro-American society and culture. *In* Crahan, M. E. and Knight, F. W. eds. Africa and the Caribbean p 1-19

Knight, Harry Lionel
Dickens and Mrs. Stowe. *In* Dickens Studies Annual v5 p43-58

Knight, Isabel F.
Utopian dream as psychic reality. *In* Studies in eighteenth-century culture v6 p427-38

Knight, Richard Payne

About individual works
An analytical inquiry into the principles of taste

Albrecht, W. P. Knight. *In* Albrecht, W. P. The sublime pleasures of tragedy p83-95

Knight, Robert Patrick
UNESCO's role in world communication. *In* Fischer, H. D. and Merrill, J. C. eds. International and intercultural communication p377-91

Knight, Sara (Kemble)

About individual works
The journal of Madam Knight
Seelye, J. Providential passages: wherein a matron, a minister, a militiaman, and a madam display the cardinal points of the Puritan compass. *In* Seelye, J. Prophetic waters p279-309

Spengemann, W. C. The poetics of adventure. *In* Spengemann, W. C. The adventurous muse p6-67

Knight, Vere W.
Haiti and Martinique. *In* King, B. A. and Ogungbesan, K. eds. A celebration of Black and African writing p46-59

Knight, William
Some general notes on what contemporary Finnish writing is like (it's like blueberries) and what it's not like. *In* Dauenhauer, R. and Binham, P. eds. Snow in May p41-47

Knight, William Nicholas
Equity, 'The merchant of Venice' and William Lambarde. *In* Shakespeare survey 27 p93-104

Knighthood. See Knights and knighthood

Knights, Ben
The idea of the clerisy in the nineteenth century

Contents
Epilogue: Cultural studies without a clerisy
The hero as man of letters: Thomas Carlyle
The idea of a university
The idea of the clerisy: Samuel Taylor Coleridge
The majority and the remnant: Matthew Arnold
The reconstruction of opinion: John Stuart Mill

Knights, Lionel Charles
Explorations 3

Contents
All or nothing: a theme in John Donne
Ben Jonson: public attitudes and social poetry
Early Blake
George Herbert
Henry James and human liberty
Literature and the teaching of literature
Also in Niblett, W. R. ed. The sciences, the humanities and the technological threat p127-38
Shakespeare: four histories: Henry V
Shakespeare: four histories: King John
Shakespeare: four histories: Richard II
Shakespeare: four histories: Richard III
Shakespeare: four histories: The background
Shakespeare's tragedies and the question of moral judgment
The tempest
The thought of Shakespeare
Timon of Athens
Two notes on Coleridge: A tract for the times: Coleridge and The friend
Two notes on Coleridge: Coleridge as critic
The tempest. *In* Shakespeare's late plays p15-31

About individual works
Drama and society in the age of Jonson

Grene, N. L. C. Knights's drama and society in the age of Jonson. *In* Drama and society p291-98

Knights and knighthood
Evergates, T. Historiography and sociology in early feudal society: the case of Hariulf and the "milites" of Saint-Riquier. *In* Viator: medieval and Renaissance studies v6 p35-49

See also Chivalry; Ministerials

Great Britain
Harvey, S. The knight and the knight's fee in England. *In* Peasants, knights and heretics p133-73

Knights and knighthood in literature
Honeycutt, B. L. The knight and his world as instruments of humor in the fabliaux. *In* Cooke, T. D. and Honeycutt, B. L. eds. The humor of the fabliaux p75-92

Knights Templars (Monastic and religious orders) See Templars in Spain

Knipe, Elizabeth A. See Murphy, T. P. jt. auth.

Knipmeyer, William B.
Folk boats of eastern French Louisiana. *In* Yoder, D. ed. American folklife p105-49

Knisbacher, Mitchell

The Jews of Iraq and the international protection of the rights of minorities (1856-1976). *In* Sidorsky, D. ed. Essays on human rights p156-78

Knoche, Ulrich

Roman satire

Contents

Aules Persius Flaccus
Decimus Junius Juvenalis
Gaius Lucilius
Horace's Satires and Epistles
Origin and name of the satura
Petronius' novel
Satire: a Roman literary genre
The satires of Quintus Ennius
Seneca's Apocolocyntosis
Varro's Menippeans

Knock, Thomas J.

"History with lightning": the forgotten film Wilson. *In* Zenderland, L. ed. Recycling the past p95-115

Knoepflmacher, Ulrich Camillus

The counterworld of Victorian fiction and The woman in white. *In* The Worlds of Victorian fiction p351-69

Mutations of the Wordsworthian child of nature. *In* Knoepflmacher, U. C. and Tennyson, G. B. eds. Nature and the Victorian imagination p391-425

Thoughts on the aggression of daughters. *in* Levine, G. L. and Knoepflmacher, U. C. eds. The endurance of Frankenstein p88-119

Knoepflmacher, Ulrich Camillus, and Tennyson, Georg Bernhard

Afterglow and aftermath. *In* Knoepflmacher, U. C. and Tennyson, G. B. eds. Nature and the Victorian imagination p489-99

Knoll, Paul W.

The Arts faculty at the University of Cracow at the end of the fifteenth century. *In* The Copernican achievement p137-56

Echoes of the New World in the international rivalries of East Central Europe. *In* First images of America p279-84

The world of the young Copernicus: society, science, and the university. *In* Science and society: past, present, and future p19-44

About individual works

The Arts faculty at the University of Cracow at the end of the fifteenth century

Steneck, N. H. Commentary: in defense of context. *In* The Copernican achievement p157-64

Knollys, Francis

About

Thompson, W. D. J. C. Sir Francis Knollys' campaign against the jure divino theory of episcopacy. *In* The Dissenting tradition p39-77

Knopf, Alfred A.

Miss Cather. *In* The Art of Willa Cather p205-24

Knorr, Klaus Eugene

Economic interdependence and national security. *In* Knorr, K. E. and Trager, F. N. eds. Economic issues and national security p 1-18

International economic leverage and its uses. *In* Knorr, K. E. and Trager, F. N. eds. Economic issues and national security p99-26

The limits of economic and military power. *In* Vernon, R. ed. The oil crisis p229-43

Military strength: economic and non-economic bases. *in* Knorr, K. E. and Trager, F. N. eds. Economic issues and national security p183-99

Knott, Jack. See Wildavsky, A. B. jt. auth.

Know-Nothing Party. See American Party

Knowledge, Classification of. See Classification of sciences

Knowledge, Sociology of

Barber, B. Toward a new view of the sociology of knowledge. *In* The Idea of social structure p103-16

Bauman, Z. Understanding as the work of history: Karl Mannheim. *In* Bauman, Z. Hermeneutics and social science p89-110

Bauman, Z. Understanding as the work of history: Karl Marx. *In* Bauman, Z. Hermeneutics and social science p48-68

Goody, J. R. Literacy, criticism, and the growth of knowledge. *In* Culture and its creators p226-43

Book reviews

Parsons, T. Review of Harold J. Bershady, Ideology and social knowledge. *In* Parsons, T. Social systems and the evolution of action theory p122-41

Knowledge, Theory of

Cavell, S. Knowing and acknowledging. *In* Cavell, S. Must we mean what we say? p238-66

Chomsky, N. Language and unconscious knowledge. *In* Psychoanalysis and language p3-44

Clarke, W. N. Interpersonal dialogue: key to realism. *In* Roth, R. J. ed. Person and community p141-53

Cohen, C. Revolutions and Copernican revolutions. *In* Science and society: past, present, and future p86-103

Copleston, F. C. Philosophical knowledge. *In* Copleston, F. C. Philosophers and philosophies p 1-16

Elliott, R. K. Education and human being I. *In* Philosophers discuss education p45-72

Hoffmann, Y. The possibility of knowledge: Kant and Nagarjuna. *In* Philosophy East/philosophy West p269-90

Langford, G. Education and human being II. *In* Philosophers discuss education p73-84

Mandel, R. Heidegger and Wittgenstein: a second Kantian revolution. *In* Murray, M. E. ed. Heidegger and modern philosophy p259-70

Miller, J. W. On the problem of knowledge. *In* Miller, J. W. The paradox of cause, and other essays p56-63

Mora, G. Vico, Piaget, and genetic epistemology. *In* Giambattista Vico's science of humanity p365-92

Nagel, T. Linguistics and epistemology. *In* Harman, G. ed. On Noam Chomsky p219-28

O'Neill, J. The mutuality of accounts: an essay on trust. *In* McNall, S. G. ed. Theoretical perspectives in sociology p369-80

Ong, W. J. "I see what you say": sense analogues for intellect. *In* Ong, W. J. Interfaces of the word p121-44

Peckham, M. Literature and knowledge. *In* Peckham, M. Romanticism and behavior p222-45

Knowledge, Theory of—*Continued*

Percy, W. The message in the bottle. *In* Percy, W. The message in the bottle p119-49

Percy, W. Semiotic and a theory of knowledge. *In* Percy, W. The message in the bottle p243-64

Quine, W. V. The limits of knowledge. *In* Quine, W. V. The ways of paradox, and other essays p59-67

Quine, W. V. The nature of natural knowledge. *In* Guttenplan, S. D. ed. Mind and language p67-81

Quine, W. V. On mental entities. *In* Quine, W. V. The ways of paradox, and other essays p221-27

Reiss, T. J. Discursive criticism and epistemology. *In* Valdés, M. J. and Miller, O. J. eds. Interpretation of narrative p38-47

Vickers, Sir G. Rationality and intuition. *In* Wechsler, J. ed. On aesthetics in science p143-64

Wheatley, J. M. O. Knowledge, empiricism and ESP. *In* Wheatley, J. M. O. and Edge, H. L. eds. Philosophical dimensions of parapsychology p142-53

Wojciechowski, J. A. The ecology of knowledge. *In* Science and society: past, present, and future p258-302

See also Belief and doubt; Certainty; Cognition; Common sense; Comprehension; Concepts; Empiricism; Experience; Gestal psychology; Idea (Philosophy); Identity; Ideology; Immanence (Philosophy); Intellect; Intuition; Knowledge, Sociology of; Objectivity; Observation (Psychology); Other minds (Theory of knowledge); Perception; Rationalism; Reality; Self-knowledge, Theory of; Sense data; Senses and sensation; Subjectivity; Truth; Uniformity of nature; Universals (Philosophy); and subdivision Knowledge, Theory of under names of philosophers, e.g. Descartes, René—Knowledge, Theory of

Knowledge, Theory of (Hinduism)

Barlingay, S. S. Indian epistemology and logic. *In* Bishop, D. H. ed. Indian thought p148-75

Knowledge, Theory of (Sociology). See Knowledge, Sociology of

Knowledge, Tree of. See Tree of life

Knowledge of self, Theory of. See Self-knowledge, Theory of

Knowles, Albert Sydney

Dos Passos in the twenties. *In* French, W. G. ed. The twenties p123-37

Knowles, John Hilton

Introduction. *In* Knowles, J. H. ed. Doing better and feeling worse p 1-7

The responsibility of the individual. *In* Knowles, J. H. ed. Doing better and feeling worse p57-80

Knowles, John Kenneth

Luisa Josefina Hernández: the labyrinth of form. *In* Lyday, L. F. and Woodyard, G. W. eds. Dramatists in revolt p133-45

Knowles, Owen. See Brake, L. jt. auth.

Knox, Bernard MacGregor Walker

The Medea of Euripides. *In* Yale classical studies v25 p193-225

Knox, George

Francesco Guardi as an apprentice in the studio of Giambattista Tiepolo. *In* Studies in eighteenth-century culture v5 p29-39

Knust, Herbert

Piscator and Brecht: affinity and alienation. *In* Mews, S. and Knust, H. eds. Essays on Brecht p44-68

Knutson, Jeanne Nickell

Human needs constraining political activity. *In* Fitzgerald, R. ed. Human needs and politics p96-123

Kobayashi, Masako. See Matsui, Sumako

Kober, Arthur

About individual works
That man is here again

O'Hara, J. That Benny Greenspan. *In* O'Hara, J. "An artist is his own fault" p161-64

Kobrin, Solomon

The labeling approach: problems and limits. *In* Delinquency, crime, and society p239-53

Koch, Philip

Regnard and Collin d' Harleville on legacies by bachelor uncles. *In* Studies in eighteenth-century culture v8 p291-309

Koch, Stephen

Blow-job and pornography. *In* Nichols, B. ed. Movies and methods p305-09

Kochan, Lionel

Graetz and Dubnow: two Jewish historians in an alien world. *In* Essays in honour of E. H. Carr p352-66

Kochanek, Stanley A.

The Indian political system. *In* Kearney, R. N. ed. Politics and modernization in South and Southeast Asia p39-107

Kochanowski, Jan

About individual works
Laments

Birnbaum, H. The sublimation of grief: poems by two mourning fathers. *In* For Wiktor Weintraub p85-98

Kochen, Manfred

Science, isolation, and international relations. *In* Isolation or interdependence? p205-42

Kochman, Thomas

"Rapping" in the Black ghetto. *In* Henslin, J. M. ed. Deviant life-styles p39-58

Kockelmans, Joseph J.

Destructive retrieve and hermeneutic phenomenology in 'Being and time.' *In* Radical phenomenology p106-37

Husserl and Kant on the pure ego. *In* Elliston, F. A. and McCormick, P. eds. Husserl p269-85

Kocówna, Barbara

The problem of language. *In* Joseph Conrad: a commemoration p194-98

Kodzic, Peter

Armaments and development. *In* The Dynamics of the arms race p202-11

Koech, Kipng'eno

African mythology: a key to understanding African religion. *In* African religions: a symposium p117-39

Koehn, Peter H.

Urban origins and consequences of national and local political transformation in Ethiopia. *In* Walton, J. and Masotti, L. H. eds. The city in comparative perspective p155-78

Kohlberg, Lawrence

Justice as reversibility. *In* Laslett, P. and Fishkin, J. eds. Philosophy, politics and society p257-72

Moral stages and sex education. *In* Sexuality and human values p111-22

About

Ryan, K. Television as a moral educator. *In* Television as a cultural force p111-27

Köhler, Erich

Deliberations on a theory of the genre of the Old Provençal descort. *In* Italian literature: roots and branches p 1-13

Kohler, Mary

To what are children entitled? *In* Gross, B. and Gross, R. eds. The children's rights movement p217-32

Kohler, Robert E.

The Lewis-Langmuir theory of valence and the chemical community, 1920-1928. *In* Historical studies in the physical sciences v6 p431-68

Rudolf Schoenheimer, isotopic tracers, and biochemistry in the 1930's. *In* Historical studies in the physical sciences v8 p257-98

Kohls, Ernst-Wilhelm

The principal theological thoughts in the Enchiridion militis Christiani. *In* Essays on the works of Erasmus p61-82

Kohlstedt, Sally Gregory

From learned society to public museum: the Boston Society of Natural History. *In* Oleson, A. and Voss, J. eds. The organization of knowledge in modern America, 1860-1920 p386-406

Savants and professionals: the American Association for the Advancement of Science, 1848-1860. *In* Oleson, A. and Brown, S. C. eds. The pursuit of knowledge in the early American Republic p299-325

Kohnstamm, Max

Institutions for interdependence. *In* The New Atlantic challenge p355-64

Koht, Halvdan

About

Skard, S. Bjørnstjerne Bjørnson and Halvdan Koht. *In* Abroad in America: Visitors to the new Nation, 1776-1914 p195-206

Koizumi, Kenkichiro

The emergence of Japan's first physicists: 1868-1900. *In* Historical studies in the physical sciences v6 p3-108

Kol sachal

Eisenstein-Barzilay, I. Finalizing an issue: Modena's authorship of the Qol sakhal. *In* Salo Wittmayer Baron v 1 p135-66

Kołakowski, Leszek

Introduction: need of utopia, fear of utopia. *In* Radicalism in the contemporary age v2 p 3-11

Marxist roots of Stalinism. *In* Stalinism p283-98

Neutrality and academic values. *In* Montefiore, A. ed. Neutrality and impartiality p72-85

Kolankiewicz, George, and Taras, Ray

Poland: socialism for Everyman? *In* Brown, A. H. and Gray, J. eds. Political cultural and political change in Communist states p101-30

Kolb, Alfred

The art of Glenway Wescott. *In* Renaissance and modern p172-79

Kolb, Lawrence Coleman

Psychological approaches. *In* American psychiatry: past, present, and future p50-63

Kolberg (Motion picture)

Taylor, R. Kolberg. *In* Taylor, R. Film propaganda p216-29

Kolers, Paul A.

Reading pictures and reading text. *In* Perkins, D. and Leondar, B. eds. The arts and cognition p136-64

Kolin, Philip C.

"Sentiment and humor in equal measure": comic forms in The rose tattoo. *In* Tennessee Williams: a tribute p214-31

Kolko, Gabriel

About

Reinitz, R. Niebuhrian irony and historical interpretation: the relationship between consensus and New Left history. *In* Canary, R. H. and Kozicki, H. J. eds. The writing of history p93-128

Kolman, Arnŏst. See Kol'man, Ėrnest

Kol'man, Ėrnest

About

Kovály, P. Arnŏst Kolman: portrait of a Marxist-Leninist philosopher. *In* Kovály, P. Rehumanization or dehumanization? p35-64

Kolve, V. A.

Chaucer and the visual arts. *In* Brewer, D. S. ed. Geoffrey Chaucer p290-320

Komatsu, Sakyo

H. G. Wells and Japanese science fiction. *In* H. G. Wells and modern science fiction p179-90

Kommunisticheskaia partiia Sovetskogo Souiuza. See Communist Party of Russia

Kommunisticheskaia partiia Uzbekistana. See Communist Party of Uzbek

Konda Lakshman

About

Gray, H. Konda Lakshman Bapuji: a backward classes leader of the Telengana (Andhra Pradesh) *In* The Making of politicians: studies from Africa and Asia p156-65

Konde tribes. See Nyakyusa (African tribe)

Koniaris, George Leonidas

Alexander, Palamedes, Troades, Sisyphus —a connected tetralogy? A connected trilogy? *In* Harvard Studies in classical philology v77 p85-124

Michigan papyrus 2754 and the Certamen. *In* Harvard Studies in classical philology v75 p107-29

Konig, David Thomas

English legal change and the origins of local government in northern Massachusetts. *In* Daniels, B. C. ed. Town and county p12-43

Konigsburg, Elaine (Lobl)

About individual works
About the B'nai Bagels

Kimmel, E. A. Jewish identity in juvenile fiction: a look at three recommended books. *In* Horn Book Magazine. Crosscurrents of criticism p150-58

Konigson, Élie

Religious drama and urban society in France at the end of the Middle Ages. *In* Drama and society p23-36

Konrad, György

About individual works
The case worker

Howe, I. George Konrad: the traffic of suffering. *In* Howe, I. Celebrations and attacks p189-91

Konvitz, Milton Ridvas

The flower and the thorn. *In* The Pulse of freedom p211-80

Judaism and the American idea

Contents

Conscience: the movement from duty to right —from the Bible to the Bill of Rights
From Jewish rights to human rights
Human dignity: from creation to Constitution
Individual conscience or group consciousness: religious liberty in the United States and Israel
Judaism and the democratic ideal
Life and liberty for the pursuit of happiness
The rule of law: Torah and the Constitution

Koo, Vi Kyuin Wellington

About

Chu, P. V. K. Wellington Koo: the diplomacy of nationalism. *In* Burns, R. D. and Bennett, E. M. eds. Diplomats in crisis p125-51

Kootenai. See Kootenay, Canada

Kootenay, Canada

History

Scott, S. H. The origins of Kootenay society, 1890-1930. *In* Bingham, E. R. and Love, G. A. eds. Northwest perspectives p78-96

Social conditions

Scott, S. H. The origins of Kootenay society, 1890-1930. *In* Bingham, E. R. and Love, G. A. eds. Northwest perspectives p78-96

Kopcke, Günter

More about Olympia B 1701 and B 1999. *In* Studies in classical art and archaeology p17-21

Kopelev, Lev Zalmanovich

A lie is conquered only by truth. *In* Medvedev, R. A. ed. The Samizdat register p203-36

Kopit, Arthur L.

About individual works
Indians

Kauffmann, S. Indians. *In* Kauffmann, S. Persons of the drama p183-86

Kopp, Jane Baltzell

"Gone, very gone youth": Sylvia Plath at Cambridge, 1955-1957. *In* Butscher, E. ed. Sylvia Plath p61-80

Koppisch, Michael S.

The faux dévot from Molière to Marivaux. *In* Johnson, R. B.; Neumann, E. S. and Trail, G. T. eds. Molière and the commonwealth of letters: patrimony and posterity p57-67

Koran

Watt, W. M. The Queen of Sheba in Islamic tradition. *In* Pritchard, J. B. ed. Solomon & Sheba p85-103

Korbonski, Andrzej

Eastern Europe and the Soviet threat. *In* Kirk, G. L. and Wessell, N. H. eds. The Soviet threat p66-76

Kore. See Persephone

Korea

Foreign relations—United States

Gaddis, J. L. Korea in American politics, strategy, and diplomacy, 1945-50. *In* The Origins of the Cold war in Asia p277-98

Kriebel, P. W. Unfinished business—intervention under the U.N. umbrella: America's participation in the Korean War, 1950-1953. *In* Higham, R. D. ed. Intervention or abstention: the dilemma of American foreign policy p114-28

History—War and intervention, 1950-1953
See Korean War, 1950-1953

Korea (Democratic People's Republic)

History

Sun, Dae-sook: A preconceived formula for Sovietization: the Communist takeover of North Korea. *In* Hammond, T. T. ed. The anatomy of Communist takeovers p475-89

Korea (Republic)

Chungang Chŏngbobu

Lee, Jai Hyon. The activities of the Korean Central Intelligence Agency in the United States. *In* Horowitz, I. L. ed. Science, sin, and scholarship p120-47

Foreign relations—United States

Lee, Jai Hyon. The activities of the Korean Central Intelligence Agency in the United States. *In* Horowitz, I. L. ed. Science, sin, and scholarship p120-47

Korean Central Intelligence Agency. See Korea (Republic). Chungang Chŏngbobu

Korean Communist Party. See Communist Party of Korea

Korean War, 1950-1953

Kriebel, P. W. Unfinished business—intervention under the U.N. umbrella: America's participation in the Korean War, 1950-1953. *In* Higham, R. D. ed. Intervention or abstention: the dilemma of American foreign policy p114-28

Okonogi, M. The domestic roots of the Korean War. *In* The Origins of the Cold war in Asia p299-320

Simmons, R. R. The Communist side: an exploratory sketch. *In* The Korean War p197-208

Causes

Slusser, R. M. Soviet Far Eastern policy, 1945-50: Stalin's goals in Korea. *In* The Origins of the Cold war in Asia p123-46

Diplomatic history

Kaplan, L. S. The Korean War and U.S. foreign relations: the case of NATO. *In* The Korean War p36-75

Slusser, R. M. Soviet Far Eastern policy, 1945-50: Stalin's goals in Korea. *In* The Origins of the Cold war in Asia p123-46

Historiography

Leopold, R. W. The Korean War: the historian's task. *In* The Korean War p209-24

Korea (Republic)—*Continued*

United States

Wiltz. J. E. The Korean War and American society. *In* The Korean War p112-58

Koreans in the United States

Houchins, L. and Houchins, C. The Korean experience in America, 1903-1924. *In* The Asian American: the historical experience p129-56

Political activity

Baldwin, F. The Korea lobby. *In* Horowitz, I. L. ed. Science, sin, and scholarship p160-74

Crittenden, A. Moon's sect pushes pro-Seoul activities. *In* Horowitz, I. L. ed. Science, sin, and scholarship p176-91

Korg, Jacob

George Gissing: humanist in exile. *In* Levine, R. A. The Victorian experience: the novelists p239-73

Korn, Arthur, and Samuely, Felix J.

A master plan for London. *In* Sharp, D. ed. The rationalist p190-207

Korn, Bertram Wallace

German-Jewish intellectual influences on American Jewish life, 1824-1972. *In* Tradition and change in Jewish experience p106-40

Korn, Sheila M.

The formal analysis of visual systems as exemplified by a study of Abelam (Papua New Guinea) paintings. *In* Greenhalgh, M. and Megaw, J. V. S. eds. Art in society p161-73

Kornaros, Bitzentzos

Characters—Aretousa

Sherrard, P. Epilogue: the figure of Aretousa. *In* Sherrard, P. The wound of Greece p118-24

Kornaros, Bitzentzos, supposed author

About individual works

Erotokritos

Sherrard, P. Epilogue: the figure of Aretousa. *In* Sherrard, P. The wound of Greece p118-24

Kornblum, William Simon, and Williams, Terry

Life-style, leisure, and community life. *In* Handbook of contemporary urban life p58-89

Körner, Stephan

Empiricism in ethics. *In* Royal Institute of Philosophy. Impressions of empiricism p216-30

Kors, Alan Charles

François-Jean Marquis de Chastellux. *In* Abroad in America: Visitors to the new Nation, 1776-1914 p3-11

Korsakov, F. pseud.

Russian destinies. *In* From under the rubble p151-71

Korshin, Paul J.

The development of abstracted typology in England, 1650-1820. *In* Miner, E. R. ed. Literary uses of typology p147-203

Korsmeyer, Carolyn Wilker

The hidden joke: generic uses of masculine terminology. *In* Feminism and philosophy p138-53

Reason and morals in the early feminist movement: Mary Wollstonecraft. *In* Gould, C. C. and Wartofsky, M. W. eds. Women and philosophy p97-111

Korzenik, Diana

Saying it with pictures. *In* Perkins, D. and Leondar, B. eds. The arts and cognition p192-207

Korzeniowski, Apollo Nałęcz

About

Miłosz, C. Joseph Conrad's father. *In* Miłosz, C. Emperor of the earth p157-85

About individual works

Comedy

Harden, E. J. The dependence of Apollo Korzeniowski's Komedia upon Griboedov's Gore ot uma. *In* For Wiktor Weintraub p209-26

Kos-Rabcewicz-Zubkowski, Ludwik

The creation of an international criminal court. *In* International terrorism and political crimes p519-36

Kosaka, Masataka

Political immobility and the uncertain future. *In* Clapp, P. and Halperin, M. H. eds. United States-Japanese relations, the 1970's p19-34

Koselleck, Reinhart

Chance as motivation for the unexplained in historical writing: notes on Archenholtz's History of the Seven Years' War. *In* Amacher, R. E. and Lange, V. eds. New perspectives in German literary criticism p212-24

Kosinski, Jerzy N.

About individual works

Steps

Boyers, R. Language and reality in Kosinski's "Steps." *In* Boyers, R. Excursions p71-86

Koslow, Arnold

Ontological and ideological issues of the classical theory of space and time. *In* Motion and time, space and matter p224-63

Koss, Stephen Edward

Asquith versus Lloyd George: the last phase and beyond. *In* Crisis and controversy p66-89

Kossuth, Lajos

About

Bako, E. Louis Kossuth. *In* Abroad in America: Visitors to the new Nation, 1776-1914 p124-33

Kossuth, Louis. See Kossuth, Lajos

Kostelanetz, Richard

New fiction in America. *In* Federman, R. ed. Surfiction p85-100

Notes on the American short story today. *In* May, C. E. ed. Short story theories p214-25

Twenty-five fictional hypotheses. *In* Federman, R. ed. Surfiction p283-86

About individual works

The end of intelligent writing

Sheed, W. New York blues. *In* Sheed, W. The good word & other words p20-23

Koster, Jan

Why subject sentences don't exist. *In* Keyser, S. J. ed. Recent transformational studies in European languages p53-64

Kostka, Edmund K.

Glimpses of Germanic-Slavic relations from Pushkin to Heinrich Mann

Contents

Bibliography

Blok, Schiller, and the Bolshevik revolution

A literary quandary: Fyodor Sologub and Heinrich Mann

Maksim Gorky: Russian writer with a Western bent

Pushkin's third dimension: the German influence

T. N. Granovsky and the ideological lure of the West

A trailblazer of Russian Westernism: V. P. Botkin

Kostof, Spiro K.

The architect in the Middle Ages, East and West. *In* Kostof, S. ed. The architect p59-95

The Emperor and the Duce: the planning of Piazzale Augusto Imperatore in Rome. *In* Millon, H. A. and Nochlin, L. eds. Art and architecture in the service of politics p270-325

The practice of architecture in the ancient world: Egypt and Greece. *In* Kostof, S. ed. The architect p3-27

Kostomarov, Nikolai Ivanovich

About

Pogorelskin, A. E. N. I. Kostomarov and the origins of the Vestnik Evropy circle. *In* Oxford Slavonic papers, new ser. v11 p84-100

Kostoroski, Emilie P.

Molière and Voltaire. *In* Johnson, R. B.; Neumann, E. S. and Trail, G. T. eds. Molière and the commonwealth of letters: patrimony and posterity p90-99

Kostoroski-Kadish, Emilie P. See Kostoroski, Emilie P.

Koszyk, Kurt

The development of the International Press Institute. *In* Fischer, H. D. and Merrill, J. C. eds. International and intercultural communication p372-76

Kotarba, Joseph A.

The chronic pain experience. *In* Douglas, J. D. and Johnson, J. M. [eds.] Existential sociology p257-72

Existential sociology. *In* McNall, S. G. ed. Theoretical perspectives in sociology p348-68

Kothari, Rajni

World politics and world order: the issue of autonomy. *In* On the creation of a just world order p39-69

Kott, Jan

About individual works

Theatre notebook, 1947-1967

Simon, J. I. Theatrical disorder of the day. *In* Simon, J. I. Singularities p145-47

Kottler, Dorian B.

Louis Pasteur and molecular dissymmetry, 1844-1857. *In* Studies in history of biology v2 p57-98

Kotzebue, August Friedrich Ferdinand von

About

Nicoll, A. From tragedy to melodrama. *In* Nicoll, A. World drama p342-69

K'ou, Ch'ien-chih

About

Mather, R. B. K'ou Ch'ien-chih and the Taoist theocracy at the Northern Wei Court, 425-451. *In* Welch, H. and Seidel, A. K. eds. Facets of Taoism p103-22

Kourvetaris, George A. and Dobratz, Betty A.

Present status of sociology in Greece. *In* Mohan, R. P. and Martindale, D. A. eds. Handbook of contemporary developments in world sociology p307-27

Kousoulas, Dimitrios George

The Greek Communists tried three times—and failed. *In* Hammond, T. T. ed. The anatomy of Communist takeovers p293-309

Kouwenhoven, John Atlee

Art, disorder, and American experience: half a truth is better than none. *In* Mann, D. A. ed. The arts in a democratic society p70-97

Kovacs, David

Three passages from the Andromache. *In* Harvard Studies in classical philology v81 p123-56

Kovalevskiĭ, Vladimir Onufrievich

About

Todes, D. P. V. O. Kovalevskiĭ: the genesis, content, and reception of his paleontological work. *In* Studies in history of biology v2 p99-165

Kovály, Pavel

Rehumanization or dehumanization?

Contents

Adam Schaff's Marxism and the human individual

Arnŏst Kolman: portrait of a Marxist-Leninist philosopher

György Lukács: the history of an error

Is it possible to humanize Marxism?

Problems of anti-humanism and humanism in the life and work of Alexander Solzhenitsyn

Koyama, Kosuke

Barefoot in an ascending elevator: a meditation. *In* On language, culture, and religion: in honor of Eugene A. Nida p213-36

Kozinŝev, Grigoriĭ Mikhaĭlovich

About individual works

Hamlet

Jorgens, J. J. Grigori Kozintsev's Hamlet. *In* Jorgens, J. J. Shakespeare on film p218-34

King Lear

Jorgens, J. J. King Lear: Peter Brook and Grigori Kozintsev. *In* Jorgen, J. J. Shakespeare on film p235-51

Kozloff, Max

The Rivera frescoes of modern industry at the Detroit Institute of Arts: proletarian art under capitalist patronage. *In* Millon, H. A. and Nochlin, L. eds. Art and architecture in the service of politics p216-29

Kozol, Jonathan

Children of the revolution. *In* Wagschal, P. H. ed. Learning tomorrows p73-88

Kpe women (African people) See Women. Bakwiri (African people)

Kpelle

Psychology

Cole, M. Ethnographic psychology of cognition—so far. *In* Spindler, G. D. ed. The making of psychological anthropology p614-31

Krabbe, Henning

A Danish actress and her conception of the part of Lady Macbeth. *In* Shakespeare survey v29 p145-49

Kracke, Waud H.

A psychoanalyst in the field: Erikson's contributions to anthropology. *In* Homans, P. ed. Childhood and selfhood p147-88

Kraft, Robert A.

The development of the concept of "orthodoxy" in early Christianity. *In* Current issues in Biblical and patristic interpretation p47-59

Krag, Jens Otto

New openings in East-West relations. *In* The New Atlantic challenge p303-08

Kragh, Helge

Niels Bohr's second atomic theory. *In* Historical studies in the physical sciences v10 p123-86

Kraiselburd, Raul

Establishing and maintaining a free press: a Latin American viewpoint. *In* Horton, P. C. ed. The Third World and press freedom p156-61

Krakow. Uniwersytet Jagiellónski

Faculty—History

Knoll, P. W. The Arts faculty at the University of Cracow at the end of the fifteenth century. *In* The Copernican achievement p137-56

History

Knoll, P. W. The world of the young Copernicus: society, science, and the university. *In* Science and society: past, present, and future p19-44

Kramer, Edith

Art and craft. *In* Ulman, E. and Dachinger, P. eds. Art therapy p106-09

Art and emptiness: new problems in art education and therapy. *In* Ulman, E. and Dachinger, P. eds. Art therapy p33-42

The practice of art therapy with children. *In* Ulman, E. and Dachinger, P. eds. Art therapy p159-80

The problem of quality in art. *In* Ulman, E. and Dachinger, P. eds. Art therapy p43-59

Kramer, Martin

The Frankenstein fallacy. *In* Hook, S.; Kurtz, P. W. and Todorovich, M. eds. The university and the state: what role for government in higher education? p95-96

Kramer, Morton

Implications of expected changes in composition of U.S. population for the delivery of mental health services during the period 1971-85. *In* American psychiatry: past, present, and future p94-112

Kramer, Roland Laird

International advertising media. *In* Fischer, H. D. and Merrill, J. C. eds. International and intercultural communication p297-307

Kramer, Victor A.

Memoirs of self-indictment: the solitude of Tennessee Williams. *In* Tennessee Williams: a tribute p663-75

Kramnick, Isaac

Introduction: the making of a crisis. *In* Kramnick, I. ed. Is Britain dying? p11-27

Kranzberg, Melvin

From carpetbag to carpet mill: technology in the New South. *In* Lewis, W. D. and Griessman, B. E. eds. The Southern mystique p33-45

Introduction: trends in the history and philosophy of technology. *In* Bugliarello, G. and Doner, D. B. eds. The history and philosophy of technology pxiii-xxxi

Krapf, Ludwig

About

Southall, A. W. White strangers and their religion in East Africa and Madagascar. *In* Shack, W. A. and Skinner, E. P. eds. Strangers in African societies p211-26

Krash, Otto

Several humanisms and John Dewey. *In* Fairfield, R. P. ed. Humanistic frontiers in American education p116-22

Krasikov, A.

Commodity number one. *In* Medvedev, R. A. ed. The Samizdat register p93-115

Krasiński, Zygmunt, hrabia

About individual works
The un-divine comedy

Miłosz, C. Krasiński's retreat. *In* Miłosz, C. Emperor of the earth p50-61

Krasner, Stephen D.

Domestic constraints on international economic leverage. *In* Knorr, K. E. and Trager, F. N. eds. Economic issues and national security p127-59

Krass, Alfred C.

Accounting for the hope that is in me. *In* Christian faith in a religiously plural world p155-67

Kraus, Elizabeth M.

Individual and society: a Whiteheadian critique of B. F. Skinner. *In* Roth, R. J. ed. Person and community p103-32

Kraus, Karl

About

Benjamin, W. Karl Kraus. *In* Benjamin, W. Reflections p239-73

Canetti, E. Karl Kraus: the school of resistance. *In* Canetti, E. The conscience of words p29-39

Canetti, E. The new Karl Kraus. *In* Canetti, E. The conscience of words p214-35

Rogers, M. A. "Dies Österreich ist eine kleine welt." *In* Branscombe, P. ed. Austrian life and literature, 1780-1938 p72-80

About individual works
Briefe an Sidonie Nádherný von Borutin: 1913-1936

Canetti, E. The new Karl Kraus. *In* Canetti, E. The conscience of words p214-35

The last days of mankind

Pynsent, R. B. The last days of Austria: Hašek and Kraus. *In* Klein, H. M. ed. The First World War in fiction p136-48

Krause, David

Sean O'Casey. *In* Finneran, R. J. ed. Anglo-Irish literature p470-517

Krause, Florence Phyfer
Negative capability and objective correlative in Shakespeare's Sonnets. *In* Tennessee Studies in literature v 20 p17-25

Krause, Sydney J.
Romanticism in Wieland: Brown and the reconciliation of opposites. *In* Artful thunder p13-24

Krauss, Herbert H.
Suicide—a psychosocial phenomenon. *In* Wolman, B. B. ed. Between survival and suicide p26-54

Krauss, Michael E.
Eskimo-Aleut. *In* Sebeok, T. A. ed. Native languages of the Americas v 1 p175-281

Na-Dene. *In* Sebeok, T. A. ed. Native languages of the Americas v 1 p283-358

Krauss, Rosalind E.
Passages in modern sculpture

Contents

Analytic space: futurism and constructivism
The double negative: a new syntax for sculpture
Forms of readymade: Duchamp and Brancusi
A game plan: the terms of surrealism
Mechanical ballets: light, motion, theater
Narrative time: the question of the Gates of hell
Tanktotem: welded images

Kravetz, Diane F.
Women social workers and clients: common victims of sexism. *In* Roberts, J. I. ed. Beyond intellectual sexism p160-71

Krebs, Edith, and Schwarz, Margarete
Austria. *In* Kamerman, S. B. and Kahn, A. J. eds. Family policy p183-216

Krefft, James H.
A possible source for Faulkner's Indians: Oliver La Farge's Laughing boy. *In* Tulane Studies in English v23 p187-92

Kreisler, Frederic Francis
Domesday book and the Anglo-Norman synthesis. *In* Order and innovation in the Middle Ages p3-16

Krekić, Barisa
Contributions of foreigners to Dubrovnik's economic growth in the late Middle Ages. *In* Viator: medieval and Renaissance studies v9 p375-94

Four Florentine commercial companies in Dubrovnik (Ragusa) in the first half of the fourteenth century. *In* The Medieval city p25-41

Italian creditors in Dubrovnik (Ragusa) and the Balkan trade, thirteenth through fifteenth centuries. *In* The Dawn of modern banking p241-54

Krell, David Farrell
Schlag der Liebe, Schlag des Todes: on a theme in Heidegger and Trakl. *In* Radical phenomemology p238-58

Kren, George M. and Rappoport, Leon H.
Clio and psyche. *In* Kren, G. M. and Rappoport, L. H. eds. Varieties of psychohistory p63-77

Křenek, Ernst

About individual works
Über neue Musik

Sessions, R. Exposition by Krenek. *In* Sessions, R. Roger Sessions on music p249-'55

Kress, Gunther R.
Structuralism and popular culture. *In* Bigsby, C. W. E. ed. Approaches to popular culture p85-106

Kretzmann, Norman
Incipit/desinit. *In* Motion and time, space and matter p101-36

Kreutz, Barbara McLaughlin
Ships, shipping, and the implications of change in the early medieval Mediterranean. *In* Viator: medieval and Renaissance studies v7 p79-109

Kreyling, Michael
Clement and the Indians: pastoral and history in The robber bridegroom. *In* Dollarhide, L. and Abadie, A. J. eds. Eudora Welty: a form of thanks p25-45

Words into criticism: Eudora Welty's essays and reviews. *In* Prenshaw, P. W. ed. Eudora Welty p411-22

Kriebel, P. Wesley
Unfinished business—intervention under the U.N. umbrella: America's participation in the Korean War, 1950-1953. *In* Higham, R. D. ed. Intervention or abstention: the dilemma of American foreign policy p114-28

Krieger, David
A Caribbean community for ocean development. *In* Borgese, E. M. and Krieger, D. eds. The tides of change p278-301

Krieger, Leonard
Germany. *In* National consciousness, history, and political culture in early-modern Europe p67-97

Krieger, Murray
Literature as illusion, as metaphor, as vision. *In* Hernadi, P. ed. What is literature? p178-89

Shakespeare and the critic's idolatry of the word. *In* Shakespeare: aspects of influence p193-210

The theoretical contributions of Eliseo Vivas. *In* Viva Vivas! p37-63

Krim, Seymour
A backward glance o'er beatnik roads. *In* Anderson, E. and Kinzie, M. eds. The little magazine in America: a modern documentary history p324-37

Krio dialects. See Creole dialects

Kripke, Saul A.
Is there a problem about substitutional quantification? *In* Evans, G. L. and McDowell, J. H. eds. Truth and meaning p324-419

Krippendorf, Ekkehart
Revolutionary foreign policy in a capitalist environment. *In* Jahn, E. ed. Soviet foreign policy p26-40

Krisberg, Barry Alan
The gang and the community: the case of the urban leadership training program. *In* Riedel, M. and Chappell, D. eds. Issues in criminal justice: planning and evaluation p99-113

Krisberg, Barry Alan, and Takagi, Paul
Ethical issues in evaluating criminal justice demonstration projects. *In* Riedel, M. and Chappell, D. eds. Issues in criminal justice: planning and evaluation p66-74

Krishna Mēnōn, Vengalil Krishnan

About

McLeod, M. B. Audience and argument in the speeches of R. G. Menzies and Krishna Menon on the Suez Canal crisis in 1956. *In* Narasimhaiah, C. D. ed. Awakened conscience p389-400

Krispyn, Egbert

Joseph Roth and the art of adaptation. *In* Strelka, J. P.; Bell, R. F. and Dobson, E. eds. Protest—form—tradition p97-109

Kristeller, Paul Oskar

The humanities as scholarship and a branch of knowledge. *In* Hook, S.; Kurtz, P. W. and Todorovich, M. eds. The philosophy of the curriculum: the need for general education p217-20

The Latin poems of Giovanni Pico della Mirandola: a supplementary note. *In* Poetry and poetics from ancient Greece to the Renaissance p185-206

See also Part 2 under title: Philosophy and humanism

Kristeller, Paul Oskar, ed.

About individual works
Giovanni Pico della Mirandola and his sources

Kristeller, P. O. The Latin poems of Giovanni Pico della Mirandola: a supplementary note. *In* Poetry and poetics from ancient Greece to the Renaissance p185-206

Kristol, Irving

The American Revolution as a successful revolution. *In* America's continuing revolution p3-21

Also in A Public philosophy reader p289-307

A foolish American ism—utopianism. *In* A Public philosophy reader p73-91

Socialism: obituary for an idea. *In* Tyrrell, R. E. ed. The future that doesn't work p186-99

About individual works
Two cheers for capitalism

Galbraith, J. K. Defenders of the faith, II: Irving Kristol. *In* Galbraith, J. K. Annals of an abiding liberal p109-17

Križanić, Juraj

About

Heaney, M. The sources of early Križanica. *In* Oxford Slavonic papers, new ser. v8 p101-36

Kroch, Adolph

Early years in the book business. *In* Bookselling in America and the world p176-80

Kroeber, Karl

Experience as history: Shelley's Venice, Turner's Carthage. *In* ELH essays for Earl R. Wasserman p31-49

Pride and prejudice: fiction's lasting novelty. *In* Halperin, J. ed. Jane Austen p144-55

Romantic historicism: the temporal sublime. *In* Kroeber, K. and Walling, W. eds. Images of romanticism p149-65

Subverting a hypocrite lecteur. *In* Weinsheimer, J. ed. Jane Austen today p33-45

Kroef, Justus Maria Van der. See Van der Kroef, Justus Maria

Kroeger, Karl

Isaiah Thomas as a music publisher. *In* American Antiquarian Society. Proceedings v86 pt2 p321-41

Kronenberg, Philip S.

Militia in the seventies: a conflict paradigm. *In* Beaumont, R. A. and Edmonds, M. eds. War in the next decade p110-34

Kronenberger, Louis

Max Beerbohm; excerpt from "The republic of letters". *In* Riewald, J. G. ed. The surprise of excellence p21-29

Kronus, Sidney

Race, ethnicity, and community. *In* Handbook of contemporary urban life p202-32

Krook, Dorothea

Recollections of Sylvia Plath. *In* Butscher, E. ed. Sylvia Plath p49-60

Kropf, Carl Raymond

Catharsis in eighteenth-century England. *In* Tennessee Studies in literature v22 p63-72

Krueger, Albert P. and Sobel, David Stuart

Air ions and health. *In* Sobel, D. S. ed. Ways of health p413-33

Krumpelmann, John Theodore

Charles Sealsfield and Weimar. *In* The German contribution to the building of the Americas p173-80

Molière as a source of German comedy. *In* Johnson, R. B.; Neumann, E. S. and Trail, G. T. eds. Molière and the commonwealth of letters: patrimony and posterity p319-26

Kruse, Horst Hermann

Ernest Hemingway's "The end of something": its independence as a short story and its place in the "education of Nick Adams." *In* Benson, J. J. ed. The short stories of Ernest Hemingway: critical essays p210-22

Krutch, Joseph Wood

About individual works
The modern temper

Margolis, J. D. Joseph Wood Krutch: a writer's passage beyond The modern temper. *In* Bornstein, G. ed. Romantic and modern p223-40

Krutilla, John V. and Page, R. Talbot

Energy policy from an environmental perspective. *In* Kalter, R. J. and Vogely, W. A. eds. Energy supply and government policy p76-98

Krzyżanowski, Jerzy Ryszard

Men at war: the Polish version. *In* For Wiktor Weintraub p239-50

Krzyżanowski, Julian

The Polish-Californian background of H. Sienkiewicz's burlesque "A comedy of errors." *In* For Wiktor Weintraub p251-56

Ktorova, Alla. See Ktorowa, Alla

Ktorowa, Alla

About

Hughes, O. R. Alla Ktorova: a new face. *In* The Bitter air of exile p394-407

Ku, Wei-chün. See Koo, Vi Kyuin Wellington

Kubal, David L.

The secret agent and the mechanical chaos. *In* Garvin, H. R. ed. Makers of the twentieth-century novel p93-102

Kubler, George
Drawings by G. A. Montorsoli in Madrid. *In* Collaboration in Italian Renaissance art p143-64

Kubo, Masaaki
The norm of myth: Euripides' Electra. *In* Harvard Studies in classical philology v71 p15-31

Kubrick, Stanley

About

Clarke, A. C. Son of Dr Strangelove; or, How I learned to stop worrying and love Stanley Kubrick; excerpt from "Report on Planet Three and other speculations." *In* Knight, D. F. ed. Turning points p277-84

Taylor, J. R. Stanley Kubrick. *In* Taylor, J. R. Directors and directions p100-35

About individual works
A clockwork orange
Kauffmann, S. A clockwork orange. *In* Kauffmann, S. Living images p88-90

Samuels, C. T. The context of A clockwork orange. *In* Samuels, C. T. Mastering the film, and other essays p171-78

Paths of glory
Truffaut, F. Stanley Kubrick: Paths of glory. *In* Truffaut, F. The films in my life p116-18

Kuehl, Jerry
History on the public screen II. *In* Smith, P. ed. The historian and film p177-85

Kuehl, Warren F.
Internationalism. *In* Encyclopedia of American foreign policy p443-54

Kuehne, Alyce de
The spectacular in the theater of Agustín Cuzzani. *In* Lyday, L. F. and Woodyard, G. W. eds. Dramatists in revolt p37-58

Kuh, Edwin
An essay on aggregation theory and practice. *In* Econometrics and economic theory p57-99

Kuhn, Albert J.
Nature spiritualized: aspects of anti-Newtonianism. *In* ELH essays for Earl R. Wasserman p110-22

Kuhn, Helmut
Germany—divided once more. *In* Prospects for constitutional democracy p101-17

Kuhn, Philip A.
Local self-government under the Republic: problems of control, autonomy, and mobilization. *In* Conflict and control in late imperial China p257-98

Kuhn, Thomas S.
Metaphor in science. *In* Ortony, A. ed. Metaphor and thought p409-19

About

Sclafani, R. J. The theory of art. *In* Aagaard-Mogensen, L. ed. Culture and art p146-70

About individual works
The structure of scientific theories
Haskell, T. L. Deterministic implications of intellectual history. *In* Higham, J. and Conkin, P. K. eds. New directions in American intellectual history p132-48

Kuist, James M.
The Gentleman's magazine in the Folger Library. the history and significance of the Nichols family collection. *In* Virginia. University. Bibliographical Society. Studies in bibliography v29 p307-22

Kujamaat. See Diola (African people)

Kūkai

About
Kitagawa, J. M. Kūkai as master and savior. *In* Reynolds, F. E. and Capps, D. eds. The biographical process p319-41

Kuklick, Bruce
Congress and foreign policy. *In* Encyclopedia of American foreign policy p141-50

Tradition and diplomatic talent: the case of the cold warriors. *In* Zenderland, L. ed. Recycling the past p116-31

Kula, Witold
The seigneury and the peasant family in eighteenth-century Poland. *In* Family and society p192-203

Kulchur (Periodical)
Hornick, L. Kulchur: a memoir. *In* Anderson, E. and Kinzie, M. eds. The little magazine in America: a modern documentary history p281-97

Sorrentino, G. Neon, Kulchur, etc. *In* Anderson, E. and Kinzie, M. eds. The little magazine in America: a modern documentary history p298-323

Kummer, George Nicholas
Who wrote "The harp of a thousand strings?" *In* Inge, M. T. ed. The frontier humorists p219-29

Kundera, Milan

About individual works
The joke
Doležel, L. A scheme of narrative time. *In* Matejka, L. and Titunik, I. R. eds. Semiotics of art p209-17

Roth, P. Imagining the erotic: three introductions. *In* Roth, P. Reading myself and others p195-214

Laughable loves
Roth, P. Imagining the erotic: three introductions. *In* Roth, P. Reading myself and others p195-214

Kunene, Daniel P.
Towards an aesthetic of Sesotho prose. *In* Exile and tradition p98-115

Kunene, Mazisi
South African oral traditions. *In* Heywood, C. ed. Aspects of South African literature p24-41

Kunert, Günter
Why write; excerpt translated from "Warum schreiben? Notizen zur Literatur." *In* Gibbons, R. ed. The poet's work: 29 masters of 20th century poetry on the origins and practice of their art p136-38

Küng, Guido
The phenomenological reduction as epoche and explication. *In* Elliston, F. A. and McCormick, P. eds. Husserl p338-49

!Kung (African people)

Psychology
Draper, P. The learning environment for aggression and anti-social behavior among the !Kung. *In* Montagu, A. ed. Learning non-aggression p31-53

Kurosawa, Akira—About individual works
—*Continued*

Throne of blood

Jorgens, J. J. Defining Macbeth: Schaefer, Welles, and Kurosawa. *In* Jorgens, J. J. Shakespeare on film p148-60

Kurth-Voight, Lieselotte E.

The reception of C. M. Wieland in America. *In* The German contribution to the building of the Americas p97-133

Wieland and the French Revolution: the writings of the first year. *In* Studies in eighteenth-century culture v7 p79-103

Kurtz, Paul W.

Education for the future: the liberating arts. *In* Hook, S.; Kurtz, P. W. and Todorovich, M. eds. The philosophy of the curriculum: the need for general education p197-204

The ethics of free inquiry. *In* Hook, S.; Kurtz, P. and Todorovich, M. eds. The ethics of teaching and scientific research p203-07

Naturalism in American philosophy. *In* Philosophy and the civilizing arts p178-212

Should the patron be the master?: the autonomy of public universities and colleges. *In* Hook, S.; Kurtz, P. W. and Todorovich, M. eds. The university and the state: what role for government in higher education? p287-91

See also Kohl, M. jt. auth.

Kuryłowicz, Jerzy

A remark on Lachmann's law. *In* Harvard Studies in classical philology v72 p295-99

Kurz, Paul Konrad

On modern German literature v 1

Contents

Doomed existence
Hermann Broch's trilogy Die Schlafwandler
Hundejahre
Journey into dustlessness
Literature and science
Literature and theology today
Perspectives in Kafka interpretation
Skeletons of the sayable—demonstrations of a world
Vicissitudes of the modern novel

On modern German literature v2

Contents

Bertolt Brecht: the man and his work
Hans Mayer: on German literature today
Identity and society: the world of Max Frisch
Thomas Mann and irony

On modern German literature v3

Contents

Fences and camps
Group 47
The individual's awareness of self and world as manifested in German lyric poetry since 1945
Lyric poetry today?
Wind hens interrogated

On modern German literature v4

Contents

Beat—Pop—underground
The contemporary novel about Jesus
The fool and doubt: on one aspect of the work of Friedrich Dürrenmatt
German lesson in New York: Uwe Johnson's novel Days of the year
Heinrich Böll: not reconciled

The insecure heraldic animal: on Günter Grass's Uptight and Local anaesthetic
The priest in the modern novel
Tendencies observable in the most recent literature
Wolves and lambs: Friedrich Dürrenmatt's dramaturgy of politics
Why is Christian literature at an end?

Kusch, Polykarp

A personal view of science and the future. *In* The Future of science p39-55

Kushner, Eva (Dubska)

About individual works

'Le "Solitaire premier" de Pontus de Tyard: prolégomènes à une interprétation'

Hall, K. M. Pontus de Tyard: a reply to a recent article. *In* French Renaissance studies, 1540-70 p185-93

Kusikov, Alexandr Borisovich

About

McVay, G. The tree-stump and the horse: the poetry of Alexander Kusikov. *In* Oxford Slavonic papers, new ser. v11 p101-31

Kutner, Luis

A philosophical perspective on rebellion; excerpts from "Due process of rebellion". *In* International terrorism and political crimes p51-64

Kutscher, Austin H. See Kutscher, A. H. 1923- jt. auth.

Kutscher, Austin H. 1923- **and Kutscher, Austin H.**

Medical school curriculum and anticipatory grief: faculty attitudes. *In* Anticipatory grief p213-17

Kuttner, Henry

About

Gunn, J. E. Henry Kuttner, C. L. Moore, Lewis Padgett et al. *In* Clareson, T. D. ed. Voices for the future: essays on major science fiction writers v 1 p185-215

Kuttner, Stephan Georg. See Kuttner, Stephen George

Kuttner, Stephen George

Gratian and Plato. *In* Church and government in the Middle Ages p93-118

See also Part 2 under title: Law, church and society

Kuvalayananda, Swami, and Vinekar, S. L.

Principles of yogic therapy; excerpt from "Yogic therapy: its basic principles and methods." *In* Sobel, D. S. ed. Ways of health p319-29

Kuz, Lubow

Children's books and multiculturalism in Canada. *In* Egoff, S. A. ed. One ocean touching p221-31

Kuzmin, Mikhail Alexeyevich

About individual works

The trout breaking through the ice

Malmstad, J. E. and Shmakov, G. Kuzmin's "The trout breaking through the ice." *In* Gibian, G. and Tjalsma, H. W. eds. Russian modernism p133-64

Kuznets, Simon Smith

Demographic aspects of the distribution of income among families: recent trends in the United States. *In* Econometrics and economic theory p223-45

Kuznetsov, Boris Grigor'evich
Einstein, science and culture. *In* Einstein p167-83

Kvaløy, Sigmund
The Mardøla Waterfall development. *In* Against pollution and hunger p289-92

Kwazulu. See Zululand

Kweli women (African people) See Women, Bakwiri (African people)

Kwiatowska, Hanna Yaxa
Family art therapy: experiments with a new technique. *In* Ulman, E. and Dachinger, P. eds. Art therapy p113-25
See also Day, J. jt. auth.

Kwili women (African people) See Women, Bakwiri (African people)

Kwiri women (African people) See Women, Bakwiri (African people)

Kyd, Thomas

About individual works
The Spanish tragedy
Altman, J. B. Tragic perspectives among the Elizabethans. *In* Altman, J. B. The Tudor play of mind p249-320

Hunter, G. K. Ironies of justice in The Spanish tragedy. *In* Hunter, G. K. Dramatic identities and cultural tradition p214-29

Rowan, D. F. The staging of The Spanish tragedy. *In* The Elizabethan theatre, V p112-23

Stilling, R. The Spanish tragedy. *In* Stilling, R. Love and death in Renaissance tragedy p26-40

Wineke, D. R. Hieronimo's garden and "the fall of Babylon": culture and anarchy in The Spanish tragedy. *In* Aeolian harps p65-79

Kyoto

Buildings—Conservation and restoration
Itó, T. and Nishikawa, K. Japan: two ancient capitals and the menace to them. *In* United Nations Educational, Scientific and Cultural Organization. The conservation of cities p107-24

City planning
Itō, T. and Nishikawa, K. Japan: two ancient capitals and the menace to them. *In* United Nations Educational, Scientific, and Cultural Organization. The conservation of cities p107-24

Kyper, John
Coming out: toward a social analysis. *In* Crew, L. ed. The gay academic p387-414

Kyranides. See Virtutes aquile

L

LEF. See Left Front in Art

LMT. See Lowenfeld mosaic test

LSD. See Lysergic acid diethylamide

Labalme, Patricia H.
The last will of a Venetian patrician (1489) *In* Philosophy and humanism p483-501

La Barre, Weston
The clinic and the field. *In* Spindler, G. D. ed. The making of psychological anthropology p259-99

Labarthe, Philippe Lacoue- See Lacoue-Labarthe, Philippe

La Belle, Jenijoy
Blake's visions and re-visions of Michaelangelo. *In* Essick, R. N. and Pearce, D. R. eds. Blake in his time p13-22

Labini, Paolo Sylos. See Sylos Labini, Paolo

Labor (Obstetrics) See Childbirth

Labor, Conscription of. See Service, Compulsory non-military

Labor, Migrant. See Migrant labor

Labor, Organized. See Trade-unions

Labor and capital. See Industrial relations

Labor and laboring classes
Bakan, M. Hannah Arendt's concepts of labor and work. *In* Hannah Arendt: the recovery of the public world p49-65

Clayre, A. Habits and customs of working people. *In* Clayre, A. Work and play p113-29

Frampton, K. The status of man and the status of his objects: a reading of The human condition. *In* Hannah Arendt: the recovery of the public world p101-30

Major, R. W. A reading of Hannah Arendt's "unusual" distinction between labor and work. *In* Hannah Arendt: the recovery of the public world p131-55

Markus, M. and Hegedüs, A. Free time and the division of labour. *In* The Humanisation of socialism p106-23

Parekh, B. C. Hannah Arendt's critique of Marx. *In* Hannah Arendt: the recovery of the public world p67-100

See also Artisans; Capital; Children—Employment; Friendly societies; Industrial relations; Middle classes; Peasantry; Servants; Socialism; Trade-unions; Unemployed; Women—Employment

Dwellings—Netherlands—Amsterdam
Searing, H. With red flags flying: housing in Amsterdam, 1915-1923. *In* Millon, H. A. and Nochlin, L. eds. Art and architecture in the service of politics p230-69

Education—England
Laqueur, T. W. Working-class demand and the growth of English elementary education, 1750-1850. *In* Schooling and society p192-205

Songs and music
See Work-songs

Wages
See Wages

Jews
Dawidowicz, L. S. The Jewishness of the American Jewish labor movement. *In* Dawidowicz, L. S. The Jewish presence p116-30

Szajkowski, Z. East European Jewish workers in Germany during World War I. *In* Salo Wittmayer Baron v2 p887-918

Chile—Political activity
Santa Lucia, P. pseud. The industrial working class and the struggle for power in Chile. *In* O'Brien, P. J. ed. Allende's Chile p128-66

Labor and laboring classes—Chile—Political activity—*Continued*

Threlfall, M. Shantytown dwellers and people's power. *In* O'Brien, P. J. ed. Allende's Chile p167-91

China

Parish, W. L. The view from the factory. *In* Terrill, R. ed. The China difference p183-98

Cuba

MacEwan, A. Incentives, equality, and power in revolutionary Cuba. *In* Radosh, R. ed. The new Cuba: paradoxes and potentials p74-101

England—Stockport

Litchfield, R. B. The family and mill: cotton mill work, family work patterns, and fertility in mid-Victorian Stockport. *In* Wohl, A. S. ed. The Victorian family p180-96

Great Britain

Kiernan, E. V. G. Working class and nation in nineteenth-century Britain. *In* Rebels and their causes p122-39

Supple, B. E. Legislation and virtue: an essay on working class self-help and the state in the early nineteenth century. *In* Historical perspectives p211-54

Wohl, A. S. Sex and the single room: incest among the Victorian working classes. *In* Wohl, A. S. ed. The Victorian family p197-216

Worsthorne, P. The trade unions: new lads on top. *In* Tyrrell, R. E. ed. The future that doesn't work p5-21

Great Britain—Religious life

Chadwick, O. The attitudes of the worker. *In* Chadwick, O. The secularization of the European mind in the nineteenth century p88-106

Milwaukee—Political activity

Miller, S. M. Milwaukee: of ethnicity and labor. *In* Stave, B. M. ed. Socialism and the cities p41-71

New York (City)—History

Ward, D. Some locational implications of the ethnic division of labor in mid-nineteenth-century American cities. *In* Pattern and process p258-70

Oklahoma City—Political activity

Burbank, G. Socialism in an Oklahoma boom-town: "Milwaukeeizing" Oklahoma City. *In* Stave, B. M. ed. Socialism and the cities p99-115

Southern States

Weeks, B. The union contribution. *In* The Rising South v 1 p25-34

Spain

Ellwood, S. The working class under the Franco régime. *In* Preston, P. ed. Spain in crisis p157-82

United States

Coles, R. Work and self-respect. *In* Erikson, E. H. ed. Adulthood p217-26

Form, W. H. Conflict within the working class: the skilled as a special-interest group. *In* The Uses of controversy in sociology p51-73

Gutman, H. G. Protestantism and the American labor movement: the Christian spirit in the Gilded Age. *In* Mulder, J. M. and Wilson, J. F. eds. Religion in American history p318-41

Mason, P. P. Working in America. *In* Alderson, W. T. ed. American issues p65-80

See also Afro-Americans—Employment

United States—Political activity

Shostak, A. B. Politics, conflict, and young blue-collarites: old dissensus and new consciousness. *In* The Uses of controversy in sociology p74-94

United States—1970-

Kanter, R. M. Work in a new America. *In* A New America? p47-78

Labor and laboring classes in literature

Lucas, W. J. Engels, Mrs Gaskell and Manchester. *In* Lucas, W. J. The literature of change p34-56

See also Proletariats in literature

Labor and state. See Labor policy

Labor and the church. See Church and labor

Labor arbitration. See Arbitration, Industrial

Labor conscription. See Service, Compulsory non-military

Labor costs. See Wages

Labor economics

Rees, A. E. Compensating wage differentials. *In* Skinner, A. S. and Wilson, T. eds. Essays on Adam Smith p336-49

See also Labor and laboring classes

Labor force. See Labor supply

Labor incentives. See Incentives in industry

Labor laws and legislation

Myers, C. A. Management and the employee. *In* McKie, J. W. ed. Social responsibility and the business predicament p311-49

See also Factory laws and legislation; Trade-unions

Labor-management relations. See Industrial relations

Labor market. See Labor supply

Labor market research. See Labor supply—Research

Labor negotiations. See Arbitration, Industrial

Labor organizations. See Trade-unions

Labor Party (Great Britain) See Labour Party (Great Britain)

Labor policy

See also Labor laws and legislation; Manpower planning

Spain

Ellwood, S. The working class under the Franco régime. *In* Preston, P. ed. Spain in crisis p157-82

United States

Derber, M. The New Deal and labor. *In* Braeman, J.; Bremer, R. H. and Brody, D. eds. The New Deal v 1 p110-32

Labor relations. See Industrial relations

Labor supply

Brown, E. H. P. The labour market. *In* The Market and the state p243-59

See also Employment forecasting; Human capital; Unemployed

Labor supply—*Continued*
Research—India
Visaria, P. M. The importance of labour-force structure in relation to employment and unemployment in less-developed countries. *In* Economic factors in population growth p411-38

France
Hayward, J. E. S. Planning and the French labour market: incomes and industrial training. *In* Planning, politics and public policy p159-76

Great Britain
Corina, J. Planning and the British labour market: incomes and manpower policy, 1965-70. *In* Planning, politics and public policy p177-201

Italy
Mariani, I. F. Incomes and employment policies in Italian economic planning. *In* Planning, politics and public policy p202-13

Underdeveloped areas
See Underdeveloped areas—Labor supply

Labor-unions. See Trade-unions

Laboratories, Physical. See Physical laboratories

Laborers. See Labor and laboring classes

Labour Party (Great Britain)
Cook, C. Labour and the downfall of the Liberal Party, 1906-14. *In* Crisis and controversy p38-65
Cook, C. Liberals, Labour and local elections. *In* Peele, G. and Cook, C. eds. The politics of reappraisal, 1918-1939 p166-88

LaBranche, Anthony
'Blanda elegeia': the background to Donne's 'Elegies.' *In* Roberts, J. R. ed. **Essential articles for the study of John** Donne's poetry p399-410
Samuel Daniel: a voice of thoughtfulness. *In* Sloan, T. O. and Waddington, R. B. eds. The rhetoric of Renaissance poetry p123-39

La Brosse, Guy de

About
Guerlac, H. Guy de La Brosse: botanist, chemist, and libertine. *In* Guerlac, H. Essays and papers in the history of modern science p440-50

Labrunie, Gérard. See Gérard de Nerval, Gérard Labrunie, known as

La Bruyère, Jean de

About individual works
The characters
Horowitz, L. K. La Bruyère. *In* Horowitz, L. K. Love and language p145-60
Koppisch, M. S. The faux dévot from Molière to Marivaux. *In* Johnson, R. B.; Neumann, E. S. and Trail, G. T. eds Molière and the commonwealth of letters: patrimony and posterity p57-67

Lacan, Jacques

About
Hartman, G. H. Psychoanalysis: the French connection. *In* Hartman, G. H. ed. Psychoanalysis and the question of the text p86-113
Leavy, S. A. The significance of Jacques Lacan. *In* Psychoanalysis and language p271-92

About individual works
Seminar on The purloined letter
Johnson, B. The frame of reference: Poe, Lacan, Derrida. *In* Hartman, G. H. ed. Psychoanalysis and the question of the text p149-71

Lace and lace making

History
Stanley, E. G. Directions for making many sorts of laces. *In* Chaucer and Middle English studies in honour of Rossell Hope Robbins p89-103

La Chaussée, Pierre Claude Nivelle de

About
Brereton, G Bourgeois comedy: sentiment and moralization. *In* Brereton, G. French comic drama p214-36

Lachs, John
The omnicolored sky: Baylis on perception. *In* Fact, value, and perception p139-50

Lachterman, David R.
The physics of Spinoza's Ethics. *In* Shahan, R. W. and Biro, J. I. eds. Spinoza: new perspectives p71-111

Lackington, James

About
Landon, R. G. Small profits do great things: James Lackington and eighteenth-century bookselling. *In* Studies in eighteenth-century culture v5 p387-99

Lackner, Bede Karl
Hans Bohm: shepherd, piper, prophet. *In* Essays on medieval civilization p73-107

Lackner, James R. See Bever, T. G. jt. auth.

Lacombe, Lucien (Motion picture)
Sarris, A. The nasty Nazis: history or mythology. *In* Sarris, A. Politics and cinema p85-91

Lacoue-Labarthe, Philippe
The caesura of the speculative. *In* Glyph 4 p57-84
Theatrum analyticum. *In* Glyph 2 p122-43

Lacourcière, Luc
A survey of folk medicine in French Canada from early times to the present. *In* American folk medicine p203-14

Lacustrine peoples and the coast, Connections between the. Posnansky, M. *In* Chittick, H. N. and Rotberg, R. I. eds. East Africa and the Orient p216-25

Lacy, Dan Mabry
Libraries and the freedom of access to information. *In* Libraries and the life of the mind in America p19-37

Lacy, Norris J.
Types of esthetic distance in the fabliaux. *In* Cooke, T. D. and Honeycutt, B. L. eds. The humor of the fabliaux p107-17

Ladd, George Eldon
Apocalyptic and New Testament theology. *In* Reconciliation and hope p285-96
The Holy Spirit in Galatians. *In* Current issues in Biblical and patristic interpretation p211-16

Ladd, Joseph Brown

About
Leary, L. G. Joseph Brown Ladd of Charleston. *In* Leary, L. G. Soundings p112-30

Laden, Richard A.
"Les relais du verbe": Perse's reticular rhetoric. *In* Glyph 4 p156-88

Ladipo, Duro

About individual works

Oba kò so (The king did not hang)

Soyinka, W. Drama and the African worldview. *In* Exile and tradition p173-90

Ladner, Gerhart Burian
On Roman attitudes toward barbarians in late antiquity. *In* Viator: medieval and Renaissance studies v7 p 1-26

Ladurie, Emmanuel Le Roy. See Le Roy Ladurie, Emmanuel

Lafarge, Catherine
Paris and myth: one vision of horror. *In* Studies in eighteenth-century culture v5 p281-91

LaFarge, John, 1835-1910

About

Auchincloss, L. In search of innocence: Henry Adams and John LaFarge in the South Seas. *In* Auchincloss, L. Life, law and letters p131-40

La Farge, Oliver

About individual works

Laughing boy

Krefft, J. H. A possible source for Faulkner's Indians: Oliver La Farge's Laughing boy. *In* Tulane Studies in English v23 p187-92

LaFave, Wayne R.
"Case-by-case adjudication" versus "standardized procedures": the Robinson dilemma. *In* The Supreme Court review, 1974 p127-63

La Fayette, Marie Madeleine (Pioche de La Vergne) comtesse de

About

Horowitz, L. K. Madame de Lafayette. *In* Horowitz, L. K. Love and language p51-72

LaFeber, Walter
American policy-makers, public opinion, and the outbreak of the Cold war, 1945-50. *In* The Origins of the Cold war in Asia p43-65

The Truman doctrine. *In* Encyclopedia of American foreign policy p980-85

LaFleur, Richard A.
Amicitia and the unity of Juvenal's first book. *In* Illinois classical studies v4, 1979 p158-77

La Fleur, William
The death and 'lives' of the poet-monk Saigyō: the genesis of a Buddhist sacred biography. *In* Reynolds, F. E. and Capps, D. eds. The biographical process p343-61

La Fontaine, Jean de

About individual works

The crow and the fox

Shell, M. The lie of the fox: Rousseau's theory of verbal, monetary, and political representation. *In* Shell, M. The economy of literature p113-28

Laforgue, Jules

Influence

Cowley, M. Laforgue in America: a testimony. *In* Cowley, M. —And I worked at the writer's trade p69-81

LaFrance, Marston. See Part 2 under title: The Stoic strain in American literature

La Garza, Rudolph O. de. See De la Garza, Rudolph O.

Lago, Carmelo Mesa-. See Mesa-Lago, Carmelo

Lagorio, Valerie Marie
The Joseph of Arimathie: English hagiography in transition. *In* Medievalia et humanistica no. 6 p91-101

Lagos, Gustavo. See Lagos Matus, Gustavo

Lagos Matus, Gustavo
The revolution of being. *In* On the creation of a just world order p71-109

La Guma, Alex

About individual works

A walk in the night

Gakwandi, S. A. La Guma's A walk in the night. *In* Gakwandi, S. A. The novel and contemporary experience in Africa p21-26

Wade, M. Art and morality in Alex La Guma's A walk in the night. *In* Parker, K. ed. The South African novel in English p164-91

Lahey, Kathleen A. and Sang, Lewis M.
Control of terrorism through a broader interpretation of Article 3 of the four Geneva Conventions of 1949. *In* International terrorism and political crimes p191-200

Laird, Marshall
Osiris, Asklepios, and the Harpies: the development of an African river basin. *In* A Time to hear and answer: essays for the Bicentennial season p103-40

Laissez-faire
Clausen, A. W. The future of our freedom-based economy. *In* Prochnow, H. V. ed. Dilemmas facing the nation p32-40

Howard, J. A. The plight of private enterprise and a possible way out. *In* Prochnow, H. V. ed. Dilemmas facing the nation p82-95

Lauer, R. H. Determinants of type of strategy. *In* Lauer, R. H. ed. Social movements and social change p85-96

Murphy, T. A. Are we losing the freedom to decide? *In* Prochnow, H. V. ed. Dilemmas facing the nation p125-33

Porter, M. C. The commerce shall be free: a new look at the old laissez-faire Court. *In* The Supreme Court review, 1976 p135-59

See also Competition; Industry and state

Laitinen, Kai
From the forest to the city: the great tradition in Finnish prose. *In* Dauenhauer, R. and Binham, P. eds. Snow in May p21-28

Lakatos, Imre, and Zahar, Elie
Why did Copernicus' research program supersede Ptolemy's? *In* The Copernican achievement p354-83

About individual works

Why did Copernicus' research program supersede Ptolemy's?

Toulmin, S. Commentary [on Why did Copernicus' research program supersede Ptolemy's]? *In* The Copernican achievement p384-91

Lake, Michael

About individual works

Michael Lake describes what the executioner actually faces

Lodge, D. George Orwell's 'A hanging', and Michael Lake describes . . .' *In* Lodge, D. The modes of modern writing p9-17

Lakes

Temperature

See Thermal pollution of rivers, lakes, etc.

Lakoff, Robin T.

Language and society. *In* Wardhaugh, R. and Brown, H. D. eds. A survey of applied linguistics p207-28

About

Valian, V. Linguistics and feminism. *In* Feminism and philosophy p154-66

Lakoff, Sanford A.

Scientists, technologists and political power. *In* Science, technology and society p355-91

Lakshin, Vladimir ĬAkovlevich

Mikhail Bulgakov's The master and Margarita. *In* Erlich, V. ed. Twentieth-century Russian literary criticism p247-83

Lakshmi (Indian goddess)

Coomaraswamy, A. K. On the Loathly Bride. *In* Coomaraswamy, A. K. Selected papers v 1 p353-70

Lally, James, and Baldock, Cora Vellekoop

Contemporary sociology in Australia and New Zealand. *In* Mohan, R. P. and Martindale, D. A. eds. Handbook of contemporary developments in world sociology p453-69

La Mama, Etc (Experimental theater club) New York (City)

Kauffmann, S. Trilogy. *In* Kauffmann, S. Persons of the drama p108-11

Lamarck, Jean Baptiste Pierre Antoine de Monet de

About

Boesiger, E. Evolutionary theories after Lamarck and Darwin. *In* Ayala, F. J. and Dobzhansky, T. G. eds. Studies in the philosophy of biology p21-43

Koestler, A. Lamarck revisited. *In* Koestler, A. Janus p193-204

Mandel'shtam, O. E. Around the naturalists. *In* Mandel'shtam, O. E. Selected essays p196-200

La Mare, Walter John de. See De La Mare, Walter John

Lamartine, Alphonse Marie Louis de

About

Ages, A. Lamartine and the philosophes. *In* Literature and history in the age of ideas p321-40

Lamb, Ursula S.

Cosmographers of Seville: nautical science and social experience. *In* First images of America p675-86

Lambarde, William

About

Knight, W. N. Equity, 'The merchant of Venice' and William Lambarde. *In* Shakespeare survey 27 p93-104

Lamberg-Karlovsky, C. C.

Third millennium modes of exchange and modes of production. *In* Ancient civilization and trade p341-68

Lambert, Francis

Cuba: Communist state or personal dictatorship? *In* Brown, A. H. and Gray, J. eds. Political culture and political change in Communist states p231-52

Lambert, Gavin

The dangerous edge

Contents

The benefits of shock
The double agent
Enemy country
Final problems: G. K. Chesterton
Final problems: Sir Arthur Conan Doyle
Night vision
A private eye
The thin protection: Eric Ambler
The thin protection: John Buchan

Lambert, Wilfred George

The historical development of the Mesopotamian pantheon: a study in sophisticated polytheism. *In* Unity and diversity p191-200

The problem of the love lyrics. *In* Unity and diversity p98-135

The Lament of Holy Mary. See Żale Matki Boskiej pod krzyżem

The Lament of the Mother of God at the foot of the Cross. See Żale Matki Boskiej pod krzyzem

Lamentations. See Elegiac poetry; Laments

Laments

Woolf, R. The wanderer, The seafarer, and the genre of planctus. *In* Anglo-Saxon poetry: essays in appreciation p192-207

Lameyer, Gordon Amis

The double in Sylvia Plath's The bell jar. *In* Butscher, E. ed. Sylvia Plath p143-65

Sylvia at Smith. *In* Butscher, E. ed. Sylvia Plath p32-41

Lamm, Norman

The phase of dialogue and reconciliation. *In* Király, B. K. ed. Tolerance and movements of religious dissent in Eastern Europe p115-29

Lamming, George

The peasant roots of the West Indian novel; excerpt from "The pleasures of exile." *In* Baugh, E. ed. Critics on Caribbean literature p24-26

About

Wynter, S. 'The necessary background.' *In* Baugh, E. ed. Critics on Caribbean literature p19-23

About individual works

In the castle of my skin

Abrahams, C. A. George Lamming and Chinua Achebe: tradition and the literary chroniclers. *In* Narasimhaiah, C. D. ed. Awakened conscience p294-306

Ngugi Wa Thiong'o. George Lamming's In the castle of my skin. *In* Baugh, E. ed. Critics on Caribbean literature p47-57

Lamont, Rosette C.

Elie Wiesel: in search of a tongue. *In* Rosenfeld, A. H. and Greenberg, I. eds. Confronting the Holocaust p80-98

Solzhenitsyn's nationalism. *In* Dunlop, J. B.; Haugh, R. and Klimoff, A. eds. Aleksandr Solzhenitsyn: critical essays and documentary materials 2d ed. p94-116

Lamorisse, Albert
About individual works
The red balloon
Truffaut, F. Albert Lamorisse: Le ballon rouge. *In* Truffaut, F. The films in my life p220-22

La Motte, Antoine Houdar, de
About
Simonsuuri, K. The interpretation of early Greek epic: Mme Dacier and the Homeric war. *In* Simonsuuri, K. Homer's original genius p46-56

About individual works
Fables nouvelles
Noel, T. Theories of the fable: La Motte and Richer. *In* Noel, T. Theories of the fable in the eighteenth century p38-46

Lampedusa, Giuseppe Tomasi di. See Tomasi di Lampedusa, Giuseppe

Lamphear, John
Reconstructing the African past. *In* Martin, P. M. and O'Meara, P. eds. Africa p53-61

Two basic themes in African history: migration and state formation. *In* Martin, P. M. and O'Meara, P. eds. Africa p83-97

Lamps
Identification
Goldstein, S. M. A terracotta lamp in the McDaniel collection. *In* Harvard Studies in classical philology v73 p291-303

Rome
Bailey, D. M. Pottery lamps. *In* Strong, D. E. and Brown, D. eds. Roman crafts p93-103

Lancashire, Anne Begor, and Levenson, Jill L.
Anonymous plays. *In* Logan, T. P. and Smith, D. S. eds. The new intellectuals p302-22

Anonymous plays [another essay] *In* Logan, T. P. and Smith, D. S. eds. The popular school p148-249

Lancaster, Diana
The price of progress in Thailand. *In* Gerbner, G. ed. Mass media policies in changing cultures p165-83

Lancaster, Jane B.
Sex and gender in evolutionary perspective. *In* Katchadourian, H. A. ed. Human sexuality p51-80

Lancaster, Marjorie S.
Middleton's use of the upper stage in Women beware women. *In* Tulane studies in English v22 p69-85

Lancaster, Otis Ewing
The future of engineering education in land-grant universities. *In* Land-grant universities and their continuing challenge p104-31

Land, Hilary, and Parker, Roy
United Kingdom. *In* Kamerman, S. B. and Kahn, A. J. eds. Family policy p331-66

Land
Samuelson, P. A. Land and the rate of interest. *In* Theory for economic efficiency: essays in honor of Abba P. Lerner p167-85
See also Agriculture—Economic aspects

Ontario
Wall, G. Ninetenth-century land use and settlement on the Canadian Shield frontier. *In* Miller, D. H. and Steffen, J. O. eds. The frontier p227-41

United States
Carstensen, V. R. The Land of Plenty. *In* Alderson, W. T. ed. American issues p17-31

Land-grant colleges. See State universities and colleges

Land question. See Land tenure

Land reform
See also Agriculture and state

Chile
Kay, C. Agrarian reform and the transition to socialism. *In* O'Brien, P. J. ed. Allende's Chile p79-105

Mexico
Katz, F. Peasants in the Mexican Revolution of 1910. *In* Forging nations: a comparative view of rural ferment and revolt p61-85

Land settlement
Canada—Case studies
Green, S. W. The agricultural colonization of temperate forest habitats: an ecological model. *In* The Frontier v2 p69-103

Finland—Case studies
Green, S. W. The agricultural colonization of temperate forest habitats: an ecological model. *In* The Frontier v2 p69-103

New Mexico—History
Simmons, M. Settlement patterns and village plans in colonial New Mexico. *In* Weber, D. J. ed. New Spain's far northern frontier p97-115

Ontario
Osborne, B. S. Frontier settlement in eastern Ontario in the nineteenth century. a study in changing perceptions of land and opportunity. *In* Miller, D. H. and Steffen, J. O. eds. The frontier p201-25
Wall, G. Nineteenth-century land use and settlement on the Canadian Shield frontier. *In* Miller, D. H. and Steffen, J. O. eds. The frontier p227-41

Texas—History
Jordan, T. G. Vegetational perception and choice of settlement site in frontier Texas. *In* Pattern and process p244-57

United States—History—Sources
Smith, J. F. Settlement on the public domain as reflected in federal records: suggested research approaches. *In* Pattern and process p290-304

Land subdivision
Evers, H. D. Urban expansion and land-ownership in underdeveloped societies. *In* Walton, J. and Masotti, L. H. eds. The city in comparative perspective p67-79

United States
Johnson, H. B. The United States land survey as a principle of order. *In* Pattern and process p114-30
Pattison, W. D. Reflections on the American rectangular land survey system. *In* Pattern and process p131-38

Land tenure
See also Commons; Peasantry; Village communities

Law
See Inclosures

Brazil
Katzman, M. T. Social relations of production on the Brazilian frontier. *In* Miller, D. H. and Steffen, J. O. eds. The frontier p275-96

England—Essex
McIntosh, M. K. The privileged villeins of the English ancient demesne. *In* Viator: medieval and Renaissance studies v7 p295-328

Europe—History
Herlihy, D. Land, family, and women in continental Europe, 701-1200. *In* Stuard, S. M. ed. Women in medieval society p13-45

Spring, D. Landed elites compared. *In* Spring, D. ed. European landed elites in the nineteenth century p 1-21

France—History
Zeldin, T. France. *In* Spring, D. ed. European landed elites in the nineteenth century p127-39

Germany—History
Berkner, L. K. Inheritance, land tenure and peasant family structure: a German regional comparison. *In* Family and inheritance p71-95

Stern, F. R. Prussia. *In* Spring, D. ed. European landed elites in the nineteenth century p45-67

Great Britain
McCloskey, D. N. The persistence of English common fields. *In* Parker, W. N. and Jones, E. L. eds. European peasants and their markets p73-119

Martin, D. Land reform. *In* Hollis, P. ed. Pressure from without p131-58

Great Britain—History
Hilton, R. H. Freedom and villeinage in England. *In* Peasants, knights and heretics p174-91

Thirsk, J. The common fields. *In* Peasants, knights and heretics p10-32

Thirsk, J. The origin of the common fields. *In* Peasants, knights and heretics p51-56

Thompson, F. M. L. Britain. *In* Spring, D. ed. European landed elites in the nineteenth century p22-44

Titow, J. Z. Medieval England and the open-field system. *In* Peasants, knights and heretics p33-50

Palestine
Aumann, M. Land ownership in Palestine, 1880-1948. *In* The Palestinians p21-29

Russia—History
Blum, J. Russia. *In* Spring, D. ed. European landed elites in the nineteenth century p68-97

Spain—History
Herr, R. Spain. *In* Spring, D. ed. European landed elites in the nineteenth century p98-126

Tanzania
Gulliver, P. H. A land dispute in Arusha, Tanzania. *In* African dimensions p 1-14

Land use
See also Agriculture

Planning
See Regional planning

Land utilization. See Land

Landar, Herbert Jay
Historiography of native Ibero-American linguistics. *In* Sebeok, T. A. ed. Native languages of the Americas v2 p185-203

Native North America. *In* Sebeok, T. A. ed. Native languages of the Americas v 1 p93-118

Landau, Mark Aleksandrovich
The enigma of Tolstoy. *In* Erlich, V. ed. Twentieth-century Russian literary criticism p201-11

Lander, Dawn
Eve among the Indians. *In* Diamond, A. and Edwards, L. R. eds. The authority of experience p194-211

Landers, Daniel M. See Madison, D. R. jt. auth.

Landes, David Solomon
Bleichröders and Rothschilds: the problem of continuity in the family firm. *In* Rosenberg, C. E. ed. The family in history p95-114

Landesman, Charles
Dreams: two types of explanations. *In* Dunlop, C. E. M. ed. Philosophical essays on dreaming p309-16

Landforms

United States
Mikesell, M. W. The rise and decline of "sequent occupance": a chapter in the history of American geography. *In* Geographies of the mind p149-69

Landgrebe, Ludwig
Phenomenology as transcendental theory of history. *In* Elliston, F. A. and McCormick, P. eds. Husserl p101-17

Landini, Francesco. See Landino, Francesco

Landino, Francesco

Performances
Craft, R. Musical R for a political season. *In* Craft, R. Current convictions p159-68

Landis, Elizabeth S.
Namibia: impending independence? *In* Carter, G. M. and O'Meara, P. eds. Southern Africa in crisis p163-99

Landis, Elizabeth S. and Davis, Michael I.
Namibia: impending independence? *In* Carter, G. M. and O'Meara, P. eds. Southern Africa: the continuing crisis p141-74

Landis, Joan Hutton
A "wild severity": toward a reading of Ben Belitt. *In* Boyers, R. ed. Contemporary poetry in America p221-39

Landlord and tenant
Meyers, C. J. The covenant of habitability and the American Law Institute. *In* Stanford legal essays p355-79

Great Britain—History
Dyer, C. A redistribution of incomes in fifteenth-century England? *In* Peasants, knights and heretics p192-215

Harris, B. J. Landlords and tenants in England in the later Middle Ages: the Buckingham estates. *In* Peasants, knights and heretics p216-20

Landon Richard, G.

Small profits do great things: James Lackington and eighteenth-century bookselling. *In* Studies in eighteenth-century culture v5 p387-99

Landor, Walter Savage

Influence—Pound

Witemeyer, H. Walter Savage Landor and Ezra Pound. *In* Bornstein, G. ed. Romantic and modern p147-63

Landow, George P.

Introduction. *In* Landow, G. P. Approaches to Victorian autobiography pxiii-xlvi

Moses striking the rock: typological symbolism in Victorian poetry. *In* Miner, E. R. ed. Literary uses of typology p315-44

The rainbow: a problematic image. *In* Knoepflmacher, U. C. and Tennyson, G. B. eds. Nature and the Victorian imagination p341-69

There began to be a great talking about the fine arts. *In* Altholz, J. L. ed. The mind and art of Victorian England p124-45

Landsberg, Hans Herman. See Darmstadter, J. jt. auth.

Landsberger, Henry A.

The sources of rural radicalism. *In* Radicalism in the contemporary age v 1 p247-91

Landscape. See Mountains in literature; Nature (Aesthetics); Nature in literature

Landscape (criticism) Pinter, H. *In* Kauffmann, S. Persons of the drama p201-04

Landscape architecture

England

Fabricant, C. Binding and dressing nature's loose tresses: the ideology of Augustan landscape design. *In* Studies in eighteenth-century culture v8 p109-35

Landscape design. See Landscape architecture

Landscape gardening

See also Landscape architecture

England

Willis, P. The visual arts. *In* Rogers, P. ed. The eighteenth century p208-39

Landscape in literature. See Nature in literature

Landscape painters

Great Britain

Hadfield, J. The moonlighters. *In* The Saturday book 34 p216-21

Landscape painting

Berger, J. Painting a landscape. *In* Berger, J. The look of things p172-77

19th century—Great Britain

Axton, W. F. Victorian landscape painting: a change in outlook. *In* Knoepflmacher, U. C. and Tennyson, G. B. eds. Nature and the Victorian imagination p281-308

Landscape painting, Chinese

Edwards, R. The orthodoxy of the unorthodox. *In* Artists and traditions p185-99

History

Cahill, J. F. The Orthodox movement in early Ch'ing painting. *In* Artists and traditions p169-81

Li, Chu-tsing. The uses of the past in Yüan landscape painting. *In* Artists and traditions p73-88

Vanderstappen, H. A. The style of some seventeenth-century Chinese paintings. *In* Artists and traditions p149-68

Landscape protection

Southern States

Horne, V. The fragile, threatened landscapes of the South. *In* The Rising South v 1 p35-49

Landy, Marcia

The silent woman: towards a feminist critique. *In* Diamond, A. and Edwards, L. R. eds. The authority of experience p16-27

Lane, Frederic Chapin

The first infidelities of the Venetian lire. *In* The Medieval city p43-63

Lane, Gary

Influence and originality in Plath's poems. *In* Lane, G. ed. Sylvia Plath p116-37

Lane, Jeremy

His master's voice? The questioning of authority in literature. *In* Josipovici, G. ed. The modern English novel: the reader, the writer and the work p113-29

Lane, Michael

Shapers of culture: the editor in book publishing. *In* Altbach, P. G. and McVey, S. eds. Perspectives on publishing p27-35

Lane, Ralph

Catholic Charismatic Renewal. *In* The New religious consciousness p162-79

Lane, Robert Edwards

Capitalist man, Socialist man. *In* Laslett, P. and Fishkin, J. eds. Philosophy, politics and society p57-77

Lane-Pool, Edward Humphrey

The discovery of Africa: a history of the exploration of Africa as reflected in the maps in the collection of the Rhodes-Livingstone Museum. *In* The Occasional papers of the Rhodes-Livingstone Museum p215-48

Lanec. See Chilongo, Lanec

Lanes, Jerrold

Art criticism and the authorship of the Chef-d'œuvre inconnu: a preliminary study. *In* The Artist and the writer in France p86-99

Lang, Fritz

About

Truffaut, F. Fritz Lang in America. *In* Truffaut, F. The films in my life p64-68

About individual works

M

Troy, W. M. *In* Denby, D. ed. Awake in the dark p105-07

Langbaum, Robert Woodrow

The art of Victorian literature. *In* Altholz, J. L. ed. The mind and art of Victorian England p16-34

The mysteries of identity

Contents

Arnold: waning energy

Beckett: zero identity

Eliot: the walking dead

Exteriority of self

Identity and sexuality

The rainbow: the way through hope

The self as a work of art

The self as God

Women in love: the way through doom

Wordsworth: the self as process

Langbaum, Robert W.—*Continued*
About individual works
The modern spirit
Hartman, G. H. Signs of the times. *In* Hartman, G. H. The fate of reading p303-14

Langdon, Harry
About
Gilliatt, P. Langdon; excerpt from 'Unholy fools." *In* Derby, D. ed. Awake in the dark p356-61

Lange, Peter
The French and Italian Communist parties: postwar strategy and domestic society. *In* Radicalism in the contemporary age v 3 p159-99

Lange, Victor
Perspectives of contemporary German criticism. *In* The Frontiers of literary criticism p53-73

Reflections on the "classical age" of German literature. *In* Studies in eighteenth-century culture v7 p 1-21

Langendoen, D. Terence
The problem of linguistic theory in relation to language behavior: a tribute and reply to Paul Goodman. *In* Bloomfield, M. W. and Haugen, E. I. eds. Language as a human problem p197-203

Speak and talk: a vindication of syntactic deep structure. *In* On language, culture, and religion: in honor of Eugene A. Nida p237-40

Langer, Lawrence L.
The age of atrocity
Contents
Albert Camus and the limits of the possible
Aleksandr Solzhenitsyn and the journey through humiliation
Charlotte Delbo and a heart of ashes
Dying voices
The examined death
Thomas Mann and death on the mountain

The divided voice: Elie Wiesel and the challenge of the Holocaust. *In* Rosenfeld, A. H. and Greenberg, I. eds. Confronting the Holocaust p31-48

Langer, Lawrence N.
The medieval Russian town. *In* Hamm, M. F. ed. The city in Russian history p11-33

Langer, Susanne Katherina (Knauth)
About individual works
Feeling and form
Frye, N. Art in a new modulation. *In* Frye, N. Northrop Frye on culture and literature p111-16
Philosophy in a new key
Percy, W. Symbol as need. *In* Percy, W. The message in the bottle p288-97

Langer, William Leonard
Infanticide: a historical survey. *In* De-Mause, L. ed. The new psychohistory p55-67

Langford, Glenn
Education and human being II. *In* Philosophers discuss education p73-84

Langford, Thomas A.
The conveyance of personal knowledge. *In* Buxton, T. H. and Prichard, K. W. eds. Excellence in university teaching p147-53

Langland, William
About individual works
Piers Plowman
Barney, S. A. The dream of history: Langland's Piers Plowman. *In* Barney, S. A. Allegories of history, allegories of love p82-104

Bowers, A. J. The Tree of Charity in Piers Plowman: its allegorical and structural significance. *In* Literary monographs v6 p 1-34

Clopper, L. M. Langland's Trinitarian analogies as key to meaning and structure. *In* Medievalia et humanistica; new ser. no. 9 p87-110

Higgs, E. D. The path of involvement: the centrality of the Dreamer in Piers Plowman. *In* Tulane Studies in English v21 p 1-34

Hobsbaum, P. Piers Plowman through modern eyes. *In* Hobsbaum, P. Tradition and experiment in English poetry p 1-29

Jennings, M. Piers Plowman and Holychurch. *In* Viator: medieval and Renaissance studies v9 p367-74

Kaske, R. E. Holy Church's speech and the structure of Piers Plowman. *In* Chaucer and Middle English studies in honour of Rossell Hope Robbins p320-27

Mann, J. Eating and drinking in 'Piers Plowman.' *In* English Association. Essays and studies, 1979 p26-43

Nolan, B. Will's dark visions of Piers the Plowman. *In* Nolan, B. The Gothic visionary perspective p205-58

Salter, E. Langland and the contexts of 'Piers Plowman.' *In* English Association. Essays and studies, 1979 p19-25

Characters—Lady Holy Church
Kaske, R. E. Holy Church's speech and the structure of Piers Plowman. *In* Chaucer and Middle English studies in honour of Rossell Hope Robbins p320-27

Langley, Batty
About
Rowan, A. J. Batty Langley's Gothic. *In* Studies in memory of David Talbot Rice p197-215

Langlois, Walter G.
Indochina: the initiation. *In* Courcel, M. H. de, ed. Malraux p19-29

Langmuir, Irving
About
Kohler, R. E. The Lewis-Langmuir theory of valence and the chemical community, 1920-1928. *In* Historical studies in the physical sciences v6 p431-68

Langner, Herman Paul
The making of a murderer. *In* Kren, G. M and Rappoport, L. H. eds. Varieties of psychohistory p257-63

Langner, Myra Honore Bluebond-. See Bluebond-Langner, Myra Honore

Langness, Lewis L.
Margaret Mead and the study of socialization. *In* Schwartz, T. ed. Socialization as cultural communication p5-20

Langston, John Mercer

About

Bloomfield, M. H. John Mercer Langston and the training of Black lawyers. *In* Bloomfield, M. H. American lawyers in a changing society, 1776-1876 p302-39

Langton, Jane

The weak place in the cloth: a study of fantasy for children. *In* Horn Book Magazine. Crosscurrents of criticism p185-96

Language, Philosophy of. See Languages—Philosophy

Language, Psychology of. See Psycholinguistics

Language acquisition. See Children—Language

Language and culture

Zwicky, F. Essay 11. *In* Fitzgerald, R. ed. What it means to be human p209-20
See also Socio-linguistics

Language and ethics

Glossop, R. J. Hume, Stevenson, and Hare on moral language. *In* Livingston, D. W. and King, J. T. eds. Hume p362-85

Language and languages

Bronowski, J. Human and animal languages. *In* Bronowski, J. A sense of the future p104-31

Bronowski, J. Language in a biological frame. *In* Bronowski, J. A sense of the future p132-54

Clark, M. M. Language and reading: research trends. *In* Davies, A. ed. Problems of language and learning p89-112

Halle, M. Knowledge unlearned and untaught: what speakers know about the sounds of their language. *In* Linguistic theory and psychological reality p294-303

Hass, W. A. Pragmatic structures of language: historical, formal and developmental issues. *In* Riegel, K. F. and Rosenwald, G. C. eds. Structure and transformation p193-213

Haugen, E. I. The curse of Babel. *In* Bloomfield, M. W. and Haugen, E. I. eds. Language as a human problem p33-43

Illich, I. Language as a commodity. *In* Wagschal, P. H. ed. Learning tomorrows p41-61

Lenneberg, E. H. The neurology of language. *In* Bloomfield, M. W. and Haugen, E. I. eds. Language as a human problem p101-19

Lewis, D. B. Languages, language, and grammar. *In* Harman, G. ed. On Noam Chomsky p253-66

Moulton, W. G. The nature of language. *In* Bloomfield, M. W. and Haugen, E. I. eds. Language as a human problem p3-21

Pondy, L. R. Leadership is a language game. *In* Leadership p87-99

Rivers, E. L. Prolegomena grammatologica: literature as the disembodiment of speech. *In* Hernadi, P. ed. What is literature? p79-88

Scharfstein, B. A. Cultures, contexts, and comparisons. *In* Philosophy East/philosophy West p9-47
See also Bilingualism; Children—Languages; Communication; Conversation; Languages—Philosophy; Linguistic change; Linguistics; Philology; Psycho-linguistics; Rhe-

toric; Semantics; Semantics (Philosophy); Sign language; Sociolinguistics; Speech; Speech and social status; Translating and interpreting; Writing; and subdivision Languages under names of continents, countries, cities, etc. e.g. India—Languages

Analogy

See Analogy (Linguistics)

Etymology

Kahane, H. R. and Kahane, R. The role of the papyri in etymological reconstruction. *In* Illinois classical studies v3, 1978 p207-20

Tennyson, G. B. Etymology and meaning. *In* Evolution of consciousness p168-82

Thomas, L. On etymons and hybrids. *In* Thomas, L. The medusa and the snail p57-64

Tuttle, E. F. Borrowing versus semantic shift: New World nomenclature in European languages. *In* First images of America p595-611

Examinations, questions, etc.

Oller, J. W. Language testing. *In* Wardhaugh, R. and Brown, H. D. eds. A survey of applied linguistics p275-300

Foreign elements

Tuttle, E. F. Borrowing versus semantic shift. New World nomenclature in European languages. *In* First images of America p595-611
See also Language and languages—Foreign words and phrases

Foreign words and phrases

Crystal, D. American English in Europe. *In* Bigsby, C. W. E. Superculture p57-68

History

Watkins, C. Language and its history. *In* Bloomfield, M. W. and Haugen, E. I. eds. Language as a human problem p85-97

Lexicology

See Lexicology

Philosophy

See Languages—Philosophy

Political aspects

See Languages—Political aspects

Psychology

See Psycholinguistics

Religious aspects

See Religion and language

Research

See Linguistic research

Sentences

See Grammar, Compartive and general—Sentences

Study and teaching

Cazden, C. B. Problems for education: language as curriculum content and learning environment. *In* Bloomfield, M. W. and Haugen, E. I. eds. Language as a human problem p137-50

Nagel, T. Linguistics and epistemology. *In* Harman, G. ed. On Noam Chomsky p219-28

Richards, J. C. Second language learning. *In* Wardhaugh, R. and Brown, H. D. eds. A survey of applied linguistics p113-37

Languages—Philosophy—*Continued*

Peacocke, C. Truth definitions and actual languages. *In* Evans, G. L. and McDowell, J. H. eds. Truth and meaning p162-88

Quine, W. V. Linguistics and philosophy. *In* Quine, W. V. The ways of paradox, and other essays p56-58

Quine, W. V. Mind and verbal dispositions. *In* Guttenplan, S. D. ed. Mind and language p83-95

Quirk, R. Thinking of words. *In* Quirk, R. The linguist and the English language p128-43

Reddy, M. J. The conduit metaphor—a case of frame conflict in our language about language. *In* Ortony, A. ed. Metaphor and thought p284-324

Ricoeur, P. Violence and language. *In* Ricoeur, P. Political and social essays p88-101

Sayers, D. L. Creative mind; excerpt from "Unpopular opinions." *In* Sayers, D. L. The whimsical Christian p92-112

Scharfstein, B. A. Cultures, contexts, and comparisons. *In* Philosophy East/philosophy West p9-47

Searle, J. R. Reiterating the differences: a reply to Derrida. *In* Glyph I p198-208

Shell, M. Introduction. *In* Shell, M. The economy of literature p 1-10

Shell, M. The lie of the fox: Rousseau's theory of verbal, monetary, and political representation. *In* Shell, M. The economy of literature p113-28

Steiner, G. Whorf, Chomsky, and the student of literature. *In* Steiner, G. On difficulty and other essays p137-63

Stewart, M. A. Locke, Steiner and understanding. *In* Royal Institute of Philosophy. Communication and understanding p20-45

Vendler, Z. Words in thought. *In* Thought, consciousness, and reality p25-48

Weber, S. It. *In* Glyph 4 p 1-31

Wright, C. Language-mastery and the Sorites paradox. *In* Evans, G. L. and McDowell, J. H. eds. Truth and meaning p223-47

See also Analysis (Philosophy); Pragmatics

Political aspects

Banjo, A. Language policy in Nigeria. *In* Smock, D. R. and Bentsi-Enchill, K. eds. The search for national integration in Africa p206-19

Fonlon, B. The language problem in Cameroon: a historical perspective. *In* Smock, D. R. and Bentsi-Enchill, K. eds. The search for national integration in Africa p189-205

Howe, J. Carrying the village: Cuna political metaphors. *In* The Social use of metaphor p132-63

Jones, R. Indonesia: language and nation-building. *In* The Year book of world affairs, 1976 p190-204

Sharma, A. K. Linguistic nationalism and India's national development. *In* Said, A. A. and Simmons, L. R. eds. Ethnicity in an international context p218-34

Smock, D. R. Language policy in Ghana. *In* Smock, D. R. and Bentsi-Enchill, K. eds. The search for national integration in Africa p169-88

Wenner, M. W. The politics of equality among European linguistic minorities. *In* Claude, R. P. ed. Comparative human rights p184-213

Psychoanalysis

See Psycholinguistics

Religious aspects

See Bible—Language, style; Religion and language

Sociological aspects

See Sociolinguistics

Study and teaching (Higher)—
United States

Weiger, J. G. Teaching foreign language and literature. *In* Cahn, S. M. ed. Scholars who teach p163-91

Languages, Mixed. See Creole dialects

Languages, Modern

Study and teaching

Cazden, C. B. Problems for education: language as curriculum content and learning environment. *In* Bloomfield, M. W. and Haugen, E. I. eds. Language as a human problem p137-50

Strevens, P. Second language learning. *In* Bloomfield, M. W. and Haugen, E. I. eds. Language as a human problem p151-62

Languages, National. See Languages—Political aspects

Languages, Official. See Languages—Political aspects

Languages, Semitic. See Semitic languages

Languages in contact

Bright, W. O. North American Indian languages contact. *In* Sebeok, T. A. ed. Native languages of the Americas v 1 p59-72

See also Bilingualism

Languedoc

Antiquities

Cheyette, F. L. The castles of the Trencavels: a preliminary aerial survey. *In* Order and innovation in the Middle Ages p255-72

Population—Historiography

Le Roy Ladurie, E. Demography and the "sinful secrets": the case of Languedoc in the late eighteenth and early nineteenth centuries. *In* Le Roy Ladurie, E. The territory of the historian p239-54

Lanham, Richard A.
The motives of eloquence

Contents

The dramatic present: Shakespeare's Henriad
The fundamental strategies: Plato and Ovid
Games and high seriousness: Chaucer
The Ovidian Shakespeare: Venus and Adonis and Lucrece
The rhetorical ideal of life
The self as middle style: Cortegiano
Superposed plays: Hamlet
Superposed poetics: The sonnets
The war between play and purpose: Gargantua and Pantagruel

Lanier, Sidney

About

Rubin, L. D. The passion of Sidney Lanier. *In* Rubin, L. D. William Elliott shoots a bear p107-44

Lantzke, Ulf
The OECD and its International Energy Agency. *In* Vernon, R. ed. The oil crisis p217-27

Laos (Tai people)
Keyes, C. F. Kin groups in a Thai-Lao community. *In* Change and persistence in Thai society p274-97

Religion
Condominas, G. Phĭbān cults in rural Laos. *In* Change and persistence in Thai society p252-73

Laotians. See Laos (Tai people)

Laotse. See Lao-tzŭ

Lao-Tze. See Lao-tzŭ

Lao-tzŭ

About individual works
Tao te ching
Tiffin, H. Tourmaline and the Tao te ching: Randolph Stow's Tourmaline. *In* Hamilton, K. G. ed. Studies in the recent Australian novel p84-120

Laou-Tze. See Lao-tzŭ

Laow Tze. See Lao-tzŭ

Lapenna, Ivo
The Soviet concept of "Socialist" international law. *In* The Year book of world affairs, 1975 p242-64

La Peyrère, Isaac de

About
Popkin, R. H. La Peyrère, the Abbé Grégoire, and the Jewish question in the eighteenth century. *In* Studies in eighteenth-century culture v4 p209-22
Popkin, R. H. The pre-Adamite theory in the Renaissance, *In* Philosophy and humanism p50-69
Popkin, R. H. Spinoza and La Peyrère. *In* Shahan, R. W. and Biro, J. I. eds. Spinoza: new perspectives p175-95

About individual works
Men before Adam
Popkin, R. H. The development of religious scepticism and the influence of Isaac La Peyrère's pro-Adamism and Bible criticism. *In* Classical influences on European culture A.D. 1500-1700 p271-80

Influence—Spinoza
Popkin, R. H. Spinoza and La Peyrère. *In* Shahan, R. W. and Bora, J. I. eds. Spinoza: new perspectives p175-95

Lapidaries (Medieval literature)
Kitson, P. Lapidary traditions in Anglo-Saxon England: part I, the background; the Old English lapidary. *In* Anglo-Saxon England 7 p9-60

Lapidge, Michael
The hermeneutic style in tenth-century Anglo-Latin literature. *In* Anglo-Saxon England 4 p67-111
Stoic cosmology *In* Rist, J. M. ed. The Stoics p161-85

Lapidus, Gail Warshofsky
Educational strategies and cultural revolution: the politics of Soviet development. *In* Cultural revolution in Russia, 1928-1931 p78-104
Sexual equality in Soviet policy: a developmental perspective. *In* Women in Russia p113-38
Socialism and modernity: education, industrialization, and social change in the USSR. *In* Cocks, P.; Daniels, R. V. and Heer, N. W. eds. The dynamics of Soviet politics p195-220

Lapidus, Ira Marvin
Adulthood in Islam: religious maturity in the Islamic tradition. *In* Erikson, E. H. ed. Adulthood p97-112
Hierarchies and networks: a comparison of Chinese and Islamic societies. *In* Conflict and control in late imperial China p26-42

Laplace, Pierre Simon, marquis de

About
Guerlac, H. Chemistry as a branch of physics: Laplace's collaboration with Lavoisier. *In* Historical studies in the physical sciences v7 p193-276
Guerlac, H. Laplace's collaboration with Lavoisier. *In* Guerlac, H. Essays and papers in the history of modern science p399-404
Merleau-Ponty, J. Laplace as a cosmologist. *In* Cosmology, history, and theology p283-91

Laplanche, Jean

About individual works
Hölderlin et la question de père
Foucault, M. The father's "no." *In* Foucault, M. Language, counter-memory, practice p68-86

Laporte, Jean
Philo in the tradition of Biblical wisdom literature. *In* Aspects of wisdom in Judaism and early Christianity p103-41

LaPorte, Robert
Pakistan and Bangladesh. *In* Kearney, R. N. ed. Politics and modernization in South and Southeast Asia p109-52

Laporte, Roy Simon Bryce- See Bryce-Laporte, Roy Simon

Lapp, John Clarke

About individual works
Aspects of Racinian tragedy
Edelman, N. Book reviews. *In* Edelman, N. The eye of the beholder p166-205

The **Lapua** movement: the threat of rightist takeover in Finland, 1930-32. Alapuro, R. and Allardt, E. *In* The Breakdown of democratic regimes pt2 p122-41

Laqueur, Thomas W.
Working-class demand and the growth of English elementary education, 1750-1850. *In* Schooling and society p192-205

Laqueur, Walter Ze'ev
Footnotes to the Holocaust. *In* Arendt, H. The Jew as pariah: Jewish identity and politics in the modern age p252-59
The issue of human rights. *In* Sidorsky, D. ed. Essays on human rights p5-20
A reply to Hannah Arendt. *In* Arendt, H. The Jew as pariah: Jewish identity and politics in the modern age p277-79

About individual works
Footnotes to the Holocaust
Arendt, H. "The formidable Dr. Robinson": a reply by Hannah Arendt. *In* Arendt, H. The Jew as pariah: Jewish identity and politics in the modern age p260-76

Laquian, Aprodicio Arcilla
Appropriate building systems. *In* Strategies for human settlements: habitat and environment p115-20

Lara, Claude Autant-. See Autant-Lara, Claude

La Ramée, Pierre de

About

Ong, W. J. Ramus: rhetoric and the pre-Newtonian mind. *In* Wimsatt, W. K. ed. Literary criticism: idea and act p128-48

Sharatt, P. Peter Ramus and the reform of the university: the divorce of philosophy and eloquence? *In* French Renaissance studies, 1540-70 p4-20

Sloan, T. O. The crossing of rhetoric and poetry in the English Renaissance. *In* Sloan, T. O. and Waddington, R. B. eds. The rhetoric of Renaissance poetry p212-42

Smith, A. J. An examination of some claims for Ramism. *In* Roberts, J. R. ed. Essential articles for the study of John Donne's poetry p178-88

Influence

Daly, R. J. Ars poetica. *In* Daly, R. J. God's altar p40-81

La Raza Unida

Shockley, J. S. Landless laborers and the Chicano movement in south Texas. *In* Forging nations: a comparative view of rural ferment and revolt p128-49

Lardner, Ring, 1915-

About individual works

The Lardners: my family remembered

Sheed, W. Ring Lardner, Jr.: The Lardners: remembering my family. *In* Sheed, W. The good word & other words p254-58

Lardner, Ring Wilmer

About

Berryman, J. Enslavement: Three American cases; the case of Ring Lardner. *In* Berryman, J. The freedom of the poet p204-16

Holmes, C. S. Ring Lardner: reluctant artist. *In* Filler, L. ed. A question of quality: popularity and value in modern creative writing p26-39

Ingram, F. L. **Fun at the incinerating plant: Lardner's wry waste land.** *In* French, W. G. ed. The twenties p111-22

Morris, W. Ring Lardner. *In* Morris, W. Earthly delights, unearthly adornments p89-94

Spatz, J. Ring Lardner: not an **escape**, but a reflection. *In* French, W. G. ed. The twenties p101-10

Large, David

William Lovett. *In* Hollis, P. ed. Pressure from without p105-30

Larimore, L. Keith

Break-even analysis for higher education. *In* Managing nonprofit organizations p95-101

Larionoff, Nina

The first circle of Alexsandr Solzhenitsyn: symbolic visions. *In* California Slavic studies v10 p173-92

Larkin, Maurice

Man and society in nineteenth-century realism

Contents

Beating the bounds

La bête humaine

Determinist thought: Stendhal and the eighteenth-century inheritance

The dismal science: economic man

Experience versus the intellect: Tolstoy

Hope and despair

The Industrial Revolution

Man and beast: the Balzacian jungle

A modus vivendi? George Eliot

More pessimism: Flaubert

Pessimism

Russia and the realist response: Turgenev

The shaping forces of society: Stendhal's Europe

Une société embourgeoisée? Balzac's France

Society versus the individual

The ubiquitous doctor

Larkin, Philip

About

Bayley, J. The importance of elsewhere. *In* Bayley, J. The uses of division p171-82

Bayley, J. The self as available reality. *In* Bayley, J. The uses of division p157-71

Fraser, G. S. Philip Larkin: the lyric note and the grand style. *In* Fraser, G. S. Essays on twentieth-century poets p243-53

Lodge, D. Philip Larkin. *In* Lodge, D. The modes of modern writing p212-20

Press, J. The poetry of Philip Larkin. *In* Royal Society of Literature of the United Kingdom, London. Essays by divers hands v39 p76-91

Thurley, G. The legacy of Auden: the poetry of Roy Fuller, Philip Larkin and Peter Porter. *In* Thurley, G. The ironic harvest p137-62

Wain, J. The poetry of Philip Larkin. *In* Wain, J. Professing poetry p113-33

About individual works

The Whitsun weddings

Holbrook, D. Modern poetry and the death of sympathy. *In* Holbrook, D. Lost bearings in English poetry p164-93

Larkin, Ralph W. See Foss, D. A. jt. auth.

Larmor, Sir Joseph

About

Doran, B. G. Origins and consolidation of field theory in nineteenth-century Britain: from the mechanical to the electromagnetic view of nature. *In* Historical studies in the physical sciences v6 p133-260

Larnach, S. L. See Oettle, T. H. G. jt. auth.

Larnach, S. L. and Macintosh, Neil William George

A comparative study of Solo and Australian aboriginal crania. *In* Grafton Elliot Smith p95-102

Laroche, Maximilien

The myth of the zombi. *In* Exile and tradition p44-61

La Rochefoucauld, François VI, duc de, prince de Marsillac

About

Horowitz, L. K. La Rochefoucauld. *In* Horowitz, L. K. Love and language p29-49

La Rochelle, Pierre Drieu. See Drieu La Rochelle, Pierre

La Rosa, Ralph Charles

Necessary truths: the poetics of Emerson's proverbs. *In* Literary monographs v8 p129-92

Laroui, Abdallah

Sands and dreams. *In* Arab and American cultures p 3-13

Larsen, June Bennett

Tennessee Williams: optimistic symbolist. *In* Tennessee Williams: a tribute p413-28

Larson, Charles R.

American Indian fiction

Contents

Assimilation: estrangement from the land
The children of Pocahontas
Cogewea: the half-blood
The emergence of American Indian fiction
The figure in the dark forest
History of the people
Rejection: the reluctant return
Survivors of the relocation
The Wokosani road

About individual works

The emergence of African fiction

Iyasere, S. O. Charles R. Larson: The emergence of African literature. *In* African literature today no 7: Focus on criticism p143-46

Larson, Kathryn M. See Benassi, V. A. jt. auth.

LaRue, Asenath, and Jarvik, Lissy F.

Aging and intellectual functioning: great expectations? *In* Jarvik, L. F. ed. Aging into the 21st century p79-96

Lascelles, Mary

Jane Austen and the novel. *In* Halperin, J. ed. Jane Austen p235-46

'King Lear' and doomsday. *In* Shakespeare survey 26 p69-79

Lasers

Carman, R. L. Lasers—evolution and technological use. *In* Neyman, J. ed. The heritage of Copernicus: theories "pleasing to the mind" p508-25

Laski, Marghanita

Harriet Martineau. *In* Abroad in America: Visitors to the new Nation, 1776-1914 p62-71

Laslett, Barbara

The significance of family membership. *In* Tufte, V. and Myerhoff, B. G. eds. Changing images of the family p231-50

Laslett, Peter

The conversation between the generations. *In* Laslett, P. and Fishkin, J. eds. Philosophy, politics and society p36-56

Lasswell, Harold Dwight

Building as political communication: the signature of power on environment. *In* Lerner, D. and Nelson, L. M. eds. Communication research—a half-century appraisal p280-94

About

Eulau, H. Elite analysis and democratic theory: the contribution of Harold D. Lasswell. *In* Eulau, H. and Czudnowski, M. M. eds. Elite recruitment in democratic polities p7-28

The last detail (Motion picture)

Kauffmann, S. The last detail. *In* Kauffmann, S. Living images p260-63

The last hurrah (Motion picture)

Taylor, R. John Ford's Boston. *In* Peary, G. and Shatzkin, R. eds. The modern American novel and the movies p215-23

Last of the red hot lovers (criticism)
Simon, N. *In* Kauffmann, S. Persons of the drama p187-90

The last picture show (Motion picture)

Kauffmann, S. The last picture show. *In* Kauffmann, S. Living images p82-84

Last Supper

Art

Williams, J. Marcialis Pincerna and the provincial in Spanish medieval art. *In* Enggass, R. C. and Stokstad, M. eds. Hortus imaginum p29-36

Last tango in Paris (Motion picture)

Kauffmann, S. Last tango in Paris. *In* Kauffmann, S. Living images p173-76

Late spring (Motion picture)

Kauffmann, S. Late spring. *In* Kauffmann, S. Living images p127-29

Latham, Jacqueline E. M.

'The tempest' and King James's 'Daemonologie.' *In* Shakespeare survey 28 p117-23

Latham, Robert Gordon

About

Quirk, R. The study of the mother-tongue. *In* Quirk, R. The linguist and the English language p77-96

Lathen, Emma, pseud.

Cornwallis's revenge. *In* Agatha Christie: first lady of crime p79-94

Latin America

Commerce—United States

Rogers, S. H. Trade relations in the inter-American system. *In* Farer, T. J. ed. The future of the inter-American system p54-65

Discovery and exploration

See America—Discovery and exploration

Economic integration

Milenky, E. S. The Cartagena Agreement in transition. *In* The Year book of world affairs, 1979 p167-79

Parkinson, F. International economic integration in Latin America and the Caribbean: a survey. *In* The Year book of world affairs, 1977 p236-56

Reed, S. L. Participation in multinational organizations and programs in the hemisphere. *In* Cuba in the world p297-312

Economic relations—United States

Farer, T. J. Toward regional accommodation: is there anything to negotiate? *In* Farer, T. J. ed. The future of the inter-American system p66-72

Emigration and immigration

Boyd-Bowman, P. M. Spanish emigrants to the Indies, 1595-98: a profile. *In* First images of America p723-35

Lockhart, J. M. Letters and people to Spain. *In* First images of America p783-96

Mörner, M. Spanish migration to the New World prior to 1810: a report on the state of research. *In* First images of America p737-82

Emigration and immigration—Bibliography

Mörner, M. A bibliography on Spanish migration. *In* First images of America p797-804

Foreign economic relations—Cuba

Reed, S. L. Participation in multinational organizations and programs in the hemisphere. *In* Cuba in the world p297-312

Foreign economic relations— United States

Baer, W. and Coes, D. V. Changes in the inter-American economic system. *In* Farer, T. J. ed. The future of the inter-American system p35-53

Latin America—Foreign economic relations
—United States—*Continued*

Bergsten, C. F. U.S.-Latin American economic relations to 1980: the international framework and some possible new approaches. *In* The Americas in a changing world p173-95

Carey, J. C. The consequences of economic intervention: Peru & Chile. *In* Higham, R. D. ed. Intervention or abstention: the dilemma of American foreign policy p144-65

Hansen, R. D. U.S.-Latin American economic relationships: bilateral, regional or global? *In* The Americas in a changing world p196-238

Foreign relations

Cuevas Cancino, F. Bolivar's commonwealth of nations. *In* [Truth and tragedy]: a tribute to Hans Morgenthau p322-32

Farer, T. J. Limiting intraregional violence: the costs of regional peacekeeping. *In* Farer, T. J. ed. The future of the inter-American system p195-203

Roett, R. The changing nature of Latin American international relations: geopolitical realities. *In* The Americas in a changing world p95-111

Foreign relations—United States

Hill, R. C. The United States and Latin America: looking ahead. *In* Prochnow, H. V. ed. Dilemmas facing the nation p238-47

Hoffman, S. The international system and U.S. policy toward Latin America. *In* The Americas in a changing world p78-94

Lowenthal, A. F. The United States and Latin America: ending the hegemonic presumption. *In* Two hundred years of American foreign policy p181-208

Silvert, K. H. The changing dynamics of hemispheric politics. *In* Baldwin, D. A. ed. America in an interdependent world p275-92

Silvert, K. H. The relevance of Latin American domestic politics to North American foreign policy. *In* The Americas in a changing world p62-77

Trask, R. R. Missionary diplomacy. *In* Encyclopedia of American foreign policy p575-83

Historiography

Borah, W. W. Latin American history in world perspective. *In* The Future of history p151-72

Smith, P. H. History. *In* Quantitative social science research on Latin America p14-61

History—To 1830

Bolton, H. E. The mission as a frontier institution in the Spanish American colonies. *In* Weber, D. J. ed. New Spain's far northern frontier p49-65

Rodríguez, M. The impact of the American Revolution on the Spanish- and Portuguese-speaking world. *In* The Impact of the American Revolution abroad p101-25

Zavala, S. A. The frontiers of Hispanic America. *In* Weber, D. J. ed. New Spain's far northern frontier p179-99

Intellectual life—American influences

Rodríguez, M. The impact of the American Revolution on the Spanish- and Portuguese-speaking world. *In* The Impact of the American Revolution abroad p101-25

Politics and government

Cuevas Cancino, F. Bolivar's commonwealth of nations. *In* [Truth and tragedy]: a tribute to Hans Morgenthau p322-32

Dussel, E. D. The political and ecclesial context of liberation theology in Latin America. *In* The Emergent gospel p175-92

Linz Storch de Gracia, J. J. The breakdown of democratic regimes: crisis, breakdown, & reequilibration. *In* The Breakdown of democratic regimes pt 1 p 1-124

Silvert, K. H. The relevance of Latin American domestic politics to North American foreign policy. *In* The Americas in a changing world p62-77

Relations (general) with the United States

Bloomfield, R. J. The inter-American system: does it have a future? *In* Farer, T. J. ed. The future of the inter-American system p3-19

Farer, T. J. The changing context of inter-American relations. *In* Farer, T. J. ed. The future of the inter-American system p xv-xxiii

Rogers, W. D. A note on the future of the inter-American system. *In* Farer, T. J. ed. The future of the inter-American system p20-29

Relations (military) with United States

Child, J. The Inter-American Military System: historical development, current status, and implications for U.S. policy. *In* Farer, T. J. ed. The future of the inter-American system p155-94

Ronfeldt, D. F. Future U.S. security assistance in the Latin American context. *In* The Americas in a changing world p156-72

Religion

Couch, B. M. New visions of the Church in Latin America: a Protestant view. *In* The Emergent gospel p193-226

Social conditions

Lagos Matus, G. The revolution of being. *In* On the creation of a just world order p71-109

Willems, E. Social change on the Latin American frontier. *In* Miller, D. H. and Steffen, J. O. eds. The frontier p259-73

Social conditions—1945-

Beltrán, S. L. R. TV etchings in the minds of Latin Americans: conservatism, materialism and conformism. *In* Fischer, H. D. and Melnik, S. R. eds. Entertainment: a cross-cultural examination p190-95

Statistics, Vital

Smith, P. H. History. *In* Quantitative social science research on Latin America p14-61

Latin American fiction

History and criticism

Brotherston, G. Settings and people. *In* Brotherston, G. The emergence of the Latin American novel p 5-24

20th century—History and criticism

Brotherston, G. A permanent home? *In* Brotherston. G. The emergence of the Latin American novel p136-40

Latin American literature

See also Spanish American literature

Black authors

Olliz Boyd, A. The concept of Black awareness as a thematic approach in Latin American literature. *In* DeCosta, M. ed. Blacks in Hispanic literature p65-73

Ortiz, A. Negritude in Latin American culture. *In* DeCosta, M. ed. Blacks in Hispanic literature p74-82

20th century—History and criticism

Forster, M. H. Latin American vanguardismo: chronology and terminology. *In* Forster, M. H. ed. Tradition and renewal p12-50

Latin ballads. See Ballads, Latin

Latin drama (Comedy)

History and criticism

Anderson, M. J. The comedy of Greece and Rome. *In* Howarth, W. D. ed. Comic drama p22-39

Beck, E. Terence improved: the paradigm of the Prodigal son in English Renaissance comedy. *In* Renaissance drama [1973] p107-22

Fantham, E. Adaptation and survival: a genre study of Roman comedy in relation to its Greek sources. *In* Ruggiers, P. G. ed. Versions of medieval comedy p29-49

Sandbach, F. H. Drama at Rome. *In* Sandbach, F. H. The comic theatre of Greece and Rome p103-17

Sandbach, F. H. Epilogue. *In* Sandbach, F. H. The comic theatre of Greece and Rome p149-52

Thomson, I. Latin "elegiac comedy" of the twelfth century. *In* Ruggiers, P. G. ed. Versions of medieval comedy p51-66

Latin drama, Medieval and modern

History and criticism

Thomson, I. Latin "elegiac comedy" of the twelfth century. *In* Ruggiers, P. G. ed. Versions of medieval comedy p51-66

Latin elegiac poetry. See Elegiac poetry, Latin

Latin hymns. See Hymns, Latin

Latin inscriptions. See Inscriptions, Latin

Latin language

Gaeng, P. A. Interpreting second declension singular forms in -u. *In* Illinois classical studies v4, 1979 p214-19

Alphabet

Harvey, F. D. Greeks and Romans learn to write. *In* Havelock, E. A. and Hershbell, J. P. eds. Communication arts in the ancient world p63-78

Etymology

Watkins, C. Etyma Enniana. *In* Harvard Studies in classical philology v77 p195-206

Watkins, C. On the family of *arceō*, ἀρκέω and Hittite *hark-. In* Harvard Studies in classical philology v74 p67-74

See also Duellum (The Latin word); Heminarium (The Latin word); Vero (The Latin word)

Grammar, Historical

Nussbaum, A. J. Ennian Laurentis terra. *In* Harvard Studies in classical philology v77 p207-15

Numerals

Willis, J. A. The multiples of the as. *In* Harvard Studies in classical philology v76 p233-44

Phonology

Kuryłowicz, J. A remark on Lachmann's law. *In* Harvard Studies in classical philology v72 p295-99

Watkins, C. A further remark on Lachmann's law. *In* Harvard Studies in classical philology v74 p55-65

Punctuation

Parkes, M. B. The impact of punctuation: punctuation, or pause and effect. *In* Murphy, J. J. ed. Medieval eloquence p127-42

Style

Winterbottom, M. Aldhelm's prose style and its origins. *In* Anglo-Saxon England 6 p39-76

Syntax

Watkins, C. An Indo-European construction in Greek and Latin. *In* Harvard Studies in classical philology v71 p115-19

Terms and phrases

Watkins, C. An Indo-European agricultural term: Latin ador, Hittite hat-. *In* Harvard Studies in classical philology v77 p187-93

Watkins, C. Latin ador, Hittite hat- again: addenda to HSCP 77 (1973) 187-193. *In* Harvard Studies in classical philology v79 p181-87

Latin letters

Patt, W. D. The early "ars dictaminis" as response to a changing society. *In* Viator: medieval and Renaissance studies v9 p133-55

Latin literature

See also Classical literature

Criticism, Textual

Skutsch, O. Readings in early Latin. *In* Harvard Studies in classical philology v76 p169-71

History and criticism

Harbert, B. Chaucer and the Latin classics. *In* Brewer, D. S. ed. Geoffrey Chaucer p137-53

Zetzel, J. E. G. On the history of Latin scholia. *In* Harvard Studies in classical philology v79 p335-54

Sources

West, M. L. Near Eastern material in Hellenistic and Roman literature. *In* Harvard Studies in classical philology v73 p113-34

Latin literature, Medieval and modern

Witke, C. Aspects of Roman poetic technique in a Carolingian Latin satiric text. *In* Illinois classical studies v4, 1979 p220-31

History and criticism

Ijsewijn, J. Neo-Latin satire: Sermo and Satyra Menippea. *In* Classical influences on European culture A.D. 1500-1700 p41-55

Lapidge, M. The hermeneutic style in tenth-century Anglo-Latin literature. *In* Anglo-Saxon England 4 p67-111

History and criticism—Bibliography

Ryan, L. V. Neo-Latin literature. *In* Jones, W. M. ed. The present state of scholarship in sixteenth-century literature p197-257

Latin love poetry. See Love poetry, Latin

Latin manuscripts. See Manuscripts, Latin

Latin Orient. See Crusades

Latin paleography. See Paleography, Latin

Latin philology. See Inscriptions, Latin

Latin poetry

See also Elegiac poetry, Latin

History and criticism

Clausen, W. Duellum. *In* Harvard Studies in classical philology v75 p69-72

Luck, G. The woman's role in Latin love poetry. *In* Perspectives of Roman poetry p15-31

Ross, D. O. Conclusions. *In* Ross, D. O. Backgrounds to Augustan poetry: Gallus, elegy and Rome p163-68

Ross, D. O. Introduction: From Catullus to Gallus. *In* Ross, D. O. Backgrounds to Augustan poetry: Gallus, elegy and Rome p 1-17

Rudd, N. Theory: sincerity and mask. *In* Rudd, N. Lines of enquiry p145-81

Latin poetry, Medieval and modern

Collected works

Sparrow, J. H. A. An anthology of Renaissance Latin verse: problems confronting the editor and compiler. *In* Classical influences on European culture A.D. 1500-1700 p57-64

History and criticism

Dronke, P. and Mann, J. Chaucer and the medieval Latin poets. *In* Brewer, D. S. ed. Geoffrey Chaucer p154-83

Hughes, D. G. Music and meter in liturgical poetry. *In* Medievalia et humanistica no. 7 p29-43

Jones, C. W. Carolingian aesthetics: why modular verse? *In* Viator: medieval and Renaissance studies v6 p309-40

Latin rhetoric. See Rhetoric, Ancient

Latin satire. See Satire, Latin

Latouche, Henri de

About

Borowitz, A. Henri de Latouche and the murder memoirs of Clarisse Manson. *In* Borowitz, A. Innocence and arsenic p132-62

Latt, David J.

Praising virtuous ladies: the literary image and historical reality of women in seventeenth-century England. *In* Springer, M. A. ed. What manner of women p39-64

Latter, D. A.

Sight-lines in a conjectural reconstruction of an Elizabethan playhouse. *In* Shakspeare survey 28 p125-35

Latter-Day Saints. See Mormons and Mormonism

Lau, Solomon Islands

Social life and customs

Maranda, E. K. Lau, Malaita: "a woman is an alien spirit." *In* Matthiasson, C. J. ed. Many sisters p177-202

Laub, Jakob

About

Pyenson, L. Einstein's early scientific collaboration. *In* Historical studies in the physical sciences v7 p83-123

Laudan, Laurens

The methodological foundations of Mach's anti-atomism and their historical roots. *In* Motion and time, space and matter p390-417

Laue, James Howard

Unanticipated change. *In* Lauer, R. H. ed. Social movements and social change p190-96

Lauer, Quentin

Philosophy and social change. *In* Roth, R. J. ed. Person and community p 1-24

Lauer, Robert H.

Afterword: Summary and directives for the future. *In* Lauer, R. H. ed. Social movements and social change p259-64

Determinants of type of strategy. *In* Lauer, R. H. ed. Social movements and social change p85-96

Introduction: Social movements and social change: the interrelationships. *In* Lauer, R. H. ed. Social movements and social change p xi-xxviii

Movement ideology, program, recruitment. *In* Lauer, R. H. ed. Social movements and social change p46-60

Lauer, Robert H. and Chen, Katy

Status/role change. *In* Lauer, R. H. ed. Social movements and social change p144-55

Lauer, Roger

A medium for mental health. *In* Zaretsky, I. I. and Leone, M. P. eds. Religious movements in contemporary America p338-54

Laughter

Girard, R. Perilous balance: A comic hypothesis. *In* Girard, R. "To double business bound" p121-35

Laumer, Keith

How to collaborate without getting your head shaved. *In* Knight, D. F. ed. Turning points p215-17

Laurent, Auguste

About

Brooke, J. H. Laurent, Gerhardt, and the philosophy of chemistry. *In* Historical studies in the physical sciences v6 p405-30

Laurie, Bruce; Hershberg, Theodore, and Alter, George

Immigrants and industry: the Philadelphia experience, 1850-1880. *In* Immigrants in industrial America, 1850-1920 p123-50

Lautman, Françoise

Differences or changes in family organization. *In* Family and society p251-61

Lautréamont, comte de, pseud. See Ducasse, Isidore Lucien

Laux, James Michael

Managerial structures in France. *In* Evolution of international management structures p95-113

LaValley, Albert J.

The stage and film children of Frankenstein: a survey. *In* Levine, G. L. and Knoepflmacher, U. C. eds. The endurance of Frankenstein p243-89

Lavater, Johann Casper

About individual works

Essays on physiognomy

Mellor, A. K. Physiognomy, phrenology, and Blake's visionary heads. *In* Essick, R. N. and Pearce, D. R. eds. Blake in his time p53-74

La Vergne, Marie Madeleine. See La Fayette, Marie Madeleine (Pioche de La Vergne) comtesse de

La Vey, Anton Szandor

About

Alfred, R. H. The Church of Satan. *In* The New religious consciousness p180-202

Lavoisier, Antoine Laurent

About

Guerlac, H. Chemistry as a branch of physics: Laplace's collaboration with Lavoisier. *In* Historical studies in the physical sciences v7 p193-276

Guerlac, H. A curious Lavoisier episode. *In* Guerlac. H. Essays and papers in the history of modern science p393-98

Guerlac, H. Laplace's collaboration with Lavoisier. *In* Guerlac, H. Essays and papers in the history of modern science p399-404

Guerlac, H. Lavoisier and his biographers. *In* Guerlac, H. Essays and papers in the history of modern science p314-26

Guerlac, H. A lost memoir of Lavoisier. *In* Guerlac, H. Essays and papers in the history of modern science p334-39

Guerlac, H. A note on Lavoisier's scientific education. *In* Guerlac, H. Essays and papers in the history of modern science p327-33

Guerlac, H. The origin of Lavoisier's work on combustion. *In* Guerlac, H. Essays and papers in the history of modern science p375-92

Law, Andrew

About

Hamm, C. E. The ecstatic and the didactic: a pattern in American music. *In* Current thought in musicology p41-62

Law, Vivien

The Latin and Old English glosses in the Ars Tatuini. *In* Anglo-Saxon England 6 p77-89

Law, William

About

Kuhn, A. J. Nature spiritualized: aspects of anti-Newtonianism. *In* ELH essays for Earl R. Wasserman p110-22

Rack, H. D. 'Christ's Kingdom not of this world:' the case of Benjamin Hoadly versus William Law reconsidered. *In* Church, society and politics p275-91

Law

Nader, L. and Serber, D. Law and the distribution of power. *In* The Uses of controversy in sociology p273-91

See also Jurisprudence; Justice; Lawyers; Natural law; Statutes

Continuing education

See Law—Study and teaching (Continuing education)

History and criticism

See Comparative law; Law and socialism

Interpretation and construction

See Judicial process

Philosophy

Barry, B. M. Is democracy special? *In* Laslett, P. and Fishkin, J. eds. Philosophy, politics and society p155-96

Dworkin, R. M. Is law a system of rules? *In* Summers, R. S. ed. Essays in legal philosophy p25-60

Kamenka, E. and Tay, A. E. S. Beyond bourgeois individualism: the contemporary crisis in law and legal ideology. *In* Kamenka, E. and Neale, R. S. eds. Feudalism, capitalism and beyond p126-44

Kistyakovsky, B. In the defense of law: the intelligentsia and legal consciousness. *In* Landmarks p112-37

Konvitz, M. R. Conscience: the movement from duty to right—from the Bible to the Bill of Rights. *In* Konvitz, M. R. Judaism and the American idea p91-137

MacLeish, A. Art and law. *In* MacLeish, A. Riders on the earth p82-88

Morris, H. Punishment for thoughts. *In* Summers, R. S. ed. Essays in legal philosophy p95-120

Summers, R. S. Legal philosophy today— an introduction. *In* Summers, R. S. ed. Essays in legal philosophy p 1-21

Tay, A. E. S. Law, the citizen and the state. *In* Law and society p 1-17

Wasserstrom, R. A. The obligation to obey the law. *In* Summers, R. S. ed. Essays in legal philosophy p274-304

Zaw, S. K. 'Irresistible impulse' and moral responsibility. *In* Royal Institute of Philosophy. Human values p99-134

See also Jurisprudence; Law and socialism

Sociology

See Sociological jurisprudence

Study and teaching (Continuing education)

Hochberg, J. A. The drive to specialization. *In* Nader, R. and Green, M. J. eds. Verdicts on lawyers p118-26

Study and teaching—United States

Frankel, M. E. Legal ethics and the ethics of law teaching. *In* Hook, S.; Kurtz, P. and Todorovich, M. eds. The ethics of teaching and scientific research p87-91

Merryman, J. H. Legal education there and here: a comparison. *In* Stanford legal essays p335-54

Wallach, A. A view from the law school. *In* Women and the power to change p81-125

Vocational guidance

Auerbach, J. S. Lawyers and social change in the Depression decade. *In* Braeman, J.; Bremner, R. H. and Brody, D. eds. The New Deal v 1 p133-69

Jews

See Jewish law

China

Cohen, J. A. Due process? *In* Terrill, R. ed. The China difference p237-59

Ethiopia

Beckstrom, J. H. Handicaps of legal social engineering in a developing nation. *In* African themes p195-212

Great Britain

Wilhelmsen, F. D. Sir John Fortescue and the English tradition. *In* Wilhelmsen, F. D. Christianity and political philosophy p111-38

Russia

Butler, W. E. Methodological innovation in Soviet international legal doctrine. *In* The Year book of world affairs, 1978 p334-41

Law—Russia—Continued

Juviler, P. H. Women and sex in Soviet law. In Women in Russia p243-65

Kamenka, E. and Tay, A. E. S. Socialism, anarchism and law. In Law and society p48-80

Kistyakovsky, B. In the defense of law: the intelligentsia and legal consciousness. In Landmarks p112-37

Sharlet, R. S. Pashukanis and the withering away of law in the USSR In Cultural revolution in Russia, 1928-1931 p169-88

Sharlet, R. S. Stalinism and Soviet legal culture. In Stalinism p155-79

Russia—History

Kleimola, A. M. Law and social change in medieval Russia: the Zakon sudnyi lyudem as a case study. In Oxford Slavonic papers, new ser. v9 p17-27

Scotland—History and criticism

Robertson, J. J. The development of the law. In Brown, J. M. ed. Scottish society in the fifteenth century p136-52

Underdeveloped areas

See Underdeveloped areas—Law

United States

Barton, J. H. Behind the legal explosion. In Stanford legal essays p43-60

United States—History and criticism

Bloomfield, M. H. William Sampson and the codification movement. In Bloomfield, M. H. American lawyers in a changing society, 1776-1876 p59-90

Ely, J. W. Law in a republican society: continuity and change in the legal system of postrevolutionary America. In Perspectives on revolution and evolution p46-65

Law (Theology)

Biblical teaching

Banks, R. The eschatological role of law in pre- and post-Christian Jewish thought. In Reconciliation and hope p173-85

Law, Arab. See Islamic law

Law, Byzantine

Kleimola, A. M. Law and social change in medieval Russia: the Zakon sudnyi lyudem as a case study. In Oxford Slavonic papers, new ser. v9 p17-27

Law, Civil. See Civil law

Law, Comparative. See Comparative law

Law, Corporation. See Corporation law

Law, Criminal. See Criminal law

Law, Factory. See Factory laws and legislation

Law, Fishery. See Fishery law and legislation

Law, Industrial. See Factory laws and legislation; Industrial laws and legislation; Labor laws and legislation

Law, International. See International law

Law, Islamic. See Islamic law

Law, Jewish. See Jewish law

Law, Labor. See Labor laws and legislation

Law, Marriage. See Marriage law

Law, Medieval

Kelley, D. R. Clio and the lawyers: forms of historical consciousness in medieval jurisprudence. In Medievalia et humanistica no. 5 p25-49

Law, Mosaic. See Jewish law

Law, Natural. See Natural law

Law, Oriental. See Islamic law; Jewish law

Law, Patent. See Patent laws and legislation

Law, Practice of. See Practice of law

Law, Semitic. See Islamic law

Law and communism. See Law and socialism

Law and Equity Court, Richmond, Va.

Tucker v. Lower. In Weir, R. F. ed. Ethical issues in death and dying p125-28

Law and ethics

Barry, B. M. Is democracy special? In Laslett, P. and Fishkin, J. eds. Philosophy, politics and society p155-96

Hughes, G. Morals and the criminal law. In Summers, R. S. ed. Essays in legal philosophy p183-207

Morris, H. Punishment for thoughts. In Summers, R. S. ed. Essays in legal philosophy p95-120

See also Judicial ethics; Legal ethics

Law and gospel. See Freedom (Theology)

Law and mental illness. See Insanity—Jurisprudence

Law and morals. See Law and ethics

Law and politics

Califano, J. A. The Washington lawyer: when to say no. In Nader, R. and Green, M. J. eds. Verdicts on lawyers p187-96

Law and sex. See Sex and law

Law and socialism

Juviler, P. H. Women and sex in Soviet law. In Women in Russia p243-65

Kamenka, E. and Tay, A. E. S. Socialism, anarchism and law. In Law and society p48-80

Sharlet, R. S. Pashukanis and the withering away of law in the USSR. In Cultural revolution in Russia, 1928-1931 p169-88

Sharlet, R. S. Stalinism and Soviet legal culture. In Stalinism p155-79

Law and society. See Sociological jurisprudence

Law as a profession See Law—Vocational guidance

Law enforcement

Audi, R. Violence, legal sanctions, and law enforcement. In Stanage, S. M. ed. Reason and violence p29-50

Whisenand, P. and Ferguson, R. F. Controlling: the use of authority, power, and influence; excerpt from "The managing of police organizations." In Armstrong, T .R. and Cinnamon, K. M. eds. Power and authority in law enforcement p56-74

Great Britain—History

Ousby, I. Thief-taking and thief-making. In Ousby, I. Bloodhounds of heaven p3-18

South Africa

Sachs. A. L. The instruments of domination in South Africa. In Thompson, L. M. and Butler, J. eds. Change in contemporary South Africa p223-49

Law enforcement—*Continued*

United States

Becker, G. S. and Stigler, G. J. Law enforcement, malfeasance, and compensation of enforcers. *In* Capitalism and freedom p230-52

Law in literature

Knight, W. N. Equity, 'The merchant of Venice' and William Lambarde. *In* Shakespeare survey 27 p93-104

Tucker, E. F. J. The letter of the law in 'The merchant of Venice.' *In* Shakespeare survey v29 p93-101

Law of nations. See International law

Law of nature. See Natural law

Law of the sea. See Maritime law

Law reform

Chirelstein, M. A. Corporate law reform. *In* McKie, J. W. ed. Social responsibility and the business predicament p41-77

United States

Tunney, J. V. and Frank, J. L. Epilogue: a congressional role in lawyer reform? *In* Nader, R. and Green, M. J. eds. Verdicts on lawyers p295-304

Law reports, digests, etc.

United States

Jacobstein, J. M. Some reflections on the control of the publication of Appellate Court opinions. *In* Stanford legal essays p267-75

Law schools

Admission

Greenawalt, R. K. Judicial scrutiny of "benign" racial preference in law school admissions. *In* Gross, B. R. ed. Reverse discrimination p217-38

Nickel, J. W. Preferential policies in hiring and admissions: a jurisprudential approach. *In* Gross, B. R. ed. Reverse discrimination p324-47

Sandalow, T. Racial preferences in higher education: political responsibility and the judicial role. *In* Gross, B. R. ed. Reverse discrimination p239-64

United States—Admission

Thomas, J. A. Heavy traffic on the purple brick road: the route to law school. *In* Hurdles p212-38

Lawal, Babatunde

Yoruba-Sango ram symbolism: from ancient Sahara or dynastic Egypt? *In* African images p225-51

Lawendowski, Bogusław

On semiotic aspect of translations. *In* Sebeok, T. A. ed. Sight, sound, and sense p264-82

Lawes, Henry

About

Martz, L. L. The music of Comus. *In* Illustrious evidence p93-113

Lawick-Goodall, Barones Jane van

The chimpanzee. *In* Goodall, V. M. ed. The quest for man p131-69

Lawler, Donald L.

The sirens of Titan: Vonnegut's metaphysical shaggy-dog story. *In* Klinkowitz, J. and Lawler, D. L. eds. Vonnegut in America p61-86

Lawler, Traugott Francis

The Aeneid. *In* Seidel, M. A. and Mendelson, E. eds. Homer to Brecht p53-75

Lawrence, Barbara

Four-letter words can hurt you. *In* Baker, R. and Elliston, F. A. eds. Philosophy & sex p31-33

Lawrence, Christopher

The nervous system and society in the Scottish Enlightenment. *In* Barnes, B. and Shapin, S. eds. Natural order p19-40

Lawrence, David Herbert

About

Alcorn, J. Hardy and Lawrence. *In* Alcorn, J. The nature novel from Hardy to Lawrence p78-89

Alcorn, J. Lawrence: a version of pastoral. *In* Alcorn, J. The nature novel from Hardy to Lawrence p90-106

Bayley, J. Dogma and fantasy. *In* Bayley, J. The uses of division p42-50

Gillie, C. D. H. Lawrence (1885-1930). *In* Gillie, C. Movements in English literature, 1900-1940 p47-64

Goonetilleke, D. C. R. A. D. H. Lawrence: primitivism? *In* Goonetilleke, D. C. R. A. Developing countries in British fiction p170-98

Kinkead-Weekes, M. Eros and metaphor: sexual relationship in the fiction of Lawrence. *In* Smith, A. ed. Lawrence and women p101-21

Langbaum, R. W. Identity and sexuality. *In* Langbaum, R. W. The mysteries of identity p251-97

Lewis, W. D. H. Lawrence; excerpt from "Paleface." *In* Lewis, W. Enemy salvoes p118-26

May, K. M. The living self. *In* May, K. M. Out of the maelstrom p43-61

May, K. M. The nature of the unconscious. *In* May, K. M. Out of the maelstrom p24-42

Meyers, J. D. H. Lawrence: The white peacock, Women in love, Aaron's rod, The plumed serpent. *In* Meyers, J. Homosexuality and literature, 1890-1930 p131-61

Meyers, J. Mark Gertler and Women in love. *In* Meyers, J. Painting and the novel p65-82

Moynahan, J. Lawrence, woman and the Celtic fringe. *In* Smith, A. ed. Lawrence and women p122-35

Mudrick, M. Lawrence. *In* Mudrick, M. The man in the machine p37-60

Oates, J. C. The hostile sun: the poetry of D. H. Lawrence. *In* Oates, J. C. New heaven, new earth: the visionary experience in literature p37-81

Ober, W. B. Lady Chatterley's what? *In* Ober, W. B. Boswell's clap and other essays p89-117

Paterson, J. Lawrence's vital source: nature and character in Thomas Hardy. *In* Knoepflmacher, U. C. and Tennyson, G. B. eds. Nature and the Victorian imagination p455-69

Pritchard, W. H. D. H. Lawrence: 1920-1930. *In* Pritchard, W. H. Seeing through everything p70-89

Ragussis, M. Epilogue: the word. *In* Ragussis, M. The subterfuge of art p226-29

Ragussis, M. The subterfuge of art: Lawrence, Freud, and "verbal consciousness." *In* Ragussis, M. The subterfuge of art p 1-5

Lawrence, David H.—About—Continued

Rahv, P. On F. R. Leavis and D. H. Lawrence. In Rahv, P. Essays on literature and politics, 1932-1972 p263-77

Vivas, E. The two Lawrences. In Garvin, H. R. ed. Makers of the twentieth-century novel p103-17

Walker, R. G. The "dark blood" of America. In Walker, R. G. Infernal paradise p28-78

Watson, G. The politics of D. H. Lawrence. In Watson, G. Politics and literature in modern Britain p110-19

Wicker, B. Lawrence and the unseen presences. In Wicker, B. The story-shaped world p120-33

About individual works
England, my England

Lodge, D. D. H. Lawrence. In Lodge, D. The modes of modern writing p160-76

Kangaroo

Alter, R. Eliot, Lawrence, and the Jews: two versions of Europe. In Alter, R. Defenses of the imagination p137-51

Russell, J. D. D. H. Lawrence: the lost girl, Kangaroo. In Russell, J. D. Style in modern British fiction p43-88

Lady Chatterley's lover

Ober, W. B. Lady Chatterley's what? In Ober, W. B. Boswell's clap and other essays p89-117

Spilka, M. On Lawrence's hostility to wilful women: the Chatterley solution. In Smith, A. ed. Lawrence and women p189-211

The Ladybird

Cowan, J. C. D. H. Lawrence's dualism: the Apollonian-Dionysian polarity and The Ladybird. In Forms of modern British fiction p73-99

The lost girl

Russell, J. D. D. H. Lawrence: The lost girl, Kangaroo. In Russell, J. D. Style in modern British fiction p43-88

The man who died

Kunkel, F. L. Lawrence's The man who died: the heavenly cock. In Kunkel, F. L. Passion and the Passion p37-57

Phoenix

Spender, S. D. H. Lawrence: Phoenix In Spender, S. The thirties and after p26-29

The plumed serpent

Apter, T. E. Let's hear what the male chauvinist is saying: The plumed serpent. In Smith, A. ed. Lawrence and women p156-77

Clark, L. D. The making of a novel: the search for the definitive text of D. H. Lawrence's "The plumed serpent." In Voices from the Southwest p113-30

Walker, R. G. The plumed serpent: Lawrence's Mexican nightmare. In Walker, R. G. Infernal paradise p79-104

The Prussian officer, and other stories—Manuscripts

Finney, B. H. D. H. Lawrence's progress to maturity: from holograph manuscript to final publication of The Prussian officer and other stories. In Virginia. University. Bibliographical Society. Studies in bibliography v28 p321-32

The rainbow

Blanchard, L. Mothers and daughters in D. H. Lawrence: The rainbow and selected shorter works. In Smith, A. ed. Lawrence and women p75-100

Cockshut, A. O. J. The optimists: Lawrence. In Cockshut, A. O. J. Man and woman: a study of love and the novel, 1740-1940 p152-60

Langbaum, R. W. The rainbow: the way through hope. In Langbaum, R. W. The mysteries of identity p298-327

Meyers, J. Fra Angelico and The rainbow. In Meyers, J. Painting and the novel p53-64

Stewart, G. Lawrence, "being," and the allotropic style. In Spilka, M. ed. Towards a poetics of fiction p331-56

Tobin, P. D. The cycle dance: D. H. Lawrence, The rainbow. In Tobin, P. D. Time and the novel p81-106

The rocking-horse winner

Snodgrass, W. D. A rocking horse: the symbol, the pattern, the way to live. In Snodgrass, W. D. In radical pursuit p128-40

Sons and lovers

Pullin, F. Lawrence's treatment of women in Sons and lovers. In Smith, A. ed. Lawrence and women p49-74

Tomlinson, T. B. D. H. Lawrence: Sons and lovers, Women in love. In Tomlinson, T. B. The English middle-class novel p185-98

Study of Thomas Hardy

Kinkead-Weekes, M. Lawrence on Hardy. In Butler, L. S. ed. Thomas Hardy after fifty years p90-103

Tickets, please

Trilling, L. D. H. Lawrence: Tickets, please. In Trilling, L. Prefaces to The experience of literature p123-27

The white peacock

Meyers, J. Maurice Greiffenhagen and The white peacock. In Meyers, J. Painting and the novel p46-52

Women in love

Bayley, J. 'Art speech.' In Bayley, J. The uses of division p25-42

Cockshut, A. O. J. The optimists: Lawrence. In Cockshut, A. O. J. Man and woman: a study of love and the novel, 1740-1940 p152-60

Langbaum, R. W. Women in love: the way through doom. In Langbaum, R. W. The mysteries of identity p328-53

Meyers, J. Mark Gertler and Women in love. In Meyers, J. Painting and the novel p65-82

Ragussis, M. D. H. Lawrence: silence in Women in love. In Ragussis, M. The subterfuge of art p197-225

Ragussis, M. D. H. Lawrence: the new vocabulary of Women in love: speech and art-speech. In Ragussis, M. The subterfuge of art p172-97

Salgado, G. Taking a nail for a walk: on reading Women in love. In Josipovici, G. ed. The modern English novel: the reader, the writer and the work p95-112

Stewart, G. Lawrence, "being," and the allotropic style. In Spilka, M. ed. Towards a poetics of fiction p331-56

Lawrence, David H.—About individual works—Women in love—*Continued*

Tatar, M. M. From science fiction to psychoanalysis: Henry James's "Bostonians," D. H. Lawrence's "Women in love," and Thomas Mann's "Mario and the magician." *In* Tatar, M. M. Spellbound p230-71

Tomlinson, T. B. Conclusion. *In* Tomlinson, T. B. The English middle-class novel p198-202

Tomlinson, T. B. D. H. Lawrence: Sons and lovers, Women in love. *In* Tomlinson, T. B. The English middle-class novel p185-98

Characters

Bersani, L. Lawrentian stillness. *In* Bersani, L. A future for Astyanax p156-85

Criticism and interpretation

Kirk, R. Vivas, Lawrence, Eliot, and the demon. *In* Viva Vivas! p225-49

H. Lawrence's "Women in love," and Tonsor, S. J. Eliseo Vivas: philosopher in spite of himself. *In* Viva Vivas! p251-72

Tristram, P. Eros and death (Lawrence, Freud and women). *In* Smith, A. ed. Lawrence and women p136-55

Influence

Trilling, D. Lawrence and the movements of modern culture. *In* Trilling, D. We must march my darlings p295-303

Influence—Huxley, Aldous

Walker, R. G. Mexico as scapegoat: Huxley, Lawrence and Beyond the Mexique bay. *In* Walker, R. G. Infernal paradise p105-38

Plots

Caserio, R. L. The family plot: Conrad, Joyce, Lawrence, Woolf, and Faulkner. *In* Caserio, R. L. Plot, story, and the novel p232-79

Poetic works

Hyman, S. E. The Lawrence mob. *In* Hyman, S. E. The critic's credentials p130-34

Pritchard, W. H. English poetry in the 1920s: Graves and Lawrence. *In* Pritchard, W. H. Seeing through everything p114-33

Richards, I. A. Lawrence as a poet. *In* Richards, I. A. Complementarities p198-200

Relationship with women

Apter, T. E. Bert Lawrence and Lady Jane. *In* Smith, A. ed. Lawrence and women p178-88

Smith, A. A new Adam and a new Eve—Lawrence and women: a biographical overview. *In* Smith, A. ed. Lawrence and women p9-48

Style

Stewart, G. Lawrence, "being," and the allotropic style. *In* Spilka, M. ed. Towards a poetics of fiction p331-56

Technique

See Lawrence, David Herbert—Style

Women

See Lawrence, David Herbert—Relationship with women

Lawrence, Francis L.

Le misanthrope reprised: four versions of Molière's theme. *In* Johnson, R. B.; Neumann, E. S. and Trail, G. T. eds. Molière and the commonwealth of letters: patrimony and posterity p82-89

Lawrence, Frieda (von Richthofen)

About

Smith, A. A new Adam and a new Eve—Lawrence and women: a biographical overview. *In* Smith, A. ed. Lawrence and women p9-48

Lawrence, James Cooper

A theory of the short story. *In* May, C. E. ed. Short story theories p60-71

Lawrence, Philip

Heaven and earth—the relation of the nebular hypothesis to geology. *In* Cosmology, history, and theology p253-81

Lawrence, Seymour

Memoir of a 50-year-old publisher on his voyage to outer space. *In* Anderson, E. and Kinzie, M. eds. The little magazine in America: a modern documentary history p143-53

Lawrence, Thomas Edward

About

Meyers, J. T. E. Lawrence. *In* Meyers, J. A fever at the core p113-42

Rutherford, A. The intellectual as hero: Lawrence of Arabia. *In* Rutherford, A. The literature of war p38-63

About individual works
Seven pillars of wisdom

Meyers, J. T. E. Lawrence: Seven pillars of wisdom. *In* Meyers, J. Homosexuality and literature, 1890-1930 p114-30

Rutherford, A. The intellectual as hero: Lawrence of Arabia. *In* Rutherford, A. The literature of war p38-63

Lawson, Alan

"Where a man belongs": Hal Porter's The paper chase and George Johnston's Clean straw for nothing. *In* Hamilton, K. G. ed. Studies in the recent Australian novel p168-93

Lawson, Henry Archibald Hertzberg

About

Roderick, C. A. Lawson the poet. *In* Bards, bohemians, and bookmen p203-17

About individual works
While the billy boils

Matthews, B. E. Henry Lawson's fictional world. *In* Bards, bohemians, and bookmen p170-202

Lawson, Lewis A.

The moviegoer and the Stoic heritage *In* The Stoic strain in American literature p180-91

Lawson, Lewis A. comp.

Bibliography. *In* Friedman, M. J. and Lawson, L. A. eds. The added dimension p235-56

Lawton, Ben

Giuseppe Giacosa and Giacomo Puccini. *In* Abroad in America: Visitors to the new Nation, 1776-1914 p247-59

Lawyers

Lieberman, J. K. How to avoid lawyers. *In* Nader, R. and Green, M. J. eds. Verdicts on lawyers p105-17

Riley, D. P. The mystique of lawyers. *In* Nader, R. and Green, M. J. eds. Verdicts on lawyers p80-93

Lawyers—*Continued*

Tunney, J. V. and Frank, J. L. Epilogue: a congressional role in lawyer reform? *In* Nader, R. and Green, M. J. eds. Verdicts on lawyers p295-304

See also Admission to the bar; Corporate legal departments; Legal ethics; Practice of law; Right to counsel; Women lawyers

Discipline

Califano, J. A. The Washington lawyer: when to say no. *In* Nader, R. and Green, M. J. eds. Verdicts on lawyers p187-96

Garbus, M. and Seligman, J. Sanctions and disbarment: they sit in judgment. *In* Nader, R. and Green, M. J. eds. Verdicts on lawyers p47-60

Specialties and specialists

Hochberg, J. A. The drive to specialization. *In* Nader, R. and Green, M. J. eds. Verdicts on lawyers p118-26

New York (State)—History

Klein, M. M. New York lawyers and the coming of the American Revolution. *In* Studies in eighteenth-century culture v7 p23-47

United States

Auerbach, J. S. Lawyers and social change in the Depression decade. *In* Braeman, J.; Bremner, R. H. and Brody, D. eds. The New Deal v 1 p133-69

Bloomfield, M. H. Antilawyer sentiment in the early Republic. *In* Bloomfield, M. H. American lawyers in a changing society, 1776-1876 p32-58

Bloomfield, M. H. Conclusion. *In* Bloomfield, M. H. American lawyers in a changing society, 1776-1876 p340-48

Bloomfield, M. H. Upgrading the professional image. *In* Bloomfield, M. H. American lawyers in a changing society, 1776-1876 p136-90

United States—Fees

Green, M. J. The gross legal product: "How much justice can you afford?" *In* Nader, R. and Green, M. J. eds. Verdicts on lawyers p63-79

Lawyers (Canon law)

Brundage, J. A. Holy war and the medieval lawyers. *In* The Holy war p99-140

Lay leadership. See Christian leadership

Laycock, Douglas

Federal interference with state prosecutions the need for prospective relief. *In* The Supreme Court review, 1977 p193-238

Laye, Camara

About

King, A. Camara Laye. *In* King, B. A. and Ogungbesan, K. eds. A celebration of Black and African writing p112-23

About individual works

The African child

Okeh, P. I. Two ways of explaining Africa: an insight into Camara Laye's L'enfant noir and Ferdinand Oyono's Le vieux nègre et la médaille. *In* Exile and tradition p74-84

Laying on of hands. See Imposition of hands

Layish, Aharon

Social and political changes in Arab society in Israel. *In* The Palestinians p81-87

Laymon, Ronald L.

The Michelson-Morley experiment: descriptive dependence on to-be tested theories. *In* Motion and time, space and matter p436-64

Newton's advertised precision and his refutation of the received laws of refraction. *In* Studies in perception p231-58

Lays

History and criticism

Beston, J. B. How much was known of the Breton lai in fourteenth-century England? *In* The Learned and the lewed p319-36

Layton, Edwin T.

Conditions of technological development. *In* Science, technology and society p197-222

Layton, Irving

About

Woodcock, G. A grab at Proteus: notes on Irving Layton. *In* Woodcock, G. ed. Poets and critics p53-70

Layton, Robert

Art and visual communication. *In* Greenhalgh, M. and Megaw, J. V. S. eds. Art in society p21-30

Laytrim, Lord. See Leitrim, William Clements, 3d Earl

Layzer, David

Heritability analyses of IQ scores: science or numerology? *In* Montagu, A. ed. Race and IQ p193-219

Lazare, Bernard

About

Arendt, H. Herzl and Lazare. *In* Arendt, H. The Jew as pariah: Jewish identity and politics in the modern age p125-30

Lazarev, Viktor Nikitich

The bipartite tablets of St Sophia in Novgorod. *In* Studies in memory of David Talbot Rice p68-82

Lazarillo de Tormes

About individual works

The life of Lazarillo de Tormes, his fortunes and adversities

Bjornson, R. The birth of the picaresque: Lazarillo de Tormes and the socializing process. *In* Bjornson, R. The picaresque hero in European fiction p21-42

Lazarsfeld, Paul Felix

Communication research and its applications: a postscript. *In* Lerner, D. and Nelson, L. M. eds. Communication research—a half-century appraisal p257-60

The prognosis for international communications research. *In* Fischer, H. D. and Merrill, J. C. eds. International and intercultural communication p485-92

Working with Merton. *In* The Idea of social structure p35-66

Lazerson, Marvin

Consensus and conflict in American education: historical perspectives. *In* Parents, teachers, and children: prospects for choice in American education p15-36

Laziness

Altschule, M. D. Acedia—its evolution from deadly sin to psychiatric syndrome. *In* Altschule, M. D. Origins of concepts in human behavior p75-83

Lea, F. R. See Lea, Frank Alfred

Lea, Frank Alfred

What's the good? *In* Abbs, P. ed. The black rainbow p189-210

Leab, Daniel J.

The blue collar ethnic in Bicentennial America: Rocky. *In* OConnor, J. E. and Jackson, M. A. eds. American history/American film p257-72

Leach, Edmund Roland

Cultural components in the concept of race. *In* Racial variation in man p27-54

Leach, Gerald

About individual works
The biocrats

Koestler, A. Benighted attitudes. *In* Koestler, A. The heel of Achilles p67-71

Leacock, Stephen Butler

About

Bush, D. Stephen Leacock. *In* Staines, D. ed. The Canadian imagination p123-51

Lead, Jane (Ward)

About

Smith, C. F. Jane Lead: mysticism and the woman cloathed with the sun. *In* Gilbert, S. M. and Gubar, S. eds. Shakespeare's sisters p3-18

Lead mines and mining

Middle West

Kay, J. Indian responses to a mining frontier. *In* The Frontier v2 p193-203

Leadership

Babbitt, I. Democracy and leadership; excerpt. *In* Crunden, R. M. ed. The superfluous men p212-21

Barton, J. J. Eastern and southern Europeans. *In* Ethnic leadership in America p150-75

Christopher, T. W. The role of leadership. *In* The Rising South v2 p48-69

Goble, R. L. Leadership for a society in transition. *In* Benton, L. R. ed. Management for the future p125-38

Higham, J. Introduction: the forms of ethnic leadership. *In* Ethnic leadership in America p 1-18

Horton, T. R. Leadership of the spirit: a present and future need. *In* Benton, L. R. ed. Management for the future p148-63

Kelly, A. H. American political leadership: the optimistic ethical world view and the Jeffersonian synthesis. *In* Library of Congress Symposia on the American Revolution, 3d, 1974. Leadership in the American Revolution p7-39

Lundberg, C. C. The unreported leadership research of Dr. G. Hypothetical: six variables in need of recognition. *In* Leadership p65-83

McCall, M. W. and Lombardo, M. M. Where else can we go? *In* Leadership p151-65

Mazlish, B. Leadership in the American Revolution: the psychological dimension. *In* Library of Congress Symposia on the American Revolution, 3d, 1974. Leadership in the American Revolution p113-33

Mintz, S. W. Ethnicity and leadership: an afterword. *In* Ethnic leadership in America p198-205

Pfeffer, J. The ambiguity of leadership. *In* Leadership p13-34

Pondy, L. R. Leadership is a language game. *In* Leadership p87-99

Richardson, F. L. W. The elusive nature of cooperation and leadership: discovering a primitive process that regulates human behavior. *In* Eddy, E. M. and Partridge, W. L. eds. Applied anthropology in America p87-111

Weick, K. E. The spines of leaders. *In* Leadership p37-61

Yates, D. The roots of American leadership: political style and policy consequences. *In* Burnham, W. D. and Weinberg, M. W. eds. American politics and public policy p140-68

See also Command of troops; Elite (Social sciences)

Leadership, Afro-American. See Afro-American leadership

Leadership, Indian. See Indian leadership

Leadership, Irish-American. See Irish-American leadership

Leadership, Japanese American. See Japanese American leadership

Leadership, Jewish. See Jewish leadership

Leaf, Mark. See Lee, B. jt. auth.; Messent, P. jt. auth.

League of Arab States

Boutros-Ghali, B. Arab diplomacy: failures and successes. *In* Arab and American cultures p221-36

Boutros-Ghali, B. The League of Arab States and the Organization of African Unity. *In* El-Ayouty, Y. ed. The Organization of African Unity after ten years p47-61

League of Nations

Corwin, E. S. Wilson and the Senate. *In* Corwin, E. S. Presidential power and the Constitution p28-31

Hula, E. Fifty years of international government: reflections on the League of Nations and the United Nations. *In* [Truth and tragedy]: a tribute to Hans Morgenthau p179-98

Mandatory system
See Mandates

Leahy, John J.

On the civil liberties of sect members: Part 3. *In* Horowitz, I. L. ed. Science, sin, and scholarship p208-16

Leal, Juan de Valdés. See Valdés Leal, Juan de

Leal, Luis

Native and foreign influences in contemporary Mexican fiction: a search for identity. *In* Forster, M. H. ed. Tradition and renewal p102-28

Lear, Edward

About

Prickett, S. Consensus and nonsense: Lear and Carroll. *In* Prickett, S. Victorian fantasy p114-49

Learning

Psychological aspects
See Learning, Psychology of

Learning, Psychology of

Bettelheim, B. The decision to fail. *In* Bettelheim, B. Surviving, and other essays p142-68

Howard, V. A. Artistic practice and skills. *In* Perkins, D. and Leondar, B. eds. The arts and cognition p208-40

Learning, Psychology of—*Continued*

Levy, R. I. A conjunctive pattern in middle class informal and formal education. *In* Schwartz, T. ed. Socialization as cultural communication p177-87

Richards, I. A. The secret of "feedforward." *In* Richards, I. A. Complementarities p246-53

See also Comprehension; Learning ability; Learning disabilities; Programmed instruction

Learning ability

Biesheuvel, S. An examination of Jensen's theory concerning educability, heritability and population differences. *In* Montagu, A. ed. Race and IQ p59-72

See also Learning, Psychology of; Learning disabilities

Learning and scholarship

Adler, M. J. Teaching and learning. *In* From Parnassus p57-65

Ahlstrom, S. E. Thought and social change: reflections on cultural studies. *In* Luedtke, L. S. ed. The study of American culture p63-75

Bazerman, C. The grant, the scholar and the university community. *In* Hook, S.; Kurtz, P. W. and Todorovich, M. eds. The university and the state: what role for government in higher education? p221-25

Caplow, T. How many books? *In* From Parnassus p66-74

Eurich, N. Learning in America. *In* From Parnassus p75-83

Gibson, M. The continuity of learning, circa 850-circa 1050. *In* Viator: medieval and Renaissance studies v6 p 1-13

Gilkey, L. B. The structure of academic revolutions. *In* The Nature of scientific discovery p538-46

Green, T. F. Learning without metaphor. *In* Ortony, A. ed. Metaphor and thought p462-73

Halle, L. J. General education and the understanding of politics: the case of Hans J. Morgenthau. *In* [Truth and tragedy]: a tribute to Hans Morgenthau p55-65

Highet, G. The pleasures of learning. *In* Highet, G. The immortal profession p 1-19

Highet, G. The scholarly life. *In* Highet, G. The immortal profession p57-74

Knights, B. Epilogue: Cultural studies without a clerisy. *In* Knights, B. The idea of the clerisy in the nineteenth century p214-32

Miller, J. W. The scholar as man of the world. *In* Miller, J. W. The paradox of cause, and other essays p174-92

Petrie, H. G. Metaphor and learning. *In* Ortony, A. ed. Metaphor and thought p438-61

Sticht, T. G. Educational uses of metaphor. *In* Ortony, A. ed. Metaphor and thought p474-85

Wiles, R. M. The ivory tower, new style. *In* Studies in eighteenth-century culture v4 p3-11

See also Ciceronianism; Culture; Education; Humanism; Research; Scholarly publishing; Wisdom

China—History

Struve, L. A. Ambivalence and action: some frustrated scholars of the K'ang-hsi period. *In* Spence, J. D. and Wills, J. E. eds. From Ming to Ch'ing p321-65

Germany

Ringer, F. K. The German academic community. *In* Oleson, A. and Voss, J. eds. The organization of knowledge in modern America, 1860-1920 p409-29

Great Britain

Knights, B. The idea of a university. *In* Knights, B. The idea of the clerisy in the nineteenth century p178-213

Spain—Seville

Brown, J. A community of scholars. *In* Brown, J. Images and ideas in seventeenth-century Spanish painting p21-43

United States

Galambos, L. The American economy and the reorganization of the sources of knowledge. *In* Oleson, A. and Voss, J. eds. The organization of knowledge in modern America, 1860-1920 p269-82

Harris, N. The lamp of learning: popular lights and shadows. *In* Oleson, A. and Voss, J. eds. The organization of knowledge in modern America, 1860-1920 p430-39

Hawkins, H. University identity: the teaching and research functions. *In* Oleson, A. and Voss, J. eds. The organization of knowledge in modern America, 1860-1920 p285-312

Higham, J. The matrix of specialization. *In* Oleson, A. and Voss, J. eds. The organization of knowledge in modern America, 1860-1920 p3-18

Oleson, A. and Voss, J. Introduction. *In* Oleson, A. and Voss, J. eds. The organization of knowledge in modern America, 1860-1920 p vii-xxi

Rosenberg, C. Toward an ecology of knowledge: on discipline, context, and history. *In* Oleson, A. and Voss, J. eds. The organization of knowledge in modern America, 1860-1920 p440-55

Ross, D. The development of the social sciences. *In* Oleson, A. and Voss, J. eds. The organization of knowledge in modern America, 1860-1920 p107-38

Shils, E. A. The order of learning in the United States: the ascendancy of the university. *In* Oleson, A. and Voss, J. eds. The organization of knowledge in modern America, 1860-1920 p19-47

Veysey, L. R. The plural organized worlds of the humanities. *In* Oleson, A. and Voss, J. eds. The organization of knowledge in modern America, 1860-1920 p51-106

Learning center approach to teaching. See Open plan schools

Learning disabilities

Elkind, D. The curriculum-disabled child. *In* Elkind, D. The child and society p223-36

Learning disorders. See Learning disabilities

Leary, Lewis Gaston

Soundings

Contents

Leary, Lewis G.

Soundings

Contents—Continued

The literary opinions of Joseph Dennie

Nathaniel Tucker: expatriate patriot

Philip Freneau: a reassessment

Royall Tyler: first gentleman of the American theater

Samuel Low: New York's first poet

Thomas Branagan: Republican rhetoric and romanticism in America

Washington Irving: an end and a new beginning

Leary, Timothy Francis

About

Glicksberg, C. I. The politics of madness. *In* Glicksberg, C. I. The literature of commitment p163-85

Trilling, D. Celebrating with Dr Leary. *In* Trilling, D. We must march my darlings p15-38

Leary, Virginia

The implementation of the human rights provision of the Helsinki Final Act: a preliminary assessment: 1975-1977. *In* Human rights, international law and the Helsinki Accord p111-60

Leather work, Roman

Waterer, J. W. Leatherwork. *In* Strong, D. E. and Brown, D. eds. Roman crafts p179-93

Leavell, Frank Hartwell

Dualism in Stuart's Trees of heaven. *In* LeMaster, J. R. and Clarke, M. W. eds. Jesse Stuart p54-69

Leavis, Frank Raymond

About

Bilan, R. P. The basic concepts and criteria of F. R. Leavis's novel criticism. *In* Spilka, M. ed. Towards a poetics of fiction p157-76

Goodheart, E. The organic society of F. R. Leavis. *In* Goodheart, E. The failure of criticism p69-83

Pritchard, W. H. The literature of criticism. *In* Pritchard, W. H. Seeing through everything p134-53

Rahv, P. On F. R. Leavis and D. H. Lawrence. *In* Rahv, P. Essays on literature and politics, 1932-1972 p263-77

Sadock, G. J. Dickens and Dr Leavis: a critical commentary on Hard times. *In* Dickens Studies Annual v 2 p208-16

Thurley, G. F. R. Leavis and the English existential tradition. *In* Thurley, G. The ironic harvest p23-37

About individual works

The common pursuit

Fergusson, F. On F. R. Leavis. *In* Fergusson, F. Literary landmarks p131-36

The great tradition

Page, N. The great tradition revisited. *In* Jane Austen's achievement p44-63

Trilling, L. Dr. Leavis and the moral tradition. *In* Trilling, L. A gathering of fugitives p108-14

New bearings in English poetry

Holbrook, D. Criticism has lost confidence in itself. *In* Holbrook, D. Lost bearings in English poetry p25-47

Leavis, Frank Raymond, and Leavis, Queenie Dorothy

About individual works

Dickens, the novelist

Bayley, J. Dickens and his critics. *In* Bayley, J. The uses of division p90-103

Mudrick, M. Leavis on Dickens. *In* Mudrick, L. The man in the machine p111-22

Leavis, Queenie Dorothy

Melville: the 1853-6 phase. *In* Pullin, F. ed. New perspectives on Melville p197-228

See also Leavis, F. R. jt. auth.

Leavitt, Harold J. See Lipman-Blumen, J. jt. auth.

Leavitt, Ruby Rohrlich- See Rohrlich-Leavitt, Ruby

Leavy, Stanley A.

The significance of Jacques Lacan. *In* Psychoanalysis and language p271-92

Lebanese in Sierra Leone

Leighton, N. O. The political economy of a stranger population: the Lebanese of Sierra Leone. *In* Shack, W. A. and Skinner, E. P. eds. Strangers in African societies p85-103

Lebeau de Schosne, Augustin Théodore Vincent

About individual works

L'assembleé

Gravit, F. W. The first centenary of Molière's death. *In* Johnson, R. B.; Neumann, E. S. and Trail, G. T. eds. Molière and the commonwealth of letters: patrimony and posterity p547-56

Lebek, W. D.

Heminarium: Quintilian Institutio oratoria 6.3.52 and CIL IV 10566. *In* Harvard Studies in classical philology v82 p271-75

Lebnikov, Velimir. See Khlebnikov, Velemir

Le Bovier, Bernard, sieur de Fontenelle. See Fontenelle, Bernard Le Bovier de

Lebow, Ned. See Lebow, Richard Ned

Lebow, Richard Ned

British images of poverty in pre-famine Ireland. *In* Casey, D. J. and Rhodes, R. E. eds. Views of the Irish peasantry, 1800-1916 p57-83

Lebra, Takie Sugiyama

Social psychological change. *In* Lauer, R. H. ed. Social movements and social change p127-43

Le Breton, André-François

About

Kafker, F. A. The fortunes and misfortunes of a leading French bookseller-printer: André-François Le Breton, chief publisher of the Encyclopédie. *In* Studies in eighteenth-century culture v5 p371-85

Lebrun, François

About individual works

Les hommes et la mort en Anjou aux XVIIᵉ et XVIIIᵉ siècles

Le Roy Ladurie, E. Chaunu, Lebrun, Vovelle: the new history of death. *In* Le Roy Ladurie, E. The territory of the historian p273-84

Leca, Miguel Mañara y Vicentelo de. See Mañara y Vicentelo de Leca, Miguel

Lecar, Myron

The asteroids. *In* Man and cosmos p136-42

Le Caron, Louis
About
Kelley, D. R. Louis Le Caron philosophe. *In* Philosophy and humanism p30-49

About individual works
Les dialogues de Loys Le Caron parisien
Barron, B. Poet and orator in Louis le Caron's Dialogue de la poësie (1556). *In* French Renaissance studies, 1540-70 p21-35

Le Carré, John. See Cornwell, David John Moore

Lechtman, Heather, and Steinberg, Arthur
The history of technology: an anthropological point of view. *in* Bugliarello, G. and Doner, D. B. eds. The history and philosophy of technology p135-60

Leclaire, Serge
Unconscious inscription: another memory. *In* Roland, A. ed. Psychoanalysis, creativity, and literature p72-84

Leclant, Jean
Coffee and cafés in Paris, 1644-1693. *In* Food and drink in history p86-108

LeClercq, Richard V.
Crashaw's Epithalamium: pattern and vision. *In* Literary monographs v6 p71-108

Le Clézio, Jean Marie Gustave
About
Cagnon, M. A. and Smith, S. L. J. M. G. Le Clézio: fiction's double bind. *In* Federman, R. ed. Surfiction p215-26

About individual works
Fever
Oxenhandler, N. Nihilism in Le Clézio's La Fièvre. *In* Symbolism and modern literature p264-73

Le Comte, Edward Semple
Poets' riddles
Contents
The ending of Hamlet as a farewell to Essex
The 'haemony' passage in Comus
Hamlet's second utterance: forty-three interpretations
Jack Donne: from rake to husband
Marvell's "The nymph complaining for the death of her fawn"
New objections to a pre-Restoration date for Samson Agonistes
"That two-handed engine" and Savonarola and the Blackfriars fatal vespers

About individual works
Milton and sex
Wittreich, J. A. The new Milton criticism. *In* Review, v 1 1979 p123-64

Le Corbusier, pseud. See Jeanneret-Gris, Charles Édouard

Lectures and lecturing
United States
Vidal, G. The state of the Union. *In* Vidal, G. Matters of fact and of fiction p265-85

Lecythi
Clairmont, C. W. The lekythos of Myrrhine. *In* Studies in classical art and archaeology p103-10
Phillips, K. M. and Ashmead, A. H. Three goddesses and a falcon. *In* Studies in classical art and archaeology p45-52

Ledeen, Michael Arthur
Italy: war as a style of life. *In* The War generation p104-34

Lederer, Josef
John Donne and the emblematic practice. *In* Roberts, J. R. ed. Essential articles for the study of John Donne's poetry p107-21

Ledger, Marshall
Ring around A Christmas garland. *In* Aeolian harps p227-46

Le Duc, Eugène Emmanuel Viollet- See Viollet-Le Duc, Eugène Emmanuel

Lee, A. Robert
Moby-Dick: the tale and the telling. *In* Pullin, F. ed. New perspectives on Melville p86-127

Lee, Alvin A.
Toward a critique of The dream of the rood. *In* Anglo-Saxon poetry: essays in appreciation p163-91

Lee, Andrew
International suppression of hijacking. *In* International terrorism and political crimes p248-56

Lee, Anne Thompson
Le bone Florence of Rome: a Middle English adaptation of a French romance. *In* The Learned and the lewed p343-54

Lee, Brian S.
A poem 'Clepid the sevene ages.' *In* An English miscellany p72-92

Lee, Brian S. and Leaf, Mark
American literature: the twentieth century. *In* English Association. The year's work in English studies v54 p425-65

Lee, Brian S. and Murray, David J.
American literature: the twentieth century. *In* English Association. The year's work in English studies v53 p434-77

Lee, Charles, 1731-1782
About
Shy, J. W. American strategy: Charles Lee and the radical alternative. *In* Shy, J. W. A people numerous and armed p133-62

Lee, David N.
Visual information during locomotion. *In* Perception p250-67

Lee, Dorothy D.
Linguistic reflection of Wintu thought; excerpt from "Freedom and culture." *In* Tedlock, D. E. and Tedlock, B. eds. Teachings from the American earth p130-40

Lee, Edward N.
The sense of an object: Epicurus on seeing and hearing. *In* Studies in perception p27-59

Lee, Gary R.
A federal equal-employment-opportunity program. *In* Henderson, G. ed. Human relations in the military p237-48

Lee, Guy
Otium cum indignitate: Tibullus I.I. *In* Woodman, T. and West, D. eds. Quality and pleasure in Latin poetry p94-114

Lee, Harper
About individual works
To kill a mockingbird
Going, W. T. Store and Mockingbird: two Pulitzer novels about Alabama. *In* Going, W. T. Essays on Alabama literature p9-31

Lee, Hermione
'Taste' and 'tenderness' as moral values in the novels of Jane Austen. *In* Davies, R. T. and Beatty, B. G. eds. Literature of the romantic period, 1750-1850 p82-95

Lee, J. J.
Aspects of urbanization and economic development in Germany, 1815-1914. *In* Towns in societies p279-93

Lee, Jai Hyon
The activities of the Korean Central Intelligence Agency in the United States. *In* Horowitz, I. L. ed. Science, sin, and scholarship p120-47

Lee, James
Migration and expansion in Chinese history. *In* Human migration p20-47

Lee, John Alan
Meeting males by mail. *In* Crew, L. ed. The gay academic p415-27

Lee, Joseph
Administrators and agriculture: aspects of German agricultural policy in the First World War. *In* War and economic development p229-38

Lee, Leo Ou-fan
Genesis of a writer: notes on Lú Xun's educational experience, 1881-1909. *In* Modern Chinese literature in the May Fourth era p161-88

Lee, Peter K. H.
Between the old and the new. *In* The Emergent gospel p124-36

Lee, Robert Edward

About

Castel, A. E. The historian and the General: Thomas L. Connelly versus Robert E. Lee. *In* Hubbell, J. T. ed. Battles lost and won p215-28

Connelly, T. L. Robert E. Lee and the western Confederacy: a criticism of Lee's strategic ability. *In* Hubbell, J. T. ed. Battles lost and won p197-213

Lee, Robin
The fictional topography of Samuel Beckett. *In* Josipovici, G. ed. The modern English novel: the reader, the writer and the work p206-24

Lee, Thomas A.
The Middle Grijalva regional chronology and ceramic relations: a preliminary report. *In* Mesoamerican archaeology p 1-20

Lee, Vernon, pseud. See Paget, Violet

Lee-Painter, Susan. See Lewis, M. jt. auth.

Leech, Clifford
Masking and unmasking in the last plays. *In* Shakespeare's romances reconsidered p40-59

The moral tragedy of Romeo and Juliet. *In* English Renaissance drama p59-75

Studies in Shakespearian and other Jacobean tragedy, 1918-1972: a retrospect. *In* Shakespeare survey 26 p 1-9

Leeds, Anthony, and Leeds, Elizabeth R.
Accounting for behavioral differences: three political systems and the responses of squatters in Brazil, Peru, and Chile. *In* Walton, J. and Masotti, L. H. eds. The city in comparative perspective p193-248

Leeds, Elizabeth R. See Leeds, A. jt. auth.

Leenhardt, Jacques
Ideologies and trends in contemporary French sociology. *In* Mohan, R. P. and Martindale, D. A. eds. Handbook of contemporary developments in world sociology p9-18

Lees, Robert B.
Review of Syntactic structures. *In* Harman, G. ed. On Noam Chomsky p34-79

Le Fanu, Joseph Sheridan

About

Barclay, G. S. Vampires and ladies: Sheridan Le Fanu. *In* Barclay, G. S. Anatomy of horror: the masters of occult fiction p22-38

Briggs, J. Ancestral voices: the ghost story from Lucian to Le Fanu. *In* Briggs, J. Night visitors p25-51

Sullivan, J. Beginnings: Sheridan Le Fanu. *In* Sullivan, J. Elegant nightmares p32-68

Sullivan, J. "Green tea": the archetypal ghost story. *In* Sullivan, J. Elegant nightmares p11-31

Lefebvre, Georges
The place of the Revolution in the agrarian history of France. *In* Rural society in France p31-49

Lefebvre, Kenneth
Problems and considerations for effective home care of the cancer patient. *In* Home care p165-71

Le Fèvre, Jacques, d'Étaples

About individual works

De magia naturali

Rice, E. F. The de magia naturali of Jacques Lefèvre d'Étaples. *In* Philosophy and humanism p19-29

Le Fèvre de la Boderie, Guy

About individual works

Encyclie des secrets de l'éternité

Wilson, D. B. The quadrivium in the scientific poetry of Guy Lefèvre de la Boderie. *In* French Renaissance studies, 1540-70 p95-108

Le Fèvre d'Étaples, Jacques. See Le Fèvre, Jacques, d'Étaples

Leff, Michael C.
The logician's rhetoric: Boethius' De differentiis topicis, Book IV. *In* Murphy, J. J. ed. Medieval eloquence p3-24

Lefferts, H. Leedom
Frontier demography: an introduction. *In* Miller, D. H. and Steffen, J. O. eds. The frontier p33-55

Lefkadia, Macedonia. See Naousa, Greece

Lefkowitz, Mary R.
Bacchylides' Ode 5: imitation and originality. *In* Harvard Studies in classical philology v73 p45-96

Left (Political science) See Right and left (Political science)

Left Front in Art
Thomson, B. The redundancy of art: Soviet and Marxist views of art in the 1920s. *In* Thomson, B. Lot's wife and the Venus of Milo p53-74

Leftwich, Adrian
The constitution and continuity of South African inequality: some conceptual questions. *In* Leftwich, A. ed. South Africa: economic growth and political change p125-85

Legal assistance to the poor

United States

Conyers, J. R. Undermining poverty lawyers. *In* Nader, R. and Green, M. J. eds. Verdicts on lawyers p129-43

Tucker, M. S. Pro bono ABA? *In* Nader, R. and Green, M. J. eds. Verdicts on lawyers p20-32

Legal assistants

Lieberman, J. K. How to avoid lawyers. *In* Nader, R. and Green, M. J. eds. Verdicts on lawyers p105-17

Legal documents

Arabia

Lewis, N. Two Greek documents from provincia Arabia. *In* Illinois classical studies v3, 1978 p100-14

Egypt

Bingen, J. The third-century B.C. landleases from Tholthis. *In* Illinois classical studies v3, 1978 p74-80

Legal education. See Law—Study and teaching

Legal ethics

See also Advertising—Lawyers; Lawyers—Discipline

United States

Dorsey, G. L. Legal ethics and the adversary system. *In* Hook, S.; Kurtz, P. and Todorovich, M. eds. The ethics of teaching and scientific research p99-115

Frankel, M. E. Legal ethics and the ethics of law teaching. *In* Hook, S.; Kurtz, P. and Todorovich, M. eds. The ethics of teaching and scientific research p87-91

Redlich, N. Legal ethics: a problem of role definition. *In* Hook, S.; Kurtz, P. and Todorovich, M. eds. The ethics of teaching and scientific research p93-97

Legal fictions. See Fictions (Law)

Legal holidays. See Holidays

Legal literature

History and criticism

Dunlop, D. M. H. M. Baratz and his view of Khazar influence on the earliest Russian literature, juridical and historical. *In* Salo Wittmayer Baron v 1 p345-67

Legal profession. See Lawyers

Legal representation of the poor. See Legal assistance to the poor

Legal services, Prepaid. See Prepaid legal services

Legal services for the poor. See Legal assistance to the poor

Legal services insurance. See Prepaid legal services

Legal status of women. See Women—Legal status, laws, etc.

Legates, Papal

Somerville, R. E. Cardinal Stephan of St Gristogono: some remarks on legates and legatine councils in the eleventh century. *In* Law, church, and society p157-66

Le Gaufey, Guy. See Bleandonu, G. jt. auth.

Legends

Dégh, L. and Vázsonyï, A. Legend and belief. *In* Folklore genres p93-123

Lüthi, M. Aspects of the Märchen and the legend. *In* Folklore genres p17-33

Runciman, Sir S. History and legend. *In* Royal Society of Literature of the United Kingdom, London. Essays by divers hands v39 p112-25

See also Chansons de geste; Fairy tales; Folk-lore; Romances; and subdivision Legends under special subjects, e.g. Grail—Legends; Joseph of Arimathea—Legends

Jews

See Legends, Jewish

Legends, Ethiopic

Ullendorff, E. The Queen of Sheba in Ethiopian tradition. *In* Pritchard, J. B. ed. Solomon & Sheba p104-14

Legends, Islamic

Watt, W. M. The Queen of Sheba in Islamic tradition. *In* Pritchard, J. B. ed. Solomon & Sheba p85-103

Legends, Jewish

Leviant, C. Jewish influence upon Arthurian legends. *In* Salo Wittmayer Baron v2 p639-56

Silberman, L. H. The Queen of Sheba in Judaic tradition. *In* Pritchard, J. B. ed. Solomon & Sheba p65-84

Legends, Muslim. See Legends, Islamic

Legends, Roman

Mitchell, R. E. Roman coins as historical evidence: the Trojan legends of Rome. *In* Illinois classical studies, v 1 1976 p65-85

Léger, Aléxis Saint-Léger

About

Little, R. The world and the word in Saint-John Perse. *In* Cardinal, R. ed. Sensibility and creation p122-35

Paz, O. A modern hymn. *In* Paz, O. The siren & the seashell, p137-43

Tate, A. Homage to St. John Perse. *In* Tate, A. Memoirs and opinions, 1926-1974 p76-81

About individual works

Winds

Laden, R. A. "Les relais du verbe": Perse's reticular rhetoric. *In* Glyph 4 p156-88

Léger, Fernand

About

Berger, J. Fernand Léger. *In* Berger, J. The look of things p107-21

Legge, John David

Southeast Asian history and the social sciences. *In* Southeast Asian history and historiography p388-404

Legge, Mary Dominica

Anglo-Norman hagiography and the romances. *In* Medievalia et humanistica no. 6 p41-49

Leggett, John

About

Milne, G. Recent exemplars. *In* Milne, G. The sense of society p254-71

Leggitt, Hunter. See Myers, L. jt. auth.

Legislation, Comparative. See Comparative law

Legislative auditing

United States

Sharkansky, I. The politics of auditing. *In* Smith, B. L. R. ed. The new political economy: the public use of the private sector p278-318

Legislative bodies. See Legislators; also names of individual legislative bodies; e.g. United States. Congress

Legislative bodies as courts. See Impeachments

Legislative power

See also Federal government; Judicial review; Separation of powers; State governments; Treaty-making power; War and emergency powers

United States

Dry, M. Congress. *In* Graham, G. J. and Graham, S. G. eds. Founding principles of American government p223-57

Ornstein, N. J. and Rohde, D. W. Seniority and future power in Congress. *In* Ornstein, N. J. ed. Congress in change p72-87

Legislative printing. See Printing, Legislative

Legislators

United States

Fenno, R. F. If, as Ralph Nader says, Congress is "the broken branch," how come we love our Congressmen so much? *In* Ornstein, N. J. ed. Congress in change p277-87

Kim, Chong Lim; Green, J. J. and Patterson, S. C. Partisanship in the recruitment and performance of American state legislators. *In* Eulau, H. and Czudnowski, M. M. eds. Elite recruitment in democratic polities p79-103

Legitimation of children

Senegal

Sapir, J. D. The fabricated child. *In* The Social use of metaphor p193-223

Legnano, Giovanni da

About individual works
Questio disputata

Kirshner, J. Conscience and public finance: a Questio disputata of John of Legnano on the public debt of Genoa. *In* Philosophy and humanism p434-53

Legnanus Joannes. See Legnano, Giovanni da

Le Goff, Jacques

The usurer and Purgatory. *In* The Dawn of modern banking p25-52

See also Biraben, J. N. jt. auth.

Le Goff, Timothy J. A. and Sutherland, D. M. G.

The Revolution and the rural community in eighteenth-century Brittany. *In* French society and the Revolution p29-52

Legouis, Pierre

'Titus Andronicus', III, i, 298-9. *In* Shakespeare survey 28 p71-74

Le Guin, Ursula K.

Science fiction and Mrs. Brown. *In* Nicholls, P. ed. Science fiction at large p13-33

This fear of dragons. *In* Blishen, E. ed. The thorny paradise p87-92

About

Wood, S. Discovering worlds: the fiction of Ursula K. Le Guin. *In* Clareson, T. D. ed. Voices for the future: essays on major science fiction writers v2 p154-79

About individual works
A wizard of Earthsea

- Cameron, E. High fantasy: A wizard of Earthsea. *In* Horn Book Magazine. Crosscurrents of criticism p333-41

Legum, Colin

Conclusion: Looking to the future. *In* Carter, G. M. and O'Meara, P. eds. Southern Africa in crisis p258-67

International rivalries in the Southern African conflict. *In* Carter, G. M. and O'Meara, P. eds. Southern Africa: the continuing crisis p3-17

Introduction: The international dimension of the crisis in Southern Africa. *In* Carter, G. M. and O'Meara, P. eds. Southern Africa in crisis p3-13

Southern Africa: the politics of detente. *In* The Year book of world affairs, 1976 p14-29

Lehman, J. Lee

Gay students. *In* Crew, L. ed. The gay academic p57-63

Lehmann, John

The myth and the writer. *In* Courcel, M. H. de, ed. Malraux p141-52

About individual works
A nest of tigers

Connolly, C. The Sitwells. *In* Connolly, C. The evening colonnade p251-54

Lehmann, Paul Louis

About

Allen, H. T. The life and ministry of Paul L. Lehmann: a personal tribute. *In* The Context of contemporary theology p15-22

About individual works
Ethics in a Christian context

Reist, B. A. Beyond ideological theology. *In* The Context of contemporary theology p171-86

Bibliography

Mathewson, R. C. A Paul Lehmann bibliography. *In* The Context of contemporary theology p253-67

Lehmann, Phyllis Lourene Williams

Lefkadia and the second style. *In* Studies in classical art and archaeology p225-29

Lehmann, Rosamond

Characters—Women

Kaplan, S. J. Rosamond Lehmann. *In* Kaplan, S. J. Feminine consciousness in the modern British novel p110-35

Lehning, Arthur

Bakunin's conceptions of revolutionary organisations and their role: a study of his 'secret societies'. *In* Essays in honour of E. H. Carr p57-81

Lehnsen, Erika

Correlation between clinical course and pictorial expression of a schizophrenic patient. *In* Ulman, E. and Dachinger, P. eds. Art therapy p286-310

Leibenstein, Harvey

Efficiency wages, X-efficiency, and urban unemployment. *In* Economic development and planning p168-85

Leibniz, Gottfried Wilhelm, Freiherr von

About

Cassirer, E. Descartes, Leibniz, and Vico. *In* Cassirer, E. Symbol, myth, and culture p95-107

Hausman, A. M. Innate ideas. *In* Studies in perception p200-30

**Leibniz, Gottfried W., Freiherr von—About
—Continued**

Krieger, L. Germany. *In* National consciousness, history, and political culture in early-modern Europe p67-97

McGuire, J. E. "Labyrinthus continui": Leibniz on substance, activity, and matter. *In* Motion and time, space and matter p290-326

Sebeok, T. A. The seventeenth century Cheremis: the evidence from Witsen. *In* On language, culture, and religion: in honor of Eugene A. Nida p301-14

Wilson, M. D. Leibniz's dynamics and contingency in nature. *In* Motion and time, space and matter p264-89

Leibowitz, Lila
Perspectives on the evolution of sex differences. *In* Reiter, R. R. ed. Toward an anthropology of women p20-35

Leighton, Neil Owen
The political economy of a stranger population: the Lebanese of Sierra Leone. *In* Shack, W. A. and Skinner, E. P. eds. Strangers in African societies p85-103

Leinster, Murray, pseud. See Jenkins, William Fitzgerald

Leiris, Michel
Race and culture. *In* United Nations Educational, Scientific and Cultural Organization. Race, science and society p135-72

Leisure
Chaney, D. C. and Chaney, J. H. The audience for mass leisure. *In* Fischer, H. D. and Melnik, S. R. eds. Entertainment: a cross-cultural examination p129-43

Markus, M. and Hegedüs, A. Free time and the division of labour. *In* The Humanisation of socialism p106-23

Melnik, S. R. The "uses and gratifications" approach in the study of "entertainment" and leisure use. *In* Fischer, H. D. and Melnik, S. R. eds. Entertainment: a cross-cultural examination p144-52

Psychological aspects

Clayre, A. Some effects of repetitive work on leisure. *In* Clayre, A. Work and play p171-80

Plaut, W. G. The Sabbath as protest: thoughts on work and leisure in the automated society. *In* Tradition and change in Jewish experience p169-83

Japan

Linhart, S. The use and meaning of leisure in present-day Japan. *In* Modern Japan p198-208

Japan—Public opinion

Linhart, S. The use and meaning of leisure in present-day Japan. *In* Modern Japan p198-208

United States

Kornblum, W. and Williams, T. Life-style, leisure, and community life. *In* Handbook of contemporary urban life p58-89

Leitrim, William Clements, 3d Earl

Assassination

Lloyd, A. L. On an unpublished Irish ballad. *In* Rebels and their causes p177-207

Lekachman, Robert
The inevitability of planning. *In* Planning, politics, and the public interest p143-60

The radical Keynes. *In* Skidelsky, R. J. A. ed. The end of the Keynesian era p59-66

About individual works
The inevitability of planning

Bowden, G. T. A response: planning—yes, but by whom? *In* Planning, politics, and the public interest p161-66

Lekythoi. See Lecythi

Leland, John

About

Buckalew, R. E. Leland's transcript of Ælfric's Glossary. *In* Anglo-Saxon England 7 p149-64

Leland, Marine Elizabeth
Quebec literature in its American context. *In* Staines, D. ed. The Canadian imagination p188-225

Lelchuk, Alan
Philip Rahv: the last years. *In* Images and ideas in American culture p204-19

About individual works
American mischief

Roth, P. Imagining the erotic: three introductions. *In* Roth, P. Reading myself and others p195-214

Lely, Gilbert

About individual works
The Marquis de Sade, a biography

Connolly, C. Sade. *In* Connolly, C. The evening colonnade p125-27

LeMaster, J. R.
Jesse Stuart's poetry as Fugitive-Agrarian synthesis. *In* LeMaster, J. R. and Clarke, M. W. eds. Jesse Stuart p19-39

Lemay, Edna Hindie
Thomas Hérier, a country surgeon outside Angoulême at the end of the XVIIIth century: a contribution to social history. *In* Branca, P. ed. The medicine show p229-42

Lemay, Joseph A. Leo
The frontiersman from lout to hero: notes on the significance of the comparative method and the stage theory in early American literature and culture. *In* American Antiquarian Society. Proceedings v88 pt2 p187-223

Literature to 1800. *In* American literary scholarship, 1973 p179-207

The text, rhetorical strategies, and themes of "The speech of Miss Polly Baker." *In* Lemay, J. A. L. ed. The oldest revolutionary p91-120

Lemay, Richard Joseph
The fly against the elephant: Flandinus against Pomponazzi on fate. *In* Philosophy and humanism p70-99

The Hispanic origin of our present numeral forms. *In* Viator: medieval and Renaissance studies v8 p435-59

Lemert, Charles Clay
Sociology and the twilight of man

Contents

Analytic realism: Talcott Parsons
Axiomatic explanation: George Homans
Critical theory: Juergen Habermas
Ethnomethodology: Aaron Cicourel
Homocentric sociology in the twilight
Homocentrism and sociological discourse
Phenomenological sociology: Schutz, Berger, Luckmann
Symbolic interactionism: Herbert Blumer
Theory constructionism: Hubert Blalock

Lemert, Charles C.—*Continued*
Structuralist semiotics and the decentering of sociology. *In* McNall, S. G. ed. Theoretical perspectives in sociology p96-111

Lemert, Edwin McCarthy
Response to critics: feedback and choice. *In* The Uses of controversy in sociology p244-49

Lemon, James T.
The weakness of place and community in early Pennsylvania. *In* European settlement and development in North America: essays on geographical change in honour and memory of Andrew Hill Clark p190-207

Lenaghan, Robert Thomas
The clerk of Venus: Chaucer and medieval romance. *In* The Learned and the lewed p31-43

Lenard, Philipp Eduard Anton

About

Wheaton, B. R. Philipp Lenard and the photoelectric effect, 1889-1911. *In* Historical studies in the physical sciences v9 p299-322

Lence, Ross Marlo
The American Declaration of Independence: the majority and the right of political power. *In* Graham, G. J. and Graham, S. G. eds. Founding principles of American government p29-59

Lenczowski, George
The oil-producing countries. *In* Vernon, R. ed. The oil crisis p59-72

Lenhardt, Christian K.
The wanderings of enlightenment. *In* O'Neill, J. ed. On critical theory p34-57

Lenin, Nikolai. See Lenin, Vladimir Il'ich

Lenin, Vladimir Il'ich

About

Mathewson, R. W. Lenin and Gorky: the turning point. *In* Mathewson. R. W. The positive hero in Russian literature p156-76

Mihajlov, M. On responsibility: Marx and Lenin in their personal lives. *In* Mihajlov, M. Underground notes p37-42

Parry, A. Lenin: high priest of terror. *In* Parry, A. Terrorism: from Robespierre to Arafat p131-45

Parry, A. Now is the time. *In* Parry, A. Terrorism: from Robespierre to Arafat p146-60

Parry, A. Thought waves of hatred. *In* Parry, A. Terrorism: from Robespierre to Arafat p161-70

About individual works

Imperialism, the highest stage of capitalism

Holdsworth, M. Lenin's Imperialism in retrospect. *In* Essays in honour of E. H. Carr p341-51

Materialism and empirio-criticism

Flew, A. G. N. Lenin and the Cartesian inheritance. *In* Flew, A. G. N. A rational animal p196-221

Art patronage

Bowlt, J. E. Russian sculpture and Lenin's plan of monumental propaganda. *In* Millon, H. A. and Nochlin, L. eds. Art and architecture in the service of politics p182-93

Leningrad

Social conditions

Lincoln, W. B. The daily life of St Petersburg officials in the mid nineteenth century. *In* Oxford Slavonic papers, new ser. v8 p82-100

Lenkowsky, Leslie
Welfare in the welfare state. *In* Tyrrell, R. E. ed. The future that doesn't work p144-66

Lenneberg, Eric Heinz
The neurology of language. *In* Bloomfield, M. W. and Haugen, E. I. eds. Language as a human problem p101-19

Lennon, Hugh Ormsby-. See Ormsby-Lennon, Hugh

Lennox, Charlotte (Ramsay)

About individual works

The female Quixote; or, The adventures of Arabella

Auty, S. G. Fielding's followers: The female Quixote. *In* Auty, S. G. The comic spirit of eighteenth-century novels p66-78

Lenny (Motion picture)
Sarris, A. Lenny. *In* Sarris, A. Politics and cinema p52-56

Lenny (criticism) Barry, J. *In* Brustein, R. S. The culture watch p14-17

Lenormand, Henri René

About

Muir, K. The plays of Henri René Lenormand. *In* Muir, K. The singularity of Shakespeare, and other essays p180-97

Lenski, Gerhard Emmanuel
Social structure in evolutionary perspective. *In* Blau, P. M. ed. Approaches to the study of social structure p135-53

About individual works

Social structure in evolutionary perspective

Bierstedt, R. S. Comment on Lenski's evolutionary perspective. *In* Blau, P. M. ed. Approaches to the study of social structure p154-58

Lenson, David R.
Achilles' choice

Contents

Afterword
A case of migration through genres
Choric equivalents in modern drama
Classical analogy: Giraudoux versus Faulkner
The other tragedy
Paradoxes of tragedy
Toward lyric tragedy: W. B. Yeats
Tragedy in prose fiction: Moby-Dick

Lenz, Widukind
Chemicals as a cause of human malformations. *In* Against pollution and hunger p89-96

Leo III, Saint, Pope

About

Wallach, L. The genuine and the forged oath of Pope Leo III. *In* Wallach, L. Diplomatic studies in Latin and Greek documents from the Carolingian age p299-327

Wallach, L. The Roman synod of December 800 and the alleged trial of Leo III. *In* Wallach, L. Diplomatic studies in Latin and Greek documents from the Carolingian age p328-52

Leo III, Pope. See Leo III, Saint, Pope

The Leofric missal and tenth-century English art. Deshman, R. *In* Anglo-Saxon England 6 p145-73

León, Eusebio M. Mujal-. See Mujal-León, Eusebio M.

Léon, Luis Ponce de

About individual works
The life removed

Poggioli, R. Pastoral and soledad. *In* Poggioli, R. The oaten flute p182-93

Leon, Spain. San Isidoro el Real (church). Panteón de los Reyes

Williams, J. Marcialis Pincerna and the provincial in Spanish medieval art. *In* Enggass, R. C. and Stokstad, M. eds. Hortus imaginum p29-36

Leonard, Irving Albert

Domingo Faustino Sarmiento. *In* Abroad in America: Visitors to the new Nation, 1776-1914 p104-13

Leonardo da Vinci

About individual works
Leda and the swan

Bertolini, J. A. Ecphrasis and dramaturgy: Leonardo's Leda in Rucellai's Oreste. *In* Renaissance drama [1976] p151-76

Madonna of the rocks

Brown, D. A. The London Madonna of the rocks in light of two Milanese adaptations. *In* Collaboration in Italian Renaissance art p167-86

Mona Lisa (La Gioconda)

Alphand, N. M. Escorting the Mona Lisa. *In* Courcel, M. H. de, ed. Malraux p95-99

Leondar, Barbara

Hatching plots: genesis of storymaking. *In* Perkins, D. and Leondar, B. eds. The arts and cognition p172-91

Leone, Mark P.

The economic basis for the evolution of Mormon religion. *In* Zaretsky, I. I. and Leone, M. P. eds. Religious movements in contemporary America p722-66

Leone da Modena

Authorship

Eisenstein-Barzilay, I. Finalizing an issue: Modena's authorship of the Qol sakhal. *In* Salo Wittmayer Baron v 1 p135-66

Leoniceno, Niccolò

About individual works
De tribus doctrinis ordinatis

Edwards, W. F. Niccolò Leoniceno and the origins of humanist discussion of method. *In* Philosophy and humanism p283-305

Leonicenus, Nicolaus. See Leoniceno, Niccolò

Leonov, Leonid Maksimovich

About

Thomson, B. The fact of art: Leonard Leonov. *In* Thomson, B. Lot's wife and the Venus of Milo p123-38

About individual works
Road to the ocean

Mathewson, R. W. Four novels. *In* Mathewson, R. W. The positive hero in Russian literature p233-53

Leopardi, Giacomo, conte

About

Nelson, L. Leopardi first and last. *In* Italian literature: roots and branches p333-62

Perella, N. J. The nineteenth century. *In* Perella, N. J. Midday in Italian literature p70-113

Leopold, Richard William

The history of United States foreign policy: past, present, and future. *In* The Future of history p231-46

The Korean War: the historian's task. *In* The Korean War p209-24

Le Page, R. B.

Dialect in West Indian literature. *In* Baugh, E. ed. Critics on Caribbean literature p123-29

Le Pellec, Yves

Rabbit underground. *In* Johnson, I. D. and Johnson, C. [eds.] Les américanistes p94-109

Le Petit, Jehan. See Petit, Jean

Lepsius, Mario Rainer

From fragmented party democracy to government by emergency decree and National Socialist takeover: Germany. *In* The Breakdown of democratic regimes pt2 p34-79

Lerenbaum, Miriam

Moll Flanders: "a woman on her own account." *In* Diamond, A. and Edwards, L. R. eds. The authority of experience p101-17

Leridon, Henri

The role of economic factors in birth-rate trends and fluctuations. *In* Economic factors in population growth p179-97

Lerman, Paul

American concerns: keeping order versus fighting crime. *In* Empey, L. T. ed. Juvenile justice p150-79

Lermontov, Mikhail Iúr'evich

About

Katz, M. R. Lermontov's literary ballads. *In* Katz, M. R. The literary ballad in early nineteenth-century Russian literature p166-82

About individual works
A hero of our time

Calder, A. Literature and serfdom: Gogol, Lermontov and Goncharov, *In* Calder, A. Russia discovered p37-72

Rowe, W. W. Duality and symmetry in Lermontov's A hero of our time. *In* Rowe, W. W. Nabokov & others: patterns in Russian literature p27-36

Lerner, Abba Ptachya

Black studies: the universities in moral crisis. *In* Fairfield, R. P. ed. Humanistic frontiers in American education p127-33

Demography, economics, and technology and the Middle East conflict. *In* The New world balance and peace in the Middle East: reality or mirage? p98-104

Money, debt and wealth. *In* Econometrics and economic theory p247-59

Wages, profits, and marginal analysis. *In* Inflation, trade and taxes p23-28

About

Mundell, R. A. Abba Lerner and the theory of foreign trade. *In* Theory for economic efficiency: essays in honor of Abba P. Lerner p144-50

Lerner, Barbara
Washington v. Davis: quantity, quality and equality in employment testing. *In* The Supreme Court review, 1976 p263-316

Lerner, Daniel
Communication and development. *In* Lerner, D. and Nelson, L. M. eds. Communication research—a half-century appraisal p148-66

Lerner, Laurence
An essay on Dombey and son, *In* Lerner, L. The Victorians p 195-208
An essay on The Princess. *In* Lerner, L. ed. The Victorians p209-22
Literature and money. *In* English Association. Essays and studies, 1975 p106-22
Poetry. *In* Lerner, L. ed. The Victorians p25-45

Lerner, Robert E.
An "Angel of Philadelphia" in the reign of Philip the Fair: the case of Guiard of Cressonessart. *In* Order and innovation in the Middle Ages p343-64

Lerner, Warren
Attempting a revolution from without: Poland in 1920. *In* Hammond, T. T. ed. The anatomy of Communist takeovers p94-106

Le Roy Ladurie, Emmanuel
Family structures and inheritance customs in sixteenth-century France. *In* Family and inheritance p37-70
Famine amenorrhoea (seventeenth-twentieth centuries) *In* Biology of man in history p163-78
Same as Amenorrhoea in time of famine (seventeenth-twentieth centuries) *In* The Territory of the historian p255-71
Rural revolts and protest movements in France from 1675-1788. *In* Studies in eighteenth-century culture v5 p423-51
A system of customary law: family structures and inheritance customs in sixteenth-century France. *In* Family and society p75-103
The territory of the historian
Contents
Amenorrhoea in time of famine (seventeenth to twentieth century)
Same as Le Roy Ladurie, E. Famine amenorrhoea (seventeenth-twentieth centuries) *In* Biology of man in history p163-78
Changes in Parisian rents from the end of the Middle Ages to the eighteenth century
Chaunu, Lebrun, Vovelle: the new history of death
The chief defects of Gregory King
The conscripts of 1868: a study of the correlation between geographical mobility, delinquency and physical stature, and other aspects of the situation of the young Frenchmen called to do military service in that year
Demography and the "sinful secrets": the case of Languedoc in the late eighteenth and early nineteenth centuries
The "event" and the "long term" in social history: the case of the Chouan uprising
From Brantôme to Paul VI
From Waterloo to Colyton
The historian and the computer
The history of rain and fine weather
In Normandy's woods and fields
Mélusine down on the farm: metamorphosis of a myth

Quantitative history: the 6th section of the École Pratique des Hautes Études
The quantitative revolution and French historians: record of a generation (1932-1968)
Rural civilization
Tithes and net agricultural output (fifteenth to eighteenth century)
Writing the history of the climate
See also Pesez, J. M. jt. auth.

Le Sage, Alain René

About
Brereton, G. The cynical generation: Dancourt, Regnard, Dufresny, Lesage. *In* Brereton, G. French comic drama p163-93

About individual works
Gil Blas
Bjornson, R. The picaresque hero arrives: sentiment and success in LeSage's Gil Blas. *In* Bjornson, R. The picaresque hero in European fiction p207-27

Lesbian love. See Lesbianism

Lesbianism
Rich, A. C. "It is the lesbian in us. . . ." *In* Rich, A. C. On lies, secrets, and silence p199-202
Stanley, J. P. Lesbian separatism: the linguistic and social sources of separatist politics. *In* Crew, L. ed. The gay academic p121-31
See also Lesbians

Personal narratives
Brown, R. M. The lesbian woman: two points of view: A woman's place is wherever she wants it to be. *In* Gochros, H. L. and Gochros, J. S. eds. The sexually oppressed p152-59

United States
Brown, R. M. The lesbian woman: two points of view: A woman's place is wherever she wants it to be. *In* Gochros, H. L. and Gochros, J. S. eds. The sexually oppressed p152-59
Goodman, B. The lesbian woman: two points of view: The problems of lesbians. *In* Gochros, H. L. and Gochros, J. S. eds. The sexually oppressed p145-51

Lesbianism in literature
Cockshut, A. O. J. The lesbian theme. *In* Cockshut, A. O. J. Man and woman: a study of love and the novel, 1740-1940 p186-208

Lesbians
Rich, A. C. The meaning of our love for women is what we have constantly to expand. *In* Rich, A. C. On lies, secrets, and silence p223-30

Lesbians in literature
Rich, A. C. "It is the lesbian in us. . . ." *In* Rich, A. C. On lies, secrets, and silence p199-202

Lesch, Ann Mosley
The origins of Palestine Arab nationalism. *In* Nationalism in a non-national state p265-90

Leser, Paul W.
No man, having put his hand to the plow . . . *In* On language, culture, and religion: in honor of Eugene A. Nida p241-58

LeShan, Lawrence Lee

Individual realities: commonsense, science, and mysticism; excerpts from "Toward a general theory of the paranormal." *In* Wheatley, J. M. O. and Edge, H. L. eds. Philosophical dimensions of parapsychology p425-40

What it feels like to be a parapsychologist. *In* Parapsychology: its relation to physics, biology, psychology, and psychiatry p162-66

Lesko, Kathleen M.

A rare Restoration manuscript promptbook: John Wilson's Belphegor, corrected by the author. *In* Virginia. University. Bibliographical Society. Studies in bibliography v32 p215-19

Leskov, Nicholas. See Leskov, Nikolaĭ Semenovich

Leskov, Nikolaĭ Semenovich

About

Calder, A. Literature and morality: Leskov, Chekhov, late Tolstoy. *In* Calder, A. Russia discovered p238-75

Lesky, Albin

On the Heraclidae of Euripides. *In* Yale classical studies v25 p227-38

Leslau, Wolf

Taamrat Emmanuel's notes of Falasha monks and holy places. *In* Salo Wittmayer Baron v2 p623-37

Leslie, Larry Lee

Updating education for the professions: the new mission. *In* Land-grant universities and their continuing challenge p237-65

Leśmian, Bolesław

About

Stone, R. Metapoetics and structure in Bolesaw Leśmian's Russian poetry. *In* California Slavic studies v10 p137-72

Lesotho

Politics and government

Vilakazi, A. L. Swaziland and Lesotho: from traditionalism to modernity. *In* Carter, G. M. and O'Meara, P. eds. Southern Africa in crisis p226-57

Weisfelder, R. F. Lesotho: changing patterns of dependence. *In* Carter, G. M. and O'Meara, P. eds. Southern Africa: the continuing crisis p249-68

Less developed countries. See Underdeveloped areas

Lesser, Simon O.

The whispered meanings

Contents

Act One, Scene One, of Lear
The attitude of fiction
L'Avventura
Freud and Hamlet again
Hawthorne's "My kinsman, Major Molineux"
Macbeth: drama and dream
A note on Pamela
The Odyssey: the hidden dreams
Oedipus the King: the two dramas, the two conflicts
Reflections on Pinter's The birthday party
The role of unconscious understanding in Flaubert and Dostoevsky
"Sailing to Byzantium": another voyage, another reading
Saint and sinner: Dostoevsky's "Idiot"
The source of guilt and the sense of guilt: Kafka's The trial

Lesser vehicle (Buddhism) See Hinayana Buddhism

Lessing, Alfred Cook Tayler

About

Lessing, D. M. My father. *In* Lessing, D. M. A small personal voice p83-93

Lessing, Doris May

A small personal voice

Contents

Afterword to The story of an African farm by Olive Schreiner
Allah be praised
Ant's eye view: a review of The soul of the white ant by Eugène Marais
Being prohibited
A deep darkness: a review of Out of Africa by Karen Blixen
The fruits of humbug
In the world, not of it
My father
Preface to The golden notebook
The small personal voice
Vonnegut's responsibility

About

Hardin, N. S. Doris Lessing and the Sufi way. *In* Pratt, A. and Dembo, L. S. eds. Doris Lessing p148-64

Kaplan, S. J. The limits of consciousness in the novels of Doris Lessing. *In* Pratt, A. V. and Dembo, L. S. eds. Doris Lessing p119-32

Lessing, D. M. Being prohibited. *In* Lessing, D. M. A small personal voice p155-60

Showalter, E. Beyond the female aesthetic: contemporary women novelists. *In* Showalter, E. A literature of their own p298-319

Sukenick, L. Feeling and reason in Doris Lessing's fiction. *In* Pratt, A. V. and Dembo, L. S. eds. Doris Lessing p98-118

About individual works

Briefing for a descent into hell

Bolling, D. T. Structure and theme in Briefing for a descent into hell. *In* Pratt, A. V. and Dembo, L. S. eds. Doris Lessing p133-47

Sale, R. H. Mailer & Lessing. *In* Sale, R. H. On not being good enough p21-30

Children of violence

Kaplan, S. J. Doris Lessing. *In* Kaplan, S. J. Feminine consciousness in the modern British novel p136-72

The four-gated city

Barnouw, D. Disorderly company: from The golden notebook to The four-gated city. *In* Pratt, A. V. and Dembo, L. S. eds. Doris Lessing p74-97

Rigney, B. H. "A rehearsal for madness": hysteria as sanity in The four-gated city. *In* Rigney, B. H. Madness and sexual politics in the feminist novel p65-89

Sale, R. H. Mailer & Lessing. *In* Sale, R. H. On not being good enough p21-30

The golden notebook

Barnouw, D. Disorderly company: from The golden notebook to The four-gated city. *In* Pratt, A. V. and Dembo, L. S. eds. Doris Lessing p74-97

Carey, J. L. Art and reality in The golden notebook. *In* Pratt, A. V. and Dembo, L. S. eds. Doris Lessing p20-39

Lessing, Doris M.—About individual works—
The golden notebook—*Continued*

Cohen, M. "Out of the chaos, a new kind of strength": Doris Lessing's The golden notebook. *In* Diamond, A. and Edwards, L. R. eds. The authority of experience p178-93

Hinz, E. J. and Teunissen, J. J. The Pietà as icon in The golden notebook. *In* Pratt, A. V. and Dembo, L. S. eds. Doris Lessing p40-53

Howe, I. Doris Lessing: no compromise, no happiness. *In* Howe, I. Celebrations and attacks p112-17

Kaplan, S. J. Doris Lessing. *In* Kaplan, S. J. Feminine consciousness in the modern British novel p136-72

Lessing, D. M. Preface to The golden notebook. *In* Lessing, D. M. A small personal voice p23-43

Morgan, E. Alienation of the woman writer in The golden notebook. *In* Pratt, A. V. and Dembo, L. S. eds. Doris Lessing p54-63

The grass is singing

Gottlieb, L. C. and Keitner, W. Colonialism as metaphor and experience in 'The grass is singing' and 'Surfacing.' *In* Narasimhaiah, C. D. ed. Awakened conscience p307-14

Zak, M. W. The grass is singing: a little novel about the emotions. *In* Pratt, A. V. and Dembo, L. S. eds. Doris Lessing p64-73

Characters—Anna Wulf

Cohen, M. "Out of the chaos, a new kind of strength": Doris Lessing's The golden notebook. *In* Diamond, A. and Edwards, L. R. eds. The authority of experience p178-93

Characters—Women

Kaplan, S. J. Doris Lessing. *In* Kaplan, S. J. Feminine consciousness in the modern British novel p136-72

Lessing, Gotthold Ephraim

About

Michael, W. F. Lessing and Molière. *In* Johnson, R. B.; Neumann, E. S. and Trail, G. T. eds. Molière and the commonwealth of letters: patrimony and posterity p271-75

Nicoll, A. From tragedy to melodrama. *In* Nicoll, A. World drama p342-69

Ryder, F. G. Lessing on liberty: the literary work as autobiography. *In* Studies in eighteenth-century culture v6 p229-44

Sjogren, C. O. The status of women in several of Lessing's dramas. *In* Studies in eighteenth-century culture v6 p347-59

About individual works

Abhandlungen über die Fabel

Noel, T. Lessing's Aesopian fables and the anti-Lessing. *In* Noel, T. Theories of the fable in the eighteenth century p85-101

The education of the human race

Allison, H. E. Lessing's conception of revelation as education. *In* Studies in eighteenth-century culture v4 p183-93

Influence—Herder

Noel, T. Herder and the romantic turn. *In* Noel, T. Theories of the fable in the eighteenth century p122-39

Lester, David
The use of the telephone in counseling and crisis intervention. *In* The Social impact of the telephone p454-72

Lester, Marianne
Profits, politics, power: the heart of the controversy. *In* Horowitz, I. L. ed. Science, sin, and scholarship p148-59

Lester, Richard Allen

About individual works

Antibias regulation of universities

Hook, S. The bias in anti-bias regulations. *In* Gross, B. R. ed. Reverse discrimination p88-96

Lesthaeghe, Ron, and Van de Walle, Etienne
Economic factors and fertility decline in France and Belgium. *In* Economic factors in population growth p205-28

Le Sueur, Jean François

About

Dent, E. J. The school of Paris—II. *In* Dent, E. J. The rise of romantic opera p64-79

Dent, E. J. The school of Paris—III. *In* Dent, E. J. The rise of romantic opera p80-94

Lesy, Michael, comp.

About individual works

Wisconsin death trip

Gass, W. H. Wisconsin death trip. *In* Gass, W. H. The world within the word p39-44

Letelier, Jenaro Prieto. See Prieto, Jenaro

Lethaby, William Richard

About

Watkin, D. The theme in the twentieth century: Lethaby. *In* Watkin, D. Morality and architecture p33-37

Letiche, John M.
Dependent monetary systems and economic development: the case of sterling East Africa. *In* Economic development and planning p186-236

Letman, Sloan T.
Some sociological aspects of terror-violence in a colonial setting. *In* International terrorism and political crimes p33-42

Letter pictures. See Concrete poetry

Letter-writing

History

Constable, G. The structure of medieval society according to the dictatores of the twelfth century. *In* Law, church, and society p253-67

Letters. See English letters; Latin letters; and similar headings

Letters, English. See English letters

Letters in literature
Jeffrey, D. K. The epistolary format of Pamela and Humphry Clinker. *In* A Provision of human nature p145-54

Letters of obscure men
Schäffer, P. Letters of obscure men. *In* Hoffmeister, G. ed. The Renaissance and Reformation in Germany p129-40

Lettvin, Jerome Y.
The Gorgon's eye. *In* Brecher, K. and Feirtag, M. eds. Astronomy of the ancients p133-51

Letwin, Shirley Robin

The achievement of Friedrich A. Hayek. *In* Essays on Hayek p147-67

Nature, history and morality. *In* Royal Institute of Philosophy. Nature and conduct p229-50

Leucadia, Macedonia. See Naousa, Greece

Leuchtenburg, William Edward

The American perception of the Arab world. *In* Arab and American cultures p15-25

The White House and Black America: from Eisenhower to Carter. *In* Have we overcome? Race relations since Brown p121-45

Leuilliot, Paul

Frédéric Zuber's visits to England. 1834-41. *In* Great Britain and her world, 1750-1914 p87-98

A manifesto: the defense and illustration of local history. *In* Rural society in France p6-30

Leukadia, Macedonia. See Naousa, Greece

Leukemia

Personal narratives

Jaffe, L. and Jaffe, A. Terminal candor and the coda syndrome: a tandem view of fatal illness. *In* Feifel, H. [ed.] New meanings of death p195-211

Leukemia, Radiation-induced

Sternglass, E. J. Nuclear radiation and human health. *In* Against pollution and hunger p121-79

Leukemia in children

Bluebond-Langner, M. I know, do you? A study of awareness, communication, and coping in terminally ill children. *In* Anticipatory grief p171-81

Comerford, B. Parental anticipatory grief and guidelines for caregivers. *In* Anticipatory grief p147-57

Kerney, L. G. The ministry and a parents' sharing group: preliminary report. *In* Anticipatory grief p315-19

Levanda, Lev Osipovich

About

Perlmann, M. Levanda's last year. *In* Salo Wittmayer Baron v2 p717-24

Levant. See Near East

LeVee, Luella Nash

Per ardua ad astra. *In* Frost: centennial essays III p83-104

Levellers

George, C. H. Gerrard Winstanley: a critical retrospect. *In* The Dissenting tradition p191-225

Heinemann, M. Popular drama and Leveller style—Richard Overton and John Harris. *In* Rebels and their causes p69-92

Hill, J. E. C. From Lollards to Levellers. *In* Rebels and their causes p49-67

Levenson, Jacob Clavner

Remarks at the memorial service in Cambridge, April 25, 1969. *In* Meisner, M. J. and Murphey, R. eds. The Mozartian historian p47-49

Levenson, Jill L.

Shakespeare's Troilus and Cressida and the monumental tradition in tapestries and literature. *In* Renaissance drama [1976] p43-84

See also Lancashire, A. B. jt. auth.

Levenson, Joseph Richmond

The choice of Jewish identity. *In* Meisner, M. J. and Murphey, R. eds. The Mozartian historian p180-93

About

Croizier, R. C. China's worlds: cosmopolitanism, nationalism, and the "problem of Chinese identity." *In* Meisner, M. J. and Murphey, R. eds. The Mozartian historian p157-74

Fairbank, J. K. J.R.L.—getting started. *In* Meisner, M. J. and Murphey, R. eds. The Mozartian historian p27-42

Keene, D. Remarks at the memorial service in Berkeley, April 13, 1969. *In* Meisner, M. J. and Murphey, R. eds. The Mozartian historian p43-46

Levenson, J. C. Remarks at the memorial service in Cambridge, April 25, 1969. *In* Meisner, M. J. and Murphey, R. eds. The Mozartian historian p47-49

McDonald, A. The historian's quest. *In* Meisner, M. J. and Murphey, R. eds. The Mozartian historian p76-88

Schurmann, H. F. Joseph Levenson on China and the world. *In* Meisner, M. J. and Murphey, R. eds. The Mozartian historian p58-75

Schwartz, B. I. History and culture in the thought of Joseph Levenson. *In* Meisner, M. J. and Murphey, R. eds. The Mozartian historian p100-12

Spence, J. D. Tensions. *In* Meisner, M. J. and Murphey, R. eds. The Mozartian historian p113-22

Van Slyke, L. P. Joseph Levenson's approach to history. *In* Meisner, M. J. and Murphey, R. eds. The Mozartian historian p91-99

About individual works

The choice of Jewish identity

Levenson, R. Notes on "The choice of Jewish identity." *In* Meisner, M. J. and Murphey, R. eds. The Mozartian historian p177-79

Confucian China and its modern fate

Kahn, H. L. An unreconstructed review of Levenson's trilogy. *In* Meisner, M. J. and Murphey, R. eds. The Mozartian historian p50-57

Confucian China and its modern fate v 1 The problem of intellectual continuity

Cahill, J. F. Style as idea in Ming-Ch'ing painting. *In* Meisner, M. J. and Murphey, R. eds. The Mozartian historian p137-56

Confucian China and its modern fate v 2 The problem of monarchical decay

Wakeman, F. E. A note on the development of the theme of bureaucratic-monarchic tension in Joseph R. Levenson's work. *In* Meisner, M. J. and Murphey, R. eds. The Mozartian historian p123-33

Levenson, Rosemary

Notes on "The choice of Jewish identity." *In* Meisner, M. J. and Murphey, R. eds. The Mozartian historian p177-79

Leventhal, Herbert, and Mooney, James E. (eds.)

A bibliography of loyalist source material in the United States, Part I. *In* American Antiquarian Society. Proceedings v85 pt 1 p73-308

Leventhal, Herbert, and Mooney, James E.
—*Continued*

A bibliography of loyalist source material in the United States, Part II. *In* American Antiquarian Society. Proceedings v85 pt2 p405-60

A bibliography of loyalist source material in the United States, Part III. *In* American Antiquarian Society. Proceedings v86 pt2 p343-90

Lever, Charles James

About

Sutherland, J. A. Lever and Ainsworth: missing the first rank. *In* Sutherland, J. A. Victorian novelists and publishers p152-65

About individual works
Lord Kilgobbin

Jeffares, A. N. Lever's 'Lord Kilgobbin.' *In* English Association. Essays and studies, 1975 p47-57

Lever, Julius Walter

Shakespeare and the ideas of his time. *In* Shakespeare survey v29 p79-91

Levere, Trevor H.

The rich economy of nature: chemistry in the nineteenth century. *In* Knoepflmacher, U. C. and Tennyson, G. B. eds. Nature and the Victorian imagination p189-200

Levertov, Denise

Some notes on organic form; excerpt from "The poet in the world." *In* Gibbons, R. ed. The poet's work: 29 masters of 20th century poetry on the origins and practice of their art p254-59

About

Altieri, C. F. Denise Levertov and the limits of the aesthetics of presence. *In* Altieri, C. F. Enlarging the temple p225-44

Blau DuPlessis, R. The critique of consciousness and myth in Levertov, Rich, and Rukeyser. *In* Gilbert, S. M. and Gubar, S. eds. Shakespeare's sisters p280-300

Thurley, G. Phenomenalist idioms: Doolittle, Moore, Levertov. *In* Thurley, G. The American moment p109-25

About individual works
O taste and see

Harris, V. The incorporative consciousness: Levertov's journey from discretion to unity. *In* Kagle, S. E. ed. America: exploration and travel p166-90

Levey, Martin

Methodology and the history of science. *In* Essays on Islamic philosophy and science p136-46

Levi ben Gershon

About individual works
Milhamot hashem

Feldman, S. N. O. Platonic themes in Gersonides' cosmology. *In* Salo Wittmayer Baron v 1 p383-405

Levi, Anthony Herbert Tigar

Erasmus, the early Jesuits and the classics. *In* Classical influences on European culture A.D. 1500-1700 p223-38

Ethics and the encyclopedia in the sixteenth century. *In* French Renaissance studies, 1540-70 p170-84

Levi, Carlo

About

Pacifici, S. Carlo Levi: the essayist as novelist. *In* Pacifici, S. The modern Italian novel: from Pea to Moravia p90-98

Levi, Rozita

Cuba and the nonaligned movement. *In* Cuba in the world p147-51

Levi, Werner

Are developing states more equal than others? *In* The Year book of world affairs, 1978 p286-302

Lévi-Strauss, Claude

Race and history. *In* United Nations Educational, Scientific and Cultural Organization. Race, science and society p95-134

About

Derrida, J. Structure, sign and play in the discourse of the human sciences. *In* Derrida, J. Writing and difference p278-93

Girard, R. Differentiation and reciprocity in Lévi-Strauss and contemporary theory. *In* Girard, R. "To double business bound" p155-77

Same as Gerard, R. Differentiation and undifferentiation in Lévi-Strauss and current critical theory. *In* Krieger, M. and Dembo, L. S. eds. Directions for criticism p111-36

About individual works
The raw and the cooked

Girard, R. Violence and representation in the mythical text. *In* Girard, R. "To double business bound" p178-98

Totemism

Girard, R. Violence and representation in the mythical text. *In* Girard, R. "To double business bound" p178-98

Leviant, Curt

Jewish influence upon Arthurian legends. *In* Salo Wittmayer Baron v2 p639-56

Levin, Arthur A.

Andrey Bely, M. O. Gershenzon, and Vekhi: a rejoinder to N. Valentinov. *In* Janecek, G. ed. Andrey Bely p169-80

Levin, David Michael

Husserl's notion of self-evidence. *In* Pivčević, E. ed. Phenomenology and philosophical understanding p53-77

Levin, Harry

Excursus: the example of Cervantes: the novel as parody. *In* Wimsatt, W. K. ed. Literary criticism: idea and act p330-45

Shakespeare's misanthrope. *In* Shakespeare survey 26 p89-94

The uncles of Dickens. *In* The Worlds of Victorian fiction p 1-35

About individual works
The overreacher, a study of Christopher Marlowe

Berryman, J. Marlowe's damnations. *In* Berryman, J. The freedom of the poet p3-8

The power of blackness

Marcus, S. Three obsessed critics. *In* Marcus, S. Representations p102-17

Levin, Henry M.

Education and earnings of Blacks and the Brown decision. *In* Have we overcome? Race relations since Brown p79-119

Levin, Kim

The ersatz object. *In* Battcock, G. ed. Super realism p96-110

Malcolm Morley: post-style illusionism. *In* Battcock, G. ed. Super realism p170-86

Levin, Martin

Ask not what our presidents are "really like"; ask what we and our political institutions are like: a call for a politics of institutions, not men. *In* Burnham, W. D. and Weinberg, M. W. eds. American politics and public policy p109-39

Levin, Meyer

About individual works
Compulsion

Filler, L. Meyer Levin's Compulsion. *In* Filler, L. ed. A question of quality: popularity and value in modern creative writing p148-59

Levin, Samuel R.

Standard approaches to metaphor and a proposal for literary metaphor. *In* Ortony, A. ed. Metaphor and thought p124-35

About

Hill, A. A. Two views of poetic language and meaning: the poem as cryptogram and as example of deviant grammar. *In* Hill, A. A. Constituent and pattern in poetry p115-22

Levinas, Emmanuel

Ideology and idealism. *In* Modern Jewish ethics p121-38

About

Derrida, J. Violence and metaphysics: an essay on the thought of Emmanuel Levinas. *In* Derrida, J. Writing and difference p79-153

About individual works
Ideology and idealism

Weiss, A. Ethics as transcendence and the contemporary world: a response to Emmanuel Levinas. *In* Modern Jewish ethics p139-52

Levine, Daniel H.

Venezuela since 1958: the consolidation of democratic politics. *In* The Breakdown of democratic regimes p3 p82-109

Levine, Daniel U.

Urban teaching training. *In* Murphy, T. P. ed. Universities in the urban crisis p259-84

Levine, Donald Nathan

Simmel at a distance: on the history and systematics of the sociology of the stranger. *In* Shack, W. A. and Skinner, E. P. eds. Strangers in African societies p21-36

Levine, George Lewis

The ambiguous heritage of Frankenstein. *In* Levine, G. L. and Knoepflmacher, U. C. eds. The endurance of Frankenstein p3-30

High and low: Ruskin and the novelists. *In* Knoepflmacher, U. C. and Tennyson, G. B. eds. Nature and the Victorian imagination p137-52

Levine, Herbert M.

Summary of proceedings. *In* Arms control and technological innovation p11-35

Levine, Jo Ann

Three in enterprise. *In* Gross, B. and Gross, R. eds. The children's rights movement p283-86

Levine, Madeline Geltman

Orpheus in exile: some reflections on Tuwim's Kwiaty polskie. *In* For Wiktor Weintraub p267-75

Levine, Philip, 1928-

About

Mills, R. J. "The true and earthy prayer": Philip Levine's poetry. *In* Mills, R. J. Cry of the human p251-65

Levine, Robert

The pearl-child: topos and archetype in the Middle English Pearl. *In* Medievalia et humanistica no. 8 p243-51

LeVine, Robert Alan

Anthropology and sex: developmental aspects. *In* Katchadourian, H. A. ed. Human sexuality p309-19

Le Vine, Victor T.

Political integration and the United Republic of Cameroon. *In* Smock, D. R. and Bentsi-Enchill, K. eds. The search for national integration in Africa p270-84

Levitan, William

Plexed artistry: Aratean acrostics. *In* Glyph 5 p55-68

Levitation

Ducasse, C. J. The philosophical importance of "psychic phenomena." *In* Ludwig, J. K. ed. Philosophy and parapsychology p128-41

Also in Wheatley, J. M. O. and Edge, H. L. eds. Philosophical dimensions of parapsychology p30-45

Levith, Murray Jay

Edwin M. Moseley. *In* Renaissance and modern p vii-x

Juliet's question and Shakespeare's names. *In* Renaissance and modern p21-32

Leviton, Daniel

Death education. *In* Feifel, H. [ed.] New meanings of death p253-72

Levitt, Annette S.

Roger Vitrac and the drama of surrealism. *In* Aeolian harps p247-72

Levitt, Morton

That bouillabaisse: medical school admissions. *In* Hurdles p239-67

Le Vot, André

New modes of story-telling in recent American writings: the dismantling of contemporary fiction. *In* Johnson, I. D. and Johnson, C. [eds.] Les américanistes p110-29

Levy, Bernard Isaac. See Ulman, E. jt. auth.

Levy, David

The ethical life and the political life. *In* Viva Vivas! p65-86

Levy, Frank

What Ronald Reagan can teach the United States about welfare reform. *In* Burnham, W. D. and Weinberg, M. W. eds. American politics and public policy p336-63

Levý, Jiří

The translation of verbal art. *In* Matejka, L. and Titunik, I. R. eds. Semiotics of art p218-28

Levy, Laurie

Outside the bell jar. *In* Butscher, E. ed. Sylvia Plath p42-48

Levy, Marion Joseph

Clarence E. Ayres as a university teacher. *In* Science and ceremony p181-86

Levy, Paul

The Bloomsbury group. *In* Keynes, M. ed. Essays on John Maynard Keynes p60-72

Levy, Robert Isaac

A conjunctive pattern in middle class informal and formal education. *In* Schwartz, T. ed. Socialization as cultural communication p177-87

Tahitian gentleness and redundant controls. *In* Montague, A. ed. Learning non-aggression p222-35

Levy, Walter James

An Atlantic-Japanese energy policy. *In* The New Atlantic challenge p119-49

World oil cooperation or international chaos. *In* Bundy, W. P. ed. The world economic crisis p206-29

Lewalski, Barbara Kiefer

Protestant poetics and the seventeenth-century religious lyric

Contents

Art and the sacred subject: sermon theory, Biblical personae, and Protestant poetics

Biblical genre theory: precepts and models for the religious lyric

The Biblical symbolic mode: typology and the religious lyric

Edward Taylor:lisps of praise and strategies for self-dispraise

George Herbert: artful psalms from the temple in the heart

Henry Vaughan: pleading in groans of my Lord's penning

"Is there in truth no beautie?" Protestant poetics and the Protestant paradigm of salvation

John Donne: writing after the copy of a metaphorical God

The poetic texture of scripture: tropes and figures for the religious lyric

Protestant emblematics: sacred emblems and religious lyrics

Protestant meditation: kinds, structures, and strategies of development for the meditative lyric

Thomas Traherne: naked truth, transparent words, and the renunciation of metaphor

Typology and poetry: a consideration of Herbert, Vaughan, and Marvell. *In* Illustrious evidence p41-69

Typological symbolism and the "progress of the soul" in seventeenth-century literature. *In* Miner, E. R. ed. Literary uses of typology p79-114

Lewes, George Henry

About

Baker, W. Leigh Hunt, George Henry Lewes and Henry Hallam's Introduction to the literature of Europe. *In* Virginia. University. Bibliographical Society. Studies in bibliography v32 p252-73

Haight, G. S. The Carlyles and the Leweses. *In* Carlyle and his contemporaries p181-204

Lewin, Moshe

The social background of Stalinism. *In* Stalinism p111-36

Society, state, and ideology during the First Five-Year Plan. *In* Cultural revolution in Russia, 1928-1931 p41-77

'Taking grain': Soviet policies of agricultural procurements before the War. *In* Essays in honour of E. H. Carr p281-323

Lewis, Alun

About

Scannell, V. Alun Lewis. *In* Scannell, V. Not without glory p52-73

Lewis, Archibald Ross

Northern European sea power and the Straits of Gibraltar, 1031-1350 A.D. *In* Order and innovation in the Middle Ages p139-64

Lewis, Barbara Caroline

Economic activity and marriage among Ivoirian urban women. *In* Schlegel, A. E. ed. Sexual stratification p161-91

Lewis, Bernard

The African diaspora and the civilization of Islam. *In* Kilson, M. L. and Rotberg, R. I. eds. The African diaspora p37-56

An anti-Jewish ode: the qasida of Abu Ishaq against Joseph ibn Nagrella. *In* Salo Wittmayer Baron v2 p657-68

Epilogue. *In* Lewis, B. ed. Islam and the Arab world p345-47

The faith and the faithful. *In* Lewis, B. ed. Islam and the Arab world p25-56

Gibbon on Muhammad. *In* Edward Gibbon and The decline and fall of the Roman Empire p61-73

Lewis, Carolyn Baker

Agricultural evolution on secondary frontiers: a Florida model. *In* The Frontier v2 p205-33

Lewis, Cecil Day- See Day-Lewis, Cecil

Lewis, Clive Staples

On science fiction; excerpt from "Of other worlds: essays and stories." *In* Knight, D. F. ed. Turning points p119-31

About

Hooper, W. Narnia: the author, the critics, and the tale. *In* Schakel, P. J. ed. The longing for a form p105-18

Huttar, C. A. C. S. Lewis' Narnia and the "grand design." *In* Schakel, P. J. ed. The longing for a form p119-35

Manlove, C. N. C. S. Lewis (1898-1963) and Perelandra. *In* Manlove, C. N. Modern fantasy p99-151

Oury, R. S. "The thing itself": C. S. Lewis and the value of something other. *In* Schakel, P. J. ed. The longing for a form p 1-19

Schumaker, W. The cosmic trilogy of C. S. Lewis. *In* Schakel, P. J. ed. The longing for a form p51-63

Tixier, E. Imagination baptized, or "Holiness" in the chronicles of Narnia. *In* Schakel, P. J. ed. The longing for a form p136-58

Zogby, E. G. Triadic patterns in Lewis's life and thought. *In* Schakel, P. J. ed. The longing for a form p20-39

About individual works

Out of the silent planet

Walsh, C. The reeducation of the fearful pilgrim. *In* Schakel, P. J. ed. The longing for a form p64-72

Perelandra

Hannay, M. P. A preface to Perelandra. *In* Schakel, P. J. ed. The longing for a form p73-90

Manlove, C. N. C. S. Lewis (1898-1963) and Perelandra. *In* Manlove, C. N. Modern fantasy p99-151

The silver chair

Cox, J. D. Epistemological release in The silver chair. *In* Schakel, P. J. ed. The longing for a form p159-68

That hideous strength

Purtill, R. L. That hideous strength: a double story. *In* Schakel, P. J. ed. The longing for a form p91-102

Lewis, Clive S.—About individual works
—*Continued*

Till we have faces

Christopher, J. R. Archetypal patterns in Till we have faces. *In* Schakel, P. J. ed. The longing for a form p193-212

Kilby, C. S. Till we have faces: an interpretation. *In* Schakel, P. J. ed. The longing for a form p171-81

Van Der Weele, S. J. From Mt. Olympus to Glome: C. S. Lewis's dislocation of Apuleius's "Cupid and Psyche" in Till we have faces. *In* Schakel, P. J. ed. The longing for a form p182-92

Lewis, David B.

Languages, language, and grammar. *In* Harman, G. ed. On Noam Chomsky p253-66

Lewis, David K.

Psychophysical and theoretical identifications. *In* Philosophical aspects of the mind-body problem p43-53

Survival and identity. *In* Rorty, A. O. ed. The identities of persons p17-40

About individual works
Survival and identity

Parfit, D. Lewis, Perry, and what matters. *In* Rorty, A. O. ed. The identities of persons p91-107

Lewis, Douglas

On the aims and method of Spinoza's philosophy. *In* Shahan, R. W. and Biro, J. I. eds. Spinoza: new perspectives p217-34

The Washington relief of Peace and its pendant. *In* Collaboration in Italian Renaissance art p233-44

Lewis, Geneviève Rodis- See Rodis-Lewis, Geneviève

Lewis, Gilbert Newton

About

Kohler, R. E. The Lewis-Langmuir theory of valence and the chemical community, 1920-1928. *In* Historical studies in the physical sciences v6 p431-68

Stuewer, R. H. G. N. Lewis on detailed balancing, the symmetry of time, and the nature of light. *In* Historical studies in the physical sciences v6 p469-511

Lewis, Gwynn

The White Terror of 1815 in the department of the Gard: counter-revolution, continuity and the individual. *In* French society and the Revolution p286-313

Lewis, Hanna Ballin

Molière and Hofmannsthal. *In* Johnson, R. B.; Neumann, E. S. and Trail, G. T. eds. Molière and the commonwealth of letters: patrimony and posterity p345-51

Lewis, Henry Taliaferro, supposed author.
See The harp of a thousand strings

Lewis, Hywel David

The elusive self and practice. *In* The Personal universe p64-73

Immortality and dualism. *In* Reason and religion p282-300

Religion and the paranormal. *In* Thakur, S. C. ed. Philosophy and psychical research p142-56

Lewis, I. M.

The nation, state, and politics in Somalia. *In* Smock, D. R. and Bentsi-Enchill, K. eds. The search for national integration in Africa p285-306

Lewis, John

The fantasy world of Sidney Sime. *In* The Saturday book 34 p202-15

Lewis, John S.

The outer planets. *In* Man and cosmos p117-30

Lewis, Kenneth E.

An archaeological perspective on social change—the Virginia frontier. *In* Miller, D. H. and Steffen, J. O. eds. The frontier p139-59

Lewis, Mary Christianna (Milne)

Miss Marple—a portrait. *In* Agatha Christie: first lady of crime p193-204

Lewis, Matthew Gregory

About

Berryman, J. The monk and its author. *In* Berryman, J. The freedom of the poet p129-43

About individual works
The monk

Berryman, J. The monk and its author. *In* Berryman, J. The freedom of the poet p129-43

Howells, C. A. M. G. Lewis, The monk. *In* Howells, C. A. Love, mystery, and misery p62-79

Madoff, M. The useful myth of Gothic ancestry. *In* Studies in eighteenth-century culture v8 p337-50

Lewis, Maureen Warner

The African impact on language and literature in the English-speaking Caribbean. *In* Crahan, M. E. and Knight, F. W. eds. Africa and the Caribbean p101-23

Lewis, Michael, and Lee-Painter, Susan

The origin of interactions: methodological issues. *In* Riegel, K. F. and Rosenwald, G. C. eds. Structure and transformation p119-31

Lewis, Naphtali

Two Greek documents from provincia Arabia. *In* Illinois classical studies v3, 1978 p100-14

Lewis, P. B.

Wittgenstein on seeing and interpreting. *In* Royal Institute of Philosophy. Impressions of empiricism p93-108

Lewis, Peter Shervey

Of Breton alliances and other matters. *In* War, literature, and politics in the late Middle Ages p122-43

Lewis, Robert A. and Rowland, Richard H.

Urbanization in Russia and the USSR, 1897-1970. *In* Hamm, M. F. ed. The city in Russian history p205-21

Lewis, Robert William

Hemingway's concept of sport and "Soldier's home." *In* Benson, J. J. ed. The short stories of Ernest Hemingway: critical essays p170-80

Lewis, Roger

Captain America meets the Bash Street Kids: the comic form in Britain and the United States. *In* Bigsby, C. W. E. Superculture p175-89

Lewis, Sinclair

About

Farrell, J. T. Sinclair Lewis. *In* Farrell, J. T. Literary essays, 1954-1974 p65-69

Holman, C. H. Anodyne for the village virus. *In* Holman, C. H. Windows on the world p48-60

Lewis, Sinclair—About—_Continued_

Hyman, S. E. Anthropologist of Gopher Prairie. _In_ Hyman, S. E. The critic's credentials p97-101

Marcus, S. Sinclair Lewis. _In_ Marcus, S. Representations p41-60

Milne, G. Practitioners, 1920-1960. _In_ Milne, G. The sense of society p205-35

About individual works
Babbitt

Pugh, D. G. Baedekers, Babbittry, and Baudelaire. _In_ French, W. G. ed. The twenties p87-99

Main Street

Goist, P. D. The ideal questioned but not abandoned: Sherwood Anderson, Sinclair Lewis, and Floyd Dell. _In_ Goist, P. D. From Main Street to State Street p21-34

Watkins, F. C. Main Street: culture through the periscope of ego. _In_ Watkins, F. C. In time and place p193-213

Lewis, Suzanne

Problems of architectural style and the Ambrosian liturgy in late fourth-century Milan. _In_ Enggass, R. C. and Stokstad, M. eds. Hortus imaginum p11-19

Lewis, Tayler

About

Greene, J. C. Science and religion. _In_ The Rise of Adventism p50-69

Lewis, Walter David

Technology, community, and humanity: the big picture. _In_ Lewis, W. D. and Griessman, B. E. eds. The Southern mystique p15-32

Lewis, Warren Harmon

About

Harvey, A. M. Johns Hopkins—the birthplace of tissue culture: the story of Ross G. Harrison, Warren H. Lewis, and George O. Gey. _In_ Harvey, A. M. Adventures in medical research p114-23

Lewis, Sir William Arthur

The diffusion of development. _In_ The Market and the state p135-56

Lewis, Wilmarth Sheldon

Edmond Malone, Horace Walpole, and Shakespeare. _In_ Evidence in literary scholarship p353-62

A house-party at Stowe. _In_ The Dress of words p117-25

Lewis, Wyndham

Enemy salvoes

Contents

André Malraux
Camus and Sartre
Cervantes
Charles Péguy
D. H. Lawrence
'Detachment' and the writer
Ernest Hemingway
The external approach to writing
Ezra Pound
George Bernard Shaw
George Orwell
Gertrude Stein
Gustave Flaubert
Henry James
James Joyce
The machine poets
Matthew Arnold

Russian novelists and Trollope
The Russians
Satire defended
Shakespeare
Sherwood Anderson
The solitary outlaw
T. S. Eliot and I. A. Richards
The Transition writers
Truth and the writer's freedom
Virginia Woolf
The war writers
William Faulkner

About

Frye, N. Neoclassical agony. _In_ Frye, N. Northrop Frye on culture and literature p178-87

Glicksberg, C. I. Wyndham Lewis: the reactionary artist and his commitment. _In_ Glicksberg, C. I. The literature of commitment p84-99

Pritchard, W. H. The literature of criticism. _In_ Pritchard, W. H. Seeing through everything p134-53

About individual works
The revenge for love

Pritchard, W. H. Satire and fiction: examples from the 1930s. _In_ Pritchard, W. H. Seeing through everything p178-208

Self condemned

Russell, J. D. Wyndham Lewis: Tarr, Self condemned. _In_ Russell, J. D. Style in modern British fiction p123-57

Tarr

Russell, J. D. Wyndham Lewis: Tarr, Self condemned. _In_ Russell, J. D. Style in modern British fiction p123-57

Contemporaries

See Lewis, Wyndham—Friends and associates

Friends and associates

Holroyd, M. Damn and 'blast'! the friendship of Wyndham Lewis and Augustus John. _In_ Royal Society of Literature of the United Kingdom, London. Essays by divers hands v38 p48-57

Poetic works

Spender, S. Wyndham Lewis as poet. _In_ Spender, S. The thirties and after p23-25

Lewis and Clark Expedition

Allen, J. L. Thomas Jefferson and the passage to India: a pre-exploratory image. _In_ Pattern and process p103-13

Lewontin, Richard Charles

Darwin and Mendel—the materialist revolution. _In_ Neyman, J. ed. The heritage of Copernicus: theories "pleasing to the mind" p166-83

Race and intelligence. _In_ Montagu, A. ed. Race and IQ p175-91

Lexicography

Nida, E. A.; Louw, J. P. and Smith, R. B. Semantic domains and componential analysis of meaning. _In_ Current issues in linguistic theory p139-67

Data processing

Cassidy, F. G. Use of computers in one lexicographical project: DARE. _In_ James B. McMillan: essays in linguistics by his friends and colleagues p133-42

Lexicology

Fillmore, C. J. Topics in lexical semantics. *In* Current issues in linguistic theory p76-138

Nida, E. A.; Louw, J. P. and Smith, R. B. Semantic domains and componential analysis of meaning. *In* Current issues in linguistic theory p139-67

See also Language and languages—Etymology

Ley, Ralph J.

Francis Bacon, Galileo, and the Brechtian theater. *In* Mews, S. and Knust, H. eds. Essays on Brecht p174-89

Leyerle, John

The game and play of hero. *In* Concepts of the hero in the Middle Ages and the Renaissance p49-82

The heart and the chain. *In* The Learned and the lewed p113-45

Thematic interlace in 'The Canterbury tales.' *In* English Association. Essays and studies, 1976 p107-21

Leymarie, Jean

Malraux and the creative process. *In* Courcel, M. H. de, ed. Malraux p184-203

Leys, Wayne Albert Risser

Political and moral pluralism. *In* The Abdication of philosophy: philosophy and the public good p93-107

Lezama Lima, José

About individual works

Paradiso

Adams, R. M. Counterparts. *In* Adams, R. M. Afterjoyce p162-93

MacAdam, A. J. Juan Carlos Onetti & José Lezama Lima: a double portrait of the artist. *In* MacAdam, A. J. Modern Latin American narratives p102-09

Lhombreaud, Roger

About individual works

Arthur Symons, a critical biography

Connolly, C. Arthur Symons. *In* Connolly, C. The evening colonnade p155-58

Li, Chu-tsing

The uses of the past in Yüan landscape painting. *In* Artists and traditions p73-88

Li, Ju-chên

About individual works

Ching hua yuan

Hsia, Chih-tsing. The scholar-novelist and Chinese culture: a reappraisal of Ching-hua yuan. *In* Chinese narrative p266-305

Li, Kung-lin

About

Barnhart, R. Li Kung-lin's use of past styles. *In* Artists and traditions p51-71

Li, Peter

Narrative patterns in San-kuo and Shui-hu. *In* Chinese narrative p73-84

Li, Victor Hai

China and off-shore oil: the Tiao-yü dispute. *In* China's changing role in the world economy p143-62

Human rights in a Chinese context. *In* Terrill, R. ed. The China difference p219-35

Politics and health care in China: the barefoot doctors. *In* Stanford legal essays p303-16

Liang, Chi

About

Lin, Yü-sheng. The suicide of Liang Chi: an ambiguous case of moral conservatism. *In* The Limits of change p151-68

Liang, Ch'i-ch'ao

About

Grieder, J. B. Liang Ch'i-ch'ao and Hu Shih. *In* Abroad in America: Visitors to the new Nation, 1776-1914 p279-92

Hsia, Chih-tsing. Yen Fu and Liang Ch'i-ch'ao as advocates of new fiction. *In* Chinese approaches to literature from Confucius to Liang Ch'i-ch'ao p221-57

Liang, Shu-ming

About

Alitto, G. The conservative as sage: Liang Shu-ming. *In* The Limits of change p213-41

Liapunov, Vadim

Limbo and the sharashka. *In* Dunlop, J. B.; Haugh, R. and Klimoff, A. eds. Aleksandr Solzhenitsyn: critical essays and documentary materials 2d ed. p231-40

Libby, Willard Frank

Radiocarbon dating. *In* The Frontiers of knowledge p325-58

Libel and slander

See also Liberty of speech

Great Britain

Brustein, R. S. Reflections on privacy. *In* Brustein, R. S. The culture watch p59-63

Liber epigrammatum heroico metro; excerpt from Urbanesis (MS)

Wallach, L. The Urbana Anglo-Saxon sylloge of Latin inscriptions. *In* Poetry and poetics from ancient Greece to the Renaissance p134-51

Liberal education. See Education, Humanistic

Liberal Judaism. See Reform Judaism

Liberal Party (Great Britain)

Arnold, M. The nadir of liberalism. *In* Arnold, M. The last word p54-77

Campbell, J. The renewal of liberalism: liberalism without Liberals. *In* Peele, G. and Cook, C. eds. The politics of reappraisal, 1918-1939 p88-113

Cook, C. Labour and the downfall of the Liberal Party, 1906-14. *In* Crisis and controversy p38-65

Cook, C. Liberals, Labour and local elections. *In* Peele, G. and Cook, C. eds. The politics of reappraisal, 1918-1939 p166-88

Grigg, J. Liberals on trial. *In* Crisis and controversy p23-37

Liberalism

Bay, C. From contract to community: thoughts on liberalism and postindustrial society. *In* Dallmayr, F. R. ed. From contract to community p29-45

Howe, I. Literature and liberalism. *In* Howe, I. Celebrations and attacks p239-54

Ketchum, S. A. Liberalism and marriage law. *In* Feminism and philosophy p264-76

Lippmann, W. The good society; excerpt. *In* Crunden, R. M. ed. The superfluous men p238-48

Rahv, P. Liberal anticommunism revisited. *In* Rahv, P. Essays on literature and politics, 1932-1972 p341-45

See also Laissez-faire

Liberty of information. See Freedom of information

Liberty of religion. See Religious liberty

Liberty of speech

Polsby, D. D. Buckley v. Valeo: the special nature of political speech. *In* The Supreme Court review, 1976 p 1-43

Schiro, R. Commercial speech: the demise of a chimera. *In* The Supreme Court review, 1976 p45-98

See also Freedom of information; Liberty of the press

Japan

Beer, L. W. Freedom of expression in Japan with comparative reference to the United States. *In* Claude, R. P. ed. Comparative human rights p99-126

United States

Arkes, H. P. Civility and the restriction of speech: rediscovering the defamation of groups. *In* The Supreme Court review, 1974 p281-335

Bedau, H. A. Free speech, the right to listen, and disruptive interference. *In* The Concept of academic freedom p191-211

Bedau, H. A. Reply to Alan Pasch. *In* The Concept of academic freedom p217-25

Gunther, G. Learned Hand and the origins of modern first amendment doctrine: some fragments of history. *In* Stanford legal essays p195-249

Pasch, A. Comments on Bedau's "Free speech, the right to listen, and disruptive interference." *In* The Concept of academic freedom p212-16

Pasch, A. Comments on Bedau's reply. *In* The Concept of academic freedom p226-34

Stone, G. R. Fora Americana: speech in public places. *In* The Supreme Court review, 1974 p233-80

Liberty of the press

Blanchard, M. A. The institutional press and its First Amendment privileges. *In* The Supreme Court review, 1978 p225-96

Lewis, W. Truth and the writer's freedom; excerpt from "The writer and the absolute." *In* Lewis, W. Enemy salvoes p31-34

Lowenstein, R. L. Press freedom as a barometer of political democracy. *In* Fischer, H. D. and Merrill, J. C. eds. International and intercultural communication p136-47

Merrill, J. C. Freedom of the press: changing concept? *In* Fischer, H. D. and Merrill, J. C. eds. International and intercultural communication p125-35

Nixon, R. B. Factors related to freedom in national press systems. *In* Fischer, H. D. and Merrill, J. C. eds. International and intercultural communication p148-60

Royster, V. C. The American press and the Revolutionary tradition. *In* America's continuing revolution p205-25

Salomone, F. Terrorism and the mass media. *In* International terrorism and political crimes p43-46

See also Censorship; Freedom of information

India

Verghese, G. Press censorship under Indira Gandhi. *In* Horton, P. C. ed. The Third World and press freedom p220-30

Japan—History

Altman, A. A. Shinbunshi: the early Meiji adaptation of the Western-style newspaper. *In* Modern Japan p52-66

South Africa

Qoboza, P. Press censorship in South Africa. *In* Horton, P. C. ed. The Third World and press freedom p231-37

United States

Oakes, J. B. The responsibility of the press. *In* Tomorrow's American p171-88

Liberty of the will. See Free will and determinism

Librarians

New Mexico

Horgan, P. An amateur librarian. *In* Voices from the Southwest p65-75

Librarians, Education of. See Library education

Librarians, Training of. See Library education

Libraries

Foucault, M. Fantasia of the library. *In* Foucault, M. Language, counter-memory, practice p87-109

MacLeish, A. The premise at the center. *In* MacLeish, A. Riders on the earth p40-47

Censorship

Berninghausen, D. K. Asheim's liberal approach to intellectual freedom. *In* As much to learn as to teach p38-50

Federal aid

See Federal aid to libraries

History

Connolly, C. Great libraries. *In* Connolly, C. The evening colonnade p415-18

Law and legislation

See Library legislation

Europe—Influence

Liebaers, H. The impact of American and European librarianship upon each other. *In* Libraries and the life of the mind in America p67-83

United States

Boorstin, D. J. The indivisible community. *In* Libraries and the life of the mind in America p115-30

Cole, J. Y. Storehouses and workshops: American libraries and the uses of knowledge. *In* Oleson, A. and Voss, J. eds. The organization of knowledge in modern America, 1860-1920 p364-85

Molz, R. K. Libraries and the development and future of tax support. *In* Libraries and the life of the mind in America p41-63

Pilpel, H. F. Libraries and the First Amendment. *In* Libraries and the life of the mind in America p87-106

United States—History

Franklin, J. H. Libraries in a pluralistic society. *In* Libraries and the life of the mind in America p3-15

Lacy, D. M. Libraries and the freedom of access to information. *In* Libraries and the life of the mind in America p19-37

United States—Influence

Liebaers, H. The impact of American and European librarianship upon each other. *In* Libraries and the life of the mind in America p67-83

Libraries, International
Rayward, W. B. The literature of international and comparative librarianship. *In* As much to learn as to teach p217-35
Libraries, Private. See Book collectors
Libraries, State. See State libraries
Libraries, University and college

United States
Downs, R. B. Changing trends in academic libraries. *In* As much to learn as to teach p203-16
Libraries and adult education
Houle, C. O. Seven adult educational roles of the public library. *In* As much to learn as to teach p94-116
Libraries and community
Ihrig, A. B. Librarians and the political process. *In* As much to learn as to teach p83-93
See also Libraries and adult education
Libraries and education. See Libraries and adult education
Libraries and Mexican Americans
Trejo, A. D. Of books and libraries. *In* Trejo, A. D. ed. The Chicanos p167-86
Libraries and readers
McMullen, C. H. American librarians and the pursuit of happiness. *In* As much to learn as to teach p51-82
Libraries and society
Franklin, J. H. Libraries in a pluralistic society. *In* Libraries and the life of the mind in America p3-15
Holley, E. G. Library issues in the seventies. *In* As much to learn as to teach p25-37
Libraries and state. See Federal aid to libraries
Library adult education. See Libraries and adult education
Library censorship. See Libraries—Censorship
Library cooperation. See Libraries, International
Library education
Heim, K. M. Professional education: some comparisons. *In* As much to learn as to teach p128-76
Lieberman, I. Library education—changing goals. *In* As much to learn as to teach p177-202
Library legislation
Ihrig, A. B. Librarians and the political process. *In* As much to learn as to teach p83-93
See also Federal aid to libraries
Library of Congress. See United States. Library of Congress
Library resources
McMullen, C. H. American librarians and the pursuit of happiness. *In* As much to learn as to teach p51-82
Library school education. See Library education
Library science
See also Bibliography; Cataloging

Study and teaching
See Library education
Library science literature
Rayward, W. B. The literature of international and comparative librarianship. *In* As much to learn as to teach p217-35

Library use studies

United States
McMullen, C. H. American librarians and the pursuit of happiness. *In* As much to learn as to teach p51-82
Libretto
Josipovici, G. Words and music today. *In* Josipovici, G. The lessons of modernism p143-50
Libri Carolini
Henry, P. Images of the Church in the Second Nicene Council and in the Libri Carolini. *In* Law, church, and society p237-52
Wallach, L. Actus Silvestri, Libri Carolini and the Constantine Donation: the solution of a pseudo-problem. *In* Wallach, L. Diplomatic studies in Latin and Greek documents from the Carolingian age p152-59
Wallach, L. Alcuin as the author of the Libri Carolini: epilogue to Part III. *In* Wallach, L. Diplomatic studies in Latin and Greek documents from the Carolingian age p287-94
Wallach, L. Ambrosiaster and the Libri Carolini. *In* Wallach, L. Diplomatic studies in Latin and Greek documents from the Carolingian age p140-51
Wallach, L. The Libri Carolini and patristics, Latin and Greek. *In* Wallach, L. Diplomatic studies in Latin and Greek documents from the Carolingian age p59-122
Wallach, L. On "Spanish symptoms" in the Libri Carolini. *In* Wallach, L. Diplomatic studies in Latin and Greek documents from the Carolingian age p222-47
Wallach, L. Origin and composition of the Libri Carolini. *In* Wallach, L. Diplomatic studies in Latin and Greek documents from the Carolingian age p47-58
Wallach, L. The origins, corrections, and Tironian notes of the Vaticanus Latinus 7207. *In* Wallach, L. Diplomatic studies in Latin and Greek documents from the Carolingian age p187-208
Wallach, L. Philological and historical evidence disproving Theodulph of Orléans' alleged authorship. *In* Wallach, L. Diplomatic studies in Latin and Greek documents from the Carolingian age p248-71
Wallach, L. The textual history of a Greek Ambrose text: Libri Carolini II.15. *In* Wallach, L. Diplomatic studies in Latin and Greek documents from the Carolingian age p123-39
Wallach, L. Valid and invalid argumentation concerning "Spanish symptoms." *In* Wallach, L. Diplomatic studies in Latin and Greek documents from the Carolingian age p209-21
Wallach, L. The Vaticanus Latinus 7207 and paleographical problems. *In* Wallach, L. Diplomatic studies in Latin and Greek documents from the Carolingian age p165-86

Lichtenstadter, Ilse
Religion as a cultural and political factor in the Middle East—past and present. *In* The New world balance and peace in the Middle East: reality or mirage? p137-42

Lichtenstein, Aharon
Does Jewish tradition recognize an ethic independent of Halakha? *In* Modern Jewish ethics p62-88

Lichtenstein, David S.
The alienated intellectual and government bureaucracy. *In* Hook, S.; Kurtz, P. W. and Todorovich, M. eds. The university and the state: what role for government in higher education? p249-64

Lide, Barbara
Strindberg and Molière: parallels, influence, image. *In* Johnson, R. B.; Neumann, E. S. and Trail, G. T. eds. Molière and the commonwealth of letters: patrimony and posterity p259-68

Lidz, Theodore
The family, myth, and ethics. *In* Psychiatry and the humanities v 1 p173-90

Lidz, Victor M.
Secularization, ethical life, and religion in modern societies. *In* Johnson, H. M. ed. Religious change and continuity p191-217
See also Parsons, T. jt. auth. The "gift of life" and its reciprocation

Liebaers, Herman
The impact of American and European librarianship upon each other. *In* Libraries and the life of the mind in America p67-83

Liebenow, J. Gus
Africa in world affairs. *In* Martin, P. M. and O'Meara, P. eds. Africa p395-414

Lieberman, Irving
Library education—changing goals. *In* As much to learn as to teach p177-202

Lieberman, Jethro Koller
How to avoid lawyers. *In* Nader, R. and Green, M. J. eds. Verdicts on lawyers p105-17

Lieberman, Laurence
The church of ash. *In* Boyers, R. ed. Contemporary poetry in America p256-66
Same as: Lieberman, L. W. S. Merwin: the church of ash. *In* Unassigned frequencies p122-32

Unassigned frequencies

Contents

A. R. Ammons: of mind and world
David Wagoner: the cold speech of the earth
Derek Walcott and Michael S. Harper: the muse of history
Howard Moss: bitter and sweet, dread and desire
James Dickey: The deepening of being
James Dickey: The worldly mystic
James Wright: words of grass
Jean Garrigue: the body of the dream
John Ashbery: unassigned frequencies: whispers out of time
John Berryman, William Stafford, and James Dickey: the expansional poet: a return to personality
M. B. Tolson and A. R. Ammons: book-length poems
Mark Strand: the book of mourning
Richard Howard: the archeologist poet
W. S. Merwin: the church of ash
Same as: Lieberman, L. The church of ash. *In* Boyers, R. ed. Contemporary poetry in America p256-66
W. S. Merwin and Anthony Hecht: risks and faiths
William Stafford and Frederick Morgan: the shocks of normality

Lieberman, Leonard
The debate over race: a study in the sociology of knowledge. *In* Montagu, A. ed. Race and IQ p19-41

Lieberman, Leonard M.
An attempt to decentralize adult correctional services. *In* Riedel, M. and Chappell, D. eds. Issues in criminal justice: planning and evaluation p114-25

Lieberman, Morton A.
Group therapies. *In* Overview of the psychotherapies p92-117
Relocation research and social policy. *In* Gubrium, J. F. ed. Late life p215-34

Liebling, Abbot Joseph

About individual works
The most of A. J. Liebling
Hyman, S. E. A multitude of Lieblings. *In* Hyman, S. E. The critic's credentials p74-78

Lienhardt, Godfrey
Getting your own back: themes in Nilotic myth. *In* Studies in social anthropology p213-37
Social anthropology of Africa. *In* African studies since 1945 p179-85

Lienhardt, Peter
The interpretation of rumour. *In* Studies in social anthropology p105-31

Li Érh. See Lao-tzŭ

Lievsay, John Leon. See Part 2 under title: Studies in the continental background of Renaissance English literature: essays presented to John L. Lievsay

Life. See Conduct of life; Death; Old age; Ontology; Philosophical anthropology

Life (Biology)
Brody, B. A. Fetal humanity and the theory of essentialism. *In* Baker, R. and Elliston, F. A. eds. Philosophy & sex p338-55
Holbrook, D. Essay 10. *In* Fitzgerald, R. ed. What it means to be human p186-208
Jonas, D. F. Life, death, awareness, and concern: a progression. *In* Life after death p169-81
Ospovat, D. Perfect adaptation and teleological explanation: approaches to the problem of the history of life in the mid-nineteenth century. *In* Studies in history of biology, v2 p33-56
Thomas, L. The medusa and the snail. *In* Thomas, L. The medusa and the snail p 1-6
Thomas, L. The youngest and brightest thing around. *In* Thomas, L. The medusa and the snail p12-18
See also Death (Biology); Reproduction; Vitalism

Life, Elixir of. See Elixir of life

Life, Future. See Future life

Life, Spiritual. See Spiritual life

Life, Tree of. See Tree of life

Life after death. See Future life; Immortality

Life and death, Power over
Cantor, N. L. A patient's decision to decline life-saving medical treatment: bodily integrity versus the preservation of life. *In* Weir, R. F. ed. Ethical issues in death and dying p241-70
Duff, R. S. and Campbell, A. G. M. Moral and ethical dilemmas in the special-care nursery. *In* Weir, R. F. ed. Ethical issues in death and dying p133-44

Limited war

Garnett, J. C. Limited conventional war in the nuclear age. *In* Howard, M. ed. Restraints on war p79-102

Martin, L.W. Limited nuclear war. *In* Howard, M. ed. Restraints on war p103-21

O'Connell, D. P. Limited war at sea since 1945. *In* Howard, M. ed. Restraints on war p123-34

Rathjens, G. W. Nuclear war between the super-powers. *In* Griffiths, F. and Polanyi, J. C. eds. The dangers of nuclear war p135-46

Lin, Han-sheng

Chou Fo-hai: the diplomacy of survival. *In* Burns, R. D. and Bennett, E. M. eds. Diplomats in crisis p171-99

Lin, Paul T. K.

Development guided by values: comments on China's road and its implications. *In* On the creation of a just world order p259-94

Lin, Shuen-fu

Ritual and narrative structure in Ju-lin wai-shih. *In* Chinese narrative p244-65

Lin, Yü-sheng

The suicide of Liang Chi: an ambiguous case of moral conservatism. *In* The Limits of change p151-68

Lincoln, Abraham, President U.S.

About

Capps, D, Lincoln's martyrdom: a study of exemplary mythic patterns. *In* Reynolds, F. E. and Capps, D. eds. The biographical process p393-412

Swierenga, R. P. The ethnic voter and the first Lincoln election. *In* Swierenga, R. P. ed. Beyond the Civil War synthesis p99-115

Wright, E. Lincoln before his election. *In* Burton, D. H ed. American history—British historians p221-37

Assassination

Capps, D. Lincoln's martyrdom: a study of exemplary mythic patterns. *In* Reynolds, F. E. and Capps, D. eds. The biographical process p393-412

Lincoln, Andrew. See Dodd, P. jt. auth.

Lincoln, Charles Eric

The new Black estate: the coming of age of Blackamerica. *In* Have we overcome? Race relations since Brown p3-30

Lincoln, W. Bruce

The daily life of St Petersburg officials in the mid nineteenth century. *In* Oxford Slavonic papers, new ser. v8 p82-100

Lincoln Center Repertory Theater Company

Miller, A. Arthur Miller vs. Lincoln Center. *In* Miller, A. The theater essays of Arthur Miller p354-61

Lind, Ilse Dusoir

The effect of painting on Faulkner's poetic form. *In* Faulkner, modernism, and film: Faulkner and Yoknapatawpha, 1978 p127-48

Faulkner's uses of poetic drama. *In* Faulkner, modernism, and film: Faulkner and Yoknapatawpha, 1978 p66-81

Faulkner's women. *In* The Maker and the myth: Faulkner and Yoknapatawpha, 1977 p89-104

Lindberg, Carter Harry

Mask of God and Prince of Lies: Luther's theology of the demonic. *In* Disguises of the demonic p87-103

Lindberg, David C.

The intromission-extramission controversy in Islamic visual theory: Alkindi versus Avicenna. *In* Studies in perception p137-59

The science of optics. *In* Lindberg, D. C. ed. Science in the Middle Ages p338-68

The transmission of Greek and Arabic learning to the West. *In* Lindberg, D. C. ed. Science in the Middle Ages p52-90

Linden, Glenn Marston

"Radical" political and economic policies: the Senate, 1873-1877. *In* Swierenga, R. P. ed. Beyond the Civil War synthesis p233-42

Linder, Robert Dean

The resurgence of evangelical social concern (1925-75). *In* Wells, D. F. and Woodbridge, J. D. eds. The evangelicals p189-210

Linderski, Jerzy

The aedileship of Favonius, Curio the Younger and Cicero's election to the augurate. *In* Harvard Studies in classical philology v76 p181-200

Lindfors, Bernth

The blind men and the elephant. *In* African literature today no. 7: Focus on criticism p53-64

"East is East and West is West": points of divergence in African literary history. *In* Narasimhaiah, C. D. ed. Awakened conscience p42-49

Lindgren, Astrid (Ericsson)

A short talk with a prospective children's writer. *In* Horn Book Magazine. Crosscurrents of criticism p 3-6

Lindgren, Jarl

Finland. *In* Kamerman, S. B. and Kahn, A. J. eds. Family policy p270-94

Lindheim, Roslyn

Designs for living. *In* Jarvik, L. F. ed. Aging into the 21st century p153-68

Lindner, Robert Mitchell

About individual works

The jet-propelled couch

Predmore, R. L. On interpreting Don Quixote's character. *In* Studies in the continental background of Renaissance English literature: essays presented to John L. Lievsay p186-201

Lindsay, Jack

Ebenezer Jones, 1820-1860—an English symbolist. *In* Rebels and their causes p151-75

Norman Lindsay as novelist. *In* Bards, bohemians, and bookmen p251-65

Lindsay, John Vliet

The great American drift. *In* Warner, S. B. ed. The American experiment p110-24

Lindsay, Nicholas Vachel

Thirty differences between the photoplays and the stage; excerpt from "The art of the moving picture." *In* Denby, D. ed. Awake in the dark p9-18

About

Viereck, P. R. E. Vachel Lindsay: the Dante of the Fundamentalists. *In* Filler, L. ed. A question of quality: popularity and value in modern creative writing p124-47

Lindsay, Norman
About
Lindsay, J. Norman Lindsay as novelist. *In* Bards, bohemians, and bookmen p251-65

Lindsay, Robert George
International communication: a need for new priorities. *In* Fischer, H. D. and Merrill, J. C. eds. International and intercultural communication p493-99

Lindsay, Vachel. See Lindsay, Nicholas Vachel

Lindstrom, Carl
Innovative building technologies: water-free waste disposal. *In* Strategies for human settlements: habitat and environment p152-56

Line of demarcation of Alexander VI. See Demarcation line of Alexander VI

Linear perspective. See Perspective

Ling, Mêng-ch'u
About
Hanan, P. The nature of Ling Meng-ch'u's fiction. *In* Chinese narrative p85-114

Ling, Roger
Stuccowork. *In* Strong, D. E. and Brown, D. eds. Roman crafts p209-21

Linguistic analogy. See Analogy (Linguistics)

Linguistic analysis (Linguistics)
Hodge, R. W. Linguistics and popular culture. *In* Bigsby, C. W. E. ed. Approaches to popular culture p107-28
Lakoff, R. Language and society. *In* Wardhaugh, R. and Brown, H. D. eds. A survey of applied linguistics p207-28
Langendoen, D. T. The problem of linguistic theory in relation to language behavior: a tribute and reply to Paul Goodman. *In* Bloomfield, M. W. and Haugen, E. I. eds. Language as a human problem p197-203
Quine, W. V. Methodological reflections on current linguistic theory. *In* Harman, G. ed. On Noam Chomsky p104-17
Silberstein, M. Shifters, linguistic categories, and cultural description. *In* Basso, K. H. and Selby, H. A. eds. Meaning in anthropology p11-55
See also Systemic grammar

Linguistic analysis (Philosophy) See Analysis (Philosophy)

Linguistic atlas of New England; ed. by Hans Kurath
Duckert, A. R. The winds of change. *In* James B. McMillan: essays in linguistics by his friends and colleagues p21-28

Linguistic atlas of the Gulf States (proposed)
Pederson, L. A. Grassroots grammar in the Gulf States. *In* James B. McMillan: essays in linguistics by his friends and colleagues p91-112

Linguistic atlas of the North Central States (proposed)
McDavid, V. The social distribution of selected verb forms in the Linguistic atlas of the North Central States. *In* James B. McMillan: essays in linguistics by his friends and colleagues p41-50

Linguistic atlas of the Upper Midwest
Allen, H. B. The Linguistic atlas of the Upper Midwest as a source of sociolinguistic information. *In* James B. McMillan: essays in linguistics by his friends and colleagues p 3-19

Linguistic change
Wells, R. S. Metonymy and misunderstanding: an aspect of language change. *In* Current issues in linguistic theory p195-214

Linguistic research
Katz, J. J. The relevance of linguistics to philosophy. *In* Harman, G. ed. On Noam Chomsky p229-41

History
Bloom, L. Language development. *In* Wardhaugh, R. and Brown, H. D. eds. A survey of applied linguistics p8-43
Hoijer, H. History of American Indian linguistics. *In* Sebeok, T. A. ed. Native languages of the Americas v 1 p3-22
Landar, H. J. Historiography of native Ibero-American linguistics. *In* Sebeok, T. A. ed. Native languages of the Americas v2 p185-203

Methodology
See Linguistics—Methodology

Linguistic science. See Linguistics

Linguistics
Gleason, H. A. Linguistics and philology. *In* On language, culture, and religion: in honor of Eugene A. Nida p199-212
Kiparsky, R. P. V. The role of linguistics in a theory of poetry. *In* Bloomfield, M. W. and Haugen, E. I. eds. Language as a human problem p233-49
Richards, I. A. Factors and functions in linguistics. *In* Richards, I. A. Poetries p 1-16
Sadock, J. M. Figurative speech and linguistics. *In* Ortony, A. ed. Metaphor and thought p46-63
Steiner, G. Whorf, Chomsky, and the student of literature. *In* Steiner, G. On difficulty and other essays p137-63
Also in Wimsatt, W. K. ed. Literary criticism: idea and act p242-62
See also Analogy (Linguistics); Anaphora (Linguistics); Applied linguistics; Areal linguistics; Biolinguistics; Grammar, Comparative and general; Historical linguistics; Psycholinguistics; Reference (Linguistics); Sociolinguistics; Structural linguistics; Universals (Linguistics); Word (Linguistics)

Methodology
Blumstein, S. Structuralism in linguistics: methodological and theoretical perspectives: *In* Riegel, K. F. and Rosenwald, G. C. eds. Structure and transformation p153-65
Lakoff, R. Language and society. *In* Wardhaugh, R. and Brown, H. D. eds. A survey of applied linguistics p207-28

Linguistics, Mathematical. See Mathematical linguistics

Linguistics, Statistical. See Mathematical linguistics

Linguistics, Structural. See Structural linguistics

Linguostylistics. See Language and languages—Style

Linhart, Sepp
The use and meaning of leisure in present-day Japan. *In* Modern Japan p198-208

Link, Perry
Traditional-style popular urban fiction in the teens and twenties. *In* Modern Chinese literature in the May Fourth era p327-49

The **Link** model of world trade, with applications to 1972-73. Klein, L. R.; Moriguchi, C. and Van Peeterssen, A. *In* Kenen, P. B. ed. International trade and finance p453-83

Linklater, Eric

About

Hart, F. R. Novelists of survival. *In* Hart, F. R. The Scottish novel p246-86

Linn, John Blair

About

Leary, L. G. John Blair Linn, 1777-1805. *In* Leary, L. G. Soundings p175-207

Linna, Väinö

About individual works
The unknown soldier

Dauenhauer, R. The view from the Aspen Grove: Paavo Haavikko in national and international context. *In* Dauenhauer, R. and Binham, P. eds. Snow in May p67-97

Linnér, Sven

The hero in Swedish fiction after World War II. *In* The Hero in Scandinavian literature p107-23

Lins do Rego, José

About individual works
O moleque Ricardo

Preto-Rodas, R. A. The Black presence and two Brazilian modernists: Jorge de Lima and José Lins do Rêgo. *In* Forster, M. H. ed. Tradition and renewal p81-101

Linsley, Austin

U.S.-Cuban relations: the role of Puerto Rico. *In* Cuba in the world p119-30

Lint, Gregg L.

The law of nations and the American Revolution. *In* The American Revolution and "a candid world" p111-33

Linz, Juan J. See Linz Storch de Gracia, Juan José

Linz Storch de Gracia, Juan José

The breakdown of democratic regimes: Crisis, breakdown, & reequilibration. *In* The Breakdown of democratic regimes pt 1 p 1-124

From great hopes to civil war: the breakdown of democracy in Spain. *In* The Breakdown of democratic regimes pt2 p142-215

Some notes toward a comparative study of fascism in sociological historical perspective. *In* Laqueur, W. Z. ed. Fascism: a reader's guide p3-121

Lipking, Lawrence Erwin

A history of the future. *In* Harth, J. P. ed. New approaches to eighteenth-century literature p157-76

Lipman-Blumen, Jean, and Leavitt, Harold J.

Sexual behavior as an expression of achievement orientation. *In* Katchadourian, H. A. ed. Human sexuality p246-56

Lippard, Lucy R.

Introduction to surrealists on art. *In* Kaplan, P. and Manso, S. eds. Major European art movements, 1900-1945 p325-36

Lippi, Filippino

About individual works
Strozzi chapel frescoes

Winternitz, E. Muses and music in a burial chapel: an interpretation of Filippino Lippi's window wall in the Cappella Strozzi. *In* Winternitz, E. Musical instruments and their symbolism in Western art p166-84

Lippmann, Walter

The good society; excerpt. *In* Crunden, R. M. ed. The superfluous men p238-48

The public interest; excerpt from "Essays in the public philosophy." *In* A Public philosophy reader p198-201

About individual works
Essays in the public philosophy

Coffey, J. W. Epilogue: faith, reason, and the scientific method. *In* Coffey, J. W. Political realism in American thought p159-70

Cuervo, R. F. The definition of public philosophy: Lippmann and Murray. *In* A Public philosophy reader p97-102

Lipset, David

Gregory Bateson: early biography. *In* About Bateson p21-54

Lipset, Seymour Martin

The American university—1964-1974: from activism to austerity. *In* Universities in the Western world p143-56

The end of ideology and the ideology of the intellectuals. *In* Culture and its creators p15-42

Opportunity and welfare in the first new nation. *In* America's continuing revolution p333-59

Revolution and counterrevolution—some comments at a conference analyzing the Bicentennial of a celebrated North American divorce. *In* Perspectives on revolution and evolution p22-45

Social structure and social change. *In* Blau, P. M. ed. Approaches to the study of social structure p172-209

Why no socialism in the United States? *In* Radicalism in the contemporary age v 1 p31-149

Lipset, Seymour Martin, and Basu, Asoke

Intellectual types and political roles. *In* The Idea of social structure p433-70

Lipsey, Roger

Introduction. *In* Coomaraswamy, A. K. Selected papers v 1 pxxix-xxxviii

Lipsius, Justus

About

Momigliano, A. The first political commentary on Tacitus: appendix. *In* Momigliano, A. Essays in ancient and modern historiography p218-29

Lipsky, Michael

Standing the study of public policy implementation on its head. *In* Burnham, W. D. and Weinberg, M. W. eds. American politics and public policy p391-402

Lipton, Morris A. and Nemeroff, Charles B.

The biology of aging and its role in depression. *In* Aging: the process and the people p47-95

Liquidity (Economics) See International liquidity

Liquor problem

See also Indians of North America—Liquor problem; Temperance

Russia

Krasikov, A. Commodity number one. *In* Medvedev, R. A. ed. The Samizdat register p93-115

Lira, Pablo, pseud.

The crisis of hegemony in the Chilean Left. *In* O'Brien, P. J. ed. Allende's Chile p27-50

The **lira** da braccio. Winternitz, E. *In* Winternitz, E. Musical instruments and their symbolism in Western art p86-98

Lisca, Peter
The structure of Hemingway's Across the river and into the trees. *In* Wagner, L. W. ed. Ernest Hemingway p288-306

Lisio, Donald John
United States: bread and butter politics. *In* The War generation p38-58

Liska, George
Morgenthau vs. Machiavelli: political realism and power politics. *In* [Truth and tragedy]: a tribute to Hans Morgenthau p104-11

Liskofsky, Sidney
The United Nations and human rights: "alternative approaches." *In* Sidorsky, D. ed. Essays on human rights p46-67

Lister, Larry. See Lister, Lawrence H.

Lister, Lawrence H.
Adolescents. *In* Gochros, H. L. and Gochros, J. S. eds. The sexually oppressed p41-53

Liston, Maureen
Chester Himes, A nigger. *In* Bruck, P. ed. The Black American short story in the 20th century p85-97

Liszt, Franz
About
Craft, R. Lisztomania. *In* Craft, R. Current convictions p168-83

Litchfield, Robert Burr
The family and the mill: cotton mill work, family work patterns, and fertility in mid-Victorian Stockport. *In* Wohl, A. S. ed. The Victorian family p180-96

Literacy. See Illiteracy

Literal (The English word)
Barfield, O. The meaning of "literal." *In* Barfield, O. The rediscovery of meaning, and other essays p32-43

Literary awards. See Literary prizes

Literary characters. See Characters and characteristics in literature

Literary collaboration. See Authorship—Collaboration

Literary criticism. See Criticism

Literary form
Abrahams, R. D. The complex relations of simple forms. *In* Folklore genres p193-214

Ben-Amos, D. Analytical categories and ethnic genres. *In* Folklore genres p215-42

Ben-Amos, D. Introduction. *In* Folklore genres p ix-xlv

Bogan, L. The pleasures of formal poetry; excerpt from "A poet's alphabet." *In* Gibbons, R. ed. The poet's work: 29 masters of 20th century poetry on the origins and practice of their art p203-14

Burke, K. On literary form. *In* Young, T. D. ed. The New Criticism and after p80-90

Cawelti, J. G. Literary formulas and their cultural significance. *In* Luedtke, L. S. ed. The study of American culture p177-217

Cawelti, J. G. Notes toward a typology of literary formulas. *In* Cawelti, J. G. Adventure, mystery, and romance p37-50

Cawelti, J. G. The study of literary formulas. *In* Cawelti, J. G. Adventure, mystery, and romance p5-36

Cohen, R. On the interrelations of eighteenth-century literary forms. *In* Harth, J. P. ed. New approaches to eighteenth-century literature p33-78

Cunningham, J. V. The problem of form. *In* Cunningham, J. V. The collected essays of J. V. Cunningham p247-50

Duncan, R. E. Notes on poetic form. *In* Gibbons, R. ed. The poet's work: 29 masters of 20th century poetry on the origins and practice of their art p260-62

Fowler, A. The life and death of literary forms. *In* Cohen, R. ed. New directions in literary history p77-94

Frye, N. Charms and riddles. *In* Frye, N. Spiritus mundi p123-47

Levertov, D. Some notes on organic form; excerpt from "The poet in the world." *In* Gibbons, R. ed. The poet's work: 29 masters of 20th century poetry on the origins and practice of their art p254-59

Rader, R. W. The concept of genre and eighteenth-century studies. *In* Harth, J. P. ed. New approaches to eighteenth-century literature p79-115

Scholes, R. E. An approach through genre. *In* Spilka, M. ed. Towards a poetics of fiction p41-51

Watkins, E. Dialectic and form. *In* Watkins, E. The critical act p158-87

Literary influence. See Influence (Literary, artistic, etc.)

Literary prizes
Clark, P. P. and Clark, T. N. Patrons, publishers, and prizes: the writer's estate in France. *In* Culture and its creators p197-225

Literary property. See Copyright

Literary research
Osborn, J. M. The search for English literary documents. *In* Wimsatt, W. K. ed. Literary criticism: idea and act p15-31

Sutherland, J. R. Down Chancery Lane. *In* Evidence in literary scholarship p165-78

Literary sketch. See Essay

Literary style. See Style, Literary

Literary tradition. See Influence (Literary, artistic, etc.)

Literary transmission. See Transmission of texts

Literature
See also Apple in literature; Art and literature; Authorship; Autobiography; Books and reading; Characters and characteristics in literature; Children's literature; Christian literature, Early; Classical literature; Classicism; Copyright; Creation (Literary, artistic, etc.); Critcism; Drama; Fairy tales; Family in literature; Fantastic fiction; Folk literature; Gothic literature; Health in literature; Heroes in literature; Influence (Literary, artistic, etc.); Jews in literature; Magic in literature; Modernism (Literature); Mothers and daughters in literature; Music and literature; Myth in literature; Mythology in literature; Pastoral literature; Peasants in literature; Picaresque literature; Plots (Drama, novel, etc.); Poetry; Realism in literature; Religious literature; Romances; Romanticism; Semiotics and literature; Sports in literature; Style, Literary; Trees in literature; Will in literature; Wit and humor; Women in literature; also national literatures, e.g. English literature

Literature—*Continued*

Aesthetics

Beardsley, M. C. Aesthetic intentions and fictive illocutions. *In* Hernadi, P. ed. What is literature? p161-77

Iser, W. The reading process: a phenomenological approach. *In* Cohen, R. ed. New directions in literary history p125-45

Lodge, D. Metaphor and metonymy. *In* Lodge, D. The modes of modern writing p73-124

Stankiewicz, E. Poetics and verbal art. *In* Sebeok, T. A. ed. A perfusion of signs p54-76

Strelka, J. The literary work: its structure, unity, and distinction from forms of nonliterary expression. *In* Hernadi, P. ed. What is literature? p115-26

Vodička, F. Response to verbal art. *In* Matejka, L. and Titunik, I. R. eds. Semiotics of art p197-208

See also Style, Literary

Awards

See Literary prizes

Censorship

See Censorship

Economic aspects

Shell, M. Conclusion. *In* Shell, M. The economy of literature p152-56

Shell, M. The lie of the fox: Rousseau's theory of verbal, monetary, and political representation. *In* Shell, M. The economy of literature p113-28

Evaluation

See Books and reading; Criticism

Forms

See Literary form

History and criticism

Abrams, M. H. Belief and the suspension of disbelief. *In* Wimsatt, W. K. ed. Literary criticism: idea and act p149-69

Brombert, V. H. Introduction: The prison dream. *In* Brombert, V. H. The romantic prison p3-17

Downs, R. B. Ideas in the flow of civilization. *In* Downs, R. B. Books that changed the world p 1-25

Fiedler, L. A. Towards a definition of popular literature. *In* Bigsby, C. W. E. Superculture p28-42

Fowler, R. Literature as discourse. *In* Royal Institute of Philosophy. Communication and understanding p174-94

Frye, N. Charms and riddles. *In* Frye, N. Spiritus mundi p123-47

Hartman, G. H. From the sublime to the hermeneutic. *In* Hartman, G. H. The fate of reading p114-23

Jauss, H. R. History of art and pragmatic history. *In* Amacher, R. E. and Lange, V. eds. New perspectives in German literary criticism p432-64

Kurz, P. K. Literature and science. *In* Kurz, P. K. On modern German literature v 1 p56-79

Lerner, L. Literature and money. *In* English Association. Essays and studies, 1975 p106-22

Lodge, D. What is realism? *In* Lodge, D. The modes of modern writing p22-27

Ong, W. J. From mimesis to irony: writing and print as integuments of voice. *In* Ong, W. J. Interfaces of the word p272-302

Ong, W. J. Maranatha: death and life in the text of the Book. *In* Ong, W. J. Interfaces of the word p230-71

Ong, W. J. The writer's audience is always a fiction. *In* Ong, W. J. Interfaces of the word p53-81

Riffaterre, M. The stylistic approach to literary history. *In* Cohen, R. ed. New directions in literary history p147-64

Schneider, D. J. The symbolic system and the authority of the literary work. *In* Schneider, D. J. Symbolism: the Manichean vision p204-17

Taylor, A. Conclusion. *In* Taylor, A. Magic and English romanticism p251-55

Taylor, A. Introduction. *In* Taylor, A. Magic and English romanticism p 1-14

Torrance, R. M. Introduction: Comic butt and comic hero. *In* Torrance, R. M. The comic hero p 1-11

Trilling, L. The fate of pleasure: Wordsworth to Dostoevski; excerpt from "Beyond culture". *In* Wimsatt, W. K. ed. Literary criticism: idea and act p189-211

Vodička, F. Response to verbal art. *In* Matejka, L. and Titunik, I. R. eds. Semiotics of art p197-208

Watkins, E. Criticism and community: on literary value. *In* Watkins, E. The critical act p213-51

Watson, P. F. The Queen of Sheba in Christian tradition. *In* Pritchard, J. B. ed. Solomon & Sheba p115-45

Weimann, R. Past significance and present meaning in literary history. *In* Cohen, R. ed. New directions in literary history p43-61

Wellek, R. The fall of literary history. *In* Amacher, R. E. and Lange, V. eds. New perspectives in German literary criticism 418-31

Wilder, T. N. Goethe and world literature. *In* Wilder, T. N. American characteristics, and other essays p137-48

Wimsatt, J. I. The mirror as metaphor for literature. *In* Hernadi, P. ed. What is literature? p127-40

See also Authors

History and criticism—Theory, etc.

Altieri, C. F. A procedural definition of literature. *In* Hernadi, P. ed. What is literature? p62-78

Beardsley, M. C. Aesthetic intentions and fictive illocutions. *In* Hernadi, P. ed. What is literature? p161-77

Davenport, E. Why theorize about literature? *In* Hernadi, P. ed. What is literature? p35-46

Fowler, A. Intention floreat. *In* On literary intention p242-55

Guillén, C. The aesthetics of literary influence; excerpt from "Literature as system." *In* Primeau, R. ed. Influx p49-73

Hartman, G. H. The fate of reading. *In* Hartman, G. H. The fate of reading p248-74

Hartman, G. H. History writing as answerable style. *In* Hartman, G. H. The fate of reading p101-13

Also in Cohen, R. ed. New directions in literary history p95-105

Hartman, G. H. I. A. Richards and the dream of communication. *In* Hartman, G. H. The fate of reading p20-40

Hassan, I. H. The problem of influence in literary history: notes towards a definition. *In* Primeau, R. ed. Influx p34-46

Literature—History and criticism—Theory, etc.—Continued

Hirsch, E. D. In defense of the author; excerpt from "Validity in interpretation." *In* On literary intention p87-103

Hirsch, E. D. Objective interpretation. *In* On literary intention p26-54

Hirsch, E. D. What isn't literature? *In* Hernadi, P. ed. What is literature? p24-34

Holland, N. N. Literature as transaction. *In* Hernadi, P. ed. What is literature? p206-18

Hough, G. G. An eighth type of ambiguity. *In* On literary intention p222-41

Jauss, H. R. Literary history as a challenge to literary theory. *In* Cohen, R. ed. New directions in literary history p11-41

McFadden, G. M. "Literature": a many-sided process. *In* Hernadi, P. ed. What is literature? p49-61

Markiewicz, H. **The limits of literature.** *In* Cohen, R. ed. New directions in literary history p189-98

Shell, M. The Golden Fleece and the voice of the shuttle: economy in literary theory. *In* Shell, M. The economy of literature p89-112

Skinner, Q. Motives, intentions and the interpretation of texts. *In* On literary intention p210-21

Watson, G. The literary past; excerpt from "The story of literature." *In* On literary intention p158-73

Wellek, R. What is literature? *In* Hernadi, P. ed. What is literature? p16-23

Moral and religious aspects

See Literautre and morals; Religion and literature

Philosophy

Abrams, M. H. Belief and the suspension of disbelief. *In* Wimsatt, W. K. ed. Literary criticism: idea and act p149-69

Altieri, C. F. A procedural definition of literature. *In* Hernadi, P. ed. What is literature? p62-78

Amirthanayagam, G. Literature as culture. *In* Narasimhaiah, C. D. ed. Awakened conscience p433-40

Barthes, R. The death of the author. *In* Barthes, R. Image, music, text p142-48

Barthes, R. From work to text. *In* Barthes, R. Image, music, text p155-64

Beardsley, M. C. Aesthetic intentions and fictive illocutions. *In* Hernadi, P. ed. What is literature? p161-77

Bronowski, J. Imagination as plan and as experiment. *In* Bronowski, J. The visionary eye p133-47

Brown, R. L. and Steinmann, M. Native readers of fiction: a speech-act and genre-rule approach to defining literature. *In* Hernadi, P. ed. What is literature? p141-60

Burke, K. (Nonsymbolic) motion/(symbolic) action. *In* Roland, A. ed. Psychoanalysis, creativity, and literature p117-43

Cawelti, J. G. The study of literary formulas. *In* Cawelti, J. G. Adventure, mystery, and romance p5-36

Coomaraswamy, A. K. Intention; excerpt from "Figures of speech or figures of thought: collected essays on the traditional or 'normal' view of art." *In* Coomaraswamy, A. K. Selected papers v 1 p266-75

Coxe, L. O. After words. *In* Coxe, L. O. Enabling acts p161-64

Davenport, E. Why theorize about literature? *In* Hernadi, P. ed. What is literature? p35-46

Donato, E. The idioms of the text: notes on the language of philosophy and the fictions of literature. *In* Glyph 2 p 1-13

Ehrmann, J. The death of literature. *In* Federman, R. ed. Surfiction p229-53

Farrell, J. T. The value of literature in modern society. *In* Farrell, J. T. Literary essays, 1954-1974 p50-53

Foucault, M. Language to infinity. *In* Foucault, M. Language, counter-memory, practice p53-67

Fowler, R. Literature as discourse. *In* Royal Institute of Philosophy. Communication and understanding p174-94

Gass, W. H. Groping for trouts. *In* Gass, W. H. The world within the word p262-79

Hill, A. A. Principles governing semantic parallels. *In* Hill, A. A. Constituent and pattern in poetry p95-103

Hill, A. A. A program for the definition of literature. *In* Hill, A. A. Constituent and pattern in poetry p3-9

Hirsch, E. D. What isn't literature? *In* Hernadi, P. ed. What is literature? p24-34

Holland, N. N. Literature as transaction. *In* Hernadi, P. ed. What is literature? p206-18

Howell, W. S. Literature as an enterprise in communication. *In* Howell, W. S. Poetics, rhetoric. and logic p215-33

Knights, L. C. Literature and the teaching of literature. *In* Knights, L. C. Explorations 3 p9-23

Also in Niblett, W. R. ed. The sciences, the humanities and the technological threat p127-38

Krieger, M. Literature as illusion, as metaphor, as vision. *In* Hernadi, P. ed. What is literature? p178-89

Kurz, P. K. Literature and theology today. *In* Kurz, P. K. On modern German literature v 1 p80-104

Lane, J. His master's voice? The questioning of authority in literature. *In* Josipovici, G. ed. The modern English novel: the reader, the writer and the work p113-29

Lodge, D. What is literature? *In* Lodge, D. The modes of modern writing p 1-9

McCanles, M. "All discourse aspires to the analytic proposition." *In* Hernadi, P. ed. What is literature? p190-205

McFadden, G. M. "Literature": a many-sided process. *In* Hernadi, P. ed. What is literature? p49-61

Malraux, A. Anti-critique. *In* Courcel, M. H. de, ed. Malraux p223-57

Matthews, R. J. Literary works express propositions. *In* Hernadi, P. ed. What is literature? p102-12

Mink, L. O. History and fiction as modes of comprehension. *In* Cohen, R. ed. New directions in literary history p107-24

Pasternak, B. L. Some statements. *In* Proffer, C. R. ed Modern Russian poets on poetry p81-85

Peckham, M. Literature and knowledge. *In* Peckham, M. Romanticism and behavior p222-45

Peckham, M. "Literature": disjunction and redundancy. *In* Hernadi, P. ed. What is literature? p219-30

Poirier, R. The difficulties of modernism and the modernism of difficulty. *In* Images and ideas in American culture p124-40

Literature—Philosophy—Continued

Richards, I. A. Literature, oral-aural and optical. In Richards, I. A. Complementarities p201-08

Rivers, E. L. Prolegomena grammatologica: literature as the disembodiment of speech. In Hernadi, P. ed. What is literature? p79-88

Scholes, R. E. Toward a semiotics of literature. In Hernadi, P. ed. What is literature? p231-50

Shell, M. Introduction. In Shell, M. The economy of literature p 1-10

Sims, J. H. Milton, literature as a Bible, and the Bible as literature. In Patrick, J. M. and Sundell, R. H. eds. Milton and the art of sacred song p3-21

Solzhenitsyn, A. I. Nobel lecture. In Dunlop, J. B.; Haugh, R. and Klimoff, A. eds. Aleksandr Solzhenitsyn: critical essays and documentary materials 2d ed. p557-75

Sparshott, F. E. On the possibility of saying what literature is. In Hernadi, P. ed. What is literature? p3-15

Steadman, J. M. The iconographical approach. In Steadman, J. M. Nature into myth p23-45

Strelka, J. The literary work: its structure, unity, and distinction from forms of non-literary expression. In Hernadi, P. ed. What is literature? p115-26

Trilling, L. The sense of the past; excerpt from "The liberal imagination." In Primeau, R. ed. Influx p22-33

Wellek, R. What is literature? In Hernadi, P. ed. What is literature? p16-23

Williams, R. Literature in society. In Contemporary approaches to English studies p24-37

Wimsatt, J. I. The mirror as metaphor for literature. In Hernadi, P. ed. What is literature? p127-40

Political aspects

See Politics and literature

Prizes

See Literary prizes

Psychology

Crews, F. C. Reductionism and its discontents. In Crews, F. C. Out of my system p165-85

Fish, S. E. Literature in the reader: affective stylistics. In Primeau, R. ed. Influx p154-79

Holland, N. N. Literature as transformation; excerpt from "The dynamics of literary response." In Primeau, R. ed. Influx p137-53

Rosenblatt, L. M. Towards a transactional theory of reading. In Primeau, R. ed. Influx p121-36

See also Literature—Philosophy

Research

See Literary research

Study and teaching

Coleman, E. Values in the arts and sciences: a course. In Aeolian harps p15-36

Crews, F. C. Do literary studies have an ideology? In Crews, F. C. Out of my system p105-20

Crews, F. C. Offing culture: literary study and the Movement. In Crews, F. C. Out of my system p121-44

Frye, N. The search for acceptable words. In Frye, N. Spiritus mundi p3-26

Knights, L. C. Literature and the teaching of literature. In Knights, L. C. Explorations 3 p9-23

Rich, A. C. Teaching language in open admissions. In Rich, A. C. On lies, secrets, and silence p51-68

Richards, I. A. Literature for the unlettered. In Richards, I. A. Poetries p149-64

Richards, I. A. Sources of our common aim. In Richards, I. A. Poetries p165-214

Robertson, D. W. Some observations on method in literary studies. In Cohen, R. ed. New directions in literary history p63-75

Study and teaching (Higher)—
United States

Weiger, J. G. Teaching foreign language and literature. In Cahn, S. M. ed. Scholars who teach p163-91

Style

See Style, Literary

Translating

See Translating and interpreting

Exiled authors

Nandan, S. The immigrant Indian experience in literature: Trinidad and Fiji. In Narasimhaiah, C. D. ed. Awakened conscience p346-59

Souza, E. de. The expatriate experience. In Narasimhaiah, C. D. ed. Awakened conscience p339-45

19th century—History and criticism

Mudford, P. Richard Wagner: an afterword. In Mudford, P. The art of celebration p187-89

Literature, Ancient. See Classical literature

Literature, Apocalyptic. See Apocalyptic literature

Literature, Classical. See Classical literature

Literature, Comic. See Burlesque (Literature); Comedy; Commedia dell'arte; Farce; Parody; Satire

Literature, Comparative

Block, H. M. The concept of influence in comparative literature. In Primeau, R. ed. Influx p74-81

American and Canadian

Smith, A. J. M. Evolution and revolution as aspects of English-Canadian and American literature. In Perspectives on revolution and evolution p213-37

Canadian and American

Smith, A. J. M. Evolution and revolution as aspects of English-Canadian and American literature. In Perspectives on revolution and evolution p213-37

Chinese and European

Eber, I. Images of oppressed peoples and modern Chinese literature. In Modern Chinese literature in the May Fourth era p127-41

McDougall, B. S. The impact of Western literary trends. In Modern Chinese literature in the May Fourth era p37-61

Chinese and Japanese

Cheng, Ching-mao. The impact of Japanese literary trends on modern Chinese writers. In Modern Chinese literature in the May Fourth era p63-88

Literature, Comparative—*Continued*

Chinese and Russian

Fokkema, D. W. Lu Xun: the impact of Russian literature. *In* Modern Chinese literature in the May Fourth era p89-101

Widmer, E. Qu Qiubai and Russian literature. *In* Modern Chinese literature in the May Fourth era p103-25

English and French

Prescott, A. L. Afterword. *In* Prescott, A. L. French poets and the English Renaissance p235-39

European and Chinese

Eber, I. Images of oppressed peoples and modern Chinese literature. *In* Modern Chinese literature in the May Fourth era p127-41

McDougall, B. S. The impact of Western literary trends. *In* Modern Chinese literature in the May Fourth era p37-61

French and English

Prescott, A. L. Afterword. *In* Prescott, A. L. French poets and the English Renaissance p235-39

Japanese and Chinese

Cheng, Ching-mao. The impact of Japanese literary trends on modern Chinese writers. *In* Modern Chinese literature in the May Fourth era p63-88

Russian and Chinese

Fokkema, D. W. Lu Xun: the impact of Russian literature. *In* Modern Chinese literature in the May Fourth era p89-101

Widmer, E. Qu Qiubai and Russian literature. *In* Modern Chinese literature in the May Fourth era p103-25

Themes, motives

Ure, P. The Widow of Ephesus: some reflections on an international comic theme. *In* Ure, P. Elizabethan and Jacobean drama p221-36

Literature, Crime in. See Crime in literature

Literature, Epic. See Epic literature

Literature, Gothic. See Gothic revival (Literature)

Literature, Immoral

See also Censorship; Sex in literature

History and criticism

Cooke, T. D. Pornography, the comic spirit, and the fabliaux. *In* Cooke, T. D. and Honeycutt, B. L. eds. The humor of the fabliaux p137-62

Garrison, D. Immoral fiction in the late Victorian library. *In* Howe, D. W. ed. Victorian America p141-59

Lyons, J. O. Whores and rakes in the gardens of delight. *In* Lyons, J. O. The invention of the self p176-96

Law and legislation

See Obscenity (Law)

Literature, Legal. See Legal literature

Literature, Library science. See Library science literature

Literature, Medieval

See also Romances

History and criticism

Bloomfield, M. W. The problem of the hero in the later medieval period. *In* Concepts of the hero in the Middle Ages and the Renaissance p27-48

Economou, G. D. The two Venuses and courtly love. *In* In pursuit of perfection p17-50

Ferrante, J. M. Allegory. *In* Ferrante, J. M. Woman as image in medieval literature p37-64

Ferrante, J. M. The conflict of lyric conventions and romance form. *In* In pursuit of perfection p135-78

Ferrante, J. M. Courtly literature. *In* Ferrante, J. M. Woman as image in medieval literature p65-97

Ferrante, J. M. In the thirteenth century. *In* Ferrante, J. M. Woman as image in medieval literature p99-127

Gibson, M. The continuity of learning, circa 850-circa 1050. *In* Viator: medieval and Renaissance studies v6 p 1-13

Green, D. H. On damning with faint praise in medieval literature. *In* Viator: medieval and Renaissance studies v6 p117-69

Hardison, O. B. Toward a history of medieval literary criticism. *In* Medievalia et humanistica no. 7 p 1-12

Reiss, E. Fin'amors: its history and meaning in medieval literature. *In* Medieval and Renaissance studies 1976 p74-99

Ruggiers, P. G. Introduction: Some theoretical considerations of comedy in the Middle Ages. *In* Ruggiers, P. G. ed. Versions of medieval comedy p 1-17

Sayre, R. F. Antiquity and the Middle Ages. *In* Sayre, R. F. Solitude in society p13-33

Stevens, M. The performing self in twelfth-century culture. *In* Viator: medieval and Renaissance studies v9 p193-212

Theiner, P. The medieval Terence. *In* The Learned and the lewed p231-47

Vance, E. Pas de trois: narrative, hermeneutics, and structure in medieval poetics. *In* Valdés, M. J. and Miller, O. J. eds. Interpretation of narrative p118-34

Literature, Modern

See also European literature; Gothic revival (Literature); Neoclassicism (Literature)

History and criticism

Bell, D. Beyond modernism, beyond self. *In* Art, politics, and will p213-53

Bersani, L. Murderous lovers. *In* Bersani, L. A future for Astyanax p3-14

Glicksberg, C. I. Literature and social responsibility. *In* Glicksberg, C. I. The literature of commitment p37-48

Josipovici, G. 'But time will not relent': modern literature and the experience of time. *In* Josipovici, G. ed. The modern English novel: the reader, the writer and the work p252-72

Josipovici, G. The lessons of modernism. *In* Josipovici, G. The lessons of modernism p109-23

Josipovici, G. Linearity and fragmentation. *In* Josipovici, G. The lessons of modernism p124-39

Literature, Modern—History and criticism
—*Continued*

Lane, J. His master's voice? The questioning of authority in literature. *In* Josipovici, G. ed. The modern English novel: the reader, the writer and the work p113-29

Lenson, D. R. The other tragedy. *In* Lenson, D. R. Achilles' choice p137-58

Smith, A. D. Neo-classicist and romantic elements in the emergence of nationalist conceptions. *In* Smith, A. D. ed. Nationalist movements p74-87

Tatar, M. M. Salvation by electricity: science, poetry, and "Naturphilosophie." *In* Tatar, M. M. Spellbound p45-81

15th and 16th centuries—History and criticism

Greene, T. M. Renaissance warfare: a metaphor in conflict. *In* The Holy war p157-80

18th century—History and criticism

Lyons, J. O. Out of the void. *In* Lyons, J. O. The invention of the self p 1-17

Lyons, J. O. The traveler at home. *In* Lyons, J. O. The invention of the self p156-75

Lyons, J. O. Whores and rakes in the gardens of delight. *In* Lyons, J. O. The invention of the self p176-96

May, G. C. Autobiography and the eighteenth century. *In* Martz, L. L. and Williams, A. L. eds. The author in his work p319-35

19th century—History and criticism
See Decadence (Literary movement)

20th century

Graff, G. The myth of the postmodern breakthrough. *In* Graff, G. Literature against itself p31-62

20th century—History and criticism

Adams, R. M. Three thematic interludes. *In* Adams, R. M. Afterjoyce p36-64

Auerbach, N. A world at war: one big Miss Brodie. *In* Auerbach, N. Communities of women p159-91

Connolly, C. The modern movement. *In* Connolly, C. The evening colonnade p197-201

Forster, M. H. Latin American vanguardismo: chronology and terminology. *In* Forster, M. H. ed. Tradition and renewal p12-50

Glicksberg, C. I. From surrealism to communism. *In* Glicksberg, C. I. The literature of commitment p150-62

Glicksberg, C. I. The mystique of commitment. *In* Glicksberg, C. I. The literature of commitment p49-66

Heller, E. Observations on psychoanalysis and modern literature. *In* Psychiatry and the humanities v 1 p35-50

Kennedy, A. Dramatic action, the modern and the post-modern. *In* Kennedy, A. The protean self p27-61

Kurz, P. K. Beat—Pop—underground. *In* Kurz, P. K. On modern German literature v4 p202-41

Kurz, P. K. Fences and camps. *In* Kurz, P. K. On modern German literature v3 p95-127

MacLeish, A. Return from the excursion. *In* MacLeish, A. Riders on the earth p 3-12

McMillan, D. Transition's revolutionaries. *In* McMillan, D. Transition p113-24

Peyre, H. Is literature dead? Or dying? *In* Peyre, H. French literary imagination and Dostoevsky, and other essays p138-56

Poirier, R. The difficulties of modernism and the modernism of difficulty. *In* Images and ideas in American culture p124-40

Rahv, P. Twilight of the thirties: passage from an editorial. *In* Rahv, P. Essays on literature and politics, 1932-1972 p305-09

Read, Sir H. E. The limits of permissiveness. *In* Abbs, P. ed. The black rainbow p4-18

Ziolkowski, T. Some features of religious figuralism in twentieth-century literature. *In* Miner, E. R. ed. Literary uses of typology p345-69

See also Dadaism

Literature, Pastoral. See Pastoral literature

Literature, Picaresque. See Picaresque literature

Literature, Popular. See Popular literature

Literature, Primitive. See Folk literature

Literature, Renaissance. See Literature, Modern—15th and 16th centuries

Literature, Rococo. See Rococo literature

Literature, Underground. See Underground literature

Literature and art. See Art and literature

Literature and Christianity. See Christianity and literature

Literature and communism. See Communism and literature

Literature and fascism. See Fascism and literature

Literature and folk-lore

Mandel'shtam, O. E. Literary Moscow: birth of the fabula. *In* Mandel'shtam, O. E. Selected essays p138-43

Utley, F. L. Oral genres as a bridge to written literature. *In* Folklore genres p3-15

See also Folk-lore in literature

Literature and history

Brooks, C. The modern writer and the burden of history. *In* Tulane studies in English v22 p155-68

Canary, R. H. Science fiction as fictive history. *In* Clareson, T. D. ed. Many futures, many worlds p164-81

Coxe, L. O. History and imagination. *In* Coxe, L. O. Enabling acts p114-24

Cunningham, J. V. The ancient quarrel between history and poetry. *In* Cunningham, J. V. The collected essays of J. V. Cunningham p120-27

Gilman, S. Literature and historical insight. *In* Américo Castro and the meaning of Spanish civilization p317-24

Gossman, L. History and literature: reproduction or signification. *In* Canary, R. H. and Kozicki, H. J. eds. The writing of history p3-40

Holman, C. H. Barren ground and the shape of history. *In* Holman, C. H. Windows on the world p118-28

Hughes, P. Creativity and history in Vico and his contemporaries. *In* Giambattista Vico's science of humanity p155-69

Kermode, J. F. An approach through history. *In* Spilka, M. ed. Towards a poetics of fiction p23-30

Luedtke, L. S. Not so common ground: controversies in contemporary American studies. *In* Luedtke, L. S. ed. The study of American culture p323-67

Literature and history—*Continued*

Miller, J. H. Narrative and history. *In* ELH essays for Earl R. Wasserman p165-83

Mink, L. O. Narrative form as a cognitive instrument. *In* Canary, R. H. and Kozicki, H. J. eds. The writing of history p129-49

Nemerov, H. What was modern poetry? Three lectures: Poetry and history. *In* Nemerov, H. Figures of thought p166-83

Terdiman, R. Conclusion. *In* Terdiman, R. The dialectics of isolation p227-48

White, H. V. The burden of history. *In* White, H. V. Tropics of discourse p27-50

White, H. V. The fictions of factual representation. *In* Fletcher, A. J. S. ed. The literature of fact p21-44

Also in White, H. V. Tropics of discourse p121-34

White, H. V. The historical text as literary artifact. *In* Canary, R. H. and Kozicki, H. J. eds. The writing of history p41-62

Also in White, H. V. Tropics of discourse p81-100

See also History in literature

Literature and homosexuality. See Homosexuality and literature

Literature and liturgy. See Liturgy and literature

Literature and mental illness

Foucault, M. The father's "no." *In* Foucault, M. Language, counter-memory, practice p68-86

Glicksberg, C. I. The politics of madness. *In* Glicksberg, C. I. The literature of commitment p163-85

Ober, W. B. Madness and poetry: a note on Collins, Cowper, and Smart. *In* Ober, W. B. Boswell's clap and other essays p137-92

Thurley, G. The poetry of breakdown: Robert Lowell and Anne Sexton. *In* Thurley, G. The American moment p70-90

Literature and morals

Beyer, J. The morality of the amoral. *In* Cooke, T. D. and Honeycutt, B. L. eds. The humor of the fabliaux p15-42

Cowley, M. Rebels, artists, and scoundrels. *In* Cowley, M. —And I worked at the writer's trade p249-66

Trilling, L. Dr Leavis and the moral tradition. *In* Trilling, L. A gathering of fugitives p108-14

Trilling, L. The morality of inertia. *In* Trilling, L. A gathering of fugitives p34-44

See also Literature, Immoral

Literature and moving-pictures. See Moving-pictures and literature

Literature and music. See Music and literature

Literature and painting. See Art and literature

Literature and politics. See Politics and literature

Literature and psychoanalysis. See Psychoanalysis and literature

Literature and religion. See Religion and literature

Literature and revolutions

Mills, H. C. Lu Xun: literature and revolution—from Mara to Marx. *In* Modern Chinese literature in the May Fourth era p189-220

Peyre, H. Literature and revolution. *In* Peyre, H. French literary imagination and Dostoevsky, and other essays p74-92

Smith, E. E. From romantic revolution to welfare state. *In* Smith, E. E. The angry young men of the thirties p134-53

Literature and science

Bronowski, J. The imaginative mind in science; excerpt from "Imagination and the university." *In* Bronowski, J. The visionary eye p20-32

Bronowski, J. The logic of the mind. *In* Bronowski, J. A sense of the future p56-73

Frye, N. The times of the signs. *In* Frye, N. Spiritus mundi p66-96

Grieve, C. M. Poetry and science; excerpt from "Selected essays of Hugh MacDiarmid." *In* Gibbons, R. ed. The poet's work: 29 masters of 20th century poetry on the origins and practice of their art p121-35

Kurz, P. K. Literature and science. *In* Kurz, P. K. On modern German literature v 1 p56-79

Morgan, E. A glimpse of Petavius. *In* Morgan, E. Essays p3-15

Robinson, C. Science, reason and the material world. *In* Robinson, C. French literature in the nineteenth century p50-107

Mudford, P. The backcloth changes. . .' *In* Mudford, P. The art of celebration p21-33

Taylor, J. G. Scientific thought in fiction and in fact. *In* Nicholls, P. ed. Science fiction at large p57-72

See also Literature and technology; Science fiction

Literature and sculpture. See Art and literature

Literature and society

Achebe, C. Africa and her writers. *In* Achebe, C. Morning yet on creation day p29-45

Achebe, C. The African writer and the Biafran cause. *In* Achebe, C. Morning yet on creation day p137-47

Achebe, C. The novelist as teacher. *In* Achebe, C. Morning yet on creation day p67-73

Balakian, N. The decline of "mass markets." *In* Balakian, N. Critical encounters p225-29

Bellow, S. Writers and literature in American society. *In* Culture and its creators p172-96

Benamou, M. The concept of marginality in ethno-poetics. *In* Minority language and literature p150-60

Colmer, J. The writer as critic of society. *In* Colmer, J. Coleridge to Catch-22 p 1-17

Donaldson, S. and Massa, A. Individual and society. *In* Donaldson, S. and Massa, A. American literature: nineteenth and early twentieth centuries p120-51

Elliott, M. S. Respecting our organs. *In* Gold, J. ed. In the name of language! p161-204

Glicksberg, C. I. Literature and social responsibility. *In* Glicksberg, C. I. The literature of commitment p37-48

Glicksberg, C. I. The mystique of commitment. *In* Glicksberg, C. I. The literature of commitment p49-66

Glicksberg, C. I. The unpolitical writer. *In* Glicksberg, C. I. The literature of commitment p113-30

Graff, G. Babbitt at the abyss. *In* Graff, G. Literature against itself p207-39

Literature and society—*Continued*

Graff, G. Culture, criticism and unreality. *In* Graff, G. Literature against itself p 1-29

Graff, G. English in America. *In* Graff, G. Literature against itself p103-27

Graff, G. The politics of anti-realism. *In* Graff, G. Literature against itself p63-101

Greene, M. The rational and the emancipatory: towards a role for imaginative literature. *In* Greene, M. Landscapes of learning p22-41

Harris, N. Utopian fiction and its discontents. *in* Uprooted Americans p209-44

Hassan, I. H. Models of transformation: ideology, utopia, and fantasy in America. *In* Hassan, I. H. Paracriticisms p151-76

Hemstedt, G. The novel. *In* Lerner, L. ed. The Victorians p4-24

Hyman, S. E. Eight propositions about literature and society. *In* Hyman, S. E. The critic's credentials p38-41

Mäding, K. Popular literature in dependent society: the case of colonial Hong Kong. *In* Fischer, H. D. and Melnik, S. R. eds. Entertainment: a cross cultural examination p180-89

Middleton, J. C. Remarks at the Québec international meeting of writers, October 1974. *In* Middleton, J. C. Bolshevism in art p151-57

Muir, K. The pursuit of relevance. *In* Muir, K. The singularity of Shakespeare, and other essays p198-211

Peyre, H. Literature and revolution. *In* Peyre, H. French literary imagination and Dostoevsky, and other essays p74-92

Rogers, P. Introduction: the writer and society. *In* Rogers, P. ed. The eighteenth century p 1-80

Smith, H. N. The issues. *In* Smith, H. N. Democracy and the novel p3-15

Thompson, D. Maid of all work. *In* Thompson, D. The uses of poetry p70-111

Thompson, D. Rites, bards, ballads. *In* Thompson, D. The uses of poetry p43-69

Tillotson, G. 'Earnestness.' *In* Tillotson, G. A view of Victorian literature p23-54

Trilling, L. The sense of the past; excerpt from "The liberal imagination." *In* Primeau, R. ed. Influx p22-33

Welty, E. Must the novelist crusade? *In* Welty. E. The eye of the story p146-58

Williams, R. Literature in society. *In* Contemporary approaches to English studies p24-37

Wimsatt, W. K. Day of the leopards. *In* Wimsatt, W. K. Day of the leopards p3-10

Great Britain

Goodheart, E. English social criticism and the spirit of Reformation. *In* Goodheart, E. The failure of criticism p28-50

Literature and sociology. See Literature and society

Literature and state

Kunitz, S. J. Poet and state. *In* Kunitz, S. J. A kind of order, a kind of folly p47-58

See also Politics and literature

Russia

Brown, D. B. The literary situation. *In* Brown, D. B. Soviet Russian literature since Stalin p 1-22

South Africa

Moyana, T. T. Problems of a creative writer in South Africa. *In* Heywood, C. ed. Aspects of South African literature p85-98

Literature and technology

Bellow, S. Literature in the age of technology. *In* The Frontiers of knowledge p3-25

Also in Technology and the frontiers of knowledge p1-22

Clarke, A. C. Technology and the limits of knowledge. *In* The Frontiers of knowledge p117-40

Cunningham, J. V. Technology and poetry. *In* Cunningham, J. V. The collected essays of J. V. Cunningham p439-42

Dick, P. K. Man, android and machine. *In* Nicholls, P. ed. Science fiction at large p199-224

Lewis, W. The machine poets. *In* Lewis, W. Enemy salvoes p173-76

Tashjian, D. L. Hart Crane and the machine. *In* Tashjian, D. L. Skyscraper primitives p143-64

Warrick, P. S. Images of the man-machine intelligence relationship in science fiction. *In* Clareson, T. D. ed. Many futures, many worlds p182-223

Lithography

History

Ristow, W. W. Lithography and maps, 1796-1850. *In* Woodward, D. A. ed. Five centuries of map printing p77-112

Litowitz, Bonnie E.

On overdetermination. *In* Psychoanalysis and language p355-94

Littell, Franklin Hamlin

The Radical Reformation and the American experience. *In* America in theological perspective p71-86

Little, Lester Knox

The personal development of Peter Damian. *In* Order and innovation in the Middle Ages p317-41

Little, Malcolm. See Malcolm X

Little, Paul E.

Some reflections on evangelism in the New Testament. *In* Current issues in Biblical and patristic interpretation p318-23

Little, Roger

The world and the word in Saint-John Perse. *In* Cardinal, R. ed. Sensibility and creation p122-35

Little Big Man (Motion picture)

Bezanson, M. Berger and Penn's West: visions and revisions. *In* Peary, G. and Shatzkin, R. eds. The modern American novel and the movies p272-81

Kauffmann, S. Little Big Man. *In* Kauffmann, S. Living images p31-33

Little magazines

History

Connolly, C. Little magazines. *In* Connolly, C. The evening colonnade p375-86

United States

Anania, M. Of living belfry and rampart: on American literary magazines since 1950. *In* Anderson, E. and Kinzie, M. eds. The little magazine in America: a modern documentary history p6-23

Boyers, R. The little magazine in its place: literary culture and anarchy. *In* Anderson, E. and Kinzie, M. eds. The little magazine in America: a modern documentary history p50-67

Little magazines—United States—_Continued_

Michelson, P. On The Purple Sage, Chicago Review, and Big Table. _In_ Anderson, E. and Kinzie, M. eds. The little magazine in America: a modern documentary history p341-75

Montag, T. The little magazine small press connection: some conjectures. _In_ Anderson, E. and Kinzie, M. eds. The little magazine in America: a modern documentary history p575-93

Redmond, E. Stridency and the sword: literary and cultural emphasis in Afro-American magazines. _In_ Anderson, E. and Kinzie, M. eds. The little magazine in America: a modern documentary history p538-73

Robinson, C. Academia and the little magazine. _In_ Anderson, E. and Kinzie, M. eds. The little magazine in America: a modern documentary history p27-49

Stefanile, F. The little magazine today. _In_ Anderson, E. and Kinzie, M. eds. The little magazine in America: a modern documentary history p649-63

United States—Bibliography

Martin, P. A. An annotated bibliography of selected little magazines. _In_ Anderson, E. and Kinzie, M. eds. The little magazine in America: a modern documentary history p666-750

Little murders (Motion picture)

Kauffmann, S. Little murders. _In_ Kauffmann, S. Living images p35-38

Little presses

United States

Balakian, N. Poets, printers and pamphleteers. _In_ Balakian, N. Critical encounters p239-42

Henderson, B. Independent publishing: today and yesterday. _In_ Altbach, P. G. and McVey, S. eds. Perspectives on publishing p217-29

Montag, T. The little magazine small press connection: some conjectures. _In_ Anderson, E. and Kinzie, M. eds. The little magazine in America: a modern documentary history p575-93

Little vehicle (Buddhism) See Hinayana Buddhism

Littlefield, Thomson H.

A Ripton afternoon. _In_ Frost: centennial essays III p3-6

Littlejohn, David

Communicating ideas by television. _In_ Television as a social force: new approaches to TV criticism p63-79

Thoughts on television criticism. _In_ Television as a cultural force p147-73

Littlewood, A. R.

The symbolism of the apple in Greek and Roman literature. _In_ Harvard Studies in classical philology v72 p147-81

Liturgical architecture. See Liturgy and architecture

Liturgical drama

Bevington, D. M. Discontinuity in medieval acting traditions. _In_ The Elizabethan theatre, V p 1-16

History and criticism

Nicoll, A. Religious drama and profane during the Middle Ages. _In_ Nicoll, A. World drama p103-31

Liturgics

Werner, E. Two types of ritual and their music. _In_ Salo Wittmayer Baron v2 p975-1008

See also Christian art and symbolism; Liturgy and drama; Liturgy and literature

Liturgies. See Liturgics

Liturgy. See Liturgics

Liturgy and architecture

Lewis, S. Problems of architectural style and the Ambrosian liturgy in late fourth-century Milan. _In_ Enggass, R. C. and Stokstad, M. eds. Hortus imaginum p11-19

Liturgy and drama

Dunn, E. C. French medievalists and the saint's play: a problem for American scholarship. _In_ Medievalia et humanistica no.6 p51-62

Liturgy and literature

Gatch, M. M. Old English literature and the liturgy: problems and potential. _In_ Anglo-Saxon England 6 p237-47

Loerke, W. C. The monumental miniature. _In_ The Place of book illumination in Byzantine art p61-97

Litvinov, Pavel Mikhaïlovich

The human-rights movement in the Soviet Union. _In_ Sidorsky, D. ed. Essays on human rights p113-25

Litz, A. Walton

'A development of self': character and personality in Jane Austen's fiction. _In_ Jane Austen's achievement p64-78

Persuasion: forms of estrangement. _In_ Halperin, J. ed. Jane Austen p221-32

"That strange abstraction, 'nature' ": T. S. Eliot's Victorian inheritance. _In_ Knoepflmacher, U. C. and Tennyson, G. B. eds. Nature and the Victorian imagination p470-88

Wallace Stevens' defense of poetry: La poésie pure, the new romantic and the pressure of reality. _In_ Bornstein, G. ed. Romantic and modern p111-32

Litz, Walton. See Litz, A. Walton

Litzinger, Boyd

Kenneth Leslie Knickerbocker. _In_ Tennessee Studies in literature v20 p xi-xviii

The new vision of Judgment: the case of St Guido. _In_ Tennessee Studies in literature v20 p69-75

Liu, James J. Y. See Liu, Jo-yü

Liu, Jo-yü

Some literary qualities of the lyric (Tz'u). _In_ Birch, C. ed. Studies in Chinese literary genres p133-53

Tradition and creativity in early Ch'ing poetics. _In_ Artists and traditions p17-19

Liu, Nien-ling. See Chin, Ai-li S. jt. auth.

Liu, Shih-p'ei

About

Bernal, M. Liu Shih-p'ei and National Essence. _In_ The Limits of change p90-112

Liu, Tsung-chou

About

T'ang, Chün-i. Liu Tsung-chou's doctrine of moral mind and practice and his critique of Wang Yang-ming. _In_ The Unfolding of Neo-Confucianism p305-31

Lively, Penelope
Children and memory. *In* Horn Book Magazine. Crosscurrents of criticism p226-33

About

Rees, D. The narrative art of Penelope Lively. *In* Horn Book Magazine. Crosscurrents of criticism p342-48

Liversidge, Joan E. A.
Woodwork. *In* Strong, D. E. and Brown, D. eds. Roman crafts p155-65

Livesay, Dorothy

About

Stevens, P. Dorothy Livesay: the love poetry. *In* Woodcock, G. ed. Poets and critics p33-52

Living, Standard of. See Cost and standard of living

Livingston, Donald Wilson
Hume's conservatism. *In* Studies in eighteenth-century culture v7 p213-33
Hume's historical theory of meaning. *In* Livingston, D. W. and King, J. T. eds. Hume p213-38

Livingstone, David

About

Fletcher, I. M. David Livingstone: a short portrait of the great missionary-explorer. *In* The Occasional papers of the Rhodes-Livingstone Museum p297-333

Livingstone, Frank Brown. See Brace, C. L. jt. auth.

Livius, Titus

About

Whitfield, J. H. Livy, Tacitus. *In* Classical influences on European culture A.D. 1500-1700 p281-93

Livy. See Livius, Titus

Llewellyn, John. See Eatwell, J. jt. auth.

Llosa, Mario Vargas. See Vargas Llosa, Mario

Lloyd, A. C.
Emotion and decision in Stoic psychology. *In* Rist, J. M. ed. The Stoics p233-46

Lloyd, Albert Lancaster
On an unpublished Irish ballad. *In* Rebels and their causes p177-207

Lloyd, Barbara Bloom (LeVine)
Culture and colour coding. *In* Royal Institute of Philosophy. Communication and understanding p140-61

Lloyd, David Demarest
John Loughborough Pearson: noble seriousness. *In* Seven Victorian architects p66-83

Lloyd, Marie

About

Eliot, T. S. Marie Lloyd. *In* Eliot, T. S. Selected prose of T. S. Eliot p172-74

Lloyd, Trevor
Browning and politics. *In* Armstrong, I. ed. Robert Browning p142-67

Lloyd George, David Lloyd George, 1st Earl

About

Koss, S. E. Asquith versus Lloyd George: the last phase and beyond. *In* Crisis and controversy p66-89

Lloyd-Jones, Hugh
Agamemnonea. *In* Harvard Studies in classical philology v73 p97-104

Nietzsche and the study of the ancient world. *In* O'Flaherty, J. C.; Sellner, T. F. and Helm, R. M. eds. Studies in Nietzsche and the classical tradition p 1-15
Pindar Fr. 169. *In* Harvard Studies in classical philology v76 p45-56

Lloyd-Jones, Hugh, and Rea, John
Callimachus, fragments 260-261. *In* Harvard Studies in classical philology v72 p125-45

Lo, Kuan-chung, supposed author

About individual works

San Kuo

Li, P. Narrative patterns in San-kuo and Shui-hu. *In* Chinese narrative p73-84

Shui hu chuan

Li, P. Narrative patterns in San-kuo and Shui-hu. *In* Chinese narrative p73-84

Loans. See Bank loans; Interest and usury

Loanwords. See Language and languages—Foreign elements

Loar, Brian
Two theories of meaning. *In* Evans, G. L. and McDowell, J. H. eds. Truth and meaning p138-61

Loathly Bride, On the Coomaraswamy, A. K. *In* Coomaraswamy, A. K. Selected papers v 1 p353-70

Lobachevskiĭ, Nikolaĭ Ivanovich

About

Lukacs, E. Non-Euclidean geometry. *In* Neyman, J. ed. The heritage of Copernicus: theories "pleasing to the mind" p359-77

Lobban, Carolyn Fluehr- See Fluehr-Lobban, Carolyn

Lobbying
Galnoor, I. The information marketplace. *In* Galnoor, I. ed. Government secrecy in democracies p77-92
See also Lobbyists

Lobbyists
Pertschuk, M. The lawyer-lobbyist. *In* Nader, R. and Green, M. J. eds. Verdicts on lawyers p197-207
See also Foreign propagandists in the United States

Lobenthal, Joseph S. See Luger, M. jt. auth.

Lobitz, Gretchen K. See Johnson, S. M. jt. auth.

Lobkowicz, Nicholas. See Lobkowicz, Nikolaus

Lobkowicz, Nikolaus
On the history of theory and praxis. *In* Political theory and praxis p13-27

Local administration. See Local government

Local color in literature
Alcorn, J. Spirit of place: The novel. *In* Alcorn, J. The nature novel from Hardy to Lawrence p60-77
Welty, E. Place in fiction. *In* Welty, E. The eye of the story p116-33

Local elections

Connecticut—Bridgeport

Stave, B. M. The Great Depression and urban political continuity: Bridgeport chooses socialism. *In* Stave, B. M. ed. Socialism and the cities p157-83

Local elections—*Continued*
Great Britain
Cook, C. Liberals, Labour and local elections. *In* Peele, G. and Cook, C. eds. The politics of reappraisal, 1918-1939 p166-88
New Jersey—Passaic
Ebner, M. H. Socialism and progressive political reform: the 1911 change-of-government in Passaic. *In* Stave, B. M. ed. Socialism and the cities p116-40
Oklahoma—Oklahoma City
Burbank, G. Socialism in an Oklahoma boom-town: "Milwaukeeizing" Oklahoma City. *In* Stave, B. M. ed. Socialism and the cities p99-115

Local finance. See Grants-in-aid; Metropolitan finance

Local government
See also Mayors; Metropolitan government; Municipal government

Connecticut—History
Daniels, B. C. The political structure of local government in colonial Connecticut. *In* Daniels, B. C. ed. Town and county p44-71

Ethiopia
Koehn, P. H. Urban origins and consequences of national and local political transformation in Ethiopia. *In* Walton, J. and Masotti, L. H. eds. The city in comparative perspective p155-78

Great Britain—History
Konig, D. T. English legal change and the origins of local government in northern Massachusetts. *In* Daniels, B. C. ed. Town and county p12-43

Maryland—History
Carr, L. G. The foundations of social order: local government in colonial Maryland. *In* Daniels, B. C. ed. Town and county p72-110

Massachusetts—History
Konig, D. T. English legal change and the origins of local government in northern Massachusetts. *In* Daniels, B. C. ed. Town and county p12-43

New York (State)
Caso, R. G. Managing the unmanageable *In* Benton, L. R. ed. Management for the future p47-62

New York (State)—History
Varga, N. The development and structure of local government in colonial New York. *In* Daniels, B. C. ed. Town and county p186-215

Pennsylvania—History
Bockelman, W. L. Local government in colonial Pennsylvania. *In* Daniels, B. C. ed. Town and county p216-37

Philadelphia—History
Diamondstone, J. M. The government of eighteenth-century Philadelphia. *In* Daniels, B. C. ed. Town and county p238-63

South Carolina—History
Waterhouse, R. The responsible gentry of colonial South Carolina: a study in local government, 1670-1770. *In* Daniels, B. C. ed. Town and county p160-85

United States
Street, D. and Davidson, J. L. Community and politics in city and suburb. *In* Handbook of contemporary urban life p468-93

Weber, R. E. The political responsiveness of the American states and their local governments. *In* Rieselbach, L. N. ed. People vs. government: the responsiveness of American institutions p189-225

Virginia—History
Seiler, W. H. The Anglican Church: a basic institution of local government in colonial Virginia. *In* Daniels, B. C. ed. Town and county p134-59

Wheeler, R. A. The county court in colonial Virginia. *In* Daniels, B. C. ed. Town and county p111-33

Local history
Leuilliot, P. A manifesto: the defense and illustration of local history. *In* Rural society in France p6-30

Nevins, A. The universal and the local. *In* Nevins, A. Allan Nevins on history p123-29

Thrupp, S. L. The pedigree and prospects of local history. *In* Thrupp, S. L. Society and history p256-68

Loch, Wolfgang
Some comments on the subject of psychoanalysis and truth. *In* Thought, consciousness, and reality p217-55

Lochman, Jan Milic
Toward a theology of Christological concentration. *In* The Context of contemporary theology p209-23

Locke, Alain Le Roy
About individual works
The new Negro
Cruse, H. The creative and performing arts and the struggle for identity and credibility. *In* Johnson, H. A. ed. Negotiating the mainstream p47-102

Locke, Elsie
Book trails in a small country (New Zealand) *In* Egoff, S. A. ed. One ocean touching p93-109

Locke, John
About
Grant, P. Conclusion. John Norris and Mr Locke: bodies and the uses of imagination. *In* Grant, P. Images and ideas in literature of the English Renaissance p192-209

Hacker, P. M. S. Locke and the meaning of colour words. *In* Royal Institute of Philosophy. Impressions of empiricism p23-46

Langbaum, R. W. Wordsworth: the self as process. *In* Langbaum, R. W. The mysteries of identity p25-47

Patterson, R. L. An analysis of faith. *In* Fact, value, and perception p85-105

Wiggins, D. Locke, Butler and the stream of consciousness: and men as a natural kind. *In* Rorty, A. O. ed. The identities of persons p139-73

About individual works
An essay concerning human understanding
Kittel, H. A. The book of Urizen and An essay concerning human understanding. *In* Phillips, M. C. ed. Interpreting Blake p111-44

O'Donnell, S. Mr Locke and the ladies: the indelible words on the tabula rasa. *In* Studies in eighteenth-century culture v8 151-64

Loewenberg, Peter
The psychohistorical origins of the Nazi youth cohort. *In* Kren, G. M. and Rappoport, L. H. eds. Varieties of psychohistory p219-47

Löffelholz, Franz

About individual works
Grundgriss
Middleton, J. C. On translating a text by Franz Mon. *In* Middleton, J. C. Bolshevism in art p160-72

Translations
Middleton, J. C. On translating a text by Franz Mon. *In* Middleton, J. C. Bolshevism in art p160-72

Lofgren, Charles Augustin
Missouri v. Holland in historical perspective. *In* The Supreme Court review, 1975 p77-122

Log cabins
Roberts, W. E. The Whitaker-Waggoner log house from Morgan County, Indiana. *In* Yoder, D. ed. American folklife p185-207

Logan, Joshua

About individual works
Picnic
Truffaut, F. Joshua Logan: Picnic. *In* Truffaut, F. The films in my life p125-26

Logan, Terence Patrick
George Chapman. *In* Logan, T. P. and Smith, D. S. eds. The new intellectuals p117-70

Logan, Terence Patrick, and Smith, Denzell Stewart
Other dramatists. *In* Logan, T. P. and Smith, D. S. eds. The new intellectuals p323-40
Other dramatists [another essay] *In* Logan, T. P. and Smith, D. S. eds. The popular school p250-74

Logic
Ayer, A. J. Self-evidence. *In* Pivčević, E. ed. Phenomenology and philosophical understanding p79-92
Berlin, Sir I. Logical translation. *In* Berlin, Sir I. Concepts and categories p56-80
Daor, D. Modes of argument. *In* Philosophy East/philosophy West p162-95
Foot, P. Moral arguments. *In* Foot, P. Virtues and vices, and other essays in moral philosophy p96-109
Mueller, I. An introduction to Stoic logic. *In* Rist, J. M. ed. The Stoics p 1-26
Quine, W. V. Carnap and logical truth. *In* Quine, W. V. The ways of paradox, and other essays p107-32
Quine, W. V. Mr Strawson on logical theory. *In* Quine, W. V. The ways of paradox, and other essays p137-57
Tejera, V. Dialogue and dialectic. *In* Philosophy and the civilizing arts p49-59
Willard, D. A. The paradox of logical psychologism: Husserl's way out. *In* Elliston, F. A. and McCormick, P. eds. Husserl p10-17

See also Certainty; Evidence; Hypothesis; Induction (Logic); Intention (Logic); Judgment (Logic); Knowledge, Theory of; Logical positivism; Modality (Logic); Nominalism; Probabilities; Proposition (Logic); Reasoning; Thought and thinking; Uniformity of nature; Universals (Philosophy); Verification (Logic)

History
Jardine, L. Humanism and dialectic in sixteenth-century Cambridge: a preliminary investigation. *In* Classical influences on European culture A.D. 1500-1700 p141-54

Logic, Deductive. See Logic

Logic, Deontic. See Deontic logic

Logic, Hindu. See Hindu logic

Logic, Inductive. See Induction (Logic)

Logic, Medieval
Armstrong, C. J. R. The dialectical road to truth: the dialogue. *In* French Renaissance studies, 1540-70 p36-51
Kretzmann, N. Incipit/desinit. *In* Motion and time, space and matter p101-36
Moody, E. A. The medieval contribution to logic. *In* Moody, E. A. Studies in medieval philosophy, science, and logic p371-90

Logic, Modern
Quine, W. V. On the application of modern logic. *In* Quine, W. V. The ways of paradox, and other essays p33-39
Weinberg, J. R. The universal affirmative. *In* Weinberg, J. R. Ockham, Descartes, and Hume p163-69

See also First-order logic

Logic, Symbolic and mathematical
Borgmann, A. Heidegger and symbolic logic. *In* Murray, M. E. ed. Heidegger and modern philosophy p 3-22
Cocchiarella, N. B. Formal ontology and the foundations of mathematics. *In* Nakhnikian, G. ed. Bertrand Russell's philosophy p29-46
Evans, G. L. Semantic structure and logical form. *In* Evans, G. L. and McDowell, J. H. eds. Truth and meaning p199-222
Hammersley, J. M. The technology of thought. *In* Neyman, J. ed. The heritage of Copernicus: theories "pleasing to the mind" p394-415
Hiz, H. Logical basis of semiotics. *In* Sebeok, T. A. ed. A perfusion of signs p40-53
Quine, W. V. Logic as a source of syntactical insights. *In* Quine, W. V. The ways of paradox, and other essays p44-49
Quine, W. V. A logistical approach to the ontological problem. *In* Quine, W. V. The ways of paradox, and other essays p197-202
Quine, W. V. Truth by convention. *In* Quine, W. V. The ways of paradox, and other essays p77-106
Quine, W. V. The variable. *In* Quine, W. V. The ways of paradox, and other essays p272-82
Stenius, E. 'All men are mortal.' *In* Fact, value, and perception p31-41
Weinberg, J. R. Relation and qualities. *In* Weinberg, J. R. Ockham, Descartes, and Hume p147-50

See also First-order logic; Predicate calculus; Probabilities; Propositional calculus; Science—Methodology; Semantics (Philosophy); Set theory

Logic, Transcendental. See Transcendental logic

Logic, Universal. See Logic, Symbolic and mathematical

Logic and faith. See Faith and reason

Logic machines. See Artificial intelligence

Logical analysis. See Analysis (Philosophy)

Logical empircism. See Logical positivism

Logical positivism

Carnap, R. The overcoming of metaphysics through logical analysis of language. *In* Murray, M. E. ed. Heidegger and modern philosophy p23-34

Ellis, B. D. Physicalism and the contents of sense experience. *In* Philosophical aspects of the mind-body problem p64-77

Gunderson, K. Asymmetries and mind-body perplexities. *In* Philosophical aspects of the mind-body problem p99-130

Suppe, F. R. Afterword—1977. *In* Suppe, F. R. ed. The structure of scientific theories p615-730

See also Analysis (Philosophy)

Lok Sevak Mandal

Pandey, G. The Shastris of Kashi and Lahore: the making of Congress leaders. *In* The Making of politicians: studies from Africa and Asia p116-25

Lokāyata

Chattopadhyaya, D. Lokāyata materialism. *In* Bishop, D. H. ed. Indian thought p101-14

Lola Montes (Motion picture)

Truffaut, F. Max Ophuls: Lola Montes. *In* Truffaut, F. The films in my life p225-29

Lolita (Motion picture)

French, B. The celluloid Lolita: a not-so-crazy quilt. *In* Peary, G. and Shatzkin, R. eds. The modern American novel and the movies p224-35

Lollards

Aston, M. E. Lollardy and sedition, 1381-1431. *In* Peasants, knights and heretics p273-318

Hill, J. E. C. From Lollards to Levellers. *In* Rebels and their causes p49-67

Lombard architecture. See Architecture, Lombard

Lombardi, John V.

The abolition of slavery in Venezuela: a nonevent. *In* Toplin, R. B. ed. Slavery and race relations in Latin America p228-52

Lombardo, Antonio I.

About individual works

Peace establishing her reign

Lewis, D. The Washington relief of Peace and its pendant. *In* Collaboration in Italian Renaissance art p233-44

Lombardo, Michael M. See McCall, M. W. jt. auth.

Lombards. See Barbarian invasions of Rome

Lomonosov, Mikhail Vasil'evich

About

Stacy, R. H. Mikhail Lomonosov. *In* Stacy, R. H. Russian literary criticism p13-24

London, Bruce

Ecology as macrosociology: a new look at an old perspective. *In* McNall, S. G. ed. Theoretical perspectives in sociology p494-513

London, Bruce, and Flanagan, William G.

Comparative urban ecology: a summary of the field. *In* Walton, J. and Masotti, L. H. eds. The city in comparative perspective p41-66

London, Herbert I.

Questions of viability in nontraditional education. *In* Hook, S.; Kurtz, P. W. and Todorovich, M. eds. The philosophy of the curriculum: the need for general education p221-26

London, Howard B.

The perils of opportunity: the working-class community college student in sociological perspective. *In* Hurdles p145-92

London, Jack

About

Sarotte, G. M. Latent homosexuality: short of and beyond true heterosexuality: Jack London: the hypervirile syndrome. *In* Sarotte, G. M. Like a brother, like a lover p240-61

Walcutt, C. C. Jack London. *In* Walcutt, C. C. ed. Seven novelists in the American naturalist tradition p131-67

Biography—Character

Sarotte, G. M. Latent homosexuality: short of and beyond true heterosexuality: Jack London: the hypervirile syndrome. *In* Sarotte, G. M. Like a brother, like a lover p240-61

Psychology

See London, Jack—Biography—Character

London

City planning

Korn, A. and Samuely, F. J. A master plan for London. *In* Sharp, D. ed. The rationalists p190-207

Commerce

Dietz, B. Antwerp and London: the structure and balance of trade in the 1560s. *In* Wealth and power in Tudor England p186-203

Description—1801-1900

Greaves, J. Going astray. *In* Dickens Studies Annual v3 p144-61

Economic conditions

Longstreth, F. H. The city, industry and the state. *In* Crouch, C. ed. State and economy in contemporary capitalism p157-90

Foreign population—History

Thrupp, S. L. Aliens in and around London in the fifteenth century. *In* Thrupp, S. L. Society and history p101-27

History

Power, M. J. The East and West in early-modern London. *In* Wealth and power in Tudor England p167-85

Wrigley, E. A. A simple model of London's importance in changing English society and economy, 1650-1750. *In* Towns in societies p215-43

Intellectual life

Levy, P. The Bloomsbury group. *In* Keynes, M. ed. Essays on John Maynard Keynes p60-72

Social conditions

Miskimin, H. A. The legacies of London: 1259-1330. *In* The Medieval city p209-27

Suburbs and environs

Creese, W. L. Imagination in the suburb. *In* Knoepflmacher, U. C. and Tennyson, G. B. eds. Nature and the Victorian imagination p49-67

London—*Continued*

Theaters

Bradbrook, M. C. Shakespeare and the multiple theaters of Jacobean London. *In* The Elizabethan theatre, VI p88-104

London. Royal College of Chemistry

History

Roberts, G. K. The establishment of the Royal College of Chemistry: an investigation of the social context of early-Victorian chemistry. *In* Historical studies in the physical sciences v7 p437-85

London. St Paul's Cathedral

Gair, W. R. The presentation of plays at Second Paul's: the early phase (1599-1602). *In* The Elizabethan theatre, VI p21-47

London in literature

Burke, A. R. The house of Chuzzlewit and the architectural city. *In* Dickens Studies Annual v3 p14-40

Skilton, D. Dickens and the literature of London. *In* Skilton, D. The English novel p99-119

Thompson, E. P. 'London.' *In* Phillips, M. C. ed. Interpreting Blake p5-31

Weitzman, A. J. Dr. Johnson's philurbanism. *In* Aeolian harps p95-109

London Journal; and Weekly Record of Literature, Science, and Art

Mitchell, S. The forgotten woman of the period: penny weekly family magazines of the 1840's and 1850's. *In* Vicinus, M. ed. A widening sphere p29-51

Lonelyhearts (Motion picture)

Klein, M. Miss L. gets married. *In* Peary, G. and Shatzkin, R. eds. The modern American novel and the movies p19-28

Long, A. A.

Dialectic and the Stoic sage. *In* Rist, J. M. ed. The Stoics p101-24

Long, Charles H.

Primitive religion. *In* Adams, C. J. ed. A reader's guide to the great religions p 1-38

Long, Franklin A.

Arms control from the perspective of the nineteen-seventies. *In* Long, F. A. and Rathjens, G. W. eds. Arms, defense policy, and arms control p 1-13

Long, Richard A. See Whalum, W. jt. auth.

Long, Rose-Carol Washton

Kandinsky and abstraction: the role of the hidden image. *In* Kaplan, P. and Manso, S. eds. Major European art movements, 1900-1945 p275-98

Long, Theodore Dixon

The dynamics of Japanese science policy. *In* Science policies of industrial nations p133-68

Long, Theodore Dixon, and Wright, Christopher

Science policy institutions in six countries. *In* Science policies of industrial nations p 1-11

Long, Timothy

The parados of Aristophanes' Wasps. *In* Illinois classical studies, v 1 1976 p15-21

The long goodbye (Motion picture)

Kauffmann, S. The long goodbye. *In* Kauffmann, S. Living images p231-33

Longacre, Robert E.

Comparative reconstruction of indigenous languages. *In* Sebeok, T. A. ed. Native languages of the Americas v2 p99-139

Longacre, William A.

Population dynamics at the Grasshopper pueblo, Arizona. *In* Zubrow, E. B. W. ed. Demographic anthropology p169-84

Longenecker, Richard N.

Literary criteria in life of Jesus research: an evaluation and proposal. *In* Current issues in Biblical and patristic interpretation p217-29

The obedience of Christ in the theology of the early Church. *In* Reconciliation and hope p142-52

Longevity

Comfort, A. A biologist laments and exhorts. *In* Jarvik, L. F. ed. Aging into the 21st century p41-60

Morison, R. S. Misgivings about life-extending technologies. *In* Holton, G. J. and Morison, R. S. eds. Limits of scientific inquiry p211-26

See also Aging; Old age

Longford, Frank Pakenham, 7th Earl of

About individual works

The grain of wheat

Vidal, G. Contagious self-love. *In* Vidal, G. Matters of fact and of fiction p149-52

Longhena, Baldassare

About individual works

Santa Maria della Salute (Church)

Wittkower, R. Santa Maria della Salute. *In* Wittkower, R. Studies in the Italian baroque p125-52

Longinus, Cassius

About individual works

On the sublime

Olson, E. The argument of Longinus's On the sublime. *In* Olson, E. On value judgments in the arts, and other essays p157-85

Olson, E. Longinus and Reynolds. *In* Olson, E. On value judgments in the arts, and other essays p107-17

Longomontanus, Christian Sørensen

About

Moesgaard, K. P. Cosmology in the wake of Tycho Brahe's astronomy. *In* Cosmology, history, and theology p293-305

Longomontanus, Christianus Severini. See Longomontanus, Christian Sørensen

Longstreet, Augustus Baldwin

About

Wade, J. D. Augustus Baldwin Longstreet: a Southern cultural type. *In* Inge, M. T. ed. The frontier humorists p94-104

About individual works

Georgia scenes, characters, incidents, etc., in the first half century of the Republic, by a native Georgian

Downs, R. B. Yarns of frontier life. *In* Downs, R. B. Books that changed the South p74-81

Gray, R. J. The good farmer: some variations on a historical theme. *In* Gray, R. J. The literature of memory p106-49

Poe, E. A. Georgia scenes. *In* Inge, M. T. ed. The frontier humorists p85-93

Longstreth, Frank Hoover

The city, industry and the state. *In* Crouch, C. ed. State and economy in contemporary capitalism p157-90

Longstreth Thompson, Francis Michael. See Thompson, Francis Michael Longstreth

Longsworth, Robert.
Chaucer's clerk as teacher. *In* The Learned and the lewed p61-66

Longus
About individual works
Daphnis and Chloe
Heiserman, A. R. Antonine comedy. *In* Heiserman, A. R. The novel before the novel p117-66

Longworth (T.) Firm
Stoddard, R. E. A catalogue of the dramatic imprints of David and Thomas Longworth, 1802-1821. *In* American Antiquarian Society. Proceedings v84 pt2 p317-98

Lonsdale, Roger H.
Dr. Burney, 'Joel Collier', and Sabrina. *In* Evidence in literary scholarship p281-308
"A garden, and a grave": the poetry of Oliver Goldsmith. *In* Martz, L. L. and Williams, A. L. eds. The author in his work p3-30

Looft, William R. and Svoboda, Cyril P.
Structuralism in cognitive developmental psychology: past, contemporary and future perspectives. *In* Riegel, K. F. and Rosenwald, G. C. eds. Structure and transformation p49-60

The Looker-on
Willey, E. P. A late-century Spectatorial essayist and his personae. *In* The Dress of words p209-18

Loomis, Chauncey C.
The Arctic sublime. In Knoepflmacher, U. C. and Tennyson, G. B. eds. Nature and the Victorian imagination p95-112

Loos, Adolf
About
Banham, R. Adolf Loos: ornament and crime. *In* Sharp, D. ed. The rationalists p26-33
About individual works
Ornament and crime
Banham, R. Adolf Loos: ornament and crime. *In* Sharp, D. ed. The rationalists p26-33

Lope de Vega. See Vega Carpio, Lope Félix de

López, Emilio González. See González López, Emilio

López, Jorge F. Pérez- See Pérez-López, Jorge F.

Lopez, Robert S.
The culture of the medieval merchant. *In* Medieval and Renaissance studies 1976 p52-73
The dawn of medieval banking. *In* The Dawn of modern banking p 1-23
The practical transmission of medieval culture. *In* Jeffrey, D. L. ed. By things seen: reference and recognition in medieval thought p125-42
Proxy in medieval trade. *In* Order and innovation in the Middle Ages p187-94
See also Part 2 under title: The medieval city

López Palanco, Rafael. See Palanco, Rafael López

López-Rey y Arrojo, Manuel
United Nations social defence policy and the problem of crime. *In* Crime, criminology and public policy p489-508

López Velarde, Ramón
About
Paz, O. The road of passion. *In* Paz, O. The siren & the seashell p67-112

Lora, Ronald
By love possessed: the Cozzens-Macdonald affair. *In* Filler, L. ed. A question of quality: popularity and value in modern creative writing p57-79

Lorca, Federico García. See García Lorca, Federico

Lorch, Maristella de Panizza. See De Panizza Lorch, Maristella

Lord, Albert Bates
Homer as oral poet. *In* Harvard Studies in classical philology v72 p 1-46
Perspectives on recent work on oral literature. *In* Duggan, J. J. ed. Oral literature p 1-24
About individual works
The singer of tales
Gunn, D. M. Thematic composition and Homeric authorship. *In* Harvard Studies in classical philology v75 p 1-31

Lord, George De Forest
Milton's dialogue with omniscience in Paradise lost. *In* Martz, L. L. and Williams, A. L. eds. The author in his work p31-50

Lord North. See North, Frederick, 2d Earl of Guilford

Lord's Day. See Sabbath

Lord's prayer
Sharpe, E. J. The Old English runic Paternoster. *In* Symbols of power p41-60

Lord's Supper
Martin, J. H. The Eucharistic treatise of John Quidort of Paris. *In* Viator: medieval and Renaissance studies v6 p195-240
See also Last Supper

Lorentz, Hendrik Antoon
About
Hirosige, T. The ether problem, the mechanistic worldview, and the origins of the theory of relativity. *In* Historical studies in the physical sciences v7 p3-82
Schaffner, K. F. Space and time in Lorentz, Poincaré, and Einstein: divergent approaches to the discovery and development of the special theory of relativity. *In* Motion and time, space and matter p465-507

Lorenz, James
State of siege: group legal services for the middle class. *In* Nader, R. and Green, M. J. eds. Verdicts on lawyers p144-57

Lorenz, Jim. See Lorenz, James

Lorenzen, David N.
The life of Śaṅkarācārya. *In* Reynolds, F. E. and Capps, D. eds. The biographical process p87-107

Lorenzetto
About individual works
Saint Peter
Chastel, A. Two Roman statues: Saints Peter and Paul. *In* Collaboration in Italian Renaissance art p59-73

Lorenzo di Ludovico di Guglielmo Lotti. See Lorenzetto

Loria, Arturo
Einstein and education. *In* Einstein p215-27

Lorin, Martin I.
Implications for therapy in the pediatric patient. *In* Anticipatory grief p182-86

Lorris, Guillaume de. See Guillaume de Lorris

Losey, Joseph

About individual works
The assassination of Trotsky
Kauffmann, S. The assassination of Trotsky. *In* Kauffmann, S. Living images p140-42

Loss of loved ones by death. See Bereavement

Los Silos, Spain. Silos abbey
Schapiro, M. From Mozarabic to Romanesque in Silos. *In* Schapiro, M. Selected papers v 1 p28-101

Lotarski, Susanne S.
The Communist takeover in Poland. *In* Hammond, T. T. ed. The anatomy of Communist takeovers p339-67

Loti, Pierre. See Viaud, Julien

Lotichius, Petrus Secundus

About
Ludwig, W. Petrus Lotichius Secundus and the Roman elegists: prolegomena to a study of Neo-Latin elegy. *In* Classical influences on European culture A.D. 1500-1700 p171-90

Lotti, Lorenzo. See Lorenzetto

Lotz, Wolfgang
Studies in Italian Renaissance architecture

Contents
Italian architecture in the later sixteenth century
Notes on the centralized church of the Renaissance
The Piazza Ducale in Vigevano: a princely forum of the late fifteenth century
The rendering of the interior in architectural drawings of the Renaissance
The Roman legacy in Sansovino's Venetian buildings
Sixteenth-century Italian squares
Three essays on Palladio: Observations on Palladio's drawings
Three essays on Palladio: Reflections on Palladio as town planner
Three essays on Palladio: The Rotonda: a secular building with a dome

Lougy, Robert Edward
Dickens' Hard times: the romance as radical literature. *In* Dickens Studies Annual v2 p237-54
Remembrances of death past and future: a reading of David Copperfield. *In* Dickens Studies Annual v6 p72-101

Louis IX, Saint, King of France

About
Jordan, W. C. Supplying Aigues-Mortes for the Crusade of 1248: the problem of restructuring trade. *In* Order and innovation in the Middle Ages p165-72

Louis XIII, King of France

About
Marvick, E. W. Childhood history and decisions of state: the case of Louis XIII. *In* DeMause, L. ed. The new psychohistory p199-244

Louis XIV, King of France

Monuments, etc.
Wittkower, R. The vicissitudes of a dynastic monument: Bernini's equestrian statue of Louis XIV. *In* Wittkower, R. Studies in the Italian baroque p83-102

Louisiana

Politics and government—
1865-1950
Moore, J. R. The New Deal in Louisiana. *In* Braeman, J.; Bremner, R. H. and Brody, D. eds. The New Deal v2 p137-65

Louria, Yvette
Molière and Griboiedov. *In* Johnson, R. B.; Neumann, E. S. and Trail, G. T. eds. Molière and the commonwealth of letters: patrimony and posterity p379-82

Lourié, Helen, pseud. See Storr, Catherine

Louw, Johannes P. See Nida, E. A. jt. auth.

Love, Harold
The argument of Donne's First anniversary. *In* Roberts, J. R. ed. Essential articles for the study of John Donne's poetry p355-62
Preacher and publisher: Oliver Heywood and Thomas Parkhurst. *In* Virginia. University. Bibliographical Society. Studies in bibliography v31 p227-35

Love
Bateson, M. C. Daddy, can a scientist be wise? *In* About Bateson p57-73
Bowden, B. The art of courtly copulation. *In* Medievalia et humanistica; new ser. no. 9 p67-85
Rapaport, E. On the future of love: Rousseau and the radical feminists. *In* Gould, C. C. and Wartofsky, M. W. eds. Women and philosophy p185-205
See also Courtly love

Love (Motion picture)
Kauffmann, S. Love. *In* Kauffmann, S. Living images p185-88

Love (Theology)
Bethge, E. Love without limits. *In* The Context of contemporary theology p243-49

Love (The word)
Walker, L. L. "Love" in the Old Testament: some lexical observations. *In* Current issues in Biblical and patristic interpretation p277-88

Love, Courtly. See Courtly love

Love in literature
Brody, S. N. The comic rejection of courtly love. *In* In pursuit of perfection p221-61
Cockshut, A. O. J. Jane Austen. *In* Cockshut, A. O. J. Man and woman: a study of love and the novel, 1740-1940 p54-71
Cockshut, A. O. J. Love and the novel. *In* Cockshut, A. O. J. Man and woman: a study of love and the novel, 1740-1940 p 9-31
Cockshut, A. O. J. The optimists: Lawrence. *In* Cockshut, A. O. J. Man and woman: a study of love and the novel, 1740-1940 p152-60
Cockshut, A. O. J. The pessimists: Emily Brontë. *In* Cockshut, A. O. J. Man and woman: a study of love and the novel, 1740-1940 p107-11
Cockshut, A. O. J. The pessimists: George Gissing. *In* Cockshut, A. O. J. Man and woman: a study of love and the novel, 1740-1940 p131-35

Love in literature—*Continued*

Cockshut, A.O. J. The pessimists: J. A. Froude. *In* Cockshut, A. O. J. Man and woman: a study of love and the novel, 1740-1940 p100-07

Cockshut, A O. J. The pessimists: Thomas Hardy. *In* Cockshut, A. O. J. Man and woman: a study of love and the novel, 1740-1940 p116-30

Cockshut, A. O. J. The realists: Mrs Gaskell. *In* Cockshut, A. O. J. Man and woman: a study of love and the novel, 1740-1940 p86-99

Cockshut, A. O. J. The realists: Thackeray. *In* Cockshut, A. O. J. Man and woman: a study of love and the novel, 1740-1940 p73-86

Cockshut, A. O. J. Richardson and Fielding. *In* Cockshut, A. O. J. Man and woman: a study of love and the novel, 1740-1940 p32-45

Ferrante, J. M. Dante. *In* Ferrante, J. M. Woman as image in medieval literature p129-52

Garrety, M. Love and war: R. H. Mottram, The Spanish farm trilogy and Ernest Hemingway, A farewell to arms. *In* Klein, H. M. ed. The First World War in fiction p10-22

Johnson, W. S. Sexual attitudes: secular, sacramental, and ideal. *In* Johnson, W. S. Sex and marriage in Victorian poetry p34-109

Kennard, J. E. Aristocrat versus commoner. *In* Kennard, J. E. Victims of convention p46-79

Kennard, J. E. Capital punishment. *In* Kennard, J. E. Victims of convention p63-79

Kennard, J. E. Her transitory self. *In* Kennard, J. E. Victims of convention p136-57

Kennard, J. E. Introduction. *In* Kennard, J. E. Victims of convention p 9-20

Kennard, J. E. Jane Austen: the establishment. *In* Kennard, J. E. Victims of convention p21-54

Kennard, J. E. A question of mastery: the novels of Charlotte Brontë. *In* Kennard, J. E. Victims of convention p80-107

Kennard, J. E. A wife who waddles: the novels of George Eliot. *In* Kennard, J. E. Victims of convention p108-35

Lucas, W. J. A note on the treatment of love and marriage in later Victorian fiction. *In* Lucas, W. J. The literature of change p192-207

Manlove, C. M. 'Rooteles moot grene soone deye': the helplessness of Chaucer's Troilus and Criseyde. *In* English Association. Essays and studies, 1978 p 1-22

Morse, S. "The subverted flower": an exercise in triangulation. *In* Frost: centennial essays II p170-76

Poggioli, R. Pastoral love. *In* Poggioli, R. The oaten flute p 42-63

Polk, N. E. Water, wanderers, and weddings: love in Eudora Welty. *In* Dollarhide, L. and Abadie, A. J. eds. Eudora Welty: a form of thanks p95-122

Quinn, E. C. Beyond courtly love: religious elements in Tristan and La queste del Saint Graal. *In* In Pursuit of perfection p179-219

Reiss, E. Chaucer's courtly love. *In* The Learned and the lewed p95-111.

Sabin, M. "Love" in The prelude. *In* Sabin, M. English romanticism and the French tradition p33-47

Sabin, M. Rousseau and the vocabulary of feeling. *In* Sabin, M. English romanticism and the French tradition p17-32

Smith, A. J. Sense and innocence: two love episodes in Dante and Milton. *In* An English miscellany p119-30

Terdiman, R. Conclusion. *In* Terdiman, R. The dialects of isolation p227-48

Tristram, P. Eros and death (Lawrence, Freud and women). *In* Smith, A. ed. Lawrence and women p136-55

See also Sentimentalism in literature; Sex in literature

Love in motion pictures

French, B. The hard and the soft. *In* French, B. On the verge of revolt p48-60

Love poetry. See Minnesingers

Love poetry, English

Hardy, B. N. Passion and contemplation in Yeats's love poetry. *In* Hardy, B. N. The advantage of lyric p67-83

History and criticism

Armstrong, I. Browning and Victorian poetry of sexual love. *In* Armstrong, I. ed. Robert Browning p267-98

Love poetry, French

History and criticism

Kelly, D. Imagination and the Second Rhetoric. *In* Kelly, D. Medieval imagination p96-120

Kelly, D. Rhetoric and poetry. *In* Kelly, D. Medieval imagination p3-12

Kelly, D. Verisimilitude and imagination: the crisis in late courtly poetry. *In* Kelly, D. Medieval imagination p177-203

Love poetry, Latin

History and criticism

Luck, G. The woman's role in Latin love poetry. *In* Perspectives of Roman poetry p15-31

Love stories

Mann, P. H. Romantic fiction and its readers. *In* Fischer, H. D. and Melnik, S. R. eds. Entertainment: a cross-cultural examination p34-42

Lovecraft, Howard Phillips

About

Barclay, G. S. The myth that never was: Howard P. Lovecraft. *In* Barclay, G. S. Anatomy of horror: the masters of occult fiction p81-96

Lovell, Alan

The Western. *In* Nichols, B. ed. Movies and methods p164-75

Lovelock, Julian. See Dyson, A. E. jt. auth.

Lovers and thieves (Motion picture)

Truffaut, F. Sacha Guitry: Assassins et voleurs. *In* Truffaut, F. The films in my life p214-16

Lovett, William

About

Large, D. William Lovett. *In* Hollis, P. ed. Pressure from without p105-30

Lovink, Johannes Anton Alexander

Prospects for democratic control. *In* Prospects for constitutional democracy p36-52

Low, Samuel
About
Leary, L. G. Samuel Low: New York's first poet. *In* Leary, L. G. Soundings p67-82

Low income housing. See Housing

Lowance, Mason Ira
Typology and millennial eschatology in early New England. *In* Miner, E. R. ed. Literary uses of typology p228-73

Lowance, Mason Ira, and Watters, David
Increase Mather's 'New Jerusalem', millennialism in late seventeenth-century New England. *In* American Antiquarian Society. Proceedings v87 pt2 p343-408

Lowe, Adolph
Adam Smith's system of equilibrium growth. *In* Skinner, A. S. and Wilson, T. eds. Essays on Adam Smith p415-25

Lowe, Gareth W.
The Mixe-Zoque as competing neighbors of the early Lowland Maya. *In* The Origins of Maya civilization p197-248

Lowell, Elizabeth Hardwick. See Hardwick, Elizabeth

Lowell, Robert
About
Altieri, C. F. Robert Lowell and the difficulties of escaping modernism. *In* Altieri, C. F. Enlarging the temple p53-77
Bayley, J. The self as available reality. *In* Bayley, J. The uses of division p157-71
Kalstone, D. Robert Lowell: the uses of history. *In* Kalstone, D. Five temperaments p41-76
Kunitz, S. J. Poet: "A slightly laughable and glamorous word": a conversation with Robert Lowell. *In* Kunitz, S. J. A kind of order, a kind of folly p153-60
Kunitz, S. J. Poet of terribilità. *In* Kunitz, S. J. A kind of order, a kind of folly p247-50
Martin, J. Robert Lowell. *In* Donoghue, D. ed. Seven American poets from MacLeish to Nemerov p209-49
Miller, J. E. Poetic metamorphoses: Lowell and Berryman (a prologue). *In* Miller, J. E. The American quest for a supreme fiction p2-11
Pearson, G. Robert Lowell: the middle years. *In* Boyers, R. ed. Contemporary poetry in America p43-58
Simpson, L. Robert Lowell's indissoluble-bride. *In* Simpson, L. A revolution in taste p129-67
Thurley, G. The poetry of breakdown: Robert Lowell and Anne Sexton. *In* Thurley, G. The American moment p70-90
About individual works
For the Union dead
Holbrook, D. Paralysis as "space is nearer": Robert Lowell's For the Union dead. *In* Holbrook, D. Lost bearings in English poetry p48-57
Trilling, L. Robert Lowell: For the Union dead. *In* Trilling, L. Prefaces to The experience of literature p296-302
History
Kalstone, D. Robert Lowell: the uses of history. *In* Kalstone, D. Five temperaments p41-76
Imitations
Belitt, B. Imitations: translation as personal mode. *In* Belitt, B. Adam's dream p54-66

Lord Weary's castle
Berryman, J. Robert Lowell and others. *In* Berryman, J. The freedom of the poet p286-96
Notebook
Connolly, C. Robert Lowell. *In* Connolly, C. The evening colonnade p361-64
Notebook, 1967-68
Boyers, R. On Robert Lowell. *In* Boyers, R. Excursions p147-55
The Old Glory
Simon, J. I. Strange devices on the banner. *In* Simon, J. I. Singularities p181-84
Skunk hour
Berryman, J. Despondency and madness: on Lowell's "Skunk hour." *In* Berryman, J. The freedom of the poet p316-22

Lowen, Alexander
Human nature. *In* Hanna, T. ed. Explorers of humankind p33-47

Lowenfeld mosaic test
Métraux, R. B. Eidos and change: continuity in process, discontinuity in product. *In* Schwartz, T. ed. Socialization as cultural communication p201-16

Lowenstein, Ralph Lynn
Press freedom as a barometer of political democracy. *In* Fischer, H. D. and Merrill, J. C. eds. International and intercultural communication p136-47
Use of foreign media by developing nations. *In* Fischer, H. D. and Merrill, J. C. eds. International and intercultural communication p210-17

Lowenthal, Abraham Frederic
The United States and Latin America: ending the hegemonic presumption. *In* Two hundred years of American foreign policy p181-208

Lowenthal, David
The place of the past in the American landscape. *In* Geographies of the mind p89-117

Lowenthal, Richard
The university's autonomy versus social priorities. *In* Universities in the Western world p75-84

Lower, Arthur Reginald Marsden
About
Berger, C. Arthur Lower and a national community. *In* Berger, C. The writing of Canadian history p112-36

Lowi, Theodore J.
The information revolution, politics, and the prospects for an open society. *In* Galnoor, I. ed. Government secrecy in democracies p40-61

Löwith, Karl
About individual works
Meaning in history
Frye, N. The rhythm of growth and decay. *In* Frye, N. Northrop Frye on culture and literature p141-46

Lowman, Al
A chronology of LCP keepsakes. *In* Voices from the Southwest p132-45

Lowry, Malcolm
About
Dodson, D. B. Malcolm Lowry. *In* Stade, G. ed. Six contemporary British novelists p115-64

Gass, W. H. Malcolm Lowry. *In* Gass, W. H. The world within the word p16-38

Walker, R. G. Under Under the volcano: the Mexicans voyages of Malcolm Lowry. *In* Walker, R. G. Infernal paradise p281-321

About individual works
Under the volcano

Walker, R. G. The barranca of history: Mexico as nexus of doom in Under the volcano. *In* Walker, R. G. Infernal paradise p237-80

Technique
Bradbrook, M. C. Narrative form in Conrad and Lowry. *In* Joseph Conrad: a commemoration p129-42

Lowry, Wilson McNeil
The arts in America: evolution and tradition. *In* The American Revolution: a continuing commitment p41-52

Loy, John W.
Race and sport: a reaction to the McPherson and Madison and Landers papers. *In* Social problems in athletics p157-67

Loyalists, American. See American loyalists

Loyalty
Woolf, R. The ideal of men dying with their lord in the Germania and in The Battle of Maldon. *In* Anglo-Saxon England 5 p63-81

See also Patriotism

Loyalty, Political. See Allegiance

Loyn, Henry Royston
Kinship in Anglo-Saxon England. *In* Anglo-Saxon England 3 p197-209

Loyola, Ignacio de, Saint
About
Levi, A. H. T. Erasmus, the early Jesuits and the classics. *In* Classical influences on European culture A.D. 1500-1700 p223-38

Ložar, Tom
Before the brave: portrait of man as a young artist. *In* Morgan, R. G. ed. Kenneth Patchen: a collection of essays p193-207

Lu Xun. See Chow, Shu-jên

Luba (Bantu people). See Baluba

Lubetkin, Berthold
About
Jordan, R. Berthold Lubetkin. *In* Sharp, D. ed. The rationalists p101-17

Lubieniecki, Stanislaw
About individual works
Historia Reformationis Polonicae

Williams, G. H. The Sarmatian myth sublimated in the Historia Reformationis Polonicae (1664/1685) of Stanislas Lubieniecki and related documents. *In* For Wiktor Weintraub p571-83

Lubin, Bernard. See Neff, F. W. jt. auth.

Lubitsch, Ernst
About
Truffaut, F. Lubitsch was a prince. *In* Truffaut, F. The films in my life p50-53

Lucas, Colin Renshaw
Nobles, bourgeois and the origins of the French Revolution. *In* French society and the Revolution p88-131

Lucas, Elizabeth. See Pinckney, Eliza (Lucas)

Lucas, George R.
Political and economic dimensions of hunger: strategies to combat famine in the 1970's. *In* Lucas, G. R. and Ogletree, T. W. eds. Lifeboat ethics p 1-28

Lucas, John Randolph
On processes for resolving disputes; excerpt from "The principles of politics." *In* Summers, R. S. ed. Essays in legal philosophy p167-82

Lucas, Paul Robert
"An appeal to the learned": the mind of Solomon Stoddard. *In* Vaughan, A. T. and Bremer, F. J. eds. Puritan New England p326-45

Lucas, Victoria, pseud. See Plath, Sylvia

Lucas, William John
The literature of change
Contents

Engels, Mrs Gaskell and Manchester

Hardy's women

Mrs Gaskell and the nature of social change

A note on the treatment of love and marriage in later Victorian fiction

William Hale White and the problems of deliverance

Lucca, Italy
Commerce—History
Blomquist, T. W. The dawn of banking in an Italian commune: thirteenth century Lucca. *In* The Dawn of modern banking p53-75

Luce, Gay G.
Biological rhythms in health and disease. *In* Sobel, D. S. ed. Ways of health p397-411

Luce, Gordon Hannington
Sources of early Burma history. *In* Southeast Asian history and historiography p31-42

Luce, Henry Robinson
About
Sheed, W. More light on Luce. *In* Sheed, W. The good word & other words p132-36

Luce, John Victor
The sources and literary form of Plato's Atlantis narrative. *In* Ramage, E. S. ed. Atlantis, fact or fiction? p49-78

Lucia, Patricia Santa, pseud. See Santa Lucia, Patricia, pseud.

Lucie-Smith, Edward
About individual works
Eroticism in Western art

Rosenberg, H. Trials of Eros. *In* Rosenberg, H. Art on the edge p216-26

Lucilius, Caius
About
Knoche, U. Gaius Lucilius. *In* Knoche, U. Roman satire p31-52

About individual works
Satires

Knoche, U. Gaius Lucilius. *In* Knoche, U. Roman satire p31-52

Ramage, E. S. Lucilius, the discoverer of the genre. *In* Roman satirists and their satire p27-52

Lucilius, Gaius. See Lucilius, Caius

Luck, Edward C.

The Soviet Union and conventional arms control. *In* Kirk, G. L. and Wessell, N. H. eds. The Soviet threat p57-65

Luck, Georg

Disiecta membra: on the arrangement of Claudian's Carmina minora. *In* Illinois classical studies v4, 1979 p200-13

An interpretation of Horace's Eleventh Epode. *In* Illinois classical studies, v 1 1976 p122-26

The textual history of Juvenal and the Oxford lines. *In* Harvard Studies in classical philology v76 p217-31

The woman's role in Latin love poetry. *In* Perspectives of Roman poetry p15-31

Luckett, Richard

Exotick but rational entertainments: the English dramatick operas. *In* English drama: forms and development p123-41

'Meaning motion': old music and some modern writers. *In* English Association. Essays and studies, 1977 p88-97

Luckmann, Thomas

About

Lemert, C. C. Phenomenological sociology: Schutz, Berger, Luckmann. *In* Lemert, C. C. Sociology and the twilight of man p135-64

Lucretius Carus, Titus

About individual works
On the nature of things

Avotins, I. Lucretius 2.16-2.33. *In* Harvard Studies in classical philology v82 p167-73

Stewart, D. J. The silence of Magna Mater. *In* Harvard Studies in classical philology v74 p75-84

On the nature of things (Book I, Lines 62-101)

Kenney, E. J. Vivida vis: Polemic and pathos in Lucretius I.62-101. *In* Woodman, T. and West, D. eds. Quality and pleasure in Latin poetry p18-30

On the nature of things (Book III, 1-30)

Stokes, M. C. A Lucretian paragraph: III. 1-30. *In* Poetry and poetics from ancient Greece to the Renaissance p91-104

Manuscripts

Brown, V. The "insular intermediary" in the tradition of Lucretius. *In* Harvard Studies in classical philology v72 p301-08

The Ludovisi head. Ridgway, B. S. *In* Studies in classical art and archaeology p153-61

Ludwig, Jan Keith

Philosophy & parapsychology. *In* Ludwig, J. K. ed. Philosophy and parapsychology p17-40

Ludwig, Richard Milton

Pound and Eliot. *In* American literary scholarship, 1974 p101-21

Ludwig, Walther

Petrus Lotichius Secundus and the Roman elegists: prolegomena to a study of Neo-Latin elegy. *In* Classical influences on European culture A.D. 1500-1700 p171-90

Ludwig (Motion picture)

Kauffmann, S. Ludwig. *In* Kauffmann, S. Living images p183-85

Luebke, Frederick C.

The Germans. *In* Ethnic leadership in America p64-90

Luecke, Jane-Marie

Measuring Old English rhythm: Applying the method to Beowulf. *In* Literary monographs v9 p49-74

Measuring Old English rhythm: Measuring the rhythm of the Five Types. *In* Literary monographs v9 p75-95

Measuring Old English rhythm: Surveying the history of Old English prosody. *In* Literary monographs v9 p4-30

Measuring Old English rhythm: The suspect verses and a summary. *In* Literary monographs v9 p96-111

Measuring Old English rhythm: The unequal measures of Gregorian chant. *In* Literary monographs v9 p31-48

Luedtke, Luther Stephen

Not so common ground: controversies in contemporary American studies. *In* Luedtke, L. S. ed. The study of American culture p323-67

Luehrs, Robert Boice

The problematical compromise: the early deism of Anthony Collins. *In* Studies in eighteenth-century culture v6 p59-77

Luenas (Bantu tribe)

White, C. M. N. The material culture of the Lunda-Lovale peoples. *In* The Occasional papers of the Rhodes-Livingstone Museum p53-70

Lueschen, Guenther

Cheating in sport. *In* Social problems in athletics p67-77

Luger, Milton, and Lobenthal, Joseph S.

Cushioning future shock in corrections. *In* Riedel, M. and Chappel, D. eds. Issues in criminal justice: planning and evaluation p126-33

Lūghd, Jānit Abū- See Abū-Lūghd, Jānit

Luhmann, Niklas. See Habermas, J. jt. auth.

Luis de Léon. See Léon, Luis Ponce de

Lukacs, Eugene

Non-Euclidean geometry. *In* Neyman, J. ed. The heritage of Copernicus: theories "pleasing to the mind" p359-77

Lukács, Georg. See Lukács, György

Lukács, György

About

Watkins, E. Raymond Williams and Marxist criticism. *In* Watkins, E. The critical act p141-57

About individual works
History and class consciousness

Kovály, P. György Lukács: the history of an error. *In* Kovály, P. Rehumanization or dehuminization? p65-100

Solzhenitsyn

Howe, I. Lukacs and Solzhenitsyn. *In* Dunlop, J. B.; Haugh, R. and Klimoff, A. eds. Aleksandr Solzhenitsyn: critical essays and documentary materials 2d ed. p147-55

Theory of the novel

Good, G. Lukács' Theory of the novel. *In* Spilka, M. ed. Towards a poetics of fiction p125-35

Luke, David
"How is it that you live, and what is it that you do?: the question of old age in English romantic poetry. *In* Spicker, S. F.; Woodward, K. M. and Van Tassel, D. D. eds. Aging and the elderly p221-40

Luke, F. D.
Nietzsche and the imagery of height. *In* Pasley, J. M. S. ed. Nietzsche: imagery and thought p104-22

Lukermann, Fred E. See Porter, P. W. jt. auth.

Lully, Jean Baptiste de
About
Harned, A. R. Molière and Lully. *In* Johnson, R. B.; Neumann, E. S. and Trail, G. T. eds. Molière and the commonwealth of letters: patrimony and posterity p31-48

Lumbee Indians
Evans, W. M. The North Carolina Lumbees: from assimilation to revitalization. *In* Williams, W. L. ed. Southeastern Indians since the removal era p49-71

Lumsdaine, Arthur A.
On mass communication experiments and the like. *In* Lerner, D. and Nelson, L. M. eds. Communication research—a half-century appraisal p37-69

Lumsden, William Hepburn Russell
Impact of independence and nationalism on tropical medicine. *In* Cahill, K. M. ed. Health and development p23-35

Lunar bases
Asimov, I. The moon as threshold. *In* The Frontiers of knowledge p359-99

Lunda (Bantu tribe)
Turner, V. W. Lunda rites and ceremonies. *In* The Occasional papers of the Rhodes-Livingstone Museum p335-88
White, C. M. N. The material culture of the Lunda-Lovale peoples. *In* The Occasional papers of the Rhodes-Livingstone Museum p53-70

Lundberg, Craig Carl
The unreported leadership research of Dr. G. Hypothetical: six variables in need of recognition. *In* Leadership p65-83

Lundén, Rolf
Foreign scholarship: Scandinavian contributions. *In* American literary scholarship, 1975 p498-501
Foreign scholarship: Scandinavian contributions [another essay] *In* American literary scholarship, 1976 p459-62
Foreign scholarship: Scandinavian contributions [another essay] *In* American literary scholarship, 1977 p505-15

Lundgreen, Peter
Educational expansion and economic growth in nineteenth-century Germany: a quantitative study. *In* Schooling and society p20-66
See also Fischer, W. jt. auth.

Lundquist, Anne S.
Ludvig Holberg and Molière: imitation or constructive emulation? *In* Johnson, R. B.; Neumann, E. S. and Trail, G. T. eds. Molière and the commonwealth of letters: patrimony and posterity p245-51

Lunds Universitet
Curricula
Emmelin, L. An environmental studies program. *In* Against pollution and hunger p256-59

Lunn, George Richard
About
Hendrickson, K. E. Tribune of the people: George R. Lunn and the rise and fall of Christian Socialism in Schenectady. *In* Stave, B. M. ed. Socialism and the cities p72-98

Luo (Nilotic tribe)
Mazrui, A. A. Casualties of an underdeveloped class structure: the expulsion of Luo workers and Asian bourgeoisie from Uganda. *In* Shack, W. A. and Skinner, E. P. eds. Strangers in African societies p261-88
Southall, A. W. From segmentary lineage to ethnic association—Luo, Luhya, Ibo, and others. *In* Colonialism and change p203-29

Lur'e, Íakov Solomonovich
An unpublished epigram on an English ambassador to Russia. *In* Oxford Slavonic papers new ser. v7 p13-17

Luria, Gina. See Tayler, I. B. S. jt. auth.

Luria, J. See Lur'e, Íakov Solomonovich

Luria, Salvador Edward
What can biologists solve? *In* Montagu, A. ed. Race and IQ p42-51

Luria, Zella
Psychosocial determinants of gender identity, role, and orientation. *In* Katchadourian, H. A. ed. Human sexuality p163-93

Lurie, Abraham. See Dean, A. jt. auth.

Lurie, Nancy Oestreich
The world's oldest on-going protest demonstration: North American Indian drinking patterns. *In* The American Indian p55-76

Luscombe, David E.
The 'lex divinitatis' in the bull 'Unam sanctam' of Pope Boniface VIII. *In* Church and government in the Middle Ages p205-21

Lustig, Irma S.
The friendship of Johnson and Boswell: some biographical considerations. *In* Studies in eighteenth-century culture v6 p199-214

Luther, David G.
China, lump sum settlements, and executive agreements. *In* China's changing role in the world economy p213-22

Luther, Martin
About
Gerrish, B. A. De libero arbitrio (1524): Erasmus on piety, theology, and the Lutheran dogma. *In* Essays on the works of Erasmus p187-209
Haile, H. G. Luther as Renaissance writer. *In* Hoffmeister, G. ed. The Renaissance and Reformation in Germany p141-56
Lindberg, C. H. Mask of God and Prince of Lies: Luther's theology of the demonic. *In* Disguises of the demonic p87-103
Sellin, P. R. The hidden God: Reformation awe in Renaissance English literature. *In* The Darker vision of the Renaissance p147-96
Thompson, W. D. J. C. Luther and the right of resistance to the Emperor. *In* Church, society and politics p159-202

Biography
Bornkamm, H. Luther and his father: observations on Erik H. Erikson's Young man Luther: a study in psychoanalysis and history. *In* Homans, P. ed. Childhood and selfhood p59-88

Luther, Martin—*Continued*
Psychology
Bornkamm, H. Luther and his father: observations on Erik H. Erikson's Young man Luther: a study in psychoanalysis and history. *In* Homans, P. ed. Childhood and selfhood p59-88

Edwards, M. U. Erikson, experimental psychology, and Luther's identity. *In* Homans, P. ed. Childhood and selfhood p89-112

Lutheran Church
Education—History
Strauss, G. The state of pedagogical theory c. 1530: what Protestant reformers knew about education. *In* Schooling and society p69-94

Lüthi, Max
Aspects of the Märchen and the legend. *In* Folklore genres p17-33

Luttwak, Edward N.
The failure to understand strategy. *In* Decline of the West? George Kennan and his critics p97-111

Lutyens, Sir Edwin Landseer
About
Gradidge, R. Edwin Lutyens: the last High Victorian. *In* Seven Victorian architects p122-36

Lutz, Cora Elizabeth
Essays on manuscripts and rare books
Contents
Aesticampianus' Commentary on the De grammatica of Martianus Capella
Aesticampianus' edition of the Tabula attributed to Cebes
The Apocryphal Abgarus-Jesus Epistles in England in the Middle Ages
A bifolium from a Sacramentarium Gregorianum
Bishop Dubravius on fishponds
A diamond and a Dürer in Dubravius' commentary on Martianus Capella
A fourteenth-century argument for an international date line
Johannes Climacus' Ladder of divine ascent
A manuscript fragment from Bede's monastery
A manuscript of Charlemagne's Homiliarium
Manuscripts copied from printed books
A medieval textbook
Note on St. Basil's address on reading Greek literature
The Theriobulia of Jan Dubravius
An unusual educational device of Aldus Manutius
Walter Burley's De vita et moribus philosophorum

Lutz, Donald S.
Popular consent and popular control: 1776-1789. *In* Graham, G. J. and Graham, S. G. eds. Founding principles of American government p60-97

Lux, Guillermo, and Vigil, Maurilio E.
Return to Aztlan: the Chicano rediscovers his Indian past. *In* Trejo, A. D. ed. The Chicanos p 1-17

Lwenas (Bantu tribe) See Luenas (Bantu tribe)

Lwo (Nilotic tribe) See Luo (Nilotic tribe)

Lyall, W. A. L. See Vachon, M. L. S. jt. auth.

Lyas, Colin
Danto and Dickie on art. *In* Aagaard-Mogensen, L. ed. Culture and art p170-93
The groundlessness of religious belief. *In* Reason and religion p158-80

Lyautey, Louis Hubert Gonzalve
About
Abū Lughd, J. Moroccan cities: apartheid and the serendipity of conservation. *In* African themes p77-111

Lyday, Leon F.
The theater of Alfredo Dias Gomes. *In* Lyday, L. F. and Woodyard, G. W. eds. Dramatists in revolt p221-42

Lydgate, John
About
Walsh, E. John Lydgate and the proverbial tiger. *In* The Learned and the lewed p291-303
About individual works
St Edmund and Fremund
Miller, J. I. Lydgate the hagiographer as literary artist. *In* The Learned and the lewed p279-90

Lyell, Sir Charles, 1st bart.
About individual works
Principles of geology
Gould, S. J. Agassiz's marginalia in Lyell's Principles, or the perils of uniformity and the ambiguity of heroes. *In* Studies in history of biology v3 p119-38

Lying. See Truthfulness and falsehood

Lyle, E. B.
The Wee wee man and Als y yod on ay Mounday. *In* Ballad studies p21-28

Lyle, Jack
Public television: too much ambition and overcommitment? *In* Lerner, D. and Nelson, L. M. eds. Communication research—a half-century appraisal p193-209

Lyly, John
About
Altman, J. B. Quaestiones copiosae: pastoral and courtly in John Lyly. *In* Altman, J. B. The Tudor play of mind p196-228
Helgerson, R. Lyly. *In* Helgerson, R. The Elizabethan prodigals p58-78
About individual works
Endimion
Saccio, P. The oddity of Lyly's Endimion. *In* The Elizabethan theatre, V p92-111
Gallathea
Scragg, L. Shakespeare, Lyly and Ovid: the influence of 'Gallathea' on 'A midsummer night's dream.' *In* Shakespeare survey 30 p125-34
Influence—Shakespeare
Scragg, L. Shakespeare, Lyle and Ovid: the influence of 'Gallathea' on 'A midsummer night's dream.' *In* Shakespeare survey 30 p125-34

Lyman, Stanford Morris
The acceptance, rejection, and reconstruction of histories: on some controversies in the study of social and cultural change. *In* Brown, R. H. and Lyman, S. M. eds. Structure, consciousness, and history p53-105
Conflict and the web of group affiliation in San Francisco's Chinatown, 1850-1910. *In* The Asian American: the historical experience p26-52
Japanese-American generation gap. *In* Henslin, J. M. ed. Deviant life-styles p25-38

Lynch, Joseph Howard

A Carolingian borrowing from Second Nicaea (787). *In* Medievalia et humanistica no. 5 p127-38

Lynch, Michael

The life below the life. *In* Crew, L. ed. The gay academic p178-92

Lynd, Helen Merrell. See Lynd, R. S. jt. auth.

Lynd, Robert Staughton, and Lynd, Helen Merrell

About individual works
Middletown

Goist, P. O. Middletown and the "eclipse of community": Robert and Helen Lynd. *In* Goist, P. D. From Main Street to State Street p46-56

Middletown in transition

Goist, P. D. Middletown and the "eclipse of community": Robert and Helen Lynd. *In* Goist, P. D. From Main Street to State Street p46-56

Lyne, R. O. A. M.

Scilicet et tempus veniet. . . : Virgil, Georgics I.463-514. *In* Woodman, T. and West, D. eds. Quality and pleasure in Latin poetry p47-66

Lynn, Kenneth Schuyler

Adulthood in American literature. *In* Erikson, E. H. ed. Adulthood p237-47

Lynn, Richard John

Orthodoxy and enlightenment: Wang Shih-chen's theory of poetry and its antecedents. *In* The Unfolding of Neo-Confucianism p217-69

Lyon, Eleanor. See Sanders, C. R. jt. auth.

Lyon, James K.

Kipling's "Soldiers three" and Brecht's A man's a man. *In* Mews, S. and Knust, H. eds. Essays on Brecht p99-113

Lyon, Stewart

Some problems in interpreting Anglo-Saxon coinage. *In* Anglo-Saxon England 5 p173-224

Lyons, Bonnie

David Levinsky: modern man as orphan. *In* Tulane Studies in English v23 p85-93

Lyons, Francis Stewart Leland

The Parnell theme in literature. *In* Place, personality and the Irish writer p69-95

Lyons, Gene

Report on the Fiction Collective. *In* Anderson, E. and Kinzie, M. eds. The little magazine in America: a modern documentary history p625-34

Lyons, John

About individual works
Noam Chomsky

Hymes, D. H. Review of Noam Chomsky. *In* Harman, G. ed. On Noam Chomsky p316-33

Lyons, John O.

The invention of the self

Contents

Autobiography
Biography
The circumference of the self
Confessional high tide
Dancing on the head of a pin
Into our age
Once upon a time
Out of the void

Rogues and adventurers
The traveler at home
Travelers East
Whores and rakes in the gardens of delight

On Lie down in darkness. *In* Morris, R. K. and Malin, I. eds. The achievement of William Styron p88-99

Lyons, Paul

The New Left and the Cuban Revolution. *In* Radosh, R. ed. The new Cuba: paradoxes and potentials p211-46

Lyra, F.

Foreign scholarship: East European contributions. *In* American literary scholarship, 1977 p463-67

Lyre

History

Winternitz, E. The lira da braccio. *In* Winternitz, E. Musical instruments and their symbolism in Western art p86-98

Lyre in art

Winternitz, E. The lira da braccio. *In* Winternitz, E. Musical instruments and their symbolism in Western art p86-98

Lyric poetry

Hardy, B. N. The advantage of lyric. *In* Hardy, B. N. The advantage of lyric p 1-17

Olson, E. The lyric. *In* Olson, E. On value judgments in the arts, and other essays p212-19

Olson, E. "Sailing to Byzantium": prolegomena to a poetics of the lyric. *In* Olson, E. On value judgments in the arts, and other essays p3-14

Shaffer, E. S. The visionary character. Revelation and the lyrical ballad. *In* Shaffer, E. S. 'Kubla Khan' and The fall of Jerusalem p62-95

See also Albas; Ballads; Elegiac poetry

History and criticism

Hough, G. G. The modernist lyric. *In* Hough, G. G. Selected essays p237-47

Lysergic acid diethylamide

Dahlberg, C. C. LSD therapy: a case study. *In* Anticipatory grief p296-310

Lauer, R. H. Movement ideology, program, recruitment. *In* Lauer, R. H. ed. Social movements and social change p46-60

Trilling, D. Celebrating with Dr Leary. *In* Trilling, D. We must march my darlings p15-38

Lysosomes

De Duve, C. R. Cells age: are lysosomes among the villains? *In* Jarvik, L. F. ed. Aging into the 21st century p25-31

Lythe, Samuel George Edgar

Economic life. *In* Brown, J. M. ed. Scottish society in the fifteenth century p66-84

Lytle, Guy Fitch

Patronage patterns and Oxford colleges, c.1300-c.1530. *In* The University in society v 1 p111-49

Lyttelton, Adrian

Italian fascism. *In* Laqueur, W. Z. ed. Fascism: a reader's guide p125-50

Lytton, Edward George Earle Lytton Bulwer-Lytton, 1st Baron

About individual works
Harold

Sanders, A. The new seriousness: Edward Bulwer-Lytton's Harold. *In* Sanders, A. The Victorian historical novel, 1840-1880 p47-67

M

M (Motion picture)
Troy, W. M. *In* Denby, D. ed. Awake in the dark p105-07

M*A*S*H (Television program)
Fass, P. S. Television as cultural document: promises and problems. *In* Television as a cultural force p37-57

MIRV. See Multiple independently targetable reentry vehicles

Maalot, Israel
Massacre, 1974
Watad, M. Insufferable silence. *In* The Palestinians p133-35

Mabillon, Jean
About
Momigliano, A. Mabillon's Italian disciples. *In* Momigliano, A. Essays in ancient and modern historiography p277-93

MacAdam, Alfred J.
Modern Latin American narratives
Contents
Adolfo Bioy Casares: Satire & self-portrait
Adolfo Bioy Casares: The lying compass
Gabriel Garcia Márquez: a commodius vicus of recirculation
Guillermo Cabrera Infante: the vast fragment
João Guimarães Rosa: honneur des hommes
José Donoso: endgame
Juan Carlos Onetti & José Lezama Lima: a double portrait of the artist
Juan Rulfo: the secular myth
Julio Cortázar: self-explanation & self-destruction
Machado de Assis: satire & madness
Manuel Puig: things as they are
Severo Sarduy: vital signs

McAleer, Edward C.
Empedocles, Omar Khayyám and Rabbi Ben Ezra. *In* Tennessee Studies in literature v20 p76-84

McAllister, William. See Prewitt, K. jt. auth.

McAlmon, Robert
About
Ford, H. D. Robert McAlmon's Contact publishing company. *In* Ford, H. D. Published in Paris p34-94

McAnany, Patrick D.
Recommendations for improving the ailing probation system. *In* Contemporary issues in criminal justice p76-93

MacAndrew, Elizabeth
Courtly-genteel or moral-didactic?—A response to Carey McIntosh. *In* Studies in eighteenth-century culture v4 p155-59

Macaques
Behavior
Kaufman, I. C. Learning what comes naturally: the role of life experience in the establishment of species typical behavior. *In* Schwartz, T. ed. Socialization as cultural communication p37-50

Macaulay, Rose
About
Babington-Smith, C. Rose Macaulay in her writings. *In* Royal Society of Literature of the United Kingdom, London. Essays by divers hands v38 p143-58

Macaulay, Thomas Babington Macaulay, 1st Baron
About
Dawson, C. Poetics: the hero as poet. *In* Dawson, C. Victorian noon p16-35

McAuley, James Philip
The condition of Australian universities. *In* Universities in the Western world p264-67

Macauley, Robie
The Kenyon Review, 1939-1970. *In* Anderson, E. and Kinzie, M. eds. The little magazine in America: a modern documentary history p71-77

McAuliffe, William E.
Beyond secondary deviance: negative labelling and its effects on the heroin addict. *In* Gove, W. R. ed. The labelling of deviance p205-42

MacAvoy, Paul W. See Breyer, S. G. jt. auth.

McAvoy, Thomas Timothy
The formation of the Catholic minority in the United States, 1820-1860. *In* Mulder, J. M. and Wilson, J. F. eds. Religion in American history p254-69

MacBean, James Roy
Vent d'Est or Godard and Rocha at the crossroads. *In* Nichols, B. ed. Movies and methods p91-106

Macbeth (Motion picture by George Schaefer)
Jorgens, J. J. Defining Macbeth: Schaefer, Welles, and Kurosawa. *In* Jorgens, J. J. Shakespeare on film p148-60

Macbeth (Motion picture by Orson Welles)
Jorgens, J. J. Defining Macbeth: Schaefer, Welles, and Kurosawa. *In* Jorgens, J. J. Shakespeare on film p148-60

Macbeth (Motion picture by Roman Polanski)
Jorgens, J. J. Roman Polanski's Macbeth. *In* Jorgens, J. J. Shakespeare on film p161-74
Kauffmann, S. Macbeth. *In* Kauffmann, S. Living images p90-92

Macbird! (criticism) Garson, B. *In* Kauffmann, S. Persons of the drama p178-81

McBride, Mary
Prisoners of illusion: surrealistic escape in The milk train doesn't stop here anymore. *In* Tennessee Williams: a tribute p341-48

McBride, Theresa M.
'As the twig is bent': the Victorian nanny. *In* Wohl, A. S. ed. The Victorian family p44-58

McCabe, John
The condition of music. *In* Abbs, P. ed. The black rainbow p114-33

Maccabees
Cohen, M. A. The Hasmonean revolution politically considered. *In* Salo Wittmayer Baron v 1 p263-85

MacCaffrey, Isabel Gamble
The scope of imagination in Upon Appleton House. *In* Friedenreich, K. ed. Tercentenary essays in honor of Andrew Marvell p224-44

McCaffrey, Phillip
The adder at Malory's battle of Salisbury: sources, symbols, and themes. *In* Tennessee Studies in literature v22 p17-27

MacCaig, Norman

About

Fraser, G. S. Norman MacCaig: four poems examined. *In* Fraser, G. S. Essays on twentieth-century poets p204-14

McCall, Charles H.

Political parties and popular government. *In* Graham, G. J. and Graham, S. G. eds Founding principles of American government p280-304

McCall, Daniel Francis

The hornbill and analogous forms in West African sculpture. *In* African images p269-324

McCall, George J.

The social looking-glass: a sociological perspective on self-development. *In* Mischel, T. ed. The self p274-87

McCall, Marsh Howard. See Hillers, D. R. jt. auth.

McCall, Morgan W. and Lombardo, Michael M.

Where else can we go? *In* Leadership p151-65

MacCallum, Gerald Cushing

Legislative intent. *In* Summers, R. S. ed. Essays in legal philosophy p237-73

McCallum, James Dow

Introduction to Java Head by Joseph Hergesheimer. *In* Praise from famous men: an anthology of introductions p94-103

MacCallum, John Bruce

About

Harvey, A. M. A new school of anatomy: the story of Franklin P. Mall, Florence R. Sabin, and John B. MacCallum. *In* Harvey, A. M. Adventures in medical research p97-113

MacCallum, William George

About

Harvey, A. M. Medical students on the march: Brown, MacCallum, and Opie. *In* Harvey, A. M. Adventures in medical research p18-31

McCanles, Michael

"All discourse aspires to the analytic proposition." *In* Hernadi, P. ed. What is literature? p190-205

Dialectical criticism and Renaissance literature

Contents

The dialectic of right and power in eight plays of Shakespeare, 1595-1604
Dialectical criticism and beyond
The dialectical structure of the metaphysical lyric: Donne, Herbert, Marvell
Myth and method in the scientific philosophy of Francis Bacon
Paradise lost and the dialectic of Providence
Paradox in Donne. *In* Roberts, J. R. ed. Essential articles for the study of John Donne's poetry p220-35

The rhetoric of the sublime in Crashaw's poetry. *In* Sloan, T. O. and Waddington, R. B. eds. The rhetoric of Renaissance poetry p189-211

McCann, William

Kin Hubbard and journalistic humor in the Midwest. *In* Essays in honor of Russel B. Nye p129-40

McCarran-Walter Act. See Immigration and nationality Act (1952; revised 1965)

McCarron, Robert M.

Folly and wisdom: three Dickensian wise fools. *In* Dickens Studies Annual v6 p40-56

MacCarthy, Sir Charles

About

Walls, A. F. A colonial concordat: two views of Christianity and civilisation. *In* Church, society and politics p293-302

McCarthy, Frederick David

Relationships between Australian aboriginal material culture, and Southeast Asia and Melanesia. *In* Grafton Elliot Smith p210-26

McCarthy, John A.

Shaftesbury and Wieland: the question of enthusiasm. *In* Studies in eighteenth-century culture v6 p79-95

McCarthy, Joseph Raymond

About

Caughey, J. W. McCarthyism rampant. *In* The Pulse of freedom p154-210

McCarthy, Mary Therese

Philip Rahv, 1908-1973. *In* Rahv, P. Essays on literature and politics, 1932-1972 pvii-x

The Tolstoy connection. *In* Dunlop, J. B; Haugh, R. and Klimoff, A. eds. Aleksandr Solzhenitsyn: critical essays and documentary materials 2d ed. p332-50

About

Martin, W. The satire and moral vision of Mary McCarthy. *In* Cohen, S. B. ed. Comic relief p187-206

Stock, I. Mary McCarthy. *In* Howard, M. ed. Seven American women writers of the twentieth century p214-64

About individual works
The group

Connolly, C. Mary McCarthy. *In* Connolly, C. The evening colonnade p296-99

McCarthy, Michael

The education in architecture of the man of taste. *In* Studies in eighteenth-century culture v5 p337-53

McCarthyism. See McCarthy, Joseph Raymond

McCaughey, John Davis

The death of death (I Corinthians 15:26). *In* Reconciliation and hope p246-61

McClanahan, Thomas

Frost's theodicy: "word I had no one left but God." *In* Frost: centennial essays II p112-26

McClaran, Marlys

Mexico. *In* Sebeok, T. A. ed. Native languages of the Americas v2 p141-61

McClatchy, Joseph D.

Short circuits and folding mirrors. *In* Lane, G. ed. Sylvia Plath p19-32

McClear, James F.

The Republic and the millennium. *In* Mulder, J. M. and Wilson, J. F. eds. Religion in American history p181-98

McCleery, William. See Beye, H. jt. auth.

McClellan, George Brinton

About

Harsh, J. L. On the McClellan-go-round. *In* Hubbell, J. T. ed. Battles lost and won p55-72

McClellan, James Paul. See Carey, G. W. jt. auth.

McClelland, Charles E.
The aristocracy and university reform in eighteenth-century Germany. *In* Schooling and society p146-73

McClintick, David

About individual works
Stealing from the rich: the Home-stake oil swindle
Galbraith, J. K. Should stealing from the rich be punished? *In* Galbraith, J. K. Annals of an abiding liberal p323-30

McClintock, Frederick Hemming
Facts and myths about the state of crime. *In* Crime, criminology and public policy p33-46

McCloskey, Donald N.
The economics of enclosure: a market analysis. *In* Parker, W. N. and Jones, E. L. eds. European peasants and their markets p123-60
The persistence of English common fields. *In* Parker, W. N. and Jones, E. L. eds. European peasants and their markets p73-119

McCloskey, Henry John
Essay 12. *In* Fitzgerald, R. ed. What it means to be human p221-40

McClure, Michael
About
Thurley, G. The development of the new language: Wieners, Jones, McClure, Whalen, Corso. *In* Thurley, G. The American moment p187-209

McClusky, Howard Yale
Designs for learning. *In* Jarvik, L. F. ed. Aging into the 21st century p169-84

Maccoby, Eleanor E.
Current changes in the family and their impact upon the socialization of children. *In* Major social issues p195-207
Gender identity and sex-role adoption. *In* Katchadourian, H. A. ed. Human sexuality p194-203

MacColla, Fionn
About individual works
And the cock crew
Hart, F. R. The tragedy of the Clearances. *In* Hart, F. R. The Scottish novel p325-35

McCombie, Frank
'Hamlet' and the 'Moriae encomium'. *In* Shakespeare survey 27 p59-69

McConica, James K.
Scholars and commoners in Renaissance Oxford. *In* The University in society v 1 p151-81

McConkey, Dale Durant
Applying management by objectives to nonprofit organizations. *In* Managing nonprofit orgaizations p141-54
The future: its challenge and its promise; excerpt from "MBO for nonprofit organizations." *In* Managing nonprofit organizations p199-206
MBO in church organizations; excerpt from "MBO for nonprofit organizations." *In* Managing nonprofit organizations p164-75

McConnell, Frank D.
"Death among the apple trees": The waves and the world of things. *In* Garvin, H. R. ed. Makers of the twentieth-century novel p49-61

McConnell, Thomas Raymond
Surfeit or dearth of highly educated people? *In* McMurrin, S. M. ed. On the meaning of the university p63-80

McCool, Gerald A.
Person and community in Karl Rahner. *In* Roth, R. J. ed. Person and community p63-86

McCorison, Marcus Allen
The nature of humanistic societies in early America. *In* Oleson, A. and Brown, S. C. eds. The pursuit of knowledge in the early American Republic p248-60

McCormick, P.
Phenomenology and metaphilosophy. *In* Elliston, F. A. and McCormick, P. eds. Husserl p350-64

McCormick, Richard A.
To save or let die: the dilemma of modern medicine. *In* Weir, R. F. ed. Ethical issues in death and dying p173-84

McCoy, Donald R. and Ruetten, Richard T.
Towards equality: Blacks in the United States during the Second World War. *In* Hepburn, A. C. ed. Minorities in history p135-53

McCoy, Horace
About individual works
They shoot horses, don't they?
Warshow, P. The unreal McCoy. *In* Peary, G. and Shatzkin, R. eds. The modern American novel and the movies p29-39

McCoy, Kathleen
The femininity of Moll Flanders. *In* Studies in eighteenth-century culture v7 p413-22

McCoy, W. James
Aristotle's Athenaion Politeia and the establishment of the Thirty Tyrants. *In* Yale classical studies v24 p131-45

McCracken, Paul Winston
Can capitalism survive? *In* Prochnow, H. V. ed. Dilemmas facing the nation p134-52

McCrank, Lawrence J.
The foundation of the confraternity of Tarragona by Archbishop Oleguer Bonestruga, 1126-1129. *In* Viator: medieval and Renaissance studies v9 p157-77

McCrea, William Hunter
Models, laws, and the universe. *In* Cosmology, history, and theology p59-73

McCready, William Charles
Parochial schools: the "free choice" alternative. *In* Parents, teachers, and children: prospects for choice in American education p67-75
Social utilities in a pluralistic society. *In* The Diverse society: implications for social policy p13-25
See also Greeley, A. M. jt. auth.

McCready, William David
Papalists and antipapalists: aspects of the church/state controversy in the later Middle Ages. *In* Viator: medieval and Renaissance studies v6 p241-73

McCredie, James R.
The architects of the Parthenon. *In* Studies in classical art and archaeology p69-73

McCullers, Carson (Smith)

About

Balakian, N. Carson McCullers: love perverse and perfect. *In* Balakian, N. Critical encounters p109-15

Graver, L. S. Carson McCullers. *In* Howard, M. ed. Seven American women writers of the twentieth century p265-310

Gray, R. J. Aftermath: Southern literature since World War II. *In* Gray, R. J. The literature of memory p257-305

About individual works
The heart is a lonely hunter

Aldridge, R. Two planetary systems. *In* Peary, G. and Shatzkin, R. eds. The modern American novel and the movies p119-30

Style

Morris, W. Carson McCullers. *In* Morris, M. Earthly delights, unearthly adornments p163-68

McCulley, Cecil M.

John Marston. *In* Logan, T. P. and Smith, D. S. eds. The new intellectuals p171-247

McCurry, Charles

Religious careers and religious devotion in thirteenth-century Metz. *In* Viator: medieval and Renaissance studies v9 p325-33

Utilia metensia: local benefices for the papal Curia, 1212—c.1370. *In* Law, church, and society p311-23

McDaniel, Walton Brooks

About

Goold, G. P. Walton Brooks McDaniel: a biographical note. *In* Harvard Studies in classical philology v76 p xi-xvii

McDaniel v. Paty. *In* The Supreme Court review, 1978 p171-90

McDaniel collection, A terracotta lamp in the. Goldstein, S. M. *In* Harvard Studies in classical philology v73 p291-303

McDavid, Raven Ioor, ed. See Linguistic atlas of the North Central States (proposed)

McDavid, Raven Ioor, and O'Cain, Raymond K.

"Existential" there and it: an essay on method and interpretation of data. *In* James B. McMillan: essays in linguistics by his friends and colleagues p29-40

McDavid, Virginia

The social distribution of selected verb forms in the Linguistic atlas of the North Central States. *In* James B. McMillan: essays in linguistics by his friends and colleagues p41-50

McDermott, Walsh

Evaluating the physician and his technology. *In* Knowles, J. H. ed. Doing better and feeling worse p135-57

MacDiarmid, Hugh, pseud. See Grieve, Christopher Murray

McDonald, Angus

The historian's quest. *In* Meisner, M. J. and Murphey, R. eds. The Mozartian historian p76-88

McDonald, Christie V.

The model of reading in Rousseau's Dialogues. *In* Valdés, M. J. and Miller, O. J. eds. Interpretation of narrative p11-18

Macdonald, Dwight

8½: Fellini's obvious masterpiece; excerpt from "Dwight Macdonald on movies." *In* Denby, D. ed. Awake in the dark p113-27

The greatest story ever told; excerpt from "Dwight Macdonald on movies." *In* Denby, D. ed. Awake in the dark p382-88

About

Murray, E. Dwight Macdonald, "congenital critic". *In* Murray, E. Nine American film critics p205-31

About individual works
By Cozzens possessed

Lora, R. By love possessed: the Cozzens-Macdonald affair. *In* Filler, L. ed. A question of quality: popularity and value in modern creative writing p57-79

MacDonald, Edgar E.

An essay in bibliography. *In* Ellen Glasgow p191-224

Glasgow, Cabell, and Richmond. *In* Ellen Glasgow p25-45

McDonald, Geoffrey

The defeat of the General Strike. *In* Peele, G. and Cook, C. eds. The politics of reappraisal, 1918-1939 p64-87

Macdonald, George

About

Hart, F. R. Mid-Victorians. *In* Hart, F. R. The Scottish novel p93-113

Manlove, C. N. George Macdonald (1824-1905). *In* Manlove, C. N. Modern fantasy p55-98

Prickett, S. Adults in allegory land: Kingsley and Macdonald. *In* Prickett, S. Victorian fantasy p150-97

Prickett, S. Demythologising and mythmaking: Arnold versus Macdonald. *In* Prickett, S. Romanticism and religion p211-48

Macdonald, Hugh

"Un pays où tous sont musiciens. . ." *In* From Parnassus p285-94

Macdonald, John Ross, pseud. See Millar, Kenneth

MacDonald, Margaret

Sleeping and waking. *In* Dunlop, C. E. M. ed. Philosophical essays on dreaming p64-80

About individual works
Language of political theory

Pateman, C. Political obligation and conceptual analysis. *In* Laslett, P. and Fishkin, J. eds. Philosophy, politics and society p227-56

Sleeping and waking

Yost, R. M. and Kalish, D. Miss MacDonald on sleeping and waking. *In* Dunlop, C. E. M. ed. Philosophical essays on dreaming p81-102

McDonald, Marianne

Does Euripides call the gods μακάριοι? *In* Illinois classical studies v4, 1979 p27-33

Macdonald, Ross, pseud. See Millar, Kenneth

McDonald, Stephen L.

Taxation system and market distortion. *In* Kalter, R. J. and Vogely, W. A. eds. Energy supply and government policy p26-50

MacDonald, William Graham

Christology and "The angel of the Lord." *In* Current issues in Biblical and patristic interpretation p324-35

MacDonald, William Lloyd
Roman architects. *In* Kostof, S. ed. The architect p28-58

McDougal, Stuart Yeatman
Pound and Eliot. *In* American literary scholarship, 1975 p131-42
Pound and Eliot [another essay] *In* American literary scholarship, 1976 p109-18

McDougall, Bonnie S.
The impact of Western literary trends. *In* Modern Chinese literature in the May Fourth era p37-61

MacDougall, David
Prospects of the ethnographic film. *In* Nichols, B. ed. Movies and methods p135-50

MacDougall, Norman A. T.
Foreign relations: England and France. *In* Brown, J. M. ed. Scottish society in the fifteenth century p101-11
The sources: a reappraisal of the legend. *In* Brown, J. M. ed. Scottish society in the fifteenth century p10-32

McDowell, Frederick Peter Woll
The prewar novels. *In* Ellen Glasgow p82-107

McDowell, John Henry
On 'The reality of the past.' *In* Hookway, C. and Pettit, P. eds. Action and interpretation p127-44
Truth conditions, bivalance, and verificationism. *In* Evans, G. L. and McDowell, J. H. eds. Truth and meaning p42-66

Mace, David Robert
Delinquent sex and marriage counselors. *In* Gross, L. ed. Sexual issues in marriage p53-63

Mace, William M. See Shaw, R. jt. auth.

Macedonia
History—Sources
Badian, E. A king's notebooks. *In* Harvard Studies in classical philology v72 p183-204

McElderry, Bruce Robert
Max Beerbohm: essayist, caricaturist, novelist. *In* Riewald, J. G. ed. The surprise of excellence p215-28

McEvoy, John G. and McGuire, James Edward
God and nature: Priestley's way of rational dissent. *In* Historical studies in the physical sciences v6 p325-404

MacEwan, Arthur
Incentives, equality, and power in revolutionary Cuba. *In* Radosh, R. ed. The new Cuba: paradoxes and potentials p74-101

McEwen, Gilbert D.
"A turn of thinking": Benjamin Franklin, Cotton Mather, and Daniel Defoe on "doing good." *In* The Dress of words p53-65

MacEwen, Gwendolyn
About
Atwood, M. E. MacEwen's Muse. *In* Woodcock, G. ed. Poets and critics p215-24

Macey, Samuel L.
Hogarth and the iconography of time. *In* Studies in eighteenth-century culture v5 p41-53

McFadden, George Middleton
"Literature": a many-sided process. *In* Hernadi, P. ed. What is literature? p49-61

McFarland, David Diedrik
The aged in the 21st century: a demographer's view. *In* Jarvik, L. F. ed. Aging into the 21st century p5-22

McFarland, Ronald E.
The rhetoric of optics in Lord Herbert's poems to Diana Cecil. *In* Medievalia et humanistica no. 5 p215-28

McFarlane, Ian Dalrymple
The history of George Buchanan's Sphæra. *In* French Renaissance studies, 1540-70 p194-212
Reflections on Ravisius Textor's Specimen epithetorum. *In* Classical influences on European culture A.D. 1500-1700 p81-90

McFarlane, James Walter
Ronald Gray's Ibsen—a dissenting view. *In* Drama and society p299-311

McGalliard, John Calvin. See Part 2 under title: Anglo-Saxon poetry: essays in appreciation

McGann, Jerome J.
Rossetti's significant details. *In* Sambrook, J. ed. Pre-Raphaelitism p230-42
The significance of biographical context: two poems by Lord Byron. *In* Martz, L. L. and Williams, A. L. eds. The author in his work p347-64

McGann, Kevin
Ayn Rand in the stockyard of the spirit. *In* Peary, G. and Shatzkin, R. eds. The modern American novel and the movies p325-35

McGee, Michael C.
The rhetorical process in eighteenth century England. *In* Rhetoric: a tradition in transition p99-121

McGee, T. G.
Rural-urban mobility in South and Southeast Asia: different formulations, different answers. *In* Human migration p199-224

McGee, Timothy J.
The role of the Quem quaeritis dialogue in the history of Western drama. *In* Renaissance drama [1976] p177-91

Mc Ghee, Dorothy Madeleine
Encyclopedism and its conscience: evolution and revolution. *In* Literature and history in the age of ideas p377-86

McGill, Arthur Chute
Structures of inhumanity. *In* Disguises of the demonic p116-33

McGill, William James
Government regulation and academic freedom. *In* Hook, S.; Kurtz, P. W. and Todorovich, M. eds. The university and the state: what role for government in higher education? p139-54

About individual works
Government regulation and academic freedom

Bloom, A. A response to President McGill. *In* Hook, S.; Kurtz, P. W. and Todorovich, M. eds. The university and the state: what role for government in higher education? p155-61

McGilligan, Patrick
Mr. Saroyan's thoroughly Amercan movie. *In* Peary, G. and Shatzkin, R. eds. The modern American novel and the movies p156-67

McGinn, Bernard
Iter sancti Sepulchri: the piety of the first Crusaders. *In* Essays on medieval civilization p33-71

McGlathery, James M.

Kleist's version of Molière's Amphitryon: Ølympian cuckolding and unio mystica. *In* Johnson, R. B.; Neumann, E. S. and Trail, G. T. eds. Molière and the commonwealth of letters: patrimony and posterity p327-33

McGlinn, Jeanne M.

Tennessee Williams' women: illusion and reality, sexuality and love. *In* Tennessee Williams: a tribute p510-24

McGovern, George Stanley

About

Sheed, W. Miami: 1972. *In* Sheed, W. The good word & other words p279-88

MacGowran, Jack

About individual works
Jack MacGowran in the works of Samuel Beckett

Kauffmann, S. MacGowran in Beckett. *In* Kauffmann, S. Persons of the drama p211-13

McGraw, Robert F.

Minutemen of '61: the pre-Civil War Massachusetts milita. *In* Hubbell, J. T. ed. Battles lost and won p141-55

McGrory, Kathleen

The Yeats industry: scholarship frowned into littleness? *In* Yeats, Joyce, and Beckett p52-70

McGuinness, Brian

The Grundgedanke of the Tractatus. *In* Royal Institute of Philosophy. Understanding Wittgenstein p49-61

McGuire, James Edward

"Labyrinthus continui"; Leibniz on substance, activity, and matter. *In* Motion and time, space and matter p290-326

See also McEvoy, J. G. jt. auth.

McGuire, John

Kristo Das Pal: politician as intermediary. *In* The Making of politicians: studies from Africa and Asia p93-102

Mach, Ernst

About

Hiebert, E. N. An appraisal of the work of Ernst Mach: scientist-historian-philosopher. *In* Motion and time, space and matter p360-89

Laudan, L. The methodological foundations of Mach's anti-atomism and their historical roots. *In* Motion and time, space and matter p390-417

Mácha, Karel Hynek

About

Jakobson, R. What is poetry? *In* Matejka, L. and Titunik, I. R. eds. Semiotics of art p164-75

Machado, Antonio. See Machado y Ruiz, Antonio

Machado de Assis, Joaquim Maria

About

Pritchett, V. S. Machado de Assis: a Brazilian. *In* Pritchett, V. S. The myth makers p158-63

About individual works
Epitaph of a small winner

MacAdam, A. J. Machado de Assis: satire & madness. *In* MacAdam, A. J. Modern Latin American narratives p11-28

Machado y Ruiz, Antonio

About

Paz, O. Antonio Machado. *In* Paz, O. The siren & the seashell p145-51

Shaw, D. L. Machado: the road to emptiness. *In* Shaw, D. L. The generation of 1898 in Spain p127-60

About individual works
Juan de Mairena (Translated by Ben Belitt)

Belitt, B. Translator's preface: Juan de Mairena. *In* Belitt, B. Adam's dream p84-90

Machala, Pavel

Eastern Europe, Eurocommunism, and the problems of détente. *In* Kaplan, M. A. ed. The many faces of communism p228-65

Machamer, Peter K.

Causality and explanation in Descartes' natural philosophy. *In* Motion and time, space and matter p168-99

Commentary: fictionalism and realism in 16th century astronomy. *In* The Copernican achievement p346-53

Gibson and the conditions for perception. *In* Studies in perception p435-66

McHaney, Thomas Lafayette

Brooks on Faulkner: the end of the long view: *In* Review, v 1 1979 p29-45

McHardy, A. K.

The alien priories and the expulsion of aliens from England in 1378. *In* Church, society and politics p133-41

Machaut, Guillaume de. See Guillaume de Machaut

Machen, Arthur

About

Briggs, J. A scientific spirit: mesmerism, drugs and psychic doctors. *In* Briggs, J. Night visitors p52-75

Machiavelli, Niccolò

About

Aron, R. Machiavelli and Marx. *In* Aron, R. Politics and history p87-101

Cairns, C. The political conscience. *In* Cairns, C. Italian literature p45-90

Gilbert, F. Machiavellism. *In* Gilbert, F. History p155-76

Whitfield, J. H. Livy Tacitus. *In* Classical influences on European culture A.D. 1500-1700 p281-93

About individual works
The discourses on Titus Livius

Gilbert, F. The composition and structure of Machiavelli's Discorsi. *In* Gilbert, F. History p115-33

The Florentine histories

Gilbert, F. Machiavelli's Istorie Fiorentine: an essay in interpretation. *In* Gilbert, F. History p135-53

The prince

Downs, R. B. Anatomy of power politics. *In* Downs, R. B. Books that changed the world p163-74

Gilbert, F. The humanist concept of the prince and The prince of Machiavelli. *In* Gilbert, F. History p91-114

Influence

Adams, R. P. Opposed Tudor myths of power: Machiavellian tyrants and Christian kings. *In* Studies in the continental background of Renaissance English literature: essays presented to John L. Lievsay p67-90

Machiavelli, Zanobi di Jacopo
About individual works
Coronation of the Virgin
Winternitz, E. On angel concerts in the 15th century: a critical approach to realism and symbolism in sacred painting. *In* Winternitz, E. Musical instruments and their symbolism in Western art p137-49

Machine theory. See Artificial intelligence

Machine translating
Kay, M. Automatic translation of natural languages. *In* Bloomfield, M. W. and Haugen, E. I. eds. Language as a human problem p219-32
Smith, P. H. The failure of the machine and the triumph of the mind. *In* Gold, J. ed. In the name of language! p205-09

Machinery
Models
Rodis-Lewis, G. Limitations of the mechanical model in the Cartesian conception of the organism. *In* Hooker, M. ed. Descartes p152-70

Machinery and civilization. See Technology and civilization

Machinery in art
Richards, J. M. Towards a rational aesthetic. *In* Sharp, D. ed. The rationalists p130-42
Skolimowski, H. Rationality in architecture and in the design process. *In* Sharp, D. ed. The rationalists p160-72

Mackinder, Sir Halford John
About individual works
The geographical pivot of history
Downs, R. B. Heartland and world-island. *In* Downs, R. B. Books that changed the world p263-73

Machinery in industry
Clayre, A. Early criticisms of modern society. *In* Clayre, A. Work and play p30-44
Clayre, A. Pastoral and machinery. *In* Clayre, A. Work and play p89-102
See also Technological innovations; Unemployment, Technological

Machlup, Fritz
The effects of fiscal policy and the choice of definitions. *In* Theory for economic efficiency: essays in honor of Abba P. Lerner p76-91
Hayek's contribution to economics. *In* Essays on Hayek p13-59

Macías Nguema Byogo
Sundiata, I. K. Creolization on Fernando Po: the nature of society. *In* Kilson, M. L. and Rotberg, R. I. eds. The African diaspora p391-413

McIllwraith, Maureen Mollie Hunter (McVeigh)
The last lord of Redhouse Castle. *In* Blishen, E. ed. The thorny paradise p128-39

McInnes, Neil
The politics of needs—or, Who needs politics? *In* Fitzgerald, R. ed. Human needs and politics p229-43

McInnis, Noel F. See Theobald, R. jt. auth.

McIntosh, Carey
Quantities of qualities: nominal style and the novel. *In* Studies in eighteenth-century culture v4 p139-53

About individual works
Quantities of qualities: nominal style and the novel
MacAndrew, E . Courtly-genteel or moral-didactic?—A response to Carey McIntosh. *In* Studies in eighteenth-century culture v4 p155-59

McIntosh, Maria Jane
About
Baym, N. Z. Maria McIntosh. *In* Baym, N. Z. Woman's fiction p86-109

McIntosh, Marjorie Keniston
The privileged villeins of the English ancient demesne. *In* Viator: medieval and Renaissance studies v7 p295-328

Macintosh, Neil William George
Early man and the dog in Australia. *In* Grafton Elliot Smith p83-94
See also Larnach, S. L. jt. auth.

McIntyre, Alasdair C.
Has science any future? *In* Science and society: past, present, and future p356-62

About
Flew, A. G. N. A rational animal. *In* Flew, A. G. N. A rational animal p89-122

McIntyre, Michael. See Shaw, R. jt. auth.

McIntyre, William David
Malaya from the 1850's to the 1870's, and its historians, 1950-1970: from strategy to sociology. *In* Southeast Asian history and historiography p262-84

Mack, Maynard
Pope's books: a biographical survey with a finding list. *In* English literature in the age of disguise p209-305
Pope's copy of Chaucer. *In* Evidence in literary scholarship p105-21

The mack (Motion picture)
Kauffmann, S. The mack. *In* Kauffmann, S. Living images p190-94

McKane, William
Observations on the tiḳḳûnê sôpᵉrim. *In* On language, culture, and religion: in honor of Eugene A. Nida p53-77

McKay, Claude
About
Bone, R. A. Three versions of pastoral. *In* Bone, R. A. Down home p139-70
Timothy, H. P. Claude McKay: individualism and group consciousness. *In* King, B. A. and Ogungbesan, K. eds. A celebration of Black and African writing p15-29

About individual works
Banana Bottom
Ramchand, K. The vision of a 'sustaining community' in Claude McKay's Banana Bottom. *In* Baugh, E. ed. Critics on Caribbean literature p93-102

McKay, David P. See Crawford, R. A. jt. auth.

McKay, Henry Donald
About
Finestone, H. The delinquent and society: the Shaw and McKay tradition. *In* Delinquency, crime, and society p23-49
Weinberg, S. K. Shaw-McKay theories of delinquency in cross-cultural context. *In* Delinquency, crime, and society p167-85

McKean, Roland N.

Collective choice. *In* McKie, J. W. ed. Social responsibility and the business predicament p109-34

Property rights, pollution, and power. *In* Capitalism and freedom p92-111

MacKellar, Walter

On two English metamorphoses. *In* Poetry and poetics from ancient Greece to the Renaissance p207-17

McKelway, Alexander J.

Eden revisited: hope beyond tragedy. *In* The Context of contemporary theology p25-42

McKendrick, Neil

Home demand and economic growth: a new view of the role of women and children in the Industrial Revolution. *In* Historical perspectives p152-210

J. H. Plumb: a valedictory tribute. *In* Historical perspectives p 1-18

MacKenna, Sir Bernard Joseph Maxwell

General deterrence. *In* Progress in penal reform p182-95

MacKenna, Sir Brian. See MacKenna, Sir Bernard Joseph Maxwell

McKenna, John W.

Piety and propaganda: the cult of King Henry VI. *In* Chaucer and Middle English studies in honour of Rossell Hope Robbins p72-88

McKenna, Richard

Journey with a little man; excerpt from "The sons of Martha, and other stories." *In* Knight, D. F. ed. Turning points p285-300

About

McKenna, R. Journey with a little man; excerpt from "The sons of Martha, and other stories." *In* Knight, D. F. ed. Turning points p285-300

McKenzie, Barbara A.

The eye of time: the photographs of Eudora Welty. *In* Prenshaw, P. W. ed. Eudora Welty p386-400

Mackenzie, Sir Compton

About

Hart, F. R. Highlands of the humorists. *In* Hart, F. R. The Scottish novel p374-84

Hart, F. R. Novelists of the modern renaissance. *In* Hart, F. R. The Scottish novel p207-45

MacKenzie, Donald, and Barnes, Barry

Scientific judgment: the biometry-Mendelism controversy. *In* Barnes, B. and Shapin, S. eds. Natural order p191-210

MacKenzie, Henry

About

Butler, M. Sentimentalism: the radical inheritance. *In* Butler, M. Jane Austen and the war of ideas p7-28

About individual works

Julia de Roubigné

Butler, M. Sentimentalism: the radical inheritance. *In* Butler, M. Jane Austen and the war of ideas p7-28

MacKenzie, John P.

Of judges and the ABA. *In* Nader, R. and Green, M. J. eds. Verdicts on lawyers p33-46

McKenzie, Robert H.

Introduction: Of new Souths rising. *In* The Rising South v2 p 1-10

McKeown, Elizabeth K.

Catholic identity in America. *In* America in theological perspective p56-68

McKie, Douglas

About individual works

Antoine Lavoisier: scientist, economist, social reformer

Guerlac, H. Lavoisier and his biographers. *In* Guerlac, H. Essays and papers in the history of modern science p314-26

McKie, James Warren

Changing views. *In* McKie, J. W. ed. Social responsibility and the business predicament p17-40

The United States. *In* Vernon, R. ed. The oil crisis p73-90

Mackie, John Leslie

Problems of intentionality. *In* Pivčević, E. ed. Phenomenology and philosophical understanding p37-52

Mackie, William Soutar. See Part 2 under title: An English miscellany

MacKillop, James J.

Finn MacCool: the hero and the anti-hero in Irish folk tradition. *In* Casey, D. J. and Rhodes, R. E. eds. Views of the Irish peasantry, 1800-1916 p86-106

MacKinder, Sir Halford John

About individual works

The geographical pivot of history

Downs, R. B. Heartland and world-island. *In* Downs, R. B. Books that changed the world p263-73

MacKinnon, Edward Michael

Heisenberg, models, and the rise of matrix mechanics. *In* Historical studies in the physical sciences v8 p137-88

McKinnon, Ronald I.

America's role in stabilizing the world's monetary system. *In* A New America? p305-24

Mackintosh, Catharine Winkworth

Some pioneer missions of Northern Rhodesia and Nyasaland. *In* The Occasional papers of the Rhodes-Livingstone Museum p249-95

Mackintosh, John Malcolm

Stalin's policies towards Eastern Europe, 1939-1948: the general picture. *In* Hammond, T. T. ed. The anatomy of Communist takeovers p229-43

Mackintosh, Malcolm. See Mackintosh, John Malcolm

Macklin, Barbara June

Belief, ritual, and healing: New England spiritualism and Mexican-American spiritism compared. *In* Zaretsky, I. I. and Leone, M. P. eds. Religious movements in contemporary America p383-417

Macklin, J. J.

B. Pérez Galdós: Fortunata and Jacinta. *In* Williams, D. A. ed. The monster in the mirror p179-203

Macklin, June. See Macklin, Barbara June

MacLachlan, Colin Mackey

African slave trade and economic development in Amazonia, 1700-1800. *In* Toplin, R. B. ed. Slavery and race relations in Latin America p112-45

McLachlan, James
The choice of Hercules: American student societies in the early 19th century. *In* The University in society v2 p449-94

McLachlan, Noel
Penal reform and penal history: some reflections. *In* Progress in penal reform p 1-24

Maclagan, Michael
A Byzantine princess in Portugal. *In* Studies in memory of David Talbot Rice p284-93

MacLaren, Ian, pseud. See Watson, John, 1850-1907

Maclaren, Peter I. R.
The fishing devices of Central and Southern Africa. *In* The Occasional papers of the Rhodes-Livingstone Museum p427-88

McLauchlan, Juliet
The Prince of Denmark and Claudius's court. *In* Shakespeare survey 27 p43-57

McLaughlin, Virginia Yans- See Yans-McLaughlin, Virginia

MacLaurin, Evan Colin Briarcliffe
Cultural diffusion in the Middle East during the second millennium BC. *In* Grafton Eliot Smith p175-96

McLaverty, James
Lawton Gilliver: Pope's bookseller. *In* Virginia. University. Bibliographical Society. Studies in bibliography v32 p101-24

Maclean, Norman F.

About individual works

A river runs through it, and other stories

Sale, R. H. Bradley & Maclean. *In* Sale, R. H. On not being good enough p84-93

MacLean, Paul D.
The imitative-creative interplay of our three mentalities. *In* Harris, H. A. ed. Astride the two cultures p187-213

Maclear, James F.
New England and the Fifth Monarchy: the quest for the millennium in early American Puritanism. *In* Vaughan, A. T. and Bremer, F. J. eds. Puritan New England p66-91

MacLeish, Archibald
Bicentennial of what? *In* Aspects of American liberty p 1-7

"A memorial tribute to Carl Sandburg." *In* Praise from famous men: an anthology of introductions p104-08

Riders on the earth
Contents
Art and law
Autobiographical information
Eden in Hartford
Expatriates in Paris
Gerald Murphy
The ghost of Thomas Jefferson
A lay sermon for the hill towns
Mark Van Doren
Master or man
Moonlighting on Yale Field
New England's Frost and Frost's New England
News from the horse and wagon
The premise at the center
President Johnson alive and Carl Sandburg dead
Remarks on the Pulitzer prize
Return from the excursion
The revolt of the diminished man
The Venetian grave

About

MacLeish, A. Autobiographical information. *In* MacLeish, A. Riders on the earth p69-81

Smith, G. C. Archibald MacLeish. *In* Donoghue, D. ed. Seven American poets from MacLeish to Nemerov p16-54

McLeod, Alan L.
The creation of national images in Indian and Pakistani speeches to the United States Congress. *In* Narasimhaiah, C. D. ed. Awakened conscience p378-88

MacLeod, Duncan J.
Fanny Kemble. *In* Abroad in America: Visitors to the new Nation, 1776-1914 p72-81

Towards caste: Blacks in eighteenth-century America. *In* Hepburn, A. C. ed. Minorities in history p102-15

McLeod, Fiona, pseud. See Sharp, William

MacLeod, Kay. See MacLeod, R. M. jt. auth.

McLeod, Malcolm D.
Aspects of Asante images. *In* Greenhalgh, M. and Megaw, J. V. S. eds. Art in society p305-16

McLeod, Marian B.
Audience and argument in the speeches of R. G. Menzies and Krishna Menon on the Suez Canal crisis in 1956. *In* Narasimhaiah, C. D. ed. Awakened conscience p389-400

McLeod, Randall
A technique of headline analysis, with application to Shakespeares Sonnets, 1609. *In* Virginia. University. Bibliographical Society. Studies in bibliography v32 p197-210

MacLeod, Roy M.
Changing perspectives in the social history of science. *In* Science, technology and society p149-95

MacLeod, Roy M. and MacLeod, Kay
War and economic development: government and the optical industry in Britain, 1914-18. *In* War and economic development p165-203

McLevy, Jasper
About
Stave, B. M. The Great Depression and urban political continuity: Bridgeport chooses socialism. *In* Stave, B. M. ed. Socialism and the cities p157-83

MacLochlainn, Alf
Gael and peasant—a case of mistaken identity? *In* Casey, D. J. and Rhodes, R .E. eds. Views of the Irish peasantry, 1800-1916 p17-36

McLoughlin, William Gerald
Cherokee anomie, 1794-1809: new roles for Red men, Red women, and Black slaves. *In* Uprooted Americans p125-60

'Enthusiasm for liberty': the Great Awakening as the key to the Revolution. *In* American Antiquarian Society. Proceedings v87 pt 1 p69-95

Revivalism. *In* The Rise of Adventism p119-53

McLuhan, Herbert Marshall
Canada: the borderline case. *In* Staines, D. ed. The Canadian imagination p226-48

The implications of cultural uniformity. *In* Bigsby, C. W. E. Superculture p43-56

McLuhan, Herbert M.—*Continued*

About

Cameron, E. McLuhan, youth, and literature. *In* Horn Book Magazine. Crosscurrents of criticism p98-120

McLuhan, Marshall. See McLuhan, Herbert Marshall

McManners, John

Jansenism and the politics in the eighteenth century. *In* Church, society and politics p253-73

McMaster, John Bach

About

Nevins, A. John Bach McMaster. *In* Nevins, A. Allan Nevins on history p359-72

McMaster, Juliet

Love and pedagogy. *In* Weinsheimer, J. ed. Jane Austen today p64-91

Thackeray's things: time's local habitation. *In* Levine, R. A. The Victorian experience: the novelists p49-86

McMillan, Dougald, 1937-

Transition

Contents

Dadaism

Dylan Thomas

Expressionism

Gertrude Stein

Getting into print

Hart Crane

Revolution and synthesis: the growth of a theory

Samuel Beckett

Subversion and quest: the first year

Surrealism

Transition in the Wake: friends and the enemy

Transition's revolutionaries

Verticalism

'Work in progress' in Transition

MacMillan, Duane Johnson

His 'magnum o': stoic humanism in Faulkner's A fable. *In* The Stoic strain in American literature p136-76

McMillan, James Benjamin

About

Raymond, J. C. and Russell, I. W. James B. McMillan. *In* James B. McMillan: essays in linguistics by his friends and colleagues p vii-xiii

McMorran, Ian

The patriot and the partisans: Wang Fu-chih's involvement in the politics of the Yung-li court. *In* Spence, J. D. and Wills, J. E. eds. From Ming to Ch'ing p133-66

Wang Fu-chih and the Neo-Confucian tradition. *In* The Unfolding of Neo-Confucianism p413-67

McMullen, Charles Haynes

American librarians and the pursuit of happiness. *In* As much to learn as to teach p51-82

McMullen, Haynes. See McMullen, Charles Haynes

McMullin, B. J.

The direction line as bibliographical evidence: Sheet K in Crowne's City politiques, 1683. *In* Virginia. University. Bibliographical Society. Studies in bibliography v31 p178-84

Macmurray, John

Science and objectivity. *In* The Personal universe p7-23

About

Duncan, A. R. C. No man is an island... *In* The Personal universe p40-53

Nephew, A. H. The personal universe. *In* The Personal universe p99-108

Wren, T. E. John Macmurray's search for reality: introduction. *In* The Personal universe p 1-6

MacMurray, John Van Antwerp

About

Buckley, T. H. John Van Antwerp MacMurray: the diplomacy of an American mandarin. *In* Burns, R. D. and Bennett, E. M. eds. Diplomats in crisis p27-48

McMurrin, Sterling M.

Ideas and the processes of history. *In* The Abdication of philosophy: philosophy and the public good p109-28

The philosophy of education. *In* McMurrin, S. M. ed. On the meaning of the university p 1-12

McMurry, Richard M.

Rise to glory: a speculative essay on the early career of John Bell Hood. *In* Rank and file p39-54

McMurtry, John

Monogamy: a critique. *In* Baker, R. and Elliston, F. A. eds. Philosophy & sex p166-77

About individual works

Monogamy: a critique

Bayles, M. D. Marriage, love, and procreation. *In* Baker, R. and Elliston, F. A. eds. Philosophy & sex p190-206

McNab, Bruce

Obligations of the Church in English society: military arrays of the clergy, 1369-1418. *In* Order and innovation in the Middle Ages p293-314

MacNabb, D. G. C. See Khamara, E. J. jt. auth.

McNall, Scott G.

Introduction: alternative theoretical perspectives in modern sociology. *In* McNall, S. G. ed. Theoretical perspectives in sociology p 1-14

McNally, James Richard

Melanchton's earliest rhetoric. *In* Rhetoric: a tradition in transition p33-48

McNamara, Jo Ann, and Wemple, Suzanne, F.

Marriage and divorce in the Frankish kingdom. *In* Stuard, S. M. ed. Women in medieval society p95-124

McNamara, Robert Strange

The world population problem. *In* World change and world security p117-58

McNamara, William

Psychology and the Christian mystical tradition. *In* Tart, C. T. ed. Transpersonal psychologies p389-430

Macnaughton, William Robert

The narrator in Henry James's The sacred fount. *In* Literature and ideas in America p155-81

McNeal, Peter

Non-custodial supervision. *In* Progress in penal reform p255-67

McNeal, Robert Hatch

Trotskyist interpretations of Stalinism. *In* Stalinism p30-52

MacNeice, John Frederick

About

Brown, T. MacNeice: father and son. *In* Time was away p21-34

MacNeice, Louis

See also Auden, W. H. jt. auth.

About

Allen, W. E. MacNeice as critic. *In* Time was away p55-61

Andrews, K. Time and the will lie side-stepped: Athens, the interval. *In* Time was away p103-09

Auden, W. H. Louis MacNeice: a memorial address. *In* Time was away p5-10

Bower, D. MacNeice: sound and vision. *In* Time was away p97-102

Brown, T. MacNeice: father and son. *In* Time was away p21-34

Dodds, E. R. Louis MacNeice at Birmingham. *In* Time was away p35-38

Fraser, G. S. Evasive honesty: the poetry of Louis MacNeice. *In* Fraser, G. S. Essays on twentieth-century poets p152-61

Mahon, D. MacNeice in England and Ireland. *In* Time was away p113-22

Montague, J. Despair and delight. *In* Time was away p123-27

Nicholson, C. E. Trees were green. *In* Time was away p11-20

Pritchard, W. H. Auden & Co. *In* Pritchard, W. H. Seeing through everything p154-77

Reid, A. MacNeice in the theatre. *In* Time was away p73-85

Skelton, R. Celt and classicist: the verse-craft of Louis MacNeice. *In* Time was away p43-53

Smith, E. E. Louis MacNeice: the circular movement. *In* Smith, E. E. The angry young men of the thirties p69-93

Smith, R. D. Castle on the air. *In* Time was away p87-95

About individual works

Collected poems

Connolly, C. Louis MacNeice. *In* Connolly, C. The evening colonnade p327-30

Bibliography

Smith, R. D. Radio scripts, 1941-1963. *In* Time was away p141-48

MacNeice, Louis, tr.

About individual works

The Agamemnon of Aeschylus

Stanford, W. B. The translation of the 'Agamemnon' of Aeschylus. *In* Time was away p63-66

Faust

Stahl, E. L. The 'Faust' translation: a personal account. *In* Time was away p67-71

MacNeice family

Nicholson, C. E. Trees were green. *In* Time was away p11-20

McNeill, Janet

When the magic has to stop. *In* Horn Book Magazine. Crosscurrents of criticism p35-40

McNeill, Terry

State and nationality under communism. *In* Hayward, J. E. S. and Berki, R. N. eds. State and society in contemporary Europe p118-40

McNeill, William Hardy

Human migration: a historical overview. *In* Human migration p3-19

On national frontiers: ethnic homogeneity and pluralism. *In* Small comforts for hard times p207-19

McNelly, John T.

Media exposure in developing urban societies. *In* Fischer, H. D. and Merrill, J. C. eds. International and intercultural communication p218-25

McNelly, Willis Everett

Kurt Vonnegut as science-fiction writer. *In* Klinkowitz, J. and Lawler, D. L. eds. Vonnegut in America p87-96

Two views: Ray Bradbury—past, present, and future. *In* Clareson, T. D. ed. Voices for the future: essays on major science fiction writers v 1 p167-75

McNemar, Donald W.

The United States and the United Nations. *In* Baldwin, D. A. ed. America in an interdependent world p315-46

MacNicholas, John

Williams' power of the keys. *In* Tennessee Williams: a tribute p581-605

McNickle, D'Arcy

About individual works

The surrounded

Larson, C. R. Rejection: the reluctant return. *In* Larson, C. R. American Indian fiction p66-96

McNulty, Michael Leigh

The contemporary map of Africa. *In* Martin, P. M. and O'Meara, P. eds. Africa p24-49

McPherson, Barry David

The Black athlete: an overview and analysis. *In* Social problems in athletics p122-50

About individual works

The Black athlete: an overview and analysis

Loy, J. W. Race and sport: a reaction to the McPherson and Madison and Landers papers. *In* Social problems in athletics p157-67

Macpherson, Crawford Brough

Capitalism and the changing concept of property. *In* Kamenka, E. and Neale, R. S. eds. Feudalism, capitalism and beyond p104-24

The false roots of Western democracy. *In* Dallmayr, F. R. ed. From contract to community p17-27

Needs and wants: an ontological or historical problem? *In* Fitzgerald, R. ed. Human needs and politics p26-35

About

Weinstein, M. A. C. B. Macpherson: the roots of democracy and liberalism. *In* De Crespigny, A. and Minogue, K. R. eds. Contemporary political philosophers p253-71

McPherson, Hugo

How hot is The scarlet letter? *In* Essays in honor of Russel B. Nye p141-50

Macpherson, James

About

Greenway, J. L. The gateway to innocence: Ossian and the Nordic bard as myth. *In* Studies in eighteenth-century culture v4 p161-70

Wain, J. Alternative poetry. *In* Wain, J. Professing poetry p13-44

Macpherson, James—*Continued*

About individual works
The works of Ossian

Simonsuuri, K. Notions of poetry and society in the controversy about Ossian. *In* Simonsuuri, K. Homer's original genius p108-18

McPherson, James M.
The new Puritanism: values and goals of freedmen's education in America. *In* The University in society v2 p611-42

McPherson, Thomas

About individual works
Political obligation

Pateman, C. Political obligation and conceptual analysis. *In* Laslett, P. and Fishkin, J. eds. Philosophy, politics and society p227-56

McQuade, Walter
Management problems enter the picture at art museums. *In* Managing nonprofit organizations p261-69

MacQueen, John
The literature of fifteenth-century Scotland. *In* Brown, J. M. ed. Scottish society in the fifteenth century p184-208

McQuillan, D. Aidan
Territory and ethnic identity: some new measures of an old theme in the cultural geography of the United States. *In* European settlement and development in North America: essays on geographical change in honour and memory of Andrew Hill Clark p136-69

MacRae, Donald Gunn
The British position. *In* Universities in the Western world p176-80

McReynolds, James Clark

About
White, G. E. The Four Horsemen: the sources of judicial notoriety. *In* White, G. E. The American judicial tradition p178-99

Macroeconomics
Friedlaender, A. F. Absolute poverty and macroeconomic activity. *In* Inflation, trade and taxes p194-217

McShea, Robert J.
Spinoza: human nature and history. *In* Freeman, E. and Mandelbaum, M. H. eds. Spinoza p101-15

McTurk, R. W. and Williams, D. J.
Middle English: excluding Chaucer. *In* English Association. The year's work in English studies v55 p92-147

Middle English: excluding Chaucer [another essay] *In* English Association. The year's work in English studies v56 p81-117

See also Dolan, T. P. jt. auth.

McVay, Gordon
The tree-stump and the horse: the poetry of Alexander Kusikov. *In* Oxford Slavonic papers, new ser. v11 p101-31

McVey, Sheila
Nineteenth century America: publishing in a developing country. *In* Altbach, P. G. and McVey, S. eds. Perspectives on publishing p187-201

McWhiney, Grady
The Confederacy's first shot. *In* Hubbell, J. T. ed. Battles lost and won p73-82

Who whipped whom? Confederate defeat reexamined. *In* Hubbell, J. T. ed. Battles lost and won p261-82

McWilliams, John Probasco
Fictions of Merry Mount. *In* Zenderland, L. ed. Recycling the past p 1-28

Great expectations: the beacon, the gibbet, and the ship. *In* Dickens Studies Annual v2 p255-66

McWilliams, Wilson Carey
On equality as the moral foundation for community. *In* The Moral foundations of the American Republic p188-213

See also Bathory, P. D. jt. auth.

McWilliams-Tullberg, Rita
Women and degrees at Cambridge University, 1862-1897. *In* Vicinus, M. ed. A widening sphere p117-45

Madagascar
Southall, A. W. White strangers and their religion in East Africa and Madagascar. *In* Shack, W. A. and Skinner, E. P. eds. Strangers in African societies p211-26

Antiquities
Vérin, P. Austronesian contributions to the culture of Madagascar: some archaeological problems. *In* Chittick, H. N. and Rotberg, R. I. eds. East Africa and the Orient p164-91

Civilization
Vérin, P. Austronesian contributions to the culture of Madagascar: some archaeological problems. *In* Chittick, H. N. and Rotberg, R. I. eds. East Africa and the Orient p164-91

Madden, David
The American writer as public icon. *In* Browne, R. B. and Fishwick, M. W. eds. Icons of America p87-99

About individual works
Night shift

Kirby, T. A. An analogue (?) to The reeve's tale. *In* Chaucer and Middle English studies in honour of Rossell Hope Robbins p381-83

Madden, William Anthony
Arnold the poet: (i) lyric and elegiac poems. *In* Allott, K. ed. Matthew Arnold p39-69

Maddox, Brenda
Women and the switchboard. *In* The Social impact of the telephone p262-80

Maddox, George L.
The social and cultural context of aging. *In* Aging: the process and the people p20-46

Sociology, aging, and guided social change: relating alternative organization of helping resources to well-being. *In* Major social issues p323-37

Will senior power become a reality? *In* Jarvik, L. F. ed. Aging into the 21st century p185-96

Maddox, Jerald C.
Photography as folk art. *In* One hundred years of photographic history p103-08

Maddox, Robert
The function of the Son of Man in the Gospel of John. *In* Reconciliation and hope p186-204

Maddy, Yulisa Amadu

About individual works
No past, no present, no future

Palmer, E. T. Yulisa Amadu Maddy: No past, no present, no future. *In* African literature today no. 7: Focus on criticism p163-66

Madge, Charles
The relevance of family patterns in the process of modernization in East Asia. *In* Social organization and the applications of anthropology p161-95

Madhusudan Reddy, V.
The Vedas. *In* Bishop, D. H. ed. Indian thought p23-37

Madhya Pradesh, India

Social conditions

Jain, R. K. Bendela genealogy and legends: the past of an indigenous ruling group of central India. *In* Studies in social anthopology p238-72

Mäding, Klaus
Popular literature in dependent society: the case of colonial Hong Kong. *In* Fischer, H. D. and Melnik, S. R. eds. Entertainment: a cross-cultural examination p180-89

Madison, Bernice
Social services for women: problems and priorities. *In* Women in Russia p307-32

Madison, Donna R. and Landers, Daniel M.
Racial discrimination in football: a test of the "stacking" of playing positions hypothesis. *In* Social problems in athletics p151-56

About individual works

Racial discrimination in football: a test of the "stacking" of playing positions hypothesis

Loy, J. W. Race and sport: a reaction to the McPherson and Madison and Landers papers. *In* Social problems in athletics p157-67

Madison, Gary Brent
Phenomenology and existentialism: Husserl and the end of idealism. *In* Elliston, F. A. and McCormick, P. eds. Husserl p247-68

Madison, James, President U.S.

About

Adair, D. G. "That politics may be reduced to a science": David Hume, James Madison, and the tenth Federalist. *In* Livingston, D. W. and King, J. T. eds. Hume p404-17

Diamond, M. Ethics and politics: the American way. *In* The Moral foundations of the American Republic p39-72

Madison, Wis.

Schools

Sampson, H. L. Model for participation. *In* Managing nonprofit organizations p109-11

Madkour, Ibrahim. See Madkūr, Ibrahim

Madkūr, Ibrahim
Past, present, and future. *In* The Genius of Arab civilization p215-18

Madness. See Insanity; Mental illness

Madoff, Mark
The useful myth of Gothic ancestry. *In* Studies in eighteenth-century culture v8 p337-50

Madsen, David Lawrence
The land-grant university: myth and reality. *In* Land-grant universities and their continuing challenge p23-48

Maestlin, Michael

About

Westman, R. S. Three responses to the Copernican theory: Johannes Praetorius, Tycho Brahe, and Michael Maestlin. *In* The Copernican achievement p285-345

Maeterlinck, Maurice

About

Nicoll, A. Neo-romanticism in the theatre. *In* Nicoll, A. World drama p515-30

Worth, K. J. Maeterlinck. *In* Worth, K. J. The Irish drama of Europe from Yeats to Beckett p72-98

Worth, K. J. Towards modernism: a new theatrical syntax. *In* Worth, K. J. The Irish drama of Europe from Yeats to Beckett p11-47

Worth, K. J. Yeats, Maeterlinck and Synge. *In* Worth, K. J. The Irish drama of Europe from Yeats to Beckett p140-57

Maeztu, Ramiro de

About

Shaw, D. L. Maeztu: from Left to Right. *In* Shaw, D. L. The generation of 1898 in Spain p75-94

Mafia
Ianni, F. A. J. Organized crime and the Italo-American family. *In* Studies in Italian American social history p28-39

Vassalli, G. An Italian enquiry concerning the Mafia. *In* Crime, criminology and public policy p595-622

Magazines. See Periodicals

Magee, Stephen P.
Prices, incomes, and foreign trade. *In* Kenen, P. B. ed. International trade and finance p175-252

Magendie, François

About

Albury, W. R. Experiment and explanation in the physiology of Bichat and Magendie. *In* Studies in history of biology v 1 p47-131

Temkin, O. The philosophical background of Magendie's physiology. *In* Temkin, O. The double face of Janus p317-39

Maggs, Peter B.
Legal controls on American publication of heterodox Soviet writings. *In* Tokes, R. L. ed. Dissent in the USSR p310-25

Maghribis in Cairo 1527, The agreement between the Musta 'ribs' and the. Hirschberg, J. W. *In* Salo Wittmayer Baron v2 p577-90

Magic
Gray, W. G. Patterns of Western magic: a psychological appreciation. *In* Tart, C. T. ed. Transpersonal psychologies p431-72

Sagan, E Religion and magic: a developmental view. *In* Johnson, H. M. ed. Religious change and continuity p87-116

Taylor, A. Introduction. *In* Taylor, A. Magic and English romanticism p 1-14

See also Alchemy; Medicine, Magic, mystic, and spagiric; Occult sciences; Science and magic; Witchcraft

Magic, Anglo-Saxon
Hill, T. D. The æcerbot charm and its Christian user. *In* Anglo-Saxon England 6 p213-21

Magic, Jewish
Goldin, J. The magic of magic and superstition. *In* Aspects of religious propaganda in Judaism and early Christianity p115-47

Magic, Semitic. See Magic, Jewish

Magic and poetry
Romilly, J. de. Gorgias and magic. *In* Romilly, J. de. Magic and rhetoric in ancient Greece p 1-22

Magic and poetry—*Continued*

Romilly, J. de. Logic versus magic: Aristotle and later writers. *In* Romilly, J. de. Magic and rhetoric in ancient Greece p67-88

Romilly, J. de. Plato and conjurers. *In* Romilly, J. de. Magic and rhetoric in ancient Greece p23-43

Taylor, A. Coleridge and the potent voice. *In* Taylor, A. Magic and English romanticism p99-133

Taylor, A. Magical language and poetic analogy. *In* Taylor, A. Magic and English romanticism p38-63

Taylor, A. Self-destroying enthrallments: Byron and Keats. *in* Taylor, A. Magic and English romanticism p221-50

Taylor, A. Shelley's political enchantments. *In* Taylor, A. Magic and English romanticism p184-220

Taylor, A. Wordsworth's arguments against magical words. *In* Taylor, A. Magic and English romanticism p134-83

The magic flute (Motion picture)

Craft, R. Playing with the magic flute. *In* Craft, R. Current convictions p34-48

Magic in literature

Cooper, H. Magic that does not work. *In* Medievalia et humanistica no. 7 p131-46

Taylor, A. Coleridge and the magical power of the imagination. *In* Taylor, A. Magic and English romanticism p64-98

Taylor, A. Conclusion. *In* Taylor, A. Magic and English romanticism p251-55

Taylor, A. An eighteenth-century metaphor. *In* Taylor, A. Magic and English romanticism p15-37

Taylor, A. Introduction. *In* Taylor, A. Magic and English romanticism p 1-14

Wicker, B. Metaphor and "fiction." *In* Wicker, B. The story-shaped world p33-49

Magnetic healing. See Mesmerism

Magnetism. See Animal magnetism; Electricity; Electromagnetic theory; Electromagnetism

Magnetism, Animal. See Animal magnetism

Magnetism, Human. See Animal magnetism

Magnitizdat: uncensored songs of dissent. Sosin, G. *In* Tokes, R. L. ed. Dissent in the USSR p276-309

Maguire, Daniel C.

Catholic ethics with an American accent. *In* America in theological perspective p13-36

A Catholic view of mercy killing. *In* Kohl, M. ed. Beneficent euthanasia p12-33

Deciding for yourself: the objections. *In* Weir, R. F. ed. Ethical issues in death and dying p320-47

Mahābhārata

Van Nooten, B. A. The Sanskrit epics. *In* Oinas, F. J. ed. Heroic epic and saga p49-75

Mahābhārata. Bhagavadgītā

Barfield, O. Imagination and inspiration. *In* Barfield, O. The redscovery of meaning, and other essays p111-29

Bishop, D. H. The Bhagavad Gītā. *In* Bishop, D. H. ed. Indian thought p62-80

Mahadevan, T. K.

Gandhi—a modernist heresy. *In* Bishop, D. H. ed. Indian thought p357-63

Mahadevan, Telliyavaram Mahadevan Ponnambalam

Śaṅkara. *In* Bishop, D. H. ed. Indian thought p283-300

Mahajani, Usha

Sino-American rapprochement and the new configurations in Southeast Asia. *In* The Year book of world affairs, 1975 p106-20

Sino-Soviet conflict and rivalry in South-East Asia in the post-Vietnam phase. *In* The Year book of world affairs, 1978 p153-74

Mahan, Alfred Thayer

About individual works

The influence of sea power upon history, 1660-1783

Downs, R. B. Leviathan against elephant. *In* Downs, R. B. Books that changed the world p252-62

Mahan, Dennis Hart

About

Hagerman, E. H. From Jomini to Dennis Hart Mahan: the evolution of trench warfare and the American Civil War. *In* Hubbell, J. T. ed. Battles lost and won p31-54

Maharaj Ji

About

Messer, J. Guru Maharaj Ji and the Divine Light Mission. *In* The New religious consciousness p52-72

Mahatma Gandhi. See Gandhi, Mohandas Karamchand

Mahayana Buddhism

Dumoulin, H. Buddhism in modern Japan. *In* Dumoulin, H. ed. Buddhism in the modern world p215-76

Dumoulin, H. Contemporary Buddhism in Korea. *In* Dumoulin, H. ed. Buddhism in the modern world p202-14

Locke, J. K. Present-day Buddhism in Nepal. *In* Dumoulin, H. ed. Buddhism in the modern world p294-301

Raguin, Y. Buddhism in Taiwan. *In* Dumoulin, H. ed. Buddhism in the modern world p179-85

Snellgrove, D. L. Tibetan Buddhism today. *In* Dumoulin, H. ed. Buddhism in the modern world p277-93

Wayman, A. Buddhism in Malaysia. *In* Dumoulin, H. ed. Buddhism in the modern world p194-201

Welch, H. H. Buddhism in China today. *In* Dumoulin, H. ed. Buddhism in the modern world p164-78

See also Tantric Buddhism; Zen Buddhism

Mahdi, Muhsin

Remarks on Alfarabi's Attainment of happiness. *In* Essays on Islamic philosophy and science p47-66

Maher, Vanessa

Women and social change in Morocco. *In* Beck, L. and Keddie, N. R. eds. Women in the Muslim world p100-23

Mahigel, E. Louis, and Stone, Gregory P.

Hustling as a career. *In* Social problems in athletics p78-85

Mahler, Fred

Adolescents' ethics and morals in the year 2000. *In* Adolescence and youth in prospect p79-94

Mahler, Raphael

A Jewish memorandum to the Viceroy of the kingdom of Poland, Paskiewicz. *In* Salo Wittmayer Baron v2 p669-96

Mahmoud, Zaki Naguib

The intellectual life in contemporary Egypt. *In* Arab and American cultures p201-08

Rational aspects of the classical Arabic culture. *In* Arab and American cultures p87-92

Mahmud Sevket, paşa. See Sevket, Mahmut, paşa

Mahon, Derek

MacNeice in England and Ireland. *In* Time was away p113-22

Mahoney, Dhira B.

Malory's "Tale of Sir Tristram": source and setting reconsidered. *In* Medievalia et humanistica; new ser. no. 9 p175-98

Mahoney, Edward P.

Nicoletto Vernia on the soul and immortality. *In* Philosophy and humanism p144-63

Mahoney, Michael S.

Mathematics. *In* Lindberg, D. C. ed. Science in the Middle Ages p145-78

Mahony, Patrick Joseph

The anniversaries: Donne's rhetorical approach to evil. *In* Roberts, J. R. ed. Essential articles for the study of John Donne's poetry p363-67

Maĩakovskiĭ, Vladimir Vladimirovich

How to make verse. *In* Proffer, C. R. ed. Modern Russian poets on poetry p103-43

About

Brown, E. J. Mayakovsky's Futurist period. *In* Gibian, G. and Tjalsma, H. W. eds. Russian modernism p107-32

Glicksberg, C. I. Mayakovsky: the suicide of a committed poet. *In* Glicksberg, C. I. The literature of commitment p339-58

Jakobson, R. The contours of The safe conduct. *In* Matejka, L. and Titunik, I. R. eds. Semiotics of art p188-96

Jakobson, R. On a generation that squandered its poets. *In* Erlich, V. ed. Twentieth-century Russian literary criticism p138-66

Morgan, E. Introduction to Wi the haill voice: 25 poems by Vladimir Mayakovsky translated into Scots. *In* Morgan, E. Essays p58-66

Striedter, J. The "new myth" of revolution—a study of Mayakovsky's early poetry. *In* Amacher, R. E. and Lange, V. eds. New perspectives in German literary criticism p357-85

Trotskiĭ, L. Majakovskij and Russian futurism. *In* Erlich, V. ed. Twentieth-century Russian literary criticism p169-81

About individual works
Brooklyn Bridge

Morgan, E. Three views of Brooklyn Bridge. *In* Morgan, E. Essays p43-57

Maidment, B. E. See Watson, J. R. jt. auth.

Maier, Charles Steven

Beyond revolution? Resistance and vulnerability to radicalism in advanced Western societies. *In* Radicalism in the contemporary age v3 p241-67

The politics of inflation in the twentieth century. *In* The Political economy of inflation p37-72

Maier, Pauline

Early Revolutionary leaders in the South and the problem of Southern distinctiveness. *In* The Southern experience in the American Revolution p3-24

Mailer, Norman

About

Brustein, R. S. Cultural schizophrenia. *In* Brustein, R. S. The culture watch p17-25

Elliott, S. J. Homosexuality in the crucial decade: three novelists' views. *In* Crew, L. ed. The gay academic p164-77

Oates, J. C. The teleology of the unconscious: the art of Norman Mailer. *In* Oates, J. C. New heaven; new earth: the visionary experience in literature p177-203

Sarotte, G. M. Latent homosexuality: short of and beyond true heterosexuality: Norman Mailer: the overt latent homosexual. *In* Sarotte, G. M. Like a brother, like a lover p279-92

Wicker, B. Mailer and the big plot being hatched by nature. *In* Wicker, B. The story-shaped world p195-207

About individual works
An American dream

Fetterley, J. An American dream: "Hula, hula," said the witches. *In* Fetterley, J. The resisting reader p154-89

Rahv, P. Crime without punishment. *In* Rahv, P. Essays on literature and politics, 1932-1972 p67-74

Sadoff, D. F. Norman Mailer to posterity. *In* Filler, L. ed. A question of quality: popularity and value in modern creative writing p181-92

The armies of the night

Couser, G. T. Three contemporaries: Malcolm X, Norman Mailer, and Robert Pirsig. *In* Couser, G. T. American autobiography p164-96

Trilling, D. On the steps of Low Library. *In* Trilling, D. We must march my darlings p77-153

Barbary shore

Howe, I. Mailer's political novel. *In* Howe, I. Celebrations and attacks p39-40

Marilyn, a biography

Sarris, A. Marilyn, by Norman Mailer. *In* Sarris, A. Politics and cinema p162-67

Miami and the siege of Chicago

Sheed, W. Norman Mailer: Miami and the siege of Chicago. *In* Sheed, W. The good word & other words p275-78

Of a fire on the moon

Sale, R. H. Mailer & Lessing. *In* Sale, R. H. On not being good enough p21-30

The Presidential papers

Connolly, C. Norman Mailer. *In* Connolly, C. The evening colonnade p358-60

The prisoner of sex

Trilling, D. Women's liberation: The prisoner of sex. *In* Trilling, D. We must march my darlings p199-210

Maimbourg, Louis

About individual works
The history of the League

Roper, A. Characteristics of Dryden's prose. *In* ELH essays for Earl R. Wasserman p375-99

Translations, English

Roper, A. Characteristics of Dryden's prose. *In* ELH essays for Earl R. Wasserman p375-99

Maimonides, Moses. See Moses ben Maimon

Maine

Civilization

White, E. B. Letter from the East. *In* White, E. B. Essays of E. B. White p71-79

Description and travel

White, E. B. Once more to the lake. *In* White, E. B. Essays of E. B. White p197-202

Social conditions

White, E. B. Letter from the East. *In* White, E. B. Essays of E. B. White p71-79

Maine. Superior Court

Maine Medical Center v. Houle. *In* Weir, R. F. ed. Ethical issues in death and dying p185-86

Maine Medical Center v. Houle

Maine. Superior Court. Maine Medical Center v. Houle. *In* Weir, R. F. ed. Ethical issues in death and dying p185-86

Mair, Lucy Philips. See Part 2 under title: Colonialism and change

Mairan, Jean Jacques Dortous de

About

Guerlac, H. The Newtonianism of Dortous de Mairan. *In* Guerlac, H. Essays and papers in the history of modern science p479-90

Mais, Roger

About individual works

Brother Man

Brathwaite, E. K. Roger Mais's Brother Man as jazz novel. *In* Baugh, E. ed. Critics on Caribbean literature p103-12

Majakovskij, Vladimir. See Maĭakovskiĭ, Vladimir Vladimirovich

Majakowski, Wladimir. See Maĭakovskiĭ, Vladimir Vladimirovich

Majdiak, Daniel

The romantic self and Henderson the rain king. *In* Garvin, H. R. ed. Makers of the twentieth-century novel p276-89

Major, Robert W.

A reading of Hannah Arendt's "unusual" distinction between labor and work. *In* Hannah Arendt: the recovery of the public world p131-55

Majorities. See Minorities

Makaukau (African people) See !Kung (African people)

Makavejev, Dusan

About

Taylor, J. R. Dušan Makavejev. *In* Taylor, J. R. Directors and directions p228-50

Makielski, Sally Kimball

Population policy for the United States: the role of applied anthropology. *In* Eddy, E. M. and Partridge, W. L. eds. Applied anthropology in America p373-89

Makiesky-Barrow, Susan. See Sutton, C. R. jt. auth.

Makita, Tetsuo

Television drama and Japanese culture with special emphasis on historical drama. *In* Fischer, H. D. and Melnik, S. R. eds. Entertainment: a cross-cultural examination p63-73

Makriyannis, Strategou. See Makrygiannes, Iōannēs

Makrygiannes, Iōnnēs

About individual works

Apomnēmoneumata

Sherrard, P. General Makriyannis: the portrait of a Greek. *In* Sherrard, P. The wound of Greece p51-71

Malabar, India

History

Pearson, M. N. Corruption and corsairs in sixteenth-century western India. *In* Kling, B. B. and Pearson, M. N. eds. The age of partnership p15-41

Maladjusted children. See Problem children

Malagasy language

Southall, A. W. The problem of Malagasy origins. *In* Chittick, H. N. and Rotberg, R. I. eds. East Africa and the Orient p192-215

Malagasy Republic. See Madagascar

Malamud, Bernard

About

Benson, J. J. An introduction: Bernard Malamud and the haunting of America. *In* The Fiction of Bernard Malamud p13-42

Field, L. A. Bernard Malamud and the marginal Jew. *In* The Fiction of Bernard Malamud p97-116

Hassan, I. H. Bernard Malamud: 1976 fictions within our fictions. *In* The Fiction of Bernard Malamud p43-64

Roth, P. Imagining Jews. *In* Roth, P. Reading myself and others p215-46

Siegel, B. Through a glass darkly: Bernard Malmaud's painful views of the self. *In* The Fiction of Bernard Malamud p117-47

About individual works

The magic barrel

Howe, I. The stories of Bernard Malamud. *In* Howe, I. Celebrations and attacks p32-34

Trilling, L. Bernard Malamud: The magic barrel. *In* Trilling, L. Prefaces to The experience of literature p170-74

A new life

Fiedler, L. A. The many names of S. Levin: an essay in genre criticism. *In* The Fiction of Bernard Malamud p149-61

Pictures of Fidelman

Scholes, R. E. Comedy and grotesquerie. *In* Scholes, R. E. Fabulation and metafiction p139-92

The tenants

Alter, R. Updike, Malamud, and the fire this time. *In* Alter, R. Defenses of the imagination p233-48

Sale, R. H. Hawkes, Malamud, Richler, Oates. *In* Sale, R. H. On not being good enough p30-42

Bibliography

Risty, D. A comprehensive checklist of Malamud criticism. *In* The Fiction of Bernard Malamud p163-90

Characters

Hays, P. L. Malamud's Yiddish-accented medieval stories. *In* The Fiction of Bernard Malamud p87-96

Characters—Heroes

Handy, W. J. The Malamud hero: a quest for existence. *In* The Fiction of Bernard Malamud p65-86

Criticism and interpretation

Benson, J. J. An introduction: Bernard Malamud and the haunting of America. *In* The Fiction of Bernard Malamud p13-42

Malaspina, Alejandro. See Malaspina, Alessandro

Malaspina, Alessandro

About

Cutter, D. C. Spanish scientific exploration along the Pacific Coast. *In* Weber, D. J. ed. New Spain's far northern frontier p35-47

Malawi

Politics and government

Proctor, J. H. Communal representation in the Republic of Malawi. *In* Prospects for constitutional democracy p146-64

Religion

Kalilombe, P. A. The presence of the Church in Africa. *In* The Emergent gospel p22-30

Malay language

See also Indonesian language

Etymology

Wolff, J. U. Malay borrowings in Tagalog. *In* Southeast Asian history and historiography p345-67

Malay Peninsula

Commerce—Netherlands

Arasaratnam, S. Dutch commercial policy and interests in the Malay Peninsula, 1750-1795. *In* Kling, B. B. and Pearson, M. N. eds. The age of partnership p159-89

Malay race

Firth, R. W. Relations between personal kin (waris) among Kelantan Malays. *In* Social organization and the applications of anthropology p23-61

Malaya

Historiography

McIntyre, W. D. Malaya from the 1850's to the 1870's, and its historians, 1950-1970: from strategy to sociology. *In* Southeast Asian history and historiography p262-84

History

McIntyre, W. D. Malaya from the 1850's to the 1870's, and its historians, 1950-1970: from strategy to sociology. *In* Southeast Asian history and historiography p262-84

Malayan languages. See Malay language

Malays. See Malay race

Malaysia

Politics and government

Jupp, J. Modernization and pluralism: Ceylon and Malaysia. *In* Leftwich, A. ed. South Africa: economic growth and political change p187-211

Means, G. P. Malaysia. *In* Kearney, R. N. ed. Politics and modernization in South and Southeast Asia p153-214

Social conditions

Jupp, J. Modernization and pluralism: Ceylon and Malaysia. *In* Leftwich, A. ed. South Africa: economic growth and political change p187-211

Malcolm, Norman

Dreaming and skepticism. *In* Dunlop, C. E. M. ed. Philosophical essays on dreaming p103-26

The groundlessness of belief. *In* Reason and religion p143-57

Memory as direct awareness of the past. *In* Royal Institute of Philosophy. Impressions of empiricism p 1-22

About

Curley, E. M. Dreaming and conceptual revision. *In* Dunlop, C. E. M. ed. Philosophical essays on dreaming p317-46

About individual works

Dreaming

Ayer, Sir A. J. Professor Malcolm on dreams. *In* Dunlop, C. E. M. ed. Philosophical essays on dreaming p127-48

Caldwell, R. L. Malcolm and the criterion of sleep. *In* Dunlop, C. E. M. ed. Philosophical essays on dreaming p157-73

Canfield, J. V. Judgments in sleep. *In* Dunlop, C. E. M. ed. Philosophical essays on dreaming p149-56

Chappell, V. C. The concept of dreaming. *In* Dunlop, C. E. M. ed. Philosophical essays on dreaming p280-308

Chihara, C. S. What dreams are made on. *In* Dunlop, C. E. M. ed. Philosophical essays on dreaming p251-64

Dennett, D. C. Are dreams experiences? *In* Dunlop, C. E. M. ed. Philosophical essays on dreaming p227-50

Landesman, C. Dreams: two types of explanations. *In* Dunlop, C. E. M. ed. Philosophical essays on dreaming p309-16

Pears, D. F. Dreaming. *In* Dunlop, C. E. M. ed Philosophical essays on dreaming p205-26

Siegler, F. A. Remembering dreams. *In* Dunlop, C. E. M. ed. Philosophical essays on dreaming p265-79

The groundlessness of belief

Lyas, C. The groundlessness of religious belief. *In* Reason and religion p158-80

The privacy of experience

Cavell, S. Knowing and acknowledging. *In* Cavell, S. Must we mean what we say? p238-66

Scientific materialism and the identity theory

Flew, A. G. N. Mind/Brain identity and the Cartesian framework. *In* Flew, A. G. N. A rational animal p123-50

Malcolm X

About individual works

The autobiography of Malcolm X

Couser, G. T. Three contemporaries: Malcolm X, Norman Mailer, and Robert Pirsig. *In* Couser, G. T. American autobiography p164-96

Lessing, D. M. Allah be praised. *In* Lessing, D. M. A small personal voice p121-27

Maldon (Anglo-Saxon poem)

Blake, N. F. The genesis of The Battle of Maldon. *In* Anglo-Saxon England 7 p119-29

Doane, A. N. Legend, history and artifice in "The Battle of Maldon." *In* Viator: medieval and Renaissance studies v9 p39-66

Huppé, B. F. The concept of the hero in the early Middle Ages. *In* Concepts of the hero in the Middle Ages and the Renaissance p 1-26

Woolf, R. The ideal of men dying with their lord in the Germania and in The Battle of Maldon. *In* Anglo-Saxon England 5 p63-81

Male homosexuality. See Homosexuals, Male

Male sex hormone. See Hormones, Sex

Malebranche, Nicolas

About

Grant, P. John Norris and the Oratorians: belief and the images in God. *In* Grant, P. Images and ideas in literature of the English Renaissance p154-91

Radner, D. M. C. Malebranche's refutation of Spinoza. *In* Shahan, R. W. and Biro, J. I. eds. Spinoza: new perspectives p113-28

Malek, Frederic Vincent

Managing for results in the Federal government. *In* Managing nonprofit organizations p48-56

Malekin, P. and Crane, D. E. L.

The later seventeenth century. *In* English Association. The year's work in English studies v53 p250-72

Malesherbes, Chrétien Guillaume de Lamoignon de

About

Shaw, E. P. Censorship and subterfuge in eighteenth-century France. *In* Literature and history in the age of ideas p287-309

Maletzke, Gerhard

Intercultural and international communication. *In* Fischer, H. D. and Merrill, J. C. eds. International and intercultural communication p409-16

Malgonkar, Manohar

About

Singh, R. S. Historian turned fabulist: Manohar Malgonkar. *In* Singh, R. S. Indian novel in English p119-35

Malia, Martin E.

Adulthood refracted: Russia and Leo Tolstoi. *In* Erikson, E. H. ed. Adulthood p173-87

Malin, Irving

Flannery O'Connor and the grotesque. *In* Friedman, M. J. and Lawson, L. A. eds. The added dimension p108-22

The symbolic march. *In* Morris, R. K. and Malin, I. eds. The achievement of William Styron p122-33

See also Morris, R. K. jt. auth.

Malinowski, Bronislaw

About

Parsons, T. Malinowski and the theory of social systems. *In* Parsons, T. Social systems and the evolution of action theory p82-99

Malins, Edward Greenway

Lucca quartet. *In* Prentki, T. ed. Francis Warner p148-54

Malitz, Sidney. See Goldstein, E. G. jt. auth.

Malkiel, Yakov

Changes in the European languages under a new set of sociolinguistic circumstances. *In* First images of America p581-93

Mall, Franklin Paine

About

Harvey, A. M. A new school of anatomy: the story of Franklin P. Mall, Florence R. Sabin, and John B. MacCallum. *In* Harvey, A. M. Adventures in medical research p97-113

Mallac, Guy de

A Russian impressionist: Leonid Osipovich Pasternak, 1862-1945. *In* California Slavic studies v10 p87-120

Mallakh, Dorothea. See Mallakh, R. jt. auth.

Mallakh, Raja'i and Mallakh, Dorothea

Trade and commerce. *In* The Genius of Arab civilization p193-210

Mallarmé, Stéphane

About

Nalbantian, S. The Symbolists: the failing soul. *In* Nalbantian, S. The symbol of the soul from Hölderlin to Yeats p66-85

Parker, P. A. Epilogue. *In* Parker, P. A. Inescapable romance p219-43

About individual works

A la nue accablante

Stempel, W. D. Syntax and obscurity in poetry: on Mallarme's A la nue accablante. *in* Amacher, R. E. and Lange, V. eds. New perspectives in German literary criticism p134-49

The afternoon of a fawn

Poggioli, R. "L'Heure du berger": Mallarmé's grand eclogue. *In* Poggioli, R. The oaten flute p283-311

Malleo, Eduardo

About individual works

The bay of silence

Foster, D. W. Eduardo Mallea and the dilemma of the prophetic observer. *In* Foster, D. W. Currents in the contemporary Argentine novel: Arlt, Mallea, Sabato, and Cortázar p46-69

Mallison, Sally V. See Mallison, W. T. jt. auth.

Mallison, William Thomas, and Mallison, Sally V.

The concept of public purpose terror in international law: doctrines and sanctions to reduce the destruction of human and material values. *In* International terrorism and political crimes p67-85

An international law appraisal of the juridical characteristics of the resistance of the people of Palestine: the struggle for human rights. *In* International terrorism and political crimes p173-90

Mallowan, Agatha (Miller) Christie. See Christie, Agatha (Miller)

Malmstad, John E. and Shmakov, Gennady

Kuzmin's "The trout breaking through the ice." *In* Gibian, G. and Tjalsma, H. W. eds. Russian modernism p133-64

Malmstrom, Jean

First language teaching. *In* Wardhaugh, R. and Brown, H. D. eds. A survey of applied linguistics p44-68

Malone, Dumas

Mr Jefferson's private life. *In* American Antiquarian Society. Proceedings v84 pt 1 p65-72

Malone, Edmond

About

Lewis, W. S. Edmond Malone, Horace Walpole, and Shakespeare. *In* Evidence in literary scholarship p353-62

Malone, Henry Thompson

Bell Irvin Wiley: uncommon soldier. *In* Rank and file p 1-20

Malone, Marvin

The gall of Wormwood in printing over 66 issues and still continuing. *In* Anderson, E. and Kinzie, M. eds. The little magazine in America: a modern documentary history p389-404

Maltese dialect

Massa, D. The politics of cross-cultural dependence in language and poetry. *In* Narasimhaiah, C. D. ed. Awakened conscience p14-28

Maltese language. See Maltese dialect

Malthus, Thomas Robert

About

Flew, A. G. N. Powers, checks, and choice in Malthus. *In* Flew, A. G. N. A rational animal p34-48

About individual works

An essay on the principle of population

Downs, R. B. Too many mouths. *In* Downs, R. B. Books that changed the world p206-16

Influence—Darwin

Shapin, S. and Barnes, B. Darwin and social Darwinism: purity and history. *In* Barnes, B. and Shapin, S. eds. Natural order p125-42

Malthusianism

Flew, A. G. N. Powers, checks, and choice in Malthus. *In* Flew, A. G. N. A rational animal p34-48

See also Population

Maly, Kenneth

To re-awaken the matter of being. *In* Radical phenomenology p282-98

Mambuti. See Bambute

Mamelukes

Ayalon, D. Preliminary remarks on the mamlūk military institution in Islam. *In* War, technology and society in the Middle East p44-58

Rabie, H. The training of the mamlūk fāris. *In* War, technology and society in the Middle East p153-63

Mammals. See Marsupialia; Monotremata

Mammoth (the word)

Heaney, M. The implications of Richard James's maimanto. *In* Oxford Slavonic papers, new ser. v9 p102-09

Man, Paul de. See De Man, Paul

Man

Fletcher, J. F. Humanness. *In* Fletcher, J. F. Humanhood: essays in biomedical ethics p7-19

Herbert, X. Essay 13. *In* Fitzgerald, R. ed. What it means to be human p241-46

Holbrook, D. Essay 10. *In* Fitzgerald, R. ed. What it means to be human p186-208

McCloskey, H. J. Essay 12. *In* Fitzgerald, R. ed. What it means to be human p221-40

Rosen, E. The impact of Copernicus on man's conception of his place in the world. *In* Science and society: past, present, and future p52-67

Rucker, E. D. Institutions and the alienated man. *In* Philosophy and the civilizing arts p283-315

See also Anthropology; Anthropometry; Ethnology; Human biology; Persons; Philosophical anthropology

Animal nature

Benson, J. Hog in sloth, fox in stealth: man and beast in moral thinking. *In* Royal Institute of Philosophy. Nature and conduct p265-80

Dubos, R. J. The bestiality of the human species. *In* Dubos, R. J. Beast or angel? p41-44

Dubos, R. J. Humanity and the beast. *In* Dubos, R. J. Beast or angel? p61-66

Koestler, A. Prologue: the new calendar. *In* Koestler, A. Janus p 1-20

See also Sociobiology

Economic value

See Human capital

Influence of climate

Weiner, J. S. Physiological variation. *In* Racial variation in man p65-69

Influence of environment

Dubos, R. J. Human ecology. *In* Sobel, D. S. ed. Ways of health p387-96

Green, S. W. The agricultural colonization of temperate forest habitats: an ecological model. *In* The Frontier v2 p69-103

Hess, D. W. Pioneering as ecological process: a model and test case of frontier adaptation. *In* The Frontier v2 p123-51

Skinner, B. F. The steep and thorny way to a science of behaviour. *In* Harré, R. ed. Problems of scientific revolution p58-71

See also Architecture—Human factors; Dwellings—Psychological aspects; Man—Influence of climate

Influence on nature

Dubos, R. J. Social adaptations. *In* Dubos, R. J. Beast or angel? p33-38

Hartshorne, C. The environmental results of technology. *In* Philosophy & environmental crisis p69-78

Huxley, A. L. Man and his planet. *In* Huxley, A. L. The Human situation p12-27

Jaberg, R. L. Search for a center. *In* America in theological perspective p230-46

Mikesell, M. W. The rise and decline of "sequent occupance": a chapter in the history of American geography. *In* Geographies of the mind p149-69

Orr, D. W. Modernization and the ecological perspective. *In* Orr, D. W. and Soroos, M. S. eds. The global predicament p75-89

Thomas, L. A trip abroad. *In* Thomas, L. The medusa and the snail p106-09

Wald, G. The human condition. *In* Sociobiology and human nature p277-82

See also Environmental policy

Migrations

Dubos, R. J. The camp and the open road. *In* Dubos, R. J. Beast or angel? p130-34

McNeill, W. H. Human migration: a historical overview. *In* Human migration p3-19

Stewart, T. D. Perspectives on some problems of early man common to America and Australia. *In* Grafton Elliot Smith p114-35

See also Migration, Internal

Origin

Dubos, R. The saga of the human species. *In* Dubos, R. J. Beast or angel? p16-22

Popkin, R. H. The development of religious scepticism and the influence of Isaac La Peyrère's pre-Adamism and Bible criticism. *In* Classical influences on European culture A.D. 1500-1700 p271-80

See also Evolution; Human evolution

Man (Hinduism)

Reddy, V. N. K. Concepts of man. *In* Bishop, D. H. ed. Indian thought p252-73

The man (Motion picture)
Sarris, A. The man. *In* Sarris, A. Politics and cinema p21-23

Man (Philosophy) See Philosophical anthropology

Man (Theology)
Popkin, R. H. The pre-Adamite theory in the Renaissance. *In* Philosophy and humanism p50-69
See also Fall of man; Image of God; Man (Hinduism); Soul

Man, Antiquity of. See Man—Origin

Man, Doctrine of. See Man (Theology)

Man, Fall of. See Fall of man

Man, Fossil. See Fossil man

Man, Prehistoric
Larnach, S. L. and Macintosh, N. W. G. A comparative study of Solo and Australian aboriginal crania. *In* Grafton Elliot Smith p95-102
Napier, J. R. The talented primate. *In* Goodall, V. M. ed. The quest for man p79-103
Steward, J. H. The evolution of prefarming societies. *In* Steward, J. H. Evolution and ecology p103-27
See also Fossil man; Man—Origin

Food
Bender, B. The first revolution. *In* Goodall, V. M. ed. The quest for man p105-28

Population
Ammerman, A. J.; Cavalli-Sforza, L. L. and Wagener, D. K. Toward the estimation of population growth in Old World prehistory. *In* Zubrow, E. B. W. ed. Demographic anthropology p27-61

America
See Paleo-Indians

Australia
McCarthy, F. D. Relationships between Australian aboriginal material culture, and Southeast Asia and Melanesia. *In* Grafton Elliott Smith p210-26
Macintosh, N. W. G. Early man and the dog in Australia. *In* Grafton Elliot Smith p83-94

New Guinea
White, J. P. Early man in New Guinea. *In* Grafton Elliot Smith p109-13

Oceanica
McCarthy, F. D. Relationships between Australian aboriginal material culture, and Southeast Asia and Melanesia. *In* Grafton Elliot Smith p210-26

South America
Steward, J. H. Cultural evolution in South America. *In* Steward, J. H. Evolution and ecology p128-50

Man, Primitive
Coomaraswamy, A. K. Primitive mentality; excerpt from "Figures of speech or figures of thought: collected essays on the traditional or 'normal' view of art." *In* Coomaraswamy, A. K. Selected papers v 1 p286-307
See also Ethnology; Society, Primitive

Man and wife. See Husband and wife

A man escaped (Motion picture)
Truffaut, F. Robert Bresson: Un condamné à mort s'est échappé. *In* Truffaut, F. The films in my life p190-96

The man with the golden arm (Motion picture)
Rosen, R. C. Anatomy of a junkie movie. *In* Peary, G. and Shatzkin, R. eds. The modern American novel and the movies p189-98

Management
Affleck, J. G. The constructive orchestration of chaos. *In* Benton, L. R. ed. Management for the future p 1-8
Akula, W. G. and Vora, J. A. Systems planning tomorrow's hospitals today. *In* Managing nonprofit organizations p118-23
Brevoord, C. Effective management in the future. *In* Benton, L. R. ed. Management for the future p27-46
Davis, K. Some fundamental trends affecting management in the future. *In* Benton, L. R. ed. Management for the future p63-76
Debutts, J. D. The management of complexity. *In* Benton, L. R. ed. Management for the future p77-86
Elkin, R. A systems approach to planning and managing programs for the handicapped. *In* Managing nonprofit organizations p71-77
Fallon, K. P. Participatory management: an alternative in human service delivery systems. *In* Managing nonprofit organizations p244-51
Gray, J. L. Matrix organizational design as a vehicle for effective delivery of public health care and social services. *In* Managing nonprofit organizations p209-19
Horton, T. R. Leadership of the spirit: a present and future need. *In* Benton, L. R. ed. Management for the future p148-63
Jenks, J. M. Industrial democracy: a new challenge for management. *In* Benton, L. R. ed. Management for the future p175-88
McQuade, W. Management problems enter the picture at art museums. *In* Managing nonprofit organizations p261-69
Mazze, E. M. Management toward the year 2000: the challenges and the opportunities. *In* Benton, L. R. ed. Management for the future p219-28
Mitroff, I. I. Systemic problem solving. *In* Leadership p129-43
Newman, W. H. Control: past or future. *In* Benton, L. R. ed. Management for the future p229-37
Ronan, W. J. The new dimensions of management. *In* Benton, L. R. ed. Management for the future p247-56
Schelling, T. C. Command and control. *In* McKie, J. W. ed. Social responsibility and the business predicament p79-108
Zoffer, H. J. The road ahead for management: evolution or obsolescence. *In* Benton, L. R. ed. Management for the future p317-29
See also Bank management; Business; jectives; Organizational behavior; School management and organization; and subdivision Management under specific subjects, e.g. Corporations—Management

Management by objectives
Hacker, T. Management by objectives for schools. *In* Managing nonprofit organizations p155-63
Hand, H. H. and Hollingsworth, A. T. Tailoring MBO to hospitals. *In* Managing nonprofit organizations p176-86

Management by objectives—Continued

McConkey, D. D. Applying management by objectives to nonprofit organizations. In Managing nonprofit organizations p141-54

McConkey, D. D. The future: its challenge and its promise; excerpt from "MBO for nonprofit organizations." In Managing nonprofit organizations p199-206

McConkey, D. D. MBO in church organizations; excerpt from "MBO for nonprofit organizations." In Managing nonprofit organizations p164-75

Malek, F. V. Managing for results in the Federal government. In Managing nonprofit organizations p48-56

Shetty, Y. K. and Carlisle, H. M. A study of management by objectives in a professional organization. In Managing nonprofit organizations p187-98

Mañara y Vicentelo de Leca, Miguel

About

Brown, J. Hieroglyphs of death and salvation: the decoration of the Church of the Hermandad de la Caridad, Seville. In Brown, J. Images and ideas in seventeenth-century Spanish painting p128-46

Manchester, England

City planning

Goodrich, P. S. Manchester's urban univer-city. In Murphy, T. P. ed. Universities in the urban crisis p161-78

Social conditions

Lucas, W. J. Engels, Mrs. Gaskell and Manchester. In Lucas, W. J. The literature of change p34-56

University

See Victoria University of Manchester

Manchester, England in literature

Lucas, W. J. Engels, Mrs Gaskell and Manchester. In Lucas, W. J. The literature of change p34-56

Manchester metropolitan area, England

Goodrich, P. S. Manchester's urban univer-city. In Murphy, T. P. ed. Universities in the urban crisis p161-78

Manchuria

History—Incident, 1931

See Mukden Incident, 1931

Manchurian Incident, 1931. See Mukden Incident, 1931

Manchus

Roth, G. The Manchu-Chinese relationship, 1618-1636. In Spence, J. D. and Wills, J. E. eds. From Ming to Ch'ing p 1-38

See also China—History—Ch'ing dynasty, 1644-1912

Mandari (African people)

Buxton, J. C. Initiation and bead-sets in western Mandari. In Studies in social anthropology p310-27

Mandates

Bennett, E. M. Mandates and trusteeships. In Encyclopedia of American foreign policy p521-25

See also Protectorates

Mandates, Colonial. See Mandates

Mande (African people) See Mandingo (African people)

Mandel, Eli

About

Ower, J. Black and secret poet: notes on Eli Mandel. In Woodcock, G. ed. Poets and critics p138-50

Mandel, Frank. See Harbach, O. A. jt. auth.

Mandel, Ross

Heidegger and Wittgenstein: a second Kantian revolution. In Murray, M. E. ed. Heidegger and modern philosophy p259-70

Mandel'shtam, Osip Emil'evich

On the addressee. In Proffer, C. R. ed. Modern Russian poets on poetry p52-59

On the nature of the word. In Proffer, C. R. ed. Modern Russian poets on poetry p33-50

Same as Mandel'shtam, O. E. About the nature of the word. In Mandel'shtam, O. E. Selected essays p65-79

Selected essays

Contents

About an interlocutor

About the nature of the word

Same as: Mandel'shtam, O. E. On the nature of the word. In Proffer, C. R. ed. Modern Russian poets in poetry p33-50

Alagez

Around the naturalists

Ashot Ovanesian

Ashtarak

Attack

Badger's burrow

Conversation about Dante

The end of the novel

Fourth prose

François Villon

The French

Humanism & modern life

Literary Moscow

Literary Moscow: Birth of the fabula

The morning of acmeism

The nineteenth century

Notes about Chénier

Notes about poetry

Peter Chaadaev

Pushkin & Scriabin (fragments)

Sevan

Storm & stress

Sukhum

The word & culture

also in Gibbons, R. ed. The poets work: 29 masters of 20th century poetry on the origins and practice of their art p16-22

Zamoskvorech'e

About

Alter, R. Osip Mandelstam: the poet as witness. In Alter, R. Defenses of the imagination p25-46

Ginzburg, L. S. The poetics of Osip Mandelstam. In Erlich, V. ed. Twentieth-century Russian literary criticism p284-312

Slonim, M. L. The fate of poets: Mandelstam, Akhmatova, Tsvetayeva. In Slonim, M. L. Soviet Russian literature p248-67

Struve, G. Osip Mandelstam and Auguste Barbier. In California Slavic studies v8 p131-66

About individual works
Tristia

Gillis, D. C. The Persephone myth in Mandelstam's Tristia. In California Slavic studies v9 p139-59

Mandelstam, Osip. See Mandel'shtam, Osip Emil'evich

Mander, Raymond, and Mitchenson, Joe

Pin-ups of the past. *In* The Saturday book 34 p80-96

Mandeville, Bernard

About individual works

The fable of the bees

Clayre, A. An early instrumentalist theory: Mandeville. *In* Clayre, A. Work and play p103-12

A modest defence of publick stews

Rogal, S. J. The selling of sex: Mandeville's Modest defence of publick stews. *In* Studies in eighteenth-century culture v5 p141-50

Mandeville, Sir John

About individual works

The travels of Sir John Mandeville

Seymour, M. C. Medieval America and 'Sir John Mandeville.' *In* An English miscellany p46-53

Zacher, C. K. The pilgrim as curious traveler: Mandeville's Travels. *In* Zacher, C. K. Curiosity and pilgrimage p130-57

Mandingo (African people)

Bravmann, R. A. Masking tradition and figurative art among the Islamized Mande. *In* African images p144-69

Mangelsdorf, Paul Christoph

Foreword to Experiments in plant hybridisation by Gregor Mendel. *In* Praise from famous men: an anthology of introductions p109-13

Mangione, Jerre Gerlando

On being a Sicilian American. *In* Studies in Italian American social history p40-49

About

Mangione, J. G. On being a Sicilian American. *In* Studies in Italian American social history p40-49

Manheim, Leonard Falk

Dickens' fools and madmen. *In* Dickens Studies Annual v2 p69-97

Dickens' heroes, heroes, and heroids. *In* Dickens Studies Annual v5 p 1-22

A tale of two characters: a study in multiple projection. *In* Dickens Studies Annual v 1 p225-37

Mani

About

Henrichs, A. Mani and the Babylonian Baptists: a historical confrontation. *In* Harvard Studies in classical philology v77 p23-59

Mania. See Psychoses

Manichaeism

Henrichs, A. Mani and the Babylonian Baptists: a historical confrontation. *In* Harvard Studies in classical philology v77 p23-59

Koenen, L. Augustine and Manichaeism in light of the Cologne Mani Codex. *In* Illinois classical studies v3, 1978 p154-95

Manichaeism in literature

Schneider, D. J. The dream and the knitting machine: Joseph Conrad's symbolism. *In* Schneider, D. J. Symbolism: the Manichean vision p40-61

Schneider, D. J. The Manichean vision and the reading of symbolist works. *In* Schneider, D. J. Symbolism: the Manichean vision p 1-39

Schneider, D. J. "Orts, scraps, fragments" and the circle of wholeness: the symbolism of Virginia Woolf. *In* Schneider, D. J. Symbolism: the Manichean vision p118-53

Schneider, D. J. The symbolic system and the authority of the literary work. *In* Schneider, D. J. Symbolism: the Manichean vision p204-17

Schneider, D. J. "A terrible mixture in things": the symbolism of Henry James. *In* Schneider, D. J. Symbolism: the Manichean vision p62-117

Schneider, D. J. "The war that never ends": patterns of proliferation in Wallace Stevens's poetry. *In* Schneider, D. J. Symbolism: the Manichean vision p154-203

Manifest destiny (United States) See United States—Territorial expansion

Maniquis, Robert Manuel

Lonely empires: personal and public visions of Thomas De Quincey. *In* Literary monographs v8 p47-127

Manjirō. See Nakahama, Manjirō

Mankiewicz, Joseph Leo

About individual works

The barefoot contessa

Truffaut, F. Joseph Mankiewicz: The barefoot contessa. *In* Truffaut, F. The films in my life p129-32

Julius Caesar

Jorgens, J. J. Joseph Mankiewicz's Julius Caesar. *In* Jorgens, J. J. Shakespeare on film p92-105

Mankind (Morality play)

Jones, R. C. Dangerous sport: the audience's engagement with vice in the moral interludes. *In* Renaissance drama [1973] p45-64

Weimann, R. Moralities and interludes. *In* Weimann, R. Shakespeare and the popular tradition in the theater: studies in the social dimension of dramatic form and function p98-160

Manlove, Colin Nicholas

Literature and reality, 1600-1800

Contents

Conclusion
Cowper
Defoe
Donne and Marvell
Dryden
Fielding
Goldsmith and Crabbe
Gray: Elegy written in a country churchyard
Johnson
Jonson and Herrick
Milton
Pope
Swift
Thomson: The seasons

Modern fantasy

Contents

C. S. Lewis (1898-1963) and Perelandra
Charles Kingsley (1819-75) and The water-babies
George MacDonald (1824-1905)
J. R. R. Tolkien (1892-1973) and The Lord of the Rings
Mervyn Peake (1911-68)-The 'Titus' trilogy

Manlove, Colin N.—*Continued*

An organic hesitancy: theme and style in Billy Budd. *In* Pullin, F. ed. New perspectives on Melville p275-300

'Rooteles moot grene soone deye': the helplessness of Chaucer's Troilus and Criseyde. *In* English Association. Essays and studies, 1978 p 1-22

Mann, Arthur

The melting pot. *In* Uprooted Americans p288-318

Mann, Dennis Alan

Architectural icons: the best surprise is no surprise. *In* Browne, R. B. and Fishwick, M. W. eds. Icons of America p35-56

Conclusions. *In* Mann, D. A. ed. The arts in a democratic society p140-50

Introduction: the arts in a democratic society. *In* Mann, D. A. ed. The arts in a democratic society p 3-18

Mann, Heinrich

About individual works
Professor Unrat

Kostka, E. K. A literary quandary: Fyodor Sologub and Heinrich Mann. *In* Kostka, E. K. Glimpses of Germanic-Slavic relations from Pushkin to Heinrich Mann p21-37

Mann, Jill

Eating and drinking in 'Piers Plowman.' *In* English Association. Essays and studies, 1979 p26-43

See also Dronke, P. jt. auth.

Mann, Peter H.

Romantic fiction and its readers. *In* Fischer, H. D. and Melnik, S. R. eds. Entertainment: a cross-cultural examination p34-42

Mann, Phillip A.

Psychology of police organization: reward structure and group dynamics; excerpt from "Psychological consultation with a police department." *In* Armstrong, T. R. and Cinnamon, K. M. eds. Power and authority in law enforcement p104-14

Mann, Richard Dewey

The multiple goals of teaching. *In* Buxton, T. H. and Prichard, K. W. eds. Excellence in university teaching p39-47

Mann, Thomas

About

Craft, R. The discreet charm of the bourgeoisie. *In* Craft, R. Current convictions p256-68

Daemmrich, H. S. Mann's portrait of the artist: archetypal patterns. *In* Garvin, H. R. ed. Makers of the twentieth-century novel p166-78

Kurz, P. K. Thomas Mann and irony. *In* Kurz, P. K. On modern German literature v2 p3-21

Mudford, P. Thomas Mann. *In* Mudford, P. The art of celebration p72-87

Reed, T. J. Nietzsche's animals: idea, image and influence. *In* Pasley, J. M. S. ed. Nietzsche: imagery and thought p159-219

Wilder, T. N. Thomas Mann, 1875-1955. *In* Wilder, T. N. American characteristics, and other essays p240-44

About individual works
Buddenbrooks

Tobin, P. D. "Links in a chain": Thomas Mann, Buddenbrooks. *In* Tobin, P. D. Time and the novel p54-80

Death in Venice

Heller, E. Thomas Mann in Venice. *In* Heller, E. The poet's self and the poem p73-91

Meyers, J. Mann and Musil: Death in Venice and Young Törless. *In* Meyers, J. Homosexuality and literature, 1890-1930 p42-57

Schmidgall, G. Benjamin Britten. *In* Schmidgall, G. Literature as opera p321-55

Disorder and early sorrow

Trilling, L. Thomas Mann: Disorder and early sorrow. *In* Trilling, L. Prefaces to The experience of literature p131-35

Doctor Faustus

Craft, R. The Doctor Faustus case. *In* Craft, R. Current convictions p269-82

Dolan, P. J. Mann: art, politics, and the apocalypse. *In* Dolan, P. J. Of war and war's alarms p145-80

Hughes, H. S. Conclusion: The sea change. *In* Hughes, H. S. The sea change p240-72

Johnson, E. B. An unpublished letter of Thomas Mann concerning a nonsource for Doctor Faustus. *In* Strelka, J.P.; Bell, R. F. and Dobson, E. eds. Protest—form—tradition p15-34

Meyers, J. Dürer and Doctor Faustus. *In* Meyers, J. Painting and the novel p157-74

Gespräch in Briefen [von] Thomas Mann [und] Karl Kerényi

Middleton, J. C. Thomas Mann's letters to Paul Amann and Karl Kerényi. *In* Middleton, J. C. Bolshevism in art p252-57

Letters to Paul Amann, 1915-1952

Middleton, J. C. Thomas Mann's letters to Paul Amann and Karl Kerényi. *In* Middleton, J. C. Bolshevism in art p252-57

The magic mountain

Bruford, W. H. Thomas Mann: Der Zauberberg (1924). *In* Bruford, W. H. The German tradition of self-cultivation p206-25

Langer, L. L. Thomas Mann and death on the mountain. *In* Langer, L. L. The age of atrocity p69-112

Swales, M. Mann: The magic mountain (1924). *In* Swales, M. The German Bildungsroman from Wieland to Hesse p105-28

Webb, E. The perilous journey to wholeness in Thomas Mann. *In* Webb, E. The dark dove p157-93

Mario and the magician

Dolan, P. J. Mann: art, politics, and the apocalypse. *In* Dolan, P. J. Of war and war's alarms p145-80

Tatar, M. M. From science fiction to psychoanalysis: Henry James's "Bostonians," D. H. Lawrence's "Women in love," and Thomas Mann's "Mario and the magician." *In* Tatar, M. M. Spellbound p230-71

Characters—Felix Krull

Torrance, R. M. Ulysses and Hermes in modern times. *In* Torrance, R. M. The comic hero p240-73

Political and social views

Bruford, W. H. The conversion of an unpolitical man. *In* Bruford, W. H. The German tradition of self-cultivation p226-63

Manne, Henry G.
Corporate altruism and individualistic methodology. *In* Capitalism and freedom p128-42

Manned space flight. See Outer space—Exploration

Mannella, Charles J. See Schwartz, D. C. jt. auth.

Manner, Eeva Liisa

About

Sala, K. Eeva-Liisa Manner: a literary portrait. *In* Dauenhauer, R. and Binham, P. eds. Snow in May p58-59

Mannerism (Architecture)
Rowe, C. Mannerism and modern architecture. *In* Sharp, D. ed. The rationalists p174-89

Mannerism (Art)
Barolsky, P. Mannerist bizzarrie. *In* Barolsky, P. Infinite jest: wit and humor in Italian Renaissance art p101-38

Hoy, C. H. Jacobean tragedy and the mannerist style. *In* Shakespeare survey 26 p49-67

Manners and customs. See Caste; Festivals; Popular culture; Rites and ceremonies; Salutations

Mannheim, Karl

About

Bauman, Z. Understanding as the work of history: Karl Mannheim. *In* Bauman, Z. Hermeneutics and social science p89-110

Hughes, H. S. The critique of fascism. *In* Hughes, H. S. The sea change p70-133

Manning, Duane
In search of substantive change. *In* Buxton, T. H. and Prichard, K. W. eds. Excellence in university teaching p239-45

Manning, Frederic

About individual works

Her privates we

Smith, C. N. The very plain song of it: Frederic Manning, Her privates we. *In* Klein, H. M. ed. The First World War in fiction p174-82

Manning, Martha. See Blechman, E. A. jt. auth.

Manning, Sylvia
Families in Dickens. *In* Tufte, V. and Myerhoff, B. G. eds. Changing images of the family p141-53

Manning, W. H.
Blacksmithing. *In* Strong, D. E. and Brown, D. eds. Roman crafts p143-53

Manor, James
The lesser leader amid political transformation: the Congress Party in Mysore state in 1941 and 1951. *In* The Making of politicians: studies from Africa and Asia p140-55

Manor, Yohanan
France. *In* Galnoor, I. ed. Government secrecy in democracies p234-54

Manpower. See Labor supply

Manpower planning

United States

Ginzberg, E. Manpower planning in a pluralistic economy. *In* Planning, politics, and the public interest p28-37

Manpower policy
Marshall, F. R. Human resources and changing values in the South. *In* Lewis, W. D. and Griessman, B. E. eds. The Southern mystique p47-62

See also Vocational education

Underdeveloped areas

See Underdeveloped areas—Manpower policy

Manpower utilization. See Manpower policy

Manser, Anthony Richard
Austin's 'linguistic phenomenology.' *In* Pivčević, E. ed. Phenomenology and philosophical understanding p109-24

Mansfeld, Jaap
Alcmaeon: 'physikos' or physician? With some remarks on Calcidius' 'On vision' compared to Galen's Plac. Hipp. Plat. VII. *In* Kephalaion p26-38

Mansfield, Harvey Claflin, 1905-
Independence and accountability for federal contractors and grantees. *In* Smith, B. L. R. ed. The new political economy: the public use of the private sector p319-35

Mansfield, Joseph
Que viva prohibition? *In* Peary, G. and Shatzkin, R. eds. The modern American novel and the movies p308-16

Mansfield, Katherine

About

Rankin, W. Ineffability in the fiction of Jean Toomer and Katherine Mansfield. *In* Renaissance and modern p160-71

Mansfield, Michael Joseph

About

Glass, A. J. Mike Mansfield, Majority Leader. *In* Ornstein, N. J. ed. Congress in change p142-54

Manson, Marie Françoise Clarisse (Enjalran)

About individual works

Memoirs of Madame Manson, explanatory of her conduct, on the trial for the assassination of M. Fualdès

Borowitz, A. Henri de Latouche and the murder memoirs of Clarisse Manson. *In* Borowitz, A. Innocence and arsenic p132-62

Mansson, Helge Hilding
Justifying the Final Solution. *In* Weir, R. F. ed. Ethical issues in death and dying p308-19

Mansur, Abdul Kasim. See Firdawsī

Mansurov, Nikolai Sergeevich
The study of the mass communications and cultural establishments in the USSR. Some results of sociological research. *In* Fischer, H. D. and Melnik, S. R. eds. Entertainment: a cross-cultural examination p153-78

Mantegna, Andrea

About individual works

St James led to martyrdom

Meyers, J. Bellini, Giotto, Mantegna, Botticelli and Swann's way. *In* Meyers, J. Painting and the novel p96-111

Mantrayāna Buddhism. See Tantric Buddhism

Manuel, Frank Edward
Edward Gibbon: historien-philosophe. *In* Edward Gibbon and The decline and fall of the Roman Empire p167-81

Manuel, Frank E.—*Continued*

The use and abuse of psychology in history. *In* Kren, G. M. and Rappoport, L. H. eds. Varieties of psychohistory p38-62

Manufacture royale des glaces. See Saint-Gobain, s.a.

Manus tribe

Psychology

Mead, M. The evocation of psychologically relevant responses in ethnological field work. *In* Spindler, G. D. ed. The making of psychological anthropology p89-139

Manuscript depositories. See Archives

Manuscript transmission. See Transmission of texts

Manuscripts

Lutz, C. E. Manuscripts copied from printed books. *In* Lutz, C. E. Essays on manuscripts and rare books p129-38

See also Diplomatics; Illumination of books and manuscripts; Marginalia; Music—Manuscripts; Paleography; Transmission of texts; also subdivision Manuscripts under subjects and names of authors and individual works e.g. Ambrose, Saint Bp. of Milan—Manuscripts

Book reviews

Colker, M. L. Recent books about medieval manuscripts. *In* Medievalia et humanistica no. 5 p229-32

Collectors and collecting

Nevins, A. The role of the manuscript collector. *In* Nevins, A. Allan Nevins on history p254-62

Osborn, J. M. The search for English literary documents. *In* Wimsatt, W. K. ed. Literary criticism: idea and act p15-31

Depositories

See Archives

Egypt

Browne, G. M. Ostraca Harvardiana. *In* Harvard Studies in classical philology v76 p245-58

Russia

Waugh, D. C. Asbuka znakami lits: Egyptian hieroglyphs in the Privy Chancellery Archive. *In* Oxford Slavonic papers, new ser. v10 p46-50

Manuscripts (Papyri)

Kahane, H. R. and Kahane, R. The role of the papyri in etymological reconstruction. *In* Illinois classical studies v3, 1978 p207-20

See also Manuscripts, Greek (Papyri)

Manuscripts, Anglo-Saxon

Brownrigg, L. L. Manuscripts containing English decoration 871-1066, catalogued and illustrated: a review. *In* Anglo-Saxon England 7 p239-66

Cameron, A. F. Middle English in Old English manuscripts. *In* Chaucer and Middle English studies in honour of Rossell Hope Robbins p218-29

Godden, M. R. Old English composite homilies from Winchester. *In* Anglo-Saxon England 4 p57-65

Ker, N. R. A supplement to Catalogue of manuscripts containing Anglo-Saxon. *In* Anglo-Saxon England 5 p121-31

Mitchell, B. C.; Ball, C. and Cameron, A. F. Short titles of Old English texts. *In* Anglo-Saxon England 4 p207-21

Parkes, M. B. The palaeography of the Parker manuscript of the Chronicle, laws and Sedulius, and historiography at Winchester in the late ninth and tenth centuries. *In* Anglo-Saxon England 5 p149-71

Rigg, A. G. and Wieland, G. R. A Canterbury classbook of the mid-eleventh century (The 'Cambridge songs' manuscript) *In* Anglo-Saxon England 4 p113-30

Robinson, P. R. Self-contained units in composite manuscripts of the Anglo-Saxon period. *In* Anglo-Saxon England 7 p231-38

Manuscripts, Arabic (Judeo Arabic)

Goitein, S. D. F. A mansion in Fustat: a twelfth-century description of a domestic compound in the ancient capital of Egypt. *In* The Medieval city p163-78

Manuscripts, Church Slavic

Birnbaum, H. The New York Croato-Glagolitic missal and its background (preliminary communication). *In* California Slavic studies v10 p225-40

Manuscripts, Coptic (Papyri)

Browne, G. M. The Sahidic version of Kingdoms IV. *In* Illinois classical studies v3, 1978 p196-205

Manuscripts, English

Keiser, G. R. Lincoln Cathedral Library MS 91: life and milieu of the scribe. *In* Virginia. University. Bibliographical Society. Studies in bibliography v32 p158-79

Manuscripts, Greek

Browne, G. M. Ostraca Harvardiana. *In* Harvard Studies in classical philology v76 p245-58

Vaio, J. A new manuscript of Babrius: fact or fable? *In* Illinois classical studies, v2 1977 p173-83

Manuscripts, Greek (Papyri)

Browne, G. M. Harpocration panegyrista. *In* Illinois classical studies, v2 1977 p184-96

Browne, G. M. Late Roman papyri from the Michigan collection. *In* Harvard Studies in classical philology v75 p177-90

Browne, G. M. Three papyri from fourth-century Karanis. *In* Harvard Studies in classical philology v74 p317-31

Koniaris, G. L. Michigan papyrus 2754 and the Certamen. *In* Harvard Studies in classical philology v75 p107-29

Lloyd-Jones, H. and Rea, J. Callimachus, fragments 260-261. *In* Harvard Studies in classical philology v72 p125-45

Oates, J. F. More of Nemesion's notes: P. Corn. inv. 18. *In* Illinois classical studies v3, 1978 p81-87

Pearl, O. M. Rules for musical contests. *In* Illinois classical studies v3, 1978 p132-38

Renehan, R. The Michigan Alcidamas-papyrus: a problem in methodology. *In* Harvard Studies in classical philology v75 p85-105

Weinstein, M. E. An unpublished papyrus fragment of new comedy. *In* Harvard Studies in classical philology v75 p131-34

Willis, W. H. Two literary papyri in an archive from Panopolis. *In* Illinois classical studies v3, 1978 p140-51

Youtie, H. C. Grenfell's gift to Lumbroso. *In* Illinois classical studies v3, 1978 p90-99

Manuscripts, Illuminated. See Illumination of books and manuscripts; Illumination of books and manuscripts, Medieval; and similar headings

Map printing—History—*Continued*

Ristow, W. W. Lithography and maps, 1796-1850. *In* Woodward, D. A. ed. Five centuries of map printing p77-112

Robinson, A. H. Mapmaking and map printing: the evolution of a working relationship. *In* Woodward, D. A. ed. Five centuries of map printing p 1-23

Verner, C. Copperplate printing. *In* Woodward, D. A. ed. Five centuries of map printing p51-75

Woodward, D. A. The woodcut technique. *In* Woodward, D. A. ed. Five centuries of map printing p25-50

Maps

History

See Cartography—History

Printing

See Map printing

Maps, Printing of. See Map printing

Marais, Eugène Nielsen

About individual works

The soul of the white ant

Lessing, D. M. Ant's eye view: a review of The soul of the white ant by Eugène Marais. *In* Lessing, D. M. A small personal voice p143-52

Maranda, Elli Köngäs

Lau, Malaita: "a woman is an alien spirit". *In* Matthiasson, C. J. ed. Many sisters p177-202

Marandel, Jean Patrice

The deductive image. *In* Battcock, G. ed. Super realism p36-48

Maranos

Fischel, W. J. Garcia de Orta—a militant Marrano in Portuguese-India in the 16th century. *In* Salo Wittmayer Baron v 1 p407-32

Marans, Robert W. and Rodgers, Willard Lineus

Toward an understanding of community satisfaction. *In* Hawley, A. H. and Rock, V. P. eds. Metropolitan America in contemporary perspective p299-352

Marantz, Paul Joseph

Peaceful coexistence: from heresy to orthodoxy. *In* Cocks, P.; Daniels, R. V. and Heer, N. W. eds. The dynamics of Soviet politics p293-308

Maratsos, Michael

New models in linguistics and language acquisition. *In* Linguistic theory and psychological reality p246-63

Marble sculpture, Classical

Turkey—Izmir (City)

Dwyer, E. J. On the meaning of the griffin pelta. *In* Studies in classical art and archaeology p235-38

Marble sculpture, Hellenistic

England—London

Herrmann, A. The biter: a late Hellenistic astragal player. *In* Studies in classical art and archaeology p163-73

Marble sculpture, Roman

Dwyer, E. J. On the meaning of the griffin pelta. *In* Studies in classical art and archaeology p235-38

Strong, D. E. and Claridge, A. Marble sculpture. *In* Strong, D. E. and Brown, D. eds. Roman crafts p195-207

Marbury, Anne. See Hutchinson, Anne (Marbury)

Marcabru. See Marcabrun

Marcabrun

About

Topsfield, L. T. Marcabru and Fin'Amors. *In* Topsfield, L. T. Troubadours and love p70-107

About individual works

Dire vos vuoill ses doptansa

Nichols, S. G. Toward an aesthetic of the Provençal lyric II: Marcabru's Dire vos vuoill ses doptansa (BdT 293, 18). *In* Italian literature: roots and branches p15-37

March, William, pseud. See Campbell, William Edward March

Marckwardt, Albert Henry, ed. See Linguistic atlas of the North Central States (proposed)

Marco Polo. See Polo, Marco

Marcos, Plínio

About

Schoenbach, P. J. Plinio Marcos: reporter of bad times. *In* Lyday, L. F. and Woodyard, G. W. eds. Dramatists in revolt p243-57

Marcovich, Miroslav. See Markovîc, Miroslav

Marcum, John A.

Angola: division or unity? *In* Carter, G. M. and O'Meara, P. eds. Southern Africa in crisis p136-62

Angola: perilous transition to independence. *In* Carter, G. M. and O'Meara, P. eds. Southern Africa: the continuing crisis p175-98

Marcus, David Donald

Symbolism and mental process in Dombey and son. *In* Dickens Studies Annual v6 p57-71

Marcus, Harold G.

The British and the Ethiopian railway. *In* African dimensions p29-51

Marcus, Irwin Murray

Observations on teaching. *In* Buxton, T. H. and Prichard, K. W. eds. Excellence in university teaching p67-69

Marcus, Jacob Rader

The American colonial Jew: a study in acculturation. *In* Tradition and change in Jewish experience p75-88

Marcus, Mordecai

What is an initiation story? *In* May, C. E. ed. Short story theories p189-201

Marcus, Phillip L.

The Celtic revival: literature and the theatre. *In* De Breffny, B. ed. The Irish world p199-226

Marcus, Steven

Lionel Trilling, 1905-1975. *In* Art, politics, and will p265-78

Representations

Contents

Authority and obedience
Awakening from the nightmare? Notes on the historical novel
Dashiell Hammett and the Continental Op
Evelyn Waugh and the art of entertainment
Freud and Dora: story, history, case history
Hunger and ideology
An ideal reviewer

Marcus, Steven

Representations

Contents—Continued

Language into structure: Pickwick papers
The limits of literary history
Literature and social theory: starting in
with George Eliot
Madness, literature, and society
Mt Everest and the British national spirit
Sinclair Lewis
Snopes revisited
Stalky & Co.
Three obsessed critics

Some questions in general education today.
In From Parnassus p84-104

also in Sinall comforts for hard times
p281-302

Their brothers' keepers: an episode from
English history. *In* Doing good p39-66

Marcuse, Herbert

On science and phenomenology. *In* Giddens, A. ed. Positivism and sociology p225-36

About

Agger, B. On happiness and the damaged
life. *In* O'Neill, J. ed. On critical theory p12-33

Graff, G. The politics of anti-realism. *In*
Graff, G. Literature against itself p63-101

Hughes, H. S. The critique of mass society. *In* Hughes, H. S. The sea change
p134-88

Kettler, D. Herbert Marcuse: alienation
and negativity. *In* De Crespigny, A. and
Minogue, K. R. eds. Contemporary political
philosophers p 1-48

About individual works

Eros and civilization

Harries, K. Death and utopia: towards a
critique of the ethics of satisfaction. *In*
Radical phenomenology p138-52

Marder, Herbert

Beyond the lighthouse: The years. *In* Garvin, H. R. ed. Makers of the twentieth-century novel p62-69

Mardi Gras. See subdivision Carnival under
names of cities and towns, e.g. New Orleans—Carnival

The **Mardøla** Waterfall development. Kvaløy, S. *In* Against pollution and hunger
p289-92

Marduk

Lambert, W. G. The historical development of the Mesopotamian pantheon: a study
in sophisticated polytheism. *In* Unity and
diversity p191-200

Mare, W. Harold

A study of the New Testament concept of
the Parousia. *In* Current issues in Biblical
and patristic interpretation p336-45

Maresca, Thomas E.

The context of Dryden's Absalom and
Achitophel. *In* ELH essays for Earl R. Wasserman p50-68

Epic to novel

Contents

Dryden
Fielding
Pope
Swift

Marey, Étienne-Jules

About

Scharf, A. Max Ernst, Étienne-Jules
Marey, and the poetry of scientific illustration. *In* One hundred years of photographic
history p117-26

Marginal peoples. See Marginality, Social

Marginal productivity

Lerner, A. P. Wages, profits, and marginal analysis. *In* Inflation, trade and taxes
p23-28

Marginalia

Cameron, A. F. Middle English in Old
English manuscripts. *In* Chaucer and Middle English studies in honour of Rossell
Hope Robbins p218-29

Marginality, Social

Benamou, M. The concept of marginality
in ethno-poetics. *In* Minority language and
literature p150-60

United States

Glaser, D. Marginal workers: some antecedents and implications of an idea from
Shaw and McKay. *In* Delinquency, crime,
and society p254-66

Margoliash, Emanuel

Informational macromolecules and biological evolution. *In* Neyman, J. ed. The heritage of Copernicus: theories "pleasing to the
mind" p184-206

Margolin, Jean-Claude

The method of "words and things" in
Erasmus's De pueris instituendis (1529) and
Comenius's Orbis sensualium pictus (1658)
In Essays on the works of Erasmus p221-38

Margolin, Uri

Conclusion: literary structuralism and hermeneutics in significant convergence, 1976.
In Valdés, M. J. and Miller, O. J. eds.
Interpretation of narrative p177-85

Margolis, Clorinda. See Margolis, J. Z. jt.
auth.

Margolis, John D.

Joseph Wood Krutch: a writer's passage
beyond The modern temper. *In* Bornstein, G.
ed. Romantic and modern p223-40

Margolis, Joseph Zalman

The ontological peculiarity of works of art.
In Margolis, J. Z. ed. Philosophy looks at
the arts p213-24

The question of homosexuality. *In* Baker, R. and Elliston, F. A. eds. Philosophy &
sex p288-302

The relevance of Dewey's epistemology. *In*
Cahn, S. M. ed. New studies in the philosophy of John Dewey p117-48

Robust relativism. *In* Margolis, J. Z. ed.
Philosophy looks at the arts p387-437

Works of art are physically embodied and
culturally emergent entities. *In* Aagaard-Mogensen, L. ed. Culture and art p32-45

Margolis, Joseph Zalman, and Margolis, Clorinda

The separation of marriage and family. *In*
Feminism and philosophy p291-307

Marguérite d'Angoulême, queen of Navarre

About

Auld, L. E. Music as dramatic device in
the secular theater of Marguerite de Navarre.
In Renaissance drama [1976] p193-217

Marguérite of Navarre. See Marguérite
d'Angoulême, queen of Navarre

Marguerite Porette. See Marguerite Porrette

Marguerite Porrette

About

Lerner, R. E. An "Angel of Philadelphia" in the reign of Philip the Fair: the case of Guiard of Cressonessart. *In* Order and innovation in the Middle Ages p343-64

Mariani, Isidoro Franco

Incomes and employment policies in Italian economic planning. *In* Planning, politics and public policy p202-13

Mariano, Nicky

About individual works
Forty years with Berenson

Connolly, C. Berenson. *In* Connolly, C. The evening colonnade p26-29

Marichal, Juan Augusto

The New World from within: the Inca Garcilaso. *In* First images of America p57-61

Marighella, Carlos

About

Parry, A. Wanton romantics: Guevara, Debray, Marighella. *In* Parry, A. Terrorism: from Robespierre to Arafat p244-60

Marin, John

About

Wilder, T. N. John Marin, 1870-1953. *In* Wilder, T. N. American characteristics, and other essays p234-39

Marin, Louis

An American event on the French stage: notes on an eighteenth-century engraving. *In* Glyph 3 p 1-17

Disneyland: a degenerate utopia. *In* Glyph I p50-66

'Le neutre' and philosophical discourse. *In* Montefiore, A. ed. Neutrality and impartiality p86-127

Marine pollution

Law and legislation

Craven, J. P. A legal regime for arms control and pollution control in the oceans. *In* Borgese, E. M. and Krieger, D. eds. The tides of change p100-09

Mediterranean Sea

Ritchie-Calder, P. R. Baron Ritchie Calder. The pollution of the Mediterranean. *In* Borgese, E. M. and Krieger, D. eds. The tides of change p144-65

Marine resources

Jouvenel, B. de. An economic view of marine problems. *In* Borgese, E. M. and Krieger, D. eds. The tides of change p4-32

Kaplan, I. Mater omnium: automated energy and material wealth from the sea. *In* Borgese, E. M. and Krieger, D. eds. The tides of change p48-75

See also Fisheries

International cooperation

Varon, B. Ocean issues on the international agenda. *In* Erb, G. F. and Kalab, V. eds. Beyond dependency p120-31

Marine resources. See Fisheries

Marine surveying. See Hydrographic surveying

Marinelli, Peter V.

Redemptive laughter: comedy in the Italian romances. *In* Ruggiers, P. G. ed. Versions of medieval comedy p227-48

Marinetti, Filippo Tomasso

About individual works
L'alcòva d'acciaio

Wagstaff, C. Dead man erect: F. T. Marinetti, L'alcova d'acciaio. *In* Klein, H. M. ed. The First World War in fiction p149-59

Marino, Matthew

Toward a modal paradigm. *In* James B. McMillan: essays in linguistics by his friends and colleagues p73-89

Marinow, Al

The self-portraits of a schizophrenic patient. *In* Ulman, E. and Dachinger, P. eds. Art therapy p325-27

Marionettes. See Puppets and puppet-plays

Maritain, Jacques

About individual works
Creative intuition in art and poetry

Fergusson, F. Maritain's Creative intuition. *In* Fergusson, F. Literary landmarks p37-47

Marital counseling. See Marriage counseling

Marital status. See Married people

Maritime law

Egge, B. An international multipurpose surveillance system. *In* Borgese, E. M. and Krieger, D. eds. The tides of change p121-39

Schwarzenberger, G. Trends in the law of the sea. *In* The Year book of world affairs, 1979 p328-73

See also Freedom of the seas; Territorial waters

Maritime war. See War, Maritime (International law)

Marivaux, Pierre Carlet de Chamblain de

About

Brereton, G. Marivaux. *In* Brereton, G. French comic drama p194-213

Cismaru, A. Molière's presence in selected plays of Marivaux. *In* Johnson, R. B.; Neumann, E. S. and Trail, G. T. eds. Molière and the commonwealth of letters: patrimony and posterity p68-81

Turnell, M. Marivaux. *In* Turnell, M. The rise of the French novel p29-70

About individual works
The fortunate peasant

Koppisch, M. S. The faux dévot from Molière to Marivaux. *In* Johnson, R. B.; Neumann, E. S. and Trail, G. T. eds. Molière and the commonwealth of letters: patrimony and posterity p57-67

Mark, Carson J.

Consequences of nuclear war. *In* Griffiths, F. and Polanyi, J. C. eds. The dangers of nuclear war p7-21

Mark, Eduard

Mr. "X" is inconsistent and wrong. *In* Decline of the West? George Kennan and his critics p157-72

Mark, Thomas Carson

Truth and adequacy in Spinozistic ideas. *In* Shahan, R. W. and Biro, J. I. eds. Spinoza: new perspectives p11-34

Mark Twain, pseud. See Clemens, Samuel Langhorne

Markandaya, Kamala, pseud. See Taylor, Kamala (Purnaiya)

Marked woman (Motion picture)

Kay, K. Sisters of the night. *In* Nichols, B. ed. Movies and methods p185-94

Markiewicz, Henryk
The limits of literature. *In* Cohen, R. ed. New directions in literary history p189-98

Markov, Vladimir
Georgy Ivanov: nihilist as light-bearer. *In* The Bitter air of exile p139-63
Mozart: theme and variations. *In* The Bitter air of exile p441-70

Marković, Mihailo. See Marković, Mihajlo

Marković, Mihajlo
Stalinism and Marxism. *In* Stalinism p299-319
Women's liberation and human emancipation. *In* Gould, C. C. and Wartofsky, M. W. eds. Women and philosophy p145-67

Marković, Miroslav
Euclio, Cnemon, and the Peripatos. *In* Illinois classical studies, v2 1977 p197-218
Hephaestion, Apotelesmatica, Book 1. *In* Illinois classical studies, v 1 1976 p59-64
Theophilus of Antioch: fifty-five emendations. *In* Illinois classical studies v4, 1979 p76-93
Xenophanes on drinking-parties and Olympic Games. *In* Illinois classical studies v3, 1978 p 1-26

Markovits, Richard S.
Some preliminary notes on the American antitrust laws' economic tests of legality. *In* Stanford legal essays p317-34

Marks, John D. See Borosage, R. L. jt. auth.

Marks, Mollyanne
Renovation of form: time as hero in Blake's major prophecies. *In* Studies in eighteenth-century culture v5 p55-66

Marks, Morton Allen
Uncovering ritual structures in Afro-American music. *In* Zaretsky, I. I. and Leone, M. P. eds. Religious movements in contemporary America p60-134

Marks, Shula
South African studies since World War Two. *In* African studies since 1945 p186-99

Marks, Potters'. See Pottery—Marks

Marks in paper. See Water-marks

Markus, Maria
Women and work: emancipation at a dead end. *In* The Humanisation of socialism p76-90

Markus, Maria, and Hegedüs, András
Community and individuality. *In* The Humanisation of socialism p91-105
Free time and the division of labour. *In* The Humanisation of socialism p106-23
The role of values in the long-range planning of distribution and consumption. *In* The Humanisation of socialism p140-60
Tendencies in Marxist sociology in the Socialist countries. *In* The Humanisation of socialism p124-39

Marlborough, Helen
Herrick's epigrams of praise. *In* Rollin, R. B. and Patrick, J. M. eds. "Trust to good verses": Herrick tercentenary essays p159-69

Marler, Peter
Affective and symbolic meaning: some zoosemiotic speculations. *In* Sebeok, T. A. ed. Sight, sound, and sense p113-23

Marlies, Mike
Doubt, reason, and Cartesian therapy. *In* Hooker, M. ed. Descartes p89-113

Marlow, James Elliott
Dickens' romance: the novel as other. *In* Dickens Studies Annual v5 p23-42

Marlowe, Christopher

About

Altman, J. B. "If words might serve"; Marlowe's supposes. *In* Altman, J. B. The Tudor play of mind p321-88
Berryman, J. Marlowe's damnations. *In* Berryman, J. The freedom of the poet p3-8
Craik, T. W. The reconstruction of stage action from early dramatic texts. *In* The Elizabethan theatre, V p76-91
Garber, M. B. "Infinite riches in a little room": closure and enclosure in Marlowe. *In* Kernan, A. B. ed. Two Renaissance mythmakers p 3-21
Goldman, M. Marlowe and the histrionics of ravishment. *In* Kernan, A. B. ed. Two Renaissance mythmakers p22-40
Greenblatt, S. J. Marlowe and Renaissance self-fashioning. *In* Kernan, A. B. ed. Two Renaissance mythmakers p41-69

About individual works
Doctor Faustus

Hunter, G. K. Five-act structure in Doctor Faustus. *In* Hunter, G. K. Dramatic identities and cultural tradition p335-49
Snow, E. A. Marlowe's Doctor Faustus and the ends of desire. *In* Kernan, A. B. ed. Two Renaissance mythmakers p70-110
Young, D. P. Where the bee sucks: A triangular study of Doctor Faustus, The alchemist, and The tempest. *In* Shakespeare's romances reconsidered p149-66

Edward II

Boyette, P. E. Wanton humour and wanton poets: homosexuality in Marlowe's Edward II. *In* Tulane studies in English v22 p33-50
Cushner, A. W. Some observations on Marlowe's Edward II. *In* Renaissance and modern p11-20

The Jew of Malta

Hunter, G. K. The theology of Marlowe's The Jew of Malta. *In* Hunter, G. K. Dramatic identities and cultural tradition p60-102

Tamburlaine the Great

Battenhouse, R. W. The relation of Henry V to Tamburlaine. *In* Shakespeare survey 27 p71-79

The tragedy of Dido, Queen of Carthage

Stilling, R. The tragedy of Dido, Queen of Carthage. *In* Stilling, R. Love and death in Renaissance tragedy p41-55

Characters

Hawkins, H. 'If this be error': imagination and truth in Shakespeare and Marlowe. *In* Hawkins, H. Poetic freedom and poetic truth p78-104

Characters—Faustus

Snow, E. A. Marlowe's Doctor Faustus and the ends of desire. *In* Kernan, A. B. ed. Two Renaissance mythmakers p70-110

Influence—Shakespeare

Battenhouse, R. W. The relation of Henry V to Tamburlaine. *In* Shakespeare survey 27 p71-79

Marmaras, Apostolos, and Marmaras, Lilika
An English translation of the ancient Greek dedicatory verses to Atalanta in Calydon. *In* Aeolian harps p179-89

Marmaras, Lilika. See Marmaras, A. jt. auth.

Marmor, Judd
Homosexuality. *In* Sexuality and human values p24-33

Marmura, Ella
Arabic literature: a living heritage. *In* Savory, R. M. ed. Introduction to Islamic civilisation p61-70

Marmura, Michael E.
Avicenna's chapter, "On the relative," in the Metaphysics of the Shifā. *In* Essays on Islamic philosophy and science p83-99
Ghazali's attitude to the secular sciences and logic. *In* Essays on Islamic philosophy and science p100-11
God and his creation: two medieval Islamic views. *In* Savory, R. M. ed. Introduction to Islamic civilisation p46-53

Marot, Clément

Appreciation—England
Prescott, A. L. Marot. *In* Prescott, A. L. French poets and the English Renaissance p 1-36

Influence
Prescott, A. L. Marot. *In* Prescott, A. L. French poets and the English Renaissance p 1-36

Marotti, Arthur Francis
Donne and "The extasie". *In* Sloan, T. O. and Waddington, R. B. eds. The rhetoric of Renaissance poetry p140-73

Marovitz, Sanford E.
Old man Ahab. *In* Artful thunder p139-61

Marquand, John Phillips, 1893-1960

About
Holman, C. H. Marquand, novelist of manners. *In* Holman, C. H. Windows on the world p61-97
Milne, G. John P. Marquand. *In* Milne, G. The sense of society p168-204

Marquard, Odo
On the importance of the theory of the unconscious for a theory of no longer fine art. *In* Amacher, R. E. and Lange, V. eds. New perspectives in German literary criticism p260-78

Marquardt, Friedrich-Wilhelm
Socialism in the theology of Karl Barth. *In* Hunsinger, G. ed. Karl Barth and radical politics p47-76

About individual works
Theologie und Sozialismus
Diem, H. Karl Barth as Socialist: controversy over a new attempt to understand him. *In* Hunsinger, G. ed. Karl Barth and radical politics p121-38
Schellong, D. On reading Karl Barth from the left. *In* Hunsinger, G. ed. Karl Barth and radical politics p139-57

Marqués, René

About
Holzapfel, T. The theater of René Marqués: in search of identity and form. *In* Lyday, L. F. and Woodyard, G. W. eds. Dramatists in revolt p146-66

Marquetry

Italy
Winternitz, E. The importance of quattrocento intarsias for the history of musical instruments. *In* Winternitz, E. Musical instruments and their symbolism in Western art p116-19

Italy—Gubbio
Winternitz, E. Quattrocento science in the Gubbio study. *In* Winternitz, E. Musical instruments and their symbolism in Western art p120-28

Márquez, Gabriel García. See García Márquez, Gabriel

Marquis, Don

About individual works
Archy and Mehitabel
White, E. B. Don Marquis. *In* White, E. B. Essays of E. B. White p250-55

Marquis, Donald Bagley
Ethics and the elderly: some problems. *In* Spicker, S. F.; Woodward, K. M. and Van Tassel, D. D. eds. Aging and the elderly p341-55

Marrakesh, Morocco
Koestler, A. Marrakech. *In* Koestler, A. The heel of Achilles p192-205

Marranos. See Maranos

Marriage
Barnhart, J. E. and Barnhart, M. A. The myth of the complete person. *In* Feminism and philosophy p277-90
Bayles, M. D. Marriage, love, and procreation. *In* Baker, R. and Elliston, F. A. eds. Philosophy & sex p190-206
Blum, L. and others. Altruism and women's oppression. *In* Gould, C. C. and Wartofsky, M. W. eds. Women and philosophy p222-47
Cohen, C. Sex, birth control, and human life. *In* Baker, R. and Elliston, F. A. eds. Philosophy & sex p150-65
Herlihy, D. The medieval marriage market. *In* Medieval and Renaissance studies [1974] p3-27
McMurtry, J. Monogamy: a critique. *In* Baker, R. and Elliston, F. A. eds. Philosophy & sex p166-77
Margolis, J. Z. and Margolis, C. The separation of marriage and family. *In* Feminism and philosophy p291-307
O'Driscoll, L. H. On the nature and value of marriage. *In* Feminism and philosophy p249-63
Palmer, D. The consolation of the wedded. *In* Baker, R. and Elliston, F. A. eds. Philosophy & sex p178-89
Paulus VI, Pope. Humanae vitae. *In* Baker, R. and Elliston, F. A. eds. Philosophy & sex p131-49
Whiting, J. W. M. and Whiting, B. B. Aloofness and intimacy of husbands and wives: a cross-cultural study. *In* Schwartz, T. ed. Socialization as cultural communication p91-115
See also Divorce; Domestic relations; Family; Husbands; Marriage counseling; Sex in marriage; Sexual ethics

Annulment
See Divorce

Case studies
Peterson, J. A. Nagging and sex. *In* Gross, L. ed. Sexual issues in marriage p85-92

Europe
Flandin, J. L. Contraception, marriage, and sexual relations in the Christian West. *In* Biology of man in history p23-47

Marriage—*Continued*

Formosa

Wolf, A. P. Marriage and adoption in northern Taiwan. *In* Social organization and the applications of anthropology p128-60

France

Baulant, M. The scattered family: another aspect of seventeenth-century demography. *In* Family and society p104-16

Burguière, A. From Malthus to Max Weber: belated marriage and the spirit of enterprise. *In* Family and society p237-50

France—Béarn

Bourdieu, P. Marriage strategies as strategies of social reproduction. *In* Family and society p117-44

Germany

McNamara, J. A. and Wemple, S. F. Marriage and divorce in the Frankish kingdom. *In* Stuard, S. M. ed. Women in medieval society p95-124

Islam

See Marriage (Islamic law)

United States

Cuber, J. F. Age-discrepant marriages. *In* Gross, L. ed. Sexual issues in marriage p245-58

Schwab, J. J. Antipathy to marriage. *In* Gross, L. ed. Sexual issues in marriage p105-13

Marriage (Islamic law)

Coulson, N. J. and Hinchcliffe, D. Women and law reform in contemporary Islam. *In* Beck, L. and Keddie, N. R. eds. Women in the Muslim world p37-51

Marriage, Sacred (Mythology) See Sacred marriage (Mythology)

Marriage counseling

Martin, P. A. The psychotherapy of marital partners: old or new? *In* Overview of the psychotherapies p125-50

Pomeroy, W. B. The sex interview in counseling. *In* Sexuality and human values p36-47

Voegeli, H. T.; Goldberg, M. L. and Schneider, I. A marital crisis precipated by art therapy. *In* Ulman, E. and Dachinger, P. eds. Art therapy p276-85

United States

DeBurger, J. E. Sex in troubled marriages. *In* Gross, L. ed. Sexual issues in marriage p65-72

Mace, D. R. Delinquent sex and marriage counselors. *In* Gross, L. ed. Sexual issues in marriage p53-63

Marriage customs and rites, Amahuaca

Dole, G. E. The marriages of Paco: a woman's life among the Amahuaca. *In* Matthiasson, C. J. ed. Many sisters p3-35

Marriage customs and rites, Bantu

O'Brien, D. Female husbands in southern Bantu societies. *In* Schlegel, A. E. ed. Sexual stratification p109-26

Marriage customs and rites, Indian. See Indians of Mexico—Marriage customs and rites

Marriage guidance. See Marriage counseling

Marriage in Cana (Miracle)

Smith, M. On the Wine God in Palestine (Gen. 18, Jn. 2, and Achilles Tatius) *In* Salo Wittmayer Baron v2 p815-29

Marriage in literature

ApRoberts, R. Emily and Nora and Dorothy and Priscilla and Jemima and Carry. *In* Levine, R. A. The Victorian experience: the novelists p87-120

Brown, L. W. The business of marrying and mothering. *In* Jane Austen's achievement p27-43

Gilbert, S. M. and Gubar, S. George Eliot as the Angel of Destruction. *In* Gilbert, S. M. and Gubar, S. The madwoman in the attic p478-535

Glasser, M. D. Marriage and The second nun's tale. *In* Tennessee Studies in literature v23 p 1-14

Hall, D. R. Molière: critic and victim of the social institution of marriage. *In* Johnson, R. B.; Neumann, E. S. and Trail, G. T. eds. Molière and the commonwealth of letters: patrimony and posterity p49-53

Hardy, J. E. Marrying down in Eudora Welty's novels. *In* Prenshaw, P. W. ed. Eudora Welty p93-119

Heilbrun, C. G. Marriage perceived: English literature, 1873-1941. *In* Springer, M. A. ed. What manner of woman p160-83

Johnson, W. S. Marriage and divorce in Browning. *In* Johnson, W. S. Sex and marriage in Victorian poetry p185-251

Johnson, W. S. Marriage and divorce in Tennyson. *In* Johnson, W. S. Sex and marriage in Victorian poetry p110-84

Lucas, W. J. A note on the treatment of love and marriage in later Victorian fiction. *In* Lucas, W. J. The literature of change p192-207

Olson, C. C. The interludes of the Marriage Group in the Canterbury tales. *In* Chaucer and Middle English studies in honour of Rossell Hope Robbins p164-72

Tobin, P. D. The cycle dance: D. H. Lawrence, The rainbow. *In* Tobin, P. D. Time and the novel p81-106

See also Family in literature

Marriage in moving-pictures

French, B. The eleven-year itch. *In* French, B. On the verge of revolt p73-83

French, B. The joys of marriage. *In* French, B. On the verge of revolt p13-22

French, B. Some pretty natural noises. *In* French, B. On the verge of revolt p23-34

Marriage law

See also Adultery; Dowry

Russia

Farnsworth, B. B. Bolshevik alternatives and the Soviet family: the 1926 marriage law debate. In Women in Russia p139-65

United States

Ketchum, S. A. Liberalism and marriage law. *In* Feminism and philosophy p264-76

Marriage law (Islamic law) See Marriage (Islamic law)

Married people

Palson, C. and Palson, R. Swinging in wedlock. *In* Henslin, J. M. ed. Deviant lifestyles p231-54

See also Married women

Married persons. See Married people

Married women

See also Husband and wife; Widows

Egypt—Conduct of life

Mohsen, S. K. The Egyptian woman: between modernity and tradition. *In* Matthiasson, C. J. ed. Many sisters p37-58

Married women—*Continued*

England

Holcombe, L. Victorian wives and property: reform of the Married Women's Property Law, 1857-1882. *In* Vicinus, M. ed. A widening sphere p3-28

Guatemala

Maynard, E. Guatemalan women: life under tw_ types of patriarchy. *In* Matthiasson, C. J. ed. Many sisters p77-98

Syria

Sweet, L. E. In reality: some Middle Eastern women. *In* Matthiasson, C. J. ed. Many sisters p379-97

Marris, Robin Lapthorn

Britain's relative economic decline: a reply to Stephen Blank. *In* Kramnick, I. ed. Is Britain dying? p89-94

Marrison, A. J.

Great Britain and her rivals in the Latin American cotton piece-goods market, 1880-1914. *In* Great Britain and her world, 1750-1914 p309-48

Marryat, Frederick

About

Hawes, D. Marryat and Dickens: a personal and literary relationship. *In* Dickens Studies Annual v2 p39-68

The marrying kind (Motion picture)

French, B. Some pretty natural noises. *In* French, B. On the verge of revolt p23-34

Marschak, Jacob

Efficient organizational design. *In* Theory for economic efficiency: essays in honor of Abba P. Lerner p110-19

Marsden, Brian G.

The comets. *In* Man and cosmos p152-64

Marsden, George M.

From fundamentalism to evangelicalism: a historical analysis. *In* Wells, D. F. and Woodbridge, J. D. eds. The evangelicals p122-42

Marsden, Michael T.

Iconology of the Western romance. *In* Browne, R. B. and Fishwick, M. W. eds. Icons of America p284-91

Marsé, Juan

About individual works

Ultimas tardes con Teresa

Schwartz, R. Juan Marse and Ultimas tardes con Teresa (Last afternoons with Teresa) (1966). *In* Schwartz, R. Spain's New Wave novelists, 1950-1974 p205-16

Marseilles

Description

Benjamin, W. Hashish in Marseilles. *In* Benjamin, W. Reflections p137-45

Benjamin, W. Marseilles. *In* Benjamin, W. Reflections p131-36

Marsh, Caryl

A framework for describing subjective states of consciousness. *In* Alternate states of consciousness p121-44

Marsh, Ngaio

About

Panek, L. L. Ngaio Marsh. *In* Panek, L. L. Watteau's shepherds: the detective novel in Britain, 1914-1940 p185-97

Marsh, Reginald

About

Rosenberg, H. Reginald Marsh: decline and fall. *In* Rosenberg, H. Art on the edge p190-94

Marshack, Alexander

The Chamula calendar board: an internal and comparative analysis. *In* Mesoamerican archaeology p255-70

Marshall, Arthur

The perfect lady. *In* The Saturday book 34 p127-33

Marshall, Charles Burton

American foreign policy as a dimension of the American Revolution. *In* America's continuing revolution p363-84

Continuity and discontinuity: dour reflections on the national security. *In* Havard, W. C. and Bernd, J. L. eds. 200 years of the Republic in retrospect p258-75

Marshall, Eli Kennerly

About

Harvey, A. M. The story of chemotherapy at Johns Hopkins: Perrin H. Long, Eleanor A. Bliss, and E. Kennerly Marshall, Jr. *In* Harvey, A. M. Adventures in medical research p390-400

Marshall, F. Ray

Black employment in the South since 1954. *In* Two decades of change p27-46

Human resources and changing values in the South. *In* Lewis, W. D. and Griessman, B. E. eds. The Southern mystique p47-62

Marshall, I. Howard

The development of the concept of redemption in the New Testament. *In* Reconciliation and hope p153-69

Marshall, John, 1755-1835

About

White, G. E. John Marshall and the genesis of the tradition. *In* White, G. E. The American judicial tradition p7-34

Marshall, Peter

Masters and banians in eighteenth-century Calcutta. *In* Kling, B. B. and Pearson, M. N. eds. The age of partnership 191-213

Marshall, Ray. See Marshall, F. Ray

Marshall plan. See Economic assistance, American

Marson, Charles C.; Crosby, Margaret C. and Schlosser, Alan L.

On the civil liberties of sect members: Part 1. *In* Horowitz, I. L. ed. Science, sin, and scholarship p192-97

Marsot, Afaf Lutfi al-Sayyid. See al-Sayyid Marsot, Afaf Lutfi

Marston, John

About

Hunter, G. K. English folly and Italian vice. *In* Hunter, G. K. Dramatic identities and cultural tradition p103-32

Huntley, F. L. Joseph Hall, John Marston, and The returne from Parnassus. *In* Illustrious evidence p3-22

About individual works

Antonio and Mellida

Stilling, R. Antonio and Mellida: I & II. *In* Stilling, R. Love and death in Renaissance tragedy p82-96

Martson, John—About individual works
—*Continued*

Antonio's revenge

Stilling, R. Antonio and Mellida: I & II.
In Stilling, R. Love and death in Renaissance
tragedy p82-96

The malcontent

Babula, W. The avenger and the satirist:
John Marston's Malevole. *In* The Elizabethan
theatre, VI p48-58

Foakes, R. A. On Marston, The malcontent, and The revenger's tragedy. *In* The
Elizabethan theatre, VI p59-75

The wonder of women

Ure, P. John Marston's Sophonisba: a
reconsideration. *In* Ure, P. Elizabethan and
Jacobean drama p75-92

Bibliography

McCulley, C. M. John Marston. *In* Logan,
T. P. and Smith, D. S. eds. The new intellectuals p171-247

Characters—Malevole (Altofronto)

Babula, W. The avenger and the satirist:
John Marston's Malevole. *In* The Elizabethan theatre, VI p48-58

Characters—Sophonisba

Ure, P. John Marston's Sophonisba: a
reconsideration. *In* Ure, P. Elizabethan and
Jacobean drama p75-92

Marsupialia

Simons, J. R. The brain and evolution of
lower mammals. *In* Grafton Elliot Smith
p39-49

Marsyas

Art

Hanfmann, G. M. A. The crucified donkey
man: Achaios and Jesus. *In* Studies in classical art and archaeology p205-07

Winternitz, E. The curse of Pallas Athena.
In Winternitz, E. Musical instruments and
their symbolism in Western art p150-65

Martel, Suzanne (Chouinard)

Ring-around-a-roses of French-Canadian
book marketing. *In* Egoff, S. A. ed. One
ocean touching p202-11

Martens, Rainer

Competition: in need of a theory. *In* Social problems in athletics p9-17

Marter, Shirley van. See Van Marter,
Shirley

Marti, José

About

De Onís, J. José Marti. *In* Abroad in
America: Visitors to the new Nation, 1776-
1914 p218-27

Martial. See Martialis, Marcus Valerius

Martialis, Saint, Bp. of Limoges

Art

Williams, J. Marcialis Pincerna and the
provincial in Spanish medieval art. *In* Enggass, R. C. and Stokstad, M. eds. Hortus
imaginum p29-36

Martialis, Marcus Valerius

About individual works

The epigrams of Martial

Fredericks, S. C. Juvenal: a return to invective. *In* Roman satirists and their satire
p136-69

Friends and associates

White, P. The friends of Martial, Statius,
and Pliny, and the dispersal of patronage. *In*
Harvard Studies in classical philology v79
p265-300

Martianus Capella

About individual works

De nuptiis philologae et Mercurii

Lutz, C. E. Aesticampianus' Commentary
on the De grammatica of Martianus Capella.
In Lutz, C. E. Essays on manuscripts and
rare books p87-96

Lutz, C. E. A diamond and a Dürer in
Dubravius' commentary on Martianus
Capella. *In* Lutz, C. E. Essays on manu-
scripts and rare books p105-13

Martin, Abe, pseud. See Hubbard, Frank
McKinney

Martin, Andrew

The dynamics of change in a Keynesian
political economy: the Swedish case and its
implications. *In* Crouch, C. ed. State and
economy in contemporary capitalism p88-121

Martin, Angus

From Marmontel to Berquin: the dynamic
concept of morality in eighteenth-century
French fiction. *In* Studies in eighteenth-century culture v6 p285-302

Martin, Bernice

The mining of the ivory tower. *In* Universities in the Western world p95-115

Martin, Bradford G.

The spread of Islam. *In* Martin, P. M. and
O'Meara, P. eds. Africa p98-113

Martin, Bruce Kirk

Vanity fair: narrative ambivalence and
comic form. *In* Tennessee Studies in literature v20 p37-49

Martin, David

Land reform. *In* Hollis, P. ed. Pressure
from without p131-58

Martin, David, 1915-

About individual works

The hero of Too

Hadgraft, C. Indulgence: David Martin's
The hero of Too, Frank Dalby Davidson's
[sic] The white thorntree, Dal Stivens's
A horse of air, David Malouf's Johnno, and
Frank Hardy's But the dead are many. *In*
Hamilton, K. G. ed. Studies in the recent
Australian novel p194-224

Martin, David A.

Mutations: religio-political crisis and the
collapse of Puritanism and humanism. *In*
Universities in the Western world p85-97

Martin, Graham Dunstan

Jules Supervielle: a poetry of diffidence. *In*
Cardinal, R. ed. Sensibility and creation
p103-21

Martin, Henry Newell

About

Harvey, A. M. Fountainhead of American
physiology: H. Newell Martin and his pupil
William Henry Howell. *In* Harvey, A. M.
Adventures in medical research p84-96

Martin, Jay

Erskine Caldwell's singular devotions. *In*
Filler, L. ed. A question of quality: popularity and value in modern creative writing
p40-56

Martin, Jay—*Continued*

National development and ethnic poetics: the function of literature in the liberation of peoples. *In* Luedtke, L. S. ed. The study of American culture p219-40

Robert Lowell. *In* Donoghue, D. ed. Seven American poets from MacLeish to Nemerov p209-49

About individual works
Nathanael West

Hyman, S. E. Prince Myshkin in Hollywood. *In* Hyman, S. E. The critic's credentials p102-06

Martin, Jeanne S.

History and paradigm in the Towneley cycle. *In* Medievalia et humanistica no. 8 p125-45

Martin, John, 1789-1854

About

Meisel, M. The material sublime: John Martin, Byron, Turner, and the theater. *In* Kroeber, K. and Walling, W. eds. Images of romanticism p211-32

Martin, John A. See Katchadourian, H. A. jt. auth.

Martin, John Bartlow

About individual works
Adlai Stevenson and the world: the life of Adlai E. Stevenson

Galbraith, J. K. John Bartlow Martin and Adlai Stevenson. *In* Galbraith, J. K. Annals of an abiding liberal p295-300

Adlai Stevenson of Illinois: the life of Adlai E. Stevenson

Galbraith, J. K. John Bartlow Martin and Adlai Stevenson. *In* Galbraith, J. K. Annals of an abiding liberal p295-300

Martin, John Hilary

The Eucharistic treatise of John Quidort of Paris. *In* Viator: medieval and Renaissance studies v6 p195-240

Martin, John Powell

The scope of police manpower studies. *In* Crime, criminology and public policy p197-211

Martin, John Stephen

The novels of Oliver Wendell Holmes: a re-interpretation. *In* Literature and ideas in America p111-27

Martin, Laurence W.

Limited nuclear war. *In* Howard, M. ed. Restraints on war p103-21

Martin, Leslie John

The contradiction of cross-cultural communication. *In* Fischer, H. D. and Merrill, J. C. eds. International and intercultural communication p424-34

Effectiveness of international propaganda. *In* Fischer, H. D. and Merrill, J. C. eds. International and intercultural communication p262-72

Prospects for international communication. *In* Fischer, H. D. and Merrill, J. C. eds. International and intercultural communication p447-56

Martin, Michael L.

Pedagogical arguments for preferential hiring and tenuring of women teachers in the university. *In* Gould, C. C. and Wartofsky, M. W. eds. Women and philosophy p325-33

Martin, Peter A.

An annotated bibliography of selected little magazines. *In* Anderson, E. and Kinzie, M. eds. The little magazine in America: a modern documentary history p666-750

Martin, Peter Aaron

The psychotherapy of marital partners: old or new? *In* Overview of the psychotherapies p125-50

Martin, Phyllis M. and O'Meara, Patrick

Africa: problems and perspectives. *In* Martin, P. M. and O'Meara, P. eds. Africa p 3-8

Martin, Ralph P.

Reconciliation and forgiveness in the letter to the Colossians. *In* Reconciliation and hope p104-24

Martin, Richard. See Edmunds, L. jt. auth.

Martin, Robert A.

Editor's introduction. *In* Miller, A. The theater essays of Arthur Miller pxv-xxxix

Martin, Sander, and others

The comparability of behavioral data in laboratory and natural settings. *In* Behavior modification and families p189-203

Martin, Wendy

Anne Bradstreet's poetry: a study of subversive piety. *In* Gilbert, S. M. and Gubar, S. eds. Shakespeare's sisters p19-31

The satire and moral vision of Mary McCarthy. *In* Cohen, S. B. ed. Comic relief p187-206

Martin-Santos, Luis

About individual works
Time of silence

Schwartz, R. Luis Martin-Santos and Tiempo de silencio (Time of silence) (1962). *In* Schwartz, R. Spain's New Wave novelists, 1950-1974 p153-70

Martine, James John

Hemingway's "Fifty grand": the other fight(s). *In* Benson, J. J. ed. The short stories of Ernest Hemingway: critical essays p198-203

A little light on Hemingway's "The light of the world." *In* Benson, J. J. ed. The short stories of Ernest Hemingway: critical essays p196-98

Martineau, Harriet

About

Laski, M. Harriet Martineau. *In* Abroad in America: Visitors to the new Nation, 1776-1914 p62-71

Martines, Lauro

The gentleman in Renaissance Italy: strains of isolation in the body politic. *In* The Darker vision of the Renaissance p77-93

Martínez, Roberto R. Bacalski- See Bacalski-Martinez, Roberto R.

Martínez Bonati, Félix. See Bonati, Félix Martínez

Martínez Ruiz, José

About

Shaw, D. L. Azorin: the rediscovery of a tradition. *In* Shaw, D. L. The generation of 1898 in Spain p161-85

Martini, Carlo M.

Eclecticism and Atticism in the textual criticism of the Greek New Testament. *In* On language, culture, and religion: in honor of Eugene A. Nida p149-56

Marty, Martin E.

The American tradition and the American tomorrow. *In* Tomorrow's American p133-55

The changing role of religion in American society. *In* The National purpose reconsidered p29-51

Migration: the moral framework. *In* Human migration p387-403

Of darters and schools and clergymen: the religion clauses worse confounded. *In* The Supreme Court review, 1978 p171-90

Reinhold Niebuhr: public theology and the American experience. *In* Scott, N. A. ed. The legacy of Reinhold Niebuhr p8-35

Tensions within contemporary evangelicalism: a critical appraisal. *In* Wells, D. F. and Woodbridge, J. D. eds. The evangelicals p170-88

Marty (Motion picture)

French, B. Dogs like us. *In* French, B. On the verge of revolt p84-91

Martz, Louis Lohr

Donne and the meditative tradition. *In* Roberts, J. R. ed. Essential articles for the study of John Donne's poetry p142-49

The music of Comus. *In* Illustrious evidence p93-113

Paradise lost: the solitary way. *In* Martz, L. L. and Williams, A. L. eds. The author in his work p71-84

The rising poet, 1645. *In* Wimsatt, W. K. ed. Literary criticism: idea and act p402-22

Martz, William J.

John Berryman. *In* Donoghue, D. ed. Seven American poets from MacLeish to Nemerov p171-208

Marvell, Andrew

About

Bradbrook, M. C. Marvell and the masque. *In* Friedenreich, K. ed. Tercentenary essays in honor of Andrew Marvell p204-23

Clayton, T. "It is marvel he outdwells his hour": some perspectives on Marvell's medium. *In* Friedenreich, K. ed. Tercentenary essays in honor of Andrew Marvell p47-75

Donno, E. S. The unhoopable Marvell. *In* Friedenreich, K. ed. Tercentenary essays in honor of Andrew Marvell p21-46

Eliot, T. S. Andrew Marvell. *In* Eliot, T. S. Selected prose of T. S. Eliot p161-71

Empson, W. Natural magic and populism in Marvell's poetry. *In* Andrew Marvell p36-61

Everett, B. The shooting of the bears: poetry and politics in Andrew Marvell. *In* Andrew Marvell p62-103

Friedenreich, K. The mower mown: Marvell's Dances of death. *In* Friedenreich, K. ed. Tercentenary essays in honor of Andrew Marvell p153-79

McCanles, M. The dialectical structure of the metaphysical lyric: Donne, Herbert, Marvell. *In* McCanles, M. Dialectical criticism and Renaissance literature p54-119

Manlove, C. N. Donne and Marvell. *In* Manlove, C. N. Literature and reality, 1600-1800 p3-15

Summers, J. H. Some apocalyptic strains in Marvell's poetry. *In* Friedenreich, K. ed. Tercentenary essays in honor of Andrew Marvell p180-203

Toliver, H. E. Marvell's songs and pictorial exhibits. *In* Friedenreich, K. ed. Tercentenary essays in honor of Andrew Marvell p105-20

Zwicker, S. N. Politics and panegyric: the figural mode from Marvell to Pope. *In* Miner, E. R. ed. Literary uses of typology p115-46

About individual works

A dialogue between the resolved soul and created pleasure

Pequigney, J. Marvell's "soul" poetry. *In* Friedenreich, K. ed. Tercentenary essays in honor of Andrew Marvell p76-104

A dialogue between the soul and body

Pequigney, J. Marvell's "soul" poetry. *In* Friedenreich, K. ed. Tercentenary essays in honor of Andrew Marvell p76-104

The garden

Poggioli, R. The pastoral of the self. *In* Poggioli, R. The oaten flute p166-81

Richards, I. A. "The garden." *In* Richards, I. A. Poetries p95-111

Horatian ode

Brooks, C. Literary criticism: Marvell's "Horatian ode". *In* Wimsatt, W. K. ed. Literary criticism: idea and act p423-43

Last instructions to a painter

Farley-Hills, D. Last instructions to a painter. *In* Farley-Hills, D. The benevolence of laughter: comic poetry of the Commonwealth and Restoration p72-98

Messina, J. The heroic image in the Last instructions to a painter. *In* Friedenreich, K. ed. Tercentenary essays in honor of Andrew Marvell p297-310

Mourning

Clayton, T. "It is marvel he outdwells his hour": some perspectives on Marvell's medium. *In* Friedenreich, K. ed. Tercentenary essays in honor of Andrew Marvell p47-75

The nymph complaining for the death of her faun

Le Comte, E. S. Marvell's "The nymph complaining for the death of her fawn". *In* Le Comte, E. S. Poets' riddles p161-79

On a drop of dew

Pequigney, J. Marvell's "soul" poetry. *In* Friedenreich, K. ed. Tercentenary essays in honor of Andrew Marvell p76-104

The picture of little T.C. in a prospect of flowers

Dyson, A. E. and Lovelock, J. Serpent in Eden: Marvell's 'The picture of little T.C. in a prospect of flowers.' *In* Dyson, A. E. and Lovelock, J. Masterful images p37-46

Satires

Chernaik, W. L. Marvell's Satires: the artist as Puritan. *In* Friedenreich, K. ed. Tercentenary essays in honor of Andrew Marvell p268-96

Edwards, A. S. G. New texts of Marvell's Satires: II. *In* Virginia. University. Bibliographical Society. Studies in bibliography v31 p221-26

Edwards, A. S. G. and Schuler, R M. New texts of Marvell's Satires. *In* Virginia. University. Bibliographical Society. Studies in bibliography v30 p180-85

Marx, Karl—About—*Continued*

Parry, A. In the name of Marx. *In* Parry, A. Terrorism: from Robespierre to Arafat p67-77

Piccone, P. Beyond identity theory. *In* O'Neill, J. ed. On critical theory p129-44

Shapiro, J. J. The slime of history: embeddedness in nature and critical theory. *In* O'Neill, J. ed. On critical theory p145-63

Springborg, P. Karl Marx on human needs. *In* Fitzgerald, R. ed. Human needs and politics p157-73

Voegelin, E. Marx: Inverted dialects. *In* Voegelin, E. From Enlightenment to revolution p240-72

Voegelin, E. Marx: The genesis of gnostic socialism. *In* Voegelin, E. From Enlightenment to revolution p273-302

Wellmer, A. Communications and emancipation: reflections on the linguistic turn in critical theory. *In* O'Neill, J. ed. On critical theory p231-63

About individual works
Capital

Downs, R. B. Prophet of the proletariat. *In* Downs, R. B. Books that changed the world p239-51

The eighteenth Brumaire of Louis Bonaparte

Saïd, E. W. On repetition. *In* Fletcher A. J. S. ed. The literature of fact p134-58

Marx, Leo

The American Revolution and the American landscape. *In* America's continuing revolution p247-69

Reflections on the neo-romantic critique of science. *In* Holton, G. J. and Morison, R. S. eds. Limits of scientific inquiry p61-73

Technology and the study of man. *In* Niblett, W. R. ed. The sciences, the humanities and the technological threat p3-20

Marx, Werner

Thought and issue in Heidegger. *In* Radical phenomenology p12-30

Marxian economics

Bakan, M. Hannah Arendt's concepts of labor and work. *In* Hannah Arendt: the recovery of the public world p49-65

Burawoy, M. Contemporary currents in Marxist theory. *In* McNall, S. G. ed. Theoretical perspectives in sociology p16-39

Dobb, M. H. Some historical reflections on planning and the market. *In* Essays in honour of E. H. Carr p324-38

Erlich, A. Stalinism and Marxian growth models. *In* Stalinism p137-54

Holland, S. Keynes and the Socialists. *In* Skidelsky, R. J. A. ed. The end of the Keynesian era p67-77

Krippendorff, E. Revolutionary foreign policy in a capitalist environment. *In* Jahn, E. ed. Soviet foreign policy p26-40

Ollman, B. Marx's vision of communism: a reconstruction. *In* Radicalism in the contemporary age v2 p35-83

Parekh, B. C. Hannah Arendt's critique of Marx. *In* Hannah Arendt: the recovery of the public world p67-100

Parsons, T. Religious and economic symbolism in the Western world. *In* Johnson, H. M. ed. Religious change and continuity p 1-48

Zimin, A. On the question of the place in history of the social structure of the Soviet Union. *In* Medvedev, R. A. ed. The Samizdat register p116-46

Methodology

Applebaum, R. P. Marxist method: structural constraints and social praxis. *In* McNall, S. G. ed. Theoretical perspectives in sociology p200-13

Marxian school of sociology

Burawoy, M. Contemporary currents in Marxist theory. *In* McNall, S. G. ed. Theoretical perspectives in sociology p16-39

Goering, J. M. The Marxist perspective and urban sociology. *In* McNall, S. G. ed. Theoretical perspectives in sociology p479-93

Wardell, M. L. and Benson, J. K. A dialectical view: foundation for an alternative sociological method. *In* McNall, S. G. ed. Theoretical perspectives in sociology p232-48

See also Frankfurt school of sociology

Marxian sociology. See Communism and society; Marxian school of sociology

Marxism. See Communism

Marxism. See Communism; Marx, Karl; Socialism

Marxism. See Communism; Socialism

Marxist sociology. See Marxian school of sociology

Mary, Virgin

Art

Middeldorf, U. Some Florentine painted Madonna reliefs. *In* Collaboration in Italian Renaissance art p77-90

Proske, B. I. G. Two ivory Madonnas. *In* Enggass, R. C. and Stokstad, M. eds. Hortus imaginum p37-44

Snyder, J. E. The mosaic in Santa Maria Nova and the original apse decoration of Santa Maria Maggiore. *In* Enggass, R. C. and Stokstad, M. eds. Hortus imaginum p 1-9

See also Icons

Mary, Virgin, in fiction, drama, poetry, etc.

Pietrkiewicz, J. Simultaneity in a sequence: the time pattern of a mediaeval poem. *In* For Wiktor Weintraub p333-44

Mary Magdalene, Saint in fiction, drama, poetry, etc.

Jennings, M. The art of the Pseudo-Origen homily De Maria Magdalena. *In* Medievalia et humanistica no. 5 p139-52

Woolf, R. English imitations of the Homelia Origenis de Maria Magdalena. *In* Chaucer and Middle English studies in honour of Rossell Hope Robbins p384-91

Mary Stuart, Queen of the Scots

About

Wiley, W. L. Mary, Queen of Scots, in France. *In* Studies in the continental background of Renaissance English literature: essays presented to John L. Lievsay p133-54

Mary Stuart, Queen of the Scots, in fiction, drama, poetry, etc.

Wiley, W. L. Mary, Queen of Scots, in France. *In* Studies in the continental background of Renaissance English literature: essays presented to John L. Lievsay p133-54

Mary Hartman, Mary Hartman (Television program)

Craft, R. Elegy for Mary Hartman, Mary Hartman. *In* Craft, R. Current convictions p306-15

The Mary Tyler Moore Show (Television program)
Fass, P. S. Television as cultural document: promises and problems. *In* Television as a cultural force p37-57

Maryland

History—Civil War, 1861-1865—Campaigns and battles
Duncan, R. R. Marylanders and the invasion of 1862. *In* Hubbell, J. T. ed. Battles lost and won p183-96

Militia—History
Aldrich, D. M. Frontier militias: militia laws on the North American and South African frontiers. *In* The Frontier v2 p153-66

Politics and government—Colonial period, ca. 1600-1775
Carr, L. G. The foundations of social order: local government in colonial Maryland. *In* Daniels, B. C. ed. Town and county p72-110

Masanja, Patrick
Neocolonialism and revolution in Africa. *In* The Emergent gospel p 9-21

Masculinity (Psychology)
Baker, R. "Pricks" and "chicks": a plea for "persons." *In* Baker, R. and Elliston, F. A. eds. Philosophy & sex p45-64

Frye, M. Male chauvinism: a conceptual analysis. *In* Baker, R. and Elliston, F. A. eds. Philosophy & sex p65-79

Rich, A. C. Caryatid: Two columns: Vietnam and sexual violence. *In* Rich, A. C. On lies, secrets, and silence p107-16

Rich, A. C. Disloyal to civilization: feminism, racism, gynephobia. *In* Rich, A. C. On lies, secrets, and silence p275-310

Sarotte, G. M. The circumstances of the homosexual as reflected in the novel and theater: Between the American woman and the American virile ideal. *In* Sarotte, G. M. Like a brother, like a lover p185-92

Masek, Rosemary
Women in an age of transition, 1485-1714. *In* Kanner, B. ed. The women of England p138-82

Masers, Optical. See Lasers

Masferrer, Marianne, and Mesa Lago, Carmelo
The gradual integration of the Black in Cuba: under the Colony, the Republic, and the Revolution. *In* Toplin, R. B. ed. Slavery and race relations in Latin America p348-84

Māshā'allāh

About
Pingree, D. E. Māshā'allāh: some Sasanian and Syriac sources. *In* Essays on Islamic philosophy and science p5-14

Masheck, Joseph Daniel Cahill
Verist sculpture: Hanson and De Andrea. *In* Battcock, G. ed. Super realism p187-211

Masinton, Charles G. See Masinton, M. jt. auth.

Masinton, Martha, and Masinton, Charles G.
Second-class citizenship: the status of women in contemporary American fiction. *In* Springer, M. A. ed. What manner of woman p297-315

Masks. See Mumming

Masks (Plays) See Masques

Masks, African
Bravmann, R. A. Masking tradition and figurative art among the Islamized Mande. *In* African images p144-69

Masks, Etruscan
Oleson, J. An Etruscan satyr mask in the Fogg Art Museum. *In* Harvard Studies in classical philology v76 p259-69

Maslow, Abraham Harold
Education, art, and peak experiences. *In* Fairfield, R. P. ed. Humanistic frontiers in American education p185-93

About
Fitzgerald, R. Abraham Maslow's hierarchy of needs—an exposition and evaluation. *In* Fitzgerald, R. ed. Human needs and politics p36-51

Smith, M. B. Metapsychology, politics, and human needs. *In* Fitzgerald, R. ed. Human needs and politics p124-41

Masochism

Cases, clinical reports, statistics
Ober, W. B. Swinburne's masochism: neuropathology and psychopathology. *In* Ober, W. B. Boswell's clap and other essays p43-88

Masochism in literature
Sarotte, G. M. Latent homosexuality: short of and beyond true heterosexuality: Henry James: the feminine masochist syndrome. *In* Sarotte, G. M. Like a brother, like a lover p197-211

Sarotte, G. M. Latent homosexuality: short of and beyond true heterosexuality: The feminine-masochist temperament in certain Jewish characters. *In* Sarotte, G. M. Like a brother, like a lover p229-39

Mason, Alpheus Thomas
America's political heritage: revolution and free government—a Bicentennial tribute. *In* Essays on the Constitution of the United States p11-31

Mason, Harold Andrew
The first setting of Tennyson's 'Morte D'Arthur.' *In* English Association. Essays and studies, 1978 p98-114

About individual works
Shakespeare's tragedies of love

Bayley, J. Send for Macbeth. *In* Bayley, J. The uses of division p217-23

Bayley, J. The 'serious character.' *In* Bayley, J. The uses of division p224-34

Mason, Michael
Browning and the dramatic monologue. *In* Armstrong, I. ed. Robert Browning p231-66

Mason, Philip Parker
Working in America. *In* Alderson, W. T. ed. American issues p65-80

Masoret
Edelmann, R. מסורת and its historical background. *In* Salo Wittmayer Baron v 1 p369-82

Masotti, Louis H. and Walton, John
Comparative urban research: the logic of comparisons and the nature of urbanism. *In* Walton, J. and Masotti, L. H. eds. The city in comparative perspective p 1-15

Masques

Axton, M. The Tudor mask and Elizabethan court drama. *In* English drama: forms and development p24-47

Bradbrook, M. C. Marvell and the masque. *In* Friedenreich, K. ed. Tercentenary essays in honor of Andrew Marvell p204-23

Frye, N. Romance as masque. *In* Frye, N. Spiritus mundi p148-78

also in Shakespeare's romances reconsidered p11-39

Gordon, D. J. Poet and architect: the intellectual setting of the quarrel between Ben Jonson and Inigo Jones. *In* Gordon, D. J. The Renaissance imagination p77-101

Gordon, D. J. Roles and mysteries. *In* Gordon, D. J. The Renaissance imagination p3-23

Leech, C. Masking and unmasking in the last plays. *In* Shakespeare's romances reconsidered p40-59

Wickham, G. W. G. Masque and antimasque in 'The tempest.' *In* English Association. Essays and studies, 1975 p 1-14

Mass, Regina Dionisopoulos-. See Dionisopoulos-Mass, Regina

Mass (Music)

Wardropper, B. W. The religious conversion of profane poetry. *In* Studies in the continental background of Renaissance English literature: essays presented to John L. Lievsay p203-22

Mass (Physics) See Atomic mass; Weight (Physics)

Mass (Physics) See Atomic mass

Mass casualties

Treatment

See Emergency medical services

Mass communication. See Communication; Mass media

Mass culture. See Popular culture

Mass media

Bogart, L. Mass media today and tomorrow. *In* Fischer, H. D. and Merrill, J. C. eds. International and intercultural communication p63-70

Edelstein, A. New variables for cross-cultural study. *In* Gerbner, G. ed. Mass media policies in changing cultures p207-21

Hester, A. International information flow. *In* Fischer, H. D. and Merrill, J. C. eds. International and intercultural communication p242-50

Janowitz, M. The journalistic profession and the mass media. *In* Culture and its creators p72-96

Lindsay, R. G. International communication: a need for new priorities. *In* Fischer, H. D. and Merrill, J. C. eds. International and intercultural communication p493-99

Merrill, J. C. Media and national development. *In* Fischer, H. D. and Merrill, J. C. eds. International and intercultural communication p186-99

Moeller, L. G. Mass media and national goals. *In* Fischer, H. D. and Merrill, J. C. eds. International and intercultural communication p200-09

Mowlana, H. A paradigm for comparative mass media analysis. *In* Fischer, H. D. and Merrill, J. C. eds. International and intercultural communication p474-84

Mowlana, H. and Robinson, A. E. Ethnic mobilization and communication theory. *In* Said, A. A. and Simmons, L. R. eds. Ethnicity in an international context p48-63

Ong, W. J. Media transformation: the talked book. *In* Ong, W. J. Interfaces of the word p82-91

Ong, W. J. Voice and the opening of closed systems. *In* Ong, W. J. Interfaces of the word p305-41

Schramm, W. L. World distribution of the mass media; excerpt from "Mass media and national development". *In* Fischer, H. D. and Merrill, J. C. eds. International and intercultural communication p179-85

Williams, R Communications as cultural science. *In* Bigsby, C. W. E. ed. Approaches to popular culture p27-38

See also Communism and mass media; Newspapers; Television broadcasting; Violence in mass media

History

Nicoll, A. Changes and chances. *In* Nicoll, A. World drama p765-90

Law and legislation—Peru

Perrett, H. E. de Sagasti. Mass media revolution in Peru. *In* Gerbner, G. ed. Mass media policies in changing cultures p135-46

Law and legislation—Sweden

Ivre, I. Conflict and resolution in Sweden. *In* Gerbner, G. ed. Mass media policies in changing cultures p119-30

Political aspects

Davison, W. P. The role of communication in democracies; excerpt from "International political communication." *In* Fischer, H. D. and Merrill, J. C. eds. International and intercultural communication p29-36

Sussman, L. R. Developmental journalism: the ideological factor. *In* Horton, P. C. ed. The Third World and press freedom p74-92

Political aspects—Hungary

Szecskö, T. The development of a Socialist communication theory. *In* Gerbner, G. ed. Mass media policies in changing cultures p223-34

Political aspects—Peru

Perrett, H. E. de S. Mass media revolution in Peru. *In* Gerbner, G. ed. Mass media policies in changing cultures p135-46

Political aspects—United States

Polsby, N. W. Interest groups and the Presidency: trends in political intermediation in America. *In* Burnham, W. D. and Weinberg, M. W. eds. American politics and public policy p41-52

Schiller, H. I. The free flow of information—for whom? *In* Gerbner, G. ed. Mass media policies in changing cultures p105-15

Social aspects

Allen, I. L. Social integration as an organizing principle. *In* Gerbner, G. ed. Mass media policies in changing cultures p235-50

Brustein, R. S. News theatre. *In* Brustein, R. S. The culture watch p173-89

Chaffee, S. H. Mass media effects: new research perspectives. *In* Lerner, D. and Nelson, L. M. eds. Communication research—a half-century appraisal p210-41

Fischer, H. D. Entertainment—an underestimated central function of communication. *In* Fischer, H. D. and Melnik, S. R. eds. Entertainment: a cross-cultural examination p2-19

Mass media—Social aspects—*Continued*

Haacke, W. Mass media—the playground for grown-ups. *In* Fischer, H. D. and Melnik, S. R. eds. Entertainment: a cross-cultural examination p94-98

Hood, S. C. The dilemma of the communicators. *In* Bigsby, C. W. E. ed. Approaches to popular culture p201-12

Melnik, S. R. The "uses and gratifications" approach in the study of "entertainment" and leisure use. *In* Fischer, H. D. and Melnik, S. R. eds. Entertainment: a cross-cultural examination p144-52

Pool, I. de S. Technology and policy in the information age. *In* Lerner, D. and Nelson, L. M. eds. Communication research—a half-century appraisal p261-79

Social aspects—United States

Minow, N. N. Electronics and the future. *In* Tomorrow's American p157-70

Wahlstrom, B. J. Images of the family in the mass media: an American iconography? *In* Tufte, V. and Myerhoff, B. G. eds. Changing images of the family p193-227

Africa

Head, S. W. Trends in tropical African societies. *In* Gerbner, G. ed. Mass media policies in changing cultures p83-103

China

Chu, G. C. Popular media: a glimpse of the new Chinese culture. *In* Chu, G. C. ed. Popular media in China p 1-15

See also Television broadcasting

India

Parmer, S. Traditional folk forms in India and their use in national development; excerpt from "Traditional folk media in India." *In* Fischer, H. D. and Melnik, S. R. eds. Entertainment: a cross-cultural examination p74-82

Singh, K. Elite control and challenge in changing India. *In* Gerbner, G. ed. Mass media policies in changing cultures p147-58

Iran

Nejad, K. M. The story-teller and mass media in Iran. *In* Fischer, H. D. and Melnik, S. R. eds. Entertainment: a cross-cultural examination p43-62

Kenya

Neher, W. W. and Condon, J. C. The mass media and nation-building in Kenya and Tanzania. *In* Smock, D. R. and Bentsi-Enchill, K. eds. The search for national integration in Africa p220-39

Malaysia

Guimary, D. L. Broadcasting in Malaysia. *In* Gerbner, G. ed. Mass media policies in changing cultures p159-63

Near East

Mowlana, H. Trends in Middle Eastern societies. *In* Gerbner, G. ed. Mass media policies in changing cultures p73-82

Russia

Mansurov, N. S. The study of the mass communications and cultural establishments in the USSR. Some results of sociological research. *In* Fischer, H. D. and Melnik, S. R. eds. Entertainment: a cross-cultural examination p153-78

Scandinavia

Nordenstreng, K. From mass media to mass consciousness. *In* Gerbner, G. ed. Mass media policies in changing cultures p269-83

Tanzania

Neher, W. W. and Condon, J. C. The mass media and nation-building in Kenya and Tanzania. *In* Smock, D. R. and Bentsi-Enchill, K. eds. The search for national integration in Africa p220-39

Underdeveloped areas

See Underdeveloped areas—Mass media

United States

Barnouw, E The media revolution. *In* The American Revolution: a continuing commitment p27-39

Tunstall, J. The American role in worldwide mass communication. *In* Gerbner, G. ed. Mass media policies in changing cultures p3-12

Mass media and children. See Television and children

Mass media and minorities

St Leger, F. Y. The mass media and minority cultures. *In* Alcock, A. E.; Taylor, B. K. and Welton, J. M. eds. The future of cultural minorities 63-81

See also Mass media and race relations

Mass media and race relations

Great Britain

Husband, C. Some aspects of the interaction of the British entertainment media with contemporary race relations. *In* Fischer, H. D. and Melnik, S. R. eds. Entertainment: a cross-cultural examination p196-207

Mass media and the arts

Banham, R. Mediated environments or: You can't build that here. *In* Bigsby, C. W. E. Superculture p69-82

See also Popular culture

Mass psychology. See Social psychology

Mass society

Allen, I. L. Social integration as an organizing principle. *In* Gerbner, G. ed. Mass media policies in changing cultures p235-50

Chiaromonte, N. The mass situation and noble values. *In* Chiaromonte, N. The worm of consciousness, and other essays p236-65

Hunter, A. Persistence of local sentiments in mass society. *In* Handbook of contemporary urban life p133-62

See also Mass media; Popular culture

Massa, Ann. See Donaldson, S. jt. auth.

Massa, Daniel

The politics of cross-cultural dependence in language and poetry. *In* Narasimhaiah, C. D. ed. Awakened conscience p14-28

Massachusetts

Charters

Simmons, R. C. The Massachusetts Charter of 1691. *In* Allen, H. C. and Thompson, R. eds. Contrast and connection p66-87

Church history

Stoever, W. K. B. The nature of New England antinomianism. *In* Stoever, W. K. B. 'A faire and easie way to heaven' p161-83

Stoever, W. K. B. The New England controversy. *In* Stoever, W. K. B. 'A faire and easie way to heaven' p21-33

Massachusetts—*Continued*

Commerce

Rutman, D. B. Governor Winthrop's garden crop: the significance of agriculture in the early commerce of Massachusetts Bay. *In* Vaughan, A. T. and Bremer, F. J. eds. Puritan New England p155-71

Historiography

Brown, B. K. T. The controversy over the franchise in Puritan Massachusetts, 1954 to 1974. *In* Vaughan, A. T. and Bremer, F. J. eds. Puritan New England p128-54

History—Colonial period, ca. 1600-1775

Breen, T. H. and Foster, S. The Puritans' greatest achievement: a study of social cohesion in seventeenth-century Massachusetts. *In* Vaughan, A. T. and Bremer, F. J. eds. Puritan New England p110-27

Cohen, R. D. Church and state in seventeenth-century Massachusetts: another look at the antinomian controversy. *In* Vaughan, A. T. and Bremer, F. J. eds. Puritan New England p174-86

McWilliams, J. P. Fictions of Merry Mount. *In* Zenderland, L. ed. Recycling the past p 1-28

Rutman, D. B. Governor Winthrop's garden crop: the significance of agriculture in the early commerce of Massachusetts Bay. *In* Vaughan, A. T. and Bremer, F. J. eds. Puritan New England p155-71

Twombly, R. C. and Moore, R. H. Black Puritan: the Negro in seventeenth-century Massachusetts. *In* Vaughan, A. T. and Bremer, F. J. eds. Puritan New England p187-200

History—New Plymouth, 1620-1691

See Pilgrims (New Plymouth Colony)

Learned institutions and societies—History

Whitehill, W. M. Early learned societies in Boston and vicinity. *In* Oleson, A. and Brown, S. C. eds. The pursuit of knowledge in the early American Republic p151-73

Militia—History

Aldrich, D. M. Frontier militias: militia laws on the North American and South African frontiers. *In* The Frontier v2 p153-66

McGraw, R. F. Minutemen of '61: the pre-Civil War Massachusetts militia. *In* Hubbell, J. T. ed. Battles lost and won p141-55

Politics and government—Colonial period, ca. 1600-1775

Konig, D. T. English legal change and the origins of local government in northern Massachusetts. *In* Daniels, B. C. ed. Town and county p12-43

Politics and government—1775-1865

Goodman, P. The politics of industrialism: Massachusetts, 1830-1870. *In* Uprooted Americans p161-207

Politics and government—1865-1950

Gorvine, H. The New Deal in Massachusetts. *In* Braeman, J.; Bremmer, R. H. and Brody, D. eds. The New Deal v2 p3-44

Social life and customs—Colonial period, ca.1600-1775

Allen, D. G. A tale of two towns: persistent English localism in seventeenth-century Massachusetts. *In* Allen, H. C. and Thompson, R. eds. Contrast and connection p 1-35

Massage. See Massage parlors

Massage parlors

United States

Velarde, A. J. and Warlick, M. Massage parlors: the sensuality business. *In* Henslin, J. M. ed. Deviant life-styles p209-29

Massell, Gregory J.

Modernization and national policy in Soviet Central Asia: problems and prospects. *In* Cocks, P.; Daniels, R. V. and Heer, N. W. eds. The dynamics of Soviet politics p265-90

Massey, Irving

The gaping pig

Contents

Aspects of metamorphosis in Alice

Flaubert and "La légende de Saint-Julien l'hospitalier"

The golden ass: character versus structure

Metamorphosis in Gogol: "The nose"

Postscript

Singles and doubles: Frankenstein

Singles and doubles: Narcissism in Hoffmann's "The sandman"

Singles and doubles: Peter Schlemihl

The third self: Dracula, Jekyll and Hyde, "Lokis"

Massinger, Philip

About

Eliot, T. S. From Philip Massinger. *In* Eliot, T. S. Selected prose of T. S. Eliot p153-60

About individual works

Believe as you list

Edwards, P. The royal pretenders in Massinger and Ford. *In* English Association. Essays and studes, 1974 p18-36

Masson, David

Pre-Raphaelitism in art and literature. *In* Sambrook, J. ed. Pre-Raphaelitism p71-91

Masson, Margaret W.

Pessimism surpassed: new colleges as bastions against barbarism in colonial America. *In* Studies in eighteenth-century culture v8 p69-86

Masson, Peter, and Thorburn, Andrew

Advertising: the American influence in Europe. *In* Bigsby, C. W. E. Superculture p96-106

Master of the Griselda legend

Mode, R. L. Ancient paragons in a Piccolomini scheme. *In* Enggass, R. C. and Stokstad, M. eds. Hortus imaginum p73-83

Master of the St. Lucy Legend

About individual works

Assumption of the Virgin

Winternitz, E. On angel concerts in the 15th century: a critical approach to realism and symbolism in sacred painting. *In* Winternitz, E. Musical instruments and their symbolism in Western art p137-49

Masters, Edgar Lee

Farrell, J. T. A chance meeting with Mencken and Masters. *In* Farrell, J. T. Literary essays, 1954-1974 p79-83

About individual works

Spoon River anthology

Hyman, S. E. Truths from the grave. *In* Hyman, S. E. The critic's credentials p91-96

Masters, William H. and Johnson, Virginia E.
The role of religion in sexual dysfunction. *In* Sexuality and human values p86-96

Mästlin, Michael. See Maestlin, Michael

Masuda, Kichisaburō. See Nomura, Kichisaburō

Matejka, Ladislav
Postscript. Prague school semiotics. *In* Matejka, L. and Titunik, I. R. eds. Semiotics of art p265-90

Materia medica. See Materia medica, Vegetable

Materia medica, Arabic. See Medicine, Arabic

Materia medica, Vegetable
Talbot, C. H. America and the European drug trade. *In* First images of America p833-44

See also Botany, Medical; Medicine, Medieval

Materialism
Cooper, D. E. ESP and the materialist theory of mind. *In* Thakur, S. C. ed. Philosophy and psychical research p59-80

Robinson, C. Science, reason and the material world. *In* Robinson, C. French literature in the nineteenth century p50-107

Temkin, O. Materialism in French and German physiology of the early nineteenth century. *In* Temkin, O. The double face of Janus p340-44

See also Dualism; Idealism; Lokāyata; Monism; Realism

Materialism, Dialectical. See Dialectical materialism

Mathematical ability
Papert, S. A. The mathematical unconscious. *In* Wechsler, J. ed. On aesthetics in science p105-19

Mathematical crystallography. See Crystallography, Mathematical

Mathematical linguistics
Davidson, D. H. Semantics for natural languages. *In* Harman, G. ed. On Noam Chomsky p242-52

Maratsos, M. New models in linguistics and language acquisition. *In* Linguistic theory and psychological reality p246-63

See also Semantics—Mathematical models

Mathematical logic. See Logic, Symbolic and mathematical

Mathematical physics
Wise, M. N. William Thomson's mathematical route to energy conservation: a case study of the role of mathematics in concept formation. *In* Historical studies in the physical sciences v10 p49-83

Mathematical research

France—History
Shinn, T. W. The French science faculty system, 1808-1914: institutional change and research potential in mathematics and the physical sciences. *In* Historical studies in the physical sciences v10 p271-332

Mathematical sets. See Set theory

Mathematical statistics
Robbins, H. The statistical mode of thought. *In* Neyman, J. ed. The heritage of Copernicus: theories "pleasing to the mind" p419-32

See also Regression analysis

Mathematics
Holland, R. F. Absolute ethics, mathematics and the impossibility of politics. *In* Royal Institute of Philosophy. Human values p172-88

Quine, W. V. Foundations of mathematics. *In* Quine, W. V. The ways of paradox, and other essays p22-32

See also Groups; Theory of; Logic, Symbolic and mathematical; Mensuration; Metric system; Set theory; Variables (Mathematics)

History
Taton, R. The mathematical revolution of the seventeenth century. *In* Bonelli, M. L. R. and Shea, W. R. eds. Reason, experiment, and mysticism in the scientific revolution p283-90

History—Europe
Mahoney, M. S. Mathematics. *In* Lindberg, D. C. ed. Science in the Middle Ages p145-78

History—Great Britain
Richards, J. L. The reception of a mathematical theory: non-Euclidean geometry in England, 1868-1883. *In* Barnes, B. and Shapin, S. eds. Natural order p143-66

History—United States
Kevles, D. J. The physics, mathematics, and chemistry communities: a comparative analysis. *In* Oleson, A. and Voss, J. eds. The organization of knowledge in modern America, 1860-1920 p139-72

Philosophy
Papert, S. A. The mathematical unconscious. *In* Wechsler, J. ed. On aesthetics in science p105-19

Quine, W. V. Truth by convention. *In* Quine, W. V. The ways of paradox, and other essays p77-106

See Continuity

Research
See Mathematical research

Study and teaching—
Germany—Saxony—History
Jungnickel, C. Teaching and research in the physical sciences and mathematics in Saxony, 1820-1850. *In* Historical studies in the physical sciences v10 p3-47

Study and teaching (Higher)—
United States
Gurland, R. H. Teaching mathematics. *In* Cahn, S. M. ed. Scholars who teach p75-100

Mathematics, Arabic
Sabra, A. I. The scientific enterprise. *In* Lewis, B. ed. Islam and the Arab world p181-200

Mathematics, Greek. See Geometry—Early works to 1800

Mather, Cotton

About
Breitwieser, M. R. Cotton Mather's crazed wife. *In* Glyph 5 p88-113

McEwen, G. D. "A turn of thinking": Benjamin Franklin, Cotton Mather, and Daniel Defoe on "doing good." *In* The Dress of words p53-65

Middlekauff, R. M. Piety and intellect in Puritanism. *In* Mulder, J. M. and Wilson, J. F. eds. Religion in American history p74-85

Mather, Cotton—About—*Continued*

Seelye, J. A fabric huge: Cotton Mather's masterpiece: or, The original errand betrayed. *In* Seelye, J. Prophetic waters p253-77

Stein, S. J. Cotton Mather and Jonathan Edwards on the number of the beast: eighteenth-century speculation about the Antichrist. *In* American Antiquarian Society. Proceedings v84 pt2 p293-315

About individual works
Magnalia Christe Americana

Seelye, J. A fabric huge: Cotton Mather's masterpiece: or, The original errand betrayed. *In* Seelye, J. Prophetic waters p253-77

Mather, Increase

About

Couser, G. T. Piety and prophecy in Puritan spiritual autobiography. *In* Couser, G. T. American autobiography p10-27

Elliott, E. From father to son: the evolution of typology in Puritan New England. *In* Miner, E. R. ed. Literary uses of typology p204-27

About individual works
New Jerusalem

Lowance, M. I. and Watters, D. Increase Mather's 'New Jerusalem', millenialism in late seventeenth-century New England. *In* American Antiquarian Society. Proceedings v87 pt2 p343-408

Manuscripts

Joyce, W. L. and Hall, M. G. Three manuscripts of Increase Mather. *In* American Antiquarian Society. Proceedings v86 pt 1 p113-23

Lowance, M. I. and Watters, D. Increase Mather's 'New Jerusalem', millenialism in late seventeenth-century New England. *In* American Antiquarian Society. Proceedings v87 pt2 p343-408

Mather, Richard B.

K'ou Ch'ien-chih and the Taoist theocracy at the Northern Wei Court, 425-451. *In* Welch, H. and Seidel, A. K. eds. Facets of Taoism p103-22

Mathers, S. Liddell MacGregor

About

Fennelly, L. W. W. B. Yeats and S. L. MacGregor Mathers. *In* Yeats and the occult p285-306

Matheson, William

American literary bibliography—FPAA style. *In* Review, v 1 1979 p173-81

Matheus, John Frederic

African footprints in Hispanic-American literature. *In* DeCosta, M. ed. Blacks in Hispanic literature p53-64

Mathew, Gervase

The aesthetic theories of Gregory of Nyssa. *In* Studies in memory of David Talbot Rice p217-22

The dating and the significance of the Periplus of the Erythrean Sea. *In* Chittick, H. N. and Rotberg, R. I. eds. East Africa and the Orient p147-63

Mathews, David

Coming to terms with another new South. *In* The Rising South v 1 p92-105

A Southern university and the South. *In* The Rising South v2 p178-86

Mathews, Donald G.

The second Great Awakening as an organizing process, 1780-1830. *In* Mulder, J. M. and Wilson, J. F. eds. Religion in American history p199-217

Mathews, Shailer

About

Fiorenza, F. S. American culture and Modernism: Shailer Mathews's interpretation of American Christianity. *In* America in theological perspective p163-86

Mathews, Thomas G.

Historical patterns of Caribbean communication. *In* Borgese, E. M. and Krieger, D. eds. The tides of change p222-38

The question of color in Puerto Rico. *In* Toplin, R. B. ed. Slavery and race relations in Latin America p299-323

Mathews v. Diaz. *In* The Supreme Court review, 1977 p275-339

Mathewson, Robert C.

A Paul Lehmann bibliography. *In* The Context of contemporary theology p253-67

Mathewson, Rufus W.

The positive hero in Russian literature
Contents

Andrei Sinyavsky: conclusions
Belinsky: "My heroes are the destroyers"
Chernyshevsky: "The salt of the salt of the earth"
Complete and incomplete men
Dobrolyubov: beyond the superfluous man
Four novels
The hero and the heritage
Leather men
Lenin and Gorky: the turning point
Marxism, realism, and the hero
Pasternak: "An inward music"
Rebuttal I: The theory
Rebuttal II: Hamlet and Don Quixote
Rebuttal III: The dissident vision
Solzhenitsyn I: Marx proposes, Stalin disposes
Solzhenitsyn II: "Just like that!"
Solzhenitsyn III: Positive Colonels and a tragic General
Two bureaucracies

Mathias, Peter

Conflicts of function in the rise of big business: the British experience. *In* Evolution of international management structures p40-58

Swords and ploughshares: the armed forces, medicine and public health in the late eighteenth century. *In* War and economic development p73-90

Mathieu, Vittorio

Truth as the mother of history. *In* Giambattista Vico's science of humanity p113-24

Mathy, Francis

Shusaku Endo: the second period. *In* Postwar trends in Japan p3-14

Matisse, Henri

About

Gowing, L. Matisse: the harmony of light. *In* Kaplan, P. and Manso, S. eds. Major European art movements, 1900-1945 p5-41

Matlack, Cynthia Sutherland

"Spectatress of the mischief which she made": tragic woman perceived and perceiver. *In* Studies in eighteenth-century culture v6 p317-30

Matlub Ali, S.
DEPTHnews: a model for a Third World feature agency. *In* Horton, P. C. ed. The Third World and press freedom p187-96

Matos, Luis Palés. See Palés Matos, Luis

Matriarchy
Hyman, S. E. Myths and mothers. *In* Hyman, S. E. The critic's credentials p298-304

Webster, P. Matriarchy: a vision of power. *In* Reiter, R. R. ed. Toward an anthropology of women p141-56

Matrilineal kinship. See Matriarchy

Matrimony. See Marriage

Matrix mechanics
MacKinnon, E. M. Heisenberg, models, and the rise of matrix mechanics. *In* Historical studies in the physical sciences v8 p137-88

See also Quantum theory

The **Matron** of Ephesus in eighteenth-century France: the lady and the legend. Runte, R. *In* Studies in eighteenth-century culture v6 p361-75

Matsen, Herbert Stanley
Giovanni Garzoni (1419-1505) to Alessandro Achillini (1463-1512): an unpublished letter and defense. *In* Philosophy and humanism p518-30

Matson, Wallace I.
Spinoza's theory of mind. *In* Freeman, E. and Mandelbaum, M. H. eds. Spinoza p49-60

Matsui, Sumako
About
Powell, B. Matsui Sumako: actress and woman. *In* Modern Japan p135-46

Matsuo, Bashō
About
Foard, J. H. The loneliness of Matsuo Bashō. *In* Reynolds, F. E. and Capps, D. eds. The biographical process p363-91

Matsuoka, Yōsuke
About
Teters, B. Matsuoka Yōsuke: the diplomacy of bluff and gesture. *In* Burns, R. D. and Bennett, E. M. eds. Diplomats in crisis p275-96

The Mattei affair (Motion picture)
Sarris, A. The Mattei affair. *In* Sarris, A. Politics and cinema p78-79

Mattei Sarcophagus
Winternitz, E. Musical archaeology of the Renaissance in Raphael's Parnassus. *In* Winternitz, E. Musical instruments and their symbolism in Western art p185-201

Matteotti, Giacomo
About
Nazzaro, P. Fascist and anti-Fascist reaction in the United States to the Matteotti murder. *In* Studies in Italian American social history p50-65

Matter
Barfield, O. Matter, imagination, and spirit. *In* Barfield, O. The rediscovery of meaning, and other essays p143-54

Multhauf, R. P. The science of matter. *In* Lindberg, D. C. ed. Science in the Middle Ages p369-90

See also Substance (Philosophy)

Constitution
See Atoms; Ether (of space); Molecular theory

Matter and form. See Hylomorphism

Mattern, Ruth
Descartes's correspondence with Elizabeth: concerning both the union and distinction of mind and body. *In* Hooker, M. ed. Descartes p212-22

Matthew, David C. C.
"Toward Bethlehem": Battle of angels and Orpheus descending. *In* Tennessee Williams: a tribute p172-91

Matthews, Brander
The philosophy of the short-story; excerpt. *In* May, C. E. ed. Short story theories p52-59

Matthews, Brian Ernest
Henry Lawson's fictional world. *In* Bards, bohemians, and bookmen p170-202

Matthews, Gareth Blanc
A medieval theory of vision. *In* Studies in perception p186-99

On talking philosophy with children. *In* Royal Institute of Philosophy. Communication and understanding p46-62

Matthews, James Tilly
About
Altschule, M. D. The singular case of James Tilly Matthews, a clear paranoid. *In* Altschule, M. D. Origins of concepts in human behavior p85-87

Haslam, J. Illustrations of madness. *In* Altschule, M. D. Origins of concepts in human behavior p88-121

Matthews, John Joseph
About individual works
Sundown
Larson, C. R. Assimilation: estrangement from the land. *In* Larson, C. R. American Indian fiction p34-65

Matthews, Robert Charles Oliver
Public policy and monetary expenditure. *In* The Market and the state p330-45

Matthews, Robert J.
Literary works express propositions. *In* Hernadi, P. ed. What is literature? p102-12

Matthews, William, 1905-
The wife of Bath and all her sect. *In* Viator: medieval and Renaissance studies v5 p413-43

Matthiasson, Carolyn J.
Conclusion. *In* Matthiasson, C. J. ed. Many sisters p421-37

Matthiessen, Francis Otto
About individual works
Theodore Dreiser
Berryman, J. Enslavement: Three American cases; Theodore Dreiser. *In* Berryman, J. The freedom of the poet p185-89

Mattick, Hans W.
Reflections of a former prison warden. *In* Delinquency, crime, and society p287-315

Maturation (Psychology)
Day, W. F. On the behavioral analysis of self-deception and self-development. *In* Mischel, T. ed. The self p224-49

See also Adulthood

Maturin, Charles Robert
About individual works
Melmoth the wanderer
Howells, C. A. C. R. Maturin, Melmoth the wanderer. *In* Howells, C. A. Love, mystery, and misery p131-58

Matus, Gustavo Lagos. See Lagos Matus, Gustavo

Matute, Ana Maria

About individual works

Primera memoria

Schwartz, R. Ana Maria Matute and Primera memoria. *In* Schwartz, R. Spain's New Wave novelists, 1950-1974 p113-31

Matza, David

The disreputable poor. *In* Davis, F. J. and Stivers, R. eds. The collective definition of deviance p197-221

Maud, Ruan

The future of an illusion: the myth of white meliorism in South Africa. *In* Leftwich, A. ed. South Africa: economic growth and political change p287-318

Maugham, William Somerset

About individual works

The treasure

Trilling, L. William Somerset Maugham: The treasure. *In* Trilling, L. Prefaces to The experience of literature p89-91

Maull, Hanns

Oil and influence: the oil weapon examined. *In* Knorr, K. E. and Trager, F. N. eds. Economic issues and national security p259-88

Maupassant, Guy de

About individual works

Duchoux

Trilling, L. Guy de Maupassant: *In* Trilling, L. Prefaces to The experience of literature p92-95

Maupertuis, Pierre Louis Moreau de

About

Brown, H. From London to Lapland: Maupertuis, Johann Bernoulli I, and La Terre applatie, 1728-1738. *In* Literature and history in the age of ideas p69-94

Maurer, Armand Augustine

Some aspects of fourteenth-century philosophy. *In* Medievalia et humanistica no. 7 p175-88

Maurer, David Joseph

Relief problems and politics in Ohio. *In* Braeman, J.; Bremmer, R. H. and Brody, D. eds. The New Deal v2 p77-102

Mauretania Tingitana (Roman province)

Eadie, J. W. Civitates and clients: Roman frontier policies in Pannonia and Mauretania Tingitana. *In* Miller, D. H. and Steffen, J. O. eds. The frontier p57-80

Maurice, Frederick Denison

About

Prickett, S. Newman versus Maurice: development of doctrine and the growth of the mind. *In* Prickett, S. Romanticism and religion p152-73

About individual works

The Kingdom of Christ

Prickett, S. F. D. Maurice: The Kingdom of Christ. *In* Prickett, S. Romanticism and religion p120-51

Mauritius

Simmons, A. Class or communalism? A study of the politics of Creoles in Mauritius. *In* Kilson, M. L. and Rotberg, R. I. eds. The African diaspora p366-90

Economic conditions

Tinker, H. Arthur Phayre in Mauritius, 1874-1878: social policy and economic reality. *In* Southeast Asian history and historiography p59-85

History, Economic

See Mauritius—Economic conditions

Mauron, Charles

About individual works

L'inconscient dans l'oeuvre et la vie de La Racine

Bersani, L. Racine, psychoanalysis and Oedipus. *In* Bersani, L. A future for Astyanax p17-50

Mausoleums. See Tombs

Les mauvaises rencontres (Motion picture)

Truffaut, F. Alexandre Astruc: Les mauvaises rencontres. *In* Truffaut, F. The films in my life p305-07

Mauvelain, Bruzard de

About

Darnton, R. Trade in the taboo: the life of a clandestine book dealer in prerevolutionary France. *In* Korshin, P. J. ed. The widening circle p11-83

Mauzy, Richard. See Morris, R. P. jt. auth.

Mavor, Osborne Henry

About

Morgan, E. James Bridie. *In* Morgan, E. Essays p232-41

Mawhinney, John J.

H. Richard Niebuhr and reshaping American Christianity. *In* America in theological perspective p140-62

Maxfield Miller, Elizabeth. See Miller, Elizabeth Maxfield

Maximianus, Cornelius. See Maximianus Etruscus

Maximianus Etruscus

About

Szövérffy, J. Maximianus a satirist? *In* Harvard Studies in classical philology v72 p351-67

Maxims

Screech, M. A. Commonplaces of law, proverbial wisdom and philosophy: their importance in Renaissance scholarship (Rabelais, Joachim du Bellay, Montaigne). *In* Classical influences on European culture A.D. 1500-1700 p127-34

See also Aphorisms and apothegms; Proverbs

Maxwell, Clerk. See Maxwell, James Clerk

Maxwell, Grover

The later Bertrand Russell: philosophical revolution. *In* Nakhnikian, G. ed. Bertrand Russell's philosophy p169-82

Russell on perception and mind-body: a study in philosophical method. *In* Philosophical aspects of the mind-body problem p131-53

Maxwell, James Clerk

About

Doran, B. G. Origins and consolidation of field theory in nineteenth-century Britain: from the mechanical to the electromagnetic view of nature. *In* Historical studies in the physical sciences v6 p133-260

May, C. J.
Some lesser leaders of the Communist movement in Kerala. *In* The Making of politicians: studies from Africa and Asia p166-82

May, Charles E.
Brick Pollitt as homo ludens: "three players of a summer game" and Cat on a hot tin roof. *In* Tennessee Williams: a tribute p277-91

A survey of short story criticism in America. *In* May, C. E. ed. Short story theories p3-12

May, Charles E. comp.
A selected, annotated bibliography of the short story. *In* May, C. E. ed. Short story theories p226-51

May, Georges Claude
Autobiography and the eighteenth century. *In* Martz, L. L. and Williams, A. L. eds. The author in his work 319-35

Probability and improbability in eighteenth-century research. *In* Studies in eighteenth-century culture v5 p3-10

About individual works
Tragédie cornélienne, tragédie racinienne

Edelman, N. Book reviews. *In* Edelman, N. The eye of the beholder p166-205

May, Gita
. Molière and Stendhal. *In* Johnson, R. B.; Neumann, E. S. and Trail, G. T. eds. Molière and the commonwealth of letters: patrimony and posterity p125-32

Stendhal and the age of ideas. *In* Literature and history in the age of ideas p343-57

May, Henry Farnham
Intellectual history and religious history. *In* Higham, J. and Conkin, P. K. eds. New directions in American intellectual history p105-15

May, J. Gary
Personality development and ethnic identity. *In* The Diverse society: implications for social policy p43-58

May, James Boyer
On Trace. *In* Anderson, E. and Kinzie, M. eds. The little magazine in America: a modern documentary history p376-87

May, John R.
American literary variations on the demonic. *In* Disguises of the demonic p31-47

May, Keith M.
Out of the maelstrom
Contents

Attack on the unconscious
The burden of consciousness
The living self
The nature of the unconscious
A new synthesis
The search for identity

May, Rollo
Gregory Bateson and humanistic psychology. *In* About Bateson p77-99
Psychology and the human dilemma
Contents

Anxiety and values
The context of psychotherapy
Dangers in the relation of existentialism to psychotherapy
Freedom and responsibility reexamined
Historical roots of modern anxiety theories

Jean-Paul Sartre and psychoanalysis
The man who was put in a cage
Modern man's loss of significance
Personal identity in an anonymous world
A phenomenological approach to psychotherapy
Questions for a science of man
Social responsibilities of psychologists
What is the human dilemma?

About individual works
Love and will

Fitzgerald, R. Essay 3. *In* Fitzgerald, R. ed. What it means to be human p44-63

May, Steven W.
William Hunnis and the 1577 Paradise of dainty devices. *In* Virginia. University. Bibliographical Society. Studies in bibliography v28 p63-80

May, William F.
Attitudes toward the newly dead. *In* Death inside out p139-49
The metaphysical plight of the family. *In* Death inside out p49-60

Maya art. See Mayas—Art

Maya calendar. See Calendar, Maya

Maya hieroglyphics. See Mayas—Writing

Maya mythology. See Mayas—Religion and mythology

Mayakovsky, Vladimir. See Maĭakovskiĭ, Vladimir Vladimirovich

Mayapan, Mexico
Rathje, W. L. The last tango in Mayapán: a tentative trajectory of production-distribution systems. *In* Ancient civilization and trade p409-48

Sabloff, J. A. and others. Trade and power in postclassic Yucatan: initial observations. *In* Mesoamerican archaeology p397-416

Mayas
Coe, M. D. Olmec and Maya: a study in relationships. *In* The Origins of Maya civilization p183-95

Lowe, G. W. The Mixe-Zoque as competing neighbors of the early Lowland Maya. *In* The Origins of Maya civilization p197-248

Netting, R. M. Maya subsistence: mythologies, analogies, possibilities. *In* The Origins of Maya civilization p299-333

Sanders, W. T. Environmental heterogeneity and the evolution of Lowland Maya civilization. *In* The Origins of Maya civilization p287-97

See also Tzotzil Indians

Antiquities
Adams, R. E. W. Rio Bec archaeology and the rise of Maya civilization. *In* The Origins of Maya civilization p77-99

Adams, R. E. W. A trial estimation of classic Maya palace populations at Uaxactun. *In* Mesoamerican archaeology p285-96

Adams, R. E. W. and Culbert, T. P. The origins of civilization in the Maya Lowlands. *In* The Origins of Maya civilization p3-24

Ball, J. W. The rise of the northern Maya chiefdoms: a socioprocessual analysis. *In* The Origins of Maya civilization p101-32

Culbert, T. P. Early Maya development at Tikal, Guatemala. *In* The Origins of Maya civilization p27-43

Feldman, L. H. Shells from afar: 'Panamic' molluscs in Mayan sites. *In* Mesoamerican archaeology p129-33

Mayas—Antiquities—*Continued*

Hammond, N. The distribution of late classic Maya major ceremonial centres in the central area. *In* Mesoamerican archaeology p313-34

Hammond, N. Ex oriente lux: a view from Belize. *In* The Origins of Maya civilization p45-76

Molloy, J. P. and Rathje, W. L. Sexploitation among the late classic Maya. *In* Mesoamerican archaeology p431-44

Puleston, D. E. Intersite areas in the vicinity of Tikal and Uaxactun. *In* Mesoamerican archaeology p303-11

Rands, R. L. The ceramic sequence at Palenque, Chiapas. *In* Mesoamerican archaeology p51-75

Rands, R. L. The rise of Classic Maya civilization in the Northwestern Zone: isolation and integration. *In* The Origins of Maya civilization p159-80

Rathje, W. L. The last tango in Mayapán: a tentative trajectory of production-distribution systems. *In* Ancient civilization and trade p409-48

Rathje, W. L. The Tikal connection. *In* The Origins of Maya civilization p373-82

Sabloff, J. A. and Freidel, D. A. A model of a pre-Columbian trading center. *In* Ancient civilization and trade p369-408

Webster, D. L. Warfare and the evolution of Maya civilization. *In* The Origins of Maya civilization p335-71

Willey, G. R. The classic Maya hiatus: a rehearsal for the collapse? *In* Mesoamerican archaeology p417-30

Willey, G. R. The rise of classic Maya civilization: a Pasión Valley perspective. *In* The Origins of Maya civilization p133-57

Willey, G. R. The rise of Maya civilization: a summary view. *In* The Origins of Maya civilization p383-423

See also Calendar, Maya

Art

Miller, A. G. The iconography of the painting in the Temple of the Diving God, Tulum, Quintana Roo; Mexico: the twisted cords. *In* Mesoamerican archaelogy p167-86

Quirarte, J. Early art styles of Mesoamerica and Early classic Maya art. *In* The Origins of Maya civilization p249-83

Calendar

See Calendar, Maya

Civilization

See Mayas—Culture

Culture

Gifford, J. C. Recent thought concerning the interpretation of Maya prehistory. *In* Mesoamerican archaeology p77-98

History

Adams, R. E. W. and Culbert, T. P. The origins of civilization in the Maya Lowlands. *In* The Origins of Maya civilization p3-24

Ball, J. W. The rise of the northern Maya chiefdoms: a socioprocessual analysis. *In* The Origins of Maya civilization p101-32

Webster, D. L. Warfare and the evolution of Maya civilization. *In* The Origins of Maya civilization p335-71

History—Historiography

Adams, R. E. W. and Culbert, T. P The origins of civilization in the Maya Lowlands. *In* The Origins of Maya civilization p3-24

Religion and mythology

Miller, A. G. The iconography of the painting in the Temple of the Diving God, Tulum, Quintana Roo, Mexico: the twisted cords. *In* Mesoamerican archaeology p167-86

Rites and ceremonies

Furst, P. T. "High states" in culture-historical perspective. *In* Alternate states of consciousness p53-88

Social life and customs

Molloy, J. P. and Rathje, W. L. Sexploitation among the late classic Maya. *In* Mesoamerican archaeology p431-44

Price, B. J. The burden of the cargo: ethnographical models and archaeological inference. *In* Mesoamerican archaeology p445-65

Wars

Webster, D. L. Warfare and the evolution of Maya civilization. *In* The Origins of Maya civilization p335-71

Writing

Barthel, T. S Writing systems. *In* Sebeok, T. A. ed. Native languages of the Americas v2 p27-53

Mayer, Arno J.

The lower middle class as historical problem. *In* Small comforts for hard times p220-45

Mayer, Hans

Brecht's Drums, a dog, and Beckett's Godot. *In* Mews, S. and Knust, H. eds. Essays on Brecht p71-78

About

Demetz, P. Transformations of recent Marxist criticism: Hans Mayer, Ernst Fischer, Lucien Goldmann. *In* The Frontiers of literary criticism p75-92

Mayer, Julius Robert von

About

Heimann, P. M. Mayer's concept of "force": the "axis" of a new science of physics. *In* Historical studies in the physical sciences v7 p277-96

Mayer, Martin

Higher education for all? The case of open admissions. *In* Murphy, T. P. ed. Universities in the urban crisis p215-39

The telephone and the uses of time. *In* The Social impact of the telephone p225-45

Mayer, Philip

Class, status, and ethnicity as perceived by Johannesburg Africans. *In* Thompson, L. M. and Butler, J. eds. Change in contemporary South Africa p138-67

Mayers, Marvin Keene

Indigenous dialectology. *In* Sebeok, T. A. ed. Native languages of the Americas v2 p89-98

Mayhew, Henry

About

Humpherys, A. Dickens and Mayhew on the London poor. *In* Dickens Studies Annual v4 p78-90

Mayhew, Lewis B.
Lessening influence and the search for purpose. *In* The Third century p44-51

Maynard, Eileen
Guatemalan women: life under two types of patriarchy. *In* Matthiasson, C. J. ed. Many sisters p77-98

Maynard, John Rogers
Broad canvas, narrow perspective: the problem of the English historical novel in the nineteenth century. *In* The Worlds of Victorian fiction p237-65

Maynard, Patrick
Depiction, vision, and convention. *In* Margolis, J. Z. ed. Philosophy looks at the arts p273-306

Maynard, Reid Norris
Autotelism in Henry James's aesthetic. *In* Tennessee Studies in literature v21 p35-42

Maynell, Hugo Anthony

About individual works
The intelligibility of the universe
Stopes-Roe, H. V. The intelligibility of the universe. *In* Reason and religion p44-71

Maynes, Charles William
The United Nations: out of control or out of touch, *In* The Year book of world affairs, 1977 p98-111

Maynes, Edwin Scott
Attitudes, behavior, and economics. *In* Major social issues p390-411

Mayo, Bernard
Moral integrity. *In* Royal Institute of Philosophy. Human values p27-43

Mayo, Edith
Ladies and liberation: icon and iconoclast in the women's movement. *In* Browne, R. B. and Fishwick, M. W. eds. Icons of America p209-27

Mayors

France
Tarrow, S. G. and Smith, V. L. Crisis recruitment and the political involvement of local elites: some evidence from Italy and France. *In* Eulau, H. and Czudnowski, M. M. eds. Elite recruitment in democratic polities p205-37

Italy
Tarrow, S. G. and Smith, V. L. Crisis recruitment and the political involvement of local elites: some evidence from Italy and France. *In* Eulau, H. and Czudnowski, M. M. eds. Elite recruitment in democratic polities p205-37

United States
Brown, L. D. Mayors and models: notes on the study of urban politics. *In* Burnham, W. D. and Weinberg, M. W. eds. American politics and public policy p251-79

Mayow, John

About
Guerlac, H. The poets' nitre: studies in the chemistry of John Mayow—II. *In* Guerlac, H. Essays and papers in the history of modern science p260-74

About individual works
Medico-physical works
Guerlac, H. John Mayow and the aerial nitre: studies in the chemistry of John Mayow—I. *In* Guerlac, H. Essays and papers in the history of modern science p245-59

Mayr, Ernst. See Part 2 under title: Studies in history of biology v3

Mays, Benjamin Elijah

About individual works
Born to rebel
Reed, I. Born to rebel. *In* Reed, I. Shrovetide in old New Orleans p67-71

Mays, Wolfe
Phenomenology and Marxism. *In* Pivčević, E. ed. Phenomenology and philosophical understanding p231-50

Mazlish, Bruce
Leadership in the American Revolution: the psychological dimension. *In* Library of Congress Symposia on the American Revolution, 3d, 1974. Leadership in the American Revolution p113-33

The Mills: father and son. *In* Explorations in psychohistory p136-48

What is psycho-history? *In* Kren, G. M. and Rappoport, L. H. eds. Varieties of psychohistory p17-37

Mazrui, Ali Al'amin
The Afro-Saxons. *In* Said, A. A. and Simmons, L. R. eds. Ethnicity in an international context p203-17

Casualties of an underdeveloped class structure: the expulsion of Luo workers and Asian bourgeoisie from Uganda. *In* Shack, W. A. and Skinner, E. P. eds. Strangers in African societies p261-88

The de-Indianization of Uganda: who is a citizen? *In* Smock, D. R. and Bentsi-Enchill, K. eds. The search for national integration in Africa p77-90

Ethnic stratification and the military-agrarian complex: the Uganda case. *In* Glazer, N. and Moynahan, D. P. eds. Ethnicity p420-49

The new interdependence. *In* Erb, G. F. and Kallab, V. eds. Beyond dependency p38-54

World culture and the search for human consensus. *In* On the creation of a just world order p 1-37

Mazur, Michael Paul
The developing countries in the world economy: a question of bargaining power? *In* Baldwin, D. A. ed. America in an interdependent world p137-61

Interdependence, flexible exchange rates, and capital controls: the international monetary order in transition. *In* Baldwin, D. A. ed. America in an interdependent world p63-89

Mazzara, Richard Alfred
The theater of Jorge Andrade. *In* Lyday, L. F. and Woodyard, G. W. eds. Dramatists in revolt p205-20

Mazzaro, Jerome
Between two worlds: the post-modernism of Randall Jarrell. *In* Boyers, R. ed. Contemporary poetry in America p78-98

The fact of Beatrice in The vita nuova. *In* Fletcher, A. J. S. ed. The literature of fact p83-108

Sylvia Plath and the cycles of history. *In* Lane, G. ed. Sylvia Plath p218-40

Mazze, Edward M.
Management toward the year 2000: the challenges and the opportunities. *In* Benton, L. R. ed. Management for the future p219-28

Mazzeo, Joseph Anthony
Varieties of interpretation
Contents
Interpretation and its occasions
Interpretation, humanistic culture, and cultural change
Myth and science in the theology of Rudolf Bultmann
New wine in old bottles: reflections on historicity and the problem of allegory
The Platonic debate over myth, truth, and virtue
Style as interpretation

Mazzotta, Giuseppe Francesco
The Decameron: the marginality of literature. *In* Dombroski, R. S. ed. Critical perspectives on The Decameron p129-48

Mba-tivi. See Tivi (African people)

Mbata, Jeremiah Congress
Profile of change: the cumulative significance of changes among Africans. *In* Thompson, L. M. and Butler, J. eds. Change in contemporary South Africa p201-20

Mead, Carl David
A scholar's profile. *In* Essays in honor of Russel B. Nye p 1-6

M'Bow, Amadou-Mahtar
The role of universities in the developing countries. *In* The Frontiers of human knowledge p201-14

Mbughuni, L. A.
Old and new drama from East Africa. *In* African literature today no. 8: Drama in Africa p85-98

Mbuti. See Bambute

Mead, Margaret
End linkage: a tool for cross-cultural analysis. *In* About Bateson p171-231
Ethnicity and anthropology in America. *In* Ethnic identity p173-97
The evocation of psychologically relevant responses in ethnological field work. *In* Spindler, G. D. ed. The making of psychological anthropology p89-139
The evolving ethics of applied anthropology. *In* Eddy, E. M. and Partridge, W. L. eds. Applied anthropology in America p425-37
The heritage of our children. *In* Gross, B. and Gross, R. eds. The children's rights movement p150-58
Individual responsibility within a new technological framework. *In* The Frontiers of human knowledge p159-62
Styles of American womanhood through 200 years of history. *In* The American Revolution: a continuing commitment p55-65
The transforming power of culture. *In* Hanna, T. ed. Explorers of humankind 140-47

About
Langness, L. L. Margaret Mead and the study of socialization. *In* Schwartz, T. ed. Socialization as cultural communication p5-20

About individual works
Continuities in cultural evolution
Bronowski, J. Where do we go from here? *In* Bronowski, J. A sense of the future p155-62

Mead, Sidney Earl
American Protestantism during the Revolutionary epoch. *In* Mulder, J. M. and Wilson, J. F. eds. Religion in American history p162-80

Mead, Walter J.
Petroleum: an unregulated industry? *In* Kalter, R. J. and Vogely, W. A. eds. Energy supply and government policy p130-60

Meade, James Edward
The Keynesian revolution. *In* Keynes, M. ed. Essays on John Maynard Keynes p82-88

Meadows, Donella Hager
Food and population: policies for the United States. *In* Baldwin, D. A. ed. America in an interdependent world p163-220

Mean streets (Motion picture)
Kauffmann, S. Mean streets. *In* Kauffmann, S. Living images p229-31

Meaning (Philosophy)
Barfield, O. The rediscovery of meaning. *In* Barfield, O. The rediscovery of meaning, and other essays p11-21
Burke, K. Rhetoric, poetics, and philosophy. *In* Burks, D. M. ed. Rhetoric, philosophy, and literature: an exploration p15-33
Cavell, S. Must we mean what we say? *In* Cavell, S. Must we mean what we say? p 1-43
Cleveland, H. Words and meanings. *In* The Abdication of philosophy: philosophy and the public good p237-42
Close, A. J. Don Quixote and the 'intentionalist fallacy.' *In* On literary intention p174-93
Dummett, M. A. E. What is a theory of meaning? *In* Guttenplan, S. D. ed. Mind and language p97-138
Dummett, M. A. E. What is a theory of meaning? (II). *In* Evans, G. L. and McDowell, J. H. eds. Truth and meaning p66-137
Føllesdal, D. Meaning and experience. *In* Guttenplan, S. D. ed. Mind and language p25-44
Foster, J. A. Meaning and truth theory. *In* Evans, G. L. and McDowell, J. H. eds. Truth and meaning p 1-32
Foster, J. A. Reply to Foster [on Meaning and truth theory]. *In* Evans, G. L. and McDowell, J. H. eds. Truth and meaning p33-41
Graeser, A. The Stoic theory of meaning. *In* Rist, J. M. ed. The Stoics p77-100
Hirsch, E. D. In defense of the author; excerpt from "Validity in interpretation." *In* On literary intention p87-103
Hirsch, E. D. Objective interpretation. *In* On literary intention p26-54
Hirsch, E. D. Three dimensions of hermeneutics. *In* On literary intention p194-209
Hough, G. G. An eighth type of ambiguity. *In* Hough, G. G. Selected essays p23-45
Livingston, D. W. Hume's historical theory of meaning. *In* Livingston, D. W. and King, J. T. eds. Hume p213-38
Loar, B. Two theories of meaning. *In* Evans, G. L. and McDowell, J. H. eds. Truth and meaning p138-61
McDowell, J. H. Truth conditions, bivalence, and verificationism. *In* Evans, G. L. and McDowell, J. H. eds. Truth and meaning p42-66
Matthews, R. J. Literary works express propositions. *In* Hernadi, P. ed. What is literature? p102-12
Mohanty, J. N. Husserl's theory of meaning. *In* Elliston, F. A. and McCormick, P. eds. Husserl p18-37
Natanson, M. A. The arts of indirection. *In* Burks, D. M. ed. Rhetoric, philosophy, and literature: an exploration p35-47

Meaning (Philosophy)—*Continued*

Peckham, M. The intentional? Fallacy? *In* On literary intention p139-57

Percy, W. The Delta factor. *In* Percy, W. The message in the bottle p3-45

Percy, W. The mystery of language. *In* Percy, W. The message in the bottle p150-58

Redpath, T. The meaning of a poem. *In* On literary intention p14-25

Richards, I. A. Meaning and change of meaning. *In* Richards, I. A. Complementarities p73-87

Richards, I. A. Multiple definition. *In* Richards, I. A. Complementarities p56-72

Skorupski, J. The meaning of another culture's beliefs. *In* Hookway, C. and Pettti, P. eds. Action and interpretation p83-106

Tennyson, G. B. Etymology and meaning. *In* Evolution of consciousness p168-82

See also Semantics (Philosophy)

Meaning (Psychology)

Peckham, M. The virtues of superficiality. *In* Peckham, M. Romanticism and behavior p249-62

Richards, I. A. Meaning and change of meaning. *In* Richards, I. A. Complementarities p73-87

Rumelhart, D. E. Some problems with the notion of literal meanings. *In* Ortony, A. ed. Metaphor and thought p78-90

See also Definition (Logic); Logical positivism; Semantics; Thought and thinking

Means, Gordon Paul

Malaysia. *In* Kearney, R. N. ed. Politics and modernization in South and Southeast Asia. p153-214

Meany, George

Challenges to the labor movement. *In* Prochnow, H. V. ed. Dilemmas facing the nation p166-78

Measurements, Mental. See Mental tests

Measuring. See Mensuration

Mechanical models. See Machinery—Models

Mechanical translating. See Machine translating

Mechanics

Funkenstein, A. The dialectical preparation for scientific revolutions. *In* The Copernican achievement p165-203

Hirosige, T. The ether problem, the mechanistic worldview, and the origins of the theory of relativity. *In* Historical studies in the physical sciences v7 p3-82

See also Balance; Force and energy; Inertia (Mechanics); Mathematical physics; Motion; Statics

History—Arab countries

Hill, D. R. Mechanical technology. *In* The Genius of Arab civilization p175-88

Mechanics, Celestial

Mulholland, J. D. Movements of celestial bodies—Velikovsky's fatal flaw. *In* Goldsmith, D. ed. Scientists confront Velikovsky p105-15

Mechanism (Philosophy)

Beckner, M. Reduction, hierarchies and organicism. *In* Ayala, F. J. and Dobzhansky, T. G. eds. Studies in the philosophy of biology p163-76

Birch, L. C. Chance, necessity and purpose. *In* Ayala, F. J. and Dobzhansky, T. G. eds. Studies in the philosophy of biology p225-39

Campbell, D. T. 'Downward causation' in hierarchically organised biological systems. *In* Ayala, F. J. and Dobzhansky, T. G. eds. Studies in the philosophy of biology p179-86

Duchesneau, F. Malpighi, Descartes, and the epistemological problems of iatro-mechanism. *In* Bonelli, M. L. R. and Shea, W. R. eds. Reason, experiment, and mysticism in the scientific revolution p111-30

Goodfield, G. J. Changing strategies: a comparison of reductionist attitudes in biological and medical research in the nineteenth and twentieth centuries. *In* Ayala, F. J. and Dobzhansky, T. G. eds. Studies in the philosophy of biology p65-86

Popper, K. R. Scientific reduction and the essential incompleteness of all science. *In* Ayala, F. J. and Dobzhansky, T. G. eds. Studies in the philosophy of biology p259-83

Thorpe, W. H. Reductionism in biology. *In* Ayala, F. J. and Dobzhansky, T. G. eds. Studies in the philosophy of biology p109-36

See also Materialism; Vitalism

Mechanistic philosophy. See Mechanism (Philosophy)

Mechling, Jay Edmund

In search of an American ethnophysics. *In* Luedtke, L. S. ed. The study of American culture p241-77

Meckier, Jerome

The faint image of Eden: the many worlds of Nicholas Nickleby. *In* Dickens Studies Annual v1 p129-46

Waugh as diarist. *In* Review, v 1 1979 p333-45

Mecom, Jane (Franklin)

About

Scott, A. F. Self-portraits: three women. *In* Uprooted Americans p43-76

Medawar, Sir Peter Brian

A geometric model of reduction and emergence. *In* Ayala, F. J. and Dobzhansky, T. G. eds. Studies in the philosophy of biology p57-63

Technology and evolution. *In* The Frontiers of knowledge p105-15

Also in Technology and the frontiers of knowledge p99-110

Medcalf, Stephen

The innocence of P. G. Wodehouse. *In* Josipovici, G. ed. The modern English novel: the reader, the writer and the work p186-205

Medeiros, Patricia M.

Three travelers: Carver, Bartram, and Woolman. *In* Emerson, E. H. ed. American literature, 1764-1789 p195-211

Mediation, International

Ashmore, H. S. An exercise in demi-diplomacy: the case of Vietnam. *In* Unofficial diplomats p130-41

Freymond, J. The International Committee of the Red Cross as a neutral intermediary. *In* Unofficial diplomats p142-51

Talbot, P. The Cyprus seminar. *In* Unofficial diplomats p159-67

See also Arbitration, International

Mediation and conciliation, Industrial. See Arbitration, Industrial

Medical and health care industry. See Medical care

Medical anthropology. See Folk medicine; Medicine, Primitive

Medical assistance. See Public health—International cooperation

Medical assistance, American
Carey, H. L. A humane mission for American foreign policy. *In* Cahill, K. M. ed. Health and development p15-22

Medical astrology
White, L. T. Medical astrologers and late medieval technology. *In* Viator: medieval and Renaissance studies v6 p295-308

Medical botany. See Botany, Medical

Medical care
Anderson, O. W. The model health service —a search for utopia. *In* The Frontiers of human knowledge p29-43
Callahan, D. J. Biomedical progress and the limits of human health. *In* Small comforts for hard times p170-81
Haggerty, R. J. The boundaries of health care. *In* Sobel, D. S. ed. Ways of health p45-60
Waldheim, K. Health in a world perspective. *In* Cahill, K. M. ed. Health and development p 1-3
See also Child health services; Home care services

Administration
See Health services administration

Management
See Health services administration

Planning
See Health planning

Political aspects
Frei Montalva, E. President Chile. The political realities of health in a developing nation. *In* Cahill, K. M. ed. Health and development p4-14

Psychological aspects
Illich, I. The political uses of natural death. *In* Death inside out p25-42

Research
See Medical research

Underdeveloped areas
See Underdeveloped areas—Medical care

United States
Densen, P. M. Public accountability and reporting systems in Medicare and other health programs. *In* Smith, B. L. R. ed. The new political economy: the public use of the private sector p229-44
Duval, M. K. The provider, the government, and the consumer. *In* Knowles, J. H. ed. Doing better and feeling worse p185-92
Eisenberg, L. The search for care. *In* Knowles, J. H. ed. Doing better and feeling worse p235-46
Fox, R. C. The medicalization and demedicalization of American society. *In* Knowles, J. H. ed. Doing better and feeling worse p9-22
Ginzberg, E. Health services, power centers, and decision-making mechanisms. *In* Knowles, J. H. ed. Doing better and feeling worse p203-13
Grossman, L. Ethnicity and health delivery systems. *In* The Diverse society: implications for social policy p129-48

Knowles, J. H. Introduction. *In* Knowles, J. H. ed. Doing better and feeling worse p 1-7
Knowles, J. H. The responsibility of the individual. *In* Knowles, J. H. ed. Doing better and feeling worse p57-80
McDermott, W. Evaluating the physician and his technology. *In* Knowles, J. H. ed. Doing better and feeling worse p135-57
Rogers, D. E. The challenge of primary care. *In* Knowles, J. H. ed. Doing better and feeling worse p81-103
Saward, E. W. Institutional organization, incentives, and change. *In* Knowles, J. H. ed. Doing better and feeling worse p193-202
Starr, P. Medicine and the waning of professional sovereignty. *In* A New America? p175-93
Thomas, L. The health-care system. *In* Thomas, L. The medusa and the snail p45-50
Thomas, L. On the science and technology of medicine. *In* Knowles, J. H. ed. Doing better and feeling worse p35-46
Warner, D. C. Government initiatives and controls in American medical care. *In* Smith, B. L. R. ed. The new political economy: the public use of the private sector p214-28

Medical care, Cost of

United States
Klarman, H. E. The financing of health care. *In* Knowles, J. H. ed. Doing better and feeling worse p215-34

Medical care, State. See Medicine, State

Medical centers. See Medical colleges

Medical colleges

Curricula
Kutscher, A. H. 1923- and Kutscher, A. H. Medical school curriculum and anticipatory grief: faculty attitudes. *In* Anticipatory grief p213-17
Thomas, L. How to fix the premedical curriculum. *In* Thomas, L. The medusa and the snail p137-41

Europe
Bell, W. J. Philadelphia medical students in Europe, 1750-1800. *In* Bell, W. J. The colonial physician & other essays p41-69

United States
Ebert, R. H. Medical education in the United States. *In* Knowles, J. H. ed. Doing better and feeling worse p171-84

United States—Admission
Levitt, M. That bouillabaisse: medical school admissions. *In* Hurdles p239-67

United States—Entrance requirements
See Medical colleges—United States—Admission

Medical delusions
Price, D. B. Miraculous restoration of lost body parts: relationship to the phantom limb phenomenon and to limb-burial superstitions and practices. *In* American folk medicine p49-71
Thomas, L. On magic in medicine. *In* Thomas, L. The medusa and the snail p19-26

Medical diagnosis. See Diagnosis

Medical economics
Costanzo, G. A. Economics and health. *In* Cahill, K. M. ed. Health and development p69-82
See also Medical care, Cost of

Medical economics—*Continued*
United States

Starr, P. Medicine, economy and society in nineteenth-century America. *In* Branca, P. ed. The medicine show p47-66

Thomas, L. A brief historical note on medical economics. *In* Thomas, L. The medusa and the snail p142-44

Medical education

Ellis, J. R. Medical education—a personal view. *In* The Frontiers of human knowledge p69-78

Kendall, P. L. Theory and research: the case of studies in medical education. *In* The Idea of social structure p301-21

Pellegrino, E. D. The academic role of the vice president for health sciences. *In* Managing nonprofit organizations p38-47

See also Medical colleges; Paramedical education

United States

Ebert, R. H. Medical education in the United States. *In* Knowles, J. H. ed. Doing better and feeling worse p171-84

Medical education. See Medical colleges; Paramedical education

Medical emergencies. See Emergency medical services

Medical ethics

Callahan, D. J. Health and society: some ethical imperatives. *In* Knowles, J. H. ed. Doing better and feeling worse p23-33

Duff, R. S. and Campbell, A. G. M. Moral and ethical dilemmas in the special-care nursery. *In* Weir, R. F. ed. Ethical issues in death and dying p133-44

Fletcher, G. P. Prolonging life. *In* Weir, R. F. ed. Ethical issues in death and dying p226-40

Fletcher, J. F. Distributive justice. *In* Fletcher, J. F. Humanhood: essays in biomedical ethics p41-53

Fletcher, J. F. Experiments on humans. *In* Fletcher, J. F. Humanhood: essays in biomedical ethics p176-89

Fletcher, J. F. Genetic engineering. *In* Fletcher, J. F. Humanhood: essays in biomedical ethics p79-92

Fletcher, J. F. Medical diagnosis: our right to know the truth. *In* Weir, R. F. ed. Ethical issues in death and dying p26-41

Fletcher, J. F. Wasting human bodies. *In* Fletcher, J. F. Humanhood: essays in biomedical ethics p65-78

Gaylin, W. The technology of life and death. *In* Small comforts for hard times p152-69

McCormick, R. A. To save or let die: the dilemma of modern medicine. *In* Weir, R. F. ed. Ethical issues in death and dying p173-84

Meyer, B. C. Truth and the physician. *In* Weir, R. F. ed. Ethical issues in death and dying p42-54

Oken, D. What to tell cancer patients: a study of medical attitudes. *In* Weir, R. F. ed. Ethical issues in death and dying p 9-25

Parsons, T. Research with human subjects and the "professional complex." *In* Parsons, T. Action theory and the human condition p35-65

Reiser, S. J. Therapeutic choice and moral doubt in a technological age. *In* Knowles, J. H. ed. Doing better and feeling worse p47-56

Veatch, R. M. and Draper, T. F. The values of physicians. *In* Population policy and ethics p377-408

Williams, G. L. Euthanasia and the physician. *In* Kohl, M. ed. Beneficent euthanasia p145-68

See also Euthanasia

Medical experiments on humans. See Human experimentation in medicine

Medical fees

United States

Thomas, L. A brief historical note on medical economics. *In* Thomas, L. The medusa and the snail p142-44

Medical folk-lore. See Folk medicine

Medical genetics

Carlson, E. A. Genetics and the biological basis of the human condition. *In* The Tricentennial people p3-17

See also Genetic counseling

Medical illustration

Harvey, A. M. The second professor of gynecology and the Department of Art as applied to medicine. *In* Harvey, A. M. Adventures in medical research p173-87

Medical jurisprudence

Oettle, T. H. G. and Larnach, S. L. The identification of aboriginal traits in forensic medicine. *In* Grafton Elliot Smith p103-08

Medical laws and legislation

Drinan, R. F. Should there be a legal right to die? *In* Weir, R. F. ed. Ethical issues in death and dying p297-307

See also Physicians—Licenses

France

Ramsey, M. Medical power and popular medicine: illegal healers in nineteenth-century France. *In* Branca, P. ed. The medicine show p183-210

Medical logic. See Medicine—Philosophy

Medical microbiology. See Infection

Medical personnel

See also Physicians; Surgeons

Legal status, laws, etc.

See Medical laws and legislation

France

Goubert, J. P. The extent of medical practice in France around 1780. *In* Branca, P. ed. The medicine show p211-28

Medical personnel and patient

Benoliel, J. Q. Anticipatory grief in physicians and nurses. *In* Anticipatory grief p218-28

Carpenter, J. O. and Hall, G. Anticipatory grief and the disciplined professions. *In* Anticipatory grief p229-36

Garfield, C. A. Impact of death on the health-care professional. *In* Feifel, H. [ed.] New meanings of death p143-51

See also Nurse and patient

Medical policy

See also Medicine, State

United States

Duval, M. K. The provider, the government, and the consumer. *In* Knowles, J. H. ed. Doing better and feeling worse p185-92

Saward, E. W. Institutional organization, incentives, and change. *In* Knowles, J. H. ed. Doing better and feeling worse p193-202

Medical policy—United States—_Continued_

Wildavsky, A. B. Doing better and feeling worse: the political pathology of health policy. _In_ Knowles, J. H. ed. Doing better and feeling worse p105-23

Medical profession. See Medicine; Physicians

Medical research

Bodmer, W. F. Biomedical advances: a mixed blessing? _In_ Harré, R. ed. Problems of scientific revolution p25-41

Burchenal, J. H. The relevance of research in tropical medicine today. _In_ Cahill, K. M. ed. Health and development p59-68

Parsons, T. Research with human subjects and the "professional complex." _In_ Parsons, T. Action theory and the human condition p35-65

See also Pharmaceutical research

Moral and religious aspects

Davis, B. D. The scientific versus the adversary approach in bio-medical research. _In_ Hook, S.; Kurtz, P. and Todorovich, M. eds. The ethics of teaching and scientific research p165-68

Fletcher, J. F. Experiments on humans. _In_ Fletcher, J. F. Humanhood: essays in biomedical ethics p176-89

Fletcher, J. F. Fetal research. _In_ Fletcher, J. F. Humanhood: essays in biomedical ethics p93-105

Siegel, S. An ethical approach to bio-medical research. _In_ Hook, S.; Kurtz, P. and Todorovich, M. eds. The ethics of teaching and scientific research p169-73

Africa, East

Lumsden, W. H. R. Impact of independence and nationalism on tropical medicine. _In_ Cahill, K. M. ed. Health and development p23-35

United States

Bennett, I. L. Technology as a shaping force. _In_ Knowles, J. H. ed. Doing better and feeling worse p125-33

Fredrickson, D. S. Health and the search for new knowledge. _In_ Knowles, J. H. ed. Doing better and feeling worse p159-70

Patrick, E. A. Medical science and tomorrow's American. _In_ Tomorrow's American p47-68

Medical research ethics. See Medical ethics

Medical schools. See Medical colleges

Medical service, Cost of. See Medical care, Cost of

Medical services. See Medical care

Medical social work

Caroff, P. and Dobrof, R. Social work: its institutional role. _In_ Anticipatory grief p251-63

Pritchard, E. R. The social worker's responsibility. _In_ Anticipatory grief p237-45

Medical societies

United States—History

Cassedy, J. H. Medicine and the learned society in the United States, 1660-1850. _In_ Oleson, A. and Brown, S. C. eds. The pursuit of knowledge in the early American Republic p261-78

Medical sociology. See Social medicine

Medical students

Political activity

Resnick, J. L. The emerging physician: from political activist to professional vanguard. _In_ Gerstl, J. E. and Jacobs, G. eds. Professions for the people p175-213

Europe

Bell, W. J. Philadelphia medical students in Europe, 1750-1800. _In_ Bell, W. J. The colonial physician & other essays p41-69

Medical superstitions. See Medical delusions

Medical technology

Bennett, I. L. Technology as a shaping force. _In_ Knowles, J. H. ed. Doing better and feeling worse p125-33

McDermott, W. Evaluating the physician and his technology. _In_ Knowles, J. H. ed. Doing better and feeling worse p135-57

Thomas, L. On the science and technology of medicine. _In_ Knowles, J. H. ed. Doing better and feeling worse p35-46

See also Medicine; Clinical

Medici, Cosimo I, 1519-1574. See Cosimo I, de Medici, il Grande, grand-duke of Tuscany

Medici, Lorenzino de'

About individual works

L'Aridiosia

Wadsworth, P. A. From the commedia erudita to Molière. _In_ Johnson, R. B.; Neumann, E. S. and Trail, G. T. eds. Molière and the commonwealth of letters: patrimony and posterity p443-53

Medici, Lorenzo di Pier Francesco (called Lorenzino) de'. See Medici, Lorenzino de'

Medici, House of

Gilbert, F. Bernardo Rucellai and the Orti Oricellari: a study of the origin of modern political thought. _In_ Gilbert, F. History p215-46

Medicine, Beatrice

Learning to be an anthropologist and remaining "native." _In_ Eddy, E. M. and Partridge, W. L. eds. Applied anthropology in America p182-96

Medicine

Dubos, R. J. Hippocrates in modern dress. _In_ Sobel, D. S. ed. Ways of health p205-30

Dubos, R. J. Medicine evolving; excerpts from "Man adapting." _In_ Sobel, D. S. ed. Ways of health p21-44

Powles, J. G. On the limitations of modern medicine. _In_ Sobel, D. S. ed. Ways of health p61-86

See also Botany, Medical; Histology; Pathology

Biography

See Physicians

Cost of medical care

See Medical care, Cost of

Economic aspects

See Medical economics

Economics

See Medical economics

Historiography

Temkin, O. The historiography of ideas in medicine. _In_ Temkin, O. The double face of Janus p110-25

Medicine—*Continued*

History

Branca, P. Towards a social history of medicine. *In* Branca, P. ed. The medicine show p89-101

Gebhard, B. The interrelationship of scientific and folk medicine in the United States of America since 1850. *In* American folk medicine p87-98

Kinsman, R. S. Folly, melancholy, and madness: a study in shifting styles of medical analysis and treatment, 1450-1675. *In* The Darker vision of the Renaissance p273-320

Morantz, R. A. M. Making women modern: middle class women and health reform in 19th century America. *In* Branca, P. ed. The medicine show p103-20

Staum, M. S. Medical components in Cabanis's science of man. *In* Studies in history of biology, v2 p 1-31

Temkin, O. Basic science, medicine, and the romantic era. *In* Temkin, O. The double face of Janus p345-72

Temkin, O. Comparative study in the history of medicine. *In* Temkin, O. The double face of Janus p126-34

Temkin, O. The era of Paul Ehrlich. *In* Temkin, O. The double face of Janus p261-68

Temkin, O. An essay on the usefulness of medical history for medicine. *In* Temkin, O. The double face of Janus p68-100

Temkin, O. German concepts of ontogeny and history around 1800. *In* Temkin, O. The double face of Janus p373-89

Temkin, O. The meaning of medicine in historical perspective. *In* Temkin, O. The double face of Janus p41-49

Temkin, O. On the interrelationship of the history and the philosophy of medicine. *In* Temkin, O. The double face of Janus p101-09

Temkin, O. Wunderlich, Schelling and the history of medicine. *In* Temkin, O. The double face of Janus p246-51

Thomas, L. Medical lessons from history. *In* Thomas, L. The medusa and the snail p158-75

See also Medicine, Arabic; Medicine, Medieval; and similar headings

Laws and legislation

See Medical laws and legislation

Moral and religious aspects

See Medical ethics

Periodicals—Bibliography

Harvey, A. M. Johns Hopkins and biomedical communication. *In* Harvey, A. M. Adventures in medical research p364-89

Philosophy

Shands, H. C. and Meltzer, J. D. Unexpected semiotic implications of medical inquiry. *In* Sebeok, T. A. ed. A perfusion of signs p77-89

Temkin, O. Basic science, medicine, and the romantic era. *In* Temkin, O. The double face of Janus p345-72

Temkin, O. Greek medicine as science and craft. *In* Temkin, O. The double face of Janus p137-53

Temkin, O. Health and disease. *In* Temkin, O. The double face of Janus p419-40

Temkin, O. Medicine and the problem of moral responsibility. *In* Temkin, O. The double face of Janus p50-67

Temkin, O. On the interrelationship of the history and the philosophy of medicine. *In* Temkin, O. The double face of Janus p101-09

Temkin, O. The philosophical background of Magendie's physiology. *In* Temkin, O. The double face of Janus p317-39

Temkin, O. The scientific approach to disease: specific entity and individual sickness. *In* Temkin, O. The double face of Janus p441-55

Temkin, O. Zimmermann's philosophy of the physician. *In* Temkin, O. The double face of Janus p239-45

Practice

See Therapeutics

Research

See Medical research

Social aspects

See Social medicine

Study and teaching

Temkin, O. Comparative study in the history of medicine. *In* Temkin, O. The double face of Janus p126-34

See also Medical colleges

Social aspects

See Social medicine

Superstitions

See Medical delusions

Early works to 1800

See Medicine, Medieval

France—History

Goubert, J. P. The extent of medical practice in France around 1780. *In* Branca, P. ed. The medicine show p211-28

Peter, J. P. Disease and the sick at the end of the eighteenth century. *In* Biology of man in history p81-124

Ramsey, M. Medical power and popular medicine: illegal healers in nineteenth-century France. *In* Branca, P. ed. The medicine show p183-210

Great Britain—History

Ormsby-Lennon, H. Radical physicians and conservative poets in Restoration England: Dryden among the doctors. *In* Studies in eighteenth-century culture v7 p389-411

Near East—History

Wickens, G. M. The Middle East as a world centre of science and medicine. *In* Savory, R. M. ed. Introduction to Islamic civilisation p111-19

Tropics

See Tropical medicine

United States

Callahan, D. J. Health and society: some ethical imperatives. *In* Knowles, J. H. ed. Doing better and feeling worse p23-33

Patrick, E. A. Medical science and tomorrow's American. *In* Tomorrow's American p47-68

Rogers, D. E. The challenge of primary care. *In* Knowles, J. H. ed. Doing better and feeling worse p81-103

Starr, P. Medicine and the waning of professional sovereignty. *In* A New America? p175-93

Medicine—*Continued*

United States—History

Bell, W. J. The Fielding H. Garrison lecture; a portrait of the colonial physician. *In* Bell, W. J. The colonial physician & other essays p5-25

Grob, G. N. The social history of medicine and disease in America: problems and possibilities. *In* Branca, P. ed. The medicine show p 1-19

Starr, P. Medicine, economy and society in nineteenth-century America. *In* Branca, P. ed. The medicine show p47-66

Medicine, Ancient

Dubos, R. J. Medicine evolving; excerpts from "Man adapting." *In* Sobel, D. S. ed. Ways of health p21-44

Hippocrates. From The works of Hippocrates. *In* Sobel, D. S. ed. Ways of health p189-203

See also Medicine, Greek and Roman

Medicine, Arabic

Hamarneh, S. K. The life sciences. *In* The Genius of Arab civilization p145-72

Levey, M. Methodology and the history of science. *In* Essays on Islamic philosophy and science p136-46

Medicine, Byzantine

Temkin, O. Byzantine medicine: tradition and empiricism. *In* Temkin, O. The double face of Janus p202-22

Temkin, O. The Byzantine origin of the names for the basilic and cephalic veins. *In* Temkin, O. The double face of Janus p198-201

Medicine, Chinese

Huang-ti nei ching su wên: From The Yellow Emperor's classic of internal medicine. *In* Sobel, D. S. ed. Ways of health p173-87

Porkert, M. Chinese medicine: a traditional healing science. *In* Sobel, D. S. ed. Ways of health p147-72

Medicine, Clinical

Harvey, A. M. Classical descriptions of disease. *In* Harvey, A. M. Adventures in medical research p152-72

Harvey, A. M. Creators of clinical medicine's scientific base: Franklin Paine Mall, Lewellys Franklin Barker, and Rufus Cole. *In* Harvey, A. M. Adventures in medical research p124-38

Medicine, Experimental

Parsons, T. Research with human subjects and the "professional complex." *In* Parsons, T. Action theory and the human condition p35-65

See also Medical research

Medicine, Greek and Roman

Mansfeld, J. Alcmaeon: 'physikos' or physician? With some remarks on Calcidius' 'On vision' compared to Galen's Plac. Hipp. Plat. VII. *In* Kephalaion p26-38

Simon, B. The Hippocratic corpus. *In* Simon, B. Mind and madness in ancient Greece p215-27

Temkin, O. Greek medicine as science and craft. *In* Temkin, O. The double face of Janus p137-53

Temkin, O. History of Hippocratism in late antiquity: the third century and the Latin West. *In* Temkin, O. The double face of Janus p167-77

Tracy, T. J. Plato, Galen, and the center of consciousness. *In* Illinois classical studies v 1 1976 p43-52

Medicine, Magic, mystic, and spagiric

Frank, J. D. Nonmedical healing: religious and secular; excerpt from "Persuasion and healing." *In* Sobel, D. S. ed. Ways of health p231-66

Grad, B. R. Healing by the laying on of hands: a review of experiments. *In* Sobel, D. S. ed. Ways of health p267-87

Gray, D. Notes on some Middle English charms. *In* Chaucer and Middle English studies in honour of Rossell Hope Robbins p56-71

Yoder, D. Hohman and Romanus: origins and diffusion of the Pennsylvania German powwow manual. *In* American folk medicine p235-48

See also Folk medicine; Medical delusions; Precious stones—Therapeutic use

Medicine, Medieval

Hippocrates. From the works of Hippocrates. *In* Sobel, D. S. ed. Ways of health p189-203

Riddle, J. M. Theory and practice in medieval medicine. *In* Viator: medieval and Renaissance studies v5 p157-4

Talbot, C. H. Medicine. *In* Lindberg, D. C. ed. Science in the Middle Ages p391-428

See also Medicine, Arabic

Medicine, Occult. See Medicine, Magic, mystic, and spagiric

Medicine, Oriental. See Medicine, Arabic

Medicine, Popular. See Folk medicine

Medicine, Preventive. See Public health

Medicine, Primitive

Turner, V. W. Lunda medicine and the treatment of disease. *In* The Occasional papers of the Rhodes-Livingstone Museum p649-719

See also Folk medicine; Indians of North America—Medicine; Medicine-man

Medicine, Psychosomatic

History

Altschule, M. D. Swedenborg and Stahl: opposite—and wrong—sides of the same coin. *In* Altschule, M. D. Origins of concepts in human behavior p183-92

Medicine, Roman. See Medicine, Greek and Roman

Medicine, Social. See Social medicine

Medicine, State

Great Britain

Schwartz, H. The infirmity of British medicine. *In* Tyrrell, R. E. ed. The future that doesn't work p22-41

Medicine, Tropical. See Tropics—Disease and hygiene

Medicine and art. See Medical illustration

Medicine and Islam

Wickens, G. M. The Middle East as a world centre of science and medicine. *In* Savory, R. M. ed. Introduction to Islamic civilisation p111-19

Medicine and psychology. See Psychiatry

Medicine and religion

Drinan, R. F. Should there be a legal right to die? *In* Weir, R. F. ed. Ethical issues in death and dying p297-307

See also Hallucinogenic drugs and religious experience; Healing (in religion, folklore, etc.)

Medicine and state. See Medical policy

Medicine in literature

Ormsby-Lennon, H. Radical physicians and conservative poets in Restoration England: Dryden among the doctors. *In* Studies in eighteenth-century culture v7 p389-411

Pasley, J. M. S. Nietzsche's use of medical terms. *In* Pasley, J. M. S. ed. Nietzsche: imagery and thought p123-58

See also Physicians in literature

Medicine-man

Barbeau, M. The career of a medicine-man; excerpt from "Medicine-men on the North Pacific coast." *In* Tedlock, D. E. and Tedlock, B. eds. Teachings from the American earth p3-12

Sandner, D. F. Navaho Indian medicine and medicine men. *In* Sobel, D. S. ed. Ways of health p117-46

See also Shamanism

Medicine wheels and Plains Indian astronomy. Eddy, J. A. *In* Brecher, K. and Feirtag, M. eds. Astronomy of the ancients p 1-24

Medieval aesthetics. See Aesthetics, Medieval

Medieval and modern Latin manuscripts. See Manuscripts, Latin (Medieval and modern)

Medieval architecture. See Architecture, Medieval

Medieval art. See Art, Medieval

Medieval astronomy. See Astronomy, Medieval

Medieval cities and towns. See Cities and towns, Medieval

Medieval civilization. See Civilization, Medieval

Medieval education. See Education, Medieval

Medieval literature. See Literature, Medieval

Medieval music. See Music—History and criticism—Medieval, 400-1500

Medieval poetry. See Poetry, Medieval

Medieval science. See Science, Medieval

Medievalism in Renaissance Germany. Borchardt, F. L. *In* Creative encounter p73-85

Medievalists

Ray, R. D. Medieval historiography through the twelfth century: problems and progress of research. *In* Viator; medieval and Renaissance studies v5 p33-59

Meditation

Lewalski, B. K. Protestant meditation: kinds, structures, and strategies of development for the meditative lyric. *In* Lewalski, B. K. Protestant poetics and the seventeenth-century religious lyric p147-78

See also Recollection (Theology)

Meditation in literature

Cain, T. G. S. "Times trans-shifting": Herrick in meditation. *In* Rollin, R. B. and Patrick, J. M. eds. "Trust to good verses": Herrick tercentenary essays p103-23

Mediterranean region

Badurina, B. Military force in the Mediterranean. *In* Borgese, E. M. and Krieger, D. eds. The tides of change p197-209

Gonen, A. Mediterranean tourism: some geographic perspectives. *In* Borgese, E. M. and Krieger, D. eds. The tides of change p179-96

Foreign economic relations—European Economic Community countries

Shlaim, A. The Community and the Mediterranean basin. *In* Twitchett, K. J. ed. Europe and the world p77-120

Naval history

Kreutz, B. M. Ships, shipping, and the implications of change in the early medieval Mediterranean. *In* Viator: medieval and Renaissance studies v7 p79-109

Politics and government

Friedlander, R. A. Problems of the Mediterranean: a geopolitical perspective. *In* The Year book of world affairs, 1978 p175-90

Relations (military) with Russia

Zoppo, C. E. Arms control in the Mediterranean and European security. *In* International terrorism and world security p248-76

Relations (military) with the United States

Zoppo, C. E. Arms control in the Mediterranean and European security. *In* International terrorism and world security p248-76

Religion—Bibliography

Oxtoby, W. G. The ancient world. *In* Adams, C. J. ed. A reader's guide to the great religions p39-77

Mediterranean Sea

Borgese, E. M. A Mediterranean Council to Combat Pollution. *In* Borgese, E. M. and Krieger, D. eds. The tides of change p210-17

Holt, S. J. Mediterranean and Black Sea fisheries. *In* Borgese, E. M. and Krieger, D. eds. The tides of change p166-78

Ritchie-Calder, P. R. Baron Ritchie Calder. The pollution of the Mediterranean. *In* Borgese, E. M. and Krieger, D. eds. The tides of change p144-65

Mediums

Ducasse, C. J. How stands the case for the reality of survival; excerpt from "A critical examination of the belief in a life after death." *In* Wheatley, J. M. O. and Edge, H. L. eds. Philosophical dimensions of parapsychology p282-94

Harper, G. M. and Kelly, J. S. Preliminary examination of the script of E[lizabeth] R[adcliffe]. *In* Yeats and the occult p130-71

Lauer, R. A medium for mental health. *In* Zaretsky, I. I. and Leone, M. P. eds. Religious movements in contemporary America p338-54

Price, H. H. Mediumship and human survival. *In* Wheatley, J. M. O. and Edge, H. L. eds. Philosophical dimensions of parapsychology p262-81

Medusa in literature

Freccero, J. Dante's Medusa: allegory and autobiography. *In* Jeffrey, D. L. ed. By things seen: reference and recognition in medieval thought p33-46

Medvedev, Roǐ Aleksandrovich

New pages from the political biography of Stalin. *In* Stalinism p199-235

The October Revolution and the problem of history as a law-governed process. *In* Medvedev, R. A. ed. The Samizdat register p 1-71

On Solzhenitsyn's The Gulag Archipelago. *In* Dunlop, J. B.; Haugh, R. and Klimoff, A. eds. Aleksandr Solzhenitsyn: critical essays and documentary materials 2d ed. p460-76

Medvedev, Roy. See Medvedev, Roǐ Aleksandrovich

Medwall, Henry

About individual works

Fulgens and Lucres

Altman, J. B. Demonstrative and explorative: two paradigms. *In* Altman, J. B. The Tudor play of mind p13-30

Nature

Altman, J. B. Demonstrative and explorative: two paradigms. *In* Altman, J. B. The Tudor play of mind p13-30

Medwin, Alisoun Gardner- See Gardner-Medwin, Alisoun

Meehan, Bernard

Outsiders, insiders, and property in Durham around 1100. *In* Church, society and politics p45-58

Meehan, Thomas Clarke

Jenaro Prieto: the man and his work. *In* Forster, M. H. ed. Tradition and renewal p157-207

Meehl, Paul Everett, and Scriven, Michael

Compatibility of science and ESP. *In* Ludwig, J. K. ed. Philosophy and parapsychology p187-90

Also in Wheatley, J. M. O. and Edge, H. L. eds. Philosophical dimensions of parapsychology p405-08

Meeks, Wayne A.

The divine agent and his counterfeit in Philo and the Fourth Gospel. *In* Aspects of religious propaganda in Judaism and early Christianity p43-67

Meerse, David E.

The northern Democratic Party and the Congressional elections of 1858. *In* Swierenga, R. P. ed. Beyond the Civil War synthesis p79-97

Meerson-Aksenov, Michael Georgievich. See Meerson-Aksenov, Mikhail Georgievich

Meerson-Aksenov, Mikhail Georgievich

The influence of the Jewish exodus on the democratization of Soviet society. *In* Sidorsky, D. ed. Essays on human rights p144-56

Meese, Elizabeth A.

Constructing time and place: Eudora Welty in the thirties. *In* Prenshaw, P. W. ed. Eudora Welty p401-10

Meessen, Karl Matthias

The application of the antitrust rules of the EEC Treaty by the Commission of the European Communities. *In* Davis, K. C. Discretionary justice in Europe and America p75-99

Megalithic monuments

Evans, E. E. Prehistoric Ireland: from the earliest migrations to about AD 500. *In* De Breffny, B. ed. The Irish world p20-46

Megarian decree, Plutarch and the. Fornara, C. W. *In* Yale classical studies v24 p213-28

Megaw, Arthur H. S.

An early thirteenth-century Aegean glazed ware. *In* Studies in memory of David Talbot Rice p34-45

Meggyesy, Dave

About individual works

Out of their league

Sheed, W. Unnecessary roughness. *In* Sheed, W. The good word & other words p148-53

Meher Baba

About

Anthony, D. and Robbins, T. The Meher Baba movement: its affect [sic] on postadolescent social alienation. *In* Zaretsky, I. I. and Leone, M. P. eds. Religious movements in contemporary America p479-511

Mehl, Dieter

The audience of Chaucer's Troilus and Criseyde. *In* Chaucer and Middle English studies in honour of Rossell Hope Robbins p173-89

Mehlman, Jeffrey

Cataract: Diderot's discursive politics, 1749-1751. *In* Glyph 2 p37-63

Mehta, Jarava Lal

Finding Heidegger. *In* Radical phenomenology p5-11

Méhul, Étienne Henri

About

Dent, E. J. The school of Paris—II. *In* Dent, E. J. The rise of romantic opera p64-79

Dent, E. J. The school of Paris—III. *In* Dent, E. J. The rise of romantic opera p80-94

Méhul, Étienne Nicolas. See Méhul, Étienne Henri

Mei, Tsu-lin. See Kao, Yu-kung, jt. auth.

Meier, August

Negroes in the first and second reconstructions of the South. *In* Swierenga, R. P. ed. Beyond the Civil War synthesis p275-91

Meier, Friedrich Max

The mystic path. *In* Lewis, B. ed. Islam and the Arab world p117-40

Meier, Fritz. See Meier, Friedrich Max

Meiji Restoration. See Japan—History—Restoration, 1853-1870

Meiklejohn, Norman Arthur

The implementation of slave legislation in eighteenth-century New Granada. *In* Toplin, R. B. ed. Slavery and race relations in Latin America p176-201

Meine, Franklin Julius

Tall tales of the Southwest. *In* Inge, M. T. ed. The frontier humorists p15-31

Meinecke, Friedrich

About

Gilbert, F. Friedrich Meinecke. *In* Gilbert, F. History p67-87

Meiners, R. K.

On modern poetry, poetic consciousness, and the madness of poets. *In* Evolution of consciousness p106-20

Meinhard, H. H.

The patrilineal principle in early Teutonic kinship. *In* Studies in social anthropology p 1-29

Meinig, Donald William

Prologue: Andrew Hill Clark, historical geographer. *In* European settlement and development in North America: essays on geographical change in honour and memory of Andrew Hill Clark p3-26

Meinke, Peter

Howard Nemerov. *In* Donoghue, D. ed. Seven American poets from MacLeish to Nemerov p250-86

Meinong, Alexius, Ritter von Handschuchsheim

About

Findlay, J. N. Axiological ethics. *In* New studies in ethics v2 p119-213

Meisel, Martin

"Half sick of shadows": the aesthetic dialogue in pre-Raphaelite painting. *In* Knoepflmacher, U. C. and Tennyson, G. B. eds. Nature and the Victorian imagination p309-40

The material sublime: John Martin, Byron, Turner, and the theater. *In* Kroeber, K. and Walling, W. eds. Images of romanticism p211-32

Meiser, Enya P. Flores- . See Flores-Meiser, Enya P.

Meisner, Maurice J.

Marxism and Chinese values. *In* Terrill, R. ed. The China difference p99-116

Utopian and dystopian elements in the Maoist vision of the future. *In* Radicalism in the contemporary age v2 p85-126

Meissner, William W.

Cognitive aspects of the paranoid process —prospectus. *In* Thought, consciousness, and reality p159-216

Melanau (Malaysian people)

Morris, H. S. In the wake of mechanization: sago and society in Sarawak. *In* Social organization and the applications of anthropology p273-301

Melancholia. See Depression, Mental

Melancholy

Kinsman, R. S. Folly, melancholy, and madness: a study in shifting styles of medical analysis and treatment, 1450-1675. *In* The Darker vision of the Renaissance p273-320

Melancholy in literature

Greene, D. J. From accidie to neurosis: The castle of indolence revisted. *In* English literature in the age of disguise p131-56

Radzinowicz, M. A. N. Medicinable tragedy: the structure of Samson Agonistes and seventeenth-century psychopathology. *In* English drama: forms and development p94-122

Melanchthon, Philip

About

Westman, R. S. The Wittenberg interpretation of the Copernican theory. *In* The Nature of scientific discovery p393-429

About individual works

De rhetorica libri tres

McNally, J. R. Melanchton's earliest rhetoric. *In* Rhetoric: a tradition in transition p33-48

Melander, Ingrid

Experimental sonnets: a study of rhyme. *In* Prentki, T. ed. Francis Warner p131-39

Melcher, Frederic Gershom

Bookselling in Boston. *In* Bookselling in America and the world p156-62

Melchiori, Barbara

Browning in Italy. *In* Armstrong, I. ed Robert Browning p168-83

Melchiori, Giorgio

The Wandering Rocks, or, The rejection of Stephen Dedalus. *In* English Association. Essays and studies, 1975 p58-75

Melchor, Alejandro

Assessing ASEAN's viability in a changing world. *In* Pacific Asia and U.S. policies: a political-economic-strategic assessment p67-79

Meldrum, Barbara

Vardis Fisher's Antelope people: pursuing an elusive dream. *In* Bingham, E. R. and Love, G. A. eds. Northwest perspectives p152-66

Melendy, Howard Brett

Filipinos in the United States. *In* The Asian American: the historical experience p101-28

Melia, Daniel Frederick

Parallel versions of "The boyhood deeds of Cuchulainn." *In* Duggan, J. J. ed. Oral literature p25-40

Melito, Saint, Bp. of Sardis

About individual works

The homily on the Passion

Hawthorne, G. F. A new English translation of Melito's paschal homily. *In* Current issues in Biblical and patristic interpretation p147-75

Melito Sardium. See Melito, Saint, Bp. of Sardis

Mellard, James M.

Faulkner's "golden book": The reivers as romantic comedy. *In* Garvin, H. R. ed. Makers of the twentieth-century novel p218-27

Mellette, Susan J.

Connotations of hospitalization. *In* Home care p268-72

Melling, Philip

American popular culture in the thirties: ideology, myth, genre. *In* Bigsby, C. W. E. ed. Approaches to popular culture p241-63

The death ship: B. Traven's cradle. *In* French, W. G. ed. The twenties p139-56

Mellinkoff, David

Right to counsel: the message from America. *In* First images of America p405-13

Mellor, Anne Kostelanetz

Physiognomy, phrenology, and Blake's visionary heads. *In* Essick, R. N. and Pearce, D. R. eds. Blake in his time p53-74

Melnik, Stefan Reinhard

The "uses and gratifications" approach in the study of "entertainment" and leisure use. *In* Fischer, H. D. and Melnik, S. R. eds. Entertainment: a cross-cultural examination p144-52

Melodrama

Cawelti, J. G. The best-selling social melodrama. *In* Cawelti, J. G. Adventure, mystery, and romance p260-95

Rosador, K. T. von. Myth and Victorian melodrama. *In* English Association. Essays and studies, 1979 p97-114

Thorburn, D. Television melodrama. *In* Television as a cultural force p77-94

Meltzer, James D. See Shands, H. C. jt. auth.

Meltzer, Milton

Where do all the prizes go? The case for nonfiction. *In* Horn Book Magazine. Crosscurrents of criticism p51-57

Meltzer, Ronald I.

Contemporary security dimensions of international trade relations. *In* Knorr, K. E. and Trager, F. N. eds. Economic issues and national security p200-30

Mélusine

Le Roy Ladurie, E. Mélusine down on the farm: metamorphosis of a myth. *In* Le Roy Ladurie, E. The territory of a historian p203-20

Melville, Herman

About

Dew, M. C. Black-hearted Melville: "geniality" reconsidered. *In* Artful thunder p177-94

Homberger, E. Melville, Lt Guert Gansevoort and authority: an essay in biography. *In* Pullin, F. ed. New perspectives on Melville p255-74

Leavis, Q. D. Melville: the 1853-6 phase. *In* Pullin, F. ed. New perspectives on Melville p197-228

Moss, S. P. Hawthorne and Melville: an inquiry into their art and the mystery of their friendship. *In* Literary monographs v7 p45-84

Mottram, E. Orpheus and measured forms: law, madness and reticence in Melville. *In* Pullin, F. ed. New perspectives on Melville p229-54

Pops, M. L. Melville: to him. *In* Boyers, R. ed. Contemporary poetry in America p189-220

Richardson, R. D. Melville. *In* Richardson, R. D. Myth and literature in the American renaissance p195-233

Spengemann, W. C. Herman Melville. *In* Spengemann, W. C. The adventurous muse p178-212

Zif, L. Shakespeare and Melville's America. *In* Pullin, F. ed. New perspectives on Melville p54-67

About individual works

Bartleby the scrivener

Stern, M. R. Towards 'Bartleby the scrivener.' *In* The Stoic strain in American literature p19-41

Trilling, L. Bartleby the scrivener: a story of Wall Street. *In* Trilling, L. Prefaces to The experience of literature p74-78

Billy Budd

Manlove, C. N. An organic hesitancy: theme and style in Billy Budd. *In* Pullin, F. ed. New perspectives on Melville p275-300

Mottram, E. Orpheus and measured forms: law, madness and reticence in Melville. *In* Pullin, F. ed. New perspectives on Melville p229-54

The confidence-man

Alter, R. The self-conscious novel in eclipse. *In* Alter, R. Partial magic p84-137

Barney, S. A. The sun's a thief: Melville's The confidence-man. *In* Barney, S. A. Allegories of history, allegories of love p144-71

Leavis, Q. D. Melville: the 1853-6 phase. *In* Pullin, F. ed. New perspectives on Melville p197-228

Sussman, H. The deconstructor as politician: Melville's Confidence-man. *In* Glyph 4 p32-56

The Encantadas

Coxe, L. O. Herman Melville's The Encantadas. *In* Coxe, L. O. Enabling acts p143-49

Israel Potter: his fifty years of exile

Goldman, A. Melville's England. *In* Pullin, F. ed. New perspectives on Melville p68-85

Mardi

Brodhead, R. H. Mardi: creating the creative. *In* Pullin, F. ed. New perspectives on Melville p29-53

Yannella, D. J. "Seeing the elephant" in Mardi. *In* Artful thunder p105-17

Moby Dick

Caserio, R. L. The divine inert: Melville. *In* Caserio, R. L. Plot, story, and the novel p133-66

Hayford, H. Unnecessary duplicates: a key to the writing of Moby-Dick. *In* Pullin, F. ed. New perspectives on Melville p128-61

Hirsch, D. H. Hamlet, Moby-Dick, and passional thinking. *In* Shakespeare: aspects of influence p135-62

Lee, A. R. Moby-Dick: the tale and the telling. *In* Pullin, F. ed. New perspectives on Melville p86-127

Lenson, D. R. Tragedy in prose fiction: Moby-Dick. *In* Lenson, D. R. Achilles' choice p40-64

Pryse, M. Moby-Dick: social physics and metaphysics. *In* Pryse, M. The mark and the knowledge p49-91

Smith, H. N. The madness of Ahab. *In* Smith, H. N. Democracy and the novel p35-55

Wilder, T. N. Toward an American language. *In* Wilder, T. N. American characteristics, and other essays p3-33

Moby Dick (Chapter 1)

Hayford, H. "Loomings": yarns and figures in the fabric. *In* Artful thunder p119-37

Moby Dick (Chapter 32: Cetology)

Gasché, R. The scene of writing: a deferred outset. *In* Glyph I p150-71

Moby Dick (Chapter 54)

Heflin, W. L. Sources from the whale-fishery and "The Town-ho's story." *In* Artful thunder p163-76

Pierre; or, The ambiguities

Higgins, B. and Parker, H. The flawed grandeur of Melville's Pierre. *In* Pullin, F. ed. New perspectives on Melville p162-96

Tobin, P. D. Subverting the father: some nineteenth-century precursors. *In* Tobin, P. D. Time and the novel p29-53

Redburn

Goldman, A. Melville's England. *In* Pullin, F. ed. New perspectives on Melville p68-85

Typee

Pullin, F. Melville's Typee: the failure of Eden. *In* Pullin, F. ed. New perspectives on Melville p 1-28

Spengemann, W. C. Herman Melville. *In* Spengemann, W. C. The adventurous muse p178-212

Melville, Hermann—*Continued*

Bibliography

Parker, H. Melville. *In* American literary scholarship, 1973 p65-84

Parker, H. Melville [another essay]. *In* American literary scholarship, 1974 p43-59

Parker, H. Melville [another essay]. *In* American literary scholarship, 1975 p59-82

Parker, H. Melville [another essay]. *In* American literary scholarship, 1976 p47-59

Parker, H. Melville [another essay]. *In* American literary scholarship, 1977 p49-63

Characters

Pryse, M. Moby-Dick: social physics and metaphysics. *In* Pryse, M. The mark and the knowledge p49-91

Characters—Ahab

Lenson, D. R. Tragedy in prose fiction: Moby-Dick. *In* Lenson, D. R. Achilles' choice p40-64

Marovitz, S. E. Old man Ahab. *In* Artful thunder p139-61

Smith, H. N. The madness of Ahab. *In* Smith, H. N. Democracy and the novel p35-55

Characters—Bartleby

Barber, P. What if Bartleby were a woman? *In* Diamond, A. and Edwards, L. R. eds. The authority of experience p212-23

Stern, M. R. Towards 'Bartleby the scrivener.' *In* The Stoic strain in American literature p19-41

Characters—Isabel Banford

Fryer, J. The temptress: In which the ambiguities of the Dark Lady are compounded by the appearance of the Pale Maiden: Melville's Isabel. *In* Fryer, J. The faces of Eve p47-54

Characters—Ishmael

Hayford, H. "Loomings": yarns and figures in the fabric. *In* Artful thunder p119-37

Characters—Lucy Tartan

Fryer, J. The American princess: The Pale Maiden. *In* Fryer, J. The faces of Eve p87-97

Plots

Caserio, R. L. The divine inert: Melville. *In* Caserio, R. L. Plot, story, and the novel p133-66

Sources

Heflin, W. L. Sources from the whale-fishery and "The Town-ho's story." *In* Artful thunder p163-76

Yannella, D. J. "Seeing the elephant" in Mardi. *In* Artful thunder p105-17

Style

Morris, W. Melville. *In* Morris, W. Earthly delights, unearthly adornments p19-23

Memmi, Albert

About individual works

Portrait of a Jew

Kedourie, E. Mr Memmi on Jewishness and the Jews. *In* Kedourie, E. Arabic political memoirs and other studies p101-06

Memoirs. See Autobiography; Biography

Memorial tablets. See Sepulchral monuments

Memorials. See Monuments

Memories of underdevelopment (Motion picture)

Kauffmann, S. Memories of underdevelopment. *In* Kauffmann, S. Living images p198-200

Memory

Arnheim, R. Space as an image of time. *In* Kroeber, K. and Walling, W. eds. Images of romanticism p 1-12

Bricke, J. Hume on self-identity, memory and causality. *In* David Hume p167-74

Chafe, W. L. The recall and verbalization of past experience. *In* Current issues in linguistic theory p215-46

Coomaraswamy, A. K. Recollection, Indian and platonic. *In* Coomaraswamy, A. K. Selected papers v2 p49-65

Leclaire, S. Unconscious inscription: another memory. *In* Roland, A. ed. Psychoanalysis, creativity, and literature p72-84

Lively, P. Children and memory. *In* Horn Book Magazine. Crosscurrents of criticism p226-33

Malcolm, N. Memory as direct awareness of the past. *In* Royal Institute of Philosophy. Impressions of empiricism p 1-22

Morris, W. Of memory, emotion and imagination. *In* Morris, W. Earthly delights, unearthly adornments p 1-6

Noxon, J. H. Remembering and imagining the past. *In* Livingston, D. W. and King, J. T. eds. Hume p270-95

Palombo, S. R. Dreams, memory, and the origin of thought. *In* Thought, consciousness, and reality p49-83

Roll, W. G. ESP and memory. *In* Wheatley, J. M. O. and Edge, H. L. eds. Philosophical dimensions of parapsychology p154-84

See also Eidetic imagery; Mnemonics

Memory, Disorders of. See Aphasia

Memory as a theme in literature. See Memory in literature

Memory in literature

Dawson, C. "The lamp of memory": Wordsworth and Dickens. *In* Dawson, C. Victorian noon p123-43

Hardy, B. N. Memory and memories. *In* Hardy, B. N. Tellers and listeners p56-101

Sabin, M. The charm of memory. *In* Sabin, M. English romanticism and the French tradition p78-102

Simpson, L. P. The Southern aesthetic of memory. *In* Tulane Studies in English, v23 p207-27

Men

Psychology

See Masculinity (Psychology)

Lebanon

Chatty, D. Changing sex roles in Bedouin society in Syria and Lebanon. *In* Beck, L. and Keddie, N. R. eds. Women in the Muslim world p399-415

Syria

Chatty, D. Changing sex roles in Bedouin society in Syria and Lebanon. *In* Beck, L. and Keddie, N. R. eds. Women in the Muslim world p399-415

United States—Sexual behavior

Pittman, D. J. The male house of prostitution. *In* Henslin, J. M. ed. Deviant lifestyles p151-65

Men (God)

Hiesinger, U. W. Three images of the god Men. *In* Harvard Studies in classical philology v71 p303-10

Men (Psychology). See Masculinity (Psychology)

Men in motion pictures

French, B. The amiable spouse. *In* French, B. On the verge of revolt p35-47

French, B. Dogs like us. *In* French, B. On the verge of revolt p84-91

Menaechmus

About

Brown, M. A pre-Aristotelian mathematician on deductive order. *In* Philosophy and humanism p258-74

Menaker, Esther

Creativity as the central concept in the psychology of Otto Rank. *In* Roland, A. ed. Psychoanalysis, creativity, and literature p162-77

Menander, of Athens

About

Anderson, W. D. Menander and Molière. *In* Johnson, R. B.; Neumann, E. S. and Trail, G. T. eds. Molière and the commonwealth of letters: patrimony and posterity p413-16

Fantham, E. Adaptation and survival: a genre study of Roman comedy in relation to its Greek sources. *In* Ruggiers, P. G. ed. Versions of medieval comedy p19-49

Nicoll, A. From Menander to the mimes. *In* Nicoll, A. World drama p74-99

Sandbach, F. H. Menander. *In* Sandbach, F. H. The comic theatre of Greece and Rome p76-102

About individual works

Epitrepontes

Weinstein, M. E. Menander Epitrepontes 44 and 139. *In* Harvard Studies in classical philology v75 p135-38

Samia

Sandbach, F. H. Menander. *In* Sandbach, F. H. The comic theatre of Greece and Rome p76-102

Mencken, Henry Louis

James Huneker; excerpt from "A book of prefaces." *In* Crunden, R. M. ed. The superfluous men p108-16

Lo, the poor bookseller. *In* **Bookselling in America and the world** p163-70

The need for an aristocracy; excerpt from "Prejudices: second series." *In* Crunden, R. M. ed. The superfluous men p73-79

Notes on democracy; excerpt. *In* Crunden, R. M. ed. The superfluous men p223-30

Paul Elmer More; excerpt from "Prejudices: third series." *In* Crunden, R. M. ed. The superfluous men p147-48

About

Farrell, J. T. A chance meeting with Mencken and Masters. *In* Farrell, J. T. Literary essays, 1954-1974 p79-83

Farrell, J. T. A Mencken revival: introduction to Prejudices. *In* Farrell, J. T. Literary essays, 1954-1974 p5-15

Wagner, P. M. H. L. Mencken. *In* Ross, R. G. ed. Makers of American thought p85-119

About individual works

Notes on democracy

Davidson, D. H. L. Mencken. *In* Crunden, R. M. ed. The superfluous men p232-35

Mencken, Mrs Sara (Haardt) See Haardt, Sara

Mendel, Gregor Johann

About

Lewontin, R. C. Darwin and Mendel—the materialist revolution. *In* Neyman, J. ed. The heritage of Copernicus: theories "pleasing to the mind" p166-83

About individual works

Experiments in plant hybridisation

Mangelsdorf, P. C. Foreword to Experiments in plant hybridisation by Gregor Mendel. *In* Praise from famous men: an anthology of introductions p109-13

Mendels, Franklin Frits

Agriculture and peasant industry in eighteenth-century Flanders. *In* Parker, W. N. and Jones, E. L. eds. European peasants and their markets p179-204

Mendel's law

Lewontin, R. C. Darwin and Mendel—the materialist revolution. *In* Neyman, J. ed. The heritage of Copernicus: theories "pleasing to the mind" p166-83

Mendelson, Edward

Authorized biography and its discontents. *In* Studies in biography p9-26

The Caucasian chalk circle and Endgame. *In* Seidel, M. A. and Mendelson, E. eds. Homer to Brecht p336-52

The sacred, the profane, and The crying of lot 49. *In* Baldwin, K. H. and Kirby, D. K. eds. Individual and community p182-222

Mendelssohn, Moses

About

Altmann, A. Letters from Dohm to Mendelssohn. *In* Salo Wittmayer Baron v 1 p39-62

Mendenhall, Dorothy Reed

About

Harvey, A. M. Johns Hopkins—its role in medical education for women. *In* Harvey, A. M. Adventures in medical research p225-47

Mendenhall, George E.

The conflict between value systems and social control. *In* Unity and diversity p169-80

Mendes, Helen A. See Solomon, B. B. jt. auth.

Mengel, R. William. See Karber, P. A. jt. auth.

Menilek II, King of Ethiopia

About

Marcus, H. G. The British and the Ethiopian railway. *In* African dimensions p29-51

Mennonites. See Amish

Mēnōn, V. K. Krishna. See Krishna Mēnōn, Vengalil Krishnan

The Menorah journal

Trilling, L. A novel of the thirties. *In* Trilling, L. The last decade p3-24

Men's etiquette. See Etiquette for men

Mensah, Atta Annan

Cultural activities and the mass media in Uganda and Zambia. *In* Smock, D. R. and Bentsi-Enchill, K. eds. The search for national integration in Africa p240-47

Menstruation disorders. See Amenorrhea

Mensuration

Gass, W. H. Groping for trouts. *In* Gass, W. H. The world within the word p262-79

Mental ability and age. See Age and intelligence

Mental chronometry. See Time perception

Mental culture. See Mental discipline

Mental deficiency. See Mentally handicapped

Mental depression. See Depression, Mental

Mental discipline

Elliott, R. K. Education and human being I. *In* Philosophers discuss education p45-72

See also Ability, Influence of age on, Self-culture

Mental diseases. See Mental illness; Psychology, Pathological; Psychoses

Mental disorders. See Mental illness

Mental healing. See Psychotherapy

Mental health. See Emotions

Mental health research. See Psychiatric research

Mental health services

Case studies

Anderson, J. P. Practical reasoning in action. *In* Douglas, J. D. and Johnson, J. M. [eds]. Existential sociology p174-98

Mental hospitals. See Psychiatric hospitals

Mental illness

Davis, K. Mental hygiene and the class structure. *In* Davis, F. J. and Stivers, R. eds. The collective definition of deviance p99-113

Gove, W. R. Labelling and mental illness: a critique. *In* Gove, W. R. ed. The labelling of deviance p35-81

Kinsman, R. S. Folly, melancholy, and madness: a study in shifting styles of medical analysis and treatment, 1450-1675. *In* The Darker vision of the Renaissance p273-320

Simon, B. The development of models of mental illness. *In* Simon, B. Mind and madness in ancient Greece p31-42

Szasz, T. S. The mental health ethic; excerpt from "Ideology and insanity". *In* Davis, F. J. and Stivers, R. eds. The collective definition of deviance p114-29

Szasz, T. S. Society's internal enemies and protectors; excerpt from "The manufacture of madness". *In* Davis, F. J. and Stivers, R. eds. The collective definition of deviance p177-96

See also Paranoia

Cases, clinical reports, statistics

Menaker, E. Creativity as the central concept in the psychology of Otto Rank. *In* Roland, A. ed. Psychoanalysis, creativity, and literature p162-77

Péraldi, F. The crane-child. *In* Roland, A. ed. Psychoanalysis, creativity, and literature p96-102

Diagnosis

Goffman, E. The insanity of place; excerpt from "Relations in public". *In* Davis, F. J. and Stivers, R. eds. The collective definition of deviance p325-33

Physiological aspects

Altschule, M. D. The calcified pineal gland: nature mimics art—almost. *In* Altschule, M. D. Origins of concepts in human behavior p165-81

Wallace, A. F. C. Basic studies, applied projects, and eventual implementation: a case history of biological and cultural research in mental health. *In* Spindler, G. D. ed. The making of psychological anthropology p203-16

Research

See Psychiatric research

Europe

White, L. T. Death and the Devil. *In* The Darker vision of the Renaissance p25-46

Massachusetts—Statistics

Rosenkrantz, B. G. and Vinovskis, M. A. The invisible lunatics: old age and insanity in mid-nineteenth-century Massachusetts. *In* Spicker, S. F.; Woodward, K. M. and Van Tassel, D. D. eds. Aging and the elderly p95-125

United States—Statistics

Kramer, M. Implications of expected changes in composition of U.S. population for the delivery of mental health services during the period 1971-85. *In* American psychiatry: past, present, and future p94-112

Mental illness and law. See Insanity—Jurisprudence

Mental illness and literature. See Literature and mental illness

Mental illness in literature

Biasin, G. P. From anatomy to criticism. *In* Biasin, G. P. Literary diseases p3-35

Manheim, L. Dickens' fools and madmen. *In* Dickens Studies Annual v2 p69-97

Predmore, R. L. On interpreting Don Quixote's character. *In* Studies in the continental background of Renaissance English literature: essays presented to John L. Lievsay p186-201

Rigney, B. H. "The frenzied moment": sex and insanity in Jane Eyre. *In* Rigney, B. H. Madness and sexual politics in the feminist novel p13-37

Rigney, B. H. "A rehearsal for madness": hysteria as sanity in The four-gated city. *In* Rigney, B. H. Madness and sexual politics in the feminist novel p65-89

Rigney, B. H. "The sane and the insane": psychosis and mysticism in Mrs. Dalloway. *In* Rigney, B. H. Madness and sexual politics in the feminist novel p39-63

Rigney, B. H. The self-created other: integration and survival. *In* Rigney, B. H. Madness and sexual politics in the feminist novel p117-27

Simon, B. Mental life in Greek tragedy. *In* Simon, B. Mind and madness in ancient Greece p89-121

Simon, B. Mental life in the Homeric epics. *In* Simon, B. Mind and madness in ancient Greece p53-77

Simon, B. Tragedy and therapy. *In* Simon, B. Mind and madness in ancient Greece p122-54

Mental images. See Imagery (Psychology)

Mental philosophy. See Psychology

Mental stereotype. See Stereotype (Psychology)

Mental suggestion. See Therapeutics, Suggestive

Mental telepathy. See Thought-transference

Mental tests. See Intelligence tests

Mental work
Arendt, H. Mental activities in a world of appearances. *In* Arendt, H. The life of the mind v 1 p67-125
Arendt, H. The philosophers and the will. *In* Arendt, H. The life of the mind v2 p11-51

Mentally handicapped
Gordon, R. A. Examining labelling theory: the case of mental retardation. *In* Gove, W. R. ed. The labelling of deviance p83-146

Care and treatment—United States
Tylor, P. L. "Denied the power to choose the good:" sexuality and mental defect in American medical practice, 1850-1920. *In* Branca, P. ed. The medicine show 165-82

Institutional care—United States
Ginsberg, L. H. The institutionalized mentally disabled. *In* Gochros, H. L. and Gochros, J. S. eds. The sexually oppressed p215-24

United States—Sexual behavior
Ginsberg, L. H. The institutionalized mentally disabled. *In* Gochros, H. L. and Gochros, J. S. eds. The sexually oppressed p215-24
Kempton, W. The mentally retarded person. *In* Gochros, H. L. and Gochros, J. S. eds. The sexually oppressed p239-56
Tylor, P. L. "Denied the power to choose the good:" sexuality and mental defect in American medical practice, 1850-1920. *In* Branca, P. ed. The medicine show p165-82

Mentally handicapped children
Terdal, L. G.; Jackson, R. H. and Garner, A. M. Mother-child interactions: a comparison between normal and developmentally delayed groups. *In* Behavior modification and families p249-64
Ulman, E. and Dachinger, P. Therapeutic art programs around the world. *In* Ulman, E. and Dachinger, P. eds. Art therapy p208-12
See also Slow learning children

Cases, clinical reports, statistics
Crawford, J. W. Art for the mentally retarded; directed or creative. *In* Ulman, E. and Dachinger, P. eds. Art therapy p387-92

Education
Gitter, L. L. Montessori and the compulsive cleanliness of severely retarded children. *In* Ulman, E. and Dachinger, P. eds. Art therapy p181-90

Education—Case studies
Bolgen, K. There are no hopeless children. *In* Fairfield, R. P. ed. Humanistic frontiers in American education p220-36

Mentally ill
Care and treatment
Spiegel, J. P. Conflicts in ideologies and values. *In* American psychiatry: past, present, and future p8-14

Care and treatment—History
Altschule, M. D. The early history of psychiatric treatment. *In* Altschule, M. D. Origins of concepts in human behavior p123-51
Dain, N. American psychiatry in the 18th century. *In* American psychiatry: past, present, and future p15-27

Care and treatment—France
Bleandonu, G. and Le Gaufey, G. The creation of the insane asylums of Auxerre and Paris. *In* Deviants and the abandoned in French society p180-212
Weiner, D. B. Three champions of the handicapped in Revolutionary France. *In* From Parnassus p161-76

Care and treatment—United States
Berger, P. A.; Hamburg, B. and Hamburg, D. A. Mental health: progress and problems. *In* Knowles, J. H. ed. Doing better and feeling worse p261-76

Legal status, laws, etc.
See Insanity—Jurisprudence

Rehabilitation
Ulman, E. Therapy is not enough: the contribution of art to general hospital psychiatry. *In* Ulman, E. and Dachinger, P. eds. Art therapy p14-32

Suicidal behavior
Szasz, T. S. The ethics of suicide. *In* Weir, R. F. ed. Ethical issues in death and dying p374-86
Wolman, B. B. The anticulture of suicide. *In* Wolman, B. B. ed. Between survival and suicide p77-94

Mentally retarded. See Mentally handicapped

Mentally retarded children. See Mentally handicapped children

Menzies, Robert Gordon
About
McLeod, M. B. Audience and argument in the speeches of R. G. Menzies and Krishna Menon on the Suez Canal crisis in 1956. *In* Narasimhaiah, C. D. ed. Awakened conscience p389-400

Mepham, John
Figures of desire: narration and fiction in To the lighthouse. *In* Josipovici, G. ed. The modern English novel: the reader, the writer and the work p149-85

Mercantile system
Coats, A. W. Adam Smith and the mercantile system. *In* Skinner, A. S. and Wilson, T. eds. Essays on Adam Smith p218-36
Fleming, J. M. Mercantilism and free trade today. *In* The Market and the state p164-85

Mercenary troops. See Condottieri

Merchants
Prakash, O. Asian trade and European impact: a study of the trade from Bengal, 1630-1720. *In* Kling, B. B. and Pearson, M. N. eds. The age of partnership p43-70

Europe—History
Lopez, R. S. The culture of the medieval merchant. *In* Medieval and Renaissance studies 1976 p52-73

Merchants—*Continued*

Great Britain—History

Ruiz, T. F. Castilian merchants in England, 1248-1350. *In* Order and innovation in the Middle Ages p173-85

India

Brennig, J. J. Joint-stock companies of Coromandel. *In* Kling, B. B. and Pearson, M. N. eds. The age of partnership p71-96

Das Gupta, A. Gujarati merchants and the Red Sea trade, 1700-1725. *In* Kling, B. B. and Pearson, M. N. eds. The age of partnership p123-58

Marshall, P. Masters and banians in eighteenth-century Calcutta. *In* Kling, B. B. and Pearson, M. N. eds. The age of partnership p191-213

Thailand—History

Moerman, M. Chīangkham's trade in the "old days." *In* Change and persistence in Thai society p151-71

Mercier, Louis Sébastien

About

Jones, T. B. and Nicol, B. de B. Diderot and Mercier. *In* Jones, T. B. and Nicol, B. de B. Neo-classical dramatic criticism, 1560-1770 p145-76

About individual works
Memoirs of the year two thousand five hundred

Knight, I. F. Utopian dream as psychic reality. *In* Studies in eighteenth-century culture v6 p427-38

Mercier, Sébastien. See Mercier, Louis Sébastien

Mercier, Vivian
The Irishness of Beckett: Ireland/the world: Beckett's Irishness. *In* Yeats, Joyce, and Beckett p147-52

Mercure de France. Paris. 1672-1820
Wilkins, K. Attitudes toward women in two eighteenth-century French periodicals. *In* Studies in eighteenth-century culture v6 p393-406

Mercurius
Ramage, N. H. Draped herm from Sardis. *In* Harvard Studies in classical philology v78 p253-56

Mercy killing. See Euthanasia

Méré, Antoine Gombaud, chevalier de

About

Horowitz, L. K. The chevalier de Méré. *In* Horowitz, L. K. Love and language p15-28

Meredith, Dennis L. See Biller, H. B. jt. auth.

Meredith, George

About

Skilton, D. New approaches: Meredith, Hardy and Butler. *In* Skilton, D. The English novel p163-77

Stevenson, L. Carlyle and Meredith. *In* Carlyle and his contemporaries p256-79

Stevenson, L. Meredith and the art of implication. *In* Levine, R. A. The Victorian experience: the novelists p177-201

About individual works
The egoist

Haley, B. The athlete as barbarian: Richard Feverel and Willoughby Patterne. *In* Haley, B. The healthy body and Victorian culture p227-51

Kennard, J. E. Her transitory self. *In* Kennard, J. E. Victims of convention p136-57

Parrill, A. S. Portraits of ladies. *In* Tennessee Studies in literature v20 p92-99

Modern love

Ball, P. M. 'If I be dear to someone else.' *In* Ball, P. M. The heart's events p105-66

The ordeal of Richard Feverel

Haley, B. The athlete as barbarian: Richard Feverel and Willoughby Patterne. *In* Haley, B. The healthy body and Victorian culture p227-51

Stevenson, R. C. Comedy, tragedy, and the spirit of critical intelligence in Richard Feverel. *In* The Worlds of Victorian fiction p205-22

Sandra Belloni

Rance, N. George Meredith: Sandra Belloni (1864) and Vittoria (1866). *In* Rance, N. The historical novel and popular politics in nineteenth-century England p155-71

Vittoria

Rance, N. George Meredith: Sandra Belloni (1864) and Vittoria (1866). *In* Rance, N. The historical novel and popular politics in nineteenth-century England p155-71

Meregalli, Franco
A parallel observer and innovator: José Ortega y Gasset. *In* Américo Castro and the meaning of Spanish civilization p267-91

Merezhkovskiĭ, Dmitrĭ Sergeevich
Gogol and the Devil. *In* Maguire, R. A. ed. Gogol from the twentieth century p55-102

About

Stammler, H. A. Russian metapolitics: Merezhkovsky's religious understanding of the historical process. *In* California Slavic studies v9 p123-38

Merezhkovsky, Dmitry. See Merezhkovskiĭ, Dmitrĭ Sergeevich

Merideth, Robert
"It's a small world": high school, American culture studies, and cultural revolution. *In* Luedtke, L. S. ed. The study of American culture p279-322

Meridian lines. See International date line

Mérimée, Prosper

About

Massey, I. The third self: Dracula, Jekyll and Hyde, "Lokis." *In* Massey, I. The gaping pig p98-114

Merisi, Michelangelo. See Caravaggio, Michelangelo Merisi da

Meriwether, James B.
Faulkner. *In* American literary scholarship, 1973 p135-49

Faulkner's essays on Anderson. *In* Faulkner: fifty years after The marble faun p159-81

Merkabah. See Throne of God

Merkelbach, Reinhold
The girl in the rosebush: a Turkish tale and its roots in ancient ritual. *In* Harvard Studies in classical philology v82 p 1-15

Merleau-Ponty, Jacques
Laplace as a cosmologist. *In* Cosmology, history, and theology p283-91

Merleau-Ponty, Maurice

About

Fontana, A. and Van de Water, R. The existential thought of Jean-Paul Sartre and Maurice Merleau-Ponty. *In* Douglas, J. D. and Johnson, J. M. [eds.] Existential sociology p101-29

Grene, M. G. The aesthetic dialogue of Sartre and Merleau-Ponty. *In* Grene, M. G. Philosophy in and out of Europe p87-107

Mays, W. Phenomenology and Marxism. *In* Pivčević, E. ed. Phenomenology and philosophical understanding p231-50

Silverman, H. J. Heidegger and Merleau-Ponty: interpreting Hegel. *In* Radical phenomenology p209-24

Merli, Frank J. and Ferrell, Robert Hugh
Blockades and quarantines. *In* Encyclopedia of American foreign policy p90-103

Merlin
Ford, P. K. The death of Merlin in the Chronicle of Elis Gruffydd. *In* Viator: medieval and Renaissance studies v7 p379-90

Merlin, Christian
Tax relief contracts in France. *In* Davis, K. C. Discretionary justice in Europe and America p161-78

Merlin, Samuel
Summation and projections. *In* The New world balance and peace in the Middle East: reality or mirage? p227-40

Mermier, Guy R.
The grotesque in French medieval literature: a study in forms and meanings. *In* Ruggiers, P. G. ed. Versions of medieval comedy p101-34

Meroë
Shinnie, P. L. The development of Meroitic studies since 1945. *In* African studies since 1945 p169-78

Merrem, Daniel Carl Theodor

About

Temkin, O. Merrem's youthful dream: the early history of experimental pylorectomy. *In* Temkin, O. The double face of Janus p497-509

Merrens, Harry Roy
Settlement of the colonial Atlantic seaboard. *In* Pattern and process p235-43

Merriam, Alan P.
Traditional music of Black Africa. *In* Martin, P. M. and O'Meara, P. eds. Africa p243-58

Merrick, Gordon

About

Elliott, S. J. Homosexuality in the crucial decade: three novelists' views. *In* Crew, L. ed. The gay academic p164-77

Merrick, Leonard

About individual works
Conrad in quest of his youth
Barrie, J. M. bart. Introduction to Conrad in search of his youth. *In* Praise from famous men: an anthology of introductions p14-18

Merrill, James Ingram

About

Kalstone, D. James Merrill: transparent things. *In* Kalstone, D. Five temperaments p77-128

Merrill, John Calhoun
A conceptual overview of world journalism; excerpts from "Imperative of freedom." *In* Fischer, H. D. and Merrill, J. C. eds. International and intercultural communication p18-28

Freedom of the press: changing concept? *In* Fischer, H. D. and Merrill, J. C. eds. International and intercultural communication p125-35

Global patterns of elite daily journalism. *In* Fischer, H. D. and Merrill, J. C. eds. International and intercultural communication p90-98

Media and national development. *In* Fischer, H. D. and Merrill, J. C. eds. International and intercultural communication p186-99

Merritt, Karen
Women and higher education: voices from the sexual Siberia. *In* Roberts, J. I. ed. Beyond intellectual sexism p353-64

Merryman, John Henry
Legal education there and here: a comparison. *In* Stanford legal essays p335-54

Merrymount, Mass. See Quincy, Mass.

The Mersey sound: Adrian Henri, Roger McGough, Brian Patten
Robinson, I. Paper tygers, or, The circus animals' desertion in the new pop poetry. *In* Abbs, P. ed. The black rainbow p19-31

Mertens, Joan R.
A white-ground cup by Euphronios. *In* Harvard Studies in classical philology v76 p271-81

Merton, Robert King
Structural analysis in sociology. *In* Blau, P. M. ed. Approaches to the study of social structure p21-52

About

Coser, L. A. Merton's uses of the European sociological tradition. *In* The Idea of social structure p85-100

Goode, W. J. Homans' and Merton's structural approach. *In* Blau, P. M. ed. Approaches to the study of social structure p66-75

Lazarsfeld, P. F. Working with Merton. *In* The Idea of social structure p35-66

Stinchcombe, A. L. Merton's theory of social structure. *In* The Idea of social structure 11-33

Merwin, William Stanley

About

Altieri, C. F. The struggle with absence: Robert Creeley and W. S. Merwin. *In* Altieri, C. F. Enlarging the temple p170-224

Watkins, E. Criticism and community: on literary value. *In* Watkins, E. The critical act p213-51

About individual works
The lice
Lieberman, L. W. S. Merwin and Anthony Hecht: risks and faiths. *In* Lieberman, L. Unassigned frequencies p257-62

Merwin, William S.—About individual works
—*Continued*

Writings to an unfinished accompaniment
Lieberman, L. The church of ash. *In* Boyers, R. ed. Contemporary poetry in America p256-66

Same as: Lieberman, L. W. S. Merwin: the church of ash. *In* Lieberman, L. Unassigned frequencies p122-32

Lieberman, L. W. S. Merwin: the church of ash. *In* Lieberman, L. Unassigned frequencies p122-32

Mesa-Lago, Carmelo
The economics of U.S.-Cuban rapprochement. *In* Cuba in the world p199-224

The economy and international economic relations. *In* Cuba in the world p169-98

See also Masferrer, M. jt. auth.

Meserve, Walter J.
Drama. *In* American literary scholarship, 1973 p369-81

Mesmer, Franz Anton. See Mesmer, Friedrich Anton

Mesmer, Friedrich Anton

About
Tatar, M. M. From Mesmer to Freud: animal magnetism, hypnosis, and suggestion. *In* Tatar, M. M. Spellbound p3-44

Mesmerism
Fancher, R. E. Early hypnotists and the psychology of social influence. *In* Fancher, R. E. Pioneers of psychology p170-204

See also Animal magnetism

History
Tatar, M. M. Masters and slaves: the creative process in Hawthorne's fiction. *In* Tatar, M. M. Spellbound p189-229

Mesmerism in literature
Briggs, J. A scientific spirit: mesmerism, drugs and psychic doctors. *In* Briggs, J. Night visitors p52-75

Tatar, M. M. Blindness and insight: visionary experience in the tales of E. T. A. Hoffmann. *In* Tatar, M. M. Spellbound p121-51

Tatar, M. M. From science fiction to psychoanalysis: Henry James's "Bostonians," D. H. Lawrence's "Women in love," and Thomas Mann's "Mario and the magician." *In* Tatar, M. M. Spellbound p230-71

Tatar, M. M. Masters and slaves: the creative process in Hawthorne's fiction. *In* Tatar, M. M. Spellbound p189-229

Tatar, M. M. The metaphysics of the will: voyeurs and visionaries in Balzac's "Comédie humaine." *In* Tatar, M. M. Spellbound p152-88

Tatar, M. M. Salvation by electricity: science poetry and "Naturphilosophie." *In* Tatar, M. M. Spellbound p45-81

Mesopotamia. See Iraq

Messahala. See Māshā'allāh

Messenger, John Cowan
Bibliography. *In* Casey, D. J. and Rhodes, R. E. eds. Views of the Irish peasantry, 1800-1916 p203-17

Messent, Pete, and Leaf, Mark
American literature: the twentieth century. *In* English Association. The year's work in English studies v55 p505-69

Messer, Jeanne
Guru Maharaj Ji and the Divine Light Mission. *In* The New religious consciousness p52-72

Messerli, Douglas
"A battle with both sides using the same tactics": the language of time in Losing battles. *In* Prenshaw, P. W. ed. Eudora Welty p351-66

Messianic era (Judaism) in literature
Wohlfarth, I. On the messianic structure of Walter Benjamin's last reflections. *In* Glyph 3 p148-212

Messina, Joseph
The heroic image in the Last instructions to a painter. *In* Friedenreich, K. ed. Tercentenary essays in honor of Andrew Marvell p297-310

Messing, Gordon M.
Pound's Propertius: the homage and the damage. *In* Poetry and poetics from ancient Greece to the Renaissance p105-33

The status of [æ] in Attic Greek. *In* Illinois classical studies, v 1 1976 p 1-6

Messiri, Sawsan el. See el-Messiri, Sawsan

Metabasis, Vico as philosopher of. Fáj, A. *In* Giambattista Vico's science of humanity p87-109

Metal trade. See Iron industry and trade

Metal-work
See also Silversmithing

England
Hinton, D. A. Late Anglo-Saxon metal-work: and assessment. *In* Anglo-Saxon England 4 p171-80

Metallurgy

Technological innovations
Smith, C. S. Remarks on the discovery of techniques and on sources for the study of their history. *In* Bugliarello, G. and Doner, D. B. eds. The history and philosophy of technology p31-37

Metamathematics. See Logic, Symbolic and mathematical

Metamorphosis in literature
Bersani, L. Desire and metamorphosis. *In* Bersani, L. A future for Astyanax p189-229

Massey, I. Aspects of metamorphosis in Alice. *In* Massey, I. The gaping pig p76-97

Massey, I. Flaubert and "La légende de Sainte-Julien l'hospitalier." *In* Massey, I. The gaping pig p156-84

Massey, I. The golden ass; character versus structure. *In* Massey, I. The gaping pig p34-75

Massey, I. Introduction. *In* Massey, I. The gaping pig p 1-33

Massey, I. Metamorphosis in Gogol: "The nose." *In* Massey, I. The gaping pig p59-75

Massey, I. Postscript. *In* Massey, I. The gaping pig p185-97

Massey, I. Singles and doubles narcissism in Hoffmann's "The sandman." *In* Massey, I. The gaping pig p115-23

Massey, I. The third self: Dracula, Jekyll and Hyde, "Lokis." *In* Massey, I. The gaping pig p98-114

Shea, D. B. Emerson and the American metamorphosis. *In* Levin, D. ed. Emerson: prophecy, metamorphosis, and influence p29-56

Metaphilosophy, Phenomenology and. McCormick, P. *In* Elliston, F. A. and McCormick, P. eds. Husserl p350-64

Metaphor

Basso, K. H. 'Wise words' of the Western Apache: metaphor and semantic theory. *In* Basso, K. H. and Selby, H. A. eds. Meaning in anthropology p93-121

Black, M. More about metaphor. *In* Ortony, A. ed. Metaphor and thought p19-43

Boyd, R. N. Metaphor and theory change: what is "metaphor" a metaphor for? *In* Ortony, A. ed. Metaphor and thought p356-408

Cohen, L. J. The semantics of metaphor. *In* Ortony, A. ed. Metaphor and thought p64-77

Crocker, J. C. The social functions of rhetorical forms. *In* The Social use of metaphor p33-66

Edge, D. Technological metaphor and social control. *In* Bugliarello, G. and Doner, D. B. eds. The history and philosophy of technology p309-24

Fernandez, J. W. The performance of ritual metaphors. *In* The Social use of metaphor p100-31

Fraser, B. The interpretation of novel metaphors. *In* Ortony, A. ed. Metaphor and thought p172-85

Green, T. F. Learning without metaphor. *In* Ortony, A. ed. Metaphor and thought p462-73

Howe, J. Carrying the village: Cuna political metaphors. *In* The Social use of metaphor p132-63

Kuhn, T. S. Metaphor in science. *In* Ortony, A. ed. Metaphor and thought p409-19

Levin, S. R. Standard approaches to metaphor and a proposal for literary metaphor. *In* Ortony, A. ed. Metaphor and thought p124-35

Lodge, D. Metaphor and metonymy. *In* Lodge, S. The modes of modern writing p73-124

Mazrui, A. A. The Afro-Saxons. *In* Said, A. A. and Simmons, L. R. eds. Ethnicity in an international context p203-17

Miller, G. A. Images and models, similes and metaphors. *In* Ortony, A. ed. Metaphor and thought p202-50

Morgan, J. L. Observations on the pragmatics of metaphor. *In* Ortony, A. ed. Metaphor and thought p136-47

Nemerov, H. What was modern poetry? Three lectures: Image and metaphor. *In* Nemerov, H. Figures of thought p149-66

Ortony, A. Metaphor: a multidimensional problem. *In* Ortony, A. ed. Metaphor and thought p 1-16

Ortony, A. The role of similarity in similes and metaphors. *In* Ortony, A. ed. Metaphor and thought p186-201

Percy, W. Metaphor as mistake. *In* Percy, W. The message in the bottle p64-82

Petrie, H. G. Metaphor and learning. *In* Ortony, A. ed. Metaphor and thought p438-61

Pylyshyn, Z. W. Metaphorical imprecision and the "top-down" research strategy. *In* Ortony, A. ed. Metaphor and thought p420-36

Rumelhart, D. E. Some problems with the notion of literal meanings. *In* Ortony, A. ed. Metaphor and thought p78-90

Sadock, J. M. Figurative speech and linguistics. *In* Ortony, A. ed. Metaphor and thought p46-63

Sapir, J. D. The anatomy of metaphor. *In* The Social use of metaphor p3-32

Searle, J. R. Metaphor. *In* Ortony, A. ed. Metaphor and thought p92-123

Stern, J. P. Nietzsche and the idea of metaphor. *In* Pasley, J. M. S. ed. Nietzsche: imagery and thought p64-82

Sticht, T. G. Educational uses of metaphor. *In* Ortony, A. ed. Metaphor and thought p474-85

Temkin, O. Metaphors of human biology. *In* Temkin, O. The double face of Janus p271-83

Wells, R. S. Metonymy and misunderstanding: an aspect of language change. *In* Current issues in linguistic theory p195-214

Wicker, B. Metaphor and 'analogy.' *In* Wicker, B. The story-shaped world p11-32

Wicker, B. Metaphor and 'fiction.' *In* Wicker, B. The story-shaped world p33-49

Wicker, B. Metaphor and 'God.' *In* Wicker, B. The story-shaped world p71-106

Wicker, B. Metaphor and 'nature.' *In* Wicker, B. The story-shaped world p50-70

Psychological aspects

Paivio, A. Psychological processes in the comprehension of metaphor. *In* Ortony, A. ed. Metaphor and thought p150-71

Social aspects

Reddy, M. J. The conduit metaphor—a case of frame conflict in our language about language. *In* Ortony, A. ed. Metaphor and thought p284-324

Schon, D. A. Generative metaphor: a perspective on problem-setting in social policy. *In* Ortony, A. ed. Metaphor and thought p254-83

Sternberg, R. J.; Tourangeau, R. and Nigro, G. Metaphor, induction, and social policy: the convergence of macroscopic and microscopic views. *In* Ortony, A. ed. Metaphor and thought p325-53

Metaphysics

Carnap, R. The overcoming of metaphysics through logical analysis of language. *In* Murray, M. E. ed. Heidegger and modern philosophy p23-34

Derrida, J. La parole soufflée. *In* Derrida, J. Writing and difference p169-95

Derrida, J. Violence and metaphysics: an essay on the thought of Emmanuel Levinas. *In* Derrida, J. Writing and difference p79-153

Grant, P. The matter of roots: belief, images, and bodies. *In* Grant, P. Images and ideas in literature of the English Renaissance p 1-26

Harris, E. E. Science, metaphysics, and teleology. *In* The Personal universe p24-39

Holbrook, D. Essay 10. *In* Fitzgerald, R. ed. What it means to be human p186-208

Koestler, A. Physics and metaphysics. *In* Koestler, A. Janus p242-73

Moody, E. A. Empiricism and metaphysics in medieval philosophy. *In* Moody, E. A. Studies in medieval philosophy, science, and logic p287-304

Weinberg, J. R. The argument of Anselm and some medieval critics. *In* Weinberg, J. R. Ockham, Descartes, and Hume p 3-14

See also Causation; Cosmology; Immanence (Philosophy); Knowledge, Theory of; Ontology; Space and time; Substance (Philosophy); and subdivision Metaphysics under names of philosophers

Metapsychology. See Psychical research; Spiritualism

Metcalf, Keyes DeWitt
Introduction of Daniel J. Boorstin. *In* Libraries and the life of the mind in America p109-13

Metelli, Fabio
Achromatic color conditions in the perception of transparency. *In* Perception p95-116

Metempsychosis. See Transmigration

Meteorology
Hughes, J. D. The Copernican legacy for meteorology. *In* Neyman, J. ed. The heritage of Copernicus: theories "pleasing to the mind" p332-54

Meter. See Versification

Metford, J. C. J.
Comedy in Spain and the Spanish comedia. *In* Howarth, W. D. ed. Comic drama p81-101

Methodism
Davie, D. Dissent and the Wesleyans, 1740-1800. *In* Davie, D. A gathered Church p37-54

History
Rogal, S. J. John Wesley on war and peace. *In* Studies in eighteenth-century culture v7 p329-44

Methodology
Harris, E. E. Empiricism in science and philosophy. *In* Royal Institute of Philosophy. Impressions of empiricism p154-67

Marin, L. 'Le neutre' and philosophical discourse. *In* Montefiore, A. ed. Neutrality and impartiality p86-127

See also Classification of sciences; Problem solving; subdivision Methodology under special subjects, e.g. Science—Methodology

Metonymy
Wells, R. S. Metonymy and misunderstanding: an aspect of language change. *In* Current issues in linguistic theory p195-214

Métraux, Rhoda Bubendey
Eidos and change: continuity in process, discontinuity in product. *In* Schwartz, T. ed. Socialization as cultural communication p201-16

Metric system
Trager, G. L. Think metric. *In* On language, culture, and religion: in honor of Eugene A. Nida p373-80

Metropolitan areas
See also Metropolitan government; Municipal powers and services beyond corporate limits; Urban renewal

United States
Abler, R. The telephone and the evolution of the American metropolitan system. *In* The Social impact of the telephone p318-41

Foley, D. L. Accessibility for residents in the metropolitan environment. *In* Hawley, A. H. and Rock, V. P. eds. Metropolitan America in contemporary perspective p157-98

Gottdiener, M. D. Social planning and metropolitan growth. *In* Handbook of contemporary urban life p494-518

Janowitz, M. and Street, D. Changing social order of the metropolitan area. *In* Handbook of contemporary urban life p90-128

Kasarda, J. D. Urbanization, community, and the metropolitan problem. *In* Handbook of contemporary urban life p27-57

Kornblum, W. S. and Williams, T. Lifestyle, leisure, and community life. *In* Handbook of contemporary urban life p58-89

Pearce, D. and Street, D. Welfare in the metropolitan area. *In* Handbook of contemporary urban life p319-51

Perin, C. The symbolic landscape: authority and the American way. *In* Mann, D. A. ed. The arts in a democratic society p43-57

Zimmer, B. G. The urban centrifugal drift. *In* Hawley, A. H. and Rock, V. P. eds. Metropolitan America in contemporary perspective p23-91

Metropolitan finance

United States
Fitch, L. C. Fiscal and productive efficiency in urban government systems. *In* Hawley, A. H. and Rock, V. P. eds. Metropolitan America in contemporary perspective p397-429

Metropolitan government
See also Metropolitan finance

United States
Campbell, A. K. and Dollenmayer, J. A. Governance in a metropolitan society. *In* Hawley, A. H. and Rock, V. P. eds. Metropolitan America in contemporary perspective p355-96

Street, D. and Davidson, J. L. Community and politics in city and suburb. *In* Handbook of contemporary urban life p468-93

Zimmerman, J. F. The patchwork approach: adaptive responses to increasing urbanization. *In* Hawley, A. H. and Rock, V. P. eds. Metropolitan America in contemporary perspective p431-73

Metropolitan Hospital Center. See New York (City) Metropolitan Hospital Center

Metternich-Winneburg, Clemens Lothar Wenzel, Fürst von

About
Sked, A. Metternich and the federalist myth. *In* Crisis and controversy p 1-22

Metwalli, Ahmed M.
Americans abroad: the popular art of travel writing in the nineteenth century. *In* Kagle, S. E. ed. America: exploration and travel p68-82

Metz, Christian
Current problems of film theory: Mitry's L'Esthetique et psychologie du cinema, vol. II. *In* Nichols, B. ed. Movies and methods p568-78

On the notion of cinematographic language. *In* Nichols, B. ed. Movies and methods p582-89

About individual works
Le cinema: langue ou langage?
Wollen, P. Cinema and semiology: some points of contact. *In* Nichols, B. ed. Movies and methods p481-92

Metz (Diocese)

Church history
McCurry, C. Religious careers and religious devotion in thirteenth-century Metz. *In* Viator: medieval and Renaissance studies v9 p325-33

McCurry, C. Utilia metensia: local benefices for the papal Curia, 1212—c.1370. *In* Law, church, and society p311-23

Metzger, Bruce Manning
Early Arabic versions of the New Testament. *In* On language, culture, and religion: in honor of Eugene A. Nida p157-68

Metzger, Walter P.
Academic freedom and scientific freedom. *In* Holton, G. J. and Morison, R. S. eds. Limits of scientific inquiry p93-114

Metzger, Wolfgang
Can the subject create his world? *In* Perception p57-71

Mews, Siegfried
The dramatic Dioscuri: Moilère's German reception in the late nineteenth century. *In* Johnson, R. B.; Neumann, E. S. and Trail, G. T. eds. Molière and the commonwealth of letters: patrimony and posterity p334-44

Mews, Siegfried, and English, Raymond
The Jungle transcended: Brecht and Zuckmayer. *In* Mews, S. and Knust, H. eds. Essays on Brecht p79-98

Mexican American literature (English) See American literature—Mexican American authors

Mexican American literature (Spanish)
Trejo, A. D. As we see ourselves in Chicano literature. *In* Trejo, A. D. ed. The Chicanos p187-211

History and criticism
De la Garza, R. O. and Rivera, R. The socio-political world of the Chicano: a comparative analysis of social scientific and literary perspectives. *In* Minority language and literature p42-64
Paredes, R. A. The promise of Chicano literature. *In* Minority language and literature p29-41

Mexican American women
Gonzales, S. A. The Chicana perspective: a design for self-awareness. *In* Trejo, A. D. ed. The Chicanos p81-99

New Mexico
Gallegos y Cháves, E. The northern New Mexican woman: a changing silhouette. *In* Trejo, A. D. ed. The Chicanos p67-79

Mexican Americans
Arvizu, S. F. Education for constructive marginality. *In* Smithsonian Institution. The cultural drama p123-35
Beardsley, T. S. The Hispanic impact upon the United States. *In* The Immigrant experience in America p 9-43
De la Garza, R. O. and Rivera, R. The socio-political world of the Chicano: a comparative analysis of social scientific and literary perspectives. *In* Minority language and literature p42-64

Books and reading
Trejo, A. D. Of books and libraries. *In* Trejo, A. D. ed. The Chicanos p167-86

Civil rights
De la Garza, R. O. The politics of Mexican Americans. *In* Trejo, A. D. ed. The Chicanos p101-20

Education
Ballesteros, D. Bilingual-bicultural education: a must for Chicanos. *In* Trejo, A. D. ed. The Chicanos p151-65
Guerra, M. H. Bilingualism and biculturalism: assets for Chicanos. *In* Trejo, A. D. ed. The Chicanos p121-32

Education—Spanish language
Fallis, G. V. Spanish language programs for Hispanic minorities: current needs and priorities. *In* Minority language and literature p86-98

Ethnic identity
Lux, G. and Vigil, M. E. Return to Aztlan: the Chicano rediscovers his Indian past. *In* Trejo, A. D. eds. The Chicanos p 1-17
Ramos, R. The Mexican American: am I who they say I am? *In* Trejo, A. D. ed. The Chicanos p49-66
Velez-I, C. G. Ourselves through the eyes of an anthropologist. *In* Trejo, A. D. ed. The Chicanos p37-48

History
Bacalski-Martínez, R. R. Aspects of Mexican American cultural heritage. *In* Trejo, A. D. ed. The Chicanos p19-35

Politics and suffrage
De la Garza, R. O. The politics of Mexican Americans. *In* Trejo, A. D. ed. The Chicanos p101-20

Social life and customs
Bacalski-Martínez, R. R. Aspects of Mexican American cultural heritage. *In* Trejo, A. D. ed. The Chicanos p19-35
Gonzales, S A. The Chicana perspective: a design for self-awareness. *In* Trejo, A. D. ed. The Chicanos p81-99

Suffrage
See Mexican Americans—Politics and suffrage

Women
See Mexican American women

Arizona
Granger, B. H. Some aspects of folk medicine among Spanish-speaking people in southern Arizona. *In* American folk medicine p191-202

New Mexico—Santa Fe
Bailey, D. T. and Haulman, B. E. Ethnic differences on the Southwestern United States frontier, 1860. *In* Miller, D. H. and Steffen, J. O. eds. The frontier p243-57

Rio Grande Valley
Evans, J. L. Ethnic tensions in the Lower Rio Grande Valley to 1860. *In* Yoder, D. ed. American folklife p239-55

Texas
Graham, J. S. The role of the curandero in the Mexican American folk medicine system in west Texas. *In* American folk medicine p175-89

Texas—Politics and suffrage
Shockley, J. S. Landless laborers and the Chicano movement in south Texas. *In* Forging nations: a comparative view of rural ferment and revolt p128-49

Texas—San Antonio
Bailey, D. T. and Haulman, B. E. Ethnic differences on the Southwestern United States frontier, 1860. *In* Miller, D. H. and Steffen, J. O. eds. The frontier p243-57

Mexican Americans and libraries. See Libraries and Mexican Americans

Mexican Americans in literature

De la Garza, R. O. and Rivera, R. The socio-political world of the Chicano: a comparative analysis of social scientific and literary perspectives. *In* Minority language and literature p42-64

Mexican art objects. See Art objects, Mexican

Mexican fiction

History and criticism

Leal, L. Native and foreign influence in contemporary Mexican fiction: a search for identity. *In* Forster, M. H. ed. Tradition and renewal p102-28

Mexican folk-lore. See Folk-lore, Mexican

Mexican hieroglyphics. See Indians of Mexico—Writing

Mexican literature

History and criticism

Meyer, V. J. The images of women in contemporary Mexican literature. *In* Roberts, J. I. ed. Beyond intellectual sexism p210-28

Mexican national characteristics. See National characteristics, Mexican

Mexicans in California

Servín, M. P. California's Hispanic heritage: a view into the Spanish myth. *In* Weber, D. J. ed. New Spain's far northern frontier p117-33

Mexicans in the United States

Bustamante, J. A. The "Wetback" as deviant: an application of labeling theory. *In* Davis, F. J. and Stivers, R. eds. The collective definition of deviance p256-67

See also Mexican Americans

Mexico

Antiquities

Grove, D. C. The highland Olmec manifestation: a consideration of what it is and isn't. *In* Mesoamerican archaeology p109-28

Pailes, R. A. and Whitecotton, J. W. The greater Southwest and the Mesoamerican "world" system: an exploratory model of frontier relationships. *In* The Frontier v2 p105-21

Willey, G. R. The rise of Maya civilization: a summary view. *In* The Origins of Maya civilization p383-423

Williams, G. External influences and the upper RioVerde drainage basin at Los Altos, West Mexico. *In* Mesoamerican archaeology p21-50

Constitution

Baldwin, F. N. Constitutional limitations on government in Mexico, the United States, and Uganda. *In* Claude, R. P. ed. Comparative human rights p76-98

Constitutional law

Baldwin, F. N. Constitutional limitations on government in Mexico, the United States, and Uganda. *In* Claude, R. P. ed. Comparative human rights p76-98

Economic conditions

Cockcroft, J. D. Mexico. *In* Chilcote, R. H. and Edelstein, J. C. eds. Latin America: the struggle with dependency and beyond p222-303

Foreign relations—United States

Haley, P. E. Comparative intervention: Mexico in 1914 & Dominica in 1965. *In* Higham, R. D. ed. Intervention or abstention: the dilemma of American foreign policy p40-59

History—Spanish colony, 1540-1810

Faulk, O. B. The presidio: fortress or farce? *In* Weber, D. J. ed. New Spain's far northern frontier p67-76

García Navarro, L. The North of New Spain as a political problem in the eighteenth century. *In* Weber, D. J. ed. New Spain's far northern frontier p201-15

Park, J. F. Spanish Indian policy in northern Mexico, 1765-1810. *In* Weber, D. J. ed. New Spain's far northern frontier p217-34

History—1910-1946

Katz, F. Peasants in the Mexican Revolution of 1910. *In* Forging nations: a comparative view of rural ferment and revolt p61-85

Politics and government—1910-1946

Katz, F. Peasants in the Mexican Revolution of 1910. *In* Forging nations: a comparative view of rural ferment and revolt p61-85

Religion—Bibliography

Vázquez, J. A. The religions of Mexico and of Central and South America. *In* Adams, C. J. ed. A reader's guide to the great religions p78-89

Social conditions

Cockcroft, J. D. Mexico. *In* Chilcote, R. H. and Edelstein, J. C. eds. Latin America: the struggle with dependency and beyond p222-303

Social life and customs

Kearney, M. A world-view explanation of the evil eye. *In* The Evil eye p175-92

Mexico in literature

Walker, R. G. The fascination of Mexico. *In* Walker, R. G. Infernal paradise p 1-27

Meyendorff, Jean

The Church. *In* Auty, R. and Obolensky, D. eds. An introduction to Russian history p315-30

Meyendorff, John. See Meyendorff, Jean

Meyer, Alfred G.

Marxism and the women's movement. *In* Women in Russia p84-112

Meyer, Bernard C.

Truth and the physician. *In* Weir, R. F. ed. Ethical issues in death and dying p42-54

About individual works

Joseph Conrad

Crews, F. C. Conrad's uneasiness—and ours. *In* Crews, F. C. Out of my system p41-62

Meyer, Conrad Ferdinand

About individual works

A boy suffers

Swales, M. Meyer: Das Leiden eines Knaben. *In* Swales, M. The German Novelle p180-201

Meyer, Donald Harvey

American intellectuals and the Victorian crisis of faith. *In* Howe, D. W. ed. Victorian America p59-77

The democratic Enlightenment

Contents

The American achievement
Benjamin Franklin and the art of virtue
The civilized Americans
The critical period in American intellectual history

Meyer, Donald H.
The democratic Enlightenment
Contents—Continued
The ethics of belief and the conduct of the mind
From piety to moralism
John Adams and the scenery of politics
John Witherspoon and the education of the public conscience
Jonathan Edwards and the reality of the unseen
Political mechanics and the new consciousness
Religion and the experimental method of reasoning
Science, rhetoric, and revolution
Thomas Jefferson and the rhetoric of republicanism
William Ellery Channing and the inward enlightenment

Meyer, Ernest
The bilateral and multilateral meetings of the International Press Institute. *In* Unofficial diplomats p56-65

Meyer, Hans

About individual works
Zur deutschen Literatur der Zeit
Kurz, P. K. Hans Mayer: on German literature today. *In* Kurz, P. K. On modern German literature v2 p155-60

Meyer, Heinrich
Some remarks about German-American relations. *In* The German contribution to the building of the Americas p359-72

Meyer, Leonard B.
Forgery and the anthropology of art; excerpt from "Music, the arts and ideas." *In* Aagaard-Mogensen, L. ed. Culture and art p53-66

Meyer, Marc Anthony
Land charters and the legal position of Anglo-Saxon womn. *In* Kanner, B. ed. The women of England p57-82

Meyer, Victoria Junco
The images of women in contemporary Mexican literature. *In* Roberts, J. I. ed. Beyond intellectual sexism p210-28

Meyer-Dohm, Peter
Investments in communication and the development process. *In* Fischer, H. D. and Merrill, J. C. eds. International and intercultural communication p226-35

Meyerowitz, Joseph H.
Dying: dromenon versus drama. *In* Anticipatory grief p79-93

Meyers, B. David
An analysis of OAU's effectiveness at regional collective defense. *In* El-Ayouty, Y. ed. The Organization of African Unity after ten years p118-32

Meyers, Charles J.
The covenant of habitability and the American Law Institute. *In* Stanford legal essays p355-79

Meyers, Jeffrey
A fever at the core
Contents
André Malraux
Gabriele D'Annunzio
Robert Bontine Cunninghame Graham
Roger Casement
T. E. Lawrence
Wilfred Scawen Blunt

Homosexuality and literature, 1890-1930
Contents
Conrad: Victory
D. H. Lawrence: The white peacock, Women in love, Aaron's rod, The plumed serpent
Forster: A room with a view, Maurice, The life to come
Gide: The immoralist
Mann and Musil: Death in Venice and Young Törless
Proust: Cities of the plain
T. E. Lawrence: Seven pillars of wisdom
Wilde: The picture of Dorian Gray
Painting and the novel
Contents
Bellini, Giotto, Mantegna, Botticelli and Swann's way
Bronzino, Veronese and The wings of the dove
Dürer and Doctor Faustus
Fra Angelico and The rainbow
Ghirlandaio and Where angels fear to tread; Giotto and A room with a view
Greuze and The Leopard
Guido Reni and The marble faun
Gustave Moreau and Against nature
Holbein and The idiot
Mark Gertler and Women in love
Maurice Greiffenhagen and The white peacock
Van Eyck and The Fall
Vermeer and The captive

Meyers, Mary Ann
Gates ajar: death in Mormon thought and practice. *In* Death in America p112-33

Meyersohn, Rolf B.
Abundance reconsidered. *In* On the making of Americans p87-104

Meynell, Hugo Anthony
The intelligibility of the universe. *In* Reason and religion p23-43

Michael, Nancy C.
The relationship between the 1609 quarto of Pericles and Wilkins' Painful aduentures. *In* Tulane studies in English v22 p51-68

Michael, Wolfgang Friedrich
Lessing and Molière. *In* Johnson, R. B.; Neumann, E. S. and Trail, G. T. eds. Molière and the commonwealth of letters: patrimony and posterity p271-75

Michaelis, Christian Friedrich

About

Temkin, O. A postscript to "Merrem's youthful dream." *In* Temkin, O. The double face of Janus p510-11

Michaels, James Williams, and Green, Dan S.
Behavioral sociology: emergent forms and issues. *In* McNall, S. G. ed. Theoretical perspectives in sociology p187-98

Michaels, Ruth. See Buckley, I. G. jt. auth.

Michaels, Walter Benn
Walden's false bottoms. *In* Glyph I p132-49

Michaelsen, Robert
The Beecher family: microcosm of a chapter in the evolution of religious sensibility in America. *In* Reynolds, F. E. and Capps, D. eds. The biographical process p253-71

Michaelson, Katherine
  The first photographic record of a scientific conference. *In* One hundred years of photographic history p109-16

Michałowski, Kazimierz
  Deir el Bahari. *In* The Frontiers of human knowledge p163-69

Michals, Duane

About individual works
Journey of the spirit after death
  Barrow, T . Three photographers and their books. *In* One hundred years of photographic history p7-14

Michelangelo. See Buonarroti, Michel Angelo

Michelet, Jules

About
  Haac, O. A. Faith in the Enlightenment: Voltaire and Rousseau seen by Michelet. *In* Studies in eighteenth-century culture v7 p475-90

Michelini, Ann
  ΥΒΡΙΣ and plants. *In* Harvard Studies in classical philology v82 p35-44

Michelson, Peter
  On The Purple Sage, Chicago Review, and Big Table. *In* Anderson, E. and Kinzie, M. eds. The little magazine in America: a modern documentary history p341-75

  The **Michelson**-Morley experiment: descriptive dependence on to-be-tested theories. Laymon, R. L. *In* Motion and time, space and matter p436-64

Michi. See Tivi (African people)

The **Michigan** Alcidamas-papyrus: a problem in methodology. Renehan, R. *In* Harvard Studies in classical philology v75 p85-105

Michigan papyrus 2754 and the Certamen. Koniaris, G. L. *In* Harvard Studies in classical philology v75 p107-29

Mickelsen, A. Berkeley
  The metaphorical language of theology: its experiential base—Biblical and contemporary. *In* Current issues in Biblical and patristic interpretation p346-54

Mickelson, Anne Z.
  Reaching out: sensitivity and order in recent American fiction by women

Contents
Erica Jong: flying or grounded?
Gail Godwin: order and accommodation
Joan Didion: the hurting woman
Lois Gould: the musical chairs of power
Piecemeal liberation: Marge Piercy, Sara Davidson, Marilyn French, Grace Paley
Sexual love in the fiction of Joyce Carol Oates
Winging upward: Black women: Sarah E. Wright, Toni Morrison, Alice Walker

Mickiewicz, Adam

About individual works
The books of the Polish nation and of the Polish pilgrimage
  Duker, A. G. Adam Mickiewicz's antiJewish period: studies in "The books of the Polish nation and of the Polish pilgrimage." *In* Salo Wittmayer Baron v 1 p311-43

Crimean sonnets
  Stankiewicz, E. Sound and sight in the Sonety krymskie of Adam Mickiewicz. *In* For Wiktor Weintraub p493-503

Forefathers
  Giergielewicz, M. Priests and exorcists in Mickiewicz's Forefathers. *In* For Wiktor Weintraub p135-50

Characters
  Giergielewicz, M. Priests and exorcists in Mickiewicz's Forefathers. *In* For Wiktor Weintraub p135-50

Microeconomics
  Richardson, G. B. Adam Smith on competition and increasing returns. *In* Skinner, A. S. and Wilson, T. eds. Essays on Adam Smith p350-60

Microscope and microscopy. See Histology

Microscopic anatomy. See Histology

Middeldorf, Ulrich
  Some Florentine painted Madonna reliefs. *In* Collaboration in Italian Renaissance art p77-90

Middendorf, John Harlan
  Johnson on the couch. *In* Review, v 1 1979 p 1-12

Middle Ages
  Hallam, H. E. The medieval social picture. *In* Kamenka, E. and Neale, R. S. eds. Feudalism, capitalism and beyond p28-49

  Lopez, R. S. The culture of the medieval merchant. *In* Medieval and Renaissance studies 1976 p52-73

  See also Architecture, Medieval; Church history—Middle Ages, 600-1500; Civilization, Medieval; Literature, Medieval; Renaissance; Science, Medieval; and similar headings

Biography
See Biography—Middle Ages, 500-1500

Historiography
  Aston, M. E. Huizinga's harvest: England and The waning of the Middle Ages. *In* Medievalia et humanistica; new ser. no. 9 p 1-24

  Funkenstein, A. Periodization and self-understanding in the Middle Ages and early modern times. *In* Medievalia et humanistica no. 5 p3-23

  Ray, R. D. Medieval historiography through the twelfth century: problems and progress of research. *In* Viator: medieval and Renaissance studies v5 p33-59

  Sullivan, R. E. The Middle Ages in the Western tradition: some reconsiderations. *In* Essays on medieval civilization p3-31

History
  Lewis, A. R. Northern European sea power and the Straits of Gibraltar, 1031-1350 A.D. *In* Order and innovation in the Middle Ages p139-64

  Lopez, R. S. The practical transmission of medieval culture. *In* Jeffrey, D. L. ed. By things seen: reference and recognition in medieval thought p125-42

  White, L. T. The Crusades and the technological thrust of the West. *In* War, technology and society in the Middle East p97-112

  See also Chivalry; Church history—Middle Ages, 600-1500; Civilization, Medieval; Crusades; Feudalism; Knights and knighthood; Monasticism and religious orders—Middle Ages, 600-1500; Twelfth century; Thirteenth century

Middle Ages—*Continued*

History—Data processing

Herlihy, D. Computer-assisted analysis of the statistical documents of medieval society. *In* Powell, J. M. ed. Medieval studies p185-211

Middle Ages (The phrase)

Edelman, N. The early uses of medium aevum, moyen age, Middle Ages. *In* Edelman, N. The eye of the beholder p58-81

Edelman, N. Other early uses of moyen age and moyen temps. *In* Edelman, N. The eye of the beholder p82-85

Middle classes

Mayer, A. J. The lower middle class as historical problem. *In* Small comforts for hard times p220-45

Neale, R. S. 'The bourgeoisie, historically, has played a most revolutionary part.' *In* Kamenka, E. and Neale, R. S. eds. Feudalism, capitalism and beyond p84-102

Smithey, R. A. The new militancy and its impact on the Afro-American middle class. *In* Johnson, H. A. ed. Negotiating the mainstream p196-216

France—History

Larkin, M. Une société embourgeoisée? Balzac's France. *In* Larkin, M. Man and society in nineteenth-century realism p42-51

Lucas, C. R. Nobles, bourgeois and the origins of the French Revolution. *In* French society and the Revolution p88-131

Middle classes in literature

Tomlinson, T. B. The novel and middle-class England. *In* Tomlinson, T. B. The Engilsh middle-class novel p7-20

Middle East. See Near East

Middle East in literature. See Near East in literature

Middle English. See English language—Middle English, 1100-1500; English literature—Middle English, 1100-1500

Middle West

Antiquities

Ford, R. I. Evolutionary ecology and the evolution of human ecosystems: a case study from the Midwestern U.S.A. *In* Explanation of prehistoric change p153-84

Middle West in literature

Holman, C. H. Anodyne for the village virus. *In* Holman, C. H. Windows on the world p48-60

Middleburg Psalms. Temperley, N. *In* Virginia. University. Bibliographical Society. Studies in bibliography v30 p162-70

Middlekauff, Robert M.

Piety and intellect in Puritanism. *In* Mulder, J. M. and Wilson, J. F. eds. Religion in American history p74-85

Middleton, Charles. See Barham, Charles Middleton, 1st Baron

Middleton, Drew

Russian presence and economic interests in the Mediterranean and the Indian Ocean. *In* The New world balance and peace in the Middle East: reality or mirage? p43-49

Middleton, John Christopher

Bolshevism in art

Contents

The alienated self

The art of unreason

'Bolshevism in art': dada and politics

Dada versus expressionism, or The red king's dream

An enigma transfigured in Hermann Hesse's Glasperlenspiel

Hermann Hesse's Morgenlandfahrt

Mörike's moonchild: a reading of the poem 'Auf eine Christblume'

Notes on rhythm

Notes on some poems 1964/5

On translating a text by Franz Mon

Paragraphs on translation

Pattern without predictability, or Pythagoras saved: a comment on Kurt Schwitters' 'Gedicht 25'

The picture of nobody: some remarks on Robert Walser

Remarks at the Québec international meeting of writers, October 1974

Rilke's Birth of Venus

The rise of primitivism and its relevance to the poetry of expressionism and dada

Thomas Mann's letters to Paul Amann and Karl Kerényi

Two mountain scenes in Novalis and the question of symbolic style

Middleton, Thomas

See also Dekker, T. jt. auth.

About

Eliot, T. S. From Thomas Middleton. *In* Eliot, T. S. Selected prose of T. S. Eliot p189-95

Paster, G. K. The city in Plautus and Middleton. *In* Renaissance drama [1973] p29-44

About individual works

A chaste maid in Cheapside

Hibbard, G. R. Love, marriage and money in Shakespeare's theatre and Shakespeare's England. *In* The Elizabethan theatre, VI p134-55

Women beware women

Champion, L. S. Middleton: Women beware women, The changeling. *In* Champion, L. S. Tragic patterns in Jacobean and Caroline drama p152-79

Lancaster, M. S. Middleton's use of the upper stage in Women beware women. *In* Tulane studies in English v22 p69-85

Stilling, R. Thomas Middleton. *In* Stilling, R. Love and death in Renaissance tragedy p247-65

Bibliography

Brooks, J. B. Thomas Middleton. *In* Logan, T. P. and Smith, D. S. ed. The popular school p51-84

Dramaturgy

See Middleton, Thomas—Technique

Style

See Middleton, Thomas—Technique

Technique

Lancaster, M. S. Middleton's use of the upper stage in Women beware women. *In* Tulane studies in English v22 p69-85

Middleton, Thomas, and Rowley, William

About individual works

The changeling

Champion, L. S. Middleton: Women beware women, The changeling. *In* Champion, L. S. Tragic patterns in Jacobean and Caroline drama p152-79

Middleton, Thomas, and Rowley, William—
About individual works—The changeling—
Continued

Salingar, L. 'The changeling' and the drama of domestic life. *In* English Association. Essays and studies, 1979 p80-96

Stilling, R. Thomas Middleton. *In* Stilling, R. Love and death in Renaisance tragedy p247-65

A faire quarrell

Johnson, G. D. The printing of A faire quarrell, Q2. *In* Virginia. University. Bibliographical Society. Studies in bibliography v29 p288-92

Kistner, A. L. and Kistner, M. K. The themes and structures of a A fair quarrel. *In* Tennessee Studies in literature v23 p31-46

Midgley, E. B. F.
Natural law and the renewal of the philosophy of international relations. *In* The Year book of world affairs, 1975 p121-36

Midrash
Fischel, H. A. The transformation of wisdom in the world of Midrash. *In* Aspects of wisdom in Judaism and early Christianity p67-101

Leviant, C. Jewish influence upon Arthurian legends. *In* Salo Wittmayer Baron v2 p639-56

Folk-lore

See Folk-lore—Jews

A midsummer night's dream (criticism)
Shakespeare, W. *In* Kauffmann, S. Persons of the drama p51-62

A midsummer night's dream (Motion picture by Max Reinhardt and William Dieterle)
Jorgens, J. J. Max Reinhardt and William Dieterle's A midsummer night's dream. *In* Jorgens, J.J. Shakespeare on film p36-50

A midsummer night's dream (Motion picture by Peter Hall)
Jorgens, J. J. Peter Hall's A midsummer night's dream. *In* Jorgens, J. J. Shakespeare on film p51-65

Midwest. See Middle West

Midwestern States. See Middle West

Midwives

United States

Donegan, J. B. Man-midwifery and the delicacy of the sexes. *In* "Remember the ladies": new perspectives on women in American history p90-109

Mies van der Rohe, Ludwig

About

Carter, P. Mies van der Rohe. *In* Sharp, D. ed. The rationalists p59-72

Miettinen, Jorma K.
Can conventional new technologies and new tactics replace tactical nuclear weapons in Europe? *In* Arms control and technological innovation p52-69

Mignard, Pierre

About

Miller, E. M. Molière and the court painters, especially Pierre Mignard. *In* Johnson, R. B.; Neumann, E. S. and Trail, G. T. eds. Molière and the commonwealth of letters: patrimony and posterity p5-30

Migrant labor

United States

Coles, R. "God save them, those children: and for allowing such a state of affairs to continue, God save us, too"; excerpt from "Uprooted children." *In* Gross, B. and Gross, R. eds. The children's rights movement p118-22

Migration, Internal
See also Cities and towns—Growth; Land settlement; Residential mobility

Research—United States

Merrens, H. R. Settlement of the colonial Atlantic seaboard. *In* Pattern and process p235-43

Africa

Lamphear, J. Two basic themes in African history: migration and state formation. *In* Martin, P. M. and O'Meara, P. eds. Africa p83-97

Argentine Republic—History

Solberg, C. Mass migrations in Argentina, 1870-1970. *In* Human migration p146-70

China

Lee, J. Migration and expansion in Chinese history. *In* Human migration p20-47

Europe

Hume, I. M. Some economic aspects of labour migration in Europe since the Second World War. *In* Economic factors in population growth p491-509

Russia

Bennigsen, A. A. and Wimbush, S. E. Migration and political control: Soviet Europeans in Soviet Central Asia. *In* Human migration p173-87

United States

Morrison, P. A. and Wheeler, J. P. The image of "elsewhere" in the American tradition of migration. *In* Human migration p75-84

Taeuber, K. E. and Taeuber, A. F. The Black population in the United States. *In*

Migration, Rural-urban. See Rural-urban migration

Migrations of man. See Man—Migrations
The Black American reference book p159-206

Mihajlov, Mihajlo
Underground notes
Contents
The absurdity of nonideology
The artist as the enemy
Comments on The unperfect society
Djilas versus Marx: the theory of alienation
Dostoyevsky on the Catholic "Left"
Letter to a friend in the West
Mystical experiences of the labor camps
A new approach to Anna Karenina
On responsibility: Marx and Lenin in their personal lives
The phenomenology of the Kingdom of Lies
Religious rebirth
Russia and communism
The shoots of hope
Some timely thoughts (concerning Letter to the Soviet leaders by A. Solzhenitsyn)
Three paradoxes
Two convergences
The way into the impasse

Mije Indians. See Mixe Indians

Mikalson, Jon Dennis
Ennius' usage of is ea id. *In* Harvard Studies in classical philology v80 p171-77

Mikdashi, Zuhayr M.
The OPEC process. *In* Vernon, R. ed. The oil crisis p203-15

Mikesell, Marvin W.
The rise and decline of "sequent occupance": a chapter in the history of American geography. *In* Geographies of the mind p149-69

Milani, Ken
It doesn't add up: the role of human resource accounting in effecting work humanization. *In* Heisler, W. J. and Houck, J. W. eds. A matter of dignity p179-95

Milani-Comparetti, Marco
Genetics and adolescent development: perspectives for the future. *In* Adolescence and youth in prospect p137-47

Milenky, Edward S.
The Cartagena Agreement in transition. *In* The Year book of world affairs, 1979 p167-79

Miles, Rosalind
A baby god: the creative dynamism of Emily Brontë's poetry. *In* Smith, A. ed. The art of Emily Brontë p68-93
The women of Wessex. *In* Smith, A. ed. The novels of Thomas Hardy p23-44

Milford, Nancy

About individual works
Zelda
Connolly, C. Scott and Zelda Fitzgerald. *In* Connolly, C. The evening colonnade p273-76

Milgram, Stanley

About
Koestler, A. Ad majorem gloriam . . . . *In* Koestler, A. Janus p77-97

About individual works
Obedience to authority
Marcus, S. Authority and obedience. *In* Marcus, S. Representations p17-27

Miliband, Ralph
A state of desubordination. *In* Kramnick, I. ed. Is Britain dying? p152-65

Milieu therapy. See Therapeutic community

Militarism

United States
Kamman, W. Militarism. *In* Encyclopedia of American foreign policy p545-56

Military aid. See Military assistance

Military and civilian power. See Civil supremacy over the military

Military architecture. See Limes (Roman boundary)

Military art and science
Guerlac, H. Vauban: the impact of science on war. *In* Guerlac, H. Essays and papers in the history of modern science p413-39
Miettinen, J. K. Can conventional new technologies and new tactics replace tactical nuclear weapons in Europe? *In* Arms control and technological innovation p52-69
Williams, R. Science, technology, and the future of warfare. *In* Beaumont, R. A. and Edmonds, M. eds. War in the next decade p157-79

See also Armaments; Armies; Biological warfare; Chemical warfare; Command of troops; Intrenchments; Ordnance; Spies; Strategy; War

History
Bosworth, C. E. Armies of the Prophet. *In* Lewis, B. ed. Islam and the Arab world p201-24
Collins, L. J. D. The military organization and tactics of the Crimean Tatars, 16th-17th centuries. *In* War, technology and society in the Middle East p257-76
Parry, V. S. La manière de combattre. *In* War, technology and society in the Middle East p218-56

Early works to 1800—History and criticism
Hale, J. R. Printing and military culture of Renaissance Venice. *In* Medievalia et humanistica no. 8 p21-62

Military assistance, American

Great Britain
Carlton, D. The British independent nuclear deterrent and the future of European security. *In* International terrorism and world security p277-94

Military assistance, Cuban

Angola
Valdés, N. P. Revolutionary solidarity in Angola. *In* Cuba in the world p87-117

Military assistance, Russian

Near East
Ofer, G. Economic aspects of Soviet involvement in the Middle East. *In* Ro'i, Y. ed. The limits to power p67-93

Military capitulations. See Capitulations, Military

Military-civil relations. See Civil supremacy over the military

Military government
Dudley, B. J. Military government and national integration in Nigeria. *In* Smock, D. R. and Bentsi-Enchill, K. eds. The search for national integration in Africa p28-46

Military history
Brett, M. The military interest of the Battle of Haydarān. *In* War, technology and society in the Middle East p78-88
Hill, D. R. The role of the camel and the horse in the early Arab conquests. *In* War, technology and society in the Middle East p32-43

See also Military art and science—History; Military policy; also subdivision History, Military under names of countries, cities, etc., e.g. Venice—History, Military

Military history, Medieval
Bosworth, C. E. Recruitment, muster, and review in medieval Islamic armies. *In* War, technology and society in the Middle East p59-77
McNab, B. Obligations of the Church in English society: military arrays of the clergy, 1369-1418. *In* Order and innovation in the Middle Ages p293-314
White, L. T. The Crusades and the technological thrust of the West. *In* War, technology and society in the Middle East p97-112

Military history, Modern

19th century

Yapp, M. E. The modernization of Middle Eastern armies in the nineteenth century: a comparative view. *In* War, technology and society in the Middle East p330-66

20th century

Kendel, I. 116 wars in 30 years. *In* Arms control and technological innovation p303-21

The military-industrial complex. Trask, D. F. *In* Encyclopedia of American foreign policy p557-66

Military intervention. See Intervention (International law)

Military law. See Air Force law

Military personnel. See Soldiers

Military personnel and drugs. See Drugs and military personnel

Military policy
Packard, D. Perceptions of the military balance. *In* The New Atlantic challenge p203-16

Sapolsky, H. M. Science, technology and military policy. *In* Science, technology and society p443-71

See also Deterrence (Strategy); Limited war; National security

Underdeveloped areas

See Underdeveloped areas—Military policy

Military posts

Spain—Colonies—America

Faulk, O. B. The presidio: fortress or farce? *In* Weber, D. J. ed. New Spain's far northern frontier p67-76

Military power. See Armies; Disarmament

Military research
Brooks, H. The military innovation system and the qualitative arms race. *In* Long, F. A. and Rathjens, G. W. eds. Arms, defense policy, and arms control p75-97

Steinbruner, J. D. and Carter, B. Organizational and political dimensions of the strategic posture: the problems of reform. *In* Long, F. A. and Rathjens, G. W. eds. Arms, defense policy, and arms control p131-54

United States

Rapoport, A. Classified military research and the university. *In* Fairfield, R. P. ed. Humanistic frontiers in American education p54-60

Military science. See Military art and science

Military service, Compulsory

United States

Kennedy, T. C. Conscription. *In* Encyclopedia of American foreign policy p151-57

Military service as a profession. See Armed Forces—Vocational guidance

Military strategy. See Strategy

Milky Way
Bok, B. J. Harlow Shapley and the discovery of the center of our galaxy. *In* Neyman, J. ed. The heritage of Copernicus: theories "pleasing to the mind" p26-62

Goldsmith, D. W. Edwin Hubble and the universe outside our galaxy. *In* Neyman, J. ed. The heritage of Copernicus: theories "pleasing to the mind" p63-94

Mill, James

About

Mazlish, B. The Mills: father and son. *In* Explorations in psychohistory p136-48

Mill, John Stuart
Essays on poetry

Contents
Browning's Pauline
Poems and romances of Alfred de Vigny
Tennyson's poems
The two kinds of poetry
What is poetry?

About

Chadwick, O. On liberalism. *In* Chadwick, O. The secularization of the European mind in the nineteenth century p21-47

Colmer, J. The utilitarian approach. *In* Colmer, J. Coleridge to Catch-22 p30-43

Dworkin, G. Paternalism. *In* The Abdication of philosophy: philosophy and the public good p209-27

Also in Laslett, P. and Fishkin, J. eds. Philosophy politics and society p78-96

Knights, B. The reconstruction of opinion: John Stuart Mill. *In* Knights, B. The idea of the clerisy in the nineteenth century p140-77

Mazlish, B. The Mills: father and son. *In* Explorations in psychohistory p136-48

Quinton, A. Utilitarian ethics. *In* New studies in ethics v2 p 1-118

Sanders, C. R. The letters of John Stuart Mill. *In* Sanders, C. R. Carlyle's friendships, and other studies p282-86

Spivey, E. Carlyle and the logic-choppers: J. S. Mill and Diderot. *In* Carlyle and his contemporaries p60-73

About individual works

Autobiography

Fleishman, A. Personal myth: three Victorian autobiographers. *In* Landow, G. P. ed. Approaches to Victorian autobiography p215-34

Gelpi, B. C. The innocent I: Dickens' influence on Victorian autobiography. *In* The Worlds of Victorian fiction p57-71

Griffin, A. The interior garden and John Stuart Mill. *In* Knoepflmacher, U. C. and Tennyson, G. B. eds. Nature and the Victorian imagination p171-86

On liberty

Wollheim, R. Bertrand Russell and the liberal tradition. *In* Nakhnikian, G. ed. Bertrand Russell's philosophy p209-20

Political science

Knights, B. The reconstruction of opinion: John Stuart Mill. *In* Knights, B. The idea of the clerisy in the nineteenth century p140-77

Millais, Sir John Everett, bart.

About

Williamson, A. Hunt and Millais: retreat to respectibility. *In* Williamson, A. Artist and writers in revolt p62-84

Millar, Kenneth

About

Hartman, G. H. Literature high and low: the case of the mystery story. *In* Hartman, G. H. The fate of reading p203-22

About individual works

The underground man

Welty, E. Ross Macdonald's The underground man. *In* Welty, E. The eye of the story p251-60

Millay, Edna St Vincent

About

Eckman, F. Edna St Vincent Millay: notes toward a reappraisal. *In* Filler, L. ed. A question of quality: popularity and value in modern creative writing p193-203

Stanbrough, J. Edna St. Vincent Millay and the language of vulnerability. *In* Gilbert, S. M. and Gubar, S. eds. Shakespeare's sisters p183-99

Millay, Edna St. Vincent. See Dillon, G. jt. tr.

Millenarianism. See Millenialism

Millennialism

Lebra, T. S. Social psychological change. *In* Lauer, R. H. ed. Social movements and social change p127-43

Rosen, G. An analgesic strategy. *In* Lauer, R. H. ed. Social movements and social change p97-106

Bibliography

Smith, T. L. Social reform: some reflections on causation and consequence. *In* The Rise of Adventism p18-29

History

Butler, J. M. Adventism and the American experience. *In* The Rise of Adventism p173-206

Sandeen, E. R. Millennialism. *In* The Rise of Adventism p104-18

United States

Maclear, J. F. The Republic and the millennium. *In* Mulder, J. M. and Wilson, J. F. eds. Religion in American history p181-98

Millennianism. See Millennialism

Millennium

Maclear, J. F. New England and the Fifth Monarchy: the quest for the millennium in early American Puritanism. *In* Vaughan, A. T. and Bremer, F. J. eds. Puritan New England p66-91

See also Millenialism

History of doctrines

Lowance, M. I. Typology and millennial eschatology in early New England. *In* Miner, E. R. ed. Literary uses of typology p228-73

Miller, Abraham H.

The ethics of teaching political science: another perspective. *In* Hook, S.; Kurtz, P. and Todorovich, M. eds. The ethics of teaching and scientific research p43-48

Miller, Aloysius J. See Part 2 under title: Postwar trends in Japan

Miller, Arthur, 1915-

The theater essays of Arthur Miller

Contents

The American theater
Arthur Miller vs. Lincoln Center
Brewed in The crucible
Broadway, from O'Neill to now
The family in modern drama
Foreword to After the fall
Introduction to A view from the bridge (Two-act version)
Introduction to the Collected plays
It could happen here—and did
Journey to The crucible
Many writers: few plays
The nature of tragedy
1956 and all this
On adaptations

On recognition
On social plays
On the theater in Russia
Preface to an adaptation of Ibsen's An enemy of the people
The Salesman has a birthday
The shadows of the gods
Tragedy and the common man
What makes plays endure?

About

Brashear, W. R. The empty bench: Arthur Miller and social drama. *In* Brashear, W. R. The gorgon's head p134-49

Martin, R. A. Editor's introduction. *In* Miller, A. The theater essays of Arthur Miller p xv-xxxix

Miller, A. Introduction to the Collected plays. *In* Miller, A. The theater essays of Arthur Miller p113-70

Schwarz, A. After the fall. *In* Schwarz, A. From Büchner to Beckett p161-82

Schwarz, A. Society and human passion as a tragic motive. *In* Schwarz, A. From Büchner to Beckett p100-60

About individual works
After the fall

Miller, A. Foreword to After the fall. *In* Miller, A. The theater essays of Arthur Miller p255-57

The creation of the world and other business

Kauffmann, S. The creation of the world and other business. *In* Kauffmann, S. Persons of the drama p230-33

The crucible

Kauffmann, S. The crucible. *In* Kauffmann, S. Persons of the drama p139-42

Miller, A. Brewed in The crucible. *In* Miller, A. The theater essays of Arthur Miller p171-74

Miller, A. It could happen here—and did. *In* Miller, A. The theater essays of Arthur Miller p294-300.

Miller, A. Journey to The crucible. *In* Miller, A. The theater essays of Arthur Miller p27-30

Schwarz, A. The experience of history as fateful. *In* Schwarz, A. From Büchner to Beckett p61-99

Death of a salesman

Kauffmann, S. Death of a salesman. *In* Kauffmann, S. Persons of the drama p142-45

Miller, A. The Salesman has a birthday. *In* Miller, A. The theater essays of Arthur Miller p12-15

A view from the bridge

Miller, A. Introduction to A view from the bridge (Two-act version) *In* Miller, A. The theater essays of Arthur Miller p218-22

Miller, A. What makes play endure? *In* Miller, A. The theater essays of Arthur Miller p258-63

Books and reading

Miller, A. The shadows of the gods. *In* Miller, A. The theater essays of Arthur Miller p175-94

Miller, Arthur Green

The iconography of the painting in the Temple of the Diving God, Tulum, Quintana Roo, Mexico: the twisted cords. *In* Mesoamerican archaeology p167-86

Miller, Arthur I.
Visualization lost and regained: the genesis of the quantum theory in the period 1913-27. *In* Wechsler, J. ed. On aesthetics in science p73-102

Miller, Clarence H.
Donne's "A nocturnall upon S. Lucies day" and the nocturns of matins. *In* Roberts, J. R. ed. Essential articles for the study of John Donne's poetry p305-10

The logic and rhetoric of proverbs in Erasmus's Praise of Folly. *In* Essays on the works of Erasmus p83-98

Miller, David Bolton
The Lübeckers Bartholomäus Ghotan and Nicolaus Bülow in Novgorod and Moscow and the problem of early Western influences on Russian culture. *In* Viator: medieval and Renaissance studies v9 p395-412

Miller, David Harry
State and city in seventeenth-century Muscovy. *In* Hamm, M. F. ed. The city in Russian history p34-52

Miller, David Harry, and Savage, William W.
Ethnic stereotypes and the frontier: a comparative study of Roman and American experience. *In* Miller, D. H. and Steffen, J. O. eds. The frontier p109-37

Miller, David Humphreys
The fur men and explorers meet the Indians. *In* Red Men and hat-wearers p25-45

Miller, David L.
Dominion of the eye in Frost. *In* Frost: centennial essays II p141-58

Miller, Edward
War, taxation and the English economy in the late thirteenth and early fourteenth centuries. *In* War and economic development p11-31

Miller, Elizabeth Maxfield
Molière and the court painters, especially Pierre Mignard. *In* Johnson, R. B.; Neumann, E. S. and Trail, G. T. eds. Molière and the commonwealth of letters: patrimony and posterity p5-30

Miller, Eugene F.
Leo Strauss: the recovery of political philosophy. *In* De Crespigny, A. and Minogue, K. R. eds. Contemporary political philosophers p67-99

Miller, George Armitage
Images and models, similes and metaphors. *In* Ortony, A. ed. Metaphor and thought p202-50

Semantic relations among words. *In* Linguistic theory and psychological reality p60-118

Miller, Gerald E.
An evaluation of the Soviet navy. *In* Kirk, G. L. and Wessell, N. H. eds. The Soviet threat p47-56

Existing systems of command and control. *In* Griffiths, F. and Polanyi, J. C. eds. The dangers of nuclear war p50-66

Miller, Gerald R.
Toward a rhetoric of counterattitudinal advocacy. *In* Rhetoric: a tradition in transition p279-99

Miller, Helen
Henry VIII's unwritten will: grants of lands and honours in 1547. *In* Wealth and power in Tudor England p87-105

Miller, Henry
Patchen: man of anger and light; excerpt from "Stand still like the hummingbird." *In* Morgan, R. G. ed. Kenneth Patchen: a collection of essays p33-42

About

Allen, M. Henry Miller: Yea-sayer. *In* Tennessee Studies in literature v23 p100-10

Ford, H. D. Jack Kahane and the guardian Obelisk. *In* Ford, H. D. Published in Paris p345-84

Shapiro, K. J. The greatest living Patagonian. *In* Shapiro, K. J. The poetry wreck p175-200

About individual works
Genius and lust: a journey through the major writings of Henry Miller, edited by Norman Mailer

Gass, W. H. Food and beast language. *In* Gass, W. H. The world within the word p253-61

Tropic of Cancer

Connolly, C. Henry Miller. *In* Connolly, C. The evening colonnade p293-95

Miller, Howard
Evangelical religion and colonial Princeton. *In* Schooling and society p115-45

Miller, James
The pathos of novelty: Hannah Arendt's image of freedom in the modern world. *In* Hannah Arendt: the recovery of the public world p177-208

Miller, James Edwin
The American quest for a supreme fiction

Contents

The American bard/embarrassed Henry heard himself a-being: John Berryman's "Dream songs"

Bards of the great idea: seekers of the supreme fiction

The care & feeding of long poems: the American epic from Barlow to Berryman

Dreaming of the lost America of love: Allen Ginsberg's "Fall of America"

An epic is a poem containing history: Ezra Pound's "Cantos"

An epic of the modern consciousness: Hart Cranes "Bridge"

How shall I be mirror to this modernity? William Carlos Williams's "Paterson"

Making a mappemunde to include my being: Charles Olson's Maximus poems

Meditations on a recipe for a modern American epic: Wallace Stevens's "Notes toward a supreme fiction"

Personal mood transmuted into epic: T. S. Eliot's "Waste land"

Poetic metamorphoses: Lowell and Berryman (a prologue)

She's here, install'd amid the kitchen ware: Walt Whitman's epic creation

Fitzgerald's Gatsby: the world as ash heap. *In* French, W. G. ed. The twenties p181-202

Sanctuary: Yoknapatawpha's Waste land. *In* Baldwin, K. H. and Kirby, D. K. eds. Individual and community p137-59

Also in French, W. G. ed. The twenties p249-67

Willa Cather and the art of fiction. *In* The Art of Willa Cather p121-55

Miller, James Ivan
Lydgate the hagiographer as literary artist. *In* The Learned and the lewed p279-90

Miller, Jim Wayne
The gift outright: W-Hollow. *In* Le-Master, J. R. and Clarke, M. W. eds. Jesse Stuart p103-16

Miller, John

About
Barnes, J. J. John Miller: first trans-atlantic publisher's agent. *In* Virginia. University. Bibliographical Society. Studies in bibliography v29 p373-79

Miller, John Hawkins
'Temple and sewer': childbirth, prudery, and Victoria Regina. *In* Wohl, A. S. ed. The Victorian family p23-43

Miller, John William
The paradox of cause, and other essays
Contents
Accidents will happen
The ahistoric ideal
Freedom as a characteristic of man in a democratic society
Functioning objects, facts, and artifacts
History and humanism
Idealism and freedom
A meditation on a painting
The midworld
On the problem of knowledge
The paradox of cause
The scholar as man of the world
Utopia and the state
What does art do?

Miller, Jordan Yale
Drama. *In* American literary scholarship, 1974 p373-86
Drama [another essay] *In* American literary scholarship, 1975 p399-416
Expressionism: The waste land enacted. *In* French, W. G. ed. The twenties p439-54
The other O'Neill. *In* French, W. G. ed. The twenties p455-73

Miller, Joseph Calder
The slave trade in Congo and Angola. *In* Kilson, M. L. and Rotberg, R. I. eds. The African diaspora p75-113

Miller, Joseph Hillis, 1928-
Ariadne's thread: repetition and the narrative line. *In* Valdés, M. J. and Miller, O. J. eds. Interpretation of narrative p148-66
Fiction and repetition: Tess of the d'Urbervilles. *In* Forms of modern British fiction p43-71
The linguistic moment in "The wreck of the Deutschland." *In* Young, T. D. ed. The New Criticism and after p47-60
Narrative and history. *In* ELH essays for Earl R. Wasserman p165-83
Nature and the linguistic moment. *In* Knoepflmacher, U. C. and Tennyson, G. B. eds. Nature and the Victorian imagination p440-51
Optic and semiotic in Middlemarch. *In* The Worlds of Victorian fiction p125-45

Miller, Karl
V. S. Naipaul and the new order: a view of The mimic men. *In* Baugh, E. ed. Critics on Caribbean literature p75-83

Miller, L. Keith, and others
The positive community: a strategy for applying behavioral engineering to the redesign of family and community. *In* Behavior modification and families p91-112

Miller, Lewis Holmes
William James, Robert Frost, and "The black cottage." *In* Frost: centennial essays III p368-81

Miller, Nancy K.
Justine, or, The vicious circle. *In* Studies in eighteenth-century culture v5 p215-28

Miller, Owen J.
Reading as a process of reconstruction: a critique of recent structuralist formulations. *In* Valdés, M. J. and Miller, O. J. eds. Interpretation of narrative p19-27

Miller, Paul A.
Administrative orientations from anthropology: thoughts of a college president. *In* Eddy, E. M. and Partridge, W. L. eds. Applied anthropology in America p147-64

Miller, Perry
From the covenant to the revival. *In* Mulder, J. M. and Wilson, J. F. eds. Religion in American history p145-61
The marrow of Puritan divinity. *In* Vaughan, A. T. and Bremer, F. J. eds. Puritan New England p44-65

About individual works
Errand into the wilderness
Bercovitch, S. New England's errand reappraised. *In* Higham, J. and Conkin, P. K. eds. New directions in American intellectual history p85-104

The New England mind: from colony to province
Stoever, W. K. B. "Preparation for salvation." *In* Stoever, W. K. B. 'A faire and easie way to heaven' p192-99

"Preparation for salvation" in seventeenth-century New England
Stoever, W. K. B. "Preparation for salvation." *In* Stoever, W. K. B. 'A faire and easie way to heaven' p192-99

Miller, R. H.
Sir John Harrington's Irish journals. *In* Virginia. University. Bibliographical Society. Studies in bibliography v32 p179-86

Miller, Richard G.
Fort Worth and the Progressive Era: the movement for charter revision, 1899-1907. *In* Essays on urban America p89-125

Miller, Robert F.
The scientific-technical revolution and the Soviet administrative debate. *In* Cocks, P.; Daniels, R. V. and Heer, N. W. eds. The dynamics of Soviet politics p137-55

Miller, Robert H.
Sir John Harington's A supplie or addicion to the catalogue of bishops, to the yeare 1608: composition and text. *In* Virginia. University. Bibliographical Society. Studies in bibliography v30 p145-61

Miller, Ruth, and Katopes, Peter J.
The Harlem Renaissance: Arna W. Bontemps, Countee Cullen, James Weldon Johnson, Claude McKay, and Jean Toomer. *In* Inge, M. T.; Duke, J. M. and Bryer, J. R. eds. Black American writers v 1 p161-86
Modern beginnings: William Wells Brown, Charles Waddell Chesnutt, Martin R. Delany, Paul Laurence Dunbar, Sutton E. Griggs, Frances Ellen Watkins Harper, and Frank J. Webb. *In* Inge, M. T.; Duke, J. M. and Bryer, J. R. eds. Black American writers v 1 p133-60
Slave narratives. *In* Inge, M. T.; Duke, J. M. and Bryer, J. R. eds. Black American writers v 1 p21-46

Miller, Sally M.

Milwaukee: of ethnicity and labor. *In* Stave, B. M. ed. Socialism and the cities p41-71

Miller, Samuel Freeman

About

White, G. E. Miller, Bradley, Field and the reconstructed Constitution. *In* White, G. E. The American judicial tradition p84-108

Miller, Stanley L.

The first laboratory synthesis of organic compounds under primitive earth conditions. *In* Neyman, J. ed. The heritage of Copernicus: theories "pleasing to the mind" p228-42

Miller, Susan

Eighteenth-century play and the game of Tom Jones. *In* A Provision of human nature p83-93

Miller, Walter Benson

White gangs. *In* Henslin, J. M. ed. Deviant life-styles p261-88

Youth gangs in the urban crisis era. *In* Delinquency, crime, and society p91-128

Miller, Walter M.

About

Samuelson, D. N. The lost canticles of Walter M. Miller, Jr. *In* Clareson, T. D. ed. Voices for the future: essays on major science fiction writers v2 p56-81

Miller, William

About

Arthur, D. T. Millerism. *In* The Rise of Adventism p154-72

Miller, William Vaughn

Portraits of the artist: Anderson's fictional storytellers. *In* Anderson, D. D. ed. Sherwood Anderson: dimensions of his literary art p 1-23

Millerites. See Adventists

Millett, John David

Money and other trifles. *In* The Third century p64-71

Millgate, Michael

Faulkner and history. *In* The South and Faulkner's Yoknapatawpha p22-39

Faulkner and the South: some reflections. *In* The South and Faulkner's Yoknapatawpha p195-210

Faulkner's masters. *In* Tulane Studies in English, v23 p143-55

Millhauser, Milton

Great expectations: the three endings. *In* Dickens Studies Annual v2 p267-77

Millhouse; a white comedy (Motion picture)

Kauffmann, S. Millhouse. *In* Kauffmann, S. Living images p77-78

Millikan, Robert Andrews

About

Holton, G. J. Subelectrons, presuppositions, and the Millikan-Ehrenhaft dispute. *In* Historical studies in the physical sciences v9 p161-224

Kargon, R. H. Temple to science: cooperative research and the birth of the California Institute of Technology. *In* Historical studies in the physical sciences v8 p3-31

Millin, Sara Gertrude (Liebson)

About individual works

God's stepchildren

Rabkin, D. Race and fiction: God's stepchildren and Turbott Wolfe. *In* Parker, K. ed. The South African novel in English p77-94

Millon, Henry A.

Some new towns in Italy in the 1930s. *In* Millon, H. A. and Nochlin, L. eds. Art and architecture in the service of politics p326-41

Millon, René Francis

The study of urbanism at Teotihuacan, Mexico. *In* Mesoamerican archaeology p335-62

Mills, David

The two versions of Chester play V: Balaam and Balak. *In* Chaucer and Middle English studies in honour of Rossell Hope Robbins p366-71

See also Bazire, J. jt. auth.

Mills, Harriet C.

Literature in fetters. *In* Terrill, R. ed. The China difference p285-304

Lu Xun: literature and revolution—from Mara to Marx. *In* Modern Chinese literature in the May Fourth era p189-220

Mills, Michael. See Morris, N. jt. auth.

Mills, Ralph J.

Cry of the human

Contents

Creation's very self: on the personal element in recent American poetry

Donald Hall's poetry

Earth hard: David Ignatow's poetry

In the way of becoming: Theodore Roethke's last poems

A reading of Galway Kinnell

"The true and earthy prayer": Philip Levine's poetry

Richard Eberhart. *In* Donoghue, D. ed. Seven American poets from MacLeish to Nemerov p55-91

Theodore Roethke. *In* Donoghue, D. ed. Seven American poets from MacLeish to Nemerov p92-131

Mills, Richard Martin

The virgin lands since Khrushchev: choices and decisions in Soviet policy making. *In* Cocks, P.; Daniels, R. V. and Heer, N. W. eds. The dynamics of Soviet politics p178-92

Mills, Ted

Leadership from abroad: European developments in industrial democracy. *In* Heisler, W. J. and Houck, J. W. eds. A matter of dignity p115-29

Millward, W. G.

Iran. *In* Savory, R. M. ed. Introduction to Islamic civilisation p169-77

Milne, Alan Alexander

About individual works

The red house mystery

Panek, L. L. A. A. Milne. *In* Panek, L. L. Watteau's shepherds: the detective novel in Britain, 1914-1940 p64-71

Milne, Fred L.

Shelley's The Cenci: the ice motif and the ninth circle of Dante's Hell. *In* Tennessee Studies in literature v22 p117-32

Milner, Joseph O.
Autonomy and communion in A death in the family. *In* Tennessee Studies in literature v21 p105-13

Milner-Gulland, Robin R.
Art and architecture in the Petersburg age, 1700-1860. *In* Auty, R. and Obolensky, D. eds. An introduction to Russian art and architecture p71-111

Art and architecture of Old Russia, 988-1700. *In* Auty, R. and Obolensky, D. eds. An introduction to Russian art and architecture p 1-70

Miłosz, Czesław
Bronisława Ostrowska and Miguel Mañara. *In* For Wiktor Weintraub p293-306
Emperor of the earth
Vilnius, Lithuania: an ethnic agglomerate. *In* Ethnic identity p339-52

Milosz, O. V. de L. See Milosz, Oscar Vladislas

Milosz, Oscar Vladislas
About
Miłosz, C. Bronisława Ostrowska and Miguel Mañara. For Wiktor Weintraub p293-306

About individual works
Miguel Manara
Miłosz, C. Bronisława Ostrowska and Miguel Mañara. *In* For Wiktor Weintraub p293-306

Milstein, Michael A.
Strategic arms limitation and military strategic concepts. *In* Arms control and technological innovation p198-209

Milton, John
About
Arnold, M. Milton. *In* Arnold, M. The last word p328-33

Eliot, T. S. From Milton II. *In* Eliot, T. S. Selected prose of T. S. Eliot p265-74
Eliot, T. S. Milton I. *In* Eliot, T. S. Selected prose of T. S. Eliot p258-64

Grant, P. Time and temptation in Paradise regained: belief and the single image. *In* Grant, P. Images and ideas in literature of the English Renaissance p129-53

Heninger, S. K. Sidney and Milton: the poet as maker. *In* Wittreich, J. A. ed. Milton and the line of vision p57-95

Manlove, C. N. Milton. *In* Manlove, C. N. Literature and reality, 1600-1800 p30-56

Martz, L. L. The rising poet, 1645. *In* Wimsatt, W. K. ed. Literary criticism: idea and act p402-22

Mollenkott, V. R. The pervasive influence of the Apocrypha in Milton's thought and art. *In* Patrick, J. M. and Sundell, R. H. eds. Milton and the art of sacred song p23-43

Oram, W. A. Nature, poetry, and Milton's genii. *In* Patrick, J. M. and Sundell, R. H. eds. Milton and the art of sacred song p47-64

Parker, P. A. Milton. *In* Parker, P. A. Inescapable romance p114-58

Sims, J. H. Milton, literature as a Bible, and the Bible as literature. *In* Patrick, J. M. and Sundell, R. H. eds. Milton and the art of sacred song p3-21

Trickett, R. Shakespeare and Milton. *In* English Association. Essays and studies, 1978 p23-35

Webber, J. Walking on water: Milton, Stevens, and contemporary American poetry. *In* Wittreich, J. A. ed. Milton and the line of vision p231-68

Williams, K. Milton, greatest Spenserian. *In* Wittreich, J. A. ed. Milton and the line of vision p25-55

Wittreich, J. A. "A poet amongst poets": Milton and the tradition of prophecy. *In* Wittreich, J. A. ed. Milton and the line of vision p97-142

About individual works
Comus
Fish, S. E. Problem solving in Comus. *In* Illustrious evidence p115-31

Le Comte, E. S. The 'haemony' passage in Comus. *In* Le Comte, E. S. Poets' riddles p67-99

Martz, L. L. The music of Comus. *In* Illustrious evidence p93-113

Piehler, P. Milton's iconoclasm. *In* Evolution of consciousness p121-35

Steadman, J. M. A mask at Ludlow: Comus and Dionysiac revel. *In* Steadman, J. M. Nature into myth p213-40

Wain, J. Reflections on the first night of Comus. *In* Wain, J. Professing poetry p134-56

Lycidas
Hill, A. A. Imagery and meaning: a passage from Lycidas and a poem by Blake. *In* Hill, A. A. Constituent and pattern in poetry p71-82

Poggioli, R. Milton's Lycidas. *In* Poggioli, R. The oaten flute p83-104

Trilling, L. John Milton: Lycidas. *In* Trilling, L. Prefaces to The experience of literature p194-200

Wittreich, J. A. "A poet amongst poets": Milton and the tradition of prophecy. *In* Wittreich, J. A. ed. Milton and the line of vision p97-142

Lycidas (Lines 130-131)
Le Comte, E. S. "That two-handed engine" and Savonarola and the Blackfriars fatal vespers. *In* Le Comte, E. S. Poets' riddles p100-28

Milton, John—About individual works—*Cont.*

A maske presented at Ludlow Castle

Barber, C. L. A mask presented at Ludlow Castle: the masque as a masque. *In* Wimsatt, W. K. ed. Literary criticism: idea and act p382-401

On the morning of Christ's Nativity

Chambers, A. B. Christmas: the liturgy of the Church and English verse of the Renaissance. *In* Literary monographs v6 p109-53

Davies, H. N. Laid artfully together: stanzaic design in Milton's 'On the morning of Christ's Nativity.' *In* Røstvig, M. S. ed. Fair forms p85-117

Røstvig, M. S. Elaborate song: conceptual structure in Milton's 'On the morning of Christ's Nativity.' *In* Røstvig, M. S. ed. Fair forms p54-84

Paradise lost

Adams, R. M. A little look into Chaos. *In* Illustrious evidence p71-89

Adelman, J. Creation and the place of the poet in Paradise lost. *In* Martz, L. L. and Williams, A. L. eds. The author in his work p51-69

Bloom, L. D. Addison's popular aesthetic: the rhetoric of the Paradise lost papers. *In* Martz, L. L. and Williams, A. L. eds. The author in his work p263-81

Bloom, H. Clinamen, or Poetic misprision; excerpt from "The anxiety of influence." *In* Primeau, R. ed. Influx p82-99

Curran, S. The siege of hateful contraries: Shelley, Mary Shelley, Byron, and Paradise lost. *In* Wittreich, J. A. ed. Milton and the line of vision p209-30

DiSalvo, J. Blake encountering Milton: politics and the family in Paradise lost and The four Zoas. *In* Wittreich, J. A. ed. Milton and the line of vision p143-34

Dyson, A. E. and Lovelock, J. Event perverse: Milton's epic of exile. *In* Dyson, A. E. and Lovelock, J. Masterful images p47-70

Gilbert, S. M. and Gubar, S. Horror's twin: Mary Shelley's monstrous Eve. *In* Gilbert, S. M. and Gubar, S. The madwoman in the attic p213-47

Gilbert, S. M. and Gubar, S. Looking oppositely: Emily Brontë's Bible of Hell. *In* Gilbert, S. M. and Gubar, S. The madwoman in the attic p248-308

Gilbert, S. M. and Gubar, S. Milton's bogey: patriarchal poetry and women readers. *In* Gilbert, S. M. and Gubar, S. The madwoman in the attic p187-212

Hannay, M. P. A preface to Perelandra. *In* Schakel, P. J. ed. The longing for a form p73-90

Hawkins, H. 'Of their vain contest': poetic and critical deadlocks in Paradise lost and Spenser's bower of bliss. *In* Hawkins, H. Poetic freedom and poetic truth p55-77

Howard, D. R. Flying through space: Chaucer and Milton. *In* Wittreich, J. A. ed. Milton and the line of vision p3-23

Kennedy, W. J. The epic genre and varieties of form. *In* Kennedy, W. J. Rhetorical norms in Renaissance literature p128-88

Lord, G. D. Milton's dialogue with omniscience in Paradise lost. *In* Martz, L. L. and Williams, A. L. eds. The author in his work p31-50

McCanles, M. Paradise lost and the dialectic of Providence. *In* McCanles, M. Dialectical criticism and Renaissance literature p120-58

MacKellar, W. On two English metamorphoses. *In* Poetry and poetics from ancient Greece to the Renaissance p207-17

Martz, L. L. Paradise lost: the solitary way. *In* Martz, L. L. and Williams, A. L. eds. The author in his work p71-84

Ong, W. J. From epithet to logic: Miltonic epic and the closure of existence. *In* Ong, W. J. Interfaces of the word p189-212

Parker, P. A. Milton. *In* Parker, P. A. Inescapable romance p114-58

Piehler, P. Milton's iconoclasm. *In* Evolution of consciousness p121-35

Ricks, C. B. Sound and sense in Paradise lost. *In* Royal Society of Literature of the United Kingdom. London. Essays by divers hands v39 p92-111

Rollin, R. B. Milton's "I's": the narrator and the reader in Paradise lost. *In* Renaissance and modern p33-55

Shawcross, J. T. The hero of Paradise lost one more time. *In* Patrick, J. M. and Sundell, R. H. eds. Milton and the art of sacred song p137-47

Steadman, J. M. The arming of an archetype. *In* Concepts of the hero in the Middle Ages and the Renaissance p147-96

Steadman, J. M. Paradise lost: Milton's "Sin." The problem of literary indebtedness. *In* Steadman, J. M. Nature into myth p174-84

Paradise lost (Book I, lines 306-11)

Steadman, J. M. Paradise lost: the Devil and Pharaoh's chivalry. Etymological and typological imagery and Renaissance chronography. *In* Steadman, J. M. Nature into myth p185-212

Paradise lost (Book IV, lines 492-511)

Smith, A. J. Sense and innocence: two love episodes in Dante and Milton. *In* An English miscellany p119-30

Paradise lost (Book VI)

Revard, S. H. P. The Renaissance Michael and the Son of God. *In* Patrick, J. M. and Sundell, R. H. eds. Milton and the art of sacred song p121-35

Paradise lost (Prologues)

Sundell, R. H. The singer and his song in the Prologues of Paradise lost. *In* Patrick, J. M. and Sundell, R. H. eds. Milton and the art of sacred song p65-80

Paradise regained

Grant, P. Time and temptation in Paradise regained: belief and the single image. *In* Grant, P. Images and ideas in literature of the English Renaissance p129-53

Steadman, J. M. The arming of an archetype. *In* Concepts of the hero in the Middle Ages and the Renaissance p147-96

Samson Agonistes

Bowers, F. T. Samson Agonistes: justice and reconciliation. *In* The Dress of words p 1-23

Frye, N. Agon and logos. *In* Frye, N. Spiritus mundi p201-27

Le Comte, E. S. New objections to a pre-Restoration date for Samson Agonistes. *In* Le Comte, E. S. Poets' riddles p129-60

Milton, John—About individual works—Samson Agonistes—*Continued*

Radzinowicz, M. A. N. Medicinable tragedy: the structure of Samson Agonistes and seventeenth-century psychopathology. *In* English drama: forms and development p94-122

Bibliography

Fallon, R. T. Miltonic documents in the Public Record Office, London. *In* Virginia. University. Bibliographical Society. Studies in bibliography v32 p82-100

Patrides, C. A. Milton. *In* English Association. The year's work in English studies v53 p239-49

Patrides, C. A. Milton [another essay]. *In* English Association. The year's work in English studies v54 p242-51

Patrides, C. A. Milton [another essay]. *In* English Association. The year's work in English studies v55 p282-96

Patrides, C. A. Milton [another essay]. *In* English Association. The year's work in English studies p56 p210-20

Patrides, C. A. Milton [another essay]. *In* English Association. The year's work in English studies v57 p178-84

Characters

Hawkins, H. 'Of their vain contest': poetic and critical deadlocks in Paradise lost and Spenser's bower of bliss. *In* Hawkins, H. Poetic freedom and poetic truth p55-77

Characters—(Archangel) Michael

Revard, S. H. P. The Renaissance Michael and the Son of God. *In* Patrick, J. M. and Sundell, R. H. eds. Milton and the art of sacred song p121-35

Characters—Satan

Shawcross, J. T. The hero of Paradise lost one more time. *In* Patrick, J. M. and Sundell, R. H. eds. Milton and the art of sacred song p137-47

Characters—Sin

Steadman, J. M. Paradise lost: Milton's "Sin." The problem of literary indebtedness. *In* Steadman, J. M. Nature into myth p174-84

Criticism and interpretation

Bloom, L. D. Addison's popular aesthetic: the rhetoric of the Paradise lost papers. *In* Martz, L. L. and Williams, A. L. eds. The author in his work p263-81

Influence

Gilbert, S. M. and Gubar, S. Milton's bogey: patriarchal poetry and women readers. *In* Gilbert, S. M. and Gubar, S. The madwoman in the attic p187-212

Webber, J. Walking on water: Milton, Stevens, and contemporary American poetry. *In* Wittreich, J. A. ed. Milton and the line of vision p231-68

Influence—Blake

DiSalvo, J. Blake encountering Milton: politics and the family in Paradise lost and The four Zoas. *In* Wittreich, J. A. ed. Milton and the line of vision p143-84

Influence—Shelley, Mary Wollstonecraft (Godwin)

Gilbert, S. M. and Gubar, S. Horror's twin: Mary Shelley's monstrous Eve. *In* Gilbert, S. M. and Gubar, S. The madwoman in the attic p213-47

Influence—Shelley, Percy Bysshe

Curran, S. The siege of hateful contraries: Shelley, Mary Shelley, Byron, and Paradise lost. *In* Wittreich, J. A. ed. Milton and the line of vision p209-30

Influence—Wordsworth

Rieger, J. Wordsworth unalarm'd. *In* Wittreich, J. A. ed. Milton and the line of vision p185-208

Knowledge—Music

Frank, M. H. Milton's knowledge of music: some speculations. *In* Patrick, J. M. and Sundell, R. H. eds Milton and the art of sacred song p83-98

Language

Sherbo, A. Milton. *In* Sherbo, A. English poetic diction from Chaucer to Wordsworth p86-104

Musical settings

Martz, L. L. The music of Comus. *In* Illustrious evidence p93-113

Sources

Le Comte, E. S. "That two-handed engine" and Savonarola and the Blackfriars fatal vespers. *In* Le Comte, E. S. Poets' riddles p100-28

Steadman, J. M. Paradise lost: Milton's "Sin." The problem of literary indebtedness. *In* Steadman, J. M. Nature into myth p174-84

Style

Sherbo, A. Milton. *In* Sherbo, A. English poetic diction from Chaucer to Wordsworth p86-104

See also Milton, John—Technique

Technique

Patrick, J. M. Milton's revolution against rime, and some of its implications. *In* Patrick, J. M. and Sundell, R. H. eds. Milton and the art of sacred song p99-117

Milton, John in fiction, drama, poetry, etc.

Butter, P. H. Milton: the final plates. *In* Phillips, M. C. ed. Interpreting Blake p145-63

Milton, Theodore Ross

Thoughts on our national strategy for the future. *In* Grand strategy for the 1980s p57-71

Milward, Alan S.

Fascism and the economy. *In* Laqueur, W. Z. ed. Fascism: a reader's guide p379-412

Milwaukee

Politics and government

Miller, S. M. Milwaukee: of ethnicity and labor. *In* Stave, B. M. ed. Socialism and the cities p41-71

Mimesis in literature

Alter, R. Mimesis and the motive for fiction. *In* Images and ideas in American culture p99-123

Dieckmann, H. The transformation of the concept of imitation in eighteenth-century French esthetics. *In* Amacher, R. E. and Lange, V. eds. New perspectives in German literary criticism p49-85

Girard, R. The mimetic desire of Paolo and Francesca. *In* Girard, R. "To double business bound" p 1-8

Girard, R. The underground critic. *In* Girard, R. "To double business bound" p36-60

Mimetic faculty, On the. Benjamin W. *In* Benjamin, W. Reflections p333-36

Minces, Juliette

Women in Algeria. *In* Beck, L. and Keddie, N. R. eds. Women in the Muslim world p159-71

Mind. See Intellect; Psychology

Mind and body

Anscombe, G. E. M. The first person. *In* Guttenplan, S. D. ed. Mind and language p45-65

Arendt, H. Appearance. *In* Arendt, H. The life of the mind v 1 p17-65

Brown, B. B. On the nature of the human mind. *In* Hanna, T. ed. Explorers of humankind p73-86

Cheng, Chung-ying. Mind and body: aspects of identity. *In* Philosophical aspects of the mind-body problem p78-98

Cooper, D. E. ESP and the materialist theory of mind. *In* Thakur, S. C. ed. Philosophy and psychical research p59-80

Donagan, A. Descartes's "synthetic" treatment of the real distinction between mind and body. *In* Hooker, M. ed. Descartes p186-96

Eccles, Sir J. C. Cerebral activity and consciousness. *In* Ayala, F. J. and Dobzhansky, T. G. eds. Studies in the philosophy of biology p87-105

Economos, J. J. Identity and "the difference." *In* Philosophical aspects of the mind-body problems p154-61

Feigl, H. Some crucial issues of mind-body monism. *In* Philosophical aspects of the mind-body problem p20-34

Flew, A. G. N. Mind/brain identity and the Cartesian framework. *In* Flew, A. G. N. A rational animal p123-50

Flew, A. G. N. A rational animal. *In* Flew, A. G. N. A rational animal p89-122

Gunderson, K. Asymmetries and mind-body perplexities. *In* Philosophical aspects of the mind-body problem p99-130

Hanna, T. Introduction: the Sphinx and the soma. *In* Hanna, T. ed. Explorers of humankind p 1-15

Holborow, L. The 'prejudice in favour of psychophysical parallelism'. *In* Royal Institute of Philosophy. Understanding Wittgenstein p193-207

Hooker, M. Descartes's denial of mind-body identity. *In* Hooker, M. ed. Descartes p171-85

Huxley, A. L. The ego. *In* Huxley, A. L. The Human situation p137-51

Huxley, A. L. How original is original sin? *In* Huxley, A. L. The Human situation p59-73

Lewis, D. K. Psychophysical and theoretical identifications. *In* Philosophical aspects of the mind-body problem p43-53

Lowen, A. Human nature. *In* Hanna, T. ed. Explorers of humankind p33-47

Matson, W. I. Spinoza's theory of mind. *In* Freeman, E. and Mandelbaum, M. H. eds. Spinoza p49-60

Mattern, R. Descartes's correspondence with Elizabeth: concerning both the union and distinction of mind and body. *In* Hooker, M. ed. Descartes p212-22

Maxwell, G. Russell on perception and mind-body: a study in philosophical method. *In* Philosophical aspects of the mind-body problem p131-53

Odegard, D. A. The body identical with the human mind: a problem in Spinoza's philosophy. *In* Freeman, E. and Mandelbaum, M. H. eds. Spinoza p61-83

Quine, W. V. Mind and verbal dispositions. *In* Guttenplan, S. D. ed. Mind and language p83-95

Rensch, B. Polynomistic determination of biological processes. *In* Ayala, F. J. and Dobzhansky, T. G. eds. Studies in the philosophy of biology p241-55

Shoemaker, S. Embodiment and behavior. *In* Rorty, A. O. ed. The identities of persons p109-37

Townsend, J. T. The mind-body equation revisited. *In* Philosophical aspects of the mind-body problem p200-18

Tracy, T. J. Plato, Galen, and the center of consciousness. *In* Illinois classical studies, v 1 1976 p43-52

Watanabe, S. Logic of the empirical world, with reference to the identity theory and reductionism. *In* Philosophical aspects of the mind-body problem p162-81

Weinberg, J. R. Descartes on the distinction of mind and body. *In* Weinberg, J. R. Ockham, Descartes, and Hume p71-82

See also Biofeedback training; Consciousness; Nervous system; Other minds (Theory of knowledge); Phrenology; Psychology, Physiological; Rolfing; Self; Sleep

Mind-distorting drugs. See Hallucinogenic drugs

Mind-reading. See Thought-transference

Minds of others (Theory of knowledge) See Other minds (Theory of knowledge)

Miner, Anne S.

Affirmative action at Stanford University; introductory notes. *In* Women in academia p139-62

Miner, Earl Roy

Afterword. *In* Miner, E. R. ed. Literary uses of typology p370-94

The poetics of the critical act: Dryden's dealings with rivals and predecessors. *In* Evidence in literary scholarship p45-62

Time, sequence, and plot in Restoration literature. *In* Studies in eighteenth-century culture v5 p67-85

Mineral industries

Taxation—United States

McDonald, S. L. Taxation system and market distortion. *In* Kalter, R. J. and Vogely, W. A. eds. Energy supply and government policy p26-50

Mineral resources. See Mines and mineral resources

Miners. See Coal-miners

Mines and mineral resources

Noble, S. B. Resources and the political options facing the United States. *In* Isolation or interdependence? p167-92

See also Raw materials

Underdeveloped areas

See Underdeveloped areas—Mines and mineral resources

Mingay, G. E. See Bagwell, P. S. jt. auth.

Mingrelia, Georgia (Transcaucasia)

History

Allen, W. E. D. A Russian embassy to Mingrelia (1639-40). *In* Studies in memory of David Talbot Rice p294-316

Miniature painting

Influence

Kitzinger, E. The role of miniature painting in mural decoration. *In* The Place of book illumination in Byzantine art p99-142

Miniature painting, Byzantine

Buchthal, H. Toward a history of Palaeologan illumination. *In* The Place of book illumination in Byzantine art p143-77

Loerke, W. C. The monumental miniature. *In* The Place of book illumination in Byzantine art p61-97

Weitzmann, K. The study of Byzantine book illumination, past, present, and future. *In* The Place of book illumination in Byzantine art p 1-60

Miniatures (Illumination of books and manuscripts) See Illumination of books and manuscripts

Minimal art

Osborne, H. The new sensibility of the 1960s. *In* Osborne, H. Abstraction and artifice in twentieth-century art p149-62

Minimum income. See Income maintenance programs

Ministerials

Freed, J. B. The formation of the Salzburg ministerialage in the tenth and eleventh centuries: an example of upward social mobility in the early Middle Ages. *In* Viator: medieval and Renaissance studies v9 p67-102

Freed, J. B. The origins of the European nobility: the problem of the ministerials. *In* Viator: medieval and Renaissance studies v7 p211-41

Mink, Louis O.

History and fiction as modes of comprehension. *In* Cohen, R. ed. New directions in literary history p107-24

Narrative form as a cognitive instrument. *In* Canary, R. H. and Kozicki, H. J. eds. The writing of history p129-49

Minkowski, Hermann

About

Galison, P. L. Minkowski's space-time: from visual thinking to the absolute world. *In* Historical studies in the physical sciences v10 p85-121

Minneapolis

Schools

Arendt, J. D. Promoting pluralism in the public schools. *In* Minority language and literature p121-29

Minnesingers

Goldin, F. The array of perspectives in the early courtly love lyric. *In* In pursuit of perfection p51-100

See also Troubadours

Minoans

Fears, J. R. Atlantis and the Minoan thalassocracy: a study in modern mythopoeism. *In* Ramage, E. S. ed. Atlantis, fact or fiction? p103-34

Minogue, Kenneth R.

Michael Oakeshott: the boundless sea of politics. *In* De Crespigny, A. and Minogue, K. R. eds. Contemporary political philosophers p120-46

Nationalism and the patriotism of city-states. *In* Smith, A. D. ed. Nationalist movements p54-73

Natural rights, ideology and the game of life. *In* Human rights p13-35

Minor planets. See Planets, Minor

Minorities

Alcock, A. E. A reappraisal of existing theory and practice in the protection of minorities. *In* Hepburn, A. C. ed. Minorities in history p226-41

Alcock, A. E.; Taylor, B. K. and Welton, J. M. Conclusions. *In* Alcock, A. E.; Taylor, B. K. and Welton, J. M. eds. The future of cultural minorities p177-99

Deloria, V. The future of racial minorities in American society. *In* Bundy, R. F. ed. Images of the future: the twenty-first century and beyond p159-65

Lijphart, A. Political theories and the explanation of ethnic conflict in the Western world: falsified predictions and plausible postdictions. *In* Esman, M. J. ed. Ethnic conflict in the Western world p46-64

O'Brien, T. A. Economic support for minority languages. *In* Alcock, A. E.; Taylor, B. K. and Welton, J. M. eds. The future of cultural minorities p82-101

Price, G. The present position and viability of minority languages. *In* Alcock, A. E.; Taylor, B. K. and Welton, J M. eds. The future of cultural minorities p30-43

Taylor, B. K. Culture: whence, whither and why? *In* Alcock, A. E.; Taylor, B. K. and Welton, J. M. eds. The future of cultural minorities p9-29

Van Dyke, V. The individual, the state, and ethnic communities in political theory. *In* Kommers, D. P. and Loescher, G. D. eds. Human rights and American foreign policy p36-62

Whitaker, B. C. G. Minority rights and self-determination. *In* Kommers, D. P. and Loescher, G. D. eds. Human rights and American foreign policy p63-76

See also Assimilation (Sociology); Discrimination; Ethnic attitudes; Mass media and minorities; Nationalism; Race discrimination; Race relations; Segregation; names of individual races or peoples, e.g. East Indians in South Africa; also subdivision Foreign population under names of countries, cities, etc., e.g. Ghana—Foreign population

Education

Sutherland, M. B. Comparative perspectives on the education of cultural minorities. *In* Alcock, A. E.; Taylor, B. K. and Welton, J. M. eds. The future of cultural minorities p44-62

See also Education, Bilingual

Education—Minneapolis

Arendt, J. D. Promoting pluralism in the public schools. *In* Minority language and literature p121-29

Education (Higher)—United States

Heslep, R. D. Preferential treatment in admitting racial minority students. *In* Social justice & preferential treatment p33-51

O'Neil, R. M. The case for preferential admissions; excerpt from "Discriminating against discrimination: preferential admissions in the DeFunis case." *In* Gross, B. R. ed. Reverse discrimination p66-83

Wasserstrom, R. A. The university and the case for preferential treatment. *In* Social justice & preferential treatment p16-32

Employment

See Affirmative action programs

Minorities—*Continued*

Employment—New York (City)—History

Ward, D. Some locational implications of the ethnic division of labor in mid-nineteenth-century American cities. *In* Pattern and process p258-70

Employment—United States

Murphy, T. P. Minority faculty recruitment. *In* Murphy, T. P. ed. Universities in the urban crisis p325-51

History

Hepburn, A. C. Minorities in history. *In* Hepburn, A. C. ed. Minorities in history p 1-10

Law and legislation

Palley, C. The role of law in relation to minority groups. *In* Alcock, A. E.; Taylor, B. K. and Welton, J. M. eds. The future of cultural minorities p120-60

Political activity

Alcock, A. E. The development of governmental attitudes to cultural minorities in Western industrial states. *In* Alcock, A. E.; Taylor, B. K. and Welton, J. M. eds. The future of cultural minorities p102-19

Political aspects

Gladdish, K. R. The political dynamics of cultural minorities. *In* Alcock, A. E.; Taylor, B. K. and Welton, J. M. eds. The future of cultural minorities p161-76

Study and teaching

See Ethnic studies

Bolzano (Province)

Alcock, A E. Three case-studies in minority protection: South Tyrol, Cyprus, Quebec. *In* Hepburn, A. C. ed. Minorities in history p189-225

China

Pye, L. W. China: ethnic minorities and national security. *In* Glazer, N. and Moynihan, D. P. eds. Ethnicity p489-512

Europe

Alcock, A. E. The development of governmental attitudes to cultural minorities in Western industrial states. *In* Alcock, A. E.; Taylor, B. K. and Welton, J. M. eds. The future of cultural minorities p102-19

Connor, W. F. Ethnonationalism in the First world: the present in historical perspective. *In* Esman, M. J. ed. Ethnic conflict in the Western world p20-45

Esman, M. J. Perspectives on ethnic conflict in industrialized societies. *In* Esman, M. J. ed. Ethnic conflict in the Western world p371-90

Klein, T. Minorities in Central Europe in the sixteenth and early seventeenth centuries. *In* Hepburn, A. C. ed. Minorities in history p31-50

Wenner, M. W. The politics of equality among European linguistic minorities. *In* Claude, R. P. ed. Comparative human rights p184-213

Europe, Eastern

McNeill, T. State and nationality under communism. *In* Hayward, J. E. S. and Berki, R. N. eds State and society in contemporary Europe p118-40

France

Beer, W. R. The social class of ethnic activists in contemporary France. *In* Esman, M. J. ed. Ethnic conflict in the Western world p143-58

Great Britain

Sharp, A. J. Britain and the protection of minorities at the Paris Peace Conference, 1919. *In* Hepburn, A. C. ed. Minorities in history p170-88

Ireland

Canny, N. P. Dominant minorities: English settlers in Ireland and Virginia, 1550-1650. *In* Hepburn, A. C. ed. Minorities in history p51-69

Milwaukee

Miller, S. M. Milwaukee: of ethnicity and labor. *In* Stave, B. M. ed. Socialism and the cities p41-71

Russia

McNeill, T. State and nationality under communism. *In* Hayward, J. E. S. and Berki, R. N. eds. State and society in contemporary Europe p118-40

Pipes, R. Reflections on the nationality problems in the Soviet Union. *In* Glazer, N. and Moynihan, D. P. eds. Ethnicity p453-65

Rakowska-Harmstone, T. Ethnic autonomy in the Soviet Union. *In* Said, A. A. and Simmons, L. R. eds. Ethnicity in an international context p150-66

Shafarevich, I. R. Separation or reconciliation? The nationalities question in the USSR. *In* From under the rubble p88-104

Uganda

Kuper, J. "Goan" and "Asian" in Uganda: an analysis of racial identity and cultural categories. *In* Shack, W. A. and Skinner, E. P. eds. Strangers in African societies p243-59

Mazrui, A. A. Casualties of an underdeveloped class structure: the expulsion of Luo workers and Asian bourgeoisie from Uganda. *In* Shack, W. A. and Skinner, E. P. eds. Strangers in African societies p261-88

United States

Blackwell, J. E. The power basis of ethnic conflict in American society. *In* The Uses of controversy in sociology p179-96

Deloria, V. The new Exodus. *In* Smithsonian Institution. The cultural drama p89-105

Gans, H. J. Symbolic ethnicity: the future of ethnic groups and cultures in America. *In* On the making of Americans p193-220

Gerson, L. L. Ethnics in American politics. *In* Havard, W. C. and Bernd, J. L. eds. 200 years of the Republic in retrospect p336-46

Glazer, N. The emergence of an American ethnic pattern; excerpt from "Affirmative discrimination: ethnic inequality and public policy." *In* Gross, B. R. ed. Reverse discrimination p132-55

Greeley, A. M. Why study ethnicity? *In* The Diverse society: implications for social policy p3-12

Grossman, L. Ethnicity and health delivery systems. *In* The Diverse society: implications for social policy p129-48

Higham, J. Introduction: the forms of ethnic leadership. *In* Ethnic leadership in America p 1-18

Minorities—United States—*Continued*

McCready, W. C. Social utilities in a pluralistic society. *In* The Diverse society: implications for social policy p13-25

Sheed, W. The subject of ethnics. *In* Sheed, W. The good word & other words p142-47

Snetsinger, J. G. Ethnicity and foreign policy. *In* Encyclopedia of American foreign policy p322-29

Sowell, T. Ethnicity in a changing America. *In* A New America? p213-37

Virginia

Canny, N. P. Dominant minorities: English settlers in Ireland and Virginia, 1550-1650. *In* Hepburn, A. C. ed. Minorities in history p51-69

Yugoslavia

Stavrou, N. A. Ethnicity in Yugoslavia: roots and impact. *In* Said, A. A. and Simmons, L. R. eds. Ethnicity in an international context p134-49

Minorities in television

Great Britain

Husband, C. Some aspects of the interaction of the British entertainment media with contemporary race relations. *In* Fischer, H. D. and Melnik, S. R. eds. Entertainment: a cross-cultural examination p196-207

Minorities on television. See Minorities in television

Minority groups. See Minorities

Minority literature (American) See American literature—Minority authors

Minow, Newton Norman

Electronics and the future. *In* Tomorrow's American p157-70

Minstrel shows

Jackson, B. The minstrel mode. *In* Jackson, B. The waiting years p155-64

See also Afro-Americans in the performing arts

Minstrels. See Bards and bardism

Minton, William Warren

The frequency and structuring of traditional formulas in Hesiod's Theogony. *In* Harvard Studies in classical philology v79 p25-54

Mints

See also Coinage

Rome

Sellwood, D. Minting. *In* Strong, D. E. and Brown, D. eds. Roman crafts p63-73

Mintz, Sidney Wilfred

The Caribbean region. *In* Mintz, S. W. ed. Slavery, colonialism, and racism p45-71

Ethnicity and leadership: an afterword. *In* Ethnic leadership in America p198-205

Miracle-plays. See Mysteries and miracle-plays

Miracles

Achtemeier, P. J. Jesus and the disciples as miracle workers in the Apocryphal New Testament. *In* Aspects of religious propaganda in Judaism and early Christianity p149-86

See also Supernatural

Mirak, Robert

Selected bibliography of the published works of Oscar Handlin. *In* Uprooted Americans p349-65

Miranda doctrine in the Burger Court, The. Stone, G. R. *In* The Supreme Court review, 1977 p99-169

Miró, Joan

About

Ashton, D. Stripping down to cosmos; excerpt from "A reading of modern art." *In* Kaplan, P. and Manso, S. eds. Major European art movements, 1900-1945 p337-52

Rosenberg, H. Miró. *In* Rosenberg, H. Art on the edge p22-38

Mirskiĭ, Dmitriĭ Petrovich

Marina Tsvetaeva. *In* The Bitter air of exile p88-93

Mirsky, Dmitry Svyatopolk, Prince. See Mirskiĭ, Dmitriĭ Petrovich

Mirsky, Mark Jay

On Fiction. *In* Anderson, E. and Kinzie, M. eds. The little magazine in America: a modern documentary history p515-23

Misanthropy in literature

Lawrence, F. L. Le misanthrope reprised: four versions of Molière's theme. *In* Johnson, R. B.; Neumann, E. S. and Trail, G. T. eds. Molière and the commonwealth of letters: patrimony and posterity p82-89

Miscarriage. See Abortion

Miscegenation

Morton, N. E. Interracial crosses and group differences. *In* Racial variation in man p151-69

United States

Bolt, C. Red, Black and white in nineteenth-century America. *In* Hepburn, A. C. ed. Minorities in history p116-34

Mischel, Harriet Nerlove. See Mischel, W. jt. auth.

Mischel, Theodore

Conceptual issues in the psychology of the self: an introduction. *In* Mischel, T. ed. The self p3-28

Mischel, Walter, and Mischel, Harriet Nerlove

Self-control and the self. *In* Mischel, T. ed. The self p31-64

Misconduct in office

Nagel, T. Ruthlessness in public life. *In* Hampshire, S. ed. Public and private morality p75-91

Also in Nagel, T. Mortal questions p75-90

Misdemeanors (Law) See Criminal law

The misfortunes of Fyfe (Limerick)

Bouissac, P. A semiotic approach to nonsense: clowns and limericks. *In* Sebeok, T. A. ed. Sight, sound, and sense p244-63

Misgeld, Dieter

Critical theory and hermeneutics: the debate between Habermas and Gadamer. *In* O'Neill, J. ed. On critical theory p164-83

Mishan, Edward Joshua. See Mishan, Ezra Joshua

Mishan, Ezra Joshua

Does perfect competition in mining produce an optimal rate of exploitation? *In* Theory for economic efficiency: essays in honor of Abba P. Lerner p120-43

Mishima, Yukio, pseud.

About

Iga, M. Personal situation as a factor in suicide, with reference to Yasunari Kawabata and Yukio Mishima. *In* Wolman, B. B. ed. Between survival and suicide p103-28

Mishima, Yukio, pseud.—About—*Continued*

Keene, D. The death of Mishima. *In* Smithsonian Institution. **The cultural drama** p271-87

Miwa, K. In the shadow of leaves and Mishima's death. *In* Postwar trends in Japan p229-49

Ueda, M. Mishima Yukio. *In* Ueda, M. Modern Japanese writers p219-59

Yamanouchi, H. A phantasy world: Mishima Yukio. *In* Yamanouchi, H. The search for authenticity in modern Japanese literature p137-52

About individual works

The temple of the golden pavilion

Ueda, M. Mishima Yukio. *In* Ueda, M. Modern Japanese writers p219-59

Miskimin, Harry A.

The legacies of London: 1259-1330. *In* The Medieval city p209-27

Misner, Charles W.

Cosmology and theology. *In* Cosmology, history, and theology p75-100

Missals. See Illumination of books and manuscripts

Missile warheads. See Multiple independently targetable reentry vehicles

Missiles, Cruise. See Cruise missiles

Missing link. See Neanderthal race

Missiology. See Missions—Theory

Mission of the church. See Church and the world

Mission to Moscow (Motion picture)

Culbert, D. H. Our awkward ally: Mission to Moscow. *In* O'Connor, J. E. and Jackson, M. A. eds. American history/American film p121-45

Missionaries, American

Varg, P. A. Missionaries. *In* Encyclopedia of American foreign policy p567-74

Missions

Anderson, G. H. Religion as a problem for the Christian mission. *In* Christian faith in a religiously plural world p104-16

See also subdivision Missions under names of churches, denominations, religious orders, etc.; e.g. Catholic Church—Missions

Biblical teaching

Howard, D. M. Some reflections on the mission of the Church. *In* Current issues in Biblical and patristic interpretation p309-17

Theory

Howard, D. M. Some reflections on the mission of the Church. *In* Current issues in Biblical and patristic interpretation p309-17

Africa, Central

Mackintosh, C. W. Some pioneer missions of Northern Rhodesia and Nyasaland. *In* The Occasional papers of the Rhodes-Livingstone Museum p249-95

Africa, East

Southall, A. W. White strangers and their religion in East Africa and Madagascar. *In* Shack, W. A. and Skinner, E. P. eds. Strangers in African societies p211-26

America

Bolton, H. E. The mission as a frontier institution in the Spanish American colonies. *In* Weber, D. J. ed. New Spain's far northern frontier p49-65

Borneo

Taylor, B. Church and state in Borneo: the Anglican bishopric. *In* Church, society and politics p357-68

Caucasus

Jones, M. V. The sad and curious story of Karass. *In* Oxford Slavonic papers, new ser. v8 p53-81

Madagascar

Southall, A. W. White strangers and their religion in East Africa and Madagascar. *In* Shack, W. A. and Skinner, E. P. eds. Strangers in African societies p211-26

Philippine Islands

Anderson, G. H. The Philippines: reluctant beneficiary of the missionary impulse in Europe. *In* First images of America p391-403

Sierra Leone

Walls, A. F. A colonial concordat: two views of Christianity and civilisation. *In* Church, society and politics p293-302

Missions, American

Varg, P. Missionaries. *In* Encyclopedia of American foreign policy p567-74

Missions, British

Harrison, B. The Anglo-Chinese College at Malacca, 1818-1843. *In* Southeast Asian history and historiography p246-61

Taylor, B. Church and state in Borneo: the Anglican bishopric. *In* Church, society and politics p357-68

Walls, A. F. A colonial concordat: two views of Christianity and civilisation. *In* Church, society and politics p293-302

Missions, Indian. See Indians—Missions

Missions, Spanish

Anderson, G. H. The Philippines: reluctant beneficiary of the missionary impulse in Europe. *In* First images of America p391-403

Bolton, H. E. The mission as a frontier institution in the Spanish American colonies. *In* Weber, D. J. ed. New Spain's far northern frontier p49-65

History

Phillips, G. H. Indians and the breakdown of the Spanish mission system in California. *In* Weber, D. J. ed. New Spain's far northern frontier p257-70

Missions to Afro-Americans

McPherson, J. M. The new Puritanism: values and goals of freedmen's education in America. *In* The University in society v2 p611-42

Missions to Chinese

Malacca, Malaya

Harrison, B. The Anglo-Chinese College at Malacca, 1818-1843. *In* Southeast Asian history and historiography p246-61

Mississippi

Description and travel—Views

Welty, E. One time, one place; excerpt. *In* Welty, E. The eye of the story p349-55

Mississippi in literature

Brown, C. S. Faulkner's localism. *In* The Maker and the myth: Faulkner and Yoknapatawpha, 1977 p3-24

Bryant, J. A. The recovery of the confident narrator: A curtain of green to Losing battles. *In* Prenshaw, P. W. ed. Eudora Welty p68-82

Mississippi in literature—*Continued*

Devlin, A. J. Eudora Welty's Mississippi. *In* Prenshaw, P. W. ed. Eudora Welty p157-78

Noyes, C. E. Welcome to Faulkner and Yoknapatawpha, 1977. *In* The Maker and the myth: Faulkner and Yoknapatawpha, 1977 pxi-xiv

Phillips, R. L. A structural approach to myth in the fiction of Eudora Welty. *In* Prenshaw, P. W. ed. Eudora Welty p56-67

Mississippi River

Hilliard, S. B. Antebellum interregional trade: the Mississippi River as an example. *In* Pattern and process p202-14

Mississippi Valley. See Middle West

Missouri

Foreign population

Schroeder, A. E. The survival of German traditions in Missouri. *In* The German contribution to the building of the Americas p289-313

History—Civil War, 1861-1865—Guerrillas

Castel, A. E. Quantrill's bushwhackers: a case study in partisan warfare. *In* Hubbell, J. T. ed. Battles lost and won p171-81

Missouri compromise. See Kansas-Nebraska bill

Missouri River

Allen, J. L. Thomas Jefferson and the passage to India: a pre-exploratory image. *In* Pattern and process p103-13

Missouri v. Holland. *In* The Supreme Court review, 1975 p77-122

Mistakes. See Errors

Mr Arkadin (Motion picture)

Truffaut, F. Orson Welles: Confidential report. *In* Truffaut, F. The films in my life p285-87

Mr Deeds goes to town (Motion picture)

Rohdie, S. Totems and movies. *In* Nichols, B. ed. Movies and methods p469-81

Mistletoe (in religion, folklore, etc.)

Belmont, N. Levana; or, How to raise up children. *In* Family and society p 1-15

Mitcham, Carl

Philosophy and the history of technology. *In* Bugliarello, G. and Doner, D. B. eds. The history and philosophy of technology p163-201

Mitchell, Bonner. See Corrigan, B. jt. auth.

Mitchell, Breon

A portrait and the Bildungsroman tradition. *In* Staley, T. F. and Benstock, B. eds. Approaches to Joyce's Portrait p61-74

Mitchell, Bruce Colston

Linguistic facts and the interpretation of Old English poetry. *In* Anglo-Saxon England 4 p11-28

Mitchell, Bruce Colston; Ball, Christopher, and Cameron, Angus Fraser

Short titles of Old English texts. *In* Anglo-Saxon England 4 p207-21

Mitchell, C. R.

Peace keeping: the police function. *In* The Year book of world affairs, 1976 p150-73

Mitchell, Charles

'Very like a whale': the spectator's role in modern art. *In* Concerning contemporary art p35-88

Mitchell, Harvey

Resistance to the Revolution in western France. *In* French society and the Revolution p248-85

The world between the literate and oral traditions in eighteenth-century France: ecclesiastical instructions and popular mentalities. *In* Studies in eighteenth-century culture v8 p33-67

Mitchell, James Leslie

About

Hart, F. R. Novelists of the modern renaissance. *In* Hart, F. R. The Scottish novel p207-45

Mitchell, Joan

About

Rosenberg, H. Joan Mitchell: artist against background. *In* Rosenberg, H. Art on the edge p79-86

Mitchell, Joseph, 1908-

About

Hyman, S. E. The art of Joseph Mitchell. *In* Hyman, S. E. The critic's credentials p79-85

Mitchell, L. E. See Dolan, T. P. jt. auth.

Mitchell, Margaret

About individual works
Gone with the wind

Rubin, L. D. Scarlett O'Hara and the two Quentin Compsons. *In* The South and Faulkner's Yoknapatawpha p168-94

Watkins, F. C. Gone with the wind as vulgar literature. *In* Watkins, F. C. In time and place p33-48

Characters—Scarlett O'Hara

Rubin, L. D. Scarlett O'Hara and the two Quentin Compsons. *In* The South and Faulkner's Yoknapatawpha p168-94

Mitchell, Richard Eugene

Roman coins as historical evidence: the Trojan legends of Rome. *In* Illinois classical studies, v 1 1976 p65-85

Mitchell, Robert D.

The formation of early American cultural regions: an interpretation. *In* European settlement and development in North America: essays on geographical change in honour and memory of Andrew Hill Clark p66-90

Mitchell, Sally

The forgotten women of the period: penny weekly family magazines of the 1840's and 1850's. *In* Vicinus, M. ed. A widening sphere p29-51

Mitchenson, Joe. See Mander, R. jt. auth.

Mitchison, Naomi Margaret (Haldane)

About

Hart, F. R. Mitchison and later romancers. *In* Hart, F. R. The Scottish novel p182-97

Mitford, Mary Russell

About individual works
Our village

Doubleday, N. F. Miss Mitford's village sketches. *In* Doubleday, N. F. Variety of attempt p95-112

Mitford, Nancy

About

Auchincloss, L. Nancy Mitford's Versailles. *In* Auchincloss, L. Life, law and letters p105-10

Mitford, Nancy—*Continued*

About individual works
Voltaire in love

Connolly, C. Voltaire: 1. *In* Connolly, C. The evening colonnade p118-21

Mitford, Rupert Leo Scott Bruce- See Bruce-Mitford, Rupert Leo Scott

Mitroff, Ian Irving
Systemic problem solving. *In* Leadership p129-43

Mitry, Jean

About individual works
Esthétique et psychologie du cinéma

Metz, C. Current problems of film theory: Mitry's L'Esthetique. et psychologie du cinema, vol. II. *In* Nichols, B. ed. Movies and methods p568-78

Mitscherlich, Alexander, and Mitscherlich, Margarete
The inability to mourn. *In* Explorations in psychohistory p257-70

Mitscherlich, Axel Ludwig Stern- See Stern-Mitscherlich, Axel Ludwig

Mitscherlich, Margarete. See Mitscherlich, A. jt. auth.

Mitten, David Gordon, and Yügrüm, Güldem
The Gygean Lake, 1969: Eski Balikhane, preliminary report. *In* Harvard Studies in classical philology v75 p191-95

Miwa, Kimitada
In the shadow of leaves and Mishima's death. *In* Postwar trends in Japan p229-49

Japanese images of war with the United States. *In* Iriye, A. ed. Mutual images p115-37

Mix, Katherine Lyon
Max on Shaw. *In* Riewald, J. G. ed. The surprise of excellence p131-37

Mixe Indians
Lowe, G. W. The Mixe-Zoque as competing neighbors of the early Lowland Maya. *In* The Origins of Maya civilization p197-248

Mixtures. See Solution (Chemistry)

Miyakawa, Hisayuki
Local cults around Mount Lu at the time of Sun En's rebellion. *In* Welch, H. and Seidel, A. K. eds. Facets of Taoism p83-101

Miyamoto, Kenji

About
Fukui, H. The Japanese Communist Party: the Miyamoto line and its problems. *In* Kaplan, M. A. ed. The many faces of communism p279-332

Mizener, Arthur Moore
Poetic drama and the well-made play. *In* Wimsatt, W. K. ed. Literary criticism: idea and act p576-89

About individual works
The saddest story: a biography of Ford Madox Ford

Welty, E. Arthur Mizener's The saddest story: a biography of Ford Madox Ford. *In* Welty, E. The eye of the story p241-50

Mizuta, Hiroshi
Moral philosophy and civil society. *In* Skinner, A. S. and Wilson, T. eds. Essays on Adam Smith p114-31

Mnemonics
See also Memory

History
Zinn, G. A. Hugh of Saint Victor and the art of memory. *In* Viator: medieval and Renaissance studies v5 p211-34

Mo, Ti

About
Rubin, V. A. "State machine for the general welfare." *In* Rubin, V. A. Individual and state in ancient China p33-54

Mo Tzu. See Mo, Ti

Moberg, David O.
Fundamentalists and evangelicals in society. *In* Wells, D. F. and Woodbridge, J. D. eds. The evangelicals p143-69

Spiritual well-being in late life. *In* Gubrium, J. F. ed. Late life p256-79

Mobility. See Migration, Internal; Residential mobility; Social mobility

Mobutu, Joseph Désiré. See Mobutu, Sese Seko

Mobutu, Sese Seko

About
Kanza, T. R. Zaire's foreign policy. *In* Aluko, O. ed. The foreign policies of African states p235-43

Mocek, Reinhard

About individual works
Wilhelm Roux-Hans Driesch:zur Geschichte der Entwicklungsphysiologie der Tiere ("Entwicklungsmechanik")

Haraway, D. J. Reinterpretation or rehabilitation: an exercise in contemporay Marxist history of science. *In* Studies in history of biology v2 p193-209

Moch, Jules Salvador
Verification and control. *In* The Dynamics of the arms race p116-22

Mockingbird, Jon

About individual works
The Wokosani road

Larson, C. R. The Wokosani road. *In* Larson, C. R. American Indian fiction p181-89

Modality (Logic)
Clark, R. L. Facts, fact-correlates, and fact-surrogates. *In* Fact, value, and perception p3-17

Quine, W. V. Reply to Professor Marcus. *In* Quine, W. V. The ways of paradox, and other essays p177-84

Quine, W. V. Three grades of modal involvement. *In* Quine, W. V. The ways of paradox, and other essays p158-76

Rescher, N. and Vander Nat, A. The Arabic theory of temporal modal syllogistic. *In* Essays on Islamic philosophy and science p189-221

Wiggins, D. The De re 'must': a note on the logical form of essentialist claims. *In* Evans, G. L. and McDowell, J. H. eds. Truth and meaning p285-312

See also Deontic logic

Mode, Robert L.
Ancient paragons in a Piccolomini scheme. *In* Enggass, R. C. and Stokstad, M. eds. Hortus imaginum p73-83

Model cities. See Urban renewal

Modell, John
Class or ethnic solidarity: the Japanese American company union. *In* The Asian American: the historical experience p67-80

Models, Astronomical. See Astronomical models

Models, Mechanical. See Machinery—Models

Modelski, George A.
World order-keeping: some alternative structures. *In* New dimensions of world politics p54-72

Modena, Leo. See Leone de Modena

Modern art. See Art, Modern; Modernism (Art)

Modern civilization. See Civilization, Modern

Modern ethics. See Ethics, Modern

Modern Language Association of America. Center for Editions of American Authors
Tanselle, G. T. Greg's theory of copytext and the editing of American literature. *In* Virginia. University. Bibliographical Society. Studies in bibliography v28 p167-229

Modern logic. See Logic, Modern

Modern music. See Music—History and criticism—20th century

Modern painting. See Painting, Modern

Modern philosophy. See Philosophy, Modern

Modern poetry. See Poetry, Modern

Modernism
Fiorenza, F. S. American culture and Modernism: Shailer Mathews's interpretation of American Christianity. *In* America in theological perspective p163-86
See also Fundamentalism

Modernism (Art)
Hassan, I. H. POSTmodernISM: a paracritical bibliography. *In* Hassan, I. H. Paracriticisms p39-59
Rosenberg, H. The old age of modernism. *In* Rosenberg, H. Art on the edge p281-87
See also Art, Abstract; Art, Modern—20th century; Avant-garde (Aesthetics); Cubism; Dadaism; Expressionism (Art); Fauvism; Futurism (Art); Surrealism

Modernism (Literature)
Altieri, C. F. Modern and post modern: symbolist and immanentist modes of poetic thought. *In* Altieri, C. F. Enlarging the temple p29-52
Bell, D. Beyond modernism, beyond self. *In* Art, politics, and will p213-53
Carden, P. J. Ornamentalism and modernism. *In* Gibian, G. and Tjalsma, H. W. eds. Russian modernism p49-64
French, W. G. "The death of the hired man": modernism and transcendence. *In* Frost: centennial essays III p382-401
Friedman, A. W. The once and future age of modernism: an introduction. *In* Forms of modern British fiction p3-14
Goodheart, E. Modernism and the critical spirit. *In* Goodheart, E. The failure of criticism p8-27
Gustafsson, L. Strindberg as a forerunner of Scandinavian modernism. *In* The Hero in Scandinavian literature p125-41
Hassan, I. H. POSTmodernISM: a paracritical bibliography. *In* Hassan, I. H. Paracriticisms p39-59

Howe, I. Endgame: the fate of modernism. *In* Howe, I. Celebrations and attacks p166-69
Ivask, G. Russian modernist poets and the mystic sectarians. *In* Gibian, G. and Tjalsma, H. W. eds. Russian modernism p85-106
Josipovici, G. The lessons of modernism. *In* Josipovici, G. The lessons of modernism p109-23
Kalbouss, G. Andrey Bely and the Modernist movement in Russian drama. *In* Janecek, G. ed. Andrey Bely p146-55
Kennedy, A. Dramatic action, the modern and the post-modern. *In* Kennedy, A. The protean self p27-61
Kenner, H. Faulkner and the avant-garde. *In* Faulkner, modernism, and film: Faulkner and Yoknapatawpha, 1978 p182-96
Poirier, R. The difficulties of modernism and the modernism of difficulty. *In* Images and ideas in American culture p124-40
Stacy, R. H. The modernists. *In* Stacy, R. H. Russian literary criticism p105-62
Tjalsma, H. W. The Petersburg poets. *In* Gibian, G. and Tjalsma, H. W. eds. Russian modernism p65-84
Weidle, W. The poison of modernism. *In* Gibian, G. and Tjalsma, H. W. eds. Russian modernism p18-30

Modernism in art. See Modernism (Art)

Modernist art. See Modernism (Art)

Modernist-fundamentalist controversy
Linder, R. D. The resurgence of evangelical social concern (1925-75). *In* Wells, D. F. and Woodbridge, J. D. eds. The evangelicals p189-210
Sandeen, E. R. The origins of Fundamentalism. *In* Mulder, J. M. and Wilson, J. F. eds. Religion in American history p415-30
See also Fundamentalism

Modlin, Charles Ernest
The loyalists' reply. *In* Emerson, E. H. ed. American literature, 1764-1789 p59-71

Moellendorf, Ulrich von Wilamowitz- See Wilamowitz-Moellendorf, Ulrich von

Moeller, Leslie G.
Mass media and national goals. *In* Fischer, H. D. and Merrill, J. C eds International and intercultural communication p200-09

Moerman, Michael
Chīangkham's trade in the "old days." *In* Change and persistence in Thai society p151-71

Moers, Ellen
Female Gothic. *In* Levine, G. L. and Knoepflmacher, U. C. eds. The endurance of Frankenstein p77-87
Performing heroinism: the myth of Corinne. *In* The Worlds of Victorian fiction p319-50

About individual works
The dandy, Brummel to Beerbohm
Connolly, C. The dandy: 2. *In* Connolly, C. The evening colonnade p133-35

Moesgaard, Kristian P.
Cosmology in the wake of Tycho Brahe's astronomy. *In* Cosmology, history, and theology p293-305

Mofolo, Thomas

About
Kunene, D. P. Towards an aesthetic of Sesotho prose. *In* Exile and tradition p98-115

Mofolo, Thomas—*Continued*

About individual works
Chaka

Ikonne, C. Purpose versus plot: the double vision of Thomas Mofolo's narrator. *In* Heywood, C. ed. Aspects of South African literature p54-65

Moggridge, Donald Edward

Economic policy in the Second World War. *In* Keynes, M. ed. Essays on John Maynard Keynes p177-201

The influence of Keynes on the economics of his time. *In* Keynes, M. ed. Essays on John Maynard Keynes p73-81

Mohamet. See Muhammad, the prophet

Mohammed, the prophet. See Muhammad, the prophet

Mohammedanism. See Islam

Mohan, Raj Pal

Contemporary sociology in India. *In* Mohan, R. P. and Martindale, D. A. eds. Handbook of contemporary developments in world sociology p423-38

See also Roucek, J. S. jt. auth.

Mohanty, Jitendranath N.

Husserl's theory of meaning. *In* Elliston, F. A. and McCormick, P. eds. Husserl p18-37

Mohawk Indians

Education

Cook, S. Akwesasne education. *In* Roots of open education in America p7-12

Mohawk language. See Iroquoian languages

Mohsen, Safia K.

The Egyptian woman: between modernity and tradition. *In* Matthiasson, C. J. ed. Many sisters p37-58

Moir, David Macbeth

About individual works
The life of Mansie Wauch, tailor in Dalkeith

Hart, F. R. The other Blackwoodians. *In* Hart, F. R. The Scottish novel p53-84

Moissac, France. Saint Pierre (Abbey)

Schapiro, M. The Romanesque sculpture of Moissac. *In* Schapiro, M. Selected papers v 1 p131-264

Moki language. See Hopi language

Mokpe women (African people) See Women, Bakwiri (African people)

Moldavian S.S.R.

History

Fischer-Galati, S. F. The Moldavian Soviet Republic in Soviet domestic and foreign policy. *In* Szporluk, R. ed. The influence of East Europe and the Soviet West on the USSR p229-50

Molecular asymmetry. See Stereochemistry

Molecular biochemistry. See Molecular biology

Molecular biology

Dupree, A. H. Biological and social theories—a new opportunity for a union of systems. *In* Science and society: past, present, and future p136-74

Sinsheimer, R. L. The molecular basis of life. *In* Neyman, J. ed. The heritage of Copernicus: theories "pleasing to the mind" p143-65

See also Molecular genetics

Molecular genetics

Monod, J. L. On the molecular theory of evolution. *In* Harré, R. ed. Problems of scientific revolution p11-24

Molecular models. See Molecules—Models

Molecular physics and its relations with other sciences, Structure of. Daudel, R. *In* The Frontiers of human knowledge p243-53

Molecular theory

Laudan, L. The methodological foundations of Mach's anti-atomism and their historical roots. *In* Motion and time, space and matter p390-417

Quine, W. V. Posits and reality. *In* Quine, W. V. The ways of paradox, and other essays p246-54

Molecular weights. See Atomic weights

Molecules

Models

Garber, E. Molecular science in late-nineteenth-century Britain. *In* Historical studies in the physical sciences v9 p265-97

Moler, Kenneth L.

The two voices of Fanny Price. *In* Halperin, J. ed. Jane Austen p172-79

Moles (Animals) (in religion, folklore, etc.)

Hand, W. D. The mole in folk medicine: a survey from Indic antiquity to modern America II. *In* American folk medicine p37-48

Puhvel, J. The mole in folk medicine: a survey from Indic antiquity to modern America, I. *In* American folk medicine p31-35

Molesworth, Charles

James Wright and the dissolving self. *In* Boyers, R. ed. Contemporary poetry in America p267-78

Molière, Jean Baptiste Poquelin

About

Anderson, W. D. Menander and Molière. *In* Johnson, R. B.; Neumann, E. S. and Trail, G. T. eds. Molière and the commonwealth of letters: patrimony and posterity p413-16

Brereton, G. Molière: life and theatrical career. *In* Brereton, G. French comic drama p85-101

Brereton, G. Molière's comedy. *In* Brereton, G. French comic drama p102-49

Fergusson, F. Molière. *In* Fergusson, F. Literary landmarks p76-88

Hanak, M. J. Molière's dialectics of the grotesque and the struggle for natural order. *In* Johnson, R. B.; Neumann, E. S. and Trail, G. T. eds. Molière and the commonwealth of letters: patrimony and posterity p499-506

Kern, E. G. Molière and the tradition of the grotesque. *In* Johnson, R. B.; Neumann, E. S. and Trail, G. T. eds. Molière and the commonwealth of letters: patrimony and posterity p507-20

Mould, W. A. Illusion and reality: a new resolution of an old paradox. *In* Johnson, R. B.; Neumann, E. S. and Trail, G. T. eds. Molière and the commonwealth of letters: patrimony and posterity p521-26

Nicoll, A. Molière and the comedy of manners. *In* Nicoll, A. World drama p258-74

Pellissier, S. L. Ionesco and Molière. *In* Johnson, R. B.; Neumann, E. S. and Trail, G. T. eds. Molière and the commonwealth of letters: patrimony and posterity p145-59

Stambler, B. Terence and Molière. *In* Johnson, R. B.; Neumann, E. S. and Trail, G. T. eds. Molière and the commonwealth of letters: patrimony and posterity p417-29

Molière, Jean B. P.—About—*Continued*

Sumberg, L. A. M. From farce in the âge buorgeois (1440-1500) to farce Molièresque: the structure of generic change. *In* Johnson, R. B.; Neumann, E. S. and Trail, G. T. eds. Molière and the commonwealth of letters: patrimony and posterity p430-42

Wilbur, R. Introductions to Molière. *In* Wilbur, R. Responses p224-38

About individual works

Amphitryon

McGlathery, J. M. Kleist's version of Molière's Amphitryon: Olympian cuckolding and unio mystica. *In* Johnson, R. B.; Neumann, E. S. and Trail, G. T. eds. Molière and the commonwealth of letters: patrimony and posterity p327-33

Don Juan

Bloch, A. Dom Juan and Don Giovanni. *In* Johnson, R. B.; Neumann, E. S. and Trail, G. T. eds. Molière and the commonwealth of letters: patrimony and posterity p287-98

Wiingaard, J. Dom Juan, a reassessment in view of modern existentialism. *In* Johnson, R. B.; Neumann, E. S. and Trail, G. T. eds. Molière and the commonwealth of letters: patrimony and posterity p639-44

The misanthrope

DiBattista, M. A. The misanthrope. *In* Seidel, M. A. and Mendelson, E. eds. Homer to Brecht p255-72

Hamilton, J. F. Molière and Rousseau: the confrontation of art and politics. *In* Johnson, R. B.; Neumann, E. S. and Trail, G. T. eds. Molière and the commonwealth of letters: patrimony and posterity p100-08

Hutman, N. L. Célimène as anti-ingenue: Molière and the transformation of comic types. *In* Johnson, R. B.; Neumann, E. S. and Trail, G. T. eds. Molière and the commonwealth of letters: patrimony and posterity p457-61

Lawrence, F. L. Le misanthrope reprised: four versions of Molière's theme. *In* Johnson, R. B.; Neumann, E. S. and Trail, G. T. eds. Molière and the commonwealth of letters: patrimony and posterity p82-89

Simon, J. I. Translation or adaptation? *In* From Parnassus p147-57

The rehearsal at Versailles

Sogliuzzo, A. R. Theater of the theater: Molière and Pirandello. *In* Johnson, R. B.; Neumann, E. S. and Trail, G. T. eds. Molière and the commonwealth of letters: patrimony and posterity p183-89

Tartuffe

Koppisch, M. S. The faux dévot from Molière to Marivaux. *In* Johnson, R. B.; Neumann, E. S. and Trail, G. T. eds. Molière and the commonwealth of letters: patrimony and posterity p57-67

The would-be gentleman

White, K. S. Hypnotic language and its apotheoses: Molière and Ionesco. *In* Johnson, R. B.; Neumann, E. S. and Trail, G. T. eds. Molière and the commonwealth of letters: patrimony and posterity. p160-68

Acting

See Molière, Jean Baptiste Poquelin—Dramatic production

Adaptations

Durer, C. S. Molière and Polish comedy. *In* Johnson, R. B.; Neumann, E. S. and Trail, G. T. eds. Molière and the commonwealth of letters: patrimony and posterity p365-78

Fiedler, L. M. Molière on Max Reinhardt's stage. *In* Johnson, R. B.; Neumann, E. S. and Trail, G. T. eds. Molière and the commonwealth of letters: patrimony and posterity p591-602

Kauffmann, S. Scapino. *In* Kauffmann, S. Persons of the drama p130-33

Kearful, F. J. Molière among the English, 1660-1737. *In* Johnson, R. B.; Neumann, E. S. and Trail, G. T. eds. Molière and the commonwealth of letters: patrimony and posterity p199-217

McGlathery, J. M. Kleist's version of Molière's Amphitryon: Olympian cuckolding and unio mystica. *In* Johnson, R. B.; Neumann, E. S. and Trail, G. T. eds. Molière and the commonwealth of letters: patrimony and posterity p327-33

Anniversaries, etc., 1773

Gravit, F. W. The first centenary of Molière's death. *In* Johnson, R. B.; Neumann, E. S. and Trail, G. T. eds. Molière and the commonwealth of letters: patrimony and posterity p547-56

Appreciation—Germany

Mews, S. The dramatic Dioscuri: Molière's German reception in the late nineteenth century. *In* Johnson, R. B.; Neumann, E. S. and Trail, G. T. eds. Molière and the commonwealth of letters: patrimony and posterity p334-44

Appreciation—Hungary

Katona, A. Molière in Hungary: his reputation. *In* Johnson, R. B.; Neumann, E. S. and Trail, G. T. eds. Molière and the commonwealth of letters: patrimony and posterity p355-64

Bibliography

Hall, H. G. The present state of Molière studies. *In* Johnson, R. B.; Neumann, E. S. and Trail, G. T. eds. Molière and the commonwealth of letters: patrimony and posterity p728-46

Biography—Marriage

Hall, D. R. Molière: critic and victim of the social institution of marriage. *In* Johnson, R. B.; Neumann, E. S. and Trail, G. T. eds. Molière and the commonwealth of letters: patrimony and posterity p49-53

Centennial celebrations, etc., 1773

See Molière, Jean Baptiste Poquelin—Anniversaries, etc., 1773

Characters

Vogler, F. W. Molière and the comical Teuton. *In* Johnson, R. B.; Neumann, E. S. and Trail, G. T. eds. Molière and the commonwealth of letters: patrimony and posterity p527-32

Characters—Célimène

Hutman, N. L. Célimène as anti-ingenue: Molière and the transformation of comic types. *In* Johnson, R. B.; Neumann, E. S. and Trail, G. T. eds. Molière and the commonwealth of letters: patrimony and posterity p457-61

Molière, Jean B. P.—*Continued*

Language

Vogler, F. W. Molière and the comical Teuton. *In* Johnson, R. B.; Neumann, E. S. and Trail, G. T. eds. Molière and the commonwealth of letters: patrimony and posterity p527-32

Moving-pictures

See Molière, Jean Baptiste Poquelin—Film adaptations

Musical settings

Harned, A. R. Molière and Lully. *In* Johnson, R. B.; Neumann, E. S. and Trail, G. T. eds. Molière and the commonwealth of letters: patrimony and posterity p31-48

Poetic works

Conroy, P. V. Songs and sonnets: patterns of characterization. *In* Johnson, R. B.; Neumann, E. S. and Trail, G. T. eds. Molière and the commonwealth of letters: patrimony and posterity p533-41

Relationship with women

See Molière, Jean Baptiste Poquelin—Biography—Marriage

Religion and ethics

Romero, L. Molière's morale: debates in criticism. *In* Johnson, R. B.; Neumann, E. S. and Trail, G. T. eds. Molière and the commonwealth of letters: patrimony and posterity p706-27

Songs and music

Conroy, P. V. Songs and sonnets: patterns of characterization. *In* Johnson, R. B.; Neumann, E. S. and Trail, G. T. eds. Molière and the commonwealth of letters: patrimony and posterity p533-41

Sources

Wadsworth, P. A. From the commedia erudita to Molière. *In* Johnson, R. B.; Neumann, E. S. and Trail, G. T. eds. Molière and the commonwealth of letters: patrimony and posterity p443-53

Stage history—Brazil

Stevens, W. K. Recent Brazilian productions of Le bourgeois gentilhomme and Les femmes savantes. *In* Johnson, R. B.; Neumann, E. S. and Trail, G. T. eds. Molière and the commonwealth of letters: patrimony and posterity p407-09

Stage history—Canada

Fitzpatrick, M. A. Molière and the early years of French-Canadian theater. *In* Johnson, R. B.; Neumann, E. S. and Trail, G. T. eds. Molière and the commonwealth of letters: patrimony and posterity p385-99

Stage history—Denmark

Jensen, A. E. Molière in Denmark in the 18th century. *In* Johnson, R. B.; Neumann, E. S. and Trail, G. T. eds. Molière and the commonwealth of letters: patrimony and posterity p252-58

Stage history—Germany

Fiedler, L. M. Molière on Max Reinhardt's stage. *In* Johnson, R. B.; Neumann, E. S. and Trail, G. T. eds. Molière and the commonwealth of letters: patrimony and posterity p591-602

Stage history—Hungary

Katona, A. Molière in Hungary: his reputation. *In* Johnson, R. B.; Neumann, E. S. and Trail, G. T. eds. Molière and the commonwealth of letters: patrimony and posterity p355-64

Stage history—New York (City)

Keating, L. C. Molière in New York. *In* Johnson, R. B.; Neumann, E. S. and Trail, G. T. eds. Molière and the commonwealth of letters: patrimony and posterity p400-06

Stage history—Spain

Holt, M. P. Contemporary translations and stagings of Molière's plays in Spain. *In* Johnson, R. B.; Neumann, E. S. and Trail, G. T. eds. Molière and the commonwealth of letters: patrimony and posterity p190-95

Stage presentation

See Molière, Jean Baptiste Poquelin—Dramatic production

Translations, English

Simon, J. I. Translation or adaptation? *In* From Parnassus p147-57

Solomon, S. Problems and suggested solutions in translating Molière. *In* Johnson, R. B.; Neumann, E. S. and Trail, G. T. eds. Molière and the commonwealth of letters: patrimony and posterity p603-16

Translations, Hungarian

Katona, A. Molière in Hungary: his reputation. *In* Johnson, R. B.; Neumann, E. S. and Trail, G. T. eds. Molière and the commonwealth of letters: patrimony and posterity p355-64

Translations, Portuguese

Stevens, W. K. Recent Brazilian productions of Le bourgeois gentilhomme and Les femmes savantes. *In* Johnson, R. B.; Neumann, E. S. and Trail, G. T. eds. Molière and the commonwealth of letters: patrimony and posterity p407-09

Translations, Spanish

Holt, M. P. Contemporary translations and stagings of Molière's plays in Spain. *In* Johnson, R. B.; Neumann, E. S. and Trail, G. T. eds. Molière and the commonwealth of letters: patrimony and posterity p190-95

Molière, Jean Baptiste Poquelin, in fiction, drama, poetry, etc.

Howarth, W. D. The playwright as hero: biographical plays with Molière as protagonist: 1673-1972. *In* Johnson, R. B.; Neumann, E. S. and Trail, G. T. eds. Molière and the commonwealth of letters: patrimony and posterity p557-72

Moll, Bernhard Albrecht

About

Andre, J. and Fröschle, H. The American expedition of Emperor Joseph II and Bernhard Moll's silhouettes. *In* The German contribution to the building of the Americas p135-72

Mollenkott, Virginia Ramey

Herrick and the cleansing of perception. *In* Rollin, R. B. and Patrick, J. M. eds. "Trust to good verses": Herrick tercentenary essays p197-209

The pervasive influence of the Apocrypha in Milton's thought and art. *In* Patrick, J. M. and Sundell, R. H. eds. Milton and the art of sacred song p23-43

Moller, Caroline Ifeka· See Ifeka-Moller, Caroline

Mollinger, Robert Neal
Wallace Stevens' search for the central man. *In* Tennessee Studies in literature v21 p66-79

Molloy, John P. and Rathje, William Laurens
Sexploitation among the late classic Maya. *In* Mesoamerican archaeology p431-44

Molnar, Thomas Steven
On authority; excerpt from "Authority and its enemies." *In* A Public philosophy reader p219-27

Moloney, Michael Francis
Donne's metrical practice. *In* Roberts, J. R. ed. Essential articles for the study of John Donne's poetry p171-77

Moltmann, Jürgen
Liberation in the light of hope. *In* The Context of contemporary theology p127-46

Molz, Redmond Kathleen
Libraries and the development and future of tax support. *In* Libraries and the life of the mind in America p41-63

Momaday, Natachie Scott
Native American attitudes to the environment. *In* Seeing with a native eye p79-85

About individual works
House made of dawn
Larson, C. R. Rejection: the reluctant return. *In* Larson, C. R. American Indian fiction p66-96
Watkins, F. C. Culture versus anonymity in House made of dawn. *In* Watkins, F. C. In time and place p133-71

Mombasa, Kenya
Social conditions
Edari, R. S. Social change in Mombasa, Kenya. *In* Walton, J. and Masotti, L. H. eds. The city in comparative perspective p179-92

Momberger, Philip
Faulkner's "country" as ideal community. *In* Baldwin, K. H. and Kirby, D. K. eds. Individual and community p112-36

Momigliano, Arnaldo
Essays in ancient and modern historiography
Contents
The ancient city of Fustel de Coulanges
Athens in the third century B.C. and the discovery of Rome in the histories of Timaeus of Tauromenium
Did Fabius Pictor lie?
Eastern elements in Post-exilic Jewish, and Greek, historiography
The fault of the Greeks
The first political commentary on Tacitus
The first political commentary on Tacitus: appendix
The historian's skin
Historicism revisited
Introduction to the Griechische Kulturgeschichte by Jacob Burckhardt
J. G. Droysen between Greeks and Jews
The lonely historian Ammianus Marcellinus
Mabillon's Italian disciples
Pagan and Christian historiography in the fourth century A.D.
Perizonius, Niebuhr and the character of early Roman tradition

A Piedmontese view of the history of ideas
Polybius' reappearance in Western Europe
Popular religious beliefs and the late Roman historians
Reconsidering B. Croce (1866-1952)
Time in ancient historiography
Tradition and the classical historian
Vico's Scienza nuova: Roman 'bestioni' and Roman 'eroi'
Gibbon from an Italian point of view. *In* Edward Gibbon and The decline and fall of the Roman Empire p75-85

Mommsen, Hans
National socialism: continuity and change. *In* Laqueur, W. Z. ed. Fascism: a reader's guide p179-210

Mon, Franz. See Löffelholz, Franz

Monaco, James
The New Wave
Contents
Chabrol: films noirs in color
Godard: Modes of discourse
Godard: Returning to zero (picture and act)
Godard: A season in hell: icy poetry
Godard: Theory and practice: the Dziga-Vertov period
Godard: Women and the outsider
Introduction: The camera writes
Rivette: the process of narrative
Rohmer: Moral tales: the art of courtly love
Truffaut: Intimate politics
Truffaut: The Antoine Doinel cycle
Truffaut: The explosion of genres
Truffaut: The statement of genres

Monaco, Paul
The popular cinema as reflection of the group process in France, 1919-1929. *In* DeMause, L. ed. The new psychohistory p151-79

Monarchs. See Kings and rulers

Monarchy, French
Renna, T. J. Aristotle and the French monarchy, 1260-1303. *In* Viator: medieval and Renaissance studies v9 p309-24

Monastery of Guadalupe. See Guadalupe, Spain. Santa Maria (Hieronymite monastery)

Monastic and religious life of women. See Celibacy

Monasticism and religious orders
See also Cluniacs; Franciscans; Friars

Middle Ages, 600-1500
Sims-Williams, P. Continental influence at Bath monastery in the seventh century. *In* Anglo-Saxon England 4 p 1-28
Smalley, B. Ecclesiastical attitudes to novelty, c. 1100-c. 1250. *In* Church, society and politics p113-31
Sullivan, R. E. The medieval monk as frontiersman. *In* The Frontier v2 p25-49

England
Meehan, B. Outsiders, insiders, and property in Durham around 1100. *In* Church, society and politics p45-58
Sayers, J. Monastic archdeacons. *In* Church and government in the Middle Ages p177-203

Monasticism and religious orders, Taoist
Yoshioka, Y. Taoist monastic life. *In* Welch, H. and Seidel, A. K. eds. Facets of Taoism p229-52

Monasticism and religious orders for women. See Nuns in literature

Mondale, Walter Frederick
Beyond detente: toward international economic security. *In* Bundy, W. P. ed. The world economic crisis p230-52

Mondriaan, Pieter Cornelis

About
Rosenberg, H. Mondrian: meaning in abstract art I. *In* Rosenberg, H. Art on the edge p39-49
Schapiro, M. Mondrian. *In* Schapiro, M. Selected papers v2 p233-61
Welsh, R. P. Mondrian and theosophy. *In* Kaplan, P. and Manso, S. eds. Major European art movements, 1900-1945 p250-74

Moneta, Carlos Juan. See Moneta Testa, Carlos

Moneta Testa, Carlos
Argentine foreign policy in the Cold war. *In* Siracusa, J. M. and Barclay, G. S. eds. The impact of the Cold war p101-24

Monetary management. See Monetary policy

Monetary policy
Mazur, M. P. Interdependence, flexible exchange rates, and capital controls: the international monetary order in transition. *In* Baldwin, D. A. ed. America in an interdependent world p63-89
McKinnon, R. I. America's role in stabilizing the world's monetary system. *In* A New America? p305-24
Segré, C. The future of international monetary management. *In* The New Atlantic challenge p103-12
See also Fiscal policy

United States
Cagan, P. and Schwartz, A. J. How feasible is a flexible monetary policy? *In* Capitalism and freedom p262-93
McKinnon, R. I. America's role in stabilizing the world's monetary system. *In* A New America? p305-24

Monetary question. See Currency question; Money

Money
Lerner, A. P. Money, debt and wealth. *In* Econometrics and economic theory p247-59
Matthews, R. C. O. Public policy and monetary expenditure. *In* The Market and the state p330-45
Reed, I. Image and money. *In* Reed, I. Shrovetide in old New Orleans p53-59
Shell, M. The Ring of Gyges. *In* Shell, M. The economy of literature p11-62
Triffin, R. Basic considerations on international monetary reform. *In* Inflation, trade and taxes p119-36
Vickers, D. Adam Smith and the status of the theory of money. *In* Skinner, A. S. and Wilson, T. eds. Essays on Adam Smith p482-503
See also Bills of exchange; Coinage; Foreign exchange; Gold; Inflation (Finance); Mints; Purchasing power; Silver

Africa, East
Letiche, J. M. Dependent monetary systems and economic development: the case of sterling East Africa. *In* Economic development and planning p186-236

Venice—History
Lane, F. C. The first infidelities of the Venetian lire. *In* The Medieval city p43-63

Money in literature
Lerner, L. Literature and money. *In* English Association. Essays and studies, 1975 p106-22
Shell, M. The language of character: an introduction to a poetics of monetary inscriptions. *In* Shell, M. The economy of literature p63-88

Money supply. See Monetary policy

Mongkut, King of Thailand

Bibliography
Wilson, C. M. Toward a bibliography of the life and times of Mongkut, King of Thailand, 1851-1868. *In* Southeast Asian history and historiography p164-89

Mongolia (Mongolian People's Republic)

History
Hammond, T. T. The Communist takeover of Outer Mongolia: model for Eastern Europe? *In* Hammond, T. T. ed. The anatomy of Communist takeovers p107-44

Mongolism
Gustafson, J. M. Mongolism, parental desires, and the right to life. *In* Weir, R. F. ed. Ethical issues in death and dying p145-72

Mongols. See Tatars

Monig, Christopher, pseud. See Crossen, Kendell Foster

Monism
Todd, R. B. Monism and immanence: the foundations of Stoic physics. *In* Rist, J. M. ed. The Stoics p137-60
See also Dualism; Idealism; Materialism; Pluralism

The Monitor
Granger, B. I. Early Southern serials. *In* Granger, B. I. American essay serials from Franklin to Irving p70-96

Monkeys
See also Macaques

Behavior
Lancaster, J. B. Sex and gender in evolutionary perspective. *In* Katchadourian, H. A. ed. Human sexuality p51-80
Rowell, T. E. Growing up in a monkey group. *In* Schwartz, T. ed. Socialization as cultural communication p21-36

Monkman, Leslie
Kenya and the New Jerusalem in A grain of wheat. *In* African literature today no. 7: Focus on criticism p111-16

Mönks, Franz J. See Hill, J. P. jt. auth.

Monks
Sullivan, R. E. The medieval monk as frontiersman. *In* The Frontier v2 p25-49

Monod, Jacques L.
On chance and necessity. *In* Ayala, F. J. and Dobzhansky, T. G. eds. Studies in the philosophy of biology p357-61
On the molecular theory of evolution. *In* Harré, R. ed. Problems of scientific revolution p11-24

About individual works
Chance and necessity
Monod, J. L. On chance and necessity. *In* Ayala, F. J. and Dobzhansky, T. G. eds. Studies in the philosophy of biology p357-61

Monod, Sylvère
Confessions of an unrepentant Chestertonian. *In* Dickens Studies Annual v3 p214-28

Monologue

Hobsbaum, P. The rise of the dramatic monologue. *In* Hobsbaum, P. Tradition and experiment in English poetry p233-54

Mason, M. Browning and the dramatic monologue. *In* Armstrong, I. ed. Robert **Browning p231-66**

Pascal, R. Conclusions. *In* Pascal, R The dual voice p135-41

Pascal, R. The narrator problem. *In* Pascal, R. The dual voice p 1-36

Monopolies

See also Oligopolies

Mathematical models

Bergson, A. Consumer's and producer's surplus and general equilibrium. *In* Theory for economic efficiency: essays in honor of Abba P. Lerner p12-23

Monotheism

Coomaraswamy, A. K. Vedic "monotheism." *In* Coomaraswamy, A. K. Selected papers v2 p166-76

Petersen, D. L. Max Weber and the sociological study of ancient Israel. *In* Johnson, H. M. ed. Religious change and continuity p117-49

Radin, P. Monotheism among American Indians. *In* Tedlock, D. E. and Tedlock, B. eds. Teachings from the American earth p219-47

Monotremata

Cimons, J. R. The brain and evolution of lower mammals. *In* Grafton Elliot Smith p39-49

Monroe, James T.

The Hispanic-Arabic world. *In* Américo Castro and the meaning of Spanish civilization p69-90

Studies on the "ḥargas": the Arabic and the romance "ḥargas." *In* Viator: medieval and Renaissance studies v8 p95-125

Monroe, Marilyn

About

Sarris, A. Marilyn, by Norman Mailer. *In* Sarris, A. Politics and cinema p162-67

Monroe doctrine

Van Alstyne, R. W. The Monroe doctrine. *In* Encyclopedia of American foreign policy p584-96

Monsters. See Gorgons

Monsters in literature

Brooks, P. "Godlike science/unhallowed arts": language, nature, and monstrosity. *In* Levine, G. L. and Knoepflmacher, U. C. eds. The endurance of Frankenstein p205-20

Ellis, K. Monsters in the garden: Mary Shelley and the bourgeois family. *In* Levine, G. L. and Knoepflmacher, U. C. eds. The endurance of Frankenstein p123-42

Griffin, A. Fire and ice in Frankenstein. *In* Levine, G. L. and Knoepflmacher, U. C. eds. The endurance of Frankenstein p49-73

Knoepflmacher, U. C. Thoughts on the aggression of daughters. *In* Levine, G. L. and Knoepflmacher, U. C. eds. The endurance of Frankenstein p88-119

Levine, G. L. The ambiguous heritage of Frankenstein. *In* Levine, G. L. and Knoepflmacher, U. C. eds. The endurance of Frankenstein p3-30

Moers, E. Female Gothic. *In* Levine, G. L. and Knoepflmacher, U. C. eds. The endurance of Frankestein p77-87

Prickett, S. Dreams and nightmares: monsters under the hill. *In* Prickett, S. Victorian fantasy p75-113

Scott, P. D. Vital artifice: Mary, Percy, and the psychopolitical integrity of Frankenstein. *In* Levine, G. L. and Knoepflmacher, U. C. eds. The endurance of Frankenstein p172-202

Sterrenburg, L. W. Mary Shelley's monster: politics and psyche in Frankenstein. *In* Levine, G. L. and Knoepflmacher, U. C. eds. The endurance of Frankenstein p143-71

Stevick, P. Frankenstein and comedy. *In* Levine, G. L. and Knoepflmacher, U. C. eds. The endurance of Frankenstein p221-39

Wilt, J. Frankenstein as Mystery play. *In* Levine, G. L. and Knoepflmacher, U. C. eds. The endurance of Frankenstein p31-48

Montag, Tom

The little magazine small press connection: some conjectures. *In* Anderson, E. and Kinzie, M. eds. The little magazine in America: a modern documentary history p575-93

Montagu, Ashley

Introduction. *In* Montagu, A. ed. Learning nonaggression p3-11

My conception of the nature of human nature. *In* Hanna, T. ed. Explorers of humankind p90-102

See also Dobzhansky, T. J. jt. auth.

Montagu, Elizabeth

About individual works

This side of the truth

Balakian, N. Three post-psychological novels. *In* Balakian, N. Critical encounters p95-104

Montagu, Lady Mary (Pierrepont) Wortley

About

Halsband, R. "Condemned to petticoats": Lady Mary Wortley Montagu as feminist and writer. *In* The Dress of words p35-52

Halsband, R. New anecdotes of Lady Mary Wortley Montagu. *In* Evidence in literary scholarship p241-46

Montagu, Lady Mary (Pierrepoint) Wortley, and Hervey, John Hervey, Baron

About individual works

Verses address'd to the imitator of the First satire of the Second book of Horace

Grundy, I. Verses address'd to the imitator of Horace: a skirmish between Pope and some persons of rank and fortune. *In* Virginia. University. Bibliographical Society. Studies in bibliography v30 p96-119

Montagu, Montague Francis Ashley- See Montagu, Ashley

Montague, John

Despair and delight. *In* Time was away p123-27

Montaigne, Michel Eyquem de

About

Screech, M. A. Medicine and literature: aspects of Rabelais and Montaigne (with a glance at the law). *In* French Renaissance studies, 1540-70 p156-69

Thomas, L. Why Montaigne is not a bore. *In* Thomas, L. The medusa and the snail p145-50

Montaigne, Michel E. de—*Continued*

About individual works
The education of children

Phillips, M.M. From the Ciceronianus to Montaigne. *In* Classical influences on European culture A.D. 1500-1700 p191-97

Essays

Lyons, J. O. Autobiography. *In* Lyons, J. O. The invention of the self p55-74

O'Neill, J. Essay 2. *In* Fitzgerald, R. ed. What it means to be human p25-43

Screech, M. A. Commonplaces of law, proverbial wisdom and philosophy: their importance in Renaissance scholarship (Rabelais, Joachim du Bellay, Montaigne). *In* Classical influences on European culture A.D. 1500-1700 p127-34

On cannibals

Scaglione, A. D. A note on Montaigne's Des cannibales and the humanist tradition. *In* First images of America p63-70

Upon some verses of Virgil

Coleman, D. G. Montaigne's 'Sur des vers de Virgile': taboo subject, taboo author. *In* Classical influences on European culture A.D. 1500-1700 p135-40

Influence—Donne

Ornstein, R. Donne, Montaigne, and natural law. *In* Roberts, J. R. ed. Essential articles for the study of John Donne's poetry p129-41

Influence—Shakespeare

Elrodt, R. Self-consciousness in Montaigne and Shakespeare. *In* Shakespeare survey 28 p37-50

Montale, Eugenio

About

Perella, N. J. Eugenio Montale. *In* Perella, N. J. Midday in Italian literature p240-62

Characters—Arsenio

Biasin, G. P. Strategies of the anti-hero: Svevo, Pirandello, and Montale. *In* Italian literature: roots and branches p363-81

Montalenti, Giuseppe

From Aristotle to Democritus via Darwin: a short survey of a long historical and logical journey. *In* Ayala, F. J. and Dobzhansky, T. G. eds. Studies in the philosophy of biology p3-19

Montalva, Eduardo Frei. See Frei Montalva, Eduardo, President Chile

Montana

Politics and government

Malone, M. P. The Montana New Dealers. *In* Braeman, J.; Bremner, R. H. and Brody, D. eds. The New Deal v2 p240-68

Montanhagol, Guilhem de. See Guilhem de Montanhagol

Monte Cassino (Benedictine Monastery)

Newton, F. L. Some Monte Cassino scribes in the eleventh century *In* Medieval and Renaissance studies [1975] p3-19

Montefeltro, Federigo, Count of. See Federigo, Count of Montefeltro, Duke of Urbino

Montefiore Hospital of Western Pennsylvania

Hailperin, C. M. Twenty-five years of home care services. *In* Home care p137-47

Montes de Oca, Marco Antonio

About

Forster, M. H. Four contemporary Mexican poets: Marco Antonio Montes de Oca, Gabriel Zaid, José Emilio Pacheco, Homero Aridjis. *In* Forster, M. H. ed. Tradition and renewal p139-56

Montesquieu, Charles Louis de Secondat, baron de La Brede et de

About

Shackleton, R. Allies and enemies: Voltaire and Montesquieu. *In* Royal Society of Literature of the United Kingdom, London. Essays by divers hands v39 p126-45

Shackleton, R. John Black and Montesquieu—the search for a correspondence. *In* Evidence in literary scholarship p215-27

About individual works
The Persian letters

Crisafulli, A. S. The Journal des Sçavans and The Lettres persanes. *In* Literature and history in the age of ideas p59-66

The spirit of the laws

Chamley, P. E. The conflict between Montesquieu and Hume: a study of the origins of Adam Smith's universalism. *In* Skinner, A. S. and Wilson, T. eds. Essays on Adam Smith p274-305

Guerlac, H. Three eighteenth-century social philosophers: scientific influences on their thought. *In* Guerlac, H. Essays and papers in the history of modern science p451-64

Hughes, P. Creativity and history in Vico and his contemporaries. *In* Giambattista Vico's science of humanity p155-69

Montessori method of education

Elkind, D. Piaget and Montessori in the classroom. *In* Elkind, D. The child and society p143-55

Gitter, L. L. Montessori and the compulsive cleanliness of severely retarded children. *In* Ulman, E. and Dachinger, P. eds. Art therapy p181-90

Montgomery, David

Immigrant workers and managerial reform. *In* Immigrants in industrial America, 1850-1920 p96-110

Montgomery, John Dickey

The infrastructure of technical assistance: American aid experience in Africa. *In* African dimensions p137-53

Montgomery, Marion

Hemingway's "The gambler, the nun, and the radio": a reading and a problem. *In* Benson, J. J. ed. The short stories of Ernest Hemingway: critical essays p203-10

Robert Frost: one who shrewdly pretends. *In* Frost: centennial essays II p213-22

Montgomery, Robert

About individual works
Subject to fits

Kauffmann, S. Subject to fits. *In* Kauffmann, S. Persons of the drama p216-18

Montgomery, Sarah Southworth

United States direct investment in Europe and Canada, 1955-1970: a regression study. *In* Inflation, trade and taxes p137-62

Montherlant, Henry de

About

Glicksberg, C. I. Henry de Montherlant: hedonism and the Absurd. *In* Glicksberg, C. I. The literature of nihilism p155-78

About individual works

Chaos and night

Glicksberg, C. I. Henry de Montherlant: hedonism and the Absurd. *In* Glicksberg, C. I. The literature of nihilism p155-78

Montini, Giovanni Battista, Cardinal. See Paulus, VI, Pope

Montorsoli, Fra Giovanni Angelo

About

Kubler, G. Drawings by G. A. Montorsoli in Madrid. *In* Collaboration in Italian Renaissance art p143-64

Monts, Elizabeth A. and Burger, Laura J.
The status of home economics and the status of women. *In* Roberts, J. I. ed. Beyond intellectual sexism p381-86

Monty, Jeanne Ruth
Voltaire's debt to the Encyclopédie in the Opinion en alphabet. *In* Literature and history in the age of ideas p153-67

Monuments
Dubos, R. J. Hauts lieux and monuments. *In* Dubos, R. J. Beast or angel? p107-15

See also Megalithic monuments; Tombs

United States

Geist, C. D. Historic sites and monuments as icons. *In* Browne, R. B. and Fishwick, M. W. eds. Icons of America p57-66

Moodley, Kogila A.
South African Indians: the wavering minority. *In* Thompson, L. M. and Butler, J. eds. Change in contemporary South Africa p250-79

Moody, Anthony David
'To fill all the desert with inviolable voice.' *In* The Waste land in different voices p47-66

Moody, Edward J.
Magical therapy: an anthropological investigation of contemporary Satanism. *In* Zaretsky, I. I. and Leone, M. P. eds. Religious movements in contemporary America p355-82

Moody, Ernest Addison
Studies in medieval philosophy, science, and logic

Contents

The age of analysis
Buridan and a dilemma of nominalism
Empiricism and metaphysics in medieval philosophy
Galileo and Avempace: the dynamics of the Leaning Tower Experiment
Galileo and his precursors
Jean Buridan
John Buridan on the habitability of the earth
Laws of motion in medieval physics
The medieval contribution to logic
Ockham and Aegidius of Rome
Ockham, Buridan, and Nicholas of Autrecourt
A quodlibetal question of Robert Holkot, O.P. on the problem of the objects of knowledge and of belief
William of Auvergne and his treatise De anima
William of Ockham

Moody, Michael E.
Religion in the life of Charles Middleton, First Baron Barham. *In* The Dissenting tradition p140-63

Moody, Michael Weston
A small whirlpool: narrative structure in The green house. *In* Rossman, C. R. and Friedman, A. W. eds. Mario Vargas Llosa p15-35

Mookerjee, Girija
Malraux and the Hindu vision. *In* Courcel, M. H. de, ed. Malraux p112-19

Moon, Sun Myung
God's hope for America: Keynote speech at Yankee Stadium, June 1, 1976. *In* Horowitz, I. L. ed. Science, sin, and scholarship p2-11

The search for absolute values: harmony among the sciences: Founder's address, Fifth International Conference on the Unity of the Sciences, November 26, 1976, Washington, D. C. *In* Horowitz, I. L. ed. Science, sin, and scholarship p12-18

About

Anthony, D. and Robbins, T. L. The effect of detente on the growth of new religions: Reverend Moon and the Unification Church. *In* Needleman, J. and Baker, G. eds. Understanding the new religions p80-100

Lester, M. Profits, politics, power: the heart of the controversy. *In* Horowitz, I. L. ed. Science, sin, and scholarship p148-59

Welles, C. The eclipse of Sun Myung Moon. *In* Horowitz, I. L. ed. Science, sin, and scholarship p242-58

Moon
Wood, J. A. The moon. *In* Man and cosmos p50-62

Observations

Gingerich, O. Dissertation cum Professore Righini et Sidereo nuncio. *In* Bonelli, M. L. R. and Shea, W. R. eds. Reason, experiment, and mysticism in the scientific revolution p77-88

Righini, G. New light on Galileo's lunar observations. *In* Bonelli, M. L. R. and Shea, W. R. eds. Reason, experiment, and mysticism in the scientific revolution p59-76

Surface

Righini, G. Terrestrial interpretations of lunar spots. *In* Bonelli, M. L. R. and Shea, W. R. eds. Reason, experiment, and mysticism in the scientific revolution p89-94

Moon bases. See Lunar bases

Moon settlements. See Lunar bases

Mooney, James
The doctrine of the Ghost dance; excerpt from "The ghost-dance religion and the Sioux outbreak of 1890." *In* Tedlock, D. E. and Tedlock, B. eds. Teachings from the American earth p75-95

Mooney, James E.
Loyalist imprints printed in America, 1774-1785. *In* American Antiquarian Society. Proceedings v84 pt 1 p105-218

See also Leventhal, H. jt. auth

Moore, Beverly C. and Harris, Fred R.
Class actions: let the people in. *In* Nader, R. and Green, M. J. eds. Verdicts on lawyers p172-84

Moore, C. L. See Moore, Catherine Lucile

Moore, Carlisle

Carlyle and Goethe as scientist. *In* Carlyle and his contemporaries p21-34

Carlyle, mathematics and "mathesis." *In* Fielding, K. J. and Tarr, R. L. eds. Carlyle past and present p61-95

Moore, Catherine Lucile

About

Gunn, J. E. Henry Kuttner, C. L. Moore, Lewis Padgett et al. *In* Clareson, T. D. ed. Voices for the future: essays on major science fiction writers v 1 p185-215

Moore, Don D.

John Webster. *In* Logan, T. P. and Smith, D. S. eds. The popular school p85-104

Moore, Emily Campbell

Native American Indian values. *In* Population policy and ethics p237-75

Moore, Erna Marie

Friedrich Torberg's Mein ist die Rache as a literary work of art. *In* Strelka, J. P.; Bell, R. F. and Dobson, E. eds. Protest—form—tradition p111-21

Moore, Florence M.

Homemaker-home health aides—essential thanatologists. *In* Home care p208-14

Moore, George

About

Caserio, R. L. Plot, purpose, and the modern self. *In* Caserio, R. L. Plot, story, and the novel p167-97

Henn, T. R. George Moore. *In* Henn, T. R. Last essays p173-90

About individual works
The brook Kerith

Richards, I. A. Jesus' other life. *In* Richards, I. A. Complementarities p209-14

Bibliography

Gerber, H. E. George Moore. *In* Finner-ran, R. J. ed. Anglo-Irish literature p138-66

Moore, George Edward

About

Richards, I. A. Complementarities. *In* Richards, I. A. Complementarities p108-26

Skilton, D. Late-Victorian choices: James, Wilde, Gissing and Moore. *In* Skilton, D. The English novel p178-91

Moore, Gerald

The language of West Indian poetry. *In* Baugh, E. ed. Critics on Caribbean literature p130-36

About individual works
Wole Soyinka

Banham, M. Eldred Durosimi Jones: The writing of Wole Soyinka; Gerald Moore: Wole Soyinka. *In* African literature today no. 7: Focus on criticism p153-54

Moore, Harry Thornton

E. M. Forster. *In* Stade, G. ed. Six modern British novelists p219-68

About

Apter, T. E. Bert Lawrence and Lady Jane. *In* Smith, A. ed. Lawrence and women p178-88

About individual works
The priest of love

Mudrick, M. Lawrence. *In* Mudrick, M. The man in the machine p37-60

Moore, John A.

The dissembling-speech of Ajax. *In* Yale classical studies v25 p47-66

Moore, John Robert, 1936-

The New Deal in Louisiana. *In* Braeman, J.; Bremner, R. H. and Brody, D. eds. The New Deal v2 p137-65

Moore, Joseph Earle

About

Harvey, A. M. Contributions of the part-time staff of the Johns Hopkins Hospital: Moore, King, and Gay. *In* Harvey, A. M. Adventures in medical research p248-60

Moore, Marianne

Idiosyncrasy and technique. *In* Gibbons, R. ed. The poet's work: 29 masters of 20th century poetry on the origins and practice of their art p215-29

About

Kammer, J. The art of silence and the forms of women's poetry. *In* Gilbert, S. M. and Gubar, S. eds. Shakespeare's sisters p153-64

Kenner, H. Disliking it. *In* Kenner, H. A homemade world p91-118

Kunitz, S. J. Responses, glosses, refractions. *In* Kunitz, S. J. A kind of order, a kind of folly p223-27

Thurley, G. Phenomenalist idioms: Doolittle, Moore, Levertov. *In* Thurley, G. The American moment p109-25

About individual works
Like a bulwark

Olson, E. The poetry of Marianne Moore. *In* Olson, E. On value judgments in the arts, and other essays p50-54

What are years

Kunitz, S. J. Pangolin of poets. *In* Kunitz, S. J. A kind of order, a kind of folly p220-22

Moore, Mary B.

Poseidon in the Gigantomachy. *In* Studies in classical art and archaeology p23-27

Moore, Maxine

Asimov, Calvin, and Moses. *In* Clareson, T. D. ed. Voices for the future: essays on major science fiction writers v 1 p88-103

Moore, Robert Hamilton. See Twombly, R. C. jt. auth.

Moore, Robert Laurence

Spiritualism. *In* The Rise of Adventism p79-103

Moore, Thomas

About individual works
The loves of the angels

Bentley, G. E. A jewel in an Ethiop's ear. *In* Essick, R. N. and Pearce, D. R. eds. Blake in his time p213-40

Moorhouse, Frank

About individual works
The electrical experience

Cantrell, L. The new novel: David Ireland's The unknown industrial prisoner, Michael Wilding's The short story embassy, and Frank Moorhouse's The electrical experience. *In* Hamilton, K. G. ed. Studies in the recent Australian novel p225-57

Moorish architecture. See Architecture, Islamic

Moorish art. See Art, Islamic

Moorman, Charles

The night of the iguana: a long introduction, a general essay, and no explication at all. *In* Tennessee Williams: a tribute p318-24

Moos, Stanislaus von

The palace as a fortress: Rome and Bologna under Pope Julius II. *In* Millon, H. A. and Nochlin, L. eds. Art and architecture in the service of politics p46-79

The politics of the open hand: notes on Le Corbusier and Nehru at Chandigarh. *In* Walden, R. ed. The open hand p412-57

Mora, George

Vico, Piaget and genetic epistemology. *In* Giambattista Vico's science of humanity p365-92

Moraes, Dom F.

About

Souza, E. de. The expatriate experience. *In* Narasimhaiah, C. D. ed. Awakened conscience p339-45

Moral conditions. See Sex customs; and subdivision Moral conditions under names of countries, cities, etc. e.g. United States—Moral conditions

Moral development

Bettelheim, B. Education and the reality principle. *In* Bettelheim, B. Surviving, and other essays p127-41

Moral education

Butler, C. Tragedy and moral education. *In* Contemporary approaches to English studies p77-93

Greene, M. Wide-awakeness and the moral life. *In* Greene, M. Landscapes of learning p42-52

Kohlberg, L. Moral stages and sex education. *In* Sexuality and human values p111-22

See also Moral development

Moral judgment. See Judgment (Ethics)

Moral philosophy. See Ethics

Moral theology. See Christian ethics

Moralities

History and criticism

Nicoll, A. Religious drama and profane during the Middle Ages. *In* Nicoll, A. World drama p103-31

Moralities, English

History and criticism

Jones, R. C. Dangerous sport: the audience's engagement with vice in the moral interludes. *In* Renaissance drama [1973] p45-64

Somerset, J. A. B. "Fair is foul and foul is fair": vice-comedy's development and theatrical effects. *In* The Elizabethan theatre, V **p54-75**

Weimann, R. Moralities and interludes. *In* Weimann, R. Shakespeare and the popular tradition in the theater: studies in the social dimension of dramatic form and function p98-160

Morality. See Ethics

Morality and religion. See Religion and ethics

Morality plays. See Moralities

Morals. See Conduct of life; Ethics

Morals and literature. See Literature and morals

Moran, Maureen; Painter, Susan, and Redmond, James

The twentieth century [another essay] *In* English Association. The year's work in English studies v57 p315-81

The twentieth century. *In* English Association. The year's work in English studies v57 p315-81

Moran, Theodore Harvey

The international political economy of Cuban nickel development. *In* Cuba in the world p257-72

Moran, William L.

An Assyriological gloss on the new Archilochus fragment. *In* Harvard Studies in classical philology v82 p17-19

The Syrian scribe of the Jerusalem Amarna letters. *In* Unity and diversity p146-66

Morantz, Regina Ann Markell

Making women modern: middle class women and health reform in 19th century America. *In* Branca, P. ed. The medicine show p103-20

Moratín, Leandro Fernández de

Contemporaries

See Moratín, Leandro Fernández de—Friends and associates

Friends and associates

Dowling, J. C. Moratín's circle of friends: intellectual ferment in Spain, 1780-1800. *In* Studies in eighteenth-century culture v5 p165-83

Moravia, Alberto

Boccaccio; excerpt from "Man as an end, a defense of humanism." *In* Dombroski, R. S. ed. Critical perspectives on The Decameron p99-112

The short story and the novel; excerpt from "Man as an end, a defense of humanism." *In* May, C. E. ed. Short story theories p147-51

About

Pacifici, S. Alberto Moravia: sex, money, and love in the novel. *In* Pacifici, S. The modern Italian novel: from Pea to Moravia p200-39

Ragusa, O. Alberto Moravia; voyeurism and storytelling (1). *In* Ragusa, O. Narrative and drama p122-33

About individual works
The empty canvas

Chiaromonte, N. The worm of consciousness. *In* Chiaromonte, N. The worm of consciousness, and other essays p153-59

Moravians. See Bohemian Brethren

More, Hannah

About individual works
Coelebs in search of a wife

Pickering, S. Coelebs in Search of a wife, and Waverley. *In* Pickering, S. The moral tradition in English fiction, 1785-1850 p89-105

More, Paul Elmer

Irving Babbitt. *In* Crunden, R. M. ed. The superfluous men p136-45

Rationalism and faith: excerpt from "The skeptical approach to religion." *In* Crunden, R. M. ed. The superfluous men p252-60

More, Paul E.—*Continued*

About

Tate, A. Humanism and naturalism. *In* Tate, A. Memoirs and opinions, 1926-1974 p170-94

West, T. R. The divided consciousness: Allen Tate, John Crowe Ransom, Paul Elmer More. *In* West, T. R. Nature, community & will p40-96

About individual works

Shelburne essays

Mencken, H. L. Paul Elmer More; excerpt from "Prejudices: third series." *In* Crunden, R. M. ed. The superfluous men p147-48

More, Sir Thomas, Saint

About

Sylvester, R. S. Conscience and consciousness. *In* Martz, L. L. and Williams, A. L. eds. The author in his work p163-74

About individual works

Utopia

Altman, J. B. Propaedeutic for drama: questions as fiction. *In* Altman, J. B. The Tudor play of mind p64-106

Gordon, W. M. The monastic achievement and More's utopian dream. *In* Medievalia et humanistica; new ser. no. 9 p199-214

Kennedy, W. J. The style of ironic discourse. *In* Kennedy, W. J. Rhetorical norms in Renaissance literature p79-127

Slavin, A. J. The American principle from More to Locke. *In* First images of America p139-64

Suvin, D. The time machine versus Utopia as structural models for SF. *In* Suvin, D. Metamorphoses of science fiction p222-42

Suvin, D. The alternative island. *In* Suvin, D. Metamorphoses of science fiction p90-114

More, Sir Thomas, Saint, in fiction, drama, poetry, etc.

Corrigan, B. Sir Thomas More: personage and symbol on the Italian stage. *In* Studies in the continental background of Renaissance English literature: essays presented to John L. Lievsay p91-108

Moreau, Gustave

About

Meyers, J. Gustave Moreau and Against nature. *In* Meyers, J. Painting and the novel p84-95

Moreau de Maupertuis, Pierre Louis. See Maupertuis, Pierre Louis Moreau de

Morel, Alain

Power and ideology in the village community of Picardy: past and present. *In* Rural society in France p107-25

Morelly

About individual works

Code de la nature

Knight, I. F. Utopian dream as psychic reality. *In* Studies in eighteenth-century culture v6 p427-38

Morelos, Mexico

Antiquities

Grennes-Ravitz, R. A. The Olmec presence at Iglesia Vieja, Morelos. *In* Mesoamerican archaeology p99-108

Moretti, Marino

About

Pacifici, S. Voices from the provinces: Grazia Deledda and Marino Moretti. *In* Pacifici, S. The modern Italian novel: from Capuana to Tozzi p86-107

Moretus, Balthasar

About

Judson, J. R. Rubens and Moretus. *In* Medieval and Renaissance studies 1976 p141-59

Morewedge, Parviz

The analysis of "substance" in Tūsī's Logic and in the Ibn Sīnian tradition. *In* Essays on Islamic philosophy and science p158-88

Morf, Gustav

Ethnic groups and developmental models: the case of Quebec. *In* Said, A. A. and Simmons, L. R. eds. Ethnicity in an international context p76-91

Morgan, Alice Bank

"Honour & right" in Arthur of Little Britain. *In* The Learned and the lewed p371-84

Morgan, Bruce

Theology in the context of the social sciences. *In* The Context of contemporary theology p157-70

Morgan, David

Woman suffrage in Britain and America in the early twentieth century. *In* Allen, H. C. and Thompson, R. eds. Contrast and connection p272-95

Morgan, E. Philip

Botswana: development, democracy, and vulnerability. *In* Carter, G. M. and O'Meara, P. eds. Southern Africa: the continuing crisis p288-48

Morgan, Edmund Sears

The Halfway covenant; excerpt from "Visible saints." *In* Mulder, J. M. and Wilson, J. F. eds. Religion in American history p29-44

The problem of popular sovereignty. *In* Aspects of American liberty p95-113

The Puritan ethic and the American Revolution. *In* Vaughan, A. T. and Bremer, F. J. eds. Puritan New England p364-84

Morgan, Edwin

Essays

Contents

The beatnik in the Kailyaird

Dryden's drudging

Dunbar and the language of poetry

Edwin Muir

A glimpse of Petavius

Heraclitus in Gorky Street: the theme of metamorphosis in the poetry of Andrei Voznesensky

Into the constellation: some thoughts on the origin and nature of concrete poetry

Introduction to Wi the haill voice: 25 poems by Vladimir Mayakovsky translated into Scots

James Bridie

MacDiarmid at seventy-five

MacDiarmid embattled

The novels of Robin Jenkins

Poetry and knowledge in MacDiarmid's later work

The poetry of Robert Louis Stevenson

A prelude to The prelude

Morgan, Edwin
  Essays
    Contents—Continued
  The raging and the grace: some notes on the
    poetry of Iain Crichton Smith
  Registering the reality of Scotland
  The resources of Scotland
  Scottish poetry in the 1960s
  Three views of Brooklyn Bridge
  The walls of Gormenghast: an introduction
    to the novels of Mervyn Peake
  Wordsworth in 1970
  Zbigniew Herbert

Morgan, Edwin Philip
  Botswana: democratic politics and development. *In* Carter, G. M. and O'Meara, P.
  eds. Southern Africa in crisis p200-25

Morgan, Elaine
  Women and the future. *In* Bundy, R. F.
  ed. Images of the future: the twenty-first
  century and beyond p143-51

Morgan, Ellen
  Alienation of the woman writer in The
  golden notebook. *In* Pratt, A. V. and
  Dembo, L. S. eds. Doris Lessing p54-63

Morgan, Frederick

About individual works

A book of change

  Lieberman, L. William Stafford and Frederick Morgan: the shocks of normality. *In*
  Lieberman, L. Unassigned frequencies p272-
  83

Morgan, Jerry L.
  Observations on the pragmatics of metaphor. *In* Ortony, A. ed. Metaphor and
  thought p136-47

Morgan, John, 1735-1789

About

  Bell, W. J. John Morgan, founder of the
  medical school. *In* Bell, W. J. The colonial
  physician & other essays p194-204

Morgan, Kenneth O.
  The future at work: Anglo-American progressivism, 1890-1917. *In* Allen, H. C. and
  Thompson, R. eds. Contrast and connection
  p245-71

Morgan, Richard G.
  The journal of Albion Moonlight: its form
  and meaning. *In* Morgan, R. G. ed. Kenneth
  Patchen: a collection of essays p152-80

Morgan, Robert J.
  "Time hath found us": the Jeffersonian
  revolutionary vision. *In* Havard, W. C. and
  Bernd, J. L. eds. 200 years of the Republic in retrospect p20-36

Morgan, Roger Pearce
  E. H. Carr and the study of international
  relations. *In* Essays in honour of E. H. Carr
  p171-80
  The transatlantic relationship. *In* Twitchett, K. J. ed. Europe and the world p35-56

Morgan, Thomas Hunt

About

  Allen, G. E. The transformation of a science: T. H. Morgan and the emergence of
  a new American biology. *In* Oleson, A. and
  Voss, J. eds. The organization of knowledge in modern America, 1860-1920 p173-
  210

Morgan, Victor
  Cambridge University and "the country,"
  1560-1640. *In* The University in society v 1
  p183-245

Morgan, William W.
  The partial vision: Hardy's idea of dramatic poetry. *In* Tennessee Studies in literature v20 p100-08

Morgan County, Ind.

Historic houses, etc.

  Roberts, W. E. The Whitaker-Waggoner
  log house from Morgan County, Indiana. *In*
  Yoder, D. ed. American folklife p185-207

Morgann, Maurice

About individual works

An essay on the dramatic character of Sir John Falstaff

  Bayley, J. The meaning of impression.
  In Bayley, J. The uses of division p211-17

Morgenthau, Hans Joachim
  Big power confrontations in the Middle
  East. *In* The New world balance and peace
  in the Middle East: reality or mirage? p69-
  73
  The fallacy of thinking conventionally
  about nuclear weapons. *In* Arms control and
  technological innovation p255-64
  Fragment of an intellectual autobiography:
  1904-1932. *In* [Truth and tragedy]: a trib-
  ute to Hans Morgenthau p 1-17
  Some political aspects of disarmament.
  In The Dynamics of the arms race p57-64
  World politics and the politics of oil. *In*
  Eppen, G. D. ed. Energy: the policy issues
  p43-51

About

  Coffey, J. W. Hans Morgenthau and the
  Western political tradition. *In* Coffey, J. W.
  Political realism in American thought p125-
  57
  Falk, R. A. Normative constraints on
  statecraft: some comments on Morgenthau's
  perspective. *In* [Truth and tragedy]: a tribute to Hans Morgenthau p77-84
  Graebner, N. A. Morgenthau as historian.
  In [Truth and tragedy]: a tribute to Hans
  Morgenthau p66-76
  Halle, L. J. General education and the
  understanding of politics: the case of Hans
  J. Morgenthau. *In* [Truth and tragedy]: a
  tribute to Hans Morgenthau p55-65
  Hardin, C. M. The problem of political
  power in the United States. *In* [Truth and
  tragedy]: a tribute to Hans Morgenthau
  p142-52
  Liska, G. Morgenthau vs. Machiavelli: po-
  litical realism and power politics. *In* [Truth
  and tragedy]: a tribute to Hans Morgenthau p104-11
  Morgenthau, H. J. Fragment of an intellectual autobiography: 1904-1932. *In* [Truth
  and tragedy]: a tribute to Hans Morgenthau p 1-17
  Myers, R. J. An approximation of justice.
  In [Truth and tragedy]: a tribute to Hans
  Morgenthau p125-29
  Osgood, R. E. The mission of Morgenthau. *In* [Truth and tragedy]: a tribute to
  Hans Morgenthau p32-40
  Raskin, M. G. Morgenthau: the idealism
  of a realist. *In* [Truth and tragedy]: a tribute to Hans Morgenthau p85-94
  Shinn, R. L. Realism and ethics in political philosophy. *In* [Truth and tragedy]: a
  tribute to Hans Morgenthau p95-103

Morgenthau, Hans J.—About—*Continued*

Stoessinger, J. G. The statesman and the critic: Kissinger and Morgenthau. *In* [Truth and tragedy]: a tribute to Hans Morgenthau p220-36

Thompson, K. W. Philosophy and politics: the two commitments of Hans J. Morgenthau. *In* [Truth and tragedy]: a tribute to Hans Morgenthau p21-31

Watson, A. Morgenthau's concept of the national interest and the new states of the Third world. *In* [Truth and tragedy]: a tribute to Hans Morgenthau p305-15

About individual works
Politics among nations

Rakove, M. L. Power, self-interest, and Chicago politics: a comparison of the theory of Politics among nations and the reality of politics in Chicago. *In* [Truth and tragedy]: a tribute to Hans Morgenthau p112-24

Scientific man vs. power politics

Tsou, Tang. "Scientific man vs. power politics" revisited. *In* [Truth and tragedy]: a tribute to Hans Morgenthau p41-52

Influence

Hotz, A. J. Morgenthau's influence on the study of international relations. *In* [Truth and tragedy]: a tribute to Hans Morgenthau p316-21

Morgenthau, Henry, 1891-1967

About

Kimball, W. F. The Morgenthau plan. *In* Encyclopedia of American foreign policy p597-602

Morgenthau, Ruth Schachter

Strangers, nationals, and multinationals in contemporary Africa. *In* Shack, W. A. and Skinner, E. P. eds. Strangers in African societies p105-20

Mori, Ōgai

About individual works
Sanshō the steward

Rimer, J. T. Nagai Kafū and Mori Ōgai: the past versus the present. *In* Rimer, J. T. Modern Japanese fiction and its traditions p138-61

Moriguchi, Chikashi. See Klein, L. R. jt. auth.

Mörike, Eduard Friedrich

About individual works
Auf eine Christblume

Middleton, J. C. Mörike's moonchild: a reading of the poem 'Auf eine Christblume.' *In* Middleton, J. C. Bolshevism in art p190-208

Morillo, Marvin George

Donne's "The relique" as satire. *In* Tulane studies in English v21 p47-55

Morin, Edgar

About individual works
Rumor in Orleans

Koestler, A. Anatomy of a canard. *In* Koestler, A. The heel of Achilles p87-90

Morineau, Michel

The potato in the eighteenth century. *In* Food and drink in history p17-36

Morínigo, Marcos Augusto

The Hispanic inheritance of Iberoamerica. *In* Américo Castro and the meaning of Spanish civilization p295-307

Moriscos. See Mudéjares

Morison, Robert Swain

Death: process or event? *In* Death inside out p63-70

Also in Weir, R. F. ed. Ethical issues in death and dyiing p57-69

Misgivings about life-extending technologies. *In* Holton, G. J. and Morison, R. S. eds. Limits of scientific inquiry p211-26

About

Kass, L. R. Death as an event: a commentary on Robert Morison. *In* Weir, R. F. ed. Ethical issues in death and dying p70-81

Morison, William L.

Frames of reference for legal ideals. *In* Law and society p18-47

Morita, Akio

Creativity in modern industry. *In* The Frontiers of knowledge p143-56

Morley, Christopher Darlington

Introduction to Nine answers by G. Bernard Shaw. *In* Praise from famous men: an anthology of introductions p116-23

Morley, Malcolm

About

Levin, K. Malcolm Morley: post-style illusionism. *In* Battcock, G. ed. Super realism p170-86

Morley, Patricia A.

'In God's name': ironic forms of religious drama in Canada and Australia. *In* Narasimhaiah, C. D. ed. Awakened conscience p275-83

Mormon Church. See Mormons and Mormonism

Mormons and Mormonism

Leone, M. P. The economic basis for the evolution of Mormon religion. *In* Zaretsky, I. I. and Leone, M. P. eds. Religious movements in contemporary America p722-66

Meyers, M. A. Gates ajar: death in Mormon thought and practice. *In* Death in America p112-33

See also Church of Jesus Christ of Latter-Day Saints

Mörner, Magnus

A bibliography on Spanish migration. *In* First images of America p797-804

Spanish migration to the New World prior to 1810: a report on the state of research. *In* First images of America p737-82

Morocco

Social conditions

Maher, V. Women and social change in Morocco. *In* Beck, L. and Keddie, N. R. eds. Women in the Muslim world p100-23

Morphine. See Heroin

Morphology (Animals)

Technique

Simons, J. R. The brain and evolution of lower mammals. *In* Grafton Elliot Smith p39-49

Morpurgo, J. E.

Richer in esteem: a reappraisal of John Burgoyne. *In* Essays in honor of Russel B. Nye p151-67

Morpurgo, Vittorio Ballio
About
Kostof, S. K. The Emperor and the Duce: the planning of Piazzale Augusto Imperatore in Rome. *In* Millon, H. A. and Nochlin, L. eds. Art and architecture in the service of politics p270-325

Morris, Allison
Scottish juvenile justice: a critique. *In* Crime, criminology and public policy p347-74

Morris, Ben
On discovering what it means to be human. *In* Niblett, W. R. ed. The sciences, the humanities and the technological threat p90-105

Morris, Bertram
On Hobbes' humanism. *In* Philosophy and the civilizing arts p89-102

Morris, Colin
Judicium Dei: the social and political significance of the ordeal in the eleventh century. *In* Church, society and politics p95-111

Morris, Cynthia Taft. See Adelman, I. jt. auth.

Morris, Desmond
About individual works
Intimate behaviour
Koestler, A. The naked touch. *In* Koestler, A. The heel of Achilles p72-76

Morris, Frederic A. See Allison, G. T. jt. auth.

Morris, H. Stephen
In the wake of mechanization: sago and society in Sarawak. *In* Social organization and the applications of anthropology p273-301

Morris, Herbert
Punishment for thoughts. *In* Summers, R. S. ed. Essays in legal philosophy p95-120

Morris, John
Richard Aldington and Death of a hero—or life of an anti-hero? *In* Klein, H. M. ed. The First World War in fiction p183-92

Morris, Leon Lamb. See Part 2 under title: Reconciliation and hope

Morris, Mervyn
The dialect poetry of Louise Bennett. *In* Baugh, E. ed. Critics on Caribbean literature p137-48

Morris, Norval, and Mills, Michael
Prisoners as laboratory animals. *In* Contemporary issues in criminal justice p129-43

Morris, Richard Brandon
Historical prologue. *In* The National purpose reconsidered p 1-9

Morris, Robert
Long-term severe disability. *In* Home care p237-44
About
Krauss, R. E. The double negative: a new syntax for sculpture. *In* Krauss, R. E. Passages in modern sculpture p243-88

Morris, Robert K.
In the clap shack: comedy in the charnel house. *In* Morris, R. K. and Malin, I. eds. The achievement of William Styron p227-41

Morris, Robert K. and Malin, Irving
Vision and value: the achievement of William Styron. *In* Morris, R. K. and Malin, I. eds. The achievement of William Styron p 1-50

Morris, Robert L.
Biology and psychical research. *In* Parapsychology: its relation to physics, biology, psychology, and psychiatry p48-75

Morris, Roger P. and Mauzy, Richard
Following the scenario: reflections on five case histories in the mode and aftermath of CIA intervention. *In* Borosage, R. L. and Marks, J. D. eds. The CIA file p28-45

Morris, Wesley Abram
Friday's footprint
Contents
The centrality of language
The pilgrimage of being
Stylistics
Toward a literary hermeneutics

Morris, William, 1834-1896
About
Clayre, A. William Morris and his English predecessors. *In* Clayre, A. Work and play p63-78

Pater, W. H. Poems by William Morris. *In* Sambrook, J. ed. Pre-Raphaelitsm p105-17

Quirk, R. Dasent, Morris, and aspects of translation. *In* Quirk, R. The linguist and the English language p97-109

Trilling, L. Aggression and utopia. *In* Trilling, L. The last decade p148-59

Williamson, A. Burne-Jones: the stained-glass influence. *In* Williamson, A. Artists and writers in revolt p132-60

Williamson, A. Morris: craft and saga. *In* Williamson, A. Artists and writers in revolt p85-102

Williamson, A. Ruskin and Morris: the Socialist legacy. *In* Williamson, A. Artists and writers in revolt p103-31

About individual works
Journals of travel in Iceland
1871, 1873
Kirchhoff, F. Travel as anti-autobiography: William Morris's Icelandic journals. *in* Landow, G. P. ed. Approaches to Victorian autobiography p292-310

News from nowhere

Suvin, D. Anticipating the sunburst: dream, vision—or nightmare? *In* Suvin, D. Metamorphoses of science fiction p170-207

Trilling, L. Aggression and utopia. *In* Trilling, L. The last decade p148-59

Morris, Wright
Earthly delights, unearthly adornments
Contents
Carson McCullers
Closing the gap
Ernest Hemingway
Gertrude Stein
The ghostly rumble among the drums
Henry James
An image sampler
James Agee
John Dos Passos
Katherine Anne Porter
Mark Twain
Melville
Of memory, emotion and imagination
Origins: the self-imaged image-maker
Richard Wright: real and imagined Black voices
Ring Lardner

Morris, Wright
Earthly delights, unearthly adornments
Contents—Continued
Scott Fitzgerald
Sherwood Anderson
Stephen Crane
T. S. Eliot
Unearthly adornments
Whitman
Willa Cather
William Faulkner
About
Morris, W. Origins: the self-imaged image-maker. *In* Morris, W. Earthly delights, unearthly adornments p169-79

Morris-Hale, Walter
From empire to nation: the African experience. *In* Aftermath of empire p85-101

Morrison, Clyde Arthur
Solar energy for dwellings. *In* Strategies for human settlements: habitat and environment p91-99

Morrison, David
Planetary astronomy and Velikovsky's catastrophism. *In* Goldsmith, D. ed. Scientists confront Velikovsky p145-76

Morrison, Fred L.
The right to fish for seacoast products: Gibbons v. Ogden resurrected. *In* The Supreme Court review, 1977 p239-56

Morrison, James Lunsford
The struggle between sectionalism and nationalism at ante-bellum West Point, 1830-1861. *In* Hubbell, J. T. ed. Battles lost and won p19-29

Morrison, Karl Frederick
The structure of holiness in Othloh's Vita Bonifatii and Ebo's Vita Ottonis. *In* Law, church, and society p131-56

Morrison, Peter A. and Wheeler, Judith P.
The image of "elsewhere" in the American tradition of migration. *In* Human migration p75-84

Morrison, Philip
On broken symmetries. *In* Wechsler, J. ed. On aesthetics in science p55-70

Morrison, Toni
About individual works
Song of Solomon
Mickelson, A. Z. Winging upward: Black women: Sarah E. Wright, Toni Morrison, Alice Walker. *In* Mickelson, A. Z. Reaching out: sensitivity and order in recent American fiction by women p112-74

Sula
Mickelson, A. Z. Winging upward: Black women: Sarah E. Wright, Toni Morrison, Alice Walker. *In* Mickelson, A. Z. Reaching out: sensitivity and order in recent American fiction by women p112-74

Morrissey, Paul
About
Taylor, J. R. Andy Warhol/Paul Morrissey. *In* Taylor, J. R. Directors and directions p136-64

Morse, Arthur D.
About individual works
While six million died
Koestler, A. Sins of omission. *In* Koestler, A. The heel of Achilles p49-55

Morse, Edward L.
The Atlantic economy in crisis. *In* Atlantis lost p149-82
The new Europe: a unified bloc or blocked unity? *In* The Interaction of economics and foreign policy p102-29

Morse, Josiah Mitchell
Baudelaire, Stephen Dedalus, and Shem the Penman. *In* Garvin, H. R. ed. Makers of the twentieth-century novel p19-27

Morse, Richard McGhee
Brazil's urban development: colony and empire. *In* From colony to nation p155-81

Morse, Stearns
"The subverted flower": an exercise in triangulation. *In* Frost: centennial essays II p170-76

Morse, Stephen J.
Family law in transition: from traditional families to individual liberty. *In* Tufte, V. and Myerhoff, B. G. eds. Changing images of the family p319-60

Morsy, Soheir A.
Sex differences and folk illness in an Egyptian village. *In* Beck, L. and Keddie, N. R. eds. Women in the Muslim world p599-616

Mort Artu
Segre, C. Deconstruction and reconstruction of a tale: from La mort le roi Artu to the Novellino. *In* Segre, C. Structures and time p58-64

Mortain, France
Genealogy
Hill, B. D. The Counts of Mortain and the origins of the Norman congregation of Savigny. *In* Order and innovation in the Middle Ages p237-53

Mortality
Arnheim, R. Space as an image of time. *In* Kroeber, K. and Walling, W. eds. Images of romanticism p 1-12
Engelhardt, H. T. The counsels of finitude. *In* Death inside out p115-25
Vinovskis, M. A. Angels' heads and weeping willows: death in early America. *In* American Antiquarian Society. Proceedings v86 pt2 p273-302
See also Children—Mortality; Death (Biology)

Mortality in literature
Cain, T. G. S. "Times trans-shifting": Herrick in meditation. *In* Rollin, R. B. and Patrick, J. M. eds. "Trust to good verses": Herrick tercentenary essays p103-23

Mortimer, Kenneth Paul. See Anderson, G. L. jt. auth.

Mortimer, Kenneth Paul, and Johnson, Mark D.
External degree programs: the current educational frontier. *In* Land-grant universities and their continuing challenge p286-308

Mortimer, Roger de, Earl of March
About
Wood, C. T. Queens, queans, and kingship: an inquiry into theories of royal legitimacy in late medieval England and France. *In* Order and innovation in the Middle Ages p385-400

Morton, Arthur Leslie
About
Cornforth, M. C. A. L. Morton—portrait of a Marxist historian. *In* Rebels and their causes p7-19

Morton, Cynthia Neverdon-. See Neverdon-Morton, Cynthia

Morton, Donald A.
The naval shore establishment and Parkinson's laws. *In* Managing nonprofit organizations p289-302

Morton, Louis
Who next? The spread of nuclear weapons. *In* Baldwin, D. A. ed. America in an interdependent world p29-60

Morton, Miriam
Young Soviet readers and their literature. *In* Egoff, S. A. ed. One ocean touching p38-59

Morton, Newton E.
Interracial crosses and group differences. *In* Racial variation in man p151-69

Morton, Richard
Roy McKeen Wiles, 1903-1974. *In* Studies in eighteenth-century culture v4 p xv-xxii

Morton, Thomas

About
McWilliams, J. P. Fictions of Merry Mount. *In* Zenderland, L. ed. Recycling the past p 1-28

About individual works
New English Canaan or New Canaan
Seelye, J. Womb of nature: Thomas Morton and the call of the wild. *In* Seelye, J. Prophetic waters p159-85

Morton, William Lewis

About
Berger, C. William Morton: the delicate balance of region and nation. *In* Berger, C. The writing of Canadian history p238-58

Mortuary customs. See Funeral rites and ceremonies; Mourning customs

Mortuary statistics. See Infants—Mortality; Mortality

Mosaic law. See Jewish law

Mosaic pavements. See Pavements, Mosaic

Mosaics
Kitzinger, E. The role of miniature painting in mural decoration. *In* The Place of book illumination in Byzantine art p99-142
See also Pavements, Mosaic

Mosaics, Early Christian

Influence
Loerke, W. C. The monumental miniature. *In* The Place of book illumination in Byzantine art p61-97

Rome (City)
Snyder, J. E. The mosaic in Santa Maria Nova and the original apse decoration of Santa Maria Maggiore. *In* Enggass, R. C. and Stoakstad, M. eds. Hortus imaginum p 1-9

Mosaics, Greco-Roman
Neal, D. S. Floor mosaics. *In* Strong, D. E. and Brown, D. eds. Roman crafts p241-52
Sear, F. Wall and vault mosaics. *In* Strong, D. E. and Brown, D. eds. Roman crafts p231-39

Moscivici, Serge
The reenchantment of the world. *In* Beyond the crisis p133-68

Moscow

City planning
Frolic, B. M. The new Moscow city plan. *In* Hamm, M. F. ed. The city in Russian history p276-88

Commerce
Gohstand, R. The shaping of Moscow by nineteenth-century trade. *In* Hamm, M. F. ed. The city in Russian history p160-81

Description
Benjamin, W. Moscow. *In* Benjamin, W. Reflections p97-130

Intellectual life
Mandel'shtam, O. E. Literary Moscow. *In* Mandel'shtam, O. E. Selected essays p133-37

Moscow Art Theatre
Kauffmann, S. The Moscow Art Theater. *In* Kauffmann, S. Persons of the drama p48-51

Moscow Trials, 1936-1937
Rahv, P. Trials of the mind. *In* Rahv, P. Essays on literature and politics, 1932-1972 p284-92

Moseley, Edwin M. See Part 2 under title: Renaissance and modern

Moser, Gerald M.
Luís Bernardo Honwana's place among the writers in Mozambique. *In* King, B. A. and Ogungbesan, K. eds. A celebration of Black and African writing p189-203

Moser, Thomas Colborn
Conrad and The good soldier. *In* Joseph Conrad: a commemoration p174-82

Moser, Walter
Kant: origin and utopia. *In* Studies in eighteenth-century culture v8 p253-68

Moses

About
Meeks, W. A. The divine agent and his counterfeit in Philo and the Fourth Gospel. *In* Aspects of religious propaganda in Judaism and early Christianity p43-67

Moses ben Maimon

About individual works
Mishneh Torah
Dienstag, J. I. Christian translators of Maimonides' Mishneh Torah into Latin. *In* Salo Wittmayer Baron v 1 p287-309

Translations, Latin—Bibliography
Dienstag, J. I. Christian translators of Maimonides' Mishneh Torah into Latin. *In* Salo Wittmayer Baron v 1 p287-309

Moses, Joel Charles
Women in political roles. *In* Women in Russia p333-53

Moses, John Anthony
Germany and the Cold war: historiographical consequences. *In* Siracusa, J. M. and Barclay, G. S. eds. The impact of the Cold war p64-83

Moses, Robert

About
Vidal, G. What Robert Moses did to New York City. *In* Vidal, G. Matters of fact and of fiction p237-51

Moses in fiction, drama, poetry, etc.
Landow, G. P. Moses striking the rock: typological symbolism in Victorian poetry. *In* Miner, E. R. ed. Literary uses of typology p315-44

Moshe Ibn Ezra. See Ibn Ezra, Moses ben Jacob

Moss, Howard

About

Lieberman, L. Howard Moss: bitter and sweet, dread and desire. *In* Lieberman, L. Unassigned frequencies p133-39

Moss, Leonard Wallace, and Cappannari, Stephen C.

Mal'occhio, ayin ha ra, oculus fascinus, Judenblick: the evil eye hovers above. *In* The Evil eye p 1-15

Moss, Roger

Difficult language: the justification of Joyce's syntax in Ulysses. *In* Josipovici, G. ed. The modern English novel: the reader, the writer and the work p130-48

Moss, Sidney Phil

Hawthorne and Melville: an inquiry into their art and the mystery of their friendship. *In* Literary monographs v7 p45-84

Moss, Steven A.

Home is not necessarily "home." *In* Home care p77-83

Moss, Walter Gerald

Why the anxious fear? Aging and death in the works of Turgenev. *In* Spicker, S. F.; Woodward, K. M. and Van Tassel, D. D. eds. Aging and the elderly p241-60

Mossner, Ernest Campbell

Hume and the legacy of the Dialogues. *In* David Hume p 1-22

The most-favored-nation principle. Doencke, J. D. *In* Encyclopedia of American foreign policy p603-09

Mostaert, Jan

About individual works

West Indies landscape

Snyder, J. E. Jan Mostaert's West Indies landscape. *In* First images of America p495-502

Mostel, Zero

About

Kauffmann, S. Ulysses in Nighttown. *In* Kauffmann, S. Persons of the drama p149-52

Motamed-Nejad, Kazem

The story-teller and mass media in Iran. *In* Fischer, H. D. and Melnik, S. R. eds. Entertainment: a cross-cultural examination p43-62

Mote, Frederick W.

The arts and the 'theorizing mode' of the civilization. *In* Artists and traditions p 3-8

Mother (Motion picture)

Taylor, R. Mother. *In* Taylor, R. Film propaganda p81-91

Mother and child

Bruner, J. S. Learning how to do things with words. *In* Human growth and development p62-84

Hinde, R. A. Social development: a biological approach. *In* Human growth and development p 1-32

Kagan, J. The child in the family. *In* Rossi, A. S.; Kagan, J. and Hareven, T. K. eds. The family p33-56

Morgan, E. Women and the future. *In* Bundy, R. F. ed. Images of the future: the twenty-first century and beyond p143-51

Shorter, E. Maternal sentiment and death in childbirth: a new agenda for psycho-medical history. *In* Branca, P. ed. The medicine show p67-88

Terdal, L. G.; Jackson, R. H. and Garner, A. M. Mother-child interactions: a comparison between normal and developmentally delayed groups. *In* Behavior modification and families p249-64

The mother and the whore (Motion picture)

Kauffmann, S. The mother and the whore. *In* Kauffmann, S. Living images p257-60

Mother-child relationship. See Mother and child

Mothers

Rich, A. C. Motherhood: the contemporary emergency and the quantum leap. *In* Rich, A. C. On lies, secrets, and silence p259-73

Rich, A. C. Motherhood in bondage. *In* Rich, A. C. On lies, secrets, and silence p195-97

See also Parent and child

Employment—Europe

Scott, J. W. and Tilly, L. A. Women's work and the family in nineteenth century Europe. *In* Rosenberg, C. E. ed. The family in history p145-78

Mothers (in religion, folklore, etc.) See Women (in religion, folklore, etc)

Mothers and daughters in literature

Blanchard, L. Mothers and daughters in D. H. Lawrence: The rainbow and selected shorter works. *In* Smith, A. ed. Lawrence and women p75-100

Mothers in literature

Bienstock, B. G. The changing image of the American Jewish mother. *In* Tufte, V. and Myerhoff, B. G. eds. Changing images of the family p173-91

Brown, L. W. The business of marrying and mothering. *In* Jane Austen's achievement p27-43

Knoepflmacher, U. C. Thoughts on the aggression of daughters. *In* Levine, G. L. and Knoepflmacher, U. C. eds. The endurance of Frankenstein p88-119

Motion

Anderson, W. E. Cartesian motion. *In* Motion and time, space and matter p200-23

Drake, S. Galileo's new science of motion. *In* Bonelli, M. L. R. and Shea, W. R. eds. Reason, experiment, and mysticism in the scientific revolution p131-56

Furley, D. J. Aristotle and the Atomists on motion in a void. *In* Motion and time, space and matter p83-100

Moody, E. A. Laws of motion in medieval physics. *In* Moody, E. A. Studies in medieval philosophy, science, and logic p189-201

Murdoch, J. E. and Sylla, E. D. The science of motion. *In* Lindberg, D. C. ed. Science in the Middle Ages p206-64

See also Acceleration (Mechanics); Force and energy; Mechanics; Movement, Psychology of

Motion of the solar system in space. See Solar system—Motion in space

Motion-picture industry. See Moving-picture industry

Motion pictures. See Moving-pictures

Motivation (Psychology)

Alston, W. P. Self-intervention and the structure of motivation. *In* Mischel, T. ed. The self p65-102

Flew, A. G. N. Motives and Freud's unconscious. *In* Flew, A. G. N. A rational animal p 151-71

See also Competition (Psychology) Dissonance (Psychology); Need (Psychology)

Motivation in sports. See Sports—Psychological aspects

Motley, Constance Baker

Criminal law: "law and order" and the criminal justice system. *In* Perspectives on justice p39-72

The legal status of the Black American. *In* The Black American reference book p90-127

Motley, John Lothrop

About

Nevins, A. John Lothrop Motley. *In* Nevins, A. Allan Nevins on history p320-32

Motor psychology. See Movement, Psychology of

Motsch, Markus F.

The forgotten genre: the poetic epistle in eighteenth-century German literature. *In* Studies in eighteenth-century culture v4 p119-24

Mott, Stephen Charles

The power of giving and receiving: reciprocity in Hellenistic benevolence. *In* Current issues in Biblical and patristic interpretation p60-72

Motteux, Peter Anthony

About individual works

Love's a jest

Bowers, F. T. Motteux's "Love's a jest" (1696): a running-title and presswork problem *In* Bowers, F. T. Essays in bibliography, text, and editing p269-74

Criticism, Textual

Bowers, F. T. Motteux's "Love's a jest" (1696): a running-title and presswork problem. *In* Bowers, F. T. Essays in bibliography, text, and editing p269-74

Motto, Anna Lydia, and Clark, John R.

Senecan tragedy: a critique of scholarly trends. *In* Renaissance drama [1973] p219-35

Mottoes

Rosenthal, E. S. Plus Oultre: the idea imperial of Charles V in his columnar device on the Alhambra. *In* Enggass, R .C. and Stokstad, M. eds. Hortus imaginum p85-93

Mottram, Eric

Orpheus and measured forms: law, madness and reticence in Melville. *In* Pullin, F. ed. New perspectives on Melville p229-54

Poe's Pym and the American social imagination. *In* Artful thunder p25-53

Mottram, Ralph Hall

About individual works

The Spanish farm trilogy

Garrety, M. Love and war: R. H. Mottram, The Spanish farm trilogy and Ernest Hemingway, A farewell to arms. *In* Klein, H. M. ed. The First World War in fiction p10-22

Mould, William A.

Illusion and reality: a new resolution of an old paradox. *In* Johnson, R. B.; Neumann, E. S. and Trail, G. T. eds. Molière and the commonwealth of letters: patrimony and posterity p521-26

Moulton, Janice Marie

The myth of the neutral "man." *In* Feminism and philosophy p124-37

Sex and reference. *In* Baker, R. and Elliston, F. A. eds. Philosophy and sex p34-44

Moulton, William Gamwell

The nature of language. *In* Bloomfield, M. W. and Haugen, E. I. eds. Language as a human problem p3-21

Mouly, Ruth Widmayer

Values and aspirations of Soviet youth. *In* Cocks, P.; Daniels, R. V. and Heer, N. W. eds. The dynamics of Soviet politics p221-38

Mounds

Friesland

TeBrake, W. H. Ecology and economy in early medieval Frisia. *In* Viator: medieval and Renaissance studies v9 p 1-29

Mount, A. J.

H. de Balzac: Lost illusions. *In* Williams, D. A. ed. The monster in the mirror p17-39

Mount Auburn Cemetery

French, S. G. The cemetery as cultural institution: the establishment of Mount Auburn and the "rural cemetery" movement. *In* Death in America p69-91

Mount Wollaston. See Quincy, Mass.

Mountain climbing. See Mountaineering

Mountain whites (Southern States) in literature

Flanagan, J. T. Jesse Stuart, regional novelist. *In* LeMaster, J. R. and Clarke, M. W. eds. Jesse Stuart p70-88

Mountaineering

Richards, I. A. The lure of high mountaineering. *In* Richards, I. A. Complementarities p233-45

Robertson, D. A. Mid-Victorians amongst the Alps. *In* Knoepflmacher, U. C. and Tennyson, G. B. eds. Nature and the Victorian imagination p113-36

Mountains. See Mountaineering

Mountains in literature

Levine, G. L. High and low: Ruskin and the novelists. *In* Knoepflmacher, U. C. and Tennyson, G. B. eds. Nature and the Victorian imagination p137-52

Middleton, J. C. Two mountain scenes in Novalis and the question of symbolic style. *In* Middleton, J. C. Bolshevism in art p258-73

Mouridiya. See Murīdīyah

Mourids. See Murīdīyah

Mourning customs

Goody, J. R. Death and the interpretation of culture: a bibliographic overview. *In* Death in America p 1-8

United States

Raether, H. C. and Slater, R. C. Immediate postdeath activities in the United States. *In* Feifel, H. [ed.] New meanings of death p233-48

See also Funeral rites and ceremonies

Moving-picture producers and directors

Corliss, R. Introduction: notes on a screenwriter's theory, 1973—introduction to Talking pictures. *In* Denby, D. ed. Awake in the dark p215-26

Farber, M. Underground films; excerpt from "Negative space." *In* Denby, D. ed. Awake in the dark p65-77

Kael, P. Circles and squares: joys and Sarris; excerpt from "I lost it at the movies." *In* Denby, D. ed. Awake in the dark p146-68

Sarris, A. Toward a theory of film history; excerpt from "The American cinema." *In* Denby, D. ed. Awake in the dark p183-200

Also in Nichols, B. ed. Movies and methods p237-51

Wollen, P. The auteur theory; excerpt from "Signs and meanings in the cinema." *In* Nichols, B. ed. Movies and methods p529-42

France

Monaco, J. Introduction: The camera writes. *In* Monaco, J. The New Wave p3-12

Truffaut, F. Jacques Rivette: Paris nous appartient. *In* Truffaut, F. The films in my life p320-23

Moving-picture production. See Moving-picture production and direction

Moving-picture reviews. See Moving-pictures—Reviews

Moving-picture writing. See Moving-picture authorship

Moving-pictures

Jakobson, R. Is the cinema in decline? *In* Matejka, L. and Titunik, I. R. eds. Semiotics of art p145-52

Schrader, P. Notes on film noir. *In* Denby, D. ed. Awake in the dark p278-90

United Nations Educational, Scientific and Cultural Organization. Film as a universal mass medium. *In* Fischer, H. D. and Merill, J. C. eds. International and intercultural communication p115-20

See also Antisemitism in motion pictures; Characters and characteristics in moving-pictures; Color moving-pictures; Experimental films; Gangster films; Historical films; Love in motion pictures; Marriage in moving-pictures; Men in motion pictures; Nonverbal communication in motion pictures; Politics in motion pictures; Science fiction films; Sex in moving-pictures; Violence in moving-pictures; Western films; Women in moving-pictures; and subdivision Moving-pictures under subjects e.g. Ethnology—Moving-pictures; Fascism—Moving-pictures; Nuns—Moving-pictures

Aesthetics

Abramson, R. Structure and meaning in the cinema. *In* Nichols, B. ed. Movies and methods p558-68

Dayan, D. The tutor-code of classical cinema. *In* Nichols, B. ed. Movies and methods p438-51

Eco, U. Articulations of the cinematic code. *In* Nichols, B. ed. Movies and methods p590-607

Ferguson, O. Life goes to the pictures; excerpt from "The film criticism of Otis Ferguson." *In* Denby, D. Awake in the dark p49-59

Henderson, B. Two types of film theory. *In* Nichols, B. ed. Movies and methods p388-400

Lindsay, N. V. Thirty differences between the photoplays and the stage; excerpt from "The art of the moving picture." *In* Denby, D. ed. Awake in the dark p9-18

Lodge, D. Metaphor and metonymy. *In* Lodge, D. The modes of modern writing p73-124

Metz, C. Current problems of film theory: Mitry's L'Esthetique et psychologie du cinema, vol. II. *In* Nichols, B. ed. Movies and methods p568-78

Metz, C. On the notion of cinematographic language. *In* Nichols, B. ed. Movies and methods p582-89

Mukařovský, J. A note on the aesthetics of film. *In* Mukařovský, J. Structure, sign and function p178-90

Mukařovský, J. Time in film. *In* Mukařovský, J. Structure, sign, and function p191-200

Nichols, B. Style, grammar, and the movies. *In* Nichols, B. ed. Movies and methods p607-28

Panofsky, E. Style and medium in the motion pictures. *In* Denby, D. ed. Awake in the dark p30-48

Pasolini, P. P. The cinema of poetry. *In* Nichols, B. ed. Movies and methods p542-58

Place, J. A. and Peterson, L. S. Some visual motifs of film noir. *In* Nichols, B. ed. Movies and methods p325-38

Rohdie, S. Totems and movies. *In* Nichols, B. ed. Movies and methods p469-81

Rothman, W. Against "the system of the suture." *In* Nichols, B. ed. Movies and methods p451-59

Wollen, P. Cinema and semiology: some points of contact. *In* Nichols, B. ed. Movies and methods p481-92

Aesthetics—History

Perkins, V. F. A critical history of early film theory; excerpt from "Film as film." *In* Nichols, B. ed. Movies and methods p401-22

Biography

See Moving-picture producers and directors

Censorship

Sarris, A. Porn versus Puritanism. *In* Sarris, A. Politics and cinema p138-47

Criticism

See Moving-picture criticism

Editing

Rothman, W. Against "the system of the suture." *In* Nichols, B. ed. Movies and methods p451-59

Evaluation

See Moving-picture criticism

History

Kauffmann, S. Foreign and domestic: exchanges through film history. *In* Kauffmann, S. Living images p362-79

Sarris, A. Sixties cinema: zoomshots, jumpcuts, freeze frames, and girls, girls, girls! *In* Sarris, A. Politics and cinema p181-95

Moving-pictures—History—*Continued*

Sarris, A. Toward a theory of film history; excerpt from "The American cinema." *In* Denby, D. ed. Awake in the dark p183-200

Also in Nichols, B. ed. Movies and methods p237-51

News films

See Newsreel

Philosophy

Kjørup, S. Film as a meetingplace of multiple codes. *In* Perkins, D. and Leondar, B. eds. The arts and cognition p20-47

Play-writing

See Moving-picture authorship

Plots, themes, etc.

Griffith, R. Cycles and genres. *In* Nichols, B. ed. Movies and methods p111-18

Tudor, A. Genre and critical methodology; excerpt from "Theories of film." *In* Nichols, B. ed. Movies and methods p118-26

Political aspects

Comolli, J. L. and Narboni, J. Cinema/ideology/criticism. *In* Nichols, B. ed. Movies and methods p22-30

Dayan, D. The tutor-code of classical cinema. *In* Nichols, B. ed. Movies and methods p438-51

MacBean, J. R. Vent d'Est or Godard and Rocha at the crossroads. *In* Nichols, B. ed. Movies and methods p91-106

Sarris, A. Politics and cinema. *In* Sarris, A. Politics and cinema p9-15

Sarris, A. State of siege. *In* Denby, D. ed. Awake in the dark p200-14

Solanas, F. and Gettino, O. Towards a third cinema. *In* Nichols, B. ed. Movies and methods p44-64

Production and direction

Grenville, J. A. S. The historian as filmmaker II. *In* Smith, P. ed. The historian and film p132-41

Henderson, B. The long take. *In* Nichols, B. ed. Movies and methods p314-24

Kuehl, J. History on the public screen II. *In* Smith, P. ed. The historian and film p177-85

Watt, D. C. History on the public screen I. *In* Smith, P. ed. The historian and film p169-76

See also Moving-picture producers and directors

Research

Pontecorvo, L. Film resources. *In* Smith, P. ed. The historian and film p15-31

Reviews

Agee, J. Comedy's greatest era; excerpt from "Agee on film v 1." *In* Denby, D. ed. Awake in the dark p230-48

Agee, J. Three short reviews; excerpt from "Agee on film v 1." *In* Denby, D. ed. Awake in the dark p378-82

Kael, P. Three program notes; excerpt from "Kiss kiss bang bang." *In* Denby, D. ed. Awake in the dark p388-91

Sontag, S. The imagination of disaster; excerpt from "Against interpretation." *In* Denby, D. ed. Awake in the dark p263-78

Warshow, R. The Westerner. *In* Denby, D. ed. Awake in the dark p248-63

Social aspects

Richards, J. Frank Capra and the cinema of Populism. *In* Nichols, B. ed. Movies and methods p65-77

Themes, motives

See Moving-pictures—Plots, themes, etc.

France

Truffaut, F. A certain tendency of the French cinema. *In* Nichols, B. ed. Movies and methods p224-37

Truffaut, F. Jacques Rivette: Paris nous appartient. *In* Truffaut, F. The films in my life p320-23

Germany—History

Taylor, R. Germany; The historical background. *In* Taylor, R. Film propaganda p133-55

Taylor, R. Germany: The needs of revolution. *In* Taylor, R. Film propaganda p156-68

Taylor, R. Germany: Themes and variations. *In* Taylor, R. Film propaganda p169-76

Latin America

Solanas, F. and Gettino, O. Towards a third cinema. *In* Nichols, B. ed. Movies and methods p44-64

Russia—History

Taylor, R. Russia: The historical background. *In* Taylor, R. Film propaganda p35-43

Taylor, R. Russia: The needs of revolution. *In* Taylor, R. Film propaganda p44-68

Taylor, R. Russia: Themes and variations. *In* Taylor, R. Film propaganda p69-80

United States

Appel, A. Nabokov's dark cinema: a diptych. *In* The Bitter air of exile p196-273

Ferguson, O. Life goes to the pictures; excerpt from "The film criticism of Otis Ferguson." *In* Denby, D. ed. Awake in the dark p49-59

Griffith, R. Cycles and genres. *In* Nichols, B. ed. Movies and methods p111-18

Melling, P. American popular culture in the thirties: ideology, myth, genre. *In* Bigsby, C. W. E. ed. Approaches to popular culture p241-63

Panofsky, E. Style and medium in the motion pictures. *In* Denby, D. ed. Awake in the dark p30-48

Place, J. A. and Peterson, L. S. Some visual motifs of film noir. *In* Nichols, B. ed. Movies and methods p325-38

Seldes, G. The Keystone the builders rejected; excerpt from "The seven lively arts." *In* Denby, D. ed. Awake in the dark p18-30

Warshow, R. The Westerner. *In* Denby, D. ed. Awake in the dark p248-63

United States—History

Agee, J. Comedy's greatest era; excerpt from "Agee on film v 1." *In* Denby, D. ed. Awake in the dark p230-48

Griffith, R. Cycles and genres. *In* Nichols, B. ed. Movies and methods p111-18

Moving-pictures, American

Europe

Guback, T. H. The international film industry. *In* Gerbner, G. ed. Mass media policies in changing cultures p21-40

Moving-pictures, American—*Continued*

France

Elsasser, T. Two decades in another country: Hollywood and the cinéphiles. *In* Bigsby, C. W. E. Superculture p199-216

Moving-pictures, Documentary

Hughes, W. C. The evaluation of film as evidence. *In* Smith, P. ed. The historian and film p49-79

MacDougall, D. Prospects of the ethnographic film. *In* Nichols, B. ed. Movies and methods p135-50

Moving-pictures, Experimental. See Experimental films

Moving-pictures, French

Monaco, P. The popular cinema as reflection of the group process in France, 1919-1929. *In* DeMause, L. ed. The new psychohistory p151-79

Moving-pictures, Russian

Murray, E. Potemkin. *In* Murray, E. Ten film classics p 1-17

Moving-pictures, Swedish

Steene, B. Bergman's movement toward nihilism: the antiheroic stance in Secrets of women, Brink of life, The seventh seal, and the Chamber Film trilogy. *In* The Hero in Scandinavian literature p87-105

Moving-pictures and literature

Appel, A. Nabokov's dark cinema: a diptych. *In* The Bitter air of exile p196-273

Lodge, D. Thomas Hardy as a cinematic novelist. *In* Butler, L. S. ed. Thomas Hardy after fifty years p78-89

Paroissien, D. H. Dickens and the cinema. *In* Dickens Studies Annual v7 p68-80

Turnell, M. Flaubert. *In* Turnell, M. The rise of the French novel p169-218

See also Film adaptations

Moving-pictures and theater

Kauffmann, S. Notes on theater-and-film. *In* Kauffmann, S. Living images p353-62

Moving-pictures for children. See Children's films

Moving-pictures in education

Grenville, J. A. S. The historian as filmmaker II. *In* Smith, P. ed. The historian and film p132-41

Haworth, B. Film in the classroom. *In* Smith, P. ed. The historian and film p157-68

Schuursma, R. L. The historian as filmmaker, I. *In* Smith, P. ed. The historian and film p121-31

See also Moving-pictures in higher education

Moving-pictures in ethnology

Greenhill, L. P. Film documentation of folklife. *In* Yoder, D. ed. American folklife p71-104

Moving-pictures in higher education

Marwick, A. Film in university teaching. *In* Smith, P. ed. The historian and film p142-56

Moving-pictures in historiography

Hughes, W. C. The evaluation of film as evidence. *In* Smith, P. ed. The historian and film p49-79

Moving-pictures in literature

Kalson, A. E. Tennessee Williams at the Delta Brilliant. *In* Tennessee Williams: a tribute p774-94

Moving-pictures in propaganda

Culbert, D. H. Our awkward ally: Mission to Moscow. *In* O'Connor, J. E. and Jackson, M. A. eds. American history/American film p121-45

Taylor, R. Conclusions. *In* Taylor, R. Film propaganda p230-33

Taylor, R. Germany: The needs of revolution. *In* Taylor, R. Film propaganda p156-68

Taylor, R. Germany: Themes and variations. *In* Taylor, R. Film propaganda p169-76

Taylor, R. Propaganda and film. *In* Taylor, R. Film propaganda p19-32

Taylor, R. Russia: The historical background. *In* Taylor, R. Film propaganda p35-43

Taylor, R. Russia: The needs of revolution. *In* Taylor, R. Film propaganda p44-68

Taylor, R. Russia: Themes and variations. *In* Taylor, R. Film propaganda p69-80

Mowen, John. See Shuman, I. G. jt. auth.

Mowlana, Hamid

A paradigm for comparative mass media analysis. *In* Fischer, H. D. and Merrill, J. C. eds. International and intercultural communication p474-84

Trends in Middle Eastern societies. *In* Gerbner, G. ed. Mass media policies in changing cultures p73-82

Mowlana, Hamid, and Robinson, Ann Elizabeth

Ethnic mobilization and communication theory. *In* Said, A. A. and Simmons, L. R. eds. Ethnicity in an international context p48-63

Moyana, T. T.

Problems of a creative writer in South Africa. *In* Heywood, C. ed. Aspects of South African literature p85-98

Moyer, J. Alan

Urban growth and the development of the telephone: some relationships at the turn of the century. *In* The Social impact of the telephone p342-69

Moynahan, Julian

Lawrence, woman and the Celtic fringe. *In* Smith, A. ed. Lawrence and women p122-35

Pastoralism as culture and counter-culture in English fiction, 1800-1928: from a view to a death. *In* Spilka, M. ed. Towards a poetics of fiction p239-54

Moynihan, Daniel Patrick

The significance of the Zionism-as-racism resolution for international human rights. *In* Sidorsky, D. ed. Essays on human rights p37-45

Mozambique

Foreign relations

Hodges, T. Mozambique: the politics of liberation. *In* Carter, G. M. and O'Meara, P. eds. Southern Africa in crisis p48-88

Also in Carter, G. M. and O'Meara, P. eds. Africa: the continuing crisis p57-92

Historiography

Bender, G. and Isaacman, A. F. The changing historiography of Angola and Mozambique. *In* African studies since 1945 p220-48

Mudrick, Marvin—*Continued*
About
Sale, R. H. Marvin Mudrick. *In* Sale,
R. H. On not being good enough p166-74

Mueller, Ian
An introduction to Stoic logic. *In* Rist,
J. M. ed. The Stoics p 1-26

Mueller, Martin, 1939-
Knowledge and delusion in the Iliad. *In*
Wright, J. H. ed. Essays on the Iliad p105-27

Mugomba, Agrippah T.
Small developing states and the external
operational environment. *In* The Year book
of world affairs, 1979 p201-16

Mugridge, Ian
Armed neutralities. *In* Encyclopedia of
American foreign policy p43-48

Muhammad, the prophet
Lewis, B. Gibbon on Muhammad. *In* Ed-
ward Gibbon and The decline and fall of the
Roman Empire p61-73

Waugh, E. H. Following the beloved:
Muhammad as model in the Ṣūfī tradition.
In Reynolds, F. E. and Capps, D. eds. The
biographical process p63-85

Muhammad Ali
About individual works
The Greatest, my own story
Reed, I. The Greatest, my own story. *In*
Reed, I. Shrovetide in old New Orleans p120-
25

**Muhammad ibn 'Umar, Fakhr al-Dīn, al-
Rāzī.** See al-Rāzī, Fakhr al-Dīn Muhammad ibn 'Umar

Muhammad ibn Zakarīyā, Abu Bakr, al-Rāzī.
See al-Rāzī, Abu Bakr Muhammad ibn
Zakarīyā

Muhammadinism. See Islam

Muhando, Penina
About individual works
Tambuein Haki Zetu
Mbughuni, L. A. Old and new drama
from East Africa. *In* African literature today
no. 8: Drama in Africa p85-98

Mühlberg, Battle of, 1547
Iconography
Rosenthal, E. S. Plus Oultre: the idea
imperial of Charles V in his columnar device on the Alhambra. *In* Enggass, R. C.
and Stokstad, M. eds. Hortus imaginum
p85-93

Muir, Edwin
About
Hamburger, M. Edwin Muir. *In* Hamburger, M. Art as second nature p86-102

Morgan, E. Edwin Muir. *In* Morgan, E.
Essays p186-93

About individual works
Selected letters of Edwin Muir
Hamburger, M. Edwin Muir's Letters. *In*
Hamburger, M. Art as second nature p103-
06

Muir, John
About individual works
My first summer in the Sierra
Xiques, D. John Muir's My first summer
in the Sierra. *In* Kagle, S. E. ed. America:
exploration and travel p102-12

Travels in Alaska
Tallmadge, J. John Muir, Emerson, and
the book of nature: the explorer as prophet.
In Kagle, S. E. ed. America: exploration
and travel p113-25

Muir, Kenneth
The singularity of Shakespeare, and other
essays
Contents
The comedies of Calderón
The conclusion of The winter's tale
Congreve on the modern stage
Edward III
The plays of Henri René Lenormand
Poetry as a criticism of life
The pursuit of relevance
Robert Greene as dramatist
Shakespeare and the tragic pattern
The singularity of Shakespeare
Some Freudian interpretations of Shake-
speare
This side idolatry
Timon of Athens and the cash-nexus
The uncomic pun

Theophames in the last plays. *In* Shakespeare's late plays p32-43

Muir, William Ker
The state legislature as a school of
political capacity. *In* Burnham, W. D. and
Weinberg, W. M. eds. American politics
and public policy p222-47

Mujal-León, Eusebio M.
Portuguese and Spanish communism in
comparative perspective. *In* Kaplan, M. A.
ed. The many faces of communism p122-45

Mukařovský, Jan
Art as semiotic fact. *In* Matejka, L. and
Titunik, I. R. eds. Semiotics of art p3-9

Same as Mukařovský, J. Art as a semiotic
fact. *In* Mukařovský, J. Structure and function p82-88

The essence of the visual arts. *In*
Matejka, L. and Titunik, I. R. eds. Semiotics
of art p229-44

Also in Mukařovský, J. Structure, sign and
function p220-35

Poetic reference. *In* Matejka, L. and Titu-
nik, I. R. eds. Semiotics of art p155-63
Structure, sign, and function
Contents
The aesthetic norm
Art as a semiotic fact

Same as Mukařovský, J. Art as semiotic
fact. *In* Matejka, L. and Titunik, I. R. ed.
Semiotics of art p3-9

An attempt at a structural analysis of a
dramatic figure
Can there be a universal aesthetic value
in art
The concept of the whole in the theory
of art
Dialectic contradictions in modern art
Intentionality and unintentionality in art
Jan Mukařovský's structural aesthetics
A note on the aesthetics of film
On structuralism
On the current state of the theory of theater
On the problem of functions in architecture
Personality in art
The place of the aesthetic function among
the other functions
The significance of aesthetics
Time in film

Mukařovský, Jan—*Continued*

About

Mukařovský, J. Jan Mukařovský's structural aesthetics. *In* Mukařovský, J. Structure, sign, and function p ix-xxxix

Mukden Incident, 1931

Graebner, N. A. The Manchurian crisis, 1931-1932. *In* Higham, R. D. ed. Intervention or abstention: the dilemma of American foreign policy p60-78

Mukherjee, Meenakshi

Inside the outsider. *In* Narasimhaiah, C. D. ed. Awakened conscience p86-91

Mukirane, Isaya

About

Kasfir, N. Seizing half a loaf: Isaya Mukirane and self-recruitment for secession. *In* The Making of politicians: studies from Africa and Asia p66-77

Mules (in religion, folklore, etc.)

Corbin, D. A. Mine mules and coal tipples: icons of the coalfields. *In* Browne, R. B. and Fishwick, M. W. eds. Icons of America p253-62

Mulhallen, Karen G.

'For friendship's sake: some additions to Blake's sheets for Designs to a series of ballads (1802). *In* Virginia. University. Bibliographical Society. Studies in bibliography v29 p331-41

Mulholland, J. Derral

Movements of celestial bodies—Velikovsky's fatal flaw. *In* Goldsmith, D. ed. Scientists confront Velikovsky p105-15

Mulk-Raj, Anand. See Anand, Mulk Raj

Mulkay, Michael J.

Sociology of the scientific research community. *In* Science, technology and society p93-148

Mullā Sadrā, Muhammad ibn Ibrāhīm

About

Rahman, F. The God-world relationship in Mullā Sadrā. *In* Essays on Islamic philosophy and science p238-53

Mullan, W. N. B.

Grillparzer and the realist tradition. *In* Branscombe, P. ed. Austrian life and literature, 1780-1938 p26-39

Mullen, Richard D.

"I told you so": Wells's last decade, 1936-1945. *In* H. G. Wells and modern science fiction p116-25

Muller, Steven

A new American university? *In* A New America? p31-45

Mulligan, James A.

About

Swart, S. L. The military examination board in the Civil War: a case study. *In* Hubbell, J. T. ed. Battles lost and won p241-59

Mullin, Michael

British Caribbean and North American slaves in an era of war and revolution, 1775-1807. *In* The Southern experience in the American Revolution p235-67

Mulqueen, James E.

Emersonian transcendentalism: over-soul or over-self? *In* Tennessee Studies in literature v 21 p21-27

Mulryne, J. R.

Printer's copy for part of volume seven of the W. B. Yeats Collected works in verse and prose (1908). *In* Virginia. University. Bibliographical Society. Studies in bibliography v30 p235-40

Multhauf, Robert P.

The science of matter. *In* Lindberg, D. C. ed. Science in the Middle Ages p369-90

Multilingualism. See Bilingualism

Multinational corporations. See International business enterprises

Multiple independently targetable reentry vehicles

Rathjens, G. W. Slowing down the arms race. *In* The Dynamics of the arms race p82-91

York, H. F. The origins of MIRV. *In* The Dynamics of the arms race p23-35

Multiple personality

De Sousa, R. B. Rational homunculi. *In* Rorty, A. O. ed. The identities of persons p217-38

Mulvey, Christopher

David Copperfield: the folk-story structure. *In* Dickens Studies Annual v5 p74-94

Mumford, Lewis

About

Goist, P. D. Regionalism and community: the urbanism of Lewis Mumford. *In* Goist, P. D. From Main Street to State Street p143-57

Sale, R. H. Mumford & Fuller. *In* Sale, R. H. On not being good enough p202-18

Mumming

Abrahams, R. D. and Bauman, R. Ranges of festival behavior. *In* Babcock, B. A. ed. The reversible world p193-208

Mumming plays

History and criticism

Weimann, R. The folk play and social custom. *In* Weimann, R. Shakespeare and the popular tradition in the theater; studies in the social dimension of dramatic form and function p15-48

Munazzamat al-Tahrir al-Filastiniyah

Caroz, Y. The Palestinians: who they are. *In* The Palestinians p77-80

Freedman, R. O. Soviet policy toward international terrorism. *In* International terrorism p115-47

Harkabi, Y. The debate at the 12th Palestinian National Council. *In* The Palestinians p159-65

Harkabi, Y. A Palestinian democratic state as the political goal of the Palestinians. *In* The Palestinians p154-58

Harkabi, Y. The Palestinian National Covenant. *In* The Palestinians p143-53

Norton, A. R. Moscow and the Palestinians: a new tool of Soviet policy in the Middle East. *In* The Palestinians p228-48

Parry, A. Arafat and other sacrificers. *In* Parry, A. Terrorism: from Robespierre to Arafat p449-68

Prittie, T. C. F. Israel and the Palestinian question. *In* The Palestinians p213-27

Weisband, E. and Roguly, D. Palestinian terrorism: violence, verbal strategy, and legitimacy. *In* International terrorism p258-319

Munby, Alan Noel Latimer

The book collector. *In* Keynes, M. ed. Essays on John Maynard Keynes p290-98

Munby, Alan N. L.—*Continued*

About individual works

Essays and papers

Todd, W. B. The diversions of an ardent bibliophile. *In* Review, v 1 1979 p329-32

Munch, Edvard

About

Craft, R. Edvard Munch: self-portraitist. *In* Craft, R. Current convictions p315-28

Munday, Anthony

Bibliography

Haaker, A. Anthony Munday. *In* Logan, T. P. and Smith, D. S. eds. The popular school p122-36

Mundell, Robert A.

Abba Lerner and the theory of foreign trade. *In* Theory for economic efficiency: essays in honor of Abba P. Lerner p144-50

Mundhenk, Norm

The subjectivity of anachronism. *In* On language, culture, and religion: in honor of Eugene A. Nida p259-73

Mundle, Clement W. K.

Does the concept of precognition make sense? *In* Ludwig, J. K. ed. Philosophy and parapsychology p327-40

On the 'psychic' powers of nonhuman animals. *In* Thakur, S. C. ed. Philosophy and psychical research p157-80

Strange facts in search of a theory. *In* Wheatley, J. M. O. and Edge, H. L. eds. Philosophical dimensions of parapsychology p76-97

See also Kneale, M. H. jt. auth.

About individual works

Does the concept of precognition make sense?

Brier, R. Mundle, Broad, Ducasse and the precognition problem. *In* Ludwig, J. K. ed. Philosophy and parapsychology p341-49

Mundurucu Indians

Steward, J. H. Tappers and trappers: parallel processes in acculturation. *In* Steward, J. H. Evolution and ecology p151-79

Mundy, Anthony. See Munday, Anthony

Mundy, John Hine

The origins of the College of Saint-Raymond at the University of Toulouse. *In* Philosophy and humanism p454-61

Municipal administration. See Municipal government

Municipal charters. See Charters of American cities, e.g. Boston. Charters

Municipal corporations

Russia

Hanchett, W. S. Tsarist statutory regulation of municipal government in the nineteenth century. *In* Hamm, M. F. ed. The city in Russian history p91-114

Municipal elections. See Local elections

Municipal engineering. See Housing; Public buildings

Municipal finance. See Metropolitan finance

Municipal government

Brown, L. D. Mayors and models: notes on the study of urban politics. *In* Burnham, W. D. and Weinberg, M. W. eds. American politics and public policy p251-79

Ginsburg, S. G. Management for the future: a prognosis and prescription with specific concern for university and governmental management. *In* Benton, L. R. ed. Management for the future p109-24

See also Federal-city relations; Local elections; Mayors; Metropolitan government

Law and legislation

See Municipal corporations

Belgium

Aiken, M. T. Urban social structure and political competition: a comparative study of local politics in four European nations. *In* Walton, J. and Masotti, L. H. eds. The city in comparative perspective p119-53

France

Aiken, M. T. Urban social structure and political competition: a comparative study of local politics in four European nations. *In* Walton, J. and Masotti, L. H. eds. The city in comparative perspective p119-53

Italy

Aiken, M. T. Urban social structure and political competition: a comparative study of local politics in four European nations. *In* Walton, J. and Masotti, L. H. eds. The city in comparative perspective p119-53

Netherlands

Aiken, M. T. Urban social structure and political competition: a comparative study of local politics in four European nations. *In* Walton, J. and Masotti, L. H. eds. The city in comparative perspective p119-53

Irwin, G. A. Party, accountability and the recruitment of municipal councilmen in the Netherlands. *In* Eulau, H. and Czudnowski, M. M. eds. Elite recruitment in democratic polities p163-204

San Francisco

Irwin, G. A. Party, accountability and the recruitment of municipal councilmen in the Netherlands. *In* Eulau, H. and Czudnowski, M. M. eds. Elite recruitment in democratic polities p163-204

Municipal powers and services beyond corporate limits

United States

Zimmerman, J. F. The patchwork approach: adaptive responses to increasing urbanization. *In* Hawley, A. H. and Rock, A. P. eds. Metropolitan America in contemporary perspective p431-73

Municipal research

Masotti, L. H. and Walton, J. Comparative urban research: the logic of comparisons and the nature of urbanism. *In* Walton, J. and Masotti, L. H. eds. The city in comparative perspective p 1-15

Walton, J. Political economy of world urban systems: directions for comparative research. *In* Walton, J. and Masotti, L. H. eds. The city in comparative perspective p301-13

Municipal services beyond corporate limits. See Municipal powers and services beyond corporate limits

Municipal universities and colleges

United States

Murphy, T. P. and Seyffert, M. G. The future urban university. *In* Murphy, T. P. ed. Universities in the urban crisis p381-400

Murdoch, John E.
The development of a critical temper: new approaches and modes of analysis in four-teenth-century philosophy, science, and theology. *In* Medieval and Renaissance studies [1975] p51-79

Euclides Graeco-Latinus: a hitherto un-known medieval Latin translation of the Elements made directly from the Greek. *In* Harvard Studies in classical philology v71 p249-302

Murdoch, John E. and Sylla, Edith Dudley
The science of motion. *In* Lindberg, D. C. ed. Science in the Middle Ages p206-64

Murdock, Clark A.
Economic factors as objects of security: economics, security and vulnerability. *In* Knorr, K. E. and Trager, F. N. eds. Economic issues and national security p67-98

Murdock, Graham, and Halloran, James Dermont
Contexts of creativity in television drama: an exploratory study in Britain. *In* Fischer, H. D. and Melnik, S. R. eds. Entertainment: a cross-cultural examination p273-85

Murena, A. Terentius Varro

About

Sumner, G. V. Varrones Murenae. *In* Harvard Studies in classical philology v82 p187-95

Swan, M. The consular fasti of 23 B.C. and the conspiracy of Varro Murena. *In* Harvard Studies in classical philology v71 p235-47

Murena, L. (Terentius) Varro. See Murena, Varro

Murena, Varro

About

Swan, M. The consular fasti of 23 B.C. and the conspiracy of Varro Murena. *In* Harvard Studies in classical philology v71 p235-47

Murgia, Charles Edward
Critical notes on the text of Servius' com-mentary on Aeneid III-V. *In* Harvard Studies in classical philology v72 p311-50

Muridīyah
Karp, M. The "Protestant ethic" of the Mourids of Senegal. *In* African dimensions p197-213

Murnau, Friedrich Wilhelm

About

Henderson, B. The long take. *In* Nichols, B. ed. Movies and methods p314-24

Murphey, Murray G.
The place of beliefs in modern culture. *In* Higham, J. and Conkin, P. K. eds. New directions in American intellectual history p151-65

Murphy, Avon Jack
Robert Herrick: the self-conscious critic in Hesperides. *In* Rollin, R. B. and Patrick, J. M. eds. "Trust to good verses": Herrick tercentenary essays p53-63

Murphy, Gardner
Are there any solid facts in psychical re-search? *In* Wheatley, J. M. O. and Edge, H. L. eds. Philosophical dimensions of parapsychology p388-404

The problem of repeatability in psychical research. *In* Ludwig, J. K. ed. Philosophy and parapsychology p270-83

Murphy, Gerald

About

MacLeish, A. Gerald Murphy. *In* Mac-Leish, A. Riders on the earth p123-26

Murphy, James
The role of international law in the pre-vention of terrorist kidnapping of diplomatic personnel. *In* International terrorism and political crimes p285-313

Murphy, James Jerome
Rhetoric in early Middle English: rhetoric and dialectic in The owl and the nightingale. *In* Murphy, J. J. ed. Medieval eloquence p198-230

Murphy, John F.
United Nations proposals on the control and repression of terrorism. *In* International terrorism and political crimes p493-506

Murphy, Paul L.
"Certain unalienable rights." *In* Alderson, W. T. ed. American issues p33-48

Communities in conflict. *In* The Pulse of freedom p23-64

Murphy, Richard

About

Harmon, M. Introduction: the poet and his background. *In* Harmon. M. ed. Richard Murphy: poet of two traditions p7-9

Heaney, S. The poetry of Richard Murphy. *In* Harmon, M. ed. Richard Murphy: poet of two traditions p18-30

About individual works
The Battle of Aughrim

Sims, J. G. The Battle of Aughrim: his-tory and poetry. *In* Harmon, M. ed. Richard Murphy: poet of two traditions p36-51

Bibliography

FitzGerald, M. M. A Richard Murphy bibliography. *In* Harmon, M. ed. Richard Murphy: poet of two traditions p104-17

Style

Harmon, M. Beginning with words. *In* Harmon, M. ed. Richard Murphy: poet of two traditions p118-28

Murphy, Robert Francis
Introduction: The anthropological theories of Julian H. Steward. *In* Steward, J. H. Evolution and ecology p 1-39

Murphy, Stan
The meaning of Greene County. *In* The Rising South v2 p78-94

Murphy, Thomas Aquinas
Are we losing the freedom to decide? *In* Prochnow, H. V. ed. Dilemmas facing the nation p125-33

Murphy, Thomas Paul
Free universities and urban higher educa-tion. *In* Murphy, T. P. ed. Universities in the urban crisis p113-35

Internships in urban government. *In* Murphy, T. P. ed. Universities in the urban crisis p71-92

Minority faculty recruitment. *In* Murphy, T. P. ed. Universities in the urban crisis p325-51

University bureaucracy and the urban thrust. *In* Murphy, T. P. ed. Universities in the urban crisis p287-313

Urban governmental manpower. *In* Mur-phy, T. P. ed. Universities in the urban crisis p49-70

See also Zarnowiecki, J. jt. auth.

Murphy, Thomas Paul, and Knipe, Elizabeth A.
The federal government and urban higher education. In Murphy, T. P. ed. Universities in the urban crisis p353-79

Murphy, Thomas Paul, and Seyffert, M. Gordon
The future urban university. In Murphy, T. P. ed. Universities in the urban crisis p381-400

Murphy, Thomas Paul, and Zarnowiecki, James
The urban observatory: a university—city research venture. In Murphy, T. P. ed. Universities in the urban crisis p15-47

Murphy, Walter F.
The art of constitutional interpretation. In Essays on the Constitution of the United States p130-59

Murphy, William M.
Psychic daughter, mystic son, sceptic father. In Yeats and the occult p11-26

Murray, David J. See Lee, B. jt. auth.

Murray, Edward
Nine American film critics
Contents
Andrew Sarris and auteur criticism
Dwight Macdonald, "congenital critic"
James Agee, "amateur critic"
John Simon, judicial critic
Parker Tyler and psychoanalytic-mythological criticism
Pauline Kael and pluralistic, nonaesthetic criticism
Robert Warshow and sociological criticism
Stanley Kauffmann and pluralistic, aesthetic criticism
Vernon Young, ethnological-aesthetic critic
Ten film classics
Contents
L'Avventura
The bicycle thief
Bonnie and Clyde
Citizen Kane
The 400 blows
Ikiru
On the waterfront
Potemkin
La strada
Wild strawberries

Murray, George Raymond Beasley- See Beasley-Murray, George Raymond

Murray, Gilbert
About
Gilbert Murray. In Highet, G. The immortal profession p145-74

Murray, Henry Alexander
Dedication. In Artful thunder p3-7

Murray, John
About
Faulkner, T. C. George Crabbe: Murray's 1834 edition of the life and poems. In Virginia. University. Bibliographical Society. Studies in bibliography v32 p246-52

Murray, John, publisher, London
Bennett, S. B. John Murray's family library and the cheapening of books in early nineteenth century Britain. In Virginia. University. Bibliographical Society. Studies in bibliography v29 p139-66

Murray, John Courtney
The civilization of the pluralist society; excerpt from "We hold these truths: Catholic reflections on the American proposition." In A Public philosophy reader p143-51
Two cases for the public consensus; excerpt from "We hold these truths: Catholic reflections on the American proposition." In A Public philosophy reader p103-11
About
Cuervo, R. F. The definition of public philosophy: Lippmann and Murray. In A Public philosophy reader p97-102

Murray, Judith (Sargent)
About individual works
The gleaner
Granger, B. I. Judith Sargent Murray. In Granger, B. I. American essay serials from Franklin to Irving p164-81

Murray, Lawrence Leo
Hollywood, nihilism, and the youth culture of the sixties: Bonnie and Clyde. In O'Connor, J. E. and Jackson, M. A. eds. American history/American film p237-56

Murray, Michael E.
Heidegger and Ryle: two versions of phenomenology. In Murray, M. E. ed. Heidegger and modern philosophy p271-90

Murray, Robert F.
The ethical and moral values of Black Americans and population policy. In Population policy and ethics p197-207
Genetic counseling: boon or bane? In The Tricentennial people p29-46
The perspective of the population geneticist. In Population policy and ethics p365-75

Murray, Timothy C.
Kenneth Burke's logology: a mock logomachy. In Glyph 2 p144-61

Murray, W. A.
Donne and Paracelsus: an essay in interpretation. In Roberts, J. R. ed. Essential articles for the study of John Donne's poetry p122-28
What was the soul of the apple? In Roberts, J. R. ed. Essential articles for the study of John Donne's poetry p462-74

Murrin, Michael
The rhetoric of fairyland. In Sloan, T. O. and Waddington, R. S. eds. The rhetoric of Renaissance poetry p73-95

Murrow, Edward R.
About individual works
This is London
Davis, E. H. Introduction to This is London by Edward R. Murrow. In Praise from famous men: an anthology of introductions p45-48

Murry, John Middleton
About
Richards, I. A. Between truth and truth. In Richards, I. A. Complementarities p37-48

Mursia, Ugo
The true birthplace of Joseph Conrad. In Joseph Conrad: a commemoration p199-205

Murvar, Vatro
Integrative and revolutionary capabilities of religion. In Johnson, H. M. ed. Religious change and continuity p74-86

Muscovy Company

Baron, S. H. Osip Nepea and the opening of Anglo-Russian commercial relations. *In* Oxford Slavonic papers, new ser. v11 p42-63

Muses in art

Winternitz, E. The inspired musician: a 16th-century musical pastiche. *In* Winternitz, E. Musical instruments and their symbolism in Western art p202-10

Winternitz, E. Muses and music in a burial chapel: an interpretation of Filippino Lippi's window wall in the Cappella Strozzi. *In* Winternitz, E. Musical instruments and their symbolism in Western art p166-84

Winternitz, E. Musical archaeology of the Renaissance in Raphael's Parnassus. *In* Winternitz, E. Musical instruments and their symbolism in Western art p185-201

Musette. See Bagpipe

Museum directors

Palmer, A. M. Through the glass case: the curator and the object. *In* Material culture and the study of American life p219-44

Museum techniques

Skramstad, H. K. Interpreting material culture: a view from the other side of the glass. *In* Material culture and the study of American life p175-200

Museums. See Museum techniques

Musgrave, Richard Abel

Adam Smith on public finance and distribution. *In* The Market and the state p296-319

Taxation, inflation, and growth. *In* Inflation, trade and taxes p181-93

Mushakoji, Kinhide

A note on trilateral crisis diplomacy: the irritants in the Japan-U.S.-E.C. relations. *In* Postwar trends in Japan p15-36

Mushete, Ngindu

Unity of faith and pluralism in theology. *In* The Emergent gospel p50-55

Mushkat, Marion

The diffusion of economic and military power and its impact on the Middle East conflict. *In* Arms control and technological innovation p247-54

Music

Sessions, R. The composer and his message. *In* Sessions, R. Roger Sessions on music p3-26

Sessions, R. Song and pattern in music today. *In* Sessions, R. Roger Sessions on music p53-70

See also Composition (Music); Computer music; Folk-songs; Opera; Singing

Aesthetics

See Music—Philosophy and aesthetics

Bibliography

Duckles, V. H. The library of the mind: observations on the relationship between musical scholarship and bibliography. *In* Current thought in musicology p277-96

Bibliography—Manuscripts

See Music—Manuscripts

Composition

See Composition (Music)

Economic aspects

Sessions, R. Music in a business economy. *In* Sessions, R. Roger Sessions on music p157-68

Historiography

Winternitz, E. Appendix: images as records for the history of music. *In* Winternitz, E. Musical instruments and their symbolism in Western art p227-33

See also Musical criticism; Musicology

History and criticism

Sessions, R. Composer and critic. *In* Sessions, R. Roger Sessions on music p120-22

Sessions, R. The scope of music criticism. *In* Sessions, R. Roger Sessions on music p146-56

Werner, E. Two types of ritual and their music. *In* Salo Wittmayer Baron v2 p975-1008

History and criticism—Methods

See Music—Historiography; Musical criticism

History and criticism—Sources

Winternitz, E. Appendix: images as records for the history of music. *In* Winternitz, E. Musical instruments and their symbolism in Western art p227-33

Winternitz, E. The visual arts as a source for the historian of music. *In* Winternitz, E. Musical instruments and their symbolism in Western art p25-42

History and criticism—Theory, etc.

See Music—Historiography; Musical criticism

History and criticism—Medieval, 400-1500

Crocker, R. L. The early Frankish sequence: a new musical form. *In* Viator: medieval and Renaissance studies v6 p341-49

Pattison, B. Renaissance music. *In* Background to the English Renaissance p57-66

Pirrotta, N. "Musica de sono humano" and the musical poetics of Guido of Arezzo. *In* Medievalia et humanistica no. 7 p13-27

Reaney, G. The irrational and late medieval music. *In* The Darker vision of the Renaissance p197-219

Reaney, G. The prospects for research in medieval music in the 1970's. *In* Current thought in musicology p247-76

Smith, B. R. The contest of Apollo and Marsyas: ideas about music in the Middle Ages. *In* Jeffrey, D. L. ed. By things seen: reference and recognition in medieval thought p81-107

History and criticism—Medieval, 400-1500—Bibliography

Karp, T. C. Medieval music in perspective. *In* Powell, J. M. ed. Medieval studies p343-72

History and criticism—16th century

Pattison, B. Renaissance music. *In* Background to the English Renaissance p57-66

History and criticism—19th century

See Romanticism in music

History and criticism—20th century

Cavell, S. Music discomposed. *In* Cavell, S. Must we mean what we say? p180-212

Sessions, R. Music in crisis. *In* Sessions, R. Roger Sessions on music p27-44

Sessions, R. The new musical horizon. *In* Sessions, R. Roger Sessions on music p45-52

See also Jazz music

Music—*Continued*

Instruction and study

Sessions, R. The composer in the university. *In* Sessions, R. Roger Sessions on music p193-203

Sessions, R. New vistas in musical education. *In* Sessions, R. Roger Sessions on music p187-92

Sessions, R. What can be taught? *In* Sessions, R. Roger Sessions on music p204-27

Instruction and study—United States

Griffel, L. M. Teaching music. *In* Cahn S. M. ed. Scholars who teach p193-216

Manuscripts

Hartzell, K. D. An unknown English Benedictine gradual of the eleventh century. *In* Anglo-Saxon England 4 p131-44

Pennington, A. E. Music in sixteenth-century Moldavia: new evidence. *In* Oxford Slavonic papers new ser. v11 p64-83

Manuscripts—Massachusetts

Crawford, R. A. and McKay, D. P. Music in manuscript: a Massachusetts tune-book of 1782. *In* American Antiquarian Society. Proceedings v84 pt 1 p43-64

Performance

Barthes, R. Musica practica. *In* Barthes, R. Image, music, text p149-54

Philosophy and aesthetics

Cavell, S. Music discomposed. *In* Cavell, S. Must we mean what we say? p180-212

Hollander, J. Musica mundana and Twelfth night. *In* Wimsatt, W. K. ed. Literary criticism: idea and act p265-83

Nattiez, J. J. The contribution of musical semiotics to the semiotic discussion in general. *In* Sebeok, T. A. ed. A perfusion of signs p121-42

Sessions, R. How a "difficult" composer gets that way. *In* Sessions, R. Roger Sessions on music p169-71

Sessions, R. Music and the crisis of the arts. *In* Sessions, R. Roger Sessions on music p175-86

See also Style, Musical

Poetry—History and criticism

Silver, I. The marriage of poetry and music in France: Ronsard's predecessors and contemporaries. *In* Poetry and poetics from ancient Greece to the Renaissance p152-84

Political aspects

Sessions, R. American music and the crisis. *In* Sessions, R. Roger Sessions on music p295-303

Sessions, R. Artists and this war. *In* Sessions, R. Roger Sessions on music p313-18

Sessions, R. Music and nationalism. *In* Sessions, R. Roger Sessions on music p271-81

Sessions, R. No more business-as-usual. *In* Sessions, R. Roger Sessions on music p304-12

Sessions, R. On the American future. *In* Sessions, R. Roger Sessions on music p288-94

Sessions, R. Vienna—vale, ave. *In* Sessions, R. Roger Sessions on music p282-87

Psychology

Carter, E. Music and the time screen. *In* Current thought in musicology p63-88

Study and teaching

See Music—Instruction and study

Theory

Sessions, R. Escape by theory. *In* Sessions, R. Roger Sessions on music p256-62

Sessions, R. Exposition by Křenek. *In* Sessions, R. Roger Sessions on music p249-55

Sessions, R. The function of theory. *In* Sessions, R. Roger Sessions on music p263-68

Sessions, R. Heinrich Schenker's contribution. *In* Sessions, R. Roger Sessions on music p231-40

Sessions, R. Hindemith on theory. *In* Sessions, R. Roger Sessions on music p241-48

See also Composition (Music); Music—Philosophy and aesthetics; Musical temperament

Theory—Medieval, 400-1500

Reaney, G. The irrational and late medieval music. *In* The Darker vision of the Renaissance p197-219

Theory—Medieval, 400-1500— Bibliography

Karp, T. C. Medieval music in perspective. *In* Powell, J. M. ed. Medieval studies p343-72

Afro-Americans

See Afro-American music

Jews

Werner, E. Two types of ritual and their music. *In* Salo Wittmayer Baron v2 p975-1008

Africa

See Music, African

Brazil

Béhague, G. H. Notes on regional and national trends in Afro-Brazilian cult music. *In* Forster, M. H. ed. Tradition and renewal p68-80

France—History and criticism

Macdonald, H. "Un pays où tous sont musiciens . . ." *In* From Parnassus p285-94

Germany

Sessions, R. Music and nationalism. *In* Sessions, R. Roger Sessions on music p271-81

Great Britain

McCabe, J. The condition of music. *In* Abbs, P. ed. The black rainbow p114-33

Moldavia

Pennington, A. E. Music in sixteenth-century Moldavia: new evidence. *In* Oxford Slavonic papers new ser. v11 p64-83

United States

Sessions, R. America moves to the avant-scene. *In* Sessions, R. Roger Sessions on music p123-36

Vienna

Sessions, R. Vienna—vale, ave. *In* Sessions, R. Roger Sessions on music p282-87

Music, African

Béhague, G. H. Notes on regional and national trends in Afro-Brazilian cult music. *In* Forster, M. H. ed. Tradition and renewal p68-80

Music, African—*Continued*

Jones, A. M. African music in Northern Rhodesia and some other places. *In* The Occasional papers of the Rhodes-Livingstone Museum p71-144

Kaemmer, J. E. Changing music in contemporary Africa. *In* Martin, P. M. and O'Meara, P. eds. Africa p367-77

Merriam, A. P. Traditional music of Black Africa. *In* Martin, P. M. and O'Meara, P. eds. Africa p243-58

Nketia, J. H. K. The musical heritage of Africa. *In* Mintz, S. W. ed. Slavery, colonialism, and racism p151-61

Music, Afro-American. See Afro-American music

Music, American

History and criticism

Hamm, C. E. The ecstatic and the didactic: a pattern in American music. *In* Current thought in musicology p41-62

Music, Brazilian. See Music—Brazil

Music, Computer. See Computer music

Music, Dramaitc. See Music in theaters; Opera

Music, English

History and criticism

Luckett, R. 'Meaning motion': old music and some modern writers. *In* English Association. Essays and studies, 1977 p88-97

Music, French

History and criticism

Macdonald, H. "Un pays où tous sont musiciens . . ." *In* From Parnassus p285-94

Music, German

Influence

Macdonald, H. "Un pays où tous sont musiciens . . ." *In* From Parnassus p285-94

Music, Hebrew. See Music—Jews

Music, Islamic

History and criticism

Shiloah, A. The dimension of sound. *In* Lewis, B. ed. Islam and the Arab world p161-80

Music, Jewish. See Music—Jews

Music, Medieval. See Music—History and criticism—Medieval, 400-1500; Music—Theory—Medieval, 400-1500

Music, Muslim. See Music. Islamic

Music, Negro. See Afro-American music

Music, Popular (Songs, etc.)

Schwartz, D. C. and Mannella, C. J. Popular music as an agency of political socialization: a study in popular culture and politics. *In* Schwartz, D. C. and Schwartz, S. K. eds. New directions in political socialization p289-316

Recording

See Music, Popular (Songs, etc.)—Writing and publishing

Social aspects

Schmidtchen, G. Light music and the radio listener. *In* Fischer, H. D. and Melnik, S. R. eds. Entertainment: a cross-cultural examination p286-98

Europe

Watts, M. The call and response of popular music: the impact of American pop music in Europe. *In* Bigsby, C. W. E. Superculture p123-39

Germany, West—
Writing and publishing

Zeppenfeld, W. The economics and structure of the record and tape industry: the example of West Germany. *In* Fischer, H. D. and Melnik, S. R. eds. Entertainment: a cross-cultural examination p248-57

Great Britain

Parker, C. Pop song, the manipulated ritual. *In* Abbs, P. ed. The black rainbow p134-67

Watts, M. The call and response of popular music: the impact of American pop music in Europe. *In* Bigsby, C. W. E. Superculture p123-39

United States

Watts, M. The call and response of popular music: the impact of American pop music in Europe. *In* Bigsby, C. W. E. Superculture p123-39

Music, Primitive

Jones, A. M. African music in Northern Rhodesia and some other places. *In* The Occasional papers of the Rhodes-Livingstone Museum p71-144

See also Drum language

Music, Theatrical. See Music in theaters; Opera

Music and literature

Ciardi, J. Kenneth Patchen: poetry and poetry with jazz. *In* Morgan, R. G. ed. Kenneth Patchen: a collection of essays p29-30

Elmore, A. E. Herrick and the poetry of song. *In* Rollin, R. B. and Patrick, J. M. eds. "Trust to good verses": Herrick tercentenary essays p65-75

Gay, P. Browning and music. *In* Armstrong, I. ed. Robert Browning p211-30

Hawkes, T. 'That Shakespeherian rag.' *In* English Association. Essays and studies, 1977 p22-38

Hughes, D. G. Music and meter in liturgical poetry. *In* Medievalia et humanistica no. 7 p29-43

Luckett, R. 'Meaning motion': old music and some modern writers. *In* English Association. Essays and studies, 1977 p88-97

Martz, L. L. The music of Comus. *In* Illustrious evidence p93-113

Neil, A. Kenneth Patchen reads with jazz in Canada. *In* Morgan, R. G. ed. Kenneth Patchen: a collection of essays p54-58

Peyre, H. Poets against music in the age of symbolism. *In* Symbolism and modern literature p179-92

Schmidgall, G. Afterword. *In* Schmidgall, G. Literature as opera p357-70

Schmidgall, G. An opening perspective. *In* Schmidgall, G. Literature as opera p 1-28

See, C. The jazz musician as Patchen's hero. *In* Morgan, R. G. ed. Kenneth Patchen: a collection of essays p218-28

Silver, I. Ronsard on the marriage of poetry, music, and the dance. *In* Studies in the continental background of Renaissance English literature: essays presented to John L. Lievsay p155-69

Thompson, D. In the beginning. *In* Thompson, D. The uses of poetry p19-42

Yates, P. Patchen's poetry and jazz. *In* Morgan, R. G. ed. Kenneth Patchen: a collection of essays p208-17

See also Music—Poetry

Music and poetry. See Music and literature

Music and race

Sessions, R. Music and nationalism. *In* Sessions, R. Roger Sessions on music p271-81

Music and radio. See Radio and music

Music and romanticism. See Romanticism in music

Music and society. See Music—Economic aspects

Music and war. See World War, 1939-1945— Music and the war

Music in art

Winternitz, E. The inspired musician: a 16th-century musical pastiche. *In* Winternitz, E. Musical instruments and their symbolism in Western art p202-10

See also Musical instruments in art

Music in literature

Frank, M. H. Milton's knowledge of music: some speculations. *In* Patrick, J. M. and Sundell, R. H. eds. Milton and the art of sacred song p83-98

Toliver, H. E. Marvell's songs and pictorial exhibits. *In* Friedenreich, K. ed. Tercentenary essays in honor of Andrew Marvell p105-20

Weaver, W. T. Music and mystery. *In* Agatha Christie: first lady of crime p183-92

See also Music and literature

Music in theaters

Auld, L. E. Music as dramatic device in the secular theater of Marguerite de Navarre. *In* Renaissance drama [1976] p193-217

Music printing

Kroeger, K. Isaiah Thomas as a music publisher. *In* American Antiquarian Society. Proceedings v86 pt2 p321-41

Music publishers. See Music printing

Music trade. See Music—Economic aspects

Musical composition. See Composition (Music)

Musical criticism

Barthes, R. The grain of the voice. *In* Barthes, R. Image, music, text p179-89

Barthes, R. Musica practica. *In* Barthes, R. Image, music, text p149-54

Isherwood, R. M. The third war of the musical Enlightenment. *In* Studies in eighteenth-century culture v4 p223-45

Musical education. See Music—Instruction and study

Musical iconography. See Music in art

Musical instruments

History

Brown, H. M. Instruments and voices in the fifteenth-century chanson. *In* Current thought in musicology p89-137

Winternitz, E. Appendix: images as records for the history of music. *In* Winternitz, E. Musical instruments and their symbolism in Western art p227-33

Winternitz, E. The importance of quattrocento intarsias for the history of musical instruments. *In* Winternitz, E. Musical instruments and their symbolism in Western art p116-19

Winternitz, E. The visual arts as a source for the historian of music. *In* Winternitz, E. Musical instruments and their symbolism in Western art p25-42

Italy—History

Winternitz, E. Musical instruments for the stage in paintings by Filippino Lippi, Piero di Cosimo, and Lorenzo Costa. *In* Winternitz, E. Musical instruments and their symbolism in Western art p211-25

Musical instruments, Primitive. See Music, Primitive

Musical instruments in art

Winternitz, E. Appendix: images as records for the history of music. *In* Winternitz, E. Musical instruments and their symbolism in Western art p227-33

Winternitz, E. Bagpipes for the Lord. *In* Winternitz, E. Musical instruments and their symbolism in Western art p129-36

Winternitz, E. The curse of Pallas Athena. *In* Winternitz, E. Musical instruments and their symbolism in Western art p150-65

Winternitz, E. The importance of quattrocento intarsias for the history of musical instruments. *In* Winternitz, E. Musical instruments and their symbolism in Western art p116-19

Winternitz, E. The knowledge of musical instruments as an aid to the art historian. *In* Winternitz, E. Musical instruments and their symbolism in Western art p43-56

Winternitz, E. Muses and music in a burial chapel: an interpretation of Filippino Lippi's window wall in the Cappella Strozzi. *In* Winternitz, E. Musical instruments and their symbolism in Western art p166-84

Winternitz, E. Musical archaeology of the Renaissance in Raphael's Parnassus. *In* Winternitz, E. Musical instruments and their symbolism in Western art p185-201

Winternitz, E. Musical instruments for the stage in paintings by Filippino Lippi, Piero di Cosimo, and Lorenzo Costa. *In* Winternitz, E. Musical instruments and their symbolism in Western art p211-25

Winternitz, E. On angel concerts in the 15th century: a critical approach to realism and symbolism in sacred painting. *In* Winternitz, E. Musical instruments and their symbolism in Western art p137-49

Winternitz, E. The survival of the kithara and the evolution of the English cittern: a study in morphology. *In* Winternitz, E. Musical instruments and their symbolism in Western art p57-65

Winternitz, E. The visual arts as a source for the historian of music. *In* Winternitz, E. Musical instruments and their symbolism in Western art p25-42

Musical performance. See Music—Performance

Musical research. See Musicology

Musical style. See Style, Musical

Musical temperament

Ellsworth, O. B. A fourteenth-century proposal for equal temperament. *In* Viator: medieval and Renaissance studies v5 p445-53

Musical travels through England

Lonsdale, R. H. Dr. Burney, 'Joel Collier', and Sabrina. *In* Evidence in literary scholarship p281-308

Musicians in literature. See Music and literature

Musicology

Chase, G. Musicology, history, and anthropology: current thoughts. *In* Current thought in musicology p231-46

Duckles, V. H. The library of the mind: observations on the relationship between musical scholarship and bibliography. *In* Current thought in musicology p277-96

Reaney, G. The prospects for research in medieval music in the 1970's. *In* Current thought in musicology p247-76

See also Musical criticism

Musil, Robert

About

Henninger, P. On literature and condensation: Robert Musil's early novellas. *In* Glyph 5 p114-32

About individual works

Young Törless

Meyers, J. Mann and Musil: Death in Venice and Young Törless. *In* Meyers, J. Homosexuality and literature, 1890-1930 p42-57

Musinga, Victor Eleame

About

Etherton, M. The dilemma of the popular playwright: the work of Kabwe Kasoma and V. E. Musinga. *In* African literature today no. 8: Drama in Africa p26-41

Muskogee Indians. See Creek Indians

Muskoki Indians. See Creek Indians

Muslim architecture. See Architecture, Islamic

Muslim art. See Art, Islamic

Muslim cities and towns. See Cities and towns, Islamic

Muslim civilization. See Civilization, Islamic

Muslim countries. See Islamic countries

Muslim Empire. See Islamic Empire

Muslim ethics. See Islamic ethics

Muslim holy war. See Jihad

Muslim legends. See Legends, Islamic

Muslim literature. See Islamic literature

Muslim music. See Music, Islamic

Muslim philosophy. See Philosophy, Islamic

Muslim psychology. See Islam—Psychology

Muslim theology. See Islamic theology

Muslim women. See Women, Muslim

Muslimism. See Islam

Muslims

Women

See Women, Muslim

Muslims, Black

History

Lewis, B. The African diaspora and the civilization of Islam. *In* Kilson, M. L. and Rotberg, R. I. eds. The African diaspora p37-56

Muslims in Africa

Hunwick, J. O. The study of Muslim Africa: retrospect and prospect. *In* African studies since 1945 p136-55

Muslims in China

Pillsbury, B. L. K. Being female in a Muslim minority in China. *In* Beck, L. and Keddie, N. R. eds. Women in the Muslim world p651-73

History

Rossabi, M. Muslim and Central Asian revolts. *In* Spence, J. D. and Wills, J. E. eds. From Ming to Ch'ing p167-99

Muslims in India

Rizvi, S. A. A. Muslim India. *In* Lewis, B. ed. Islam and the Arab world p301-20

Muslims in Indonesia

Johns, A. H. Islam in Southeast Asia: problems of perspective. *In* Southeast Asian history and historiography p304-20

Muslims in Russia

Bennigsen, A. The Bolshevik conquest of the Moslem borderlands. *In* Hammond, T. T. ed. The anatomy of Communist takeovers p61-70

Carlisle, D. S. Modernization, generations, and the Uzbek Soviet intelligentsia. *In* Cocks, P.; Daniels, R. V. and Heer, N. W. eds. The dynamics of Soviet politics p239-64

Muslims in Senegal

Karp, M. The "Protestant ethic" of the Mourids of Senegal. *In* African dimensions p197-213

Muslims in Spain. See Arabs in Spain

Mussolini, Benito

About

Kostof, S. K. The Emperor and the Duce: the planning of Piazzale Augusto Imperatore in Rome. *In* Millon, H. A. and Nochlin, L. eds. Art and architecture in the service of politics p270-325

Musson, Albert Edward

Continental influences on the Industrial Revolution in Great Britain. *In* Great Britain and her world, 1750-1914 p71-85

Mussulmanism. See Islam

Mustanoja, Tauno F.

Verbal rhyming in Chaucer. *In* Chaucer and Middle English studies in honour of Rossell Hope Robbins p104-10

Musta 'Ribs and the Maghribis in Cairo 1527, The agreement between the. Hirschberg, J. W. *In* Salo Wittmayer Baron v2 p577-90

Mutagenesis. See Chemical mutagenesis

Mutation (Biology) See Evolution; Genetic load

Muth, Richard F.

Economic policy and urban problems. *In* Capitalism and freedom p158-82

Mutual benefit associations. See Friendly societies

Mutual housing. See Housing, Cooperative

Mutual security program, 1951- See Economic assistance, American

Muwashshah

Monroe, J. T. Studies on the "ḥarğas": the Arabic and the romance "ḥarğas." *In* Viator: medieval and Renaissance studies v8 p95-125

Mwase, George Simeon

About individual works

Strike a blow and die

Hyman, S. E. A blow with a maize stalk. *In* Hyman, S. E. The critic's credentials p185-91

My darling Clementine (Motion picture)

Nichols, B. Style, grammar, and the movies. *In* Nichols, B. ed. Movies and methods p607-28

My life to live (Motion picture)
Beh, S. H. Vivre sa vie. *In* Nichols, B. ed.
Movies and methods p180-85

My uncle (Motion picture)
Truffaut, F. Jacques Tati: Mon oncle. *In*
Truffaut, F. The films in my life p235-37

My uncle Antoine (Motion picture)
Sarris, A. My uncle Antoine. *In* Sarris, A.
Politics and cinema p159-61

Mycosis. See Blastomycosis

Myerhoff, Barbara G.
Return to Wirikuta: ritual reversal and
symbolic continuity on the Peyote hunt of
the Huichol Indians. *In* Babcock, B. A. ed.
The reversible world p225-39

Shamanic equilibrium: balance and mediation in known and unknown worlds. *In*
American folk medicine p99-108

Myers, Alexander Reginald
George William Coopland: a biographical
appreciation. *In* War, literature, and politics
in the late Middle Ages p 1-11

Myers, Charles Andrews
Management and the employee. *In* McKie,
J. W. ed. Social responsibility and the
business predicament p311-49

Myers, Frederic William Henry

About
Kahn, S. D. "Myers' problem" revisited.
In Parapsychology: its relation to physics,
biology, psychology, and psychiatry p208-34

Myers, Leopold Hamilton

About
Gillie, C. The critical decade, 1930-1940.
In Gillie, C. Movements in English litera-
ture, 1900-1940 p122-49

About individual works
The near and the far
Cockshut, A. O. J. The male homosexual:
Satire. *In* Cockshut, A. O. J. Man and
woman: a study of love and the novel,
1740-1940 p181-85

Myers, Lonny, and Leggitt, Hunter
A positive view of adultery. *In* Gross, L.
ed. Sexual issues in marriage p165-80

Myers, Mitzi
Mary Wollstonecraft's Letters written . . .
in Sweden: toward romantic autobiography.
In Studies in eighteenth-century culture v8
p165-85

Politics from the outside: Mary Wollstonecraft's first Vindication. *In* Studies in
eighteenth-century culture v6 p113-32

Myers, Robert James
An approximation of justice. *In* [Truth
and tragedy]: a tribute to Hans Morgenthau p125-29

Myhill, John
The undefinability of the set of natural
numbers in the ramified Principia. *In*
Nakhnikian, G. ed. Bertrand Russell's philosophy p19-27

About individual works
*The undefinability of the set of
natural numbers in the
ramified Principia*
Cocchiarella, N. B. Formal ontology
and the foundations of mathematics. *In*
Nakhnikian, G. ed. Bertrand Russell's philosophy p29-46

Mylne, Vivienne
Social realism in the dialogue of eighteenth-century French fiction. *In* Studies in
eighteenth-century culture v6 p265-84

Myrdal, Alva (Reimer)
An "outsider's" view of the arms race. *In*
Ethics and nuclear strategy? p82-91

Myrdal, Gunnar
Race and class in a welfare state. *In* The
National purpose reconsidered p73-95

About individual works
An American dilemma
Grantham, D. W. Ralph J. Bunche and
the making of a documentary classic. *In*
Grantham, D. W. The regional imagination
p133-52

Myres, Sandra L.
The ranching frontier: Spanish institutional
backgrounds of the Plains cattle industry.
In Weber, D. J. ed. New Spain's far northern frontier 79-94

Myrrhine

About
Clairmont, C. W. The lekythos of Myrrhine. *In* Studies in classical art and archaeology p103-10

Mysore. See Karnataka, India

Mysteries and miracle-plays
See also Drama, Medieval

History and criticism
Nicoll, A. Religious drama and profane
during the Middle Ages. *In* Nicoll, A. World
drama p103-31

Mysteries and miracle plays, English

History and criticism
Brockman, B. A. Cain and Abel in the
Chester creation: narrative tradition and
dramatic potential. *In* Medievalia et humanistica no. 5 p169-82

Kahrl, S. J. The civic religious drama of
medieval England: a review of recent scholarship. *In* Renaissance drama [1973] p237-48

Weimann, R. The mystery cycles. *In* Weimann, R. Shakespeare and the popular tradition in the theater: studies in the social dimension of dramatic form and function p49-
97

Woolf, R. The influence of the mystery
plays upon the popular tragedies of the
1560's. *In* Renaissance drama [1973] p89-105

Mystery and detective stories. See Detective
and mystery stories

Mystery in literature
Grossvogel, D. I. Introduction. *In* Gross-
vogel, D. I. Mystery and its fictions: from
Oedipus to Agatha Christie p 1-21

Grossvogel, D. I. "The purloined letter":
the mystery of the text. *In* Grossvogel,
D. I. Mystery and its fictions: from Oedipus to Agatha Christie p93-107

The mystery of Picasso (Motion picture)
Truffaut, F. Henri-Georges Clouzot: Le
mystère Picasso. *In* Truffaut, F. The films
in my life p201-03

Mystery stories. See Detective and mystery
stories

Mystical theology. See Mysticism

Mysticism

Clarke, J. J. Mysticism and the paradox of survival. *In* Donnelly, J. P. ed. Language, metaphysics, and death p216-27

Dupré, L. K. The mystical experience of the self and its philosophical significance. *In* Psychiatry and the humanities v 1 p101-25

Huxley, A. L. Man and religion. *In* Huxley, A. L. The Human situation p198-215

LeShan, L. L. Individual realities: commonsense, science, and mysticism; excerpts from "Toward a general theory of the paranormal." *In* Wheatley, J. M. O. and Edge, H. L. eds. Philosophical dimensions of parapsychology p425-40

McNamara, W. Psychology and the Christian mystical tradition. *In* Tart, C. T. ed. Transpersonal psychologies p389-430

Prince, R. H. Cocoon work: an interpretation of the concern of contemporary youth with the mystical. *In* Zaretsky, I. I. and Leone, M. P. eds. Religious movements in contemporary America p255-71

History

Bolle, K. W. Structures of Renaissance mysticism. *In* The Darker vision of the Renaissance p119-45

History of doctrines

See Mysticism—History

Psychology

McNamara, W. Psychology and the Christian mystical tradition. *In* Tart, C. T. ed. Transpersonal psychologies p389-430

Islam

See Sufism

Judaism

Alter, R. Gershom Scholem: history and the abyss. *In* Alter, R. Defenses of the imagination p67-89

Arendt, H. Jewish history, revised. *In* Arendt, H. The Jew as pariah: Jewish identity and politics in the modern age p96-105

Lamm, N. The phase of dialogue and reconciliation. *In* Király, B. K. ed. Tolerance and movements of religious dissent in Eastern Europe p115-29

See also Hasidism

Middle Ages

Sunderland, E. R. The system of proportion of Filippo Brunelleschi. *In* Enggass, R. C. and Stokstad, M. eds. Hortus imaginum p65-72

Great Britain

Kuhn, A. J. Nature spiritualized: aspects of anti-Newtonianism. *In* ELH essays for Earl R. Wasserman p110-22

Mysticism and literature

Grant, P. Richard Crashaw and the Capucins: images and the force of belief. *In* Grant, P. Images and ideas in literature of the English Renaissance p89-128

Myth

Barfield, O. Dream, myth, and philosophical double vision. *In* Barfield, O. The rediscovery of meaning, and other essays p22-31

Barthes, R. Change the object itself. *In* Barthes, R. Image, music, text p165-69

Cantelli, G. Myth and language in Vico. *In* Giambattista Vico's science of humanity p47-63

Cassirer, E. Judaism and the modern political myths. *In* Cassirer, E. Symbol, myth, and culture p233-41

Cassirer, E. The technique of our modern political myths. *In* Cassirer, E. Symbol, myth, and culture p242-67

Hyman, S. E. Jessie Weston and the Forest of Broceliande. *In* Hyman, S. E. The critic's credentials p284-97

Lidz, T. The family, myth, and ethics. *In* Psychiatry and the humanities v 1 p173-90

Luedtke, L. S. Not so common ground: controversies in contemporary American studies. *In* Luedtke, L. S. ed. The study of American culture p323-67

Mazzeo, J. A. Myth and science in the theology of Rudolf Bultmann. *In* Mazzeo, J. A. Varieties of interpretation p129-53

Mazzeo, J. A. The Platonic debate over myth, truth, and virtue. *In* Mazzeo, J. A. Varieties of interpretation p71-94

See also Myth in the Bible

Myth in literature

Anderson, D. D. Anderson and myth. *In* Anderson, D. D. ed. Sherwood Anderson: dimensions of his literary art p118-41

Bennett, B. H. Williams and European drama: infernalists and forgers of modern myths. *In* Tennessee Williams: a tribute p429-59

Brown, C. S. Faulkner's universality. *In* The Maker and the myth: Faulkner and Yoknapatawpha, 1977 p146-69

Calvino, I. Myth in the narrative. *In* Federman, R. ed. Surfiction p75-81

Castile, P. Women and myth in Faulkner's first novel. *In* Tulane Studies in English, v23 p175-86

Cowley, M. Magic in Faulkner. *In* Faulkner, modernism, and film: Faulkner and Yoknapatawpha, 1978 p3-19

Gilbert, S. M. and Gubar, S. Milton's bogey: patriarchal poetry and women readers. *In* Gilbert, S. M. and Gubar, S. The madwoman in the attic p187-212

Greenway, J. L. The gateway to innocence: Ossian and the Nordic bard as myth. *In* Studies in eighteenth-century culture v4 p161-70

Morris, W. A. The pilgrimage of being. *In* Morris, W. A. Friday's footprint p 1-83

Ragussis, M. W. B. Yeats: "Her vision in the wood" as tragic art: a "hollow image of fulfilled desire." *In* Ragussis, M. The subterfuge of art p109-32

Richardson, R. D. Emerson. *In* Richardson, R. D. Myth and literature in the American renaissance p65-89

Richardson, R. D. Hawthorne. *In* Richardson, R. D. Myth and literature in the American renaissance p165-94

Richardson, R. D. Melville. *In* Richardson, R. D. Myth and literature in the American renaissance p195-233

Richardson, R. D. Parker and Alcott. *In* Richardson, R. D. Myth and literature in the American renaissance p34-64

Richardson, R. D. Thoreau. *In* Richardson, R. D. Myth and literature in the American renaissance p90-137

Richardson, R. D. Whitman. *In* Richardson, R. D. Myth and literature in the American renaissance p138-64

Stauffer, D. A. The modern myth of the modern myth. *In* Wimsatt, W. K. ed. Literary criticism: idea and act p66-82

Myth in literature—*Continued*

Wolfe, G. K. The known and the unknown: structure and image in science fiction. *In* Clareson, T. D. ed. Many futures, many worlds p94-116

Myth in the Bible

Frye, N. History and myth in the Bible. *In* Fletcher, A. J. S. ed. The literature of fact p 1-19

Richardson, R. D. Parker and Alcott. *In* Richardson, R. D. Myth and literature in the American renaissance p34-64

Myth in the Old Testament

Fiorenza, E. S. Wisdom mythology and the Christological hymns of the New Testament. *In* Aspects of wisdom in Judaism and early Christianity p17-41

Mythical places. See Geographical myths

Mythology

Coomaraswamy, A. K. Symplegades. *In* Coomaraswamy, A. K. Selected papers v 1 p521-44

Green, T. F. Stories and images of the future. *In* Bundy, R. F. ed. Images of the future: the twenty-first century and beyond p35-44

See also Art and mythology; Geographical myths; Myth; Myth in the Bible; Myth in the Old Testament; Religion, Primitive; Sacred marriage (Mythology); Symbolism; Totemism; *also:* Fire (in religion, folklore, etc.) and similar headings

Mythology, African

Koech, K. African mythology: a key to understanding African religion. *In* African religions: a symposium p117-39

Mythology, Assyro-Babylonian

Lambert, W. G. The historical development of the Mesopotamian pantheon: a study in sophisticated polytheism. *In* Unity and diversity p191-200

Mythology, Aztec. See Aztecs—Religion and mythology

Mythology, Classical

Reiche, H. A. T. The language of archaic astronomy: a clue to the Atlantis myth? *In* Brecher, K. and Feirtag, M. eds. Astronomy of the ancients p153-89

See also Gorgons; Mythology, Greek; and names of mythological persons and objects, e.g. Cupid

Mythology, Classical, in art

Vermeule, C. C. Interactions and reflections of painting, mosaic and sculpture: complex mythological scenes in Greek and Roman imperial numismatic art. *In* Studies in classical art and archaeology p275-82

Mythology, Egyptian

Lawal, B. Yoruba-Sango ram symbolism: from ancient Sahara or dynastic Egypt? *In* African images p225-51

Mythology, Greek

Fredericks, S. C. Plato's Atlantis: a mythologist looks at myth. *In* Ramage, E. S. ed. Atlantis, fact or fiction? p81-99

Pearson, L. I. C. Myth and archaeologia in Italy and Sicily—Timaeus and his predecessors. *In* Yale classical studies v24 p171-95

Mythology, Greek, in art

Harrison, E. B. Apollo's cloak. *In* Studies in classical art and archaeology p91-98

Moore, M. B. Poseidon in the Gigantomachy. *In* Studies in classical art and archaeology p23-27

Phillips, K. M. and Ashmead, A. H. Three goddesses and a falcon. *In* Studies in classical art and archaeology p45-52

Richardson, E. H. The story of Ariadne in Italy. *In* Studies in classical art and archaeology p189-95

Robertson, M. Two question-marks on the Parthenon. *In* Studies in classical art and archaeology p75-87

Mythology, Greek in literature

Siemens, W. L. Apollo's metamorphosis in Pantaleón y las visitadoras. *In* Rossman, C. R. and Friedman, A. W. eds. Mario Vargas Llosa p88-100

Willcock, M. M. Some aspects of the gods in the Iliad. *In* Wright, J. H. ed. Essays on the Iliad p58-69

Mythology, Haitian

Laroche, M. The myth of the zombi. *In* Exile and tradition p44-61

Mythology, Hindu

Coomaraswamy, A. K. On the Loathly Bride. *In* Coomaraswamy, A. K. Selected papers v 1 p353-70

Mythology, Hittite

Hoffner, H. A. Hittite mythological texts: a survey. *In* Unity and diversity p136-45

Mythology, Indian (American Indian). See Indians of North America—Religion and mythology

Mythology, Indo-European. See Soma

Mythology, Irish

Smith, R. J. Irish mythology. *In* Orel, H. ed. Irish history and culture p 1-24

Mythology, Maya. See Mayas—Religion and mythology

Mythology, Nahautl. See Nahuas—Religion and mythology

Mythology, Yoruba

Bascom, W. R. Oba's ear: a Yoruba myth in Cuba and Brazil. *In* Crowley, D. J. ed. African folklore in the New World p3-19

Elder, J. D. Morality in a Yoruba ritual in Trinidad. *In* Yoder, D. ed. American folklife p281-91

Lawal, B. Yoruba-Sango ram symbolism: from ancient Sahara or dynastic Egypt? *In* African images p225-51

Mythology in art. See Art and mythology

Mythology in literature

Adams, R. M. Three thematic interludes. *In* Adams, R. M. Afterjoyce p36-64

Alexander, L. High fantasy and heroic romance. *In* Horn Book Magazine. Crosscurrents of criticism p170-77

Allen, J. A. The other way to live: demigods in Eudora Welty's fiction. *In* Prenshaw, P. W. ed. Eudora Welty p26-55

Bertolini, J. A. Ecphrasis and dramaturgy: Leonardo's Leda in Rucellai's Oreste. *In* Renaissance drama [1976] p151-76

Bryant, J. A. The recovery of the confident narrator: A curtain of green to Losing battles. *In* Prenshaw, P. W. ed. Eudora Welty p68-82

Cowan, J. C. D. H. Lawrence's dualism: the Apollonian-Dionysian polarity and The Ladybird. *In* Forms of modern British fiction p73-99

Mythology in literature—*Continued*

David, A. How Marcia lost her skin: a note on Chaucer's mythology. *In* The Learned and the lewed p19-29

Demmin, J. and Curley, D. Golden apples and silver apples. *In* Prenshaw, P. W. ed. Eudora Welty p242-57

Emmitt, R. J. Love, death, and resurrection in The great Gatsby. *In* Aeolian harps p273-89

Fredericks, S. C. Revivals of ancient mythologies in current science fiction and fantasy. *In* Clareson, T. D. ed. Many futures, many worlds p50-65

Frye, N. Expanding eyes. *In* Frye, N. Spiritus mundi p99-122

Fuhrmann, M. Myth as a recurrent theme in Greek tragedy and twentieth-century drama. *In* Amacher, R. E. and Lange, V. eds. New perspectives in German literary criticism p295-319

Galinsky, G. K. Ovid's metamorphosis of myth. *In* Perspectives of Roman poetry p105-27

Johnson, B. H. Classical allusions in the poetry of Donne. *In* Roberts, J. R. ed. Essential articles for the study of John Donne's poetry p85-92

Nestrick, W. V. Spenser and the Renaissance mythology of love. *In* Literary monographs v6 p35-70

Ower, J. Erotic mythology in the poetry of Tennessee Williams. *In* Tennessee Williams: a tribute p609-23

Phillips, R. L. A structural approach to myth in the fiction of Eudora Welty. *In* Prenshaw, P. W. ed. Eudora Welty p56-67

Pitavy-Souques, D. Technique as myth: the structure of The golden apples. *In* Prenshaw, P. W. ed. Eudora Welty p258-68

Richardson, R. D. Emerson. *In* Richardson, R. D. Myth and literature in the American renaissance p65-89

Richardson, R. D. Hawthorne. *In* Richardson, R. D. Myth and literature in the American renaissance p195-233

Richardson, R. D. Melville. *In* Richardson, R. D. Myth and literature in the American renaissance p90-137

Richardson, R. D. Thoreau. *In* Richardson, son, R. D. Myth and literature in the American renaissance p165-94

Richardson, R. D. The two traditions. *In* Richardson, R. D. Myth and literature in the American renaissance p9-33

Richardson, R. D. Whitman. *In* Richardson, son, R. D. Myth and literature in the American renaissance p138-64

Rosador, K. T. von. Myth and Victorian melodrama. *In* English Association. Essays and studies, 1979 p97-114

Rose, P. W. The myth of Pindar's First Nemean: sportsmen, poetry, and paideia. *In* Harvard Studies in classical philology v78 p145-75

Shaffer, E. S. Hölderlin's 'Patmos' ode and 'Kubla Khan': mythological doubling. *In* Shaffer, E. S. 'Kubla Khan' and The fall of Jerusalem p145-90

Skaggs, M. M. Morgana's apples and pears. *In* Prenshaw, P. W. ed. Eudora Welty p220-41

Stauffer, D. A. The modern myth of the modern myth. *In* Wimsatt, W. K. ed. Literary criticism: idea and act p66-82

Steadman, J. M. The Faerie Queene: "Errour" and the Renaissance. *In* Steadman, J. M. Nature into myth p159-73

Steadman, J. M. "The merry wives of Windsor:" Falstaff as Actaeon. A dramatic emblem. *In* Steadman, J. M. Nature into myth p117-30

Thompson, J. J. Symbol, myth, and ritual in The glass menagerie, The rose tattoo, and Orpheus descending. *In* Tennessee Williams: a tribute p679-711

Turner, D. E. The mythic vision in Tennessee Williams' Camino Real. *In* Tennessee Williams: a tribute p237-51

Ziolkowski, T. Some features of religious figuralism in twentieth-century literature. *In* Miner, E. R. ed. Literary uses of typology p345-69

Myths. See Mythology

N

NATO. See North Atlantic Treaty Organization

NIRA. See National Industrial Recovery Act, 1933

NPT. See Treaty on the non-proliferation of nuclear weapons

NRA. See National Industrial Recovery Act, 1933

NSF. See United States. National Science Foundation

NUWM. See National Unemployed Workers' Movement

Na Nagara Prasert. See Prasert na Nagara

Nabokov, Vladimir Vladimirovich

On Khodasevich. *In* The Bitter air of exile p83-87

About

Adamovich, G. V. Vladimir Nabokov. *In* Erlich, V. ed. Twentieth-century Russian literary criticism p219-31

Adams, R. M. Vladimir Nabokov. *In* Adams, R. M. Afterjoyce p146-61

Alter, R. Defenses of the imagination. *In* Alter, R. Defenses of the imagination p 3-22

Appel, A. Nabokov's dark cinema: a diptych. *In* The Bitter air of exile p196-273

Carroll, W. Nabokov's signs and symbols. *In* A Book of things about Vladimir Nabokov p203-17

Couturier, M. Nabokov's performative writing. *In* Johnson, I. D. and Johnson, C. [eds.] Les américanistes p156-81

Donald, M. Fantasy. *In* Donald, M. The American novel in the twentieth century p108-40

Gass, W. H. Upright among staring fish *In* Gass, W. H. The world within the word p203-07

Johnson, D. B. Contrastive phonoaesthetics; or, Why Nabokov gave up translating poetry as poetry. *In* A Book of things about Vladimir Nabokov p28-41

Johnson, D. B. Synesthesia, polychromatism, and Nabokov. *In* A Book of things about Vladimir Nabokov p84-103

Rowe, W. W. The honesty of Nabokovian deception. *In* A Book of things about Vladimir Nabokov p171-81

Na-Déné languages. See Tinne languages

Nader, Laura, and Serber, David
Law and the distribution of power. *In* The Uses of controversy in sociology p273-91

Nader, Ralph
The responsibility of the professional. *In* Against pollution and hunger p19-24

Naerssen, Frits Herman van
Tribute to the god and tribute to the king. *In* Southeast Asian history and historiography p296-303

Naess, Arne. See Ness, Arne

Naess, Harald S.
Who was Hamsun's hero? *In* The Hero in Scandinavian literature p63-86

Naesselund, Gunnar R.
UNESCO and the press in the Third World. *In* Horton, P. C. ed. The Third World and press freedom p210-19

Nag Hammadi texts (The teachings of Silvanus)
Schoedel, W. R. Jewish wisdom and the formation of the Christian ascetic. *In* Aspects of wisdom in Judaism and early Christianity p169-99

Nagai, Kafū

About
Ueda, M. Nagai Kafū. *In* Ueda, M. Modern Japanese writers p26-53

About individual works
The river Sumida
Rimer, J. T. Nagai Kafū and Mori Ōgai: the past versus the present. *In* Rimer, J. T. Modern Japanese fiction and its traditions p138-61

Nagai, Michio, and Nishijima, Takeo
Postwar Japanese education and the United States. *In* Iriye, A. ed. Mutual images p169-87

Nagai, Yōnosuke
The roots of Cold war doctrine: the esoteric and the exoteric. *In* The Origins of the Cold war in Asia p15-42

Nagaoka, Hantarō

About
Koizumi, K. The emergence of Japan's first physicists: 1868-1900. *In* Historical studies in the physical sciences v6 p3-108

Nagara Prasert na. See Prasert na Nagara

Nagarjuna, Siddha

About
Hoffmann, Y. The possibility of knowledge: Kant and Nagarjuna. *In* Philosophy East/philosophy West p269-90

Nagel, Ernest
In defense of scientific knowledge. *In* Hook, S.; Kurtz, P. W. and Todorovich, M. eds. The philosophy of the curriculum p119-26

Nagel, Thomas
Linguistics and epistemology. *In* Harman, G. ed. On Noam Chomsky p219-28
Mortal questions
Contents
The Absurd
Also in Donnelly, J. P. Language, metaphysics and death p106-15
Brain bisection and the unity of consciousness

Death
Also in Donnelly, J. P. ed. Language, metaphysics and death p62-68
Equality
Ethics without biology
The fragmentation of value
Moral luck
Panpsychism
The policy of preference
Ruthlessness in public life
Also in Hampshire, S. ed. Public and private morality p75-91
Sexual perversion
Also in Baker, R. and Elliston, F. A. eds. Philosophy & sex p247-60
Subjective and objective
War and massacre
What is it like to be a bat?

Nägele, Rainer
The discourse of the other: Hölderlin's ode "Stimme des Volks" and the dialectic of the Enlightenment. *In* Glyph 5 p 1-33

Nagy, Gregory John
On the death of. Actaeon. *In* Harvard Studies in classical philology v77 p179-80
Phaethon, Sappho's Phaon, and the White Rock of Leukas. *In* Harvard Studies in classical philology v77 p137-77
Six studies of sacral vocabulary relating to the fireplace. *In* Harvard Studies in classical philology v78 p71-106

Nagy, Ivan Boszormenyi· See Boszormenyi-Nagy, Ivan

Nahemow, Nina, and Adams, Bert N.
Old age among the Baganda: continuity and change. *In* Gubrium, J. F. ed. Late life p147-66

Nahuas

Religion and mythology
De Gerez, T. A basket of fireflies: Quetzalcoatl and the Nahuatl poetry of Mexico. *In* Egoff, S. A. ed. One ocean touching p138-46

Nahuatl literature. See Aztec literature

Nahuatl mythology. See Nahuas—Religion and mythology

Nailor, Peter
The military bureaucracy: a case study of a civilian contribution. *In* Beaumont, R. A. and Edmonds, M. eds. War in the next decade p180-202

Naipaul, Vidiadhar Surajprasad

About
Blaise, C. The Commonwealth writer and his material. *In* Narasimhaiah, C. D. ed. Awakened conscience p118-26
Ramraj, V. J. Diminishing satire: a study of V. S. Naipaul and Mordecai Richler. *In* Narasimhaiah, C. D. ed. Awakened conscience p261-74

About individual works
A house for Mr Biswas
Nandan, S. The immigrant Indian experience in literature: Trinidad and Fiji. *In* Narasimhaiah, C. D. ed. Awakened conscience p346-59
Ormerod, D. 'Unaccommodated man': Naipaul's B. Wordsworth and Biswas. *In* Baugh, E. ed. Critics on Caribbean literature p87-92
Raghavacharyulu, D. V. K. Naipaul and Narayan: the sense of life. *In* Narasimhaiah, C. D. ed. Awakened conscience p216-25

Nancréde, Paul Joseph Guérard de

About

Stern, M. B. Brissot de Warville and the Franco-American press. *In* Virginia. University. Bibliographical Society. Studies in bibliography v29 p362-72

Nancy, Jean Luc

Larvatus pro deo. *In* Glyph 2 p14-36

Nanda, Ved P.

Racial discrimination and the law: recent legislation in Great Britain, Canada, and the United States. *In* Claude, R. P. ed. Comparative human rights p214-50

Nandan, Satendra

The immigrant Indian experience in literature: Trinidad and Fiji. *In* Narasimhaiah, C. D. ed. Awakened conscience p346-59

Nantes

Social conditions

Depauw, J. Illicit sexual activity and society in eighteenth-century Nantes. *In* Family and society p145-91

Naoumides, Mark

The v-recension of St. Cyril's Lexicon. *In* Illinois classical studies v4, 1979 p94-135

Naousa, Greece

Tombs

Lehmann, P. L. W. Lefkadia and the second style. *In* Studies in classical art and archaeology p225-29

Naoussa, Greece. See Naousa, Greece

Napea, Osip. See Nepea, Osip

Napier, Arthur Sampson

About

Scragg, D. G. Napier's 'Wulfstan' homily xxx: its sources, its relationship to the Vercelli Book and its style. *In* Anglo-Saxon England p197-211

Napier, John Russell

The talented primate. *In* Goodall, V. M. ed. The quest for man p79-103

The tree of evolution. *In* Goodall, V. M. ed. The quest for man p57-78

Naples

Description

Benjamin, W. Naples. *In* Benjamin, W. Reflections p163-73

Blunt, A. Naples as seen by French travellers, 1630-1780. *In* The Artist and the writer in France p 1-14

Napoleon, Continental system of. See Continental system of Napoleon

Napoleonic Wars. See France—History—Revolution, 1789-1799

Naqshbandi (Islamic order)

Bibliography

Algar, H. Bibliographical notes on the Naqshbandi tariqat. *In* Essays on Islamic philosophy and science p254-59

Naqshbandīyah. See Naqshbandi (Islamic order)

Nara, Japan

Buildings—Conservation and restoration

Itō, T., and Nishikawa, K. Japan: two ancient capitals and the menace to them. *In* United Nations Educational, Scientific and Cultural Organizations. The conservation of cities p107-24

City planning

Ito, T. and Nishikawa, K. Japan: two ancient capitals and the menace to them. *In* United Nations Educational, Scientific and Cultural Organization. The conservation of cities p107-24

Narasimhaiah, C. D.

Introduction. *In* Narasimhaiah, C. D. ed. Awakened conscience pxv-xxxi

Narayan, R. K.

About

Raghavacharyulu, D. V. K. Naipaul and Narayan: the sense of life. *In* Narasimhaiah, C. D. ed. Awakened conscience p216-25

Singh, R. S. "Without illusions and hysterics": R. K. Narayan. *In* Singh, R. S. Indian novel in English p55-72

Narboni, Jean. See Comolli, J. L. jt. auth.

Narcissism

Selzer, M. Narcissism and the quest for power. *In* [Truth and tragedy]: a tribute to Hans Morgenthau p130-41

Wolf, E. S. The disconnected self. *In* Roland, A. ed. Psychoanalysis, creativity, and literature p103-14

Narcissism in literature

Girard, R. Narcissism: The Freudian myth demythified by Proust. *In* Roland, A. ed. Psychoanalysis, creativity, and literature p293-311

Massey, I. Singles and doubles: Narcissism in Hoffmann's "The sandman." *In* Massey, I. The gaping pig p115-23

Narcissus (Mythological figure) in literature

Ragussis, M. Epilogue: the echo. *In* Ragussis, M. The subterfuge of art p230-33

Narcotic addicts

Jackson, B. Deviance as success: the double inversion of stigmatized roles. *In* Babcock, B. A. ed. The reversible world p258-73

McAuliffe, W. E. Beyond secondary deviance: negative labelling and its effects on the heroin addict. *In* Gove, W. R. ed. The labelling of deviance p205-42

Rehabilitation—United States

Eisenhart, T. S. Rehabilitation: one man's opinion. *In* Henderson, G. ed. Human relations in the military p177-86

Sugarman, B. Reluctant converts: social control, socialization and adaptation in therapeutic communities. *In* Wallis, R. ed. Sectarianism p141-61

Thornton, O. D. The Vietnam connection. *In* Henderson, G. ed. Human relations in the military p163-75

Narcotics. See Heroin

Naremore, James Otis

Consciousness and society in A portrait of the artist. *In* Staley, T. F. and Benstock, B. eds. Approaches to Joyce's Portrait p113-34

Narodnichestvo. See Populism in Russia

Narration (Rhetoric)

Barthes, R. Introduction to the structural analysis of narratives. *In* Barthes, R. Image, music, text p79-124

Caserio, R. L. The featuring of act as "the rescue": story in Dickens and George Eliot. *In* Caserio, R. L. Plot, story, and the novel p91-132

Caserio, R. L. Narrative reason: the sense of plot and historical experience. *In* Caserio, R. L. Plot, story, and the novel p27-56

Narration (Rhetoric)—*Continued*

Cowley, M. A defense of storytelling. *In* Cowley, M.—And I worked at the writer's trade p194-213

Doležel, L. A scheme of narrative time. *In* Matejka, L. and Titunik, I. R. eds. Semiotics of art p209-17

Hamlin, C. Strategies of reversal in literary narrative. *In* Valdés, M. J. and Miller, O. J. eds. Interpretation of narrative p61-77

Hardy, B. N. An approach through narrative. *In* Spilka, M. ed. Towards a poetics of fiction p31-40

Hardy, B. N. Good stories, good listeners. *In* Hardy, B. N. Tellers and listeners p131-62

Hardy, B. N. Narrative imagination. *In* Hardy, B. N. Tellers and listeners p3-18

Iser, W. Narrative strategies as a means of communication. *In* Valdés, M. J. and Miller, O. J. eds. Interpretation of narrative p100-17

Kao, Yu-kung. Lyric vision in Chinese narrative tradition: a reading of Hung-lou meng and Ju-lin wai-shih. *In* Chinese narrative p227-43

Miller, J. H. Ariadne's thread: repetition and the narrative line. *In* Valdés, M. J. and Miller, O. J. eds. Interpretation of narrative p148-66

Plaks, A. H. Towards a critical theory of Chinese narrative. *In* Chinese narrative p309-52

Riffaterre, M. The reader's perception of narrative: Balzac's Paix du ménage. *In* Valdés, M. J. and Miller, O. J. eds. Interpretation of narrative p28-37

Segre, C. Analysis of the tale, narrative logic, and time. *In* Segre, C. Structures and time p 1-56

Stierle, K. H. Story as exemplum—exemplum as story: on the pragmatics and poetics of narrative texts. *In* Amacher, R. E. and Lange, V. eds. New perspectives in German literary criticism p389-417

Vance, E. Pas de trois: narrative, hermeneutics, and structure in medieval poetics. *In* Valdés, M. J. and Miller, O. J. eds. Interpretation of narrative p118-34

Wang, J. C. Early Chinese narrative: the Tso-chuan as example. *In* Chinese narrative p3-20

Wong, Kam-ming. Point of view, norms, and structure: Hung-lou meng and lyrical fiction. *In* Chinese narrative p203-26

Narrative painting

Great Britain—History

Waldfogel, M. Narrative painting. *In* Altholz, J. L. ed. The mind and art of Victorian England p159-74

Narrative poetry

See also Epic poetry

History and criticism

Coxe, L. O. The narrative poem: novel of the future? *In* Coxe, L. O. Enabling acts p70-87

Narrative writing. See Narration (Rhetoric)

Narveson, Jan

Morality and starvation. *In* Aiken, W. and La Follette, H. eds. World hunger and moral obligation p49-65

Nash, Paul

Some economic questions. *In* Roots of open education in America p126-30

Nash, Roderick

Do rocks have rights? Thoughts on environmental ethics. *In* Small comforts for hard times p120-34

Machines and Americans. *In* Luedtke, L. S. ed. The study of American culture p99-119

Nash, Thomas

About

Berryman, J. Thomas Nashe and The unfortunate traveller. *In* Berryman, J. The freedom of the poet p9-28

About individual works

Adieu, farewell, earth's bliss

Cunningham, J. V. Logic and lyric: Marvell, Dunbar, and Nashe. *In* Cunningham, J. V. The collected essays of J. V. Cunningham p162-79

The unfortunate traveller; or, The life of Jack Wilson

Berryman, J. Thomas Nashe and The unfortunate traveller. *In* Berryman, J. The freedom of the poet p9-28

Nashe, Thomas. See Nash, Thomas

Nasīr al-Dīn, Muhammad ibn Muhammad, al-Tūsī. See al-Tūsī, Nasīr al-Dīn Muhammad ibn Muhammad

Naso, Julius. See Julius Naso

Nasr, Seyyed Hossein

The significance of Persian philosophical works in the tradition of Islamic philosophy. *In* Essays on Islamic philosophy and science p67-75

Nassau Co., N.Y.

Politics and government

Caso, R. G. Managing the unmanageable. *In* Benton, L. R. ed. Management for the future p47-62

Nassef, Abdel-Fattah

Problems of maintaining employment in developing countries in the face of rapid population growth. *In* Economic factors in population growth p394-410

Nasser, Gamal Abdel, President United Arab Republic

About

Safran, N. Egypt's search for ideology: the Nasser era. *In* Kilson, M. ed. New states in the modern world p37-56

Nasser, Gamal Abdul. See Nasser, Gamal Abdel, President United Arab Republic

Natanson, Maurice Alexander

The arts of indirection. *In* Burks, D. M. ed. Rhetoric, philosophy, and literature: an exploration p35-47

Natchez, Miss.

Description

Welty, E. Some notes on river country. *In* Welty, E. The eye of the story p286-99

Natchez Trace

Welty, E. Some notes on river country. *In* Welty, E. The eye of the story p286-99

Natchez Trace in literature

Welty, E. Fairy tale of the Natchez Trace. *In* Welty, E. The eye of the story p300-14

Nath, Kamla

Education and employment among Kuwaiti women. *In* Beck, L. and Keddie, N. R. eds. Women in the Muslim world p172-88

Nathan, George John

The existence and nature of God in Hume's theism. *In* Livingston, D. W. and King, J. T. eds. Hume p126-49

Nathan, Leonard Edward

Gascoigne's "Lullabie" and structures in the Tudor lyric. *In* Sloan, T. O. and Waddington, R. S. eds. The rhetoric of Renaissance poetry p58-72

Nathanson, Iric. See Fraser, D. M. jt. auth.

National Academy of Sciences, Washington, D. C.

Dupree, A. H. The National Academy of Sciences and the American definition of science. *In* Oleson, A. and Voss, J. eds. The organization of knowledge in modern America, 1860-1920 p342-63

National characteristics

Altenbernd, L. A. The idea of national character: inspiration or fallacy? *In* Kagle, S. E. ed. America: exploration and travel p9-17

De Vos, G. and Romanucci-Ross, L. Ethnicity: vessel of meaning and emblem of contrast. *In* Ethnic identity p363-90

Dubos, R. J. The diversity of human life. *In* Dubos, R. J. Beast or angel? p171-80

National characteristics, American

Arnold, M. Civilisation in the United States. *In* Arnold, M. The last word p350-69

Biallas, L. J. America: the myth of the hunter. *In* America in theological perspective p206-29

Brogan, Sir D. W. The character of American life; excerpt from "America in the modern world." *In* Burton, D. H. ed. American history—British historians p3-23

Browning, D. S. Erikson and the search for a normative image of man. *In* Homans, P. ed. Childhood and selfhood p264-92

Cropsey, J. The United States as regime and the sources of the American way of life. *In* The Moral foundations of the American Republic p86-101

DeLeon, D. Space and community. *In* DeLeon, D. The American as anarchist p37-44

Diamond, M. Ethics and politics: the American way. *In* The Moral foundations of the American Republic p39-72

Featherstone, J. John Dewey and David Riesman: from the lost individual to the lonely crowd. *In* On the making of Americans p3-39

Fortin, R. A. Life, liberty, and the pursuit of happiness. *In* Alderson, W. T. ed. American issues p129-44

Glazer, N. Individualism and equality in the United States. *In* On the making of Americans p127-42

Jencks, C. S. The social basis of unselfishness. *In* On the making of Americans p63-86

Kazin, A. The drama of good and evil in American writing. *In* An Almost chosen people p51-66

Konvitz, M. R. Introduction: the American-Hebraic idea. *In* Konvitz, M. R. Judaism and the American idea p15-32

Lowenthal, D. The place of the past in the American landscape. *In* Geographies of the mind p89-117

MacLeish, A. Master or man. *In* MacLeish, A. Riders on the earth p27-39

Marty, M. E. The American tradition and the American tomorrow. *In* Tomorrow's American p133-55

Marx, L. The American Revolution and the American landscape. *In* America's continuing revolution p247-69

Mead, M. Ethnicity and anthropology in America. *In* Ethnic identity p173-97

Meyersohn, R. B. Abundance reconsidered. *In* On the making of Americans p87-104

Novak, M. The Nation with the soul of a church; excerpt from "Choosing our king: powerful symbols in Presidential politics." *In* A Public philosophy reader p92-96

Rescher, N. The environmental crisis and the quality of life. *In* Philosophy & environmental crisis p90-104

Santayana, G. Materialism and idealism; excerpt from "Character and opinion in the United States." *In* Crunden, R. M. ed. The superfluous men p48-54

Sarotte, G. M. The circumstances of the homosexual as reflected in the novel and theater: Between the American woman and the American virile ideal. *In* Sarotte, G. M. Like a brother, like a lover p185-92

Saum, L. O. Death in the popular mind of pre-Civil War America. *In* Death in America p30-48

Sennett, R. What Tocqueville feared. *In* On the making of Americans p105-25

Spencer, B. T. Gertrude Stein: non-expatriate. *In* Literature and ideas in America p204-27

Trilling, L. Two notes on David Riesman. *In* Trilling, L. A gathering of fugitives p91-107

Veysey, L. R. Growing up in America. *In* Alderson, W. T. ed. American issues p113-28

Warren, R. P. The use of the past. *In* A Time to hear and answer: essays for the Bicentennial season p 1-35

Welter, R. On studying the national mind. *In* Higham, J. and Conkin, P. K. eds. New directions in American intellectual history p64-82

Wilder, T. N. The American loneliness. *In* Wilder, T. N. American characteristics, and other essays p34-47

Wilder, T. N. Toward an American language. *In* Wilder, T. N. American characteristics, and other essays p3-33

Wood, G. S. The democratization of mind in the American Revolution. *In* The Moral foundations of the American Republic p102-28

National characteristics, Canadian

McLuhan, H. M. Canada: the borderline case. *In* Staines, D. ed. The Canadian imagination p226-48

National characteristics, Chinese

Hsu, F. L. K. Passage to understanding. *In* Spindler, G. D. ed. The making of psychological anthropology p142-73

Rin, H. The synthesizing mind in Chinese ethnocultural adjustment. *In* Ethnic identity p137-55

Schell, O. Private life in a public culture. *In* Terrill, R ed. The China difference p23-35

Wang, Gungwu. The Chinese. *In* Wilson, R. G. ed. Mao Tse-tung in the scales of history p272-99

National characteristics, German

Mitscherlich, A. and Mitscherlich, M. The inability to mourn. *In* Explorations in psychohistory p257-70

National characteristics, Indic
McLeod, A. L. The creation of national images in Indian and Pakistani speeches to the United States Congress. *In* Narasimhaiah, C. D. ed. Awakened conscience p378-88

Walsh, W. The Indian sensibility in English. *In* Narasimhaiah, C. D. ed. Awakened conscience p63-72

National characteristics, Japanese
DeVos, G. A. The Japanese adapt to change. *In* Spindler, G. D. ed. The making of psychological anthropology p219-57

Wagatsuma, H. Problems of cultural identity in modern Japan. *In* Ethnic identity p307-34

See also Bushido

National characteristics, Mexican

Public opinion

Weber, D. J. "Scare more than apes." Historical roots of Anglo-American stereotypes of Mexicans. *In* Weber, D. J. ed. New Spain's far northern frontier p293-307

National characteristics, Pakistani
McLeod, A. L. The creation of national images in Indian and Pakistani speeches to the United States Congress. *In* Narasimhaiah, C. D. ed. Awakened conscience p378-88

National characteristics, Spanish
Castro, A. The meaning of Spanish civilization. *In* Américo Castro and the meaning of Spanish civilization p23-40

National characteristics in literature
Amirthanayagam, G. Literature as culture. *In* Narasimhaiah, C. D. ed. Awakened conscience p433-40

National consciousness. See Nationalism

National debts. See Debts, Public

National domain. See Public domain

National Endowment for the Arts
Hanks, N. Design for America's third century. *In* The Uneasy coalition: design in corporate America p91-105

National Essence Journal. See Kuo-ts'ui hsüeh-pao

National Guard (U.S.) See United States. National Guard

The **national health** (criticism) Nichols, P. *In* Kauffmann, S. Persons of the drama p242-44

National Health Service, Great Britain. See Great Britain. National Health Service

National holidays. See Holidays

National images. See National characteristics

National Industrial Recovery Act, 1933
Corwin, E. S. Some probable repercussions of "Nira" on our constitutional system. *In* Corwin, E. S. Presidential power and the Constitution p55-63

National Institute of Arts and Letters. See American Academy of Arts and Letters

National Institute of Mental Health. See United States. National Institute of Mental Health

National League of Cities
Murphy, T. P. and Zarnowiecki, J. The urban observatory: a university—city research venture. *In* Murphy, T. P. ed. Universities in the urban crisis p15-47

National League of Cities v. Usery. *In* The Supreme Court review, 1976 p161-82

National Liberation Front (Greece)
LaFeber, W. The Truman doctrine. *In* Encyclopedia of American foreign policy p980-85

National Mutual Life Assurance Society
Davenport, N. E. H. Keynes in the City. *In* Keynes, M. ed. Essays on John Maynard Keynes p224-29

National planning. See Economic policy

National psychology. See Ethnopsychology; National characteristics

National Republican Party. See Whig Party

National resources. See Mines and mineral resources

National Science Foundation. See United States. National Science Foundation

National security
Christensen, C. J. Food and national security. *In* Knorr, K. E. and Trager, F. N. eds. Economic issues and national security p289-320

Christensen, C. J. Structural power and national security. *In* Knorr, K. E. and Trager, F. N. eds. Economic issues and national security p127-59

Gilpin, R. G. Economic interdependence and national security in historical perspective.. *In* Knorr, K. E. and Trager, F. N. eds. Economic issues and national security p19-66

Kelly, J. S. International monetary systems and national security. *In* Knorr, K. E. and Trager, F. N. eds. Economic issues and national security p231-58

Knorr, K. E. Economic interdependence and national security. *In* Knorr, K. E. and Trager, F. N. eds. Economic issues and national security p 1-18

Knorr, K. E. Military strength: economic and non-economic bases. *In* Knorr, K. E. and Trager, F. N. eds. Economic issues and national security p183-99

Meltzer, R. I. Contemporary security dimensions of international trade relations. *In* Knorr, K. E. and Trager, F. N. eds. Economic issues and national security p200-30

Murdock, C. A. Economic factors as objects of security: economics, security and vulnerability. *In* Knorr, K. E. and Trager, F. N. eds. Economic issues and national security p67-98

See also International relations; Military policy; also subdivision National security under names of countries, e.g. United States —National security

National self-determination. See Self-determination, National

National socialism
Arendt, H. Organized guilt and universal responsibility. *In* Arendt, H. The Jew as pariah: Jewish identity and politics in the modern age p225-36

Bettelheim, B. Remarks on the psychological appeal of totalitarianism. *In* Bettelheim, B. Surviving, and other essays p317-32

Bracher, K. D. The role of Hitler: perspectives of interpretation. *In* Laqueur, W. Z. ed. Fascism: a reader's guide p211-25

Cassirer, E. Judaism and the modern political myths. *In* Cassirer, E. Symbol. myth, and culture p233-41

Nationalism—*Continued*

Syria

Khalidi, R. Arab nationalism in Syria: the formative years, 1908-1914. *In* Nationalism in a non-national state p207-37

Ukraine

Bilinsky, Y. The incorporation of Western Ukraine and its impact on politics and society in Soviet Ukraine. *In* Szporluk, R. ed. The influence of East Europe and the Soviet West on the USSR p180-228

United States

Kaplan, L. S. Nationalism. *In* Encyclopedia of American foreign policy p610-22

Meyer, D. H. The American achievement. *In* Meyer, D. H. The democratic Enlightenment p210-15

Nationalism and religion

Robbins, T. and others. The last civil religion: Reverend Moon and the Unification Church. *In* Horowitz, I. L. ed. Science, sin, and scholarship p46-73

See also Jews—Election, Doctrine of; Religion and state

Nationalism and socialism

McNeill, T. State and nationality under communism. *In* Hayward, J. E. S. and Berki, R. N. eds. State and society in contemporary Europe p118-40

Shafarevich, I. R. Separation or reconciliation? The nationalities question in the USSR. *In* From under the rubble p88-104

Nationalism in literature

Innes, C. L. Through the looking glass: African and Irish nationalist writing. *In* African literature no. 9: Africa, America and the Caribbean p10-24

Lamont, R. C. Solzhenitsyn's nationalism. *In* Dunlop, J. B.; Haugh, R. and Klimoff, A. eds. Aleksandr Solzhenitsyn: critical essays and documentary materials 2d ed. p94-116

Nationalism in music. See Music and race

Nationalization of alien property. See Eminent domain (International law)

Nationalities, Principle of. See Self-determination, National

Nationalsozialistische Deutsche Arbeiter-Partei

Lepsius, M. R. From fragmented party democracy to government by emergency decree and National Socialist takeover: Germany. *In* The Breakdown of democratic regimes pt2 p34-79

Nations, Law of. See International law

Nations, Small. See States, Small

Native American Party. See American Party

Native races. See Ethnology; Race relations

Native son (Motion picture)

Brunette, P. Two Wrights, one wrong. *In* Peary, G. and Shatzkin, R. eds. The modern American novel and the movies p131-42

Nativism

Bloomfield, M. H. Riot control in Philadelphia. *In* Bloomfield, M. H. American lawyers in a changing society, 1776-1876 p191-234

Smith, G. S. Nativism. *In* Encyclopedia of American foreign policy p651-67

See also American Party

Nativistic movements

Bond, G. Minor prophets and Yombe cultural dynamics. *In* Colonialism and change p145-62

See also Ghost dance

Natsume, Kinnosuke. See Natsume, Sōseki

Natsume, Sōseki

About

Ueda, M. Natsume Sōseki. *In* Ueda, M. Modern Japanese writers p 1-25

Yamanouchi, H. The agonies of individualism: Natsume Soseki. *In* Yamanouchi, H. The search for authenticity in modern Japanese literature p40-81

About individual works

Kusamakura

Rimer, J. T. Natsume Soseki: the past as style. *In* Rimer, J. T. Modern Japanese fiction and its traditions p38-61

Nattiez, Jean-Jacques

The contribution of musical semiotics to the semiotic discussion in general. *In* Sebeok, T. A. ed. A perfusion of signs p121-42

Natural history

Wilson, D. S. The nature reporter in the presence of nature and culture. *In* Wilson, D. S. In the presence of nature p 1-12

Early works to 1735

See Natural history—Pre-Linnean works

Pre-Linnean works

Stannard, J. W. Natural history. *In* Lindberg, D. C. ed. Science in the Middle Ages p429-60

United States

Wilson, D. S. Epilogue. *In* Wilson, D. S. In the presence of nature p187-95

Natural history literature

United States

Wilson, D. S. The nature reporter in colonial American culture. *In* Wilson, D. S. In the presence of nature p13-45

Natural law

Arnold, C. Analyses of right. *In* Human rights p74-86

Corwin, E. S. The natural law and constitutional law. *In* Corwin, E. S. Presidential power and the Constitution p 1-22

Funkenstein, A. Natural science and social theory: Hobbes, Spinoza, and Vico. *In* Giambattista Vico's science of humanity p187-212

Kauper, P. G. The higher law and the rights of man in a revolutionary society. *In* America's continuing revolution p45-69

Kemp, J. Ethical naturalism. *In* New studies in ethics v 1 p173-228

Kleinig, J. Human rights, legal rights and social change. *In* Human rights p36-47

Midgley, E. B. F. Natural law and the renewal of the philosophy of international relations. *In* The Year book of world affairs, 1975 p121-36

Minogue, K. R. Natural rights, ideology and the game of life. *In* Human rights p 13-35

O'Connor, D. J. Aquinas and natural law. *In* New studies in ethics v 1 p79-172

O'Leary, B. Global famine and the sense of justice. *In* The Personal universe p91-98

Osborn, E. F. Four problems. *In* Osborn, E. F. Ethical patterns in early Christian thought p183-213

Natural law—*Continued*

Sidorsky, D. Contemporary reinterpretations of the concept of human rights. *In* Sidorsky, D. ed. Essays on human rights p88-109

Suganami, H. Why ought treaties to be kept? *In* The Year book of world affairs, 1979 p243-56

Wasserstrom, R. A. The obligation to obey the law. *In* Summers, R. S. ed. Essays in legal philosophy p274-304

Wilhelmsen, F. D. The limits of natural law. *In* Wilhelmsen, F. D. Christianity and political philosophy p10-24

Wilhelmsen, F. D. The natural law tradition and the American political experience. *In* Wilhelmsen, F. D. Christianity and political philosophy p174-92

See also Ethics; International law; Jurisprudence; Law—Philosophy; Liberty; Political ethics

History

Ornstein, R. Donne, Montaigne, and natural law. *In* Roberts, J. R. ed. Essential articles for the study of John Donne's poetry p129-41

Natural philosophy. See Physics

Natural resources. See Conservation of natural resources; Marine resources; Power resources

Natural rights. See Natural law

Natural science. See Natural history; Physics; Science

Natural selection

Campbell, D. T. Unjustified variation and selective retention in scientific discovery. *In* Ayala, F. J. and Dobzhansky, T. G. eds. Studies in the philosophy of biology p139-61

Dobzhansky, T. G. and Montagu, A. Natural selection and the mental capacities of mankind. *In* Montagu, A. ed. Race and IQ p104-13

Hamilton, W. D. Innate social aptitudes of man: an approach from evolutionary genetics. *In* Biosocial anthropology p133-55

Spuhler, J. N. The maximum opportunity for natural selection in some human populations. *In* Zubrow, E. B. W. ed. Demographic anthropology p185-226

See also Evolution; Heredity

Natural theology

Kuhn, A. J. Nature spiritualized: aspects of anti-Newtonianism. *In* ELH essays for Earl R. Wasserman p110-22

See also Philosophy of nature; Religion and science; Teleology

History of doctrines

Nelson, B. N. The quest for certitude and the books of Scripture, nature, and conscience. *In* The Nature of scientific discovery p355-72

Natural theology in literature

Hough, G. G. The natural theology of In memoriam. *In* Hough, G. G. Selected essays p110-25

Naturalism

Kurtz, P. W. Naturalism in American philosophy. *In* Philosophy and the civilizing arts p178-212

See also Mechanism (Philosophy)

Naturalism in art. See Idealism in art; Realism in art; Romanticism in art

Naturalism in literature

Cheuse, A. Mario Vargas Llosa and Conversation in the cathedral: the question of naturalism. *In* Rossman, C. R. and Friedman, A. W. eds. Mario Vargas Llosa p52-58

Grimm, R. Naturalism and epic drama. *In* Mews, S. and Knust, H. eds. Essays on Brecht p3-27

Kauffmann, S. Notes on naturalism: truth is stranger as fiction. *In* Kauffmann, S. Persons of the drama p329-35

Williams, R. Social environment and theatrical environment: the case of English naturalism. *In* English drama: forms and development p203-23

See also Idealism in literature; Realism in literature; Romanticism

Naturalistic ethics. See Ethics, Evolutionary

Naturalists

Mandel'shtam, O. E. Around the naturalists. *In* Mandel'shtam, O. E. Selected essays p196-200

Wilson, D. S. The nature reporter in the presence of nature and culture. *In* Wilson, D. S. In the presence of nature p 1-12

United States

Wilson, D. S. The nature reporter in colonial American culture. *In* Wilson, D. S. In the presence of nature p13-45

Naturalization

Florence

Kirshner, J. "Ars imitatur naturam": a consilium of Baldus on naturalization in Florence. *In* Viator: medieval and Renaissance studies v5 p289-331

Nature

Wicker, B. Metaphor and 'nature.' *In* Wicker, B. The story-shaped world p50-70

See also Man—Influence on nature

Nurture

See Nature and nurture

Philosophy

See Philosophy of nature

Nature (Aesthetics)

Huxley, A. L. More nature in art. *In* Huxley, A. L. The Human situation p28-41

Wilbur, R. Regarding places. *In* Wilbur, R. Responses p152-60

Nature (in religion, folklore, etc.) See Geographical myths

Nature, Effect of man on. See Man—Influence on nature

Nature, Law of. See Natural law

Nature, Philosophy of. See Philosophy of nature

Nature, Uniformity of. See Uniformity of nature

Nature and nurture

Bronfenbrenner, U. Nature with nurture: a reinterpretation of the evidence. *In* Montagu, A. ed. Race and IQ p114-44

Cowan, R. S. Nature and nurture: the interplay of biology and politics in the work of Francis Galton. *In* Studies in history of biology v 1 p133-208

Dubos, R. J. Biological Freudianism. *In* Dubos, R. J. Beast or angel? p30-32

Harwood, J. Heredity, environment, and the legitimation of social policy. *In* Barnes, B. and Shapin, S. eds. Natural order p231-51

Nature and nurture—*Continued*

Klineberg, O. Race and psychology. *In* United Nations Educational, Scientific and Cultural Organization. Race, science and society p173-207

Tizard, B. The environment and intellectual functions. *In* Racial variation in man p109-20

Nature conservation. See Landscape protection

Nature in art. See Nature (Aesthetics)

Nature in literature

Alcorn, J. Butler: the new spirit. *In* Alcorn, J. The nature novel from Hardy to Lawrence p25-41

Alcorn, J. Epilogue: Is Great Pan dead? *In* Alcorn, J. The nature novel from Hardy to Lawrence p113-23

Alcorn, J. Hardy: a better world. *In* Alcorn, J. The nature novel from Hardy to Lawrence p 1-24

Alcorn, J. Hardy and Lawrence. *In* Alcorn, J. The nature novel from Hardy to Lawrence p78-89

Alcorn, J. Lawrence: a version of pastoral. *In* Alcorn, J. The nature novel from Hardy to Lawrence p90-106

Barbeau, A. T. The wild and the garden: a double focus on reality in Pope's An essay on man. *In* Tennessee Studies in literature v22 p73-84

Blythe, R. The dangerous idyll: sweet Auburn to Akenfield. *In* Royal Society of Literature of the United Kingdom, London. Essays by divers hands v38 p15-32

Booth, M. R. Irish landscape in the Victorian theatre. *In* Place, personality and the Irish writer p159-72

Drabble, M. Hardy and the natural world. *In* Drabble, M. ed. The genius of Thomas Hardy p162-69

Fabricant, C. Binding and dressing nature's loose tresses: the ideology of Augustan landscape design. *In* Studies in eighteenth-century culture v8 p109-35

Gill, J. E. Discovery and alienation, nature and reason in Gulliver's Travels, Parts I-III. *In* Tennessee Studies in literature v22 p85-104

Jeffares, A. N. Place, space and personality and the Irish writer. *In* Place, personality and the Irish writer p11-40

Lyons, J. O. The traveler at home. *In* Lyons, J. O. The invention of the self p156-75

Manlove, C. N. Cowper. *In* Manlove, C. N. Literature and reality, 1600-1800 p193-208

Manlove, C. N. Thomson: The seasons. *In* Manlove, C. N. Literature and reality, 1600-1800 p125-35

Miller, J. H. Nature and the linguistic moment. *In* Knoepflmacher, U. C. and Tennyson, G. B. eds. Nature and the Victorian imagination p440-51

Oram, W. A. Nature, poetry, and Milton's genii. *In* Patrick, J. M. and Sundell, R. H. eds. Milton and the art of sacred song p47-64

Pilkington, J. Nature's legacy to William Faulkner. *In* The South and Faulkner's Yoknapatawpha p104-27

Prickett, S. Wordsworth and the language of nature. *In* Prickett, S. Romanticism and religion p70-90

Seelye, J. Womb of nature: Thomas Morton and the call of the wild. *In* Seelye, J. Prophetic waters p159-85

Tichi, C. A kingdom unto the world. *In* Tichi, C. New World, new earth p 1-36

Ware, M. The telescope reversed: Ann Radcliffe and natural scenery. *In* A Provision of human nature p169-89

See also Mountains in literature

Nature in poetry. See Nature in literature

Nature study. See Animals, Habits and behavior of

Nature versus nurture. See Nature and nurture

Naumberg Margaret. See Naumburg, Margaret

Naumburg, Margaret

Spontaneous art in education and psychotherapy. *In* Ulman, E. and Dachinger, P. eds. Art therapy p221-39

Nautical surveying. See Hydrographic surveying

Navaho Indians

Sandner, D. F. Navaho Indian medicine and medicine men. *In* Sobel, D. S. ed. Ways of health p117-46

Toelken, J. B. Seeing with a native eye: how many sheep will it hold? *In* Seeing with a native eye p9-24

Education (Higher)

Ackley, R. The Navajo college-level-literacy program: a holistic response to language development for the "outsider." *In* Minority language and literature p99-106

Legends

Toelken, J. B. The "pretty languages" of Yellowman: genre, mode, and texture in Navaho coyote narratives. *In* Folklore genres p145-70

Navaho language. See Athapascan languages

Navajo Community College

Ackley, R. The Navajo college-level-literacy program: a holistic response to language development for the "outsider." *In* Minority language and literature p99-106

Navajo Indians. See Navaho Indians

Navajo language. See Navaho language

Naval history

Kreutz, B. M. Ships, shipping and the implications of change in the early medieval Mediterranean. *In* Viator: medieval and Renaissance studies v7 p79-109

Lewis, A. R. Northern European sea power and the Straits of Gibraltar, 1031-1350 A.D. *In* Order and innovation in the Middle Ages p139-64

See also Privateering

Naval law. See Maritime law

Naval ordnance. See Ordnance, Naval

Naval warfare. See War, Maritime (International law)

Navarro, Luis García. See García Navarro, Luis

Navigation

See also Hydrographic surveying

History

Lamb, U. S. Cosmographers of Seville: nautical science and social experience. *In* First images of America p675-86

Rogers, F. M. Celestial navigation: from local systems to a global conception. *In* First images of America p687-704

Navy. See Russia. Navy

Nayak, G. C.
Survival, reincarnation, and the problem of personal identity. *In* Wheatley, J. M. O. and Edge, H. L. eds. Philosophical dimensions of parapsychology p295-307

Nazareth, Peter
Time in the Third World: a fictional exploration. *In* Narasimhaiah, C. D. ed. Awakened conscience p195-205

About individual works
In a brown mantle
Amur, G. S. Peter Nazareth's 'In a brown mantle': novel as revolutionary art. *In* Narasimhaiah, C. D. ed. Awakened conscience p111-17

Nazi architecture. See National socialism and architecture

Nazi-Soviet pact, 1939. See Russo-German treaty, 1939

Nazism. See National socialism

Nazzaro, Pellegrino
Fascist and anti-Fascist reaction in the United States to the Matteotti murder. *In* Studies in Italian American social history p50-65

Ndembu (African tribe)
Turner, V. W. Lunda medicine and the treatment of disease. *In* The Occasional papers of the Rhodes-Livingstone Museum p649-719

Psychology
Turner, V. W. Encounter with Freud: the making of a comparative symbologist. *In* Spindler, G. D. ed. The making of psychological anthropology p558-83

Rites and ceremonies
Turner, V. W. Encounter with Freud: the making of a comparative symbologist. *In* Spindler, G. D. ed. The making of psychological anthropology p558-83
See also Chihamba

Ndonga (African tribe) See Ambo (African tribe)

Neal, David S.
Floor mosaics. *In* Strong, D. E. and Brown, D. eds. Roman crafts p241-52

Neal, Larry
The Black contribution to American letters: Part II, The writer as activist—1960 and after. *In* The Black American reference book p767-90

Neal, Marie Augusta
Civil religion, theology, and politics in America. *In* America in theological perspective p99-122
Women in religious symbolism and organization. *In* Johnson, H. M. ed. Religious change and continuity p218-50

Neale, Robert Edward
Initiatory grief. *In* Anticipatory grief p331-42

Neale, Ronald Stanley
'The bourgeoisie, historically, has played a most revolutionary part.' *In* Kamenka, E. and Neale, R. S. eds. Feudalism, capitalism and beyond p84-102

Neanderthal race
Stewart, T. D. Recent developments in understanding the relationship between the Neanderthals and modern man. *In* Grafton Elliot Smith p67-82

Near East
Wickens, G. M. Introduction to the Middle East. *In* Savory, R. M. ed. Introduction to Islamic civilisation p 1-13
See also Arab countries

Armed Forces
AlRoy, G. C. Military capabilities in the Middle East. *In* The New world balance and peace in the Middle East: reality or mirage? p50-60
Hurewitz, J. W. Soldiers and social change in plural societies: the contemporary Middle East. *In* War, technology and society in the Middle East p400-11
Janowitz, M. Some observations on the comparative analysis of Middle Eastern military institutions. *In* War, technology and society in the Middle East p412-40

Civilization
Wickens, G. M. Khātimah. *In* Savory, R. M. ed. Introduction to Islamic civilisation p189-94
Wickens, G. M. What the West borrowed from the Middle East. *In* Savory, R. M. ed. Introduction to Islamic civilisation p120-25

Defenses
Mushkat, M. The diffusion of economic and military power and its impact on the Middle East conflict. *In* Arms control and technological innovation p247-54

Foreign economic relations—
Russia
Middleton, D. Russian presence and economic interests in the Mediterranean and the Indian Ocean. *In* The New world balance and peace in the Middle East: reality or mirage? p43-49

Foreign economic relations—
United States
Perlmutter, A. American strategic and economic interests in the area. *In* The New world balance and peace in the Middle East: reality or mirage? p143-54

Foreign relations
Morgenthau, H. J. Big power confrontations in the Middle East. *In* The New world balance and peace in the Middle East: reality or mirage? p69-73

Foreign relations—Russia
Freedman, R. O. The Soviet conception of a Middle East peace settlement. *In* Ro'i, Y. ed. The limits to power p282-327
Golan, G. The Arab-Israeli conflict in Soviet-US relations. *In* Ro'i, Y. ed. The limits to power p7-31
Gurevitz, B. The Soviet Union and the Palestinian organisations. *In* Ro'i, Y. ed. The limits to power p254-81
Norton, A. R. Moscow and the Palestinians: a new tool of Soviet policy in the Middle East. *In* The Palestinians p228-48
Sella, A. Changes in Soviet political-military policy in the Middle East after 1973. *In* Ro'i, Y. ed. The limits to power p32-64
Smolansky, O. M. The United States and the Soviet Union in the Middle East. *In* Kirk, G. L. and Wessell, N. H. eds. The Soviet threat p99-109
Spechler, D. R. The Soviet Union in the Middle East: problems, policies and prospective trends. *In* Ro'i, Y. ed. The limits to power p331-65

Near East—*Continued*

Foreign relations—United States

Campbell, J. C. American efforts for peace. *In* The Elusive peace in the Middle East p249-310

DeNovo, J. A. The Eisenhower doctrine. *In* Encyclopedia of American foreign policy p292-301

History

Davison, R. H. Nationalism as an Ottoman problem and the Ottoman response. *In* Nationalism in a non-national state p25-56

Haddad, W. W. Nationalism in the Ottoman Empire. *In* Nationalism in a non-national state p3-24

Kedourie, É. The fate of constitutionalism in the Middle East. *In* Kedourie, É. Arabic political memoirs and other studies p 1-27

Rustow, D. A. Political ends and military means in the late Ottoman and post-Ottoman Middle East. *In* War, technology and society in the Middle East p386-99

History—622-1517

See Islamic Empire

History—20th century

Haddad, R. M. The Ottoman Empire in the contemporary Middle East. *In* Aftermath of empire p39-61

Literatures

See Near Eastern literature

Politics aid government

Avineri, S. Political and social aspects of Israeli and Arab nationalism. *In* The Palestinians p97-111

Avnery, U. The Palestinian option. *In* The Palestinians p187-93

Bolling, L. R. Quaker work in the Middle East following the June 1967 War. *In* Unofficial diplomats p80-88

Campbell, J. C. American efforts for peace. *In* The Elusive peace in the Middle East p249-310

Dinstein, Y. Terrorism and war of liberation: an Israeli perspective of the Arab-Israeli conflict. *In* International terrorism and political crimes p155-72

Dowty, A. International guarantees with special reference to the Middle East. *In* The Dynamics of the arms race p215-30

Friedlander, R. A. Problems of the Mediterranean: a geopolitical perspective. *In* The Year book of world affairs, 1978 p175-90

Harbottle, M. Simulating peace-making in the Middle East: an exercise in reality. *In* Unofficial diplomats p241-49

Mallison, W. T. and Mallison, S. V. An international law appraisal of the juridical characteristics of the resistance of the people of Palestine: the struggle for human rights. *In* International terrorism and political crimes p173-90

Ma'oz, M. A Palestinian state—where? *In* The Palestinians p194-96

Norton, A. R. Moscow and the Palestinians: a new tool of Soviet policy in the Middle East. *In* The Palestinians p228-48

Pryce-Jones, D. On Israel's East. *In* The Palestinians p209-12

Rubinstein, A. Palestinian nationalism: an established fact. *In* The Palestinians p183-86

Rustow, D. A. Political ends and military means in the late Ottoman and post-Ottoman Middle East. *In* War, technology and society in the Middle East p386-99

Smolansky, O. M. The United States and the Soviet Union in the Middle East. *In* Kirk, G. L. and Wessell, N. H. eds. The Soviet threat p99-109

Syrkin, M. Palestinian nationalism: its development and goal. *In* The Palestinians p199-208

Tachau, F. Conclusion. *In* Political elites and political development in the Middle East p293-305

Tachau, F. Introduction: Political elites and political development in the Middle East. *In* Political elites and political development in the Middle East p 1-21

Waxman, C. I. Varieties of Palestinian nationalism. *In* The Palestinians p112-20

Politics and government—20th century

Arendt, H. Peace or armistice in the Near East? *In* Arendt, H. The Jew as pariah: Jewish identity and politics in the modern age p193-222

Golan, G. The Arab-Israeli conflict in Soviet-US relations. *In* Ro'i, Y. ed. The limits to power p7-31

Spechler, D. R. The Soviet Union in the Middle East: problems, policies and prospective trends. *In* Ro'i, Y. ed. The limits to power p331-65

Relations (military) with Russia

Middleton, D. Russian presence and economic interests in the Mediterranean and the Indian Ocean. *In* The New world balance and peace in the Middle East: reality or mirage? p43-49

Relations (military) with the United States

Perlmutter, A. American strategic and economic interests in the area. *In* The New world balance and peace in the Middle East: reality or mirage? p143-54

Religion

Crehan, J. Near Eastern societies. *In* Life after death p97-122

Lichtenstadter, I. Religion as a cultural and political factor in the Middle East—past and present. *In* The New world balance and peace in the Middle East: reality or mirage? p137-42

Religion—Bibliography

Oxtoby, W. G. The ancient world. *In* Adams, C. J. ed. A reader's guide to the great religions p39-77

Social conditions

Ashtor, E. An essay on the diet of the various classes in the medieval Levant. *In* Biology of man in history p125-62

Hurewitz, J. W. Soldiers and social change in plural societies: the contemporary Middle East. *In* War, technology and society in the Middle East p400-11

Social life and customs

Spooner, B. The evil eye in the Middle East. *In* The Evil eye p76-84

Near East in literature

Lyons, J. O. Travelers East. *In* Lyons, J. O. The invention of the self p121-55

Near Eastern literature

History and criticism

West, M. L. Near Eastern material in Hellenistic and Roman literature. *In* Harvard Studies in classical philology v73 p113-34

Nearchus

About

Badian, E. Nearchus the Cretan. *In* Yale classical studies v24 p147-70

Neavill, Gordon B.

Role of the publisher in the dissemination of knowledge. *In* Altbach, P. G. and McVey, S. eds. Perspectives on publishing p47-57

Nebel, Sylvia Sue

Hamann's views on human reason. *In* Studies in eighteenth-century culture v4 p125-30

Nebulae. See Crab Nebula; Galaxies

Nebular hypothesis

Lawrence, P. Heaven and earth—the relation of the nebular hypothesis to geology. *In* Cosmology, history, and theology p253-81

See also Cosmogony

Necessity (Philosophy)

Flew, A. G. N. Hume and historical necessity. *In* Flew, A. G. N. A rational animal p49-74

Quine, W. V. Necessary truth. *In* Quine, W. V. The ways of paradox, and other essays p68-76

Quine, W. V. Reply to Professor Marcus. *In* Quine, W. V. The ways of paradox, and other essays p177-84

Quine, W. V. Three grades of modal involvement. *In* Quine, W. V. The ways of paradox, and other essays p158-76

Reesor, M. E. Necessity and fate in Stoic philosophy. *In* Rist, J. M. ed. The Stoics p187-202

Robinson, G. S. Nature and necessity. *In* Royal Institute of Philosophy. Impressions of empiricism p200-15

Trilling, L. Art, will, and necessity. *In* Trilling, L. The last decade p129-47

Vartanian, A. Necessity or freedom? The politics of an eighteenth-century metaphysical debate. *In* Studies in eighteenth-century culture v7 p153-74

Wiggins, D. The De re 'must': a note on the logical form of essentialist claims. *In* Evans, G. L. and McDowell, J. H. eds. Truth and meaning p285-312

See also Causation; Chance; Fate and fatalism; Free will and determinism; Teleology; Truth

Nederlandsche Oost-Indische Compagnie

Arasaratnam, S. Dutch commercial policy and interests in the Malay Peninsula, 1750-1795. *In* Kling, B. B. and Pearson, M. N. eds. The age of partnership p159-89

Prakash, O. Asian trade and European impact: a study of the trade from Bengal, 1630-1720. *In* Kling, B. B. and Pearson, M. N. eds. The age of partnership p43-70

Need (Psychology)

Bay, C. Human needs and political education. *In* Fitzgerald, R. ed. Human needs and politics p 1-25

Condren, C. The quest for a concept of needs. *In* Fitzgerald, R. ed. Human needs and politics p244-60

Fitzgerald, R. Abraham Maslow's hierarchy of needs—an exposition and evaluation. *In* Fitzgerald, R. ed. Human needs and politics p36-51

Fitzgerald, R. The ambiguity and rhetoric of 'need.' *In* Fitzgerald, R. ed. Human needs and politics p195-212

Flew, A. G. N. Wants or needs, choices or commands. *In* Fitzgerald, R. ed. Human needs and politics p213-28

Holbrook, D. Politics and the need for meaning. *In* Fitzgerald, R. ed. Human needs and politics p174-94

Knutson, J. N. Human needs constraining political activity. *In* Fitzgerald, R. ed. Human needs and politics p96-123

McInnes, N. The politics of needs—or, Who needs politics? *In* Fitzgerald, R. ed. Human needs and politics p229-43

Macpherson, C. B. Needs and wants: an ontological or historical problem? *In* Fitzgerald, R. ed. Human needs and politics p26-35

Nielsen, K. True needs, rationality and emancipation. *In* Fitzgerald, R. ed. Human needs and politics p142-56

Renshon, S. A. Human needs and political analysis: an examination of a framework. *In* Fitzgerald, R. ed. Human needs and politics p52-73

Smith, M. B. Metapsychology, politics, and human needs. *In* Fitzgerald, R. ed. Human needs and politics p124-41

Springborg, P. Karl Marx on human needs. *In* Fitzgerald, R. ed. Human needs and politics p157-73

Wollheim, R. Needs, desires and moral turpitude. *In* Royal Institute of Philosophy. Nature and conduct p162-79

Needham, Joseph

Alchemy and early chemistry in China. *In* The Frontiers of human knowledge p171-81

Needham, Rodney

Charles Staniland Wake, 1835-1910: a biographical record. *In* Studies in social anthropology p354-83

Needleman, Jacob

Psychiatry and the sacred. *In* Needleman, J. and Lewis, D. eds. On the way to self knowledge p3-25

Neel, Bege B.

The rule of reverse in "Mr Sludge, 'The medium.'" *In* Tennessee Studies in literature v20 p60-68

Neely, Sharlotte

Acculturation and persistence among North Carolina's eastern band of Cherokee Indians. *In* Williams, W. L. ed. Southeastern Indians since the removal era p154-73

Neera, pseud. See Radius, Anna (Zuccari)

Nef, John Ulrich, 1899-

Background paper: the interplay of literature, art, and science in the time of Copernicus. *In* The Nature of scientific discovery p462-67

Neff, Franklin W. and Lubin, Bernard

Observations on power and authority from a training program for police managers. *In* Armstrong, T. R. and Cinnamon, K. M. eds. Power and authority in law enforcement p115-30

Negotiable instruments. See Bills of exchange

Negotiations in international disputes. See Diplomatic negotiations in international disputes

Negri, Enrico de'. See De'Negri, Enrico

Negro minstrel shows. See Minstrel shows

Negro spirituals. See Spirituals (Songs)

Negroes. See Blacks; Afro-Americans

Negroponte, Nicholas

About individual works
The architecture machine

Sale, R. H. Toynbee, Ellul, Safdie, Negroponte. *In* Sale, R. H. On not being good enough p188-202

Neher, André
Shaddai: the God of the broken arch (a theological approach to the Holocaust) *In* Rosenfeld, A. H. and Greenberg, I. eds. Confronting the Holocaust p150-58

Neher, Clark D.
Thailand. *In* Kearney, R. N. ed. Politics and modernization in South and Southeast Asia p215-52

Neher, William Walter, and Condon, John C.
The mass media and nation-building in Kenya and Tanzania. *In* Smock, D. R. and Bentsi-Enchill, K. eds. The search for national integration in Africa p220-39

Nehra, Krishan S. See Hutton, E. J. jt. auth.

Nehru, Jawaharlal

About
Moos, S. von. The politics of the open hand: notes on Le Corbusier and Nehru at Chandigarh. *In* Walden, R. ed. The open hand p412-57

Neidhardt, Friedhelm
The Federal Republic of Germany. *In* Kamerman, S. B. and Kahn, A. J. eds. Family policy p217-38

Neidhart von Reuental

About
Karlin, R. The challenge to courtly love. *In* In pursuit of perfection p101-33

Neil, Alan
Kenneth Patchen reads with jazz in Canada. *In* Morgan, R. G. ed. Kenneth Patchen: a collection of essays p54-58

Neill, Alexander Sutherland

About
Barrow, R. A. S. Neill (1883-1973). *In* Barrow, R. Radical education p64-91

About individual works
The problem child

Bettelheim, B. About Summerhill. *In* Bettelheim, B. Surviving, and other essays p169-84

Neill, Michael
"Anticke pageantrie": the mannerist art of Perkin Warbeck. *In* Renaissance drama [1976] p117-50

Neiman, Fraser
A reader's guide to Arnold. *In* Allott, K. ed. Matthew Arnold p 1-38

Nejad, Kazem Motamed- See Motamed-Nejad, Kazem

Nelkin, Dorothy
Technology and public policy. *In* Science, technology and society p393-441

Threats and promises: negotiating the control of research. *In* Holton, G. J. and Morison, R. S. eds. Limits of scientific inquiry p191-209

Nell, Onora (O'Neill)
How do we know when opportunities are equal? *In* Gould, C. C. and Wartofsky, M. W. eds. Women and philosophy p334-46

Also in Feminism and philosophy p177-89

Lifeboat earth. *In* Aiken, W. and La Follette, H. eds. World hunger and moral obligation p148-64

Some inconsistent educational aism. *In* Small comforts for hard times p303-07

Nelli, Humbert S.
Chicago's Italian-language press and World War I. *In* Studies in Italian American social history p66-80

Nellist, Brian
Narrative modes in the Waverley novels. *In* Davies, R. T. and Beatty, B. G. eds. Literature of the romantic period, 1750-1850 p56-71

Nelson, Benjamin N.
The quest for certitude and the books of Scripture, nature, and conscience. *In* The Nature of scientific discovery p355-72

Nelson, Cary
The psychology of criticism, or what can be said. *In* Hartman, G. H. ed. Psychoanalysis and the question of the text p45-61

Nelson, Garrison
Change and continuity in the recruitment of U.S. House leaders, 1789-1975. *In* Ornstein, N. J. ed. Congress in change p155-83

Nelson, Harland S.
Stagg's gardens: the railway through Dickens' world. *In* Dickens Studies Annual v3 p41-53

Nelson, J. Walter
War and peace and the British poets of sensibility. *In* Studies in eighteenth-century culture v7 p345-66

Nelson, Jack L.
Nationalistic education and the free man. *In* Fairfield, R. P. ed. Humanistic frontiers in American education p139-47

Nelson, John Charles
Love and sex in The Decameron. *In* Philosophy and humanism p339-51

Nelson, L. D. M.
The Andean common market. *In* The Year book of world affairs, 1975 p208-21

Nelson, Lowry, 1926-
Leopardi first and last. *In* Italian literature: roots and branches p333-62

Nelson, Lyle M.
The Stanford years. *In* Lerner, D. and Nelson, L. M. eds. Communication research —a half-century appraisal p317-24

Nelson, Mary Jean. See Stokstad, M. jt. auth.

Nelson, Ray
The moral prose of Kenneth Patchen. *In* Morgan, R. G. ed. Kenneth Patchen: a collection of essays p229-52

Nemeroff, Charles B. See Lipton, M. A. jt. auth.

Nemerov, Howard
Figures of thought
Contents
About time
The dream of Dante
Exceptions and rules
Also in Evolution of consciousness p42-47
Figures of thought
On poetry and painting, with a thought of music
On the resemblances between science and religion
Poetry and meaning
Also in Boyers, R. ed. Contemporary poetry in America p 1-15
Quidnunc the poet and Mr Gigadibs
Speaking silence
Speculation turning to itself
Thirteen ways of looking at a skylark
Thoughts on first passing the hundredth page of Finnegans wake
What was modern poetry? Three lectures: Image and metaphor
What was modern poetry? Three lectures: Poetry and history
What was modern poetry? Three lectures: What will suffice
The winter addresses of Kenneth Burke

The first county of places. *In* Images and ideas in American culture p158-68

About
Boyers, R. Howard Nemerov's true voice of feeling. *In* Boyers, R. Excursions p217-41
Kiehl, J. M. The poems of Howard Nemerov: where loveliness adorns intelligible things. *In* Boyers, R. ed. Contemporary poetry in America p279-302
Meinke, P. Howard Nemerov. *In* Donoghue, D. ed. Seven American poets from MacLeish to Nemerov p250-86
Young, G. L. "The fountainhead of all forms": poetry and the unconscious in Emerson and Howard Nemerov. *In* Artful thunder p241-67

Nemiah, John C.
Psychodynamic psychotherapy. *In* Overview of the psychotherapies p36-50

Nemoy, Leon
The attitude of the early Karaites towards Christianity. *In* Salo Wittmayer Baron v2 p697-715

Nemser, Cindy
The closeup vision. *In* Battcock, G. ed. Super realism p49-63

Neoclassicism (Art)
Wennberg, B. G. On education and the impact of neo-classicism on tuition. *In* Wennberg, B. G. French and Scandinavian sculpture in the nineteenth century p194-97
Wennberg, B. G. On neo-classicism. *In* Wennberg, B. G. French and Scandinavian sculpture in the nineteenth century p10-53

France
Whiteley, J. Homer abandoned: a French neo-classical theme. *In* The Artist and the writer in France p40-51

Great Britain
Goodreau, D. Pictorial sources of the neo-classical style: London or Rome? *In* Studies in eighteenth-century culture v4 p247-70

Neoclassicism (Literature)
History and criticism
Cooke, M. G. The extremes of self and system: The symbiosis of self and system in the neoclassical regime. *In* Cooke, M. G. The romantic will p57-76
Ijsewijn, J. Neo-Latin satire: Sermo and Satyra Menippea. *In* Classical influences on European culture A.D. 1500-1700 p41-55
Jones, T. B. and Nicol, B. de B. The English scene—Restoration and early eighteenth-century criticism. *In* Jones, T. B. and Nicol, B. de B. Neo-classical dramatic criticism, 1560-1770 p95-123
Jones, T. B. and Nicol, B. de B. French neo-classicism. *In* Jones, T. B. and Nicol, B. de B. Neo-classical dramatic criticism, 1560-1770 p49-94
Jones, T. B. and Nicol, B. de B. From Robortello to Ben Jonson. *In* Jones, T. B. and Nicol, B. de B. Neo-classical dramatic criticism, 1560-1770 p18-48
Jones, T. B. and Nicol, B. de B. Introduction: Aristotle and Horace. *In* Jones, T. B. and Nicol, B. de B. Neo-classical dramatic criticism, 1560-1770 p 1-17
Simonsuuri, K. Epic genius: the departure from the neoclassical model. *In* Simonsuuri, K. Homer's original genius p77-89
Smith, A. D. Neo-classicist and romantic elements in the emergence of nationalist conceptions. *In* Smith, A. D. ed. Nationalist movements p74-87

Neo-Confucianism
Chan, Wing-tsit. The Hsing-li ching-i and the Ch'eng-Chu school of the seventeenth century. *In* The Unfolding of Neo-Confucianism p543-79
Cheng, Chung-ying. Reason, substance, and human desires in seventeenth-century Neo-Confucianism. *In* The Unfolding of Neo-Confucianism p469-509
De Bary, W. T. Neo-Confucian cultivation and the seventeenth-century "enlightenment." *In* The Unfolding of Neo-Confucianism p141-216
McMorran, I. Wang Fu-chih and the Neo-Confucian tradition. *In* The Unfolding of Neo-Confucianism p413-67
Tu, Wei-ming. 'Inner experience': the basis of creativity in Neo-Confucian thinking. *In* Artists and traditions p 9-15
Tu, Wei-ming. Yen Yüan: from inner experience to lived concreteness. *In* The Unfolding of Neo-Confucianism p511-41

Neo-fascism. See Fascism

Neologisms. See Words, New

Neon (Periodical)
Sorrentino, G. Neon, Kulchur, etc. *In* Anderson, E. and Kinzie, M. eds. The little magazine in America: a modern documentary history p298-323

Neo-orthodoxy. See Fundamentalism

Neoplasticism
Osborne, H. Constructivism. *In* Osborne, H. Abstraction and artifice in twentieth-century art p125-48

Neoplatonism. See Alexandrian school

Neo-positivism. See Logical positivism

Nepea, Osip
Baron, S. H. Osip Nepea and the opening of Anglo-Russian commercial relations. *In* Oxford Slavonic papers, new ser. v11 p42-63

Nephew, Albert H.

The personal universe. *In* The Personal universe p99-108

Nepos, Cornelius

About

Elder, J. P. Catullus I, his poetic creed, and Nepos. *In* Harvard Studies in classical philology v71 p143-49

Neptune. See Neptunus

Neptunus

Brower, R. A. Visual and verbal translation of myth: Neptune in Virgil, Rubens, Dryden. *In* Brower, R. A. Mirror on mirror p17-45

Art

Moore, M. B. Poseidon in the Gigantomachy. *In* Studies in classical art and archaeology p23-27

Neroccio di Bartolomeo (di Benedetto de') Landi

About

Carli, E. Two stucco reliefs by Neroccio di Bartolomeo. *In* Collaboration in Italian Renaissance art p21-29

Neruda, Pablo

About

Belitt, B. The moving finger and the unknown Neruda. *In* Belitt, B. Adam's dream p138-53

Belitt, B. Pablo Neruda: A revaluation. *In* Belitt, B. Adam's dream p108-37

Belitt, B. Pablo Neruda: Splendor and death. *In* Belitt, B. Adam's dream p175-83

About individual works

Memoirs

Belitt, B. Neruda's Memoirs: a reading from Homer. *In* Belitt, B. Adam's dream p157-74

Residence in earth (Translated by Donald D. Walsh)

Belitt, B. The translator as nobody in particular. *In* Belitt, B. Adam's dream p45-53

Selected poems (Translated by Ben Belitt)

Belitt, B. Translator's preface: The selected poems of Pablo Neruda. *In* Belitt, B. Adam's dream p101-07

Splendor and death of Joaquín Murieta (Translated by Ben Belitt)

Belitt, B. Neruda's Joaquín Murieta: a note on the poetics of translation. *In* Belitt, B. Adam's dream p67-78

Nerval, Gérard de. See Gérard de Nerval, Gerald Labrunie, known as

Nerve-cells. See Nerves

Nerves

Hubel, D. Neurobiology: a science in need of a Copernicus. *In* Neyman, J. ed. The heritage of Copernicus: theories "pleasing to the mind" p243-60

See also Nervous system

Diseases

See Nervous system—Diseases

Surgery

See Nervous system—Surgery

Nervous system

Feldenkrais, M. Man and the world. *In* Hanna, T. ed. Explorers of mankind p19-29

Lawrence, C. The nervous system and society in the Scottish Enlightment. *In* Barnes, B. and Shapin, S. eds. Natural order p19-40

See also Brain; Nerves; Neurophysiology

Diseases

Harvey, A. M. Discoveries at Johns Hopkins related to the nervous system and its diseases. *In* Harvey, A. M. Adventures in medical research p401-24

Diseases—Psychosomatic aspects

Shands, H. C. Verbal patterns and medical disease: prophylactic implications of learning. *In* Sebeok, T. A. ed. Sight, sound, and sense p175-201

Hygiene

See Relaxation

Surgery

Harvey, A. M. Neurosurgical genius: Walter Edward Dandy. *In* Harvey, A. M. Adventures in medical research p60-68

Nesbit, Edith. See Bland, Edith (Nesbit)

Ness, Arne

The place of joy in a world of fact. *In* Against pollution and hunger p297-307

Ness, Frederic William

Consensus and preservation. *In* The Third century p135-40

Nestrick, William Virgil

Coming to life: Frankenstein and the nature of film narrative. *In* Levine, G. L. and Knoepflmacher, U. C. eds. The endurance of Frankenstein p290-315

Spenser and the Renaissance mythology of love. *In* Literary monographs v6 p35-70

Nestroy, Johann Nepomuk

About

Rogers, M. A. "Dies Osterreich ist eine kleine welt." *In* Branscombe, P. ed. Austrian life and literature, 1780-1938 p72-80

About individual works

Zu ebener Erde und erster Stock, oder: die Launen des Glücks

Potter, P. M. Nestroy's Zu ebener Erde und erster Stock: a reappraisal. *In* Branscombe, P. ed. Austrian life and literature, 1780-1938 p40-48

Netherlands

Commerce—Malay Peninsula

Arasaratnam, S. Dutch commercial policy and interests in the Malay Peninsula, 1750-1795. *In* Kling, B. B. and Pearson, M. N. eds. The age of partnership p159-89

History—Wars of Independence, 1556-1648

Parker, G. War and economic change: the economic costs of the Dutch revolt. *In* War and economic development p49-71

History—1714-1795

Schulte Nordholt, J. W. The impact of the American Revolution on the Dutch Republic. *In* The impact of the American Revolution abroad p41-63

Netherlands—*Continued*

History—1795-1815

Schama, S. The exigencies of war and the politics of taxation in the Netherlands, 1795-1810. *In* War and economic development p103-37

Laws, statutes, etc.—Nuisance Act, 1953

Staatsen, A. A. M. F. Enforcement of the Nuisance Act in the Netherlands. *In* Davis, K. C. Discretionary justice in Europe and America p100-14

Netting, Robert McCorkle

Maya subsistence: mythologies, analogies, possibilities. *In* The Origins of Maya civilization p299-333

Nettler, Gwynn

Description, prescription, and science: on differences between knowing something and knowing enough, promising and predicting. *In* Major social issues p156-71

Nettleship, Martin A.

Weaving in its social context among the Atayal of Taiwan. *In* Greenhalgh, M. and Megaw, J. V. S. eds. Art in society p175-91

Networks, Information. See Information networks

Neugarten, Bernice Levin

The future and the young-old. *In* Jarvik, L. F. ed. Aging into the 21st century p137-52

Neumann, Franz Leopold

About

Hughes, H. S. The critique of fascism. *In* Hughes, H. S. The sea change p70-133

Neumeier v. Kuehner. *In* Stanford legal essays p251-65

Neurobiology

Eccles, J. C. Cerebral activity and consciousness. *In* Ayala, F. J. and Dobzhansky, T. G. eds. Studies in the philosophy of biology p87-105

Hubel, D. Neurobiology: a science in need of Copernicus. *In* Neyman, J. ed. The heritage of Copernicus: theories "pleasing to the mind" p243-60

Neurology

Lenneberg, E. H. The neurology of language. *In* Bloomfield, M. W. and Haugen, E. I. eds. Language as a human problem p101-19

See also Neurobiology; Neuropsychiatry

Research

Harvey, A. M. Discoveries at Johns Hopkins related to the nervous system and its diseases. *In* Harvey, A. M. Adventures in medical research p401-24

Neuropathology. See Nervous system—Diseases

Neurophysiology

Pribram, K. H. Some observations on the organization of studies of mind, brain, and behavior. *In* Alternate states of consciousness p220-29

Neuropsychiatry

Ehrenwald, J. Parapsychology and the seven dragons: a neuropsychiatric model of psi phenomena. *In* Parapsychology: its relation to physics, biology, psychology, and psychiatry p246-63

Neuroses. See Depression, Mental; Psychoses

Neurosurgery. See Nervous system—Surgery

Neurotics Nomine

Jones, R. K. Some sectarian characteristics of therapeutic groups with special reference to Recovery, inc. and Neurotics Nomine. *In* Wallis, R. ed. Sectarianism p190-210

Neusner, Jacob

Politics and theology in Talmudic Babylonia. *In* Tradition and change in Jewish experience p46-74

Neutralism. See Neutrality

Neutrality

Barlett, R. J. Neutrality. *In* Encyclopedia of American foreign policy p679-87

Jankowitsch, P. Neutrality and nonalignment: foreign policies of independence in the twentieth century. *In* [Truth and tragedy]: a tribute to Hans Morgenthau p237-58

Sudjatmoko. Reflections on nonalignment in the 1970s. *In* Erb, G. F. and Kallab, V. eds. Beyond dependency p28-37

See also Intervention (International law); and subdivision Neutrality under names of countries and of neutralized areas, e.g. United States—Neutrality

Neutrality, Armed

Mugridge, I. Armed neutralities. *In* Encyclopedia of American foreign policy p43-48

Neutrons. See Electrons

Neverdon-Morton, Cynthia

The Black woman's struggle for equality in the South, 1895-1925. *In* Harley, S. and Terborg-Penn, R. eds. The Afro-American woman p43-57

Neville, Emily Cheney

About individual works

Berries Goodman

Kimmel, E. A. Jewish identity in juvenile fiction: a look at three recommended books. *In* Horn Book Magazine. Crosscurrents of criticism p150-58

Neville, Gwen Kennedy

Marginal communicant: the anthropologist in religious groups and agencies. *In* Eddy, E. M. and Partridge, W. L. eds. Applied anthropology in America p197-209

Nevins, Allan

Allan Nevins on history

Contents

Nevins Allan

Allan Nevins on history

Contents—Continued

Oral history: how and why it was born

Reading in a book-crowded age

Recent progress of American social history

The role of the manuscript collector

The universal and the local

What the scientist and historian can teach each other

What's the matter with history?

Why public men keep diaries

Foreword to Profiles in courage by John F. Kennedy. *In* Praise from famous men: an anthology of introductions p124-30

About

Billington, R. A. Allan Nevins, historian: a personal reminiscence. *In* Nevins, A. Allan Nevins on history p ix-xxvii

New, Melvyn

Sterne as editor: the "Abuses of conscience" sermon. *In* Studies in eighteenth-century culture v8 p243-51

New, Melvyn, and Fry, Norman

Some borrowings in Tristram Shandy: the textual problem. *In* Virginia. University. Bibliographical Society. Studies in bibliography v29 p322-30

New, W. H.

New language, new world. *In* Narasimhaiah, C. D. ed. Awakened conscience p360-77

New, The

Simon, J. I. New, newer, newest. *In* Simon, J. I. Singularities p119-25

New Archangel, Alaska. See Sitka, Alaska

New Criticism

Graff, G. Culture, criticism and unreality. *In* Graff, G. Literature against itself p 1-29

Graff, G. What was New Criticism? *In* Graff, G. Literature against itself p129-49

Kenner, H. The pedagogue as critic. *In* Young, T. D. ed. The New Criticism and after p36-46

Morris, W. A. Stylistics. *In* Morris, W. A. Friday's footprint p147-87

Ong, W. J. The poem as a closed field: the once New Criticism and the nature of literature. *In* Ong, W. J. Interfaces of the word p213-29

Watkins, E. Introduction: Poetics, poetry, and the practice of criticism. *In* Watkins, E. The critical act p3-23

New England

Intellectual life

Hall, D. D. The world of print and collective mentality in seventeenth-century New England. *In* Higham, J. and Conkin, P. K. eds. New directions in American intellectual history p166-80

New England in literature

Eakin, P. J. Henry James and the New England consciousness: Roderick Hudson, The Europeans, Hawthorne. *In* Eakin, P. J. The New England girl p131-67

Eakin, P. J. The Howells heroine: from The lady of the Aroostook to April hopes. *In* Eakin, P. J. The New England girl p83-130

Eakin, P. J. Introduction: History and the heroines of fiction. *In* Eakin, P. J. The New England girl p3-24

Eakin, P. J. New England in extremis: The Bostonians. *In* Eakin, P. J. The New England girl p195-217

Eakin, P. J. Renunciation in New England: Harriet Beecher Stowe and The minister's wooing. *In* Eakin, P. J. The New England girl p27-48

Eakin, P. J. Self-culture: Margaret Fuller and Hawthorne's heroines. *In* Eakin, P. J. The New England girl p49-79

Eakin, P. J. The tragedy of self-culture: The portrait of a lady. *In* Eakin, P. J. The New England girl p168-94

MacLeish, A. New England's Frost and Frost's New England. *In* MacLeish, A. Riders on the earth p143-53

Seelye, J. Glorious enterprise: Governor John Winthrop's wonderful wall. *In* Seelye, J. Prophetic waters p131-58

New England theology

Influence

Grabo, N. S. Colonial American theology: holiness and the lyric impulse. *In* Essays in honor of Russel B. Nye p74-91

New England witchcraft. See Witchcraft—New England

New Guinea

Native races

Jacobs, W. R. The fatal confrontation: early native-white relations on the frontiers of Australia, New Guinea, and America—a comparative study. *In* The American Indian p27-54

Wood-carving

See Wood-carving—New Guinea

New Hampshire

History

Demos, J. Witchcraft and local culture in Hampton, New Hampshire. *In* Uprooted Americans p9-42

New Jersey

Census—History

Wacker, P. O. Patterns and problems in the historical geography of the Afro-American population of New Jersey, 1726-1860. *In* Pattern and process p25-72

New Jersey. Superior Court

In the matter of Karen Quinlan, an alleged incompetent. *In* Weir, R. F. ed. Ethical issues in death and dying p271-77

The new land (Motion picture)

Kauffmann, S. The new land. *In* Kauffmann, S. Living images p222-26

New Left. See College students—Political activity; Communism—1945- ; Radicalism; Right and left (Political science)

New Mexico

Antiquities

Glassow, M. A. Population aggregation and systemic change: examples from the American Southwest. *In* Explanation of prehistoric change p185-214

History—To 1848

Simmons, M. Settlement patterns and village plans in colonial New Mexico. *In* Weber, D. J. ed. New Spain's far northern frontier p97-115

Politics and government— 1848-1950

Pickens, W. The New Deal in New Mexico. *In* Braeman, J.; Bremner, R. H. and Brody, D. eds. The New Deal v2 p311-54

New Orleans

Carnival

Reed, I. Shrovetide in old New Orleans. *In* Reed, I. Shrovetide in old New Orleans p 9-33

Commerce—History

Hilliard, S. B. Antebellum interregional trade: the Mississippi River as an example. *In* Pattern and process p202-14

New Orleans in literature

Richardson, T. J. The city of day and the city of night: New Orleans and the exotic unreality of Tennessee Williams. *In* Tennessee Williams: a tribute p631-46

New products. See Design, Industrial

New Review publications

Ford, H. D. Four new directions: content over form: New Review. *In* Ford, H. D. Published in Paris p318-22

New states. See States, New

New Testament Greek. See Greek language, Biblical

New words. See Words, New

New Year

North Carolina

Robbins, W. L. Wishing in and shooting in the New Year among the Germans in the Carolinas. *In* Yoder, D. ed. American folklife p257-79

New York v. Cathedral Academy. *In* The Supreme Court review, 1978 p171-90

New York (City)

Description

White, E. B. Here is New York. *In* White, E. B. Essays of E. B. White p118-33

Human Resources Administration

Harris, K. L. Organizing to overhaul a mess. *In* Managing nonprofit organizations p229-43

Intellectual life

Sheed, W. New York blues. *In* Sheed, W. The good word & other words p20-23

Learned institutions and societies—History

Hindle, B. The underside of the learned society in New York, 1754-1854. *In* Oleson, A. and Brown, S. C. eds. The pursuit of knowledge in the early American Republic p84-116

Metropolitan Hospital Center

Eichwald, H. An organized home care program. *In* Home care p148-52

New York (City) City University of New York

Skurnick, B. J. A basic writing program at an urban university. *In* Minority language and literature p80-85

Admission

Rich, A. C. Teaching language in open admissions. *In* Rich, A. C. On lies, secrets, and silence p51-68

Curricula

Mayer, M. Higher education for all? The case of open admissions. *In* Murphy, T. P. ed. Universities in the urban crisis p215-39

Entrance requirements

Mayer, M. Higher education for all? The case of open admissions. *In* Murphy, T. P. ed. Universities in the urban crisis p215-39

New York (City) International Exhibition of Modern Art, 1913

Schapiro, M. The introduction of modern art in America: the Armory Show. *In* Schapiro, M. Selected papers v2 p135-77

New York (City) Off-Track Betting Corporation

Shagan, M. D. Is gambling worth enforcement gamble? *In* Contemporary issues in criminal justice p16-39

New York (City) St. Luke's Hospital. See St. Luke's Hospital, New York

New York (City) World Trade Center

Billington, D. P. Technology and the structuring of cities. *In* Small comforts for hard times p182-98

New York (City) World's Fair, 1939-1940

White, E. B. The World of Tomorrow. *In* White, E. B. Essays of E. B. White p111-17

New York (State)

Church history

Hudson, W. S. A time of religious ferment. *In* The Rise of Adventism p 1-17

History—Colonial period, ca. 1600-1775

Klein, M. M. New York lawyers and the coming of the American Revolution. *In* Studies in eighteenth-century culture v7 p23-47

Politics and government—Colonial period, ca. 1600-1775

Varga, N. The development and structure of local government in colonial New York. *In* Daniels, B. C. ed. Town and county p186-215

New York City College. See New York (City) City University of New York

New York. Metropolitan Opera

Craft, R. Figaro at the Met: a marriage on the rocks. *In* Craft, R. Current convictions p49-59

New York Shakespeare Festival

Kauffmann, S. Much ado about nothing. *In* Kauffmann, S. Persons of the drama p99-102

Simon, J. I. Mugging the Bard in Central Park. *In* Simon, J. I. Singularities p107-11

New York Shakespeare Festival Public Theater

Kauffmann, S. The stages of Joseph Papp. *In* Kauffmann, S. Persons of the drama p3-28

New Zealand

Foreign relations

Chapman, C. Towards a new Pacific alliance. *In* The Year book of world affairs, 1975 p88-105

Social conditions

Chapman, C. Towards a new Pacific alliance. *In* The Year book of world affairs, 1975 p88-105

New Zealand children's literature. See Children's literature, New Zealand

New Zealand in literature

Tiffin, C. Mates, mum, and Maui: the theme of maturity in three antipodean novels. *In* Narasimhaiah, C. D. ed. Awakened conscience p127-45

Newall, Venetia

Icons as symbols of power. *In* Symbols of power p61-99

Newark, N.J. Free Public Library

Roth, P. The Newark Public Library. *In* Roth, P. Reading myself and others p175-77

Newbery, John

About

Buck, J. D. C. The motives of puffing: John Newbery's advertisements 1742-1767. *In* Virginia. University. Bibliographical Society. Studies in bibliography v30 p196-210

Newell, Alex

Early modern English idiom in a prose passage from King Lear. *In* Shakespeare's late plays p56-75

Newey, Vincent

The steadfast self: an aspect of Wordsworth. *In* Davies, R. T. and Beatty, B. G. eds. Literature of the romantic period, 1750-1850 p36-55

Newfield, Jack

The ten worst judges. *In* Nader, R. and Green, M. J. eds. Verdicts on lawyers p269-84

Newhall, Beaumont

About

Coke, F. V. Introduction: Beaumont Newhall. *In* One hundred years of photographic history p viii-x

Newman, Barnett

About

Rosenberg, H. Newman: meaning in abstract art II. *In* Rosenberg, H. Art on the edge p50-59

Newman, Dorothy K.

The Black American worker. *In* The Black American reference book p251-83

Newman, Francis William

About individual works

Phases of faith

Dawson, C. Phases of the soul: the Newman brothers. *In* Dawson, C. Victorian noon p105-22

Newman, Frank

Taking the helm. *In* The Third century p116-26

Newman, John Henry, Cardinal

About

Capps, D. Newman's illness in Sicily: the reformer as biographer. *In* Reynolds, F. E. and Capps, D. eds. The biographical process p201-18

Dawson, C. Phases of the soul: the Newman brothers. *In* Dawson, C. Victorian noon p105-22

Haley, B. Types of healthy Christianity: Newman and Kingsley. *In* Haley, B. The healthy body and Victorian culture p95-119

About individual works

Apologia pro vita sua

Ryan, M. A grammatology of assent: Cardinal Newman's Apologia pro vita sua. *In* Landow, G. P. ed. Approaches to Victorian autobiography p128-57

Callista

Sanders, A. The argument from tradition: Hypatia, Fabiola and Callista. *In* Sanders, A. The Victorian historical novel, 1840-1880 p120-48

An essay in aid of a grammar of assent

Prickett, S. Newman: imagination and assent. *In* Prickett, S. Romanticism and religion p174-210

An essay on the development of Christian doctrine

Prickett, S. Newman versus Maurice: development of doctrine and the growth of the mind. *In* Prickett, S. Romanticism and religion p152-73

Newman, Stephen J.

Barnaby Rudge: Dickens and Scott. *In* Davies, R. T. and Beatty, B. G. eds. Literature of the romantic period, 1750-1850 p171-88

Newman, William Herman

Control: past or future. *In* Benton, L. R. ed. Management for the future p229-37

News, Foreign. See Foreign news

News agencies

Aggarwala, N. K. News with Third World perspectives: a practical suggestion. *In* Horton, P. C. ed. The Third World and press freedom p197-209

Boyd-Barrett, O. The global news wholesalers. *In* Gerbner, G. ed. Mass media policies in changing cultures p13-20

Galliner, P. Improving news flow in the Third World. *In* Horton, P. C. ed. The Third World and press freedom p93-103

Gawad, M. A. Attempts of the Arab world to participate in balancing the flow of information. *In* Horton, P. C. ed. The Third World and press freedom p173-86

Olasope, B. The Nonaligned News Agencies Pool and the free flow of meaningful news: an African viewpoint. *In* Horton, P. C. ed. The Third World and press freedom p162-72

Rosenblum, M. The Western wire services and the Third World. *In* Horton, P. C. ed. The Third World and press freedom p104-26

Tatarian, R. News flow in the Third World: an overview. *In* Horton, P. C. ed. The Third World and press freedom p 1-54

News broadcasts. See Television broadcasting of news

News-gathering organizations. See News agencies

News photography. See Photography, Journalistic

News services. See News agencies

Newsom, Robert

About individual works

Dickens on the romantic side of familiar things: Bleak House and the novel tradition

Dunn, R. J. "Illuminating distortions" and the Dickens critics. *In* Review, v 1 1979 p91-104

Newson, Elisabeth

Unreasonable care: the establishment of selfhood. *In* Royal Institute of Philosophy. Human values p 1-26

Newspaper publishing

United States—Historiography

Nevins, A. American journalism and its historical treatment. *In* Nevins, A. Allan Nevins on history p82-102

Ngugi Wa Thiong'o—*Continued*

About individual works
A grain of wheat

Gakwandi, S. A. Commitment: Ngugi's A grain of wheat. *In* Gakwandi, S. A. The novel and contemporary experience in Africa p108-19

Monkman, L. Kenya and the New Jerusalem in A grain of wheat. *In* African literature today no. 7: Focus on criticism p111-16

Nguni

Wilson, M. Strangers in Africa: reflections on Nyakyusa, Nguni, and Sotho evidence. *In* Shack, W. A. and Skinner, E. P. eds. Strangers in African society p51-66

Ng'weno, Hilary

All freedom is at stake. *In* Horton, P. C. ed. The Third World and press freedom p127-34

Niaousta, Greece. See Naousa, Greece

Nibelungenlied

Bäuml, F. H. and Spielmann, E. From illiteracy to literacy: prolegomena to a study of the Nibelungenlied. *In* Duggan, J. J. ed. Oral literature p62-73

Curschann, M. The concept of the oral formula as an impediment to our understanding of medieval oral poetry. *In* Medievalia et humanistica no. 8 p63-76

Wailes, S. L. The Nibelungenlied as heroic epic. *In* Oinas, F. J. ed. Heroic epic and saga p120-43

Niblett, William Roy

The individual and the social future. *In* Niblett, W. R. ed. The sciences, the humanities and the technological threat p157-65

Nicaea, Council of, 2d, 787

Henry, P. Images of the Church in the Second Nicene Council and in the Libri Carolini. *In* Law, church, and society p237-52

Lynch, J. H. A Carolingian borrowing from Second Nicaea (787). *In* Medievalia et humanistica no. 5 p127-38

Wallach, L. The Greek and Latin versions of II Nicaea, 787, and the Synodica of Hadrian I (JE 2448). *In* Wallach, L. Diplomatic studies in Latin and Greek documents from the Carolingian age p3-26

Nicene Creed

Sayers, D. L. What do we believe? Excerpt from "Unpopular opinions." *In* Sayers, D. L. The whimsical Christian p29-33

Nicgorski, Walter, and Weber, Ronald Edward

Afterword. *In* An Almost chosen people p147-60

Nichol, B. P.

About individual works
The true eventual story of Billy the Kid

Scobie, S. Two authors in search of a character: bp Nichol and Michael Ondaatje. *In* Woodcock, G. ed. Poets and critics p225-46

Nicholas of Autrecourt. See Nicolaus de Autricuria

Nicholas of Cusa. See Nicolaus Causanius, Cardinal

Nicholas of Lynne
About

Eisner, S. Chaucer's use of Nicholas of Lynn's Calendar. *In* English Association. Essays and studies, 1976 p 1-22

Nicholas, Herbert George

The wartime alliance and after; the Cold war alliance; excerpt from "Britain and the U.S.A. *In* Burton, D. H. ed. American history—British historians p93-124

Nicholls, Peter

Science fiction: the monsters and the critics. *In* Nicholls, P. ed. Science fiction at large p157-83

Nichols, Bill

Style, grammar, and the movies. *In* Nichols, B. ed. Movies and methods p607-28

Nichols, Charles Harold

Comic modes in Black America (a ramble through Afro-American humor). *In* Cohen, S. B. ed. Comic relief p105-26

Nichols, David C.

Federal City College: a model for new urban universities? *In* Land-grant universities and their continuing challenge p205-22

Land-grant university services and urban policy. *In* Land-grant universities and their continuing challenge p223-36

Nichols, Fred Joseph

Faust. *In* Seidel, M. A. and Mendelson, E. eds. Homer and Brecht p292-316

Nichols, Marie Hochmuth

Rhetoric and the humane tradition. *In* Rhetoric: a tradition in transition p178-91

Nichols, Peter

About individual works
The national health

Kauffman, S. The national health. *In* Kauffmann, S. Persons of the drama p242-44

Nichols, Raymond L.

Rebels, beginners, and buffoons: politics as action. *In* Political theory and praxis p159-99

Nichols, Ruth

Something of myself. *In* Egoff, S. A. ed. One ocean touching p189-94

About

Nichols, R. Something of myself. *In* Egoff, S. A. ed. One ocean touching p189-94

Nichols, Stephen G.

Old French narrative poetry: some recent studies. *In* Medievalia et humanistica no. 5 p233-37

A poetics of historicism? Recent trends in medieval literary study. *In* Medievalia et humanistica no. 8 p77-101

Toward an aesthetic of the Provençal lyric II: Marcabru's Dire vos vuoill ses doptansa (BdT 293, 18). *In* Italian literature: roots and branches p15-37

Nichols family

Kuist, J. M. The Gentleman's magazine in the Folger Library: the history and significance of the Nichols family collection. *In* Virginia. University. Bibliographical Society. Studies in bibliography v29 p307-22

Nicholson, Caroline Elizabeth

Trees were green. *In* Time was away p11-20

Nicholson, Elizabeth. See Nicholson, Caroline Elizabeth

Nicholson, Henry Bigger

Tepepolco, the locale of the first stage of Fr. Bernardino de Sahagún's great ethnographic project: historical and cultural notes. *In* Mesoamerican archaeology p145-54

Nicholson, Michael

Aleksandr Soylzhenitsyn: a bibliography of responses in the official Soviet press from November 1962 to April 1973. *In* Dunlop, J. B.; Haugh, R. and Klimoff, A. eds. Aleksandr Solzhenitsyn: critical essays and documentary materials 2d ed. p579-610

The Gulag Archipelago: a survey of Soviet responses. *In* Dunlop, J. B.; Haugh, R. and Klimoff, A. eds. Aleksandr Solzhenitsyn: critical essays and documentary materials 2d ed. p477-500

Peace education: a sceptic's view. *In* International terrorism and world security p296-307

Solzhenitsyn and samizdat. *In* Dunlop, J. B.; Haugh, R. and Klimoff, A. eds. Aleksandr Solzhenitsyn: critical essays and documentary materials 2d ed. p63-93

Nicholson, Simon

Children as planners. *In* Gross, B. and Gross, R. eds. The children's rights movement p287-95

Nicholson, Susan T.

The Roman Catholic doctrine of therapeutic abortion. *In* Feminism and philosophy p385-407

Nickel, James Wesley

Discrimination and morally relevant characteristics. *In* Gross, B. R. ed. Reverse discrimination p288-90

Preferential policies in hiring and admissions: a jurisprudential approach. *In* Gross, B. R. ed. Reverse discrimination p324-47

Should reparations be to individuals or to groups? *In* Gross, B. R. ed. Reverse discrimination p314-20

Nickel

Moran, T. H. The international political economy of Cuban nickel development. *In* Cuba in the world p257-72

Nickels, Cameron Charles

Franklin's Poor Richard's almanacs: "the humblest of his labors." *In* Lemay, J. A. L. ed. The oldest revolutionary p77-89

Nicol, Bernard de Bear. See Jones, T. B. jt. auth.

Nicolaus Causanius, Cardinal

About

Joda, R. Nicholas of Cusa: precursor of humanism. *In* Hoffmeister, G. ed. The Renaissance and Reformation in Germany p33-49

Nicolaus de Autricuria

About

Copleston, F. C. The logical empiricism of Nicholas of Autrecourt. *In* Copleston, F. C. Philosophers and philosophies p79-89

Moody, E. A. Ockham, Buridan, and Nicholas of Autrecourt. *In* Moody, E. A. Studies in medieval philosophy, science, and logic p127-60

Weinberg, J. R. Fourteenth- and twentieth-century positivism. *In* Weinberg, J. R. Ockham, Descartes, and Hume p50-67

Nicole, Roger Robert

Some comments on Hebrews 6:4-6 and the doctrine of the perseverance of God with the saints. *In* Current issues in Biblical and patristic interpretation p355-64

Nicoll, Allardyce

World drama

(See note in: List of books indexed)

Contents

The American advent and dramatic revolution in Poland

Aristophanes and the Old Comedy

Changes and chances

Comedy and extravaganza

Comedy, tragedy, and melodrama in Italy

The comic spirit and social unrest

The coming of realism

The dawn of realism: Euripides

The drama of China

The drama of the individual

Early seventeenth-century tragedy and comedy

Eugene O'Neill

The expressionistic movement

The extension of the realistic

The first dramatist: Aeschylus

French romanticism and classicism

From Menander to the mimes

From tragedy to melodrama

The glory of the Greek theatre: Sophocles

The growth of bourgeois comedy

The independent theatre in Germany

The international theatre of the Jesuits

The Japanese drama

Molière and the comedy of manners

Neo-romanticism in the theatre

The play of ideas in France

The poetic stage

The popular beginnings

The popular play: the commedia dell'arte

Post-war drama in Italy

Purposeful laughter: George Bernard Shaw

Racine and the tragedy of sentiment

Realism in diverse lands: Italy, Spain, England, Russia

Realism, social and otherwise

The realm of fancy

The relics of the older realism

Religious drama and profane during the Middle Ages

The Restoration comedy of manners

The revival of poetic drama

The Sanskrit drama

Shakespeare and his predecessors

The Spanish stage under Lope de Vega and Calderón

Strindberg and the play of the subconscious

The theatre symbolic and theatrical

Tragedy and opera

The triumph of realism: Ibsen

The vogue of the historical play

The wave of sentimentalism

Nicoll, John Ramsay Allardyce. See Nicoll, Allardyce

Nicolson, Sir Harold George

Zuleika Dobson—a revaluation. *In* Riewald, J. G. ed. The surprise of excellence p30-37

Nicolson, I. F.

Nigeria: wars cold and hot, and lukewarm ideas. *In* Siracusa, J. M. and Barclay, G. S. eds. The impact of the Cold war p84-100

Nicolson, Nigel

About individual works

Portrait of a marriage

Trilling, D. Portrait of a marriage. *In* Trilling, D. We must march my darlings p307-15

Nida, Eugene Albert. See Part 2 under title: On Language, culture, and religion: in honor of Eugene A. Nida

Nida, Eugene Albert; Louw, Johannes P. and Smith, Rondal B.
Semantic domains and componential analysis of meaning. *In* Current issues in linguistic theory p139-67

Niebuhr, Barthold Georg

About

Momigliano, A. Perizonius, Niebuhr and the character of early Roman tradition. *In* Momigliano, A. Essays in ancient and modern historiography p231-51

Niebuhr, Helmut Richard

About

Mawhinney, J. J. H. Richard Niebuhr and reshaping American Christianity. *In* America in theological perspective p140-62

Niebuhr, Reinhold

About

Brown, R. M. Reinhold Niebuhr: a study in humanity and humility. *In* Scott, N. A. ed. The legacy of Reinhold Niebuhr p 1-7
Gilkey, L. B. Reinhold Niebuhr's theology of history. *In* Scott, N. A. ed. The legacy of Reinhold Niebuhr p36-62
Marty, M. E. Reinhold Niebuhr: public theology and the American experience. *In* Scott, N. A. ed. The legacy of Reinhold Niebuhr p8-35
Scott, N. A. Introduction. *In* Scott, N. A. ed. The legacy of Reinhold Niebuhr p ix-xxiv
Scott, N. A. Reinhold Niebuhr. *In* Ross, R. G. ed. Makers of American thought p227-61
Shinn, R. L. Realism, radicalism, and eschatology in Reinhold Niebuhr: a reassessment. *In* Scott, N. A. ed. The legacy of Reinhold Niebuhr p85-99
Thompson, K. W. Niebuhr as thinker and doer. *In* Scott, N. A. ed. The legacy of Reinhold Niebuhr p100-10

About individual works
Faith and history
Frye, N. The rhythm of growth and decay. *In* Frye, N. Northrop Frye on culture and literature p141-46

Ethics
Coffey, J. W. The Christian realism of Reinhold Niebuhr. *In* Political realism in American thought p79-124
Gamwell, F. I. Reinhold Niebuhr's theistic ethic. *In* Scott, N. A. ed. The legacy of Reinhold Niebuhr p63-84

Political science
Coffey, J. W. The Christian realism of Reinhold Niebuhr. *In* Political realism in American thought p79-124

Nielsen, Kai
True needs, rationality and emancipation. *In* Fitzgerald, R. ed. Human needs and politics p142-56

About

Flew, A. G. N. Wants or needs, choices or commands. *In* Fitzgerald, R. ed. Human needs and politics p213-28

Niemeyer, Gerhart
The commitments of political education. *In* A Public philosophy reader p246-56
The loss and recovery of history. *In* A Public philosophy reader p203-17

Niesen, George
The artist against the reality in the plays of Tennessee Williams. *In* Tennessee Williams: a tribute p463-93

Niess, Robert Judson
Zola's Au bonheur des dames: the making of a symbol. *In* Symbolism and modern literature p130-50

Nietzsche, Friedrich Wilhelm
Glicksberg, C. I. Introduction. *In* Glicksberg, C. I. The literature of nihilism p9-33

About

Andrew, E. The unity of theory and practice: the science of Marx and Nietzsche. *In* Political theory and praxis p117-37
Arendt, H. Conclusions. *In* Arendt, H. The life of the mind v2 p147-217
Baeumer, M. L. Nietzsche and the tradition of the Dionysian. *In* O'Flaherty, J. C.; Sellner, T. F. and Helm, R. M. eds. Studies in Nietzsche and the classical tradition p165-89
Biser, E. Between Inferno and Purgatorio: thoughts on a structural comparison of Nietzsche with Dante. *In* O'Flaherty, J. C.; Sellner, T. F. and Helm, R. M. eds. Studies in Nietzsche and the classical tradition p55-70
Boulby, M Nietzsche and the finis Latinorum. *In* O'Flaherty, J. C.; Sellner, T. F. and Helm, R. M. eds. Studies in Nietzsche and the classical tradition p214-33
Brashear, W. R. Nietzsche and Spengler on Hamlet. *In* Brashear, W. R. The gorgon's head p15-26
Copleston, F. C. Foreground and background in Nietzsche. *In* Copleston, F. C. Philosophers and philosophies p117-30
Foucault, M. Nietzsche, genealogy, history. *In* Foucault, M. Language, counter-memory, practice p139-64
Fraser, R. S. Nietzsche, Byron, and the classical tradition. *In* O'Flaherty, J. C.; Sellner, T. F. and Helm, R. M. eds. Studies in Nietzsche and the classical tradition p190-98
Gilman, S. L. Parody and parallel: Heine, Nietzsche, and the classical world. *In* O'Flaherty, J. C.; Sellner, T. F. and Helm, R. M. eds. Studies in Nietzsche and the classical tradition p199-213
Girard, R. Strategies of madness—Nietzsche, Wagner, and Dostoevski. *In* Girard, R. "To double business bound" p61-83
Heller, E. Nietzsche in the waste land. *In* Heller, E. The poet's self and the poem p28-50
Helm, R. M. Plato in the thought of Nietzsche and Augustine. *In* O'Flaherty, J. C.; Sellner, T. F. and Helm, R. M. eds. Studies in Nietzsche and the classical tradition p16-32
Jacobs, C. Nietzsche: the stammering text: the fragmentary studies preliminary to The birth of tragedy. *In* Jacobs, C. The dissimulating harmony p 1-22
Kaufmann, W. A. Nietzsche and the death of tragedy: a critique. *In* O'Flaherty, J. C.; Sellner, T. F. and Helm, R. M. eds. Studies in Nietzsche and the classical tradition p234-54
Lloyd-Jones, H. Nietzsche and the study of the ancient world. *In* O'Flaherty, J. C.; Sellner, T. F. and Helm, R. M. eds. Studies in Nietzsche and the classical tradition p 1-15

Nietzsche, Friedrich W.—About—*Continued*

Pütz, H. P. Nietzsche: art and intellectual inquiry. *In* Pasley, J. M. S. ed. Nietzsche: imagery and thought p 1-32

Rehder, H. The reluctant disciple: Nietzsche and Schiller. *In* O'Flaherty, J. C.; Sellner, T. F. and Helm, R M. eds. Studies in Nietzsche and the classical tradition p156-64

Said, E. W. Conrad and Nietzsche. *In* Joseph Conrad: a commemoration p65-76

Schlechta, K. The German "classicist" Goethe as reflected in Nietzsche's works. *In* O'Flaherty, J. C.; Sellner, T. F. and Helm, R. M. eds. Studies in Nietzsche and the classical tradition p144-55

Scott, N. A. Friedrich Nietzsche—evangelist of the death of God. *In* Scott, N. A. Mirrors of man in existentialism p60-87

Stern, J P. Nietzsche and the idea of metaphor. *In* Pasley, J. M. S. ed. Nietzsche: imagery and thought p64-82

Williams, W. D. Nietzsche's masks. *In* Pasley, J. M. S ed Nietzsche: imagery and thought p83-103

Wingler, H. Aristotle in the thought of Nietzsche and Thomas Aquinas. *In* O'Flaherty, J. C.; Sellner, T. F. and Helm, R. M. eds. Studies in Nietzsche and the classical tradition p33-54

About individual works
The birth of tragedy

Cordle, T. H. Malraux and Nietzsche's Birth of tragedy. *In* Garvin, H. R. ed. Makers of the twentieth-century novel p133-43

Hester, M. The structure of tragedy and the art of painting. *In* O'Flaherty, J. C.; Sellner, T. F. and Helm, R. M. eds. Studies in Nietzsche and the classical tradition p71-88

Jacobs, C. Nietzsche: the stammering text: the fragmentary studies preliminary to The birth of tragedy. *In* Jacobs, C The dissimulating harmony p 1-22

Lenson, D. R. The other tragedy. *In* Lenson, D. R. Achilles' choice p137-58

O'Flaherty, J. C. Socrates in Hamann's Socratic memorabilia and Nietzsche's Birth of tragedy. *In* O'Flaherty, J. C. ; Sellner, T. F. and Helm, R. M. eds. Studies in Nietzsche and the classical tradition p134-43

Weinberg, K. The impact of ancient Greece and of French classicism on Nietzsche's concept of tragedy. *In* O'Flaherty, J. C.; Sellner, T. F. and Helm, R. M. eds. Studies in Nietzsche and the classical tradition p89-108

Ecce homo

Ryan, M. The act. *In* Glyph 2 p64-87

Human, all-too-human

Heller, P. Nietzsche in his relation to Voltaire and Rousseau. *In* O'Flaherty, J. C.; Sellner, T. F. and Helm, R. M. eds. Studies in Nietzsche and the classical tradition p109-33

Thus spake Zarathustra

Bruford, W. H. Friedrich Nietzsche: Also sprach Zarathustra (1883-5). *In* Bruford, W. H. The German tradition of self-cultivation p164-89

Heller, E. Nietzsche in the waste land. *In* Heller, E. The poet's self and the poem p28-50

Luke, F. D. Nietzsche and the imagery of height. *In* Pasley, J. M. S. ed. Nietzsche: imagery and thought p104-22

Webb, E. The ambiguities of secularization: modern transformations of the Kingdom in Nietzsche, Ibsen, Beckett, and Stevens. *In* Webb, E. The dark dove p34-87

Aesthetics

Pütz, H. P. Nietzsche: art and intellectual inquiry. *In* Pasley, J. M. S. ed. Nietzsche: imagery and thought p 1-32

Ethics

Foot, P. Nietzsche: the revaluation of values. *In* Foot, P. Virtues and vices, and other essays in moral philosophy p81-95

Influence

Bridgwater, P. English writers and Nietzsche. *In* Pasley, J. M. S. ed. Nietzsche: imagery and thought p220-58

Reed, T. J. Nietzsche's animals: idea, image and influence. *In* Pasley, J. M S. ed. Nietzsche: imagery and thought p159-219

Influence—Malraux

Cordle, T. H. Malraux and Nietzsche's Birth of tragedy. *In* Garvin, H. R. ed. Makers of the twentieth-century novel p133-43

Influence—O'Neill, Eugene
Gladstone, 1888-1953

Brashear, W. R. The wisdom of Silenus: O'Neill's spiritual ancestors. *In* Brashear, W. R. The gorgon's head p104-33

Knowledge, Theory of

Warnock, M. Nietzsche's conception of truth. *In* Pasley, J. M S. ed. Nietzsche: imagery and thought p33-63

Language

Luke, F. D. Nietzsche and the imagery of height. *In* Pasley, J. M. S. ed. Nietzsche: imagery and thought p104-22

Pasley, J. M. S. Nietzsche's use of medical terms. *In* Pasley, J. M. S. ed. Nietzsche: imagery and thought p123-58

Stern, J. P. Nietzsche and the idea of metaphor. *In* Pasley, J. M. S. ed. Nietzsche: imagery and thought p64-82

Nigeria
Achebe, C. Named for Victoria, Queen of England. *In* Achebe, C. Morning yet on creation day p115-24

Constitutional history

Ojo, A. Law and government in Nigeria. *In* Smock, D. R. and Bentsi-Enchill, K. eds. The search for national integration in Africa p47-67

Foreign relations

Aluko, O. Nigerian foreign policy. *In* Aluko, O. ed. The foreign policies of African states p163-95

Nicolson, I. F. Nigeria: wars cold and hot, and lukewarm ideas. *In* Siracusa, J. M. and Barclay, G. S. eds. The impact of the Cold war p84-100

History

Ifeka-Moller, C. Female militancy and colonial revolt: the women's war of 1929, Eastern Nigeria. *In* Ardener, S. G. ed. Perceiving women p127-57

Nigeria—*Continued*

History—Civil War, 1967-1970

Achebe, C. The African writer and the Biafran cause. *In* Achebe, C. Morning yet on creation day p137-47

Červenka, Z. The OAU and the Nigerian Civil War. *In* El-Ayouty, Y. ed. The Organization of African Unity after ten years p152-73

Languages

Banjo, A. Language policy in Nigeria. *In* Smock, D. R. and Bentsi-Enchill, K. eds. The search for national integration in Africa p206-19

Military policy

Dudley, B. J. Military government and national integration in Nigeria. *In* Smock, D. R. and Bentsi-Enchill, K. eds. The search for national integration in Africa p28-46

Politics and government

Achebe, C. The African writer and the Biafran cause. *In* Achebe, C. Morning yet on creation day p137-47

Akinyemi, A. B. National unity within the context of regional relations: the Nigerian experience. *In* Smock, D. R. and Bentsi-Enchill, K. eds. The search for national integration in Africa p68-76

Cohen, R. The pull of opposites: incorporation and autonomy in Nigeria. *In* African themes p149-73

Dudley, B. J. Military government and national integration in Nigeria. *In* Smock, D. R. and Bentsi-Enchill, K. eds. The search for national integration in Africa p28-46

Otite, O. Encapsulated political systems *In* Colonialism and change p67-84

Politics and government—1960-

Nicolson, I. F. Nigeria: wars cold and hot, and lukewarm ideas. *In* Siracusa, J. M. and Barclay, G. S. eds. The impact of the Cold war p84-100

Social conditions

O'Flinn, J. P. Towards a sociology of the Nigerian novel. *In* African literature today no. 7: Focus on criticism p34-52

Nigeria in literature

Goonetilleke, D. C. R. A. Joyce Cary: the clash of cultures in Nigeria. *In* Goonetilleke, D. C. R. A. Developing countries in British fiction p199-244

Taiwo, O. Historical and cultural influences on the Nigerian novelists. *In* Taiwo, O. Culture and the Nigerian novel p 1-33

Nigerian bronzes. See Bronzes, Nigerian

Nigerian Civil War. See Nigeria—History—Civil War, 1967-1970

Nigerian fiction

History and criticism

Taiwo, O. Historical and cultural influence on the Nigerian novelists. *In* Taiwo, O. Culture and the Nigerian novel p 1-33

Nigerian fiction (English)

O'Flinn, J. P. Towards a sociology of the Nigerian novel. *In* African literature today no. 7: Focus on criticism p34-52

Nigerian literature

History and criticism

Achebe, C. The African writer and the Biafran cause. *In* Achebe, C. Morning yet on creation day p137-47

Achebe, C. Where angels fear to tread. *In* Achebe, C. Morning yet on creation day p75-79

Taiwo, O. Conclusion. *In* Taiwo, O. Culture and the Nigerian novel p210-14

Nigerians in Ghana

Eades, J. S. Kinship and entrepreneurship among Yoruba in northern Ghana. *In* Shack, W. A. and Skinner, E. P. eds. Strangers in African societies p169-82

Sudarkasa, N. From stranger to alien: the sociopolitical history of the Nigerian Yoruba in Ghana, 1900-1970. *In* Shack, W. A. and Skinner, E. P. eds. Strangers in African societies p141-67

Nighswonger, Carl A.

The vectors and vital signs in grief synchronization. *In* Anticipatory grief p267-75

Night in literature

Caistor, N. The image of night in Rene Char's poetry. *In* Cardinal, R. ed. Sensibility and creation p168-82

The night of the hunter (Motion picture)

Wood, R. Charles Laughton on Grubb Street. *In* Peary, G. and Shatzkin, R. eds. The modern American novel and the movies p204-14

The night porter (Motion picture)

Sarris, A. The nasty Nazis: history or mythology. *In* Sarris, A. Politics and cinema p85-91

Nightmares

Hufford, D. J. A new approach to the "old hag": the nightmare tradition reexamined. *In* American folk medicine p73-85

Nigro, Georgia. See Sternberg, R. J. jt. auth.

Nigro, Kirsten F.

From criollismo to the grotesque: approaches to José Donoso. *In* Forster, M. H. ed. Tradition and renewal p208-32

Nihilism. See Anarchism and anarchists; Terrorism

Nihilism (Philosophy)

Frank, S. L. The ethic of nihilism: a characterization of the Russian intelligentsia's moral outlook. *In* Landmarks p155-84

Glicksberg, C. I. Conclusion. *In* Glicksberg, C. I. The literature of nihilism p303-15

Glicksberg, C. I. Introduction. *In* Glicksberg, C. I. The literature of nihilism p9-33

Glicksberg, C. I. Religion and nihilism. *In* Glicksberg, C. I. The literature of nihilism p39-52

Glicksberg, C. I. Unamuno and the quest for faith. *In* Glicksberg, C. I. The literature of nihilism p53-70

See also Nothing (Philosophy)

Nihilism in literature

Glicksberg, C. I. Albert Camus: from nihilism to revolt. *In* Glicksberg, C. I. The literature of nihilism p198-209

Glicksberg, C. I. The battle against the Absurd in France. *In* Glicksberg, C. I. The literature of nihilism p142-54

Glicksberg, C. I. Conclusion. *In* Glicksberg, C. I. The literature of nihilism p303-15

Nissan Island

Social policy

Chan, G. and Saini, B. S. Integrated farming system and settlement plan for Nissan Island, Papua New Guinea. *In* Strategies for human settlements: habitat and environment p45-66

Nitchie, George Wilson

Robert Frost: some reflections on poetry and power. *In* Frost: centennial essays II p40-47

Niter in literature. See Saltpeter in literature

Nitze, Paul Henry

The global military balance. *In* Kirk, G. L. and Wessell, N. H. eds. The Soviet threat p4-14

Nitze, William Albert

Influence—Mann

Johnson, E. B. An unpublished letter of Thomas Mann concerning a nonsource for Doctor Faustus. *In* Strelka, J. P.; Bell, R. F. and Dobson, E. eds. Protest—form—tradition p15-34

Niven, Alastair

The Scottish element in Commonwealth literature. *In* Narasimhaiah, C. D. ed. Awakened conscience p29-41

Niven, Frederick John

About

Singleton, M. K. Frederick Niven redivivus: a Scots-Canadian's Pacific Northwest. *In* Bingham, E. R. and Love, G. A. eds. Northwest perspectives p122-35

Nivernais

Social conditions

Thuillier, G. Water supplies in nineteenth-century Nivernais. *In* Food and drink in history p109-25

Nixon, John William

To live and die in Dixie. *In* The Rising South v2 p95-116

Nixon, Raymond Blalock

Factors related to freedom in national press systems. *In* Fischer, H. D. and Merrill, J. C. eds. International and intercultural communication p148-60

Nixon, Richard Milhous, President U.S.

About

Atherton, A. L. The Nixon administration and the Arab-Israeli conflict. *In* The New world balance and peace in the Middle East: reality or mirage? p196-208

Brustein, R. S. Thebes and Watergate. *In* Brustein, R. S. The culture watch p94-96

Finger, S. M. The Nixon Doctrine and the Middle East. *In* The New world balance and peace in the Middle East: reality or mirage? p209-16

Johnson, J. T. Just war, the Nixon Doctrine and the future shape of American military policy. *In* The Year book of world affairs, 1975 p137-54

About individual works

The memoirs of Richard Nixon

Galbraith, J. K. RN: the memoirs of Richard Nixon. *In* Galbraith, J. K. Annals of an abiding liberal p346-50

Nizard, Lucien

Planning as the regulatory reproduction of the status quo. *In* Planning, politics and public policy p433-44

Njau, Rebecca

About

Mbughuni, L. A. Old and new drama from East Africa. *In* African literature today no. 8: Drama in Africa p85-98

Nketia, J. H. Kwabena

The musical heritage of Africa. *In* Mintz, S. W. ed. Slavery, colonialism, and racism p151-61

Nkosi, Lewis

Post-war drama in Africa. *In* Nicoll, A. World drama p895-99

Nmolim, Charles E.

Jungian archetypes and the main characters in Oyono's Une vie de boy. *In* African literature today no. 7: Focus on criticism p117-22

No, no, Nanette (criticism) Harbach, O. A. and Mandel, F. *In* Simon, J. I. Singularities p126-32

Nō plays

Rimer, J. T. Source books II: The tale of the Heike and the nō drama. *In* Rimer, J. T. Modern Japanese fiction and its traditions p97-122

History and criticism

Nicoll, A. The Japanese drama. *In* Nicoll, A. World drama p546-61

Nobel prizes

Connolly, C. My Nobel prize. *In* Connolly, C. The evening colonnade p437-40

Nobility

Freed, J. B. The origins of the European nobility: the problem of the ministerials. *In* Viator: medieval and Renaissance studies v7 p211-41

See also Aristocracy; and subdivision Nobility under names of countries e.g. France—Nobility

Noble, Stedman B.

Resources and the political options facing the United States. *In* Isolation or interdependence? p167-92

Noble savage

Echeruo, M. J. C. The exo-cultural hero of the Enlightenment. *In* Echeruo, M. J. C. The conditioned imagination from Shakespeare to Conrad p71-92

Washburn, W. E. The clash of morality in the American forest. *In* First images of America p335-50

White, H. V. The Noble savage theme as fetish. *In* First images of America p121-35

Also in White, H. V. Tropics of discourse p183-96

Nochlin, Linda

Realism now. *In* Battcock, G. ed. Super realism p111-25

Some women realists. *In* Battcock, G. ed. Super realism p64-78

Nock, Albert Jay

American education; excerpt from "Free speech and plain language." *In* Crunden, R. M. ed. The superfluous men p60-71

Anarchist's progress; excerpt from "On doing the right thing, and other essays." *In* Crunden, R. M. ed. The superfluous men p28-43

Pantagruelism. *In* Crunden, R. M. ed. The superfluous men p98-106

Nock, Albert J.—*Continued*

About

Nock, A. J. Anarchist's progress; excerpt from "On doing the right thing, and other essays." *In* Crunden, R. M. ed. The superfluous men p28-43

Noel, Thomas

Theories of the fable in the eighteenth century

Contents

Aesop as a popular figure and the fable in England

Dissolution of a functioning literary genre

Dodsley and England at mid-century

The fable in Germany during the first half-century

French ideas at mid-century

Herder and the romantic turn

La Fontaine and the seventeenth-century forerunners

Lessing's Aesopian fables and the anti-Lessing

The popularity of the fable and the rationale

Rousseau and the fable in education

Samaniego, Iriarte, and the fable in Spain

Theories of the fable: La Motte and Richer

Noel Hume, Ivor

Material culture with the dirt on it: a Virginian perspective. *In* Material culture and the study of American life p21-40

Noema, Husserl's concept of the. Solomon, R. C. *In* Elliston, F. A. and McCormick, P. eds. Husserl p168-81

Noguchi, Tetsurō. See Sakai, T. jt. auth.

Nohrnberg, James Carson

The Iliad. *In* Seidel, M. A. and Mendelson, E. eds. Homer to Brecht p3-29

The Inferno. *In* Seidel, M. A. and Mendelson, E. eds. Homer to Brecht p76-104

Nokes, Peter L.

The evaluation of penal systems. *In* Progress in penal reform p68-82

Nolan, Barbara

The Gothic visionary perspective

Contents

Anagogy, aevum and two later medieval visionary arts

The later medieval spiritual quest: through time to aevum

New directions in twelfth-century spirituality

Pearl: a fourteenth-century vision in August

The vita nuova: Dante's Book of Revelation

Will's dark visions of Piers the Plowman

Nolan, Thomas

Ritual and therapy. *In* Anticipatory grief p358-64

Nolen, John

About

Goist, P. D. Planning the American city: Charles Mulford Robinson and John Nolen. *In* Goist, P. D. From Main Street to State Street p121-42

Nolte, Richard H.

American relations with the Arab states and Israel. *In* The New world balance and peace in the Middle East: reality or mirage? p181-89

Nolutshungu, Sam C.

The impact of external opposition on South African politics. *In* Thompson, L. M. and Butler, J. eds. Change in contemporary South Africa p369-99

Nomenclature. See Names

Nominalism

Gilbert, N. W. Richard de Bury and the "quires of yesterday's sophisms." *In* Philosophy and humanism p229-57

Moody, E. A. Buridan and a dilemma of nominalism. *In* Moody, E. A. Studies in medieval philosophy, science, and logic p353-70

See also Reality

Nominations for office. See Political conventions

Nomura, Kichisaburō

About

Conroy, H. F. Nomura Kichisaburō: the diplomacy of drama and desperation. *In* Burns, R. D. and Bennett, E. M. eds. Diplomats in crisis p297-316

The **Nonaligned** News Agencies Pool and the free flow of meaningful news: an African viewpoint. Olasope, B. *In* Horton, P. C. ed. The Third World and press freedom p162-72

Non-alignment. See Neutrality

Noncombatants (International law) See Combatants and noncombatants (International law)

Nonconformists. See Dissenters

Nonconformists, Religious. See Dissenters, Religious

Nonconformity (Religion) See Dissenters, Religious

Non-Euclidean geometry. See Geometry, Non-Euclidean

Non-objective art. See Art, Abstract

Nonprofit corporations. See Corporations, Nonprofit

Nonproliferation, Nuclear. See Nuclear nonproliferation

Nonproliferation of nuclear weapons. See Atomic weapons and disarmament

Nonrecognition of governments. See Recognition (International law)

Nonselfgoverning territories. See Colonies; International trusteeships

Nonsense literature. See Nonsense-verses

Nonsense literature, English

History and criticism

Prickett, S. Consensus and nonsense: Lear and Carroll. *In* Prickett, S. Victorian fantasy p114-49

Nonsense-verses

Rother, J. Wallace Stevens as a nonsense poet. *In* Tennessee Studies in literature v21 p80-90

Nonsense-verses, English

History and criticism

Smith, A. J. M. Nonsense poetry and romanticism. *In* Essays in honor of Russel B. Nye p180-94

Nonverbal communication

Argyle, M. Non-verbal communication and language. *In* Royal Institute of Philosophy. Communication and understanding p63-78

Nonverbal communication in motion pictures

Eco, U. Articulations of the cinematic code. *In* Nichols, B. ed. Movies and methods p590-607

Metz, C. Current problem of film theory: Mitry's L'Esthetique et psychologie du cinema, vol. II. *In* Nichols, B. ed. Movies and methods p568-78

Pasolini, P. P. The cinema of poetry. *In* Nichols, B. ed. Movies and methods p542-58

Nonviolence

Eschen, D. von; Kirk, J. R. and Pinard, M. The problems of success—violence legitimized. *In* Laure, R. H. ed. Social movements and social change p203-26

See also Pacifism

Nonviolence. See Pacifism

Nook Farm

MacLeish, A. Eden in Hartford. *In* MacLeish, A. Riders on the earth p132-38

Noon in literature

Perella, N. J. Conclusion. *In* Perella, N. J. Midday in Italian literature p263-65

Perella, N. J. Eugenio Montale. *In* Perella, N. J. Midday in Italian literature p240-62

Perella, N. J. From Dante to Pindemonte. *In* Perella, N. J. Midday in Italian literature p33-69

Perella, N. J. Gabriele D'Annunzio. *In* Perella, N. J. Midday in Italian literature p114-44

Perella, N. J. Giuseppe Ungaretti. *In* Perella, N. J. Midday in Italian literature p201-39

Perella, N. J. Introduction. *In* Perella, N. J. Midday in Italian literature p3-32

Perella, N. J. The nineteenth century. *In* Perella, N. J. Midday in Italian literature p70-113

Perella, N. J. Some twentieth-century voices. *In* Perella, N. J. Midday in Italian literature p145-200

Noonan, John Thomas, 1926-

Marriage in Michoacán. *In* First images of America p351-62

Who was Rolandus? *In* Law, church, and society p21-48

Nooten, Barend A. Van. See Van Nooten, Barend, A.

Nora, Pierre

America and the French intellectuals. *In* A New America? p325-37

Norberg, Anders See Akerman, S. jt. auth.

Nordenstreng, Kaarle

From mass media to mass consciousness. *In* Gerbner, G. ed. Mass media policies in changing cultures p269-83

Recent developments in European communications theory. *In* Fischer, H. D. and Merrill, J. C. eds. International and intercultural communication p457-65

Nordholt, J. W. Schulte. See Schulte Nordholt, J. W.

Norfolk, England

Social life and customs

Allen, D. G. A tale of two towns: persistent English localism in seventeenth-century Massachusetts. *In* Allen, H. C. and Thompson, R. eds. Contrast and connection p 1-35

Norfolk, Va.

History

Roeber, A. G. A New England woman's perspective on Norfolk, Virginia, 1801-1802: excerpts from the diary of Ruth Henshaw Bascom. *In* American Antiquarian Society. Proceedings v88 pt2 p277-328

Norford, George E.

The popular media: Part II, The Black role in radio and television. *In* The Black American reference book p875-88

Norman, Charles

About individual works

The magic-maker, E. E. Cummings

Connolly, C. E. E. Cummings. *In* Connolly, C. The evening colonnade p281-84

Norman, Richard

The neutral teacher? *In* Philosophers discuss education p172-87

Normandy

Charters, grants, privileges

Chibnall, M. Charter and chronicle: the use of archive sources by Norman historians. *In* Church and government in the Middle Ages p 1-17

History

Breese, L. W. The persistence of Scandinavian connections in Normandy in the tenth and early eleventh centuries. *In* Viator: medieval and Renaissance studies v8 p47-61

Radding, C. M. The administrators of the aids in Normandy, 1360-1380. *In* Order and innovation in the Middle Ages p41-53

Rural conditions

Le Roy Ladurie, E. In Normandy's woods and fields. *In* Le Roy Ladurie, E. The territory of the historian p133-71

Norris, Frank

About

Frohock, W. M. Frank Norris. *In* Walcutt, C. C. ed. Seven novelists in the American naturalist tradition p55-91

About individual works

The octopus

Davison, R. A. Frank Norris' The octopus: some observations on Vanamee, Shelgrim and St Paul. *In* Literature and ideas in America p182-203

Frohock, W. M. Frank Norris. *In* Walcutt, C. C. ed. Seven novelists in the American naturalist tradition p55-91

The pit

Davison, R. A. A reading of Frank Norris's The pit. *In* The Stoic strain in American literature p77-94

Characters

Davison, R. A. Frank Norris' The octopus: some observations on Vanamee, Shelgrim and St Paul. *In* Literature and ideas in America p182-203

Norris, John

About

Grant, P. Conclusion. John Norris and Mr Locke: bodies and the uses of imagination. *In* Grant, P. Images and ideas in literature of the English Renaissance p192-209

Grant, P. John Norris and the Oratorians: belief and the images in God. *In* Grant, P. Images and ideas in literature of the English Renaissance p154-91

Norris, John—*Continued*

About individual works

An essay towards the theory of the ideal or intelligible world

Grant, P. John Norris and the Oratorians: belief and the images in God. *In* Grant, P. Images and ideas in literature of the English Renaissance p154-91

North, Christopher, pseud. See Wilson, John, 1785-1854

North, Frederick, 2d Earl of Guilford

About

Brown, A. S. The impossible dream: the North ministry, the structure of politics, and conciliation. *In* The American Revolution and "a candid world" p17-39

North, Helen F.

The mare, the vixen, and the bee: sophrosyne as the virtue of women in antiquity. *In* Illinois classical studies, v2 1977 p35-48

North, John David

Chronology and the age of the world. *In* Cosmology, history, and theology p307-33

North Africa

History

Spencer, W. Ottoman North Africa. *In* Nationalism in a non-national state p103-27

North African fiction (French)

History and criticism

Accad, E. The theme of sexual oppression in the North African novel. *In* Beck, L. and Keddie, N. R. eds. Women in the Muslim world p617-28

Yetiv, I. Alienation in the modern novel of French North Africa before independence. *In* Exile and tradition p85-97

North American Conference on the Social Implications of Industrialization and Technological Change, Chicago, 1960

About individual works

Industrialization and society

Thrupp, S. L. Tradition and development: a choice of views. *In* Thrupp, S. L. Society and history p198-206

North American Indians. See Indians of North America

North American Review

Doubleday, N. F. Doctrine for fiction in the North American Review: 1815-1826. *In* Literature and ideas in America p20-39

North Atlantic Treaty Organization

Blau, T. Consultations in NATO during and after the October War. *In* International terrorism and world security p234-47

Brown, S. A world of multiple relationships. *In* Atlantis lost p103-18

Carlton, D. The doctrine of tactical nuclear warfare and some alternatives. *In* The Dynamics of the arms race p135-42

Cavalletti, F. Contributions of Western Europe to disarmament. *In* The Dynamics of the arms race p143-59

Erickson, J. The European military balance. *In* Kirk, G. L. and Wessell, N. H. eds. The Soviet threat p110-21

Garnett, J. C. Limited conventional war in the nuclear age. *In* Howard, M. ed. Restraints on war p79-102

Holst, J. W. NATO, the European Community, and the transatlantic order. *In* The New Atlantic challenge p265-77

Kaplan, L. S. The Korean War and U.S. foreign relations: the case of NATO. *In* The Korean War p36-75

Packard, D. Perceptions of the military balance. *In* The New Atlantic challenge p203-16

Ravenal, E. C. Alliance dissolution and American disengagement. *In* Atlantis lost p205-24

Schmidt, H. H. W. New tasks for the Atlantic Alliance. *In* The Year book of world affairs, 1975 p22-33

Steel, R. The abdication of Europe. *In* Atlantis lost p47-63

North Carolina

Social life and customs

Robbins, W. L. Wishing in and shooting in the New Year among the Germans in the Carolinas. *In* Yoder, D. ed. American folklife p257-79

Social life and customs—Colonial period, ca. 1600-1775

Kay, M. L. M. and Cary, L. L. Class, mobility, and conflict in North Carolina. *In* The Southern experience in the American Revolution p109-51

Northam, John Richard

Waiting for Prospero. *In* English drama: forms and development p186-202

Northedge, Frederick Samuel

British foreign policy in a Community context. *In* Twitchett, K. J. ed. Europe and the world p175-95

Northern Buddhism. See Mahayana Buddhism

Northern Ireland

History—1969-

Bell, J. B. Strategy, tactics, and terror: an Irish perspective. *In* International terrorism p65-89

Politics and government

Schmitt, D. E. Ethnic conflict in Northern Ireland: international aspects of conflict management. *In* Esman, M. J. ed. Ethnic conflict in the Western world p228-50

Northern vehicle. See Mahayana Buddhism

Northern Wei dynasty. See China—History—Northern Wei dynasty, 386-534

Northfield Mount Hermon School

Jones, H. L. Breaking the synergism barrier. *In* Managing nonprofit organizations p252-57

Northmen in England

Fellows Jensen, G. The Vikings in England: a review. *In* Anglo-Saxon England 4 p181-206

Northrop, Filmer Stuart Cuckow

About individual works

The meeting of East and West

Frye, N. Total identification. *In* Frye, N. Northrop Frye on culture and literature p107-10

Northwest, Pacific

Bibliography

Tonsfeldt, W. The Pacific Northwest: a selected and annotated bibliography. *In* Bingham, E. R. and Love, G. A. eds. Northwest perspectives p219-35

Northwest, Pacific—*Continued*

History

Clark, N. H. Notes for a tricentennial historian. *In* Bingham, E. R. and Love, G. A eds. Northwest perspectives p44-58

Northwest, Pacific in literature

Etulain, R. W. Ernest Haycox: popular novelist of the Pacific Northwest. *In* Bingham, E. R. and Love, G. A. eds. Northwest perspectives p136-50

Singleton, M. K. Frederick Niven redivivus: a Scots-Canadian's Pacific Northwest. *In* Bingham, E. R. and Love, G. A. eds. Northwest perspectives p122-35

Vanderbilt, K. Theodore Roethke as a Northwest poet. *In* Bingham, E. R. and Love, G. A. eds. Northwest perspectives p186-216

Northwest Passage

Allen, J. L. Thomas Jefferson and the passage to India: a pre-exploratory image. *In* Pattern and process p103-13

Nortje, Arthur

About

Dameron, C. Arthur Nortje: craftsman for his muse. *In* Heywood, C. ed. Aspects of South African literature p155-62

Norton, Augustus R.

Moscow and the Palestinians: a new tool of Soviet policy in the Middle East. *In* The Palestinians p228-48

Norton, Dolores G.

Residential environment and Black self-image. *In* The Diverse society: implications for social policy p75-89

Norton, James Adolphus

The interaction of state and Federal policy. *In* Hook, S.; Kurtz, P. W. and Todorovich, M. eds. The university and the state: what role for government in higher education? p73-76

Notes from a diary. *In* The Third century p181-87

Norton, Mary Beth

"What an alarming crisis is this": Southern women and the American Revolution. *In* The Southern experience in the American Revolution p203-34

Norway

Economic conditions

Erichsen, E. Norway: twenty years after the Marshall plan. *In* Inflation, trade and taxes p163-77

Norwegian Americans

Bjork, K. O. The Norwegians in America: "giants in the earth." *In* The Immigrant experience in America p63-94

Norwegian sculpture. See Sculpture, Norwegian

Norwegians in the United States. See Norwegian Americans

Norwich, England

History

Carter, A. The Anglo-Saxon origins of Norwich: the problems and approaches. *In* Anglo-Saxon England 7 p175-204

Norwid, Cyprian

About individual works

Krakus

Sławińska, I. Two concepts of time in dramatic structure: Turgenev and Norwid. *In* For Wiktor Weintraub p479-92

Norwid, Kamil Cyprian. See Norwid, Cyprian

Notaries

Genoa—History

Kedar, B. Z. The Genoese notaries of 1382: the anatomy of an urban occupational group. *In* The Medieval city p73-94

Nothing (Philosophy)

Frings, M. S. Nothingness and being: a Schelerian comment. *In* Radical phenomenology p182-89

Rosen, S. Thinking about nothing. *In* Murray, M. E. ed. Heidegger and modern philosophy p116-37

Nothingness (Philosophy). See Nothing (Philosophy)

Notice (Law)

Dam, K. W. Class action notice: who needs it? *In* The Supreme Court review, 1974 p97-126

Noticias Argentinas

Kraiselburd, R. Establishing and maintaining a free press: a Latin American viewpoint. *In* Horton, P. C. ed. The Third World and press freedom p156-61

Nott, Kathleen

Ideology and poetry. *In* The Waste land in different voices p203-20

The Trojan horses: Koestler and the behaviourists. *In* Harris, H. A. ed. Astride the two cultures p162-74

Nottebohm, Gustav

About

Lockwood, L. Nottebohm revisited. *In* Current thought in musicology p139-91

Nova Scotia

Race question

Walker, J. W. S. The establishment of a free Black community in Nova Scotia, 1783-1840. *In* Kilson, M. L. and Rotberg, R. I. eds. The African diaspora p205-36

Novae. See Stars, New

Novak, Maximillian E.

Criticism, adaptation, politics, and the Shakespearean model of Dryden's All for love. *In* Studies in eighteenth-century culture v7 p375-87

Novak, Michael

The banality of evil. *In* Decline of the West? George Kennan and his critics p71-74

Conclusion: social trust. *In* Parents, teachers, and children: prospects for choice in American education p257-78

The Nation with the soul of a church; excerpt from "Choosing our king: powerful symbols in Presidential politics." *In* A Public philosophy reader p92-96

Rooting, agon; excerpt from "The joy of sports: end zones, bases, baskets, balls, and the consecration of the American spirit." *In* A Public philosophy reader p279-87

Television shapes the soul. *In* Television as a social force: new approaches to TV criticism p9-21

About individual works

The use of the unmeltable ethnics

Sheed, W. The subject of ethnics. *In* Sheed, W. The good word & other words p142-47

Novak, Robert D. See Evans, R. jt. auth.

Novalis, pseud. See Hardenberg, Friedrich Leopold, Freiherr

Novarr, David
Donne's 'Epithalamion made at Lincoln's Inn': context and date. *In* Roberts, J. R. ed. Essential articles for the study of John Donne's poetry p439-50

Nove, Alec
Agriculture. *In* Brown, A. H. and Kaser, M. eds. The Soviet Union since the fall of Khrushchev p 1-15
The political economy of the Allende regime. *In* O'Brien, P. I. ed. Allende's Chile p51-78
Some observations on Bukharin and his ideas. *In* Essays in honour of E. H. Carr p181-203
The structure of the Soviet state: the economy. *In* Auty, R. and Obolensky, D. eds. An introduction to Russian history p350-65

Novelists
Graham, W. The novelist as a human being. *In* Royal Society of Literature of the United Kingdom, London. Essays by divers hands v39 p47-66

Novelists, English

19th century
Sutherland, J. A. Craft versus trade: novelists and publishers. *In* Sutherland, J. A. Victorian novelists and publishers p72-98

Il novellino
Segre, C. Deconstruction and reconstruction of a tale: from La mort le roi Artu to the Novellino. *In* Segre, C. Structures and time p58-64

Novels. See Fiction; Plots (Drama, novel, etc.)

Novelty books. See Toy and movable books

Novgorod, Russia (Duchy)

History
Birnbaum, H. Lord Novgorod the Great: its place in medieval culture. *In* Viator: medieval and Renaissance studies v8 p215-54

Novgorod. Museum of History and Architecture. See Sophia church calendar (Icons)

Novogrod, John C.
Internal strife, self-determination, and world order. *In* International terrorism and political crimes p98-119

Novotny, Henry Rudolph Frank
The logic of the social sciences: to be, to do, or to describe? *In* Hook, S.; Kurtz, P. W. and Todorovich, M. eds. The philosophy of the curriculum: the need for general education p235-46
The New Class, and "Professor Bill." *In* Hook, S.; Kurtz, P. W., and Todorovich, M. eds. The university and the state: what role for government in higher education? p277-85
Objectivity and biased skepticism in higher education. *In* Hook, S.; Kurtz, P. and Todorovich, N. eds. The ethics of teaching and scientific research p61-69

Novum, SF and the. Suvin, D. *In* Suvin, D. Metamophoses of science fiction p63-89

Novy Mir. See Novyï Mir (Periodical)

Novyï Mir (Periodical)
Spechler, D. Permitted dissent in the decade after Stalin: criticism and protest in Novy Mir, 1953-1964. *In* Cocks, P.; Daniels, R. V. and Heer, N. W. eds. The dynamics of Soviet politics p28-50

Nowak, John E. See Glennon, R. J. jt. auth.

Nowell, Charles Edward
Old World origins of the Spanish-American viceregal system. *In* First images of America p221-30

Nowell, Elizabeth

About individual works
Thomas Wolfe, a biography
Connolly, C. Thomas Wolfe. *In* Connolly, C. The evening colonnade p277-80

Nowell, Laurence

About
Grant, R. J. S. Laurence Nowell's transcript of BM Cotton Otho B. xi. *In* Anglo-Saxon England 3 p111-24

Nowell-Smith, Geoffrey
Shape and a black point. *In* Nichols, B. ed. Movies and methods p354-63

Nowell-Smith, Patrick Horace

About individual works
Ethics
Couch, W. T. The sacred and golden cord. *In* Viva Vivas! p87-137

Nowitz, Leonie
Dying and the aged person: process and implications for social work practice. *In* Home care p185-95

Nowlan, Kevin B.
Modern Ireland: the birth and growth of the new state. *In* De Breffny, B. ed. The Irish world p255-80

Nowotny, Hans-Joachim Hoffmann- See Hoffmann-Nowotny, Hans-Joachim

Noxon, James Herbert
Remembering and imagining the past. *In* Livingston, D. W. and King, J. T. eds. Hume p270-95

Noyes, Arthur Amos

About
Kargon, R. H. Temple to science: cooperative research and the birth of the California Institute of Technology. *In* Historical studies in the physical sciences v8 p3-31

Noyes, Charles Edward
Welcome to Faulkner and Yoknapatawpha, 1977. *In* The Maker and the myth: Faulkner and Yoknapatawpha, 1977 pxi-xiv

Noyes, John Humphrey

About
Klass, D. Psychohistory and communal patterns: John Humphrey Noyes and the Oneida Community. *In* Reynolds, F. E. and Capps, D. eds. The biographical process p273-96

Ntshona, Winston. See Fugard, A. jt. auth.

Nuclear chemistry. See Nuclear physics

Nuclear energy. See Atomic energy

Nuclear-free zones. See Atomic-weapon-free zones

Nuclear fuels

Estimates and costs
Gilinsky, V. Fuelling the Western world's reactors: problems and issues. *In* International terrorism and world security p140-57

Nuclear masses. See Atomic mass

Nuclear nonproliferation
Schütze, W. A world of many nuclear powers. *In* Griffiths, F. and Polanyi, J. C. eds. The dangers of nuclear war p85-92

See also Arms control; Atomic power—International control; Atomic-weapon-free zones; Atomic weapons and disarmament

Nuclear particles. See Particles (Nuclear physics)

Nuclear physics
Serwer, D. Unmechanischer Zwang: Pauli, Heisenberg, and the rejection of the mechanical atom, 1923-1925. *In* Historical studies in the physical sciences v8 p189-256

See also Chemistry, Physical and theoretical; Particles (Nuclear physics)

History
Garber, E. Molecular science in late-nineteenth century Britain. *In* Historical studies in the physical sciences v9 p265-97

Nuclear reactors
Baker, S. J. The international political economy of proliferation. *In* Arms control and technological innovation p70-101

See also Fusion reactors

Fuel
See Nuclear fuels

Nuclear structure. See Atomic structure

Nuclear technology. See Nuclear nonproliferation

Nuclear warfare. See Atomic warfare

Nuclear-weapon-free zones. See Atomic-weapon-free zones

Nuclear weapons. See Atomic weapons

Nucleic acid synthesis
Cohen, S. S. On the origins of cells: the development of a Copernican revolution. *In* Neyman, J. ed. The heritage of Copernicus: theories "pleasing to the mind" p207-27

Nucleic acids
Margoliash, E. Informational macromolecules and biological evolution. *In* Neyman, J. ed. The heritage of Copernicus: theories "pleasing to the mind" p184-206

Nucleons. See Particles (Nuclear physics)

Nuclides. See Isotopes

Nuisances
Netherlands
Staatsen, A. A. M. F. Enforcement of the Nuisance Act in the Netherlands. *In* Davis, K. C. Discretionary justice in Europe and America p100-14

Nukunya, G. K.
The family and social change. *In* Colonialism and change p163-77

Number concept
Quine, W. V. Ontological reduction and the world of numbers. *In* Quine, W. V. The ways of paradox, and other essays p212-20

Number study. See Numbers, Theory of

Number symbolism. See Symbolism of numbers

Number theory. See Numbers, Theory of

Numbers, Natural. See Numbers, Theory of

Numbers, Theory of
Quine, W. V. Ontological reduction and the world of numbers. *In* Quine, W. V. The ways of paradox, and other essays p212-20

Numeraires, The case of the three. Harberger, A. C. *In* Economic development and planning p142-56

Numerals
History
Lemay, R. J. The Hispanic origin of our present numeral forms. *In* Viator: medieval and Renaissance studies v8 p435-59

Numerology. See Symbolism of numbers

Numismatics, Anglo-Saxon
Dolley, R. H. M. Towards a revision of the internal chronology of the coinages of Edward the Elder and Plegmund. *In* Anglo-Saxon England 3 p175-77

Lyon, S. Some problems in interpreting Anglo-Saxon coinage. *In* Anglo-Saxon England 5 p173-224

Smart, V. Corrections to Hildebrand's corpus of Anglo-Saxon moneyers: from Cnut to Edward the Confessor. *In* Anglo-Saxon England 4 p155-70

Numismatics, Greek
Vermeule, C. C. Interactions and reflections of painting, mosaic and sculpture: complex mythological scenes in Greek and Roman imperial numismatic art. *In* Studies in classical art and archaeology p275-82

Numismatics, Medieval
Historiography
Grierson, P. Numismatics. *In* Powell, J. M. ed. Medieval studies p103-50

Numismatics, Roman
Mitchell, R. E. Roman coins as historical evidence: the Trojan legends of Rome. *In* Illinois classical studies, v 1 1976 p65-85

Vermeule, C. C. Interactions and reflections of painting, mosaic and sculpture: complex mythological scenes in Greek and Roman imperial numismatic art. *In* Studies in classical art and archaeology p275-82

Nummi, Lassi
At the sea gate of the palace. *In* Dauenhauer, R. and Binham, P. eds. Snow in May p98-101

Nunamiut (Eskimo tribe)
Population
Binford, L. R. and Chasko, W. J. Nunamiut demographic history: a provocative case. *In* Zubrow, E. B. W. ed. Demographic anthropology p63-143

Núñez, Carlota Carvallo de. See Carvallo de Núñez, Carlota

Nunnerley, David
JFK: assassination, martyrdom, impact; excerpt from "President Kennedy and Britain." *In* Burton, D. H. ed. American history—British historians p239-54

Nuns
Moving-pictures
French, B. Brides of Christ. *In* French, B. On the verge of revolt p121-36

Nuns in literature
Bennett, D. H. Women and the Nativist movement. *In* "Remember the ladies": new perspectives on women in American history p61-89

The nun's story (Motion picture)
French, B. Brides of Christ. *In* French, B. On the verge of revolt p121-36

Nurse and patient

Benoliel, J. Q. Nurses and the human experience of dying. *In* Feifel, H. [ed.] New meanings of death p123-42

Jackson, E. E. Effective communication in nurse-patient relationships. *In* Henderson, G. ed. Human relations in the military p203-17

Nurse-patient relationship. See Nurse and patient

Nursery schools. See Education, Preschool

Nurses

See also Nurse and patient

United States

Wessells, V. G. The nurse and home care of the terminally ill. *In* Home care p49-59

Nurses and nursing. See Nurses; Nursing

Nursing

See also Nurse and patient

United States

Wessells, V. G. The nurse and home care of the terminally ill. *In* Home care p49-59

Nursing homes

Gubrium, J. F. On multiple realities in a nursing home. *In* Gubrium, J. F. ed. Late life p61-98

Nurture and nature. See Nature and nurture

Nussbaum, Alan J.

Ennian Laurentis terra. *In* Harvard Studies in classical philology v77 p207-15

Nussbaum, Martha C.

The text of Aristotle's De motu animalium. *In* Harvard Studies in classical philology v80 p111-59

Nussbaumer, Adolf

The economic systems of Socialist Eastern Europe: principles, development, and operation. *In* The Year book of world affairs, 1975 p222-41

Industrial co-operation and East-West trade. *In* The Year book of world affairs, 1978 p64-75

The market economies of the West. *In* The Year book of world affairs, 1976 p223-42

Nutrition

Williams, R. and others. A renaissance of nutritional science. *In* Sobel, D. S. ed. Ways of health p459-77

Aging effect

See Aging—Nutritional aspects

Historiography

Aymard, M. Toward the history of nutrition: some methodological remarks. *In* Food and drink in history p 1-16

Nutrition disorders

Le Roy Ladurie, E. Amenorrhoea in time of famine (seventeenth to twentieth century). *In* Le Roy Ladurie, E. The territory of the historian p255-71

Same as Le Roy Ladurie, E. Famine amenorrhoea (seventeenth-twentieth centuries) *In* Biology of man in history p163-78

Nuttal, Anthony David

'Measure for measure': the bed-trick. *In* Shakespeare survey 28 p51-56

Nutter, G. Warren

Freedom in a revolutionary economy. *In* America's continuing revolution p183-201

Nwanko, Nkem

About individual works

Danda

Taiwo, O. Social criticism. *In* Taiwo, O. Culture and the Nigerian novel p34-73

Nwapa, Flora

About individual works

Idu

Emenyonu, E. N. Who does Flora Nwapa write for? *In* African literature today no. 7: Focus on criticism p28-33

Nwoga, Donatus Ibe

The limitations of universal critical criteria. *In* Exile and tradition p8-30

See also Egudu, R. N. jt. auth.

Nyakyusa (African tribe)

Wilson, M. Strangers in Africa: reflections on Nyakyusa, Nguni, and Sotho evidence. *In* Shack, W. A. and Skinner, E. P. eds. Strangers in African societies p51-66

Nyamiti, Charles

Approaches to African theology. *In* The Emergent gospel p31-45

Nyamwezi (African people)

Bennett, N. R. Isike, Ntemi of Unyanyembe. *In* African dimensions p53-67

Nye, Joseph S.

Nationalism, statesmen, and the size of African states. *In* Kilson, M. ed. New states in the modern world p158-68

Transnational and transgovernmental relations. *In* New dimensions of world politics p36-53

Nye, Russel Blaine

About

Mead, C. D. A scholar's profile. *In* Essays in honor of Russel B. Nye p 1-6

Nygaard, Agnar Petter

The ethical problem of human genetics. *In* Against pollution and hunger p218-19

Nygard, Holger Olof

Popular ballad and medieval romance. *In* Ballad studies p 1-19

Nyikiusa (African tribe) See Nyakyusa (African tribe)

Nykrog, Per

Courtliness and the townspeople: the fabliaux as a courtly burlesque. *In* Cook, T. D. and Honeycutt, B. L. eds. The humor of the fabliaux p59-73

Nyoro (Bantu people) See Banyoro

Nzekwu, Onuora

About

Taiwo, O. Onuora Nzekwu and Elechi Amadi. *In* Taiwo, O. Culture and the Nigerian novel p181-209

O

OAS. See Organization of American States

OECD. See Organization for Economic Co-operation and Development

O.E.D. See The Oxford English dictionary

OEO. See United States. Office of Economic Opportunity

OPEC. See Organization of Petroleum Exporting Countries

OSA. See Society of Modern Architects

O lucky man! (Motion picture)
Kauffmann, S. O lucky man! *In* Kauffmann, S. Living images p204-07

Oakes, John B.
The responsibility of the press. *In* Tomorrow's American p171-88

Oakeshott, Michael Joseph
Rationalism in politics

Contents
The activity of being an historian
The moral life in the writings of Thomas Hobbes
On being conservative
The political economy of freedom
Political education
Rational conduct
Rationalism in politics
The study of 'politics' in a university
The Tower of Babel
The voice of poetry in the conversation of mankind

About
Minogue, K. R. Michael Oakeshott: the boundless sea of politics. *In* De Crespigny, A. and Minogue, K. R. eds. Contemporary political philosophers p120-46

Oaks, Robert Francis
The city under military occupation: Philadelphia, 1777-1778. *In* Essays on urban America p21-54

Oates, John F.
More of Nemesion's notes: P. Corn. inv. 18. *In* Illinois classical studies v3, 1978 p81-87

Oates, Joyce Carol
New heaven, new earth: the visionary experience in literature

Contents
Anarchy and order in Beckett's Trilogy
The art of relationships: Henry James and Virginia Woolf
The death throes of romanticism: the poetry of Sylvia Plath
Also in Boyers, R. ed. Contemporary poetry in America p139-56
Also in Butscher, E. ed. Sylvia Plath p206-24
The hostile sun: the poetry of D. H. Lawrence
Kafka's paradise
The nightmare of naturalism: Harriette Arnow's "The dollmaker"
Out of stone, into flesh: the imagination of James Dickey
The teleology of the unconscious: the art of Norman Mailer
The visionary art of Flannery O'Connor

About
Allen, M. The terrified women of Joyce Carol Oates. *In* Allen, M. The necessary blankness p133-59
Mickelson, A. Z. Sexual love in the fiction of Joyce Carol Oates. *In* Mickelson, A. Z. Reaching out: sensitivity and order in recent American fiction by women p15-34

About individual works
The edge of impossibility
Balakian, N. The tragedy of delusion: criticism by Joyce Carol Oates. *In* Balakian, N. Critical encounters p139-42

Wonderland
Sale, R. H. Hawkes, Malamud, Richler, Oates. *In* Sale, R. H. On not being good enough p30-42

Oates, Stephen B.
John Brown and his judges: a critique of the historical literature. *In* Swierenga, R. P. ed. Beyond the Civil War synthesis p57-76

Oba's ear: a Yoruba myth in Cuba and Brazil. Bascom, W. R. *In* Crowley, D. J. ed. African folklore in the New World p3-19

Obatala, J. K.
Black consciousness and American policy in Africa. *In* Said, A. A. and Simmons, L. R. eds. Ethnicity in an international context p64-75

Obbo, Christine
Village strangers in Buganda society. *In* Shack, W. A. and Skinner, E. P. eds. Strangers in African societies p227-41

Obedience
Koestler, A. Ad majorem gloriam. . . . *In* Koestler, A. Janus p77-97
Longenecker, R. N. The obedience of Christ in the theology of the early Church. *In* Reconciliation and hope p142-52

Ob'edinenie Sovremennykh Arkitektorov. See Society of Modern Architects

Obelisk Press
Ford, H. D. Jack Kahane and the guardian Obelisk. *In* Ford, H. D. Published in Paris p345-84

Obelisks
Waugh, D. C. Azbuka znakami lits: Egyptian hieroglyphs in the Privy Chancellery Archive. *In* Oxford Slavonic papers, new ser. v10 p46-50

Ober, William B.
Boswell's clap and other essays

Contents
Boswell's clap
Chekhov among the doctors: the doctor's dilemma
Did Socrates die of hemlock poisoning?
Drowsed with the fume of poppies: opium and John Keats
The Earl of Rochester and ejaculatio praecox
Lady Chatterley's what?
Madness and poetry: a note on Collins, Cowper, and Smart
Swinburne's masochism: neuropathology and psychopathology
Thomas Shadwell: his exitus revis'd
William Carlos Williams, M.D.: physician as poet

Oberembt, Kenneth J.
Lord Berners' translation of Artus de la petite Bretagne. *In* Medievalia et humanistica no. 5 p191-99

Oberg, Arthur Kenneth
Sylvia Plath and the new decadence. *In* Butscher, E. ed. Sylvia Plath p177-85

Oberman, Heiko Augustinus
Reformation and revolution: Copernicus discovery in an era of change. *In* The Nature of scientific discovery p134-69

Oberth, Hermann
About
Horwath, P. Hermann J. Oberth. The father of space travel: American perspectives. *In* The German contribution to the building of the Americas p343-58

Obesity

Control

See Reducing

Obeyesekere, Gananath

Personal identity and cultural crisis: the case of Anagārika Dharmapala of Sri Lanka. *In* Reynolds, F. E. and Capps, D. eds. The biographical process p221-52

Sinhalese-Buddhist identity in Ceylon. *In* Ethnic identity p231-58

Obitts, Stanley R.

Historical explanation and Barth on Christ's Resurrection. *In* Current issues in Biblical and patristic interpretation p365-77

Object (Philosophy)

Miller, J. W. Functioning objects, facts, and artifacts. *In* Miller, J. W. The paradox of cause, and other essays p124-29

Miller, J. W. The midworld. *In* Miller, J. W. The paradox of cause, and other essays p106-23

Quine, W. V. On mental entities. *In* Quine, W. V. The ways of paradox, and other essays p221-27

Quine, W. V. On multiplying entities. *In* Quine, W. V. The ways of paradox, and other essays p259-64

Objectivity

Baumann, F. Objectivity and indoctrination. *In* Hook, S.; Kurtz, P. and Todorovich, M. eds. The ethics of teaching and scientific research p53-59

Macmurray, J. Science and objectivity. *In* The Personal universe p7-23

Nagel, T. Subjective and objective. *In* Nagel, T. Mortal questions p196-213

Novotny, H. R. F. Objectivity and biased skepticism in higher education. *In* Hook, S.; Kurtz, P. and Todorovich, M. eds. The ethics of teaching and scientific research p61-69

Zimmerman, M. Objectivity in education. *In* Hook, S.; Kurtz, P. and Todorovich, M. eds. The ethics of teaching and scientific research p49-51

Obler, Jeffrey. See Steiner, J. jt. auth.

Obligation. See Duty; Responsibility

Obolensky, Dimitri

Early Russian literature (1000-1300). *In* Auty, R. and Obolensky, D. eds. An introduction to Russian language and literature p56-89

Medieval Russian culture in the writings of D. S. Likhachev. *In* Oxford Slavonic papers, new ser. v9 p 1-16

O'Brady, Frédéric

On staging Molière today. *In* Johnson, R. B.; Neumann, E. S. and Trail, G. T. eds. Molière and the commonwealth of letters: patrimony and posterity p628-38

O'Briant, Walter H.

Man, nature, and the history of philosophy. *In* Philosophy & environmental crisis p79-89

O'Brien, Conor Cruise. See Cruise O'Brien, Conor

O'Brien, Darcy

In Ireland after A portrait. *In* Staley, T. F. and Benstock, B. eds. Approaches to Joyce's Portrait p213-35

O'Brien, David J.

American Catholicism and American religion. *In* Mulder, J. M. and Wilson, J. F. eds. Religion in American history p397-414

O'Brien, Denise

Female husbands in southern Bantu societies. *In* Schlegel, A. E. ed. Sexual stratification p109-26

O'Brien, Donal Brian Cruise. See Cruise O'Brien, Donal Brian

O'Brien, George. See Hoving, W. jt. auth.

O'Brien, Ken

Death and revolution: a reappraisal of identity theory. *In* O'Neill, J. ed. On critical theory p104-28

O'Brien, Michael

The idea of the American South, 1920-1941

Contents

Allen Tate: "the punctilious abyss"
Donald Davidson: "the creed of memory"
Frank Owsley: "the immoderate past"
The idea of the South: an interpretation
John Ransom: the cycle of commitment
Odum: Sociology in the South
Odum: Southern sociology
Odum: The failure of regionalism
On the idea of the South: origins, mutation, and fragmentation
Wade: a turning inward

O'Brien, Philip J.

The military in power and the lessons of Chile. *In* O'Brien, P. J. ed. Allende's Chile p273-94

Was the United States responsible for the Chilean coup? *In* O'Brien, P. J. ed. Allende's Chile p217-43

O'Brien, Terence A.

Economic support for minority languages. *In* Alcock, A. E.; Taylor, B. K. and Welton, J. M. eds. The future of cultural minorities p82-101

Obscene literature. See Literature, Immoral

Obscenity (Law)

United States

Gerber, R. J. Obscenity-lust's labors lost and won. *In* Contemporary issues in criminal justice p40-56

Observation (Psychology)

Tart, C. T. Science, states of consciousness, and spiritual experiences: the need for state-specific sciences. *In* Tart, C. T. ed. Transpersonal psychologies p9-58

See also Introspection

Observations, Astronomical. See Astronomy—Observations

Obsolescence (Accounting) See Depreciation

Obstetrics

See also Abortion

History

Branca, P. Towards a social history of medicine. *In* Branca, P. ed. The medicine show p89-101

Harvey, A. M. John Whitridge Williams—his contributions to obstetrics. *In* Harvey, A. M. Adventures in medical research p188-94

United States—History

Donegan, J. B. Man-midwifery and the delicacy of the sexes. *In* "Remember the ladies": new perspectives on women in American history p90-109

O'Cain, Raymond K. See McDavid, R. I. jt. auth.

Ocampo, Victoria

Malraux's world and ours. *In* Courcel, M. H. de, ed. Malraux p212-21

O'Casey, Sean

About

Worth, K. J. O'Casey. *In* Worth, K. J. The Irish drama of Europe from Yeats to Beckett p220-40

Bibliography

Krause, D. Sean O'Casey. *In* Finneran, R. J. ed. Anglo-Irish literature p470-517

Occam, William. See Ockham, William

Occidental civilization. See Civilization, Occidental

Occult medicine. See Medicine, Magic, mystic and spagiric

Occult sciences

Burke, J. G. Hermetism as a Renaissance world view. *In* The Darker vision of the Renaissance p95-117

Truzzi, M. Towards a sociology of the occult: notes on modern witchcraft. *In* Zaretsky, I. I. and Leone, M. P. eds. Religious movements in contemporary America p628-45

Whitehead, H. Reasonably fantastic: some perspectives on scientology, science fiction, and occultism. *In* Zaretsky, I. I. and Leone, M. P. eds. Religious movements in contemporary America p547-87

See also Alchemy; Demonology; Magic; Mediums; Satanism; Spiritualism; Superstition

Occultism. See Occultism in literature

Occultism in literature

Barclay, G. S. The lure of the occult. *In* Barclay, G. S. Anatomy of horror: the masters of occult fiction p7-21

Briggs, J. A scientific spirit: mesmerism, drugs and psychic doctors. *In* Briggs, J. Night visitors p52-75

Occupational aptitude tests. See Employment tests

Occupational crimes. See White collar crimes

Occupational mobility

New York (State)—Buffalo

Glasco, L. Ethnicity and occupation in the mid-ninteenth century: Irish, Germans, and native-born whites in Buffalo, New York. *In* Immigrants in industrial America, 1850-1920 p151-75

New York (State)—Poughkeepsie

Griffen, C. The "old" immigration and industrialization: a case study. *In* Immigrants in industrial America p176-210

Pennsylvania—Philadelphia

Laurie, B.; Hershberg, T. and Alter, G. Immigrants and industry: the Philadelphia experience, 1850-1880. *In* Immigrants in industrial America, 1850-1920 p123-50

Occupational tests. See Employment tests

Occupational therapy. See Art therapy

Occupations. See Professions

Ocean

Economic aspects

See Marine resources

Research

See Oceanographic research

Taxation

Eatwell, J.; Llewellyn, J. and Tarling, R. An ocean development tax. *In* Borgese, E. M. and Krieger, D. eds. The tides of change p33-47

Ocean bottom (Maritime law) See Continental shelf

Ocean pollution. See Marine pollution

Oceanographic research

Fye, P. M. Scientific research in the ocean. *In* Borgese, E. M. and Krieger, D. eds. The tides of change p306-09

Wooster, W. S. Conditions for ocean research. *In* Borgese, E. M. and Krieger, D. eds. The tides of change p310-17

Oceanography

Borgese, E. M. A constitution for the oceans. *In* Borgese, E. M. and Krieger, D. eds. The tides of change p340-52

Pardo, A. New institutions for ocean space. *In* Borgese, E. M. and Krieger, D. eds. The tides of change p324-27

See also Marine resources

Research

See Oceanographic research

Ochipawa Indians. See Chippewa Indians

Ochs, Donovan J.

Charles Butler on methods of persuasion: a translation. *In* Rhetoric: a tradition in transition p66-98

Ochsenwald, William Leo

The financial basis of Ottoman rule in the Hijaz, 1840-1877. *In* Nationalism in a non-national state p129-49

Ockham, William

About

Moody, E. A. Ockham, Buridan, and Nicholas of Autrecourt. *In* Moody, E. A. Studies in medieval philosophy, science, and logic p127-60

Moody, E. A. William of Ockham. *In* Moody, E. A. Studies in medieval philosophy, science, and logic p409-38

Weinberg, J. R. Ockham's theory of scientific method. *In* Weinberg, J. R. Ockham, Descartes, and Hume p22-32

About individual works

Exposito super libros physicorum

Moody, E. A. Ockham and Aegidius of Rome. *In* Moody, E. A. Studies in medieval philosophy, science and logic p161-88

Quaestiones super libros physicorum

Moody, E. A. Ockham and Aegidius of Rome. *In* Moody, E. A. Studies in medieval philosophy, science, and logic p161-88

Ó Coileáin, Seán

Irish saga literature. *In* Oinas, F. J. ed. Heroic epic and saga p172-92

O'Connell, Daniel

About

O'Connell, M. R. Daniel O'Connell and the Irish eighteenth century. *In* Studies in eighteenth-century culture v5 p475-95

O'Connell, Donald Patrick

Limited war at sea since 1945. *In* Howard, M. ed. Restraints on war p123-34

O'Connell, Maurice R.

Daniel O'Connell and the Irish eighteenth century. *In* Studies in eighteenth-century culture v5 p475-95

O'Connor, Daniel John

Aquinas and natural law. *In* New studies in ethics v 1 p79-172

The status of sense data. *In* Royal Institute of Philosophy. Impressions of empiricism p79-92

O'Connor, Edwin

About individual works
The last hurrah
Taylor, R. John Ford's Boston. *In* Peary, and Shatzkin, R. eds. The modern American novel and the movies p215-23

O'Connor, Flannery

About
Bleikasten, A. The heresy of Flannery O'Connor. *In* Johnson, I. D. and Johnson, C. [eds.] Les américanistes p53-70

Friedman, M. J. Introduction. *In* Friedman, M. J. and Lawson, L. A. eds. The added dimension p 1-31

Gardiner, H. C. Flannery O'Connor's clarity of vision. *In* Friedman, M. J. and Lawson, L. A. eds. The added dimension p184-206

Gordon, C. An American girl. *In* Friedman, M. J. and Lawson, L. A. eds. The added dimension p123-37

Hoffman, F. J. The search for redemption: Flannery O'Connor's fiction. *In* Friedman, M. J. and Lawson, L. A. eds. The added dimension p32-48

Holman, C. H. Detached laughter in the South. *In* Holman, C. H. Windows on the world p27-47

Holman, C. H. Her rue with a difference: Flannery O'Connor and the Southern literary tradition. *In* Friedman, M. J. and Lawson, L. A. eds. The added dimension p73-87

Howe, I. Flannery O'Connor's stories. *In* Howe, I. Celebrations and attacks p97-101

Hyman, S. E. Flannery O'Connor. *In* Howard, M. ed. Seven American women writers of the twentieth century p311-55

Malin, I. Flannery O'Connor and the grotesque. *In* Friedman, M. J. and Lawson, L. A. eds. The added dimension p108-22

Oates, J. C. The visionary art of Flannery O'Connor. *In* Oates, J. C. New heaven, new earth: the visionary experience in literature p141-76

Quinn, M. B. Flannery O'Connor, a realist of distances. *In* Friedman, M. J. and Lawson, L. A. eds. The added dimension p157-83

Rubin, L. D. Flannery O'Connor and the Bible Belt. *In* Friedman, M. J. and Lawson, L. A. eds. The added dimension p49-72

Scott, N. A. Flannery O'Connor's testimony: the pressure of glory. *In* Friedman, M. J. and Lawson, L. A. eds. The added dimension p138-56

About individual works
A memory of Mary Ann
Gardiner, H. C. Flannery O'Connor's clarity of vision. *In* Friedman, M. J. and Lawson, L. A. eds. The added dimension p184-206

The violent bear it away
Duhamel, P. A. The novelist as prophet. *In* Friedman, M. J. and Lawson, L. A. eds. The added dimension p88-107

Wise blood
Gray, R. J. Aftermath: Southern literature since World War II. *In* Gray, R. J. The literature of memory p257-305

Kunkel, F. L. Wrestlers with Christ and Cupid. *In* Kunkel, F. L. Passion and the Passion p129-56

Bibliography
Lawson, L. A. Bibliography. *In* Friedman, M. J. and Lawson, L. A. eds. The added dimension p235-56

Criticism and interpretation
Friedman, M. J. "The perplexing business": Flannery O'Connor and her critics enter the 1970s. *In* Friedman, M. J. and Lawson, L. A. eds. The added dimension p207-34

O'Connor, Francis V.

Philip Guston and political humanism. *In* Millon, H. A. and Nochlin, L. eds. Art and architecture in the service of politics p342-55

O'Connor, Francis V. ed.

About individual works
The New Deal Art projects
Rosenberg, H. The profession of art: the W.P.A. Art Project. *In* Rosenberg, H. Art on the edge p195-205

O'Connor, Frank. See O'Donovan, Michael

O'Connor, John E.

A reaffirmation of American ideals: Drums along the Mohawk. *In* O'Connor, J. E. and Jackson, M. A. eds. American history/American film p97-119

O'Connor, John S.

Compositors D and F of the Shakespeare First folio. *In* Virginia. University. Bibliographical Society. Studies in bibliography v28 p81-117

A qualitative analysis of compositors C and D in the Shakespeare First folio. *In* Virginia. University. Bibliographical Society. Studies in bibliography v30 p57-74

O'Connor, Margaret Anne

Fiction: the 1930s to the 1950s. *In* American literary scholarship, 1974 p253-78

Fiction: the 1930s to the 1950s [another essay] *In* American literary scholarship, 1975 p295-326

Fiction: the 1930s to the 1950s. *In* American literary scholarship, 1976 p251-85

Fiction: the 1930s to the 1950s [another essay] *In* American literary scholarship, 1977 p273-302

O'Connor, Stanley J.

Reflections on a problem sculpture from Jaiyā in peninsular Siam. *In* Southeast Asian history and historiography p100-06

Octavian Caesar, Emperor of Rome. See Augustus, Emperor of Rome

October (Motion picture)

Taylor, R. October. *In* Taylor, R. Film propaganda p92-102

October Middle East War, 1973. See Israel-Arab War, 1973

Oculomotor system. See Eye—Movements

Odegard, Douglas Andrew

The body identical with the human mind: a problem in Spinoza's philosophy. *In* Freeman, E. and Mandelbaum, M. H. eds. Spinoza p61-83

Odell, Peter R.

The international oil companies in the new world oil market. *In* The Year book of world affairs, 1978 p76-92

Odessa

City planning
Skinner, F. W. Trends in planning practices: the building of Odessa, 1794-1917. *In* Hamm, M. F. ed. The city in Russian history p139-59

Odets, Clifford

About

Brenman-Gibson, M. The creation of plays: with a specimen analysis. *In* Roland, A. ed. Psychoanalysis, creativity, and literature p178-230

About individual works

The country girl

Simon, J. I. The aesthetics of the actor's appearance. *In* Simon, J. I. Singularities p195-209

Rocket to the moon

Brenman-Gibson, M. The creation of plays: with a specimen analysis. *In* Roland, A. ed. Psychoanalysis. creativity, and literature p178-230

Odonata. See Dragonflies

O'Donnell, Guillermo A.

Permanent crisis and the failure to create a democratic regime: Argentina, 1955-66. *In* The Breakdown of democratic regimes pt3 p138-77

O'Donnell, James Howlett

The Southern Indians in the War for American Independence, 1775-1783. *In* Hudson, C. M. ed. **Four centuries of Southern Indians** p46-64

O'Donnell, Sheryl

Mr Locke and the ladies: the indelible words on the tabula rasa. *In* Studies in eighteenth-century culture v8 p151-64

O'Donnell, William Hugh

Yeats as adept and artist: The speckled bird, The secret rose, and The wind among the reeds. *In* Yeats and the occult p55-79

O'Donovan, Michael

A clean well-lighted place. *In* Benson, J. J. ed. **The short stories of Ernest Hemingway: critical essays** p85-92

The lonely voice; excerpt. *In* May, C. E. ed. Short story theories p83-93

O'Dowd, Michael

South Africa in the light of the stages of economic growth. *In* Leftwich, A. ed. South Africa: economic growth and political change p29-43

O'Driscoll, Lyla H.

On the nature and value of marriage. *In* Feminism and philosophy p249-63

O'Driscoll, Robert

Return to the hearthstone: ideals of the Celtic Literary Revival. *In* Place, personality and the Irish writer p41-68

Odum, Eugene Pleasants

Environmental ethic and the attitude revolution. *In* Philosophy & environmental crisis p10-15

Odum, Howard Washington

About

Downs, R. B. Regional inventory. *In* Downs, R. B. Books that changed the South p237-47

O'Brien, M. Odum: Sociology in the South. *In* O'Brien, M. The idea of the American South, 1920-1941 p31-50

O'Brien, M. Odum: Southern sociology. *In* O'Brien, M. The idea of the American South, 1920-1941 p51-69

O'Brien, M. Odum: The failure of regionalism. *In* O'Brien, M. The idea of the American South, 1920-1941 p70-93

About individual works

Southern regions of the United States

Downs, R. B. Regional inventory. *In* Downs, R. B. Books that changed the South p237-47

O'Dwyer, John P.

Classroom collage: one perspective. *In* Parents, teachers, and children: prospects for choice in American education p37-58

Oe, Kenzaburō

About

Yamanouchi, H. Abe Kōbō and Oe Kenzaburō: the search for identity in contemporary Japanese literature. *In* Modern Japan p166-86

Yamanouchi, H. In search of identity: Abé Kōbō and Ōe Kenzaburō. *In* Yamanouchi, H. The search for authenticity in modern Japanese literature p153-74

Oedipus

Fergusson, F. Oedipus according to Freud, Sophocles, and Cocteau. *In* Fergusson, F. Literary landmarks p101-13

Oedipus complex

Girard, R. Delirium as system. *In* Girard, R. "To double business bound" p84-120

Girard, R. Strategies of madness—Nietzsche, Wagner, and Dostoevski. *In* Girard, R. "To double business bound" p61-83

Oedipus complex in literature

Bersani, L. Racine, psychoanalysis and Oedipus. *In* Bersani, L. A future for Astyanax p17-50

Oettle, T. H. G. and Larnach, S. L.

The identification of aboriginal traits in forensic medicine. *In* Grafton Elliot Smith p103-08

Of mice and men (criticism) Steinbeck, J. *In* Kauffmann, S. Persons of the drama p156-59

Of mice and men (Motion picture)

Everson, W. K. Thoughts on a great adaptation. *In* Peary, G. and Shatzkin, R. eds. The modern American novel and the movies p63-69

O'Feeney, Sean. See Ford, John, 1895-1973

Ofer, Gur

Economic aspects of Soviet involvement in the Middle East. *In* Ro'i, Y. ed. The limits to power p67-93

Offenders, Female. See Female offenders

Offenses against property

Kampala, Uganda

Clinard, M. B. and Abbott, D. J. Community organization and property crime: a comparative study of social control in the slums of an African city. *In* Delinquency, crime, and society p186-206

Offenses against the person. See Abduction; Homicide; Kidnapping; Rape; Sex crimes

Office of Economic Opportunity. See United States. Office of Economic Opportunity

Office of the United Nations High Commissioner for Refugees. See United Nations. Office of the United Nations High Commissioner for Refugees

Office practice in government

Howlett, M. J. Strategic planning in state government. *In* Managing nonprofit organizations p124-37

Officer, Lawrence H.
Demand conditions under multidimensional pricing. *In* Econometrics and economic theory p261-84

Offshore oil fields. See Petroleum in submerged lands

O'Flaherty, James Carneal
Language and reason in the thought of Hamann. *In* Creative encounter p86-104

Socrates in Hamann's Socratic memorabilia and Nietzsche's Birth of tragedy. *In* O'Flaherty, J. C.; Sellner, T. F. and Helm, R. M. eds. Studies in Nietzsche and the classical tradition p134-43

O'Flinn, J. P.
Towards a sociology of the Nigerian novel. *In* African literature today no. 7: Focus on criticism p34-52

Ofshe, Richard
Synanon: the people business. *In* The New religious consciousness p116-37

Ōfuchi, Ninji
The formation of the Taoist Canon. *In* Welch, H. and Seidel, A. K. eds. Facets of Taoism p253-67

Ogallalla Indians. See Oglala Indians

Ogawa, Dennis Masaaki
Asian Americans. *In* Gochros, H. L. and Gochros, J. S. eds. The sexually oppressed p192-201

Ogden, James
The later seventeenth century. *In* English Association. The year's work in English studies v55 p297-321

The later seventeenth century. [another essay] *In* English Association. The year's work in English studies v56 p221-41

The later seventeenth century [another essay] *In* English Association. The year's work in English studies v57 p185-204

See also Brake, L. jt. auth.

Ogibenin, Boris Leonidovich
A semiotic approach to religion. *In* Sebeok, T. A. ed. Sight, sound, and sense p232-43

Oglala Indians

Religion and mythology
Walker, J. R. Oglala metaphysics. *In* Tedlock, D. E. and Tedlock, B. eds. Teachings from the American earth p205-18

Rites and ceremonies
Brown, J. E . Hanblecheyapi: crying for a vision; excerpt from "The sacred pipe." *In* Tedlock, D. E. and Tedlock, B. eds. Teachings from the American earth p20-41

O'Gorman, Edmundo
History, technology, and the pursuit of happiness. *In* The Frontiers of knowledge p79-103

Also in Technology and the frontiers of knowledge p73-97

Ogungbesan, Kolawole
Symbol and meaning in The beautiful ones are not yet born. *In* African literature today no. 7: Focus on criticism p93-110

Wole Soyinka: the past and the visionary writer. *In* King, B. A. and Ogungbesan, K. eds. A celebration of Black and African writing p175-88

Ogunsanwo, Alaba
The foreign policy of Algeria. *In* Aluko, O. ed. The foreign policies of African states p24-40

Ogunyemi, Chikwenye Okonjo
Iconoclasts both: Wole Soyinka and LeRoi Jones. *In* African literature no. 9: Africa, America and the Caribbean p25-28

O'Hagan, Timothy
Quality and equality in education: a critique of David Cooper. *In* Philosophers discuss education p130-43

O'Hara, Frank

About
Altieri, C. F. Varieties of immanentist experience: Robert Bly, Charles Olson, and Frank O'Hara. *In* Altieri, C. F. Enlarging the temple p78-127

Blasing, M. K. Frank O'Hara and the poetics of love. *In* Blasing, M. K. The art of life p139-56

O'Hara, J. D.
Plath's comedy. *In* Lane, G. ed. Sylvia Plath p74-96

O'Hara, John
"An artist is his own fault"
Contents
An artist is his own fault
The author's name is Hemingway
Characters in search
Dialog, detail, and type
Don't say it never happened
Dorothy Parker, hip pocket size
Every great writer of fiction was a great social historian
I was determined to make plain what I had seen
In memory of Scott Fitzgerald: certain aspects
Logistics of the novel
Method and technique of the novel
The prize is a good one
Remarks on the novel
Scott Fitzgerald—odds and ends
That Benny Greenspan
We all know how good we are
What makes a writer?
Writing—what's in it for me?

About
Farrell, J. T. The eternal question of John O'Hara. *In* Farrell, J. T. Literary essays, 1954-1974 p90-92

Milne, G. Practitioners, 1920-1960. *In* Milne, G. The sense of society p205-35

O'Hara, J. Don't say it never happened. *In* O'Hara, J. "An artist is his own fault" p212-16

O'Hara, J. Every great writer of fiction was a great social historian. *In* O'Hara, J. "An artist is his own fault" p105-18

O'Hara, J. Method and technique of the novel. *In* O'Hara, J. "An artist is his own fault" p37-52

O'Hara, J. Remarks on the novel. *In* O'Hara, J. "An artist is his own fault" p82-103

O'Hara, J. We all know how good we are. *In* O'Hara, J. "An artist is his own fault" p103-05

About individual works
Butterfield 8

O'Hara, J. I was determined to make plain what I had seen. *In* O'Hara, J. "An artist is his own fault" p122-26

Summer's day

Trilling, L. John O'Hara: Summer's day. *In* Trilling, L. Prefaces to The experience of literature p156-59

O'Hara, John—About individual works—
Continued
Ten North Frederick
O'Hara, J. The prize is a good one. *In* O'Hara, J. "An artist is his own fault" p80-82

Technique
O'Hara, J. Dialog, detail, and type. *In* O'Hara, J. "An artist is his own fault" p3-20
O'Hara, J. Logistics of the novel. *In* O'Hara, J. "An artist is his own fault" p20-37

O'Higgins, Paul
Unlawful seizure of persons by states. *In* International terrorism and political crimes p336-42

Ohio
Economic conditions
Maurer, D. J. Relief problems and politics in Ohio. *In* Braeman, J.; Bremner, R. H. and Brody, D. eds. The New Deal v2 p77-102

Politics and government—1865-1950
Maurer, D. J. Relief problems and politics in Ohio. *In* Braeman, J.; Bremner, R. H. and Brody, D. eds. The New Deal v2 p77-102

Ohlin, Goran
Economic theory confronts population growth. *In* Economic factors in population growth p3-16

Ohmann, Carol Burke. See Bell, B. C. jt. auth.

Ohmann, Richard Malin
The social definition of literature. *In* Hernadi, P. ed. What is literature? p89-101

About individual works
English in America: a radical view of the profession
Graff, G. English in America. *In* Graff, G. Literature against itself p103-27

Oikonomia (The Greek word)
Erickson, J. H. Oikonomia in Byzantine canon law. *In* Law, church, and society p225-36

Oil fields. See Petroleum in submerged lands
Oil fields, Offshore. See Petroleum in submerged lands
Oil-fuel. See Petroleum as fuel
Oil industries. See Petroleum industry and trade
Oil-painting. See Painting

Oinas, Felix J.
The Balto-Finnic epics. *In* Oinas, F. J. ed. Heroic epic and saga p286-309
Russian byliny. *In* Oinas, F. J. ed. Heroic epic and saga p236-56

Oisin. See Ossian
Ojibwa Indians. See Chippewa Indians

Ojo, Abiola
Law and government in Nigeria. *In* Smock, D. R. and Bentsi-Enchill, K. eds. The search for national integration in Africa p47-67

Ojo-Ade, Femi
De origen Africano, soy cubano: African elements in the literature of Cuba. *In* African literature today no. 9: Africa, America and the Caribbean p47-57

Okabe, Tatsumi
The Cold war and China. *In* The Origins of the Cold war in Asia p224-51

Okara, Gabriel
About individual works
The voice
Taiwo, O. Social criticism. *In* Taiwo, O. Culture and the Nigerian novel p34-73

Okeh, Peter Igbonekwu
Two ways of explaining Africa: an insight into Camara Laye's L'enfant noir and Ferdinand Oyono's Le vieux nègre et la médaille. *In* Exile and tradition p74-84

Okely, Judith
Gypsy women: models in conflict. *In* Ardener, S. G. ed. Perceiving women p55-86

Oken, Donald
What to tell cancer patients: a study of medical attitudes. *In* Weir, R. F. ed. Ethical issues in death and dying p 9-25

Okinagan language. See Salishan languages

Oklahoma
Economic conditions
Bryant, K. L. Oklahoma and the New Deal. *In* Braeman, J.; Bremner, R. H. and Brody, D. eds. The New Deal v2 p166-97

Politics and government
Bryant, K. L. Oklahoma and the New Deal. *In* Braeman, J.; Bremner, R. H. and Brody, D. eds. The New Deal v2 p166-97

Oklahoma City
Politics and government
Burbank, G. Socialism in an Oklahoma boom-town: "Milwaukeeizing" Oklahoma City. *In* Stave, B. M. ed. Socialism and the cities p99-115

Okonogi, Masao
The domestic roots of the Korean War. *In* The Origins of the Cold war in Asia p299-320

Oksenberg, Michel
The political leader. *In* Wilson, R. G. ed. Mao Tse-tung in the scales of history p70-116

Okumu, John
Kenya's foreign policy. *In* Aluko, O. ed. The foreign policies of African states p136-62

Olafson, Frederick A.
Humanism and the humanities. *In* Hook, S.; Kurtz, P. W. and Todorovich, M. eds. The philosophy of the curriculum: the need for general education p51-74
Husserl's theory of intentionality in contemporary perspective. *In* Elliston, F. A. and McCormick, P. eds. Husserl p160-67
The school and society: reflections on John Dewey's philosophy of education. *In* Cahn, S. M. ed. New studies in the philosophy of John Dewey p172-203

About individual works
Humanism and the humanities
Abrams, M. H. The language and methods of humanism. *In* Hook, S.; Kurtz, P. W. and Todorovich, M. eds. The philosophy of the curriculum: the need for general education p89-97
Himmelfarb, G. Observations on humanism and history. *In* Hook, S.; Kurtz, P. W. and Todorovich, M. eds. The philosophy of the curriculum: the need for general education p81-87

Olafson, Robert Bruce

B. Traven and The death ship as high culture. *In* Filler, L. ed. A question of quality: popularity and value in modern creative writing p160-71

Olasope, Biola

The Nonaligned News Agencies Pool and the free flow of meaningful news: an African viewpoint. *In* Horton, P. C. ed. The Third World and press freedom p162-72

Olcott, Anthony

The author's special intention: a study of The real life of Sebastian Knight. *In* A Book of things about Vladimir Nabokov p104-21

Poplavsky: the heir presumptive of Montparnasse. *In* The Bitter air of exile p274-88

Olcott, Henry Steel

About

Ellwood, R. S. Colonel Olcott and Madame Blavatsky journey to the East. *In* Ellwood, R. S. Alternative altars p104-35

Old age

Hareven, T. K. The last stage: historical adulthood and old age. *In* Erikson, E. H. ed. Adulthood p201-15

Nowitz, L. Dying and the aged person: process and implications for social work practice. *In* Home care p185-95

See also Ability, Influence of age on

Psychological aspects

See Aged—Psychology

Research

Graney, M. J. The aged and their environment: the study of intervening variables. *In* Gubrium, J. F. ed. Late life p5-17

Smith, D. S. Old age and the 'great transformation': a New England case study. *In* Spicker, S. F.; Woodward, K. M. and Van Tassel, D.D. eds. Aging and the elderly p285-302

Spicker, S. F. Gerontogenetic mentation: memory, dementia and medicine in the penultimate years. *In* Spicker, S. F.; Woodward, K. M. and Van Tassel, D. D. eds. Aging and the elderly p153-80

Old age homes

Psychological aspects

Lieberman, M. A. Relocation research and social policy. *In* Gubrium, J. F. ed. Late life p215-34

Old age in art

Berg, G. and Gadow, S. Toward more human meanings of aging: ideals and images from philosophy and art. *In* Spicker, S. F.; Woodward, K. M. and Van Tassel, D. D. eds. Aging and the elderly p83-92

Old age in literature

Freedman, R. Sufficiently decayed: gerontophobia in English literature. *In* Spicker, S. F.; Woodward, K. M. and Van Tassel, D. D. eds. Aging and the elderly p49-61

Luke, D. "How is it that you live, and what is it that you do?": the question of old age in English romantic poetry. *In* Spicker, S. F.; Woodward, K. M. and Van Tassel, D. D. eds. Aging and the elderly p221-40

Moss, W. G. Why the anxious fear? Aging and death in the works of Turgenev. *In* Spicker, S. F.; Woodward, K. M. and Van Tassel, D. D. eds. Aging and the elderly p241-60

Stahmer, H. M. The aged in two ancient oral cultures: the ancient Hebrews and Homeric Greece. *In* Spicker, S. F.; Woodward, K. M. and Van Tassel, D. D. eds. Aging and the elderly p23-36

Steadman, J. M. "The pardoner's tale": old age and contemptus mundi. *In* Steadman, J. M. Nature into myth p104-14

Tamke, S. S. Human values and aging: the perspective of the Victorian nursery. *In* Spicker, S. F.; Woodward, K. M. and Van Tassel, D. D. eds. Aging and the elderly p63-81

Woodward, K. M. Master songs of meditation: the late poems of Eliot, Pound, Stevens, and Williams. *In* Spicker, S. F.; Woodward, K. M. and Van Tassel, D. D. eds. Aging and the elderly p181-202

The old bachelor

Granger, B. I. Early Philadelphia serials. *In* Granger, B. I. American essay serials from Franklin to Irving p41-69

Old English language. See Anglo-Saxon language

Old English literature. See Anglo-Saxon literature; English literature—Middle English, 1100-1500

Old English poetry. See Anglo-Saxon poetry

Old French literature. See French literature—To 1500

Old French poetry. See French poetry—To 1500

Old Icelandic literature. See Icelandic and Old Norse literature

The old man and the sea (Motion picture)

Nadeau, R. L. Film and mythic heroism: Sturges's Old man. *In* Peary, G. and Shatzkin, R. eds. The modern American novel and the movies p199-203

Old Order Amish. See Amish

Old Russian literature. See Russian literature—To 1700

Old Saxon language. See Anglo-Saxon language

Old times (criticism) Pinter, H. *In* Kauffmann, S. Persons of the drama p335-48

Oldenburg, Claes

About

Krauss, R. E. Mechanical ballets: light, motion, theater. *In* Krauss, R. E. Passages in modern sculpture p201-42

Olds, Glenn A.

Introduction: the good man and the good. *In* The Abdication of philosophy: philosophy and the public good p 1-13

O'Leary, Basil

Global famine and the sense of justice. *In* The Personal universe p91-98

O'Leary, John F.

Nuclear energy and public policy issues. *In* Kalter, R. J. and Vogely, W. A. eds. Energy supply and government policy p235-54

Olegarius, Saint, Bp. of Barcelona

About

McCrank, L. J. The foundation of the confraternity of Tarragona by Archbishop Oleguer Bonestruga, 1126-1129. *In* Viator: medieval and Renaissance studies v9 p157-77

Oleguer Bonestruga. See Olegarius, Saint, Bp. of Barcelona

Olesha, Ĭŭriĭ Karlovich

About

Glicksberg, C. I. Commitment, coercion, and conformity. *In* Glicksberg, C. I. The literature of commitment p359-80

Slonim, M. L. Soviet romantics: from Grin, Paustovsky, and Olesha to Tikhonov and Bagritsky. *In* Slonim, M. L. Soviet Russian literature p116-33

Olesha, Yuri. See Olesha, Ĭŭriĭ Karlovich

Oleson, Alexandra

Introduction: To build a new intellectual order. *In* Oleson, A. and Brown, S. C. eds. The pursuit of knowledge in the early American Republic pxv-xxv

Oleson, Alexandra, and Voss, John

Introduction. *In* Oleson, A. and Voss, J. eds. The organization of knowledge in modern America, 1860-1920 p vii-xxi

Oleson, John

An Etruscan satyr mask in the Fogg Art Museum. *In* Harvard Studies in classical philology v76 p259-69

Oligopolies

Esposito, F. F. and Esposito, L. Industry price changes, market structure and inflation. *In* Inflation, trade and taxes p29-49

Oliphant, Margaret Oliphant (Wilson)

About

Cunningham, V. Mrs Oliphant and the tradition. *In* Cunningham, V. Everywhere spoken against p231-48

Hart, F. R. Mid-Victorians. *In* Hart, F. R. The Scottish novel p93-113

About individual works
The autobiography and letters of Mrs. M. O. W. Oliphant

Peterson, L. H. Audience and the autobiographers's art: an approach to the autobiography of Mrs. M. O. W. Oliphant. *In* Landow, G. P ed. Approaches to Victorian autobiography p158-74

Olitski, Jules

About

Rosenberg, H. Olitski, Kelly, Hamilton: dogma and talent. *In* Rosenberg, H. Art on the edge p60-70

Oliver, Barbara, and Robinson, K. E.

The eighteenth century. *In* English Association. The year's work in English studies v54 p276-300

Oliver, Donald William

Utilitarian perfectionism and education: a critique of underlying forces of innovative education. *In* Social forces and schooling p250-81

Oliver, Harry

About

Ritchie, W. "Give this place a little class"; the saga of a desert rat. *In* Voices from the Southwest p76-81

Oliver, Paul

Blue-eyed blues: the impact of blues on European popular culture. *In* Bigsby, C. W. E. ed. Approaches to popular culture p227-39 39

Jazz is where you find it: the European experience of jazz. *In* Bigsby, C. W. E. Superculture p140-51

Oliver, Revilo Pendleton

Did Tacitus finish the Annales? *In* Illinois classical studies, v2 1977 p289-314

The Second Medicean ms. and the text of Tacitus. *In* Illinois classical studies, v 1 1976 p190-225

Tacitean nobilitas. *In* Illinois classical studies v3, 1978 p238-61

Olivier, Sir Laurence Kerr

About individual works
Hamlet

Jorgens, J. J. Laurence Olivier's Hamlet. *In* Jorgens, J. J. Shakespeare on film p207-17

Henry V

Jorgens, J. J. Laurence Olivier's Henry V. *In* Jorgens, J. J. Shakespeare on film p122-35

Richard III

Jorgens, J. J. Laurence Olivier's Richard III. *In* Jorgens, J. J. Shakespeare on film p136-47

Oller, John W.

Language testing. *In* Wardhaugh, R. and Brown, H. D. eds. A survey of applied linguistics p275-300

Olliz Boyd, Antonio

The concept of Black awareness as a thematic approach in Latin American literature. *In* DeCosta, M. ed. Blacks in Hispanic literature p65-73

Ollman, Bertell

Marx's vision of communism: a reconstruction. *In* Radicalism in the contemporary age v2 p35-83

Olmecas. See Olmecs

Olmecs

Coe, M. D. Olmec and Maya: a study in relationships. *In* The Origins of Maya civilization p183-95

Lowe, G. W. The Mixe-Zoque as competing neighbors of the early Lowland Maya. *In* The Origins of Maya civilization p197-248

Antiquities

Grennes-Ravitz, R. A. The Olmec presence at Iglesia Vieja, Morelos. *In* Mesoamerican archaeology p99-108

Grove, D. C. The highland Olmec manifestation: a consideration of what it is and isn't. *In* Mesoamerican archaeology p109-28

Olmsted, Frederick Law

About

Downs, R. B. Southern traveler. *In* Downs, R. B. Books that changed the South p125-37

About individual works
The cotton kingdom: a traveller's observations on cotton and slavery in the American slave states

Downs, R. B. Southern traveler. *In* Downs, R. B. Books that changed the South p125-37

Olney, James Leslie

The esoteric flower: Yeats and Jung. *In* Yeats and the occult p27-54

O'Loughlin, Michael Jerome Kevin

The Odyssey. *In* Seidel, M. A. and Mendelson, E. eds. Homer to Brecht p30-52

Olson, Alan M.

The mythic language of the demonic: an introduction. *In* Disguises of the demonic p9-16

Olson, Charles
About

Altieri, C F. Varieties of immanentist experience: Robert Bly, Charles Olson, and Frank O'Hara. *In* Altieri, C. F. Enlarging the temple p78-127

Pops, M. L. Melville: to him, Olson. *In* Boyers, R. ed. Contemporary poetry in America p189-220

Thurley, G. Black Mountain academy: Charles Olson as critic and poet. *In* Thurley, G. The American moment p126-38

About individual works
Call me Ishmael

Pops, M. L. Melville: to him, Olson. *In* Boyers, R. ed. Contemporary poetry in America p189-220

The Maximus poems

Miller, J. E. Making a mappermunde to include my being: Charles Olson's Maximus poems. *In* Miller, J. E. The American quest for a supreme fiction p202-32

Olson, Clair Colby
The interludes of the Marriage Group in the Canterbury tales. *In* Chaucer and Middle English studies in honour of Rossell Hope Robbins p164-72

Olson, Elder
On value judgments in the arts, and other essays
Contents
The argument of Longinus's On the sublime
Art and science
The dialectical foundations of critical pluralism
A dialogue on symbolism
A dialogue on the function of art in society
Hamlet and the hermeneutics of drama
A letter on teaching drama
Longinus and Reynolds
Louise Bogan and Léonie Adams
The lyric
"Mighty opposites": remarks on the plot of Hamlet
On value judgments in the arts
An outline of poetic theory
The poetic method of Aristotle: its powers and limitations
The poetic process
The poetry of Dylan Thomas
The poetry of Marianne Moore
The poetry of Wallace Stevens
Rhetoric and the appreciation of Pope
"Sailing to Byzantium": prolegomena to a poetics of the lyric
William Empson, contemporary criticism, and poetic diction

Olsson, Kurt O.
Rhetoric, John Gower, and the late medieval exemplum. *In* Medievalia et humanistica no. 8 p185-200

Olympic games
Fischer, H. D. From cooperation to quasi-congruency—interdependencies between the Olympic games and television. *In* Fischer, H. D. and Melnik, S. R. eds. Entertainment: a cross-cultural examination p208-33

O'Malley, Glenn
Dante, Shelley, and T. S. Eliot. *In* Bornstein, G. ed. Romantic and modern p165-76

O'Malley, John W.
The discovery of America and reform thought at the Papal Court in the early Cinquecento. *In* First images of America p185-200

Omar Alejandro Goicoechea. See Goicoechea Omar, Alejandro

Ombudsman
Connecticut
Hollander, B. L. A private ombudsman for a public agency: planning and development of the Connecticut correctional system ombudsman. *In* Riedel, M. and Chappell, D. eds. Issues in criminal justice: planning and evaluation p87-98

O'Meally, Robert G.
Frederick Douglass' 1845 Narrative: the text was meant to be preached. *in* Fisher, D. and Stepto, R. B. eds. Afro-American literature p192-211

Riffs and rituals: folklore in the work of Ralph Ellison. *In* Fisher, D. and Stepto, R. B. eds. Afro-American literature p153-69

O'Meara, Joseph
Abortion: the court decides a non-case. *In* The Supreme Court review, 1974 p337-60

O'Meara, Patrick
Rhodesia: from white rule to independent Zimbabwe. *In* Carter, G. M. and O'Meara, P. eds. Southern Africa in crisis p15-47

Rhodesia/Zimbabwe: guerrilla warfare or political settlement? *In* Carter, G. M. and O'Meara, P. eds. Southern Africa: the continuing crisis p18-56

See also Martin, P. M. jt. auth.

Omotoso, Kole
Arabic drama and Islamic belief-system in Egypt. *In* African literature today no. 8: Drama in Africa p99-105

On the waterfront (Motion picture)
Murray, E. On the waterfront. *In* Murray, E. Ten film classics p86-101

Onat, Etta S.
Gladly would she learn and gladly teach: the female graduate student. *In* Hurdles p288-317

Ondaatje, Michael
About individual works
The collected works of Billy the Kid

Scobie, S. Two authors in search of a character: bp Nichol and Michael Ondaatje. *In* Woodcock, G. ed. Poets and critics p225-46

One (The One in philosophy)
Coomaraswamy, A. K. Vedic exemplarism. *In* Coomaraswamy, A. K. Selected papers v2 p177-97

One-act plays
Simon, J. I. A brief for brevity. *In* Simon, J. I. Singularities p68-70

One flew over the cuckoo's nest (Motion picture)
Haskell, M. Kesey cured: Forman's sweet insanity. *In* Peary, G. and Shatzkin, R. eds. The modern American novel and the movies p266-71

One-parent family. See Single-parent family

One-room schools. See Rural schools

One-teacher schools. See Rural schools

Oneida Community

Klass, D. Psychohistory and communal patterns: John Humphrey Noyes and the Oneida Community. *In* Reynolds, F. E. and Capps, D. eds. The biographical process p273-96

Oneida language. See Iroquoian languages

O'Neil, Robert M.

The case for preferential admissions; excerpt from "Discriminating against discrimination: preferential admissions in the DeFunis case." *In* Gross, B. R. ed. Reverse discrimination p66-83

O'Neill, Eugene Gladstone, 1888-1953

About

Brashear, W. R. The play as will and idea: Shaw and O'Neill. *In* Brashear, W. R. The gorgon's head p88-103

Brashear, W. R. The wisdom of Silenus: O'Neill's spiritual ancestors. *In* Brashear, W. R. The gorgon's head p104-33

Miller, J. Y. The other O'Neill. *In* French, W. G. ed. The twenties p455-73

Nicoll, A. Eugene O'Neill. *In* Nicoll, A. World drama p750-61

Schwarz, A. Society and human passion as a tragic motive. *In* Schwarz, A. From Büchner to Beckett p100-60

About individual works

Ah, wilderness!

Kauffmann, S. Ah, wilderness! *In* Kauffmann, S. Persons of the drama p136-39

Bound East for Cardiff

Voelker, P. D. The uncertain origins of Eugene O'Neill's "Bound East for Cardiff." *In* Virginia. University. Bibliographical Society. Studies in bibliography v32 p273-83

Children of the sea

Voelker, P. D. The uncertain origins of Eugene O'Neill's "Bound East for Cardiff." *In* Virginia. University. Bibliographical Society. Studies in bibliography v32 p277-83

Desire under the elms

Ehrlich, A. A streetcar named Desire under the elms: a study of dramatic space in A streetcar named Desire and Desire under the elms. *In* Tennessee Williams: a tribute p126-36

Long day's journey into night

D'Andrea, P. P. "Thou starre of poets": Shakespeare as DNA. *In* Shakespeare: aspects of influence p163-91

O'Neill, John

Critique and remembrance. *In* O'Neill, J. ed. On critical theory p 1-11

Essay 2. *In* Fitzgerald, R. ed. What it means to be human p25-43

The mutuality of accounts: an essay on trust. *In* McNall, S. G. ed. Theoretical perspectives in sociology p369-80

Time's body: Vico on the love of language and institution. *In* Giambattista Vico's science of humanity p333-39

Violence, technology, and the body politic. *In* Stanage, S. M. ed. Reason and violence p5-26

About individual works

Making sense together: an introduction to wild sociology

Agger, B. On happiness and the damaged life. *In* O'Neill, J. ed. On critical theory p12-33

O'Neill, Onora. See Nell, Onora O'Neill

O'Neill, William L.

Divorce as a moral issue: a hundred years of controversy. *In* "Remember the ladies": new perspectives on women in American history p127-43

Onetti, Juan Carlos

About individual works

A brief life

MacAdam, A. J. Juan Carlos Onetti & José Lezama Lima: a double portrait of the artist. *In* MacAdam, A. J. Modern Latin American narratives p102-09

Corpsegatherer

Brotherston, G. Survival in the sullied city: Juan Carlos Onetti. *In* Brotherston, G. The emergence of the Latin American novel p60-70

Ong, Walter Jackson

Commonplace rhapsody: Ravisius Textor, Zwinger and Shakespeare. *In* Classical influences on European culture A.D. 1500-1700 p91-126

Same as Ong, W. J. Typographic rhapsody: Raviasius Textor, Zwinger, and Shakespeare. *In* Ong, W. J. Interfaces of the word p 147-88

From rhetorical culture to new criticism: the poem as a closed field. *In* Simpson, L. P. ed. The possibilities of order: Cleanth Brooks and his work p150-67

Interfaces of the word

Contents

African talking drums and oral noetics

From epithet to logic: Miltonic epic and the closure of existence

From mimesis to irony: writing and print as integuments of voice

"I see what you say": sense analogues for intellect

Maranatha: death and life in the text of the Book

Media transformation: the talked book

The poem as a closed field: the once New Criticism and the nature of literature

Transformations of the word and alienation

Typographic rhapsody: Ravisius Textor, Zwinger, and Shakespeare

Same as Ong, W. J. Commonplace rhapsody: Ravisius Textor, Zwinger and Shakespeare. *In* Classical influence on European culture A.D. 1500-1700 p91-126

Voice and the opening of closed systems

The writer's audience is always a fiction

Oral culture and the literate mind. *In* Minority language and literature p134-49

Ramus: rhetoric and the pre-Newtonian mind. *In* Wimsatt, W. K. ed. Literary criticism: idea and act p128-48

Onîs, José de. See De Onís, José

Onitsha, Nigeria

Achebe, C. Onitsha, gift of the Niger. *In* Achebe, C. Morning yet on creation day p153-57

Onley, Gloria Elizabeth

Power politics in Bluebeard's castle. *In* Woodcock, G. ed. Poets and critics p191-214

Onofri, Arturo

About

Perella, N. J. Some twentieth-century voices. *In* Perella, N. J. Midday in Italian literature p145-200

Onondaga Indians

Reservations

Richards, C. E. Onondaga women: among the liberated. *In* Matthiasson, C. J. ed. Many sisters p401-19

Women—Case studies

Richards, C. E. Onondaga women: among the liberated. *In* Matthiasson, C. J. ed. Many sisters p401-19

Onondaga language. See Iroquoian languages

Ontario

Economic conditions

Osborne, B. S. Frontier settlement in eastern Ontario in the nineteenth century: a study in changing perceptions of land and opportunity. *In* Miller, D. H. and Steffen, J. O. eds. The frontier p201-25

Ontogenesis. See Ontogeny

Ontogeny

Temkin, O. German concepts of ontogeny and history around 1800. *In* Temkin, O. The double face of Janus p373-89

Ontological argument. See God—Proof, Ontological

Ontological-Hysteric Theater

Kauffmann, S. Ontological-Hysteric Theater. *In* Kauffmann, S. Persons of the drama p35-39

Ontology

Chisholm, R. M. Coming into being and passing away: can the metaphysician help? *In* Donnelly, J. P. ed. Language, metaphysics, and death p 1-24

Coomaraswamy, A. K. Does "Socrates is old" imply that "Socrates is"? *In* Coomaraswamy, A. K. Selected papers v2 p408-25

Quine, W. V. A logistical approach to the ontological problem. *In* Quine, W. V. The ways of paradox, and other essays p197-202

Quine, W. V. On multiplying entities. *In* Quine, W. V. The ways of paradox, and other essays p259-64

Scharfstein, B. A. 'Cogito ergo sum': Descartes, Augustine, and Sankara. *In* Philosophy East/philosophy West p199-217

Shehadi, F. A. Arabic and the concept of being. *In* Essays on Islamic philosophy and science p147-57

Vick, G. R. Heidegger's linguistic rehabilitation of Parmenides' "Being." *In* Murray, M. E. ed. Heidegger and modern philosophy p203-21

See also Existentialism; God—Proof, Ontological; Identity; Metaphysics; Necessity (Philosophy); Nothing (Philosophy); Philosophical anthropology

Open classroom approach to teaching. See Open plan schools

Open door policy (Far East) See Eastern question (Far East)

Open education. See Open plan schools

Open plan schools

Hawkridge, D. G. Communication and education in open learning systems. *In* Lerner, D. and Nelson, L. M. eds. Communication research—a half-century appraisal p70-103

See also Free schools

History

Perrone, V. A view of school reform. *In* Roots of open education in America p173-90

Open Theatre, New York (City)

Brustein, R. S. Back to the wilderness: The Open Theatre. *In* Brustein, R. S. The culture watch p118-22

Kauffmann, S. The Open Theater. *In* Kauffmann, S. Persons of the drama p28-31

Opera

Schmidgall, G. Afterword. *In* Schmidgall, G. Literature as opera p357-70

Sessions, R. To revitalize opera. *In* Sessions, R. Roger Sessions on music p137-45

Dramaturgy

Schmidgall, G. An opening perspective. *In* Schmidgall, G. Literature as opera p 1-28

History and criticism

Dent, E. J. Conclusion. *In* Dent, E. J. The rise of romantic opera p176-89

Dent, E. J. The conventions of opera. *In* Dent, E. J. The rise of romantic opera p17-32

Dent, E. J. The heritage of Gluck. *In* Dent, E. J. The rise of romantic opera p33-46

Dent, E. J. Introduction. *In* Dent, E. J. The rise of romantic opera p 1-16

Nicoll, A. Tragedy and opera. *In* Nicoll, A. World drama p294-306

England

See Opera, English

France

Isherwood, R. M. The third war of the musical Enlightenment. *In* Studies in eighteenth-century culture v4 p223-45

See also Opera, French

Germany

See Opera, German

Italy

See Opera, Italian

Opera, Chinese

Cheng, P. H. A comparative value analysis: traditional versus revolutionary opera. *in* Chu, G. C. Popular media in China p104-23

Chu, G. C. and Cheng, P. H. Revolutionary opera: an instrument for cultural change. *In* Chu, G. C. ed. Popular media in China p73-103

Opera, English

Luckett, R. Exotick but rational entertainments: the English dramatick operas. *In* English drama: forms and development p123-41

Opera, French

Dent, E. J. The school of Paris—II. *In* Dent, E. J. The rise of romantic opera p64-79

Dent, E. J. The school of Paris—III. *In* Dent, E. J. The rise of romantic opera p80-94

See also Opera—France

Opera, German

Dent, E. J. Beethoven and Schubert. *In* Dent, E. J. The rise of romantic opera p125-44

Opera, Italian

Dent, E. J. Rossini. *In* Dent, E. J. The rise of romantic opera p110-24

Operant behavior

Michaels, J. W. and Green, D. S. Behavioral sociology: emergent forms and issues. *In* McNall, S. G. ed. Theoretical perspectives in sociology p187-98

Secord, P. F. Making oneself behave: a critique of the behavioral paradigm and an alternative conceptualization. *In* Mischel, T. ed. The self p250-73

Operas

Librettos

Josipovici, G. Words and music today. *In* Josipovici, G. The lessons of modernism p143-50

Operating rooms

Charnley, Sir J. K. Experiences in the development of a clean air operating room. *In* The Frontiers of human knowledge p45-58

Operationalism

Chihara, C. S. and Fodor, J. A. Operationalism and ordinary language: a critique of Wittgenstein. *In* Dunlop, C. E. M. ed. Philosophical essays on dreaming p174-204

Ophuls, Max

About

Henderson, B. The long take. *In* Nichols, B. ed. Movies and methods p314-24

Truffaut, F. Max Ophuls is dead. *In* Truffaut, F. The films in my life p229-34

About individual works
Lola Montes

Truffaut, F. Max Ophuls: Lola Montes. *In* Truffaut, F. The films in my life p225-29

Opie, Eugene Lindsay

About

Harvey, A. M. Medical students on the march: Brown, MacCallum, and Opie. *In* Harvey, A. M. Adventures in medical research p18-31

Opie, Iona (Archibald) and Opie, Peter

Books that come to life. *In* The Saturday book 34 p61-79

Opie, Peter. See Opie, I. A. jt. auth.

Opinion (The word)

Ure, P. A note on 'opinion' in Daniel, Greville, and Chapman. *In* Ure, P. Elizabethan and Jacobean drama p209-20

Opinion, Public. See Public opinion

Opinions, Judicial. See Judicial opinions

Opium habit

Ober, W. B. Drowsed with the fume of poppies: opium and John Keats. *In* Ober, W. B. Boswell's clap and other essays p118-36

Opium trade

China—History

Spence, J. D. Opium smoking in Ch'ing China. *In* Conflict and control in late imperial China p143-73

Oppen, George

About individual works
Collected poems

Hamburger, M. George Oppen's Collected poems. *In* Hamburger, M. Art as second nature p153-56

Oppenheimer, Julius Robert

On Albert Einstein. *In* Einstein p44-49

Oppression (Psychology)

Tormey, J. F. Exploitation, oppression and self-sacrifice. *In* Gould, C. C. and Wartofsky, M. W. eds. Women and philosophy p206-21

Optical illusions

Gregory, R. L. The confounded eye. *In* Gregory, R. L. and Gombrich, Sir E. H. J. eds. Illusion in nature and art p49-95

Optical instruments. See Astronomical instruments; Optical trade

Optical masers. See Lasers

Optical trade

Great Britain—History

MacLeod, R. M. and MacLeod, K. War and economic development: government and the optical industry in Britain, 1914-18. *In* War and economic development p165-203

Optics

See also Achromatism; Color; Light; Night, Wave theory of; Perspective, Refraction

Early works to 1800

Lindberg, D. C. The science of optics. *In* Lindberg, D. C. ed. Science in the Middle Ages p338-68

Optics, Physiological

Lee, D. N. Visual information during locomotion. *In* Perception p250-67

See also Color vision; Optical illusions; Visual perception

Oral communication

Cronkhite, G. L. Rhetoric, communication, and psycho-epistemology. *In* Rhetoric: a tradition in transition p261-78

Ervin-Tripp, S. M. Speech acts and social learning. *In* Basso, K. H. and Selby, H. A. eds. Meaning in anthropology p123-53

Silverstein, M. Shifters, linguistic categories, and cultural description. *In* Basso, K. H. and Selby, H. A. eds. Meaning in anthropology p11-55

See also Oral tradition; Speech

Research

See Speech—Research

Africa

Ong, W. J. African talking drums and oral noetics. *In* Ong, W. J. Interfaces of the word p92-120

Oral communication. See Oral tradition

Oral history

Nevins, A. History this side the horizon. *In* Nevins, A. Allan Nevins on history p275-87

Nevins, A. Oral history: how and why it was born. *In* Nevins, A. Alan Nevins on history p288-93

See also Oral tradition

Oral intercourse

Humphreys, L. Tearoom trade: impersonal sex in public places. *In* Henslin, J. M. ed. Deviant life-styles p123-50

Oral interpretation

Winters, Y. The audible reading of poetry; excerpt from "The function of criticism." *In* Gross, H. S. ed. The structure of verse p129-46

See also Chants (Plain, Gregorian, etc.); Story-telling

Oral literature. See Folk literature

Oral poetry. See Folk poetry

The **Oresteia** (criticism) Aeschylus. *In* Kauffmann, S. Persons of the drama p102-04

Orestes

Art

Vermeule, E. T. More sleeping furies. *In* Studies in classical art and archaeology p185-88

Organism (Philosophy)

Rodis-Lewis, G. Limitations of the mechanical model in the Cartesian conception of the organism. *In* Hooker, M. ed. Descartes p152-70

Organization

See also Management; Organizational behavior

Research

See Organizational research

Organization, Industrial. See Industrial organization

Organization, Social. See Social structure

Organization for Economic Cooperation and Development

Lantzke, U. The OECD and its International Energy Agency. *In* Vernon, R. ed. The oil crisis p217-27

Organization of African Unity

Andemicael, B. OAU collaboration with the United Nations in economic and social development. *In* El-Ayouty, Y. ed. The Organization of African Unity after ten years p213-36

Boutros-Ghali, B. The League of Arab States and the Organization of African Unity. *In* El-Ayouty, Y. ed. The Organization of African Unity after ten years p47-61

Cervenka, Z. The OAU and the Nigerian Civil War. *In* El-Ayouty, Y. ed. The Organization of African Unity after ten years p152-73

El-Ayouty, Y. The OAU and the Arab-Israeli conflict: a case of mediation that failed. *In* El-Ayouty, Y. ed. The Organization of African Unity after ten years p189-212

Kapungu, L. T. The OAU's support for the liberation of Southern Africa. *In* El-Ayouty, Y. ed. The Organization of African Unity after ten years p135-51

Meyers, B. D. An analysis of OAU's effectiveness at regional collective defense. *In* El-Ayouty, Y. ed. The Organization of African Unity after ten years p118-32

Salih, G. M. The role of OAU in public administration and management. *In* El-Ayouty, Y. ed. The Organization of African Unity after ten years p237-50

Thompson, W. S. and Zartman, I. W. The development of norms in the African system. *In* El-Ayouty, Y. ed. The Organization of African Unity after ten years p3-46

Welch, C. E. The OAU and international recognition: lessons from Uganda. *In* El-Ayouty, Y. ed. The Organization of African Unity after ten years p103-17

Woronoff, J. The OAU and sub-Saharan regional bodies. *In* El-Ayouty, Y. ed. The Organization of African Unity after ten years p62-78

Yakemtchouk, R. The OAU and international law. *In* El-Ayouty Y. ed. The Organization of African Unity after ten years p79-102

Organization of American States

Bloomfield, R. J. The inter-American system: does it have a future? *In* Farer, T. J. ed. The future of the inter-American system p3-19

Rogers, W. D. A note on the future of the inter-American system. *In* Farer, T. J. ed. The future of the inter-American system p20-29

Wood, B. The Organisation of American States. *In* The Year book of world affairs, 1979 p148-66

Organization of Petroleum Exporting Countries

Doran, C. F. Oil politics and the rise of codependence. *In* Orr, D. S. and Soroos, M. S. eds. The global predicament p195-208

Girvan, N. Economic nationalism. *In* Vernon, R. ed. The oil crisis p145-58

Knorr, K. E. The limits of economic and military power. *In* Vernon, R. ed. The oil crisis p229-43

Lenczowski, G. The oil-producing countries. *In* Vernon, R. ed. The oil crisis p59-72

Mikdashi, Z. M. The OPEC process. *In* Vernon, R. ed. The oil crisis p203-15

Odell, P. R. The international oil companies in the new world oil market. *In* The Year book of world affairs, 1978 p76-92

Smart, I. Uniqueness and generality. *In* Vernon, R. ed. The oil crisis p259-81

Organizational behavior

Vaill, P. B. Toward a behavioral description of high-performing systems. *In* Leadership p103-25

Organizational effectiveness

Affleck, J. G. The constructive orchestration of chaos. *In* Benton, L. R. ed. Management for the future p 1-8

Brevoord, C. Effective management in the future. *In* Benton, L. R. ed. Management for the future p27-46

Organizational research

Vaill, P. B. Toward a behavioral description of high-performing systems. *In* Leadership p103-25

Organized crime. See Mafia

Orgasm

Moulton, J. M. Sex and reference. *In* Baker, R. and Elliston, F. A. eds. Philosophy & sex p34-44

Orgies. See Group sex

Ori, Kan

Japanese public opinion and Sino-Japanese relations, 1969-1972. *In* Postwar trends in Japan p37-60

Oriental art. See Art, Oriental

Oriental literature

History and criticism

Johns, A. H. Islam in Southeast Asia: problems of perspective. *In* Southeast Asian history and historiography p304-20

Oriental philosophy. See Philosophy, Oriental

Oriental poetry

Shaffer, E. S. The oriental idyll. *In* Shaffer, E. S. 'Kubla Khan' and The fall of Jerusalem p96-144

Orientation. See Orientation (Psychology)

Orientation (Psychology)

Peckham, M. The virtues of superficiality. *In* Peckham, M. Romanticism and behavior p249-62

Oriented (The word)
Porter, M. G. On redefining—oriented. *In* James B. McMillan: essays in linguistics by his friends and colleagues p163-80

Origen. See Origenes

Origenes
About individual works
Homelia Origenis de Maria Magdalena
Jennings, M. The art of the Pseudo-Origen homily De Maria Magdalena. *In* Medievalia et humanistica no. 5 p139-52

Woolf, R. English imitations of the Homelia Origenis de Maria Magdalena. *In* Chaucer and Middle English studies in honour of Rossell Hope Robbins p384-91

Origin (Periodical)
Corman, C. Origin. *In* Anderson, E. and Kinzie, M. eds. The little magazine in America: a modern documentary history p239-47

Origin of man. See Man—Origin

Origin of species
Sulloway, F. J. Geographic isolation in Darwin's thinking: the vicissitudes of a crucial idea. *in* Studies in history of biology v3 p23-65
See also Natural selection

Originality
Meyer, L. B. Forgery and the anthropology of art; excerpt from "Music, the arts, and ideas." *In* Aagaard-Mogensen, L. ed. Culture and art p53-66
See also Creation (Literary, artistic, etc.)

Orlov, Ann
Demythologizing scholarly publishing. *In* Altbach, P. G. and McVey, S. eds. Perspectives on publishing p231-45

Ormerod, David
'Unaccommodated man': Naipaul's B. Wordsworth and Biswas. *In* Baugh, E. ed. Critics on Caribbean literature p87-92

Ormond, Leonée
Browning and painting. *In* Armstrong, I. ed. Robert Browning p184-210

Ormsby-Lennon, Hugh
Poetic standards on the early Augustan battleground. *In* Studies in eighteenth-century culture v5 p253-80

Radical physicians and conservative poets in Restoration England: Dryden among the doctors. *In* Studies in eighteenth-century culture v7 p389-411

Ornament. See Decoration and ornament

Ornamental boxes. See Boxes, Ornamental

Ornamentalism and modernism. Carden, P. J. *In* Gibian, G. and Tjalsma, H. W. eds. Russian modernism p49-64

Ornstein, Norman J.
Causes and consequences of congressional change: subcommittee reforms in the House of Representatives, 1970-73. *In* Ornstein, N. J. ed. Congress in change p88-114

What makes Congress run? *In* Ornstein, N. J. ed. Congress in change p203-07

Ornstein, Norman J. and Rohde, David W.
Seniority and future power in Congress. *In* Ornstein, N. J. ed. Congress in change p72-87

Ornstein, Robert
Bourgeois morality and dramatic convention in A woman killed with kindness. *In* English Renaissance drama p128-41

Donne, Montaigne, and natural law. *In* Roberts, J. R. ed. Essential articles for the study of John Donne's poetry p129-41

Ornstein, Robert Evans
Contemporary sufism. *In* Tart, C. T. ed. Transpersonal psychologies p353-88

Oropesa, Tomàs de Iriarte y. See Iriarte y Oropesa, Tomàs de

O'Rourke, John F. and Chevan, Albert
A factorial ecology of age groups in the United States, 1960. *In* Gubrium, J. F. ed. Late life p32-58

Orpheus (formerly attributed to Giovanni Bellini)
Sheard, W. S. The Widener Orpheus: attribution, type, invention. *In* Collaboration in Italian Renaissance art p189-231

Orr, David Gerald
The icon in the time tunnel. *In* Browne, R. B. and Fishwick, M. W. eds. Icons of America p13-23

Orr, David W.
Modernization and the ecological perspective. *In* Orr, D. W. and Soroos, M. S. eds. The global predicament p75-89

Orr, David W. and Hill, Stuart
Leviathan, the open society, and the crisis of ecology. *In* Orr, D. W. and Soroos, M. S. eds. The global predicament p308-26

Orr, John Berk
The changing family: a social ethical perspective. *In* Tufte, V. and Myerhoff, B. G. eds. Changing images of the family p377-88

Orr, Linda
The limit of limits: aphorism in Char's Feuillets d'Hypnos. *In* Symbolism and modern literature p248-63

Orrantia, Dagoberto
The function of myth in Fernando del Paso's José Trigo. *In* Forster, M. H. ed. Tradition and renewal p129-38

Orrell, John
Inigo Jones at the Cockpit. *In* Shakespeare survey 30 p157-68

Orta, Garcia de
About
Fischel, W. J. Garcia de Orta—a militant Marrano in Portuguese-India in the 16th century. *In* Salo Wittmayer Baron v 1 p407-32

Ortega, Alvaro
Simple water technologies. *In* Strategies for human settlements: habitat and environment p79-83

Ortega y Gasset, José
About
Copleston, F. C. Ortega y Gasset and philosophical relativism. *In* Copleston, F. C. Philosophers and philosophies p172-84

Cowley, M. "And Jesse begat . . ." a note on literary generations. *In* Cowley, M. —And I worked at the writer's trade p 1-20

Meregalli, F. A parallel observer and innovator: José Ortega y Gasset. *In* Américo Castro and the meaning of Spanish civilization p267-91

Shaw, D. L. New directions. *In* Shaw, D. L. The generation of 1898 in Spain p186-205

Otchipwe Indians. See Chippewa Indians

Othello (Motion picture by Orson Welles)
Jorgens, J. J. Orson Welles's Othello. *In* Jorgens, J. J. Shakespeare on film p175-90

Othello (Motion picture by Stuart Burge and John Dexter)
Jorgens, J. J. Stuart Burge and John Dexter's Othello. *In* Jorgens, J. J. Shakespeare on film p191-206

Other minds (Theory of knowledge)
Cavell, S. Knowing and acknowledging. *In* Cavell, S. Must we mean what we say? p238-66
Elliston, F. A. Husserl's phenomenology of empathy. *In* Elliston, F. A. and McCormick, P. eds. Husserl p213-46
Swiggart, P. A note on telepathy. *In* Wheatley, J. M. O. and Edge, H. L. eds. Philosophical dimensions of parapsychology p139-41
Thalberg, I. Telepathic awareness of another's feelings. *In* Wheatley, J. M. O. and Edge, H. L. eds. Philosophical dimensions of parapsychology p133-38
Vesey, G. N. A. Other minds. *In* Royal Institute of Philosophy. Understanding Wittgenstein p149-61

Othlo, Monk of St Emmeram

About individual works
Vita S. Bonifacii
Morrison, K. F. The structure of holiness in Othloh's Vita Bonifatii and Ebo's Vita Ottonis. *In* Law, church, and society p131-56

Othloh. See Othlo, Monk of St Emmeram

Othlonus, Monk. See Othlo, Monk of St Emmeram

Otho B. xi, Laurence Nowell's transcript of BM Cotton. Grant, R. J. S. *In* Anglo-Saxon England 3 p111-24

Otite, Onigu
Encapsulated political systems. *In* Colonialism and change p67-84

Oto language. See Siouan languages

Otomian languages
Rensch, C. R. Otomanguean isoglosses. *In* Sebeok, T. A. ed. Native languages of the Americas v2 p163-84

O'Toole, L. M.
Analytic and synthetic approaches to narrative structure: Sherlock Holmes and 'The Sussex vampire.' *In* Fowler, R. ed. Style and structure in literature p143-76

O'Toole, Roger
Sectarianism in politics: case studies of Maoists and De Leonists. *In* Wallis, R. ed. Sectarianism p162-89

Otte, James Karl
The role of Alfred of Sareshel (Alfredus Anglicus) and his commentary on the Metheora in the reacquisition of Aristotle. *In* Viator: medieval and Renaissance studies v7 p197-209

Otto, Patricia Courtney
Women in the mirror: using novels to study Victorian women. *In* Kanner, B. ed. The women of England p296-344

Ottoman Empire. See Turkey—History—Ottoman Empire, 1288-1918

The **Ottoman** millet system: an evaluation. Shaw, S. J. *In* Király, B. K. ed. Tolerance and movements of religious dissent in Eastern Europe p183-84

Ó Tuathaigh, Gearóid
The distressed society: the struggle for emancipation and independence, 1801-1918. *In* De Breffny, B. ed. The Irish world p171-98

Oudart, Jean-Pierre
About
Dayan, D. The tutor-code of classical cinema. *In* Nichols, B. ed. Movies and methods p438-51

Oudh, India
Politics and government
Reeves, P. D. Pathways to political advancement: problems of choice for taluqdar politicians in late British India. *In* The Making of politicians: studies from Africa and Asia p103-15

Our Gang films
Appel, A. Tristram in movielove: Lolita at the movies. *In* A Book of things about Vladimir Nabokov p123-70

Oury, R. Scott
"The thing itself": C. S. Lewis and the value of something other. *In* Schakel, P. J. ed. The longing for a form p 1-19

Oury, Scott. See Oury, R. Scott

Ousby, Ian
Bloodhounds of heaven
Contents
Arthur Conan Doyle
Caleb Williams
Charles Dickens
Thief-taking and thief-making
Vidocq translated
Wilkie Collins and other sensation novelists

Ousmane, Sembene
About
Bestman, M. T. Sembène Ousmane: social commitment and the search for an African identity. *In* King, B. A. and Ogungbesan, K. eds. A celebration of Black and African writing p139-49

About individual works
God's bits of wood
Gakwandi, S. A. Commitment: Ousmane's God's bits of wood. *In* Gakwandi, S. A. The novel and contemporary experience in Africa p119-25
Hyman, S. E. Waiting for Bakayoko. *In* Hyman, S. E. The critic's credentials p192-97

Outdoor life. See Camping

Outer space
Exploration
Asimov, I. The moon as threshold. *In* The Frontiers of knowledge p359-99
Salmon, J. D. Resupplying spaceship earth: prospects for space industrialization. *In* Orr, D. W. and Soroos, M. S. eds. The global predicament p209-29

Ou-yang, Hsiu
About
Chen, Yü-shih. The literary theory and practice of Ou-yang Hsiu. *In* Chinese approaches to literature from Confucius to Liang Ch'i-ch'ao p67-96

Ovambo (African tribe) See Ambo (African tribe)

Ovanesian, Ashot
About
Mandel'shtam, O. E. Ashot Ovanesian. *In* Mandel'shtam, O. E. Selected essays p179-80

Ovenden, Michael W.
Intimations of unity. *In* Science and society: past, present, and future p363-74

Ovens. See Stoves

Overfield, James H.
Scholastic opposition to humanism in pre-Reformation Germany. *In* Viator: medieval and Renaissance studies v7 p391-420

Overholt, William H.
Sources of radicalism and revolution: a survey of the literature. *In* Radicalism in the contemporary age v1 p293-335

Overton, Richard
About
Heinemann, M. Popular drama and Leveller style—Richard Overton and John Harris. *In* Rebels and their causes p69-92

Overton, Willis F.
General systems, structure and development. *In* Riegel, K. F. and Rosenwald, G. C. eds. Structure and transformation p61-81

Oviatt, Alton B.
Reflections on effective teaching. *In* Buxton, T. H. and Prichard, K. W. eds. Excellence in university teaching p48-54

Ovid. See Ovidius Naso, Publius

Ovidius Naso, Publius
About
Lanham, R. A. The fundamental strategies: Plato and Ovid. *In* Lanham, R. A. The motives of eloquence p36-64

About individual works
Amores 1.5 (Aestus erat)
Rudd, N. Translation. *In* Rudd, N. Lines of enquiry p182-210

The art of love
Rudd, N. History: Ovid and the Augustan myth. *In* Rudd, N. Lines of enquiry p 1-31

Heroides
Fisher, E. A. Two notes on the Heroides. *In* Harvard Studies in classical philology v74 p193-205
Kenney, E. J. Notes on Ovid: III. *In* Harvard Studies in classical philology v74 p169-85
Trowbridge, F. H. Pope's Eloisa and the Heroides of Ovid. *In* Trowbridge, F. H. From Dryden to Jane Austen p135-53
White, D. G. Ovid, Heroides 16.45-46. *In* Harvard Studies in classical philology v74 p187-91

Metamorphoses
Anderson, W. S. Studies on the Naples Ms. IV F 3 of Ovid's Metamorphoses. *In* Illinois classical studies, v2 1977 p255-79
MacKellar, W. On two English metamorphoses. *In* Poetry and poetics from ancient Greece to the Renaissance p207-17

Metamorphoses (Book III)
Galinsky, G. K. Ovid's metamorphosis of myth. *In* Perspectives of Roman poetry p105-27

Metamorphoses (Book VIII)
Galinsky, G. K. Ovid's metamorphosis of myth. *In* Perspectives of Roman poetry p105-27

Influence—Chaucer
Harbert, B. Chaucer and the Latin classics. *In* Brewer, D. S. ed. Geoffrey Chaucer p137-53

Translations, English
Rudd, N. Translation. *In* Rudd, N. Lines of enquiry p182-210

Ovidius Naso, Publius in fiction, drama, poetry, etc.
Jahn, J. D. Chapman's enargia and the popular perspective on Ovids banquet of sence. *In* Tennessee Studies in literature v23 p15-30

Oviedo, José Miguel
La tia Julia y el escribidor, or the coded self-portrait. *In* Rossman, C. R. and Friedman, A. W. eds. Mario Vargas Llosa p166-81

Owen, Charles A.
Minor changes in Chaucer's Troilus and Criseyde. *In* Chaucer and Middle English studies in honour of Rossell Hope Robbins p303-19

Owen, Dawud G. Rosser- See Rosser-Owen, Dawud G.

Owen, Dean H.
The psychophysics of prior experience. *In* Studies in perception p467-524

Owen, Dorothy
The muniments of Ely Cathedral priory. *In* Church and government in the Middle Ages p157-76

Owen, Eric Trevor
The farewell of Hector and Andromache; excerpt from "The story of the Iliad." *In* Wright, J. H. ed. Essays on the Iliad p93-104

Owen, Guy
Robert Frost and The waste land. *In* French, W. G. ed. The twenties p351-63

Owen, Gwilym Ellis Lane
Aristotle on time. *In* Motion and time, space and matter p3-27

Owen, Robert
About
Saville, J. Robert Owen on the family and the marriage system of the old immoral world. *In* Rebels and their causes p107-21

About individual works
A new view of society
Ausubel, H. Robert Owen and his New view of society. *In* Salo Wittmayer Baron v 1 p129-34

Owens, Claire Myers
Zen Buddhism. *In* Tart, C. T. ed. Transpersonal psychologies p153-202

Owens, Joseph
Naming in Parmenides. *In* Kephalaion p16-25

Owens, William A.
From Isaac Watts to "heaven's radio." *In* From Parnassus p295-310

Ower, John
Black and secret poet: notes on Eli Mandel. *In* Woodcock, G. ed. Poets and critics p138-50
Erotic mythology in the poetry of Tennessee Williams. *In* Tennessee Williams: a tribute p609-23

The owl and the nightingale
Murphy, J. J. Rhetoric in early Middle English: rhetoric and dialectic in The owl and the nightingale. *In* Murphy, J. J. ed. Medieval eloquence p198-230

The owl and the pussycat (Motion picture)
Kauffmann, S. The owl and the pussycat. *In* Kauffmann, S. Living images p26-27

Ownership. See Property

Owomoyela, Oyekan
African literatures: an introduction
Contents
Drama
European language poetry
The novel
Traditional oral art: folklore
Vernacular literatures

Owsley, Frank Lawrence
The foundations of democracy. *In* Crunden, R. M. ed. The superfluous men p118-27
The pillars of agrarianism. *In* Crunden, R. M. ed. The superfluous men p184-94

About
O'Brien, M. Frank Owsley: "the immoderate past." *In* O'Brien, M. The idea of the American South, 1920-1941 p162-84

Owusu, Maxwell
Comparative politics, history, and political anthropology. *In* Colonialism and change p25-65

Oxenhandler, Neal
Listening to Burroughs' voice. *In* Federman, R. ed. Surfiction p181-201
Nihilism in Le Clézio's La Fièvre. *In* Symbolism and modern literature p264-73

Oxford. University
Connolly, C. Oxford in our twenties. *In* Connolly, C. The evening colonnade p8-11
Sutherland, L. S. William Blackstone and the legal chairs at Oxford. *In* Evidence in literary scholarship p229-40

Faculty
Engel, A. Emerging concepts of the academic profession at Oxford, 1800-1854. *In* The University in society v 1 p305-52

History
Engel, A. Emerging concepts of the academic profession at Oxford, 1800-1854. *In* The University in society v 1 p305-52
Lytle, G. F. Patronage patterns and Oxford colleges, c1300-c.1530. *In* The University in society v 1 p111-49
McConica, J. K. Scholars and commoners in Renaissance Oxford. *In* The University in society v 1 p151-81
Stone, L. J. The size and composition of the Oxford student body, 1580-1910. *In* The University in society v 1 p3-110

Students
Stone, L. J. The size and composition of the Oxford student body, 1580-1910. *In* The University in society v 1 p3-110

Oxford and Asquith, Herbert Henry Asquith, 1st Earl of
About
Koss, S. E. Asquith versus Lloyd George: the last phase and beyond. *In* Crisis and controversy p66-89

The Oxford English dictionary
Burchfield, R. W. Some thoughts on the revision of the O.E.D. *In* An English miscellany p208-18

The Oxford English dictionary. A supplement to the Oxford English dictionary
Burchfield, R. W. Further aspects of short-term historical lexicography. *In* James B. McMillan: essays in linguistics by his friends and colleagues p115-31

Oxford movement
Tennyson, G. B. The sacramental imagination. *In* Knoepflmacher, U. C. and Tennyson, G. B. eds. Nature and the Victorian imagination p370-90

Oxnam, Robert B.
The past is still present. *In* Terrill, R. ed. The China difference p57-77

Oxtoby, Willard G.
The ancient world. *In* Adams, C. J. ed. A reader's guide to the great religions p39-77

Oxyrhynchus, Egypt
Turner, E. G. Oxyrhynchus and Rome. *In* Harvard Studies in classical philology v79 p 1-24

Oxyrhynchus papyri
Turner, E. G. Oxyrhynchus and Rome. *In* Harvard Studies in classical philology v79 p 1-24

Oyono, Ferdinand
About individual works
Boy (Houseboy)
Gakwandi, S. A. Colonial injustice: Oyono's Houseboy. *In* Gakwandi, S. A. The novel and contemporary experience in Africa p13-21
Nnolim, C. E. Jungian archetypes and the main characters in Oyono's Une vie de boy. *In* African literature today no. 7: Focus on criticism p117-22

The old man and the medal
Okeh, P. I. Two ways of explaining Africa: an insight into Camara Laye's L'enfant noir and Ferdinand Oyono's Le vieux nègre et la médaille. *In* Exile and tradition p74-84

Oz, Amos
About
Alter, R. Fiction in a state of siege. *In* Alter, R. Defenses of the imagination p213-31
Alter, R. A problem of horizons. *In* Alter, R. Defenses of the imagination p249-62

Ozick, Cynthia
About
Cohen, S. B. The Jewish literary comediennes. *In* Cohen, S. B. ed. Comic relief p172-86

Ozu, Yasujirō
About individual works
Late spring
Kauffmann, S. Late spring. *In* Kauffmann, S. Living images p127-29

Tokyo story
Kauffmann, S. Tokyo story. *In* Kauffmann, S. Living images p100-03

P

PCE. See Communist Party of Spain

PCF. See Communist Party of France

PCI. See Communist Party of Italy

PCP. See Communist Party of Portugal

P.E.N. clubs, International Congress of the. See International Congress of the P.E.N. clubs, Barcelona

PFA. See Press Foundation of Asia

PKI. See Communist Party of Indonesia

PLO. See Munazzamat al-Tahrīr al-Filastīnīyah

PSI. See Psychical research

Paarlberg, Don
Agriculture—stumbling block or stepping stone? *In* Prochnow, H. V. ed. Dilemmas facing the nation p179-201

Pace, George B. See Doyle, A. I. jt. auth.

Pacem in Maribus IV to the United Nations Committee on the Peaceful Uses of the Sea-Bed, Recommendations from. Borgese, E. M. ed. *In* Borgese, E. M. and Krieger, D. eds. The tides of change p353-57

Pacheco, Francisco
About
Brown, J. A community of scholars. *In* Brown, J. Images and ideas in seventeenth-century Spanish painting p21-43

About individual works
Arte de la pintura, su antiguedad y grandezas
Brown, J. El Arte de la pintura as an academic document. *In* Brown, J. Images and ideas in seventeenth-century Spanish painting p44-62

Pacheco, José Emilio
About
Forster, M. H. Four contemporary Mexican poets: Marco Antonio Montes de Oca, Gabriel Zaid, José Emilio Pacheco, Homero Aridjis. *In* Forster, M. H. ed. Tradition and renewal p139-56

Pacific area
Economic conditions
Wu, Yuan-li. Economic trends in the future of the western Pacific. *In* Pacific Asia and U.S. policies: a political-economic-strategic assessment p95-107

Foreign relations—United States
Pfaltzgraff, R. L. and Davis, J. K. The Asian/Pacific region—implications for U.S. global strategy. *In* Pacific Asia and U.S. policies: a political-economic-strategic assessment p16-27
Tsunoda, J. America's future role in the Northwest Pacific area. *In* Pacific Asia and U.S. policies: a political-economic-strategic assessment p58-62

Pacific coast (Canada) in literature
Singleton, M. K. Frederick Niven redivivus: a Scots-Canadian's Pacific Northwest. *In* Bingham, E. R. and Love, G. A. eds. Northwest perspectives p122-35

Pacific relations. See Pan-Pacific relations

Pacific settlement of international disputes
Gross, L. On the justiciability of international disputes. *In* [Truth and tragedy]: a tribute to Hans Morgenthau p203-19
See also Arbitration, International; International courts; Mediation, International

Pacifici, Sergio
The modern Italian novel: from Capuana to Tozzi
Contents
Alfred Panzini: the bourgeois novel
Background of the modern Italian novel
Federigo Tozzi: the novel reborn
Gabriele d'Annunzio: the birth of superman
Giuseppe A. Borgese: the ideological void

Luigi Capuana: the theorist as novelist
Luigi Pirandello: man and his masks
Voices from the provinces: Grazia Deledda and Marino Moretti
Women writers: Neera and Aleramo
The modern Italian novel: from Pea to Moravia
Contents
Alberto Moravia: sex, money, and love in the novel
Background of the modern Italian novel
Carlo Emilio Gadda: the experimental novel
Carlo Levi: the essayist as novelist
Cesare Pavese: symbols, myths, and the novel
Dino Buzzati: the Gothic novel
Elio Vittorini: the poetization of ideology
The "southern" novel
Three writers in search of the novel

Pacifism
Chatfield, C. Pacifism. *In* Encyclopedia of American foreign policy p722-29
Gallie, W. B. Tolstoy: from 'War and peace' to 'The kingdom of God is within you.' *In* Gallie, W. B. Philosophers of peace and war p100-32

History
Brock, P. The Hutterites and war, 1530-1800. *In* Király, B. K. ed. Tolerance and movements of religious dissent in Eastern Europe p43-51

Packard, Cynthia, and Browne, Ray Broadus
Pinball machine: marble icon. *In* Browne, R. B. and Fishwick, M. W. eds. Icons of America p177-89

Packard, David
Perceptions of the military balance. *In* The New Atlantic challenge p203-16

Packwood, Robert William
The Senate seniority system. *In* Ornstein, N. J. ed. Congress in change p60-71

Paden, John N.
Dimensions of national integration in Africa. *In* African themes p175-93

Paden, William Doremus
Bertran de Born in Italy. *In* Italian literature: roots and branches p39-65

Padgett, Lewis, pseud. See Kuttner, Henry

Paganism
Momigliano, A. Pagan and Christian historiography in the fourth century A.D. *In* Momigliano, A. Essays in ancient and modern historiography p107-26
Roberts, J. J. M. Divine freedom and cultic manipulation in Israel and Mesopotamia. *In* Unity and diversity p181-90

Bibliography
Oxtoby, W. G. The ancient world. *In* Adams, C. J. ed. A reader's guide to the great religions p39-77

Page, Benjamin
Cooling the legislative tea. *In* Burnham, W. D. and Weinberg, M. W. eds. American politics and public policy p171-87

Page, Bruce. See Raw, C. jt. auth.

Page, Norman
The great tradition revisited. *In* Jane Austen's achievement p44-63
Orders of merit. *In* Weinsheimer, J. ed. Jane Austen today p92-108

Page, Philip

The Princess Casamassima: suicide and "The penetrating imagination." *In* Tennessee Studies in literature v22 p162-69

Page, R. Talbot. See Krutilla, J. V. jt. auth.

Page, Sally R.

Faulkner's sense of the sacred. *In* Faulkner: fifty years after The marble faun p101-21

Page, Thomas Nelson

About individual works
In ole Virginia

Downs, R. B. Moonlight and magnolia. *In* Downs, R. B. Books that changed the South p176-85

Pageants

Welty, E. A pageant of birds. *In* Welty, E. The eye of the story p315-20

See also Festivals; Masques

Paget, Violet

About

Briggs, J. A sense of the past: Henry James and Vernon Lee. *In* Briggs, J. Night visitors p111-23

Paget, William, 1st Baron of Beaudesert

About

Miller, H. Henry VIII's unwritten will: grants of lands and honours in 1547. *In* Wealth and power in Tudor England p87-105

Pai, Chih-ang

The central contradiction in Mao Dun's earliest fiction. *In* Modern Chinese literature in the May Fourth era p233-59

Pa'il, Meir

The dynamics of power: morality in armed conflict after the Six Day War. *In* Modern Jewish ethics p191-220

Pailes, Richard A. and Whitecotton, Joseph W.

The greater Southwest and the Mesoamerican "world" system: an exploratory model of frontier relationships. *In* The Frontier v2 p105-21

Pain, Philip

About

Daly, R. Gnostics and naturalists. *In* Daly, R. J. God's altar p128-61

Pain

Kotarba, J. A. The chronic pain experience. *In* Douglas, J. D. and Johnson, J. M. [eds.] Existential sociology p257-72

Paine, Thomas

About

Granger, B. I. Early Philadelphia serials. *In* Granger, B. I. American essay serials from Franklin to Irving p41-69

Hinz, E. J. Thomas Paine. *In* Emerson, E. H. ed. American literature, 1764-1789 p39-57

About individual works
Common sense

Downs, R. B. American firebrand. *In* Downs, R. B. Books that changed the world p175-88

Painter, George Duncan

About individual works
Marcel Proust

Auchincloss, L. Marcel Proust: the autobiography in the novel. *In* Auchincloss, L. Life, law and letters p39-45

Proust v 1: The early years

Connolly, C. Marcel Proust: 2. *In* Connolly, C. The evening colonnade p186-88

Painter, Jack. See Painter, John

Painter, John

Eschatological faith in the Gospel of John. *In* Reconciliation and hope p36-52

Painter, Susan. See Moran, M. jt. auth.

Painter, Susan Lee- See Lee-Painter, Susan

Painters

See also Artists

France

Miller, E. M. Molière and the court painters, especially Pierre Mignard. *In* Johnson, R. B.; Neumann, E. S. and Trail, G. T. eds. Molière and the commonwealth of letters: patrimony and posterity p5-30

Great Britain

Hunt, W. H. Pre-Raphaelitism and the pre-Raphaelite brotherhood; excerpts. *In* Sambrook, J. ed. Pre-Raphaelitism p27-44

Painting

Berger, J. Past seen from a possible future. *In* Berger, J. The look of things p211-21

Grene, M. G. The aesthetic dialogue of Sartre and Merleau-Ponty. *In* Grene, M. G. Philosophy in and out of Europe p87-107

Veltruský, J. Some aspects of the pictorial sign (1973). *In* Matejka, L. and Titunik, I. R. eds. Semiotics of art p245-64

Wollheim, R. Style now. *In* **Concerning contemporary art** p133-53

See also Cubism; Landscape painting; Narrative painting; Portrait painting; Preraphaelitism; Realism in art

Early works to 1800

Brown, J. El Arte de la pintura as an academic document. *In* Brown, J. Images and ideas in seventeenth-century Spanish painting p44-62

History

Gilman, E. B. The curious perspective in England. *In* Gilman, E. B. The curious perspective p50-66

History—19th century

See Painting, Modern—19th century—History

Poetry

Ormond, L. Browning and painting. *In* Armstrong, I. ed. Robert Browning p184-210

Snodgrass, W. D. Poems about paintings. *In* Snodgrass, W. D. In radical pursuit p63-97

Psychological aspects

Garai, J. E. The use of painting to resolve an artist's identity conflicts. *In* Ulman, E. and Dachinger, P. eds. Art therapy p311-24

Ulman, E. and Levy, B. I. An experimental approach to the judgment of psychopathology from painting. *In* Ulman, E. and Dachinger, P. eds. Art therapy p393-402

Painting, Abelam (New Guinea tribe)

Korn, S. M. The formal analysis of visual systems as exemplified by a study of Abelam (Papua New Guinea) paintings. *In* Greenhalgh, M. and Megaw, J. V. S. eds. Art in society p161-73

Painting, Abstract

Long, R. C. W. Kandinsky and abstraction: the role of the hidden image. *In* Kaplan, P. and Manso, S. eds. Major European art movements, 1900-1945 p275-98

See also Abstract expressionism; Constructivism (Art)

Painting, Baroque

Spain

Brown, J. Theory into practice: the arts and the academy. *In* Brown, J. Images and ideas in seventeenth-century Spanish painting p63-83

Spain—Historiography

Brown, J. Introduction: observations on the historiography of seventeenth-century Spanish painting. *In* Brown, J. Images and ideas in seventeenth-century Spanish painting p3-18

Painting, British

Goodreau, D. **Pictorial sources of the neo-classical style: London or Rome?** *In* Studies in eighteenth-century culture v4 p247-70

Painting, Chinese

Coomaraswamy, A. K. Chinese painting at Boston. *In* Coomaraswamy, A. K. Selected papers v 1 p308-15

Loewe, M. The world to come. A two-thousand year old painting from China. *In* Symbols of power p35-40

History

Fong, Wen C. Archaism as a 'primitive' style. *In* Artists and traditions p89-109

Soper, A. C. The relationship of early Chinese painting to its own past. *In* Artists and traditions p21-47

Sung-Yüan dynasties, 960-1368

Li, Chu-tsing. The uses of the past in Yüan landscape painting. *In* Artists and traditions p73-88

Ming-Manchu (Ch'ing) dynasties, 1368-1912

Cahill, J. F. The Orthodox movement in early Ch'ing painting. *In* Artists and traditions p169-81

Cahill, J. F. Style as idea in Ming-Ch'ing painting. *In* Meisner, M. J. and Murphey, R. eds. The Mozartian historan p137-56

Edwards, R. The orthodoxy and the unorthodox. *In* Artists and traditions p185-99

Ho, Wai-kam. Tung Ch'i-ch'ang's new orthodoxy and the Southern School theory. *In* Artists and traditions p113-29

Vanderstappen, H. A. The style of some seventeenth-century Chinese paintings. *In* Artists and traditions p149-68

20th century

Sullivan, M. Orthodoxy and individualism in twentieth-century Chinese art. *In* Artists and traditions p201-05

Painting, Dutch

History

Chiarenza, C. Notes on aesthetic relationships between seventeenth-century Dutch paintings and nineteenth-century photography. *In* One hundred years of photographic history p19-34

Painting, English

See also Painting, British

History

Hemstedt, G. Painting and illustration. *In* Lerner, L. ed. The Victorians p139-52

Painting, French

Mandel'shtam, O. E. The French. *In* Mandel'shtam, O. E. Selected essays p193-95

See also Fauvism

History

Sobieszek, R. A. Photography and the theory of realism in the Second Empire: a reexamination of a relationship. *In* One hundred years of photographic history p145-59

Painting, Italian

History

Barolsky, P. Facetiae by Raphael and his friends. *In* Barolsky, P. Infinite jest: wit and humor in Italian Renaissance art p75-100

Barolsky, P. The grotesque and mock-heroic in north Italy. *In* Barolsky, P. Infinite jest: wit and humor in Italian Renaissance art p183-208

Winternitz, E. Musical instruments for the stage in paintings by Filippino Lippi, Piero di Cosimo, and Lorenzo Costa. *In* Winternitz, E. Musical instruments and their symbolism in Western art p211-25

Painting, Modern

Peckham, M. Iconography and iconology in the arts of the nineteenth and twentieth centuries. *In* Peckham, M. Romanticism and behavior p90-108

19th century

See Painting, Victorian

19th century—History

Fairlie, A. Flaubert and some painters of his time. *In* The Artist and the writer in France p111-25

Reff, T. Images of Flaubert's Queen of Sheba in later nineteenth-century art. *In* The Artist and the writer in France p126-33

20th century—History

Danto, A. C. The artworld. *In* Margolis, J. Z. ed. Philosophy looks at the arts p132-44

20th century—United States

Tashjian, D. L. Painting the machine. *In* Tashjian, D. L. Skyscraper primitives p204-26

Painting, Narrative. See Narrative painting

Painting, Religious. See Christian art and symbolism

Painting, Renaissance

Barolsky, P. Facetiae by Raphael and his friends. *In* Barolsky, P. Infinite jest: wit and humor in Italian Renaissance art p75-100

Bensimon, M. J. Modes of perception of reality in the Renaissance. *In* The Darker vision of the Renaissance p221-72

Italy—History

Barolsky, P. The grotesque and mock-heroic in north Italy. *In* Barolsky, P. Infinite jest: wit and humor in Italian Renaissance art p183-208

Tuscany

Wilkins, D. The meaning of space in four-teenth-century Tuscan painting. *In* Jeffrey, D. L. ed. By things seen: reference and recognition in medieval thought p109-21

Painting, Renaissance—*Continued*
Venice—History
Barolsky, P. Laughter from the Venetian boudoir. *In* Barolsky, P. Infinite jest: wit and humor in Italian Renaissance art p158-82

Painting, Russian
History
Hilton, A. The revolutionary theme in Russian realism. *In* Millon, H. A. and Nochlin, L. eds. Art and architecture in the service of politics p108-27

Painting, Spanish
Brown, J. Theory into practice: the arts and the academy. *In* Brown, J. Images and ideas in seventeenth-century Spanish painting p63-83

Historiography
Brown, J. Introduction: observations on the historiography of seventeenth-century Spanish painting. *In* Brown, J. Images and ideas in seventeenth-century Spanish painting p3-18

Painting, Venetian
History
Barolsky, P. Laughter from the Venetian boudoir. *In* Barolsky, P. Infinite jest: wit and humor in Italian Renaissance art p158-82

Painting, Victorian
England
Waldfogel, M Narrative painting. *In* Altholz, J. L. ed. The mind and art of Victorian England p159-74

Painting and literature. See Art and literature

Paintings. See Painting

Pais, Abraham
Einstein, Newton, and success. *In* Einstein p35-37

Paivio, Allan
Psychological processes in the comprehension of metaphor. *In* Ortony, A. ed. Metaphor and thought p150-71

Pakistan
Foreign relations—United States
Richter, W. L. Relative abstention: India & Pakistan. *In* Higham, R. D. ed. Intervention or abstention: the dilemma of American foreign policy p202-17

Military policy
Bellany, I. The acquisition of arms by poor states. *In* The Year book of world affairs, 1976 p174-89

Politics and government—1971-
Choudhury, G. W. Roles and careers of middle-rank politicians: some cases from East Bengal. *In* The Making of politicians: studies from Africa and Asia p195-206

LaPorte, R. Pakistan and Bangladesh. *In* Kearney, R. N. ed. Politics and modernization in South and Southeast Asia p109-52

Pakistan-Indian Conflict, 1971- See India-Pakistan Conflict, 1971-

Pakistan orations (English)
McLeod, A. L. The creation of national images in Indian and Pakistani speeches to the United States Congress. *In* Narasimhaiah, C. D. ed. Awakened conscience p378-88

Pakizegi, Behnaz
Legal and social position of Iranian women. *In* Beck, L. and Keddie, N. R. eds. Women in the Muslim world p216-26

Pakot (African people) See Suks

Pal, Kristo Das
About
McGuire, J. Kristo Das Pal: politician as intermediary. *In* The Making of politicians: studies from Africa and Asia p93-102

Palaces
Great Britain
Hembry, P. Episcopal palaces, 1535 to 1660. *In* Wealth and power in Tudor England p146-66

Italy—Bologna
Moos, S. von. The palace as a fortress: Rome and Bologna under Pope Julius II. *In* Millon, H. A. and Nochlin, L. eds. Art and architecture in the service of politics p46-79

Italy—Rome (City)
Moos, S. von. The palace as a fortress: Rome and Bologna under Pope Julius II. *In* Millon, H. A. and Nochlin, L. eds. Art and architecture in the service of politics p46-79

Turkey
See Istanbul. Blachernae Palace

Palaeologan illumination, Toward a history of. Buchthal, H. *In* The Place of book illumination in Byzantine art p143-77

Palamari, Demetra
The shark who swallowed his epoch: family, nature, and society in the novels of Emile Zola. *In* Tufte, V. and Myerhoff, B. G. eds. Changing images of the family p155-72

Palanco, Rafael López
Evolution of building technology. *In* Bugliarello, G. and Doner, D. B. eds. The history and philosophy of technology p344-57

Palazzeschi, Aldo
About
Pacifici, S. Three writers in search of the novel. *In* Pacifici, S. The modern Italian novel: from Pea to Moravia p18-46

Palenque, Mexico
Antiquities
Rands, R. L. The ceramic sequence at Palenque, Chiapas. *In* Mesoamerican archaeology p51-75

Rands, R. L. The rise of Classic Maya civilization in the Northwestern Zone: isolation and integration. *In* The Origins of Maya civilization p159-80

Paleography
Colker, M. L. Some recent works for palaeographers. *In* Medievalia et humanistica no. 8 p235-42

See also Manuscripts; Ostraka

Russia
Auty, R. Russian writing and printing: writing. *In* Auty, R. and Obolensky, D. eds. An introduction to Russian language and literature p41-47

Paleography, Latin
History
John, J. J. Latin paleography. *In* Powell, J. M. ed. Medieval studies p 1-68

Paleography, Musical. See Music—Manuscripts

Paleo-Indians

North America

Stewart, T. D. Perspectives on some problems of early man common to America and Australia. *In* Grafton Elliot Smith p114-35

Paleontology

History

Todes, D. P. V. O. Kovalevskii: the genesis, content, and reception of his paleontological work. *In* Studies in history of biology v2 p99-165

Palés Matos, Luis

About

Johnson, L. A. El tema negro: the nature of primitivism in the poetry of Luis Palés Matos. *In* DeCosta, M. ed. Blacks in Hispanic literature p123-36

Palestine

Economic conditions

Gottheil, F. M. Arab immigration into pre-state Israel: 1922-1931. *In* The Palestinians p30-40

Emigration and immigration

Gottheil, F. M. Arab immigration into pre-state Israel: 1922-1931. *In* The Palestinians p30-40

Foreign relations— United States

Deutsch, D. The Palestine question: domestic pressures on the President for intervention, 1944-1948. *In* Higham, R. D. ed. Intervention or abstention: the dilemma of American foreign policy p79-94

History—To 70 A.D.

Pritchard, J. B. The age of Solomon. *In* Pritchard, J. B. ed. Solomon & Sheba p17-39

See also Judaism—History—Post-exilic period, 586 B.C.-210 A.D.

History—70-

Aumann, M. Land ownership in Palestine, 1880-1948. *In* The Palestinians p21-29

Sharon, M. Palestine in the Islamic and Ottoman period. *In* The Palestinians p9-20

History—638-1917

Kedourie, É. Sir Mark Sykes and Palestine, 1915-16. *In* Kedourie, É. Arabic political memoirs and other studies p236-42

See also Crusades

History—1917-1948

Alexander, Y. From terrorism to war: the anatomy of the birth of Israel. *In* International terrorism p211-57

Lesch, A. M. The origins of Palestine Arab nationalism. *In* Nationalism in a non-national state p265-90

Weizmann, C. The Jewish people and Palestine; excerpts. *In* The Palestinians p46-50

Palestine Liberation Organization. See Munazzamat al-Tahrīr al-Filastīnīyah

Palestine problem, 1917- See Jewish-Arab relations—1917-

Palestinian Arabs

Gottheil, F. M. Arab immigration into pre-state Israel: 1922-1931. *In* The Palestinians p30-40

Gurevitz, B. The Soviet Union and the Palestinians. *In* Ro'i, Y. ed. The limits to power p254-81

Lesch, A. M. The origins of Palestine Arab nationalism. *In* Nationalism in a non-national state p265-90

Porat, Y. The Palestinian-Arab nationalist movement. *In* The Palestinians p121-27

Pryce-Jones, D. On Israel's East. *In* The Palestinians p209-12

Sharon, M. Palestine in the Islamic and Ottoman period. *In* The Palestinians p9-20

Syrkin, M. Palestinian nationalism: its development and goal. *In* The Palestinians p199-208

See also Jewish-Arab relations

Palestinians. See Palestinian Arabs

Palestrina. Temple of Fortune

Wittkower, R. Pietro da Cortona's project for reconstructing the Temple of Palestrina. *In* Wittkower, R. Studies in the Italian baroque p115-24

Palewski, Gaston

A surprising friendship: Malraux and De Gaulle. *In* Courcel, M. H. de, ed. Malraux p68-78

Paley, Grace

About

Mickelson, A. Z. Piecemeal liberation: Marge Piercy, Sara Davidson, Marilyn French, Grace Paley. *In* Mickelson, A. Z. Reaching out: sensitivity and order in recent American fiction by women p175-234

Paley, Morton D.

"Wonderful originals"—Blake and ancient sculpture. *In* Essick, R. N. and Pearce, D. R. eds. Blake in his time p170-97

Pali Buddhism. See Hinayana Buddhism

Pāli language

Lexicology

Coomaraswamy, A. K. Some Pāli words. *In* Coomaraswamy, A. K. Selected papers v2 p264-329

Palihawadana, Mahinda

A Buddhist response: religion beyond ideology and power. *In* Christian faith in a religiously plural world p34-45

Is there a Theravada Buddhist idea of grace? *In* Christian faith in a religiously plural world p181-95

Palladio, Andrea

About

Lotz, W. Three essays on Palladio: Observations on Palladio's drawings. *In* Lotz, W. Studies in Italian Renaissance architecture p181-86

Lotz, W. Three essays on Palladio: Reflections on Palladio as town planner. *In* Lotz, W. Studies in Italian Renaissance architecture p187-90

About individual works
Villa Rotonda, Vicenza

Lotz, W. Three essays on Palladio: The Rotonda: a secular building with a dome. *In* Lotz, W. Studies in Italian Renaissance architecture p190-208

Palley, Claire

The role of law in relation to minority groups. *In* Alcock, A. E.; Taylor, B. K. and Welton, J. M eds. The future of cultural minorities p120-60

Palmer, Arlene M.

Through the glass case: the curator and the object. *In* Material culture and the study of American life p219-44

Palmer, Bruce

Codification of terrorism as an international crime. *In* International terrorism and political crimes p507-18

Strategic guidelines for the United States in 1980s. *In* Grand strategy for the 1980s p73-112

Palmer, Darryl W.

The Resurrection of Jesus and the mission of the Church. *In* Reconciliation and hope p205-23

Palmer, David

The consolation of the wedded. *In* Baker, R. and Elliston, F. A. eds. Philosophy & sex p178-89

Palmer, David John

Critical studies. *In* Shakespeare survey 27 p155-72

Critical studies [another essay] *In* Shakespeare survey 28 p149-64

Critical studies [another essay] *In* Shakespeare survey 29 p157-67

Palmer, Elihu

About

French, R. S. Elihu Palmer, radical deist, radical republican: a reconsideration of American free thought. *In* Studies in eighteenth-century culture v8 p87-108

Palmer, Eustace Taiwo

The development of Sierra Leone writing. *In* King, B. A. and Ogungbesan, K. eds. A celebration of Black and African writing p245-57

Yulisa Amadu Maddy: No past, no present, no future. *In* African literature today no. 7: Focus on criticism p163-66

About individual works

An introduction to the African novel

James, A. A. Eustace Palmer: An introduction to the African novel. *In* African literature today no. 7: Focus on criticism p147-52

Palmer, John Joseph Norman, and Wells, A. P.

Ecclesiastical reform and the politics of the Hundred Years War during the pontificate of Urban V (1362-70). *In* War, literature, and politics in the late Middle Ages p169-89

Palmer, Leslie Howard

The ironic word in Hardy's novels. *In* Tennessee Studies in literature v20 p109-23

Palmer, Nettie

About

Smith, V. B. Australia of the spirit: some aspects of the work of Vance and Nettie Palmer, 1938-48. *In* Bards, bohemians, and bookmen p236-50

Palmer, Robert Roswell

The European Enlightenment in its American setting. *In* Aspects of American liberty p47-55

The fading dream: how European revolutionaries have seen the American Revolution. *In* Essays on modern European revolutionary history p89-104

The impact of the American Revolution abroad. *In* The Impact of the American Revolution abroad p5-18

Palmer, Stanley H.

Rebellion, emancipation, starvation: the dilemma of peaceful protest in Ireland, 1798-1848. *In* Essays on modern European revolutionary history p 3-38

Palmer, Vance

About

Smith, V. B. Australia of the spirit: some aspects of the work of Vance and Nettie Palmer, 1938-48. *In* Bards, bohemians, and bookmen p236-50

Palmer, William J.

Dickens and the eighteenth century. *In* Dickens Studies Annual v6 p15-39

Palombo, Stanley R.

Dreams, memory, and the origin of thought. *In* Thought, consciousness, and reality p40-83

Palson, Charles, and Palson, Rebecca

Swinging in wedlock. *In* Henslin, J. M. ed. Deviant life-styles p231-54

Palson, Rebecca. See Palson, C. jt. auth.

Pan-Africanism

Reid, I. S. Black Americans and Africa. *In* The Black American reference book p648-83

See also African cooperation

Pan-Americanism

Karnes, T. L. Pan-Americanism. *In* Encyclopedia of American foreign policy p730-41

See also Monroe doctrine

Pan-Arabism. See Panarabism

Pan-Germanism. See Pangermanism

Pan-Pacific relations

Chapman, C. Towards a new Pacific alliance. *In* The Year book of world affairs, 1975 p88-105

Panagia Phorbiotissa (Church) See Asinou. Panagia Phorbiotissa (Church)

Panama

Foreign relations—United States

Cox, R. G. Choices for partnership or bloodshed in Panama. *In* The Americas in a changing world p132-55

Panama Canal

Cox, R. G. Choices for partnership or bloodshed in Panama. *In* The Americas in a changing world p132-55

Rubinoff, I. A sea-level canal in Panama. *In* Borgese, E. M. and Krieger, D. eds. The tides of change p254-63

Panarabism

Boutros-Ghali, B. Arab diplomacy: failures and successes. *In* Arab and American cultures p221-36

Laroui, A. Sands and dreams. *In* Arab and American cultures p 3-13

Pandey, Gyanendra

The Shastris of Kashi and Lahore: the making of Congress leaders. *In* The Making of politicians: studies from Africa and Asia p116-25

Panek, Leroy Lad

Watteau's shepherds

Contents

A. A. Milne

Agatha Christie

Anthony Berkeley Cox

Backgrounds and approaches

Panek, Leroy L.
Watteau's shepherds
Contents—Continued
Dorothy Sayers
E. C. Bentley
The end
John Dickson Carr
Margery Allingham
Ngaio Marsh

Pangenesis. See Heredity

Pangermanism
Kann, R. A. Protestantism and German nationalism in the Austro-German Alpine lands (1). *In* Király, B. K. ed. Tolerance and movements of religious dissent in Eastern Europe p11-25

Panić, M.
The origin of increasing inflationary tendencies in contemporary society. *In* The Political economy of inflation p137-60

Panić, Mica. See Panić, M.

Panić, Milivoje. See Panić, M.

Paniker, K. Ayyappa
Folk humour: a comparison of the comic ballads of Australia and Kerala (India). *In* Narasimhaiah, C. D. ed. Awakened conscience p236-50

Panislamism. See Panarabism

Panizza Lorch, Maristella de. See De Panizza Lorch, Maristella

Pannell, William E.
The religious heritage of Blacks. *In* Wells, D. F. and Woodbridge, J. D. eds. The evangelicals p96-107

Pannonia (Roman province)
Eadie, J. W. Civitates and clients: Roman frontier policies in Pannonia and Mauretania Tingitana. *In* Miller, D. H. and Steffen, J. O. eds. The frontier p57-80

Panofsky, Erwin
Style and medium in the motion pictures. *In* Denby, D. ed. Awake in the dark p30-48

Panpsychism
Nagel, T. Panpsychism. *In* Nagel, T. Mortal questions p181-95

Panteón de los Reyes. See Leon, Spain. San Isidoro el Real (Church) Panteón de los Reyes

Pantham, Thomas
The formation of the politically active stratum: evidence from the career origins of party activists in an Indian city. *In* The Making of politicians: studies from Africa and Asia p207-26

Pantheism. See Monotheism; Theism

Pantheon of the Kings of the Church of San Isidoro. See Leon, Spain. San Isidoro el Real (Church) Panteón de los Reyes

Pantomime

England

Speaight, G. Pantomime. *In* The Saturday book 34 p10-23

Pantzer, Katherine F. See Jackson, W. A. jt. auth.

Panuska, Joseph A.
Open-endedness as an educational goal. *In* Buxton, T. H. and Prichard, K. W. eds. Excellence in university teaching p94-102

Panzini, Alfredo

About

Pacifici, S. Alfredo Panzini: the bourgeois novel. *In* Pacifici, S. The modern Italian novel: from Capuana to Tozzi p68-77

Paoletti, John T.
The Bargello David and public sculpture in fifteenth-century Florence. *In* Collaboration in Italian Renaissance art 99-111

Paoli, Cesare

About individual works
Documenti di ser Ciappelletto

Benton, J. F. The accounts of Cepperello da Prato for the tax on nouveaux acquêts in the bailliage of Troyes. *In* Order and innovation in the Middle Ages p111-35

Paolo Romano

About individual works
Saint Paul

Chastel, A. Two Roman statues: Saints Peter and Paul. *In* Collaboration in Italian Renaissance art p59-73

Paolo Taccone. See Paolo Romano

Papacy

History

McCready, W. D. Papalists and antipapalists: aspects of the church/state controversy in the later Middle Ages. *In* Viator: medieval and Renaissance studies v6 p241-73

Papago Indians

Rites and ceremonies

Underhill, R. M. The salt pilgrimage; excerpt from "Papago Indian religion." *In* Tedlock, D. E. and Tedlock, B. eds. Teachings from the American earth p42-74

Papal infallibility. See Popes—Infallibility

Papal legates. See Legates, Papal

Papal States

History

Blumenthal, U. R. Patrimonia and regalia in 1111. *In* Law, church, and society p 9-20

Paper making and trade

Trade-marks
See Water-marks

United States—History

Bidwell, J. The size of the sheet in America: paper-moulds manufactured by N. & D. Sellers of Philadelphia. *In* American Antiquarian Society. Proceedings v87 pt2 p299-342

Paper moon (Motion picture)
Kauffmann, S. Paper moon. *In* Kauffmann, S. Living images p202-04

Papermaking and trade. See Paper making and trade

Papert, Seymour A.
The mathematical unconscious. *In* Wechsler, J. ed. On aesthetics in science p105-19

Paphos

Antiquities

Megaw, A. H. S. An early thirteenth-century Aegean glazed ware. *In* Studies in memory of David Talbot Rice p34-45

Papp, Joseph

About

Kauffmann, S. The stages of Joseph Papp. *In* Kauffmann, S. Persons of the drama p3-28

Pappas, George Sotiros
Broad, sensa, and explanation. *In* Studies in perception p402-21

Papua-New Guinea (Territory) See Nissan Island

Papuans
Faithorn, E. The concept of pollution among the Káfe of the Papua New Guinea Highlands. *In* Reiter, R. R. ed. Toward an anthropology of women p127-40

History
Jacobs, W. R. The fatal confrontation: early native-white relations on the frontiers of Australia, New Guinea, and America—a comparative study. *In* The American Indian p27-54

Papyrus manuscripts. See Manuscripts (Papyri)

Papyrus Michigan 1447
Renner, T. A papyrus dictionary of metamorphoses. *In* Harvard Studies in classical philology v82 p277-93

Parabole. See Metaphor; Simile

Paracelsus

About
Temkin, O. The elusiveness of Paracelus. *In* Temkin, O. The double face of Janus p225-38

Influence—Donne
Murray, W. A. Donne and Paracelsus: an essay in interpretation. *In* Roberts, J. R. ed. Essential articles for the study of John Donne's poetry p122-28

Paradise in literature
Bleeth, K. A. The image of paradise in The merchant's tale. *In* The Learned and the lewed p45-60

Fryer, J. The myth of America as New World Garden of Eden: The Garden. *In* Fryer, J. The faces of Eve p3-5

Hannay, M. P. A preface to Perelandra. *In* Schakel, P. J. ed. The longing for a form p73-90

Scheerer, C. The deathly paradise of Sylvia Plath. *In* Butscher, E. ed. Sylvia Plath p166-76

The paradise of dainty devices
May, S. W. William Hunnis and the 1577 Paradise of dainty devices. *In* Virginia. University. Bibliographical Society. Studies in bibliography v28 p63-80

Paradox
Bowers, J. W. and Sanders, R. E. Paradox as a rhetorical strategy. *In* Rhetoric: a tradition in transition p300-15

Quine, W. V. The ways of paradox. *In* Quine, W. V. The ways of paradox, and other essays p 1-18

Paradox in literature
Colie, R. L. The rhetoric of transcendence. *In* Roberts, J. R. ed. Essential articles for the study of John Donne's poetry p199-219

McCanles, M. Paradox in Donne. *In* Roberts, J. R. ed. Essential articles for the study of John Donne's poetry p220-35

Paralegal personnel. See Legal assistants

Parallax
Henderson, J. A. Erasmus Reinhold's determination of the distance of the sun from the earth. *In* The Copernican achievement p108-29

Sun
Abers, E. S. and Kennel, C. F. Commentary: the role of error in ancient methods for determining the solar distance. *In* The Corpernican achievement p130-36

Parallels (Geometry)
Lukas, E. Non-Euclidean geometry. *In* Neyman, J. ed. The heritage of Copernicus: theories "pleasing to the mind" p359-77

See also Geometry, Non-Euclidean

Paramedical education

China (People's Republic of China, 1949-)
Li, V. H. Politics and health care in China: the barefoot doctors. *In* Stanford legal essays p303-16

Paranoia
Altschule, M. D. The singular case of James Tilly Matthews, a clear paranoid. *In* Altschule, M. D. Origins of concepts in human behavior p85-87

Kearney, M. A world-view explanation of the evil eye. *In* The Evil eye p175-92

Meissner, W. W. Cognitive aspects of the paranoid process—prospectus. *In* Thought, consciousness, and reality p159-216

Cases, clinical reports, statistics
Haslam, J. Illustrations of madness. *In* Altschule, M. D. Origins of concepts in human behavior p88-121

'Paranormal', On the meaning of. Braude, S. E. *In* Ludwig, J. K. ed. Philosophy and parapsychology p227-44

Parapsychology. See Psychical research

Parapsychology and animals
Morris, R. L. Biology and psychical research. *In* Parapsychology: its relation to physics, biology, psychology, and psychiatry p48-75

Parapsychology and philosophy
Broad, C. D. The philosophical implications of foreknowledge. *In* Ludwig, J. K. ed. Philosophy and parapsychology p287-312

Also in Wheatley, J. M. O. and Edge, H. L. eds. Philosophical dimensions of parapsychology p198-226

Broad, C. D. The relevance of psychical research to philosophy. *In* Ludwig, J. K. ed. Philosophy and parapsychology p43-63

Also in Wheatley, J. M. O. and Edge, H. L. eds. Philosophical dimensions of parapsychology p10-29

Ducasse, C. J. The philosophical importance of "psychic phenomena." *In* Wheatley, J. M. O. and Edge, H. L. eds. Philosophical dimensions of parapsychology p30-45

Kneale, M. H.; Robinson, R. G. F. and Mundle, C. W. K. Symposium: Is psychical research relevant to philosophy? *In* Ludwig, J. K. ed. Philosophy and parapsychology p64-109

Ludwig, J. K. Philosophy and parapsychology. *In* Ludwig, J. K. ed. Philosophy and parapsychology p17-40

Price, H. H. Some philosophical questions about telepathy and clairvoyance. *In* Wheatley, J. M. O. and Edge, H. L. eds. Philosophical dimensions of parapsychology p105-32

Parapsychology and philosophy—*Continued*

Tart, C. T. The physical universe, the spiritual universe, and the paranormal. *In* Tart, C. T. ed. Transpersonal psychologies p113-51

Wheatley, J. M. O. Knowledge, empiricism and ESP. *In* Wheatley, J. M. O. and Edge, H. L. eds. Philosophical dimensions of parapsychology p142-53

Parapsychology and religion. See Religion and parapsychology

Pardo, Arvid

New institutions for ocean space. *In* Borgese, E. M. and Krieger, D. eds. The tides of change p324-27

Paredes, J. Anthony

Back from disappearance: the Alabama Creek Indian community. *In* Williams, W. L. ed. Southeastern Indians since the removal era p123-41

Paredes, Raymund Arthur

The promise of Chicano literature. *In* Minority language and literature p29-41

Parekh, Bhikhu C.

Hannah Arendt's critique of Marx. *In* Hannah Arendt: the recovery of the public world p67-100

Parekh, Bikhu. See Parekh, Bhikhu C.

Parent and child

Benassi, V. A. and Larson, K. M. Modification of family interaction with the child as the behavior-change agent. *In* Behavior modification and families p331-37

Elkind, D. Culture, change, and children. *In* Elkind, D. The child and society p3-16

Elkind, D. Exploitation and the generational conflict. *In* Elkind, D. The child and society p80-89

Elkind, D. Middle-class delinquency. *In* Elkind, D. The child and society p167-74

Entwisle, D. R. Socialization and the young family. *In* Major social issues p208-16

Horowitz, F. D. Directions for parenting. *In* Behavior modification and families p7-33

Kagan, J. The child in the family. *In* Rossi, A. S.; Kagan, J. and Hareven, T. K. eds. The family p33-56

Peterson, R. F. Power, programming, and punishment: could we be overcontrolling our children? *In* Behavior modification and families p338-52

Zuckerman, M. Dr. Spock: the confidence man. *In* Rosenberg, C. E. ed. The family in history p179-207

See also Adolescence; Child abuse; Children—Management; Father and child; Fathers; Mother and child; Single-parent family

Case studies

Bernal, M. E. and others. Comparison of boys' behaviors in homes and classrooms. *In* Behavior modification and families p204-27

Martin, S. and others. The comparability of behavioral data in laboratory and natural settings. *In* Behavior modification and families p189-203

Parent and child (Law) See Children—Law; Custody of children

Parent-teacher relationships. See Home and school

Parental behavior in animals. See Animals, Infancy of

Parental custody. See Custody of children

Parenti, Michael John

The blessings of private enterprise: a personal reminiscence. *In* Studies in Italian American social history p81-83

About

Parenti, M. J. The blessings of private enterprise: a personal reminiscence. *In* Studies in Italian American social history p81-83

Parents' advisory committees in education

Singleton, R. California: the Self-Determination in Education Act, 1968. *In* Parents, teachers, and children: prospects for choice in American education p77-83

Parents without partners. See Single-parent family

Parfit, Derek

Lewis, Perry, and what matters. *In* Rorty, A. O. ed. The identities of persons p91-107

Parikh, Kirit S.

India in 2001. *In* Economic factors in population growth p303-23

Paris, Bernard J.

Experiences of Thomas Hardy. *In* Levine, R. A. The Victorian experience: the novelists p203-37

Paris

Description

Benjamin, W. Paris, capital of the nineteenth century. *In* Benjamin, W. Reflections p146-62

Chiaromonte, N. Paris, 1951. *In* Chiaromonte, N. The worm of consciousness, and other essays p41-49

Connolly, C. Shades of spleen. *In* Connolly, C. The evening colonnade p143-47

Economic conditions—Historiography

Le Roy Ladurie, E. Changes in Parisian rents from the end of the Middle Ages to the eighteenth century. *In* Le Roy Ladurie, E. The territory of the historian p61-75

History

Benjamin, W. Paris, capital of the nineteenth century. *In* Benjamin, W. Reflections p146-62

Intellectual life

Showalter, E. Madame de Graffigny and her salon. *In* Studies in eighteenth-century culture v6 p377-91

Tate, A. Miss Toklas' American cake. *In* Tate, A. Memoirs and opinions, 1926-1974 p46-66

Social conditions

Leclant, J. Coffee and cafés in Paris, 1644-1693. *In* Food and drink in history p86-108

Paris. Arc de triomphe de l'Étoile

Butler, R. Long live the Revolution, the Republic, and especially the Emperor: the political sculpture of Rude. *In* Millon, H. A. and Nochlin, L. eds. Art and architecture in the service of politics p92-107

Paris. Comédie-Française

Kauffmann, S. The Comédie Française. *In* Kauffmann, S. Persons of the drama p72-74

Paris. École nationale supérieure des beaux-arts

Draper, J. The Ecole des beaux-arts and the architectural profession in the United States: the case of John Galen Howard. *In* Kostof, S. ed. The architect p209-37

Paris. Opéra
Craft, R. The Paris Opéra in New York. *In* Craft, R. Current convictions p59-68

Paris. Peace Conference, 1919
Elcock, H. J. J. M. Keynes at the Paris Peace Conference. *In* Keynes, M. ed. Essays on John Maynard Keynes p162-76

Sharp, A. J. Britain and the protection of minorities at the Paris Peace Conference, 1919. *In* Hepburn, A. C. ed. Minorities in history p170-88

Paris. Université
Bernstein, A. E. Magisterium and license: corporate autonomy against papal authority in the medieval University of Paris. *In* Viator: medieval and Renaissance studies v9 p291-307

Gilbert, N. W. Richard de Bury and the "quires of yesterday's sophisms." *In* Philosophy and humanism p229-57

Sharratt, P. Peter Ramus and the reform of the university: the divorce of philosophy and eloquence? *In* French Renaissance studies, 1540-70 p4-20

About individual works
Chartularium Universitatis parisiensis
Moody, E. A. Ockham, Buridan, and Nicholas of Autrecourt. *In* Moody, E. A. Studies in medieval philosophy, science, and logic p127-60

Paris, Declaration of, 1856
Ferris, N. B. Transatlantic misunderstanding: William Henry Seward and the Declaration of Paris negotiation of 1861. *In* Rank and file p55-78

Paris in literature
Lafarge, C. Paris and myth: one vision of horror. *In* Studies in eighteenth-century culture v5 p281-91

The Paris Review
About individual works
Writers at work: The Paris Review interviews (series)
Cowley, M. How writers write. *In* Cowley, M.—And I worked at the writer's trade p176-93

Sheed, W. The interview as art. *In* Sheed, W. *In* Sheed, W. The good word & other words p206-11

Parish, William Lucious
The view from the factory. *In* Terrill, R. ed. The China difference p183-98

Parisi, Frank M.
Emblems of melancholy: For children: The gates of paradise. *In* Phillips, M. C. ed. Interpreting Blake p70-110

Parisi, Joseph A.
The care and funding of Pegasus. *In* Anderson, E. and Kinzie, M. eds. The little magazine in America: a modern documentary history p216-35

Park, Joseph F.
Spanish Indian policy in northern Mexico, 1765-1810. *In* Weber, D. J. ed. New Spain's far northern frontier p217-34

Park, Robert Ezra
About
Goist, P. D. A sociologist and the city: the experience of Robert Park. *In* Goist, P. D. From Main Street to State Street p110-20

Park, Rosemary
The disestablished humanities. *In* Small comforts for hard times p308-20

Liberal education: a chameleon. *In* From Parnassus p105-18

About individual works
The disestablished humanities
Hanning, R. W. A view from the Ivory Tower: in response to Rosemary Park. *In* Small comforts for hard times p321-31

Park, William
Ironist and moralist: the two readers of Tom Jones. *In* Studies in eighteenth-century culture v8 p233-42

Parke, Catherine N.
Imlac and autobiography. *In* Studies in eighteenth-century culture v6 p183-98

Parke, Thomas, 1749-1835
About
Bell, W. J. Thomas Parke, M.D., physician and friend. *In* Bell, W. J. The colonial physician & other essays p71-97

Parker, Bird. See Parker, Charles Christopher

Parker, Brian. See Parker, R. B.

Parker, Charles
Pop song, the manipulated ritual. *In* Abbs, P. ed. The black rainbow p134-67

Parker, Charles Christopher
About
Reed, I. Bird lives! *In* Reed, I. Shrovetide in old New Orleans p105-09

Parker, David
The Huguenots in seventeenth-century France. *In* Hepburn, A. C. ed. Minorities in history p11-30

Parker, David L.
From sound believer to practical preparationist: some Puritan harmonics in Franklin's Autobiography. *In* Lemay, J. A. L. ed. The oldest revolutionary p67-75

Parker, Dorothy (Rothschild)
About
Sheed, W. The wit of George S. Kaufman and Dorothy Parker. *In* Sheed, W. The good word & other words p159-63

About individual works
The portable Dorothy Parker
O'Hara, J. Dorothy Parker, hip pocket size. *In* O'Hara, J. "An artist is his own fault" p158-61

Parker, Geoffrey
War and economic change: the economic costs of the Dutch revolt. *In* War and economic development p49-71

Parker, Hershel
Melville. *In* American literary scholarship, 1973 p65-84

Melville [another essay] *In* American literary scholarship, 1974 p43-59

Melville [another essay] *In* American literary scholarship, 1975 p59-82

Melville [another essay] *In* American literary scholarships, 1976 p47-59

Melville [another essay] *In* American literary scholarship, 1977 p49-63

Tromping through fairyland: two books on Melville's tales. *In* Review v 1 1979 p183-93

Parker, Kenneth

Nadine Gordimer and the pitfalls of liberalism. *In* Parker, K. ed. The South African novel in English p114-30

The South African novel in English. *In* Parker, K. ed. The South African novel in English p 1-26

Parker, Patricia A.

Inescapable romance

Contents

Ariosto

Keats

Milton

Spenser

Parker, R. B.

Is there a Canadian drama? *In* Staines, D. ed. The Canadian imagination p152-87

Volpone and Reynard the Fox. *In* Renaissance drama [1976] p3-42

Parker, Roy. See Land, H. jt. auth.

Parker, Theodore

About

Richardson, R. D. Parker and Alcott. *In* Richardson, R. D. Myth and literature in the American renaissance p34-64

Parker, William Nelson

Introduction. *In* Parker, W. N. and Jones, E. L. eds. European peasants and their markets p3-22

Parkes, Malcolm Beckwith

The impact of punctuation: punctuation, or pause and effect. *In* Murphy, J. J. ed. Medieval eloquence p127-42

The palaeography of the Parker manuscript of the Chronicle, laws and Sedulius, and historiography at Winchester in the late ninth and tenth centuries. *In* Anglo-Saxon England 5 p149-71

Parkhurst, Thomas

About

Love, H. Preacher and publisher: Oliver Heywood and Thomas Parkhurst. *In* Virginia. University. Bibliographical Society. Studies in bibliography v31 p227-35

Parkinson, F.

International economic integration in Latin America and the Caribbean: a survey. *In* The Year book of world affairs, 1977 p236-56

Parkinson, George Henry Radcliffe

Spinoza on the power and freedom of man. *In* Freeman, E. and Mandelbaum, M. H. eds. Spinoza p7-33

The translation theory of understanding. *In* Royal Institute of Philosophy. Communication and understanding p 1-19

"Truth is its own standard": aspects of Spinoza's theory of truth. *In* Shahan, R. W. and Biro, J. I. eds. Spinoza: new perspectives p35-55

Parkman, Francis

About

Nevins, A. Francis Parkman. *In* Nevins, A. Allan Nevins on history p333-47

Parks, George Bruner

Italian tributes to Cardinal Pole. *In* Studies in the continental background of Renaissance English literature: essays presented to John L. Lievsay p43-66

Pico della Mirandola in Tudor translation. *In* Philosophy and humanism p352-69

Parliamentary government. See Representative government and representation

Parman, Donald Lee

The Indian and the Civilian Conservation Corps. *In* The American Indian p127-45

Parmar, Samuel L.

Self-reliant development in an "interdependent" world. *In* Erb, G. F. and Kallab, V. eds. Beyond dependency p3-27

Parmar, Shyam

Traditional folk forms in India and their use in national development; excerpt from "Traditional folk media in India." *In* Fischer, H. D. and Melnik, S. R. eds. Entertainment: a cross-cultural examination p74-82

Parmenides Eleates

About

Owens, J. Naming in Parmenides. *In* Kephalaion p16-25

Vick, G. R. Heidegger's linguistic rehabilitation of Parmenides' "Being." *In* Murray, M. E. ed. Heidegger and modern philosophy p203-21

Parnell, Charles Stewart, in fiction, drama, poetry, etc.

Lyons, F. S. L. The Parnell theme in literature. *In* Place, personality and the Irish writer p69-95

Parody

Brody, S. N. The comic rejection of courtly love. *In* In pursuit of perfection p221-61

Brower, R. A. Introduction: Translation as parody. *In* Brower, R. A. Mirror on mirror p 1-16

Kenney, W. Parodies and imitations of Johnson in the eighteenth century. *In* Studies in eighteenth-century culture v7 p463-73

Ledger, M. Ring around A Christmas garland. *In* Aeolian harps p227-46

Ross, D. O. The Culex and Moretum as post-Augustan literary parodies. *In* Harvard Studies in classical philology v79 p235-64

See also Burlesque (Literature)

Paroissien, David H.

Charles Dickens and the Weller family. *In* Dickens Studies Annual v2 p 1-38

Dickens and the cinema. *In* Dickens Studies Annual v7 p68-80

Parrill, Anna Sue

Portraits of ladies. *In* Tennessee Studies in literature v20 p92-99

Parrinder, Edward Geoffrey

Religions of the East. *In* Life after death p80-96

Parrinder, Geoffrey. See Parrinder, Edward Geoffrey

Parrinder, Patrick

Imagining the future: Wells and Zamyatin. *In* H. G. Wells and modern science fiction p126-43

Parrini, Carl P.

Reparations. *In* Encyclopedia of American foreign policy p893-99

Parrish, Bernie

About individual works

They call it a game

Sheed, W. Unnecessary roughness. *In* Sheed, W. The good word & other words p148-53

Parrots (in religion, folklore, etc.)

Crocker, J. C. My brother the parrot. *In* The Social use of metaphor p164-92

Parry, Adam Milman

Have we Homer's Iliad? *In* Wright, J. H. ed. Essays on the Iliad p 1-27

Language and characterization in Homer. *In* Harvard Studies in classical philology v76 p 1-22

About

Havelock, E. A. In memoriam Adam and Anne Parry. *In* Yale classical studies v24 p ix-xv

Parry, Albert

Terrorism: from Robespierre to Arafat

Contents

America's pie
Anarchists: philosophers with bombs
Arafat and other sacrificers
Azef: terror chief as double agent
Canada's white niggers
Crimson in the Irish Green and Orange
The Days of Rage and after
Fanon and the Black Panthers
The Final Solution
Fire in the African bush
Five minutes to midnight
Genghis Khan with the telephone
The guillotine athirst
Heirs to Tupac-Amaru
Hitler's Holocaust
Hunting the Tsar
In the name of Marx
Lenin: high priest of terror
Mao's muzzle
The morbid tango
New Europe's old hatreds
The new international
The new Robin Hoods, the media, and the police
Now is the time
Red samurai and Turkey's nihilists
Right-wing terror
Robespierre's bloody virtue
Siempre la violencia!
Stalin's Archipelago
The Symbionese and Patty Hearst
Terror: an overall view
Terror as aberration
Terrorists then and now
Thought waves of hatred
Three innovations
Trotsky: target of boomerang
Vietnam and other jungles, other pyres
Violence: genesis of terror
Wanton romantics: Guevara, Debray, Marighella
The Weathermen

Parry, Anne

About

Havelock, E. A. In memoriam Adam and Anne Parry. *In* Yale classical studies v24 p ix-xv

Parry, John Horace

A secular sense of responsibility. *In* First images of America p287-304

Parry, Vernon S.

La manière de combattre. *In* War, technology and society in the Middle East p218-56

Parsons, Robert

About individual works

A memorial of the reformation of England

Scarisbrick, J. J. Robert Persons's plans for the 'true' reformation of England. *In* Historical perspectives p19-42

Parsons, Talcott

Action theory and the human condition

Contents

Belief, unbelief, and disbelief
Christianity
Death in the Western world
Durkheim on religion revisited: another look at The elementary forms of the religious life
The future of the university
The "gift of life" and its reciprocation [co-authored with Renée C. Fox and Victor M. Lidz]
Health and disease: a sociological and action perspective
The interpretation of dreams by Sigmund Freud
A paradigm of the human condition
Religion in postindustrial America: the problem of secularization
Research with human subjects and the "professional complex"
The sick role and the role of the physician reconsidered
Some considerations on the growth of the American system of higher education and research

Also in Culture and its creator p266-84

Stability and change in the American university
The university "bundle": a study of the balance between differentiation and integration

Clarence Ayre's economics and sociology. *In* Science and ceremony p175-79

Religious and economic symbolism in the Western world. *In* Johnson, H. M. ed. Religious change and continuity p 1-48

Social systems and the evolution of action theory

Contents

Comparative studies and evolutionary change
Equality and inequality in modern society, or social stratification revisited
Malinowski and the theory of social systems
On building social system theory: a personal history
The present status of "structural-functional" theory in sociology

Also in The idea of social structure p67-83

The relations between biological and socio-cultural theory
Review of Harold J. Bershady, Ideology and social knowledge
Review of L. T. Hobhouse, Sociology and philosophy: a centenary collection of essays and articles
Social interaction
Social structure and the symbolic media of interchange

Also in Blau, P. M. ed. Approaches to the study of social structure p94-120

Social systems
Some problems of general theory in sociology
Some theoretical considerations on the nature and trends of change of ethnicity

Also in Glazer, N. and Moynihan, D. P. eds. Ethnicity p53-83

Parsons, Talcott—*Continued*
About
Creelan, P. G. Social theory as confession: Parsonsian sociology and the symbolism of evil. *In* Brown, R. H. and Lyman, S. M. eds. Structure, consciousness, and history p173-96

Lemert, C. C. Analytic realism: Talcott Parsons. *In* Lemert, C. C. Sociology and the twilight of man p80-108

Parsons, T. On building social system theory: a personal history. *In* Parsons, T. Social systems and the evolution of action theory p22-76

About individual works
Social structure and the symbolic media of interchange

Wallace, W. L. Structure and action in the theories of Coleman and Parsons. *In* Blau, P. M. ed. Approaches to the study of social structure p121-34

Knowledge, Theory of
Bauman, Z. Understanding as the work of reason: Talcott Parsons. *In* Baumann, Z. Hermeneutics and social science p131-47

Part-songs, French
Brown, H. M. Instruments and voices in the fifteenth-century chanson. *In* Current thought in musicology p89-137

Heartz, D. The chanson in the humanist era. *In* Current thought in musicology p193-230

Partai Komunis Indonesia. See Communist Party of Indonesia

Partee, Barbara Hall
Linguistic metatheory. *In* Harman, G. ed. On Noam Chomsky p303-15

Parthenon. See Athens. Parthenon

Participation, Political. See Political participation

Participation, Social. See Social participation

Participation books. See Toy and movable books

Particle beams. See Particles (Nuclear physics)

Particles (Nuclear physics)
Bromberg, J. L. The concept of particle creation before and after quantum mechanics. *In* Historical studies in the physical sciences v7 p161-91

Partido Communista de Cuba. See Communist Party of Cuba

Parties. See Entertaining

Parties, Political. See Political parties

Partiîâ Sofsialistov-revoliûfsionerov
Parry, A. Azef: terror chief as double agent. *In* Parry, A. Terrorism: from Robespierre to Arafat p120-30

Partisan Review
Phillips, W. On Partisan Review. *In* Anderson, E. and Kinzie, M. eds. The little magazine in America: a modern documentary history p131-41

Partonopeus de Blois
Hanning, R. W. Critical moments: individuality in chivalric romance. *In* Hanning, R. W. The individual in twelfth-century romance p53-104

Hanning, R. W. The romance plot and the crisis of inner awareness. *In* Hanning, R. W. The individual in twelfth-century romance p194-233

Partridge, Astley Cooper
Form and language in English neo-classical poetry. *In* An English miscellany p131-48

Partridge, Edward Bellamy
Teaching English. *In* Cahn, S. M. ed. Scholars who teach p37-73

Partridge, Monica
Alexander Herzen: his last phase. *In* Essays in honour of E. H. Carr p36-56

Partridge, William L.
Uses and nonuses of anthropological data on drug abuse. *In* Eddy, E. M. and Partridge, W. L. eds. Applied anthropology in America p350-72

See also Eddy, E. M. jt. auth.

Partridge, William L. and Eddy, Elizabeth M.
The development of applied anthropology in America. *In* Eddy, E. M. and Partridge, W. L. eds. Applied anthropology in America p3-45

Party affiliation
Illinois
Jensen, R. J. The religious and occupational roots of party identification: Illinois and Indiana in the 1870's. *In* Swierenga, R. P. ed. Beyond the Civil War synthesis p255-73

Indiana
Jensen, R. J. The religious and occupational roots of party identification: Illinois and Indiana in the 1870's. *In* Swierenga, R. P. ed. Beyond the Civil War synthesis p255-73

Pascal, Blaise
About
Brombert, V. H. Pascal's dungeon. *In* Brombert, V. H. The romantic dungeon p18-29

Voegelin, E. Helvétius and the heritage of Pascal. *In* Voegelin, E. From Enlightenment to Revolution p53-73

Pascal, Roy
The dual voice
Contents
Conclusions
Dostoyevsky and the flux of experience: The idiot
Early accomplishment: Georg Büchner: Lenz
Early accomplishment: Goethe: The elective affinities
Early accomplishment: Jane Austen
The French masters: Emile Zola—use and abuse
The French masters: Gustave Flaubert: Madame Bovary
The narrator problem
Victorians: Dickens and mimicry: Bleak House
Victorians: The Thackeray-type narrator; Anthony Trollope—confusions of perspective
Victorians: The Thackeray-type narrator: George Eliot—author and narrator

Pasch, Alan
Comments on Bedau's "Free speech, the right to listen, and disruptive interference." *In* The Concept of academic freedom p212-16

Comments on Bedau's reply. *In* The Concept of academic freedom p226-34

Paschal II, Pope. See Paschalis II, Pope

Paschal, Carlo
About
Momigliano, A. The first political commentary on Tacitus. *In* Momigliano, A. Essays in ancient and modern historigoraphy p205-18

Paschalis II, Pope
About
Blumenthal, U. R. Patrimonia and regalia in 1111. *In* Law, church, and society p 9-20

Paschalius, Carolus. See Paschal, Carlo

Paschkis, Victor
Education for our changing technology. *In* Against pollution and hunger p249-55

Pascoe, Louis Bernard
Gerson and the Donation of Constantine: growth and development within the Church. *In* Viator: medieval and Renaissance studies v5 p469-85

Pashukanis, Evgenil Bronislavich
About
Sharlet, R. Pashukanis and the withering away of law in the USSR. *In* Cultural revolution in Russia, 1928-1931 p169-88

Pasigraphy
Walker, D. P. Esoteric symbolism. *In* Poetry and poetics from ancient Greece to the Renaissance p218-32

Pasión Valley, Guatemala. See Petén Guatemala (Dept.)

Pasley, John Malcolm Sabine
Nietzsche's use of medical terms. *In* Pasley, J. M. S. ed. Nietzsche: imagery and thought p123-58

Pasley, Malcolm. See Pasley, John Malcolm Sabine

Paso, Fernando del
About individual works
José Trigo
Orrantia, D. The function of myth in Fernando del Paso's José Trigo. *In* Forster, M. H. ed. Tradition and renewal p129-38

Pasolini, Pier Paolo
The cinema of poetry. *In* Nichols, B. ed. Movies and methods p542-58
About
Eco, U. Articulations of the cinematic code. *In* Nichols, B. ed. Movies and methods p590-607
Ragusa, O. Gadda, Pasolini, and experimentalism: form or ideology? *In* Ragusa, O. Narrative and drama p134-54
Taylor, J. R. Pier Paolo Pasolini. *In* Taylor, J. R. Directors and directions p44-68
About individual works
The cinema of poetry
Abramson, R. Structure and meaning in the cinema. *In* Nichols, B. ed. Movies and methods p558-68

Pasquale, Carlo. See Paschal, Carlo

Pasquino, Gianfranco, and Pecchini, Umberto
Italy. *In* Planning, politics and public policy p70-92

Passaic, N. J.
Politics and government
Ebner, M. H. Socialism and progressive political reform: the 1911 change-of-government in Passaic. *In* Stave, B. M. ed. Socialism and the cities p116-40

Passenger accommodation. See Steamboats—Passenger accommodation

The passion of Anna (Motion picture)
Simon, J. I. The passion of Anna; excerpt from "Movies into film." *In* Denby, D. ed. Awake in the dark p128-36

The passion of Joan of Arc (Motion picture)
Potamkin, H. A. The passion of Jeanne D'Arc. *In* Denby, D. ed. Awake in the dark p102-05

Passion-plays. See Mysteries and miracle-plays

Passions. See Emotions

Passive resistance. See Nonviolence

Passmore, John Arthur
Attitudes to nature. *In* Royal Institute of Philosophy. Nature and conduct p251-64
Hume and the ethics of belief. *In* David Hume p77-92
A note on care. *In* Niblett, W. R. ed. The sciences, the humanities and the technological threat p106-15

Passos, John Dos. See Dos Passos, John

Paster, Gail Kern
The city in Plautus and Middleton. *In* Renaissance drama [1973] p29-44

Pasternak, Boris Leonidovich
From A safe-conduct. *In* Proffer, C. R. ed. Modern Russian poets on poetry p87-95
From Notes of a translator. *In* Proffer, C. R. ed. Modern Russian poets on poetry p96-101
Some statements. *In* Gibbons, R. ed. The poet's work: 29 masters of 20th century poetry on the origins and practice of their art p23-27
Also in Proffer, C. R. ed. Modern Russian poets on poetry p81-85
About
Anning, N. J. Pasternak. *In* Freeborn, R. ed. Russian literary attitudes from Pushkin to Solzhenitsyn p99-119
Barnes, C. J. Boris Pasternak's revolutionary year. *In* Barnes, C. J. ed. Studies in twentieth century Russian literature p46-60
Jakobson, R. The contours of The safe conduct. *In* Matejka, L. and Titunik, I. R. eds. Semiotics of art p188-96
Pasternak, B. L. From A safe-conduct. *In* Proffer, C. R. ed. Modern Russian poets on poetry p87-95
Pritchett, V. S. Boris Pasternak: unsafe conduct. *In* Pritchett, V. S. The myth makers p9-20
Sinîavskiĭ, A. D. On Boris Pasternak. *In* Erlich, V. ed. Twentieth-century Russian literary criticism p235-46
Stacy, R. H. Reaction. *In* Stacy, R. H. Russian literary criticism p231-55
About individual works
Doctor Zhivago
Mathewson, R. W. Pasternak: "An inward music." *In* Mathewson, R. W. The positive hero in Russian literature p259-78
Miłosz, C. On Pasternak soberly. *In* Miłosz, C. Emperor of the earth p62-78
Pritchett, V. S. Boris Pasternak: unsafe conduct. *In* Pritchett, V. S. The myth makers p9-20

Pasternak, Boris L.—*Continued*

My sister life

Barnes, C. J. Boris Pasternak's revolutionary year. *In* Barnes, C. J. ed. Studies in twentieth century Russian literature p46-60

Safe conduct

Jakobson, R. The contours of The safe conduct. *In* Matejka, L. and Titunik, I. R. eds. Semiotics of art p188-96

Poetic works

Miłosz, C. On Pasternak soberly. *In* Miłosz, C. Emperor of the earth p62-78

Pasternak, Leonid Osipovich

About

Mallac, G. de. A Russian impressionist: Leonid Osipovich Pasternak, 1862-1945. *In* California Slavic studies v10 p87-120

Pasteur, Louis

About

Kottler, D. B. Louis Pasteur and molecular dissymmetry, 1844-1857. *In* Studies in history of biology v2 p57-98

Pasti, Nino

The military balance between East and West in Europe. *In* International terrorism and world security p189-233

Pastner, Carroll M.

The status of women and property on a Baluchistan oasis in Pakistan. *In* Beck, L. and Keddie, N. R. eds. Women in the Muslim world p434-50

Pasto, Jerome K. See Fortman, H. R. jt. auth.

Pastoral counseling. See Pastoral psychology

Pastoral fiction, American

History and criticism

Bone, R. A. The Harlem Renaissance: a reappraisal. *In* Bone, R. A. Down home p109-38

Bone, R. A. Three versions of pastoral. *In* Bone, R. A. Down home p139-70

Pastoral fiction, English

History and criticism

Moynahan, J. Pastoralism as culture and counter-culture in English fiction, 1800-1928: from a view to a death. *In* Spilka, M. ed. Towards a poetics of fiction p239-54

Pastoral literature

See also Country life in literature

History and criticism

Poggioli, R. The Christian pastoral. *In* Poggioli, R. The oaten flute p105-34

Poggioli, R. Naboth's vineyard: the pastoral view of the social order. *In* Poggioli, R. The oaten flute p194-219

Poggioli, R. Pastoral love. *In* Poggioli, R. The oaten flute p42-63

Pastoral medicine. See Pastoral psychology

Pastoral poetry

History and criticism

Feingold, R. Introduction. *In* Feingold, R. Nature and society p 1-17

Poggioli, R. The funeral elegy. *In* Poggioli, R. The oaten flute p64-82

Poggioli, R. The oaten flute. *In* Poggioli, R. The oaten flute p 1-41

Poggioli, R. The poetics of the pastoral. *In* Poggioli, R. The oaten flute p153-65

Pastoral poetry, English

History and criticism

Feingold, R. Art divorced from nature: The task and bucolic tradition. *In* Feingold, R. Nature and society p155-92

Feingold, R. Epilogue: eighteenth-century endings, romantic beginnings. *In* Feingold, R. Nature and society p193-200

Feingold, R. Introduction. *In* Feingold, R. Nature and society p 1-17

Feingold, R. Two worlds of work: John Dyer's The fleece. *In* Feingold, R. Nature and society p83-119

Tillman, J. S. Herrick's georgic encomia. *In* Rollin, R. B. and Patrick, J. M. eds. "Trust to good verses": Herrick tercentenary essays p149-57

Pastoral psychology

Nolan, T. Ritual and therapy. *In* Anticipatory grief p358-64

Pastore, Nicholas

Helmholtz on the projection or transfer of sensation. *In* Studies in perception p355-76

Pastusiak, Longin

Henryk Sienkiewicz. *In* Abroad in America: Visitors to the new Nation, 1776-1914 p176-85

Pat Garrett and Billy the Kid (Motion picture)

Kauffmann, S. Pat Garrett and Billy the Kid. *In* Kauffmann, S. Living images p207-08

Patchen, Kenneth

About

Beye, H. and McCleery, W. The most mysterious people in the Village. *In* Morgan, R. G. ed. Kenneth Patchen: a collection of essays p45-51

Breit, H. Kenneth Patchen and the critical blind alley. *In* Morgan, R. G. ed. Kenneth Patchen: a collection of essays p136-43

Ciardi, J. Kenneth Patchen: poetry, and poetry with jazz. *In* Morgan, R. G. ed. Kenneth Patchen: a collection of essays p29-30

Gascoyne, D. Introducing Kenneth Patchen. *In* Morgan, R. G. ed. Kenneth Patchen: a collection of essays p144-51

Glicksberg, C. I. The world of Kenneth Patchen. *In* Morgan, R. G. ed. Kenneth Patchen: a collection of essays p181-92

Hack, R. Memorial poetry reading for Kenneth Patchen. *In* Morgan, R. G. ed. Kenneth Patchen: a collection of essays p91-97

Miller, H. Patchen: man of anger and light; excerpt from "Stand still like the humming-bird." *In* Morgan, R. G. ed. Kenneth Patchen: a collection of essays p33-42

Neil, A. Kenneth Patchen reads with jazz in Canada. *In* Morgan, R. G. ed. Kenneth Patchen: a collection of essays p54-58

Nelson, R. The moral prose of Kenneth Patchen. *In* Morgan, R. G. ed. Kenneth Patchen: a collection of essays p229-52

Rexroth, K. Kenneth Patchen: naturalist of the public nightmare. *In* Morgan, R. G. ed. Kenneth Patchen: a collection of essays p20-28

Schevill, J. E. Kenneth Patchen: the search for wonder and joy. *In* Morgan, R. G. ed. Kenneth Patchen: a collection of essays p98-102

See, C. The jazz musician as Patchen's hero. *In* Morgan, R. G. ed. Kenneth Patchen: a collection of essays p218-28

Patchen, Kenneth—About—*Continued*

Thurley, G. Rexroth and Patchen: alternatives to breakdown. *In* Thurley, G. The American moment p159-71

Williams, J. Out of sight, out of conscience. *In* Morgan, R. G. ed. Kenneth Patchen: a collection of essays p59-80

Yates, P. Patchen's poetry and jazz. *In* Morgan, R. G. ed. Kenneth Patchen: a collection of essays p208-17

About individual works
Before the brave

Deutsch, B. A poet of the steel works. *In* Morgan, R. G. ed. Kenneth Patchen: a collection of essays p10-12

Ložar, T. Before the brave: portrait of man as a young artist. *In* Morgan, R. G. ed. Kenneth Patchen: a collection of essays p193-207

Wilder, A. N. Revolutionary and proletarian poetry: Kenneth Patchen; excerpt from "The spiritual aspects of the new poetry." *In* Morgan, R. G. ed. Kenneth Patchen: a collection of essays p98-102

The journal of Albion Moonlight

Morgan, R. G. The journal of Albion Moonlight: its form and meaning. *In* Morgan, R. G. ed. Kenneth Patchen: a collection of essays p152-80

Williams, W. C. A counsel of madness. *In* Morgan, R. G. ed. Kenneth Patchen: a collection of essays p3-9

Red wine and yellow hair

Hall, J. T. Patchen's angry shoes. *In* Morgan, R. G. ed. Kenneth Patchen: a collection of essays p17-19

Selected poems (1946 edition)

Taylor, F. Puck in the gardens of the sun. *In* Morgan, R. G. ed. Kenneth Patchen: a collection of essays p13-16

Pateman, Carole

Political obligation and conceptual analysis. *In* Laslett, P. and Fishkin, J. eds. Philosophy, politics and society p227-56

Patent laws and legislation

United States

Goldstein, P. Kewanee Oil Co. v. Bicron Corp.: notes on a closing circle. *In* The Supreme Court review, 1974 p81-95

Patents

See also Patent laws and legislation

Laws and legislation
See Patent laws and legislation

Pater, Walter Horatio

Poems by William Morris. *In* Sambrook, J. ed. Pre-Raphaelitism p105-17

About individual works
Studies in the history of the Renaissance

Caserio, R. L. Narrative reason: the sense of plot and historical experience. *In* Caserio, R. L. Plot, story and the novel p27-56

Patera Martelli

Winternitz, E. The inspired musician: a 16th-century musical pastiche. *In* Winternitz, E. Musical instruments and their symbolism in Western art p202-10

Paterculus, Velleius. See Velleius Paterculus, Gaius

Paternal deprivation

Biller, H. B. and Meredith, D. L. The invisible American father. *In* Gross, L. ed. Sexual issues in marriage p277-87

Paternalism. Dworkin, G. *In* The Abdication of philosophy and the public good p209-27

Paternoster, The Old English runic. Sharpe, E. J. *In* Symbols of power p41-60

Paterson, John

Lawrence's vital source: nature and character in Thomas Hardy. *In* Knoepflmacher, U. C. and Tennyson, G. B. eds. Nature and the Victorian imagination p455-69

Pathological psychology. See Psychology, Pathological

Pathology

Thomas, L. Medical lessons from history. *In* Thomas, L. The medusa and the snail p158-75

Thomas, L. On disease. *In* Thomas, L. The medusa and the snail p93-101

Thomas, L. On magic in medicine. *In* Thomas, L. The medusa and the snail p19-26

Thomas, L. On meddling. *In* Thomas, L. The medusa and the snail p110-14

See also Diagnosis

Paths of glory (Motion picture)

Truffaut, F. Stanley Kubrick: Paths of glory. *In* Truffaut, F. The films in my life p116-18

Patient and medical personnel. See Medical personnel and patient

Patient and nurse. See Nurse and patient

Patient and physician. See Physician and patient

Patient and psychotherapist. See Psychotherapist and patient

Patient compliance

Cantor, N. L. A patient's decision to decline life-saving medical treatment: bodily integrity versus the preservation of life. *In* Weir, R. F. ed. Ethical issues in death and dying p241-70

Patient participation. See Patient compliance

Patinkin, Don

The development of Keynes' policy thinking. *In* Theory for economic efficiency: essays in honor of Abba P. Lerner p150-66

Patlagean, Evelyne

Birth control in the early Byzantine Empire. *In* Biology of man in history p 1-22

Patleina Monastery site, Bulgaria

Akrabovia-Zhandova, I. Preslav inlaid ceramics. *In* Studies in memory of David Talbot Rice p25-33

Patmore, Coventry Kersey Dighton

About

Ball, P. M. 'Till all my widowed race be run.' *In* Ball, P. M. The heart's events p58-104

About individual works
The angel in the house

Ball, P. M. 'To marry her and take her home.' *In* Ball, P. M. The heart's events p167-221

Christ, C. Victorian masculinity and The angel in the house. *In* Vicinus, M. ed. A widening sphere p146-62

Patočka, Jan

The Husserlian doctrine and eidetic intuition and its recent critics. *In* Elliston, F. A. and McCormick, P. eds. Husserl p150-59

Patočka, Jean. See Patočka, Jan

Paton, Alan
Roy Campbell. *In* Heywood, C. ed. Aspects of South African literature p3-23

Patriarchs (Bible)
Pocock, D. F. North and South in the Book of Genesis. *In* Studies in social anthropology p273-84

Patriarchy. See Family

Patrick, Edward A.
Medical science and tomorrow's American. *In* Tomorrow's American p47-68

Patrick, John Max
The idea of liberty in the theological writings of Sir Henry Vane the Younger. *In* The Dissenting tradition p100-07

Milton's revolution against rime, and some of its implications. *In* Patrick, J. M. and Sundell, R. H. eds. Milton and the art of sacred song p99-117

"Poetry perpetuates the poet": Richard James and the growth of Herrick's reputation. *In* Rollin, R. B. and Patrick, J. M. eds. "Trust to good verses": Herrick tercentenary essays p221-34

Patrides, C. A.
Milton. *In* English Association. The year's work in English studies v53 p239-49

Milton [another essay] *In* English Association. The year's work in English studies v54 p242-51

Milton [another essay] *In* English Association. The year's work in English studies v55 p282-96

Milton [another essay] *In* English Association. The year's work in English studies v57 p210-20

Milton [another essay] *In* English Association. The year's work in English studies v57 p178-84

A patriot for me (criticism) Osborne, J. *In* Kauffmann, S. Persons of the drama p181-83

Patriotic poetry

History and criticism
Thompson, D. Patriotism and politics. *In* Thompson, D. The uses of poetry p112-36

Patriotism
Minogue, K. R. Nationalism and the patriotism of city-states. *In* Smith, A. D. ed. Nationalist movements p54-73

Tuan, Yi-Fu. Geopiety: a theme in man's attachment to nature and to place. *In* Geographies of the mind p11-39
See also Nationalism

Study and teaching—United States
Nelson, J. L. Nationalistic education and the free man. *In* Fairfield, R. P. ed. Humanistic frontiers in American education p139-47

France
Church, W. F. France. *In* National consciousness, history, and political culture in early-modern Europe p43-66

Patriotism in art
Kammen, M. G. From liberty to prosperity: reflections upon the role of revolutionary iconography in national tradition. *In* American Antiquarian Society. Proceedings v86 pt2 p237-72

Patristics. See Fathers of the church

Patron and client
Akin Rabibhadana, M. R. Clientship and class structure in the Early Bangkok period. *In* Change and persistence in Thai society p93-123

Hanks, L. M. The Thai social order as entourage and circle. *In* Change and persistence in Thai society p197-218

Patronage, Ecclesiastical
Lytle, G. F. Patronage patterns and Oxford colleges, c.1300-c.1530. *In* The University in society v 1 p111-49

Patronage, Political

United States
Tabachnik, L. Political patronage and ethnic groups: foreign-born in the United States Customhouse Service, 1821-1861. *In* Swierenga, R. P. ed. Beyond the Civil War synthesis p245-54

Patronage of art. See Art patronage

Patronage of literature. See Authors and patrons

Patt, William D.
The early "ars dictaminis" as response to a changing society *In* Viator: medieval and Renaissance studies v9 p133-55

Patten, Robert L.
Autobiography into autobiography: the evolution of David Copperfield. *In* Landow, G. P. ed. Approaches to Victorian autobiography p269-91

Dickens time and again. *In* Dickens Studies Annual v2 p163-96

"A surprising transformation": Dickens and the hearth. *In* Knoepflmacher, U. C. and Tennyson, G. B. eds. Nature and the Victorian imagination p153-70
See also Kappel, A. J. jt auth.

Patterson, Annabel M.
Our mutual friend: Dickens as the Compleat Angler. *In* Dickens Studies Annual v 1 p252-64

Patterson, Gerald Roy
The aggressive child: victim and architect of a coercive system. *In* Behavior modification and families p267-316

Patterson, Horace Orlando
Context and choice in ethnic allegiance: a theoretical framework and Caribbean case study. *In* Glazer, N. and Moynihan, D. P. eds. Ethnicity p305-49

Migration in Caribbean societies: socioeconomic and symbolic resource. *In* Human migration p106-45

Patterson, Lee Willing
Chaucerian confession: penitential literature and the pardoner. *In* Medievalia et humanistica no. 7 p153-73

Patterson, Margaret C.

About individual works
Literary research guide
Altick, R. D. This will never do. *In* Review v 1 1979 p47-60

Patterson, Orlando. See Patterson, Horace Orlando

Patterson, Robert Leet
An analysis of faith. *In* Fact, value, and perception p85-105

Patterson, Samuel Charles. See Kim, Chong Lim, jt. auth.

Patterson, William Brown

Jean de Serres and the politics of religious pacification, 1594-8. *In* Church, society and politics p223-44

Pattison, Bruce

Renaissance music. *In* Background to the English Renaissance p57-66

Pattison, E. Mansell

Ideological support for the marginal middle class: faith healing and glossolalia. *In* Zaretsky, I. I. and Leone, M. P. eds. Religious movements in contemporary America p418-55

Pattison, William David

Reflections on the American rectangular land survey system. *In* Pattern and process p131-38

Patton, William C.

The leader as a counselor. *In* Henderson, G. ed. Human relations in the miltary p33-39

Paul, Saint, apostle

About

Arendt, H. Quaestio mihi factus sum: the discovery of the inner man. *In* Arendt, H. The life of the mind v2 p53-110

Betz, H. D. In defense of the spirit: Paul's letter to the Galatians as a document of early Christian apologetics. *In* Aspects of religious propaganda in Judaism and early Christianity p99-114

Elwell, W. A. The deity of Christ in the writings of Paul. *In* Current issues in Biblical and patristic interpretation p297-308

Jarrott, C. A. L. Erasmus's annotations and Colet's commentaries on Paul: a comparison of some theological themes. *In* Essays on the works of Erasmus p125-44

Kaiser, W. C. The weightier and lighter matters of the law: Moses, Jesus and Paul. *In* Current issues in Biblical and patristic interpretation p176-92

Pearson, B. A. Hellenistic-Jewish wisdom speculation and Paul. *In* Aspects of wisdom in Judaism and early Christianity p43-66

Tarachow, S. St Paul and early Christianity. *In* Wolman, B. B. ed. Psychoanalysis and Catholicism p143-207

Paul of Tarsus. See Paul, Saint, apostle

Paul VI, Pope. See Paulus VI, Pope

Paul, Sherman

Repossessing and renewing

Contents

Alfred Kazin

Emerson's Essays

From lookout to ashram: the way of Gary Snyder

The identities of John Jay Chapman

An introduction to William Carlos Williams

Louis Sullivan and organic architecture

Paul Rosenfeld

Randolph Bourne

Also in Ross, R. G. ed. Makers of American thought p120-56

Thoreau's Walden

Van Wyck Brooks's ordeal and pilgrimage

Pauli, Wolfgang

About

Serwer, D. Unmechanischer Zwang: Pauli, Heisenberg, and the rejection of the mechanical atom, 1923-1925. *In* Historical studies in the physical sciences v8 p189-256

Paulson, Ronald

Rochester: the body politic and the body private. *In* Martz, L. L. and Williams, A. L. eds. The author in his work p103-21

The simplicity of Hogarth's Industry and idleness. *In* ELH essays for Earl R. Wasserman p 1-30

Turner's graffiti: the sun and its glosses. *In* Kroeber, K. and Walling, W. eds. Images of romanticism p167-88

Paulus VI, Pope

Humanae vitae. *In* Baker, R. and Elliston, F. A. eds. Philosophy & sex p131-49

About individual works

Humanae vitae

Cohen C. Sex, birth control, and human life. *In* Baker, R. and Elliston, F. A. eds. Philosophy & sex p150-65

Margolis, J. Z. and Margolis, C. The separation of marriage and family. *In* Feminism and philosophy p291-307

Paulus Diaconus

About

Lutz, C. E. A manuscript of Charlemagne's Homiliarium. *In* Lutz, C. E. Essays on manuscripts and rare books p24-27

Pauly, Thomas H.

In search of "The spirit of '76." *In* Zenderland, L. ed. Recycling the past p29-49

Pauperism. See Poor

Paustovskiĭ, Konstantin Georgievich

About

Slonim, M. L. Soviet romantics: from Grin, Paustovsky, and Olesha to Tikhonov and Bagritsky. *In* Slonim, M. L. Soviet Russian literature p116-33

Paustovsky, Konstantin. See Paustovskiĭ, Konstantin Georgievich

Pavements, Mosaic

Rome

Neal, D. S. Floor mosaics. *In* Strong, D. E. and Brown, D. eds. Roman crafts p241-52

Pavese, Carlo

The new Heracles poem of Pindar. *In* Harvard Studies in classical philology v72 p47-88

Pavese, Cesare

About

Pacifici, S. Cesare Pavese: symbols, myths, and the novel. *In* Pacifici, S. The modern Italian novel: from Pea to Moravia p118-59

Rimanelli, G. Pavese's Diario: why suicide? Why not? *In* Italian literature: roots and branches p383-405

About individual works

The burning brand: diaries 1935-1950

Rimanelli, G. Pavese's Diario: why suicide? Why not? *In* Italian literature: roots and branches p383-405

Selected works

Hyman, S. E. Sad encounters. *In* Hyman, S. E. The critic's credentials p198-205

Pavia

Social conditions

Cipolla, C. M. A plague doctor. *In* The Medieval city p65-72

Pavlov, Ivan Petrovich

About

Fancher, R. E. Psychology as the science of behavior: Ivan Pavlov and John B. Watson. *In* Fancher, R. E. Pioneers of psychology p295-338

Payday (Motion picture)

Kauffmann, S. Payday. *In* Kauffmann, S. Living images p181-83

Payne, Harry Charles

Elite versus popular mentality in the eighteenth century. *In* Studies in eighteenth-century culture v8 p3-32

Payne, Robert O.

Rhetoric in Chaucer: Chaucer's realization of himself as rhetor. *In* Murphy, J. J. ed. Medieval eloquence p270-87

Payne, Stanley G.

Fascism in Western Europe. *In* Laqueur, W. Z. ed. Fascism: a reader's guide p295-311

Paz, Octavio

Marcel Duchamp, or, The castle of purity; excerpt. *In* Kaplan, P. and Manso, S. eds. Major European art movements, 1900-1945 p353-96

The siren & the seashell

Contents

Antonio Machado
E. E. Cummings
Jorge Guillén
José Juan Tablada
A literature of foundations
A modern hymn
Poetry of solitude and poetry of communion
The rider of the air
The road of passion
The siren and the seashell
Sor Juana Inés de la Cruz

About

Howe, I. Octavio Paz: Mexican modernist. *In* Howe, I. Celebrations and attacks p225-29

p'Bitek, Okot. See Bitek, Okot p'

Pea, Enrico

About

Pacifici, S. Three writers in search of the novel. *In* Pacifici, S. The modern Italian novel: from Pea to Moravia p18-46

Peace, Richard Arthur

The logic of madness: Gogol''s Zapiski sumasshedshego. *In* Oxford Slavonic papers, new ser. v9 p28-45

Peace

Carroll, B. A. Peacemaking. *In* Encyclopedia of American foreign policy p742-51

Curle, A. Peace studies. *In* The Year book of world affairs, 1976 p5-13

Gallie, W. B. Kant on perpetual peace. *In* Gallie, W. B. Philosophers of peace and war p 8-36

Galtung, J. Nonterritorial actors and the problem of peace. *In* **On the creation of a just world order p151-88**

White, E. B. Unity. *In* White, E. B. Essays of E. B. White p100-08

See also International education; International organization; Pacifism; Security, International; War

Societies, etc.

See Peace societies

Peace (Philosophy)

Donnelly, J. The metaphysics of peace. *In* Roth, R. J. ed. Person and community p25-41

Peace societies

Ferrell, R. H. Peace movements. *In* Encyclopedia of American foreign policy p752-62

Peace treaties

Carroll, B. A. Peacemaking. *In* Encyclopedia of American foreign policy p742-51

Peaceful change (International relations)

Gallie, W. B. Concluding remarks. *In* Gallie, W. B. Philosophers of peace and war p133-41

Peaceful coexistence. See World politics—1945-

Peacekeeping forces. See International police; United Nations—Armed Forces

Peacock, Alan Turner

The treatment of the principles of public finance in The wealth of nations. *In* Skinner, A. S. and Wilson, T. eds. Essays on Adam Smith p553-67

Peacock, Alan Turner, and Ricketts, Martin

The growth of the public sector and inflation. *In* The Political economy of inflation p117-36

Peacock, James L.

Symbolic reversal and social history: transvestites and clowns of Java. *In* Babcock, B. A. ed. The reversible world p209-24

Peacock, Ronald

Eliot's contribution to criticism of drama. *In* The Literary criticism of T. S. Eliot p89-110

Peacock, Thomas Love

About

Colmer, J. The comic spirit. *In* Colmer, J. Coleridge to Catch-22 p44-56

Crabbe, J. K. The harmony of her mind: Peacock's emancipated women. *In* Tennessee Studies in literature v23 p75-86

Peacocke, Arthur Robert

Cosmos and creation. *In* Cosmology, history, and theology p365-81

Peacocke, Christopher

An appendix to David Wiggins' 'note.' *In* Evans, G. L. and McDowell, J. H. eds. Truth and meaning p313-24

Truth definitions and actual languages. *In* Evans, G. L. and McDowell, J. H. eds. Truth and meaning p162-88

Peake, Mervyn Laurence

About

Morgan, E. The walls of Gormenghast: an introduction to the novels of Mervyn Peake. *In* **Morgan, E. Essays p35-42**

About individual works

The Gormenghast trilogy

Manlove, C. N. Mervyn Peake (1911-68)-The 'Titus' trilogy. *In* Manlove, C. N. Modern fantasy p207-57

Pearce, Ann Philippa

Writing a book: A dog so small. *In* Blishen, E. ed. The thorny paradise p140-45

About individual works

A dog so small

Pearce, A. P. Writing a book: A dog so small. *In* Blishen, E. ed. The thorny paradise p140-45

Pearce, Diana, and Street, David
Welfare in the metropolitan area. *In* Handbook of contemporary urban life p319-51

Pearce, Philippa. See Pearce, Ann, Philippa

Pearce, Richard A.
Enter the frame. *In* Federman, R. ed. Surfiction p47-57

Nabokov's black (hole) humor: Lolita and Pale fire. *In* Cohen, S. B. ed. Comic relief p28-44

Pearce, Roy Harvey
Day-dream and fact: the import of The Blithedale romance. *In* Baldwin, K. H. and Kirby, D. K. eds. Individual and community p49-63

Pearcy, Roy J.
Investigations into the principles of fabliau structure. *In* Ruggiers, P. G. ed. Versions of medieval comedy p67-100

Modes of signification and the humor of obscene diction in the fabliaux. *In* Cooke, T. D. and Honeycutt, B. L. eds. The humor of the fabliaux p163-96

Pearl, Orsamus Merrill
Rules for musical contests. *In* Illinois classical studies v3, 1978 p132-38

Pearl (Middle English poem)
Eldredge, L. M. The state of "Pearl" studies since 1933. *In* Viator: medieval and Renaissance studies v6 p171-94

Levine, R. The pearl-child: topos and archetype in the Middle English Pearl. *In* Medievalia et humanistica no. 8 p243-51

Nolan, B. Pearl: a fourteenth-century vision in August. *In* Nolan, B. The Gothic visionary perspective p156-204

Pears, David Francis
Dreaming. *In* Dunlop, C. E. M. ed. Philosophical essays on dreaming p205-26

Russell's theories of memory, 1912-1921. *In* Nakhnikian, G. ed. Bertrand Russell's philosophy p117-37

Pearsall, Derek Albert
The English romance in the fifteenth century. *In* English Association. Essays and studies, 1976 p56-83

John Capgrave's Life of St Katharine and popular romance style. *In* Medievalia et humanistica no.6 p121-37

Pearson, Birger Albert
Hellenistic-Jewish wisdom speculation and Paul. *In* Aspects of wisdom in Judaism and early Christianity p43-66

Pearson, Gabriel
Robert Lowell: the middle years. *In* Boyers, R. ed. Contemporary poetry in America p43-58

Towards a reading of Dombey and son. *In* Josipovici, G. ed. The modern English novel: the reader, the writer and the work p54-76

Pearson, John George
About individual works
The life of Ian Fleming
Connolly, C. Ian Fleming. *In* Connolly, C. The evening colonnade p350-53

Pearson, John Loughborough
About
Lloyd, D. D. John Loughborough Pearson: noble seriousness. *In* Seven Victorian architects p66-83

Pearson, Karl
About individual works
The grammar of science
Wilson, D. B. Concepts of physical nature: John Herschel to Karl Pearson. *In* Knoepflmacher, U. C. and Tennyson, G. B. eds. Nature and the Victorian imagination p201-15

Pearson, Lionel Ignacius Cusack
The dynamics of Pindar's music: Ninth Nemean and Third Olympian. *In* Illinois classical studies v2 1977 p54-69

Myth and archaeologia in Italy and Sicily —Timaeus and his predecessors. *In* Yale classical studies v24 p171-95

Pearson, Michael Naylor
Corruption and corsairs in sixteenth-century western India: a functional analysis. *In* Kling, B. B. and Pearson, M. N. eds. The age of partnership p15-41

Pearson, Willie
Race and universalism in the scientific community. *In* Gaston, J. ed. Sociology of science p38-53

Peasant art. See Folk art

Peasant uprisings
Le Roy Ladurie, E. Rural revolts and protest movements in France from 1675-1788. *In* Studies in eighteenth-century culture v5 p423-51

Europe
Tilly, C. Rural collective action in modern Europe. *In* Forging nations: a comparative view of rural ferment and revolt p9-40

Peasantry
Adams, R. N. Rural collective action and the state: a discussion. *In* Forging nations: a comparative view of rural ferment and revolt p150-67

Landsberger, H. A. The sources of rural radicalism. *In* Radicalism in the contemporary age v 1 p247-91

See also Agricultural laborers; Land tenure; Rural conditions; Villeinage

Africa
Saul, J. S. African peasantries and revolutionary change. *In* Forging nations: a comparative view of rural ferment and revolt p86-127

Belgium—Flanders
Mendels, F. F. Agriculture and peasant industry in eighteenth-century Flanders. *In* Parker, W. N. and Jones, E. L. eds. European peasants and their markets p179-204

Bengal
Broomfield, J. H. Peasant mobilization in twentieth-century Bengal. *In* Forging nations: a comparative view of rural ferment and revolt p41-60

Brazil
Schwartz, S. B. Elite politics and the growth of a peasantry in late colonial Brazil. *In* From colony to nation p133-54

Chile
Kay, C. Agrarian reform and the transition to socialism. *In* O'Brien, P. J. ed. Allende's Chile p79-105

Peasantry—*Continued*

Europe—History

Hoffmann, R. C. Medieval origins of the common fields. *In* Parker, W. N. and Jones, E. L. eds. European peasants and their markets p23-71

Tilly, C. Rural collective action in modern Europe. *In* Forging nations: a comparative view of rural ferment and revolt p9-40

France

Grantham, G. W. Scale and organization in French farming, 1840-1880. *In* Parker, W. N. and Jones, E. L. eds. European peasants and their markets p293-326

Le Roy Ladurie, E. Rural revolts and protest movements in France from 1675-1788. *In* Studies in eighteenth-century culture v5 p423-51

Germany

Berkner, L. K. Inheritance, land tenure and peasant family structure: a German regional comparison. *In* Family and inheritance p71-95

Great Britain—History

Howell, C. Peasant inheritance customs in the Midlands, 1280-1700. *In* Family and inheritance p112-55

Spufford, M. Peasant inheritance customs and land distribution in Cambridgeshire from the sixteenth to the eighteenth centuries. *In* Family and inheritance p156-76

Greece

Dionisopoulas-Mass, R. The evil eye and bewitchment in a peasant village. *In* The Evil eye p42-62

Ireland—History

Evans, E. E. Peasant beliefs in nineteenth-century Ireland. *In* Casey, D. J. and Rhodes, R. S. eds. Views of the Irish peasantry, 1800-1916 p37-56

Lebow, R. N. British images of poverty in pre-famine Ireland. *In* Casey, D. J. and Rhodes, R. E. eds. Views of the Irish peasantry, 1800-1916 p57-83

Mexico

Katz, F. Peasants in the Mexican Revolution of 1910. *In* Forging nations: a comparative view of rural ferment and revolt p61-85

Netherlands—Friesland

De Vries, J. Peasant demand patterns and economic development: Friesland, 1550-1750. *In* Parker, W. N. and Jones, E. L. eds. European peasants and their markets p205-66

Spain

Sevilla-Guzman, E. The peasantry and the Franco régime. *In* Preston, P. ed. Spain in crisis p101-24

Peasants. See Peasantry

Peasants in art

Rose, M. G. Jack B. Yeats's picture of the peasant. *In* Casey, D. J. and Rhodes, R. E. eds. Views of the Irish peasantry, 1800-1916 p192-202

Peasants in literature

Brown, D. B. The village writers. *In* Brown, D. B. Soviet Russian literature since Stalin p218-52

Dash, J. M. The peasant novel in Haiti. *In* African literature today no. 9: Africa, America and the Caribbean p77-90

Harmon, M. Cobwebs before the wind: aspects of the peasantry in Irish literature from 1800 to 1916. *In* Casey, D. J. and Rhodes, R. E. eds. Views of the Irish peasantry, 1800-1916 p129-59

Lamming, G. The peasant roots of the West Indian novel; excerpt from "The pleasures of exile." *In* Baugh, E. ed. Critics on Caribbean literature p24-26

Rohlehr, G. The folk in Caribbean literature. *In* Baugh, E. ed. Critics on Caribbean literature p27-30

Peasants' uprisings. See Peasant uprisings

Pease, Donald E.

The bridge: emotional dynamics of an epic of consciousness. *In* French, W. G. ed. The twenties p387-403

Reflections on Moon Lake: the presences of the playwright. *In* Tennessee Williams: a tribute p829-47

Peat, David W.

Creation and redemption. *In* Cosmology, history, and theology p383-86

Pebworth, Ted-Larry, comp.

Selected and annotated bibliography. *In* Rollin, R. B. and Patrick, J. M. eds. "Trust to good verses": Herrick tercentenary essays p237-39

Pecchini, Umberto. See Pasquino, G. jt. auth. franco

Peck, Russell A.

Number as cosmic language. *In* Jeffrey, D. L. ed. By things seen: reference and recognition in medieval thought p47-80

Peck, Samuel Minturn

About

Going, W. T. Samuel Minturn Peck, gentleman of letters. *In* Going, W. T. Essays on Alabama literature p61-79

Peckham, Howard Henry

Independence: the view from Britain. *In* American Antiquarian Society. Proceedings v85 pt.2 p387-403

Peckham, Morse

Browning and romanticism. *In* Armstrong, I. ed. Robert Browning p47-76

Edgar Saltus and the heroic decadence. *In* Tulane Studies in English v23 p61-69

Frederick the Great. *In* Fielding, K. J. and Tarr, R. L. eds. Carlyle past and present p198-215

The intentional? Fallacy? *In* On literary intention p139-57

"Literature": disjunction and redundancy. *In* Hernadi, P. ed. What is literature? p219-30

Romanticism and behavior

Contents

The arts and the centers of power

Arts for the cultivation of radical sensitivity

The corporation's role in today's crisis of cultural incoherence

The cultural crisis of the 1970s

Cultural stagnation in American universities and colleges

The deplorable consequences of the idea of creativity

Ernest Hemingway: sexual themes in his writing

The function of history in nineteenth-century European culture

Pelloutier, Fernand Léonce Émile

About

Baker, A. S. Fernand Pelloutier and the making of a revolutionary syndicalism. *In* Essays on modern European revolutionary history p39-68

Pellowe, John. See Strang, B. M. H. jt. auth.

Peloponnesian War, 431-404 B.C. See Greece —History—Peloponnesian War, 431-404 B.C.

Pelta, On the meaning of the griffin. Dwyer, E. J. *In* Studies in classical art and archaeology p235-38

Peluso, Emil. See Simon, W. jt. auth.

Pelz, Donald Campbell
Some expanded perspectives on use of social science in public policy. *In* Major social issues p346-57

Pemberton, Vivian H.
Hart Crane's heritage. *In* Artful thunder p221-40

Pembroke's Company. See Pembroke's Men

Pembroke's Men
Pinciss, G. M. Shakespeare, Her Majesty's players and Pembroke's Men. *In* Shakespeare survey 27 p129-36

Peña, Félix
Multinational enterprises and North-South relations. *In* Erb, G. F. and Kallab, V. eds. Beyond dependency p57-74

Penal codes. See Criminal law

Penal institutions. See Prisons

Penal law. See Criminal law

Penalties (Criminal law) See Punishment

Pendry, E. D.
Shakespeare's life, times, and stage. *In* Shakespeare survey v31 p177-91

Penelhum, Terence
Self-identity and self-regard. *In* Rorty, A. O. ed. The identities of persons p253-80

Survival and disembodied existence; excerpts. *In* Wheatley, J. M. O. and Edge, H. L. eds. Philosophical dimensions and parapsychology p308-29

Penella, Robert Joseph
An unpublished letter of Apollonius of Tyana to the Sardians. *In* Harvard Studies in classical philology v79 p305-11

Penitence. See Repentance

Penitentiaries. See Prisons

Penley, Constance
Cries and whispers. *In* Nichols, B. ed. Movies and methods p204-08

Penn, Arthur

About individual works

Bonnie and Clyde

Murray, E. Bonnie and Clyde. *In* Murray, E. Ten film classics p149-66

Samuels, C. T. Bonnie and Clyde. *In* Samuels, C. T. Mastering the film, and other essays p136-43

Penn, Rosalyn Terborg-. See Terborg-Penn, Rosalyn

Penn, William

About

Robbins, C. The efforts of William Penn to lay a foundation for future ages. *In* Aspects of American liberty p68-80

Pennington, Anne Elizabeth
Music in sixteenth-century Moldavia: new evidence. *In* Oxford Slavonic papers, new ser. v11 p64-83

Pennington, Kenneth James
Pope Innocent III's views on church and state: a gloss to Per venerabilem. *In* Law, church, and society p49-67

Pennsylvania

Historical geography

Lemon, J. T. The weakness of place and community in early Pennsylvania. *In* European settlement and development in North America: essays on geographical change in honour and memory of Andrew Hill Clark p190-207

History—Civil War, 1861-1865

Shankman, A. M. For the Union as it was and the Constitution as it is: a Copperhead views the Civil War. *In* Rank and file p93-111

Politics and government—Colonial period, ca. 1600-1775

Bockelman, W. L. Local government in colonial Pennsylvania. *In* Daniels, B. C. ed. Town and county p216-37

Robbins, C. The efforts of William Penn to lay a foundation for future ages. *In* Aspects of American liberty p68-80

Politics and government—1865-1950

Keller, R. C. Pennsylvania's Little New Deal. *In* Braeman, J.; Bremner, R. H. and Brody, D. eds. The New Deal v2 p45-76

Pennsylvania. State University. College of Human Development
Vallance, T. R. Home economics and the development of new forms of human service education. *In* Land-grant universities and their continuing challenge p79-103

Pennsylvania. University

Department of Architecture

Esherick, J. Architectural education in the thirties and seventies: a personal view. *In* Kostof, S. ed. The architect p238-79

School of Fine Arts. Department of Architecture

See Pennsylvania. University. Department of Architecture

Pennsylvania Dutch. See Pennsylvania Germans

Pennsylvania Germans
Yoder, D. Hohman and Romanus: origins and diffusion of the Pennsylvania German powwow manual. *In* American folk medicine p235-48

History

Waldenrath, A. The Pennsylvania-Germans: development of their printing and their newspress in the War for American Independence. *In* The German contribution to the building of the Americas p47-74

Penology. See Prisons; Punishment

Penrith, Mary C.
Plain and contorted speech in Emma. *In* An English miscellany p149-62

Penrod, James H.
Harden Taliaferro, folk humorist of North Carolina. *In* Inge, M. T. ed. The frontier humorists p187-93

Penrose, Edith Tilton
The development of crisis. *In* Vernon, R. ed. The oil crisis p39-57

Penrose, Sir Roland
In praise of illusion. *In* Gregory, R. L. and Gombrich, Sir E. H. J. eds. Illusion in nature and art p245-84

The Pentagon papers
Curzon, D. The generic secrets of government decision making. *In* Galnoor, I. ed. Government secrecy in democracies p93-109

Pentecostal churches
Garrison, V. E. Sectarianism and psychosocial adjustment: a controlled comparison of Puerto Rican Pentecostals and Catholics. *In* Zaretsky, I. I. and Leone, M. P. eds. Religious movements in contemporary America p298-329

Gerlach, L. P. Pentecostalism: revolution or counter-revolution? *In* Zaretsky, I. I. and Leone, M. P. eds. Religious movements in contemporary America p669-99

Hine, V. H. The deprivation and disorganization theories of social movements. *In* Zaretsky, I. I. and Leone, M. P. eds. Religious movements in contemporary America p646-61

Pentecostal movement. See Pentecostalism

Pentecostalism
Lane, R. Catholic Charismatic Renewal. *In* The New religious consciousness p162-79

See also Jesus People; Pentecostal churches

Penutian languages
Shipley, W. F. California. *In* Sebeok, T. A. ed. Native languages of the Americas v 1 p427-59

Thompson, L. C. The Northwest. *In* Sebeok, T. A. ed. Native languages of the Americas v 1 p359-425

Penzias, Arno Allan
An observational view of the cosmos. *In* Cosmology, history, and theology p101-12

People's democracies
Brus, W. Stalinism and the "peoples' democracies." *In* Stalinism p239-56

Pepper, Stephen Coburn
A split in the identity theory. *In* Philosophical aspects of the mind-body problem p35-42

Pepys, Samuel

About individual works

The diary of Samuel Pepys; edited by Robert Latham and William Matthews (v I-IX)

Mudrick, M. Su cosa mi cosa; or, Busy busy busy. *In* Mudrick, M. Books are not life but then what is? p12-26

Pequigney, Joseph
Marvell's "soul" poetry. *In* Friedenrich, K. ed. Tercentenary essays in honor of Andrew Marvell p76-104

Pequot War, 1636-1638
Seelye, J. By way of Newton: how Thomas Hooker crossed his Rubicon and started the Pequot War: a Hudibrastic interlude. *In* Seelye, J. Prophetic waters p187-216

Vaughan, A. T. Pequots and Puritans: the causes of the War of 1637. *In* Vaughan, A. T. and Bremer, F. J. eds. Puritan New England p201-14

Péraldi, François
American psychoanalysis. *In* Roland A. ed. Psychoanalysis, creativity, and literature p22-38

The crane-child. *In* Roland, A. ed. Psychoanalysis, creativity, and literature p96-102

Perception
Anderson, R. F. The location, extension, shape, and size of Hume's perceptions. *In* Livingston, D. W. and King, J. T. eds. Hume p153-71

Bohm, D. Imagination, fancy, insight, and reason in the process of thought. *In* Evolution of consciousness p51-68

Butler, R. J. Hume's impressions. *In* Royal Institute of Philosophy. Impressions of empiricism p122-36

Cassirer, E. Reflections on the concept of group and the theory of perception. *In* Cassirer, E. Symbol, myth, and culture p271-91

Clark, R. L. Considerations for a logic for naive realism. *In* Studies in perception p525-56

Fieandt, K. von. Some psychological constituents and aspects of object perception. *In* Perception p72-83

Hirst, R. J. Science and anti-science in the philosophy of perception. *In* Studies in perception p377-401

Hobbs, A. C. New phenomenalism as an account of perceptual knowledge. *In* Royal Institute of Philosophy. Impressions of empiricism p109-21

Lee, E. N. The sense of an object: Epicurus on seeing and hearing. *In* Studies in perception p27-59

Lewis, P. B. Wittgenstein on seeing and interpreting. *In* Royal Institute of Philosophy. Impressions of empiricism p93-108

Maxwell, G. Russell on perception and mind-body: a study in philosophical method. *In* Philosophical aspects of the mind-body problems p131-53

Owen, D. H. The psychophysics of prior experience. *In* Studies in perception p467-524

Pappas, G. S. Broad, sensa, and explanation. *In* Studies in perception p402-21

Pastore, N. Helmholtz on the projection or transfer of sensation. *In* Studies in perception p355-76

Schofield, R. E. Joseph Priestley on sensation and perception. *In* Studies in perception p336-54

Turnbull, R. G. The role of the "special sensibles" in the perception theories of Plato and Aristotle. *In* Studies in perception p3-26

Von Staden, H. The Stoic theory of perception and its "Platonic" critics. *In* Studies in perception p96-136

See also Awareness; Body image; Cognition; Consciousness; Gestalt psychology; Ideology; Space perception; Time perception; Visual perception; Whole and parts (Psychology)

Perception, Extrasensory. See Extrasensory perception

Perceval (Romances)
Tax, P. W. The Grail kingdom and Parzival's first visit: intrigue, minne, despair. *In* Medieval and Renaissance studies [1975] p20-36

Percy, Thomas Bp. of Dromore

About

Brooks, C. Thomas Percy, Don Quixote, and Don Bowle. *In* Evidence in literary scholarship p247-61

Percy, Walker
The message in the bottle
Contents
Culture: the antimony of the scientific method
The Delta factor
The loss of the creature
The man on the train
The message in the bottle
Metaphor as mistake
The mystery of language
Notes for a novel about the end of the world
Semiotic and a theory of knowledge
Symbol as hermeneutic in existentialism
Symbol as need
Symbol, consciousness, and intersubjectivity
The symbolic structure of interpersonal process
A theory of language
Toward a triadic theory of meaning

About individual works
Love in the ruins
Sheed, W. Walker Percy redivivus. *In* Sheed, W. The good word & other words p127-31

The moviegoer
Lawson, L. A. The moviegoer and the stoic heritage. *In* The Stoic strain in American literature p180-91
Tanner, T. Afterword: Wonder and alienation—the mystic and the moviegoer. *In* Tanner, T. The reign of wonder p336-61
Vauthier, S. Narrative triangle and triple alliance: a look at "The moviegoer." *In* Johnson, I. D. and Johnson, C. [eds.] Les américanistes p71-93

Perella, Nicolas James
Midday in Italian literature
Contents
Eugenio Montale
From Dante to Pindemonte
Gabriele D'Annunzio
Giuseppe Ungaretti
The nineteenth century
Some twentieth-century voices

Perelman, Sidney Joseph

About individual works
Baby, it's cold inside
Welty, E. S. J. Perelman's The most of S. J. Perelman; Baby, it's cold inside. *In* Welty, E. The eye of the story p235-40

The most of S. J. Perelman
Welty, E. S. J. Perelman's The most of S. J. Perelman; Baby, it's cold inside. *In* Welty, E. The eye of the story p235-40

Perényi, Eleanor Spencer Stone

About individual works
Liszt: the artist as romantic hero
Craft, R. Lisztomania. *In* Craft, R. Current convictions p168-83

Peretz, Don
The Kennedy and Johnson administrations and the Six-Day War. *In* The New world balance and peace in the Middle East: reality or mirage p190-95

Pereverzev, Valerian Fedorovich
The evolution of Gogol's art; excerpt from "The art of Gogol". *In* Maguire, R. A. ed. Gogol from the twentieth century p133-54

Pérez de Ayala, Ramon

About
Shaw, D. L. New directions. *In* Shaw, D. L. The generation of 1898 in Spain p186-205

Pérez Galdós, Benito

About
Pritchett, V. S. Benito Perez Galdos: a Spanish Balzac. *In* Pritchett, V. S. The myth makers p152-57
Snow, C. P. Baron Snow. Galdós. *In* Snow, C. P. Baron Snow. The realists p217-55

About individual works
El amigo Manso
Rutherford, J. Story, character, setting, and narrative mode in Galdos's El amigo Manso. *In* Fowler, R. ed. Style and structure in literature p177-212

Fortunata and Jacinta
Macklin, J. J. B. Pérez Galdós: Fortunata and Jacinta. *In* Williams, D. A. ed. The monster in the mirror p179-203

Pérez-López, Jorge F.
Sugar and petroleum in Cuban-Soviet terms of trade. *In* Cuba in the world p273-96

Performance
Vaill, P. B. Toward a behavioral description of high-performing systems. *In* Leadership p103-25

Performing arts

Social aspects
Petur, I. Some aspects of entertainment theory and practice. *In* Fischer, H. D. and Melnik, S. R. eds. Entertainment: a cross-cultural examination p306-14

Study and teaching—United States
Brustein, R. S. Theatre and the university. *In* Brustein, R. S. The culture watch p166-73

China
Witke, R. The performing arts. *In* Terrill, R. ed. The China difference p263-83

United States
See Afro-Americans in the performing arts

United States—Finance
Brustein, R. S. The money crisis and the performing arts. *In* Brustein, R. S. The culture watch p158-65

Perga. See Perge

Pergamene sculpture. See Sculpture, Pergamene

Pergamon. See Pergamum. Altar of Zeus. Frieze

Pergamum. Altar of Zeus. Frieze
Carter, J. C. The date of the sculptured coffer lids from the Temple of Athene Polias at Priene. *In* Studies in classical art and archaeology p139-51
Ridgway, B. S. The Ludovisi head. *In* Studies in classical art and archaeolgy p153-61

Perge

Genealogy
Jones, C. P. The Plancii of Perge and Diana Planciana. *In* Harvard Studies in classical philology v80 p231-37

Peri, Peter L.

About

Berger, J. Peter Peri. *In* Berger, J. The look of things p61-65

Perin, Constance

The symbolic landscape; authority and the American way. *In* Mann, D. A. ed. The arts in a democratic society p43-57

Periodicals

Fischer, H. D. Periodicals and the international communication system. *In* Fischer, H. D. and Merrill, J. C. eds. International and intercultural communication p99-114

See also English periodicals; Little magazines; Newspapers; Press

Circulation

See American periodicals—Circulation

Periodicals, Afro-American. See Afro-American periodicals

The periods of man's life; or, Bids of the virtues and vices for the soul of man
Lee, B. S. A poem 'Clepid the sevene ages.' *In* An English miscellany p72-92

Periplus maris. Erythræ

Mathew, G. The dating and the significance of the Periplus of the Erythrean Sea. *In* Chittick, H. N. and Rotberg, R. I. eds. East Africa and the Orient p147-63

Peristiany, Jean G.

The ideal and the actual: the role of prophets in the Pokot political system. *In* Studies in social anthropology p167-212

Peristiany, John G. See Peristiany, Jean G.

Perizonius, Jacobus

About

Momigliano, A. Perizonius, Niebuhr and the character of early Roman tradition. *In* Momigliano, A. Essays in ancient and modern historiography p231-51

Perkins, Carl D.

The view from the Hill. *In* The Third century p83-88

Perkins, David

A better word: studies of poetry editing. *In* Perkins, D. and Leondar, B. eds. The arts and cognition p246-83

Perkins, Dwight H.

Asian economic growth: the influence of the United States and Japan. *In* Clapp, P. and Halperin, M. H. eds. United States-Japanese relations, the 1970's p94-119

Perkins, Elizabeth

Towards seeing minor poets steadily and whole. *In* Bards, bohemians, and bookmen p39-55

Perkins, Jean Ashmead

The ironic mode in autobiography: Franklin and Rousseau. *In* Studies in eighteenth-century culture v6 p215-28

The Physiocrats and the Encyclopedists. *In* Studies in eighteenth-century culture v8 p323-36

Perkins, John Bryan Ward- See Ward-Perkins, John Bryan

Perkins, Maxwell Evart

About

Holman, C. H. The dwarf on Wolfe's shoulder. *In* Holman, C. H. Windows on the world p144-57

Perkins, V. F.

The cinema of Nicholas Ray. *In* Nichols, B. ed. Movies and methods p251-62

A critical history of early film theory; excerpt from "Film as film." *In* Nichols, B. ed. Movies and methods p401-22

Perlman, Daniel H.

New tools and techniques in university administration. *In* Managing nonprofit organizations p59-70

Perlman, E.

Inversion in Great expectations. *In* Dickens Studies Annual v7 p190-202

Perlman, Harvey S. and Rhinelander, Laurens Hamilton

Williams & Wilkins Co. v. United States: photocopying, copyright, and the judicial process. *In* The Supreme Court review, 1975 p355-417

Perlman, Melvin Lee

Comments on explanation, and on stability and change. *In* Explanation of prehistoric change p319-33

Perlmann, Moshe

Levanda's last year. *In* Salo Wittmayer Baron v2 p717-24

Perlmutter, Amos

American strategic and economic interests in the area. *In* The New world balance and peace in the Middle East: reality or mirage? p143-54

Perloff, Marjorie G.

On the road to Ariel: the "transitional" poetry of Sylvia Plath. *In* Butscher, E. ed. Sylvia Plath p125-42

Sylvia Plath's "Sivvy" poems: a portrait of the poet as daughter. *In* Lane, G. ed. Sylvia Plath p155-78

Permanent education. See Continuing education

Permissive will of God. See Theodicy

Perón, Juan Domingo, President Argentine Republic

About

Parry, A. The morbid tango. *In* Parry, A. Terrorism: from Robespierre to Arafat p261-73

Perrault, Charles

About

Davidson, H. M. Fontenelle, Perrault, and the realignment of the arts. *In* Literature and history in the age of ideas p3-13

About individual works

Paralelle des anciens et des modernes

Simonsuuri, K. Opposition to antiquity: Charles Perrault. *In* Simonsuuri, K. Homer's original genius p37-45

Perret, Auguste

About

Collins, P. Auguste Perret. *In* Sharp, D. ed. The nationalists p16-25

Perrett, Heli E. de Sagasti

Mass media revolution in Peru. *In* Gerbner, G. ed. Mass media policies in changing cultures p135-46

Perrin, Jean

The Actaeon myth in Shelley's poetry. *In* English Association. Essays and studies, 1975 p29-46

Perrine, Laurence

Robert Frost and the idea of immortality. *In* Frost: centennial essays II p85-98

Perrone, Vito
A view of school reform. *In* Roots of open education in America p173-90

Perrot, Michelle
Delinquency and the penitentiary system in nineteenth-century France. *In* Deviants and the abandoned in French society p213-45

Perrucci, Robert
In the service of man: radical movements in the professions. *In* Gerstl, J. E. and Jacobs, G. eds. Professions for the people p215-30

Perry, Charles R.
The British experience, 1876-1912: the impact of the telephone during the years of delay. *In* The Social impact of the telephone p69-96

Perry, John Richard
The importance of being identical. *In* Rorty, A. O. ed. The identities of persons p67-90

About individual works
The importance of being identical
Parfit, D. Lewis, Perry, and what matters. *In* Rorty, A. O. ed. The identities of persons p91-107

Perse, St John, pseud. See Léger, Aléxis Saint-Léger

Persecution. See Liberty of conscience

The **persecution** and assassination of Jean-Paul Marat as performed by the inmates of the asylum at Charenton under the direction of the Marquis de Sade (criticism) Weiss, P. *In* Kauffmann, S. Persons of the drama p51-62

Persephone
Gillis, D. C. The Persephone myth in Mandelstam's Tristia. *In* California Slavic studies v9 p139-59

Persephone in literature
Frick, D. C. The Proserpine figure in Swinburne's Poems and ballads I. *In* Aeolian harps p192-205

Persepolis
Roaf, M. A mathematical analysis of the styles of the Persepolis reliefs. *In* Greenhalgh, M. and Megaw, J. V. S. eds. Art in society p133-45

Persepolis. Apadana (Great Hall)
Porada, E. Some thoughts on the audience reliefs of Persepolis. *In* Studies in classical art and archaeology p37-43

Perseus (Mythological figure)
Lettvin, J. Y. The Gorgon's eye. *In* Brecher, K. and Feirtag, M. eds. Astronomy of the ancients p133-51

Persia. See Iran

Persian antiquities
Hanfmann, G. M. A. Sardis, Croesus, and the Persians. *In* Hanfmann, G. M. A. From Croesus to Constantine p1-21

Persian folk-lore. See Folk-lore, Persian

Persian literature

History and criticism
Wickens, G. M. Persian literature. an affirmation of identity. *In* Savory, R. M. ed. Introduction to Islamic civilisation p71-77

Persian philosophy. See Philosophy, Persian

Persius Flaccus, Aulus
About
Knoche, U. Aules Persius Flaccus. *In* Knoche, U. Roman satire p127-39
Ramage, E. S. Method and structure in the satires of Persius. *In* Illinois classical studies v4, 1979 p136-51

About individual works
The satires of Persius
Knoche, U. Aules Persius Flaccus. *In* Knoche, U. Roman satire p127-39
Ramage, E. S. Persius, the philosopher-satirist. *In* Roman satirists and their satire p114-35

Sources
Rudd, N. Imitation: association of ideas in Persius. *In* Rudd, N. Lines of enquiry p54-83

Persius Flaccus, Aules. See Persius Flaccus, Aulus

Person (Grammar) See Grammar, Comparative and general—Person

Persona (Motion picture)
Boyers, R. Bergman's "Persona": an essay on tragedy. *In* Boyers, R. Excursions p47-70
Kauffmann, S. Persona. *In* Kauffmann, S. Living images p340-50

Personal development. See Personality

Personal growth. See Self-actualization (Psychology)

Personal injuries
Franklin, M. A. Personal injury accidents in New Zealand and the United States: some striking similarities. *In* Stanford legal essays p129-48

Personal liberty. See Liberty

Personal space. See Crowding stress

Personalism. See Individualism

Personality
Broad, C. D. Personal identity and survival. *In* Wheatley, J. M. O. and Edge, H. L. eds. Philosophical dimensions of parapsychology p348-65
Lewis, D. K. Survival and identity. *In* Rorty, A. O. ed. The identities of persons p17-40
Loder, J. E. The fashioning of power: a Christian perspective on the life-style phenomenon. *In* The Context of contemporary theology p187-205
Nayak, G. C. Survival, reincarnation, and the problem of personal identity. *In* Wheatley, J. M. O. and Edge, H. L. eds. Philosophical dimensions of parapsychology p292-307
Parfit, D. Lewis, Perry, and what matters. *In* Rorty, A. O. ed. The identities of persons p91-107
Penelhum, T. Self-identity and self-regard. *In* Rorty, A. O. ed. The identities of persons p253-80
Penelhum, T. Survival and disembodied existence; excerpts. *In* Wheatley, J. M. O. and Edge, H. L. eds. Philosophical dimensions of parapsychology p308-29
Perry, J. R. The importance of being identical. *In* Rorty, A. O. ed. The identities of persons p67-90
Renshon, S. A. The role of personality development in political socialization. *In* Schwartz, D. C. and Schwartz, S. K. eds. New directions in political socialization p29-68

Pertschuk, Michael
The lawyer-lobbyist. *In* Nader, R. and Green, M. J. eds. Verdicts on lawyers p197-207

Peru

History—to 1548
Bourque, S. C. The clash of empires: Peru's enduring paradox. *In* Aftermath of empire p65-81

History—1548-1820
Bourque, S. C. The clash of empires: Peru's enduring paradox. *In* Aftermath of empire p65-81

Politics and government—1919-
Cotler, J. A structural-historical approach to the breakdown of democratic institutions: Peru. *In* The Breakdown of democratic regimes pt3 p178-206

Leeds, A. and Leeds, E. R. Accounting for behavioral differences: three political systems and the responses of squatters in Brazil, Peru, and Chile. *In* Walton, J. and Masotti, L. H. eds. The city in comparative perspective p193-248

Perumbulavil, Vilasini
Children's books and reading in a plural society—Singapore. *In* Egoff, S. A. ed. One ocean touching p60-78

Peruzzi family
Krekić, B. Four Florentine commercial companies in Dubrovnik (Ragusa) in the first half of the fourteenth century. *In* The Medieval city p25-41

Perversion, Sexual. See Sexual deviation

Pesez, Jean-Marie, and Le Roy Ladurie, Emmanuel
The deserted villages of France: an overview. *In* Rural society in France p72-106

Pessac, France. Quartiers modernes Frugès
Taylor, B. B. Le Corbusier at Pessac: professional and client responsibilities. *In* Walden, R. ed. The open hand p162-85

Pessoa, Fernando

About
Josipovici, G. Fernando Pessoa, 1888-1935. *In* Josipovici, G. The lessons of modernism p26-50

Pesticide industry

United States
Harmer, R. M. Selling death. *In* Against pollution and hunger p97-117

Pesticide pollution. See Pesticides—Environmental aspects

Pesticides

Environmental aspects—United States
Harmer, R. M. Selling death. *In* Against pollution and hunger p97-117

Law and legislation—United States
Harmer, R. M. Selling death. *In* Against pollution and hunger p97-117

Pesticides and the environment. See Pesticides—Environmental aspects

Pestré, Abbé

About
Rex, W. E. The philosophical articles by Abbé Pestré in Diderot's Encyclopédie. *In* Studies in eighteenth-century culture v7 p251-62

Pete 'n' Tillie (Motion picture)
Kauffmann, S. Pete 'n' Tillie. *In* Kauffmann, S. Living images p162-63

Petén, Guatemala (Dept.)

Antiquities
Willey, G. R. The rise of Classic Maya civilization: a Pasión Valley perspective. *In* The Origins of Maya civilization p133-57

Peter Alboini of Mantua. See Petrus Mantuanus

Peter Damian. See Pietro Damiani, Saint

Peter Martyr. See Vermigli, Pietro Martire

Peter of Mantua. See Petrus Mantuanus

Peter, Jean-Pierre
Disease and the sick at the end of the eighteenth century. *In* Biology of man in history p81-124

Peterborough, N.H.

History—Revolution, 1775-1783
Shy, J. W. Hearts and minds in the American Revolution: the case of "Long Bill" Scott and Peterborough, New Hampshire. *In* Shy, J. W. A people numerous and armed p163-79

Peterkiewicz, Jerzy. See Pietrkiewicz, Jerzy

Peters, A. D.

About
Koestler, A. In memory of A. D. Peters. *In* Koestler, A. The heel of Achilles p112-15

Peters, August Detlev. See Peters, A. D.

Peters, Edward Murray
The Archbishop and the hedgehog. *In* Law, church, and society p167-84

Pars, parte: Dante and an urban contribution to political thought. *In* The Medieval city p113-40

Peters, Emrys L.
The status of women in four Middle East communities. *In* Beck, L. and Keddie, N. R. eds. Women in the Muslim world p311-50

Peters, Jonathan
L. S. Senghor: the mask poems of Chants d'ombre. *In* African literature today no. 7: Focus on criticism p76-92

Peters, Phillis. See Wheatley, Phillis

Peters, Richard Stanley
Subjectivity and standards. *In* Niblett, W. R. ed. The sciences, the humanities and the technological threat p139-56

About individual works
Education and the educated man
Elliott, R. K. Education and human being I. *In* Philosophers discuss education p45-72

Peters, Robert L.
Algernon Charles Swinburne and the use of integral detail. *In* Sambrook, J. ed. Pre-Raphaelitism p206-19

Peters, Ronald M.
The written Constitution. *In* Graham, G. J. and Graham, S. G. eds. Founding principles of American government p168-96

Peters, Stephen
Ingredients of the Communist takeover in Albania. *In* Hammond, T. T. ed. The anatomy of Communist takeovers p273-92

Petersen, David L.
Max Weber and the sociological study of ancient Israel. *In* Johnson, H. M. ed. Religious change and continuity p117-49

Petroleum—*Continued*

Caribbean region

Emery, K. O. and Uchupi, E. The oil potential of the Caribbean. *In* Borgese, E. M. and Krieger, D. eds. The tides of change p239-53

Petroleum as fuel

Morgenthau, H. J. World politics and the politics of oil. *In* Eppen, G. D. ed. Energy: the policy issues p43-51

Petroleum Exporting Countries, Organization of. See Organization of Petroleum Exporting Countries

Petroleum in submerged lands

Senkaku Islands

Li, V. H. China and off-shore oil: the Tiao-yü Tai dispute. *In* China's changing role in the world economy p143-62

Petroleum industry and trade

Adelman, M. A. The hinge of energy policy: relations between energy markets in the United States and abroad. *In* Eppen, G. D. ed. Energy: the policy issues p71-81

Akins, J. E. The oil crisis: this time the wolf is here. *In* Bundy, W. P. ed. The world economic crisis p21-49

Aliber, R. Z. Oil and the money crunch. *In* Eppen, G. D. ed. Energy: the policy issues p82-95

Amuzegar, J. The oil story: facts, fiction and fair play. *In* Bundy, W. P. ed. The world economic crisis p69-82

Calleo, D. P. America, Europe and the oil crisis: hegemony reaffirmed? *In* Atlantis lost p119-47

Darmstadter, J. and Landsberg, H. H. The economic background. *In* Vernon, R. ed. The oil crisis p15-37

Lantzke, U. The OECD and its International Energy Agency. *In* Vernon, R. ed. The oil crisis p217-27

Maull, H. Oil and influence: the oil weapon examined. *In* Knorr, K. E. and Trager, F. N. eds. Economic issues and national security p259-88

Odell, P. R. The international oil companies in the new world oil market. *In* The Year book of world affairs, 1978 p76-92

Penrose, E. T. The development of crisis. *In* Vernon, R. ed. The oil crisis p39-57

Smart, I. Uniqueness and generality. *In* Vernon, R. ed. The oil crisis p259-81

Smith, W. D. The energy crisis and the Middle East. *In* The New world balance and peace in the Middle East: reality or mirage? p105-17

Stobaugh, R. B. The oil companies in the crisis. *In* Vernon, R. ed. The oil crisis p179-202

Swearingen, J. E. What price dependence? *In* Prochnow, H. V. ed. Dilemmas facing the nation p96-108

Vernon, R. The distribution of power. *In* Vernon, R. ed. The oil crisis p245-57

Vernon, R. An interpretation. *In* Vernon, R. ed. The oil crisis p 1-14

Wilkins, M. The oil companies in perspective. *In* Vernon, R. ed. The oil crisis p159-78

Williams, H. R. Some ingredients of a national oil and gas policy. *In* Stanford legal essays p445-60

Political aspects

Doran, C. F. Oil politics and the rise of codependence. *In* Orr, D. S. and Soroos, M. S. eds. The global predicament p195-208

Friendlander, R. A. Problems of the Mediterranean: a geopolitical perspective. *In* The Year book of world affairs, 1978 p175-90

Spechler, D. R. and Spechler, M. C. The Soviet Union and the oil weapon: benefits and dilemmas p96-123

Prices

See Petroleum products—Prices

Arab countries

Zonis, M. Oil and politics in the Middle East. *In* Eppen, G. D. ed. Energy: the policy issues p52-68

Cuba

Pérez-López, J. F. Sugar and petroleum in Cuban-Soviet terms of trade. *In* Cuba in the world p273-96

Europe

Prodi, R. and Clô, A. Europe. *In* Vernon, R. ed. The oil crisis p91-112

Japan

Tsurumi, Y. Japan. *In* Vernon, R. ed. The oil crisis p113-27

Russia

Goldman, M. I. The Soviet Union. *In* Vernon, R. ed. The oil crisis p129-43

United States

Galbraith, J. K. Defenders of the faith, III: Wright and Slick. *In* Galbraith, J. K. Annals of an abiding liberal p118-22

McKie, J. W. The United States. *In* Vernon, R. ed. The oil crisis p73-90

Mead, W. J. Petroleum: an unregulated industry? *In* Kalter, R. J. and Vogely, W. A. eds. Energy supply and government policy p130-60

Venezuela

Tugwell, F. Venezuela and the inter-American system. *In* Farer, T. J. ed. The future of the inter-American system p256-69

Petroleum products

Prices

Aliber, R. Z. Oil and the money crunch. *In* Eppen, G. D. ed. Energy: the policy issues p82-95

Prices—United States

Johnson, W. A. The impact of price controls on the oil industry: how to worsen an energy crisis. *In* Eppen, G. D. ed. Energy: the policy issues p99-121

Petronio, Giuseppe

The place of The Decameron. *In* Dombroski, R. S. ed. Critical perspectives on The Decameron p48-60

Petronius Arbiter

About individual works

Satyricon

Fredericks, S. C. Seneca and Petronius: Menippean satire under Nero. *In* Roman satirists and their satire p89-113

Knoche, U. Petronius' novel. *In* Knoche, U. Roman satire p109-26

Lyons, J. O. Whores and rakes in the gardens of delight. *In* Lyons, J. O. The invention of the self p176-96

Petrović, Djurdjica

Fire-arms in the Balkans on the eve of and after the Ottoman conquests of the fourteenth and fifteenth centuries. *In* War, technology and society in the Middle East p164-94

Petrus Mantuanus
About
James, T. E. A fragment of An exposition of the first letter of Seneca to Lucilius attributed to Peter of Mantua. *In* Philosophy and humanism p531-41

Pettigrew, Thomas Fraser
Prejudice: Prejudice and the situation. *In* The Black American reference book p521-28

Three issues in ethnicity: boundaries, deprivations, and perceptions. *In* Major social issues p25-49

See also DeVos, G. A. jt. auth.

Pettit, Philip
The life-world and role-theory. *In* Pivčević, E. ed. Phenomenology and philosophical understanding p251-70

Rational man theory. *In* Hookway, C. and Pettit, P. eds. Action and interpretation p43-63

Petuchowski, Jakob J.
The limits of self-sacrifice. *In* Modern Jewish ethics p103-18

Petur, István
Some aspects of entertainment theory and practice. *In* Fischer, H. D. and Melnik, S. R. eds. Entertainment: a cross-cultural examination p306-14

Pevsner, Nikolaus
Frank Lloyd Wright's peaceful penetration of Europe. *In* Sharp, D. ed. The rationalists p35-41
About
Watkin, D. Pevsner. *In* Watkin, D. Morality and architecture p71-111

Pewter
Rome
Brown, D. Bronze and pewter. *In* Strong, D. E. and Brown, D. eds. Roman crafts p25-42

Pewter work. See Pewtercraft

Pewtercraft
Brown, D. Bronze and pewter. *In* Strong, D. E. and Brown, D. eds. Roman crafts p25-42

Pewtersmithing. See Pewtercraft

Peyote. See Peyotism

Peyote cult. See Peyotism

Peyote religion. See Peyotism

Peyotism
Myerhoff, B. G. Return to Wirikuta: ritual reversal and symbolic continuity on the Peyote hunt of the Huichol Indians. *In* Babcock, B. A. ed. The reversible world p225-39

Slotkin, J. S. The Peyote way. *In* Tedlock, D. E. and Tedlock, B. eds. Teachings from the American earth p96-104

Peyre, Henri
French literary imagination and Dostoevsky, and other essays
Contents
Claudel and the French literary tradition
French literary imagination and Dostoevsky
Gide and literary influences
Is literature dead? Or dying?
Literature and revolution
The notion of the Absurd in contemporary French literature
Poets against music in the age of symbolism. *In* Symbolism and modern literature p179-92

Stendhal and Balzac as admirers and followers of Molière. *In* Johnson, R. B.; Neumann, E. S. and Trail, G. T. eds. Molière and the commonwealth of letters: patrimony and posterity p133-44

Peyton, K. M. pseud.
On not writing a proper book. *In* Blishen, E. ed. The thorny paradise p123-27

Peyton, Kathleen Wendy. See Peyton, K. M. pseud.

Peyton, Michael. See Peyton, K. M. pseud.

Pfaltzgraff, Robert L. and Davis, Jacquelyn K.
The Asian/Pacific region—implications for U.S. global strategy. *In* Pacific Asia and U.S. policies: a political-economic strategic assessment p16-27

Pfeffer, Jeffrey
The ambiguity of leadership. *In* Leadership p13-34

Pfeffer, Leo
The legitimation of marginal religions in the United States. *In* Zaretsky, I. I. and Leone, M. P. eds. Religious movements in contemporary America p9-26

Pfeiffer, Eric
Sex and aging. *In* Gross, L. ed. Sexual issues in marriage p43-47

Pfeiffer, William S.
Mary Cochran: Sherwood Anderson's ten-year novel. *In* Virginia. University. Bibliographical Society. Studies in bibliography v31 p248-57

Phaethon
Nagy, G. J. Phaethon, Sappho's Phaon, and the White Rock of Leukas. *In* Harvard Studies in classical philology v77 p137-77

Pharisees
Dempsey, P. J. R. A note on the phenomenon of Pharisaism. *In* Wolman, B. B. ed. Psychoanalysis and Catholicism p111-14

Pharmaceutical research
Harvey, A. M. Pharmacology's giant: John Jacob Abel. *In* Harvey, A. M. Adventures in medical research p49-59

Morris, N. and Mills, M. Prisoners as laboratory animals. *In* Contemporary issues in criminal justice p129-43

Pharmacology
See also Chemotherapy; Psychopharmacology
Research
See Pharmaceutical research

Pharmacy
Research
See Pharmaceutical research

Pharr, Susan J.
Japan: historical and contemporary perspectives. *In* Giele, J. Z. and Smock, A. C. eds. Women: roles and status in eight countries p217-55

Phayre, Sir Arthur Purves
About
Tinker, H. Arthur Phayre in Mauritius, 1874-1878: social policy and economic reality. *In* Southeast Asian history and historiography p59-85

Phelps, Edward John
About
Campbell, C. S. Edward J. Phelps and Anglo-American relations. *In* Allen, H. C. and Thompson, R. eds. Contrast and connection p210-24

Phelps, Gilbert
The Byronic Byron. *In* Jump, J. D. ed. Byron p52-75

Phelps, Leland R.
Goethe's adaptation of Romeo and Juliet. *in* Creative encounter p17-24

Phelps, Wayne H.
Some sixteenth-century stationers' wills. *In* Virginia. University. Bibliographical Society. Studies in bibliography v32 p48-59

Phenix, Philip Henry
Teaching as celebration. *In* Buxton, T. H. and Prichard, K. W. eds. Excellence in university teaching p22-29

Phenomenalism
Hobbs, A. C. New phenomenalism as an account of perceptual knowledge. *In* Royal Institute of Philosophy. Impressions of empiricism p109-21

Quinton, A. The concept of a phenomenon. *In* Pivčević, E. ed. Phenomenology and philosophical understanding p 1-16

Phenomenological psychology
May, A. A phenomenological approach to psychotherapy. *In* May, R. Psychology and the human dilemma p111-27

Metzger, W. Can the subject create his world? *In* Perception p57-71

See also Existential psychology

Phenomenological sociology
Lemert, C. C. Phenomenological sociology: Schultz, Berger, Luckmann. *In* Lemert, C. C. Sociology and the twilight of man p135-64

See also Ethnomethdology

Phenomenology
Bauman, Z. Understanding as the work of reason: Edmund Husserl. *In* Bauman, Z. Hermeneutics and social science p111-30

Biemel, W. Husserl's Encyclopedia Britannica article and Heidegger's remarks thereon. *In* Elliston, F. A. and McCormick, P. eds. Husserl p286-303

Carr, D. Husserl's problematic concept of the life-world. *In* Elliston, F. A. and McCormick, P. eds. Husserl p202-12

Derrida, J. From restricted to general economy: a Hegelianism without reserve. *In* Derrida, J. Writing and difference p251-77

Derrida, J. "Genesis and structure" and phenomenology. *In* Derrida, J. Writing and difference p154-68

Dickens, D. R. Phenomenology. *In* McNall, S. G. ed. Theoretical perspectives in sociology p325-47

Dreyfus, H. L. and Haugeland, J. Husserl and Heidegger: philosophy's last stand. *In* Murray, M. E. ed. Heidegger and modern philosophy p222-38

Durfee, H. A. Analytic philosophy, phenomenology, and the concept of consciousness. *In* Thought, consciousness, and reality p111-30

Elliston, F. A. Husserl's phenomenology of empathy. *In* Elliston, F. A. and McCormick, P. eds. Husserl p213-46

Findlay, J. N. Phenomenology and the meaning of realism. *In* Pivčević, E. ed. Phenomenology and philosophical understanding p143-58

Heath, P. L. The idea of a phenomenological ethics. *In* Pivčević, E. ed. Phenomenology and philosophical understanding p159-72

Kern, I. The three ways to the transcendental phenomenological reduction in the philosophy of Edmund Husserl. *In* Elliston, F. A. and McCormick, P. eds. Husserl p126-49

Kockelmans, J. J. Destructive retrieve and hermeneutic phenomenology in 'Being and time.' *In* Radical phenomenology p106-37

Küng, G. The phenomenological reduction as epoche and explication. *In* Elliston, F. A. and McCormick, P. eds. Husserl p338-49

Landgrebe, L. Phenomenology as transcendental theory of history. *In* Elliston, F. A. and McCormick, P. eds. Husserl p101-17

Levin, D. M. Husserl's notion of self-evidence. *In* Pivčević, E. ed. Phenomenology and philosophical understanding p53-77

McCormick, P. Phenomenology and metaphilosophy. *In* Elliston, F. A. and McCormick, P. eds. Husserl p350-64

Madison, G. B. Phenomenology and existentialism: Husserl and the end of idealism. *In* Elliston, F. A. and McCormick, P. eds. Husserl p247-68

Mays, W. Phenomenology and Marxism. *In* Pivčević, E. ed. Phenomenology and philosophical understanding p231-50

Murray, M. E. Heidegger and Ryle: two versions of phenomenology. *In* Murray, M. E. ed. Heidegger and modern philosophy p271-90

Pivčević, E. Concepts, phenomenology and philosophical understanding. *In* Pivčević, E. ed. Phenomenology and philosophical understanding p271-86

Ricoeur, P. Phenomenology of freedom. *In* Pivčević, E. ed. Phenomenology and philosophical understanding p173-94

Tugendhat, E. Phenomenology and linguistic analysis. *In* Elliston, F. A. and McCormick, P. eds. Husserl p325-37

Warnock, M. The nature of the mental image: phenomenology, Sartre and Wittgenstein. *In* Warnock, M. Imagination p131-95

Wartofsky, M. W. Consciousness, praxis, and reality: Marxism vs. phenomenology. *In* Elliston, F. A. and McCormick, P. eds. Husserl p304-13

Welton, D. C. Structure and genesis in Husserl's phenomenology. *In* Elliston, F. A. and McCormick, P. eds. Husserl p54-69

See also Existential psychology; Existentalism; Phenomenological sociology

Methodology

Casey, E. S. Imagination and phenomenological method. *In* Elliston, F. A. and McCormick, P. eds. Husserl p70-82

Zaner, R. M. On the sense of method in phenomenology. *In* Pivčević, E. ed. Phenomenology and philosophical understanding p125-41

Philadelphia

History—Revolution, 1775-1783

Oaks, R. F. The city under military occupation: Philadelphia, 1777-1778. *In* Essays on urban America p21-54

Politics and government

Ambacher, B. I. Urban response to Jacksonian democracy: Philadelphia Democrats and the Bank War, 1832-1834. *In* Essays on urban America p55-87

Philadelphia—*Continued*

Politics and government—Colonial period, ca. 1600-1775

Diamondstone, J. M. The government of eighteenth-century Philadelphia. *In* Daniels, B. C. ed. Town and county p238-63

Riots, 1844

Bloomfield, M. H. Riot control in Philadelphia. *In* Bloomfield, M. H. American lawyers in a changing society, 1776-1876 p191-234

Social conditions

Oaks, R. F. The city under military occupation: Philadelphia, 1777-1778. *In* Essays on urban America p21-54

Philanthropy. See Charities; Endowments

Philberth, Karl
The generation of matter and the conservation of energy. *In* Cosmology, history, and theology p113-29

Philbrick, Thomas
Thomas Jefferson. *In* Emerson, E. H. ed. American literature, 1764-1789 p145-69

Philip I, Count of Flanders

About

De Gryse, L. M. Some observations on the origin of the Flemish bailiff (bailli): the reign of Philip of Alsace. *In* Viator: medieval and Renaissance studies v7 p243-94

Philip II, King of Spain

Art patronage

Trevor-Roper, H. R. Philip II and the anti-Reformation. *In* Trevor-Roper, H. R. Princes and artists p47-83

Philip IV, King of France. See Philippe IV, le Bel, King of France

Philip of Alsace, Count of Flanders. See Philip I, Count of Flanders

Philip the Fair. See Philippe, IV, le Bel, King of France

Philipp, Mangol Bayat- See Bayat-Philipp, Mangol

Philipp, Thomas
Feminism and nationalist politics in Egypt. *In* Beck, L. and Keddie, N. R. eds. Women in the Muslim world p277-94

Philippe IV, le Bel, King of France

About

Brown, E. A. R. Royal salvation and needs of state in late Capetian France. *In* Order and innovation in the Middle Ages p365-83

Philippe d'Alsace, comte de Flandre. See Philip I, Count of Flanders

Philippine Islands

Social conditions

Eggan, F. R. Applied anthropology in the Mountain Province, Philippines. *In* Social organization and the applications of anthropology p196-209

Social life and customs

Flores-Meiser, E. P. The hot mouth and evil eye. *In* The Evil eye p149-62

Philippine languages. See Tagalog language

Philips, Sir Cyril Henry
Dalhousie and the Burmese War of 1852. *In* Southeast Asian history and historiography p51-58

Philipson, Morris H.
Virginia Woolf's Orlando: biography as a work of fiction. *In* From Parnassus p237-48

Phillips, D. Z.
The problem of evil. *In* Reason and religion p103-21

About individual works

In search of the moral must

Foot, P. Are moral considerations overriding? *In* Foot, P. Virtues and vices, and other essays in moral philosophy p181-88

Phillips, George Harwood
Indians and the breakdown of the Spanish mission system in California. *In* Weber, D. J. ed. New Spain's far northern frontier p257-70

Phillips, Herbert P.
The culture of Siamese intellectuals. *In* Change and persistence in Thai society p324-57

Phillips, Jerrold A.
Kingdom of earth: some approaches. *In* Tennessee Williams: a tribute p349-53

Phillips, Kyle Meredith, and Ashmead, Ann Hardwell
Three goddesses and a falcon. *In* Studies in classical art and archaeology p45-52

Phillips, Margaret Mann
From the Ciceronianus to Montaigne. *In* Classical influences on European culture A.D. 1500-1700 p191-97

Ways with adages. *In* Essays on the works of Erasmus p51-60

Phillips, Robert L.
A structural approach to myth in the fiction of Eudora Welty. *In* Prenshaw, P. W. ed. Eudora Welty p56-67

Phillips, Robert S.
The dark funnel: a reading of Sylvia Plath; excerpt from "The confessional poets." *In* Butscher, E. ed. Sylvia Plath p186-205

Mask and symbol in Set this house on fire. *In* Morris, R. K. and Malin, I. eds. The achievement of William Styron p134-49

Phillips, Ulrich Bonnell

About

Downs, R. B. Antebellum South. *In* Downs, R. B. Books that changed the South p218-28

About individual works

Life and labor in the old South

Downs, R. B. Antebellum South. *In* Downs, R. B. Books that changed the South p218-28

Phillips, William
On Partisan Review. *In* Anderson, E. and Kinzie, M. eds. The little magazine in America: a modern documentary history p131-41

Phillips curve
Gordon, R. A. A skeptical look at the "natural rate" hypothesis. *In* Theory for economic efficiency: essays in honor of Abba P. Lerner p46-61

Solow, R. M. Down the Phillips curve with gun and camera. *In* Inflation, trade and taxes p3-22

Phillipson, Nicholas T.
Culture and society in the 18th century province: the case of Edinburgh and the Scottish Enlightenment. *In* The University in society v2 p407-48

Philmus, Robert M.

Borges and Wells and the labyrinths of time. *In* H. G. Wells and modern science fiction p159-78

Philo Judaeus

About

Daube, D. The rabbis and Philo on human rights. *In* Sidorsky, D. ed. Essays on human rights p234-46

Laporte, J. Philo in the tradition of Biblical wisdom literature. *In* Aspects of wisdom in Judaism and early Christianity p103-41

Meeks, W. A. The divine agent and his counterfeit in Philo and the Fourth Gospel. *In* Aspects of religious propaganda in Judaism and early Christianity p43-67

Philo of Alexandria. See Philo Judaeus

Philology

Barfield, O. Philology and the Incarnation. *In* Barfield, O. The rediscovery of meaning, and other essays p228-36

Philology, Comparative. See Comparative linguistics

Philomel in literature

Thompson, A. Philomel in 'Titus Andronicus' and 'Cymbeline'. *In* Shakespeare survey v31 p23-32

Philosophers

Aron, R. The social responsibility of the philosopher. *in* Aron, R. Politics and history p249-59

Russell, B. R. 3d Earl. The duty of a philosopher in this age. *In* The Abdication of philosophy: philosophy and the public good p15-22

Philosophers' stone. See Alchemy

Philosophical analysis. See Analysis (Philosophy)

Philosophical anthropology

Bambrough, R. Essay on man. *In* Royal Institute of Philosophy. Nature and conduct p 1-13

Bruner, J. S. Psychology and the image of man. *In* Bruner, J. S. On knowing p167-89

Copleston, F. C. The existentialist concept of man. *In* Copleston, F. C. Philosophers and philosophies p160-71

Copleston, F. C. Man, transcendence and the absence of God. *In* Copleston, F. C. Philosophers and philosophies p57-67

Cram, R. A. Why we do not behave like human beings; excerpt from "Convictions and controversies." *In* Crunden, R. M. ed. The superfluous men p86-94

Davies, J. C. Essay 4. *In* Fitzgerald, R. ed. What it means to be human p64-82

Dobzhansky, T. G. Evolution and man's self-image. *In* Goodall, V. M. ed. The quest for man p189-220

Dubos, R. J. Humanity and the beast. *In* Dubos, R. J. Beast or angel? p61-66

Dubos, R. J. The humanness of the human species. *In* Dubos, R. J. Beast or angel? p45-50

Economos, J. J. Identity and "the difference." *In* Philosophical aspects of the mind-body problem p154-61

Flew, A. G. N. Epilogue. *In* Flew, A. G. N. A rational animal p222-25

Flew, A. G. N. A rational animal. *In* Flew, A. G. N. A rational animal p89-122

Gould, C. C. The woman question: philosophy of liberation and the liberation of philosophy. *In* Gould, C. C. and Wartofsky, M. W. eds. Women and philosophy p5-44

Holbrook, D. Politics and the need for meaning. *In* Fitzgerald, R. ed. Human needs and politics p174-94

Huxley, A. L. How original is original sin? *In* Huxley, A. L. The Human situation p59-73

Huxley, A. L. The problem of human nature. *In* Huxley, A. L. The Human situation p123-36

Jaberg, R. L. Search for a center. *In* America in theological perspective p230-46

Koestler, A. A glance through the keyhole. *In* Koestler, A. Janus p274-86

Koestler, A. Prologue: the new calendar. *In* Koestler, A. Janus p 1-20

Koestler, A. The urge to self-destruction. *In* Koestler, A. The heel of Achilles p3-19

Letwin, S. R. Nature, history and morality. *In* Royal Institute of Philosophy. Nature and conduct p229-50

O'Briant, W. H. Man, nature, and the history of philosophy. *In* Philosophy & environmental crisis p79-89

O'Neill, J. Time's body: Vico on the love of language and institution. *In* Giambattista Vico's science of humanity p333-39

Quinton, A. Has a man an essence? *In* Royal Institute of Philosophy. Nature and conduct p14-35

Shapiro, J. J. The slime of history: embeddedness in nature and critical theory. *In* O'Neill, J. ed. On critical theory p145-63

Smith, M. B. Essay I. *In* Fitzgerald, R. ed. What it means to be human p3-24

Thomas, L. The youngest and brightest thing around. *In* Thomas, L. The medusa and the snail p12-18

Van Peursen, C. A. The horizon. *In* Elliston, F. A. and McCormick, P. eds. Husserl p182-201

Wolff, R. P. There's nobody here but us persons. *In* Gould, C. C. and Wartofsky, M. W. eds. Women and philosophy p128-44

See also Humanism; Man (Theology); Man—Animal nature; Mind and body; Persons

Methodology

Derrida, J. Structure, sign and play in the discourse of the human sciences. *In* Derrida, J. Writing and difference p278-93

Philosophical grammar. See Grammar, Comparative and general

Philosophy

Arendt, H. The philosophers and the will. *In* Arendt, H. The life of the mind v2 p11-51

Aron, R. The social responsibility of the philosopher. *In* Aron, R. Politics and history p249-59

Barfield, O. Dream, myth, and philosophical double vision. *In* Barfield, O. The rediscovery of meaning, and other essays p22-31

Berlin, Sir I. The purpose of philosophy. *In* Berlin, Sir I. Concepts and categories p 1-11

Bitzer, L. F. Rhetoric and public knowledge. *In* Burks, D. M. ed. Rhetoric, philosophy, and literature: an exploration p67-93

Broad, C. D. The relevance of psychical research to philosophy. *In* Ludwig, J. K. ed. Philosophy and parapsychology p43-63

Philosophy—*Continued*

Burke, K. Rhetoric, poetics, and philosophy. *In* Burks, D. M. ed. Rhetoric, philosophy, and literature: an exploration p15-33

Cassirer, E. The concept of philosophy as a philosophical problem. *In* Cassirer, E. Symbol, myth, and culture p49-63

Cassirer, E. Philosophy and politics. *In* Cassirer, E. Symbol, myth, and culture p219-32

Copleston, F. C. Philosophical knowledge. *In* Copleston, F. C. Philosophers and philosophies p 1-16

Donato, E. The idioms of the text: notes on the language of philosophy and the fictions of literature. *In* Glyph 2 p 1-13

Dunn, J. Practising history and social science on 'realist' assumptions. *In* Hookway, C. and Pettit, P. eds. Action and interpretation p145-75

Grene, M. G. Still philosophy? *In* Grene, M. G. Philosophy in and out of Europe p 1-10

Johnstone, H. W. From philosophy to rhetoric and back. *In* Burks, D. M. ed. Rhetoric, philosophy, and literature: an exploration p49-66

Kneale, M. H.; Robinson, R. G. F. and Mundle, C. W. K. Symposium: Is psychical research relevant to philosophy? *In* Ludwig, J. K. ed. Philosophy and parapsychology p64-109

Lauer, Q. Philosophy and social change. *In* Roth, R. J. ed. Person and community p 1-24

Matthews, G. B. On talking philosophy with children. *In* Royal Institute of Philosophy. Communication and understanding p46-62

Miller, J. W. The ahistoric ideal. *In* Miller, J. W. The paradox of cause, and other essays p130-60

Natanson, M. A. The arts of indirection. *In* Burks, D. M. ed. Rhetoric, philosophy, and literature: an exploration p35-47

Rintelen, F. J. von. The public good and the attainment and loss of reality in science and philosophy. *In* The Abdication of philosophy: philosophy and the public good p251-66

Russell, B. R. 3d Earl. The duty of a philosopher in this age. *In* The Abdication of philosophy: philosophy and the public good p15-22

Schneider, H. W. The American Establishment, the civilizing arts, and philosophy. *In* Philosophy and the civilizing arts p433-45

Schneider, H. W. Philosophy will never be a science. *In* Philosophy and the civilizing arts p467-73

See also Absurd (Philosophy); Act (Philosophy); Aesthetics; Analysis (Philosophy); Authenticity (Philosophy); Belief and doubt; Causation; Consciousness; Cosmology; Criticism (Philosophy); Cycles; Difference (Philosophy); Dualism; Ends and means; Ethics; Experience; Facts (Philosophy); Fate and fatalism; Free will and determinism; Humanism; Idea (Philosophy); Idealism; Ideology; Immortality (Philosophy); Individuation; Intuition; Irrationalism (Philosophy); Knowledge, Theory of; Logic; Meaning (Philosophy); Metaphysics; Mind and body; Mysticism; Naturalism; Nominalism; Ontology; Operationalism; Organism (Philosophy); Parapsychology and philosophy; Perception;

Pluralism; Positivism; Practice (Philosophy); Pragmatism; Rationalism; Realism; Reality; Repetition (Philosophy); Self (Philosophy); Soul; Structuralism; Style (Philosophy); Theory (Philosophy); Thomists; Thought and thinking; Truth; Universals (Philosophy); Utilitarianism; Will

History

Copleston, F. C. The history of philosophy: relativism and recurrence. *In* Copleston, F. C. Philosophers and philosophies p17-28

Foucault, M. History of systems of thought. *In* Foucault, M. Language, counter-memory, practice p199-217

Lobkowicz, N. On the history of theory and praxis. *In* Political theory and praxis p13-27

History—Germany

Koenne, W. On the relationship between philosophy and technology in the German-speaking countries. *In* Bugliarello, G. and Doner, D. B. eds. The history and philosophy of technology p282-93

History—Italy

Randall, J. H. Paduan Aristotelianism reconsidered. *In* Philosophy and humanism p275-82

Methodology

See Methodology

Study and teaching

Gray, J. G. The moral responsibilities of teachers of philosophy. *In* Philosophy and the civilizing arts p370-77

Hahn, L. E. Advice to the new philosophy teacher. *In* Philosophy and the civilizing arts p356-69

Therapeutic use

Simon, B. The philosopher as therapist. *In* Simon, B. Mind and madness in ancient Greece p180-99

Philosophy, American

Kurtz, P. W. Naturalism in American philosophy. *In* Philosophy and the civilizing arts p178-212

Santayana, G. A brief history of my opinions. *In* Crunden, R. M. ed. The superfluous men p5-18

20th century

Grene, M. G. Philosophy in and out of Europe: The European sources of recent Anglo-American philosophy. *In* Grene, M. G. Philosophy in and out of Europe p11-23

Grene, M. G. Philosophy in and out of Europe: The reception of Continental philosophy in America. *In* Grene, M. G. Philosophy in and out of Europe p24-37

Philosophy, Analytical. See Analysis (Philosophy)

Philosophy, Ancient

Anton, J. P. Tragic vision and philosophic theoria in classical Greece. *In* Philosophy and the civilizing arts p 1-23

Arendt, H. Quaestio mihi factus sum: the discovery of the inner man. *In* Arendt, H. The life of the mind v2 p53-110

Arendt, H. What makes us think? *In* Arendt, H. The life of the mind v 1 p127-93

Coomaraswamy, A. K. Recollection, Indian and platonic. *In* Coomaraswamy, A. K. Selected papers v2 p49-65

Furley, D. J. Aristotle and the Atomists on motion in a void. *In* Motion and time, space and matter p83-100

Philosophy, Ancient—*Continued*

Hahm, D. E. Early Hellenistic theories of vision and the perception of color. *In* Studies in perception p60-95

Hermassi, K. C. What theatre means. *In* Hermassi, K. C. Polity and theater in historical perspective p3-24

McWilliams, W. C. On equality as the moral foundation for community. *In* The Moral foundations of the American Republic p183-213

Olney, J. L. The esoteric flower: Yeats and Jung. *In* Yeats and the occult p27-54

Popper, Sir K. R. The myth of the framework. *In* The Abdication of philosophy: philosophy and the public good p23-48

Romilly, J. de. Rhetoric and the classification of arts in the fourth century B.C. *In* Romilly, J. de. Magic and rhetoric in ancient Greece p45-66

Simon, B. The philosopher as therapist. *In* Simon, B. Mind and madness in ancient Greece p180-99

Tejera, V. Dialogue and dialectic. *In* Philosophy and the civilizing arts p49-59

Wilken, R. L. Wisdom and philosophy in early Christianity. *In* Aspects of wisdom in Judaism and early Christianity p143-68

See also Gnosticism; Manichaeism; Platonists; Science, Ancient; Sophists (Greek philosophy); Stoics

Philosophy, Arab

Mahmoud, Z. N. Rational aspects of the classical Arabic culture. *In* Arab and American cultures p87-92

See also Philosophy Islamic

Philosophy, Arabic. See Philosophy, Arab

Philosophy, Asean. See Philosophy, Oriental

Philosophy, Buddhist. See Buddhist doctrines; Philosophy, Indic

Philosophy, Chinese

Chang Mei Yuan. Malraux and Chinese thinking. *In* Courcel, M. H. de, ed. Malraux p103-11

Rubin, V. A. The theory and practice of a totalitarian state. *In* Rubin, V. A. Individual and state in ancient China p55-87

See also Neo-Confucianism; Philosophy, Chinese; Philosophy, Taoist

History

Araki, K. Confucianism and Buddhism in the late Ming. *In* The Unfolding of Neo-Confucianism p39-66

Ch'ien, E. T. Chiao Hung and the revolt against Ch'eng-Chu orthodoxy. *In* The Unfolding of Neo-Confucianism p271-303

T'ang, Chün-i. Liu Tsung-chou's doctrine of moral mind and practice and his critique of Wang Yang-ming. *In* The Unfolding of Neo-Confucianism p305-31

Philosophy, Comparative

Biderman, S. Scriptures, revelation, and reason. *In* Philosophy East/philosophy West p128-61

Bishop, D. H. Epilogue. *In* Bishop, D. H. ed. Indian thought p364-83

Daor, D. Modes of argument. *In* Philosophy East/philosophy West p162-95

Scharfstein, B. A. Cultures, contexts, and comparisons. *In* Philosophy East/philosophy West p9-47

Scharfstein, B. A. Three philosophical civilizations: a preliminary comparison. *In* Philosophy East/philosophy West p48-127

Philosophy, Confucian

Rubin, V. A. Tradition and human personality. *In* Rubin, V. A. Individual and state in ancient China p 1-31

Philosophy, English

Khamara, E. J. and Macnabb, D. G. C. Hume and his predecessors on the causal maxim. *In* David Hume p146-55

18th century

Palmer, W. J. Dickens and the eighteenth century. *In* Dickens Studies Annual v6 p15-39

Price, J. V. Religion and ideas. *In* Rogers, P. ed. The eighteenth century p120-52

20th century

Grene, M. G. Philosophy in and out of Europe: The European sources of recent Anglo-American philosophy. *In* Grene, M. G. Philosophy in and out of Europe p11-23

Hirst, R. J. Science and anti-science in the philosophy of perception. *In* Studies in perception p377-401

Philosophy, French

Starobinski, J. From the decline of erudition to the decline of nations: Gibbon's response to French thought. *In* Edward Gibbon and The decline and fall of the Roman Empire p139-57

19th century

Robinson, C. Science, reason and the material world. *In* Robinson, C. French literature in the nineteenth century p50-107

Philosophy, German

Weber, S. M. Aesthetic experience and self-reflection as emancipatory processes: two complementary aspects of critical theory. *In* O'Neill, J. ed. On critical theory p78-103

Philosophy, Greek. See Philosophy, Ancient

Philosophy, Hindu

Bhatt, G. S. Social philosophy. *In* Bishop, D. H. ed. Indian thought p197-232

Scharfstein, B. A. Three philosophical civilizations: a preliminary comparison. *In* Phlisophy East/philosophy West p48-127

See also Ātman; Hindu logic; Philosophy, Indic; Yoga

Philosophy, Indic

Barlingay, S. S. Indian epistemology and logic. *In* Bishop, D. H. ed. Indian thought p148-75

Coomaraswamy, A. K. Kha and other words denoting "zero," in connection with the Indian metaphysics of space. *In* Coomaraswamy, A. K. Selected papers v2 p220-30

Coomaraswamy, A. K. Recollection, Indian and platonic. *In* Coomaraswamy, A. K. Selected papers v2 p49-65

Joshi, G. N. Metaphysics. *In* Bishop, D. H. ed. Indian thought p176-96

Sharma, I. C. Indian ethics. *In* Bishop, D. H. ed. Indian thought p233-51

20th century

Bishop, D. H. Epilogue. *In* Bishop D. H. ed. Indian thought p364-83

Philosophy, Islamic

Fakhry, M. Philosophy and history. *In* The Genius of Arab civilization p55-73

Grunebaum, G. E. von. Relations of philosophy and science: a general view. *In* Essays on Islamic philosophy and science p 1-4

Philosophy, Islamic—*Continued*

Marmura, M. E. God and his creation: two medieval Islamic views. *In* Savory, R. M. ed. Introduction to Islamic civilisation p46-53

Nasr, S. H. The significance of Persian philosophical works in the tradition of Islamic philosophy. *In* Essays on Islamic philosophy and science p67-75

Rahman, F. The eternity of the world and the heavenly bodies in post-Avicennan philosophy. *In* Essays on Islamic philosophy and science p222-37

Rescher, N. and Vander Nat, A. The Arabic theory of temporal modal syllogistic. *In* Essays on Islamic philosophy and science p189-221

See also Islamic ethics

Greek influences

Shehadi, F. A. Arabic and the concept of being. *In* Essays on Islamic philosophy and science p147-57

Philosophy, Jewish

Copleston, F. C. Philosophy and religion in Judaism and Christianity. *In* Copleston, F. C. Philosophers and philosophies p29-42

Goitein, S. D. Human rights in Jewish thought and life in the Middle Ages. *In* Sidorsky, D. ed. Essays on human rights p247-64

Philosophy, Mechanistic. See Mechanism (Philosophy)

Philosophy, Medieval

Funkenstein, A. Periodization and self-understanding in the Middle Ages and early modern times. *In* Medievalia et humanistica no. 5 p3-23

Jeffrey, D. L. Breaking up the synthesis: from Plato's academy to the "school of Athens." *In* Jeffrey, D. L. ed. By things seen: reference and recognition in medieval thought p227-52

Moody, E. A. Empiricism and metaphysics in medieval philosophy. *In* Moody, E. A. Studies in medieval philosophy, science, and logic p287-304

Murdoch, J. E. The development of a critical temper: new approaches and modes of analysis in fourteenth-century philosophy, science, and theology. *In* Medieval and Renaissance studies [1975] p51-79

Post, G. Philosophy and citizenship in the thirteenth century-laicisation, the two laws and Aristotle. *In* Order and innovation in the Middle Ages p401-08

See also Scholasticism; Thomists

Historiography

Synan, E. A. Latin philosophies of the Middle Ages. *In* Powell, J. M. ed. Medieval studies p277-311

Philosophy, Modern

Cavell, S. Aesthetic problems of modern philosophy. *In* Cavell, S. Must we mean what we say? p73-96

Derrida, J. Structure, sign and play in the discourse of the human sciences. *In* Derrida, J. Writing and difference p278-93

See also Evolution; Existentialism; Humanism—20th century; Phenomenology; Philosophy, English; Philosophy, German; Positivism; Semantics (Philosophy)

History

May, R. Historical roots of modern anxiety theories. *In* May, R. Psychology and the human dilemma p55-71

16th century

See Philosophy, Renaissance

18th century

Barnouw, J. Materialism and freedom: commentary on papers by Robert E. Schofield and Aram Vartanian. *In* Studies in eighteenth-century culture v7 p193-212

Popkin, R. H. The philosophical bases of modern racism. *In* Philosophy and the civilizing arts p126-65

Schofield, R. E. An evolutionary taxonomy of eighteenth-century Newtonianisms. *In* Studies in eighteenth-century culture v7 p175-92

See also Enlightenment

20th century

Fallico, A. B. Philosophy and human commitment. *In* The Abdication of philosophy: philosophy and the public good p81-87

Grene, M. G. Philosophy in and out of Europe: The reception of Continental philosophy in America. *In* Grene, M. G. Philosophy in and out of Europe p24-37

Holbrook, D. Conclusions. *In* Holbrook, D. Lost bearings in English poetry p217-44

Holbrook, D. Poetry has lost confidence in itself. *In* Holbrook, D. Lost bearings in English poetry p11-24

Salmon, W. C. Russell on scientific inference. *In* Nakhnikian, G. ed. Bertrand Russell's philosophy p183-208

Straus, E. W. The existential approach to psychiatry. *In* Psychiatry and the humanities v 1 p127-43

Philosophy, Moral. See Ethics

Philosophy, Muslim. See Philosophy, Islamic

Philosophy, Natural. See Physics

Philosophy, Oriental

Browning, R. W. The study of Asian philosophy: for history; for comparison; for synthesis? *In* Viva Vivas! p289-330

See also Philosophy Comparative

Philosophy, Patristic. See Fathers of the church

Philosophy, Persian

Nasr, S. H. The significance of Persian philosophical works in the tradition of Islamic philosophy. *In* Essays on Islamic philosophy and science p67-75

Philosophy, Polish

History

Knoll, P. W. The world of the young Copernicus: society, science, and the university. *In* Science and society: past, present, and future p19-44

Philosophy, Renaissance

Bensimon, M. J. Modes of perception of reality in the Renaissance. *In* The Darker vision of the Renaissance p221-72

Colie, R. L. The rhetoric of transcendence. *In* Roberts, J. R. ed. Essential articles for the study of John Donne's poetry p199-219

Rosen, E. The impact of Copernicus on man's conception of his place in the world. *In* Science and society: past, present, and future p52-67

Philosophy, Roman. See Philosophy, Ancient

Philosophy, Russian

Berdíaev, N. A. Philosophic truth and the moral truth of the intelligentsia. *In* Landmarks p3-22

Kline, G. L. Recent uncensored Soviet philosophical writings. *In* Tokes, R. L. ed. Dissent in the USSR p158-90

Philosophy, Taoist

Daor, D. Two metaphysical concepts: Li and idea. *In* Philosophy East/philosophy West p235-46

Philosophy and astronomy. See Astronomy—Philosophy

Philosophy and Judaism. See Judaism and philosophy

Philosophy and religion

Alon, I. Between fatalism and causality: Al-Ash'ari and Spinoza. *In* Philosophy East/philosophy West p218-34

Biderman, S. Scriptures, revelation, and reason. *In* Philosophy East/philosophy West p128-61

Copleston, F. C. Philosophy and religion in Judaism and Christianity. *In* Copleston, F. C. Philosophers and philosophies p29-42

See also Faith and reason; Religion—Philosophy

Philosophy and science. See Science—Philosophy

Philosophy in literature

Carpenter, F. I. Hemingway achieves the fifth dimension; excerpt from "American literature and the dream". *In* Wagner, L. W. ed. Ernest Hemingway p279-87

Drew, P. Browning and philosophy. *In* Armstrong, I. ed. Robert Browning p104-41

See also Existentialism in literature

Philosophy of history. See History—Philosophy

Philosophy of language. See Languages—Philosophy

Philosophy of law. See Law—Philosophy

Philosophy of literature. See Literature—Philosophy

Philosophy of medicine. See Medicine—Philosophy

Philosophy of nature

Bell, D. Technology, nature, and society. *In* The Frontiers of knowledge p27-78

Also in Technology and the frontiers of knowledge p23-71

Doran, B. G. Origins and consolidation of field theory in nineteenth-century Britain: from the mechanical to the electromagnetic view of nature. *In* Historical studies in the physical sciences v6 p133-260

Goldberg, S. Max Planck's philosophy of nature and his elaboration of the special theory of relativity. *In* Historical studies in the physical sciences v7 p125-60

Huxley, A. L. More nature in art. *In* Huxley, A. L. The Human situation p28-41

Letwin, S. R. Nature, history and morality. *In* Royal Institute of Philosophy. Nature and conduct p229-50

O'Briant, W. H. Man, nature, and the history of philosophy. *In* Philosophy & environmental crisis p79-89

Passmore, J. A. Attitudes to nature. *In* Royal Institute of Philosophy. Nature and conduct p251-64

Ricoeur, P. Nature and freedom. *In* Ricoeur, P. Political and social essays p23-45

Robinson, G. S. Nature and necessity. *In* Royal Institute of Philosophy. Impressions of empiricism p200-15

Tatar, M. M. Salvation by electricity: science, poetry, and "Naturphilosophie." *In* Tatar, M. M. Spellbound p45-81

Wicker, B. Metaphor and 'nature.' *In* Wicker, B. The story-shaped world p50-70

Wilson, M. D. Leibniz's dynamics and contingency in nature. *In* Motion and time, space and matter p264-89

Wojciechowski, J. A. The ecology of knowledge. *In* Science and society: past, present, and future p258-302

See also Cosmology; Nature (Aesthetics); Uniformity of nature

Philosophy of rhetoric. See Rhetoric—Philosophy

Philosophy of teaching. See Education—Philosophy

Phips, Sir William

About

Seelye, J. A fabric huge: Cotton Mather's masterpiece: or, The original errand betrayed. *In* Seelye, J. Prophetic waters p253-77

Phiz, pseud. See Browne, Hablot Knight

Phonology. See Grammar, Comparative and general—Phonology

Phonorecords

Reviews

Craft, R. Musical R for a political season. *In* Craft, R. Current convictions p159-68

Photius I, Saint, Patriarch of Constantinople

About individual works

Bibliotheca

Heiserman, A. R. Bits and epitomes. *In* Heiserman, A. R. The novel before the novel p41-63

Photoelectricity

Wheaton, B. R. Philipp Lenard and the photoelectric effect, 1889-1911. *In* Historical studies in the physical sciences v9 p299-322

Photoelectrons. See Photoelectricity

Photoemission. See Photoelectricity

Photoengraving. See Photomechanical process

Photographic composition. See Composition (Photography)

Photographic duplication. See Photomechanical process

Photography

Barthes, R. The photographic message. *In* Barthes, R. Image, music, text p15-31

Berger, J. Understanding a photograph. *In* Berger, J. The look of things p178-82

Forth, R. F. On appreciation. *In* One hundred years of photographic history p53-58

See also Cameras; Photomechanical process

Aesthetics

See Photography, Artistic

Composition

See Composition (Photography)

History

Chiarenza, C. Notes on aesthetic relationships between seventeenth-century Dutch painting and nineteenth-century photography. *In* One hundred years of photographic history p19-34

Photography—*Continued*

History—France
Sobieszek, R. A. Photography and the theory of realism in the Second Empire: a reexamination of a relationship. *In* One hundred years of photographic history p145-59

History—Hamburg
Kempe, F. A historical sketch of photography in Hamburg. *In* One hundred years of photographic history p91-102

Moving-pictures
See Cinematography; Moving-pictures

Museums
Fern, A. M. Remarks toward an ideal museum of photography. *In* One hundred years of photographic history p47-52

Portraits
Michaelson, K. The first photographic record of a scientific conference. *In* One hundred years of photographic history p109-16

See also Glamour photography

Printing processes
Borcoman, J. W. Notes on the early use of combination printing. *In* One hundred years of photographic history p15-18

Scientific applications
See Scientific illustration

Photography, Aerial. See Aerial photography in archaeology

Photography, Artistic
Smith, H. H. Models for critics. *In* One hundred years of photographic history p139-43

Tashjian, D. L. Camera Work and the anti-art of photography. *In* Tashjian, D. L. Skyscraper primitives p15-28

White, M. Silence of seeing. *In* One hundred years of photographic history p169-73

See also Glamour photography

Photography, Composite
Berger, J. The political uses of photomontage. *In* Berger, J. The look of things p183-89

Borcoman, J. W. Notes on the early use of combination printing. *In* One hundred years of photographic history p15-18

Keim, J. A. Photomontage after World War I. *In* One hundred years of photographic history p83-90

Photography, Documentary
Taylor, W. R. Psyching out the city. *In* Uprooted Americans p245-87

Photography, Erotic. See Glamour photography

Photography, Glamour. See Glamour photography

Photography, Journalistic
Barthes, R. The photographic message. *In* Barthes, R. Image, music, text p15-31

See also Newsreel

Photography, Stereoscopic
Darrah, W. C. Stereographs: a neglected source of history of photography. *In* One hundred years of photographic history p43-46

Photography and art. See Art and photography

Photojournalism. See Photography, Journalistic

Photolithography. See Photomechanical processes

Photomechanical processes
Koeman, C. The application of photography to map printing and the transition to offset lithography. *In* Woodward, D. A. ed. Five centuries of map printing p137-55

Photomontage after World War I. Keim, J. A. *In* One hundred years of photographic history p83-90

Photons. See Lasers

Phrenology
Fancher, R. E. The physiology of mind: conceptions of the brain from Gall to Penfield. *In* Fancher, R. E. Pioneers of psychology p43-86

Hull, D. L. Scientific bandwagon or traveling medicine show? *In* Sociobiology and human nature p136-63

Mellor, A. K. Physiognomy, phrenology, and Blake's visionary heads. *In* Essick, R. N. and Pearce, D. R. eds. Blake in his time p53-74

See also Mind and body; Physiognomy

History
Shapin, S. Homo phrenologicus: anthropological perspectives on an historical problem. *In* Barnes, B. and Shapin, S. eds. Natural order p41-71

Physical anthropology
Hanna, T. Introduction: the Sphinx and the soma. *In* Hanna, T. ed. Explorers of humankind p 1-15

Tiger, L. Somatic factors and social behaviour. *In* Biosocial anthropology p115-32

See also Blood groups; Fossil man; Human behavior; Human genetics; Race

Physical education and training

Moral and religious aspects
Blake, J. B. Health reform. *In* The Rise of Adventism p30-49

Physical education for children. See Sports for children

Physical education for women

United States
Brown, J. M. Women in physical education: the dribble index of liberation. *In* Roberts, J. I. ed. Beyond intellectual sexism p365-80

Physical fitness
Haskell, W. L. Physical activity in health maintenance. *In* Sobel, D. S. ed. Ways of health p435-57

Physical geography. See Landforms; Man—Influence on nature

Physical laboratories

Great Britain—History
Sviedrys, R. The rise of physics laboratories in Britain. *In* Historical studies in the physical sciences v7 p405-36

Physical mathematics. See Mathematical physics

Physical research. See Physics—Research

Physicalism. See Logical positivism

Physically handicapped

See also Deaf

Sexual behavior

Romano, M. D. The physically handicapped. *In* Gochros, H. L. and Gochros, J. S. eds. The sexually oppressed p257-67

Physically handicapped services

United States

Morris, R. Long-term severe disability. *In* Home care p237-44

Physician and patient

Eisenberg, L. The search for care. *In* Knowles, J. H. ed. Doing better and feeling worse p235-46

Fletcher, J. F. Medical diagnosis: our right to know the truth. *In* Weir, R. F. ed. Ethical issues in death and dying p26-41

Meyer, B. C. Truth and the physician. *In* Weir, R. F. ed. Ethical issues in death and dying p42-54

See also Psychotherapist and patient

Physicians

White, L. P. Death and the physician: mortuis vivos docent. *In* Feifel, H. [ed.] New meanings of death p91-106

See also Surgeons

Licenses—United States

Tabachnik, L. Licensing in the legal and medical professions, 1820-1860: a historical case study. *In* Gerstl, J. E. and Jacobs, G. eds. Professions for the people p25-42

Salaries, pensions, etc.

See Medical fees

France—Lyon

Faure, O. Physicians in Lyon during the nineteenth century: an extraordinary social success. *In* Branca, P. ed. The medicine show p243-58

Great Britain

Ormsby-Lennon, H. Radical physicians and conservative poets in Restoration England: Dryden among the doctors. *In* Studies in eighteenth-century culture v7 p389-411

Pavia

Cipolla, C. M. A plague doctor. *In* The Medieval city p65-72

Philadelphia

Bell, W. J. Philadelphia medical students in Europe, 1750-1800. *In* Bell, W. J. The colonial physician & other essays p41-69

Russia

Frieden, N. M. The Russia cholera epidemic, 1892-93, and medical professionalization. *In* Branca, P. ed. The medicine show p259-80

United States

Bell, W. J. The Fielding H. Garrison lecture: a portrait of the colonial physician. *In* Bell, W. J. The colonial physician & other essays p5-25

McDermott, W. Evaluating the physician and his technology. *In* Knowles, J. H. ed. Doing better and feeling worse p135-57

Physicians in literature

Larkin, M. The ubiquitous doctor. *In* Larkin, M. Man and society in nineteenth-century realism p134-38

Ober, W. B. Chekhov among the doctors: the doctor's dilemma. *In* Ober, W. B. Boswell's clap and other essays p193-205

See also Medicine in literature

Physicists

Germany

Pyenson, L. Einstein's early scientific collaboration. *In* Historical studies in the physical sciences v7 p83-123

Japan

Koizumi, K. The emergence of Japan's first physicists: 1868-1900. *In* Historical studies in the physical sciences v6 p3-108

Physics

Chauvin, R. To reconcile psi and physics. *In* Wheatley, J. M. O. and Edge, H. L. eds. Philosophical dimensions of parapsychology p409-12

Daudel, R. Structure of molecular physics and its relations with other sciences. *In* The Frontiers of human knowledge p243-53

Koestler, A. Physics and metaphysics. *In* Koestler, A. Janus p242-73

Todd, R. B. Monism and immanence: the foundations of Stoic physics. *In* Rist, J. M. ed. The Stoics p137-60

See also Electricity; Field theory (Physics); Force and energy; General relativity (Physics); Gravitation; Mathematical physics; Mechanics; Meteorology; Motion; Optics; Quantum theory; Symmetry (Physics)

Early works to 1800

Donahue, W. H. The solid planetary spheres in post-Copernican natural philosophy. *In* The Copernican achievement p244-75

Grant, E. Place and space in medieval physical thought. *In* Motion and time, space and matter p137-67

Hahm, D. E. Weight and lightness in Aristotle and his predecessors. *In* Motion and time, space and matter p56-82

Kretzmann, N. Incipit/desinit. *In* Motion and time, space and matter p101-36

Moody, E. A. Galileo and Avempace: the dynamics of the Leaning Tower Experiment. *In* Moody, E. A. Studies in medieval philosophy, science, and logic p203-86

Moody, E. A. Laws of motion in medieval physics. *In* Moody, E. A. Studies in medieval philosophy, science, and logic p189-201

Experiments

Holton, G. J. Subelectrons, presuppositions, and the Millikan-Ehrenhaft dispute. *In* Historical studies in the physical sciences v9 p161-224

Laymon, R. L. The Michelson-Morley experiment: descriptive dependence on to-be-tested theories. *In* Motion and time, space and matter p436-64

Experiments—History

Frankel, E. J. B. Biot and the mathematization of experimental physics in Napoleonic France. *In* Historical studies in the physical sciences v8 p33-72

History

Crosland, M. P. and Smith, C. The transmission of physics from France to Britain: 1800-1840. *In* Historical studies in the physical sciences v9 p1-61

Heimann, P. M. Mayer's concept of "force": the "axis" of a new science of physics. *In* Historical studies in the physical sciences v7 p277-96

Physics—History—*Continued*

Hirosige, T. The ether problem, the mechanistic worldview, and the origins of the theory of relativity. *In* Historical studies in the physical sciences v7 p3-82

Pyenson, L. Einstein's early scientific collaboration. *In* Historical studies in the physical sciences v7 p83-123

History—England

Wilson, D. B. Concepts of physical nature: John Herschel to Karl Pearson. *In* Knoepflmacher, U. C. and Tennyson, G. B. eds. Nature and the Victorian imagination p201-15

Wynne, B. Physics and psychics: science, symbolic action, and social control in late Victorian England. *In* Barnes, B. and Shapin, S. eds. Natural order p167-86

History—France

Guerlac, H. Chemistry as a branch of physics: Laplace's collaboration with Lavoisier. *In* Historical studies in the physical sciences v7 p193-276

History—Germany

Caneva, K. L. From galvanism to electrodynamics: the transformation of German physics and its social context. *In* Historical studies in the physical sciences v9 p63-159

History—Japan

Koizumi, K. The emergence of Japan's first physicists: 1868-1900. *In* Historical studies in the physical sciences v6 p3-108

History—United States

Kevles, D. J. The physics, mathematics, and chemistry communities: a comparative analysis. *In* Oleson, A. and Voss, J. eds. The organization of knowledge in modern America, 1860-1920 p139-72

Philosophy

McGuire, J. E. "Labyrinthus continui": Leibniz on substance, activity, and matter. *In* Motion and time, space and matter p290-326

See also Causality (Physics)

Research

Heisenberg, W. Tradition in science. *In* The nature of scientific discovery p219-36

Research—France—History

Shinn, T. W. The French science faculty system, 1808-1914: institutional change and research potential in mathematics and the physical sciences. *In* Historical studies in the physical sciences v10 p271-332

Study and teaching—Germany—Saxony—History

Jungnickel, C. Teaching and research in the physical sciences and mathematics in Saxony, 1820-1850. *In* Historical studies in the physical sciences v10 p3-47

Physics, Astronomical. See Astrophysics

Physics, Nuclear. See Nuclear physics

Physics research. See Physics—Research

Physiocrats

Perkins, J. A. The Physiocrats and the Encyclopedists. *In* Studies in eighteenth-century culture v8 p323-36

Physiognomy

Mellor, A. K. Physiognomy, phrenology, and Blake's visionary heads. *In* Essick, R. N. and Pearce, D. R. eds. Blake in his time p53-74

Summers, D. David's scowl. *In* Collaboration in Italian Renaissance art p113-24

See also Facial expression; Face; Phrenology

Physiological chemistry. See Biological chemistry

Physiological optics. See Optics, Physiological

Physiological psychology. See Psychology, Physiological

Physiological stress. See Stress (Physiology)

Physiology

See also Animal heat; Neurophysiology; Reproduction; Senses and sensation

History

Temkin, O. Materialism in French and German physiology of the early nineteenth century. *In* Temkin, O. The double face of Janus p340-44

Research

Harvey, A. M. Fountainhead of American physiology: H. Newell Martin and his pupil William Henry Howell. *In* Harvey, A. M. Adventures in medical research p84-96

Great Britain—History

Cooter, R. The power of the body: the early nineteenth century. *In* Barnes, B. and Shapin, S. eds. Natural order p73-92

Scotland—History

Lawrence, C. The nervous system and society in the Scottish Enlightment. *In* Barnes, B. and Shapin, S. eds. Natural order p19-40

Physiology, Experimental

History

Albury, W. R. Experiment and explanation in the physiology of Bichat and Magendie. *In* Studies in history of biology, v 1 p47-131

Phythian-Adams, Charles

Urban decay in late medieval England. *In* Towns in societies p159-85

Phytogeography

Sauer, J. D. Changing perception and exploitation of New World plants in Europe, 1492-1800. *In* First images of America p813-32

See also Plant introduction

Piachaud, David

Inflation and income distribution. *In* The Political economy of inflation p88-116

Piaget, Jean

About

Elkind, D. The origins of religion in the child. *In* Elkind, D. The child and society p269-80

Elkind, D. Piaget and Montessori in the classroom. *In* Elkind, D. The child and society p143-55

Elkind, D. The study of spontaneous religion in the child. *In* Elkind, D. The child and society p255-68

Fancher, R. E. Modern pioneers: Jean Piaget and B. F. Skinner. *In* Fancher, R. E. Pioneers of psychology p339-72

Mora, G. Vico, Piaget, and genetic epistemology. *In* Giambattista Vico's science of humanity p365-92

Piaget, Jean—About—*Continued*

Rosenau, N. The sources of children's political concepts: an application of Piaget's theory. *In* Schwartz, D. C. and Schwartz, S. K. eds. New directions in political socialization p163-87

Wilden, A. Piaget and the structure as law and order. *In* Riegel, K. F. and Rosenwald, G. C. eds. Structure and transformation p83-117

Wozniak, R. H. Dialecticism and structuralism: the philosophical foundation of Soviet psychology and Piagetian cognitive developmental theory. *In* Riegel, K. F. and Rosenwald, G. C. eds. Structure and transformation p25-45

About individual works
The child's conception of the world

Matthews, G. B. On talking philosophy with children. *In* Royal Institute of Philosophy. Communication and understanding p46-62

Piazza, Thomas

Jewish identity and the counterculture. *In* The New religious consciousness p245-64

Picabia, Francis

About

Tashjian, D. L. 291 and Francis Picabia. *In* Tashjian, D. L. Skyscraper primitives p29-48

Picardy

Social conditions

Morel, A. Power and ideology in the village community of Picardy: past and present. *In* Rural society in France p107-25

Picaresque literature

History and criticism

Babcock, B. A. "Liberty's a whore": inversions, marginalia, and picaresque narrative. *In* Babcock, B. A. ed. The reversible world p95-116

Bjornson, R. El buscón: Quevedo's annihilation of the picaresque. *In* Bjornson, R. The picaresque hero in European fiction p106-26

Bjornson, R. In the wake of Guzmán: variations on the picaresque-life theme. *In* Bjornson, R. The picaresque hero in European fiction p66-105

Bjornson, R. Introduction. *In* Bjornson, R. The picaresque hero in European fiction p3-20

Bjornson, R. Translations & transitions. *In* Bjornson, R. The picaresque hero in European fiction p139-65

Bjornson, R. The waning of the Spanish picaresque: El diablo cojuelo and Estebanillo González. *In* Bjornson, R. The picaresque hero in European fiction p127-38

Lyons, J. O. Rogues and adventurers. *In* Lyons, J. O. The invention of the self p75-88

Skilton, D. Quixotic and picaresque fiction. *In* Skilton, D. The English novel p32-44

Picaresque novel. *See* Picaresque literature

Picasso, Pablo

About

Fry, E. Introduction, the history of cubism, cubism as a stylistic and historical phenomenon; excerpt from "Cubism." *In* Kaplan, P. and Manso, S. eds. Major European art movements, 1900-1945 p101-46

Greenberg, C. Collage; excerpt from "Art and culture (Revised edition)" *In* Kaplan, P. and Manso, S. eds. Major European art movements, 1900-1945 p147-63

Steinberg, L. Drawing as if to possess; excerpt from "Other criteria." *In* Kaplan, P. and Manso, S. eds. Major European art movements, 1900-1945 p193-221

About individual works
Woman with a fan

Schapiro, M. Picasso's Woman with a fan. *In* Schapiro, M. Selected papers v2 p111-20

Piccolomini, House of

Mode, R. L. Ancient paragons in a Piccolomini scheme. *In* Enggass, R. C. and Stokstad, M. eds. Hortus imaginum p73-83

Piccone, Paul

Beyond identity theory. *In* O'Neill, J. ed. On critical theory p129-44

Pick, Herbert L.

Visual coding of nonvisual spatial information. *In* Perception p153-65

Pickens, William

The New Deal in New Mexico. *In* Braeman, J.; Bremner, R. H. and Brody, D. eds. The New Deal v2 p311-54

Pickens, Fort

McWhiney, G. The Confederacy's first shot. *In* Hubbell, J. T. ed. Battles lost and won p73-82

Pickering, Percival Spencer Umfreville

About

Dolby, R. G. A. Debates over the theory of solution: a study of dissent in physical chemistry in the English-speaking world in the late nineteenth and early twentieth centuries. *In* Historical studies in the physical sciences v7 p297-404

Pickering, Samuel

The moral tradition in English fiction, 1785-1850

Contents

Afterword
The Christian Observer and the novel
Coelebs in search of a wife, and Waverley
Dombey and son and Unitarianism
The Old Curiosity Shop, and Legh Richmond's tracts
Protestantism in Barnaby Rudge
The Sunday school movement: new readers and the novel

Pickowicz, Paul Gene

Qu Qiubai's critique of the May Fourth generation: early Chinese Marxist literary criticism. *In* Modern Chinese literature in the May Fourth era p351-84

Pickvance, Christopher G.

Housing: reproduction of capital and reproduction of labour power: some recent French work. *In* Walton, J. and Masotti, L. H. eds. The city in comparative perspective p271-89

Picnic (Motion picture)

French, B. A minimal feast. *In* French, B. On the verge of revolt p105-20

Truffaut, F. Joshua Logan: Picnic. *In* Truffaut, F. The films in my life p125-26

Pico della Mirandola, Giovanni

About

Kristeller, P. O. The Latin poems of Giovanni Pico della Mirandola: a supplementary note. *In* Poetry and poetics from ancient Greece to the Renaissance p185-206

Pico della Mirandola, Giovanni—*Continued*

Translations, English

Parks, G. B. Pico della Mirandola in Tudor translation. *In* Philosophy and humanism p352-69

Pictographs. *See* Picture-writing, Indian

Pictor, Quintus Fabius. See Fabius Pictor, Quintus

Picture-books for children

Hwang, J. C. Lien-huan-hua: revolutionary serial pictures. *In* Chu, G. C. ed. Popular media in China p51-72

History and criticism

Johnston, M. E. Surprised by joy: the world of picture-books. *In* Egoff, S. A. ed. One ocean touching p147-54

Picture story books. See Stories without words

Picture-writing, Indian

Brandt, J. C. Pictographs and petroglyphs of the Southwest Indians. *In* Brecher, K. and Feirtag, M. eds. Astronomy of the ancients p25-38

Picture-writing, Maya. See Mayas—Writing

Picture-writing, Mexican. See Indians of Mexico—Writing

Pictures

Kennedy, J. M. and Fox, N. Pictures to see and pictures to touch. *In* Perkins, D. and Leondar, B. eds. The arts and cognition p118-35

Roupas, T. G. Information and pictorial representation. *In* Perkins, D. and Leondar, B. eds. The arts and cognition p48-79

Piehler, Paul

Milton's iconoclasm. *In* Evolution of consciousness p121-35

About individual works

The visionary landscape: a study in medieval allegory

Barfield, O. The rediscovery of allegory (I) *In* Barfield, O. The rediscovery of meaning, and other essays p93-100

Levine, R. The pearl-child: topos and archetype in the Middle English Pearl. *In* Medievalia et humanistica no. 8 p243-51

Pierce, Christine. See Collins, M. L. jt. auth.

Pierce, John Robinson

The telephone and society in the past 100 years. *In* The Social impact of the telephone p159-95

Pierce, Kenneth M.

The Bunkers, the critics and the news. *In* Television as a cultural force p59-75

Piercy, Marge

About individual works

Small changes

Mickelson, A. Z. Piecemeal liberation: Marge Piercy, Sara Davidson, Marilyn French, Grace Paley. *In* Mickelson, A. Z. Reaching out: sensitivity and order in recent American fiction by women p175-234

Pierre, Andrew J.

America faces Western Europe in the 1980s: Atlanticism preserved, disengagement, or devolution? *In* Atlantis lost p183-204

Pierre, George

About individual works

Autumn's bounty

Larson, C. R. Survivors of the relocation. *In* Larson, C. R. American Indian fiction p133-64

Pierre d'Auvergne. See Peire d'Auvergne

Piersen, William D.

Puttin' down Ole Massa: African satire in the New World. *In* Crowley, D. J. ed. African folklore in the New World p20-34

Pierson, George Wilson

The university and American society. *In* Small comforts for hard times p263-76

About individual works

The university and American society

De Bary, W. T. The university, society, and the critical temper: in response to George W. Pierson. *In* Small comforts for hard times p277-80

Pietersma, Henry

Husserl's views on the evident and the true. *In* Elliston, F. A. and McCormick, P. eds. Husserl p38-53

Pietism

See also Evangicalism

United States

Mead, S. E. American Protestantism during the Revolutionary epoch. *In* Mulder, J. M. and Wilson, J. F. eds. Religion in American history p162-80

Pietrkiewicz, Jerzy

Simultaneity in a sequence: the time pattern of a mediaeval poem. *In* For Wiktor Weintraub p333-44

Pietro, Robert J. di. See Di Pietro, Robert J.

Pietro Damiani, Saint

About

Little, L. K. The personal development of Peter Damian. *In* Order and innovation in the Middle Ages p317-41

Piety

Middlekauff, R. M. Piety and intellect in Puritanism. *In* Mulder, J. M. and Wilson, J. F. eds. Religion in American history p74-85

Tuan, Yi-Fu. Geopiety: a theme in man's attachment to nature and to place. *In* Geographies of the mind p11-39

Pifer, Alan J.

A clash of tangled forces. *In* The Third century p58-63

The jeopardy of private institutions. *In* Smith, B. L. R. ed. The new political economy: the public use of the private sector p68-82

Pignatari, Décio

The contiguity illusion. *In* Sebeok, T. A. ed. Sight, sound, and sense p84-97

Pigs. See Swine

Pike, David

A camp through the eyes of a peasant: Solzhenitsyn's One day in the life of Ivan Denisovich. *In* California Slavic studies v10 p193-223

Pike, Kenneth Lee

Agreement types dispersed into a ninecell spectrum. *In* On language, culture, and religion: in honor of Eugene A. Nida p275-86

Piker, Steven Isaac

The post-peasant village in Central Plain Thai society. *In* Change and persistence in Thai society p298-323

Pilgrim Fathers. See Pilgrims (New Plymouth Colony)

Pilgrims (New Plymouth Colony)

Seelye, J. A model of Moses: the Pilgrims lend a prophetic presence to the land. *In* Seelye, J. Prophetic waters p97-130

Pilgrims and pilgrimages

See also Christian pilgrims and pilgrimages

Europe—History

McGinn, B. Iter sancti Sepulchri: the piety of the first Crusaders. *In* Essays on medieval civilization p33-71

Pilgrims and pilgrimages in literature

Zacher, C. K. A new sense of the world. *In* Zacher, C. K. Curiosity and pilgrimage p3-17

Zacher, C. K. The pilgrim as curious traveler: Mandeville's Travels. *In* Zacher, C. K. Curiosity and pilgrimage p130-57

Piliavin, Jane Allyn

On feminine self-presentation in groups. *In* Roberts, J. I. ed. Beyond intellectual sexism p138-59

Pilkington, John

Nature's legacy to William Faulkner. *In* The South and Faulkner's Yoknapatawpha p104-27

Pillars of Islam. See Jihad

Pillinger, Hugh Edward

Some Callimachean influences on Propertius, Book 4. *In* Harvard Studies in classical philology v73 p171-99

Pillsbury, Barbara L. K.

Being female in a Muslim minority in China. *In* Beck, L. and Keddie, N. R. eds. Women in the Muslim world p651-73

Pillsbury, Edmund P.

Vasari's staircase in the Palazzo Vecchio. *In* Collaboration in Italian Renaissance art p125-41

Pil'nyak, Boris, pseud. See Vogav, Boris Andreevich

Pilot guides

Florida Straits

De Vorsey, L. La Florida revealed: the De Brahm surveys of British East Florida, 1765-1771. *In* Pattern and process p87-102

Pilpel, Harriet Fleischl

Libraries and the First Amendment. *In* Libraries and the life of the mind in America p87-106

Piman Indians

Fontana, B. L. The faces and forces of Pimeria Alta. *In* Voices from the Southwest p45-54

Pinard, Maurice. See Eschen, D. von, jt. auth.

Pinball machines

Packard, C. and Browne, R. B. Pinball machine: marble icon. *In* Browne, R. B. and Fishwick, M. W. eds. Icons of America p177-89

Pincherle, Alberto. See Moravia, Alberto

Pinciss, Gerald Martin

The old honor and the new courtesy: '1 Henry IV.' *In* Shakespeare survey v31 p85-91

Shakespeare, Her Majesty's players and Pembroke's Men. *In* Shakespeare survey 27 p129-36

Pinckney, Eliza (Lucas)

About

Scott, A. F. Self-portraits: three women. *In* Uprooted Americans p43-76

Pindar. See Pindarus

Pindarus

About individual works

First Pythian ode

Brower, R. A. The Theban eagle in English plumage. *In* Brower, R. A. Mirror on mirror p46-54

[Fragment 169]

Lloyd-Jones, H. Pindar Fr. 169. *In* Harvard Studies in classical philology v76 p45-56

Nemean 1

Rose, P. W. The myth of Pindar's First Nemean: sportsmen, poetry, and paideia. *In* Harvard Studies in classical philology v78 p145-75

Nemean 7

Kirkwood, G. M. Nemean 7 and the theme of vicissitude in Pindar. *In* Poetry and poetics from ancient Greece to the Renaissance p56-90

Nemean 9

Pearson, L. I. C. The dynamics of Pindar's music: Ninth Nemean and Third Olympian. *In* Illinois classical studies, v2 1977 p54-69

Olympian (Ode I, lines 8-11)

Nisetich, F. J. Olympian 1:8-11: an epinician metaphor. *In* Harvard Studies in classical philology v79 p55-68

Olympian (Ode III)

Pearson, L. I. C. The dynamics of Pindar's music: Ninth Nemean and Third Olympian. *In* Illinois classical studies, v2 1977 p54-69

Manuscripts

Pavese, C. The new Heracles poem of Pindar. *In* Harvard Studies in classical philology v72 p47-88

Translations, English

Brower, R. A. The Theban eagle in English plumage. *In* Brower, R. A. Mirror on mirror p46-54

Pinder, John

The Community and the state trading countries. *In* Twitchett, K. J. ed. Europe and the world p57-76

Pinderhughes, Charles A.

Black personality in American society. *In* The Black American reference book p128-58

Pine, Martin

Pietro Pomponazzi and the medieval tradition of God's foreknowledge. *In* Philosophy and humanism p100-15

Pine, Sandra

Fostering growth through art education, art therapy, and art in psychotherapy. *In* Ulman, E. and Dachinger, P. eds. Art therapy p60-94

Pine, Vanderlyn R.

Dying, death, and social behavior. *In* Anticipatory grief p31-47

Pineal body
Calcification
Altschule, M. D. The calcified pineal gland: nature mimics art—almost. *In* Altschule, M. D. Origins of concepts in human behavior p165-81

Pinedo, Baltasar de
About
Wilder, T. N. Lope, Pinedo, some child actors, and a lion. *In* Wilder, T. N. American characteristics, and other essays p267-77

Pinel, Philippe
About
Weiner, D. B. Three champions of the handicapped in Revolutionary France. *In* From Parnassus p161-76

Pingree, David Edwin
The Indian and pseudo-Indian passages in Greek and Latin astronomical and astrological texts. *In* Viator: medieval and Renaissance studies v7 p141-95

Māshā'allāh: some Sasanian and Syriac sources. *In* Essays on Islamic philosophy and science p5-14

Pinhey, Elliot C. G.
Dragonflies (Odonata) of Central Africa. *In* The Occasional papers of the Rhodes-Livingstone Museum p539-648

Pinion, F. B.
The ranging vision. *In* Butler, L. S. ed. Thomas Hardy after fifty years p 1-12

Pinker, James Brand
About
Karl. F. R. Conrad and Pinker. *In* Joseph Conrad: a commemoration p156-73

Pinsker, Sanford
On David Wagoner. *In* Boyers, R. ed. Contemporary poetry in America p360-68

Ulysses as ghost story. *In* Renaissance and modern p119-32

The urban tall tale: frontier humor in a contemporary key. *In* Cohen, S. B. ed. Comic relief p249-62

Pinter, Frances
Changes in the South Tyrol issue. *In* The Year book of world affairs, 1977 p64-74

Pinter, Harold
About
Alexander, N. 'Past, present and Pinter. *In* English Association. Essays and studies, 1974 p 1-17

Kennedy, A. K. Pinter. *In* Kennedy, A. K. Six dramatists in search of a language p165-91

About individual works
The birthday party
Lesser, S. O. Reflections on Pinter's The birthday party. *In* Lesser, S. O. The whispered meanings p203-11

The homecoming
Kauffmann, S. The homecoming. *In* Kauffmann, S. Living images p242-46

Landscape
Kauffmann, S. Landscape/Silence. *In* Kauffmann, S. Persons of the drama p201-04

Old times
Kauffmann, S. Pinter and sexuality: notes, mostly on Old times. *In* Kauffmann, S. Persons of the drama p335-48

Silence
Kauffmann, S. Landscape/Silence. *In* Kauffmann, S. Persons of the drama p201-04

Pinup photography. See Glamour photography

Pioneer life. See Frontier and pioneer life

Pioneers
See also Frontier and pioneer life

United States
Bryant, P. T. The family journey to the West. *In* Kagle, S. E. ed. America: exploration and travel p153-65

Piore, Michael Joseph
Immigration, work expectations, and labor market structure. *In* The Diverse society: implications for social policy p109-27

Piotrowski, Jerzy
Family and adolescents in the near future. *In* Adolescence and youth in prospect p159-70

Piovani, Pietro
Apoliticality and politicality in Vico. *In* Giambattista Vico's science of humanity p395-408

Piozzi, Hester Lynch (Salusbury) Thrale
About
Wimsatt, W. K. Images of Samuel Johnson. *In* ELH essays for Earl R. Wasserman p69-84

Piper, David
The Chesterfield House Library portraits. *In* Evidence in literary scholarship p179-95

Piper, Don C.
Unilateral acts of states with regard to environmental protection. *In* Orr, D. W. and Soroos, M. S. eds. The global predicament p264-81

Piperek, Maximilian. See Foramitti, H. jt. auth.

Pipes, Richard
Basic Soviet institutions have not changed. *In* Decline of the West? George Kennan and his critics p61-69

Reflections on the nationality problems in the Soviet Union. *In* Glazer, N. and Moynihan, D. P. eds. Ethnicity p453-65

Pippi, Giulio. See Giulio Romano

Pirages, Dennis C.
The unbalanced revolution. *In* Science and society: past, present, and future p231-49

Pirandello, Luigi
About
Nicoll, A. The extension of the realistic. *In* Nicoll, A. World drama p577-607

Pacifici, S. Luigi Pirandello: man and his masks. *In* Pacifici, S. The modern Italian novel: from Capuana to Tozzi p108-35

Ragusa, O. Pirandello and Verga. *In* Ragusa, O. Narrative and drama p58-82

About individual works
Henry IV
Roland, A. and Rizzo, G. Psychoanalysis in search of Pirandello: six characters and Henry IV. *In* Roland, A. ed. Psychoanalysis, creativity, and literature p323-51

Schlueter, J. Pirandello's Henry IV. *In* Schlueter, J. Metafictional characters in modern drama p19-34

Pirandello, Luigi—About individual works
—*Continued*

La patente [one-act play]

Ragusa, O. Pirandello's La patente: play and story (1). *In* Ragusa, O. Narrative and drama p83-108

La patente [story]

Ragusa, O. Pirandello's La patente: play and story (1). *In* Ragusa, O. Narrative and drama p83-108

One, none and a hundred-thousand

Biasin, G. P. Moscarda's mirror. *In* Biasin, G. P. Literary diseases p100-26

Short stories

Howe, I. The stories of Pirandello. *In* Howe, I. Celebrations and attacks p118-26

Six characters in search of an author

Grossvogel, D. I. Pirandello: the mask as evidence and limit. *In* Grossvogel, D. I. Mystery and its fiction: from Oedipus to Agatha Christie p109-26

Roland, A. and Rizzo, G. Psychoanalysis in search of Pirandello: six characters and Henry IV. *In* Roland, A. ed. Psychoanalysis, creativity, and literature p323-51

Trilling, L. Luigi Pirandello: Six characters in search of an author: a comedy in the making. *In* Trilling, L. Prefaces to The experience of literature p45-50

Tonight we improvise

Sogliuzzo, A. R. Theater of the theater: Molière and Pirandello. *In* Johnson, R. B.; Neumann, E. S. and Trail, G. T. eds. Molière and the commonwealth of letters: patrimony and posterity p183-89

L'umorismo

Chiaromonte, N. Pirandello and humor. *In* Chiaromonte, N. The worm of consciousness, and other essays p80-93

Characters—Henry IV

Schlueter, J. Pirandello's Henry IV. *In* Schlueter, J. Metafictional characters in modern drama p19-34

Characters—Vitangelo Moscarda

Biasin, G. P. Strategies of the anti-hero: Svevo, Pirandello, and Montale. *In* Italian literature: roots and branches p363-81

Piranesi, Giambattista. See Piranesi, Giovanni Battista

Piranesi, Giovanni Battista

About

Eitner, L. E. A. Cages, prisons, and captives in eighteenth-century art. *In* Kroeber, K. and Walling, W. eds. Images of romanticism p13-38

Wittkower, R. Piranesi and eighteenth-century Egyptomania. *In* Wittkower, R. Studies in the Italian baroque p259-73

Wittkower, R. Piranesi as architect. *In* Wittkower, R. Studies in the Italian baroque p247-58

Wittkower, R. Piranesi's architectural creed. *In* Wittkower, R. Studies in the Italian baroque p235-46

About individual works

Carceri d'invenzione

Reed, A. Abysmal influence: Baudelaire, Coleridge, De Quincey, Piranesi, Wordsworth. *In* Glyph 4 189-206

Influence

Reed, A. Abysmal influence: Baudelaire, Coleridge, De Quincey, Piranesi, Wordsworth. *in* Glyph 4 p189-206

Pirates

Pearson, M. N. Corruption and corsairs in sixteenth-century western India. *In* Kling, B. B. and Pearson, M. N. eds. The age of partnership p15-41

See also Privateering

Pirenne, Henri

About

Hibbert, A. B. The origins of the medieval town patriciate. *In* Towns in societies p91-104

Pirrotta, Nino

"Musica de sono humano" and the musical poetics of Guido of Arezzo. *In* Medievalia et humanistica no. 7 p13-27

Pirsig, Robert M.

About individual works

Zen and the art of motorcycle maintenance

Couser, G. T. Three contemporaries: Malcolm X, Norman Mailer, and Robert Pirsig. *In* Couser, G. T. American autobiography p164-96

Pisan, Christine de

About individual works

The epistle of Othea to Hector

Ignatius, M. A. Christine de Pizan's Epistre Othea: an experiment in literary form. *In* Medievalia et humanistica; new ser. no.9 p127-42

Pisarev, Dimitrii Ivanovich

About

Stacy, R. H. The civic critics. *In* Stacy, R. H. Russian literary criticism p55-65

Piscator, Erwin

About

Chiaromonte, N. The political theater. *In* Chiaromonte, N. The worm of consciousness, and other essays p127-52

Knust, H. Piscator and Brecht: affinity and alienation. *In* Mews, S. and Knust, H. eds. Essays on Brecht p44-68

Pischel, Enrica Collotti. See Collotti Pischel, Enrica

Pitavy-Souques, Daniele

Technique as myth: the structure of The golden apples. *In* Prenshaw, P. W. ed. Eudora Welty p258-68

Pitkin, Hanna Fenichel

About individual works

Obligation and consent

Pateman, C. Political obligation and conceptual analysis. *In* Laslett, P. and Fishkin, J. eds. Philosophy, politics and society p227-56

Pittenger, Norman. See Pittenger, William Norman

Pittenger, William Norman

Evils and God—from a 'process' perspective. *In* Crew, L. ed. The gay academic p361-66

Pittman, David Joshua

The male house of prostitution. *In* Henslin, J. M. ed. Deviant life-styles p151-65

Pittsburgh

Politics and government

Stave, B. M. Pittsburgh and the New Deal. *In* Braeman, J.; Bremner, R. H. and Brody, D. eds. The New Deal v2 p376-406

Pivčević, Edo

Concepts, phenomenology and philosophical understanding. *In* Pivčević, E. ed. Phenomenology and philosophical understanding p271-86

Plaatje, Solomon Tshekisho

About individual works

The Boer War diary of Sol T. Plaatje: an African at Mafeking

Ravenscroft, A. African, Boer, and Indian attitudes to an imperialist war. *In* Narasimhaiah, C. D. ed. Awakened conscience p315-26

Mhudi

Couzens, T. J. Sol Plaatje's Mhudi. *In* Parker, K. ed. The South African novel in English p57-76

Place, J. A. and Peterson, L. S.

Some visual motifs of film noir. *In* Nichols, B. ed. Movies and methods p325-38

Place-names. See Names, Geographical

Places, Imaginary. See Geographical myths

Plague

Biraben, J. N. and Le Goff, J. The plague in the early Middle Ages. *In* Biology of man in history p48-80

Cipolla, C. M. A plague doctor. *In* The Medieval city p65-72

See also Black death

Europe

Thrupp, S. L. Plague effects in medieval Europe. *In* Thrupp, S. L. Society and history p150-62

Great Britain

Russell, J. C. The earlier medieval plague in the British Isles. *In* Viator: medieval and Renaissance studies v7 p65-78

Plague in literature

Girard, R. The plague in literature and myth. *In* Girard, R. "To double business bound" p136-54

Plain Editions

Ford, H. D. Gertrude Stein's Plain Editions. *In* Ford, H. D. Published in Paris p231-52

Plains

United States

Bowden, M. J. The Great American Desert in the American mind: the historiography of a geographical notion. *In* Geographies of the mind p119-47

Plains Indians. See Indians of North America—Great Plains

Plaks, Andrew H.

Allegory in Hsi-yu chi and Hung-lou meng. *In* Chinese narrative p163-202

Towards a critical theory of Chinese narrative. *In* Chinese narrative p309-52

Plamenatz, John Petrov

About

Cohen, G. A. Being, consciousness and roles: on the foundations of historical materialism. *In* Essays in honour of E. H. Carr p82-97

Planck, Max Karl Ernst Ludwig

About

Goldberg, S. Max Planck's philosophy of nature and his elaboration of the special theory of relativity. *In* Historical studies in the physical sciences v7 p125-60

Planetary meteorology. See Planets—Atmospheres

Planetoids. See Planets, Minor

Planets

Lewis, J. S. The outer planets. *In* Man and cosmos p117-30

Morrison, D. Planetary astronomy and Velikovsky's catastrophism. *In* Goldsmith, D. ed. Scientists confront Velikovsky p145-76

Sagan, C. The planets. *In* Man and cosmos p68-84

Atmospheres

Rasool, S. I. Planetary atmospheres. *In* Man and cosmos p101-10

Planets, Minor

Lecar, M. The asteroids. *In* Man and cosmos p136-42

Planets, Theory of. See Mechanics, Celestial

Planets in literature

Anderson, P. How to build a planet. *In* Knight, D. F. ed. Turning points p205-14

Planned parenthood. See Birth control

Planning

Howlett, M. J. Strategic planning in state government. *In* Managing nonprofit organizations p124-37

See also Health planning; Regional planning

Plant classification. See Botany—Classification

Plant geography. See Phytogeography

Plant introduction

Europe

Hamilton, E. J. What the New World gave the economy of the Old. *In* First images of America p853-84

Plant lore. See Ethnobotany

Plant taxonomy. See Botany—Classification

Plantation life

America

Szwed, J. F. and Abrahams, R. D. After the myth: studying Afro-American cultural patterns in the plantation literature. *In* Crowley, D. J. ed. African folklore in the New World p65-86

Southern States

Bargainnier, E. F. The plantation: Southern icon. *In* Browne, R. B. and Fishwick, M. W. eds. Icons of America p271-83

Plantation life in literature

Gray, R. J. Back to the old plantation: the recovery and reexamination of a dream. *In* Gray, R. J. The literature of memory p150-96

Plantation songs. See Afro-American songs

Plantations. See Plantation life

Plantin, family of printers

Judson, J. R. Rubens and Moretus. *In* Medieval and Renaissance studies 1976 p141-59

Plantinga, Alvin

Possible but unactual objects: on what there isn't; excerpt from "The nature of necessity." *In* Margolis, J. Z. ed. Philosophy looks at the arts p438-81

Plants

Classification

See Botany—Classification

Plants, Cultivated. See Plants, Edible

Plants, Edible

Africa, Eastern

Gwynne, M. D. The origin and spread of some domestic food plants of Eastern Africa. *In* Chittick, H. N. and Rotberg, R. I. eds. East Africa and the Orient p248-71

Plants, Medicinal. See Botany, Medical

Plants, Poisonous. See Poisonous plants

Plants, Useful. See Botany, Medical; Plants, Edible

Plaques, plaquettes

Bank, A. V. A copper-gilt plaque of the archangel Gabriel. *In* Studies in memory of David Talbot Rice p6-9

Plaster. See Stucco

Plate-glass

Harris, J. R. Saint-Gobain and Ravenhead. *In* Great Britain and her world, 1750-1914 p27-70

Plate-printing. See Engravings—Printing

Plath, Sylvia

About

Bedient, C. Sylvia Plath, romantic. . . . *In* Lane, G. ed Sylvia Plath p3-18

Butscher, E. In search of Sylvia: an introduction. *In* Butscher, E. ed. Sylvia Plath p3-29

Diggory, T. Armored women, naked men: Dickinson, Whitman, and their successors. *In* Gilbert, S. M. and Gubar, S. eds. Shakespeare's sisters p135-50

Ferrier, C. The beekeeper's apprentice. *In* Lane, G. ed. Sylvia Plath p203-17

Gilbert, S. M. A fine, white flying myth: the life/work of Sylvia Plath. *In* Gilbert, S. M. and Gubar, S. eds. Shakespeare's sisters p245-60

Guttenberg, B. Plath's cosmology and the house of Yeats. *In* Lane, G. ed. Sylvia Plath p138-52

Hardy, B. N. The poetry of Sylvia Plath. *In* Hardy, B. N. The advantage of lyric p121-40

Howe, I. The Plath celebration: a partial dissent; excerpt from "The critical point." *In* Butscher, E. ed. Sylvia Plath p225-35

Kenner, H. Sincerity kills. *In* Lane, G. Sylvia Plath p33-44

Kopp, J. B. "Gone, very gone youth": Sylvia Plath at Cambridge, 1955-1957. *In* Butscher, E. ed. Sylvia Plath p61-80

Krook, D. Recollections of Sylvia Plath. *In* Butscher, E. ed. Sylvia Plath p49-60

Lameyer, G. A. Sylvia at Smith. *In* Butscher, E. ed. Sylvia Plath p32-41

Lane, G. Influence and originality in Plath's poems. *In* Lane, G. ed. Sylvia Plath p116-37

Levy, L. Outside the bell jar. *In* Butscher, E. ed. Sylvia Plath p42-48

McClatchy, J. D. Short circuits and folding mirrors. *In* Lane, G. ed. Sylvia Plath p19-32

Mazzaro, J. Sylvia Plath and the cycles of history. *In* Lane, G. ed. Sylvia Plath p218-40

Oates, J. C. The death throes of romanticism; the poems of Sylvia Plath. *In* Boyers, R. ed. Contemporary poetry in America p139-56

Also in Oates, J. C. New haven, new earth: the visionary experience in literature p111-40

Same as Oates, J. C. The death throes of romanticism: the poetry of Sylvia Plath. *In* Butscher, E. ed. Sylvia Plath p206-24

Oberg, A. K. Sylvia Plath and the new decadence. *In* Butscher, E. ed. Sylvia Plath p177-85

O'Hara, J. D. Plath's comedy. *In* Lane, G. ed. Sylvia Plath p74-96

Perloff, M. G. Sylvia Plath's "Sivvy" poems: a portrait of the poet as daughter. *In* Lane, G. ed. Sylvia Plath p155-78

Phillips, R. S. The dark funnel: a reading of Sylvia Plath; excerpt from "The confessional poets." *In* Butscher, E. ed. Sylvia Plath p186-205

Quinn, M. B. Medusan imagery in Sylvia Plath. *in* Lane, G. ed. Sylvia Plath p97-115

Ries, L. R. Sylvia Plath: the internalized response. *In* Ries, L. R. Wolf masks p33-58

Roche, C. Sylvia Plath: vignettes from England. *In* Butscher, E. ed. Sylvia Plath p81-96

Scheerer, C. The deathly paradise of Sylvia Plath. *In* Butscher, E. ed. Sylvia Plath p166-76

Schwartz, M. M. and Bollas, C. The absence at the center: Sylvia Plath and suicide. *In* Lane, G. ed. Sylvia Plath p179-202

Shapiro, D. Sylvia Plath: drama and melodrama. *In* Lane, G. ed. Sylvia Plath p45-53

Sigmund, E. Sylvia in Devon: 1962. *In* Butscher, E. ed. Sylvia Plath p100-07

Simpson, L. Black, banded with yellow. *In* Simpson, L. A revolution in taste p83-127

About individual works

Ariel

Blessing, R. A. The shape of the psyche: vision and technique in the late poems of Sylvia Plath. *In* Lane, G. ed. Sylvia Plath p57-73

Boyers, R. Sylvia Plath: the trepanned veteran. *In* Boyers, R. Excursions p156-67

The bell jar

Allen, M. Sylvia Plath's defiance: The bell jar. *In* Allen, M. The necessary blankness p160-78

Lameyer, G. A. The double in Sylvia Plath's The bell jar. *In* Butscher, E. ed. Sylvia Plath p143-65

The colossus

Smith, P. Architectonics: Sylvia Plath's Colossus. *In* Butscher, E. ed. Sylvia Plath p111-24

Crossing the water

Boyers, R. More on Sylvia Plath. *In* Boyers, R. Excursions p168-75

Perloff, M. G. On the road to Ariel: the "transitional" poetry of Sylvia Plath. *In* Butscher, E. ed. Sylvia Plath p125-42

Winter trees

Perloff, M. G. On the road to Ariel: the "transitional" poetry of Sylvia Plath. *In* Butscher, E. ed. Sylvia Plath p125-42

Plato

About

Arendt, H. What makes us think? *In* Arendt, H. The life of the mind v 1 p127-93

Dickason, A. Anatomy and destiny: the role of biology in Plato's view of women. *In* Gould, C. C. and Wartofsky, M. W. eds. Women and philosophy p45-53

Downs, R. B. Judge of nature and mankind. *In* Downs, R. B. Books that changed the world p49-68

Fears, J. R. Atlantis and the Minoan thalassocracy: a study in modern mythopoeism. *In* Ramage, E. S. ed. Atlantis, fact or fiction? p103-34

Fredericks, S. C. Plato's Atlantis: a mythologist looks at myth. *In* Ramage, E. S. ed. Atlantis, fact or fiction? p81-99

Havelock, E. A. The justice of Plato. *In* Havelock, E. A. The Greek concept of justice p308-23

Havelock, E. A. A philosophy of the written word. *In* Havelock, E. A. The Greek concept of justice p324-34

Helm, R. M. Plato in the thought of Nietzsche and Augustine. *In* O'Flaherty, J. C.; Sellner, T. F. and Helm, R. M. eds. Studies in Nietzsche and the classical tradition p16-32

Herter, H. The problematic mention of Hippocrates in Plato's Phaedrus. *In* Illinois classical studies, v 1 1976 p22-42

Holland, R. F. Absolute ethics, mathematics and the impossibility of politics. *In* Royal Institute of Philosophy. Human values p172-88

Huby, P. M. Greek ethics. *In* New studies in ethics v 1 p 1-78

Luce, J. V. The sources and literary form of Plato's Atlantis narrative. *In* Ramage, E. S. ed. Atlantis, fact or fiction? p49-78

Mazzeo, J. A. The Platonic debate over myth, truth, and virtue. *In* Mazzeo, J. A. Varieties of interpretation p71-94

Olney, J. L. The esoteric flower: Yeats and Jung. *In* Yeats and the occult p27-54

Ramage, E. S. Perspectives ancient and modern. *In* Ramage, E. S. ed. Atlantis, fact or fiction? p3-45

Reiche, H. A. T. The language of archaic astronomy: a clue to the Atlantis myth? *In* Brecher, K. and Feirtag, M. eds. Astronomy of the ancients p153-89

Richards, I. A. Sources of our common aim. *In* Richards, I. A. Poetries p165-214

Romilly, J. de. Plato and conjurers. *In* Romilly, J. de. Magic and rhetoric in ancient Greece p23-43

Sayers, D. L. Toward a Christian esthetic; excerpt from "Unpopular opinions." *In* Sayers, D. L. The whimsical Christian p73-91

Turnbull, R. G. The role of the "special sensibles" in the perception theories of Plato and Aristotle. *In* Studies in perception p3-26

Waldman, T. A key to Plato's early dialogues. *In* Philosophy and the civilizing arts p60-88

About individual works

Apology

Strycker, E. de. The oracle given to Chaerephon about Socrates. *In* Kephalaion p39-49

Phaedo

Ober, W. B. Did Socrates die of hemlock poisoning? *In* Ober, W. B. Boswell's clap and other essays p262-70

Phaedrus

Herter, H. The problematic mention of Hippocrates in Plato's Phaedrus. *In* Illinois classical studies, v 1 1976 p22-42

Vries, G. J. de. A general theory of literary composition in the Phaedrus. *In* Kephalaion p50-52

The republic

Hermassi, K. C. Theatre of political memory. *In* Hermassi, K. C. Polity and theatre in historical perspective p65-94

Shell, M. The Ring of Gyges. *In* Shell, M. The economy of literature p11-62

Symposium

Lanham, R. A. The fundamental strategies: Plato and Ovid. *In* Lanham, R. A. The motives of eloquence p36-64

Timaeus

Kuttner, S. G. Gratian and Plato. *In* Church and government in the Middle Ages p93-118

Tracy, T. J. Plato, Galen, and the center of consciousness. *In* Illinois classical studies, v 1 1976 p43-52

Zeyl, D. J. Plato and talk of a world in flux: Timaeus. *In* Harvard Studies in classical philology v79 p125-48

Aesthetics

Coomaraswamy, A. K. A figure of speech or a figure of thought? Excerpt from "Figures of speech or figures of thought: collected essays on the traditional or 'normal' view of art." *In* Coomaraswamy, A. K. Selected papers v 1 p13-42

Influence

Simon, B. Plato and Freud. *In* Simon, B. Mind and madness in ancient Greece p200-12

Influence—Galenus

Tracy, T. J. Plato, Galen, and the center of consciousness. *In* Illinois classical studies, v 1 1976 p43-52

Influence—Gratianus, the Canonist

Kuttner, S. G. Gratian and Plato. *In* Church and government in the Middle Ages p93-118

Influence—Swift

Trowbridge, F. H. Swift and Socrates. *In* Trowbridge, F. H. From Dryden to Jane Austen p81-123

Metaphysics

Daor, D. Two metaphysical concepts: Li and idea. *In* Philosophy East/philosophy West p235-46

Political science

Ball, T. Plato and Aristotle: the unity versus the autonomy of theory and practice. *In* Political theory and praxis p57-69

Psychology

Simon, B. The philosopher as therapist. *In* Simon, B. Mind and madness in ancient Greece p180-99

Simon, B. Plato's concept of mind and its disorders. *In* Simon, B. Mind and madness in ancient Greece p157-79

Platonism. See Platonists

Platonists

Rijk, L. M. de. Quaestio de ideis. Some notes on an important chapter of Platonism. *In* Kephalaion p204-13

Trowbridge, F. H. Platonism and Sir Joshua Reynolds. *In* Trowbridge, F. H. From Dryden to Jane Austen p200-09

Von Staden, H. The Stoic theory of perception and its "Platonic" critics. *In* Studies in perception p96-136

Platonov, Andreï Platonovich

About

Slonim, M. L. Posthumous revivals: Bulgakov, Platonov, Zabolotsky. *In* Slonim, M. L. Soviet Russian literature p352-62

Thomson, B. The difference of art: some Soviet writers of the 1920s and 1930s. *In* Thomson, B. Lot's wife and the Venus of Milo p98-122

Plaut, W. Gunther

The Sabbath as protest: thoughts on work and leisure in the automated society. *In* Tradition and change in Jewish experience p169-83

Plautus, Titus Maccius

About

Fantham, E. Adaptation and survival: a genre study of Roman comedy in relation to its Greek sources. *In* Ruggiers, P. G. ed. Versions of medieval comedy p19-49

Nicoll, A. From Menander to the mimes. *In* Nicoll, A. World drama p74-99

Paster, G. K. The city in Plautus and Middleton. *In* Renaissance drama [1973] p29-44

Sandbach, F. H. Plautus. *In* Sandbach, F. H. The comic theatre of Greece and Rome p118-34

Segal, E. The business of Roman comedy. *In* Perspectives of Roman poetry p93-103

Smith, B. R. Sir Amorous Knight and the indecorous Romans; or, Plautus and Terence play court in the Renaissance. *In* Renaissance drama [1973] p3-27

About individual works

Aulularia

Markovic, M. Euclio, Cnemon, and the Peripatos. *In* Illinois classical studies, v2 1977 p197-218

Bacchides (Lines 925-978)

Jocelyn, H. D. Chrysalus and the Fall of Troy (Plautus, Bacchides 925-978). *In* Harvard Studies in classical philology v73 p135-52

Characters—Pseudolus

Torrance, R. M. Bondservant and beast of burden. *In* Torrance, R. M. The comic hero p60-82

Play

Coomaraswamy, A. K. Līlā. *In* Coomaraswamy, A. K. Selected papers v2 p148-55

Coomaraswamy, A. K. Play and seriousness. *In* Coomaraswamy, A. K. Selected papers v2 p156-58

Erikson, E. H. Play and actuality. *In* Explorations in psychohistory p109-35

Wimsatt, W. K. Belinda ludens. *In* Wimsatt, W. K. Day of the leopards p99-116

England

Miller, S. Eighteenth-century play and the game of Tom Jones. *In* A Provision of human nature p83-93

United States

Devereux, E. C. Backyard versus Little League baseball: the impoverishment of children's games. *In* Social problems in athletics p37-56

Mahigel, E. L. and Stone, G. P. Hustling as a career. *In* Social problems in athletics p78-85

Play direction (Theater) See Theater—Production and direction

Play in literature

Sanders, D. A. Revelation as child's play in Frost's "Directive." *In* Frost: centennial essays II p267-77

Warner, S. D. The control of play and the play of control in Robert Frost's poetry. *In* Frost: centennial essays II p262-66

Play it as it lays (Motion picture)

Kauffmann, S. Play it as it lays. *In* Kauffmann, S. Living images p156-58

Play of The talents. See The talents

Play within a play

Bergeron, D. M. The play-within-the play in 3 Henry VI. *In* Tennessee Studies in literature v22 p37-45

Play-writing. See Playwriting

The **playboy** of the Western world (criticism) Synge, J. *In* Kauffmann, S. Persons of the drama p117-20

Playhouses. See Theaters

Plays. See Drama

Plays, Fairy. See Fairy plays

Plays, Medieval. See Drama, Medieval; Moralities; Mysteries and miracle-plays

Plays, Television. See Television plays

Playtime (Motion picture)

Kauffmann, S. Playtime. *In* Kauffmann, S. Living images p212-13

Playwrights. See Dramatists

Playwriting

Wilder, T. N. Some thought on playwriting. *in* Wilder, T. N. American characteristics, and other essays p115-26

See also Drama—Technique

Plazas

Italy

Lotz, W. Sixteenth-century Italian squares. *In* Lotz, W. Studies in Italian Renaissance architecture p74-116

Ple, Albert

Christian morality and Freudian morality. *In* Wolman, B. B. ed. Psychoanalysis and Catholicism p97-110

Pleasure

Sutherland, S. R. Hume and the concept of pleasure. *In* David Hume p218-24

Trilling, L. The fate of pleasure: Wordsworth to Dostoevski; excerpt from "Beyond culture". *In* Wimsatt, W. K. ed. Literary criticism: idea and act p189-211

See also Happiness

Pletcher, David M.

Manifest destiny. *In* Encyclopedia of American foreign policy p526-34

Presidential power in foreign affairs. *In* Encyclopedia of American foreign policy p805-26

Pleynet, Marcelin

About

Greene, R. W. Marcelin Pleynet. *In* Greene, R. W. Six French poets of our time p159-75

Plinius Caecilius Secundus, C.

About individual works

Letters

Syme, Sir R. Pliny the procurator. *In* Harvard Studies in classical philology v73 p201-36

Friends and associates

White, P. The friends of Martial, Statius, and Pliny, and the dispersal of patronage. *In* Harvard Studies in classical philology v79 p265-300

Plinius Secundus, C.

About

Syme, Sir R. Pliny the procurator. *In* Harvard Studies in classical philology v73 p201-36

Pliny, the Elder. See Plinius Secundus, C.

Pliny, the Younger. See Plinius Caecilius Secundus, C.

Ploch, Donald Raymond

Research funding for sociology in the National Science Foundation. *In* Gaston, J. ed. Sociology of science p54-62

Plog, Fred

Explaining change. *In* Explanation of prehistoric change p17-57

Systems theory and simulation: the case of Hawaiian warfare and redistribution. *In* Explanation of prehistoric change p259-318

Plomer, William Charles Franklin

Francis Kilvert and his Diary. *In* Royal Society of Literature of the United Kingdom, London. Essays by divers hands v38 p78-92

About individual works

Turbott Wolfe

Rabkin, D. Race and fiction: God's stepchildren and Turbott Wolfe. *In* Parker, K. ed. The South African novel in English p77-94

Plotinus

About

Schwyzer, H. R. The intellect in Plotinus and the archetypes of C. G. Jung. *In* Kephalaion p214-22

About individual works

Enneades

Armstrong, A. H. Beauty and the discovery of divinity in the thought of Plotinus. *In* Kephalaion p155-63

Sinnige, T. G. Metaphysical and personal religion in Plotinus. *In* Kephalaion p147-54

Enneades (IV)

Straaten, M. van. On Plotinus IV, 7[2], 8³. *In* Kephalaion p164-70

Aesthetics

Armstrong, A. H. Beauty and the discovery of divinity in the thought of Plotinus. *In* Kephalaion p155-63

Metaphysics

Armstrong, A. H. Beauty and the discovery of divinity in the thought of Plotinus. *In* Kephalaion p155-63

Sinnige, T. G. Metaphysical and personal religion in Plotinus. *In* Kephalaion p147-54

Plots (Drama, novel, etc.)

Brower, R. A. The heresy of plot. *In* Brower, R. A. Mirror on mirror p123-38

Caserio, R. L. Narrative reason: the sense of plot and historical experience. *In* Caserio, R. L. Plot, story, and the novel p27-56

Caserio, R. L. Plot, purpose, and the modern self. *In* Caserio, R. L. Plot, story, and the novel p167-97

Caserio, R. L. The sense of plot. *In* Caserio, R. L. Plot, story, and the novel p3-26

Cawelti, J. G. Notes toward a typology of literary formulas. *In* Cawelti, J. G. Adventure, mystery, and romance p37-50

Cawelti, J. G. The study of literary formulas. *In* Cawelti, J. G. Adventure, mystery, and romance p5-36

Culler, J. D. Defining narrative units. *In* Fowler, R. ed. Style and structure in literature p123-42

Leondar, B. Hatching plots: genesis of storymaking. *In* Perkins, D. and Leondar, B. eds. The arts and cognition p172-91

Riggs, D. "Plot" and "episode" in early neoclassical criticism. *In* Renaissance drama [1973] p149-75

Weimann, R. Moralities and interludes. *In* Weimann, R. Shakespeare and the popular tradition in the theater: studies in the social dimension of dramatic form and function p98-160

See also Plots under names of literary authors, e.g. Dickens, Charles—Plots

Plumb, John Harold

The impact of the American Revolution on Great Britain. *In* The Impact of the American Revolution abroad p65-78

About

McKendrick, N. J. H. Plumb: a valedictory tribute. *In* Historical perspectives p 1-18

Plumb, Marjorie M. and Holland, Jimmie C. B.

Cancer in adolescents: the symptom is the thing. *In* Anticipatory grief p193-209

Plumptre, Arthur FitzWalter Wynne

Maynard Keynes as a teacher. *In* Keynes, M. ed. Essays on John Maynard Keynes p247-53

Plumstead, A. W.

The election sermons; excerpt from "The wall and the garden." *In* Mulder, J. M. and Wilson, J. F. eds. Religion in American history p57-73

Hector St John de Crèvecoeur. *In* Emerson, E. H. ed. American literature, 1764-1789 p213-31

Pluralism

Gordon, M. M. Toward a general theory of racial and ethnic group relations. *In* Glazer, N. and Moynihan, D. P. eds. Ethnicity p84-110

Leys, W. A. R. Political and moral pluralism. *In* The Abdication of philosophy: philosophy and the public good p93-107

See also Atomism; Monism

Pluralism (Social sciences)

Dillon, W. S. E pluribus unum? *In* Smithsonian Institution. The cultural drama p33-67

Dubos, R. J. Pluralism and world order. *In* Dubos, R. J. Beast or angel? p181-89

Pluralism (Social sciences)—*Continued*

Fortes, M. The plural society in Africa. *In* Leftwich, A. ed. South Africa: economic growth and political change p 1-27

Jupp, J. Modernization and pluralism: Ceylon and Malaysia. *In* Leftwich, A. ed. South Africa: economic growth and political change p187-211

Leftwich, A. The constitution and continuity of South African inequality: some conceptual questions. *In* Leftwich, A. ed. South Africa: economic growth and political change p125-85

McCready, W. C. Social utilities in a pluralistic society. *In* The Diverse society: implications for social policy p13-25

Wax, M. L. Cultural pluralism, political power, and ethnic studies. *In* Smithsonian Institution. The cultural drama p107-20

See also Ethnicity

Plutarch. See Plutarchus

Plutarchus

About individual works
Lives

Fornara, C. W. Plutarch and the Megarian decree. *In* Yale classical studies v24 p213-28

Pneuma. See Soul; Spirit

Pneumatology (Philosophy) See Spirit

Pneumatology (Theology) See Spirit

Pocahontas

About

Larson, C. R. The children of Pocahontas. *In* Larson, C. R. American Indian fiction p17-33

Pocket money (Motion picture)

Kauffmann, S. Pocket money. *In* Kauffmann, S. Living images p110-12

Pocock, David Francis

North and South in the Book of Genesis. *In* Studies in social anthropology p273-84

Pocock, John Greville Agard

Between Machiavelli and Hume: Gibbon as civic humanist and philosophical historian. *In* Edward Gibbon and The decline and fall of the Roman Empire p103-19

Early modern capitalism—the Augustan perception. *In* Kamenka, E. and Neale, R. S. eds. Feudalism, capitalism and beyond p62-83

England. *In* National consciousness, history, and political culture in early-modern Europe p98-117

Modes of political and historical time in early eighteenth-century England. *In* Studies in eighteenth-century culture v5 p87-102

About individual works
The Macchiavellian moment: Florentine political thought and the Atlantic republic tradition

Hexter, J. H. Republic, virtue, liberty, and the political universe of J. G. A. Pocock. *In* Hexter, J. H. On historians p255-303

Ross, D. The liberal tradition revisited and the republican tradition addressed. *In* Higham, J. and Conkin, P. K. eds. New directions in American intellectual history p116-31

Podgórecki, Adam

Jurisprudence empirically tested. *In* Crime, criminology and public policy p297-317

Podhoretz, Norman

About individual works
Making it

Balakian, N. Crossing the ethnic barrier. *In* Balakian, N. Critical encounters p183-93

Poe, Edgar Allan

Georgia scenes. *In* Inge, M. T. ed. The frontier humorists p85-93

Review of Twice-told tales. *In* May, C. E. ed. Short story theories p45-51

About

Cawelti, J. G. The formula of the classical detective story. *In* Cawelti, J. G. Adventure, mystery, and romance p80-105

Hough, G. G. Edgar Allan Poe. *In* Hough, G. G. Selected essays p126-43

Suvin, D. The shift to anticipation: radical rhapsody and romantic recoil. *In* Suvin, D. Metamorphoses of science fiction p115-44

Tate, A. The poetry of Edgar Allan Poe. *In* Tate, A. Memoirs and opinions, 1926-1974 p115-27

Wilbur, R. Edgar Allan Poe. *In* Wilbur, R. Responses p39-66

About individual works
The fall of the House of Usher

Roppolo, J. P. Undercurrents in Poe's "The fall of the House of Usher." *In* Tulane Studies in English v23 p 1-16

Tate, A. Three commentaries: Poe, James, and Joyce. *In* Tate, A. Memoirs and opinions, 1926-1974 p155-69

The narrative of Arthur Gordon Pym of Nantucket

Mottram, E. Poe's Pym and the American social imagination. *In* Artful thunder p25-53

Rowe, J. C. Writing and truth in Poe's The narrative of Arthur Gordon Pym. *In* Glyph 2 p102-21

Spengemann, W. C. The adventurous muse: "The Algerine captive" and "Arthur Gordon Pym." *In* Spengemann, W. C. The adventurous muse p119-50

Wilbur, R. "The narrative of Arthur Gordon Pym." *In* Wilbur, R. Responses p190-214

The purloined letter

Grossvogel, D. I. "The purloined letter": the mystery of the text. *In* Grossvogel, D. I. Mystery and its fictions: from Oedipus to Agatha Christie p93-107

Johnson, B. The frame of reference: Poe, Lacan, Derrida. *In* Hartman, G. H. ed. Psychoanalysis and the question of the text p149-71

Bibliography

Stauffer, D. B. Poe. *In* American literary scholarship, 1975 p35-58

Stauffer, D. B. Poe [another essay] *In* American literary scholarship, 1976 p33-46

Stauffer, D. B. Poe [another essay] *In* American literary scholarship, 1977 p35-47

Thompson, G. R. Poe. *In* American literary scholarship, 1973 p32-64

Thompson, G. R. Poe [another essay] *In* American literary scholarship, 1974 p29-42

Characters—Roderick Usher

Wright, N. Roderick Usher: Poe's turn-of-the-century artist. *In* Artful thunder p55-67

Poe, Edgar A.—*Continued*

Criticism and interpretation

Bollier, E. P. Against the American grain: William Carlos Williams between Whitman and Poe. *In* Tulane Studies in English v23 p123-42

Johnson, B. The frame of reference: Poe, Lacan, Derrida. *In* Hartman, G. H. ed. Psychoanalysis and the question of the text p149-71

Wilbur, R. The Poe mystery case. *In* Wilbur, R. Responses p127-38

Film adaptations

Weaver, M. Edgar Allan Poe and the early avant-garde film. *In* English Association. Essays and studies, 1977 p73-85

Moving-pictures

See Poe, Edgar Allan—Film adaptations

Plots

Caserio, R. L. Plot and the point of reversal: Dickens and Poe. *In* Caserio, R. L. Plot, story, and the novel p57-90

Poema del Cid

Duggan, J. J. Formulaic diction in the Cantar de mio Cid and the old French epic. *In* Duggan, J. J. ed. Oral literature p74-83

Poetic drama. See Verse drama

Poetics

Bronowski, J. Music, metaphor, and meaning. *In* Bronowski, J. The visionary eye p93-108

Cunningham, J. V. How shall the poem be written? *In* Cunningham, J. V. The collected essays of J. V. Cunningham p256-71

Goring, M. The sound of poetry. *In* Royal Society of Literature of the United Kingdom, London. Essays by divers hands v39 p 1-23

Maiâkovskiĭ, V. V. How to make verse. *In* Proffer, C. R. ed. Modern Russian poets on poetry p103-43

Moore, M. Idiosyncrasy and technique. *In* The poet's work: 29 masters of 20th century poetry on the origins and practice of their art p215-29

Olson, E. The poetic process. *In* Olson, E. On value judgments in the arts, and other essays p220-25

Perkins, D. A better word: studies of poetry editing. *In* Perkins, D. and Leondar, B. eds. The arts and cognition p246-83

Shapiro, K. J. The true artificer. *In* Shapiro, K. J. The poetry wreck p245-67

Sinclair, J. M. When is a poem like a sunset? *In* Ballad studies p153-69

Taylor, A. Magical language and poetic analogy. *In* Taylor, A. Magic and English romanticism p38-63

Taylor, A. Wordsworth's arguments against magical words. *In* Taylor, A. Magic and English romanticism p134-83

Wilbur, R. The bottles become new, too. *In* Wilbur, R. Responses p215-23

Wimsatt, W. K. In search of verbal mimesis (supplement to "Laokoon: an oracle reconsulted"). *In* Wimsatt, W. K. Day of the leopards p57-73

See also Children's poetry—Authorship; Poetry—Authorship; Rhythm

Poetry

Abrams, M. H. Coleridge, Baudelaire, and modernist poetics. *In* Amacher, R. E. and Lange, V. eds. New perspectives in German literary criticism p150-81

Blok, A. A. On the mission of the poet. *In* Proffer, C. R. ed. Modern Russian poets on poetry p71-80

Bloom, H. Poetry, revisionism, repression. *In* Bloom, H. Poetry and repression p 1-27

Bogan, L. The pleasures of formal poetry; excerpt from "A poet's alphabet." *In* Gibbons, R. ed. The poet's work: 29 masters of 20th century poetry on the origins and practice of their art p203-14

Bronowski, J. The act of recognition. *In* Bronowski, J. The visionary eye p114-27

Bronowski, J. The imaginative mind in art; excerpt from "Imagination and the university." *In* Bronowski, J. The visionary eye p6-19

Bronowski, J. The nature of art; excerpt from "The poet's defence." *In* Bronowski, J. The visionary eye p 1-5

Bronowski, J. The speaking eye, the visionary ear. *In* Bronowski, J. The visionary eye p75-87

Cernuda, L. Words before a reading. *In* Gibbons, R. ed. The poet's work: 29 masters of 20th century poetry on the origins and practice of their art p42-47

Cioffi, F. Intention and interpretation in criticism. *In* On literary intention p55-73

Crane, H. General aims and theories; excerpt from "The complete poetry and selected letters and prose of Hart Crane." *In* Gibbons, R. ed. The poet's work: 29 masters of 20th century poetry on the origins and practice of their art p179-82

Cunningham, J. V. The ancient quarrel between history and poetry. *In* Cunningham, J. V. The collected essays of J. V. Cunningham p120-27

Cunningham, J. V. Poetry, structure, and tradition. *In* Cunningham, J. V. The collected essays of J. V. Cunningham p133-46

Cunningham, J. V. The problem of form. *In* Cunningham, J. V. The collected essays of J. V. Cunningham p247-50

DeLaura, D. J. The poetry of thought. *In* Altholz, J. L. ed. The mind and art of Victorian England p35-57

Duncan, R. E. Notes on poetic form. *In* Gibbons, R. ed. The poet's work: 29 masters of 20th century poetry on the origins and practice of their art p260-62

Eberhart, R. Notes on poetry. *In* Eberhart, R. Of poetry and poets p3-5

Eberhart, R. The poet as teacher. *In* Eberhart, R. Of poetry and poets p52-58

Eberhart, R. Poetry as a creative principle. *In* Eberhart, R. Of poetry and poets p8-18

Eberhart, R. Why I write poetry. *In* Eberhart, R. Of poetry and poets p30-32

Eberhart, R. Will and psyche in poetry. *In* Eberhart, R. Of poetry and poets p59-75

Eliot, T. S. From The music of poetry. *In* Eliot, T. S. Selected prose of T. S. Eliot p107-14

Eliot, T. S. From The use of poetry and the use of criticism. *In* Eliot, T. S. Selected prose of T. S. Eliot p79-96

Eliot, T. S. Tradition and the individual talent. *In* Eliot, T. S. Selected prose of T. S. Eliot p37-44

Poetry—*Continued*

Squires, G. Poetry and the future. *In* Bundy, R. F. ed. Images of the future: the twenty-first century and beyond p16-23

Stankiewicz, E. Poetics and verbal art. *In* Sebeok, T. A. ed. A perfusion of signs p54-76

Starobinski, J. André Chénier and the allegory of poetry. *In* Kroeber, K. and Walling, W. eds. Images of romanticism p39-60

Stevens, W. The irrational element in poetry; excerpt from "Opus posthumous." *In* Gibbons, R. ed. The poet's work: 29 masters of 20th century poetry on the origins and practice of their art p48-58

Thompson, D. The nature of poetry. *In* Thompson, D. The uses of poetry p 1-18

Thompson, D. Uses of poetry. *In* Thompson, D. The uses of poetry p194-225

Tsvetaeva, M. I. E. Art in the light of conscience. *In* Proffer, C. R. ed. Modern Russian poets on poetry p145-84

Watkins, E. Introduction: Poetics, poetry, and the practice of criticism. *In* Watkins, E. The critical act p3-23

Watkins, E. Poetic autonomy. *In* Watkins, E. The critical act p24-55

Wilbur, R. On my own work. *In* Wilbur, R. Responses p115-26

Wimsatt, W. K. Genesis: a fallacy revisited. *In* On literary intention p116-38

Wimsatt, W. K. and Beardsley, M. C. The intentional fallacy; excerpt from "The verbal icon." *In* On literary intention p 1-13

Winters, Y. The audible reading of poetry; excerpt from "The function of criticism." *In* Gross, H. S. ed. The structure of verse p129-46

See also Albas; Concrete poetry; Elegiac poetry; Free verse; Imagist poetry; Lays; Lyric poetry; Magic and poetry; Pastoral poetry; Protest poetry

Authorship

Berry, W. The specialization of poetry. *In* Gibbons, R. ed. The poet's work: 29 masters of 20th century poetry on the origins and practice of their art p139-56

Eberhart, R. The theory of poetry. *In* Eberhart, R. Of poetry and poets p76-85

Eliot, T. S. Tradition and the individual talent. *In* Eliot, T. S. Selected prose of T. S. Eliot p37-44

Heaney, S. Feelings into words. *In* Gibbons, R. ed. The poet's work: 29 masters of 20th century poetry on the origins and practice of their art p263-82

Moore, M. Idiosyncrasy and technique. *In* Gibbons, R. ed. The poet's work: 29 masters of 20th century poetry on the origins and practice of their art p215-29

Schwartz, D. The vocation of the poet in the modern world; excerpts from "Selected essays of Delmore Schwartz." *In* Gibbons, R. ed. The poet's work: 29 masters of 20th century poetry on the origins and practice of their art p82-91

Collections—History and criticism

Balakian, N. Realists of the interior: women poets of today. *In* Balakian, N. Critical encounters p156-58

History and criticism

Adams, P. G. Definitions and the tradition. *In* Adams, P. G. Graces of harmony p 1-56

Barfield, O. Poetic diction and legal fiction. *In* Barfield, O. The rediscovery of meaning, and other essays p44-64

Cavell, S. Aesthetic problems of modern philosophy. *In* Cavell, S. Must we mean what we say? p73-96

Cunningham, J. V. Several kinds of short poem. *In* Cunningham, J. V. The collected essays of J. V. Cunningham p431-38

Cunningham, J. V. Technology and poetry. *In* Cunningham, J. V. The collected essays of J. V. Cunningham p439-42

Eberhart, R. Pure poetry. *In* Eberhart, R. Of poetry and poets p19-29

Eliot, T. S. Tradition and the individual talent; excerpt from "Selected essays; new edition." *In* Primeau, R. ed. Influx p15-21

Fergusson, F. Poetry and drama. *In* Symbolism and modern literature p13-25

Freedman, R. Intentionality and the literary object. *In* Krieger, M. and Dembo, L. S. eds. Directions for criticism p137-59

Graves, R. Harp, anvil, oar; excerpt from "The crowning privilege." *In* Gross, H. S. ed. The structure of verse p21-39

Hill, A. A. Two views of poetic language and meaning: the poem as cryptogram and as example of deviant grammar. *In* Hill, A. A. Constituent and pattern in poetry p115-22

Holbrook, D. Conclusions. *In* Holbrook, D. Lost bearings in English poetry p217-44

Nemerov, H. Figures of thought. *In* Nemerov, H. Figures of thought p18-29

Nemerov, H. The winter addresses of Kenneth Burke. *In* Nemerov, H. Figures of thought p126-35

Ong, W. J. From rhetorical culture to new criticism: the poem as a closed field. *In* Simpson, L. P. ed. The possibilities of order: Cleanth Brooks and his work p150-67

Richards, I. A. Notes on the practice of interpretation. *In* Richards, I. A. Complementarities p189-97

Richards, I. A. Reversals in poetry. *In* Richards, I. A. Poetries p59-70

Roethke, T. What do I like? *In* Gross, H. S. ed. The structure of verse p241-55

Steiner, G. On difficulty. *In* Steiner, G. On difficulty and other essays p18-47

Thompson, D. In the beginning. *In* Thompson, D. The uses of poetry p19-42

Thompson, D. Maid of all work. *In* Thompson, D. The uses of poetry p70-111

Thompson, D. The printed poem. *In* Thompson, D. The uses of poetry p173-93

Thompson, D. Rites, bards, ballads. *In* Thompson, D. The uses of poetry p43-69

Tsvetaeva, M. I. E. A poet on criticism. *In* The Bitter air of exile p103-34

Wain, J. Poetry and social criticism. *In* Wain, J. Professing poetry p157-76

Wilbur, R. Poetry's debt to poetry. *In* Wilbur, R. Responses p161-84

Wimsatt, W. K. Organic form: some questions about a metaphor. *In* Wimsatt, W. K. Day of the leopards p205-33

Philosophy

See Poetry

Study and teaching

Eberhart, R. The poet as teacher. *In* Eberhart, R. Of poetry and poets p52-58

Technique

See Poetics

Poetry—*Continued*

Therapeutic use

Thompson, D. Uses of poetry. *In* Thompson, D. The uses of poetry p194-225

Translating

Tate, A. Translation or imitation? *In* Tate, A. Memoirs and opinions, 1926-1974 p195-207

Poetry (Periodical)

Parisi, J. A. The care and funding of Pegasus. *In* Anderson, E. and Kinzie, M. eds. The little magazine in America: a modern documentary history p216-35

Poetry, Medieval

Hughes, D. G. Music and meter in liturgical poetry. *In* Medievalia et humanistica no. 7 p29-43

Jackson, W. T. H. The politics of a poet: the Archipoeta as revealed by his imagery. *In* Philosophy and humanism p320-38

Pietrkiewicz, J. Simultaneity in a sequence: the time pattern of a mediaeval poem. *In* For Wiktor Weintraub p333-44

Wetherbee, W. The theme of imagination in medieval poetry and the allegorical figure "Genius." *In* Medievalia et humanistica no. 7 p45-64

History and criticism

Gallo, E. The grammarian's rhetoric: the Poetria nova of Geoffrey of Vinsauf. *In* Murphy, J. J. ed. Medieval eloquence p68-84

Kelly, D. Imagination. *In* Kelly, D. Medieval imagination p26-56

Nichols, S. G. A poetics of historicism? Recent trends in medieval literary study. *In* Medievalia et humanistica no. 8 p77-101

Wardropper, B. W. The religious conversion of profane poetry. *In* Studies in the continental background of Renaissance English literature: essays presented to John L. Lievsay p203-22

Poetry, Modern

Simpson, M. A. Death and modern poetry. *In* Feifel, H. [ed.] New meanings of death p313-33

History and criticism

Hough, G. G. The modernist lyric. *In* Hough, G. G. Selected essays p237-47

Luckett, R. 'Meaning motion': old music and some modern writers. *In* English Association. Essays and studies, 1977 p88-97

Nalbantian, S. The philosophical evolution. *In* Nalbantian, S. The symbol of the soul from Hölderlin to Yeats p119-38

Ong, W. J. The poem as a closed field: the once New Criticism and the nature of literature. *In* Ong, W. J. Interfaces of the word p213-29

Snodgrass, W. D. A poem's becoming. *In* Snodgrass, W. D. In radical pursuit p33-62

19th century—History and criticism

Nalbantian, S. The soul concept as a poetic device. *In* Nalbantian, S. The symbol of the soul from Hölderlin to Yeats p 1-12

Nalbantian, S. The stylistic alchemy. *In* Nalbantian, S. The symbol of the soul from Hölderlin to Yeats p100-18

Nalbantian, S. Wordsworth, Hölderlin and their contemporaries: the imperial soul. *In* Nalbantian, S. The symbol of the soul from Hölderlin to Yeats p13-37

20th century—History and criticism

Abrams, M. H. Coleridge, Baudelaire, and modernist poetics. *In* Amacher, R. E. and Lange, V. eds. New perspectives in German literary criticism p150-81

Berryman, J. Robert Lowell and others. *In* Berryman, J. The freedom of the poet p286-96

Holbrook, D. Poetry has lost confidence in itself. *In* Holbrook, D. Lost bearings in English poetry p11-24

Meiners, R. K. On modern poetry, poetic consciousness, and the madness of poets. *In* Evolution of consciousness p106-20

Morgan, E. A glimpse of Petavius. *In* Morgan, E. Essays p3-15

Poetry, Political. See Political poetry

Poetry, Translating of. See Poetry—Translating

Poetry and history. See Literature and history

Poetry and Islam. See Islam and poetry

Poetry and music. See Music and literature

Poetry and religion. See Religion and poetry

Poetry and science. See Literature and science

Poetry and society. See Literature and society

Poets

Shapiro, K. J. The career of the poem. *In* Shapiro, K. J. The poetry wreck p300-22

See also Women poets

Poets, Insane. See Literature and mental illness

Poets, Irish

Eberhart, R. Memory of meeting Yeats, Æ, Gogarty, James Stephens. *In* Eberhart, R. Of poetry and poets p148-52

Poets, Women. See Women poets

Poets in literature

Kinneavy, G. B. Metaphors of the poet and his craft in William Dunbar. *In* Aeolian harps p57-64

Pöggeler, Otto

Being as appropriation. *In* Murray, M. E. ed. Heidegger and modern philosophy p84-115

Poggioli, Renato

The oaten flute

Contents

Poggioli, Renato—*Continued*

About individual works

· The theory of the avant-garde

Howe, I. Endgame: the fate of modernism. *In* Howe, I. Celebrations and attacks p166-69

Pogorelskin, Alexis E.

N. I. Kostomarov and the origins of the Vestnik Evropy circle. *In* Oxford Slavonic papers, new ser. v11 p84-00

Pogue, Forrest Carlisle

The Revolutionary transformation of the art of war. *In* America's continuing revolution p309-29

Pohl, Constance

The "unmaking" of a political film. *In* Peary, G. and Shatzkin, R. eds. The modern American novel and the movies p317-24

Pohl, Reynaldo Galindo. See Galindo Pohl, Reynaldo

Poincaré, Henri

About

Hirosige, T. The ether problem, the mechanistic worldview, and the origins of the theory of relativity. *In* Historical studies in the physical sciences v7 p3-82

Papert, S. A. The mathematical unconscious. *In* Wechsler, J. ed. On aesthetics in science p105-19

Schaffner, K. F. Space and time in Lorentz, Poincaré, and Einstein: divergent approaches to the discovery and development of the special theory of relativity. *In* Motion and time, space and matter p465-507

Poincaré, Jules Henri. See Poincaré, Henri

Poinsot, Juan de Sancto Tomas. See João de Santo Thomaz

La pointe courte (Motion picture)

Truffaut, F. Agnès Varda: La pointe courte. *In* Truffaut, F. The films in my life p308-10

Poirier, Richard

The difficulties of modernism and the modernism of difficulty. *In* Images and ideas in American culture p124-40

About individual works

The performing self

Hartman, G. H. Signs of the times. *In* Hartman, G. H. The fate of reading p303-14

Poirier, William Richard. See Poirier, Richard

Pois, Joseph

Trends in General Accounting Office audits. *In* Smith, B. L. R. ed. The new political economy: the public use of the private sector p245-77

Poisonous plants

Africa

Gilges, W. Some African poison plants and medicines of Northern Rhodesia. *In* The Occasional papers of the Rhodes-Livingstone Museum p389-426

Pokagon, Simon

About individual works

O-gî-mäw-kwĕ mit-gwä-kî (Queen of the woods)

Larson, C. R. Assimilation: estrangement from the land. *In* Larson, C. R. American Indian fiction p34-65

Pokot (African people) See Suks

Polachek, James M.

Gentry hegemony: Soochow in the T'ung-chih restoration. *In* Conflict and control in late imperial China p211-56

Polak, Frederick Lodewijk

Responsibility for the future. *In* Bundy, R. F. ed. Images of the future: the twenty-first century and beyond p9-15

Poland

Church history

Klocowski, J. The Polish church. *In* Callahan, W. J. and Higgs, D. eds. Church and society in Catholic Europe of the eighteenth century p122-37

Williams, G. H. The Sarmatian myth sublimated in the Historia Reformationis Polonicae (1664/1685) of Stanislas Lubieniecki and related documents. *In* For Wiktor Weintraub p571-83

History

Knoll, P. W. Echoes of the New World in the international rivalries of East Central Europe. *In* First images of America p279-84

History—First partition, 1772

Wandycz, P. S. Partitions of Poland and the diplomacy of the partitioning powers: some reflections on the Bicentennial of 1772. *In* For Wiktor Weintraub p559-70

History—Wars of 1918-1921

Lerner, W. Attempting a revolution from without: Poland in 1920. *In* Hammond, T. T. ed. The anatomy of Communist takeovers p94-106

History—Occupation, 1939-1945

Itō, T. The genesis of the Cold war: confrontation over Poland, 1941-44. *In* The Origins of the Cold war in Asia p147-202

Lotarski, S. S. The Communist takeover in Poland. *In* Hammond, T. T. ed. The anatomy of Communist takeovers p339-67

History—1945-

Lotarski, S. S. The Communist takeover in Poland. *In* Hammond, T. T. ed. The anatomy of Communist takeovers p339-67

Politics and government

Kolankiewicz, G. and Taras, R. Poland: socialism for Everyman? *In* Brown, A. H. and Gray, J. eds. Political culture and political change in Communist states p101-30

Social conditions

Kula, W The seigneury and the peasant family in eighteenth-century Poland. *In* Family and society p192-203

Polanski, Roman

About individual works

Macbeth

Jorgens, J. J. Roman Polanski's Macbeth. *In* Jorgens, J. J. Shakespeare on film p161-74

Kauffmann, S. Macbeth. *In* Kauffmann, S. Living images. p90-92

Polanyi, John Charles

The dangers of nuclear war. *In* Griffiths, F. and Polanyi, J. C. eds. The dangers of nuclear war p182-93

Polanyi, Karl

Traders and trade. *In* Ancient civilization and trade p133-54

Polanyi, Karl—*Continued*

About

Dalton, G. Karl Polanyi's analysis of long-distance trade and his wider paradigm. *In* Ancient civilization and trade p63-132

Polanyi, Michael

About

Gelwick, R. Essay 8. *In* Fitzgerald, R. ed. What it means to be human p142-63

Polar expeditions. See Arctic regions

Polar regions. See Arctic regions; South Pole

Polaris (Missile)

Tsipis, K. M. Anti-submarine warfare and missile submarines. *In* The Dynamics of the arms race p36-46

Polarity (in religion, folklore, etc.)

Myerhoff, B. G. Return to Wirikuta: ritual reversal and symbolic continuity on the peyote hunt of the Huichol Indians. *In* Babcock, B. A. ed. The reversible world p225-39

See also Good and evil

Polarity (Philosophy) See Dialectic

Pole, Jack Richon

The American past: is it still usable? *In* Burton, D. H. ed. American history—British historians p27-49

Pole, Reginald, Cardinal

About

Parks, G. B. Italian tributes to Cardinal Pole. *In* Studies in the continental background of Renaissance English literature: essays presented to John L. Lievsay p43-66

Polenberg, Richard

The decline of the New Deal, 1937-1940. *In* Braeman, J.; Bremner, R. H. and Brody, D. eds. The New Deal v 1 p246-66

Poles in the United States

Golab, C. The impact of the industrial experience on the immigrant family: the huddled masses reconsidered. *In* Immigrants in industrial America, 1850-1920 p 1-32

Police

See also Traffic police

Europe

Bayley, D. H. The police and political development in Europe. *In* Tilly, C. ed. The formation of national states in Western Europe p328-79

Great Britain

Martin, J. P. The scope of police manpower studies. *In* Crime, criminology and public policy p197-211

Williams, D. G. T. Prosecution, discretion and the accountability of the police. *In* Crime, criminology and public policy p161-95

Wilson, J. Q. Crime and punishment in England. *In* Tyrrell, R. E. ed. The future that doesn't work p64-94

South Africa

Sachs, A. L. The instruments of domination in South Africa. *In* Thompson, L. M. and Butler, J. eds. Change in contemporary South Africa p223-49

United States

Mann, P. A. Psychology of police organization: reward structure and group dynamics; excerpt from "Psychological consultation with a police department." *In* Armstrong, T. R. and Cinnamon, K. M. eds. Power and authority in law enforcement p104-14

Neff, F. W. and Lubin, B. Observations on power and authority from a training program for police managers. *In* Armstrong, T. R. and Cinnamon, K. M. eds. Power and authority in law enforcement p115-30

Ostrom, E. The design of institutional arrangements and the responsiveness of the police. *In* Rieselbach, L. N. ed. People vs. government: the responsiveness of American institutions p274-99

Skolnick, J. H. The police in protest: National Commission on the Causes and Prevention of Violence (a staff report); excerpt from "The politics of protest." *In* Armstrong, T. R. and Cinnamon, K. M. eds. Power and authority in law enforcement p131-90

Police, International. See International police

Police community relations. See Public relations—Police

Policy, Medical. See Medical policy

Policy sciences

Adams, W. The contribution of economics to public policy formulation. *In* Major social issues p358-69

Bardach, E. Reason, responsibility, and the new social regulation. *In* Burnham, W. D. and Weinberg, M. W. eds. American politics and public policy p364-90

Lipsky, M. Standing the study of public policy implementation on its head. *In* Burnham, W. D. and Weinberg, M. W. eds. American politics and public policy p391-402

Pelz, D. C. Some expanded perspectives on use of social science in public policy. *In* Major social issues p346-57

Rein, M. and Rabinovitz, F. F. Implementation: a theoretical perspective. *In* Burnham, W. D. and Weinberg, M. W. eds. American politics and public policy p307-35

Polier, Justine Wise

Banished children. *In* Gross, B. and Gross, R. eds. The children's rights movement p71-73

Prescriptions for reform: doing what we set out to do? *In* Empey, L. T. ed. Juvenile justice p213-44

Polis (The Greek word)

Tassi, A. Communitas and polis. *In* Roth, R. J. ed. Person and community p133-40

Polish Communist Party. See Communist Party of Poland

Polish drama (Comedy)

History and criticism

Durer, C. S. Molière and Polish comedy. *In* Johnson, R. B.; Neumann, E. S. and Trail, G. T. eds. Molière and the commonwealth of letters: patrimony and posterity p365-78

Polish Laboratory Theater

Kauffmann, S. Grotowski's theater. *In* Kauffmann, S. Persons of the drama p63-72

Polish literature

20th century—History and criticism

Brown, D. B. Czechoslovak and Polish influences on Soviet literature. *In* Szporluk, R. ed. The influence of East Europe and the Soviet West on the USSR p117-46

Krzyżanowski, J. R. Men at war: the Polish version. *In* For Wiktor Weintraub p239-50

Polish question

Wandycz, P. S. Partitions of Poland and the diplomacy of the partitioning powers: some reflections on the Bicentennial of 1772. *In* For Wiktor Weintraub p559-70

Polish-Russian War, 1920-1921. See Poland —History—Wars of 1918-1921

Politian, Angelo. See Poliziano, Angelo

Political affiliation. See Party affiliation

Political atrocities. See Jews—Persecutions

Polish-Russian War, 1920-1921. See Poland poetry

Political ballads and songs, Russian

Sosin, G. Magnitizdat: uncensored songs of dissent. *In* Tokes, R. L. ed. Dissent in the USSR p276-309

Political behavior. See Political psychology; Politics, Practical

Political boundaries. See Boundaries

Political communication. See Communication in politics

Political conventions

Nakamura, R. T. and Sullivan, D. G. Party democracy and democratic control. *In* Burnham, W. D. and Weinberg, M. W. eds. American politics and public policy p26-40

Political corruption in literature. See Corruption (in politics) in literature

Political crimes and offenses

Bassiouni, M. C. The political offense exception in extradition law and practice. *In* International terrorism and political crimes p398-447

Evans, A. E. Aircraft hijacking: what is being done. *In* International terrorism and political crimes p219-47

Kittrie, N. N. Reconciling the irreconcilable: the quest for international agreement over political crime and terrorism. *In* The Year book of world affairs, 1978 p208-36

Lee, A. International suppression of hijacking. *In* International terrorism and political crimes p248-56

Sewell, A. F. Political crime: a psychologist's perspective. *In* International terrorism and political crimes p11-26

Vogler, T. Perspectives on extradition and terrorism. *In* International terrorism and political crimes p391-97

Zlataric, B. History of international terrorism and its legal control. *In* International terrorism and political crimes p474-84

See also Anarchism and anarchists; Assassination; Assaulting a foreign official; Extradition; Impeachments; Terrorism

Political economy. See Economics

Political ethics

Apel, K. O. The conflicts of our time and the problem of political ethics. *In* Dallmayr, F. R. ed. From contract to community p81-101

Benn, S. I. The problematic rationality of political participation. *In* Laslett, P. and Fishkin, J. eds. Philosophy, politics and society p291-312

Diamond, M. Ethics and politics: the American way. *In* The Moral foundations of the American Republic p39-72

Dworkin, G. Paternalism. *In* Laslett, P. and Fishkin, J. eds. Philosophy, politics and society p78-96

Fishkin, J. Tyranny and democratic theory. *In* Laslett, P. and Fishkin, J. eds. Philosophy, politics and society p197-226

Ford, H. P. Politics, ethics, and the arms race. *In* Ethics and nuclear strategy? p51-71

Goldwin, R. A. Of men and angels: a search for morality in the Constitution. *In* The Moral foundations of the American Republic p 1-18

Hofstadter, R. The Founding Fathers: an age of realism; excerpt from "The American political tradition and the men who made it." *In* The Moral foundations of the American Republic p73-85

McWilliams, W. C. On equality as the moral foundation for community. *In* The Moral foundations of the American Republic p183-213

Nagel, T. Ruthlessness in public life. *In* Nagel, T. Mortal questions p75-90

Pateman, C. Political obligation and conceptual analysis. *In* Laslett, P. and Fishkin, J. eds. Philosophy, politics and society p227-56

Shinn, R. L. Realism and ethics in political philosophy. *In* [Truth and tragedy]: a tribute to Hans Morgenthau p95-103

Solzhenitsyn, A. I. Repentance and self-limitation in the life of nations. *In* From under the rubble p105-43

Williams, B. A. O. Politics and moral character. *In* Hampshire, S. ed. Public and private morality p55-73

Winters, F. X. Ethics, diplomacy, and defense. *In* Ethics and nuclear strategy? p14-50

See also Civics; Corruption (in politics); Government, Resistance to; Political crimes and offenses

Political murder. See Assassination

Political offenses. See Political crimes and offenses

Political oratory

Kristol, I. A foolish American ism—utopianism. *In* A Public philosophy reader p73-91

Political participation

Benn, S. I. The problematic rationality of political participation. *In* Laslett, P. and Fishkin, J. eds. Philosophy, politics and society p291-312

Cruise O'Brien, C. Actors, roles, and stages. *In* Smithsonian Institution. The cultural drama p71-85

Fay, B. C. How people change themselves: the relationship between critical theory and its audience. *In* Political theory and praxis p200-33

Lipset, S. M. and Basu, A. Intellectual types and political roles. *In* The Idea of social structure p433-70

Lobkowicz, N. On the history of theory and praxis. *In* Political theory and praxis p13-27

Nichols, R. L. Rebels, beginners, and buffoons: politics as action. *In* Political theory and praxis p159-99

See also Minorities—Political activity; Politics, Practical

China

Baum, R. Politics and the citizen. *In* Terrill, R. ed. The China difference p161-81

France

Tarrow, S. G. and Smith, V. L. Crisis recruitment and the political involvement of local elites: some evidence from Italy and France. *In* Eulau, H. and Czudnowski, M. M. eds. Elite recruitment in democratic polities p205-37

Political participation—*Continued*

Germany, West

Kaltefleiter, W. The recruitment market of the German political elite. *In* Eulau, H. and Czudnowski, M. M. eds. Elite recruitment in democratic polities p239-62

India

Marvick, D. Recruitment patterns of campaign activities in India: legislative candidates, public notables, and the organizational personnel of rival parties. *In* Eulau, H. and Czudnowski, M. M. eds. Elite recruitment in democratic polities p133-62

Pantham, T. The formation of the politically active stratum: evidence from the career origins of party activists in an Indian city. *In* The Making of politicians: studies from Africa and Asia p207-26

Italy

Tarrow, S. G. and Smith, V. L. Crisis recruitment and the political involvement of local elites: some evidence from Italy and France. *In* Eulau, H. and Czudnowski, M. M. eds. Elite recruitment in democratic polities p205-37

Netherlands

Irwin, G. A. Party, accountability and the recruitment of municipal councilmen in the Netherlands. *In* Eulau, H. and Czudnowski, M. M. eds. Elite recruitment in democratic polities p163-204

San Francisco

Irwin, G. A. Party, accountability and the recruitment of municipal councilmen in the Netherlands. *In* Eulau, H. and Czudnowski, M. M. eds. Elite recruitment in democratic polities p163-204

Uganda

Twaddle, M. The politician as agitator in eastern Uganda. *In* The Making of politicians: studies from Africa and Asia p78-92

United States

Burnham, W. D. Revitalization and decay: looking toward the third century of American electoral politics. *In* Havard, W. C. and Bernd, J. L. eds. 200 years of the Republic in retrospect p146-72

Gerson, L. L. Ethnics in American politics. *In* Havard, W. C. and Bernd, J. L. eds. 200 years of the Republic in retrospect p336-46

Kim, Chong Lim; Green, J. J. and Patterson, S. C. Partisanship in the recruitment and performance of American state legislators. *In* Eulau, H. and Czudnowski, M. M. eds. Elite recruitment in democratic polities p79-103

Marvick, D. Continuities in recruitment theory and research: toward a new model. *In* Eulau, H. and Czudnowski, M. M. eds. Elite recruitment in democratic polities p29-44

Political parties

See also Communist parties; Party affiliation; Political conventions; Right and Left (Political science); names of parties, e.g. Democratic Party; and subdivision Politics and government under names of countries, cities, etc., e.g. United States—Politics and government

Arab countries

Kedourie, É. Political parties in the Arab world. *In* Kedourie, É. Arabic political memoirs and other studies p28-58

Europe

Wheaton, M. A. Political parties and government decision-making. *In* Hayward, J. E. S. and Berki, R. N. eds State and society in contemporary Europe p42-57

Great Britain

Miliband, R. A state of desubordination. *In* Kramnick, I. ed. Is Britain dying? p152-65

Rasmussen, J. S. Was Guy Fawkes right? *In* Kramnick, I. ed. Is Britain dying? p97-125

Japan—History

Sims, R. L. National elections and electioneering in Akita Ken, 1930-1942. *In* Modern Japan p89-112

Netherlands

Irwin, G. A. Party, accountability and the recruitment of municipal councilmen in the Netherlands. *In* Eulau, H. and Czudnowski, M. M. eds. Elite recruitment in democratic polities p163-204

San Francisco

Irwin, G. A. Party, accountability and the recruitment of municipal councilmen in the Netherlands. *In* Eulau, H. and Czudnowski, M. M. eds. Elite recruitment in democratic polities p163-204

United States

Burnham, W. D. American politics in the 1970's: beyond party? *In* The American party systems p308-57

Burnham, W. D. Revitalization and decay: looking toward the third century of American electoral politics. *In* Havard, W. C. and Bernd, J. L. eds. 200 years of the Republic in retrospect p146-72

King, M. R. and Seligman, L. G. Critical elections, Congressional recruitment and public policy. *In* Eulau, H. and Czudnowski, M. M. eds. Elite recruitment in democratic polities p263-99

McCall, C. H. Political parties and popular government. *In* Graham, G. J. and Graham, S. G. eds. Founding principles of American government p280-304

Shannon, J. B. Bicentennial reflections on party government. *In* Havard, W. C. and Bernd, J. L. eds. 200 years of the Republic in retrospect p128-45

Political patronage. See Patronage, Political

Political plays. See Theater—Political aspects

Political poetry

History and criticism

Eberhart, R. Poetry and politics. *In* Eberhart, R. Of poetry and poets p86-88

Goodwin, K. L. Invective and obliqueness in political poetry: Kasaipwalova, Brathwaite, and Soyinka. *In* Narasimhaiah, C. D. ed. Awakened conscience p251-60

Thompson, D. Patriotism and politics. *In* Thompson, D. The uses of poetry p112-36

Political poetry, English

History and criticism

Everett, B. The shooting of the bears: poetry and politics in Andrew Marvell. *In* Andrew Marvell p62-103

Glicksberg, C. I. Poetry and radicalism in England. *In* Glicksberg, C. I. The literature of commitment p250-76

Summers, C. J. Herrick's political poetry: the strategies of his art. *In* Rollin, R. B. and Patrick, J. M. eds. "Trust to good verses": Herrick tercentenary essays p171-83

Political poetry, Finnish

History and criticism

Svedberg, I. Political poetry in modern Finnish literature. *In* Dauenhauer, R. and Binham, P. eds. Snow in May p53-57

Political poetry, Russian. See Political ballads and songs, Russian

Political posters, Chilean

Kunzle, D. Art of the new Chile: mural, poster, and comic book in a "revolutionary process." *In* Millon, H. A. and Nochlin, L. eds. Art and architecture in the service of politics p356-81

Political prisoners

Russia

Mihajlov, M. Mystical experiences of the labor camps. *In* Mihajlov, M. Underground notes p169-200

Parry, A. Stalin's Archipelago. *In* Parry, A. Terrorism: from Robespierre to Arafat p187-202

Political psychology

Bay, C. Human needs and political education. *In* Fitzgerald, R. ed. Human needs and politics p 1-25

Czudnowski, M. M. Aspiring and established politicians: the structure of value systems and role profiles. *In* Eulau, H. and Czudnowski, M. M. eds. Elite recruitment in democratic polities p45-78

Feifer, G. No protest: the case of the passive minority. *In* Tokes, R. L. ed. Dissent in the USSR p418-37

Frank, S. L. The ethic of nihilism: a characterization of the Russian intelligentsia's moral outlook. *In* Landmarks p155-84

Girvetz, H. K. An anatomy of violence. *In* Stanage, S. M. ed. Reason and violence p183-204

Knutson, J. N. Human needs constraining political activity. *In* Fitzgerald, R. ed. Human needs and politics p96-123

McInnes, N. The politics of needs—or, Who needs politics? *In* Fitzgerald, R. ed. Human needs and politics p229-43

Renshon, S. A. Human needs and political analysis: an examination of a framework. *In* Fitzgerald, R. ed. Human needs and politics p52-73

Rosen, G. An analgesic strategy. *In* Lauer, R. H. ed. Social movements and social change p97-106

Smith, M. B. Metapsychology, politics, and human needs. *In* Fitzgerald, R. ed. Human needs and politics p124-41

See also Political participation; Political socialization; Public opinion

Political refugees. See Refugees, Political

Political representation. See Representative government and representation

Political rights. See Citizenship; Suffrage

Political satire, English

Hunter, K. M. H. The informing word: verbal strategies in visual satire. *In* Studies in eighteenth-century culture v4 p271-96

Political scandals. See Corruption (in politics)

Political science

Andrew, E. The unity of theory and practice: the science of Marx and Nietzsche. *In* Political theory and praxis p117-37

Aron, R. History and politics. *In* Aron, R. Politics and history p237-48

Bay, C. Essay 7. *In* Fitzgerald, R. ed. What it means to be human p128-41

Berlin, Sir I. Does political theory still exist? *in* Berlin, Sir I. Concepts and categories p143-72

Bernstein, R. J. Hannah Arendt: the ambiguities of theory and practice. *In* Political theory and praxis p141-58

Bishirjian, R. J. The nature of public philosophy. *In* A Public philosophy reader p17-70

Butterfield, Sir H. Global good and evil: the moderate cupidity of Everyman. *In* [Truth and tragedy]: a tribute to Hans Morgenthau p199-202

Cassirer, E. Philosophy and politics. *In* Cassirer, E. Symbol, myth, and culture p219-32

Cassirer, E. The technique of our modern political myths. *In* Cassirer, E. Symbol, myth, and culture p242-67

Condren, C. The quest for a concept of needs. *In* Fitzgerald, R. ed. Human needs and politics p244-60

Cropsey, J. Adam Smith and political philosophy. *In* Skinner, A. S. and Wilson, T. eds. Essays on Adam Smith p132-53

Cuervo, R. F. The definition of public philosophy: Lippmann and Murray. *In* A Public philosophy reader p97-102

Davies, J. C. The development of individuals and the development of politics. *In* Fitzgerald, R. ed. Human needs and politics p74-95

Euben, J. P. Creatures of a day: thought and action in Thucydides. *In* Political theory and praxis p28-56

Fitzgerald, R. The ambiguity and rhetoric of 'need.' *In* Fitzgerald, R. ed. Human needs and politics p195-212

Fuss, P. L. Theory and practice in Hegel and Marx: an unfinished dialogue. *In* Political theory and praxis p97-116

Holbrook, D. Politics and the need for meaning. *In* Fitzgerald, R. ed. Human needs and politics p174-94

Lippmann, W. The good society; excerpt. *In* Crunden, R. M. ed. The superfluous men p238-48

Liska, G. Morgenthau vs. Machiavelli: political realism and power politics. *In* [Truth and tragedy]: a tribute to Hans Morgenthau p104-11

Oakeshott, M. J. Political education. *In* Oakeshott, M. J. Rationalism in politics p111-36

Oakeshott, M. J. Rationalism in politics. *In* Oakeshott, M. J. Rationalism in politics p 1-36

Ostrom, V. The American contribution to a theory of constitutional choice. *In* Havard, W. C. and Bernd, J. L. eds. 200 years of the Republic in retrospect p56-78

Peters, E. M. Pars, parte: Dante and an urban contribution to political thought. *In* The Medieval city p113-40

Shklar, J. N. Politics and the intellect. *In* Studies in eighteenth-century culture v7 p139-51

Political science—*Continued*

Tonsor, S. J. What is the purpose of politics? *In* A Public philosophy reader p267-77

Tsou, Tang. "Scientific man vs. power politics" revisited. *In* [Truth and tragedy]: a tribute to Hans Morgenthau p41-52

Wilhelmsen, F. D. Cicero and the politics of the public orthodoxy. *In* Wilhelmsen, F. D. Christianity and political philosophy p251-59

Wilhelmsen, F. D. Donoso Cortés and the meaning of political power. *In* Wilhelmsen, F. D. Christianity and political philosophy p139-73

Wilhelmsen, F. D. Professor Voegelin and the Christian tradition. *In* Wilhelmsen, F. D. Christianity and political philosophy p193-208

See also Anarchism and anarchists; Authoritarianism; Authority; Autonomy; Bureaucracy; Citizenship; Civics; Civil rights; Clans and clan system; Communication in politics; Communism; Conservatism; Constitutional history; Decision-making in political science; Democracy; Equality; Executive power; Geopolitics; Individualism; Jurisprudence; Liberalism; Liberty; Nationalism; Natural law; Political conventions; Poliitcal crimes and offenses; Political ethics; Political psychology; Political sociology; Politics, Practical; Power (Social sciences); Pressure groups; Public administration; Public opinion; Radicalism; Representative government and representation; Revolutions; Right and Left (Political science); Separation of powers; Social contract; Socialism; Sovereignty; State, The; State governments; Tribal government; Utopias; Village communities; World politics; and subdivision Politics and government under names of countries, states, etc.

History

Coffey, J. W. Hans Morgenthau and the Western political tradition. *In* Coffey, J. W. Political realism in American thought p125-57

Hexter, J. H. Republic, virtue, liberty, and the political universe of J. G. A. Pocock. *In* Hexter, J. H. On historians p255-303

Wright, H. T. Toward an explanation of the origin of the state. *In* Explanation of prehistoric change p215-30

History—China

Rubin, V. A. The theory and practice of a totalitarian state. *In* Rubin, V. A. Individual and state in ancient China p55-87

History—Florence

Hexter, J. H. Republic, virtue, liberty, and the political universe of J. G. A. Pocock. *In* Hexter, J. H. On historians p255-303

History—Great Britain

Pocock, J. G. A. England. *In* National consciousness, history, and political culture in early-modern Europe p98-117

Pocock, J. G. A. Modes of political and historical time in early eighteenth-century England. *In* Studies in eighteenth-century culture v5 p87-102

Thomas, W. The philosophic radicals. *In* Hollis, P. ed. Pressure from without p52-79

Watson, G. Acton's 'History of liberty.' *In* Watson, G. Politics and literature in modern Britain p153-72

History—Italy

Gilbert, F. Italy. *In* National consciousness, history, and political culture in early modern Europe p21-42

History—United States

Coffey, J. W. Epilogue: faith, reason, and the scientific method. *In* Coffey, J. W. Political realism in American thought p159-70

Kelly, A. H. American political leadership: the optimistic ethical world view and the Jeffersonian synthesis. *In* Library of Congress Symposia on the American Revolution, 3d, 1974. Leadership in the American Revolution p7-39

Methodology

Strong, T. B. Dramaturgical discourse and political enactments: toward an artistic foundation for political space. *In* Brown, R. H. and Lyman, S. M. eds. Structure, conciousness, and history p237-60

Thrupp, S. L. Diachronic methods in comparative politics. *In* Thrupp, S. L. Society and history p309-27

Research

See Political science research

Study and teaching

Bay, C. Human needs and political education. *In* Fitzgerald, R. ed. Human needs and politics p 1-25

Niemeyer, G. The commitments of political education. *In* A Public philosophy reader p246-56

Oakeshott, M. J. Political education. *In* Oakeshott, M. J. Rationalism in politics p111-36

Oakeshott, M. J. The study of 'politics' in a university. *In* Oakeshott, M. J. Rationalism in politics p301-33

Ricoeur, P. The tasks of the political educator. *In* Ricoeur, P. Political and social essays p271-93

Study and teaching—United States

Dunner, J. On the condition of political science. *In* Hook, S.; Kurtz, P. W. and Todorovich, M. eds. The philosophy of the curriculum: the need for general education p253-55

Study and teaching (Secondary)—United States

Caplow, T. How many books? *In* From Parnassus p66-74

Diamond, M. Teaching about politics as a vocation. *In* Hook, S.; Kurtz, P. and Todorovich, M. eds. The ethics of teaching and scientific research p3-22

Miller, A. H. The ethics of teaching political science: another perspective. *In* Hook, S.; Kurtz, P. and Todorovich, M. eds. The ethics of teaching and scientific research p43-48

United States

Bishirjian, R. J. The nature of public philosophy. *In* A Public philosophy reader p17-70

Murray, J. C. The civilization of the pluralist society; excerpt from "We hold these truths: Catholic reflections on the American proposition." *In* A Public philosophy reader p143-51

Political science—United States—*Continued*

Murray, J. C. Two cases for the public consensus; excerpt from "We hold these truths: Catholic reflections on the American proposition." *In* A Public philosophy reader p103-11

Nisbet, R. A. Public opinion versus popular opinion. *In* A Public philosophy reader p169-97

Political science research

Latin America

Kaufman, C. L. Political science. *In* Quantitative social science research on Latin America p162-207

United States

Baar, C. Judicial behavior and comparative rights policy. *In* Claude, R. P. ed. Comparative human rights p353-81

Political socialization

Cutler, N. E. Toward a generational conception of political socialization. *In* Schwartz, D. C. and Schwartz, S. K. eds. New directions in political socialization p254-88

Pollock, J. C. Early socialization and elite behavior. *In* Schwartz, D. C. and Schwartz, S. K. eds. New directions in political socialization p203-26

Renshon, S. A. Birth order and political socialization. *In* Schwartz, D. C. and Schwartz, S. K. eds. New directions in political socialization p69-95

Renshon, S. A. The role of personality development in political socialization. *In* Schwartz, D. C. and Schwartz, S. K. eds. New directions in political socialization p29-68

Rohter, I. S. A social-learning approach to political socialization. *In* Schwartz, D. C. and Schwartz, S. K. eds. New directions in political socialization p129-62

Rosenau, N. The sources of children's political concepts: an application of Piaget's theory. *In* Schwartz, D. C. and Schwartz, S. K. eds. New directions in political socialization p163-87

Schwartz, D. C. and Mannella, C. J. Popular music as an agency of political socialization: a study in popular culture and politics. *In* Schwartz, D. C. and Schwartz, S. K. eds. New directions in political socialization p289-316

Schwartz, D. C.; Garrison, J. and Alouf, J. Health, body images, and political socialization. *In* Schwartz, D. C. and Schwartz, S. K. eds. New directions in political socialization p96-126

Schwartz, S. K. Patterns of cynicism: differential political socialization among adolescents. *In* Schwartz, D. C. and Schwartz, S. K. eds. New directions in political socialization p188-202

Schwartz, S. K. Preschoolers and politics. *In* Schwartz, D. C. and Schwartz, S. K. eds. New directions in political socialization p229-53

Political sociology

Bell, D. Ethnicity and social change. *In* Glazer, N. and Moynihan, D. P. eds. Ethnicity p141-74

Fay, B. C. How people change themselves: the relationship between critical theory and its audience. *In* Political theory and praxis p200-33

Strong, T. B. Dramaturgical discourse and political enactments: toward an artistic foundation for political space. *In* Brown, R. H. and Lyman, S. M. eds. Structure, consciousness, and history p237-60

See also Political participation; Political socialization

Political violence. See Assassination; Revolutions; Terrorism; Violence

Politicians. See Women in politics

Politics. See Political science; Politics, Practical

Politics, Practical

Gusfield, J. R. A dramatistic theory of status politics; excerpt from "Symbolic crusade". *In* Davis, F. J. and Stivers, R. eds. The collective definition of deviance p22-39

Tonsor, S. J. What is the purpose of politics? *In* A Public philosophy reader p267-77

See also Aged—Political activity; Business and politics; Lobbying; Political participation; Politics and education; Voting

Psychological aspects

See Political psychology

Politics and architecture. See Architecture and state

Politics and children. See Children and politics

Politics and Christianity. See Christianity and politics

Politics and education

Bickel, A. M. The aims of education and the proper standards of the university. *In* Universities in the Western world p3-11

Dahrendorf, R. The educational class. *In* Universities in the Western world p47-57

Giner, S. Power, freedom and social change in the Spanish university, 1939-75. *In* Preston, P. ed. Spain in crisis p183-211

Kolakowski, L. Neutrality and academic values. *In* Montefiore, A. ed. Neutrality and impartiality p72-85

Taylor, C. Neutrality in the university. *In* Montefiore, A. ed. Neutrality and impartiality p128-48

Ten, C. L. Politics in the academe. *In* Montefiore, A. ed. Neutrality and impartiality p149-64

Weinstein, W. L. The academic and the political. *In* Montefiore, A. ed. Neutrality and impartiality p165-95

Politics and labor unions. See Trade unions—Political activity

Politics and law. See Law and politics

Politics and literature

Achebe, C. The African writer and the Biafran cause. *In* **Achebe, C. Morning yet on creation day p137-47**

Crews, F. C. Do literary studies have an ideology? *In* **Crews, F. C. Out of my system p105-20**

Cruise O'Brien, C. Actors, roles, and stages. *In* Smithsonian Institution. The cultural drama p71-85

Glicksberg, C. I. Albert Camus: art versus politics. *In* Glicksberg, C. I. The literature of commitment p236-49

Glicksberg, C. I. André Malraux: tragic humanism and the political imperative. *In* Glicksberg, C. I. The literature of commitment p208-21

Politics in literature—*Continued*

Dolan, P. J. Dostoyevsky: the political gospel. *In* Dolan, P. J. Of war and war's alarms p36-69

Dolan, P. J. Hawthorne: the politics of puberty. *In* Dolan, P. J. Of war and war's alarms p16-35

Dolan, P. J. James: the aesthetics of politics. *In* Dolan, P. J. Of war and war's alarms p70-95

Dolan, P. J. Kafka: the political machine. *In* Dolan, P. J. Of war and war's alarms p125-44

Dolan, P. J. The lamps of Europe. *In* Dolan, P. J. Of war and war's alarms p 1-15

Dolan, P. J. Mann: art, politics, and the apocalypse. *In* Dolan, P. J. Of war and war's alarms p145-80

Glicksberg, C. I. George Orwell and the morality of politics. *In* Glicksberg, C. I. The literature of commitment p289-318

Gurr, A. J. 'Coriolanus' and the body politic. *In* Shakespeare survey 28 p63-69

Heffernan, J. A. W. Politics and freedom: refractions of Blake in Joyce Cary and Allen Ginsberg. *In* Bornstein, G. ed. Romantic and modern p177-95

Henn, T. R. The weasel's tooth. *In* Henn, T. R. Last essays p26-50

Kelly, G. Conclusion. *In* Kelly, G. The English Jacobin novel, 1780-1805 p261-69

Kelly, G. Introduction. *In* Kelly, G. The English Jacobin novel, 1780-1805 p 1-19

Lessing. D. M. The small personal voice. *In* Lessing, D. M. A small personal voice p3-21

Levin, A. A. Andrey Bely, M. O. Gershenzon, and Vekhi: a rejoinder to N. Valentinov. *In* Janecek, G. ed. Andrey Bely p169-80

Lloyd, T. Browning and politics. *In* **Armstrong, I. ed. Robert Browning** p142-67

Rance, N. Popular politics in George Eliot's historical novels of the 1860s. *In* Rance, N. The historical novel and popular politics in nineteenth-century England p102-36

Schonhorn, M. Defoe: the literature of politics and the politics of some fictions. *In* English literature in the age of disguise p15-56

Sterrenburg, L. W. Mary Shelley's monster: politics and psyche in Frankenstein. *In* Levine, G. L. and Knoepflmacher, U. C. eds. The endurance of Frankenstein p143-71

Stineback, D. C. Visiting the "engine-room": Henry Adams's Democracy. *In* Stineback, D. C. Shifting world p61-74

Taylor, A. Shelley's political enchantments. *In* Taylor, A. Magic and English romanticism p184-220

Terdiman, R. Flaubert and after: failure formalized. *In* Terdiman, R. The dialectics of isolation p60-95

Tomlinson, T. B. Love and politics in the English novel, 1840s-1860s. *In* Tomlinson, T. B. The English middle-class novel p69-82

Zwicker, S. N. Politics and panegyric: the figural mode from Marvell to Pope. *In* Miner, E. R. ed. Literary uses of typology p115-46

See also Communism in literature; Political poetry

Politics in motion pictures

Comolli, J. L. and Narboni, J. Cinema/ideology/criticism. *In* Nichols, B. ed. Movies and methods p22-30

Monaco, J. Godard: Returning to zero (picture and act). *In* Monaco, J. The New Wave p187-212

Monaco, J. Godard: Theory and practice: the Dziga-Vertov period. *In* Monaco, J. The New Wave p213-52

Solanas, F. and Gettino, O. Towards a third cinema. *In* Nichols, B. ed. Movies and methods p44-64

Poliziano, Angelo

About individual works
Miscellaneorum centuria secunda

Gilbert, F. History and philology: Politian. *In* Gilbert, F. History p379-86

Polk, Noel Earl

Water, wanderers, and weddings: love in Eudora Welty. *In* Dollarhide, L. and Abadie, A. J. eds. Eudora Welty: a form of thanks p95-122

Pollack, Gerald Alexander

The economic consequences of the energy crisis. *In* Bundy, W. P. ed. The world economic crisis p120-39

Pollack, H. See Vachon, M. L. S. jt. auth.

Pollack, Jonathan D.

Sino-Soviet relations. *In* Kirk, G. L. and Wessell, N. H. eds. The Soviet threat p30-46

Pollard, Braxton

International advertising: practical considerations. *In* Fischer, H. D. and Merrill, J. C. eds. International and intercultural communication p286-96

Pollard, David E.

Ch'i in Chinese literary theory. *In* Chinese approaches to literature from Confucius to Liang Ch'i-ch'ai p43-66

Chou Tso-jen: a scholar who withdrew. *In* The Limits of change p332-56

Pollination. See Fertilization of plants

Pollman, Jim

CB radio as icon. *In* Browne, R. B. and Fishwick, M. W. eds. Icons of America p161-76

Pollock, Jean-Yves

Trace theory and French syntax. *In* Keyser, S. J. ed. Recent transformational studies in European languages p65-112

Pollock, John C.

Early socialization and elite behavior. *In* Schwartz, D. C. and Schwartz, S. K. eds. New directions in political socialization p203-26

Pollock, John C.; White, Dan, and Gold, Frank

When soldiers return: combat and political alienation among white Vietnam veterans. *In* Schwartz, D. C. and Schwartz, S. K. eds. New directions in political socialization p317-33

Pollution

Thring, M. W. Physical and chemical aspects of pollution. *In* Against pollution and hunger p63-88

See also Pollution control industry; Refuse and refuse disposal

Economic aspects

McKean, R. N. Property rights, pollution, and power. *In* Capitalism and freedom p92-111

Rothenberg, J. The physical environment. *In* McKie, J. W. ed. Social responsibility and the business predicament p191-215

Economic aspects—United States

Commoner, B. Energy, environment, and economics. *In* Eppen, G. D. ed. Energy: the policy issues p25-40

Pontius Pilate in literature

Weimann, R. The mystery cycles. *In* Weimann, R. Shakespeare and the popular tradition in the theater: studies in the social dimension of dramatic form and function p49-97

Ponty, Jacques Merleau- See Merleau-Ponty, Jacques

Ponty, Maurice Merleau- See Merleau-Ponty, Maurice

Pool, Edward Humphrey Lane- See Lane-Pool, Edward Humphrey

Pool, Ithiel de Sola

Technology and policy in the information age. *In* Lerner, D. and Nelson, L. M. eds. Communication research—a half-century appraisal p261-79

Pool, Ithiel de Sola, and others

Foresight and hindsight: the case of the telephone. *In* The Social impact of the telephone p127-57

Poole, Ernest

About

Goist, P. D. Alternative perspective: the "radical" journalism of Hutchins Hapgood and Ernest Poole. *In* Goist, P. D. From Main Street to State Street p94-109

Poole, Roger

Essay 9. *In* Fitzgerald, R. ed. What it means to be human p164-85

Poon, David Jim-tat

Tatzepao: its history and significance as a communication medium. *In* Chu, G. C. ed. Popular media in China p184-221

Poor

Friedlaender, A. F. Absolute poverty and macroeconomic activity. *In* Inflation, trade and taxes p194-217

Matza, D. The disreputable poor. *In* Davis, F. J. and Stivers, R. eds. The collective definition of deviance p197-221

See also Labor and laboring classes; Population; also subdivision Poor under names of cities, e.g. Bordeaux—Poor

Health and hygiene

Goulet, D. World health and world hunger: putting development ethics to the test. *In* Cahill, K. M. ed. Health and development p83-101

Medical care

See Poor—Health and hygiene

England—History

Marcus, S. Their brothers' keepers: an episode from English history. *In* Doing good p39-66

United States

Chilman, C. S. The poor. *In* Gochros, H. L. and Gochros, J. S. eds. The sexually oppressed p202-12

Muth, R. F. Economic policy and urban problems. *In* Capitalism and freedom p158-82

Poor laws

England

Marcus, S. Their brothers' keepers: an episode from English history. *In* Doing good p39-66

Poor priests. See Lollards

Pop art

Kurz, P. K. Beat—Pop—underground. *In* Kurz, P. K. On modern German literature v4 p202-41

Pope, Alexander

About

Adams, P. G. "Music resembles poetry": the auditory appeal of Pope's meter. *In* Adams, P. G. Graces of harmony p87-117

Cohen, R. Pope's meanings and the strategies of interrelation. *In* English literature in the age of disguise p101-30

Mack, M. Pope's copy of Chaucer. *In* Evidence in literary scholarship p105-21

McLaverty, J. Lawton Gilliver: Pope's bookseller. *In* Virginia. University. Bibliographical Society. Studies in bibliography v32 p101-24

Manlove, C. N. Pope. *In* Literature and reality, 1600-1800 p76-98

Partridge, A. C. Form and language in English neo-classical poetry. *In* An English miscellany p131-48

Simonsuuri, K. Pope's view of Homer: 'fire' and invention. *In* Simonsuuri, K. Homer's original genius p57-64

Trowbridge, F. H. Pope, Gay, and The shepherd's week. *In* Trowbridge, F. H. From Dryden to Jane Austen p124-34

Williams, A. L. What Pope did to Donne. *In* A Provision of human nature p111-19

Williams, K. The moralized song: some Renaissance themes in Pope. *In* ELH essays for Earl R. Wasserman p285-308

Zwicker, S. N. Politics and panegyric: the figural mode from Marvell to Pope. *In* Miner, E. R. ed Literary uses of typology p115-46

About individual works

The Dunciad

Cunningham, J. S. Pope, Eliot, and 'The mind of Europe.' *In* The Waste land in different voices p67-85

Maresca, T. E. Pope. *In* Maresca, T. E. Epic to novel p79-131

Eloisa to Abelard

Trowbridge, F. H. Pope's Eloisa and the Heroides of Ovid. *In* Trowbridge, F. H. From Dryden to Jane Austen p135-53

Epistle to Bathhurst

Feingold, R. The good society and the bucolic mode: Virgil and Pope. *In* Feingold, R. Nature and society p19-49

Epistle to Burlington

Feingold, R. The good society and the bucolic mode: Virgil and Pope. *In* Feingold, R. Nature and society p19-49

Epistle to Dr Arbuthnot

Olson, E. Rhetoric and the appreciation of Pope. *In* Olson, E. On value judgments in the arts, and other essays p15-35

An essay on man

Barbeau, A. T. The wild and the garden: a double focus on reality in Pope's An essay on man. *In* Tennessee Studies in literature v22 p73-84

An essay on man (Epistle I)

Trilling, L. An essay on man: Epistle I. *In* Trilling, L. Prefaces to The experience of literature p206-14

The First satire of the Second book of Horace, imitated

Grundy, I. Verses address'd to the imitator of Horace: a skirmish between Pope and some persons of rank and fortune. *In* Virginia. University. Bibliographical Society. Studies in bibliography v30 p96-119

Pope, Alexander—About individual works
—*Continued*

The rape of the lock

Brower, R. A. From the Iliad to Jane Austen, via The rape of the lock. *In* Halperin, J. ed. Jane Austen p43-60

Same as: Brower, R. A. From the Illiad to the novel via The rape of the lock. *In* Brower, R. A. mirror on mirror p77-95

Brower, R. A. From the Iliad to the novel, via The rape of the lock. *In* Brower, R. A. Mirror on mirror p77-95

Same as: Brower, R. A. From the Illiad to Jane Austen, via The rape of the lock. *In* Halperin,, J. ed. Jane Austen p43-60

Dyson, A. E. and Lovelock, J. In spite of all her art: Pope's The rape of the lock. *In* Dyson, A. E. and Lovelock, J. Masterful images p97-123

Maresca, T. E. Pope. *In* Maresca, T. E. Epic to novel p79-131

Wimsatt, W. K. Belinda ludens. *In* Wimsatt, W. K. Day of the leopards p99-116

Windsor Forest

MacKellar, W. On two English metamorphoses. *In* Poetry and poetics from ancient Greece to the Renaissance p207-17

Influence—Byron

England, A. B. The style of Don Juan and Augustan poetry. *In* Jump, J. D. ed. Byron p94-112

Language

Sherbo, A. Pope. *In* Sherbo, A. English poetic diction from Chaucer to Wordsworth p132-57

Library

Mack, M. Pope's books: a biographical survey with a finding list. *In* English literature in the age of disguise p209-305

Portraits, etc.

Riely, J. C. and Wimsatt, W. K. A supplement to the portraits of Alexander Pope. *In* Evidence in literary scholarship p123-64

Style

Sherbo, A. Pope. *In* Sherbo, A. English poetic diction from Chaucer to Wordsworth p132-57

Pope, Alexander, tr.

About individual works

The Iliad

Brower, R. A. Pope's Iliad for twentieth-century readers. *In* Brower, R. A. Mirror on mirror p55-76

Hodgart, M. J. C. The subscription list for Pope's Iliad, 1715. *In* The Dress of words p25-34

Pope, John Collins

Second thoughts on the interpretation of The seafarer. *In* Anglo-Saxon England 3 p75-86

Pope, Robert G.

The myth of declension. *In* Mulder, J. M. and Wilson, J. F. eds. Religion in American history p45-56

New England versus the New England mind: the myth of declension. *In* Vaughan, A. T. and Bremer, F. J. eds. Puritan New England p314-25

Pope-Hennessy, James

About individual works

Anthony Trollope

Mudrick, M. Trollope. *In* Mudrick, M. The man in the machine p97-109

Monckton Milnes

Trilling, L. Profession: man of the world. *In* Trilling, L. A gathering of fugitives p115-25

Pope-Hennessy, Richard James Arthur. See Pope-Hennessy, James

Popes

Infallibility

Izbicki, T. M. Infallibility and the erring pope: Guido Terreni and Johannes de Turrecremata. *In* Law, church, and society p97-111

Temporal power

McCready, W. D. Papalists and antipapalists: aspects of the church/state controversy in the later Middle Ages. *In* Viator: medieval and Renaissance studies v6 p241-73

Pennington, K. J. Pope Innocent III's views on church and state: a gloss to Per venerabilem. *In* Law, church, and society p49-67

Popkin, Richard Henry

The development of religious scepticism and the influence of Isaac La Peyrère's pre-Adamism and Bible criticism. *In* Classical influences on European culture A.D. 1500-1700 p271-80

La Peyrère, the Abbé Grégoire, and the Jewish question in the eighteenth century. *In* Studies in eighteenth-century culture v4 p209-22

The philosophical bases of modern racism. *In* Philosophy and the civilizing arts p126-65

The pre-Adamite theory in the Renaissance. *In* Philosophy and humanism p50-69

Spinoza and La Peyrère. *In* Shahan, R. W. and Biro, J. I. eds. Spinoza: new perspectives p 175-95

Poplavskiĭ, Boris Iŭlianovich

About

Karlinsky, S. In search of Poplavsky: a collage. *In* The Bitter air of exile p311-33

Olcott, A. Poplavsky: the heir presumptive of Montparnasse. *In* The Bitter air of exile p274-88

Poplavsky, Boris. See Poplavskiĭ, Boris Iŭlianovich

Popovic, Nenad D.

Yugoslavia's crucial place in world politics. *In* Kaplan, M. A. ed. The many faces of communism p266-78

Popper, Sir Karl Raimund

The myth of the framework. *In* The Abdication of philosophy: philosophy and the public good p23-48

The rationality of scientific revolutions. *In* Harré, R. ed. Problems of scientific revolution p72-101

Scientific reduction and the essential incompleteness of all science. *In* Ayala, F. J. and Dobzhansky, T. G. eds. Studies in the philosophy of biology p259-83

About

Albert, H. The myth of total reason: dialectical claims in the light of undialectical criticism. *In* Giddens, A. ed. Positivism and sociology p157-94

Popper, Sir Karl R.—About—*Continued*

Habermas, J. Rationalism divided in two: a reply to Albert. *In* Giddens, A. ed. Positivism and sociology p195-223

Quinton, A. Karl Popper: politics without essences. *In* De Crespigny, A. and Minogue, K. R. eds. Contemporary political philosophers p147-67

Wilson, H. T. Science, critique, and criticism: the "open society" revisited. *In* O'Neill, J. ed. On critical theory p205-30

About individual works

Conjectures and refutations

Bronowski, J. Humanism and the growth of knowledge. *In* Bronowski, J. A sense of the future p74-103

The logic of scientific discovery

Bronowski, J. Humanism and the growth of knowledge. *In* Bronowski, J. A sense of the future p74-103

Pops, Martin Leonard

Melville: to him, Olson. *In* Boyers, R. ed. Contemporary poetry in America p189-220

Popular arts. See Popular culture

Popular culture

Barbu, Z. Popular culture: a sociological approach. *In* Bigsby, C. W. E. ed. Approaches to popular culture p39-68

Bigsby, C. W. E. Europe, America and the cultural debate. *In* Bigsby, C. W. E. Superculture p 1-27

Chaney, D. C. and Chaney, J. H. The audience for mass leisure. *In* Fischer, H. D. and Melnik, S. R. eds. Entertainment: a cross-cultural examination p129-43

Craig, D. Marxism and popular culture. *In* Bigsby, C. W. E. ed. Approaches to popular culture p129-49

Fiedler, L. Elite literature and mass society. *In* Mann, D. A. ed. The arts in a democratic society p118-39

Fiedler, L. A. Towards a definition of popular literature. *In* Bigsby, C. W. E. Superculture p28-42

Filler, L. Introduction: a question of quality. *In* Filler, L. ed. A question of quality: popularity and value in modern creative writing p 1-7

Fishwick, M. W. The thingness of things. *In* Essays in honor of Russel B. Nye p65-73

Goodlad, S. Mass entertainment in perspective: the need for a theory of the middle range. *In* Fischer, H. D. and Melnik, S. R. eds. Entertainment: a cross-cultural examination p120-28

Hodge, R. W. Linguistics and popular culture. *In* Bigsby, C. W. E. ed. Approaches to popular culture p107-28

Kato, H. Popular culture. *In* Lerner, D. and Nelson, L. M. eds. Communication research—a half-century appraisal p242-53

Kress, G. R. Structuralism and popular culture. *In* Bigsby, C. W. E. ed. Approaches to popular culture p85-106

McLuhan, H. M. The implications of cultural uniformity. *In* Bigsby, C. W. E. Superculture p43-56

Mann, D. A. Conclusions. *In* Mann, D. A. ed. The arts in a democratic society p140-50

Mann, D. A. Introduction: the arts in a democratic society. *In* Mann, D. A. The arts in a democratic society p 3-18

Payne, H. C. Elite versus popular mentality in the eighteenth century. *In* Studies in eighteenth-century culture v8 p3-32

Schmidt, J. Humanism and popular culture. *In* Hoffmeister, G. ed. The Renaissance and Reformation in Germany p177-88

See also Popular literature; Street literature; also subdivision Popular culture under names of countries, cities, etc. e.g. United States—Popular culture

History

Burke, P. Oblique approaches to the history of popular culture. *In* Bigsby, C. W. E. ed. Approaches to popular culture p69-84

Political aspects

Bigsby, C. W. E. The politics of popular culture. *In* Bigsby, C. W. E. ed. Approaches to popular culture p3-25

Psychological aspects

Homans, P. The uses and limits of psychobiography as an approach to popular culture: the case of 'the Western.' *In* Reynolds, F. E. and Capps, D. eds. The biographical process p297-316

Popular literature

History and criticism

Cawelti, J. G. Literary formulas and their cultural significance. *In* Luedtke, L. S. ed. The study of American culture p177-217

Social aspects

Kaupp, P. The misunderstood best-seller: the social function of entertainment literature. *In* Fischer, H. D. and Melnik, S. R. eds. Entertainment: a cross-cultural examination p234-46

Hongkong

Mäding, K. Popular literature in dependent society: the case of colonial Hong Kong. *In* Fischer, H. D. and Melnik, S. R. eds. Entertainment: a cross-cultural examination p180-89

Popular music. See Music, Popular (Songs, etc.)

Popular songs. See Music, Popular (Songs, etc.)

Popular Unity. See Unidad Popular

Population

Burton, R. G. A philosopher looks at the population bomb. *In* Philosophy & environmental crisis p105-16

Engelhardt, H. T. Individuals and communities, present and future: towards a morality in a time of famine. *In* Lucas, G. R. and Ogletree, T. W. eds. Lifeboat ethics p70-83

Guillaumont, P. The optimum rate of population growth. *In* Economic factors in population growth p29-62

Hardin, G. J. Carrying capacity as an ethical concept. *In* Lucas, G. R. and Ogletree, T. W. eds. Lifeboat ethics p120-37

Hilton, A. M. Against pollution and hunger: environment and development. *In* Against pollution and hunger p27-59

Hinds, S. W. On the relations of medical triage to world famine: an historical survey. *In* Lucas, G. R. and Ogletree, T. W. eds. Lifeboat ethics p29-51

Huxley, A. L. The population explosion. *In* Huxley, A. L. The Human situation p42-58

Leridon, H. The role of economic factors in birth-rate trends and fluctuations. *In* Economic factors in population growth p179-97

Population—*Continued*

McNamara, R. S. The world population problem. *In* World change and world security p117-58

Meadows, D. H. Food and population: policies for the United States. *In* Baldwin, D. A. ed. America in an interdependent world p163-220

Ohlin, G. Economic theory confronts population growth. *In* Economic factors in population growth p3-16

Schultz, T. P. Determinants of fertility: a micro-economic model of choice. *In* Economic factors in population growth p89-124

See also Birth control; Demography; Malthusianism; Man—Migrations; Mortality; Population forecasting; Population policy; and subdivision Population under names of countries, cities, etc., e.g. Russia—Population

Law and legislation—United States
Brown, P. G. and Corfman, E. L. Moral-political values: an historical analysis. *In* Population policy and ethics p55-126

Research
See Population research

Population forecasting
Clinton, R. L. Population dynamics and future prospects for development. *In* Orr, D. W. and Soroos, M. S. eds. The global predicament p56-74

Guillaumont, P. The optimum rate of population growth. *In* Economic factors in population growth p29-62

McFarland, D. D. The aged in the 21st century: a demographer's view. *In* Jarvik, L. F. ed. Aging into the 21st century p5-22

India
Parikh, K. S. India in 2001. *In* Economic factors in population growth p303-23

United States
Ridker, R. G. Population growth, economic growth and the environment in the United States. *In* Economic factors in population growth p324-51

Population genetics
Murray, R. F. The perspective of the population geneticist. *In* Population policy and ethics p365-75

Mathematical models
Provine, W. B. The role of mathematical population geneticists in the evolutionary synthesis of the 1930s and 1940s. *In* Studies in history of biology v2 p167-92

Terminology
Adams, M. B. From "gene fund" to "gene pool": on the evolution of evolutionary language. *In* Studies in history of biology v3 p241-85

Population geography. See Residential mobility

Population policy
Leridon, H. The role of economic factors in birth-rate trends and fluctuations. *In* Economic factors in population growth p179-97

Sauvy, A. The optimal change of a population. *In* Economic factors in population growth p63-73

Stolnitz, G. J. International migration policies: some demographic and economic contexts. *In* Human migration p307-16

Veatch, R. M. An ethical analysis of population policy proposals. *In* Population policy and ethics p445-75

Veatch, R. M. Justice. *In* Population policy and ethics p31-39

Warwick, D. P. Freedom. *In* Population policy and ethics p17-29

Zolberg, A. R. International migration policies in a changing world system. *In* Human migration p241-86

See also Birth control; and subdivision Population policy under countries, e.g. United States—Population policy

Moral and religious aspects
Dyck, A. J. Religious views. *In* Population policy and ethics p277-323

Population projections. See Population forecasting

Population research
O'Rourke, J. F. and Chevan, A. A factorial ecology of age groups in the United States, 1960. *In* Gubrium, J. F. ed. Late life p32-58

Sauvy, A. The optimal change of a population. *In* Economic factors in population growth p63-73

Stone, J. R. N. Demographic variables in the economics of education. *In* Economic factors in population growth p521-52

Israel
Ben Porath, Y. Fertility in Israel: a mini-survey and some new findings. *In* Economic factors in population growth p136-72

Sweden
Akerman, S. and Norberg, A. Employment opportunities, family-building and internal migration in the late nineteenth century: some Swedish case studies. *In* Economic factors in population growth p453-86

Populism

Latin America
Hennessy, C. A. M. Fascism and Populism in Latin America. *In* Laqueur, W. Z. ed. Fascism: a reader's guide p255-94

Russia
Berlin, Sir I. Russian Populism. *In* Berlin, Sir I. Russian thinkers p210-37

Parry, A. Hunting the Tsar. *In* Parry, A. Terrorism: from Robespierre to Arafat p107-19

Porada, Edith
Some thoughts on the audience reliefs of Persepolis. *In* Studies in classical art and archaeology p37-43

Porat, Yehoshua
The Palestinian-Arab nationalist movement. *In* The Palestinians p121-27

Porath, Yoram Ben. See Ben Porath, Yoram

Porcelain, Sèvres. See Sèvres porcelain

Porkert, Manfred
Chinese medicine: a traditional healing science. *In* Sobel, D. S. ed. Ways of health p147-72

Pornography
Dawidowicz, L. S. Smut and anti-Semitism. *In* Dawidowicz, L. S. The Jewish presence p216-24

Lodge, D. William Burroughs: 'The naked lunch.' *In* Lodge, D. The modes of modern writing p35-38

Sheed, W. Dirty business. *In* Sheed, W. The good word & other words p82-85

See also Literature, Immoral; Obscenity (Law); Sex in moving-pictures

Pornography in motion pictures. See Sex in moving picture

Porte, Joel
Emerson in 1838: essaying to be. *In* Studies in biography p183-99

Porter, Cole

About

Sheed, W. Rhapsodist in blue. *In* Sheed, W. The good word & other words p154-58

Porter, David Hugh
The recurrent motifs of Horace, Carmina IV. *In* Harvard Studies in classical philology v79 p189-228

Porter, Hal

About individual works

The paper chase

Lawson, A. "Where a man belongs": Hal Porter's The paper chase and George Johnston's Clean straw for nothing. *In* Hamliton, K. G. ed. Studies in the recent Australian novel p168-93

Porter, John A.
Ethnic pluralism in Canadian perspective. *In* Glazer, N. and Moynihan, D. P. eds. Ethnicity p267-304

Porter, John R.
Melting pot or mosaic: revolution or reversion? *In* Perspectives on revolution and evolution p152-79

Porter, Katherine Anne

About

Gray, R. J. Back to the old plantation: the recovery and reexamination of a dream. *In* Gray, R. J. The literature of memory p150-96

Morris, W. Katherine Anne Porter. *In* Morris, W. Earthly delights, unearthly adornments p105-11

Welty, E. Katherine Anne Porter: the eye of the story. *In* Welty, E. The eye of the story p30-40

West, R. B. Katherine Anne Porter. *In* Howard, M. ed. Seven American women writers of the twentieth century p122-65

Characters—Women

Carson, B. H. Winning: Katherine Anne Porter's women. *In* Diamond, A. and Edward, L. R. eds. The authority of experience p239-56

Porter, Mary Cornelia
That commerce shall be free: a new look at the old laissez-faire Court. *In* The Supreme Court review, 1976 p135-59

Porter, Mary Gray
On redefining-oriented. *In* James B. McMillan: essays in linguistics by his friends and colleagues p163-80

Porter, Melinda Camber
The use of structure in the plays. *In* Prentki, T. ed. Francis Warner p32-38

Porter, Peter

About

Thurley, G. The legacy of Auden: the poetry of Roy Fuller, Philip Larkin and Peter Porter. *In* Thurley, G. The ironic harvest p137-62

Porter, Philip Wayland, and Lukermann, Fred E.
The geography of Utopia. *In* Geographies of the mind p197-223

Porter, Raymond J.
The Irishness of Joyce: the cracked lookingglass. *In* Yeats, Joyce, and Beckett p87-91

Porter, Roy
Creation and credence: the career of theories of the earth in Britain 1660-1820. *In* Barnes, B. and Shapin, S. eds. Natural order p97-123

Porter, Vincent
Television and film production strategies in the European community. *In* Fischer, H. D. and Melnik, S. R. eds. Entertainment: a cross-cultural examination p258-72

Portes, Alejandro
Sociology and the use of secondary data. *In* Quantitative social science research on Latin America p208-70

Portes, Richard
Inflation under central planning. *In* The Political economy of inflation p73-87

Portrait drawing. See Portrait painting

Portrait painting

History

Berger, J. The changing view of man in the portrait. *In* Berger, J. The look of things p35-41

Portrait sculpture
Kunitz, S. J. Meditations of a sitter. *In* Kunitz, S. J. A kind of order, a kind of folly p135-38

Portraits
Coomaraswamy, A K. The meeting of eyes; excerpt from "Figures of speech or figures of thought: collected essays in the traditional or 'normal' view of art." *In* Coomaraswamy, A. K. Selected papers v 1 p233-37

See also Photography—Portraits; subdivision Portraits under classes of persons, e.g. Authors, English—Portraits; and subdivision Portraits under names of persons

Portugal

Colonies—Angola

Wheeler, D. L. Rebels and rebellions in Angola, 1672-1892. *In* African dimensions p81-93

Colonies—Brazil

Russell-Wood, A. J. R. Preconditions and precipitants of the independence movement in Portuguese America. *In* From colony to nation p3-40

Colonies—India

Pearson, M. N. Corruption and corsairs in sixteenth-century western India: a functional analysis. *In* Kling, B. B. and Pearson, M. N. eds. The age of partnership p15-41

History

Cardozo, M. da S. S. The modernization of Portugal and the independence of Brazil. *In* From colony to nation p185-210

Portuguese Communist Party. See Communist Party of Portugal

Portuguese in India
Pearson, M. N. Corruption and corsairs in sixteenth-century western India: a functional analysis. *In* Kling, B. B. and Pearson, M. N. eds. The age of partnership p15-41

Portuguese literature

African authors

See African literature (Portuguese)

Brazil

See Brazilian literature

Poseidon. See Neptunus

Positivism

Barfield, O. The rediscovery of meaning. *In* Barfield, O. The rediscovery of meaning, and other essays p11-21

Brown, R. H. The emergence of existential thought: philosophical perspectives on positivist and humanist forms of social theory. *In* Douglas, J. D. and Johnson, J. M. [eds.] Existential sociology p77-100

Voegelin, E. The apocalypse of man: Comte. *In* Voegelin, E. From Enlightenment to revolution p136-59

Voegelin, E. Positivism and its antecedents. *In* Voegelin, E. From Enlightenment to revolution p74-109

Voegelin, E. The religion of humanity and the French Revolution. *In* Voegelin, E. From Enlightenment to revolution p160-94

Weinberg, J. R. Fourteenth- and twentieth-century positivism. *In* Weinberg, J. R. Ockham, Descartes, and Hume p50-67

See also Idealism; Logical positivism; Materialism

Positivism, Logical. See Logical positivism

Posnansky, Merrick

Connections between the Lacustrine peoples and the coast. *In* Chittick, H. N. and Rotberg, R. I. eds. East Africa and the Orient p216-25

Posner, Richard A.

The DeFunis case and the constitutionality of preferential treatment of racial minorities. *In* The Supreme Court review, 1974 p 1-32

See also Casper, G. jt. auth.

Possession (Law) See Property

Possession, Spirit. See Spirit possession

Possible art. See Conceptual art

Post, Gaines

Philosophy and citizenship in the thirteenth century; laicisation, the two laws and Aristotle. *In* Order and innovation in the Middle Ages p401-08

Post, Kenneth William John

Individuals and the dialectic: a Marxist view of political biographies. *In* The Making of politicians: studies from Africa and Asia p17-27

Post-Angel (Periodical)

Jenkins, A. Dunton's Post-Angel: messenger of remarkable providences. *In* The Dress of words p151-65

Post-impressionism (Art) See Cubism; Dadaism; Expressionism (Art); Surrealism

Post-object art. See Conceptual art

Postage-stamps

United States

Skaggs, D. C. Postage stamps as icons. *In* Browne, R. B. and Fishwick, M. W. eds. Icons of America p198-208

Postl, Carl. See Sealsfield, Charles

Postlethwait, Samuel N.

Students, teachers, and technology. *In* Buxton, T. H. and Prichard, K. W. eds. Excellence in university teaching p220-31

Postman, Neil, and Weingartner, Charles

About individual works

Teaching as a subversive activity

Barrow, R. Neil Postman and Charles Weingartner. *In* Barrow, R. Radical education p154-76

Post-millennialism. See Millennialism

Poston, Lawrence

Browning and the altered romantic landscape. *In* Knoepflmacher, U. C. and Tennyson, G. B. eds. Nature and the Victorian imagination p426-40

Potamkin, Harry Alan

The passion of Jeanne D'Arc. *In* Denby, D. ed. Awake in the dark p102-05

Potatoes

Europe

Morineau, M. The potato in the eighteenth century. *In* Food and drink in history p17-36

Potemkin (Motion picture)

Kauffmann, S. Potemkin. *In* Kauffmann, S. Living images p290-98

Murray, E. Potemkin. *In* Murray, E. Ten film classics p1-17

Potholm, Christian P.

The effects on South Africa of changes in contiguous territories. *In* Thompson, L. M. and Butler, J. eds. Change in contemporary South Africa p329-48

Potlatch in literature

Donahue, C. Potlatch and charity: notes on the heroic in Beowulf. *In* Anglo-Saxon poetry: essays in appreciation p23-40

Potsherds (Ostraka) See Ostraka

Potter, Francis

About individual works

An interpretation of the number 666

Stein, S. J. Cotton Mather and Jonathan Edwards on tse number of the best; eighteenth-century speculation about the Antichrist. *In* American Antiquarian Society. Proceedings v84 pt2 p293-315

Potter, Jack Myers

About

Dobie, J. F. Belling the lead steer. *In* Dobie, J. F. Prefaces p35-47

Potter, Jim

Some British reflections on Turner and the frontier. *In* Burton, D. H. ed. American history—British historians p127-48

Potter, Lois

The antic disposition of Richard II. *In* Shakespeare survey 27 p33-41

Potter, P. M.

Nestroy's Zu ebener Erde und erster Stock: a reappraisal. *In* Branscombe, P. ed. Austrian life and literature, 1780-1938 p40-48

Potter, Ralph Benajah

The simple structure of the population debate: the logic of the ecology movement. *In* Population policy and ethics p347-63

Potters' marks. See Pottery—Marks

Pottery

See also Faience; Indians of Mexico—Pottery

Marks

Grace, V. R. Exceptional amphora stamps. *In* Studies in classical art and archaeology p115-27

Hirschland, N. L. and Hammond, M. Stamped potters' marks and other stamped pottery in the McDaniel collection. *In* Harvard Studies in classical philology v72 p369-82

Paphos

Megaw, A. H. S. An early thirteenth-century Aegean glazed ware. *In* Studies in memory of David Talbot Rice p34-45

Pottery—*Continued*

Preslav, Bulgaria

Akrabova-Zhandova, I. Preslav inlaid ceramics. *In* Studies in memory of David Talbot Rice p25-33

Pottery, Greek

Mertens, J. R. A white-ground cup by Euphronios. *In* Harvard Studies in classical philology v76 p271-81

Pottery, Maya

Culbert, T. P. Early Maya development at Tikal, Guatemala. *In* The Origins of Maya civilization p27-43

Rands, R. L. The rise of Classic Maya civilization in the Northwestern Zone: isolation and integration. *In* The Origins of Maya civilization p159-80

Pottery, Roman

Brown, D. Pottery. *In* Strong, D. E. and Brown, D. eds. Roman crafts p75-91

Wrabetz, J. F. A new Serenus stamping from Sardis and the origins of the Eastern Sigillata B ware. *In* Harvard Studies in classical philology v81 p195-97

Pottery craft

Bailey, D. M. Pottery lamps. *In* Strong, D. E. and Brown, D. eds. Roman crafts p93-103

Brown, D. Pottery. *In* Strong, D. E. and Brown, D. eds. Roman crafts p75-91

Pottery dating. See Pottery—Marks

Pottery figures

Egypt—Alexandria

Thompson, D. B. A faience fellah. *In* Studies in classical art and archaeology p175-78

Pottery making (Handicraft) See Pottery craft

Pottinger, John Stanley

The drive toward equality. *In* Gross, B. R. ed. Reverse discrimination p41-49

Race, sex, and jobs: the drive toward equality. *In* Women in academia p37-44

Potts, Timothy Cyril

The place of structure in comunication. *In* Royal Institute of Philosophy. Communication and understanding p91-115

Pouched animals. See Marsupialia

Poulard, Jean Victor

The French Communist Party and the popular union. *In* Kaplan, M. A. ed. The many faces of communism p72-121

Poulet, Georges

The role of improvisation in Corinne. *In* ELH essays for Earl R. Wasserman p309-19

Pound, Ezra Loomis

Treatise on metre; excerpt from "ABC of reading." *In* Gross, H. S. ed. The structure of verse p234-40

About

Berryman, J. The poetry of Ezra Pound. *In* Berryman, J. The freedom of the poet p253-69

Connolly, C. Ezra Pound: 2. *In* Connolly, C. The evening colonnade p222-25

Eliot, T. S. From Ezra Pound: his metric and poetry. *In* Eliot, T. S. Selected prose of T. S. Eliot p149-50

Fraser, G. S. Pound: masks, myth, man. *In* Fraser, G. S. Essays on twentieth-century poets p80-88

Frye, N. Phalanx of particulars. *In* Frye, N. Northrop Frye on culture and literature p197-203

Glicksberg, C. I. Ezra Pound and the commitment to fascism. *In* Glicksberg, C. I. The literature of commitment p100-10

Holbrook, D. The lack of a creative theme: Ezra Pound's stone mouths biting empty air and Eliot's Hollow men. *In* Holbrook, D. Lost bearings in English poetry p58-100

Lewis, W. Ezra Pound; excerpt from "Time and Western man." *In* Lewis, W. Enemy salvoes p161-72

MacLeish, A. The Venetian grave. *In* MacLeish, A. Riders on the earth p115-22

Schneidau, H. N. Pound and Wordsworth on poetry and prose. *In* Bornstein, G. ed. Romantic and modern p133-45

Shapiro, K. J. Ezra Pound: the scapegoat of modern poetry. *In* Shapiro, K. J. The poetry wreck p29-54

Sheed, W. Honoring Ezra Pound. *In* Sheed, W. The good word & other words p58-61

Wilhelm, J. J. Arnaut Daniel's legacy to Dante and to Pound. *In* Italian literature: roots and branches p67-83

Witemeyer, H. Walter Savage Landor and Ezra Pound. *In* Bornstein, G. ed. Romantic and modern p147-63

About individual works

The cantos

Halperen, M. How to read a canto. *In* French, W. G. ed. The twenties p335-50

Miller, J. E. An epic is a poem containing history: Ezra Pound's "Cantos." *In* Miller, J. E. The American quest for a supreme fiction p68-98

Homage to Sextus Propertius

Messing, G. M. Pound's Propertius: the homage and the damage. *In* Poetry and poetics from ancient Greece to the Renaissance p105-33

Hugh Selwyn Mauberley

Holbrook, D. The lack of a creative theme: Ezra Pound's stone mouths biting empty air and Eliot's Hollow men. *In* Holbrook, D. Lost bearings in English poetry p58-100

The Pisan cantos

Eberhart, R. Pound's new cantos. *In* Eberhart, R. Of poetry and poets p126-40

Bibliography

Bornstein, G. Pound and Eliot. *In* American literary scholarship, 1977 p119-33

Ludwig, R. M. Pound and Eliot. *In* American literary scholarship, 1974 p101-21

McDougal, S. Y. Pound and Eliot. *In* American literary scholarship, 1975 p131-42

McDougal, S. Y. Pound and Eliot [another essay] *In* American literary scholarship, 1976 p109-18

Influence—Hemingway

Hurwitz, H. M. Hemingway's tutor, Ezra Pound. *In* Wagner, L. W. ed. Ernest Hemingway p8-21

Poussin, Nicholas

About

Wittkower, R. The role of classical models in Bernini's and Poussin's preparatory work. *In* Wittkower, R. Studies in the Italian baroque p103-14

Poverty

Brown, S. E. Love unites and hunger separates them: poor women in the Dominican Republic. *In* Reiter, R. R. ed. Toward an anthropology of women p322-32

Humpherys, A. Dickens and Mayhew on the London poor. *In* Dickens Studies Annual v4 p78-90

See also Income maintenance programs; Poor; Public welfare; and subdivisions Economic conditions and Social conditions under names of countries, e.g. Ireland—Economic conditions; United States—Social conditions

United States

Benson, J. K. A power strategy. *In* Lauer, R. H. ed. Social movements and social change p107-20

Powell, Anthony

About

Pritchard, W. H. Satire and fiction: examples from the 1930s. *In* Pritchard, W. H. Seeing through everything p178-208

Powell, Arthur G.

Harvard's School of Education and the Federal government: institutional effects of interaction in the 1960s. *In* Hook, S.; Kurtz, P. W. and Todorovich, M. eds. The university and the state: what role for government in higher education? p51-72

Powell, Barry B.

Poeta ludens: thrust and counter-thrust in Eclogue 3. *In* Illinois classical studies, v 1 1976 p113-21

Powell, Brian

Communits kabuki: a contradiction in terms? *In* Drama and society p147-67

Matsui Sumako: actress and woman. *In* Modern Japan p135-46

Powell, Dilys. See Powell, Elizabeth Dilys

Powell, Elizabeth Dilys

The film of the book. *In* Royal Society óf Literature of the United Kingdom, London. Essays by divers hands v38 p93-111

Powell, Lawrence Clark

Bibliography

Lowman, A. A chronology of LCP keepsakes. *In* Voices from the Southwest p132-45

Books and reading

Lowman, A. A chronology of LCP keepsakes. *In* Voices from the Southwest p132-45

Powell, Lawrence N.

Rejected Republican incumbents in the 1866 Congressional nominating convention: a study in Reconstruction politics. *In* Swierenga, R. P. ed. Beyond the Civil War synthesis p117-35

Power, Crawford

About individual works

The encounter

Howe, I. Treacheries of faith. *In* Howe, I. Celebrations and attacks p102-08

Power, Francis Crawford. See Power, Crawford

Power, Michael John

The East and West in early-modern London. *In* Wealth and power in Tudor England p167-85

Power (Mechanics) See Force and energy

Power (Psychology) See Control (Psychology)

Power (Social sciences)

Anderson, M. Power and inflation. *In* The Political economy of inflation p240-62

Armstrong, T. R. The roots of power. *In* Armstrong, T. R. and Cinnamon, K. M. eds. Power and authority in law enforcement p5-12

Aron, R. Macht, power, puissance: democratic prose or demoniac poetry? *In* Aron, R. Politics and history p102-21

Blackwell, J. E. The power basis of ethnic conflict in American society. *In* The Uses of controversy in sociology p179-96

Blum, J. Russia. *In* Spring, D. ed. European landed elites in the nineteenth century p68-97

Christensen, C. J. Structural power and national security. *In* Knorr, K. E. and Trager, F. N. eds. Economic issues and national security p127-59

Coleman, J. S. Legitimate and illegitimate use of power. *In* The Idea of social structure p221-36

Crozier, M. The problem of power. *In* Armstrong, T. R. and Cinnamon, K. M. eds. Power and authority in law enforcement p23-38

Fairfield, R. P. The paradox of power. *In* Armstrong, T. R. and Cinnamon, K. M. eds. Power and authority in law enforcement p13-22

Geertz, C. Centers, kings, and charisma: reflections on the symbolics of power. *in* Culture and its creators p150-71

Geschwender, J. A. On power and powerlessness: or with a little help from our friends. *In* Major social issues p439-54

Glasser, I. Prisoners of benevolence: power versus liberty in the welfare state. *In* Doing good p97-170

Gotesky, R. Social force, social power, and social violence. *In* Stanage, S. M. ed. Reason and violence p145-79

Hardin, C. M. The problem of political power in the United States. *In* [Truth and tragedy]: a tribute to Hans Morgenthau p142-52

Herr, R. Spain. *In* Spring, D. European landed elites in the nineteenth century p98-126

Liska, G. Morgenthau vs. Machiavelli: political realism and power politics. *In* [Truth and tragedy]: a tribute to Hans Morgenthau p104-11

McKean, R. N. Property rights, pollution, and power. *In* Capitalism and freedom p92-111

Nader, L. and Serber, D. Law and the distribution of power. *In* The Uses of controversy in sociology p273-91

Neff, F. W. and Lubin, B. Observations on power and authority from a training program for police managers. *In* Armstrong, T. R. and Cinnamon, K. M. eds. Power and authority in law enforcement p115-30

Peckham, M. The arts and the centers of power. *In* Peckham, M. Romanticism and behavior p328-50

Schacht, R. On power and powerlessness. *In* Major social issues p425-38

Spring, D. Landed elites compared. *In* Spring, D. ed. European landed elites in the nineteenth century p 1-21

Stern, F. R. Prussia. *In* Spring, D. ed. European landed elites in the nineteenth century p45-67

Power (Social sciences)—*Continued*

Stinchcombe, A. L. Marxist theories of power and empirical research. *In* The Uses of controversy in sociology p301-14

Thompson, F. M. L. Britain. *In* Spring, D. ed. European landed elites in the nineteenth century 22-44

Whisenand, P. and Ferguson, R. F. Controlling: the use of authority, power, and influence; excerpt from "The managing of police organizations." *In* Armstrong, T. R. and Cinnamon, K. M. eds. Power and authority in law enforcement p56-74

Wilhelmsen, F. D. Donoso Cortés and the meaning of political power. *In* Wilhelmsen, F. D. Christianity and political philosophy p139-73

Wilhelmsen, F. D. The problem of political power and the forces of darkness. *In* Wilhelmsen, F. D. Christianity and political philosophy p60-110

Zeldin, T. France. *In* Spring, D. ed. European landed elites in the nineteenth century p127-39

See also Consensus (Social science); Elite (Social sciences); Social status

Power (Theology). See Authority (Religion)

Power, Balance of. See Balance of power

Power, Executive. See Executive power

Power, Legislative. See Legislative power

Power politics. See Balance of power

Power resources

Pollack, G. A. The economic consequences of the energy crisis. *In* Bundy, W. P. ed. The world economic crisis p120-39

Shinn, R. L. Living with scarcity. *In* Small comforts for hard times p137-51

Wilson, C. L. A plan for energy independence. *In* Bundy, W. P. ed. The world economic crisis p50-68

See also Energy policy; Solar energy

Law and legislation—United States

Vogely, W. A. Federal government energy organization. *In* Kalter, R. J. and Vogely, W. A. eds. Energy supply and government policy p306-25

Research—United States

Tilton, J. E. The public role in energy research and development. *In* Kalter, R. J. and Vogely, W. A. eds. Energy supply and government policy p99-129

Timenes, N. Beyond the crisis: transitional, efficient, and ultimate resources. *In* Kalter, R. J. and Vogely, W. A. eds. Energy supply and government policy p326-45

United States

Kalter, R. J. and Vogely, W. A. Introduction. *In* Kalter, R. J. and Vogely, W. A. eds. Energy supply and government policy p11-25

Ronall, J. O. The energy crisis and its potential effects upon American policy. *In* The New world balance and peace in the Middle East: reality or mirage? p119-24

Sachs, R. G. Our energy options—so what else is new? *In* Eppen, G. D. ed. Energy: the policy issues p3-24

Smith, W. D. The energy crisis and the Middle East. *In* The New world balance and peace in the Middle East: reality or mirage? p105-17

Timenes, N. Beyond the crisis: transitional, efficient, and ultimate resources. *In* Kalter, R. J. and Vogely, W. A. eds. Energy supply and government policy p326-45

Power resources research. See Power resources—Research

Power supply. See Power resources

Powers, Separation of. See Separation of powers

Powles, John G.

On the limitations of modern medicine. *In* Sobel, D. S. ed. Ways of health p61-86

Powlick, Leonard

Cymbeline and the comedy of anticlimax. *In* Shakespeare's late plays p131-41

Pownall, Thomas

About

Shy, J. W. The spectrum of imperial possibilities: Henry Ellis and Thomas Pownall, 1763-1775. *In* Shy, J. W. A people numerous and armed p35-72

Powys, Llewelyn

About

Cavaliero, G. The land of lost content: Henry Williamson, Llewelyn Powys. *In* Cavaliero, G. The rural tradition in the English novel, 1900-1939 p118-32

Powys, Theodore Francis

About

Cavaliero, G. Rural symbolism: T. F. Powys. *In* Cavaliero, G. The rural tradition in the English novel, 1900-1939 p173-95

Pozzi, Dora C.

A note on δυσχείρωμα. *In* Harvard Studies in classical philology v75 p63-67

Pozzuoli

Genealogy

D'Arms, J. H. CIL X, 1792: a municipal notable of the Augustan age. *In* Harvard Studies in classical philology v76 p207-16

Practical politics. See Politics, Practical

Practice (Philosophy)

Andrew, E. The unity of theory and practice: the science of Marx and Nietzsche. *In* Political theory and praxis p117-37

Applebaum, R. P. Marxist method: structural constraints and social praxis. *In* McNall, S. G. ed. Theoretical perspectives in sociology p200-13

Ball, T. Plato and Aristotle: the unity versus the autonomy of theory and practice. *In* Political theory and praxis p57-69

Bernstein, R. J. Hannah Arendt: the ambiguities of theory and practice. *In* Political theory and praxis p141-58

Euben, J. P. Creatures of a day: thought and action in Thucydides. *In* Political theory and praxis p28-56

Fuss, P. L. Theory and practice in Hegel and Marx: an unfinished dialogue. *In* Political theory and praxis p97-116

Lobkowicz, N. On the history of theory and praxis. *In* Political theory and praxis p13-27

Raschke, C. Kant on theory and practice. *In* Political theory and praxis p73-96

Wartofsky, M. W. Consciousness, praxis, and reality: Marxism vs. phenomenology. *In* Elliston, F. A. and McCormick, P. eds. Husserl p304-13

Practice of law

See also Admission to the bar; Law—Vocational guidance; Legal assistants; Legal ethics

United States

Bloomfield, M. H. Conclusion. *In* Bloomfield, M. H. American lawyers in a changing society, 1776-1876 p340-48

Bloomfield, M. H. Upgrading the professional image. *In* Bloomfield, M. H. American lawyers in a changing society, 1776-1876 p136-90

Kidder, R. L. Lawyers for the people: dilemmas of legal activists. *In* Gerstl, J. E. and Jacobs, G. eds. Professions for the people p153-74

Praetorius, Johannes

About

Westman, R. S. Three responses to the Copernican theory: Johannes Praetorius, Tycho Brahe, and Michael Maestlin. *In* The Copernican achievement p285-345

Pragmatics

Stenning, K. Anaphora as an approach to pragmatics. *In* Linguistic theory and psychological reality p162-200

Pragmatism

Deininger, W. T. Promise and peril in pragmatic historical thought: a contemporary dialogue. *In* Philosophy and the civilizing arts p264-82

See also Experience; Reality; Truth; Utilitarianism

Prague Linguistic Circle. See Pražský linguistický kroužek

Prairies

United States

Birch, B. P. British evaluations of the forest openings and prairie edges of the North-Central states. 1800-1850. *In* The Frontier v2 p167-92

Prakash, Om

Asian trade and European impact: a study of the trade from Bengal, 1630-1720. *In* Kling, B. B. and Pearson, M. N. eds. The age of partnership 43-70

Prakke, Hendricus Johannes

The "socius" function of the press. *In* Fischer, H. D. and Melnik, S. R. eds. Entertainment: a cross-cultural examination p99-104

Towards a philosophy of publicistics. *In* Fischer, H. D. and Merrill, J. C. eds. International and intercultural communication p466-73

Prakke, Henk. See Prakke, Hendricus Johannes

Pranger, Robert John

Domestic politics in Fortress America. *In* Isolation or interdependence? p115-30

Prasert na Nagara. See Griswold, A. B. jt. auth.

Pratt, Annis Vilas

The new feminist criticism: exploring the history of the new space. *In* Roberts, J. I. ed. Beyond intellectual sexism p175-95

Pratt, Edwin John

About

Buitenhuis, P. E. J. Pratt. *In* Staines, D. ed. The Canadian imagination p46-68

Davey, T. F. E. J. Pratt: apostle of corporate man. *In* Woodcock, G. ed. Poets and critics p 1-13

Pratt, Pamela

Wall painting. *In* Strong, D. E. and Brown, D. eds. Roman crafts p223-29

Pratt, William C.

"Jimmie Higgins" and the Reading Socialist community: an exploration of the Socialist rank and file. *In* Stave, B. M. ed. Socialism and the cities p141-56

The Prattler

Granger, B. I. Early Philadelphia serials. *In* Granger, B. I. American essay serials from Franklin to Irving p41-69

Prawer, Joshua

Crusader cities. *In* The Medieval city p179-99

Prayer-books

Raw, B. C. The prayers and devotions in the Ancrene wisse. *In* Chaucer and Middle English studies in honour of Rossell Hope Robbins p260-71

Prayer groups

Bateson, M. C. Ritualization: a study in texture and texture change. *In* Zaretsky, I. I. and Leone, M. P. eds. Religious movements in contemporary America p150-65

Prayer-meetings. See Prayer groups

Prayers. See Lord's prayer

Praz, Mario

The critical importance of the revived interest in seventeenth-century metaphysical poetry. *In* Roberts, J. R. ed. Essential articles for the study of John Donne's poetry p3-10

Two masters of the absurd: Grandville and Carroll. *In* The Artist and the writer in France p134-37

About individual works

The romantic agony

Woodard, C. R. Wordsworth and The romantic agony. *In* Tennessee Studies in literature v20 p 1-10

Pražský linguistický kroužek

Matejka, L. Postscript. Prague school semiotics. *In* Matejka, L. and Titunik, I. R. eds. Semiotics of art p265-90

Preaching

Lewalski, B. K. Art and the sacred subject: sermon theory, Biblical personae, and Protestant poetics. *In* Lewalski, B. K. Protestant poetics and the seventeenth-century religious lyric p213-50

History—Middle Ages, 600-1500

Wenzel, S. Vices, virtues, and popular preaching. *In* Medieval and Renaissance studies [1974] p28-54

History—Great Britain

Haines, R. M. Church, society and politics in the early fifteenth century as viewed from an English pulpit. *In* Church, society and politics p143-57

History—United States

Ulrich, L. T. Vertuous women found: New England ministerial literature, 1668-1735. *In* Vaughan, A. T. and Bremer, F. J. eds. Puritan New England p215-31

Preaching, Extemporaneous

Rosenberg, B. A. The psychology of the spiritual sermon. *In* Zaretsky, I. I. and Leone, M. P. eds. Religious movements in contemporary America p135-49

Preaching to children
Stannard, D. E. Death and the Puritan child. *In* Vaughan, A. T. and Bremer, F. J. eds. Puritan New England p232-49

Prebish, Charles S.
Reflections on the transmission of Buddhism to America. *In* Needleman, J. and Baker, G. eds. Understanding the new religions p153-72

Precedence

Russia
Bennett, H. A. Evolution of the meanings of chin: an introduction to the Russian institution of rank ordering and niche assignment from the time of Peter the Great's Table of Ranks to the Bolshevik Revolution. *In* California Slavic studies v10 p 1-43

Precession
Swerdlow, N. M. On Copernicus' theory of precession. *In* The Copernican achievement p49-98

Precious stones

Therapeutic use
Forbes, T. R. The madstone. *In* American folk medicine p11-19

Precisians. See Puritans

Predestination
Pine, M. Pietro Pomponazzi and the medieval tradition of God's foreknowledge. *In* Philosophy and humanism p100-15
See also Free will and determinism; Necessity (Philosophy)

Predicate (Logic) See Definition (Logic)

Predicate and subject (Grammar) See Grammar, Comparative and general—Topic and comment

Predicate calculus
Kripke, S. A. Is there a problem about substitutional quantification? *In* Evans, G. L. and McDowell, J. H. eds. Truth and meaning p324-419
Quine, W. V. Algebraic logic and predicate functors. *In* Quine, W. V. The ways of paradox, and other essays p283-307
Quine, W. V. Quantifiers and propositional attitudes. *In* Quine, W. V. The ways of paradox, and other essays p185-96
Quine, W. V. Reply to Professor Marcus *In* Quine, W. V. The ways of paradox, and other essays p177-84
Quine, W. V. Three grades of modal involvement. *In* Quine, W. V. The ways of paradox, and other essays p158-76
Quine, W. V. Truth and disquotation. *In* Quine, W. V. The ways of paradox, and other essays p308-21

Prediction. See Forecasting

Prediction (Logic)
Woolhouse, R. S. The empiricist account of dispositions. *In* Royal Institute of Philosophy. Impressions of empiricism p184-99

Prediction, Social. See Social prediction

Predmore, Richard Lionel
On interpreting Don Quixote's character. *In* Studies in the continental background of Renaissance English literature: essays presented to John L. Lievsay p186-201

Pre-existence. See Reincarnation

Prefaces
Guinagh, K. A preface on prefaces. *In* Praise from famous men: an anthology of introductions p ix-xiv

Pregler, Hilde Haider- See Haider-Pregler, Hilde

Prehistoric man. See Man, Prehistoric

Preisendanz, Wolfgang
Bridging the gap between Heine the poet and Heine the journalist. *In* Amacher, R. E. and Lange, V. eds. New perspectives in German literary criticism p225-59

Preiswerk, Adrian Roy
The place of intercultural relations in the study of international relations. *In* The Year book of world affairs, 1978 p251-67

Prejudices and antipathies
Allport, G. W. Prejudice: Prejudice and the individual. *In* The Black American reference book p515-21
Pettigrew, T. F. Prejudice: Prejudice and the situation. *In* The Black American reference book p521-28
Williams, R. M. Prejudice: Prejudice and society. *In* The Black American reference book p528-36
See also Antisemitism; Racism

United States
Weber, D. J. "Scarce more than apes." Historical roots of Anglo-American stereotypes of Mexicans. *In* Weber, D. J. ed. New Spain's far northern frontier p293-307

Premarital counseling. See Marriage counseling

Premarital sex
Bettelheim, B. About the sexual revolution. *In* Bettelheim, B. Surviving, and other essays p370-86

Premillennialism. See Millennialism

Preminger, Otto

About individual works
Bonjour tristesse
Truffaut, F. Otto Preminger: Bonjour tristesse. *In* Truffaut, F. The films in my life p137-40

Prenshaw, Peggy Whitman
The paradoxical Southern world of Tennessee Williams. *In* Tennessee Williams: a tribute p5-29
Woman's world, man's place: the fiction of Eudora Welty. *In* Dollarhide, L. and Abadie, A. J. eds. Eudora Welty: a form of thanks p46-77

Prentki, Tim
Requiem for the living. *In* Prentki, T. ed. Francis Warner p88-109

Prepaid legal services
Lorenz, J. State of siege: group legal services for the middle class. *In* Nader, R. and Green, M. J. eds. Verdicts on lawyers p144-57

Preraphaelites
Dawson, C. The Germ: aesthetic manifesto. *In* Dawson, C. Victorian noon p203-23

Preraphaelitism
Axton, W. F. Victorian landscape painting: a change in outlook. *In* Knoepflmacher, U. C. and Tennyson, G. B. eds. Nature and the Victorian imagination p281-308
Buckley, J. H. The fear of art; excerpt from "The Victorian temper". *In* Sambrook, J. ed. Pre-Raphaelitism p186-205
Heath-Stubbs, J. F. A. Pre-Raphaelitism and the aesthetic withdrawal; excerpt from "The darkling plain". *In* Sambrook, J. ed. Pre-Raphaelitism p166-85

Preraphaelitism—*Continued*

Hough, G. G. The aesthetic of pre-Raphaelitism; excerpt from "The last romantics". *In* Sambrook, J. ed. Pre-Raphaelitism p133-52

House, H. Pre-Raphaelite poetry; excerpt from "All in due time". *In* Sambrook, J. ed. Pre-Raphaelitism p126-32

Hunt, J. D. A moment's monument: reflections on pre-Raphaelite vision in poetry and painting. *In* Sambrook, J. ed. Pre-Raphaelitism p243-64

Hunt, W. H. Pre-Raphaelitism and the pre-Raphaelite brotherhood; excerpts. *In* Sambrook, J. ed. Pre-Raphaelitism p27-44

Masson, D. Pre-Raphaelitism in art and literature. *In* Sambrook, J. ed. Pre-Raphaelitism p71-91

Meisel, M. "Half sick of shadows": the aesthetic dialogue in Pre-Raphaelite painting. *In* Knoepflmacher, U. C. and Tennyson, G. B. eds. Nature and the Victorian imagination p309-40

Rossetti, D. G. Hand and soul. *In* Sambrook, J. ed. Pre-Raphaelitism p45-56

Rossetti, W. M. Pre-Raphaelitism. *In* Sambrook, J. ed. Pre-Raphaelitism p64-70

Ruskin, J. Pre-Raphaelitism. *In* Sambrook, J. ed. Pre-Raphaelitism p92-104

Spender, S. The Pre-Raphaelite literary painters. *In* Sambrook, J. ed. Pre-Raphaelitism p118-25

Stephens, F. G. The purpose and tendency of early Italian art. *In* Sambrook, J. ed. Pre-Raphaelitism p57-63

Williamson, A. Hunt and Millais: retreat to respectability. *In* Williamson, A. Artists and writers in revolt p62-84

Williamson, A. Rossetti and Pre-Raphaelitism. *In* Williamson, A. Artists and writers in revolt p37-61

Influence

Williamson, A. Whistler, Wilde and the aesthetic influence. *In* Williamson, A. Artists and writers in revolt p182-96

Prerogative, Royal. See Regalia

Presbyterians in Ireland

Barkley, J. M. The Presbyterian Church in Ireland and the Government of Ireland Act (1920) *In* Church, society and politics p393-403

Preschool education. See Education, Preschool

Prescott, Anne Lake

French poets and the English Renaissance

Contents

Afterword
Desportes
Du Bartas
Du Bellay
Marot
Ronsard

Preservation of moving-picture film. See Moving-picture film—Preservation and storage

Presidents

United States

Drucker, P. F. How to make the Presidency manageable. *In* Managing nonprofit organizations p280-88

Ebel, H. But what kind of baby is Jimmy Carter? *In* DeMause, L. and Ebel, H. eds. Jimmy Carter and American fantasy p117-27

Eckart, D. R. and Ries, J. C. The American Presidency. *In* Rieselbach, L. N. ed. People vs. government: the responsiveness of American institutions p15-65

Levin, M. Ask not what our presidents are "really like"; ask what we and our political institutions are like: a call for a politics of institutions, not men. *In* Burnham, W. D. and Weinberg, M. W. eds. American politics and public policy p109-39

Reedy, G. E. The Presidency in 1976: focal point of political unity? *In* Havard, W. C. and Bernd, J. L. eds. 200 years of the Republic in retrospect p228-38

Wildavsky, A. B. and Knott, J. Jimmy Carter's theory of governing. *In* Burnham, W. D. and Weinberg, M. W. eds. American politics and public policy p55-76

United States—Election—1860

Swierenga, R. P. The ethnic voter and the first Lincoln election. *In* Swierenga, R. P. ed. Beyond the Civil War synthesis p99-115

United States—Election—1976

Burnham, W. D. The 1976 election: has the crisis been adjourned? *In* Burnham, W. D. and Weinberg, M. W. eds. American politics and public policy p 1-25

United States—Powers

See Executive power—United States

United States—Racial attitudes

Leuchtenburg, W. E. The White House and Black America: from Eisenhower to Carter. *In* Have we overcome? Race relations since Brown p121-45

United States—Staff

Bowman, A. H. Presidential advisers. *In* Encyclopedia of American foreign policy p790-804

United States—Views on race question

See Presidents—United States—Racial attitudes

Presidents, College. See College presidents

Presley, Delma Eugene

Little acts of grace. *In* Tennessee Williams: a tribute p571-80

Press, John

The poetry of Philip Larkin. *In* Royal Society of Literature of the United Kingdom, London. Essays by divers hands v39 76-91

Press

Nevins, A. The newspaperman and the scholar. *In* Nevins, A. Allan Nevins on history p36-42

See also Government and the press; Liberty of the press; News agencies; Newspapers; Periodicals; Public opinion; Street literature

Societies, etc.

See Journalism—Societies, etc.

Africa, West

Jones-Quartey, K. A. B. The West African press since the Second World War—a bibliographical review. *In* African studies since 1945 p106-24

Press and government. See Government and the press

Press and politics
Merrill, J. C. A conceptual overview of world journalism; excerpts from "Imperative of freedom." *In* Fischer, H. D. and Merrill, J. C. eds. International and intercultural communication p18-28

See also Journalism—Politcal aspects

Chicago—History

Nelli, H. S. Chicago's Italian-language press and World War I. *In* Studies in Italian American social history p66-80

Great Britain

Seymour-Ure, C. The press and the party system between the Wars. *In* Peele, G. and Cook, C. eds. The politics of reappraisal, 1918-1939 p232-57

Press associations. See Journalism—Societies, etc.

Press censorship. See Liberty of the press

Press clubs. See Journalism—Societies, etc.

Press councils
Fischer, H. D. Press councils throughout the world: an empirical approach. *In* Fischer, H. D. and Merrill, J. C. eds. International and intercultural communication p161-74

Press Foundation of Asia
Matlub Ali, S. DEPTHnews: a model for a Third World feature agency. *In* Horton, P. C. ed. The Third World and press freedom p187-96

Presses, Little. See Little presses

Pressure groups
See also Lobbying

Europe

Hayward, J. E. S. Interest groups and the demand for state action. *In* Hayward, J. E. S. and Berki, R. N. eds. State and society in contemporary Europe p23-41

Great Britain—History

Hollis, P. Pressure from without: an introduction. *In* Hollis, P. ed. Pressure from without p 1-26

United States

Polsby, N. W. Interest groups and the Presidency: trends in political intermediation in America. *In* Burnham, W. D. and Weinberg, M. W. eds. American politics and public policy p41-52

Presthus, Robert Vance
Evolution and Canadian political culture: the politics of accommodation. *In* Perspectives on revolution and evolution p103-32

Prestige. See Social classes; Social status

Preston, Jean F.
Books before printing: a codicological catalogue. *In* Review, v 1, 1979 p223-31

Preston, Paul
The anti-Francoist opposition: the long march to unity. *In* Preston, P. ed. Spain in crisis p125-56

Preston, Richard Arthur
Some conclusions about the revolution-evolution problem. *In* Perspectives on revolution and evolution p268-87

Preston, William
Shadows of war and fear. *In* The Pulse of freedom p105-53

Prestwich, Michael
Italian merchants in late thirteenth and early fourteenth century England. *In* The Dawn of modern banking p77-104

Presumptions (Law) See Fictions (Law)

Preto-Rodas, Richard Anthony
The Black presence and two Brazilian modernists: Jorge de Lima and José Lins do Rêgo. *In* Forster, M. H. ed. Tradition and renewal p81-101

Pretzel, Paul W.
Philosophical and ethical considerations of suicide prevention. *In* Weir, R. F. ed. Ethical issues in death and dying p387-400

Prevention of crime. See Crime prevention

Prevention of suicide. See Suicide—Prevention

Prévost, Antoine François, called Prévost d'Exiles

About individual works

Manon Lescaut
Francis, R. A. The first-person narrator in the Abbé Prévost's Memoires d'un homme de qualité. *In* Studies in eighteenth-century culture v6 p303-16

Memoirs of a man of quality
Francis, R. A. The first-person narrator in the Abbé Prévost's Memoires d'un homme de qualité. *In* Studies in eighteenth-century culture v6 p303-16

Prewer, Richard R.
The contribution of prison medicine. *In* Progress in penal reform p116-28

Prewitt, Kenneth, and McAllister, William
Changes in the American executive elite, 1930-1970. *In* Eulau, H. and Czudnowski, M. M. eds. Elite recruitment in democratic polities p105-32

Preyer, Robert O.
The burden of culture and the dialectic of literature. *In* Evolution of consciousness p98-105

Preziosi, Patricia G.
The Homeric Hymn to Aphrodite: an oral analysis. *In* Harvard Studies in classical philology v71 p171-240

Pribram, Karl H.
From infinities to no-thing: an exploration of brain function. *In* Hanna, T. ed. Explorers of humankind p106-17

The linguistic act. *In* Psychoanalysis and language p75-98

Some observations on the organization of studies of mind, brain, and behavior. *In* Alternate states of consciousness p220-29

Price, Barbara J.
The burden of the cargo: ethnographical models and archaeological inference. *In* Mesoamerican archaeology p445-65

Price, Cecil John Layton
Pursuing Sheridan. *In* Evidence in literary scholarship p309-20

Price, Charles P.
Religion and revelation. *In* Christian faith in a religiously plural world p117-22

Price, Derek John de Solla
Ups and downs in the pulse of science and technology. *In* Gaston, J. ed. Sociology of science p162-71

Price, Don K.
Endless frontier or bureaucratic morass? *In* Holton, G. J. and Morison, R. S. eds. Limits of scientific inquiry p74-92

Price, Douglas B.

Miraculous restoration of lost body parts: relationship to the phantom limb phenomenon and to limb-burial superstitions and practices. *In* American folk medicine p49-71

Price, George Robert

Science and the supernatural. *In* Ludwig, J. K. ed. Philosophy and parapsychology p145-71

Where is the definitive experiment? *In* Ludwig, J. K. ed. Philosophy and parapsychology p196-202

About individual works
Science and the supernatural

Meehl, P. E. and Scriven, M. Compatibility of science and ESP. *In* Ludwig, J. K. ed. Philosophy and parapsychology p187-90

Also in Wheatley, J. M. O. and Edge, H. L. eds. Philosophical dimensions of parapsychology p405-08

Rhine, J. B. Comments on "Science and the supernatural." *In* Ludwig, J. K. ed. Philosophy and parapsychology p178-86

Soal, S. G. On "Science and the supernatural." *In* Ludwig, J. K. ed. Philosophy and parapsychology p172-77

Price, Glanville

The present position and viability of minority languages. *In* Alcock, A. E.; Taylor, B. K. and Welton, J. M. eds. The future of cultural minorities p30-43

Price, Henry Habberley

Mediumship and human survival. *In* Wheatley, J. M. O. and Edge, H. L. eds. Philosophical dimensions of parapsychology p262-81

Parapsychology and human nature. *In* Ludwig, J. K. ed. Philosophy and parapsychology p371-86

Some philosophical questions about telepathy and clairvoyance. *In* Wheatley, J. M. O. and Edge, H. L. eds. Philosophical dimensions of parapsychology p105-32

Survival and the idea of 'another world.' *In* Donnelly, J. P. ed. Language, metaphysics, and death p176-95

Price, Hugh Douglas

Congress and the evolution of legislative "professionalism". *In* Ornstein, N. J. ed. Congress in change p2-23

Price, Jennifer

Glass. *In* Strong, D. E. and Brown, D. eds. Roman crafts p111-25

Price, John D.

Yves Bonnefoy: the sense of things. *In* Cardinal, R. ed. Sensibility and creation p204-19

Price, John Vladimir

Religion and ideas. *In* Rogers, P. ed. The eighteenth century p120-52

Price, Martin

The irrelevant detail and the emergence of form. *In* Wimsatt, W. K. ed. Literary criticism: idea and act p521-36

Price, Reynolds

A form of thanks. *In* Dollarhide, L. and Abadie, A. J. eds. Eudora Welty: a form of thanks p123-28

Price-Williams, Douglas

Cognition: anthropological and psychological nexus. *In* Spindler, G. D. ed. The making of psychological anthropology p586-611

Price policy

Mathematical models

Officer, L. H. Demand conditions under multidimensional pricing. *In* Econometrics and economic theory p261-84

Price regulation. See Wage-price policy

Price theory. See Prices

Prices

Caves, R. E. Looking at inflation in the open economy. *In* Inflation, trade and taxes p75-95

Rostow, W. W. Technology and the price system. *In* Science and ceremony p75-113

See also Oligopolies; Purchasing power; Wages; and subdivision Prices under names of products and other objects e.g. Ores—Prices

Mathematical models

Esposito, F. F. and Esposito, L. Industry price changes, market structure and inflation. *In* Inflation, trade and taxes p29-49

Magee, S. P. Prices, incomes, and foreign trade. *In* Kenen, P. B. ed. International trade and finance p175-252

Prichard, Elizabeth R.

The social worker's responsibility. *In* Anticipatory grief p237-45

Prichard, Keith W.

Teaching education courses: the other side of the tracks. *In* Buxton, T. H. and Prichard, K. W. eds. Excellence in university teaching p70-79

Prickett, Stephen

Romanticism and religion

Contents

Demythologising and myth-making: Arnold versus MacDonald

F. D. Maurice: The Kingdom of Christ

Keble's 'two worlds'

'A liberty of speculation which no Christian can tolerate'—the later Coleridge

'The living educts of the imagination': Coleridge on religious language

Newman: imagination and assent

Newman versus Maurice: development of doctrine and the growth of the mind

Summary: tradition and the Church

Wordsworth and the language of nature

Victorian fantasy

Contents

Adults in allegory land: Kingsley and Macdonald

Christmas at Scrooge's

Consensus and nonsense: Lear and Carroll

Dreams and nightmares: monsters under the hill

The evolution of a word

Worlds within worlds: Kipling and Nesbit

Priene, Asia Minor. Temple of Athena Polias

Carter, J. C. The date of the sculptured coffer lids from the Temple of Athene Polias at Priene. *In* Studies in classical art and archaeology p139-51

Priesthood

Biblical teaching

Robinson, D. W. B. The priesthood of Paul in the gospel of hope. *In* Reconciliation and hope p231-45

Priestley, F. E. L.

English: an obsolete industry? *In* Gold, J. ed. In the name of language! p18-45

Priestley, Joseph

About

Guerlac, H. Joseph Priestley's first papers on gases and their reception in France. *In* Guerlac, H. Essays and papers in the history of modern science p304-13

McEvoy, J. G. and McGuire, J. E. God and nature: Priestley's way of rational dissent. *In* Historical studies in the physical sciences v6 p325-404

Schofield, R. E. Joseph Priestley on sensation and perception. *In* Studies in perception p336-54

Priests in literature. See Clergy in literature

Prieto, Genaro. See Prieto, Jenaro

Prieto, Jenaro

About

Meehan, T. C. Jenaro Prieto: the man and his work. *In* Forster, M. H. ed. Tradition and renewal p157-207

Primary school students. See School children

Primates

See also Man

Behavior

Fox, R. Primate kin and human kinship. *In* Biosocial anthropology p9-35

Primers, Russian

Rosenhan, M. S. Images of male and female in children's readers. *In* Women in Russia p293-305

Primitive agriculture. See Agriculture, Primitive

Primitive art. See Art, Primitive

Primitive Christianity. See Church history—Primitive and early church, ca. 30-600

Primitive literature. See Folk literature

Primitive man. See Man, Primitive

Primitive religion. See Religion, Primitive

Primitivism in art

Goldwater, R. The primitivism of the Fauves, the Brücke, the primitivism of the Blaue Reiter; excerpt from "Primitivism in modern art." *In* Kaplan, P. and Manso, S. eds. Major European art movements, 1900-1945 p42-90

Middleton, J. C. The rise of primitivism and its relevance to the poetry of expressionism and dada. *In* Middleton, J. C. Bolshevism in art p23-37

Primitivism in literature

Goonetilleke, D. C. R. A. D. H. Lawrence: primitivism? *In* Goonetilleke, D. C. R. A. Developing countries in British fiction p170-98

Middleton, J. C. The rise of primitivism and its relevance to the poetry of expressionism and dada. *In* Middleton, J. C. Bolshevism in art p23-37

Simonsuuri, K. Notions of poetry and society in the controversy about Ossian. *In* Simonsuuri, K. Homer's original genius p108-18

See also Noble savage

Prince, Oliver Hilhouse, pseud. See Longstreet, Augustus Baldwin

Prince, Raymond H.

Cocoon work: an interpretation of the concern of contemporary youth with the mystical. *In* Zaretsky, I. I. and Leone, M. P. eds. Religious movements in contemporary America p255-71

Princeton. University

History

McLachlan, J. The choice of Hercules: American student societies in the early 19th century. *In* The University in society v2 p449-94

Miller, H. Evangelical religion and colonial Princeton. *In* Schooling and society p115-45

Principals, School. See School superintendents and principals

Principle of the uniformity of nature. See Uniformity of nature

Prins, Anton Adriaan

The dating in the Canterbury tales. *In* Chaucer and Middle English studies in honour of Rossell Hope Robbins p342-47

Printing

See also Bibliography; Book industries and trade; Water-marks

History

Bowers, F. T. Bibliographical evidence from the printer's measure. *In* Bowers, F. T. Essays in bibliography, text, and editing p258-68

Bowers, F. T. Old wine in new bottles: problems of machine printing. *In* Bowers, F. T. Essays in bibliography, text, and editing p392-411

Bowers, F. T. Running-title evidence for determining half-sheet imposition. *In* Bowers, F. T. Essays in bibliography, text, and editing p254-57

See also Bibliography—Early printed books; Incunabula; and subdivision Imprints under names of countries, states, cities, etc. e.g. Venice—Imprints

History—America

Adams, T. R. Some bibliographical observations on and questions about the relationship between the discovery of America and the invention of printing. *In* First images of America p529-36

History—Antwerp

Judson, J. R. Rubens and Moretus. *In* Medieval and Renaissance studies 1976 p141-59

History—England

Bowers, F. T. Elizabethan proofing. *In* Bowers, F. T. Essays in bibliography, text, and editing p240-53

History—Great Britain

Garbáty, T. J. Wynkyn de Worde's "Sir Thopas" and other tales. *In* Virginia. University. Bibliographical Society. Studies in bibliography v31 p57-67

Williams, W. P. Chetwin, Crooke, and the Jonson folios. *In* Virginia. University. Bibliographical Society. Studies in bibliography v30 p75-95

History—Pennsylvania

Waldenrath, A. The Pennsylvania-Germans: development of their printing and their newspress in the War for American Independence. *In* The German contribution to the building of the Americas p47-74

History—Russia

Simmons, J. S. G. Russian writing and printing: printing. *In* Auty, R. and Obolensky, D. eds. An introduction to Russian language and literature p47-55

Printing—*Continued*

History—United States

Silver, R. G. Flash of the comet: the typographical career of Samuel N. Dickinson. *In* Virginia. University. Bibliographical Society. Studies in bibliography v31 p68-89

History—Venice

Dunston, A. J. Venetian 'woodcut' capitals. *In* Virginia. University. Bibliographical Society. Studies in bibliography v30 p136-44

Little presses

See Little presses

Printing, Copperplate. See Engravings—Printing

Printing, Legislative

United States—History

Silver, R. G. Aprons instead of uniforms: the practice of printing, 1776-1787. *In* American Antiquarian Society. Proceedings v87 pt 1 p111-94

Printing, Public

United States—History

Silver, R. G. Aprons instead of uniforms: the practice of printing, 1776-1787. *In* American Antiquarian Society. Proceedings v87 pt 1 p111-94

Prints. See Lithography

Prior, Roger

George Wilkins and the young heir. *In* Shakespeare survey v29 p33-39

Prison hospitals. See Prisoners—Medical care

Prison psychology

Trasler, G. The role of psychologists in the penal system. *In* Progress in penal reform p129-41

See also Holocaust, Jewish (1939-1945)—Psychological aspects

Prison sentences

Great Britain

Blom-Cooper, L. J. Sentencing structure: a paradigm for the future. *In* Progress in penal reform p174-81

James, Sir A. E. The sentencing process: present practice and future policy. *In* Progress in penal reform p165-73

MacKenna, Sir B. J. M. General deterrence. *In* Progress in penal reform p182-95

Prisoners

Eitner, L. E. A. Cages, prisons, and captives in eighteenth-century art. *In* Kroeber, K. and Walling, W. eds. Images of romanticism p13-38

Hermann, H. A prisoner's perspective. *In* Progress in penal reform p209-20

See also Rehabilitation of criminals; Women prisoners

Education

See Education of prisoners

Legal status, laws, etc.

Morris, N. and Mills, M. Prisoners as laboratory animals. *In* Contemporary issues in criminal justice p129-43

Medical care—Great Britain

Prewer, R. R. The contribution of prison medicine. *In* Progress in penal reform p116-28

Psychiatric care—Great Britain

Prewer, R. R. The contribution of prison medicine. *In* Progress in penal reform p116-28

See also Prison psychology

Sexual behavior

Jackson, B. Deviance as success: the double inversion of stigmatized roles. *In* Babcock, B. A. ed. The reversible world p258-75

Rothenberg, D. Prisoners. *In* Gochros, H. L. and Gochros, J. S. eds. The sexually oppressed p225-36

Prisoners, Political. See Political prisoners

Prisoners in literature

Eitner, L. E. A. Cages, prisons, and captives in eighteenth-century art. *In* Kroeber, K. and Walling, W. eds. Images of romanticism p13-38

Prisons

Hawkins, G. The new penology. *In* Law and society p108-27

Nokes, P. L. The evaluation of penal systems. *In* Progress in penal reform p68-82

See also Imprisonment; Prison psychology; Prison sentences; Prisoners

California

Conrad, J. P. Winners and losers: a perspective on penal change. *In* Progress in penal reform p196-208

Europe

Bishop, N. Aspects of European penal systems. *In* Progress in penal reform p83-100

France

Perrot, M. Delinquency and the penitentiary system in nineteenth-century France. *In* Deviants and the abandoned in French society p213-45

Great Britain

Thomas, J. E. Policy and administration in penal establishments. *In* Progress in penal reform p54-67

Great Britain—Laws and regulations

McLachlan, N. Penal reform and penal history: some reflections. *In* Progress in penal reform p 1-24

United States

Fogel, D. Prison: the fortress model vs. the justice model. *In* Contemporary issues in criminal justice p119-28

Sayles, M. Behind locked doors. *In* Eddy, E. M. and Partridge, W. L. eds. Applied anthropology in America p210-28

Prisons in literature

Brombert, V. H. Epilogue: The borderline zone. *In* Brombert, V. H. The romantic prison p200-09

Brombert, V. H. Introduction: The prison dream. *In* Brombert, V. H. The romantic prison p3-17

Brombert, V. H. Nerval's privileged enclosures. *In* Brombert, V. H. The romantic prison p120-32

Brombert, V. H. Pascal's dungeon. *In* Brombert, V. H. The romantic prison p18-29

Brombert, V. H. Pétrus Borel: prison and the Gothic tradition. *In* Brombert, V. H. The romantic prison p49-61

Prisons in literature—*Continued*

Brombert, V. H. Sartre and the drama of ensnarement. *In* Brombert, V. H. The romantic prison p185-99

Brombert, V. H. Servitude and solidarity. *In* Brombert, V. H. The romantic prison p173-84

Brombert, V. H. Stendhal: the happy prison. *In* Brombert, V. H. The romantic prison p62-87

Brombert, V. H. Victor Hugo: the spaceless prison. *In* Brombert, V. H. The romantic prison p88-119

Easson, A. Marshalsea prisoners: Mr Dorrit and Mr Hemens. *In* Dickens Studies Annual v 3 p77-86

Reed, J. R. Confinement and character in Dickens' novels. *In* Dickens Studies Annual v 1 p41-54

Pritchard, Edward Evan Evans. See Evans-Pritchard, Edward Evan

Pritchard, James Bennett

The age of Solomon. *In* Pritchard, J. B. ed. Solomon & Sheba p17-39

Conclusion. *In* Pritchard, J. B. ed. Solomon & Sheba p146-51

Introduction. *In* Pritchard, J. B. ed. Solomon & Sheba p7-15

Pritchard, Linda K.

Religious change in nineteenth-century America. *In* The New religious consciousness p297-330

Pritchard, William H.

Seeing through everything

Contents

Auden & Co.
D. H. Lawrence: 1920-1930
England seen through
English poetry in the 1920s: Graves and Lawrence
Last things: 'Four quartets'
The literature of criticism
Satire and fiction: examples from the 1930s
Some 1920s fiction: Ford, Forster, Woolf, T. S. Eliot: 1918-1922

Pritchett, Charles Hermann

Judicial supremacy from Marshall to Burger. *In* Essays on the Constitution of the United States p99-112

Pritchett, Victor Sawdon

The myth makers

Contents

Alexander Pushkin: founding father
Alexander Solzhenitsyn: The Gulag Circle
Anton Chekhov: a doctor
August Strindberg: a bolting horse
Benito Perez Galdos: a Spanish Balzac
Boris Pasternak: unsafe conduct
Eça de Queiroz: a Portuguese diplomat
Emile Zola's life
Franz Kafka: estranged
Fyodor Dostoevsky: the early Dostoevsky
Gabriel Garcia Marquez: the myth makers
George Sand: George Sand
Gustave Flaubert: the quotidian
Ivan Goncharov: the dream of a censor
Jean Genet: a modern nihilist
Jorge Luis Borges: medallions
Leo Tolstoy: the despot
Machado de Assis: a Brazilian
Stendhal: an early outsider

About indivdual works

Books in general

Balakian, N. Criticism par excellence: V. S. Pritchett. *In* Balakian, N. Critical encounters p136-38

The living novel and later appreciations

Marcus, S. An ideal reviewer. *In* Marcus, S. Representations p118-28

Midnight oil

Sheed, W. V. S. Pritchett: Midnight oil. *In* Sheed, W. The good word & other words p223-27

Prittie, Terence Cornelius Farmer

Israel and the Palestinian question. *In* The Palestinians p213-27

Middle East refugees. *In* The Palestinians p51-73

Privacy, Right of

Bettelheim, B. Some comments on privacy. *In* Bettelheim, B. Surviving, and other essays p399-411

Capouya, E. On privacy and community. *In* Small comforts for hard times p109-19

Huxley, A. L. The individual life of man. *In* Huxley, A. L. The Human situation p108-22

Wellman, C. A new conception of human rights. *In* Human rights p48-58

Great Britain

Brustein, R. S. Reflections on privacy. *In* Brustein, R. S. The culture watch p59-63

Hutton, E. J.; Nehra, K. S. and Sastri, D. S. The right of privacy in the United States, Great Britain, and India. *In* Claude, R. P. ed. Comparative human rights p127-60

India

Hutton, E. J.; Nehra, K. S. and Sastri, D. S. The right of privacy in the United States, Great Britain, and India. *In* Claude, R. P. ed. Comparative human rights p127-60

United States

Hutton, E. J.; Nehra, K. S. and Sastri, D. S. The right of privacy in the United States, Great Britain, and India. *In* Claude, R. P. ed. Comparative human rights p127-60

Private presses. See Privately printed books; also names of individual presses

Private property, Right of. See Right of property

Private schools. See State aid to private schools

Privateering

Symcox, G. W. The battle of the Atlantic, 1500-1700. *In* First images of America p265-77

Privately printed books

Henderson, B. Independent publishing: today and yesterday. *In* Altbach, P. G. and McVey, S. eds. Perspectives on publishing p217-29

Privilege against self-incrimination. See Self-incrimination

Probabilism

Trowbridge, F. H. White of Selborne: the ethos of probabilism. *In* Trowbridge, F. H. From Dryden to Jane Austen p249-72

Probabilities

Robbins, H. The statistical mode of thought. *In* Neyman, J. ed. The heritage of Copernicus: theories "pleasing to the mind" p419-32

Stove, D. C. Why should probability be the guide of life? *In* Livingston, D. W. and King, J. T. eds. Hume p50-68

Trowbridge, F. H. Scattered atoms of probability. *In* Trowbridge, F. H. From Dryden to Jane Austen p213-48

See also Sampling (Statistics)

Probate law and practice. See Estates (Law)

Probation

Great Britain

McNeal, P. Non-custodial supervision. *In* Progress in penal reform p255-67

United States

McAnany, P. D. Recommendations for improving the ailing probation system. *In* Contemporary issues in criminal justice p76-93

Problem children

See also Juvenile delinquency

Education

Bettelheim, B. About Summerhill. *In* Bettelheim, B. Surviving, and other essays p169-84

Education—Case studies

Bolgen, K. There are no hopeless children. *In* Fairfield, R. P. ed. Humanistic frontiers in American education p220-36

United States

Delfini, L. F.; Bernal, M. E. and Rosen, P. M. Comparison of deviant and normal boys in home settings. *In* Behavior modification and families p228-48

Johnson, S. M.; Bolstad, O. D. and Lobitz, G. K. Generalization and contrast phenomena in behavior modification with children. *In* Behavior modification and famlies p160-88

Patterson, G. R. The aggressive child: victim and architect of a coercive system. *In* Behavior modification and families p267-316

Problem solving

Foltz, W. J. Two forms of unofficial conflict intervention: the problem-solving and the process-promoting workshops. *In* Unofficial diplomats p201-21

Kelman, H. C. The problem-solving workshop in conflict resolution. *In* Unofficial diplomats p168-200

Mitroff, I. I. Systemic problem solving. *In* Leadership p129-43

Sayers, D. L. Problem picture; excerpt from "The mind of the Maker." *In* Sayers, D. L. The whimsical Christian p122-50

Procedure (Law) See Civil procedure; Judicial process

Processions. See Festivals

Proctor, J. Harris

Communal representation in the Republic of Malawi. *In* Prospects for constitutional democracy p146-64

Proctor, Samuel DeWitt

Land-grant universities and the Black presence. *In* Land-grant universities and their continuing challenge p190-204

Prodi, Romano, and Clô, Alberto

Europe. *In* Vernon, R. ed. The oil crisis p91-112

Prodicus of Ceos

About

Henrichs, A. Two doxographical notes: Democritus and Prodicus on religion. *In* Harvard Studies in classical philology v79 p93-123

Prodigal son (Parable)

Drama

Beck, E. Terence improved: the paradigm of the Prodigal son in English Renaissance comedy. *In* Renaissance drama [1973] p107-22

Producers, Moving-picture. See Moving-picture producers and directors

Production (Economic theory)

Mathematical models

See Production functions (Economic theory)

Production functions (Economic theory)

Tinbergen, J. Changing factor shares and the translog production function. *In* Theory for economic efficiency: essays in honor of Abba P. Lerner p195-216

Production-line methods. See Assembly-line methods

Productivity, Marginal. See Marginal productivity

Profession of arms. See Armed Forces—Vocational guidance

Professional education

Tolley, G. S. Higher education and the professions. *In* Niblett, W. R. ed. The sciences, the humanities and the technological threat p65-76

See also Special types of professional education, e.g. Library education; Professional education of women; and the subdivision Study and teaching under particular fields, e.g. Political science—Study and teaching

United States

Leslie, L. L. Updating education for the professions: the new mission. *In* Land-grant universities and their continuing challenge p237-65

Professional education of women

United States

Trilling, D. We must march my darlings: Daughters of the middle class. *In* Trilling, D. We must march my darlings p272-91

See also Higher education of women

Professional ethics

Horowitz, I. L. Science, sin, and sponsorship. *In* Horowitz, I. L. ed. Science, sin, and scholarship p260-81

See also Anthropological ethics; Medical ethics; Teachers, Professional ethics for

Professional socialization

Perrucci, R. In the service of man: radical movements in the professions. *In* Gerstl, J. E. and Jacobs, G. eds. Professions for the people p215-30

Professional sports

Social aspects

Juliani, R. N. Social change and the athlete. *In* Gerstl, J. E. and Jacobs, G. eds. Professions for the people p61-94

Professions

Bender, T. The cultures of intellectual life: the city and the professions. *In* Higham, J. and Conkin, P. K. eds. New directions in American intellectual history p181-95

See also Professional socialization

Great Britain

Tolley, G. S. Higher education and the professions. *In* Niblett, W. R. ed. The sciences, the humanities and the technological threat p65-76

United States

Smythe, H. H. The Black professional. *In* The Black American reference book p453-79

Yarmolinsky, A. What future for the professional in American society? *In* A New America? p159-74

Professors. See College teachers

Profit

Lerner, A. P. Wages, profits, and marginal analysis. *In* Inflation, trade and taxes p23-28

Rosenberg, N. Adam Smith on profits—paradox lost and regained. *In* Skinner, A. S. and Wilson, T. eds. Essays on Adam Smith p377-89

See also Capitalism

Programmed instruction

Jones, T. F. Discovery laboratories: an alternative to "cookbook labs". *In* Buxton, T. H. and Prichard, K. W. eds. Excellence in university teaching p103-08

Postlethwait, S. N. Students, teachers, and technology. *In* Buxton, T. H. and Prichard, K. W. eds. Excellence in university teaching p220-31

Programmed learning. See Programmed instruction

Programs, Radio. See Radio programs

Programs, Television. See Television programs

Progress

Hesburgh, T. M. The civil rights revolution: from confrontation to education. *In* Hesburgh, T. M. The Hesburgh papers p121-25

Highet, G. The illusion of progress. *In* Highet, G. The immortal profession p21-35

Moscivici, S. The reenchantment of the world. *In* Beyond the crisis p133-68

Stockton, C. N. Economics and the mechanism of historical progress in Hume's History. *In* Livingston, D. W. and King, J. T. eds. Hume p296-320

Voegelin, E. The conflict between progress and political existence after Turgot. *In* Voegelin, E. From Enlightenment to Revolution p110-35

See also Science and civilization; Social change

Progressive Party (Founded 1948)

Gill, G. R. "Win or lose—we win": the 1952 Vice Presidential campaign of Charlotta A. Bass. *In* Harley, S. and Terborg-Penn, R. eds. The Afro-American woman p109-18

Progressivism (United States politics)

Davis, G. Theodore Roosevelt and the Progressive Era: a study in individual and group psychohistory. *In* DeMause, L. ed. The new psychohistory p245-305

Miller, R. G. Fort Worth and the Progressive Era: the movement for charter revision, 1899-1907. *In* Essays on urban America p89-125

Morgan, K. O. The future at work: Anglo-American progressivism, 1890-1917. *In* Allen, H. C. and Thompson, R. eds. Contrast and connection p245-71

Rothman, D. J. The state as parent: social policy in the Progressive Era. *In* Doing good p67-96

Thompson, J. A. American Progressive publicists and the First World War 1914-1917. *In* Burton, D. H. ed. American history —British historians p187-217

Prohibited books

Darnton, R. Trade in the taboo: the life of a clandestine book dealer in prerevolutionary France. *In* Korshin, P. J. ed. The widening circle p11-83

See also Censorship; Liberty of the press

Prohibited books (Canon law) See Index librorum prohibitorum

Prohibition. See Temperance

Project Independence (U.S. Energy Supply Effort)

Adelman, M. A. The hinge of energy policy: relations between energy markets in the United States and abroad. *In* Eppen, G. D. ed. Energy: the policy issues p71-81

Project method in teaching. See Field work (Educational method)

Projection. See Perspective

Prokhorov, Yevgeny

The Marxist press concept. *In* Fischer, H. D. and Merrill, J. C. eds. International and intercultural communication p51-58

Prokopovich, Feofan. See Feofan, Abp. of Novgorod

Proletariat in literature

Rahv, P. Proletarian literature: a political autopsy. *In* Rahv, P. Essays on literature and politics, 1932-1972 p293-304

Proliferation, Nuclear. See Nuclear non-proliferation

Prologues and epilogues. See Prefaces

Prolongation of life span. See Longevity

Promiscuity

Elliston, F. A. In defense of promiscuity. *In* Baker, R. and Elliston, F. A. eds. Philosophy & sex p222-43

Promised land (Motion picture)

Sarris, A. Promised lands. *In* Sarris, A. Politics and cinema p96-101

Pronay, Nicholas

The newsreels: the illusion of actuality. *In* Smith, P. ed. The historian and film p95-119

Proof. See Evidence

Propaganda

Gordon, G. N. Aristotle as a modern propagandist. *In* Havelock, E. A. and Hershbell, J. P. eds. Communication arts in the ancient world p55-61

Taylor, R. Propaganda and film. *In* Taylor, R. Film propaganda p19-32

See also Moving-pictures in propaganda; Propaganda, International; Public opinion; Rumor

Propaganda, Communist

Taylor, R. Conclusions. *In* Taylor, R. Film propaganda p230-33

Taylor, R. Russia: The needs of revolution. *In* Taylor, R. Film propaganda p44-68

Taylor, R. Russia: Themes and variations *In* Taylor, R. Film propaganda p69-80

Propaganda, German

Taylor, R. Conclusions. *In* Taylor, R. Film propaganda p230-33

Taylor, R. Germany: The needs of revolution. *In* Taylor, R. Film propaganda p156-68

Taylor, R. Germany: Themes and variations. *In* Taylor, R. Film propaganda p169-76

Propaganda, International

Ellul, J. International propaganda and myths. *In* Fischer, H. D. and Merrill, J. C. eds. International and intercultural communication p273-79

Martin, L. J. Effectiveness of international propaganda. *In* Fischer, H. D. and Merrill, J. C. eds. International and intercultural communication p262-72

Propaganda, Russian

Taylor, R. Conclusions. *In* Taylor, R. Film propaganda p230-33

Taylor, R. Russia: The historical background. *In* Taylor, R. Film propaganda p35-43

Taylor, R. Russia: The needs of revolution. *In* Taylor, R. Film propaganda p44-68

Taylor, R. Russia: Themes and variations. *In* Taylor, R. Film propaganda p69-80

Propaganda in moving-pictures. See Moving-pictures in propaganda

Propertius, Sextus Aurelius

About

Ross, D. O. Propertius: from ardoris poeta to Romanus Callimachus. *In* Ross, D. O. Backgrounds to Augustan poetry: Gallus, elegy and Rome p107-30

Skutsch, O. The Second book of Propertius. *In* Harvard Studies in classical philology v79 p229-33

About individual works

The elegies

Messing, G. M. Pound's Propertius: the homage and the damage. *In* Poetry and poetics from ancient Greece to the Renaissance p105-33

The elegies (Book I, number 8)

Pucci, P. Lingering on the threshold. *In* Glyph 3 p52-73

The elegies (Book 3)

Jacobson, H. Structure and meaning in Propertius Book 3. *In* Illinois classical studies, v 1 1976 p160-73

Putnam, M. C. J. Propertius 3.22: Tullus' return. *In* Illinois classical studies v2 1977 p240-54

The elegies [Book 4]

Pillinger, H. E. Some Callimachean influences on Propertius, Book 4. *In* Harvard Studies in classical philology v73 p171-99

Hylas

Bramble, J. C. Cui non dictus Hylas puer? Propertius I.20. *In* Woodman, T. and West, D. eds. Quality and pleasure in Latin poetry p81-93

Monobiblos

Ross, D. O. Propertius' Monobiblos. *In* Ross, D. O. Backgrounds to Augustan poetry: Gallus, elegy and Rome p51-84

Criticism, Textual

Goold, G. P. Noctes-Propertianae. *In* Harvard Studies in classical philology v71 p59-106

Property

Macpherson, C. B. Capitalism and the changing concept of property. *In* Kamenka, E. and Neale, R. S. eds. Feudalism, capitalism and beyond p104-24

Tay, A. E. S. Law, the citizen and the state. *In* Law and society p 1-17

See also Right of property; Wealth

History

Kiernan, E. V. G. Private property in history. *In* Family and inheritance p361-98

Property (Canon law)

Ste Croix, G. E. M. de. Early Christian attitudes to property and slavery. *In* Church, society and politics p 1-38

Property (Islamic Law)

Pastner, C. M. The status of women and property on a Baluchistan oasis in Pakistan. *In* Beck, L. and Keddie, N. R. eds. Women in the Muslim world p434-50

Property, Crimes against. See Offenses against property

Property, Literary. See Copyright

Property, Right of. See Right of property

Property in literature

Hardy, B. N. Properties and possessions in Jane Austen's novels p79-105

Prophecy

Wittreich, J. A. "A poet amongst poets": Milton and the tradition of prophecy. *In* Wittreich, J. A. ed. Milton and the line of vision p97-142

Prophecies. See Apocalyptic literature; Twentieth century—Forecasts

Prophecy in literature

Sayers, D. L. Oedipus simplex: freedom and fate in folklore and fiction; excerpt from "The poetry of search and the poetry of statement and other posthumous essays on literature, religion, and language." *In* Sayers, D. L. The whimsical Christian p235-57

Prophets

Petersen, D. L. Max Weber and the sociological study of ancient Israel. *In* Johnson, H. M. ed. Religious change and continuity p117-49

Proportion. See Symmetry

Proportion (Art). See Perspective

Proposition (Logic)

Berlin, Sir I. Empirical propositions and hypothetical statements. *In* Berlin, Sir I. Concepts and categories p32-55

Berlin, Sir I. Logical translation. *In* Berlin, Sir I. Concepts and categories p56-80

Castañeda Calderón, H. N. Goodness, intentions, and propositions. *In* Fact, value, and perception p67-83

Matthews, R. J. Literary works express propositions. *In* Hernadi, P. ed. What is literature? p102-12

Plantinga, A. Possible but unactual objects on what there isn't; excerpt from "The nature of necessity.." *In* Margolis, J. Z. ed. Philosophy looks at the arts p438-81

Propositional calculus

Quine, W. V. Ontological remarks on the propositional calculus. *In* Quine, W. V. The ways of paradox, and other essays p265-71

Quine, W. V. Quantifiers and propositional attitudes. *In* Quine, W. V. The ways of paradox, and other essays p185-96

Prose poems, French

Shattuck, R. Vibratory organism: crise de prose. *In* Symbolism and modern literature p193-204

Prosecution

See also Double jeopardy

Great Britain

Williams, D. G. T. Prosecution, discretion and the accountability of the police. *In* Crime, criminology and public policy p161-95

Great Britain—History

Caenegem, R. C. van. Public prosecution of crime in twelfth-century England. *In* Church and government in the Middle Ages p41-76

United States

Laycock, D. Federal interference with state prosecutions: the need for prospective relief. *In* The Supreme Court review, 1977 p193-238

Prosecutors, Public. See Public prosecutors

Proserpine. See Persephone

Proserpine in literature. See Persephone in literature

Proske, Beatrice Irene Gilman

Two ivory Madonnas. *In* Enggass, R. C. and Stokstad, M. eds. Hortus imaginum p37-44

Prosody. See Versification

Prosopography. Beech, G. T. *In* Powell, J. M. ed. Medieval studies p151-84

Prosser, Michael Hubert

The cultural communicator. *In* Fischer, H. D. and Merrill, J. C. eds. International and intercultural communication p417-23

Prostitutes

England

Walkowitz, J. The making of an outcast group: prostitutes and working women in nineteenth-century Plymouth and Southampton. *In* Vicinus, M. ed. A widening sphere p72-93

Prostitution

England—Law and legislation

Walkowitz, J. The making of an outcast group: prostitutes and working women in nineteenth-century Plymouth and Southampton. *In* Vicinus, M. ed. A widening sphere p72-93

France

Rossiaud, J. Prostitution, youth, and society in the towns of southeastern France in the fifteenth century. *In* Deviants and the abandoned in French society p 1-46

Great Britain

Rogal, S. J. The selling of sex: Mandeville's Modest defence of publick stews. *In* Studies in eighteenth-century culture v5 p141-50

United States

Pittman, D. J. The male house of prostitution. *In* Henslin, J. M. ed. Deviant lifestyles p151-65

United States—History

Johnson, C. D. That guilty third tier: prostitution in nineteenth-century American theaters. *In* Howe, D. W. ed. Victorian America p111-20

Protagoras

About

Trinkaus, C. Protagoras in the Renaissance: an exploration. *In* Philosophy and humanism p190-213

Protection. See Free trade and protection

Protection of citizens abroad. See Diplomatic protection

Protective coloration (Biology)

Hinton, H. E. Natural deception. *In* Gregory, R. L. and Gombrich, Sir E. H. J. eds. Illusion in nature and art p97-159

Protectorates

Esthus, R. A. Protectorates and spheres of influence. *In* Encyclopedia of American foreign policy p836-43

Protest movements (Vietnamese Conflict, 1961-1975) See Vietnamese Conflict, 1961-1975—Protest movements

Protest poetry

History and criticism

Thompson, D. Dissent and protest. *In* Thompson, D. The uses of poetry p137-72

Protestant churches

California—San Francisco Bay Region

Wolfe, J. Three congregations. *In* The New religious consciousness p227-44

France—History

Parker, D. The Huguenots in seventeenth-century France. *In* Hepburn, A. C. ed. Minorities in history p11-30

United States—History

Banner, L. W. Religious benevolence as social control: a critique of an interpretation. *In* Mulder, J. M. and Wilson, J. F. eds. Religion in American history p218-35

Maclear, J. F. The Republic and the millennium. *In* Mulder, J. M. and Wilson, J. F. eds. Religion in American history p181-98

Mathews, D. G. The second Great Awakening as an organizing process, 1780-1830. *In* Mulder, J. M. and Wilson, J. F. eds. Religion in American history p199-217

Mead, S. E. American Protestantism during the Revolutionary epoch. *In* Mulder, J. M. and Wilson, J. F. eds. Religion in American history p162-80

Protestant dissenters. See Dissenters, Religious

The Protestant Post-Boy

Snyder, H. L. The contributions of Abel Boyer as Whig journalist and writer of The Protestant Post-Boy, 1711-1712. *In* The Dress of words p139-49

Protestant Reformation. See Reformation

Protestant sects. See Protestant churches

Protestant theology. See Theology, Protestant

Protestantism

Garrett, G. P. Ladies in Boston have their hats: notes on WASP humor. *In* Cohen, S. B. ed. Comic relief p207-37

Martin, D. A. Mutations: religio-political crisis and the collapse of Puritanism and humanism. *In* Universities in the Western world p85-97

Parsons, T. Religious and economic symbolism in the Western world. *In* Johnson, H. M. ed. Religious change and continuity p 1-48

See also Evangelicalism; Protestant churches, Reformation

Protestantism—Continued

History

Banner, L. W. Religious benevolence as social control: a critique of an interpretation. In Mulder, J. M. and Wilson, J. F. eds. Religion in American history p218-35

Handy, R. T. The American religious depression, 1925-1935. In Mulder, J. M. and Wilson, J. F. eds. Religion in American history p431-44

Király, B. K. Protestantism in Hungary between the Revolution and the Ausgleich. In Király, B. K. ed. Tolerance and movements of religious dissent in Eastern Europe p65-85

Littell, F. H. The Radical Reformation and the American experience. In America in theological perspective p71-86

Influence

Kann, R. A. Protestantism and German nationalism in the Austro-German Alpine lands (1). In Király, B. K. ed. Tolerance and movements of religious dissent in Eastern Europe p11-25

Protestantism, Evangelical. See Evangelicalism

Protestantism and capitalism

Anthony D. and Robbins, T. L. The effect of detente on the growth of new religions: Reverend Moon and the Unification Church. In Needleman, J. and Baker, G. eds. Understanding the new religions p80-100

Protestantism in literature

Lewalski, B. K. Edward Taylor: lisps of praise and strategies for self-dispraise. In Lewalski, B. K. Protestant poetics and the seventeenth-century religious lyric p388-426

Lewalski, B. K. George Herbert: artful psalms from the temple in the heart. In Lewalski, B. K. Protestant poetics and the seventeenth-century religious lyric p283-316

Lewalski, B. K. Henry Vaughan: pleading in groans of my Lord's penning. In Lewalski, B. K. Protestant poetics and the seventeenth-century religious lyric p317-51

Lewalski, B. K. "Is there in truth no beautie?" Protestant poetics and the Protestant paradigm of salvation. In Lewalski, B. K. Protestant poetics and the seventeenth-century religious lyric p3-27

Lewalski, B. K. John Donne: writing after the copy of a metaphorical God. In Lewalski, B. K. Protestant poetics and the seventeenth-century religious lyrics p253-82

Lewalski, B. K. Thomas Traherne: naked truth, transparent words, and the renunciation of metaphor. In Lewalski, B. K. Protestant poetics and the seventeenth-century religious lyric p352-87

Pickering, S. Protestantism in Barnaby Rudge. In Pickering, S. The moral tradition in English fiction, 1785-1850 p123-48

Protestants

Hungary

Király, B. K. Protestantism in Hungary between the Revolution and the Ausgleich. In Király, B. K. ed. Tolerance and movements of religious dissent in Eastern Europe p65-85

Ireland

D'Alton, I. A contrast in crises: southern Irish Protestantism, 1820-43 and 1885-1910. In Hepburn, A. C. ed. Minorities in history p70-83

United States

DeLeon, D. Conscience and community. In DeLeon, D. The American as anarchist p14-23

Garrett, G. P. Ladies in Boston have their hats: notes on WASP humor. In Cohen, S. B. ed. Comic relief p207-37

Littell, F. H. The Radical Reformation and the American experience. In America in theological perspective p71-86

Mawhinney, J. J. H. Richard Niebuhr and reshaping American Christianity. In America in theological perspective p140-62

Schneider, M. L. A Catholic perspective on American civil religion. In America in theological perspective p123-39

Sheed, W. The subject of ethnics. In Sheed, W. The good word & other words p142-47

Singleton, G. H. Protestant voluntary organizations and the shaping of Victorian America. In Howe, D. W. ed. Victorian America p47-58

Proteus Echo

Granger, B. I. Early Boston serials. In Granger, B. I. American essay serials from Franklin to Irving p13-40

Prott, Lyndel V.

The future of the International Court of Justice. In The Year book of world affairs, 1979 p284-303

Proudfoot, Richard

Textual studies. In Shakespeare survey 26 p177-84

Textual studies [another essay] In Shakespeare survey 27 p179-92

Textual studies [another essay] In Shakespeare survey 28 p173-81

Textual studies [another essay] In Shakespeare survey v29 p177-85

Textual studies [another essay] In Shakespeare survey 30 p203-10

Verbal reminiscence and the two-part structure of 'The winter's tale.' In Shakespeare survey v29 p67-78

Proust, Marcel

About

Breé, G. From Jean Santeuil to Time regained. In Garvin, H. R. ed. Makers of the twentieth-century novel p144-48

Church, M. Kafka and Proust: a contrast in time. In Garvin, H. R. ed. Makers of the twentieth-century novel p149-53

Gass, W. H. Proust at 100. In Gass, W. H. The world within the word p147-57

Girard, R. Narcissism: the Freudian myth demythified by Proust. In Roland, A. ed. Psychoanalysis, creativity, and literature p293-311

Jay, K. Male homosexuality and lesbianism in the works of Proust and Gide. In Crew, L. ed. The gay academic p216-43

Snow, C. P. Baron Snow. Proust. In Snow, C. P. Baron Snow. The realists p297-333

About individual works

By way of Sainte-Beuve (Contre Sainte-Beuve)

Connolly, C. Marcel Proust: 1. In Connolly, C. The evening colonnade p182-85

The captive

Meyers, J. Vermeer and The captive. In Meyers, J. Painting and the novel p112-23

Cities of the plain

Meyers, J. Cities of the plain. In Meyers, J. Homosexuality and literature, 1890-1930 p58-75

Proust, Marcel—About individual works
—*Continued*

Remembrance of things past

Auchincloss, L. Marcel Proust: the autobiography in the novel. *In* Auchincloss, L. Life, law and letters p39-45

Auchincloss, L. Swann, male chauvinist and Albertine, boy-girl. *In* Auchincloss, L. Life, law and letters p97-104

Hardy, B. N. Memory and memories. *In* Hardy, B. N. Tellers and listeners p56-101

Jones, P. Knowledge and illusion in A la recherche du temps perdu. *In* Jones, P. Philosophy and the novel p147-80

May K. M. The search for identity. *In* May, K. M. Out of the maelstrom p62-77

Terdiman, R. Conclusion. *In* Terdiman, R. The dialectics of isolation p227-48

Terdiman, R. The depreciation of the event. *In* Terdiman, R. The dialectics of isolation p96-198

Swann's way

Meyers, J. Bellini, Giotto, Mantegna, Botticelli and Swann's way. *In* Meyers, J. Painting and the novel p96-111

Sayre, R. F. Du côté de chez Swann: the unknowable other. *In* Sayre, R. F. Solitude in society p91-116

The sweet cheat gone

Terdiman, R. Narration in La fugitive. *In* Terdiman, R. The dialectics of isolation p199-225

Criticism and interpretation

Jacobs, C. Benjamin: Walter Benjamin: Image of Proust. *In* Jacobs, C. The dissimulating harmony p87-110

Provençal poetry

History and criticism

Köhler, E. Deliberations on a theory of the genre of the Old Provençal descort. *In* Italian literature: roots and branches p 1-13

Nichols, S. G. Toward an aesthetic of the Provençal lyric II: Marcabru's Dire vos vuoill ses doptansa (BdT 293, 18). *In* Italian literature: roots and branches p15-37

Provence

Description and travel

Connolly, C. Farewell to Provence. *In* Connolly, C. The evening colonnade p20-25

Social conditions

Roubin, L. A. Male space and female space within the Provençal community. *In* Rural society in France p152-80

Social life and customs

Roubin, L. A. Male space and female space within the Provençal community. *In* Rural society in France p152-80

Proverbs

Friedman, A. B. "When Adam delved. . .": contexts of an historic proverb. *In* The Learned and the lewed p213-30

La Rosa, R. C. Necessary truths: the poetics of Emerson's proverbs. *In* Literary monographs v8 p129-92

Miller, C. H. The logic and rhetoric of proverbs in Erasmus's Praise of Folly. *In* Essays on the works of Erasmus p83-98

Nemerov, H. Exceptions and rules. *In* Nemerov, H. Figures of thought p42-48

Phillips, M. M. Ways with adages. *In* Essays on the works of Erasmus p51-60

Sands, D. B. Reynard the Fox and the manipulation of the popular proverb. *In* The Learned and the lewed p265-78

Seitel, P. I. Proverbs: a social use of metaphor. *In* Folklore genres p125-43

See also Aphorisms and apothegms; Maxims

Proverbs, Assyro-Babylonian

Moran, W. L. An Assyriological gloss on the new Archilochus fragment. *In* Harvard studies in classical philology v82 p17-19

Proverbs, Haya. See Proverbs, Ziba

Proverbs, Hebrew

Gruenewald, M. "It is enough for the servant to be like his master." *In* Salo Wittmayer Baron v2 p573-76

Proverbs, Jewish. See Proverbs, Hebrew

Proverbs, Ziba

Seitel, P. Saying Haya sayings: two categories of proverb use. *In* The Social use of metaphor p75-99

Providence and government of God

Chadwick, O. On a sense of providence. *In* Chadwick, O. The secularization of the European mind in the nineteenth century p250-66

Provine, William B.

Francis B. Sumner and the evolutionary synthesis. *In* Studies in history of biology v3 p211-40

The role of mathematical population geneticists in the evolutionary synthesis of the 1930s and 1940s. *In* Studies in history of biology, v2 p167-92

Provisional Irish Republican Army. See Irish Republican Army

Proxy

Lopez, R. S. Proxy in medieval trade. *In* Order and innovation in the Middle Ages p187-94

Prudence. See Common sense

Prudentius Clemens, Aurelius

About individual works

Psychomachia

Barney, S. A. The siege of paradise: Prudentius's Psychomachia. *In* Barney, S. A. Allegories of history, allegories of love p61-81

Hollander, R. Typology and secular literature: some medieval problems and examples. *In* Miner, E. R. ed. Literary uses of typology p3-19

Průšek, Jaroslav

Urban centers: the cradle of popular fiction. *In* Birch, C. ed. Studies in Chinese literary genres p259-98

Prussia

Economic conditions

Dickler, R. A. Organization and change in productivity in Eastern Prussia. *In* Parker, W. N. and Jones, E. L. ed. European peasants and their markets p269-92

Pryce-Jones, David

On Israel's East. *In* The Palestinians p209-12

Pryor, Taylor A.

Growing seafood on shore. *In* Strategies for human settlements: habitat and environment p67-78

Pryse, Marjorie
The mark and the knowledge

Contents

Faulkner's "Dry September" and "Red leaves": caste and outcast
Invisible man: the world in a man-of-war
Light in August: violence and excommunity
Moby-Dick: social physics and metaphysics
Postscript
The scarlet letter: social stigma and art
The transcendental imagination: the mark as focus

Psychedelic drugs. See Hallucinogenic drugs

Psychiatric hospitals

Massachusetts

Rosenkrantz, B. G. and Vinovskis, M. A. The invisible lunatics: old age and insanity in mid-nineteenth-century Massachusetts. *In* Spicker, S. F.; Woodward, K. M. and Van Tassel, D. D. eds. Aging and the elderly p95-125

United States—History

Dain, N. American psychiatry in the 18th century. *In* American psychiatry: past, present, and future p15-27

Psychiatric research

Wallace, A. F. C. Basic studies, applied projects, and eventual implementation: a case history of biological and cultural research in mental health. *In* Spindler, G. D. ed.. The making of psychological anthropology p203-16

Psychiatric social work. See Medical social work

Psychiatry

Ullman, M. Psychiatry and parapsychology: the consummation of an uncertain romance. *In* Parapsychology: its relation to physics, biology, psychology, and psychiatry p171-207

See also Adolescent psychiatry; Geriatric psychiatry; Mental illness; Neuropsychiatry; Psychology, Pathological; Psychotherapy; Social psychiatry

Cases, clinical reports, statistics

Birtchnell, J. An analysis of the art productions of a psychiatric patient who was preoccupied with his nose. *In* Ulman, E. and Dachinger, P. eds. Art therapy p328-41

Dewdney, S. H. Elda's art therapy in the context of a quarter century of psychiatric treatment. *In* Ulman, E. and Dachinger, P. eds. Art therapy p240-75

Schwarz, B. E. Psi and the life cycle. *In* Parapsychology: its relation to physics, biology, psychology, and psychiatry p235-45

History

Altschule, M. D. Miscellanea. *In* Altschule, M. D. Origins of concepts in human behavior p193-200

Simon, B. The development of models of mental illness. *In* Simon, B. Mind and madness in ancient Greece p31-42

Simon, B. On the babel of tongues in contemporary psychiatry. *In* Simon, B. Mind and madness in ancient Greece p1-30

Methodology

Elkes, J. Subjective and objective observation in psychiatry: a note toward discussion. *In* Alternate states of consciousness p242-63

Research

See Psychiatric research

Social aspects

Bazelon, D. L. The role of psychiatry in society: a jurist's viewpoint. *In* American psychiatry: past, present, and future p157-69

Grinker, R. R. The role of psychiatry in society. *In* American psychiatry: past, present, and future p170-82

Rosenberg, C. E. The crisis in psychiatric legitimacy: reflections on psychiatry, medicine, and public policy. *In* American psychiatry: past, present, and future p135-48

Schwartz, M. S. A role for psychiatry in the future: a proposal. *In* American psychiatry: past, present, and future p149-56

Russia

Joravsky, D. The construction of the Stalinist psyche. *In* Cultural revolution in Russia, 1928-1931 p105-28

United States—History

Romano, J. American psychiatry: past, present, and future. *In* American psychiatry: past, present, and future p28-44

United States—Statistics

Kramer, M. Implications of expected changes in composition of U.S. population for the delivery of mental health services during the period 1971-85. *In* American psychiatry: past, present, and future p94-112

Psychiatry, Geriatric. See Geriatric psychiatry

Psychiatry, Social. See Social psychiatry

Psychiatry and art. See Art therapy

Psychiatry and religion

De Salzmann, M. Man's ever new and eternal challenge. *In* Needleman, J. and Lewis, D. eds. On the way to self knowledge p54-75

Frankl, V. E. Man's search for ultimate meaning. *In* Needleman, J. and Lewis, D. eds. On the way to self knowledge p182-203

Hillman, J. Peaks and vales. *In* Needleman, J. and Lewis, D. eds. On the way to self knowledge p114-41

Malone, T. P. The Christian sacred tradition and psychotherapy. *In* Needleman, J. and Lewis, D. eds. On the way to self knowledge p26-45

Needleman, J. Psychiatry and the sacred. *In* Needleman, J. and Lewis, D. eds. On the way to self knowledge p3-25

Skynner, A. C. R. The relationship of psychotherapy to sacred tradition. *In* Needleman, J. and Lewis, D. eds. On the way to self knowledge p204-25

Psychic trauma

Bettelheim, B. Schizophrenia as a reaction to extreme situations. *In* Bettelheim, B. Surviving, and other essays p112-24

Bettelheim, B. Trauma and reintegration. *In* Bettelheim, B. Surviving, and other essays p19-37

Psychical research

Beloff, J. Explaining the paranormal, with Epilogue—1977. *In* Ludwig, J. K. ed. Philosophy and parapsychology p353-70

Beloff, J. Parapsychology and its neighbors. *In* Wheatley, J. M. O. and Edge, H. L. eds. Philosophical dimensions of parapsychology p374-87

Braude, S. E. On the meaning of 'paranormal.' *In* Ludwig, J. K. ed. Philosophy and parapsychology p227-44

Psychical research—_Continued_

Broad, C. D. The relevance of psychical research to philosophy; excerpt from "Religion, philosophy and psychical research." _In_ Wheatley, J. M. O. and Edge, H. L. eds. Philosophical dimensions of parapsychology p10-29

Chauvin, R. To reconcile psi and physics. _In_ Wheatley, J. M. O. and Edge, H. L. eds. Philosophical dimensions of parapsychology p409-12

Child, I. L. Parapsychology and the rest of psychology: a mutual challenge. _In_ Parapsychology: its relation to physics, biology, psychology, and psychiatry p95-121

Ehrenwald, J. Parapsychology and the seven dragons: a neuropsychiatric model of psi phenomena. _In_ Parapsychology: its relation to physics, biology, psychology, and psychiatry p246-63

Flew, A. G. N. Describing and explaining; excerpt from "A new approach to psychical research." _In_ Ludwig, J. K. ed. Philosophy and parapsychology p207-26

Flew, A. G. N. Parapsychology revisited: laws, miracles, and repeatability. _In_ Ludwig, J. K. ed. Philosophy and parapsychology p263-69

Foster, L. A. The causal objection to precognition. _In_ Ludwig, J. K. ed. Philosophy and parapsychology p313-26

Godbey, J. W. Central-state materialism and parapsychology. _In_ Ludwig, J. K. ed. Philosophy and parapsychology p401-04

Haynes, R. Wrestling Jacob: Koestler and the paranormal. _In_ Harris, H. A. ed. Astride the two cultures p175-86

James, W. Final impressions of a psychical researcher; excerpt from "Memories and studies." _In_ Ludwig, J. K. ed. Philosophy and parapsychology p407-20

Kahn, S. D. "Myers' problem" revisited. _In_ Parapsychology: its relation to physics, biology, psychology, and psychiatry p208-34

Koestler, A. Physics and metaphysics. _In_ Koestler, A. Janus p242-73

Koestler, A. Science and para-science. _In_ Koestler, A. The heel of Achilles p138-54

Koestler, A. Science and reality. _In_ Koestler, A. The heel of Achilles p155-57

LeShan, L. L. What it feels like to be a parapsychologist. _In_ Parapsychology: its relation to physics, biology, psychology, and psychiatry p162-66

Morris, R. L. Biology and psychical research. _In_ Parapsychology: its relation to physics, biology, psychology, and psychiatry p48-75

Mundle, C. W. K. Does the concept of precognition make sense? _In_ Ludwig, J. K. ed. Philosophy and parapsychology p327-40

Mundle, C. W. K. Strange facts in search of a theory. _In_ Wheatley, J. M. O. and Edge, H. L. eds. Philosophical dimensions of parapsychology p76-97

Murphy, G. Are there any solid facts in psychical research? _In_ Wheatley, J. M. O. and Edge, H. L. eds. Philosophical dimensions of parapsychology p388-404

Murphy, G. The problem of repeatability in psychical research. _In_ Ludwig, J. K. ed. Philosophy and parapsychology p270-83

Roberts, R. B. A theory for psi. _In_ Parapsychology: its relation to physics, biology, psychology, and psychiatry p40-44

Rogers, C. R. Some new directions: a personal view. _In_ Hanna, T. ed. Explorers of humankind p123-35

Rush, J. H. Physical aspects of psi phenomena. _In_ Parapsychology: its relation to physics, biology, psychology, and psychiatry p6-39

Schmeidler, G. R. The relation between psychology and parapsychology. _In_ Parapsychology: its relation to physics, biology, psychology, and psychiatry p122-50

Schwarz, B. E. Psi and the life cycle. _In_ Parapsychology: its relation to physics, biology, psychology, and psychiatry p235-45

Scriven, M. The frontiers of psychology: psychoanalysis and parapsychology. _In_ Wheatley, J. M. O. and Edge, H. L. eds. Philosophical dimensions of parapsychology p46-75

Scriven, M. New frontiers of the brain. _In_ Ludwig, J. K. ed. Philosophy and parapsychology p387-400

Shewmaker, K. L. and Berenda, C. W. Science and the problem of psi. _In_ Wheatley, J. M. O. and Edge, H. L. eds. Philosophical dimensions of parapsychology p413-24

Tart, C. T. The physical universe, the spiritual universe, and the paranormal. _In_ Tart, C. T. ed. Transpersonal psychologies p113-51

Ullman, M. Psychiatry and parapsychology: the consummation of an uncertain romance. _In_ Parapsychology: its relation to physics, biology, psychology, and psychiatry p171-207

Van de Castle, R. L. Some possible anthropological contributions to the study of parapsychology. _In_ Parapsychology: its relation to physics, biology, psychology, and psychiatry p151-61

See also Clairvoyance; Extrasensory perception; Mediums; Parapsychology and animals; Psychology Religions; Religion and parapsychology; Second sight; Thought-transference

Great Britain—History

Wynne, B. Physics and psychics: science, symbolic action, and social control in late Victorian England. _In_ Barnes, B. and Shapin S. eds. Natural order p167-86

Psychoanalysis

Danto, A. C. Freudian explanations and the language of the unconscious. _In_ Psychoanalysis and language p325-53

Edelson, M. What is the psychoanalyst talking about? _In_ Psychoanalysis and language p99-170

Fancher, R. E. Man in conflict: the psychoanalytic psychology of Sigmund Freud. _In_ Fancher, R. E. Pioneers of psychology p205-49

Flew, A. G. N. Psychoanalysis and free-will. _In_ Flew, A. G. N. A rational animal p172-95

Franck, I. Spinoza, Freud, and Hampshire on psychic freedom. _In_ Thought, consciousness, and reality p257-309

Gass, W. H. The anatomy of mind. _In_ Gass, W. H. The world within the word p208-52

Green, A. The double and the absent. _In_ Roland, A. ed. Psychoanalysis, creativity, and literature p271-92

Gregory, I. Psycho-analysis, human nature and human conduct. _In_ Royal Institute of Philosophy. Nature and conduct p99-120

Psychoanalysis—*Continued*

Holland, N. N. What can a concept of identity add to psycholinguistics? *In* Psychoanalysis and language p171-234

Homans, P. Introduction. *In* Homans, P. ed. Childhood and selfhood p13-54

Kafka, J. S. On reality: an examination of object constancy, ambiguity, paradox, and time. *In* Thought, consciousness, and reality p133-58

Lacoue-Labarthe, P. Theatrum analyticum. *In* Glyph 2 p122-43

Leavy, S. A. The significance of Jacques Lacan. *In* Psychoanalysis and language p271-92

Leclaire, S. Unconscious inscription: another memory. *In* Roland, A. ed. Psychoanalysis, creativity, and literature p72-84

Litowitz, B. E. On overdetermination. *In* Psychoanalysis and language p355-94

Loch, W. Some comments on the subject of psychoanalysis and truth. *In* Thought, consciousness, and reality p217-55

Loewald, H. W. Primary process, secondary process, and language. *In* Psychoanalysis and language p235-70

O'Brien, K. Death and revolution: a reappraisal of identity theory. *In* O'Neill, J. ed. On critical theory p104-28

Palombo, S. R. Dreams, memory, and the origins of thought. *In* Thought, consciousness, and reality p49-83

Pontalis, J. B. On death-work in Freud, in the self, in culture. *In* Roland, A. ed. Psychoanalysis, creativity, and literature p85-95

Ricoeur, P. Image and language in psychoanalysis. *In* Psychoanalysis and language p293-324

Schwartz, M. M. Critic, define thyself. *In* Hartman, G. H. ed. Psychoanalysis and the question of the text p 1-17

Scriven, M. The frontiers of psychology: psychoanalysis and parapsychology. *In* Wheatley, J. M. O. and Edge, H. L. eds. Philosophical dimensions of parapsychology p46-75

Simon, B. The psychoanalytic and social psychiatric models. *In* Simon, B. Mind and madness in ancient Greece p271-89

Steiner, G. A remark on language and psychoanalysis. *In* Steiner, G. On difficulty and other essays p48-60

Tatar, M. M. From Mesmer to Freud: animal magnetism, hypnosis, and suggestion. *In* Tatar, M. M. Spellbound p3-44

Weber, S. It. *In* Glyph 4 p 1-31

Wolf, E. S. The disconnected self. *In* Roland, A. ed. Psychoanalysis, creativity, and literature p103-14

Wolf, E. S. 'Irrationality' in a psychoanalytic psychology of the self. *In* Mischel, T. ed. The self p203-23

See also Catharsis; Dreams; Existential psychology; Oedipus complex; Psychohistory; Subconsciousness

History

Hughes, H. S. The advent of ego psychology. *In* Hughes, H. S. The sea change p189-239

France

Bigras, J. French psychoanalysis. *In* Roland, A. ed. Psychoanalysis, creativity, and literature p11-21

France—Social aspects

Turkle, S. French psychoanalysis: a sociological perspective. *In* Roland, A. ed. Psychoanalysis, creativity, and literature p39-71

United States

Péraldi, F. American psychoanalysis. *In* Roland, A. ed. Psychoanalysis, creativity, and literature p22-38

Psychoanalysis and art

Marquard, O. On the importance of the theory of the unconscious for a theory of no longer fine art. *In* Amacher, R. E. and Lange, V. eds. New perspectives in German literary criticism p260-78

Ricoeur, P. Psychoanalysis and the work of art. *In* Psychiatry and the humanities v 1 p3-33

Psychoanalysis and literature

Anderson, C. G. Baby Tuckoo: Joyce's "features of infancy." *In* Staley, T. F. and Benstock, B. eds. Approaches to Joyce's Portrait p135-68

Bersani, L. Artaud, defecation and birth. *In* Bersani, L. A future for Astyanax p259-72

Bersani, L. Murderous lovers. *In* Bersani, L. A future for Astyanax p3-14

Bersani, L. Racine, psychoanalysis and Oedipus. *In* Bersani, L. A future for Astyanax p17-50

Brenman-Gibson, M. The creation of plays: with a specimen analysis. *In* Roland, A. ed. Psychoanalysis, creativity, and literature p178-230

Crews, F. C. Anaesthetic criticism. *In* Crews, F. C. Out of my system p63-87

Crews, F. C. Can literature be psychoanalyzed? *In* Crews, F. C. Out of my system p3-18

Crews, F. C. Reductionism and its discontents. *In* Crews, F. C. Out of my system p165-85

Green, A. The double and the absent. *In* Roland, A. ed. Psychoanalysis, creativity, and literature p271-92

Hartman, G. H. Psychoanalysis: the French connection. *in* Hartman, G. H. ed. Psychoanalysis and the question of the text p86-113

Heller, E. Observations on psychoanalysis and modern literature. *In* Psychiatry and the humanities v 1 p35-50

Holland, N. N. Literary interpretation and three phases of psychoanalysis. *In* Roland, A. ed. Psychoanalysis, creativity, and literature p232-47

Johnson, B. The frame of reference: Poe, Lacan, Derrida. *In* Hartman, G. H. ed. Psychoanalysis and the question of the text p149-71

Lesser, S. O. Freud and Hamlet again. *In* Lesser, S. O. The whispered meanings p20-31

May, K. M. The burden of consciousness. *In* May, K. M. Out of the maelstrom p 1-23

May, K. M. The living self. *In* May, K. M. Out of the maelstrom p43-61

May, K. M. The nature of the unconscious.. *In* May, K. M. Out of the maelstrom p24-42

May, K. M. A new synthesis. *In* May, K. M. Out of the maelstrom p98-121

May, K. M. The search for identity. *In* May, K. M. Out of the maelstrom p62-77

Psychoanalysis and literature—*Continued*

Muir, K. Some Freudian interpretations of Shakespeare. *In* Muir, K. The singularity of Shakespeare, and other essays p110-23

Ragussis, M. The subterfuge of art: Lawrence, Freud, and "verbal consciousness." *In* Ragussis, M. The subterfuge of art p1-5

Ragussis, M. The subterfuge of art: Literature and regression. *In* Ragussis, M. The subterfuge of art p5-16

Rigney, B. H. Introduction. *In* Rigney, B. H. Madness and sexual politics in the feminist novel p 1-12

Roland, A. Toward a reorientation of psychoanalytic literary criticism. *In* Roland, A. ed. Psychoanalysis, creativity, and literature p248-70

Roland, A. and Rizzo, G. Psychoanalysis in search of Pirandello: six characters and Henry IV. *In* Roland, A. ed. Psychoanalysis, creativity, and literature p323-51

Wasiolek, E. The future of psychoanalytic criticism. *In* The Frontiers of literary criticism p149-68

Psychoanalysis and religion

Ancona, L. Considerations on Christian vocations seen from the point of view of psychoanalysis. *In* Wolman, B. B. ed. Psychoanalysis and Catholicism p65-96

Bartemeier, L. H. Psychoanalysis and religion. *In* Wolman, B. B. ed. Psychoanalysis and Catholicism p7-18

Beirnaert, L. Introduction to the reading of Freud's texts on religion. *In* Wolman, B. B. ed. Psychoanalysis and Catholicism p19-30

Cousins, E. H. The many-leveled psyche: correlation between psychotherapy and the spiritual life. *In* Wolman, B. B. ed. Psychoanalysis and Catholicism p31-64

Homans, P. The significance of Erikson's psychology for modern understandings of religion. *In* Homans, P. ed. Childhood and selfhood p231-63

See also Catholic Church and psychoanalysis

Psychoanalysis in historiography. See Psychohistory

Psychoanalysis in literature

Nicoll, A. The drama of the individual. *In* Nicoll, A. World drama p654-73

Tatar, M. M. From science fiction to psychoanalysis: Henry James's "Bostonians," D. H. Lawrence's "Women in love," and Thomas Mann's "Mario and the magician." *In* Tatar, M. M. Spellbound p230-71

Psychoanalyst and patient. See Psychotherapist and patient

Psychoanalytic literary criticism. See Psychoanalysis and literature

Psychobiology. See Developmental psychobiology

Psychobiology, Experimental

Grad, B. R. The biological effects of the "laying on of hands" on animals and plants: implications for biology. *In* Parapsychology: its relation to physics, biology, psychology, and psychiatry p76-89

Morris, R. L. Biology and psychical research. *In* Parapsychology: its relation to physics, biology, psychology, and psychiatry p48-75

Psychogenic needs. See Need (Psychology)

Psychohistory

Capps, D. Psychohistory and historical genres: the plight and promise of Eriksonian biography. *In* Homans, P. ed. Childhood and selfhood p189-228

DeMause, L. The independence of psychohistory. *In* DeMause, L. ed. The new psychohistory p7-27

DeMause, L. Psychohistory and psychotherapy. *In* DeMause, L. ed. The new psychohistory p307-13

Kren, G. M. and Rappoport, L. H. Clio and psyche. *In* Kren, G. M. and Rappoport, L. H. eds. Varieties of psychohistory p63-77

Lifton, R. J. On psychohistory. *In* Explorations in psychohistory p21-41

Mazlish, B What is psycho-history? *In* Kren, G. M. and Rappoport, L. H. eds. Varieties of psychohistory p17-37

Shorter, E. Maternal sentiment and deaths in childbirth: a new agenda for psychomedical history. *In* Branca, P. ed. The medicine show p67-88

Psychokinesis. See Levitation

Psycholinguistics

Beardsley, E. L. Referential genderization. *In* Gould, C. C. and Wartofsky, M. W. eds. Women and philosophy p285-93

Beardsley, E. L. Traits and genderization. *In* Feminism and philosophy p117-23

Bever, T. G. The psychology of language and structuralist investigation of nativism *In* Harman, G. ed. On Noam Chomsky p146-64

Blumenthal, A. L. Psycholinguistics: some historical issues. *In* Riegel, K. F. and Rosenwald, G. C. eds. Structure and transformation p135-52

Bruner, J S. Language as an instrument of thought. *In* Davies, A. ed. Problems of language and learning p61-88

Chomsky, N. Language and unconscious knowledge. *In* Psychoanalysis and language p3-44

Danto, A. C. Freudian explanations and the language of the unconscious. *In* Psychoanalysis and language p325-53

Edelson, M. What is the psychoanalyst talking about? *In* Psychoanalysis and language p99-170

Greene, J. Psycholinguistics: competence and performance. *In* Royal Institute of Philosophy. Communication and understanding p79-90

Holland, N. N. What can a concept of identity add to psycholinguistics? *In* Psychoanalysis and language p171-234

Korsmeyer, C. W. The hidden joke: generic uses of masculine terminology. *In* Feminism and philosophy p138-53

Litowitz, B. E. On overdetermination. *In* Psychoanalysis and language p355-94

Loewald, H. W. Primary process, secondary process, and language. *In* Psychoanalysis and language p235-70

Moulton, J. M. The myth of the neutral "man." *In* Feminism and philosophy p124-37

Paivio, A. Psychological processes in the comprehension of metaphor. *In* Ortony, A. ed. Metaphor and thought p150-71

Pribram, K. H. The linguistic act. *In* Psychoanalysis and language p75-98

Psycholinguistics

Richards, I. A. Emotive language still. *In* Richards, I. A. Complementarities p88-97

Ricoeur, P. Image and language in psychoanalysis. *In* Psychoanalysis and language p293-324

Rosenberg, B. A. The psychology of the spiritual sermon *In* Zaretsky, I. I. and Leone, M. P. eds. Religious movements in contemporary America p135-49

Rumelhart, D. E. Some problems with the notion of literal meanings. *In* Ortony, A. ed. Metaphor and thought p78-90

Smith, J. H. Language and the genealogy of the absent object. *In* Psychiatry and the humanities v 1 p145-70

Steiner, G. A remark on language and psychoanalysis. *In* Steiner, G. On difficulty and other essays p48-60

Valian, V. Linguistics and feminism. *In* Feminism and philosophy p154-66

Wanner, E. Do we understand sentences from the outside-in or from the inside-out? *In* Bloomfield, M. W. and Haugen, E. I. eds. Language as a human problem p165-85

Whitaker, H. and Whitaker, H. Language disorders. *In* Wardhaugh, R. and Brown, H. D. eds. A survey of applied linguistics p250-74

See also Generative grammar; Thought and thinking

Psychological anthropology. See Ethnopsychology

Psychological manifestations of general diseases. See Mental illness—Physiological aspects

Psychological phenomenology. See Phenomenological psychology

Psychological research

Cole, M. and Scribner, S. Theorizing about socialization of cognition. *In* Schwartz, T. ed. Socialization as cultural communication p157-76

Psychological testing of children. See Psychological tests for children

Psychological tests for children

Elkind, D. Borderline retardation in low- and middle-income adolescents. *In* Elkind, D. The child and society p175-201

Psychologists

Great Britain

Trasler, G. The role of psychologists in the penal system. *In* Progress in penal reform p129-41

Psychology

Bruner J. S. Psychology and the image of man. *In* Bruner J. S. On knowing p167-89

Flew, A. G. N. Human psychology and Skinnerian behaviourism. *In* Flew, A. G. N. A rational animal p140-50

Huxley, A. L. Latent human potentialities. *In* Huxley, A. L. The Human situation p236-53

McInnes, N. The politics of needs—or, Who needs politics? *In* Fitzgerald, R. ed. Human needs and politics p229-43

May, R. What is the human dilemma? *In* May, R. Psychology and the human dilemma p3-22

Rosenhan, D. L. Moral character. *In* Stanford legal essays p401-11

Schmeidler, G. R. The relation between psychology and parapsychology. *In* Parapsychology: its relation to physics, biology, psychology, and psychiatry p122-50

Skinner, B. F. The steep and thorny way to a science of behaviour. *In* Harré, R. ed. Problems of scientific revolution p58-71

Tart, C. T. Some assumptions of orthodox, Western psychology. *In* Tart, C. T. ed. Transpersonal psychologies p59-111

Ulanov, A. B. The psychological reality of the demonic. *In* Disguises of the demonic. *In* Disguises of the demonic p135-49

See also Aggressiveness (Psychology); Aging—Psychological aspects; Attention; Behavior genetics; Behaviorism (Psychology); Belief and doubt; Choice (Psychology); Cognition; Consciousness; Developmental psychology; Deprivation (Psychology); Drawing, Psychology of; Educational psychology; Ego (Psychology); Eidetic imagery; Emotions; Ethnopsychology; Experience; Gestalt psychology; Human behavior; Humanistic psychology; Imagination; Imitation; Intellect; Intentionalism; Knowledge, Theory of; Logic; Memory; Motivation (Psychology); Orientation (Psychology); Perception; Personality; Phrenology; Political psychology; Problem solving; Psychical research; Psychoanalysis; Psycholinguistics; Rhetoric and psychology; Senses and sensation; Social interaction; Social psychology; Subconsciousness; Temperament; Thought and thinking; Values; Will

Comparative studies

See Ethnopsychology

History

Altschule, M. D. Miscellanea. *In* Altschule, M. D. Origins of concepts in human behavior p193-200

Fancher, R. E. Psychology in the university: Wilhelm Wundt and William James. *In* Fancher, R. E. Pioneers of psychology p126-69

May, R. Questions for a science of man. *In* May, R. Psychology and the human dilemma p182-200

Moral and religious aspects

May, R. Social responsibilities of psychologists. *In* May, R. Psychology and the human dilemma p201-21

Research

See Psychological research

Psychology, Abnormal. See Psychology, Pathological

Psychology, Applied. See Amputees—Psychology; Behavior modification; Persuasion (Psychology)

Psychology, Buddhist. See Buddhism—Psychology

Psychology, Child. See Child psychology

Psychology, Comparative. See Animals, Habits and behavior of; Human behavior; Sociobiology

Psychology, Educational. See Educational psychology

Psychology, Ethnic. See Ethnopsychology

Psychology, Existential. See Existential psychology

Psychology, Experimental. See Psychobiology, Experimental

Psychology, Hindu. See Hinduism—Psychology

Psychology, Islamic. See Islam—Psychology

Psychology, Military. See Deterrence (Strategy)

Psychology, Muslim. See Islam—Psychology

Psychology, National. See Ethnopsychology; National characteristics

Psychology, Pastoral. See Pastoral psychology

Psychology, Pathological

Rosen, G. An analgesic strategy. *In* Lauer, R. H. ed. Social movements and social change p97-106

See also Aphasia; Depression, Mental; Hysteria; Medicine, Psychosomatic; Mental illness; Psychic trauma; Psychiatry; Psychoanalysis; Subconsciousness

Cases, clinical reports, statistics

See Psychiatry—Cases, clinical reports, statistics

Classification

Koestler, A. Can psychiatrists be trusted? *In* Koestler, A. The heel of Achilles p33-40

History

Simon, B. The Greeks and the irrational. *In* Simon, B. Mind and madness in ancient Greece p43-49

Simon, B. The Hippocratic corpus. *In* Simon, B. Mind and madness in ancient Greece p215-27

Simon, B. Plato and Freud. *In* Simon, B. Mind and madness in ancient Greece p200-12

Philosophy

Simon, B. Plato's concept of mind and its disorders. *In* Simon, B. Mind and madness in ancient Greece p157-79

Research

See Psychiatric research

Psychology, Phenomenological. See Phenomenological psychology

Psychology, Physiological

Haley, B. Mens sana in corpore sano: Victorian psychophysiology. *In* Haley, B. The healthy body and Victorian culture p23-45

Schwartz, D. C.; Garrison, J. and Alouf, J. Health, body images, and political socialization. *In* Schwartz, D. C. and Schwartz, S. K. eds. New directions in political socialization p96-126

See also Amputees—Psychology; Behaviorism (Psychology); Memory; Mental illness—Physiological aspects; Mind and body; Optical illusions; Psychoanalysis; Senses and sensation; Sleep; Time perception

Psychology, Political. See Political psychology

Psychology, Prison. See Prison psychology

Psychology, Racial. See Ethnopsychology

Psychology, Religious

Adams, R. M. Religion of man, religion of woman. *In* Art, politics, and will p173-90

Adler, N. Ritual, release, and orientation: maintenance of the self in the antinomian personality. *In* Zaretsky, I. I. and Leone, M. P. eds. Religious movements in contemporary America p283-97

Ellwood, R. S. Inner worlds: the psychology of excursus religion. *In* Ellwood, R. S. Alternative altars p42-61

Homans, P. The significance of Erikson's psychology for modern understandings of religion. *In* Homans, P. ed. Childhood and selfhood p231-63

Pattison, E. M. Ideological support for the marginal middle class: faith healing and glossolalia. *In* Zaretsky, I. I. and Leone, M. P. eds. Religious movements in contemporary America p418-55

Tart, C. T. Some assumptions of orthodox, Western psychology. *In* Tart, C. T. ed. Transpersonal psychologies p59-111

Psychology, Sexual. See Sex (Psychology)

Psychology, Social. See Social psychology

Psychology, Structural. See Gestalt psychology

Psychology and religion

Cox, H. G. Deep structures in the study of new religions. *In* Needleman, J. and Baker, G. eds. Understanding the new religions p122-30

Goleman, D. The impact of the new religions on psychology. *In* Needleman, J. and Baker, G. eds. Understanding the new religions p113-21

See also Psychology, Religious

Psychology of language. See Psycholinguistics

Psychology of learning. See Learning Psychology of

Psychopathology. See Psychology, Pathological

Psychopathology in literature. See Mental illness in literature

Psychopathy. See Psychology, Pathological

Psychopharmacology

Berger, P. A.; Hamburg, B. and Hamburg, D. A. Mental health: progress and problems. *In* Knowles, J. H. ed. Doing better and feeling worse p261-76

Frazier, S. H. Psychopharmacology in a psychotherapeutic setting. *In* Overview of the psychotherapies p118-24

See also Schizophrenia—Chemotheraphy

Psychophysiology. See Psychology, Physiological

Psychoses

Kety, S. S. Biological approaches to treatment and understanding of the major psychoses. *In* American psychiatry: past, present, and future p64-77

Péraldi, F. The crane-child. *In* Roland, A. ed. Psychoanalysis, creativity, and literature p96-102

See also Paranoia

Psychoses in children. See Schizophrenia in children

Psychosomatic medicine. See Medicine, Psychosomatic

Psychosomatic neuropathology. See Nervous system—Diseases—Psychosomatic aspects

Psychotherapist and patient

Friedman, M. S. Healing through meeting: a dialogical approach to psychotherapy and family therapy. *In* Psychiatry and the humanities v 1 p191-233

Percy, W. The symbolic structure of interpersonal process. *In* Percy, W. The message in the bottle p189-214

Weisman, A. D. The psychiatrist and the inexorable. *In* Feifel, H. [ed.] New meanings of death p107-22

Psychotherapists

Torrey, E. F. Spiritualists and shamans as psychotherapists: an account of original anthropological sin. *In* Zaretsky, I. I. and Leone, M. P. eds. Religious movements in contemporary America p330-37

Psychotherapy

Birk, L. and Brinkley-Birk, A. The learning therapies. *In* Overview of the psychotherapies p51-67

DeMause, L. Psychohistory and psychotherapy. *In* DeMause, L. ed. The new psychohistory p307-13

De Salzmann, M. Man's ever new and eternal challenge. *In* Needleman, J. and Lewis, D. eds. On the way to self knowledge p54-75

Frank, J. D. An overview of psychotherapy. *In* Overview of the psychotherapies p3-21

Frankl, V. E. Man's search for ultimate meaning. *In* Needleman, J. and Lewis, D. eds. On the way to self knowledge p182-203

Friedman, M. S. Healing through meeting: a dialogical approach to psychotherapy and family therapy. *In* Psychiatry and the humanities v 1 p191-233

Lauer, R. A medium for mental health. *In* Zaretsky, I. I. and Leone, M. P. eds. Religious movements in contemporary America p338-54

Malone, T. P. The Christian sacred tradition and psychotherapy. *In* Needleman, J. and Lewis, D. eds. On the way to self knowledge p26-45

Martin, P. A. The psychotherapy of marital partners: old or new? *In* Overview of the psychotherapies p125-50

May, R. The context of psychotherapy. *In* May, R. Psychology and the human dilemma p87-110

Needleman, J. Psychiatry and the sacred. *In* Needleman, J. and Lewis, D. eds. On the way to self knowledge p3-25

Nemiah, J. C. Psychodynamic psychotherapy. *In* Overview of the psychotherapies p36-50

Skynner, A. C. R. The relationship of psychotherapy to sacred tradition. *In* Needleman, J. and Lewis, D. eds. On the way to self knowledge p204-25

Zubin, J. A biometric approach to diagnosis and evaluation of therapeutic intervention in schizophrenia. *In* Overview of the psychotherapies p153-204

See also Adolescent psychotherapy; Art therapy; Child psychotherapy; Group psychotherapy; Psycho-pharmacology; Psychotherapists; Rolfing; Therapeutics, Suggestive

History

Altschule, M. D. The early history of psychiatric treatment. *In* Altschule, M. D. Origins of concepts in human behavior p123-51

Social aspects

Rieff, P. The triumph of the therapeutic; excerpt. *In* Davis, F. J. and Stivers, R. The collective definition of deviance p392-410

Stivers, R. Social control in the technological society. *In* Davis, F. J. and Stivers, R. eds. The collective definition of deviance p376-91

Szasz, T. S. Society's internal enemies and protectors; excerpt from "The manufacture of madness". *In* Davis, F. J. and Stivers, R. eds. The collective definition of deviance p177-96

United States—History

Kolb, L. C. Psychological approaches. *In* American psychiatry: past, present, and future p50-63

Psychotomimetic drugs. See Hallucinogenic drugs

Psychotropic drugs. See Hallucinogenic drugs

Ptolemaeus, Claudius

About

Wilson, C. A. Rheticus, Ravetz, and the "necessity" of Copernicus' innovation. *In* The Copernican achievement p17-39

Influence

Lakatos, I. and Zahar, E. Why did Copernicus' research program supersede Ptolemy's? *In* The Copernican achievement p354-83

Ptolemy, Claudius. See Ptolemaeus, Claudius

Public accommodations, Discrimination in. See Discrimination in public accommodations

Public administration

Becker, H. K. Historical-philosophical development of administration: excerpt from "Issues in police administration." *In* Armstrong, T. R. and Cinnamon, K. M. eds. Power and authority in law enforcement p77-103

Salih, G. M. The role of OAU in public administration and management. *In* El-Ayouty, Y. ed. The Organization of African Unity after ten years p237-50

See also Bureaucracy; Civil service; Decentraliaztion in government; Impeachments; also subdivision Politics and government under names of countries, cities, etc. e.g. Illinois—Politics and government

Study and teaching—Africa

Kirk-Greene, A. H. M. Public administration and African studies. *In* African studies since 1945 p125-35

Public assistance. See Public welfare

Public buildings

Billington, D. P. Technology and the structuring of cities. *In* Small comforts for hard times p182-98

Salvadori, M. G. The aesthetics of technology: in response to David P. Billington. *In* Small comforts for hard times p199-203

See also School buildings

Public contracts

United States

Smith, B. L. R. The public use of the private sector. *In* Smith, B. L. R. ed. The new political economy: the public use of the private sector p 1-45

Staats, E. B. New problems of accountability for federal programs. *In* Smith, B. L. R. ed. The new political economy: the public use of the private sector p46-67

Public debts. See Debts, Public

Public demonstrations. See Demonstrations

Public opinion—*Continued*

Japan

Kamei, S. The sacred land of liberty: images of America in nineteenth century Japan. *In* Iriye, A. ed. Mutual images p55-72

Katō, H. America as seen by Japanese travelers. *In* Iriye, A. ed. Mutual images p188-201

Miwa, K. Japanese images of war with the United States. *In* Iriye, A. ed. Mutual images p115-37

Saeki, S. Images of the United States as a hypothetical enemy. *In* Iriye, A. ed. Mutual images p100-14

North America

Radosh, R. The Cuban Revolution and Western intellectuals. *In* Radosh, R. ed. The new Cuba: paradoxes and potentials p37-55

Rome

Yavetz, Z. Existimatio, fama, and the ides of March. *In* Harvard Studies in classical philology v78 p35-65

Russia

Hollander, G. D. Political communication and dissent in the Soviet Union. *In* Tokes, R. L. ed. Dissent in the USSR p233-75

San Francisco

Wuthnow, R. The new religions in social context. *In* The New religious consciousness p267-93

United States

Barton, J. H. An educational strategy for arms control. *In* International terrorism and world security p308-13

Clapp, P. A. and Halperin, M. H. U.S. elite images of Japan: the postwar period. *In* Iriye, A. ed. Mutual images p202-22

Glazer, N. From Ruth Benedict to Herman Kahn: the postwar Japanese image in the American mind. *In* Iriye, A. ed. Mutual images p138-68

Hutt, P. B. Public criticism of health science policy. *In* Holton, G. J. and Morison, R. S. eds. Limits of scientific inquiry p157-69

Isaacs, H. R. Some concluding remarks: the turning mirrors. *In* Iriye, A. ed. Mutual images p258-65

Nazzaro, P. Fascist and anti-Fascist reaction in the United States to the Matteotti murder. *In* Studies in Italian American social history p50-65

Nelli, H. S. Chicago's Italian-language press and World War I. *In* Studies in Italian American social history p66-80

Temperley, H. Anglo-American images. *In* Allen, H. C. and Thompson, R. eds. Contrast and connection p321-47

Public policy management. See Policy sciences

Public printing. See Printing, Public

Public prosecutors

Rabinowitz, V. The prosecutor: the duty to seek justice. *In* Nader, R. and Green, M. J. eds. Verdicts on lawyers p231-41

Public relations

Baerns. B. International business public relations. *In* Fischer, H. D. and Merrill, J. C. eds. International and intercultural communication p316-28

See also Advertising; Public opinion; Publicity

Police

Ostrom, E. The design of institutional arrangements and the responsiveness of the police. *In* Rieselbach, L. N. ed. People vs. government: the responsiveness of American institutions p274-99

Public schools

Europe

Arnold, M. Common schools abroad. *In* Arnold, M. The last word p88-105

United States

Kozol, J. Children of the revolution. *In* Wagschal, P. H. ed. Learning tomorrows p73-88

Public speaking. See Debates and debating; Lectures and lecturing

Public squares. See Plazas

Public television. See Television in education; Television programs, Public service

Public theater. See New York Shakespeare Festival Public Theater

Public two-year colleges. See Community colleges

Public utilities

Porter, M. C. That commerce shall be free: a new look at the old laissez-faire Court. *In* The Supreme Court review, 1976 p135-59

Public welfare

Huber, J. The politics of public assistance: Western Europe and the United States. *In* Major social issues p109-25

See also Day care centers; Family policy; Food relief; Income maintenance programs; Poor; Social workers

Law

See Poor laws

Philosophy

Rothman, D. J. The state as parent: social policy in the Progressive Era. *In* Doing good p67-96

California

Levy, F. What Ronald Reagan can teach the United States about welfare reform. *In* Burnham, W. D. and Weinberg, M. W. eds. American politics and public policy p336-63

Colorado

Wickens, J. F. Depression and the New Deal in Colorado. *In* Braeman, J.; Bremner, R. H. and Brody, D. eds. The New Deal v2 p269-310

Louisiana

Moore, J. R. The New Deal in Louisiana. *In* Braeman, J.; Bremner, R. H. and Brody, D. eds. The New Deal v2 p137-65

Netherlands

Staatsen, A. A. M. F. General assistance in the Netherlands. *In* Davis, K. C. Discretionary justice in Europe and America p133-48

United States

Glasser, I. Prisoners of benevolence: power versus liberty in the welfare state. *In* Doing good p97-170

United States—Finance

Reagan, M. D. Accountability and independence in federal grants-in-aid. *In* Smith, B. L. R. ed. The new political economy: the public use of the private sector p181-213

Public welfare—*Continued*

United States—History

Pearce, D. and Street, D. Welfare in the metropolitan area. *In* Handbook of contemporary urban life p319-51

Publicity

Prakke, H. J. Towards a philosophy of publicistics. *In* Fischer, H. D. and Merrill, J. C. eds. International and intercultural communication p466-73

See also Advertising

Publishers and authors. See Authors and publishers

Publishers and publishing

Altbach, P. G. Publishing and the intellectual system. *In* Altbach, P. G. and McVey, S. eds. Perspectives on publishing p3-15

Neavill, G. B. Role of the publisher in the dissemination of knowledge. *In* Altbach, P. G. and McVey, S. eds. Perspectives on publishing p47-57

See also Book industries and trade; Booksellers and bookselling; Copyright; Little presses; Music printing; Scholarly publishing

Africa

Achebe, C. Publishing in Africa: a writer's view. *In* Achebe, C. Morning yet on creation day p105-12

Rea, J. Aspects of African publishing, 1945-1974. *In* African studies since 1945 p96-105

Smith, K. Who controls book publishing in Anglophone middle Africa? *In* Altbach, P. G. and McVey, S. eds. Perspectives on publishing p129-40

France

Shaw, E. P. Censorship and subterfuge in eighteenth-century France. *In* Literature and history in the age of ideas p287-309

Great Britain

Lightfoot, M. The distribution of books: weak link in the publishing chain. *In* Altbach, P. G. and McVey, S. eds. Perspectives on publishing p71-79

Great Britain—History

Bennett, S. B. John Murray's family library and the cheapening of books in early nineteenth century Britain. *In* Virginia. University. Bibliographical Society. Studies in bibliography v29 p139-66

Booth, J. Rationalization and crisis: a quarter century of British publishing. *In* Altbach, P. G. and McVey, S. eds. Perspectives on publishing p59-69

Sutherland, J. A. Craft versus trade: novelists and publishers. *In* Sutherland, J. A. Victorian novelists and publishers p72-98

Sutherland, J. A. Mass market and big business: novel publishing at midcentury *In* Sutherland, J. A. Victorian novelists and publishers p41-71

Sutherland, J. A. Novel publishing, 1830-1870. *In* Sutherland, J. A. Victorian novelists and publishers p9-40

India

Altbach, P. G. Publishing in a transitional society: the case of India. *In* Altbach, P. G. and McVey, S. eds. Perspectives on publishing p141-55

Russia

Booher, E. E. Publishing in the USSR and Yugoslavia. *In* Altbach, P. G. and McVey, S. eds. Perspectives on publishing p173-86

Singapore

Gopinathan, S. Publishing in a plural society: the case of Singapore. *In* Altbach, P. G. and McVey, S. eds. Perspectives on publishing p157-71

Underdeveloped areas

See Underdeveloped areas—Publishers and publishing

United States

Coser, L. A. Publishers as gatekeepers of ideas. *In* Altbach, P. G. and McVey, S. eds. Perspectives on publishing p17-25

Dessauer, J. P. Pity poor Pascal: some sobering reflections on the American book scene. *In* Altbach, P. G. and McVey, S. eds. Perspectives on publishing p205-16

Johnson, G. Women in publishing. *In* Altbach, P. G. and McVey, S. eds. Perspectives on publishing p259-72

Lightfoot, M. The distribution of books: weak link in the publishing chain. *In* Altbach, P. G. and McVey, S. eds. Perspectives on publishing p71-79

Whitten, P. The changing world of college textbook publishing. *In* Altbach, P. G. and McVey, S. eds. Perspectives on publishing p247-58

United States—History

McVey, S. Nineteenth century America: publishing in a developing country. *In* Altbach, P. G. and McVey, S. eds. Perspectives on publishing p187-201

Yugoslavia

Booher, E. E. Publishing in the USSR and Yugoslavia. *In* Altbach, P. G. and McVey, S. eds. Perspectives on publishing p173-86

Puccetti, Roland

The conquest of death. *In* Donnelly, J. P. ed. Language, metaphysics, and death p163-75

Pucci, Piero

Lingering on the threshold. *In* Glyph 3 p52-73

True and false discourse in Hesiod. *In* Poetry and poetics from ancient Greece to the Renaissance p29-55

Puccini, Giacomo

About

Lawton, B. Giuseppe Giacosa and Giacomo Puccini. *In* Abroad in America: Visitors to the new Nation, 1776-1914 p247-59

Pucelle, Jean

About individual works

Book of hours of Jeanne d'Évreux

Winternitz, E. Bagpipes for the Lord. *In* Winternitz, E. Musical instruments and their symbolism in Western art p129-36

Puche, José Luis Castillo. See Castillo Puche, José Luis

Pudovkin, Vsevolod Īllarionovīch

About individual works

Mother

Taylor, R. Mother. *In* Taylor, R. Film propaganda p81-91

Pueblo Indians

See also Tewa Indians

Antiquities

See Basket-Maker Indians

Puerto Rican children

Hentoff, N. Turning kids into waste. *In* Gross, B. and Gross, R. eds. The children's rights movement p78-81

Puerto Rican literature

Bibliography

Babín, M. T. Contemporary Puerto Rican literature in translation. *In* Minority language and literature p115-20

Puerto Ricans

Children

See Puerto Rican children

Puerto Ricans in Boston

Case studies

Piore, M. J. Immigration, work expectations, and labor market structure. *In* The Diverse society: implications for social policy p109-27

Puerto Ricans in New York (City)

Garrison, V. E. Sectarianism and psychosocial adjustment: a controlled comparison of Puerto Rican Pentecostals and Catholics. *In* Zaretsky, I. I. and Leone, M. P. eds. Religious movements in contemporary America p298-329

Puerto Ricans in the United States

Fitzpatrick, J. P. Transitional values of Puerto Ricans. *In* The Diverse society: implications for social policy p93-107

Education

Hill-Burnett, J. Developing anthropological knowledge through application. *In* Eddy, E. M. and Partridge, W. L. eds. Applied anthropology in America p112-28

Education—Spanish language

Fallis, G. V. Spanish language programs for Hispanic minorities: current needs and priorities. *In* Minority language and literature p86-98

Puerto Rico

Linsley, A. U.S.-Cuban relations: the role of Puerto Rico. *In* Cuba in the world p119-30

Description and travel

Brower, R. A. With Gibbon in Puerto Rico. *In* Edward Gibbon and The decline and fall of the Roman Empire p247-49

Race question

Mathews, T. G. The question of color in Puerto Rico. *In* Toplin, R. B. ed. Slavery and race relations in Latin America p299-323

Social conditions

Steward, J. H. The people of Puerto Rico. *In* Steward, J. H. Evolution and ecology p240-96

Puértolas, Julio Rodríguez. See Rodríguez Puértolas, Julio

Pugh, David G.

Baedekers, Babbittry, and Baudelaire. *In* French, W. G. ed. The twenties p87-99

Pugin, Augustus Welby Northmore

About

Watkin, D. The theme in the nineteenth century: Pugin. *In* Watkin, D. Morality and architecture p17-23

Puhvel, Jaan

The mole in folk medicine: a survey from Indic antiquity to modern America I. *In* American folk medicine p31-35

Puig, Manuel

About individual works
Betrayed by Rita Hayworth

MacAdam, A. J. Manuel Puig: things as they are. *In* MacAdam, A. J. Modern Latin American narratives p91-101

The Buenos Aires affair

Alter, R. Mimesis and the motive for fiction. *In* Images and ideas in American culture p99-123

Heartbreak tango: a serial

MacAdam, A. J. Manuel Puig: things as they are. *In* MacAdam, A. J. Modern Latin American narratives p91-101

Pulcher Claudius. See Clodius Pulcher, Publius

Pulci, Luigi

About individual works
Il Morgante

Giamatti, A. B. Headlong horses, headless horsemen: an essay on the chivalric epics of Pulci, Boiardo, and Ariosto. *In* Italian literature: roots and branches p265-307

Puleston, Dennis E.

Intersite areas in the vicinity of Tikal and Uaxactun. *In* Mesoamerican archaeology p303-11

Pulitzer prizes

MacLeish, A. Remarks on the Pulitzer prize. *In* MacLeish, A. Riders on the earth p109-11

Simon, J. I. Should Albee have said "No, thanks"? *In* Simon, J. I. Singularities p58-64

Pullin, Faith

Lawrence's treatment of women in Sons and lovers. *In* Smith, A. ed. Lawrence and women p49-74

Melville's Typee: the failure of Eden. *In* Pullin, F. ed. New perspectives on Melville p 1-28

Pulmonary circulation

Temkin, O. Was Serventus influenced by Ibn an-Nafîs? *In* Temkin, O. The double face of Janus p284-86

Punctuation. See subdivision Punctuation under names of languages, e.g. Latin language—Punctuation

Punishment

Christie, N. Utility and social values in court decisions on punishment. *In* Crime, criminology and public policy p281-96

Hawkins, G. The new penology. *In* Law and society p108-27

See also Criminal law; Imprisonment; Prison sentences; Sentences (Criminal procedure)

China—History

Chen-Chang, Fu-mei. Local control of convicted thieves in eighteenth-century China. *In* Conflict and control in late imperial China p121-42

Punishment—*Continued*

South Africa

Steyn, J. H. The punishment scene in South Africa—developments over the past decade and the prospects for reform. *In* Crime, criminology and public policy p527-70

United States

Wolfgang, M. E. Real and perceived changes of crime and punishment. *In* A New America? p143-57

Punishment in crime deterrence

Ehrlich, I. and Mark, R. Deterrence and economics: a perspective on theory and evidence. *In* Major social issues p172-88

Punishment in literature

Reaves R. B. Crime and punishment in the detective fiction of Dorothy L. Sayers. *In* Hannay, M. P. ed. As her whimsey took her p 1-13

Puns and punning

Kline, G. L. Philosophical puns. *In* Philosophy and the civilizing arts p213-35

Puns and punning in literature

Muir, K. The uncomic pun. *In* Muir, K. The singularity of Shakespeare, and other essays p20-37

Puntil, Joseph E. See Simon, W. jt. auth.

Pupil-teacher relationships. See Teacher-student relationships

Puppets and puppet-plays

Japan

Barthes, R. Lesson in writing. *In* Barthes, R. Image, music, text p170-78

Purchas, Samuel

About individual works

Hakluytus posthumus, or Purchas his pilgrimes

Seelye, J. A model of Moses: the Pilgrims lend a prophetic presence to the land. *In* Seelye, J. Prophetic waters p97-130

Purchasing power

Zabinski, Z. The biological index of the buying power of money. *In* Biology of man in history p179-90

Purdy, Alfred W.

About

Doyle, M. Proteus at Roblin Lake: Al Purdy's transformations. *In* Woodcock, G. ed. Poets and critics p92-109

Purdy, James

About

Allen, M. Women of the fabulators: Barth, Pynchon, Purdy, Kesey. *In* Allen, M. The necessary blankness p14-69

Kennard, J. E. James Purdy: fidelity to failure. *In* Kennard, J. E. Number and nightmare p82-100

Purdy, Martin

Le Corbusier and the theological program. *In* Walden, R. ed. The open hand p286-321

Purgatory

Le Goff, J. The usurer and Purgatory. *In* The Dawn of modern banking p25-52

Purism (Art)

Osborne, H. Futurism and the representation of movement. *In* Osborne, H. Abstraction and artifice in twentieth-century art p77-93

Puritan theology. See Theology, Puritan

Puritans

Ahlstrom, S. E. Diversity in religion as a force for liberty: a quadricentennial view of the problem. *In* Aspects of American liberty p56-67

Collinson, P. Towards a broader understanding of the early dissenting tradition. *In* The Dissenting tradition p3-38

Hall, D. D. Understanding the Puritans. *In* Mulder, J. M. and Wilson, J. F. eds. Religion in American history p 1-16

Morgan, E. S. The Puritan ethic and the American Revolution. *In* Vaughan, A. T. and Bremer, F. J. eds. Puritan New England p364-84

Stannard, D. E. Death and the Puritan child. *In* Death in America p9-29

Also in Vaughan, A. T. and Bremer, F. J. eds. Puritan New England p232-49

Tichi, C. A kingdom unto the world. *In* Tichi, C. New World, new earth p 1-36

Vander Molen, R. J. Anglican against Puritan: ideological origins during the Marian exile. *In* Vaughan, A. T. and Bremer, F. J. eds. Puritan New England p2-18

See also Church of England; Pilgrims (New Plymouth Colony)

Influence

Ahlstrom, S. E. From Puritanism to evangelicalism: a critical perspective. *In* Wells, D. F. and Woodbridge, J. D. eds. The evangelicals p269-89

Great Britain

Fisch, H. Shakespeare and the Puritan dynamic. *In* Shakespeare survey 27 p81-92

Thompson, R. The Puritans and prurience: aspects of the Restoration book trade. *In* Allen, H. C. and Thompson, R. eds. Contrast and connection p36-65

Walzer, M. Puritanism as a revolutionary ideology. *In* Vaughan, A. T. and Bremer, F. J. eds. Puritan New England p19-41

Zinberg, C. The usable dissenting past: John Strype and Elizabethan Puritanism. *In* The Dissenting tradition p123-39

Massachusetts

Breen, T. H. and Foster, S. The Puritans' greatest achievement: a study of social cohesion in seventeenth-century Massachusetts. *In* Vaughan, A. T. and Bremer, F. J. eds. Puritan New England p110-27

Brown, B. K. T. The controversy over the franchise in Puritan Massachusetts, 1954 to 1974. *In* Vaughan, A. T. and Bremer, F. J. eds. Puritan New England p128-54

Lockridge, K. A. The history of a Puritan church, 1637-1736. *In* Vaughan, A. T. and Bremer, F. J. eds. Puritan New England p92-108

New England

Bercovitch, S. Emerson the prophet: romanticism, Puritanism, and auto-American-biography. *In* Levin, D. ed. Emerson: prophecy, metamorphosis, and influence p 1-27

Bercovitch, S. New England's errand reappraised. *In* Higham, J. and Conkin, P. K. eds. New directions in American intellectual history p85-104

Daly, R. G. Introduction: Puritanism and poetry. *In* Daly, R. J. God's altar p 1-5

Puritans—New England—_Continued_

Eakin, P. J. Renunciation in New England: Harriet Beecher Stowe and The minister's wooing. _In_ Eakin, P. J. The New England girl p27-48

Hall, M. G. and Joyce, W. L. The Halfway covenant of 1662: some new evidence. _In_ American Antiquarian Society. Proceedings v87 pt 1 p97-110

Maclear, J. F. New England and the Fifth Monarchy: the quest for the millennium in early American Puritanism. _In_ Vaughan, A. T. and Bremer, F. J. eds. Puritan New England p66-91

Middlekauff, R. M. Piety and intellect in Puritanism. _In_ Mulder, J. M. and Wilson, J. F. eds. Religion in American history p74-85

Morgan, E. S. The Halfway covenant; excerpt from "Visible saints." _In_ Mulder, J. M. and Wilson, J. F. eds. Religion in American history p29-44

Plumstead, A. W. The election sermons; excerpt from "The wall and the garden." _In_ Mulder, J. M. and Wilson, J. F. eds. Religion in American history p57-73

Pope, R. G. The myth of declension. _In_ Mulder, J. M. and Wilson, J. F. eds. Religion in American history p45-56

Pope, R. G. New England versus the New England mind: the myth of declension. _In_ Vaughan, A. T. and Bremer, F. J. eds. Puritan New England p314-25

Seelye, J. Ecclesiastic drums: Puritan theocrats, despairing of the present generation, reform the past. _In_ Seelye, J. Prophetic waters p217-52

Simpson, A. The covenanted community; excerpt from "Puritanism in old and New England." _In_ Mulder, J. M. and Wilson, J. F. eds. Religion in American history p17-28

Thompson, R. The Puritans and prurience: aspects of the Restoration book trade. _In_ Allen, H. C. and Thompson, R. eds. Contrast and connection p36-65

United States

Hansen, M. L. Immigration and Puritanism. _In_ Mulder, J. M. and Wilson, J. F. eds. Religion in American history p342-57

Puritans in literature

Daly, R. J. Anne Bradstreet and the practice of weaned affections. _In_ Daly, R. J. God's altar p82-127

Daly, R. J. Edward Taylor: Christ's creation and the dissatisfactions of metaphor. _In_ Daly, R. J. God's altar p162-99

Daly, R. J. Gnostics and naturalists. _In_ Daly, R. J. God's altar p128-61

Daly, R. J. The world's body. _In_ Daly, R. J. God's altar p6-39

History and criticism—Bibliography

Daly, R. J. Appendix: In critic's hands: a bibliographical essay. _In_ Daly, R. J. God's altar p201-23

Purity, Ritual. See Scapegoat

Purkart, Josef

Rhetoric in later Latin: Boncompagno of Signa and the rhetoric of love. In Murphy, J. J. ed. Medieval eloquence p319-31

The Purple Sage

Michelson, P. On The Purple Sage, Chicago Review, and Big Table. _In_ Anderson, E. and Kinzie, M. eds The little magazine in America: a modern documentary history p341-75

Pursglove, Glyn

Erected wit and infected will: some notes towards a reading of Meeting ends. _In_ Prentki, T. ed. Francis Warner p39-52

Purtill, Richard L.

That hideous strength: a double story. _In_ Schakel, P. J. ed. The longing for a form p91-102

Puschmann-Nalenz, Barbara

Ernest J. Gaines, A long day in November. _In_ Bruck, P. ed. The Black American short story in the 20th century p157-69

The Pushcart Press

Henderson, B. On Pushcart Press. _In_ Anderson, E. and Kinzie, M. eds. The little magazine in America: a modern documentary history p614-23

Pushkin, Aleksandr Sergeevich

About

Blok, A. A. On the mission of the poet. _In_ Proffer, C. R. ed. Modern Russian poets on poetry p71-80

Calder, A. Pushkin's Russia. _In_ Calder, A. Russia discovered p3-34

Donchin, G. Pushkin. _In_ Freeborn, R. ed. Russian literary attitudes from Pushkin to Solzhenitsyn p19-38

Eikhenbaum, B. M. Pushkin's path to prose. _In_ Erlich, V. ed. Twentieth-century Russian literary criticism p86-96

Katz, M. R. Pushkin's literary ballads. _In_ Katz, M. R. The literary ballad in early nineteenth-century Russian literature p139-65

Khodasevich, V. F. The shaken tripod. _In_ Proffer, C. R. ed. Modern Russian poets on poetry p61-70

Kostka, E. K. Pushkin's third dimension: the German influence. _In_ Kostka, E. K. Glimpses of Germanic-Slavic relations from Pushkin to Heinrich Mann p101-21

Mandel'shtam, O. E. Pushkin & Scriabin (fragments). _In_ Mandel'shtam, O. E. Selected essays p123-27

Mudrick, M. Pushkin in English. _In_ Mudrick, M. Books are not life but then what is? p65-86

Pritchett, V. S. Alexander Pushkin: founding father. _In_ Pritchett, V. S. The myth makers p77-88

Stacy, R. H. The age of Pushkin. _In_ Stacy, R. H. Russian literary criticism p25-37

Warner, E. A. Pushkin in the Russian folk-plays. _In_ Duggan, J. J. ed. Oral literature p101-07

About individual works
Eugene Onegin

Gregg, L. Slava snabokovu. _In_ A Book of things about Vladimir Nabokov p11-27

Rowe, W. W. Pushkinian impatient expectation and its function in Eugene Onegin. _In_ Rowe, W. W. Nabokov & others: patterns in Russian literature p15-26

Schmidgall, G. Peter Ilyich Tchaikovsky _In_ Schmidgall, G. Literature as opera p217-46

Shklovskiĭ, V. B. Pushkin and Sterne: Eugene Onegin. _In_ Erlich, V. ed. Twentieth-century Russian literary criticism p63-80

Criticism and interpretation

Pritchett, V. S. Alexander Pushkin: founding father. _In_ Pritchett, V. S. The myth makers p77-88

Pushkin, Alexsandr S.—*Continued*

Translations, English

Mudrick, M. Pushkin in English. *In* Mudrick, M. Books are not life but then what is? p65-86

Puteoli. See Pozzuoli

Putnam, Hilary W.

Some issues in the theory of grammar. *In* Harman, G. ed. On Noam Chomsky p80-103

Putnam, Howard Phelps

About

Coxe, L. O. Romance of the rose: John Peale Bishop and Phelps Putnam. *In* Coxe, L. O. Enabling acts p150-60

Putnam, Michael C. J.

Propertius 3.22: Tullus' return. *In* Illinois classical studies v2 1977 p240-54

Putnam, Phelps. See Putnam, Howard Phelps

Pütz, Heinz Peter

Nietzsche: art and intellectual inquiry. *In* Pasley, J. M. S. ed. Nietzsche: imagery and thought p 1-32

Pütz, Peter. See Pütz, Heinz Peter

Puzo, Mario

About individual works
The godfather

Cawelti, J. G. The mythology of crime and its formulaic embodiments. *In* Cawelti, J. G. Adventure, mystery, and romance p51-79

Puzzles. See Riddles

Pye, Lucian W.

Building a relationship on the sands of cultural exchanges. *In* China and America p109-48

China: ethnic minorities and national security. *In* Glazer, N. and Moynihan, D. P. eds. Ethnicity p489-512

Pyenson, Lewis

Einstein's early scientific collaboration. *In* Historical studies in the physical sciences v7 p83-123

Pygmies. See Bambute

Pyke, Magnus

The influence of American foods and food technology in Europe. *In* Bigsby, C. W. E. Superculture p83-95

Pylyshyn, Zenon W.

Metaphorical imprecision and the "top-down" research strategy. *In* Ortony, A. ed. Metaphor and thought p420-36

Pynchon, Thomas

About

Adams, R. M. Counterparts. *In* Adams, R. M. Afterjoyce p162-93

Allen, M. Women of the fabulators: Barth, Pynchon, Purdy, Kesey. *In* Allen, M. The necessary blankness p14-69

Vidal, G. American plastic: the matter of fiction. *In* Vidal, G. Matters of fact and of fiction p99-126

About individual works
The crying of lot 49

Mendelson, E. The sacred, the profane, and The crying of lot 49. *In* Baldwin, K. H. and Kirby, D. K. eds. Individual and community p182-222

V.

Richter, D. H. The failure of completeness: Pynchon's V. *In* Richter, D. H. Fable's end p101-35

Pynsent, Robert B.

Contemporary German fiction: the dimensions of experimentation. *In* Federman, R. ed. Surfiction p135-61

The last days of Austria: Hašek and Kraus. *In* Klein, H. M. ed. The First World War in fiction p136-48

Q

Q document (Biblical criticism)

Robinson, J. M. Jesus as Sophos and Sophia: wisdom tradition and the Gospels. *In* Aspects of wisdom in Judaism and early Christianity p 1-16

Qashqai tribe. See Kashkai tribe

al Qazwini al-Kātibī. See al-Kātibī 'Ali ibn 'Umar

Qhung (African people) See !Kung (African people)

Qoboza, Percy

Press censorship in South Africa. *In* Horton, P. C. ed. The Third World and press freedom p231-37

Qol säkhal. See Kol sachal

Qu Qiubai. See Ch'ü, Ch'iu-pai

Quacks and quackery

France

Ramsey, M. Medical power and popular medicine: illegal healers in nineteenth-century France. *In* Branca, P. ed. The medicine show p183-210

Quakers. See Friends, Society of

Quality (Philosophy)

Barfield, O. Science and quality. *In* Barfield, O. The rediscovery of meaning, and other essays p176-86

Cooper, D. E. Quality and equality in education. *In* Philosophers discuss education p113-29

O'Hagan, T. Quality and equality in education: a critique of David Cooper. *In* Philosophers discuss education p130-43

Quantification theory. See Predicate calculus

Quantrill, William Clarke

About

Castel, A. E. Quantrill's bushwhackers: a case study in partisan warfare. *In* Hubbell, J. T. ed. Battles lost and won p171-81

Quantum dynamics. See Quantum theory

Quantum mechanics. See Quantum theory

Quantum statistics. See Matrix mechanics

Quantum theory

Barut, A. O. Elementary particles, universes, and singularity surfaces. *In* Cosmology, history, and theology p15-21

Bromberg, J. L. The concept of particle creation before and after quantum mechanics. *In* Historical studies in the physical sciences v7 p161-91

Heelan, P. A. Quantum relativity and the cosmic observer. *In* Cosmology, history, and theology p29-37

Quantium theory—*Continued*

Klein, M. J. Einstein and the development of quantum physics. *In* Einstein p133-51

Koestler, A. Physics and metaphysics. *In* Koestler, A. Janus p242-73

Miller, A. I. Visualization lost and regained: the genesis of the quantum theory in the period 1913-27. *In* Wechsler, J. ed. On aesthetics in science p73-102

Weisskopf, V. F. The impact of quantum theory on modern physics. *In* Neyman, J. ed. The heritage of Copernicus: theories "pleasing to the mind" p311-31

Wheeler, J. A. The universe as home for man. *In* The Nature of scientific discovery p261-96

See also Atomic theory; Chemistry, Physical and theoretical; Force and energy; Heisenberg uncertainty principle; Relativity (Physics); Statistical thermodynamics

Quarles, Benjamin

Black history unbound. *In* Mintz, S. W. ed. Slavery, colonialism, and racism p163-78

Quarreling

Charny, I. W. and others. How does marital quarreling affect sexual relations? *In* Gross, L. ed. Sexual issues in marriage p121-28

Quarterly Review of Literature

Weiss, T. QRL: hallelujah on a straw. *In* Anderson, E. and Kinzie, M. eds. The little magazine in America: a modern documentary history p164-83

Quartey, K. A. B. Jones-. See Jones-Quartey, K. A. B.

Quartz

Beckwith, J. Some early Byzantine rock crystals. *In* Studies in memory of David Talbot Rice p 1-5

Quasars

Schmidt, M. Quasars and the universe. *In* The Nature of scientific discovery p246-60

Quasi-judicial agencies. See Independent regulatory commissions

Quasi-stellar radio sources. See Quasars

Québec (Province)

History—Autonomy and independence movements

Morf, G. Ethnic groups and developmental models: the case of Quebec. *In* Said, A. A. and Simmons. L. R. eds. Ethnicity in an international context p76-91

Rocher, G. The quiet revolution and revolutionary movements among Quebec French Canadians. *In* Perspectives on revolution and evolution p238-67

Warburton, T. R. Nationalism and language in Switzerland and Canada. *In* Smith, A. D. ed. Nationalist movements p88-109

History—Separatist movement

See Québec (Province)—History—Autonomy and independence movements

Separatist movement

See Québec (Province)—History—Autonomy and independence movements

Québec (Province) in literature

Joyaux, G. J. Roch Carrier's trilogy: a second look at Quebec's dark years. *In* Essays in honor of Russel B. Nye p105-28

Québec Liberation Front. See Front de Libération du Québec

Queen Elizabeth's Men

Pinciss, G. M. Shakespeare, Her Majesty's players and Pembroke's Men. *In* Shakespeare survey 27 p129-36

Queen of the woods. See Pokagon, S. O-gi-mäw-kwe mit-gwä-ki (Queen of the woods)

Queens. See Kings and rulers

Queens in art. See Kings and rulers in art

Queen's Men. See Queen Elizabeth's Men

Queiroz, José Maria de Eça de. See Eça de Queiroz, José Maria de

Quem quaeritis dialogue in the history of Western drama, The role of the. McGee, T. J. *In* Renaissance drama [1976] p177-91

Quennell, Peter

About individual works

Alexander Pope

Connolly, C. Pope: 1. *In* Connolly, C. The evening colonnade p112-14

La queste del Saint Graal

Quinn, E. C. Beyond courtly love: religious elements in Tristan and La queste del Saint Graal. *In* In pursuit of perfection p179-219

Questiaux, Nicole, and Fournier, Jacques

France. *in* Kamerman, S. B. and Kahn, A. J. eds. Family policy p117-82

Quevedo y Villegas, Francisco Gomez de

About individual works

The life and adventures of Don Pablos, the sharper

Bjornson, R. El buscón: Quevedo's annihilation of the picaresque. *In* Bjornson, R. The picaresque hero in European fiction p106-26

Quichés

Cosminsky, S. The evil eye in a Quiché community. *In* The Evil eye p163-74

Quie, Albert Harold

The tyranny of the urgent. *In* The Third century p147-52

The quiet man (Motion picture)

French, B. The joys of marriage. *In* French, B. On the verge of revolt p13-22

Quiggin, Alison Hingston

Trade routes, trade and currency in East Africa. *In* The Occasional papers of the Rhodes-Livingstone Museum p145-65

Quincey, Thomas de. See De Quincey, Thomas

Quincy, Mass.

History

McWilliams, J. P. Fictions of Merry Mount. *In* Zenderland, L. ed. Recycling the past p 1-28

Quine, Willard Van Orman

Methodological reflections on current linguistic theory. *In* Harman, G. ed. On Noam Chomsky p104-17

Mind and verbal dispositions. *In* Guttenplan, S. D. ed. Mind and language p83-95

The nature of natural knowledge. *In* Guttenplan, S. D. ed. Mind and language p67-81

The ways of paradox, and other essays

Contents

Algebraic logic and predicate functors
Carnap and logical truth
Foundations of mathematics

Quine, Willard V.
The ways of paradox, and other essays
Contents—Continued
Homage to Rudolf Carnap
Implicit definition sustained
The limits of knowledge
Linguistics and philosophy
Logic as a source of syntactical insights
A logistical approach to the ontological problem
Mr Strawson on logical theory
Necessary truth
On a supposed antinomy
On Carnap's views on ontology
On mental entities
On multiplying entities
On simple theories of a complex world
On the application of modern logic
Ontological reduction and the world of numbers
Ontological remarks on the propositional calculus
Posits and reality
Quantifiers and propositional attitudes
Reply to Professor Marcus
The scope and language of science
Three grades of modal involvement
Truth and disquotation
Truth by convention
Vagaries of definition
The variable
The ways of paradox

About

Føllesdal, D. Meaning and experience. *In* Guttenplan, S. D. ed. Mind and language p25-44

Hookway, C. Indeterminacy and interpretation. *In* Hookway, C. and Pettit, P. eds. Action and interpretation p17-42

Margolis, J. Z. The relevance of Dewey's epistemology. *In* Cahn, S. M. ed. New studies in the philosophy of John Dewey p117-48

Quinlan, In re (N.J.)
New Jersey. Superior Court. In the matter of Karen Quinlan, an alleged incompetent. *In* Weir, R. F. ed. Ethical issues in death and dying p271-77

Quinn, Bernetta. See Quinn, Mary Bernetta

Quinn, David Beers
New geographical horizons: literature. *In* First images of America p635-58

Quinn, Dennis Bruce
Donne's Anniversaries as celebration. *In* Roberts, J. R. ed. Essential articles for the study of John Donne's poetry p368-73

Quinn, Esther Casier
Beyond courtly love: religious elements in Tristan and La queste del Saint Graal. *In* In pursuit of perfection p179-219

Quinn, Mary Bernetta
Flannery O'Connor, a realist of distances. *In* Friedman, M. J. and Lawson, L. A. eds. The added dimension p157-83

Medusan imagery in Sylvia Plath. *In* Lane, G. ed. Sylvia Plath p97-115

Quinney, Richard
A sociological theory of criminal law. *In* Davis, F. J. and Stivers, R. eds. The collective definition of deviance p40-49

Quinones, Ricardo J.

About individual works

The Renaissance discovery of time

Mudrick, M. A thrust in the hand is worth two in the bush. *In* Mudrick, M. Books are not life but then what is? p234-41

Quintilian. See Quintilianus, Marcus Fabius

Quintilianus, Marcus Fabius

About individual works

Institutio oratoria

Bailey, D. R. S. Emendations of pseudo-Quintilian's longer declamations. *In* Harvard Studies in classical philology v80 p187-217

Lebek, W. D. Heminarium: Quintilian Institutio oratoria 6.3.52 and CIL IV 10566. *In* Harvard Studies in classical philology v82 p271-75

Quinton, Anthony
The concept of a phenomenon. *In* Pivčević, E. ed. Phenomenology and philosophical understanding p 1-16

Has man an essence? *In* Royal Institute of Philosophy. Nature and conduct p14-35

Karl Popper: politics without essences. *In* De Crespigny, A. and Minogue, K. R. eds. Contemporary political philosophers p147-67

Utilitarian ethics. *In* New studies in ethics v2 p 1-118

Quirarte, Jacinto
Early art styles of Mesoamerica and Early Classic Maya art. *In* The Origins of Maya civilization p249-83

Quirino, Leonard
The cards indicate a voyage on A streetcar named Desire. *In* Tennessee Williams: a tribute p77-96

Quirk, Randolph
The linguist and the English language
Contents
Bon-mots from places
Charles Dickens, linguist
A commodity of good names
Dasent, Morris, and aspects of translation
A glimpse of eighteenth-century prescriptivism
The image of the dictionary
The 'language' of language and literature
Our knowledge of English
Shakespeare and the English language
The study of the mother-tongue
Thinking of words
Third international

Quiroga, Elena

About individual works

Algo pasa en la calle

Schwartz, R. Quiroga and Algo pasa en la calle (Something happens on the street) (1954). *In* Schwartz, R. Spain's New Wave novelists, 1950-1974 p66-73

Quiroga de Abarca, Elene. See Quiroga, Elena

Qumran scrolls. See Dead Sea scrolls

Quotations. See Maxims

Qureshi, Saleem
Political violence in the South Asian subcontinent. *In* International terrorism p151-93

R

ROTC. See United States. Air Force. Reserve Officers' Training Corps; United States. Army. Reserve Officers' Training Corps; United States. Navy. Reserve Officers' Training Corps

Raamsdonk, Wouter van
Promoting the sense of social responsibility in Dutch education. *In* Against pollution and hunger p260-69

Rabbinical literature
Goldin, J. The magic of magic and superstition. *In* Aspects of religious propaganda in Judaism and early Christianity p115-47
Gruenewald, M. "It is enough for the servant to be like his master." *In* Salo Wittmayer Baron v2 p573-76
See also Midrash

Animals
See Rabbinical literature—Natural history

History and criticism
Daube, D. The rabbis and Philo on human rights. *In* Sidorsky, D. ed. Essays on human rights p234-46

Natural history
Berger, A. Ayalta: from the doe in the field to the mother of the messiahs. *In* Salo Wittmayer Baron v 1 p209-17

Rabbinical seminaries
Goitein, S. D. F. New sources on the Palestinian gaonate. *In* Salo Wittmayer Baron v 1 p503-37

Rabbis. See Geonim

Rabbit, run (Motion picture)
Siegel, G. Rabbit runs down. *In* Peary, G. and Shatzkin, R. eds. The modern American novel and the movies p247-55

Rabcewicz-Zubkowski, Ludwik Kos- See Kos-Rabcewicz-Zubkowski, Ludwik

Rabelais, François
About
Screech, M. A. Medicine and literature: aspects of Rabelais and Montaigne (with a glance at the law). *In* French Renaissance studies, 1540-70 p156-69

About individual works
Gargantua and Pantagruel
Kennedy, W. J. The style of ironic discourse. *In* Kennedy, W. J. Rhetorical norms in Renaissance literature p79-127
Lanham, R. A. The war between play and purpose: Gargantua and Pantagruel. *In* Lanham, R. A. The motives of eloquence p165-89
Screech, M. A. Commonplaces of law, proverbial wisdom and philosophy: their importance in Renaissance scholarship (Rabelais, Joachim du Bellay, Montaigne). *In* Classical influences on European culture A.D. 1500-1700 p127-34
Wasserman, J. The word as object: the Rabelaisian novel. *In* Spilka, M. ed. Towards a poetics of fiction p316-30

Characters—Pantagruel
Nock, A. J. Pantagruelism. *In* Crunden, R. M. ed. The superfluous men p98-106

Rabie, Hassanein
The training of the mamlūk fāris. *In* War, technology and society in the Middle East p153-63

Rabil, Albert
Erasmus's Paraphrases of the New Testament. *In* Essays on the works of Erasmus p145-61

Rabin, Michael
The uses and limitations of science teaching. *In* Hook, S.; Kurtz, P. W. and Todorovich, M. eds. The philosophy of the curriculum: the need for general education p127-36

Rabin, Robert Leonard
Preclusion of judicial review in the processing of claims for veterans' benefits: a preliminary analysis. *In* Stanford legal essays p381-99

Rabinovich, Itamar. See Golan, G. jt. auth.

Rabinovitch, Nachum L.
Halakha and other systems of ethics: attitudes and interactions. *In* Modern Jewish ethics p89-102

Rabinovitz, Francine F. See Rein, M. jt. auth.

Rabinovitz, Rubin
The craftsmanship of Beckett: the deterioration of outside reality in Samuel Beckett's fiction. *In* Yeats, Joyce, and Beckett p167-71
Iris Murdoch. *In* Stade, G. ed. Six contemporary British novelists p271-332

Rabinowitz, Howard N.
Continuity and change: Southern urban development, 1860-1900. *In* Brownell, B. A. and Goldfield, D. R. eds. The city in Southern history p92-122
George Washington as icon, 1865-1900. *In* Browne, R. B. and Fishwick, M. W. eds. Icons of America p67-86

Rabinowitz, Shalom
About
Kaufman, B. Sholom Aleichem. *In* Abroad in America: Visitors to the new Nation, 1776-1914 p270-78

Rabinowitz, Solomon J. See Rabinowitz, Shalom

Rabinowitz, Stanley J.
Bely and Sologub: toward the history of a friendship. *In* Janecek, G. ed. Andrey Bely p156-68

Rabinowitz, Victor
The prosecutor: the duty to seek justice. *In* Nader, R. and Green, M. J. eds. Verdicts on lawyers p231-41

Rabkin, David
Race and fiction: God's stepchildren and Turbott Wolfe. *In* Parker, K. ed. The South African novel in English p77-94

Raccoons
White, E. B. Coon tree. *In* White, E. B. Essays of E. B. White p34-45

Race
Béteille, A. Race, caste and ethnic identity. *In* United Nations Educational, Scientific and Cultural Organization. Race, science and society p211-33
Bodmer, W. F. Race and IQ: the genetic background. *In* Montagu, A. ed. Race and IQ p252-86
Bottoms, A. E. and Wiles, P. Race, crime and violence. *In* Racial variation in man p131-49
Brace, C. L. and Livingstone, F. B. On creeping Jensenism. *In* Montagu, A. ed. Race and IQ p151-73

Race—*Continued*

Dobzhansky, T. G. and Montagu, A. Natural selection and the mental capacities of mankind. *In* Montagu, A. ed. Race and IQ p104-13

Dubinin, N. P. Race and contemporary genetics. *In* United Nations Educational, Scientific and Cultural Organization. Race, science and society p68-94

Dubos, R. J. The races of man. *In* Dubos, R. J. Beast or angel? p23-29

Dunn, L. C. Race and biology. *In* United Nations Educational, Scientific and Cultural Organization. Race, science and society p31-67

Klineberg, O. Race and psychology. *In* United Nations Educational, Scientific and Cultural Organization. Race, science and society p173-207

Leach, E. R. Cultural components in the concept of race. *In* Racial variation in man p27-54

Leiris, M. Race and culture. *In* United Nations Educational, Scientific and Cultural Organization. Race, science and society p135-72

Lieberman, L. The debate over race: a study in the sociology of knowledge. *In* Montagu, A. ed. Race and IQ p19-41

Sunderland, E. Biological components of the races of man. *In* Racial variation in man p9-25

See also Religion and race

Race and music. See Music and race

Race awareness

Kronus, S. Race, ethnicity, and community. *In* Handbook of contemporary urban life p202-32

Raveau, F. H. M. Role of color in identification processes. *In* Ethnic identity p353-59

See also Afro-Americans—Race identity; Blacks—Race identity; Ethnic attitudes; Ethnicity; Racism

Race discrimination

Brown, R. C. A commentary on racial myths and the Black athlete. *In* Social problems in athletics p168-73

Essien-Udom, E. U. Tribalism and racism. *In* United Nations Educational, Scientific and Cultural Organization. Race, science and society p234-61

Posner, R. A. The DeFunis case and the constitutionality of preferential treatment of racial minorities. *In* The Supreme Court review, 1974 p 1-32

Reed, I. Crushing the mutiny. *In* Reed, I. Shrovetide in old New Orleans p237-45

Rich, A. C. Disloyal to civilization: feminism, racism, gynephobia. *In* Rich, A. C. On lies, secrets, and silence p275-310

See also Discrimination in education; Discrimination in employment; Discrimination in public accommodations

History

Rose, S. P. R. Scientific racism and ideology. *In* Racial variation in man p191-210

Law and legislation—Canada

Nanda, V. P. Racial discrimination and the law: recent legislation in Great Britain, Canada, and the United States. *In* Claude, R. P. ed. Comparative human rights p214-50

Law and legislation—Great Britain

Nanda, V. P. Racial discrimination and the law: recent legislation in Great Britain, Canada, and the United States. *In* Claude, R. P. ed. Comparative human rights p214-50

Law and legislation—United States

Cox, A. Harvard College amicus curiae, DeFunis v. Odegaard. *In* Gross, B. R. ed. Reverse discrimination p184-97

Douglas, W. O. DeFunis v. Odegaard, dissenting opinion (April 23,1974). *In* Gross, B. R. ed. Reverse discrimination p198-207

Ely, J. H. The constitutionality of reverse racial discrimination. *In* Gross, B. R. ed. Reverse discrimination p208-16

Freund, P. A. Equality, race, and preferential treatment. *In* Small comforts for hard times p26-33

Greenawalt, R. K. Judicial scrutiny of "benign" racial preference in law school admissions. *In* Gross, B. R. ed. Reverse discrimination p217-38

Nanda, V. P. Racial discrimination and the law: recent legislation in Great Britain, Canada, and the United States. *In* Claude, R. P. ed. Comparative human rights p214-50

Nickel, J. W. Preferential policies in hiring and admissions: a jurisprudential approach. *In* Gross, B. R. ed. Reverse discrimination p324-47

Sandalow, T. Racial preferences in higher education: political responsibility and the judicial role. *In* Gross, B. R. ed. Reverse discrimination p239-64

United States

McPherson, B. D. The Black athlete: an overview and analysis. *In* Social problems in athletics p122-50

Nagel, T. The policy of preference. *In* Nagel, T. Mortal questions p91-105

See also Afro-Americans—Civil rights

Race improvement. See Eugenics

Race prejudice. See Race discrimination; Racism

Race problems. See Race relations

Race psychology. See Ethnopsychology

Race question. See Race relations

Race relations

Banton, M. P. 1960: a turning point in the study of race relations. *In* Mintz, S. W. ed. Slavery, colonialism, and racism p31-44

Deloria, V. The future of racial minorities in American society. *In* Bundy, R. F. ed. Images of the future: the twenty-first century and beyond p159-65

Gordon, M. M. Toward a general theory of racial and ethnic group relations. *In* Glazer, N. and Moynihan, D. P. eds. Ethnicity p84-110

Harwood, J. Heredity, environment, and the legitimation of social policy. *In* Barnes, B. and Shapin, S. eds. Natural order p231-51

Henriques, F. Contemporary racial problems. *In* Racial variation in man p211-32

Hudson, D. The World Council of Churches and racism. *In* The Year book of world affairs, 1975 p155-72

Popkin, R. H. The philosophical bases of modern racism. *In* Philosophy and the civilizing arts p126-65

Race relations—*Continued*

Watson, G. Race and the Socialists. *In* Watson, G. Politics and literature in modern Britain p120-37

See also Antisemitism; Mass media and race relations; Minorities; Race discrimination; Racism; also subdivision Race relations under names of regions, couunties, cities, etc. e.g. Virginia—Race relations

History

Deighton, H. S. Multiracial societies—an historical perspective. *In* Racial variation in man p179-90

Race relations in literature

Alexander, M. A. W. Faulkner & race. *In* The Maker and the myth: Faulkner and Yoknapatawpha, 1977 p105-21

Goonetilleke, D. C. R. A. Difficulties of connection in India: Kipling and Forster. *In* Goonetilleke, D. C. R. A. Developing countries in British fiction p134-69

Rose, A. H. Recent American writings: the leveling of racial vision. *In* Rose, A. H. Demonic vision p119-36

Sarotte, G. M. Four archetypes of the homosexual couple: The white and the Black. *In* Sarotte, G. M. Like a brother, like a lover p92-104

Races of man. See Ethnology

Racevskis, Karlis

The French Academy as a proponent of egalitarianism. *In* Studies in eighteenth-century culture v7 p105-16

Rachels, James

John Dewey and the truth about ethics. *In* Cahn, S. M. ed. New studies in the philosophy of John Dewey p149-71

Vegetarianism and "the other weight problem." *In* Aiken, W. and La Follette, H. eds. World hunger and moral obligation p180-93

Racial amalgamation. See Miscegenation

Racial attitudes of American presidents. See Presidents—United States—Racial attitudes

Racial crossing. See Miscegenation

Racial discrimination. See Race discrimination

Racial identity of Afro-Americans. See Afro-Americans—Race identity

Racial identity of Blacks. See Blacks—Race identity

Racial issues. See Race problems; and subdivision Race question under names of countries, states, cities, etc.

Racine, Jean Baptiste

About

Auchincloss, L. Racine and Port-Royal. *In* Auchincloss, L. Life, law and letters p121-30

Nicoll, A. Racine and the tragedy of sentiment. *In* Nicoll, A. World drama p243-57

About individual works

Esther, a tragedy

Knapp, B. L. Jean Racine's Esther and two Hebrew translations of this drama. *In* Salo Wittmayer Baron v2 p591-621

Phèdre

Edelman, N. The central image in Phèdre. *In* Edelman, N. The eye of the beholder p130-41

Edelman, N. The motion of Phèdre from Act III into Act IV: an alternative reading. *In* Edelman, N. The eye of the beholder p121-29

Fry, P. H. Phaedra. *In* Seidel, M. A. and Mendelson, E. eds. Homer to Brecht p273-91

Characters

Bersani, L. Racine, psychoanalysis and Oedipus. *In* Bersani, L. A future for Astyanax p17-50

Translations, Hebrew

Knapp, B. L. Jean Racine's Esther and two Hebrew translations of this drama. *In* Salo Wittmayer Baron v2 p591-621

Racism

Moynihan, D. P. The significance of the Zionism-as-racism resolution for international human rights. *In* Sidorsky, D. ed. Essays on human rights p37-45

See also Antisemitism; Race discrimination

Rack, Henry Denman

'Christ's Kingdom not of this world:' the case of Benjamin Hoadly versus William Law reconsidered. *In* Church, society and politics p275-91

Rack, Johannes. See Aesticampianus, Johannes Rhagius

Raconteurs. See Storytellers

Radbill, Samuel X.

The role of animals in infant feeding. *In* American folk medicine p21-30

Radcliffe, Ann (Ward)

About

Ware, M. The telescope reversed: Ann Radcliffe and natural scenery. *In* A Provision of human nature p169-89

About individual works

The mysteries of Udolpho

Howells, C. A. Ann Radcliffe, The mysteries of Udolpho. *In* Howells, C. A. Love, mystery, and misery p28-61

Radcliffe, Elizabeth

About

Harper, G. M. and Kelly, J. S. Preliminary examination of the script of E[lizabeth] R[adcliffe]. *In* Yeats and the occult p130-71

Radcliffe, Mary Ann

About individual works

Manfroné; or, The one-handed monk

Howells, C. A. Minerva Press fiction, 1796-1819: Regina Maria Roche, The children of the abbey and Mary-Anne Radcliffe, Manfroné; or The one-handed monk. *In* Howells, C. A. Love, mystery, and misery p80-113

Radcliffe College

Students

Trilling, D. We must march my darlings: A return to the past. *In* Trilling, D. We must march my darlings p213-50

Trilling, D. We must march my darlings: Daughters of the middle class. *In* Trilling, D. We must march my darlings p272-91

Radding, Charles Michael

The administrators of the aids in Normandy, 1360-1380. *In* Order and innovation in the Middle Ages p41-53

Rader, Ralph Wilson

The concept of genre and eighteenth-century studies. *In* Harth, J. P. ed. New approaches to eighteenth-century literature p79-115

Radest, Howard B.

On interdisciplinary education. *In* Hook, S.; Kurtz, P. W. and Todorovich, M. eds. The philosophy of the curriculum: the need for general education p227-33

Radhasoami Satsang

Juergensmeyer, M. Radhasoami as a transnational movement. *In* Needleman, J. and Baker, G. eds. Understanding the new religions p190-200

Radiation

Physiological effect

Sternglass, E. J. Nuclear radiation and human health. *In* Against pollution and hunger p121-79

Toxicology

See Leukemia, Radiation-induced

Radiation-induced leukemia. See Leukemia, Radiation-induced

Radiation mutagenesis. See Radiogenetics

Radicalism

Dreitzel, H. P. On the political meaning of culture. *In* Beyond the crisis p83-129

Frye, N. The university and personal life. *In* Frye, N. Spiritus mundi p27-48

Graff, G. The politics of anti-realism. *In* Graff, G. Literature against itself p63-101

Overholt, W. H. Sources of radicalism and revolution: a survey of the literature. *In* Radicalism in the contemporary age v1 p293-335

Stepan, A. C. Inclusionary and exclusionary military responses to radicalism: with special attention to Peru; excerpt from "The state and society: Peru in comparative perspective." *In* Radicalism in the contemporary age v3 p221-39

History

Bialer, S. On the meanings, sources, and carriers of radicalism in contemporary industrialized societies: introductory remarks. *In* Radicalism in the contemporary age v1 p 3-29

Bialer, S. The resurgence and changing nature of the Left in industrialized democracies. *In* Radicalism in the contemporary age v3 p 3-81

Landsberger, H. A. The sources of rural radicalism. *In* Radicalism in the contemporary age v1 p247-91

Jews

Rothman, S. and others. Ethnic variation in student radicalism: some new perspectives. *In* Radicalism in the contemporary age v1 p151-211

Europe

Maier, C. S. Beyond revolution? Resistance and vulnerability to radicalism in advanced Western societies. *In* Radicalism in the contemporary age v3 p241-67

Teodori, M. The New Lefts in Europe. *In* Radicalism in the contemporary age v3 p201-19

Tucker, R. C. The perils of success—deradicalization. *In* Lauer, R. H. ed. Social movements and social change p227-55

Europe—History

Nisbet, R. A. The function of the vision of the future in radical movements. *In* Radicalism in the contemporary age v2 p13-33

France—History

Tarrow, S. G. From Cold war to historic compromise: approaches to French and Italian radicalism. *In* Radicalism in the contemporary age v1 p213-45

Germany, West

Kuhn, H. Germany—divided once more. *In* Prospects for constitutional democracy p101-17

Nipperdey, T. The German university in crisis. *In* Universities in the Western world p119-42

Italy—History

Tarrow, S. G. From Cold war to historic compromise: approaches to French and Italian radicalism. *In* Radicalism in the contemporary age v1 p213-45

San Francisco Bay Region

Bellah, R. N. The new consciousness and the Berkeley New Left. *In* The New religious consciousness p77-92

United States

DeLeon, D. The future of the radical past. *In* DeLeon, D. The American as anarchist p134-57

Howard, D. The future as present: political and theoretical implications. *In* Radicalism in the contemporary age v2 p129-52

Ingham, A. G. Sport and the "New Left"; some reflections upon opposition without praxis. *In* Social problems in athletics p238-48

Lipset, S. M. Why no socialism in the United States? *In* Radicalism in the contemporary age v1 p31-149

Parry, A. The Weathermen. *In* Parry, A. Terrorism: from Robespierre to Arafat p322-29

Perrucci, R. In the service of man: radical movements in the professions. *In* Gerstl, J. E. and Jacobs, G. eds. Professions for the people p215-30

Rothman, S. and others. Ethnic variation in student radicalism: some new perspectives. *In* Radicalism in the contemporary age v1 p151-211

Whitfield, S. J. "Totalitarianism" in eclipse: the recent fate of an idea. *In* Images and ideas in American culture p60-95

United States—History

DeLeon, D. Conscience and community. *In* DeLeon, D. The American as anarchist p14-23

DeLeon, D. Left libertarianism. *In* DeLeon, D. The American as anarchist p85-101

DeLeon, D. Overview. *In* DeLeon, D. The American as anarchist p3-13

DeLeon, D. Statist radicalism. *In* DeLeon, D. The American as anarchist p102-14

Radicals

Psychology

Overholt, W. H. Sources of radicalism and revolution: a survey of the literature. *In* Radicalism in the contemporary age v1 p293-335

Rothman, S. and others. Ethnic variations in student radicalism: some new perspectives. *In* Radicalism in the contemporary age v1 p151-211

Radiguet, Raymond

About

Turnell, M. Raymond Radiguet. *In* Turnell, M. The rise of the French novel p257-96

About individual works

The Count's ball

Turnell, M. Raymond Radiguet. *In* Turnell, M. The rise of the French novel p257-96

Devil in the flesh

Turnell, M. Raymond Radiguet. *In* Turnell, M. The rise of the French novel p257-96

Radin, Paul

Monotheism among American Indians. *In* Tedlock, D. E. and Tedlock, B. eds. Teachings from the American earth p219-47

Radio

See also Telephone wireless

Broadcasting

See Radio broadcasting

United States—Laws and regulations

Polsby, D. D. F.C.C. v. National Citizens Committee for Broadcasting and the judicious uses of administrative discretion. *In* The Supreme Court review, 1978 p 1-38

Radio, Citizens band. See Citizens band radio

Radio and music

Schmidtchen, G. Light music and the radio listener. *In* Fischer, H. D. and Melnik, S. R. eds. Entertainment: a crosscultural examination p286-98

Radio broadcasting

Follath, E. An international comparison of broadcasting systems. *In* Fischer, H. D. and Merrill, J. C. eds. International and intercultural communication p71-82

See also International broadcasting

Social aspects

Schmidtchen, G. Light music and the radio listener. *In* Fischer, H. D. and Melnik, S. R. eds. Entertainment: a cross-cultural examination p286-98

Nigeria

Ugboajah, F. O. Some issues in Nigerian broadcasting. *In* Gerbner, G. ed. Mass media policies in changing cultures p185-87

Sweden

Ivre, I. Conflict and resolution in Sweden. *In* Gerbner, G. ed. Mass media policies in changing cultures p119-30

Radio industry and trade

United States

See Afro-Americans in the radio industry

Radio programs

Nigeria

Ugboajah, F. O. Some issues in Nigerian broadcasting. *In* Gerbner, G. ed. Mass media policies in changing cultures p185-87

Radio sources (Astronomy) See Quasars

Radioactive dating. See Radiocarbon dating

Radioactive dust. See Radioactive fallout

Radioactive fallout

White, E. B. Sootfall and fallout. *In* White, E. B. Essays of E. B. White p90-99

Radioactive pollution. See Radioactive fallout

Radioactive substances. See Isotopes

Radioactivity. See Alpha rays; Transuuranium elements

Radiocarbon dating

Libby, W. F. Radiocarbon dating. *In* The Frontiers of knowledge p325-58

Radiogenetics

Sternglass, E. J. Nuclear radiation and human health. *In* Against pollution and hunger p121-79

Radius, Anna (Zuccari)

About

Pacifici, S. Women writers: Neera and Aleramo. *In* Pacifici, S. The modern Italian novel: from Capuana to Tozzi p49-67

Radner, Daisie Missouri Crumling

Malebranche's refutation of Spinoza. *In* Shahan, R. W. and Biro, J. I. eds. Spinoza: new perspectives p113-28

Radosh, Ronald

Cuba: a personal report. *In* Radosh, R. ed. The new Cuba: paradoxes and potentials p56-73

The Cuban Revolution and Western intellectuals. *In* Radosh, R. ed. The new Cuba: paradoxes and potentials p37-55

About individual works

Cuba: a personal report

Radosh, R. The Cuban Revolution and Western intellectuals. *In* Radosh, R. ed. The new Cuba: paradoxes and potentials p37-55

Radoyce, Lubomir

Writer in hell: notes on Dostoevsky's Letters. *In* California Slavic studies v9 p71-122

Radway, Laurence I.

Domestic attitudes as constraints on American foreign policy leaders. *In* Baldwin, D. A. ed. America in an interdependent world p295-313

The future of the Reserve Officer Training Corps. *In* Beaumont, R. A. and Edmonds, M. eds. War in the next decade p55-68

Radzinowicz, Sir Leon

About

Anttila, I. The foundation of co-operation in European criminological research: Sir Leon Radzinowicz and the Criminological Scientific Council at the Council of Europe. *In* Crime, criminology and public policy p25-32

Bibliography

Hawkins, K. O. An annotated bibliography of the writings of Leon Radzinowicz. *In* Crime, criminology and public policy p623-35

Radzinowicz, Mary Ann

Medicinable tragedy: the structure of Samson Agonistes and seventeenth-century psychopathology. *In* English drama: forms and development p94-122

About individual works

Toward Samson Agonistes: the growth of Milton's mind

Wittreich, J. A. The new Milton criticism. *In* Review, v 1 1979 p123-64

Rae, Douglas W.

A principle of simple justice. *In* Laslett, P. and Fishkin, J. eds. Philosophy, politics and society p134-54

Rae, John Bell

The application of science to industry. *In* Oleson, A. and Voss, J. eds. The organization of knowledge in modern America, 1860-1920 p249-68

Raeff, Marc

The Empress and the Vinerian Professor: Catherine II's projects of government reforms and Blackstone's Commentaries. *In* Oxford Slavonic papers, new ser. v7 p18-41

Imperial Russia: Peter I to Nicholas I. *In* Auty, R. and Obolensky, D. eds. An introduction to Russian history p121-95

Raether, Howard C. and Slater, Robert C.

Immediate postdeath activities in the United States. *In* Feifel, H. [ed.] New meanings of death p238-48

Rafeq, Abdul-Karím

The local forces in Syria in the seventeenth and eighteenth centuries. *In* War, technology and society in the Middle East p277-307

Raffaele Sanzio. See Raphael

Raffel, Burton

Judith: hypermetricity and rhetoric. *In* Anglo-Saxon poetry: essays in appreciation p124-34

Raghavachar, S. S.

Śaiva-Siddhānta, Viśistadvaita, Dvaita. *In* Bishop, D. H. ed. Indian thought p301-15

Raghavacharyulu, D. V. K.

Naipaul and Narayan: the sense of life. *In* Narasimhaiah, C. D. ed. Awakened conscience p216-25

Ragtime music

Hawkes, T. 'That Shakespeherian rag.' *In* English Association. Essays and studies, 1977 p22-38

Raguin, Yves

Buddhism in Taiwan. *In* Dumoulin, H. ed. Buddhism in the modern world p179-85

Ragusa, Olga

Narrative and drama

Contents

Alberto Moravia: voyeurism and storytelling (1)

Gadda, Pasolini, and experimentalism: form or ideology?

"The light is split in the prism . . .": Svevo's unfinished play, Con la penna d'oro

Narrative vs stylistic structure in I Malavoglia

Pirandello and Verga

Pirandello's La patente: play and story (1)

Stendhal, Tomasi di Lampedusa, and the novel

Ragusa. See Dubrovnik, Yugoslavia

Ragussis, Michael

The subterfuge of art

Contents

D. H. Lawrence: Silence in Women in love

D. H. Lawrence: The new vocabulary of Women in love: speech and art-speech

E. M. Forster: the vision of evil in fiction: the narrative structure of A passage to India

Epilogue: The echo

Epilogue: The word

Keats: "awake sweet dreamer!": Narrator and reader in "The eve of St. Agnes"

Keats:: The language of gods and men: the fragmented world of the Hyperion poems

The subterfuge of art: Lawrence, Freud, and "verbal consciousness"

The subterfuge of art: Literature and regression

W. B. Yeats: "Her vision in the wood" as tragic art: a "hollow image of fulfilled desire"

W. B. Yeats: The vision of evil and poetic objectivity in "Nineteen hundred and nineteen"

Wordsworth: the Arab dream: the language behind nature and art

Rahman, Fazlur

The eternity of the world and the heavenly bodies in post-Avicennan philosophy. *In* Essays on Islamic philosophy and science p222-37

The God-world relationship in Mullā Sadrā. *In* Essays on Islamic philosophy and science p238-53

A Muslim response: Christian particularity and the faith of Islam. *In* Christian faith in a religiously plural world p69-79

Rahner, Karl

About

McCool, G. A. Person and community in Karl Rahner. *In* Roth, R. J. ed. Person and community p63-86

Rahtz, Philip, and Bullough, Donald A.

The parts of an Anglo-Saxon mill. *In* Anglo-Saxon England 6 p15-37

Rahv, Philip

Essays on literature and politics, 1932-1972

Contents

American intellectuals in the postwar situation

Crime without punishment

The cult of experience in American writing

The Dark Lady of Salem

Delmore Schwartz: the paradox of precocity

Dostoevsky: descent into the underground

Dostoevsky in Crime and punishment

Dostoevsky in The possessed

The education of Anton Chekhov

Excerpts from "the literary class war"

F. Scott Fitzgerald on the Riviera

Gogol as a modern instance

The great outsider

The heiress of all the ages

Henry James and his cult

In dubious battle

Also in Dunlop, J. B; Haugh, R. and Klimoff; A. eds. Aleksandr Solzhenitsyn: critical essays and documentary materials 2d ed p356-64

An introduction to Kafka

The legend of the Grand Inquisitor

Liberal anticommunism revisited

Mrs. Woolf and Mrs. Brown

On F. R. Leavis and D. H. Lawrence

The other Dostoevsky

Paleface and Redskin

The princess

Proletarian literature: a political autopsy

Religion and the intellectuals

Saul Bellow's progress

The sense and nonsense of Whittaker Chambers

T. S. Eliot in his posthumous essays

Trials of the mind

Twilight of the thirties: passage from an editorial

Two subversive Russians

What and where is the New Left?

Ramage, Edwin S.—*Continued*

Lucilius, the discoverer of the genre. *In* Roman satirists and their satire p27-52

Method and structure in the satires of Persius. *In* Illinois classical studies v4, 1979 p136-51

Persius, the philosopher-satirist. *In* Roman satirists and their satire p114-35

Perspectives ancient and modern. *In* Ramage, E. S. ed. Atlantis, fact or fiction? p3-45

Ramage, Nancy Hirschland

Draped herm from Sardis. *In* Harvard Studies in classical philology v78 p253-56

Ramakrishna

About

Chatterji, P. Ramakrishna. *In* Bishop, D. H. ed. Indian thought p346-56

Coomaraswamy, A. K. Śrī Ramakrishna and religious tolerance. *In* Coomaraswamy, A. K. Selected papers v2 p34-42

Ramakrishna Rao, K. B.

Jainism. *In* Bishop, D. H. ed. Indian thought p85-100

Rāmāyāna. See Valmīki Rāmāyanā

Ramazani, Rouhollah K.

The autonomous Republic of Azerbaijan and the Kurdish People's Republic: their rise and fall. *In* Hammond, T. T. ed. The anatomy of Communist takeovers p448-74

Ramchand, Kenneth

The vision of a 'sustaining community' in Claude McKay's Banana Bottom. *In* Baugh, E. ed. Critics on Caribbean literature p93-102

Ramcharan, B. G.

Equality and discrimination in international economic law (VIII): the United Nations Regional Economic Commissions. *In* The Year book of world affairs, 1978 p268-85

The International Law Commission. *In* The Year book of world affairs, 1975 p283-300

Ramírez, Román

About

Harvey, L. P. Oral composition and the performance of novels of chivalry in Spain. *In* Duggan, J. J. ed. Oral literature p84-100

Ramism. See La Ramée, Pierre de

Ramon de Caldes

About

Bisson, T. N. Ramon de Caldes (c. 1135-c. 1200): Dean of Barcelona and King's Minister. *In* Law, church, and society p281-92

Ramos, Mel

About

Truewoman, H. Realism in drag. *In* Battcock, G. ed. Super realism p223-29

Ramos, Reyes

The Mexican American: am I who they say I am? *In* Trejo, A. D. ed. The Chicanos p49-66

Ramraj, Victor J.

Diminishing satire: a study of V. S. Naipaul and Mordecai Richler. *In* Narasîmhaiah, C. D. ed. Awakened conscience p261-74

Rams (in religion, folklore, etc.)

Lawal, B. Yoruba-Sango ram symbolism: from ancient Sahara or dynastic Egypt? *In* African images p225-51

Rams in art

Lawal, B. Yoruba-Sango ram symbolism: from ancient Sahara or dynastic Egypt? *In* African images p225-51

Ramsay, James Andrew Broun, 1st marquess of Dalhousie. See Dalhousie, James Andrew Broun Ramsay, 1st marquess of

Ramsdonk, Wouter van. See Raamsdonk, Wouter van

Ramsey, Clifford Earl

A midsummer night's dream. *In* Seidel, M. A. and Mendelson, E. eds. Homer to Brecht p214-37

Ramsey, Jarold

The Indian literature of Oregon. *In* Bingham, E. R. and Love, G. A. eds. Northwest perspectives p2-19

Ramsey, Matthew

Medical power and popular medicine: illegal healers in nineteenth-century France. *In* Branca, P. ed. The medicine show p183-210

Ramsey, Paul, 1913-

The indignity of 'death with dignity.' *In* Death inside out p81-96

On (only) caring for the dying. *In* Weir, R. F. ed. Ethical issues in death and dying p189-225

Ramshorn, Mary T.

Selected tasks for the dying patient and family members. *In* Anticipatory grief p246-50

Ramus, Peter. See La Ramée, Pierre de

Rance, Nicholas

The historical novel and popular politics in nineteenth-century England

Contents

Charles Dickens: A tale of two cities (1859)

Elizabeth Gaskell: Sylvia's lovers (1863)

George Meredith: Sandra Belloni (1864) and Vittoria (1866)

The historical novel after Scott

Popular politics in George Eliot's historical novels of the 1860s

The sensational calm, 1848-67

Ranches

Great Plains

Myres, S. L. The ranching frontier: Spanish institutional backgrounds of the Plains cattle industry. *In* Weber, D. J. ed. New Spain's far northern frontier p79-94

Latin America

Myres, S. L. The ranching frontier: Spanish institutional background of the Plains cattle industry. *In* Weber, D. J. ed. New Spain's far northern frontier p79-94

Spain

Myres, S. L. The ranching frontier: Spanish institutional backgrounds of the Plains cattle industry. *In* Weber, D. J. ed. New Spain's far northern frontier 79-94

Ranchos. See Ranches

Rand, Ayn

About individual works

The fountainhead

McGann, K. Ayn Rand in the stockyard of the spirit. *In* Peary, G. and Shatzkin, R. eds. The modern American novel and the movies p325-35

Rand, Richard A.

Geraldine. *In* Glyph 3 p74-97

Randall, John Herman, 1899-

Paduan Aristotelianism reconsidered. *In* Philosophy and humanism p275-82

Randall, Margaret

El corno emplumado, 1961-1969: some notes in retrospect, 1975. *In* Anderson, E. and Kinzie, M. eds. The little magazine in America: a modern documentary history p405-22

Randall, Mark. See Ehrlich, I. jt. auth.

Randers, Jørgen, and Behrens, William

Watch for the foothills: signaling the end to growth in a finite world. *In* Orr, D. W. and Soroos, M. S. eds. The global predicament p18-38

Rands, Robert Lawrence

The ceramic sequence at Palenque, Chiapas. *In* Mesoamerican archaeology p51-75

The rise of Classic Maya civilization in the Northwestern Zone: isolation and integration. *In* The Origins of Maya civilization p159-80

Ranft, Bryan

Restraints on war at sea before 1945. *In* Howard, M. ed. Restraints on war p39-56

Ranger, Robin

Arms control in theory and practice. *In* The Year book of world affairs, 1977 p112-37

Ranger, Terence O.

Towards a usable African past. *In* African studies since 1945 p17-30

Ranis, Gustav. See Fei, J. C. H. jt. auth.

Rank, Otto

About

Menaker, E. Creativity as the central concept in the psychology of Otto Rank. *In* Roland, A. ed. Psychoanalysis, creativity, and literature p162-77

Rank. See Social classes

Rank, Order of. See Precedence

Rankin, William

Ineffability in the fiction of Jean Toomer and Katherine Mansfield. *In* Renaissance and modern p160-71

Ransom, John Crowe

God without thunder; excerpt. *In* Crunden, R. M. ed. The superfluous men p262-68

The South defends its heritage. *In* Crunden, R. M. ed. The superfluous men p172-82

About

Gray, R. J. The Nashville Agrarians. *In* Gray, R. J. The literature of memory p40-105

Hough, G. G. John Crowe Ransom: the poet and the critic. *In* Hough, G. G. Selected essays p217-36

Kenner, H. The pedagogue as critic. *In* Young, T. D. ed. The New Criticism and after p36-46

O'Brien, M. John Ransom: the cycle of commitment. *In* O'Brien, M. The idea of the American South, 1920-1941 p117-35

Rubin, L. D. A critic almost anonymous: John Crowe Ransom goes North. *In* Young, T. D. ed. The New Criticism and after p 1-21

Tate, A. Reflections on the death of John Crowe Ransom. *In* Tate, A. Memoirs and **opinions, 1926-1974 p39-45**

Young, T. D. The evolution of Ransom's critical theory: image and ideas *In* Young, T. D. ed. The New Criticism and after p22-35

Young, T. D. Introduction. *In* Young, T D. ed. The New Criticism and after p xv-xxi

Young, T. D. A little divergence: the critical theories of John Crowe Ransom and Cleanth Brooks. *In* Simpson, L. P. ed. The possibilities of order: Cleanth Brooks and his work p168-95

About individual works
Captain Carpenter

Berryman, J. The sorrows of Captain Carpenter. *In* Berryman, J. The freedom of the poet p279-81

Master's in the garden again

Snodgrass, W. D. Master's in the verse patch: John Crowe Ransom. *In* Snodgrass, W. D. In radical pursuit p117-27

The world's body

West, T. R. The divided consciousness: Allen Tate, John Crowe Ransom, Paul Elmer More. *In* West, T. R. Nature, community, & will p40-96

Friends and associates—
Robert Frost

Young, T. D. Our two worthies: Robert Frost and John Crowe Ransom. *In* Frost: centennial essays II p281-90

Ransom, Roger L. See Sutch, R. C. jt. auth.

Rao, K. L. Seshagiri

A Hindu response: the value of religious pluralism. *In* Christian faith in a religiously plural world p46-58

Rao, Paladugu V.

Telephone and instructional communications. *In* The Social impact of the telephone p473-86

Rao, Potluri

Specification bias in seemingly unrelated regressions. *In* Econometrics and economic theory p101-13

Rao, Raja. See Raja Rao

Rapaport, Elizabeth

On the future of love: Rousseau and the radical feminists. *In* Gould, C. C. and Wartofsky, M. W. eds. Women and philosophy p185-205

Rapaport, Elizabeth, and Sagal, Paul T.

One step forward, two steps backward: abortion and ethical theory. *In* Feminism and philosophy p408-16

Rape

Foa, P. What's wrong with rape. *In* Feminism and philosophy p347-59

Peterson, S. R. Coercion and rape: the state as a male protection racket. *In* Feminism and philosophy p360-71

Shafer, C. M. and Frye, M. Rape and respect. *In* Feminism and philosophy p333-46

France

Rossiaud, J. Prostitution, youth, and society in the towns of southeastern France in the fifteenth century. *In* Deviants and the abandoned in French society p 1-46

United States

Griffin, S. Rape: the all-American crime. *In* Feminism and philosophy p313-32

Schultz, L. G. Sexual victims. *In* Gochros, H. L. and Gochros, J. S. eds. The sexually oppressed p110-25

Raphael

About

Barolsky, P. Facetiae by Raphael and his friends. *In* Barolsky, P. Infinite jest: wit and humor in Italian Renaissance art p75-100

About individual works

Parnassus

Winternitz, E. Musical archaeology of the Renaissance in Raphael's Parnassus. *In* Winternitz, E. Musical instruments and their symbolism in Western art p185-201

Raphael, David Daiches

The impartial spectator. *In* Skinner, A. S. and Wilson, T. eds. Essays on Adam Smith p83-99

'The true old Humean philosophy' and its influence on Adam Smith. *In* David Hume p23-38

Raphael, Max

About individual works

The demands of art

Berger, J. Revolutionary undoing. *In* Berger, J. The look of things p201-10

Rapoport, Anatol

Classified military research and the university. *In* Fairfield, R. P. ed. Humanistic frontiers in American education p54-60

Rappaport, Armin

Freedom of the seas. *In* Encyclopedia of American foreign policy p387-97

Rappaport, Roy A.

Biology, meaning, and the quality of life. *In* Major social issues p265-76

Rare books. See Bibliography—Rare books

Raschke, Carl

Kant on theory and practice. *In* Political theory and praxis p73-96

Rashomon (Motion picture)

Kauffmann, S. Rashomon. *In* Kauffmann, S. Living images p316-24

Raskin, Marcus G.

Futurology and its radical critique. *In* Radicalism in the contemporary age v2 p155-73

Morgenthau: the idealism of a realist. *In* [Truth and tragedy]: a tribute to Hans Morgenthau p85-94

Rasmussen, Jorgen Scott

Was Guy Fawkes right? *In* Kramnick, I. ed. Is Britain dying? p97-125

Rasmussen, Knud Johan Victor

A Shaman's journey to the sea spirit Takänakapsâluk; excerpt from "Report of the fifth Thule expedition, 1921-24." *In* Tedlock, D. E. and Tedlock, B. eds. Teachings from the American earth p13-19

Rasool, S. I.

Planetary atmospheres. *In* Man and cosmos p101-10

Raspe, Rudolf Erich

About

Dawson, R. F. Rudolf Erich Raspe: the geologist Captain Cook refused. *In* Studies in eighteenth-century culture v8 p269-90

Raspelbrot (The word)

Shub, E. An adventure in translation. *In* Horn Book Magazine. Crosscurrents of criticism p287-89

Rast, David F. K. Steindl. See Steindl-Rast, David F. K.

Rastall, John. See Rastell, John

Rastell, John

About individual works

Gentleness and nobility

Altman, J. B. The method staged: debate plays by Heywood and Rastell. *In* Altman, J. B. The Tudor play of mind p107-29

Ratcliffe, Barrie M.

The origins of the Anglo-French commercial treaty of 1860: a reassessment. *In* Great Britain and her world, 1750-1914 p125-51

Rathje, William Laurens

The last tango in Mayapán: a tentative trajectory of production-distribution systems. *In* Ancient civilization and trade p409-48

The Tikal connection. *In* The Origins of Maya civilization p373-82

See also Molloy, J. P. jt. auth.

Rathjens, George W.

Changing perspectives on arms control. *In* Long, F. A. and Rathjens, G. W. eds. Arms, defense policy, and arms control p201-14

Nuclear war between the super-powers. *In* Griffiths, F. and Polanyi, J. C. eds. The dangers of nuclear war p135-46

Slowing down the arms race. *In* The Dynamics of the arms race p82-91

Rathmell, John C. A.

The later sixteenth century, excluding drama. *In* English Association. The year's work in English studies v53 p207-21

Rationalism

Bronowski, J. The fulfillment of man. *In* Bronowski, J. A sense of the future p249-62

Donnelly, J. P. Suicide and rationality. *In* Donnelly, J. P. Language, metaphysics, and death p88-105

Oakeshott, M. J. Rationalism in politics. *In* Oakeshott, M. J. Rationalism in politics p 1-36

Popper, Sir K. R. The myth of the framework. *In* The Abdication of philosophy: philosophy and the public good p23-48

Skolimowski, H. Problems of rationality in biology. *In* Ayala, F. J. and Dobzhansky, T. G. eds. Studies in the philosophy of biology p205-23

See also Belief and doubt; Deism; Empiricism; Enlightenment; Intuition; Irrationalism (Philosophy); Positivism; Reason; Skepticism

Ratisbon

History

Kearney, M. E. Regensburg burgher factions and the failure of the Swabian Town League in 1389. *In* Viator: medieval and Renaissance studies v6 p275-94

Politics and government

Kearney, M. E. Regensburg burgher factions and the failure of the Swabian Town League in 1389. *In* Viator: medieval and Renaissance studies v6 p275-94

Raveau, François H. M.

Role of color in identification processes. *In* Ethnic identity p353-59

Ravel, Maurice

About

Craft, R. The nostalgic kingdom of Maurice Ravel. *In* Craft, R. Current convictions p184-95

Ravenal, Earl C.

Alliance dissolution and American disengagement. *In* Atlantis lost p205-24

Ravenhead, Saint-Gobain and. Harris, J. R.
In Great Britain and her world, 1750-1914
p27-70

Ravennas, Anonymus

About

Staab, F. Ostrogothic geographers at the court of Theodoric the Great: a study of some sources of the anonymus cosmographer of Ravenna. *In* Viator: medieval and Renaissance studies v7 p27-64

Ravenscroft, Arthur
African, Boer, and Indian attitudes to an imperialist war. *In* Narasimhaiah, C. D. ed. Awakened conscience p315-26
The novels of Bessie Head. *In* Heywood, C. ed. Aspects of South African literature p174-86
Pauline Smith. *in* Parker, K. ed. The South African novel in English p46-56

Ravetz, Jerome Raymond
Criticisms of science. *In* Science, technology and society p71-89
'. . . et augebitur scientia.' *In* Harré, R. ed. Problems of scientific revolution p42-57

About

Wilson, C. A. Rheticus, Ravetz, and the "necessity" of Copernicus' innovation. *In* The Copernican achievement p17-39

Ravin, Arnold Warren
The gene as catalyst; the gene as organism. *In* Studies in history of biology, v 1 p 1-45

Ravindranatha Thākura. See Tagore, Sir Rabindranath

Ravisius Textor, Joannes. See Tixier, Jean, Seigneur de Ravisy

Ravitz, Abe C.
Ballyhoo, gargoyles, & firecrackers: Ben Hecht's aesthetic calliope. *In* Filler, L. ed. A question of quality: popularity and value in modern creative writing p229-43

Ravitz, Justin C.
Reflections of a radical judge: beyond the courtroom. *In* Nader, R. and Green, M. J. eds. Verdicts on lawyers p255-68

Ravitz, Ronald A. Grennes- See Grennes-Ravitz, Ronald A.

Raw, Barbara Catherine
The prayers and devotions in the Ancrene wisse. *In* Chaucer and Middle English studies in honour of Rossell Hope Robbins p260-71
The probable derivation of most of the illustrations in Junius II from an illustrated Old Saxon Genesis. *In* Anglo-Saxon England 5 p133-48

Raw, Charles; Page, Bruce, and Hodgson, Godfrey

About individual works
"Do you sincerely want to be rich?"
The full story of Bernard Cornfeld
and the IOS
Galbraith, J. K. Bernard Cornfeld: benefactor. *In* Galbraith, J. K. Annals of an abiding liberal p311-16

Raw materials
Winberg, A. R. Resource politics: the future of international markets for raw materials. *In* Orr, D. W. and Soroos, M. S. eds. The global predicament p178-94

Rawls, John
. A well-ordered society. *In* Laslett, P. and Fishkin, J. eds. Philosophy, politics and society p6-20

About

Gorovitz, S. John Rawls: a theory of justice. *In* De Crespigny, A. and Minogue, K. R. eds. Contemporary political philosophers p272-89

About individual works
Outline of a decision procedure
for ethics
Sclafani, R. J. The theory of art. *In* Aagaard-Mogensen, L. ed. Culture and art p146-70

A theory of justice
Buchanan, J. M. The justice of natural liberty. *In* Glahe, F. R. ed. Adam Smith and The wealth of nations p61-81
Nisbet, R. A. The costs of equality. *In* Small comforts for hard times p34-49
Rae, D. W. A principle of simple justice. *In* Laslett, P. and Fishkin, J. eds. Philosophy, politics and society p134-54
Reiman, J. H. Doing justice to criminology: reflections on the implications for criminology of recent developments in the philosophy of justice. *In* Riedel, M. and Chappell, D. eds. Issues in criminal justice: planning and evaluation p134-43
Taylor, T. The concept of justice and the laws of war. *In* Perspectives on justice p3-35

Rawson, Claude Julien
The nightmares of Strephon: nymphs of the city in the poems of Swift, Baudelaire, Eliot. *In* English literature in the age of disguise p57-97

Ray, Arthur J.
The Hudson's Bay company fur trade in the eighteenth century: a comparative economic study. *In* European settlement and development in North America: essays on geographical change in honour and memory of Andrew Hill Clark p116-35

Ray, Benoy Gopal
Rabindranath Tagore. *In* Bishop, D. H. ed. Indian thought p337-45

Ray, Dennis Michael
Chinese perceptions of social imperialism and economic dependency: the impact of Soviet aid. *In* China's changing role in the world economy p36-82

Ray, Man

About

Tashjian, D. L. Marcel Duchamp and Man Ray. *In* Tashjian, D. L. Skyscraper primitives p49-70

Ray, Nicholas

About

Perkins, V. F. The cinema of Nicholas Ray. *In* Nichols, B. ed. Movies and methods p251-62

About individual works
Bigger than life
Truffaut, F. Nicholas Ray: Bigger than life. *In* Truffaut, F. The films in my life p143-47

Johnny Guitar
Truffaut, F. Nicholas Ray: Johnny Guitar. *In* Truffaut, F. The films in my life p141-43

Ray, Roger D.
Medieval historiography through the twelfth century: problems and progress of research. *In* Viator: medieval and Renaissance studies v5 p33-59

Ray, Satyajit

About

Taylor, J. R. Satyajit Ray. *In* Taylor, J. R. Directors and directions p165-203

Rayfield, Donald

Little tragedies: Russia's other drama. *In* Drama and society p99-116

Raymond, H. D.

Beyond freedom, dignity, and ridicule. *In* Battcock, G. ed. Super realism p126-34

Raymond, James C. and Russell, I. Willis

James B. McMillan. *In* James B. McMillan: essays in linguistics by his friends and colleagues p vii-xiii

Raynauld, André

The implications of an evolutionary tradition for the structure and functioning of Canada's economic development. *In* Perspectives on revolution and evolution p133-51

Rayward, W. Boyd

The literature of international and comparative librarianship. *In* As much to learn as to teach p217-35

al-Rāzī, Abu Bakr Muhammad ibn Zakarīyā

About

Iskandar, A. Z. The medical bibliography of al-Rāzī. *In* Essays on Islamic philosophy and science p41-46

al-Rāzī, Fakhr al-Dīn Muhammad ibn 'Umar

About

Goodman, L. E. Rāzī's myth of the fall of soul: its function in his philosophy. *In* Essays on Islamic philosophy and science p25-40

Razumnik Vasil'evich, Ivanov. See Ivanov, Razumnik Vasil'evich

Rea, John. See Lloyd-Jones, H. jt. auth.

Rea, Julian

Aspects of African publishing, 1945-1974. *In* African studies since 1945 p96-105

Reactor fuels. See Nuclear fuels

Read, Sir Herbert Edward

The limits of permissiveness. *In* Abbs, P. ed. The black rainbow p4-18

About individual works
English prose style

Richards, I. A. Herbert Read's English prose style. *In* Richards, I. A. Complementarities p178-88

The true voice of feeling

Frye, N. Ministry of angels. *In* Frye, N. Northrop Frye on culture and literature p130-40

Readability (Literary style)

Nevins, A. What's the matter with history? *In* Nevins, A. Allan Nevins on history p3-12

Readers and libraries. See Libraries and readers

Reading, Pa.

Politics and government

Pratt, W. C. "Jimmie Higgins" and the Reading Socialist community: an exploration of the Socialist rank and file. *In* Stave, B. M. ed. Socialism and the cities p141-56

Reading

Clark, M. M. Language and reading: research trends. *In* Davies, A. ed. Problems of language and learning p89-112

Iser, W. The reading process: a phenomenological approach. *In* Cohen, R. ed. New directions in literary history p125-45

Weber, R. M. Reading. *In* Wardhaugh, R. and Brown, H. D. eds. A survey of applied linguistics p92-112

Study and teaching
See Reading; Reading (Elementary)

Reading (Elementary)

Bettelheim, B. The decision to fail. *In* Bettelheim, B. Surviving, and other essays p142-68

Elkind, D. We can teach reading better. *In* Elkind, D. The child and society p156-64

Reading, Choice of. See Books and reading; Reading interests

Reading, Psychology of

Kolers, P. A. Reading pictures and reading text. *In* Perkins, D. and Leondar, B. eds. The arts and cognition p136-64

Reading habits. See Books and reading; Reading interests

Reading interests

See also Books and reading

Africa

Achebe, C. What do African intellectuals read? *In* Achebe, C. Morning yet on creation day p61-66

Great Britain

Mann, P. H. Romantic fiction and its readers. *In* Fischer, H. D. and Melnik, S. R. eds. Entertainment: a cross-cultural examination p34-42

Pickering, S. The Sunday school movement: new readers and the novel. *In* Pickering, S. The moral tradition in English fiction, 1785-1850 p11-64

Reading interests of children. See Books and reading for children

Reagan, Michael D.

Accountability and independence in federal grants-in-aid. *In* Smith, B. L. R. ed. The new political economy: the public use of the private sector p181-213

Reagan, Ronald Wilson

About

Levy, F. What Ronald Reagan can teach the United States about welfare reform. *In* Burnham, W. D. and Weinberg, M. W. eds. American politics and public policy p336-63

Réage, Pauline

About individual works
Story of O

Bersani, L. Persons in pieces. *In* Bersani, L. A future for Astyanax p286-315

Real, Willi

Ralph Ellison, King of the bingo game. *In* Bruck, P. ed. The Black American short story in the 20th century p111-27

Real estate subdivision. See Land subdivision

Real property. See Inclosures; Inheritance and succession; Land tenure

Realism

Clark, R. L. Considerations for a logic for naïve realism. *In* Studies in perception p525-56

Jardine, N. 'Realistic' realism and the progress of science. *In* Hookway, C. and Pettit, P. eds. Action and interpretation p107-25

Realism in literature—_Continued_

Schwartz, R. Summary: major trends and writers (1950-1970's). _In_ Schwartz, R. Spain's New Wave novelists, 1950-1974 p228-305

Schwartz, R. What is the Spanish New Wave? _In_ Schwartz, R. Spain's New Wave novelists, 1950-1974 p7-31

Simon, J. I. Is this the right way to rebel? _In_ Simon, J. I. Singularities p84-91

Smith, H. N. William Dean Howells: the theology of realism. _In_ Smith, H. N. Democracy and the novel p75-103

Snow, C. P. Baron Snow. Balzac. _In_ Snow, C. P. Baron Snow. The realists p35-71

Snow, C. P. Baron Snow. Dickens. _In_ Snow, C. P. Baron Snow. The realists p72-101

Snow, C. P. Baron Snow. Dostoevsky. _In_ Snow, C. P. Baron Snow. The realists p102-77

Snow, C. P. Baron Snow. Galdós. _In_ Snow, C. P. Baron Snow. The realists p217-55

Snow, C. P. Baron Snow. Henry James. _In_ Snow, C. P. Baron Snow. The realists p256-96

Snow, C. P. Baron Snow. Proust. _In_ Snow, C. P. Baron Snow. The realists p297-333

Snow, C. P. Baron Snow. Stendhal. _In_ Snow, C. P. Baron Snow. The realists p 1-34

Snow, C. P. Baron Snow. Tolstoy. _In_ Snow, C. P. Baron Snow. The realists p178-216

Stoneman, P. G. Eliot: Middlemarch. _In_ Williams, D. A. ed. The monster in the mirror p102-30

Terdiman, R. Balzac: the logic of failure. _In_ Terdiman, R. The dialectics of isolation p39-59

Terdiman, R. The coherence of the tradition. _In_ Terdiman, R. The dialectics of isolation p3-15

Turner, D. Theodor Fontane: Effi Briest. _In_ Williams, D. A. ed. The monster in the mirror p234-56

Williams, D. A. G. Flaubert: Sentimental education. _In_ Williams, D. A. ed. The monster in the mirror p75-101

Williams, D. A. The practice of realism. _In_ Williams, D. A. ed. The monster in the mirror p257-79

See also Idealism in literature; Mimesis in literature

Reality

Barfield, O. Self and reality. _In_ Barfield, O. The rediscovery of meaning, and other essays p155-75

Blumenberg, H. The concept of reality and the possibility of the novel. _In_ Amacher, R. E. and Lange, V. eds. New perspectives in German literary criticism p29-48

Graff, G. Culture, criticism and unreality. _In_ Graff, G. Literature against itself p 1-29

Kafka, J. S. On reality: an examination of object constancy, ambiguity, paradox, and time. _In_ Thought, consciousness, and reality p133-58

LeShan, L. L. Individual realities: commonsense, science, and mysticism; excerpt from "Toward a general theory of the paranormal." _In_ Wheatley, J. M. O. and Edge, H. L. eds. Philosophical dimensions of parapsychology p425-40

Rintelen, F. J. von. The public good and the attainment and loss of reality in science and philosophy. _In_ The Abdication of philosophy; philosophy and the public good p251-66

Wartofsky, M. W. Consciousness, praxis, and reality: Marxism vs. phenomenology. _In_ Elliston, F. A. and McCormick, P. eds. Husserl p304-13

See also Experience; Knowledge, Theory of; Monism; Objectivity

Reaney, Gilbert

The irrational and late medieval music.. _In_ The Darker vision of the Renaissance p197-219

The prospects for research in medieval music in the 1970's. _In_ Current thought in musicology p247-76

Reaney, James

About

Atwood, M. E. Reaney collected. _In_ Woodcock, G. ed. Poets and critics p151-58

Rear window (Motion picture)

Truffaut, F. Alfred Hitchcock: Rear window. _In_ Truffaut, F. The films in my life p77-79

Reardon, John

Hemingway's esthetic and ethical sportsmen. _In_ Wagner, L. W. ed. Ernest Hemingway p131-44

Reason

Franck, I. Spinoza, Freud, and Hampshire on psychic freedom. _In_ Thought, consciousness, and reality p257-309

Frankfurt, H. G. Descartes on the consistency of reason. _In_ Hooker, M. ed. Descartes p26-39

Marlies, M. Doubt, reason, and Cartesian therapy. _In_ Hooker, M. ed. Descartes p89-113

Oakeshott, M. J. Rational conduct. _In_ Oakeshott, M. J. Rationalism in politics p80-110

Scruton, R. Reason and happiness. _In_ Royal Institute of Philosophy. Nature and conduct p139-61

See also Common sense; Reasoning; Wisdom

Reason and faith. See Faith and reason

Reason in literature

Gill, J. E. Discovery and alienation, nature and reason in Gulliver's Travels, Parts I-III. _In_ Tennessee Studies in literature v22 p85-104

Reasoning

Bohm, D. Imagination, fancy, insight, and reason in the process of thought. _In_ Evolution of consciousness p51-68

Hammersley, J. M. The technology of thought. _In_ Neyman, J. ed. The heritage of Copernicus: theories "pleasing to the mind" p394-415

Hampshire, S. On having a reason. _In_ Royal Institute of Philosophy. Human values p86-98

Johnstone, H. W. From philosophy to rhetoric and back. _In_ Burks, D. M. ed. Rhetoric, philosophy, and literature: an exploration p49-66

See also Hypothesis; Induction (Logic); Intention (Logic); Judgment (Logic); Logic

Reasoning (Psychology) See Intellect

Reasoning in children
Matthews, G. B. On talking philosophy with children. *In* Royal Institute of Philosophy. Communication and understanding p46-62

Reaves, R. B.
Crime and punishment in the detective fiction of Dorothy L. Sayers. *In* Hannay, M. P. ed. As her whimsey took her p 1-13

Rebellions. See Civil War; Revolutions

Rebels (Social psychology). See Alienation (Social psychology)

Reber, Calvin Henry
Traditional Christianity as an African religion. *In* African religions: a symposium p255-74

Rebhorn, Wayne Alexander
Desiderius Erasmus: cosmopolitan Christian humanism. *In* Hoffmeister, G. ed. The Renaissance and Reformation in Germany p83-97

Rebirth. See Reincarnation

Rebora, Clemente Maria

About
Perella, N. J. Some twentieth-century voices. *In* Perella, N. J. Midday in Italian literature p145-200

Recidivists

United States
Cressey, D. R. Restraint of trade, recividism, and delinquent neighborhoods. *In* Delinquency, crime, and society p209-38

Reciprocity
Smith, R. F. Reciprocity. *In* Encyclopedia of American foreign policy p867-81

Reckford, Kenneth Joseph
Some trees in Virgil and Tolkien. *In* Perspectives of Roman poetry p57-91
Teaching the heroic journey. *In* Buxton, T. H. and Prichard, K. W. eds. Excellence in university teaching p11-21

Recognition (International law)
Coletta, P. E. Recognition policy. *In* Encyclopedia of American foreign policy p882-92

Recollection (Theology)
Coomaraswamy, A. K. Recollection, Indian and platonic. *In* Coomaraswamy, A. K. Selected papers v2 p49-65

Recombinant DNA
Baltimore, D. Limiting science: a biologist's perspective. *In* Holton, G. J. and Morison, R. S. eds. Limits of scientific inquiry p37-45
Culliton, B. J. Science's restive public. *In* Holton, G. J. and Morison, R. S. eds. Limits of scientific inquiry p147-56
Graham, L. R. Concerns about science and attempts to regulate inquiry. *In* Holton, G. J. and Morison, R. S. eds. Limits of scientific inquiry p 1-21
Nelkin, D. Threats and promises: negotiating the control of research. *In* Holton, G. J. and Morison, R. S. eds. Limits of scientific inquiry p191-209

Reconstruction
Benedict, M. L. Preserving Federalism: Reconstruction and the judicious uses of administrative discretion. *In* The Supreme Court review, 1978 p39-79
Benedict, M. L. The rout of radicalism: Republicans and the elections of 1867. *In* Swierenga, R. P. ed. Beyond the Civil War synthesis p137-47

Brock, W. R. The nature of the Reconstruction crisis; excerpt from "An American crisis: Congress and Reconstruction, 1865-67." *In* Burton, D. H. ed. American history—British historians p169-86
Curry, R. O. The Civil War and Reconstruction, 1861-1877: a critical overview of recent trends and interpretations. *In* Swierenga, R. P. ed. Beyond the Civil War synthesis p33-56
Linden, G. M. "Radical" political and economic policies: the Senate, 1873-1877. *In* Swierenga, R. P. ed. Beyond the Civil War synthesis p233-42
Rose, W. L. N. Jubilee & beyond: what was freedom? *In* What was freedom's price? p3-20
Sutch, R. C. and Ransom, R. L. Sharecropping: market response or mechanism of race control? *In* What was freedom's price? p51-69
See also Freedmen; Southern States—History—1865-

Reconstruction (1914-1939)

Great Britain
Ward, S. R. Great Britain: land fit for heroes lost. *In* The War generation p10-37

United States
Lisio, D. J. United States: bread and butter politics. *In* The War generation p38-58

Reconstruction (1939-1951)

Germany
Kimball, W. F. The Morgenthau plan. *In* Encyclopedia of American foreign policy p597-602

Recovery, inc., the Association of Former mental Patients and Their Relatives
Jones, R. K. Some sectarian characteristics of therapeutic groups with special reference to Recovery, inc. and Neurotics Nomine. *In* Wallis, R. ed. Sectarianism p190-210

Recovery of waste materials. See Recycling (Waste, etc.)

Recreation
Haacke, W. Mass media—the playground for grown-ups. *In* Fischer, H. D. and Melnik, S. R. eds. Entertainment: a cross-cultural examination p94-98
See also Leisure

Recycling (Waste, etc.)
Stanford, G. Recycling in human settlements. *In* Strategies for human settlements: habitat and environment p40-44

The red balloon (Motion picture)
Truffaut, F. Albert Lamorisse: Le ballon rouge. *In* Truffaut, F. The films in my life p220-22

Red Cross. International Committee, Geneva
Freymond, J. The International Committee of the Red Cross as a neutral intermediary. *In* Unofficial diplomats p142-51
Veuthey, M. A survey of international humanitarian law in noninternational armed conflicts: 1949-1974. *In* International terrorism and political crimes p86-97

Red river (Motion picture)
Sklar, R. Empire to the West: Red river. *In* O'Connor, J. E. and Jackson, M. A. eds. American history/American films p167-81

Red Sea

Das Gupta, A. Gujarati merchants and the Red Sea trade, 1700-1725. *In* Kling, B. B. and Pearson, M. N. eds. The age of partnership p123-58

Red shift

Vigier, J. P. Cosmological implications of nonvelocity redshifts—a tired-light mechanism. *In* Cosmology, history, and theology p141-57

Reddaway, Peter

The development of dissent and opposition. *In* Brown, A. H. and Kaser, M. eds. The Soviet Union since the fall of Khrushchev p121-56

Theory and practice of human rights in the Soviet Union. *In* Kommers, D. P. and Loescher, G. D. eds. Human rights and American foreign policy p115-29

Reddy, Michael J.

The conduit metaphor—a case of frame conflict in our language about language. *In* Ortony, A. ed. Metaphor and thought p284-324

Reddy, V. Madhusudan. See Madhusudan Reddy, V.

Reddy, V. Narayan Karan

Concepts of man. *In* Bishop, D. H. ed. Indian thought p252-73

Redemption

Biblical teaching

Marshall, I. H. The development of the concept of redemption in the New Testament. *In* Reconciliation and hope p153-69

History of doctrines

Stoever, W. K. B. The order of redemption and the ground of assurance. *In* Stoever, W. K. B. 'A faire and easie way to heaven' p119-37

Redevelopment, Urban. See City planning

Redfern, W. D.

Against nature: Jean Giono and Le grand troupeau. *In* Klein, H. M. ed. The First World War in fiction p73-83

Redfield, James M.

The wrath of Achilles as tragic error; excerpt from "Nature and culture in the Iliad: the tragedy of Hector." *In* Wright, J. H. ed. Essays on the Iliad p85-92

Redford, Emmette Shelburn

Watergate: a test of constitutional democracy. *In* Prospects for constitutional democracy p183-97

Redgrove, Peter

About

Hobsbaum, P. The poetry of barbarism. *In* Hobsbaum, P. Tradition and experiment in English poetry p308-30

Redlich, Norman

Legal ethics: a problem of role definition. *In* Hook, S.; Kurtz, P. and Todorovich, M. eds. The ethics of teaching and scientific research p93-97

Redlikh, Roman N.

About individual works

Stalinshchina kak dukhovnyi fenomen

Mihajlov, M. The phenomenology of the Kingdom of Lies. *In* Mihajlov, M. Underground notes p32-36

Redman, John, 1722-1808

About

Bell, W. J. John Redman, medical preceptor (1722-1808). *In* Bell, W. J. The colonial physician & other essays p27-39

Redmond, Eugene

Stridency and the sword: literary and cultural emphasis in Afro-American magazines. *In* Anderson, E. and Kinzie, M. eds. The little magazine in America: a modern documentary history p538-73

Redmond, James. See Davidson, E. J. jt. auth.; Moran, M. jt. auth.

Redpath, Theodore

The meaning of a poem. *In* On literary intention p14-25

Some textual problems in Donne's 'Songs and sonets.' *in* English Association. Essays and studies, 1979 p57-79

Redshift. See Red shift

Reducing

Allon, N. Group-dieting rituals. *In* Henslin, J. M. ed. Deviant life-styles p101-14

Reductionism

Koestler, A. The holarchy. *In* Koestler, A. Janus p23-56

Watanabe, S. Logic of the empirical world, with reference to the identity theory and reductionism. *In* Philosophical aspects of the mind-body problem p162-81

See also Logical positivism

Reductionism in biology. Thorpe, W. H. *In* Ayala, F. J. and Dobzhansky, T. G. eds. Studies in the philosophy of biology p109-36

Reed, Allan W.

Anticipatory grief work. *In* Anticipatory grief p346-57

Reed, Arden

Abysmal influence: Baudelaire, Coleridge, De Quincey, Piranesi,; Wordsworth. *In* Glyph 4 p189-206

Reed, Carol

About

Samuels, C. T. Carol Reed and the novelistic film. *In* Samuels, C. T. Mastering the film, and other essays p12-41

Reed, Henry

About

Scannell, V. Henry Reed and others. *In* Scannell, V. Not without glory p134-71

Reed, Ishmael

Shrovetide in old New Orleans

Contents

An American romance
Before the War, poems as they happened
Bird lives!
Born to rebel
Chester Himes: writer
The children of Ham
Crushing the mutiny
De mayor of Harlem
Gliberals
The Greatest, my own story
Harlem Renaissance day
I hear you, Doc
Image and money
The "liberal" in us all
The multi-cultural artist: a new phase in American writing
Music: Black, white and blue

About

Nichols, C. H. Comic modes in Black America (a ramble through Afro-American humor). *In* Cohen, S. B. ed. Comic relief p105-26

Reed, James
Confinement and character in Dickens' novels. *In* Dickens Studies Annual v 1 p41-54

Reed, John
Léopold Sédar Senghor's poetry. *In* King, B. A. and Ogungbesan, K. eds. A celebration of Black and African writing p102-11

Reed, Peter J.
The later Vonnegut. *In* Klinkowitz, J. and Lawler, D. L. eds. Vonnegut in America p150-86

Reed, Richard
The animal world in Robert Frost's poetry. *In* Frost: centennial essays II p159-69

Reed, Simeon Gannett

About

Singer, B. Oregon's nineteenth-century notables: Simeon Gannett Reed and Thomas Lamb Eliot. *In* Bingham, E. R. and Love, G. A. eds. Northwest perspectives p61-76

Reed, Steven L.
Participation in multinational organizations and programs in the hemisphere. *In* Cuba in the world p297-312

Reed, Terence James
Nietzsche's animals: idea, image and influence. *In* Pasley, J. M. S. ed. Nietzsche: imagery and thought p 159-219

Reed, Walter Lewis
The cherry orchard and Hedda Gabler. *In* Seidel, M. A. and Mendelson, E. eds. Homer to Brecht p317-35

The problem with a poetics of the novel. *In* Spilka, M. ed. Towards a poetics of fiction p62-74

Reedy, George E.
The Presidency in 1976: focal point of political unity? *In* Havard, W. C. and Bernd, J. L. eds. 200 years of the Republic in retrospect p228-38

Rees, Albert Everett
Compensating wage differentials. *In* Skinner, A. S. and Wilson, T. eds. Essays on Adam Smith p336-49

Rees, David
The narrative art of Penelope Lively. *In* Horn Book Magazine. Crosscurrents of criticism p342-48

Rees, Elfan
Exercises in private diplomacy: selected activities of the Commission of the Churches on International Affairs. *In* Unofficial diplomats p111-29

Rees, Goronwy
Darkness at noon and the 'grammatical fiction.' *In* Harris, H. A. ed. Astride the two cultures p102-22

Rees, Mina Spiegel
The ivory tower and the marketplace. *In* McMurrin, S. M. ed. On the meaning of the university p81-101

Rees, Owen Geoffrey
The Barmen Declaration (May 1934) *In* Church, society and politics p405-17

Rees, Sir Richard, bart.

About individual works
*George Orwell, fugitive from the
    camp of victory*
Connolly, C. George Orwell: 2. *In* Connolly, C. The evening colonnade p340-42

Reese, Juergen
The Federal Republic of Germany. *In* Galnoor, I. ed. Government secrecy in democracies p216-33

Reesor, Margaret E.
Necessity and fate in Stoic philosophy. *In* Rist, J. M. ed. The Stoics p187-202

Reeve, Clara

About individual works
The old English baron
Madoff, M. The useful myth of Gothic ancestry. *In* Studies in eighteenth-century culture v8 p337-50

Reeve, M. D. and Rouse, Richard H.
New light on the transmission of Donatus's "commentum Terentii." *In* Viator: medieval and Renaissance studies v9 p235-49

Reeves, Albert Compton
Thomas Hoccleve, bureaucrat. *In* Medievalia et humanistica no. 5 p201-14

Reeves, Marjorie
History and prophecy in medieval thought. *In* Medievalia et humanistica no. 5 p51-75

Why history? *In* Niblett, W. R. ed. The sciences, the humanities and the technological threat p116-26

Reeves, Peter D.
Pathways to political advancement: problems of choice for taluqdar politicians in late British India. *In* The Making of politicians: studies from Africa and Asia p103-15

Reeves, Robert B.
Reflections on two false expectations. *In* Anticipatory grief p281-84

Reference (Linguistics)
Boyd, R. N. Metaphor and theory change: what is "metaphor" a metaphor for? *In* Ortony, A. ed. Metaphor and thought p356-408

Kuhn, T. S. Metaphor in science. *In* Ortony, A. ed. Metaphor and thought p409-19

Reference groups
Hyman, H. H. Reference individuals and reference idols. *In* The Idea of social structure p265-82

Reff, Theodore
Images of Flaubert's Queen of Sheba in later nineteenth-century art. *In* The Artist and the writer in France p126-33

Reflexive knowledge. See Self-knowledge, Theory of

Reform, Social. See Social problems

Reform Judaism

United States

Dawidowicz, L. S. When Reform was young. *In* Dawidowicz, L. S. The Jewish presence p92-104

Reform of criminals. See Rehabilitation of criminals

Reformation

Kingdon, R. M. Was the Protestant Reformation a revolution? The case of Geneva. *In* Church, society and politics p203-22

Littell, F. H. The Radical Reformation and the American experience. *In* America in theological perspective p71-86

Thompson, W. D. J. C. Luther and the right of resistance to the Emperor. *In* Church, society and politics p159-202

See also Calvinism; Protestantism

Book reviews

Slavin, A. J. Some oblique light: three studies in Reformation history. *In* Medievalia et humanistica no. 6 p203-07

Early movements

Smith, D. Reaction and revolution: antihumanism in the reform movements. *In* Hoffmeister, G. ed. The Renaissance and Reformation in Germany p157-76

Historiography

Hillerbrand, H. J. The popular dimension of the Reformation: an essay in methodology and historiography. *In* Medieval and Renaissance studies [1974] p55-86

Spitz, L. W. Periodization in history: Renaissance and Reformation. *In* The Future of history p189-217

History

See Reformation

Great Britain

Dickens, A. G. The ambivalent English Reformation. *In* Background to the English Renaissance p43-56

Hungary

Király, B. K. The Sublime Porte, Vienna, Transylvania and the dissemination of Protestant Reformation in royal Hungary. *In* Király, B. K. ed. Tolerance and movements of religious dissent in Eastern Europe p199-221

Reformatories. See Juvenile detention homes

Reformers, Social. See Social reformers

Refraction

Laymon, R. L. Newton's advertised precision and his refutation of the received laws of refraction. *In* Studies in perception p231-58

Refugees, Arab

Caroz, Y. The Palestinians: who they are. *In* The Palestinians p77-80

Mallison, W. T. and Mallison, S. V. An international law appraisal of the juridical characteristics of the resistance of the people of Palestine: the struggle for human rights. *In* International terrorism and political crimes p173-90

Prittie, T. C. F. Israel and the Palestinian question. *In* The Palestinians p213-27

Prittie, T. C. F. Middle East refugees. *In* The Palestinians p51-73

Rubinstein, A. Palestinian nationalism: an established fact. *In* The Palestinians p183-86

Refugees, Italian

Chiaromonte, N. Lost Italians. *In* Chiaromonte, N. The worm of consciousness, and other essays p31-40

Refugees, Jewish

Arendt, H. We refugees. *in* Arendt, H. The Jew as pariah: Jewish identity and politics in the modern age p55-66

Prittie, T. C. F. Middle East refugees. *In* The Palestinians p51-73

Refugees, Political

Goormaghtigh, J. How an INGO contributed to broadening the scope and competence of an IGO. *In* Unofficial diplomats p250-58

Hughes, H. S. Conclusion: The sea change. *In* Hughes, H. S. The sea change p240-72

Hughes, H. S. The great migration. *In* Hughes, H. S. The sea change p 1-34

Pellegrino, J. An effective school of patriotism. *In* Studies in Italian American social history p84-104

Slonim, M. L. The third emigration. *In* Slonim, M. L. Soviet Russian literature p408-18

See also Refugees, Arab; Refugees, Jewish

Legal status, laws, etc.—Sweden

Sundberg, J. W. F. Thinking the unthinkable or the case of Dr Tsironis. *In* International terrorism and political crimes p448-59

Refuse and refuse disposal

Lindstrom, C. Innovative building technologies: water-free waste disposal. *In* Strategies for human settlements: habitat and environment p152-56

Regalia

Holy Roman Empire

Blumenthal, U. R. Patrimonia and regalia in 1111. *In* Law, church, and society p9-20

Regency

Great Britain

Gronbeck, B. E. Edmund Burke and the Regency Crisis of 1788-89. *In* Rhetoric: a tradition in transition p142-77

Regensburg. See Ratisbon

Regional planning

Chinitz, B. Regional development. *In* McKie, J. W. ed. Social responsibility and the business predicament p247-73

Gottdiener, M. D. Social planning and metropolitan growth. *In* Handbook of contemporary urban life p494-518

France

Gremion, P. and Worms, J. P. The French regional planning experiments. *In* Planning, politics and public policy p217-36

Watson, M. The regional dimension of planning. *In* Planning, politics and public policy p285-94

Great Britain

Watson, M. The regional dimension of planning. *In* Planning, politics and public policy p285-94

Wright, M. and Young, S. Regional planning in Britain. *In* Planning, politics and public policy p237-68

Italy

Selan, V. and Donnini, R. Regional planning in Italy. *In* Planning, politics and public policy p269-84

Watson, M. The regional dimension of planning. *In* Planning, politics and public policy p285-94

Regional planning—*Continued*

Japan

Sargent, J. Regional development policy in Japan: some aspects of the plan for re-modelling the Japanese archipelago. *In* Modern Japan p227-43

United States

Goist, P. D. Regionalism and community: the urbanism of Lewis Mumford. *In* Goist, P. D. From Main Street to State Street p143-57

Regionalism

Africa

Woronoff, J. The OAU and sub-Saharan regional bodies. *In* El-Ayouty, Y. ed. The Organization of African Unity after ten years p62-78

Europe

Scheinman, L. The interfaces of regional-ism in Western Europe: Brussels and the peripheries. *In* Esman, M. J. ed. Ethnic con-flict in the Western world p65-78

France

Beer, W. R. The social class of ethnic activists in contemporary France. *In* Esman, M. J. ed. Ethnic conflict in the Western world p143-58

Berger, S. D. Bretons and Jacobins: re-flections on French regional ethnicity. *In* Esman, M. J. ed. Ethnic conflict in the Western world p159-78

Ghana

Schildkrout, E. The ideology of regional-ism in Ghana. *In* Shack, W. A. and Skinner, E. P. eds. Strangers in African societies p183-207

United States

Jordy, W. H. Four approaches to region-alism in the visual arts of the 1930s. *In* Luedtke, L. S. ed. The study of American culture p19-48

Wertheim, A. F. Constance Rourke and the discovery of American culture in the 1930s. *In* Luedtke, L. S. ed. The study of American culture p49-61

Regionalism (International organization)

Carnegie, A. R. Commonwealth Caribbean regionalism: legal aspects. *In* The Year book of world affairs, 1979 p180-200

Yalem, R. J. Regional security communi-ties and world order. *In* The Year book of world affairs, 1979 p217-42

Regionalism in literature

Cavaliero, G. Literary regionalism: Hugh Walpole, Sheila Kaye-Smith. *In* Cavaliero, G. The rural tradition in the English novel, 1900-1939 p66-80

Flanagan, J. T. Jesse Stuart, regional novelist. *In* LeMaster, J. R. and Clarke, M. W. eds. Jesse Stuart p70-88

Register, Cheri. See Register, Cheryl

Register, Cheryl

American feminist literary criticism: a bib-liographical introduction. *In* Donovan, J. C. ed. Feminist literary criticism p 1-28

Regnard, Jean Françoise

About

Brereton, G. The cynical generation: Dan-court, Regnard, Dufresny, Lesage. *In* Brere-ton, G. French comic drama p163-93

About individual works
The sole heir

Koch, P. Regnard and Collin d'Harleville on legacies by bachelor uncles. *In* Studies in eighteenth-century culture v8 p291-309

Regnault, Victor

About

Jammes, A. Victor Regnault, calotypist. *In* One hundred years of photographic his-tory p77-82

Regnery, Henry

Introduction: For and about Eliseo Vivas. *In* Viva Vivas! p11-22

Regression (Civilization)

Burke, P. Tradition and experience: the idea of decline from Bruni to Gibbon. *In* Edward Gibbon and The decline and fall of the Roman Empire p87-102

See also Progress

Regression (Psychology)

Ragussis, M. The subterfuge of art: Litera-ture and regression. *In* Ragussis, M. The subterfuge of art p5-16

Regression analysis

Rao, P. Specification bias in seemingly unrelated regressions. *In* Econometrics and economic theory p101-13

Zellner, A. The quality of quantitative economic policy-making when targets and costs of change are mis-specified. *In* Econo-metrics and economic theory p147-64

Regressive behavior. See Regression (Psy-chology)

Regulated industries. See Public utilities

Regulatory agencies. See Administrative agencies; Independent regulatory commis-sions

Regulatory commissions. See Independent regulatory commissions

Rehabilitation of criminals

Conrad, J. P. Winners and losers: a per-spective on penal change. *In* Progress in penal reform p196-208

See also Probation; Rehabilitation of ju-venile delinquents

Great Britain

Stirling, W. R. The role of education in the penal system. *In* Progress in penal re-form p142-54

See also Social work with delinquents and criminals

Great Britain

Hinton, N. Intermediate treatment. *In* Progress in penal reform p238-44

Rehberg, Richard A. and Cohen, Michael A.

Political attitudes and participation in ex-tracurricular activities. *In* Social problems in athletics p201-11

About individual works
Political attitudes and participation in extracurricular activities

Spady, W. G. A commentary on sport and the New Left. *In* Social problems in athletics p212-23

Rehder, Helmut

The reluctant disciple: Nietzsche and Schiller. *In* O'Flaherty, J. C.; Sellner, T. F. and Helm, R. M. eds. Studies in Nietzsche and the classical tradition p156-64

Rehder, Robert M.
The form of Hardy's novels. *In* Butler, L. S. ed. Thomas Hardy after fifty years p13-27

Reich, Charles A.
Countercultural forces: emerging divergence in American culture; excerpt from "The greening of America." *In* Social forces and schooling p82-99

About individual works
The greening of America
Koestler, A. The Abishag complex. *In* Koestler, A. The heel of Achilles p91-96

Reich, Wilhelm
About
Crews, F. C. Anxious energetics. *In* Crews, F. C. Out of my system p145-64

Reich-Soviet nonaggression pact, 1939. See Russo-German treaty, 1939

Reiche, Harald Anton Thrap
The language of archaic astronomy: a clue to the Atlantis myth? *In* Brecher, K. and Feirtag, M. eds. Astronomy of the ancients p153-89

Reichel-Dolmatoff, Gerardo
Drug-induced optical sensations and their relationship to applied art among some Colombian Indians. *In* Greenhalgh, M. and Megaw, J. V. S. eds. Art in society p289-304

Reichert, Victor Emanuel
The Robert Frost I knew. *In* Frost: centennial essays III p105-22

Reid, Alec
MacNeice in the theatre. *In* Time was away p73-85

Reid, Alex A. L.
Comparing telephone with face-to-face contact. *In* The Social impact of the telephone p386-414

Reid, Inez Smith
Black Americans and Africa. *In* The Black American reference book p648-83

Reid, James M.
The literary years. *In* Lerner, D. and Nelson, L. M. eds. Communication research—a half-century appraisal p302-04

Reid, Louis Arnaud
About individual works
A study in aesthetics
Trilling, L. Criticism and aesthetics. *In* Trilling, L. A gathering of fugitives p143-52

Reid, Mayne
About
Miłosz, C. On Thomas Mayne Reid. *In* Miłosz, C. Emperor of the earth p144-56

Reid, S. W.
Some spellings of compositor B in the Shakespeare First Folio. *In* Virginia. University. Bibliographical Society. Studies in bibliography v29 p102-38

Reid, Thomas
About
Schofield, R. E. Joseph Priestley on sensation and perception. *In* Studies in perception p336-54

Reid, Thomas Mayne. See Reid, Mayne

The Reign of King Edward III
Muir, K. Edward III. *In* Muir, K. The singularity of Shakespeare, and other essays p38-55

Reik, Theodor
About individual works
Ritual
Freud, S. Preface to Ritual: psychoanalytic studies by Theodor Reik. *In* Praise from famous men: an anthology of introductions p82-88

Reilly, John M.
Richard Wright. *In* Inge, M. T.; Duke, J. M. and Bryer, J. R. eds. Black American writers v2 p 1-46

Reilly, R. J.
A note on Barfield, romanticism and time. *In* Evolution of consciousness p183-90

Reiman, Donald H.
Trelawny and decay of lying. *In* Review v 1 1979 p275-94

Reiman, Jeffrey H.
Doing justice to criminology: reflections on the implications for criminology of recent developments in the philosophy of justice. *In* Riedel, M. and Chappell, D. eds. Issues in criminal justice: planning and evaluation p134-43

Reimarus, Hermann Samuel
About
Grossmann, W. Edelmann and the silent Reimarus. *In* Studies in eighteenth-century culture v4 p195-203

Reimer, Everett H.
About
Barrow, R. Everett Reimer (b. 1922) and Ivan Illich (b. 1926). *In* Barrow, R. Radical education p127-53

Rein, Martin, and Rabinovitz, Francine F.
Implementation: a theoretical perspective. *In* Burnham, W. D. and Weinberg, M. W. eds. American politics and public policy p307-35

Reincarnation
Nayak, G. C. Survival, reincarnation, and the problem of personal identity. *In* Wheatley, J. M. O. and Edge, H. L. eds. Philosophical dimensions of parapsychology p295-307

See also Transmigration

Reinecke, George F.
Speculation, intention, and the teaching of Chaucer. *In* The Learned and the lewed p81-93

Reinert, Paul Clare
Three reforms. *In* The Third century p141-46

Reinforcement (Psychology)
Corson, J. A. Families as mutual control systems: optimization by systemization of reinforcement. *In* Behavior modification and families p317-30

Peterson, R. F. Power, programming, and punishment: could we be overcontrolling our children? *In* Behavior modification and families p338-52

Rohter, I. S. A social-learning approach to political socialization. *In* Schwartz, D. C. and Schwartz, S. K. eds. New directions in political socialization p129-62

Reingold, Nathan
Definitions and speculations: the professionalization of science in America in the nineteenth century. *In* Oleson, A. and Brown, S. C. eds. The pursuit of knowledge in the early American Republic p33-69

Reingold, Nathan—*Continued*

National science policy in a private foundation: the Carnegie Institution of Washington. *In* Oleson, A. and Voss, J. eds. The organization of knowledge in modern America, 1860-1920 p313-41

Reinhardt, Max

About

Fiedler, L. M. Molière on Max Reinhardt's stage. *In* Johnson, R. B.; Neumann, E. S. and Trail, G. T. eds. Molière and the commonwealth of letters: patrimony and posterity p591-602

Simon, J. I. Ham of genius. *In* Simon, J. I. Singularities p32-34

Reinhardt, Max, and Dieterle, William

About individual works

A midsummer night's dream

Jorgens, J. J. Max Reinhardt and William Dieterle's A midsummer night's dream. *In* Jorgens, J. J. Shakespeare on film p36-50

Reinhartz, Dennis

Milovan Djilas: the transcendence of a revolutionary. *In* Essays on modern European revolutionary history p69-88

Reinhold, Erasmus

About individual works

Commentarius in opus revolutionum Copernici

Henderson, J. A. Erasmus Reinhold's determination of the distance of the sun from the earth. *In* The Copernican achievement p108-29

Reinitz, Richard

Niebuhrian irony and historical interpretation: the relationship between consensus and New Left history. *In* Canary, R. H. and Kozicki, H. J. eds. The writing of history p93-128

Reischauer, Edwin Oldfather

Introduction: An overview. *In* Clapp, P. and Halperin, M. H. eds. United States-Japanese relations, the 1970's p 1-18

Reiser, Stanley Joel

Therapeutic choice and moral doubt in a technological age. *In* Knowles, J. H. ed. Doing better and feeling worse p47-56

Reiss, Albert John

Settling the frontiers of a pioneer in American criminology: Henry McKay. *In* Delinquency, crime, and society p64-88

Reiss, Edmund

Chaucer's courtly love. *In* The Learned and the lewed p95-111

Fin'amors: its history and meaning in medieval literature. *In* Medieval and Renaissance studies 1976 p74-99

Reiss, Timothy J.

Discursive criticism and epistemology. *In* Valdés, M. J. and Miller, O. J. eds. Interpretation of narrative p38-47

Reist, Benjamin A.

Beyond ideological theology. *In* The Context of contemporary theology p171-86

Reiter, Rayna R.

Men and women in the south of France: public and private domains. *In* Reiter, R. R. ed. Toward an anthropology of women p252-82

Reitman, Alan

Past, present, and future. *In* The Pulse of freedom p281-342

Reitz, Deneys

About individual works

Commando: a Boer journal of the Boer War

Ravenscroft, A. African, Boer, and Indian attitudes to an imperialist war. *In* Narasimhaiah, C. D. ed. Awakened conscience p315-26

Relationism. *See* Logical positivism

Relativism, Cultural. *See* Cultural relativism

Relativistic theory of gravitations. *See* General relativity (Physics)

Relativity. *See* Subjectivity

Relativity (Ethics) *See* Ethical relativism

Relativity (Physics)

Bergia, S. Einstein and the birth of special relativity. *In* Einstein p65-89

Bondi, H. Relativity theory and gravitation. *In* Einstein p113-29

Galison, P. L. Minkowski's space-time: from visual thinking to the absolute world. *In* Historical studies in the physical sciences v10 p85-121

Goldberg, S. Max Planck's philosophy of nature and his elaboration of the special theory of relativity. *In* Historical studies in the physical sciences v7 p125-60

Hirosige, T. The ether problem, the mechanistic worldview, and the origins of the theory of relativity. *In* Historical studies in the physical sciences v7 p3-82

Sachs, R. K. Relativity. *In* Neyman, J. ed. The heritage of Copernicus: theories "pleasing to the mind" p297-310

Salmon, W. C. Clocks and simultaneity in special relativity or, Which twin has the Timex? *In* Motion and time, space and matter p508-45

Siegel, D. M. Classical-electromagnetic and relativistic approaches to the problem of non-integral atomic masses. *In* Historical studies in the physical sciences v9 p323-60

See also General relativity (Physics); Quantum theory; Space and time

Study and teaching

Dorling, G. Approaches to the teaching of special relativity. *In* Einstein p245-60

Relativity theory, General. *See* General relativity (Physics)

Relaxation

Benson, H. The relaxation response: techniques and clinical applications. *In* Sobel, D. S. ed. Ways of health p331-51

Relief (Aid) *See* Public welfare

Relief (Sculpture)

Akrabova-Zhandova, I. Preslav inlaid ceramics. *In* Studies in memory of David Talbot Rice p25-33

Asia Minor—Priene

Carter, J. C. The date of the sculptured coffer lids from the Temple of Athene Polias at Priene. *In* Studies in classical art and archaeology p139-51

Iran—Persepolis

Porada, E. Some thoughts on the audience reliefs of Persepolis. *In* Studies in classical art and archaeology p37-43

Religion

Carman, J. B. Religion as a problem for Christian theology. *In* Christian faith in a religiously plural world p83-103

Religion—*Continued*

Dawe, D. G. Christian faith in a religiously plural world. *In* Christian faith in a religiously plural world p13-33

Palihawadana, M. A Buddhist response: religion beyond ideology and power. *In* Christian faith in a religiously plural world p34-45

Poole, R. Essay 9. *In* Fitzgerald, R. ed. What it means to be human p164-85

Rahv, P. Religion and the intellectuals. *In* Rahv, P. Essays on literature and politics, 1932-1972 p310-16

Sagan, E. Religion and magic: a developmental view. *In* Johnson, H. M. ed. Religious change and continuity p87-116

Schneider, H. W. Radical empiricism and religion. *In* Philosophy and the civilizing arts p446-66

Schneider, L. Dialectical orientation and the sociology of religion. *In* Johnson, H .M. ed. Religious change and continuity p49-73

Smith, W. C. An historian of faith reflects on what we are doing here. *In* Christian faith in a religiously plural world p139-48

Steindl-Rast, D. F. K. Defining religion from within. *In* Christian faith in a religiously plural world p123-35

See also Belief and doubt; Cult; Cultus; Deism; Faith; God; Monotheism; Mysticism; Myth; Positivism; Polytheism; Psychology, Religious; Psychology and religion; Rationalism; Religious; Revelation; Satanism; Supernatural; Superstition; Theism; Theology; Women and religion; also subdivision Religion or Religion and mythology under names of countries, races, people, etc. e.g. Egypt—Religion; Indians of North America—Religion and mythology; and headings beginning with the word Religious

Historiography

Momigliano, A. Popular religious beliefs and the late Roman historians. *In* Momigliano, A. Essays in ancient and modern historiography p141-59

History

Ahlstrom, S. E. From Sinai to the Golden Gate: the liberation of religion in the Occident. *In* Needleman, J. and Baker, G. eds. Understanding the new religions p3-22

Philosophy

Curley, E. M. Spinoza and recent philosophy of religion. *In* Shahan, R. W. and Biro, J. I. eds. Spinoza: new perspectives p161-75

Ellwood, R. S. Excursus religion. *In* Ellwood, R. S. Alternative altars p20-41

Huxley, A. L. Man and religion. *In* Huxley, A. L. The Human situation p198-215

Ogibenin, B. L. A semiotic approach to religion. *In* Sebeok, T. A. ed. Sight, sound, and sense p232-43

Psychological aspects

See Psychology, Religious

Study and teaching

Baker, G. Language and mind in the study of new religious movements. *In* Needleman, J. and Baker, G. eds. Understanding the new religions p285-98

Bellah, R. N. Religious studies as "new religion." *In* Needleman, J. and Baker, G. eds. Understanding the new religions p106-12

Capps, W. H. The interpenetration of new religion and religious studies. *In* Needleman, J. and Baker, G. eds. Understanding the new religions p101-05

Cox, H. G. Deep structures in the study of new religions. *In* Needleman, J. and Baker, G. eds. Understanding the new religions p122-30

Gilkey, L. B. Toward a religious criterion of religion. *In* Needleman, J. and Baker, G. eds. Understanding the new religions p131-37

Hutchison, J. A. Religion among the liberal arts. *In* Philosophy and the civilizing arts p378-88

Study and teaching—Methodology

Richardson, J. T.; Stewart, M. W. and Simmonds, R. B. Researching a fundamentalist commune. *In* Needleman, J. and Baker, G. eds. Understanding the new religions p235-51

Stone, D. On knowing how we know about the new religions. *In* Needleman, J. and Baker, G. eds. Understanding the new religions p141-52

20th century

Boulding, E. Religion, futurism, and models of social change. *In* Bundy, R. F. ed. Images of the future: the twenty-first century and beyond p169-81

Capps, W. H. The interpenetration of new religion and religious studies. *In* Needleman, J. and Baker, G. eds. Understanding the new religions p101-05

Lidz, V. M. Secularization, ethical life, and religion in modern societies. *In* Johnson, H. M. ed. Religious change and continuity p191-217

Ransom, J. C. God without thunder; excerpt. *In* Crunden, R. M. ed. The superfluous men p262-68

Roszak, T. Ethics, ecstasy, and the study of new religions. *In* Needleman, J. and Baker, G. eds. Understanding the new religions p49-62

Religion, Prehistoric. See Megalithic monuments

Religion, Primitive

Burland, C. A. Primitive societies. *In* Life after death p39-53

Frye, N. Symbolism of the unconscious. *In* Frye, N. Northrop Frye on culture and literature p84-94

See also Dancing (in religion, folklore, etc.); Fetishism; Fire (in religion, folklore, etc.); Initiations (in religion, folklore, etc.) Nativistic movements; Sacrifice; Sun (in religion, folklore, etc.); Superstition; Voodooism; also subdivision Religion and mythology under Indians of North America, etc.

Bibliography

Long, C. H. Primitive religion. *In* Adams, C. J. ed. A reader's guide to the great religions p 1-38

Religion and architecture. See Architecture and religion

Religion and art. See Art and religion

Religion and communism. See Communism and religion

Religion and culture

Bishirjian, R. J. The nature of public philosophy. *In* A Public philosophy reader p17-70

Koyama, K. Barefoot in an ascending elevator: a meditation. *In* On language, culture, and religion: in honor of Eugene A. Nida p213-36

Religion and culture—*Continued*

Novak, M. The Nation with the soul of a church; excerpt from "Choosing our king: powerful symbols in Presidential politics." *In* A Public philosophy reader p92-96

Peckham, M. The deplorable consequences of the idea of creativity. *In* Peckham, M. Romanticism and behavior p206-21

See also Christianity and culture

Religion and drama. See Religious drama

Religion and education. See Church and education

Religion and ethics

Meyer, D. H. The ethics of belief and the conduct of the mind. *In* Meyer, D. H. The democratic Enlightenment p82-93

Sidorsky, D. The autonomy of moral objectivity. *In* Modern Jewish ethics p153-73

See also Christian ethics; Ethics, Jewish; Islamic ethics

Religion and evolution. See Evolution and religion

Religion and international affairs

Wuthnow, R. Religious movements and the transition il world order. *In* Needleman, J. and Baker, G. eds. Understanding the new religions p63-79

Religion and labor. See Church and labor

Religion and language

Bateson, M. C. Ritualization: a study in texture and texture change. *In* Zaretsky, I. I. and Leone, M. P. eds. Religious movements in contemporary America p150-65

Brown, S. C. Religion and the limits of language. *In* Reason and religion p233-55

Copleston, F. C. Aquinas and the autonomy of religious language. *In* Copleston, F. C. Philosophers and philosophies p43-56

Crystal, D. The problem of language variety: an example from religious language. *In* Royal Institute of Philosophy. Communication and understanding p195-207

Durrant, M. Some comments on "Meaning and religious language." *In* Reason and religion p222-32

Prickett, S. 'The living educts of the imagination': Coleridge on religious language. *In* Prickett, S. Romanticism and religion p9-33

Winch, P. Meaning and religious language. *In* Reason and religion p193-221

Religion and literature

Eliot, T. S. Religion and literature. *In* Eliot, T. S. Selected prose of T. S. Eliot p97-106

Heiserman, A. R. Divine romance. *In* Heiserman, A. R. The novel before the novel p183-219

King, J. N. Theology, science fiction, and man's future orientation. *In* Clareson, T. D. ed. Many futures, many worlds p237-59

Pickering, S. Afterword. *In* Pickering, S. The moral tradition in English fiction, 1785-1850 p169-73

Pickering, S. The Christian Observer and the novel. *In* Pickering, S. The moral tradition in English fiction, 1785-1850 p65-87

Pickering, S. Coelebs in search of a wife, and Waverly. *In* Pickering, S. The moral tradition in English fiction, 1785-1850 p89-105

Pickering, S. The Old Curiosity Shop, and Legh Richmond's tracts. *In* Pickering, S. The moral tradition in English fiction, 1785-1850 p107-22

Pickering, S. The Sunday school movement: new readers and the novel. *In* Pickering, S. The moral tradition in English fiction, 1785-1850 p11-64

Scott, N. A. Criticism and the religious prospect. *In* English Association. Essays and studies, 1977 p98-108

See also Christianity and literature; Mysticism and literature; Religion in literature; Religion in poetry

Religion and parapsychology

Harrison, J. Religion and psychical research. *In* Thakur, S. C. ed. Philosophy and psychical research p97-121

Lewis, H. D. Religion and the paranormal. *In* Thakur, S. C. ed. Philosophy and psychical research p142-56

Religion and philosophy. See Philosophy and religion

Religion and poetry

Coxe, L. O. Poetry and—religion? *In* Coxe, L. O. Enabling acts p96-113

Daly, R. J. Anne Bradstreet and the practice of weaned affections. *In* Daly, R. J. God's altar p82-127

Daly, R. J. Ars poetica. *In* Daly, R. J. God's altar p40-81

Daly, R. J. Edward Taylor: Christ's creation and the dissatisfactions of metaphor. *In* Daly, R. J. God's altar p162-99

Daly, R. J. Gnostics and naturalists. *In* Daly, R. J. God's altar p128-61

Daly, R. J. Introduction: Puritanism and poetry. *In* Daly, R. J. God's altar p 1-5

Daly, R. J. The world's body. *In* Daly, R. J. God's altar p6-39

DeLaura, D. J. The future of poetry: a context for Carlyle and Arnold. *In* Carlyle and his contemporaries p148-80

Jones, D. Use and sign. *In* Jones, D. The dying Gaul, and other writings p177-85

Thompson, D. Rites, bards, ballads. *In* Thompson, D. The uses of poetry p43-69

See also Islam and poetry; Magic and poetry; Religion in poetry

Religion and politics

Ahlstrom, S. E. Diversity in religion as a force for liberty: a quadricentennial view of the problem. *In* Aspects of American liberty p56-67

See also Christianity and politics

Illinois

Jensen, R. J. The religious and occupational roots of party identification: Illinois and Indiana in the 1870's. *In* Swierenga, R. P. ed. Beyond the Civil War synthesis p255-73

Indiana

Jensen, R. J. The religious and occupational roots of party identification: Illinois and Indiana in the 1870's. *In* Swierenga, R. P. ed. Beyond the Civil War synthesis p255-73

Religion and psychiatry. See Psychiatry and religion

Religion and psychoanalysis. See Psychoanalysis and religion

Religion and race

Smith, A. Black reflections on the study of new religious consciousness. *In* Needleman, J. and Baker, G. eds. Understanding the new religions p209-19

Religion and science

Altholz, J. L. The warfare of conscience with theology. *In* Altholz, J. L. ed. The mind and art of Victorian England p58-77

Burrow, J. W. Faith, doubt and unbelief. *In* Lerner, L. ed. The Victorians p153-73

Hefner, P. J. Basic Christian assumptions about the cosmos. *In* Cosmology, history, and theology p347-64

Misner, C. W. Cosmology and theology. *In* Cosmology, history, and theology p75-100

Nemerov, H. On the resemblances between science and religion. *In* Nemerov, H. Figures of thought p49-54

Oberman, H. A. Reformation and revolution: Copernicus' discovery in an era of change. *In* The Nature of scientific discovery p134-69

Thomas, D. M. American technocracy and the religious spirit: an unholy alliance? *In* America in theological perspective p189-205

White, L. T. Science and the sense of self: the medieval background of a modern confrontation. *In* Holton, G. J. and Morison, R. S. eds. Limits of scientific inquiry p47-59

See also Evolution and Christianity; Evolution and religion; Faith and reason; Islam and science; Man—Origin; Natural theology

Anecdotes, facetiae, satire, etc.

Burhoe, R. W. A cosmic perspective on man's future. *In* Bundy, R. F. ed. Images of the future: the twenty-first century and beyond p182-92

History of controversy

Greene, J. C. Science and religion. *In* The Rise of Adventism p50-69

See also Modernist-fundamentalist controversy

1800-1859

Chadwick, O. Science and religion. *In* Chadwick, O. The secularization of the European mind in the nineteenth century p161-88

1860-1899

Chadwick, O. Science and religion. *In* Chadwick, O. The secularization of the European mind in the nineteenth century p161-88

Meyer, D. H. American intellectuals and the Victorian crisis of faith. *In* Howe, D. W. ed. Victorian America p59-77

1900-

See Modernist-fundamentalist controversy

Religion and sex. See Sex and religion

Religion and social problems. See Religion and sociology

Religion and society. See Religion and sociology

Religion and sociology

Berger, P. L. Religion in a revolutionary society. *In* America's continuing revolution p143-58

Chadwick, O. Karl Marx. *In* Chadwick, O. The secularization of the European mind in the nineteenth century p48-87

Eister, A. W. Culture crises and new religious movements: a paradigmatic statement of a theory of cults. *In* Zaretsky, I. I. and Leone, M. P. eds. Religious movements in contemporary America p612-27

Ellwood, R. S. Emergent religion in America: an historical perspective. *In* Needleman, J. and Baker, G. eds. Understanding the new religions p267-84

El-Shamy, H. African world view and religion. *In* Martin, P. M. and O'Meara, P. eds. Africa p208-20

Hargrove, B. Integrative and transformative religions. *In* Needleman, J. and Baker, G. eds. Understanding the new religions p257-66

Hine, V. H. The deprivation and disorganization theories of social movements. *In* Zaretsky, I. I. and Leone, M. P. eds. Religious movements in contemporary America p646-61

Johnson, H. M. Religion in social change and social evolution. *In* Johnson, H. M. ed. Religious change and continuity p313-39

Johnson, H. M. Religion in urban society. *In* Handbook of contemporary urban life p233-57

Marty, M. E. The changing role of religion in American society. *In* The National purpose reconsidered p29-51

See also Sociology, Biblical; Sociology, Christian

Religion and state

Murvar, V. Integrative and revolutionary capabilities of religion. *In* Johnson, H. M. ed. Religious change and continuity p74-86

Wilhelmsen, F. D. and Kendall, W. Cicero and the politics of the public orthodoxy. *In* A Public philosophy reader p112-41

See also Nationalism and religion

New England

Plumstead, A. W. The election sermons; excerpt from "The wall and the garden." *In* Mulder, J. M. and Wilson, J. F. eds. Religion in American history p57-73

Zaire—Katanga

Bustin, E. Government policy toward African cult movements: the case of Katanga. *In* African dimensions p113-35

Religion and technology. See Religion and science

Religion and war. See War and religion

Religion in drama

Hewison, P. Theology in the plays. *In* Prentki, T. ed. Francis Warner p53-66

See also Religious drama

Religion in literature

Dawson, C. Phases of the soul: the Newman brothers. *In* Dawson, C. Victorian noon p105-22

Donaldson, S. and Massa, A. Religion and irreligion: Doubts and certainties. *In* Donaldson, S. and Massa, A. American literature: nineteenth and early twentieth centuries p212-27

Donaldson, S. and Massa, A. Religion and irreligion: God and Mammon. *In* Donaldson, S. and Massa, A. American literature: nineteenth and early twentieth centuries p190-211

Kurz, P. K. Hermann Broch's trilogy Die Schlafwandler. *In* Kurz, P. K. On modern German literature v 1 p105-30

Presley, D. E. Little acts of grace. *In* Tennessee Williams: a tribute p571-80

Robinson, C. The idealist revolt. *In* Robinson, C. French literature in the nineteenth century p13-49

See also Bible in literature; Christianity in literature; Religion and literature; Religion in drama; Religion in poetry

Religion in poetry

Hough, G. G. Vision and doctrine in Four quartets. *In* Hough, G. G. Selected essays p173-99

Kau, J. L. C. "Trust . . . to go by contraries": incarnation and the paradox of belief in the poetry of Frost. *In* Frost: centennial essays II p99-111

Martin, W. Anne Bradstreet's poetry: a study of subversive piety. *In* Gilbert, S. M. and Gubar, S. eds. Shakespeare's sisters p19-31

Mollenkott, V. R. Herrick and the cleansing of perception. *In* Rollin, R. B. and Patrick, J. M. eds. "Trust to good verses": Herrick tercentenary essays p197-209

Oram, W. A. Herrick's use of sacred materials. *In* Rollin, R. B. and Patrick, J. M. eds. "Trust to good verses": Herrick tercentenary essays p211-18

Shepherd, G. Religion and philosophy in Chaucer. *In* Brewer, D. S. ed. Geoffrey Chaucer p262-89

See also Religion and poetry

Religions

Baker, G. Language and mind in the study of new religious movements. *In* Needleman, J. and Baker, G. eds. Understanding the new religions p285-98

Coomaraswamy, A. K. The sea. *In* Coomaraswamy, A. K. Selected papers v 1 p405-11

Hick, J. H. Christian theology and interreligious dialogue. *In* The Frontiers of human knowledge p 1-14

Hultkrantz, A. The contribution of the study of North American Indian religions to the history of religions. *In* Seeing with a native eye p86-106

Tuan, Yi-Fu. Geopiety: a theme in man's attachment to nature and to place. *In* Geographies of the mind p11-39

See also Buddhism; Confucianism; Cults; Gnosticism; Islam; Judaism; Mythology; Paganism; Polytheism; Religion; Sects; Shamanism; Spiritualism; Taoism

African influences

Barrett, L. E. African religion in the Americas: the "islands in between." *In* African religions: a symposium p183-215

Sturm, F. G. Afro-Brazilian cults. *In* African religions: a symposium p217-39

Bibliography

Oxtoby, W. G. The ancient world. *In* Adams, C. J. ed. A reader's guide to the great religions p39-77

Religions, Comparative. See Religions

Religions, Modern. See Cults; Sects

Religious art. See Christian art and symbolism; Church architecture

Religious belief. See Belief and doubt; Faith

Religious denominations. See Religions; Sects; and particular denominations or sects

Religious drama

Dunn, E. C. French medievalists and the saint's play: a problem for American scholarship. *In* Medievalia et humanistica no. 6 p51-62

See also Liturgical drama; Moralities

History and criticism

Morley, P. A. 'In God's name': ironic forms of religious drama in Canada and Australia. *In* Narasimhaiah, C. D. ed. Awakened conscience p275-83

Nicoll, A. The drama of the individual. *In* Nicoll, A. World drama p654-73

Religious drama, French

Presentation, etc.

Konigson, É. Religious drama and urban society in France at the end of the Middle Ages. *In* Drama and society p23-36

Religious education

Law and legislation

Greenawalt, R. K. Voucher plans and sectarian schools: the constitutional problem. *In* Parents, teachers, and children: prospects for choice in American education p207-25

Religious freedom. See Religious liberty

Religious liberty

Ahlstrom, S. E. Diversity in religion as a force for liberty: a quadricentennial view of the problem. *In* Aspects of American liberty p56-67

Danzig, R. How questions begot answers in Felix Frankfurter's first flag salute opinion. *In* The Supreme Court review, 1977 p257-74

Judah, J. S. New religions and religious liberty. *In* Needleman, J. and Baker, G. eds. Understanding the new religions p201-08

Leahy, J. J. On the civil liberties of sect members: Part 3. *In* Horowitz, I. L. ed. Science, sin, and scholarship p208-16

Marson, C. C.; Crosby, M. C. and Schlosser, A. L. On the civil liberties of sect members: Part 1. *In* Horowitz, I. L. ed. Science, sin, and scholarship p192-97

See also Religious tolerance

Israel

Konvitz, M. R. Individual conscience or group consciousness: religious liberty in the United States and Israel. *In* Konvitz, M. R. Judaism and the American idea p139-59

Shetreet, S. Freedom of conscience and religion in Israel. *In* Sidorsky, D. ed. Essays on human rights p179-92

United States

Berns, W. F. Religion and the founding principle. *In* The Moral foundations of the American Republic p157-82

Marty, M. E. Of darters and schools and clergymen: the religion clauses worse confounded. *In* The Supreme Court review, 1978 p171-90

Religious life (Christianity) See Christian life

Religious literature

See also Christian literature, Early; Liturgy and literature

Censorship

Youngs, F. J. The Tudor governments and dissident religious books. *In* The Dissenting tradition p167-90

History

Webb, E. The tradition of the sacred in the West. *In* Webb, E. The dark dove p12-33

Religious literature, Jewish

History and criticism

Silberman, L. H. The Queen of Sheba in Judaic tradition. *In* Pritchard, J. B. ed. Solomon & Sheba p65-84

Religious painting. See Christian art and symbolism

Religious poetry, English

History and criticism

Wardropper, B. W. The religious conversion of profane poetry. *In* Studies in the continental background of Renaissance English literature: essays presented to John L. Lievsay p203-22

Middle English (1100-1500)—
History and criticism

Wenzel, S. The English verses in the **Fasciculus morum.** *In* Chaucer and Middle English studies in honour of Rossell Hope Robbins p230-48

Early modern, 1500-1700
History and criticism

Chambers, A. B. Christmas: the liturgy of the Church and English verse of the Renaissance. *In* Literary monographs, v6 p109-53

Religious psychology. See Psychology, Religious

Religious rites. See Rites and ceremonies

Religious sociology. See Religion and sociology

Religious thought

Middle Ages, 600-1500

Kinsman, R. S. Introduction. *In* The Darker vision of the Renaissance p 1-23

Modern period, 1500-

Kinsman, R. S. Introduction. *In* The Darker vision of the Renaissance p 1-23

Webb, E. The paradox of the sacred. *In* Webb, E. The dark dove p3-11

16th century

Nelson, B. N. The quest for certitude and the books of Scripture, nature, and conscience. *In* The Nature of scientific discovery p355-72

17th century

Nelson, B. N. The quest for certitude and the books of Scripture, nature, and conscience. *In* The Nature of scientific discovery p355-72

20th century

Whitehead, E. E. Religious images of aging: an examination of themes in contemporary Christian thought. *In* Spicker, S. F.; Woodward, K. M. and Van Tassel, D. D. eds. Aging and the elderly p37-48

Great Britain

Prickett, S. Summary: tradition and the Church. *In* Prickett, S. Romanticism and religion p249-67

Shepherd, G. Religion and philosophy in Chaucer. *In* Brewer, D. S. ed. Geoffrey Chaucer p262-89

Religious tolerance

Coomaraswamy, A. K. Srī Ramakrishna and religious tolerance. *In* Coomaraswamy, A. K. Selected papers v2 p34-42

See also Religious liberty

Europe, Eastern—History

Hillerbrand, H. J. Religious dissent and toleration: introductory reflections. *In* Király, B. K. ed. Tolerance and movements of religious dissent in Eastern Europe p 1-8

Religious vocation. See Vocation (in religious orders, congregations, etc.)

Relocation of business. See Business relocation

Remand homes. See Juvenile detention homes

Remarque, Erich Maria

About individual works
All quiet on the Western front

Rowley, B. A. Journalism into fiction: In Western nichts Neues. *In* Klein, H. M. ed. The First World War in fiction p101-11

Remarriage in literature

Rudd, N. Idea: Dido's culpa. *In* Rudd, N. Lines of enquiry p32-53

Remedial English. See English language—Remedial teaching

Remedial teaching. See English language—Remedial teaching

Remi de Beauvais

About individual works
La Magdeleine

Grant, P. Richard Crashaw and the Capucins: images and the force of belief. *In* Grant, P. Images and ideas in literature of the English Renaissance p89-128

Remington, Frederic

About

Dobie, J. F. A summary introduction to Frederic Remington. *In* Dobie, J. F. Prefaces p175-86

Reminick, Ronald A.

The evil eye belief among the Amhara. *In* The Evil eye p85-101

Remizov, Alekseĭ Mikhaĭlovich

About

Shane, A. M. An introduction to Alexei Remizov. *In* The Bitter air of exile p10-16

Remy, Dorothy

Underdevelopment and the experience of women: a Nigerian case study. *In* Reiter, R. R. ed. Toward an anthropology of women p358-71

Renaissance

Bolle, K. W. Structures of Renaissance mysticism. *In* The Darker vision of the Renaissance p119-45

Bouwsma, W.J. Changing assumptions in later Renaissance culture. *In* Viator: medieval and Renaissance studies v7 p421-40

Burke, J. G. Hermetism as a Renaissance world view. *In* The Darker vision of the Renaissance p95-117

Gombrich, E. H. J. The Renaissance—period or movement? *In* Background to the English Renaissance p9-30

Hale, J. R. The Renaissance label. *In* Background to the English Renaissance p31-42

Hexter, J. H. Wallace K. Ferguson and Hiram Hayden [sic]: the Renaissance again —and again. *In* Hexter, J. H. On historians p45-59

Renaissance—*Continued*

Hoffmeister, G. The pagan influence of the Italian Renaissance on German life and letters, 1450-1520. *In* Hoffmeister, G. ed. The Renaissance and Reformation in Germany p51-67

Trinkaus, C. E. Renaissance and discovery. *In* First images of America p3-9

See also Humanism; Sixteenth century

Historiography

Nisbet, R. A. The myth of the Renaissance. *In* The Idea of social structure p471-96

Spitz, L. W. Periodization in history: Renaissance and Reformation. *In* The Future of history p189-217

England

Cunningham, J. V. The Renaissance in England. *In* Cunningham, J. V. The collected essays of J. V. Cunningham p282-310

Europe

See Renaissance

France

Wightman, W. P. D. Cosmological and technological trends in the French Renaissance. *In* French Renaissance studies, 1540-70 p70-80

Germany

Borchardt, F. L. Medievalism in Renaissance Germany. *In* Creative encounter p73-85

Jantz, H. E. S. Images of America in the German Renaissance. *In* First images of America p91-106

Great Britain

McCanles, M. Dialectical criticism and beyond. *In* McCanles, M. Dialectical criticism and Renaissance literature p214-73

Italy

Altschul, M. Culture and community in the Italian Renaissance: four recent studies. *In* Medievalia et humanistica no. 5 p247-52

Goldstein, T. E. Impulses of Italian Renaissance culture behind the age of discoveries. *In* First images of America p27-35

Nisbet, R. A. The myth of the Renaissance. *In* The Idea of social structure p471-96

Renaissance architecture. See Architecture, Renaissance

Renaissance art. See Art, Renaissance

Renaissance cities and towns. See Cities and towns, Renaissance

Renaissance painting. See Painting, Renaissance

Renaissance philosophy. See Philosophy, Renaissance

Renaissance sculpture. See Sculpture, Renaissance

Renan, Ernest

About

Said, E. W. Renan's philological laboratory. *In* Art, politics, and will p59-98

About individual works

The life of Jesus

Shaffer, E. S. Browning's St John: the casuistry of the higher criticism. *In* Shaffer, E. S. 'Kubla Khan' and The fall of Jerusalem p191-224

Renaud de Beaujeu

About individual works

Le bel inconnu

Hanning, R. W. The romance plot and the crisis of inner awareness. *In* Hanning, R. W. The individual in twelfth-century romance p194-233

Renault, Mary

About

Heilbrun, C. G. Axiothea's grief; the disability of the female imagination. *In* From Parnassus p227-36

René, of Anjou, King of Naples. See René I, d'Anjou, King of Naples and Jerusalem

René I, d'Anjou, King of Naples and Jerusalem

About

Kelly, D. Imagination in poetry of Charles d'Orléans and René d'Anjou. *In* Kelly, D. Medieval imagination p204-29

Renehan, Robert

The Michigan Alcidamas-papyrus: a problem in methodology. *In* Harvard Studies in classical philology v75 p85-105

Renfrew, Colin

Trade as action at a distance: questions of integration and communication. *In* Ancient civilization and trade p3-59

Renger, Johannes M.

Mesopotamian epic literature. *In* Oinas, F. J. ed. Heroic epic and saga p27-48

Rengo Sekigun

Parry, A. Red samurai and Turkey's nihilists. *In* Parry, A. Terrorism: from Robespierre to Arafat p433-48

Reni, Guido

About

Meyers, J. Guido Reni and The marble faun. *In* Meyers, J. Painting and the novel p6-18

Renna, Thomas Julius

Aristotle and the French monarchy, 1260-1303. *In* Viator: medieval and Renaissance studies v9 p309-24

Renner, Timothy

A papyrus dictionary of metamorphoses. *In* Harvard Studies in classical philology v82 p277-93

Renoir, Alain

Beowulf: a contextual introduction to its contents and techniques. *In* Oinas, F. J. ed. Heroic epic and saga p99-119

A reading context for The wife's lament. *In* Anglo-Saxon poetry: essays in appreciation p224-41

The terror of the dark waters: a note on Virgilian and Beowulfian techniques. *In* The Learned and the lewed p147-60

Renoir, Jean

About

Samuels, C. T. Jean Renoir and the theatrical film. *In* Samuels, C. T. Mastering the film, and other essays p42-68

Truffaut, F. A Jean Renoir festival. *In* Truffaut, F. The films in my life p36-47

About individual works

La grande illusion

Kauffmann, S. La grande illusion. *In* Kauffmann, S. Living images p307-16

Rensch, Bernard. See Rensch, Bernhard

Rensch, Bernhard

Polynomistic determination of biological processes. *In* Ayala, F. J. and Dobzhansky, T. G. eds. Studies in the philosophy of biology p241-55

Rensch, Calvin Ross

Otomanguean isoglosses. *In* Sebeok, T. A. ed. Native languages of the Americas v2 p163-84

Renshon, Stanley Allen

Birth order and political socialization. *In* Schwartz, D. C. and Schwartz, S. K. eds. New directions in political socialization p69-95

Human needs and political analysis: an examination of a framework. *In* Fitzgerald, R. ed. Human needs and politics p52-73

The role of personality development in political socialization. *In* Schwartz, D. C. and Schwartz, S. K. eds. New directions in political socialization p29-68

Rent

Paris

Le Roy Ladurie, E. Changes in Parisian rents from the end of the Middle Ages to the eighteenth century. *In* Le Roy Ladurie, E. The territory of the historian p61-75

Reparation

United States

Geis, G. Compensation to victims of violent crime. *In* Contemporary issues in criminal justice p94-115

Reparations

Parrini, C. P. Reparations. *In* Encyclopedia of American foreign policy p893-99

Repentance

Elagin, S. Repentance: its theory, history and prescription for today. *In* Medvedev, R. A. ed. The Samizdat register p237-66

Peterson, D. L. John Donne's Holy sonnets and the Anglican doctrine of contrition. *In* Roberts, J. R. ed. Essential articles for the study of John Donne's poetry p313-23

Solzhenitsyn, A. I. Repentance and self-limitation in the life of nations. *In* From under the rubble p105-43

Repetition (Philosophy)

Foucault, M. Theatrum philosophicum. *In* Foucault, M. Language, counter-memory, practice p165-96

Repin, Il'ià- Efimovich

About

Hilton, A. The revolutionary theme in Russian realism. *In* Millon, H. A. and Nochlin, L. eds. Art and architecture in the service of politics p108-27

Replacement of industrial equipment

Jorgenson, D. W. The economic theory of replacement and depreciation. *In* Econometrics and economic theory p190-221

Reppert, James Donald

F. J. Child and the ballad. *In* The Learned and the lewed p197-212

Representation. See Representative government and representation

Representation (Philosophy)

Goodman, N. Reality remade; excerpt from "Languages of art". *In* Margolis, J. Z. ed. Philosophy looks at the arts p225-48

Maynard, P. Depiction, vision, and convention. *In* Margolis, J. Z. ed. Philosophy looks at the arts p273-306

Wollheim, R. On drawing an object. *In* Margolis, J. Z. ed. Philosophy looks at the arts p249-72

Representative government and representation

Nisbet, R. A. Public opinion versus popular opinion. *In* A Public philosophy reader p169-97

See also Democracy; Pressure groups; Suffrage

Canada

Berger, C. The rise of liberty. *In* Berger, C. The writing of Canadian history p32-53

United States

Caldwell, L. K. Responsiveness and responsibility: the anomalous problem of the environment. *In* Rieselbach, L. N. ed. People vs. government: the responsiveness of American institutions p300-27

Eckart, D. R. and Ries, J. C. The American Presidency. *In* Rieselbach, L. N. ed. People vs. government: the responsiveness of American institutions p15-65

Meyer, D. H. Thomas Jefferson and the rhetoric of republicanism. *In* Meyer, D. H. The democratic Enlightenment p109-28

Morgan, E. S. The problem of popular sovereignty. *In* Aspects of American liberty p95-113

Niskanen, W. A. The pathology of politics. *In* Capitalism and freedom p20-35

Rieselbach, L. N. After Watergate, what? *In* Rieselbach, L. N. ed. People vs. government: the responsiveness of American institutions p66-118

Weber, R. E. The political responsiveness of the American states and their local governments. *In* Rieselbach, L. N. ed. People vs. government: the responsiveness of American institutions p189-225

Repression (Psychology)

Bloom, H. Emerson and Whitman: the American sublime. *In* Bloom, H. Poetry and repression p235-66

Bloom, H. Keats: romance revised. *In* Bloom, H. Poetry and repression p112-42

Bloom, H. Poetry, revisionism, repression. *In* Bloom, H. Poetry and repression p 1-27

Bloom, H. Tennyson: in the shadow of Keats. *In* Bloom, H. Poetry and repression p143-74

Bloom, H. Wallace Stevens: the transcendental strain. *In* Bloom, H. Poetry and repression p267-93

Bloom, H. Yeats, Gnosticism, and the sacred void. *In* Bloom, H. Poetry and repression p205-34

Reproduction

Churchill, F. B. Sex and the single organism: biological theories of sexuality in mid-nineteenth century. *In* Studies in history of biology v3 p139-77

Walters, L. Genetics, reproductive biology, and bioethics. *In* The Tricentennial people p66-74

See also Fetus; Human reproduction; Isolating mechanisms

Reproduction (Psychology) See Imagination; Memory

Reproduction, Asexual. See Cloning

Reps, John William

Bonanza towns: urban planning on the Western mining frontier. *In* Pattern and process p271-89

Republican Party

Benedict, M. L. The rout of radicalism: Republicans and the elections of 1867. *In* Swierenga, R. P. ed. Beyond the Civil War synthesis p137-47

Gambill, E. L. Who were the Senate radicals? *In* Swierenga, R. P. ed. Beyond the Civil War synthesis p225-32

Powell, L. N. Rejected Republican incumbents in the 1866 Congressional nominating convention: a study in Reconstruction politics. *In* Swierenga, R. P. ed. Beyond the Civil War synthesis p117-35

Massachusetts

Goodman, P. The politics of industrialism: Massachusetts, 1830-1870. *In* Uprooted Americans p161-207

New York (State)

Field, P. F. Republicans and Black suffrage in New York State: the grass roots response. *In* Swierenga, R. P. ed. Beyond the Civil War synthesis p149-62

Republics. See Democracy; Federal government; Representative government and representation

Rescher, Nicholas

The environmental crisis and the quality of life. *In* Philosophy & environmental crisis p90-104

Rescher, Nicholas, and Vander Nat, Arnold

The Arabic theory of temporal modal syllogistic. *In* Essays on Islamic philosophy and science p189-221

Research

Baltimore, D. Limiting science: a biologist's perspective. *In* Holton, G. J. and Morison, R. S. eds. Limits of scientific inquiry p37-45

Bok, S. Freedom and risk. *In* Holton, G. J. and Morison, R. S. eds. Limits of scientific inquiry p115-27

Bronowski, J. The disestablishment of science. *In* Bronowski, J. A sense of the future p235-48

Brooks, H. The problems of research priorities. *In* Holton, G. J. and Morison, R. S. eds. Limits of scientific inquiry p171-90

Gieryn, T. F. Problem retention and problem change in science. *In* Gaston, J. ed. Sociology of science p96-115

Graham, L. R. Concerns about science and attempts to regulate inquiry. *In* Holton, G. J. and Morison, R. S. eds. Limits of scientific inquiry p 1-21

Hargens, L. L. Theory and method in the sociology of science. *In* Gaston, J. ed. Sociology of science p121-39

Holton, G. J. From the endless frontier to the ideology of limits. *In* Holton, G. J. and Morison, R. S. eds. Limits of scientific inquiry p227-41

Kurtz, P. W. The ethics of free inquiry. *In* Hook, S.; Kurtz, P. and Todorovich, M. eds. The ethics of teaching and scientific research p203-07

Metzger, W. P. Academic freedom and scientific freedom. *In* Holton, G. J. and Morison, R. S. eds. Limits of scientific inquiry p93-114

Mulkay, M. J. Sociology of the scientific research community. *In* Science, technology and society p93-148

Nelkin, D. Threats and promises: negotiating the control of research. *In* Holton, G. J. and Morison, R. S. eds. Limits of scientific inquiry p191-209

Salomon, J. J. Science policy studies and the development of science policy. *In* Science, technology and society p43-70

Sinsheimer, R. L. The presumptions of science. *In* Holton, G. J. and Morison, R. S. eds. Limits of scientific inquiry p23-35

Spiegel-Rösing, I. S. The study of science, technology and society (SSTS): recent trends and future challenges. *In* Science, technology and society p7-42

Swazey, J. P. Protecting the "animal of necessity": limits to inquiry in clinical investigation. *In* Holton, G. J. and Morison, R. S. eds. Limits of scientific inquiry p129-45

Thomas, L. The hazards of science. *In* Thomas, L. The medusa and the snail p65-75

Watson, J. D. The dissemination of unpublished information. *In* The Frontiers of knowledge p157-75

Zuckerman, H. A. Theory choice and problem choice in science. *In* Gaston, J. ed. Sociology of science p65-95

See also Anthropological research; Biological research; Cardiovascular research; Educational research; Family research; Historical research; Learning and scholarship; Literary research; Mathematical research; Military research; Political science research; Psychical research; Research, Industrial; Sex research; Social science research; Sociological research; Vision research

Citizen participation

Culliton, B. J. Science's restive public. *In* Holton, G. J. and Morison, R. S. eds. Limits of scientific inquiry p147-56

Nelkin, D. Threats and promises: negotiating the control of research. *In* Holton, G. J. and Morison, R. S. eds. Limits of scientific inquiry p191-209

Economic aspects

Freeman, C. Economics and research and development. *In* Science, technology and society p223-75

Federal aid

See Federal aid to research

Moral and religious aspects

Brennan, D. G. Ethical principles and national security research. *In* Hook, S.; Kurtz, P. and Todorovich, M. eds. The ethics of teaching and scientific research p175-77

Hibbs, A. R. An engineer's approach to the ethics of research. *In* Hook, S.; Kurtz, P. and Todorovich, M. eds. The ethics of teaching and scientific research p179-86

Hook, S. Rejoinder: Dr Hibbs and the ethics of discussion. *In* Hook, S.; Kurtz, P. and Todorovich, M. eds. The ethics of teaching and scientific research p187-90

Horn, J. L. The ethics of research: a case history and its lessons. *In* Hook, S.; Kurtz, P. and Todorovich, M. eds. The ethics of teaching and scientific research p135-59

Humphreys, L. G. The fallout of the legal mind in research. *In* Hook, S.; Kurtz, P. and Todorovich, M. eds. The ethics of teaching and scientific research p161-64

Todorovich, M. Wanted: a rational decision procedure for value conflicts in science. *In* Hook, S.; Kurtz, P. and Todorovich, M. eds. The ethics of teaching and scientific research p191-201

Research—*Continued*

Psychological aspects

Fisch, R. Psychology of science. *In* Science, technology and society p277-318

Germany—Saxony—History

Jungnickel, C. Teaching and research in the physical sciences and mathematics in Saxony, 1820-1850. *In* Historical studies in the physical sciences v10 p3-47

United States

Parsons, T. Some considerations on the growth of the American system of higher education and research. *In* Culture and its creators p266-84

Also in Parsons, T. Action theory and the human condition p115-32

United States—History

Kargon, R. H. Temple to science: cooperative research and the birth of the California Institute of Technology. *In* Historical studies in the physical sciences v8 p3-31

Research, Endowment of. See Endowment of research

Research, Historical. See Historical research

Research, Industrial

United States—History

Rae, J. B. The application of science to industry. *In* Oleson, A. and Voss, J. eds. The organization of knowledge in modern America, 1860-1920 p249-68

Research, Medical. See Medical research

Research, Military. See Military research

Research, Musical. See Musicology

Research, Psychological. See Psychological research

Research grants

Bazerman, C. The grant, the scholar and the university community. *In* Hook, S.; Kurtz, P. W. and Todorovich, M. eds. The university and the state: what role for government in higher education? p221-25

See also Federal aid to research

Evaluation

Ploch, D. R. Research funding for sociology in the National Science Foundation. *In* Gaston, J. ed. Sociology of science p54-62

Research in higher education. See Education, Higher—Research

Research libraries. See Libraries, University and college

Resemblance (Philosophy) See Identity

Reservations, Indian. See Indians of North America—Reservations

Residences. See Architecture, Domestic; Dwellings

Residential mobility

Gottmann, J. Megalopolis and antipolis: the telephones and the structure of the city. *In* The Social impact of the telephone p303-17

Asia, Southeastern

McGee, T. G. Rural-urban mobility in South and Southeast Asia: different formulations, different answers. *In* Human migration p199-224

New Jersey—History

Wacker, P. O. Patterns and problems in the historical geography of the Afro-American population of New Jersey, 1726-1860. *In* Pattern and process p25-72

New York (City)—History

Ward, D. Some locational implications of the ethnic division of labor in mid-nineteenth-century American cities. *In* Pattern and process p258-70

San Francisco—History

Bowden, M. J. Persistence, failure, and mobility in the inner city: preliminary notes. *In* Pattern and process p169-92

United States

Edel, M.; Harris, J. R. and Rothenberg, J. Urban concentration and deconcentration. *In* Hawley, A. H. and Rock, V. P. eds. Metropolitan America in contemporary perspective p123-56

Resistance to government. See Government, Resistance to

Reskin, Barbara F.

Sex differentiation and the social organization of science. *In* Gaston, J. ed. Sociology of science p6-37

Resnick, Idrian N.

Manpower requirements and allocation of educational resources in underdeveloped countries. *In* African dimensions p155-69

Resnick, James L.

The emerging physician: from political activist to professional vanguard. *In* Gerstl, J. E. and Jacobs, G. eds. Professions for the people p175-213

Resource management. See Conservation of natural resources

Resource recovery. See Recycling (Waste, etc.)

Resources, Marine. See Marine resources

Responsibility

Boden, M. A. Human values in the mechanistic universe. *In* Royal Institute of Philosophy. Human values p135-71

Flew, A. G. N. Sartre and unconditional responsibility. *In* Flew, A. G. N. A rational animal p75-88

May, R. Freedom and responsibility reexamined. *In* May, R. Psychology and the human dilemma p168-81

Polak, F. L. Responsibility for the future. *In* Bundy, R. F. ed. Images of the future: the twenty-first century and beyond p9-15

Stough, C. L. Stoic determinism and moral responsibility. *In* Rist, J. M. ed. The Stoics p203-31

Taylor, C. Responsibility for self. *In* Rorty, A. O. ed. The identities of persons p281-99

Taylor, C. What is human agency? *In* Mischel, T. ed. The self p103-35

Zaw, S. K. 'Irresistible impulse' and moral responsibility. *In* Royal Institute of Philosophy. Human values p99-134

See also Duty; Free will and determinism

Political aspects

Jacob, P. E. Autonomy and political responsibility: the enigmatic verdict of a cross-national comparative study of community dynamics. *In* Walton, J. and Masotti, L. H. eds. The city in comparative perspective p97-118

Rest. See Sleep

Restif de la Bretonne, Nicolas Edme

About

Knight, I. F. Utopian dream as psychic reality. *In* Studies in eighteenth-century culture v6 p427-38

Reston, James R.
America in a changing world. *In* A Time to hear and answer: essays for the Bicentennial season p141-55

Restorations, Political. See France—History—Restoration, 1814-1830

Restraint of trade

United States

Bork, R. H. Vertical restraints: Schwinn overruled. *In* The Supreme Court review, 1977 p171-92

Cressey, D. R. Restraint of trade, recidivism, and delinquent neighborhoods, *In* Delinquency, crime, and society p209-38

Restrictive trade practices. See Restraint of trade

Resurrection
Simon, U. E. Resurrection in a post-religious age. *In* Life after death p144-53

Sutherland, S. R. Immortality and resurection. *In* Donnelly, J. P. ed. Language, metaphysics, and death p196-207

See also Jesus Christ—Resurrection

Resurrection of Christ. See Jesus Christ—Resurrection

Retail trade. See Central business districts

Retarded children. See Mentally handicapped children; Slow learning children

Retention (Psychology) See Memory

The return from Parnassus
Huntley, F. L. Joseph Hall, John Marston, and The returne from Parnassus. *In* Illustrious evidence p3-22

Reuental, Neidhart von. See Neidhart von Reuental

Reutov, Oleg Aleksandrovich
Some modern problems concerning the prohibition of the development, production and stockpiling of chemical warfare agents. *In* The Dynamics of the arms race p185-91

Revard, Stella Hill Purce
The Renaissance Michael and the Son of God. *In* Patrick, J. M. and Sundell, R. H. eds. Milton and the art of sacred song p121-35

Revel, Jacques
A capital city's privileges: food supplies in early-modern Rome. *In* Food and drink in history p37-49

Revelation
Price, C. P. Religion and revelation. *In* Christian faith in a religiously plural world p117-22

See also Apocalyptic literature

Revenue. See Taxation

Revenue sharing. See Intergovernmental fiscal relations

Rever, Philip R.
The dynamics of admission to the less-selective public and private sector colleges. *In* Hurdles p111-44

Reverdy, Pierre
About
Bishop, M. Eyes and seeing in the poetry of Pierre Reverdy. *In* Cardinal, R. ed. Sensibility and creation p57-71

Greene, R. W. Pierre Reverdy. *In* Greene, R. W. Six French poets of our time p23-58

Review, Judicial. See Judicial review

Reviewing (Books) See Book reviewing

Revisionism. Theoharis, A. G. *In* Encyclopedia of American foreign policy p900-13

Revival (Religion) See Revivals

Revival, Evangelical. See Evangelical revival

Revival movements (Art) See Neoclassicism (Art)

Revival of letters. See Renaissance

Revivalists. See Evangelists

Revivals
Hudson, W. S. A time of religious ferment. *In* The Rise of Adventism p 1-17

McLoughlin, W. G. Revivalism. *In* The Rise of Adventism p119-53

See also Jesus People

United States
Pritchard, L. K. Religious change in nineteenth-century America. *In* The New religious consciousness p297-330

Revivals. See Jesus People

Revolution (Theology)
Walzer, M. Puritanism as a revolutionary ideology. *In* Vaughan, A. T. and Bremer, F. J. eds. Puritan New England p19-41

Revolution, American. See United States—History—Revolution, 1775-1783

Revolution, French. See France—History—Revolution, 1789-1799

Revolution of 1848 in France. See France—History—February Revolution, 1848

Revolutionary poetry, American
History and criticism
Ložar, T. Before the brave: portrait of man as a young artist. *In* Morgan, R. G. ed. Kenneth Patchen: a collection of essays p193-207

Wilder, A. N. Revolutionary and proletarian poetry: Kenneth Patchen; excerpt from "The spiritual aspects of the new poetry. *In* Morgan, R. G. ed. Kenneth Patchen: a collection of essays p123-35

Revolutionary poetry, English
Smith, E. E. From romantic revolution to welfare state. *In* Smith, E. E. The angry young men of the thirties p134-53

Revolutionary poetry, Russian
Striedter, J. The "new myth" of revolution—a study of Mayakovsky's early poetry. *In* Amacher, R. E. and Lange, V. eds. New perspectives in German literary criticism p357-85

Revolutionary War, American. See United States—History—Revolution, 1775-1783

Revolutionists
Bell, J. B. Proliferation: sophisticated weapons and revolutionary options—the sub-state perspective. *In* Arms control and technological innovation p146-60

Psychology
Overholt, W. H. Sources of radicalism and revolution: a survey of the literature. *In* Radicalism in the contemporary age v 1 p293-335

Europe
Palmer, R. R. The fading dream: how European revolutionaries have seen the American Revolution. *In* Essays on modern European revolutionary history p89-104

Revolutions

Cohen, C. Revolutions and Copernican revolutions. *In* Science and society: past, present, and future p86-103

Dallin, A. Retreat from optimism: on Marxian models of revolution. *In* Radicalism in the contemporary age v3 p117-57

Dunn, J. M. The success and failure of modern revolutions. *In* Radicalism in the contemporary age v3 p83-114

Foot, M. R. D. Resistance, war and revolution. *In* The Year book of world affairs, 1977 p158-75

Gallie, W. B. Marx and Engels on revolution and war. *In* Gallie, W. B. Philosophers of peace and war p66-99

Hammond, T. T. The history of Communist takeovers. *In* Hammond, T. T. ed. The anatomy of Communist takeovers p 1-45

Hammond, T. T. A summing up. *In* Hammond, T. T. ed. The anatomy of Communist takeovers p638-43

Kristol, I. The American Revolution as a successful revolution. *In* America's continuing revolution p3-21

Kutner, L. A philosophical perspective on rebellion; excerpts from "Due process of rebellion". *In* International terrorism and political crimes p51-64

Overholt, W. H. Sources of radicalism and revolution: a survey of the literature. *In* Radicalism in the contemporary age v 1 p293-335

Skocpol, T Explaining revolutions: in quest of a social-structural approach. *In* The Uses of controversy in sociology p155-75

Struve, P. B. The intelligentsia and revolution. *In* Landmarks p138-54

Weber, E. J. Revolution? Counterrevolution? What revolution? *In* Laqueur, W. Z. ed. Fascism: a reader's guide p435-67

Welch, R. E. Revolution and foreign policy. *In* Encyclopedia of American foreign policy p914-23

See also Civil war; France—History—Revolution, 1789-1799; Insurgency; Peasant uprising; Terrorism; United States—History —Revolution, 1775-1783; and similar headings

Africa

Saul, J. S. African peasantries and revolutionary change. *In* Forging nations: a comparative view of rural ferment and revolt p86-127

Angola

Wheeler, D. L. Rebels and rebellions in Angola, 1672-1892. *In* African dimensions p81-93

Europe—History

Berlin, Sir I. Russia and 1848. *In* Berlin, Sir I. Russian thinkers p 1-21

Revolutions and art. See Art and revolutions

Revolutions and literature. See Literature and revolutions

Revolutions in literature

Rosenthal, B. G. Revolution as apocalypse: the case of Bely. *In* Janecek, G. ed. Andrey Bely p181-92

Rewak, William John

James Agee's Let us now praise famous men: the shadow over America. *In* Tennessee Studies in literature v21 p91-104

Rex, John

The plural society: the South African case. *In* Leftwich, A. ed. South Africa: economic growth and political change p45-60

Racialism and the urban crisis. *In* United Nations Educational, Scientific and Cultural Organization. Race, science and society p262-300

Rex, Walter E.

The philosophical articles by Abbé Pestré in Diderot's Encyclopédie. *In* Studies in eighteenth-century culture v7 p251-62

Rexroth, Kenneth

Kenneth Patchen: naturalist of the public nightmare. *In* Morgan, R. G. ed. Kenneth Patchen: a collection of essays p20-28

About

Thurley, G. Rexroth and Patchen: alternatives to breakdown. *In* Thurley, G. The American moment p159-71

Rey, Alain

Communication vs. semiosis: two conceptions of semiotics. *In* Sebeok, T. A. ed. Sight, sound, and sense p98-110

Rey, Georges

Survival. *In* Rorty, A. O. ed. The identities of persons p41-66

Rey y Arrojo, Manuel López-. See López-Rey y Arrojo, Manuel

Reyburn, William David

Secular culture, missions, and spiritual values. *In* On language, culture, and religion: in honor of Eugene A. Nida p287-99

Reyes, Alfonso

About

Paz, O. The rider of the air. *In* Paz, O. The siren & the seashell p113-22

Reykjavik. National Theater

Kauffmann, S. Report from Iceland. *In* Kauffmann, S. Persons of the drama p85-88

Reynard the Fox

Parker, R. B. Volpone and Reynard the Fox. *In* Renaissance drama [1976] p3-42

Sands, D. B. Reynard the Fox and the manipulation of the popular proverb. *In* The Learned and the lewed p265-78

Torrance, R. M. Renegade vassal. *In* Torrance, R. M. The comic hero p83-110

Reynaud, Jean-Daniel, and Bourdieu, Pierre

Is a sociology of action possible? *In* Giddens, A. ed. Positivism and sociology p101-13

Reynolds, Barbara

Dorothy L. Sayers, interpreter of Dante. *In* Hannay, M. P. ed. As her whimsey took her p123-32

Reynolds, David Parham

Business management in an age of change. *In* Benton, L. R. ed. Management for the future p239-45

Reynolds, Frank E.

Buddhism. *In* Adams, C. J. ed. A reader's guide to the great religions p156-222

The many lives of Buddha: a study of sacred biography and Theravāda tradition. *In* Reynolds, F. E. and Capps, D. eds. The biographical process p37-61

See also Kitagawa, J. M. jt. auth.

Reynolds, John Hamilton

About

Jones, L. M. Hazlitt, Reynolds, and the Edinburgh Review. *In* Virginia. University. Bibliographical Society. Studies in bibliography v29 p342-46

Reynolds, Sir Joshua

About

Olson, E. Longinus and Reynolds. *In* Olson, E. On value judgments in the arts, and other essays p107-17

Trowbridge, F. H. Platonism and Sir Joshua Reynolds. *In* Trowbridge, F. H. From Dryden to Jane Austen p200-09

About individual works

Discourses

Adams, H. Revisiting Reynold's [sic] Discourses and Blake's annotations. *In* Essick, R. N. and Pearce, D. R. eds. Blake in his time p128-44

Reynolds, Mack

About

Warrick, P. S. Mack Reynolds: the future as socio-economic possibility. *In* Clareson, T. D. ed. Voices for the future: essays on major science fiction writers v2 p136-53

Reynolds, Mary Trackett

Dante's Francesca and James Joyce's "Sirens." *In* Italian literature: roots and branches p155-200

Reynolds, Roger Edward

Marginalia on a tenth-century text on the ecclesiastical officers. *In* Law, church, and society p115-29

Reynolds, Walter, Abp. of Canterbury

About

Denton, J. Walter Reynolds and ecclesiastical politics, 1313-1316: a postscript to 'Councils & synods, II.' *In* Church and government in the Middle Ages p247-74

Reynolds, William

Dorothy Sayers and the drama of orthodoxy. *In* Hannay, M. P. ed. As her whimsey took her p91-106

Reznikoff, Charles

About

Alter, R. Charles Reznikoff: between present and past. *In* Alter, R. Defenses of the imagination p119-35

Rhagius, Johannes. See Aesticampianus, Johannes Rhagius

Rhäticus, George Joachim

About individual works

De libris revolutionum Nicolai Copernici narratio prima

Wilson, C. A. Rheticus, Ravetz, and the "necessity" of Copernicus' innovation. *In* The Copernican achievement p17-39

Rhees, Rush

Questions on logical inference. *In* Royal Institute of Philosophy. Understanding Wittgenstein p30-48

Rheticus, George Joachim. See Rhäticus, George Joachim

Rheticus, Joachimus. See Rhäticus, George Joachim

Rhetoric

Burke, K. Rhetoric, poetics, and philosophy. *In* Burks, D. M. ed. Rhetoric, philosophy, and literature: an exploration p15-33

Crocker, J. C. The social functions of rhetorical forms. *In* The Social use of metaphor p33-66

Giuliani, A. Vico's rhetorical philosophy and the new rhetoric. *In* Giambattista Vico's science of humanity p31-46

Howell, W. S. Adam Smith's lectures on rhetoric: an historical assessment; excerpt from "Eighteenth-century British logic and rhetoric." *In* Skinner, A. S. and Wilson, T. eds. Essays on Adam Smith p11-43

Howell, W. S. The arts of literary criticism in Renaissance Britain: a comprehensive view. *In* Howell, W. S. Poetics, rhetoric, and logic p73-122

Howell, W. S. Kenneth Burke's "Lexicon rhetoricae": a critical examination. *In* Howell, W. S. Poetics, rhetoric, and logic p234-55

Howell, W. S. Literature as an enterprise in communication. *In* Howell, W. S. Poetics, rhetoric, and logic p215-33

Howell, W. S. Renaissance rhetoric and modern rhetoric: a study in change. *In* Howell, W. S. Poetics, rhetoric, and logic p141-62

Johnstone, H. W. From philosophy to rhetoric and back. *In* Burks, D. M. ed. Rhetoric, philosophy, and literature: an exploration p49-66

Kennedy, W. J. Conclusion. *In* Kennedy, W. J. Rhetorical norms in Renaissance literature p189-91

Kennedy, W. J. The epic genre and varieties of form. *In* Kennedy, W. J. Rhetorical norms in Renaissance literature p128-88

Kennedy, W. J. Introduction: rhetorical criticism and literary theory. *In* Kennedy, W. J. Rhetorical norms in Renaissance literature p1-19

Kennedy, W. J. The Petrarchan mode in lyric poetry. *In* Kennedy, W. J. Rhetorical norms in Renaissance literature p20-78

Kennedy, W. J. The style of ironic discourse. *In* Kennedy, W. J. Rhetorical norms in Renaissance literature p79-127

Natanson, M. A. The arts of indirection. *In* Burks, D. M. ed. Rhetoric, philosophy, and literature: an exploration p35-47

Nichols, M. H. Rhetoric and the humane tradition. *In* Rhetoric: a tradition in transition p178-91

Romilly, J. de. Gorgias and magic. *In* Romilly, J. de. Magic and rhetoric in ancient Greece p 1-22

Romilly, J. de. Logic versus magic: Aristotle and later writers. *In* Romilly, J. de. Magic and rhetoric in ancient Greece p67-88

Romilly, J. de. Plato and conjurers. *In* Romilly, J. de. Magic and rhetoric in ancient Greece p23-43

Romilly, J. de. Rhetoric and the classification of arts in the fourth century B.C. *In* Romilly, J. de. Magic and rhetoric in ancient Greece p45-66

See also Criticism; Debates and debating; Diction; Figures of speech; Irony; Narration (Rhetoric); Persuasion (Rhetoric); Style, Literary

Rhetoric—*Continued*

Philosophy

Bitzer, L. F. The rhetorical situation. *In* Rhetoric: a tradition in transition p247-60

Lanham, R. A. The rhetorical ideal of life. *In* Lanham, R. A. The motives of eloquence p 1-35

Wallace, K. R. Bacon, rhetoric, and ornament of words. *In* Rhetoric: a tradition in transition p49-65

Political aspects

Bitzer, L. F. Rhetoric and public knowledge. *In* Burks, D. M. ed. Rhetoric, philosophy, and literature: an exploration p67-93

Bryant, D. C. Literature and politics. *In* Burks, D. M. ed. Rhetoric, philosophy, and literature: an exploration p95-107

See also Political oratory

Psychological aspects

See Rhetoric and psychology

Study and teaching—History

Altman, J. B. The moral cultivation of ambivalence. *In* Altman, J. B. The Tudor play of mind p31-63

1500-1800

Altman, J. B. The moral cultivation of ambivalence. *In* Altman, J. B. The Tudor play of mind p31-63

Altman, J. B. Propaedeutic for drama: questions as fiction. *In* Altman, J. B. The Tudor play of mind p64-106

Howell, W. S. Poetics, rhetoric and modern rhetoric: a study in change. *In* Howell, W. S. Poetics, rhetoric, and logic p141-62

McGee, M. C. The rhetorical process in eighteenth century England. *In* Rhetoric: a tradition in transition p99-121

Phillips, M. M. From the Ciceronianus to Montaigne. *In* Classical influences on European culture A.D. 1500-1700 p191-97

Trapp, J. B. Rhetoric and the Renaissance. *In* Background to the English Renaissance p90-108

Rhetoric, Ancient

Campbell, J. J. Rhetoric in old English literature: adaptation of classical rhetoric in old English literature. *In* Murphy, J. J. ed. Medieval eloquence p173-97

Keuls, E. Rhetoric and visual aids in Greece and Rome. *In* Havelock, E. A. and Hershbell, J. P. eds. Communication arts in the ancient world p121-34

Trapp, J. B. Rhetoric and the Renaissance. *In* Background to the English Renaissance p90-108

Ward, J. O. The commentator's rhetoric: from antiquity to the Renaissance: glosses and commentaries on Cicero's Rhetorica. *In* Murphy, J. J. ed. Medieval eloquence p25-67

Rhetoric, Medieval

Banker, J. R. The ars dictaminis and rhetorical textbooks at the Bolognese University in the fourteenth century. *In* Medievalia et humanistica no. 5 p153-68

Cave, T. C. Copia and cornucopia. *In* French Renaissance studies, 1540-70 p52-69

Payne, R. O. Rhetoric in Chaucer: Chaucer's realization of himself as rhetor. *In* Murphy, J. J. ed. Medieval eloquence p270-87

Trapp, J. B. Rhetoric and the Renaissance. *In* Background to the English Renaissance p90-108

Rhetoric and psychology

Crocker, J. C. The social functions of rhetorical forms. *In* The Social use of metaphor p33-66

Rhetorica ad Herennium

Gotoff, H. C. The concept of periodicity in the Ad Herennium. *In* Harvard Studies in classical philology v77 p217-23

Rhine, Joseph Banks

Comments on "Science and the supernatural." *In* Ludwig, J. K. ed. Philosophy and parapsychology p178-86

The experiment should fit the hypothesis. *In* Ludwig, J. K. ed. Philosophy and parapsychology p202-04

The science of nonphysical nature. *In* Ludwig, J. K. ed. Philosophy and parapsychology p117-27

About

Ducasse, C. J. The philosophical importance of "psychic phenomena." *In* Wheatley, J. M. O. and Edge, H. L. eds. Philosophical dimensions of parapsychology p30-45

Rhinelander, Laurens Hamilton. See Perlman, H. S. jt. auth.

Rhoads, James Berton

The role of the National Archives. *In* Pattern and process p5-8

Rhodes, Carolyn Hodgson

Tyranny by computer: automated data processing and oppressive government in science fiction. *In* Clareson, T. D. ed. Many futures, many worlds p66-93

Rhodes, Eugene Manlove

About

Dobie, J. F. A salute to Gene Rhodes. *In* Dobie, J. F. Prefaces p48-66

Rhodes, Frank Howard Trevor

Nicholas Copernicus: the gentle revolutionary. *In* Science and society: past, present, and future p377-405

Rhodes, James Ford

Nevins, A. James Ford Rhodes as man and historian. *In* Nevins, A. Allan Nevins on history p393-412

Rhodes, Michael

The earlier sixteenth century. *In* English Association. The year's work in English studies v56 p130-35

The earlier sixteenth century [another essay] *In* English Association. The year's work in English studies v57 p101-07

Rhodesia, Southern. See Zimbabwe

Rhodesia and Nyasaland

Race question

Lessing, D. M. The fruits of humbug. *In* Lessing, D. M. A small personal voice p161-71

Rhyme. See Alliteration; Rhythm

Rhys, Jean

About

Souza, E. de. The expatriate experience. *In* Narasimhaiah, C. D. ed. Awakened conscience p339-45

Rhythm

Middleton, J. C. Notes on rhythm. *In* Middleton, J. C. Bolshevism in art p225-29

Richards, I. A. Rhythm and metre; excerpt from "Principles of literary criticism." *In* Gross, H. S. ed. The structure of verse p68-76

Rhythm—*Continued*

Roethke, T. What do I like? *In* Gross, H. S. ed. The structure of verse p241-55

Stevenson, C. L. The rhythm of English verse. *In* Gross, H. S. ed. The structure of verse p194-224

Weissenberger, K. Poetic rhythm and the exile situation. *In* Strelka, J. P.; Bell, R. F. and Dobson, E. eds. Protest—form—tradition p133-44

Winters, Y. The audible reading of poetry; excerpt from "The function of criticism." *In* Gross, H. S. ed. The structure of verse p129-46

Ribman, Ronald

About individual works

The journey of the fifth horse

Kauffmann, S. The journey of the fifth horse. *In* Kauffmann, S. Persons of the drama p173-75

Ricardo, David

About

Dobb, M. H. Ricardo and Adam Smith. *In* Skinner, A. S. and Wilson, T. eds. Essays on Adam Smith p324-35

Ricardou, Jean

Nouveau roman, Tel Quel. *In* Federman, R. ed. Surfiction p101-33

Writing between the lines. *In* Federman, R. ed. Surfiction p263-77

Riccardi (Firm)

Kaeuper, R. W. The Societas Riccardorum and economic change. *In* Jeffrey, D. L. ed. By things seen: reference and recognition in medieval thought p161-72

Rice, Berkeley

The pull of Sun Moon. *In* Horowitz, I. L. ed. Science, sin, and scholarship p226-41

Rice, David G.

Xenophon, Diodorus and the year 379/378 B.C. Reconstruction and reappraisal. *In* Yale classical studies v24 p95-130

Rice, David Talbot. See Part 2 under title: Studies in memory of David Talbot Rice

Rice, Eugene F.

The De magia naturali of Jacques Lefèvre d'Etaples. *In* Philosophy and humanism p19-29

The humanist idea of Christian antiquity and the impact of Greek patristic work on sixteenth-century thought. *In* Classical influences on European culture A.D. 1500-1700 p199-203

Rice, Lee C.

Spinoza on individuation. *In* Freeman, E. and Mandelbaum, M. H. eds. Spinoza p195-214

Rice, Robert C.

The penitential motif in Cynewulf's Fates of the Apostles and in his epilogues. *In* Anglo-Saxon England 6 p105-19

Rice, Stuart Alan

A private view of teaching science. *In* Buxton, T. H. and Prichard, K. W. eds. Excellence in university teaching p128-31

Rice, Tamara Talbot

Animal combat scenes in Byzantine art. *In* Studies in memory of David Talbot Rice p17-23

Rice, Thomas J.

Barnaby Rudge: a vade mecum for the theme of domestic government in Dickens. *In* Dickens Studies Annual v7 p81-102

Rice

Southern States—History

Hilliard, S. B. Antebellum tidewater rice culture in South Carolina and Georgia. *In* European settlement and development in North America: essays on geographical change in honour and memory of Andrew Hill Clark p91-115

Thailand—Marketing

Moerman, M. Chīangkham's trade in the "old days." *In* Change and persistence in Thai society p151-71

Rich, Adrienne Cecile

On lies, secrets, and silence

Contents

Anne Sexton: 1928-1974

The antifeminist woman

Caryatid: Two columns: Natalya Gorbanevskaya

Caryatid: Two columns: Vietnam and sexual violence

Claiming an education

Conditions for work: the common world of women

Disloyal to civilization: feminism, racism, gynephobia

Husband-right and father-right

"It is the lesbian in us . . ."

Jane Eyre: the temptations of a motherless woman

The meaning of our love for women is what we have constantly to expand

Motherhood in bondage

Motherhood: the contemporary emergency and the quantum leap

Power and danger: works of a common woman

Taking women students seriously

Teaching language in open admissions

The tensions of Anne Bradstreet

Toward a woman-centered university

Also in Women and the power to change p1-46

Vesuvius at home: the power of Emily Dickinson

Also in Gilbert, S. M. and Gubar, S. eds. Shakespeare's sisters p99-121

When we dead awaken: writing as re-vision

Woman observing, preserving, conspiring, surviving: the poems of Eleanor Ross Taylor

Women and honor: some notes on lying

About

Blau Duplessis, R. The critique of consciousness and myth in Levertov, Rich, and Rukeyser. *In* Gilbert, S. M. and Gubar, S. eds. Shakespeare's sisters p280-300

Boyers, R. On Adrienne Rich: intelligence and will. *In* Boyers, R. ed. Contemporary poetry in America p157-73

Also in Boyers, R. Excursions p201-16

Kalstone, D. Adrienne Rich: face to face. *In* Kalstone, D. Five temperaments p129-69

Rich, Arnold Rice

About

Harvey, A. M. Compleat clinician and Renaissance pathologist: Louis Hamman and Arnold R. Rich. *In* Harvey, A. M. Adventures in medical research p139-51

Richard III (Motion picture)

Jorgens, J. J. Laurence Oliver's Richard III. *In* Jorgens, J. J. Shakespeare on film p136-47

Richard of Bury. See Aungerville, Richard, known as Richard de Bury, Bp. of Durham

Richards, Cara Elizabeth
Onondaga women: among the liberated. *In* Matthiasson, C. J. ed. Many sisters p401-19

Richards, Howard
Productive justice. *In* Aiken, W. and La Follette, H. eds. World hunger and moral obligation p165-79

Richards, Ivor Armstrong
Complementarities
Contents
Art and science
Beauty and truth
Belief
Between truth and truth
Complementarities
The conduct of verse
Emotion and art
Emotive language still
The enlightening eye
Gerard Hopkins
The God of Dostoevsky
Herbert Read's English prose style
The instruments of criticism: expression
Jesus' other life
John Watson's Behaviorism
Lawrence as a poet
Literature, oral-aural and optical
The lure of high mountaineering
Max Eastman's The literary mind: its place in an age of science
Meaning and change of meaning
Multiple definition
Nineteen hundred and now
Notes on the practice of interpretation
A passage to Forster
The secret of "feedforward"
Semantics
Poetries
Contents
Coleridge's other poems
The ever-new discovery
"The exstasie"
Factors and functions in linguistics
"The garden"
The interinanimations of words
Linguistics into poetics
Literature for the unlettered
"The phoenix and the turtle"
Poetry as an instrument of research
Poetry as paideia
Powers and limits of signs
Reversals in poetry
Sources of our common aim
The vulnerable poet and the friend
What is belief?
What is saying?
Rhythm and metre; excerpt from "Principles of literary criticism." *In* Gross, H. S. ed. The structure of verse p68-76

About
Hartman, G. I. A. Richards and the dream of communication. *In* Hartman, G. The fate of reading p20-40
Lewis, W. T. S. Eliot and I. A. Richards; excerpt from "Men without art." *In* Lewis, W. Enemy salvoes p184-200
Wimsatt, W. K. I.A.R.: what to say about a poem. *In* Wimsatt, W. K. Day of the leopards p234-49

About individual works
Practical criticism
Eliot, T. S. From The use of poetry and the use of criticism. *In* Eliot, T. S. Selected prose of T. S. Eliot p79-96

Richards, Jack C.
Second language learning. *In* Wardhaugh, R. and Brown, H. D. eds. A survey of applied linguistics p113-37

Richards, James Maude
Towards a rational aesthetic. *In* Sharp, D. ed. The rationalists p130-42
Wells Coates, 1893-1958. *In* Sharp, D. ed. The rationalists p93-99

Richards, Jeffrey
Frank Capra and the cinema of Populism. *In* Nichols, B. ed. Movies and methods p65-77

Richards, Joan L.
The reception of a mathematical theory: non-Euclidean geometry in England, 1868-1883. *In* Barnes, B. and Shapin, S. eds. Natural order p143-66

Richards, Mary Caroline
The vessel and the fire. *In* Evolution of consciousness p211-24

Richards, Robert O.
Urbanization of rural areas. *In* Handbook of contemporary urban life p551-91

Richard's cork-leg (criticism) Behan, B. *In* Brustein, R. S. The culture watch p53-56

Richardson, Dorothy Miller

About
Showalter, E. The female aesthetic. *In* Showalter, E. A literature of their own p240-62

About individual works
Pilgrimage
Kaplan, S. J. Dorothy M. Richardson. *In* Kaplan, S. J. Feminine consciousness in the modern British novel p8-46

Richardson, Edgar Preston
George Washington: the evidence of the portraits. *In* Aspects of American liberty p196-225

Richardson, Emeline Hill
The story of Ariadne in Italy. *In* Studies in classical art and archaeology p189-95

Richardson, Frederick Leopold William
The elusive nature of cooperation and leadership: discovering a primitive process that regulates human behavior. *In* Eddy, E. M. and Partridge, W. L. eds. Applied anthropology in America p87-111

Richardson, George Barclay
Adam Smith on competition and increasing returns. *In* Skinner, A. S. and Wilson, T. eds. Essays on Adam Smith p350-60

Richardson, Harold Edward
Stuart country: the man-artist and the myth. *In* LeMaster, J. R. and Clarke, M. W. eds. Jesse Stuart p 1-18

Richardson, Harry V.
Afro-American religion: The origin and development of the established churches. *In* The Black American reference book p492-506

Richardson, James T.; Stewart, Mary W. and Simmonds, Robert B.
Researching a fundamentalist commune. *In* Needleman, J. and Baker, G. eds. Understanding the new religions p235-51

Richardson, Lawrence

Basilica Fulvia, modo Aemilia. *In* Studies in classical art and archaeology p209-15

Richardson, Robert D.

Myth and literature in the American renaissance

Contents

Emerson
Hawthorne
Melville
Parker and Alcott
Thoreau
The two traditions
Whitman

Richardson, Samuel

About

Rogers, P. Samuel Richardson and Defoe's Tour (1738): the evidence of bibliography. *In* Virginia. University. Bibliographical Society. Studies in bibliography v28 p305-07

Skilton, D. Richardson and Fielding. *In* Skilton, D. The English novel p19-31

Torrance, R. M. Moral rake and masterful lackey. *In* Torrance, R. M. The comic hero p177-205

About individual works
Clarissa Harlowe

Braudy, L. B. Penetration and impenetrability in Clarissa. *In* Harth, J. P. ed. New approaches to eighteenth-century literature p177-206

Cockshut, A. O. J. Richardson and Fielding. *In* Cockshut, A. O. J. Man and woman: a study of love and the novel, 1740-1940 p32-45

Karl, F. R. Samuel Richardson and Clarissa. *In* Karl, F. R. The adversary literature p99-145

MacAndrew, E. Courtly-genteel or moral-didactic?—A response to Carey McIntosh. *In* Studies in eighteenth-century culture v4 p155-59

McIntosh, C. Quantities of qualities: nominal style and the novel. *In* Studies in eighteenth-century culture v4 p139-53

Spacks, P. A. M. Early fiction and the frightened male. *In* Spilka, M. ed. Towards a poetics of fiction p255-65

Traugott, J. Clarissa's Richardson: an essay to find the reader. *In* English literature in the age of disguise p157-208

Van Marter, S. Richardson's revisions of Clarissa in the third and fourth editions. *In* Virginia. University. Bibliographical Society. Studies in bibliography v28 p119-52

Pamela

Jeffrey, D. K. The epistolary format of Pamela and Humphry Clinker. *In* A Provision of human nature p145-54

Karl, F. R. Samuel Richardson and Clarissa. *In* Karl, F. R. The adversary literature p99-145

Lesser, S. O. A note on Pamela. *In* Lesser, S. O. The whispered meanings p14-19

Roussel, R. Reflections on the letter: the reconciliation of distance and presence in Pamela. *In* ELH essays for Earl R. Wasserman p85-109

Spacks, P. A. M. The sense of audience: Samuel Richardson, Colley Cibber. *In* Spacks, P. A. M. Imagining a self p193-226

Sir Charles Grandison

Harris, J. The reviser observed: the last volume of Sir Charles Grandison. *In* Virginia. University. Bibliographical Society. Studies in bibliography v29 p 1-31

Characters—Women

Rogers, K. Richardson's empathy with women. *In* Diamond, A. and Edwards, L. R. eds. The authority of experience p118-36

Influence—Fielding

Eaves, T. C. D. Amelia and Clarissa. *In* A Provision of human nature p95-110

Influence—Friedel

Horwath, P. Richardsonian characters and motifs in Johann Friedel's novel Eleonore. *In* Branscombe, P. ed. Austrian life and literature, 1780-1938 p 1-11

Richardson, Thomas J.

The city of day and the city of night: New Orleans and the exotic unreality of Tennessee Williams. *In* Tennessee Williams: a tribute p631-46

Richer, Henri

About individual works
Fables nouvelles

Noel, T. Theories of the fable: La Motte and Richer. *In* Noel, T. Theories of the fable in the eighteenth century p38-46

Riches. See Wealth

Richetti, John J.

The portrayal of women in Restoration and eighteenth-century English literature. *In* Springer, M. A. ed. What manner of woman p65-97

Richler, Mordecai

About

Ramraj, V. J. Diminishing satire: a study of V. S. Naipaul and Mordecai Richler. *In* Narasimhaiah, C. D. ed. Awakened conscience p261-74

About individual works
St Urbain's horseman

Sale, R. H. Hawkes, Malamud, Richler, Oates. *In* Sale, R. H. On not being good enough p30-42

Richmond, Julius Benjamin

The needs of children. *In* Knowles, J. H. ed. Doing better and feeling worse p247-59

Richmond, Lee John

The education of Vardaman Bundren in Faulkner's As I lay dying. *In* Renaissance and modern p133-42

Richmond, Legh

About

Pickering, S. The Old Curiosity Shop, and Legh Richmond's tracts. *In* Pickering, S. The moral tradition in English fiction, 1785-1850 p107-22

Richmond

Social life and customs—History

MacDonald, E. E. Glasgow, Cabell, and Richmond. *In* Ellen Glasgow p25-45

Richmond, Va. Law and Equity Court. See Law and Equity Court, Richmond, Va.

Richter, Curt Paul

About

Harvey, A. M. More bright stars in the Johns Hopkins galaxy. *In* Harvey, A. M. Adventures in medical research p333-63

Richter, David H.
  Fable's end
    Contents
The achievement of shape in the twentieth-
century fable: Joseph Heller's Catch-22
Allegory versus fable: Golding's Lord of
the flies
Aspects of the eighteenth-century rhetorical
  novel: Johnson's Rasselas and Voltaire's
  Candide
Bellow's Herzog
Conclusions
The failure of completeness: Pynchon's V.
Novel forms of thesis: Camus's The
  stranger
Open form and the fable

Richter, William Louis
  Relative abstention: India & Pakistan. *In*
Higham, R. D. ed. Intervention or abstention: the dilemma of American foreign policy
p202-17

Rickels, Milton
  The imagery of George Washington Harris. *In* Inge, M. T. ed. The frontier humorists p155-69

Rickett, Adele Austin
  Method and intuition: the poetic theories
of Huang, T'ing-chien. *In* Chinese approaches
to literature from Confucius to Liang Ch'i-
ch'ao p97-119

Ricketts, Martin. See Peacock, A. T. jt. auth.

Ricklefs, Merle C.
  Javanese sources in the writing of modern
Javanese history. *In* Southeast Asian history
and historiography p332-44

Ricks, Christopher B.
  Sound and sense in Paradise lost. *In* Royal
Society of Literature of the United Kingdom,
London. Essays by divers hands v39 p92-111
  See also Shannon, E. F. jt. auth.

    About individual works
      Keats and embarrassment
Bayley, J. Another view of the question.
In Bayley, J. The uses of division p145-56

Rickword, Edgell
  William Cobbett's Twopenny trash. *In*
Rebels and their causes p141-49

Ricoeur, Paul
  Image and language in psychoanalysis. *In*
Psychoanalysis and language p293-324
  Phenomenology of freedom. *In* Pivče-
vić, E. ed. Phenomenology and philosoph-
ical understanding p173-94
  Political and social essays
    Contents
Adventures of the state and the task of
Christians
A critique of B. F. Skinner's Beyond free-
dom and dignity
Ethics and culture: Habermas and Gadamer
in dialogue
Faith and culture
From Marxism to contemporary communism
From nation to humanity: task of Christians
Nature and freedom
The project of a social ethic
Socialism today
The tasks of the political educator
Urbanization and secularization
Violence and language
What does humanism mean?
Ye are the salt of the earth

Psychoanalysis and the work of art. *In*
Psychiatry and the humanities v 1 p3-33
  The task of hermeneutics. *In* Murray, M. E. ed. Heidegger and modern philosophy p141-60

Ridderbos, Herman N.
  The earliest confession of the atonement
in Paul. *In* Reconciliation and hope p76-89

Riddle, John M.
  Theory and practice in medieval medicine.
In Viator: medieval and Renaissance studies
v5 p157-84

Riddles
  Frye, N. Charms and riddles. *In* Frye, N.
Spiritus mundi p123-47
  Scott, C. T. On defining the riddle: the
problem of a structural unit. *In* Folklore
genres p77-90

Riddles in literature
  Gorfain, P. Puzzle and artifice: the riddle
as metapoetry in 'Pericles.' *In* Shakespeare
survey v29 p11-20

The ride across Lake Constance (criticism)
  Handke, P. *In* Kauffmann, S. Persons of
the drama p198-201

Rideout, Walter Bates
  Talbot Whittingham and Anderson: a
passage to Winesburg, Ohio. *In* Anderson,
D. D. ed. Sherwood Anderson: dimensions
of his literary art p41-60

Ridgely, Joseph Vincent
  The empty world of Wieland. *In* Baldwin, K. H. and Kirby, D. K. eds. Individual
and community p3-16

Ridgway, Brunildes
  The Ludovisi head. *In* Studies in classical
art and archaeology p153-61

Ridington, Tonia. See Ridington, W. R. jt.
ed.

Ridington, William Robin, and Ridington,
Tonia
  The inner eye of Shamanism and Totem-
ism. *In* Tedlock, D. E. and Tedlock, B. eds.
Teachings from the American earth p190-204

Ridker, Ronald Gene
  Population growth, economic growth and
the environment in the United States. *In*
Economic factors in population growth p324-
51

Ridley, Florence H.
  Gawain Douglas re-catalogued. *In* Review.
v 1 1979 p255-63
  A plea for the Middle Scots. *In* The
Learned and the lewed p175-96

Rieber, Roger A.
  Public information and political leadership
in international organisations: the United
Nations Secretary General. *In* The Year
book of world affairs, 1976 p42-68

Riefenstahl, Leni
    About
Sarris, A. Fascinating fascism meets leering
leftism. *In* Sarris, A. Politics and cinema
p107-15
  Sontag, S. Fascinating fascism. *In*
Nichols, B. ed. Movies and methods p31-43
    About individual works
      The last of the Nuba
Sontag, S. Fascinating fascism. *In*
Nichols, B. ed. Movies and methods p31-43
      Triumph of the will
Taylor, R. Triumph of the will. *In* Tay-
lor, R. Film propaganda p177-89

Rieff, Philip
Freud and the authority of the past; excerpt from "Freud: the mind of the moralist". *In* Explorations in psychohistory p78-108

The triumph of the therapeutic; excerpt. *In* Davis, F. J. and Stivers, R. eds. The collected definition of deviance p392-410

About
Goodheart, E. A postscript to the higher criticism: the case of Philip Rieff. *In* Goodheart, E. The failure of criticism p84-104

Riegel, Klaus F.
Semantic basis of language: language as labor. *In* Riegel, K. F. and Rosenwald, G. C. eds. Structure and transformation p167-92

Structure and transformation in modern intellectual history. *In* Riegel, K. F. and Rosenwald, G. C. eds. Structure and transformation p3-24

Riegel, Oscar Wetherhold
Satellite communication and national power. *In* Gerbner, G. ed. Mass media policies in changing cultures p63-72

Rieger, James
Wordsworth unalarm'd. *In* Wittreich, J. A. ed. Milton and the line of vision p185-208

Riegl, Alois

About individual works
Die spätrömische Kunstindustrie
Harlow, B. Realignment: Alois Riegl's image of late Roman art industry. *In* Glyph 3 p118-36

Riely, John C. and Wimsatt, Wililam Kurtz
A supplement to the portraits of Alexander Pope. *In* Evidence in literary scholarship p123-64

Riemsdijk, Henk van
On the diagnosis of Wh movement. *In* Keyser, S. J. ed. Recent transformational studies in European languages p189-206

Rienzo, Cola di

About
Borchardt, F. L. First contacts with Italy. *In* Hoffmeister, G. ed. The Renaissance and Reformation in Germany p 1-16

Ries, John C. See Eckart, D. R. jt. auth.

Ries, Lawrence R.
Wolf masks
Contents
John Wain: the evasive answer
Literature and violence
Sylvia Plath: the internalized response
Ted Hughes: acceptance and accommodation
Thom Gunn: the retreat from violence

Rieselbach, Leroy N.
After Watergate, what? *In* Rieselbach, L. N. ed. People vs. government: the responsiveness of American institutions p66-118

Riesenberg, Peter N.
Citizenship at law in late medieval Italy. *In* Viator: medieval and Renaissance studies v5 p333-46

Riesman, David, 1909-
Small steps to a larger vision. *In* The Third century p24-32

Some questions about discontinuities in American society. *In* The Uses of controversy in sociology p3-29

About
Featherstone, J. John Dewey and David Riesman: from the lost individual to the lonely crowd. *In* On the making of Americans p3-39

Hughes, E. C. Epilogue. *In* On the making of Americans p315-17

About individual works
Individualism reconsidered
Trilling, L. Two notes on David Riesman. *In* Trilling, L. A gathering of fugitives p91-107

The lonely crowd
Trilling, L. Two notes on David Riesman. *In* Trilling, L. A gathering of fugitives p91-107

Rieti, Italy

Church history
Brentano, R. Localism and longevity: the example of the chapter of Rieti in the thirteenth and fourteenth centuries. *In* Law, church, and society p293-310

Riewald, Jacobus Gerhardus
Max Beerbohm and Oscar Wilde; excerpt from "Sir Max Beerbohm, man and writer". *In* Riewald, J. G. ed. The surprise of excellence p47-64

Riffaterre, Michael
French formalism. *In* The Frontiers of literary criticism p93-119

The reader's perception of narrative: Balzac's Paix du ménage. *In* Valdés, M. J. and Miller, O. J. eds. Interpretation of narrative p28-37

The stylistic approach to literary history. *In* Cohen, R. ed. New directions in literary history p147-64

Rigby, Thomas Harold
Stalinism and the mono-organizational society. *In* Stalinism p53-76

Rigg, A. G. and Wieland, G. R.
A Canterbury classbook of the mid-eleventh century (The 'Cambridge songs' manuscript) *In* Anglo-Saxon England 4 p113-30

Rigg, Diana

About
Brustein, R. S. In defense of repertory theatre. *In* Brustein, R. S. The culture watch p96-102

Riggio, Thomas P.
Uncle Tom reconstructed: a neglected chapter in the history of a book. *In* Zanderland, L. ed. Recycling the past p66-80

Riggs, David
"Plot" and "episode" in early neoclassical criticism. *In* Renaissance drama [1973] p149-75

Righini, Guglielmo
New light on Galileo's lunar observations. *In* Bonelli, M. L. R. and Shea, W. R. eds. Reason, experiment, and mysticism in the scientific revolution p59-76

Righini Bonelli, M. L. See Bonelli, M. L. R.

Right (Political science) See Right and left (Political science)

Right and left (Political science)
DeLeon, D. The future of the radical past. *In* DeLeon, D. The American as anarchist p134-57

Dworkin, R. M. Liberalism. *In* Hampshire, S. ed. Public and private morality p113-43

Ritual—*Continued*

Turner, V. W. Comments and conclusions. In Babcock, B. A. ed. The reversible world p276-96

Weimann, R. The mimus. *In* Weimann, R. Shakespeare and the popular tradition in the theater: studies in the social dimension of dramatic form and function p 1-14

See also Liturgics; Rites and ceremonies; and subheading Liturgy and ritual under church bodies, e.g. Catholic Church. Liturgy and ritual

Ritualism. See Ritual

Riu, Manuel

Banking and society in late medieval and early modern Aragon. *In* The Dawn of modern banking p131-67

The **River** Niger (criticism) Walker, J. A. *In* Kauffmann, S. Persons of the drama p234-36

Rivera, Diego

About

Catlin, S. L. Political iconography in the Diego Rivera frescoes at Cuernavaca, Mexico. *In* Millon, H. A. and Nochlin, L. eds. Art and architecture in the service of politics p194-215

Kozloff, M. The Rivera frescoes of modern industry at the Detroit Institute of Arts: proletarian art under capitalist patronage. *In* Millon, H. A. and Nochlin, L. eds. Art and architecture in the service of politics p216-29

Rivera, Rowena. See De la Garza, R. O. jt. auth.

Rivers, Elias L.

Prolegomena grammatologica: literature as the disembodiment of speech. *In* Hernadi, P. ed. What is literature? p79-88

Rivers

Temperature

See Thermal pollution of rivers, lakes, etc.

New England

Seelye, J. Ecclesiastic drums: Puritan theocrats, despairing of the present generation, reform the past. *In* Seelye, J. Prophetic waters p217-52

Rivers in literature

Seelye, J. By way of Newtown: how Thomas Hooker crossed his Rubicon and started the Pequot War: a Hudibrastic interlude. *In* Seelye, J. Prophetic waters p187-216

Seelye, J. Captain courageous: Captain John Smith, father of us all. *In* Seelye, J. Prophetic waters p57-95

Seelye, J. Divine tobacco: Hakluyt and the Virginia business. *In* Seelye, J. Prophetic waters p23-56

Seelye, J. Epilogue. *In* Seelye, J. Prophetic waters p383-88

Seelye, J. Glorious enterprise: Governor John Winthrop's wonderful wall. *In* Seelye, J. Prophetic waters p131-58

Seelye, J. On His Majesty's service: Robert Beverley, William Byrd, and the Palladian version of American pastoral. *In* Seelye, J. Prophetic waters p341-81

Seelye, J. Prologue. *In* Seelye, J. Prophetic waters p3-7

Seelye, J. Return Alpheus: Taylor, Sewall, Wolcott, and Company: some poetic fabrics from the linsey-woolsey loom. *In* Seelye, J. Prophetic waters p311-39

Riverso, Emanuele

Vico and Wittgenstein. *In* Giambattista Vico's science of humanity p263-73

Rivette, Jacques

About

Monaco, J. Rivette: the process of narrative. *In* Monaco, J. The New Wave p305-33

Truffaut, F. Jacques Rivette: Paris nous appartient. *In* Truffaut, F. The films in my life p320-23

Rivière, Charles Dufresny, sieur de la. See Durfresny, Charles, sieur de la Rivière

Rivière, Jean

Foreign scholarship: French contributions. *In* American literary scholarship, 1975 p473-76

Foreign scholarship: French contributions [another essay] *In* American literary scholarship, 1976 431-34

Rivière, Jean, and others

Foreign contributions. *In* American literary scholarship, 1973 p439-57

Foreign scholarship. *In* American literary scholarship, 1974 p433-58

Rizvi, S. A. A.

Muslim India. *In* Lewis, B. ed. Islam and the Arab world p301-20

Rizzi, Luigi

A restructuring rule in Italian syntax. *In* Keyser, S. J. ed. Recent transformational studies in European languages p113-58

Rizzo, Gino. See Roland, A. jt. auth.

Rizzuto, A.

About

Maddox, J. C. Photography as folk art. *In* One hundred years of photographic history p103-08

Roads, Toll. See Toll roads

Roaf, Michael

A mathematical analysis of the styles of the Perseolis reliefs. *In* Greenhalgh, M. and Megaw, J. V. S. eds. Art in society p133-45

Roazen, Paul

About individual works

Freud and his followers

Gass, W. H. The anatomy of mind. *In* Gass, W. H. The world within the word p208-52

Robb, Kevin W.

Poetic sources of the Greek alphabet: rhythm and abecedarium from Phoenician to Greek. *In* Havelock, E. A. and Hershbell, J. P. eds. Communication arts in the ancient world p23-36

Robbe-Grillet, Alain

About

Vidal, G. French letters: theories of the new novel. *In* Vidal, G. Matters of fact and of fiction p65-88

Wicker, B. Robbe-Grillet and the one-dimensional novel. *In* Wicker, B. The story-shaped world p184-94

Wylie, H. A. Alain Robbe-Grillet: scientific humanist. *In* Garvin, H. R. ed. Makers of the twentieth-century novel p245-52

About individual works

The erasers

Grossvogel, D. I. Robbe-Grillet: structure as mystery (II). *In* Grossvogel, D. I. Mystery and its fiction: from Oedipus to Agatha Christie p165-79

Robertson, Durant Waite, and Huppé, Bernard Felix

About individual works

Piers Plowman and scriptural tradition

Donaldson, E. T. Patristic exegesis in the criticism of medieval literature: the opposition. *In* Wimsatt, W. K. ed. Literary criticism: idea and act p170-88

Robertson, Eleanor

The Rome casket. *In* Studies in memory of David Talbot Rice p11-15

Robertson, James I.

Chaplain William E. Wiatt: soldier of the cloth. *In* Rank and file p113-36

Robertson, James Joseph

The development of the law. *In* Brown, J. M. ed. Scottish society in the fifteenth century p136-52

Robertson, John Henry, 1909-

About individual works

Wavell, scholar and soldier

Kedourie, É. Wavell and Iraq, April-May 1941. *In* Kedourie, É. Arabic political memoirs and other studies p273-82

Robertson, Martin

Two question-marks on the Parthenon. *In* Studies in classical art and archaeology p75-87

Robeson, Paul

About

Cruse, H. The creative and performing arts and the struggle for identity and credibility. *In* Johnson, H. A. ed. Negotiating the mainstream p47-102

Robespierre, Maximilien Marie Isadore de

About

Parry, A. The guillotine athirst. *In* Parry, A. Terrorism: from Robespierre to Arafat p55-66

Parry, A. Robespierre's bloody virtue. *In* Parry, A. Terrorism: from Robespierre to Arafat p39-54

Robin Hood

Aston, T. H. Robin Hood. *In* Peasants, knights and heretics p270-72

Bessinger, J. B. The Gest of Robin Hood revisited. *In* The Learned and the lewed p355-69

Hilton, R. H. The origins of Robin Hood. *In* Peasants, knights and heretics p221-35

Holt, J. C. The origins and audience of the ballads of Robin Hood. *In* Peasants, knights and heretics p236-57

Holt, J. C. Robin Hood: some comments. *In* Peasants, knights and heretics p267-69

Keen, M. H. Robin Hood—peasant or gentleman? *In* Peasants, knights and heretics p258-66

Robins, Lee N.

Alcoholism and labelling theory. *In* Gove, W. R. ed. The labelling of deviance p21-33

Robinson, Ann Elizabeth. See Mowlana, H. jt. auth.

Robinson, Arthur Howard

Mapmaking and map printing: the evolution of a working relationship. *In* Woodward, D. A. ed. Five centuries of map printing p 1-23

Robinson, Austin. See Robinson, Edward Austin Gossage

Robinson, Charles

Academia and the little magazine. *In* Anderson, E. and Kinzie, M. eds. The little magazine in America: a modern documentary history p27-49

Robinson, Charles Mulford

About

Goist, P. D. Planning the American city: Charles Mulford Robinson and John Nolen. *In* Goist, P. D. From Main Street to State Street p121-42

Robinson, Christopher

French literature in the nineteenth century

Contents

Collective values

Conclusion

The idealist revolt

Science, reason and the material world

Subjective reality

Robinson, Denys Kay- See Kay-Robinson, Denys

Robinson, Donald William Broadley, Bp.

The priesthood of Paul in the gospel of hope. *In* Reconciliation and hope p231-45

Robinson, Edward Austin Gossage

A personal view. *In* Keynes, M. ed. Essays on John Maynard Keynes p9-23

Robinson, Edwin Arlington

About

Coxe, L. O. Edwin Arlington Robinson: the lost tradition. *In* Coxe, L. O. Enabling acts p7-26

Cunningham, J. V. Edwin Arlington Robinson: a brief biography. *In* Cunningham, J. V. The collected essays of J. V. Cunningham p375-78

About individual works

The Wandering Jew

Stanford, D. E. Edwin Arlington Robinson's "The Wandering Jew." *In* Tulane Studies in English v23 p95-108

Robinson, Eric

The transference of British technology to Russia, 1760-1820: a preliminary enquiry. *In* Great Britain and her world, 1750-1914 p 1-26

Robinson, Fred C.

Artful ambiguities in the Old English "book-moth" riddle. *In* Anglo-Saxon poetry: essays in appreciation p355-62

Robinson, Guy Schuyler

Nature and necessity. *In* Royal Institute of Philosophy. Impressions of empiricism p200-15

Robinson, Ian

Paper tygers or, The circus animals' desertion in the new pop poetry. *In* Abbs, P. ed. The black rainbow p19-31

Robinson, Ian Stuart

"Periculosus homo": Pope Gregory VII and episcopal authority. *In* Viator: medieval and Renaissance studies v9 p103-31

Robinson, Jacob

About individual works

And the crooked shall be made straight: the Eichmann trial, the Jewish catastrophe and Hannah Arendt's narrative

Arendt, H. "The formidable Dr. Robinson": a reply by Hannah Arendt. *In* Arendt, H. The Jew as pariah: Jewish identity and politics in the modern age p260-76

Robinson, Jacob—About individual works—
And the crooked shall be made straight:
the Eichmann trial, the Jewish catastrophe
and Hannah Arendt's narrative—*Continued*
Laqueur, W. Z. Footnotes to the Holo-
caust. *In* Arendt, H. The Jew as pariah:
Jewish identity and politics in the modern
age p252-59
Laqueur, W. Z. A reply to Hannah
Arendt. *In* Arendt, H. The Jew as pariah:
Jewish identity and politics in the modern
age p277-79
Robinson, James McConkey
Jesus as Sophos and Sophia: wisdom tra-
dition and the Gospels. *In* Aspects of wis-
dom in Judaism and early Christianity p 1-16
Robinson, Joan
What has become of the Keynesian revo-
lution? *In* Keynes, M. ed. Essays on John
Maynard Keynes p123-31
Robinson, K. E.
The eighteenth century. *In* English Asso-
ciation. The year's work in English studies
v55 p322-58
The eighteenth century [another essay] *In*
English Association. The year's work in
English studies v56 p242-76
The eighteenth century [another essay] *In*
English Association. The year's work in
English studies v57 p205-35
See also Oliver, B. jt. auth.
Robinson, Michael J.
American political legitimacy in an era of
electronic journalism: reflections on the eve-
ning news. *In* Television as a social force:
new approaches to TV criticism p97-139
A twentieth-century medium in a nine-
teenth-century legislature: the effects of tele-
vision on the American Congress. *In*
Ornstein, N. J. ed. Congress in change
p240-60
Robinson, P. R.
Self-contained units in composite manu-
scripts of the Anglo-Saxon period. *In* Anglo-
Saxon England 7 p231-38
Robinson, Richard George Frederick. See
Kneale, M. H. jt. auth
Robinson, Thomas More
A Sophist on omniscience, polymathy, and
omnicompetence: Δ.Λ.8.I—I3¹. *In* Illinois
classical studies v2 1977 p125-35
Robison, Wade Lee
David Hume: naturalist and meta-sceptic.
In Livingston, D. W. and King, J. T. eds.
Hume p23-49
Hume's causal skepticism. *In* David Hume
p150-66
Robson, John M.
Our mutual friend: a rhetorical approach
to the first number. *In* Dickens Studies
Annual v3 p198-213
Thoughts on social change and political
accommodation in Victorian Britain. *In* Al-
tholz, J. L. ed. The mind and art of Victor-
ian England p78-93
Robson, William Wallace
A poet's notebook: The use of poetry and
the use of criticism. *In* The Literary crit-
icism of T. S. Eliot p139-59
Rocha, Glauber

About

MacBean, J. R. Vent d'East or Godard
and Rocha at the crossroads. *In* Nichols, B.
ed. Movies and methods p91-106
Roche, Clarissa
Sylvia Plath: vignettes from England. *In*
Butscher. E. ed. Sylvia Plath p81-96

Roche, George Charles
The relevance of Friedrich A. Hayek. *In*
Essays on Hayek p 1-11
Roche, Pete, comp.

About individual works

Love, love, love: the new love poetry

Robinson, I. Paper tygers or, The circus
animals' desertion in the new pop poetry.
In Abbs, P. ed. The black rainbow p19-31
Roche, Regina Maria

About individual works

The children of the abbey

Howells, C. A. Minerva Press fiction,
1796-1819: Regina Maria Roche, The children of the abbey and Mary-Anne Radcliffe,
Manfroné; or, The one-handed monk. *In*
Howells, C. A. Love, mystery, and misery
p80-113
Roche, Thomas P.
Tasso's enchanted woods. *In* Miner, E. R.
ed. Literary uses of typology p49-78
**Rochefoucauld, François VI, duc de la,
prince de Marsillac.** See La Rochefoucauld,
François VI, duc de, prince de Marsillac
Rocher, Guy
The quiet revolution and revolutionary
movements among Quebec French Can-
adians. *In* Perspectives on revolution and
evolution p238-67
Rocher, Rosane
Alien and empathic: the Indian poems of
N. B. Halhed. *In* Kling, B. B. and Pearson,
M. N. eds The age of partnership p215-35
Rochester, John Wilmot, 2d Earl of

About

Farley-Hills, D. John Wilmot, Earl of
Rochester. *In* Farley-Hills, D. The benevo-
lence of laughter: comic poetry of the Commonwealth and Restoration p132-55
Mudrick, M. The offending member. *In*
Mudrick, M. Books are not life but then
what is? p27-38
Ober, W B. The Earl of Rochester and
ejaculatio praecox. *In* Ober, W. B. Boswell's
clap and other essays p233-52
Paulson, R. Rochester: the body politic
and the body private. *In* Martz, L. L. and
Williams, A. L. eds. The author in his
work p103-21
Wilcoxon, R. Rochester's sexual politics.
In Studies in eighteenth-century culture v8
p137-49

About individual works

Satyr against mankind

Farley-Hills, D. Rochester: the major
satires. *In* Farley-Hills, D. The benevolence
of laughter: comic poetry of the Commonwealth and Restoration p156-83

Timon

Farley-Hills, D. Rochester: the major
satires. *In* Farley-Hills, D. The benevolence
of laughter: comic poetry of the Commonwealth and Restoration p156-83

Tunbridge Wells

Farley-Hills, D. Rochester: the major
satires. *In* Farley-Hills, D. The benevolence
of laughter: comic poetry of the Commonwealth and Restoration p156-83

Rock carvings. See Petroglyphs
Rock-crystal. See Quartz

Rocke, Alan J.
Atoms and equivalents: the early development of the chemical atomic theory. *In* Historical studies in the physical sciences v9 p225-63

Rockefeller, Nelson Aldrich
Towards a new relationship. *In* **The New** Atlantic challenge p53-58

Rocks, James Engel
Louis Sullivan's The autobiography of an idea: "spring song" and "autumn reverie." *In* Tulane Studies in English v23 p109-21

Rocky (Motion picture)
Leab, D. J. The blue collar ethnic in Bicentennial America: Rocky. *In* O'Connor, J. E. and Jackson, M. A. eds. American history/American film p257-72

Rococo art. See Art, Rococo

Rococo literature
Brady, P. A sweet disorder: atomistic empiricism and the rococo mode of vision. *In* Studies in eighteenth-century culture v7 p451-61

Rodas, Richard A. Preto- See Preto-Rodas, Richard A.

Roddick, Jacqueline F.
Class structure and class politics in Chile. *In* O'Brien, P. J. ed. Allende's Chile p 1-26

Roderick, Colin Arthur
Lawson the poet. *In* Bards, bohemians, and bookmen p203-17

Roderick, John M.
From "Tarantula Arms" to "Della Robbia blue": the Tennessee William tragicomic transit authority. *In* Tennessee Williams: a tribute p116-25

Rodes, Robert Emmet. See Shaffer, T. L. jt. auth.

Rodgers, Willard Lineus. See Marans, R. W. jt. auth.

Rodgers, William Robert

About individual works
Irish literary portraits
Balakian, N. The charmed circle: the Irish writers. *In* Balakian, N. Critical encounters p219-22

Rodin, Auguste

About
Krauss, R. E. Narrative time: the question of the Gates of hell. *In* Krauss, R. E. Passages in modern sculpture p7-37

Rodino, Peter Wallace
The compact with the people. *In* Warner, S. B. ed. The American experiment p89-100

Rodis-Lewis, Geneviève
Limitations of the mechanical model in the Cartesian conception of the organism. *In* Hooker, M. ed. Descartes p152-70

Rodley, Nigel S.
Monitoring human rights by the U.N. system and nongovernmental organizations. *In* Kommers, D. P. and Loescher, G. D. eds. Human rights and American foreign policy p157-78

Rodríguez, Mario
The impact of the American Revolution on the Spanish-and Portuguese-speaking world. *In* The Impact of the American Revolution abroad p101-25

Rodríguez Cepeda, Enrique
The Spanishness of the eighteenth century. *In* Américo Castro and the meaning of Spanish civilization p223-38

Rodríguez Puértolas, Julio
A comprehensive view of medieval Spain. *In* Américo Castro and the meaning of Spanish civilization p113-34

Roe, Harry V. Stopes- See Stopes-Roe, Harry V.

Roe, John
The later sixteenth century: excluding drama. *In* English Association. The year's work in English studies v54 p200-17
The later sixteenth century: excluding drama [another essay] *In* English Association. The year's work in English studies v55 p248-62
The later sixteenth century, excluding drama [another essay] *In* English Association. The year's work in English studies v56 p182-94
The later sixteenth century: excluding drama [another essay] *In* English Association. The year's work in English studies v57 p154-63

Roeber, A. G.
A New England woman's perspective on Norfolk, Virginia, 1801-1802: excerpts from the diary of Ruth Henshaw Bascom. *In* American Antiquarian Society. Proceedings v88 pt2 p277-328

Roethke, Theodore
What do I like? *In* Gross, H. S. ed. The structure of verse p241-55

About
Eberhart, R. On Theodore Roethke's poetry. *In* Eberhart, R. Of poetry and poets p172-78
Kunitz, S. J. Poet of transformations. *In* Kunitz, S. J. A kind of order, a kind of folly p96-109
Kunitz, S. J. Remembering Roethke. *In* Kunitz, S. J. A kind of order, a kind of folly p77-82
Kunitz, S. J. Roethke: poet of transformations. *In* Boyers, R. ed. Contemporary poetry in America p99-109
Mills, R. J. Theodore Roethke. *In* **Donoghue, D. ed. Seven American poets from MacLeish to Nemerov p92-131**
Snodgrass, W. D. "That anguish of concreteness"—Theodore Roethke's career. *In* Snodgrass, W. D. In radical pursuit p101-16
Thurley, G. Theodore Roethke: Lost son. *In* Thurley, G. The American moment p91-105
Vanderbilt, K. Theodore Roethke as a Northwest poet. *In* Bingham, E. R. and Love, G. A. eds. Northwest perspectives p186-216

About individual works
Collected poems
Boyers, R. A very separate peace: on Roethke. *In* Boyers, R. Excursions p131-38

The far field
Mills, R. J. In the way of becoming: Theodore Roethke's last poems. *In* Mills, R. J. Cry of the human p47-66

In a dark time
Kunitz, S. J. The taste of self. *In* Kunitz, S. J. A kind of order, a kind of folly p87-95

Roethke, Theodore—About individual works
—*Continued*

The lost son (poem)

Thurley, G. Theodore Roethke: Lost son. *In* Thurley, G. The American moment p91-105

The lost son, and other poems

Kunitz, S. J. News of the root. *In* Kunitz, S. J. A kind of order, a kind of folly p83-86

Selected letters of Theodore Roethke

Boyers, R. The Roethke Letters. *In* Boyers, R. Excursions p139-46

Roett, Riordan

Brazil and the inter-American system. *In* Farer, T. J. ed. The future of the inter-American system p235-55

The changing nature of Latin American international relations: geopolitical realities. *In* The Americas in a changing world p95-111

Rogal, Samuel J.

John Wesley on war and peace. *In* Studies in eighteenth-century culture v7 p329-44

The selling of sex: Mandeville's Modest defence of publick stews. *In* Studies in eighteenth-century culture v5 p141-50

Rogel, Carole

The wandering monk and the Balkan national awakening. *In* Nationalism in a non-national state p77-101

Rogers, Carl Ransom

Some new directions: a personal view. *In* Hanna, T. ed. Explorers of humankind p123-35

Rogers, David Elliott

The challenge of primary care. *In* Knowles, J. H. ed. Doing better and feeling worse p81-103

Rogers, Everett M.

Network analysis of the diffusion of innovations: family planning in Korean villages. *In* Lerner, D. and Nelson, L. M. eds. Communication research—a half-century appraisal p117-47

Rogers, Francis Millet

Celestial navigation: from local systems to a global conception. *In* First images of America p687-704

Rogers, Katherine

Anne Finch, Countess of Winchilsea: an Augustan woman poet. *In* Gilbert, S. M. and Gubar, S. eds. Shakespeare's sisters p32-46

Richardson's empathy with women. *In* Diamond, A. and Edwards, L. R. eds. The authority of experience p118-36

Rogers, M. A.

"Dies Österreich ist eine kleine Welt." *In* Branscombe, P. ed. Austrian life and literature, 1780-1938 p72-80

Rogers, Pat

Introduction: the writer and society. *In* Rogers, P. ed. The eighteenth century p1-80

Samuel Richardson and Defoe's Tour (1738): the evidence of bibliography. *In* Virginia. University. Bibliographical Society. Studies in bibliography v28 p305-07

Rogers, Stephen H.

Trade relations in the inter-American system. *In* Farer, T. J. ed. The future of the inter-American system p54-65

Rogers, Will

About

Rollins, P. C. Will Rogers and the relevance of nostalgia: Steamboat 'round the bend. *In* O'Connor, J. E. and Jackson, M. A. eds. American history/American film p77-96

Rogers, William Dill

A note on the future of the inter-American system. *In* Farer, T. J. ed. The future of the inter-American system p20-29

Rogers, Winslow

Thackeray's self-consciousness. *In* The Worlds of Victorian fiction p149-63

Rogger, Hans

Russian ministers and the Jewish question, 1881-1917. *In* California Slavic studies v8 p15-76

The Skobelev phenomenon: the hero and his worship. *In* Oxford Slavonic papers v9, new ser. p46-78

Rogozinski, Jan

Ennoblement by the Crown and social stratification in France, 1285-1322: a prosopographical survey. *In* Order and innovation in the Middle Ages p273-91

Rogues and vagabonds in literature

Lyons, J. O. Rogues and adventures. *In* Lyons, J. O. The invention of the self p75-88

See also Picaresque literature

Roguly, Damir. See Weisband, E. jt. auth.

Rohde, David W. See Fiorina, M. P.; Ornstein, N. J. jt. auths.

Rohdie, Sam

Totems and movies. *In* Nichols, B. ed. Movies and methods p469-81

Rohlehr, Gordon

Blues and rebellion: Edward Brathwaite's Rights of passage. *In* Baugh, E. ed. Critics on Caribbean literature p63-74

The folk in Caribbean literature. *In* Baugh, E. ed. Critics on Caribbean literature p27-30

Samuel Selvon and the language of the people. *In* Baugh, E. ed. Critics on Caribbean literature p153-61

Rohlen, Thomas P.

The promise of adulthood in Japanese spiritualism. *In* Erikson, E. H. ed. Adulthood p129-47

Rohmer, Eric

About

Monaco, J. Rohmer: Moral tales: the art of courtly love. *In* Monaco, J. The New Wave p286-304

About individual works

Chloe in the afternoon

Kauffmann, S. Chloe in the afternoon. *In* Kauffmann, S. Living images p142-45

Claire's knee

Kauffmann, S. Claire's knee. *In* Kauffmann, S. Living images p45-48

La collectionneuse

Kauffmann, S. La collectionneuse. *In* Kauffmann, S. Living images p55-57

Rohrbach, Günter

Why television entertainment, for whom and how? *In* Fischer, H. D. and Melnik, S. R. eds. Entertainment: a cross-cultural examination p299-305

Rohrberger, Mary

The short story: a proposed definition; excerpt from "Hawthorne and the modern short story: a study in genre." *In* May, C. E. ed. Short story theories p80-82

Rohrlich-Leavitt, Ruby; Sykes, Barbara, and Weatherford, Elizabeth

Aboriginal woman: male and female anthropological perspectives. *In* Reiter, R. R. ed. Toward an anthropology of women p110-26

Rohter, Ira S.

A social-learning approach to political socialization. *In* Schwartz, D. C. and Schwartz, S. K. eds. New directions in political socialization p129-62

Ro'i, Yaacov

The Soviet attitude to the existence of Israel. *in* Ro'i, Y. ed. The limits to power p213-31

The Soviet Union and Egypt: the constraints of a power-client relationship. *In* Ro'i, Y. ed. The limits to power p181-212

Rokeach, Milton

About individual works

The three Christs of Ypsilanti

Marcus, S. Madness, literature, and society. *In* Marcus, S. Representations p137-60

Rokkan, Stein

Dimensions of state formation and nation-building: a possible paradigm for research on variations within Europe. *In* Tilly, C. ed. The formation of national states in Western Europe p562-600

Roland, Alan

Toward a reorientation of psychoanalytic literary criticism. *In* Roland, A. ed. Psychoanalysis, creativity, and literature p248-70

Roland, Alan, and Rizzo, Gino

Psychoanalysis in search of Pirandello: six characters and Henry IV. *In* Roland, A. ed. Psychoanalysis, creativity, and literature p323-51

Roland, Mary, pseud. See Lewis, Mary Christianna (Milne)

Rolandus, Magister. See Alexander III, Pope

Role, Social. See Social role

Rolf, Ida Pauline

Structure: a new factor in understanding the human condition. *In* Hanna, T. ed. Explorers of humankind p51-56

Rolfing

Rolf, I. P. Structure: a new factor in understanding the human condition. *In* Hanna, T. ed. Explorers of humankind p51-56

Röling, Bert V. A.

The function of miliary power. *In* Arms control and technological innovation p288-302

Roll, William George

ESP and memory. *In* Wheatley, J. M. O. and Edge, H. L. eds. Philosophical dimensions of parapsychology p154-84

Rollason, D. W.

Lists of saints' resting-places in Anglo-Saxon England. *In* Anglo-Saxon England 7 p61-93

Rolle, Andrew F.

The American Italians: psychological and social adjustments. *In* Studies in Italian American social history p105-17

Rolleston, James L.

The usable future: Franz Werfel's Star of the unborn as exile literature. *In* Strelka, J. P.; Bell, R. F. and Dobson, E. eds. Protest—form—tradition p57-80

Rollin, Roger B.

Milton's "I's": the narrator and the reader in Paradise lost. *In* Renaissance and modern p33-55

Sweet numbers and sour readers: trends and perspectives in Herrick criticism. *In* Rollin, R. B. and Patrick, J. M. eds. "Trust to good verses": Herrick tercentenary essays p3-11

Rollins, Peter C.

Will Rogers and the relevance of nostalgia: Steamboat 'round the bend. *In* O'Connor, J. E. and M. A. eds. American history/American film p77-96

Rollins, Richard M.

Words as social control: Noah Webster and the creation of the American dictionary. *In* Zenderland, L. ed. Recycling the past p50-65

Roma, Emilio L.

The scope of the intentional fallacy. *In* On literary intention p74-86

Roma (Motion picture)

Kauffmann, S. Fellini's Roma. *In* Kauffmann, S. Living images p148-50

Roman, Paul Michael. See Trice, H. M. jt. auth.

Roman architecture. See Architecture, Roman

Roman art. See Art, Roman

Roman bronzes. See Bronzes, Roman

Roman Catholic Church. See Catholic Church

Roman coins. See Coins, Roman

Roman consuls. See Consuls, Roman

Roman d'Eneas. See Eneas (Romance)

Roman de la Rose

Barney, S. A. Adornment: the Romance of the Rose. *In* Barney, S. A. Allegories of history, allegories of love p179-215

David, A. How Marcia lost her skin: a note on Chaucer's mythology. *In* The Learned and the lewed p19-29

Kelly, D. Guillaume de Lorris and imagination in the Roman de la Rose. *In* Kelly, D. Medieval imagination p57-95

Roman de Renart

Torrance, R. M. Renegade vassal. *In* Torrance, R. M. The comic hero p83-110

Roman enamel and enameling. See Enamel and enameling, Roman

Roman jewelry. See Jewelry, Roman

Roman law. See Aliens (Roman law); Civil law

Roman leather work. See Leather work, Roman

Roman legends. See Legends, Roman

Roman literature. See Latin literature

Roman marble sculpture. See Marble sculpture, Roman

Roman medicine. See Medicine, Greek and Roman

Roman mosaics. See Mosaics, Roman

Roman mural painting and decoration. See Mural painting and decoration, Roman

Roman philosophy. See Philosophy, Ancient

Roman pottery. See Pottery, Roman

Roman satire. See Satire, Roman

Roman terra-cottas. See Terra-cottas, Roman

Romance fiction

History and criticism

Hart, F. R. Mitchison and later romancers. *In* Hart, F. R. The Scottish novel p182-97

Hart, F. R. Romance after the Enlightenment. *In* Hart, F. R. The Scottish novel p143-53

Hart, F. R. Stevenson, Munro, and Buchan. *In* Hart, F. R. The Scottish novel p154-81

Romance of the three kingdoms. See San Kuo

Romances

Lenaghan, R. T. The clerk of Venus: Chaucer and medieval romance. *In* The Learned and the lewed p31-43

See also Guy of Warwick (Romance)

History and criticism

Bieler, L. Hagiography and romance in medieval Ireland. *In* Medievalia et humanistica no. 6 p13-24

Cooper, H. Magic that does not work. *In* Medievalia et humanistica no. 7 p131-46

Green, D. H. The pathway to adventure. *In* Viator: medieval and Renaissance studies v8 p145-88

Hanning, R. W. Afterword: the evolution of chivalric romance in the early thirteenth century. *In* Hanning, R. W. The individual in twelfth-century romance p234-42

Hanning, R. W. Critical moments: individuality in chivalric romance. *In* Hanning, R. W. The individual in twelfth-century romance p53-104

Hanning, R. W. The individual and mimesis, II: multiple perspectives on reality. *In* Hanning, R. W. The individual in twelfth-century romance p171-93

Hanning, R. W. Introduction. *In* Hanning, R. W. The individual in twelfth-century romance p 1-16

Hanning, R. W. The romance plot and the crisis of inner awareness. *In* Hanning, R. W. The individual in twelfth-century romance p194-233

Heist, W. W. Irish saints' lives, romance, and cultural history. *In* Medievalia et humanistica no. 6 p25-40

Hornstein, L. H. Medieval romance. *In* Medievalia et humanistica no. 7 p189-94

Lagorio, V. M. The Joseph of Arimathie: English hagiography in transition. *In* Medievalia et humanistica no. 6 p91-101

Legge, M. D. Anglo-Norman hagiography and the romances. *In* Medievalia et humanistica no. 6 p41-49

Influence

Hays, P. L. Malamud's Yiddish-accented medieval stories. *In* The Fiction of Bernard Malamud p87-96

Romances, English

History and criticism

Pearsall, D. A. The English romance in the fifteenth century. *In* English Association. Essays and studies, 1976 p56-83

Romances, French. See Romances

Romances, German

History and criticism

Green, D. H. On damning with faint praise in medieval literature. *In* Viator: medieval and Renaissance studies v6 p117-69

Romances, Greek

History and criticism

Heiserman, A. R. Divine romance. *In* Heiserman, A. R. The novel before the novel p183-219

Romances, Italian

History and criticism

Marinelli, P. V. Redemptive laughter: comedy in the Italian romances. *In* Ruggiers, P. G. ed. Versions of medieval comedy p227-48

Romanesque art. See Art, Romanesque

Romanesque illumination of books and manuscripts. See Illumination of books and manuscripts, Romanesque

Romanesque sculpture. See Sculpture, Romanesque

Romania

Politics and government—1944-

Fischer-Galati, S. A. The Communist takeover of Rumania: a function of Soviet power. *In* Hammond, T. T. ed. The anatomy of Communist takeovers p310-20

Romanian Communist Party. See Communist Party of Romania

Romanian literature

History and criticism

Florescu, R. R. The Devil in Romanian literature and folklore. *In* Disguises of the demonic p69-86

Romano, Giulio. See Giulio Romano

Romano, John, 1908-

American psychiatry: past, present, and future. *In* American psychiatry: past, present, and future p28-44

Romano, John, 1948-

About individual works

Dickens and reality

Dunn, R. J. "Illuminating distortions" and the Dickens critics. *In* Review, v 1 1979 p91-104

Romano, Mary D.

The physically handicapped. *In* Gochros, H. L. and Gochros, J. S. eds. The sexually oppressed p257-67

Romanov, V. Ya. See Gippenreiter, Y. B. jt. auth.

Romans

Mauretania Tingitana

Eadie, J. W. Civitates and clients: Roman frontier policies in Pannonia and Mauretania Tingitana. *In* Miller, D. H. and Steffen, J. O. eds. The frontier p57-80

Pannonia

Eadie, J. W. Civitates and clients: Roman frontier policies in Pannonia and Maurentania Tingitana. *In* Miller, D. H. and Steffen, J. O. eds. The frontier p57-80

Romanticism

Altieri, C. F. Modern and post modern: symbolist and immanentist modes of poetic thought. *In* Altieri, C. F. Enlarging the temple p29-52

Romanticism—*Continued*

Bawcutt, N. W. The revival of Elizabethan drama and the crisis of romantic drama. *In* Davies, R. T. and Beatty, B. G. eds. Literature of the romantic period, 1750-1850 p96-113

Bercovitch, S. Emerson the prophet: romanticism, Puritanism, and auto-Americanbiography. *In* Levin, D. ed. Emerson: prophecy, metamorphosis, and influence p 1-27

Blotner, J. L. Romantic elements in Faulkner. *In* Bornstein, G. ed. Romantic and modern p207-21

Cooke, M. G. The extremes of self and system: volatile self and system in the romantic complex. *In* Cooke, M. G. The romantic will p76-84

Cooke, M. G. The will in English romanticism: Introduction: consciousness and conduct. *In* Cooke, M. G. The romantic will p 1-4

Cooke, M. G. The will in English romanticism: The question of the will. *In* Cooke, M. G. The romantic will p5-29

Davies, R. T. Samuel Johnson, James Boswell, and the romantic. *In* Davies, R. T. and Beatty, B. G. eds. Literature of the romantic period, 1750-1850 p 1-18

Evert, W. H. Coadjutors of oppression: a romantic and modern theory of evil. *In* Bornstein, G. ed. Romantic and modern p29-52

Goldman, M. The ghost of joy: reflections on romanticism and the forms of modern drama. *In* Bornstein, G. ed. Romantic and modern p53-68

Kroeber, K. Experience as history: Shelley's Venice, Turner's Carthage. *In* ELH essays for Earl R. Wasserman p31-49

Litz, A. W. Wallace Stevens' defense of poetry: La poésie pure, the new romantic, and the pressure of reality. *In* Bornstein, G. ed. Romantic and modern p111-32

Nicoll, A. French romanticism and classicism. *In* Nicoll, A. World drama p154-60

Nicoll, A. The realm of fancy. *In* Nicoll, A. World drama p387-405

Parker, P. A. Introduction. *In* Parker, P. A. Inescapable romance p3-15

Peckham, M. Rebellion and deviance. *In* Peckham, M. Romanticism and behavior p67-89

Peckham, M. Browning and romanticism. *In* Armstrong, I. ed. Robert Browning p47-76

Peckham, M. Romanticism and behavior. *In* Peckham, M. Romanticism and behavior p3-31

Reilly, R. J. A note on Barfield, romanticism, and time. *In* Evolution of consciousness p183-90

Skilton, D. Gothic, romantic and heroic. *In* Skilton, D. The English novel p59-79

Slonim, M. L. Soviet romantics: from Grin, Paustovsky, and Olesha to Tikhonov and Bagritsky. *In* Slonim, M. L. Soviet Russian literature p116-33

Smith, A. J. M. Nonsense poetry and romanticism. *In* Essays in honor of Russel B. Nye p180-94

Yamanouchi, H. From romanticism to naturalism: Kitamura Tōkoku and Shimazaki Tōson. *In* Yamanouchi, H. The search for authenticity in modern Japanese literature p20-39

See also Gothic revival (Literature); Realism in literature

England

Albrecht, W. P. The sublime of vision. *In* Albrecht, W. P. The sublime pleasures of tragedy p97-114

Allott, K. Victorian poetry and the legacy of romanticism. *In* Davies, R. T. and Beatty, B. G. eds. Literature of the romantic period, 1750-1850 p181-206

Bornstein, G. Yeats and the greater romantic lyric. *In* Bornstein, G. ed. Romantic and modern p91-110

Brisman, L. Introduction. *In* Brisman, L. Romantic origins p11-20

Cooke, M. G. The will in English romanticism: The will in romantic poetry. *In* Cooke, M. G. The romantic will p29-51

Cooke, M. G. The will to art. *In* Cooke, M. G. The romantic will p145-50

Cooke, M. G. The will to art: Conclusion. *In* Cooke, M. G. The romantic will p216-22

Cooke, M. G. The will to art: Excursus: the will to art in romanticism. *In* Cooke, M. G. The romantic will p182-87

Heffernan, J. A. W. The English romantic perception of color. *In* Kroeber, K. and Walling, W. eds. Images of romanticism p133-48

Sperry, S. M. Toward a definition of romantic irony in English literature. *In* Bornstein, G. ed. Romantic and modern p3-28

Storch, R. F. Abstract idealism in English romantic poetry and painting. *In* Kroeber, K. and Walling, W. eds. Images of romanticism p189-209

Taylor, A. An eighteenth-century metaphor. *In* Taylor, A. Magic and English romanticism p15-37

England—Bibliography

Dodd, P.; Lincoln, A. and Watson, J. R. The nineteenth century; romantic period. *In* English Association. The year's work in English studies v57 p236-61

Europe

Smith, A. D. Neo-classicist and romantic elements in the emergence of nationalist conceptions. *In* Smith, A. D. ed. Nationalist movements p74-87

France

Sayre, R. F. Modern times. *In* Sayre, R. F. Solitude in society p56-87

Germany

Tal, U. Young German intellectuals on romanticism and Judaism—spiritual turbulence in the early 19th century. *In* Salo Wittmayer Baron v2 p919-38

Germany—Influence

Berlin, Sir I. A remarkable decade: German romanticism in Petersburg and Moscow. *In* Berlin, Sir I. Russian thinkers p136-49

Russia

Berlin, Sir I. A remarkable decade: German romanticism in Petersburg and Moscow. *In* Berlin, Sir I. Russian thinkers p136-49

Romanticism in art

Kroeber, K. Experience as history: Shelley's Venice, Turner's Carthage. *In* ELH essays for Earl R. Wasserman p31-49

Rosenblum, R. Other romantic currents: Klee to Ernst; excerpt from "Modern painting and the northern romantic tradition, Friedrich to Rothko." *In* Kaplan, P. and Manso, S. eds. Major European art movements, 1900-1945 p91-100

Romanticism in art—*Continued*

Wennberg, B. G. On romanticism. *In* Wennberg, B. G. French and Scandinavian sculpture in the nineteenth century p54-90

Exhibitions

Berger, J. Romantic notebooks. *In* Berger, J. The look of things p97-102

England—History

Heffernan, J. A. W. The English romantic perception of color. In Kroeber, K. and Walling, W. eds. Images of romanticism p133-48

Kroeber, K. Romantic historicism: the temporal sublime. *In* Kroeber, K. and Walling, W. eds. Images of romanticism p149-65

Storch, R. F. Abstract idealism in English romantic poetry and painting. *In* Kroeber, K. and Walling, W. eds. Images of romanticism p189-209

Romanticism in literature. See Romanticism

Romanticism in music

Dent, E. J. Beethoven and Schubert. *In* Dent, E. J. The rise of romantic opera p125-44

Dent, E. J. Conclusion. *In* Dent, E. J. The rise of romantic opera p176-89

Dent, E. J. The conventions of opera. *In* Dent, E. J. The rise of romantic opera p17-32

Dent, E. J. The heritage of Gluck. *In* Dent, E. J. The rise of romantic opera p33-46

Dent, E. J. Introduction. *In* Dent, E. J. The rise of romantic opera p 1-16

Dent, E. J. Rossini. *In* Dent, E. J. The rise of romantic opera p110-24

Dent, E. J. The school of Paris—I. *In* Dent, E. J. The rise of romantic opera p47-63

Dent, E. J. The school of Paris—II. *In* Dent, E. J. The rise of romantic opera p64-79

Dent, E. J. The school of Paris—III. *In* Dent, E. J. The rise of romantic opera p80-94

Romanucci-Ross, Lola

Italian ethnic identity and its transformations. *In* Ethnic identity p198-226

See also De Vos, G. jt. auth.

Romasco, Albert U.

Hoover-Roosevelt and the Great Depression: a historiographic inquiry into a perennial comparison. *In* Braeman, J.; Bremner, R. H. and Brody, D. eds. The New Deal v 1 p3-26

Rome

Civilization—Egyptian influences

Koenen, L. Egyptian influence in Tibullus. *In* Illinois classical studies, v 1 1976 p127-59

Economic conditions

Hopkins, K. Economic growth and towns in classical antiquity. *In* Towns in societies p35-77

Foreign relations—Spain

Sumner, G. V. Roman policy in Spain before the Hannibalic War. *In* Harvard Studies in classical philology v72 p205-46

Frontier troubles

Burns, T. S. The Alpine frontiers and early medieval Italy to the middle of the seventh century. *In* The Frontier v2 p51-68

Genealogy

Jones, C. P. Julius Naso and Julius Secundus. *In* Harvard Studies in classical philology v72 p279-88

Jones, C. P. A leading family of Roman Thespiae. *In* Harvard Studies in classical philology v74 p223-55

Weinrib, E. J. The family connections of M. Livius Drusus Libo. *In* Harvard Studies in classical philology v72 p247-78

Wiseman, T. P. Pulcher Claudius. *In* Harvard Studies in classical philology v74 p207-21

Historiography

Downs, R. B. Sense of the past. *In* Downs, R. B. Books that changed the world p121-50

Momigliano, A. Did Fabius Pictor lie? *In* Momigliano, A. Essays on ancient and modern historiography p99-105

History

Walbank, F. W. Nationality as a factor in Roman history. *In* Harvard Studies in classical philology v76 p145-68

History—Chronology

Barnes, T. D. Constans and Gratian in Rome. *In* Harvard Studies in classical philology v79 p325-33

Barnes, T. D. Origen, Aquila, and Eusebius. *In* Harvard Studies in classical philology v74 p313-16

Bowersock, G. W. The proconsulate of Albus. *In* Harvard Studies in classical philology v72 p289-94

History—To 510 B.C.—Historiography

Mitchell, R. E. Roman coins as historical evidence: the Trojan legends of Rome. *In* Illinois classical studies, v 1 1976 p65-85

History—Republic, 265-30 B.C.

Gabba, E. The Perusine War and triumviral Italy. *In* Harvard Studies in classical philology v75 p139-60

Oliver, R. P. Tacitean nobilitas. *In* Illinois classical studies v3, 1978 p238-61

History—Republic, 265-30 B.C. —Historiography

Momigliano, A. The historian's skin. *In* Momigliano, A. Essays in ancient and modern historiography p67-77

History—30 B.C.-284 A.D.

Syme, Sir R. Pliny the procurator. *In* Harvard Studies in classical philology v73 p201-36

History—30 B.C.-284 A.D. —Historiography

Swan, M. The consular fasti of 23 B.C. and the conspiracy of Varro Murena. *In* Harvard Studies in classical philology v71 p235-47

History—Nero, 54-68

Bradley, K. R. Nero's retinue in Greece, A.D. 66/67. *In* Illinois classical studies v4, 1979 p152-57

History—284-476

Ladner, G. B. On Roman attitudes toward barbarians in late antiquity. *In* Viator: medieval and Renaissance studies v7 p 1-26

Momigliano, A. Popular religious beliefs and the late Roman historians. *In* Momigliano, A. Essays in ancient and modern historiography p141-59

Rome—*Continued*

History—284-476
—Historiography
Momigliano, A. The lonely historian Ammianus Marcellinus. *In* Momigliano, A. Essays in ancient and modern historiography p127-40

Nobility
Oliver, R. P. Tacitean nobilitas. *In* Illinois classical studies v3, 1978 p238-61

Officials and employees
Syme, Sir R. Pliny the procurator. *In* Harvard Studies in classical philology v73 p201-36

Politics and government
Gruen, E. S. Cicero and Licinius Calvus. *In* Harvard Studies in classical philology v71 p215-33

Linderski, J. The aedileship of Favonius, Curio the Younger and Cicero's election to the augurate. *In* Harvard Studies in classical philology v76 p181-200

Politics and government— 265-30 B.C.
Yavetz, Z. Existimatio, fama, and the ides of March. *In* Harvard Studies in classical philology v78 p35-65

Politics and government—284-476
Cameron, A. Theodosius the Great and the regency of Stilico. *In* Harvard Studies in classical philology v73 p247-80

Provinces
Burns, T. S. The Alpine frontiers and early medieval Italy to the middle of the seventh century. *In* The Frontier v2 p51-68

Cooter, W. S. Preindustrial frontiers and interaction spheres: prolegomenon to a study of Roman frontier regions. *In* Miller, D. H. and Steffen, J. O. eds. The frontier p81-107

Provinces—Administration
Eadie, J. W. Civitates and clients: Roman frontier policies in Pannonia and Mauretania Tingitana. *In* Miller, D. H. and Steffen, J. O. eds. The frontier p57-80

Syme, Sir R. Pliny the procurator. *In* Harvard Studies in classical philology v73 p201-36

Relations (general) with Germanic tribes
Miller, D. H. and Savage, W. W. Ethnic stereotypes and the frontier: a comparative study of Roman and American experience. *In* Miller, D. H. and Steffen, J. O. eds. The frontier p109-37

Religion
Fishwick, D. Flamen Augustorum. *In* Harvard Studies in classical philology v74 p299-312

Wilhelmsen, F. D. and Kendall, W. Cicero and the politics of the public orthodoxy. *In* A Public philosophy reader p112-41

Social conditions
Brown, P. D. Gibbon's views on culture and society in the fifth and sixth centuries. *In* Edward Gibbon and The decline and fall of the Roman Empire p37-52

Rome (City)
Social conditions
Revel, J. A capital city's privileges: food supplies in early-modern Rome. *In* Food and drink in history p37-49

Rome (City) Basilica Aemilia
Richardson, L. Basilica Fulvia, modo Aemilia. *In* Studies in classical art and archaeology p209-15

Rome (City) Basilica Fulvia. See Rome (City) Basilica Aemilia

Rome (City) Basilica Paulli. See Rome (City) Basilica Aemilia

Rome (City) Mausoleum of Augustus
Kostof, S. K. The Emperor and the Duce: the planning of Piazzale Augusto Imperatore in Rome. *In* Millon, H. A. and Nochlin, L. eds. Art and architecture in the service of politics p270-325

Rome (City) Palazzo delle Finanze
Schroeter, E. Rome's first national state architecture: the Palazzo delle Finanze. *In* Millon, H. A. and Nochlin, L. eds. Art and architecture in the service of politics p128-49

Rome (City) Piazzale Augusto Imperatore
Kostof, S. K. The Emperor and the Duce: the planning of Piazzale Augusto Imperatore in Rome. *in* Millon, H. A. and Nochlin, L. eds. Art and architecture in the service of politics p270-325

Rome (City) San Girolamo della Carità (Church)
Varriano, J. L. Domenico Castelli's façade for San Girolamo della Carità in Rome. *In* Enggass, R. C. and Stokstad, M. eds. Hortus imaginum p139-45

Rome (City) Santa Maria Maggiore (Church)
Kitzinger, E. The role of miniature painting in mural decoration. *In* The Place of book illumination in Byzantine art p99-142

Snyder, J. E. The mosaic in Santa Maria Nova and the original apse decoration of Santa Maria Maggiore. *In* Enggass, R. C. and Stokstad, M. eds. Hortus imaginum p 1-9

Rome (City) Santa Maria Nova (Church)
Snyder, J. E. The mosaic in Santa Maria Nova and the original apse decoration of Santa Maria Maggiore. *In* Enggass, R. C. and Stokstad, M. eds. Hortus imaginum p 1-9

Rome in literature
Hunter, G. K. A Roman thought: Renaissance attitudes to history exemplified in Shakespeare and Jonson. *In* An English miscellany p93-118

Velz, J. W. The ancient world in Shakespeare: authenticity or anachronism? A retrospect. *In* Shakespeare survey v31 p 1-12

Romeo, Rosario
The Jesuit sources and the Italian political Utopia in the second half of the sixteenth century. *In* First images of America p165-84

Romeo and Juliet (Motion picture)
Jorgens, J. J. Franco Zeffirelli's Romeo and Juliet. *In* Jorgens, J. J. Shakespeare on film p79-91

Romero, Laurence
Molière's morale: debates in criticism. *In* Johnson, R. B.; Neumann, E. S. and Trail, G. T. eds. Molière and the commonwealth of letters: patrimony and posterity p706-27

Romilly, Jacqueline de
Magic and rhetoric in ancient Greece
Contents
Gorgias and magic
Logic versus magic: Aristotle and later writers
Plato and conjurers
Rhetoric and the classification of arts in the fourth century B.C.

Romney, George

Influence
Hagstrum, J. H. Romney and Blake: gifts of grace and terror. *In* Essick, R. N. and Pearce, D. R. eds. Blake in his time p201-12

Romney, George Wilcken
The greatest threats to our society. *In* Prochnow, H. V. ed. Dilemmas facing the nation p153-65

Romónum. *See* Truk Islands

Ronall, Joachim O.
The energy crisis and its potential effects upon American policy. *In* The New world balance and peace in the Middle East: reality or mirage? p119-24

Ronan, William John
The new dimensions of management. *In* Benton, L. R. ed. Management for the future p247-56

Ronfeldt, David F.
Future U.S. security assistance in the Latin American context. *In* The Americas in a changing world p156-72

Ronsard, Pierre de

About
Silver, I. Ronsard on the marriage of poetry, music, and the dance. *In* Studies in the continental background of Renaissance English literature: essays presented to John L. Lievsay p155-69
Wiley, W. L. Mary, Queen of Scots, in France. *In* Studies in the continental background of Renaissance English literature: essays presented to John L. Lievsay p133-54

About individual works
Les amours
Kennedy, W. J. The Petrarchan mode in lyric poetry. *In* Kennedy, W. J. Rhetorical norms in Renaisssance literature p20-78

Appreciation—England
Prescott, A. L. Ronsard. *In* Prescott, A. L. French poets and the English Renaissance p76-131

Influence
Prescott, A. L. Ronsard. *In* Prescott, A. L. French poets and the English Renaissance p76-131

Rood, Harold William. See Haley, P. E. jt. auth.

Rood, Karen Lane
Robert Frost's "sentence sounds": wildness opposing the sonnet form. *In* Frost: centennial essays II p196-210

Roofs. See Domes

Rooney, William Joseph
"The canonization"—the language of pardox reconsidered. *In* Roberts, J. R. ed. Essential articles for the study of John Donne's poetry p271-78

Roopnaraine, R. Rupert
Time and the circle in Little Dorrit. *In* Dickens Studies Annual v3 p54-76

Roosevelt, Franklin Delano, President U.S.

About
Corwin, E. S. President and Court: a crucial issue. *In* Corwin, E. S. Presidential power and the Constitution p63-71
Corwin, E. S. The war and the Constitution: President and Congress. *In* Corwin, E. S. Presidential power and the Constitution p112-20
Romasco, A. U. Hoover-Roosevelt and the Great Depression: a historiographic inquiry into a perennial comparison. *In* Braeman, J.; Bremner, R. H. and Brody, D. eds. The New Deal v 1 p3-26
Siracusa, J. M. FDR, Truman, and Indochina, 1941-1952: the forgotten years. *In* Siracusa, J. M. and Barclay, G. S. eds. The impact of the Cold war p163-83

Roosevelt, Theodore, President U.S.

About
Davis, G. Theodore Roosevelt and the Progressive Era: a study in individual and group psychohistory. *In* DeMause, L. ed. The new psychohistory p245-305
Grantham, D. W. Dinner at the White House: Theodore Roosevelt, Booker T. Washington, and the South. *In* Grantham, D. W. The regional imagination p33-52

Roosters in literature
Steadman, J. M. "The nun's priest's tale": Chauntecleer and medieval natural history. *In* Steadman, J. M. Nature into myth p86-94

Root, Robert Kilburn

About individual works
The poetical career of Alexander Pope
Olson, E. Rhetoric and the appreciation of Pope. *In* Olson, E. On value judgments in the arts, and other essays p15-35

Rooth, Signe Alice
Fredrika Bremer. *In* Abroad in America: Visitors to the new Nation, 1776-1914 p114-23

Roover, Raymond Adrien de. See De Roover, Raymond Adrien

Roper, Alan
Characteristics of Dryden's prose. *In* ELH essays for Earl R. Wasserman p375-99

Roper, Hugh Redwald Trevor- See Trevor-Roper, Hugh Redwald

Roppolo, Joseph Patrick
Undercurrents in Poe's "The fall of the House of Usher." *In* Tulane Studies in English v23 p 1-16

Rorty, Amélie Oksenberg
Dilemmas of academic and intellectual freedom. *In* The Concept of academic freedom p97-110
A literary postscript: Characters, persons, selves, individuals. *In* Rorty, A. O. ed. The identities of persons p301-23
Some comments on Sartorius's paper on tenure. *In* The Concept of academic freedom p180-83

Rorty, Richard
Dewey's metaphysics. *In* Cahn, S. M. ed. New studies in the philosophy of John Dewey p45-74
Overcoming the tradition: Heidegger and Dewey. *In* Murray, M. E. ed. Heidegger and modern philosophy p239-58

Rosa, João Guimarães

About individual works

The devil to pay in the backlands

MacAdam, A. J. João Guimarães Rosa: honneur des hommes. *In* MacAdam, A. J. Modern Latin American narratives p69-77

Rosa, Mario

The Italian churches. *In* Callahan, W. J. and Higgs, D. eds. Church and society in Catholic Europe of the eighteenth century p66-76

Rosa, Ralph Charles la. See La Rosa, Ralph Charles

Rosador, Kurt Tetzeli von

Myth and Victorian melodrama. *In* English Association. Essays and studies, 1979 p97-114

Rosaldo, Renato Ignacio

The rhetoric of control: Ilongots viewed as natural bandits and wild Indians. *In* Babcock, B. A. ed. The reversible world p240-57

The story of Tukbaw: 'they listen as he orates.' *In* Reynolds, F. E. and Capps, D. eds. The biographical process p121-51

Rosán, Laurence J.

Philosophies of homophobia and homophilia. *In* Crew, L. ed. The gay academic p255-81

Rosberg, Gerald Mark

Legal regulation of the migration process: the "crisis" of illegal immigration. *In* Human migration p336-76

The protection of aliens from discriminatory treatment by the national government. *In* The Supreme Court review, 1977 p275-339

Rosbottom, Ronald C.

A matter of competence: the relationship between reading and novel-making in eighteenth-century France. *In* Studies in eighteenth-century culture v6 p245-63

Rose, Alan Henry

Demonic vision

Contents

Blackness in the fantastic world of old Southwestern humor

Demonic vision and the conventions of antebellum Southern fiction

The limits of humanity in the fiction of William Faulkner

"A plan to wake the devil": race and aesthetics in the tales of George Washington Harris

"A prisoner of style": the uses of art in Huckleberry Finn and Pudd'nhead Wilson

Recent American writings: the leveling of racial vision

Tom Sawyer: the making of a safe world

Rose, Edward J.

The "Gothicized imagination" of "Michelangelo Blake." *In* Essick, R. N. and Pearce, D. R. eds. Blake in his time p155-69

Rose, Marilyn Gaddis

Jack B. Yeats's picture of the peasant. *In* Casey, D. J. and Rhodes, R. E. eds. Views of the Irish peasantry, 1800-1916 p192-202

Rose, Mark

Hamlet. *In* Seidel, M. A. and Mendelson, E. eds. Homer to Brecht p238-54

Rose, Peter Wires

The myth of Pindar's First Nemean: sportsmen, poetry, and paideia. *In* Harvard Studies in classical philology v78 p145-75

Sophocles' Philoctetes and the teachings of the Sophists. *In* Harvard Studies in classical philology v80 p49-105

Rose, Steven Peter Russell

Scientific racism and ideology. *In* Racial variation in man p191-210

Rose, Willie Lee Nichols

Jubilee & beyond: what was freedom? *In* What was freedom's price? p3-20

Rosecrance, Richard N.

American influence in world politics. *In* Rosecrance, R. N. ed. America as an ordinary country p224-44

International interdependence. *In* New dimensions of world politics p20-35

New directions? *In* Rosecrance, R. N. ed. America as an ordinary country p245-66

The Pax Britannica and British foreign policy. *In* Kramnick, I. ed. Is Britain dying? p215-30

Rosen, Charles

About individual works

Arnold Schoenberg

Craft, R. Towards Schoenberg. *In* Craft, R. Current convictions p195-210

Rosen, Edward

The impact of Copernicus on man's conception of his place in the world. *In* Science and society: past, present, and future p52-67

Kepler's mastery of Greek. *In* Philosophy and humanism p310-19

Rosen, George, 1910-

A slaughter of innocents: aspects of child health in the eighteenth-century city. *In* Studies in eighteenth-century culture v5 p293-316

Rosen, George, 1920-

An analgesic strategy. *In* Lauer, R. H. ed. Social movements and social change p97-106

Rosen, Lawrence

The negotiation of reality: male-female relations in Sefrou, Morocco. *in* Beck, L. and Keddie, N. R. eds. Women in the Muslim world p561-84

Rosen, Paul M. See Delfini, L. F. jt. auth.

Rosen, Robert C.

Anatomy of a junkie movie. *In* Peary, G. and Shatzkin, R. eds. The modern American novel and the movies p189-98

Rosen, Stanley

Thinking about nothing. *In* Murray, M. E. ed. Heidegger and modern philosophy p116-37

Rosen, Steven J. and Frank, Robert

Measures against international terrorism. *In* International terrorism and world security p60-68

Rosenau, James N.

Decision-making approaches and theories. *In* Encyclopedia of American foreign policy p219-28

Rosenau, Norah

The sources of children's political concepts: an application of Piaget's theory. *In* Schwartz, D. C. and Schwartz, S. K. eds. New directions in political socialization p163-87

Rosenberg, Bruce A.

The psychology of the spiritual sermon. *In* Zaretsky, I. I. and Leone, M. P. eds. Religious movements in contemporary America p135-49

Rosenberg, Charles E.

And heal the sick: hospital and patient in 19th century America. *In* Branca, P. ed. The medicine show p121-40

The crisis in psychiatric legitimacy: reflections on psychiatry, medicine, and public policy. *In* American psychiatry: past, present, and future p135-48

Introduction: History and experience. *In* Rosenberg, C. E. ed. The family in history p 1-11

Toward an ecology of knowledge: on discipline, context, and history. *In* Oleson, A. and Voss, J. eds. The organization of knowledge in modern America, 1860-1920 p440-55

Rosenberg, Edgar

A preface to Great expectations: the Pale Usher dusts his lexicons. *In* Dickens Studies Annual v2 p294-335

Rosenberg, Harold

Art on the edge

Contents

Adding up: the reign of the art market
Art and the crowd
Collage: philosophy of put-togethers
Criticism and its premises
The cubist epoch
Dubuffet: shockers and fairy tales
Duchamp: private and public
Futurism
Giacometti: reality at cockcrow
Joan Mitchell: artist against background
Lester Johnson's abstract men
Miró
Mondrian: meaning in abstract art I
Newman: meaning in abstract art II
The old age of modernism
Olitski, Kelly, Hamilton: dogma and talent
On the edge: Documenta 5
The peaceable kingdom: American folk art
Place patriotism and the New York mainstream
The profession of art: the W.P.A. Art Project
Reality again: the new photorealism
Reginald Marsh: decline and fall
Shall these bones live?: art movement ghosts
Steinberg: self and style
Thoughts in off-season
Trials of Eros
Warhol: art's other self
What's new: ritual revolution

Reality again. *In* Battcock, G. ed. Super realism p135-42

About individual works
The de-definition of art

Trilling, L. Art, will, and necessity. *In* Trilling, L. The last decade p129-47

Rosenberg, Isaac
About

Howe, I. The poetry of Isaac Rosenberg. *In* Howe, I. Celebrations and attacks p195-201

Rosenberg, Nathan

Adam Smith on profits—paradox lost and regained. *In* Skinner, A. S. and Wilson, T. eds. Essays on Adam Smith p377-89

Technology, economy, and values. *In* Bugliarello, G. and Doner, D. B. eds. The history and philosophy of technology p81-111

Rosenblatt, Louise Michelle

Towards a transactional theory of reading. *In* Primeau, R. ed. Influx p121-36

Rosenblum, Dolores

Christina Rossetti: the inward pose. *In* Gilbert, S. M. and Gubar, S. eds. Shakespeare's sisters p82-98

Rosenblum, Mort

The Western wire services and the Third World. *In* Horton, P. C. ed. The Third World and press freedom p104-26

Rosenblum, Robert

Other romantic currents: Klee to Ernst; excerpt from "Modern painting and the northern romantic tradition, Friedrich to Rothko." *In* Kaplan, P. and Manso, S. eds. Major European art movements, 1900-1945 p91-100

Rosenfeld, Alvin Hirsch

The problematics of Holocaust literature. *In* Rosenfeld, A. H. and Greenberg, I. eds. Confronting the Holocaust p 1-30

Rosenfeld, Gerry

Urban education: the Establishment's last stand. *In* Social forces and schooling p282-309

Rosenfeld, Myra Nan

The Royal Building Administration in France from Charles V to Louis XIV. *In* Kostof, S. ed. The architect p161-79

Rosenfeld, Paul
About

Paul, S. Paul Rosenfeld. *In* Paul, S. Repossessing and renewing p71-110

Rosenfield, Leonora Davidson (Cohen)

The rights of women in the French Revolution. *In* Studies in eighteenth-century culture v7 p117-37

Rosengren, Karl Erik

International news: time and type of report. *In* Fischer, H. D. and Merrill, J. C. eds. International and intercultural communication p251-56

Rosenhan, David Leonard

Moral character. *In* Stanford legal essays p401-11

Rosenhan, Mollie Schwartz

Images of male and female in children's readers. *In* Women in Russia p293-305

Rosenkrantz, Barbara Gutmann

Early American learned societies as informants on our past: some conclusions and suggestions for further research. *In* Oleson, A. and Brown, S. C. eds. The pursuit of knowledge in the early American Republic p345-53

Rosenkrantz, Barbara Gutmann, and Vinovskis, Maris A.

The invisible lunatics: old age and insanity in mid-nineteenth-century Massachusetts. *In* Spicker, S. F.; Woodward, K. M. and Van Tassel, D. D. eds. Aging and the elderly p95-125

Rosenmayr, Hilde, and Rosenmayr, Leopold

The social plasticity of youth. *In* Adolescence and youth in prospect p95-113

Rosenmayr, Leopold. See Rosenmayr, H. jt. auth.

Rosenstock, Morton

The Jews: from the ghettos of Europe to the suburbs of the United States. *In* The Immigrant experience in America p147-71

Rosenthal, Bernice Glatzer

Revolution as apocalypse: the case of Bely. *In* Janecek, G. ed. Andrey Bely p181-92

Rosenthal, Earl S.
Plus Oultre: the idea imperial of Charles V in his columnar device on the Alhambra. *In* Enggass, R. C. and Stokstad, M. eds. Hortus imaginum p85-93

Rosenthal, Erwin Isak Jacob
Hermann Cohen and Heinrich Graetz. *In* Salo Wittmayer Baron v2 p725-43

Rosenthal, Macha Louis
Randall Jarrell. *In* Donoghue, D. ed. Seven American poets from MacLeish to Nemerov p132-70

Some thoughts on American poetry today. *In* Boyers, R. ed. Contemporary poetry in America p16-29

Rosenwald, George C.
Epilogue: Reflections on the universalism of structure. *In* Riegel, K. F. and Rosenwald, G. C. eds. Structure and transformation p215-19

Rosenzweig, Franz
About
Kaufman, W. E. Franz Rosenzweig: toward an existential Jewish theology. *In* Kaufman, W. E. Contemporary Jewish philosophies p27-54

Rosenzweig, Robert M.
Faculty and standards of ethical conduct. *In* Hook, S.; Kurtz, P. and Todorovich, M. eds. The ethics of teaching and scientific research p73-82

Rösing, Ina Susanne Spiegel- See Spiegel-Rösing, Ina Susanne

Rosivach, Vincent J.
The two worlds of the Antigone. *In* Illinois classical studies v4, 1979 p16-26

Rosovsky, Henry
Japan and the United States: notes from the devil's advocate. *In* Clapp, P. and Halperin, M. H. eds. United States-Japanese relations, the 1970's p79-93

Ross, Alan
About
Scannell, V. Alan Ross and Charles Causley. *In* Scannell, V. Not without glory p113-33

Ross, David J. See Block, R. L. jt. auth.

Ross, David O.
Background to Augustan poetry: Gallus, elegy and Rome
Contents
Conclusions
Gallus and the Tenth Eclogue
Gallus the elegist
Introduction: From Catullus to Gallus
Propertius: from ardoris poeta to Romanus Callimachus
Propertius' Monobiblos
The Roman poetry of Horace and Tibullus
The Sixth Eclogue: Virgil's poetic genealogy

The Culex and Moretum as post-Augustan literary parodies. *In* Harvard Studies in classical philology v79 p235-64

Ross, Dorothy
The development of the social sciences. *In* Oleson, A. and Voss, J. eds. The organization of knowledge in modern America, 1860-1920 p107-38

The liberal tradition revisited and the republican tradition addressed. *In* Higham, J. and Conkin, P. K. eds. New directions in American intellectual history p116-31

Ross, Gary Meredith
W. Cameron Forbes: the diplomacy of a Darwinist. *In* Burns, R. D. and Bennett, E. M. eds. Diplomats in crisis p49-64

Ross, James F.
About individual works
Philosophical theology
Curley, E. M. Spinoza and recent philosophy of religion. *In* Shahan, R. W. and Biro, J. I. eds. Spinoza: new perspectives p161-75

Ross, Jennie-Keith
Life goes on: social organization in a French retirement residence. *In* Gubrium, J. F. ed. Late life p99-120

Ross, John Robert
Excerpts from Constraints on variables in syntax. *In* Harman, G. ed. On Noam Chomsky p165-200

Ross, L. W.
Flexible exchange rates. *In* The Year book of world affairs, 1976 p258-72

Ross, Lola Romanucci- See Romanucci-Ross, Lola

Ross, Ralph Gilbert
The experience of value. *In* Philosophy and the civilizing arts p316-44

Some puzzles in Hobbes. *In* Ross, R. G.; Schneider, H. W. and Waldman, T. eds. Thomas Hobbes in his time p43-60

Ross, Thomas B.
Surreptitious entry: the CIA's operations in the United States. *In* Borosage, R. L. and Marks, J. D. eds. The CIA file p93-108

Rossabi, Morris
Muslim and Central Asian revolts. *In* Spence, J. D. and Wills, J. E. eds. From Ming to Ch'ing p167-99

Rossano Gospels. See Codex rossanensis

Rossellini, Roberto
About
Truffaut, F. Roberto Rossellini prefers real life. *In* Truffaut, F. The films in my life p273-77

About individual works
The rise of Louis XIV
Kauffmann, S. The rise of Louis XIV. *In* Kauffmann, S. Living images p8-11

Rosser-Owen, Dawud G. See Sardar, Z. jt. auth.

Rossetti, Christina Georgina
About
Gilbert, S. M. and Gubar, S. The aesthetics of reunuciation. *In* Gilbert, S. M. and Gubar, S. The madwoman in the attic p539-80

Rosenblum, D. Christina Rossetti: the inward pose. *In* Gilbert, S. M. and Gubar, S. eds. Shakespeare's sisters p82-98

Rossetti, Dante Gabriel
Hand and soul. *In* Sambrook, J. ed. Pre-Raphaelitism p45-56

About
Buckley, J. H. The fear of art; excerpt from "The Victorian temper". *In* Sambrook, J. ed. Pre-Raphaelitism p186-205

Doughty, O. Rossetti's conception of the "poetic" in poetry and painting. *In* Sambrook, J. ed. Pre-Raphaelitism p153-65

Rossetti, Dante G.—About—*Continued*

Johnson, W. S. D. G. Rossetti as painter and poet. *In* Sambrook, J. ed. Pre-Raphaelitism p220-29

McGann, J. J. Rossetti's significant details. *In* Sambrook, J. ed. Pre-Raphaelitism p230-42

Williamson, A. Rossetti and Pre-Raphaelitism. *In* Williamson, A. Artists and writers in revolt p37-61

About individual works
Sir Hugh the Heron

Greene, M. E. Rossetti's "absurd trash": "Sir Hugh the Heron" reconsidered. *In* Tennessee Studies in literature v20 p85-91

Rossetti, William Michael
Pre-Raphaelitism. *In* Sambrook, J. ed. Pre-Raphaelitism p64-70

About

Dawson, C. Dramatic elegists: Arnold, Clough, and Browning at mid-century. *In* Dawson, C. Victorian noon p63-104

Rossi, Alice S.
A biosocial perspective on parenting. *In* Rossi, A. S.; Kagan, J. and Hareven, T. K. eds. The family p 1-32

Rossi, Giambattista di Jacopo di Guasparre

About

Barolsky, P. Mannerist bizzarrie. *In* Barolsky, P. Infinite jest: wit and humor in Italian Renaissance art p101-38

Rossi, Joan Warchol
Cymbeline's debt to Holinshed: the richness of III.1. *In* Shakespeare's romances reconsidered p104-12

Rossi, Paolo
Hermeticism, rationality and the scientific revolution. *In* Bonelli, M. L. R. and Shea, W. R. eds. Reason, experiment, and mysticism in the scientific revolution p247-73

Rossi, Peter Henry
Conventional wisdom, common sense, and empirical knowledge: the case of stratification research and views of American society. *In* The Uses of controversy in sociology p30-47

Rossiaud, Jacques
Prostitution, youth, and society in the towns of southeastern France in the fifteenth century. *In* Deviants and the abandoned in French society p 1-46

Rossini, Gioacchino Antonio

About

Dent, E. J. Rossini. *In* Dent, E. J. The rise of romantic opera p110-24

Rossiter, Frank R.

About individual works
Charles Ives and his America

Craft, R. Ives's world. *In* Craft, R. Current convictions p211-14

Rossiter, Margaret Walsh
The organization of agricultural improvement in the United States, 1785-1865. *In* Oleson, A. and Brown, S. C. eds. The pursuit of knowledge in the early American Republic p279-98

The organization of the agricultural sciences. *In* Oleson, A. and Voss, J. eds. The organization of knowledge in modern America, 1860-1920 p211-48

Rossman, Charles
Stephen Dedalus and the spiritual-heroic refrigerating apparatus: art and life in Joyce's Portrait. *In* Forms of modern British fiction p101-31

Rossman, Isadore
Home care of the cancer patient. *In* Home care p60-69

Rossman, Michael
Declaration on the birth of the child Lorca. *In* Gross, B. and Gross, R. eds. The children's rights movement p276-78

Rosso, Fiorentino. See Rossi, Giambattista di Jacopo di Guasparre

Rosso of Florence. See Rossi, Giambattista di Jacopo di Guasparre

Rostand, Edmond

About

Nicoll, A. Neo-romanticism in the theatre. *In* Nicoll, A. World drama p515-30

About individual works
Cyrano de Bergerac

Simon, J. I. Cyrano de Bergerac. *In* Simon, J. I. Singularities p17-19

Rostow, Eugene Victor
Future world systems. *In* The New Atlantic challenge p285-99

Kennan's grand design. *In* Decline of the West? George Kennan and his critics p113-31

Rostow, Walt Whitman
Technology and the price system. *In* Science and ceremony p75-113

Røstvig, Maren-Sofie
Elaborate song: conceptual structure in Milton's 'On the morning of Christ's Nativity.' *In* Røstvig, M. S. ed. Fair forms p54-84

In ordine di ruota: circular structure in "The unfortunate lover" and Upon Appleton House. *In* Friedenreich, K. ed. Tercentenary essays in honor of Andrew Marvell p245-67

Tom Jones and the choice of Hercules. *In* Røstvig, M. S. ed. Fair forms p147-77

Roszak, Theodore
Ethics, ecstasy, and the study of new religions. *In* Needleman, J. and Baker, G. eds. Understanding the new religions p49-62

About

Marx, L. Reflections on the neo-romantic critique of science. *In* Holton, G. J. and Morison, R. S. eds. Limits of scientific inquiry p61-73

West, T. R. Nature and artifice: Hannah Arendt, Theodore Roszak, Paul Goodman. *In* West, T. R. Nature, community, & will p97-137

About individual works
Where the wasteland ends

Barfield, O. The coming trauma of materialism. *In* Barfield, O. The rediscovery of meaning, and other essays p187-200

Rotberg, Robert I.
Vodun and the politics of Haiti. *In* Kilson, M. L. and Rotberg, R. I. eds. The African diaspora p342-65

Rotelande, Hue de. See Hue de Rotelande

Rotenstreich, Nathan
Vico and Kant. *In* Giambattista Vico's science of humanity p221-40

Rotermundt, Rainer, and Schmiederer, Ursula
Social structure and foreign policy in the Soviet Union. *In* Jahn, E. ed. Soviet foreign policy p91-113

Roth, Catharine Prince
Thematic s-aorists in Homer. *In* Harvard Studies in classical philology v77 p181-86

Roth, Gertraude
The Manchu-Chinese relationship, 1618-1636. *In* Spence, J. D. and Wills, J. E. eds. From Ming to Ch'ing p 1-38

Roth, John K.
Telling a tale that cannot be told: reflections on the authorship of Elie Wiesel. *In* Rosenfeld, A. H. and Greenberg, I. eds. Confronting the Holocaust p58-79

Roth, Joseph

About individual works
Legende vom heiligen Trinker
Browning, B. W. Joseph Roth's Legende vom heiligen Trinker: essence and elixir. *In* Strelka, J. P.; Bell, R. F. and Dobson, E. eds. Protest—form—tradition p81-95

Roth, Joseph, tr.

About individual works
Jawohl, mein Herr, ich bin ein Katholik!
Krispyn, E. Joseph Roth and the art of adaptation. *In* Strelka, J. P.; Bell, R. F. and Dobson, E. eds. Protest—form—tradition p97-109

Roth, Philip
Reading myself and others
Contents
Cambodia: a modest proposal
"I always wanted you to admire my fasting"; or, Looking at Kafka
Imagining Jews
Imagining the erotic: three introductions
In response to those who have asked me: "how did you come to write that book, anyway?"
My baseball years
The Newark Public Library
Our castle
Some new Jewish stereotypes
The story of three stories
Writing about Jews
Writing American fiction

About
Roth, P. "I always wanted you to admire my fasting"; or, Looking at Kafka. *In* Roth, P. Reading myself and others p247-[70]

Roth, P. My baseball years. *In* Roth, P. Reading myself and others p179-84

About individual works
Defender of the faith
Roth, P. The story of the three stories. *In* Roth, P. Reading myself and others p171-74

Roth, P. Writing about Jews. *In* Roth, P. Reading myself and others p149-69

Eli, the fanatic
Roth, P. The story of three stories. *In* Roth, P. Reading myself and others p171-74

Epstein
Roth, P. The story of three stories. *In* Roth, P. Reading myself and others p171-74

Roth, P. Writing about Jews. *In* Roth, P. Reading myself and others p149-69

Goodbye, Columbus
Howe, I. The suburbs of Babylon. *In* Howe, I. Celebrations and attacks p35-38

Letting go
Allen, M. Philip Roth: when she was good she was horrid. *In* Allen, M. The necessary blankness p70-96

Portnoy's complaint
Bettelheim, B. Portnoy psychoanalyzed. *In* Bettelheim, B. Surviving, and other essays p387-98

Grebstein, S. N. The comic anatomy of Portnoy's complaint. *In* Cohen, S. B. ed. Comic relief p152-71

Hyman, S. E. The book of the year? *In* Hyman, S. E. The critic's credentials p112-17

Roth, P. Imagining Jews. *In* Roth, P. Reading myself and others p215-46

Roth, P. In response to those who have asked me: "how did you come to write that book, anyway?" *In* Roth, P. Reading myself and others p33-41

Trilling, D. Our uncomplaining homosexuals. *In* Trilling, D. We must march my darlings p157-71

Reading myself and others
Sale, R. H. Philip Roth. *In* Sale, R. H. On not being good enough p81-84

When she was good
Allen, M. Philip Roth: when she was good she was horrid. *In* Allen, M. The necessary blankness p70-96

Criticism and interpretation
Hyman, S. E. The book of the year? *In* Hyman, S. E. The critic's credentials p112-17

Sheed, W. Howe's complaint. *In* Sheed, W. The good word & other words p12-15

Sources
Roth, P. In response to those who have asked me: "how did you come to write that book, anyway?" *In* Roth, P. Reading myself and others p33-41

Roth, Robert J.
Person and technology: a Deweyan perspective. *In* Roth, R. J. ed. Person and community p87-102

Rothblatt, Sheldon
The student sub-culture and the examination system in early 19th century Oxbridge. *In* The University in society v 1 p247-303

Rothenberg, Albert
The unconscious and creativity. *In* Roland, A. ed. Psychoanalysis, creativity, and literature p144-61

Rothenberg, David
Prisoners. *In* Gochros, H. L. and Gochros, J. S. eds. The sexually oppressed p225-36

Rothenberg, Jerome
The physical environment. *In* McKie, J. W. ed. Social responsibility and the business predicament p191-215

See also Edel, M. jt. auth.

Rothenstein, Sir John Knewstub Maurice
Introduction to The poets' corner. *In* Riewald, J. G. ed. The surprise of excellence p 1-5

Rother, James
Wallace Stevens as a nonsense poet. *In* Tennessee Studies in literature v21 p80-90

Rothermere, Harold Sidney Harmsworth, 1st Viscount

About

Addison, P. Patriotism under pressure: Lord Rothermere and British foreign policy. *In* Peele, G. and Cook, C. eds. The politics of reappraisal, 1918-1939 p189-208

Rothman, David J.

The challenge of crime; excerpt from "The discovery of the asylum". *In* Davis, F. J. and Stivers, R. eds. The collective definition of deviance p130-46

The Progressive legacy: development of American attitudes toward juvenile delinquency. *In* Empey, L. T. ed. Juvenile justice p34-68

The state as parent: social policy in the Progressive Era. *In* Doing good p67-96

Rothman, Rozann Cole

The symbolic uses of public information. *In* Galnoor, I. ed. Government secrecy in democracies p62-76

Rothman, Stanley, and others

Ethnic variation in student radicalism: some new perspectives. *In* Radicalism in the contemporary age v 1 p151-211

Rothman, William

Against "the system of the suture." *In* Nichols, B. ed. Movies and methods p451-59

To have and have not adapted a novel. *In* Peary, G. and Shatzkin, R. eds. The modern American novel and the movies p70-79

Rothschild family

Landes, D. S. Bleichröders and Rothschilds: the problem of continuity in the family firm. *In* Rosenberg, C. E. ed. The family in history p95-114

Rothstein, Eric

Systems of order and inquiry in later eighteenth-century fiction

Contents

Amelia
Caleb Williams
The historical hypothesis
Humphry Clinker
Rasselas
Tristram Shandy

Rothstein, Robert Allen

The linguist as dissenter: Jan Baudouin de Courtenay. *In* For Wiktor Weintraub p391-405

Rotrou, Jean

About

Brereton, G. Rotrou and romantic comedy. *In* Brereton, G. French comic drama p44-50

Rotter, Pat, ed.

About individual works

Bitches & sad ladies: an anthology of fiction by and about women

Balakian, N. Bitches and sad ladies. *In* Balakian, N. Critical encounters p159-61

Rotundas. See Domes

Rotz, Rhiman A.

Investigating urban uprisings with examples from Hanseatic towns, 1374-1416. *In* Order and innovation in the Middle Ages p215-33

Roubin, Lucienne A.

Male space and female space within the Provençal community. *In* Rural society in France p152-80

Roucek, Joseph Slabey

Contemporary sociology in Czechoslovakia. *In* Mohan, R. P. and Martindale, D. A. eds. Handbook of contemporary developments in world sociology p193-202

Roucek, Joseph Slabey, and Mohan, Raj Pal

Contemporary sociology in Hungary. *In* Mohan, R. P. and Martindale, D. A. eds. Handbook of contemporary developments in world sociology p247-59

Contemporary sociology in Romania. *In* Mohan, R. P. and Martindale, D. A. eds. Handbook of contemporary developments in world sociology p261-72

Contemporary sociology in the Soviet Union. *In* Mohan, R. P. and Martindale, D. A. eds. Handbook of contemporary developments in world sociology p287-301

Rouen (Province)

Church history

Foreville, R. The synod of the province of Rouen in the eleventh and twelfth centuries. *In* Church and government in the Middle Ages p19-39

Rougemont, Louis de, pseud. See Grin, Henry Louis

Rouleau, Eric

Peace without the Palestinians? *In* The New world balance and peace in the Middle East: reality or mirage p155-64

Roumain, Jacques

Translations, English

Dixon, M. Rivers remembering their source: comparative studies in Black literary history—Langston Hughes, Jacques Roumain, and négritude. *In* Fisher, D. and Stepto, R. B. eds. Afro-American literature p25-43

Rountree, Helen C.

The Indians of Virginia: a third race in a biracial state. *In* Williams, W. L. ed. Southeastern Indians since the removal era p27-48

Roupas, T. Graham

Information and pictorial representation. *In* Perkins, D. and Leondar, B. eds. The arts and cognition p48-79

Rourke, Constance Mayfield

About

Rubin, J. S. Constance Rourke in context: the uses of myth. *In* Zenderland, L. ed. Recycling the past p81-94

Wertheim, A. F. Constance Rourke and the discovery of American culture in the 1930s. *In* Luedtke, L. S. ed. The study of American culture p49-61

Rourke, Francis Edward

The United States. *In* Galnoor, I. ed. Government secrecy in democracies p113-28

Rouse, Blair H.

Ellen Glasgow's civilized men. *In* Ellen Glasgow p132-66

Rousseau, G. S.

Science. *In* Rogers, P. ed. The eighteenth century p153-207

Rousseau, Jean Jacques

About

Ages, A. Lamartine and the philosophes. *In* Literature and history in the age of ideas p321-40

Rousseau, Jean J.—About—*Continued*

Barrow, R. A critical look at certain themes in Rousseau. *In* Barrow, R. Radical education p39-63

Clayre, A. Rousseau. *In* Clayre, A. Work and play p7-14

Haac, O. A. Faith in the Enlightenment: Voltaire and Rousseau seen by Michelet. *In* Studies in eighteenth-century culture v7 p475-90

Heller, P. Nietzsche in his relation to Voltaire and Rousseau. *In* O'Flaherty, J. C.; Sellner, T. F. and Helm, R. M. eds. Studies in Nietzsche and the classical tradition p109-33

Noel, T. Rousseau and the fable in education. *In* Noel, T. Theories of the fable in the eighteenth century p102-13

Rapaport, E. On the future of love: Rousseau and the radical feminists. *In* Gould, C. C. and Wartofsky, M. W. eds. Women and philosophy p185-205

Sabin, M. Rousseau and the vocabulary of feeling. *In* Sabin, M. English romanticism and the French tradition p17-32

Sabin, M. The sentiment of being. *In* Sabin, M. English romanticism and the French tradition p103-24

Sabin, M. The story of a life. *In* Sabin, M. English romanticism and the French tradition p3-16

Shell, M. The lie of the fox: Rousseau's theory of verbal, monetary, and political representation. *In* Shell, M. The economy of literature p113-28

Topazio, V. W. A reevaluation of Rousseau's political doctrine. *In* Literature and history in the age of ideas p179-92

About individual works
The confessions
De Man, P. The purloined ribbon. *In* Glyph I p28-49

Grosskurth, P. Where was Rousseau? *In* Landow, G. P. ed. Approaches to Victorian autobiography p26-38

Lyons, J. O. Confessional high tide. *In* Lyons, J. O. The invention of the self p89-120

Perkins, J. A. The ironic mode in autobiography: Franklin and Rousseau. *In* Studies in eighteenth-century culture v6 p215-28

Sabin, M. The charm of memory. *In* Sabin, M. English romanticism and the French tradition p78-102

Sabin, M. The sources of imagination. *In* Sabin, M. English romanticism and the French tradition p51-77

Dialogues
McDonald, C. V. The model of reading in Rousseau's Dialogues. *In* Valdés, M. J. and Miller, O. J. eds. Interpretation of narrative p11-18

Emile
Barrow, R. Jean-Jacques Rousseau (1712-88) *In* Barrow, R. Radical education p12-38

Brooks, R. A. Rousseau's antifeminism in the Lettre à d' Alembert and Emile. *In* Literature and history in the age of ideas p209-27

Hamilton, J. F. Literature and the "natural man" in Rousseau's Emile. *In* Literature and history in the age of ideas p195-206

Julia: or, The new Eloisa
Turnell, M. Rousseau. *In* Turnell, M. The rise of the French novel p107-44

Letter to d'Alembert on the theatre
Brooks, R. A. Rousseau's antifeminism in the Lettre à d' Alembert and Emile. *In* Literature and history in the age of ideas p209-27

Hamilton, J. F. Molière and Rousseau: the confrontation of art and politics. *In* Johnson, R. B.; Neumann, E. S. and Trail, G. T. eds. Molière and the commonwealth of letters: patrimony and posterity p100-08

The reveries of a solitary
De Man, P. The purloined ribbon. *In* Glyph I p28-49

Katz, E. The problem of the environment in Les Rêveries du promeneur solitaire. *In* Studies in eighteenth-century culture v4 p95-107

The social contract
Barrow, R. Jean-Jacques Rousseau (1712-88) *In* Barrow, R. Radical education p12-38

Schneider, M. L. A Catholic perspective on American civil religion. *In* America in theological perspective p123-39

Influence
Grosskurth, P. Where was Rousseau? *In* Landow, G. P. ed. Approaches to Victorian autobiography p26-38

Political and social views
Najder, Z. Conrad and Rousseau: concepts of man and society. *In* Joseph Conrad: a commemoration p77-90

Roussel, Roy. See Roussel, Royal

Roussel, Royal

Reflections on the letter: the reconciliation of distance and presence in Pamela. *In* ELH essays for Earl R. Wasserman p85-109

Rousset, Jean

About individual works
Forme et signification: essais sur les structures littéraires de Corneille à Claudel
Derrida, J. Force and signification. *In* Derrida, J. Writing and difference p3-30

Rout, Leslie Brennan

The African in colonial Brazil. *In* Kilson, M. L. and Rotberg, R. I. eds. The African diaspora p132-71

Routes of travel. See Railroad travel

Rouveret, Alain

Result clauses and conditions on rules. *In* Keyser, S. J. ed. Recent transformational studies in European languages p159-87

Roux, Wilhelm

About
Haraway, D. J. Reinterpretation or rehabilitation: an exercise in contemporary Marxist history of science. *In* Studies in history of biology v2 p193-209

Roving Eye Press

Ford, H. D. Four new directions: fourth-dimensional writing: the Roving Eye. *In* Ford, H. D. Published in Paris p302-11

Rovit, Earl Herbert

College humor and the modern audience. *In* Cohen, S. B. ed. Comic relief p238-48

Of human dignity: "In another country." *In* Benson, J. J. ed. The short stories of Ernest Hemingway: critical essays p167-70

Rowan, Alistair John
Batty Langley's Gothic. *In* Studies in memory of David Talbot Rice p197-215

Rowan, Donald Frederick
The staging of The Spanish tragedy. *In* The Elizabethan theatre, V p112-23

Rowdon, Maurice

About individual works
The fall of Venice
Connolly, C. Venice: 1. *In* Connolly, C. The evening colonnade p30-33

Rowe, Colin
Mannerism and modern architecture. *In* Sharp, D. ed. The rationalists p174-89

Rowe, John A.
The pattern of political administration in precolonial Buganda. *In* African themes p65-76

Rowe, John Carlos
Writing and truth in Poe's The narrative of Arthur Gordon Pym. *In* Glyph 2 p102-21

Rowe, Nicholas
About
Matlack, C. S. "Spectatress of the mischief which she made": tragic woman perceived and perceiver. *In* Studies in eighteenth-century culture v6 p317-30

Rowe, William Woodin
The honesty of Nabokovian deception. *In* A Book of things about Vladimir Nabokov p171-81

Nabokov & others: patterns in Russian literature
Contents
Crime and punishment and The brothers Karamazov: some comparative observations
Dostoevskian patterned antinomy and its function in Crime and punishment
Duality and symmetry in Lermontov's A hero of our time
Gogol's descriptive double image and its use in Dead souls
Nabokov: the hounds of fate
Nabokovian shimmers of meaning
Nabokovian superimposed and alternative realities
Nabokov's bonus effects
Nabokov's ghosts: some notes on Transparent things
Pnin's uncanny looking glass
Also in A Book of things about Vladimir Nabokov p182-92
Pushkinian impatient expectation and its function in Eugene Onegin
Russian oaks and Nabokov's "Ballad"
Some fateful patterns in Tolstoi

Rowell, Thelma E.
Growing up in a monkey group. *In* Schwartz, T. ed. Socialization as cultural communication p21-36

Rowland, Beryl
Chaucer's blasphemous churl: a new interpretation of The miller's tale. *In* Chaucer and Middle English studies in honour of Rossell Hope Robbins p43-55

Rowland, Richard H.
Urban in-migration in late nineteenth-century Russia. *In* Hamm, M. F. ed. The city in Russian history p115-24
See also Lewis, R. A. jt. auth.

Rowlandson, Mary (White)
About individual works
The sovereignity and goodness of God
Seelye, J. Providential passages: wherein a matron, a minister, a militiaman, and a madam display the cardinal points of the Puritan compass. *In* Seelye, J. Prophetic waters p279-309

Rowley, Brian Alan
Journalism into fiction: Im Westen nichts Neues. *In* Klein, H. M. ed. The First World War in fiction p101-11

Rowley, William. See Middleton, T. jt. auth.

Rowse, Alfred Leslie
Byron's Cornish ancestry. *In* Jump, J. D. ed. Byron p 1-15
Hardy and Cornwall. *In* Drabble, M. ed. The genius of Thomas Hardy p119-38

Roxborough, Ian
Reversing the Revolution: the Chilean opposition to Allende. *In* O'Brien, P. J. ed. Allende's Chile p192-216

Roy, David Todd
Chang Chu-p'o's Commentary on the Chin p'ing mei. *In* Chinese narrative p115-23

Roy, Krishna
Population policy from the southern perspective. *In* Erb, G. F. and Kallab, V. eds. Beyond dependency p95-110

Royal Building Administration. See France. Administration des bâtiments royaux

Royal College of Chemistry, London. See London. Royal College of Chemistry

Royal demesne. See Crown lands

The Royal Shakespeare Theatre Company
Crick, B. R. The political in Britain's two national theatres. *In* Drama and society p169-94
Thomson, P. No Rome of safety: the Royal Shakespeare season 1972 reviewed. *In* Shakespeare survey 26 p139-50
Thomson, P. Shakespeare straight and crooked: a review of the 1973 season at Stratford. *In* Shakespeare survey 27 p143-54
Thomson, P. The smallest season: The Royal Shakespeare Company at Stratford in 1974. *In* Shakespeare survey 28 p137-48
Thomson, P. Towards a poor Shakespeare: The Royal Shakespeare Company at Stratford in 1975. *In* Shakespeare survey v29 p151-56
Warren, R. Comedies and histories at two Stratfords, 1977. *In* Shakespeare survey v31 p141-53
Warren, R. Theory and practice: Stratford 1976. *In* Shakespeare survey 30 p169-79

Royal Society of Canada, Ottawa
Bowler, P. J. The early development of scientific societies in Canada. *In* Oleson, A. and Brown, S. C. eds. The pursuit of knowledge in the early American Republic p326-39

Royal Society of London
Frick, G. F. The Royal Society in America. *In* Oleson, A. and Brown, S. C. eds. The pursuit of knowledge in the early American Republic p70-83

Royot, Daniel
Aspects of the American picaresque in "Little Big Man." *In* Johnson, I. D. and Johnson, C. [eds.] Les américanistes p37-52

Royster, Vermont Connecticut
The American press and the Revolutionary tradition. *In* America's continuing revolution p205-25

Rozman, Gilbert

Comparative approaches to urbanization: Russia, 1750-1800. *In* Hamm, M. F. ed. The city in Russian history p69-85

Rubber

Zambia

Hobson, R. H. Rubber: a footnote to Northern Rhodesian history. *In* The Occasional papers of the Rhodes-Livingstone Museum p489-538

Rubber industry and trade

Zambia—History

Hobson, R. H. Rubber: a footnote to Northern Rhodesian history. *In* The Occasional papers of the Rhodes-Livingstone Museum p489-538

Rubbo, Anna

The spread of capitalism in rural Colombia: effects on poor women. *In* Reiter, R. R. ed. Toward an anthropology of women p333-57

Rubens, Sir Peter Paul

About

Gordon, D. J. Roles and mysteries. *In* The Renaissance imagination p3-23

Gordon, D. J. Rubens and the Whitehall ceiling. *In* Gordon, D. J. The Renaissance imagination p24-50

Judson, J. R. Rubens and Moretus. *In* Medieval and Renaissance studies 1976 p141-59

Trevor-Roper, H. R. The Archdukes and Rubens. *In* Trevor-Roper, H. R. Princes and artists p127-63

About individual works

Quos ego

Brower, R. A. Visual and verbal translation of myth: Neptune in Virgil, Rubens, Dryden. *In* Brower, R. A. Mirror on mirror p17-45

Rubenstein, Richard Lowell

About

Kaufman, W. E. Richard L. Rubenstein: the encounter with nothingness. *In* Kaufman, W. E. Contemporary Jewish philosophies p78-93

Rubia Barcia, José

What's in a name: Américo Castro (y Quesada) *In* Américo Castro and the meaning of Spanish civilization p3-22

Rubin, Gayle

The traffic in women: notes on the "political economy" of sex. *In* Reiter, R. R. ed. Toward an anthropology of women p157-210

Rubin, Joan Shelley

Constance Rourke in context: the uses of myth. *In* Zenderland, L. ed. Recycling the past p81-94

Rubin, Louis Decimus

A critic almost anonymous: John Crowe Ransom goes North. *In* Young, T. D. ed. The New Criticism and after p 1-21

Flannery O'Connor and the Bible Belt. *In* Friedman, M. J. and Lawson, L. A. eds. The added dimension p49-72

Is the Southern literary renascence over?: a sort of cautionary epistle. *In* The Rising South v 1 p72-91

Notes on a Southern writer in our time. *In* Morris, R. K. and Malin, I. eds. The achievement of William Styron p51-87

Scarlet O'Hara and the two Quentin Compsons. *In* The South and Faulkner's Yoknapatawpha p168-94

William Elliott shoots a bear

Contents

"The Begum of Bengal": Mark Twain and the South

Also in Baldwin, K. H. and Kirby, D. K. eds. Individual and community p64-93

Everything brought out into the open: Eudora Welty's Losing battles

Fugitives as agrarians: the impulse behind I'll take my stand

The passion of Sidney Lanier

Politics and the novel: George W. Cable and the genteel tradition

Second thoughts on the Old Gray Mare

Southern literature: a Piedmont art

Thomas Wolfe once again

Uncle Remus and the ubiquitous Rabbit

William Elliott shoots a bear

William Styron and human bondage

William Faulkner: the discovery of a man's vocation. *In* Faulkner: fifty years after The marble faun p43-68

Rubin, Vitaly Aronovich

Individual and state in ancient China

Contents

Nature against civilization

"State machine for the general welfare"

The theory and practice of a totalitarian state

Tradition and human personality

Rubinoff, Ira

A sea-level canal in Panama. *In* Borgese, E. M. and Krieger, D. eds. The tides of change p254-63

Rubinoff, Lionel

Violence and the retreat from reason. *In* Stanage, S. M. ed. Reason and violence p73-118

Rubinoff, M. Lionel. See Rubinoff, Lionel

Rubinstein, Amnon

Palestinian nationalism: an established fact. *In* The Palestinians p183-86

Rucellai, Bernardo

About

Gilbert, F. Bernardo Rucellai and the Orti Oricellari: a study on the origin of modern political thought. *In* Gilbert, F. History p215-46

Rucellai, Giovanni

About individual works

L'Oreste

Bertolini, J. A. Ecphrasis and dramaturgy: Leonardo's Leda in Rucellai's Oreste. *In* Renaissance drama [1976] p151-76

Rucker, Darnell. See Rucker, Egbert Darnell

Rucker, Egbert Darnell

Institutions and the alienated man. *In* Philosophy and the civilizing arts p283-315

Rucker, Mary E.

Benjamin Franklin. *In* Emerson, E. H. ed. American literature, 1764-1789 p105-25

Rudd, Niall
Lines of enquiry
Contents
Architecture: theories about Virgil's Eclogues
History: Ovid and the Augustan myth
Idea: Dido's culpa
Imitation: association of ideas in Persius
Theory: sincerity and mask
Tone: poets and patrons in Juvenal's Seventh Satire
Translation

Ruddick, Sara
Better sex. *In* Baker, R. and Elliston, F. A. eds. Philosophy & sex p83-104

Ruddick, William
Don Juan in search of freedom: Byron's emergence as a satirist. *In* Jump, J. D. ed. Byron p113-37

Rude, Donald W. See Davis, K. W. jt. auth

Rude, François
About
Butler, R. Long live the Revolution, the Republic, and especially the Emperor: the political sculpture of Rude. *In* Millon, H. A. and Nochlin, L. eds. Art and architecture in the service of politics p92-107

Rudin, A. James
Jews and Judaism in Reverend Moon's Divine principle. *In* Horowitz, I. L. ed. Science, sin, and scholarship p74-83

Rudner, Martin
Traditionalism and socialism in Burma's political development. *In* Eisenstadt, S. N. and Azmon, Y. eds. Socialism and tradition p105-39

Rudolph II, Emperor of Germany
Art patronage
Trevor-Roper, H. R. Rudolf II in Prague. *In* Trevor-Roper, H. R. Princes and artists p85-125

Rudolph, Lloyd I. See Rudolph, S. H. jt. auth.

Rudolph, Susanne Hoeber, and Rudolph, Lloyd I.
Rajput adulthood: reflections on the Amar Singh Diary. *In* Erikson, E. H. ed. Adulthood p 149-71

Rudy, John George
Structure and unity in The white doe of Rylstone. *In* Aeolian harps p133-48

Ruetten, Richard T. See McCoy, D. R. jt. auth.

Ruggiers, Paul G.
Introduction: some theoretical considerations of comedy in the Middle Ages. *In* Ruggiers, P. G. ed. Versions of medieval comedy p 1-17

Ruhle, Hermann
Innovative building technologies: productivity. *In* Strategies for human settlements: habitat and environment p145-47

Ruina, Jack
The arms race and SALT. *In* The Dynamics of the arms race p47-56

Ruins. See Excavations (Archaeology)

Ruiz, Antonio Machado y. See Machado y Ruiz, Antonio

Ruiz, José Martínez. See Martínez Ruiz, José

Ruiz, Juan arcipreste de Hita
About individual works
The book of good love
Gilman, S. Literature and historical insight. *In* Américo Castro and the meaning of Spanish civilization p317-24

Ruiz, Teofilo F.
Castilian merchants in England, 1248-1350. *In* Order and innovation in the Middle Ages p173-85

Rukeyser, Muriel
About
Blau Duplessis, R. The critique of consciousness and myth in Levertov, Rich, and Rukeyser. *In* Gilbert, S. M. and Gubar, S. eds. Shakespeare's sisters p280-300

Rule of law
Dietze, G. Hayek on the rule of law. *In* Essays on Hayek p107-46
Strayer, J. R. The rule of law. *In* Aspects of American liberty p16-36
See also Due process of law; Judicial review

Rulfo, Juan
About individual works
Pedro Páramo
Brotherston, G. Province of dead souls: Juan Rulfo. *In* Brotherston, G. The emergence of the Latin American novel p71-80
MacAdam, A. J. Juan Rulfo: the secular myth. *In* MacAdam, A. J. Modern Latin American narratives p88-90

The ruling class (Motion picture)
Kauffmann, S. The ruling class. *In* Kauffmann, S. Living images p132-35

Rumania. See Romania

Rumanian literature. See Romanian literature

Rumelhart, David E.
Some problems with the notion of literal meanings. *In* Ortony, A. ed. Metaphor and thought p78-90

Rumor
Lienhardt, P. The interpretation of rumour. *In* Studies in social anthropology p105-31

Runciman, Sir Steven
Blachernae Palace and its decoration. *In* Studies in memory of David Talbot Rice p277-83
Gibbon and Byzantium. *In* Edward Gibbon and The decline and fall of the Roman Empire p53-60
History and legend. *In* Royal Society of Literature of the United Kingdom, London. Essays by divers hands v39 p112-25

Rundell, Walter
Webb the schoolteacher. *In* Essays on Walter Prescott Webb p95-123

Runes
Frese, D. W. The art of Cynewulf's runic signatures. *In* Anglo-Saxon poetry: essays in appreciation p312-34
Sharpe, E. J. The Old English runic Paternoster. *In* Symbols of power p41-60

Runic alphabets. See Runes

Runte, Roseann
The Matron of Ephesus in eighteenth century France: the lady and the legend. *In* Studies in eighteenth-century culture v6 p361-75

Ruoff, Gene W.
Faulkner: the way out of the waste land. *In* French, W. G. ed. The twenties p235-48

Rupen, Robert Arthur
The absorption of Tuva. *In* Hammond, T. T. ed. The anatomy of Communist takeovers p145-62

Rural conditions
Clayre, A. Pastoral and machinery. *In* Clayre, A. Work and play p89-102
See also Peasantry; also subdivision Rural conditions under names of countries, states, etc. e.g. Russia—Rural conditions

Rural economic development. See Community development

Rural exodus. See Rural-urban migration

Rural life. See Country life; Peasantry

Rural poetry. See Pastoral poetry

Rural population. See Rural-urban migration

Rural schools
United States
Schroeder, F. E. H. The little red schoolhouse. *In* Browne, R. B. and Fishwick, M. W. eds. Icons of America p139-60

Vermont
Howrigan, N. L. The one-room schoolhouse—North. *In* Roots of open education in America p67-72

Virginia
Burks, M. The one-room schoolhouse—South. *In* Roots of open education in America p59-66

Rural sociology. See Sociology, Rural

Rural-urban migration
Todaro, M. P. Rural-urban migration, unemployment and job probabilities: recent theoretical and empirical research. *In* Economic factors in population growth p367-85
See also Urbanization

Mexico (City)
Cornelius, W. A. The impact of cityward migration on urban land and housing markets: problems and policy alternatives in Mexico City. *In* Walton, J. and Masotti, L. H. eds. The city in comparative perspective p249-70

Russia
Rowland, R. H. Urban in-migration in late nineteenth century Russia. *In* Hamm, M. F. ed. The city in Russian history p115-24

United States
Campbell, R. R. Beyond the suburbs: the changing rural scene. *In* Hawley, A. H. and Rock, V. P. eds. Metropolitan America in contemporary perspectives p93-122
Zimmer, B. G. The urban centrifugal drift. *In* Hawley, A. H. and Rock, V. P. eds. Metropolitan America in contemporary perspective p23-91

Rural women
Russia
Dunn, E. Russian rural women. *In* Women in Russia p167-87

Rush, Benjamin
About
Tichi, C. Worried celebrants of the American Revolution. *In* Emerson, E. H. ed. American literature, 1764-1789 p275-91

Rush, Benjamin F.
A surgical oncologist's observations. *In* Anticipatory grief p98-106

Rush, Joseph Harold
Physical aspects of psi phenomena. *In* Parapsychology: its relation to physics, biology, psychology, and psychiatry p6-39

Rushing, Andrea Benton
Images of Black women in Afro-American poetry. *In* Harley, S. and Terborg-Penn, R. eds. The Afro-American woman p74-84

Rusk, Dean
The American Revolution and the future. *In* America's continuing revolution p387-98
Preferential treatment: some reflections. *In* Social justice & preferential treatment p154-60

Ruskin, John
Pre-Raphaelitism. *In* Sambrook, J. ed. Pre-Raphaelitism p92-104

About
Cate, G. A. Ruskin's discipleship to Carlyle: a revaluation. *In* Carlyle and his contemporaries p227-56
Landow, G. P. There began to be a great talking about the fine arts. *In* Altholz, J. L. ed. The mind and art of Victorian England p124-45
Levine, G. L. High and low: Ruskin and the novelists. *In* Knoepflmacher, U. C. and Tennyson, G. B. eds. Nature and the Victorian imagination p137-52
Shell, M. John Ruskin and the political economy of literature. *In* Shell, M. The economy of literature p129-51
Williamson, A. Ruskin and Morris: the Socialist legacy. *In* Williamson, A. Artists and writers in revolt p103-31
Williamson, A. Ruskin: art and the critic. *In* Williamson, A. Artists and writers in revolt p16-34

About individual works
Praeterita
Columbus, C. K. Ruskin's Praeterita as thanatography. *In* Landow, G. P. ed. Approaches to Victorian autobiography p109-27
Helsinger, E. K. The structure of Ruskin's Praeterita. *In* Landow, G. P. ed. Approaches to Victorian autobiography p87-108

Proserpina
Kirchhoff, F. A. A science against sciences: Ruskin's floral mythology. *In* Knoepflmacher, U. C. and Tennyson, G. B. eds. Nature and the Victorian imagination p246-58

The stones of Venice
Caserio, R. L. Narrative reason: the sense of plot and historical experience. *In* Caserio, R. L. Plot, story, and the novel p27-56

Influence—Jeanneret-Gris
Sekler, M. P. M. Le Corbusier, Ruskin, the tree and the open hand. *In* Walden, R. ed. The open hand p42-95

Ruskin family
Brooks, M. Love and possession in a Victorian household: the example of the Ruskins. *In* Wohl, A. S. ed. The Victorian family p82-100

Russ, Joanna Ruth
Alien monsters. *In* Knight, D. F. ed. Turning points p132-43

Russak, Ben

Scholarly publishing in Western Europe and Great Britain: a survey and analysis. *In* Altbach, P. G. and McVey, S. eds. Perspectives on publishing p103-16

Russell, Bertrand Russell, 3d Earl

The duty of a philosopher in this age. *In* The Abdication of philosophy: philosophy and the public good p15-22

See also Whitehead, A. N. jt. auth.

About

Clark, R. Ontology and the philosophy of mind in Sellars' critique of Russell. *In* Nakhnikian, G. ed. Bertrand Russell's philosophy p101-16

Couch, W. T. The sacred and golden cord. *In* Viva Vivas! p87-137

Maxwell, G. The later Bertrand Russell: philosophical revolutionary. *In* Nakhnikian, G. ed. Bertrand Russell's philosophy p169-82

Maxwell, G. Russell on perception and mind-body: a study in philosophical method. *In* Philosophical aspects of the mind-body problem p131-53

Mudrick, M. Agèd eagles and dirty old men. *In* Mudrick, M. Books are not life but then what is? p132-42

Nakhnikian, G. Some questions about Bertrand Russell's liberalism. *In* Nakhnikian, G. ed. Bertrand Russell's philosophy p221-26

Pears, D. F. Russell's theories of memory, 1912-1921. *In* Nakhnikian, G. ed. Bertrand Russell's philosophy p117-37

Schoenman, R. B. Bertrand Russell and the peace movement. *In* Nakhnikian, G. ed. Bertrand Russell's philosophy p227-52

Sellars, W. S. Ontology and the philosophy of mind in Russell. *In* Nakhnikian, G. ed. Bertrand Russell's philosophy p57-100

Sherman, E. F. Bertrand Russell and the peace movement: liberal consistency or radical change? *In* Nikhnikian, G. ed. Bertrand Russell's philosophy p253-63

Stock, G. Wittgenstein on Russell's theory of judgment. *In* Royal Institute of Philosophy. Understanding Wittgenstein p62-75

Wollheim, R. Bertrand Russell and the liberal tradition. *In* Nakhnikian, G. ed. Bertrand Russell's philosophy p209-20

About individual works
Human knowledge, its scope and limits

Salmon, W. C. Memory and perception in Human knowledge. *In* Nakhnikian, G. ed. Bertrand Russell's philosophy p139-67

Knowledge, Theory of

Chisholm, R. M. On the nature of acquaintance: a discussion of Russell's theory of knowledge. *In* Nakhnikian, G. ed. Bertrand Russell's philosophy p47-56

Russell, Charles Marion

About

Dobie, J. F. The conservatism of Charles M. Russell. *In* Dobie, J. F. Prefaces p67-74

Russell, George William

About

Henn, T. R. The sainthood of A.E. *In* Henn, T. R. Last essays p137-56

Bibliography

Carens, J. F. Four Revival figures: Lady Gregory, A. E. (George W. Russell), Oliver St. John Gogarty, and James Stephens. *In* Finneran, R. J. ed. Anglo-Irish literature p436-69

Russell, I. Willis. See Raymond, J. C. jt. auth.

Russell, John

About individual works
Max. Ernst

Connolly, C. Max Ernst. *In* Connolly, C. The evening colonnade p398-401

Russell, John David

Style in modern British fiction

Contents

Advance aim

D. H. Lawrence: The lost girl, Kangaroo

E. M. Forster: Howards End, A passage to India

Henry Green: Back, Concluding

James Joyce: Dubliners

Wyndham Lewis: Tarr, Self condemned

Russell, Josiah Cox

The earlier medieval plague in the British Isles. *In* Viator: medieval and Renaissance studies v7 p65-78

Russell, Ken

About individual works
The devils

Kauffmann, S. The devils. *In* Kauffmann, S. Living images p72-73

Russell, Robert

The problem of self-expression in the later works of Valentin Kataev. *In* Barnes, C. J. ed. Studies in twentieth century Russian literature p78-91

Russell, Ross

About individual works
Bird lives!

Reed, I. Bird lives! *In* Reed, I. Shrovetide in old New Orleans p105-09

Russell, William Howard

About

Wright, E. William Howard Russell and Edward Dicey. *In* Abroad in America: Visitors to the new Nation, 1776-1914 p145-56

Russell-Wood, A. J. R.

Preconditions and precipitants of the independence movement in Portuguese America. *In* From colony to nation p3-40

Russett, Bruce M.

A countercombatant alternative to nuclear MADness. *In* Ethics and nuclear strategy? p124-43

Elite perceptions and theories of world politics. *In* New dimensions of world politics p86-108

Russia

Army—History

Erickson, J. Some military and political aspects of the 'militia army' controversy, 1919-1920. *In* Essays in honour of E. H. Carr p204-28

Civilization

A.B. pseud. The direction of change. *In* From under the rubble p144-50

Cherniavsky, M. Russia. *In* National consciousness, history, and political culture in early-modern Europe p118-43

Russia—Foreign relations—United States
—*Continued*

Novak, M. The banality of evil. *In* Decline of the West? George Kennan and his critics p71-74

Pipes, R. Basic Soviet institutions have not changed. *In* Decline of the West? George Kennan and his critics p61-69

Sigur, G. The strategic triangle: the U.S., the U.S.S.R. and the P.R.C. *In* Pacific Asia and U.S. policies: a political-economic-strategic assessment p28-35

Weiss, S. Is Brezhnev a man of peace? *In* Decline of the West? George Kennan and his critics p75-78

Foreign relations—Yugoslavia

Wilson, Sir D. Yugoslavia and Soviet policy. *In* Kirk, G. L. and Wessell, N. H. eds. The Soviet threat p77-87

Historiography

Enteen, G. M. Marxist historians during the cultural revolution: a case study of professional in-fighting. *In* Cultural revolution in Russia, 1928-1931 p154-68

Heer, N. W. Political leadership in Soviet historiography: cult or collective? *In* Cocks, P.; Daniels, R. V. and Heer, N. W. eds. The dynamics of Soviet politics p11-27

Keenan, E. L. The trouble with Muscovy: some observations upon problems of the comparative study of form and genre in historical writing. *In* Medievalia et humanistica no. 5 p103-26

History

Bolkhovitinov, N. N. The American Revolution and the Russian Empire. *In* The Impact of the American Revolution abroad p81-97

Cherniavsky, M. Russia. *In* National consciousness, history, and political culture in early-modern Europe p118-43

Kellogg, G. Alienation and solidarity: interlocking opposites. *In* Kellogg, G. Dark prophets of hope p5-15

History—Kievan period, 862-1237

Langer, L. N. The medieval Russian town. *In* Hamm, M. F. ed. The city in Russian history p11-33

Stokes, A. D. Kievan Russia. *In* Auty, R. and Obolensky, D. eds. An introduction to Russian history p49-77

History—1237-1480

Andreyev, N. Appanage and Muscovite Russia. *In* Auty, R. and Obolensky, D. eds. An introduction to Russian history p78-120

History—1237-1480—Sources

Fennell, J. L. I. The struggle for power in north-east Russia, 1246-9; an investigation of the sources. *In* Oxford Slavonic papers, new ser. v7 p112-21

History—Period of consolidation, 1462-1605

Miller, D. B. The Lübeckers Bartholomäus Ghotan and Nicolaus Bülow in Novgorod and Moscow and the problem of early Western influences on Russian culture. *In* Viator: medieval and Renaissance studies v9 p395-412

History—1613-1689

Miller, D. H. State and city in seventeenth-century Muscovy. *In* Hamm, M. F. ed. The city in Russian history p34-52

History—1689-1800

Hittle, J. M. The service city in the eighteenth century. *In* Hamm, M. F. ed. The city in Russian history p53-68

Raeff, M. Imperial Russia: Peter I to Nicolas I. *In* Auty, R. and Obolensky, D. eds. An introduction to Russian history p121-95

History—Catherine II, 1762-1796

Brown, A. H. S. E. Desnitsky, Adam Smith, and the Nakaz of Catherine II. *In* Oxford Slavonic papers, new ser. v7 p42-59

Raeff, M. The Empress and the Vinerian Professor: Catherine II's projects of government reforms and Blackstone's Commentaries. *In* Oxford Slavonic papers, new ser. v7 p18-41

History—19th century

Keep, J. L. H. Imperial Russia: Alexander II to the Revolution. *In* Auty, R. and Obolensky, D. eds. An introduction to Russian history p196-271

Raeff, M. Imperial Russia: Peter I to Nicholas I. *In* Auty, R. and Obolensky, D. eds. An introduction to Russian history p121-95

History—Alexander II, 1855-1881

Parry, A. Hunting the Tsar. *In* Parry, A. Terrorism: from Robespierre to Arafat p107-19

History—Revolution of 1905

Epstein, B. W. The Revolution of 1905 and Russian foreign policy. *In* Essays in honour of E. H. Carr p98-125

Struve, P. B. The intelligentsia and revolution. *In* Landmarks p138-54

History—Revolution of 1905— Foreign public opinion

Harrison, W. The British press and the Russian Revolution of 1905-1907. *In* Oxford Slavonic papers, new ser. v7 p75-95

History—Revolution, 1917-1921

Bennigsen, A. The Bolshevik conquest of the Moslem borderlands. *In* Hammond, T. T. eds. The anatomy of Communist takeovers p61-70

Keep, J. L. H. The Bolshevik revolution: prototype or myth? *In* Hammond, T. T. ed. The anatomy of Communist takeovers p46-60

Medvedev, R. A. The October Revolution and the problem of history as a law-governed process. *In* Medvedev, R. A. ed. The Samizdat register p 1-71

Parry, A. Now is the time. *In* Parry, A. Terrorism: from Robespierre to Arafat p146-60

Tucker, R. C. Stalinism as revolution from above. *In* Stalinism p77-108

Yakubovich, M. P. From the history of ideas. *In* Medvedev, R. A. ed. The Samizdat register p147-202

History—Revolution, 1917-1921—Fiction

Alter, R. Shtetl and revolution. *In* Alter, R. Defenses of the imagination p199-212

History—Revolution, 1917-1921— Influence on literature

Kostka, E. K. Blok, Schiller, and the Bolshevik revolution. *In* Kostka, E. K. Glimpses of Germanic-Slavic relations from Pushkin to Heinrich Mann p55-68

Russia—*Continued*

History—1917-
Willetts, H. T. Soviet Russia. *In* Auty, R. and Obolensky, D. eds. An introduction to Russian history p272-314

History—1925-1953
Fitzpatrick, S. Cultural revolution as class war. *In* Cultural revolution in Russia, 1928-1931 p8-40

Lewin, M. Society, state, and ideology during the First Five-Year Plan. *In* Cultural revolution in Russia, 1928-1931 p41-77

History, Naval
Bartlett, R. P. Scottish cannon-founders and the Russian Navy, 1768-85. *In* Oxford Slavonic papers, new ser. v10 p51-72

Industries—History
Robinson, E. The transference of British technology to Russia, 1760-1820: a preliminary enquiry. *In* Great Britain and her world, 1750-1914 p 1-26

Thiede, R. L. Industry and urbanization in New Russia from 1860 to 1910. *In* Hamm, M. F. ed. The city in Russian history p125-38

Intellectual life
Fitzpatrick, S. Cultural revolution as class war. *In* Cultural revolution in Russia, 1928-1931 p 8-40

Kunitz, S. J. A visit to Russia. *In* Kunitz, S. J. A kind of order, a kind of folly p18-38

Malia, M. E. Adulthood refracted: Russia and Leo Tolstoi. *In* Erikson, E. H. ed. Adulthood p173-87

Pogorelskin, A. E. N. I. Kostomarov and the origins of the Vestnik Evropy circle. *In* Oxford Slavonic papers, new ser. v11 p84-100

Intellectual life—American influences
Bolkhovitinov, N. N. The American Revolution and the Russian Empire. *In* The Impact of the American Revolution abroad p81-97

Intellectual life—History
Berlin, Sir I. A remarkable decade: The birth of the Russian intelligentsia. *In* Berlin, Sir I. Russian thinkers p114-35

Berlin, Sir I. Russia and 1848. *In* Berlin, Sir I. Russian thinkers p 1-21

Laws, statutes, etc.
Hanchett, W. S. Tsarist statutory regulation of municipal government in the nineteenth century. *In* Hamm, M. F. ed. The city in Russian history p91-114

Military policy
Holloway, D. Foreign and defence policy. *In* Brown, A. H. and Kaser, M. eds. The Soviet Union since the fall of Khrushchev p49-76

Ruina, J. The arms race and SALT. *In* The Dynamics of the arms race p47-56

Schelling, T. C. The importance of agreements. *In* The Dynamics of the arms race p65-77

Tiedtke, J. and Tiedtke, S. The Soviet Union's internal problems and the development of the Warsaw Treaty Organisation. *In* Jahn, E. ed. Soviet foreign policy p114-57

Tsipis, K. M. The arms race as posturing. *In* The Dynamics of the arms race p78-81

Zumwalt, E. R. Soviet strategy and U.S. counter-strategy. *In* Grand strategy for the 1980s p37-55

Moral conditions
Mihajlov, M. Religious rebirth. *In* Mihajlov, M. Underground notes p23-25

Navy
Miller, G. E. An evaluation of the Soviet navy. *In* Kirk, G. L. and Wessell, N. H. eds. The Soviet threat p47-56

Nobility
Blum, J. Russia. *In* Spring, D. ed. European landed elites in the nineteenth century p68-97

Politics and government
Brzezinski, Z. K. Soviet politics: from the future to the past? *In* Cocks, P.; Daniels, R. V. and Heer, N. W. eds. The dynamics of Soviet politics p337-51

White, S. The USSR: patterns of autocracy and industrialism. *In* Brown, A. H. and Gray, J. eds. Political culture and political change in Communist states p25-65

Politics and government—19th century
Rogger, H. Russian ministers and the Jewish question, 1881-1917. *In* California Slavic studies v8 p15-76

Politics and government—1825-1855
Berlin, Sir I. Russia and 1848. *In* Berlin, Sir I. Russian thinkers p 1-21

Politics and government—1894-1917
Emmons, T. Russia's banquet campaign. *In* California Slavic studies v10 p45-86

Parry, A. Azef: terror chief as double agent. *In* Parry, A. Terrorism: from Robespierre to Arafat p120-30

Politics and government—20th century
Rogger, H. Russian ministers and the Jewish question, 1881-1917. *In* California Slavic studies v8 p15-76

Politics and government—1917-
Agursky, M. The Soviet legitimacy crisis and its international implications. *In* Kaplan, M. A. ed. The many faces of communism p146-93

Heer, N. W. Political leadership in Soviet historiography: cult or collective? *In* Cocks, P.; Daniels, R. V. and Heer, N. W. eds. The dynamics of Soviet politics p11-27

Medvedev, R. A. New pages from the political biography of Stalin. *In* Stalinism p199-235

Parry, A. Stalin's Archipelago. *In* Parry, A. Terrorism: from Robespierre to Arafat p187-202

Rigby, T. H. Stalinism and the mono-organizational society. *In* Stalinism p53-76

Schapiro, L. B. The structure of the Soviet state: government and politics. *In* Auty, R. and Obolensky, D. eds. An introduction to Russian history p331-49

Slusser, R. M. History and the democratic opposition. *In* Tokes, R. L. ed. Dissent in the USSR p329-53

Politics and government—1917-1936
Connor, W. D. The manufacture of deviance: the case of the Soviet purge, 1936-1938. *In* Davis, F. J. and Stivers, R. eds. The collective definition of deviance p241-55

Russia—*Continued*

Politics and government—1936-1953

Connor, W. D. The manufacture of deviance: the case of the Soviet purge, 1936-1938. *In* Davis, F. J. and Stivers, R. eds. The collective definition of deviance p241-55

Politics and government—1945-

Hardt, J. P. Soviet commercial relations and political change. *In* The Interaction of economics and foreign policy p48-83

Politics and government—1953-

Barghoorn, F. C. The post-Khrushchev campaign to suppress dissent: perspectives, strategies, and techniques of repression. *In* Tokes, R. L. ed. Dissent in the USSR p35-95

Biddulph, H. L. Protest strategies of the Soviet intellectual opposition. *In* Tokes, R. L. ed. Dissent in the USSR p96-115

Brown, A. H. Political developments: some conclusions and an interpretation. *In* Brown, A. H. and Kaser, M. eds. The Soviet Union since the fall of Khrushchev p218-75

Cocks, P. The policy process and bureaucratic politics. *In* Cocks, P.; Daniels, R. V. and Heer, N. W. eds. The dynamics of Soviet politics p156-78

Connor, W. D. Differentiation, integration, and political dissent in the USSR. *In* Tokes, R. L. ed. Dissent in the USSR p139-57

Daniels, R. V. Office holding and elite status: the Central Committee of the CPSU. *In* Cocks, P.; Daniels, R. V. and Heer, N. W. eds. The dynamics of Soviet politics p77-95

Feifer, G. No protest: the case of the passive minority. *In* Tokes, R. L. ed. Dissent in the USSR p418-37

Frank, P. J. The changing composition of the Communist Party. *In* Brown, A. H. and Kaser, M. eds. The Soviet Union since the fall of Khrushchev p96-120

Friedgut, T. H. The democratic movement: dimensions and perspectives. *In* Tokes, R. L. ed. Dissent in the USSR p116-36

Hodgson, J. H. The problem of succession. *In* Cocks, P.; Daniels, R. V. and Heer, N. W. eds. The dynamics of Soviet politics p96-116

Hollander, G. D. Political communication and dissent in the Soviet Union. *In* Tokes, R. L. ed. Dissent in the USSR p233-75

Juviler, P. H. and Zawadska, H. J. Détente and Soviet domestic politics. *In* Kirk, G. L. and Wessell, N. H. eds. The Soviet threat p158-67

Litvinov, P. M. The human-rights movement in the Soviet Union. *In* Sidorsky, D. ed. Essays on human rights p113-25

Massell, G. J. Modernization and national policy in Soviet Central Asia: problems and prospects. *In* Cocks, P.; Daniels, R. V. and Heer, N. W. eds. The dynamics of Soviet politics p265-90

Meerson-Aksenov, M. G. The influence of the Jewish exodus on the democratization of Soviet society. *In* Sidorsky, D. ed. Essays on human rights p144-56

Miller, R. F. The scientific-technical revolution and the Soviet administrative debate. *In* Cocks, P.; Daniels, R. V. and Heer, N. W. eds. The dynamics of Soviet politics p137-55

Rakowska-Harmstone, T. Toward a theory of Soviet leadership maintenance. *In* Cocks, P.; Daniels, R. V. and Heer, N. W. eds. The dynamics of Soviet politics p51-76

Reddaway, P. The development of dissent and oposition. *In* Brown, A. H. and Kaser, M. eds. The Soviet Union since the fall of Khrushchev p121-56

Ulam, A. B. Do we know all there is to know about the USSR? *In* Cocks, P.; Daniels, R. V. and Heer, N. W. eds. The dynamics of Soviet politics p3-8

Population

Bennigsen, A. A. and Wimbush, S. E. Migration and political control: Soviet Europeans in Soviet Central Asia. *In* Human migration p173-87

Newth, J. A. Demographic developments. *In* Brown, A. H. and Kaser, M. eds. The Soviet Union since the fall of Khrushchev p79-95

Relations (general) with Europe, Eastern

Gitelman, Z. Y. The diffusion of political innovation: from East Europe to the Soviet Union. *In* Szporluk, R. ed. The influence of East Europe and the Soviet West on the USSR p11-67

Korbonski, A. Eastern Europe and the Soviet threat. *In* Kirk, G. L. and Wessell, N. H. eds. The Soviet threat p66-76

Relations (general) with Great Britain

Robinson, E. The transference of British technology to Russia, 1760-1820: a preliminary enquiry. *In* Great Britain and her world, 1750-1914 p 1-26

Relations (general) with the Baltic States

Vardys, V. S. The role of the Baltic republics in Soviet society. *In* Szporluk, R. ed. The influence of East Europe and the Soviet West on the USSR p147-79

Relations (military) with Europe

Pasti, N. The military balance between East and West in Europe. *In* International terrorism and world security p189-233

Relations (military) with the Mediterranean region

Zoppo, C. E. Arms control in the Mediterranean and European security. *In* International terrorism and world security p248-76

Relations (military) with the Near East

Middleton, D. Russian presence and economic interests in the Mediterranean and the Indian Ocean. *In* The New world balance and peace in the Middle East; reality or mirage p43-49

Relations (military) with the United States

Rathjens, G. W. Nuclear war between the super-powers. *In* Griffiths, F. and Polanyi, J. C. eds. The dangers of nuclear war p135-46

Religion

Bourdeaux, M Religion. *In* Brown, A. H. and Kaser, M. eds. The Soviet Union since the fall of Khrushchev p157-80

Russian literature

Bibliography

Kostka, E. K. comp. Bibliography. *In* Kostka, E. K. Glimpses of Germanic-Slavic relations from Pushkin to Heinrich Mann p144-54

History and criticism

Freeborn, R. Russian literary attitudes from Pushkin to Solzhenitsyn. *In* Freeborn, R. ed. Russian literary attitudes from Pushkin to Solzhenitsyn p 1-18

Glicksberg, C. I. Nihilism in the Russian soul. *In* Glicksberg, C. I. The literature of nihilism p73-94

Mandel'shtam, O. E. About the nature of the word. *In* Mandel'shtam, O. E. Selected essays p65-78

Same as: Mandel'shtam, O. E. On the nature of the word. *In* Proffer, C. R. ed. Modern Russian poets on poetry p33-50

Mandel'shtam, O. E. On the nature of the word. *In* Proffer, C. R. ed. Modern Russian poets on poetry p33-50

Same as: Mandel'shtam, O. E. About the nature of the word. *In* Mandel'shtam, O. E. Selected essays p65-79

West, J. D. The poetic landscape of the Russian symbolists. *In* Barnes, C. J. ed. Studies in twentieth century Russian literature p 1-16

Old Russian

See Russian literature—To 1700

Translations into English

Polushkin, M. A few words on translation. *In* Horn Book Magazine. Crosscurrents of criticism p283-86

To 1700—History and criticism

Andreyev, N. Literature in the Muscovite period (1300-1700). *In* Auty, R. and Obolensky, D. eds. An introduction to Russian language and literature p90-110

Obolensky, D. Early Russian literature (1000-1300). *In* Auty, R. and Obolensky, D. eds. An introduction to Russian language and literature p56-89

17th century

See Russian literature—To 1700

18th century—History and criticism

Burgess, M. A. S. The age of classicism (1700-1820). *In* Auty, R. and Obolensky, D. eds. An introduction to Russian language and literature p111-32

19th century—History and criticism

Mathewson, R. W. Rebuttal I: The theory. *In* Mathewson, R. W. The positive hero in Russian literature p84-96

Mathewson, R. W. Rebuttal II: Hamlet and Don Quixote. *In* Mathewson, R. W. The positive hero in Russian literature p97-112

Setchkarev, V. From the golden to the silver age (1820-1917). *In* Auty, R. and Obolensky, D. eds. An introduction to Russian language and literature p133-84

Stacy, R. H. The aesthetic critics. *In* Stacy, R. H. Russian literary criticism p66-79

Stacy, R. H. The modernists. *In* Stacy, R. H. Russian literary criticism p105-62

Stacy, R. H. Tolstoy and Dostoevsky. *In* Stacy, R. H. Russian literary criticism p80-104

20th century

See Acmeism

20th century—History and criticism

Bowlt, J. E. The "Union of Youth." *In* Gibian, G. and Tjalsma, H. W. eds. Russian modernism p165-87

Brown, D. B. Conclusion. *In* Brown, D. B. Soviet Russian literature since Stalin p373-78

Brown, D. B. Czechoslovak and Polish influences on Soviet literature. *In* Szporluk, R. ed. The influence of East Europe and the Soviet West on the USSR p117-46

Brown, D. B. The literary situation. *In* Brown, D. B. Soviet Russian literature since Stalin p 1-22

Brown, D. B. Underground literature. *In* Brown, D. B. Soviet Russian literature since Stalin p352-72

Carden, P. J. Ornamentalism and modernism. *In* Gibian, G. and Tjalsman, H. W. eds. Russian modernism p49-64

Clark, K. Little heroes and big deeds: literature responds to the First Five-Year Plan. *In* Cultural revolution in Russia, 1928-1931 p189-206

Clark, K. Utopian anthropology as a context for Stalinist literature. *In* Stalinism p180-98

Dewhirst, M. Soviet Russian literature and literary policy. *In* Brown, A. H. and Kaser, M. eds. The Soviet Union since the fall of Khrushchev p181-95

Glicksberg, C. I. Commitment, coercion, and conformity. *In* Glicksberg, C. I. The literature of commitment p359-80

Hayward, M. Literature in the Soviet period (1917-1975). *In* Auty, R. and Obolensky, D. eds. An introduction to Russian language and literature p185-230

Mandel'shtam, O. E. Literary Moscow. *In* Mandel'shtam, O. E. Selected essays p133-37

Mathewson, R. W. Leather men. *In* Mathewson, R. W. The positive hero in Russian literature p179-210

Mathewson, R. W. Rebuttal III: The dissident vision. *In* Mathewson, R. W. The positive hero in Russian literature p255-58

Mathewson, R. W. Two bureaucracies. *In* Mathewson, R. W. The positive hero in Russian literature p211-32

Miller, A. On the theater in Russia; excerpt from "In Russia." *In* Miller, A. The theater essays of Arthur Miller p319-46

Miłosz, C. On modern Russian literature and the West. *In* Miłosz, C. Emperor of the earth p79-84

Slonim, M. L. Fluctuations and trials. *In* Slonim, M. L. Soviet Russian literature p394-407

Slonim, M. L. Soviet romantics: from Grin, Paustovsky, and Olesha to Tikhonov and Bagritsky. *In* Slonim, M. L. Soviet Russian literature p116-33

Slonim, M. L. The third emigration. *In* Slonim, M. L. Soviet Russian literature p408-18

Stacy, R. H. Marxist and Soviet criticism. *In* Stacy, R. H. Russian literary criticism p185-230

Stacy, R. H. The modernists. *In* Stacy, R. H. Russian literary criticism p105-62

Russian literature—20th century—History and criticism—*Continued*

Thomson, B. The redundancy of art: Soviet and Marxist views of art in the 1920s. *In* Thomson, B. Lot's wife and the Venus of Milo p53-74

Weidlé, W. The poison of modernism. *In* Gibian, G. and Tjalsma, H. W. eds. Russian modernism p18-30

See also Constructivism (Russian literature); Formalism (Russian literature)

Russian Orthodox Eastern Church. See Orthodox Eastern Church, Russian

Russian philosophy. See Philosophy, Russian

Russian poetry

See also Bylini

History and criticism

Katz, M. R. The influence of folk ballads and the ballad revival on Russian literary ballads. *In* Katz, M. R. The literary ballad in early nineteenth-century Russian literature p3-18

Mandel'shtam, O. E. About an interlocutor. *In* Mandel'shtam, O. E. Selected essays p58-64

Mandel'shtam, O. E. Attack. *In* Mandel'shtam, O. E. Selected essays p54-57

18th century—History and criticism

Katz, M. R. Russian literary ballads of the 1790s. *In* Katz, M. R. The literary ballad in early nineteenth-century Russian literature p19-36

19th century—History and criticism

Katz, M. R. Polemics. *In* Katz, M. R. The literary ballad in early nineteenth-century Russian literature p101-20

Katz, M. R. Zhukovsky's imitators. *In* Katz, M. R. The literary ballad in early nineteenth-century Russian literature p121-38

20th century—History and criticism

Brown, D. B. The first Soviet generation of poets. *In* Brown, D. B. Soviet Russian literature since Stalin p62-79

Brown, D. B. The oldest poets. *In* Brown, D. B. Soviet Russian literature since Stalin p23-61

Brown, D. B. Poets formed during the war. *In* Brown, D. B. Soviet Russian literature since Stalin p80-105

Brown, D. B. The younger generation of poets. *In* Brown, D. B. Soviet Russian literature since Stalin p106-44

Ivask, G. Russian modernist poets and the mystic sectarians. *In* Gibian, G. and Tjalsma, H. W. eds. Russian modernism p85-106

Kunitz, S. J. A visit to Russia. *In* Kunitz, S. J. A kind of order, a kind of folly p18-38

Mandel'shtam, O. E. Notes about poetry. *In* Mandel'shtam, O. E. Selected essays p80-84

Mandel'shtam, O. E. Storm & stress. *In* Mandel'shtam, O. E. Selected essays p144-53

Tjalsma, H. W. The Petersburg poets. *In* Gibian, G. and Tjalsma, H. W. eds. Russian modernism p65-84

See also Constructivism (Russian literature)

Russian-Polish War, 1920-1921. See Poland—History—Wars of 1918-1921

Russian primers. See Primers, Russian

Russian propaganda. See Propaganda, Russian

Russian prose literature

20th century—History and criticism

Brown, D. B. Literature reexamines the past. *In* Brown, D. B. Soviet Russian literature since Stalin p253-84

Brown, D. B. The village writers. *In* Brown, D. B. Soviet Russian literature since Stalin p218-52

Russian revolutionary poetry. See Revolutionary poetry, Russian

Russian satellites. See Communist countries

Russian sculpture. See Sculpture, Russian

Russians in Alaska

Gibson, J. R. Old Russia in the New World: adversaries and adversities in Russian America. *In* European settlement and development in North America: essays on geographical change in honour and memory of Andrew Hill Clark p46-65

Russians in literature

Crankshaw, E. Conrad and Russia. *In* Joseph Conrad: a commemoration p91-104

Russians in Paris

Cole, E. A. Paris 1848: a Russian ideological spectrum. *In* California Slavic studies v8 p 1-13

Russo, Joseph

How, and what, does Homer communicate? The medium and message of Homeric verse. *In* Havelock, E. A. and Hershbell, J. P. eds. Communication arts in the ancient world p39-52

Russo, Joseph, and Simon, Bennett

Homeric psychology and the oral epic tradition. *In* Wright, J. H. ed. Essays on the Iliad p41-57

Russo, Nicholas John

From Mezzogiorno to metropolis: Brooklyn's new Italian immigrants. *In* Studies in Italian American social history p118-31

Russo-German pact. See Russo-German treaty, 1939

Russo-German treaty, 1939

Watt, D. C. The initiation of the negotiations leading to the Nazi-Soviet pact: a historical problem. *In* Essays in honour of E. H. Carr p152-70

Russo-Japanese Border Conflicts, 1932-1941

Coox, A. D. Shigemitsu Mamoru: the diplomacy of crisis. *In* Burns, R. D. and Bennett, E. M. eds. Diplomats in crisis p251-73

Rust, Richard Dilworth

Coverdale's confession, a key to meaning in The Blithedale romance. *In* Literature and ideas in America p96-110

Rusten, Jeffrey S.

Wasps 1360-1369: Philokleon's ΤΩΘΑΣΜΟΣ. *In* Harvard Studies in classical philology v81 p157-61

Rustow, Dankwart Alexander

Political ends and military means in the late Ottoman and post-Ottoman Middle East. *In* War, technology and society in the Middle East p386-99·

Rutherford, Andrew
The literature of war
Contents
The Christian as hero: Waugh's Sword of honour
The common man as hero: literature of the Western Front
The intellectual as hero: Lawrence of Arabia
The spy as hero: Le Carré and the Cold War
The subaltern as hero: Kipling and frontier war
Rutherford, Ernest Rutherford, 1st Baron

About

Trenn, T. J. Rutherford and recoil atoms: the metamorphosis and success of a once stillborn theory. *In* Historical studies in the physical sciences v6 p513-47
Rutherford, John
Story, character, setting, and narrative mode in Galdós's El amigo Manso. *In* Fowler, R. ed. Style and structure in literature p177-212
Rutherford, Mark, pseud. See White, William Hale
Rutherford, William E.
Second language teaching. *In* Wardhaugh, R. and Brown, H. D. eds. A survey of applied linguistics p138-63

Rutman, Darrett Bruce
Governor Winthrop's garden crop: the significance of agriculture in the early commerce of Massachusetts Bay. *In* Vaughan, A. T. and Bremer, F. J. eds. Puritan New England p155-71

Rutman, Leonard
Evaluating explorations and demonstrations for planning in criminal justice. *In* Riedel, M. and Chappell, D. eds. Issues in criminal justice: planning and evaluation p48-58

Rutter, John Gatt- See Gatt-Rutter, John

Rutter, Michael
Early sources of security and competence. *In* Human growth and development p33-61

Ruysschaert, José

About individual works
Juste Lipse et les Annales de Tacite
Momigliano, A. The first political commentary on Tacitus: appendix. *In* Momigliano, A. Essays in ancient and modern historiography p218-29

Ruzzante. See Beolco, Angelo, called Ruzzante

Ryals, Clyde de L.
"Analyzing humanity back into its elements": Browning's Aristophanes' apology and Carlyle. *In* Carlyle and his contemporaries p280-97

Ryan, Alan
Maximising, moralising and dramatising. *In* Hookway, C. and Pettit, P. eds. Action and interpretation p65-81

Ryan, John Julian
Humanistic work: its philosophical and cultural implications. *In* Heisler, W. J. and Houck, J. W. eds. A matter of dignity p11-22

Ryan, Kevin
Television as a moral educator. *In* Television as a cultural force p111-27

Ryan, Lawrence V.
Neo-Latin literature. *In* Jones, W. M. ed. The present state of scholarship in sixteenth-century literature p197-257
Ryan, Michael
The act. *In* Glyph 2 p64-87
A grammatology of assent: Cardinal Newman's Apologia pro vita sua. *In* Landow, G. P. ed. Approaches to Victorian autobiography p128-57
Ryan, Michael, 1946-

About individual works
Threats instead of trees
Kunitz, S. J. Michael Ryan. *In* Kunitz, S. J. A kind of order, a kind of folly p289-93
Ryder, Frank Glessner
Lessing on liberty: the literary work as autobiography. *In* Studies in eighteenth-century culture v6 p229-44
Ryf, Robert Stanley
Joseph Conrad. *In* Stade, G. ed. Six modern British novelists p131-74
Rylands, George Humphrey Wolfestan
The Kingsman. *In* Keynes, M. ed. Essays on John Maynard Keynes p39-48
Ryle, Gilbert
Heidegger's Sein und Zeit. *In* Murray, M. E. ed. Heidegger and modern philosophy p53-64

About individual works
The concept of mind
Murray, M. E. Heidegger and Ryle: two versions of phenomenology. *In* Murray, M. E. ed. Heidegger and modern philosophy p271-90

Heidegger's Sein und Zeit
Murray, M. E. Heidegger and Ryle: two versions of phenomenology. *In* Murray, M. E. ed. Heidegger and modern philosophy p271-90

S

SABRA. See South African Bureau of Racial Affairs

SALT. See Strategic Arms Limitation Talks

SAP. See Socialdemo Kratiska Arbetarepartier

SDS. See Students for a Democratic Society

SEEK (Search for education, elevation and knowledge) See New York (City) City University of New York—Admission

SKP. See Communist Party of Finland

SLA. See Symbionese Liberation Army

Saadiah ben Joseph, gaon

About
Wolfson, H. A. Saadia on the semantic aspects of the problem of attribute. *In* Salo Wittmayer Baron v2 p1009-22

About individual works
The book of beliefs and opinions
Fox, M. On the rational commandments in Saadia's philosophy: a reexamination. *In* Modern Jewish ethics p174-87

Saadyah Gaon. See Saadiah ben Joseph, gaon

Sabah

Historiography

Tarling, N. Some notes on the historiography of British Borneo. *In* Southeast Asian history and historiography p285-95

Sábato, Ernesto R.

About individual works

On heroes and bombs

Foster, D. W. Ernesto Sabato and the anatomy of a national unconscious. *In* Foster, D. W. Currents in the contemporary Argentine novel: Arlt, Mallea, Sabato, and Cortázar p70-97

Sabbatarians. See Seventh-Day Adventists

Sabbath

Plaut, W. G. The Sabbath as protest: thoughts on work and leisure in the automated society. *In* Tradition and change in Jewish experience p169-83

Sabean, David Warren

Aspects of kinship behaviour and property in rural Western Europe before 1800. *In* Family and inheritance p96-111

Sabers

Starr, S. Z. Cold steel: the saber and the Union cavalry. *In* Hubbell, J. T. ed. Battles lost and won p107-24

Sabin, Florence Rena

About

Harvey, A. M. A new school of anatomy: the story of Franklin P. Mall, Florence R. Sabin, and John B. MacCallum. *In* Harvey, A. M. Adventures in medical research p97-113

Sabin, Margery

English romanticism and the French tradition

Contents

Beauty and taste
The charm of memory
The language of nature
"Love" in The prelude
The lovely behavior of things: Hopkins and Baudelaire
Middlemarch: beyond the voyage to Cythera
The poverty of nature in Madame Bovary
Rousseau and the vocabulary of feeling
The sentiment of being
The sources of imagination
The story of a life
Symbolic light
Victor Hugo and Wordsworthian perception
Victor Hugo: from spectacle to symbol

Sabloff, Jeremy A. and Friedel, David A.

A model of a pre-Columbian trading center. *In* Ancient civilization and trade p369-408

Sabloff, Jeremy A. and others

Trade and power in postclassic Yucatan: initial observations. *In* Mesoamerican archaeology p397-416

Sabra, A. I.

The exact sciences. *In* The Genius of Arab civilization p121-41

The scientific enterprise. *In* Lewis, B. ed. Islam and the Arab world p181-200

Sensation and inference in Alhazen's theory of visual perception. *In* Studies in perception 160-85

Sabres. See Sabers

Sabshin, Melvin

Social-community approaches in psychiatry. *In* American psychiatry: past, present, and future p78-93

Saccio, Peter

The oddity of Lyly's Endimion. *In* The Elizabethan theatre, V p92-111

Sacco and Vanzetti (Motion picture)

Sarris, A. Sacco and Vanzetti. *In* Sarris, A. Politics and cinema p59-60

Saccone, Eduardo

Grazia, sprezzatura, and affettazione in Castiglione's Book of the courtier. *In* Glyph 5 p34-54

Sachar, Abram Leon

At the threshold of the third century. *In* Tradition and change in Jewish experience p257-72

Sachs, Albert Louis

The instruments of domination in South Africa. *In* Thompson, L. M. and Butler, J. eds. Change in contemporary South Africa p223-49

Sachs, Albie. See Sachs, Albert Louis

Sachs, Nelly

About

Kurz, P. K. Journey into dustlessness. *In* Kurz, P. K. On modern German literature v 1 p194-215

Sachs, Rainer K.

Relativity. *In* Neyman, J. ed. The heritage of Copernicus: theories "pleasing to the mind" p297-310

Sachs, Robert G.

Our energy options—so what else is new? *In* Eppen, G. D. ed. Energy: the policy issues p3-24

Sacks, Herbert S.

"Bloody Monday": the crisis of the high school seniors. *In* Hurdles p10-47

Sacks, Karen

Engels revisited: women, the organization of production, and private property. *In* Reiter, R. R. ed. Toward an anthropology of women p211-34

Sacks, Michael Paul

Women in the industrial labor force. *In* Women in Russia p189-204

Sacksteder, William

Spinoza on democracy. *In* Freeman, E. and Mandelbaum, M. H. eds. Spinoza p117-38

Spinoza on part and whole: the worm's eye view *In* Shahan, R. W. and Biro, J. I. eds. Spinoza: new perspectives p139-59

Sackville-West, Victoria Mary

About

Fone, B. R. S. Sons and lovers: three English portraits. *In* Crew, L. ed. The gay academic p200-15

Sacrament of the Altar. See Lord's Supper

Sacraments

See also Lord's Supper

Catholic Church

Jones, D. A Christmas message, 1960. *In* Jones, D. The dying Gaul, and other writings p167-76

Sacred marriage (Mythology)

Jacobsen, T. Religious drama in ancient Mesopotamia. *In* Unity and diversity p65-97

Sacred numbers. See Symbolism of numbers

Sacrifice

Nagy, G. J. Six studies of sacral vocabulary relating to the fireplace. *In* Harvard Studies in classical philology v78 p71-106

Werner, E. Two types of ritual and their music. *In* Salo Wittmayer Baron v2 p975-1008

See also Scapegoat

Saddlemyer, Ann

Synge and the doors of perception. *In* Place, personality and the Irish writer p97-120

Sade, Donatien Alphonse François, comte, called marquis de

About individual works

Justine

Miller, N. K. Justine, or, The vicious circle. *In* Studies in eighteenth-century culture v5 p215-28

Sadism in literature

Scholes, R. E. Comedy and grotesquerie. *In* Scholes, R. E. Fabulation and metafiction p139-92

Sadler, Blair L.

Legal and ethical implications of reducing immigration. *In* Population policy and ethics p411-29

Sadock, Geoffrey Johnston

Dickens and Dr Leavis: a critical commentary on Hard times. *In* Dickens Studies Annual v2 p208-16

Sadock, Jerrold M.

Figurative speech and linguistics. *In* Ortony, A. ed. Metaphor and thought p46-63

Sadoff, Dianne Fallon

Norman Mailer to posterity. *In* Filler, L. ed. A question of quality: popularity and value in modern creative writing p181-92

Sadr ad-Dīn ash-Shīrazī. See Mullā Sadrā, Muhammad ibn Ibrāhīm

Sadrā, Muhammad ibn Ibrāhīm Mullā. See Mullā Sadrā, Muhammad ibn Ibrāhīm

Sadrā, Mullā. See Mullā Sadrā, Muhammad ibn Ibrāhīm

Saeki, Kiichi

Japan's security in a multipolar world. *In* Clapp, P. and Halperin, M. H. eds. United States-Japanese relations, the 1970's p183-202

Saeki, Shōichi

Images of the United States as a hypothetical enemy. *In* Iriye, A. ed. Mutual images p100-14

Safdie, Moshe

Collective consciousness in making environment. *In* The Frontiers of knowledge p201-34

About individual works

Beyond Habitat

Sale, R. H. Toynbee, Ellul, Safdie, Negroponte. *In* Sale, R H. On not being good enough p188-202

Safran, Nadav

Egypt's search for ideology: the Nasser era. *In* Kilson, M. ed. New states in the modern world p37-56

The War and the future of the Arab-Israeli conflict. *In* Bundy, W. P. ed. The world economic crisis p83-104

Sagal, Paul T. See Rapaport, E. jt. auth.

Sagan, Carl

An analysis of Worlds in collision. *In* Goldsmith, D. ed. Scientists confront Velikovsky p41-104

The planets. *In* Man and cosmos p68-84

Sagan, Eli

Religion and magic: a developmental view. *In* Johnson, H. M. ed. Religious change and continuity p87-116

Sagar, Keith M.

The originality of Wuthering Heights. *In* Smith, A. ed. The art of Emily Brontë p121-59

Sagarin, Edward, and Kelly, Robert J.

Sexual deviance and labelling perspectives. *In* Gove, W. R. ed. The labelling of deviance p243-71

Sagas. See Icelandic and Old Norse literature; Játvarðar saga Helga

Sagasti Perrett, Heli E. de. See Perrett, Heli E. de Sagasti

Sahagún, Bernardino de

About

Nicholson, H. B. Tepepolco, the locale of the first stage of Fr. Bernardino de Sahagún's great ethnographic project: historical and cultural notes. *In* Mesoamerican archaeology p145-54

Sahović, Milan

Disarmament and international law. *In* The Dynamics of the arms race p160-68

Said, Abdul Aziz, and Simmons, Luiz R.

The ethnic factor in world politics. *In* Said, A. A. and Simmons, L. R. eds. Ethnicity in an international context p15-47

Said, Edward W.

Conrad and Nietzsche. *In* Joseph Conrad: a commemoration p65-76

On repetition. *In* Fletcher, A. J. S. ed. The literature of fact p134-58

Renan's philological laboratory. *In* Art, politics, and will p59-98

Roads taken and not taken in contemporary criticism. *In* Krieger, M. and Dembo, L. S. eds. Directions for criticism p33-54

Saigyō

About

La Fleur, W. The death and 'lives' of the poet-monk Saigyō: the genesis of a Buddhist sacred biography. *In* Reynolds, F. E. and Capps, D. eds. The biographical process p343-61

Sailing

White, E. B. The sea and the wind that blows. *In* White, E. B. Essays of E. B. White p205-07

Sailors in literature. See Seamen in literature

Saini, Balwant Singh. See Chan, G. jt. auth.

St Aubyn, Giles

Queen Victoria as an author. *In* Royal Society of Literature of the United Kingdom, London. Essays by divers hands v38 p127-42

Saint Catherine (Basilian monastery) See Sinai. Saint Catherine (Basilian monastery)

St Christopher's Hospice, London

Saunders, C. Dying they live: St Christopher's Hospice. *In* Feifel, H. [ed.] New meanings of death p153-79

St Clair, William Linn

About individual works

Trelawny: the incurable romancer

Reiman, D. H. Trelawny and the decay of lying. *In* Review, v 1 1979 p275-94

Saint-Étienne (Cathedral) See Auxerre, France. Saint-Étienne (Cathedral)

Saint-Évremond, Charles de. See Saint-Évremond, Charles de Marguetel de Saint Denis, seigneur de

Saint-Évremond, Charles de Marguetel de Saint Denis, seigneur de

About

Horowitz, L. K. Saint-Evremond. *In* Horowitz, L. K. Love and language p73-89

Saint-Exupéry, Antoine de

About

Balakian, N. Poet of the air—and earth: Antoine de Saint-Exupéry. *In* Balakian, N. Critical encounters p142-45

Saint-Gilles, France (Gard) Abbey church of Saint-Gilles

Schapiro, M. New documents on Saint-Gilles. *In* Schapiro, M. Selected papers v 1 p328-46

Saint-Gobain, s.a.

History

Harris, J. R. Saint-Gobain and Ravenhead. *In* Great Britain and her world, 1750-1914 p27-70

St James's Chronicle

Bond, R. P. and Bond, M. N. The minute books of the St James's Chronicle. *In* Virginia. University. Bibliographical Society. Studies in bibliography v28 p17-40

St John de Crèvecoeur, Jean Hector. See Crèvecoeur, Michel Guillaume St Jean de, called Saint John de Crèvecoeur

St John's Apocalypse no. 786 (Icons)

Cutler, A. The Apocalypse icon in the Byzantine Museum, Athens. *In* Studies in memory of David Talbot Rice p94-112

St Leger, Frederick Y.

·The mass media and minority cultures. *In* Alcock, A. E.; Taylor, B. K. and Welton, J. M. eds. The future of cultural minorities p63-81

St. Luke's Hospital, New York

Woodring, S. Hospice pilot project in an acute-care general hospital 1975-1976. *In* Home care p159-64

St Mary's City, Md.

Carson, C. Doing history with material culture. *In* Material culture and the study of American life p41-64

St Nicholas (Periodical)

White, E. B. The St Nicholas League. *In* White, E. B. Essays of E. B. White p225-33

St Nicholas League

White, E. B. The St Nicholas League. *In* White, E. B. Essays of E. B. White p225-33

St Peter's (Basilica) See Vatican City. San Pietro in Vaticano (Basilica)

Saint Peter's Square. See Vatican City. Piazza San Pietro

St Petersburg. See Leningrad

Saint Pierre (Abbey). See Moissac, France. Saint Pierre (Abbey)

Saint-Riquier, France (Benedictine abbey)

Evergates, T. Historiography and sociology in early feudal society: the case of Hariulf and the "milites" of Saint-Riquier. *In* Viator: medieval and Renaissance studies v6 p35-49

Saint-Simon, Claude Henri, comte de

About

Voegelin, E. The religion of humanity and the French Revolution. *In* Voegelin, E. From Enlightenment to revolution p160-94

Saint-Simon, Louis de Rouvroy, duc de

About individual works

Historical memoirs of the duc de Saint-Simon: a shortened version

Mudrick, M. Saint-Simon. *In* Mudrick, M. The man in the machine p123-36

Memoirs

Auchincloss, L. Saint-Simon: novelist or historian? *In* Auchincloss, L. Life, law and letters p147-50

Saint-Simonianism

Fielding, K. J. Carlyle and the Saint-Simonians (1830-1832): new considerations. *In* Carlyle and his contemporaries p35-59

St Tammany Parish, La.

Antiquities

Peterson, J. H. Louisiana Choctaw life at the end of the nineteenth century. *In* Hudson, C. M. ed. Four centuries of Southern Indians p101-12

Sainte-Beuve, Charles Augustin

About

Arnold, M. Sainte-Beuve. *In* Arnold, M. The last word p106-19

Ste Croix, Geoffrey E. M. de

Early Christian attitudes to property and slavery. *In* Church, society and politics p 1-38

Sainte Marie (Abbey church). See Souillac, France. Sainte Marie (Abbey church)

Saints

See also Hagiography

Psychology

Goodich, M. Childhood and adolescence among the thirteenth-century saints. *In* Kren, G. M. and Rappoport, L. H. eds. Varieties of psychohistory p193-218

England

Rollason, D. W. Lists of saints' resting-places in Anglo-Saxon England. *In* Anglo-Saxon England 7 p61-93

Saints, Irish

Bieler, L. Hagiography and romance in medieval Ireland. *In* Medievalia et humanistica no.6 p13-24

Heist, W. W. Irish saints' lives, romance, and cultural history. *In* Medievalia et humanistica no.6 p25-40

Saints, Women

Legends

Anson, J. S. The female transvestite in monasticism: the origin and development of a motif. *In* Viator: medieval and Renaissance studies v5 p 1-32

Saints in art

Chastel, A. Two Roman statues: Saints Peter and Paul. *In* Collaboration in Italian Renaissance art p59-73

Sakai, Tadao, and Noguchi, Tetsurō
Taoist studies in Japan. *In* Welch, H. and Seidel, A. K. eds. Facets of Taoism p269-87

Sakai

Children

Dentan, R. K. Notes on childhood in a nonviolent context: the Semai case. *In* Montagu, A. ed. Learning non-aggression p94-143

Psychology

Dentan, R. K. Notes on childhood in a nonviolent context: the Semai case. *In* Montagu, A. ed. Learning non-aggression p94-143

Sakamoto, Yoshikazu
Toward global identity. *In* On the creation of a just world order p189-210

Sakharov, Andrei Dmitrievich

About

Dornan, P. Andrei Sakharov: the conscience of a liberal scientist. *In* Tokes, R. L. ed. Dissent in the USSR p354-417

Mihajlov, M. Two convergences. *In* Mihajlov, M. Underground notes p 1-5

About individual works

Progress, coexistence, and intellectual freedom

Solzhenitsyn, A. I. As breathing and consciousness return. *In* From under the rubble p3-25

Sala, Kaarina
Eeva Liisa Manner: a literary portrait. *In* Dauenhauer, R. and Binham, P. eds. Snow in May p58-59

La salamandre (Motion picture)
Kauffmann, S. La salamandre; Charles, dead or alive. *In* Kauffmann, S. Living images p118-21

Salamon, Lester Milton, and Wamsley, Gary L.
The Federal bureaucracy: responsive to whom? *In* Rieselbach, L. N. ed. People vs. government: the responsiveness of American institutions p151-88

Sale, Roger H.
On not being good enough
Contents
Alfred Kazin
Bradley & Maclean
Dashiell Hammett
The golden age of the American novel
Hawkes, Malamud, Richler, Oates
Hugh Kenner
Huxley & Bennett, Bedford & Drabble
Irving Howe
Jane Jacobs
Kurt Vonnegut, Jr.
Leslie Fiedler
Lionel Trilling
Mailer & Lessing
Marvin Mudrick
Mumford & Fuller
Novelists, readers, critics
Philip Roth
René Wellek
Robert Stone
Toynbee, Ellul, Safdie, Negroponte
Unknown novels
Williams, Weesner, Drabble

Salehar, Anna Maria
Nabokov's Gift: an apprenticeship in creativity. *In* A Book of things about Vladimir Nabokov p70-83

Sales

United States

Danzig, R. A comment on the jurisprudence of the Uniform Commercial Code. *In* Stanford legal essays p97-111

Sales promotion. See Advertising

Salgādo, Gāmini. See Salgādo, Ramsay Gāmini Norton

Salgādo, Ramsay Gāmini Norton
Taking a nail for a walk: on reading Women in love. *In* Josipovici, G. ed. The modern English novel: the reader, the writer and the work p95-112

Salieri, Antonio

About

Borowitz, A. Salieri and the "murder" of Mozart. *In* Borowitz, A. Innocence and arsenic p63-86

Dent, E. J. The heritage of Gluck. *In* Dent, E. J. The rise of romantic opera p33-46

Salih, Galobawi Mohammed
The role of OAU in public administration and management. *In* El-Ayouty, Y. ed. The Organization of African Unity after ten years p237-50

Salingar, Leo
'The changeling' and the drama of domestic life. *In* English Association. Essays and studies, 1979 p80-96

Comic form in Ben Jonson: Volpone and the philosopher's stone. *In* English drama: forms and development p48-68

Salinger, Herman. See Part 2 under title: Creative encounter

Salinger, Jerome David

About

Howe, I. The Salinger cult. *In* Howe, I. Celebrations and attacks p93-96

Tanner, T Afterword: Wonder and alienation—the mystic and the moviegoer. *In* Tanner, T. The reign of wonder p336-61

Salishan languages
Thompson, L. C. The Northwest. *In* Sebeok, T. A. ed. Native languages of the Americas v 1 p359-425

Sallis, John
The origins of Heidegger's thought. *In* Radical phenomenology p43-57

Salmagundi
Boyers, R. The little magazine in its place: literary culture and anarchy. *In* Anderson, E. and Kinzie, M. eds. The little magazine in America: a modern documentary history p50-67

Salmon, Jack D.
Resupplying spaceship earth: prospects for space industrialization. *In* Orr, D. W. and Soroos, M. S. eds. The global predicament p209-29

Salmon, Wesley C.
Clocks and simultaneity in special relativity or, Which twin has the Timex? *In* Motion and time, space and matter p508-45

Memory and perception in Human knowledge. *In* Nakhnikian, G. ed. Bertrand Russell's philosophy p139-67

Russell on scientific inference; or, Will the real deductivist please stand up? *In* Nakhnikian, G. ed. Bertrand Russell's philosophy p183-208

Salmond, John A.
Aubrey Williams: atypical New Dealer? *In* Braeman, J.; Bremner, R. H. and Brody, D. eds. The New Deal v 1 p218-45

Salomé, Lou Andreas- See Andreas-Salomé, Lou

Salomon, Jean-Jacques
Science policy studies and the development of science policy. *In* Science, technology and society p43-70

Salomon, Roger B.
The mock-heroics of desire: some stoic personae in the work of William Carlos Williams. *In* The Stoic strain in American literature p97-112

Salomon and Saturn
Sharpe, E. J. The Old English runic Paternoster. *In* Symbols of power p41-60

Salomone, Franco
Terrorism and the mass media. *In* International terrorism and political crimes p43-46

Salons
Showalter, E. Madame de Graffigny and her salon. *In* Studies in eighteenth-century culture v6 p377-91

Salt, M. J.
Romanus Egudu and Donatus Nwoga: Igbo traditional verse. *In* African literature today no. 7: Focus on criticism p156-58

Syl Cheyney-Coker: Concerto for an exile. *In* African literature today no. 7: Focus on criticism p159-62

Salter, Elizabeth
Langland and the contexts of 'Piers Plowman.' *In* English Association. Essays and studies, 1979 p19-25

Saltpeter in literature
Guerlac, H. The poets' nitre: studies in the chemistry of John Mayow—II. *In* Guerlac, H. Essays and papers in the history of modern science p260-74

Saltus, Edgar Evertson

About
Peckham, M. Edgar Saltus and the heroic decadence. *In* Tulane Studies in English, v23 p61-69

Saltykōv, Mikhail Evgrafovich

About individual works
The Golovlyov family
Calder, A. Fiction and politics: the art of Turgenev. *In* Calder, A. Russia discovered p73-107

Saltykov-Shchedrin, Mikhail Evgrafovich. See Saltykōv, Mikhail Evgrafovich

Salutations

History
Constable, G. The structure of medieval society according to the dictatores of the twelfth century. *In* Law, church, and society p253-67

Salutin, Marilyn
Stripper morality. *In* Henslin, J. M. ed. Deviant life-styles p191-208

Salvadori, Mario George
The aesthetics of technology: in response to David P. Billington. *In* Small comforts for hard times p199-203

Salvadori, Massimo
Aftermath of empire. *In* Aftermath of empire p105-52

Salvadori, Max William. See Salvadori, Massimo

Salvation
Brown, J. Hieroglyphs of death and salvation: the decoration of the Church of the Hermandad de la Caridad, Seville. *In* Brown, J. Images and ideas in seventeenth-century Spanish painting p128-46

See also Assurance (Theology); Covenants (Theology); Justification; Repentance

History of doctrines
Johnson, P. J. Hobbes's Anglican doctrine of salvation. *In* Ross, R. G.; Schneider, H. W. and Waldman, T. eds. Thomas Hobbes in his time p102-25

Salvemini, Gaetano

About
Hughes, H. S. The critique of fascism. *In* Hughes, H. S. The sea change p70-133

Salzburg

History
Freed, J. B. The formation of the Salzburg ministerialage in the tenth and eleventh centuries: an example of upward social mobility in the early Middle Ages. *In* Viator: medieval and Renaissance studies v9 p67-102

Salzburg festival
Craft, R. Salzburg, Mozart, and Cosi. *In* Craft, R. Current convictions p13-24

Salzmann, Michel de. See De Salzmann, Michel

Samaniego, Félix María

About individual works
Fábulas en verso castellano, para el uso del Real seminario vascongado
Noel, T. Samaniego, Iriarte, and the fable in Spain. *In* Noel, T. Theories of the fable in the eighteenth century p140-44

Sambrook, Arthur James. See Sambrook, James

Samizdat. See Underground literature—Russia

Sampling (Statistics)
Cochran, W. G. The vital role of randomization in experiments and surveys. *In* Neyman, J. ed. The heritage of Copernicus: theories "pleasing to the mind" p445-63

Sampson, Anthony

About individual works
The sovereign state of ITT
Vidal, G. Conglomerates. *In* Vidal, G. Matters of fact and of fiction p253-58

Sampson, Howard L.
Model for participation. *In* Managing non-profit organizations p109-17

Sampson, William

About
Bloomfield, M. H. William Sampson and the codification movement. *In* Bloomfield, M. H. American lawyers in a changing society, 1776-1876 p59-90

Samson, Allan A.
Indonesia. *In* Kearney, R. N. ed. Politics and modernization in South and Southeast Asia p253-77

Samuel, Maurice

Race, nation, and people in the Jewish Bible. *In* Tradition and change in Jewish experience p26-45

About individual works
In praise of Yiddish

Dawidowicz, L. S. Yiddish and its translation. *In* Dawidowicz, L. S. The Jewish presence p154-62

Samuels, Charles Thomas

Mastering the film, and other essays
Contents

The blow-up: sorting things out
Bonnie and Clyde
Carol Reed and the novelistic film
The context of A clockwork orange
Federico Fellini: juxtaposition
Hitchcock
How not to film a novel
Hyphens of the self
Jean Renoir and the theatrical film
Notes for an introduction
Puppets: from Z to Zabriskie Point
Tampering with reality

Samuels, Stuart

The age of conspiracy and conformity: Invasion of the body snatchers. *In* O'Connor, J. E. and Jackson, M. A. eds. American history/American film p203-17

Samuelson, David N.

The frontier worlds of Robert A. Heinlein. *In* Clareson, T. D. ed. Voices for the future: essays on major science fiction writers v 1 p104-52

The lost canticles of Walter M. Miller, Jr. *In* Clareson, T. D. ed. Voices for the future: essays on major science fiction writers v2 p56-81

Samuelson, Paul Anthony

Illogic of neo-Marxian doctrine of unequal exchange. *In* Inflation, trade and taxes p96-107

Land and the rate of interest. *In* Theory for economic efficiency: essays in honor of Abba P. Lerner p167-85

Samuely, Felix J. See Korn, A. jt. auth.

Samurai. See Bushido

Samvega (The Indic word)

Coomaraswamy, A. K. Samvega: aesthetic shock; excerpt from "Figures of speech or figures of thought: collected essays on the traditional or 'normal' view of art." *In* Coomaraswamy, A. K. Selected papers v 1 p179-85

San (African people)

Eibl-Eibesfeldt, I. The Bushmen. *In* Goodall, V. M. ed. The quest for man p171-86

See also !Kung (African people)

San Antonio

Race question

Bailey, D. T. and Haulman, B. E. Ethnic differences on the Southwestern United States frontier, 1860. *In* Miller, D. H. and Steffen, J. O. eds. The frontier p243-57

San Benito County

History

Friedman, L. M. San Benito 1890: legal snapshot of a county. *In* Stanford legal essays p163-77

San Blas Indians. See Cuna Indians

San Francisco

Lyman, S. M. Conflict and the web of group affiliation in San Francisco's Chinatown, 1850-1910. *In* The Asian American: the historical experience p26-52

City planning

Bowden, M. J. Persistence, failure, and mobility in the inner city: preliminary notes. *In* Pattern and process p169-92

Social conditions

Becker, H. S. and Horowitz, I. L. The culture of civility. *In* Henslin, J. M. ed Deviant life-styles p337-48

San Francisco. American Conservatory Theater

Kauffmann, S. The American Conservatory Theater. *In* Kauffmann, S. Persons of the drama p31-35

San Girolamo della Carità (Church) See Rome (City) San Girolamo della Carità (Church)

San Isidoro el Real (Church) See Leon, Spain. San Isidoro el Real (Church) Panteón de los Reyes

San kuo

Li, P. Narrative patterns in San-kuo and Shui-hu. *In* Chinese narrative p73-84

San Marco (Basilica) Mosaici della Genesi. See Venice. San Marco (Basilica) Mosaici della Genesi

Sánchez Ferlosio, Rafael

About individual works
El Jarama

Schwartz, R. Rafael Sanchez Ferlosio and El Jarama (1956). *In* Schwartz, R. Spain's New Wave novelists, 1950-1974 p87-99

Sanctification. See Holiness

Sanctions (International law)

Vinson, J. C. Sanctions. *In* Encyclopedia of American foreign policy p924-35

See also Embargo

Sanctis, Francesco de

Boccaccio's human comedy; excerpt from "History of Italian literature." *In* Dombroski, R. S. ed. Critical perspectives on The Decameron p26-37

Sand, George, pseud. of Mme Dudevant

About

Pritchett, V. S. George Sand: George Sand. *In* Pritchett, V. S. The myth makers p115-27

Sandalow, Terrance

Racial preferences in higher education: political responsibility and the judicial role. *In* Gross, B. R. ed. Reverse discrimination p239-64

Sanday, Peggy R.

On the causes of IQ differences between groups and implications for social policy. *In* Montagu, A. ed. Race and IQ p220-51

Sandbach, F. H.

The comic theatre of Greece and Rome
Contents

Aristophanes
An Athenian comedy
Drama at Rome
Epilogue
Menander
New Comedy

Sandbach, F. H.
The comic theatre of Greece and Rome
Contents—Continued
Old Comedy
Plautus
Terence

Five textual notes. *In* Illinois classical studies, v2 1977 p49-53

Sandburg, Carl

About

MacLeish, A. "A memorial tribute to Carl Sandburg." *In* Praise from famous men: an anthology of introductions p104-08

MacLeish, A. President Johnson alive and Carl Sandburg dead. *In* MacLeish, A. Riders on the earth p127-31

Sandeen, Ernest Robert
Millennialism. *In* The Rise of Adventism p104-18

The origins of Fundamentalism. *In* Mulder, J. M. and Wilson, J. F. eds. Religion in American history p415-30

Sanders, Andrew
The Victorian historical novel, 1840-1880
Contents
The argument from tradition: Hypatia, Fabiola and Callista
Clio's heroes and Thackeray's heroes: Henry Esmond and The Virginians
A Gothic revival: William Harrison Ainsworth's The Tower of London
Last of the English: Charles Kingsley's Hereward the Wake
Marching into the night: Thomas Hardy's The trumpet-major
The new seriousness: Edward Bulwer-Lytton's Harold
'Romola's waking': George Eliot's historical novel
Suffering a sea-change: Mrs Gaskell's Sylvia's lovers
The track of a storm: Charles Dickens' historical novels
See also Daniell, D. jt. auth.

Sanders, Charles Richard
Carlyle's friendships, and other studies
Contents
The ancient mariner and Coleridge's theory of poetic art
The background of Carlyle's portrait of Coleridge in The life of John Sterling
Carlyle and Tennyson
The Carlyles and Byron
The Carlyles and Thackeray
The correspondence and friendship of Thomas Carlyle and Leigh Hunt
The letters of John Stuart Mill
Retracing Carlyle's journey of 1849 through Ireland
Tennyson and the human hand
Two kinds of poetry
The Victorian Rembrandt: Carlyle's portraits of his contemporaries
• Carlyle's pen portraits of Queen Victoria and Prince Albert. *In* Fielding, K. J. and Tarr, R. L. eds. Carlyle past and present p216-38

About

Clubbe, J. Charles Richard Sanders. *In* Carlyle and his contemporaries pxiii-xxiii

Sanders, Clinton R. and Lyon, Eleanor
The humanistic professional: the reorientation of artistic production. *In* Gerstl, J. E. and Jacobs, G. eds. Professions for the people p43-59

Sanders, David Alan
John Dos Passos as conservative. *In* Filler, L. ed. A question of quality: popularity and value in modern creative writing p115-23

Revelation as child's play in Frost's "Directive." *In* Frost: centennial essays II p267-77

Sanders, James Alvin
The Qumran Psalms scroll (11QPs^a) reviewed. *In* On language, culture, and religion: in honour of Eugene A. Nida p79-99

Sanders, Jim Alvin. See Sanders, James Alvin

Sanders, Joe
Zelazny: unfinished business. *In* Clareson, T. D. ed. Voices for the future: essays on major science fiction writers v2 p180-96

Sanders, Norman Joseph
Critical studies. *In* Shakespeare survey 26 p151-68

An overview of critical approaches to the romances. *In* Shakespeare's romances reconsidered p 1-10

The true prince and the false thief: Prince Hal and the shift of identity. *In* Shakespeare survey 30 p29-34

Sanders, Robert E. See Bowers, J. W. jt. auth.

Sanders, William T.
Environmental heterogeneity and the evolution of Lowland Maya civilization. *In* The Origins of Maya civilization p287-97

Resource utilization and political evolution in the Teotihuacan Valley. *In* Explanation of prehistoric change p231-59

Sandler, Bernice
Sex discrimination, educational institutions, and the law: a new issue on campus. *In* Women in academia p20-36

Sandler, R.
The changing concept of the individual. *In* Savory, R. M. ed. Introduction to Islamic civilisation p137-45

Islamic art: variations on themes of arabesque. *In* Savory, R. M. ed. Introduction to Islamic civilisation p89-109

Sandmel, Samuel
After the ghetto: Jews in Western culture, art, and intellect. *In* Tradition and change in Jewish experience p198-210

Sandner, Donald F.
Navaho Indian medicine and medicine men. *In* Sobel, D. S. ed. Ways of health p117-46

Sands, Donald B.
Reynard the Fox and the manipulation of the popular proverb. *In* The Learned and the lewed p265-78

Sandwich Islands. See Hawaii

Sang, Lewis M. See Lahey, K. A. jt. auth.

Sango. See Shango

Sanguinetti, Elise (Ayers)

About

Emerson, O. B. Some contemporary literary views of the newest South. *In* The Rising South v2 p117-25

Saṅka Achārya. See Saṅkarācārya

Saṅkara Achārya. See Saṅkarācārya

Saṅkarācārya

About

Lorenzen, D. N. The life of Saṅkarācārya. *In* Reynolds, F. E. and Capps, D. eds. The biographical process p87-107

Mahadevan, T. M. P. Śaṅkara. *In* Bishop, D. H. ed. Indian thought p283-300

Scharfstein, B. A. 'Cogito ergo sum': Descartes, Augustine, and Śankara. *In* Philosophy East/philosophy West p199-217

Sano di Pietro

About

Eisenberg, M. An antiphonal page of the Sienese Quattrocento. *In* Enggass, R. C. and Stokstad, M. eds. Hortus imaginum p51-55

Sansculottes

Andrews, R. M. The justices of the peace of Revolutionary Paris, September 1792-November 1794 (Frimaire Year III). *In* French society and the Revolution p167-216

Sanskrit drama

History and criticism

Nicoll, A. The Sanskrit drama. *In* Nicoll, A. World drama p531-38

Sansone, David

The Bacchae as satyr-play? *In* Illinois classical studies v3, 1978 p40-46

Sansovino, Jacopo

About

Lotz, W. The Roman legacy in Sansovino's Venetian buildings. *In* Lotz, W. Studies in Italian Renaissance architecture p140-51

Santa Fe, N.M.

Race question

Bailey, D. T. and Haulman, B. E. Ethnic differences on the Southwestern United States frontier, 1860. *In* Miller, D. H. and Steffen, J. O. eds. The frontier p243-57

Santa Francesca Romana (Church) See Rome (City) Santa Maria Nova (Church)

Santa Lucia, Patricia, pseud.

The industrial working class and the struggle for power in Chile. *In* O'Brien, P. J. ed. Allende's Chile p128-66

Santa Maria della Salute. See Venice. Santa Maria della Salute (Church)

Santa Maria Maggiore (Church) See Rome (City) Santa Maria Maggiore (Church)

Santa Maria Nova (Church) See Rome (City) Santa Maria Nova (Church)

Santangelo, Gennaro

The dark snows of Kilimanjaro. *In* Benson, J. J. ed. The short stories of Ernest Hemingway: critical essays p251-61

Santayana, George

A brief history of my opinions. *In* Crunden, R. M. ed. The superfluous men p5-18

A long way round to Nirvana. *In* Crunden, R. M. ed. The superfluous men p278-84

Materialism and idealism; excerpt from "Character and opinion in the United States." *In* Crunden, R. M. ed. The superfluous men p48-54

About

Santayana, G. A brief history of my opinions. *In* Crunden, R. M. ed. The superfluous men p5-18

Trilling, L. "That smile of Parmenides made me think." *In* Trilling, L. A gathering of fugitives p164-79

About individual works

Letters

Trilling, L. "That smile of Parmenides made me think." *In* Trilling, L. A gathering of fugitives p164-79

Santiago de Compostela, Spain

González López, E. The myth of Saint James and its functional reality. *In* Américo Castro and the meaning of Spanish civilization p91-111

Santo Domingo de Silos. See Los Silos, Spain. Silos abbey

Santos, Jesús Fernández. See Fernández Santos, Jesús

Santos, Luis Martín-. See Martín-Santos, Luis

Santos, Theotonio dos

Brazil: the origins of a crisis. *In* Chilcote, R. H. and Edelstein, J. C. eds. Latin America: the struggle with dependency and beyond p409-90

Santos (Art)

New Mexico

Wroth, W. H. The flowering and decline of the New Mexican santero: 1780-1900. *In* Weber, D. J. ed. New Spain's far northern frontier p273-82

Sapadin, Eugene

Hume's Law, Hume's way. *In* David Hume p210-17

Sapiny (African tribe)

Goldschmidt, W. R. Absent eyes and idle hands: socialization for low affect among the Sebei. *In* Schwartz, T. ed. Socialization as cultural communication p65-71

Sapir, J. David

The anatomy of metaphor. *In* The Social use of metaphor p3-32

The fabricated child. *In* The Social use of metaphor p193-223

Sapolsky, Harvey M.

Science, technology and military policy. *In* Science, technology and society p443-71

Sappho

About

Nagy, G. J. Phaethon, Sappho's Phaon, and the White Rock of Leukas. *In* Harvard Studies in classical philology v77 p137-77

Saracenic architecture. See Architecture, Islamic

Sarawak

Historiography

Tarling, N. Some notes on the historiography of British Borneo. *In* Southeast Asian history and historiography p285-95

Social conditions

Morris, H. S. In the wake of mechanization: sago and society in Sarawak. *In* Social organization and the applications of anthropology p273-301

Sarcasm. See Irony

Sardar, Ziauddin, and Rosser-Owen, Dawud G.

Science policy and developing countries. *In* Science, technology and society p535-75

Sardes. See Sardis

Sardis

Antiquities

Ramage, N. H. Draped herm from Sardis. *In* Harvard Studies in classical philology v78 p253-56

City planning

Hanfmann, G. M. A. Sardis, Croesus, and the Persians. *In* Hanfmann, G. M. A. From Croesus to Constantine p 1-21

Sarduy, Severo

About individual works

From Cuba with a song

MacAdam, A. J. Severo Sarduy: vital signs. *In* MacAdam, A. J. Modern Latin American narratives p44-50

Sargent, John

Regional development policy in Japan: some aspects of the plan for remodelling the Japanese archipelago. *In* Modern Japan p227-43

Sarin, Madhu

Chandigarh as a place to live in. *In* Walden, R. ed. The open hand p374-410

Sarkar, Chanchal

Journalists' organizations in Socialist society. *In* Fischer, H. D. and Merrill, J. C. eds. International and intercultural communication p37-50

Sarmatians. See Alani

Sarmiento, Domingo Faustino, President Argentine Republic

About

Ducey, C. A. Travel narratives of D. F. Sarmiento: a seminal frontier thesis. *In* Kagle, S. E. ed. America: exploration and travel p50-66

Leonard, I. A. Domingo Faustino Sarmiento. *In* Abroad in America: Visitors to the new Nation, 1776-1914 p104-13

Sarotte, Georges Michel
Like a brother, like a lover

Contents

The circumstances of the homosexual as reflected in the novel and theater: Between the American woman and the American virile ideal

The circumstances of the homosexual as reflected in the novel and theater: Small town and big city

The circumstances of the homosexual as reflected in the novel and theater: Three categories of homosexuals

Conclusion: another country

The evolution of the American sexual "establishment"

The evolution of the homosexual in the American novel—Melville to Baldwin

Four archetypes of the homosexual couple: Adolescents

Four archetypes of the homosexual couple: Teacher and pupil

Four archetypes of the homosexual couple: The captain and the soldier

Four archetypes of the homosexual couple: The white and the Black

The homosexual character on the stage

Homosexuality and the theater: Edward Albee: homosexual playwright in spite of himself

Homosexuality and the theater: Tennessee Williams: theater as psychotherapy

Homosexuality and the theater: William Inge: "Homosexual spite" in action

Latent homosexuality: short of and beyond true heterosexuality: Ernest Hemingway: the (almost) total sublimation of the homosexual instinct

Latent homosexuality: short of and beyond true heterosexuality: Francis Scott Fitzgerald: self-virilization and its failure

Latent homosexuality: short of and beyond true heterosexuality: Henry James: the feminine masochist syndrome

Latent homosexuality: short of and beyond true heterosexuality: Jack London: the hypervirile syndrome

Latent homosexuality: short of and beyond true heterosexuality: Norman Mailer: the overt homosexual

Latent homosexuality: short of and beyond true heterosexuality: The feminine-masochist temperament in certain Jewish characters

Saroyan, William

About

Balakian, N. The world of William Saroyan. *In* Balakian, N. Critical encounters p162-76

About individual works

The human comedy

McGilligan, P. Mr. Saroyan's thoroughly American movie. *In* Peary, G. and Shatzkin, R. eds. The modern American novel and the movies p156-67

The time of your life

Kauffmann, S. The time of your life. *In* Kauffmann, S. Persons of the drama p111-14

Sarraute, Nathalie

About

Vidal, G. French letters: theories of the new novel. *In* Vidal, G. Matters of fact and of fiction p65-88

Wright, M. Nathalie Sarraute: alienated or alienator? *In* Garvin, H. R. ed. Makers of the twentieth-century novel p253-58

About individual works

The planetarium, a novel

Sayre, R. F. Le planétarium: solitude in the world of commodities. *In* Sayre, R. F. Solitude in society p176-94

Portrait of a man unknown

Balakian, N. Three post-psychological novels. *In* Balakian, N. Critical encounters p95-104

Sarrel, Lorna J. and Sarrel, Philip Martin

The college subculture. *In* Sexuality and human values p71-84

Sarrel, Philip Martin. See Sarrel, L. J. jt. auth.

Sarris, Andrew

John Ford: The grapes of wrath. *In* Denby, D. ed. Awake in the dark p320-25

Politics and cinema

Contents

The assassination of Trotsky

Avant-garde films are more boring than ever

The candidate

The case of the Naves brothers

Cock-tale parties on the East Side

The conversation

Dog day afternoon

Fascinating fascism meets leering leftism

The front

Sartre, Jean P.—About individual works—
Nausea—*Continued*

Doubrovsky, S. "The nine of hearts": fragment of a psychoreading of La nausée. *In* Roland, A. ed. Psychoanalysis, creativity, and literature p313-22

Glicksberg, C. I. Sartre: from Nausea to communism. *In* Glicksberg, C. I. The literature of nihilism p210-21

The psychology of imagination

Warnock, M. The nature of the mental image: phenomenology, Sartre and Wittgenstein. *In* Warnock, M. Imagination p131-95

Sartre on theater

Gass, W. H. Sartre on theater. *In* Gass, W. H. The world within the word p177-202

Ethics

Warnock, M. Existentialist ethics. *In* New studies in ethics v2 p361-420

Psychology

Collins, M. L. and Pierce, C. Holes and slime: sexism in Sartre's psychoanalysis. *In* Gould, C. C. and Wartofsky, M. W. eds. Women and philosophy p112-27

Saslow, Edward Louis

Shaftesbury cursed: Dryden's revision of the Achitophel lines. *In* Virginia. University. Bibliographical Society. Studies in bibliography v28 p276-83

Saslow, George

Application of behavior therapy. *In* Overview of the psychotherapies p68-91

Sasseen, Robert F.

Patronage and the academy. *In* Hook, S.; Kurtz, P. W. and Todorovich, M. eds. The university and the state: what role for government in higher education? p87-93

Sassoon, Sir Philip, bart.

About individual works
The third route

Wilder, T. N. Sir Philip Sassoon's The Third route. *In* Wilder, T. N. American characteristics, and other essays p251-54

Sastri, Durvasula S. See Hutton, E. J. jt. auth.

Sastry, Manikonda V Rama. See Rama Sastry, Manikonda V.

Satan. See Devil

Satan in literature. See Devil in literature

Satanism

Moody, E. J. Magical therapy: an anthropological investigation of contemporary Satanism. *In* Zaretsky, I. I. and Leone, M. P. eds. Religious movements in contemporary America p355-82

Truzzi, M. Towards a sociology of the occult: notes on modern witchcraft. *In* Zaretsky, I. I. and Leone, M. P. eds. Religious movements in contemporary America p628-45

Satellite vehicles. See Artificial satellites

Satellites. See Moon

Satellites, Artificial. See Artificial satellites

Sater, William F.

The Black experience in Chile. *In* Toplin, R. B. ed. Slavery and race relations in Latin America p13-50

Satire

Fitz Gerald, G. The satiric short story: a definition. *In* May, C. E. ed. Short story theories p182-88

See also Burlesque (Literature); Grotesque; Irony; Parody

History and criticism

Lewis, W. Satire defended. *In* Lewis, W. Enemy salvoes p41-49

Satire, American

History and criticism

Tilton, J. W. On learning by going where the critic has to go. *In* Tilton, J. W. Cosmic satire in the contemporary novel p13-20

Wymer, T. L. The Swiftian satire of Kurt Vonnegut, Jr. *In* Clareson, T. D. ed. Voices for the future: essays on major science fiction writers v 1 p238-62

Satire, English

History and criticism

Chernaik, W. L. Marvell's Satires: the artist as Puritan. *In* Friedenreich, K. ed. Tercentenary essays in honor of Andrew Marvell p268-96

Manlove, C. N. Dryden. *In* Manlove, C. N. Literature and reality, 1600-1800 p57-75

Manlove, C. N. Fielding. *In* Manlove, C. N. Literature and reality, 1600-1800 p136-48

Manlove, C. N. Swift. *In* Manlove, C. N. Literature and reality, 1600-1800 p114-24

Pritchard, W. H. Satire and fiction: examples from the 1930s. *In* Pritchard, W. H. Seeing through everything p178-208

Thompson, A. Shelley and 'Satire's scourge.' *In* Davies, R. T. and Beatty, B. G. eds. Literature of the romantic period, 1750-1850 p135-50

Satire, Latin

History and criticism

Abbott, K. M. Satira and satiricus in late Latin. *In* Illinois classical studies v4, 1979 p192-99

Fredericks, S. C. Irony of overstatement in the satires of Juvenal. *In* Illinois classical studies v4, 1979 p178-91

Ijsewijn, J. Neo-Latin satire: Sermo and Satyra Menippea. *In* Classical influences on

Knoche, U. Satire: a Roman literary genre. *In* Knoche, U. Roman satire p3-6 European culture A.D. 1500-1700 p41-55

LaFleur, R. A. Amicitia and the unity of Juvenal's first book. *In* Illinois classical studies v4, 1979 p158-77

Ramage, E. S. Ennius and the origins of Roman satire. *In* Roman satirists and their satire p8-26

Ramage, E. S. Method and structure in the satires of Persius. *In* Illinois classical studies v4, 1979 p136-51

Witke, C. Aspects of Roman poetic technique in a Carolingian Latin satiric text. *In* Illinois classical studies v4, 1979 p220-31

Sources

Knoche, U. Origin and name of the satura. *In* Knoche, U. Roman satire p7-16

Satirical songs, African

Piersen, W. D. Puttin' down Old Massa: African satire in the New World. *In* Crowley, D. J. ed. African folklore in the New World p20-34

Satirical songs, Afro-American

Piersen, M. E. Puttin' down Ole Massa: African satire in the New World. *In* Crowley, D. J. ed. African folklore in the New World p20-34

Sato, Hiroko

Willa Cather in Japan. *In* The Art of Willa Cather p84-102

Satura (The Latin word)

Knoche, U. Origin and name of the satura. *In* Knoche, U. Roman satire p7-16

Saturn (Planet)

Lewis, J. S. The outer planets. *In* Man and cosmos p117-30

Satyric drama, Greek. See Greek drama (Satyr play)

Saubolle, Louis E.

The economic face of communism in Asia. *In* Pacific Asia and U.S. policies: a political-economic-strategic assessment p108-14

Saudi Arabia

Politics and government

Wenner, M. W. Saudi Arabia: survival of traditional elites. *In* Political elites and political development in the Middle East p157-91

Sauer, Jonathan Deininger

Changing perception and exploitation of New World plants in Europe, 1492-1800. *In* First images of America p813-32

Saul, John S.

African peasantries and revolutionary change. *In* Forging nations: a comparative view of rural ferment and revolt p86-127

Saum, Lewis O.

Death in the popular mind of pre-Civil War America. *In* Death in America p30-48

Saunders, Cicely

Dying they live: St Christopher's Hospice. *In* Feifel, H. [ed.] New meanings of death p153-79

Sautet, Claude

About individual works

Vincent, François, Paul and the others

Truffaut, F. Claude Sautet: Vincent, François, Paul et les autres. *In* Truffaut, F. The films in my life p340-42

Sauvy, Alfred

The optimal change of a population. *In* Economic factors in population growth p63-73

Savage, Michael

Major patterns of group interaction in South African society. *In* Thompson, L. M. and Butler, J. eds. Change in contemporary South Africa p280-302

Savage, Richard

About individual works

Sir Thomas Overbury: a tragedy

Ellis, F. H. Johnson and Savage: two failed tragedies and a failed tragic hero. *In* Martz, L. L. and Williams, A. L. eds. The author in his work p337-46

Savage, William W. See Miller, D. H. jt. auth.

Savage, William W. and Thompson, Stephen I.

The comparative study of the frontier: an introduction. *In* The Frontier v2 p3-24

Savage, Noble. See Noble savage

Save the tiger (Motion picture)

Kauffmann, S. Save the tiger. *In* Kauffmann, S. Living images p177-79

Savigny, France (Cistercian abbey)

History

Hill, B. D. The Counts of Mortain and the origins of the Norman congregation of Savigny. *In* Order and innovation in the Middle Ages p237-53

Saville, John

Robert Owen on the family and the marriage system of the old immoral world. *In* Rebels and their causes p107-21

Saving and thrift. See Savings-banks

Savings-banks

Scott, I. O. Thrift institution management: tomorrow and today. *In* Benton, L. R. ed. Management for the future p271-82

Great Britain

Supple, B. E. Legislation and virtue: an essay on working class self-help and the state in the early nineteenth century. *In* Historical perspectives p211-54

Savoie, Norman Richard

Molière and French television. *In* Johnson, R. B.; Neumann, E. S. and Trail, G. T. eds. Molière and the commonwealth of letters: patrimony and posterity p645-62

Savonarola, Girolamo Maria Francesco Matteo

About

Le Comte, E. S. "That two-handed engine" and Savonarola and the Blackfriars fatal vespers. *In* Le Comte, E. S. Poets' riddles p100-28

Savory, Roger Mervyn

Christendom vs. Islam: interaction and coexistence. *In* Savory, R. M. ed. Introduction to Islamic civilisation p127-35

Land of the lion and the sun. *In* Lewis, B. ed. Islam and the Arab world p245-72

Law and traditional society. *In* Savory, R. M. ed. Introduction to Islamic civilisation p54-60

Saw, Ruth Lydia

The task of metaphysics for Spinoza. *In* Freeman, E. and Mandelbaum, M. H. eds. Spinoza p235-43

Saw you my father? (English ballad) See The grey cock (English ballad)

Saward, Ernest W.

Institutional organization, incentives, and change. *In* Knowles, J. H. ed. Doing better and feeling worse p193-202

Sawhill, Isabel VanDevanter

Economic perspectives on the family. *In* Rossi, A. S.; Kagan, J. and Hareven, T. K. eds. The family p115-26

Saxe, Arthur A.

On the origin of evolutionary processes: state formation in the Sandwich Islands, a systemic approach. *In* Explanation of prehistoric change p105-51

Sayaco Indians. See Amahuaca Indians

Sayers, Dorothy Leigh

The whimsical Christian

Contents

Christian morality
Creative mind
Creed or chaos?
Dante and Charles Williams
The dates in The Red-Headed League
The dogma is the drama

Sayers, Dorothy L.

The whimsical Christian

Contents—Continued

The Faust legend and the idea of the Devil
The greatest drama ever staged
The image of God
Oedipus simplix: freedom and fate in folk-
lore and fiction
The other six deadly sins
Problem picture
Strong meat
Toward a Christian esthetic
A vote of thanks to Cyrus
What do we believe?
The writing and reading of allegory

About

Dunn, R. P. "The laughter of the universe": Dorothy L. Sayers and the whimsical vision. *In* Hannay, M. P. ed. As her
whimsey took her p200-12

Gregory, E. R. Wilkie Collins and Dorothy L. Sayers. *In* Hannay, M. P. ed As
her whimsey took her p51-64

Hannay, M. P. Introduction. *In* Hannay,
M. P. ed. As her whimsey took her p xi-xvi

Panek, L. L. Dorothy Sayers. *In* Panek,
L. L. Watteau's shepherd: the detective
novel in Britain, 1914-1940 p72-110

Reaves, R. B. Crime and punishment in
the detective fiction of Dorothy L. Sayers.
In Hannay, M. P. ed. As her whimsey took
her p 1-13

Reynolds, W. Dorothy L. Sayers, interpreter of Dante. *In* Hannay, M. P. ed. As
her whimsey took her p 123-32

Reynolds, W. Dorothy Sayers and the
drama of orthodoxy. *In* Hannay, M. P. ed.
As her whimsey took her p91-106

Stock, R. D. and Stock, B. The agents
of evil and justice in the novels of Dorothy
L. Sayers. *In* Hannay, M. P. ed. As her
whimsey took her p14-22

Tischler, N. M. Artist, artifact, and audience: the aesthetics and practice of Dorothy L. Sayers. *In* Hannay, M. P. ed. As
her whimsey took her p153-64

About individual works

The man born to be king

Curran, T. The word made flesh: the
Christian aesthetic in Dorothy L. Sayers's
The man born to be king. *In* Hannay, M. P.
ed. As her whimsey took her p67-77

Dale, A. S. The man born to be king:
Dorothy L. Sayers's best mystery plot. *In*
Hannay, M. P. ed. As her whimsey took
her p78-90

The mind of the Maker

Harp, R. L. The mind of the Maker: the
theological aesthetic of Dorothy Sayers and
its application to poetry. *In* Hannay, M. P.
ed. As her whimsey took her p176-99

Webster, R. T. The mind of the Maker:
logical construction, creative choice and the
Trinity. *In* Hannay, M. P. ed. As her whimsey took her p165-75

The nine tailors

Basney, L. The nine tailors and the complexity of innocence. *In* Hannay, M. P. ed.
As her whimsey took her p23-35

Cawelti, J. G. The art of the classical detective story. *In* Cawelti, J. G. Adventure,
mystery, and romance p106-38

Characters—Harriet Vane

Hannay, M. P. Harriet's influence on the
characterization of Lord Peter Wimsey. *In*
Hannay M. P. ed. As her whimsey took
her p36-50

Characters—Lord Peter Wimsey

Hannay, M. P. Harriet's influence on the
characterization of Lord Peter Wimsey. *In*
Hannay, M. P. ed. As her whimsey took
her p36-50

Sayers, Dorothy Leigh, tr.

About individual works

The Comedy of Dante Alighieri

Dunlap, B. J. Through a dark wood of
criticism: the rationale and reception of
Dorothy L. Sayers's translation of Dante.
In Hannay, M. P. ed. As her whimsey took
her p133-49

Tristan in Brittany

Thorpe, L. Dorothy L. Sayers as a translator of Le roman de Tristan and La chanson de Roland. *In* Hannay, M. P. ed. As
her whimsey took her p109-22

Sayers, Jane

Monastic archdeacons. *In* Church and government · in the Middle Ages p177-203

Sayings. See Aphorisms and apothegms;
Maxims; Proverbs

Sayles, Myrna

Behind locked doors. *In* Eddy, E. M. and
Partridge, W. L. eds. Applied anthropology
in America p210-28

Sayre, Robert F.

Solitude in society

Contents

Afterword
L'Ancien régime: agreeable wilderness,
pleasant solitude
Antiquity and the Middle Ages
La chute: the egocentric individual
La condition humaine: solitude or solidarity?
Du côté de chez Swann: the unknowable
other
Journal d'un curé de campagne: the saint's
Gethsemane
Modern times
Le planétarium: solitude in the world of
commodities

al-Sayyid Marsot, Afaf Lutfi

The revolutionary gentlewomen in Egypt.
In Beck, L. and Keddie, N. R. eds. Women
in the Muslim world p261-76

Scaglione, Aldo Domenico

A note on Montaigne's Des cannibales and
the humanist tradition. *In* First images of
America p63-70

Rhetoric in Italian literature: Dante and
the rhetorical theory of sentence structure.
In Murphy, J. J. ed. Medieval eloquence
p252-69

Scalapino, Robert Anthony

Competitive strategic perceptions underlying U.S. policy in Asia. *In* Pacific Asia
and U.S. policies: a political-economic-
strategic assessment p 1-15

Scalds and scaldic poetry. See Bards and
bardism

Scalia, Antonin

Vermont Yankee: the A P A, the D.C.
Circuit, and the Supreme Court. *In* The
Supreme Court review, 1978 p345-409

Scandinavia
Antiquities
Cohen, S. L. The earliest Scandinavian towns. *In* The Medieval city p313-25

Foreign relations—Scotland
Crawford, B. E. Scotland's foreign relations: Scandinavia. *In* Brown, J. M. ed. Scottish society in the fifteenth century p85-100

Scandinavian literature. See Icelandic and Old Norse literature

Scanlon, Thomas Michael
Academic freedom and the control of research. *In* The Concept of academic freedom p237-54

Rights, goals, and fairness. *In* Hampshire, S. ed. Public and private morality p93-111

About individual works
Academic freedom and the control of research
Thomson, J. J. Academic freedom and research. *In* The Concept of academic freedom p255-62

Scannell, Vernon
Not without glory

Contents
Alan Ross and Charles Causley
Alun Lewis
American poets of the Second World War
Henry Reed and others
Keith Douglas
Roy Fuller
Setting the scene
Sidney Keyes

Scapegoat
Szasz, T. S. The expulsion of evil; excerpt from "The manufacture of madness". *In* Davis, F. J. and Stivers, R. eds. The collective definition of deviance p60-84

Scapegoat in literature
Davis, M. E. Mario Vargas Llosa: the necessary scapegoat. *In* Rossman, C. R. and Friedman, A. W. eds. Mario Vargas Llosa p136-50

Scapino (criticism) Dunlop, F. *In* Kauffmann, S. Persons of the drama p130-33

The scar of shame (Motion picture)
Cripps, T. R. "Race movies" as voices of the Black bourgeoisie: The scar of shame. *In* O'Connor, J. E. and Jackson, M. A. eds. American history/American film p39-55

Scarcity
Shinn, R. L. Living with scarcity. *In* Small comforts for hard times p137-51

Scarecrow (Motion picture)
Kauffmann, S. Scarecrow. *In* Kauffmann, S. Living images p195-97

Scarfe, Laurence
The baroque of Salento. *In* The Saturday book 34 p172-84

Scarisbrick, John Joseph
Cardinal Wolsey and the common weal. *In* Wealth and power in Tudor England p45-67

Robert Persons's plans for the 'true' reformation of England. *In* Historical perspectives p19-42

Scarpaci, Jean Ann
Immigrants in the new South: Italians in Louisiana's sugar parishes, 1880-1910. *In* Studies in Italian American social history p132-52

Scarron, Paul
About
Brereton, G Scarron and burlesque comedy. *In* Brereton, G. French comic drama p51-84

Scarrow, Howard A.
Participation through decentralization: the case of Britain. *In* Prospects for constitutional democracy p134-45

Scarry, Elaine
Henry Esmond: the rookery at Castlewood. *In* Literary monographs v7 p 1-43

Scenarios. See Moving-picture plays

Scenery (Stage) See Theaters—Stage-setting and scenery

Scepticism. See Skepticism

Scève, Maurice
About individual works
Délie
Tetel, M. Renaissance aborted and renascences: Scève's Délie. *In* Medieval and Renaissance studies 1976 p100-18

Schacht, Richard
On power and powerlessness. *In* Major social issues p425-38

Schachterle, Lance E.
American bibliographical notes. *In* American Antiquarian Society. Proceedings v84 pt 1 p219-32

Bleak House as a serial novel. *In* Dickens Studies Annual v 1 p212-24

Oliver Twist and its serial predecessors. *In* Dickens Studies Annual v3 p 1-13

Schaefer, George
About individual works
Macbeth
Jorgens, J. J. Defining Macbeth: Schaefer, Welles, and Kurosawa. *In* Jorgens, J. J. Shakespeare on film p148-60

Schafer, Walter E.
Sport and youth counterculture: contrasting socialization themes. *In* Social problems in athletics p183-200

Schaff, Adam
About individual works
Marxism and the human individual
Kovály, P. Adam Schaff's Marxism and the human individual. *In* Kovály, P. Rehumanization or dehumanization? p101-19

Schäffer, Peter
Letters of obscure men. *In* Hoffmeister, G. ed. The Renaissance and Reformation in Germany p129-40

Schaffner, Kenneth F.
Space and time in Lorentz, Poincaré, and Einstein: divergent approaches to the discovery and development of the special theory of relativity. *In* Motion and time, space and matter p465-507

Schaffner, Robert Michael
Can a scientific/technical executive from industry find happiness in a government agency? *In* Managing nonprofit organizations p32-37

Schama, Simon
The exigencies of war and the politics of taxation in the Netherlands, 1795-1810. *In* War and economic development p103-37

Schamberg, Morton Livingston
About
Coke, F. V. The cubist photographs of Paul Strand and Morton Schamberg. *In* One hundred years of photographic history p35-42

Schanzer, Ernest
Shakespeare and the doctrine of the unity of time. *In* Shakespeare survey 28 p57-61

Schapiro, Leonard Bertram
The structure of the Soviet state: government and politics. *In* Auty, R. and Obolensky, D. eds. An introduction to Russian history p331-49

Schapiro, Meyer
Selected papers v 1
Contents
From Mozarabic to Romanesque in Silos
New documents on Saint-Gilles
On geometrical schematism in Romanesque art
On the aesthetic attitude in Romanesque art
A relief in Rodez and the beginnings of Romanesque sculpture in southern France
The Romanesque sculpture of Moissac
The sculptures of Souillac
Two Romanesque drawings in Auxerre and some iconographic problems
Selected papers v2
Contents
The apples of Cézanne: an essay on the meaning of still-life
Arshile Gorky
Chagall's Illustrations for the Bible
Courbet and popular imagery
The introduction of modern art in America: the Armory Show
Mondrian
Nature of abstract art
On a painting of Van Gogh
Picasso's Woman with a fan
Seurat

Scharf, Aaron
Max Ernst, Étienne-Jules Marey, and the poetry of scientific illustration. *In* One hundred years of photographic history p117-26

Scharfstein, Ben-Ami
'Cogito ergo sum': Descartes, Augustine, and Śankara. *In* Philosophy East/philosophy West p199-217
Cultures, contexts, and comparisons. *In* Philosophy East/philosophy West p9-47
Three philosophical civilizations: a preliminary comparison. *In* Philosophy East/philosophy West p48-127

Schechner, Richard
About
Simon, J. I. "What can I do in the water?" *In* Simon, J. I. Singularities p133-36

Schechter, Harold
Comicons. *In* Browne, R. B. and Fishwick, M. W. eds. Icons of America p263-70

Scheerer, Constance
The deathly paradise of Sylvia Plath. *In* Butscher, E. ed. Sylvia Plath p166-76

Scheff, Thomas J.
Social conditions for rationality: how urban and rural courts deal with the mentally ill. *In* Davis, F. J. and Stivers, R. eds. The collective definition of deviance p317-24

Scheffauer, Hermann George
Walter Gropius. *In* Sharp, D. ed. The rationalists p42-49

Scheffler, Harold Walter
The "meaning" of kinship in American culture: another view. *In* Basso, K. H. and Selby, H. A. eds. Meaning in anthropology p57-91

Schegloff, Emanuel Abraham
Identification and recognition in interactional openings. *In* The Social impact of the telephone p415-50

Scheiber, Harry N.
The pay of Confederate troops and problems of demoralization: a case of administrative failure. *In* Hubbell, J. T. ed. Battles lost and won p229-39

Scheick, William J.
"An intercourse not well designed": talk and touch in the plays of Tennessee Williams. *In* Tennessee Williams: a tribute p763-73

Schein, Richard David
The land-grant university and environmental affairs. *In* Land-grant universities and their continuing challenge p178-89

Scheindlin, Raymond Paul
Rabbi Moshe Ibn Ezra on the legitimacy of poetry. *In* Medievalia et humanistica no. 7 p101-15

Scheinman, Lawrence
The interfaces of regionalism in Western Europe: Brussels and the peripheries. *In* Esman, M. J. ed. Ethnic conflict in the Western world p65-78

Scheler, Max Ferdinand
About
Frings, M. S. Nothingness and being: a Schelerian comment. *In* Radical phenomenology p182-89
Ethics
Heath, P. L. The idea of a phenomenological ethics. *In* Pivčević, E. ed. Phenomenology and philosophical understanding p159-72

Schell, Orville
Private life in a public culture. *In* Terrill, R. ed. The China difference p23-35

Schelling, Friedrich Wilhelm Joseph von
About
Warnock, M. Imagination and creative art: Hume, Kent and Schelling. *In* Warnock, M. Imagination p35-71

Schelling, Thomas C.
Command and control. *In* McKie, J. W. ed. Social responsibility and the business predicament p79-108
A framework for the evaluation of arms-control proposals. *In* Long, F. A. and Rathjens, G. W. eds. Arms, defense policy, and arms control p187-200
The importance of agreements. *In* The Dynamics of the arms race p65-77

Schellong, Dieter
On reading Karl Barth from the left. *In* Hunsinger, G. ed. Karl Barth and radical politics p139-57

Schenck, Benjamin Robinson
About
Harvey, A. M. Two mycoses first described at Johns Hopkins. *In* Harvey, A. M. Adventures in medical research p32-38

Schenectady, N.Y.

Politics and government

Hendrickson, K. E. Tribune of the people: George R. Lunn and the rise and fall of Christian Socialism in Schenectady. *In* Stave, B. M. ed. Socialism and the cities p72-98

Schenker, Heinrich

About

Sessions, R. Heinrich Schenker's contribution. *In* Sessions, R. Roger Sessions on music p231-40

About individual works
Der freie Satz

Sessions, R. Escape by theory. *In* Sessions, R. Roger Sessions on music p256-62

Schertz, Lyle P.

World food: prices and the poor. *In* Bundy, W. P. ed. The world economic crisis p179-205

Scheuner, Ulrich

The future of the European Community. *In* The Year book of world affairs, 1979 p32-54

Schevill, James Erwin

Kenneth Patchen: the search for wonder and joy. *In* Morgan, R. G. ed. Kenneth Patchen: a collection of essays p98-102

Scheye, Thomas E.

The glass menagerie: "It's no tragedy, Freckles." *In* Tennessee Williams: a tribute p207-13

Schickel, Richard

About individual works
His picture in the papers

Sarris, A. His picture in the papers: a speculation on celebrity in America, based on the life of Douglas Fairbanks, Sr. *In* Sarris, A. Politics and cinema p168-71

Schiele, Egon

About

Hamburger, M. Egon Echiele: the background. *In* Hamburger, M. Art as second nature p107-11

Schildkrout, Enid

The ideology of regionalism in Ghana. *In* Shack, W. A. and Skinner, E. P. eds. Strangers in African societies p183-207

Schiller, Herbert I.

The free flow of information—for whom? *In* Gerbner, G. ed. Mass media policies in changing cultures p105-15

Schiller, Johann Christoph Friedrich von

About

Clayre, A. Schiller. *In* Clayre, A. Work and play p15-21

Lange, V. Reflections on the "classical age" of German literature. *In* Studies in eighteenth-century culture v7 p 1-21

Nicoll, A. From tragedy to melodrama. *In* Nicoll, A. World drama p342-69

Rehder, H. The reluctant disciple: Nietzsche and Schiller. *In* O'Flaherty, J. C.; Sellner, T. F. and Helm, R. M. eds. Studies in Nietzsche and the classical tradition p156-64

About individual works
Mary Stuart

Schmidgall, G. Gaetano Donizetti. *In* Schmidgall, G. Literature as opera p109-47

Influence—Blok

Kostka, E. K. Blok, Schiller, and the Bolshevik revolution. *In* Kostka, E. K. Glimpses of Germanic-Slavic relations p55-68

Influence—Pushkin

Kostka, E. K. Pushkin's third dimension: the German influence. *In* Kostka, E. K. Glimpses of Germanic-Slavic relations from Pushkin to Heinrich Mann p101-21

Schilling, Bernard Nicholas

The apotheosis of Voltaire. *In* Evidence in literary scholarship p363-77

Schilpp, Paul Arthur

About

Olds, G. A. Introduction: the good man and the good. *In* The Abdication of philosophy: philosophy and the public good p 1-13

Steinkraus, W. E. Paul Schilpp and the social relevance of philosophy. *In* The Abdication of philosophy: philosophy and the public good p279-98

Schindler, Marvin S.

The history of Dr. Johann Faustus. *In* Hoffmeister, G. ed. The Renaissance and Reformation in Germany p189-202

Schiro, Richard

Commercial speech: the demise of a chimera. *In* The Supreme Court review, 1976 p45-98

Schism

Eastern and Western Church

Henry, P. Images of the Church in the Second Nicene Council and in the Libri Carolini. *In* Law, church, and society p237-52

Greek and Latin Church
See Schism—Eastern and Western Church

Latin and Greek Church
See Schism—Eastern and Western Church

Schizophrenia

Bettelheim, B. Schizophrenia as a reaction to extreme situations. *In* Bettelheim, B. Surviving, and other essays p112-24

Cases, clinical reports, statistics

Lehnsen, E. Correlation between clinical course and pictorial expression of a schizophrenic patient. *In* Ulman, E. and Dachinger, P. eds. Art therapy p286-310

Marinow, A. The self-portraits of a schizophrenic patient. *In* Ulman, E. and Dachinger, P. eds. Art therapy p325-27

Chemotherapy

Kety, S. S. Biological approaches to treatment and understanding of the major psychoses. *In* American psychiatry: past, present, and future p64-77

Diagnosis

Zubin, J. A biometric approach to diagnosis and evaluation of therapeutic intervention in schizophrenia. *In* Overview of the psychotherapies p153-204

Schizophrenia in children

Bettelheim, B. Schizophrenia as a reaction to extreme situations. *In* Bettelheim, B. Surviving, and other essays p112-24

Schlauch, Margaret

A Polish analogue of The man of law's tale. *In* Chaucer and Middle English studies in honour of Rossell Hope Robbins p372-80

Schlechta, Karl
The German "classicist" Goethe as reflected in Nietzsche's works. *In* O'Flaherty, J. C.; Sellner, T. F. and Helm, R. M. eds. Studies in Nietzsche and the classical tradition p144-55

Schlegel, Alice Elizabeth
Male and female in Hopi thought and action. *In* Schlegel, A. E. ed. Sexual stratification p245-69

An overview. *In* Schlegel, A. E. ed. Sexual stratification p344-57

Toward a theory of sexual stratification. *In* Schlegel, A. E. ed. Sexual stratification p 1-40

Schleiermacher, Friedrich Ernst Daniel

About individual works

Soliloquies

Bruford, W. H. Friedrich Schleiermacher: Monologen (1801). *In* Bruford, W. H. The German tradition of self-cultivation p58-87

Schlemmer, Lawrence, and Muil, Tim J.
Social and political change in the African areas: a case study of KwaZulu. *In* Thompson, L. M. and Butler, J. eds. Change in contemporary South Africa p107-37

Schlesinger, Arthur Meier, 1888-1965
A critical period in American religion, 1875-1900. *In* Mulder, J. M. and Wilson, J. F. eds. Religion in American history p302-17

Schlesinger, James Rodney

About

King, P. All at sea? A critique of the American strategic force structure. *In* Arms control and technological innovation p265-87

Schless, Howard H.
Dante: comedy and conversion. *In* Ruggiers, P. G. ed. Versions of medieval comedy p135-49

Transformations: Chaucer's use of Italian. *In* Brewer, D. S. ed. Geoffrey Chaucer p184-223

Schlögl, Friedrich

About

Bailey, L. H. Ferdinand Kürnberger, Friedrich Schlögl and the feuilleton in Gründerzeit Vienna. *In* Branscombe, P. ed. Austrian life and literature, 1780-1938 p59-71

Schlossberg, Edwin
For my father. *In* About Bateson p145-67

Schlosser, Alan L. See Marson, C. C. jt. auth.

Schlueter, June
Metafictional characters in modern drama

Contents

Albee's Martha and George
Beckett's Didi and Gogo, Hamm and Clov
Genet's maids, brothel patrons, and Blacks
Metafictional theater: Handke's The ride across Lake Constance
Pirandello's Henry IV
Stoppard's Moon and Birdboot, Rosencrantz and Guildenstern
Weiss's inmates at Charenton

Schmandt, Jurgen
United States science policy in transition. *In* Science policies of industrial nations p191-212

Schmeidler, Gertrude Raffel
The relation between psychology and parapsychology. *In* Parapsychology: its relation to physics, biology, psychology, and psychiatry p122-50

Schmelz, Oskar, and Bachi, Roberto
Hebrew as everyday language of the Jews in Israel—statistical appraisal. *In* Salo Wittmayer Baron v2 p745-85

Schmelz, Usiel. See Schmelz, Oskar

Schmemann, Alexander
A lucid love. *In* Dunlop, J. B.; Haugh, R. and Klimoff, A. eds. Aleksandr Solzhenitsyn: critical essays and documentary materials 2d ed. p382-92

On Solzhenitsyn. *In* Dunlop, J. B.; Haugh, R. and Klimoff, A. eds. Aleksandr Solzhenitsyn: critical essays and documentary materials 2d ed. p28-44

Reflections on The Gulag Archipelago. *In* Dunlop, J. B.; Haugh, R. and Klimoff, A. eds. Aleksandr Solzhenitsyn: critical essays and documentary materials 2d ed. p515-26

Schmertz, Eric J.
Compulsory arbitration revisited: the relevance of the public sector experience in private sector management. *In* Benton, L. R. ed. Management for the future p257-69

Schmidgall, Gary
Literature as opera

Contents

Afterword
Alban Berg
Benjamin Britten
Gaetano Donizetti
George Frederic Handel
Giuseppe Verdi
Hector Berlioz
An opening perspective
Peter Ilyich Tchaikovsky
Richard Strauss
Wolfgang Amadeus Mozart

Schmidt, Donald L.
The theater of Osvaldo Dragún. *In* Lyday, L. F. and Woodyard, G. W. eds. Dramatists in revolt p77-94

Schmidt, Helmut H. W.
New tasks for the Atlantic Alliance. *In* The Year book of world affairs, 1975 p22-33

The struggle for the world product. *In* Bundy, W. P. ed. The world economic crisis p105-19

Schmidt, John R.
Lawyers on judges: competence and selection. *In* Nader, R. and Green, M. J. eds. Verdicts on lawyers p285-94

Schmidt, Josef
Humanism and popular culture. *In* Hoffmeister, G. ed. The Renaissance and Reformation in Germany p177-88

Schmidt, Maarten
Quasars and the universe. *In* The Nature of scientific discovery p246-60

Schmidt, Stanley
The science in science fiction. *In* Clareson, T. D. ed. Many futures, many worlds p27-49

Schmidtchen, Gerhard
Light music and the radio listener. *In* Fischer, H. D. and Melnik, S. R. eds. Entertainment: a cross-cultural examination p286-98

Schmiederer, Ursula. See Rotermundt, R. jt. auth.

Schmitt, Charles B.

The correspondence of Jacques Daléchamps. *In* Viator: medieval and Renaissance studies v8 p399-434

Girolamo Borro's Multae sunt nostrarum ignorationum causae (Ms. Vat. Ross. 1009) *In* Philosophy and humanism p462-76

Schmitt, David E.

Ethnic conflict in Northern Ireland: international aspects of conflict management. *In* Esman, M. J. ed. Ethnic conflict in the Western world p228-50

Schmitt, Hans A.

Landed and moneyed princes: the harvest of tradition and conflict in German business and politics. *In* Evolution of international management structures p67-88

Schmitt, Richard

Academic freedom: the future of a confusion. *In* The Concept of academic freedom p111-24

About individual works

Academic freedom: the future of a confusion

Rorty, A. O. Dilemmas of academic and intellectual freedom. *In* The Concept of academic freedom p97-110

Schmitz, Ettore

About individual works

Con la penna d'oro

Ragusa, O. "The light is split in the prism . . . ": Svevo's unfinished play, Con la penna d'oro. *In* Ragusa, O. Narrative and drama p109-21

The confessions of Zeno

Biasin, G. P. Zeno's last bomb. *In* Biasin, G. P. Literary diseases p63-99

Characters—Zeno Cosini

Biasin, G. P. Strategies of the anti-hero: Svevo, Pirandello, and Montale. *In* Italian literature: roots and branches p363-81

Schmitz, Götz

Cresseid's trial: a revision. Fame and defamation in Henryson's 'Testament of Cresseid.' *In* English Association. Essays and studies, 1979 p44-56

Schneewind, Jerome B.

Sociobiology, social policy, and Nirvana. *In* Sociobiology and human nature p225-39

Schneidau, Herbert N.

Pound and Wordsworth on poetry and prose. *In* Bornstein, G. ed. Romantic and modern p133-45

Schneider, Claude

Cynewulf's devaluation of heroic tradition in Juliana. *In* Anglo-Saxon England 7 p107-18

Schneider, Daniel John

Hemingway's A farewell to arms: the novel as pure poetry. *In* Wagner, L. W. ed. Ernest Hemingway p252-66

Symbolism: the Manichean vision

Contents

The dream and the knitting machine: Joseph Conrad's symbolism
The Manichean vision and the reading of symbolist works
"Orts, scraps, fragments" and the circle of wholeness: the symbolism of Virginia Woolf

The symbolic system and the authority of the literary work
"A terrible mixture in things": the symbolism of Henry James
"The war that never ends": patterns of proliferation in Wallace Stevens's poetry

Schneider, David M.

Depopulation and the Yap tabinau. *In* Social organization and the applications of anthropology p94-113

Notes toward a theory of culture. *In* Basso, K. H. and Selby, H. A. eds. Meaning in anthropology p197-220

About

Scheffler, H. W. The "meaning" of kinship in American culture: another view. *In* Basso, K. H. and Selby, H. A. eds. Meaning in anthropology p57-91

Schneider, Harold K.

Economic man in Africa. *In* Martin, P. M. and O'Meara, P. eds. Africa p189-207

Schneider, Herbert Wallace

The American Establishment, the civilizing arts, and philosophy. *In* Philosophy and the civilizing arts p433-45

Community, communication, and communion. *In* Philosophy and the civilizing arts p487-94

Declaration, theory, and existence of human rights. *In* The Abdication of philosophy: philosophy and the public good p89-92

Philosophy will never be a science. *In* Philosophy and the civilizing arts p467-73

The piety of Hobbes. *In* Ross, R. G.; Schneider, H. W. and Waldman, T. eds. Thomas Hobbes in his time p84-101

Radical empiricism and religion. *In* Philosophy and the civilizing arts p446-66

"Reasonable rationalism: the heritage of the Enlightenment." *In* Philosophy and the civilizing arts p474-86

Schneider, Irving. See Voegeli, H. T. jt. auth.

Schneider, Laurence Allen

National Essence and the new intelligentsia. *In* The Limits of change p57-89

Schneider, Louis

Dialectical orientation and the sociology of religion. *In* Johnson, H. M. ed. Religious change and continuity p49-73

Ironic perspective and sociological thought. *In* The Idea of social structure p323-37

Schneider, Mary Lea

A Catholic perspective on American civil religion. *In* America in theological perspective p123-39

Schneider, Ronald M.

Guatemala: an aborted Communist takeover. *In* Hammond, T. T. ed. The anatomy of Communist takeovers p563-82

Schnorrenberg, Barbara B.

The eighteenth-century Englishwoman. *In* Kanner, B. ed. The women of England p183-228

Schoeck, Richard J.

English literature. *In* Jones, W. M. ed. The present state of scholarship in sixteenth-century literature p111-68

The historian as dissenter: the function of criticism in Lord Acton's "Inaugural lecture on the study of history." *In* The Dissenting tradition p262-69

Schoedel, William Richard
Jewish wisdom and the formation of the Christian ascetic. *In* Aspects of wisdom in Judaism and early Christianity p169-99

Schoenbach, Peter Julian
Plinio Marcos: reporter of bad times. *In* Lyday, L. F. and Woodyard, G. W. eds. Dramatists in revolt p243-57

Schoenberg, Arnold See Schönberg, Arnold

Schoenberg, Hans W.
The partition of Germany and the neutralization of Austria. *In* Hammond, T. T. ed. The anatomy of Communist takeovers p368-84

Schoener, Allon, ed.

About individual works
Portal to America
Mudrick, M. The smell of mortality. *In* Mudrick, M. Books are not life but then what is? p157-73

Schoenheimer, Rudolf

About
Kohler, R. E. Rudolf Schoenheimer, isotopic tracers, and biochemistry in the 1930's. *In* Historical sutdies in the physical sciences-v8 p257-98

Schoenman, Ralph Benedict
Bertrand Russell and the peace movement. *In* Nakhnikian, G. ed. Bertrand Russell's philosophy p227-52

About individual works
Bertrand Russell and the peace movement
Sherman, E. F. Bertrand Russell and the peace movement: liberal consistency of radical change? *In* Nakhnikian, G. ed. Bertrand Russell's philosophy p253-63

Schoeps, Karl-Heinz
Epic structures in the plays of Bernard Shaw and Bertolt Brecht. *In* Mews, S. and Knust, H. eds. Essays on Brecht p28-43

Schoettle, Enid Curtis Bok
Arms limitation and security policies required to minimise the proliferation of nuclear weapons. *In* Arms control and technological innovation p102-31

Schofield, Robert Edwin
An evolutionary taxonomy of eighteenth-century Newtonianisms. *In* Studies in eighteenth-century culture v7 p175-92

Joseph Priestley on sensation and perception. *In* Studies in perception p336-54

About individual works
An evolutionary taxonomy of eighteenth-century Newtonianisms
Barnouw, J. Materialism and freedom: commentary on papers by Robert E. Schofield and Aram Vartanian. *In* Studies in eighteenth-century culture v7 p193-212

Scholander, Per Frederik
Water under tension, its fundamental role in capillarity, osmosis and colligative properties. *In* The Frontiers of human knowledge p297-308

Scholarly publishing
Orlov, A. Demythologizing scholarly publishing. *In* Altbach, P. G. and McVey, S. eds. Perspectives on publishing p231-45

Europe
Russak, B. Scholarly publishing in Western Europe and Great Britain: a survey and analysis. *In* Altbach, P. G. and McVey, S. eds. Perspectives on publishing p103-16

Scholars, Jewish. See Historians, Jewish

Scholarship. See Learning and scholarship

Scholasticism
Wallace, W. A. The philosophical setting of medieval science. *In* Lindberg, D. C. ed. Science in the Middle Ages p91-119
See also Nominalism; Thomists

Scholem, Gershom Gerhard

About
Alter, R. Gershom Scholem: history and the abyss. *In* Alter, R. Defenses of the imagination p67-89

About individual works
Major trends in Jewish mysticism
Arendt, H. Jewish history, revised. *In* Arendt, H. The Jew as pariah: Jewish identity and politics in the modern age p96-105

Scholer, David
Sins within and sins without: an interpretation of 1 John 5:16-17. *In* Current issues in Biblical and patristic interpretation p230-46

Scholes, Robert E.
An approach through genre. *In* Spilka, M. ed. Towards a poetics of fiction p41-51

The contributions of formalism and structuralism to the theory of fiction. *In* Spilka, M. ed. Towards a poetics of fiction p107-24

Fabulation and metafiction
Contents
Comedy and grotesquerie
Fabulation and reality
Metafiction
Modern allegory
The nature of romance

Toward a semiotics of literature. *In* Hernadi, P. ed. What is literature? p231-50

About individual works
The illiberal imagination
Trilling, L. Art, will, and necessity. *In* Trilling, L. The last decade p129-47

Scholia
Zetzel, J. E. G. On the history of Latin scholia. *In* Harvard Studies in classical philology v79 p335-54

Scholte, Henricus Petrus

About
Swierenga, R. P. The ethnic voter and the first Lincoln election. *In* Swierenga, R. P. ed. Beyond the Civil War synthesis p99-115

Scholte, Henry Peter. See Scholte, Henricus Petrus

Schon, Donald A.
Generative metaphor: a perspective on problem-setting in social policy. *In* Ortony, A. ed. Metaphor and thought p254-83

Schon, Donald A.—*Continued*

About individual works

Generative metaphor: a perspective on problem-setting in social policy

Reddy, M. J. The conduit metaphor—a case of frame conflict in our language about language. *In* Ortony, A. ed. Metaphor and thought p284-324

Sternberg, R. J.; Tourangeau, R. and Nigro, G. Metaphor, induction, and social policy: the convergence of macroscopic and microscopic views. *In* Ortony, A. ed. Metaphor and thought p325-53

Schönberg, Arnold

About

Craft, R. Towards Schoenberg. *In* Craft, R. Current convictions p195-210

Dawidowicz, L. S. Arnold Schoenberg: a search for Jewish identity. *In* Dawidowicz, L. S. The Jewish presence p32-45

Sessions, R. Schoenberg in the United States. *In* Sessions, R. Roger Sessions on music p353-69

Sessions, R. Some notes on Schoenberg and the "method of composing with twelve tones." *In* Sessions, R. Roger Sessions on music p370-75

About individual works

Moses and Aaron

Dawidowicz, L. S. Arnold Schoenberg: a search for Jewish identity *In* Dawidowicz, L. S. The Jewish presence p32-45

Style and idea

Craft, R. Towards Schoenberg. *In* Craft, R. Current convictions p195-210

Schonhorn, Manuel

Defoe: the literature of politics and the politics of some fictions. *In* English literature in the age of disguise p15-56

School, Choice of

Coons, J. E. and Sugarman, S. D. A case for choice; excerpt from "Education by choice: the case for family control." *In* Parents, teachers, and children: prospects for choice in American education p129-48

Doyle, D. P. The politics of choice: a view from the bridge. *In* Parents, teachers, and children: prospects for choice in American education p227-55

Greeley, A. M. Freedom of choice: "our commitment to integration." *In* Parents, teachers, and children: prospects for choice in American education p183-205

McCready, W. C. Parochial schools: the "free choice" alternative. *In* Parents, teachers, and children: prospects for choice in American education p67-75

Sowell, T. Choice in education and parental responsibility. *In* Parents, teachers, and children: prospects for choice in American education p165-82

Wagner, R. E. American education and the economics of caring. *In* Parents, teachers, and children: prospects for choice in American education p111-25

School administration. See School management and organization

School administrators. See School superintendents and principals

School and community. See Community and school

School and home. See Home and school

School architecture. See School buildings

School attendance. See Dropouts; Student expulsion

School-books. See Text-books

School buildings

Bettelheim, B. Mental health and urban design. *In* Bettelheim, B. Surviving, and other essays p201-20

School children

United States

Bernal, M. E. and others. Comparison of boys' behaviors in homes and classrooms. *In* Behavior modification and families p204-27

Delfini, L. F.; Bernal, M. E. and Rosen, P. M. Comparison of deviant and normal boys in home settings. *In* Behavior modification and families p228-48

School clubs. See Students' societies

School desegregation. See School integration

School discipline. See Student expulsion; Students—Legal status, laws, etc.

School dropouts. See Dropouts

School endowments. See Endowments

School finance. See Education—Finance

School-houses. See School buildings

School integration

Greeley, A. M. Freedom of choice: "our commitment to integration." *In* Parents, teachers, and children: prospects for choice in American education p183-205

See also Segregation in education

Arkansas—Little Rock

Grantham, D. W. The Little Rock school crisis: Negro rights and the struggle for an integrated America. *In* Grantham, D. W. The regional imagination p185-97

United States

See Afro-Americans—Education

School management and organization

Hacker, T. Management by objectives for schools. *In* Managing nonprofit organizations p155-63

Jones, H. L. Breaking the synergism barrier. *In* Managing nonprofit organizations p252-57

Sampson, H. L. Model for participation. *In* Managing nonprofit organizations p109-17

Scrupski, A. Educational management: promise and failure. *In* Social forces and schooling p223-49

Vandermyn, G. and Smith, H. D. Finding answers to school problems. *In* Managing nonprofit organizations p220-28

See also Teaching

School principals. See School superintendents and principals

School sports

Case studies

Rehberg, R. A. and Cohen, M. A. Political attitudes and participation in extracurricular activities. *In* Social problems in athletics p201-11

Social aspects—United States

Petrie, B. M. The athletic group as an emerging deviant subculture. *In* Social problems in athletics p224-37

Schramm, Wilbur L.—*Continued*

Bibliography

Chu, G. C. Bibliography of the works of Wilbur Schramm. *In* Lerner, D. and Nelson, L. M. eds. Communication research—a half-century appraisal p331-40

Schreiber, Anna P.

The status of women in the United States and the Scandinavian countires. *In* Claude, R. P. ed. Comparative human rights p251-66

Schreiner, Olive

About

Edmands, U. Olive Schreiner. *In* Parker, K. ed. The South African novel in English p27-45

Lessing, D. M. Afterword to The story of an African farm by Olive Schreiner. *In* Lessing, D. M. A small personal voice p97-120

Showalter, E. The feminist novelists. *In* Showalter, E. A literature of their own p182-215

About individual works

The story of an African farm

Cockshut, A. O. J. The optimists. *In* Cockshut, A. O. J. Man and woman: a study of love and the novel, 1740-1940 p136-52

Lessing, D. M. Afterword to The story of an African farm by Olive Schreiner. *In* Lessing, D. M. A small personal voice p97-120

Influence—Lawrence

Heywood, C. Oliver Schreiner's influence on George Moore and D. H. Lawrence. *In* Heywood, C. ed. Aspects of South African literature p42-53

Influence—Moore

Heywood, C. Oliver Schreiner's influence on George Moore and D. H. Lawrence. *In* Heywood, C. ed. Aspects of South African literature p42-53

Schrickx, Willem

'Pericles' in a book-list of 1619 from the English Jesuit mission and some of the play's special problems. *In* Shakespeare survey v29 p21-32

Schröder, Brigitte

Science, technology and foreign policy. *In* Science, technology and society p473-506

Schrödinger, Erwin

About

Hanle, P. A. Indeterminacy before Heisenberg: the case of Franz Exner and Erwin Schrödinger. *In* Historical studies in the physical sciences v10 p225-69

Schroeder, Adolf Ernst

The survival of German traditions in Missouri. *In* The German contribution to the building of the Americas p289-313

Schroeder, Albert H.

Shifting for survival in the Spanish Southwest. *In* Weber, D. J. ed. New Spain's far northern frontier p237-55

Schroeder, Fred E. H.

The little red schoolhouse. *In* Browne, R. B. and Fishwick, M. W. eds. Icons of America p139-60

Schroeder, Peter Reinhold

Stylistic analogies between old English art and poetry. *In* Viator: medieval and Renaissance studies v5 p185-97

Schroeder-Gudehus, Brigitte. See Schröder, Brigitte

Schroeter, Eberhard

Rome's first national state architecture: the Palazzo delle Finanze. *In* Millon, H. A. and Nochlin, L. eds. Art and architecture in the service of politics p128-49

Schubert, Franz Peter

About

Dent, E. J. Beethoven and Schubert. *In* Dent, E. J. The rise of romantic opera p125-44

Schuler, Monica

Myalism and the African religious tradition in Jamaica. *In* Crahan, M. E. and Knight, F. W. eds. Africa and the Caribbean p65-79

Schuler, Robert M. See Edwards, A. S. G. jt. auth.

Schulte Nordholt, J. W.

The impact of the American Revolution on the Dutch Republic. *In* The Impact of the American Revolution abroad p41-63

Schultz, Elizabeth A.

"Free in fact and at last": the image of the Black woman in Black American fiction. *In* Springer, M. A. ed. What manner of woman p316-44

Schultz, LeRoy G.

Sexual victims. *In* Gochros, H. L. and Gochros, J. S. eds. The sexually oppressed p110-25

Schultz, T. Paul

Determinants of fertility: a micro-economic model of choice. *In* Economic factors in population growth p89-124

Schultz, Theodore William

Migration: an economist's view. *In* Human migration p377-86

Schulz, Esther D.

Education for human sexuality; excerpt from "Family life and sex education: curriculum and instruction." *In* Fairfield, R. P. ed. Humanistic frontiers in American education p69-74

Schulz, Max F.

Toward a definition of black humor; excerpt from "Black humor fiction of the sixties." *In* Cohen, S. B. ed. Comic relief p14-27

Schumacher, Dorin

Subjectivities: a theory of the critical process. *In* Donovan, J. C. ed. Feminist literary criticism p29-37

Schumacher, Ernst Friedrich

Using intermediate technologies. *In* Strategies for human settlements: habitat and environment p121-25

Schuman, Howard

Introduction: ambiguities in the attitude-behavior relation. *In* Major social issues p373-76

Schumpeter, Joseph Alois

About individual works

Capitalism, socialism, and democracy

Brittan, S. Can democracy manage an economy? *In* Skidelsky, R. J. A. ed. The end of the Keynesian era p41-46

Schurmann, Franz. See Schurmann, Herbert Franz

Schurmann, Herbert Franz

Joseph Levenson on China and the world. *In* Meisner, M. J. and Murphey, R. eds. The Mozartian historian p58-75

Schutz, Alfred

Subjective and objective meaning. *In* Giddens, A. ed. Positivism and sociology p33-52

About

Altheide, D. L. The sociology of Alfred Schutz. *In* Douglas, J. D. and Johnson, J. M. [eds.] Existential sociology p133-52

Garfinkel, H. The rational properties of scientific and common-sense activities. *In* Giddens, A. ed. Positivism and sociology p53-73

Lemert, C. C. Phenomenological sociology: Schutz, Berger, Luckmann. *In* Lemert, C. C. Sociology and the twilight of man p135-64

Pettit, P. The life-world and role-theory. *In* Pivčević, E. ed. Phenomenology and philosophical understanding p251-70

Knowledge, Theory of

Bauman, Z. Understanding as the work of life: From Schutz to ethnomethodology. *In* Bauman, Z. Hermeneutics and social science p172-93

Schütze, Walter

A world of many nuclear powers. *In* Griffiths, F. and Polanyi, J. C. eds. The dangers of nuclear war p85-92

Schuursma, Rolf L.

The historian as film-maker I. *In* Smith, P. ed. The historian and film p121-31

Schuwer, André L.

Nature and the holy: on Heidegger's interpretation of Holderlin's hymn "Wie wenn am Feiertage." *In* Radical phenomenology p225-37

Schwab, John J.

Antipathy to marriage. *In* Gross, L. ed. Sexual issues in marriage p105-13

Schwab, Joseph Jackson

On reviving liberal education—in the seventies. *In* Hook, S.; Kurtz, P. W. and Todorovich, M. eds. The philosophy of the curriculum: the need for general education p37-48

Schwartz, Alvin

Children, humor, and folklore. *In* Horn Book Magazine. Crosscurrents of criticism p205-16

Schwartz, Anna Jacobson. See Cagan, P. jt. auth.

Schwartz, Benjamin Isadore

History and culture in the thought of Joseph Levenson. *In* Meisner, M. J. and Murphey, R. eds The Mozartian historian p100-12

Notes on conservatism in general and in China in particular. *In* The Limits of change p3-21

The philosopher. *In* Wilson, R. G. ed. Mao Tse-tung in the scales of history p9-34

Schwartz, Bernard

The United States: the doctrine of executive privilege. *In* Galnoor, I. ed. Government secrecy in democracies p129-42

About individual works
The American Heritage History of the law in America

Wiener, F. B. American law for the coffee table—an impossible dream. *In* The Supreme Court review, 1975 p423-42

Schwartz, David C. and Mannella, Charles J.

Popular music as an agency of political socialization: a study in popular culture and politics. *In* Schwartz, D. C. and Schwartz, S. K. eds. New directions in political socialization p289-316

Schwartz, David C.; Garrison, Joseph, and Alouf, James

Health, body images, and political socialization. *In* Schwartz, D. C. and Schwartz, S. K. eds. New directions in political socialization p96-126

Schwartz, Delmore

The vocation of the poet in the modern world; excerpts from "Selected essays of Delmore Schwartz." *In* Gibbons, R. ed. The poet's work: 29 masters of 20th century poetry on the origins and practice of their art p82-91

About

Howe, I. Delmore Schwartz: an appreciation. *In* Howe, I. Celebrations and attacks p183-88

About individual works
Selected essays of Delmore Schwartz

Rahv, P. Delmore Schwartz: the paradox of precocity. *In* Rahv, P. Essays on literature and politics, 1932-1972 p85-92

Schwartz, Gary Edward

Biofeedback and the treatment of disregulation disorders. *In* Sobel, D. S. ed. Ways of health p353-86

Schwartz, Harry

The infirmity of British medicine. *In* Tyrrell, R. E. ed. The future that doesn't work p22-41

Schwartz, Morris S.

A role for psychiatry in the future: a proposal. *In* American psychiatry: past, present, and future p149-56

Schwartz, Murray M.

Critic, define thyself. *In* Hartman, G. H. ed. Psychoanalysis and the question of the text p 1-17

Schwartz, Murray M. and Bollas, Christopher

The absence at the center: Sylvia Plath and suicide. *In* Lane, G. ed. Sylvia Plath p179-202

Schwartz, Ronald

Spain's New Wave novelists, 1950-1974

Contents

Alfonso Grosso and Guarnición de silla (Troop of cavalry) (1971)

Ana Maria Matute and Primera memoria (First memories) (1960)

Cela and La colmena (The hive) (1951)

Daniel Sueiro and La criba (The sieve) (1958)

Gironella and Los cipreses creen en Dios (The cypresses believe in God) (1953)

Ignacio Aldecoa and Parte de una historia (Part of a story) (1967)

Jesús Fernández Santos and Los bravos (The savage ones) (1954)

José Luis Castillo-Puche and Paralelo 40 (The fortieth parallel) (1963)

José Maria Carrascal and Groovy (1973)

Juan Benet and Volverás á Región (You'll probably return to Región) (1967)

Juan Garcia Hortelano and Tormenta de verano (Summer storm) (1962)

Juan Goytisolo and Senãs de identidad (Marks of identity) (1966)

Schwartz, Ronald
Spain's New Wave novelists, 1950-1974
Contents—Continued
Juan Marsé and Ultimas tardes con Teresa (Last afternoons with Teresa) (1966)
The literary and historical background
Luis Goytisolo-Gay and Las afueras (The outskirts) (1958)
Luis Martin-Santos and Tiempo de silencio (Time of silence) (1962)
Miguel Delibes and Parábola del náufrago (Parable of the drowning man) (1969)
Quiroga and Algo pasa en la calle (Something happens on the street) (1954)
Rafael Sánchez Ferlosio and El Jarama (1956)
The seventies: critics, exiles, new writers, the "boom" and predictions
Summary: major trends and writers (1950-1970's)
What is the Spanish New Wave?

Schwartz, Sandra Kenyon
Patterns of cynicism: differential political socialization among adolescents. *In* Schwartz, D. C. and Schwartz, S. K. eds. New directions in political socialization p188-202

Preschoolers and politics. *In* Schwartz, D. C. and Schwartz, S. K. eds. New directions in political socialization p229-53

Schwartz, Stuart Barry
Elite politics and the growth of a peasantry in late colonial Brazil. *In* From colony to nation p133-54

Schwartz, Theodore
Cultural totemism: ethnic identity primitive and modern. *In* Ethnic identity p106-31

Relations among generations in time-limited cultures. *In* Schwartz, T. ed. Socialization as cultural communication p217-30

Where is the culture? Personality as the distributive locus of culture. *In* Spindler, G. D. ed. The making of psychological anthropology p419-41

Schwartz, Warren F.
Zenith Radio Corp. v. United States: countervailing duties and the regulation of international trade. *In* The Supreme Court review, 1978 p297-312

Schwarz, Alfred
From Büchner to Beckett
Contents
After the Fall
"Condemned to be free": the will in action and paralysis
Condemned to exist
The demonic will in a bourgeois setting
The emerging poetic of modern realism and naturalism
The experience of history as fateful
The outmoded individual
The purgation of the will: tragic theater in the Christian tradition
Society and human passion as a tragic motive
Tragedy in the theater of realism

Schwarz, Berthold Eric
Psi and the life cycle. *In* Parapsychology: its relation to physics, biology, psychology, and psychiatry p235-45

Schwarz, Heinrich
An eighteenth-century English poem on the camera obscura. *In* One hundred years of photographic history p127-38

Schwarz, Leo Walder
Mutations of Jewish values in contemporary American fiction. *In* Tradition and change in Jewish experience p184-97

Schwarz, Margarete. See Krebs, E. jt. auth.

Schwarzenberger, Georg
Civitas maxima? *In* The Year book of world affairs, 1975 p337-63
The principles of the United Nations. *In* The Year book of world affairs, 1976 p307-37
Trends in the law of the sea. *In* The Year book of world affairs, 1979 p328-73

Schweik, Robert C.
Thomas Hardy: fifty years of textual scholarship. *In* Butler, L. S. ed. Thomas Hardy after fifty years p135-48

Schweitzer, Albert
About
Highet, G. Albert Schweitzer. *In* Highet, G. The immortal profession p175-97

Schwendinger, Herman, and Schwendinger, Julia
Delinquency and social reform: a radical perspective. *In* Empey, L. T. ed. Juvenile justice p245-87

Schwimmer, Erik
Semiotics and culture. *In* Sebeok, T. A. ed. A perfusion of signs p153-79

Schwitters, Kurt
About individual works
Gedicht 25
Middleton, J. C. Pattern without predictability, or Pythagoras saved: a comment on Kurt Schwitters' 'Gedicht 25.' *In* Middleton, J. C. Bolshevism in art p209-13

Schwyzer, Hans-Rudolf
The intellect in Plotinus and the archetypes of C. G. Jung. *In* Kephalaion p214-22

Science
Gingerich, O. Introduction: Does science have a future? *In* The Nature of scientific discovery p237-45
Harris, E. E. Science, metaphysics, and teleology. *In* The Personal universe p24-39
Holton, G. J. From the endless frontier to the ideology of limits. *In* Holton, G. J. and Morison, R. S. eds. Limits of scientific inquiry p227-41
Holton, G. J. Mainsprings of scientific discovery. *In* The Nature of scientific discovery p199-217
Koestler, A. The art of discovery. *In* Koestler, A. Janus p131-36
MacIntyre, A. C. Has science any future? *In* Science and society: past, present, and future p356-62
Price, G. R. Science and the supernatural. *In* Ludwig, J. K. ed. Philosophy and parapsychology p145-71
Shewmaker, K. L. and Berenda, C. W. Science and the problem of psi. *In* Wheatley, J. M.O. and Edge, H. L. eds. Philosophical dimensions of parapsychology p413-24
Wheeler, J. A. The universe as home for man. *In* The Nature of scientific discovery p261-96

See also Ethnology; Mathematics; Physics; Technology; Women in science

Classification
See Classification of sciences

Science—*Continued*

Early works to 1800

Lindberg, D. C. The transmission of Greek and Arabic learning to the West. *In* Lindberg, D. C. ed. Science in the Middle Ages p52-90

Moody, E. A. Galileo and his precursors. *In* Moody, E. A. Studies in medieval philosophy, science, and logic p393-408

See also Science, Medieval

Fiction

See Science fiction

Historiography

Cohen, I. B. The many faces of the history of science. *In* The Future of history p65-110

Guerlac, H. Some historical assumptions of the history of science. *In* Guerlac, H. Essays and papers in the history of modern science p27-39

MacLeod, R. M. Changing perspectives in the social history of science. *In* Science, technology and society p149-95

Shapin, S. Homo phrenologicus: anthropological perspectives on an historical problem. *In* Barnes, B. and Shapin, S. eds. Natural order p41-71

History

Barfield, O. The coming trauma of materialism. *In* Barfield, O. The rediscovery of meaning, and other essays p187-200

Barnouw, J. Materialism and freedom: commentary on papers by Robert E. Schofield and Aram Vartanian. *In* Studies in eighteenth-century culture v7 p193-212

Beaver, D. D. Possible relationships between the history and sociology of science. *In* Gaston, J. ed. Sociology of science p140-61

Ben-David, J. Organization, social control, and cognitive change in science. *In* Culture and its creators p244-65

Böhme, G. Models for the development of science. *In* Science, technology and society p319-51

Cardwell, D. S. L. Problems of the data base. *In* Bugliarello, G. and Doner, D. B. eds. The history and philosophy of technology p3-18

Clarke, A. C. Technology and the limits of knowledge. *In* The Frontiers of knowledge p117-40

Also in Technology and the frontiers of knowledge p111-34

Cohen, I. B. The many faces of the history of science. *In* The Future of history p65-110

Gilkey, L. B. The structure of academic revolutions. *In* The Nature of scientific discovery p538-46

Goodall, V. M. Setting the scene. *In* Goodall, V. M. ed. The quest for man p11-25

Guerlac, H. A backward view. *In* Guerlac, H. Essays and papers in the history of modern science p54-65

Guerlac, H. Science and the historian. *In* Guerlac, H. Essays and papers in the history of modern science p40-53

Haraway, D. J. Reinterpretation or rehabilitation: an exercise in contemporary Marxist history of science. *In* Studies in history of biology v2 p193-209

Iwanowska, W. The assimilation of science into our ways of thinking and living. *In* Science and society: past, present, and future p73-81

Jaki, S. L. The history of science and the idea of an oscillating universe. *In* Cosmology, history, and theology p233-51

Popper, Sir K. R. The rationality of scientific revolutions. *In* Harré, R. ed. Problems of scientific revolution p72-101

Schofield, R. E. An evolutionary taxonomy of eighteenth-century Newtonianisms. *In* Studies in eighteenth-century culture v7 p175-92

Tatar, M. M. Salvation by electricity: science, poetry, and "Naturphilosophie." *In* Tatar, M. M. Spellbound p45--81

Toulmin, S. E. Introduction: The end of the Copernican era? *In* The Nature of scientific discovery p189-98

Toulmin, S. E. The twin moralities of science. *In* Science and society: past, present, and future p111-24

See also Science, Ancient

History—Study and teaching

Guerlac, H. Teaching and research in the history of science. *In* Guerlac, H. Essays and papers in the history of modern science p19-26

History—Arab countries

Levey, M. Methodology and the history of science. *In* Essays on Islamic philosophy and science p136-46

Sabra, A. I. The exact sciences. *In* The Genius of Arab civilization p121-41

History—England

Rousseau, G. S. Science. *In* Rogers, P. ed. The eighteenth century p153-207

History—Europe

Hall, A. R. Introduction: The nature of scientific discovery in the sixteenth century. *In* The Nature of scientific discovery p91-105

Hall, A. R. Magic, metaphysics and mysticism in the scientific revolution. *In* Bonelli, M. L. R. and Shea, W. R. eds. Reason, experiment, and mysticism in the scientific revolution p275-82

Nef, J. U. Background paper: the interplay of literature, art, and science in the time of Copernicus. *In* The Nature of scientific discovery p462-67

Nelson, B. N. The quest for certitude and the books of Scripture, nature, and conscience. *In* The Nature of scientific discovery p355-72

Rossi, P. Hermeticism, rationality and the scientific revolution. *In* Bonelli, M. L. R. and Shea, W. R. eds. Reason, experiment, and mysticism in the scientific revolution p247-73

Temkin, O. Science and society in the Age of Copernicus. *In* The Nature of scientific discovery p106-33

History—France

Crosland, M. P. and Smith, C. The transmission of physics from France to Britain: 1800-1840. *In* Historical studies in the physical sciences v9 p 1-61

Guerlac, H. Science and French national strength. *In* Guerlac, H. Essays and papers in the history of modern science p491-512

Guerlac, H. Some aspects of science during the French Revolution. *In* Guerlac, H. Essays and papers in the history of modern science p465-78

Science—History—France—*Continued*

Robinson, C. Science, reason and the material world. *In* Robinson, C. French literature in the nineteenth century p50-107

Williams, L. P. A comparative study of two nineteenth-century educational systems. *In* Science and society: past, present, and future p211-16

History—Germany

Caneva, K. L. From galvanism to electrodynamics: the transformation of German physics and its social context. *In* Historical studies in the physical sciences v9 p63-159

Williams, L. P. A comparative study of two nineteenth-century educational systems. *In* Science and society: past, present, and future p211-16

History—Great Britain

Cantor, G. The reception of the wave theory of light in Britain: a case study illustrating the role of methodology in scientific debate. *In* Historical studies in the physical sciences v6 p109-32

Crosland, M. P. and Smith, C. The transmission of physics from France to Britain: 1800-1840. *In* Historical studies in the physical sciences v9 p 1-61

Garber, E. Molecular science in late-nineteenth-century Britain. *In* Historical studies in the physical sciences v9 p265-97

Hall, A. R. What did the Industrial Revolution in Britain owe to science? *In* Historical perspectives p129-51

Wilson, L. G. Science by candlelight. *In* Altholz, J. L. ed. The mind and art of Victorian England p94-106

History—Greece

Downs, R. B. Greek and Roman scientists. *In* Downs, R. B. Books that changed the world p287-306

History—Islamic countries

Sabra, A. I. The scientific enterprise. *In* Lewis, B. ed. Islam and the Arab world p181-200

History—Near East

Wickens, G. M. The Middle East as a world centre of science and medicine. *In* Savory, R. M. ed. Introduction to Islamic civilisation p111-19

History—Ohio Valley

Shapiro, H. D. The Western Academy of Natural Sciences of Cincinnati and the structure of science in the Ohio Valley 1810-1850. *In* Oleson, A. and Brown, S. C. eds. The pursuit of knowledge in the early American Republic p219-47

History—Poland

Knoll, P. W. The world of the young Copernicus: society, science, and the university. *In* Science and society: past, present, and future p19-44

History—Rome

Downs, R. B. Greek and Roman scientists. *In* Downs, R. B. Books that changed the world p287-306

History—Russia

Joravsky, D. The construction of the Stalinist psyche. *In* Cultural revolution in Russia, 1928-1931 p105-28

History—United States

Cohen, I. B. Science and the growth of the American Republic. *In* An Almost chosen people p67-106

Frick, G. F. The Royal Society in America. *In* Oleson, A. and Brown, S. C. eds. The pursuit of knowledge in the early American Republic p70-83

Rae, J. B. The application of science to industry. *In* Oleson, A. and Voss, J. eds. The organization of knowledge in modern America, 1860-1920 p249-68

Reingold, N. Definitions and speculations: the professionalization of science in America in the nineteenth century. *In* Oleson, A. and Brown, S. C. eds. The pursuit of knowledge in the early American Republic p33-69

Language

Quine, W. V. The scope and language of science. *In* Quine, W. V. The ways of paradox, and other essays p228-45

Methodology

Barfield, O. Science and quality. *In* Barfield, O. The rediscovery of meaning, and other essays p176-86

Ben-David, J. Organization, social control, and cognitive change in science. *In* Culture and its creators p244-65

Bronowski, J. The logic of experiment. *In* Bronowski, J. A sense of the future p42-55

Cantor, G. The reception of the wave theory of light in Britain: a case study illustrating the role of methodology in scientific debate. *In* Historical studies in the physical sciences v6 p109-32

Cohen, L. J. Why should the science of nature be empirical? *In* Royal Institute of Philosophy. Impressions of empiricism p168-83

Garber, D. Science and certainty in Descartes. *In* Hooker, M. ed. Descartes p114-51

Guerlac, H. Newton and the method of analysis. *In* Guerlac, H. Essays and papers in the history of modern science p193-216

Harris, E. E. Empiricism in science and philosophy. *In* Royal Institute of Philosophy. Impressions of empiricism p154-67

Heisenberg, W. Tradition in science. *In* The nature of scientific discovery p219-36

Holton, G. J. Science, science teaching, and rationality. *In* Hook, S.; Kurtz, P. W. and Todorovich, M. eds. The philosophy of the curriculum: the need for general education p101-18

Holton, G. J. 'What, precisely, is "thinking"?' *In* Einstein p153-64

Macmurray, J. Science and objectivity. *In* The Personal universe p7-23

Marx, L. Reflections on the neo-romantic critique of science. *In* Holton, G. J. and Morison, R. S. eds. Limits of scientific inquiry p61-73

Nevins, A. What the scientist and historian can teach each other. *In* Nevins, A. Allan Nevins on history p133-50

O'Neill, J. The mutuality of accounts: an essay on trust. *In* McNall, S. G. ed. Theoretical perspectives in sociology p369-80

Ovenden, M. W. Intimations of unity. *In* Science and society: past, present, and future p363-74

Percy, W. Culture: the antinomy of the scientific method. *In* Percy, W. The message in the bottle p215-42

Science—Methodology—*Continued*

Popper, Sir K. R. The myth of the framework. *In* The Abdication of philosophy: philosophy and the public good p23-48

Quine, W. V. Posits and reality. *In* Quine, W. V. The ways of paradox, and other essays p246-54

Shenfield, A. A. Scientism and the study of society. *In* Essays on Hayek p61-72

Tart, C. T. States of consciousness and state-specific sciences. *In* Wheatley, J. M. O. and Edge, H. L. eds. Philosophical dimensions of parapsychology p441-63

See also Classification of sciences; Creative ability in science; Hypothesis

Moral aspects
See Science and ethics

Philosophy

Andrew, E. The unity of theory and practice: the science of Marx and Nietzsche. *In* Political theory and praxis p117-37

Böhme, G. Models for the development of science. *In* Science, technology and society p319-51

Bondi, Sir H. What is progress in science? *In* **Harré, R. ed. Problems of scientific revolution p 1-10**

Bronowski, J. The creative process. *In* Bronowski, J. A sense of the future p 6-15

Bronowski, J. The fulfillment of man. *In* Bronowski, J. A sense of the future p249-62

Bronowski, J. The logic of nature. *In* Bronowski, J. A sense of the future p32-41

Bronowski, J. The logic of the mind. *In* Bronowski, J. A sense of the future p56-73

Bronowski, J. The principle of tolerance. *In* Bronowski, J. A sense of the future p221-34

Bronowski, J. The reach of imagination. *In* Bronowski, J. A sense of the future p22-31

Bunge, M. A. Philosophical inputs and outputs of technology. *In* Bugliarello, G. and Doner, D. B. eds. The history and philosophy of technology p262-81

Campbell, D. T. Unjustified variation and selective retention in scientific discovery. *In* Ayala, F. J. and Dobzhansky, T. G. eds. Studies in the philosophy of biology p139-61

Couch, W. T. The sacred and golden cord. *In* Viva Vivas! p87-137

Cowan, D. A. Science, history and the evidence of things not seen. *In* From Parnassus p313-23

Gilkey, L. B. The future of science. *In* The Future of science p105-28

Gruber, H. E. Darwin's "tree of nature" and other images of wide scope. *In* Wechsler, J. ed. On aesthetics in science p121-40

Guerlac, H. Science and the historian. *In* Guerlac, H. Essays and papers in the history of modern science p40-53

Hirst, R. J. Science and anti-science in the philosophy of perception. *In* Studies in perception p377-401

Hoffmann, B. Magic, science and evaluation. *In* From Parnassus p324-33

Holbrook, D. Politics and the need for meaning. *In* Fitzgerald, R. ed. Human needs and politics p174-94

Holton, G. J. Science, science teaching, and rationality. *In* Hook, S.; Kurtz, P. W. and Todorovich, M. eds. The philosophy of the curriculum: the need for general education p101-18

Hook, S. Rejoinder: Dr Hibbs and the ethics of discussion. *In* Hook, S.; Kurtz, P. and Todorovich, M. eds. The ethics of teaching and scientific research p187-90

Huxley, A. L. Integrate education. *In* Huxley, A. L. The Human situation p 1-11

Jardine, N. 'Realistic' realism and the progress of science. *In* Hookway, C. and Pettit, P. eds. Action and interpretation p107-25

Joravsky, D. The construction of the Stalinist psyche. *In* Cultural revolution in Russia, 1928-1931 p105-28

Kisiel, T. J. Heidegger and the new images of science. *In* Radical phenomenology p163-81

Kusch, P. A personal view of science and the future. *In* The Future of science p39-55

Kuznetsov, B. G. Einstein, science and culture. *In* Einstein p167-83

Lakatos, I. and Zahar, E. Why did Copernicus' research program supersede Ptolemy's? *In* The Copernican achievement p354-83

LeShan, L. L. Individual realities: commonsense, science, and mysticism; excerpts from "Toward a general theory of the paranormal." *In* Wheatley, J. M. O. and Edge, H. L. eds. Philosophical dimensions of parapsychology p425-40

Mazzeo, J. A. Myth and science in the theology of Rudolf Bultmann. *In* Mazzeo, J. A. Varieties of interpretation p129-53

Medawar, Sir P. B. A geometric model of reduction and emergence. *In* Ayala, F. J. and Dobzhansky, T. G. eds. Studies in the philosophy of biology p57-63

Moon, Sun Myung. The search for absolute values: harmony among the sciences: Founder's address, Fifth International Conference on the Unity of the Sciences. November 26, 1976, Washington, D. C. *In* Horowitz, I. L. ed. Science, sin, and scholarship p12-18

Ovenden, M. W. Intimations of unity. *In* Science and society: past, present, and future p363-74

Percy, W. Culture: the antinomy of the scientific method. *In* Percy, W. The message in the bottle p215-42

Percy, W. The Delta factor. *In* Percy, W. The message in the bottle p3-45

Popper, Sir K. R. The rationality of scientific revolutions. *In* **Harré, R. ed. Problems of scientific revolution p72-101**

Popper, Sir K. R. Scientific reduction and the essential incompleteness of all science. *In* Ayala, F. J. and Dobzhansky, T. G. eds. Studies in the philosophy of biology p259-83

Quine, W. V. The nature of natural knowledge. *In* Guttenplan, S. D. ed. Mind and language p67-81

Quine, W. V. The scope and language of science. *In* Quine, W. V. The ways of paradox, and other essays p228-45

Ravetz, J. R. Criticisms of science. *In* Science, technology and society p71-89

Ravetz, J. R. '. . . et augebitur scientia.' *In* **Harré, R. ed. Problems of scientific revolution p42-57**

Shapere, D. On the relations between compositional and evolutionary theories. *In* Ayala, F. J. and Dobzhansky, T. G. eds. Studies in the philosophy of biology p187-201

Toulmin, S. Commentary [on Why did Copernicus' research program supersede Ptolemy's]? *In* The Copernican achievement p384-91

Science—Philosophy—*Continued*

Vickers, Sir G. Rationality and intuition. *In* Wechsler, J. ed. On aethetics in science p143-64

Weinberg, J. R. Ockham's theory of scientific method. *In* Weinberg, J. R. Ockham, Descartes, and Hume p22-32

Wightman, W. P. D. Adam Smith and the history of ideas. *In* Skinner, A. S. and Wilson, T. eds. Essays on Adam Smith p44-67

Wigner, E. The scope and promise of science. *In* Hook, S.; Kurtz, P. and Todorovich, M. eds. The ethics of teaching and scientific research p131-33

Wilson, H. T. Science, critique, and criticism: the "open society" revisited. *In* O'Neill, J. ed. On critical theory p205-30

Wojciechowski, J. A. The ecology of knowledge. *In* Science and society: past, present, and future p258-302

See also Mechanism (Philosophy); Naturalism; System theory

Philosophy—History

Suppe, F. A. Afterword—1977. *In* Suppe, F. R. ed. The structure of scientific theories p615-730

Public opinion

Hutt, P. B. Public criticism of health science policy. *In* Holton, G. J. and Morison, R. S. eds. Limits of scientific inquiry p157-69

Research

See Research

Social aspects

Anderson, V. E. Evangelicals and science: fifty years after the Scopes trial (1925-75). *In* Wells, D. F. and Woodbridge, J. D. eds. The evangelicals p249-68

Beaver, D. D. Possible relationships between the history and sociology of science. *In* Gaston, J. ed. Sociology of science p140-61

Ben-David, J. Emergence of national traditions in the sociology of science: the United States and Great Britain. *In* Gaston, J. ed. Sociology of science p197-218

Ben-David, J. Organization, social control, and cognitive change in science. *In* Culture and its creators p244-65

Bronowski, J. The values of science. *In* Bronowski, J. A sense of the future p211-20

Cole, J. R. and Zuckerman, H. A. The emergence of a scientific specialty: the self-exemplifying case of the sociology of science. *In* The Idea of social structure p139-74

Cooter, R. The power of the body: the early nineteenth century. *In* Barnes, B. and Shapin, S. eds. Natural order p73-92

Cottle, T. J. "Show me a scientist who's helped poor folks and I'll kiss her hand." *In* Science and society: past, present, and future p216-27

Culliton, B. J. Science's restive public. *In* Holton, G. J. and Morison, R. S. eds Limits of scientific inquiry p147-56

Gieryn, T. F. Problem retention and problem change in science. *In* Gaston, J. ed. Sociology of science p96-115

Gilkey, L. B. The future of science. *In* The Future of science p105-28

Haas, E. B. An international 'scientific society'? *In* New dimensions of world politics p73-85

Hargens, L. L. Theory and method in the sociology of science. *In* Gaston, J. ed. Sociology of science p121-39

Hooker, C. A. Has the scientist any future in the brave new world? *In* Science and society: past, present, and future p306-56

Iwanowska, W. The assimilation of science into our ways of thinking and living. *In* Science and society: past, present, and future p73-81

Kusch, P. A personal view of science and the future. *In* The Future of science p39-55

Lakoff, S. A. Scientists, technologists and political power. *In* Science, technology and society p355-91

Lawrence, C. The nervous system and society in the Scottish Enlightenment. *In* Barnes, B. and Shapin, S. eds. Natural order p19-40

Marx, L. Reflections on the neo-romantic critique of science. *In* Holton, G. J. and Morison, R. S. eds. Limits of scientific inquiry p61-73

Morison, R. S. Misgiving about life-extending technologies. *In* Holton, G. J. and Morison, R. S. eds. Limits of scientific inquiry p211-26

Nelkin, D. Technology and public policy. *In* Science, technology and society p393-441

Pearson, W. Race and universalism in the scientific community. *In* Gaston, J. ed. Sociology of science p38-53

Pirages, D. C. The unbalanced revolution. *In* Science and society: past, present, and future p231-49

Ploch, D. R. Research funding for sociology in the National Science Foundation. *In* Gaston, J. ed. Sociology of science p54-62

Porter, R. Creation and credence: the career of theories of the earth in Britain, 1660-1820. *In* Barnes, B. and Shapin, S. eds. Natural order p97-123

Price, D. J. D. Ups and downs in the pulse of science and technology. *In* Gaston, J. ed. Sociology of science p162-71

Ravetz, J. R. Criticisms of science. *In* Science, technology and society p71-89

Reskin, B. F. Sex differentiation and the social organization of science. *In* Gaston, J. ed. Sociology of science p6-37

Rintelen, F. J. von. The public good and the attainment and loss of reality in science and philosophy. *In* The Abdication of philosophy: philosophy and the public good p251-66

Salomon, J. J. Science policy studies and the development of science policy. *In* Science, technology and society p43-70

Sapolsky, H. M. Science, technology and military policy. *In* Science, technology and society p443-71

Schröder, B. Science, technology and foreign policy. *In* Science, technology and society p473-506

Seaborg, G. T. New signposts for science. *In* The Future of science p 1-19

Shapin, S. Homo phrenologicus: anthropological perspectives on an historical problem. *In* Barnes, B. and Shapin, S. eds. Natural order p41-71

Sinsheimer, R. L. The presumptions of science. *In* Holton, G. J. and Morison, R. S. eds. Limits of scientific inquiry p23-35

Skolnikoff, E. B. Science, technology and the international system. *In* Science, technology and society p507-33

Science—Social aspects—*Continued*

Spiegel-Rösing, I. S. The study of science, technology and society (SSTS): recent trends and future challenges. *In* Science, technology and society p7-42

Stehr, N. The ethos of science revisited: social and cognitive norms. *In* Gaston, J. ed. Sociology of science p172-96

Storer, N. W. The sociological context of the Velikovsky controversy. *In* Goldsmith, D. ed. Scientists confront Velikovsky p29-39

Thomas, L The hazards of science. *In* Thomas, L. The medusa and the snail p65-75

Toulmin, S. E. Introduction: The end of the Copernican era? *In* The Nature of scientific discovery p189-98

Science and society: past, present, and fulan Nevins on history p133-50

Wynne, B. Physics and psychics: science, symbolic action, and social control in late Victorian England. *In* Barnes, B. and Shapin, S. eds. Natural order p167-86

Zuckerman, H. A. Theory choice and problem choice in science. *In* Gaston, J. ed. Sociology of science p65-95

Social aspects—Historiography

MacLeod, R. M. Changing perspectives in the social history of science. *In* Science, technology and society p149-95

Study and teaching

Rabin, M. The uses and limitations of science teaching. *In* Hook, S.; Kurtz, P. W. and Todorovich, M. eds. The philosophy of the curriculum: the need for general education p127-36

Williams, L. P. A comparative study of two nineteenth-century educational systems. *In* Science and society: past, present, and future p211-16

Study and teaching—United States

Kevles, D. J. The physics, mathematics, and chemistry communities: a comparative analysis. *In* Oleson, A. and Voss, J. eds. The organization of knowledge in modern America, 1860-1920 p139-72

Study and teaching (Higher)

Coleman, E. Values in the arts and sciences: a course. *In* Aeolian harps p15-36

Dainton, Sir F. S. A note on science in higher education. *In* Niblett, W. R. ed. The sciences, the humanities and the technological threat p36-41

Edge, D. On the purity of science. *In* Niblett, W. R. ed. The sciences, the humanities and the technological threat p42-64

Study and teaching (Higher)— Netherlands

Raamsdonk, W. van. Promoting the sense of social responsibility in Dutch education. *In* Against pollution and hunger p260-69

Study and teaching (Higher)— United States

Arons, A. B. Teaching science. *In* Cahn, S. M. ed. Scholars who teach p101-30

Fowler, J. M. Science education and the new heretics. *In* Science and society: past, present, and future p200-11

Holton, G. J. Science, science teaching, and rationality. *In* Hook, S.; Kurtz, P. W. and Todorovich, M. eds. The philosophy of the curriculum: the need for general education p101-18

Nagel, E. In defense of scientific knowledge. *In* Hook, S.; Kurtz, P. W. and Todorovich, M. eds. The philosophy of the curriculum: the need for general education p119-26

Paschkis, V. Education for our changing technology. *In* Against pollution and hunger p249-55

Rice, S. A. A private view of teaching science. *In* Buxton, T. H. and Prichard, K. W. eds. Excellence in university teaching p128-31

Todorovich, M. Multilevel teaching of the natural sciences. *In* Hook, S.; Kurtz, P. W. and Todorovich, M. eds. The philosophy of the curriculum: the need for general education p137-42

Terminology

Boyd, R. N. Metaphor and theory change: what is "metaphor" a metaphor for? *In* Ortony, A. ed. Metaphor and thought p356-408

Kuhn, T. S. Metaphor in science. *In* Ortony, A. ed. Metaphor and thought p409-19

Pylyshyn, Z. W. Metaphorical impression and the "top-down" research strategy. *In* Ortony, A. ed. Metaphor and thought p420-36

See also Science—Language

Text-books—History

Heninger, S. K. Oronce Finé and English textbooks for the mathematical sciences. *In* Studies in the continental background of Renaissance English literature: essays presented to John L. Lievsay p170-85

Vocational guidance

Bunting, M. I. Creating opportunities for women in science. *In* Women in academia p115-19

United States—Historiography

Storr, R. J. Commentary: an historian of education looks at the Newagen study. *In* Oleson, A. and Brown, S. C. eds. The pursuit of knowledge in the early American Republic p340-44

Science, Ancient

Stock, C. B. Science, technology, and economic progress in the early Middle Ages. *In* Lindberg, D. C. ed. Science in the Middle Ages p 1-51

Science, Applied. See Technology

Science, Medieval

Dales, R. C. A twelfth-century concept of the natural order. *In* Viator: medieval and Renaissance studies v9 p179-92

Murdoch, J. E. The development of a critical temper: new approaches and modes of analysis in fourteenth-century philosophy, science, and theology. *In* Medieval and Renaissance studies [1975] p51-79

Stock, C. B. Science, technology, and economic progress in the early Middle Ages. *In* Lindberg, D. C. ed. Science in the Middle Ages p 1-51

Wallace, W. A. The philosophical setting of medieval science. *In* Lindberg, D. C. ed Science in the Middle Ages p91-119

White, L. T. Science and the sense of self: the medieval background of a modern confrontation. *In* Holton, G. J. and Morison, R. S. eds. Limits of scientific inquiry p47-59

Wightman, W. P. D. Cosmological and technological trends in the French Renaissance. *In* French Renaissance studies, 1540-70 p70-80

Science, Mental. See Psychology

Science, Moral. See Ethics

Science, Political. See Political science

Science, Social. See Sociology

Science and art. See Art and science

Science and civilization

Blau, J. L. Science and social progress. *In* Philosophy and the civilizing arts p166-77

Bronowski, J. A sense of the future. *In* Bronowski, J. A sense of the future p 1-5

Gilkey, L. B. The future of science. *In* The Future of science p105-28

Gillispie, C. C. The liberating influence of science in history. *In* Aspects of American liberty p37-46

Kuznetsov, B. G. Einstein, science and culture. *In* Einstein p167-83

Stock, C. B. Science, technology, and economic progress in the early Middle Ages. *In* Lindberg, D. C. ed. Science in the Middle Ages p 1-51

Science and ethics

Bok, S. Freedom and risk. *In* Holton, G. J. and Morison, R. S. eds. Limits of scientific inquiry p115-27

Bronowski, J. The disestablishment of science. *In* Bronowski, J. A sense of the future p235-48

Bronowski, J. The fulfillment of man. *In* Bronowski, J. A sense of the future p249-62

Bronowski, J. A moral for an age of plenty. *In* Bronowski, J. A sense of the future p196-205

Hesburgh, T. M. Science and technology in modern perspective. *In* Hesburgh, T. M. The Hesburgh papers p91-99

Kurtz, P. W. The ethics of free inquiry. *In* Hook, S.; Kurtz, P. and Todorovich, M. eds. The ethics of teaching and scientific research p203-07

Mansson, H. H. Justifying the Final Solution. *In* Weir, R. F. ed. Ethical issues in death and dying p308-19

Nader, R. The responsibility of the professional. *In* Against pollution and hunger p19-24

Swazey, J. P. Protecting the "animal of necessity": limits to inquiry in clinical investigation. *In* Holton, G. J. and Morison, R. S. eds. Limits of scientific inquiry p129-45

Todorovich, M. Wanted: a rational decision procedure for value conflicts in science. *In* Hook, S.; Kurtz, P. and Todorovich, M. eds. The ethics of teaching and scientific research p191-201

Toulmin, S. E. The twin moralities of science. *In* Science and society: past, present, and future p111-24

See also Bioethics

Science and history. See Science and civilization

Science and Islam. See Islam and science

Science and Judaism. See Judaism and science

Science and literature. See Literature and science

Science and magic

Hansen, B. Science and magic. *In* Lindberg, D. C. ed. Science in the Middle Ages p483-506

Science and poetry. See Literature and science

Science and religion. See Religion and science

Science and society. See Science—Social aspects; Science and civilization

Science and state

Böhme, G. Models for the development of science. *In* Science, technology and society p319-51

Bronowski, J. The disestablishment of science. *In* Bronowski, J. A sense of the future p235-48

Long, T. D. and Wright, C. Science policy institutions in six countries. *In* Science policies of industrial nations p 1-11

Nelkin, D. Technology and public policy. *In* Science, technology and society p393-441

Ravetz, J. R. Criticisms of science. *In* Science, technology and society p71-89

Salomon, J. J. Science policy studies and the development of science policy. *In* Science, technology and society p43-70

Spiegel-Rösing, I. S. The study of science, technology and society (SSTS): recent trends and future challenges. *In* Science, technology and society p7-42

France

Gilpin, R. G. Science, technology, and French independence. *In* Science policies of industrial nations p110-32

Great Britain

Vig, N. J. Policies for science and technology in Great Britain: postwar development and reassessment. *In* Science policies of industrial nations p59-109

Japan

Long, T. D. The dynamics of Japanese science policy. *In* Science policies of industrial nations p133-68

Russia

Graham, L. R. The development of science policy in the Soviet Union. *In* Science policies of industrial nations p12-58

Sweden

Dorfer, I. N. H. Science and technology policy in Sweden. *In* Science polices of industrial nations p169-90

Underdeveloped areas

See Underdeveloped areas—Science and state

United States

Brooks, H. The problem of research priorities. *In* Holton, G. J. and Morison, R. S. eds. Limits of scientific inquiry p157-69

Hutt, P. B. Public criticism of health science policy. *In* Holton, G. J. and Morison, R. S eds. Limits of scientific inquiry p157-69

Kochen, M. Science, isolation, and international relations. *In* Isolation or interdependence? p205-42

Nelkin, D. Threats and promises: negotiating the control of research. *In* Holton, G. J. and Morison, R. S. eds. Limits of scientific inquiry p191-209

Schmandt, J. United States science policy in transition. *In* Science policies of industrial nations p191-212

Science and the arts

Bronowski, J. Architecture as a science and architecture as an art. *In* Bronowski, J. The visionary eye p45-56

Bronowski, J. The creative process. *In* Bronowski, J. A sense of the future p6-15

Bronowski, J. On art and science. *In* Bronowski, J. A. A sense of the future p16-21

Science and the arts—*Continued*

Bronowski, J. The power of artifacts. *In* Bronowski, J. The visionary eye p59-70

Bronowski, J. The shape of things. *In* Bronowski, J. The visionary eye p33-44

Science and the humanities

Guerlac, H. Humanism in science. *In* Guerlac, H. Essays and papers in the history of modern science p3-18

Marx, L. Reflections on the neo-romantic critique of science. *In* Holton, G. J. and Morison, R. S. eds. Limits of scientific inquiry p61-73

Sayers, D. L. Creative mind; excerpt from "Unpopular opinions." *In* Sayers, D. L. The whimsical Christian p92-112

See also Art and science; Literature and science

Science fiction

Asimov, I. There's nothing like a good foundation. *In* Knight, D. F. ed. Turning points p273-76

Bester, A. Gourmet dining in outer space. *In* Knight, D. F. ed. Turning points p259-66

Campbell, J. W. No copying allowed; excerpt from "Collected editorials from Analog." *In* Knight, D. F. ed. Turning points p171-74

Heinlein, R. A. Pandora's box; excerpt from "The worlds of Robert A. Heinlein." *In* Knight, D. F. ed. Turning points p238-58

Heinlein, R. A. Science fiction: its nature, faults and virtues. *In* Knight, D. F. ed. Turning points p3-28

Russ, J. R. Alien monsters. *In* Knight, D. F. ed. Turning points p132-43

Waldo, E. H. Why so much syzygy? *In* Knight, D. F. ed. Turning points p269-72

Whitehead, H. Reasonably fantastic: some perspectives on scientology, science fiction, and occultism. *In* Zaretsky, I. I. and Leone, M. P. eds. Religious movements in contemporary America p547-87

Authorship

Knight, D. F. Writing and selling science fiction. *In* Knight, D. F. ed. Turning points p218-28

Laumer, K. How to collaborate without getting your head shaved. *In* Knight, D. F. ed. Turning points p215-17

History and criticism

Aldiss, B. W. Pilgrim fathers: Lucian and all that; excerpt from "Billion year spree." *In* Knight, D. F. ed. Turning points p73-95

Amis, K. The situation today; excerpt from "New maps of hell." *In* Knight, D. F. ed. Turning points p100-16

Asimov, I. Social science fiction. *In* Knight, D. F. ed. Turning points p29-61

Blish, J. Cathedrals in space; excerpt from "The issue at hand." *In* Knight, D. F. ed. Turning points p144-62

Brunner, J. Science fiction and the larger lunacy. *In* Nicholls, P. ed. Science fiction at large p73-103

Canary, R. H. Science fiction as fictive history. *In* Clareson, T. D. ed. Many futures, many worlds p164-81

Chernysheva, T. The folktale, Wells, and modern science fiction. *In* H. G. Wells and modern science fiction p35-47

Clareson, T. D. Lost lands, lost races: a pagan princess of their very own. *In* Clareson, T. D. ed. Many futures, many worlds p117-39

Clareson, T. D. Many futures, many worlds. *In* Clareson, T. D. ed. Many futures, many worlds p14-26

Colmer, J. Science fiction. *In* Colmer, J. Coleridge to Catch-22 p197-209

Delany, S. R. Critical methods: speculative fiction. *In* Clareson, T. D. ed. Many futures, many worlds p278-91

Dick, P. K. Man, android and machine. *In* Nicholls, P. ed. Science fiction at large p199-224

Disch, T. M. The embarrassments of science fiction. *In* Nicholls, P. ed. Science fiction at large p139-55

Fredericks, S. C. Revivals of ancient mythologies in current science fiction and fantasy. *In* Clareson, T. D. ed. Many futures, many worlds p50-65

Friend, B. Virgin territory: the bonds and boundaries of women in science fiction. *In* Clareson, T. D. ed. Many futures, many worlds p140-63

Garner, A. Inner time. *In* Nicholls, P. ed. Science fiction at large p119-38

Harrison, H. Worlds beside worlds. *In* Nicholls, P. ed. Science fiction at large p105-14

Hogan, P. G. The philosophical limitations of science fiction. *In* Clareson, T. D. ed. Many futures, many worlds p260-77

Kagle, S. E. Science fiction as simulation game. *In* Clareson, T. D. ed. Many futures, many worlds p224-36

King, J. N. Theology, science fiction, and man's future orientation. *In* Clareson, T. D. ed. Many futures, many worlds p237-59

Knight, D. F. What is science fiction? *In* Knight, D. F. ed. Turning points p62-69

Le Guin, U. K. Science fiction and Mrs Brown. *In* Nicholls, P. ed. Science fiction at large p13-33

Lewis, C. S. On science fiction; excerpt from "Of other worlds: essays and stories." *In* Knight, D. F. ed. Turning points p119-31

Miłosz, C. Science fiction and the coming of the Antichrist. *In* Miłosz, C. Emperor of the earth p15-31

Nicholls, P. Science fiction: the monsters and the critics. *In* Nicholls, P. ed. Science fiction at large p157-83

Rhodes, C. H. Tyranny by computer: automated data processing and oppressive government in science fiction. *In* Clareson, T. D. ed. Many futures, many worlds p66-93

Schmidt, S. The science in science fiction. *In* Clareson, T. D. ed. Many futures, many worlds p27-49

Suvin, D. Estrangement and cognition. *In* Suvin, D. Metamorphoses of science fiction p3-15

Suvin, D. Introduction. *In* H. G. Wells and modern science fiction p9-32

Suvin, D. SF and the genelogical jungle. *In* Suvin, D. Metamorphoses of science fiction p16-36

Suvin, D. SF and the novum. *In* Suvin, D. Metamorphoses of science fiction p63-89

Taylor, J. G. Scientific thought in fiction and in fact. *In* Nicholls, P. ed. Science fiction at large p57-72

Warrick, P. S. Images of the man-machine intelligence relationship in science fiction. *In* Clareson, T. D. ed. Many futures, many worlds p182-223

Science fiction—*Continued*

Moral and religious aspects

Blish, J. Cathedrals in space; excerpt from "The issue at hand." *In* Knight, D. F. ed. Turning points p144-62

Social aspects

Asimov, I. Social science fiction. *In* Knight, D. F. ed. Turning points p29-61

Toffler, A. Science fiction and change. *In* Nicholls, P. ed. Science fiction at large p115-18

Technique

Anderson, P. How to build a planet. *In* Knight, D. F. ed. Turning points p205-14

Heinlein, R. A. On the writing of speculative fiction. *In* Knight, D. F. ed. Turning points p199-204

Knight, D. F. Writing and selling science fiction. *In* Knight, D. F. ed. Turning points p218-28

McKenna, R. Journey with a little man; excerpt from "The sons of Martha, and other stories." *In* Knight, D. F. ed. Turning points p285-300

Sheckley, R. The search for the marvellous. *In* Nicholls, P. ed. Science fiction at large p185-98

Wolfe, G. K. The known and the unknown: structure and image in science fiction. *In* Clareson, T. D. ed. Many futures, many worlds p94-116

Science fiction, American

History and criticism

Cordess, G. The impact of American science fiction on Europe. *In* Bigsby, C. W. E. Superculture p161-74

Donald, M. Popular fiction. *In* Donald, M. The American novel in the twentieth century p176-95

Favier, J. Space and settor in short science fiction. *In* Johnson, I. D. and Johnson, C. [eds.] Les américanistes p182-201

Franklin, H. B. Science fiction before Gernsback; excerpt from "Future perfect." *In* Knight, D. F. ed. Turning points p96-99

Ketterer, D. Take-off to cosmic irony: science fiction humor and the Absurd. *In* Cohen, S. B. ed. Comic relief p70-86

Versins, P. Contact. *In* Knight, D. F. ed. Turning points p163-67

Europe

Cordess, G. The impact of American science fiction on Europe. *In* Bigsby, C. W. E. Superculture p161-74

Science fiction, English

History and criticism

Hillegas, M. R. Victorian "extraterrestrials." *In* The Worlds of Victorian fiction p391-414

Science fiction, Japanese

History and criticism

Komatsu, S. H. G. Wells and Japanese science fiction. *In* H. G. Wells and modern science fiction p179-90

Science fiction, Russian

History and criticism

Suvin, D. Russian SF and its utopian tradition. *In* Suvin, D. Metamorphoses of science fiction p243-69

Versins, P. Contact. *In* Knight, D. F. ed. Turning points p163-67

Science fiction films

Clarke, A. C. Son of Dr Strangelove; or, How I learned to stop worrying and love Stanley Kubrick; excerpt from "Report on Planet Three and other speculations." *In* Knight, D. F. ed. Turning points p277-84

History and criticism

Sontag, S The imagination of disaster; excerpt from "Against interpretation." *In* Denby, D. ed. Awake in the dark p263-78

Science illustration. See Scientific illustration

Science in literature

Brunner, J. Science fiction and the larger lunacy. *In* Nicholls, P. ed. Science fiction at large p73-103

Manzalaoui, M. Chaucer and science. *In* Brewer, D. S. ed. Geoffrey Chaucer p224-61

Ponko, V. Science in the exploration narratives authored by U.S. naval officers. *In* Kagle, S. E. ed. America: exploration and travel p92-100

Schmidt, S. The science in science fiction. *In* Clareson, T. D. ed. Many futures, many worlds p27-49

Science of language. See Linguistics

Science policy. See Science and state

Science research. See Research

Science stories. See Science fiction

Sciences, Classification of. See Classification of sciences

Sciences, Occult. See Occult sciences

Sciences, Social. See Social sciences

Scientific apparatus and instruments. See Astronomical instruments

Scientific creativity. See Creative ability in science

Scientific expeditions

America

Cutter, D. C. Spanish scientific exploration along the Pacific Coast. *In* Weber, D. J. ed. New Spain's far northern frontier p35-47

Scientific illustration

Scharf, A. Max Ernst, Étienne-Jules Marey, and the poetry of scientific illustration. *In* One hundred years of photographic history p117-26

See also Medical illustration

Scientific literature

Illustration

See Scientific illustration

Scientific method. See Science—Methodology

Scientific research. See Research

Scientific societies

Canada—History

Bowler, P. J. The early development of scientific societies in Canada. *In* Oleson, A. and Brown, S. C. eds. The pursuit of knowledge in the early American Republic p326-39

South Carolina—Charleston—History

Ewan, J. A. The growth of learned and scientific societies in the southeastern United States to 1860. *In* Oleson, A. and Brown, S. C. eds. The pursuit of knowledge in the early American Republic p208-18

Scientific societies—*Continued*

Southern States—History

Ewan, J. A. The growth of learned and scientific societies in the southeastern United States to 1860. *In* Oleson, A. and Brown, S. C. eds. The pursuit of knowledge in the early American Republic p208-18

United States—History

Dupree, A. H. The national pattern of American learned societies, 1769-1863. *In* Oleson, A. and Brown, S. C. eds. The pursuit of knowledge in the early American Republic p21-32

Greene, J. C. Science, learning, and utility: patterns of organization in the early American Republic. *In* Oleson, A. and Brown, S. C. eds. The pursuit of knowledge in the early American Republic p 1-20

Oleson, A. Introduction: To build a new intellectual order. *In* Oleson, A. and Brown, S. C. eds. The pursuit of knowledge in the early American Republic pxv-xxv

Scientists

Hooker, C. A. Has the scientist any future in the brave new world? *In* Science and society: past, present, and future p306-56

Lakoff, S. A. Scientists, technologists and political power. *In* Science, technology and society p355-91

Mulkay, M. J. Sociology of the scientific research community. *In* Science, technology and society p93-148

Nader, R. The responsibility of the professional. *In* Against pollution and hunger p19-24

Schröder, B. Science, technology and foreign policy. *In* Science, technology and society p473-506

Psychology

Barron, F. X. Bisociates: artist and scientist in the act of creation. *In* Harris, H. A. ed. Astride the two cultures p37-49

Fisch, R. Psychology of science. *In* Science, technology and society p277-318

Greece

Downs, R. B. Greek and Roman scientists. *In* Downs, R. B. Books that changed the world p287-306

Rome

Downs, R. B. Greek and Roman scientists. *In* Downs, R. B. Books that changed the world p287-306

United States

Reingold, N. Definitions and speculations: the professionalization of science in America in the nineteenth century. *In* Oleson, A. and Brown, S. C. eds. The pursuit of knowledge in the early American Republic p33-69

Scientists, Afro-American. See Afro-American scientists

Scientists, Austrian

Andre, J. and Froschle, H. The American expedition of Emperor Joseph II and Bernhard Moll's silhouettes. *In* The German contribution to the building of the Americas p135-72

Scientology

Wallis, R. Societal reaction to scientology: a study in the sociology of deviant religion. *In* Wallis, R. ed. Sectarianism p86-116

Whitehead, H. Reasonably fantastic: some perspectives on scientology, science fiction, and occultism. *In* Zaretsky, I. I. and Leone, M. P. eds. Religious movements in contemporary America p547-87

Scipio Aemilianus Africanus Minor, Publius Cornelius

Friends and associates

Zetzel, J. E. G. Cicero and the Scipionic Circle. *In* Harvard Studies in classical philology v76 p173-79

Scipio, the younger. See Scipio Aemilianus Africanus Minor, Publius Cornelius

Sclafani, Richard J.

The theory of art. *In* Aagaard-Mongensen, L. ed. Culture and art p146-70

Scobie, Stephen

Two authors in search of a character: bp Nichol and Michael Ondaatje. *In* Woodcock, G. ed. Poets and critics p225-46

Scoble, Harry M. See Wiseberg, L. S. jt. auth.

Scodel, Ruth

Apollo's perfidy: Iliad Ω 59-63. *In* Harvard Studies in classical philology v81 p55-57

Scopes, John Thomas

About

Linder, R. D. The resurgence of evangelical social concern (1925-75). *In* Wells, D. F. and Woodbridge, J. D. eds. The evangelicals p189-210

Scorel, Jan van

About individual works

Allegory

Winternitz, E. The inspired musician: a 16th-century musical pastiche. *In* Winternitz, E. Musical instruments and their symbolism in Western art p202-10

Scotch-Irish in the United States

Gower, H. The Scottish element in traditional ballads collected in America. *In* Ballad studies p117-51

Scotland

Esman, M. J. Scottish nationalism, North Sea oil, and the British response. *In* Esman, M. J. ed. Ethnic conflict in the Western world p251-86

Church history—Medieval period, 1057-1567

Cowan, I. B. Church and society. *In* Brown, J. M. ed. Scottish society in the fifteenth century p112-35

Church history—17th century

Thompson, W. The Kirk and the Cameronians. *In* Rebels and their causes p93-106

Civilization—20th century

Hart, F. R. Contemporary Scotland in fact and myth. *In* Hart, F. R. The Scottish novel p201-06

Economic conditions

Lythe, S. G. E. Economic life. *In* Brown, J. M. ed. Scottish society in the fifteenth century p66-84

Foreign relations—England

Macdougall, N. A. T. Foreign relations: England and France. *In* Brown, J. M. ed. Scottish society in the fifteenth century p101-11

Scotland—*Continued*

Foreign relations—France

Macdougall, N. A. T. Foreign relations: England and France. *In* Brown, J. M. ed. Scottish society in the fifteenth century p101-11

Foreign relations—Scandinavia

Crawford, B. E. Scotland's foreign relations: Scandinavia. *In* Brown, J. M. ed. Scottish society in the fifteenth century p85-100

History—15th century

Bannerman, J. W. M. The Lordship of the Isles. *In* Brown, J. M. ed. Scottish society in the fifteenth century p209-40

Lythe, S. G. E. Economic life. *In* Brown, J. M. ed. Scottish society in the fifteenth century p66-84

History—15th century—Sources

Macdougall, N. A. T. The sources: a reappraisal of the legend. *In* Brown, J. M. ed. Scottish society in the fifteenth century p10-32

History—James III, 1460-1488

Macdougall, N. A. T. The sources: a reappraisal of the legend. *In* Brown, J. M. ed. Scottish society in the fifteenth century p10-32

History—18th century

Phillipson, N. T. Culture and society in the 18th century province: the case of Edinburgh and the Scottish Enlightenment. *In* The University in society v2 p407-48

Intellectual life

Brown, A. H. Adam Smith's first Russian followers. *In* Skinner, A. S. and Wilson, T. eds. Essays on Adam Smith p247-73

Lawrence, C. The nervous system and society in the Scottish Enlightenment. *In* Barnes, B. and Shapin, S. eds. Natural order p19-40

Languages

Morgan, E. Registering the reality of Scotland. *In* Morgan, E. Essays p153-57

Politics and government—15th century

Brown, J. M. The exercise of power. *In* Brown, J. M. ed. Scottish society in the fifteenth century p33-65

Politics and government—20th century

Brand, J. From Scotland with love. *In* Kramnick, I. ed. Is Britain dying? p169-82

Esman, M. J. Erosion of the periphery. *In* Kramnick, I. ed. Is Britain dying? p183-99

Social conditions

Hart, F. R. Contemporary Scotland in fact and myth. *In* Hart, F. R. The Scottish novel p201-06

Scotland in literature

Briggs, J Far away and long ago: Stevenson's Scotland and Kipling's India. *In* Briggs, J. Night visitors p98-110

Hart, F. R. Kennaway, Spark and after. *In* Hart, F. R. The Scottish novel p287-321

Hart, F. R. Novelists of survival. *In* Hart, F. R. The Scottish novel p246-86

Hart, F. R. Novelists of the modern renaissance. *In* Hart, F. R. The Scottish novel p207-45

Scots law. See Law—Scotland

Scott, Andrew McKay

The logic of international interaction. *In* Orr, D. W. and Soroos, M. S. eds. The global predicament 284-307

Scott, Anne Firor

Self-portraits: three women. *In* Uprooted Americans p43-76

Scott, Bonnie K. See Hogan, R. G. jt. auth.

Scott, Charles T.

On defining the riddle: the problem of a structural unit. *In* Folklore genres p77-90

Scott, Elizabeth L.

Developing criteria and measures of equal opportunities for women. *In* Women in academia p82-114

Scott, Francis Reginald

About

Smith, A. J. M. F. R. Scott and some of his poems. *In* Woodcock, G. ed. Poets and critics p14-25

Scott, Franklin Daniel

Leland Henry Carlson: man and career. *In* The Dissenting tradition p xi-xx

Scott, Ira Oscar

Thrift institution management: tomorrow and today. *In* Benton, L. R. ed. Management for the future p271-82

Scott, Joan Wallach, and Tilly, Louise A.

Women's work and the family in nineteenth century Europe. *In* Rosenberg, C. E. ed. The family in history p145-78

Scott, Kenneth E.

Two models of the civil process. *In* Stanford legal essays p413-26

Scott, Nathan A.

Criticism and the religious prospect. *In* English Association. Essays and studies, 1977 p98-108

Ernest Hemingway, a critical essay; excerpt. *In* Wagner, L. W. ed. Ernest Hemingway p212-21

Flannery O'Connor's testimony: the pressure of glory. *In* Friedman, M. J. and Lawson, L. A. eds. The added dimension p138-56

Introduction. *In* Scott, N. A. ed. The legacy of Reinhold Niebuhr p ix-xxiv

Mirrors of man in existentialism

Contents

The achievement of existentialism
Albert Camus—resistance, rebellion. . . .
Existentialism and the tragic sense of reality
Friedrich Nietzsche—evangelist of the death of God
Heidegger's path—towards the recovery of being
Jean-Paul Sartre—advocate of "responsibility in solitude"
Kierkegaard's strait gate
Martin Buber—guide to the world of Thou

"New heav'ns, new earth"—the landscape of contemporary apocalypse. *In* Philosophy and the civilizing arts p389-432

Reinhold Niebuhr. *In* Ross, R. G. ed. Makers of American thought p227-61

Scott, Osborne E.

Pre-and post- Emancipation schools. *In* Roots of open education in America p13-20

Scott, Peter Dale

Vital artifice: Mary, Percy, and the psychopolitical integrity of Frankenstein. *In* Levine, G. L. and Knoepflmacher, U. C. eds. The endurance of Frankenstein p172-202

Scott, Stanley H.

The origins of Kootenay society, 1890-1930. *In* Bingham, E. R. and Love, G. A. eds. Northwest perspectives p78-96

Scott, Sir Walter, bart.

About

Hart, F. R. Romance after the Enlightenment. *In* Hart, F. R. The Scottish novel p143-53

Hart, F. R. Scottish variations of the Gothic novel. *In* Hart, F. R. The Scottish novel p13-30

Skilton, D. Austen, Scott and the Victorians. *In* Skilton, D. The English novel p80-98

About individual works

The bride of Lammermoor

Schmidgall, G. Gaetano Donizetti. *In* Schmidgall, G. Literature as opera p109-47

Wandering Willie's tale

Doubleday, N. F. Wandering Willie's tale. *In* Doubleday, N. F. Variety of attempt p49-60

Waverley

Iser, W. Fiction—the filter of history: a study of Sir Walter Scott's Waverley. *In* Amacher, R. E. and Lange, V. eds. New perspectives in German literary criticism p86-104

Pickering, S. Coelebs in Search of a wife, and Waverley. *In* Pickering, S. The moral tradition in English fiction, 1785-1850 p89-105

The Waverley novels

Nellist, B. Narrative modes in the Waverley novels. *In* Davies, R. T. and Beatty, B. G. eds. Literature of the romantic period, 1750-1850 p56-71

Influence—Dickens

Newman, S. J. Barnaby Rudge: Dickens and Scott. *In* Davies, R. T. and Beatty, B. G. eds. Literature of the romantic period, 1750-1850 p171-88

Scottish ballads. See Ballads, Scottish

Scottish fiction

History and criticism

Hart, F. R. Kennaway, Spark and after. *In* Hart, F. R. The Scottish novel p287-321

Hart, F. R. Novelists of the modern renaissance. *In* Hart, F. R. The Scottish novel p207-45

Hart, F. R. Retrospect: notes for a theory of Scottish fiction. *In* Hart, F. R. The Scottish novel p398-408

Scottish literature

History and criticism

Morgan, E. The beatnik in the Kailyaird. *In* Morgan, E. Essays p166-76

Walling, W. More than sufficient room: Sir David Wilkie and the Scottish literary tradition. *In* Kroeber, K. and Walling, W. eds. Images of romanticism p107-31

Influence

Niven, A. The Scottish element in Commonwealth literature. *In* Narasimhaiah, C. D. ed. Awakened conscience p29-41

20th century—History and criticism

Morgan, E. The resources of Scotland. *In* Morgan, E. Essays p158-65

Scottish poetry

To 1700—History and criticism

MacQueen, J. The literature of fifteenth-century Scotland. *In* Brown, J. M. ed. Scottish society in the fifteenth century p184-208

Morgan, E. Dunbar and the language of poetry. *In* Morgan, E. Essays p81-99

20th century—History and criticism

Morgan, E. Scottish poetry in the 1960s. *In* Morgan, E. Essays p177-85

Scoville, Herbert

A different approach to arms control—reciprocal unilateral restraint. *In* Arms control and technological innovation p170-75

Flexible MADness? The case against counterforce. *In* Ethics and nuclear strategy? p113-23

The role of technology in covert intelligence collection. *In* Borosage, R. L. and Marks, J. D. eds. The CIA file p109-22

Scragg, D. G.

Napier's 'Wulfstan' homily xxx: its sources, its relationship to the Vercelli Book and its style. *In* Anglo-Saxon England 6 p197-211

Old English literature. *In* English Association. The year's work in English studies v53 p67-83

Old English literature [another essay] *In* English Association. The year's work in English studies v54 p69-82

Old English literature [another essay] *In* English Association. The year's work in English studies v55 p76-91

Scragg, Leah

Macbeth on horseback. *In* Shakespeare survey 26 p81-88

Shakespeare, Lyly and Ovid: the influence of 'Gallathea' on 'A midsummer night's dream.' *In* Shakespeare survey 30 p125-34

Screech, Michael Andrew

Commonplaces of law, proverbial wisdom and philosophy: their importance in Renaissance scholarship (Rabelais, Joachim du Bellay, Montaigne). *In* Classical influences on European culture A.D. 1500-1700 p127-34

Medicine and literature: aspects of Rabelais and Montaigne (with a glance at the law). *In* French Renaissance studies, 1540-70 p156-69

Screen writers

Corliss, R. Introduction: notes on a screenwriter's theory, 1973—introduction to Talking pictures. *In* Denby, D. ed. Awake in the dark p215-26

Screenplays. See Moving-picture plays

Scriabine, Alexander Nicholas. See Skriabin. Aleksandr Nikolaevich

Scribner, Sylvia. See Cole, M. jt. auth.

Scriven, Michael

Explanations of the supernatural. *In* Thakur, S. C. ed. Philosophy and psychical research p181-94

The frontiers of psychology: psychoanalysis and parapsychology. *In* Wheatley, J. M. O. and Edge, H. L. eds. Philosophical dimensions of parapsychology p46-75

New frontiers of the brain. *In* Ludwig, J. K. ed. Philosophy and parapsychology p387-400

See also Meehl, P. E. jt. auth.

Scruggs, Otey M.

The meaning of Harriet Tubman. *In* "Remember the ladies": new perspectives on women in American history p110-21

Scrupski, Adam

Educational horizon: promise, challenge, vulnerability. *In* Social forces and schooling p361-68

Educational management: promise and failure. *In* Social forces and schooling p223-49

The social system of the school. *In* Social forces and schooling p141-86

Scruton, Roger

Reason and happiness. *In* Royal Institute of Philosophy. Nature and conduct p139-61

Sculpture

See also Bronzes; Carving (Art industries); Portrait sculpture; Relief (Sculpture)

Color

See Polychromy

Africa

See Sculpture, African

Africa, West

Bravmann, R. A. Masking tradition and figurative art among the Islamized Mande. *In* African images p144-69

McCall, D. F. The hornbill and analogous forms in West African sculpture. *In* African images p269-324

Asia Minor

Hiesinger, U. W. Three images of the god Mên. *In* Harvard Studies in classical philology v71 p303-10

Asia Minor—History

Hanfmann, G. M. A. Sardis, Croesus, and the Persians. *In* Hanfmann, G. M. A. From Croesus to Constantine p 1-21

Hanfmann, G. M. A. The social role of sculpture in Roman cities of western Asia Minor. *In* Hanfmann, G. M. A. From Croesus to Constantine p57-74

Central Europe

See Sculpture, Bohemian

Nigeria

Cole, H. M. The history of Ibo mbari houses—facts and theories. *In* African images p104-32

Foss, W. P. Images of aggression: ivwri sculpture of the Urhobo. *In* African images p133-43

Nigeria—Benin City

Ben-Amos, P. Professionals and amateurs in Benin court carving. *In* African images p170-89

Dark, P. J. C. Benin bronze heads: styles and chronology. *In* African images p25-103

Turkey

See Pergamum. Altar of Zeus. Frieze

Sculpture, Achaemenid

Iran—Persepolis

Porada, E. Some thoughts on the audience reliefs of Persepolis. *In* Studies in classical art and archaeology p37-43

Sculpture, African

Bay, E. G. The heart-shaped face in African art. *In* African images p252-67

Grottanelli, V. L. The Lugard Lecture of 1961. *In* African images p3-22

Sculpture, Ancient

See also Sculpture, Greco-Roman; Sculpture, Greek

Influence

Paley, M. D. "Wonderful originals"—Blake and ancient sculpture. *In* Essick, R. N. and Pearce, D. R. eds. Blake in his time p170-97

Sculpture, Bohemian

Frinta, M. S. A statue of St. Christopher at the M. H. de Young Memorial Museum at San Francisco. *In* Enggass, R. C. and Stokstad, M. eds. Hortus imaginum p57-63

Sculpture, Byzantine

Beckwith, J. Some early Byzantine rock crystals. *In* Studies in memory of David Talbot Rice p 1-5

Istanbul

Hanfmann, G. M. A. Instinctu divinitatis: the Tetrarchs, Constantine, and Constaninople. *In* Hanfmann, G. M. A. From Croesus to Constantine p75-97

Sculpture, Classical. See Marble sculpture, Classical

Sculpture, Early Christian

Istanbul

Hanfmann, G. M. A. Instinctu divinitatis: the Tetrarchs, Constantine, and Constaninople. *In* Hanfmann, G. M. A. From Croesus to Constantine p75-97

Sculpture, French

Wennberg, B. G. The spirit of exuberance. *In* Wennberg, B. G. French and Scandinavian sculpture in the nineteenth century p125-50

Sculpture, Greco-Roman

Hanfmann, G. M. A. The social role of sculpture in Roman cities of western Asia Minor. *In* Hanfmann, G. M. A. From Croesus to Constantine p57-74

Sculpture, Greek

Carter, J. C. The date of the sculptured coffer lids from the Temple of Athene Polias at Priene. *In* Studies in classical art and archaeology p139-51

Robertson, M. Two question-marks on the Parthenon. *In* Studies in classical art and archaeology p75-87

See also Sculpture, Greco-Roman

Influence

Hanfmann, G. M. A. Hellenization takes command. *In* Hanfmann, G. M. A. From Croesus to Constantine p22-40

Sculpture, Hellenistic

See also Sculpture, Greco-Roman; Marble sculpture, Hellenistic

Asia Minor

Hanfmann, G. M. A. Hellenization takes command. *In* Hanfmann, G. M. A. From Croesus to Constantine p22-40

Sculpture, Italian

History

Spencer, T. J. B. The statue of Hermione. *In* English Association. Essays and studies, 1977 p39-49

Sculpture, Medieval

Basford, K. H. Quest for the Green Man. *In* Symbols of power p101-20

See also Sculpture, Romanesque

Sculpture, Modern

Wennberg, B. G. On neo-classicism. *In* Wennberg, B. G. French and Scandinavian sculpture in the nineteenth century p10-53

Sculpture, Modern—*Continued*

19th century

Wennberg, B. G. On education and the impact of neo-classicism on tuition. *In* Wennberg, B. G. French and Scandinavian sculpture in the nineteenth century p194-97

Wennberg, B. G. On neo-Renaissance. *In* Wennberg, B. G. French and Scandinavian sculpture in the nineteenth century p151-80

Wennberg, B. G. On romanticism. *In* Wennberg, B. G. French and Scandinavian sculpture in the nineteenth century p54-90

Wennberg, B. G. On the use of different materials. *In* Wennberg, B. G. French and Scandinavian sculpture in the nineteenth century p202-08

Wennberg, B. G. The roads to reality. *In* Wennberg, B. G. French and Scandinavian sculpture in the nineteenth century p91-124

19th century—France

Wennberg, B. G. The spirit of exuberance. *In* Wennberg, B. G. French and Scandinavian sculpture in the nineteenth century p125-50

20th century—Europe

Krauss, R. E. Analytic space: futurism and constructivism. *In* Krauss, R. E. Passages in modern sculpture p39-67

Krauss, R. E. A game plan: the terms of surrealism. *In* Krauss, R. E. Passages in modern sculpture p105-46

20th century—France

Krauss, R. E. Forms of readymade: Duchamp and Brancusi. *In* Krauss, R. E. Passages in modern sculpture p69-103

20th century—United States

Krauss, R. E. The double negative: a new syntax for sculpture. *In* Krauss, R. E. Passages in modern sculpture p243-88

Krauss, R. E. Mechanical ballets: light, motion, theater. *In* Krauss, R. E. Passages in modern sculpture p201-42

Krauss, R. E. Tanktotem: welded images. *In* Krauss, R. E. Passages in modern sculpture p147-200

Sculpture, Nigerian. See Sculpture—Nigeria

Sculpture, Norwegian

Wennberg, B. G. Paris in Oslo—Gustav Vigeland. *In* Wennberg, B. G. French and Scandinavian sculpture in the nineteenth century p181-93

Sculpture, Pergamene

Ridgway, B. S. The Ludovisi head. *In* Studies in classical art and archaeology p153-61

Sculpture, Renaissance

Florence

Paoletti, J. T. The Bargello David and public sculpture in fifteenth-century Florence. *In* Collaboration in Italian Renaissance art p99-111

Sculpture, Roman. See Marble sculpture, Roman; Sculpture, Greco-Roman

Sculpture, Romanesque

Schapiro, M. From Mozarabic to Romanesque in Silos. *In* Schapiro, M. Selected papers v 1 p28-101

Schapiro, M. The Romanesque sculpture of Moissac. *In* Schapiro, M. Selected papers v 1 p131-264

Europe

Seidel, L. V. Holy warriors: the Romanesque rider and the fight against Islam. *In* The Holy war p33-77

France—Rodez

Schapiro, M. A relief in Rodez and the beginnings of Romanesque sculpture in southern France. *In* Schapiro, M. Selected papers v 1 p285-305

France—Souillac

Schapiro, M. The sculptures of Souillac. *In* Schapiro, M. Selected papers v 1 p102-30

France (Gard)—Saint-Gilles

Schapiro, M. New documents on Saint-Gilles. *In* Schapiro, M. Selected papers v 1 p328-46

Sculpture, Russian

Bowlt, J. E. Russian sculpture and Lenin's plan of monumental propaganda. *In* Millon, H. A. and Nochlin, L. eds. Art and architecture in the service of politics p182-93

Sculpture, Thai

O'Connor, S. J. Reflections on a problem sculpture from Jaiyä in peninsular Siam. *In* Southeast Asian history and historiography p100-06

Sculpture, West African. See Sculpture—Africa, West

Sculpture and literature. See Art and literature

Scura, Dorothy

Glasgow and the Southern Renaissance. *In* Ellen Glasgow p46-64

Scythians. See Alani

Sea (in religion, folklore, etc.)

Coomaraswamy, A. K. The sea. *In* Coomaraswamy, A. K. Selected papers v 1 p405-11

Sea fisheries. See Fisheries

Sea food

Pryor, T. A. Growing seafood on shore. *In* Strategies for human settlements: habitat and environment p67-78

Sea Peoples

MacLaurin, E. C. B. Cultural diffusion in the Middle East during the second millennium BC. *In* Grafton Elliot Smith p175-96

Sea pollution. See Marine pollution

Sea-power. See Naval history

Seaborg, Glenn Theodore

From Mendeleev to Mendelevium—and beyond. *In* Neyman, J. ed. The heritage of Copernicus: theories "pleasing to the mind" p267-96

New signposts for science. *In* The Future of science p 1-19

Seabury, Paul

HEW and the universities. *In* Gross, B. R. ed. Reverse discrimination p97-112

Ideology and foreign policy. *In* Encyclopedia of American foreign policy p398-408

Realism and idealism. *In* Encyclopedia of American foreign policy p856-66

The seafarer (Anglo-Saxon poem)

Green, B. K. Spes viva: structure and meaning in The seafarer. *In* An English miscellany p28-45

Klein, W. F. Purpose and the "poetics" of The wanderer and The seafarer. *In* Anglo-Saxon poetry: essays in appreciation p208-23

The seafarer (Anglo-Saxon poem)—*Cont.*

Pope, J. C. Second thoughts on the interpretation of The seafarer. *In* Anglo-Saxon England 3 p75-86

Woolf, R. The wanderer, The seafarer, and the genre of planctus. *In* Anglo-Saxon poetry: essays in appreciation p192-207

Seafood. See Sea food

Seale, Morris S.

Islamic society. *In* Life after death p123-31

Seale, Patrick

About individual works
The struggle for Syria

Kedourie, É. Arabs ancient and modern. *In* Kedourie, É. Arabic political memoirs and other studies p162-69

Seals (Numismatics)

Greece

Grace, V. R. Exceptional amphora stamps. *In* Studies in classical art and archaeolgy p115-27

India

Coomaraswamy, A. K. The rape of a Nāgī: an Indian Gupta seal. *In* Coomaraswamy, A. K. Selected papers v 1 p331-40

Sealsfield, Charles

About

Feest, C. F. Charles Sealsfield (Karl Postl). *In* Abroad in America: Visitors to the new Nation, 1776-1914 p22-31

Krumpelmann, J. T. Charles Sealsfield and Weimar. *In* The German contribution to the building of the Americas p173-80

Steeves, E. L. "No time for fainting"; the frontier woman in some early American novels. *In* Kagle, S. E. ed. America: exploration and travel p191-205

Sealts, Merton M.

Emerson on the scholar, 1838: a study of "Literary ethics." *In* Literature and ideas in America p40-57

Seamen in literature

Sarotte, G. M. Four archetypes of the homosexual couple: The captain and the soldier. *In* Sarotte, G. M. Like a brother, like a lover p70-91

Sear, Frank

Wall and vault mosaics. *In* Strong, D. E. and Brown, D. eds. Roman crafts p231-39

Searches and seizures

United States

LaFave, W. R. "Case-by-case adjudication" versus "standardized procedures": the Robinson dilemma. *In* The Supreme Court review, 1974 p127-63

White, J. B. The fourth amendment as a way of talking about people: a study of Robinson and Matlock. *In* The Supreme Court review, 1974 p165-232

Searing, Helen

With red flags flying: housing in Amsterdam, 1915-1923. *In* Millon, H. A. and Nochlin, L. eds. Art and architecture in the service of politics p230-69

Searle, John R.

Chomsky's revolution in linguistics. *In* Harman, G. ed. On Noam Chomsky p2-33

Metaphor. *In* Ortony, A. ed. Metaphor and thought p92-123

A more balanced view. *In* Hook, S.; Kurtz, P. W. and Todorovich, M. eds. The university and the state: what role for government in higher education? p205-13

Reiterating the differences: a reply to Derrida. *In* Glyph I p198-208

Sociobiology and the explanation of behavior. *In* Sociobiology and human nature p164-82

Two concepts of academic freedom. *In* The Concept of academic freedom p86-96

About individual works
Metaphor

Levin, S. R. Standard approaches to metaphor and a proposal for literary metaphor. *In* Ortony, A. ed. Metaphor and thought p124-35

Morgan, J. L. Observations on the pragmatics of metaphor. *In* Ortony, A. ed. Metaphor and thought p136-47

Reiterating the differences: a reply to Derrida

Derrida, J. Limited Inc. *In* Glyph 2 p162-254

Weber, S. It. *In* Glyph 4 p 1-31

Two concepts of academic freedom

Schmitt, R. Academic freedom: the future of a confusion. *In* The Concept of academic freedom p111-24

Sears, Robert Richard

Sex-typing, object choice, and child rearing. *In* Katchadourian, H. A. ed. Human sexuality p204-22

Seas, Freedom of. See Freedom of the seas

Seascape (criticism) Albee, E. *In* Kauffmann, S. Persons of the drama p222-24

Sebald, Winfried Georg

Humanitarianism and law: Arnold Zweig, Der Streit um den Sergeanten Grischa. *In* Klein, H. M. ed. The First World War in fiction p126-35

Sebastian, Saint

Art

Zupnick, I. L. Saint Sebastian. *In* Concepts of the hero in the Middle Ages and the Renaissance p239-67

Sebei (African tribe). See Sapiny (African tribe)

Sebeok, Thomas Albert

Ecumenicalism in semiotics. *In* Sebeok, T. A. ed. A perfusion of signs p180-206

The seventeenth century Cheremis: the evidence from Witsen. *In* On language, culture, and religion: in honor of Eugene A. Nida p301-14

Secession (Periodical)

Tashjian, D. L. Broom and Secession. *In* Tashjian, D. L. Skyscraper primitives p116-42

Second Advent

Aune, D. E. The significance of the delay of the Parousia for early Christianity. *In* Current issues in Biblical and patristic interpretation p87-109

Mare, W. H. A study of the New Testament concept of the Parousia. *In* Current issues in Biblical and patristic interpretation p336-45

See also Millennium

Second Adventists. See Adventists

Second shepherds' play (Towneley ms.)
Weimann, R. The mystery cycles. *In* Weimann, R. Shakespeare and the popular tradition in the theater: studies in the social dimension of dramatic form and function p49-97

Second sight
Brier, R. Magicians, alarm clocks, and backward causation. *In* Wheatley, J. M. O. and Edge, H. L. eds. Philosophical dimensions of parapsychology p235-44
Brier, R. The metaphysics of precognition. *In* Thakur, S. C. ed. Philosophy and psychical research p46-58
Broad, C. D. The philosophical implications of foreknowledge. *In* Wheatley, J. M. O. and Edge, H. L. eds. Philosophical dimensions of parapsychology p198-226
Ducasse, C. J. Knowing the future. *In* Wheatley, J. M. O. and Edge, H. L. eds. Philosophical dimensions of parapsychology p193-97
Ducasse, C. J. A theory of the relation of causality to precognition; excerpt from "Broad on the relevance of psychical research to philosophy." *In* Wheatley, J. M. O. and Edge, H. L. eds. Philosophical dimensions of parapsychology p227-34
See also Clairvoyance; Extrasensory perception

Secondary school teaching. See High school teaching

Secondary schools. See Public schools

Secord, Paul F.
Making oneself behave: a critique of the behavioral paradigm and an alternative conceptualization. *In* Mischel, T. ed. The self p250-73

Secrecy (Law) See Privacy, Right of

Secret service
See also Intelligence service

Confederate States of America
See United States—History—Civil War, 1861-1865 — Secret service — Confederate States

United States—Civil War, 1861-1865
See United States—History—Civil War, 1861-1865—Secret service

Secretaries

Sexual behavior
Peterson, J. A. The office wife. *In* Gross, L. ed. Sexual issues in marriage p199-206

Sectionalism (United States)
Bartley, N. V. The South and sectionalism in American politics. *In* Havard, W. C. and Bernd, J. L. eds. 200 years of the Republic in retrospect p239-57
Grantham, D. W. The South and the politics of sectionalism. *In* Grantham, D. W. The regional imagination p 1-22
Morrison, J. L. The struggle between sectionalism and nationalism at ante-bellum West Point, 1830-1861. *In* Hubbell, J. T. ed. Battles lost and won p19-29
Silbey, J. H. The Civil War synthesis in American political history. *In* Swierenga, R. P. ed. Beyond the Civil War synthesis p3-13

Sects
Beckford, J. A. Two contrasting types of sectarian organization. *In* Wallis, R. ed. Sectarianism p70-85
See also Cults

Public opinion
Wuthnow, R. The new religions in social context. *In* The New religious consciousness p267-93

Europe
Wilson, B. R. American religious sects in Europe. *In* Bigsby, C. W. E. Superculture p107-22

India
Juergensmeyer, M. Radhasoami as a trans-national movement. *In* Needleman, J. and Baker, G. eds. Understanding the new religions p190-200

Japan
Rajana, E. W. New religions in Japan: an appraisal of two theories. *In* Modern Japan p187-97

United States
Juergensmeyer, M. Radhasoami as a trans-national movement. *In* Needleman, J. and Baker, G. eds. Understanding the new religions p190-200
Wilson, J. F. The historical study of marginal American religious movements. *In* Zaretsky, I. I. and Leone, M. P. eds. Religious movements in contemporary America p596-611
Wuthnow, R. The new religions in social context. *In* The New religious consciousness p267-93

United States—History
Pritchard, L. K. Religious change in nineteenth-century America. *In* The New religious consciousness p297-330

Sects, Hindu. See Hindu sects

Sects, Sikh. See Sikh sects

Secularism
Chadwick, O. History and the secular. *In* Chadwick, O. The secularization of the European mind in the nineteenth century p189-228
Chadwick, O. The moral nature of man. *In* Chadwick, O. The secularization of the European mind in the nineteenth century p229-49
Chadwick, O. On a sense of providence. *In* Chadwick, O. The secularization of the European mind in the nineteenth century p250-66
Lidz, V. M. Secularization, ethical life, and religion in modern societies. *In* Johnson, H. M. ed. Religious change and continuity p191-217
Roszak, T. Ethics, ecstasy, and the study of new religions. *In* Needleman, J. and Baker, G. eds. Understanding the new religions p49-62
See also Anti-clericalism; Secularization (Theology)

Great Britain
Chadwick, O. The attitudes of the worker. *In* Chadwick, O. The secularization of the European mind in the nineteenth century p88-106

Secularization
Reyburn, W. D. Secular culture, missions, and spiritual values. *In* On language, culture, and religion: in honor of Eugene A. Nida p287-99

United States
Parsons, T. Religion in postindustrial America: the problem of secularization. *In* Parsons, T. Action theory and the human condition p300-22

Secularization (Theology)

See also Secularism

History

Wilkes, J. W. The transformation of dissent: a review of the change from the seventeenth to the eighteenth centuries. *In* The Dissenting tradition p108-22

Secundus, Julius. See Julius Secundus

Security, International

Brandt, W. Security in a changing world. *In* World change and world security p17-27

Brown, N. Threats to security in Europe. *In* The New Atlantic challenge p219-28

Edmonds, M. The horizons of war: problems of projection. *In* Beaumont, R. A. and Edmonds, M. eds. War in the next decade p 1-20

Krag, J. O. New openings in East-West relations. *In* The New Atlantic challenge p303-08

Nacht, M. L. Arms and politics: old issues, new perceptions. *In* Arms control and technological innovation p161-69

Schmidt, H. H. W. New tasks for the Atlantic Alliance. *In* The Year book of world affairs, 1975 p22-33

Schoettle, E. C. B. Arms limitation and security policies required to minimise the proliferation of nuclear weapons. *In* Arms control and technological innovation p102-31

Stromberg, R. N. Collective security. *In* Encyclopedia of American foreign policy p124-33

Wohlstetter, A. Nuclear threats and Allied responses in an era of negotiation. *In* The New Atlantic challenge p235-60

Yalem, R. J. Regional security communities and world order. *In* The Year book of world affairs, 1979 p217-42

Yergin, D. Order and survival. *In* A New America? p263-87

See also Arms control; Disarmament; International organization; Peace

Sedge, Douglas. See Corbin, P. jt. auth.

Sedgwick, Catharine Maria

About

Baym, N. Z. Catharine Sedgwick and other early novelists. *In* Baym, N. Z. Woman's fiction p31-85

About individual works
Redwood

Doubleday, N. F. Redwood and Bryant's review. *In* Doubleday, N. F. Variety of attempt p147-59

See, Carolyn

The jazz musician as Patchen's hero. *In* Morgan, R. G. ed. Kenneth Patchen: a collection of essays p218-28

Seeger, Charles Louis

Tractatus esthetico-semioticus: model of the systems of human communication. *In* Current thought in musicology p 1-39

Seelye, John

Prophetic waters

Contents

By way of Newtown: how Thomas Hooker crossed his Rubicon and started the Pequot War: a Hudibrastic interlude

Captain courageous: Captain John Smith, father of us all

Diverse voyages: Columbus, Cartier, and the Conradian shape of adventure in America

Divine tobacco: Hakluyt and the Virginia business

Ecclesiastic drums: Puritan theocrats, despairing of the present generation, reform the past

Epilogue

Ex libris

A fabric huge: Cotton Mather's masterpiece: or, The original errand betrayed

Glorious enterprise: Governor John Winthrop's wonderful wall

A model of Moses: the Pilgrims lend a prophetic presence to the land

On His Majesty's service: Robert Beverley, William Byrd, and the Palladian version of American pastoral

Prologue

Providential passages: wherein a matron, a minister, a militiaman, and a madam display the cardinal points of the Puritan compass

Return, Alpheus: Taylor, Sewall, Wolcott, and Company: some poetic fabrics from the linsey-woolsey loom

Womb of nature: Thomas Morton and the call of the wild

Seferis, George, pseud. See Sepheriadēs, Geōrgios

Sefrou, Morocco

Social life and customs

Rosen, L. The negotiation of reality: male-female relations in Sefrou, Morocco. *In* Beck, L. and Keddie, N. R. eds. Women in the Muslim world p561-84

Segal, Charles Paul

Andromache's anagnorisis: formulaic artistry in Iliad 22.437-476. *In* Harvard Studies in classical philology v75 p33-57

Sophocles' Trachiniae: myth, poetry, and heroic values. *In* Yale classical studies v25 p99-158

Synaesthesia in Sophocles. *In* Illinois classical studies, v2 1977 p88-96

Segal, Erich W.

The business of Roman comedy. *In* Perspectives of Roman poetry p93-103

The φύσις of comedy. *In* Harvard Studies in classical philology v77 p129-36

About individual works
Love story

Spilka, M. Erich Segal as Little Nell, or The real meaning of Love story. *In* Filler, L. ed. A question of quality: popularity and value in modern creative writing p8-25

Segal, Marcia Texler, and Berheide, Catherine White

Towards a women's perspective in sociology: directions and prospects. *In* McNall, S. G. ed. Theoretical perspectives in sociology p69-82

Segre, Cesare

Structures and time

Contents

Analysis of the tale, narrative logic, and time

The Canção do exilio of Gonçalves Dias, or Structure in time

Comical structure in the tale of Alatiel

A conceptual analysis of the First eclogue of Garcilaso

Deconstruction and reconstruction of a tale: from La mort le roi Artu to the Novellino

The function of language in Samuel Beckett's Acte sans paroles

Selvon, Samuel

About individual works

A brighter sun

Rohlehr, G. Samuel Selvon and the language of the people. *In* Baugh, E. ed. Critics on Caribbean literature p153-61

Lonely Londoners

Rohlehr, G. Samuel Selvon and the language of the people. *In* Baugh, E. ed. Critics on Caribbean literature p153-61

Selzer, Michael

Narcissism and the quest for power. *In* [Truth and tragedy]: a tribute to Hans Morgenthau p130-41

Semai. See Sakai

Semantics

Cohen, L. J. The semantics of metaphor. *In* Ortony, A. ed. Metaphor and thought p65-77

Fillmore, C. J. Topics in lexical semantics. *In* Current issues in linguistic theory p76-138

Franklin, W. Speaking and touching: the problem of inexpressibility in American travel books. *In* Kagle, S. E. ed. America: exploration and travel p18-38

Grim, P. Sexism and semantics. *In* Feminism and philosophy p109-16

Nida, E. A.; Louw, J. P. and Smith, R. B. Semantic domains and componential analysis of meaning. *In* Current issues in linguistic theory p139-67

Richards, I. A. Meaning and change of meaning. *In* Richards, I. A. Complementarities p73-87

Richards, I. A. Semantics. *In* Richards, I. A. Complementarities p98-107

Riegel, K. F. Semantic basis of language: language as labor. *In* Riegel, K. F. and Rosenwald, G. C. eds. Structure and transformation p167-92

Silverstein, M. Shifters, linguistic categories, and cultural description. *In* Basso, K. H. and Selby, H. A. eds. Meaning in anthropology p11-55

Veltruský, J. Construction of semantic contexts. *In* Matejka, L. and Titunik, I. R. eds. Semiotics of art p134-44

See also Definition (Logic); Discourse analysis; Reference (Linguistics); Semiotics; and subdivision Semantics under names of languages, e.g. English language—Semantics

Mathematical models

Wanner, E. and Maratsos, M. P. An ATN approach to comprehension. *In* Linguistic theory and psychological reality p119-61

Semantics (Philosophy)

Derrida, J. Freud and the scene of writing. *In* Derrida, J. Writing and difference p196-231

Derrida, J. From restricted to general economy: a Hegelianism without reserve. *In* Derrida, J. Writing and difference p251-77

Derrida, J. La parole soufflée. *In* Derrida, J. Writing and difference p169-95

Evans, G. L. Semantic structure and logical form. *In* Evans, G. L. and McDowell, J. H. eds. Truth and meaning p199-222

Hookway, C. Indeterminacy and interpretation. *In* Hookway, C. and Pettit, P. eds. Action and interpretation p17-42

Katz, J. J. The relevance of linguistics to philosophy. *In* Harman, G. ed. On Noam Chomsky p229-41

Keenan, E. L. Logic and language. *In* Bloomfield, M. W. and Haugen, E. I. eds. Language as a human problem p187-96

Moody, E. A. The age of analysis. *In* Moody, E. A. Studies in medieval philosophy, science, and logic p305-20

Mukařovský, J. Intentionality and unintentionality in art. *In* Mukařovský, J. Structure, sign, and function p89-128

Partee, B. H. Linguistic metatheory. *In* Harman, G. ed. On Noam Chomsky p303-15

Peckham, M. The virtues of superficiality. *In* Peckham, M. Romanticism and behavior p249-62

Putnam, H. W. Some issues in the theory of grammar. *In* Harman, G. ed. On Noam Chomsky p80-103

Schutz, A. Subjective and objective meaning. *In* Giddens, A. ed. Positivism and sociology p33-52

Stampe, D. W. Toward a grammar of meaning. *In* Harman, G. ed. On Noam Chomsky p267-302

Strawson, P. F. On understanding the structure of one's language. *In* Evans, G. L. and McDowell, J. H. eds. Truth and meaning p189-98

See also Analysis (Philosophy); Communication; Meaning (Philosophy); Pragmatics

Semantics (Religion) See Religion and language

Semasiology. See Semantics

Semeiotics. See Semantics (Philosophy); Semiotics; Signs and symbols

Semil-Jakubowicz, Malgorzata

Post-war drama in Eastern Europe. *In* Nicoll, A. World drama p861-71

Seminole Indians

Kersey, H. A. Those left behind: the Seminole Indians of Florida. *In* Williams, W. L. ed. Southeastern Indians since the removal era p174-90

Semiology (Linguistics) See Semiotics

Semiology (Semantics) See Semantics

Semiotics

Agrest, D. and Gandelsonas, M. Semiotics and the limits of architecture. *In* Sebeok, T. A. ed. A perfusion of signs p90-120

Bogatyrev, P. G. Semiotics in the folk theater. *In* Matejka, L. and Titunik, I. R. eds. Semiotics of art p33-50

Bouissac, P. A semiotic approach to nonsense: clowns and limericks. *In* Sebeok, T. A. ed. Sight, sound, and sense p244-63

Bouissac, P. Semiotics and spectacles: the circus institution and representations. *In* Sebeok, T. A. ed. A perfusion of signs p143-52

Brušák, K. Signs in the Chinese theater. *In* Matejka, L. and Titunik, I. R. eds. Semiotics of art p59-73

Eco, U. Semiotics: a discipline or an interdisciplinary method? *In* Sebeok, T. A. ed. Sight, sound, and sense p73-83

Hiż, H. Logical basis of semiotics. *In* Sebeok, T. A. ed. A perfusion of signs p40-53

Honzl, J. Dynamics of the sign in the theater. *In* Matejka, L. and Titunik, I. R. eds. Semiotics of art p74-93

Jakobson, R. Is the cinema in decline? *In* Matejka, L. and Titunik, I. R. eds. Semiotics of art p145-52

Kjørup, S. Film as a meetingplace of multiple codes. *In* Perkins, D. and Leondar, B. eds. The arts and cognition p20-47

Seneca, Lucius A.—*Continued*

Influence—Juvenalis

Dick, B. F. Seneca and Juvenal 10. *In* Harvard Studies in classical philology v73 p237-46

Seneca, Lucius Annaeus (the younger) See Seneca, Lucius Annaeus

Seneca language. See Iroquoian languages

Senegal

Description and travel

Connolly, C. Destination Atlantis. *In* Connolly, C. The evening colonnade p85-103

Politics and government

Cruise O'Brien, D. B. Clan, community, nation: dimensions of political loyalty in Senegal. *In* Smock, D. R. and Bentsi-Enchill, K. eds. The search for national integration in Africa p255-69

Senescence. See Aging; Old age

Senghaas, Dieter. See Deutsch, K. W. jt. auth.

Senghor, Leópold Sédar, President Senegal

About

Case, F. I. Négritude and utopianism. *In* African literature today no. 7: Focus on criticism p65-75

Dorsinville, M. Senghor or the song of exile. *In* Exile and tradition p62-73

Reed, J. Léopold Sédar Senghor's poetry. *In* King, B. A. and Ogungbesan, K. eds. A celebration of Black and African writing p102-11

About individual works

Chants d'ombre

Peters, J. L. S. Senghor: the mask poems of Chants d'ombre. *In* African literature today no. 7: Focus on criticism p76-92

Sengupta, Jati K.

Economic policy simulation in dynamic control models under econometric estimation. *In* Econometrics and economic theory p114-37

Senior centers. See Aged—Societies and clubs

Senior citizens. See Aged

Senior power. See Aged—Political activity

Seniors, High school. See High school seniors

Senkaku Islands

Li, V. H. China and off-shore oil: the Tiao-yü Tai dispute. *In* China's changing role in the world economy p143-62

Sennett, Richard

Destructive Gemeinschaft. *In* Beyond the crisis p171-97

What Tocqueville feared. *In* On the making of Americans p105-25

Senoi. See Sakai

Senoufo (African people) See Senufo (African people)

Sensation. See Senses and sensation

Sense data

O'Connor, D. J. The status of sense data. *In* Royal Institute of Philosophy. Impressions of empiricism p79-92

Quine, W. V. Posits and reality. *In* Quine, W. V. The ways of paradox, and other essays p246-54

Sixel, F. W. The problem of sense: Habermas v. Luhmann. *In* O'Neill, J. ed. On critical theory p184-204

Sense-organs. See Senses and sensation

Senses and sensation

Bouwsma, O. K. Descartes' skepticism of the senses. *In* Dunlop, C. E. M. ed. Philosophical essays on dreaming p52-63

Bower, T. G. R. The evolution of sensory systems. *In* Perception p141-52

Ellis, B. D. Physicalism and the contents of sense experience. *In* Philosophical aspects of the mind-body problem p64-77

Ong, W. J. "I see what you say": sense analogues for intellect. *In* Ong, W. J. Interfaces of the word p121-44

Quine, W. V. On mental entities. *In* Quine, W. V. The ways of paradox, and other essays p221-27

Schofield, R. E. Joseph Priestley on sensation and perception. *In* Studies in perception p336-54

Selver, C. and Brooks, C. V. Notes about the human potential. *In* Hanna, T. ed. Explorers of humankind p60-69

Turnbull, R. G. The role of the "special sensibles" in the perception theories of Plato and Aristotle. *In* Studies in perception p3-26

See also Amputees—Psychology; Gestalt psychology; Hearing; Pain; Sense data; Time perception; Touch; Vision

Sensitivity training. See Group relations training

Sentences (Criminal procedure)

Great Britain

Hood, R. G. Criminology and penal change: a case study of the nature and impact of some recent advice to governments. *In* Crime, criminology and public policy p375-417

United States

Motley, C. B. Criminal law: "law and order" and the criminal justice system. *In* Perspectives on justice p39-72

Sentences, Prison. See Prison sentences

Sentencing. See Sentences (Criminal procedure)

Sentimentalism in literature

Butler, M. The Jacobin novel I: revolution and reason. *In* Butler, M. Jane Austen and the war of ideas p29-56

Butler, M. Sentimentalism: the radical inheritance. *In* Butler, M. Jane Austen and the war of ideas p7-28

Karl, F. R. Tristram Shandy, the sentimental novel, and sentimentalists. *In* Karl, F. R. The adversary literature p205-34

Nicoll, A. The wave of sentimentalism. *In* Nicoll, A. World drama p330-36

Skilton, D. Sterne, sentiment and its opponents. *In* Skilton, D. The English novel p45-58

See also Love in literature

Senufo (African people)

McCall, D. F. The hornbill and analogous forms in West African sculpture. *In* African images p269-324

Separation (Law) See Divorce

Separation of powers

See also Judicial review

United States

Carey, G. W. The separation of powers. *In* Graham, G. J. and Graham, S. G. eds. Founding principles of American government p98-134

Servius, grammarian, fl. ca. 400—*Continued*
Manuscripts
Murgia, C. E. Critical notes on the text of Servius' commentary on Aeneid III-V. *In* Harvard Studies in classical philology v72 p311-50

Servius Honoratus, Maurus. See Servius, grammarian, fl. ca. 400

Serwer, Daniel
Unmechanischer Zwang: Pauli, Heisenberg, and the rejection of the mechanical atom, 1923-1925. *In* Historical studies in the physical sciences v8 p189-256

Sessions, Roger
Roger Sessions on music
Contents
America moves to the avant-scene
American music and the crisis
Art, freedom, and the individual
Artists and this war
Composer and critic
The composer and his message
The composer in the university
Ernest Bloch
Escape by theory
Europe comes to America
Exposition by Krenek
The function of theory
Heinrich Schenker's contribution
Hindemith on theory
Hindemith's Mathis der Maler
How a "difficult" composer gets that way
Music and nationalism
Music and the crisis of the arts
Music in a business economy
Music in crisis
The new musical horizon
New vistas in musical education
No more business-as-usual
On Oedipus Rex
On the American future
Problems and issues facing the composer today
Schoenberg in the United States
The scope of music criticism
Some notes on Schoenberg and the "method of composing with twelve tones"
Song and pattern in music today
Style and "styles" in music
Thoughts on Stravinsky
To revitalize opera
Vienna—vale, ave
What can be taught?

Set theory
Quine, W. V. Foundations of mathematics. *In* Quine, W. V. The ways of paradox, and other essays p22-32
Quine, W. V. On multiplying entities. *In* Quine, W. V. The ways of paradox, and other essays p259-64
Ulam, S. M. Infinities. *In* Neyman, J. ed. The heritage of Copernicus: theories "pleasing to the mind" p378-93
See also Logic, Symbolic and mathematical

Setchkarev, Vsevolod
From the golden to the silver age (1820-1917). *In* Auty, R. and Obolensky, D. eds. An introduction to Russian language and literature p133-84

Seton-Watson, Hugh
How right the old Kennan was! *In* Decline of the West? George Kennan and his critics p39-48

The Soviet Union and its neighbours. *In* Auty, R. and Obolensky, D. eds. An introduction to Russian history p366-87

Sets (Mathematics) See Set theory

Setting (Literature)
Johnson, E. D. H. "The truer measure": setting in Emma, Middlemarch, and Howards End. *In* Bornstein, G. ed. Romantic and modern p197-205

Settlement of land. See Land settlement

Seung, Thomas Kaehao
Bonaventure's figural exemplarism in Dante. *In* Italian literature: roots and branches p117-54

Seurat, Georges Pierre
About
Schapiro, M. Seurat. *In* Schapiro, M. Selected papers v2 p101-09

Sevan, Armenia
Mandel'shtam, O. E. Journey to Armenia. *In* Mandel'shtam, O. E. Selected essays p173-78

Seven beauties (Motion picture)
Bettelheim, B. Surviving. *In* Bettelheim, B. Surviving, and other essays p274-314

Seven Cities of Gold. See Cibola

Seven deadly sins. See Deadly sins

The seven year itch (Motion picture)
Truffaut, F. Billy Wilder: The seven year itch. *In* Truffaut, F. The films in my life p159-61

Seventeenth century. See Civilization, Modern—17th century

Seventh-Day Adventists
Bibliography
Carner, V. D.; Kubo, S. and Rice, C. Bibliographical essay. *In* The Rise of Adventism p207-317
History
Butler, J. M. Adventism and the American experience. *In* The Rise of Adventism p173-206

Severs, J. Burke
Chaucer's clerks. *In* Chaucer and Middle English studies in honour of Rossell Hope Robbins p140-52

Sévigné, Marie (de Rabutin Chantal) marquis de
About individual works
Letters
Horowitz, L. K. Madame De Sévigné. *In* Horowitz, L. K. Love and language p91-111

Sevilla-Guzman, Eduardo
The peasantry and the Franco régime. *In* Preston, P. ed. Spain in crisis p101-24

Seville
Intellectual life
Brown, J. A community of scholars. *In* Brown, J. Images and ideas in seventeenth-century Spanish painting p21-43
Brown, J. Theory into practice: the arts and the academy. *In* Brown, J. Images and ideas in seventeenth-century Spanish painting p63-83

Seville. La Caridad (Church)
Brown, J. Hieroglyphs of death and salvation: the decoration of the Church of the Hermandad de la Caridad, Seville. *In* Brown, J. Images and ideas in seventeenth-century Spanish painting p128-46

Sevket, Mahmut, pasa

About

Swanson, G. W. War, technology, and society in the Ottoman Empire from the reign of Abdülhamid II to 1913: Mahmud Sevket and the German military mission. *In* War, technology and society in the Middle East p367-85

Sèvres porcelain

Taylor, S. Artists and philosophes as mirrored by Sèvres and Wedgwood. *In* The Artist and the writer in France p21-39

Sewall, Samuel

About individual works

Upon the drying up that ancient river, the River Merrymak

Seelye, J. Return, Alpheus: Taylor, Sewall, Wolcott, and Company: some poetic fabrics from the linsey-woolsey loom. *In* Seelye, J. Prophetic waters p311-39

Seward, John, pseud. See Stephens, Frederic George

Seward, William Henry

About

Ferris, N. B. Transatlantic misunderstanding: William Henry Seward and the Declaration of Paris negotiation of 1861. *In* Rank and file p55-78

Sewart, John J.

Critical theory and the critique of conservative method. *In* McNall, S. G. ed. Theoretical perspectives in sociology p310-22

Sewell, Alan Francis

Political crime: a psychologist's perspective. *In* International terrorism and political crimes p11-26

Sewell, Elizabeth Missing

About

Frerichs, S. C. Elizabeth Missing Sewell: concealment and revelation in a Victorian everywoman. *In* Landow, G. P. ed. Approaches to Victorian autobiography p175-99

About individual works

The autobiography of Elizabeth M. Sewell

Frerichs, S. C. Elizabeth Missing Sewell: concealment and revelation in a Victorian everywoman. *In* Landow, G. P. ed. Approaches to Victorian autobiography p175-99

Sex

Alexander, R. D. Sexuality and sociality in humans and other primates. *In* Katchadourian, H. A. ed. Human sexuality p81-97

Gagnon, J. H. The interaction of gender roles and sexual conduct. *In* Katchadourian, H. A. ed. Human sexuality p225-45

Rainwater, L. Sociological perspectives on sex and its psychosocial derivatives. *In* Katchadourian, H. A. ed. Human sexuality p257-64

Ruddick, S. Better sex. *In* Baker, R. and Elliston, F. A. eds. Philosophy & sex p83-104

Solomon, R. C. Sex and perversion. *In* Baker, R. and Elliston, F. A. eds. Philosophy & sex p268-87

Staples, R. Black sexuality. *In* Sexuality and human values p62-70

See also Group sex; Homosexuality; Lesbianism; Reproduction; Sex (Biology)

Physiological aspects

See Sex (Biology)

Psychological aspects

See Sex (Psychology)

Research

See Sex research

Terminology

Baker, R. "Pricks" and "chicks": a plea for "persons." *In* Baker, R. and Elliston, F. A. eds. Philosophy & sex p45-64

Katchadourian, H. A. The terminology of sex and gender. *In* Katchadourian, H. A. ed. Human sexuality p8-34

Lawrence, B. Four-letter words can hurt you. *In* Baker, R. and Elliston, F. A. eds. Philosophy & sex p31-33

Moulton, J. M. Sex and reference. *In* Baker, R. and Elliston, F. A. eds. Philosophy & sex p34-44

Sex (Biology)

Churchill, F. B. Sex and the single organism: biological theories of sexuality in mid-nineteenth century. *In* Studies in history of biology v3 p139-77

Davidson, J. M. Biological determinants of sex: their scope and limitations. *In* Katchadourian, H. A. ed. Human sexuality p134-49

Dickason, A. Anatomy and destiny: the role of biology in Plato's view of women. *In* Gould, C. C. and Wartofsky, M. W. eds. Women and philosophy p45-53

Ehrhardt, A. A. The interactional model of sex hormones and behavior. *In* Katchadourian, H. A. ed. Human sexuality p150-60

Green, R. Biological influences on sexual identity. *In* Katchadourian, H. A. ed. Human sexuality p115-33

Hall, D. L. Biology, sex hormones and sexism in the 1920's. *In* Gould, C. C. and Wartofsky, M. W. eds. Women and philosophy p81-96

Sex (Physiology). See Sex (Biology)

Sex (Psychology)

Beach, F. A. Animal models and psychological inference. *In* Katchadourian, H. A. ed. Human sexuality p98-112

De Vos, G. A. Affective dissonance and primary socialization: implications for a theory of incest avoidance. *In* Schwartz, T. ed. Socialization as cultural communication p73-90

Katchadourian, H. A. and Martin, J. A. Analyses of human sexual behavior. *In* Katchadourian, H. A. ed. Human sexuality p35-48

Lipman-Blumen, J. and Leavitt, H. J. Sexual behavior as an expression of achievement orientation. *In* Katchadourian, H. A. ed. Human sexuality p246-56

Peterson, J. A. Nagging and sex. *In* Gross, L. ed. Sexual issues in marriage p85-92

Rapaport, E. On the future of love: Rousseau and the radical feminists. *In* Gould, C. C. and Wartofsky, M. W. eds. Women and philosophy p185-205

See also Femininity (Psychology); Masculinity (Psychology); Oedipus complex; Sex differences (Psychology); Sex role; Sexism; Sexual disorders

Sex (Theology) See Homosexuality and Christianity

Sex, Change of. See Change of sex

Sex, Oral. See Oral intercourse

Sex and Islam

Vieille, P. Iranian women in family alliance and sexual politics. *In* Beck, L. and Keddie, N. R. eds. Women in the Muslim world p451-72

Sex and law

See also Abortion; Domestic relations; Homosexuality—Law and legislation; Sex crimes

United States

Skolnick, J. H. Should sexual relations be treated as crimes? *In* Contemporary issues in criminal justice p5-15

Sex and religion

Flandrin, J. L. Contraception, marriage, and sexual relations in the Christian West. *In* Biology of man in history p23-47

Haeberle, E. J. Historical roots of sexual oppression. *In* Gochros, H. L. and Gochros, J. S. eds. The sexually oppressed p3-27

Masters, W. H. and Johnson, V. E. The role of religion in sexual dysfunction. *In* Sexuality and human values p86-96

Thomas, J. L. The road ahead. *In* Sexuality and human values p132-51

See also Homosexuality and Christianity; Sex and Islam

Sex and religion in literature

Kunkel, F. L. Conclusion. *In* Kunkel, F. L. Passion and the Passion p169-83

Kunkel, F. L. Golding's The spire: the prayer and the phallus. *In* Kunkel, F. L. Passion and the Passion p58-74

Kunkel, F. L. John Updike: between heaven and earth. *In* Kunkel, F. L. Passion and the Passion p75-98

Kunkel, F. L. Lawrence's The man who died: the heavenly cock. *In* Kunkel, F. L. Passion and the Passion p37-57

Kunkel, F. L. The sexy Cross. *In* Kunkel, F. L. Passion and the Passion p157-68

Kunkel, F. L. Tennessee Williams: God, sex, and death. *In* Kunkel, F. L. Passion and the Passion p99-107

Kunkel, F. L. Wrestlers with Christ and Cupid. *In* Kunkel, F. L. Passion and the Passion p129-56

Sex behavior in animals. See Sexual behavior in animals

Sex bias. See Sexism

Sex crimes

Sutherland, E. H. The diffusion of sexual psychopath laws. *In* Davis, F. J. and Stivers, R. eds. The collective definition of deviance p281-95

West, D. J. Thoughts on sex law reform. *In* Crime, criminology and public policy p469-87

See also Child molesting; Rape; Sex and law

Sex customs

Faithorn, E. The concept of pollution among the Káfe of the Papua New Guinea Highlands. *In* Reiter, R. R. ed. Toward an anthropology of women p127-40

Gochros, H. L. and Gochros, J. S. Introduction: Who are the sexually oppressed? *In* Gochros, H. L. and Gochros, J. S. eds. The sexually oppressed p xix-xxiii

Heller, A. The future of relations between the sexes. *In* The Humanisation of socialism p27-41

See also Group sex; Premarital sex; Sex and religion; Sex in literature

History

Haeberle, E. J. Historical roots of sexual oppression. *In* Gochros, H. L. and Gochros, J. S. eds. The sexually oppressed p3-27

Great Britain

Smith, F. B. Sexuality in Britain, 1800-1900: some suggested revisions. *In* Vicinus, M. ed. A widening sphere p182-98

Iran

Vieille, P. Iranian women in family alliance and sexual politics. *In* Beck, L. and Keddie, N. R. eds. Women in the Muslim world p451-72

Nantes

Depauw, J. Illicit sexual activity and society in eighteenth-century Nantes. *In* Family and society p145-91

United States

Chilman, C. S. The poor. *In* Gochros, H. L. and Gochros, J. S. eds. The sexually oppressed p202-12

Johnson, L. B. Blacks. *In* Gochros, H. L. and Gochros, J. S. eds. The sexually oppressed p173-91

Ogawa, D. M. Asian Americans. *In* Gochros, H. L. and Gochros, J. S. eds. The sexually oppressed p192-201

Sex differences

Leibowitz, L. Perspectives on the evolution of sex differences. *In* Reiter, R. R. ed. Toward an anthropology of women p20-35

Whitbeck, C. Theories of sex difference. *In* Gould, C. C. and Wartofsky, M. W. eds. Women and philosophy p54-80

Sex differences (Psychology)

Green, R. Biological influences on sexual identity. *In* Katchadourian, H. A. ed. Human sexuality p115-33

Sherman, J. A. Some psychological "facts" about women: will the real Ms. please stand up? *In* Roberts, J. I. ed. Beyond intellectual sexism p113-37

Whitbeck, C. Theories of sex differences. *In* Gould, C. C. and Wartofsky, M. W. eds. Women and philosophy p54-80

See also Androgyny (Psychology); Sex role

Sex discrimination

See also Sex discrimination against women

Law and legislation—United States

Ginsburg, R. B. Gender in the Supreme Court: the 1973 and 1974 terms. *In* The Supreme Court review, 1975 p 1-24

Sex discrimination against women

Bundy, M. L. A nonmale image of the future. *In* Bundy, R. F. ed. Images of the future: the twenty-first century and beyond p152-58

Reskin, B. F. Sex differentiation and the social organization of science. *In* Gaston, J. ed. Sociology of science p6-37

Rubin, G. The traffic in women: notes on the "political economy" of sex. *In* Reiter, R. R. ed. Toward an anthropology of women p157-210

Case studies

Beach, R. I. A case history of affirmative action. *In* Women in academia p128-38

Sex discrimination against women—*Continued*

United States

Barasch, F. K. HEW, the university, and women. *In* Gross, B. R. ed. Reverse discrimination p54-65

Bunting, M. I. Creating opportunities for women in science. *In* Women in academia p115-19

Cook, A. H. Sex discrimination at universities: an ombudsman's view. *In* Women in academia p120-27

Crocker, L. Preferential treatment. *In* Feminism and philosophy p190-209

Fullinwider, R. K. On preferential hiring. *In* Feminism and philosophy p210-24

Ginsburg, R. B. Realizing the equality principle. *In* Social justice & preferential treatment p135-53

Goldman, A. H. Limits to the justification of reverse discrimination. *In* Feminism and philosophy p225-41

Kravetz, D. F. Women social workers and clients: common victims of sexism. *In* Roberts, J. I. ed. Beyond intellectual sexism p160-71

Nagel, T. The policy of preference. *In* Nagel, T. Mortal questions p91-105

Scott, E. L. Developing criteria and measures of equal opportunities for women. *In* Women in academia p82-114

Seidman, A. W. Women who work for wages. *In* Roberts, J. I. ed. Beyond intellectual sexism p265-73

Weitzman, L. J. Legal requirements, structures, and strategies for eliminating sex discrimination in academe. *In* Women in academia p45-81

Sex discrimination in education

Greene, M. Sexism in the schools. *In* Greene, M. Landscapes of learning p244-55

Law and legislation—United States

Sandler, B. Sex discrimination, educational institutions, and the law: a new issue on campus. *In* Women in academia p20-36

United States

Fennema, E. Women and girls in the public schools: defeat or liberation? *In* Roberts, J. I. ed. Beyond intellectual sexism p343-52

Hornig, L. S. Affirmative action through affirmative attitudes. *In* Women in academia p8-19

Sex education. See Sex instruction

Sex hormones. See Hormones, Sex

Sex in art. See Erotic art

Sex in literature

Alcorn, J. Toward Freud. *In* Alcorn, J. The nature novel from Hardy to Lawrence p107-12

Armstrong, I. Browning and Victorian poetry of sexual love. *In* Armstrong, I. ed. Robert Browning p267-98

Bayley, J. Keats and sex. *In* Bayley, J. The uses of division p130-45

Bersani, L. Emma Bovary and the sense of sex. *In* Bersani, L. A future for Astyanax p89-105

Bersani, L. Lawrentian stillness. *In* Bersani, L. A future for Astyanax p156-85

Bersani, L. Persons in pieces. *In* Bersani, L. A future for Astyanax p286-315

Boyers, R. Attitudes toward sex in American "high culture." *In* Boyers, R. Excursions p109-28

Christian, D. Inversion and the erotic: the case of William Blake. *In* Babcock, B. A. ed. The reversible world p117-28

Cockshut, A. O. J. The optimists. *In* Cockshut, A. O. J. Man and woman: a study of love and the novel, 1740-1940 p136-52

Fetterley, J. An American dream: "Hula, hula," said the witches. *In* Fetterley, J. The resisting reader p154-89

Fetterley, J. A farewell to arms: Hemingway's "resentful cryptogram." *In* Fetterley, J. The resisting reader p46-71

Fetterley, J. Palpable designs: four American short stories: Growing up male in America: "I want to know why." *In* Fetterley, J. The resisting reader p12-22

Johnson, W. S. Sexual attitudes: secular, sacramental, and ideal. *In* Johnson, W. S. Sex and marriage in Victorian poetry p34-109

Johnson, W. S. Victorian and modern. *In* Johnson, W. S. Sex and marriage in Victorian poetry p252-62

Kinkead-Weekes, M. Eros and metaphor: sexual relationship in the fiction of Lawrence. *In* Smith, A. ed. Lawrence and women p101-21

Langbaum, R. W. Identity and sexuality. *In* Langbaum, R. W. The mysteries of identity p251-97

Langbaum, R. W. The rainbow: the way through hope. *In* Langbaum, R. W. The mysteries of identity p298-327

Langbaum, R. W. Women in love: the way through doom. *In* Langbaum, R. W. The mysteries of identity p328-53

Mickelson, A. Z. Sexual love in the fiction of Joyce Carol Oates. *In* Mickelson, A. Z. Reaching out: sensitivity and order in recent American fiction by women p15-34

Ower, J. Erotic mythology in the poetry of Tennessee Williams. *In* Tennessee Williams: a tribute p609-23

Peckham, M. Ernest Hemingway: sexual themes in his writing. *In* Peckham, M. Romanticism and behavior p139-58

Peckham, M. The place of sex in the work of William Faulkner. *In* Peckham, M. Romanticism and behavior p159-76

Prickett, S. Dreams and nightmares: monsters under the hill. *In* Prickett, S. Victorian fantasy p75-113

Simpson, L. P. Sex & history: origins of Faulkner's apocrypha. *In* The Makers and the myth: Faulkner and Yoknapatawpha, 1977 p43-70

Skaggs, M. M. Morgana's apples and pears. *In* Prenshaw, P. W. ed. Eudora Welty p220-41

Spacks, P. A. M. Early fiction and the frightened male. *In* Spilka, M. ed. Towards a poetics of fiction p255-65

Steiner, G. Eros and idiom. *In* Steiner, G. On difficulty and other essays p95-136

Tobin, P. D. The cycle dance: D. H. Lawrence, The rainbow. *In* Tobin, P. D. Time and the novel p81-106

Trilling, D. Our uncomplaining homosexuals. *In* Trilling, D. We must march my darlings p157-71

Sex in literature—*Continued*

White, R. L. The warmth of desire: sex in Anderson's novels. *In* Anderson, D. D ed. Sherwood Anderson dimensions of his literary art p24-40

Wilcoxon, R. Rochester's sexual politics. *In* Studies in eighteenth-century culture v8 p137-49

See also Homosexuality in literature; Love in literature; Sexual deviation in literature

Sex in marriage

Bernard, J. S. and others. How to make marital sex more exciting—5 views. *In* Gross, L. ed. Sexual issues in marriage p17-24

Charney, I. and others. How does marital quarreling affect sexual relations? *In* Gross, L. ed. Sexual issues in marriage p121-28

Cuber, J. F. Sex in five types of marriages. *In* Gross, L. ed. Sexual issues in marriage p3-10

DeBurger, J. E. Sex in troubled marriages. *In* Gross, L. ed. Sexual issues in marriage p65-72

Sex in mass media. See Sex in literature; Sex in moving-pictures

Sex in moving-pictures

Koch, S. Blow-job and pornography. *In* Nichols, B. ed. Movies and methods p305-09

Sarris, A. Cock-tale parties on the East Side. *In* Sarris, A. Politics and cinema p135-37

Sarris, A. The politics of pornography. *In* Sarris, A. Politics and cinema p128-34

Sarris, A. Porn versus Puritanism. *In* Sarris, A. Politics and cinema p138-47

Tyler, P. The awful fate of the sex goddess; excerpt from "Sex psyche etcetera in the film." *In* Denby, D. ed. Awake in the dark p349-56

Sex in prisons. See Prisoners—Sexual behavior

Sex in the arts. See Sex in literature

Sex in the performing arts. See Sex in moving-pictures; Sex in the theater

Sex in the theater

Johnson, C. D. That guilty third tier: prostitution in nineteenth-century American theaters. *In* Howe, D. W. ed. Victorian America p111-20

Kauffmann, S. Homosexual drama and its disguises. *In* Kauffmann, S. Persons of the drama p291-94

Kauffmann, S. On the acceptability of the homosexual. *In* Kauffmann, S. Persons of the drama p295-98

Sex instruction

Great Britain

Smith, F. B. Sexuality in Britain, 1800-1900: some suggested revisions. *In* Vicinus, M. ed. A widening sphere p182-98

United States

Schulz, E. D. Education for human sexuality; excerpt from "Family life and sex education: curriculum and instruction." *In* Fairfield, R. P. ed. Humanistic frontiers in American education p69-74

Spring, J. H. The American high school and the development of social character. *In* Feinberg, W. and Rosemont, H. eds. Work, technology, and education p41-59

Sex perversion. See Sexual deviation

Sex research

Boorstin, D. J. Statistical morality; excerpt from "The Americans: the democratic experience". *In* Davis, F. J. and Stivers, R. eds. The collective definition of deviance p156-61

Whiting, B. B. Contributions of anthropology to the study of gender identity, gender role, and sexual behavior. *In* Katchadourian, H. A. ed. Human sexuality p320-31

Sex role

Bacdayan, A. S. Mechanistic cooperation and sexual equality among the western Bontoc. *In* Schlegel, A. E. ed. Sexual stratification p270-91

Beardsley, E. L. Referential genderization. *In* Gould, C. C. and Wartofsky, M. W. eds. Women and philosophy p285-93

Bettelheim, B. Growing up female. *In* Bettelheim, B. Surviving, and other essays p221-38

Blum, L. and others. Altruism and women's oppression. *In* Gould, C. C. and Wartofsky, M. W. eds. Women and philosophy p222-47

Broderick, C. B. Heterosexuality. *In* Sexuality and human values p12-23

Chatty, D. Changing sex roles in Bedouin society in Syria and Lebanon. *In* Beck, L. and Keddie, N. R. eds. Women in the Muslim world p399-415

Christ, C. Victorian masculinity and The angel in the house. *In* Vicinus, M. ed. A widening sphere p146-62

Cronin, C. Illusion and reality in Sicily. *In* Schlegel, A. E. ed. Sexual stratification p67-93

Datan, N. Ecological antecedents and sex-role consequences in traditional and modern Israeli subcultures. *In* Schlegel, A. E. ed. Sexual stratification p326-43

Davis, N. A. Z. Women on top; symbolic sexual inversion and political disorder in early modern Europe. *In* Babcock, B. A. ed. The reversible world p147-90

Draper, P. !Kung women: contrasts in sexual egalitarianism in foraging and sedentary contexts. *In* Reiter, R. R. ed. Toward an anthropology of women p77-109

Gagnon, J. H. The interaction of gender roles and sexual conduct. *In* Katchadourian, H. A. ed. Human sexuality p225-45

Gilbert, S. M. and Gubar, S. Infection in the sentence: the woman writer and the anxiety of authorship. *In* Gilbert, S. M. and Gubar, S. The madwoman in the attic p45-92

Gilbert, S. M. and Gubar, S. The queen's looking glass: female creativity, male images of women, and the metaphor of literary paternity. *In* Gilbert, S. M. and Gubar, S. The madwoman in the attic p3-44

Gould, C. C. The woman question: philosophy of liberation and the liberation of philosophy. *In* Gould, C. C. and Wartofsky, M. W. eds. Women and philosophy p5-44

Greene, M. The lived world. *In* Greene, M. Landscapes of learning p213-24

Harkess, S. Family and sex roles in urban society. *In* Handbook of contemporary urban life p163-201

Hein, H. On reaction and the women's movement. *In* Gould, C. C. and Wartofsky, M. W eds. Women and philosophy p248-70

Sex role—*Continued*

Held, V. Marx, sex, and the transformation of society. *In* Gould, C. C. and Wartofsky, M. W. eds. Women and philosophy p168-84

Katchadourian, H. A. The terminology of sex and gender. *In* Katchadourian, H. A. ed. Human sexuality p8-34

Leibowitz, L. Perspectives on the evolution of sex differences. *In* Reiter, R. R. ed. Toward an anthropology of women p20-35

LeVine, R. A. Anthropology and sex: developmental aspects. *In* Katchadourian, H. A. ed. Human sexuality p309-19

Lipman-Blumen, J. and Leavitt, H. J. Sexual behavior as an expression of achievement orientation. *In* Katchadourian, H. A. ed. Human sexuality p246-56

Luria, Z. Psychosocial determinants of gender identity, role, and orientation. *In* Katchadourian, H. A. ed. Human sexuality p163-93

Maccoby, E. E. Gender identity and sex-role adoption. *In* Katchadourian, H. A. ed. Human sexuality p194-203

Morgan, E. Women and the future. *In* Bundy, R. F. ed. Images of the future: the twenty-first century and beyond p143-51

Morsy, S. A. Sex differences and folk illness in an Egyptian village. *In* Beck, L. and Keddie, N. R. eds. Women in the Muslim world p599-616

Rainwater, L. Sociological perspectives on sex and its psychosocial derivatives. *In* Katchadourian, H. A. ed. Human sexuality p257-64

Rohrlich-Leavitt, R.; Sykes, B. and Weatherford, E. Aboriginal woman: male and female anthropological perspectives. *In* Reiter, R. R. ed. Toward an anthropology of women p110-26

Rosen, L. The negotiation of reality: male-female relations in Sefrou, Morocco. *In* Beck, L. and Keddie, N. R. eds. Women in the Muslim world p561-84

Rosenhan, M. S. Images of male and female in children's readers. *In* Women in Russia p293-305

Schlegel, A. E. An overview. *In* Schlegel, A. E. ed. Sexual stratification p344-57

Schlegel, A. E. Male and female in Hopi thought and action. *In* Schlegel, A. E. ed. Sexual stratification p245-69

Schlegel, A. E. Toward a theory of sexual stratification. *In* Schlegel, A. E. ed. Sexual stratification p 1-40

Sears, R. R. Sex-typing, object choice, and child rearing. *In* Katchadourian, H. A. ed. Human sexuality p204-22

Shapiro, J. Cross-cultural perspectives on sexual differentiation. *In* Katchadourian, H. A. ed. Human sexuality p269-308

Sutton, C. and Makiesky-Barrow, S. Social inequality and sexual status in Barbados. *In* Schlegel, A. E. ed. Sexual stratification p292-325

Trilling, D. Women's liberation: Female biology in a male culture. *In* Trilling, D. We must march my darlings p189-98

Whiting, B. B. Contributions of anthropology to the study of gender identity, gender role, and sexual behavior. *In* Katchadourian, H. A. ed. Human sexuality p320-31

See also Androgyny (Psychology); Sexism

Sex role in literature

Demmin, J. and Curley, D. Golden apples and silver apples. *In* Prenshaw, P. W. ed. Eudora Welty p242-57

Feustle, J. A. Mario Vargas Llosa: a labyrinth of solitude. *In* Rossman, C. R. and Friedman, A. W. eds. Mario Vargas Llosa p128-35

Gilbert, S. M. and Gubar, S. George Eliot as the Angel of Destruction. *In* Gilbert, S. M. and Gubar, S. The madwoman in the attic p478-535

Gilbert, S. M. and Gubar, S. Looking oppositely: Emily Brontë's Bible of Hell. *In* Gilbert, S. M. and Gubar, S. The madwoman in the attic p248-308

Gilbert, S. M. and Gubar, S. Made keen by loss: George Eliot's veiled vision. *In* Gilbert, S. M. and Gubar, S. The madwoman in the attic p443-77

Gilbert, S. M. and Gubar, S. The queen's looking glass: female creativity, male images of women, and the metaphor of literary paternity. *In* Gilbert, S. M. and Gubar, S. The madwoman in the attic p3-44

Gilbert, S. M. and Gubar, S. A secret, inward wound: The professor's pupil. *In* Gilbert, S. M. and Gubar, S. The madwoman in the attic p311-35

Gilbert, S. M. and Gubar, S. Shut up in prose: gender and genre in Austen's juvenilia. *In* Gilbert, S. M. and Gubar, S. The madwoman in the attic p107-45

Jones, R. E. Sexual roles in the works of Tennessee Williams. *In* Tennessee Williams: a tribute p545-57

Rigney, B. H. "After the failure of logic": descent and return in Surfacing. *In* Rigney, B. H. Madness and sexual politics in the feminist novel p91-115

Rigney, B. H. "The frenzied moment": sex and insanity in Jane Eyre. *In* Rigney, B. H. Madness and sexual politics in the feminist novel p13-37

Rigney, B. H. "A rehearsal for madness": hysteria as sanity in The four-gated city. *In* Rigney, B. H. Madness and sexual politics in the feminist novel p65-89

Rigney, B. H. "The sane and the insane": psychosis and mysticism in Mrs. Dalloway. *In* Rigney, B. H. Madness and sexual politics in the feminist novel p39-63

Rigney, B. H. The self-created other: integration and survival. *In* Rigney, B. H. Madness and sexual politics in the feminist novel p117-27

Sex-role inversion. See Change of sex

Sexism

Beardsley, E. L. Traits and genderization. *In* Feminism and philosophy p117-23

Greene, M. Sexism in the schools. *In* Greene, M. Landscapes of learning p244-55

Grim, P. Sexism and semantics. *In* Feminism and philosophy p109-16

Korsmeyer, C. W. The hidden joke: generic uses of masculine terminology. *In* Feminism and philosophy p 138-53

Moulton, J. M. The myth of the neutral "man." *In* Feminism and philosophy p124-37

See also Sex role

Sexton, Anne

About

Juhasz, S. Seeking the exit or the home: poetry and salvation in the career of Anne Sexton. *In* Gilbert, S. M. and Gubar, S. eds. Shakespeare's sisters p261-68

Sexton, Anne—About—*Continued*

Rich, A. C. Anne Sexton: 1928-1974. *In* Rich, A. C. On lies, secrets, and silence p121-23

Thurley, G. The poetry of breakdown: Robert Lowell and Anne Sexton. *In* Thurley, G. The American moment p70-90

Sexton, Robert Fenimore. See Stephenson, J. B. jt. auth.

Sexton, William P.

Work humanization in practice: what should business do? *In* Heisler, W. J. and Houck, J. W. eds. A matter of dignity p131-45

Sextus, Pythagoroeus

About individual works

The sentences of Sextus

Wilken, R. L. Wisdom and philosophy in early Christianity. *In* Aspects of wisdom in Judaism and early Christianity p143-68

Sexual behavior. See Sex; Sex customs; Sexual ethics

Sexual behavior. See Sexual ethics

Sexual behavior, Psychology of. See Sex (Psychology)

Sexual behavior in animals

Beach, F. A. Animal models and psychological inference. *In* Katchadourian, H. A. ed. Human sexuality p98-112

Lancaster, J. B. Sex and gender in evolutionary perspective. *In* Katchadourian, H. A. ed. Human sexuality p51-80

Leibowitz, L. Perspectives on the evolution of sex differences. *In* Reiter, R. R. ed. Toward an anthropology of women p20-35

Sexual crimes. See Sex crimes

Sexual deviation

Nagel, T. Sexual perversion. *In* Baker, R. and Elliston, F. A. eds. Philosophy & sex p247-60

Also in Nagel, T. Mortal questions p39-52

Sagarin, E. and Kelly, R. J. Sexual deviance and labelling perspectives. *In* Gove, W. R. ed. The labelling of deviance p243-71

Slote, M. A. Inapplicable concepts and sexual perversion. *In* Baker, R. and Elliston, F. A. eds. Philosophy & sex p261-67

Solomon, R. C. Sex and perversion. *In* Baker, R. and Elliston, F. A. eds. Philosophy & sex p268-87

Social aspects

Kirk, S. A. Society and sexual deviance. *In* Gochros, H. L. and Gochros, J. S. eds. The sexually oppressed p28-37

United States

Humphreys, L. Tearoom trade: impersonal sex in public places. *In* Henslin, J. M. ed. Deviant life-styles p123-50

Sexual deviation in literature

Kunkel, F. L. Jean Genet: counterfeit saint. *In* Kunkel, F. L. Passion and the Passion p108-28

Sexual dimorphism in humans. See Sex differences

Sexual discrimination. See Sex discrimination

Sexual disorders

Masters, W. H. and Johnson, V. E. The role of religion in sexual dysfunction. *In* Sexuality and human values p86-96

See also Sexual deviation

Sexual ethics

Baumrin, B. H. Sexual immorality delineated. *In* Baker, R. and Elliston, F. A. eds. Philosophy & sex p116-28

Bettelheim, B. About the sexual revolution. *In* Bettelheim, B. Surviving, and other essays p370-86

Cohen, C. Sex, birth control, and human life. *In* Baker, R. and Elliston, F. A. eds. Philosophy & sex p150-65

Johnson, W. S. Sexual attitudes: "Victorian" and Victorian. *In* Johnson, W. S. Sex and marriage in Victorian poetry p13-33

Palson, C. and Palson, R. Swinging in wedlock. *In* Henslin, J. M. ed. Deviant life-styles p231-54

Paulus VI, Pope. Humanae vitae. *In* Baker, R. and Elliston, F. A. eds. Philosophy & sex p131-49

Rapaport, E. and Sagal, P. T. One step forward, two steps backward: abortion and ethical theory. *In* Feminism and philosophy p408-16

Ruddick, S. Better sex. *In* Baker, R. and Elliston, F. A. eds. Philosophy & sex p83-104

Sennett, R. Destructive Gemeinschaft. *In* Beyond the crisis p171-97

Skolnick, J. H. Should sexual relations be treated as crimes? *In* Contemporary issues in criminal justice p5-15

Thomas, J. L. The road ahead. *In* Sexuality and human values p132-51

Verene, D. P. Sexual love and moral experience. *In* Baker, R. and Elliston, F. A. eds. Philosophy & sex p105-15

See also Promiscuity; Sex and religion

Sexual ethics for youth

Broderick, C. B. Adolescence. *In* Sexuality and human values p50-61

Gilligan, C. F. Sexual dilemmas at the high-school level. *In* Sexuality and human values p98-110

Sexual intercourse. See Oral intercourse

Sexual offenses. See Sex crimes

Sexual perversion. See Sexual deviation

Sexual psychology. See Sex (Psychology)

Seyffert, M. Gordon

The university as an urban neighbor. *In* Murphy, T. P. ed. Universities in the urban crisis p137-59

See also Murphy, T. P. jt. auth.

Seymour, Charles, 1912-1977. See Part 2 under title: Collaboration in Italian Renaissance art

Seymour, Forrest W.

A look back at Wounded Knee. *In* American Antiquarian Society. Proceedings v84 pt 1 p33-42

Seymour, Michael C.

Medieval America and 'Sir John Mandeville.' *In* An English miscellany p46-53

Seymour-Ure, Colin

Great Britain. *In* Galnoor, I. ed. Government secrecy in democracies p157-75

The press and the party system between the Wars. *In* Peele, G. and Cook, C. eds. The politics of reappraisal, 1918-1939 p232-57

Seznec, Jean. See Part 2 under title: The Artist and the writer in France

Sforza, Luigi Luca Cavalli- See Cavalli-Sforza, Luigi Luca

Sgraffito decoration. See Graffito decoration

Shack, William A.

Open systems and closed boundaries: the ritual process of stranger relations in new African states. *In* Shack, W. A. and Skinner, E. P. eds. Strangers in African society p37-47

Shackford, James Atkins

David Crockett, the legend and the symbol; excerpt from "David Crockett, the man and the legend." *In* Inge, M. T. ed. The frontier humorists p208-18

Shackleton, Robert

Allies and enemies: Voltaire and Montesquieu. *In* Royal Society of Literature of the United Kingdom, London. Essays by divers hands v39 p126-45

The impact of French literature on Gibbon. *In* Edward Gibbon and The decline and fall of the Roman Empire p207-18

John Black and Montesquieu—the search for a correspondence. *In* Evidence in literary scholarship p215-27

Shaddai. See God (Judaism)—Name

Shades and shadows. See Perspective

Shadick, Robert G. See Gullo, S. V. jt. auth.

Shadwell, Thomas

About

Ober, W. B. Thomas Shadwell: his exitus revis'd. *In* Ober, W. B. Boswell's clap and other essays p253-61

Vieth, D. M. The discovery of the date of Mac Flecknoe. *in* Evidence in literary scholarship p63-87

Shafarevich, Igor Rostislavovich

Does Russia have a future? *In* From under the rubble p279-94

Separation or reconciliation? The nationalities question in the USSR. *In* From under the rubble p88-104

Socialism in our past and future. *In* From under the rubble p26-66

Shafer, Carolyn M. and Frye, Marilyn

Rape and respect. *In* Feminism and philosophy p333-46

Shaffer, E. S.

'Kubla Khan' and The fall of Jerusalem
Contents

Browning's St John: the casuistry of the higher criticism

Daniel Deronda and the conventions of fiction

The fall of Jerusalem: Coleridge's unwritten epic

Hölderlin's 'Patmos' ode and 'Kubla Khan': mythological doubling

The oriental idyll

The visionary character: Revelation and the lyrical ballad

Shaffer, Peter

About individual works

Equus

Kauffmann, S. Equus. *In* Kauffmann, S. Persons of the drama p249-51

Shaffer, Thomas L. and Rodes, Robert Emmet

Law for those who are to die. *In* Feifel, H. [ed.] New meanings of death p291-311

Shaftesbury, Anthony Ashley Cooper, 3d Earl of

About individual works

A letter concerning enthusiasm

McCarthy, J. A. Shaftesbury and Wieland: the question of enthusiasm. *In* Studies in eighteenth-century culture v6 p79-95

Wolf, R. B. The publication of Shaftesbury's Letter concerning enthusiasm. *In* Virginia. University. Bibliographical Society. Studies in bibliography v32 p237-41

Influence—Fielding

Røstvig, M. S. Tom Jones and the choice of Hercules. *In* Røstvig, M. S. ed. Fair forms p147-77

Influence—Wieland

McCarthy, J. A. Shaftesbury and Wieland: the question of enthusiasm. *In* Studies in eighteenth-century culture v6 p79-95

Shaftesbury, Anthony Ashley Cooper, 7th Earl of

About

Finlayson, G. B. A. M. Shaftesbury. *In* Hollis, P. ed. Pressure from without p159-82

Shagan, Michael D.

Is gambling worth enforcement gamble? *In* Contemporary issues in criminal justice p16-39

Shahsevan nomads of Iran; The women's subsociety among the. Tapper, N. *In* Beck, L. and Keddie, N. R. eds. Women in the Muslim world p374-98

Shaker furniture. See Furniture, Shaker

Shakers

United States

Ellwood, R. S. Shakers and spiritualists. *In* Ellwood, R. S. Alternative altars p65-103

Whitworth, J. M. Communitarian groups and the world. *In* Wallis, R. ed. Sectarianism p117-37

Shakespeare, William

About

Bayley, J. Living in the present. *In* Bayley, J. The uses of division p185-89

Bayley, J. The meaning of impression. *In* Bayley, J. The uses of division p211-17

Bayley, J. The Troilus atmosphere. *In* Bayley, J. The uses of division p189-201

Berryman, J. Shakespeare at thirty. *In* Berryman, J. The freedom of the poet p29-55

Bradbrook, M. C. Shakespeare and the multiple theatres of Jacobean London. *In* The Elizabethan theatre, VI p88-104

Childress, D. T. Are Shakespeare's late plays really romances? *In* Shakespeare's late plays p44-55

Cunningham, J. V. The Donatan tradition. *In* Cunningham, J. V. The collected essays of J. V. Cunningham p30-52

Cunningham, J. V. In Shakespeare's day. *In* Cunningham, J. V. The collected essays of J. V. Cunningham p342-45

Cunningham, J. V. Reason panders will. *In* Cunningham, J. V. The collected essays of J. V. Cunningham p97-119

Cunningham, J. V. Wonder. *In* Cunningham, J. V. The collected essays of J. V. Cunningham p53-96

Donoghue, D. Writing against time. *In* Donoghue, D. The sovereign ghost p207-29

Edwards, P. Shakespeare and the healing power of deceit. *In* Shakespeare survey v31 p115-25

Shakespeare, William—About—Continued

Emden, C. S. Shakespeare and the eye. *In* Shakespeare survey 26 p129-37

Fiedler, L. A. The defense of the illusion and the creation of myth; device and symbol in the plays of Shakespeare. *In* Wimsatt, W. K. ed. Literary criticism: idea and act p97-109

Hermassi, K. C. The play within the play. *In* Hermassi, K. C. Polity and theater in historical perspective p128-36

Hermassi, K. C. Theatre as the city of man. *In* Hermassi, K. C. Polity and theater in historical perspective p137-51

Hibbard, G. R. Love, marriage and money in Shakespeare's theatre and Shakespeare's England. *In* The Elizabethan theatre, VI p134-55

Hoy, C. H. Jacobean tragedy and the mannerist style. *In* Shakespeare survey 26 p49-67

Hurstfield, J. The politics of corruption in Shakespeare's England. *In* Shakespeare survey 28 p15-28

Jorgensen, P. A. Shakespeare's brave new world. *In* First images of America p83-89

Kernan, A. B. Shakespeare's essays on dramatic poesy: the nature and function of theater within the sonnets and the plays. *In* Martz, L. L. and Williams, A. L. eds. The author in his work p175-96

Levith, M. J. Juliet's question and Shakespeare's names. *In* Renaissance and modern p21-32

Lewis, W. Shakespeare; excerpt from "The lion and the fox." *In* Lewis, W. Enemy salvoes p53-65

McCanles, M. The dialectic of right and power in eight plays of Shakespeare, 1595-1604. *In* McCanles, M. Dialectical criticism and Renaissance literature p159-213

Muir, K. The pursuit of relevance. *In* Muir, K. The singularity of Shakespeare, and other essays p198-211

Muir, K. The singularity of Shakespeare. *In* Muir, K. The singularity of Shakespeare, and other essays p124-37

Muir, K. Theophanies in the last plays. *In* Shakespeare's late plays p32-43

Muir, K. This side idolatry. *In* Muir, K. The singularity of Shakespeare, and other essays p92-109

Nicoll, A. Shakespeare and his predecessors. *In* Nicoll, A. World drama p206-23

Pasternak, B. L. From Notes of a translator. *In* Proffer, C. R. ed. Modern Russian poets on poetry p96-101

Schanzer, E. Shakespeare and the doctrine of the unity of time. *In* Shakespeare survey 28 p57-61

Wickham, G. W. G. From tragedy to tragi-comedy: 'King Lear' as prologue. *In* Shakespeare survey 26 p33-48

About individual works

All's well that ends well

Bowers, F. T. Foul papers, Compositor B, and the speech-prefixes of All's well that ends well. *In* Virginia. University. Bibliographical Society. Studies in bibliography v32 p60-81

Brooke, N. 'All's well that ends well.' *In* Shakespeare survey 30 p73-84

Antony and Cleopatra

Bayley, J. 'Antony and Cleopatra' and 'Coriolanus.' *In* Bayley, J. The uses of division p234-44

Coates, J. 'The choice of Hercules' in 'Antony and Cleopatra'. *In* Shakespeare survey v31 p45-52

Novak, M. E. Criticism, adaptation, politics, and the Shakespearean model of Dryden's All for love. *In* Studies in eighteenth-century culture v7 p375-87

Simmons, J. L. 'Antony and Cleopatra' and 'Coriolanus', Shakespeare's heroic tragedies: a Jacobean adjustment. *In* Shakespeare survey 26 p95-101

Stilling, R. Shakespeare and the poetry of earth. *In* Stilling, R. Love and death in Renaissance tragedy p277-92

Weitz, M. Literature without philosophy: 'Antony and Cleopatra.' *In* Shakespeare survey 28 p29-36

The comedy of errors

Altman, J. B. Inventing answers in English comedy. *In* Altman, J. B. The Tudor play of mind p148-95

Coriolanus

Bayley, J. 'Antony and Cleopatra' and 'Coriolanus.' *In* Bayley, J. The uses of division p234-44

Crowley, R. C. Coriolanus and the epic genre. *In* Shakespeare's late plays p114-30

Gordon, D. J. Name and fame: Shakespeare's Coriolanus. *In* Gordon, D. J. The Renaissance imagination p203-19

Gurr, A. J. 'Coriolanus' and the body politic. *In* Shakespeare survey 28 p63-69

Simmons, J. L. 'Antony and Cleopatra' and 'Coriolanus', Shakespeare's heroic tragedies: a Jacobean adjustment. *In* Shakespeare survey 26 p95-101

Van Dyke, J. Making a scene: language and gesture in 'Coriolanus.' *In* Shakespeare survey 30 p135-46

Cymbeline

Powlick, L. Cymbeline and the comedy of anticlimax. *In* Shakespeare's late plays p131-41

Siemon, J. E. Noble virtue in 'Cymbeline.' *In* Shakespeare survey v29 p51-61

Thompson, A. Philomel in 'Titus Andronicus' and 'Cymbeline'. *In* Shakespeare survey v31 p23-32

Warren, R. Theatrical virtuosity and poetic complexity in 'Cymbeline.' *In* Shakespeare survey v29 p41-49

Cymbeline (Act III, Scene 1)

Rossi, J. W. Cymbeline's debt to Holinshed: the richness of III.1. *In* Shakespeare's romances reconsidered p104-12

Hamlet

Adey, L. Enjoyment, contemplation, and hierarchy in Hamlet. *In* Evolution of consciousness p149-67

Berry, R. 'To say one': an essay on 'Hamlet.' *In* Shakespeare survey 28 p107-15

Booth, S. On the value of Hamlet. *In* Wimsatt, W. K. ed. Literary criticism: idea and act p284-310

Brashear, W. R. Nietzsche and Spengler on Hamlet. *In* Brashear, W. R. The gorgon's head p15-26

Brockbank, J. P. Hamlet the Bonesetter. *In* Shakespeare survey 30 p103-15

Brown, K. 'Form and cause conjoin'd': 'Hamlet' and Shakespeare's workshop. *In* Shakespeare survey 26 p11-20

Shakespeare, William—About individual works—Hamlet—*Continued*

Cunningham, J. V. Aught of woe or wonder. *In* Cunningham, J. V. The collected essays of J. V. Cunningham p9-29

Cunningham, J. V. The heart of his mystery. *In* Cunningham, J. V. The collected essays of J. V. Cunningham p346-52

Cunningham, J. V. Plots and errors: Hamlet and King Lear. *In* Cunningham, J. V. The collected essays of J. V. Cunningham p210-24

Eliot, T. S. Hamlet. *In* Eliot, T. S. Selected prose of T. S. Eliot p45-49

Everett, B. 'Hamlet': a time to die. *In* Shakespeare survey 30 p117-23

Ewbank, I. S. 'Hamlet' and the power of words. *In* Shakespeare survey 30 p85-102

Fiedler, L. A. The defense of the illusion and the creation of myth; device and symbol in the plays of Shakespeare. *In* Wimsatt, W. K. ed. Literary criticism: idea and act p97-109

Greene, R. L. Hamlet's skimmington. *In* Evidence in literary scholarship p 1-11

Hermassi, K. C. The play within the play. *In* Hermassi, K. C. Polity and theater in historical perspective p128-36

Hibbard, G. R. 'Henry IV' and 'Hamlet.' *In* Shakespeare survey 30 p 1-12

Hunter, G. K. The heroism of Hamlet. *In* Hunter, G. K. Dramatic identities and cultural tradition p230-50

Jorgens, J. J. Grigori Kozintsev's Hamlet. *In* Jorgens, J. J. Shakespeare on film p218-34

Jorgens, J. J. Laurence Olivier's Hamlet. *In* Jorgens, J. J. Shakespeare on film p207-17

Kauffmann, S. Hamlet. *In* Kauffmann, S. Persons of the drama p91-93

Lanham, R. A. Superposed plays: Hamlet. *In* Lanham, R. A. The motives of eloquence p129-43

Le Comte, E. S. The ending of Hamlet as a farewell to Essex. *In* Le Comte, E. S. Poets' riddles p10-43

McCombie, F. 'Hamlet' and the 'Moriae encomium'. *In* Shakespeare survey 27 p59-69

McLauchlan, J. The Prince of Denmark and Claudius's court. *In* Shakespeare survey 27 p43-57

Olson, E. Hamlet and the hermeneutics of drama. *In* Olson, E. On value judgments in the arts, and other essays p73-89

Olson, E. "Mighty opposites": remarks on the plot of Hamlet. *In* Olson, E. On value judgments in the arts, and other essays p90-104

Rose, M. Hamlet. *In* Seidel, M. A. and Mendelson, E. eds. Homer to Brecht p238-54

Stilling, R. Hamlet. *In* Stilling, R. Love and death in Renaissance tragedy p103-22

Ure, P. Character and role from Richard III to Hamlet. *In* Ure, P. Elizabethan and Jacobean drama p22-43

Webber, J. Hamlet and the freeing of the mind. *In* English Renaissance drama p76-99

Weimann, R. Moralities and interludes. *In* Weimann, R. Shakespeare and the popular tradition in the theater: studies in the social dimension of dramatic form and function p98-160

Henry IV

Hibbard, G. R. 'Henry IV' and 'Hamlet.' *In* Shakespeare survey 30 p 1-12

Hunter, G. K. Henry IV and the Elizabethan two-part play. *In* Hunter, G. K. Dramatic identities and cultural tradition p303-18

Jorgens, J. J. Orson Welles's Chimes at midnight (Falstaff) *In* Jorgens, J. J. Shakespeare on film p106-21

Henry IV, Part 1

Pinciss, G. M. The old honor and the new courtesy: '1 Henry IV'. *In* Shakespeare survey v31 p85-91

Henry IV, Part 2

Somerset, J. A. B. Falstaff, the Prince, and the pattern of '2 Henry IV.' *In* Shakespeare survey 30 p35-45

Henry V

Babula, W. Whatever happened to Prince Hal? An essay on 'Henry V.' *In* Shakespeare survey 30 p47-59

Barnard, J. The murder of Falstaff, David Jones, and the 'disciplines of war.' *In* Evidence in literary scholarship p13-27

Battenhouse, R. W. The relation of Henry V to Tamburlaine. *In* Shakespeare survey 27 p71-79

Gurr, A. 'Henry V' and the bees' commonwealth. *In* Shakespeare survey 30 p61-72

Jones, G. P. 'Henry V': the chorus and the audience. *In* Shakespeare survey v31 p93-104

Jorgens, J. J. Laurence Olivier's Henry V. *In* Jorgens, J. J. Shakespeare on film p122-35

Kauffmann, S. A note on Shakespeare program notes. *In* Kauffmann, S. Persons of the drama p93-96

Knights, L. C. Shakespeare: four histories: Henry V. *In* Knights, L. C. Explorations 3 p181-86

Henry VI

Daniell, D. J. Opening up the text: Shakespeare's Henry VI plays in performance. *In* Drama and society p247-77

Kauffmann, S. A note on Shakespeare program notes. *In* Kauffmann, S. Persons of the drama p93-96

Henry VI, Part III

Bergeron, D. M. The play-within-the-play in 3 Henry VI. *In* Tennessee Studies in literature v22 p37-45

Julius Caesar

Hunter, G. K. A Roman thought: Renaissance attitudes to history exemplified in Shakespeare and Jonson. *In* An English miscellany p93-118

Jorgens, J. J. Joseph Mankiewicz's Julius Caesar. *In* Jorgens, J. J. Shakespeare on film p92-105

King John

Knights, L. C. Shakespeare: four histories: King John. *In* Knights, L. C. Explorations 3 p171-80

King Lear

Cavell, S. The avoidance of love: a reading of King Lear. *In* Cavell, S. Must we mean what we say? p267-353

Cunningham, J. V. Plots and errors: Hamlet and King Lear. *In* Cunningham, J. V. The collected essays of J. V. Cunningham p210-24

Shakespeare, William—About individual works—Othello—*Continued*

Hunter, G. K. Othello and colour prejudice. *In* Hunter, G. K. Dramatic identities and cultural tradition p31-59

Jorgens, J. J. Orson Welles's Othello. *In* Jorgens, J. J. Shakespeare on film p175-90

Jorgens, J. J. Stuart Burge and John Dexter's Othello. *In* Jorgens, J. J. Shakespeare on film p191-206

Stilling, R. Othello. *In* Stilling, R. Love and death in Renaissance tragedy p145-65

Othello (Act I, Scene 1)

Willson, R. F. Brabantio seduced: the opening scene of Othello. *In* Tennessee Studies in literature v22 p28-36

Pericles, Prince of Tyre

Gorfain, P. Puzzle and artifice: the riddle as metapoetry in 'Pericles.' *In* Shakespeare survey v29 p11-20

Michael, N. C. The relationship between the 1609 quarto of Pericles and Wilkins' Painful aduentures. *In* Tulane studies in English v22 p51-68

Schrickx, W. 'Pericles' in a book-list of 1619 from the English Jesuit mission and some of the play's special problems. *In* Shakespeare survey v29 p21-32

Welsh, A. Heritage in Pericles. *In* Shakespeare's late plays p89-113

"The phoenix and the turtle"

Cunningham, J. V. Idea as structure: The phoenix and turtle. *In* Cunningham, J. V. The collected essays of J. V. Cunningham p196-209

Richards, I. A. "The phoenix and the turtle." *In* Richards, I. A. Poetries p50-58

The rape of Lucrece

Hulse, S. C. 'A piece of skilful painting' in Shakespeare's 'Lucrece'. *In* Shakespeare survey v31 p13-22

Lanham, R. A. The Ovidian Shakespeare: Venus and Adonis and Lucrece. *In* Lanham, R. A. The motives of eloquence p82-110

Richard II

Gilman, E. B. Richard II and the perspectives of history. *In* Gilman, E. B. The curious perspective p88-128

Also in Renaissance drama [1976] p85-115

Knights, L. C. Shakespeare: four histories: Richard II. *In* Knights, L. C. Explorations 3 p175-80

Shoenbaum, S. 'Richard II' and the realities of power. *In* Shakespeare survey 28 p 1-13

Richard III

Jorgens, J. J. Laurence Olivier's Richard III. *In* Jorgens, J. J. Shakespeare on film p136-47

Knights, L. C. Shakespeare: four histories: Richard III. *In* Knights, L. C. Explorations 3 p163-71

Toole, W. B. The motif of psychic division in 'Richard III'. *In* Shakespeare survey 27 p21-32

Romeo and Juliet

Hunter, G. K. Shakespeare's earliest tragedies: 'Titus Andronicus' and 'Romeo and Juliet'. *In* Shakespeare survey 27 p 1-9

Also in Hunter, G. K. Dramatic identities and cultural tradition p319-34

Jorgens, J. J. Franco Zeffirelli's Romeo and Juliet. *In* Jorgens, J. J. Shakespeare on film p79-91

Leech, C. The moral tragedy of Romeo and Juliet. *In* English Renaissance drama p59-75

Phelps, L. R. Goethe's adaptation of Romeo and Juliet. *In* Creative encounter p17-24

The sonnets

Boyette, P. E. Shakespeare's Sonnets: homosexuality and the critics. *In* Tulane Studies in English v21 p35-46

Krause, F. P. Negative capability and objective correlative in Shakespeare's Sonnets. *In* Tennessee Studies in literature v20 p17-25

Lanham, R. A. Superposed poetics: The sonnets. *In* Lanham, R. A. The motives of eloquence p111-28

McLeod, R. A technique of headline analysis, with application to Shakespeares Sonnets, 1609. *In* Virginia. University. Bibliographical Society. Studies in bibliography v32 p197-210

Sonnet XV: When I consider everything that grows

Waddington, R. B. Shakespeare's Sonnet 15 and the art of memory. *In* Sloan, T. O. and Waddington, R. B. eds. The rhetoric of Renaissance poetry p96-122

Sonnet XXIX: When in disgrace with Fortune and men's eyes

Schwartz, M. M. Critic, define thyself. *In* Hartman, G. H. ed. Psychoanalysis and the question of the text p 1-17

Sonnet LXXIII: That time of year thou mayst in me behold

Fowler, R. Language and the reader: Shakespeare's Sonnet 73. *In* Fowler, R. ed. Style and structure in literature p79-122

Sonnets (CXXVI to CLIV)

Allen, M. J. B. Shakespeare's man descending a staircase: Sonnets 126 to 154. *In* Shakespeare survey v31 p127-38

Sonnet CXXIX: Th' expense of spirit in a waste of shame

Ong, W. J. Commonplace rhapsody: Ravisius Textor, Zwinger and Shakespeare. *In* Classical influences on European culture A.D. 1500-1700 p91-126

Same as: Ong, W. J. Typographic rhapsody: Ravisius Textor, winger, and Shakespeare. *In* Ong, W. J. Interfaces of the word p147-88

Richards, I. A. Linguistics into poetics. *In* Richards, I. A. Poetries p39-49

The taming of the shrew

Forker, C. R. Immediacy and remoteness in The taming of the shrew and The winter's tale. *In* Shakespeare's romances reconsidered p134-48

Jorgens, J. J. Franco Zeffirelli's Taming of the shrew. *In* Jorgens, J. J. Shakespeare on film p66-78

Kahn, C. The taming of the shrew: Shakespeare's mirror of marriage. *In* Diamond, A. and Edwards, L. R. eds. The authority of experience p84-100

Shakespeare, William—About individual works—*Continued*

The tempest

Berryman, J. Shakespeare's last word. *In* Berryman, J. The freedom of the poet p72-87

Coletti, T. Music and The tempest. *In* Shakespeare's late plays p185-99

Felperin, H. M. Romance and romanticism: some reflections on The tempest and Heart of darkness, or When is romance no longer romance? *In* Shakespeare's romances reconsidered p60-76

Frank, M. Shakespeare's existential comedy. *In* Shakespeare's late plays p142-65

Grant, P. The tempest and the magic of charity: believing the images. *In* Grant, P. Images and ideas in literature of the English Renaissance p63-88

Hibbard, G. R. Adumbrations of 'The tempest' in 'A midsummer night's dream'. *In* Shakespeare survey v31 p77-83

Higgs, E. D. Post-creation freedom in The tempest. *In* Shakespeare's late plays p200-12

Kennedy, A. From Shakespeare to Congreve: between drama and novel. *In* Kennedy, A. Meaning and signs in fiction p17-29

Kermode, J. F. Can we say absolutely anything we like? *In* Art, politics, and will p159-72

Knights, L. C. The tempest. *In* Knight, L. C. Explorations 3 p145-56

Also in Shakespeare's late plays p 15-31

Northam, J. R. Waiting for Prospero. *In* English drama: forms and development p186-202

Roberts, J. A. "Wife" or "wise"—The tempest 1. 1786. *In* Virginia. University. Bibliographical Society. Studies in bibliography v31 p203-08

Schorin, G. Approaching the genre of The tempest. *In* Shakespeare's late plays p166-84

Shrimpton, N. Directing 'The tempest.' *In* Shakespeare survey v29 p63-67

Siskin, C. Freedom and loss in 'The tempest.' *In* Shakespeare survey 30 p147-55

Solomon, A. A reading of The tempest. *In* Shakespeare's late plays p213-34

Wickham, G. W. G. Masque and antimasque in 'The tempest.' *In* English Association. Essays and studies, 1975 p 1-14

Young, D. P. Where the bee sucks: A triangular study of Doctor Faustus, The alchemist, and The tempest. *In* Shakespeare's romances reconsidered p149-66

The tempest—Sources

Latham, J. E. M. 'The tempest' and King James's 'Daemonologie.' *In* Shakespeare survey 28 p117-23

Timon of Athens

Bulman, J. C. The date and production of 'Timon' reconsidered. *In* Shakespeare survey 27 p111-27

Bulman, J. C. Shakespeare's use of the 'Timon' comedy. *In* Shakespeare survey v29 p103-16

Knights, L. C. Timon of Athens. *In* Knights, L. C. Explorations 3 p129-44

Levin, H. Shakespeare's misanthrope. *In* Shakespeare survey 26 p89-94

Muir, K. Timon of Athens and the cashnexus. *In* Muir, K. The singularity of Shakespeare, and other essays p56-75

Tinker, M. Theme in Timon of Athens. *In* Shakespeare's late plays p76-88

Titus Andronicus

Hunter, G. K. Shakespeare's earliest tragedies. *In* Shakespeare survey 27 p 1-9

Also in Hunter, G. K. Dramatic identities and cultural tradition p319-34

Thompson, A. Philomel in 'Titus Andronicus' and 'Cymbeline'. *In* Shakespeare survey v31 p23-32

Tricomi, A. H. The aesthetics of mutilation in 'Titus Andronicus'. *In* Shakespeare survey 27 p11-19

Titus Andronicus (III, i, 298-9)

Legouis, P. 'Titus Andronicus', III, i, 298-9. *In* Shakespeare survey 28 p71-74

Troilus and Cressida

Bayley, J. The divisions of rhetoric. *In* Bayley, J. The uses of division p201-04

Bayley, J. The Troilus atmosphere. *In* Bayley, J. The uses of division p189-201

Gass, W. H. Groping for trouts. *In* Gass, W. H. The world within the word p262-79

Girard, R. The plague in literature and myth. *In* Girard, R. "To double business bound" p136-54

Levenson, J. L. Shakespeare's Troilus and Cressida and the monumental tradition in tapestries and literature. *In* Renaissance drama [1976] p43-84

Stilling, R. Troilus and Cressida. *In* Stilling, R. Love and death in Renaissance tragedy p123-44

Troilus and Cressida—Sources

Whitaker, V. K. Still another source for Troilus and Cressida. *In* English Renaissance drama p100-07

Twelfth night

Gilman, E. B. The "natural perspective" of Shakespearean comedy: Twelfth night and A midsummer night's dream. *In* Gilman, E. B. The curious perspective p129-66

Hollander, J. Musica mundana and Twelfth night. *In* Wimsatt, W. K. ed. Literary criticism: idea and act p265-83

Venus and Adonis

Hobday, C. H. Shakespeare's Venus and Adonis sonnets. *In* Shakespeare survey 26 p103-09

Kane, G. Some reflections on critical method. *In* English Association. Essays and studies, 1976 p23-38

Lanham, R. A. The Ovidian Shakespeare: Venus and Adonis and Lucrece. *In* Lanham, R. A. The motives of eloquence p82-110

The winter's tale

Bateson, F. W. How old was Leontes? *In* English Association. Essays and studies, 1978 p65-74

Bellette, A. F. Truth and utterance in 'The winter's tale'. *In* Shakespeare survey v31 p65-75

Bergeron, D. M. The restoration of Hermoine [sic] in The winter's tale. *In* Shakespeare's romances reconsidered p125-33

Dash, I. G. A penchant for Perdita on the eighteenth-century English stage. *In* Studies in eighteenth-century culture v6 p331-46

Forker, C. R. Immediacy and remoteness in The taming of the shrew and The winter's tale. *In* Shakespeare's romances reconsidered p134-48

Shakespeare, William—About individual works—The winter's tale—*Continued*

Fowler, A. Leontes' contrition and the repair of nature. *In* English Association. Essays and studies, 1978 p36-64

Frey, C. Tragic structure in The winter's tale: the affective dimension. *In* Shakespeare's romances reconsidered p113-24

Muir, K. The conclusion of The winter's tale. *In* Muir, K. The singularity of Shakespeare, and other essays p76-91

Proudfoot, R. Verbal reminiscence and the two-part structure of 'The winter's tale.' *In* Shakespeare survey v29 p67-78

Spencer, T. J. B. The statue of Hermione. *In* English Association. Essays and studies, 1977 p39-49

Stilling, R. Shakespeare and the poetry of earth. *In* Stilling, R. Love and death in Renaissance tragedy p277-92

Adaptations

Novak, M. E. Criticism, adaptation, politics, and the Shakespearean model of Dryden's All for love. *In* Studies in eighteenth-century culture v7 p375-87

Bibliography

Alexander, N. Shakespeare's life, times, and stage. *In* Shakespeare survey 26 p168-76

Alexander, N. Shakespeare's life, times, and stage [another essay] *In* Shakespeare survey 27 p172-79

Corbin, P. and Sedge, D. Shakespeare. *In* English Asociation. The year's work in English studies v53 p147-92

Daniell, D. J. and Easson, A. Shakespeare. *in* English Association. The year's work in English studies v57 p108-45

Daniell, D. J. and others. Shakespeare. *In* English Association. The year's work in English studies v55 p193-230

Daniell, D. J. and others [another essay] Shakespeare. *In* English Association. The year's work in English studies v54 p 153-84

Daniell, D. J.; Easson, A. and Sanders, A. Shakespeare. *In* English Association. The year's work in English studies v56 p136-75

Leech, C. Studies in Shakespearian and other Jacobean tragedy, 1918-1972: a retrospect. *In* Shakespeare survey 26 p 1-9

McLeod, R. A technique of headline analysis, with application to Shakespeares Sonnets, 1609. *In* Virginia. University. Bibliographical Society. Studies in bibliography v32 p197-210

Sherbo, A. George Steevens's 1785 variorum Shakespeare. *In* Virginia. University. Bibliographical Society. Studies in bibliography v32 p241-46

Woodson, W. C. The printer's copy for the 1785 Variorum Shakespeare. *In* Virginia. University. Bibliographical Society. Studies in bibliography v31 p208-10

Woodson, W. C. The 1785 Variorum Shakespeare. *In* Virginia. University. Bibliographical Society. Studies in bibliography v28 p318-20

Bibliography—Folios

Bowers, F. T. The folio Othello: compositor E. *In* Bowers, F. T. Essays in bibliography, text, and editing p326-58

Bibliography—Folios. 1623

O'Connor, J. J. Compositors D and F of the Shakespeare First folio. *In* Virginia. University. Bibliographical Society. Studies in bibliography v28 p81-117

O'Connor, J. S. A qualitative analysis of compositors C and D in the Shakespeare First folio. *In* Virginia. University. Bibliographical Society. Studies in bibliography v30 p57-74

Reid, S. W. Some spellings of compositor B in the Shakespeare First folio. *In* Virginia. University. Bibliographical Society. Studies in bibliography v29 p102-38

Bibliography—Quartos

Bowers, F. T. An examination of the method of proof correction in King Lear Q1. *In* Bowers, F. T. Essays in bibliography, text, and editing p212-39

Michael, N. C. The relationship between the 1609 quarto of Pericles and Wilkins' painful aduentures. *In* Tulane Studies in English v22 p51-68

Biography—Bibliography

Bawcutt, N. W. Shakespeare's life, times, and stage. *In* Shakespeare survey 28 p164-73

Bawcutt, N. W. Shakespeare's life, times, and stage [another essay] *In* Shakespeare survey v29 p168-77

Bawcutt, N. W. Shakespeare's life, times, and stage [another essay] *In* Shakespeare survey 30 p191-203

Pendry, E. D. Shakespeare's life, times, and stage. *In* Shakespeare survey v31 p177-91

Characters

Edwards, P. Shakespeare and the healing power of deceit. *In* Shakespeare survey v31 p115-25

Ellrodt, R. Self-consciousness in Montaigne and Shakespeare. *In* Shakespeare survey 28 p37-50

Fisch, H. Shakespeare and the Puritan dynamic. *In* Shakespeare survey 27 p81-92

Hawkins, H. 'If this be error': imagination and truth in Shakespeare and Marlowe. *In* Hawkins, H. Poetic freedom and poetic truth p78-104

Hawkins, H. Introduction: Poetic injustice: some winners and losers in medieval and Renaissance literature. *In* Hawkins, H. Poetic freedom and poetic truth p 1-25

Hoy, C. H. Fathers and daughters in Shakespeare's romances. *In* Shakespeare's romances reconsidered p77-90

Lewis, W. S. Edmond Malone, Horace Walpole, and Shakespeare. *In* Evidence in literary scholarship p353-62

Siemon, J. E. Noble virtue in 'Cymbeline.' *In* Shakespeare survey v29 p51-61

Ure, P. Character and role from Richard III to Hamlet. *In* Ure, P. Elizabethan and Jacobean drama p22-43

Ure, P. Shakespeare and the inward self of the tragic hero. *In* Ure, P. Elizabethan and Jacobean drama p 1-21

Characters—Autolycus

Hartwig, J. Cloten, Autolycus, and Caliban: bearers of parodic burdens. *In* Shakespeare's romances reconsidered p91-103

Characters—Brabantio

Willson, R. F. Brabantio seduced: the opening scene of Othello. *In* Tennessee Studies in literature v22 p28-36

Characters—Brutus

Walzer, M. Consenting to one's own death: the case of Brutus. *In* Kohl, M. ed. Beneficent euthanasia p100-05

Shakespeare, William—*Continued*

Characters—Women

Clubb, L. G. Woman as wonder: a generic figure in Italian and Shakespearean comedy. *In* Studies in the continental background of Renaissance English literature: essays presented to John L. Lievsay p109-32

Dash, I. G. A penchant for Perdita on the eighteenth-century English stage. *In* Studies in eighteenth-century culture v6 p331-46

Speaight, R. Shakespeare's heroines. *In* Royal Society of Literature of the United Kingdom, London. Essays by divers hands v39 p146-62

Contemporary England

Hibbard, G. R. Love, marriage and money in Shakespeare's theatre and Shakespeare's England. *In* The Elizabethan theatre, VI p134-55

Hurstfield, J. The politics of corruption in Shakespeare's England. *In* Shakespeare survey 28 p15-28

Wickham, G. W. G. From tragedy to tragi-comedy: 'King Lear' as prologue. *In* Shakespeare survey 26 p33-48

Bowers, F. T. An examination of the method of proof correction in King Lear Q1. *In* Bowers, F. T. Essays in bibliography, text, and editing p212-39

Bowers, F. T. The folio Othello: compositor E. *In* Bowers, F. T. Essays in bibliography, text, and editing p326-58

Criticism, Textual

Bowers, F. T. Foul papers, Compositor B, and the speech-prefixes of All's well that ends well. *In* Virginia. University. Bibliographical Society. Studies in bibliography v32 p60-81

Craven, A. E. The reliability of Simmes's Compositor A. *In* Virginia. University. Bibliographical Society. Studies in bibliography v32 p186-97

Honigmann, E. A. J. Re-enter the stage direction: Shakespeare and some contemporaries. *In* Shakespeare survey v29 p117-25

Hunter, G. K. Were there act-pauses on Shakespeare's stage? *In* English Renaissance drama p15-35

O'Connor, J. J. Compositors D and F of the Shakespeare first folio. *In* Virginia. University. Bibliographical Society. Studies in bibliography v28 p81-117

O'Connor, J. S. A qualitative analysis of compositors C and D in the Shakespeare First folio. *In* Virginia. University. Bibliographical Society. Studies in bibliography v30 p57-74

Roberts, J. A. "Wife" or "wise"—The tempest 1. 1786. *In* Virginia. University. Bibliographical Society. Studies in bibliography v31 p203-08

Criticism, Textual—Bibliography

Proudfoot, R. Textual studies. *In* Shakespeare survey 26 p177-84

Proudfoot, R. Textual studies. [another essay] *In* Shakespeare survey 27 p179-92

Proudfoot, R. Textual studies. [another essay] *In* Shakespeare survey 28 p173-81

Proudfoot, R. Textual studies. [another essay] *In* Shakespeare survey v29 p177-85

Proudfoot, R. Textual studies. [another essay] *In* Shakespeare survey 30 p203-10

Williams, G. W. Textual studies. *In* Shakespeare survey v31 p191-98

Criticism and interpretation

Bayley, J. Send for Macbeth. *In* Bayley, J. The uses of division p217-23

Brashear, W. R. Nietzsche and Spengler on Hamlet. *In* Brashear, W. R. The gorgon's head p15-26

Hoeniger, F. D. Shakespeare's romances since 1958: a retrospect. *In* Shakespeare survey v29 p 1-10

Holland, N. N. How can Dr. Johnson's remarks on Cordelia's death add to my own response? *In* Hartman, G. H. ed. Psychoanalysis and the question of the text p18-44

Hunter, G. K. T. S. Eliot and the creation of a symbolist Shakespeare. *In* Hunter, G. K. Dramatic identities and cultural tradition p286-99

Jones, T. B. and Nicol, B. D. Rowe. Pope and Johnson on Shakespeare. *In* Jones, T. B. and Nicol, B. D. Neo-classical dramatic criticism. 1560-1770 p124-44

Kermode, J. F. Can we say absolutely anything we like? *In* Art, politics, and will p159-72

Krieger, M. Shakespeare and the critic's idolatry of the word. *In* Shakespeare: aspects of influence p193-210

Lever, J. W. Shakespeare and the ideas of his time. *In* Shakespeare survey v29 p79-91

Mudrick, M. Twenty-three stone-deaf theologians. *In* Mudrick, M. Books are not life but then what is? p193-210

Muir, K. Some Freudian interpretations of Shakespeare. *In* Muir, K. The singularity of Shakespeare, and other essays p110-23

Sanders, N. J. An overview of critical approaches to the romances. *In* Shakespeare's romances reconsidered p 1-10

Velz, J. W. The ancient world in Shakespeare: authenticity or anachronism? A retrospect. *In* Shakespeare survey v31 p 1-12

Wells, S. W. Shakespeare in Max Beerbohm's theatre criticism. *In* Shakespeare survey v29 p133-44

Criticism and interpretation—
Bibliography

Hill, R. F. Critical studies. *In* Shakespeare survey 30 p181-90

Hill, R. F. Critical studies [another essay] *In* Shakespeare survey v31 p163-77

Palmer, D. J. Critical studies. *In* Shakespeare survey 27 p155-72

Palmer, D. J. Critical studies [another essay] *In* Shakespeare survey 28 p149-64

Palmer, D. J. Critical studies [another essay] *In* Shakespeare survey v29 p157-67

Sanders, N. J. Critical studies. *In* Shakespeare survey 26 p151-68

Dramatic production

Seltzer, D. Shakespeare's texts and modern productions. *In* Wimsatt, W. K. ed. Literary criticism: idea and act p311-29

Shrimpton, N. Directing 'The tempest.' *In* Shakespeare survey v29 p63-67

Weimann, R. Shakespeare's theater: tradition and experiment. *In* Weimann, R. Shakespeare and the popular tradition in the theater: studies in the social dimension of dramatic form and function p208-52

Dramaturgy

See Shakespeare, William—Dramatic production; Shakespeare, William—Technique

Shakespeare, William—*Continued*

Editors

Sherbo, A. George Steevens's 1785 variorum Shakespeare. *In* Virginia. University. Bibliographical Society. Studies in bibliography v32 p241-46

Ethical ideas

See Shakespeare, William—Religion and ethics

Film adaptations

Jorgens, J. J. Franco Zeffirelli's Romeo and Juliet. *In* Jorgens, J. J. Shakespeare on film p79-91

Jorgens, J. J. Franco Zeffirelli's Taming of the shrew. *In* Jorgens, J. J. Shakespeare on film p66-78

Jorgens, J. J. Grigori Kozintsev's Hamlet. *In* Jorgens, J. J. Shakespeare on film p218-34

Jorgens, J. J. Laurence Olivier's Hamlet. *In* Jorgens, J. J. Shakespeare on film p207-17

Jorgens, J. J. Laurence Olivier's Richard III *In* Jorgens, J. J. Shakespeare on film p136-47

Jorgens, J. J. Max Reinhardt and William Dieterle's A midsummer night's dream. *In* Jorgens, J. J. Shakespeare on film p36-50

Jorgens, J. J. Orson Welles's Chimes at midnight (Falstaff) *In* Jorgens, J. J. Shakespeare on film p106-21

Jorgens, J. J. Orson Welles's Othello. *In* Jorgens, J. J. Shakespeare on film p175-90

Jorgens, J. J. Peter Hall's A midsummer night's dream. *In* Jorgens, J. J. Shakespeare on film p51-65

Jorgens, J. J. Realizing Shakespeare on film. *In* Jorgens, J. J. Shakespeare on film p 1-35

Jorgens, J. J. Stuart Burge and John Dexter's Othello *In* Jorgens, J. J. Shakespeare on film p191-206

Seltzer, D. Shakespeare's texts and modern productions. *In* Wimsatt, W. K. ed. Literary criticism: idea and act p311-29

Histories

Hermassi, K. C. Power without love. *In* Hermassi, K. C. Polity and theater in historical perspective p102-27

Knights, L. C. Shakespeare: four histories: The background. *In* Knights, L. C. Explorations 3 p157-63

Lanham, R. A. The dramatic present: Shakespeare's Henriad. *In* Lanham, R. A. The motives of eloquence p190-223

Humor

See Shakespeare, William—Humor, satire, etc.

Humor, satire, etc.

Muir, K. The uncomic pun. *In* Muir, K. The singularity of Shakespeare, and other essays p20-37

Influence

Bloomfield, M. W. Quoting and alluding: Shakespeare in the English language. *In* Shakespeare: aspects of influence p 1-20

Charney, M. M. Webster vs. Middleton, or the Shakespearean yardstick in Jacobean tragedy. *In* English Renaissance drama p118-27

D'Andrea, P. P. "Thou starre of poets": Shakespeare as DNA. *In* Shakespeare: aspects of influence p163-91

Hoy, C. H. Shakespeare and the drama of his time. *In* Shakespeare: aspects of influence p21-41

Influence—Dickens

Harbage, A. Shakespeare and the early Dickens. *In* Shakespeare: aspects of influence p109-34

Influence—Eliot, Thomas Stearns

Harris, B. 'This music crept by me': Shakespeare and Wagner. *In* The Waste land in different voices p105-16

Influence—Keats

Bush, D. Keats and Shakespeare. *In* Shakespeare: aspects of influence p71-89

Influence—Melville

Hirsch, D. H. Hamlet, Moby-Dick, and passional thinking. *In* Shakespeare: aspects of influence p135-62

Ziff, L. Shakespeare and Melville's America. *In* Pullin, F. ed. New perspectives on Melville p54-67

Influence—Milton

Trickett, R. Shakespeare and Milton. *In* English Association. Essays and studies, 1978 p23-35

Influence—Shelley

Cantor, P. A. "A distorting mirror": Shelley's The Cenci and Shakespearean tragedy. *In* Shakespeare: aspects of influence p91-108

Knowledge—Law

Knight, W. N. Equity, 'The merchant of Venice' and William Lambarde. *In* Shakespeare survey 27 p93-104

Knowledge—Music

Carpenter, N. C. Shakespeare and music: unexplored areas. *In* Renaissance drama [1976] p243-55

Coletti, T. Music and The tempest. *In* Shakespeare's late plays p185-99

Knowledge—Philosophy

See Shakespeare, William—Philosophy

Language

Hawkes, T. 'That Shakespeherian rag.' *In* English Association. Essays and studies, 1977 p22-38

Newell, A. Early modern English idiom in a prose passage from King Lear. *In* Shakespeare's late plays p56-75

Quirk, R. Shakespeare and the English language. *In* Quirk, R. The linguist and the English language p46-64

Sherbo, A. Shakespeare. *In* Sherbo, A. English poetic diction from Chaucer to Wordsworth p69-85

Moral ideas

See Shakespeare, William—Religion and ethics

Moving-pictures

See Shakespeare, William—Film adaptations

Music

See Shakespeare, William—Knowledge—Music

Musical settings

Carpenter, N. C. Shakespeare and music: unexplored areas. *In* Renaissance drama [1976] p243-55

Shakespeare, William—*Continued*

Philosophy

Knights, L. C. The thought of Shakespeare. *In* Knights, L. C. Explorations 3 p115-28

Lever, J. W. Shakespeare and the ideas of his time. *In* Shakespeare survey v29 p79-91

Weitz, M. Literature without philosophy: 'Antony and Cleopatra.' *In* Shakespeare survey 28 p29-36

Poetic works

Smith, H. D. The nondramatic poems. *In* Shakespeare: aspects of influence p43-53

Wilbur, R. Shakespeare's poems. *In* Wilbur, R. Responses p78-90

Religion and ethics

Fisch, H. Shakespeare and the Puritan dynamic. *In* Shakespeare survey 27 p81-92

Romances (Tragicomedies)

See Shakespeare, William—Tragicomedies

Sources

Bulman, J. C. Shakespeare's use of the 'Timon' comedy. *In* Shakespeare survey v29 p103-16

Hobsbaum, P. Shakespeare's handling of his sources. *In* Hobsbaum, P. Tradition and experiment in English poetry p89-125

Hunter, G. K. Italian tragicomedy on the English stage. *In* Renaissance drama [1973] p123-48

McCombie, F. 'Hamlet' and the 'Moriae encomium'. *In* Shakespeare survey 27 p59-69

Rossi, J. W. Cymbeline's debt to Holinshed: the richness of III.1. *In* Shakespeare's romances reconsidered p104-12

Tobin, J. J. M. Apuleius and the Bradleian tragedies. *In* Shakespeare survey v31 p33-43

Weimann, R. The folk play and social custom. *In* Weimann, R. Shakespeare and the popular tradition in the theater: studies in the social dimension of dramatic form and function p15-48

Stage history

Weimann, R. Shakespeare's theater: tradition and experiment. *In* Weimann, R. Shakespeare and the popular tradition in the theater: studies in the social dimension of dramatic form and function p208-52

Stage history—Bibliography

Bawcutt, N. W. Shakespeare's life, times, and stage. *In* Shakespeare survey 28 p164-73

Bawcutt, N. W. Shakespeare's life, times, and stage [another essay] *In* Shakespeare survey v29 p168-77

Bawcutt, N. W. Shakespeare's life, times, and stage [another essay] *In* Shakespeare survey 30 p191-203

Pendry, E. D. Shakespeare's life, times, and stage. *In* Shakespeare survey v31 p177-91

Stage history—To 1625

Hunter, G. K. Were there act-pauses on Shakespeare's stage? *In* English Renaissance drama p15-35

Pinciss, G. M. Shakespeare, Her Majesty's players and Pembroke's Men. *In* Shakespeare survey 27 p129-36

Scragg, L. Macbeth on horseback. *In* Shakespeare survey 26 p81-88

Stage history—1800-1950

Daniell, D. J. Opening up the text: Shakespeare's Henry VI plays in performance. *In* Drama and society p247-77

Stage history—1950-

Brustein, R. S. No more masterpieces revisited: a speech to the Shakespeare '74 Convention at Brooklyn College. *In* Brustein, R. S. The culture watch p131-37

Stage history—Canada

Warren, R. Comedies and histories at two Stratfords, 1977. *In* Shakespeare survey v31 p141-53

Stage history—Great Britain

Schrickx, W. 'Pericles' in a book-list of 1619 from the English Jesuit mission and some of the play's special problems. *In* Shakespeare survey v29 p21-32

Seltzer, D. Shakespeare's texts and modern productions. *In* Wimsatt, W. K. ed. Literary criticism: idea and act p311-29

Thomson, P. Towards a poor Shakespeare: The Royal Shakespeare Company at Stratford in 1975. *In* Shakespeare survey v29 p151-56

Trewin, J. C. Brought up with Shakespeare. *In* Royal Society of Literature of the United Kingdom, London. Essays by divers hands v39 p163-80

Warren, R. Comedies and histories at two Stratfords, 1977. *In* Shakespeare survey v31 p141-53

Warren, R. Theory and practice: Stratford 1976. *In* Shakespeare survey 30 p169-79

Stage history— United States

Brustein, R. S. No more masterpieces revisited: a speech to the Shakespeare '74 Convention at Brooklyn College. *In* Brustein, R. S. The culture watch p131-37

Stage presentation

See Shakespeare, William—Dramatic production; Shakespeare, William—Stage history

Stage setting and scenery

See Shakespeare, William—Stage history

Study and teaching

Alexander, N. Shakespeare's life, times, and stage. *In* Shakespeare survey 26 p168-76

Alexander, N. Shakespeare's life, times, and stage [another essay] *In* Shakespeare survey 27 p172-79

Style

Sherbo, A. Shakespeare. *In* Sherbo, A. English poetic diction from Chaucer to Wordsworth p69-85

Technique

Beckerman, B. Shakespeare and the life of the scene. *In* English Renaissance drama p36-45

Brown, K. 'Form and cause conjoin'd': 'Hamlet' and Shakespeare's workshop. *In* Shakespeare survey 26 p11-20

Erlich, B. S. Structure, inversion, and game in Shakespeare's classical world. *In* Shakespeare survey v31 p53-63

Hunter, G. K. Were there act-pauses on Shakespeare's stage? *In* English Renaissance drama p15-35

Jones, G. P. 'Henry V': the chorus and the audience. *In* Shakespeare survey v31 p93-104

Shakespeare, William—*Continued*

Tragedies

Champion, L. S. Shakespeare: from Elizabethan to Jacobean. *In* Champion, L. S. Tragic patterns in Jacobean and Caroline drama p19-61

Knights, L. C. Shakespeare's tragedies and the question of moral judgement. *In* Knights, L. C. Explorations 2 p101-14

Muir, K. Shakespeare and the tragic pattern. *In* Muir, K. The singularity of Shakespeare, and other essays p 1-19

Seltzer, D. Prince Hal and tragic style. *In* Shakespeare survey 30 p 13-27

Tobin, J. J. M. Apuleius and the Bradleian tragedies. *In* Shakespeare survey v31 p33-43

Ure, P. Shakespeare and the inward self of the tragic hero. *In* Ure, P. Elizabethan and Jacobean drama p 1-21

Tragicomedies

Frye, N. Romance as masque. *In* Shakespeare's romances reconsidered p11-39

Hogan, J. J. Lear: a tragedy with a difference; and Shakespeare's tragicomedies or romances. *In* The Frontiers of human knowledge p153-57

Hoy, C. H. Fathers and daughters in Shakespeare's romances. *In* Shakespeare's romances reconsidered p77-90

Leech, C. Masking and unmasking in the last plays. *In* Shakespeare's romances reconsidered p40-59

Sanders, N. J. An overview of critical approaches to the romances. *In* Shakespeare's romances reconsidered p 1-10

Tragicomedies—Bibliography

Kay, C. M. and Jacobs, H. E. comps. A selected bibliography on Shakespeare's romances. *In* Shakespeare's romances reconsidered p181-215

Translations

Brower, R. A. Poetic and dramatic design in versions and translations of Shakespeare. *In* Brower, R. A. Mirror on mirror p139-58

Translations, French

Denommé, R. T. French theater reform and Vigny's translation of Othello in 1829. *In* Symbolism and modern literature p81-102

Translations, German

Phelps, L. R. Goethe's adaptation of Romeo and Juliet. *In* Creative encounter p17-24

Shakespeare and company

Beach, S. Shakespeare and company. *In* Bookselling in America and the world p149-55

Ford, H. D. From Princeton to Paris: Sylvia Beach. *In* Ford, H. D. Published in Paris p3-33

Shakespeare Festival, New York. See New York. Shakespeare Festival

Shakespeare Festival, Stratford, Ontario. See Stratford, Ontario. Shakespeare Festival

Shallowness. See Superficiality

Shamai, Nira. See Honig, M. H. jt. auth.

Shamanism

Bean, L. J. California Indian shamanism and folk curing. *In* American folk medicine p109-23

Furst, P. T. "High states" in culture-historical perspective. *In* Alternate states of consciousness p53-88

Rasmussen, K. J. V. A shaman's journey to the sea spirit Takánakapsâluk; excerpt from "Report of the fifth Thule expedition, 1921-24." *In* Tedlock, D. E. and Tedlock, B. eds. Teachings from the American earth p13-19

Ridington, W. R. and Ridington, T. The inner eye of shamanism and totemism. *In* Tedlock, D. E. and Tedlock, B. eds. Teachings from the American earth p190-204

Walker, J. R. Oglala metaphysics. *In* Tedlock, D. E. and Tedlock, B. eds. Teachings from the American earth p205-18

See also Medicine-man

Shamanistic symbolism

Myerhoff, B. G. Shamanic equilibrium: balance and mediation in known and unknown worlds. *In* American folk medicine p99-108

Shame (the word)

Kee, H. C. The linguistic background of "shame" in the New Testament. *In* On language, culture, and religion: in honor of Eugene A. Nida p133-47

Shamir, Shimon

Arab socialism and Egyptian-Islamic tradition. *In* Eisenstadt, S. N. and Azmon, Y. eds. Socialism and tradition p193-218

el-Shamy, Hasan

African world view and religion. *In* Martin, P. M. and O'Meara, P. eds. Africa p208-20

Shand, Philip Morton

Peter Behrens. *In* Sharp, D. ed. The rationalists p6-15

Shands, Harley Cecil

Verbal patterns and medical disease: prophylactic implications of learning. *In* Sebeok, T. A. ed. Sight, sound, and sense p175-201

Shands, Harley Cecil, and Meltzer, James D.

Unexpected semiotic implications of medical inquiry. *In* Sebeok, T. A. ed. A perfusion of signs p77-89

Shane, Alex M.

An introduction to Alexei Remizov. *In* The Bitter air of exile p10-16

About individual works

The life and works of Evgenij Zamjatin

Hyman, S. E. A Scythian humanist. *In* Hyman, S. E. The critic's credentials p248-52

Shane (Motion picture)

French, B. The amiable spouse. *In* French, B. On the verge of revolt p35-47

Shang Yang. See Kung-sun, Yang

Shango

Lawal, B. Yoruba-Sango ram symbolism: from ancient Sahara or dynastic Egypt? *In* African images p225-51

Shankar. See Saṅkarācārya

Shankland, Graeme

Why trouble with historic towns? *In* United Nations Educational, Scientific and Cultural Organization. The conservation of cities p24-42

Shankland, Robert Sherwood

Conversations with Albert Einstein. *In* Einstein p38-39

Shankman, Arnold Michel

For the Union as it was and the Constitution as it is: a Copperhead views the Civil War. *In* Rank and file p93-111

Shannon, Edgar Finley, and Ricks, Christopher B.

A further history of Tennyson's Ode on the death of the Duke of Wellington: the manuscript at Trinity College and the galley proof at Lincoln. *In* Virginia. University. Bibliographical Society. Studies in bibliography v32 p125-57

Shannon, Jasper Berry

Bicentennial reflections on party government. *In* Havard, W. C. and Bernd, J. L. eds. 200 years of the Republic in retrospect p128-45

Shannon, Richard T.

David Urquhart and the Foreign Affairs Committees. *In* Hollis, P. ed. Pressure from without p239-61

Shannon, William Vincent

The Irish in America: starvation, struggle and success. *In* De Breffny, B. ed. The Irish world p235-54

Our lost children. *In* Gross, B. and Gross, R. eds. The children's rights movement p148-50

Shao-ch'uan. See Koo, Vi Kyuin Wellington

Shapere, Dudley

On the relations between compositional and evolutionary theories. *In* Ayala, F. J. and Dobzhansky, T. G. eds. Studies in the philosophy of biology p187-201

Shapin, Steven

Homo phrenologicus: anthropological perspectives on an historical problem. *In* Barnes, B. and Shapin, S. eds. Natural order p41-71

Shapin, Steven, and Barnes, Barry

Darwin and social Darwinism: purity and history. *In* Barnes, B. and Shapin, S. eds. Natural order p125-42

Shapira, Yoram David

Cuba and the Arab-Israeli conflict. *In* Cuba in the world p153-66

Shapiro, David

A biofeedback strategy in the study of consciousness. *In* Alternate states of consciousness p145-57

Sylvia Plath: drama and melodrama. *In* Lane, G. ed. Sylvia Plath p45-53

Shapiro, Henry D.

The Western Academy of Natural Sciences of Cincinnati and the structure of science in the Ohio Valley 1810-1850. *In* Oleson, A. and Brown, S. C. eds. The pursuit of knowledge in the early American Republic p219-47

Shapiro, Jeremy J.

The slime of history: embeddedness in nature and critical theory. *In* O'Neill, J. ed. On critical theory p145-63

Shapiro, Judith

Cross-cultural perspectives on sexual differentiation. *In* Katchadourian, H. A. ed. Human sexuality p269-308

Shapiro, Karl Jay

The poetry wreck

Contents

American poet?
The career of the poem
The death of Randall Jarrell
The decolonization of American literature
Dylan Thomas
Ezra Pound: the scapegoat of modern poetry
The first white aboriginal

The greatest living Patagonian
Is poetry an American art?
The retreat of W. H. Auden
T. S. Eliot: the death of literary judgment
The true artificer
W. B. Yeats: trial by culture
William Carlos Williams: the true contemporary

What is not poetry? Excerpt from "In defense of ignorance." *In* Gibbons, R. ed. The poet's work: 29 masters of 20th century poetry on the origins and practice of their art p92-109

About

Scannell, V. American poets of the Second World War. *In* Scannell, V. Not without glory p172-237

Shapiro, K. J. American poet? *In* Shapiro, K. J. The poetry wreck p323-52

Shapiro, Martin M.

The Constitution and economic rights. *In* Essays on the Constitution of the United States p74-98

Shapley, Fern Rusk

Tiepolo's Zenobia cycle. *In* Enggass, R. C. and Stokstad, M. eds. Hortus imaginum p193-98

Shapley, Harlow

About

Bok, B. J. Harlow Shapley and the discovery of the center of our galaxy. *In* Neyman, J. ed. The heritage of Copernicus: theories "pleasing to the mind" p26-62

Share, Bernard

'A fancy turn, you know.' *In* Time was away p39-42

Share-cropping

Sutch, R. C. and Ransom, R. L. Sharecropping: market response or mechanism of race control? *In* What was freedom's price? p51-69

Sharia (Islamic law) See Islamic law

Sharits, Paul J.

About

Cornwell, R. Paul Sharits: illusion and object. *In* Nichols, B. ed. Movies and methods p363-73

Sharkansky, Ira

The politics of auditing. *In* Smith, B. L. R. ed. The new political economy: the public use of the private sector p278-318

Sharlet, Robert S.

Pashukanis and the withering away of law in the USSR. *In* Cultural revolution in Russia, 1928-1931 p169-88

Stalinism and Soviet legal culture. *In* Stalinism p155-79

Sharma, Ajit Kumar

Linguistic nationalism and India's national development. *In* Said, A. A. and Simmons, L. R. eds. Ethnicity in an international context p218-34

Sharma, Ishwar Chandra

Indian ethics. *In* Bishop, D. H. ed. Indian thought p233-51

Sharon, Mosheh

Palestine in the Islamic and Ottoman period. *In* The Palestinians p9-20

Sharp, Alan J.

Britain and the protection of minorities at the Paris Peace Conference, 1919. *In* Hepburn, A. C. ed. Minorities in history p170-88

Sharp, Lauriston. See Part 2 under title: Social organization and the applications of anthropology

Sharp, William

About

Hart, F. R. Late Victorian Celticisms. *In* Hart, F. R. The Scottish novel p336-47

Sharp, William F.

Manumission, 'libres' and Black resistance: the Colombian Chocó, 1680-1810. *In* Toplin, R. B. ed. Slavery and race relations in Latin America p89-111

Sharpe, Eric J.

The Old English runic Paternoster. *In* Symbols of power p41-60

Sharpe, Jim

Innovation and change in British land-use planning. *In* Planning, politics and public policy p316-57

Sharratt, Peter

Peter Ramus and the reform of the university: the divorce of philosophy and eloquence? *In* French Renaissance studies, 1540-70 p4-20

Sharrock, Roger

Browning and history. *In* Armstrong, I. ed. Robert Browning p77-103

Eliot's 'tone.' *In* The Literary criticism of T. S. Eliot p160-83

Shattuck, Roger

Vibratory organism: crise de prose. *In* Symbolism and modern literature p193-204

Shatzkin, Roger

Who cares who killed Owen Taylor? *In* Peary, G. and Shatzkin, R. eds. The modern American novel and the movies p80-94

Shaw, Bernard. See Shaw, George Bernard

Shaw, C. A.

Dilemmas of supergrowth: depleting irreplaceable raw materials. *In* The Year book of world affairs, 1976 p273-91

Shaw, Clifford Robe

About

Finestone, H. The delinquent and society: the Shaw and McKay tradition. *In* Delinquency, crime, and society p23-49

Weinberg, S. K. Shaw-McKay theories of delinquency in cross-cultural context. *In* Delinquency, crime, and society p167-85

Shaw, Donald Leslie

The generation of 1898 in Spain

Contents

Azorín: the rediscovery of a tradition
Baroja: anguish, action, and ataraxia
Conclusion
Ganivet and the emergence of the generation
Machado: the road to emptiness
Maeztu: from Left to Right
New directions
Origins and definitions
Unamuno: the giant of the generation

Shaw, Douglas V.

Political leadership in the industrial city: Irish development and nativist response in Jersey City. *In* Immigrants in industrial America, 1850-1920 p85-95

Shaw, Edward Pease

Censorship and subterfuge in eighteenth-century France. *In* Literature and history in the age of ideas p287-309

Shaw, Ezel Kural

The Ottoman aspects of Pax Ottomanica: the political, practical and psychological aspects of Pax Ottomanica. *In* Király, B. K. ed. Tolerance and movements of religious dissent in Eastern Europe p165-82

Shaw, George Bernard

About

Balakian, N. Shaw and his Boswell. *In* Balakian, N. Critical encounters p124-28

Brashear, W. R. The play as will and idea: Shaw and O'Neill. *In* Brashear, W. R. The gorgon's head p88-103

Coxe, L. O. You never can tell: George Bernard Shaw reviewed. *In* Coxe, L. O. Enabling acts p125-42

Gillie, C. Drama, 1900-1940. *In* Gillie, C. Movements in English literature, 1900-1940 p164-82

Kennedy, A. K. Shaw. *In* Kennedy, A. K. Six dramatists in search of a language p38-86

Kettle, A. Bernard Shaw and the new spirit. *In* Rebels and their causes p209-20

Lewis, W. George Bernard Shaw; excerpt from "The art of being ruled." *In* Lewis, W. Enemy salvoes p66-72

Mizener, A. M. Poetic drama and the well-made play. *In* Wimsatt, W. K. ed. Literary criticism: idea and act p576-89

Mudford, P. George Bernard Shaw. *In* Mudford, P. The art of celebration p153-64

Nicoll, A. Purposeful laughter: George Bernard Shaw. *In* Nicoll, A. World drama p627-46

Schoeps, K. H. Epic structures in the plays of Bernard Shaw and Bertolt Brecht. *In* Mews, S. and Knust, H. eds. Essays on Brecht p28-43

Wilder, T. N. George Bernard Shaw. *In* Wilder, T. N. American characteristics, and other essays p88-94

About individual works

Collected letters, 1874-1897

Kauffmann, S. Bernard Shaw: collected letters, 1874-1897. *In* Kauffmann, S. Persons of the drama p305-12

Collected letters, 1898-1910

Balakian, N. Memo: to Bernard Shaw. *In* Balakian, N. Critical encounters p129-32

Kauffmann, S. Bernard Shaw: collected letters, 1898-1910. *In* Kauffmann, S. Persons of the drama p312-17

The doctor's dilemma

Trilling, L. George Bernard Shaw: The doctor's dilemma. *In* Trilling, L. Prefaces to The experience of literature p37-44

Nine answers

Morley, C. D. Introduction to Nine answers by G. Bernard Shaw. *In* Praise from famous men: an anthology of introductions p116-23

Saint Joan

Schwarz, A. The experience of history as fateful. *In* Schwarz, A. From Büchner to Beckett p61-99

Bibliography

Weintraub, S. Bernard Shaw. *In* Finneran, R. J. ed. Anglo-Irish literature p167-215

Friends and associates

Mix, K. L. Max on Shaw. *In* Riewald, J. G. ed. The surprise of excellence p131-37

Shaw, George B.—*Continued*

Relations with contemporaries

See Shaw, George Bernard—Friends and associates

Shaw, James R.

Albertus Magnus and the rise of an empirical approach in medieval philosophy and science. *In* Jeffrey, D. L. ed. By things seen: reference and recognition in medieval thought p175-85

Shaw, Lemuel

About

White, G. E. Kent, Story, and Shaw: the judicial function and property rights. *In* White, G. E. The American judicial tradition p35-63

Shaw, Margery Wayne Schlamp

Genetics and the law. *In* The Tricentennial people p48-57

Shaw, Robert; McIntyre, Michael, and Mace, William M.

The role of symmetry in event perception. *In* Perception p276-310

Shaw, Russell B.

The changing Catholic school. *In* Fairfield, R. P. ed. Humanistic frontiers in American education p84-93

Shaw, Stanford J.

The Ottoman millet system: an evaluation. *In* Király, B. K. ed. Tolerance and movements of religious dissent in Eastern Europe p183-84

Shaw, Thurstan

The art of Benin through the eyes of the artist, the art historian, the ethnographer and the archaeologist. *In* Greenhalgh, M. and Megaw, J. V. S. eds. Art in society p207-23

Changes in African archaeology in the last forty years. *In* African studies since 1945 p156-68

Shaw, Timothy M.

Southern Africa: from détente to deluge? *In* The Year book of world affairs, 1978 p117-38

Zambia's foreign policy. *In* Aluko, O. ed. The foreign policies of African states p220-34

Shaw, Timothy M. and Anglin, Douglas George

Zambia: the crises of liberation. *In* Carter, G. M. and O'Meara, P. eds. Southern Africa: the continuing crisis p199-227

Shawcross, John T.

The hero of Paradise lost one more time. *In* Patrick, J. M. and Sundell, R. H. eds. Milton and the art of sacred song p137-47

The names of Herrick's mistresses in Hesperides. *In* Rollin, R. B. and Patrick, J. M. eds. "Trust to good verses": Herrick tercentenary essays p89-102

The poet as orator: one phase of his judicial pose. *In* Sloan, T. O. and Waddington, R. B. eds. The rhetoric of Renaissance poetry p5-36

Shayon, Robert Lewis

Television international. *In* Gerbner, G. ed. Mass media policies in changing cultures p41-55

Shea, Daniel Bartholomew

The art and instruction of Jonathan Edwards's Personal narrative. *In* Vaughan, A. T. and Bremer, F. J. eds. Puritan New England p299-311

Emerson and the American metamorphosis. *In* Levin, D. ed. Emerson: prophecy, metamorphosis, and influence p29-56

Sheard, Wendy Stedman

The Widener Orpheus: attribution, type, invention. *In* Collaboration in Italian Renaissance art p189-231

Sheba, Queen of

Legend

Pritchard, J. B. Conclusion. *In* Pritchard, J. B. ed. Solomon & Sheba p146-51

Pritchard, J. B. Introduction. *In* Pritchard, J. B. ed. Solomon & Sheba p7-15

Silberman, L. H. The Queen of Sheba in Judaic tradition. *In* Pritchard, J. B. ed. Solomon & Sheba p65-84

Ullendorff, E. The Queen of Sheba in Ethiopian tradition. *In* Pritchard, J. B. ed. Solomon & Sheba p104-14

Watson, P. F. The Queen of Sheba in Christian tradition. *In* Pritchard, J. B. ed. Solomon & Sheba p115-45

Watt, W. M. The Queen of Sheba in Islamic tradition. *In* Pritchard, J. B. ed. Solomon & Sheba p85-103

Sheba (Kingdom)

Beek, G. W. van. The land of Sheba. *In* Pritchard, J. B. ed. Solomon & Sheba p40-63

Sheckley, Robert

The search for the marvellous. *In* Nicholls, P. ed. Science fiction at large p185-98

Shedd, Russell

Multiple meanings in the Gospel of John. *In* Current issues in Biblical and patristic interpretation p247-58

Sheed, Francis Joseph

About

Sheed, W. Frank Sheed and Maisie Ward: writers, publishers, and parents. *In* Sheed, W. The good word & other words p164-70

Sheed, Wilfrid

The good word & other words

Contents

Sheed, Wilfrid
  The good word & other words
    Contents—Continued
Mary Gordon: Final payments
Men's women, women's men
Miami: 1972
A moral problem
More light on Luce
New York blues
Norman Mailer: Miami and the siege of Chi-
  cago
The novel of manners
Now that men can cry . . .
On keeping closets closed
P. G. Wodehouse: Leave it to Psmith
Rhapsodist in blue
Ring Lardner, Jr.: The Lardners: remem-
  bering my family
Spock mugged
The subject of ethnics
There is no (Irish) Mafia
Toward the Black Pussy Cafe
The twin urges of James Baldwin
Unnecessary roughness
V. S. Pritchett: Midnight oil
Walker Percy redivivus
Watergate as literature
The wit of George S. Kaufman and Dorothy
  Parker
Writer as something else
Writers' politics

Sheed & Ward (Publishers)
  Sheed, W. Frank Sheed and Maisie Ward:
  writers, publishers, and parents. *In* Sheed, W.
  The good word & other words p164-70

Sheehan, Thomas
  Getting to the topic: the new edition of
  Wegmarken. *In* Radical phenomenology
  p299-313

Sheehan, Vincent

About individual works
Dorothy and Red
  Marcus, S. Sinclair Lewis. *In* Marcus, S.
  Representations p41-60

Sheehy, Jeanne
  The Celtic revival: the visual arts. *In* De
  Breffny, B. ed. The Irish world p226-34

Shehadi, Fadlou A.
  Arabic and the concept of being. *In* Essays on Islamic philosophy and science p147-
  57

Sheldon, Charles David
  The politics of the Civil War of 1868. *In*
  Modern Japan p27-51

Sheldon, Sue Eastman
  The eagle: bird of magic and medicine
  in a Middle English translation of the Kyranides. *In* Tulane studies in English v22 p 1-31

Shell, Marc
  The economy of literature
    Contents
Conclusion
The Golden Fleece and the voice of the
  shuttle: economy in literary theory
John Ruskin and the political economy of
  literature
The language of character: an introduction
  to a poetics of monetary inscriptions
The lie of the fox: Rousseau's theory of ver-
  bal, monetary, and political representation
The Ring of Gyges

Shelley, Mary Wollstonecroft (Godwin)
About
  Gilbert, S. M. and Gubar, S. The parables
  of the cave. *In* Gilbert, S. M. and Gubar, S.
  The madwoman in the attic p93-104
  Scott, P D. Vital artifice: Mary, Percy,
  and the psychopolitical integrity of Frankenstein. *In* Levine, G. L. and Knoepflmacher,
  U. C. eds. The endurance of Frankenstein
  p172-202

About individual works
Frankenstein
  Brooks, P. "Godlike science/unhallowed
  arts": language, nature, and monstrosity. *In*
  Levine, G. L. and Knoepflmacher, U. C. eds.
  The endurance of Frankenstein p205-20
  Ellis, K. Monsters in the garden: Mary
  Shelley and the bourgeois family. *In* Levine,
  G. L. and Knoepflmacher, U. C. eds. The
  endurance of Frankenstein p123-42
  Gilbert, S. M. and Gubar, S. Horror's
  twin: Mary Shelley's monstrous Eve. *In*
  Gilbert, S. M. and Gubar, S. The madwoman
  in the attic p213-47
  Griffin, A. Fire and ice in Frankenstein.
  In Levine, G. L. and Knoepflmacher, U. C.
  eds. The endurance of Frankenstein p49-73
  Knoepflmacher, U. C. Thoughts on the ag-
  gression of daughters. *In* Levine, G. L. and
  Knoepflmacher, U. C. eds. The endurance
  of Frankenstein p88-119
  LaValley, A. J. The stage and film chil-
  dren of Frankenstein: a survey. *In* Levine,
  G. L. and Knoepflmacher, U. C. eds. The
  endurance of Frankenstein p243-89
  Levine, G. L. The ambiguous heritage of
  Frankenstein. *In* Levine, G. L. and Knoepflmacher, U. C. eds. The endurance of Frankenstein p3-30
  Massey, I. Singles and doubles: Frankenstein. *In* Massey, I. The gaping pig p124-37
  Moers, E. Female Gothic. *In* Levine, G. L.
  and Knoepflmacher, U. C. eds. The endurance of Frankenstein p77-87
  Nestrick, W. V. Coming to life: Frankenstein and the nature of film narrative. *In*
  Levine, G. L. and Knoepflmacher, U. C.
  eds. The endurance of Frankenstein p290-
  315
  Scott, P. D. Vital artifice: Mary, Percy,
  and the psychopolitical integrity of Frankenstein. *In* Levine, G. L. and Knoepflmacher,
  U. C. eds. The endurance of Frankenstein
  p172-202
  Sterrenburg, L. W. Mary Shelley's mon-
  ster: politics and psyche in Frankenstein. *In*
  Levine, G. L. and Knoepflmacher, U. C.
  eds. The endurance of Frankenstein p143-71
  Stevick, P. Frankenstein and comedy. *In*
  Levine, G. L. and Knoepflmacher, U. C. eds.
  The endurance of Frankenstein p221-39
  Suvin, D. The shift to anticipation: radi-
  cal rhapsody and romantic recoil. *In* Suvin, D.
  Metamorphoses of science fiction p115-44
  Wilt, J. Frankenstein as Mystery play. *In*
  Levine, G. L. and Knoepflmacher, U. C. eds.
  The endurance of Frankenstein p31-48

Adaptations
  LaValley, A. J. The stage and film children of Frankenstein: a survey. *In* Levine,
  G. L. and Knoepflmacher, U. C. eds. The
  endurance of Frankenstein p243-89

Shepherd, William C.

Conversion and adhesion. *In* Johnson, H. M. ed. Religious change and continuity p251-63

"The Shepherd of Hermas" and the development of medieval visionary allegory. Bogdanos, T. *In* Viator: medieval and Renaissance studies v8 p33-46

The shepherds' play

Stock, L. K. Comedy in the English Mystery Cycles: three comic scenes in the Chester Shepherds' play. *In* Ruggiers, P. G. ed. Versions of medieval comedy p211-26

Sheppard, Carl D.

The bronze doors of Augsburg Cathedral. *In* Enggass, R. C. and Stokstad, M. eds. Hortus imaginum p21-27

Shepperson, George

H. G. Wells. *In* Abroad in America: Visitors to the new Nation, 1776-1914 p293-301

Sherbo, Arthur

English poetic diction from Chaucer to Wordsworth

Contents

Chaucer to Spenser
Dryden
Milton
Pope
Prolegomena
Shakespeare
Some origins of poetic diction
Thomson
Wordsworth

George Steevens's 1785 variorum Shakespeare. *In* Virginia. University. Bibliographical Society. Studies in bibliography v32 p241-46

Johnson's Shakespeare and the dramatic criticism in The lives of the English poets. *In* Shakespeare: aspects of influence p55-69

Sheridan, Richard Brinsley Butler

About

Price, C. J. L. Pursuing Sheridan. *In* Evidence in literary scholarship p309-20

About individual works

The school for scandal

Bateson, F. W. The application of thought to an eighteenth-century text: The school for scandal. *In* Evidence in literary scholarship p321-35

Criticism, Textual

Bateson, F. W. The application of thought to an eighteenth-century text: The school for scandal. *In* Evidence in literary scholarship p321-35

Sherif, Carolyn Wood

The social context of competition. *In* Social problems in athletics p18-36

Sheringham, Michael

From the labyrinth of language to the language of the senses: the poetry of Andre Breton. *In* Cardinal, R. ed. Sensibility and creation p72-102

Sherlock, David

Silver and silversmithing. *In* Strong, D. E. and Brown, D. eds. Roman crafts p11-23

Sherman, Claire Richter

The Queen in Charles V's "Coronation Book": Jeanne de Bourbon and the "Ordo ad reginam benedicendam." *In* Viator: medieval and Renaissance studies v8 p255-98

Sherman, Edward F.

Accountability and responsiveness of the military establishment. *In* Rieselbach, L. N. ed. People vs. government: the responsiveness of American institutions p226-73

Bertrand Russell and the peace movement: liberal consistency or radical change? *In* Nakhnikian, G. ed. Bertrand Russell's philosophy p253-63

Sherman, Julia Ann

Some psychological "facts" about women: will the real Ms. please stand up? *In* Roberts, J. I. ed. Beyond intellectual sexism p113-37

Sherrard, Philip

The wound of Greece

Contents

Andreas Kalvos and the eighteenth-century ethos
Anghelos Sikelianos and his vision of Greece
Epilogue: the figure of Aretousa
General Makriyannis: the portrait of a Greek
George Seferis 1900-1971: the man and his poetry
Introduction: who are the Greeks?

Sherry, Norman

The essential Conrad. *In* English Association. Essays and studies, 1974 p98-113

About individual works

Conrad's Eastern world

Mudrick, M. Conrad. *In* Mudrick, M. The man in the machine p137-43

Conrad's Western world

Mudrick, M. Conrad. *In* Mudrick, M. The man in the machine p137-43

Sherry, Peggy Meyer

The "predicament" of the autograph: "William Blake." *In* Glyph 4 p131-55

Sherwin, Byron L.

Jewish views of euthanasia. *In* Kohl, M. ed. Beneficent euthanasia p3-11

Wiesel's Midrash: the writings of Elie Wiesel and their relationship to Jewish tradition. *In* Rosenfeld, A. H. and Greenberg, I. eds. Confronting the Holocaust p117-32

Sherwin, Robert C.

The presentation of educational self in the classroom. *In* Buxton, T. H. and Prichard, K. W. eds. Excellence in university teaching p30-38

Sherzer, Dina

De-construction in Waiting for Godot. *In* Babcock, B. A. ed. The reversible world p129-46

Sherzer, Joel

Areal linguistics in North America. *In* Sebeok, T. A. ed. Native languages of the Americas v 1 p121-73

Shestack, Jerome J.

Human-rights issues in Israel's rule of the West Bank and Gaza. *In* Sidorsky, D. ed. Essays on human rights p193-209

Shestov, Leo

About

Bayley, J. Shestov's law. *In* Bayley, J. The uses of division p84-90

Miłosz, C. Shestov, or The purity of despair. *In* Miłosz, C. Emperor of the earth p99-119

Shetreet, Shimon

Freedom of conscience and religion in Israel. *In* Sidorsky, D. ed. Essays on human rights p179-92

Shetty, Y. Krishna, and Carlisle, Howard M.
A study of management by objectives in a professional organization. *In* Managing nonprofit organizations p187-98

Shevelov, George Y.
On lexical Polonisms in literary Ukrainian. *In* For Wiktor Weintraub p449-63

Shewmaker, Kenneth L. and Berenda, Carlton Warren
Science and the problem of psi. *In* Wheatley, J. M. O. and Edge, H. L. eds. Philosophical dimensions of parapsychology p413-24

Shichor, Yitzhak
The basic assumptions and sources of Maoism. *In* Eisenstadt, S. N. and Azmon, Y. eds. Socialism and tradition p77-103

Shidahara, Kijūrō
About
Brown, S. D. Shidehara Kijūrō: the diplomacy of the yen. *In* Burns, R. D. and Bennett, E. M. eds. Diplomats in crisis p201-25

Shidehara, Kijūrō. See Shidahara, Kijūrō

Shields, Hugh
The grey cock: dawn song or revenant ballad? *In* Ballad studies p67-92

Shields, Nancy, comp.
Bibliography of the publications of Wiktor Weintraub. *In* For Wiktor Weintraub p605-21

Shiga, Naoya
About
Ueda, M. Shiga Naoya. *In* Ueda, M. Modern Japanese writers p85-110
Yamanouchi, H. The rivals: Shiga Naoya and Akutagawa Ryūnosuke. *In* Yamanouchi, H. The search for authenticity in modern Japanese literature p82-106

Shigemitsu, Mamoru
About
Coox, A. D. Shigemitsu Mamoru: the diplomacy of crisis. *In* Burns, R. D. and Bennett, E. M. eds. Diplomats in crisis p251-73

Shih-Chih. See Hu, Shih

Shih ching
Chen, Shih-hsiang. The Shih-ching: its generic significance in Chinese literary history and poetics. *In* Birch, C. ed. Studies in Chinese literary genres p8-41

Shikes, Ralph E.
Five artists in the service of politics in the pages of L'Assiette au beurre. *In* Millon, H. A. and Nochlin, L. eds. Art and architecture in the service of politics p162-81

Shillony, Ben-Ami
Myth and reality in Japan of the 1930s. *In* Modern Japan p81-88

Shiloah, Amnon
The dimension of sound. *In* Lewis, B. ed. Islam and the Arab world p161-80

Shils, Edward Albert
The academic ethos under strain. *In* Universities in the Western world p16-46
Governments and universities. *In* Hook, S.; Kurtz, P. W. and Todorovich, M. eds. The university and the state: what role for government in higher education? p177-204

The order of learning in the United States: the ascendancy of the university. *In* Oleson, A. and Voss, J. eds. The organization of knowledge in modern America, 1860-1920 p19-47
Roots—the sense of place and past: the cultural gains and losses of migration. *In* Human migration p404-26
See also Part 2 under title: Culture and its creators

Shimada, Noriko, and others
Ume Tsuda and Motoko Hani: echoes of American cultural feminism in Japan. *In* "Remember the ladies": new perspectives on women in American history p161-78

Shimahara, Nobuo Kenneth
American society, culture, and socialization. *In* Social forces and schooling p49-81
Cultural evolution: technology as a converging force. *In* Social forces and schooling p15-48

Shimazaki, Tōson
About
Yamanouchi, H. From romanticism to naturalism: Kitamura Tōkoku and Shimazaki Tōson. *In* Yamanouchi, H. The search for authenticity in modern Japanese literature p20-39

Shiner, Roger Alfred
Individuals, groups, and inverse discrimination. *In* Gross, B. R. ed. Reverse discrimination p310-13

Shinjo, K. See Johnston, H. N. jt. auth.

Shinn, Roger Lincoln
Living with scarcity. *In* Small comforts for hard times p137-51
Realism and ethics in political philosophy. *In* [Truth and tragedy]: a tribute to Hans Morgenthau p95-103
Realism, radicalism, and eschatology in Reinhold Niebuhr: a reassessment. *In* Scott, N. A. ed. The legacy of Reinhold Niebuhr p85-99

Shinn, Terry W.
The French science faculty system, 1808-1914: institutional change and research potential in mathematics and the physical sciences. *In* Historical studies in the physical sciences v10 p271-332

Shinnie, Peter L.
The development of Meroitic studies since 1945. *In* African studies since 1945 p169-78

Shipley, William F.
California. *In* Sebeok, T. A. ed. Native languages of the Americas v 1 p427-59

Shippey, T. A.
Old English literature. *In* English Association. The year's work in English studies v56 p63-80
Old English literature [another essay] *In* English Association. The year's work in English studies v57 p43-59

Shipping
See also Steamboat lines

History
Kreutz, B. M. Ships, shipping, and the implications of change in the early medieval Mediterranean. *In* Viator: medieval and Renaissance studies v7 p79-109

Ships

History

Kreutz, B. M. Ships, shipping, and the implications of change in the early medieval Mediterranean. *In* Viator: medieval and Renaissance studies v7 p79-109

al-Shirwānī, Muhammad ibn Fayd Allāh ibn Muhammad Amīn

About

Rescher, N. and Vander Nat, A. The Arabic theory of temporal modal syllogistic. *In* Essays on Islamic philosophy and science p189-221

Shively, Michael G. See De Cecco, J. P. jt. auth.

Shklar, Judith N.

Politics and the intellect. *In* Studies in eighteenth-century culture v7 p139-51

Shklovskiĭ, Viktor Borisovich

Parallels in Tolstoy. *In* Erlich, V. ed. Twentieth-century Russian literary criticism p81-85

Pushkin and Sterne: Eugene Onegin. *In* Erlich, V. ed. Twentieth-century Russian literary criticism p63-80

Some reflections on The Decameron. *In* Dombroski, R. S. ed. Critical perspectives on The Decameron p61-68

See also Brik, O. M. jt. auth.

Shklovsky, Viktor. See Shklovskiĭ, Viktor Borisovich

Shlaim, Avi

The Community and the Mediterranean basin. *In* Twitchett, K. J. ed. Europe and the world p77-120

Shmueli, Efraim. See Shmueli, Ephraim

Shmueli, Ephraim

The geometrical method, personal caution, and the idea of tolerance. *In* Shahan, R. W. and Biro, J. I. eds. Spinoza: new perspectives p197-215

Shneidman, Edwin S.

The college student and death. *In* Feifel, H. [ed.] New meanings of death p67-86

Preventing suicide. *In* Weir, R. F. ed. Ethical issues in death and dying p363-73

Shock corridor (Motion picture)

Elsaesser, T. Shock corridor by Sam Fuller. *In* Nichols, B. ed. Movies and methods p290-97

Shockley, John Stapels

Landless laborers and the Chicano movement in south Texas. *In* Forging nations: a comparative view of rural ferment and revolt p128-49

Shoemaker, Francis

New dimensions for world cultures. *In* Fairfield, R. P. ed. Humanistic frontiers in American education p289-301

Shoemaker, Sydney

Embodiment and behavior. *In* Rorty, A. O. ed. The identities of persons p109-37

Immortality and dualism. *In* Reason and religion p259-81

About individual works

Immortality and dualism

Lewis, H. D. Immortality and dualism. *In* Reason and religion p282-300

Shoenbaum, Samuel

'Richard II' and the realities of power. *In* Shakespeare survey 28 p 1-13

Sholokhov, Mikhail Aleksandrovich

About individual works

The silent Don

Mathewson, R. W. Four novels. *In* Mathewson, R. W. The positive hero in Russian literature p233-53

Virgin soil uprooted

Mathewson, R. W. Two bureaucracies. *In* Mathewson, R. W. The positive hero in Russian literature p211-32

Sholom Aleichem, pseud. See Rabinowitz, Shalom

Shone, Richard, and Grant, Duncan James Corrowr

The picture collector. *In* Keynes, M. ed. Essays on John Maynard Keynes p280-89

Short, James F.

Gangs, politics, and the social order. *In* Delinquency, crime, and society p129-63

Short films. See Moving-picture cartoons

Short plays. See One-act plays

Short stories

See also Story-telling

History and criticism

See Short story

Short stories, American

See also Western stories

History and criticism

Bader, A. L. The structure of the modern short story. *In* May, C. E. ed. Short story theories p107-15

Bone, R. A. Literary forebears. *In* Bone, R. A. Down home p3-18

Bone, R. A. Paul Dunbar. *In* Bone, R. A. Down home p42-73

Favier, J. Space and settor in short science fiction. *In* Johnson, I. D. and Johnson, C. [eds.] Les américanistes p182-201

Gullason, T. A. The short story: underrated art. *In* May, C. E. ed. Short story theories p13-31

Kostelanetz, R. Notes on the American short story today. *In* May, C. E. ed. Short story theories p214-25

May, C. E. A survey of short story criticism in America. *In* May, C. E. ed. Short story theories p3-12

Afro-American authors—History and criticism

Bruck, P. Black American short fiction in the 20th century: problems of audience, and the evolution of artistic stances and themes. *In* Bruck, P. ed. The Black American short story in the 20th century p 1-19

Short stories, Chinese

Chin, Ai-li S. and Liu, Nien-ling. Short stories in China: theory and practice, 1973-1975. *In* Chu, G. C. ed. Popular media in China p124-83

Short stories, Finnish

History and criticism

Ahokas, J. A. The short story in Finnish literature. *In* Dauenhauer, R. and Binham, P. eds. Snow in May p29-40

Short stories, German

History and criticism

Swales, M. Conclusion. *In* Swales, M. The German Novelle p202-14

Short stories, German—History and criticism
—Continued

Swales, M. The Novelle as historical genre. *In* Swales, M. The German Novelle p8-18

Swales, M. The theory of the Novelle. *In* Swales, M. The German Novelle p19-58

Short story

Bader, A. L. The structure of the modern short story. *In* May, C. E. ed. Short story theories p107-15

Baldeshwiler, E. The lyric short story: the sketch of a history. *In* May, C. E. ed. Short story theories p202-13

Bates, H. E. The modern short story: retrospect. *In* May, C. E. ed. Short story theories p72-79

Bowen, E. The Faber Book of modern short stories. *In* May, C. E. ed. Short story theories p152-58

Fitz Gerald, G. The satiric short story. *In* May, C. E. ed. Short story theories p182-88

Friedman, N. What makes a short story short? *In* May, C. E. ed. Short story theories p131-46

Going, W. T. Alabama in the short story: notes for an anthology. *In* Going, W. T. Essays on Alabama literature p39-60

Gordimer, N. "The flash of fireflies." *In* May, C. E. ed. Short story theories p178-81

Gullason, T. A. The short story: an underrated art. *In* May, C. E. ed. Short story theories p13-31

Hanan, P. The early Chinese short story: a critical theory in outline. *In* Birch, C. ed. Studies in Chinese literary genres p299-338

Jarrell, R. Stories. *In* May, C. E. ed. Short story theories p32-44

Lawrence, J. C. A theory of the short story. *In* May, C. E. ed. Short story theories p60-71

Marcus, M. What is an initiation story? *In* May, C. E. ed. Short story theories p189-201

Matthews, B. The philosophy of the short-story; excerpt. *In* May, C. E. ed. Short story theories p52-59

May, C. E. A survey of short story criticism in America. *In* May, C. E. ed. Short story theories p3-12

Moravia, A. The short story and the novel; excerpt from "Man as an end, a defense of humanism." *In* May, C. E. ed. Short story theories p147-51

O'Donovan, M. The lonely voice; excerpt. *In* May, C. E. ed. Short story theories p83-93

Rohrberger, M. The short story: a proposed definition; excerpt from "Hawthorne and the modern short story: a study in genre." *In* May, C. E. ed. Short story theories p80-82

Stroud, T. A. A critical approach to the short story. *In* May, C. E. ed. Short story theories p116-30

Welty, E. Looking at short stories. *In* Welty, E. The eye of the story p85-106

Welty, E. The reading and writing of short stories. *In* May, C. E. ed. Short story theories p159-77

Welty, E. Writing and analyzing a story. *In* Welty, E. The eye of the story p107-15

Shorter, Edward

Maternal sentiment and death in childbirth: a new agenda for psycho-medical history. *In* Branca, P. ed. The medicine show p67-88

Shortt, Adam

About

Berger, C. The founders of critical history: George M. Wrong and Adam Shortt. *In* Berger, C. The writing of Canadian history p 1-31

Shoshonean Indians

Steward, J. H. The foundations of Basin-Plateau Shoshonean society. *In* Steward, J. H. Evolution and ecology p366-406

Shoshonean languages. See Hopi language

Shostak, Arthur B.

Politics, conflict, and young blue-collarites: old dissensus and new consciousness. *In* The Uses of controversy in sociology p74-94

Shott, Susan

The sociology of emotion: some starting points. *In* McNall, S. G. ed. Theoretical perspectives in sociology p450-62

Showalter, Elaine

Family secrets and domestic subversion: rebellion in the novels of the 1860s. *In* Wohl, A. S. ed. The Victorian family p101-16

A literature of their own

Contents

Beyond the female aesthetic: contemporary women novelists

The double critical standard and the feminine novel

The female aesthetic

The female tradition

Feminine heroes: The woman's man

Feminine heroines: Charlotte Brontë and George Eliot

The feminine novelists and the will to write

The feminist novelists

Subverting the feminine novel: sensationalism and feminine protest

Virginia Woolf and the flight into androgyny

Women writers and the suffrage movement

Showalter, English

Madame de Graffigny and her salon. *In* Studies in eighteenth-century culture v6 p377-91

Shrimpton, Nick

Directing 'The tempest.' *In* Shakespeare survey v29 p63-67

Hell's hymnbook: Blake's Songs of innocence and of experience and their models. *In* Davies, R. T. and Beatty, B. G. eds. Literature of the romantic period, 1750-1850 p19-35

Shrines

Nigeria

Cole, H. M. The history of Ibo mbari houses—facts and theories. *In* African images p104-32

Shriver, Donald W.

Lifeboaters and mainlanders: a response. *In* Lucas, G. R. and Ogletree, T. W. eds. Lifeboat ethics p141-50

Shub, Elizabeth

An adventure in translation. *In* Horn Book Magazine. Crosscurrent of criticism p287-89

Shui-hu chuan

Li, P. Narrative patterns in San-kuo and Shui-hu. *In* Chinese narrative p73-84

Shulman, Abraham

About individual works

The old country

Dawidowicz, L. S. Picturing the past. *In* Dawidowicz, L. S. The Jewish presence p177-90

Shulman, Colette

The individual and the collective. *In* Women in Russia p375-84

Shulman, Marshall Darrow

Arms control in an international context. *In* Long, F. A. and Rathjens, G. W. eds. Arms, defense policy, and arms control p53-61

Shumaker, Wayne

The cosmic trilogy of C. S. Lewis. *In* Schakel, P. J. ed. The longing for a form p51-63

Shuman, I. Gayle and Mowen, John

The jury system: old problems and a new alternative. *In* Contemporary issues in criminal justice p59-75

Shuy, Roger W.

Dialectology. *In* Wardhaugh, R. and Brown, H. D. eds. A survey of applied linguistics p182-206

Shweder, Richard Allen, and LeVine, Robert Alan

Dream concepts of Hausa children: a critique of the "doctrine of invariant sequence" in cognitive development. *In* Schwartz, T. ed. Socialization as cultural communication p117-38

Shy, John W.

British strategy for pacifying the Southern colonies, 1778-1781. *In* The Southern experience in the American Revolution p155-73

A people numerous and armed

Contents

The American military experience: history and learning

The American Revolution today

American strategy: Charles Lee and the radical alternative

Armed loyalism: the case of the lower Hudson Valley

The Empire militant: Thomas Gage and the coming of war

The Empire remembered: Lawrence Gipson, historian

Hearts and minds in the American Revolution: the case of "Long Bill" Scott and Peterborough, New Hampshire

The military conflict considered as a revolutionary war

A new look at the colonial militia

The spectrum of imperial possibilities: Henry Ellis and Thomas Pownall, 1763-1775

Siam. See Thailand

Sibley, Mulford Quickert

Political theory, peace, and the problem of world order. *In* Dallmayr, F. R. ed. From contract to community p127-65

Sibling sequence. See Birth order

Sicard, Roch Ambroise Cucurron

About

Weiner, D. B. Three champions of the handicapped in Revolutionary France. *In* From Parnassus p161-76

Sichard, Johannes. See Sichardus, Johannes

Sichardus, Johannes

About

Kisch, G. An unpublished consilium of Johannes Sichardus. *In* Philosophy and humanism p477-82

Sicherl, M.

The tragic issue in Sophocles' Ajax. *In* Yale classical studies v25 p67-98

Sicherman, Carol Marks

Donne's timeless Anniversaries. *In* Roberts, J. R. ed. Essential articles for the study of John Donne's poetry p374-86

Sicilian American, On being a. Mangione, J. G. *In* Studies in Italian social history p40-49

Sicily

History—To 800—Historiography

Pearson, L. I. C. Myth and archaeologia in Italy and Sicily—Timaeus and his predecessors. *In* Yale classical studies v24 p171-95

Sick

See also Medical personnel and patient

Cooperation

See Patient compliance

Psychology

Shands, H. C. Verbal patterns and medical disease: prophylactic implications of learning. *In* Sebeok, T. A. ed. Sight, sound, and sense p175-201

Sick, Care of. See Care of the sick

Sick children

Psychology

Rutter, M. Early sources of security and competence. *In* Human growth and development p33-61

Siddartha, Prince. See Gautama Buddha

Sidman, Charles Francis

From the Act of Union to the fall of Parnell. *In* Orel, H. ed. Irish history and culture p225-50

From the fall of Parnell to modern Ireland. *In* Orel, H. ed. Irish history and culture p329-46

Sidnell, Michael J.

Mr Yeats, Michael Robartes and their circle. *In* Yeats and the occult p225-54

Sidney, Sir Philip

About

Helgerson, R. Sidney. *In* Helgerson, R. The Elizabethan prodigals p124-55

About individual works

Arcadia

Altman, J. B. Propaedeutic for drama: questions as fiction. *In* Altman, J. B. The Tudor play of mind p64-106

Astrophel and Stella

Kennedy, W. J. The Petrarchan mode in lyric poetry. *In* Kennedy, W. J. Rhetorical norms in Renaissance literature p20-78

The defence of poesy

Heninger, S. K. Sidney and Milton: the poet as maker. *In* Wittreich, J. A. ed. Milton and the line of vision p57-95

Bibliography—Quartos

Jackson, M. P. The printer of the first quarto of Astrophil and Stella (1591). *In* Virginia. University. Bibliographical Society. Studies in bibliography v31 p201-03

Influence—Milton

Heninger, S. K. Sidney and Milton: the poet as maker. *In* Wittreich, J. A. ed. Milton and the line of vision p57-95

Sidons, C. pseud. See Sealsfield, Charles

Sidorsky, David
The autonomy of moral objectivity. *In* Modern Jewish ethics p153-73
Contemporary reinterpretations of the concept of human rights. *In* Sidorsky, D. ed. Essays on human rights p88-109

Sieber, Roy
Some aspects of religion and art in Africa. *In* African religions: a symposium p141-57
Traditional arts of Black Africa. *In* Martin, P. M. and O'Meara, P. eds. Africa p221-42

Siegel, Ben
Through a glass darkly: Bernard Malamud's painful views of the self. *In* The Fiction of Bernard Malamud p117-47

Siegel, Daniel Menahem
Classical-electromagnetic and relativistic approaches to the problem of nonintegral atomic masses. *In* Historical studies in the physical sciences v9 p323-60

Siegel, Gary
Rabbit runs down. *In* Peary, G. and Shatzkin, R. eds. The modern American novel and the movies p247-55

Siegel, James T.
Awareness of the past in the Hikajat Potjoet Moehamat. *In* Southeast Asian history and historiography p321-31
Curing rites, dreams, and domestic politics in a Sumatran society. *In* Glyph 3 p18-31

Siegel, Seymour
An ethical approach to bio-medical research. *In* Hook, S.; Kurtz, P. and Todorovich, M. eds. The ethics of teaching and scientific research p169-73

Siegler, Frederick Adrian
Remembering dreams. *In* Dunlop, C. E. M. ed. Philosophical essays on dreaming p265-79

Siemens, William Lee
Apollo's metamorphosis in Pantaleón y las visitadoras. *In* Rossman, C. R. and Friedman, A. W. eds. Mario Vargas Llosa p88-100

Siemon, James Edward
Noble virtue in 'Cymbeline.' *In* Shakespeare survey v29 p51-61

Siena

History

Bowsky, W. M. Italian diplomatic history: a case for the smaller commune. *In* Order and innovation in the Middle Ages p55-74

Siena (African people) See Senufo (African people)

Sienkiewicz, Henryk

About

Pastusiak, L. Henryk Sienkiewicz. *In* Abroad in America: Visitors to the new Nation, 1776-1914 p176-85

About individual works
Komedia pomylek

Krzyżanowski, J. The Polish-Californian background of H. Sienkiewicz's burlesque "A comedy of errors." *In* For Wiktor Weintraub p251-56

Sierck, Detlef. See Sirk, Douglas

Sierra Leone
Leighton, N. O. The political economy of a stranger population: the Lebanese of Sierra Leone. *In* Shack, W. A. and Skinner, E. P. eds. Strangers in African societies p85-103

Siertsema, Berthe
Linguistic de-stigmatization? *In* On language, culture, and religion: in honor of Eugene A. Nida p315-36

Siew Hwa Beh. See Beh, Siew Hwa

Sight. See Vision

Sigillography. See Seals (Numismatics)

Sigler, Jay Adrian
Research resources on comparative rights policies. *In* Claude, R. P. ed. Comparative human rights p286-94

Sigmund, Elizabeth
Sylvia in Devon: 1962. *In* Butscher, E. ed. Sylvia Plath p100-07

Sign language
Stokoe, W. C. Sign languages and the verbal/nonverbal distinction. *In* Sebeok, T. A. ed. Sight, sound, and sense p157-72
See also Signs and symbols

Signals and signaling. See Drum language

Signets. See Seals (Numismatics)

Signification (Linguistics) See Reference (Linguistics)

Signs. See Signs and symbols

Signs and symbols
Barthes, R. Change the object itself. *In* Barthes, R. Image, music, text p165-69
Barthes, R. Rhetoric of the image. *In* Barthes, R. Image, music, text p32-51
Fisch, M. H. Peirce's general theory of signs. *In* Sebeok, T. A. ed. Sight, sound, and sense p31-70
Fishwick, M. W. Icons of America. *In* Browne, R. B. and Fishwick, M. W. eds. Icons of America p3-12
Gardner, H. Senses, symbols, operations: an organization of artistry. *In* Perkins, D. and Leondar, B. eds. The arts and cognition p88-117
Goethals, G. Sacred-secular icons. *In* Browne, R. B. and Fishwick, M. W. eds. Icons of America p24-34
Orr, D. G. The icon in the time tunnel. *In* Browne, R. B. and Fishwick, M. W. eds. Icons of America p13-23
Roupas, T. G. Information and pictorial representation. *In* Perkins, D. and Leondar, B. eds. The arts and cognition p48-79
Zeman, J. J. Peirce's theory of signs. *In* Sebeok, T. A. ed. A perfusion of signs p22-39
See also Semiotics; Sign language; Symbolism

Sigsbee, David Lee
The disciplined satire of Horace. *In* Roman satirists and their satire p64-88
Varro and Menippean satire. *In* Roman satirists and their satire p53-63

Sigur, Gaston
The strategic triangle: the U.S., the U.S.S.R. and the P.R.C. *in* Pacific Asia and U.S. policies: a political-economic-strategic assessment p28-35

Sigworth, Oliver F.
A way of looking at some baroque poems. *In* Studies in eighteenth-century culture v4 p31-41

Sikelianos, Angelos

About

Sherrard, P. Anghelos Sikelianos and his vision of Greece. *In* Sherrard, P. The wound of Greece p72-93

Sikh sects
Tobey, A. The Summer Solstice of the Healthy-Happy-Holy Organization. *In* The New religious consciousness p5-30

Sikhism

Bibliography
Singh, K. The Sikhs. *In* Adams, C. J. ed. A reader's guide to the great religions p223-30

Sects
See Sikh sects

Sikhs in the United States
Tobey, A. The Summer Solstice of the Healthy-Happy-Holy Organization. *In* The New religious consciousness p5-30

Silber, Irwin
Serpico. *In* Nichols, B. ed. Movies and methods p78-81

Silber, John Robert
The rest was history. *In* The Third century p194-96

Silberman, Lou H.
American impact: Judaism in the United States in the early nineteenth century. *In* Tradition and change in Jewish experience p89-105
The Queen of Sheba in Judaic tradition. *In* Pritchard, J. B. ed. Solomon & Sheba p65-84

Silbey, Joel H.
The Civil War synthesis in American political history. *In* Swierenga, R. P. ed. Beyond the Civil War synthesis p3-13
Silence (criticism) Pinter, H. *In* Kauffmann, S. Persons of the drama p201-04

Silence in literature
Kammer, J. The art of silence and the forms of women's poetry. *In* Gilbert, S. M. and Gubar, S. eds. Shakespeare's sisters p153-64
Ragussis, M. D. H. Lawrence: silence in Women in love. *In* Ragussis, M. The subterfuge of art p197-225
Ward, J. A. James Agee's aesthetic of silence: Let us now praise famous men. *In* Tulane Studies in English v23 p193-206

Silhol, Robert
Portrait of an ideal critic. *In* Johnson, I. D. and Johnson, C. [eds.] Les américanistes p202-15

Silk, Leonard Solomon
America in the world economy. *In* Rosecrance, R. N. ed. America as an ordinary country p158-73

Silko, Leslie

About individual works
Ceremony
Larson, C. R. Survivors of the relocation. *In* Larson, C. R. American Indian fiction p133-64

Silos abbey. See Los Silos, Spain. Silos abbey

Silver, Catherine Bodard
France: contrasts in familial and societal roles. *In* Giele, J. Z. and Smock, A. C. eds. Women: roles and status in eight countries p257-99

Silver, Isidore
The marriage of poetry and music in France: Ronsard's predecessors and contemporaries. *In* Poetry and poetics from ancient Greece to the Renaissance p152-84

Ronsard on the marriage of poetry, music, and the dance. *In* Studies in the continental background of Renaissance English literature: essays presented to John L. Lievsay p155-69

Silver, Rollo Gabriel
Aprons instead of uniforms: the practice of printing, 1776-1787. *In* American Antiquarian Society. Proceedings v87 pt 1 p111-94
Flash of the comet: the typographical career of Samuel N. Dickinson. *In* Virginia. University. Bibliographical Society. Studies in bibliography v31 p68-89

Silver
Belsley, D. A. United States silver coinage: what remains of an extinct specie. *In* Inflation, trade and taxes p50-72
See also Coinage

Silverberg, Robert

About
Clareson, T. D. The fictions of Robert Silverberg. *In* Clareson, T. D. ed. Voices for the future: essays on major science fiction writers v2 p 1-33

Silverman, Hugh Jerald
Heidegger and Merleau-Ponty: interpreting Hegel. *In* Radical phenomenology p209-24

Silverman, Joseph H.
The Spanish Jews: early references and later effects. *In* Américo Castro and the meaning of Spanish civilization p137-65

Silverman, Phyllis R.
Anticipatory grief from the perspective of widowhood. *In* Anticipatory grief p320-30

Silverman, Sydel Finfer
The life crisis as a clue to social function: the case of Italy. *In* Reiter, R. R. ed. Toward an anthropology of women p309-21

Silversmithing. See Silverwork

Silverstein, Michael
Shifters, linguistic categories, and cultural description. *In* Basso, K. H. and Selby, H. A. eds. Meaning in anthropology p11-55

Silverstein, Norman
James Dickey's muscular eschatology. *In* Boyers, R. ed. Contemporary poetry in America p303-13

Silvert, Kalman Hirsch
The changing dynamics of hemispheric politics. *In* Baldwin, D. A. ed. America in an interdependent world p275-92
The relevance of Latin American domestic politics to North American foreign policy. *In* The Americas in a changing world p62-77

Silverwork

Rome
Sherlock, D. Silver and silversmithing. *In* Strong, D. E. and Brown, D. eds. Roman crafts p11-23

Silvia, Daniel S.
Some fifteenth-century manuscripts of the Canterbury tales. *In* Chaucer and Middle English studies in honour of Rossell Hope Robbins p153-63

Simak, Clifford Donald

About
Clareson, T. D. Clifford D. Simak: the inhabited universe. *In* Clareson, T. D. ed. Voices for the future: essays on major science fiction writers v 1 p64-87

Sime, Sidney H.
About
Lewis, J. The fantasy world of Sidney Sime. *In* The Saturday book 34 p202-15

Simenon, Georges
About
Cawelti, J. G. The art of the classical detective story. *In* Cawelti, J. G. Adventure, mystery, and romance p106-38

Lambert, G. Night vision. *In* Lambert, G. The dangerous edge p171-209

Simeon manuscript
Doyle, A. I. The shaping of the Vernon and Simeon manuscripts. *In* Chaucer and Middle English studies in honour of Rossell Hope Robbins p328-41

Simes, Dimitri K.
Human rights and détente. *In* Kirk, G. L. and Wessell, N. H. eds. The Soviet threat p135-47

Simić, Andrei
White ethnic and Chicano families: continuity and adaptation in the New World. *In* Tufte, V. and Myerhoff, B. G. eds. Changing images of the family p251-69

Simic, Charles
About
Thurley, G. Devices among words: Kinnell, Bly, Simic. *In* Thurley, G. The American moment p210-28

Simile
Miller, G. A. Images and models, similes and metaphors. *In* Ortony, A. ed. Metaphor and thought p202-50

Ortony, A. The role of similarity in similes and metaphors. *In* Ortony, A. ed. Metaphor and thought p186-201

See also Metaphor

Simmel, Georg
About
Levine, D. N. Simmel at a distance: on the history and systematics of the sociology of the stranger. *In* Shack, W. A. and Skinner, E. P. eds. Strangers in African society p21-36

Simmes, Valentine
About
Craven, A. E. The reliability of Simmes's Compositor A. *In* Virginia. University. Bibliographical Society. Studies in bibliography v32 p186-97

Simmonds, Robert B. See Richardson, J. T. jt. auth.

Simmons, Adele
Class or communalism? A study of the politics of Creoles in Mauritius. *In* Kilson, M. L. and Rotberg, R. I. eds. The African diaspora p366-90

Simmons, John Simon Gabriel
Russian writing and printing: printing. *In* Auty, R. and Obolensky, D. eds. An introduction to Russian language and literature p47-55

Simmons, Joseph Larry
'Antony and Cleopatra' and 'Coriolanus', Shakespeare's heroic tragedies: a Jacobean adjustment. *In* Shakespeare survey 26 p95-101

Simmons, Luiz R. See Said, A. A. jt. auth.

Simmons, Marc
Authors and books in colonial New Mexico. *In* Voices from the Southwest p13-32

Settlement patterns and village plans in colonial New Mexico. *In* Weber, D. J. ed. New Spain's far northern frontier p97-115

Simmons, Merle Edwin
The Spanish epic. *In* Oinas, F. J. ed. Heroic epic and saga p216-35

Simmons, Richard Clive
The Massachusetts Charter of 1691. *In* Allen, H. C. and Thompson, R. eds. Contrast and connection p66-87

Simmons, Robert R.
The Communist side: an exploratory sketch. *In* The Korean War p197-208

Simms, John Gerald
The Battle of Aughrim: history and poetry. *In* Harmon, M. ed. Richard Murphy: poet of two traditions p36-51

Simms, William Gilmore
About
Rose, A. H. Demonic vision and the conventions of antebellum Southern fiction. *In* Rose, A. H. Demonic vision p39-62

Steeves, E. L. "No time for fainting": the frontier woman in some early American novels. *In* Kagel, S. E. ed. America: exploration and travel p191-205

Watson, C. S. William Gilmore Simms. *In* Watson, C. S. Antebellum Charleston dramatists p110-42

About individual works
Michael Bonham; or, The fall of Bexar

Watson, C. S. William Gilmore Simms. *In* Watson, C. S. Antebellum Charleston dramatists p110-42

Norman Maurice; or, The man of the people

Watson, C. S. William Gilmore Simms. *In* Watson, C. S. Antebellum Charleston dramatists p110-42

Simon, Alfred E. See Kimball, R. jt. auth.

Simon, Bennett
Mind and madness in ancient Greece
Contents
Aristotle on melancholy
The development of models of mental illness
Epic as therapy
The Greeks and the irrational
The Hippocratic corpus
Hysteria and social issues
Mental life in Greek tragedy
Mental life in the Homeric epics
On the babel of tongues in contemporary psychiatry
The philosopher as therapist
Plato and Freud
Plato's concept of mind and its disorders
The psychoanalytic and social psychiatric models
Tragedy and therapy
See also Russo, J. jt. auth.

Simon, Ernst
The neighbor (re'a) whom we shall love. *In* Modern Jewish ethics p29-56

About individual works
The neighbor (re'a) whom we shall love
Fisch, H. A response to Ernst Simon. *In* Modern Jewish ethics p57-61

Simon, G. Kass- See Kass-Simon, G.

Simon, Irène

Robert South and the Augustans. *In* English Association. Essays and studies, 1975 p15-28

Simon, John Ivan

A critical credo; excerpt from "Private screenings." *In* Denby, D. ed. Awake in the dark p169-82

The passion of Anna; excerpt from "Movies into film." *In* Denby, D. ed. Awake in the dark p128-36

Singularities

Contents

Advice to the hatelorn
The aesthetics of the actor's appearance
Black plays, white reviewers
A brief for brevity
Can drama be saved?
Charm: indefinable but indispensable
A critical need or two
Critical prognosis: new chaps and old boys
Cyrano de Bergerac
Danton's death
The Deputy and its metamorphoses
Grope, grapple, fulminate, lament—don't just sit there!
Grotowski's grotesqueries
Ham of genius
How many ostriches can dance on a pinhead?
How personal can a critic get?
In praise of professionalism
Is this the right way to rebel?
Lovable little people
Madness as theater
Mugging the Bard in Central Park
Must the rest be silence?
New, newer, newest
Peer Gynt
A roller-coaster ride with Kenneth Tynan
Should Albee have said "No, thanks"?
Should Shubert Alley be renamed Memory Lane?
A step in the right direction
Strange devices on the banner
Theatrical disorder of the day
Toward the conquest of inner space
"What can I do in the water"?
What is taste?
When you write that, smile!
The wild duck

Translation or adaptation? *In* From Parnassus p147-57

About

Murray, E. John Simon, judicial critic. *In* Murray, E. Nine American film critics p90-109

Simon, Neil

About individual works

The gingerbread lady

Kauffmann, S. The gingerbread lady. *In* Kauffmann, S. Persons of the drama p190-93

Simon, Pierre, marquis de Laplace. See Laplace, Pierre Simon, marquis de

Simon, Ulrich E.

Resurrection in a post-religious age. *In* Life after death p144-53

Simon, Walter B.

Democracy in the shadow of imposed sovereignty: the First Republic of Austria. *In* The Breakdown of democratic regimes pt2 p80-121

Simon, William; Puntil, Joseph E. and Peluso, Emil

Continuities in delinquency research. *In* Delinquency, crime, and society p50-63

Simon, William E.

The crucial issue is freedom. *In* Prochnow, H. V. ed. Dilemmas facing the nation p 1-31

About individual works

A time for truth

Galbraith, J. K. Defenders of the faith, I: William Simon. *In* Galbraith, J. K. Annals of an abiding liberal p103-08

Simonides of Ceos

About individual works

[*The Scopas-fragment*]

Dickie, M. W. The argument and form of Simonides 542 PMG. *In* Harvard Studies in classical philology v82 p21-33

Simons, Henry Calvert

About individual works

Economic policy for a free society

Oakeshott, M. J. The political economy of freedom. *In* Oakeshott, M. J. Rationalism in politics p37-58

Simons, J. R.

The brain and evolution of lower mammals. *In* Grafton Elliot Smith p39-49

Simonsohn, Shelomo

The Hebrew revival among early medieval European Jews. *In* Salo Wittmayer Baron v2 p831-58

Simonsohn, Shlomo. See Simonsohn, Shelomo

Simonsuuri, Kirsti

Homer's original genius

Contents

Ancients and moderns: the problem of cultural progress
Epic genius: the departure from the neoclassical model
The interpretation of early Greek epic: Mme Dacier and the Homeric war
Notions of poetry and society in the controversy about Ossian
Opposition to antiquity: Charles Perrault
The originality of Homer: some conclusions
Poetry is original 'imitation': Robert Wood's theory of the Homeric epic
Pope's view of Homer: 'fire' and invention
The primitivists and the primitive bard
Thomas Blackwell: the problem of Homer's genius
Vico's discovery of the true Homer
Voltaire and the poetry of the primitive age

Simplified spelling. See Spelling reform

Simpson, Alan

The covenanted community; excerpt from "Puritanism in old and New England." *In* Mulder, J. M. and Wilson, J. F. eds. Religion in American history p17-28

Simpson, Evan

Discrimination as an example of moral irrationality. *In* Fact, value, and perception p107-22

Simpson, George Eaton

Religions of the Caribbean. *In* Kilson, M. L. and Rotberg, R. I. eds. The African diaspora p280-311

Simpson, Harriette Louisa. See Arnow, Harriette Louisa (Simpson)

Simpson, James
Arnold and Goethe. *In* Allott, K. ed. Matthew Arnold p286-318

Simpson, Lewis Pearson
Faulkner and the legend of the artist. *In* Faulkner: fifty years after The marble faun p69-100

The printer as a man of letters: Franklin and the symbolism of the third realm. *In* Lemay, J. A. L. ed. The oldest revolutionary p3-20

Sex & history: origins of Faulkner's apocrypha. *In* The Maker and the myth: Faulkner and Yoknapatawpha, 1977 p43-70

The Southern aesthetic of memory. *In* Tulane Studies in English v23 p207-27

The Southern Review and a post-Southern American letters. *In* Anderson, E. and Kinzie, M. eds. The little magazine in America: a modern documentary history p78-99

The symbolism of literary alienation in the Revolutionary age. *In* Havard, W. C. and Bernd, J. L. eds. 200 years of the Republic in retrospect p79-100

Yoknapatawpha & Faulkner's fable of civilization. *In* The Maker and the myth. Faulkner and Yoknapatawpha, 1977 p122-45

Simpson, Louis
A revolution in taste
Contents
Black, banded with yellow
The color of saying
"The eye altering alters all"
Robert Lowell's indissoluble bride

About
Scannell, V. American poets of the Second World War. *In* Scannell, V. Not without glory p172-237

Simpson, Michael A.
Death and modern poetry. *In* Feifel, H. [ed.] New meanings of death p313-33

Sims, James H.
Milton, literature as a Bible, and the Bible as literature. *In* Patrick, J. M. and Sundell, R. H. eds. Milton and the art of sacred song p3-21

Sims, Richard L.
National elections and electioneering in Akita Ken, 1930-1942. *In* Modern Japan p89-112

Sims-Williams, Patrick
Continental influence at Bath monastery in the seventh century. *In* Anglo-Saxon England 4 p 1-28

Cuthswith, seventh-century abbess of Inkberrow, near Worcester, and the Würzburg manuscript of Jerome on Ecclesiastes. *In* Anglo-Saxon England 5 p 1-21

Simulation methods
Harbottle, M. Simulating peace-making in the Middle East: an exercise in reality. *In* Unofficial diplomats p241-49
See also subdivision Simulation methods under subjects, e.g. Social sciences—Simulation methods

Sin
Scholer, D. M. Sins within and sins without: an interpretation of 1 John 5: 16-17. *In* Current issues in Biblical and patristic interpretation p230-46
See also Repentance

Sin, Original. See Fall of man

Sinai. Saint Catherine (Basilian monastery)
Weitzmann, K. A group of early twelfth-century Sinai icons attributed to Cyprus. *In* Studies in memory of David Talbot Rice p47-63

Sincerity
Bayley, J. The authentic and the sincere. *In* Bayley, J. The uses of division p17-25

Sincerity in literature
Rudd, N. Theory: sincerity and masks. *In* Rudd, N. Lines of enquiry p145-81

Sinclair, Bruce
Science, technology, and the Franklin Institute. *In* Oleson, A. and Brown, S. C. eds. The pursuit of knowledge in the early American Republic p194-207

Sinclair, J. McH.
When is a poem like a sunset? *In* Ballad studies p153-69

Sinclair, May

About individual works
Mary Olivier
Kaplan, S. J. May Sinclair. *In* Kaplan, S. J. Feminine consciousness in the modern British novel p47-75

Sinclair, Upton Beall

About individual works
The wet parade
Mansfield, J. Que viva prohibition? *In* Peary, G. and Shatzkin, R. eds. The modern American novel and the movies p308-16

Sindbād, the philosopher

About individual works
The book of Sindibād
Steadman, J. M. The wife of Bath's Prologue: book-burning and the Veda of women's wiles. *In* Steadman, J. M. Nature into myth p95-103

Singapore

Politics and government
Ten, C. L. Politics in the academe. *In* Montefiore, A. ed. Neutrality and impartiality p149-64

Singapore (City) University
Ten, C. L. Politics in the academe. *In* Montefiore, A. ed. Neutrality and impartiality p149-64

Singapore children's literature. See Children's literature, Singapore

Singer, Barnett
Oregon's nineteenth-century notables: Simeon Gannett Reed and Thomas Lamb Eliot. *In* Bingham, E. R. and Love, G. A. eds. Northwest perspectives p61-76

Singer, Hans Wolfgang
Environmental factors in project analysis: a conceptual note. *In* Theory for economic efficiency: essays in honor of Abba P. Lerner p186-94

International policies and their effect on employment. *In* Economic development and planning p237-49

Singer, Isaac Bashevis

About individual works
Satan in Goray
Howe, I. In the day of a false messiah. *In* Celebrations and attacks p49-52

Singer, Jerome L.
Ongoing thought: the normative baseline for alternate states of consciousness. *In* Alternate states of consciousness p89-120

Singer, Joel David
The behavioral approach to diplomatic history. *In* Encyclopedia of American foreign policy p66-77

About individual works
Level-of-analysis problems in international relations
Yalem, R. J. The level-of-analysis problem reconsidered. *In* The Year book of world affairs, 1977 p306-26

Singer, Milton
For a semiotic anthropology. *In* Sebeok, T. A. ed. Sight, sound, and sense p202-31

Singer, Peter
Famine, affluence, and morality. *In* Aiken, W. and La Follette, H. eds. World hunger and moral obligation p22-36
Also in Laslett, P. and Fishkin, J. eds. Philosophy, politics and society p21-35

About individual works
Famine, affluence, and morality
Arthur, J. Rights and the duty to bring aid. *In* Aiken, W. and La Follette, H. eds. World hunger and moral obligation p37-48

Singh, Amar

About individual works
Diary
Rudolph, S. H. and Rudolph, L. I. Rajput adulthood: reflections on the Amar Singh Diary. *In* Erikson, E. H. ed. Adulthood p149-71

Singh, Harbhajan
About
Tobey, A. The Summer Solstice of the Healthy-Happy-Holy Organization. *In* The New religious consciousness p5-30

Singh, Khushwant
The Sikhs. *In* Adams, C. J. ed. A reader's guide to the great religions p223-30

Singh, Kusum
Elite control and challenge in changing India. *In* Gerbner, G. ed. Mass media policies in changing cultures p147-58

Singh, Ram Sewak
Indian novel in English
Contents
Aloneness alone: Anita Desai and Arun Joshi
"A European Brahmin": Raja Rao
Fictional technique
From resentment to social protest: Mulk Raj Anand
From social criticism to utopianism: Bhabani Bhattacharya
Historian turned fabulist: Manohar Malgonkar
Indo-English fiction: a retrospective introduction
Ironic vision of a social realist: Ruth Prawer Jhabvala
Soulful East and ratiocinative West: Kamala Markandaya
"Without illusions and hysterics": R. K. Narayan

Singhalese. See Sinhalese

Singing
Barthes, R. The grain of the voice. *In* Barthes, R. Image, music, text p179-89

Methods
See Bel canto
Single-parent family
See also Paternal deprivation

United States
Blechman, E. A. and Manning, M. A reward-cost analysis of the single-parent family. *In* Behavior modification and families p61-90

Single women. See Widows
Singleton, Gregory H.
Protestant voluntary organizations and the shaping of Victorian America. *In* Howe, D. W. ed. Victorian America p47-58

Singleton, Marvin Kenneth
Frederick Niven redivivus: a Scots-Canadian's Pacific Northwest. *In* Bingham, E. R. and Love, G. A. eds. Northwest perspectives p122-35

Singleton, Robert
California: the Self-Determination in Education Act, 1968. *In* Parents, teachers, and children: prospects for choice in American education p77-83

Sinhalese
Obeyesekere, G. Sinhalese-Buddhist identity in Ceylon. *In* Ethnic identity p231-58

Siniâvskiĭ, Andreĭ Donat'evich
On Boris Pasternak. *In* Erlich, V. ed. Twentieth-century Russian literary criticism p235-46

About
Brown, D. B. The art of Andrei Sinyavsky. *In* Brown, D. B. Soviet Russian literature since Stalin p331-51
Mathewson, R. W. Andrei Sinyavsky: conclusions. *In* Mathewson, R. W. The positive hero in Russian literature p341-55
Rahv, P. Two subversive Russians. *In* Rahv, P. Essays on literature and politics, 1932-1972 p232-37
Stacy, R. H. Reaction. *In* Stacy, R. H. Russian literary criticism p231-55

Sinjavskij, Andrej. See Siniâvskiĭ, Andreĭ Donat'evich

Sinn Fein Rebellion, 1916. See Ireland—History—Sinn Fein Rebellion, 1916

Sinnige, Theo Gerard. See Sinnige, Theodorus Gerardus

Sinnige, Theodorus Gerardus
Metaphysical and personal religion in Plotinus. *In* Kephalaion p147-54

Sino-Japanese Conflict, 1937-1945
Nish, I. H. Japan and the outbreak of war in 1941. *In* Crisis and controversy p130-47
See also China—History—1937-1945

Sins. See Deadly sins; Sin; Vices
Sins, Deadly. See Deadly sins
Sins, Mortal. See Deadly sins
Sinsheimer, Robert L.
The molecular basis of life. *In* Neyman, J. ed. The heritage of Copernicus: theories "pleasing to the mind" p143-65
The presumptions of science. *In* Holton, G. J. and Morison, R. S. eds. Limits of scientific inquiry p23-35

Sinyavsky, Andrei. See Siniavskii, Andrei Donat'evich

Siouan Indians. See Catawba Indians; Oglala Indians

Siouan languages
Chafe, W. L. Siouan, Iroquoian, and Caddoan. *In* Sebeok, T. A. ed. Native languages of the Americas v 1 p527-72

Sioux Indians. See Dakota Indians

Sir Gawain and the Green Knight. See Gawain and the Grene Knight

Siracusa, Joseph M.
FDR, Truman, and Indochina, 1941-1952: the forgotten years. *In* Siracusa, J. M. and Barclay, G. S. eds. The impact of the Cold war p163-83

Sirahniho, pseud. See Harris, John, fl. 1648

Siraisi, Nancy G. See Kibre, P. jt. auth.

Sircello, Guy J.
Expressive properties of art; excerpt from "Mind & art: an essay on the varieties of expression". *In* Margolis, J. Z. ed. Philosophy looks at the arts p325-45

Siringo, Charles

About
Dobie, J. F. Charlie Siringo, writer and man. *In* Dobie, J. F. Prefaces p75-104

Sirius
Brecher, K. Sirius enigmas. *In* Brecher, K. and Feirtag, M. eds. Astronomy of the ancients p91-115

Sirk, Douglas

About individual works
The tarnished angels
Stern, M. From the folklore of speed to Danse macabre. *In* Peary, G. and Shatzkin, R. eds. The modern American novel and the movies p40-52

Written on the wind
Truffaut, F. Douglas Sirk: Written on the wind. *In* Truffaut, F. The films in my life p148-50

Siroux, Maxine F.
Iran: the vitality of Isfahan. *In* United Nations Educational, Scientific and Cultural Organization. The conservation of cities p146-58

Siskin, Clifford
Freedom and loss in 'The tempest.' *In* Shakespeare survey 30 p147-55

Site, Myer
Art and the slow learner. *In* Ulman, E. and Dachinger, P. eds. Art therapy p191-207

Sitka, Alaska

History
Gibson, J. R. Old Russia in the New World: adversaries and adversities in Russian America. *In* European settlement and development in North America: essays on geographical change in honour and memory of Andrew Hill Clark p46-65

Six Day War, 1967. See Israel-Arab War, 1967

Sixel, Friedrich W.
The problem of sense: Habermas v. Luhmann. *In* O'Neill, J. ed. On critical theory p184-204

Sixteenth century
Hall, M. B. The spirit of innovation in the sixteenth century. *In* The Nature of scientific discovery p309-21

Levi, A. H. T. Ethics and the encyclopedia in the sixteenth century. *In* French Renaissance studies, 1540-70 p170-84
See also Reformation

The sixtene poyntis of charite
Utley, F. L. Chaucer's Troilus and St Paul's charity. *In* Chaucer and Middle English studies in honour of Rossell Hope Robbins p272-87

Sizwe Banzi is dead (criticism) Fugard, A.; Kani, J. and Ntshona, W. *In* Kauffmann, S. Persons of the drama p208-11

Sjogren, Christine Oertel
The status of women in several of Lessing's dramas. *In* Studies in eighteenth-century culture v6 p347-59

Skaggs, David Curtis
Postage stamps as icons. *In* Browne, R. B. and Fishwick, M. W. eds. Icons of America p198-208

Skaggs, Merrill Maguire
Morgana's apples and pears. *In* Prenshaw, P. W. ed. Eudora Welty p220-41

Skala, Johannes. See Dubravius, Jan, Bp. of Olomouc

Skard, Sigmund
Bjørnstjerne Bjørnson and Halvdan Koht. *In* Abroad in America: Visitors to the new Nation, 1776-1914 p195-206

Sked, Alan
Metternich and the federalist myth. *In* Crisis and controversy p 1-22

Skeletal remains. See Anthropometry; Man, Prehistoric

Skelton, Robin
Celt and classicist: the versecraft of Louis MacNeice. *In* Time was away p43-53

Skepticism
Blumenfeld, D. and Blumenfeld, J. B. Can I know that I am not dreaming? *In* Hooker, M. ed. Descartes p234-55

Doney, W. Spinoza on philosophical skepticism. *In* Freeman, E. and Mandelbaum, M. H. eds. Spinoza p139-57

Marlies, M. Doubt, reason, and Cartesian therapy. *In* Hooker, M. ed. Descartes p89-113

Miller, J. W. The ahistoric ideal. *In* Miller, J. W. The paradox of cause, and other essays p130-60

Miller, J. W. The midworld. *In* Miller, J. W. The paradox of cause, and other essays p106-23

More, P. E. Rationalism and faith; excerpt from "The skeptical approach to religion." *In* Crunden, R. M. ed. The superfluous men p252-60

Popkin, R. H. The development of religious scepticism and the influence of Isaac La Peyrère's pre-Adamism and Bible criticism. *In* Classical influences on European culture A.D. 1500-1700 p271-80
See also Belief and doubt; Truth

Sketch, Literary. See Essay

Skidelsky, Robert Jacob Alexander
The decline of Keynesian politics. *In* Crouch, C. State and economy in contemporary capitalism p55-87

The political meaning of the Keynesian revolution. *In* Skidelsky, R. J. A. ed. The end of the Keynesian era p33-40

Skidelsky, Robert J. A.—*Continued*

The reception of the Keynesian revolution. *In* Keynes, M. ed. Essays on John Maynard Keynes p89-107

The revolt against the Victorians. *In* Skidelsky, R. J. A. ed. The end of the Keynesian era p 1-9

Skidmore, David

The Chilean experience of change: the primacy of the political. *In* Leftwich, A. ed. South Africa: economic growth and political change p213-48

Skilled labor

United States

Form, W. H. Conflict within the working class: the skilled as a special-interest group. *In* The Uses of controversy in sociology p51-73

Skilling, Harold Gordon

Stalinism and Czechoslovak political culture. *In* Stalinism p257-80

Skilton, David

The English novel

Contents

Austen, Scott and the Victorians

Defoe and the Augustan age

Dickens and the literature of London

Gothic, romantic and heroic

Industrialisation and the condition of England

Late-Victorian choices: James, Wilde, Gissing and Moore

New approaches: Meredith, Hardy and Butler

Quixotic and picaresque fiction

Richardson and Fielding

Sterne, sentiment and its opponents

Victorian views of the individual: the Brontës, Thackeray, Trollope and George Eliot

Skinner, Andrew S.

Adam Smith: an economic interpretation of history. *In* Skinner, A. S. and Wilson, T. eds. Essays on Adam Smith p154-78

Skinner, Burrhus Frederic

The steep and thorny way to a science of behaviour. *In* Harré, R. ed. Problems of scientific revolution p58-71

About

Corson, J. A. Families as mutual control systems: optimization by systemization of reinforcement. *In* Behavior modification and families p317-30

Day, W. F. On the behavioral analysis of self-deception and self-development. *In* Mischel, T. ed. The self p224-49

Fancher, R. E. Modern pioneers: Jean Piaget and B. F. Skinner. *In* Fancher, R. E. Pioneers of psychology p339-72

About individual works

Beyond freedom and dignity

Flew, A. G. N. Human psychology and Skinnerian behaviourism. *In* Flew, A. G. N. A rational animal p140-50

Kraus, E. M. Individual and society: a Whiteheadian critique of B. F. Skinner. *In* Roth, R. J. ed. Person and community p103-32

Ricoeur, P. A critique of B. F. Skinner's Beyond freedom and dignity. *In* Ricoeur, P. Political and social essays p46-67

Skinner, Elliott P. See Smythe, H. H. jt. auth.

Skinner, Eugene R.

The theater of Emilio Carballido: spinning a web. *In* Lyday, L. F. and Woodyard, G. W. eds. Dramatists in revolt p19-36

Skinner, Frederick W.

Trends in planning practices: the building of Odessa, 1794-1917. *In* Hamm, M. F. ed. The city in Russian history p139-59

Skinner, Quentin

Motives, intentions and the interpretation of texts. *In* On literary intention p210-21

The principles and practice of opposition: the case of Bolingbroke versus Walpole. *In* Historical perspectives p93-128

About individual works

The principle and practice of opposition: the case of Bolingbroke versus Walpole

Hollis, M. My role and its duties. *In* Royal Institute of Philosophy. Nature and conduct p180-99

Skiotis, Dennis N.

Mountain warriors and the Greek revolution. *In* War, technology and society in the Middle East p308-29

Sklar, Robert

Empire to the West: Red river. *In* O'Connor, J E. and Jackson, M. A. eds. American history/American film p167-81

Sklare, Marshall

About individual works

America's Jews

Dawidowicz, L. S. Explaining American Jews. *In* Dawidowicz, L. S. The Jewish presence p61-66

Sklepowich, Edward A.

In pursuit of the lyric quarry: the image of the homosexual in Tennessee Williams' prose fiction. *In* Tennessee Williams: a tribute p525-44

Skobelev, Mikhail Dimitrievich

About

Rogger, H. The Skobelev phenomenon: the hero and his worship. *In* Oxford Slavonic papers, new ser. v9 p46-78

Skocpol, Theda

Explaining revolutions: in quest of a social-structural approach. *In* The Uses of controversy in sociology p155-75

Skolimowski, Henryk

Philosophy of technology as a philosophy of man. *In* Bugliarello, G. and Doner, D. B. eds. The history and philosophy of technology p325-36

Problems of rationality in biology. *In* Ayala, F. J. and Dobzhansky, T. G. eds. Studies in the philosophy of biology p205-23

Rationality in architecture and in the design process. *In* Sharp, D. ed. The rationalists p160-72

Skolnick, Arlene

Public images, private realities: the American family in popular culture and social science. *In* Tufte, V. and Myerhoff, B. G. eds. Changing images of the family p297-315

Skolnick, Jerome H.

Changing civil rights through law: can it be done? *In* Major social issues p141-48

The police in protest: National Commission on the Causes and Prevention of Violence (a staff report); excerpt from "The politics of protest." *In* Armstrong, T. R. and Cinnamon, K. M. eds. Power and authority in law enforcement p131-90

Should sexual relations be treated as crimes? *In* Contemporary issues in criminal justice p5-15

Skolnikoff, Eugene B.

Science, technology and the international system. *In* Science, technology and society p507-33

Skorupski, John

The meaning of another culture's beliefs. *In* Hookway, C. and Pettit, P. eds. Action and interpretation p83-106

Skramstad, Harold K.

Interpreting material culture: a view from the other side of the glass. *In* Material culture and the study of American life p175-200

Skriabin, Aleksandr Nikolaevich

About

Mandel'shtam, O. E. Pushkin & Scriabin (fragments). *In* Mandel'shtam, O. E. Selected essays p123-27

Skurnick, Blanche Jacqueline

A basic writing program at an urban university. *In* Minority language and literature p80-85

Skutsch, Otto

Notes on Ennian tragedy. *In* Harvard Studies in classical philology v71 p125-42

The original form of the Second Eclogue. *In* Harvard Studies in classical philology v74 p95-99

Readings in early Latin. *In* Harvard Studies in classical philology v76 p169-71

The Second book of Propertius. *In* Harvard Studies in classical philology v79 p229-33

Symmetry and sense in the Eclogues. *In* Harvard Studies in classical philology v73 p153-69

Sky hijacking. See Hijacking of aircraft

Skynner, A. C. Robin

The relationship of psychotherapy to sacred tradition. *In* Needleman, J. and Lewis, D. eds. On the way to self knowledge p204-25

Slabbert, Frederick van Zyl. See Van Zyl Slabbert, Frederick

Slabey, Robert M.

As I lay dying as an existential novel. *In* Garvin, H. R. ed. Makers of the twentieth-century novel p208-17

Slaby, Steve M.

What should we ask of the history of technology? *In* Bugliarello, G. and Doner, D. B. eds. The history and philosophy of technology p112-27

Slander (Law) See Libel and slander

Slater, James Alexander, and Caulfield, Ernest Joseph

The colonial gravestone carvings of Obadiah Wheeler. *In* American Antiquarian Society. Proceedings v84 pt 1 p73-103

Slater, Roslyn Bernice Alfin-. See Alfin-Slater, Roslyn Bernice

Slater, Robert C. See Raether, H. C. jt. auth.

Slater, William J.

Symposium at sea. *In* Harvard Studies in classical philology v80 p161-70

Slaughterhouse-Five (Motion picture)

DiMeo, S. Novel into film: so it goes. *In* Peary, G. and Shatzkin, R. eds. The modern American novel and the movies p282-92

Kauffmann, S. Slaughterhouse Five. *In* Kauffmann, S. Living images p112-13

Sarris, A. Slaughterhouse-Five. *In* Sarris, A. Politics and cinema p92-95

Slave narratives. See Slaves—United States—Biography

Slave-trade

Historiography

Fyfe, C. The dynamics of African dispersal: the transatlantic slave trade. *In* Kilson, M. L. and Rotberg, R. I. eds. The African diaspora p57-74

Angola

Miller, J. C. The slave trade in Congo and Angola. *In* Kilson, M. L. and Rotberg, R. I. eds. The African diaspora p75-113

Brazil

MacLachlan, C. M. African slave trade and economic development in Amazonia, 1700-1800. *In* Toplin, R. B. ed. Slavery and race relations in Latin America p112-45

Rout, L. B. The African in colonial Brazil. *In* Kilson, M. L. and Rotberg, R. I. eds. The African diaspora p132-71

Colombia—Cartagena

Chandler, D. L. Health conditions in the slave trade of colonial New Granada. *In* Toplin, R. B. ed. Slavery and race relations in Latin America p51-88

Congo

Miller, J. C. The slave trade in Congo and Angola. *In* Kilson, M. L. and Rotberg, R. I. eds. The African diaspora p75-113

Latin America

Chandler, D. L. Health conditions in the slave trade of colonial New Granada. *In* Toplin, R. B. ed. Slavery and race relations in Latin America p51-88

South Carolina—Charleston

Higgins, W. R. Charleston: terminus and entrepôt of the colonial slave trade. *In* Kilson, M. L. and Rotberg, R. I. eds. The African diaspora p114-31

Slavery

Sellin, J. T. Slavery and the punishment of crime. *In* Crime, criminology and public policy p93-106

See also Slave trade; Villeinage

Emancipation

Woodward, C. V. The price of freedom. *In* What was freedom's price? p93-113

Slavery and slaves in literature

Jackson, S. M. Fact from fiction: another look at slavery in three Spanish-American novels. *In* DeCosta, M. ed. Blacks in Hispanic literature p83-89

Turner, D. T. Faulkner and slavery. *In* The South and Faulkner's Yoknapatawpha p62-85

Slavery in Trinidad

Higman, B. W. African and Creole slave family patterns in Trinidad. *In* Crahan, M. E. and Knight, F. W. eds. Africa and the Caribbean p41-64

Slavery in Venezuela

Lombardi, J. V. The abolition of slavery in Venezuela: a nonevent. *In* Toplin, R. B. ed. Slavery and race relations in Latin America p228-52

Slaves

United States—Biography—Bibliography

Miller, R. and Katopes, P. J. Slave narratives. *In* Inge, M. T.; Duke, J. M. and Bryer, J. R. eds. Black American writers v 1 p21-46

United States—Nutrition

Kiple, K. F. and Kiple, V. H. Slave child mortality: some nutritional answers to a perennial puzzle. *In* Branca, P. ed. The medicine show p21-46

Slaves, Emancipation of. See Slavery in the United States—Emancipation

Slaves in literature. See Slavery and slaves in literature

Slavic languages

Golab, Z. Linguistic traces of primitive religious dualism in Slavic. *In* For Wiktor Weintraub p151-59

Heaney, M. The sources of early Križanica. *In* Oxford Slavonic papers, new ser. v8 p101-36

Slavin, Arthur Joseph

The American principle from More to Locke. *In* First images of America p139-64

Some oblique light: three studies in Reformation history. *In* Medievalia et humanistica no. 6 p203-07

Sławińska, Irena

Two concepts of time in dramatic structure: Turgenev and Norwid. *In* For Wiktor Weintraub p479-92

Sledd, James H.

We have met the enemy—and he is us. *In* Minority language and literature p65-70

Sleep

Ayer, Sir A. J. Professor Malcolm on dreams. *In* Dunlop, C. E. M. ed. Philosophical essays on dreaming p127-48

Bouwsma, O. K. Descartes' skepticism of the senses. *In* Dunlop, C. E. M. ed. Philosophical essays on dreaming p52-63

Caldwell, R. L. Macolm and the criterion of sleep. *In* Dunlop, C. E. M. ed. Philosophical essays on dreaming p157-73

Canfield, J. V. Judgments in sleep. *In* Dunlop, C. E. M. ed. Philosophical essays on dreaming p149-56

MacDonald, M. Sleeping and waking. *In* Dunlop, C. E. M. ed. Philosophical essays on dreaming p64-80

Malcolm, N. Dreaming and skepticism. *In* Dunlop, C. E. M. ed. Philosophical essays on dreaming p103-26

Pears, D. F. Dreaming. *In* Dunlop, C. E. M. ed. Philosophical essays on dreaming p205-26

Yost, R. M. and Kalish, D. Miss MacDonald on sleeping and waking. *In* Dunlop, C. E. M. ed. Philosophical essays on dreaming p81-102

See also Dreams; Nightmares

Slepfsov, Vasiliĭ Alekseevich

About

Brumfield, W. C. Sleptsov redivivus. *In* California Slavic studies v9 p27-70

Slesinger, Tess

About individual works

The unpossessed

Trilling, L. A novel of the thirties. *In* Trilling, L. The last decade p3-24

Slevin, Carl

Bertrand de Jouvenel: efficiency and amenity. *In* De Crespigny, A. and Minogue, K. R. eds. Contemporary political philosophers p168-90

Sligo, Ireland

Henn, T. R. 'The place of shells.' *In* Henn, T. R. Last essays p13-25

Sliwowski, George

Legal aspects of terrorism. *In* International terrorism and world security p69-77

Sloan, Thomas J.

A look at America's potential roles in a global food crisis. *In* Orr, D. W. and Soroos, M. S. eds. The global predicament p110-30

Sloan, Thomas O.

The crossing of rhetoric and poetry in the English Renaissance. *In* Sloan, T. O. and Waddington, R. B. eds. The rhetoric of Renaissance poetry p212-42

The persona as rhetor: an interpretation of Donne's Satyre III. *In* Roberts, J. R. ed. Essential articles for the study of John Donne's poetry p424-38

The rhetoric in the poetry of John Donne. *In* Roberts, J. R. ed. Essential articles for the study of John Donne's poetry p189-98

Slobodkin, Lawrence Basil

Sociology and ecology: the need for mutual concern. *In* Major social issues p250-64

Slocum, Sally

Woman the gatherer: male bias in anthropology. *In* Reiter, R. R. ed. Toward an anthropology of women p36-50

Slonim, Marc L'vovich

Soviet Russian literature

Contents

Alexander Solzhenitsyn: the great challenger

The fate of poets: Mandelstam, Akhmatova, Tsvetayeva

Fluctuations and trials

Posthumous revivals: Bulgakov, Platonov, Zabolotsky

Samizdat: the underground press

Soviet romantics: from Grin, Paustovsky, and Olesha to Tikhonov and Bagritsky

The third emigration

Slonimskiĭ, Aleksandr Leonidovich

The technique of the comic in Gogol. *In* Maguire, R. A. ed. Gogol from the twentieth century p323-73

Slonimsky, Alexander. See Slonimskiĭ, Aleksandr Leonidovich

Slot machines

Kallan, R. A. The one-armed bandit: a lasting icon. *In* Browne, R. B. and Fishwick, M. W. eds. Icons of America p190-97

Slote, Bernice

An appointment with the future: Willa Cather. *In* French, W. G. ed. The twenties p39-49

Slote, Bernice—*Continued*

A gathering of nations. *In* The Art of Willa Cather p248-53

Whitman and Dickinson. *In* American literary scholarship, 1973 p85-98

Whitman and Dickinson [another essay] *In* American literary scholarship, 1974 p61-74

Slote, Michael A.

Existentialism and the fear of dying. *In* Donnelly, J. P. ed. Language, metaphysics, and death p69-87

Inapplicable concepts and sexual perversion. *In* Baker, R. and Elliston, F. A. eds. Philosophy & sex p261-67

The morality of wealth. *In* Aiken, W. and La Follette, H. eds. World hunger and moral obligation p124-47

Sloth. See Laziness

Slotkin, James Sidney

The Peyote way. *In* Tedlock, D. E. and Tedlock, B. eds. Teachings from the American earth p96-104

Slovak Americans

Social life and customs

Stein, H. F. Envy and the evil eye: an essay in the psychological ontogeny of belief and ritual. *In* The Evil eye p193-222

Slow learners. See Slow learning children

Slow learning children

Site, M. Art and the slow learner. *In* Ulman, E. and Dachinger, P. eds. Art therapy p191-207

Slums

Kampala, Uganda

Clinard, M. B. and Abbott, D. J. Community organization and property crime: a comparative study of social control in the slums of an African city. *In* Delinquency, crime, and society p186-206

Slusser, Robert M.

History and the democratic opposition. *In* Tokes, R. L. ed. Dissent in the USSR p329-53

Soviet Far Eastern policy, 1945-50: Stalin's goals in Korea. *In* The Origins of the Cold war in Asia p123-46

Small, Melvin

Public opinion. *In* Encyclopedia of American foreign policy p844-55

Small countries. See States, Small

Small presses. See Little presses

Smalley, Beryl

Ecclesiastical attitudes to novelty, c. 1100-c. 1250. *In* Church, society and politics p113-31

Smalley, William Allen

Restructuring translations of the psalms as poetry. *In* On language, culture, and religion: in honor of Eugene A. Nida p337-71

Smallpox

Preventive inoculation

Bell, W. J. Dr. James Smith and the public encouragement for vaccination for smallpox. *In* Bell, W. J. The colonial physician & other essays p131-47

Smallpox, Inoculation of. See Smallpox—Preventive inoculation

Smallpox vaccine. See Smallpox—Preventive inoculation

Smart, Christopher

About

Ober, W. B. Madness and poetry: a note on Collins, Cowper, and Smart. *In* Ober, W. B. Boswell's clap and other essays p137-92

About individual works
Jubilate Agno (Rejoice in the Lamb)

Hartman, G. H. Christopher Smart's Magnificat: toward a theory of representation. *In* ELH essays for Earl R. Wasserman p139-64

Also in Hartman, G. H. The fate of reading p74-98

Smart, Ian

Uniqueness and generality. *In* Vernon, R. ed. The oil crisis p259-81

Smart, John Jamieson Coswell

On some criticisms of a physicalist theory of colors. *In* Philosophical aspects of the mind-body problem p54-63

About individual works
Materialism

Flew, A. G. N. Mind/brain identity and the Cartesian framework. *In* Flew, A. G. N. A rational animal p123-50

Smart, Veronica

Corrections to Hildebrand's corpus of Anglo-Saxon moneyers: from Cnut to Edward the Confessor. *In* Anglo-Saxon England 4 p155-70

Smedley, Audrey

Women of Udu: survival in a harsh land. *In* Matthiasson, C. J. ed. Many sisters p205-28

Smelser, Marshall

An understanding of the American Revolution. *In* An Almost chosen people p3-18

Smelstor, Marjorie Rose

Expatriation and exploration: the exiled artists of the 1920s. *In* Kagle, S. E. ed. America: exploration and travel p136-52

Smiley, Donald V.

French-English relations in Canada and consociational democracy. *In* Esman, M. J. ed. Ethnic conflict in the Western world p179-203

Smirke, Sydney

About

Crook, J. M. Sydney Smirke: the architecture of compromise. *In* Seven Victorian architects p50-65

Smirnov, IAkov Ivanovich

About

Cross, A. G. Yakov Smirnov: a Russian priest of many parts. *In* Oxford Slavonic papers, new ser. v8 p37-52

Smirnov, Yakov. See Smirnov, IAkov Ivanovich

Smith, Adam

About

Bagolini, L. The topicality of Adam Smith's notion of sympathy and judicial evaluations. *In* Skinner, A. S. and Wilson, T. eds. Essays on Adam Smith p100-13

Brown, A. H. S. E. Desnitsky, Adam Smith, and the Nakaz of Catherine II. *In* Oxford Slavonic papers, new ser. v7 p42-59

Smith, Adam—About individual works—The wealth of nations—*Continued*

Stevens, D. Adam Smith and the colonial disturbances. *In* Skinner, A. S. and Wilson, T. eds. Essays on Adam Smith p202-17

Stigler, G. J. Smith's travels on the Ship of State. *In* Skinner, A. S. and Wilson, T. eds. Essays on Adam Smith p237-46

Sylos Labini, P. Competition: the product markets. *In* The Market and the state p200-32

Vickers, D. Adam Smith and the status of the theory of money. *In* Skinner, A. S. and Wilson, T. eds. Essays on Adam Smith p482-503

West, E. G. Adam Smith and alienation: wealth increases, men decay? *In* Skinner, A. S. and Wilson, T. eds. Essays on Adam Smith p540-52

Influence

Brown, A. H. Adam Smith's first Russian followers. *In* Skinner, A. S. and Wilson, T. eds. Essays on Adam Smith p247-73

Smith, Albert Hugh

About individual works

English place-name elements

Quirk, R. Bon-mots from places. *In* Quirk, R. The linguist and the English language p110-17

Smith, Albert James

An examination of some claims for Ramism. *In* Roberts, J. R. ed. Essential articles for the study of John Donne's poetry p178-88

Sense and innocence: two love episodes in Dante and Milton. *In* An English miscellany p119-30

Smith, Ann D.

The woman offender. *In* Progress in penal reform p155-64

Smith, Anne

Introduction: Towards a new assessment. *In* Smith, A. ed. The art of Emily Brontë p7-29

A new Adam and a new Eve—Lawrence and women: a biographical overview. *In* Smith, A. ed. Lawrence and women p9-48

Smith, Anthony

"Just a pleasant way to spend an evening" —the softening embrace of American television. *In* A New America? p195-212

Smith, Anthony Douglas

Introduction: the formation of nationalist movements. *In* Smith, A. D. ed. Nationalist movements p 1-30

Neo-classicist and romantic elements in the emergence of nationalist conceptions. *In* Smith, A. D. ed. Nationalist movements p74-87

Smith, Archie

Black reflections on the study of new religious consciousness. *in* Needleman, J. and Baker, G. eds. Understanding the new religions p209-19

Smith, Arthur J. R.

Future problems of trade policy: a question of political leadership. *In* The New Atlantic challenge p79-95

Smith, Arthur James Marshall

Evolution and revolution as aspects of English-Canadian and American literature. *in* Perspectives on revolution and evolution p213-37

F. R. Scott and some of his poems. *In* Woodcock, G. ed. Poets and critics p14-25

Nonsense poetry and romanticism. *In* Essays in honor of Russel B. Nye p180-94

Smith, Barbara Herrnstein

Poetry as fiction. *In* Cohen, R. ed. New directions in literary history p165-87

Smith, Bruce L. R.

The public use of the private sector. *In* Smith, B. L. R. ed. The new political economy: the public use of the private sector p 1-45

Smith, Bruce R.

The contest of Apollo and Marsyas: ideas about music in the Middle Ages. *In* Jeffrey, D. L. ed. By things seen: reference and recognition in medieval thought p81-107

Sir Amorous Knight and the indecorous Romans; or, Plautus and the Terence play court in the Renaissance. *In* Renaissance drama [1973] p3-27

Smith, Catherine F.

Jane Lead: mysticism and the woman cloathed with the sun. *In* Gilbert, S. M. and Gubar, S. eds. Shakespeare's sisters p3-18

Smith, Cecil Blanche (Fitz Gerald) Woodham. See Woodham Smith, Cecil Blanche (Fitz Gerald)

Smith, Charles Harvard Gibbs- See Gibbs-Smith, Charles Harvard

Smith, Christopher Norman

The very plain song of it: Frederic Manning, Her privates we. *In* Klein, H. M. ed. The First World War in fiction p174-82

Smith, Clarence Jay

Soviet Russia and the Red revolution of 1918 in Finland. *In* Hammond, T. T. ed. The anatomy of Communist takeovers p71-93

Smith, Constance Babington-. See Babington-Smith, Constance

Smith, Crosbie. See Crosland, M. P. jt. auth.

Smith, Curtis C.

Olaf Stapledon's dispassionate objectivity. *In* Clareson, T. D. ed. Voices for the future: essays on major science fiction writers v 1 p44-63

Smith, Cyril Stanley

Remarks on the discovery of techniques and on sources for the study of their history. *In* Bugliarello, G. and Doner, D. B. eds. The history and philosophy of technology p31-37

Structural hierarchy in science, art, and history. *In* Wechsler, J. ed. On aesthetics in science p9-53

Smith, Daniel Malloy

The Fourteen Points. *In* Encyclopedia of American foreign policy p380-86

Smith, Daniel Scott

Old age and the 'great transformation': a New England case study. *In* Spicker, S. F.; Woodward, K. M. and Van Tassel, D. D. eds. Aging and the elderly p285-302

Smith, Datus Clifford

The bright promise of publishing in developing countries. *In* Altbach, P. G. and McVey, S. eds. Perspectives on publishing p117-28

Smith, David

About

Krauss, R. E. Tanktotem: welded images. *In* Krauss, R. E. Passages in modern sculpture p147-200

Smith, Joseph H.
Language and the genealogy of the absent object. *In* Psychiatry and the humanities v 1 p145-70

Smith, Julian Francis
"A canary for one": Hemingway in the wasteland. *In* Benson, J. J. ed. The short stories of Ernest Hemingway: critical essays p233-38
Hemingway and the thing left out. *In* Benson, J. J. ed. The short stories of Ernest Hemingway: critical essays p135-47
Also in Wagner, L. W. ed. Ernest Hemingway p188-20

Smith, Keith
Who controls book publishing in Anglophone middle Africa? *In* Altbach, P. G. and McVey, S. eds. Perspectives on publishing p129-40

Smith, Logan Pearsall
About
Connolly, C. A voice from the dead? *In* Connolly, C. The evening colonnade p441-44

Smith, Mahlon Brewster
Essay I. *In* Fitzgerald, R. ed. What it means to be human p3-24
Metapsychology, politics, and human needs. *In* Fitzgerald, R. ed. Human needs and politics p124-41

Smith, Mary Sweeney
The deaf. *In* Gochros, H. L. and Gochros, J. S. eds. The sexually oppressed p268-76

Smith, Michael H. and Carey, R.
The Nixon legacy and American foreign policy. *In* The Year book of world affairs, 1978 p23-42
See also Williams, P. jt. auth.

Smith, Morton
On the Wine God in Palestine (Gen. 18, Jn. 2, and Achilles Tatius) *In* Salo Wittmayer Baron v2 p815-29

Smith, Pamela
Architectonics: Sylvia Plath's Colossus. *In* Butscher, E. ed. Sylvia Plath p111-24

Smith, Patrick Horace Nowell- See Nowell-Smith, Patrick Horace

Smith, Pauline
About
Ravenscroft, A. Pauline Smith. *In* Parker, K. ed. The South African novel in English p46-56

Smith, Pauline Janet. See Smith, Pauline

Smith, Peter H.
The breakdown of democracy in Argentina, 1916-30. *In* The Breakdown of democratic regimes pt3 p3-27
History. *In* Quantitative social science research on Latin America p14-61

Smith, Philip H.
The failure of the machine and the triumph of the mind. *In* Gold. J. ed. In the name of language! p205-09

Smith, Ralph Bernard
England and Vietnam in the fifteenth and sixteenth centuries: an essay in historical comparison. *In* Southeast Asian history and historiography p227-45

Smith, Raymond T.
Religion in the formation of West Indian society: Guyana and Jamaica. *In* Kilson, M. L. and Rotberg, R. I. eds. The African diaspora p312-41

Smith, Reginald Donald
Castle on the air. *In* Time was away p87-95
Radio scripts, 1941-1963. *In* Time was away p141-48

Smith, Richard Thomas
Societal reaction and physical disability: contrasting perspectives. *In* Gove, W. R. ed. The labelling of deviance p147-56

Smith, Robert Freeman
Reciprocity. *In* Encyclopedia of American foreign policy p867-81

Smith, Robert Jerome
Festivals and calendar customs. *In* Orel, H. ed. Irish history and culture p129-45
Irish mythology. *In* Orel, H. ed. Irish history and culture p 1-24

Smith, Roger C.
The human significance of biology: Carpenter, Darwin, and the vera causa. *In* Knoepflmacher, U. C. and Tennyson, G. B. eds. Nature and the Victorian imagination p216-30

Smith, Rondal B. See Nida, E. A. jt. auth.

Smith, Rowland
The Johannesburg genre. *In* Exile and tradition p116-31
The plot beneath the skin: the novels of C. J. Driver. *In* Heywood, C. ed. Aspects of South African literature p145-54

Smith, Russell Yates
The British and Sa'd Zaghlul, 1906-1912. *In* Nationalism in a non-national state p195-206

Smith, Sheila Kaye- See Kaye-Smith, Sheila

Smith, Stephen L. See Cagnon, M. A. jt. auth.

Smith, Steven R.
Death, dying and the elderly in seventeenth-century England. *In* Spicker, S. F.; Woodward, K. M. and Van Tassel, D. D. eds. Aging and the elderly p205-19

Smith, Stuart Allen
Alfred Waterhouse: civic grandeur. *In* Seven Victorian architects p102-21

Smith, Timothy Lawrence
Lay initiative in the religious life of American immigrants, 1880-1950. *In* Mulder, J. M. and Wilson, J. F. eds. Religion in American history p358-78
Social reform: some reflections on causation and consequence. *In* The Rise of Adventism p18-29

Smith, Trevor
Britain. *In* Planning, politics and public policy p52-69
Industrial planning in Britain. *In* Planning, politics and public policy p111-27

Smith, Victor Lamonte. See Tarrow, S. G. jt. auth.

Smith, Vivian Brian
Australia of the spirit: some aspects of the work of Vance and Nettie Palmer, 1938-48. *In* Bards, bohemians, and bookmen p236-50

Smith, W. H.
International terrorism: a political analysis. *In* The Year book of world affairs, 1977 p138-57

Smith, Wesley Dale
Expressive form in Euripides' Suppliants. *In* Harvard Studies in classical philology v71 p151-70

Smith, Wilfred Cantwell
An historian of faith reflects on what we are doing here. *In* Christian faith in a religiously plural world p139-48

Smith, William D.
The energy crisis and the Middle East. *In* The New world balance and peace in the Middle East: reality or mirage? p105-17

Smith, William Jay
Precision and reticence: Eudora Welty's poetic vision. *In* Dollarhide, L. and Abadie, A. J. eds. Eudora Welty: a form of thanks p78-94

Smithey, Robert Arthur
The new militancy and its impact on the Afro-American middle class. *In* Johnson, H. A. ed. Negotiating the mainstream p196-216

Smock, Audrey Chapman
Bangladesh: a struggle with tradition and poverty. *In* Giele, J. Z. and Smock, A. C. eds. Women: roles and status in eight countries p81-126
Conclusion: Determinants of women's roles and status. *In* Giele, J. Z. and Smock, A. C. eds. Women: roles and status in eight countries p383-421
Education and national integration in Ghana. *In* Smock, D. R. and Bentsi-Enchill, K. eds. The search for national integration in Africa p117-38
Ghana: from autonomy to subordination. *In* Giele, J. Z. and Smock, A. C. eds. Women: roles and status in eight countries p173-216
The impact of modernization on women's position in the family in Ghana. *In* Schlegel, A. E. ed. Sexual stratification p192-214

Smock, Audrey Chapman, and Youssef, Nadia Haggag
Egypt: from seclusion to limited participation. *In* Giele, J. Z. and Smock, A. C. eds. Women: roles and status in eight countries p33-79

Smock, David R.
Language policy in Ghana. *In* Smock, D. R. and Bentsi-Enchill, K. eds. The search for national integration in Africa p169-88

Smolansky, Oles M.
The United States and the Soviet Union in the Middle East. *In* Kirk, G. L. and Wessell, N. H. eds. The Soviet threat p99-109

Smolinski, Leon
East European influences on Soviet economic thought and reform. *In* Szporluk, R. ed. The influence of East Europe and the Soviet West on the USSR p68-90

Smollett, Tobias George

About
Hart, F. R. Scottish variations of the Gothic novel. *In* Hart, F. R. The Scottish novel p13-30
Skilton, D. Quixotic and picaresque fiction. *In* Skilton, D. The English novel p32-44

About individual works
The adventures of Ferdinand Count Fathom
Jeffrey, D. K. "Ductility and dissimulation": the unity of Ferdinand Count Fathom. *In* Tennessee Studies in literature v23 p47-60

The expedition of Humphry Clinker
Auty, S. G. Smollett and Sterne and animal spirits: Humphry Clinker. *In* Auty, S. G. The comic spirit of eighteenth-century novels p158-79
Jeffrey, D. K. The epistolary format of Pamela and Humphry Clinker. *In* A Provision of human nature p145-54
Karl, F. R. Smollett's Humphry Clinker: the choleric temper. *In* Karl, F. R. The adversary literature p183-204
Rothstein, E. Humphry Clinker. *In* Rothstein, E. Systems of order and inquiry in later eighteenth-century fiction p109-53

Peregrine Pickle
Auty, S. G. Smollett and Sterne and animal spirits: Peregrine Pickle. *In* Auty, S. G. The comic spirit of eighteenth-century novels p103-19
Spacks, P. A. M. Early fiction and the frightened male. *In* Spilka, M. ed. Towards a poetics of fiction p255-65

Roderick Random
Bjornson, R. The picaresque hero as young nobleman: victimization and vindication in Smollett's Roderick Random. *In* Bjornson, R. The picaresque hero in European fiction p228-45

Smyser, Jay M.
In-house corporate counsel: the erosion of independence. *In* Nader, R. and Green, M. J. eds. Verdicts on lawyers p208-16

Smythe, Hugh H.
The Black professional. *In* The Black American reference book p453-79

Smythe, Hugh H. and Skinner, Elliott P.
Black participation in U.S. foreign relations. *In* The Black American reference book p638-47

Smythe, Hugh H. and Stokes, Carl Burton
The Black role in American politics: Part I, The present. *In* The Black American reference book p580-621

Smythe, Mabel Murphy
The Black role in the economy. *In* The Black American reference book p207-50
See also Douglass, J. H. jt. auth.

Snake cults (Holiness churches)
Daugherty, M. L. Serpent handling as sacrament. *In* Browne, R. B. and Fishwick, M. W. eds. Icons of America p124-38
Gerrard, N. L. The serpent-handling religions of West Virginia. *In* Henslin, J. M. ed. Deviant life-styles p79-86

Snake handling (Holiness churches) See Snake cults (Holiness churches)

Snakes in literature. See Serpents in literature

Snellgrove, David L.
Tibetan Buddhism today. *In* Dumoulin, H. ed. Buddhism in the modern world p277-93

Snetsinger, John Godall
Ethnicity and foreign policy. *In* Encyclopedia of American foreign policy p322-29

Snodgrass, William DeWitt
In radical pursuit
Contents
Analysis of depths: The Inferno
Crime for punishment: the tenor of part one
Finding a poem
Glorying in failure: Cervantes and Don Quixote

Snodgrass, William D.
In radical pursuit
Contents—Continued
Gods of The Iliad: memoirs of a brainpicker
Master's in the verse patch: John Crowe Ransom
Moonshine and sunny beams: ruminations on A midsummer night's dream
Poems about paintings
A poem's becoming
A rocking horse: the symbol, the pattern, the way to live
Tact and the poet's force
"That anguish of concreteness"—Theodore Roethke's career

About
Snodgrass, W. D. Poems about paintings. *In* Snodgrass, W. D. In radical pursuit p63-97

About individual works
A cardinal
Snodgrass, W. D. A poem's becoming. *In* Snodgrass, W. D. In radical pursuit p33-62

Heart's needle
Snodgrass, W. D. Finding a poem. *In* Snodgrass, W. D. In radical pursuit p23-32

Snow, Charles Percy, Baron Snow
Albert Einstein 1879-1955; excerpt from "Variety of men." *In* Einstein p3-8
The classical detective story. *In* From Parnassus p16-22

The realists
Contents
Balzac
Dickens
Dostoevsky
Galdós
Henry James
Proust
Stendhal
Tolstoy

About
Davis, R. G. C. P. Snow. *In* Stade, G. ed. Six contemporary British novelists p57-114

About individual works
The new men
Trilling, L. The novel alive or dead. *In* Trilling, L. A gathering of fugitives p135-42

The sleep of reason
Borowitz, A. The Snows on the Moors: C. P. Snow and Pamela Hansford Johnson on the Moors murder case. *In* Borowitz, A. Innocence and arsenic p 1-25

Snow, Edward Alan
Marlowe's Doctor Faustus and the ends of desire. *In* Kernan, A. B. ed. Two Renaissance mythmakers p70-110

Snowden, Frank Martin
Ethiopians and the Graeco-Roman world. *In* Kilson, M. L. and Rotberg, R. I. eds. The African diaspora p11-36

Snyder, Emile
Aimé Césaire: the reclaiming of the land. *In* Exile and tradition p31-43
Modern Africa in literature. *In* Martin, P. M. and O'Meara, P. eds. Africa p331-47

Snyder, Gary
About
Altieri, C. F. Process as plenitude: the poetry of Gary Snyder and Robert Duncan. *In* Altieri, C. F. Enlarging the temple p128-69

Ellwood, R. S. Zen journeys to the West. *In* Ellwood, R. S. Alternative altars p136-63
Paul, S. From lookout to ashram: the way of Gary Snyder. *In* Paul, S. Repossessing and renewing p195-235

Snyder, Henry Leonard
The contributions of Abel Boyer as Whig journalist and writer of The Protestant Post-Boy, 1711-1712. *In* The Dress of words p139-49
From the accession of the Tudors to the Treaty of Limerick. *In* Orel, H. ed. Irish history and culture p109-27
From the beginnings to the end of the Middle Ages. *In* Orel, H. ed. Irish history and culture p25-41
From the Treaty of Limerick to the union with Great Britain. *In* Orel, H. ed. Irish history and culture p147-64

Snyder, James Edward
Jan Mostaert's West Indies landscape. *In* First images of America p495-502
The mosaic in Santa Maria Nova and the original apse decoration of Santa Maria Maggiore. *In* Enggass, R. C. and Stokstad, M. eds. Hortus imaginum p 1-9

Soal, Samuel George
On "Science and the supernatural." *In* Ludwig, J. K. ed. Philosophy and parapsychology p172-77

Sobel, David Stuart. See Brody, H.; Krueger, A. P. jt. auths.

Sobel, Eli
German literature. *In* Jones, W. M. ed. The present state of scholarship in sixteenth-century literature p169-96

Sobieszek, Robert A.
Photography and the theory of realism in the Second Empire: a reexamination of a relationship. *In* One hundred years of photographic history p145-59

Sobo (African people)
Foss, W. P. Images of aggression: ivwri sculpture of the Urhobo. *In* African images p133-43

Soboul, Albert
Persistence of "feudalism" in the rural society of nineteenth-century France. *In* Rural society in France p50-71

Sochen, June
The new woman and twenties America: Way down east. *In* O'Connor, J. E. and Jackson, M. A. eds. American history/American film p 1-15

Social acceptance
Foot, P. Approval and disapproval. *In* Foot, P. Virtues and vices, and other essays in moral philosophy p189-207

Social action
Baumgartner, T.; Burns, T. R. and Deville, P.R. Actors, games, and systems: the dialectics of social action and system structuring. *In* McNall, S. G. ed. Theoretical perspectives in sociology p128-48
See also Environmental protection—Citizen participation

Social adjustment
Rutter, M. Early sources of security and competence. *In* Human growth and development p33-61
See also Deviant behavior; Social acceptance

Social alienation. See Alienation (Social psychology)

Social anthropology. See Ethnology

Social case work

Busck, L. The Family Guidance Center in Copenhagen. *In* Davis, K. C. Discretionary justice in Europe and America p115-31

Nowitz, L. Dying and the aged person: process and implications for social work practice. *in* Home care p185-95

See also Counseling; Interviewing

Social change

Bell, D. Ethnicity and social change. *In* Glazer, N. and Moynihan, D. P. eds. Ethnicity p141-74

Bell, W. Futuristics and social behavior. *In* Bundy, R. F. ed. Images of the future: the twenty-first century and beyond p57-65

Boulding, E. Educational structure and community transformation. *In* Wagschal, P. H. ed. Learning tomorrows p97-107

Braibanti, R. J. Context, cause, and change. *In* Prospects for constitutional democracy p165-82

Cohen, C. Revolutions and Copernican revolutions. *In* Science and society: past, present, and future p86-103

Dreitzel, H. P. On the political meaning of culture. *In* Beyond the crisis p83-129

Dubos, R. J. Revolutions and resurrection. *In* Dubos, R. J. Beast or angel? p161-67

Dubos, R. J. Yesterday's future shock. *In* Dubos, R. J. Beast or angel? p119-29

Elkind, D. Culture, change, and children. *In* Elkind, D. The child and society p3-16

Francoeur, R. T. Human nature and human relations. *In* Bundy, R. F. ed. Images of the future: the twenty-first century and beyond p125-34

Gluckman, M. New dimensions of change, conflict and settlement. *In* United Nations Educational, Scientific and Cultural Organization. Race, science and society p319-40

Goodman, F. D. Prognosis: a new religion? *In* Zaretsky, I. I. and Leone, M. P. eds. Religious movements in contemporary America p244-54

Huntington, S. P. Remarks on the meanings of stability in the modern era. *In* Radicalism in the contemporary age v3 p269-82

Inkeles, A. The future of individual modernity. *In* Major social issues p459-75

Inkeles, A. Understanding and misunderstanding individual modernity. *In* The Uses of controversy in sociology p103-30

Jackson, M. Broad societal changes. *In* Lauer, R. H ed. Social movements and social change p174-89

Johnson, H. M. Religion in social change and social evolution. *In* Johnson, H. M. ed. Religious change and continuity p313-39

Keniston, K. Psychological development and historical change. *In* Explorations in psychohistory p149-64

Keniston, K. Stranded in the present. *In* Kren, G. M. and Rappoport, L. H. eds. Varieties of psychohistory p251-56

Lagos Matus, G. The revolution of being. *In* On the creation of a just world order p71-109

Lauer, Q. Philosophy and social change. *In* Roth, R. J. ed. Person and community p 1-24

Lauer, R. H. Afterword: Summary and directives for the future. *In* Lauer, R. H. ed. Social movements and social change p259-64

Lauer, R. H. Introduction: Social movements and social change: the interrelationships. *In* Lauer, R. H. ed. Social movements and social change p xi-xxviii

Lipset, S. M. Social structure and social change. *In* Blau, P. M. ed. Approaches to the study of social structure p172-209

Lyman, S. M. The acceptance, rejection, and reconstruction of histories: on some controversies in the study of social and cultural change. *In* Brown, R. H. and Lyman, S. M. eds. Structure, consciousness, and history p53-105

Mazzeo, J. A. Interpretation, humanistic culture, and cultural change. *In* Mazzeo, J. A. Varieties of interpretation p95-128

Moscivici, S. The reenchantment of the world. *In* Beyond the crisis p133-68

Orr, D. W. Modernization and the ecological perspective. *In* Orr, D. W. and Soroos, M. S. eds. The global predicament p75-89

Parsons, T. Some theoretical considerations on the nature and trends of change of ethnicity. *In* Glazer, N. and Moynihan, D. P. eds. Ethnicity p53-83

Peckham, M. The cultural crisis of the 1970s. *In* Peckham, M. Romanticism and behavior p362-79

Perlman, M. L. Comments on explanation, and on stability and change. *In* Explanation of prehistoric change p319-33

Robson, J. M. Thoughts on social change and political accommodation in Victorian Britain. *In* Altholz, J. L. ed. The mind and art of Victorian England p78-93

Sakamoto, Y. Toward global identity. *In* On the creation of a just world order p189-210

Schlossberg, E. For my father. *In* About Bateson p145-67

Steward, J. H. Cultural evolution. *In* Steward, J. H. Evolution and ecology p58-67

Steward, J. H. Modernization in traditional societies. *In* Steward, J. H. Evolution and ecology p297-330

Taylor, B. K. Culture: whence, whither and why? *In* Alcock, A. E.; Taylor, B. K. and Welton, J. M. eds. The future of cultural minorities p9-29

Thrupp, S. L. Tradition and development: a choice of views. *In* Thrupp, S. L. Society and history p198-206

Touraine, A. Crisis or transformation? *In* Beyond the crisis p17-45

Touraine, A. Introduction. *In* Beyond the crisis p 3-13

Wallerstein, I. M. Modernization: requiescat in pace. *In* The Uses of controversy in sociology p131-35

Weizsäcker, C. F. Freiherr von. A sceptical contribution. *In* On the creation of a just world order p111-50

Yinger, J. M. Countercultures and social change. *In* Major social issues p476-97

See also Culture diffusion; Economic development—Social aspects; Industry—Social aspects; Revolution (Theology); Social Darwinism; Social evolution

Case studies

Ford, R. I. Evolutionary ecology and the evolution of human ecosystems: a case study from the Midwestern U.S.A. *In* Explanation of prehistoric change p153-84

Social change—Case studies—*Continued*

Glassow, M. A. Population aggregation and systemic change: examples from the American Southwest. *In* Explanation of prehistoric change p185-214

Sanders, W. T. Resource utilization and political evolution in the Teotihuacan Valley. *In* Explanation of prehistoric change p231-59

Saxe, A. A. On the origin of evolutionary processes: state formation in the Sandwich Islands, a systemic approach. *In* Explanation of prehistoric change p105-51

Mathematical models

Hill, J. N. Systems theory and the explanation of change. *In* Explanation of prehistoric change p59-103

Plog, F. Explaining change. *In* Explanation of prehistoric change p17-57

United States

Ahlstrom, S. E. Thought and social change: reflections on cultural studies. *In* Luedtke, L. S. ed. The study of American culture p63-75

Social change in literature

Cairns, C. Social change. *In* Cairns, C. Italian literature p91-128

Lucas, W. J. Mrs Gaskell and the nature of social change. *In* Lucas, W. J. The literature of change p 1-33

Stineback, D. C. Conclusion: The present situation. *In* Stineback, D. C. Shifting world p171-76

Social classes

Béteille, A. Race, caste and ethnic identity. *In* United Nations Educational, Scientific and Cultural Organization. Race, science and society p211-33

Davis, K. Mental hygiene and the class structure. *In* Davis, F. J. and Stivers, R. eds. The collective definition of deviance p99-113

Fisk, M. Academic freedom in class society. *In* The Concept of academic freedom p5-26

Kiernan, E. V. G. Nationalist movements and social classes. *In* Smith, A. D. ed. Nationalist movements p110-33

Parsons, T. Equality and inequality in modern society, or social stratification revisited. *In* Parsons, T. Social systems and the evolution of action theory p321-80

Touraine, A. Social identity and the formation of social movements. *In* Smithsonian Institution. The cultural drama p237-67

See also Elite (Social sciences); Middle classes; Students' socio-economic status; Upper classes

Historiography

Himmelfarb, G. Social history and the moral imagination. *In* Art, politics, and will p28-58

Chile

Roddick, J. F. Class structure and class politics in Chile. *In* O'Brien, P. J. ed. Allende's Chile p 1-26

England

Gorer, G. English identity over time and Empire. *In* Ethnic identity p156-72

France

Beer, W. R. The social class of ethnic activists in contemporary France. *In* Esman, M. J. ed. Ethnic conflict in the Western world p143-58

France—Faulquemont

Forster, R. The "world" between seigneur and peasant. *In* Studies in eighteenth-century culture v5 p401-21

France—Historiography

Rogozinski, J. Ennoblement by the Crown and social stratification in France, 1285-1322: a prosopographical survey. *In* Order and innovation in the Middle Ages p273-91

Great Britain—History

Supple, B. E. The governing framework: social class and institutional reform in Victorian Britain. *In* Lerner, L. ed. The Victorians p90-119

Thrupp, S. L. The problem of conservatism in fifteenth-century England. *In* Thrupp, S. L. Society and history p237-44

India

Berreman, G. D. Bazar behavior: social identity and social interaction in urban India. *In* Ethnic identity p71-105

Peru

Bourricaud, F. Indian, mestizo and cholo as symbols in the Peruvian system of stratification. *In* Glazer, N. and Moynihan, D. P. eds. Ethnicity p350-87

Russia

Bennett, H. A. Evolution of the meanings of chin: an introduction to the Russian institution of rank ordering and niche assignment from the time of Peter the Great's Table of Ranks to the Bolshevik Revolution. *In* California Slavic studies v10 p 1-43

South Africa

Butler, J. The significance of recent changes within the white ruling caste. *In* Thompson, L. M. and Butler, J. eds. Change in contemporary South Africa p79-103

Leftwich, A. The constitution and continuity of South African inequality: some conceptual questions. *In* Leftwich, A. ed. South Africa: economic growth and political change p125-85

Thailand—History

Akin Rabibhadana, M. R. Clientship and class structure in the Early Bangkok period. *In* Change and persistence in Thai society p93-123

United States

Rossi, P. H. Conventional wisdom, common sense, and empirical knowledge: the case of stratification research and views of American society. *In* The Uses of controversy in sociology p30-47

Social classes in literature

Friedman, A. B. "When Adam delved . . .": contexts of an historic proverb. *In* The Learned and the lewed p213-30

Kennard, J. E. Aristocrat versus commoner. *In* Kennard. J. E. Victims of convention p46-79

Miller, A. Tragedy and the common man. *In* Miller, A. The theater essays of Arthur Miller p 3-7

Milne, G. The beginnings. *In* Milne, G. The sense of society p19-42

Milne, G. Conclusion. *In* Milne, G. The sense of society p272-76

Milne, G. Edith Wharton. *In* Milne, G. The sense of society p116-49

Social evolution—*Continued*

Hamburg, D. A. Ancient man in the twentieth century. *In* Goodall, V. M. ed. The quest for man p27-54

Johnson, H. M. Religion in social change and social evolution. *In* Johnson, H. M. ed. Religious change and continuity p313-39

Lenski, G. E. Social structure in evolutionary perspective. *In* Blau, P. M. ed. Approaches to the study of social structure p135-53

Lévi-Strauss, C. Race and history. *In* United Nations Educational, Scientific and Cultural Organization. Race, science and society p95-134

Rieff, P. The triumph of the therapeutic; excerpt. *In* Davis, F. J. and Stivers, R. eds. The collected definition of deviance p392-410

Schwartz, T. Relations among generations in time-limited cultures. *In* Schwartz, T. ed. Socialization as cultural communication p217-30

Shimahara, N. K. American society, culture and socialization. *In* Social forces and schooling p49-81

Shimahara, N. K. Cultural evolution: technology. *In* Social forces and schooling p15-48

Steward, J. H. The concept and method of cultural ecology. *In* Steward, J. H. Evolution and ecology p43-57

Steward, J. H. Cultural evolution. *In* Steward, J. H. Evolution and ecology p58-67

Steward, J. H. Evolutionary principles and social types. *In* Steward, J. H. Evolution and ecology p68-86

See also Social change; Social Darwinism; Sociobiology

Social forecasting. See Social prediction

Social groups

Chance, M. R. A. Social cohesion and the structure of attention. *In* Biosocial anthropology p93-113

Dubos, R. J. Individualism and collectivity. *In* Dubos, R. J. Beast or angel? p51-60

Isaacs, H. R. Basic group identity: the idols of the tribe. *In* Glazer, N. and Moynihan, D. P. eds. Ethnicity p29-52

See also Age groups; Decision-making, Group; Elite (Social sciences); Leadership; Reference groups; Social isolation; Social mobility; Social participation; Social psychology; Social values; Subculture

Social history

Fuller, R. B. Learning tomorrows: education for a changing world. *In* Wagschal, P. H. ed. Learning tomorrows p 1-26

Himmelfarb, G. Social history and the moral imagination. *In* Art, politics, and will p28-58

Rosenberg, C. E. Introduction: History and experience. *In* Rosenberg, C. E. ed. The family in history p 1-11

See also Economic development—Social aspects; Labor and laboring classes; Social mobility; Social policy; Social problems; Social stability; Technology and civilization; Urbanization; and subdivision Social conditions under names of countries, cities, e.g. Europe—Social conditions

Methodology

Fischer, D. H. The braided narrative: substance and form in social history. *In* Fletcher, A. J. S. ed. The literature of fact p109-33

Medieval, 500-1500

Coleman, E. R. Infanticide in the early Middle Ages. *In* Stuard, S. M. ed. Women in medieval society p47-70

Herlihy, D. The generation in medieval history. *In* Viator: medieval and Renaissance studies v5 p347-64

Herlihy, D. Land, family, and women in continental Europe, 701-1200. *In* Stuard, S. M. ed. Women in medieval society p13-45

Le Goff, J. The usurer and Purgatory. *In* The Dawn of modern banking p25-52

Sabean, D. W. Aspects of kinship behaviour and property in rural Western Europe before 1800. *In* Family and inheritance p96-111

Thrupp, S. L. The dynamics of medieval society. *In* Thrupp, S. L. Society and history p44-60

Modern, 1500-

See Mass society

1945-

Cowen, Z. The way we live now. *In* Prospects for constitutional democracy p3-20

Social indicators. See Social prediction

Social institutions

See also Social structure

Great Britain

Supple, B. E. The governing framework: social class and institutional reform in Victorian Britain. *In* Lerner, L. ed. The Victorians p90-119

United States

Berger, P. L. In praise of particularity: the concept of mediating structures. *In* An Almost chosen people p107-18

Social integration

Dubos, R. J. The clan and the stranger *In* Dubos, R. J. Beast or angel? p83-91

Fortes, M. The plural society in Africa. *In* Leftwich, A. ed. South Africa: economic growth and political change p 1-27

Social interaction

Alexander, R. D. Sexuality and sociality in humans and other primates. *In* Katchadourian, H. A. ed. Human sexuality p81-97

Coleman, J. S. Social structure and a theory of action. *In* Blau, P. M. ed. Approaches to the study of social structure p76-93

Feinman, S. Biosociological approaches to social behavior. *In* McNall, S. G. ed. Theoretical perspectives in sociology p399-413

Fox, K. A. Combining economic and noneconomic objectives in development planning: problems of concept and measurement. *In* Economic development and planning p104-41

Gusfield, J. R. The sociological reality of America: an essay on mass culture. *In* On the making of Americans p41-62

Harré, R. Architectonic man: on the structuring of lived experience. *In* Brown, R. H. and Lyman, S. M. eds. Structure, consciousness, and history p139-72

Hingers, R. H. and Willer, D. Prevailing postulates of social exchange theory. *In* McNall, S. G. ed. Theoretical perspectives in sociology p169-86

Lewis, M. and Lee-Painter, S. The origin of interactions: methodological issues. *In* Riegel, K. F. and Rosenwald, G. C. eds. Structure and transformation p119-31

Social mobility

Thrupp, S. L. Hierarchy, illusion, and social mobility. *In* Thrupp, S. L. Society and history p25-28

See also Social classes

United States

Ginzberg, E. Jew and Negro: notes on the mobility of two minority groups in the United States. *In* Salo Wittmayer Baron v 1 p491-501

Social movements

Lauer, R. H. Afterword: Summary and directions for the future. *In* Lauer, R. H. ed. Social movements and social change p259-64

Lauer, R. H. Introduction: Social movements and social change: the interrelationships. *In* Lauer, R. H. ed. Social movements and social change p xi-xxviii

Rosen, G. An analgesic strategy. *In* Lauer, R. H. ed. Social movements and social change p97-106

Touraine, A. Social identity and the formation of social movements. *In* Smithsonian Institution. The cultural drama p237-67

Europe

Tucker, R. C. The perils of success—deradicalization. *In* Lauer, R. H. ed. Social movements and social change p227-55

United States

Laue, J. H. Unanticipated change. *In* Lauer, R. H. ed. Social movements and social change p190-96

Lauer, R. H. Determinants of type of strategy. *In* Lauer, R. H. ed. Social movements and social change p85-96

Lebra, T. S. Social psychological change. *In* Lauer, R. H. ed. Social movements and social change p127-43

Social participation

Barfield, O. Participation and isolation: a fresh light on present discontents. *In* Barfield, O. The rediscovery of meaning, and other essays p201-16

See also Political participation; Social groups

Social perception. See Sexism

Social planning. See Social policy

Social policy

Dubos, R. J. Creative adaptations to the future. *In* Aspects of American liberty p162-73

Fox, K. A. Combining economic and noneconomic objectives in development planning: problems of concept and measurement. *In* Economic development and planning p104-41

Keller, S. I. The planning of communities: anticipations and hindsights. *In* The Idea of social structure p283-99

Schon, D. A. Generative metaphor: a perspective on problem-setting in social policy. *In* Ortony, A. ed. Metaphor and thought p254-83

Sternberg, R. J.; Tourangeau, R. and Nigro, G. Metaphor, induction, and social policy: the convergence of macroscopic and microscopic views. *In* Ortony, A. ed. Metaphor and thought p325-53

See also Economic policy; Education and state; Family policy; Housing policy; Population policy; Social action; Welfare economics; also subdivision Social policy under names of countries, states, cities, etc.

Social prediction

Hesburgh, T. M. Problems and opportunities on a very interdependent planet. *In* Hesburgh, T. M. The Hesburgh papers p196-206

Randers, J. and Behrens, W. Watch for the foothills: signaling the end to growth in a finite world. *In* Orr, D. W. and Soroos, M. S. eds. The global predicament p18-38

Raskin, M. G. Futurology and its radical critique. *In* Radicalism in the contemporary age v2 p155-73

Social problems

Brown, L. R. Issues of human welfare. *In* Bundy, R. F. ed. Images of the future: the twenty-first century and beyond p81-95

Bundy, R. F. Up the downward path: the futures movement and the social imagination. *In* Bundy, R. F. ed. Images of the future: the twenty-first century and beyond p66-77

Harding, S. G. Feminism: reform or revolution? *In* Gould, C. C. and Wartofsky, M. W. eds. Women and philosophy p271-84

Held, V. Marx, sex, and the transformation of society. *In* Gould, C. C. and Wartofsky, M. W. eds. Women and philosophy p168-84

Short, J. F. Gangs, politics, and the social order. *In* Delinquency, crime, and society p129-63

Supple, B. E. The governing framework: social class and institutional reform in Victorian Britain. *In* Lerner, L. ed. The Victorians p90-119

Touraine, A. Crisis or transformation? *In* Beyond the crisis p17-45

Touraine, A. Introduction. *In* Beyond the crisis p3-13

See also Children—Employment; Crime and criminals; Delinquents; Divorce; Eugenics; Juvenile delinquency; Liquor problem; Poor; Progress; Public welfare; Race discrimination; Race relations; Reconstruction (1914-1939); Social action; Social ethics; Suicide; Technology and civilization

Social problems and the church. See Church and social problems

Social problems in education. See Educational sociology

Social problems in literature

Colmer, J. The writer as critic of society. *In* Colmer, J. Coleridge to Catch-22 p 1-17

Davis, E. R. Dickens and significant tradition. *In* Dickens Studies Annual v7 p49-67

Melling, P. American popular culture in the thirties: ideology, myth, genre. *In* Bigsby, C. W. E. ed. Approaches to popular culture p241-63

Miller, A. On social plays. *In* Miller, A. The theater essays of Arthur Miller p51-68

Nicoll, A. Realism, social and otherwise. *In* Nicoll, A. World drama p689-710

Poggioli, R. Naboth's vineyard: the pastoral view of the social order. *In* Poggioli, R The oaten flute p194-219

Supple, B. E. Material development: the condition of England 1830-1860. *In* Lerner, L. ed. The Victorians p49-69

Tillotson, G. 'Earnestness.' *In* Tillotson, G. A view of Victorian literature p23-54

Welty, E. Must the novelist crusade? *In* Welty, E. The eye of the story p146-58

See also Labor and laboring classes in literature

Social progress. See Progress

Social psychiatry

Simon, B. The psychoanalytic and social psychiatric models. *In* Simon, B. Mind and madness in ancient Greece p271-89

See also Psychotherapy—Social aspects; Therapeutic community

United States

Sabshin. M. Social-community approaches in psychiatry. *In* American psychiatry: past, present, and future p78-93

Social psychology

Bay, C. Essay 7. *In* Fitzgerald, R. ed. What it means to be human p128-41

Bettelheim, B. Individual and mass behavior in extreme situations. *In* Bettelheim, B. Surviving, and other essays p48-83

Butterfield, Sir H. Global good and evil: the moderate cupidity of Everyman. *In* [Truth and tragedy]: a tribute to Hans Morgenthau p199-202

Foramitti, H. and Piperek, M. Anxieties of city dwellers. *In* United Nations Educational, Scientific and Cultural Organization. The conservation of cities p43-56

Francoeur, R. T. Human nature and human relations. *In* Bundy, R. F. ed. Images of the future: the twenty-first century and beyond p125-34

Hamburg, D. A. Ancient man in the twentieth century. *In* Goodall, V. M. ed. The quest for man p27-54

Janis, I. L. Groupthink among policy makers. *In* Kren, G. M. and Rappoport, L. H. eds. Varieties of psychohistory p315-29

Koestler, A. Ad majorem gloriam. . . . *In* Koestler, A. Janus p77-97

Petti, P. Rational man theory. *In* Hookway, C. and Pettit, P. eds. Action and interpretation p43-63

Ryan, A. Maximising, moralising and dramatising. *In* Hookway, C. and Pettit, P. eds. Action and interpretation p65-81

Sennett, R. Destructive Gemeinschaft. *In* Beyond the crisis p171-97

Smith, M. B. Metapsychology, politics, and human needs. *In* Fitzgerald, R. ed. Human needs and politics p124-41

Touraine, A. The raison d'être of a sociology of action. *In* Giddens, A. ed. Positivism and sociology p115-27

Touraine, A. Towards a sociology of action. *In* Giddens, A. ed. Positivism and sociology p75-100

White, L. T. Death and the Devil. *In* The Darker vision of the Renaissance p25-46

Williams, R. M. Relative deprivation. *In* The Idea of social structure p355-78

See also Alienation (Social psychology); Attitude (Psychology); Discrimination; Emigration and immigration—Psychological aspects; Ethnopsychology; Exchange theory (Sociology); Leadership; Organizational behavior; Political psychology; Prison psychology; Public opinion; Social adjustment; Social interaction; Social movements; Social psychiatry; Social role; Stereotype (Psychology); Symbolic interactionism; Violence

Experiments

Koestler, A. Ad majorem gloriam. . . . *In* Koestler, A. Janus p77-97

History

Fancher, R. E. Early hypnotists and the psychology of social influence. *In* Fancher, R. E. Pioneers of psychology p170-204

Social reform. See Social problems

Social reformers

Spain

Zavala, I. M. Dreams of reality: enlightened hopes for an unattainable Spain. *In* Studies in eighteenth-century culture v6 p459-70

Social research. See Social science research

Social Research, inc., Chicago

Gardner, B. B. Doing business with management. *In* Eddy, E. M. and Partridge, W. L. eds. Applied anthropology in America p245-60

Social role

Coser, R. L. The complexity of roles as a seedbed of individual autonomy. *In* The Idea of social structure p237-63

DeVos, G. A. Selective permeability and reference group sanctioning: psychocultural continuities in role degradation. *In* Major social issues p7-24

Hollis, M. My role and its duties. *In* Royal Institute of Philosophy. Nature and conduct p180-99

McCall, G. J. The social looking-glass: a sociological perspective on self-development. *In* Mischel, T. ed. The self p274-87

Parsons, T. The sick role and the role of the physician reconsidered. *In* Parsons, T. Action theory and the human condition p17-34

Shapiro, J. Cross-cultural perspectives on sexual differentiation. *In* Katchadourian, H. A. ed. Human sexuality p269-308

See also Sex role

Social science. See Social sciences; Sociology

Social science research

Claude, R. P. Comparative rights research: some intersections between law and the social sciences. *In* Claude, R. P. ed. Comparative human rights p382-407

Hamilton, R. F. Old issues and new directions for research. *In* The Uses of controversy in sociology p95-99

See also Sociological research

Latin America

Cowgill, G. L. Archaeology. *In* Quantitative social science research on Latin America p103-31

Portes, A. Sociology and the use of secondary data. *In* Quantitative social science research on Latin America p208-70

Smith, P. H. History. *In* Quantitative social science research on Latin America p14-61

Southern States

Grantham, D. W. The regional imagination: social scientists and the American South. *In* Grantham, D. W. The regional imagination p153-84

United States

Friedman, R. C. and Friedman, R. S. Social and behavioral sciences in the 1970s. *In* Land-grant universities and their continuing challenge p160-77

Gardner, B. B. Doing business with management. *In* Eddy, E. M. and Partridge, W. L. eds. Applied anthropology in America p245-60

Social Science Research Council. Committee on Historical Analysis

About individual works

Generalization in the writing of history

Thrupp, S. L. Some historians on generalization. *In* Thrupp, S. L. Society and history p269-73

Social sciences

Dunn, J. Practising history and social science on 'realist' assumptions. *In* Hookway, C. and Pettit, P. eds. Action and interpretation p145-75

Gellner, E. A. The new idealism—cause and meaning in the social sciences. *In* Giddens, A. ed. Positivism and sociology p129-56

Hesburgh, T. M. Social science in an age of social revolution. *In* Hesburgh, T. M. The Hesburgh papers p101-12

Hesse, M. B. Theory and value in the social sciences. *In* Hookway, C. and Pettit, P. eds. Action and interpretation p 1-16

Misgeld, D. Critical theory and hermeneutics: the debate between Habermas and Gadamer. *In* O'Neill, J. ed. On critical theory p164-83

Morgan, B. Theology in the context of the social sciences. *In* The Context of contemporary theology p157-70

Novotny, H. R. F. The logic of the social sciences: to be, to do, or to describe? *In* Hook, S.; Kurtz, P. W. and Todorovich, M. eds. The philosophy of the curriculum: the need for general education p235-46

Ross, D. The development of the social sciences. *In* Oleson, A. and Voss, J. eds. The organization of knowledge in modern America, 1860-1920 p107-38

Thrupp, S. L. Editorial from the first issue of Comparative Studies in Society and History. *In* Thrupp, S. L. Society and history p328-31

Wallerstein, I. M. A world-system perspective on the social sciences. *In* McNall, S. G. ed. Theoretical perspectives in sociology p40-50

Wilson, H. T. Science, critique, and criticism: the "open society" revisited. *In* O'Neill, J. ed. On critical theory p205-30

Wood, G. S. Intellectual history and the social sciences. *In* Higham, J. and Conkin, P. K. eds. New directions in American intellectual history p27-41

See also Civics; Conservatism; Cross-cultural studies; Human behavior; Pluralism (Social sciences); Power (Social sciences); Social change; Statics and dynamics (Social sciences)

Comparative studies

Parsons, T. Comparative studies and evolutionary change. *In* Parsons, T. Social systems and the evolution of action theory p279-320

Field work

Johnson, J. M. Behind the rational appearances: fusion of thinking and feeling in sociological research. *In* Douglas, J. D. and Johnson, J. M. [eds.] Existential sociology p201-28

See also Anthropology—Field work

History

Featherstone, J. John Dewey and David Riesman: from the lost individual to the lonely crowd. *In* On the making of Americans p3-39

Stone, L. History and the social sciences in the twentieth century. *In* The Future of history p3-42

History—Poland

Bauman, Z. East European and Soviet social science: a case study in stimulus diffusion. *In* Szporluk, R. ed. The influence of East Europe and the Soviet West on the USSR p91-116

History—Russia

Bauman, Z. East European and Soviet social science: a case study in stimulus diffusion. *In* Szporluk, R. ed. The influence of East Europe and the Soviet West on the USSR p91-116

Solomon, S. G. Rural scholars and the cultural revolution. *In* Cultural revolution in Russia, 1928-1931 p129-53

Methodology

Lyman, S. M. The acceptance, rejection, and reconstruction of histories: on some controversies in the study of social and cultural change. *In* Brown, R. H. and Lyman, S. M. eds. Structure, consciousness, and history p53-105

Nevins, A. Advances in the social sciences. *In* Nevins, A. Allan Nevins on history p151-57

Nevins, A. The old history and the new. *In* Nevins, A. Allan Nevins on history p181-202

Shenfield, A. A. Scientism and the study of society. *In* Essays on Hayek p61-72

See also Social sciences—Field work

Research

See Social science research

Simulation methods

Plog, F. Systems theory and simulation: the case of Hawaiian warfare and redistribution. *In* Explanation of prehistoric change p259-318

Study and teaching

Bartley, R. L. A role for social science? *In* Hook, S.; Kurtz, P. W. and Todorovich, M. eds. The philosophy of the curriculum: the need for general education p169-73

Glazer, N. The social sciences in liberal education. *In* Hook, S.; Kurtz, P. W. and Todorovich, M. eds. The philosophy of the curriculum: the need for general education p145-58

Gross, F. Thoughts on a social-science curriculum. *In* Hook, S.; Kurtz, P. W. and Todorovich, M. eds. The philosophy of the curriculum: the need for general education p261-73

Issawi, C. P. The economist among the social scientists. *In* Hook, S.; Kurtz, P. W. and Todorovich, M. eds. The philosophy of the curriculum: the need for general education p159-64

Sowell, T. Social science and general education. *In* Hook, S.; Kurtz, P. W. and Todorovich, M. eds. The philosophy of the curriculum: the need for general education p165-68

Study and teaching—United States

Friedman, R. C. and Friedman, R. S. Social and behavioral sciences in the 1970s. *In* Land-grant universities and their continuing challenge p160-77

Social structure—*Continued*

Stinchcombe, A. L. Merton's theory of social structure. *In* The Idea of social structure p11-33

Wallace, W. L. Structure and action in the theories of Coleman and Parsons. *In* Blau, P. M. ed. Approaches to the study of social structure p121-34

Wright, C. R. Social structure and mass communications behavior: exploring patterns through constructional analysis. *In* The Idea of social structure p379-413

See also Social institutions

Case studies

Aiken, M. T. Urban social structure and political competition: a comparative study of local politics in four European nations. *In* Walton, J. and Masotti, L. H. eds. The city in comparative perspective p119-53

Social studies. See Social sciences

Social systems

Baumgartner, T.; Burns, T. R. and De-Villé, P. R. Actors, games, and systems: the dialectics of social action and system structuring. *In* McNall, S. G. ed. Theoretical perspectives in sociology p128-48

Dupree, A. H. Biological and social theories—a new opportunity for a union of systems. *In* Science and society: past, present, and future p136-74

Parsons, T. Social systems. *In* Parsons, T. Social systems and the evolution of action theory p177-203

Scott, A. M. The logic of international interaction. *In* Orr, D. W. and Soroos, M. S. eds. The global predicament 284-307

Sixel, F. W. The problem of sense: Habermas v. Luhmann. *In* O'Neill, J. ed. On critical theory p184-204

See also Social institutions

Social values

Bronowski, J. The human values. *In* Bronowski, J. A sense of the future p206-10

Bronowski, J. The values of science. *In* Bronowski, J. A sense of the future p211-20

Brown, P. G. and Corfman, E. L. Moral-political values: an historical analysis. *In* Population policy and ethics p55-126

Czudnowski, M. M. Aspiring and established politicians: the structure of value systems and role profiles. *In* Eulau, H. and Czudnowski, M. M. eds. Elite recruitment in democratic polities p45-78

Edgar, H. S. and Greenawalt, R. K. The legal tradition. *In* Population policy and ethics p127-66

Golding, M. P. Security/survival. *In* Population policy and ethics p47-52

Munro, D. J. The shape of Chinese values in the eye of an American philosopher. *In* Terrill, R. ed. The China difference p37-56

Self, P. Techniques and values in policy decisions. *In* Royal Institute of Philosophy. Nature and conduct p298-312

Social welfare. See Charities; Public welfare; Social service

Social work. See Social service

Social work research. See Social service—Research

Social work with Afro-Americans. See Afro-Americans—Social work with

Social work with delinquents and criminals

United States

Glaser, D. Marginal workers: some antecedents and implications of an idea from Shaw and McKay. *In* Delinquency, crime, and society p254-66

Krisberg, B. A. The gang and the community: the case of the urban leadership training program. *In* Riedel, M. and Chappell, D. eds. Issues in criminal justice: planning and evaluation p99-113

Social work with juvenile delinquents. See Social work with delinquents and criminals

Social workers

Johnson, J. M. Occasioned transcendence. *In* Douglas, J. D. and Johnson, J. M. [eds.] Existential sociology p229-53

Socialdemo Kratiska Arbetarepartier

Martin, A. The dynamics of change in a Keynesian political economy: the Swedish case and its implications. *In* Crouch, C. ed. State and economy in contemporary capitalism p88-121

Socialism

Bialer, S. The resurgence and changing nature of the Left in industrialized democracies. *In* Radicalism in the contemporary age v3 p3-81

Birnbaum, N. On the possibility of a new politics in the West. *In* Beyond the crisis p201-32

Buckley, W. F. The road to serfdom: the intellectuals and socialism. *In* Essays on Hayek p95-106

Chadwick, O. Karl Marx. *In* Chadwick, O. The secularization of the European mind in the nineteenth century p48-87

Dallin, A. Retreat from optimism: on Marxian models of revolution. *In* Radicalism in the contemporary age v 3 p117-57

Grassi, E. Marxism, humanism, and the problem of imagination in Vico's works. *In* Giambattista Vico's science of humanity p275-94

Heller, A. Theory and practice from the point of view of human needs. *In* The Humanisation of socialism p58-75

Kristol, I. Socialism: obituary for an idea. *In* Tyrrell, R. E. ed. The future that doesn't work p186-99

Lipset, S. M. Why no socialism in the United States? *In* Radicalism in the contemporary age v 1 p31-149

Markus, M. and Hegedüs, A. Community and individuality. *In* The Humanisation of socialism p91-105

Markus, M. and Hegedüs, A. Tendencies in Marxist sociology in the Socialist countries. *In* The Humanisation of socialism p124-39

Ricoeur, P. Socialism today. *In* Ricoeur, P. Political and social essays p229-42

Shafarevich, I. R. Socialism in our past and future. *In* From under the rubble p26-66

Supek, R. The visible hand and the degradation of individuality. *In* Beyond the crisis p49-80

Voegelin, E. Marx: The genesis of gnostic socialism. *In* Voegelin, E. From Enlightenment to revolution p273-302

Wartofsky, M. W. Consciousness, praxis, and reality: Marxism vs. phenomenology. *In* Elliston, F. A. and McCormick, P. eds. Husserl p304-13

Socialism—*Continued*

Watson, G. Race and the Socialists. *In* Watson, G. Politics and literature in modern Britain p120-34

See also Communism; Dialectical materialism; Equality; Individualism; Industry and state; Marxian economics; National socialism; Utopias; Women and socialism

Psychological aspects

Lane, R. E. Capitalist man, Socialist man. *In* Laslett, P. and Fishkin, J. eds. Philosophy politics and society p57-77

Socialism, Christian

Gollwitzer, H. Kingdom of God and socialism in the theology of Karl Barth. *In* Hunsinger, G. ed. Karl Barth and radical politics p77-120

Hendrickson, K. E. Tribune of the people: George R. Lunn and the rise and fall of Christian Socialism in Schenectady. *In* Stave, B. M. ed. Socialism and the cities p72-98

Marquardt, F. W. Socialism in the theology of Karl Barth. *In* Hunsinger, G. ed. Karl Barth and radical politics p47-76

Socialism and art

Kunzle, D. Art of the new Chile: mural, poster, and comic book in a "revolutionary process." *In* Millon, H. A. and Nochlin, L. eds. Art and architecture in the service of politics p356-81

See also Socialist realism in art

Socialism and Catholic Church. See Communism and Christianity—Catholic Church

Socialism and Islam

Shamir, S. Arab socialism and Egyptian-Islamic tradition. *In* Eisenstadt, S. N. and Azmon, Y. eds. Socialism and tradition p193-218

Socialism and law. See Law and socialism

Socialism and literature. See Communism and literature

Socialism and nationalism. See Nationalism and socialism

Socialism and women. See Women and socialism

Socialism in Africa

Chazan, N. Myths and realities in African socialism. *In* Eisenstadt, S. N. and Azmon, Y. eds. Socialism and tradition p141-71

Socialism in Arab countries

Shamir, S. Arab socialism and Egyptian-Islamic tradition. *In* Eisenstadt, S. N. and Azmon, Y. eds. Socialism and tradition p193-218

Socialism in Burma

Rudner, M. Traditionalism and socialism in Burma's political development. *In* Eisenstadt, S. N. and Azmon, Y. eds. Socialism and tradition p105-39

Socialism in Chile

Gonzalez, M. Ideology and culture under Popular Unity. *In* O'Brien, P. J. ed. Allende's Chile p106-27

Kay, C. Agrarian reform and the transition to socialism. *In* O'Brien, P. J. ed. Allende's Chile p79-105

Socialism in Egypt

Shamir, S. Arab socialism and Egyptian-Islamic tradition. *In* Eisenstadt, S. N. and Azmon, Y. eds. Socialism and tradition p193-218

Socialism in Europe

Hegedüs, A. The self-criticism of Socialist society: a reality and necessity. *In* The Humanisation of socialism p161-75

Socialism in Ghana

Chazan, N. Nkrumaism: Ghana's experiment with African socialism. *In* Eisenstadt, S. N. and Azmon, Y. eds. Socialism and tradition p173-92

Socialism in Great Britain

Holland, S. Keynes and the Socialists. *In* Skidelsky, R. J. A. ed. The end of the Keynesian era p67-77

Welch, C. Intellectuals have consequences. *In* Tyrrell, R. E. ed. The future that doesn't work p42-63

Williamson, A. Ruskin and Morris: the Socialist legacy. *In* Williamson, A. Artists and writers in revolt p103-31

Socialism in Hungary

Markus, M. and Hegedüs, A. The role of values in the long-range planning of distribution and consumption. *In* The Humanisation of socialism p140-60

Socialism in Russia

Yakubovich, M. P. From the history of ideas. *In* Medvedev, R. A. ed. The Samizdat register p147-202

Socialism in the Netherlands

Searing, H. With red flags flying: housing in Amsterdam, 1915-1923. *In* Millon, H. A. and Nochlin, L. eds. Art and architecture in the service of politics p230-69

Socialism in the United States

Lipset, S. M. Why no socialism in the United States? *In* Radicalism in the contemporary age v 1 p31-149

Socialist ethics. See Communist ethics

Socialist Labour Party

Canada—Toronto

O'Toole. R. Sectarianism in politics: case studies of Maoists and De Leonists. *In* Wallis, R. ed. Sectarianism p162-89

Socialist Party (U.S.)

History

Burbank, G. Socialism in an Oklahoma boom-town: "Milwaukeeizing" Oklahoma City. *In* Stave, B. M. ed. Socialism and the cities p99-115

Ebner, M. H. Socialism and progressive political reform: the 1911 change-of-government in Passaic. *In* Stave, B. M. ed. Socialism and the cities p116-40

Green, J. R. The "salesmen-soldiers" of the "appeal army": a profile of rank-and-file Socialist agitators. *In* Stave, B. M. ed. Socialism and the cities p13-40

Hendrickson, K. E. Tribune of the people: George R. Lunn and the rise and fall of Christian Socialism in Schenectady. *In* Stave. B. M. ed. Socialism and the cities p72-98

Miller, S. M. Milwaukee: of ethnicity and labor. *In* Stave, B. M. ed. Socialism and the cities p41-71

Pratt, W. C. "Jimmie Higgins" and the Reading Socialist community: an exploration of the Socialist rank and file. *In* Stave, B. M. ed. Socialism and the cities p141-56

Stave, B. M. The Great Depression and urban political continuity: Bridgeport chooses socialism. *In* Stave, B. M. ed. Socialism and the cities p157-83

Socialist realism in art

Russia

Bowlt, J. E. Art and architecture in Soviet Russia, 1917-1972. *In* Auty, R. and Obolensky, D. eds. An introduction to Russian art and architecture p145-72

Socialist Revolutionaries. See Partiia Sofsialistov-revoliutsionerov

Socialization

Bateson, G. Some components of socialization for trance. *In* Schwartz, T. ed. Socialization as cultural communication p51-63

Devereux, G. Time: history versus chronicle; socialization as cultural preexperience. *In* Schwartz, T. ed. Socialization as cultural communication p189-200

Langness, L. L. Margaret Mead and the study of socialization. *In* Schwartz, T. ed. Socialization as cultural communication p5-20

Lebra, T. S. Social psychological change. *In* Lauer, R. H. ed. Social movements and social change p127-43

Levy, R. I. Tahitian gentleness and redundant controls. *In* Montague, A. ed. Learning non-aggression p222-35

Schafer, W. E. Sport and youth counterculture: contrasting socialization themes. *In* Social problems in athletics p183-200

Shimahara, N. K. American society, culture and socialization. *In* Social forces and schooling p49-81

Spady, W. G. A commentary on sport and the New Left. *In* Social problems in athletics p212-23

Spring, J. H. The American high school and the development of social character. *In* Feinberg, W. and Rosemont, H. eds. Work, technology, and education p41-59

See also Cognition and culture; Personality and culture; Political socialization; Professional socialization

Socialization, Political. See Political socialization

Socialized medicine. See Medicine, State

Socially handicapped

Education (Higher)—United States

Rich, A. C. Teaching language in open admissions. *In* Rich, A. C. On lies, secrets, and silence p51-68

Socially handicapped children

Elkind, D. Borderline retardation in low- and middle-income adolescents. *In* Elkind, D. The child and society p175-201

Education (Preschool)—United States

Bronfenbrenner, U. Is early intervention effective? Some studies of early education in familial and extra-familial settings. *In* Montagu, A. ed. Race and IQ p287-322

New York (City)

Cole, L. Kill each other, be killed, kill yourself; excerpt from "Street kids." *In* Gross, B. and Gross, R. eds. The children's rights movement p74-78

Societies. See Agricultural societies; Technical societies

Societies, Benefit. See Friendly societies

Society, Primitive

Steward, J. H. Determinism in primitive society? *In* Steward, J. H. Evolution and ecology p180-87

Washburn, W. E. The clash of morality in the American forest. *In* First images of America p355-50

Webb, M. C. The flag follows trade: an essay on the necessary interaction of military and commercial factors in state formation. *In* Ancient civilization and trade p155-209

See also Agriculture, Primitive; Art, Primitive; Economics, Primitive; Government, Primitive; Man, Prehistoric; Music, Primitive; Religion, Primitive; Totemism; Tribal government; Tribes and tribal system

Society and architecture. See Architecture and society

Society and art. See Art and society

Society and communism. See Communism and society

Society and education. See Educational sociology

Society and energy policy. See Energy policy —Social aspects

Society and euthanasia. See Euthanasia— Social aspects

Society and language. See Sociolinguistics

Society and law. See Sociological jurisprudence

Society and libraries. See Libraries and society

Society and literature. See Literature and society

Society and religion. See Religion and sociology

Society and telecommunication. See Telecommunication—Social aspects

Society and the arts. See Arts and society

Society and the church. See Church and the world

Society and the telephone. See Telephone— Social aspects

Society and war. See War and society

Society for the Liberation of Religion from State Patronage and Control
Thompson, D. M. The Liberation Society, 1844-1868. *In* Hollis, P. ed. Pressure from without p210-38

Society of Jesus. See Jesuits

Society of Modern Architects
Starr, S. F. OSA: the union of contemporary architects. *In* Gibian, G. and Tjalsma, H. W. eds. Russian modernism p188-208

Socinianism
Williams, G. H. The Sarmatian myth sublimated in the Historia Reformationis Polonicae (1664/1685) of Stanislas Lubieniecki and related documents. *In* For Wiktor Weintraub p571-83

Sociobiology
Alper, J. S. Ethical and social implications. *In* Sociobiology and human nature p195-212

Barash, D. P. Evolution as a paradigm for behavior. *In* Sociobiology and human nature. p13-32

Beach, F. A. Sociobiology and interspecific comparisons of behavior. *In* Sociobiology and human nature p116-35

Boulding, K. E. Sociobiology or biosociology? *In* Sociobiology and human nature p260-76

Sociobiology—*Continued*

Feinman, S. Biosociological approaches to social behavior. *In* McNall, S. G. ed. Theoretical perspectives in sociology p399-413

Fuller, J. L. Genes, brains, and behavior. *In* Sociobiology and human nature p98-115

Green, P. J.; Morgan, C. J. and Barash, D. P. Sociobiology. *In* McNall, S. G. ed. Theoretical perspectives in sociology p414-30

Gregory, M. S. Epilogue. *In* Sociobiology and human nature p283-94

Grene, M. G. Sociobiology and the human mind. *In* Sociobiology and human nature p213-24

Hardin, G. J. Nice guys finish last. *In* Sociobiology and human nature p183-94

Holton, G. J. The new synthesis? *In* Sociobiology and human nature p75-97

Hull, D. L. Scientific bandwagon or traveling medicine show? *In* Sociobiology and human nature p136-63

Schneewind, J. B. Sociobiology, social policy, and Nirvana. *In* Sociobiology and human nature p225-39

Searle, J. R. Sociobiology and the explanation of behavior. *In* Sociobiology and human nature p164-82

Van den Berghe, P. L. Bridging the paradigms: biology and the social sciences. *In* Sociobiology and human nature p33-52

Washburn, S. L. Animal behavior and social anthropology. *In* Sociobiology and human nature p53-74

Wilson, E. O. Introduction: what is sociobiology? *In* Sociobiology and human nature p 1-12

Socio-economic status of students. See Students' socio-economic status

Socio-economic status of teachers. See Teachers' socio-economic status

Sociolinguistics

Achebe, C. Language and the destiny of man. *In* Achebe, C. Morning yet on creation day p47-59

Allen, H. B. The Linguistic atlas of the Upper Midwest as a source of sociolinguistic information. *In* James B. McMillan: essays in linguistics by his friends and colleagues p3-19

Capey, A. C. The language of enlightenment. *In* Abbs, P. ed. The black rainbow p92-113

Crystal, D. The problem of language variety: an example from religious language. *In* Royal Institute of Philosophy. Communication and understanding p195-207

Elliott, M. S. Respecting our organs. *In* Gold, J. ed. In the name of language! p161-204

Ervin-Tripp, S. M. Speech acts and social learning. *In* Basso, K. H. and Selby, H. A. eds. Meaning in anthropology p123-53

Ferguson, C. A. Language problems of variaion and repertoire. *In* Bloomfield, M. W. and Haugen, E. I. eds. Language as a human problem p23-32

Fishman, J. A. The sociology of language: yesterday, today, and tomorrow. *In* Current issues in linguistic theory p51-75

Greenblatt, S. J. Learning to curse: aspects of linguistic colonialism in the sixteenth century. *In* First images of America p561-80

Halliday, M. A. K. Talking one's way in. *In* Davies, A. ed. Problems of language and learning p8-33

Hays, D. G. Language and interpersonal relationships. *In* Bloomfield, M. W. and Haugen, E. I. eds. Language as a human problem p205-18

Lakoff, R. Language and society. *In* Wardhaugh, R. and Brown, H. D. eds. A survey of applied linguistics p207-28

Malkiel, Y. Changes in the European languages under a new set of sociolinguistic circumstances. *In* First images of America p581-93

Siertsema, B. Linguistic de-stigmatization? *In* On language, culture, and religion: in honor of Eugene A. Nida p315-36

Speitel, H. H. Dialect. *In* Davies, A. ed. Problems of language and learning p34-60

Teeter, K. V. Linguistics and anthropology. *In* Bloomfield, M. W. and Haugen, E. I. eds. Language as a human problem p73-84

See also Linguistic change; Literature and society

Sociological jurisprudence

Kamenka, E. and Tay, A. E. S. Beyond bourgeois individualism: the contemporary crisis and legal ideology. *In* Kamenka, E. and Neale, R. S. eds. Feudalism, capitalism and beyond p126-44

Morison, W. L. Frames of reference for legal ideals. *In* Law and society p18-47

Riley, D. P. The mystique of lawyers. *In* Nader, R. and Green, M. J. eds. Verdicts on lawyers p80-93

Tay, A. E. S. Law, the citizen and the state. *In* Law and society p 1-17

Sociological phenomenology. See Phenomenological sociology

Sociological research

Johnson, J. M. Behind the rational appearances: fusion of thinking and feeling in sociological research. *In* Douglas, J. D. and Johnson, J. M. [eds.] Existential sociology p201-28

Kendall, P. L. Theory and research: the case of studies in medical education. *In* The Idea of social structure p301-21

Lumsdaine, A. A. On mass communication experiments and the like. *In* Lerner, D. and Nelson, L. M. eds. Communication research —a half-century appraisal p37-69

Australia

Lally, J. and Baldock, C. V. Contemporary sociology in Australia and New Zealand. *In* Mohan, R. P. and Martindale, D. A. eds. Handbook of contemporary developments in world sociology p453-69

Austria

Bunzel, J. H. Contemporary sociology in Austria. *In* Mohan, R. P. and Martindale, D. A. eds. Handbook of contemporary developments in world sociology p83-89

Belgium

Bie, P. de. Contemporary sociology in Belgium. *In* Mohan, R. P. and Martindale, D. A. eds. Handbook of contemporary developments in world sociology p31-45

Bulgaria

Dobrianov, V. and Stavrov, B. Contemporary sociology in Bulgaria. *In* Mohan, R. P. and Martindale, D. A. eds. Handbook of contemporary developments in world sociology p227-45

Sociological research—*Continued*

Czechoslovakia

Roucek, J. S. Contemporary sociology in Czechoslovakia. *In* Mohan, R. P. and Martindale, D. A. eds. Handbook of contemporary developments in world sociology p193-202

Egypt

Hegazy, E. Contemporary sociology in Egypt. *In* Mohan, R. P. and Martindale, D. A. eds. Handbook of contemporary developments in world sociology p379-90

Finland

Allardt, E. Contemporary sociology in Finland. *In* Mohan, R. P. and Martindale, D. A. eds. Handbook of contemporary developments in world sociology p107-25

France

Leenhardt, J. Ideologies and trends in contemporary French sociology. *In* Mohan, R. P. and Martindale, D. A. eds. Handbook of contemporary developments in world sociology p9-18

Germany, West

Spinner, I. The development of West German sociology since 1945. *In* Mohan, R. P. and Martindale, D. A. eds. Handbook of contemporary developments in world sociology p69-81

Great Britain

Jackson, J. A. Sociology in contemporary Britain. *In* Mohan, R. P. and Martindale, D. A. eds. Handbook of contemporary developments in world sociology p19-30

Greece

Kourvetaris, G. A. and Dobratz, B. A. Present status of sociology in Greece. *In* Mohan, R. P. and Martindale, D. A. eds. Handbook of contemporary developments in world sociology p307-27

Hungary

Roucek, J. S. and Mohan, R. P. Contemporary sociology in Hungary. *In* Mohan, R. P. and Martindale, D. A. eds. Handbook of contemporary developments in world sociology p247-59

India

Mohan, R. P. Contemporary sociology in India. *In* Mohan, R. P. and Martindale, D. A. eds. Handbook of contemporary developments in world sociology p423-38

Italy

DiRenzo, G. J. Contemporary sociology in Italy. *In* Mohan, R. P. and Martindale, D. A. eds. Handbook of contemporary developments in world sociology p329-54

Japan

Ishida, T. Contemporary sociology in Japan. *In* Mohan, R. P. and Martindale, D. A. eds. Handbook of contemporary developments in world sociology p439-52

Latin America

Ianni, O. Sociology in Latin America. *In* Mohan, R. P. and Martindale, D. A. eds. Handbook of contemporary developments in world sociology p173-88

Netherlands

Valk, J. M. M. de. Contemporary sociological theory in the Netherlands. *In* Mohan, R. P. and Martindale, D. A. eds. Handbook of contemporary developments in world sociology p47-57

New Zealand

Lally, J. and Baldock, C. V. Contemporary sociology in Australia and New Zealand. *In* Mohan, R. P. and Martindale, D. A. eds. Handbook of contemporary developments in world sociology p453-69

Nigeria

Akiwowo, A. A. Contemporary sociology in Nigeria. *In* Mohan, R. P. and Martindale, D. A. eds. Handbook of contemporary developments in world sociology p391-407

Pakistan

Gardezi, H. N. Contemporary sociology in Pakistan and Bangladesh. *In* Mohan, R. P. and Martindale, D. A. eds. Handbook of contemporary developments in world sociology p413-22

Poland

Gella, A. Current developments in Polish sociology. *In* Mohan, R. P. and Martindale, D. A. eds. Handbook of contemporary developments in world sociology p203-26

Romania

Roucek, J. S. and Mohan, R. P. Contemporary sociology in Romania. *In* Mohan, R. P. and Martindale, D. A. eds. Handbook of contemporary developments in world sociology p261-72

Russia

Roucek, J. S. and Mohan, R. P. Contemporary sociology in the Soviet Union. *In* Mohan, R. P. and Martindale, D. A. eds. Handbook of contemporary developments in world sociology p287-301

Spain

Munné, F. Sociology in contemporary Spain. *In* Mohan, R. P. and Martindale, D. A. eds. Handbook of contemporary developments in world sociology p355-76

Sweden

Boalt, G. and Herlin, H. Sociology in Sweden, 1965-1973: a description based on a sociometric method. *In* Mohan, R. P. and Martindale, D. A. eds. Handbook of contemporary developments in world sociology p91-105

Switzerland

Girod, R. Contemporary sociology in Switzerland. *In* Mohan, R. P. and Martindale, D. A. eds. Handbook of contemporary developments in world sociology p59-68

United States

Frumkin, R. M. Contemporary sociology in the United States. *In* Mohan, R. P. and Martindale, D. A. eds. Handbook of contemporary developments in world sociology p131-57

Yugoslavia

Gobetz, G. E.; Goricar, J. and Jambrek, P. Yugoslav sociology. *In* Mohan, R. P. and Martindale, D. A. eds. Handbook of contemporary developments in world sociology p273-86

Sociology

Ball, R. A. Sociology and general systems theory. *In* McNall, S. G. ed. Theoretical perspectives in sociology p115-27

Bauman, Z. Understanding as the work of reason: Talcott Parsons. *In* Bauman, Z. Hermeneutics and social science p131-47

Black, D. J. A strategy of pure sociology. *In* McNall, S. G. ed. Theoretical perspectives in sociology p149-68

Sociology—*Continued*

Catton, W. R. and Dunlap, R. E. Environmental sociology: a new paradigm *In* McNall, S. G. ed. Theoretical perspectives in sociology p465-78

Coleman, J. S. The emergence of sociology as a policy science. *In* The Uses of controversy in sociology p253-61

Douglas, J. D. Existential sociology. *In* Douglas, J. D. and Johnson, J. M. [eds.] Existential sociology p 3-73

Einsenstadt, S. N. The sociological tradition: origins, boundaries, patterns of innovation, and crises. *In* Culture and its creators p43-71

Gouldner, A. W. Sociology and the everyday life. *In* The Idea of social structure p417-32

Hoult, T. F. The humanist perspective. *In* McNall, S. G. ed. Theoretical perspectives in sociology p83-95

Kotarba, J. A. Existential sociology. *In* McNall, S. G. ed. Theoretical perspectives in sociology p348-68

Lemert, C. C. Homocentric sociology in the twilight. *In* Lemert, C. C. Sociology and the twilight of man p226-31

Lemert, C. C. Homocentrism and sociological discourse. *In* Lemert, C. C. Sociology and the twilight of man p 1-22

Lemert, C. C. Structuralist semiotics and the decentering of sociology. *In* McNall, S. G. ed. Theoretical perspectives in sociology p96-111

Levine, D. N. Simmel at a distance: on the history and systematics of the sociology of the stranger. *In* Shack, W. A. and Skinner, E. P. eds. Strangers in African society p21-36

McNall, S. G. Introduction: alternative theoretical perspectives in modern sociology. *In* McNall, S. G. ed. Theoretical perspectives in sociology p1-14

O'Neill, J. The mutuality of accounts: an essay on trust. *In* McNall, S. G. ed. Theoretical perspectives in sociology p369-80

Parsons, T. On building social system theory: a personal history. *In* Parsons, T. Social systems and the evolution of action theory p22-76

Parsons, T. A paradigm of the human condition. *In* Parsons, T. Action theory and the human condition p352-433

Parsons, T. Some problems of general theory in sociology. *In* Parsons, T. Social systems and the evolution of action theory p229-69

Schneider, H. W. Community, communication, and communion. *In* Philosophy and the civilizing arts p487-94

Schneider, L. Ironic perspective and sociological thought. *In* The Idea of social structure p323-37

Segal, M. T. and Berheide, C. W. Towards a women's perspective in sociology: directions and prospects. *In* McNall, S. G. ed. Theoretical perspectives in sociology p69-82

Sixel, F. W. The problem of sense: Habermas v. Luhmann. *In* O'Neill, J. ed. On critical theory p184-204

See also Cities and towns; Communication; Community; Conservatism; Crime and criminals; Educational sociology; Equality; Ethnopsychology; Exchange theory (Sociology); Family; Heredity; Historical sociology; Human ecology; Industrial sociology; Knowledge, Sociology of; Marginality, Social; Mass society; Phenomological sociology; Political sociology; Power (Social sciences); Social change; Social conflict; Social contract; Social control; Social ethics; Social history; Social mobility; Social prediction; Social psychology; Social structure; Social systems; Socialism; Socialization; Society; Primitive; Sociolinguistics; Statics and dynamics (Social sciences); Women

Book reviews

Parsons, T. Review of L. T. Hobhouse, Sociology and philosophy: a centenary collection of essays and articles. *In* Parsons, T. Social systems and the evolution of action theory p77-81

History

Aron, R. On the historical condition of the sociologist. *In* Aron, R. Politics and history p62-82

Bauman, Z. Introduction: The challenge of hermeneutics. *In* Bauman, Z. Hermeneutics and social science p7-22

Peckham, M. Reflections on historical modes in the nineteenth century. *In* Peckham, M. Romanticism and behavior p40-66

History—Austria

Bunzel, J. H. Contemporary sociology in Austria. *In* Mohan, R. P. and Martindale, D. A. eds. Handbook of contemporary developments in world sociology p83-89

History—Belgium

Bie, P. de. Contemporary sociology in Belgium. *In* Mohan, R. P. and Martindale, D. A. eds. Handbook of contemporary developments in world sociology p31-45

History—Bulgaria

Dobrianov, V. and Stavrov, B. Contemporary sociology in Bulgaria. *In* Mohan, R. P. and Martindale, D. A. eds. Handbook of contemporary developments in world sociology p227-45

History—Canada

Anderson, A. B. and others. Sociology in Canada: a developmental overview. *In* Mohan, R. P. and Martindale, D. A. eds. Handbook of contemporary developments in world sociology p159-71

History—Czechoslovakia

Roucek, J. S. Contemporary sociology in Czechoslovakia. *In* Mohan, R. P. and Martindale, D. A. eds. Handbook of contemporary developments in world sociology p193-202

History—Egypt

Hegazy, E. Contemporary sociology in Egypt. *In* Mohan, R. P. and Martindale, D. A. eds. Handbook of contemporary developments in world sociology p379-90

History—Finland

Allardt, E. Contemporary sociology in Finland. *In* Mohan, R. P. and Martindale, D. A. eds. Handbook of contemporary developments in world sociology p107-25

History—France

Leenhardt, J. Ideologies and trends in contemporary French sociology. *In* Mohan, R. P. and Martindale, D. A. eds. Handbook of contemporary developments in world sociology p9-18

Sociology—*Continued*

History—Germany, West

Spinner, I. The development of West German sociology since 1945. *In* Mohan, R. P. and Martindale, D. A. eds. Handbook of contemporary developments in world sociology p69-81

History—Great Britain

Jackson, J. A. Sociology in contemporary Britain. *In* Mohan, R. P. and Martindale, D. A. eds. Handbook of contemporary developments in world sociology p19-30

History—Greece

Kourvetaris, G. A. and Dobratz, B. A. Present status of sociology in Greece. *In* Mohan, R. P. and Martindale, D. A. eds. Handbook of contemporary developments in world sociology p307-27

History—Hungary

Roucek, J. S. and Mohan, R. P. Contemporary sociology in Hungary. *In* Mohan, R. P. and Martindale, D. A. eds. Handbook of contemporary developments in world sociology p247-59

History—India

Mohan, R. P. Contemporary sociology in India. *In* Mohan, R. P. and Martindale, D. A. eds. Handbook of contemporary developments in world sociology p423-38

History—Italy

DiRenzo, G. J. Contemporary sociology in Italy. *In* Mohan, R. P. and Martindale, D. A. eds. Handbook of contemporary developments in world sociology p329-54

History—Japan

Ishida, T. Contemporary sociology in Japan. *In* Mohan, R. P. and Martindale, D. A. eds. Handbook of contemporary developments in world sociology p439-52

History—Latin America

Ianni, O. Sociology in Latin America. *In* Mohan, R. P. and Martindale, D. A. eds. Handbook of contemporary developments in world sociology p173-88

History—Netherlands

Valk, J. M. M. de. Contemporary sociological theory in the Netherlands. *In* Mohan, R. P. and Martindale, D. A. eds. Handbook of contemporary developments in world sociology p47-57

History—Nigeria

Akiwowo, A. A. Contemporary sociology in Nigeria. *In* Mohan, R. P. and Martindale, D. A. eds. Handbook of contemporary developments in world sociology p391-407

History—Pakistan

Gardezi, H. N. Contemporary sociology in Pakistan and Bangladesh. *In* Mohan, R. P. and Martindale, D. A. eds. Handbook of contemporary developments in world sociology p413-22

History—Poland

Gella, A. Current developments in Polish sociology. *In* Mohan, R. P. and Martindale, D. A. eds. Handbook of contemporary developments in world sociology p203-26

History—Romania

Roucek, J. S. and Mohan, R. P. Contemporary sociology in Romania. *In* Mohan, R. P. and Martindale, D. A. eds. Handbook of contemporary developments in world sociology p261-72

History—Russia

Roucek, J. S. and Mohan, R. P. Contemporary sociology in the Soviet Union. *In* Mohan, R. P. and Martindale, D. A. eds. Handbook of contemporary developments in world sociology p287-301

History—Spain

Munné, F. Sociology in contemporary Spain. *In* Mohan, R. P. and Martindale, D. A. eds. Handbook of contemporary developments in world sociology p355-76

History—Sweden

Boalt, G. and Herlin, H. Sociology in Sweden, 1965-1973: a description based on a sociometric method. *In* Mohan, R. P. and Martindale, D. A. eds. Handbook of contemporary developments in world sociology p91-105

History—Switzerland

Girod, R. Contemporary sociology in Switzerland. *In* Mohan, R. P. and Martindale, D. A. eds. Handbook of contemporary developments in world sociology p59-68

History—United States

Frumkin, R. M. Contemporary sociology in the United States. *In* Mohan, R. P. and Martindale, D. A. eds. Handbook of contemporary developments in world sociology p131-57

History—Yugoslavia

Gobetz, G. E.; Goricar, J. and Jambrek, P. Yugoslav sociology. *In* Mohan, R. P. and Martindale, D. A. eds. Handbook of contemporary developments in world sociology p273-86

Mathematical models

Selvin, H. C. On formalizing theory. *In* The Idea of social structure p339-54

Methodology

Bauman, Z. Consensus and truth. *In* Bauman, Z. Hermeneutics and social science p225-46

Bauman, Z. Understanding as the work of history: Karl Mannheim. *In* Bauman, Z. Hermeneutics and social science p89-110

Bauman, Z. Understanding as the work of history: Max Weber. *In* Bauman, Z. Hermeneutics and social science p69-88

Boalt, G. and Herlin, H. Sociology in Sweden, 1965-1973: a description based on a sociometric method. *In* Mohan, R. P. and Martindale, D. A. eds. Handbook of contemporary developments in world sociology p91-105

Brown, R. H. Symbolic realism and sociological thought: beyond the positivist-romantic debate. *In* Brown, R. H. and Lyman, S. M. eds. Structure, consciousness, and history p13-37

Brown, R. H. and Lyman, S. M. Symbolic realism and cognitive aesthetics: an invitation. *In* Brown, R. H. and Lyman, S. M. eds. Structure, consciousness, and history p 1-10

Coser, L. A. Two methods in search of a substance. *In* The Uses of controversy in sociology p329-41

Sociology—Methodology—*Continued*

Febvre, L. P. V. Man or productivity. *In* Rural society in France p 1-5

Giddens, A. Hermeneutics, ethnomethodologly, and problems of interpretative analysis. *In* The Uses of controversy in sociology p315-28

Han, Sang Jin. Ideology—critique and social science: the use of discursive method. *In* McNall, S. G. ed. Theoretical perspectives in sociology p292-309

Lemert, C. C. Analytic realism: Talcott Parsons. *In* Lemert, C. C. Sociology and the twilight of man p80-108

Lemert, C. C. Axiomatic explanation: George Homans. *In* Lemert, C. C. Sociology and the twilight of man p23-50

Lemert, C. C. Critical theory: Juergen Habermas. *In* Lemert, C. C. Sociology and the twilight of man p194-225

Lemert, C. C. Symbolic interactionism: Herbert Blumer. *In* Lemert, C. C. Sociology and the twilight of man p109-34

Lemert, C. C. Theory constructionism: Hubert Blalock. *In* Lemert, C. C. Sociology and the twilight of man p51-79

Merton, R. K. Structural analysis in sociology. *In* Blau, P. M. ed. Approaches to the study of social structure p21-52

Touraine, A. The raison d'être of a sociology of action. *In* Giddens, A. ed. Positivism and sociology p115-27

Touraine, A. Towards a sociology of action. *In* Giddens, A. ed. Positivism and sociology p75-100

Walls, D. S. Dialectical social science. *In* McNall, S. G. ed. Theoretical perspectives in sociology p214-31

Wardell, M. L. and Benson, J. K. A dialectical view: foundation for an alternative sociological method. *In* McNall, S. G. ed. Theoretical perspectives in sociology p232-48

Philosophy

Brown, R. H. Symbolic realism and sociological thought: beyond the positivist-romantic debate. *In* Brown, R. H. and Lyman, S. M. eds. Structure, consciousness, and history p13-37

Brown, R. H. and Lyman, S. M. Symbolic realism and cognitive aesthetics: an invitation. *In* Brown, R. H. and Lyman, S. M. eds. Structure, consciousness, and history p 1-10

Research

See Sociological research

Study and teaching—Belgium

Bie, P. de. Contemporary sociology in Belgium. *In* Mohan, R. P. and Martindale, D. A. eds. Handbook of contemporary developments in world sociology p31-45

Study and teaching—Canada

Anderson, A. B. and others. Sociology in Canada: a developmental overview. *In* Mohan, R. P. and Martindale, D. A. eds. Handbook of contemporary developments in world sociology p159-71

Study and teaching—Italy

DiRenzo, G. J. Contemporary sociology in Italy. *In* Mohan, R. P. and Martindale, D. A. eds. Handbook of contemporary developments in world sociology p329-54

Southern States

O'Brien, M. Odum: Sociology in the South. *In* O'Brien, M. The idea of the American South, 1920-1941 p31-50

O'Brien, M. Odum: Southern sociology. *In* O'Brien, M. The idea of the American South, 1920-1941 p51-69

O'Brien, M. Odum: The failure of regionalism. *In* O'Brien, M. The idea of the American South, 1920-1941 p70-93

Sociology, Biblical

Brichto, H. C. The Hebrew Bible on human rights. *In* Sidorsky, D. ed. Essays on human rights p215-33

Sociology, Buddhist

Bell, I. P. Buddhist sociology: some thoughts on the convergence of sociology and the Eastern paths of liberation. *In* McNall, S. G. ed. Theoretical perspectives in sociology p53-68

Sociology, Christian

Eliot, T. S. From the idea of a Christian society. *In* Eliot, T. S. Selected prose of T. S. Eliot p285-91

Lee, P. K. H. Between the old and the new. *In* The Emergent gospel p124-36

Mendenhall, G. E. The conflict between value systems and social control. *In* Unity and diversity p169-80

Moberg, D. O. Fundamentalists and evangelicals in society. *In* Wells, D. F. and Woodbridge, J. D. eds. The evangelicals p143-69

Morgan, B. Theology in the context of the social sciences. *In* The Context of contemporary theology p157-70

Neal, M. A. Civil religion, theology, and politics in America. *In* America in theological perspective p99-122

See also Christianity and economics; Revolution (Theology)

Modern period, 1500-

See Sociology, Christian

United States—History

Linder, R. D. The resurgence of evangelical social concern (1925-75). *In* Wells, D. F. and Woodbridge, J. D. eds. The evangelicals p189-210

Sociology, Descriptive. See Social history

Sociology, Educational. See Educational sociology

Sociology, Industrial. See Industrial sociology

Socology, Islamic. See Cities and towns, Islamic; Islam and economics; Women in Islam

Sociology, Jewish. See Sociology, Biblical

Sociology, Military. See Civil supremacy over the military; Military policy; War and society

Sociology, Religious. See Religion and sociology

Sociology, Rural

Richards, R. O. Urbanization of rural areas. *In* Handbook of contemporary urban life p551-91

See also Community; Peasantry; Rural conditions; Rural women

History—Europe

Tilly, C. Rural collective action in modern Europe. *In* Forging nations: a comparative view of rural ferment and revolt p9-40

Sociology, Rural—*Continued*

History—Russia

Solomon, S. G. Rural scholars and the cultural revolution. *In* Cultural revolution in Russia, 1928-1931 p129-53

History—United States

Campbell, R. R. Beyond the suburbs: the changing rural scene. *In* Hawley, A. H. and Rock, V. P. eds. Metropolitan America in contemporary perspective p93-122

Sociology, Urban

Castells, M. Urban sociology and urban politics: from a critique to new trends of research. *In* Walton, J. and Masotti, L. H. eds. The city in comparative perspective p291-300

Goering, J. M. The Marxist perspective and urban sociology. *In* McNall, S. G. ed. Theoretical perspectives in sociology p479-93

Harkness, S. Family and sex roles in urban society. *In* Handbook of contemporary urban life p163-201

Harloe, M. Marxism, the state and the urban question: critical notes on two recent French theories. *In* Crouch, C. ed. State and economy in contemporary capitalism p122-56

London, B. and Flanagan, W. G. Comparative urban ecology: a summary of the field. *In* Walton, J. and Masotti, L. H. eds. The city in comparative perspective p41-66

Rex, J. Racialism and the urban crisis. *In* United Nations Educational, Scientific and Cultural Organization. Race, science and society p262-300

Ricoeur, P. Urbanization and secularization. *In* Ricoeur, P. Political and social essays p176-97

Suttles, G. D. Community design: the search for participation in a metropolitan society. *In* Hawley, A. H. and Rock, V. P. eds. Metropolitan America in contemporary perspective p235-97

Ward, D. The early Victorian city in England and America: on the parallel development of an urban image. *In* European settlement and development in North America: essays on geographical change in honour and memory of Andrew Hill Clark p170-89

See also Cities and towns; City and town life; Community development; Urban—Social aspects; Urban renewal; Urbanization

Sociology and architecture. See Architecture and society

Sociology and art. See Art and society

Sociology and literature. See Literature and society

Sociology and religion. See Religion and sociology

Sociology and the arts. See Arts and society

Sociology of knowledge. See Knowledge, Sociology of

Sociology of language. See Sociolinguistics

Sociology of science. See Science—Social aspects

Socrates

About

Arendt, H. What makes us think? *In* Arendt, H. The life of the mind v 1 p127-93

Huby, P. M. Greek ethics. *In* New studies in ethics v 1 p 1-78

Ober, W. B. Did Socrates die of hemlock poisoning? *In* Ober, W. B. Boswell's clap and other essays p262-70

O'Flaherty, J. C. Socrates in Hamann's Socratic memorabilia and Nietzsche's Birth of tragedy. *In* O'Flaherty, J. C.; Sellner, T. F. and Helm, R. M. eds. Studies in Nietzsche and the classical tradition p134-43

Waldman, T. A key to Plato's early dialogues. *In* Philosophy and the civilizing arts p60-88

Influence—Swift

Trowbridge, F. H. Swift and Socrates. *In* Trowbridge, F. H. From Dryden to Jane Austen p81-123

Sodalities. See Confraternities

Soedjatmoko. See Sudjatmoko

Sofism. See Sufism

Sogliuzzo, A. Richard

Theater of the theater: Molière and Pirandello. *In* Johnson, R. B.; Neumann, E. S. and Trail, G. T. eds. Molière and the commonwealth of letters: patrimony and posterity p183-89

The Soil (Periodical)

Tashjian, D. L. The Soil and Contact. *In* Tashjian, D. L. Skyscraper primitives p71-90

Soils

Guatemala—Petén (Dept)

Sanders, W. T. Environmental heterogeneity and the evolution of Lowland Maya civilization. *In* The Origins of Maya civilization p287-97

Sokołowska, Magdalena

Poland. *In* Kamerman, S. B. and Kahn, A. J. eds. Family policy p239-69

Poland: women's experience under socialism. *In* Giele, J. Z. and Smock, A. C. eds. Women: roles and status in eight countries p347-81

Solanas, Fernando, and Gettino, Octavio

Towards a third cinema. *In* Nichols, B. ed. Movies and methods p44-64

Solar eclipses. See Eclipses, Solar

Solar energy

Morrison, C. A. Solar energy for dwellings. *In* Strategies for human settlements: habitat and environment p91-99

Solar parallax. See Parallax—Sun

Solar physics. See Sun

Solar power. See Solar energy

Solar system

Cameron, A. G. W. History of the solar system. *In* Man and cosmos p21-35

Whipple, F. L. Perspectives: past, present, and future. *In* Man and cosmos p169-79

See also Planets

Motion in space

Neyman, J. Introduction: Nicholas Copernicus (Mikolaj Kopernik): an intellectual revolutionary. *In* Neyman, J. ed. The heritage of Copernicus: theories "pleasing to the mind" p 1-21

Solberg, Carl

Mass migrations in Argentina, 1870-1970. *In* Human migration p146-70

Soldiers

France

Le Roy Ladurie, E. The conscripts of 1868: a study of the correlation between geographical mobility, delinquency and physical stature, and other aspects of the situation of the young Frenchmen called to do military service in that year. *In* Le Roy Ladurie, E. The territory of the historian p33-60

Soldiers in literature

Sarotte, G. M. Four archetypes of the homosexual couple: The captain and the soldier. *In* Sarotte, G. M. Like a brother, like a lover p70-91

Soler, Jean

The semiotics of food in the Bible. *In* Food and drink in history p126-38

Solid waste management. See Refuse and refuse disposal

Solitude

Sayre, R. F. Antiquity and the Middle Ages. *In* Sayre, R. F. Solitude in society p13-33

Solitude in literature

Brombert, V. H. Baudelaire: confinement and infinity. *In* Brombert, V. H. The romantic prison p133-48

Brombert, V. H. Huysmans: the prison house of decadence. *In* Brombert, V. H. The romantic prison p149-70

Brombert, V. H. Stendahl's silken prison. *In* Martz, L. L. and Williams, A. L. eds. The author in his work p365-73

Martz, L. L. Paradise lost: the solitary way. *In* Martz, L. L. and Wiliams, A. L. eds. The author in his work p71-84

Poggioli, R. Pastoral and soledad. *In* Poggioli, R. The oaten flute p182-93

Sayre, R. F. Afterword. *In* Sayre, R. F. Solitude in society p195-201

Sayre, R. F. L'Ancien régime: agreeable wilderness, pleasant solitude. *In* Sayre, R. F. Solitude in society p34-55

Sayre, R. F. Antiquity and the Middle Ages. *In* Sayre, R. F. Solitude in society p13-33

Sayre, R. F. La condition humaine: solitude or solidarity? *In* Sayre, R. F. Solitude in society p117-32

Sayre, R. F. Du côté de chez Swann: the unknowable other. *In* Sayre, R. F. Solitude in society p91-116

Sayre, R. F. Journal d'un curé de campagne: the saint's Gethsemane. *In* Sayre, R. F. Solitude in society p133-54

Sayre, R. F. Modern times. *In* Sayre, R. F. Solitude in society p56-87

Sayre, R. F. Le planétarium: solitude in the world of commodities. *In* Sayre, R. F. Solitude in society p176-94

Sollers, Philippe

The novel and the experience of limits; excerpt from "Logiques." *In* Federman, R. ed. Surfiction p59-74

About individual works

The park

Ricardou, J. Writing between the lines. *In* Federman, R. ed. Surfiction p263-77

Sollitto. Sharmon. See Viederman, S. jt. auth.

Solmsen, Friedrich

The conclusion of the Odyssey. *In* Poetry and poetics from ancient Greece to the Renaissance p13-28

Sologub, Fedor. See Teternikov, Fedor Kuz'mich

Solomon, King of Israel

About

Feldman, L. H. Josephus as an apologist to the Greco-Roman world: his portrait of Solomon. *In* Aspects of religious propaganda in Judaism and early Christianity p69-98

Pritchard, J. B. The age of Solomon. *In* Pritchard, J. B. ed. Solomon and Sheba p17-39

Pritchard, J. B. Conclusion. *In* Pritchard, J. B. ed. Solomon & Sheba p146-51

Pritchard, J. B. Introduction. *In* Pritchard, J. B. ed. Solomon & Sheba p7-15

Silberman, L. H. The Queen of Sheba in Judaic tradition. *In* Pritchard, J. B. ed. Solomon & Sheba p65-84

Ullendorff, E. The Queen of Sheba in Ethiopian tradition. *In* Pritchard, J. B. ed. Solomon & Sheba p104-14

Watson, P. F. The Queen of Sheba in Christian tradition. *In* Pritchard, J. B. ed. Solomon & Sheba p115-45

Watt, W. M. The Queen of Sheba in Islamic tradition. *In* Pritchard, J. B. ed. Solomon & Sheba p85-103

Solomon, Andrew

A reading of The tempest. *In* Shakespeare's late plays p213-34

Solomon, Barbara Bryant, and Mendes, Helen A.

Black families: a social welfare perspective. *In* Tufte, V. and Myerhoff, B. G. eds. Changing images of the family p271-95

Solomon, Barbara Miller

A portrait of Oscar Handlin. *In* Uprooted Americans p 1-8

Solomon, Eric

Fiction and the New Deal. *In* Braeman, J.; Bremner, R. H. and Brody, D. eds. The New Deal v 1 p310-25

Solomon, Margaret C.

The craftsmanship of Joyce: Striking the lost chord: the motif of "waiting" in the Sirens episode of Ulysses. *In* Yeats, Joyce, and Beckett p92-104

Solomon, Miller

"To steal a hint was never known": the Sodom apple motif and Swift's "A beautiful young nymph going to bed." *In* Tennessee Studies in literature v22 p105-16

Solomon, Peter H.

Soviet criminology—its demise and rebirth, 1928-1963. *In* Crime, criminology and public policy p571-93

Solomon, Robert C.

Husserl's concept of the noema. *In* Elliston, F. A. and McCormick, P. eds. Husserl p168-81

Sex and perversion. *In* Baker, R. and Elliston, F. A. eds. Philosophy & sex p268-87

Solomon, Samuel

Problems and suggested solutions in translating Molière. *In* Johnson, R. B.; Neumann, E. S. and Trail, G. T. eds. Molière and the commonwealth of letters: patrimony and posterity p603-16

Solomon, Susan Gross

Rural scholars and the cultural revolution. *In* Cultural revolution in Russia, 1928-1931 p129-53

Solomon and Saturn. See Salomon and Saturn

Solon

About

Havelock, E. A. The justice of Solon. *In* Havelock, E. A. The Greek concept of justice p249-62

Solov'ev, Vladimir Sergîeevîch

About individual works

The meaning of love

Barfield, O. Form in art and in society. *In* Barfield, O. The rediscovery of meaning, and other essays p217-27

War, progress, and the end of history, including a short story of the Anti-christ

Miłosz, C. Science fiction and the coming of the Antichrist. *In* Miłosz, C. Emperor of the earth p15-31

Soloviev, Vladimir. See Solov'ev, Vladimir Sergîeevîch

Solovine, Maurice

Excerpts from a memoir. *In* Einstein p9-13

Solovyof, Vladimir. See Solov'ev, Vladimir Sergîeevîch

Solow, Robert M.

Down the Phillips curve with gun and camera. *In* Inflation, trade and taxes p3-22

Solution (Chemistry)

Dolby, R. G. A. Debates over the theory of solution: a study of dissent in physical chemistry in the English-speaking world in the late nineteenth and early twentieth centuries. *In* Historical studies in the physical sciences v7 p297-404

Solženicyn, Aleksandr. See Solzhenifsyn, Aleksandr Isaevich

Solzhenifsyn, Aleksandr Isaevich

As breathing and consciousness return. *In* From under the rubble p3-25

Autobiography. *In* Dunlop, J. B.; Haugh, R. and Klimoff, A. eds. Aleksandr Solzhenitsyn: critical essays and documentary materials 2d ed. p537-40

Letter to the Fourth Congress of Soviet writers. *In* Dunlop, J. B.; Haugh, R. and Klimoff, A. eds. Aleksandr Solzhenitsyn: critical essays and documentary materials 2d ed. p541-49

Nobel lecture. *In* Dunlop, J. B.; Haugh, R. and Klimoff, A. eds. Aleksandr Solzhenitsyn: critical essays and documentary materials 2d ed. p557-75

Repentance and self-limitation in the life of nations. *In* From under the rubble p105-43

The smatterers. *In* From under the rubble p229-78

To Patriarch Pimen of Russia. *In* Dunlop, J. B.; Haugh, R. and Klimoff, A. eds. Aleksandr Solzhenitsyn: critical essays and documentary materials 2d ed. p550-56

About

Anning, J. J. Solzhenitsyn. *In* Freeborn, R. ed. Russian literary attitudes from Pushkin to Solzhenitsyn p120-40

Böll, H. Solzhenitsyn and new realism. *In* Dunlop, J. B.; Haugh, R. and Klimoff, A. eds. Aleksandr Solzhenitsyn: critical essays and documentary materials 2d ed. p185-87

Brown, D. B. Aleksandr Solzhenitsyn. *In* Brown, D. B. Soviet Russian literature since Stalin p310-30

Des Pres, T. The heroism of survival. *In* Dunlop, J. B.; Haugh, R. and Klimoff, A. eds. Aleksandr Solzhenitsyn: critical essays and documentary materials 2d ed. p45-62

Djilas, M. Indomitable faith. *In* Dunlop, J. B.; Haugh, R. and Klimoff, A. eds. Aleksandr Solzhenitsyn: critical essays and documentary materials 2d ed. p328-31

Dunlop, J. B. Solzhenitsyn's "sketches." *In* Dunlop, J. B.; Haugh, R. and Klimoff, A. eds. Aleksandr Solzhenitsyn: critical essays and documentary materials 2d ed. p317-25

Erlich, V. The writer as witness: the achievement of Aleksandr Solzhenitsyn. *In* Dunlop, J. B.; Haugh, R. and Klimoff, A. eds. Aleksandr Solzhenitsyn: critical essays and documentary materials 2d ed. p16-27

Fanger, D. Solzhenitsyn: art and foreign matter. *In* Dunlop, J. B.; Haugh, R. and Klimoff, A. eds. Aleksandr Solzhenitsyn: critical essays and documentary materials 2d ed. p156-67

Feuer, K. B. Solzhenitsyn and the legacy of Tolstoy. *In* Dunlop, J. B.; Haugh, R. and Klimoff, A. eds. Aleksandr Solzhenitsyn: critical essays and documentary materials 2d ed. p129-46

Gasiorowska, X. Solzhenitsyn's women. *In* Dunlop, J. B.; Haugh, R. and Klimoff, A. eds. Aleksandr Solzhenitsyn: critical essays and documentary materials 2d ed. p117-28

Glicksberg, C. I. The moral protest of Solzhenitsyn. *In* Glicksberg, C. I. The literature of commitment p381-401

Haugh, R. The philosophical foundations of Solzhenitsyn's vision of art. *In* Dunlop, J. B.; Haugh, R. and Klimoff, A. eds. Aleksandr Solzhenitsyn: critical essays and documentary materials 2d ed. p168-84

Kovály, P. Problems of anti-humanism and humanism in the life and work of Alexander Solzhenitsyn. *In* Kovály, P. Rehumanization or dehumanization? p120-40

Lamont, R. C. Solzhenitsyn's nationalism. *In* Dunlop, J. B.; Haugh, R. and Klimoff, A. eds. Aleksandr Solzhenitsyn: critical essays and documentary materials 2d ed. p94-116

Langer, L. L. Aleksandr Solzhenitsyn and the journey through humiliation. *In* Langer, L. L. The age of atrocity p163-200

Nicholson, M. Solzhenitsyn and samizdat. *In* Dunlop, J. B.; Haugh, R. and Klimoff, A. eds. Aleksandr Solzhenitsyn: critical essays and documentary materials 2d ed. p63-93

Poole, R. Essay 9. *In* Fitzgerald, R. ed. What it means to be human p164-85

Pritchett, V. S. Alexander Solzhenitsyn: The Gulag Circle. *In* Pritchett, V. S. The myth makers p21-36

Schmemann, A. On Solzhenitsyn. *In* Dunlop, J. B.; Haugh, R. and Klimoff, A. eds. Aleksandr Solzhenitsyn: critical essays and documentary materials 2d ed. p28-44

Slonim, M. L. Alexander Solzhenitsyn: the great challenger. *In* Slonim, M. L. Soviet Russian literature p363-75

Solzhenitsyn, Aleksandr I.—About—*Cont.*

Solzhenitsyn, A. I. Autobiography. *In* Dunlop, J. B.; Haugh, R. and Klimoff, A. eds. Aleksandr Solzhenitsyn: critical essays and documentary materials 2d ed. p537-40

Stacy, R. H. Reaction. *In* Stacy, R. H. Russian literary criticism p231-55

Struve, G. Behind the front lines: on some neglected chapters in August 1914. *In* Dunlop, J. B.; Haugh, R. and Klimoff, A. eds. Aleksandr Solzhenitsyn: critical essays and documentary materials 2d ed. p430-46

Zamoyska, H. Solzhenitsyn and the grand tradition. *In* Dunlop, J. B.; Haugh, A. and Klimoff, A. eds. Aleksandr Solzhenitsyn: critical essays and documentary materials 2d ed. p201-18

About individual works
August 1914

Atkinson,, D. August 1941: historical novel or novel history. *In* Dunlop, J. B.; Haugh, R. and Klimoff, A. eds. Aleksandr Solzhenitsyn: critical essays and documentary materials 2d ed. p408-29

Ehre, M. On August 1914. *In* Dunlop, J. B.; Haugh, R. and Klimoff, A. eds. Aleksandr Solzhenitsyn: critical essays and documentary materials 2d ed. p365-71

Erlich, V. Solzhenitsyn's quest. *In* Dunlop, J. B.; Haugh, R. and Klimoff, A. eds. Aleksandr Solzhenitsyn: critical essays and documentary materials 2d ed. p351-55

Feuer, K. B. August 1914: Solzhenitsyn and Tolstoy. *In* Dunlop, J. B.; Haugh, R. and Klimoff, A. eds. Aleksandr Solzhenitsyn: critical essays and documentary materials 2d ed. p372-81

Jakobson, R. Note on August 1914. *In* Dunlop, J. B.; Haugh, R. and Klimoff, A. eds. Aleksandr Solzhenitsyn: critical essays and documentary materials 2d ed. p326-27

McCarthy, M. T. The Tolstoy connection. *In* Dunlop, J. B.; Haugh, R. and Klimoff, A. eds. Aleksandr Solzhenitsyn: critical essays and documentary materials 2d ed. p332-50

Mathewson, R. W. Solzhenitsyn III: positive Colonels and a tragic General. *In* Mathewson, R. W. The positive hero in Russian literature p328-40

Rahv, P. In dubious battle. *In* Dunlop, J. B.; Haugh, R. and Klimoff, A. eds. Aleksandr Solzhenitsyn: critical essays and documentary materials 2d ed. p356-64

Also in Rahv, P. Essays on literature and politics, 1932-1972 p238-46

Schmemann, A. A lucid love. *In* Dunlop, J. B.; Haugh, R. and Klimoff, A. eds. Aleksandr Solzhenitsyn: critical essays and documentary materials 2d ed. p382-92

Struve, N. The debate over August 1914. *In* Dunlop, J. B.; Haugh, R. and Klimoff, A. eds. Aleksandr Solzhenitsyn: critical essays and documentary materials 2d ed. p393-407

The cancer ward

Bradley, T. Aleksandr Solzhenitsyn's Cancer ward: the failure of defiant stoicism. *In* Dunlop, J. B.; Haugh, R. and Klimoff, A. eds. Aleksandr Solzhenitsyn: critical essays and documentary materials 2d ed. p295-302

Mathewson, R. W. Solzhenitsyn II: "Just like that!" *In* Mathewson, R. W. The positive hero in Russian literature p310-27

Muchnic, H. Cancer ward: of fate and guilt. *In* Dunlop, J. B.; Haugh, R. and Klimoff, A. eds. Aleksandr Solzhenitsyn: critical essays and documentary materials 2d ed. p277-94

Candle in the wind

Zekulin, G. The plays of Aleksandr Solzhenitsyn. *In* Dunlop, J. B.; Haugh, R. and Klimoff, A. eds. Aleksandr Solzhenitsyn: critical essays and documentary materials 2d ed p303-16

The first circle

Böll, H. The imprisoned world of Solzhenitsyn's The first circle. *In* Dunlop, J. B.; Haugh, R. and Klimoff, A. eds. Aleksandr Solzhenitsyn: critical essays and documentary materials 2d ed. p219-30

Halperin, D. M. The role of the lie in The first circle. *In* Dunlop, J. B.; Haugh, R. and Klimoff, A. eds. Aleksandr Solzhenitsyn: critical essays and documentary materials 2d ed. p260-76

Larionoff, N. The first circle of Aleksandr Solzhenitsyn: symbolic visions. *In* California Slavic studies v10 p173-92

Liapunov, V. Limbo and the sharashka. *In* Dunlop, J. B.; Haugh, R. and Klimoff, A. eds. Aleksandr Solzhenitsyn: critical essays and documentary materials 2d ed. p231-40

Mathewson, R. W. Solzhenitsyn I: Marx proposes, Stalin disposes. *In* Mathewson, R. W. The positive hero in Russian literature p279-309

The Gulag Archipelago, 1918-1956

Carpovich, V. V. The Gulag Archipelago, volume one: notes on its lexical peculiarities. *In* Dunlop, J. B.; Haugh, R. and Klimoff, A. eds. Aleksandr Solzhenitsyn: critical essays and documentary materials 2d ed. p527-33

Chukovskaîa, L. K. Breakthrough. *In* Dunlop, J. B.; Haugh, R. and Klimoff, A. eds. Aleksandr Solzhenitsyn: critical essays and documentary materials 2d ed. p456-57

Djilas, M. The Gulag Archipelago. *In* Dunlop, J. B.; Haugh, R. and Klimoff, A. eds. Aleksandr Solzhenitsyn: critical essays and documentary materials 2d ed. p512-14

Kennan, G. F. Between earth and hell. *In* Dunlop, J. B.; Haugh, R. and Klimoff, A. eds. Aleksandr Solzhenitsyn: critical essays and documentary materials 2d ed. p501-11

Klimoff, A. Translating Solzhenitsyn (cont'd): The Gulag Archipelago. *In* Dunlop, J. B.; Haugh, R. and Klimoff, A. eds. Aleksandr Solzhenitsyn: critical essays and documentary materials 2d ed. p636-49

Medvedev, R. On Solzhenitsyn's The Gulag Archipelago. *In* Dunlop, J. B.; Haugh, R. and Klimoff, A. eds. Aleksandr Solzhenitsyn: critical essays and documentary materials 2d ed. p460-76

Mihajlov, M. Mystical experiences of the labor camps. *In* Mihajlov, M. Underground notes p169-200

Mudrick, M. Solzhenitsyn. *In* Mudrick, M. The man in the machine p179-90

Nicholson, M. The Gulag Archipelago: a survey of Soviet responses. *In* Dunlop, J. B.; Haugh, R. and Klimoff, A. eds. Aleksandr Solzhenitsyn: critical essays and documentary materials 2d ed. p477-500

Solzhenitsyn, Aleksandr I.—About individual works—The Gulag Archipelago, 1918-1956 —*Continued*

Schmemann, A. Reflections on The Gulag Archipelago. *In* Dunlop, J. B.; Haugh, R. and Klimoff, A. eds. Aleksandr Solzhenitsyn: critical essays and documentary materials 2d ed. p515-26

Letter to Soviet leaders

Kopelev, L. Z. A lie is conquered only by truth. *In* Medvedev, R. A. ed. The Samizdat register p203-36

Mihajlov, M. Some timely thoughts (concerning Letter to the Soviet leaders by A. Solzhenitsyyn) *In* Mihajlov, M. Underground notes p83-104

The love-girl and the innocent

Zekulin, G. The plays of Aleksandr Solzhenitsyn. *In* Dunlop, J. B.; Haugh, R. and Klimoff, A. eds. Aleksandr Solzhenitsyn: critical essays and documentary materials 2d ed. p303-16

One day in the life of Ivan Denisovich

Connolly, C. Alexander Solzhenitsyn. *In* Connolly, C. The evening colonnade p372-74

Pike, D. A camp through the eyes of a peasant: Solzhenitsyn's One day in the life of Ivan Denisovich. *In* California Slavic studies v10 p193-223

Rahv, P. Two subversive Russians. *In* Rahv, P. Essays on literature and politics, 1932-1972 p232-37

Bibliography

Dunlop, J. B. A select Solzhenitsyn bibliography. *In* Dunlop, J. B.; Haugh, R. and Klimoff, A. eds. Aleksandr Solzhenitsyn: critical essays and documentary materials 2d ed. p650-64

Nicholson, M. Aleksandr Solzhenitsyn: a bibliography of responses in the official Soviet press from November 1962 to April 1973. *In* Dunlop, J. B.; Haugh, R. and Klimoff, A. eds. Aleksandr Solzhenitsyn: critical essays and documentary materials 2d ed. p579-610

Characters—Gleb Nerzhin

Dunlop, J. B. The odyssey of a skeptic: Gleb Nerzhin. *In* Dunlop, J. B.; Haugh, R. and Klimoff, A. eds. Aleksandr Solzhenitsyn: critical essays and documentary materials 2d ed. p241-59

Characters—Women

Gasiorowska, X. Solzhenitsyn's women. *In* Dunlop, J. B.; Haugh, R. and Klimoff, A. eds. Aleksandr Solzhenitsyn: critical essays and documentary materials 2d ed. p117-28

Language

Carpovich, V. V. Lexical peculiarities of Solzhenitsyn's language. *In* Dunlop, J. B.; Haugh, R. and Klimoff, A. eds. Aleksandr Solzhenitsyn: critical essays and documentary materials 2d ed. p188-94

Unbegaun, B. O. The "language of ultimate clarity." *In* Dunlop, J. B.; Haugh, R. and Klimoff, A. eds. Aleksandr Solzhenitsyn: critical essays and documentary materials 2d ed. p195-98

Translations, English

Klimoff, A. Translating Solzenitsyn (cont'd): The Gulag Archipelago. *In* Dunlop, J. B.; Haugh, R. and Klimoff, A. eds.

Aleksandr Solzhenitsyn: critical essays and documentary materials 2d ed. p636-49

Translations, English—Bibliography

Klimoff, A. Solzhenitsyn in English: an evaluation. *In* Dunlop, J. B.; Haugh, R. and Klimoff, A. eds. Aleksandr Solzhenitsyn: critical essays and documentary materials 2d ed. p611-35

Solzhenitsyn, Aleksandr Isaevich, ed.

About individual works

From under the rubble

Andreev, G. The Christianity of L. N. Tolstoy and of the contributors to "From under the rubble." *In* Medvedev, R. A. ed. The Samizdat register p267-314

Elagin, S. Repentance: its theory, history and prescription for today. *In* Medvedev R. A. ed. The Samizdat register p237-66

Soma

Coomaraswamy, A. K. Ātmayajña: self-sacrifice. *In* Coomaraswamy, A. K. Selected papers v2 p107-47

Somalia

Politics and government

Lewis, I. M. The nation, state, and politics in Somalia. *In* Smock, D. R. and Bentsi-Enchill, K. eds. The search for national integration in Africa p285-306

Somatology. See Physical anthropology

Some like it hot (Motion picture)

French, B. Androgyny, anyone? *In* French, B. On the verge of revolt p137-54

Kauffmann, S. Some like it hot. *In* Kauffmann, S. Living images p324-32

Somer is comen ond winter gon. See Sumer is icumen in

Somerset, J. A. B.

"Fair is foul and foul is fair": vice-comedy's development and theatrical effects. *In* The Elizabethan theatre, V p54-75

Falstaff, the Prince, and the pattern of '2 Henry IV.' *In* Shakespeare survey 30 p35-45

Somerville, James W. F.

Aesthetic and sexual relativity. *In* Crew, L. ed. The gay academic p282-302

Somerville, Robert Eugene

Cardinal Stephan of St Grisogono: some remarks on legates and legatine councils in the eleventh century. *In* Law, church, and society p157-66

Sommer, Theo

Regionalism versus multilateralism. *In* The New Atlantic challenge p333-40

Sommers, Fred

Dualism in Descartes: the logical ground. *In* Hooker, M. ed. Descartes p223-33

Son of God

Barfield, O. The "Son of God" and the "Son of Man." *In* Barfield, O. The rediscovery of meaning, and other essays p249-60

Son of God in fiction, drama, poetry, etc.

Revard, S. H. P. The Renaissance Michael and the Son of God. *In* Patrick, J. M. and Sundell, R. H. eds. Milton and the art of sacred song p121-35

Son of Man

Barfield, O. The "Son of God" and the "Son of Man." *In* Barfield, O. The rediscovery of meaning, and other essays p249-60

Maddox, R. The function of the Son of Man in the Gospel of John. *In* Reconciliation and hope p186-204

Sonderkötter, Friedrich. See Goldsmith, P. jt. auth.

The song of Roland. See Chanson de Roland

Songs. See Folk-songs; Work-songs

Songs, Afro-American. See Afro-American songs

Songs, Popular. See Music, Popular (Songs, etc.)

Sonne, Isaiah
About
Eisenstein-Barzilay, I. Finalizing an issue: Modena's authorship of the Qol sakhal. *In* Salo Wittmayer Baron v 1 p135-66

Sonoran Desert
Fontana, B. L. The faces and forces of Pimeria Alta. *In* Voices from the Southwest p45-54

Sons and fathers. See Fathers and sons

Sontag, Frederick Earl
Sun Myung Moon and the Unification Church: charges and responses. *In* Horowitz, I. L. ed. Science, sin, and scholarship p20-43

Sontag, Susan
Fascinating fascism. *In* Nichols, B. ed. Movies and methods p31-43

The imagination of disaster; excerpt from "Against interpretation." *In* Denby, D. ed. Awake in the dark p263-78
About individual works
Fascinating fascism
Sarris, A. Fascinating fascism meets leering leftism. *In* Sarris, A. Politics and cinema p107-15

Soochow, China
History
Polachek, J. M. Gentry hegemony: Soochow in the T'ung-chih restoration. *In* Conflict and control in late imperial China p211-56

Soper, Alexander Coburn
The relationship of early Chinese painting to its own past. *In* Artists and traditions p21-47

Sophia church calendar (Icons)
Lazarev, V. N. The bipartite tablets of St Sophia in Novgorod. *In* Studies in memory of David Talbot Rice p68-82

Sophists (Greek philosophy)
Avotins, I. The holders of the chairs of rhetoric at Athens. *In* Harvard Studies in classical philology v79 p313-24

Robinson, T. M. A Sophist on omniscience, polymathy, and omnicompetence: Δ. Λ. 8.1—13¹ *In* Illinois classical studies, v2 1977 p125-35

Rose, P. W. Sophocles' Philoctetes and the teachings of the Sophists. *In* Harvard Studies in classical philology v80 p49-105

Sophocles
About
Finley, J. H. Politics and early Attic tragedy. *In* Harvard Studies in classical philology v71 p 1-13

Nicoll, A. The glory of the Greek theatre: Sophocles. *In* Nicoll, A. World drama p26-41
About individual works
Ajax
Kitto, H. D. F. The Rhesus and related matters. *In* Yale classical studies v25 p317-50

Moore, J. A. The dissembling-speech of Ajax. *In* Yale classical studies v25 p47-66

Sicherl, M. The tragic issue in Sophocles' Ajax. *In* Yale classical studies v25 p67-98

Simon, B. Tragedy and therapy. *In* Simon, B. Mind and madness in ancient Greece p122-54
Ajax (Lines 815-824)
Whitman, C. H. Sophocles: Ajax, 815-824. *In* Harvard Studies in classical philology v78 p67-69
Antigone
Pozzi, D. C. A note on δυσχείρωμα. *In* Harvard Studies in classical philology v75 p63-67

Rosivach, V. J. The two worlds of the Antigone. *In* Illinois classical studies v4, 1979 p16-26
Electra
Falk, E. H. Some concepts of the tragic in versions of Electra. *In* Creative encounter p3-16
Oedipus the King
Brustein, R. S. Thebes and Watergate. *In* Brustein, R. S. The culture watch p94-96

Fergusson, F. Oedipus according to Freud, Sophocles, and Cocteau. *In* Fergusson, F. Literary landmarks p101-13

Fry, P. H. Oedipus the King. *In* Seidel, M. A. and Mendelson, E. eds. Homer to Brecht p171-90

Girard, R. The plague in literature and myth. *In* Girard, R. "To double business bound" p136-54

Grossvogel, D. I. Oedipus the King: discovering only the discoverer. *In* Grossvogel, D. I. Mystery and its fictions p23-38

Lesser, S. O. Oedipus the King: the two dramas, the two conflicts. *In* Lesser, S. O. The whispered meanings p149-80

Segal, C. P. Synaesthesia in Sophocles. *In* Illinois classical studies, v2 1977 p88-96

Trilling, L. Sophocles: Oedipus Rex. *In* Trilling, L. Prefaces to The experience of literature p3-8

Wilder, T. N. Sophocles's Oedipus Rex. *In* Wilder, T. N. American characteristics, and other essays p77-87
Oedipus Tyrannus
Edmunds, L. Sophocles Oedipus Tyrannus 80-81. *In* Harvard Studies in classical philology v80 p41-44

Shell, M. The Golden Fleece and the voice of the shuttle: economy in literary theory. *In* Shell, M. The economy of literature p89-112
Philoctetes
Easterling, P. E. Philoctetes and modern criticism. *In* Illinois classical studies v3, 1978 p27-39

Rose, P. W. Sophocles' Philoctetes and the teachings of the Sophists. *In* Harvard Studies in classical philology v80 p49-105
The women of Trachis
Segal, C. P. Sophocles' Trachiniae: myth, poetry, and heroic values. *In* Yale classical studies v25 p99-158

Sorcery. See Magic; Witchcraft

Sorel, Georges
About
Berlin, Sir I. Georges Sorel. *In* Essays in honour of E. H. Carr p3-35

Sørensen, Christian. See Longomontanus, Christian Sørensen

Sorites-paradox, Language-mastery and the.
Wright, C. *In* Evans, G. L. and McDowell, J. H. eds. Truth and meaning p223-47

Sorlin, François
Europe: the comprehensive effort. *In* United Nations Educational, Scientific and Cultural Organization. The conservation of cities p66-80

Soroos, Marvin S.
Ecology and the time dimension in human relationships. *In* Orr, D. W. and Soroos, M. S. eds. The global predicament p327-43

Exploring global ecological futures. *In* Orr, D. W. and Soroos, M. S. eds. The global predicament p39-53

Lifeboat ethics versus one-worldism in international food and resource policy. *In* Orr, D. W. and Soroos, M. S. eds. The global predicament p131-49

Sorrentino, Gilbert
Neon, Kulchur, etc. *In* Anderson, E. and Kinzie, M. eds. The little magazine in America: a modern documentary history p298-323

Sorrow. See Grief

The sorrow and the pity (Motion picture)
Kauffmann, S. The sorrow and the pity. *In* Kauffmann, S. Living images p107-10

Sarris, A. The sorrow and the pity. *In* Sarris, A. Politics and cinema p80-84

Sōseki Natsume. See Natsume, Sōseki

Sosin, Gene
Magnitizdat: uncensored songs of dissent. *In* Tokes, R. L. ed. Dissent in the USSR p276-309

Sotho (Bantu people)
Wilson, M. Strangers in Africa: reflections on Nyakyusa, Nguni, and Sotho evidence. *In* Shack, W. A. and Skinner, E. P. eds. Strangers in African societies p51-66

Soucy, Robert J.
France: veterans' politics between the Wars. *In* The War generation p59-103

Soudek, Josef
A fifteenth-century humanistic bestseller: the manuscript diffusion of Leonardo Bruni's annotated Latin version of the (pseudo-) Aristotelian Economics. *In* Philosophy and humanism p129-43

Souillac, France. Sainte Marie, (Abbey church)
Schapiro, M. The sculptures of Souillac. *In* Schapiro, M. Selected papers v 1 p102-30

Soul
Altschule, M. D. The pneuma concept of the soul. *In* Altschule, M. D. Origins of concepts in human behavior p5-17

Dilman, I. Wittgenstein on the soul. *In* Royal Institute of Philosophy. Understanding Wittgenstein p162-92

Dupré, L. K. The mystical experience of the self and its philosophical significance. *In* Psychiatry and the humanities v 1 p101-25

Eberhart, R. Will and psyche in poetry. *In* Eberhart, R. Of poetry and poets p59-75

Hick, J. H. Biology and the soul; excerpt from "Biology and the soul." *In* Donnelly, J. P. ed. Language, metaphysics, and death p150-62

Hillman, J. Peaks and vales. *In* Needleman, J. and Lewis, D. eds. On the way to self knowledge p114-41

Huxley, A. L. The problem of human nature. *In* Huxley, A. L. The Human situation p123-36

Mahoney, E. P. Nicoletto Vernia on the soul and immortality. *In* Philosophy and humanism p144-63

Mihajlov, M. Mystical experiences of the labor camps. *In* Mihajlov, M. Underground notes p169-200

Nalbantian, S. The philosophical evolution. *In* Nalbantian, S. The symbol of the soul from Hölderlin to Yeats p119-38

Taylor, R. De anima; excerpt from "With heart and mind." *In* Donnelly, J. P. ed. Language, metaphysics, and death p131-36

See also Atman; Future life; Immortality; Personality; Psychology; Reincarnation; Spirit; Spiritual life; Transmigration

Soul (Hinduism)
Coomaraswamy, A. K. Ākimcañña: self-naughting. *In* Coomaraswamy, A. K. Selected papers v2 p88-106

Soul in literature
Nalbantian, S. Baudelaire and his contemporaries: the mortal soul. *In* Nalbantian, S. The symbol of the soul from Hölderlin to Yeats p49-65

Nalbantian, S. The philosophical evolution. *In* Nalbantian, S. The symbol of the soul from Hölderlin to Yeats p119-38

Nalbantian, S. The post-Symbolists: the winter of the soul. *In* Nalbantian, S. The symbol of the soul from Hölderlin to Yeats p86-99

Nalbantian, S. Shelley and Keats: the battling soul. *In* Nalbantian, S. The symbol of the soul from Hölderlin to Yeats p38-48

Nalbantian, S. The soul concept as a poetic device. *In* Nalbantian, S. The symbol of the soul from Hölderlin to Yeats p 1-12

Nalbantian, S. The stylistic alchemy. *In* Nalbantian, S. The symbol of the soul from Hölderlin to Yeats p100-18

Nalbantian, S. The Symbolists: the failing soul. *In* Nalbantian, S. The symbol of the soul from Hölderlin to Yeats p66-85

Nalbantian, S. Wordsworth, Hölderlin and their contemporaries: the imperial soul. *In* Nalbantian, S. The symbol of the soul from Hölderlin to Yeats p13-37

Pequigney, J. Marvell's "soul" poetry. *In* Friedenreich, K. ed. Tercentenary essays in honor of Andrew Marvell p76-104

Soul music. See Afro-American music; Afro-American songs; Blues (Songs, etc.)

Sound. See Hearing

Sousa, Ronald B. de. See De Sousa, Ronald B.

South, Robert

About individual works
Sermons preached upon several occasions

Simon, I. Robert South and the Augustans. *In* English Association. Essays and studies, 1975 p15-28

South, The. See Southern States

South Africa

Description and travel
Connolly, C. The flawed diamond. *In* Connolly, C. The evening colonnade p45-59

South Africa—*Continued*

Economic conditions

Bromberger, N. Economic growth and political change in South Africa. *In* Leftwich, A. ed. South Africa: economic growth and political change p61-123

Butterworth, R. The future of South Africa. *In* The Year book of world affairs, 1977 p27-45

O'Dowd, M. South Africa in the light of the stages of economic growth. *In* Leftwich, A. ed. South Africa: economic growth and political change p29-43

Rex, J. The plural society: the South African case. *In* Leftwich, A. ed. South Africa: economic growth and political change p45-60

Wilson, F. The political implications for Blacks of economic changes now taking place in South Africa. *In* Thompson, L. M. and Butler, J. eds. Change in contemporary South Africa p168-200

Emigration and immigration

Lessing, D. M. Being prohibited. *In* Lessing, D. M. A small personal voice p155-60

Foreign economic relations

Barber, J. P. White rule and the outward policy. *In* Leftwich, A. ed. South Africa: economic growth and political change p319-42

Foreign relations

Barber, J. P. White rule and the outward policy. *In* Leftwich, A. ed. South Africa: economic growth and political change p319-42

Bissell, R. E. The ostracism of South Africa. *In* The Year book of world affairs, 1978 p139-52

Gutteridge, W. F. Southern Africa: a study in conflict. *In* The Dynamics of the arms race p231-39

Nolutshungu, S. C. The impact of external opposition on South African politics. *In* Thompson, L. M. and Butler, J. eds. Change in contemporary South Africa p369-99

Foreign relations—United States

Karis, T. United States policy toward South Africa. *In* Carter, G. M. and O'Meara, P. eds. Southern Africa: the continuing crisis p313-62

History

Carter, G. M. South Africa: growing Black-white confrontation. *In* Carter, G. M. and O'Meara, P. eds. Southern Africa: the continuing crisis p93-140

Militia

Aldrich, D. M. Frontier militias: militia laws on the North American and South African frontiers. *In* The Frontier v2 p153-66

Native races

Schlemmer, L. and Muil, T. J. Social and political change in the African areas: a case study of KwaZulu. *In* Thompson, L. M. and Butler, J. eds. Change in contemporary South Africa p107-37

Wilson, F. The political implications for Blacks of economic changes now taking place in South Africa. *In* Thompson, L. M. and Butler, J. eds. Change in contemporary South Africa p168-200

Politics and government

Barber, J. P. White rule and the outward policy. *In* Leftwich, A. ed. South Africa: economic growth and political change p319-42

Bromberger, N. Economic growth and political change in South Africa. *In* Leftwich, A. ed. South Africa: economic growth and political change p61-123

Butterworth, R. The future of South Africa. *In* The Year book of world affairs, 1977 p27-45

Carter, G. M. South Africa: battleground of rival nationalisms. *In* Carter, G. M. and O'Meara, P eds. Southern Africa in crisis p89-135

Du Toit, A. Ideological change, Afrikaner nationalism and pragmatic racial domination in South Africa. *In* Thompson, L. M. and Butler, J. eds. Change in contemporary South Africa p19-50

Gutteridge, W. F. Southern Africa: a study in conflict. *In* The Dynamics of the arms race p231-39

Hill, C. R. South Africa: the future of the liberal spirit. *In* Leftwich, A. ed. South Africa: economic growth and political change p343-57

Landis, E. S. Namibia: impending independence? *In* Carter, G. M. and O'Meara, P. eds. Southern Africa in crisis p163-99

Maud, R. The future of an illusion: the myth of white meliorism in South Africa. *In* Leftwich, A. ed. South Africa: economic growth and political change p287-318

Nolutshungu, S. C. The impact of external opposition on South African politics. *In* Thompson, L. M. and Butler, J. eds. Change in contemporary South Africa p369-99

Thompson, L. M. White over Black in South Africa: what of the future? *In* Thompson, L. M. and Butler, J. eds. Change in contemporary South Africa p400-14

Van Zyl Slabbert, F. Afrikaner nationalism, white politics, and political change in South Africa. *In* Thompson, L. M. and Butler, J. eds. Change in contemporary South Africa p3-18

Welsh, D. The political economy of Afrikaner nationalism. *In* Leftwich, A. ed. South Africa: economic growth and political change p249-85

Welsh, D. The politics of white supremacy. *In* Thompson, L. M. and Butler, J. eds. Change in contemporary South Africa p51-78

Politics and government—1961-1978

Carter, G. M. South Africa: growing Black-white confrontation. *In* Carter, G. M. and O'Meara, P. eds. Southern Africa: the continuing crisis p93-140

Legum, C. Conclusion: Looking to the future. Carter, G. M. and O'Meara, P. eds. Southern Africa in crisis p258-67

Race relations

Adam, H. Internal constellations and potentials for change. *In* Thompson, L. M. and Butler, J. eds. Change in contemporary South Africa p303-26

Bissell, R. E. The ostracism of South Africa. *In* The Year book of world affairs, 1978 p139-52

Bromberger, N. Economic growth and political change in South Africa. *In* Leftwich, A. ed. South Africa: economic growth and political change p61-123

South Africa—Race relations—Continued

Carter, G. M. A case study of the Republic of South Africa. *In* Martin, P. M. and O'Meara, P. eds. Africa p378-94

Carter, G. M. South Africa: battleground of rival nationalisms. *In* Carter, G. M. and O'Meara, P. eds. South Africa in crisis p89-135

Carter, G. M. South Africa: growing Black-white confrontation. *In* Carter, G. M. and O'Meara, P. eds. Southern Africa: the continuing crisis p93-140

Du Toit, A. Ideological change, Afrikaner nationalism and pragmatic racial domination in South Africa. *In* Thompson, L. M. and Butler, J. eds. Change in contemporary South Africa p19-50

Gutteridge, W. F. Southern Africa: a study in conflict. *In* The Dynamics of the arms race p231-39

Leftwich, A. The constitution and continuity of South African inequality: some conceptual questions. *In* Leftwich, A. ed. South Africa: economic growth and political change p125-85

Legum, C. Conclusion: Looking to the future. Carter, G. M. and O'Meara, P. eds. Southern Africa in crisis p258-67

Maud, R. The future of an illusion: the myth of white meliorism in South Africa. *In* Leftwich, A. ed. South Africa: economic growth and political change p287-318

Mayer, P. Class, status, and ethnicity as perceived by Johannesburg Africans. *In* Thompson, L. M. and Butler, J. eds. Change in contemporary South Africa p138-67

Mbata, J. C. Profile of change: the cumulative significance of changes among Africans. *In* Thompson, L. M. and Butler, J. eds. Change in contemporary South Africa p201-20

Rex, J. The plural society: the South African case. *In* Leftwich, A. ed. South Africa: economic growth and political change p45-60

Sachs, A. L. The instruments of domination in South Africa. *In* Thompson, L. M. and Butler, J. eds. Change in contemporary South Africa p223-49

Savage, M. Major patterns of group interaction in South African society. *In* Thompson, L. M. and Butler, J. eds. Change in contemporary South Africa p280-302

Thompson, L. M. White over Black in South Africa: what of the future? *In* Thompson, L. M. and Butler, J. eds. Change in contemporary South Africa p400-14

Welsh, D. The politics of white supremacy. *In* Thompson, L. M. and Butler, J. eds. Change in contemporary South Africa p51-78

Relations (general) with Africa, Southern

Potholm, C. P. The effects on South Africa of changes in contiguous territories. *In* Thompson, L. M. and Butler, J. eds. Change in contemporary South Africa p329-48

Social conditions

Bromberger, N. Economic growth and political change in South Africa. *In* Leftwich, A. ed. South Africa: economic growth and political change p61-123

Butler, J. The significance of recent changes within the white ruling caste. *In* Thompson, L. and Butler, J. eds. Change in contemporary South Africa p79-103

Carter, G. M. A case study of the Republic of South Africa. *In* Martin, P. M. and O'Meara, P. eds. Africa p378-94

Leftwich, A. The constitution and continuity of South African inequality: some conceptual questions. *In* Leftwich, A. ed. South Africa: economic growth and political change p125-85

Mbata, J. C. Profile of change: the cumulative significance of changes among Africans. *In* Thompson, L. M. and Butler, J. eds. Change in contemporary South Africa p201-20

Rex, J. The plural society: the South African case. *In* Leftwich, A. ed. South Africa: economic growth and political change p45-60

Study and teaching

Shula, M. South African studies since World War Two. *In* African studies since 1945 p186-99

South Africa in literature

Couzens, T. J. The social ethos of Black writing in South Africa, 1920-50. *In* Heywood, C. ed. Aspects of South African literature p66-81

Couzens, T. J. Sol Plaatje's Mhudi. *In* Parker, K. ed. The South African novel in English p57-76

Edmands, U. Olive Schreiner. *In* Parker, K. ed. The South African novel in English p27-45

Parker, K. Nadine Gordimer and the pitfalls of liberalism. *In* Parker, K. ed. The South African novel in English p114-30

Rabkin, D. Race and fiction: God's stepchildren and Turbott Wolfe. *In* Parker, K. ed. The South African novel in English p77-94

Ravenscroft, A. Pauline Smith. *In* Parker, K. ed. The South African novel in English p45-56

Wade, M. Art and morality in Alex La Guma's A walk in the night. *In* Parker, K. ed. The South African novel in English p104-91

Wade, M. Nadine Gordimer and Europe-in-Africa. *In* Parker, K. ed. The South African novel in English p131-63

Wade, M. South Africa's first proletarian writer. *In* Parker, K. ed. The South African novel in English p95-113

South African Bureau of Racial Affairs

Stultz, N. M. The separatist challenge to white domination in South Africa. *In* African dimensions p95-112

South African fiction (English)

20th century—History and criticism

Parker, K. The South African novel in English. *In* Parker, K. ed. The South African novel in English p 1-26

South African literature

Apronti, E. O. The tyranny of time: the theme of time in the artistic consciousness of South African writers. *In* African literature today no. 8: Drama in Africa p106-14

History and criticism

Moyana, T. T. Problems of a creative writer in South Africa. *In* Heywood, C. ed. Aspects of South African literature p58-98

South African literature (English)

Gordimer, N. English-language literature and politics in South Africa. *In* Heywood, C. ed. Aspects of South African literature p99-120

South African literature (English)—*Cont.*

History and criticism

Heywood, C. Introduction: The quest for identity. *In* Heywood, C. ed. Aspects of South African literature p vii-xv

Smith, R. The Johannesburg genre. *In* Exile and tradition p116-31

Black authors

Couzens, T. J. Early South African Black writing. *In* King, B. A. and Ogungbesan, K. eds. A celebration of Black and African writing p 1-14

Couzens, T. J. The social ethos of Black writing in South Africa, 1920-50. *In* Heywood, C. ed. Aspects of South African literature p66-81

South Africa poetry (English)

Black authors

Gordimer, N. Writers in South Africa: the new Black poets. *In* Exile and tradition p132-51

Mtshali, O. J. Black poetry in Southern Africa: what it means. *In* Heywood, C. ed. Aspects of South African literature p121-27

South African Republic. See Transvaal

South African War, 1899-1902

Trebilcock, C. War and the failure of industrial mobilisation: 1899 and 1914. *In* War and economic development p139-64

South African War, 1899-1902 in literature

Ravenscroft, A. African, Boer, and Indian attitudes to an imperialist war. *In* Narasimhaiah, C. D. ed. Awakened conscience p315-26

South America

Antiquities

Steward, J. H. Cultural evolution in South America. *In* Steward, J. H. Evolution and ecology p128-50

Religion—Bibliography

Vázquez, J. A. The religions of Mexico and of Central and South America. *In* Adams, C. J. ed. A reader's guide to the great religions p78-89

South American children's literature. See Children's literature, South American

South Asia

Foreign relations—United States

Erdman, H. L. The United States, India, and India's neighbors. *In* Baldwin, D. A. ed. America in an interdependent world p245-72

Politics and government

Kearney, R. N. South and Southeast Asia: a regional survey. *In* Kearney, R. N. ed. Politics and modernization in South and Southeast Asia p 1-38

Social conditions

Kearney, R. N. South and Southeast Asia: a regional survey. *In* Kearney, R. N. ed. Politics and modernization in South and Southeast Asia p 1-38

South Asians

Social life and customs

Maloney, C. Don't say "pretty baby" lest you zap it with your eye—the evil eye in South Asia. *In* The Evil eye p102-48

South Carolina

Politics and government—Colonial period, ca. 1600-1775

Waterhouse, R. The responsible gentry of colonial South Carolina: a study in local government, 1670-1770. *In* Daniels, B. C. ed. Town and county p160-85

South Pole

Exploring expeditions

Hillary, Sir E. South Pole—continent of adventure. *In* The Frontiers of knowledge p269-94

South Sea Islands. See Islands of the Pacific

South Tyrol, German. See Bolzano (Province)

Southall, Aidan William

The current state of national integration in Uganda. *In* Smock, D. R. and Bentsi-Enchill, K. eds. The search for national integration in Africa p307-31

From segmentary lineage to ethnic association—Luo, Luhya, Ibo, and others. *In* Colonialism and change p203-29

The problem of Malagasy origins. *In* Chittick, H. N. and Rotberg, R. I. eds. East Africa and the Orient p192-215

White strangers and their religion in East Africa and Madagascar. *In* Shack, W. A. and Skinner, E. P. eds. Strangers in African societies p211-26

Southall, Ivan

Depth and direction. *In* Horn Book Magazine. Crosscurrents of criticism p60-64

One man's Australia. *In* Egoff, S. A. ed. One ocean touching p18-37

About

Southall, I. Depth and direction. *In* Horn Book Magazine. Crosscurrents of criticism p60-64

Southall, I. One man's Australia. *In* Egoff, S. A. ed. One ocean touching p18-37

Southam, B. C.

Sanditon: the seventh novel. *In* Jane Austen's achievement p 1-26

Southern, Richard

Methods of presentation in pre-Shakespearian theatre. *In* The Elizabethan theatre, V p45-53

Southern Africa. See Africa, Southern

Southern Buddhism. See Hinayana Buddhism

The Southern Review

Simpson, L. P. The Southern Review and a post-Southern American letters. *In* Anderson, E. and Kinzie, M. eds. The little magazine in America: a modern documentary history p78-99

Southern Rhodesia. See Zimbabwe

Southern Society. See Nan she

Southern States

Griessman, B. E. Introduction: The South as a state of mind. *In* Lewis, W. D. and Griessman, B. E. eds. The Southern mystique p xvii-xxi

McKenzie, R. H. Introduction: Of new Souths rising. *In* The Rising South v2 p 1-10

Civilization

Doughty, J. B. One student's perspective. *In* The Rising South v 1 p117-20

Gray, R. J. The social and historical context. *In* Gray, R. J. The literature of memory p 1-39

Southern States—Civilization—*Continued*

Griessman, B. E. Will the South rise again or just roll over? *In* Lewis, W. D. and Griessman, B. E. eds. The Southern mystique p125-31

Lewis, W. D. Technology, community, and humanity: the big picture. *In* Lewis, W. D. and Griessman, B. E. eds. The Southern mystique p15-32

Mathews, D. Coming to terms with another new South. *In* The Rising South v 1 p92-105

O'Brien, M. The idea of the South: an interpretation. *In* O'Brien, M. The idea of the American South, 1920-1941p213-27

O'Brien, M. On the idea of the South: origins, mutation, and fragmentation. *In* O'Brien, M. The idea of the American South, 1920-1941 p3-27

Ransom, J. C. The South defends its heritage. *In* Crunden, R. M. ed. The superfluous men p172-82

Schrag, P. The new South—again, or the view from inside the carpetbag. *In* The Rising South v 1 p106-16

Economic conditions

Higgs, R. Race and economy in the South, 1890-1950. *In* The Age of segregation: race relations in the South, 1890-1945 p89-116

Marshall, F. R. Human resources and changing values in the South. *In* Lewis, W. D. and Griessman, B. E. eds. The Southern mystique p47-62

Tindall, G. B. The cost of segregation. *In* The Age of segregation: race relations in the South, 1890-1945 p117-32

Economic conditions—1945-

Henderson, V. W. Educational change and the Southern future. *In* Lewis, W. D. and Griessman, B. E. eds. The Southern mystique p63-72

Kranzberg, M. From carpetbag to carpet mill: technology in the New South. *In* Lewis, W. D. and Griessman, B. E. eds. The Southern mystique p33-45

Historical geography

Hilliard, S. B. Antebellum tidewater rice culture in South Carolina and Georgia. *In* European settlement and development in North America: essays on geographical change in honour and memory of Andrew Hill Clark p91-115

Historiography

Aaron, D. The South in American history. *in* The South and Faulkner's Yoknapatawpha p3-21

Frantz, J. B. Walter Prescott Webb and the South. *In* Essays on Walter Prescott Webb p3-15

Woodward, C. V. The future of Southern history. *In* The Future of history p135-49

History—Revolution, 1775-1783

Ferguson, C. R. Carolina and Georgia patriot and loyalist militia in action, 1778-1783. *In* The Southern experience in the American Revolution p174-99

Maier, P. Early Revolutionary leaders in the South and the problem of Southern distinctiveness. *In* The Southern experience in American Revolution p3-24

Shy, J. W. British strategy for pacifying the Southern colonies, 1778-1781. *In* the Southern experience in the American Revolution p155-73

Weir, R. M. Rebelliousness: personality development and the American Revolution in the Southern colonies. *In* The Southern experience in the American Revolution p25-54

History—Civil War, 1861-1865

See United States—History—Civil War, 1861-1865

History—1865-

Meier, A. Negroes in the first and second Reconstructions of the South. *In* Swierenga, R. P. ed. Beyond the Civil War synthesis p275-91

Industries

Anderson, J. D. Education as a vehicle for the manipulation of Black workers. *In* Feinberg, W. and Rosemont, H. eds. Work, technology, and education p15-40

Introduction: a statement of principles; excerpt from "I'll take my stand: the South and the agrarian tradition" by Twelve Southerners. *In* Crunden, R. M. ed. The superfluous men p164-70

Owsley, F. L. The pillars of agrarianism. *In* Crunden, R. M. ed. The superfluous men p184-94

Ransom, J. C. The South defends its heritage. *In* Crunden, R. M. ed. The superfluous men p172-82

Intellectual life

Lawson, L. A. The moviegoer and the Stoic heritage. *In* The Stoic strain in American literature p180-91

O'Brien, M. The idea of the South: an interpretation. *in* O'Brien, M. The idea of the American South, 1920-1941 p213-27

O'Brien, M. On the idea of the South: origins, mutation, and fragmentation. *In* O'Brien, M. The idea of the American South, 1920-1941 p3-27

Simpson, L. P. The Southern Review and a post-Southern American letters. *In* Anderson, E. and Kinzie, M. eds. The little magazine in America: a modern documentary history p78-99

Politics and government

Bartley, N. V. The South and sectionalism in American politics. *In* Havard, W. C. and Bernd, J. L. eds. 200 years of the Republic in retrospect p239-57

Carter, D. T. Southern political style. *In* The Age of segregation: race relations in the South, 1890-1945 p45-66

Christopher, T. W. The role of leadership. *In* The Rising South v2 p48-69

Grantham, D. W. The South and the politics of sectionalism. *In* Grantham, D. W. The regional imagination p 1-22

Strong, D. S. Southern politics are changing, too. *In* The Rising South v2 p70-77

Politics and government—1865-1950

Grantham, D. W. The Southern Bourbons revisited. *In* Grantham, D. W. The regional imagination p23-32

Grantham, D. W. Southern progressives and the racial imperative. *In* Grantham, D. W. The regional imagination p77-106

Grantham, D. W. Three violent scenes in Southern politics. *In* Grantham, D. W. The regional imagination p53-63

Politics and government—1951-

Cook, S. D. Southern politics since 1954: a note on change and continuity. *In* Two decades of change p5-19

Southern States in literature—*Continued*

Holman, C. H. Detached laughter in the South. *In* Cohen, S. B. ed. Comic relief p87-104

Also in Holman, C. H. Windows on the world p27-47

Holman, C. H. Faulkner's August avatars. *In* Holman, C. H. Windows on the world p129-43

Holman, C. H. Her rue with a difference: Flannery O'Connor and the Southern literary tradition. *In* Friedman, M. J. and Lawson, L. A. eds. The added dimension p73-87

Howe, I. The Snopes saga. *In* Howe, I. Celebrations and attacks p41-48

Lawson, L. A. The moviegoer and the Stoic heritage. *In* The Stoic strain in American literature p180-91

McDowell, F. P. W. The prewar novels. *In* Ellen Glasgow p82-107

Millgate, M. Faulkner and the South: some reflections. *In* The South and Faulkner's Yoknapatawpha p195-210

Prenshaw, P. W. The paradoxical Southern world of Tennessee Williams. *In* Tennessee Williams: a tribute p5-29

Rubin, L. D. "The Begum of Bengal": Mark Twain and the South. *In* Rubin, L. D. William Elliott shoots a bear p28-60

Rubin, L. D. Flannery O'Connor and the Bible Belt. *In* Friedman, M. J. and Lawson, L. A. eds. The added dimension p49-72

Simpson, L. P. The Southern aesthetic of memory. *In* Tulane Studies in English, v23 p207-27

Sullivan, W. Southern literature: the last twenty years. *In* Two decades of change p55-56

Tate, A. Faulkner's Sanctuary and the Southern myth. *In* Tate, A. Memoirs and opinions, 1926-1974 p144-54

Tobin, P. D. "The shadowy attenuation of time": William Faulkner, Absalom, Absalom! *In* Tobin, P. D. Time and the novel p107-32

Turner, D. T. Faulkner and slavery. *In* The South and Faulkner's Yoknapatawpha p62-85

Southern vehicle (Buddhism) See Hinayana Buddhism

Southerne, Thomas

About

Waith, E. M. Admiration in the comedies of Thomas Southerne. *In* Evidence in literary scholarship p89-103

Southwest, New

Antiquities

Pailes, R. A. and Whitecotton, J. W. The greater Southwest and the Mesoamerican "world" system: an exploratory model of frontier relationships. *In* The Frontier v2 p105-21

Discovery and exploration—Spanish

Hammond, G. P. The search for the fabulous in the settlement of the Southwest. *In* Weber, D. J. ed. New Spain's far northern frontier p17-33

Historiography

Adams, E. B. History of the Spanish Southwest: personalities and discoveries. *In* Voices from the Southwest p3-12

History—To 1848

Adams, E. B. History of the Spanish Southwest: personalities and discoveries. *In* Voices from the Southwest p3-12

García Navarro, L. The North of New Spain as a political problem in the eighteenth century. *In* Weber, D. J. ed. New Spain's far northern frontier p201-15

Hammond, G. P. The search for the fabulous in the settlement of the Southwest. *In* Weber, D. J. ed. New Spain's far northern frontier p17-33

Park, J. F. Spanish Indian policy in northern Mexico, 1765-1810. *In* Weber, D. J. ed. New Spain's far northern frontier p217-34

Schroeder, A. H. Shifting for survival in the Spanish Southwest. *In* Weber, D. J. ed. New Spain's far northern frontier p237-55

History, Military

Faulk, O. B. The presidio: fortress or farce? *In* Weber, D. J. ed. New Spain's far northern frontier p67-76

Southwest, New in literature

Simmons, M. Authors and books in colonial New Mexico. *In* Voices from the Southwest p13-32

Southwest, Old in literature

Rose, A. H. Blackness in the fantastic world of old Southwestern humor. *In* Rose, A. H. Demonic vision p19-38

Southwest Africa. See Namibia

Southworth, Emma Dorothy Eliza (Nevitte)

About

Baym, N. Z. E. D. E. N. Southworth and Caroline Lee Hentz. *In* Baym, N. Z. Woman's fiction p110-39

Southworth, Herbert Rutledge

The Falange: an analysis of Spain's Fascist heritage. *In* Preston, P. ed. Spain in crisis p 1-22

Souvenirs (Keepsakes)

Waikiki Beach, Hawaii

Whetmore, E. and Hibbard, D. J. Paradox in paradise: the icons of Waikiki. *In* Browne, R. B. and Fishwick, M. W. eds. Icons of America p241-52

Souza, Eunice de

The expatriate experience. *In* Narasimhaiah, C. D. ed. Awakened conscience p339-45

Sovani, N. V.

A comparative study of population and agricultural change in some countries of the ECAFE region. *In* Economic factors in population growth p279-92

Sovereigns. See Kings and rulers; and subdivision Kings and rulers under names of countries, e.g. France—Kings and rulers

Sovereignty

Calvert, P. On attaining sovereignty. *In* Smith, A. D. ed. Nationalist movements p134-49

Carson, G. B. National sovereignty at the bar: revolution by law? *In* Essays on modern European revolutionary history p105-32

See also Autonomy; Self-determination, National; Social contract; State

Sovereignity, Violation of. See Subversive activities

Soverosa, Bataza Anes de. See Soverosa, Vataça Anes de

Soverosa, Vataça Anes de

About

Maclagan, M. A Byzantine princess in Portugal. *In* Studies in memory of David Talbot Rice p284-93

Soviet bloc. See Communist countries

Soviet Central Asia

Politics and government

Massell, G. J. Modernization and national policy in Soviet Central Asia: problems and prospects. *In* Cocks, P.; Daniels, R. V. and Heer, N. W. eds. The dynamics of Soviet politics p265-90

Soviet fiction. See Russian fiction-20th century

Soviet-German pact. See Russo-German treaty, 1939

Soviet literature. See Russian literature—20th century

Soviets. See Communist state

Sowell, Thomas

Adam Smith in theory and practice. *In* Glahe, F. R. ed. Adam Smith and The wealth of nations p148-72

"Affirmative action" reconsidered. *In* Gross, B. R. ed. Reverse discrimination p113-31

Choice in education and parental responsibility. *In* Parents, teachers, and children: prospects for choice in American education p165-82

Ethnicity in a changing America. *In* A New America? p213-37

The plight of Black students in the United States. *In* Mintz, S. W. ed. Slavery, colonialism, and racism p179-96

Social science and general education. *In* Hook, S.; Kurtz, P. W. and Todorovich, M. eds. The philosophy of the curriculum: the need for general education p165-68

Soyinka, Wole

Drama and the African world-view. *In* Exile and tradition p173-90

About

Goodwin, K. L. Invective and obliqueness in political poetry: Kasaipwalova, Brathwaite, and Soyinka. *In* Narasimhaiah, C. D. ed. Awakened conscience p251-60

Ogungbesan, K. Wole Soyinka: the past and the visionary writer. *In* King, B. A. and Ogungbesan, K. eds. A celebration of Black and African writing p175-88

About individual works

A dance of the forests

Gibbs, J. The origins of A dance of the forests. *In* African literature today no. 8: Drama in Africa p66-71

The interpreters

Gakwandi, S. A. Disenchantment: Soyinka's The interpreters and Achebe's A man of the people. *In* Gakwandi, S. A. The novel and contemporary experience in Africa p66-86

The road

Izevbaye, D. S. Language and meaning in Soyinka's The road. *In* African literature today no. 8: Drama in Africa p52-65

The strong breed

Ogunyemi, C. O. Iconoclasts both: Wole Soyinka and LeRoi Jones. *In* African literature today no. 9: Africa, America and the Caribbean p25-38

Bibliography

Banham, M. Eldred Durosimi Jones: The writing of Wole Soyinka; Gerald Moore: Wole Soyinka. *In* African literature today no. 7: Focus on criticism p153-54

Dramatic production

Heywood, A. The fox's dance: the staging of Soyinka's plays. *In* African literature today no. 8: Drama in Africa p42-51

Dramaturgy

See Soyinka, Wole—Dramatic production

Soyuz molodezhi. See Union of Youth

Space (Art) See Perspective

Space and time

Coomaraswamy, A. K. Kha and other words denoting "zero," in connection with the Indian metaphysics of space. *In* Coomaraswamy, A. K. Selected papers v2 p220-30

Flew, A. G. The sources of serialism. *In* Thakur, S. C. ed. Philosophy and psychical research p81-96

Galison, P. L. Minkowski's space-time from visual thinking to the absolute world. *In* Historical studies in the physical sciences v10 p85-121

Grant, E. Place and space in medieval physical thought. *In* Motion and time, space and matter p137-67

Hörz, H. Philosophical concepts of space and time. *In* Einstein p229-41

Koslow, A. Ontological and ideological issues of the classical theory of space and time. *In* Motion and time, space and matter p224-63

Owen, G. E. L. Aristotle on time. *In* Motion and time, space and matter p3-27

Schaffner, K. F. Space and time in Lorentz, Poincaré, and Einstein: divergent approaches to the discovery and development of the special theory of relativity. *In* Motion and time, space and matter p465-507

Whitrow, G. J. The role of time in cosmology. *In* Cosmology, history, and theology p159-77

See also Ether (of space); Relativity (Physics)

Space and time as a theme in literature. See Space and time in literature

Space and time in art

Arnheim, R. Space as an image of time. *In* Kroeber, K. and Walling, W. eds. Images of romanticism p 1-12

Space and time in literature

Carothers, Y. M. Space and time in Milton: the "Bard's song." *in* Essick, R. N. and Pearce, D. R. eds. Blake in his time p116-27

Hanning, R. W. The individual and mimesis, I: time and space in chivalric romance. *In* Hanning, R. W. The individual in twelfth-century romance p139-70

Space colonies

Salmon, J. D. Resupplying spaceship earth: prospects for space industrialization. *In* Orr, D. W. and Soroos, M. S. eds. The global predicament p209-29

Space exploration (Astronautics) See Outer space—Exploration

Space flight in literature

Bester, A. Gourmet dining in outer space. *In* Knight, D. F. ed. Turning points p259-66

Space-perception

Hay, J. C. The ghost image: a tool for the analysis of the visual stimulus. *In* Perception p268-75

Hochberg, J. E. Higher-order stimuli and inter-response coupling in the perception of the visual world. *In* Perception p17-39

Johansson, G. Projective transformations as determining visual space perception. *In* Perception p117-38

Space research. See Outer space—Exploration

Space-times. See Space and time

Spacks, Patricia Ann (Meyer)

Early fiction and the frightened male. *In* Spilka, M. ed. Towards a poetics of fiction p255-65

Imagining a self

Contents

The beautiful oblique: Tristram Shandy
The defenses of form: Edward Gibbon
Dynamics of fear: Fanny Burney
Female identities
Identity in fiction and in fact
Laws of time: Fielding and Boswell
Selfhood, given and formed
The sense of audiences: Samuel Richardson, Colley Cibber
The soul's imaginings: Daniel Defoe, William Cowper
Young men's fancies: James Boswell, Henry Fielding

Spady, William George

A commentary on sport and the New Left. *In* Social problems in athletics p212-23

Spain

Armed Forces

Garcia, M. G. The Armed Forces: poor relation of the Franco régime. *In* Preston, P. ed. Spain in crisis p23-47

Civilization

Castro, A. The meaning of Spanish civilization. *In* Américo Castro and the meaning of Spanish civilization p23-40

García Gómez, E. Moorish Spain. *In* Lewis, B. ed. Islam and the Arab world p225-44

Koenigsberger, H. G. Spain. *In* National consciousness, history, and political culture in early-modern Europe p144-72

Rodríguez Cepeda, E. The Spanishness of the eighteenth century. *In* Américo Castro and the meaning of Spanish civilization p223-38

Rodríguez Puértolas, J. A comprehensive view of medieval Spain. *In* Américo Castro and the meaning of Spanish civilization p113-34

Colonies—Administration

Nowell, C. E. Old World origins of the Spanish-American viceregal system. *In* First images of America p221-30

Colonies—Social conditions

Parry, J. H. A secular sense of responsibility. *In* First images of America p287-304

Colonies—America

Bolton, H. E. The mission as a frontier institution in the Spanish American colonies. *In* Weber, D. J. ed. New Spain's far northern frontier p49-65

Covington, J. W. Relations between the eastern Timucuan Indians and the French and Spanish, 1564-1567. *In* Hudson, C. M. ed. Four centuries of Southern Indians p11-27

Holmes, J. D. L. Spanish policy toward the Southern Indians in the 1790s. *In* Hudson, C. M. ed. Four centuries of Southern Indians p65-82

Nowell, C. E. Old World origins of the Spanish-American viceregal system. *In* First images of America p221-30

Colonies—Latin America

Zavala, S. A. The frontiers of Hispanic America. *In* Weber, D. J. ed. New Spain's far northern frontier p179-99

Colonies—North America

García Navarro, L. The North of New Spain as a political problem in the eighteenth century. *In* Weber, D. J. ed. New Spain's far northern frontier p201-15

Commerce—Great Britain

Ruiz, T. F. Castilian merchants in England, 1248-1350. *In* Order and innovation in the Middle Ages p173-85

Economic policy

Esteban, J. The economic policy of Francoism: an interpretation. *In* Preston, P. ed. Spain in crisis p82-100

Emigration and immigration

Boyd-Bowman, P. M. Spanish emigrants to the Indies, 1595-98: a profile. *In* First images of America p723-35

Lockhart, J. M. Letters and people to Spain. *In* First images of America p783-96

Mörner, M. Spanish migration to the New World prior to 1810: a report on the state of research. *In* First images of America p737-82

Emigration and immigration—
Bibliography

Mörner, M. A bibliography on Spanish migration. *In* First images of America p797-804

Exploring expeditions

Lamb, U. S. Cosmographers of Seville: nautical science and social experience. *In* First images of America p675-86

Foreign relations—Rome

Sumner, G. V. Roman policy in Spain before the Hannibalic War. *In* Harvard Studies in classical philology v72 p205-46

Historiography

Aranguren, J. L. L. A new model for Hispanic history. *In* Américo Castro and the meaning of Spanish civilization p309-15

Benítez, R. An appraisal of the immediate past and present. *In* Américo Castro and the meaning of Spanish civilization p239-66

Rodríguez Puértolas, J. A comprehensive view of medieval Spain. *In* Américo Castro and the meaning of Spanish civilization p113-34

History

García Gómez, E. Moorish Spain. *In* Lewis, B. ed. Islam and the Arab world p225-44

Koenigsberger, H. G. Spain. *In* National consciousness, history, and political culture in early-modern Europe p144-72

Spanish drama—*Continued*

Classical period, 1500-1700
—History and criticism

Johnson, C. B. The classical theater and its reflection of life. *In* Américo Castro and the meaning of Spanish civilization p193-220

20th century—History and criticism
Cardona, R. Post-war Hispanic and Brazilian drama. *In* Nicoll, A. World drama p872-80

Spanish drama (Comedy)

History and criticism
Metford, J. C. J. Comedy in Spain and the Spanish comedia. *In* Howarth, W. D. ed. Comic drama p81-101

Spanish epic poetry. See Epic poetry, Spanish

Spanish explorers. See Explorers, Spanish

Spanish fiction

Translations into foreign languages
Bjornson, R. Translations & transitions. *In* Bjornson, R. The picaresque hero in European fiction p139-65

Classical period, 1500-1700—
History and criticism
Bjornson, R. In the wake of Guzmán: variations on the picaresque-life theme. *In* Bjornson, R. The picaresque hero in European fiction p66-105

Bjornson, R. The waning of the Spanish picaresque: El diablo cojuelo and Estebanillo González. *In* Bjornson, R. The picaresque hero in European fiction p127-38

Harvey, L. P. Oral composition and the performance of novels of chivalry in Spain. *In* Duggan, J. J. ed. Oral literature p84-100

20th century—History and criticism
Schwartz, R. The literary and historical background. *In* Schwartz, R. Spain's New Wave novelists, 1950-1974 p 1-6

Schwartz, R. The seventies: critics, exiles, new writers, the "boom" and predictions. *In* Schwartz, R. Spain's New Wave novelists, 1950-1974 p306-28

Schwartz, R. Summary: major trends and writers (1950-1970's). *In* Schwartz, R. Spain's New Wave novelists, 1950-1970 p228-305

Schwartz, R. What is the Spanish New Wave? *In* Schwartz, R. Spain's New Wave novelists, 1950-1974 p7-31

Spanish language

Study and teaching—United States
Fallis, G. V. Spanish language programs for Hispanic minorities: current needs and priorities. *In* Minority language and literature p86-98

Study and teaching (Higher)—
United States
Faber, E. Overcoming obstacles to curriculum change in foreign languages. *In* Minority language and literature p107-14

Spanish language in the Southwest, New
Avendaño, F. The Spanish language in the Southwest: past, present, and future. *In* Trejo, A. D. ed. The Chicanos p133-50

Spanish literature
See also Spanish American literature

History and criticism
Cobb, M. K. Afro-Arabs, Blackamoors and Blacks: an inquiry into race concepts through Spanish literature. *In* DeCosta, M. ed. Blacks in Hispanic literature p20-28

Jason, H. M. The Negro in Spanish literature to the end of the Siglo de Oro. *In* DeCosta, M. ed. Blacks in Hispanic literature p29-35

Silverman, J. H. The Spanish Jews: early references and later effects. *In* Américo Castro and the meaning of Spanish civilization p137-65

Spratlin, V. B. The Negro in Spanish literature. *In* DeCosta, M. ed. Blacks in Hispanic literature p47-52

Woodson, C. G. Attitudes of the Iberian Peninsula (in literature) *In* DeCosta, M. ed. Blacks in Hispanic literature p36-46

Wynter, S. The eye of the other: images of the Black in Spanish literature. *In* DeCosta, M. ed. Blacks in Hispanic literature p8-19

Classical period, 1500-1700—
History and criticism
Wardropper, B. W. The epic hero superseded. *In* Concepts of the hero in the Middle Ages and the Renaissance p197-221

Classical period, 1500-1700—History
and criticism—Bibliography
Beardsley, T. S. Spanish literature. *In* Jones, W. M. ed. The present state of scholarship in sixteenth-century literature p71-110

19th century—History and criticism
Shaw, D. L. Conclusion. *In* Shaw, D. L. The generation of 1898 in Spain p206-13

Shaw, D. L. Origins and definitions. *In* Shaw, D. L. The generation of 1898 in Spain p 1-16

20th century—History and criticism
Shaw, D. L. Conclusion. *In* Shaw, D. L. The generation of 1898 in Spain p206-13

Shaw, D. L. Origins and definitions. *In* Shaw, D. L. The generation of 1898 in Spain p 1-16

Mexican American authors
See Mexican American literature (Spanish)

Spanish missions. See Missions, Spanish

Spanish national characteristics. See National characteristics, Spanish

Spanish painting. See Painting, Spanish

Spargo, John
The bitter cry of children. *In* Gross, B. and Gross, R. eds. The children's rights movement p115-17

Spark, Eli M.
A minority report. *In* Hook, S.; Kurtz, P. W. and Todorovich, M. eds. The university and the state: what role for government in higher education? p245-48

Spark, Geraldine M. See Boszormenyi-Nagy, I. jt. auth.

Spark, Muriel

About
Harrison, B. J. Muriel Spark and Jane Austen. *In* Josipovici, G. ed. The modern English novel: the reader, the writer and the work p225-51

Hart, F. R. Kennaway, Spark and after. *In* Hart, F. R. The Scottish novel p287-321

Kennedy, A. Cannibals, okapis and self-slaughter in the novels of Muriel Spark. *In* Kennedy, A. The protean self p151-211

Spark, Muriel—*Continued*

About individual works

The prime of Miss Brodie

Auerbach, N. A world at war: one big Miss Brodie. *In* Auerbach, N. Communities of women p159-91

Sparkes, J. J.

The simulation of verbal communication activities. *In* Royal Institute of Philosophy. Communication and understanding p162-73

Sparrow, John Hanbury Angus

An anthology of Renaissance Latin verse: problems confronting the editor and compiler. *In* Classical influences on European culture A.D. 1500-1700 p57-64

Sparrow (Periodical)

Stefanile, F. The little magazine today. *In* Anderson, E. and Kinzie, M. eds. The little magazine in America: a modern documentary history p649-63

Sparshott, Francis Edward

Criticism and performance; excerpt from "The concept of criticism." *In* On literary intention p104-15

On the possibility of saying what literature is. *In* Hernadi, P. ed. What is literature? p3-15

Zeno on art: anatomy of a definition. *In* Rist, J. M. ed. The Stoics p273-90

Spasskiĭ, Boris Vasil'evich

About

Koestler, A. The glorious and bloody game: Requiem for Reykjavik. *In* Koestler, A. The heel of Achilles p214-31

Spassky, Boris. See Spasskiĭ, Boris Vasil'evich

Spatz, Jonas

Ring Lardner: not an escape, but a reflection. *In* French, W. G. ed. The twenties p101-10

Speaight, George

Pantomime. *In* The Saturday book 34 p10-23

Speaight, Robert

Shakespeare's heroines. *In* Royal Society of Literature of the United Kingdom, London. Essays by divers hands v39 p146-62

Speaking. See Debates and debating; Rhetoric

Spear, George E.

The university and adult education. *In* Murphy, T. P. ed. Universities in the urban crisis p181-96

The university public service mission. *In* Murphy, T. P. ed. Universities in the urban crisis p95-111

Spears, Monroe Kirklyndorf

Cleanth Brooks and the responsibilities of criticism. *In* Simpson, L. P. ed. The possibilities of order: Cleanth Brooks and his work p230-52

Spechler, Dina R.

Permitted dissent in the decade after Stalin: criticism and protest in Novy Mir, 1953-1964. *In* Cocks, P.; Daniels, R. V. and Heer, N. W. eds. The dynamics of Soviet politics p28-50

The Soviet Union in the Middle East: problems, policies and prospective trends. *In* Ro'i, Y, ed. The limits to power p331-65

Spechler, Dina R. and Spechler, Martin C.

The Soviet Union and the oil weapon: benefits and dilemmas. *In* Ro'i, Y. ed. The limits to power p96-123

Spechler, Martin C. See Spechler, D. R. jt. auth.

Special districts. See Municipal powers and services beyond corporate limits

Specialization among lawyers. See Lawyers —Specialties and specialists

Specialization, The matrix of. Higham, J. *In* Oleson, A. and Voss, J. eds. The organization of knowledge in modern America, 1860-1920 p3-18

Specie. See Money; Silver

Species

Winsor, M. P. Louis Agassiz and the species question. *In* Studies in history of biology v3 p89-117

Species, Origin of. See Origin of species

Specificity (Immunology) See Immuno-specificity

Speck, William Arthur

Politics. *In* Rogers, P. ed. The eighteenth century p81-119

Spector, Stephen

Symmetry in watermark sequences. *In* Virginia. University. Bibliographical Society. Studies in bibliography v31 p162-78

Speech

Barthes, R. Writers, intellectuals, teachers. *In* Barthes, R. Image, music, text p190-215

Davidson, D. H. Thought and talk. *In* Guttenplan, S. D. ed. Mind and language p7-23

Richards, I. A. What is saying? *In* Richards, I. A. Poetries p222-33

Seeger, C. L. Tractatus esthetico-semioticus: model of the systems of human communication. *In* Current thought in musicology p 1-39

Steiner, G. The distribution of discourse. *In* Steiner, G. On difficulty and other essays p61-94

See also Children—Language; Diction; Language and languages; Oral communication; Verbal behavior

Psychology

See Psycholinguistics

Research

Sparkes, J. J. The simulation of verbal communication activities. *In* Royal Institute of Philosophy. Communication and understanding p162-73

See also Linguistic research

Speech, Disorders of

Lenneberg, E. H. The neurology of language. Bloomfield, M. and Haugen, E. I. eds. Language as a human problem p101-19

See also Aphasia

Speech, Figures of. See Figures of speech

Speech, Liberty of. See Liberty of speech

Speech and social status

Hymes, D. H. Speech and language: on the origins and foundations of inequality among speakers. *In* Bloomfield, M. W. and Haugen, E. I. eds. Language as a human problem p45-71

See also Wit and social status

Speech communication. See Oral communication

The speech of Miss Polly Baker, before a court of judicature, at Connecticut near Boston in New England
Lemay, J. A. L. The text, rhetorical strategies, and themes of "The speech of Miss Polly Baker." *In* Lemay, J. A. L. ed. The oldest revolutionary p91-120

Speech processing systems
Sparkes, J. J. The simulation of verbal communication activities. *In* Royal Institute of Philosophy. Communication and understanding p162-73

Speeches, addresses, etc. See Eulogies

Speed. See Acceleration (Mechanics)

Speedy trial
Amsterdam, A. G. Speedy criminal trial: rights and remedies. *In* Stanford legal essays p 1-19

Speer, Albert

About individual works
Inside the Third Reich
Canetti, E. The Arch of Triumph. *In* Canetti, E. The conscience of words p153-70
Canetti, E. Hitler, according to Speer. *In* Canetti, E. The conscience of words p145-52
Dawidowicz, L. S. In Hitler's service: Albert Speer. *In* Dawidowicz, L. S. The Jewish presence p235-37

Speeth, Kathleen Riordan. See Riordan, Kathleen Trelair

Speitel, H. H.
Dialect. *In* Davies, A. ed. Problems of language and learning p34-60

Spelling reform
Venezky, R. L. Orthography. *In* Wardhaugh, R. and Brown, H. D. eds. A survey of applied linguistics p69-91

Spells. See Charms; Magic

Spence, Jonathan D.
Opium smoking in Ch'ing China. *In* Conflict and control in late imperial China p143-73
Tensions. *In* Meisner, M. J. and Murphy, R. eds. The Mozartian historian p113-22
The Wan-li period vs. the K'ang-hsi period: fragmentation vs. reintegration? *In* Artists and traditions p145-48

Spence, Joseph

About individual works
Polymetis [Dialogue 18]
Gordon, D. J. Ripa's fate. *In* Gordon, D. J. The Renaissance imagination p51-74

Spencer, Benjamin Townley
Gertrude Stein: non-expatriate. *In* Literature and ideas in America p204-27

Spencer, Herbert
About
Haley, B. Obeying the laws of life: Carlyle and Spencer. *In* Haley, B. The healthy body and Victorian culture p69-94

Spencer, John Robert
Filarete's bronze doors at St Peter's. *In* Collaboration in Italian Renaissance art p33-57

Spencer, Terence John Bew
The statue of Hermione. *In* English Association. Essays and studies, 1977 p39-49

Spencer, William
Ottoman North Africa. *In* Nationalism in a non-national state p103-27

Spender, Stephen
The pre-Raphaelite literary painters. *In* Sambrook, J. ed. Pre-Raphaelitism p118-25
The thirties and after
Contents
Background to the fifties
Background to the forties
Background to the sixties
Background to the thirties
Cyril Connolly
D. H. Lawrence: Phoenix
Heroes in Spain
I join the . . . Communist Party
Louis Aragon's The red front
Notes on revolutionaries and reactionaries: Reactionaries
Notes on revolutionaries and reactionaries: Revolutionaries
The poetic dramas of W. H. Auden and Christopher Isherwood
Poetry and revolution
Remembering Eliot
Rhineland journey
Spain invites the world's writers
Tangiers and Gibraltar now
W. B. Yeats's A vision
W. H. Auden memorial address
Wyndham Lewis as poet

About
Fraser, G. S. A poetry of search (Stephen Spender). *In* Fraser, G. S. Essays on twentieth-century poets p169-74
Pritchard, W. H. Auden & Co. *In* Pritchard, W. H. Seeing through everything p154-77
Smith, E. E. Stephen Spender: the proletarian poet. *In* Smith, E. E. The angry young men of the thirties p35-68
Spender, S. Background to the fifties. *In* Spender, S. The thirties and after p121-30
Thurley, G. A kind of scapegoat: a retrospect on Stephen Spender. *In* Thurley, G. The ironic harvest p79-97

About individual works
Forward from liberalism
Spender, S. I join the . . . Communist Party. *In* Spender, S. The thirties and after p58-60
World within world
Connolly, C. Stephen Spender. *In* Connolly, C. The evening colonnade p324-26

Spengemann, William C.
The adventurous muse
Contents
The adventurous muse: "The Algerine captive" and "Arthur Gordon Pym"
Henry James
Herman Melville
Mark Twain
Nathaniel Hawthorne
The poetics of adventure
The poetics of domesticity

Spengler, Joseph John
Adam Smith and society's decision-makers. *In* Skinner, A. S. and Wilson, T. eds. Essays on Adam Smith p390-414
Limits to growth: biospheric or institutional? *In* Science and ceremony p115-33
Smith versus Hobbes: economy versus polity. *In* Glahe, F. R. ed. Adam Smith and The wealth of nations p35-59
See also Braibanti, R. J. D. jt. ed.

Speyer, Wolfgang, ed.

About individual works

Carmina latina, by Giovanni Pico della Mirandola

Kristeller, P. O. The Latin poems of Giovanni Pico della Mirandola: a supplementary note. *In* Poetry and poetics from ancient Greece to the Renaissance p185-206

Spheres of influence

Esthus, R. A. Protectorates and spheres of influence. *In* Encyclopedia of American foreign policy p836-43

Sphragistics. See Seals (Numismatics)

Spicker, Stuart F.

Gerontogenetic mentation: memory, dementia and medicine in the penultimate years. *In* Spicker, S. F.; Woodward, K. M. and Van Tassel, D. D. eds. Aging and the elderly p153-80

Spiegel, John Paul

Conflicts in ideologies and values. *In* American psychiatry: past, present and future p8-14

Spiegel-Rösing, Ina Susanne

The study of science, technology and society (SSTS): recent trends and future challenges. *In* Science, technology and society p7-42

Spielmann, Edda. See Bäuml, F. H. jt. auth.

Spies

Alban, J. R. and Allmand, C. T. Spies and spying in the fourteenth century. *In* War, literature, and politics in the late Middle Ages p73-101

Spilka, Mark

Erich Segal as Little Nell, or The real meaning of Love story. *In* Filler, L. ed. A question of quality: popularity and value p8-25

Henry James and Walter Besant: "The art of fiction" controversy. *In* Spilka, M. ed. Towards a poetics of fiction p190-208

On Lawrence's hostility to wilful women: the Chatterley solution. *In* Smith, A. ed. Lawrence and women p189-211

Spillane, Frank Morrison

About

Cawelti, J. G. Hammett, Chandler, and Spillane. *In* Cawelti, J. G. Adventure, mystery, and romance p162-91

Spillane, Mickey. See Spillane, Frank Morrison

Spillers, Hortense J.

Gwendolyn the terrible: propositions on eleven poems. *In* Gilbert, S. M. and Gubar, S. eds. Shakespeare's sisters p233-44

Spindler, Louise Schaubel

Researching the psychology of culture change and urbanization. *In* Spindler, G. D. ed. The making of psychological anthropology p176-200

Spinner, Ilona

The development of West German sociology since 1945. *In* Mohan, R. P. and Martindale, D. A. eds. Handbook of contemporary developments in world sociology p69-81

Spinoza, Baruch. See Spinoza, Benedictus de

Spinoza, Benedictus de

About

Alon, I. Between fatalism and causality: Al-Ash'ari and Spinoza. *In* Philosophy East/philosophy West p218-34

Curley, E. M. Descartes, Spinoza and the ethics of belief. *In* Freeman, E. and Mandelbaum, M. H. eds. Spinoza p159-89

Curley, E. M. Spinoza and recent philosophy of religion. *In* Shahan, R. W. and Biro, J. I. eds. Spinoza: new perspectives p161-75

Doney, W. Spinoza on philosophical skepticism. *In* Freeman, E. and Mandelbaum, M. H. eds. Spinoza p139-57

Franck, I. Spinoza, Freud, and Hampshire on psychic freedom. *In* Thought, consciousness, and reality p257-309

Funkenstein, A. Natural science and social theory: Hobbes, Spinoza, and Vico. *In* Giambattista Vico's science of humanity p187-212

Hampshire, S. Spinoza's theory of human freedom. *In* Freeman, E. and Mandelbaum, M. H. eds. Spinoza p35-47

Hardin, C. L. Spinoza and immortality and time. *In* Shahan, R. W. and Biro, J. I. eds. Spinoza: new perspectives p129-38

Harris, E. E. Spinoza's theory of human immortality. *In* Freeman, E. and Mandelbaum, M. H. eds. Spinoza p245-62

Lewis, D. On the aims and method of Spinoza's philosophy. *In* Shahan, R. W. and Biro, J. I. eds. Spinoza: new perspectives p217-34

McShea, R. J. Spinoza: human nature and history. *In* Freeman, E. and Mandelbaum, M. H. eds. Spinoza p101-15

Matson, W. I. Spinoza's theory of mind. *In* Freeman, E. and Mandelbaum, M. H. eds. Spinoza p49-60

Odegard, D. A. The body identical with the human mind: a problem in Spinoza's philosophy. *In* Freeman, E. and Mandelbaum, M. H. eds. Spinoza p61-83

Parkinson, G. H. R. Spinoza on the power and freedom of man. *In* Freeman, E. and Mandelbaum, M. H. eds. Spinoza p7-33

Popkin, R. H. Spinoza and La Peyrère. *In* Shahan, R. W. and Biro, J. I. eds. Spinoza: new perspectives p175-95

Radner, D. M. C. Malebranche's refutation of Spinoza. *In* Shahan, R. W. and Biro, J. I. eds. Spinoza: new perspectives p113-28

Rice, L. C. Spinoza on individuation. *In* Freeman, E. and Mandelbaum, M. H. eds. Spinoza p195-214

Sacksteder, W. Spinoza on part and whole: the worm's eye view. *In* Shahan, R. W. and Biro, J. I. eds. Spinoza: new perspectives p139-59

Shmueli, E. The geometrical method, personal caution, and the idea of tolerance. *In* Shahan, R. W. and Biro, J. I. eds. Spinoza: new perspectives p197-215

About individual works

Ethics

Kessler, W. L. A note on Spinoza's concept of attribute. *In* Freeman, E. and Mandelbaum, M. H. eds. Spinoza p191-94

Lachterman, D. R. The physics of Spinoza's Ethics. *In* Shahan, R. W. and Biro, J. I. eds. Spinoza: new perspectives p71-111

Radner, D. M. C. Malebranche's refutation of Spinoza. *In* Shahan, R. W. and Biro, J. I. eds. Spinoza: new perspectives p113-28

Sacksteder, W. Spinoza on democracy. *In* Freeman, E. and Mandelbaum, M. H. eds. Spinoza p117-38

Spolsky, Bernard
Bilingualism. *In* Wardhaugh, R. and Brown, H. D. eds. A survey of applied linguistics p164-81

Spontini, Gasparo Luigi Pacifico
About
Dent, E. J. Spontini. *In* Dent, E. J. The rise of romantic opera p95-109

Influence
Cairns, D. Spontini's influence on Berlioz. *In* From Parnassus p25-41

Spooner, Brian
Anthropology and the evil eye. *In* The Evil eye p279-85
The evil eye in the Middle East. *In* The Evil eye p76-84

Sporotrichosis
Harvey, A. M. Two mycoses first described at Johns Hopkins. *In* Harvey, A. M. Adventures in medical research p32-38

Sports
Novak, M. Rooting, agon; excerpt from "The joy of sports: end zones, bases, baskets, balls, and the consecration of the American spirit." *In* A Public philosophy reader p279-87
See also Professional sports; School sports; Segregation in sports

Moral and religious aspects
Lueschen, G. Cheating in sport. *In* Social problems in athletics p67-77

Psychological aspects
Mahigel, E. L. and Stone, G. P. Hustling as a career. *In* Social problems in athletics p78-85
Steele, P. D. The bowling hustler: a study of deviance in sport. *In* Social problems in athletics p86-92

Social aspects
Lueschen, G. Cheating in sport. *In* Social problems in athletics p67-77
McPherson, B. D. The Black athlete: an overview and analysis. *In* Social problems in athletics p122-50
Steele, P. D. The bowling hustler: a study of deviance in sport. *In* Social problems in athletics p86-92

Great Britain—History—19th century
Haley, B. The new era: Victorian sport and training. *In* Haley, B. The healthy body and Victorian culture p123-40

Sports for children
Sherif, C. W. The social context of competition. *In* Social problems in athletics p18-36

Psychological aspects
Devereux, E. C. Backyard versus Little League baseball: the impoverishment of children's games. *In* Social problems in athletics p37-56

Sports in literature
Haley, B. The new era: Victorian sport and training. *In* Haley, B. The healthy body and Victorian culture p123-40

Sports motivation. See Sports—Psychological aspects

Sportsmanship
Faulkner, R. R. Making violence by doing work: selves, situations, and the world of professional hockey. *In* Social problems in athletics p93-112
Lueschen, G. Cheating in sport. *In* Social problems in athletics p66-77

Spradley, James Phillip
The moral career of a bum. *In* Henslin, J. M. ed. Deviant life-styles p305-30

Spratlin, Valaurez B.
The Negro in Spanish literature. *In* DeCosta, M. ed. Blacks in Hispanic literature p47-52

Sprey, Jetse
Extramarital relationships. *In* Gross, L. ed. Sexual issues in marriage p131-43

Sprigge, Elizabeth, and Kihm, Jean Jacques
About individual works
Jean Cocteau: the man and the mirror
Connolly, C. Jean Cocteau: 2. *In* Connolly, C. The evening colonnade p309-12

Spring, David
Landed elites compared. *In* Spring, D. ed. European landed elites in the nineteenth century p 1-21

Spring, Joel Henry
The American high school and the development of social character. *In* Feinberg, W. and Rosemont, H. eds. Work, technology, and education p41-59

Spring
See also Vernal equinox

Maine
White, E. B. A report in spring. *In* White, E. B. Essays of E. B. White p14-16

Springborg, Patricia
Karl Marx on human needs. *In* Fitzgerald, R. ed. Human needs and politics p157-73

Springer, Marlene Ann
Angels and other women in Victorian literature. *In* Springer, M. A. ed. What manner of woman p124-59

Spufford, Margaret
Peasant inheritance customs and land distribution in Cambridgeshire from the sixteenth to the eighteenth centuries. *In* Family and inheritance p156-76

Spuhler, James Norman
The maximum opportunity for natural selection in some human populations. *In* Zubrow, E. B. W. ed. Demographic anthropology p185-226

Spurlin, Paul Merrill
Readership in the American Enlightenment. *In* Literature and history in the age of ideas p359-74

Spurzheim, Johann Gasper
About individual works
The physiognomical system of Drs. Gall and Spurzheim
Mellor, A. K. Physiognomy, phrenology, and Blake's visionary heads. *In* Essick, R. N. and Pearce, D. R. eds. Blake in his time p53-74

Squares, Public. See Plazas

Squatters
Brazil
Leeds, A. and Leeds, E. R. Accounting for behavioral differences: three political systems and the responses of squatters in Brazil, Peru, and Chile. *In* Walton, J. and Masotti, L. H. eds. The city in comparative perspective p193-248

Squatters—*Continued*

Chile

Leeds, A. and Leeds, E. R. Accounting for behavioral differences: three political systems and the responses of squatters in Brazil, Peru, and Chile. *In* Walton, J. and Masotti, L. H. eds. The city in comparative perspective p193-248

Peru

Leeds, A. and Leeds, E. R. Accounting for behavioral differences: three political systems and the responses of squatters in Brazil, Peru, and Chile. *In* Walton, J. and Masotti, L. H. eds. The city in comparative perspective p193-248

Squawmish language. See Salishan languages

Squires, Geoffrey
Poetry and the future. *In* Bundy, R. F. ed. Images of the future: the twenty-first century and beyond p16-23

Squires, Roger
Silent soliloquy. *In* Royal Institute of Philosophy. Understanding Wittgenstein p208-25

Srī-Laksmī. See Lakshmi (Indian goddess)

Sri Lanka

Politics and government

Jupp, J. Five Sinhalese nationalist politicians. *In* The Making of politicians: studies from Africa and Asia p183-94

Jupp, J. Modernization and pluralism: Ceylon and Malaysia. *In* Leftwich, A. ed. South Africa: economic growth and political change p187-211

Population

Sovani, N. V. A comparative study of population and agricultural change in some countries of the ECAFE region. *In* Economic factors in population growth p273-92

Social conditions

Jupp, J. Modernization and pluralism: Ceylon and Malaysia. *In* Leftwich, A. ed. South Africa: economic growth and political change p187-211

Srinivas, Mysore Narasimhachar
The Indian village: myth and reality. *In* Studies in social anthropology p41-85

Staab, Franz
Ostrogothic geographers at the court of Theodoric the Great: a study of some sources of the anonymous cosmographer of Ravenna. *In* Viator: medieval and Renaissance studies v7 p27-64

Staats, Elmer Boyd
New problems of accountability for federal programs. *In* Smith, B. L. R. ed. The new political economy: the public use of the private sector p46-67

Staatsen, A. A. M. F.
Enforcement of the Nuisance Act in the Netherlands. *In* Davis, K. C. Discretionary justice in Europe and America p100-14

General assistance in the Netherlands. *In* Davis, K. C. Discretionary justice in Europe and America p133-48

Stability, Social. See Social stability

Stack, Carol B. See Blaydon, C. C. jt. auth.

Stacy, Robert H.
Russian literary criticism
Contents
The aesthetic critics
The age of Pushkin
Belinsky
The civic critics
The Formalists
Marxist and Soviet criticism
Mikhail Lomonosov
The modernists
Reaction
Tolstoy and Dostoevsky

Staden, Heinrich von. See Von Staden, Heinrich

Staël-Holstein, Anne Louise Germaine (Necker) Baronne de

About individual works
Corinne; or, Italy

Moers, E. Performing heroinism: the myth of Corinne. *In* The Worlds of Victorian fiction p319-50

Poulet, G. The role of improvisation in Corinne. *In* ELH essays for Earl R. Wasserman p309-19

Stafford, Edward, 3d Duke of Buckingham. See Buckingham, Edward Stafford, 3d Duke of

Stafford, William Edgar

About individual works
The rescued year

Lieberman, L. John Berryman, William Stafford, and James Dickey: the expansional poet: a return to personality. *In* Lieberman, L. Unassigned frequencies p263-71

Someday, maybe

Lieberman, L. William Stafford and Frederick Morgan: the shocks of normality. *In* Lieberman, L. Unassigned frequencies p272-83

Stafford, William Talmadge
Henry James. *In* American literary scholarship, 1973 p116-34

Henry James [another essay] *In* American literary scholarship. 1974 p87-100

Henry James [another essay] *In* American literary scholarship, 1975 p115-30

Henry James [another essay] *In* American literary scholarship, 1976 p93-107

Stage. See Acting; Actors; Drama; Theater

Stage adaptations
Miller, A. On adaptations. *In* Miller, A. The theater essays of Arthur Miller p215-17

Stage scenery. See Theaters—Stage-setting and scenery

Stahl, Ernst Ludwig
The 'Faust' translation: a personal account. *In* Time was away p67-71

Stahl, Georg Ernst

About

Altschule, M. D. Swedenborg and Stahl: opposite—and wrong—sides of the same coin. *In* Altschule, M. D. Origins of concepts in human behavior p183-92

Stahl, Hans-Peter
Learning through suffering? Croesus' conversations in the history of Herodotus. *In* Yale classical studies v24 p 1-36

On 'extra-dramatic' communication of characters in Euripides. *In* Yale classical studies v25 p159-76

Stahmer, Harold M.

The aged in two ancient oral cultures: the ancient Hebrews and Homeric Greece. *In* Spicker, S. F.; Woodward, K. M. and Van Tassel, D. D. eds. Aging and the elderly p23-36

Staines, David

Bartlett Jere Whiting. *In* The Learned and the lewed p 1-9

King Arthur in Victorian fiction. *In* The Worlds of Victorian fiction p267-93

Stalag 17 (Motion picture)

Truffaut, F. Billy Wilder: Stalag 17: *In* Truffaut, F. The films in my life p161-64

Staley, Thomas F.

James Joyce. *In* Finneran, R. J. ed. Anglo-Irish literature p366-435

Strings in the labyrinth: sixty years with Joyce's Portrait. *In* Staley, T. F. and Benstock, B. eds. Approaches to Joyce's Portrait p3-23

Stalin, Iosif

About

Medvedev, R. A. New pages from the political biography of Stalin. *In* Stalinism p199-235

Parry, A. Stalin's Archipelago. *In* Parry, A. Terrorism: from Robespierre to Arafat p187-202

Stalley, Roger

The long Middle Ages: from the twelfth century to the Reformation. *In* De Breffny, B. ed. The Irish world p71-98

Stam, John Edward

Charismatic theology in the apostolic tradition of Hippolytus. *In* Current issues in Biblical and patristic interpretation p267-76

Stambaugh, Joan

An inquiry into authenticity and inauthenticity in Being and time. *In* Radical phenomenology p153-61

Stambler, Bernard

Terence and Molière. *In* Johnson, R. B.; Neumann, E. S. and Trail, G. T. eds. Molière and the commonwealth of letters: patrimony and posterity p417-29

Stammler, Heinrich A.

Russian metapolitics: Merezhkovsky's religious understanding of the historical process. *In* California Slavic studies v9 p123-38

Stampe, Dennis W.

Toward a grammar of meaning. *In* Harman, G. ed. On Noam Chomsky p267-302

Stamper, Rexford

The two-character play: psychic individuation. *In* Tennessee Williams: a tribute p354-61

Stamps, Postage. See Postage-stamps

Stanage, Sherman Miller

Violatives: modes and themes of violence. *In* Stanage, S. M. ed. Reason and violence p207-38

Stanbrough, Jane

Edna St. Vincent Millay and the language of vulnerability. *In* Gilbert, S. M. and Gubar, S. eds. Shakespeare's sisters p183-99

Standard of living. See Cost and standard of living

Standard of value. See Money

Stanford, Ann

Anne Bradstreet: dogmatist and rebel. *In* Vaughan, A. T. and Bremer, F. J. eds. Puritan New England p287-98

Images of women in early American literature. *In* Springer, M. A. ed. What manner of woman p184-210

Stanford, Derek

The writings of Sir Max Beerbohm. *In* Riewald, J. G. ed. The surprise of excellence p77-91

Stanford, Donald E.

Edwin Arlington Robinson's "The Wandering Jew." *In* Tulane Studies in English, v23 p95-108

Stanford, Geoffrey

Recycling in human settlements. *In* Strategies for human settlements: habitat and environment p40-44

Stanford, William Bedell

The translation of the 'Agamemnon' of Aeschylus. *In* Time was away p63-66

About individual works

Greek metaphor, studies in theory and practice

Segal, C. P. Synaesthesia in Sophocles. *In* Illinois classical studies v2 1977 p88-96

Stanford University

Miner, A. S. Affirmative action at Stanford University; introductory notes. *In* Women in academia p139-62

Faculty

Rosenzweig, R. M. Faculty and standards of ethical conduct. *In* Hook, S.; Kurtz, P. and Todorovich, M. eds. The ethics of teaching and scientific research p73-82

Stange, George Robert

Refractions of Past and present. *In* Fielding, K. J. and Tarr, R. L. eds. Carlyle past and present p96-111

Stangl, Franz

About

Dawidowicz, L. S. An obedient killer: Franz Stangl, Commandant of Treblinka. *In* Dawidowicz, L. S. The Jewish presence p238-46

Stankiewicz, Edward

Poetics and verbal art. *In* Sebeok, T. A. ed. A perfusion of signs p54-76

Sound and sight in the Sonety krymskie of Adam Mickiewicz. *In* For Wiktor Weintraub p493-503

Stanley, Eric Gerald

About Troilus. *In* English Association. Essays and studies, 1976 p84-106

Directions for making many sorts of laces. *In* Chaucer and Middle English studies in honour of Rossell Hope Robbins p89-103

Stanley, Sir Henry Morton

About

Southall, A. W. White strangers and their religion in East Africa and Madagascar. *In* Shack, W. A. and Skinner, E. P. eds. Strangers in African societies p211-26

Stanley, Julia P.

Lesbian separatism: the linguistic and social sources of separatist politics. *In* Crew, L. ed. The gay academic p121-31

Stanley, Manfred

Beyond progress: three post-political futures. *In* Bundy, R. F. ed. Images of the future: the twenty-first century and beyond p115-24

Dignity versus survival? Reflections on the moral philosophy of social order. *In* Brown, R. H. and Lyman, S. M. eds. Structure, consciousness, and history p197-234

Stanley M. Isaacs Neighborhood Center, New York
Hildebrandt, H. The community center in the life of a dying person with no family involvement. *In* Home care p215-22

Stanlis, Peter J.
Acceptable in heaven's sight. *In* Frost: centennial essays III p179-311
The aesthetic theory of Eliseo Vivas. *In* Viva Vivas! p139-81
Robert Frost: politics in theory and practice. *In* Frost: centennial essays II p48-82

Stannard, David E.
Changes in the American family: fiction and reality. *In* Tufte, V. and Myerhoff, B. G. eds. Changing images of the family p83-96
Death and the Puritan child. *In* Death in America p9-29
Also in Vaughan, A. T. and Bremer, F. J. eds. Puritan New England p232-49
Growing up and growing old: dilemmas of aging in bureaucratic America. *In* Spicker, S. F.; Woodward, K. M. and Van Tassel, D. D. eds. Aging and the elderly p9-20

Stannard, Jerry Willmert
Natural history. *In* Lindberg, D. C. ed. Science in the Middle Ages p429-60

Stansky, Peter
Toward 1984: George Orwell and today's Britain. *In* Kramnick, I. ed. Is Britain dying? p269-76

Stansky, Peter, and Abrahams, William Miller
About individual works
The unknown Orwell
Connolly, C. George Orwell: 1. *In* Connolly, C. The evening colonnade p335-39

Stanton, Max Edward
Southern Louisiana survivors: the Houma Indians. *In* Williams, W. L. ed. Southeastern Indians since the removal era p90-109

Stanton, Phoebe B.
Architecture, history, and the spirit of age. *In* Altholz, J. L. ed. The mind and art of Victorian England p146-58

Stanwood, P. G.
"Essentiall joye" in Donne's Anniversaries. *In* Roberts, J. R. ed. Essential articles for the study of John Donne's poetry p387-96

Staple system
Baker, R. L. The government of Calais in 1363. *In* Order and innovation in the Middle Ages p207-14

Stapledon, Olaf. See Stapledon, William Olaf

Stapledon, William Olaf
About
Smith, C. C. Olaf Stapledon's dispassionate objectivity. *In* Clareson, T. D. ed. Voices for the future: essays on major science fiction writers v 1 p44-63

Stapleford, Richard
Constantinian politics and the atrium church. *In* Millon, H. A. and Nochlin, L. eds. Art and architecture in the service of politics p2-19

Staples, Robert
Black sexuality. *In* Sexuality and human values p62-70

Stapleton, Laurence
The theme of virtue in Donne's verse epistles. *In* Roberts, J. R. ed. Essential articles for the study of John Donne's poetry p451-61

Starke, Joseph Gabriel
Human rights and international law. *In* Human rights p113-31

Starkie, Enid
About individual works
Flaubert: the master
Connolly, C. Flaubert: 2. *In* Connolly, C. The evening colonnade p151-54

Starobinski, Jean
André Chénier and the allegory of poetry. *In* Krober, K. and Walling, W. eds. Images of romanticism p39-60
From the decline of erudition to the decline of nations: Gibbon's response to French thought. *In* Edward Gibbon and The decline and fall of the Roman Empire p139-57

Starr, Paul
Medicine and the waning of professional sovereignty. *in* A New America? p175-93
Medicine, economy and society in nineteenth-century America. *In* Branca, P. ed. The medicine show p47-66

Starr, S. Frederick
OSA: the union of contemporary architects. *In* Gibian, G. and Tjalsma, H. W. eds. Russian modernism p188-208
The revival and schism of urban planning in twentieth-century Russia. *In* Hamm, M. F. ed. The city in Russian history p222-42
Visionary town planning during the cultural revolution. *In* Cultural revolution in Russia, 1928-1931 p207-40

Starr, Stephen Z.
Cold steel: the saber and the Union cavalry. *In* Hubbell, J. T. ed. Battles lost and won p107-24

Starrett, Vincent
"Stephen Crane: an estimate." Introduction to Men, women and boats by Stephen Crane. *In* Praise from famous men: an anthology of introductions p136-46

Stars. See Astrophysics; Milky Way; Planets

Stars (in religion, folklore, etc.)
Hou, Ching-lang. The Chinese belief in baleful stars. *In* Welch, B. and Seidel, A. K. eds. Facets of Taoism p193-228

Stars, New
Zonn, W. Explosive events in the universe. *In* Neyman, J. ed. The heritage of Copernicus: theories "pleasing to the mind" p95-115

Stars, Variable. See Stars, New

Stars in literature
Hellman, C. D. A poem on the occasion of the nova of 1572. *In* Philosophy and humanism p306-09

Starvation
Narveson, J. Morality and starvation. *In* Aiken, W. and La Follette, H. eds. World hunger and moral obligation p49-65
See also Famines

State, The
Berki, R. N. State and society: an antithesis of modern political thought. *In* Hayward, J. E. S. and Berki, R. N. eds. State and society in contemporary Europe p 1-20
Cassirer, E. Hegel's theory of the state. *In* Cassirer, E. Symbol, myth, and culture p108-20

State universities and colleges—United States
—*Continued*

Leslie, L. L. Updating education for the professions: the new mission. *In* Land-grant universities and their continuing challenge p237-65

Madsen, D. L. The land-grant university: myth and reality. *In* Land-grant universities and their continuing challenge p23-48

Nichols, D. C. Land-grant university services and urban policy. *In* Land-grant universities and their continuing challenge p223-36

Proctor, S. D. Land-grant universities and the Black presence. *In* Land-grant universities and their continuing challenge p190-204

Schein, R. D. The land-grant university and environmental affairs. *In* Land-grant universities and their continuing challenge p178-89

Toombs, W. New colleges for new occupations. *In* Land-grant universities and their continuing challenge p266-85

Statehood (American politics) See State governments

States, Ideal. See Utopias

States, New

Calvert, P. On attaining sovereignty. *In* Smith, A. D. ed. Nationalist movements p134-49

Dei-Anang, M. Foreign policy of the independent African states. *In* African studies since 1945 p66-76

Watson, A. Morgenthau's concept of the national interest and the new states of the Third world. *In* [Truth and tragedy]: a tribute to Hans Morgenthau p305-15

See also Underdeveloped areas

States, Small

Mugomba, A. T. Small developing states and the external operational environment. *In* The Year book of world affairs, 1979 p201-16

See also Great powers; Neutrality

States' rights. See State rights

Statesmen

See also Diplomats

Biography

Post, K. W. J. Individuals and the dialectic: a Marxist view of political biographies. *In* The Making of politicians: studies from Africa and Asia p17-27

Africa

Nye, J. S. Nationalism, statesmen, and the size of African states. *In* Kilson, M. ed. New states in the modern world p158-68

India

Brown, J. M. 'Gandhi's men,' 1917-22: the role of the major leader in the careers of middle-rank politicians. *In* The Making of politicians: studies from Africa and Asia p126-39

Manor, J. The lesser leader amid political transformation: the Congress Party in Mysore state in 1941 and 1951. *In* The Making of politicians: studies from Africa and Asia p140-55

Sri Lanka

Jupp, J. Five Sinhalese nationalist politicians. *In* The Making of politicians: studies from Africa and Asia p183-94

United States

Yates, D. The roots of American leadership: political style and policy consequences. *In* Burnham, W. D. and Weinberg, M. W. eds. American politics and public policy p140-68

Static electricity. See Electrostatics

Statics

See also Electro-statics; Equilibrium

Early works to 1800

Brown, J. E. The science of weights. *In* Lindberg, D. C. ed. Science in the Middle Ages p179-205

Statics and dynamics (Social sciences)

Fox, K. A. Combining economic and non-economic objectives in development planning: problems of concept and measurement. *In* Economic development and planning p104-41

Mathematical models

Fox, K. A. Combining economic and non-economic objectives in development planning: problems of concept and measurement. *In* Economic development and planning p104-41

Stationers' wills, Some sixteenth-century. Phelps, W. H. *In* Virginia. University. Bibliographical Society. Studies in bibliography v32 p48-59

Stationery trade. See Paper making and trade

Statistical inference. See Probabilities

Statistical linguistics. See Mathematical linguistics

Statistical thermodynamics

Kac, M. The emergence of statistical thought in exact sciences. *In* Neyman, J. ed. The heritage of Copernicus: theories "pleasing to the mind" p433-44

Statistics. See Biometry; Econometrics; also subdivision Statistics, Vital under names of countries, cities, etc.; e.g Latin America—Statistics, Vital

Statistics, Mathematical. See Mathematical statistics

Statistics of sampling. See Sampling (Statistics)

Statius, Publius Papinius

About individual works

Sleep

Cunningham, J. V. Classical and medieval: Statius on sleep. *In* Cunningham, J. V. The collected essays of J. V. Cunningham p147-61

Friends and associates

White, P. The friends of Martial, Statius, and Pliny, and the dispersal of patronage. *In* Harvard Studies in classical philology v79 p265-300

Statues

Europe

Seidel, L. V. Holy warriors: the Romanesque rider and the fight against Islam. *In* The Holy war p33-77

Statuettes. See Bronzes

Status, Social. See Social status

Statutes

Great Britain—History

Elton, G. R. The sessional printing of statutes, 1484-1547. *In* Wealth and power in Tudor England p68-86

Stefanile, Felix

The little magazine today. *In* Anderson, E. and Kinzie, M. eds. The little magazine in America: a modern documentary history p649-63

Stefaniszyn, Bronislaw

The material culture of the Ambo of Northern Rhodesia. *In* The Occasional papers of the Rhodes-Livingstone Museum p721-826

Steffens, Joseph Lincoln. See Steffens, Lincoln

Steffens, Lincoln

About individual works

The autobiography of Lincoln Steffens

Cooley, T. The next generation; Future perfect: Lincoln Steffens. *In* Cooley, T. Educated lives: the rise of modern autobiography in America p125-38

Stegner, Wallace Earle

The Iowa years. *In* Lerner, D. and Nelson, L. M. eds. Communication research—a half-century appraisal p305-10

The writer and the concept of adulthood. *In* Erikson, E. H. ed. Adulthood p227-36

Stehr, Nico

The ethos of science revisited: social and cognitive norms. *In* Gaston, J. ed. Sociology of science p172-96

Steig, Michael

Iconography of sexual conflict in Dombey and son. *In* Dickens Studies Annual v 1 p161-67

Martin Chuzzlewit's progress by Dickens and Phiz. *In* Dickens Studies Annual v2 p119-48

Stein, Arnold Sidney

Meter and meaning in Donne's verse. *In* Roberts, J. R. ed. Essential articles for the study of John Donne's poetry p161-70

Stein, Gertrude

About

Cooley, T. The next generation; The continuous present: Gertrude Stein. *In* Cooley, T. Educated lives: the rise of modern autobiography in America p156-78

Couser, G. T. Gertrude Stein: the making of a prophet. *In* Couser, G. T. American autobiography p148-63

Ford, H. D. **Gertrude Stein's Plain editions.** *In* Ford, H. D. **Published in Paris** p231-52

Gass, W. H. Gertrude Stein and the geography of the sentence. *In* Gass, W. H. The world within the word p63-123

Howard, M. Editor's note on Edith Wharton and Gertrude Stein. *In* Howard, M. ed. Seven American women writers of the twentieth century p28-34

Lewis, W. Gertrude Stein; excerpt from "Time and Western man." *In* Lewis, W. Enemy salvoes p113-17

Lodge, D. Gertrude Stein. *In* Lodge, D. The modes of modern writing p145-55

McMillan, D. Gertrude Stein. *In* McMillan, D. Transition p167-78

Morris, W. Gertrude Stein. *In* Morris, W. Earthly delights, unearthly adornments p69-80

Spencer, B. T. Gertrude Stein: non-expatriate. *In* Literature and ideas in America p204-27

Tanner, T. Gertrude Stein and the complete actual present. *In* Tanner, T. The reign of wonder p187-204

Wagner, L. W. Sherwood, Stein, the sentence, and grape sugar and oranges. *In* Anderson, D. D. ed. Sherwood Anderson: dimensions of his literary art p75-89

About individual works

The autobiography of Alice B. Toklas

Cooley, T. The next generation; The continuous present: Gertrude Stein. *In* Cooley, T. Educated lives: the rise of modern autobiography in America p156-78

Four in America

Wilder, T. N. Gertrude Stein's Four in America. *In* Wilder, T. N. American characteristics, and other essays p193-222

The geographical history of America

Wilder, T. N. Gertrude Stein's The geographical history of America. *In* Wilder, T. N. American characteristics, and other essays p187-92

The making of Americans

Frieling, K. The becoming of Gertude Stein's The making of Americans. *In* French, W. G. ed. The twenties p157-70

Narration

Wilder, T. N. Gertrude Stein's Narration. *In* Wilder, T. N. American characteristics, and other essays p183-86

Tender buttons

Gass, W. H. Gertrude Stein and the geography of the sentence. *In* Gass, W. H. The world within the word p63-123

Language—Style

See Stein, Gertrude—Style

Style

Gass, W. H. Gertrude Stein and the geography of a sentence. *In* Gass, W. H. The world within a word p63-123

Technique

See Stein, Gertrude—Style

Stein, Howard F.

Envy and the evil eye: an essay in the psychological ontogeny of belief and ritual. *In* The Evil eye p193-222

Stein, Lorenz Jacob von

About

Gilbert, F. From political to social history: Lorenz von Stein and the Revolution of 1848. *In* Gilbert, F. History p411-21

Stein, Peter

Vacarius and the civil law. *In* Church and government in the Middle Ages p119-37

Stein, Rolf Alfred

Religious Taoism and popular religion from the second to seventh centuries. *In* Welch, H. and Seidel, A. K. eds. Facets of Taoism p53-81

Stein, Stephen J.

Cotton Mather and Jonathan Edwards on the number of the beast: eighteenth-century speculation about the Antichrist. *In* American Antiquarian Society. Proceedings v84 pt2 p293-315

Steinbeck, John, 1902-1968

About

Astro, R. Phlebas sails the Caribbean: Steinbeck, Hemingway, and the American waste land. *In* French, W. G. ed. The twenties p215-33

Gray, J. John Steinbeck. *In* Walcutt, C. C. ed. Seven novelists in the American naturalist tradition p205-44

Waldmeir, J. J. John Steinbeck: no Grapes of wrath. *In* Filler, L. ed. A question of quality: popularity and value in modern creative writing p219-28

About individual works

The grapes of wrath

Campbell, R. Trampling out the vintage: sour grapes. *In* Peary, G. and Shatzkin, R. eds. The modern American novel and the movies p107-18

Donald, M. The traditional novel. *In* Donald, M. The American novel in the twentieth century p13-72

Watkins, F. C. Flat wine from The grapes of wrath. *In* Watkins, F. C. In time and place p19-29

Of mice and men

Everson, W. K. Thoughts on a great adaptation. *In* Peary, G. and Shatzkin, R. eds. The modern American novel and the movies p63-69

Of mice and men (Play)

Kauffmann, S. Of mice and men. *In* Kauffmann, S. Persons of the drama p156-59

Steinberg, Arthur. See Lechtman, H. jt. auth.

Steinberg, Leo

Drawing as if to possess; excerpt from "Other criteria." *In* Kaplan, P. and Manso, S. eds. Major European art movements, 1900-1945 p193-221

Steinberg, Saul

About

Rosenberg, H. Steinberg: self and style. *In* Rosenberg, H. Art on the edge p109-19

Steinbruner, John D.

An assessment of nuclear crises. *In* Griffiths, F. and Polanyi, J. C. eds. The dangers of nuclear war p34-49

Steinbruner, John D. and Carter, Barry E.

Organizational and political dimensions of the strategic posture: the problems of reform. *In* Long, F. A. and Rathjens, G. W. eds. Arms, defense policy, and arms control p131-54

Steindl-Rast, David F. K.

Defining religion from within. *In* Christian faith in a religiously plural world p123-35

Steinen, Karl von den. See Von den Steinen, Karl

Steiner, George

On difficulty and other essays

Contents

After the book?

Dante now: the gossip of eternity

The distribution of discourse

Eros and idiom

On difficulty

A remark on language and psychoanalysis

Text and context

Whorf, Chomsky, and the student of literature

Also in Wimsatt, W. K. ed: Literary criticism: idea and act p242-62

Why English? *In* Contemporary approaches to English studies p8-23

About individual works

After Babel

Parkinson, G. H. R. The translation theory of understanding. *In* Royal Institute of Philosophy. Communication and understanding p 1-19

Stewart, M. A. Locke, Steiner and understanding. *In* Royal Institute of Philosophy. Communication and understanding p20-45

Steiner, Jürg, and Obler, Jeffrey

Does the consociational theory really hold for Switzerland? *In* Esman, M. J. ed. Ethnic conflict in the Western world p324-42

Steinhoff, Hans

About individual works

Uncle Kruger

Taylor, R. Uncle Kruger. *In* Taylor, R. Film propaganda p207-15

Steinkraus, Warren Edward

Paul Schilpp and the social relevance of philosophy. *In* The Abdication of philosophy: philosophy and the public good p279-98

Steinmann, Martin. See Brown, R. L. jt. auth.

Stell, Geoffrey

Architecture: the changing needs of society. *In* Brown, J. M. ed. Scottish society in the fifteenth century p153-83

Stella, Gianpietro

About

Gilbert, F. The last will of a Venetian Grand Chancellor. *In* Philosophy and humanism p502-17

Steloff, Frances

Censorship and the Gotham Book Mart. *In* Bookselling in America and the world p181-83

Stemmler, Theo

An interpretation of Alysoun. *In* Chaucer and Middle English studies in honour of Rossell Hope Robbins p111-18

Stempel, Wolf-Dieter

Syntax and obscurity in poetry: on Mallarmé's A la nue accablante. *In* Amacher, R. E. and Lange, V. eds. New perspectives in German literary criticism p134-49

Stendhal, pseud. See Beyle, Marie Henri

Stendhal, Krister

Judgment and mercy. *In* The Context of contemporary theology p147-54

Steneck, Nicholas H.

Commentary: in defense of context. *In* The Copernican achievement p157-64

Stenius, Erik

'All men are mortal.' *In* Fact, value, and perception p31-41

Stenning, Keith

Anaphora as an approach to pragmatics. *In* Linguistic theory and psychological reality p162-200

Stenvall, Aleksis

About individual works

Seven brothers

Laitinen, K. From the forest to the city: the great tradition in Finnish prose. *In* Dauenhauer, R. and Binham, P. eds. Snow in May p21-28

Stepan, Alfred C.
Inclusionary and exclusionary military responses to radicalism: with special attention to Peru; excerpt from "The state and society: Peru in comparative perspective." *In* Radicalism in the contemporary age v3 p221-39

Political leadership and regime breakdown: Brazil. *In* The Breakdown of democratic regimes pt3 p110-37

Stephan, Cardinal of St Grisogono. See Etienne, Cardinal

Stephens, A. G. See Stephens, Alfred George

Stephens, Alfred George

About

Cantrell, L. A. G. Stephens, the Bulletin, and the 1890s. *In* Bards, bohemians, and bookmen p98-113

Stephens, Ann Sophia (Winterbotham)

About

Baym, N. Z. Ann Stephens, Mary Jane Holmes, and Marion Harland. *In* Baym, N. Z. Woman's fiction p175-207

Stephens, Frederic George
The purpose and tendency of early Italian art. *In* Sambrook, J. ed. Pre-Raphaelitism p57-63

Stephens, James, 1882-1950

About individual works

Reincarnations—Sources

Finneran, R. J. The sources of James Stephens's Reincarnations: "alone I did it, barring for the noble assistance of the gods." *In* Tulane studies in English v22 p143-53

Bibliography

Carens, J. F. Four Revival figures: Lady Gregory, A. E. (George W. Russell), Oliver St. John Gogarty, and James Stephens. *In* Finneran, R. J. ed. Anglo-Irish literature p436-69

Stephens, Otis H.
Equal justice and counsel rights in the United States and Canada. *In* Claude, R. P. ed. Comparative human rights p161-83

Stephens, Robert Oren
Language magic and reality in For whom the bell tolls. *In* Wagner, L. W. ed. Ernest Hemingway p266-79

Stephenson, John B. and Sexton, Robert Fenimore
Experiential education and revitalization of the liberal arts. *In* Hook, S.; Kurtz, P. W. and Todorovich, M. eds. The philosophy of the curriculum: the need for general education p177-96

Stephenson, William
The ludenic theory of newsreading. *In* Fischer, H. D. and Melnik, S. R. eds. Entertainment: a cross-cultural examination p105-14

Stepto, Robert B.
Narration, authentication, and authorial control in Frederick Douglass' Narrative of 1845. *In* Fisher, D. and Stepto, R. B. eds. Afro-American literature p178-91

Teaching Afro-American literature: survey or tradition: the reconstruction of instruction. *In* Fisher, D. and Stepto, R. B. eds. Afro-American literature p8-24

Stereochemistry
Kottler, D. B. Louis Pasteur and molecular dissymmetry, 1844-1857. *In* Studies in history of biology v2 p57-98

Stereographs. See Photography, Stereoscopic

Stereoscopic photography. See Photography, Stereoscopic

Stereotype (Psychology)
McLuhan, H. M. The implications of cultural uniformity. *In* Bigsby, C. W. E. Superculture p43-56

Sterility. See Fertility, Human

Sterling, Christopher H.
Television as a cultural force: a selected reading list. *In* Television as a cultural force p175-84

Stern, Axel. See Stern-Mitscherlich, Axel Ludwig

Stern, Charlotte Daniels
The early Spanish drama: from medieval ritual to Renaissance art. *In* Renaissance drama [1973] p177-201

Stern, Fritz Richard
The burden of success: reflections on German Jewry. *In* Art, politics, and will p124-44

Capitalism and the cultural historian. *In* From Parnassus p209-24

Prussia. *In* Spring, D. ed. European landed elites in the nineteenth century p45-67

Stern, Gustaf

About individual works

Meaning and change of meaning

Richards, I. A. Meaning and change of meaning. *In* Richards, I. A. Complementarities p73-87

Stern, Joseph Peter
The embattled style: Ernst Jünger, In Stahlgewittern. *In* Klein, H. M. ed. The First World War in fiction p112-25

Nietzsche and the idea of metaphor. *In* Pasley, J. M. S. ed. Nietzsche: imagery and thought p64-82

Stern, Madeleine Bettina
Brissot de Warville and the Franco-American press. *In* Virginia. University. Bibliographical Society. Studies in bibliography v29 p362-72

Stern, Michael
From the folklore of speed to Danse macabre. *In* Peary, G. and Shatzkin, R. eds. The modern American novel and the movies p40-52

Stern, Milton R.
Nathaniel Hawthorne: "conservative after heaven's own fashion." *In* Essays in honor of Russel B. Nye p195-225

Towards 'Bartleby the scrivener.' *In* The Stoic strain in American literature p19-41

Stern, Robert Mitchell
Testing trade theories. *In* Kenen, P. B. ed. International trade and finance p3-49

Stern-Mitscherlich, Axel Ludwig
On value and human dignity. *In* The Personal universe p74-90

Sternberg, Josef von. See Von Sternberg, Josef

Sternberg, Robert J.; Tourangeau, Roger, and Nigro, Georgia
Metaphor, induction, and social policy: the convergence of macroscopic and microscopic views. *In* Ortony, A. ed. Metaphor and thought p325-53

Sterne, Laurence

About individual works

The abuses of conscience

New, M. Sterne as editor: the "Abuses of conscience" sermon. *In* Studies in eighteenth-century culture v8 p243-51

A sentimental journey

Auty, S. G. Smollett and Sterne and animal spirits: A sentimental journey. *In* Auty, S. G. The comic spirit of eighteenth-century novels p147-58

Cockshut, A. O. J. Sterne. *In* Cockshut, A. O. J. Man and woman: a study of love and the novel, 1740-1940 p46-53

Tristram Shandy

Alter, R. Sterne and the nostalgia for reality. *In* Alter, R. Partial magic p30-56

Auty, S. G. Smollett and Sterne and animal spirits: Tristram Shandy. *In* Auty, S. G. The comic spirit of eighteenth-century novels p119-47

Karl, F. R. Tristram Shandy, the sentimental novel, and sentimentalists. *In* Karl, F. R. The adversary literature p205-34

New, M. Sterne as editor: the "Abuses of conscience" sermon. *In* Studies in eighteenth-century culture v8 p243-51

New, M. and Fry, N. Some borrowings in Tristram Shandy: the textual problem. *In* Virginia. University. Bibliographical Society. Studies in bibliography v29 p322-30

Rothstein, E. Tristram Shandy. *In* Rothstein, E. Systems of order and inquiry in later eighteenth-century fiction p62-108

Shklovskiĭ, V. B. Pushkin and Sterne: Eugene Onegin. *In* Erlich, V. ed. Twentieth-century Russian literary criticism p63-80

Skilton, D. Sterne, sentiment and its opponents. *In* Skilton, D. The English novel p45-58

Spacks, P. A. M. The beautiful oblique: Tristram Shandy. *In* Spacks, P. A. M. Imagining a self p127-57

Spacks, P. A. M. Early fiction and the frightened male. *In* Spilka, M. ed. Towards a poetics of fiction p255-65

Sternglass, Ernest J.

Nuclear radiation and human health. *In* Against pollution and hunger p121-79

Sternhell, Zeev

Fascist ideology. *In* Laqueur, W. Z. ed. Fascism: a reader's guide p315-76

Sterrenburg, Lee Whitney

Mary Shelley's monster: politics and psyche in Frankenstein. *In* Levine, G. L. and Knoepflmacher, U. C. eds. The endurance of Frankenstein p143-71

Steuart, Denham, Sir James, bart.

About

Checkland, S. G. Adam Smith and the bankers. *In* Skinner, A. S. and Wilson, T. eds. Essays on Adam Smith p504-23

Stevens, David

Adam Smith and the colonial disturbances. *In* Skinner, A. S. and Wilson, T. eds. Essays on Adam Smith p202-17

Stevens, George

About individual works

The greatest story ever told

Macdonald, D. The greatest story ever told: excerpt from "Dwight Macdonald on movies." *In* Denby, D. ed. Awake in the dark p382-88

Stevens, John E.

About individual works

Medieval romance: themes and approaches

Hornstein, L. H. Medieval romance. *In* Medievalia et humanistica no. 7 p189-94

Stevens, Martin

The performing self in twelfth-century culture. *In* Viator: medieval and Renaissance studies v9 p193-212

Stevens, Peter

Dorothy Livesay: the love poetry. *In* Woodcock, G. ed. Poets and critics p33-52

Stevens, Wallace

Imagination as value. *In* Wimsatt, W. K. ed. Literary criticism: idea and act p83-96

The irrational element in poetry; excerpt from "Opus posthumous." *In* Gibbons, R. ed. The poet's work: 29 masters of 20th century poetry on the origins and practice of their art p48-58

About

Bertholf, R. J. Shelley, Stevens and Robert Duncan: the poetry of approximations. *In* Artful thunder p269-99

Bloom, H. Wallace Stevens: the transcendental strain. *In* Bloom, H. Poetry and repression p267-93

Cunningham, J. V. The styles and procedures of Wallace Stevens. *In* Cunningham, J. V. The collected essays of J. V. Cunningham p379-98

Cunningham, J. V. Tradition and modernity: Wallace Stevens. *In* Cunningham, J. V. The collected essays of J. V. Cunningham p225-43

Dauenhauer, R. The view from the Aspen Grove: Paavo Haavikko in national and international context. *In* Dauenhauer, R. and Binham, P. eds. Snow in May p67-97

Eberhart, R. Emerson and Wallace Stevens. *In* Eberhart, R. Of poetry and poets p153-71

Eberhart, R. Reflections on Wallace Stevens in 1976. *In* Eberhart, R. Of poetry and poets p214-301

Frye, N. Wallace Stevens and the variation form. *In* Frye, N. Spiritus mundi p275-94

Josipovici, G. 'But time will not relent': modern literature and the experience of time. *In* Josipovici, G. ed. The modern English novel: the reader, the writer and the work p252-72

Kenner, H. Something to say. *In* Kenner, H. A homemade world p50-90

Kunitz, S. J. The vice-president of insurance. *In* Kunitz, S. J. A kind of order, a kind of folly p233-40

Litz, A. W. Wallace Stevens' defense of poetry: La poésie pure, the new romantic, and the pressure of reality. *In* Bornstein, G. ed. Romantic and modern p111-32

Mollinger, R. N. Wallace Stevens' search for the central man. *In* Tennessee Studies in literature v 21 p66-79

Olson, E. The poetry of Wallace Stevens. *In* Olson, E. On value judgments in the arts, and other essays p55-64

Parker, P. A. Epilogue. *In* Parker, P. A. Inescapable romance p219-43

Rother, J. Wallace Stevens as a nonsense poet. *In* Tennessee Studies in literature v 21 p80-90

Stevens, Wallace—About—*Continued*

Schneider, D. J. The symbolic system and the authority of the literary work. *In* Schneider, D. J. Symbolism: the Manichean vision p204-17

Schneider, D. J. "The war that never ends": patterns of proliferation in Wallace Stevens's poetry. *In* Schneider, D. J. Symbolism: the Manichean vision p154-203

Webb, E. The ambiguities of secularization: modern transformations of the Kingdom in Nietzsche, Ibsen, Beckett, and Stevens. *In* Webb, E. The dark dove p34-87

Webber, J. Walking on water: Milton, Stevens, and contemporary American poetry. *In* Wittreich, J. A. ed. Milton and the line of vision p231-68

About individual works
Letters, selected and edited by Holly Stevens

Kunitz, S. J. The vice-president of insurance. *In* Kunitz, S. J. A kind of order, a kind of folly p233-40

Notes toward a supreme fiction

Miller, J. E. Meditations on a recipe for a modern American epic: Wallace Stevens's "Notes toward a supreme fiction." *In* Miller, J. E. The American quest for a supreme fiction p50-66

Sea surface full of clouds

Adams, R. P. Pure poetry: Wallace Stevens' "Sea surface full of clouds." *In* Tulane Studies in English v21 p91-122

Stevens, Winifred Kera

Recent Brazilian productions of Le bourgeois gentilhomme and Les femmes savantes. *In* Johnson, R. B.; Neumann, E. S. and Trail, G. T. eds. Molière and the commonwealth of letters: patrimony and posterity p407-09

Stevens-Cox, Gregory

The Hardy industry. *In* Drabble, M. ed. The genius of Thomas Hardy p170-81

Stevenson, Adlai Ewing, 1900-1965

About

Galbraith, J. K. John Bartlow Martin and Adlai Stevenson. *In* Galbraith, J. K. Annals of an abiding liberal p295-300

About individual works
Looking outward

Kennedy, J. F. President U.S. Preface to Looking outward: years of crisis at the United Nations by Adlai Stevenson. *In* Praise from famous men: an anthology of introductions p89-93

Stevenson, Charles Leslie

The rhythm of English verse. *In* Gross, H. S. ed. The structure of verse p194-224

About individual works
Ethics and language

Glossop, R. J. Hume, Stevenson, and Hare on moral language. *In* Livingston, D. W. and King, J. T. eds. Hume p362-85

Stevenson, David Harry

Irony and deception. *In* Riewald, J. G. ed. The surprise of excellence p65-76

Stevenson, Grace Thomas

Lester E. Asheim—an appreciation. *In* As much to learn as to teach p11-15

Stevenson, John

Myth and realty: Britain in the 1930s. *In* Crisis and controversy p90-109

The politics of violence. *In* Peele, G. and Cook, C. eds. The politics of reappraisal, 1918-1939 p146-65

Stevenson, Lionel

Carlyle and Meredith. *In* Carlyle and his contemporaries p256-79

Meredith and the art of implication. *In* The Victorian experience: the novelists p177-201

Stevenson, Richard Colton

Comedy, tragedy, and the spirit of critical intelligence in Richard Feverel. *In* The Worlds of Victorian fiction p205-22

Stevenson, Robert Louis

About

Briggs, J. Far away and long ago: Stevenson's Scotland and Kipling's India. *In* Briggs, J. Night visitors p98-110

Hart, F. R. The anti-Kailyard as theological furor. *In* Hart, F. R. The Scottish novel p131-39

Hart, F. R. Stevenson, Munro, and Buchan. *In* Hart, F. R. The Scottish novel p154-81

Morgan, E. The poetry of Robert Louis Stevenson. *In* Morgan, E. Essays p135-49

About individual works
The strange case of Dr Jekyll and Mr Hyde

Borowitz, A. Dr. Jekyll and Mr. Stevenson. *In* Borowitz, A. Innocence and arsenic p26-32

Briggs, J. A scientific spirit: mesmerism, drugs and psychic doctors. *In* Briggs, J. Night visitors p52-75

Massey, I. The third self: Dracula, Jekyll and Hyde, "Lokis." *In* Massey, I. The gaping pig p98-114

Stever, Horton Guyford

Man takes wings. *In* Neyman, J. ed. The heritage of Copernicus: theories "pleasing to the mind" p467-86

Stevick, Philip

Frankenstein and comedy. *In* Levine, G. L. and Knoepflmacher, U. C. eds. The endurance of Frankenstein p221-39

Prolegomena to the study of fictional dreck. *In* Cohen, S. B. ed. Comic relief p263-80

Stevick, Robert D.

Arithmetical design of the Old English Andreas. *In* Anglo-Saxon poetry: essays in appreciation p99-115

Steward, Julian Haynes

Evolution and ecology

Contents

Carrier acculturation: the direct historical approach

The ceremonial buffoon of the American Indian

The concept and method of cultural ecology

Concepts and methods of area research

Cultural evolution

Cultural evolution in South America

Determinism in primitive society?

The direct historical approach to archeology

The evolution of prefarming societies

Evolutionary principles and social types

The foundations of Basin-Plateau Shoshonean society

Function and configuration in archeology

Limitations of applied anthropology: the case of the Indian New Deal

Steward, Julian H.
Evolution and ecology
Contents—Continued
Modernization in traditional societies
The people of Puerto Rico
Tappers and trappers: parallel processes in acculturation
Wittfogel's irrigation hypothesis

About

Murphy, R. F. Introduction: The anthropological theories of Julian H. Steward. *In* Steward, J. H. Evolution and ecology p 1-39

Stewart, Alfred D.
Jack Williamson: the comedy of cosmic evolution. *In* Clareson, T. D. ed. Voices for the future: essays on major science fiction writers v 1 p14-43

Stewart, Douglas James
The silence of Magna Mater. *In* Harvard Studies in classical philology v74 p75-84

Stewart, Garrett
Lawrence, "being," and the allotropic style. *In* Spilka, M. ed. Towards a poetics of fiction p331-56

Stewart, George Rippey

About individual works
Names on the land
Welty, E. George R. Stewart's Names on the land. *In* Welty, E. The eye of the story p182-89

Stewart, J. I. M. See Stewart, John Innes Mackintosh

Stewart, James Brewer
The aim and impact of Garrisonian abolitionism, 1840-1860. *In* Swierenga, R. P. ed. Beyond the Civil War synthesis p329-41

Stewart, John Innes Mackintosh
The major novels. *In* Drabble, M. ed. The genius of Thomas Hardy p56-66

Stewart, John Lincoln

About individual works
The burden of time: the Fugitives and agrarians
Howe, I. Southern agrarians and American culture. *In* Howe, I. Celebrations and attacks p161-65

Stewart, Mary W. See Richardson, J. T. jt. auth.

Stewart, Michael Alexander
Locke, Steiner and understanding. *In* Royal Institute of Philosophy. Communication and understanding p20-45

Stewart, Randall
Tidewater and frontier. *In* Inge, M. T. ed. The frontier humorists p281-91

Stewart, Thomas Dale
Perspectives on some problems of early man common to America and Australia. *In* Grafton Elliot Smith p114-35
Recent developments in understanding the relationship between the Neanderthals and modern man. *In* Grafton Elliot Smith p67-82

Steyn, Jan Heinrik
The punishment scene in South Africa—developments over the past decade and the prospects for reform. *In* Crime, criminology and public policy p527-70

Sticht, Thomas G.
Educational uses of metaphor. *In* Ortony. A. ed. Metaphor and thought p474-85

Stiehm, Judith Hicks
Government and the family: justice and acceptance. *In* Tufte, V. and Myerhoff, B. G. eds. Changing images of the family p361-75

Stierle, Karl-Heinz
Story as exemplum—exemplum as story: on the pragmatics and poetics of narrative texts. *In* Amacher, R. E. and Lange, V. eds. New perspectives in German literary criticism p389-417

Stierlin, Helm
Liberation and self-destruction in the creative process. *In* Psychiatry and the humanities v 1 p51-72

Stifter, Adalbert

About individual works
Brigitta
Branscombe, P. The use of leitmotifs in Stifter's Brigitta. *In* Branscombe, P. ed. Austrian life and literature, 1780-1938 p49-50

Der Nachsommer
Bruford, W. H. Adalbert Stifter: Der Nachsommer (1857). *In* Bruford, W. H. The German tradition of self-cultivation p128-46
Swales, M. Stifter: Indian summer (1857). *In* Swales, M. The German Bildungsroman from Wieland to Hesse p74-85

Granit
Swales, M. Stifter: Granit. *In* Swales, M. The German Novelle p133-57

Stigler, George Joseph
Smith's travels on the Ship of State. *In* Skinner, A. S. and Wilson, T. eds. Essays on Adam Smith p237-46
See also Becker, G. S. jt. auth.

Stilicho, Flavius

About
Cameron, A. Theodosius the Great and the regency of Stilico. *In* Harvard Studies in classical philology v73 p247-80

Stilico. See Stilicho, Flavius

Still-life in art. See Still-life painting

Still-life painting
Schapiro, M. The apples of Cézanne: an essay on the meaning of still-life. *In* Schapiro, M. Selected papers v2 p 1-45

Stilling, Roger
Love and death in Renaissance tragedy
Contents
Antonio and Mellida: I & II
Cyril Tourneur
Gismond of Salern: in love
Hamlet
John Ford and the Jacobeans
John Webster
The love of King David and fair Bethsabe
Othello
Shakespeare and the poetry of earth
The Spanish tragedy
Thomas Heywood
Thomas Middleton
The tragedy of Dido, Queen of Carthage
Troilus and Cressida

Stillman, Richard Joseph
Black participation in the Armed Forces. *In* The Black American reference book p889-926

Stoddard, Solomon—*Continued*

About individual works

*Arguments for the proposition
(Manuscript)*

Davis, T. M. and Jeske, J. eds. Solomon Stoddard's 'Arguments' concerning admission to the Lord's Supper. *In* American Antiquarian Society. Proceedings v86 pt 1 p75-111

Stoessinger, John George

The statesman and the critic: Kissinger and Morgenthau. *In* [Truth and tragedy]: a tribute to Hans Morgenthau p220-36

The United Nations and the Arab-Israeli conflict. *In* The New world balance and peace in the Middle East: reality or mirage? p79-82

Stoever, William Kenneth Bristow

'A faire and easie way to heaven'

Contents

The dialectic of nature and grace
The doctrine of the two covenants: I
The doctrine of the two covenants: II
Epilogue
The nature of New England antinomianism
The New England controversy
The objectivity of regenerating grace: Thomas Shepard and Peter Bulkeley
The order of redemption and the ground of assurance
The preeminence of the spirit: John Cotton
"Preparation for salvation"
The quest for assurance: radical solutions and Puritan dialectics

Stoiber, Carlton

Equality and discrimination in international economic law (VII): the multinational enterprise. *In* The Year book of world affairs, 1977 p217-35

Stoics

Frede, M. Principles of Stoic grammar. *In* Rist, J. M. ed. The Stoics p27-75

Graeser, A. The Stoic theory of meaning. *In* Rist, J. M. ed. The Stoics p77-100

Kerferd, G. B. What does the wise man know? *In* Rist, J. M. ed. The Stoics p125-36

Kidd, I. G. Moral actions and rules in Stoic ethics. *In* Rist, J. M. ed. The Stoics p247-58

Lapidge, M. Stoic cosmology. *In* Rist, J. M. ed. The Stoics p161-85

Lloyd, A. C. Emotion and decision in Stoic psychology. *In* Rist, J. M. ed. The Stoics p233-46

Long, A. A. Dialectic and the Stoic sage. *In* Rist, J. M. ed. The Stoics p101-24

Mueller, I. An introduction to Stoic logic. *In* Rist, J. M. ed. The Stoics p 1-26

Reesor, M. E. Necessity and fate in Stoic philosophy. *In* Rist, J. M. ed. The Stoics p187-202

Rist, J. M. The Stoic concept of detachment. *In* Rist, J. M. ed. The Stoics p259-72

Stough, C. L. Stoic determinism and moral responsibility. *In* Rist, J. M. ed. The Stoics p203-31

Todd, R. B. Monism and immanence: the foundations of Stoic physics. *In* Rist, J. M. ed. The Stoics p137-60

Von Staden, H. The Stoic theory of perception and its "Platonic" critics. *In* Studies in perception p96-136

Stoics in literature

Allen, G. W. Walt Whitman and Stoicism. *In* The Stoic strain in American literature p43-60

Backman, M. Death and birth in Hemingway. *In* The Stoic strain in American literature p115-33

Beattie, M. Henry James: 'the voice of Stoicism.' *In* The Stoic strain in American literature p63-75

Buitenhuis, P. The Stoic strain in American literature. *In* The Stoic strain in American literature p3-16

Davison, R. A. A reading of Frank Norris's The pit. *In* The Stoic strain in American literature p77-94

Lawson, L. A. The moviegoer and the Stoic heritage. *In* The Stoic strain in American literature p180-91

MacMillan, D. J. His 'magnum o': Stoic humanism in Faulkner's A fable. *In* The Stoic strain in American literature p136-76

Salomon, R. B. The mock-heroics of desire: some Stoic personae in the work of William Carlos Williams. *In* The Stoic strain in American literature p97-112

Stojanović, Svetozar

An ideology of "objective meaning" and "objective responsibility." *In* Dallmayr, F. R. ed. From contract to community p103-25

Stoker, Bram

About

Barclay, G. S. Sex and horror: Bram Stoker. *In* Barclay, G. S. Anatomy of horror: the masters of occult fiction p39-57

About individual works

Dracula

Barclay, G. S. Sex and horror: Bram Stoker. *In* Barclay, G. S. Anatomy of horror: the masters of occult fiction p39-57

Massey, I. The third self: Dracula, Jekyll and Hyde, "Lokis." *In* Massey, I. The gaping pig p98-114

Stokes, Antony Derek

Kievan Russia. *In* Auty, R. and Obolensky, D. eds. An introduction to Russian history p49-77

Stokes, Carl Burton. See Smythe, H. H. jt. auth.

Stokes, Eric

'The Voice of the Hooligan': Kipling and the Commonwealth experience. *In* Historical perspectives p285-301

Stokes, John. See Fletcher, I. jt. auth.

Stokes, Michael C.

A Lucretian paragraph: III. 1-30. *In* Poetry and poetics from ancient Greece to the Renaissance p91-104

Stokes, Roy Bishop

Envoi. *In* Egoff, S. A. ed. One ocean touching p232-40

Stokoe, William C.

Sign languages and the verbal/nonverbal distinction. *In* Sebeok, T. A. ed. Sight, sound, and sense p157-72

Stokstad, Marilyn

Christ in Gethsemane: sculpture in the University of Kansas Museum of Art. *In* Enggass, R. C. and Stokstad, M. eds. Hortus imaginum p95-101

Medieval art. *In* Orel, H. ed. Irish history and culture p79-108

Stokstad, Marilyn, and Gill, Linda
Antiquarianism and architecture in eighteenth-century Ireland. *In* Orel, H. ed. Irish history and culture p165-87

Stokstad, Marilyn, and Nelson, Mary Jean
The arts in twentieth-century Ireland. *In* Orel, H. ed. Irish history and culture p271-89

Stolnitz, George J.
International migration policies: some demographic and economic contexts. *In* Human migration p307-16

Stomach
Surgery
Temkin, O. Merrem's youthful dream: the early history of experimental pylorectomy. *In* Temkin, O. The double face of Janus p497-509

Stone, Donald
The Human Potential movement. *In* The New religious consciousness p93-115

On knowing how we know about the new religions. *in* Needleman, J. and Baker, G. eds. Understanding the new religions p141-52

Stone, Donald A.
French literature. *In* Jones, W. M. ed. The present state of scholarship in sixteenth-century literature p45-69

Stone, Donald David
Trollope, Byron, and the conventionalities. *In* The Worlds of Victorian fiction p179-203

Stone, Edward
Hawthorne's House of Pyncheon: a theory of American drama. *In* Artful thunder p69-84

Stone, Geoffrey R.
Fora Americana: speech in public places. *In* The Supreme Court review, 1974 p233-80

Miranda doctrine in the Burger Court. *In* The Supreme Court review, 1977 p99-169

Stone, Gerald
Regionalisms, German loan-words, and Europeanisms in the language of Jakub Bart-Čišinski. *In* Oxford Slavonic papers, new ser. v9 p110-16

Stone, Gregory P. See Mahigel, E. L. jt. auth.

Stone, Harlan Fiske
About
White, G. E. Hughes and Stone: ironies of the Chief Justiceship. *In* White, G. E. The American judicial tradition p200-29

Stone, Harvey
The unknown Dickens: with a sampling of uncollected writings. *In* Dickens Studies Annual v 1 p 1-22

Stone, John Richard Nicholas
Demographic variables in the economics of education. *In* Economic factors in population growth p521-52

Stone, Lawrence Joseph
History and the social sciences in the twentieth century. *In* The Future of history p3-42

The rise of the nuclear family in early modern England: the patriarchal stage. *In* Rosenberg, C. E. ed. The family in history p13-57

The size and composition of the Oxford student body, 1580-1910. *In* The University in society v 1 p3-110

About individual works
The crisis of the aristocracy, 1558-1641
Hexter, J. H. Lawrence Stone and the English aristocracy. *In* Hexter, J. H. On historians p149-226

Stone, Robert
About individual works
Dog soldiers, a novel
Sale, R. H. Robert Stone. *In* Sale, R. H. On not being good enough p66-73

Stone, Rochelle
Metapoetics and structure in Bolesław Leśmian's Russian poetry. *In* California Slavic studies v10 p137-72

Stone, William Leete
About individual works
Tales and sketches—such as they are
Doubleday, N. F. William Leete Stone as storyteller. *In* Doubleday, N. F. Variety of attempt p160-75

Stonehenge
Gingerich, O. J. The basic astronomy of Stonehenge. *In* Brecher, K. and Feirtag, M. eds. Astronomy of the ancients p117-32

Stoneman, Patsy
G. Eliot: Middlemarch. *In* Williams, D. A. ed. The monster in the mirror p102-30

Stonesifer, Roy P.
The Union cavalry comes of age. *In* Hubbell, J. T. ed. Battles lost and won p125-34

Stonework, Decorative. See Decoration and ornament, Architectural

Stonier, Tom
Economic and technological prerequisites for achieving political and military stability. *In* Arms control and technological innovation p342-57

Unilateral disarmament re-examined. *In* International terrorism and world security p165-71

Stoop, Maria Wilhemina
Conjectures on the end of a sanctuary. *In* Studies in classical art and archaeology p179-83

Stopes-Roe, Harry V.
The intelligibility of the universe. *In* Reason and religion p44-71

Stoppard, Tom
About individual works
Jumpers
Kauffmann, S. Jumpers. *In* Kauffmann, S. Persons of the drama p239-42

The real Inspector Hound
Schlueter, J. Stoppard's Moon and Birdboot, Rosencrantz and Guildenstern. *In* Schlueter, J. Metafictional characters in modern drama p89-103

Rosencrantz and Guildenstern are dead
D'Andrea, P. P. "Thou starre of poets": Shakespeare as DNA. *In* Shakespeare: aspects of influence p163-91

Schlueter, J. Stoppard's Moon and Birdboot, Rosencrantz and Guildenstern. *In* Schlueter, J. Metafictional characters in modern drama p89-103

Stoppard, Tom—*Continued*

Characters

Schlueter, J. Stoppard's Moon and Birdboot, Rosencrantz and Guildenstern. *In* Schlueter, J. Metafictional characters in modern drama p89-103

Storch, Rudolph F.

Abstract idealism in English romantic poetry and painting. *In* Kroeber, K. and Walling, W. eds. Images of romanticism p189-209

Storch de Gracia, Juan José Linz. See Linz Storch de Gracia, Juan José

Storer, Norman W.

The sociological context of the Velikovsky controversy. *In* Goldsmith, D. ed. Scientists confront Velikovsky p29-39

Storey, David

About individual works
The changing room

Kauffmann, S. Notes on naturalism: truth is stranger as fiction. *In* Kauffmann, S. Persons of the drama p329-35

The contractor

Kauffmann, S. Notes on naturalism: truth is stranger as fiction. *In* Kauffmann, S. Persons of the drama p329-35

Stories. See Fiction

Stories without words

Hwang, J. C. Lien-huan-hua: revolutionary serial pictures. *In* Chu, G. C. ed. Popular media in China p51-72

Storing, Herbert J.

The Constitution and the Bill of Rights. *In* Essays on the Constitution of the United States p32-48

Slavery and the moral foundations of the American Republic. *In* The Moral foundations of the American Republic p214-33

Storm, Hyemeyohsts

About individual works
Seven arrows

Larson, C. R. History of the people. *In* Larson, C. R. American Indian fiction p97-132

Storm, Theodor

About

Alt, A. T. Escape and transformation: an inquiry into the nature of Storm's realism. *In* Creative encounter p117-32

Storm petrel

Whilde, A. A note on the storm petrel and corncrake. *In* Harmon, M. ed. Richard Murphy: poet of two traditions p70-72

Storr, Catherine

Why write? Why write for children? *In* Blishen, E. ed. The thorny paradise p25-33

Storr, Richard James

Commentary: an historian of education looks at the Newagen study. *In* Oleson, A. and Brown, S. C. eds. The pursuit of knowledge in the early American Republic p340-44

Story, Joseph

About

White, G. E. Kent, Story, and Shaw: the judicial function and property rights. *In* White, E. G. The American judicial tradition p35-63

Story, Kenneth E.

Theme and image in The Princess. *In* Tennessee Studies in literature v20 p50-59

Story, Short. See Short story

Story-telling

Iran

Nejad, K. M. The story-teller and mass media in Iran. *In* Fischer, H. D. and Melnik, S. R. eds. Entertainment: a cross-cultural examination p43-62

Japan

Hrdličková, V. Japanese professional storytellers. *In* Folklore genres p171-90

Storytellers

Japan

Hrdličková, V. Japanese professional storytellers. *In* Folklore genres p171-90

Stouck, David

Fiction: 1900 to the 1930s. *In* American literary scholarship, 1974 p227-51

Fiction: 1900 to the 1930s [another essay] *In* American literary scholarship, 1975 p267-94

Fiction: 1900 to the 1930s [another essay] *In* American literary scholarship, 1976 p227-49

Fiction: 1900 to the 1930s [another essay] *In* American literary scholarship, 1977 p245-71

Stough, Charlotte L.

Stoic determinism and moral responsibility. *In* Rist, J. M. ed. The Stoics p203-31

Stoughton, Michael

A late painting by Giovanni Battista Caracciolo: The judgement of Solomon. *In* Enggass, R. C. and Stokstad, M. eds. Hortus imaginum p125-28

Stourdze, Yves. See Attali, J. jt. auth.

Stourzh, Gerald

The American Revolution, modern constitutionalism and the protection of human rights. *In* [Truth and tragedy]: a tribute to Hans Morgenthau p162-76

Stove, David C.

Why should probability be the guide of life? *In* Livingston, D. W. and King, J. T. eds. Hume p50-68

Stoves

White, E. B. Coon tree. *In* White, E. B. Essays of E. B. White p34-45

Stow, John

Edwards, A. S. G. and Hedley, J. H. John Stowe, The craft of lovers and T. C.C. R.3.19. *In* Virginia. University. Bibliographical Society. Studies in bibliography v28 p265-68

About

Fletcher, B. Y. Printer's copy for Stow's Chaucer. *In* Virginia. University. Bibliographical Society. Studies in bibliography v31 p184-201

Stow, Randolph

About individual works
The merry-go-round in the sea

Tiffin, C. Mates, mum, and Maui: the theme of maturity in three antipodean novels. *In* Narasimhaiah, C. D. ed. Awakened conscience p127-45

To the islands

Tiffin, H. Towards place and placelessness: two journey patterns in Commonwealth literature. *In* Narasimhaiah, C. D. ed. Awakened conscience p146-63

Strauss, Gerald

The state of pedagogical theory c.1530: what Protestant reformers knew about education. *In* Schooling and society p69-94

Strauss, Leo

About

Miller, E. F. Leo Strauss: the recovery of political philosophy. *In* De Crespigny, A. and Minogue, K. R. eds. Contemporary political philosophers p67-99

Wilhelmsen, F. D. Jaffa, the school of Strauss, and the Christian tradition. *In* Wilhelmsen, F. D. Christianity and political philosophy p209-25

About individual works
On tyranny

Chiaromonte, N. Modern tyranny. *In* Chiaromonte, N. The worm of consciousness, and other essays p208-35

Strauss, Richard

About

Craft, R. Elektra and Richard Strauss. *In* Craft, R. Current convictions p145-55

About individual works
Elektra

Craft, R. Elektra and Richard Strauss. *In* Craft, R. Current convictions p145-55

Der Rosenkavalier

Craft, R. Der Rosenkavalier: "something Mozartian?" *In* Craft, R. Current convictions p136-45

Salomé

Craft, R. A "beautiful coloured, musical thing." *In* Craft, R. Current convictions p124-35

Schmidgall, G. Richard Strauss. *In* Schmidgall, G. Literature as opera p247-86

Strausz-Hupé, Robert

America and the defense of the West. *In* Prochnow, H. V. ed. Dilemmas facing the nation p271-93

Stravinskiĭ, Igor' Fedorovich

About

Sessions, R. Thoughts on Stravinsky. *In* Sessions, R. Roger Sessions on music p376-86

About individual works
Oedipus Rex

Sessions, R. On Oedipus Rex. *In* Sessions, R. Roger Sessions on music p339-46

The rake's progress

Josipovici, G. The rake's progress. *In* Josipovici, G. The lessons of modernism p151-66

Stravinsky, Igor. See Stravinskiĭ, Igor' Fedorovich

Straw dogs (Motion picture)

Kauffmann, S. Straw dogs. *In* Kauffmann, S. Living images p93-95

Strawberry Hill, England (Villa)

Ames, D. S. Strawberry Hill: architecture of the "as if." *In* Studies in eighteenth-century culture v8 p351-63

Strawson, Peter Frederick

Causation in perception. *In* Fact, value, and perception p151-67

On understanding the structure of one's language. *In* Evans, G. L. and McDowell, J. H. eds. Truth and meaning p189-98

About individual works
Introduction to logical theory

Quine, W. V. Mr Strawson on logical theory. *In* Quine, W. V. The ways of paradox, and other essays p137-57

Strayer, Joseph Reese

The costs and profits of war: the Anglo-French conflict of 1294-1303. *In* The Medieval city p269-91

The rule of law. *In* Aspects of American liberty p16-36

See also Part 2 under title: Order and innovation in the Middle Ages

Stream of consciousness fiction

Adams, R. M. Woolf and Faulkner: streams of consciousness. *In* Adams, R. M. Afterjoyce p65-89

Street, Arthur George

About

Cavaliero, G. Farmer novelists: H. W. Freeman, A. G. Street, Adrian Bell. *In* Cavaliero, G. The rural tradition in the English novel, 1900-1939 p101-17

Street, David

Conclusion: life in urbanized America. *In* Handbook of contemporary urban life p628-41

See also Janowitz, M.; Pearce, D. jt. auths.

Street, David, and Davidson, Jeffrey L.

Community and politics in city and suburb. *In* Handbook of contemporary urban life p468-93

Street, David, and Street, W. Paul

Print media in urban society. *In* Handbook of contemporary urban life p428-67

Street, W. Paul. See Street, D. jt. auth.

Street literature

China

Poon, D. J. Tatzepao: its history and significance as a communication medium. *In* Chu, G. C. ed. Popular media in China p184-221

Strelka, Joseph P.

The literary work: its structure, unity, and distinction from forms of non-literary expression. *In* Hernadi, P. ed. What is literature? p115-26

Material collectors, political rhetoricians, and amateurs: current methodological problems in German exile literature studies. *In* Strelka, J. P.; Bell, R. F. and Dobson, E. eds. Protest—form—tradition p 1-14

Stress (Physiology)

Benson, H. The relaxation response: techniques and clinical applications. *In* Sobel, D. S. ed. Ways of health p331-51

See also Crowding stress

Stress (Physiology). See Crowding stress

Strevens, Peter

Second language learning. *In* Bloomfield, M. W. and Haugen, E. I. eds. Language as a human problem p151-62

Stribling, Thomas Sigismund

About individual works
The store

Going, W. T. Store and Mockingbird: two Pulitzer novels about Alabama. *In* Going, W. T. Essays on Alabama literature p9-31

Strickland, Conwell G.
Students' rights and the teacher's obligations in the classroom. *In* Buxton, T. H. and Prichard, K. W. eds. Excellence in university teaching p80-85

Strickler, Nina
Anti-history and terrorism: a philosophical dimension. *In* International terrorism and political crimes p47-50

Strickmann, Michel
On the alchemy of T'ao Hung-ching. *In* Welch, H. and Seidel, A. K. eds. Facets of Taoism p123-92

Striedter, Jurij
The "new myth" of revolution—a study of Mayakovsky's early poetry. *In* Amacher, R. E. and Lange, V. eds. New perspectives in German literary criticism p357-85

Strinati, Dominic
Capitalism, the state and industrial relations. *In* Crouch, C. ed. State and economy in contemporary capitalism p191-236

Strindberg, August
About
Burnham, D. L. and Bergmann, S. A. August Strindberg's need-fear dilemma, as seen in his relationship with Harriet Bosse. *In* Psychiatry and the humanities v 1 p73-97

Gustafsson, L. Strindberg as a forerunner of Scandinavian modernism. *In* The Hero in Scandinavian literature p125-41

Lide, B. Strindberg and Molière: parallels, influence, image. *In* Johnson, R. B.; Neumann, E. S. and Trail, G. T. eds. Molière and the commonwealth of letters: patrimony and posterity p259-68

Nicoll, A. Strindberg and the play of the subconscious. *In* Nicoll, A. World drama p460-74

Schwarz, A. Society and human passion as a tragic motive. *In* Schwarz, A. From Büchner to Beckett p100-60

About individual works
A dream play
Holm, I. Strindberg and the theater. *In* The Hero in Scandinavian literature p143-55

Getting married
Pritchett, V. S. August Strindberg: a bolting horse. *In* Pritchett, V. S. The myth makers p89-94

The ghost sonata
Northam, J. R. Waiting for Prospero. *In* English drama: forms and development p186-202

The red room
Holmes, P. A. A. Strindberg: The red room. *In* Williams, D. A. ed. The monster in the mirror p131-48

Influence—White
Douglas, D. Influence and individuality: the indebtedness of Patrick White's The ham funeral and The season at Sarsaparilla to Strindberg and the German expressionist movement. *In* Bards, bohemians, and bookmen p266-80

Marriage
Burnham, D. L. and Bergmann, S. A. August Strindberg's need-fear dilemma, as seen in his relationship with Harriet Bosse. *In* Psychiatry and the humanities v 1 p73-97

Stage history
Holm, I. Strindberg and the theater. *In* The Hero in Scandinavian literature p143-55

Strip-tease
Salutin, M. Stripper morality. *In* Henslin, J. M. ed. Deviant life-styles p191-208

Strizower, Schifra
The Bene Israel and the Jewish people. *In* Salo Wittmayer Baron v2 p859-36

Stromberg, Roland N.
Collective security. *In* Encyclopedia of American foreign policy p124-33

Strømnæs, Øistein
The impact on human genetics. *In* Against pollution and hunger p215-17

Strong, Donald Emrys, and Claridge, Amanda
Marble sculpture. *In* Strong, D. E. and Brown, D. eds. Roman crafts p195-207

Strong, Donald Stuart
Southern politics are changing, too. *In* The Rising South v2 p70-77

Strong, Maurice F.
"Where are we growing?" *In* The Frontiers of human knowledge p229-42

Strong, Tracy B.
Dramaturgical discourse and political enactments: toward an artistic foundation for political space. *In* Brown, R. H. and Lyman, S. M. eds. Structure, consciousness, and history p237-60

Stroud, Theodore A.
A critical approach to the short story. *In* May, C. E. ed. Short story theories p116-30

Strouse, James C. and Claude, Richard P.
Empirical comparative rights research: some preliminary tests of development hypotheses. *In* Claude, R. P. ed. Comparative human rights p51-67

Strouse, Jean
Semiprivate lives. *In* Studies in biography p113-29

Structural anthropology
Girard, R. Differentiation and reciprocity in Lévi-Strauss and contemporary theory. *In* Girard, R. "To double business bound" p155-77

Same as: Girard, R. Differentiation and undifferentiation in Lévi-Strauss and current critical theory. *In* Krieger, M. and Dembo, L. S. eds. Directions for criticism p111-36

Girard, R. Differentiation and undifferentiation in Lévi-Strauss and current critical theory. *In* Krieger, M. and Dembo, L. S. eds. Directions for criticism p111-36

Singer, M. For a semiotic anthropology. *In* Sebeok, T. A. ed. Sight, sound, and sense p202-31

Structural design
Smith, C. S. Structural hierarchy in science, art, and history. *In* Wechsler, J. ed. On aesthetics in science p9-53

See also Architectural design

Structural engineering
Billington, D. P. Technology and the structuring of cities. *In* Small comforts for hard times p182-98

Salvadori, M. G. The aesthetics of technology: in response to David P. Billington. *In* Small comforts for hard times p199-203

Structural linguistics

Blumstein, S. Structuralism in linguistics: methodological and theoretical perspectives. *In* Riegel, K. F. and Rosenwald, G. C. eds. Structure and transformation p153-65

Hill, A. A. Toward a literary analysis. *In* Hill, A. A. Constituent and pattern in poetry p10-22

Kress, G. R. Structuralism and popular culture. *In* Bigsby, C. W. E. ed. Approaches to popular culture p85-106

Potts, T. C. The place of structure in communication. *In* Royal Institute of Philosophy. Communication and understanding p91-115

Searle, J. R. Chomsky's revolution in linguistics. *In* Harman, G. ed. On Noam Chomsky p2-33

Strawson, P. F. On understanding the structure of one's language. *In* Evans, G. L. and McDowell, J. H. eds. Truth and meaning p189-98

See also Systemic grammar

Structural psychology. See Gestalt psychology

Structuralism

Bauman, Z. Understanding as expansion of the form of life. *In* Bauman, Z. Hermeneutics and social science p194-224

Derrida, J. "Genesis and structure" and phenomenology. *In* Derrida, J. Writing and difference p154-68

Hass, W. A. Pragmatic structures of language: historical, formal and developmental issues. *In* Riegel, K. F. and Rosenwald, G. C. eds. Structure and transformation p193-213

Lemert, C. C. Structuralist semiotics and the decentering of sociology. *In* McNall, S. G. ed. Theoretical perspectives in sociology p96-111

Looft, W. R. and Svoboda, C. P. Structuralism in cognitive developmental psychology: past, contemporary and future perspectives. *In* Riegel, K. F. and Rosenwald, G. C. eds. Structure and transformation p49-60

Mukařovský, J. The concept of the whole in the theory of art. *In* Mukařovský, J. Structure, sign, and function p70-81

Mukařovský, J. On structuralism. *In* Mukařovský, J. Structure, sign, and function p 3-16

Overton, W. F. General systems, structure and development. *In* Riegel, K. F. and Rosenwald, G. C. eds. Structure and transformation p61-81

Rosenwald, G. C. Epilogue: Reflections on the universalism of structure. *In* Riegel, K. F. and Rosenwald, G. C. eds. Structure and transformation p215-19

Wilden, A. Piaget and the structure as law and order. *In* Riegel, K. F. and Rosenwald, G. C. eds. Structure and transformation p83-117

History

Riegel, K. F. Structure and transformation in modern intellectual history. *In* Riegel, K. F. and Rosenwald, G. C. eds. Structure and transformation p3-24

Structuralism (Literary analysis)

Adams, H. Contemporary ideas of literature: terrible beauty or rough beast? *In* Krieger, M. and Dembo, L. S. eds. Directions for criticism p55-83

Barthes, R. Introduction to the structural analysis of narratives. *In* Barthes, R. Image, music, text p79-124

Culler, J. D. Structuralism and literature. *In* Contemporary approaches to English studies p59-76

Derrida, J. Force and signification. *In* Derrida, J. Writing and difference p3-30

Foucault, M. What is an author? *In* Foucault, M. Language, counter-memory, practice p113-38

Girard, R. Differentiation and reciprocity in Lévi-Strauss and contemporary theory. *In* Girard, R. "To double business bound" p155-77

Same as: Differentiation and undifferentiation in Lévi-Strauss and current critical theory. *In* Krieger, M. and Dembo, L. S. eds. Directions for criticism p111-36

Girard, R. Differentiation and undifferentiation in Lévi-Strauss and current critical theory. *In* Krieger, M. and Dembo, L. S. eds. Directions for criticism p111-36

Graff, G. The politics of anti-realism. *In* Graff, G. Literature against itself p63-101

Margolin, U. Conclusion: literary structuralism and hermeneutics in significant convergence, 1976. *In* Valdés, M. J. and Miller, I. J. eds. Interpretation of narrative p177-85

Miller, O. J. Reading as a process of reconstruction: a critique of recent structuralist formulations. *In* Valdés, M. J. and Miller, O. J. eds. Interpretation of narrative p19-27

Morris, W. A. The centrality of language. *In* Morris, W. A. Friday's footprint p84-146

Morris, W. A. The pilgrimage of being. *In* Morris, W. A. Friday's footprint p 1-83

Morris, W. A. Toward a literary hermeneutics. *In* Morris, W. A. Friday's footprint p188-225

Mudrick, M. Adorable ideas and absent plenitudes. *In* Mudrick, M. Books are not life but then what is? p213-26

Scholes, R. E. The contributions of formalism and structuralism to the theory of fiction. *In* Spilka, M. ed. Towards a poetics of fiction p107-24

Stankiewicz, E. Poetics and verbal art. *In* Sebeok, T. A. ed. A perfusion of signs p54-76

Watkins, E. Criticism and method: Hirsch, Frye, Barthes, Derrida. *In* Watkins, E. The critical act p56-94

White, H. V. The Absurdist moment in contemporary literary theory. *In* Krieger, M. and Dembo, L. S. eds. Directions for criticism p85-110

See also Semiotics; Semiotics and literature

Structure (Philosophy) See Structuralism

Structure, Atomic. See Atomic structure

Structure psychology. See Whole and parts (Psychology)

Structures, Engineering of. See Structural engineering

Structures, Theory of. See Structural design; Structural engineering

Struever, Nancy S.

Vico, Valla, and the logic of humanist inquiry. *In* Giambattista Vico's science of humanity p173-85

Strunk, William

About individual works

The elements of style

White, E. B. Will Strunk. *In* White, E. B. Essays of E. B. White p256-61

Struve, Gleb

Andrey Bely redivivus. *In* Janecek, G. ed. Andrey Bely p21-43

Behind the front lines: on some neglected chapters in August 1914. *In* Dunlop, J. B.; Haugh, R. and Klimoff, A. eds. Aleksandr Solzhenitsyn: critical essays and documentary materials 2d ed. p430-46

Osip Mandelstam and Auguste Barbier. *In* California Slavic studies v8 p131-66

Struve, Lynn Ann

Ambivalence and action: some frustrated scholars of the K'ang-hsi period. *In* Spence, J. D. and Wills, J. E. eds. From Ming to Ch'ing p321-65

Struve, Nikita

The debate over August 1914. *In* Dunlop, J. B.; Haugh, R. and Klimoff, A. eds. Aleksandr Solzhenitsyn: critical essays and documentary materials 2d ed. p393-407

Struve, Petr Berngardovich

The intelligentsia and revolution. *In* Landmarks p138-54

Struve, Pyotr. See Struve, Petr Berngardovich

Strycker, Emile de

The oracle given to Chaerephon about Socrates. *In* Kephalaion p39-49

Stryker, Richard E.

Development strategies. *In* Martin, P. M. and O'Meara, P. eds. Africa p311-30

Strype, John

About

Zinberg, C. The usable dissenting past: John Strype and Elizabethan Puritanism. *In* The Dissenting tradition p123-39

Stuard, Susan Mosher

Women in charter and statute law: medieval Ragusa/Dubrovnik. *In* Stuard, S. M. ed. Women in medieval society p199-208

Stuart, Béraud, Lord of Aubigny

About

Contamine, P. The war literature of the late Middle Ages: the treaties of Robert de Balsac and Béraud Stuart, Lord of Aubigny. *In* War, literature, and politics in the late Middle Ages p102-21

Stuart, Dabney

Nabokov's Pnin: floating and singing. *In* Garvin, H. R. ed. Makers of the twentieth-century novel p259-75

Stuart, Jesse

About

Clarke, K. W. Jesse Stuart's use of folklore. *In* LeMaster, J. R. and Clarke, M. W. eds. Jesse Stuart p117-29

Flanagan, J. T. Jesse Stuart, regional novelist. *In* LeMaster, J. R. and Clarke, M. W. eds. Jesse Stuart p70-88

Foster, R. E. The short stories of Jesse Stuart. *In* LeMaster, J. R. and Clarke, M. W. eds. Jesse Stuart p40-53

Guthrie, V. G. Books for children by Jesse Stuart. *In* LeMaster, J. R. and Clarke, M. W. eds. Jesse Stuart p149-61

Hall, W Humor in Jesse Stuart's fiction. *In* LeMaster, J. R. and Clarke, M. W. eds. Jesse Stuart p89-102

Miller, J. W. The gift outright: W-Hollow. *In* LeMaster, J. R. and Clarke, M. W. eds. Jesse Stuart p103-16

Richardson, H E. Stuart country: the man-artist and the myth. *In* LeMaster, J. R. and Clarke, M. W. eds. Jesse Stuart p 1-18

About individual works
Trees of heaven

Leavell, F. H. Dualism in Stuart's Trees of heaven. *In* LeMaster, J. R. and Clarke, M. W. eds. Jesse Stuart p54-69

Biography

Clarke, M W. Jesse Stuart's educational saga as humanistic affirmation. *In* LeMaster, J. R. and Clarke, M. W. eds. Jesse Stuart p130-48

Education

See Stuart, Jesse—Knowledge and learning

Knowledge and learning

Clarke, M. W. Jesse Stuart's educational saga as humanistic affirmation. *In* LeMaster, J. R. and Clarke, M. W. eds. Jesse Stuart p130-48

Poetic works

LeMaster, J. R. Jesse Stuart's poetry as Fugitive-Agrarian synthesis. *In* LeMaster, J. R. and Clarke, M. W. eds. Jesse Stuart p19-39

Stubblebine, James H.

The Boston Ducciesque tabernacle, a collaboration. *In* Collaboration in Italian Renaissance art p 1-19

Stubbs, John, 1541-1590

About individual works
The discovery of a gaping gulf whereinto England is like to be swallowed by another French marriage

Adams, R. P. Opposed Tudor myths of power: Machiavellian tyrants and Christian kings. *In* Studies in the continental background of Renaissance English literature: essays presented to John L. Lievsay p67-90

Stubbs, John, 1943-

The impact of the Great War on the Conservative Party. *In* Peele, G. and Cook, C. eds. The politics of reappraisal, 1918-1939 p14-38

Stubbs, John Francis Alexander Heath- See Heath-Stubbs, John Francis Alexander

Stucco

Rome

Ling, R. Stuccowork. *In* Strong, D. E. and Brown, D. eds. Roman crafts p209-21

Stuckey, P. Sterling. *See* Stuckey, Sterling

Stuckey, Sterling

David Walker and the ideological origins of Black nationalism. *In* African themes p25-45

Student activities. See School sports

Student aid

United States

Finn, C. E. Federal patronage of the universities: a rose by many other names? *In* Hook, S.; Kurtz, P. W. and Todorovich, M. eds. The university and the state: what role for government in higher education? p7-49

Student clubs. See Students' societies

Student ethics. See College students—Conduct of life

Student expenditures. See College costs

Student expulsion

United States

Edelman, M. W. We are failing the children. *In* Gross, B. and Gross, R. eds. The children's rights movement p109-14

Student movements

Chiaromonte, N. The student revolt. *In* Chiaromonte, N. The worm of consciousness, and other essays p58-65

Frye, N. The university and personal life. *In* Frye, N. Spiritus mundi p27-48

Martin, B. The mining of the ivory tower. *In* Universities in the Western world p98-115

Martin, D. A. Mutations: religio-political crisis and the collapse of Puritanism and humanism. *In* Universities in the Western world p85-97

Spender, S. Background to the sixties. *In* Spender, S. The thirties and after p169-74

See also Youth movement

California—Berkeley

Bellah, R. N. The new consciousness and the Berkeley New Left. *In* The New religious consciousness p77-92

China

Israel, J. Movement genesis and direction. *In* Lauer, R. H. ed. Social movements and social change p7-28

France

Bourricaud, F. The French university as a "fixed society" or, the futility of the 1968 "reform." *In* Universities in the Western world p232-45

Germany

Jarausch, K. H. The sources of German student unrest, 1815-1848. *In* The University in society v2 p533-69

Germany, West

Nipperdey, T. The German university in crisis. *In* Universities in the Western world p119-42

Japan

Kato, I. Japanese universities: student revolt and reform plans. *In* Universities in the Western world p257-63

United States

Bettelheim, B. Obsolete youth. *In* Bettelheim, B. Surviving, and other essays p350-69

Bien, P. Metaphysics, myth, and politics. *In* Buxton, T. H. and Prichard, K. W. eds. Excellence in university teaching p157-88

Crews, F. C. Student protest and academic distance. *In* Crews, F. C. Out of my system p89-103

Hayakawa, S. I. Youth today: problems in achieving adulthood. *In* A Time to hear and answer: essays for the Bicentennial season p157-74

Hook, S. Prospects for the academic future. *In* Fairfield, R. P. ed. Humanistic frontiers in American education p253-60

MacLeish, A. The revolt of the diminished man. *In* MacLeish, A. Riders on the earth p13-26

Rothman, S. and others. Ethnic variation in student radicalism: some new perspectives. *In* Radicalism in the contemporary age v 1 p151-211

United States—History

Altbach, P. G. and Peterson, P. Movement goals and fortunes. *In* Lauer, R. H. ed. Social movements and social change p29-45

Student protest. See Student movements

Student societies. See Students' societies

Student-teacher relationships. See Teacher-student relationships

Student unrest. See Student movements

Students

See also Church work with students; Junior college students; Medical students; School children

Legal status, laws, etc.

Wilkinson, J. H. Goss v. Lopez: the Supreme Court as school superintendent. *In* The Supreme Court review, 1975 p25-75

Political activity

Jarausch, K. H. The sources of German student unrest, 1815-1848. *In* The University in society v2 p533-69

Sexual behavior

Lehman, J. L. Gay students. *In* Crew, L. ed. The gay academic p57-63

Societies, etc.

See Students' societies

Socioeconomic status—United States

Friedenberg, E. Z. Status and role in education. *In* Fairfield, R. P. ed. Humanistic frontiers in American education p37-47

New York (State)—Attitudes

Rehberg, R. A. and Cohen, M. A. Political attitudes and participation in extracurricular activities. *In* Social problems in athletics p201-11

New York (State)—Political activity

Rehberg, R. A. and Cohen, M. A. Political attitudes and participation in extracurricular activities. *In* Social problems in athletics p201-11

Spain—Political activity

Giner, S. Power, freedom and social change in the Spanish university, 1939-75. *In* Preston, P. ed. Spain in crisis p183-211

United States—Attitudes

Petrie, B. M. The athletic group as an emerging deviant subculture. *In* Social problems in athletics p224-37

Students, Afro-American. See Afro-American college students

Students, Jewish. See College students, Jewish

Students for a Democratic Society

Parry, A. The Weatherman. *In* Parry, A. Terrorism: from Robespierre to Arafat p322-29

Students in literature

Marcus, S. Stalky & Co. *In* Marcus, S. Representations p61-75

Sarotte, G. M. Four archetypes of the homosexual couple: Teacher and pupil. *In* Sarotte, G. M. Like a brother, like a lover p61-69

Students' societies

McLachlan, J. The choice of Hercules: American student societies in the early 19th century. *In* The University in society v2 p449-94

Study, Courses of. See Education—Curricula

Study, Independent. See Independent study

Study, Method of. See Independent study; Self-culture

Stuewer, Roger H.

G. N. Lewis on detailed balancing, the symmetry of time, and the nature of light. *In* Historical studies in the physical sciences v6 p469-511

Stultz, Newell Maynard

The separatist challenge to white domination in South Africa. *In* African dimensions p95-112

Stupple, A. James

Two views: The past, the future, and Ray Bradbury. *In* Clareson, T. D. ed. Voices for the future: essays on major science fiction writers v 1 p175-84

Sturgeon, Theodore, pseud. See Waldo, Edward Hamilton

Sturges, Preston

About

Farber, M. Preston Sturges: success in the movies. *In* Denby, D. ed. Awake in the dark p305-19

Sturm, Fred Gillette

Afro-Brazilian cults. *In* African religions: a symposium p217-39

Sturm, Terry

The structure of Brennan's The Wanderer. *In* Bards, bohemians, and bookmen p114-35

Sturtevant, William Curtis

First visual images of native America. *In* First images of America p417-54

Stycos, J. Mayone

Some minority opinions on birth control. *In* Population policy and ethics p169-96

Style (Philosophy)

Wollheim, R. Style now. *In* Concerning contemporary art p133-53

Style, Literary

Cunningham, J. V. The problem of style. *In* Cunningham, J. V. The collected essays of J. V. Cunningham p251-55

Fish, S. E. Literature in the reader: affective stylistics. *In* Primeau, R. ed. Influx p154-79

Freeman, D. C. Literature. *In* Wardhaugh, R. and Brown, H. D. eds. A survey of applied linguistics p229-49

Hill, A. A. Analogies, icons, and images. *In* Hill, A. A. Constituent and pattern in poetry p53-70

Hill, A. A. Poetry and stylistics. *In* Hill, A. A. Constituent and pattern in poetry p41-52

Josipovici, G. Linearity and fragmentation. *In* Josipovici, G. The lessons of modernism p124-39

Kunitz, S. J. The search for a style. *In* Kunitz, S. J. A kind of order, a kind of folly p14-17

McIntosh, C. Quantities of qualities: nominal style and the novel. *In* Studies in eighteenth-century culture v4 p139-53

Mazzeo, J. A. Style as interpretation. *In* Mazzeo, J. A. Varieties of interpretation p27-45

Morris, W. A. Stylistics. *In* Morris, W. A. Friday's footprints p147-87

Richter, D. H. Open form and the fable. *In* Richter, D. H. Fable's end p 1-21

Riffaterre, M. The stylistic approach to literary history. *In* Cohen, R. ed. New directions in literary history p147-64

Russell, J. D. Advance aim. *In* Russell, J. D. Style in modern British fiction p 1-16

Schneidau, H. N. Pound and Wordsworth on poetry and prose. *In* Bornstein, G. ed. Romantic and modern p133-45

Tate, A. Shadow: a parable and a polemic. *In* Tate, A. Memoirs and opinions, 1926-1974 p140-43

See also Criticism; Diction; Impressionism; Literature—Aesthetics; Literature—History and criticism; Rhetoric

Style, Musical

Sessions, R. Style and "styles" in music. *In* Sessions, R. Roger Sessions on music p88-101

See also Romanticism in music

Style in dress. See Costume; Fashion

Stylistics. See Language and languages—Style

Styron, William

About

Gray, R. J. Aftermath: Southern literature since World War II. *In* Gray, R. J. The literature of memory p257-305

Kelvin, N. The divided self: William Styron's fiction from Lie down in darkness to The confessions of Nat Turner. *In* Morris, R. K. and Malin, I. eds. The achievement of William Styron p208-26

Morris, R. K. and Malin, I. Vision and value: the achievement of William Styron. *In* Morris, R. K. and Malin, I. eds. The achievement of William Styron p 1-50

About individual works

The confessions of Nat Turner

Core, G. The confessions of Nat Turner and the burden of the past. *In* Morris, R. K. and Malin, I. eds. The achievement of William Styron p150-67

Gross, S. L. and Bender, E. History, politics, and literature: the myth of Nat Turner. *In* Morris, R. K. and Malin, I. eds. The achievement of William Styron p168-207

Rubin, L. D. William Styron and human bondage. *In* Rubin, L. D. William Elliott shoots a bear p226-49

Watkins, F. C. The confessions of Nat Turner: history and imagination. *In* Watkins, F. C. In time and place p51-70

White, J. The novelist as historian: William Styron and American Negro slavery. *In* Burton, D. H. ed. American history—British historians p149-68

In the clap shack

Morris, R. K. In the clap shack: comedy in the charnel house. *In* Morris, R. K. and Malin, I. eds. The achievement of William Styron p227-41

Lie down in darkness

Gordon, J. B. Permutations of death: a reading of Lie down in darkness. *In* Morris, R. K. and Malin, I. eds. The achievement of William Styron p100-21

Lyons, J. O. On Lie down in darkness. *In* Morris, R. K. and Malin, I. eds. The achievement of William Styron p88-99

Rubin, L. D. Notes on a Southern writer in our time. *In* Morris, R. K. and Malin, I. eds. The achievement of William Styron p51-87

The long march

Malin, I. The symbolic march. *In* Morris, R. K. and Malin, I. eds. The achievement of William Styron p122-33

Styron, William—About individual works
—*Continued*

Set this house on fire

Phillips, R. S. Mask and symbol in Set this house on fire. *In* Morris, R. K. and Malin, I. eds. The achievement of William Styron p134-49

Rubin, L. D. Notes on a Southern writer in our time. *In* Morris, R. K. and Malin, I. eds. The achievement of William Styron p51-87

Rubin, L. D. William Styron and human bondage. *In* Rubin, L. D. William Elliott shoots a bear p226-49

Bibliography

Bryer, J. R. William Styron: a bibliography. *In* Morris, R. K. and Malin, I. eds. The achievement of William Styron p242-77

Su, Shih

About

Chen, Yü-shih. The literary theory and practice of Ou-yang Hsiu. *In* Chinese approaches to literature from Confucius to Liang Ch'i-ch'ao p67-96

Suagee, Stephen

An artist's memory beats all other kinds: an essay on Despair. *In* A Book of things about Vladimir Nabokov p54-64

Suárez, Jorge A. See Suárez S , Jorge A.

Suárez S , Jorge A.

Classical languages. *In* Sebeok, T. A. ed. Native languages of the Americas v2 p3-25

Subconsciousness

Altschule, M. D. The ideas of the Huron Indians about the unconscious mind. *In* Altschule, M. D. Origins of concepts in human behavior p19-34

Danto, A. C. Freudian explanations and the language of the unconscious. *In* Psychoanalysis and language p325-53

Feldstein, L. C. Bifurcated psyche and social self: implications of Freud's theory of the unconscious. *In* Roth, R. J. ed. Person and community p43-62

Flew, A. G. N. Motives and Freud's unconscious. *In* Flew, A. G. N. A rational animal p151-71

Huxley, A. L. The unconscious. *In* Huxley, A. L. The Human situation p152-67

Leclaire, S. Unconscious inscription: another memory. *In* Roland, A. ed. Psychoanalysis, creativity, and literature p72-84

Marquard, O. On the importance of the theory of the unconscious for a theory of no longer fine art. *In* Amacher, R. E. and Lange, V. eds. New perspectives in German literary criticism p260-78

Rothenberg, A. The unconscious and creativity. *In* Psychoanalysis, creativity, and literature p144-61

See also Consciousness; Dreams; Mind and body; Psychoanalysis; Thought-transference; Trance

Subculture

Horton, J. E. Time and cool people. *In* Henslin, J. M. ed. Deviant life-styles p59-72

Taylor, B. K. Culture: whence, whither and why? *In* Alcock, A. E.; Taylor, B. K. and Welton, J. M. eds. The future of cultural minorities p9-29

Subdivision of land. See Land subdivision

Subject and predicate (Grammar) See Grammar, Comparative and general—Topic and comment

Subject to fits (criticism) Montgomery, R. *In* Kauffmann, S. Persons of the drama p216-18

Subjectivity

Nagel, T. Subjective and objective. *In* Nagel, T. Mortal questions p196-213

Sublime, The

Albrecht, W. P. Addison. *In* Albrecht, W. P. The sublime pleasures of tragedy p25-38

Albrecht, W. P. Alison. *In* Albrecht, W. P. The sublime pleasures of tragedy p69-82

Albrecht, W. P. Burke. *In* Albrecht, W. P. The sublime pleasures of tragedy p39-51

Albrecht, W. P. Dennis. *In* Albrecht, W. P. The sublime pleasures of tragedy p13-24

Albrecht, W. P. "The fierce dispute." *In* Albrecht, W. P. The sublime pleasures of tragedy p159-67

Albrecht, W. P. Gerard. *In* Albrecht, W. P. The sublime pleasures of tragedy p53-68

Albrecht, W. P. Hazlitt. *In* Albrecht, W. P. The sublime pleasures of tragedy p115-31

Albrecht, W. P. Keats. *In* Albrecht, W. P. The sublime pleasures of tragedy p133-58

Albrecht, W. P. Knight. *In* Albrecht, W. P. The sublime pleasures of tragedy p83-95

Albrecht, W. P. The sublime and the tragic. *In* Albrecht, W. P. The sublime pleasures of tragedy p 1-11

Albrecht, W. P. The sublime of vision. *In* Albrecht, W. P. The sublime pleasures of tragedy p97-114

Bloom, H. Emerson and Whitman: the American sublime. *In* Bloom, H. Poetry and repression p235-66

Hartman, G. H. From the sublime to the hermeneutic. *In* Hartman, G. H. The fate of reading p114-23

Hertz, N. The notion of blockage in the literature of the sublime. *In* Hartman, G. H. ed. Psychoanalysis and the question of the text p62-85

Submarine warfare. See Anti-submarine warfare

Submerged lands. See Petroleum in submerged lands

Subscription book trade. See Booksellers and bookselling—Colportage, subscription trade, etc.

Subsidies

Baumol, W. J. Acceleration incentives and x-efficiency. *In* Econometrics and economic theory p167-75

Substance (Philosophy)

Davis, J. W. Hume on qualitative content. *In* David Hume p175-80

Morewedge, P. The analysis of "substance" in Tūsī's Logic and in the ibn Sīnian tradition. *In* Essays on Islamic philosophy and science p158-88

See also Essence (Philosophy); Matter; Ontology

Suburban life

Psychological aspects

Fischer, C. S. The metropolitan experience. *In* Hawley, A. H. and Rock, V. P. eds. Metropolitan America in contemporary perspective p201-34

Suburban life—*Continued*

United States

Berger, B. M. American pastoralism, suburbia and the commune movement: an exercise in the microsociology of knowledge. *in* On the making of Americans p235-50

Suburbs

See also Suburban life

United States

Edel, M.; Harris, J. R. and Rothenberg, J. Urban concentration and deconcentration. *In* Hawley, A. H. and Rock, V. P. eds. Metropolitan America in contemporary perspective p123-56

Subversive activities

See also Political crimes and offenses; Terrorism

Chile

Borosage, R. L. and Marks, J. D. Destabilizing Chile. *In* Borosage, R. L. and Marks, J. D. eds. The CIA file p79-89

Success

O'Neill, O. Some inconsistent educational aims. *In* Small comforts for hard times p303-07

Succession to the crown. See subdivision Kings and rulers—Succession under names of countries, e.g. France—Kings and rulers—Succession

Such a gorgeous kid like me (Motion picture)

Kauffmann, S. Such a gorgeous kid like me. *In* Kauffmann, S. Living images p189-90

Sucksmith, Harvey Peter

Sir Leicester Dedlock, Wat Tyler, and the Chartists: the role of the Ironmaster in Bleak House. *In* Dickens Studies Annual v4 p113-31

Sudan

Antiquities

Shinnie, P. L. The development of Meroitic studies since 1945. *In* African studies since 1945 p169-78

Politics and government

Khalid, M. The southern Sudan settlement and its African implications. *In* El-Ayouty, Y. ed. The Organization of African Unity after ten years p174-88

Sudarkasa, Niara

From stranger to alien: the socio-political history of the Nigerian Yoruba in Ghana, 1900-1970. *In* Shack, W. A. and Skinner, E. P. eds. Strangers in African societies p141-67

Sudjatmoko

Reflections on nonalignment in the 1970s. *In* Erb, G. F. and Kallab, V. eds. Beyond dependency p28-37

Sueiro, Daniel

About individual works

La criba

Schwartz, R. Daniel Sueiro and La criba (The sieve (1958). *In* Schwartz, R. Spain's New Wave novelists, 1950-1974 p132-42

Suez Canal

History

McLeod, M. B. Audience and argument in the speeches of R. G. Menzies and Krishna Menon on the Suez Canal crisis in 1956. *In* Narasimhaiah, C. D. ed. Awakened conscience p389-400

Suffering (Jewish theology)

Neher, A. Shaddai: the God of the broken arch (a theological approach to the Holocaust) *in* Rosenfeld, A. H. and Greenberg, I. eds. Confronting the Holocaust p150-58

Suffrage

Brown, B. K. T. The controversy over the franchise in Puritan Massachusetts, 1954 to 1974. *In* Vaughan, A. T. and Bremer, F. J. eds. Puritan New England p128-54

See also Afro-Americans—Politics and suffrage; Women—Suffrage

Great Britain

Wilson, A. The suffrage movement. *In* Hollis, P. ed. Pressure from without p80-104

United States

Wood, G. S. Revolution and the political integration of the enslaved and disenfranchised. *In* America's continuing revolution p99-116

Sufism

Hardin, N. S. Doris Lessing and the Sufi way. *In* Pratt, A. and Dembo, L. S. eds. Doris Lessing p148-64

Lessing, D. M. In the world, not of it. *In* Lessing, D. M. A small personal voice p129-37

Meier, F. M. The mystic path. *In* Lewis, B. ed. Islam and the Arab world p117-40

Ornstein, R. E. Contemporary Sufism. *In* Tart, C. T. ed. Transpersonal psychologies p353-88

Waugh, E. H. Following the beloved: Muhammad as model in the Sūfī tradition. *In* Reynolds, F. E. and Capps, D. eds. The biographical process p63-85

See also Naqshbandī (Islamic order)

Morocco

Dwyer, D. H. Women, Sufism, and decision-making in Moroccan Islam. *In* Beck, L. and Keddie, N. R. eds. Women in the Muslim world p585-98

Suganami, Hidemi

Why ought treaties to be kept? *In* The Year book of world affairs, 1979 p243-56

Sugar growing. See Sugar workers

Sugar trade

Cuba

Pérez-López, J. F. Sugar and petroleum in Cuban-Soviet terms of trade. *In* Cuba in the world p273-96

Sugar workers

Louisiana

Scarpaci, J. A. Immigrants in the new South: Italians in Louisiana's sugar parishes 1880-1910. *In* Studies in Italian American social history p132-52

Sugarman, Barry

Reluctant converts: social control, socialization and adaptation in therapeutic communities. *In* Wallis, R. ed. Sectarianism p141-61

Sugarman, Stephen, D. See Coons, J. E. jt. auth.

Suger, abbot of Saint-Denis

About

Nolan, B. Anagogy, aevum and two later medieval visionary arts. *In* Nolan, B. The Gothic visionary perspective p35-83

Sugerman, Shirley Greene

An "essay" on Coleridge on imagination. *In* Evolution of consciousness p191-201

Suggestive therapeutics. See Therapeutics, Suggestive

Suggs, George Graham

Introduction. *In* Suggs, G. G. ed. Perspectives on the American Revolution p 1-11

Sugrue, Regina. See Wilson, M. G. jt. auth.

Suicide

Bernstein, A. My own suicide. *In* Wolman, B. B. ed. Between survival and suicide p95-102

Boss, M. Flight from death—mere survival; and flight into death—suicide. *In* Wolman, B. B. ed. Between survival and suicide p 1-23

Danto, B. L. Drug ingestion and suicide during anticipatory grief. *In* Anticipatory grief p311-14

Donnelly, J. P. Suicide and rationality. *In* Donnelly, J. P. ed. Language, metaphysics, and death p88-105

Fletcher, J. F. Suicide. *In* Fletcher, J. F. Humanhood: essays in biomedical ethics p166-75

Gass, W. H. The doomed in their sinking. *In* Gass, W. H. The world within the word p3-15

Hook, S. The ethics of suicide. *In* Kohl, M. ed. Beneficent euthanasia p57-69

Kaufmann, W. A. On death and lying. *In* Psychiatry and the humanities v 1 p235-40

Sheed, W. A. Alvarez: the savage god. *In* Sheed, W. The good word & other words p68-72

Williams, G. L. Euthanasia and the physician. *In* Kohl, M. ed. Beneficent euthanasia p145-68

See also Mentally ill—Suicidal behavior

Case studies

Iga, M. Personal situation as a factor in suicide, with reference to Yasunari Kawabata and Yukio Mishima. *In* Wolman, B. B. ed. Between survival and suicide p103-28

Moral and religious aspects

Pretzel, P. W. Philosophical and ethical considerations of suicide prevention. *In* Weir, R. F. ed. Ethical issues in death and dying p387-400

Szasz, T. S. The ethics of suicide. *In* Weir, R. F. ed. Ethical issues in death and dying p374-86

Also in Wolman, B. B. ed. Between survival and suicide p163-85

Prevention

Shneidman, E. S. Preventing suicide. *In* Weir, R. F. ed. Ethical issues in death and dying p363-73

Psychological aspects

Krauss, H. H. Suicide—a psychosocial phenomenon. *In* Wolman, B. B. ed. Between survival and suicide p26-54

Suicide in literature

Glicksberg, C. I. Nihilism and suicide. *In* Glicksberg, C. I. The literature of nihilism p95-115

Page, P. The Princess Casamassima: suicide and "The penetrating imagination." *In* Tennessee Studies in literature v22 p162-69

Suicide prevention. See Suicide—Prevention

Suid, Lawrence

The Pentagon and Hollywood: Dr Strangelove or: How I learned to stop worrying and love the bomb. *In* O'Connor, J. E. and Jackson, M. A. eds. American history/American film p219-35

Sukenick, Lynn

Feeling and reason in Doris Lessing's fiction. *In* Pratt, A. V. and Dembo, L. S. eds. Doris Lessing p98-118

On women and fiction. *In* Diamond, A. and Edwards, L. R. eds. The authority of experience p28-44

Sukenick, Ronald

The new tradition in fiction. *In* Federman, R. ed. Surfiction p35-45

Sukhodaya. See Sukhothai, Thailand

Sukhothai, Thailand

Griswold, A. B. and Prasert Na Nagara. On kingship and society at Sukhodaya. *In* Change and persistence in Thai society p29-92

Sukhum. See Sukhumi, Armenia

Sukhumi, Armenia

Mandel'shtam, O. E. Sukhum. *In* Mandel'shtam. O. E. Selected essays p190-92

Suks

Peristiany, J. G. The ideal and the actual: the role of prophets in the Pokot political system. *In* Studies in social anthropology p167-212

Sullivan, Denis G. See Nakamura, R. T. jt. auth.

Sullivan, Ernest W.

Authoritave manuscript corrections in Donne's Biathanatos. *In* Virginia. University. Bibliographical Society. Studies in bibliography v28 p268-76

Manuscript materials in the first edition of Donne's Biathanatos. *In* Virginia. University. Bibliographical Society. Studies in bibliography v31 p210-21

Marginal rules as evidence. *In* Virginia. University. Bibliographical Society. Studies in bibliography v30 p171-80

Sullivan, Henry Wells

Towards a new chronology for the dramatic eclogues of Juan del Encina. *In* Virginia. University. Bibliographical Society. Studies in bibliography v30 p257-75

Sullivan, Jack

Elegant nightmares

Contents

The antiquarian ghost story: Montague Rhodes James
Beginnings: Sheridan Le Fanu
Conclusion: Ghost stories as enigmas
Ghost stories of other antiquaries
"Green tea": the archetypal ghost story
Introduction
The visionary ghost story: Algernon Blackwood

Sullivan, Joseph Vincent, Bp.

The immorality of euthanasia. *In* Kohl, M. ed. Beneficent euthanasia p12-33

Sullivan, Louis Henry

About

Paul, S. Louis Sullivan and organic architecture. *In* Paul, S. Repossessing and renewing p111-30

About individual works

The autobiography of an idea

Couser, G. T. Two prophetic architects: Louis Sullivan and Frank Lloyd Wright. *In* Couser, G. T. American autobiography p120-47

Rocks, J. E. Louis Sullivan's The autobiography of an idea: "spring song" and "autumn reverie." *In* Tulane Studies in English, v23 p109-21

Sullivan, Michael

Orthodoxy and individualism in twentieth-century Chinese art. *In* Artists and traditions p201-05

Values through art. *In* Terrill, R. ed. The China difference p305-25

Sullivan, Richard Eugene

The medieval monk as frontiersman. *In* The Frontier v2 p25-49

The Middle Ages in the Western tradition: some reconsiderations. *In* Essays on medieval civilization p3-31

Sullivan, Sheila

Friends and critics, 1840-1928. *In* Drabble, M. ed. The genius of Thomas Hardy p32-43

Sullivan, Walter, 1924-

Southern literature: the last twenty years. *In* Two decades of change p55-66

Sulloway, Frank Jones

Geographic isolation in Darwin's thinking: the vicissitudes of a crucial idea. *In* Studies in history of biology v3 p23-65

Sulzberger, Cyrus Lee

The human condition of Malraux. *In* Courcel, M. H. de, ed. Malraux p204-11

Sumberg, Lewis A. M.

From farce in the âge bourgeois (1440-1500) to farce Molièresque: the structure of generic change. *In* Johnson, R. B.; Neumann, E. S. and Trail, G. T. eds. Molière and the commonwealth of letters: patrimony and posterity p430-42

Sumer is icumen in

Dronke, P. Two thirteenth-century religious lyrics. *In* Chaucer and Middle English studies in honour of Rossell Hope Robbins p392-406

Summer is a-coming in. See Sumer is icumen in

Summerhill School, Leicester, England

Barrow, R. A. S. Neill (1883-1973). *In* Barrow, R. Radical education p64-91

Bettelheim, B. About Summerhill. *In* Bettelheim, B. Surviving, and other essays p169-84

Summers, Claude J.

Herrick's political poetry: the strategies of his art. *In* Rollin, R. B. and Patrick, J. M. eds. "Trust to good verses": Herrick tercentenary essays p171-83

Summers, David

David's scowl. *In* Collaboration in Italian Renaissance art p113-24

Summers, Joseph Holmes

Some apocalyptic strains in Marvell's poetry. *In* Friedenreich, K. ed. Tercentenary essays in honor of Andrew Marvell p180-203

Summers, Robert S.

Legal philosophy today—an introduction. *In* Summers, R. S. ed. Essays in legal philosophy p 1-21

Summerskill, Edith

On the Voluntary Euthanasia Bill of 1969. *In* Kohl, M. ed. Beneficent euthanasia p204-08

Summit conferences. Wilson, T. A. *In* Encyclopedia of American foreign policy p936-44

Sumner, Francis Bertody

About

Provine, W. B. Francis B. Sumner and the evolutionary synthesis. *In* Studies in history of biology v3 p211-40

Sumner, Graham Vincent

Roman policy in Spain before the Hannibalic War. *In* Harvard Studies in classical philology v72 p205-46

The truth about Velleius Paterculus: prolegomena. *In* Harvard Studies in classical philology v74 p257-97

Varrones Murenae. *In* Harvard Studies in classical philology v82 p187-95

Sumter, Fort

McWhiney, G. The Confederacy's first shot. *In* Hubbell, J. T. ed. Battles lost and won p73-82

Sun, Dae-sook

A preconceived formula for Sovietization: the Communist takeover of North Korea. *In* Hammond, T. T. ed. The anatomy of Communist takeovers p475-89

Sun, E-tu (Zên)

Chinese history of technology: some points for comparison with the West. *In* Bugliarello, G. and Doner, D. B. eds. The history and philosophy of technology p38-49

Sun

Gingerich, O. The sun. *In* Man and cosmos p37-47

See also Eclipses, Solar

Parallax

See Parallax—Sun

Rotation

Thomas, L. An apology. *In* Thomas, L. The medusa and the snail p88-92

Sun (in religion, folklore, etc.)

Coomaraswamy, A. K. Svayamātrnnā: Janua coeli. *In* Coomaraswamy, A. K. Selected papers v 1 p465-520

Sun in art

Paulson, R. Turner's graffiti: the sun and its glosses. *In* Kroeber, K. and Walling, W. eds. Images of romanticism p167-88

Sun in literature

Berry, D. Apollinaire's solar imagery. *In* Cardinal, R. ed. Sensibility and creation p36-56

Sunday

Jones, W. R. The heavenly letter in medieval England. *In* Medievalia et humanistica no. 6 p163-78

Sunday bloody Sunday (Motion picture)

Kauffmann, S. Sunday bloody Sunday. *In* Kauffmann, S. Living images p78-81

Sunday-schools

England—History

Pickering, S. The Sunday school movement: new readers and the novel. *In* Pickering, S. The moral tradition in English fiction, 1785-1850 p11-64

Sundberg, Jacob W. F.
Thinking the unthinkable or the case of Dr Tsironis. *In* International terrorism and political crimes p448-59

Sundell, Roger H.
The singer and his song in the Prologues of Paradise lost. *In* Patrick, J. M. and Sundell, R. H. eds. Milton and the art of sacred song p65-80

Sunderland, Elizabeth Read
The system of proportion of Filippo Brunelleschi. *In* Enggass, R. C. and Stokstad, M. eds. Hortus imaginum p65-72

Sunderland, Eric
Biological components of the races of man. *In* Racial variation in man p9-25

Sunderland, Robert Spencer, 2d Earl of

About

Bennett, G. V. Jacobitism and the rise of Walpole. *In* Historical perspectives p70-92

Sundiata, Ibrahim K.
Creolization on Fernando Po: the nature of society. *In* Kilson, M. L. and Rotberg, R. I. eds. The African diaspora p391-413

Sunnis. See Sunnites

Sunnites
Lapidus, I. M. Adulthood in Islam: religious maturity in the Islamic tradition. *In* Erikson, E. H. ed. Adulthood p97-112

Sunset (criticism) Babel, I. E. *In* Kauffmann, S. Persons of the drama p176-78

Sunset Boulevard (Motion picture)
French, B. The scarlet "A." *In* French, B. On the verge of revolt p 1-12

Suomen Kommunistinen Puolue. See Communist Party of Finland

Supek, Rudi
The visible hand and the degradation of individuality. *In* Beyond the crisis p49-80

Super, Robert Henry
Arnold and literary criticism: (ii) critical practice. *In* Allott, K. ed. Matthew Arnold p149-77

The humanist at bay: the Arnold-Huxley debate. *In* Knoepflmacher, U. C. and Tennyson, G. B. eds. Nature and the Victorian imagination p231-45

Super-ego. See Ego (Psychology)

Superficiality
Peckham, M. The virtues of superficiality. *In* Peckham, M. Romanticism and behavior p249-62

Superior Court of New Jersey. See New Jersey. Superior Court

Superior Court of the State of Maine. See Maine. Superior Court

Supernatural
Price, G. R. Science and the supernatural. *In* Ludwig, J. K. ed. Philosophy and parapsychology p145-71

Scriven, M. Explanations of the supernatural. *In* Thakur, S. C. ed. Philosophy and psychical research p181-94

See also Psychical research; Superstition

Supernatural in literature
Atwood, M. E. Canadian monsters: some aspects of the supernatural in Canadian fiction. *In* Staines, D. ed. The Canadian imagination p97-122

See also Fantastic fiction; Occultism in literature

Superrealism. See Surrealism

Superstition
Goldin, J. The magic of magic and superstition. *In* Aspects of religious propaganda in Judaism and early Christianity p115-47

Hole, C. Protective symbols in the home. *In* Symbols of power p121-30

See also Alchemy; Evil eye: Fetishism; Magic; Voodoism; Witchcraft

Supervielle, Jules

About

Martin, G. D. Jules Supervielle: a poetry of diffidence. *In* Cardinal, R. ed. Sensibility and creation p103-21

Suppe, Frederick Roy
Afterword—1977. *In* Suppe, F. R. ed. The structure of scientific theories p615-730

Supple, Barry Emmanuel
The governing framework: social class and institutional reform in Victorian Britain. *In* Lerner, L. ed. The Victorians p90-119

Legislation and virtue: an essay on working class self-help and the state in the early nineteenth century. *In* Historical perspectives p211-54

Material development: the condition of England 1830-1860. *In* Lerner, L. ed. The Victorians p49-69

Supply and demand. See Consumption (Economics)

Supposition. See Hypothesis

Supremacy of law. See Rule of law

Suprematism in art
Osborne, H. Constructivism. *In* Osborne, H. Abstraction and artifice in twentieth-century art p125-48

Supreme courts. See names of individual supreme courts, e.g. United States. Supreme Court

Surety of the peace

International cooperation

Rosen, S. J. and Frank, R. Measures against international terrorism. *In* International terrorism and world security p60-68

Surgeons

France

Lemay, E. H. Thomas Hérier, a country surgeon outside Angoulême at the end of the XVIIIth century: a contribution to social history. *In* Branca, P. ed. The medicine show p229-42

Surgery

See also Operating rooms

History

Temkin, O. The role of surgery in the rise of modern medical thought. *In* Temkin, O. The double face of Janus p487-96

Surgery, Aseptic and antiseptic
Charnley, Sir J. K. Experiences in the development of a clean air operating room. *In* The Frontiers of human knowledge p45-58

Surrealism
Benjamin, W. Surrealism. *In* Benjamin, W. Reflections p177-92

Glicksberg, C. I. From surrealism to communism. *In* Glicksberg, C. I. The literature of commitment p150-62

Greene, R. W. René Char. *In* Greene, R. W. Six poets of our time p99-123

Krauss, R. E. A game plan: the terms of surrealism. *In* Krauss, R. E. Passages in modern sculpture p105-46

Surrealism—*Continued*

Levitt, A. S. Roger Vitrac and the drama of surrealism. *In* Aeolian harps p247-72

Lippard, L. R. Introduction to surrealists on art. *In* Kaplan, P. and Manso, S. eds. Major European art movements, 1900-1945 p325-36

McMillan, D. Surrealism. *In* McMillan, D. Transition p79-89

Nicoll, A. The drama of the individual. *In* Nicoll, A. World drama p654-73

Zweig, P. The new surrealism. *In* Boyers, R. ed. Contemporary poetry in America p314-29

See also Dadaism; Pop art

Surrender. See Capitulations, Military

Surrey, Henry Howard, Earl of, tr.

About individual works
Certain bokes of Vigiles Aenaeis, turned into English meter

Bawcutt, P. Douglas and Surrey: translators of Virgil. *In* English Association. Essays and studies, 1974 p52-67

Surveying

See also Hydrographic surveying

Public lands—United States
Johnson, H. B. The United States land survey as a principle of order. *In* Pattern and process p114-30

Pattison, W. D. Reflections on the American rectangular land survey system. *In* Pattern and process p131-38

Survival (Human ecology) See Human ecology

Susman, Warren Irving
"Personality" and the making of twentieth-century culture. *In* Higham, J. and Conkin, P. K. eds. New directions in American intellectual history p212-26

Suspended sentence. See Probation

Sussman, Henry
The all-embracing metaphor: reflections on Kafka's "The burrow." *In* Glyph I p100-31

The deconstructor as politician: Melville's Confidence-man. *In* Glyph 4 p32-56

Sussman, Leonard R.
Developmental journalism: the ideological factor. *In* Horton, P. C. ed. The Third World and press freedom p74-92

Sutch, Richard Charles, and Ransom, Roger L.
Sharecropping: market response or mechanism of race control? *In* What was freedom's price? p51-69

Sutcliff, Rosemary
Lost summer. *In* Blishen, E. ed. The thorny paradise p93-96

Sutcliffe, Anthony
A vision of utopia: optimistic foundations of Le Corbusier's doctrine d'urbanisme. *In* Walden, R. ed. The open hand p216-43

Suter, Barbara
Suicide and women. *In* Wolman, B. B. ed. Between survival and suicide p129-61

Sutherland, D. M. G. See Le Goff, T. J. A. jt. auth.

Sutherland, Donald
Willa Cather: the classic voice. *In* The Art of Willa Cather p156-82

Sutherland, Edwin Hardin
The diffusion of sexual psychopath laws. *In* Davis, F. J. and Stivers, R. eds. The collective definition of deviance p281-95

Sutherland, George

About
White, G. E. The Four Horsemen: the sources of judicial notoriety. *In* White, G. E. The American judicial tradition p178-99

Sutherland, James Runcieman
Down Chancery Lane. *In* Evidence in literary scholarship p165-78

Sutherland, John A.
Victorian novelists and publishers
Contents

Craft versus trade: novelists and publishers
Dickens as publishers
Hardy: breaking into fiction
'Henry Esmond': the shaping power of contract
Lever and Ainsworth: missing the first rank
Marketing 'Middlemarch'
Mass market and big business: novel publishing at midcentury
Novel publishing, 1830-1870
Trollope: making the first rank
'Westward ho!': 'a popularly successful book'

Sutherland, Lucy Stuart
William Blackstone and the legal chairs at Oxford. *In* Evidence in literary scholarship p229-40

Sutherland, Margaret B.
Comparative perspectives on the education of cultural minorities. *In* Alcock, A. E.; Taylor, B. K. and Welton, J. M. eds. The future of cultural minorities p44-62

Sutherland, Monica (La Fontaine)

About individual works
La Fontaine

Connolly, C. La Fontaine. *In* Connolly, C. The evening colonnade p107-08

Sutherland, Stewart R.
Hume and the concept of pleasure. *In* David Hume p218-24

Immortality and resurrection. *In* Donnelly, J. P. ed. Language, metaphysics, and death p196-207

Suttles, Gerald D.
Changing priorities for the urban heartland. *In* Handbook of contemporary urban life p519-47

Community design: the search for participation in a metropolitan society. *In* Hawley, A. H. and Rock, V. P. eds. Metropolitan America in contemporary perspective p235-97

Sutton, Alastair
Equality and discrimination in international economic law (VI): trends in the regulation of international trade in textiles. *In* The Year book of world affairs, 1977 p190-216

Sutton, Constance Rita, and Makiesky-Barrow, Susan
Social inequality and sexual status in Barbados. *In* Schlegel, A. E. ed. Sexual stratification p292-325

Sutton, Dana Ferrin
A handlist of satyr plays. *In* Harvard Studies in classical philology v78 p107-43

Sutton, Thomas

About

Gernsheim, H. Cuthbert Bede (The Rev Edward Bradley, 1827-1889), Robert Hunt F.R.S. (1807-1887), and Thomas Sutton (1819-1875). *In* One hundred years of photographic history p59-67

Sutton, William Alfred

Anderson's letters to Marietta D. Finley Hahn: a literary chronicle. *In* Anderson, D. D. ed. Sherwood Anderson: dimensions of his literary art p110-17

Sutton Hoo ship burial, England

Biddle, M. and others. Sutton Hoo published: a review. *In* Anglo-Saxon England 6 p249-65

Suvin, Darko

A grammar of form and a criticism of fact: The time machine as a structural model for science fiction. *In* H. G. Wells and modern science fiction p90-115

Introduction. *In* H. G. Wells and modern science fiction p9-32

Metamorphoses of science fiction

Contents

The alternative island
Anticipating the sunburst: dream, vision—or nightmare?
Defining the literary genre of utopia: some historical semantics, some genology, a proposal, and a plea
Estrangement and cognition
Karel Čapek, or the aliens amongst us
Liberalism mutes the anticipation: the space-binding machines
Russian SF and its utopian tradition
SF and the genological jungle
SF and the novum
The shift to anticipation: radical rhapsody and romantic recoil
The time machine versus Utopia as structural models for SF
Wells as the turning point of the SF tradition

Saint Joan of the slaughterhouses: structures of a slaughterhouse world. *In* Mews, S. and Knust, H. eds. Essays on Brecht p114-40

Svedberg, Ingmar

Political poetry in modern Finnish literature. *In* Dauenhauer, R. and Binham, P. eds. Snow in May p53-57

Svensson, Frances

The technological challenge to political theory. *In* Bugliarello, G. and Doner, D. B. eds. The history and philosophy of technology p294-308

Svevo, Italo, pseud. See Schmitz, Ettore

Sviedrys, Romualdas

The rise of physics laboratories in Britain. *In* Historical studies in the physical sciences v7 p405-36

Svin'in, Pavel Petrovich

About

Gleason, A. Pavel Svin'in. *In* Abroad in America: Visitors to the new Nation, 1776-1914 p12-21

Svoboda, Cyril P. See Looft, W. R. jt. auth.

Swados, Harvey

About individual works

On the line

Farrell, J. T. Harvey Swados: a Veblen of the novel. *In* Farrell, J. T. Literary essays, 1954-1974 p115-17

Swales, Martin

The German Bildungsroman from Wieland to Hesse

Contents

The Bildungsroman as a genre
Conclusion
Excursus: the Bildungsroman as taxonomic genre
Goethe: Wilhelm Meister's apprenticeship (1795-1796)
Hesse: The glass bead game (1943)
Keller: Green Henry (1879-1880)
Mann: The magic mountain (1924)
Stifter: Indian summer (1857)
Wieland: Agathon (1767)

The German Novelle

Contents

Büchner: Lenz
Chamisso: Peter Schlemihl
Conclusion
Goethe: Novelle
Grillparzer: Der arme Spielmann
Keller: Die drei gerechten Kammacher
Meyer: Das Leiden eines Knabn
The Novelle as historical genre
Stifter: Granit
The theory of the Novelle

Swan, Michael

The consular fasti of 23 B.C. and the conspiracy of Varro Murena. *In* Harvard Studies in classical philology v71 p235-47

Swanberg, W. A.

About individual works

Luce and his empire

Sheed, W. More light on Luce. *In* Sheed, W. The good word & other words p132-36

Norman Thomas, the last idealist

Howe, I. Tribune of socialism. *In* Howe, I. Celebrations and attacks p230-33

Swanson, Donald Roland

The observer observed: notes on the narrator of Under Western eyes. *In* Renaissance and modern p109-18

Swanson, Glen Wilfred

War, technology, and society in the Ottoman Empire from the reign of Abdülhamid II to 1913: Mahmud Sevket and the German military mission. *In* War, technology and society in the Middle East p367-85

Swanton, Michael

Heroes, heroism and heroic literature. *In* English Association. Essays and studies, 1977 p 1-21

Swart, J.

On re-reading William Dunbar. *In* Chaucer and Middle English studies in honour of Rossell Hope Robbins p201-09

Swart, Stanley L.

The military examination board in the Civil War: a case study. *In* Hubbell, J. T. ed. Battles lost and won p241-59

Swartz, Roderick G.

The library change agent: a state library role for the future. *In* As much to learn as to teach p117-27

Swazey, Judith P.

Protecting the "animal of necessity": limits to inquiry in clinical investigation. *In* Holton, G. J. and Morison, R. S. eds. Limits of scientific inquiry p129-45

Swaziland

History

Vilakazi, A. L. Swaziland and Lesotho: from traditionalism to modernity. *In* Carter, G. M. and O'Meara, P. eds. Southern Africa in crisis p226-57

Politics and government

Vilakazi, A. L. Swaziland and Lesotho: from traditionalism to modernity. *In* Carter, G. M. and O'Meara, P. eds. Southern Africa in crisis p226-57

Vilakazi, A. Swaziland: from tradition to modernity. *In* Carter, G. M. and O'Meara, P. eds. Southern Africa: the continuing crisis p269-90

Social conditions

Vilakazi, A. Swaziland: from tradition to modernity. *In* Carter, G. M. and O'Meara, P. eds. Southern Africa: the continuing crisis p269-90

Swearer, Donald Keeney

Recent developments in Thai Buddhism. *In* Dumoulin, H. ed. Buddhism in the modern world p99-108

Swearingen, John Eldred

What price dependence? *In* Prochnow, H. V. ed. Dilemmas facing the nation p96-108

Sweden

Economic conditions—1918-

Martin, A. The dynamics of change in a Keynesian political economy: the Swedish case and its implications. *In* Crouch, C. ed. State and economy in contemporary capitalism p88-121

Foreign relations—Greece

Sundberg, J. W. F. Thinking the unthinkable or the case of Dr Tsironis. *In* International terrorism and political crimes p448-59

Population

Akerman, S. and Norberg A. Employment opportunities, family-building and internal migration in the late nineteenth century: some Swedish case studies. *In* Economic factors in population growth p453-86

Swedenborg, Emanuel

About

Altschule, M. D. Swedenborg and Stahl: opposite—and wrong—sides of the same coin. *In* Altschule, M. D. Origins of concepts in human behavior p183-92

Ellwood, R. S. Shakers and spiritualists. *In* Ellwood, R. S. Alternative altars p65-103

Influence—Blake

Thompson, E. P. 'London.' *In* Phillips, M. C. ed. Interpreting Blake p5-31

Influence—Dostoevskii

Miłosz, C. Dostoevsky and Swedenborg. *In* Miłosz, C. Emperor of the earth p120-43

Swedish children's literature. See Children's literature, Swedish

Swedish drama

History and criticism

Kistrup, J. Post-war drama in Scandinavia. *In* Nicoll, A. World drama p854-60

Swedish fiction

History and criticism

Linnér, S. The hero in Swedish fiction after World War II. *In* The Hero in Scandinavian literature p107-23

Swedish moving-pictures. See Moving-pictures, Swedish

Sween, Joyce A. See Clignet, R. jt. auth.

Sweet, Louise Elizabeth

In reality: some Middle Eastern women. *In* Matthiasson, C. J. ed. Many sisters p379-97

Swenson, Esther J.

Education for a new generation. *In* The Rising South v2 p141-61

Swenson, May

About

Ostriker, A. May Swenson and the shapes of speculation. *In* Gilbert, S. M. and Gubar, S. eds. Shakespeare's sisters p221-32

Swerdlow, Noel Mark

On Copernicus' theory of precession. *In* The Copernican achievement p49-98

About individual works

On Copernicus' theory of precession

Gingerich, O. J. Commentary: remarks on Copernicus' observations. *In* The Copernican achievement p99-107

Swiderski, Richard

From folk to popular: plastic evil eye charms. *In* The Evil eye p28-41

Swierenga, Robert P.

The ethnic voter and the first Lincoln election. *In* Swierenga, R. P. ed. Beyond the Civil War synthesis p99-115

Swift, Jonathan

About

Elliott, R. C. Swift's satire: rules of the game. *In* ELH essays for Earl R. Wasserman p123-38

Maresca, T. E. Swift. *In* Maresca T. E. Epic to novel p135-78

Rawson, C. J. The nightmares of Strephon: nymphs of the city in the poems of Swift, Baudelaire, Eliot. *In* English literature in the age of disguise p57-97

Selby, H. R. The cell and the garret: fictions of confinement in Swift's satires and personal writings. *In* Studies in eighteenth-century culture v6 p133-56

Trowbridge, F. H. Swift and Socrates. *In* Trowbridge, F. H. From Dryden to Jane Austen p81-123

Wimsatt, W. K. Rhetoric and poems: the example of Swift. *In* Martz, L. L. and Williams, A. L. eds. The author in his work p229-44

About individual works

An argument against abolishing Christianity

Manlove, C. N. Swift. *In* Manlove, C. N. Literature and reality, 1600-1800 p114-24

A beautiful young nymph going to bed

Solomon, M. "To steal a hint was never known": the Sodom apple motif and Swift's "A beautiful young nymph going to bed." *In* Tennessee Studies in literature v22 p105-16

Gulliver's travels

Gill, J. E. Man and Yahoo: dialectic and symbolism in Gulliver's "Voyage to the country of the Houyhnhnms." *In* The Dress of words p67-90

Swift, Jonathan—*Continued*

Hughes, P. Creativity and history in Vico and his contemporaries. *In* Giambattista Vico's science of humanity p155-69

Suvin, D. The alternative island. *In* Suvin, D. Metamorphoses of science fiction p90-114

Gulliver's travels (Parts I-III)

Gill, J. E. Discovery and alienation, nature and reason in Gulliver's Travels, Parts I-III. *In* Tennessee Studies in literature v22 p85-104

A modest proposal

Manlove, C. N. Swift. *In* Manlove, C. N. Literature and reality, 1600-1800 p114-24

A tale of a tub

Kallich, M. Swift and the archetypes of hate: A tale of a tub. *In* Studies in eighteenth-century culture v4 p43-67

Verses on the death of Dr. Swift

Vieth, D. M. The mystery of personal identity: Swift's verses on his own death. *In* Martz, L. L. and Williams, A. L. eds. The author in his work p245-62

Woolley, J. Friends and enemies in Verses on the death of Dr. Swift. *In* Studies in eighteenth-century culture v8 p205-32

Influence—Byron

England, A. B. The style of Don Juan and Augustan poetry. *In* Jump, J. D. ed. Byron p94-112

Swiggart, Peter

A note on telepathy. *In* Wheatley, J. M. O. and Edge, H. L. eds. Philosophical dimensions of parapsychology p139-41

Swinburne, Algernon Charles

About

Harrison, A. H. The aesthetics of androgyny in Swinburne's early poetry. *In* Tennessee Studies in literature v23 p87-99

Ober, W. B. Swinburne's masochism: neuropathology and psychopathology. *In* Ober, W. B. Boswell's clap and other essays p43-88

Peters, R. L. Algernon Charles Swinburne and the use of integral detail. *In* Sambrook, J. ed. Pre-Raphaelitism p206-19

Williamson, A. Swinburne: poet and enfant terrible. *In* Williamson, A. Artists and writers in revolt p161-81

About individual works

Atalanta in Calydon

Marmaras, A. and Marmaras, L. An English translation of the ancient Greek dedicatory verses to Atalanta in Calydon. *In* Aeolian harps p179-89

Lesbia Brandon

Cockshut, A. O. J. The pessimists: Swinburne. *In* Cockshut, A. O. J. Man and woman: a study of love and the novel, 1740-1940 p111-16

Poems and ballads (First series)

Frick, D. C. The Proserpine figure in Swinburne's Poems and ballads I. *In* Aeolian harps p192-205

Swinburne, R. G. See Swinburne, Richard

Swinburne, Richard

The problem of evil. *In* Reason and religion p81-102

About individual works

The problem of evil

Phillips, D. Z. The problem of evil. *In* Reason and religion p103-21

Swine

White, E. B. Death of a pig. *In* White, E. B. Essays of E. B. White p17-24

France

Hémardinquer, J. J. The family pig of the ancien régime: myth or fact? *In* Food and drink in history p50-72

Swing music. See Jazz music

Swinging (Sexual behavior) See Group sex

Swingle, L. J.

Wordsworth's "picture of the mind." *In* Kroeber, K. and Walling, W. eds. Images of romanticism p81-90

Swinton, George S.

Touch and the real: contemporary Inuit aesthetics—theory, usage and relevance. *In* Greenhalgh, M. and Megaw, J. V. S. eds. Art in society p71-88

Swiss drama

History and criticism

Haider-Pregler, H. German-language postwar drama. *In* Nicoll, A. World drama p838-53

Switzerland

Languages

Warburton, T. R. Nationalism and language in Switzerland and Canada. *In* Smith, A. D. ed. Nationalist movements p88-109

Politics and government

Petersen, W. On the subnations of Western Europe. *In* Glazer, N. and Moynihan, D. P. eds. Ethnicity p177-208

Steiner, J. and Obler, J. Does the consociational theory really hold for Switzerland? *In* Esman, M. J. ed. Ethnic conflict in the Western world p324-42

Swords. See Sabers

Syena (African People) See Senufo (African people)

Sykes, Alrene

Jack Hibberd and the New Wave drama. *In* Bards, bohemians, and bookmen p305-19

Sykes, Barbara. See Rohrlich-Leavitt, R. jt. auth.

Sykes, Sir Mark, bart.

About

Kedourie, E. Sir Mark Sykes and Palestine, 1915-16. *In* Kedourie, E. Arabic political memoris and other studies p236-42

Sylla, Edith Dudley. See Murdoch, J. E. jt. auth.

Syllogism. See Logic, Symbolic and mathematical

Sylos Labini, Paolo

Competition: the product markets. *In* The Market and the state p200-32

Sylvester I, Saint, Pope

Legend

Wallach, L. Actus Silvestri, Libri Carolini, and the Constantine Donation: the solution of a pseudo-problem. *In* Wallach, L. Diplomatic studies in Latin and Greek documents from the Carolingian age p152-59

Symbolism in literature—*Continued*

Steadman, J. M. Paradise lost: Milton's "Sin." The problem of literary indebtedness. *In* Steadman, J. M. Nature into myth p174-84

Steadman, J. M. "The pardoner's tale": old age and contemptus mundi. *In* Steadman, J. M. Nature into myth p104-14

Thomson, B. The problem of art. *In* Thomson, B. Lot's wife and the Venus of Milo p 5-28

Thompson, J. J. Symbol, myth, and ritual in The glass menagerie, The rose tattoo, and Orpheus descending. *In* Tennessee Williams: a tribute p679-711

Waldmeir, J. J. Confiteor hominem: Ernest Hemingway's religion of man. *In* Wagner, L. W. ed. Ernest Hemingway p144-52

Watt, I. P. Impressionism and symbolism in Heart of darkness. *In* Joseph Conrad: a commemoration p37-53

West, J. D. The poetic landscape of the Russian symbolists. *In* Barnes, C. J. ed. Studies in twentieth century Russian literature p 1-16

Ziolkowski, T. Some features of religious figuralism in twentieth-century literature. *In* Miner, E. R. ed. Literary uses of typology p345-69

See also Allegory

Symbolism in the Bible

Walker, D. P. Esoteric symbolism. *In* Poetry and poetics from ancient Greece to the Renaissance p218-32

Symbolism of colors in literature

Cioran, S. D. A prism for the absolute: the symbolic colors of Andrey Bely. *In* Janecek, G. ed. Andrey Bely p103-14

Symbolism of numbers

Horn, W. W. On the selective use of sacred numbers and the creation in Carolingian architecture of a new aesthetic based on modular concepts. *In* Viator: medieval and Renaissance studies v6 p351-90

Peck, R. A. Number as cosmic language. *In* Jeffrey, D. L. ed. By things seen: reference and recognition in medieval thought p47-80

Sunderland, E. R. The system of proportion of Filippo Brunelleschi. *In* Enggass, R. C. and Stokstad, M. eds. Hortus imaginum p65-72

Symbols. See Signs and symbols

Symcox, Geoffrey Walter

The battle of the Atlantic, 1500-1700. *In* First images of America p265-77

Syme, Sir Ronald

Liberty in classical antiquity. *In* Aspects of American liberty p8-15

Pliny the procurator. *In* Harvard Studies in classical philology v73 p201-36

Symmetry

Morrison, P. On broken symmetries. *In* Wechsler, J. ed. On aesthetics in science p55-70

Shaw, R.; McIntyre, M. and Mace, W. M. The role of symmetry in event perception. *In* Perception p276-310

Symmetry (Chemistry) See Symmetry (Physics)

Symmetry (Physics)

Morrison, P. On broken symmetries. *In* Wechsler, J. ed. On aesthetics in science p55-70

Stuewer, R. H. G. N. Lewis on detailed balancing, the symmetry of time, and the nature of light. *In* Historical studies in the physical sciences v6 p469-511

Symmetry breaking (Physics). See Broken symmetry (Physics)

Symons, Arthur, 1865-1945

About

Worth, K. J. Towards modernism: a new theatrical syntax. *In* Worth, K. J. The Irish drama of Europe from Yeats to Beckett p11-47

About individual works

The memoirs of Arthur Symons: life and art in the 1890's

Weintraub, S. Three views of the nineties. *In* Review, v 1 1979 p301-08

Studies in the Elizabethan drama

Eliot, T. S. The perfect critic. *In* Eliot, T. S. Selected prose of T. S. Eliot p50-58

Symons, Julian

The mistress of complication. *In* Agatha Christie: first lady of crime p25-38

Sympathy

Bagolini, L. The topicality of Adam Smith's notion of sympathy and judicial evaluations. *In* Skinner, A. S. and Wilson, T. eds. Essays on Adam Smith p100-13

Wilson, T. Sympathy and self-interest. *In* The Market and the state p73-99

Sympathy (Physiology)

Hostetler, J. A. Folk medicine and sympathy healing among the Amish. *In* American folk medicine p249-58

Symplegades. Coomaraswamy, A. K. *In* Coomaraswamy, A. K. Selected papers v 1 p521-44

Symposium (Classical literature)

Slater, W. J. Symposium at sea. *In* Harvard Studies in classical philology v80 p161-70

Symptoms. See Diagnosis

Synagogues

New York (City)

Dawidowicz, L. S. Middle-class Judaism. *In* Dawidowicz, L. S. The Jewish presence p67-91

Dawidowicz, L. S. On being a woman in shul. *In* Dawidowicz, L. S. The Jewish presence p46-57

Synan, Edward A.

Latin philosophies of the Middle Ages. *In* Powell, J. M. ed. Medieval studies p277-311

Synanon Foundation

Ofshe, R. Synanon: the people business. *In* The New religious consciousness p116-37

Syndicalism

France—History

Baker, A. S. Fernand Pelloutier and the making of revolutionary syndicalism. *In* Essays on modern European revolutionary history p39-68

Syndicates (Finance)

Cohen, W. I. Consortia. *In* Encyclopedia of American foreign policy p167-76

Synge, John Millington

About

Armstrong, W. A. Synge's communities and dissenters. *In* Drama and society p117-28

Synge, John M.—About—*Continued*

Henn, T. R. J. M. Synge: a reconsideration. *In* Henn, T. R. Last essays p191-206

Saddlemyer, A. Synge and the doors of perception. *In* Place, personality and the Irish writer p97-120

Worth, K. J. Synge. *In* Worth, K. J. The Irish drama of Europe from Yeats to Beckett p120-39

About individual works

The playboy of the Western world

Gillie, C. Drama, 1900-1940. *In* Gillie, C. Movements in English literature, 1900-1940 p164-82

Kauffmann, S. The playboy of the Western world. *In* Kauffmann, S. Persons of the drama p117-20

The well of the saints

Yeats, W. B. Preface to the first edition of The well of the saints by J. M. Synge. *In* Praise from famous men: an anthology of introductions p182-89

Bibliography

Thornton, W. J. M. Synge. *In* Finneran, R. J. ed. Anglo-Irish literature p315-65

Synods. See Councils and synods

Syntactics. See Semantics (Philosophy)

Syntax. See Grammar, Comparative and general—Syntax; also subdivision Syntax under names of particular languages, e.g. French language—Syntax; Italian language —Syntax

Synthetic chemistry. See Chemistry, Organic —Synthesis

Syphilis

Guerra, F. The problem of syphilis. *In* First images of America p845-51

Temkin, O. On the history of "morality and syphilis." *In* Temkin, O. The double face of Janus p472-84

Temkin, O. Therapeutic trends and the treatment of syphilis before 1900. *In* Temkin, O. The double face of Janus p518-24

Syria

Foreign relations—Russia

Golan, G. and Rabinovich, I. The Soviet Union and Syria: the limits of co-operation. *In* Ro'i, Y. ed. The limits to power p213-31

History

Farah, C. E. Censorship and freedom of expression in Ottoman Syria and Egypt. *In* Nationalism in a non-national state p151-94

Rafeq, A. K. The local forces in Syria in the seventeenth and eighteenth centuries. *In* War, technology and society in the Middle East p277-307

Politics and government

Khalidi, R. Arab nationalism in Syria: the formative years, 1908-1914. *In* Nationalism in a non-national state p207-37

Van Dusen, M. H. Syria: downfall of a traditional elite. *In* Political elites and political development in the Middle East p115-55

Syrkin, Marie

Palestinian nationalism: its development and goal. *In* The Palestinians p199-208

System analysis

Ball, R. A. Sociology and general systems theory. *In* McNall, S. G. ed. Theoretical perspectives in sociology p115-27

Baumgartner, T.; Burns, T. R. and De-Ville, P. R. Actors. games, and systems: the dialectics of social action and system structuring. *In* McNall, S. G. ed. Theoretical perspectives in sociology p128-48

System theory

Ball, R. A. Sociology and general systems theory. *In* McNall, S. G. ed. Theoretical perspectives in sociology p115-27

Hooker, C. A. Has the scientist any future in the brave new world? *In* Science and society: past, present, and future p306-56

Overton, W. F. General systems, structure and development. *In* Riegel, K. F. and Rosenwald, G. C. eds. Structure and transformation p61-81

Plog, F. Systems theory and simulation: the case of Hawaiian warfare and redistribution. *In* Explanation of prehistoric change p259-318

See also Cybernetics; Social systems

Systematic botany. See Botany—Classification

Systematic painting. See Minimal art

Systematic theology. See Theology, Doctrinal

Systemic grammar

Evans, G. L. Semantic structure and logical form. *In* Evans, G. L. and McDowell, J. H. eds. Truth and meaning p199-222

See also Structural linguistics

Systemic linguistics. See Systemic grammar

Systems, Theory of. See System theory

Systems analysis. See System analysis

Systems engineering. See Weapons systems

Systems theory. *See* System theory

Syz, John

Recent North-South relations and multilateral soft loans. *In* The Year book of world affairs, 1975 p196-207

Szabady, Egon

Economic factors in the decline of fertility in Hungary in the nineteenth and early twentieth century. *In* Economic factors in population growth p238-40

Szajkowski, Zosa

East European Jewish workers in Germany during World War I. *In* Salo Wittmayer Baron v2 p887-918

Szasz, Thomas Stephen

The ethics of suicide. *In* Weir, R. F. ed. Ethical issues in death and dying p374-86

Also in Wolman, B. B. ed. Between survival and suicide p163-85

The expulsion of evil; excerpt from "The manufacture of madness". *In* Davis, F. J. and Stivers, R. eds. The collective definition of deviance p60-84

The mental health ethic; excerpt from "Ideology and insanity". *In* Davis, F. J. and Stivers, R. eds. The collective definition of deviance p114-29

Society's internal enemies and protectors; excerpt from "The manufacture of madness". *In* Davis, F. J. and Stivers, R. eds. The collective definition of deviance p177-96

Szecskö, Tamás

The development of a Socialist communication theory. *In* Gerbner, G. ed. Mass media policies in changing cultures p223-34

Szövérffy, Joseph
Maximianus a satirist? *In* Harvard Studies in classical philology v72 p351-67

Szwed, John F. and Abrahams, Roger D.
After the myth: studying Afro-American cultural patterns in the plantation literature. *In* Crowley, D. J. ed. African folklore in the New World p65-86

Szyliowicz, Joseph S.
Elites and modernization in Turkey. *In* Political elites and political development in the Middle East p23-66

T

TFX (Fighter planes) See F 111 (Fighter planes)

T.L.S. See The Times, London. Literary Supplement

TNIP. See Transkei National Independence Party

TROSCOM. See United States. Army. Troop Support Command

Taamrat Emmanuel

About

Leslau, W. Taamrat Emmanuel's notes of Falasha monks and holy places. *In* Salo Wittmayer Baron v2 p623-37

Tabachnik, Leonard
Licensing in the legal and medical professions, 1820-1860: a historical case study. *In* Gerstl, J. E. and Jacobs, G. eds. Professions for the people p25-42

Political patronage and ethnic groups: foreign-born in the United States Customhouse Service, 1821-1861. *In* Swierenga, R. P. ed. Beyond the Civil War synthesis p245-54

Tablada, José Juan

About

Paz, O. José Juan Tablada. *In* Paz, O. The siren & the seashell p57-65

Table setting and decoration. See Pottery

Tablets, Memorial. See Sepulchral monuments

Tablets, Tell-el-Amarna. See Tell-el-Amarna tablets

Tabula Capitolina
Balcer, J. M. The date of Herodotus IV.1: Darius' Scythian expedition. *In* Harvard Studies in classical philology v76 p99-132

Tachau, Frank
Conclusion. *In* Political elites and political development in the Middle East p293-305

Introduction: Political elites and political development in the Middle East. *In* Political elites and political development in the Middle East p 1-21

Tacitus, Cornelius

About

Momigliano, A. The first political commentary on Tacitus. *In* Momigliano, A. Essays in ancient and modern historiography p205-18

Momigliano, A. The first political commentary on Tacitus: appendix. *In* Momigliano, A. Essays in ancient and modern historiography p218-29

Oliver, R. P. Tacitean nobilitas. *In* Illinois classical studies v3, 1978 p238-61

Whitfield, J. H. Livy>Tacitus. *In* Classical influences on European culture A.D. 1500-1700 p281-93

About individual works

The annals
Oliver, R. P. Did Tacitus finish the Annales? *In* Illinois classical studies v2 1977 p289-314

Roper, A. Characteristics of Dryden's man p375-99

Codex Laurentianus Mediceus 68, II
Oliver, R. P. The Second Medicean ms. and the text of Tacitus. *In* Illinois classical studies, v 1 1976 p190-225

Germania
Woolf, R. The ideal of men dying with their lord in the Germania and in The Battle of Maldon. *In* Anglo-Saxon England 5 p63-81

Criticism, Textual
Oliver, R. P. The Second Medicean ms. and the text of Tacitus. *In* Illinois classical studies, v 1 1976 p190-225

Manuscripts
Oliver, R. P. The Second Medicean ms. and the text of Tacitus. *In* Illinois classical studies, v 1 1976 p190-225

Translations, English
Roper, A. Characteristics of Dryden's prose. *In* ELH essays for Earl R. Wasserman p375-99

Tackett, Timothy Neil
The citizen priest: politics and ideology among the parish clergy of eighteenth-century Dauphiné. *In* Studies in eighteenth-century culture v7 p307-28

Tadmor, Hayim
Assyria and the West: the ninth century and its aftermath. *In* Unity and diversity p36-48

Taeuber, Alma F. See Taeuber, K. E. jt. auth.

Taeuber, Karl Ernst, and Taeuber, Alma F.
The Black population in the United States. *In* The Black American reference book p159-206

Taft, William Howard, President U.S.

About

Fish, P. G. William Howard Taft and Charles Evans Hughes: conservative politicians as chief judicial reformers. *In* The Supreme Court review, 1975 p123-45

About individual works

Our chief magistrate and his powers
Graff, H. F. Presidents as penmen. *In* From Parnassus p3-15

Tagalog language

Etymology
Wolff, J. U. Malay borrowings in Tagalog. *In* Southeast Asian history and historiography p345-67

Tagore, Sir Rabindranath

About

Ray, G. G. Rabindranath Tagore. *In* Bishop, D. H. ed. Indian thought p337-45

Tai race

Griswold, A. B. and Prasert Na Nagara. On kingship and society at Sukhodaya. *In* Change and persistance in Thai society p29-92

See also Laos (Tai people)

Táin bó Cúailnge

Melia, D. F. Parallel versions of "The boyhood deeds of Cuchulainn." *In* Duggan, J. J. ed. Oral literature p25-40

T'ai p'ing ching

Kaltenmark, M. The ideology of the T'ai-p'ing ching. *In* Welch, H. and Seidel, A. K. eds. Facets of Taoism p19-52

Tait, Katharine

About individual works

My father Bertrand Russell

Mudrick, M. Agèd eagles and dirty old men. *In* Mudrick, M. Books are not life but then what is? p132-42

Taiwan

Economic conditions

Hermalin, A. I. Empirical research in Taiwan on factors underlying differences in fertility. *In* Economic factors in population growth p243-66

Foreign relations—United States

Cline, R. S. The two-China dilemma. *In* Pacific Asia and U.S. policies: a political-economic-strategic assessment p49-57

Clough, R. N. The Taiwan issue in Sino-American relations. *In* China and America p149-95

Social conditions

Hermalin, A. I. Empirical research in Taiwan on factors underlying differences in fertility. *In* Economic factors in population growth p243-66

Social life and customs

Wolf, A. P. Marriage and adoption in northern Taiwan. *In* Social organization and the applications of anthropology p128-60

Taiwanese

Wolf, A. P. Childhood association, sexual attraction and fertility in Taiwan. *In* Zubrow, E. B. W. ed. Demographic anthropology p227-44

Taiwo, Oladele

Culture and the Nigerian novel

Contents

Amos Tutuola
Chinua Achebe
Conclusion
Historical and cultural influences on the Nigerian novelists
Onuora Nzekwu and Elechi Amadi
Social criticism
T. M. Aluko

Taj Mahal

Berryman, J. Thursday out. *In* Berryman, J. The freedom of the poet p335-43

Takagi, Paul. See Krisberg, B. A. jt. auth.

Takayanagi, Shunichi

Christology and postwar theologians in Japan. *In* Postwar trends in Japan p119-67

Takemoto, Tadao

Malraux and Japan: an encounter under a cascade. *In* Courcel, M. H. de, ed. Malraux p120-26

Takeuchi, Kenji. See Varon, B. jt. auth.

Takulli Indians. See Carrier Indians

Tal, Uriel

Young German intellectuals on romanticism and Judaism—spiritual turbulence in the early 19th century. *In* Salo Wittmayer Baron v2 p919-38

Talansi (African tribe)

Religion

Fortes, M. Tallensi prayer. *In* Studies in social anthropology p132-48

Talbot, Charles H.

America and the European drug trade. *In* First images of America p833-44

The elixir of youth. *In* Chaucer and Middle English studies in honour of Rossell Hope Robbins p31-42

Folk medicine and history. *In* American folk medicine p7-10

Medicine. *In* Lindberg, D. C. ed. Science in the Middle Ages p391-428

Talbot, Phillips

The Cyprus seminar. *In* Unofficial diplomats p159-67

The tale of the Heike. See Heike monogatari

Talense. See Talansi (African tribe)

The talents

Coletti, T. Theology and politics in the Towneley Play of the talents. *In* Medievalia et humanistica; new ser. no. 9 p111-26

Tales. See Exempla; Legends; Romances

Tales, American

Dobie, J. F. A preface on authentic liars. *In* Dobie, J. F. Prefaces p23-34

Tales, French

History and criticism

Beyer, J. The morality of the amoral. *In* Cooke, T. D. and Honeycutt, B. L. eds. The humor of the fabliaux p15-42

Cooke, T. D. Pornography, the comic spirit, and the fabliaux. *In* Cooke, T. D. and Honeycutt, B. L. eds. The humor of the fabliaux p137-62

Helsinger, H. Pearls in the swill: comic allegory in the French fabliaux. *In* Cooke, T. D. and Honeycutt, B. L. eds. The humor of the fabliaux p93-105

Honeycutt, B. L. The knight and his world as instruments of humor in the fabliaux. *In* Cooke, T. D. and Honeycutt, B. L. eds. The humor of the fabliaux p75-92

Lacy, N. J. Types of esthetic distance in the fabliaux. *In* Cooke, T. D. and Honeycutt, B. L. eds. The humor of the fabliaux p107-17

Nykrog, P. Courtliness and the townspeople: the fabliaux as a courtly burlesque. *In* Cooke, T. D. and Honeycutt, B. L. eds. The humor of the fabliaux p59-73

Pearcy, R. J. Investigations into the principles of fabliau structure. *In* Ruggiers, P G. ed. Versions of medieval comedy p67-100

Pearcy, R. J. Modes of signification and the humor of obscene diction in the fabliaux. *In* Cooke, T. D. and Honeycutt, B. L. eds. The humor of the fabliaux p163-96

Theiner, P. Fabliau settings. *In* Cooke, T. D. and Honeycutt, B. L. eds. The humor of the fabliaux p119-36

Tales, French—History and criticism—*Cont.*

Togeby, K. The nature of the fabliaux. *In* Cooke, T. D. and Honeycutt, B. L. eds. The humor of the fabliaux p7-13

Wailes, S. L. Vagantes and the fabliaux. *In* Cooke, T. D. and Honeycutt, B. L. eds. The humor of the fabliaux p43-58

Tales, Germanic

History and criticism

Wailes, S. L. Vagantes and the fabliaux. *In* Cooke, T. D. and Honeycutt, B. L. eds. The humor of the fabliaux p43-58

Tales, Indian

History and criticism

Ramsey, J. The Indian literature of Oregon. *In* Bingham, E. R. and Love, G. A. eds. Northwest perspectives p2-19

Tales of Ise. See Ise monogatari

Talghatti, S. R.
The Upaniṣads and Upaniṣadic thought. *In* Bishop, D. H. ed. Indian thought p38-61

Taliaferro, Harden E.

About

Penrod, J. H. Harden Taliaferro, folk humorist of North Carolina. *In* Inge, M. T. ed. The frontier humorists p187-93

Talismans. See Amulets

Talking. See Conversation

Tallensi. See Talansi (African tribe)

Tallmadge, John
John Muir, Emerson, and the book of nature: the explorer as prophet. *In* Kagle, S. E. ed. America: exploration and travel p113-25

Tallmer, Margot
A societal response. *In* Anticipatory grief p19-25

Talmon, Jacob Leib
Mission and testimony: the universal significance of modern anti-Semitism. *In* Sidorsky, D. ed. Essays on human rights p336-59

Talmud

Folk-lore

See Folk-lore—Jews

Talon, Henri Antoine
Dombey and son: a closer look at the text. *In* Dickens Studies Annual v 1 p147-60

Space, time, and memory in Great expectations. *In* Dickens Studies Annual v3 p122-33

Tamale, Ghana

Commerce

Eades, J. S. Kinship and entrepreneurship among Yoruba in northern Ghana. *In* Shack, W. A. and Skinner, E. P. eds. Strangers in African societies p169-82

The taming of the shrew (Motion picture)
Jorgens, J. J. Franco Zeffirelli's Taming of the shrew. *In* Jorgens, J. J. Shakespeare on film p66-78

Taminiaux, Jacques
Heidegger and Husserl's Logical investigations. *In* Radical phenomenology p58-83

Tamke, Susan S.
Human values and aging: the perspective of the Victorian nursery. *In* Spicker, S. F.; Woodward, K. M. and Van Tassel, D. D. eds. Aging and the elderly p63-81

Tanaka, Kakuei

About individual works

Building a new Japan

Sargent, J. Regional development policy in Japan: some aspects of the plan for remodelling the Japanese archipelago. *In* Modern Japan p227-43

Tanakadate, Aikitsu

About

Koizumi, K. The emergence of Japan's first physicists: 1868-1900. *In* Historical studies in the physical sciences v6 p3-108

Tanenbaum, Marc H.
Addendum [to Jews and Judaism in Reverend Moon's Divine principle]. *In* Horowitz, I. L. ed. Science, sin, and scholarship p84-85

Taney, Roger Brooke

About

White, G. E. Roger Taney and the limits of judicial power. *In* White, G. E. The American judicial tradition p64-83

T'ang, Chün-i
Liu Tsung-chou's doctrine of moral mind and practice and his critique of Wang Yangming. *In* The Unfolding of Neo-Confucianism p305-31

Tanganyika. See Tanzania

Tanigawa, Yoshihiko
The Cominform and Southeast Asia. *In* The Origins of the Cold war in Asia p362-77

Tanizaki, Jun'ichirō

About

Ueda, M. Tanizaki Jun'ichirō. *In* Ueda, M. Modern Japanese writers p54-84

Yamanouchi, H. The eternal womanhood: Tanizaki Jun'ichiro and Kawabata Yasunari. *In* Yamanouchi, H. The search for authenticity in modern Japanese literature p107-36

Tanjug. See Telegrafska Agencija Nove Yugoslavije

Tannenbaum, Leslie
Blake and the iconography of Cain. *In* Essick, R. N. and Pearce, D. R. eds. Blake in his time p23-34

Tanner, Tony
'Gnawed bones' and 'artless tales'—eating and narrative in Conrad. *In* Joseph Conrad: a commemoration p17-36

The reign of wonder

Contents

Afterword: Wonder and alienation—the mystic and the moviegoer

Emerson: the unconquered eye and the enchanted circle

Ernest Hemingway's unhurried sensations

Gertrude Stein and the complete actual present

Henry James: The candid outsider

Henry James: The range of wonderment

Henry James: The subjective adventure

Mark Twain

Saints behold: the transcendentalist point of view

Sherwood Anderson's little things

Thoreau and the sauntering eye

Transcendentalism and imagism

Walt Whitman's ecstatic first step

Tanner, Tony—*Continued*
About individual works
City of words: American fiction, 1950-1970
Balakian, N. The multiform American imagination. *In* Balakian, N. Critical encounters p84-87

Tannu-Tuva
History
Rupen, R. A. The absorption of Tuva. *In* Hammond, T. T. ed. The anatomy of Communist taxeovers p145-62

Tanoan Indians. See Tewa Indians

Tanselle, George Thomas
Bowers's collected essays. *In* Review, v 1 1979 p195-204
Descriptive bibliography and library cataloguing. *In* Virginia. University. Bibliographical Society. Studies in bibliography v30 p 1-56
The editing of historical documents. *In* Virginia. University. Bibliographical Society. Studies in bibliography v31 p 1-56
The editorial problem of final authorial intention. *In* Virginia. University. Bibliographical Society. Studies in bibliography v29 p167-211
External fact as an editorial problem. *In* Virginia. University. Bibliographical Society. Studies in bibliography v32 p 1-47
Greg's theory of copy-text and the editing of American literature. *In* Virginia. University. Bibliographical Society. Studies in bibliography v28 p167-229

Tantric Buddhism
Doctrines
Coomaraswamy, A. K. The Tantric doctrine of divine biunity. *In* Coomaraswamy, A. K. Selected papers v2 p231-40

Tantrism, Buddhist. See Tantric Buddhism

Tanzania
Achebe, C. Tanganyika—jottings of a tourist. *In* Achebe, C. Morning yet on creation day p125-35

Description and travel
Connolly, C. Tanzanian sketch-book. *In* Connolly, C. The evening colonnade p73-84

Foreign relations
Johns, D. H. The foreign policy of Tanzania. *In* Aluko, O. ed. The foreign policies of African states p196-219

Politics and government
Saul, J. S. African peasantries and revolutionary change. *In* Forging nations: a comparative view of rural ferment and revolt p86-127

T'ao, Ch'ien
About
Hightower, J. R. Allusion in the poetry of T'ao Ch'ien. *In* Birch, C. ed. Studies in Chinese literary genres p108-32

T'ao, Hsi-shêng
About
Dirlik, A. T'ao Hsi-sheng: the social limits of change. *In* The Limits of change p305-31

T'ao, Hung-ching
About
Strickmann, M. On the alchemy of T'ao Hung-ching. *In* Welch, H. and Seidel, A. K. eds. Facets of Taoism p123-92

Tao-chi
About
Edwards, R. The orthodoxy of the unorthodox. *In* Artists and traditions p185-99

Tao tsang
Ōfuchi, N. The formation of the Taoist Canon. *In* Welch, H. and Seidel, A. K. eds. Facets of Taoism p253-67

Taoism
Ōfuchi, N. The formation of the Taoist Canon. *In* Welch, H. and Seidel, A. K. eds. Facets of Taoism p253-67
Rubin, V. A. Nature against civilization. *In* Rubin, V. A. Individual and state in ancient China p89-114
Sakai, T. and Noguchi, T. Taoist studies in Japan. *In* Welch, H. and Seidel, A. K. eds. Facets of Taoism p269-87

Bibliography
Sakai, T. and Noguchi, T. Taoist studies in Japan. *In* Welch, H. and Seidel, A. K. eds. Facets of Taoism p269-87

China—History
Mather, R. B. K'ou Ch'ien-chih and the Taoist theocracy at the Northern Wei Court, 425-451. *In* Welch, H. and Seidel, A. K. eds. Facets of Taoism p103-22
Miyakawa, H. Local cults around Mount Lu at the time of Sun En's rebellion. *In* Welch, H. and Seidel, A. K. eds. Facets of Taoism p83-101
Stein, R. A. Religious Taoism and popular religion from the second to seventh centuries. *In* Welch, H. and Seidel, A. K. eds. Facets of Taoism p53-81
Strickmann, M. On the alchemy of T'ao Hung-ching. *In* Welch, H. and Seidel, A. K. eds. Facets of Taoism p123-92

Taiwan
Hou, Ching-lang. The Chinese belief in baleful stars. *In* Welch, H. and Seidel, A. K. eds. Facets of Taoism p193-228

Taoist monasticism and religious orders. See Monasticism and religious orders, Taoist

Taoist philosophy. See Philosophy, Taoist

Taouism. See Taoism

Tapestry
Subjects
See Tapestry—Themes, motives

Themes, motives
Levenson, J. Shakespeare's Troilus and Cressida and the monumental tradition in tapestries and literature. *In* Renaissance drama [1976] p43-84

Taplin, Oliver
Aeschylean silences and silences in Aeschylus. *In* Harvard Studies in classical philology v76 p57-97

Taposiris Magna
Antiquities
See Abusir, Egypt—Antiquities

Tapper, Nancy
The women's subsociety among the Shahsevan nomads of Iran. *In* Beck, L. and Keddie, N. R. eds. Women in the Muslim world p374-398

Tarachow, Sidney
St Paul and early Christianity. *In* Wolman, B. B. ed. Psychoanalysis and Catholicism p143-207

Taras, Ray. See Kolankiewicz, G. jt. auth.

Tariff

Cases

Schwartz, W. F. Zenith Radio Corp. v. United States: countervailing duties and the regulation of international trade. *In* The Supreme Court reviews, 1978 p297-312

Law and legislation—Cases

See Tariff—Cases

Mathematical models

Corden, W. M. The costs and consequences of protection: a survey of empirical work. *In* Kenen, P. B. ed. International trade and finance p51-91

United States—Cases

Hellerstein, W. Michelin Tire Corp v. Wages: enhanced state power to tax imports. *In* The Supreme Court review, 1976 p99-133

Tarkington, Booth

About individual works
The gentleman from Indiana

Goist, P. D. The town as ideal community: Booth Tarkington and Zona Gale. *In* Goist, P. D. From Main Street to State Street p13-20

Tarling, Nicholas

Some notes on the historiography of British Borneo. *In* Southeast Asian history and historiography p285-95

Tarling, Roger. See Eatwell, J. jt. auth.

The tarnished angels (Motion picture)

Stern, M. From the folklore of speed to Danse macabre. *In* Peary, G. and Shatzkin, R. eds. The modern American novel and the movies p40-52

Tarr, Rodger LeRoy

The uncancelled leaf of Shepherd's Memoirs of Carlyle. *In* Virginia. University. Bibliographical Society. Studies in bibliography v29 p360-61

Tarragona, Spain (Province)

Church history

McCrank, L. J. The foundation of the confraternity of Tarragona by Archbishop Oleguer Bonestruga, 1126-1129. *In* Viator: medieval and Renaissance studies v9 p157-77

Tarrant, R. J.

The addressee of Virgil's Eighth Eclogue. *In* Harvard Studies in classical philology v82 p197-99

Senecan drama and its antecedents. *In* Harvard Studies in classical philology v82 p214-63

Tarrow, Sidney George

From Cold war to historic compromise: approaches to French and Italian radicalism. *In* Radicalism in the contemporary age v 1 p213-45

Tarrow, Sidney George, and Smith, Victor Lamonte

Crisis recruitment and the political involvement of local elites: some evidence from Italy and France. *In* Eulau, H. and Czudnowski, M. M. eds. Elite recruitment in democratic polities p205-37

Tarski, Alfred

About

Quine, W. V. Truth and disquotation. *In* Quine, W. V. The ways of paradox, and other essays p308-21

Tart, Charles T.

The physical universe, the spiritual universe, and the paranormal. *In* Tart, C. T. ed. Transpersonal psychologies p113-51

Putting the pieces together: a conceptual framework for understanding discrete states of consciousness. *In* Alternate states of consciousness p158-219

Science, states of consciousness, and spiritual experiences: the need for state-specific sciences. *In* Tart, C. T. ed. Transpersonal psychologies p9-58

Some assumptions of orthodox, Western psychology. *In* Tart, C. T. ed. Transpersonal psychologies p59-111

State of consciousness and state-specific sciences. *In* Wheatley, J. M. O. and Edge, H. L. eds. Philosophical dimensions of parapsychology p441-63

Tartars. See Tatars

Tashjian, Dickran Levon

Skyscraper primitives

Contents

Aftermath and conclusion
The art of assemblage
Broom and Secession
Camera Work and the anti-art of photography
E. E. Cummings and dada formalism
Hart Crane and the machine
Marcel Duchamp and Man Ray
Painting the machine
The Soil and Contact
291 and Francis Picabia
William Carlos Williams

Task Force on Death and Dying of the Institute of Society, Ethics, and the Life Sciences

Refinements in criteria for the determination of death: an appraisal. *In* Weir, R. F. ed. Ethical issues in death and dying p90-102

Task Force on Demonstrations, Protests, and Group Violence. See United States. Task Force on Demonstrations, Protests, and Group Violence

Tasmania

Race relations

Jacobs, W. R. The fatal confrontation: early native-white relations on the frontiers of Australia, New Guinea, and America—a comparative study. *In* The American Indian p27-54

Tassel, David D. van. See Van Tassel, David D.

Tassi, Aldo

Communitas and polis. *In* Roth, R. J. ed. Person and community p133-40

Tasso, Torquato

About

Cairns, C. The Catholic conscience. *In* Cairns, C. Italian literature p129-51

About individual works
Aminta

Poggioli, R. Pastoral love. *In* Poggioli, R. The oaten flute p42-63

Jerusalem delivered

Roche, T. P. Tasso's enchanted woods. *In* Miner, E. R. ed. Literary uses of typology p49-78

Taste (Aesthetics) See Aesthetics

Tave, Stuart Malcolm
Jane Austen and one of her contemporaries. *In* Halperin, J. ed. Jane Austen p61-74

Tax, Petrus W.
The Grail kingdom and Parzival's first visit: intrigue, minne, despair. *In* Medieval and Reiaissance studies [1975] p20-36

Taxation
See also subdivision Taxation under specific subjects, e.g. Ocean—Taxation

Brandenburg—History
Braun, R. Taxation, sociopolitical structure, and state-building: Great Britain and Brandenburg-Prussia. *In* Tilly, C. ed. The formation of national states in Western Europe p243-327

Europe—History
Ardant, G. Financial policy and economic infrastructure of modern states and nations. *In* Tilly, C. ed. The formation of national states in Western Europe p164-242

France—Troyes—History
Benton, J. F. The accounts of Cepperello da Prato for the tax on nouveaux acquêts in the bailliage of Troyes. *In* Order and innovation in the Middle Ages p111-35

Great Britain—History
Braun, R. Taxation, sociopolitical structure, and state-building: Great Britain and Brandenburg-Prussia. *In* Tilly, C. ed. The formation of national states in Western Europe p243-327
Elton, G. R. Taxation for war and peace in early-Tudor England. *In* War and economic development p33-48
Miller, E. War, taxation and the English economy in the late thirteenth and early fourteenth centuries. *In* War and economic development p11-31

Netherlands—History
Schama, S. The exigencies of war and the politics of taxation in the Netherlands, 1795-1810. *In* War and economic development p103-37

Normandy—History
Radding, C. M. The administrators of the aids in Normandy, 1360-1380. *In* Order and innovation in the Middle Ages p41-53

Taxonomy (Botany) See Botany—Classification

Tay, Alice Erh-Soon
Law, the citizen and the state. *In* Law and society p 1-17
Marxism, socialism and human rights. *In* Human rights p104-12
See also Kamenka, E. jt. auth.

Tayler, Irene Bowren Smith, and Luria, Gina
Gender and genre: women in British romantic literature. *In* Springer, M. A. ed. What manner of woman p98-123

Taylor, Alan John Percivale

About
Cole, C. R. "Hope without illusion": A. J. P. Taylor's dissent, 1955-1961. *In* The Dissenting tradition p226-61
See also Part 2 under title: Crisis and controversy

Taylor, Alfred Edward

About individual works
Aristotle
Olson, E. The poetic method of Aristotle: its powers and limitations. *In* Olson, E. On value judgments in the arts, and other essays p186-99

Taylor, Anya
Magic and English romanticism
Contents
Coleridge and the magical power of the imagination
Coleridge and the potent voice
An eighteenth-century metaphor
Magical language and poetic analogy
Self-destroying enthrallments: Byron and Keats
Shelley's political enchantments
Wordsworth's arguments against magical words

Taylor, Barry
States of affairs. *In* Evans, G. L. and McDowell, J. H. eds. Truth and meaning p263-84

Taylor, Brian
Church and state in Borneo: the Anglican bishopric. *In* Church, society and politics p357-68

Taylor, Brian Brace
Le Corbusier at Pessac: professional and client responsibilities. *In* Walden, R. ed. The open hand p162-85

Taylor, Brian K.
Culture: whence, whither and why? *In* Alcock, A. E.; Taylor, B. K. and Welton, J. M. eds. The future of cultural minorities p9-29
See also Alcock, A. E. jt. auth.

Taylor, Carol
Anthropologist-in-residence. *In* Eddy, E. M and Partridge, W. L. eds. Applied anthropology in America 229-44

Taylor, Charles
Neutrality in the university. *In* Montefiore, A. ed. Neutrality and impartiality p128-48
Responsibility for self. *In* Rorty, A. O. ed. The identities of persons p281-99
What is human agency? *In* Mischel, T. ed. The self p103-35

About individual works
Hegel
Craft, R. A new interpretation of Hegel? *In* Craft, R. Current convictions p244-55

Taylor, Daniel Malcolm
An empirical account of mind. *In* Royal Institute of Philosophy. Impressions of empiricism p66-78

Taylor, Edward

About
Daly, R. J. Edward Taylor: Christ's creation and the dissatisfactions of metaphor. *In* Daly, R. J. God's altar p162-99
Lewalski, B. K. Edward Taylor: lisps of praise and strategies for self-dispraise. *In* Lewalski, B. K. Protestant poetics and the seventeenth-century religious lyric p388-426
Seelye, J. Return, Alpheus: Taylor, Sewall, Wolcott, and Company: some poetic fabrics from the linsey-woolsey loom. *In* Seelye, J. Prophetic waters p311-39

Taylor, Eleanor Ross

About individual works

Welcome, Eumenides

Rich, A. C. Woman observing, preserving, conspiring, surviving: the poems of Eleanor Ross Taylor. *In* Rich, A. C. On lies, secrets, and silence p85-88

Taylor, Frajam

Puck in the gardens of the sun. *In* Morgan R. G. ed. Kenneth Patchen: a collection of essays p13-16

Taylor, Gordon Rattray

About individual works

The biological time bomb

Koestler, A. The future, if any. *In* Koestler, A. The heel of Achilles p56-61

The doomsday book

Koestler, A. Going down the drain. *In* Koestler, A. The heel of Achilles p62-66

Taylor, Harold

The teacher in the world. *In* Fairfield, R. P. ed. Humanistic frontiers in American education p302-10

Taylor, John Gerald

Scientific thought in fiction and in fact. *In* Nicholls, P. ed. Science fiction at large p57-72

Taylor, John Russell

Directors and directions

Contents

Andy Warhol/Paul Morrissey
Claude Chabrol
Dušan Makavejev
Lindsay Anderson
Miklós Jancsó
Pier Paolo Pasolini
Satyajit Ray
Stanley Kubrick

Taylor, Joshua Charles

The Futurist goal, the Futurist achievement. *In* Kaplan, P. and Manso, S. eds. Major European art movements, 1900-1945 p164-92

Taylor, Kamala (Purnaiya)

About

Singh, R. S. Soulful East and ratiocinative West: Kamala Markandaya. *In* Singh, R. S. Indian novel in English p136-48

Taylor, Maxwell Davenport

National policy too lightly armed. *In* Grand strategy for the 1980s p3-17

The reality of the Soviet threat. *In* Kirk, G. L. and Wessell, N. H. eds. The Soviet threat p168-78

Taylor, Paul A.

The studio audience for television situation comedies. *In* Fischer, H. D. and Melnik, S. R. eds. Entertainment: a cross-cultural examination p22-33

Taylor, Richard, 1919-

De anima; excerpt from "With heart and mind." *In* Donnelly, J. P. ed. Language, metaphysics, and death p131-36

Taylor, Richard, 1946-

Film propaganda

Contents

Alexander Nevsky
Germany: The historical background
Germany: The needs of revolution
Germany: Themes and variations

Kolberg
Mother
October
Propaganda and film
Russia: The historical background
Russia: The needs of revolution
Russia: Themes and variations
Three songs of Lenin
Triumph of the will
Uncle Kruger
The Wandering Jew

Taylor, Robert

John Ford's Boston. *In* Peary, G. and Shatzkin, R. eds. The modern American novel and the movies p215-23

Taylor, Samuel

Artists and philosophes as mirrored by Sèvres and Wedgwood. *In* The Artist and the writer in France p21-39

Taylor, Telford

The concept of justice and the laws of war. *In* Perspectives on justice p3-35

Taylor, Welford Dunaway

Anderson and the problem of belonging. *In* Anderson, D. D. ed. Sherwood Anderson: dimensions of his literary art p61-74

Taylor, Wendell Hertig. See Barzun, J. jt. auth.

Taylor, William E.

Tennessee Williams: the playwright as poet. *In* Tennessee Williams: a tribute p624-30

Taylor, William Robert

Psyching out the city. *In* Uprooted Americans p245-87

Tchaikovsky, Peter Ilyich. See Chaïkovskii, Petr Il'ich

Tchekhoff, Anton Pavlovich. See Chekhov, Anton Pavlovich

Tchernichovski, Saul

About

Alter, R. Defenses of the imagination. *In* Alter, R. Defenses of the imagination p 3-22

Teacher-administrator relationships

O'Dwyer, J. P. Classroom collage: one perspective. *In* Parents, teachers, and children: prospects for choice in American education p37-58

Teacher autonomy. See Teaching, Freedom of

Teacher Corps. See United States. National Teacher Corps

Teacher education. See Teachers, Training of

Teacher morale

O'Dwyer, J. P. Classroom collage: one perspective. *In* Parents, teachers, and children: prospects for choice in American education p37-58

Teacher-pupil relationships. See Teacher-student relationships

Teacher-student relationships

Elkind, D. Observing classroom frames. *In* Elkind, D. The child and society p135-42

Elkind, D. Piaget and Montessori in the classroom. *In* Elkind, D. The child and society p143-55

Elkind, D. Teacher-child contracts. *In* Elkind, D. The child and society p115-28

Strickland, C. G. Students' rights and the teacher's obligations in the classroom. *In* Buxton, T. H. and Prichard, K. W. eds. Excellence in university teaching p80-85

Teacher tenure. See Teachers—Tenure

Teacher training. See Teachers, Training of Teachers

Highet, G. The liberal teacher. *In* The immortal profession p37-56

See also Kindergarten teachers; Teaching

Recruiting—United States

Murphy, T. P. Minority faculty recruitment. *In* Murphy, T. P. ed. Universities in the urban crisis p325-51

Social and economic status

See Teachers' socio-economic status

Tenure—United States

Hughes, G. Tenure and academic freedom. *In* The Concept of academic freedom p170-79

Ritchie, A. Tenure and academic freedom. *In* The Concept of academic freedom p159-69

Rorty, A. O. Some comments on Sartorius's paper on tenure. *In* The Concept of academic freedom p180-83

Sartorius, R. E. Tenure, academic freedom, and the nature of the university. *In* The Concept of academic freedom p184-88

Sartorius, R. E. Tenure and academic freedom. *In* Concept of academic freedom p133-58

Teachers, Professional ethics for

Nisbet, L. The ethics of the art of teaching. *In* Hook, S.; Kurtz, P. and Todorovich, M. eds. The ethics of teaching and scientific research p125-27

Teachers, Rating of

Cornog, W. H. The options market in education. *In* Parents, teachers, and children: prospects for choice in American education p149-64

Teachers, Training of

Greene, M. The matter of mystification: teacher education in unquiet times. *In* Greene, M. Landscapes of learning p53-73

United States

Fairfield, R. P. Teacher education: a new immersion! *In* Fairfield, R. P. ed. Humanistic frontiers in American education p75-83

Headley, N. E. Early Progressive schools —I. *In* Roots of open education in America p131-34

United States—Curricula

Levine, D. U. Urban teaching training. *In* Murphy, T. P. ed. Universities in the urban crisis p259-84

Teachers in literature

Sarotte, G. M. Four archetypes of the homosexual couple: Teacher and pupil. *In* Sarotte, G. M. Like a brother, like a lover p61-69

Teachers' socio-economic status

United States

Wenger, M. G. The case of academia: demythologization in a non-profession. *In* Gerstl, J. E. and Jacobs, G. eds. Professions for the people p95-152

Teachers' tenure. See Teachers—Tenure

Teaching

Adler, M. J. Teaching and learning. *In* From Parnassus p57-65

Allen, D. W. Urban education: hope and prospect. *In* Wagschal, P. H. ed. Learning tomorrows p131-45

Barthes, R. Writers, intellectuals, teachers. *In* Barthes, R. Image, music, text p190-215

Highet, G. Communication. *In* Highet, G. The immortal profession p117-32

Highet, G. The need for renewal. *In* Highet, G. The immortal profession p75-89

Nisbet, L. The ethics of the art of teaching. *In* Hook, S.; Kurtz, P. and Todorovich, M. eds. The ethics of teaching and scientific research p125-27

Norman, R. The neutral teacher? *In* Philosophers discuss education p172-87

Richards, I. A. The ever-new discovery. *In* Richards, I. A. Poetries p242-49

Taylor, H. The teacher in the world. *In* Fairfield, R. P. ed. Humanistic frontiers in American education p302-10

Warnock, M. The neutral teacher? *In* Philosophers discuss education p159-71

Zwicky, F. Essay 11. *In* Fitzgerald, R. ed. What it means to be human p209-20

See also Audio-visual education; Classroom management; College teaching; Education of children; Educational psychology; High school teaching; Montessori method of education; Teacher-student relationships

Aids and devices

See also Moving-pictures in education; Programmed instruction; Telephone in education; Television in education

History

See Education—History

Teaching, Freedom of

Brown, S. C. Academic freedom. *In* Philosophers discuss education p205-20

Griffiths, A. P. Academic freedom: a reply to Dr Brown. *In* Philosophers discuss education p221-42

See also University autonomy

United States

Davis, B. H. Academic freedom, academic neutrality, and the social system. *In* The Concept of academic freedom p27-36

Fisk, M. Academic freedom in class society. *In* The Concept of academic freedom p5-26

Fisk, M. Comments on Hardy Jones and Bertram Davis. *In* The Concept of academic freedom p52-55

Hook, S. Academic freedom and professional responsibilities. *In* Hook, S.; Kurtz, P. and Todorovich, M. eds. The ethics of teaching and scientific research p117-23

Hughes, G. Tenure and academic freedom. *In* The Concept of academic freedom p170-79

Jones, H. E. Academic freedom as a moral right. *In* The Concept of academic freedom p37-51

Ritchie, A. Tenure and academic freedom. *In* The Concept of academic freedom p159-69

Rorty, A. O. Dilemmas of academic and intellectual freedom. *In* The Concept of academic freedom p97-110

Rorty, A. O. Some comments on Sartorius's paper on tenure. *In* The Concept of academic freedom p180-83

Sartorius, R. E. Tenure, academic freedom, and the nature of the university. *In* The Concept of academic freedom p184-88

Sartorius, R. E. Tenure and academic freedom. *In* The Concept of academic freedom p133-58

Technology—*Continued*
Historiography
Slaby, S. M. What should we ask of the history of technology? *In* Bugliarello, G. and Doner, D. B. eds. The history and philosophy of technology p112-27

History
Bugliarello, G. The engineer and the historian. *In* Bugliarello, G. and Doner, D. B. eds. The history and philosophy of technology p50-56

Burstyn, H. L. What can the history of technology contribute to our understanding? *In* Bugliarello, G. and Doner, D. B. eds. The history and philosophy of technology p57-80

Cardwell, D. S. L. Problems of the data base. *In* Bugliarello, G. and Doner, D. B. eds. The history and philosophy of technology p3-18

Clarke, A. C. Technology and the limits of knowledge. *In* The Frontiers of knowledge p117-40

Also in Technology and the frontiers of knowledge p111-34

Hall, M. B. The spirit of innovation in the sixteenth century. *In* The Nature of scientific discovery p309-21

Kranzberg, M Introduction: trends in the history and philosophy of technology. *In* Bugliarello, G. and Doner, D. B. eds. The history and philosophy of technology p xiii-xxxi

Lechtman, H. and Steinberg, A. The history of technology: an anthropological point of view. *In* Bugliarello, G. and Doner, D. B. eds. The history and philosophy of technology p135-60

Mitcham, C. Philosophy and the history of technology. *In* Bugliarello, G. and Doner, D. B. eds. The history and philosophy of technology p163-201

Palanco, R. L. Evolution of building technology. *In* Bugliarello, G. and Doner, D. B. eds. The history and philosophy of technology p344-57

Smith, C. S. Remarks on the discovery of techniques and on sources for the study of their history. *In* Bugliarello, G. and Doner, D. B. eds. The history and philosophy of technology p31-37

White, L. T. Medical astrologers and late medieval technology. *In* Viator: medieval and Renaissance studies v6 p295-308

History—China
Sun, E-tu (Zên) Chinese history of technology: some points for comparison with the West. *In* Bugliarello, G. and Doner, D. B. eds. The history and philosophy of technology p38-49

History—Germany
Koenne, W. On the relationship between philosophy and technology in the German-speaking countries. *In* Bugliarello, G. and Doner, D. B. eds. The history and philosophy of technology p282-93

History—Russia
Joravsky, D. What do we ask of the history of technology? *In* Bugliarello, G. and Doner, D. B. eds. The history and philosophy of technology p128-34

International cooperation
See Technology transfer

Moral and religious aspects
See Technology and ethics

Philosophy
Beaune, J. C. Technology from an encyclopedic point of view. *In* Bugliarello, G. and Doner, D. B. eds. The history and philosophy of technology p202-26

Bell, D. Technology, nature, and society. *In* The Frontiers of knowledge p27-78

Also in Technology and the frontiers of knowledge p23-71

Bunge, M. A. Philosophical inputs and outputs of technology. *In* Bugliarello, G. and Doner, D. B. eds. The history and philosophy of technology p262-81

Caws, P. J. Praxis and techne. *In* Bugliarello, G. and Doner, D. B. eds. The history and philosophy of technology p227-37

Curievici, I. Besieging the fortress. *In* Bugliarello, G. and Doner, D. B. eds. The history and philosophy of technology p339-43

Kranzberg, M. Introduction: trends in the history and philosophy of technology. *In* Bugliarello, G. and Doner, D. B. eds. The history and philosophy of technology pxiii-xxxi

Mitchum, C. Philosophy and the history of technology. *In* Bugliarello, G. and Doner, D. B. eds. The history and philosophy of technology p163-201

Skolimowski, H. Philosophy of technology as a philosophy of man. *In* Bugliarello, G. and Doner, D. B. eds. The history and philosophy of technology p325-36

Svensson, F. The technological challenge to political theory. *In* Bugliarello, G. and Doner, D. B. eds. The history and philosophy of technology p294-308

Von Foerster, H. Where do we go from here? *In* Bugliarello, G. and Doner, D. B. eds. The history and philosophy of technology p358-70

Zandi, I. Is there anyone else? *In* Bugliarello, G. and Doner, D. B. eds. The history and philosophy of technology p371-79

See also Technology and civilization

Political aspects
Peña, F. Multinational enterprises and North-South relations. *In* Erb, G. F. and Kallab, V. eds. Beyond dependency p57-74

Scoville, H. The role of technology in covert intelligence collection. *In* Borosage, R. L. and Marks, J. D. eds. The CIA file p109-22

Social aspects
Benne, K. D. Technology and community: conflicting bases of educational authority. *In* Feinberg, W. and Rosemont, H. eds. Work, technology, and education p142-65

Bettelheim, B. Obsolete youth. *In* Bettelheim, B. Surviving, and other essays p350-69

Boorstin, D. J. Political revolutions and revolutions in science and technology. *In* America's continuing revolution p161-80

Bundy, R. F. Up the downward path: the futures movement and the social imagination. *In* Bundy, R. F. ed. Images of the future: the twenty-first century and beyond p66-77

Burhoe, R. W. A cosmic perspective on man's future. *In* Bundy, R. F. ed. Images of the future: the twenty-first century and beyond p182-92

Technology—Social aspects—*Continued*

Burstyn, H. L. What can the history of technology contribute to our understanding? *In* Bugliarello, G. and Doner, D. B. eds. The history and philosophy of technology p57-80

Christiansen, D. Blind prophets and quick-witted kings. *In* Bundy, R. F. ed. Images of the future: the twenty-first century and beyond p45-53

Dubos, R. J. Crowds and machines. *In* Dubos, R. J. Beast or angel? p103-06

Dubos, R. J. The incarnations of humankind. *In* Dubos, R. J. Beast or angel? p150-60

Edge, D. Technological metaphor and social control. *In* Bugliarello, G. and Doner, D. B. eds. The history and philosophy of technology p309-24

Ellul, J. Search for an image. *In* Bundy, R. F. ed. Images of the future: the twenty-first century and beyond p24-34

Gluckman, M. New dimensions of change, conflict and settlement. *In* United Nations Educational, Scientific and Cultural Organization. Race, science and society p319-40

Graham, L. R. Concerns about science and attempts to regulate inquiry. *In* Holton, G. J. and Morison, R. S. eds. Limits of scientific inquiry p 1-21

Grant, G. P. The university curriculum and the technological threat. *In* Niblett, W. R. ed. The sciences, the humanities and the technological threat p21-35

Hartshorne, C. The environmental results of technology. *In* Philosophy & environmental crisis p69-78

Ihde, D. A phenomenology of man-machine relations. *In* Feinberg, W. and Rosemont, H. eds. Work, technology, and education p186-203

Jungk, R. Toward an experimental society. *In* Bundy, R. F. ed. Images of the future: the twenty-first century and beyond p135-40

Kusch, P. A personal view of science and the future. *In* The Future of science p39-55

Lakoff, S. A. Scientists, technologists and political power. *In* Science, technology and society p355-91

Layton, E. T. Conditions of technological development. *In* Science, technology and society p197-222

Lowi, T. J. The information revolution, politics, and the prospects for an open society. *In* Galnoor, I. ed. Government secrecy in democracies p40-61

Nelkin, D. Technology and public policy. *In* Science, technology and society p393-441

Paschkis, V. Education for our changing technology. *In* Against pollution and hunger p249-55

Pirages, D. C. The unbalanced revolution. *In* Science and society: past, present, and future p231-49

Pool, I. de S. Technology and policy in the information age. *In* Lerner, D. and Nelson, L. M. eds. Communication research—a half-century appraisal p261-79

Rosenberg, N. Technology, economy, and values. *In* Bugliarello, G. and Doner, D. B. eds. The history and philosophy of technology p81-111

Salomon, J. J. Science policy studies and the development of science policy. *In* Science, technology and society p43-70

Sapolsky, H. M. Science, technology and military policy. *In* Science, technology and society p443-71

Schröder, B. Science, technology and foreign policy. *In* Science, technology and society p473-506

Seaborg, G. T. New signposts for science. *In* The Future of science p 1-19

Skolnikoff, E. B. Science, technology and the international system. *In* Science, technology and society p507-33

Spiegel-Rösing, I. S. The study of science, technology and society (SSTS): recent trends and future challenges. *In* Science, technology and society p7-42

Stanley, M. Beyond progress: three post-political futures. *In* Bundy, R. F. Images of the future: the twenty-first century and beyond p115-24

Stivers, R. Social control in the technological society. *In* Davis, F. J. and Stivers, R. eds. The collective definition of deviance p376-91

Weissman, E. Rethinking a framework for settlement planning. *In* Strategies for human settlements: habitat and environment p15-18

Werkmeister, W. H. Reflections on our times. *In* The Abdication of philosophy: philosophy and the public good p243-49

Wojick, D. The structure of technological revolutions. *In* Bugliarello, G. and Doner, D. B. eds. The history and philosophy of technology p238-61

Social aspects—Germany

Koenne, W. On the relationship between philosophy and technology in the German-speaking countries. *In* Bugliarello, G. and Doner, D. B. eds. The history and philosophy of technology p282-93

Social aspects—Southern States

Kranzberg, M. From carpetbag to carpet mill: technology in the New South. *In* Lewis, W. D. and Griessman, B. E. eds. The Southern mystique p33-45

Lewis, W. D. Technology, community, and humanity: the big picture. *In* Lewis, W. D. and Griessman, B. E. eds. The Southern mystique p15-32

Social aspects—Southwest, New

Waters, F. The fifth world—the ninth planet. *In* Voices from the Southwest p55-62

Social aspects—Underdeveloped areas

See Underdeveloped areas—Technology—Social aspects

Social aspects—United States

Nash, R. Machines and Americans. *In* Luedtke, L. S. ed. The study of American culture p99-119

China—Foreign influences

Heymann, H. 'Self-reliance' revisited: China's technology dilemma. *In* China's changing role in the world economy p15-35

United States

Ayres, R. U. Fortress America or a world of hope? Technology. *In* Isolation or interdependence? p149-65

Thomas, D. M. American technocracy and the religious spirit: an unholy alliance? *In* America in theological perspective p189-205

Technology and art. See Art and technology

Technology and civilization

Abbs, P. The mechanical world-picture. *In* Abbs, P. ed. The black rainbow p211-38

Boorstin, D. J. Political revolutions and revolutions in science and technology. *In* America's continuing revolution p161-80

Dubos, R. J. Creative adaptations to the future. *In* Aspects of American liberty p162-73

Dubos, R. J. Technologic utopia. *In* Dubos, R. J. Beast or angel? p144-49

Fuller, R. B. Preparing for a small town world. *In* Strategies for human settlements: habitat and environment p5-14

Henderson, H. The politics of reconceptualization. *In* Wagschal, P. H. ed. Learning tomorrows p119-29

Koyama, K. Barefoot in an ascending elevator: a meditation. *In* On language, culture, and religion: in honor of Eugene A. Nida p213-36

Lewis, W. D. Technology, community, and humanity: the big picture. *In* Lewis, W. D. and Griessman, B. E. eds. The Southern mystique p15-32

Marx, L. Technology and the study of man. *In* Niblett, W. R. ed. The sciences, the humanities and the technological threat p3-20

Mead, M. Individual responsibility within a new technological framework. *In·* The Frontiers of human knowledge p159-62

Medawar, Sir P. B. Technology and evolution. *In* The Frontiers of knowledge p105-15

Also in Technology and the frontiers of knowledge p99-110

O'Gorman, E. History, technology, and the pursuit of happiness. *In* The Frontiers of knowledge p79-103

Also in Technology and the frontiers of knowledge p73-97

Roth, R. J. Person and technology: a Deweyan perspective. *In* Roth, R. J. ed. Person and community p87-102

Schumacher, E. F. Using intermediate technologies. *In* Strategies for human settlements: habitat and environment p121-25

Shimahara, N. K. Cultural evolution: technology as a converging force. *In* Social forces and schooling p15-48

Stanley, M. Dignity versus survival? Reflections on the moral philosophy of social order. *In* Brown, R. H. and Lyman, S. M. eds. Structure, consciousness, and history p197-234

Stonier, T. Economic and technological prerequisites for achieving political and military stability. *In* Arms control and technological innovation p342-57

Svensson, F. The technological challenge to political theory. *In* Bugliarello, G. and Doner, D. B. eds. The history and philosophy of technology p294-308

White, E. B. Coon tree. *In* White, E. B. Essays of E. B. White p34-45

White, L. T. The Crusades and the technological thrust of the West. *In* War, technology and society in the Middle East p97-112

Williams, R. Science, technology, and the future of warfare. *In* Beaumont, R. A. and Edmonds, M. eds. War in the next decade p157-79

See also Machinery in industry; Social problems; Technology—Philosophy

Technology and ethics

Bunge, M. A. Philosophical inputs and outputs of technology. *In* Bugliarello, G. and Doner, D. B. eds. The history and philosophy of technology p262-81

Ellul, J. Technological morality: excerpt from "To will & to do". *In* Davis, F. J. and Stivers, R. eds. The collective definition of deviance p162-76

Hesburgh, T. M. Science and technology in modern perspective. *In* Hesburgh, T. M. The Hesburgh papers p91-99

Svensson, F. The technological challenge to political theory. *In* Bugliarello, G. and Doner, D. B. eds. The history and philosophy of technology p294-308

Zandi, I. Is there anyone else? *In* Bugliarello, G. and Doner, D. B. eds. The history and philosophy of technology p371-79

Technology and literature. See Literature and technology

Technology and religion. See Religion and science

Technology and state

Layton, E. T. Conditions of technological development. *In* Science, technology and society p197-222

Long, T. D. and Wright, C. Science policy institutions in six countries. *In* Science policies of industrial nations p 1-11

Nelkin, D. Technology and public policy. *In* Science, technology and society p393-441

See also Industry and state

France

Gilpin, R. G. Science, technology, and French independence. *In* Science policies of industrial nations p110-32

Great Britain

Vig, N. J. Policies for science and technology in Great Britain: postwar development and reassessment. *In* Science policies of industrial nations p59-109

Japan

Long, T. D. The dynamics of Japanese science policy. *In* Science policies of industrial nations p133-68

Russia

Graham, L. R. The development of science policy in the Soviet Union. *In* Science policies of industrial nations p12-58

Sweden

Dorfer, I. N. H. Science and technology policy in Sweden. *In* Science policies of industrial nations p169-90

United States

Lowi, T. J. The information revolution, politics, and the prospects for an open society. *In* Galnoor, I. ed. Government secrecy in democracies p40-61

Schmandt, J. United States science policy in transition. *In* Science policies of industrial nations p191-212

Technology and the arts. See Computer music

Technology assessment

Wojick, D. The structure of technological revolutions. *In* Bugliarello, G. and Doner, D. B. eds. The history and philosophy of technology p238-61

Technology transfer

Brooks, H. Policies for technology transfer and international investment. *In* The New Atlantic challenge p157-79

Fei, J. C. H. and Ranis, G. Technological transfer, employment and development. *In* Economic development and planning p75-103

Hanson, P. The import of Western technology. *In* Brown, A. H. and Kaser, M. eds. The Soviet Union since the fall of Khrushchev p16-48

Sun, E-tu (Zên). Chinese history of technology: some points for comparison with the West. *In* Bugliarello, G. and Doner, D. B. eds. The history and philosophy of technology p38-49

See also Technological innovations

Tedlock, Barbara

The clown's way. *In* Tedlock, D. E. and Tedlock, B. eds. Teachings from the American earth p105-18

Tedlock, Dennis Ernest

An American Indian view of death. *In* Tedlock, D. E. and Tedlock, B. eds. Teachings from the American earth p248-71

Teen-agers. See Youth

Teeter, Karl V.

Algonquian. *In* Sebeok, T. A. ed. Native languages of the Americas v 1 p505-25

Linguistics and anthropology. *In* Bloomfield, M. W. and Haugen, E. I. eds. Language as a human problem p73-84

Teggart, Frederick John

About

Lyman, S. M. The acceptance, rejection, and reconstruction of histories: on some controversies in the study of social and cultural change. *In* Brown, R. H. and Lyman, S. M. eds. Structure, consciousness, and history p53-105

Teichman, Jenny

Wittgenstein on persons and human beings. *In* Royal Institute of Philosophy. Understanding Wittgenstein p133-48

Teichmann, Howard

About individual works

George S. Kaufman

Sheed, W. The wit of George S. Kaufman and Dorothy Parker. *In* Sheed, W. The good word & other words p159-63

Teilhard de Chardin, Pierre

About individual works

The future of man

Bronowski, J. Where do we go from here? *In* Bronowski, J. A sense of the future p155-62

Teitelbaum, Joel M.

The leer and the loom—social controls on handloom weavers. *In* The Evil eye p63-75

Tejera, Victorino

Dialogue and dialectic. *In* Philosophy and the civilizing arts p49-59

Telecommunication

See also Telephone, Wireless

International cooperation

Riegel, O. W. Satellite communication and national power. *In* Gerbner, G. ed. Mass media policies in changing cultures p63-72

Social aspects

Keller, S. I. The telephone in new (and old) communities. *In* The Social impact of the telephone p281-99

Thorngren, B. Silent actors: communication networks for development. *In* The Social impact of the telephone p374-85

Telecommunication systems. See Telephone systems

Telegony

Burkhardt, R. W. Closing the door on Lord Morton's mare: the rise and fall of telegony. *In* Studies in history of biology v3 p 1-21

Telegrafska Agencija Nove Yugoslavije

Ivacic, P. Toward a freer and multidimensional flow of information. *In* Horton, P. C. ed. The Third World and press freedom p135-50

Telegraph

History

Hershbell, J. P. The ancient telegraph: war and literacy. *In* Havelock, E. A. and Hershbell, J. P. eds. Communication arts in the ancient world p81-92

Teleology

Birch, L. C. Chance, necessity and purpose. *In* Ayala, F. J. and Dobzhansky, T. G. eds. Studies in the philosophy of biology p225-39

Harris, E. E. Science, metaphysics, and teleology. *In* The Personal universe p24-39

See also Causation; Necessity (Philosophy)

History

Ospovat, D. Perfect adaptation and teleological explanation: approaches to the problem of the history of life in the mid-nineteenth century. *In* Studies in history of biology, v2 p33-56

Telepathy. See Thought-transference

Telephone

Employees

See Telephone operators

History

Aronson, S. H. Bell's electrical toy: what's the use? The sociology of early telephone usage. *In* The Social impact of the telephone p15-39

Moyer, J. A. Urban growth and the development of the telephone: some relationships at the turn of the century. *In* The Social impact of the telephone p342-69

Perry, C. R. The British experience, 1876-1912: the impact of the telephone during the years of delay. *In* The Social impact of the telephone p69-96

Pierce, J. R. The telephone and society in the past 100 years. *In* The Social impact of the telephone p159-95

Pool, I. D. and others. Foresight and hindsight: the case of the telephone. *In* The Social impact of the telephone p127-57

Rates

Mayer, M. The telephone and the uses of time. *In* The Social impact of the telephone p225-45

Social aspects

Boettinger, H. M. Our sixth-and-a-half sense. *In* The Social impact of the telephone p200-07

Telephone—Social aspects—*Continued*

Cherry, C. The telephone system: creator of mobility and social change. *In* The Social impact of the telephone p112-26

Gottmann, J. Megalopolis and antipolis: the telephone and the structure of the city. *In* The Social impact of the telephone p303-17

Social aspects—Great Britain

Perry, C. R. The British experience, 1876-1912: the impact of the telephone during the years of delay. *In* The Social impact of the telephone p69-96

Social aspects—New York (City)

Wurtzel, A. H. and Turner, C. Latent functions of the telephone: what missing the extension means. *In* The Social impact of the telephone p246-61

Social aspects—United States

Abler, R. The telephone and the evolution of the American metropolitan system. *In* The Social impact of the telephone p318-41

Aronson, A. H. Bell's electrical toy: what's the use? The sociology of early telephone usage. *In* The Social impact of the telephone p15-39

Pool, I. D. and others. Foresight and hindsight: the case of the telephone. *In* The Social impact of the telephone p127-57

France

Attali, J. and Stourdze, Y. The birth of the telephone and economic crisis: the slow death of monologue in French society. *In* The Social impact of the telephone p97-111

Telephone, Wireless

History

Briggs, A. The pleasure telephone: a chapter in the prehistory of the media. *In* The Social impact of the telephone p40-65

Telephone in counseling. See Hotlines (Counseling)

Telephone in education

Rao, P. V. Telephone and instructional communications. *In* The Social impact of the telephone p473-86

Telephone in literature

Brooks, J. N. The first and only century of telephone literature. *In* The Social impact of the telephone p208-24

Telephone operators

Maddox, B. Women and the switchboard. *In* The Social impact of the telephone p262-80

Telephone systems

Pierce, J. R. The telephone and society in the past 100 years. *In* The Social impact of the telephone p159-95

Telephone teaching. See Telephone in education

Television

Broadcasting

See Television broadcasting

Law and legislation—United States

Polsby, D. D. F.C.C. v. National Citizens Committee for Broadcasting and the judicious uses of administrative discretion. *In* The Supreme Court review, 1978 p 1-38

Smith, A. "Just a pleasant way to spend an evening"—the softening embrace of American television. *In* A New America p195-212

Production and direction

Murdock, G. and Halloran, J. D. Contexts of creativity in television drama: an exploratory study in Britain. *In* Fischer, H. D. and Melnik, S. R. eds. Entertainment: a cross-cultural examination p273-85

Psychological aspects

See Television and children

Serials

See Television serials

Latin America—Social aspects

Beltrán, S. L. R. TV etchings in the minds of Latin Americans: conservatism, materialism and conformism. *In* Fischer, H. D. and Melnik, S. R. eds. Entertainment: a cross-cultural examination p190-95

Television and children

Himmelweit, H. T. Yesterday's and tomorrow's television research on children. *In* Lerner, D. and Nelson, L. M. eds. Communication research—a half-century appraisal p 9-36

Television and sports. See Television broadcasting of sports

Television and youth. See Television and children

Television broadcasting

Dizard, W. P. Television's global networks. *In* Fischer, H. D. and Merrill, J. C. eds. International and intercultural communication p83-89

Fischer, H. D. The contribution of Eurovision and Intervision to global television. *In* Fischer, H. D. and Merrill, J. C. eds. International and intercultural communication p350-71

Follath, E. An international comparison of broadcasting systems. *In* Fischer, H. D. and Merrill, J. C. eds. International and intercultural communication p71-82

See also Television in education; Television in politics; Television industry; Television programs

Law and legislation

See Television—Law and legislation

Moral and religious aspects

Alley, R. S. Media medicine and morality. *In* Television as a cultural force p95-110

Ryan, K. Television as a moral educator. *In* Television as a cultural force p111-27

News

See Television broadcasting of news

Social aspects

Eigner, E. M. British television drama and society in the 1970s. *In* Drama and society p209-25

Goodlad, S. On the social significance of television comedy. *In* Bigsby, C. W. E. ed. Approaches to popular culture p213-25

Social aspects—Germany, West

Hüther, J. Comments on the functional change of television viewing as a leisure pursuit. *In* Fischer, H. D. and Melnik, S. R. eds. Entertainment: a cross-cultural examination p83-91

Social aspects—United States

Adler, R. Understanding television: an overview of the literature of the medium as a social and cultural force. *In* Television as a social force: new approaches to TV criticism p23-47

Television plays

France

Savoie, N. R. Molière and French television. *In* Johnson, R. B.; Neumann, E. S. and Trail, G. T. eds. Molière and the commonwealth of letters: patrimony and posterity p645-62

Great Britain

Eigner, E. M. British television drama and society in the 1970s. *In* Drama and society p209-25

Japan

Makita, T. Television drama and Japanese culture with special emphasis on historical drama. *In* Fischer, H. D. and Melnik, S. R. eds. Entertainment: a cross-cultural examination p63-73

United States

Thorburn, D. Television melodrama. *In* Television as a cultural force p77-94

Television programs

Goodlad, S. On the social significance of television comedy. *In* Bigsby, C. W. E. ed. Approaches to popular culture p213-25

See also Comedy programs; Television serials

Social aspects

Rohrbach, G. Why television entertainment, for whom and how? *In* Fischer, H. D. and Melnik, S. R. eds. Entertainment: a cross-cultural examination p299-305

Great Britain

Wheldon, H. P. Creativity and collaboration in television programs. *In* The Frontiers of knowledge p177-99

United States

Esslin, M. The television series as folk epic. *In* Superculture p190-98

Fass, P. S. Television as cultural document: promises and problems. *In* Television as a cultural force p37-57

Wood, P. H. Television as dream. *In* Television as a cultural force p17-35

United States—Bibliography

Sterling, C. H. Television as a cultural force: a selected reading list. *In* Television as a cultural force p175-84

Television programs, Public service

Lyle, J. Public television: too much ambition and overcommitment. *In* Lerner, D. and Nelson, L. M. eds. Communication research—a half-century appraisal p193-209

Television relay systems. See Community antenna television

Television scripts. See Television programs

Television serials

Esslin, M. The television series as folk epic. *In* Bigsby, C. W. E. Superculture p190-98

Television stations. See Educational television stations

Telfer, Elizabeth

Autonomy as an educational ideal II. *In* Philosophers discuss education p19-35

Tell-el-Amarna tablets

Moran, W. L. The Syrian scribe of the Jerusalem Amarna letters. *In* Unity and diversity p146-66

Telle, Emile Villemeur

Erasmus's Ciceronianus: a comical colloquy. *In* Essays on the works of Erasmus p211-20

Temiar. See Sakai

Temkin, Owsei

The double face of Janus

Contents

Basic science, medicine, and the romantic era

Byzantine medicine: tradition and empiricism

The Byzantine origin of the names for the basilic and cephalic veins

The classical roots of Glisson's doctrine of irritation

Comparative study in the history of medicine

The double face of Janus

The elusiveness of Paracelsus

The era of Paul Ehrlich

An essay on the usefulness of medical history for medicine

The European background of the young Dr Welch

A Galenic model for quantitative physiological reasoning?

On Galen's pneumatology

German concepts of ontogeny and history around 1800

Greek medicine as science and craft

Health and disease

An historical analysis of the concept of infection

The historiography of ideas in medicine

History of Hippocratism in late antiquity: the third century and the Latin West

The idea of descent in post-romantic German biology: 1848-1858

Materialism in French and German physiology of the early nineteenth century

The meaning of medicine in historical perspective

Medicine and the problem of moral responsibility

Merrem's youthful dream: the early history of experimental pylorectomy

Metaphors of human biology

On the history of "morality and syphilis"

On the interrelationship of the history and the philosophy of medicine

The philosophical background of Magendie's physiology

A postscript to "Merrem's youthful dream"

The role of surgery in the rise of modern medical thought

The scientific approach to disease: specific entity and individual sickness

Studies on late Alexandrian medicine

Therapeutic trends and the treatment of syphilis before 1900

Vesalius on an immanent biological motor force

Was Servetus influenced by Ibn an-Nafîs?

Wunderlich, Schelling and the history of medicine

Zimmermann's philosophy of the physician

Science and society in the age of Copernicus. *In* The Nature of scientific discovery p106-33

About

Temkin, O. The double face of Janus. *In* Temkin, O. The double face of Janus p3-37

Temperament

Oakeshott, M. J. On being conservative. *In* Oakeshott, M. J. Rationalism in politics p168-96

Temperament, Musical. See Musical temperament

Temperance

Gusfield, J. R. Status conflicts and the changing ideologies of the American temperance movement. *In* Davis, F. J. and Stivers, R. eds. The collective definition of deviance p222-40

Temperance societies

United States

Gusfield, J. R. Status conflicts and the changing ideologies of the American temperance movement. *In* Davis, F. J. and Stivers, R. eds. The collective definition of deviance p222-40

Temperature. See Heat

Temperley, Howard

Anglo-American images. *In* Allen, H. C. and Thompson, R. eds. Contrast and connection p321-47

Anti-slavery. *In* Hollis, P. ed. Pressure from without p27-51

Temperley, Nicholas

Middleburg Psalms. *In* Virginia. University. Bibliographical Society. Studies in bibliography v30 p162-70

Templars in Spain

Bisson, T. N. Credit, prices and agrarian production in Catalonia: a Templar account (1180-1188) *In* Order and innovation in the Middle Ages p87-102

Temple, Shirley. See Black, Shirley (Temple)

Temple, Sir William, bart.

About individual works

Upon ancient and modern learning

Hinnant, C. H. Sir William Temple's views on science, poetry, and the imagination. *In* Studies in eighteenth-century culture v8 p187-203

Upon poetry

Hinnant, C. H. Sir William Temple's views on science, poetry, and the imagination. *In* Studies in eighteenth-century culture v8 p187-203

Temples, Greek

Holloway, R. R. Architect and engineer in archaic Greece. *In* Harvard Studies in classical philology v73 p281-90

Italy—Sybaris

Stoop, M. W. Conjectures on the end of a sanctuary. *In* Studies in classical art and archaeology p179-83

Temples, Hindu

India

Coomaraswamy, A. K. An Indian temple: the Kandarya Mahadeo. *In* Coomaraswamy, A. K. Selected papers v 1 p3-10

Ten, Chin Liew

Politics in the academe. *In* Montefiore, A. ed. Neutrality and impartiality p149-64

Ten from Your show of shows (Motion picture)

Sarris, A. Your show of shows revisited. *In* Sarris, A. Politics and cinema p172-80

Tenants. See Landlord and tenant

The tender trap (Motion picture)

French, B. Thé eleven-year itch. *In* French, B. On the verge of revolt p73-83

Tener, Robert H.

Walter Bagehot: some attributions. *In* Virginia. University. Bibliographical Society. Studies in bibliography v29 p346-59

Tennessee

History—1865-1950

Grantham, D. W. Black Patch War: the Kentucky and Tennessee night riders, 1905-1909. *In* Grantham, D. W. The regional imagination p65-75

Tenney, Merrill Chapin. See Part 2 under title: Current issues in Biblical and patristic interpretation

Tennyson, Alfred Tennyson, Baron

About

Bloom, H. Tennyson: in the shadow of Keats. *In* Bloom, H. Poetry and repression p143-74

Brashear, W. R. The boundless deep: Tennyson. *In* Brashear, W. R. The gorgon's head p27-48

Christ, C. Victorian masculinity and The angel in the house. *In* Vicinus, M. ed. A widening sphere p146-62

Johnson, W. S. Marriage and divorce in Tennyson. *In* Johnson, W. S. Sex and marriage in Victorian poetry p110-84

Mill, J. S. Tennyson's poems. *In* Mill, J. S. Essays on poetry p44-74

Preyer, R. O. The burden of culture and the dialectic of literature. *In* Evolution of consciousness p98-105

Sanders, C. R. Tennyson and the human hand. *In* Sanders, C. R. Carlyle's friendships, and other studies p287-304

Tillotson, G. Tennyson. *In* Tillotson, G. A view of Victorian literature p286-327

About individual works

In memoriam

Ball, P. M. 'Till all my widowed race be run.' *In* Ball, P. M. The heart's events p58-104

Dawson, C. In memoriam: the uses of Dante and Wordsworth. *In* Dawson, C. Victorian noon p36-51

Eliot, T. S. In memoriam. *In* Eliot, T. S. Selected prose of T. S. Eliot p239-47

Hough, G. G. The natural theology of In memoriam. *In* Hough, G. G. Selected essays p110-25

Maud

Ball, P. M. 'If I be dear to someone else.' *In* Ball, P. M. The heart's events p105-66

Morte D'Arthur

Mason, H. A. The first setting of Tennyson's 'Morte D'Arthur'. *In* English Association. Essays and studies, 1978 p98-110

Ode on the death of the Duke of Wellington

Shannon, E. F. and Ricks, C. B. A further history of Tennyson's Ode on the death of the Duke of Wellington: the manuscript at Trinity College and the galley proof at Lincoln. *In* Virginia. University. Bibliographical Society. Studies in bibliography v32 p125-57

The Princess

Lerner, L. An essay on The Princess. *In* Lerner, L. ed. The Victorians p209-22

Story, K. E. Theme and image in the Princess. *In* Tennessee Studies in literature v20 p50-59

Criticism and interpretation

Sanders, C. R. Carlyle and Tennyson. *In* Sanders, C. R. Carlyle's friendships, and other studies p192-225

Terminal care—*Continued*

Ramsey, P. On (only) caring for the dying. *In* Weir, R. F. ed. Ethical issues in death and dying p189-225

Saunders, C. Dying they live: St. Christopher's Hospice. *In* Feifel, H. [ed.] New meanings of death p153-79

White, L. P. Death and the physician: mortuis vivos docent. *In* Feifel, H. [ed.] New meanings of death p91-106

See also Terminal care facilities; Terminally ill children

United States

Benoliel, J. Q. Dying is a family affair. *In* Home care p17-34

Bluestone, N. "He's a sick man—he belongs in the hospital." *In* Home care p90-97

Budner, S. Shall we look before we leap? *In* Home care p232-36

Clifford, I. M. Comprehensive planning for care and the home health agency. *In* Home care p223-31

Craytor, J. K. Working with dying patients and their families. *In* Home care p37-48

Cyrus, E. A historical perspective on home health care. *In* Home care p12-16

Kaylor, C. Evaluation of home care for the terminal cancer patient: a proposed model. *In* Home care p247-59

Lockwood, J. A. From life to death. *In* Home care p263-67

Mellette, S. J. Connotations of hospitalization. *In* Home care p268-72

Moore, F. M. Homemaker-home health aides—essential thanatologists. *In* Home care p208-14

Wessels, V. G. The nurse and home care of the terminally ill. *In* Home care p49-59

Terminal care facilities

Dunn, M. K. Hospice-based home care services. *In* Home care p153-58

Woodring, S. Hospice pilot project in an acute-care general hospital, 1975-1976. *In* Home care p159-64

Terminally ill children

Bluebond-Langner, M. H. Meanings of death to children. *In* Feifel, H. [ed.] New meanings of death p47-66

Terminology. See Names

Terms and phrases

Screech, M. A. Commonplaces of law, proverbial wisdom and philosophy: their importance in Renaissance scholarship (Rabelais, Joachim du Bellay, Montaigne). *In* Classical influences on European culture A.D. 1500-1700 p127-34

Terra-cotta sculpture

Mexico

Williams, G. External influences and the upper RioVerde drainage basin at Los Altos, West Mexico. *In* Mesoamerican archaeology p21-50

Terra cotta sculpture, Etruscan

Oleson, J. An Etruscan satyr mask in the Fogg Art Museum. *In* Harvard Studies in classical philology v76 p259-69

Terra-cotta sculpture, Gallo-roman

Asia Minor

Goldstein, S. M. A terracotta lamp in the McDaniel collection. *In* Harvard Studies in classical philology v73 p291-303

Terra-cotta sculpture, Roman

Higgins, R. A. Terracottas. *In* Strong, D. E. and Brown, D. eds. Roman crafts p105-09

Terra-sigillata (Pottery) See Pottery, Roman

Terreni, Guido. See Guido Terreni, Bp.

Territorial waters

Borgese, E. M. A constitution for the oceans. *In* Borgese, E. M. and Krieger, D. eds. The tides of change p340-52

Galindo Pohl, R. Pacem in Maribus in the Caribbean. *In* Borgese, E. M. and Krieger, D. eds. The tides of change p264-77

Pardo, A. New institutions for ocean space. *In* Borgese, E. M. and Krieger, D. eds. The tides of change p324-27

See also Continental shelf; Fishery law and legislation

Territory, National. See Boundaries; Geopolitics; Territorial waters

Terror, Reign of. See France—History—Revolution, 1789-1799

Terrorism

Bassiouni, M. C. Methodological options for international legal control of terrorism. *In* International terrorism and political crimes p485-92

Bouthoul, G. Definitions of terrorism. *In* International terrorism and world security p50-59

DeSchutter, B. Problems of jurisdiction in the international control and repression of terrorism. *In* International terrorism and political crimes p377-90

Dinstein, Y. Terrorism and war of liberation: an Israeli perspective of the Arab-Israeli conflict. *In* International terrorism and political crimes p155-72

Epstein, W. Nuclear terrorism and nuclear war. *In* Griffiths, F. and Polanyi, J. C. eds. The dangers of nuclear war p109-24

Finger, S. M. International terrorism and the United Nations. *In* International terrorism p323-48

Hoffacker, L. The U.S. Government response to terrorism: a global approach. *In* International terrorism and political crimes p537-45

Jenkins, B. M. International terrorism: a new mode of conflict. *In* International terrorism and world security p13-49

Kittrie, N. N. Reconciling the irreconcilable: the quest for international agreement over political crime and terrorism. *In* The Year book of world affairs, 1978 p208-36

Lahey, K. A. and Sang, L. M. Control of terrorism through a broader interpretation of Article 3 of the four Geneva Conventions of 1949. *In* International terrorism and political crimes p191-200

Letman, S. T. Some sociological aspects of terror-violence in a colonial setting. *In* International terrorism and political crimes p33-42

Mallison, W. T. and Mallison, S. V. The concept of public purpose terror in international law: doctrines and sanctions to reduce the destruction of human and material values. *In* International terrorism and political crimes p67-85

Murphy, J. F. United Nations proposals on the control and repression of terrorism. *In* International terrorism and political crimes p493-506

Terrorism—*Continued*

Palmer, B. Codification of terrorism as an international crime. *In* International terrorism and political crimes p507-18

Parry, A. Five minutes to midnight. *In* Parry, A. Terrorism: from Robespierre to Arafat p545-62

Parry, A. Genghis Khan with the telephone. *In* Parry, A. Terrorism: from Robespierre to Arafat p509-15

Parry, A. The new international. *In* Parry, A. Terrorism: from Robespierre to Arafat p537-44

Parry, A. The new Robin Hoods, the media, and the police. *In* Parry, A. Terrorism: from Robespierre to Arafat p516-24

Parry, A. Right-wing terror. *In* Parry, A. Terrorism: from Robespierre to Arafat p488-506

Parry, A. Terror: an overall view. *In* Parry, A. Terrorism: from Robespierre to Arafat p12-20

Parry, A. Terror as aberration. *In* Parry, A. Terrorism: from Robespierre to Arafat p21-35

Parry, A. Terrorists then and now. *In* Parry, A. Terrorism: from Robespierre to Arafat p525-36

Rosen, S. J. and Frank, R. Measures against international terrorism. *In* International terrorism and world security p60-68

Salomone, F. Terrorism and the mass media. *In* International terrorism and political crimes p43-46

Smith, W. H. International terrorism: a political analysis. *In* The Year book of world affairs, 1977 p138-57

Strickler, N. Anti-history and terrorism: a philosophical dimension. *In* International terrorism and political crimes p47-50

Toman, J. Terrorism and the regulation of armed conflicts. *In* International terrorism and political crimes p133-54

United Nations. Secretariat. The origins and fundamental causes of international terrorism. *In* International terrorism and political crimes p5-10

Vogler, T. Perspectives on extradition and terrorism. *In* International terrorism and political crimes p391-97

Zlataric, B. History of international terrorism and its legal control. *In* International terrorism and political crimes p474-84

Chronology

Jenkins, B. M. International terrorism: a new mode of conflict. *In* International terrorism and world security p13-49

Law and legislation

Green, L. C. Terrorism—the Canadian perspective. *In* International terrorism p3-29

Sliwowski, G. Legal aspects of terrorism. *In* International terrorism and world security p69-77

Africa

Parry, A. Fire in the African bush. *In* Parry, A. Terrorism: from Robespierre to Arafat p469-87

Argentine Republic

Parry, A. The morbid tango. *In* Parry, A. Terrorism: from Robespierre to Arafat p261-73

Asia

Parry, A. Vietnam and other jungles, other pyres. *In* Parry, A. Terrorism: from Robespierre to Arafat p417-32

Canada

Green, L. C. Terrorism—the Canadian perspective. *In* International terrorism p 3-29

Parry, A. Canada's white niggers. *In* Parry, A. Terrorism: from Robespierre to Arafat p365-75

Europe, Western

Parry, A. New Europe's old hatreds. *In* Parry, A. Terrorism: from Robespierre to Arafat p395-416

Great Britain—History

Hachey, T. E. Political terrorism: the British experience. *In* International terrorism p90-114

India—History

Qureshi, S. Political violence in the South Asian subcontinent. *In* International terrorism p151-93

Israel

Weisband, E. and Roguly, D. Palestinian terrorism: violence, verbal strategy, and legitimacy. *In* International terrorism p258-319

Japan

Parry, A. Red samurai and Turkey's nihilists. *In* Parry, A. Terrorism: from Robespierre to Arafat p433-48

Latin America

Butler, R. E. Terrorism in Latin America. *In* International terrorism p46-61

Parry, A. Siempre la violencia! *In* Parry, A. Terrorism: from Robespierre to Arafat p286-300

Near East

Freedman, R. O. Soviet policy toward international terrorism. *In* International terrorism p115-47

Heradstveit, D. The role of international terrorism in the Middle East conflict and its implication for conflict resolution. *In* International terrorism and world security p93-103

Weisband, E. and Roguly, D. Palestinian terrorism: violence, verbal strategy, and legitimacy. *In* International terrorism p258-319

Northern Ireland

Bell, J. B. Strategy, tactics, and terror: an Irish perspective. *In* International terrorism p65-89

Parry, A. Crimson in the Irish Green and Orange. *In* Parry, A. Terrorism: from Robespierre to Arafat p376-94

Palestine—History

Alexander, Y. From terrorism to war: the anatomy of the birth of Israel. *In* International terrorism p211-57

South Africa

Efrat, E. S. Terrorism in South Africa. *In* International terrorism p194-208

South Asia—History

Qureshi, S. Political violence in the South Asian subcontinent. *In* International terrorism p151-93

Turkey

Parry, A. Red samurai and Turkey's nihilists. *In* Parry, A. Terrorism: from Robespierre to Arafat p433-48

Terrorism—*Continued*

United States

Johnpoll, B. K. Perspectives on political terrorism in the United States. *In* International terrorism p30-45

Uruguay

Parry, A. Heirs to Tupac-Amaru. *In* Parry, A. Terrorism: from Robespierre to Arafat p274-85

Terry, Janice J.
The consequences of economic abstention: the Aswan Dam. *In* Higham, R. D. ed. Intervention or abstention: the dilemma of American foreign policy p129-43

Tertz, Abram, pseud. See Siniâvskiĭ, Andreĭ Donat'evich

Terza, Dante Della. See Della Terza, Dante

Tesauro, Emmanuele, conte

About individual works
Il cannocchiale Aristotelico
Gilman, E. B. Tesauro on visual and verbal wit. *In* Gilman, E. B. The curious perspective p67-87

Tessler, Mark A.
Women's emancipation in Tunisia. *In* Beck, L. and Keddie, N. R. eds. Women in the Muslim world p141-58

Testament of Orpheus (Motion picture)
Truffaut, F. Jean Cocteau: Le testament d'Orphée. *In* Truffaut, F. The films in my life p204-08

Testing laboratories. See Physical laboratories

Tests, Mental. See Mental tests

Tests and measurements in education. See Educational tests and measurements

Tetel, Marcel
Renaissance aborted and renascences: Scève's Délie. *In* Medieval and Renaissance studies 1976 p100-18

Teternikov, Fedor Kuz'mich

About individual works
The little demon
Kostka, E. K. A literary quandary: Fyodor Sologub and Heinrich Mann. *In* Kostka, E. K. Glimpses of Germanic-Slavic relations from Pushkin to Heinrich Mann p21-37

Friends and associates
Rabinowitz, S. J. Bely and Sologub: toward the history of a friendship. *In* Janecek, G. ed. Andrey Bely p156-68

Relations with contemporaries
See Teternikov, Fedor Kuz'mich—Friends and associates

Teters, Barbara
Matsuoka Yōsuke: the diplomacy of bluff and gesture. *In* Burns, R. D. and Bennett, E. M. eds. Diplomats in crisis p275-96

Tetzeli von Rosador, Kurt. See Rosador, Kurt Tetzeli von

Teunissen, John James. See Hinz, E. J. jt. auth.

Teutonic race
Meinhard, H. H. The patrilineal principle in early Teutonic kinship. *In* Studies in social anthropology p 1-29

Tewa Indians

Medicine
Ford, R. I. Communication networks and information hierarchies in native American folk medicine: Tewa Pueblos, New Mexico. *In* American folk medicine p143-57

Religion and mythology
Ortiz, A. The Tewa world view. *In* Tedlock, D. E. and Tedlock, B. eds. Teachings from the American earth p179-89

Texas

Population
Tjarks, A. V. de. Comparative demographic analysis of Texas, 1777-1793. *In* Weber, D. J. ed. New Spain's far northern frontier p135-69

Race relations
Evans, J. L. Ethnic tensions in the Lower Rio Grande Valley to 1860. *In* Yoder, D. ed. American folklife p239-55

Social conditions
Tjarks, A. V. de. Comparative demographic analysis of Texas, 1777-1793. *In* Weber, D. J. ed. New Spain's far northern frontier p135-69

Statistics, Vital
Tjarks, A. V. de. Comparative demographic analysis of Texas, 1777-1793. *In* Weber, D. J. ed. New Spain's far northern frontier p135-69

Text-books

Manuscripts
Lutz, C. E. A medieval textbook. *In* Lutz, C. E. Essays on manuscripts and rare books p41-45

Great Britain—History
Heninger, S. K. Oronce Finé and English textbooks for the mathematical sciences. *In* Studies in the continental background of Renaissance English literature: essays presented to John L. Lievsay p170-85

United States
Whitten, P. The changing world of college textbook publishing. *In* Altbach, P. G. and McVey, S. eds. Perspectives on publishing p247-58

Textile fabrics

Rome
Wild, J. P. Textiles. *In* Strong, D. E. and Brown, D. eds. Roman crafts p167-77

Textile industry
Sutton, A. Equality and discrimination in international economic law (VI): trends in the regulation of international trade in textiles. *In* The Year book of world affairs, 1977 p190-216

Textiles. See Textile fabrics

Textor, Ravisius. See Tixier, Jean, Seigneur de Ravisy

Textual criticism. See Criticism, Textual

Textual transmission. See Transmission of texts

Thacher, James

About individual works
American medical biography
Bell, W. J. Lives in medicine: the biographical dictionaries of Thacher, Williams, and Gross. *In* Bell, W. J. The colonial physician & other essays p149-68

Thackeray, William Makepeace
About

Auchincloss, L. Thackeray's "struggling genius." *In* Auchincloss, L. Life, law and letters p167-75

Borowitz, A. Why Thackeray went to see a man hanged. *In* Borowitz, A. Innocence and arsenic p33-52

Cockshut, A. O. J. The realists: Thackeray. *In* Cockshut, A. O. J. Man and woman: a study of love and the novel, 1740-1940 p73-86

McMaster, J. Thackeray's things: time's local habitation. *In* Levine, R. A. The Victorian experience: the novelists p49-86

Rogers, W. Thackeray's self-consciousness. *In* The Worlds of Victorian fiction p149-63

Skilton, D. Victorian views of the individual: the Brontës, Thackeray, Trollope and George Eliot. *In* Skilton, D. The English novel p136-62

Tillotson, G. Thackeray. *In* Tillotson, G. A view of Victorian literature p152-86

About individual works
Henry Esmond

Hardy, B. N. Memory and memories. *In* Hardy, B. N. Tellers and listeners p56-101

Sanders, A. Clio's heroes and Thackeray's heroes: Henry Esmond and The Virginians. *In* Sanders, A. The Victorian historical novel, 1840-1880 p97-119

Scarry, E. Henry Esmond: the rookery at Castlewood. *In* Literary monographs v7 p 1-43

Sutherland, J. A. 'Henry Esmond': the shaping power of contract. *In* Sutherland, J. A. Victorian novelists and publishers p101-16

Vanity fair

Alter, R. The self-conscious novel in eclipse. *In* Alter, R. Partial magic p84-137

Martin, B. K. Vanity fair: narrative ambivalence and comic form. *In* Tennessee Studies in literature v20 p37-49

Williamson, J. W. Thackeray's mirror. *In* Tennessee Studies in literature v22 p133-53

The Virginians

Sanders, A. Clio's heroes and Thackeray's heroes: Henry Esmond and The Virginians. *In* Sanders, A. The Victorian historical novel, 1840-1880 p97-119

Characters—Becky Sharp

Martin, B. K. Vanity fair: narrative ambivalence and comic form. *In* Tennessee Studies in literature v20 p37-49

Friends and associates

Sanders, C. R. The Carlyles and Thackeray. *In* Sanders, C. R. Carlyle's friendships, and other studies p226-66

Thai poetry

Griswold, A. B. and Prasert na Nagara. A fifteenth-century Siamese historical poem. *In* Southeast Asian history and historiography p123-63

Thai sculpture. See Sculpture, Thai

Thailand
Antiquities

Griswold, A. B. and Prasert Na Nagara. On kingship and society at Sukhodaya. *In* Change and persistence in Thai society p29-92

Historiography

Wilson, C. M. Toward a bibliography of the life and times of Mongkut, King of Thailand, 1851-1868. *In* Southeast Asian history and historiography p164-89

Wyatt, D. K. Chronicle traditions in Thai historiography. *In* Southeast Asian history and historiography p107-22

Intellectual life

Phillips, H. P. The culture of Siamese intellectuals. *In* Change and persistence in Thai society p324-57

Politics and government

Neher, C. D. Thailand. *In* Kearney, R. N. ed. Politics and modernization in South and Southeast Asia p215-52

Popular culture

Lancaster, D. The price of progress in Thailand. *In* Gerbner, G. ed. Mass media policies in changing cultures p165-83

Rural conditions

Judd, L. C. Social change in Commune Baw, Thailand, 1958-1967. *In* Social organization and the applications of anthropology p210-34

Social conditions

Akin Rabibhadana, M. R. Clientship and class structure in the Early Bangkok period. *In* Change and persistence in Thai society p93-123

Kirsch, A. T. Economy, polity, and religion in Thailand. *In* Change and persistence in Thai society p172-96

Wyatt, D. K. Education and the modernization of Thai society. *In* Change and persistence in Thai society p125-49

Social life and customs

Lancaster, D. The price of progress in Thailand. *In* Gerbner, G. ed. Mass media policies in changing cultures p165-83

Thais

Hanks, L. M. The Thai social order as entourage and circle. *In* Change and persistence in Thai society p197-218

Ingersoll, J. Merit and identity in village Thailand. *In* Change and persistence in Thai society p219-51

Keyes, C. F. Kin groups in a Thai-Lao community. *In* Change and persistence in Thai society p274-97

Thakur, Shivesh Chandra

Telepathy, evolution and dualism. *In* Thakur, S. C. ed. Philosophy and psychical research p195-210

Thalberg, Irving

Reverse discrimination and the future. *In* Gould, C. C. and Wartofsky, M. W. eds. Women and philosophy p294-308

Telepathic awareness of another's feelings. *In* Wheatley, J. M. O. and Edge, H. L. eds. Philosophical dimensions of parapsychology p133-38

About individual works
Telepathic awareness of another's feelings

Swiggart, P. A note on telepathy. *In* Wheatley, J. M. O. and Edge, H. L. eds. Philosophical dimensions of parapsychology p139-41

Theater—*Continued*

Denmark—History

Jensen, A. E. Molière in Denmark in the 18th century. *In* Johnson, R. B.; Neumann, E. S. and Trail, G. T. eds. Molière and the commonwealth of letters: patrimony and posterity p252-58

England

Brustein, R. S. The limits of English realism. *In* Brustein, R. S. The culture watch p89-93

Brustein, R. S. Repertory in the doldrums. *In* Brustein, R. S. The culture watch p68-71

England—Bibliography

Bawcutt, N. W. Shakespeare's life, times, and stage. *In* Shakespeare survey 28 p164-73

England—History

Bevington, D. M. Discontinuity in medieval acting traditions. *In* The Elizabethan theatre, V p 1-16

Booth, M. R. Irish landscape in the Victorian theatre. *In* Place, personality and the Irish writer p159-72

Booth, M. R. The social value of nineteenth-century English drama. *In* Drama and society p59-74

Harbage, A. Copper into gold. *In* English Renaissance drama p 1-14

Hermassi, K. C. Theatre as the city of man. *In* Hermassi, K. C. Polity and theater in historical perspective p137-51

Hibbard, G. R. Love, marriage and money in Shakespeare's theatre and Shakespeare's England. *In* The Elizabethan theatre, VI p134-55

Hunter, G. K. Italian tragicomedy on the English stage. *In* Renaissance drama [1973] p123-48

Meisel, M. The material sublime: John Martin, Byron, Turner, and the theater. *In* Kroeber, K. and Walling, W. eds. Images of romanticism p211-32

Nicoll, A. The popular beginnings. *In* Nicoll, A. World drama p197-205

Smith, B. R. Sir Amorous Knight and the indecorous Romans; or, Plautus and Terence play court in the Renaissance. *In* Renaissance drama [1973] p3-27

Southern, R. Methods of presentation in pre-Shakespearian theatre. *In* The Elizabethan theatre, V p45-53

Weimann, R. The Elizabethan drama. *In* Weimann, R. Shakespeare and the popular tradition in the theater: studies in the social dimension of dramatic form and function p161-207

Weimann, R. Moralities and interludes. *In* Weimann, R. Shakespeare and the popular tradition in the theater: studies in the social dimension of dramatic form and function p98-160

Weimann, R. The mystery cycles. *In* Weimann, R. Shakespeare and the popular tradition in the theater: studies in the social dimension of dramatic form and function p49-97

Williams, R. Social environment and theatrical environment: the case of English naturalism. *In* English drama: forms and development p203-23

Europe—History

Nicoll, A. Tragedy and opera. *In* Nicoll, A. World drama p294-306

France—History

Konigson, É. Religious drama and urban society in France at the end of the Middle Ages. *In* Drama and society p23-36

Germany

Castein, H. German social drama in the 1960s. *In* Drama and society p195-207

Kauffmann, S. Report from Germany. *In* Kauffmann, S. Persons of the drama p74-85

Greece

Baldry, H. C. Theatre and society in Greek and Roman antiquity. *In* Drama and society p1-21

Honzl, J. The hierarchy of dramatic devices. *In* Matejka, L. and Titunik, I. R. eds. Semiotics of art p118-27

Sandbach, F. H. An Athenian comedy. *In* Sandbach, F. H. The comic theatre of Greece and Rome p15-25

Iceland

Kauffmann, S. Report from Iceland. *In* Kauffmann, S. Persons of the drama p85-88

Ireland—History

Marcus, P. L. The Celtic revival: literature and the theatre. *In* De Breffny, B. ed. The Irish world p199-226

Orel, H. A drama for the nation. *In* Orel, H. ed. Irish history and culture p251-69

Italy—History

Smith, B. R. Sir Amorous Knight and the indecorous Romans; or, Plautus and Terence play court in the Renaissance. *In* Renaissance drama [1973] p3-27

Italy—History—20th century

Dashwood, J. R. The Italian futurist theatre. *In* Drama and society p129-46

Japan

See Kabuki

Japan—History

Horie-Webber, A. Modernisation of the Japanese theatre: the Shingeki movement. *In* Modern Japan p147-65

Java

Peacock, J. L. Symbolic reversal and social history: transvestites and clowns of Java. *In* Babcock, B. A. ed. The reversible world p209-24

London

Brustein, R. S. The contemporary English theatre: mirror or lamp? *In* Brustein, R. S. The culture watch p111-17

Brustein, R. S. A tale of two cities. *In* Brustein, R. S. The culture watch p50-53

London—History

Gair, W. R. The presentation of plays at Second Paul's: the early phase (1599-1602) *In* The Elizabethan theatre, VI p21-47

Klinger, M. F. William Hogarth and London theatrical life. *In* Studies in eighteenth-century culture v5 p11-27

New York (City)

Brustein, R. S. A tale of two cities. *In* Brustein, R. S. The culture watch p50-53

Kauffmann, S. The stages of Joseph Papp. *In* Kauffmann, S. Persons of the drama p3-28

Simon, J. I. Lovable little people. *In* Simon, J. I. Singularities p112-18

Theater—*Continued*

Rome

Baldry, H. C. Theatre and society in Greek and Roman antiquity. *In* Drama and society p1-21

Russia—History

Burgess, M. A. S. The early theatre. *In* Auty, R. and Obolensky, D. eds. An introduction to Russian language and literature p231-46

Burgess, M. A. S. The nineteenth- and early twentieth-century theatre. *In* Auty, R. and Obolensky, D. eds. An inroduction to Russian language and literature p247-70

Glenny, M. The Soviet theatre. *In* Auty, R. and Obolensky, D. eds. An introduction to Russian language and literature p271-85

Russia—History—20th century

Miller, A. On the theater in Russia; excerpt from "In Russia." *In* Miller, A. The theater essays of Arthur Miller p319-46

United States

Brustein, R. S. Broadway and the non-profit theatre: a misalliance. *In* Brustein, R. S. The culture watch p143-50

Brustein, R. S. Freedom and constraint in the American theatre. *In* Brustein, R. S. The culture watch p31-46

Brustein, R. S. In defense of repertory theatre. *In* Brustein, R. S. The culture watch p96-102

Brustein, R. S. New fads, ancient truths. *In* Brustein, R. S. The culture watch p3-7

Brustein, R. S. The profession is not supporting the profession! *In* Brustein, R. S. The culture watch p125-30

Brustein, R. S. Seminal and consumer theatre. *In* Brustein, R. S. The culture watch p150-58

Simon, J. I. Can drama be saved? *In* Simon, J. I. Singularities p55-57

Simon, J. I. Toward the conquest of inner space. *In* Simon, J. I. Singularities p65-67

United States—History

Kauffmann, S. The idea of repertory. *In* Kauffmann, S. Persons of the drama p348-65

Winton, C. The theater and drama. *In* Emerson, E. H. ed. American literature, 1764-1789 p87-104

United States—History—20th century

Johnson, H. A. Black influences in the American theater: Part II, 1960 and after. *In* The Black American reference book p705-40

Miller, A. The American theater. *In* Miller, A. The theater essays of Arthur Miller p31-50

Miller, A. Broadway, from O'Neill to now. *In* Miller, A. The theater essays of Arthur Miller p347-53

Simon, J. I. "What can I do in the water?" *In* Simon, J. I. Singularities p133-36

Theater and moving-pictures. See Moving-pictures and theater

Theater and state

See also Theater—Political aspects

Europe

Allen, J. P. The effects of subsidy on Western European theatre in the 1970s. *In* Drama and society p227-40

Theater as a profession

Brustein, R. S. A Dean's goodbye: a speech to the graduates of the School of Drama. *In* Brustein, R. S. The culture watch p138-42

Brustein, R. S. The profession is not supporting the profession! *In* Brustein, R. S. The culture watch p125-30

Theater audiences

Hermassi, K. C. Reconstituting the audience. *In* Hermassi, K. C. Polity and theater in historical perspective p155-65

Weimann, R. The mimus. *In* Weimann, R. Shakespeare and the popular tradition in the theater: studies in the social dimension of dramatic form and function p 1-14

United States—History

Johnson, C. D. That guilty third tier: prostitution in nineteenth-century American theaters. *In* Howe, D. W. ed. Victorian America p111-20

Theater criticism. See Dramatic criticism

Theater in art. See Theaters—Stage-setting and scenery

Theater in literature

Beer, G. 'Coming wonders': uses of theatre in the Victorian novel. *In* English drama: forms and development p164-85

Kernan, A. B. Shakespeare's essays on dramatic poesy: the nature and function of theater within the sonnets and the plays. *In* Martz, L. L. and Williams, A. L. eds. The author in his work p175-96

Theater of Cruelty. See Drama—20th century

Theaters

Stage-setting and scenery

Meisel, M. The material sublime: John Martin, Byron, Turner, and the theater. *In* Kroeber, K. and Walling, W. eds. Images of romanticism p211-32

England

Latter, D. A. Sight-lines in a conjectural reconstruction of an Elizabethan playhouse. *In* Shakespeare survey 28 p125-35

London

See London—Theaters

United States—History

Johnson, C. D. That guilty third tier: prostitution in nineteenth-century American theaters. *In* Howe, D. W. ed. Victorian America p111-20

Theatrical music. See Music in theaters

Theatricals, College. See College theater

Thecla, Saint

About

Anson, J. S. The female transvestite in early monasticism: the origin and development of a motif. *In* Viator: medieval and Renaissance studies v5 p 1-32

Theft. See Thieves

Theiner, Paul F.

Fabliau settings. *In* Cooke, T. D. and Honeycutt, B. L. eds. The humor of the fabliaux p119-36

Medieval English literature *In* Powell, J. M. ed. Medieval studies p239-75

The medieval Terence. *In* The Learned and the lewed p231-47

Theism

Nathan, G. J. The existence and nature of God in Hume's theism. *In* Livingston, D. W. and King, J. T. eds. Hume p126-49

See also Deism; Monotheism

Themal, Joachim H.

Children's work as art. *In* Ulman, E. and Dachinger, P. eds. Art therapy p95-105

Theobald, Robert, and McInnis, Noel F.

A certain education for an uncertain time. *In* Fairfield, R. P. ed. Humanistic frontiers in American education p194-201

Theodicy

Phillips, D. Z. The problem of evil. *In* Reason and religion p103-21

Swinburne, R. The problem of evil. *In* Reason and religion p81-102

Theodolfus, Bp. of Orléans

About

Witke, C. Aspects of Roman poetic technique in a Carolingian Latin satiric text. *In* Illinois classical studies v4, 1979 p220-31

Authorship

Wallach, L. Alcuin as the author of the Libri Carolini: epilogue to Part III. *In* Wallach, L. Diplomatic studies in Latin and Greek documents from the Carolingian age p287-94

Wallach, L. Philological and historical evidence disproving Theodulph of Orléans' alleged authorship. *In* Wallach, L. Diplomatic studies in Latin and Greek documents from the Carolingian age p248-71

Theodoridas of Syracuse

About

Fogelmark, S. Two cases of ΑΔΥΝΑΤΟΝ: AG. 612 and Theodoridas AP XIII.21. *In* Harvard Studies in classical philology v79 p149-63

Theodosius I, Emperor of Rome

About

Cameron, A. Theodosius the Great and the regency of Stilico. *In* Harvard Studies in classical philology p247-80

Theodulph of Orléans. See Theodolfus, Bp. of Orléans

Theoharis, Athan G.

Revisionism. *In* Encyclopedia of American foreign policy p900-13

Theologians, Japanese

Takayanagi, S. Christology and postwar theologians in Japan. *In* Postwar trends in Japan p119-67

Theological belief. See Faith

Theology

Carman, J. B. Religion as a problem for Christian theology. *In* Christian faith in a religiously plural world p83-103

See also Christianity; Deism; Religion; Religion and science; Secularism

Congresses

Final statement: Ecumenical dialogue of Third World theologians, Dar es Salaam, Tanzania, August 5-12, 1976. *In* The Emergent gospel p259-71

16th century

Rice, E. F. The humanist idea of Christian antiquity and the impact of Greek patristic work on sixteenth-century thought. *In* Classical influences on European culture A.D. 1500-1700 p199-203

20th century

Dickson, K. A. The African theological task. *In* The Emergent gospel p46-49

Mushete, N. Unity of faith and pluralism in theology. *In* The Emergent gospel p50-55

Theology, Ascetical. See Asceticism

Theology, Covenant. See Covenants (Theology)

Theology, Doctrinal

Abesamis, C. H. Doing theological reflection in a Philippine context. *In* The Emergent gospel p112-23

Carvajal, O. P. The context of theology. *In* The Emergent gospel p99-111

Cunningham, A. and others. Critique of the theology of the Unification Church as set forth in Divine principle. *In* Horowitz, I. L. ed. Science, sin, and scholarship p102-18

Herzog, F. Reorientation in theology: listening to Black theology. *In* The context of contemporary theology p225-41

Hick, J. H. Christian theology and interreligious dialogue. *In* The Frontiers of human knowledge p 1-14

Mickelsen, A. B. The metaphorical language of theology: its experiential base— Biblical and contemporary. *In* Current issues in Biblical and patristic interpretation p346-54

Nyamiti, C. Approaches to African theology. *In* The Emergent gospel p31-45

Pittenger, W. N. Evils and God—from a 'process' perspective. *In* Crew, L. ed. The gay academic p361-66

Sayers, D. L. Creed or chaos? excerpt. *In* Sayers, D. L. The whimsical Christian p34-52

Sayers, D. L. The dogma is the drama; excerpt from "Creed or chaos?" *In* Sayers, D. L. The whimsical Christian p23-28

Sayers, D. L. The greatest drama ever staged; excerpt from "Creed or chaos?" *In* Sayers, D. L. The whimsical Christian p11-16

Sayers, D. L. Strong meat; excerpt from "Creed or chaos?" *In* Sayers, D. L. The whimsical Christian p17-22

Stendahl, K. Judgment and mercy. *In* The Context of contemporary theology p147-54

Takayanagi, S. Christology and postwar theologians in Japan. *In* Postwar trends in Japan p119-67

See also Antinomianism; Assurance (Theology); Black theology; Christian ethics; Devil; Eschatology; Fall of man; Freedom (Theology); God; Good and evil; Holiness; Islamic theology; Liberation theology; Love (Theology); New England theology; Predestination; Providence and government of God; Repentance; Resurrection; Revelation; Revolution (Theology); Sin; Teleology; Theodicy

History

See Theology, Protestant; Jesus Christ— History of doctrines; and similar headings

History—Early church

Kraft, R. A. The development of the concept of "orthodoxy" in early Christianity. *In* Current issues in Biblical and patristic interpretation p47-59

Theology, Doctrinal—*Continued*

History—Middle Ages, 600-1500

Tierney, B. "Only the truth has authority": the problem of "reception" in the decretists and in Johannes de Turrecremata. *In* Law, church, and society p69-96

See also Religious thought—Middle Ages, 600-1500

History—India

Thomas, M. M. Some trends in contemporary Indian Christian theology. *In* The Frontiers of human knowledge p15-28

Theology, Islamic. See Islamic theology

Theology, Jewish. See Jewish theology

Theology, Muslim. See Islamic theology

Theology, Mystical. See Mysticism

Theology, Natural. See Natural theology

Theology, New England. See New England theology

Theology, Protestant

Couch, B. M. New visions of the Church in Latin America: a Protestant view. *In* The Emergent gospel p193-226

Theology, Puritan

Miller, P. The marrow of Puritan divinity. *In* Vaughan, A. T. and Bremer, F. J. eds. Puritan New England p44-65

Stoever, W. K. B. The doctrine of the two covenants: I. *In* Stoever, W. K. B. 'A faire and easie way to heaven' p81-96

Stoever, W. K. B. The doctrine of the two covenants: II. *In* Stoever, W. K. B. 'A faire and easie way to heaven' p97-118

Stoever, W. K. B. Epilogue. *In* Stoever, W. K. B. 'A faire and easie way to heaven' p184-91

Stoever, W. K. B. The order of redemption and the ground of assurance. *In* Stoever, W. K. B. 'A faire and easie way to heaven' p119-37

England

Stoever, W. K. B. The quest for assurance: radical solutions and Puritan dialectics. *In* Stoever, W. K. B. 'A faire and easie way to heaven' p138-60

New England

Daly, R. J. Ars poetica. *In* Daly, R. J. God's altar p40-81

Delbanco, A. Thomas Shepard's America: the biography of an idea. *In* Studies in biography p159-82

Elliott, E. From father to son: the evolution of typology in Puritan New England. *In* Miner, E. R. ed. Literary uses of typology p204-27

Stannard, D. E. Death and the Puritan child. *In* Death in America p9-29

Stoever, W. K. B. The dialectic of nature and grace. *In* Stoever, W. K. B. 'A faire and easie way to heaven' p3-20

Stoever, W. K. B. The nature of New England antinomianism. *In* Stoever, W. K. B. 'A faire and easie way to heaven' p161-83

Stoever, W. K. B. The New England controversy. *In* Stoever, W. K. B. 'A faire and easie way to heaven' p21-33

Stoever, W. K. B. The objectivity of regenerating grace: Thomas Shepard and Peter Bulkeley. *In* Stoever, W. K. B. 'A faire and easie way to heaven' p58-80

Stoever, W. K. B. The preeminence of the spirit: John Cotton. *In* Stoever, W. K. B. 'A faire and easie way to heaven' p34-57

Stoever, W. K. B. "Preparation for salvation." *In* Stoever, W. K. B. 'A faire and easie way to heaven' p192-99

United States

Parker, D. L. From sound believer to practical preparationist: some Puritan harmonics in Franklin's Autobiography. *In* Lemay, J. A. L. ed. The oldest revolutionary p67-75

Theology of liberation. See Liberation theology

Theophanies. See Visions

Theophilus, Saint, Bp. of Antioch

About

Markovic, M. Theophilus of Antioch: fifty-five emendations. *In* Illinois classical studies v4, 1979 p76-93

Theophrastus

About

Burkert, W. Air-imprints or eidola: Democritus' aetiology of vision. *In* Illinois classical studies v2 1977 p97-109

Theoretical chemistry. See Chemistry, Physical and theoretical

Theory (Philosophy)

Agger, B. On happiness and the damaged life. *In* O'Neill, J. ed. On critical theory p12-33

Andrew, E. The unity of theory and practice: the science of Marx and Nietzsche. *In* Political theory and praxis p117-37

Ball, T. Plato and Aristotle: the unity versus the autonomy of theory and practice. *In* Political theory and praxis p57-69

Bernstein, R. J. Hannah Arendt: the ambiguities of theory and practice. *In* Political theory and praxis p141-58

Euben, J. P. Creatures of a day: thought and action in Thucydides. *In* Political theory and praxis p28-56

Fay, B. C. How people change themselves: the relationship between critical theory and its audience. *In* Political theory and praxis p200-33

Fuss, P. L. Theory and practice in Hegel and Marx: an unfinished dialogue. *In* Political theory and praxis p97-116

Lobkowicz, N. On the history of theory and praxis. *In* Political theory and praxis p13-27

O'Neill, J. Critique and remembrance. *In* O'Neill, J. ed. On critical theory p 1-11

Raschke, C. Kant on theory and practice. *In* Political theory and praxis p73-96

Weber, S. M. Aesthetic experience and self reflection as emancipatory processes: two complementary aspects of critical theory. *In* O'Neill, J. ed. On critical theory p78-103

Theory of combustion. See Combustion, Theory of

Theory of groups. See Groups, Theory of

Theory of ideas. See Idea (Philosophy)

Theory of knowledge. See Knowledge, Theory of

Theory of sets. See Set theory

Theosophists. See Theosophy

Theosophy

Ellwood, R. S. Colonel Olcott and Madame Blavatsky journey to the East. *In* Ellwood, R. S. Alternative altars p104-35

See also Gnosticism; Vedanta; Yoga

Influence

Welsh, R. P. Mondrian and theosophy. *In* Kaplan, P. and Manso, S. eds. Major European art movements, 1900-1945 p250-74

Theotocopuli, Dominico, called El Greco

About individual works
Holy Family

Frankfort, E. H. El Greco's Holy Family with the sleeping Christ Child and the infant Baptist: an image of silence and mystery. *In* Enggass, R. C. and Stokstad, M. eds. Hortus imaginum p103-11

Therapeutic abortion. See Abortion, Therapeutic

Therapeutic community

Sugarman, B. Reluctant converts: social control, socialization and adaptation in therapeutic communities. *In* Wallis, R. ed. Sectarianism p141-61

Therapeutic systems. See Folk medicine

Therapeutics

Reiser, S. J. Therapeutic choice and moral doubt in a technological age. *In* Knowles, J. H. ed. Doing better and feeling worse p47-56

See also Drugs

Therapeutics, Suggestive

Tatar, M. M. From Mesmer to Freud: animal magnetism, hypnosis, and suggestion. *In* Tatar, M. M. Spellbound p3-44

See also Pastoral psychology; Psychotherapy

Therapist and patient. See Psychotherapist and patient

Theravada Buddhism. See Hinayana Buddhism

Thermal pollution of rivers, lakes, etc.

Bourodimos, E. L. Thermopollution in the aquatic environment. *In* Against pollution and hunger p183-209

Environmental aspects—United States

Bourodimos, E. L. Thermopollution in the aquatic environment. *In* Against pollution and hunger p183-209

Mathematical models

Bourodimos, E. L. Thermopollution in the aquatic environment. *In* Against pollution and hunger p183-209

Thermodynamics. See Heat; Statistical thermodynamics

Thernstrom, Stephan Albert

The new urban history. *In* The Future of history p43-51

Thespiae, Greece

Genealogy

Jones, C. P. A leading family of Roman Thespiae. *In* Harvard Studies in classical philology v74 p223-55

They shoot horses, don't they? (Motion picture)

Warshow, P. The unreal McCoy. *In* Peary, G. and Shatzkin, R. eds. The modern American novel and the movies p29-39

Thiede, Roger Lee

Industry and urbanization in New Russia from 1860 to 1910. *In* Hamm, M. F. ed. The city in Russian history p125-38

Thieves

China—History

Chen-Chang, Fu-mei. Local control of convicted thieves in eighteenth-century China. *In* Conflict and control in late imperial China p121-42

Thieves like us (Motion picture)

Kauffmann, S. Thieves like us. *In* Kauffmann, S. Living images p263-65

Thinking. See Thought and thinking

Thinking, Artificial. See Artificial intelligence

Thiong'o Ngugi Wa. See Ngugi Wa Thiong'o

Third world. See Underdeveloped areas

Thirsk, Joan

The common fields. *In* Peasants, knights and heretics p10-32

The European debate on customs of inheritance, 1500-1700. *In* Family and inheritance p177-91

The origin of the common fields. *In* Peasants, knights and heretics p51-56

About individual works
The common fields

Titow, J. Z. Medieval England and the open-field system. *In* Peasants, knights and heretics p33-50

Thirteenth century

Freed, J. B. The friars and the delineation of state boundaries in the thirteenth century. *In* Order and innovation in the Middle Ages p31-40

Post, G. Philosophy and citizenship in the thirteenth century—laicisation, the two laws and Aristotle. *In* Order and innovation in the Middle Ages p401-08

Sullivan, R. E. The Middle Ages in the Western tradition: some reconsiderations. *In* Essays on medieval civilization p3-31

Thrupp, S. L. Comparison of cultures in the Middle Ages: Western standards as applied to Muslim civilization in the twelfth and thirteenth centuries. *In* Thrupp, S. L. Society and history p67-88

Thirty tyrants

McCoy, W. J. Aristotle's Athenaion Politeia and the establishment of the Thirty Tyrants. *In* Yale classical studies v24 p131-45

This man must die (Motion picture)

Kauffmann, S. This man must die. *In* Kauffmann, S. Living images p24-26

Thody, Philip Malcolm Waller

About individual works
Jean Genet

Connolly, C. Jean Genet. *In* Connolly, C. The evening colonnade p354-57

Thoenig, Jean Claude, and Despicht, Nigel Stanley

Transport policy. *In* Planning, politics and public policy p390-423

Tholthis, The third-century B.C. land-leases from. Bingen J. *In* Illinois classical studies v3, 1978 p74-80

Thomas à Becket, Saint, Abp. of Canterbury

About

Peters, E. M. The Archbishop and the hedgehog. *In* Law, church, and society p167-84

Turner, V. W. Religious paradigms and political action: the murder in the cathedral of Thomas Becket. *In* Reynolds, F. E. and Capps, D. eds. The biographical process p153-86

Thomas Aquinas, Saint

About

Arendt, H. Will and intellect. *In* Arendt, H. The life of the mind v2 p111-46

Copleston, F. C. Aquinas and the autonomy of religious language. *In* Copleston, F. C. Philosophers and philosophies p43-56

O'Connor, D. J. Aquinas and natural law. *In* New studies in ethics v 1 p79-172

Wingler, H. Aristotle in the thought of Nietzsche and Thomas Aquinas. *In* O'Flaherty, J. C.; Sellner, T. F. and Helm, R. M. eds. Studies in Nietzsche and the classical tradition p33-54

About individual works
Summa theologica

Downs, R. B. Fathers of the Church. *In* Downs, R. B. Books that changed the world p151-62

Zacher, C. K. Curiositas. *In* Zacher, C. K. Curiosity and pilgrimage p18-41

Influence

Wilhelmsen, F. D. Sir John Fortescue and the English tradition. *In* Wilhelmsen, F. D. Christianity and political philosophy p111-38

Thomas, Augustus

About individual works
Alabama

Going, W. T. The Prestons of Talladega and the Hubbards of Bowen: a dramatic note. *In* Going, W. T. Essays on Alabama literature p142-55

Thomas, Caroline C. Bedell

About

Harvey, A. M. Johns Hopkins—its role in medical education for women. *In* Harvey, A. M. Adventures in medical research p225-47

Thomas, D. A.

The control of discretion in the administration of criminal justice. *In* Crime, criminology and public policy p139-55

Thomas, David

Comedy in northern Europe. *In* Howarth, W. D. ed. Comic drama p144-64

Thomas, David Michael

American technocracy and the religious spirit: an unholy alliance? *In* America in theological perspective p189-205

Thomas, Deborah Allen

Dickens' Mrs. Lirriper and the evolution of a feminine stereotype. *In* Dickens Studies Annual v6 p154-66

The equivocal explanation of Dickens' George Silverman. *In* Dickens Studies Annual v3 p134-43

Thomas, Dylan

About

Eberhart, R. Some memories of Dylan Thomas. *In* Eberhart, R. Of poetry and poets p141-43

Fraser, G. S. Dylan Thomas. *In* Fraser, G. S. Essays on twentieth-century poets p182-203

Hardy, B. N. The personal and the impersonal in some of Dylan Thomas's lyrics. *In* Hardy, B. N. The advantage of lyric p112-20

Kunitz, S. J. Sea son of the wave. *In* Kunitz, S. J. A kind of order, a kind of folly p228-32

McMillan, D. Dylan Thomas. *In* McMillan, D. Transition p157-66

Olson, E. The poetry of Dylan Thomas. *In* Olson, E. On value judgments in the arts, and other essays p65-70

Shapiro, K. J. Dylan Thomas. *In* Shapiro, K. J. The poetry wreck p139-55

Simpson, L. The color of saying. *In* Simpson, L. A revolution in taste p 1-42

Thurley, G. Dylan Thomas: Merlin as sponger. *In* Thurley, G. The ironic harvest p121-36

About individual works
Selected writings

Berryman, J. Robert Lowell and others. *In* Berryman, J. The freedom of the poet p286-96

The world I breathe

Berryman, J. Dylan Thomas: the loud hill of Wales. *In* Berryman, J. The freedom of the poet p282-85

Language

Freeman, D. C. The strategy of fusion: Dylan Thomas's syntax. *In* Fowler, R. ed. Style and structure in literature p19-39

Thomas, Edward

About

Coxe, L. O. Edward Thomas and the real world. *In* Coxe, L. O. Enabling acts p88-95

Wain, J. Edward Thomas and Helen Thomas. *In* Wain, J. Professing poetry p224-55

Thomas, George B.

Kimbanguism: authentically African, authentically Christian. *In* African religions: a symposium p275-96

Thomas, Helen (Noble)

About

Wain, J. Edward Thomas and Helen Thomas. *In* Wain, J. Professing poetry p224-55

Thomas, Hugh

The lyrical illusion: Spain 1936. *In* Courcel, M. H. de, ed. Malraux p40-50

About individual works
The Spanish Civil War

Connolly, C. The Spanish Civil War: 1. *In* Connolly, C. The evening colonnade p313-16

Thomas, Isaiah

About

Kroeger, K. Isaiah Thomas as a music publisher. *In* American Antiquarian Society. Proceedings v86 pt2 p321-41

Thomas, James Alan

Heavy traffic on the purple brick road: the route to law school. *In* Hurdles p212-38

Thomas, James Edward

Policy and administration in penal establishments. *In* Progress in penal reform p54-67

Thomas, Jane Resh
Old worlds and new: anti-feminism in "Watership Down." *In* Horn Book Magazine. Crosscurrents of criticism p311-14

Thomas, John Lawrence
The road ahead. *In* Sexuality and human values p132-51

Thomas, Lewis
The medusa and the snail
Contents
An apology
A brief historical note on medical economics
The Deacon's masterpiece
The hazards of science
The health-care system
How to fix the premedical curriculum
Medical lessons from history
The medusa and the snail
Notes on punctuation
On cloning a human being
On committees
On disease
On embryology
On etymons and hybrids
On magic in medicine
On meddling
On natural death
On thinking about thinking
On transcendental metaworry (TMW)
On warts
Ponds
The scrambler in the mind
The selves
To err is human
A trip abroad
The Tucson zoo
Why Montaigne is not a bore
The wonderful mistake
The youngest and brightest thing around

On the science and technology of medicine. *In* Knowles, J. H. ed. Doing better and feeling worse p35-46

Thomas, Madathilparampil M.
Some trends in contemporary Indian Christian theology. *In* The Frontiers of human knowledge p15-28

Thomas, Norman Mattoon

About

Howe, I. Tribune of socialism. *In* Howe, I. Celebrations and attacks p230-33

Thomas, Richard F.
An alternative to ceremonial negligence (Catullus 68.73-78) *In* Harvard Studies in classical philology v82 p175-78

Thomas, William
The philosophic radicals. *In* Hollis, P. ed. Pressure from without p52-79

Thomism. See Thomists

Thomists
Donnelly, J. P. Calvinist Thomism. *In* Viator: medieval and Renaissance studies v7 p441-55

Thompson, Ann
Philomel in 'Titus Andronicus' and 'Cymbeline'. *In* Shakespeare survey v31 p23-32

Shelley and 'Satire's scourge.' *In* Davies, R. T. and Beatty, B. G. eds. Literature of the romantic period, 1750-1850 p135-50

Thompson, Arthur A.
Alabama's five economies. *In* The Rising South v2 p29-47

Thompson, Craig Ringwalt
Scripture for the ploughboy and some others. *In* Studies in the continental background of Renaissance English literature: essays presented to John L. Lievsay p 3-28
See also Part 2 under title: Essays on the works of Erasmus

Thompson, David Michael
The Liberation Society, 1844-1868. *In* Hollis, P. ed. Pressure from without p210-38
The politics of the Enabling Act (1919) *In* Church, society and politics p383-92

Thompson, Denys
The uses of poetry
Contents
Dissent and protest
In the beginning
Maid of all work
The nature of poetry
Patriotism and politics
The printed poem
Rites, bards, ballads
Uses of poetry

Thompson, Dorothy Burr
A faience fellah. *In* Studies in classical art and archaeology p175-78

Thompson, Edgar Tristram
The South and I: the view from the plantation. *In* Lewis, W. D. and Griessman, B. E. eds. The Southern mystique p73-87

Thompson, Edward Palmer
The grid of inheritance: a comment. *In* Family and inheritance p328-60
'London.' *In* Phillips, M. C. ed. Interpreting Blake p5-31

Thompson, Francis

About

Ober, W. B. Drowsed with the fume of poppies: opium and John Keats. *In* Ober, W. B. Boswell's clap and other essays p118-36

Thompson, Francis Michael Longstreth
Britain. *In* Spring, D. ed. European landed elites in the nineteenth century p22-44

Thompson, Gary Richard
Poe. *In* American literary scholarship, 1973 p32-64
Poe [another essay] *In* American literary scholarship, 1974 p29-42

Thompson, Geraldine
As bones to the body: the scope of inventio in the Colloquies of Erasmus. *In* Essays on the works of Erasmus p163-78

Thompson, John Alexander
American Progressive publicists and the First World War, 1914-1917. *In* Burton, D. H. ed. American history—British historians p187-217
The use of repetition in the prophecy of Joel. *In* On language, culture, and religion: in honor of Eugene A. Nida p101-10

Thompson, John Eric Sidney
'Canals' of the Rio Candelaria basin, Campeche, Mexico. *In* Mesoamerican archaeology p297-302

Thompson, Judith Jarvis
Symbol, myth, and ritual in The glass menagerie, The rose tattoo, and Orpheus descending. *In* Tennessee Williams: a tribute p679-711

Thompson, Kenneth Winfred

Niebuhr as thinker and doer. *In* Scott, N. A. ed. The legacy of Reinhold Niebuhr p100-10

Philosophy and politics: the two commitments of Hans J. Morgenthau. *In* [Truth and tragedy]: a tribute to Hans Morgenthau p21-31

Values and education: a worldwide review. *In* The Year book of world affairs, 1977 p327-41

Thompson, Laurence C.

The Northwest. *In* Sebeok, T. A. ed. Native languages of the Americas v 1 p359-425

Thompson, Lee Briscoe

Mosaic and monolith: a comparison of Canadian and Australian poetic responses to the Great Depression. *In* Narasimhaiah, C. D. ed. Awakened conscience p164-84

Thompson, Leonard Monteath

White over Black in South Africa: what of the future? *In* Thompson, L. M. and Butler, J. eds. Change in contemporary South Africa p400-14

Thompson, M. Geraldine. See Thompson, Geraldine

Thompson, Richard

Meep meep. *In* Nichols, B. ed. Movies and methods p126-35

Thompson, Roger

The Puritans and prurience: aspects of the Restoration book trade. *In* Allen, H. C. and Thompson, R. eds. Contrast and connection p36-65

Thompson, Stephen I.

The cultural ecology of pioneer agriculture in contemporary South America. *In* Miller, D. H. and Steffen, J. O. eds. The frontier p297-316

See also Savage, W. W. jt. auth.

Thompson, W. D. J. Cargill

Luther and the right of resistance to the Emperor. *In* Church, society and politics p159-202

Sir Francis Knollys' campaign against the jure divino theory of episcopacy. *In* The Dissenting tradition p39-77

Thompson, Willard Scott, and Zartman, I. William

The development of norms in the African system. *In* El-Ayouty, Y. ed. The Organization of African Unity after ten years p3-46

Thompson, Willie

The Kirk and the Cameronians. *In* Rebels and their causes p93-106

Thomson, Boris

Lot's wife and the Venus of Milo

Contents

The difference of art: some Soviet writers of the 1920s and 1930s
The fact of art: Leonard Leonov
The necessity of art: the last years of Aleksandr Blok
The problem of art
The redundancy of art: Soviet and Marxist views of art in the 1920s
The secret of art: two Soviet myths
Some properties of art

Thomson, Ian

Latin "elegiac comedy" of the twelfth century. *In* Ruggiers, P. G. ed. Versions of medieval comedy p51-66

Thomson, James, 1700-1748

About

Adams, P. G. James Thomson's luxuriant language. *In* Adams, P. G. Graces of harmony p118-35

About individual works

The castle of indolence

Greene, D. J. From accidie to neurosis: The castle of indolence revisited. *In* English literature in the age of disguise p131-56

Thomson, Rodney M.

William of Malmesbury and the letters of Alcuin. *In* Medievalia et humanistica no. 8 p147-61

The seasons

Adams, P. G. James Thomson's luxurious language. *In* Adams, P. G. Graces of harmony p118-35

Manlove, C. N. Thomson: The seasons. *In* Manlove, C. N. Literature and reality, 1600-1800 p125-35

Language

Sherbo, A. Thomson. *In* Sherbo, A. English poetic diction from Chaucer to Wordsworth p158-80

Style

Sherbo, A. Thomson. *In* Sherbo, A. English poetic diction from Chaucer to Wordsworth p158-80

Thomson, Judith Jarvis

Academic freedom and research. *In* The Concept of academic freedom p255-62

A defense of abortion. *In* Baker, R. and Elliston, F. A. eds. Philosophy & sex p305-23

Thomson, Peter

No Rome of safety: the Royal Shakespeare season 1972 reviewed. *In* Shakespeare survey 26 p139-50

Shakespeare straight and crooked: a review of the 1973 season at Stratford. *In* Shakespeare survey 27 p143-54

The smallest season: the Royal Shakespeare Company at Stratford in 1974. *In* Shakespeare survey 28 p137-48

Towards a poor Shakespeare: The Royal Shakespeare Company at Stratford in 1975. *In* Shakespeare survey v29 p151-56

Thomson, Rodney M.

The date of the Bury Bible reexamined. *In* Viator: medieval and Renaissance studies v6 p51-58

William of Malmesbury and some other Western writers on Islam. *In* Medievalia et humanistica no. 6 p179-87

Thomson, Sir William. See Kelvin, William Thomson, 1st Baron

Thonga tribe

Colson, E. Life among the cattle-owning plateau Tonga. *In* The Occasional papers of the Rhodes-Livingstone Museum p167-213

Thorburn, Andrew. See Masson, P. jt. auth.

Thorburn, David

Television melodrama. *In* Television as a cultural force p77-94

Thoreau, Henry David

About

Couser, G. T. Henry David Thoreau: retreat and pilgrimage. *In* Couser, G. T. American autobiography p62-79

Kern, A. C. Church, Scripture, nature and ethics in Henry Thoreau's religious thought. *In* Literature and ideas in America p79-95

Thoreau, Henry D.—About—*Continued*

Richardson, R. D. Thoreau. *In* Richardson, R. D. Myth and literature in the American renaissance p90-137

Tanner, T. Thoreau and the sauntering eye. *In* Tanner, T. The reign of wonder p46-63

Tichi, C. Questioning and chronicling: Thoreau, Cooper, Bancroft. *In* Tichi, C. New World, new earth p151-205

Wilder, T. N. The American loneliness. *In* Wilder, T. N. American characteristics, and other essays p34-47

About individual works
Civil disobedience

Downs, R. B. Individual versus state. *In* Downs, R. B. Books that changed the world p217-27

Walden

Blasing, M. K. The economies of Walden. *In* Blasing, M. K. The art of life p 1-23

Hoch, D. G. Walden: yoga and creation. *In* Artful thunder p85-102

Michaels, W. B. Walden's false bottoms. *In* Glyph I p132-49

Paul, S. Thoreau's Walden. *In* Paul, S. Repossessing and renewing p14-56

White, E. B. A slight sound at evening. *In* White, E. B. Essays of E. B. White p234-42

Bibliography

Buell, L. I. Emerson, Thoreau, and transcendentalism. *In* American literary scholarship, 1974 p3-14

Buell, L. Emerson, Thoreau, and transcendentalism [another essay] *In* American literary scholarship, 1975 p3-15

Glick, W. Emerson, Thoreau, and transcendentalism. *In* American literary scholarship, 1976 p5-14

Glick, W. Emerson, Thoreau, and transcendentalism [another essay] *In* American literary scholarship, 1977 p3-16

Harding, W. R. Emerson, Thoreau, and transcendentalism. *In* American literary scholarship, 1973 p3-14

Criticism and interpretation

Michaels, W. B. Walden's false bottoms. *In* Glyph I p132-49

Thorn, George Widmer
About

Harvey, A. M. More bright stars in the Johns Hopkins galaxy. *In* Harvey, A. M. Adventures in medical research p333-63

Thorngren, Bertil

Silent actors: communication networks for development. *In* The Social impact of the telephone p374-85

Thornton, Olen D.

The Vietnam connection. *In* Henderson, G. ed. Human relations in the military p163-75

Thornton, Robert, fl. 1440
About

Keiser, G. R. Lincoln Cathedral Library MS 91: life and milieu of the scribe. *In* Virginia. University. Bibliographical Society. Studies in bibliography v32 p158-79

Thornton, Robert Kelsey Rought, comp.
About individual works
Poetry of the 'nineties

Connolly, C. The nineties. *In* Connolly, C. The evening colonnade p163-66

Thornton, Weldon

J. M. Synge. *In* Finneran, R. J. ed. Anglo-Irish literature p315-65

Thorp, Willard

Suggs and Sut in modern dress: the latest chapter in Southern humor. *In* Inge, M. T. ed. The frontier humorists p292-99

Thorpe, James Ernest

Reflections and self-reflections: Outlandish proverbs as a context for George Herbert's other writings. *In* Illustrious evidence p23-37

Thorpe, Lewis

Dorothy L. Sayers as a translator of Le roman de Tristan and La chanson de Roland. *In* Hannay, M. P. ed. As her whimsey took her p109-22

Thorpe, Thomas Bangs
About individual works
The big bear of Arkansas

Blair, W. "The big bear of Arkansas": T. B. Thorpe and his masterpiece. *In* Inge, M. T. ed. The frontier humorists p105-17

Thorpe, William Homan

Arthur Koestler and biological thought. *In* Harris, H. A. ed. Astride the two cultures p50-68

Reductionism in biology. *In* Ayala, F. J. and Dobzhansky, T. G. eds. Studies in the philosophy of biology p109-36

Thought and thinking

Arendt, H. Appearance. *In* Arendt, H. The life of the mind v 1 p17-65

Arendt, H. What makes us think? *In* Arendt, H. The life of the mind v 1 p127-93

Arendt, H. Where are we when we think? *In* Arendt, H. The life of the mind v 1 p195-216

Bohm, D. Imagination, fancy, insight, and reason in the process of thought. *In* Evolution of consciousness p51-68

Davidson, D. H. ed. Thought and talk. *In* Guttenplan, S. D. Mind and language p7-23

De Bono, E. Lateral thinking and science fiction. *In* Nicholls, P. ed. Science fiction at large p35-55

Draenos, S. S. Thinking without a ground: Hannah Arendt and the contemporary situation of understanding. *In* Hannah Arendt: the recovery of the public world p209-24

Goody, J. R. Literacy, criticism, and the growth of knowledge. *In* Culture and its creators p226-43

Hampshire, S. N. The explanation of thought. *In* Thought, consciousness, and reality p 3-23

Hofstadter, A. Consciousness, thought, and enownment. *In* Thought, consciousness, and reality p85-109

Holton, G. J. 'What, precisely, is "thinking"?' *In* Einstein p153-64

Loewald, H. W. Primary process, secondary process, and language. *In* Psychoanalysis and language p235-70

Nemerov, H. Speculation turning to itself. *In* Nemerov, H. Figures of thought p87-94

Oakeshott, M. J. The voice of poetry in the conversation of mankind. *In* Oakeshott, M. J. Rationalism in politics p197-247

Palombo, S. R. Dreams, memory, and the origin of thought. *In* Thought, consciousness, and reality p49-83

Singer, J. L. Ongoing thought: the normative baseline for alternate states of consciousness. *In* Alternate states of consciousness p89-120

Thought and thinking—*Continued*

Squires, R. Silent soliloquy. *In* Royal Institute of Philosophy. Understanding Wittgenstein p208-25

Thomas, L. On thinking about thinking. *In* Thomas, L. The medusa and the snail p151-54

Vendler, Z. Words in thought. *In* Thought, consciousness, and reality p25-48

See also Attention; Cognition; Definition (Logic); Ideology; Intellect; Judgment; Logic; Meaning (Psychology); Memory; Perception, Psycholinguistics; Reasoning; Self; Stereotype (Psychology)

Thought-transference

Price, H. H. Parapsychology and human nature. *In* Ludwig, J. K. ed. Philosophy and parapsychology p371-86

Price, H. H. Some philosophical questions about telepathy and clairvoyance. *In* Wheatley, J. M. O. and Edge, H. L. eds. Philosophical dimensions of parapsychology p105-32

Schwarz, B. E. Psi and the life cycle. *In* Parapsychology: its relation to physics, biology, psychology, and psychiatry p235-45

Swiggart, P. A note on telepathy. *In* Wheatley, J. M. O. and Edge, H. L. eds. Philosophical dimensions of parapsychology p139-41

Thakur, S. C. Telepathy, evolution and dualism. *In* Thakur, S. C. ed. Philosophy and psychical research p195-210

Thalberg, I. Telepathic awareness of another's feelings. *In* Wheatley, J. M. O. and Edge, H. L. eds. Philosophical dimensions of parapsychology p133-38

Ullman, M. Psychiatry and parapsychology: the consummation of an uncertain romance. *In* Parapsychology: its relation to physics, biology, psychology, and psychiatry p171-207

The three kingdoms. See San Kuo

Three Mountains Press

Ford, H. D. Bill Bird and the Three Mountains. & Ford, H. D. Published in Paris p95-116

The three musketeers (Motion picture)

Kauffmann, S. The three musketeers. *In* Kauffmann, S. Living images p274-75

The three sisters (Motion picture)

Kauffmann, S. The three sisters. *In* Kauffmann, S. Living images p265-67

Three songs of Lenin (Motion picture)

Ferguson, O. Artists among the flickers; excerpt from "The film criticism of Otis Ferguson." *In* Denby, D. ed. Awake in the dark p375-77

Taylor, R. Three songs of Lenin. *In* Taylor, R. Film propaganda p103-15

Threlfall, Monica

Shantytown dwellers and people's power. *In* O'Brien, P. J. ed. Allende's Chile p167-91

Thring, Meredith Woolridge

Physical and chemical aspects of pollution. *In* Against pollution and hunger p63-88

Throne of blood (Motion picture)

Jorgens, J. J. Defining Macbeth: Schaefer, Welles, and Kurosawa. *In* Jorgens, J. J. Shakespeare on film p148-60

Throne of God

Bloom, H. Shelley and his precursors. *In* Bloom, H. Poetry and repression p83-111

Thrower, Norman Joseph William

New geographical horizons: maps. *In* First images of America p659-74

Thrupp, Sylvia Lettice

Society and history

Contents

Aliens in and around London in the fifteenth century

The city as the idea of social order

Comparative Studies in Society and History: a working alliance among specialists

Comparison of cultures in the Middle Ages: Western standards as applied to Muslim civilization in the twelfth and thirteenth centuries

The creativity of cities

Diachronic methods in comparative politics

The dynamics of medieval society

Economy and society in medieval England

Editorial from the first issue of Comparative Studies in Society and History

Hierarchy, illusion, and social mobility

History and sociology: new opportunities for cooperation

Medieval gilds reconsidered

The pedigree and prospects of local history

Plague effects in medieval Europe

Preface to Change in medieval society: Europe north of the Alps, 1050-1500

The problem of conservatism in fifteenth-century England

The problem of replacement-rates in late medieval English population

The role of comparison in the development of economic history

Social control in the medieval town

Some historians on generalization

A survey of the alien population of England in 1440

Tradition and development: a choice of views

What history and sociology can learn from each other

Thucydides

About

Edmunds, L. Thucydides' ethics as reflected in the description of stasis (3.82-83). *In* Harvard Studies in classical philology v79 p73-92

Edmunds, L. and Martin, R. Thucydides 2.65.8: ΕΛΕΥΘΕΡΩΣ. *In* Harvard Studies in classical philology v81 p187-93

About individual works

The history of the Peloponnesian War

Aron, R. Thucydides and the historical narrative. *In* Aron, R. Politics and history p20-46

Cawkwell, G. Thucydides' judgment of Periclean strategy. *In* Yale classical studies v24 p53-70

Egan, K. Thucydides, tragedian. *In* Canary, R. H. and Kozicki, H. J. eds. The writing of history p63-92

Euben, J. P. Creatures of a day: thought and action in Thucydides. *In* Political theory and praxis p28-56

Fornara, C. W. Plutarch and the Megarian decree. *In* Yale classical studies v24 p213-28

Kagan, D. The speeches in Thucydides and the Mytilene debate. *In* Yale classical studies v24 p71-94

Thuillier, Guy

Water supplies in nineteenth-century Nivernais. *In* Food and drink in history p109-25

Thunderstorms in literature

Tatar, M. M. Thunder, lightning, and electricity: moments of recognition in Heinrich von Kleist's dramas. *In* Tatar, M. M. Spellbound p82-120

Thurber, James

About individual works

Men, women and dogs

Sheed, W. James Thurber: Men, women and dogs. *In* Sheed, W. The good word & other words p228-33

Thurley, Geoffrey

The American moment

Contents

Allen Ginsberg: the whole man in

American poetry: sketch of a theory

Benign diaspora: the landscape of Richard Wilbur

Black Mountain academy: Charles Olson as critic and poet

Conclusion: towards decadence

The development of the new language: Wieners, Jones, McClure, Whalen, Corso

Devices among words: Kinnell, Bly, Simic

John Berryman: the struggle towards dislocation

Phenomenalist idioms: Doolittle, Moore, Levertov

The poetry of breakdown: Robert Lowell and Anne Sexton

Rexroth and Patchen: alternatives to breakdown

Robert Duncan: the myth of open form

Theodore Roethke: Lost son

The ironic harvest

Contents

Beyond positive values: Ted Hughes

David Gascoyne: phenomena of zero

Dylan Thomas: Merlin as sponger

F. R. Leavis and the English existential tradition

The intellectualist position

A kind of scapegoat: a retrospect on Stephen Spender

The legacy of Auden: the poetry of Roy Fuller, Philip Larkin and Peter Porter

The new poetry in England

'Partial fires': Empson's poetry

W. H. Auden: the image as instance

Thyroid gland

Diseases

Harvey, A. M. Research at Johns Hopkins on the thyroid gland and its diseases. *In* Harvey, A. M. Adventures in medical research p314-32

Tiao-yü Tai. See Senkaku Islands

Tibbles, Lance W.

Medical and legal aspects of competency as affected by old age. *In* Spicker, S. F.; Woodward, K. M. and Van Tassel, D. D. eds. Aging and the elderly p127-51

Tibeto-Burman languages. See Burmese language

Tibullus, Albius

About

Gotoff, H. C. Tibullus: nunc levis est tractanda Venus. *In* Harvard Studies in classical philology v78 p231-51

About individual works

Elegies (First elegy)

Koenen, L. Egyptian influence in Tibullus. *In* Illinois classical studies, v 1 1976 p127-59

Lee, G. Otium cum indignitate: Tibullus I.1. *In* Woodman, T. and West, D. eds. Quality and pleasure in Latin poetry p94-114

The elegies of Tibullus (2.5)

Ross, D. O. The Roman poetry of Horace and Tibullus. *In* Ross, D. O. Backgrounds to Augustan poetry: Gallus, elegy and Rome p131-62

Tichi, Cecelia

New World, new earth

Contents

Edward Johnson's American new earth

Joel Barlow and the engineered millennium

A kingdom unto the world

Questioning and chronicling: Thoreau, Cooper, Bancroft

The Revolution begins the world anew

Walt Whitman, the literatus of the new earth

Worried celebrants of the American Revolution. *In* Emerson, E. H. ed. American literature, 1764-1789 p275-91

Tick, Stanley

The sad end of Mr Meagles. *In* Dickens Studies Annual v3 p87-99

Toward Jaggers. *In* Dickens Studies Annual v5 p133-49

Tickell, Crispin Charles Cervantes

The civilizations of pre-Columbian America. *In* Life after death p67-79

Ticktin, Hillel

The relation between détente and Soviet economic reforms. *In* Jahn, E. ed. Soviet foreign policy p41-56

Tiedtke, Jutta, and Tiedtke, Stephan

The Soviet Union's internal problems and the development of the Warsaw Treaty Organisation. *In* Jahn, E. ed. Soviet foreign policy p114-57

Tiedtke, Stephan. See Tiedtke, J. jt. auth.

Tiepolo, Giambattista. See Tiepolo, Giovanni Battista

Tiepolo, Giovanni Battista

Shapley, F. R. Tiepolo's Zenobia cycle. *In* Enggass, R. C. and Stokstad, M. eds. Hortus imaginum p193-98

About

Knox, G. Francesco Guardi as an apprentice in the studio of Giambattista Tiepolo. *In* Studies in eighteenth-century culture v5 p29-39

Tierney, Brian

"Only the truth has authority": the problem of "reception" in the decretists and in Johannes de Turrecremata. *In* Law, church, and society p69-96

Tiffin, Chris

Mates, mum, and Maui: the theme of maturity in three antipodean novels. *In* Narasimhaiah, C. D. ed. Awakened conscience p127-45

Victims Black and white: Thomas Keneally's The chant of Jimmie Blacksmith. *In* Hamilton, K. G. ed. Studies in the recent Australian novel p121-48

Tiffin, Helen

Tourmaline and the Tao Te Ching: Randolph Stow's Tourmaline. *In* Hamilton, K. G. ed. Studies in the recent Australian novel p84-120

Towards place and placelessness: two journey patterns in Commonwealth literature. *In* Narasimhaiah, C. D. ed. Awakened conscience p146-63

Time (Theology)

Breck, A. D. John Wyclyf on time. *In* Cosmology, history, and theology p211-18

Peacocke, A. R. Cosmos and creation. *In* Cosmology, history, and theology p365-81

Reilly, R. J. A note on Barfield, romanticism, and time. *In* Evolution of consciousness p183-90

History of doctrines

Momigliano, A. Time in ancient historiography. *In* Momigliano, A. Essays in ancient and modern historiography p179-204

Time, Cognition of. See Time perception

Time allocation. See Leisure

Time and space. See Space and time

Time and space in art. See Space and time in art

Time clocks

Whitrow, G. J. The role of time in cosmology. *In* Cosmology, history, and theology p159-77

Time dilatation

Salmon, W. C. Clocks and simultaneity in special relativity or, Which twin has the Timex? *In* Motion and time, space and matter p508-45

Time estimation. See Time perception

Time in literature

Apronti, E. O. The tyranny of time: the theme of time in the artistic consciousness of South African writers. *In* African literature today no. 8: Drama in Africa p106-14

Bayley, J. Living in the present. *In* Bayley, J. The uses of division p185-89

Bayley, J. The Troilus atmosphere. *In* Bayley, J. The uses of division p189-201

Church, M. Kafka and Proust: a contrast in time. *In* Garvin, H. R. ed. Makers of the twentieth-century novel p149-53

Doležel, L. A scheme of narrative time. *In* Matejka, L. and Titunik, I. R. eds. Semiotics of art p209-17

Everett, B. 'Hamlet': a time to die. *In* Shakespeare survey 30 p117-23

Franklin, S. L. Dickens and time: the clock without hands. *In* Dickens Studies Annual v4 p 1-35

Garner, A. Inner time. *In* Nicholls, P. ed. Science fiction at large p119-38

Gottschalk, P. A. Time in Edwin Drood. *In* Dickens Studies Annual v 1 p265-72

Grant, P. Time and temptation in Paradise regained: belief and the single image. *In* Grant, P. Images and ideas in literature of the English Renaissance p129-53

Hagan, J. Déjà vu and the effect of timelessness in Faulkner's Absalom, Absalom! *In* Garvin, H. R. ed. Makers of the twentieth-century novel p192-207

Hough, G. G. Vision and doctrine in Four quartets. *In* Hough, G. G. Selected essays p173-99

Hutchens, E. N. An approach through time. *In* Spilka, M. ed. Towards a poetics of fiction p52-61

Jacobs, C. Benjamin: Walter Benjamin: Image of Proust. *In* Jacobs, C. The dissimulating harmony p87-110

Josipovici, G. 'But time will not relent': modern literature and the experience of time. *In* Josipovici, G. ed. The modern English novel: the reader, the writer and the work p252-72

Lively, P. Children and memory. *In* Horn Book Magazine. Crosscurrents of criticism p226-33

Marks, M. Renovation of form: time as hero in Blake's major prophecies. *In* Studies in eighteenth-century culture v5 p55-66

Miner, E. R. Time, sequence, and plot in Restoration literature. *In* Studies in eighteenth-century culture v5 p67-85

Nazareth, P. Time in the Third World: a fictional exploration. *In* Narasimhaiah, C. D. ed. Awakened conscience p195-205

Patten, R. L. Dickens time and again. *In* Dickens Studies Annual v2 p163-96

Philmus, R. M. Borges and Wells and the labyrinths of time. *In* H. G. Wells and modern science fiction p159-78

Roopnaraine, R. R. Time and the circle in Little Dorrit. *In* Dickens Studies Annual v3 p54-76

Schanzer, E. Shakespeare and the doctrine of the unity of time. *In* Shakespeare survey 28 p57-61

Sławińska, I. Two concepts of time in dramatic structure: Turgenev and Norwid. *In* For Wiktor Weintraub p479-92

Tobin, P. D. Introduction: whence the novel: the genealogical imperative. *In* Tobin, P. D. Time and the novel p3-28

Welty, E. Some notes on time in fiction. *In* Welty, E. The eye of the story p163-73

Zeller, N. A. The spiral of time in Ada. *In* A Book of things about Vladimir Nabokov p280-90

Time measurements. See Clocks and watches; Horology

The time of your life (criticism) Saroyan, W. *In* Kauffmann, S. Persons of the drama p111-14

Time perception

Brough, J. B. The emergence of an absolute consciousness in Husserl's early writings on time-consciousness. *In* Elliston, F. A. and McCormick, P. eds. Husserl p83-100

Carter, E. Music and the time screen. *In* Current thought in musicology p63-88

Ducasse, C. J. A theory of the relation of causality to precognition; excerpt from "Broad on the relevance of psychical research to philosophy." *In* Wheatley, J. M. O. and Edge, H. L. eds. Philosophical dimensions of parapsychology p227-34

Kafka, J. S. On reality: an examination of object constancy, ambiguity, paradox, and time. *In* Thought, consciousness, and reality p133-58

Whitrow, G. J. The role of time in cosmology. *In* Cosmology, history, and theology p159-77

Time recorders. See Time clocks

Timenes, Nicolai

Beyond the crisis: transitional, efficient, and ultimate resources. *In* Kalter, R. J. and Vogely, W. A. eds. Energy supply and government policy p326-45

Times Literary Supplement. See The Times, London. Literary Supplement

The Times, London. Literary Supplement

Balakian, N. Britain's lopsided view. *In* Balakian, N. Critical encounters p210-14

Hamburger, M. On anonymity. *In* Hamburger, M. Art as second nature p34-37

Timothy, Helen Pyne

Claude McKay: individualism and group consciousness. *In* King, B. A. and Ogung-besan, K. eds. A celebration of Black and African writing p15-29

Timpanaro-Cardini, Maria

Two questions of Greek geometrical terminology. *In* Kephalaion p183-88

Timucua Indians

History—Colonial period, ca. 1600-1775

Covington, J. W. Relations between the eastern Timucuan Indians and the French and Spanish, 1564-1567. *In* Hudson, C. M. ed. Four centuries of Southern Indians p11-27

Tin. See Pewter

Tinbergen, Jan

Changing factor shares and the translog production function. *In* Theory for economic efficiency: essays in honor of Abba P. Lerner p195-216

See also Part 2 under title: Econometrics and economic theory

About

Hansen, B. Introduction. *In* Economic development and planning p ix-xxiv

Tinbergen, Niko. See Tinbergen, Nikolaas

Tinbergen, Nikolaas

About individual works

Curious naturalists

Connolly, C. Mistaking the landmarks. *In* Connolly, C. The evening colonnade p408-11

Tindall, George Brown

The cost of segregation. *In* The Age of segregation: race relations in the South, 1890-1945 p117-32

Onward and upward with the rising South. *In* The Rising South v 1 p10-24

Tindall, William York. See part 2 under title: Yeats, Joyce, and Beckett

Ting, Ling, pseud. See Chiang, Ping-chi

Tinker, Chauncey Brewster

About

Wilder, T. N. Chauncey Brewster Tinker, 1876-1963. *In* Wilder, T. N. American characteristics, and other essays p245-48

Tinker, Hugh

Arthur Phayre in Mauritius, 1874-1878: social policy and economic reality. *In* Southeast Asian history and historiography p59-85

Indira Gandhi. *In* The Year book of world affairs, 1979 p102-25

Tinker, Michael

Theme in Timon of Athens. *In* Shakespeare's late plays p76-88

Tinne languages

Krauss, M. E. Na-Dene. *In* Sebeok, T. A. ed. Native languages of the Americas v 1 p283-358

Tintner, Gerhard; Kadekodi, Gopal, and Rama Sastry, Manikonda V.

A macro model of the economy for the explanation of trend and business cycle with applications to India. *In* Econometrics and economic theory p139-46

Tipton, Steven M.

New religious movements and the problems of a modern ethic. *In* Johnson, H. M. ed. Religious change and continuity p286-312

Tischler, Nancy M.

Artist, artifact, and audience: the aesthetics and practice of Dorothy L. Sayers. *In* Hannay, M. P. ed. As her whimsey took her p153-64

A gallery of witches. *In* Tennessee Williams: a tribute p494-509

Tissue culture

Harvey, A. M. Johns Hopkins—the birthplace of tissue culture: the story of Ross G. Harrison, Warren H. Lewis, and George O. Gey. *In* Harvey, A. M. Adventures in medical research p114-23

Tissues. See Tissue culture

Tithes

France

Le Roy Ladurie, E. Tithes and net agricultural output (fifteenth to eighteenth century) *In* Le Roy Ladurie, E. The territory of the historian p193-202

Titian

About

Barolsky, P. Laughter from the Venetian boudoir. *In* Barolsky, P. Infinite jest: wit and humor in Italian Renaissance art p158-82

About individual works

Danaë

Watson, P. F. Titian and Michelangelo: the Danae of 1545-1546. *In* Collaboration in Italian Renaisasnce art p245-50

Titow, J. Z.

Medieval England and the open-field system. *In* Peasants, knights and heretics p33-50

About individual works

Medieval England and the open-field system

Thirsk, J. The origin of the common fields. *In* Peasants, knights and heretics p51-56

Tittle, Charles R.

Labelling and crime: an empirical evaluation. *In* Gove, W. R. ed. The labelling of deviance p157-79

Titus, Edward J.

About

Ford, H. D. Edward Titus at the Sign of the Black Manikin. *In* Ford, H. D. Published in Paris p117-67

Tiv. See Tivi (African people)

Tivi (African people)

Bohannan, P. Tivi divination. *In* Studies in social anthropology p149-66

Cohen, R. The pull of opposites: incorporation and autonomy in Nigeria. *In* African themes p149-73

Tiwi. See Tivi (African people)

Tixier, Elaine

Imagination baptized, or "Holiness" in the chronicles of Narnia. *In* Schakel, P. J. ed. The longing for a form p136-58

Tixier, Jean, Seigneur de Ravisy

About

Ong, W. J. Commonplace rhapsody: Ravisius Textor, Zwinger and Shakespeare. *In* Classical influences on European culture A.D. 1500-1700 p91-126

Same as: Ong, W. J. Typographic rhapsody: Ravisius Textor, Zwinger, and Shakespeare. *In* Ong, W. J. Interfaces of the word p147-88

Tixier, Jean, Seigneur de Ravisy—*Continued*
About individual works
Epithets
McFarlane, I. D. Reflections on Ravisius Textor's Specimen epithetorum. *In* Classical influences on European culture A.D. 1500-1700 p81-90

Tizard, Barbara
The environment and intellectual functions. *In* Racial variation in man p109-20

Tizard, Jack
Nursery needs and choices. *In* Human growth and development p139-67

Tiziano, Vecelli. See Titian

Tjalsma, H. W.
The Petersburg poets. *In* Gibian, G. and Tjalsma, H. W. eds. Russian modernism p65-84

Tjarks, Alicia Vidaurreta de
Comparative demographic analysis of Texas, 1777-1793. *In* Weber, D. J. ed. New Spain's far northern frontier p135-69

Tlumak, Jeffrey
Certainty and Cartesian method. *In* Hooker, M. ed. Descartes p40-73

To catch a thief (Motion picture)
Truffaut, F. Alfred Hitchcock: To catch a thief. *In* Truffaut, F. The films in my life p80-82

To have and have not (Motion picture)
Rothman, W. To have and have not adapted a novel. *In* Peary, G. and Shatzkin, R. eds. The modern American novel and the movies p70-79
Wood, R. To have (written) and have not (directed) *In* Nichols, B. ed. Movies and methods p297-305

Tobacco
Cooperative marketing
Grantham, D. W. Black Patch War: the Kentucky and Tennessee night riders, 1905-1909. *In* Grantham, D. W. The regional imagination p65-75

Marketing
See Tobacco—Cooperative marketing
Tobacco manufacture and trade. See Tobacco —Cooperative marketing

Tobacco Road (Motion picture)
Gomery, D. Three roads taken: the novel, the play, and the film. *In* Peary, G. and Shatzkin, R. eds. The modern American novel and the movies p9-18

Tobey, Alan
The Summer Solstice of the Healthy-Happy-Holy Organization. *In* The New religious consciousness p5-30

Tobin, James
Deficit spending and crowding out in shorter and longer runs. *In* Theory for economic efficiency: essays in honor of Abba P. Lerner p217-36

Tobin, John Joseph Michael
Apuleius and the Bradleian tragedies. *In* Shakespeare survey v31 p33-43

Tobin, Patricia Drechsel
Time and the novel
Contents
"A colored spiral in a ball of glass": Vladimir Nabokov, Ada, or Ardor: a family chronicle
Conclusion: whither the novel: the wager on surface

The cycle dance: D. H. Lawrence, The rainbow
"Everything is known": Gabriel García Márquez, One hundred years of solitude
"Links in a chain": Thomas Mann, Buddenbrooks
"The shadowy attenuation of time": William Faulkner, Absalom, Absalom!
Subverting the father: some nineteenth-century precursors

Toby, Jackson
Delinquency in cross-cultural perspective. *In* Empey, L. T. ed. Juvenile justice p105-49

Toch, Rudolf
Management of parental anticipatory grief. *In* Anticipatory grief p161-63

Tocqueville, Alexis Charles Henri Maurice Clérel de
About individual works
Democracy in America
Higonnet, P. L. R. Alexis de Tocqueville. *In* Abroad in America: Visitors to the new Nation, 1776-1914 p52-61
Sennett, R. What Tocqueville feared. *In* On the making of Americans p105-25

Todaro, Michael P.
Rural-urban migration, unemployment and job probabilities: recent theoretical and empirical research. *In* Economic factors in population growth p367-85

Todd, Robert B.
Monism and immanence: the foundations of Stoic physics. *In* Rist, J. M. ed. The Stoics p137-60

Todd, William Burton
The diversions of an ardent bibliophile. *In* Review, v 1 1979 p329-32

Todes, Daniel P.
V. O. Kovalevskii: the genesis, content, and reception of his paleontological work. *In* Studies in history of biology v2 p99-165

Todini, Michele
About
Winternitz, E. The golden harpsichord and Todini's Galleria Armonica. *In* Winternitz, E. Musical instruments and their symbolism in Western art p110-15

Todorov, Tzvetan
About
Miller, O. J. Reading as a process of reconstruction: a critique of recent structuralist formulations. *In* Valdés, M. J. and Miller, O. J. eds. Interpretations of narrative p19-27
Scholes, R. E. The contributions of formalism and structuralism to the theory of fiction. *In* Spilka, M. ed. Towards a poetics of fiction p107-24

About individual works
Grammaire du Décaméron
Rutherford, J. Story, character, setting, and narrative mode in Galdós's El amigo Manso. *In* Fowler, R. ed. Style and structure in literature p177-212

Todorovich, Miro
Multilevel teaching of the natural sciences. *In* Hook, S.; Kurtz, P. W. and Todorovich, M. eds. The philosophy of the curriculum: the need for general education p137-42
Wanted: a rational decision procedure for value conflicts in science. *In* Hook, S.; Kurtz, P. and Todorovich, M. eds. The ethics of teaching and scientific research p191-201

Todorovich, Miro—*Continued*

Would a reorganized Federal Department of Education mean better higher education? *In* Hook, S.; Kurtz, P. W. and Todorovich, M. eds. The university and the state: what role for government in higher education? p265-75

Todorovich, Miro, and Glickstein, Howard Alan

Discrimination in higher education: a debate on faculty employment. *In* Gross, B. R. ed. Reverse discrimination p12-40

Todorovich, Miroslav M. See Todorovich, Miro

Toelken, Barre. See Toelken, John Barre

Toelken, John Barre

Northwest regional folklore. *In* Bingham, E. R. and Love, G. A. eds. Northwest perspectives p20-42

The "pretty languages" of Yellowman: genre, mode, and texture in Navaho coyote narratives. *In* Folklore genres p145-70

Seeing with a native eye: how many sheep will it hold? *In* Seeing with a native eye p9-24

Toffler, Alvin

Science fiction and change. *In* Nicholls, P. ed. Science fiction at large p115-18

Togeby, Knud

The nature of the fabliaux. *In* Cooke, T. D. and Honeycutt, B. L. eds. The humor of the fabliaux p7-13

Toit, André du. See Du Toit, André

Tokyo

Bombardment, 1945

Daniels, G. The great Tokyo Air Raid, 9-10 March 1945. *In* Modern Japan p113-34

Tokyo story (Motion picture)

Kauffmann, S. Tokyo story. *In* Kauffmann, S. Living images p100-03

Tolerance, Religious. See Religious tolerance

Toleration. See Liberty of conscience; Religious tolerance

Toliver, Harold E.

Marvell's songs and pictorial exhibits. *In* Friedenreich, K. ed. Tercentenary essays in honor of Andrew Marvell p105-20

Tolkien, John Ronald Revel

About individual works

The Lord of the Rings

Kirk, E. D. "I would rather have written in Elvish": language, fiction and The Lord of the Rings. *In* Spilka, M. ed. Towards a poetics of fiction p289-302

Manlove, C. N. J. R. R. Tolkien (1892-1972) and The Lord of the Rings. *In* Manlove, C. N. Modern fantasy p152-206

Reckford, K. J. Some trees in Virgil and Tolkien. *In* Perspectives of Roman poetry p57-91

Toll roads

New York (State)

Winslow, D. J. Tollgate lore from upstate New York. *In* Yoder, D. ed. American folklife p209-38

Tollett, Kenneth S.

What is all the shouting about? *In* Hook, S.; Kurtz, P. W. and Todorovich, M. eds. The university and the state: what role for government in higher education? p77-85

Tolley, George S.

Higher education and the professions. *In* Niblett, W. R. ed. The sciences, the humanities and the technological threat p65-76

Tolson, Melvin Beaunorus

About individual works

Harlem gallery

Lieberman, L. M. B. Tolson and A. R. Ammons: book-length poems. *In* Lieberman, L. Unassigned frequencies p252-56

Tolstoĭ, Aleksei Nikolaevich, Graf

About individual works

Road to Calvary

Mathewson, R. W. Four novels. *In* Mathewson, R. W. The positive hero in Russian literature p233-53

Tolstoĭ, Leo. See Tolstoĭ, Lev Nikolaevich, Graf

Tolstoĭ, Lev Nikolaevich, Graf

About

Andreev, G. The Christianity of L. N. Tolstoy and of the contributors to "From under the rubble." *In* Medvedev, R. A. ed. The Samizdat register p267-314

Arnold, M. Count Leo Tolstoi. *In* Arnold, M. The last word p282-304

Berlin, Sir I. The hedgehog and the fox. *In* Berlin, Sir I. Russian thinkers p22-81

Calder, A. Literature and morality: Leskov, Chekhov, late Tolstoy. *In* Calder, A. Russia discovered p238-75

Calder, A. Man, woman and male woman: Tolstoy's Anna and after. *In* Calder, A. Russia discovered p211-36

Calder, A. Tolstoy to War and peace: man against history. *In* Calder, A. Russia discovered p138-70

Canetti, E. Tolstoy: the final ancestor. *In* Canetti, E. The conscience of words p177-83

Eikhenbaum, B. M. On Tolstoy's crises. *In* Erlich, V. ed. Twentieth-century Russian literary criticism p97-101

Freeborn, R. Tolstoy. *In* Freeborn, R. ed. Russian literary attitudes from Pushkin to Solzhenitsyn p60-78

Landau, M. A. The enigma of Tolstoy. *In* Erlich, V. ed. Twentieth-century Russian literary criticism p201-11

Malia, M. E. Adulthood refracted: Russia and Leo Tolstoi. *In* Erikson, E. H. ed. Adulthood p173-87

Mudford, P. The case of Tolstoy. *In* Mudford, P. The art of celebration p34-43

Mudrick, M. Father knows best. *In* Mudrick, M. Books are not life but then what is? p98-117

Pritchett, V. S. Leo Tolstoy: the despot. *In* Pritchett, V. S. The myth makers p50-56

Rahv, P. Tolstoy: the green twig and the black trunk. *In* Rahv, P. Essays on literature and politics, 1932-1972 p208-21

Raleigh, J. H. Tolstoy and the ways of history. *In* Spilka, M. ed. Towards a poetics of fiction p211-24

Rowe, W. W. Some fateful patterns in Tolstoi. *In* Rowe, W. W. Nabokov & others: patterns in Russian literature p47-59

Shklovskiĭ, V. B. Parallels in Tolstoy. *In* Erlich, V. ed. Twentieth-century Russian literary criticism p81-85

Snow, C. P. Baron Snow. Tolstoy. *In* Snow, C. P. Baron Snow. The realists p178-216

Tomson, Edgar
The annexation of the Baltic States. *In* Hammond, T. T. ed. The anatomy of Communist takeovers p214-28

Tonelli, Giorgio
Kant's ethics as a part of metaphysics: a possible Newtonian suggestion? *In* Philosophy and the civilizing arts p236-63

Toner, Joseph Meredith

About

Bell, W. J. Joseph M. Toner (1825-1896) as a medical historian. *In* Bell, W. J. The colonial physician & other essays p169-92

Tonga arts. See Arts, Tonga

Tonica Indians. See Tunica Indians

Tonikan Indians. See Tunica Indians

Tonsfeldt, Ward
The Pacific Northwest: a selected and annotated bibliography. *In* Bingham, E. R. and Love, G. A. eds. Northwest perspectives p219-35

Tonsor, Stephen John
Eliseo Vivas: philosopher in spite of himself. *In* Viva Vivas! p251-72

What is the purpose of politics? *In* A Public philosophy reader p267-77

Toole, William Bell
The motif of psychic division in 'Richard III'. *In* Shakespeare survey 27 p21-32

Toombs, William
New colleges for new occupations. *In* Land-grant universities and their continuing challenge p266-85

Toomer, Jean

About

Bone, R. A. Jean Toomer. *In* Bone, R. A. Down home p204-38

Rankin, W. Ineffability in the fiction of Jean Toomer and Katherine Mansfield. *In* Renaissance and modern p160-71

About individual works
Cane

Bone, R. A. Jean Toomer. *In* Bone, R. A. Down home p204-38

Jackson, B. Jean Toomer's Cane; an issue of genre. *In* French, W. G. ed. The twenties p317-33

Also in Jackson, B. The waiting years p189-97

Fern

Jung, U. O. H. Jean Toomer, Fern. *In* Bruck, P. ed. The Black American short story in the 20th century p53-69

Toomer, Nathan Eugene. See Toomer, Jean

Topazio, Virgil W.
A reevaluation of Rousseau's political doctrine. *In* Literature and history in the age of ideas p179-92

Voltaire, "Lexicographer of the Enlightenment." *In* Studies in eighteenth-century culture v8 p311-21

Topic and comment (Grammar) See Grammar, Comparative and general—Topic and comment

Toplin, Robert Brent
Abolition and the issue of the Black freedman's future in Brazil. *In* Toplin, R. B. ed. Slavery and race relations in Latin America p253-76

Topsfield, L. T.
Troubadours and love

Contents

Arnaut Daniel
Bernart de Ventadorn
Guilhem de Montanhagol, Peire Cardenal and Guiraut Riquier
Guilhem IX of Aquitaine and the quest for joy
Jaufre Rudel and love from afar
Marcabrun and Fin'amors
Peire d'Alvernhe
Raimbaut d'Aurenga
Raimon de Miraval and the joy of the court

Torberg, Friedrich, pseud. See Kantor-Berg, Friedrich

Tordesillas, Treaty of, 1494
Batllori, M. The papal division of the world and its consequences. *In* First images of America p211-20

Torgovnik, Efraim
Israel: the persistent elite. *In* Political elites and political development in the Middle East p219-53

Tories, American. See American loyalists

Tories, English. See Conservative Party (Gt. Brit.)

Tormey, Alan
Art and expression: a critique; excerpt from "The concept of expression: a study in philosophical psychology and aesthetics." *In* Margolis, J. Z. ed. Philosophy looks at the arts p346-69

Tormey, Judith Farr
Exploitation, oppression and self-sacrifice. *In* Gould, C. C. and Wartofsky, M. W. eds. Women and philosophy p206-21

Torpie, Richard J.
The patient and prolonged terminal malignant disease: experiences from a radiation therapy center. *In* Anticipatory grief p119-23

Torquemada, Juan de, Cardinal

About

Izbicki, T. M. Infallibility and the erring pope: Guido Terreni and Johannes de Turrecremata. *In* Law, church, and society p97-111

Tierney, B. "Only the truth has authority": the problem of "reception" in the decretists and in Johannes de Turrecremata. *In* Law, church, and society p69-96

Torrance, Robert M.
The comic hero

Contents

Aberrant hidalgo
Afterword: in lieu of conclusion
Beggar man, king
Bondservant and beast of burden
Insouciant lover and insatiable stumblebums
Introduction: comic butt and comic hero
Jackanapes in the highest
Monarch of make-believe
Moral rake and masterful lackey
Renegade vassal
Ulysses and Hermes in modern times

Torrella, Guillem de
Bisson, T. N. Credit, prices and agrarian production in Catalonia: a Templar account. *In* Order and innovation in the Middle Ages p87-102

Torrey, Edwin Fuller
Spiritualists and shamans as psychotherapists: an account of original anthropological sin. *In* Zaretsky, I. I. and Leone, M. P. eds. Religious movements in contemporary America p330-37

Torts

United States

Hancock, M. Some choice-of-law problems posed by antiguest statutes: realism in Wisconsin and rule-fetishism in New York. *In* Stanford legal essays p251-65

Torvan, Traven. See Traven, B. pseud.

Totalitarian state. See Totalitarianism

Totalitarianism
Crick, B. R. On rereading The origins of totalitarianism. *In* Hannah Arendt: the recovery of the public world p27-47

Mihajlov, M. The shoots of hope. *In* Mihajlov, M. Underground notes p13-18

Supek, R. The visible hand and the degradation of individuality. *In* Beyond the crisis p49-80

Whitfield, S. J. "Totalitarianism" in eclipse: the recent fate of an idea. *In* Images and ideas in American culture p60-95

See also Collectivism; Communism; Fascism; National socialism

Psychology

Bettelheim, B. Remarks on the psychological appeal of totalitarianism. *In* Bettelheim, B. Surviving, and other essays p317-32

Des Pres, T. The heroism of survival. *In* Dunlop, J. B.; Haugh, R. and Klimoff, A. eds. Aleksandr Solzhenitsyn: critical essays and documentary materials 2d ed. p45-62

Totality (Philosophy) See Whole and parts (Philosophy)

Totemism
Girard, R. Violence and representation in the mythical text. *In* Girard, R. "To double business bound" p178-98

Ridington, W. R. and Ridington, T. The inner eye of shamanism and totemism. *In* Tedlock, D. E. and Tedlock, B. eds. Teachings from the American earth p190-204

Schwartz, T. Cultural totemism: ethnic identity primitive and modern. *In* Ethnic identity p106-31

Wicker, B. Metaphor and 'fiction.' *In* Wicker, B. The story-shaped world p33-49

See also Totems

Totems
Crocker, J. C. My brother the parrot. *In* The Social use of metaphor p164-92

Touch
Kennedy, J. M. and Fox, N. Pictures to see and pictures to touch. *In* Perkins, D. and Leondar, B. eds. The arts and cognition p118-35

The touch (Motion picture)
Kauffmann, S. The touch. *In* Kauffmann, S. Living images p64-65

A touch of class (Motion picture)
Kauffmann, S. A touch of class. *In* Kauffmann, S. Living images p201-02

Touch of evil (Motion picture)
Truffaut, F. Orson Welles: Touch of evil. *In* Truffaut, F. The films in my life p288-91

Toulmin, Stephen Edelston
Commentary [on Why did Copernicus' research program supersede Ptolemy's]? *In* The Copernican achievement p384-91

Introduction: The end of the Copernican era? *In* The Nature of scientific discovery p189-98

Self-knowledge and knowledge of the 'self.' *In* Mischel, T. ed. The self p291-317

The twin moralities of science. *In* Science and society: past, present, and future p111-24

See also Janik, A. jt. auth.

Toulouse

History

Mundy, J. H. The origins of the College of Saint-Raymond at the University of Toulouse. *In* Philosophy and humanism p454-61

Toulouse. Université

History

Mundy, J. H. The origins of the College of Saint-Raymond at the University of Toulouse. *In* Philosophy and humanism p454-61

La tour de Nesle (Motion picture)
Truffaut, F. La tour de Nesle. *In* Truffaut, F. The films in my life p33-35

Touraine, Alain
Crisis or transformation? *In* Beyond the crisis p17-45

Introduction. *In* Beyond the crisis p3-13

The raison d'etre of a sociology of action. *In* Giddens, A. ed. Positivism and sociology p115-27

Social identity and the formation of social movements. *In* Smithsonian Institution. The cultural drama p237-67

Towards a sociology of action. *In* Giddens, A. ed. Positivism and sociology p75-100

About individual works
Sociologie de l'action

Reynaud, J. D. and Bourdieu, P. Is a sociology of action possible? *In* Giddens, A. ed. Positivism and sociology p101-13

Touraine, A. The raison d'être of a sociology of action. *In* Giddens, A. ed. Positivism and sociology p115-27

Tourangeau, Roger. See Sternberg, R. J. jt. auth.

Tourism. See Tourist trade

Tourist trade

Mediterranean region

Gonen, A. Mediterranean tourism: some geographic perspectives. *In* Borgese, E. M. and Krieger, D. eds. The tides of change p179-96

Waikiki Beach, Hawaii

Whetmore, E. and Hibbard, D. J. Paradox in paradise: the icons of Waikiki. *In* Browne, R. B. and Fishwick, M. W. eds. Icons of America p241-52

Tourists. See Tourist trade

Tourneur, Cyril

About individual works
The atheist's tragedy

Champion, L. S. Tourneur: The revenger's tragedy, The atheist's tragedy. *In* Champion, L. S. Tragic patterns in Jacobean and Caroline drama p89-118

Tourneur, Cyril—About individual works—
The atheist's tragedy—*Continued*

Jackson, M. P. Compositorial practices in Tourneur's The atheist's tragedy. *In* Virginia. University. Bibliographical Society. Studies in bibliography v32 p210-15

Stilling, R. Cyril Tourneur. *In* Stilling, R. Love and death in Renaissance tragedy p197-223

The revenger's tragedy

Barish, J. A. The true and false families of The revenger's tragedy. *In* English Renaissance drama p142-54

Champion, L. S. Tourneur: The revenger's tragedy, The atheist's tragedy. *In* Champion, L. S. Tragic patterns in Jacobean and Caroline drama p89-118

Foakes, R. A. On Marston, The malcontent, and The revenger's tragedy. *In* The Elizabethan theatre, VI p59-75

Stilling, R. Cyril Tourneur. *In* Stilling, R. Love and death in Renaissance tragedy p197-223

Wells, S. W. The revenger's tragedy revived. *In* The Elizabethan theatre, VI p105-33

Bibliography

Forker, C. R. Cyril Tourneur. *In* Logan, T. P. and Smith, D. S. eds. The new intellectuals p248-80

Characters—Vendice

Foakes, R. A. The art of cruelty: Hamlet and Vindice. *In* Shakespeare survey 26 p21-31

Criticism, Textual

Jackson, M. P. Compositorial practices in Tourneur's The atheist's tragedy. *In* Virginia. University. Bibliographical Society. Studies in bibliography v32 p210-15

Dramatic production
See Tourneur, Cyril—Stage history

Stage history

Wells, S. W. The revenger's tragedy revived. *In* The Elizabethan theatre, VI p105-33

Tout va bien (Motion picture)
Kauffmann, S. Tout va bien. *In* Kauffmann, S. Living images p179-81

Toutain, Jean Claude

About individual works
Le produit de l'agriculture française de 1700 à 1958

Le Roy Ladurie, E. The chief defects of Gregory King. *In* Le Roy Ladurie, E. The territory of the historian p173-91

Towers, Tom H.
Love and power in Huckleberry Finn. *In* Tulane Studies in English v23 p17-37

Town and gown. See Community and college

Town life. See City and town life

Town-meeting. See Local government

Town planning. See City planning

Towneley plays
Coletti, T. Theology and politics in the Towneley Play of the talents. *In* Medievalia et humanistica; new ser. no. 9 p111-26

Martin, J. S. History and paradigm in the Towneley cycle. *In* Medievalia et humanistica no. 8 p125-45

See also Second shepherds' play (Towneley ms.)

Towns. See Cities and towns

Townsend, James Tarlton
The mind-body equation revisited. *In* Philosophical aspects of the mind-body problem p200-18

Townsend, John Rowe
An elusive border. *In* Horn Book Magazine. Crosscurrents of criticism p41-50

In literary terms. *In* Horn Book Magazine. Crosscurrents of criticism p65-71

A second look: "The mouse and his child." *In* Horn Book Magazine. Crosscurrents of criticism p330-32

Writing a book: Goodnight, Prof, love. *In* Blishen, E. ed. The thorny paradise p146-57

About individual works
Goodnight, Prof, love

Townsend, J. R. Writing a book: Goodnight, Prof, love. *In* Blishen, E. ed. The Thorny paradise p146-57

Toy and movable books
Opie, I. A. and Opie, P. Books that come to life. *In* The Saturday book 34 p61-79

Toynbee, Arnold Joseph
Bookselling, a way to international understanding. *In* Bookselling in America and the world p184-86

Man's concern with life after death. *In* Life after death p3-36

About individual works
Cities on the move

Sale, R. H. Toynbee, Ellul, Safdie, Negroponte. *In* Sale, R. H. On not being good enough p188-202

A study of history, v 1-4 (abridged by D.C. Somervell)

Frye, N. The shapes of history. *In* Frye, N. Northrop Frye on culture and literature p76-83

Tozzi, Federigo
About

Pacifici, S. Federigo Tozzi: the novel reborn. *In* Pacifici, S. The modern Italian novel: from Capuana to Tozzi p136-64

Trace
May, J. B. On Trace. *In* Anderson, E. and Kinzie, M. eds. The little magazine in America: a modern documentary history p376-87

Trachtenberg, Stanley
Berger and Barth: the comedy of decomposition. *In* Cohen, S. B. ed. Comic relief p45-69

Tractarianism. See Oxford movement

Tracy, Stephen Victor
Prometheus bound 114-117. *In* Harvard Studies in classical philology v75 p59-62

Tracy, Theodore James
Perfect friendship in Aristotle's Nicomachean Ethics. *In* Illinois classical studies v4, 1979 p65-75

Plato, Galen, and the center of consciousness. *In* Illinois classical studies, v 1 1976 p43-52

Trade. See Commerce

Trade, Restraint of. See Restraint of trade

Trade and professional associations. See Trade-unions

Trade barriers. See Commercial policy

Trade regulation
See also Patent laws and legislation; Restraint of trade; Trusts, Industrial—Law

United States
Weidenbaum, M. L. Government and the citizen. *In* Prochnow, H. V. ed. Dilemmas facing the nation p222-37

Trade routes
Quiggin, A. H. Trade routes, trade and currency in East Africa. *In* The Occasional papers of the Rhodes-Livingstone Museum p145-65

Trade-unions
Meany, G. Challenges to the labor movement. *In* Prochnow, H. V. ed. Dilemmas facing the nation p166-78

Agricultural laborers—United States
Modell, J. Class or ethnic solidarity: the Japanese American company union. *In* The Asian American: the historical experience p67-80

Automobile industry workers —United States
Bluestone, I. Work humanization in practice: what can labor do? *In* Heisler, W. J. and Houck, J. W. eds. A matter of dignity p165-78

Europe
Joseph, M. S. Trade unions in Western European politics. *In* Hayward, J. E. S. and Berki, R. N. eds. State and society in contemporary Europe p75-91

France—History
Baker, A. S. Fernand Pelloutier and the making of revolutionary syndicalism. *In* Essays on modern European revolutionary history p39-68

Great Britain
Dorfman, G. A. The Heath years: some further thoughts about the union influence. *In* Kramnick, I. ed. Is Britain dying? p55-65

Worsthorne, P. The trade unions: new lads on top. *In* Tyrrell, R. E. ed. The future that doesn't work p5-21

Southern States
Weeks, B. The union contribution. *In* The Rising South v 1 p25-34

United States
Dawidowicz, L. S. The Jewishness of the American Jewish labor movement. *In* Dawidowicz, L. S. The Jewish presence p116-30

Dunlop, J. T. Past and future tendencies in American labor organizations. *In* A New America? p79-96

Tradition (Literature). See Influence (Literary, artistic, etc.)

Tradition, Oral. See Oral tradition

Traditions. See Legends; Superstition

Traffic police
Cressey, D. R. Law, order and the motorist. *In* Crime, criminology and public policy p213-34

Traffic regulations
Cressey, D. R. Law, order and the motorist. *In* Crime, criminology and public policy p213-34

Tragedy
Anton, J. P. Tragic vision and philosophic theoria in classical Greece. *In* Philosophy and the civilizing arts p 1-23

Brashear, W. R. The power of negative thinking. *In* Brashear, W. R. The gorgon's head p 1-14

Butler, C. Tragedy and moral education. *In* Contemporary approaches to English studies p77-93

Cunningham, J. V. The Donatan tradition. *In* Cunningham, J. V. The collected essays of J. V. Cunningham p30-52

Cunningham, J. V. Tragedy as essence. *In* Cunningham, J. V. The collected essays of J. V. Cunningham p128-29

Cunningham, J. V. Wonder. *In* Cunningham, J. V. The collected essays of J. V. Cunningham p53-96

Hester, M. The structure of tragedy and the art of painting. *In* O'Flaherty, J. C.; Sellner, T. F. and Helm, R. M. eds. Studies in Nietzsche and the classical tradition p71-88

Kaufmann, W. A. Nietzsche and the death of tragedy: a critique. *In* O'Flaherty, J. C.; Sellner, T. F. and Helm, R. M. eds. Studies in Nietzsche and the classical tradition p234-54

Lacoue-Labarthe, P. The caesura of the speculative. *In* Glyph 4 p57-84

Lenson, D. R. Afterword. *In* Lenson, D. R. Achilles' choice p159-71

Lenson, D. R. Paradoxes of tragedy. *In* Lenson, D. R. Achilles' choice p3-23

Miller, A. The nature of tragedy. *In* Miller, A. The theater essays of Arthur Miller p 8-11

Miller, A. Tragedy and the common man. *In* Miller, A. The theater essays of Arthur Miller p3-7

Nicoll, A. Tragedy and opera. *In* Nicoll, A. World drama p294-306

See also Catharsis; Greek drama (Tragedy); Tragicomedy

History and criticism
Motto, A. L. and Clark, J. R. Senecan tragedy: a critique of scholarly trends. *In* Renaissance drama [1973] p219-35

Schwarz, A. The emerging poetic of modern realism and naturalism. *In* Schwarz, A. From Büchner to Beckett p3-40

Schwarz, A. Tragedy in the theater of realism. *In* Schwarz, A. From Büchner to Beckett p41-57

Therapeutic use
Simon, B. Tragedy and therapy. *In* Simon, B. Mind and madness in ancient Greece p122-54

Trager, George Leonard
Think metric. *In* On language, culture, and religion: in honor of Eugene A. Nida p373-80

Tragic, The
Albrecht, W. P. Addison. *In* Albrecht, W. P. The sublime pleasures of tragedy p25-38

Albrecht, W. P. Alison. *In* Albrecht, W. P. The sublime pleasures of tragedy p69-82

Albrecht, W. P. Burke. *In* Albrecht, W. P. The sublime pleasures of tragedy p39-51

Albrecht, W. P. Dennis. *In* Albrecht, W. P. The sublime pleasures of tragedy p13-24

Transition (Paris, 1927-1938)

Lewis, W. The Transition writers; excerpt from "The diabolical principle." *In* Lewis, W. Enemy salvoes p217-25

McMillan, D. Dadaism. *In* McMillan, D. Transition p102-09

McMillan, D. Dylan Thomas. *In* McMillan, D. Transition p157-66

McMillan, D. Expressionism. *In* McMillan, D. Transition p90-101

McMillan, D. Gertrude Stein. *In* McMillan, D. Transition p167-78

McMillan, D. Getting into print. *In* McMillan, D. Transition p9-26

McMillan, D. Hart Crane. *In* McMillan, D. Transition p125-47

McMillan, D. Revolution and synthesis: the growth of a theory. *In* McMillan, D. Transition p40-61

McMillan, D. Samuel Beckett. *In* McMillan, D. Transition p148-56

McMillan, D. Subversion and quest: the first year. *In* McMillan, D. Transition p27-39

McMillan, D. Surrealism. *In* McMillan, D. Transition p79-89

McMillan, D. Transition in the Wake: friend and the enemy. *In* McMillan, D. Transition p204-31

McMillan, D. Transition's revolutionaries. *In* McMillan, D. Transition p113-24

McMillan, D. Verticalism. *In* McMillan, D. Transition p62-75

McMillan, D. 'Work in progress' in Transition. *In* McMillan, D. Transition p179-203

Transjordan. See Jordan

Transkei National Independence Party

Stultz, N. M. The separatist challenge to white domination in South Africa. *In* African dimensions p95-112

Translating and interpreting

Brower, R. A. Introduction: Translation as parody. *In* Brower, R. A. Mirror on mirror p 1-16

Fenton, E. Blind idiot: the problems of translation. *In* Horn Book Magazine. Crosscurrents of criticism p290-305

Lawendowski, B. P. On semiotic aspect of translations. *In* Sebeok, T. A. ed. Sight, sound, and sense p264-82

Levý, J. The translation of verbal art. *In* Matejka, L. and Titunik, I. R. eds. Semiotics of art p218-28

Middleton, J. C. Paragraphs on translation. *In* Middleton, J. C. Bolshevism in art p123-50

Parkinson, G. H. R. The translation theory of understanding. *In* Royal Institute of Philosophy. Communication and understanding p 1-19

Pasternak, B. L. From Notes of a translator. *In* Proffer, C. R. ed. Modern Russian poets on poetry p96-101

Polushkin, M. A few words on translation. *In* Horn Book Magazine. Crosscurrents of criticism p283-86

Richards, I. A. Powers and limits of signs. *In* Richards, I. A. Poetries p17-38

Stewart, M. A. Locke, Steiner and understanding. *In* Royal Institute of Philosophy. Communication and understanding p20-45

Translating machines. See Machine translating

Translators. See Translating and interpreting

Transmigration

Coomaraswamy, A. K. On the one and only transmigrant. *In* Coomaraswamy, A. K. Selected papers v2 p66-87

See also Reincarnation

Transmisson of texts

Bowers, F. T. Transcription of manuscripts: the record of variants. *In* Virginia. University. Bibliographical Society. Studies in bibliography v29 p212-64

Lutz, C. E. Manuscripts copied from printed books. *In* Lutz, C. E. Essays on manuscripts and rare book p129-38

Newton, F. L. Some Monte Cassino scribes in the eleventh century. *In* Medieval and Renaissance studies [1975] p3-19

Sims-Williams, P. Cuthswith, seventh-century abbess of Inkberrow, near Worcester, and the Würzburg manuscript of Jerome on Ecclesiastes. *In* Anglo-Saxon England 5 p 1-21

Tanselle, G. T. The editorial problem of final authorial intention. *In* Virginia. University. Bibliographical Society. Studies in bibliography v29 p167-211

Wallach, L. The Greek and Latin versions of II Nicaea, 787, and the Synodica of Hadrian I (JE 2448). *In* Wallach, L. Diplomatic studies in Latin and Greek documents from the Carolingian age p3-26

See also Bibliography—Editions

Transmutation of metals. See Alchemy

Transplantation of organs, tissues, etc.

Moral and religious aspects

Fletcher, J. F. Wasting human bodies. *In* Fletcher, J. F. Humanhood: essays in biomedical ethics p65-78

May, W. F. Attitudes toward the newly dead. *In* Death inside out p139-49

Psychological aspects

Christopherson, L. K. and Gonda, T. A. Organ transplantation. *In* Anticipatory grief p107-14

Transportation

See also Railroad travel

Research—United States

Burch, F. W. Archives and the design of transportation research. *In* Pattern and process p215-23

France

Thoenig, J C. and Despicht, N. S. Transport policy. *In* Planning, politics and public policy p390-423

Great Britain

Thoenig, J. C. and Despicht, N. S. Transport policy. *In* Planning, politics and public policy p390-423

Italy

Thoenig, J. C. and Despicht, N. S. Transport policy. *In* Planning, politics and public policy p390-423

Transuranium elements

Seaborg, G. T. From Mendeleev to Mendelevium—and beyond. *In* Neyman, J. ed. The heritage of Copernicus: theories "pleasing to the mind" p267-96

Transvaal

Politics and government

Stultz, N. M. The separatist challenge to white domination in South Africa. *In* African dimensions p95-112

Transvaal War, 1899-1902. See South African War, 1899-1902

Transvaal War, 1899-1902 in literature. See South African War, 1899-1902 in literature

Transvestism

Anson, J. S. The female transvestite in early monasticism: the origin and development of a motif. *In* Viator: medieval and Renaissance studies v5 p 1-32

Davis, N. A. Z. Women on top: symbolic sexual inversion and political disorder in early modern Europe. *In* Babcock, B. A. ed. The reversible world p147-90

Peacock, J. L. Symbolic reversal and social history: transvestites and clowns of Java. *In* Babcock, B. A. ed. The reversible world p209-24

Transylvania

Relations (general) with Hungary

Király, B. K. The Sublime Porte, Vienna, Transylvania and the dissemination of Protestant Reformation in royal Hungary. *In* Király, B. K. ed. Tolerance and movements of religious dissent in Eastern Europe p199-221

Traoré, Soumana

An African experiment in grass roots development. *In* Erb, G. F. and Kallab, V. eds. Beyond dependency p111-19

Trapp, Joseph Burney

Education in the Renaissance. *In* Background to the English Renaissance p67-89

John Colet, his manuscripts and the ps.-Dionysius. *In* Classical influences on European culture A.D. 1500-1700 p205-21

Rhetoric and the Renaissance. *In* Background to the English Renaissance p90-108

Trapping. See Fur trade

Trash (Motion picture)

Kauffmann, S. Trash. *In* Kauffmann, S. Living images p23-24

Trask, David F.

The military-industrial complex. *In* Encyclopedia of American foreign policy p557-66

Trask, Roger R.

Missionary diplomacy. *In* Encyclopedia of American foreign policy p575-83

Trasler, Gordon

The role of psychologists in the penal system. *In* Progress in penal reform p129-41

Traugott, John

Clarissa's Richardson: an essay to find the reader. *In* English literature in the age of disguise p157-208

Travel. See Railroad travel

Travel, Medieval. See Christian pilgrims and pilgrimages

Travel in literature

Alcorn, J. Spirit of place: The travel book. *In* Alcorn, J. The nature novel from Hardy to Lawrence p42-59

Franklin, W. Speaking and touching: the problem of inexpressibility in American travel books. *In* Kagle, S. E. ed. America: exploration and travel p18-38

Metwalli, A. M. American abroad: the popular art of travel writing in the nineteenth century. *In* Kagle, S. E. ed. America: exploration and travel p68-82

Ponko, V. Science in the exploration narratives authored by U.S. naval officers. *In* Kagle, S. E. ed. America: exploration and travel p92-100

Spengemann, W. C. The poetics of adventure. *In* Spengemann, W. C. The adventurous muse p6-67

Travelers, English

Lyons, J. O. Travelers East. *In* Lyons, J. O. The invention of the self p121-55

Traven, B. pseud.

About individual works

The death ship

Melling, P. The death ship: B. Traven's cradle. *In* French, W. G. ed. The twenties p139-56

Olafson, R. B. B. Traven and The death ship as high culture. *In* Filler, L. ed. A question of quality: popularity and value in modern creative writing p160-71

The treasure of the Sierra Madre

Kaminsky, S. M. Gold hat, gold fever, silver screen. *In* Peary, G. and Shatzkin, R. eds. The modern American novel and the movies p53-62

Traver Tomas, Vincente

About individual works

Creativity in the arts

Glickman, J. Creativity in the arts. *In* Aagaard-Mogensen, L. ed. Culture and art p130-46

Also in Margolis, J. Z. Philosophy looks at the arts p145-68

Travesty. See Burlesque (Literature)

Traynor, Roger J.

About

White, G. E. Rationality and intuition in the process of judging: Roger Traynor. *In* White, G. E. The American judicial tradition p292-316

Trease, Geoffrey

The revolution in children's literature. *In* Blishen, E. ed. The thorny paradise p13-24

The treasure of Sierra Madre (Motion picture)

Kaminsky, S. M. Gold hat, gold fever, silver screen. *In* Peary, G. and Shatzkin, R. eds. The modern American novel and the movies p53-62

Treaties

Suganami, H. Why ought treaties to be kept? *In* The Year of world affairs, 1979 p243-56

See also Guaranty, Treaties of; Treaty-making power

Treaties of alliance. See Alliances

Treaties of guaranty. See Guaranty, Treaties of

Treatment and rehabilitation of narcotic addicts. See Narcotic addicts—Rehabilitation

Treaty-making power

United States

Corwin, E. S. Wilson and the Senate. *In* Corwin, E. S. Presidential power and the Constitution p28-31

Treaty on the non-proliferation of nuclear weapons

Morton, L. Who next? The spread of nuclear weapons. *In* Baldwin, D. A. ed. America in an interdependent world p29-60

Treaty power. See Treaty-making power

Trebilcock, Clive

War and the failure of industrial mobilisation: 1899 and 1914. *In* War and economic development p139-64

Trebilcot, Joyce
Two forms of androgynism. *In* Feminism and philosophy p70-78

Treblinka (Concentration camp)
Dawidowicz, L. S. An obedient killer: Franz Stangl, Commandant of Treblinka. *In* Dawidowicz, L. S. The Jewish presence p238-46

Tredway, M'Kean M. See Couloumbis, T. A. jt. auth.

Tree of knowledge. See Tree of life

Tree of life
Coomaraswamy, A. K. The inverted tree. *In* Coomaraswamy, A. K. Selected papers v 1 p376-404
Enstice, A. The fruit of the Tree of knowledge. *In* Smith, A. ed. The novels of Thomas Hardy p9-22

Tree worship. See Tree of life

Trees, Folk-lore of. See Folk-lore of trees

Trees in literature
Bowers, A. J. The Tree of Charity in Piers Plowman: its allegorical and structural significance. *In* Literary monographs v6 p 1-34
Crow, C. M. Valery and the image of the tree-top. *In* Cardinal, R. ed. Sensibility and creation p16-35
Reckford, K. J. Some trees in Virgil and Tolkien. *In* Perspectives of Roman poetry p57-91

Trees in poetry. See Trees in literature

Trejo, Arnulfo Duenes
As we see ourselves in Chicano literature. *In* Trejo, A. D. ed. The Chicanos p187-211
Of books and libraries. *In* Trejo, A. D. ed. The Chicanos p167-86

Trelawny, Edward John

About individual works

Adventures of a younger son

Reiman, D. H. Trelawny and decay of lying. *In* Review, v 1 1979 p275-94

Trench warfare. See Intrenchments

Trenn, Thaddeus J.
Rutherford and recoil atoms: the metamorphosis and success of a once stillborn theory. *In* Historical studies in the physical sciences v6 p513-47

Trethewey, Richard J.
International economics and politics: a theoretical framework. *In* The Interaction of economics and foreign policy p 1-24

Tret'iakov, Ivan Andreevich

About

Brown, A. H. Adam Smith's first Russian followers. *In* Skinner, A. S. and Wilson, T. eds. Essays on Adam Smith p247-73

Trevena, John, pseud. See Henham, Ernest George

Trevor-Roper, Hugh Redwald
Princes and artists
Contents
The Archdukes and Rubens
Charles V and the failure of humanism
Philip II and the anti-Reformation
Rudolf II in Prague

Trewin, John Courtenay
Brought up with Shakespeare. *In* Royal Society of Literature of the United Kingdom, London. Essays by divers hands v39 p163-80
A Midas gift to the theatre. *In* Agatha Christie: first lady of crime p131-54

About

Trewin, J. C. Brought up with Shakespeare. *In* Royal Society of Literature of the United Kingdom, London. Essays by divers hands v39 p163-80

Trexler, Richard C.
Measures against water pollution in fifteenth-century Florence. *In* Viator: medieval and Renaissance studies v5 p455-67

Trial by jury. See Jury

Trial by ordeal. See Ordeal

Trial by peers. See Jury

Trial practice. See Civil procedure; Evidence (Law); Jury

Triana, José

About

Dauster, F. N. The game of chance: the theater of José Triana. *In* Lyday, L. F. and Woodyard, G. W. eds. Dramatists in revolt p167-89

Tribal government
Otite, O. Encapsulated political systems. *In* Colonialism and change p67-84

Tribes and tribal system
Essien-Udom, E. U. Tribalism and racism. *In* United Nations Educational, Scientific and Cultural Organization. Race, science and society p234-61
Hamilton, W. D. Innate social aptitudes of man: an approach from evolutionary genetics. *In* Biosocial anthropology p133-55
See also Detribalization; Kinship; Society, Primitve; Totemism; Tribial government

Africa

Southall, A. W. From segmentary lineage to ethnic association—Luo, Luhya, Ibo, and others. *In* Colonialism and change p203-29

Iraq

Jwaideh, A. Tribalism and modern society: Iraq, a case study. *In* Savory, R. M. ed. Introduction to Islamic civilisation p160-67

Tribunals, International. See International courts

Trice, Harrison Miller, and Roman, Paul Michael
Delabeling, relabeling and Alcoholics Anonymous. *In* Davis, F. J. and Stivers, R. eds. The collective definition of deviance p360-75

Trickett, Rachel
Shakespeare and Milton. *In* English Association. Essays and studies, 1978 p23-35
Vitality of language in nineteenth-century fiction. *In* Josipovici, G. ed. The modern English novel: the reader, the writer and the work p37-53

Tricomi, Albert Henry
The aesthetics of mutilation in 'Titus Andronicus'. *In* Shakespeare survey 27 p11-19

Trident submarines. See Atomic submarines

Triffin, Robert
Basic considerations on international monetary reform. *In* Inflation, trade and taxes p119-36

Trigeminal nerve

Anatomy

Selby, G. Some aspects of the antomy of the trigeminal nerve: an example of changing concept since Elliot Smith's day. *In* Grafton Elliot Smith p58-63

Trilling, Diana

We must march my darlings
Contents

The assassination of President Kennedy
Celebrating with Dr Leary
Easy rider and its critics
Lawrence and the movements of modern culture
On the steps of Low Library
Our uncomplaining homosexuals
Portrait of a marriage
We must march my darlings: A return to the past
We must march my darlings: Daughters of the middle class
Women's liberation: Female biology in a male culture
Women's liberation: The prisoner of sex

Trilling, Lionel

The fate of pleasure: Wordsworth to Dostoevski; excerpt from "Beyond culture". *In* Wimsatt, W. K. ed. Literary criticism: idea and act p189-211

A gathering of fugitives
Contents

Adams at ease
Criticism and aesthetics
The Dickens of our day
Dr. Leavis and the moral tradition
Edmund Wilson: a backward glance
Freud's last book
The great-aunt of Mr. Forster
In defense of Zola
The morality of inertia
The novel alive or dead
A novel in passing
On not talking
Profession: man of the world
A ramble on Graves
The situation of the American intellectual at the present itme
"That smile of Parmenides made me think"
Two notes on David Riesman

The last decade
Contents

Aggression and utopia
Art, will, and necessity
The Freud/Jung letters
James Joyce in his Letters
Mind in the modern world
A novel of the thirties
The uncertain future of the humanistic educational ideal
What is criticism?
Whittaker Chambers' Journey
Why we read Jane Austen

A personal memoir. *In* From Parnassus p xv-xxii

Prefaces to Experience of literature
Contents

Albert Camus: The guest
Alexander Pope: an essay on man: Epistle I
Andrew Marvell: To his coy mistress
Anton Chekhov: Enemies
Anton Chekhov: The three sisters
Bernard Malamud: The magic barrel
Bertolt Brecht: Galileo

Coleridge, Samuel Taylor: Kubla Khan or a vision in a dream: a fragment
D. H. Lawrence: Tickets, please
E. E. Cummings: My father moved through dooms of love
E. M. Forster: The road from Colonus
Edward: Anonymous
Emily Dickinson: "Go tell it"—what a message—
Ernest Hemingway: Hills like white elephants
Fëdor Dostoevski: The Grand Inquisitor
Franz Kafka: The hunter Gracchus
George Bernard Shaw: The doctor's dilemma
George Gordon, Lord Byron: Don Juan: an episode from Canto II
Gerard Manley Hopkins: The Leaden Echo and the Golden Echo: Maidens' Song from St. Winefred's Well
Guy de Maupassant: Duchoux
Henrik Ibsen: The wild duck
Henry James: The pupil
Herman Melville: Bartleby the scrivener: a story of Wall Street
Isaac Babel: Di Grasso: A tale of Odessa
Isak Dinesen: The sailor-boy's tale
James Joyce: The dead
John Donne: A valediction: forbidding mourning
John Keats: Ode to a nightingale
John Milton: Lycidas
John O'Hara: Summer's day
Joseph Conrad: The secret sharer
Leo Tolstoi: The death of Ivan Ilych
Lionel Trilling: Of this time, of that place
Luigi Pirandello: Six characters in search of an author: a comedy in the making
Matthew Arnold: Dover Beach
Nathaniel Hawthorne: My kinsman, Major Molineux
Percy Bysshe Shelley: Ode to the West Wind
Robert Frost: Neither out far nor in deep
Robert Lowell: For the Union dead
Sir Thomas Wyatt: They flee from me
Sophocles: Oedipus Rex
Thomas Mann: Disorder and early sorrow
Thomas Stearns Eliot: The waste land
W. H. Auden: In memory of Sigmund Freud (d. Sept. 1939)
Walt Whitman: Out of the cradle endlessly rocking
William Blake: Tyger! Tyger!
William Butler Yeats: Purgatory
William Butler Yeats: Sailing to Byzantium
William Faulkner: Barn burning
William Shakespeare: The tragedy of King Lear
William Somerset Maugham: The treasure
William Wordsworth: Resolution and independence

The sense of the past; excerpt from "The liberal imagination." *In* Primeau, R. ed. Influx p22-33

About

Alter, R. Walter Benjamin: the aura of the past. *In* Alter, R. Defenses of the imagination p47-66

Hartman, G. H. Lionel Trilling as man in the middle. *In* Hartman, G. H. The fate of reading p294-302

Marcus, S. Lionel Trilling, 1905-1975. *In* Art, politics, and will p265-78

Sale, R. H. Lionel Trilling. *In* Sale, R. H. On not being good enough p148-57

Trilling, Lionel—*Continued*

About individual works

A gathering of fugitives

Balakian, N. Reviews by Trilling. *In* Balakian, N. Critical encounters p132-335

The middle of the journey

Anderson, Q. On The middle of the journey. *In* Art, politics, and will p254-64

Trilling, L. Whittaker Chambers' Journey. *In* Trilling, L. The last decade p185-203

Of this time, of that place

Trilling, L. Lionel Trilling: Of this time, of that place. *In* Trilling, L. Prefaces to The experience of literature p160-65

Sincerity and authenticity

Bayley, J. The authentic and the sincere. *In* Bayley, J. The uses of division p17-25

Howe, I. Lionel Trilling: Sincerity and authenticity. *In* Howe, I. Celebrations and attacks p213-20

Trimingham, John Spencer

The Arab geographers and the East African coast. *In* Chittick, H. N. and Rothberg, R. I. eds. East Africa and the Orient p115-46

Trinidad

Social conditions

Higman, B. W. African and Creole slave family patterns in Trinidad. *In* Crahan, M. E. and Knight, F. W. eds. Africa and the Caribbean p41-64

Trinity in literature

Clopper, L. M. Langland's Trinitarian analogies as key to meaning and structure. *In* Medievalia et humanistica p87-110

Trinkaus, Charles Edward

Protagoras in the Renaissance: an exploration. *In* Philosophy and humanism p190-213

Renaissance and discovery. *In* First images of America p3-9

Tripathi, C. B.

Swami Vivekananda. *In* Abroad in America: Visitors to the new Nation, 1776-1914 p238-46

Tripp, Susan Moore Ervin- See Ervin-Tripp, Susan Moore

Tristan

Jaffe, S. P. Rhetoric in German literature: Gottfried von Strassburg and the rhetoric of history. *In* Murphy, J. J. ed. Medieval eloquence p288-318

Leviant, C. Jewish influence upon Arthurian legends. *In* Salo Wittmayer Baron v2 p639-56

Mahoney, D. B. Malory's "Tale of Sir Tristram": source and setting reconsidered. *In* Medievalia et humanistica; new ser. no. 9 p175-98

Thorpe, L. Dorothy L. Sayers as a translator of Le roman de Tristan and La chanson de Roland. *In* Hannay, M. P. ed. As her whimsey took her p109-22

York, E. C. Isolt's trial in Béroul and La Folie Tristan d'Oxford. *In* Medievalia et humanistica no. 6 p157-61

Tristana (Motion picture)

Kauffmann, S. Tristana. *In* Kauffmann, S. Living images p17-19

Tristram, Philippa

"Divided sources." *In* Smith, A. ed. The art of Emily Brontë p182-204

Eros and death (Lawrence, Freud and women). *In* Smith, A. ed. Lawrence and women p136-55

Stories in stones. *In* Smith, A. ed. The novels of Thomas Hardy p145-68

Triumph of the will (Motion picture)

Taylor, R. Triumph of the will. *In* Taylor, R. Film propaganda p177-89

Troell, Jan

About individual works

The emigrants

Kauffmann, S. The emigrants. *In* Kauffmann, S. Living images p137-40

Samuels, C. T. Tampering with reality. *In* Samuels, C. T. Mastering the film, and other essays p198-210

The new land

Kauffmann, S. The new land. *In* Kauffmann, S. Living images p222-26

Troen, Selwyn K.

The discovery of the adolescent by American educational reformers, 1900-1920: an economic perspective. *In* Schooling and society p239-51

Trojans

Mitchell, R. E. Roman coins as historical evidence: the Trojan legends of Rome. *In* Illinois classical studies, v 1 1976 p65-85

Troland, Leonard Thompson

About

Ravin, A. W. The gene as catalyst; the gene as organism. *In* Studies in history of biology, v 1 p 1-45

Trollope, Anthony

About

ApRoberts, R. Carlyle and Trollope. *In* Carlyle and his contemporaries p205-26

Auchincloss, L. The clergy of Barchester. *In* Auchincloss, L. Life, law and letters p151-65

Galbraith, J. K. Anthony Trollope. *In* Galbraith, J. K. Annals of an abiding liberal p279-84

Lewis, W. Russian novelists and Trollope; excerpt from "'Detachment' and the fictionist." *In* Lewis, W. Enemy salvoes p84-87

Mudrick, M. Trollope. *In* Mudrick, M. The man in the machine p97-109

Stone, D. D. Trollope, Byron, and the conventionalities. *In* The Worlds of Victorian fiction p179-203

Sutherland, J. A. Trollope: making the first rank. *In* Sutherland. J. A. Victorian novelists and publishers p133-51

Tillotson, G. Trollope. *In* Tillotson, G. A view of Victorian literature p255-85

Tomlinson, T. B. Trollope's 'political' novels: Phineas Finn to The Duke's children. *In* Tomlinson, T. B. The English middle-class novel p83-101

About individual works

He knew he was right

ApRoberts, R. Emily and Nora and Dorothy and Priscilla and Jemima and Carry. *In* Levine, R. A. The Victorian experience: the novelists p87-120

Is he Popenjoy?

Pascal, R. Victorians: The Thackeray-type narrator; Anthony Trollope—confusions of perspective. *In* Pascal, R. The dual voice p89-97

Trollope, Anthony—About individual works
—*Continued*

The way we live now

Cowen, Z. The way we live now. *In* Prospects for constitutional democracy p3-20

Trollope, Frances Milton

About individual works

Domestic manners of the Americans

Cunliffe, M. Frances Trollope. *In* Abroad in America: Visitors to the new Nation, 1776-1914 p32-42

Troop Support Command. See United States. Army. Troop Support Command

Tropes. See Figures of speech

Tropical medicine

Burchenal, J. H. The relevance of research in tropical medicine today. *In* Cahill, K. M. ed. Health and development p59-68

Gilles, H. M. The ecology of disease in the tropics. *In* Cahill, K. M. ed. Health and development p49-58

Lumsden, W. H. R. Impact of independence and nationalism on tropical medicine. *In* Cahill, K. M. ed. Health and development p23-35

Tropics

Diseases and hygiene

See Tropical medicine

Trotskiĭ, Lev

Majakovskij and Russian futurism. *In* Erlich, V. ed. Twentieth-century Russian literary criticism p169-81

About

McNeal, R. H. Trotskyist interpretations of Stalinism. *In* Stalinism p30-52

Parry, A. Trotsky: target of boomerang. *In* Parry, A. Terrorism: from Robespierre to Arafat p171-86

Rahv, P. The great outsider. *In* Rahv, P. Essays on literature and politics, 1932-1972 p335-40

Trotsky, Leon. See Trotskiĭ, Lev

Troubadours

Goldin, F. The array of perspectives in the early courtly love lyric. *In* In pursuit of perfection p51-100

Topsfield, L. T. Guilhem de Montanhagol, Peire Cardenal and Guiraut Riquer. *In* Topsfield, L. T. Troubadours and love p241-52

See also Courtly love

Trousset de Valincour, Jean Baptiste Henri du. See Valincour, Jean Baptiste Henri du Trousset de

Trouverès. See French poetry—To 1500

Trow, Martin

Aspects of diversity in American higher education. *In* On the making of Americans p271-90

Trowbridge, Frederick Hoyt
From Dryden to Jane Austen
Contents

Dryden on the Elizabethans
Edward Gibbon, literary critic
Joseph Warton on the imagination
Joseph Warton's classification of English poets
Mind, body, and estate: Jane Austen's system of values

Perception, imagination, and feeling in Dryden's criticism
The place of rules in Dryden's criticism
Platonism and Sir Joshua Reynolds
Pope, Gay, and The shepherd's week
Pope's Eloisa and the Heroides of Ovid
Richard Hurd's Letters on chivalry and romance
Scattered atoms of probability
Swift and Socrates
White of Selborne: the ethos of probabilism

Troy, William
M. *In* Denby, D. ed. Awake in the dark p105-07

Troy
Mitchell, R. E. Roman coins as historical evidence: the Trojan legends of Rome. *In* Illinois classical studies, v 1 1976 p65-85

Troy in art
Levenson, J. L. Shakespeare's Troilus and Cressida and the monumental tradition in tapestries and literature. *In* Renaissance drama [1976] p43-84

Troyat, Henri

About individual works

Tolstoy

Pritchett, V. S. Leo Tolstoy: the despot. *In* Pritchett, V. S. The myth makers p50-56

Troyes, Chretien de. See Chrestien de Troyes

Troyes, France

History

Benton, J. F. The accounts of Cepperello da Prato for the tax on nouveaux acquêts in the bailliage of Troyes. *In* Order and innovation in the Middle Ages p111-35

True, Michael, ed.

About individual works

Worcester poets, with notes toward a literary history

Kunitz, S. J. The Worcester poets. *In* Kunitz, S. J. A kind of order, a kind of folly p118-21

Truewoman, Honey
Realism in drag. *In* Battcock, G. ed. Super realism p223-29

Truex, Van Day
The environment for creating good design. *In* The Uneasy coalition: design in corporate America p81-89

Truffaut, François
A certain tendency of the French cinema. *In* Nichols, B. ed. Movies and methods p224-37

The films in my life
Contents

Abel Gance: Napoléon
Agnès Varda: La pointe courte
Albert Lamorisse: Le ballon rouge
Alexandre Astruc: Les mauvaises rencontres
Alfred Hitchcock: Rear window
Alfred Hitchcock: The wrong man
Alfred Hitchcock: To catch a thief
Billy Wilder: Stalag 17
Billy Wilder: The seven year itch
Buñuel the builder
Charlie Chaplin: A king in New York
Charlie Chaplin: The great dictator
Charlie Chaplin: Who is Charlie Chaplin?
Claude Berri: Le vieil homme et l'entant
Claude Sautet: Vincent, François, Paul et les autres

Truth—*Continued*

Foster, J. A. Meaning and truth theory. *In* Evans, G. L. and McDowell, J. H. eds. Truth and meaning p 1-32

Foster, J. A. Reply to Foster [on Meaning and truth theory]. *In* Evans, G. L. and McDowell, J. H. eds. Truth and meaning p33-41

Kripke, S. A. Is there a problem about substitutional quantification? *In* Evans, G. L. and McDowell, J. H. eds. Truth and meaning p324-419

Loar, B. Two theories of meaning. *In* Evans, G. L. and McDowell, J. H. eds. Truth and meaning p138-61

Loch, W. Some comments on the subject of psychoanalysis and truth. *In* Thought, consciousness, and reality p217-55

McDowell, J. H. Truth conditions, bivalence, and verificationism. *In* Evans, G. L. and McDowell, J. H. eds. Truth and meaning p42-66

Mark, T. C. Truth and adequacy in Spinozistic ideas. *In* Shahan, R. W. and Biro, J. I. eds. Spinoza: new perspectives p11-34

Mazzeo, J. A. The Platonic debate over myth, truth, and virtue. *In* Mazzeo, J. A. Varieties of interpretation p71-94

Parkinson, G. H. R. "Truth is its own standard": aspects of Spinoza's theory of truth. *In* Shahan, R. W. and Biro, J. I. eds. Spinoza: new perspectives p35-55

Peacocke, C. An appendix to David Wiggins' 'note.' *In* Evans, G. L. and McDowell, J. H. eds. Truth and meaning p313-24

Peacocke, C. Truth definitions and actual languages. *In* Evans, G. L. and McDowell, J. H. eds. Truth and meaning p162-88

Pietersma, H. Husserl's views on the evident and the true. *In* Elliston, F. A. and McCormick, P. eds. Husserl p38-53

Quine, W. V. Carnap and logical truth. *In* Quine, W. V. The ways of paradox, and other essays p107-32

Quine, W. V. Truth and disquotation. *In* Quine, W. V. The ways of paradox, and other essays p308-21

Quine, W. V. Truth by convention. *In* Quine, W. V. The ways of paradox, and other essays p77-106

Warnock, M. Nietzsche's conception of truth. *In* Pasley, J. M. S. ed. Nietzsche: imagery and thought p33-63

See also Certainty; Error; Knowledge, Theory of; Necessity (Philosophy); Reality; Truthfulness and falsehood

Truthfulness and falsehood

Rich, A. C. Women and honor: some notes on lying. *In* Rich, A. C. On lies, secrets, and silence p185-94

Truzzi, Marcello

Towards a sociology of the occult: notes on modern witchcraft. *In* Zaretsky, I. I. and Leone, M. P. eds. Religious movements in contemporary America p628-45

Tsadikim. See Zaddikim

Ts'ai, Shih-shan Henry

Chinese immigration through Communist Chinese eyes: an introduction to the historiography. *In* The Asian American: the historical experience p53-66

Ts'ao, Chan
About individual works
Dream of the red chamber

Kao, Yu-kung. Lyric vision in Chinese narrative tradition: a reading of Hung-lou meng and Ju-lin wai-shih. *In* Chinese narrative p227-43

Plaks, A. H. Allegory in Hsi-yu chi and Hung-lou meng. *In* Chinese narrative p163-202

Wang, J. Ching-yu. The Chih-yen-chai Commentary and the Dream of the red chamber: a literary study. *In* Chinese approaches to literature from Confucius to Liang Ch'i-ch'ao p189-220

Wong, Kam-ming. Point of view, norms, and structure: Hung-lou meng and lyrical fiction. *In* Chinese narrative p203-26

Tsattine Indians
Religion and mythology

Ridington, W. R. and Ridington, T. The inner eye of shamanism and totemism. *In* Tedlock, D. E. and Tedlock, B. eds. Teachings from the American earth p190-204

Tschaikowsky, Peter Ilyich. See Chaĭkovskiĭ, Petr Il'ich

Tschiżewskij, Dmitri. See Chyzhevs'kyĭ, Dmytro

Tse. See Tz'u

Tsipis, Kosta M.

Anti-submarine warfare and missile submarines. *In* The Dynamics of the arms race p36-46

The arms race as posturing. *In* The Dynamics of the arms race p78-81

New technologies and new weapons systems. *In* Arms control and technological innovation p36-51

Tsironis, Vassilios
About

Sundberg, J. W. F. Thinking the unthinkable or the case of Dr Tsironis. *In* International terrorism and political crimes p448-59

Tso chuan

Wang, John Ching-yu. Early Chinese narrative: the Tso-chuan as example. *In* Chinese narrative p3-20

Tsonga tribe. See Thonga tribe

Tsou, Tang

China and the world in the Mao and post-Mao eras. *In* Kaplan, M. A. ed. The many faces of communism p333-52

"Scientific man vs. power politics" revisited. *In* [Truth and tragedy]: a tribute to Hans Morgenthau p41-52

Tsubouchi, Shōyō
About

Yamanouchi, H. Two precursors: Tsubouchi Shōyō and Futabatei Shimei. *In* Yamanouchi, H. The search for authenticity in modern Japanese literature p6-19

Tsuda, Umeko
About

Shimada, N. and others. Ume Tsuda and Motoko Hani: echoes of American cultural feminism in Japan. *In* "Remember the ladies": new perspectives on women in American history p161-78

Ts'ui, Hao

About

Mather, R. B. K'ou Ch'ien-chih and the Taoist theocracy at the Northern Wei Court, 425-451. *In* Welch, H. and Seidel, A. K. eds. Facets of Taoism p103-22

Tsunoda, Jun

America's future role in the Northwest Pacific area. *In* Pacific Asia and U.S. policies: a political-economic-strategic assessment p58-62

Tsurumi, Kazuko

Student movements in 1960 and 1969: continuity and change. *In* Postwar trends in Japan p195-227

Tsurumi, Yoshi. See Tsurumi, Yoshihiro

Tsurumi, Yoshihiro

Japan. *In* Vernon, R. ed. The oil crisis p113-27

Tsuruta, Kinya

An interpretation of The ruined map by Kōbō Abe. *In* Postwar trends in Japan p169-93

Tsushima, Shūji. See Dazai, Osamu, pseud.

Tsvetaeva, Marina Ivanovna (Efron)

Art in the light of conscience. *In* Proffer, C. R. ed. Modern Russian poets on poetry p145-84

A poet on criticism. *In* The Bitter air of exile p103-34

About

Mirskii, D. P. Marina Tsvetaeva. *In* The Bitter air of exile p88-93

Slonim, M. L. The fate of poets: Mandelstam, Akhmatova, Tsvetayeva. *In* Slonim, M. L. Soviet Russian literature p248-67

Tsvetayeva, Marina. See Tsvetaeva, Marina Ivanovna (Efron)

Tu, Wei-ming

The Confucian perception of adulthood. *In* Erikson, E. H. ed. Adulthood p113-27

Hsiung Shih-li's quest for authentic existence. *In* The Limits of change p242-75

'Inner experience': the basis of creativity in Neo-Confucian thinking. *In* Artists and traditions p 9-15

Yen Yüan: from inner experience to lived concreteness. *In* The Unfolding of Neo-Confucianism p511-41

Tuan, Yi-Fu

Geopiety: a theme in man's attachment to nature and to place. *In* Geographies of the mind p11-39

Tubman, Harriet (Ross)

About

Scruggs, O. M. The meaning of Harriet Tubman. *In* "Remember the ladies": new perspectives on women in American history p110-21

Tucano Indians

Art

Reichel-Dolmatoff, G. Drug-induced optical sensations and their relationship to applied art among some Colombian Indians. *In* Greenhalgh, M. and Megaw, J. V. S. eds. Art in sociey p289-304

Tucker, Benjamin Ricketson

About

DeLeon, D. Right libertarianism. *In* DeLeon, D. The American as anarchist p61-84

Tucker, Edward Frederick John

The letter of the law in 'The merchant of Venice.' *In* Shakespeare survey v29 p93-101

Tucker, Marna S.

Pro bono ABA? *In* Nader, R. and Green, M. J. eds. Verdicts on lawyers p20-32

Tucker, Nathaniel

About

Leary, L. G. Nathaniel Tucker: expatriate patriot. *In* Leary, L. G. Soundings p44-66

Tucker, Robert C.

The perils of success—deradicalization. *In* Lauer, R. H. ed. Social movements and social change p227-55

Stalinism and comparative communism. *In* Stalinism p xi-xx

Stalinism as revolution from above. *In* Stalinism p77-108

Tucker, St George, 1828-1863

About individual works

Hansford: a tale of Bacon's rebellion

Ward, W. H. St George Tucker's Hansford. *In* Tennessee Studies in literature v 21 p28-34

Tucker v. Lower

Law and Equity Court, Richmond, Va. Tucker v. Lower. *In* Weir, R. F. ed. Ethical issues in death and dying p125-28

Tuckerman, Frederick Goddard

About individual works

Complete poems

Howe, I. A neglected American poet. *In* Howe, I. Celebrations and attacks p145-49

Tucker's Administrator v. Lower, No 2831

Fletcher, J. F. Cerebration. *In* Fletcher, J. F. Humanhood: essays in biomedical ethics p159-65

Tudor, Andrew

Genre and critical methodology; excerpt from "Theories of film" *In* Nichols, B. ed. Movies and methods p118-26

Tugendhat, Ernst

Phenomenology and linguistic analysis. *In* Elliston, F. A. and McCormick, P. eds. Husserl p325-37

Tugwell, Franklin

Venezuela and the inter-American system. *In* Farer, T. J. ed. The future of the inter-American system p256-69

Tuition. See College costs; Education—Finance

Tukbaw

About

Rosaldo, R. I. The story of Tukbaw: 'they listen as he orates.' *In* Reynolds, F. E. and Capps, D. eds. The biographical process p121-51

Tullberg, Rita McWilliams- See McWilliams-Tullberg, Rita

Tullock, Gordon

Science's feet of clay. *In* Science and ceremony p135-45

Tulum, Mexico

Miller, A. G. The iconography of the painting in the Temple of the Diving God, Tulum, Quintana Roo, Mexico: the twisted cords. *In* Mesoamerican archaeology p167-86

Tulum, Mexico—*Continued*

Genealogy

Beattie, H. J. The alternative to resistance: the case of T'ung-ch'eng, Anhwei. *In* Spence, J. D. and Wills, J. E. eds. From Ming to Ch'ing p239-76

Tung, Ch'i-ch'ang

About

Ho, Wai-kam. Tung Ch'i-ch'ang's new orthodoxy and the Southern School theory. *In* Artists and traditions p113-29

T'ung-ch'eng, Anhwei

Tung, Mason

Whitney's A choice of emblemes revisited: a comparative study of the manuscript and the printed versions. *In* Virginia. University. Bibliographical Society. Studies in bibliography v29 p32-101

Tunica Indians

Downs, E. C. The struggle of the Louisiana Tunica Indians for recognition. *In* Williams, W. L. ed. Southeastern Indians since the removal era p72-89

Tuning. See Musical temperament

Tunis, John Roberts

What is a juvenile book? *In* Horn Book Magazine. Crosscurrents of criticism p22-26

Tunis

City planning

Tunnard, C. The United States: Federal funds for rescue. *In* United Nations Educational, Scientific and Cultural Organization. The conservation of cities p81-106

History

Kafi, J.el. Tunisia: hopes for the medina of Tunis. *In* United Nations Educational, Scientific and Cultural Organization. The conservation of cities p125-39

Tunisia

Social life and customs

Teitelbaum, J. M. The leer and the loom—social controls on handloom weavers. *In* The Evil eye p63-75

Tunnard, Christopher

The United States: Federal funds for rescue. *In* United Nations Educational, Scientific and Cultural Organization. The conservation of cities p81-106

Tunney, John Varich, and Frank, Jane Lakes

Epilogue: a congressional role in lawyer reform? *In* Nader, R. and Green, M. J. eds. Verdicts on lawyers p295-304

Tunstall, Jeremy

The American role in worldwide mass communication. *In* Gerbner, G. ed. Mass media policies in changing cultures p3-12

Tupamaros. See Movimiento de Liberacíon Nacional

Tupin, Joe Paul

Some psychiatric issues of euthanasia. *In* Kohl, M. ed. Beneficent euthanasia p193-203

Turgenev, Ivan Sergeevich

About

Berlin, Sir I. Fathers and children. *In* Berlin, Sir I. Russian thinkers p261-305

Calder, A. Fiction and politics: the art of Turgenev. *In* Calder, A. Russia discovered p73-107

Larkin, M. Russia and the realist response: Turgenev. *In* Larkin, M. Man and society in nineteenth-century realism p98-110

Moss, W. G. Why the anxious fear? Aging and death in the works of Turgenev. *In* Spicker, S. F.; Woodward, K. M. and Van Tassel, D. D. eds. Aging and the elderly p241-60

About individual works

Fathers and sons

Berlin, Sir I. Fathers and children. *In* Berlin, Sir I. Russian thinkers p261-305

Henry, P. I. S. Turgenev: Fathers and sons. *In* Williams, D. A. ed. The monster in the mirror p40-74

Hamlet and Don Quixote

Mathewson, R. W. Rebuttal II: Hamlet and Don Quixote. *In* Mathewson, R. W. The positive hero in Russian literature p97-112

A month in the country

Sławińska, I Two concepts of time in dramatic structure: Turgenev and Norwid. *In* For Wiktor Weintraub p479-92

Turgénieff, Ivan. See Turgenev, Ivan Sergeevich

Turgot, Anne Robert Jacques, baron de l'Aulne

About

Voegelin, E. The conflict between progress and political existence after Turgot. *In* Voegelin, E. From Enlightenment to Revolution p110-35

Voegelin, E. Positivism and its antecedents. *In* Voegelin, E. From Enlightenment to revolution p74-109

Turkey

Birnbaum, E. Turkey: from cosmopolitan Empire to nation state. *In* Savory, R. M. ed. Introduction to Islamic civilisation p179-88

Antiquities

Mitten, D. G. and Yügrüm, G. The Gygean Lake, 1969: Eski Balikhane, preliminary report. *In* Harvard Studies in classical philology v75 p191-95

See also Dag Pazari site. Turkey

Army—History

Rafeq, A. K. The local forces in Syria in the seventeenth and eighteenth centuries. *In* War, technology and society in the Middle East p277-307

Swanson, G. W. War, technology, and society in the Ottoman Empire from the reign of Abdülhamid II to 1913: Mahmud Sevket and the German military mission. *In* War, technology and society in the Middle East p367-85

Foreign relations—Great Britain

Kedourie, É. Young Turks, Freemasons and Jews. Kedourie, É. Arabic political memoirs and other studies p243-62

History

Vryonis, S. Byzantine and Turkish societies and their sources of manpower. *In* War, technology and society in the Middle East p125-52

History—Ottoman Empire, 1288-1918

Ankori, Z. From Zudecha to Yahudi Mahallesi: the Jewish quarter of Candia in the seventeenth century. *In* Salo Wittmayer Baron v 1 p63-127

Turkey—History—Ottoman Empire, 1288-1918—*Continued*

Fischer-Galati, S. A. Judeo-Christian aspects of Pax Ottomanica. *In* Király, B. K. ed. Tolerance and movements of religious dissent in Eastern Europe p185-97

Haddad, R. M. The Ottoman Empire in the contemporary Middle East. *In* Aftermath of empire p39-61

Itzkowitz, N. The Ottoman Empire. *In* Lewis, B. ed. Islam and the Arab world p273-300

Király, B. K. The Sublime Porte, Vienna, Transylvania and the dissemination of Protestant Reformation in royal Hungary. *In* Király, B. K. ed. Tolerance and movements of religious dissent in Eastern Europe p199-221

Shaw, E. K. The Ottoman aspects of Pax Ottomanica: the political, practical and psychological aspects of Pax Ottomanica. *In* Király, B. K. ed. Tolerance and movements of religious dissent in Eastern Europe p165-82

Shaw, S. J. The Ottoman millet system: an evaluation. *In* Király, B. K. ed. Tolerance and movements of religious dissent in Eastern Europe p183-84

History, Military

Inalcik, H. The socio-political effects of the diffusion of fire-arms in the Middle East. *In* War, technology and society in the Middle East p195-217

Parry, V. S. La manière de combattre. *In* War, technology and society in the Middle East p218-56

Politics and government

Szyliowicz, J. S. Elites and modernization in Turkey. *In* Political elites and political development in the Middle East p23-66

Politics and government—1453-1683

Fischer-Galati, S. A. Judeo-Christian aspects of Pax Ottomanica. *In* Király, B. K. ed. Tolerance and movements of religious dissent in Eastern Europe p185-97

Shaw, E. K. The Ottoman aspects of Pax Ottomanica: the political, practical and psychological aspects of Pax Ottomanica. *In* Király, B. K. ed. Tolerance and movements of religious dissent in Eastern Europe p165-82

Politics and government—1878-1909

Kedourie, É. The impact of the Young Turk Revolution on the Arabic-speaking provinces of the Ottoman Empire. *In* Kedourie, É. Arabic political memoirs and other studies p124-61

Social conditions

Cuisenier, J. Kinship and social organization in the Turko-Mongolian cultural area. *In* Family and society p204-36

Turkish epic literature. See Epic literature, Turkish

Turkish literature

History and criticism

Birnbaum, E. Turkish literature through the ages. *In* Savory, R. M. ed. Introduction to Islamic civilisation p79-87

Turkle, Sherry

French psychoanalysis: a sociological perspective. *In* Roland, A. ed. Psychoanalysis, creativity, and literature p39-71

Turks in Cyprus

Alcock, A. E. Three case-studies in minority protection: South Tyrol, Cyprus, Quebec. *In* Hepburn, A. C. ed. Minorities in history p189-225

Turks in Egypt

Farah, C. E. Censorship and freedom of expression in Ottoman Syria and Egypt. *In* Nationalism in a non-national state p151-94

Turks in Hejaz, Arabia

Ochsenwald, W. L. The financial basis of Ottoman rule in the Hijaz, 1840-1877. *In* Nationalism in a non-national state p129-49

Turks in North Africa

Spencer, W. Ottoman North Africa. *In* Nationalism in a non-national state p103-27

Turks in Syria

Farah, C. E. Censorship and freedom of expression in Ottoman Syria and Egypt. *In* Nationalism in a non-national state p151-94

Rafeq, A. K. The local forces in Syria in the seventeenth and eighteenth centuries. *In* War, technology and society in the Middle East p277-307

Turks in the Balkan Peninsula

Petrović, D. Fire-arms in the Balkans on the eve of and after the Ottoman conquests of the fourteenth and fifteenth centuries. *In* War, technology and society in the Middle East p164-94

Turks in the Crimea

Fisher, A. W. Crimean separatism in the Ottoman Empire. *In* Nationalism in a non-national state p57-76

Turnbull, Andrew Winchester

About individual works
Scott Fitzgerald

Connolly, C. A Fitzgerald entertainment. *In* Connolly, C. The evening colonnade p262-68

Turnbull, Colin M.

The politics of non-aggression. *In* Montagu, A. ed. Learning non-aggression p161-221

Turnbull, Robert George

"Physics" I: sense universals, principles, multiplicity, and motion. *In* Motion and time, space and matter p28-55

The role of the "special sensibles" in the perception theories of Plato and Aristotle. *In* Studies in perception p3-26

Turnell, Martin

The rise of the French novel

Contents

Alain-Fournier
Crébillon fils
Flaubert
From Marivaux to Raymond Radiguet
Marivaux
Raymond Radiguet
Rousseau
Stendhal's last novel

About individual works
The classical moment

Edelman, N. Book reviews. *In* Edelman, N. The eye of the beholder p166-205

Turner, Colin. See Wurtzel, A. H. jt. auth.

Turner, Darwin T.

Faulkner and slavery. *In* The South and Faulkner's Yoknapatawpha p62-85

Turner, David

Theodor Fontane: Effi Briest. *In* Williams, D. A. ed. The monster in the mirror p234-56

Turner, Diane E.

The mythic vision in Tennessee Williams' Camino Real. *In* Tennessee Williams: a tribute p237-51

Turner, Eric Gardiner

Oxyrhynchus and Rome. *In* Harvard Studies in classical philology v79 p 1-24

Turner, Ernest Sackville

The world of Jeffery Farnol. *In* The Saturday book 34 p45-52

Turner, Frederick Jackson

About

Cunliffe, M. The two or more worlds of Willa Cather. *In* The Art of Willa Cather p21-42

About individual works

The significance of the frontier in American history

Potter, J. Some British reflections on Turner and the frontier. *In* Burton, D. H. ed. American history—British historians p127-48

Turner, Joseph Mallord William

About

Kroeber, K. Romantic historicism: the temporal sublime. In Kroeber, K. and Walling, W. eds. Images of romanticism p149-65

Meisel, M. The material sublime: John Martin, Byron, Turner, and the theater. *In* Kroeber, K. and Walling, W. eds. Images of romanticism p211-32

Paulson, R. Turner's graffiti: the sun and its glosses. *In* Kroeber, K. and Walling, W. eds. Images of romanticism p167-88

Storch, R. F. Abstract idealism in English romantic poetry and painting. *In* Kroeber, K. and Walling, W. eds. Images of romanticism p189-209

About individual works

Dido building Carthage

Kroeber, K. Experience as history: Shelley's Venice, Turner's Carthage. *In* ELH essays for Earl R. Wasserman p31-49

Turner, Nat

About individual works

The confessions of Nat Turner, the leader of the late insurrection in Southampton, Virginia

Gross, S. L. and Bender, E. History; politics, and literature: the myth of Nat Turner. *In* Morris, R. K. and Malin, I. eds. The achievement of William Styron p168-207

Turner, Paul

Romanticism, rationalism, and the domino system. *In* Walden, R. ed. The open hand p14-41

Turner, R. Steven

University reformers and professorial scholarship in Germany, 1760-1806. *In* The University in society v2 p495-531

Turner, Victor Witter

African ritual and Western literature: is a comparative symbology possible? *In* Fletcher, A. J. S. ed. The literature of fact p45-81

Comments and conclusions. *In* Babcock, B. A. ed. The reversible world p276-96

Encounter with Freud: the making of a comparative symbologist. *In* Spindler, G. D. ed. The making of psychological anthropology p558-83

Lunda medicine and the treatment of disease. *In* The Occasional papers of the Rhodes-Livingstone Museum p649-719

Lunda rites and ceremonies. *In* The Occasional papers of the Rhodes-Livingstone Museum p335-88

Religious paradigms and political action: the murder in the cathedral of Thomas Becket. *In* Reynolds, F. E. and Capps, D. eds. The biographical process p153-86

Turner, W. Burghardt

The polemicists: David Walker, Frederick Douglass, Booker T. Washington, and W. E. B. Du Bois. *In* Inge, M. T.; Duke, J. M. and Bryer, J. R. eds. Black American writers v 1 p47-132

Turner hypothesis. See Frontier thesis

Turner thesis. See Frontier thesis

Turner's frontier hypothesis. See Frontier thesis

Turnpike roads. See Toll roads

Turrecremata, Juan de. See Torquemada. Juan de, Cardinal

Turville-Petre, Thorlac

About individual works

The alliterative revival

Blake, N. F. Middle English alliterative revivals. *In* Review, v 1 1979 p205-14

Tuscany

History

Osheim, D. J. Rural population and the Tuscan economy in the late Middle Ages. *In* Viator: medieval and Renaissance studies v7 p329-46

Social conditions

Klapisch, C. and Demonet, M. "A uno pane e uno vino": the rural Tuscan family at the beginning of the fifteenth century. *In* Family and society p41-74

Tuscarora Indians

Commerce

Boyce, D W. Did a Tuscarora confederacy exist? *In* Hudson, C. M. ed. Four centuries of Southern Indians p28-45

Tribal government

Boyce, D. W. Did a Tuscarora confederacy exist? *In* Hudson, C. M. ed. Four centuries of Southern Indians p28-45

Wars, 1711-1713

Boyce, D W. Did a Tuscarora confederacy exist? *In* Hudson, C. M. ed. Four centuries of Southern Indians p28-45

Tushnet, Mark Victor

The newer property: suggestion for the revival of substantive due process. *In* The Supreme Court review, 1975 p261-88

Tusi, Mukhammed Nasideddin. See al-Tūsī, Nasīr al-Dīn Muhammad ibn Muhammad

al-Tūsī, Nasīr al-Dīn Muhammad ibn Muhammad

About individual works

Principles of inference

Morewedge, P. The analysis of "substance" in Tūsī's Logic and in the ibn Sīnian tradition. *In* Essays on Islamic philosophy and science p158-88

Twitchett, Carol Cosgrove- See Cosgrove-Twitchett, Carol

Twitchett, Kenneth Joseph
External relations or foreign policy? *In* Twitchett, K. J. ed. Europe and the world p 1-34

Two English girls (Motion picture)
Kauffmann, S. Two English girls. *In* Kauffmann, S. Living images p150-52
Samuels, C. T. Hyphens of the self. *In* Samuels, C. T. Mastering the film, and other essays p179-89

"291" (Periodical)
Tashjian, D. L. 291 and Francis Picabia. *In* Tashjian, D. L. Skyscraper primitives p29-48

The two of us (Motion picture)
Truffaut, F. Claude Berri: Le vieil homme et l'enfant. *In* Truffaut, F. The films in my life p331-34

Twombly, Robert C. and Moore, Robert Hamilton
Black Puritan: the Negro in seventeenth-century Massachusetts. *In* Vaughan, A. T. and Bremer, F. J. eds. Puritan New England p187-200

Tyard, Pontus de
About
Hall, K. M. Pontus de Tyard: a reply to a recent article. *In* French Renaissance studies, 1540-70 p185-93

Tydeman, William
The earlier sixteenth century. *In* English Association. The year's work in English studies v53 p121-46
The earlier sixteenth century [another essay] *In* English Association. The year's work in English studies v54, p124-52
The earlier sixteenth century [another essay] *In* English Association. The year's work in English studies v55 p167-92

Tyler, Daniel
The Indian Weltanschaung: a summary of views expressed by Indians at the "Viewpoints in Indian History" Conference, August 1974, Colorado State University. *In* Red Men and hat-wearers p135-39

Tyler, Dorothy
Robert Frost in Michigan. *In* Frost: centennial essays III p7-69
The strong are saying nothing. *In* Frost: centennial essays II p305-16

Tyler, Parker
The awful fate of the sex goddess; excerpt from "Sex psyche etcetera in the film." *In* Denby, D. ed. Awake in the dark p349-56
About
Murray, E. Parker Tyler and psychoanalytic-mythological criticism. *In* Murray, E. Nine American film critics p67-89

Tyler, Royall, 1757-1827
About
Leary, L. G. Royall Tyler: first gentleman of the American theater. *In* Leary, L. G. Soundings p83-96
About individual works
The Algerine captive
Spengemann, W. C. The adventurous muse: "The Algerine captive" and "Arthur Gordon Pym." *In* Spengemann, W. C. The adventurous muse p119-50

Tyler, Wat
About
Sucksmith, H. P. Sir Leicester Dedlock, Wat Tyler, and the Chartists: the role of the Ironmaster in Bleak House. *In* Dickens Studies Annual v4 p113-31

Tylor, Peter L.
"Denied the power to choose the good:" sexuality and mental defect in American medical practice, 1850-1920. *In* Branca, P. ed. The medicine show p165-82

Tynan, Kenneth
About individual works
Tynan right and left: plays, poems, people, places and events
Simon, J. I. A roller-coaster ride with Kenneth Tynan. *In* Simon, J. I. Singularities p176-80

Tyndale, William
About
Thompson, C. R. Scripture for the ploughboy and some others. *In* Studies in the continental background of Renaissance English literature: essays presented to John L. Lievsay p 3-28

Tyner, Wallace E. See Kalter, R. J. jt. auth.

Tyniảov, IUriĭ Nikolaevich
Dostoevsky and Gogol. *In* Erlich, V. ed. Twentieth-century Russian literary criticism p102-16

Tynjanov, Jurij. See Tyniảnov, IUriĭ Nikolaevich

Types, Biblical. See Typology (Theology)

Typology (Psychology) See Characters and characteristics

Typology (Theology)
Hollander, R. Typology and secular literature: some medieval problems and examples. *In* Miner, E. R. ed. Literary uses of typology p3-19
Keller, K. Alephs, Zahirs, and the triumph of ambiguity: typology in nineteenth-century American literature. *In* Miner, E. R. ed. Literary uses of typology p274-314
Landow, G. P. Moses striking the rock: typological symbolism in Victorian poetry. *In* Miner, E. R. ed. Literary uses of typology p315-44
Lewalski, B. K. Typological symbolism and the "progress of the soul" in seventeenth-century literature. *In* Miner, E. R. ed. Literary uses of typology p79-114
Roche, T. P. Tasso's enchanted woods. *In* Miner, E. R. ed. Literary uses of typology p49-78
Ziolkowski, T. Some features of religious figuralism in twentieth-century literature. *In* Miner, E. R. ed. Literary uses of typology p345-69
Zwicker, S. N. Politics and panegyric: the figural mode from Marvell to Pope. *In* Miner, E. R. ed. Literary uses of typology p115-46
History of doctrines
Elliott, E. From father to son: the evolution of typology in Puritan New England. *In* Miner, E. R. ed. Literary uses of typology p204-27
Korshin, P. J. The development of abstracted typology in England, 1650-1820. *In* Miner, E. R. ed. Literary uses of typology p147-203

Uitzilopochtli. See Huitzilopochtli

Ukraine

History

Bilinsky, Y. The incorporation of Western Ukraine and its impact on politics and society in Soviet Ukraine. *In* Szporluk, R. ed. The influence of East Europe and the Soviet West on the USSR p180-228

Ukraine, Western

History

Bilinsky, Y. The incorporation of Western Ukraine and its impact on politics and society in Soviet Ukraine. *In* Szporluk, R. ed. The influence of East Europe and the Soviet West on the USSR p180-228

Ukrainian language

Foreign elements—Polish

Shevelov, G. Y. On lexical Polonisms in literary Ukrainian. *In* For Wiktor Weintraub p449-63

Ulam, Adam B.

Do we know all there is to know about the USSR? *In* Cocks, P.; Daniels, R. V. and Heer, N. W. eds. The dynamics of Soviet politics p3-8

Ulam, Stanislaw Macin

Infinities. *In* Neyman, J. ed. The heritage of Copernicus: theories "pleasing to the mind" p378-93

Ulanov, Ann Belford

The psychological reality of the demonic. *In* Disguises of the demonic p135-49

Ulasi, Adaora Lily

About individual works

Many things you no understand

Taiwo, O. Social criticism. *In* Taiwo, O. Culture and the Nigerian novel p34-73

Ullendorff, Edward

The Queen of Sheba in Ethiopian tradition. *In* Pritchard, J. B. ed. Solomon & Sheba p104-14

Ullman, Montague

Psychiatry and parapsychology: the consummation of an uncertain romance. *In* Parapsychology: its relation to physics, biology, psychology, and psychiatry p171-207

Ullmann, John E.

Tides and shallows. *In* Benton, L. R. ed. Management for the future p283-98

Ullmann, Walter

John Baconthorpe as a canonist. *In* Church and government in the Middle Ages p223-46

Ullmo, Yves

France. *In* Planning, politics and public policy p22-51

Ullrich, Helen Elizabeth

Caste differences between Brahmin and non-Brahmin women in a south Indian village. *In* Schlegel, A. E. ed. Sexual stratification p94-108

Ulman, Elinor

Art therapy: problems of definition. *In* Ulman, E. and Dachinger, P. eds. Art therapy p3-13

A new use of art in psychiatric diagnosis. *In* Ulman, E. and Dachinger, P. eds. Art therapy p361-86

Therapy is not enough: the contribution of art to general hospital psychiatry. *In* Ulman, E. and Dachinger, P. eds. Art therapy p14-32

Ulman, Elinor, and Dachinger, Penny

Therapeutic art programs around the world. *In* Ulman, E. and Dachinger, P. eds. Art therapy p208-12

Ulman, Elinor, and Levy, Bernard Isaac

An experimental approach to the judgment of psychopathology from paintings. *In* Ulman, E. and Dachinger, P. eds. Art therapy p393-402

Ulmecas. See Olmecs

Ulrich, Laurel Thatcher

Vertuous women found: New England ministerial literature, 1668-1735. *In* Vaughan, A. T. and Bremen, F. J. eds. Puritan New England p215-31

Ulysses in literature

Dubos, R. J. Ulysses and the American frontier. *In* Dubos, R. J. Beast or angel? p135-43

Ulysses in Nighttown (criticism) Barkentin, M. *In* Kauffmann, S. Persons of the drama p149-52

Umbanda (Cultus)

Sturm, F. G. Afro-Brazilian cults. *In* African religions: a symposium p217-39

Umbilical cord. See Umbilicus

Umbilicus (in religion, folklore, etc.)

Miller, A. G. The iconography of the painting in the Temple of the Diving God, Tulum, Quintana Roo, Mexico: the twisted cords. *In* Mesoamerican archaeology p167-86

Unamuno, Miguel. See Unamuno y Jugo, Miguel de

Unamuno y Jugo, Miguel de

About

Glicksberg, C. I. Unamuno and the quest for faith. *In* Glicksberg, C. I. The literature of nihilism p53-70

Shaw, D. L. Unamuno: the giant of the generation. *In* Shaw, D. L. The generation of 1898 in Spain p41-74

Unbegaun, Boris Ottokar

The "language of ultimate clarity." *In* Dunlop, J. B.; Haugh, R. and Klimoff, A. eds. Aleksandr Solzhenitsyn: critical essays and documentary materials 2d ed. p195-98

About

Auty, R. B. O. Unbegaun's contributions to Russian and Slavonic philology. *In* Oxford Slavonic papers, new ser. v7 p 1-2

Unbelief. See Skepticism

Unborn children (Law)

English, J. Abortion and the concept of a person. *In* Feminism and philosophy p417-28

Feinberg, J. The rights of animals and unborn generations. *In* Philosophy & environmental crisis p43-68

Uncertainty principle. See Heisenberg uncertainty principle

Uncle Kruger (Motion picture)

Taylor, R. Uncle Kruger. *In* Taylor, R. Film propaganda p207-15

Uncle Vanya (criticism) Chekhov, A. P. *In* Kauffmann, S. Persons of the drama p146-48

Uncle Vanya (Motion picture)

Kauffmann, S. Uncle Vanya. *In* Kauffmann, S. Living images p116-18

Unconsciousness. See Subconsciousness

Undefinability. See Definition (Logic)

Under milk wood (Motion picture)
Kauffmann, S. Under milk wood. *In* Kauffmann, S. Living images p171-73

Underdeveloped areas
Bergsten, C. F. Economic tensions: America versus the Third World. *In* Rosecrance, R. N. ed. America as an ordinary country p199-223

Bull, H. The Third World and international society. *In* The Year book of world affairs, 1979 p15-31

Clignet, R. and Sween, J. A. Some prerequisites for the planning of modernization processes. *In* African themes p113-47

Farer, T. J. On a collision course: the American campaign for human rights and the antiradical bias in the Third World. *In* Kommers, D. P. and Loescher, G. D. eds. Human rights and American foreign policy p263-77

Goulet, D. World health and world hunger: putting development ethics to the test. *In* Cahill, K. M. ed. Health and development p83-101

Hilton, A. M. Against pollution and hunger: environment and development. *In* Against pollution and hunger p27-59

Inkeles, A. Becoming modern: individual change in six developing countries. *In* Schwartz, T. ed. Socialization as cultural communication p231-50

Kasfir, N. M. Interdependence and American commitment to promote development in the Third World: Africa—the hardest case. *In* Baldwin, D. A. eds. America in an interdependent world p223-43

Levi, W. Are developing states more equal than others? *In* The Year book of world affairs, 1978 p286-302

Mazur, M. P. The developing countries in the world economy: a question of bargaining power? *In* Baldwin, D. A. ed. America in an interdependent world p137-61

Reed, I. The "liberal" in us all. *In* Reed, I. Shrovetide in old New Orleans p37-43

Yergin, D. Order and survival. *In* A New America? p263-87

See also States, New

Civil rights
Farer, T. J. Policy implications of the possible conflict between capitalist development and human rights in developing countries. *In* Farer, T. J. ed. The future of the inter-American system p115-18

Hewlett, S. A. Human rights and economic realities in developing nations. *In* Farer, T. J. ed. The future of the inter-American system p83-114

Zvobgo, E. J. M. A Third World view. *In* Kommers, D. P. and Loescher, G. D. eds. Human rights and American foreign policy p90-106

Commerce
Diaz Alejandro, C. F. Trade policies and economic development. *In* Kenen, P. B. ed. International trade and finance p93-150

Communication
Lerner, D. Communication and development. *In* Lerner, D. and Nelson, L. M. eds. Communication research—a half-century appraisal p148-66

Meyer-Dohm, P. Investments in communication and the development process. *In* Fischer, H. D. and Merrill, J. C. eds. International and intercultural communication p226-35

Yu, Tê-chi. Communication policy and planning for development: some notes on research. *In* Lerner, D. and Nelson, L. M. eds. Communication research—a half-century appraisal p167-90

Corporations, Foreign
Mazur, M. P. The developing countries in the world economy: a question of bargaining power? *In* Baldwin, D. A. ed. America in an interdependent world p137-61

Economic policy
Balassa, B. A. Project appraisal in developing countries. *In* Economic development in planning p40-60

Costanzo, G. A. Economics and health. *In* Cahill, K. M. ed. Health and development p69-82

Girvan, N. Economic nationalism. *In* Vernon, R. ed. The oil crisis p145-58

Johnson, H. G. Keynes and the developing world. *In* Skidelsky, R. J. A. ed. The end of the Keynesian era p88-94

Kodzic, P. Armaments and development. *In* The Dynamics of the arms race p202-11

Parmer, S. L. Self-reliant development in an "interdependent" world. *In* Erb, G. F. and Kallab, V. eds. Beyond dependency p3-27

Uri, P. Developing and industrialised countries: a generalisation. *In* The New Atlantic challenge p189-96

Vaitsos, C. V. Foreign investment and productive knowledge. *In* Erb, G. F. and Kallab, V. eds. Beyond dependency p75-94

Education
Jones, G. W. The influence of demographic variables on development via their impact on education. *In* Economic factors in population growth p553-80

Education (Higher)
M'Bow, A. M. The role of universities in the developing countries. *In* The Frontiers of human knowledge p201-14

Environmental policy
Juda, L. International environmental concern: perspectives of and implications for developing states. *In* Orr, D. W. and Soroos, M. S. eds. The global predicament p90-107

Finance
Syz, J. Recent North-South relations and multilateral soft loans. *In* The Year book of world affairs, 1975 p196-207

Foreign economic relations
Haq, M. ul. Negotiating a new bargain with the rich countries. *In* Erb, G. F. and Kallab, V. eds. Beyond dependency p157-62

Mazrui, A. A. The new interdependence. *In* Erb, G. F. and Kallab, V. eds. Beyond dependency p38-54

Peña, F. Multinational enterprises and North-South relations. *In* Erb, G. F. and Kallab, V. eds. Beyond dependency p57-74

Foreign economic relations—European Economic Community countries
Cosgrove-Twitchett, C. From association to partnership. *In* Twitchett, K. J. ed. Europe and the world p121-50

Cosgrove-Twitchett, C. Towards a Community development policy. *In* Twitchett, K. J. ed. Europe and the world p151-74

Underdeveloped areas—*Continued*

Foreign economic relations—
United States

Sellers, J. E. Famine and interdependence: toward a new identity for America and the West. *In* Lucas, G. R. and Ogletree, T. W. eds. Lifeboat ethics p100-19

Foreign relations

Erb, G. F. The developing world's "challenge" in perspective. *In* Erb, G. F. and Kallab, V. eds. Beyond dependency p135-56

Sudjatmoko. Reflections on nonalignment in the 1970s. *In* Erb, G. F. and Kallab, V. eds. Beyond dependency p28-37

Foreign trade promotion

Parmar, S. L. Self-reliant development in an "interdependent" world. *In* Erb, G. F. and Kallab, V. eds. Beyond dependency p3-27

Industries

Peña, F. Multinational enterprises and North-South relations. *In* Erb, G. F. and Kallab, V. eds. Beyond dependency p57-74

Investments, Foreign

Vaitsos, C. V. Foreign investment and productive knowledge. *In* Erb, G. F. and Kallab, V. eds. Beyond dependency p75-94

Vernon, R. Foreign operations. *In* McKie, J. W. ed. Social responsibility and the business predicament p275-310

Journalism

Aggarwala, N. K. News with Third World perspectives: a practical suggestion. *In* Horton, P. C. ed. The Third World and press freedom p197-209

Galliner, P. Improving news in the Third World. *In* Horton, P. C. ed. The Third World and press freedom p93-103

Naesselund, G. R. UNESCO and the press in the Third World. *In* Horton, P. C. ed. The Third World and press freedom p210-19

Ng'weno, H. All freedom is at stake. *In* Horton, P. C. ed. The Third World and press freedom p127-34

Olasope, B. The Nonaligned News Agencies Pool and the free flow of meaningful news: an African viewpoint. *In* Horton, P. C. ed. The Third World and press freedom p162-72

Rosenblum, M. The Western wire services and the Third World. *In* Horton, P. C. ed. The Third World and press freedom p104-26

Tatarian, R. News flow in the Third World: an overview. *In* Horton, P. C. ed. The Third World and press freedom p 1-54

Labor supply

Nassef, A. F. Problems of maintaining employment in developing countries in the face of rapid population growth. *In* Economic factors in population growth p394-410

Law

Beckstrom, J. H. Handicaps of legal-social engineering in a developing nation. *In* African themes p195-212

Manpower policy

Resnick, I. N. Manpower requirements and allocation of educational resources in underdeveloped countries. *In* African dimensions p155-69

Mass media

Allen, I. L. Social integration as an organizing principle. *In* Gerbner, G. ed. Mass media policies in changing cultures p235-50

Head, S. W. Trends in tropical African societies. *In* Gerbner, G. ed. Mass media policies in changing cultures p83-103

Lowenstein, R. L. Use of foreign media by developing nations. *In* Fischer, H. D. and Merrill, J. C. eds. International and intercultural communication p210-17

McNelly, J. T. Media exposure in developing urban societies. *In* Fischer, H. D. and Merrill, J. C. eds. International and intercultural communication p218-25

Medical care

Frei Montalva, E. President Chile. The political realities of health in a developing nation. *In* Cahill, K. M. ed. Health and development p4-14

Ritchie-Calder, P. R. Baron Ritchie-Calder. World health: an ethical-economic perspective. *In* Cahill, K. M. ed. Health and development p36-48

Military policy

Gutteridge, W. F. Arms control and developing countries. *In* The Dynamics of the arms race p212-14

Kodzic, P. Armaments and development. *In* The Dynamics of the arms race p202-11

Mines and mineral resources

Varon, B. and Takeuchi, K. Developing countries and non-fuel minerals. *In* Bundy, W. P. ed. The world economic crisis p165-78

Politics and government

Gutkind, P. C. W. Are the poor politically dangerous? Some thoughts on urbanism, urbanites, and political consciousness. *In* Colonialism and change p85-113

Population

Nassef, A. F. Problems of maintaining employment in developing countries in the face of rapid population growth. *In* Economic factors in population growth p394-410

Roy, K. Population policy from the southern perspective. *In* Erb, G. F. and Kallab, V. eds. Beyond dependency p95-110

Todaro, M. P. Rural-urban migration, unemployment and job probabilities: recent theoretical and empirical research. *In* Economic factors in population growth p367-85

Public health

Laird, M. Osiris, Asklepios, and the Harpies: the development of an African river basin. *In* A Time to hear and answer: essays for the Bicentennial season p103-40

Publishers and publishing

Altbach, P. G. Literary colonialism: books in the Third world. *In* Altbach, P. G. and McVey, S. eds. Perspectives on publishing p83-101

Smith, D. C. The bright promise of publishing in developing countries. *In* Altbach, P. G. and McVey, S. eds. Perspectives on publishing p117-28

Science and state

Sardar, Z. and Rosser-Owen, D. G. Science policy and developing countries. *In* Science, technology and society p535-75

Underdeveloped areas—*Continued*

Social conditions

Gutkind, P. C. W. Are the poor political-ly dangerous? Some thoughts on urbanism, urbanites, and political consciousness. *In* Colonialism and change p85-113

Technology—Social aspects

Gluckman, M. New dimensions of change, conflict and settlement. *In* United Nations Educational, Scientific and Cultural Organization. Race, science and society p319-40

Urbanization

Evers, H. D. Urban expansion and land-ownership in underdeveloped societies. *In* Walton, J. and Masotti, L. H. eds. The city in comparative perspective p67-79

London, B. and Flanagan, W. G. Comparative urban ecology: a summary of the field. *In* Walton, J. and Masotti, L. H. eds. The city in comparative perspective p41-66

Underdeveloped areas, Aid to. See Technical assistance

Underdeveloped areas in literature

Goonetilleke, D. C. R. A. Antecedents. *In* Goonetilleke, D. C. R. A. Developing countries in British fiction p13-32

Goonetilleke, D C. R. A. Between cultures. *In* Goonetilleke, D. C. R. A. Developing countries in British fiction p245-52

Underground films. See Experimental films

Underground literature

Darnton, R. Trade in the taboo: the life of a clandestine book dealer in prerevolutionary France. *In* Korshin, P. J. ed. The widening circle p11-83

Russia

Brown, D. B. Underground literature. *In* Brown, D. B. Soviet Russian literature since Stalin p352-72

Nicholson, M. Solzhenitsyn and samizdat. *In* Dunlop, J. B.; Haugh, R. and Klimoff, A. eds. Aleksandr Solzhenitsyn: critical essays and documentary materials 2d ed. p63-93

Slonim, M. L. Samizdat: the underground press. *In* Slonim, M. L. Soviet Russian literature p376-82

Slusser, R. M. History and the democratic opposition. *In* Tokes, R. L. ed. Dissent in the USSR p329-53

Sosin, G. Magnitizdat: uncensored songs of dissent. *In* Tokes, R. L. ed. Dissent in the USSR p276-309

Underhill, Frank Hawkins

About

Berger, C. Frank Underhill: history as political criticism. *In* Berger, C. The writing of Canadian history p54-84

Underhill, John

About individual works

Newes from America

Seelye, J. By way of Newtown: how Thomas Hooker crossed his Rubicon and started the Pequot War: a Hudibrastic interlude. *In* Seelye, J. Prophetic waters p187-216

Underhill, Ruth Murray

The salt pilgrimage; excerpt from "Papago Indian religion." *In* Tedlock, D. E. and Tedlock, B. eds. Teachings from the American earth p42-74

Underprivileged children. See Socially handicapped children

Understanding. See Comprehension

Unemployed

Leibenstein, H. Efficiency wages, X-efficiency, and urban unemployment. *In* Economic development and planning p168-85

Mathematical models

See Phillips curve

Great Britain

Stevenson, J. The politics of violence. *In* Peele, G. and Cook, C. eds. The politics of reappraisal, 1918-1939 p146-65

United States

Cottle, T. J. An unemployed family. *In* On the making of Americans p143-72

Unemployment. See Labor supply; Unemployed

Unemployment, Technological

Fei, J. C. H. and Ranis, G. Technological transfer, employment and development. *In* Economic development and planning p75-103

Ungaretti, Giuseppe

About

Perella, N. J. Giuseppe Ungaretti. *In* Perella, N. J. Midday in Italian literature p201-39

About individual works

Lindoro di deserto

Cambon, G. Ungaretti's "Lindoro di deserto": jongleur of the self. *In* Italian literature: roots and branches p407-19

Unger, Richard W.

The Netherlands herring fishery in the late Middle Ages: the false legend of Willem Beukels of Biervliet. *In* Viator: medieval and Renaissance studies v9 p335-56

Unidad Popular

Gonzalez, M. Ideology and culture under Popular Unity. *In* O'Brien, P. J. ed. Allende's Chile p106-27

Kay, C. Agrarian reform and the transition to socialism. *In* O'Brien, P. J. ed. Allende's Chile p79-105

Lira, P. pseud. The crisis of hegemony in the Chilean Left. *In* O'Brien, P. J. ed. Allende's Chile

Unification Church. See Holy Spirit Association for the Unification of World Christianity

The Unified Family. See Holy Spirit Association for the Unification of World Christianity

Uniform Commercial Code; a comment on the jurisprudence of the. Danzig, R. *In* Stanford legal essays p97-111

Uniformity of nature

Quine, W. V. On simple theories of a complex world. *In* Quine, W. V. The ways of paradox, and other essays p255-58

Unilever, ltd.

Wilson, C. H. Multinationals, management, and world markets: a historical view. *In* Evolution of international management structures p193-216

Union of Contemporary Architects. See Society of Modern Architects

Union of Youth

Bowlt, J. E. The "Union of Youth." *In* Gibian, G. and Tjalsma, H. W. eds. Russian modernism p165-87

Unions, Trade. See Trade-unions

Unitarianism. See Socinianism

Unitarianism in literature

Pickering, S. Dombey and son and Unitarianism. *In* Pickering, S. The moral tradition in English fiction, 1785-1850 p149-68

United Nations

Claude, I. L. Domestic jurisdiction and colonialism. *In* Kilson, M. ed. New states in the modern world p121-35

Cruise O'Brien, C. Actors, roles, and stages. *In* Smithsonian Institution. The cultural drama p71-85

Finger, S. M. International terrorism and the United Nations. *In* International terrorism p323-48

Garment, L. Majoritarianism at the United Nations and human rights. *In* Sidorsky, D. ed. Essays on human rights p30-36

Hambro, E. I. Permanent representatives to international organisations. *In* The Year book of world affairs, 1976 p30-41

Hoffmann, S. Regulating the new international systems. *In* Kilson, M. ed. New states in the modern world p171-99

Hula, E. Fifty years of international government: reflections on the League of Nations and the United Nations. *In* [Truth and tragedy]: a tribute to Hans Morgenthau p179-98

Liskofsky, S. The United Nations and human rights: "alternative approaches." *In* Sidorsky, D. ed. Essays on human rights p46-67

López-Rey y Arrojo, M. United Nations social defence policy and the problem of crime. *In* Crime, criminology and public policy p489-508

Maynes, C. W. The United Nations: out of control or out of touch? *In* The Year book of world affairs, 1977 p98-111

Moynihan, D. P. The significance of the Zionism-as-racism resolution for international human rights. *In* Sidorsky, D. ed. Essays on human rights p37-45

Rodley, N. S. Monitoring human rights by the U.N. system and nongovernmental organizations. *In* Kommers, D. P. and Loescher, G. D. eds. Human rights and American foreign policy p157-78

Armed Forces

James, A. Recent developments in United Nations peace-keeping. *In* The Year book of world affairs, 1977 p75-97

See also International police

Charter

Cassese, A. The Helsinki Declaration and self-determination. *In* Human rights, international law and the Helsinki Accord p83-110

Schwarzenberger, G. The principles of the United Nations. *In* The Year book of world affairs, 1976 p307-37

Commissions

Ramcharan, B. G. Equality and discrimination in international economic law (VIII): the United Nations Regional Economic Commissions. *In* The Year book of world affairs, 1978 p268-85

Economic Commission for Africa

Andemicael, B. OAU collaboration with the United Nations in economic and social development. *In* El-Ayouty, Y. ed. The Organization of African Unity after ten years p213-36

Economic Commission for Asia and the Far East. Population Division

Sovani, N. V. A comparative study of population and agricultural change in some countries of the ECAFE region. *In* Economic factors in population growth p273-92

General Assembly

The UN Declaration of the Rights of the Child. *In* Gross, B. and Gross, R. eds. The children's rights movement p333-39

General Assembly. Committee on the Peaceful Uses of the Sea-Bed and the Ocean Floor Beyond the Limits of National Jurisdiction

Borgese, E. M. ed. Recommendations from Pacem in Maribus IV to the United Nations Committee on the Peaceful Uses of the Sea-Bed. *In* Borgese, E. M. and Krieger, D. eds. The tides of change p353-57

Pardo, A. New institutions for ocean space. *In* Borgese, E. M. and Krieger, D. eds. The tides of change p324-27

Varon, B. Ocean issues on the international agenda. *In* Erb, G. F. and Kallab, V. eds. Beyond dependency p120-31

General Assembly. Declaration of the Rights of the Child

Bel Geddes, J. The rights of children in world perspective. *In* Gross, B. and Gross, R. eds. The children's rights movement p214-16

General Assembly. Eighteen-Nation Committee on Disarmament

Caracciolo, R. Main issues in the disarmament negotiations. *In* The Dynamics of the arms race p123-34

General Assembly. International Covenants on Human Rights

Frowein, J. A. The interrelationship between the Helsinki Final Act, the International Covenants on Human Rights, and the European Convention on Human Rights. *In* Human rights, international law and the Helsinki Accord p71-82

General Assembly. Universal Declaration of Human Rights

Hauser, R. E. A. International human rights protection: the dream and the deceptions. *In* Sidorsky, D. ed. Essays on human rights p21-29

Schneider, H. W. Declaration, theory, and existence of human rights. *In* The Abdication of philosophy: philosophy and the public good p89-92

Starke, J. G. Human rights and international law. *In* Human rights p113-31

International Law Commission

Ramcharan, B. G. The International Law Commission. *In* The Year Book of world affairs, 1975 p283-300

Office of the United Nations High Commissioner for Refugees

Goormaghtigh, J. How an INGO contributed to broadening the scope and competence of an IGO. *In* Unofficial diplomats p250-58

Resolutions

Murphy, J. F. United Nations proposals on the control and repression of terrorism. *In* International terrorism and political crimes p493-506

United Nations—*Continued*

Secretariat

The origins and fundamental causes of international terrorism. *In* International terrorism and political crimes p5-10

Secretary-General

Rieber, R. A. Public information and political leadership in international organisations: the United Nations Secretary General. *In* The Year book of world affairs, 1976 p42-68

Near East

Caradon, H. M. F. Baron. Is peace possible? What are the options? *In* The New world balance and peace in the Middle East: reality or mirage? p217-26

Khouri, F. J. United Nations peace efforts. *In* The Elusive peace in the Middle East p19-101

Stoessinger, J. G. The United Nations and the Arab-Israeli conflict. *In* The New world balance and peace in the Middle East: reality or mirage? p79-82

United States

McNemar, D. W. The United States and the United Nations. *In* Baldwin, D. A. ed. America in an interdependent world p315-46

United Nations Conference on the Human Environment, Stockholm, 1972
Juda, L. International environmental concern: perspectives of and implications for developing states. *In* Orr, D. W. and Soroos, M. S. eds. The global predicament p90-107

United Nations Conference on the Law of the Sea, 1974
Amerasinghe, H. S. Key issues in the Third United Nations Conference on the Law of the Sea. *In* Borgese, E. M. and Krieger, D. eds. The tides of change p328-39

Galindo Pohl, R. Pacem in Maribus in the Caribbean. *In* Borgese, E. M. and Krieger, D. eds. The tides of change p264-77

Kent, G. Ocean fisheries management. *In* Orr, D. W and Soroos, M. S. eds. The global predicament p232-48

Schwarzenberger, G. Trends in the law of the sea. *In* The Year book of world affairs, 1979 p328-73

United Nations Educational, Scientific and Cultural Organization
Film as a universal mass medium. *In* Fischer, H. D. and Merrill, J. C. eds. International and intercultural communication p115-20

United Nations Educational Scientific and Cultural Organization (as subject)
Knight, R. P. UNESCO's role in world communication. *In* Fischer, H. D. and Merrill, J. C. eds. International and intercultural communication p377-91

Naesselund, G. R. UNESCO and the press in the Third World. *In* Horton, P. C. ed. The Third World and press freedom p210-19

Tatarian, R. News flow in the Third World: an overview. *In* Horton, P. C. ed. The Third World and press freedom p 1-54

United Nations High Commissioner for Refugees. See United Nations—Office of the United Nations High Commissioner for Refugees

United Nations Monetary and Financial Conference, Bretton Woods, N.H. 1944
Gardner, R. N. Bretton Woods. *In* Keynes, M. ed. Essays on John Maynard Keynes p202-15

United Neighborhood Houses, New York
Wilson, M. G. and Sugrue, R. Senior companion program. *In* Home care p178-84

United Red Army. See Rengo Sekigun

United States

Air Force

See Air Force law—United States

Air Force—Afro-Americans

Dansby, J. L. Race relations at Base X. *In* Henderson, G. ed. Human relations in the military p59-75

Ford, B. L. Justice is more than a word. *In* Henderson, G. ed. Human relations in the military p127-44

Air Force—Personnel management

Hebebrand, R. C. Human relations in practice. *In* Henderson, G. ed. Human relations in the military p19-32

Air Force. Reserve Officers' Training Corps

Radway, L. I. The future of the Reserve Officer Training Corps. *In* Beaumont, R. A. and Edmonds, M. eds. War in the next decade p55-68

Aliens

See Aliens—United States

Annexations

See United States—Territorial expansion

Archives

See Archives—United States

Armed Forces

Holloway, B. K. United States grand strategy for the next ten years. *In* Grand strategy for the 1980s p19-36

Milton, T. R. Thoughts on our national strategy for the future. *In* Grand strategy for 1980s p57-71

Palmer, B. Strategic guidelines for the United States in the 1980s. *In* Grand strategy for the 1980s p73-112

Sherman, E. F. Accountability and responsiveness of the military establishment. *In* Rieselbach, L. N. ed. People vs. government: the responsiveness of American institutions p226-73

Taylor, M. D. National policy too lightly armed. *In* Grand strategy for the 1980s p3-17

Armed Forces—Afro-Americans

McCoy, D. R. and Ruetten, R. T. Towards equality: Blacks in the United States during the Second World War. *In* Hepburn, A. C. ed. Minorities in history p135-53

Stillman, R. J. Black participation in the Armed Forces. *In* The Black American reference book p889-926

Armed Forces—Appropriations and expenditures

Aspin, L. The defense budget and foreign policy: the role of Congress. *In* Long, F. A. and Rathjens, G. W. eds. Arms, defense policy, and arms control p155-74

Trask, D. F. The military-industrial complex. *In* Encyclopedia of American foreign policy p557-66

United States—*Continued*

Armed Forces—Officers

Williams, T. A. Youthful officer retirement: matrix for political action. *In* Beaumont, R. A. and Edmonds, M. eds. War in the next decade p69-88

Armed Forces—Reserves

See United States. National Guard

Army—Afro-American troops

Cadoria, S. G. Women officers in the United States Army: liberated? *In* Henderson, G. ed. Human relations in the military p95-105

Army—Officers—History

Swart, S. L. The military examination board in the Civil War: a case study. *In* Hubbell, J. T. ed. Battles lost and won p241-59

Army—Personnel management

Swart, S. L. The military examination board in the Civil War: a case study. *In* Hubbell, J. T. ed. Battles lost and won p241-59

Army—Women

Cadoria, S. G. Women officers in the United States Army: liberated? *In* Henderson, G. ed. Human relations in the military p95-105

Army. Cavalry—Equipment

Starr, S. Z. Cold steel: the saber and the Union cavalry. *In* Hubbell, J. T. ed. Battles lost and won p107-24

Army. Cavalry—History— Civil War, 1861-1865

Stonesifer, R. P. The Union cavalry comes of age. *In* Hubbell, J. T. ed. Battles lost and won p125-34

Army. Infantry—Equipment

Buechler, J. "Give 'em the bayonet"—a note on Civil War mythology. *In* Hubbell, J. T. ed. Battles lost and won p135-39

Army. 54th Regiment, Massachusetts Colored Infantry—Recruiting, enlistment, etc.

Abbott, R. H. Massachusetts and the recruitment of Southern Negroes, 1863-1865. *In* Hubbell, J. T. ed. Battles lost and won p157-70

Army. Reserve Officers' Training Corps

Radway, L. I. The future of the Reserve Officer Training Corps. *In* Beaumont, R. A. and Edmonds, M. eds. War in the next decade p55-68

Army. Troop Support Command

Lee, G. R. A federal equal-employment-opportunity program. *In* Henderson, G. ed. Human relations in the military p237-48

Army. Women's Army Corps

Cadoria, S. G. Women officers in the United States Army: liberated? *In* Henderson, G. ed. Human relations in the military p95-105

Articles of Confederation

Jones, H. W. The Articles of Confederation and the creation of a federal system. *In* Aspects of American liberty p126-45

Bibliography

Mooney, J. E. Loyalist imprints printed in America, 1774-1785. *In* American Antiquarian Society. Proceedings v84 pt 1 p105-218

Bureau of Narcotics

See United States. Bureau of Narcotics and Dangerous Drugs

Bureau of Narcotics and Dangerous Drugs

Dickson, D. T. Bureaucracy and morality: an organizational perspective on a moral crusade. *In* Davis, F. J. and Stivers, R. eds. The collective definition of deviance p334-49

Centennial celebrations, etc.

See American Revolution Bicentennial, 1776-1976

Central Intelligence Agency

Barnet, R. J. The "dirty-tricks" gap. *In* Borosage, R. L. and Marks, J. D. eds. The CIA file p214-28

Borosage, R. L. The Central Intelligence Agency: the king's men and the constitutional order. *In* Borosage, R. L. and Marks, J. D. eds. The CIA file p125-41

Borosage, R. L. Marks, J. D. Destabilizing Chile. *In* Borosage, R. L. and Marks, J. D. eds. The CIA file p79-89

Branfman, F. The President's secret army: a case study—the CIA in Laos, 1962-1972. *In* Borosage, R. L. and Marks, J. D. eds. The CIA file p46-78

Colby, W. E. The view from Langley. *In* Borosage, R. L. and Marks, J. D. eds. The CIA file p181-87

Falk, R. A. CIA covert operations and international law. *In* Borosage, R. L. and Marks, J. D. eds. The CIA file p142-58

Galbraith, J. K. The global strategic mind. *In* Galbraith, J. K. Annals of an abiding liberal p331-40

Halperin, M. H. Covert operations: effects of secrecy on decision-making. *In* Borosage, R. L. and Marks, J. D. eds. The CIA file p159-77

Kirkpatrick, L. B. Intelligence and counter-intelligence. *In* Encyclopedia of American foreign policy p417-27

Morris, R. P. and Mauzy, R. Following the scenario: reflections on five case histories in the mode and aftermath of CIA intervention. *In* Borosage, R. L. and Marks, J. D. eds. The CIA file p28-45

Ross, T. B. Surreptitious entry: the CIA's operations in the United States. *In* Borosage, R. L. and Marks, J. D. eds. The CIA file p93-108

Wise, D. Covert operations abroad: an overview. *In* Borosage, R, L, and Marks, J. D. eds. The CIA file p3-27

Children's Bureau—History

Johnson, J. E. The role of women in the founding of the United States Children's Bureau. *In* "Remember the ladies": new perspectives on women in American history p179-96

Church history

Benton, R. M. The preachers. *In* Emerson, E. H. ed. American literature, 1764-1789 p73-85

Civilian Conservation Corps

Parman, D. L. The Indian and the Civilian Conservation Corps. *In* The American Indian p127-45

United States—*Continued*

Civilization

Bigsby, C. W. E. Europe, America and the cultural debate. *In* Bigsby, C. W. E. Superculture p 1-27

Brogan, Sir D. W. The character of American life; excerpt from "America in the modern world." *In* Burton, D. H. ed. American history—British historians p3-23

Farrell, J. T. From bunk to buncombe. *In* Farrell, J. T. Literary essays, 1954-1974 p110-12

Fortin, R. A. Life, liberty, and the pursuit of happiness. *In* Alderson, W. T. ed. American issues p129-44

Harding, V. Is America in any sense chosen? A Black response. *In* An Almost chosen people p119-30

Hardison, O. B. Attempting the impossible and accomplishing the unbelievable: thoughts on two American revolutions. *In* A Time to hear and answer: essays for the Bicentennial season p37-58

Hesburgh, T. M. American aspirations and the grounds of hope. *In* An Almost chosen people p131-46

Konvitz, M. R. Introduction: the American-Hebraic idea. *In* Konvitz, M. R. Judaism and the American idea p15-32

MacLeish, A. Master or man. *In* MacLeish, A. Riders on the earth p27-39

McLuhan, H. M. The implications of cultural uniformity. *In* Bigsby, C. W. E. Superculture p43-56

Marty, M. E. The American tradition and the American tomorrow. *In* Tomorrow's American p133-55

Mencken, H. L. The need for an aristocracy; excerpt from "Prejudices: second series." *In* Crunden, R. M. ed. The superfluous men p73-79

Meyer, D. H. The American achievement. *In* Meyer, D. H. The democratic Enlightenment p210-15

Murray, J. C. The civilization of the pluralist society; except from "We hold these truths: Catholic reflections on the American proposition." *In* A Public philosophy reader p143-51

Nicgorski, W. and Weber, R. E. Afterword. *In* An Almost chosen people p147-60

Nisbet, R. A. American culture and the idea of community. *In* Arab and American cultures p93-105

Novak, M. The Nation with the soul of a church; excerpt from "Choosing our king: powerful symbols in Presidential politics." *In* A Public philosophy reader p92-96

Preston, R. A. Some conclusions about the revolution-evolution problem. *In* Perspectives on revolution and evolution p268-87

Roth, R. J. Person and technology: a Deweyan perspective. *In* Roth, R. J. ed. Person and community p87-102

Trilling, L. "That smile of Parmenides made me think." *In* Trilling, L. A gathering of fugitives p164-79

Trilling, L. Two notes on David Riesman. *In* Trilling, L. A gathering of fugitives p91-107

Veysey, L. R. Growing up in America. *In* Alderson, W. T. ed. American issues p113-28

Warren, R. P. The use of the past. *In* A Time to hear and answer: essays for the Bicentennial season p 1-35

Civilization—British influences

Allen, H. C. The cultural tie; excerpt from "Conflict and concord, the Anglo-American relationship since 1783." *In* Burton, D. H. ed. American history—British historians p75-91

Civilization—European influences

Sessions, R. Europe comes to America. *In* Sessions, R. Roger Sessions on music p319-25

Civilization—History

Davis, D. B. Cultural history and the American identity. *In* Smithsonian Institution. The cultural drama p139-56

Morris, R. B.. Historical prologue. *In* The National purpose reconsidered p 1-9

Civilization—Spanish American influences

Worcester, D. E. The significance of the Spanish borderlands to the United States. *In* Weber, D. J. ed. New Spain's far northern frontier p 1-14

Civilization—Spanish influences

Myres, S. L. The ranching frontier: Spanish institutional background of the Plains cattle industry. *In* Weber, D. J. ed. New Spain's far northern frontier p79-94

Worcester, D. E. The significance of the Spanish borderlands to the United States. *In* Weber, D. J. ed. New Spain's far northern frontier p 1-14

Civilization—Study and teaching

Kavanaugh, J. V. The artifact in American culture: the development of an undergraduate program in American studies. *In* Material culture and the study of American life p65-74

Luedtke, L. S. Not so common ground: controversies in contemporary American studies. *In* Luedtke, L. S. ed. The study of American culture p323-67

Mechling, J. E. In search of an American ethnophysics. *In* Luedtke, L. S. ed. The study of American culture p241-77

Merideth, R. "It's a small world": high school, American culture studies, and cultural revolution. *In* Luedtke, L. S. ed. The study of American culture p279-322

Wilson, D. S. Epilogue. *In* Wilson, D. S. In the presence of nature p187-95

Civilization—To 1783

Emerson, E. H. The cultural context of the American Revolution. *In* Emerson, E. H. ed. American literature, 1764-1789 p3-17

Meyer, D. H. The civilized Americans. *In* Meyer, D. H. The democratic Enlightenment p49-60

Nisbet, R. A. The social impact of the Revolution. *In* America's continuing revolution p73-95

Civilization—To 1783—Bibliography

Seelye, J. Ex libris. *In* Seelye, J. Prophetic waters p389-97

Civilization—19th century

Arnold, M. Civilisation in the United States. *In* Arnold, M. The last word p350-69

Brown, R. D. Modernization: a Victorian climax. *In* Howe, D. W. ed. Victorian America p29-44

Howe, D. W. Victorian culture in America. *In* Howe, D. W. ed. Victorian America p3-28

United States—Civilization—19th century —*Continued*

Lowenthal, D. The place of the past in the American landscape. *In* Geographies of the mind p89-117

Saum, L. O. Death in the popular mind of pre-Civil War America. *In* Death in America p30-48

Singleton, G. H. Protestant voluntary organizations and the shaping of Victorian America. *In* Howe, D. W. ed. Victorian America p47-58

Civilization—20th century

Coben, S. The assault on Victorianism in the twentieth century. *In* Howe, D. W. ed. Victorian America p160-81

MacLeish, A. News from the horse and wagon. *In* MacLeish, A. Riders on the earth p48-56

Murphey, M. G. The place of beliefs in modern culture. *In* Higham, J. and Conkin, P. K. eds. New directions in American intellectual history p151-65

Schneider, H. W. The American Establishment, the civilizing arts, and philosophy. *In* Philosophy and the civilizing arts p433-45

Susman, W. I. "Personality" and the making of twentieth-century culture. *In* Higham, J. and Conkin, P. K. eds. New directions in American intellectual history p212-26

Widmer, K. The waste land and the American breakdown. *In* French, W. G. ed. The twenties p475-96

Civilization—1918-1945

Aaron, D. An approach to the thirties. *In* Luedtke, L. S. ed. The study of American culture p 1-17

Coben, S. The assault on Victorianism in the twentieth century. *In* Howe, D. W. ed. Victorian America p160-81

Morris, W. The ghostly rumble among the drums. *In* Morris, W. Earthly delights, unearthly adornments p113-16

Civilization—1945-

Baron, D. The national purpose reconsidered: a post-Bicentennial perspective. *In* The National purpose reconsidered p119-39

Glock, C. Y. Consciousness among contemporary youth: an interpretation. *In* The New religious consciousness p353-66

MacLeish, A. The revolt of the diminished man. *In* MacLeish, A. Riders on the earth p13-26

Rahv, P. American intellectuals in the postwar situation. *In* Rahv, P. Essays on literature and politics, 1932-1972 p328-34

Rescher, N. The environmental crisis and the quality of life. *In* Philosophy & environmental crisis p90-104

Rusk, D. The American Revolution and the future. *In* America's continuing revolutio p387-98

 illing, L. The situation of the American int lectual at the present time. *In* Trilling, L. A gathering of fugitives p65-84

Vidal, G. The state of the Union. *In* Vidal, G. Matters of fact and of fiction p265-85

Civilization—1970-

Collier, A. T. On celebrating American independence. *In* Warner, S. B. ed. The American experiment p 1-10

Hardwick, E. Domestic manners. *In* A New America? p 1-11

Hassan, I. H. Models of transformation: ideology, utopia, and fantasy in America. *In* Hassan, I. H. Paracriticisms p151-76

Lilienthal, D. E. The rebirth of a nation. *In* Aspects of American liberty p187-95

Coinage

See Coinage—United States

Commerce

Johnson, A. M. The business of America. *In* Alderson, W. T. ed. American issues p81-96

Smith, R. F. Reciprocity. *In* Encyclopedia of American foreign policy p867-81

Commerce—Japan

Iriye, A. Japan as a competitor, 1895-1917. *In* Iriye, A. ed. Mutual images p73-99

Commerce—Latin America

Rogers, S. H. Trade relations in the inter-American system. *In* Farer, T. J. ed. The future of the inter-American system p54-65

Commercial law

See Commercial law—United States

Commercial policy

Diebold, W. U.S. trade policy: the new political dimensions. *In* Bundy, W. P. ed. The world economic crisis p140-64

Doenecke, J. D. The most-favored-nation principle. *In* Encyclopedia of American foreign policy p603-09

Holbo, P. S. Trade and commerce. *In* Encyclopedia of American foreign policy p945-60

Commercial treaties

Doenecke, J. D. The most-favored-nation principle. *In* Encyclopedia of American foreign policy p603-09

Congress

Aspin, L. The defense budget and foreign policy: the role of Congress. *In* Long, F. A. and Rathjens, G. W. eds. Arms, defense policy, and arms control p155-74

Bolling, R. The management of Congress. *In* Managing nonprofit organizations p102-08

Caraley, D. The Carter Congress and urban programs: first soundings. *In* Burnham, W. D. and Weinberg, M. W. eds. American politics and public policy p188-221

Cohen, W. Congressional power to interpret due process and equal protection. *In* Stanford legal essays p79-96

Dry, M. Congress. *In* Graham, G. J. and Graham, S. G. eds. Founding principles of American government p223-57

Fenno, R. F. If, as Ralph Nader says, Congress is "the broken branch," how come we love our Congressmen so much? *In* Ornstein, N. J. ed. Congress in change p277-87

Fraser, D. M. Congress's role in the making of international human rights policy. *In* Kommers, D P. and Loescher, G. D. eds. Human rights and American foreign policy p247-54

Huitt, R. K. Congress: retrospect and prospect. *In* Havard, W. C. and Bernd, J. L. eds. 200 years of the Republic in retrospect p209-27

Jones, C. O. Somebody must be trusted: an essay on leadership of the U.S. Congress. *In* Ornstein, N. J. ed. Congress in change p265-76

United States—Constitutional law—*Cont.*

Kelly, A. H. The Constitution and foreign policy. *In* Encyclopedia of American foreign policy p177-90

Konvitz, M. R. The rule of law: Torah and the Constitution. *In* Konvitz, M. R. Judaism and the American idea p53-68

Mason, A. T. America's political heritage: revolution and free government—a Bicentennial tribute. *In* Essays on the Constitution of the United States p11-31

Murphy, W. F. The art of constitutional interpretation. *In* Essays on the Constitution of the United States p130-59

Ostrom, V. The American contribution to a theory of constitutional choice. *In* Havard, W. C. and Bernd, J. L. eds. 200 years of the Republic in retrospect p56-78

Shapiro, M. M. The Constitution and economic rights. *In* Essays on the Constitution of the United States p74-98

Continental Congress—History

Cunliffe, M. Congressional leadership in the American Revolution. *In* Library of Congress Symposia on the American Revolution, 3d, 1974. Leadership in the American Revolution p41-61

Cost of Living Council

Johnson, W. A. The impact of price controls on the oil industry: how to worsen an energy crisis. *In* Eppen, G. D. ed. Energy: the policy issues p99-121

Court of Appeals for the District of Columbia Circuit

Scalia, A. Vermont Yankee: the A P A, the D.C. Circuit, and the Supreme Court. *In* The Supreme Court review, 1978 p345-409

Custom-house

See Customs administration — United States

Declaration of Independence

Bradford, M. E. The heresy of equality. *In* A Public philosophy reader p309-36

Diamond, M. The idea of equality: the view from the founding. *In* An Almost chosen people p19-37

Diamond, M. The revolution of sober expectations. *In* America's continuing revolution p25-41

Grimes, A. P. Conservative Revolution and liberal rhetoric: the Declaration of Independence. *In* Havard, W. C. and Bernd, J. L. eds. 200 years of the Republic in retrospect p 1-19

Howell, W. S. The Declaration of Independence and eighteenth-century logic. *In* Howell, W. S. Poetics, rhetoric, and logic p163-90

Jones, H. M. The Declaration of Independence: a critique. *In* American Antiquarian Society. Proceedings v85 pt. 1 p55-72

Kenyon, C. M. The Declaration of Independence: philosophy of government in a free society. *In* Aspects of American liberty p114-25

Konvitz, M. R. Life and liberty for the pursuit of happiness. *In* Konvitz, M. R. Judaism and the American idea p181-201

Lence, R. M. The American Declaration of Independence: the majority and the right of political power. *In* Graham, G. J. and Graham, S. G. eds. Founding principles of American government p29-59

MacLeish, A. Bicentennial of what? *In* Aspects of American liberty p 1-7

MacLeish, A. The ghost of Thomas Jefferson. *In* MacLeish, A. Riders on the earth p57-65

Marshall, C. B. American foreign policy as a dimension of the American Revolution. *In* America's continuing revolution p363-84

Peckham, H. H. Independence: the view from Britain. *In* American Antiquarian Society. Proceedings v85 pt.2 p387-403

Robbins, C. The pursuit of happiness. *In* America's continuing revolution p119-39

Defenses

Allison, G. T. and Morris, F. A. Armaments and arms control: exploring the determinants of military weapons. *In* Long, F. A. and Rathjens, G. W. eds. Arms, defense policy, and arms control p99-129

Carter, B. E. The strategic debate in the United States. *In* Kirk, G. L. and Wessell, N. H. eds. The Soviet threat p15-29

Dumas, L. J. National security and the arms race. *In* International terrorism and world security p158-64

Gray, C. S. Strategic ideas and defense policy: the organizational nexus. *In* Beaumont, R. A. and Edmonds, M. eds. War in the next decade p89-109

King, P. All at sea? A critique of the American strategic force structure. *In* Arms control and technological innovation p265-87

Morgenthau, H. J. The fallacy of thinking conventionally about nuclear weapons. *In* Arms control and technological innovation p255-64

Russett, G. M. A countercombatant alternative to nuclear MADness. *In* Ethics and nuclear strategy? p124-43

Trask, D. F. The military-industrial complex. *In* Encyclopedia of American foreign policy p557-66

Wheeler, G. E. National security. *In* Encyclopedia of American foreign policy p623-34

Winters, F. X. Ethics, diplomacy, and defense. *In* Ethics and nuclear strategy? p14-50

Department of Defense—Appropriations and expenditures

Steinbruner, J. D. and Carter, B. Organizational and political dimensions of the strategic posture: the problems of reform. *In* Long, F. A. and Rathjens, G. W. eds. Arms, defense policy, and arms control p131-54

Department of Defense—Budget

Aspin, L. The defense budget and foreign policy: the role of Congress. *In* Long, F. A. and Rathjens, G. W. eds. Arms, defense policy, and arms control p155-74

Department of Defense —Procurement

Edmonds, M. Accountability and the military-industrial complex. *In* Smith, B. L. R. ed. The new political economy: the public use of the private sector p149-80

Department of Health, Education and Welfare

Barasch, F. K. HEW, the university, and women. *In* Gross, B. R. ed. Reverse discrimination p54-65

Seabury, P. HEW and the universities. *In* Gross, B. R. ed. Reverse discrimination p97-112

United States—*Continued*

Economic conditions—1918-1945

Farrell, J. T. Writers of the thirties. *In* Farrell, J. T. Literary essays, 1954-1974 p34-38

Economic conditions—1945-

Meyersohn, R. B. Abundance reconsidered. *In* On the making of Americans p87-104

Economic conditions—1961-

Backman, J. Economic growth, standards of living, and quality of life. *In* Tomorrow's American p69-89

Galbraith, J. K. The valid image of the modern economy. *In* Galbraith, J. K. Annals of an abiding liberal p3-19

Ridker, R. G. Population growth, economic growth and the environment in the United States. *In* Economic factors in population growth p324-51

Simon, W. E. The crucial issue is freedom. *In* Prochnow, H. V. ed. Dilemmas facing the nation p 1-31

Warner, S. B. The two revolutions. *In* Warner, S. B. ed. The American experiment p11-29

Economic policy

Aliber, R. Z. U.S. economic policies and the costs of national security. *In* Isolation or interdependence? p131-48

Bowden, G. T. A response: planning— yes, but by whom? *In* Planning, politics, and the public interest p161-66

Commoner, B. Energy, environment, and economics. *In* Eppen, G. D. ed. Energy: the policy issues p25-40

Commoner, B. A new historic passage: energy, the economy, and the era of constraints. *In* The National purpose reconsidered p53-72

Darcy, R. L. Economic education, human values, and the quality of life. *In* Fairfield, R. P. ed. Humanistic frontiers in American education p102-11

Friedman, M. Adam Smith's relevance for 1976. *In* Glahe, F. R. ed. Adam Smith and The wealth of nations p7-20

Galbraith, J. K. The conservative majority syndrome. *In* Galbraith, J. K. Annals of an abiding liberal p47-53

Galbraith, J. K. Defenders of the faith, I: William Simon. *In* Galbraith, J. K. Annals of an abiding liberal p103-08

Galbraith, J. K. Economists and the economics of professional contentment. *In* Galbraith, J. K. Annals of an abiding liberal p20-35

Goldstein, W. The politics of planning for the public interest: the role of liberal ideology in a conservative society. *In* Planning, politics, and the public interest p181-200

Graham, S. G. Government and the economy. *In* Graham, G. J. and Graham, S. G. eds. Founding principles of American government p305-30

Hacker, A. The new rationality: the clash between the corporate and the public sector conceptions of the national interest. *In* Planning, politics, and the public interest p10-19

Javits, J. K. Government's role in economic management. *In* Benton, L. R. ed. Management for the future p165-73

Lekachman, R. The inevitability of planning. *In* Planning, politics, and the public interest p143-60

Vernon, R. National planning and the multinational enterprise: the U.S. case. *In* Planning, politics, and the public interest p77-94

Economic policy—1933-1945

Hawley, E. W. The New Deal and business. *In* Braeman, J.; Bremner, R. H. and Brody, D. eds. The New Deal v 1 p50-82

Kirkendall, R. S. The New Deal and agriculture. *In* Braeman, J.; Bremner, R. H. and Brody, D. eds. The New Deal v 1 p83-109

Shapiro, M. M. The Constitution and economic rights. *In* Essays on the Constitution of the United States p74-98

Wolters, R. The New Deal and the Negro. *In* Braeman, J.; Bremner, R. H. and Brody, D. eds. The New Deal v 1 p170-217

Economic policy—1961-

Galbraith, J. K. The valid image of the modern economy. *In* Galbraith, J. K. Annals of an abiding liberal p3-19

Emigration and immigration

Bustamante, J. A. The "Wetback" as deviant: an application of labeling theory. *In* Davis, F. J. and Stivers, R. eds. The collective definition of deviance p256-67

Hansen, M. L. Immigration and Puritanism. *In* Mulder, J. M. and Wilson, J. F. eds. Religion in American history p342-57

Hicks, G. L. and Handler, M. J. Ethnicity, public policy, and anthropologists. *In* Eddy, E. M. and Partridge, W. L. eds. Applied anthropology in America p292-325

Kammen, M. G. A nation of nations. *In* Alderson, W. T. ed. American issues p 1-15

Porter, J. R. Melting pot or mosaic: revolution or reversion? *In* Perspectives on revolution and evolution p152-79

Emigration and immigration— Historiography

Ts'ai, S. H. Chinese immigration through Communist Chinese eyes: an introduction to the historiography. *In* The Asian American: the historical experience p53-66

Emigration and immigration law

See Emigration and immigration law— United States

Executive departments

See Presidents—United States—Staff

Executive departments—Management

Drucker, P. F. How to make the Presidency manageable. *In* Managing nonprofit organizations p280-88

Federal Bureau of Investigation

Galbraith, J. K. My forty years with the FBI. *In* Galbraith, J. K. Annals of an abiding liberal p155-81

Federal Communications Commission

Polsby, D. D. F.C.C. v. National Citizens Committee for Broadcasting and the judicious uses of administrative discretion. *In* The Supreme Court review, 1978 p 1-38

Food and Drug Administration

Crout, J. R. Drug regulation by government: the nature of regulatory choices. *In* The Frontiers of human knowledge p59-68

United States—*Continued*

Foreign economic policy

Karlik, J. R. Economic factors influencing American foreign policy. *In* The Interaction of economics and foreign policy p25-47

Foreign economic relations

Bergsten, C. F. Economic tensions: America versus the Third World. *In* Rosecrance, R. N. ed. America as an ordinary country p199-223

Holbo, P. S. Trade and commerce. *In* Encyclopedia of American foreign policy p945-60

Mazuri, A. A. The new interdependence. Erb, G. F. and Kallab, V. eds. Beyond dependency p38-54

Ringbakk, K. A. Multinational corporations and foreign policy. *In* Baldwin, D. A. ed. America in an interdependent world p91-135

Silk, L. S. America in the world economy. *In* Rosecrance, R. N. ed. America as an ordinary country p158-73

Wilson, J. H. Economic foreign policy. *In* Encyclopedia of American foreign policy p281-91

Foreign economic relations—History

Kindleberger, C. P. U.S. foreign economic policy, 1776-1976. *In* Two hundred years of American foreign policy p209-51

Foreign economic relations—Africa

Kasfir, N. M. Interdependence and American commitment to promote development in the Third World: Africa—the hardest case. *In* Baldwin, D. A. ed. America in an interdependent world p223-43

Foreign economic relations—China

Eckstein, A. Sino-American economic relations. *In* China and America p53-108

Luther, D. G. China, lump sum settlements, and executive agreements. *In* China's changing role in the world economy p213-22

Foreign economic relations—Cuba

Mesa-Lago, C. The economics of U.S.-Cuban rapprochement. *In* Cuba in the world p199-224

Foreign economic relations—Great Britain

Calleo, D. P. Keynes and the 'Pax Americana.' *In* Skidelsky, R. J. A ed. The end of the Keynesian era p95-103

Foreign economic relations—Japan

Kanamori, H. Future U.S.-Japanese economic relations. *In* Clapp, P. and Halperin, M. H. eds. United States-Japanese relations, the 1970's p58-78

Yamamoto, M. The Cold war and U.S.-Japan economic cooperation. *In* The Origins of the Cold war in Asia p408-25

Foreign economic relations—Latin America

Bergsten, C. F. U.S.-Latin American economic relations to 1980: the international framework and some possible new approaches. *In* The Americas in a changing world p173-95

Carey, J. C. The consequences of economic intervention: Peru & Chile. *In* Higham, R. D. ed. Intervention or abstention: the dilemma of American foreign policy p144-65

Farer, T. J. Toward regional accommodation: is there anything to negotiate? *In* Farer, T. J. ed. The future of the inter-American system p66-72

Hansen, R. D. U.S.-Latin American economic relationships: bilateral, regional or global? *In* The Americas in a changing world p196-238

Foreign economic relations—Near East

Perlmutter, A. American strategic and economic interests in the area. *In* The New world balance and peace in the Middle East: reality or mirage? p143-54

Foreign economic relations—Underdeveloped areas

Sellers, J. E. Famine and interdependence: toward a new identity for America and the West. *In* Lucas, G. R. and Ogletree, T. W. eds. Lifeboat ethics p100-19

Foreign opinion

Bako, E. Louis Kossuth. *In* Abroad in America: Visitors to the new Nation, 1776-1914 p124-33

Bradová, L. Antonín Dvořák. *In* Abroad in America: Visitors to the new Nation, 1776-1914 p228-37

Collins, P. A. W. Charles Dickens. *In* Abroad in America: Visitors to the new Nation, 1776-1914 p82-91

Cunliffe, M. Frances Trollope. *In* Abroad in America: Visitors to the new Nation, 1776-1914 p32-42

De Onis, J. José Martí. *In* Abroad in America: Visitors to the new Nation, 1776-1914 p218-27

Donoghue, D. John Butler Yeats. *In* Abroad in America: Visitors to the new Nation, 1776-1914 p260-69

Duroselle, J. B. Georges Clemenceau. *In* Abroad in America: Visitors to the new Nation, 1776-1914 p167-75

Feest, C. F. Charles Sealsfield (Karl Postl). *In* Abroad in America: Visitors to the new Nation, 1776-1914 p22-31

Gleason, A. Pavel Svin'in. *In* Abroad in America: Visitors to the new Nation, 1776-1914 p12-21

Grieder, J. B. Liang, Ch'i-ch'ao and Hu Shih. *In* Abroad in America: Visitors to the new Nation, 1776-1914 p279-92

Higonnet, P. L. R. Alexis de Tocqueville. *In* Abroad in America: Visitors to the new Nation, 1776-1914 p52-61

Hollander, A. N. J. den. Charles Boissevain. *In* Abroad in America: Visitors to the new Nation, 1776-1914 p186-94

Houchins, L. John Manjirō. *In* Abroad in America: Visitors to the new Nation, 1776-1914 p92-103

Ions, E. S. James Bryce. *In* Abroad in America: Visitors to the new Nation, 1776-1914 p207-17

Katona, A. Sándor Farkas Bölöni and Ágoston Mokcsai Haraszthy. *In* Abroad in America: Visitors to the new Nation, 1776-1914 p43-51

Kaufman, B. Sholom Aleichem. *In* Abroad in America: Visitors to the new Nation, 1776-1914 p270-78

Kors, A. C. François-Jean Marquis de Chastellux. *In* Abroad in America: Visitors to the new Nation, 1776-1914 p3-11

Laski, M. Harriet Martineau. *In* Abroad in America: Visitors to the new Nation, 1776-1914 p62-71

United States—*Continued*

Foreign relations—Revolution,
1775-1783

Hutson, J. H. Early American diplomacy: a reappraisal. *In* The American Revolution and "a candid world" p40-68

Lint, G. L. The law of nations and the Revolution. *In* The American Revolution and "a candid world" p111-33

Marshall, C. B. American foreign policy as a dimension of the American Revolution. *In* America's continuing revolution p363-84

Stinchcombe, W. C. John Adams and the Model Treaty. *In* The American Revolution and "a candid world" p69-84

Foreign relations—1857-1861

Ferris, N. B. Transatlantic misunderstanding: William Henry Seward and the Declaration of Paris negotiation of 1861. *In* Rank and file p55-78

Foreign relations—20th century

Tompkins, C. D. Bipartisanship. *In* Encyclopedia of American foreign policy p78-89

Foreign relations—1909-1913

Trani, E. P. Dollar diplomacy. *In* Encyclopedia of American foreign policy p268-74

Foreign relations, 1945-

Aspin, L. The defense budget and foreign policy: the role of Congress. *In* Long, F. A. and Rathjens, G. W. eds. Arms, defense policy, and arms control p155-74

Baldwin, D. A. Foreign policy problems, 1975-1980: framework for analysis. *In* Baldwin, D. A. ed. America in an interdependent world p3-27

Bernstein, B. J. Containment. *In* Encyclopedia of American foreign policy p191-203

Cleveland, H. America's not-so manifest destiny. *In* The American Revolution: a continuing commitment p67-88

Galbraith, J. K. The global strategic mind. *In* Galbraith, J. K. Annals of an abiding liberal p331-40

Gregory, R. The domino theory. *In* Encyclopedia of American foreign policy p275-80

Hagan, K. J. Nuclear weapons and diplomacy. *In* Encyclopedia of American foreign policy p692-702

Herring, G. D. The Cold War.. *In* Encyclopedia of American foreign policy p111-23

Kuklick, B. Tradition and diplomatic talent: the case of the cold warriors. *In* Zenderland, L. ed. Recycling the past p116-31

Nagai, Y. The roots of Cold war doctrine: the esoteric and the exoteric. *In* The Origins of the Cold war in Asia p15-42

Schiller, H. I. The free flow of information—for whom? *In* Gerbner, G. ed. Mass media policies in changing cultures p105-15

Smith, M. H. and Carey, R. The Nixon legacy and American foreign policy. *In* The Year book of world affairs, 1978 p23-42

Zumwalt, E. R. Soviet strategy and U.S. counterstrategy. *In* Grand strategy for the 1980s p37-55

Foreign relations—1945-1953

Aruga, T. The United States and the Cold war: the Cold war era in American history. *In* The Origins of the Cold war in Asia p66-88

LaFeber, W. American policy-makers, public opinion, and the outbreak of the Cold war, 1945-50. *In* The Origins of the Cold war in Asia p43-65

LaFeber, W. The Truman doctrine. *In* Encyclopedia of American foreign policy p980-85

Warner, G. America, Russia, China and the origins of the Cold war, 1945-1950. *In* Siracusa, J. M. and Barclay, G. S. eds. The impact of the Cold war p144-62

Foreign relations—1969-1974

Etzold, T. H. The Nixon doctrine. *In* Encyclopedia of American foreign policy p688-91

Foreign relations—1974-1977

Farer, T. J. On a collision course: the American campaign for human rights and the antiradical bias in the Third World. *In* Kommers, D. P. and Loescher, G. D. eds. Human rights and American foreign policy p263-77

Lillich, R. B. A United States policy of humanitarian intervention and intercession. *In* Kommers, D. P. and Loescher, G. D. eds. Human rights and American foreign policy p278-98

Foreign relations—Africa

Obatala, J. K. Black consciousness and American policy in Africa. *In* Said, A. A. and Simmons, L. R. eds. Ethnicity in an international context p64-75

Smythe, H. H. and Skinner, E. P. Black participation in U.S. foreign relations. *In* The Black American reference book p638-47

Foreign relations—Asia

Johnson, C. A. A need for priorities. *In* Pacific Asia and U.S. policies: a political-economic-strategic assessment p36-48

Scalapino, R. A. Competitive strategic perceptions underlying U.S. policy in Asia. *In* Pacific Asia and U.S. policies: a political-economic-strategic assessment p 1-15

Foreign relations—Asia, Southeastern

Kahin, G. M. The United States and the anticolonial revolutions in Southeast Asia, 1945-50. *In* The Origins of the Cold war in Asia p338-61

Weatherbee, D. E. U.S. policy and the two Southeast Asias. *In* Pacific Asia and U.S. policies: a political-economic-strategic assessment p80-94

Foreign relations—Brazil

Hilton, S. E. The United States and Brazilian independence. *In* From colony to nation p109-29

Foreign relations—Chile

O'Brien, P. J. Was the United States responsible for the Chilean Coup? *In* O'Brien, P. J. ed. Allende's Chile p217-43

Foreign relations—China

Barnds, W. J. China in American foreign policy. *In* China and America p196-248

Buckley, T. H. John Van Antwerp MacMurray: the diplomacy of an American mandarin. *In* Burns, R. D. and Bennett, E. M. eds. Diplomats in crisis p27-48

Burns, R. D. Stanley K. Hornbeck: the diplomacy of the Open Door. *In* Burns, R. D. and Bennett, E. M. eds. Diplomats in crisis p91-123

United States—Foreign relations—China
—*Continued*

Cline, R. S. The two-China dilemma. *In* Pacific Asia and U.S. policies: a political-economic-strategic assessment p49-57

Clough, R. N. The Taiwan issue in Sino-American relations. *In* China and America p149-95

Cohen, W. I. The China lobby. *In* Encyclopedia of American foreign policy p104-10

Cohen, W. I. Consortia. *In* Encyclopedia of American foreign policy p167-76

Davies, J. P. America and East Asia. *In* Two hundred years of American foreign policy p90-141

Graebner, N. A. The Manchurian crisis, 1931-1932. *In* Higham, R. D. ed. Intervention or abstention: the dilemma of American foreign policy p60-78

Hyer, P. V. Hu Shih: the diplomacy of gentle persuasion. *In* Burns, R. D. and Bennett, E. M. eds. Diplomats in crisis p153-70

Mahajani, U. Sino-American rapprochement and the new configurations in Southeast Asia. *In* The Year book of world affairs, 1975 p106-20

Sigur, G. The strategic triangle: the U.S., and US. policies: a political-economic-strategic assessment p28-35

Van Alstyne, R. W. The Open Door policy. *In* Encyclopedia of American foreign policy p711-21

Whiting, A. S. Mao, China, and the Cold war. *In* The Origins of the Cold war in Asia p252-76

Wood, H. J. Nelson Trusler Johnson: the diplomacy of benevolent pragmatism. *In* Burns, R. D. and Bennett, E. M. eds. Diplomats in crisis p7-26

Foreign relations—Communist countries

Ørvik, N. Anticommunism and American foreign policy. *In* [Truth and tragedy]: a tribute to Hans Morgenthau p284-304

Foreign relations—Cuba

Blasier, C. The Soviet Union in the Cuban-American conflict. *In* Cuba in the world p37-51

Dominguez, J. I. U.S. policy toward Cuba: a discussion of options. *In* The Americas in a changing world p112-31

Duberman, M. B. The questions raised by Cuba. *In* Radosh, R. ed. The new Cuba: paradoxes and potentials p19-34

Linsley, A. U.S.-Cuban relations: the role of Puerto Rico. *In* Cuba in the world p119-30

Petras, J. F. The U.S.-Cuban policy debate. *In* Radosh, R. ed. The new Cuba: paradoxes and potentials p173-89

Foreign relations—Dominican Republic

Haley, P. E. Comparative intervention: Mexico in 1914 & Dominica in 1965. *In* Higham, R. D. ed. Intervention or abstention: the dilemma of American foreign policy p40-59

Foreign relations—East (Far East)

Hunt, K. America in the Far East: political & military dimensions. *In* Rosecrance, R. N. ed. America as an ordinary country p136-57

Foreign relations—Egypt

Terry, J. J. The consequences of economic abstention: the Aswan Dam. *In* Higham, R. D. ed. Intervention or abstention: the dilemma of American foreign policy p129-43

Foreign relations—Europe

Aron, R. Allies and rivals. *In* The New Atlantic challenge p37-41

Ball, G. W. The problem stated. *In* The New Atlantic challenge p17-25

Bernhart, L. F. E. J. C. K. G. P. Prince. *In* The New Atlantic challenge p31-35

Brown, S. A world of multiple relationships. *In* Atlantis lost p103-18

Brzezinski, Z. K. The European crossroads. *In* Atlantis lost p85-102

Calleo, D. P. America, Europe and the oil crisis: hegemony reaffirmed? *In* Atlantis lost p119-47

Chace, J. Europe: is there a price to be paid? *In* Atlantis lost p65-83

Craig, G. A. The United States and the European balance. *In* Two hundred years of American foreign policy p67-89

Duchêne, F. The United States and European Community. *In* Rosecrance, R. N. ed. America as an ordinary country p87-109

Hallstein, W. The need for vision. *In* The New Atlantic challenge p27-30

Hassner, P. Europe and the contradictions in American policy. *In* Rosecrance, R. N. ed. America as an ordinary country p60-86

Hoffman, S. No trumps, no luck, no will: gloomy thoughts on Europe's plight. *In* Atlantis lost p 1-46

Jenkins, R. H. The United States and a united Europe: are we now uncertain partners? *In* World change and world security p 1-16

Kirby, S. Great-Power involvement in European systems. *In* Hayward, J. E. S. and Berki, R. N. eds. State and society in contemporary Europe p181-202

Kohnstamm, M. Institutions for interdependence. *In* The New Atlantic challenge p355-64

Petrilli, G. Time for change. *In* The New Atlantic challenge p49-51

Pierre, A. J. America faces Western Europe in the 1980s: Atlanticism preserved, disengagement, or devolution? *In* Atlantis lost p183-204

Rockefeller, N. A. Towards a new relationship. *In* The New Atlantic challenge p53-58

Steel, R. The abdication of Europe. *In* Atlantis lost p47-63

Wahl, N. The autonomy of "domestic structures" in European-American relations. *In* Atlantis lost p225-48

Foreign relations—European Economic Community countries

Morgan, R. P. The transatlantic relationship. *In* Twitchett, K. J. ed. Europe and the world p35-56

Foreign relations—France

Kaplan, L. S. Toward isolationism: the rise and fall of the Franco-American alliance, 1775-1801. *In* The American Revolution and "a candid world" p134-60

Foreign relations—Germany, West

Katzenstein, P. West Germany's place in American foreign policy: pivot, anchor, or broker? *In* Rosecrance, R. N. ed. America as an ordinary country p110-35

United States—*Continued*

Foreign relations—Great Britain

Buchan, A. Mothers and daughters (Or Greeks and Romans) *In* Two hundred years of American foreign policy p20-66

Campbell, A. E. The nature of the Anglo-American rapprochement; excerpt from "Great Britain and the United States, 1895-1903." *In* Burton, D. H. ed. American history—British historians p257-88

Nicholas, H. G. The wartime alliance and after; the Cold war alliance; excerpt from "Britain and the U.S.A." *In* Burton, D. H. ed. American history—British historians p93-124

Foreign relations—Greece, Modern

Couloumbis, T. A. and Tredway, M. M. U.S. intervention & abstention in Greece, 1944-1970. *In* Higham, R. D. ed. Intervention or abstention: the dilemma of American foreign policy p95-113

LaFeber, W. The Truman doctrine. *In* Encyclopedia of American foreign policy p980-85

Foreign relations—India

Erdman, H. L. The United States, India, and India's neighbors. *In* Baldwin, D. A. ed. America in an interdependent world p245-72

Richter, W. L. Relative abstention: India & Pakistan. *In* Higham, R. D. ed. Intervention or abstention: the dilemma of American foreign policy p202-17

Foreign relations—Indochina

Siracusa, J. M. FDR, Truman, and Indochina, 1941-1952: the forgotten years. *In* Siracusa, J. M. and Barclay, G. S. eds. The impact of the Cold war p163-83

Foreign relations—Japan

Aruga, T. The first Japanese mission to the United States, 1860. *In* Abroad in America: Visitors to the new Nation, 1776-1914 p134-44

Bennett, E. M. Joseph C. Grew: the diplomacy of pacification. *In* Burns, R. D. and Bennett, E. M. eds. Diplomats in crisis p65-89

Burns, R. D. Stanley K. Hornbeck: the diplomacy of the Open Door. *In* Burns, R. D. and Bennett, E .M. eds. Diplomats in crisis p91-123

Clapp, P. U.S. domestic politics and relations with Japan. *In* Clapp, P. and Halperin, M. H. eds. United States-Japanese relations, the 1970's p35-57

Conroy, H. F. Nomura Kichisaburō: the diplomacy of drama and desperation. *In* Burns, R. D. and Bennett, E. M. eds. Diplomats in crisis p297-316

Davies, J. P. America and East Asia. *In* Two hundred years of American foreign policy p90-141

Hodgson, J. D. What lies ahead for U.S. —Japan relations? *In* Prochnow, H. V. ed. Dilemmas facing the nation p248-70

Iriye, A. Continuities in U.S.-Japanese relations, 1941-49. *In* The Origins of the Cold war in Asia p378-407

Kamiya, F. Summit talks in retrospect. *In* Clapp, P. and Halperin, M. H. eds. United States-Japanese relations, the 1970's p120-46

Mushakoji, K. A note on trilateral crisis diplomacy: the irritants in the Japan-U.S.-E. C. relations. *In* Postwar trends in Japan p15-36

Nish, I. H. Japan and naval aspects of the Washington Conference. *In* Modern Japan p67-80

Ross, G. M. W. Cameron Forbes: the diplomacy of a Darwinist. *In* Burns, R. D. and Bennett, E. M. eds. Diplomats in crisis p49-64

Foreign relations—Korea

Gaddis, J. L. Korea in American politics, strategy, and diplomacy, 1945-50. *In* The Origins of the Cold war in Asia p277-98

Kriebel, P. W. Unfinished business—intervention under the U.N. umbrella: America's participation in the Korean War, 1950-1953. *In* Higham, R. D. ed. Intervention or abstention: the dilemma of American foreign policy p114-28

Lee, Jai Hyon. The activities of the Korean Central Intelligence Agency in the United States. *In* Horowitz, I. L. ed. Science, sin, and scholarship p120-47

Foreign relations—Latin America

Baer, W. and Coes, D. V. Changes in the inter-American economic system. *In* Farer, T. J. ed. The future of the inter-American system p35-53

Hill, R. C. The United States and Latin America: looking ahead. *In* Prochnow, H. V. ed. Dilemmas facing the nation p238-47

Hoffman, S. The international system and U.S. policy toward Latin America. *In* The Americas in a changing world p78-94

Lowenthal, A. F. The United States and Latin America: ending the hegemonic presumption. *In* Two hundred years of American foreign policy p181-208

Silvert, K. H. The changing dynamics of hemispheric politics. *In* Baldwin, D. A. ed. America in an interdependent world p275-92

Silvert, K. H. The relevance of Latin American domestic politics to North American foreign policy. *In* The Americas in a changing world p62-77

Trask, R. R. Missionary diplomacy. *In* Encyclopedia of American foreign policy p575-83

Foreign relations—Mexico

Haley, P. E. Comparative intervention: Mexico in 1941 & Dominica in 1965. *In* Higham, R. D. ed. Intervention or abstention: the dilemma of American foreign policy p40-59

Foreign relations—Near East

Atherton, A. L. The Nixon administration and the Arab-Israeli conflict. *In* The New world balance and peace in the Middle East: reality or mirage? p196-208

Campbell, J. C. American efforts for peace. *In* The Elusive peace in the Middle East p249-310

DeNovo, J. A. The Eisenhower doctrine. *In* Encyclopedia of American foreign policy p292-301

Finger, S. M. The Nixon Doctrine and the Middle East. *In* The New world balance and peace in the Middle East: reality or mirage? p209-16

Nolte, R. H. American relations with the Arab states and Israel. *In* The New world balance and peace in the Middle East: reality or mirage? p181-89

Peretz, D. The Kennedy and Johnson administrations and the Six-Day War. *In* The New world balance and peace in the Middle East: reality or mirage? p190-95

United States—*Continued*

History

Hesburgh, T. M. American aspirations and the grounds of hope. *In* An Almost chosen people p131-46

Campbell, A. E. The American past as destiny. *In* Burton, D. H. ed. American history—British historians p51-72

History—Study and teaching (Higher)—United States

Bostert, R. H. Teaching history. *In* Cahn, S. M. ed. Scholars who teach p 1-35

History—Colonial period, ca. 1600-1775

Hutson, J. H. Tentative moves toward intercolonial union. *In* Aspects of American liberty p81-94

Marx, L. The American Revolution and the American landscape. *In* America's continuing revolution p247-69

Shy, J. W. A new look at the colonial militia. *In* Shy, J. W. A people numerous and armed p21-33

Smith, J. M. John Adams and the coming of the Revolution. *In* Suggs, G. G. ed. Perspectives on the American Revolution p75-98

Ulrich, L. T. Vertuous women found: New England ministerial literature, 1668-1735. *In* Vaughan, A. T. and Bremer, F. J. eds. Puritan New England p215-31

See also Pequot War, 1636-1638

History—Colonial period, ca. 1600-1775—Historiography

Shy, J. W. The spectrum of imperial possibilities: Henry Ellis and Thomas Pownall, 1763-1775. *In* Shy, J. W. A people numerous and armed p35-72

History—Colonial period, ca. 1600-1775—Sources

Merrens, H. R. Settlement of the colonial Atlantic seaboard. *In* Pattern and process p235-43

History—Revolution, 1775-1783

Bonwick, C. C. English Dissenters and the American Revolution. *In* Allen, H. C. and Thompson, R. eds. Contrast and connection p88-112

Hardison, O. B. Attempting the impossible and accomplishing the unbelievable: thoughts on two American Revolutions. *In* A Time to hear and answer: essays for the Bicentennial season p37-58

Higginbotham, D. Military leadership in the American Revolution. *In* Library of Congress Symposia on the American Revolution, 3d, 1974. Leadership in the American Revolution p91-111

Klein, M. M. New York lawyers and the coming of the American Revolution. *In* Studies in eighteenth-century culture v7 p23-47

Lipset, S. M. Revolution and counterrevolution—some comments at a conference analyzing the Bicentennial of a celebrated North American divorce. *In* Perspectives on revolution and evolution p22-45

Meyer, D. H. Science, rhetoric, and revolution. *In* Meyer, D. H. The democratic Enlightenment p97-108

Nisbet, R. A. The social impact of the Revolution. *In* America's continuing revolution p73-95

O'Donnell, J. H. The Southern Indians in the War for American independence, 1775-1783. *In* Hudson, C. M. ed. Four centuries of Southern Indians p46-63

Shy, J. W. American strategy: Charles Lee and the radical alternative. *In* Shy, J. W. A people numerous and armed p133-62

Smelser, M. An understanding of the American Revolution. *In* An Almost chosen people p3-18

See also American loyalists

History—Revolution, 1775-1783—Afro-American troops

Ferguson, C. C. Free men and revolution: a Black perspective. *In* The American Revolution: a continuing commitment p13-25

History—Revolution, 1775-1783—American forces

Shy, J. W. The American Revolution today. *In* Shy, J. W. A people numerous and armed p 1-19

Shy, J. W. Hearts and minds in the American Revolution: the case of "Long Bill" Scott and Peterborough, New Hampshire. *In* Shy, J. W. A people numerous and armed p163-79

History—Revolution, 1775-1783—Biography

Gilmore, M. T. Eulogy as symbolic biography: the iconography of revolutionary leadership, 1776-1826. *In* Studies in biography p131-57

Maier, P. Early Revolutionary leaders in the South and the problem of Southern distinctiveness. *In* The Southern experience in the American Revolution p3-24

History—Revolution, 1775-1783—British forces

Shy, J. W. The American Revolution today. *In* Shy, J. W. A people numerous and armed p 1-19

Shy, J. W. British strategy for pacifying the Southern colonies, 1778-1781. *In* The Southern experience in the American Revolution p155-73

Shy, J. W. Hearts and minds in the American Revolution: the case of "Long Bill" Scott and Peterborough, New Hampshire. *In* Shy, J. W. A people numerous and armed p163-79

History—Revolution, 1775-1783—Campaigns and battles

Pogue, F. C. The Revolutionary transformation of the art of war. *In* America's continuing revolution p309-29

See also Southern States—History—Revolution, 1775-1783

History—Revolution, 1775-1783—Causes

Brown, A. S. The impossible dream: the North ministry, the structure of politics and conciliation. *In* Kaplan, L. S. The American Revolution and "a candid world" p17-39

Cone, C, B. George III—America's unknown king. *In* Kaplan, L. S. The American Revolution and "a candid world" p 1-16

Greene, J. P. The American Revolution: an explanation. *In* Suggs, G. G. ed. Perspectives on the American Revolution p51-73

Greene, J. P. 'A posture of hostility': a reconsideration of some aspects of the origins of the American Revolution. *In* American Antiquarian Society. Proceedings v87 pt 1 p27-68

United States—Revolution, 1775-1783—
Causes—*Continued*

Greene, J. P. "Virtus et Libertas": political culture, social change, and the origins of the American Revolution in Virginia, 1763-1766. *In* The Southern experience in the American Revolution p55-108

Suggs, G. G. Introduction. *In* Suggs, G. G. ed. Perspectives on the American Revolution p 1-11

History—Revolution, 1775-1783—
Centennial celebrations, etc.

See American Revolution Bicentennial, 1776-1976

History—Revolution, 1775-1783—Foreign participation

See United States—History—Revolution, 1775-1783—French participation; United States—History—Revolution, 1775-1783—German participation

History—Revolution, 1775-1783—
Foreign public opinion, Russian

Griffiths, D. M. Catherine the Great, the British opposition and the American Revolution. *In* The American Revolution and "a candid world" p85-110

History—Revolution, 1775-1783—French participation

Fohlen, C. The impact of the American Revolution on France. *In* The Impact of the American Revolution abroad p21-38

History—Revolution, 1775-1783—
German participation

Waldenrath, A. The Pennsylvania-Germans: development of their printing and their newspress in the War for American Independence. *In* The German contribution to the building of the Americas p47-74

History—Revolution, 1775-1783—
Historiography

Allen, H. C. The American Revolution and the Anglo-American relationship in historical perspective. *In* Allen, H. C. and Thompson, R. eds. Contrast and connection p149-77

Brown, R. E. Did the American Revolution really happen? *In* Suggs, G. G. ed. Perspectives on the American Revolution p13-35

Collier, C. Johnny and Sam: old and new approaches to the American Revolution. *In* Horn Book Magazine. Crosscurrents of criticism p234-40

Shy, J. W. The Empire remembered: Lawrence Gipson, historian. *In* Shy, J. W. A people numerous and armed p109-31

Shy, J. W. The military conflict considered as a revolutionary war. *In* Shy, J. W. A people numerous and armed p193-224

Suggs, G. G. Introduction. *In* Suggs, G. G. ed. Perspectives on the American Revolution p 1-11

History—Revolution, 1775-1783—
Influence

Angermann, E. The impact of the American Revolution on Germany—a comment. *In* The Impact of the American Revolution abroad p160-63

Bolkhovitinov, N. N. The American Revolution and the Russian Empire. *In* The Impact of the American Revolution abroad p81-97

Dauer, M. J. The impact of the American independence and the American Constitution: 1776-1848; with a brief epilogue. *In* Havard, W. C. and Bernd, J. L. eds. 200 years of the Republic in retrospect p37-55

Edwards, O. D. The impact of the American Revolution on Ireland. *In* The Impact of the American Revolution abroad p127-58

Ely, J. W. Law in a republican society: continuity and change in the legal system of postrevolutionary America. *In* Perspectives on revolution and evolution p46-65

Fohlen, C. The impact of the American Revolution on France. *In* The Impact of the American Revolution abroad p21-38

Homma, N. The impact of the American Revolution on Japan. *In* The Impact of the American Revolution abroad p164-66

Palmer, R. R. The fading dream: how European revolutionaries have seen the American Revolution. *In* Essays on modern European revolutionary history p89-104

Palmer, R. R. The impact of the American Revolution abroad. *In* The Impact of the American Revolution abroad p5-18

Plumb, J. H. The impact of the American Revolution on Great Britain. *In* The Impact of the American Revolution abroad p65-78

Preston, R. A. Some conclusions about the revolution-evolution problem. *In* Perspectives on revolution and evolution p268-87

Rodríguez, M. The impact of the American Revolution on the Spanish-and Portuguese-speaking world. *In* The Impact of the American Revolution abroad p101-25

Schulte Nordholt, J. W. The impact of the American Revolution on the Dutch Republic. *In* The impact of the American Revolution abroad p41-63

Shy, J. W. The American Revolution today. *In* Shy, J. W. A people numerous and armed p 1-19

Stourzh, G. The American Revolution, modern constitutionalism, and the protection of human rights. *In* [Truth and tragedy]: a tribute to Hans Morgenthau p162-76

History—Revolution, 1775-1783—
Loyalists

See American loyalists

History—Revolution, 1775-1783—
Pamphlets

Ginsberg, E. K. The patriot pamphleteers. *In* Emerson, E. H. ed. American literature, 1764-1789 p19-38

History—Revolution, 1775-1783—
Pictorial works

Kammen, M. G. From liberty to prosperity: reflections upon the role of revolutionary iconography in national tradition. *In* American Antiquarian Society. Proceedings v86 pt2 p237-72

History—Revolution, 1775-1783—
Public opinion

Ubbelohde, C. The idea of independence. *In* Suggs, G. G. ed. Perspectives on the American Revolution p37-50

History—Revolution, 1775-1783—
Religious aspects

Benton, R. M. The preachers. *In* Emerson, E. H. ed. American literature, 1764-1789 p73-85

United States—*Continued*

History, Military—To 1900

Higginbotham, D. Military leadership in the American Revolution. *In* Library of Congress Symposia on the American Revolution, 3d, 1974. Leadership in the American Revolution p91-111

Pogue, F. C. The Revolutionary transformation of the art of war. *In* America's continuing revolution p309-29

Shy, J. W. The Empire militant: Thomas Gage and the coming of war. *In* Shy, J. W. A people numerous and armed p73-107

Shy, J. W. A new look at the colonial militia. *In* Shy, J. W. A people numerous and armed p21-33

History, Naval

Braisted, W. R. Naval diplomacy. *In* Encyclopedia of American foreign policy p668-78

Hagan, K. J. The historical significance of American naval intervention. *In* Higham, R. D. ed. Intervention or abstention: the dilemma of American foreign policy p21-39

History, Political

See United States—Politics and government

Immigration

See United States—Emigration and immigration

Indian Claims Commission

Dobyns, H. F. Taking the witness stand. *In* Eddy, E. M. and Partridge, W. L. eds. Applied anthropology in America p261-76

Industries

Commoner, B. Energy, environment, and economics. *In* Eppen, G. D. ed. Energy: the policy issues p25-40

Industries—History

Klein, M. The boys who stayed behind: Northern industrialists and the Civil War. *In* Rank and file p137-56

Intellectual life

Bender, T. The cultures of intellectual life: the city and the professions. *In* Higham, J. and Conkin, P. K. eds. New directions in American intellectual history p181-95

Berman, R. S. Intellect and education in a revolutionary society. *In* America's continuing revolution p273-91

Brustein, R. S. Cultural schizophrenia. *In* Brustein, R. S. The culture watch p17-25

Coben, S. The assault on Victorianism in the twentieth century. *In* Howe, D. W. ed. Victorian America p160-81

Emerson, E. H. The cultural context of the American Revolution. *In* Emerson, E. H. ed. American literature, 1764-1789 p3-17

Hall, D. D. The Victorian connection. *In* Howe, D. W. ed. Victorian America p81-94

Hassan, I. H. Models of transformation: ideology, utopia, and fantasy in America. *In* Hassan, I. H. Paracriticisms p151-76

Lipset, S. M. The end of ideology and the ideology of the intellectuals. *In* Culture and its creators p15-42

Meyer, D. H. American intellectuals and the Victorian crisis of faith. *In* Howe, D. W. ed. Victorian America p59-77

Meyer, D. H. The civilized Americans. *In* Meyer, D. H. The democratic Enlightenment p49-60

Meyer, D. H. The critical period in American intellectual history. *In* Meyer, D. H. The democratic Enlightenment p171-81

Meyer, D. H. The ethics of belief and the conduct of the mind. *In* Meyer, D. H. The democratic Enlightenment p82-93

Meyer, D. H. From piety to moralism. *In* Meyer, D. H. The democratic Enlightenment p35-45

Meyer, D. H. John Witherspoon and the education of the public conscience. *In* Meyer, D. H. The democratic Enlightenment p182-98

Meyer, D. H. Science, rhetoric, and revolution. *In* Meyer, D. H. The democratic Enlightenment p97-108

Meyer, D. H. William Ellery Channing and the inward enlightenment. *In* Meyer, D. H. The democratic Enlightenment p199-209

Murphey, M. G. The place of beliefs in modern culture. *In* Higham, J. and Conkin, P. K. eds. New directions in American intellectual history p151-65

Palmer, R. R. The European Enlightenment in its American setting. *In* Aspects of American liberty p47-55

Spurlin, P. M. Readership in the American Enlightenment. *In* Literature and history in the age of ideas p359-74

Trilling, L. On not talking. *In* Trilling, L. A gathering of fugitives p153-63

Wood, G. S. The democratization of mind in the American Revolution. *In* Library of Congress Symposia on the American Revolution, 3d, 1974. Leadership in the American Revolution p63-89

Also in The moral foundations of the American Republic p102-28

Intellectual life—Historiography

Conkin, P. K. Afterword. *In* Higham, J. and Conkin, P. K. eds. New directions in American intellectual history p227-34

Conkin, P. K. Intellectual history: past, present, and future. *In* The Future of history p111-33

Harris, N. Iconography and intellectual history: the half-tone effect. *In* Higham, J. and Conkin, P. K. eds. New directions in American intellectual history p196-211

May, H. F. Intellectual history and religious history. *In* Higham, J. and Conkin, P. K. eds. New directions in American intellectual history p105-15

Veysey, L. R. Intellectual history and the new social history. *In* Higham, J. and Conkin, P. K. eds. New directions in American intellectual history p3-26

Welter, R. On studying the national mind. *In* Higham, J. and Conkin, P. K. eds. New directions in American intellectual history p64-82

Laws, statutes, etc.

Scalia, A. Vermont Yankee: the A P A, the D.C. Circuit, and the Supreme Court. *In* The Supreme Court review, 1978 p345-409

Laws, statutes, etc., 1863-1864 (38th Congress, 1st session) (Bills)

Abbott, R. H. Massachusetts and the recruitment of Southern Negroes, 1863-1865. *In* Hubbell, J. T. ed. Battles lost and won p157-70

United States—*Continued*

Laws, statutes, etc. Civil Rights Act of 1964

Glazer, N. Individual rights against group rights. *In* Human rights p87-103

Learned institutions and societies—History

Cassedy, J. H. Medicine and the learned society in the United States, 1660-1850. *In* Oleson, A. and Brown, S. C. eds. The pursuit of knowledge in the early American Republic p261-78

Dupree, A. H. The national pattern of American learned societies, 1769-1863. *In* Oleson, A. and Brown, S. C. eds. The pursuit of knowledge in the early American Republic p21-32

Greene, J. C. Science, learning, and utility: patterns of organization in the early American Republic. *In* Oleson, A. and Brown, S. C. eds. The pursuit of knowledge in the early American Republic p 1-20

McCorison, M. A. The nature of humanistic societies in early America. *In* Oleson, A. and Brown, S. C. eds. The pursuit of knowledge in the early American Republic p248-60

Oleson, A. Introduction: To build a new intellectual order. *In* Oleson, A. and Brown, S. C. eds. The pursuit of knowledge in the early American Republic pxv-xxv

Rosenkrantz, B. G. Early American learned societies as informants on our past: some conclusions and suggestions for further research. *In* Oleson, A. and Brown, S. C. eds. The pursuit of knowledge in the early American Republic p345-53

Storr, R. J. Commentary: an historian of education looks at the Newagen study. *In* Oleson, A. and Brown, S. C. eds. The pursuit of knowledge in the early American Republic p340-44

Library of Congress

Cole, J. Y. Storehouses and workshops: American libraries and the uses of knowledge. *In* Oleson, A. and Voss, J. eds. The organization of knowledge in modern America, 1860-1920 p364-85

Literature (English)

See American literature

Literatures

See German-American literature; and similar headings

Marine Corps—Personnel management

Patton, W. C. The leader as a counselor. *In* Henderson, G. ed. Human relations in the military p33-39

Military Academy, West Point

Vidal, G. West Point. *In* Vidal, G. Matters of fact and of fiction p191-205

Military Academy, West Point—History

Morrison, J. L. The struggle between sectionalism and nationalism at ante-bellum West Point, 1830-1861. *In* Hubbell, J. T. ed. Battles lost and won p19-29

Military policy

Allison, G. T. and Morris, F. A. Armaments and arms control: exploring the determinants of military weapons. *In* Long, F. A. and Rathjens, G. W. eds. Arms, defense policy, and arms control p99-129

Carlton, D. The doctrine of tactical nuclear warfare and some alternatives. *In* The Dynamics of the arms race p135-42

Carter, B. E. The strategic debate in the United States. *In* Kirk, G. L. and Wessell, eds. The Soviet threat p15-29

Enthoven, A. C. 1963 nuclear strategy revisited. *In* Ethics and nuclear strategy? p72-81

Ford, H. P. The new power politics of counterforce. *In* [Truth and tragedy]: a tribute to Hans Morgenthau p259-71

Ford, H. P. Politics, ethics, and the arms race. *In* Ethics and nuclear strategy? p51-71

Ford, H. P. What these sobering essays tell us. *In* Ethics and nuclear strategy? p 1-13

Holloway, B. K. United States grand strategy for the next ten years. *In* Grand strategy for the 1980s. p19-36

Johnson, J. T. Just war, the Nixon Doctrine and the future shape of American military policy. *In* The Year book of world affairs, 1975 p137-54

Kamman, W. Militarism. *In* Encyclopedia of American foreign policy p545-56

King, P. All at sea? A critique of the American strategic force structure. *In* Arms control and technological innovation p265-87

Milton, T. R. Thoughts on our national strategy for the future. *In* Grand strategy for the 1980s p57-71

Palmer, B. Strategic guidelines for the United States in the 1980s. *In* Grand strategy for the 1980s p73-112

Ruina, J. The arms race and SALT. *In* The Dynamics of the arms race p47-56

Russett, G. M. A countercombatant alternative to nuclear MADness. *In* Ethics and nuclear strategy? p124-43

Schelling, T. C. The importance of agreements. *In* The Dynamics of the arms race p65-77

Scoville, H. Flexible MADness? The case against counterforce. *In* Ethics and nuclear strategy? p113-23

Strausz-Hupé, R. America and the defense of the West. *In* Prochnow, H. V. ed. Dilemmas facing the nation p271-93

Taylor, M. D. National policy too lightly armed. *In* Grand strategy for the 1980s p3-17

Trask, D. F. The military-industrial complex. *In* Encyclopedia of American foreign policy p557-66

Tsipis, K. M. The arms race as posturing. *In* The Dynamics of the arms race p78-81

Winters, F. X. Ethics, diplomacy, and defense. *In* Ethics and nuclear strategy? p14-50

Zumwalt, E. R. Soviet strategy and U.S. counter-strategy. *In* Grand strategy for the 1980s p37-55

Militia

Kronenberg, P. S. Militia in the seventies: a conflict paradigm. *In* Beaumont, R. A. and Edmonds, M. eds. War in the next decade p110-34

Moral conditions

Goldwin, R. A. Of men and angels: a search for morality in the Constitution. *In* The Moral foundations of the American Republic p 1-18

Romney, G. W. The greatest threats to our society. *In* Prochnow, H. V. ed. Dilemmas facing the nation p153-65

United States—*Continued*

National Archives and Records Services

Clarke, R. L. Some sources in the National Archives for studies of Afro-American population: growth and movement. *In* Pattern and process p73-80

Fishbein, M. H. Selected materials in the National Archives relating to commerce and industry. *In* Pattern and process p224-28

Friis, H. R. Original and published sources in research in historical geography: a comparison. *In* Pattern and process p139-59

Rhoads, J. B. The role of the National Archives. *In* Pattern and process p5-8

Smith, J. F. Settlement on the public domain as reflected in federal records: suggested research approaches. *In* Pattern and process p290-304

National Commission on Causes and Prevention of Violence

See United States. Task Force on Demonstrations, Protests, and Group Violence

National Guard

Kronenberg, P. S. Militia in the seventies: a conflict paradigm. *In* Beaumont, R. A. and Edmonds, M. eds. War in the next decade p110-34

National Institute of Mental Health

Horn, J. L. The ethics of research: a case history and its lessons. *In* Hook, S.; Kurtz, P. and Todorovich, M. eds. The ethics of teaching and scientific research p135-59

National Science Foundation

Ploch, D. R. Research funding for sociology in the National Science Foundation. *In* Gaston, J. ed. Sociology of science p54-62

National security

Branfman, F. The President's secret army: a case study—the CIA in Laos, 1962-1972. *In* Borosage, R. L. and Marks, J. D. eds. The CIA file p46-78

Dumas, L. J. National security and the arms race. *In* International terrorism and world security p158-64

Halperin, M. H. Covert operations: effects of secrecy on decision-making. *In* Borosage, R. L. and Marks, J. D. eds. The CIA file p159-77

Marshall, C. B. Continuity and discontinuity: dour reflections on the national security. *In* Havard, W. C. and Bernd, J. L. eds. 200 years of the Republic in retrospect p258-75

Wheeler, G. E. National security. *In* Encyclopedia of American foreign policy p623-34

National Teacher Corps

Cronin, T. E. Small program, big troubles: policy making for a small Great Society program. *In* Burnham, W. D. and Weinberg, M. W. eds. American politics and public policy p77-108

Navy

Braisted, W. R. Naval diplomacy. *In* Encyclopedia of American foreign policy p668-78

Navy—Personnel management

Morton, D. A. The naval shore establishment and Parkinson's laws. *In* Managing nonprofit organizations p289-302

Navy—Records and correspondence

Ponko, V. Science in the exploration narratives authored by U.S. naval officers. *In* Kagle, S. E. ed. America: exploration and travel p92-100

Navy—Weapons systems

See Fleet ballistic missile weapons systems

Navy. Reserve Officers' Training Corps

Radway, L. I. The future of the Reserve Officer Training Corps. *In* Beaumont, R. A. and Edmonds, M. eds. War in the next decade p55-68

Neutrality

Jonas, M. Isolationism. *In* Encyclopedia of American foreign policy p496-506

Kaplan, L. S. Toward isolationism: the rise and fall of the Franco-American alliance, 1775-1801. *In* The American Revolution and "a candid world" p134-60

Lint, G. L. The law of nations and the American Revolution. *In* The American Revolution and "a candid world" p111-33

Office of Economic Opportunity. Legal Services Program

Conyers, J. R. Undermining poverty lawyers. *In* Nader, R. and Green, M. J. eds. Verdicts on lawyers p129-43

Tucker, M. S. Pro bono ABA? *In* Nader, R. and Green, M. J. eds. Verdicts on lawyers p20-32

Office of Management and Budget

Malek, F. V. Managing for results in the Federal government. *In* Managing nonprofit organizations p48-56

Police

See Police—United States

Politics and government

Albinski, H. S. Organized politics and political temper: predisposing factors and outcomes. *In* Perspectives on revolution and evolution p66-102

Bessette, J. M. The Presidency. *In* Graham, G. J. and Graham, S. G. eds. Founding principles of American government p197-222

Carey, G. W. and McClellan, J. P. Towards the restoration of the American political tradition. *In* Havard, W. C. and Bernd, J. L. eds. 200 years of the Republic in retrospect p110-27

Cook, S. D. Democracy and tyranny in America: the radical paradox of the Bicentennial and Blacks in the American political system. *In* Havard, W. C. and Bernd, J. L. eds. 200 years of the Republic in retrospect p276-94

Cropsey, J. The United States as regime and the sources of the American way of life. *In* The Moral foundations of the American Republic p86-101

Diamond, M. Ethics and politics: the American way. *In* The Moral foundations of the American Republic p39-72

Diamond, M. The idea of equality: the view from the founding. *In* An Almost chosen people p19-37

Earle, V. A. The Federal structure. *In* Graham, G. J. and Graham, S. G. eds. Founding principles of American government p135-67

Fleming, G. J. The Black role in American politics: Part II, The past. *In* The Black American reference book p622-37

United States—Politics and government
—Continued

Gerson, L. L. Ethnics in American politics. *In* Havard, W. C. and Bernd, J. L. eds. 200 years of the Republic in retrospect p336-46

Graham, S. G. Government and the economy. *In* Graham, G. J. and Graham, S. G. eds. Founding principles of American government p305-30

Hardin, C. M. The problem of political power in the United States. *In* [Truth and tragedy]: a tribute to Hans Morgenthau p142-52

Huntington, S. P. The American opposition to government and its international implications. *In* Arab and American cultures p143-53

Hyneman, C. S. A call for political theory. *In* Graham, G. J. and Graham, S. G. eds. Founding principles of American government p331-46

Karl, B. D. Executive reorganization and Presidential power. *In* The Supreme Court review, 1977 p 1-37

Kelly, A. H. American political leadership: the optimistic ethical world view and the Jeffersonian synthesis. *In* Library of Congress Symposia on the American Revolution, 3d. 1974. Leadership in the American Revolution p7-39

Kristol, I. A foolish American ism—utopianism. *In* A Public philosophy reader p73-91

Lindsay, J. V. The great American drift. *In* Warner, S. B. ed. The American experiment p110-24

Lipset, S. M. Opportunity and welfare in the first new nation. *In* America's continuing revolution p333-59

Lipset, S. M. Revolution and counterrevolution—some comments at a conference analyzing the Bicentennial of a celebrated North American divorce. *In* Perspectives on revolution and evolution p22-45

Lipset, S. M. Why no socialism in the United States? *In* Radicalism in the contemporary age v 1 p31-149

McCall, C. H. Political parties and popular government. *In* Graham, G. J. and Graham, S. G. eds. Founding principles of American government p280-304

MacLeish, A. The ghost of Thomas Jefferson. *In* MacLeish, A. Riders on the earth p57-65

Morgan, E. S. The problem of popular sovereignty. *In* Aspects of American liberty p95-113

Murray, J. C. Two cases for the public consensus; excerpt from "We hold these truths: Catholic reflections on the American proposition." *In* A Public philosophy reader p103-11

Nisbet, R. A. Public opinion versus popular opinion. *In* A Public philosophy reader p169-97

Owsley, F. L. The foundations of democracy. *In* Crunden, R. M. ed. The superfluous men p118-27

Rodino, P. W. The compact with the people. *In* Warner, S. B. ed. The American experiment p89-100

Ross, D. The liberal tradition revisited and the republican tradition addressed. *In* Higham, J. and Conkin, P. K. eds. New directions in American intellectual history p116-31

Shannon, J. B. Bicentennial reflections on party government. *In* Havard, W. C. and Bernd, J. L. eds. 200 years of the Republic in retrospect p128-45

Smith, J. M. "A more perfect Union." *In* Alderson, W. T. ed. American issues p49-64

White, E. B. Bedfellows. *In* White, E. B. Essays of E. B. White p80-89

Wilhelmsen, F. D. The natural law tradition and the American political experience. *In* Wilhelmsen, F. D. Christianity and political philosophy p174-92

Williamson, R. de V. British and European commentaries on the American political experience. *In* Havard, W. C. and Bernd, J. L. eds. 200 years of the Republic in retrospect p101-09

Wyzanski, C. E. The rights of man. *In* Warner, S. B. ed. The American experiment p39-52

Politics and government—Colonial period, ca. 1600-1775

Bushman, R. L. "This new man": dependence and independence, 1776. *In* Uprooted Americans p77-96

Higginbotham, D. James Iredell and the origins of American Federalism. *In* Suggs, G. G. ed. Perspectives on the American Revolution p99-115

Hutson, J. H. Tentative moves toward intercolonial union. *In* Aspects of American liberty p81-94

Politics and government—Revolution, 1775-1783

Cunliffe, M. Congressional leadership in the American Revolution. *In* Library of Congress Symposia on the American Revolution, 3d, 1974. Leadership in the American Revolution p41-61

Hyneman, C. S. Republican government in America: the idea and its realization. *In* Graham, G. J. and Graham, S. G. eds. Founding principles of American government p3-28

Jones, H. W. The Articles of Confederation and the creation of a federal system. *In* Aspects of American liberty p126-45

Kristol, I. The American Revolution as a successful revolution. *In* America's continuing revolution p3-21

Also in A Public philosophy reader p289-307

Lence, R. M. The American Declaration of Independence: the majority and the right of political power. *In* Graham, G. J. and Graham, S. G. eds. Founding principles of American government p29-59

Lutz, D. S. Popular consent and popular control: 1776-1789. *In* Graham, G. J. and Graham, S. G. eds. Founding principles of American government p60-97

Mazlish, B. Leadership in the American Revolution: the psychological dimension. *In* Library of Congress Symposia on the American Revolution, 3d, 1974. Leadership in the American Revolution p113-33

Wood, G. S. The democratization of mind in the American Revolution. *In* Library of Congress Symposia on the American Revolution, 3d, 1974. Leadership in the American Revolution p63-89

Also in The moral foundations of the American Republic p102-28

United States—*Continued*

Politics and government—1933-1953

Preston, W. Shadows of war and fear. The Pulse of freedom p105-53

Politics and government—1945-

Arendt, H. Home to roost. *In* Warner, S. B. ed. The American experiment p61-79

Barber, B. R. The compromised Republic: public purposelessness in America. *In* The Moral foundations of the American Republic p19-38

Burnham, W. D. Revitalization and decay: looking toward the third century of American electoral politics. *In* Havard, W. C. and Bernd, J. L. eds. 200 years of the Republic in retrospect p146-72

Eckart, D. R. and Ries, J. C. The American Presidency. *In* Rieselbach, L. N. ed. People vs. government: the responsiveness of American institutions p15-65

Galbraith, J. K. RN: the memoirs of Richard Nixon. *In* Galbraith, J. K. Annals of an abiding liberal p346-50

Levin, M. Ask not what our presidents are "really like"; ask what we and our political institutions are like: a call for a politics of institutions, not men. *In* Burnham, W. D. and Weinberg, M. W. eds. American politics and public policy p109-39

Reedy, G. E. The Presidency in 1976: focal point of political unity? *In* Havard, W. C. and Bernd, J. L. eds. 200 years of the Republic in retrospect p228-38

Vidal, G. Political melodramas. *In* Vidal, G. Matters of fact and of fiction p259-64

Politics and government—1953-1961

Caughey, J. W. McCarthyism rampant. *In* The Pulse of freedom p154-210

Miller, A. It could happen here—and did. *In* Miller, A. The theater essays of Arthur Miller p294-300

Politics and govenment—1963-1969

Konvitz, M. R. The flower and the thorn. *In* The Pulse of freedom p211-80

Politics and government—1969-1974

Burnham, W. D. American politics in the 1970's: beyond party? *In* The American party systems p308-57

Konvitz, M. R. The flower and the thorn. *In* The Pulse of freedom p211-80

Rieselbach, L. N. After Watergate, what? *In* Rieselbach, L. N. ed. People vs. government: the responsiveness of American institutions p66-118

Smythe, H. H. and Stokes, C. B. The Black role in American politics: Part I, The present. *In* The Black American reference book p580-621

Politics and government—1974-1977

Cohen, R. Human rights decision-making in the executive branch: some proposals for a coordinated strategy. *In* Kommers, D. P. and Loescher, G. D. eds. Human rights and American foreign policy p216-46

Polsby, N. W. Interest groups and the Presidency: trends in political intermediation in America. *In* Burnham, W. D. and Weinberg, M. W. eds. American politics and public policy p41-52

Popular culture

Fishwick, M. W. Icons of America. *In* Browne, R. B. and Fishwick, M. W. eds. Icons of America p 3-12

Goethals, G. Sacred-secular icons. *In* Browne, R. B. and Fishwick, M. W. eds. Icons of America p24-34

Gusfield, J. R. The sociological reality of America: an essay on mass culture. *In* On the making of Americans p41-62

Harris, N. The lamp of learning: popular lights and shadows. *In* Oleson, A. and Voss, J. eds. The organization of knowledge in modern America, 1860-1920 p430-39

Orr, D. G. The icon in the time tunnel. *In* Browne, R. B. and Fishwick, M. W. eds. Icons of America p13-23

Popular culture—History

Melling, P. American popular culture in the thirties: ideology, myth, genre. *In* Bigsby, C. W. E. ed. Approaches to popular culture p241-63

Population

Makielski, S. K. Population policy for the United States: the role of applied anthropology. *In* Eddy, E. M. and Partridge, W. L. eds. Applied anthropology in America p373-89

Population—History—Sources

Clarke, R. L. Some sources in the National Archives for studies of Afro-American population: growth and movement. *In* Pattern and process p73-80

Population policy

Murray, R. F. The ethical and moral values of Black Americans and population policy. *In* Population policy and ethics p197-207

Potter, R. B. The simple structure of the population debate: the logic of the ecology movement. *In* Population policy and ethics p347-63

Viederman, S. and Sollitto, S. Economic groups: business, labor, welfare. *In* Population policy and ethics p325-46

Warwick, D. P. and Williamson, N. E. Population policy and Spanish-surname Americans. *In* Population policy and ethics p211-35

Presidents

See Presidents—United States

Public works

Chinitz, B. Regional development. *In* McKie, J. W. ed. Social responsibility and the business predicament p247-73

Bennett, L. Have we overcome? *In* Have we overcome? Race relations since Brown p189-200

Béteille, A. Race, caste and ethnic identity. *In* United Nations Educational, Scientific and Cultural Organization. Race, science and society p211-33

Bolt, C. Red, Black and white in nineteenth-century America. *In* Hepburn, A. C. ed. Minorities in history p116-34

Clark, K. B. The American revolution: democratic politics and popular education. *In* America's continuing revolution p295-306

Ferguson, C. C. Free men and revolution: a Black perspective. *In* The American Revolution: a continuing commitment p13-25

United States—*Continued*

Race relations

Harding, V. So much history, so much future: Martin Luther King, Jr., and the Second Coming of America. *In* Have we overcome? Race relations since Brown p31-78

Pinderhughes, C. A. Black personality in American society. *In* The Black American reference book p128-58

Terborg-Penn, R. Discrimination against Afro-American women in the woman's movement, 1830-1920. *In* Harley, S. and Terborg-Penn, R. eds. The Afro-American woman p17-27

Wiebe, R. H. White attitudes and Black rights from Brown to Bakke. *In* Have we overcome? Race relations since Brown p147-71

Race relations—Statistics

Kilson, M. Blacks and neo-ethnicity in American political life. *In* Glazer, N. and Moynihan, D. P. eds. Ethnicity p236-66

Relations (general) with Arab countries

Leuchtenburg, W. E. The American perception of the Arab world. *In* Arab and American cultures p15-25

Relations (general) with China

Pye, L. W. Building a relationship on the sands of cultural exchanges. *In* China and America p109-48

Relations (general) with foreign countries

Field, J. A. Philanthropy. *In* Encyclopedia of American foreign policy p763-72

Iriye, A. Intercultural relations. *In* Encyclopedia of American foreign policy p428-42

Relations (general) with Great Britain

Campbell, C. S. Edward J. Phelps and Anglo-American relations. *In* Allen, H. C. and Thompson, R. eds. Contrast and connection p210-24

Hall, D. D. The Victorian connection. *In* Howe, D. W. ed. Victorian America p81-94

Morgan, K. O. The future at work: Anglo-American progressivism, 1890-1917. *In* Allen, H. C. and Thompson, R. eds. Contrast and connection p245-71

Relations (general) with Japan

Harris, N. All the world a melting pot? Japan at American fairs, 1876-1904. *In* Iriye, A. ed. Mutual images p24-54

Nagai, M. and Nishijima, T. Postwar Japanese education and the United States. *In* Iriye, A. ed. Mutual images p169-87

Reischauer, E. O. Introduction: An overview. *In* Clapp, P. and Halperin, M. H. eds. United States-Japanese relations, the 1970's p 1-18

Relations (general) with Latin America

Bloomfield, R. J. The inter-American system: does it have a future? *In* Farer, T. J. ed. The future of the inter-American system p3-19

Farer, T. J. The changing context of inter-American relations. *In* Farer, T. J. ed. The future of the inter-American system p xv-xxiii

Rogers, W. D. A note on the future of the inter-American system. *In* Farer, T. J. ed. The future of the inter-American system p20-29

Relations (military) with Europe

Pasti, N. The military balance between East and West in Europe. *In* International terrorism and world security p189-233

Pierre, A. J. America faces Western Europe in the 1980s: Atlanticism preserved, disengagement, or devolution? *In* Atlantis lost p183-204

Ravenal, E. C. Alliance dissolution and American disengagement. *In* Atlantis lost p205-24

Relations (military) with Japan

Halperin, M. H. U.S.-Japanese security relations. *In* Clapp, P. and Halperin, M. H. eds. United States-Japanese relations, the 1970's p203-22

Miwa, K. Japanese images of war with the United States. *In* Iriye, A. ed. Mutual images p115-37

Relations (military) with Latin America

Child, J. The Inter-American Military System: historical development, current status, and implications for U.S. policy. *In* Farer, T. J. ed. The future of the inter-American system p155-94

Ronfeldt, D. F. Future U.S. security assistance in the Latin American context. *In* The Americas in a changing world p156-72

Relations (military) with Russia

Rathjens, G. W. Nuclear war between the super-powers. *In* Griffiths, F. and Polanyi, J. C. eds. The dangers of nuclear war p135-46

Relations (military) with the East (Far East)

Hunt, K. America in the Far East: political & military dimensions. *In* Rosecrance, R. N. ed. America as an ordinary country p136-57

Relations (military) with the Mediterranean region

Zoppo, C. E. Arms control in the Mediterranean and European security. *In* International terrorism and world security p248-76

Relations (military) with the Near East

Perlmutter, A. American strategic and economic interests in the area. *In* The New world balance and peace in the Middle East: reality or mirage? p143-54

Religion

Ahlstrom, S. E. From Sinai to the Golden Gate: the liberation of religion in the Occident. *In* Needleman, J. and Baker, G. eds. Understanding the new religions p3-22

Ahlstrom, S. E. The religious dimensions of American aspirations. *In* An Almost chosen people p39-49

Burkholder, J. R. "The law knows no heresy": marginal religious movements and the courts. *In* Zaretsky, I. I. and Leone, M. P. eds. Religious movements in contemporary America p27-50

Ellwood, R. S. Emergent religion in America: an historical perspective. *In* Needleman, J. and Baker, G. eds. Understanding the new religions p267-84

Ernst, E. G. Dimensions of new religion in American history. *In* Needleman, J. and Baker, G. eds. Understanding the new religions p34-45

United States—Religion—*Continued*

Marty, M. E. The changing role of religion in American society. *In* The National purpose reconsidered p29-51

Moon, Sun Myung. God's hope for America: Keynote speech at Yankee Stadium, June 1, 1976. *In* Horowitz, I. L. ed. Science, sin, and scholarship p2-11

Neal, M. A. Civil religion, theology, and politics in America. *In* America in theological perspective p99-122

Parsons, T. Religion in postindustrial America: the problem of secularization. *In* Parsons, T. Action theory and the human condition p300-22

Pfeffer, L. The legitimation of marginal religions in the United States. *In* Zaretsky, I. I. and Leone, M. P. eds. Religious movements in contemporary America p9-26

Schneider, M. L. A Catholic perspective on American civil religion. *In* America in theological perspective p123-39

Thomas, D. M. American technocracy and the religious spirit: an unholy alliance? *In* America in theological perspective p189-205

Religion—Historiography

May, H. F. Intellectual history and religious history. *In* Higham, J. and Conkin, P. K. eds. New directions in American intellectual history p105-15

Religion—History

Ellwood, R. S. Excursus religion. *In* Ellwood, R. S. Alternative altars p20-41

Religion—To 1800

Mead, S. E. American Protestantism during the Revolutionary epoch. *In* Mulder, J. M. and Wilson, J. F. eds. Religion in American history p162-80

Meyer, D. H. From piety to moralism. *In* Meyer, D. H. The democratic Enlightenment p35-45

Religion—19th century

Meyer, D. H. American intellectuals and the Victorian crisis of faith. *In* Howe, D. W. ed. Victorian America p59-77

Miller, P. From the covenant to the revival. *In* Mulder, J. M. and Wilson, J. F. eds. Religion in American history p145-61

Pritchard, L. K. Religious change in nineteenth-century America. *In* The New religious consciousness p297-330

Schlesinger, A. M. A critical period in American religion, 1875-1900. *In* Mulder, J. M. and Wilson, J. F. eds. Religion in American history p302-17

Religion—1901-1945

Handy, R. T. The American religious depression, 1925-1935. *In* Mulder, J. M. and Wilson, J. F. eds. Religion in American history p431-44

Religion—1945-

Ahlstrom, S. E. National trauma and changing religious values. *In* A New America? p13-29

Ahlstrom, S. E. The radical turn in theology and ethics: why it occurred in the 1960s. *In* Mulder, J. M. and Wilson, J. F. eds. Religion in American history p445-56

Bellah, R. N. New religious consciousness and the crisis in modernity. *In* The New religious consciousness p333-52

Bellah, R. N. Religious studies as "new religion." *In* Needleman, J. and Baker, G. eds. Understanding the new religions p106-12

Berger, P. L. Religion in a revolutionary society. *In* America's continuing revolution p143-58

Bird, F. Charisma and ritual in new religious movements. *In* Needleman, J. and Baker, G. eds. Understanding the new religions p173-89

Ellwood, R. S. Epilogue. *In* Ellwood, R. S. Alternative altars p167-73

Ellwood, R. S. Temple and cave in America. *In* Ellwood, R. S. Alternative altars p 1-19

Glock, C. Y. Consciousness among contemporary youth: an interpretation. *In* The New religious consciousness p353-66

Judah, J. S. New religions and religious liberty. *In* Needleman, J. and Baker, G. eds. Understanding the new religions p201-08

Prebish, C. S. Reflections on the transmission of Buddhism to America. *in* Needleman, J. and Baker, G. eds. Understanding the new religions p153-72

Shepherd, W. C. Conversion and adhesion. *In* Johnson, H. M. ed. Religious change and continuity p251-63

Smith, A. Black reflections on the study of new religious consciousness. *In* Needleman, J. and Baker, G. eds. Understanding the new religions p209-19

Wuthnow, R. The new religions in social context. *In* The New religious consciousness p267-93

Wuthnow, R. Religious movements and the transition in world order. *In* Needleman, J. and Baker, G. eds. Understanding the new religions p63-79

Social conditions

Alinsky, S. D. The double revolution. *In* Smithsonian Institution. The cultural drama p289-303

Bagwell, P. S. and Mingay, G. E. Britain and America: social progress, 1850-1939; excerpt from "Britain and America." *In* Burton, D. H. ed. American history—British historians p289-318

Brown, R. D. Modernization: a Victorian climax. *In* Howe, D. W. ed. Victorian America p29-44

Glazer, N. Individualism and equality in the United States. *In* On the making of Americans p127-42

Gusfield, J. R. The sociological reality of America: an essay on mass culture. *In* On the making of Americans p41-62

Hacker, A. The new rationality: the clash between the corporate and the public sector conceptions of the national interest. *In* Planning, politics, and the public interest p10-19

Jencks, C. S. The social basis of unselfishness. *In* On the making of Americans p63-86

Lipset, S. M. Why no socialism in the United States? *In* Radicalism in the contemporary age v 1 p31-149

Myrdal, G. Race and class in a welfare state. *In* The National purpose reconsidered p73-95

Riesman, D. Some questions about discontinuities in American society. *In* The Uses of controversy in sociology p3-29

United States—Social conditions—*Continued*

Rossi, P. H. Conventional wisdom, common sense, and empirical knowledge: the case of stratification research and views of American society. *In* The Uses of controversy in sociology p30-47

Shimahara, N. K. American society, culture and socialization. *In* Social forces and schooling p49-81

Social conditions—Historiography

Nevins, A. Recent progress of American social history. *In* Nevins, A. Allan Nevins on history p103-22

Veysey, L. R. Intellectual history and the new social history. *In* Higham, J. and Conkin, P. K. eds. New directions in American intellectual history p3-26

Social conditions—1918-1932

Coben, S. The assault on Victorianism in the twentieth century. *In* Howe, D. W. ed. Victorian America p160-81

Social conditions—1933-1945

Auerbach, J. S. Lawyers and social change in the Depression decade. *In* Braeman, J.; Bremner, R. H. and Brody, D. eds. The New Deal v 1 p133-69

Social conditions—1945-

Grantham, D. W. Contemporary American history. *In* Grantham, D. W. The regional imagination p233-58

Meyersohn, R. B. Abundance reconsidered. *In* On the making of Americans p87-104

Samuels, S. The age of conspiracy and conformity: Invasion of the body snatchers. *In* O'Connor, J. E. and Jackson, M. A. eds. American history/American film p203-17

Social conditions—1960-

Keniston, K. Stranded in the present. *In* Kren, G. M. and Rappoport, L. H. eds. Varieties of psychohistory p251-56

Lindsay, J. V. The great American drift. *In* Warner, S. B. ed. The American experiment p110-29

Reich, C. A. Countercultural forces: emerging divergence in American culture; excerpt from "The greening of America." *In* Social forces and schooling p82-99

Reston, J. R. America in a changing world. *In* A Time to hear and answer: essays for the Bicentennial season p141-55

Skolnick, J. H. The police in protest: National Commission on the Causes and Prevention of Violence (a staff report); excerpt from "The politics of protest." *In* Armstrong, T. R. and Cinnamon, K. M. eds. Power and authority in law enforcement p131-90

Warner, S. B. The two revolutions. *In* Warner, S. B. ed. The American experiment p11-29

Social life and customs

Jordan, W. D. Searching for adulthood in America. *In* Erikson. E. H. ed. Adulthood p189-99

Social life and customs—20th century

Denney, R. N. Feast of strangers: varieties of sociable experience in America. *In* On the making of Americans p251-69

Social life and customs—1971-

Hardwick, E. Domestic manners. *In* A New America? p 1-11

Social policy

Berger, P. L. In praise of particularity: the concept of mediating structures. *In* An Almost chosen people p107-18

Briggs, H. Scientific leadership and the price system. *In* Against pollution and hunger p273-77

Cleveland, H. America's not-so-manifest destiny. *In* The American Revolution: a continuing commitment p67-88

Harwood, J. Heredity, environment, and the legitimation of social policy. *In* Barnes, B. and Shapin, S. eds. Natural order p231-51

Heighton, R. H. and Heighton, C. Applying the anthropological perspective to social policy. *in* Eddy, E. M. and Partridge, W. L. eds. Applied anthropology in America p390-411

Kimball, S. T. Anthropology as a policy science. *In* Eddy, E. M. and Partridge, W. L. eds. Applied anthropology in America p277-91

King, M. R. and Seligman, L. G. Critical elections, Congressional recruitment and public policy. *In* Eulau, H. and Czudnowski, M. M. eds. Elite recruitment in democratic polities p263-99

Kristol, I. A foolish American ism—utopianism. *In* A Public philosophy reader p73-91

Supreme Court

Abrams v. United States. *In* Stanford legal essays p195-249

Ballew v. Georgia. *In* The Supreme Court review, 1978 p191-224

Board of Education v. Allen. *In* Fairfield, R. P. ed. Humanistic frontiers in American education p94-101

Brown v. Board of Education of the City of Topeka. *In* Have we overcome? Race relations since Brown p3-30

Brown v. Board of Education of the City of Topeka [another essay] *In* Have we overcome? Race relations since Brown p79-119

Brown v. Board of Education of the City of Topeka [another essay] *In* Have we overcome? Race relations since Brown p173-87

Buckley v. Valeo. *In* The Supreme Court review, 1976 p 1-43

DeFunis v. Odegaard. *In* Gross, B. R. ed. Reverse discrimination p184-97

DeFunis v. Odegaard [another essay] *In* Gross, B. R. ed. Reverse discrimination p198-207

DeFunis v. Odegaard [another essay] *In* The Supreme Court review, 1974 p 1-32

FCC v. National Citizens Committee for Broadcasting. *In* The Supreme Court review, 1978 p 1-38

Flast v. Cohen. *In* Fairfield, R. P. ed. Humanistic frontiers in American education p94-101

Furman v. Georgia. *In* Riedel, M. and Chappell, D. eds. Issues in criminal justice: planning and evaluation p75-86

Goldstein v. California. *In* The Supreme Court review, 1975 p147-87

Goss v. Lopez. *In* The Supreme Court review, 1975 p25-75

Hampton v. Mow Sun Wong. *In* The Supreme Court review, 1977 p275-339

Katzenbach v. United States. *In* Stanford legal essays p79-96

Kewanee Oil Co. v. Bicron Corp. *In* The Supreme Court review, 1974 p81-95

United States in literature—*Continued*

Fraser, R. The American background in Why are we so blest? *In* African literature today no. 9: Africa, America and the Caribbean p39-46

Leary, L. G. James Fenimore Cooper's lover's quarrel with America. *In* Leary, L. G. Soundings p271-91

United States v. Matlock. *In* The Supreme Court review, 1974 p165-232

United States v. Robinson. *In* The Supreme Court review, 1974 p127-63

United States v. Robinson [another essay] *In* The Supreme Court review, 1974 p165-232

Universal catalogs. See Bibliography, International

Universal Declaration of Human Rights. See United Nations. General Assembly. Universal Declaration of Human Rights

Universal history. See World history

Universals (Linguistics)
Verne, D. P. Vico's science of imaginative universals and the philosophy of symbolic forms. *In* Giambattista Vico's science of humanity p295-317

Universals (Logic) See Universals (Philosophy)

Universals (Philosophy)
Verne, D. P. Vico's science of imaginative universals and the philosophy of symbolic forms. *In* Giambattista Vico's science of humanity p295-317
See also Individuation

Universities and colleges
Dahrendorf, R. The educational class. *In* Universities in the Western world p47-57

Kolakowski, L. Neutrality and academic values. *In* Montefiore, A. ed. Neutrality and impartiality p72-85

Peckham, M. The corporation's role in today's crisis of cultural incoherence. *In* Peckham, M. Romanticism and behavior p263-84

Taylor, C. Neutrality in the university. *In* Montefiore, A. ed. Neutrality and impartiality p128-48
See also Afro-American universities and colleges; Agricultural colleges; Catholic universities and colleges; Church and college; Education, Higher; State universities and colleges; Students' societies; University extension

Administration
Cowen, Z. The governance of the universities. *In* Universities in the Western world p58-74

Pellegrino, E. D. The academic role of the vice president for health sciences. *In* Managing nonprofit organizations p38-47

Perlman, D. H. New tools and techniques in university administration. *In* Managing nonprofit organizations p59-70

Shetty, Y. K. and Carlisle, H. M. A study of management by objectives in a professional organization. *In* Managing nonprofit organizations p187-98
See also College presidents; Universities and colleges—Business management; University autonomy

Admission
See Law schools—Admission

Business management
Ginsburg, S. G. Management for the future: a prognosis and prescription with specific concern for university and governmental management. *In* Benton, L. R. ed. Management for the future p109-24

Larimore, L. K. Break-even analysis for higher education. *In* Managing nonprofit organizations p95-101

Cooperation
See University cooperation

Curricula
Grant, G. P. The university curriculum and the technological threat. *In* Niblett, W. R. ed. The sciences, the humanities and the technological threat p21-35

McConnell, T. R. Surfeit or dearth of highly educated people? *In* McMurrin, S. M. ed. On the meaning of the university p63-80

Manning, D. In search of substantive change. *In* Buxton, T. H. and Prichard, K. W. eds. Excellence in university teaching p239-45

Oakeshott, M. J. The study of 'politics' in a university. *In* Oakeshott, M. J. Rationalism in politics p301-33

Entrance requirements
See Universities and colleges—United States—Admission

Examinations
Rothblatt, S. The student sub-culture and the examination system in early 19th century Oxbridge. *In* The University in society v 1 p247-303

Faculty
Nevins, A. The newspaperman and the scholar. *In* Nevins, A. Allan Nevins on history p36-42
See also College teachers

Finance
See College costs; Federal aid to higher education

History
Martin, B. The mining of the ivory tower. *In* Universities in the Western world p98-115

Shils, E. A. The academic ethos under strain. *In* Universities in the Western world p16-46

Law and legislation
See State aid to higher education; University autonomy

Law and legislation—United States
Perkins, C. D. The view from the Hill. *In* The Third century p83-88

Religion
See Chaplains, University and college

Teachers
See College teachers

Australia
McAuley, J. P. The condition of Australian universities. *In* Universities in the Western world p264-67

Canada
Hanly, C. Problems of academic freedom in Canada. *In* Universities in the Western world p157-75

Universities and colleges—*Continued*

United States—Administration

Anderson, G. L. and Mortimer, K. P. Governance and control of tomorrow's university: whose values? *In* Land-grant universities and their continuing challenge p326-49

Babbidge, H. D. Leadership, legitimacy, and academic governance. *In* Murphy, T. P. ed. Universities in the urban crisis p315-24

Bonham, G. W. Who runs the show? *In* The Third century p158-65

Hornig, D. F. The costs of government regulation. *In* Hook, S.; Kurtz, P. W. and Todorovich, M. eds. The university and the state: what role for government in higher education? p103-13

Ikenberry, S. O. The public interest and institutional autonomy. *In* Land-grant universities and their continuing challenge p309-25

Murphy, T. P. University bureaucracy and the urban thrust. *In* Murphy, T. P. ed. Universities in the urban crisis p287-313

Newman, F. Taking the helm. *In* The Third century p116-26

Novotny, H. R. F. The New Class, and "Professor Bill." *In* Hook, S.; Kurtz, P. W. and Todorovich, M. eds. The university and the state: what role for government in higher education? p277-85

United States—Admission

Bonham, G. W. Opening the academic gates. *In* Hook, S.; Kurtz, P. W. and Todorovich, M. eds. The university and the state: what role for government in higher education? p163-66

Heslep, R. D. Preferential treatment in admitting racial minority students. *In* Social justice & preferential treatment p33-51

Katz, J. Epilogue: the admissions process—society's stake and the individual's interest. *In* Hurdles p318-47

O'Neil, R. M. The case for preferential admissions; excerpt from "Discriminating against discrimination: preferential admissions in the DeFunis case." *In* Gross, B. R. ed. Reverse discrimination p66-83

Rever, P. R. The dynamics of admission to the less-selective public and private sector colleges. *In* Hurdles p111-44

Sacks, H. S. "Bloody Monday": the crisis of the high school seniors. *In* Hurdles p10-47

Tilley, D. C. Opening admissions and the postselective era: a view from the public sector. *In* Hurdles p76-110

Wells, P. H. Applying to college: bulldog bibs and potency myths. *In* Hurdles p48-75

Willingham, W. W. Free-access colleges: where they are and whom they serve. *In* Murphy, T. P. ed. Universities in the urban crisis p197-213

See also Law schools—United States—Admission

United States—Curricula

Bernardo, A. S. New beginnings in general education. *In* Hook, S.; Kurtz, P. W. and Todorovich, M. eds. The philosophy of the curriculum: the need for general education p257-59

Dorsey, G. L. A proposal for a new division of the curriculum. *In* Hook, S.; Kurtz, P. W. and Todorovich, M. eds. The philosophy of the curriculum: the need for general education p247-52

Gross, F. Thoughts on a social-science curriculum. *In* Hook, S.; Kurtz, P. W. and Todorovich, M. eds. The philosophy of the curriculum: the need for general education p261-73

Hook, S. On sharpening the horns. *In* Hook, S.; Kurtz, P. W. and Todorovich, M. eds. The philosophy of the curriculum: the need for general education p211-15

Kadish, M. R. The desirability of pulling in one's horns. *In* Hook, S.; Kurtz, P. W. and Todorovich, M. eds. The philosophy of the curriculum: the need for general education p205-09

London, H. I. Questions of viability in nontraditional education. *In* Hook, S.; Kurtz, P. W. and Todorovich, M. eds. The philosophy of the curriculum: the need for general education p221-26

Marcus, S. Some questions in general education today. *In* Small comforts for hard times p281-302

Marx, L. Technology and the study of man. *In* Niblett, W. R. ed. The sciences, the humanities and the technological threat p3-20

Murphy, T. P. Free universities and urban higher education. *In* Murphy, T. P. ed. Universities in the urban crisis p113-35

Peckham, M. Cultural stagnation in American universities and colleges. *In* Peckham, M. Romanticism and behavior p313-27

Radest, H. B. On interdisciplinary education. *In* Hook, S.; Kurtz, P. W. and Todorovich, M. eds. The philosophy of the curriculum: the need for general education p227-33

Stephenson, J. B. and Sexton, R. F. Experiential education and revitalization of the liberal arts. *In* Hook, S.; Kurtz, P. W. and Todorovich, M. eds. The philosophy of the curriculum: the need for general education p177-96

Zarnowiecki, J. and Murphy, T. P. University without walls. *In* Murphy, T. P. ed. Universities in the urban crisis p241-58

United States—Faculty

Hook, S. Academic freedom and professional responsibilities. *In* Hook, S.; Kurtz, P. and Todorovich, M. eds. The ethics of teaching and scientific research p117-23

Hook, S. The bias in anti-bias regulations. *In* Gross, B. R. ed. Reverse discrimination p88-96

Kampf, L. The radical faculty: What are its goals? *In* Fairfield, R. P. ed. Humanistic frontiers in American education p61-68

Murphy, T. P. Minority faculty recruitment. *In* Murphy, T. P. ed. Universities in the urban crisis p325-51

Peckham, M. Cultural stagnation in American universities and colleges. *In* Peckham, M. Romanticism and behavior p313-27

Rosenzweig, R. M. Faculty and standards of ethical conduct. *In* Hook, S.; Kurtz, P. and Todorovich, M. eds. The ethics of teaching and scientific research p73-82

Van Alstyne, W. W. Faculty codes and professional responsibility. *In* Hook, S.; Kurtz, P. and Todorovich, M. eds. The ethics of teaching and scientific research p83-86

United States—Finance

Chambers, C. M. An institutional view of the costs of government regulation. *In* Hook, S.; Kurtz, P. W. and Todorovich, M. eds. The university and the state: what role for government in higher education? p123-32

Universities and colleges—United States—Finance—*Continued*

Finn, C. E. Federal patronage of the universities: a rose by many other names? *In* Hook, S.; Kurtz, P. W. and Todorovich, M. eds. The university and the state: what role for government in higher education? p7-49

Hornig, D. F. The costs of government regulation. *In* Hook, S.; Kurtz, P. W. and Todorovich, M. eds. The university and the state: what role for government in higher education? p103-13

McGill, W. J. Government regulation and academic freedom. *In* Hook, S.; Kurtz, P. W. and Todorovich, M. eds. The university and the state: what role for government in higher education? p139-54

Van Alstyne, C. The costs to colleges and universities of implementing federally mandated social programs. *In* Hook, S.; Kurtz, P. W. Todorovich, M. eds. The university and the state: what role for government in higher education? p115-22

United States—History

Hawkins, H. University identity: the teaching and research functions. *In* Oleson, A. and Voss, J. eds. The organization of knowledge in modern America, 1860-1920 p285-312

Masson, M. W. Pessimism surpassed: new colleges as bastions against barbarism in colonial America. *In* Studies in eighteenth-century culture v8 p69-86

Miller, H. Evangelical religion and colonial Princeton. *In* Schooling and society p115-45

Shils, E. A. The order of learning in the United States: the ascendancy of the university. *In* Oleson, A. and Voss, J. eds. The organization of knowledge in modern America, 1860-1920 p19-47

Trow, M. Aspects of diversity in American higher education. *In* On the making of Americans p271-90

Universities and colleges, Afro-American. See
Afro-American universities and colleges

University and community. See Community and college

University autonomy

Egerod, S. Freedom and equality in the universities. *In* Universities in the Western world p12-15

Hesburgh, T. M. The Catholic university and freedom. *In* Hesburgh, T. M. The Hesburgh papers p63-67

Hook, S. Prospects for the academic future. *In* Fairfield, R. P. ed. Humanistic frontiers in American education p253-60

Lowenthal, R. The university's autonomy versus social priorities. *In* Universities in the Western world p75-84

Metzger, W. P. Academic freedom and scientific freedom. *In* Holton, G. J. and Morison, R. S. eds. Limits of scientific inquiry p93-114

Shils, E. A. The academic ethos under strain. *In* Universities in the Western world p16-46

Shils, E. A. Governments and universities. *In* Hook, S.; Kurtz, P. W. and Todorovich, M. eds. The university and the state: what role for government in higher education? p177-204

See also Teaching, Freedom of

Canada

Hanly, C. Problems of academic freedom in Canada. *In* Universities in the Western world p157-75

Sweden

Wahlbäck, K. University autonomy in Sweden. *In* Universities in the Western world p268-78

United States

Baumann, F. Is the university a special case? *In* Hook, S.; Kurtz, P. W. and Todorovich, M. eds. The university and the state: what role for government in higher education? p237-44

Bloom, A. A response to President McGill. *In* Hook, S.; Kurtz, P. W. and Todorovich, M. eds. The university and the state: what role for government in higher education? p155-61

Bork, R. H. The limits of governmental regulation. *In* Hook, S.; Kurtz, P. W. and Todorovich, M. eds. The university and the state: what role for government in higher education? p169-75

Chambers, C. M. An institutional view of the costs of government regulation. *In* Hook, S.; Kurtz, P. W. and Todorovich, M. eds. The university and the state: what role for government in higher education? p123-32

Hook, S. The state and higher education. *In* Hook, S.; Kurtz, P. W. and Todorovich, M. eds. The university and the state: what role for government in higher education? p227-36

Hornig, D. F. The costs of government regulation. *In* Hook, S.; Kurtz, P. W. and Todorovich, M. eds. The university and the state: what role for government in higher education? 103-13

Huitt, R. K. Autonomy on the line. *In* The Third century p80-82

Ikenberry, S. O. The public interest and institutional autonomy. *In* Land-grant universities and their continuing challenge p309-25

Kurtz, P. Should the patron be the master?: the autonomy of public universities and colleges. *In* Hook, S.; Kurtz, P. W. and Todorovich, M. eds. The university and the state: what role for government in higher education? p287-91

Lichtenstein, D. S. The alienated intellectual and government bureaucracy. *In* Hook, S.; Kurtz, P. W. and Todorovich, M. eds. The university and the state: what role for government in higher education? p249-64

McGill, W. J. Government regulation and academic freedom. *In* Hook, S.; Kurtz, P. W. and Todorovich, M. eds. The university and the state: what role for government in higher education? p139-54

Novotny, H. R. F. The New Class, and "Professor Bill." *In* Hook, S.; Kurtz, P. W. and Todorovich, M. eds. The university and the state: what role for government in higher education? p277-85

University cooperation

United States

Ikenberry, S. O. The public interest and institutional autonomy. *In* Land-grant universities and their continuing challenge p309-25

University extension

United States

Mortimer, K. P. and Johnson, M. D. External degree programs: the current educational frontier. *In* Land-grant universities and their continuing challenge p286-308

University extension—United States—*Cont.*

Nichols, D. C. Land-grant university services and urban policy. *In* Land-grant universities and their continuing challenge p223-36

University libraries. See Libraries, University and college

University of Alabama. See Alabama. University

University of Cracow. See Krakow. Uniwersytet Jagiellónski

University of Lund. See Lunds Universitet

University of Paris. See Paris. Université

University presidents. See College presidents

University teachers. See College teachers

University teaching. See College teaching

University theater. See College theater

Unnik, William Cornelius van

The interpretation of Romans 12:8: ὁ μεταδιδοὺς ἐν ἁπλότητι. *In* On language, culture, and religion: in honor of Eugene A. Nida p169-83

The unseen hand (criticism) Shepard, S. *In* Brustein, R. S. The culture watch p82-84

Unterberger, Betty Miller

National self-determination. *In* Encyclopedia of American foreign policy p635-50

Unterecker, John Eugene

Countryman, peasant and servant in the poetry of W. B. Yeats. *In* Casey, D. J. and Rhodes, R. E. eds. Views of the Irish peasantry, 1800-1916 p178-91

Fiction at the edge of poetry: Durrell, Beckett, Green. *In* Forms of modern British fiction p165-99

Lawrence Durrell. *In* Stade, G. ed. Six contemporary British novelists p219-69

Untruthfulness. See Truthfulness and falsehood

Upanishads

Talghatti, S. R. The Upaniṣads and Upaniṣadic thought. *In* Bishop, D. H. ed. Indian thought p38-61

Updike, John

The cultural situation of the American writer. *In* Arab and American cultures p209-19

I am dying, Egypt, dying. *In* Arab and American cultures p55-63

Rhyming Max; excerpt from "Assorted prose." *In* Riewald, J. G. ed. The surprise of excellence p152-58

About

Allen, M. John Updike's love of "dull bovine beauty." *In* Allen, M. The necessary blankness p97-132

Donald, M. The fate of the traditional novel. *In* Donald, M. The American novel in the twentieth century p73-107

Kunkel, F. L. John Updike: between heaven and earth. *In* Kunkel, F. L. Passion and the Passion p75-98

About individual works

Couples

Hyman, S. E. Couplings. *In* Hyman, S. E. The critic's credentials p107-11

Rabbit redux

Alter, R. Updike, Malamud, and the fire this time. *In* Alter, R. Defenses of the imagination p233-48

Waldmeir, J. J. Rabbit redux reduced: rededicated? Redeemed? *In* Essays in honor of Russel B. Nye p247-62

Rabbit run

Le Pellec, Y. Rabbit underground. *In* Johnson, I. D. and Johnson, C. [eds.] Les américanistes p94-109

Siegel, G. Rabbit runs down. *In* Peary, G. and Shatzkin, R. eds. The modern American novel and the movies p247-55

Upper classes

See also Aristocracy

China

Eberhard, W. The upper-class family in traditional China. *In* Rosenberg, C. E. ed. The family in history p59-94

Great Britain

Hexter, J. H. Lawrence Stone and the English aristocracy. *In* Hexter, J. H. On historians p149-226

Ireland

Henn, T. R. 'The big house.' *In* Henn, T. R. Last essays p207-20

Italy—Genoa

Hughes, D. O. Domestic ideals and social behavior: evidence from medieval Genoa. *In* Rosenberg, C. E. ed. The family in history p115-43

Upper classes in literature

Holman, C. H. Marquand, novelist of manners. *In* Holman, C. H. Windows on the world p61-97

Uranium. See Transuranium elements

Urban V, Pope

About

Palmer, J. J. N. and Wells, A. P. Ecclesiastical reform and the politics of the Hundred Years War during the pontificate of Urban V (1362-70). *In* War, literature, and politics in the late Middle Ages p169-89

Urban areas. See Cities and towns; Metropolitan areas

Urban crime. See Crime and criminals

Urban design. See City planning

Urban development. See City planning

Urban economics

Abrams, P. Towns and economic growth: some theories and problems. *In* Towns in societies p 9-33

Daunton, M. J. Towns and economic growth in eighteenth-century England. *In* Towns in societies p245-77

Kain, J. F. Urban problems. *In* McKie, J. W. ed. Social responsibility and the business predicament p217-45

Leibenstein, H. Efficiency wages, X-efficiency, and urban unemployment. *In* Economic development and planning p168-85

Wrigley, E. A. Parasite or stimulus: the town in a pre-industrial economy. *In* Towns in societies p295-309

Urban education. See Education, Urban

Urban-federal relations. See Federal-city relations

Urban housing. See Housing

Urban life. See City and town life

Urban planning. See City planning

Urban politiics. See Metropolitan government; Municipal government

Urban population movements. See Residential mobility

Urban redevelopment. See Urban renewal

Urban renewal

Daifuku, H. Introduction: Urban retrieval too. *In* United Nations Educational, Scientific and Cultural Organization. The conservation of cities p9-23

See also City planning

Study and teaching

Murphy, T. P. University bureaucracy and the urban thrust. *In* Murphy, T. P. ed. Universities in the urban crisis p287-313

United States

Seyffert, M. G. The university as an urban neighbor. *In* Murphy, T. P. ed. Universities in the urban crisis p137-59

Suttles, G. D. Community design: the search for participation in a metropolitan society. *In* Hawley, A. H. and Rock, V. P. eds. Metropolitan America in contemporary perspective p235-97

United States—Finance

Caraley, D. The Carter Congress and urban programs: first soundings. *In* Burnham, W. D. and Weinberg, M. W. eds. American politics and public policy p188-221

Urban research. See Municipal research

Urban schools

Bossert, S. T. Education in urban society. *In* Handbook of contemporary urban life p288-318

Urban sociology. See Sociology, Urban

Urban transportation

United States

Foley, D. L. Accessibility for residents in the metropolitan environment. *In* Hawley, A. H. and Rock, V. P. eds. Metropolitan America in contemporary perspective p157-98

Urban universities. See Municipal universities and colleges

Urbanesis (Ms.)

Wallach, L. The Urbana Anglo-Saxon sylloge of Latin inscriptions. *In* Poetry and poetics from ancient Greece to the Renaissance p134-51

Urbani, Giuliano. See Bastianini, A. jt. auth.

Urbanism. See Cities and towns

Urbanization

Harloe, M. Marxism, the state and the urban question: critical notes on two French theories. *In* Crouch, C. ed. State and economy in contemporary capitalism p122-56

Roberts, B. R. Comparative perspectives on urbanization. *In* Handbook of contemporary urban life p592-627

Sutcliffe, A. A vision of utopia: optimistic foundations of Le Corbusier's doctrine d'urbanisme. *In* Walden, R. ed. The open hand p216-43

See also Detribalization; Rural-urban migration

Religious aspects

See City churches

Brazil

Morse, R. M. Brazil's urban development: colony and empire. *In* From colony to nation p155-81

Germany

Lee, J. J. Aspects of urbanization and economic development in Germany, 1815-1914. *In* Towns in societies p279-93

Russia

Blackwell, W. L. Modernization and urbanization in Russia: a comparative view. *In* Hamm, M. F. ed. The city in Russian history p291-330

Rozman, G. Comparative approaches to urbanization: Russia, 1750-1800. *In* Hamm, M. F. ed. The city in Russian history p69-85

Southern States

Brownell, B. A. The urban South comes of age, 1900-1940. *In* Brownell, B. A. and Goldfield, D. R. eds. The city in Southern history p123-58

Brownell, B. A. and Goldfield, D. R. Southern urban history. *In* Brownell, B. A. and Goldfield, D. R. eds. The city in Southern history p5-22

Earle, C. and Hoffman, R. The urban South: the first two centuries. *In* Brownell, B. A. and Goldfield, D. R. eds. The city in Southern history p23-51

Goldfield, D. R. Pursuing the American urban dream: cities in the Old South. *In* Brownell, B. A. and Goldfield, D. R. eds. The city in Southern history p52-91

Haas, E. F. The Southern metropolis, 1940-1976. *In* Brownell, B. A. and Goldfield, D. R. eds. The city in Southern history p159-91

Rabinowitz, H. N. Continuity and change: Southern urban development, 1860-1900. *In* Brownell, B. A. and Goldfield, D. R. eds. The city in Southern history p92-122

Underdeveloped areas

See Underdeveloped areas—Urbanization

United States

Edel, M.; Harris, J. R. and Rothenberg, J. Urban concentration and deconcentration. *In* Hawley, A. H. and Rock, V. P. eds. Metropolitan America in contemporary perspective p123-56

Goist, P. D. A sociologist and the city: the experience of Robert Park. *In* Goist, P. D. From Main Street to State Street p110-20

Hawley, A. H. Urbanization as process. *In* Handbook of contemporary urban life p3-26

MacLeish, A. A lay sermon for the hill towns. *In* MacLeish, A. Riders on the earth p103-08

Richards, R. O. Urbanization of rural areas. *In* Handbook of contemporary urban life p551-91

Street, D. Conclusion: life in urbanized America. *In* Handbook of contemporary urban life p628-41

United States—Historiography

Thernstrom, S. A. The new urban history. *In* The Future of history p43-51

Urbino. Palazzo Ducale

Westfall, C. W. Chivalric declaration: the Palazzo Ducale in Urbino as a political statement. *In* Millon, H. A. and Nochlin, L. eds. Art and architecture in the service of politics p20-45

Ure, Colin Seymour- See Seymour-Ure, Colin

Utopias in literature—*Continued*

Hansot, E. Reflections on war, utopias, and temporary systems. *In* Small comforts for hard times p246-59

Harris, N. Utopian fiction and its discontents. *In* Uprooted Americans p209-44

Porter, P. W. and Lukermann, F. E. The geography of Utopia. *In* Geographies of the mind p197-223

Suvin, D. The alternative island. *In* Suvin, D. Metamorphoses of science fiction p90-114

Suvin, D. Defining the literary genre of utopia: some historical semantics, some genology, a proposal, and a plea. *In* Suvin, D. Metamorphoses of science fiction p37-62

Suvin, D. Russian SF and its utopian tradition. *In* Suvin, D. Metamorphoses of science fiction p243-69

Uviller, Rena

Doing well by "doing good." *In* Gross, B. and Gross, R. eds. The children's rights movement p255-58

Uyeda, Akinari. See Ueda, Akinari

Uzbekistan

Social conditions

Carlisle, D. S. Modernization, generations, and the Uzbek Soviet intelligentsia. *In* Cocks, P.; Daniels, R. V. and Heer, N. W. eds. The dynamics of Soviet politics p239-64

V

Vacarius

About

Stein, P. Vacarius and the civil law. *In* Church and government in the Middle Ages p119-37

Vachon, M. L. S.; Lyall, W. A. L. and Pollack, H.

How group meetings ease the stress of cancer on patients and their families. *In* Home care p70-76

Vadim, Roger

About individual works

And God created woman

Truffaut, F. Roger Vadim: Et Dieu créa la femme. *In* Truffaut, F. The films in my life p311-12

Vagabonds. See Gypsies

Vagabondage. See Vagrancy

Vagantes. See Goliards

Vagi scholares. See Goliards

Vago, Bela

Fascism in Eastern Europe. *In* Laqueur, W. Z. ed. Fascism: a reader's guide p229-53

Vagrancy

Chambliss, W. J. A sociological analysis of the law of vagrancy. *In* David, F. J. and Stivers, R. eds. The collective definition of deviance p268-80

Vagrants. See Tramps

Vaill, Peter B.

Toward a behavioral description of high-performing systems. *In* Leadership p103-25

Vaio, John

A new manuscript of Babrius: fact or fable? *In* Illinois classical studies v2, 1977 p178-83

Vaitsos, Constantine V.

Foreign investment and productive knowledge. *In* Erb, G. F. and Kallab, V. eds. Beyond dependency p75-94

Vaizey, John Ernest

The international inflation. *In* The Year book of world affairs, 1976 p243-57

Keynes and Cambridge. *In* Skidelsky, R. J. A. ed. The end of the Keynesian era p10-17

Vajda, Mihaly. See Heller, A. jt. auth.

Vajrayāna Buddhism. See Tantric Buddhism

Valdés, Nelson P.

Revoultionary solidarity in Angola. *In* Cuba in the world p87-117

Valdés Leal, Juan de

About

Brown, J. Hieroglyphs of death and salvation: the decoration of the Church of the Hermandad de la Caridad, Seville. *In* Brown, J. Images and ideas in seventeenth-century Spanish painting p128-46

About individual works

Vanitas

Kinkead, D. T. An important Vanitas by Juan de Valdés Leal. *In* Enggass, R. C. and Stokstad, M. eds. Hortus imaginum p155-63

Vale, Malcolm Graham Allan

New techniques and old ideals: the impact of artillery on war and chivalry at the end of the Hundred Years War. *In* War, literature, and politics in the late Middle Ages p57-72

Vale, Vivian

Trusts and tycoons: British myth and American reality. *In* Allen, H. C. and Thompson, R. eds. Contrast and connection p225-44

Valence (Theoretical chemistry)

Kohler, R. E. The Lewis-Langmuir theory of valence and the chemical community, 1920-1928. *In* Historical studies in the physical sciences v6 p431-68

Valency. See Valence (Theoretical chemistry)

Valentinov, Nikolaï. See Vol'skiĭ, Nikolaĭ Vladislovich

Valenzuela, Arturo A.

The breakdown of democratic regimes: Chile. *In* The Breakdown of democratic regimes pt4 p3-81

Valerius Flaccus, Caius

About individual works

The Argonautica

Bailey, D. R. S. On Valerius Flaccus. *In* Harvard Studies in classical philology. v81 p199-215

Valéry, Paul

About

Connolly, C. The Gide-Valéry letters. *In* Connolly, C. The evening colonnade p300-03

Crow, C. M. Valery and the image of the tree-top. *In* Cardinal, R. ed. Sensibility and creation p16-35

Fergusson, F. The theater of Paul Valéry. *In* Fergusson, F. Literary landmarks p89-100

Gass, W. H. Paul Valéry. *In* Gass, W. H. The world within the word p158-76

Glicksberg, C. I. The battle against the Absurd in France. *In* Glicksberg, C. I. The literature of nihilism p142-54

Values—*Continued*

Olson, E. On value judgments in the arts. *In* Olson, E. On value judgments in the arts, and other essays p307-26

Richards, I. A. The ever-new discovery. *In* Richards, I. A. Poetries p242-49

Rosenberg, N. Technology, economy, and values. *In* Bugliarello, G. and Doner, D. B. eds. The history and philosophy of technology p81-111

Ross, R. G. The experience of value. *In* Philosophy and the civilizing arts p316-44

Stern-Mitscherlich, A. L. On value and human dignity. *In* The Personal universe p74-90

Taylor, C. What is human agency? *In* Mischel, T. ed. The self p103-35

Todorovich, M. Wanted: a rational decision procedure for value conflicts in science. *In* Hook, S.; Kurtz, P. and Todorovich, M. eds. The ethics of teaching and scientific research p191-201

Warnock, M. The neutral teacher. *In* Philosophers discuss education p159-71

vich, M. eds. The ethics of teaching and

Van der Kroef, Justus Maria

See also Social values

Values in literature

Bronowski, J. The play of values in the work of art. *In* Bronowski, J. The visionary eye p153-70

Vampires

Barclay, G. S. Vampires and ladies: Sheridan Le Fanu. *In* Barclay, G. S. Anatomy of horror: the masters of occult fiction p22-38

Van Alstyne, Carol

The costs to colleges and universities of implementing federally mandated social programs. *In* Hook, S.; Kurtz, P. W. and Todorovich, M. eds. The university and the state: what role for government in higher education? p115-22

Van Alstyne, Richard Warner

Debt collection. *In* Encyclopedia of American foreign policy p212-18

The Monroe doctrine. *In* Encyclopedia of American foreign policy p584-96

The Open Door policy. *In* Encyclopedia of American foreign policy p711-21

Van Alstyne, William W.

Faculty codes and professional responsibility. *In* Hook, S.; Kurtz, P. and Todorovich, M. eds. The ethics of teaching and scientific research p83-86

The specific theory of academic freedom and the general issue of civil liberty. *In* The Concept of academic freedom p59-85

About individual works

The specific theory of academic freedom and the general issue of civil liberty

Rorty, A. O. Dilemmas of academic and intellectual freedom. *In* The Concept of academic freedom p97-110

Schmitt, R. Academic freedom: the future of a confusion. *In* The Concept of academic freedom p111-24

Van Baron, Judith

The grand style. *In* Battcock, G. ed. Super realism p230-36

Van Beek, Gus Willard. See Beek, Gus Willard van

Van Beethoven, Ludwig. See Beethoven, Ludwig van

Van Bemmelen, Reinout Willem. See Bemmelen, Reinout Willem van

Van Beysterveldt, Antonie Adrianus. See Beysterveldt, Antonie Adrianus van

Van Beysterveldt, Antony. See Beysterveldt, Antonie Adrianus van

Van Breda, Herman Leo

A note on reduction and authenticity according to Husserl. *In* Elliston, F. A. and McCormick, P. eds. Husserl p124-25

Van Caenegem, Raoul C. See Caenegem, Raoul C. van

Vance, Eugene

Pas de trois: narrative, hermeneutics, and structure in medieval poetics. *In* Valdés, M. J. and Miller, O. J. eds. Interpretation of narrative p118-34

Van de Castle, Robert Leon

Some possible anthropological contributions to the study of parapsychology. *In* Parapsychology: its relation to physics, biology, psychology, and psychiatry p151-61

Vande Kieft, Ruth Marguerite

Looking with Eudora Welty. *In* Prenshaw, P. W. ed. Eudora Welty p423-44

Van Den Berg, Kent T.

"The counterfeit in personation": Spenser's Prosopopoia, or Mother Hubberds tale. *In* Martz, L. L. and Williams, A. L. eds. The author in his work p85-102

Van den Berghe, Pierre L.

Bridging the paradigms: biology and the social sciences. *In* Sociobiology and human nature p33-52

Vanderbilt, Kermit

Theodore Roethke as a Northwest poet. *In* Bingham, E. R. and Love, G. A. eds. Northwest perspectives p186-216

Vanderbilt family

Auchincloss, L. Two conversation pieces: the Astors and the Vanderbilts. *In* Auchincloss, L. Life, law and letters p79-89

Van Der Kroef, Justus Maria

The wages of ambiguity: the 1965 coup in Indonesia, its origins and meaning. *In* Hammond, T. T. ed. The anatomy of Communist takeovers p534-62

Vander Molen, Ronald J.

Anglican against Puritan: ideological origins during the Marian exile. *In* Vaughan, A. T. and Bremer, F. J. eds. Puritan New England p2-18

Vandermyn, Gaye, and Smith, H. Dean

Finding answers to school problems. *In* Managing nonprofit organizations p220-28

Vander Nat, Arnold. See Rescher, N. jt. auth.

Van der Rohe, Ludwig Mies. See Mies van der Rohe, Ludwig

Vanderstappen, Harrie A.

The style of some seventeenth-century Chinese paintings. *In* Artists and traditions p149-68

Van Der Weele, Steve J.

From Mt Olympus to Glome: C. S. Lewis's dislocation of Apuleius's "Cupid and Psyche" in Till we have faces. *In* Schakel, P. J. ed. The longing for a form p182-92

Vanderwood, Paul J.

An American Cold Warrior: Viva Zapata! *In* O'Connor, J. E. and Jackson, M. A. eds. American history/American film p183-201

Van Devanter, Willis

About

White, G. E. The Four Horsemen: the sources of judicial notoriety. *In* White, G. E. The American judicial tradition p178-99

Van de Walle, Etienne. See Lesthaeghe, R. jt. auth.

Van de Water, Richard. See Fontana, B. jt. auth.

Van Doren, Mark

About

MacLeish, A. Mark Van Doren. *In* MacLeish, A. Riders on the earth p139-42

Van Duinkerken, Anton, pseud. See Asselbergs, Willem Jan Marie Anton

Van Dusen, Michael H.

Syria: downfall of a traditional elite. *In* Political elites and political development in the Middle East p115-55

Van Dyke, Joyce

Making a scene: language and gesture in 'Coriolanus.' *In* Shakespeare survey 30 p135-46

Van Dyke, Vernon

The individual, the state, and ethnic communities in political theory. *In* Kommers, D. P. and Loescher, G. D. eds. Human rights and American foreign policy p36-62

Vane, Henry, 1613-1662

About

Patrick, J. M. The idea of liberty in the theological writings of Sir Henry Vane the Younger. *In* The Dissenting tradition p100-07

Van Evra, James

On death as a limit. *In* Donnelly, J. P. ed. Language, metaphysics, and death p25-31

Van Eyck, Jan. See Eyck, Jan van

Van Ghent, Dorothy (Bendon)

Willa Cather. *In* Howard, M. ed. Seven American women writers of the twentieth century p79-121

Van Gogh, Vincent. See Gogh, Vincent van

Van Helmont, Jean Baptiste. See Helmont, Jean Baptiste van

Van Lawick-Goodall, Barones Jane. See Lawick-Goodall, Barones Jane

Van Marter, Shirley

Richardson's revisions of Clarissa in the third and fourth editions. *In* Virginia. University. Bibliographical Society. Studies in bibliography v28 p119-52

Van Naerssen, Frits Herman. See Naerssen, Frits Herman van

Van Nooten, Barend A.

The Sanskrit epics. *In* Oinas, F. J. ed. Heroic epic and saga p49-75

Van Peeterssen A. See Klein, L. R. jt. auth.

Van Peursen, Cornelius A.

The horizon. *In* Elliston, F. A. and McCormick, P. eds. Husserl p182-201

Van Raamsdonk, Wouter. See Raamsdonk, Wouter van

Van Riemsdijk, Henk. See Riemsdijk, Henk van

Van Schaack, Peter

About

Bloomfield, M. H. Peter Van Schaack and the problem of allegiance. *In* Bloomfield, M. H. American lawyers in a changing society, 1776-1876 p 1-31

Van Slyke, Lyman Page

Joseph Levenson's approach to history. *In* Meisner, M. J. and Murphey, R. eds. The Mozartian historian p91-99

Van Steenburgh, Elston W.

Durationless moments in Hume's Treatise. *In* David Hume p181-85

Van Straaten, Modestus. See Straaten, Modestus van

Van Unnik, William Cornelius. See Unnik, William Cornelius van

VanZyl Slabbert, Frederick

Afrikaner nationalism, white politics, and political change in South Africa. *In* Thompson, L. M. and Butler, J. eds. Change in contemporary South Africa p3-18

Varbero, Richard A.

The politics of ethnicity: Philadelphia's Italians in the 1920's. *In* Studies in Italian American social history p164-81

Varda, Agnès

About individual works

La pointe courte

Truffaut, F. Agnès Varda: La Pointe courte. *In* Truffaut, F. The films in my life p308-10

Vardys, Vytas Stanley

The role of the Baltic republics in Soviet society. *In* Szporluk, R. ed. The influence of East Europe and the Soviet West on the USSR p147-79

Varey, J. E.

Kings and judges: Lope de Vega's El mejor alcalde, el rey. *In* Drama and society p37-58

Varg, Paul A.

Missionaries. *In* Encyclopedia of American foreign policy p567-74

Varga, Nicholas

The development and structure of local government in colonial New York. *In* Daniels, B. C. ed. Town and county p186-215

Vargas Llosa, Mario

About

Brody, R. Mario Vargas Llosa and the totalization impulse. *In* Rossman, C. R. and Friedman, A. W. eds. Mario Vargas Llosa 120-27

Davis, M. E. Mario Vargas Llosa: the necessary scapegoat. *In* Rossman, C. R. and Friedman, A. W. eds. Mario Vargas Llosa p136-50

Feustle, J. A. Mario Vargas Llosa: a labyrinth of solitude. *In* Rossman, C. R. and Friedman, A. W. eds. Mario Vargas Llosa p128-35

Filer, M. E. Vargas Llosa, the novelist as a critic. *In* Rossman, C. R. and Friedman, A. W. eds. Mario Vargas Llosa p109-19

Harss, L. A city boy. *In* Rossman, C. R. and Friedman, A. W. eds. Mario Vargas Llosa p101-08

About individual works

Conversation in the cathedral

Cheuse, A. Mario Vargas Llosa and Conversation in the cathedral: the question of naturalism. *In* Rossman, C. R. and Friedman, A. W. eds. Mario Vargas Llosa p52-58

Franco, J. Conversations and confessions: self and character in The fall and Conversation in the cathedral. *In* Rossman, C. R. and Friedman, A. W. eds. Mario Vargas Llosa p59-75

Vargas Llosa, Mario—About individual works—*Continued*

The green house

Díez, L. A. The sources of The green house: the mythical background of a fabulous novel. *In* Rossman, C. R. and Friedman, A. W. eds. Mario Vargas Llosa p36-51

Moody, M. W. A small whirlpool: narrative structure in The green house. *In* Rossman, C. R. and Friedman, A. W. eds. Mario Vargas Llosa p15-35

Pantaleón y las visitadoras

Siemens, W. L. Apollo's metamorphosis in Pantaleón y las visitadoras. *In* Rossman, C. R. and Friedman, A. W. eds. Mario Vargas Llosa p88-100

Williams, R. L. The narrative art of Mario Vargas Llosa: two organizing principles in Pantaleón y las visitadoras. *In* Rossman, C. R. and Friedman, A. W. eds. Mario Vargas Llosa p76-87

La tía Julia y el escribidor

Oviedo, J. M. La tía Julia y el escribidor, or the coded self-portrait. *In* Rossman, C. R. and Friedman, A. W. eds. Mario Vargas Llosa p166-81

The time of the hero

Baker, R. L. "Of how to be and what to see while you are being": the reader's performance in The time of the hero. *In* Rossman, C. R. and Friedman, A. W. eds. Mario Vargas Llosa p3-14

Brotherston, G. Social structures: Mario Vargas Llosa. *In* Brotherston, G. The emergence of the Latin American novel p110-21

Technique

Baker, R. L. "Of how to be and what to see while you are being": the reader's performance in The time of the hero. *In* Rossman, C. R. and Friedman, A. W. eds. Mario Vargas Llosa p3-14

Brody, R. Mario Vargas Llosa and the totalization impulse. *In* Rossman, C. R. and Friedman, A. W. eds. Mario Vargas Llosa p120-27

Moody, M. W. A small whirlpool: narrative structure in The green house. *In* Rossman, C. R. and Friedman, A. W. eds. Mario Vargas Llosa p15-35

Williams, R. L. The narrative art of Mario Vargas Llosa: two organizing principles in Pantaleón y las visitadoras. *In* Rossman, C. R. and Friedman, A. W. eds. Mario Vargas Llosa p76-87

Vargas, Mario. See Vargas Llosa, Mario

Vargo, Edward P.
Struggling with a bugaboo: the priest-character in Achebe and Greene and Keneally. *In* Narasimhaiah, C. D. ed. Awakened conscience p284-93

Variables (Mathematics)
Quine, W. V. The variable. *In* Quine, W. V. The ways of paradox, and other essays p272-82

Variation (Biology)
Dubos, R. J. The races of man. *In* Dubos, R. J. Beast or angel? p23-29

See also Adaptation (Biology); Evolution; Mendel's law; Natural selection

Varon, Bension
Ocean issues on the international agenda. *In* Erb, G. F. and Kallab, V. eds. Beyond dependency p120-31

Varon, Bension, and Takeuchi, Kenji
Developing countries and non-fuel minerals. *In* Bundy, W. P. ed. The world economic crisis p165-78

Varriano, John L.
Domenico Castelli's façade for San Girolamo della Carità in Rome. *In* Enggass, R. C. and Stokstad, M. eds. Hortus imaginum p129-38

Varro, Marcus Terentius

About individual works

Menippean satires

Knoche, U. Varro's Menippeans. *In* Knoche, U. Roman satire p53-69

Sigsbee, D. L. Varro and Menippean satire. *In* Roman satirists and their satire p53-63

Criticism, Textual

Skutsch, O. Readings in early Latin. *In* Harvard Studies in classical philology v76 p169-71

Vartanian, Aram
Necessity or freedom? The politics of an eighteenth-century metaphysical debate. *In* Studies in eighteenth-century culture v7 p153-74

About individual works

Necessity or freedom? The politics of an eighteenth-century metaphysical debate

Barnouw, J. Materialism and freedom: commentary on papers by Robert E. Schofield and Aram Vartanian. *In* Studies in eighteenth-century culture v7 p193-212

Vasari, Giorgio

About individual works

Palazzo Vecchio, Florence—Staircase

Pillsbury, E. P. Vasari's staircase in the Palazzo Vecchio. *In* Collaboration in Italian Renaissance art p125-41

Vase-painting, Greek
Clairmont, C. W. The lekythos of Myrrhine. *In* Studies in classical art and archaeology p103-10

Moore, M. B. Poseidon in the Gigantomachy. *In* Studies in classical art and archaeology p23-27

Phillips, K. M. and Ashmead, A. H. Three goddesses and a falcon. *In* Studies in classical art and archaeology p45-52

Vermeule, E. T. More sleeping furies. *In* Studies in classical art and archaeology p185-88

Vases, Cypriote
Frankel, D. Pottery decoration as an indicator of social relationships: a prehistoric Cypriot example. *In* Greenhalgh, M. and Megaw, J. V. S. eds. Art in society p147-60

Vases, Greek

See also Amphoras; Hydriae; Lecythi

Massachusetts—Boston

Vermeule, E. T. More sleeping furies. *In* Studies in classical art and archaeology p185-88

Rhode Island—Providence

Phillips, K. M. and Ashmead, A. H. Three goddesses and a falcon. *In* Studies in classical art and archaeology p45-52

Vases, Roman. See Hydriae

Vasoli, Cesare
Alchemy in the seventeenth century: the European and Italian scene. *In* Bonelli, M. L. R. and Shea, W. R. eds. Reason, experiment, and mysticism in the scientific revolution p49-58

Vassalli, Giuliano
An Italian enquiry concerning the Mafia. *In* Crime, criminology and public policy p595-622

Vastokas, Joan M.
Cognitive aspects of Northwest coast art. *In* Greenhalgh, M. and Megaw, J. V. S. eds. Art in society p243-59

Vasubandhu

About
Hoffmann, Y. 'Dream-world' philosophers: Berkeley and Vasubandhu. *In* Philosophy East/philosophy West p247-68

Vatican. Biblioteca Vaticana. Mss (Lat) 7207
Wallach, L. The marginalia of the Vaticanus Latinus 7207. *In* Wallach, L. Diplomatic studies in Latin and Greek documents from the Carolingian age p2h2-86

Wallach, L. The origins, corrections, and Tironian notes of the Vaticanus Latinus 7207. *In* Wallach, L. Diplomatic studies in Latin and Greek documents from the Carolingian age p187-208

Wallach, L. The Vaticanus Latinus 7207 and paleographical problems. *In* Wallach, L. Diplomatic studies in Latin and Greek documents from the Carolingian age p165-86

Vatican City. Piazza San Pietro
Wittkower, R. A counter-project to Bernini's Piazza S. Pietro. *In* Wittkower, R. Studies in the Italian baroque p61-82

Wittkower, R. The third arm of Bernini's Piazza S. Pietro. *In* Wittkower, R. Studies in the Italian baroque p53-60

Vatican City. San Pietro in Vaticano (Basilica)
Spencer, J. R. Filarete's bronze doors at St Peter's. *In* Collaboration in Italian Renaissance art p33-57

Vauban, Sébastien Le Prestre, marquis de

About
Guerlac, H. Vauban: the impact of science on war. *In* Guerlac, H. Essays and papers in the history of modern science p413-39

Vaudeville

United States
See Minstrel shows

Vaughan, Alden T.
Pequots and Puritans: the causes of the War of 1637. *In* Vaughan, A. T. and Bremer, F. J. eds. Puritan New England p201-14

Vaughan, Henry, 1622-1695

About
Brown, E. Henry Vaughan's Biblical landscape. *In* English Association. Essays and studies 1977 p50-60

Lewalski, B. K. Henry Vaughan: pleading in groans of my Lord's penning. *In* Lewalski, B. K. Protestant poetics and the seventeenth-century religious lyric p137-51

About individual works
Silex scintillans
Lewalski, B. K. Typology and poetry: a consideration of Herbert, Vaughan, and Marvell. *In* Illustrious evidence p41-69

Vaughan, James Herbert
Environment, population, and traditional society. *In* Martin, P. M. and O'Meara, P. eds. Africa p 9-23

Social and political organization in traditional societies. *In* Martin, P. M. and O'Meara, P. eds. Africa p169-88

Vauthier, Simone
Narrative triangle and triple alliance: a look at "The moviegoer." *In* Johnson, I. D. and Johnson, C. [eds.] Les américanistes p71-93

Vavuris, S. Lee
On the civil liberties of sect members: Part 2. *In* Horowitz, I. L. ed. Science, sin, and scholarship p198-207

Vázquez, Juan Adolfo
The religions of Mexico and of Central and South America. *In* Adams, C. J. ed. A reader's guide to the great religions p78-89

Vázsonyi, Andrew. See Dégh, L. jt. auth.

Veal, George, supposed author

About individual works
Musical travels through England
Lonsdale, R. H. Dr. Burney, 'Joel Collier', and Sabrina. *In* Evidence in literary scholarship p281-308

Veatch, Robert Marlin
An ethical analysis of population policy proposals. *In* Population policy and ethics p445-75

Justice. *In* Population policy and ethics p31-39

Veatch, Robert Marlin, and Draper, Thomas F.
The values of physicians. *In* Population policy and ethics p377-408

Veblen, Thorstein

About
Galbraith, J. K. Who was Thorstein Veblen? *In* Galbraith, J. K. Annals of an abiding liberal p123-47

About individual works
The theory of the leisure class
Galbraith, J. K. Who was Thorstein Veblen? *In* Galbraith, J. K. Annals of a abiding liberal p123-47

Vecelli, Tiziano. See Titian

Vedanta
Coomaraswamy, A. K. Mahā purusa: "Supreme Identity." *In* Coomaraswamy, A. K. Selected papers v2 p379-86

Coomaraswamy, A. K. Recollection, Indian and platonic. *In* Coomaraswamy, A. K. Selected papers v2 p49-65

Coomaraswamy, A. K. The Vedānta and Western tradition. *In* Coomaraswamy, A. K. Selected papers v2 p3-22

Coomaraswamy, A. K. Vedic exemplarism. *In* Coomaraswamy, A. K. Selected papers v2 p177-97

Vedas
Madhusudan Reddy, V. The Vedas. *In* Bishop, D. H. ed. Indian thought p23-37

Vedel-Petersen, Jacob
Denmark. *In* Kamerman, S. B. and Kahn, A. J. eds. Family policy p295-327

Veeder, William R.
Technique as recovery: Lolita and Mother night. *In* Klinkowitz, J. and Lawler, D. L. eds. Vonnegut in America p97-132

Vega, Lope de. See Vega Carpio, Lope Félix de

Vega Carpio, Lope Félix de

About
Nicoll, A. The Spanish stage under Lope de Vega and Calderón. *In* Nicoll, A. World drama p161-89

Wilder, T. N. Lope, Pinedo, some child actors, and a lion. *In* Wilder, T. N. American characteristics, and other essays p267-77

Wilder, T. N. New aids toward dating the early plays of Lope de Vega. *In* Wilder, T. N. American characteristics, and other essays p257-66

About individual works
The king, the greatest alcade
Varey, J. E. Kings and judges: Lope de Vega's El mejor alcade, el rey. *In* Drama and society p37-58

Vegetarianism
Rachels, J. Vegetarianism and "the other weight problem." *In* Aiken, W. and La Follette, H. eds. World hunger and moral obligation p180-93

Vekhi (Periodical)
Levin, A. A. Andrey Bely, M. O. Gershenzon, and Vekhi: a rejoinder to N. Valentinov. *In* Janecek, G. ed. Andrey Bely p169-80

Velarde, Albert J. and Warlick, Mark
Massage parlors: the sensuality business. *In* Henslin, J. M. ed. Deviant life-styles p209-29

Velarde, Ramón López. See López Velarde, Ramón

Velázquez, Diego Rodríguez de Silva y

About individual works
Las meninas
Brown, J. On the meaning of Las meninas. *In* Brown, J. Images and ideas in seventeenth-century Spanish painting p87-110

Gilman, E. B. Marvell's perspectives of the mind. *In* Gilman, E. B. The curious perspective p204-31

Velez de Guevara y Dueñas, Luis

About individual works
The crippled devil
Bjornson, R. The waning of the Spanish picaresque: El diablo cojuelo and Estebanillo González. *In* Bjornson, R. The picaresque hero in European fiction p127-38

Velez de Guevara y Dueñas, Luis, supposed author. See Vida y hechos de Estevanillo González

Velez-I, Carlos G.
Ourselves through the eyes of an anthropologist. *In* Trejo, A. D. ed. The Chicanos p37-48

Velikonja, Joseph
The identity and functional networks of the Italian immigrant. *In* Studies in Italian American social history p182-98

Velikovsky, Immanuel

About
Goldsmith, D. Introduction. *In* Goldsmith, D. ed. Scientists confront Velikovsky p19-28

Morrison, D. Planetary astronomy and Velikovsky's catastrophism. *In* Goldsmith, D. ed. Scientists confront Velikovsky p145-76

Mulholland, J. D. Movements of celestial bodies—Velikovsky's fatal flaw. *In* Goldsmith, D. ed. Scientists confront Velikovsky p105-15

Storer, N. W. The sociological context of the Velikovsky controversy. *In* Goldsmith, D. ed. Scientists confront Velikovsky p29-39

About individual works
Worlds in collision
Sagan, C. An analysis of Worlds in collision. *In* Goldsmith, D. ed. Scientists confront Velikovsky p41-104

Velingerová, Milena Doleželová. See Doleželová-Velingerová, Milena

Vellacott, Philip
Has good prevailed? A further study of The Oresteia. *In* Harvard Studies in classical philology v81 p113-22

Velleius Paterculus, Gaius

About
Sumner, G. V. The truth about Velleius Paterculus: prolegomena. *In* Harvard Studies in classical philology v74 p257-97

Veltruský, Jiří
Basic features of dramatic dialogue. *In* Matejka, L. and Titunik, I. R. eds. Semiotics of art p128-33

Construction of semantic contexts. *In* Matejka, L. and Titunik, I. R. eds. Semiotics of art p134-44

Dramatic text as a component of theater. *In* Matejka, L. and Titunik, I. R. eds. Semiotics of art p94-117

Some aspects of the pictorial sign (1973). *In* Matejka, L. and Titunik, I. R. eds. Semiotics of art p245-64

Velz, John W.
The ancient world in Shakespeare: authenticity or anachronism? A retrospect. *In* Shakespeare survey v31 p 1-12

Vena, Michael
Alberti's linguistic innovations. *In* Italian literature: roots and branches p243-63

Venard, Marc
Popular religion in the eighteenth century. *In* Callahan, W. J. and Higgs, D. eds. Church and society in Catholic Europe of the eighteenth century p138-54

Vendler, Helen Hennessy
The re-invented poem: George Herbert's alternatives. *In* Wimsatt, W. K. ed. Literary criticism: idea and act p362-81

About individual works
The poetry of George Herbert
Richards, I. A. The conduct of verse. *In* Richards, I. A. Complementarities p226-32

Vendler, Zeno
Words in thought. *In* Thought, consciousness, and reality p25-48

Veneration of Christian martyrs. See Christian martyrs—Cult

Venereal diseases. See Syphilis

Venezky, Richard L.
Orthography. *In* Wardhaugh, R. and Brown, H. D. eds. A survey of applied linguistics p69-91

Verene, Molly Black
Critical writings on Vico in English. *In* Giambattista Vico's science of humanity p457-80

Verey, David
George Frederick Bodley: climax of the Gothic revival. *In* Seven Victorian architects p84-101

Verga, Giovanni

About individual works
The house by the medlar tree
Ragusa, O. Narrative vs stylistic structure in I Malavoglia. *In* Ragusa, O. Narrative and drama p35-57

Mastro-don Gesualdo
Gatt-Rutter, J. G. Verga: Mastro-don Gesualdo. *In* Williams, D. A. ed. The monster in the mirror p204-33

Una peccatrice
Biasin, G. P. From anatomy to criticism. *In* Biasin, G. P. Literary diseases p36-62

Influence—Pirandello
Ragusa, O. Pirandello and Verga. *In* Ragusa, O. Narrative and drama p58-82

Vergeiner, Walter
Czechoslovakia. *In* Kamerman, S. B. and Kahn, A. J. eds. Family policy p91-116

Verghese, George
Press censorship under Indira Gandhi. *In* Horton, P. C. ed. The Third World and press freedom p220-30

Verghese, Paul. See Verghese, Thadikkal Paul

Verghese, Thadikkal Paul
Muddled metaphors: an Asian response to Garrett Hardin. *In* Lucas, G. R. and Ogletree, T. W. eds. Lifeboat ethics p151-56

Vergil. See Vergilius Maro, Publius

Vergilius Maro, Publius

About
Clausen, W. V. Juvenal and Virgil. *In* Harvard Studies in classical philology v80 p181-86
Eliot, T. S. What is a classic? *In* Eliot, T. S. Selected prose of T. S. Eliot p115-31

About individual works
The Aeneid
Brower, R. A. Visual and verbal translation of myth: Neptune in Virgil, Rubens, Dryden. *In* Brower, R. A. Mirror on mirror p17-45
Goold, G. P. Servius and the Helen episode. *In* Harvard Studies in classical philology v74 p101-68
Hardie, C. G. Two descents into the underworld. *In* Evolution of consciousness p136-48
Highet, G. Speech and narrative in The Aeneid. *In* Harvard Studies in classical philology v78 p189-229
Lawler, T. F. The Aeneid. *In* Seidel, M. A. and Mendelson, E. eds. Homer to Brecht p53-75
Maresca, T. E. Dryden. *In* Maresca, T. E. Epic to novel p3-75
Reckford, K. J. Some trees in Virgil and Tolkien. *In* Perspectives of Roman poetry p57-91
Renoir, A. The terror of the dark waters: a note on Virgilian and Beowulfian techniques. *In* The Learned and the lewed p147-60

The Aeneid (Books III-V)
Murgia, C. E. Critical notes on the text of Servius' commentary on Aeneid III-V. *In* Harvard Studies in classical philology v72 p311-50

Culex
Ross, D. O. The Culex and Moretum as post-Augustan literary parodies. *In* Harvard Studies in classical philology v79 p235-64

Eclogues
Rudd, N. Architecture: theories about Virgil's Eclogues. *In* Rudd, N. Lines of enquiry p119-44
Skutsch, O. Symmetry and sense in the Eclogues. *In* Harvard Studies in classical philology v73 p153-69

Eclogues (First Eclogue)
Clausen, W. On the date of the First Eclogue. *In* Harvard Studies in classical philology v76 p201-05

Eclogues (Second Eclogue)
Skutsch, O. The original form of the Second Eclogue. *In* Harvard Studies in classical philology v74 p95-99

Eclogues (Third Eclogue)
Powell, B. B. Poeta ludens: thrust and counter-thrust in Eclogue 3. *In* Illinois classical studies, v 1 1976 p113-21

Eclogues (Fourth Eclogue)
Poggioli, R. The Christian pastoral. *In* Poggioli, R. The oaten flute p105-34
Williams, G. W. A version of pastoral: Virgil, Eclogue 4. *In* Woodman, T. and West, D. eds. Quality and pleasure in Latin poetry p31-46

Eclogues (Sixth Eclogue)
Ross, D. O. The Sixth Eclogue: Virgil's poetic genealogy. *In* Ross, D. O. Backgrounds to Augustan poetry: Gallus, elegy and Rome p18-38

Eclogues (Eighth Eclogue)
Bowersock, G. W. The addressee of the Eighth Eclogue: a response. *In* Harvard Studies in classical philology v82 p201-02
Bowersock, G. W. A date in the Eighth Eclogue. *In* Harvard Studies in classical philology v75 p73-80
Tarrant, R. J. The addressee of Virgil's Eighth Eclogue. *In* Harvard Studies in classical philology v82 p197-99

Eclogues (Tenth Eclogue)
Ross, D. O. Gallus and the Tenth Eclogue. *In* Ross, D. O. Backgrounds to Augustan poetry: Gallus, elegy and Rome p85-106

Georgics
Feingold, R. The good society and the bucolic mode: Virgil and Pope. *In* Feingold, R. Nature and society p19-49

Georgics (Book I, Lines 463-514)
Lyne, R. O. A. M. Scilicet et tempus veniet . . .: Virgil, Georgics I. 463-514. *In* Woodman, T. and West, D. eds. Quality and pleasure in Latin poetry p47-66

Moretum
Ross, D. O. The Culex and Moretum as post-Augustan literary parodies. *In* Harvard Studies in classical philology v79 p235-64

Vergilius Maro, Publius—*Continued*

Characters—Dido
Rudd, N. Idea: Dido's culpa. *In* Rudd, N. Lines of enquiry p32-53

Influence—Cather
Sutherland, D. Willa Cather: the classic voice. *In* The Art of Willa Cather p156-82

Influence—Chaucer
Harbert, B. Chaucer and the Latin classics. *In* Brewer, D. S. ed. Geoffrey Chaucer p137-53

Influence—Dryden
Brower, R. A. Dryden's epic manner and Virgil. *In* Brower, R. A. Mirror on mirror p103-22

Sources
Ross, D. O. Gallus and the Tenth Eclogue. *In* Ross, D. O. Backgrounds to Augustan poetry: Gallus, elegy and Rome p85-106

Ross, D. O. The Sixth Eclogue: Virgil's poetic genealogy. *In* Ross, D. O. Backgrounds to Augustan poetry: Gallus, elegy and Rome p18-38

Technique
Highet, G. Speech and narrative in The Aeneid. *In* Harvard Studies in classical philology v78 p189-229

Translations
Bawcutt, P. Douglas and Surrey: translators of Virgil. *In* English Association. Essays and studies, 1974 p52-67

Translators
See Vergilius Maro, Publius—Translations

Verification (Logic)
Berlin, Sir I. Verification. *In* Berlin, Sir I. Concepts and categories p12-31

Brown, S. C. What is the verifiability criterion a criterion of? *In* Royal Institute of Philosophy. Impressions of empiricism p137-53

McDowell, J. H. Truth conditions, bivalence, and verificationism. *In* Evans, G. L. and McDowell, J. H. eds. Truth and meaning p42-66

Vérin, Pierre
Austronesian contributions to the culture of Madagascar: some archaeological problems. *In* Chittick, H. N. and Rotberg, R. I. eds. East Africa and the Orient p164-91

Verlaine, Paul Maria

About
Nalbantian, S. The Symbolists: the failing soul. *In* Nalbantian, S. The symbol of the soul from Hölderlin to Yeats p66-85

Vermeer, Jan Van Delft. See Vermeer, Johannes

Vermeer, Johannes

About individual works
View of Delft
Meyers, J. Vermeer and The captive. *In* Meyers, J. Painting and the novel p112-23

Vermeer de Delft, Jan. See Vermeer, Johannes

Vermeule, Cornelius Clarkson
Interactions and reflections of painting, mosaic and sculpture: complex mythological scenes in Greek and Roman imperial numismatic art. *In* Studies in classical art and archaeology p275-82

Vermeule, Emily Townsend
More sleeping furies. *In* Studies in classical art and archaeology p185-88

Vermigli, Peter Martyr. See Vermigli, Pietro Martire

Vermigli, Pietro Martire

About
Donnelly, J. P. Calvinist Thomism. *In* Viator: medieval and Renaissance studies v7 p441-55

Vermont Yankee Nuclear Power Corp. v. Natural Resources Defense Council, Inc.
In The Supreme Court review, 1978 p345-409

Vernal equinox
Harrison, K. Easter cycles and the equinox in the British Isles. *In* Anglo-Saxon England 7 p 1-8

Verne, Jules

About
Suvin, D. Liberalism mutes the anticipation: the space-binding machines. *In* Suvin, D. Metamorphoses of science fiction p145-69

Influence
Komatsu, S. H. G. Wells and Japanese science fiction. *In* H. G. Wells and modern science fiction p179-90

Verner, Coolie
Copperplate printing. *In* Woodward, D. A. ed. Five centuries of map printing p51-75

Vernia, Nicoletto. See Vernias, Nicolò

Vernias, Nicolò

About
Mahoney, E. P. Nicoletto Vernia on the soul and immortality. *In* Philosophy and humanism p144-63

Vernier, Jean Pierre
Evolution as a literary theme in H. G. Wells's science fiction. *In* H. G. Wells and modern science fiction p70-89

Mr Sammler's lesson. *In* Johnson, I. D. and Johnson, C. [eds.] Les américanistes p16-36

Vernon, John Edward
Fresh air: humor in contemporary American poetry. *In* Cohen, S. B. ed. Comic relief p304-23

Vernon, Raymond
The distribution of power. *In* Vernon, R. ed. The oil crisis p245-57

Foreign operations. *In* McKie, J. W. ed. Social responsibility and the business predicament p275-310

An interpretation. *In* Vernon, R. ed. The oil crisis p 1-14

National planning and the multinational enterprise: the U.S. case. *In* Planning, politics, and the public interest p77-94

Vernon manuscript
Doyle, A. I. The shaping of the Vernon and Simeon manuscripts. *In* Chaucer and Middle English studies in honour of Rossell Hope Robbins p328-41

Vero (The Latin word)
Colacildes, P. On the verb vero in Ennius. *In* Harvard Studies in classical philology v71 p121-23

Veronese, Paolo Cagliari, known as

About individual works
The marriage at Cana
Meyers, J. Bronzino, Veronese and The wings of the dove. *In* Meyers, J. Painting and the novel p19-30

Vers libre. See Free verse

Versailles

Auchincloss, L. Nancy Mitford's Versailles. *In* Auchincloss, L. Life, law and letters p105-10

Versailles. Louis XIV Statue (Bernini's)

Wittkower, R. The vicissitudes of a dynastic monument: Bernini's equestrian statue of Louis XIV. *In* Wittkower, R. Studies in the Italian baroque p83-102

Verse drama

Eliot, T. S. Poetry and drama. *In* Eliot, T. S. Selected prose of T. S. Eliot p132-47

Nicoll, A. The poetic stage. *In* Nicoll, A. World drama p616-26

Nicoll, A. The revival of poetic drama. *In* Nicoll, A. World drama p741-49

Verse drama, English

Eliot, T. S. Poetry and drama. *In* Eliot, T. S. Selected prose of T. S. Eliot p132-47

Verse translating. See Poetry—Translating

Verses, Occasion'd by the sight of a chamera obscura

Schwarz, H. An eighteenth-century English poem on the camera obscura. *In* One hundred years of photographic history p127-38

Versification

Graves, R. Harp, anvil, oar; excerpt from "The crowning privilege." *In* Gross, H. S. ed. The structure of verse p21-39

See also Alliteration; Poetry

Versins, Pierre

Contact. *In* Knight, D. F. ed. Turning points p163-67

Vertov, Dziga

About individual works

The Eleventh

Brik, O. M. and Shklovskiĭ, V. B. The Lef arena. *In* Nichols, B. ed. Movies and methods p15-22

Three songs of Lenin

Taylor, R. Three songs of Lenin. *In* Taylor, R. Film propaganda p103-15

Vesalius, Andreas

About

Temkin, O. Vesalius on an immanent biological motor force. *In* Temkin, O. The double face of Janus p287-89

About individual works

On the structure of the human body

Downs, R. B. Father of scientific anatomy; excerpt from "Molders of the modern mind." *In* Downs, R. B. Books that changed the world p320-23

Vesco, Robert

About

Galbraith, J. K. Robert Vesco: swindler. *In* Galbraith, J. K. Annals of an abiding liberal p317-22

Vesey, Godfrey Norman Agmondishan

Other minds. *In* Royal Institute of Philosophy. Understanding Wittgenstein p149-61

Vespasiano da Bistice, Fiorentino

About individual works

Renaissance princes, popes and prelates; the Vespasiano memoirs, lives of illustrious men of the XVth century

Wieruszowski, H. Jacob Burckhardt (1818-1897) and Vespasiano da Bisticci (1422-1498) *In* Philosophy and humanism p387-405

Veterans

Laws and legislation

—United States

Lisio, D. J. United States: bread and butter politics. *In* The War generation p38-58

Societies, etc.

Diehl, J. M. Germany: veterans' politics under three flags. *In* The War generation p135-86

Ledeen, M. A. Italy: war as a style of life. *In* The War generation p104-34

Soucy, R. J. France: veterans' politics between the Wars. *In* The War generation p59-103

Ward, S. R. Great Britain: land fit for heroes lost. *In* The War generation p10-37

United States

Pollock, J. C.; White, D. and Gold, F. When soldiers return: combat and political alienation among white Vietnam veterans. *In* Schwartz, D. C. and Schwartz, S. K. eds. New directions in political socialization p317-33

Veterans' benefits. See Veterans—Laws and legislation

Veterans' laws. See Veterans—Laws and legislation

Veterans' organizations. See Veterans—Societies, etc.

Veterans' rights. See Veterans—Laws and legislation

Vetterling, Mary K.

Some common sense notes on preferential hiring. *In* Gould, C. C. and Wartofsky, M. W. eds. Women and philosophy p320-24

Veuthey, Michel

A survey of international humanitarian law in noninternational armed conflicts: 1949-1974. *In* International terrorism and political crimes p86-97

Veysey, Laurence R.

Growing up in America. *In* Alderson, W. T. ed. American issues p113-28

Intellectual history and the new social history. *In* Higham, J. and Conkin, P. K. eds. New directions in American intellectual history p3-26

The plural organized worlds of the humanities. *In* Oleson, A. and Voss, J. eds. The organization of knowledge in modern America, 1860-1920 p51-106

Viaud, Julien

About

Bone, R. A. Eric Walrond. *In* Bone, R. A. Down home p171-203

Vice. See Literature, Immoral

Vice in literature

Somerset, J. A. B. "Fair is foul and foul is fair": vice-comedy's development and theatrical effects. *In* The Elizabethan theatre, V. p54-75

Vicenza. Teatro Olimpico

Gordon, D. J. Academicians build a theatre and give a play: the Accademia Olimpica. *In* Gordon, D. J. The Renaissance imagination p247-65

Vicenza. Villa Rotonda

Lotz, W. Three essays on Palladio: The Rotonda: a secular building with a dome. *In* Lotz, W. Studies in Italian Renaissance architecture p190-208

Viceroyalty

Nowell, C. E. Old World origins of the Spanish-American viceregal system. *In* First images of America p221-30

Vices

Foot, P. Virtues and vices. *In* Foot, P. Virtues and vices, and other essays in moral philosophy p 1-18

Wenzel, S. Vices, virtues and popular preaching. *In* Medieval and Renaissance studies [1974] p28-54

Vick, George Robert

Heidegger's linguistic rehabilitation of Parmenides' "Being." *In* Murray, M. E. ed. Heidegger and modern philosophy p203-21

Vickers, Douglas

Adam Smith and the status of the theory of money. *In* Skinner, A. S. and Wilson, T. eds. Essays on Adam Smith p482-503

Vickers, Sir Geoffrey

Rationality and intuition. *In* Wechsler, J. ed. On aesthetics in science p143-64

Vickrey, John Frederick

The narrative structure of Hengest's revenge in Beowulf. *In* Anglo-Saxon England 6 p91-103

Vickrey, William Spencer

Justice, equality, and the economic system. *In* Small comforts for hard times p59-71

Vico, Giambattista. See Vico, Giovanni Battista

Vico, Giovanni Battista

About

Cantelli, G. Myth and language in Vico. *In* Giambattista Vico's science of humanity p47-63

Cassirer, E. Descartes, Leibniz, and Vico. *In* Cassirer, E. Symbol, myth, and culture p95-107

Di Pietro, R. J. Humanism in linguistic theory: a lesson from Vico. *In* Giambattista Vico's science of humanity p341-50

Funkenstein, A. Natural science and social theory: Hobbes, Spinoza, and Vico. *In* Giambattista Vico's science of humanity p187-212

Giuliani, A. Vico's rhetorical philosophy and the new rhetoric. *In* Giambattista Vico's science of humanity p31-46

Goretti, M. The heterogenesis of ends in Vico's thought: premises for a comparison of ideas. *In* Giambattista Vico's science of humanity p213-19

Grassi, E. Marxism, humanism, and the problem of imagination in Vico's works. *In* Giambattista Vico's science of humanity p275-94

Hampshire, S. Joyce and Vico: the middle way. *In* Giambattista Vico's science of humanity p321-32

Jacobelli, I. A. M. The role of the intellectual in Giambattista Vico. *In* Giambattista Vico's science of humanity p409-21

Jordan, R. W. Vico and Husserl: history and historical science. *In* Giambattista Vico's science of humanity p251-61

Kelley, D. R. Vico's road: from philology to jurisprudence and back. *In* Giambattista Vico's science of humanity p15-29

Mathieu, V. Truth as the mother of history. *In* Giambattista Vico's science of humanity p113-24

Mora, G. Vico, Piaget, and genetic epistemology. *In* Giambattista Vico's science of humanity p365-92

O'Neill, J. Time's body: Vico on the love of language and institution. *In* Giambattista Vico's science of humanity p333-39

Riverso, E. Vico and Wittgenstein. *In* Giambattista Vico's science of humanity p263-73

Rotenstreich, N. Vico and Kant. *In* Giambattista Vico's science of humanity p221-40

Struever, N. S. Vico, Valla, and the logic of humanist inquiry. *In* Giambattista Vico's science of humanity p173-85

Tuttle, H. N. The epistemological status of the cultural world in Vico and Dilthey. *In* Giambattista Vico's science of humanity p241-50

Verene, D. P. Vico's science of imaginative universals and the philosophy of symbolic forms. *In* Giambattista Vico's science of humanity p295-317

White, H. V. What is living and what is dead in Croce's criticism of Vico. *In* White, H. V. Tropics of discourse p218-29

About individual works

The new science

Caponigri, A. R. The timelessness of the Scienza nuova of Giambattista Vico. *In* Italian literature: roots and branches p309-31

Fassò, G. The problem of law and the historical science of The new science. *In* Giambattista Vico's science of humanity p3-14

Hughes, P. Creativity and history in Vico and his contemporaries. *In* Giambattista Vico's science of humanity p155-69

Momigliano, A. Vico's Scienza nuova: Roman 'bestioni' and Roman 'eroi.' *In* Momigliano, A. Essays in ancient and modern historiography p253-76

Pompa, L. Vico and the presuppositions of historical knowledge. *In* Giambattista Vico's science of humanity p125-40

Said, E. W. On repetition. *In* Fletcher, A. J. S. ed. The literature of fact p134-58

Walsh, W. H. The logical status of Vico's ideal eternal history. *In* Giambattista Vico's science of humanity p141-53

White, H. V. The tropics of history: the deep structure of The new science. *In* Giambattista Vico's science of humanity p65-85

White, H. V. The tropics of history: the deep structure of The new science. *In* White, H. V. Tropics of discourse p197-217

Practic of the new science

Fisch, M. H. Vico's Pratica. *In* Giambattista Vico's science of humanity p423-30

Pons, A. Prudence and providence: the Pratica della scienza nuova and the problem of theory and practice in Vico. *In* Giambattista Vico's science and humanity p431-48

La scienza nuova seconda

Simonsuuri, K. Vico's discovery of the true Homer. *In* Simonsurri, K. Homer's original genius p90-98

Bibliography

Verene, M. B. Critical writings on Vico in English. *In* Giambattista Vico's science of humanity p457-80

Influence—Joyce

Church, M. A Portrait and Giambattista Vico: a source study. *In* Staley, T. F. and Benstock, B. eds. **Approaches to Joyce's Portrait** p77-88

Vietnam—*Continued*

History

Duncanson, D. J. Vietnam: from bolshevism to people's war. *In* Hammond, T. T. ed. The anatomy of Communist takeovers p490-515

History—To 1858

Smith, R. B. England and Vietnam in the fifteenth and sixteenth centuries: an essay in historical comparison. *In* Southeast Asian history and historiography p227-45

Wolters, O. W. Lê Văn Hu'u's treatment of Lý Thân Tôn's reign (1127-1137). *In* Southeast Asian history and historiography p203-26

Rural conditions

Kaufman, H. K. Culao—a Vietnamese fishing cooperative and its problems. *In* Social organization and the applications of anthropology p235-72

Vietnamese Conflict, 1961-1975

Arendt, H. Home to roost. *In* Warner, S. B. ed. The American experiment p61-79

Gregory, R. The domino theory. *In* Encyclopedia of American foreign policy p275-80

Myers, R. J. An approximation of justice. *In* [Truth and tragedy]: a tribute to Hans Morgenthau p125-29

Rich, A. C. Caryatid: Two columns: Vietnam and sexual violence. *In* Rich, A. C. On lies, secrets, and silence p107-16

Thornton, O. D. The Vietnam connection. *In* Henderson, G. ed. Human relations in the military p163-75

Aerial operations

Mrozek, D. J. Surrogate intervention: alliances & air power in the Vietnam War. *In* Higham, R. D. ed. Intervention or abstention: the dilemma of American foreign policy p184-201

Atrocities

Kelman, H. C. Violence without moral restraint: reflections on the dehumanization of victims and victimizers. *In* Kren, G. M. and Rappoport, L. H. eds. Varieties of psychohistory p282-314

Campaigns—Cambodia

Roth, P. Cambodia: a modest proposal. *In* Roth, P. Reading myself and others p185-90

Peace

Ashmore, H. S. An exercise in demi-diplomacy: the case of Vietnam. *In* Unofficial diplomats p130-41

Protest movements

Goertzel, T. G. Domestic pressures for abstention: Vietnam. *In* Higham, R. D. ed. Intervention or abstention: the dilemma of American foreign policy p166-83

Psychological aspects

Langner, H. P. The making of a murderer. *In* Kren, G. M. and Rappoport, L. H. eds. Varieties of psychohistory p257-63

Pollock, J. C.; White, D. and Gold, F. When soldiers return: combat and political alienation among white Vietnam veterans. *In* Schwartz, D. C. and Schwartz, S. K. eds. New directions in political socialization p317-33

Public opinion—United States

Goertzel, T. G. Domestic pressures for abstention: Vietnam. *In* Higham, R. D. ed. Intervention or abstention: the dilemma of American foreign policy p166-83

Vig, Norman J.

Policies for science and technology in Great Britian: postwar development and reassessment. *In* Science policies of industrial nations p59-109

Vigeland, Gustav

About

Wennberg, B. G. Paris in Oslo—Gustav Vigeland. *In* Wennberg, B. G. French and Scandinavian sculpture in the nineteenth century p181-93

Vigevano, Italy

Plazas—Piazza Ducale

Lotz, W. The Piazza Ducale in Vigevano: a princely forum of the late fifteenth century. *In* Lotz, W. Studies in Italian Renaissance architecture p117-39

Vigier, Jean-Pierre

Cosmological implications of non-velocity redshifts—a tired-light mechanism. *In* Cosmology, history, and theology p141-57

Vigil, Maurilio E. See Lux, G. jt. auth.

Vigny, Alfred Victor, comte de

About

Mill, J. S. Poems and romances of Alfred de Vigny. *In* Mills, J. S. Essays on poetry p75-137

Vigny, Alfred Victor, comte de, tr.

About individual works

Othello

Denommé, R. T. French theater reform and Vigny's translation of Othello in 1829. *In* Symbolism and modern literature p81-102

Vigo, Jean

About

Truffaut, F. Jean Vigo is dead at twenty-nine. *In* Truffaut, F. The films in my life p23-28

Vilakazi, Absolom

Swaziland: from tradition to modernity. *In* Carter, G. M. and O'Meara, P. eds. Southern Africa: the continuing crisis p269-90

Swaziland and Lesotho: from traditionalism to modernity. *In* Carter, G. M. and O'Meara, P. eds. Southern Africa in crisis p226-57

Villa Capra. See Vicenza. Villa Rotonda

Villa Rotonda. See Vicenza. Villa Rotonda

Village communities

See also Commons; Tribes and tribal system

Great Britain—History

Burrow, J. W. 'The village community' and the uses of history in late nineteenth-century England. *In* Historical perspectives p255-84

Village government. See Villages

Villages

Asia

Madge, C. The relevance of family patterns in the process of modernization in East Asia. *In* Social organization and the applications of anthropology p161-95

France—History

Pesez, J. M. and Le Roy Ladurie, E. The deserted villages of France: an overview. *In* Rural society in France p72-106

Villages—*Continued*

France—Picardy

Morel, A. Power and ideology in the village community of Picardy: past and present. *In* Rural society in France p107-25

India

Srinivas, M. N. The Indian village: myth and reality. *In* Studies in social anthropology p41-85

Laos

Condominas, G. Phĭbān cults in rural Laos. *In* Change and persistence in Thai society p252-73

Thailand

Ingersoll, J. Merit and identity in village Thailand. *In* Change and persistence in Thai society p219-51

Judd, L. C. Social change in Commune Baw, Thailand, 1958-1967. *In* Social organization and the applications of anthropology p210-34

Piker, S. I. The post-peasant village in Central Plain Thai society. *In* Change and persistence in Thai society p298-323

Villages in literature. See Cities and towns in literature

Villaverde, Cirilo

About individual works
Cecilia Valdes

Jackson, S. M. Fact from fiction: another look at slavery in three Spanish-American novels. *In* DeCosta, M. ed. Blacks in Hispanic literature p83-89

Villegas, Francisco Gomez de Quevedo y. See Quevedo y Villegas, Francisco Gomez de

Villeinage

England

Hilton, R. H. Freedom and villeinage in England. *In* Peasants, knights and heretics p174-91

England—Essex

McIntosh, M. K. The privileged villeins of the English ancient demesne. *In* Viator: medieval and Renaissance studies v7 p295-328

Villon, François

About

Mandel'shtam, O. E. François Villon. *In* Mandel'shtam, O. E. Selected essays p114-20

Mermier, G. R. The grotesque in French medieval literature: a study in forms and meanings. *In* Ruggiers, P. G. ed. Versions of medieval comedy p101-34

About individual works
The epitaph in form of a ballad which Villon made for himself and his comrades expecting to be hanged along with them

Edelman, N. Villon's Epitaphe: a reading. *In* Edelman, N. The eye of the beholder p49-57

The testament

Edelman, N. A scriptural key to Villon's Testament. *In* Edelman, N. The eye of the beholder p31-37

Edelman, N. The unity of Villon's Testament. *In* Edelman, N. The eye of the beholder p38-48

Criticism and interpretation

Edelman, N. The vogue of François Villon in France from 1828-1873. *In* Edelman, N. The eye of the beholder p 1-30

Vinaver, Eugène

About individual works
Racine

Edelman, N. Book reviews. *In* Edelman, N. The eye of the beholder p166-205

Vincent, Howard Paton

About

Gildzen, A. A celebration of Howard Vincent. *In* Artful thunder p9-10

Murray, H. A. Dedication. *In* Artful thunder p3-7

Vincent, Joan

Room for manœuvre: the political role of small towns in East Africa. *In* Colonialism and change p115-44

Vincent, R. J.

The idea of concert and international order. *In* The Year book of world affairs, 1975 p34-55

Kissinger's system of foreign policy. *In* The Year book of world affairs, 1977 p8-26

Vincent, François, Paul and the others (Motion picture)

Truffaut, F. Claude Sautet: Vincent, François, Paul et les autres. *In* Truffaut, F. The films in my life p340-42

Vinci, Leonardo da. See Leonardo da Vinci

Vinekar, S. L. See Kuvalayananda, S. jt. auth.

Vinovskis, Maris A.

Angels' heads and weeping willows: death in early America. *In* American Antiquarian Society. Proceedings v86 pt2 p273-302

Vinsauf, Geoffrey de

About individual works
Poetria nova

Gallo, E. The grammarian's rhetoric: the Poetria nova of Geoffrey of Vinsauf. *In* Murphy, J. J. ed. Medieval eloquence p68-84

Vinson, John Chalmers

Sanctions. *In* Encyclopedia of American foreign policy p924-35

Vio, Tommaso de, called Caetano, Cardinal

About individual works
De cambiis

De Roover, R. A. Cardinal Cajetan on "cambium" or exchange dealings. *In* Philosophy and humanism p423-33

Viol. See Hurdy-gurdy

Violence

Audi, R. Violence, legal sanctions, and law enforcement. *In* Stanage, S. M. ed. Reason and violence p29-50

Benjamin, W. Critique of violence. *In* Benjamin, W. Reflections p277-300

Bettelheim, B. Violence: a neglected mode of behavior. *In* Bettelheim, B. Surviving, and other essays p185-200

Binkley, T. Consensus and the justification of force. *In* Stanage, S. M. ed. Reason and violence p123-41

Girvetz, H. K. An anatomy of violence. *In* Stanage, S. M. ed. Reason and violence p183-204

Gotesky, R. Social force, social power, and social violence. *In* Stanage, S. M. ed. Reason and violence p145-79

Violence—*Continued*

Honderich, T. On inequality and violence, and the differences we make between them. *In* Royal Institute of Philosophy. Nature and conduct p46-82

Kelman, H. C. Violence without moral restraint: reflections on the dehumanization of victims and victimizers. *In* Kren, G. M. and Rappoport, L. H. eds. Varieties of psychohistory p282-314

Langner, H. P. The making of a murderer. *In* Kren, G. M. and Rappoport, L. H. eds. Varieties of psychohistory p257-63

O'Neill, J. Violence, technology, and the body politic. *In* Stanage, S. M. ed. Reason and violence p5-26

Parry, A. Right-wing terror. *In* Parry, A. Terrorism: from Robespierre to Arafat p488-506

Parry, A. Violence: genesis of terror. *In* Parry, A. Terrorism: from Robespierre to Arafat p3-11

Ricoeur, P. Violence and language. *In* Ricoeur, P. Political and social essays p88-101

Rubinoff, L. Violence and the retreat from reason. *In* Stanage, S. M. ed. Reason and violence p73-118

Stanage, S. M. Violatives: modes and themes of violence. *In* Stanage, S. M. ed. Reason and violence p207-38

United States

Skolnick, J. H. The police in protest: National Commission on the Causes and Prevention of Violence (a staff report); excerpt from "The politics of protest." *In* Armstrong, T. R. and Cinnamon, K. M. eds. Power and authority in law enforcement p131-90

United States—History

Parry, A. America's pie. *In* Parry, A. Terrorism: from Robespierre to Arafat p92-106

Violence (Law)

Audi, R. Violence, legal sanctions, and law enforcement. *In* Stanage, S. M. ed. Reason and violence p29-50

Binkley, T. Consensus and the justification of force. *In* Stanage, S. M. ed. Reason and violence p123-41

Gotesky, R. Social force, social power, and social violence. *In* Stanage, S. M. ed. Reason and violence p145-79

Violence in literature

Feuser, W. Prophet of violence: Chester Himes. *In* African literature today no. 9: Africa, America and the Caribbean p58-76

Kellogg, G. Existentialism, violence, and communism. *In* Kellogg, G. Dark prophets of hope p74-88

Ries, L. R. John Wain: the evasive answer. *In* Ries, L. R. Wolf masks p130-50

Ries, L. R. Literature and violence. *In* Ries, L. R. Wolf masks p3-32

Ries, L. R. Sylvia Plath: the internalized response. *In* Ries, L. R. Wolf masks p33-58

Ries, L. R. Ted Hughes: acceptance and accommodation. *In* Ries, L. R. Wolf masks p92-129

Ries, L. R. Thom Gunn: the retreat from violence. *In* Ries, L. R. Wolf masks p59-91

Wimsatt, W. K. Day of the leopards. *In* Wimsatt, W. K. Day of the leopards p3-10

Woodyard, G. W. Jorge Diaz and the liturgy of violence. *In* Lyday, L. F. and Woodyard, G. W. eds. Dramatists in revolt p59-76

Violence in mass media

Salomone, F. Terrorism and the mass media. *In* International terrorism and political crimes p43-46

See also Violence in moving-pictures

Violence in moving—pictures

Elsaesser, T. Screen violence: emotional structure and ideological function in 'A clockwork orange.' *In* Bigsby, C. W. E. ed. Approaches to popular culture p171-200

Sarris, A. Violence in movies. *In* Sarris, A. Politics and cinema p116-27

Violent deaths. See Homicide

Violin

History

Winternitz, E. Early violins in paintings by Gaudenzio Ferrari and his school. *In* Winternitz, E. Musical instruments and their symbolism in Western art p99-109

Violin in art

Winternitz, E. Early violins in paintings by Gaudenzio Ferrari and his school. *In* Winternitz, E. Musical instruments and their symbolism in Western art p99-109

Viollet-Le Duc, Eugène Emmanuel

About

Watkin, D. The theme in the nineteenth century: Viollet-Le-Duc. *In* Watkin, D. Morality and architecture p23-31

Virgil. See Vergilius Maro, Publius

Virginia

Antiquities

Lewis, K. E. An archaeological perspective on social change—the Virginia frontier. *In* Miller, D. H. and Steffen, J. O. eds. The frontier p139-59

Economic conditions

Hunter, R. F. Virginia and the New Deal. *In* Braeman, J.; Bremner, R. H. and Brody, D. eds. The New Deal v2 p103-36

Politics and government— Colonial period, ca. 1600-1775

Greene, J. P. "Virtus et Libertas": political culture, social change, and the origins of the American Revolution in Virginia, 1763-1766. *In* The Southern experience in the American Revolution p55-108

Seiler, W. H. The Anglican Church: a basic institution of local government in colonial Virginia. *In* Daniels, B. C. ed. Town and county p134-59

Wheeler, R. A. The county court in colonial Virginia. *In* Daniels, B. C. ed. Town and county p111-33

Politics and government —1865-1950

Hunter, R. F. Virginia and the New Deal. *In* Braeman, J.; Bremner, R. H. and Brody, D. eds. The New Deal v2 p103-36

Race relations

Rountree, H. C. The Indians of Virginia: a third race in a biracial state. *In* Williams, W. L. ed. Southeastern Indians since the removal era p27-48

Virginia. Eastern State Hospital, Williamsburg

Gardner, R. D. The bicentennial of Eastern State Hospital. *In* American psychiatry: past, present, and future p3-7

Virginia. Medical College, Richmond
Kaylor, C. Evaluation of home care for the terminal cancer patient: a proposed model. *In* Home care p247-59

Virginia in literature
Holman, C. H. Barren ground and the shape of history. *In* Holman, C. H. Windows on the world p118-28

Holman, C. H. April in Queenborough: Ellen Glasgow's comedies of manners. *In* Holman, C. H. Windows on the world p98-117

Seelye, J. Captain courageous: Captain John Smith, father of us all. *In* Seelye, J. Prophetic waters p57-95

Seelye, J. Divine tobacco: Hakluyt and the Virginia business. *In* Seelye, J. Prophetic waters p23-56

Virginity. See Celibacy

Virgoe, Roger
The recovery of the Howards in East Anglia, 1485-1529. *In* Wealth and power in Tudor England p1-20

Virtue
Ardal, P. S. Convention and value. *In* David Hume p51-68

Mazzeo, J. A. The Platonic debate over myth, truth, and virtue. *In* Mazzeo, J. A. Varieties of interpretation p71-94

See also Ethics

Virtues
Foot, P. Virtues and vices. *In* Foot, P. Virtues and vices, and other essays in moral philosophy p 1-18

See also Vices

Virtutes aquile
Sheldon, S. E. The eagle: bird of magic and medicine in a Middle English translation of the Kyranides. *In* Tulane studies in English v22 p 1-31

Visaria, Pravin M.
The importance of labour-force structure in relation to employment and unemployment in less-developed countries. *In* Economic factors in population growth p411-38

Viscardi, Giovanni Antonio

About
Heisner, B. F. Viscardi's Mariahilfkirche at Freystadt and the development of the central plan church in eighteenth century Germany. *In* Enggass, R. C. and Stokstadt, M. eds. Hortus imaginum p175-83

Vischer, Friedrich Theodor von

About individual works
Auch einer
Bruford, W. H. Friedrich Theodor Vischer: Auch einer (1879). *In* Bruford, W. H. The German tradition of self-cultivation p147-63

Visconti, Luchino

About individual works
Ludwig
Kauffmann, S. Ludwig. *In* Kauffmann, S. Living images p183-85

Vision
Nemerov, H. Speculation turning to itself. *In* Nemerov, H. Figures of thought p87-94

See also Color vision; Optics, Physiological; Visual discrimination; Visual perception

Psychological aspects
See Visual perception

Research
See Vision research

Vision research
Bishop, P. O. Grafton Elliot Smith's contribution to visual neurology and the influence of Thomas Henry Huxley. *In* Grafton Elliot Smith p50-57

Visions
Huxley, A. L. Natural history of visions. *In* Huxley, A. L. The Human situation p216-35

See also Dreams

Visions in literature
Nolan, B. The later medieval spiritual quest: through time to aevum. *In* Nolan, B. The Gothic visionary perspective p124-55

Nolan, B. Pearl: a fourteenth-century vision in August. *In* Nolan, B. The Gothic visionary perspective p156-204

Nolan, B. The vita nuova: Dante's Book of Revelation. *In* Nolan, B. The Gothic visionary perspective p84-123

Nolan, B. Will's dark visions of Piers the Plowman. *In* Nolan, B. The Gothic visionary perspective p205-58

Visions of eight (Motion picture)
Kauffmann, S. Visions of eight. *In* Kauffmann, S. Living images p220-21

Visual arts. See Art

Visual discrimination
Pick, H. L. Visual coding of nonvisual spatial information. *In* Perception p153-65

See also Visual perception

Visual education. See Audio-visual education; Moving—pictures in education; and similar headings

Visual perception
Berger, J. The sight of a man. *In* Berger, J. The look of things p190-97

Blakemore, C. The baffled brain. *In* Gregory, R. L. and Gombrich, Sir E. H. J. eds. Illusion in nature and art p9-47

Donagan, A. Berkeley's theory of the immediate objects of vision. *In* Studies in perception p312-35

Gibson, J. J. The perceiving of hidden surfaces. *In* Studies in perception p422-34

Gippenrieter, Y. B. and Romanov, V. Y. A method of investigation of the internal form of visual activity. *In* Perception p227-49

Gombrich, E. H. J. The sky is the limit: the vault of heaven and pictorial vision. *In* Perception p84-94

Gregory, R. L. The confounded eye. *In* Gregory, R. L. and Gombrich, Sir E. H. J. eds. Illusion in nature and art p49-95

Hahm, D. E. Early Hellenistic theories of vision and the perception of color. *In* Studies in perception p60-95

Kennedy, J. M. and Fox, N. Pictures to see and pictures to touch. *In* Perkins, D. and Leondar, B. eds. The arts and cognition p118-35

Kolers, P. A. Reading pictures and reading text. *In* Perkins, D. and Leondar, B. eds. The arts and cognition p136-64

Lachs, J. The omnicolored sky: Baylis on perception. *In* Fact, value, and perception p139-50

Voltaire, François Marie Arouet de

About

Ages, A. Lamartine and the philosophes. *In* Literature and history in the age of ideas p321-40

Aldridge, A. O. Feijoo, Voltaire, and the mathematics of procreation. *In* Studies in eighteenth-century culture v4 p131-38

Guerlac, H. Three eighteenth-century social philosophers: scientific influences on their thought. *In* Guerlac, H. Essays and papers in the history of modern science p451-64

Haac, O. A. Faith in the Enlightenment: Voltaire and Rousseau seen by Michelet. *In* Studies in eighteenth-century culture v7 p475-90

Heller, P. Nietzsche in his relation to Voltaire and Rousseau *In* O'Flaherty, J. C.; Sellner, T. F. and Helm, R. M. eds. Studies in Nietzsche and the classical tradition p109-33

Kostoroski, E. P. Molière and Voltaire. *In* Johnson, R. B.; Neumann, E. S. and Trail, G. T. eds. Molière and the commonwealth of letters: patrimony and posterity p90-99

Schilling, B. N. The apotheosis of Voltaire. *In* Evidence in literary scholarship p363-77

Shackleton, R. Allies and enemies: Voltaire and Montesquieu. *In* Royal Society of Literature of the United Kingdom, London. Essays by divers hands v39 p126-45

Simonsuuri, K. Voltaire and the poetry of the primitive age. *In* Simonsuuri, K. Homer's original genius p65-73

Voegelin, E. The emergence of secularized history: Bossuet and Voltaire. *In* Voegelin, E. From Enlightenment to revolution p3-34

Wade, I. O. Notes on the making of a philosophe: Cuenz and Bouhier. *In* Literature and history in the age of ideas p97-123

About individual works

Candide

Richter, D. H. Aspects of the eighteenth-century rhetorical novel: Johnson's Rasselas and Voltaire's Candide. *In* Richter, D. H. Fable's end p22-60

La Henriade

Herbert, R. L. Baron Gros's Napoleon and Voltaire's Henri IV. *In* The Artist and the writer in France p52-75

Love letters to his niece

Connolly, C. Voltaire: 2. *In* Connolly, C. The evening colonnade p122-24

La mort de César

Cottrell, R. D. Ulcerated hearts: love in Voltaire's La mort de César. *In* Literature and history in the age of ideas p169-77

Opinion en alphabet

Monty, J. R. Voltaire's debt to the Encyclopédie in the Opinion en alphabet. *In* Literature and history in the age of ideas p153-67

A philosophical dictionary

Topazio, V. W. Voltaire, "Lexicographer of the Enlightenment." *In* Studies in eighteenth-century culture v8 p311-21

Adaptations

Kauffmann, S. Candide. *In* Kauffmann, S. Persons of the drama p263-66

Appreciation—Europe

Chadwick, O. Voltaire in the nineteenth century. *In* Chadwick, O. The secularization of the European mind in the nineteenth century p143-60

Appreciation—Great Britain

Chadwick, O. Voltaire in the nineteenth century. *In* Chadwick, O. The secularization of the European mind in the nineteenth century p143-60

Voluptas (The Latin word)

De Panizza Lorch, M. Voluptas, molle quoddam et non invidiosum nomen: Lorenzo Valla's defense of voluptas in the preface to his De voluptate. *In* Philosophy and humanism p214-28

Von Blanckenhagen, Peter Heinrich. See Blanckenhagen, Peter Heinrich von

Von Bothmer, Dietrich Felix. See Bothmer, Dietrich Felix von

Von Chamisso, Adelbert. See Chamisso, Adelbert von

Von Clausewitz, Karl. See Clausewitz, Karl von

Von den Steinen, Karl

The discovery of women in eighteenth-century English political life. *In* Kanner, B. ed. The women of England p229-58

Von Dohm, Christian Wilhelm. See Dohm, Christian Wilhelm von

Von Eschen, Donald. See Eschen, Donald von

Von Fieandt, Kai. See Fieandt, Kai von

Von Foerster, Heinz

Where do we go from here? *In* Bugliarello, G. and Doner, D. B. eds. The history and philosophy of technology p358-70

Von Geusau, Frans A. M. Alting. See Alting von Geusau, Frans A. M.

Von Gluck, Christoph Willibald, Ritter. See Gluck, Christoph Willibald, Ritter von

Von Goethe, Johann Wolfgang. See Goethe, Johann Wolfgang von

Von Grimmelshausen, Hans Jakob Christoffel. See Grimmelshausen, Hans Jakob Christoffel von

Von Grunebaum, Gustav Edmund. See Grunebaum, Gustav Edmund von

Von Hayek, Friedrich August. See Hayek, Friedrich August von

Von Heimburg, Gregor. See Heimburg, Gregor von

Von Helmholtz, Hermann Ludwig Ferdinand. See Helmholtz, Hermann Ludwig Ferdinand von

Von Herder, Johann Gottfried. See Herder, Johann Gottfried von

Von Hofmannsthal, Hugo Hofmann, Edler. See Hofmannsthal, Hugo Hofmann, Edler von

Von Holst, Hermann Eduard. See Holst, Hermann Eduard von

Von Horváth, Odön. See Horváth, Ödön von

Von Humboldt, Wilhelm, Freiherr. See Humboldt, Wilhelm, Freiherr von

Von Kamphoevener, Else Sophia. See Kamphoevener, Else Sophia von

Von Kleist, Heinrich. See Kleist, Heinrich von

Voronskij, Aleksandr. See Voronskii, Aleksandr Konstantinovich

Vorsey, Louis de. See De Vorsey, Louis

Vorstellung (The German word)
Warminski, A. Pre-positional by-play. *In* Glyph 3 p98-117

Vos, George A. de. See De Vos, George A.

Vos, George Ade. See De Vos, George A.

Voss, John. See Oleson, A. jt. auth.

Voting
Riker, W. R. A confrontation between the theory of democracy and the theory of social choice. *In* The Frontiers of human knowledge p215-27

See also Suffrage

Vouchers, Educational. See Educational vouchers

Vovelle, Michel

About individual works

Piété baroque et déchristianisation en Provence au XVIII° siècle

Darnton, R. The history of mentalités: recent writings on revolution, criminality, and death in France. *In* Brown, R. H. and Lyman, S. M. eds. Structure, consciousness, and history p106-36

Le Roy Ladurie, E. Chaunu, Lebrun, Vovelle: the new history of death. *In* Le Roy Ladurie, E. The territory of the historian p273-84

Vowels. See subdivision Vowels under names of languages, e.g. French language—Vowels

Voyages, Imaginary
Suvin, D. The alternative island. *In* Suvin, D. Metamorphoses of science fiction p90-114

See also Space flight in literature

Voyages and travels. See Discoveries (in geography); Railroad travel

Voyages and travels in literature. See Travel in literature

Voyages to the otherworld. See Voyages, Imaginary

Voyages to the otherworld in literature
Hardie, C. G. Two descents into the underworld. *In* Evolution of consciousness p136-48

Voznesenskii, Andrei Andreevich
About
Morgan, E. Heraclitus in Gorky Street: the theme of metamorphosis in the poetry of Andrei Voznesensky. *In* Essays p71-78

Vries, Gerrit Jacob de
A general theory of literary composition in the Phaedrus. *In* Kephalaion p50-52

Vries, Jan de. See De Vries, Jan

Vryonis, Speros
Byzantine and Turkish societies and their sources of manpower. *In* War, technology and society in the Middle East p125-52

W

WHO. See World Health Organization

WPA. See United States. Works Projects Administration

Wa Thiong'o, James. See Ngugi Wa Thiong'o

Waard, Jan de
A Greek translation-technical treatment of Amos 1:15. *In* On language, culture, and religion: in honor of Eugene A. Nida p111-18

Wacker, Peter O.
Patterns and problems in the historical geography of the Afro-American population of New Jersey, 1726-1860. *In* Pattern and process p25-72

Waddington, Raymond Bruce
Shakespeare's Sonnet 15 and the art of memory. *In* Sloan T. O. and Waddington, R. B. eds. The rhetoric of Renaissance poetry p96-122

Wade, Ira Owen
Notes on the making of a philosophe: Cuenz and Bouhier. *In* Literature and history in the age of ideas p97-123

Wade, John Donald
Augustus Baldwin Longstreet: a Southern cultural type. *In* Inge, M. T. ed. The frontier humorists p94-104

Southern humor. *In* Inge, M. T. ed. The frontier humorists p32-44

About
O'Brien, M. Wade: a turning inward. *In* O'Brien, M. The idea of the American South, 1920-1941 p97-113

Wade, Michael
Art and morality in Alex La Guma's A walk in the night. *In* Parker, K. ed. The South African novel in English p164-91

Nadine Gordimer and Europe-in-Africa. *In* Parker, K. ed. The South African novel in English p131-63

South Africa's first proletarian writer. *In* Parker, K. ed. The South African novel in English p95-113

Wade, Richard C.
Historical analogies and public policy: the Black and immigrant experience in urban America. *In* Essays on urban America p127-47

Wadsworth, Philip Adrian
From the commedia erudita to Molière. *In* Johnson, R. B.; Neumann, E. S. and Trail, G. T. eds. Molière and the commonwealth of letters: patrimony and posterity p443-53

Waganda. See Baganda

Wagatsuma, Hiroshi
Problems of cultural identity in modern Japan. *In* Ethnic identity p307-34

Some aspects of the contemporary Japanese family: once Confucian, now fatherless? *In* Rossi, A. S.; Kagan, J. and Hareven, T. K. eds. The family p181-210

Wage-price controls. See Wage-price policy

Wage-price policy

United States
Friedelbaum, S. H. The 1971 wage-price freeze: unchallenged presidential power. *In* The Supreme Court review, 1974 p33-80

Wagener, Diane K. See Ammerman, A. J. jt. auth.

Wages
Leibenstein, H. Efficiency wages, X-efficiency, and urban unemployment. *In* Economic development and planning p168-85

Lerner, A. P. Wages, profits, and marginal analysis. *In* Inflation, trade and taxes p23-28

See also Equal pay for equal work; Wage-price policy

Waggoner, Hyatt Howe

The poetry of A. R. Ammons: some notes and reflections. *In* Boyers, R. ed. Contemporary poetry in America p330-38

Wagman, Fredrica

About individual works
Playing house

Roth, P. Imagining the erotic: three introductions. *In* Roth, P. Reading myself and others p195-214

Wagner, Geoffrey Atheling

About individual works
Wyndham Lewis, a portrait of the artist as the enemy

Frye, N. Neoclassical agony. *In* Frye, N. Northrop Frye on culture and literature p178-87

Wagner, Linda Welshimer

Faulkner and (Southern) women. *In* the South and Faulkner's Yoknapatawpha p128-46

John Dos Passos: reaching past poetry. *In* Essays in honor of Russel B. Nye p226-46

The marinating of For whom the bell tolls. *In* Wagner, L. W. ed. Ernest Hemingway p200-12

Poetry: the 1930s to the present. *In* American literary scholarship, 1973 p329-68

Poetry: the 1930s to the present [another essay] *In* American literary scholarship, 1974 p345-71

[Poetry: the 1930s to the present [another essay] *In* American literary scholarship, 1975 p379-98

Poetry: the 1930s to the present [another essay] *In* American literary scholarship, 1976 p339-54

Sherwood, Stein, the sentence, and grape sugar and oranges. *In* Anderson, D. D. ed. Sherwood Anderson: dimensions of his literary art p75-89

Wagner, Philip Marshall

H. L. Mencken. *In* Ross, R. G. ed. Makers of American thought p85-119

Wagner, Richard

About

Craft, R. Taking the Wagner cure. *In* Craft, R. Current convictions p71-81

Craft, R. "Winnie" and "Uncle Wolf." *In* Craft, R. Current convictions p92-104

Girard, R. Strategies of madness—Nietzsche, Wagner, and Dostoevski. *In* Girard, R. "To double business bound" p61-83

About individual works
Parsifal

Craft, R. Parsifal: the worship of Wagnerism. *In* Craft, R. Current convictions p82-92

The ring of the Nibelung

Auden, W. H. Mimesis and allegory. *In* Wimsatt, W. K. ed. Literary criticism: idea and act p32-43

Mudford, P. Richard Wagner: an afterword. *In* Mudford, P. The art of celebration p181-86

Tristan and Isolde

Harris, B. 'This music crept by me': Shakespeare and Wagner. *In* The Waste land in different voices p105-16

Wagner, Richard E.

American education and the economics of caring. *In* Parents, teachers, and children: prospects for choice in American education p111-25

Wagner family

Craft, R. "Winnie" and "Uncle Wolf." *In* Craft, R. Current convictions p92-104

Wagoner, David

About

Pinsker, S. On David Wagoner. *In* Boyers, R. ed. Contemporary poetry in America p360-68

About individual works
Collected poems (1956-1976)

Lieberman, L. David Wagoner: the cold speech of the earth. *In* Lieberman, L. Unassigned frequencies p152-81

Wagstaff, Christopher

Dead man erect: F. T. Marinetti, L'alcova d'acciaio. *In* Klein, H. M. ed. The First World War in fiction p149-59

Wahl, Nicholas

The autonomy of "domestic structures" in European-American relations. *In* Atlantis lost p225-48

Wahlbäck, Krister

University autonomy in Sweden. *In* Universities in the Western world p268-78

Wahlstrom, Billie Joyce

Images of the family in the mass media: an American iconography? *In* Tufte, V. and Myerhoff, B. G. eds. Changing images of the family p193-227

Wahrhaftig, Albert L.

Institution building among Oklahoma's traditional Cherokees. *In* Hudson, C. M. ed. Four centuries of Southern Indians p132-47

Waiahole Valley

Geschwender, J. A. On power and powerlessness: or with a little help from our friends. *In* Major social issues p439-54

Waikane Valley

Geschwender, J. A. On power and powerlessness: or with a little help from our friends. *In* Major social issues p439-54

Waikiki Beach, Hawaii

Popular culture

Whetmore, E. and Hibbard, D. J. Paradox in paradise: the icons of Waikiki. *In* Browne, R. B. and Fishwick, M. W. eds. Icons of America p241-52

Wailes, Stephen L.

The Nibelungenlied as heroic epic. *In* Oinas, F. J. ed. Heroic epic and saga p120-43

Vagantes and the fabliaux. *In* Cooke, T. D. and Honeycutt, B. L. eds. The humor of the fabliaux p43-58

Wain, John

Arnold Bennett. *In* Stade, G. ed. Six modern British novelists p 1-42

Professing poetry

Contents

Wain, John—*Continued*

About

Ries, L. R. John Wain: the evasive answer. *In* Ries, L. R. Wolf masks p130-50

Waith, Eugene M.

Admiration in the comedies of Thomas Southerne. *In* Evidence in literary scholarship p89-103

"Give me your hands": reflections on the author's agents in comedy. *In* Martz, L. L. and Williams, A. L. eds. The author in his work p197-211

Heywood's women worthies. *In* Concepts of the hero in the Middle Ages and the Renaissance p222-38

Struggle for calm: the dramatic structure of The broken heart. *In* English Renaissance drama p155-66

Wake, Charles Staniland

About

Needham, R. Charles Staniland Wake, 1835-1910: a biographical record. *In* Studies in social anthropology p354-83

Wake, Clive

Tchicaya U Tam'si. *In* King, B. A. and Ogungbesan, K. eds. A celebration of Black and African writing p124-38

Wake (Periodical)

Lawrence, S. Memoir of a 50-year-old publisher on his voyage to outer space. *In* Anderson, E. and Kinzie, M. eds. The little magazine in America: a modern documentary history p143-63

Wakefield, David

Stendahl and Delécluze at the Salon of 1824. *In* The Artist and the writer in France p76-85

Wakefield, Herbert Russell

About

Sullivan, J. Ghost stories of other antiquaries. *In* Sullivan, J. Elegant nightmares p91-111

Wakefield, John

Amiri Baraka (LeRoi Jones), The alternative. *In* Bruck, P. ed. The Black American short story in the 20th century p187-204

Paul Laurence Dunbar, The scapegoat. *In* Bruck, P. ed. The Black American short story in the 20th century p39-51

Wakefield cycle. See individual plays, e.g. Second shepherds' plays (Towneley ms.)

Wakeman, Frederic E.

Localism and loyalism during the Ch'ing conquest of Kiangnan: the tragedy of Chiang-yin. *In* Conflict and control in late imperial China p43-85

A note on the development of the theme of bureaucratic-monarchic tension in Joseph R. Levenson's work. *In* Meisner, M. J. and Murphey, R. eds. The Mozartian historian p123-33

The patriot. *In* Wilson, R. G. ed. Mao Tse-tung in the scales of history p223-45

The Shun interregnum of 1644. *In* Spence, J. D. and Wills, J. E. eds. From Ming to Ch'ing p39-87

Walbank, Frank William

Nationality as a factor in Roman history. *In* Harvard Studies in classical philology v76 p145-68

Symploke: its role in Polybius' Histories. *In* Yale classical studies v24 p197-212

About individual works
Polybius

Momigliano, A. The historian's skin. *In* Momigliano, A. Essays in ancient and modern historiography p67-77

Walcott, Derek

The muse of history; excerpt from "Is Massa Day dead?" *In* Baugh, E. ed. Critics on Caribbean literature p38-43

About individual works
Another life

Baugh, E. The poem as autobiographical novel: Derek Walcott's 'Another life' in relation to Wordsworth's 'Prelude' and Joyce's 'Portrait.' *In* Narasimhaiah, C. D. ed. Awakened conscience p226-35

Lieberman, L. Derek Walcott and Michael S. Harper: the muse of history. *In* Lieberman, L. Unassigned frequencies p284-96

Dream on Monkey Mountain, and other plays

Brown, L. W. The revolutionary dream of Walcott's Makak. *In* Baugh, E. ed. Critics on Caribbean literature p58-62

Tales of the islands (Chapter VI)

Figueroa, J. J. Derek Walcott's 'Poopa, da' was a fête! and Evan Jones's 'Lament of the Banana Man.' *In* Baugh, E. ed. Critics on Caribbean literature p149-52

Characters—Makak

Brown, L. W. The revolutionary dream of Walcott's Makak. *In* Baugh, E. ed. Critics on Caribbean literature p58-62

Walcutt, Charles Child

Jack London. *In* Walcutt, C. C. ed. Seven novelists in the American naturalist tradition p131-67

Wald, George

The human condition. *In* Sociobiology and human nature p277-82

Waldef, Abbot of Melrose. See Waltheof, Saint, Abbot of Melrose

Walden, Russell

New light on Le Corbusier's early years in Paris: the La Roche-Jeanneret houses. *In* Walden, R. ed. The open hand p116-61

Waldenrath, Alexander

The Pennsylvania-Germans: development of their printing and their newspress in the War for American Independence. *In* The German contribution to the building of the Americas p47-74

Waldfogel, Melvin

Narrative painting. *In* Altholz, J. L. ed. The mind and art of Victorian England p159-74

Waldheim, Kurt

Global economic problems and transnational corporations. *In* Benton, L. R. ed. Management for the future p299-305

Health in a world perspective. *In* Cahill, K. M. ed. Health and development p 1-3

Waldman, Theodore

Hobbes on the generation of a public person. *In* Ross, R. G.; Schneider, H. W. and Waldman, T. eds. Thomas Hobbes in his time p61-83

A key to Plato's early dialogues. *In* Philosophy and the civilizing arts p60-88

Waldmeir, Joseph J.
Confiteor hominem: Ernest Hemingway's religion of man. *In* Wagner, L. W. ed. Ernest Hemingway p144-52

John Steinbeck: no Grapes of wrath. *In* Filler, L. ed. A question of quality: popularity and value in modern creative writing p219-28

Rabbit redux reduced: rededicated? redeemed? *In* Essays in honor of Russel B. Nye p247-62

Waldo, Edward Hamilton
Why so much syzygy? *In* Knight, D. F. ed. Turning points p269-72

About

Friend, B. The Sturgeon connection. *In* Clareson, T. D. ed. Voices for the future: essays on major science fiction writers v 1 p153-66

Waldo, E. H. Why so much syzygy? *In* Knight, D. F. ed. Turning points p269-72

Wales

Civilization

Jones, D. A London artist looks at contemporary Wales. *In* Jones, D. The dying Gaul, and other writings p35-40

Jones, D. Welsh culture. *In* Jones, D. The dying Gaul, and other writings p117-22

Walker, Alice

About individual works
In love & trouble

Mickelson, A. Z. Winging upward: Black women: Sarah E. Wright, Toni Morrison, Alice Walker. *In* Mickelson, A. Z. Reaching out: sensitivity and order in recent American fiction by women p112-74

Meridian

Mickelson, A. Z. Winging upward: Black women: Sarah E. Wright, Toni Morrison, Alice Walker. *In* Mickelson, A. Z. Reaching out: sensitivity and order in recent American fiction by women p112-74

Walker, Daniel Pickering
Esoteric symbolism. *In* Poetry and poetics from ancient Greece to the Renaissance p218-32

Walker, David, 1785-1830

About

Stuckey, S. David Walker and the ideological origins of Black nationalism. *In* African themes p25-45

Bibliography

Turner, W. B. The polemicists: David Walker, Frederick Douglass, Booker T. Washington, and W. E. B. Du Bois. *In* Inge, M. T.; Duke, J. M. and Bryer, J. R. eds. Black American writers v 1 p47-132

Walker, David Morrison
William Burn: the country house in transition. *In* Seven Victorian architects p8-31

Walker, Ernestein
The Black woman. *In* The Black American reference book p341-77

Walker, Ian Malcolm. See Welland, D. S. R. jt. auth.

Walker, J. R.
Oglala metaphysics. *In* Tedlock, D. E. and Tedlock, B. eds. Teachings from the American earth p205-18

Walker, James W. St G.
The establishment of a free Black community in Nova Scotia, 1783-1840. *In* Kilson, M. L. and Rotberg, R. I. eds. The African diaspora p205-36

Walker, Joseph A.

About individual works
The River Niger

Kauffmann, S. The River Niger. *In* Kauffmann, S. Persons of the drama p234-36

Walker, Kenneth Richard. See Howe, C. B. jt. auth.

Walker, Larry L.
"Love" in the Old Testament: some lexical observations. *In* Current issues in Biblical and patristic interpretation p277-88

Walker, Nigel D.
Caution: some thoughts on the penal involvement rate. *In* Progress in penal reform p221-37

Lost causes in criminology. *In* Crime, criminology and public policy p47-62

Walker, Ronald G.
Infernal paradise
Contents
Appendix: The fields of paradise
The barranca of history: Mexico as nexus of doom in Under the volcano
The "dark blood" of America
The fascination of Mexico
Graham Greene and "life on a border"
Mexico as scapegoat: Huxley, Lawrence, and Beyond the Mexique bay
A Mexico of the mind: The power and the glory
The plumed serpent: Lawrence's Mexican nightmare
Time and the healing of wounds in Huxley's Eyeless in Gaza
Under Under the volcano: the Mexican voyages of Malcolm Lowry

Walker, Sue Sheridan
Widow and ward: the feudal law of child custody in medieval England. *In* Stuard, S. M. ed. Women in medieval society p159-72

Walker, William O.
Asylum. *In* Encyclopedia of American foreign policy. p49-57

Walking in literature
Weldon, R. F. Hawthorne's "Foot-prints on the sea-shore" and the literature of walking. *In* Kagle, S. E. ed. America: exploration and travel p127-35

Walkowitz, Judith
The making of an outcast group: prostitutes and working women in nineteenth-century Plymouth and Southampton. *In* Vicinus, M. ed. A widening sphere p72-93

Wall, Carey
Solid ground in John Hawkes's Second skin. *In* Garvin, H. R. ed. Makers of the twentieth-century novel p309-19

Wall, Geoffrey
Nineteenth-century land use and settlement on the Canadian Shield frontier. *In* Miller, D. H. and Steffen, J. O. eds. The frontier p227-41

Wall, Richard
Joyce's use of the Anglo-Irish dialect of English. *In* Place, personality and the Irish writer p121-35

Wall decoration. See Mural painting and decoration

Wall newspapers

China

Poon, D. J. Tatzepao: its history and significance as a communication medium. *In* Chu, G. C. ed. Popular media in China p184-221

Wallace, Anthony Francis Clarke

Basic studies, applied projects, and eventual implementation: a case history of biological and cultural research in mental health. *In* Spindler, G. D. ed. The making of psychological anthropology p203-16

Wallace, Irving

About

Browne, R. B. Irving Wallace: independent drummer. *In* Filler, L. ed. A question of quality: popularity and value in modern creative writing p92-107

Cawelti, J. G. The best-selling social melodrama. *In* Cawelti, J. G. Adventure, mystery, and romance p260-95

Wallace, John Malcolm

Coopers Hill: the manifesto of parliamentary royalism, 1641. *In* ELH essays for Earl R. Wasserman p201-47

Wallace, Karl Richards

Bacon, rhetoric, and ornament of words. *In* Rhetoric: a tradition in transition p49-65

Wallace, Patricia

The "estranged point of view": the thematics of imagination in Frost's poetry. *In* Frost: centennial essays II p177-95

Wallace, Ronald H.

The last laugh

Contents

Dwarfed into dignity: John Barth's The floating opera

The great American game: Robert Coover's The Universal Baseball Association, inc., J. Henry Waugh, prop

Never mind that the nag's a pile of bones: the contemporary American comic novel and the comic tradition

No harm in smiling: Vladimir Nabokov's Lolita

No more happy endings

The rarer action: John Hawkes's Second skin

What laughter can do: Ken Kesey's One flew over the cuckoo's nest

Wallace, Walter L.

Structure and action in the theories of Coleman and Parsons. *In* Blau, P. M. ed. Approaches to the study of social structure p121-34

Wallace, William A.

The philosophical setting of medieval science. *In* Lindberg, D. C. ed. Science in the Middle Ages p91-119

Wallach, Aleta

A view from the law school. *In* Women and the power to change p81-125

Wallach, Luitpold

Diplomatic studies in Latin and Greek documents from the Carolingian age

Contents

Actus Silvestri, Libri Carolini, and the Constantine Donation: the solution of a pseudo-problem

Alcuin as the author of the Libri Carolini: epilogue to Part III

Ambrosiaster and the Libri Carolini

The genuine and the forged oath of Pope Leo III

The Greek and Latin versions of II Nicaea, 787, and the Synodica of Hadrian I (JE 2448)

The Libri Carolini and patristics, Latin and Greek

The marginalia of the Vaticanus Latinus 7207

On "Spanish symptoms" in the Libri Carolini

Origin and composition of the Libri Carolini

The origins, corrections, and Tironian notes of the Vaticanus Latinus 7207

Philological and historical evidence disproving Theodulph of Orléans' alleged authorship

The Roman synod of December 800 and the alleged trial of Leo III

The testimonia of image-worship in Hadrian I's Synodica of 785 (JE 2448)

The textual history of a Greek Ambrose text: Libri Carolini II.15

Valid and invalid argumentation concerning "Spanish symptoms"

The Vaticanus Latinus 7207 and paleographical problems

The Urbana Anglo-Saxon sylloge of Latin inscriptions. *In* Poetry and poetics from ancient Greece to the Renaissance p134-51

Walle, Etienne van de. See Van de Walle, Etienne

Wallerstein, Immanuel Maurice

Modernization: requiescat in pace. *In* The Uses of controversy in sociology p131-35

A world-system perspective on the social sciences. *In* McNall, S. G. ed. Theoretical perspectives in sociology p40-50

Walling, William

In which Humpty Dumpty becomes king. *In* Peary, G. and Shatzkin, R. eds. The modern American novel and the movies p168-77

More than sufficient room: Sir David Wilkie and the Scottish literary tradition. *In* Kroeber, K. and Walling, W. eds. Images of romanticism p107-31

Wallis, Roy

The Aetherius Society: a case study in the formation of a mystagogic congregation. *In* Wallis, R. ed. Sectarianism p17-34

The cult and its transformation. *In* Wallis, R. ed. Sectarianism p35-49

Societal reaction to scientology: a study in the sociology of deviant religion. *In* Wallis, R. ed. Sectarianism p86-116

Walloons

Zolberg, A. R. Splitting the difference: federalization without federalization in Begium. *In* Esman, M. J. ed. Ethnic conflict in the Western world p103-42

Walls, Andrew Finlay

A colonial concordat: two views of Christianity and civilisation. *In* Church, society and politics p293-302

Walls, David S.

Dialectical social science. *In* McNall, S. G. ed. Theoretical perspectives in sociology p214-31

Walpole, Horace, 4th Earl of Orford
About
Ames, D. S. Strawberry Hill: architecture of the "as if." *In* Studies in eighteenth-century culture v8 p351-63

Lewis, W. S. Edmond Malone, Horace Walpole, and Shakespeare. *In* Evidence in literary scholarship p353-62

Mudrick, M. Chamber of horrors. *In* Mudrick, M. Books are not life but then what is? p303-09

Walpole, Sir Hugh
About
Cavaliero, G. Literary regionalism: Hugh Walpole, Sheila Kaye-Smith. *In* Cavaliero, G. The rural tradition in the English novel, 1900-1939 p66-80

Walpole, Sir Robert, 1st Earl of Orford
About
Bennett, G. V. Jacobitism and the rise of Walpole. *In* Historical perspectives p70-92

Skinner, Q. The principles and practice of opposition: the case of Bolingbroke versus Walpole. *In* Historical perspectives p93-128

Walrond, Eric
About
Bone, R. A. Eric Walrond. *In* Bone, R. A. Down home p171-203

Walser, Robert
About
Middleton, J. C. The picture of nobody: some remarks on Robert Walser. *In* Middleton, J. C. Bolshevism in art p95-122

Walsh, Chad
The reeducation of the fearful pilgrim. *In* Schakel, P. J. ed. The longing for a form p64-72

Walsh, Elizabeth
John Lydgate and the proverbial tiger. *In* The Learned and the lewed p291-303

Walsh, George B.
The first stasimon of Euripides' Electra. *In* Yale classical studies v25 p277-89

Walsh, Henry Horace
Christianity. *In* Adams, C. J. ed. A reader's guide to the great religions p345-406

Walsh, Jeffrey
The painful process of unthinking: E. E. Cummings' social vision in The enormous room. *In* Klein, H. M. ed. The First World War in fiction p32-42

Walsh, Jill Paton
History is fiction. *In* Horn Book Magazine. Crosscurrents of criticism p219-25

Seeing green. *In* Blishen, E. ed. The thorny paradise p58-61

Walsh, William
The Indian sensibility in English. *In* Narasimhaiah, C. D. ed. Awakened conscience p63-72

Walsh, William Henry
Hegelian ethics. *In* New studies in ethics v 1 p379-464

The logical status of Vico's ideal eternal history. *In* Giambattista Vico's science of humanity p141-53

Walt Disney World, Orlando, Fla.
Craft, R. In the mouse trap. *In* Craft, R. Current convictions p285-98

Walter, Elizabeth
The case of the escalating sales. *In* Agatha Christie: first lady of crime p11-24

Walter, Eugene Victor
Demons and disenchantment. *In* Disguises of the demonic p17-30

Walters, Leroy
Genetics, reproductive biology, and bioethics. *In* The Tricentennial people p66-74

Waltheof, Saint, Abbot of Melrose
About
Baker, D. Legend and reality: the case of Waldef of Melrose. *In* Church, society and politics p59-82

Walther, Luann
The invention of childhood in Victorian autobiography. *In* Landow, G. P. ed. Approaches to Victorian autobiography p64-83

Walther, Rudolf
About
Hellman, C. D. A poem on the occasion of the nova of 1572. *In* Philosophy and humanism p306-09

Walther von der Vogelweide
About
Karlin, R. The challenge to courtly love. *In* In pursuit of perfection p101-33

Walton, Craig
Hume and Jefferson on the uses of history. *In* Livingston, D. W. and King, J. T. eds. Hume p389-403

Also in Philosophy and the civilizing arts p103-25

The philosophia prima of Thomas Hobbes. *In* Ross, R. G.; Schneider, H. W. and Waldman, T. eds. Thomas Hobbes in his time p31-41

Walton, Izaak
Influence—Dickens
Patterson, A. M. Our mutual friend: Dickens as the Compleat Angler. *In* Dickens Studies Annual v 1 p252-64

Walton, John
Political economy of world urban systems: directions for comparative research. *In* Walton, J. and Masotti, L. H. eds. The city in comparative perspective p301-13

See also Masotti, L. H. jt. auth.

Walton, Kendall Lewis
Categories of art. *In* Margolis, J. Z. ed. Philosophy looks at the arts p88-131

Walton, Luke, pseud. See Henderson, Bill
Walton, Ortiz
About individual works
Music: Black, white and blue
Reed, I. Music: Black, white and blue. *In* Reed, I. Shrovetide in old New Orleans p100-04

Walvin, James. See Edwards, P. G. jt. auth

Walz, Terence
House decoration in Lower Nubia. *In* African images p190-222

Walzer, Michael
Consenting to one's own death: the case of Brutus. *In* Kohl, M. ed. Beneficent euthanasia p100-05

Puritanism as a revolutionary ideology. *In* Vaughan, A. T. and Bremer, F. J. eds. Puritan New England p19-41

Wambouti. See Bambute

Wamsley, Gary L. See Salamon, L. B. jt. auth

Wanda (Motion picture)
Kauffmann, S. Wanda. *In* Kauffmann, S. Living images p48-50

The wanderer (Anglo-Saxon poem)
Brown, G. H. An iconographic explanation of "The wanderer," lines 81b-82a. *In* Viator: medieval and Renaissance studies v9 p31-38

Klein, W. F. Purpose and the "poetics" of The wanderer and The seafarer. *In* Anglo-Saxon poetry: essays in appreciation p208-23

Mitchell, B. C. Linguistic facts and the interpretation of Old English poetry. *In* Anglo-Saxon England 4 p11-28

Woolf, R. The wanderer, The seafarer, and the genre of planctus. *In* Anglo-Saxon poetry: essays in appreciation p192-207

The Wandering Jew (Motion picture)
Taylor, R. The Wandering Jew. *In* Taylor, R. Film propaganda p190-206

Wandering Jew in literature
Stanford, D. E. Edwin Arlington Robinson's "The Wandering Jew." *In* Tulane Studies in English, v23 p95-108

Wandycz, Piotr Stefan
Partitions of Poland and the diplomacy of the partitioning powers: some reflections on the Bicentennial of 1772. *In* For Wiktor Weintraub p559-70

Wang, Chien

About
Vanderstappen, H. A. The style of some seventeenth-century Chinese paintings. *In* Artists and traditions p149-68

Wang, Fu-chih

About
McMorran, I. The patriot and the partisans: Wang Fu-chih's involvement in the politics of the Yung-li court. *In* Spence, J. T. and Wills, J. E. eds. From Ming to Ch'ing p133-66

McMorran, I. Wang Fu-chih and the Neo-Confucian tradition. *In* The Unfolding of Neo-Confucianism p413-67

Wong, Siu-Kit. Ch'ing and ching in the critical writings of Wang Fu-chih. *In* Chinese approaches to literature from Confucius to Liang Ch'i-ch'ao p121-50

Wang, Gungwu
The Chinese. *In* Wilson, R. G. ed. Mao Tse-tung in the scales of history p272-99

Chinese civilization and the diffusion of culture. *In* Grafton Elliot Smith p197-209

The limits of Nanyang Chinese nationalism, 1912-1937. *In* Southeast Asian history and historiography p405-23

Wang, Hui

About
Spence, J. D. The Wan-li period vs. the K'ang-hsi period: fragmentation vs. reintegration? *In* Artists and traditions p145-48

Wang, John Ching-yu
The Chih-yen-chai Commentary and the Dream of the red chamber: a literary study. *In* Chinese approaches to literature from Confucius to Liang Ch'i-ch'ao p189-220

Early Chinese narrative: the Tse-chuan as example. *In* Chinese narrative p3-20

Wang, Shan

About
Spence, J. D. The Wan-li period vs. the K'ang-hsi period: fragmentation vs. reintegration? *In* Artists and traditions p145-48

Wang, Shih-chên, 1634-1711

About
Kao, Yu-kung, and Mei, Tsu-lin. Ending lines in Wang Shih-chen's 'ch'i-chüeh': convention and creativity in the Ch'ing. *In* Artists and traditions p131-44

Lynn, R. J. Orthodoxy and enlightenment: Wang Shih-chen's theory of poetry and its antecedents. *In* The Unfolding of Neo-Confucianism p217-69

Wang, Shou-jên

About
Araki, K. Confucianism and Buddhism in the late Ming. *In* The Unfolding of Neo-Confucianism p39-66

T'ang, Chün-i. Liu Tsung-chou's doctrine of moral mind and practice and his critique of Wang Yang-ming. *In* The Unfolding of Neo-Confucianism p305-31

Wang, Yang-ming. See Wang, Shou-jên

Wanner, Eric
Do we understand sentences from the outside-in or from the inside-out? *In* Bloomfield, M. W. and Haugen, E. I. eds. Language as a human problem p165-85

Wanner, Eric, and Maratsos, Michael P.
An ATN approach to comprehension. *In* Linguistic theory and psychological reality p119-61

War
Armstrong, C. A. J. Sir John Fastolf and the law of arms. *In* War, literature, and politics in the late Middle Ages p46-56

Beaumont, R. A. Polemology: promises and a problem. *In* Beaumont, R. A. and Edmonds, M. eds. War in the next decade p203-10

Claud, I. L. The problem of evaluating war. *In* New dimensions of world politics p109-26

Edmonds, M. The horizons of war: problems of projection. *In* Beaumont, R. A. and Edmonds, M. eds. War in the next decade p 1-20

Foot, M. R. D. Resistance, war and revolution. *In* The Year book of world affairs, 1977 p158-75

Gallie, W. B. Marx and Engels on revolution and war. *In* Gallie, W. B. Philosophers of peace and war p66-99

Garnett, J. C. The concept of war. *In* The Year book of world affairs, 1976 p133-49

Howard, M. Temperamenta belli: can war be controlled? *In* Howard, M. ed. Restraints on war p 1-15

Huxley, A. L. War and nationalism. *In* Huxley, A. L. The Human situation p74-90

Koestler, A. Prologue: the new calendar. *In* Koestler, A. Janus p 1-20

Winter, J. M. Introduction: the economic and social history of war. *In* War and economic development p 1-10

Wright, N. A. R. The tree of battles of Honoré Bouvet and the laws of war. *In* War, literature, and politics in the late Middle Age p12-31

See also Air warfare; Atomic warfare; Biological warfare; Chemical warfare; Civil war; Disarmament; Limited war; Military art and science; Military policy; Peace; Strategy; War and society; also specific wars, battles, etc., e.g. Netherlands—History—Wars of Independence, 1556-1648

War in literature—*Continued*

Nelson, J. W. War and peace and the British poets of sensibility. *In* Studies in eighteenth-century culture v7 p345-66

Rutherford, A. The Christian as hero: Waugh's Sword of honour. *In* Rutherford, A. The literature of war p113-34

Rutherford, A. The common man as hero: literature of the Western Front. *In* Rutherford, A. The literature of war p64-112

Rutherford, A. The intellectual as hero: Lawrence of Arabia. *In* Rutherford, A. The literature of war p38-63

Saeki, S. Images of the United States as a hypothetical enemy. *In* Iriye, A. ed. Mutual images p100-14

War of 1914. See European War, 1914-1918

War of the American Revolution. See United States—History—Revolution, 1775-1783

War powers. See War and emergency powers

War protest movements (Vietnamese Conflict, 1961-1975) See Vietnamese Conflict, 1961-1975—Protest movements

Warburg, Aby

About

Gilbert, F. From art history to the history of civilization: Aby Warburg. *In* Gilbert, F. History p423-39

Warburton, John

About

Bliss, M. D. John Warburton as antiquary and collector: evidence from the sale catalogue of his collection. *In* Virginia. University. Bibliographical Society. Studies in bibliography v29 p296-306

Warburton, Thomas Rennie

Nationalism and language in Switzerland and Canada. *In* Smith, A. D. ed. Nationalist movements p88-109

Ward, Dana

Kissinger: a psychohistory. *In* DeMause, L. ed. The new psychohistory p69-130

Ward, David

The early Victorian city in England and America: on the parallel development of an urban image. *In* European settlement and development in North America: essays on geographical change in honour and memory of Andrew Hill Clark p170-89

Some locational implications of the ethnic division of labor in mid-nineteenth-century American cities. *In* Pattern and process p258-70

Ward, John O.

The commentator's rhetoric: from antiquity to the Renaissance: glosses and commentaries on Cicero's Rhetorica. *In* Murphy, J. J. ed. Medieval eloquence p25-67

Ward, Joseph Anthony

James Agee's aesthetic of silence: Let us now praise famous men. *In* Tulane Studies in English, v23 p193-206

Ward, Maisie

About

Sheed, W. Frank Sheed and Maisie Ward: writers, publishers, and parents. *In* Sheed, W. The good word & other words p164-70

Ward, Michael R.

Okop p'Bitek and the rise of East African writing. *In* King, B. A. and Ogungbesan, K. eds. A celebration of Black and African writing p217-31

Ward, Nicole

'Fourmillante cité': Baudelaire and 'The waste land.' *In* The Waste land in different voices p87-104

Ward, Robert Elmer

The case for German-American literature. *In* The German contribution to the building of the Americas p373-91

Ward, Stephen R.

Great Britain: land fit for heroes lost. *In* The War generation p10-37

Ward, Wilber Henry

St George Tucker's Hansford. *In* Tennessee Studies in literature v21 p28-34

Ward-Perkins, John Bryan

Taste, tradition and technology: some aspects of the architecture of late republican and early imperial central Italy. *In* Studies in classical art and archaeology p197-204

Wardell, Mark L. and Benson, Jerry Kenneth

A dialectical view: foundation for an alternative sociological method. *In* McNall, S. G. ed. Theoretical perspectives in sociology p232-48

Wardell, Nancy Needham

The corporation. *In* A New America? p97-110

Wardropper, Bruce W.

The epic hero superseded. *In* Concepts of the hero in the Middle Ages and the Renaissance p197-221

The religious conversion of profane poetry. *In* Studies in the continental background of Renaissance English literature: essays presented to John L. Lievsay p203-22

Ware, Malcolm

The telescope reversed: Ann Radcliffe and natural scenery. *In* A Provision of human nature p169-89

Ware, Ronald Dean

Medieval chronology: theory and practice. *In* Powell, J. M. ed. Medieval studies p213-37

Warhol, Andy

About

Rosenberg, H. Warhol: art's other self. *In* Rosenberg, H. Art on the edge p98-108

Taylor, J. R. Andy Warhol/Paul Morrissey. *In* Taylor, J. R. Directors and directions p136-64

About individual works

Blow-job

Koch, S. Blow-job and pornography. *In* Nichols, B. ed. Movies and methods p305-09

Warka, Iraq

Johnson, G. A. Locational analysis and the investigation of Uruk local exchange systems. *In* Ancient civilization and trade p285-339

Warkentin, John

Epilogue. *In* European settlement and development in North America: essays on geographical change in honour and memory of Andrew Hill Clark p208-20

Warlick, Mark. See Velarde, A. J. jt. auth.

Warminski, Andrzej

Pre-positional by-play. *In* Glyph 3 p98-117

Warner, Anna Bartlett

About

Baym, N. Z. Susan Warner, Anna Warner, and Maria Cummins. *In* Baym, N. Z. Woman's fiction p140-74

Warren, Robert P.—About individual works
—*Continued*

Brother to dragons

Nakadate, N. E. Voices of community: the function of colloquy in Robert Penn Warren's Brother to dragons. *In* Tennessee Studies in literature v21 p114-24

Warren, Roger

Comedies and histories at two Stratfords, 1977. *In* Shakespeare survey v31 p141-53

Theatrical virtuosity and poetic complexity in 'Cymbeline.' *In* Shakespeare survey v29 p41-49

Theory and practice: Stratford 1976. *In* Shakespeare survey 30 p169-79

Warrick, Patricia S.

Images of the man-machine intelligence relationship in science fiction. *In* Clareson, T. D. ed. Many futures, many worlds p182-223

Mack Reynolds: the future as socio-economic possibility. *In* Clareson, T. D. ed. Voices for the future: essays on major science fiction writers v2 p136-53

Wars. See Military history; War

Wars of Alexander

Duggan, H. N. The role of formulas in the dissemination of a middle English alliterative romance. *In* Virginia. University. Bibliographical Society. Studies in bibliography v29 p265-88

Warsaw Pact, 1955

Erickson, J. The European military balance. *In* Kirk, G. L. and Wessell, N. H. eds. The Soviet threat p110-21

Tiedtke, J. and Tiedtke, S. The Soviet Union's internal problems and the development of the Warsaw Treaty Organisation. *In* Jahn, E. ed. Soviet foreign policy p114-57

Warsaw Treaty, 1955. See Warsaw Pact, 1955

Warshow, Paul

The unreal McCoy. *In* Peary, G. and Shatzkin, R. eds. The modern American novel and the movies p29-39

Warshow, Robert

Preface to the immediate experience. *In* Denby, D. ed. Awake in the dark p141-45

The Westerner. *In* Denby, D. ed. Awake in the dark p248-63

About

Murray, E. Robert Warshow and sociological criticism. *In* Murray, E. Nine American film critics p24-37

Wartofsky, Marx W.

Art and technology: conflicting models of education? The uses of a cultural myth. *In* Feinberg, W. and Rosemont, H. eds. Work, technology, and education p166-85

Consciousness, praxis, and reality: Marxism vs. phenomenology. *In* Elliston, F. A. and McCormick, P. eds. Husserl p304-13

Warton, Joseph

About individual works

An essay on the genius and writings of Pope

Fairer, D. The writing and printing of Joseph Warton's Essay on Pope. *In* Virginia. University. Bibliographical Society. Studies in bibliography v30 p211-19

Trowbridge, F. H. Joseph Warton on the imagination. *In* Trowbridge, F. H. From Dryden to Jane Austen p161-74

Trowbridge, F. H. Joseph Warton's classification of English poets. *In* Trowbridge, F. H. From Dryden to Jane Austen p157-60

Criticism, Textual

Fairer, D. The writing and printing of Joseph Warton's Essay on Pope. *In* Virginia. University. Bibliographical Society. Studies in bibliography v30 p211-19

Warts

Thomas, L. On warts. *In* Thomas, L. The medusa and the snail p76-81

Warwick, Dolores. See Frese, Dolores Warwick

Warwick, Donald P.

Freedom. *In* Population policy and ethics p17-29

Warwick, Donald P. and Williamson, Nancy E.

Population policy and Spanish-surname Americans. *In* Population policy and ethics p211-35

Washburn, Sherwood Larned

Animal behavior and social anthropology. *In* Sociobiology and human nature p53-74

Washburn, Wilcomb E.

The clash of morality in the American forest. *In* First images of America p335-50

The writing of American Indian history: a status report. *In* The American Indian p3-25

Washington, Booker Taliaferro

About

Downs, R. B. The great compromiser. *In* Downs, R. B. Books that changed the South p186-96

Grantham, D. W. Dinner at the White House: Theodore Roosevelt, Booker T. Washington, and the South. *In* Grantham, D. W. The regional imagination p32-52

About individual works

Up from slavery

Downs, R. B. The great compromiser. *In* Downs, R. B. Books that changed the South p186-96

Bibliography

Turner, W. B. The polemicists: David Walker, Frederick Douglass, Booker T. Washington, and W. E. B. Du Bois. *In* Inge, M. T.; Duke, J. M. and Bryer, J R. eds. Black American writers v 1 p47-132

Washington, George, President U.S.

About

Rabinowitz, H. N. George Washington as icon, 1865-1900. *In* Browne, R. B. and Fishwick, M. W. eds. Icons of America p67-86

Portraits

Richardson, E. P. George Washington: the evidence of the portraits. *In* Aspects of American liberty p196-225

Washington, Mary Helen

Politics of the outsider: Black studies in the university, 1976. *In* Minority language and literature p130-33

Washington, D.C. Conference on the Limitation of Armament, 1921-1922. See Conference on the Limitation of Armament, Washington, D.C., 1921-1922

Washington v. Davis. *In* The Supreme Court review, 1976 p263-316

Wasiolek, Edward

The future of psychoanalytic criticism. *In* The Frontiers of literary criticism p149-68

Wasow, Mona, and Loeb, Martin Bernard

The aged. *In* Gochros, H. L. and Gochros, J. S. eds. The sexually oppressed p54-68

Wasserman, Earl Reeves. See Part 2 under title: ELH essays for Earl R. Wasserman

Wasserman, Jerry

The word as object: the Rabelaisian novel. *In* Spilka, M. ed. Towards a poetics of fiction p316-30

Wasserstrom, Richard A.

Is adultery immoral? *In* Baker, R. and Elliston, F. A. eds. Philosophy & sex p207-21

The laws of war. *In* The Abdication of philosophy: philosophy and the public good p157-73

The obligation to obey the law. *In* Summers, R. S. ed. Essays in legal philosophy p274-304

The university and the case for preferential treatment. *In* Social justice & preferential treatment p16-32

Wasserstrom, William

Van Wyck Brooks. *In* Ross, R. G. ed. Makers of American thought p157-91

Wästberg, Per

Themes in African literature today. *In* Mintz, S. W. ed. Slavery, colonialism, and racism p135-50

Waste, Disposal of. See Refuse and refuse disposal

Waste products. See Recycling (Waste, etc.); Refuse and refuse disposal

Waste recycling. See Recycling (Waste, etc.)

Watad, Muhammad

Insufferable silence. *In* The Palestinians p133-35

Watanabe, Morimichi

Gregor Heimburg and early humanism in Germany. *In* Philosophy and humanism p406-22

Watanabe, Satoshi

Can the cognitive process be totally mechanized? *In* Philosophical aspects of the mind-body problem p182-99

Logic of the empirical world, with reference to the identity theory and reductionism. *In* Philosophical aspects of the mind-body problem p162-81

Watanabe, Satosi. See Watanabe, Satoshi

Watanabe Rajana, Eimi. See Rajana, Eimi Watanabe

Watch Tower movement. See Jehovah's Witnesses

Watches. See Clocks and watches

Water, Richard van de. See Van de Water, Richard

Water

See also Ponds

Pollution

See also Thermal pollution of rivers, lakes, etc.

Pollution—Law and legislation—United States

Currie, D. P. Congress, the Court, and water pollution. *In* The Supreme Court review, 1977 p39-62

Pollution—Europe—History

Trexler, R. C. Measures against water pollution in fifteenth-century Florence. *In* Viator: medieval and Renaissance studies v5 p455-67

Water balance (Physiology) See Osmoregulation

Water-electrolyte balance (Physiology) See Osmoregulation

Water in agriculture. See Irrigation

Water-marks

Spector, S. Symmetry in watermark sequences. *In* Virginia. University. Bibliographical Society. Studies in bibliography v31 p162-78

Water mills

Great Britain

Rahtz, P. and Bullough, D. A. The parts of an Anglo-Saxon mill. *In* Anglo-Saxon England 6 p15-37

Water-power electric plants

Environmental aspects—Norway—Eikesdal

Kvaløy, S. The Mardøla waterfall development. *In* Against pollution and hunger p289-92

Water resources development. See Irrigation; Water supply

Water-supply

Ortega, A. Simple water technologies. *In* Strategies for human settlements: habitat and environment p79-83

See also Irrigation

France—Nivernais

Thuilier, G. Water supplies in nineteenth-century Nivernais. *In* Food and drink in history p109-25

Waterer, John William

Leatherwork. *In* Strong, D. E. and Brown, D. eds. Roman crafts p179-93

Watergate affair, 1972-

Arendt, H. Home to roost. *In* Warner, S. B. ed. The American experiment p61-79

Brustein, R. S. Thebes and Watergate. *In* Brustein, R. S. The culture watch p94-96

DeMott, B. Gentlemen of principle, priests of presumption. *In* Bigsby, C. W. E. ed. Approaches to popular culture p264-74

Galbraith, J. K. John Dean, ambition and the White House. *In* Galbraith, J. Annals of an abiding liberal p341-45

Redford, E. S. Watergate: a test of constitutional democracy. *In* Prospects for constitutional democracy p183-97

Roth, P. Our castle. *In* Roth, P. Reading myself and others p191-94

Sheed, W. A moral problem. *In* Sheed, W. The good word & other words p86-90

Sheed, W. Watergate as literature. *In* Sheed, W. The good word & other words p77-81

Waterhouse, Alfred

About

Smith, S. A. Alfred Waterhouse: civic grandeur. *In* Seven Victorian architects p102-21

Waterhouse, Richard

The responsible gentry of colonial South Carolina: a study in local government, 1670-1770. *In* Daniels, B. C. ed. Town and county p160-85

Waterhouse, Ruth
Ælfric's use of discourse in some saints' lives. *In* Anglo-Saxon England 5 p83-103

Affective language, especially alliterating qualifiers, in Ælfric's Life of St Alban. *In* Anglo-Saxon England 7 p131-48

Waterman, G. Henry
The Greek "verbal genitive." *In* Current issues in Biblical and patristic interpretation p289-93

Watermarks. See Water-marks

Watermills. See Water mills

Waters, Frank
The fifth world—the ninth planet. *In* Voices from the Southwest p55-62

Waters, Martin J.
Peasants and emigrants: considerations of the Gaelic League as a social movement. *In* Casey, D. J. and Rhodes, R. E. eds. Views of the Irish peasantry, 1800-1916 p160-77

Watkin, David
Morality and architecture
Contents
Pevsner
The theme in the nineteenth century: Pugin
The theme in the nineteenth century: Violett-Le-Duc
The theme in the twentieth century: Brave new world
The theme in the twentieth century: Furneaux Jordan
The theme in the twentieth century: Lethaby

Watkins, Calvert
Etyma Enniana. *In* Harvard Studies in classical philology v77 p195-206

A further remark on Lachmann's law. *In* Harvard Studies in classical philology v74 p55-65

An Indo-European agricultural term: Latin ador, Hittite hat-. *In* Harvard Studies in classical philology v77 p187-93

An Indo-European construction in Greek and Latin. *In* Harvard Studies in classical philology v71 p115-19

Language and its history. *In* Bloomfield, M. W. and Haugen, E. I. eds. Language as a human problem p85-97

Latin ador, Hittite hat- again: addenda to HSCP 77 (1973) 187-193. *In* Harvard Studies in classical philology v79 p181-87

Observations on the "Nestor's cup" inscription. *In* Harvard Studies in classical philology v80 p25-40

On the family of *arceō*, ἀρκέω, and Hittite *hark. In* Harvard Studies in classical philology v74 p67-74

Watkins, Evan
The critical act
Contents
Charles Tomlinson: the poetry of experience
Criticism and community: on literary value
Criticism and method: Hirsch, Frye, Barthes, Derrida
Dialectic and form
The fiction of intrepretation: Faulkner's Absalom, Absalom!
Introduction: Poetics, poetry, and the practice of criticism
Poetic autonomy
Raymond Williams and Marxist criticism

Watkins, Floyd C.
Habet: Faulkner and the ownership of property. *In* Faulkner: fifty years after The marble faun p123-37

In time and place.
Contents
As I lay dying: the dignity of earth
The confessions of Nat Turner: history and imagination
Culture versus anonymity in House made of dawn
Death comes for the Archbishop: worlds old and new
Flat wine from The grapes of wrath
Gone with the wind as vulgar literature
Main Street: culture through the periscope of ego
The makings of American fiction
My Antonia: "still, all day long, Nebraska"
A void New World

Watkins, Geoffrey M.
Yeats and Mr Watkins' Bookshop. *In* Yeats and the occult p307-10

Watkins, John W. N.
Three views concerning human freedom. *In* Royal Institute of Philosophy. Nature and conduct p200-28

Watson, Adam
Morgenthau's concept of the national interest and the new states of the Third world. *In* [Truth and tragedy]: a tribute to Hans Morgenthau p305-15

Watson, Charles Sullivan
Antebellum Charleston dramatists
Contents
The Charleston theater
Conclusions: Charleston dramatists and American drama
Dramatic writing, 1797 to the Civil War
John Blake White
William Gilmore Simms
William Ioor

Watson, Colin
The message of Mayhem Parva. *In* Agatha Christie: first lady of crime p95-110

Watson, Francis
Diderot and Houdon: a little-known bust. *In* The Artist and the writer in France p15-20

Watson, George
The literary past; excerpt from "The story of literature." *In* On literary intention p158-73

Politics and literature in modern Britain
Contents
Acton's 'History of liberty'
Did Stalin dupe the intellectuals?
George Orwell
Left and Right
The literature of fascism
The myth of catastrophe
The New Left
The politics of D. H. Lawrence
Race and the Socialists
The social criticism of Matthew Arnold

Watson, Hugh Seton- See Seton-Watson, Hugh

Watson, James Dewey
The dissemination of unpublished information. *In* The Frontiers of knowledge p157-75

Watson, John, 1850-1907

About

Hart, F. R. The liberals in the Kailyard. *In* Hart, F. R. The Scottish novel p114-30

Watson, John Broadus

About

Fancher, R. E. Psychology as the science of behavior: Ivan Pavlov and John B. Watson. *In* Fancher, R. E. Pioneers of psychology p295-338

About individual works

Behaviorism

Richards, I. A. John Watson's Behaviorism. *In* Richards, I. A. Complementarities p16-23

Watson, John Richard. See Brake, L. jt. auth., Dodd, P. jt. auth.

Watson, John Richard; Maidment, B. E. and Chapple, J. A. V.

The nineteenth century. *In* English Association. The year's work in English studies v53 p296-360

The nineteenth century [another essay]. *In* English Association. The year's work in English studies v54 p301-62

Watson, Michael

A comparative evaluation of planning practice in the liberal democratic state. *In* Planning, politics and public policy p445-83

The regional dimension of planning. *In* Planning, politics and public policy p285-94

Watson, Paul F.

The Queen of Sheba in Christian tradition. *In* Pritchard, J. B. ed. Solomon & Sheba p115-45

Titian and Michelangelo: the Danae of 1545-1546. *In* Collaboration in Italian Renaissance art p245-50

Watson, Richard A.

Reason and morality in a world of limited food. *In* Aiken, W. and La Follette, H. eds. World hunger and moral obligation p115-23

Watson, Thomas John, 1914-

Good design is good business. *In* The Uneasy coalition: design in corporate America p57-79

Watt, Donald Cameron

Britain and the Cold war in the Far East, 1945-58. *In* The Origins of the Cold war in Asia p89-122

The historiography of appeasement. *In* Crisis and controversy p110-29

History on the public screen I. *In* Smith, P. ed. The historian and film p169-76

The initiation of the negotiations leading to the Nazi-Soviet pact: a historical problem. *In* Essays in honour of E. H. Carr p152-70

Introduction: The historian's tasks and responsibilities. *In* The Origins of the Cold war in Asia p3-14

Restraints on war in the air before 1945. *In* Howard, M. ed. Restraints on war p57-77

Watt, Ian Pierre

Impressionism and symbolism in Heart of darkness. *In* Joseph Conrad: a commemoration p37-53

Oral Dickens. *In* Dickens Studies Annual v3 p165-81

Serious reflections on The rise of the novel. *In* Spilka, M. ed. Towards a poetics of fiction p90-103

About individual works

The rise of the novel

Watt, I. P. Serious reflections on The rise of the novel. *In* Spilka, M. ed. Towards a poetics of fiction p90-103

Watt, James

Donovan, A. L. Toward a social history of technological ideas: Joseph Black, James Watt, and the separate condenser. *In* Bugliarello, G. and Doner, D. B. eds. The history and philosophy of technology p19-30

Watt, William Montgomery

Islamic conceptions of the holy war. *In* The Holy war p141-56

The Queen of Sheba in Islamic tradition. *In* Pritchard, J. B. ed. Solomon & Sheba p85-103

Watteau, Antoine. See Watteau, Jean Antoine

Watteau, Jean Antoine

About

Berger, J. Drawings by Watteau. *In* Berger, J. The look of things p103-06

Watters, David. See Lowance, M. I. jt. auth.

Watts, Alan Wilson

About

Ellwood, R. S. Zen journeys to the West. *In* Ellwood, R. S. Alternative altars p136-63

Watts, Harold W.

Why, and how well, do we analyze inequality? *In* Major social issues p126-40

Watts, Isaac

About

Davie, D. Old dissent, 1700-1740. *In* Davie, D. A gathered Church p19-36

Watts, Michael

The call and response of popular music: the impact of American pop music in Europe. *In* Bigsby, C. W. E. Superculture p123-39

Waugh, Daniel Clarke

Azbuka znakami lits: Egyptian hieroglyphs in the Privy Chancellery Archive. *In* Oxford Slavonic papers, new ser. v10 p46-50

Waugh, Earle Howard

Following the beloved: Muhammad as model in the Sūfī tradition. *In* Reynolds, F. E. and Capps, D. eds. The biographical process p63-85

Waugh, Evelyn

Max Beerbohm: a lesson in manners. *In* Riewald, J. G. ed. The surprise of excellence p92-95

About

Lodge, D. Evelyn Waugh. *In* Stade, G. ed. Six modern British novelists p43-86

Marcus, S. Evelyn Waugh and the art of entertainment. *In* Marcus, S. Representations p88-101

Pritchard, W. H. Satire and fiction: examples from the 1930s. *In* Pritchard, W. H. Seeing through everything p178-208

Sheed, W. Evelyn Waugh: no snob like a snubbed snob. *In* Sheed, W. The good word & other words p53-57

Wicker, B. Waugh and the narrator as Dandy. *In* Wicker, B. The story-shaped world p151-68

Webb, Eugene
The dark dove
Contents

The ambiguities of secularization: modern transformations of the Kingdom in Nietzsche, Ibsen, Beckett, and Stevens
A darkness shining in brightness: James Joyce and the obscure soul of the world
The one and the many: the ambiguous challenge of Being in the poetry of Yeats and Rilke
The paradox of the sacred
The perilous journey to wholeness in Thomas Mann
The tradition of the sacred in the West
W. H. Auden: the ambiguity of the sacred
The way up and the way down: the redemption of time in T. S. Eliot's "Ash Wednesday" and Four quartets

Webb, Jane Carter
The implications of control for the human personality: Hawthorne's point of view. *In* Tulane Studies in English v21 p57-66

Webb, Malcolm Coffin
The flag follows trade: an essay on the necessary interaction of military and commercial factors in state formation. *In* Ancient civilization and trade p155-209

Webb, Mary Gladys (Meredith)

About

Cavaliero, G. Romantic landscapes: Mary Webb, E. H. Young. *In* Cavaliero, G. The rural tradition in the English novel, 1900-1939 p133-56

About individual works
Precious bane

Baldwin, S. Baldwin, 1st Earl. Introduction to Precious bane by Mary Webb. *In* Praise from famous men: an anthology of introductions p10-13

Webb, Walter Prescott
Foreword to Texas county histories: a bibliography by H. Bailey Carroll. *In* Praise from famous men: an anthology of introductions p147-57

About

Frantz, J. B. Walter Prescott Webb and the South. *In* Essays on Walter Prescott Webb p3-15
Rundell, W. Webb the schoolteacher. *In* Essays on Walter Prescott Webb p95-123

About individual works
The Great Frontier

Wolfskill, G. The Webb "Great Frontier" hypothesis and international law. *In* Essays on Walter Prescott Webb p73-93

The Great Plains

Hollon, W. E. Walter Prescott Webb's arid West: four decades later. *In* Essays on Walter Prescott Webb p53-72

Webber, A. Horie-. See Horie-Webber, A.

Webber, Joan
Hamlet and the freeing of the mind. *In* English Renaissance drama p76-99
Walking on water: Milton, Stevens, and contemporary American poetry. *In* Wittreich, J. A. ed. Milton and the line of vision p231-68

Webberley, Roy
An attempt at an overview. *In* Harris, H. A. ed. Astride the two cultures p 1-19

Webby, Elizabeth
"Parents rather than critics": some early reviews of Australian literature. *In* Bards, bohemians, and bookmen p19-38

Weber, Brom
Sherwood Anderson. *In* Walcutt, C. C. ed. Seven novelists in the American naturalist tradition p168-204
Sut Lovingood. *In* Inge, M. T. ed. The frontier humorist p135-45

Weber, Carl. See Weber, Karl Maria Friedrich Ernst, Freiherr von

Weber, David J.
"Scarce more than apes." Historical roots of Anglo-American stereotypes of Mexicans. *In* Weber, D. J. ed. New Spain's far northern frontier p293-307

Weber, Eugen Joseph
Revolution? Counterrevolution? What revolution? *In* Laqueur, W. Z. ed. Fascism: a reader's guide p435-67

Weber, Karl Maria Friedrich Ernst, Freiherr von

About

Dent, E. J. Weber and his contemporaries. *In* Dent, E. J. The rise of romantic opera p145-61

Weber, Max, 1864-1920
Subjectivity and determinism. *In* Giddens, A. ed. Positivism and sociology p23-31

About

Bauman, Z. Understanding as the work of history. *In* Bauman, Z. Hermeneutics and social science p69-88
Diamond, M. Teaching about politics as a vocation. *In* Hook, S.; Kurtz, P. and Todorovich, M. eds. The ethics of teaching and scientific research p3-22
Frankel, C. Facts, values, and responsible choice. *In* Hook, S.; Kurtz, P. and Todorovich, M. eds. The ethics of teaching and scientific research p23-28
Schutz, A. Subjective and objective meaning. *In* Giddens, A. ed. Positivism and sociology p33-52

About individual works
Ancient Judaism

Petersen, D. L. Max Weber and the sociological study of ancient Israel. *In* Johnson, H. M. ed. Religious change and continuity p117-49

The Protestant ethic and the spirit of capitalism

Karp, M. The "Protestant ethic" of the Mourids of Senegal. *In* African dimensions p197-213

Weber, Ronald Edward
The political responsiveness of the American states and their local governments. *In* Rieselbach, L. N. ed. People vs. government: the responsiveness of American institutions p189-225
See also Nicgorski, W. jt. auth.

Weber, Rose-Marie
Reading. *In* Wardhaugh, R. and Brown, H. D. eds. A survey of applied linguistics p92-112

Weber, Samuel
The divaricator: remarks on Freud's Witz. *In* Glyph I p 1-27
It. *In* Glyph 4 p 1-31

Weber, Shierry M.

Aesthetic experience and self-reflection as emancipatory processes: two complementary aspects of critical theory. *In* O'Neill, J. ed. On critical theory p78-103

Webster, David L.

Warfare and the evolution of Maya civization. *In* The Origins of Maya civilization p335-71

Webster, John

About

Carson, N. John Webster: the apprentice years. *In* The Elizabethan theatre, VI p76-87

Charney, M. M. Webster vs. Middleton, or the Shakespearean yardstick in Jacobean tragedy. *In* English Renaissance drama p118-27

About individual works

The Duchess of Malfi

Champion, L. S. Webster: The white devil, The Duchess of Malfi. *In* Champion, L. S. Tragic patterns in Jacobean and Caroline drama p119-51

Hawkins, H. 'The victim's side': Webster's Duchess of Malfi and Chaucer's Clerk's tale. *In* Hawkins, H. Poetic freedom and poetic truth p26-54

Stilling, R. John Webster. *In* Stilling, R. Love and death in Renaissance tragedy p224-46

The white devil

Champion, L. S. Webster: The white devil, The Duchess of Malfi. *In* Champion, L. S. Tragic patterns in Jacobean and Caroline drama p119-51

Stilling, R. John Webster. *In* Stilling, R. Love and death in Renaissance tragedy p224-46

Bibliography

Moore, D. D. John Webster. *In* Logan, T. P. and Smith, D. S. eds. The popular school p85-104

Webster, Noah

About individual works

An American dictionary of the English language

Rollins, R. M. Words as social control: Noah Webster and the creation of the American dictionary. *In* Zenderland, L. ed. Recycling the past p50-65

Webster, Paula

Matriarchy: a vision of power. *In* Reiter, R. R. ed. Toward an anthropology of women p141-56

Webster, Richard T.

The mind of the Maker: logical construction, creative choice and the Trinity. *In* Hannay M. P. ed. As her whimsey took her p165-75

Webster's Third new international dictionary of the English language, unabridged

Quirk, R. Third international. *In* Quirk, R. The linguist and the English language p144-47

Wechsler, Herbert

The model penal code and the codification of American criminal law. *In* Crime, criminology and public policy p419-68

Weckmann-Muñoz, Luis

The Alexandrine bulls of 1493: pseudo-Asiatic documents. *In* First images of America p201-09

Wedding in Cana. See Marriage in Cana (Miracle)

Wedgwood ware

Taylor, S. Artists and philosophes as mirrored by Sèvres and Wedgwood. *In* The Artist and the writer in France p21-39

The Wee wee man (Ballad)

Lyle, E. B. The Wee wee man and Als y yod on ay Mounday. *In* Ballad studies p21-28

Weekes, Mark Kinkead- See Kinkead-Weekes, Mark

Weeks, Barney

The union contribution. *In* The Rising South v 1 p25-34

Weeks, Edward

Foreword to Good-bye, Mr Chips by James Hilton. *In* Praise from famous men: an anthology of introductions p158-61

Weeks, Jeffrey

A survey of primary sources and archives for the history of early twentieth-century English women. *In* Kanner, B. ed. The women of England p388-418

Weeks, Richard Ralph

The energy crisis and the capital shortage. *In* Benton, L. R. ed. Management for the future p307-15

Weele, Steve J. van der. See Van Der Weele, Steve J.

Weems, Mason Locke

About

Downs, R. B. History versus legend. *In* Downs, R. B. Books that changed the South p51-62

About individual works

A history of the life and death, virtues and exploits of General George Washington

Downs, R. B. History versus legend. *In* Downs, R. B. Books that changed the South p51-62

Weesner, Theodore

About individual works

The car thief

Sale, R. H. Williams, Weesner, Drabble. *In* Sale, R. H. On not being good enough p42-53

Wei dynasty, Northern. See China—History—Northern Wei dynasty, 386-534

Weick, Karl E.

The spines of leaders *In* Leadership p37-61

Weidenbaum, Murray L.

Government and the citizen. *In* Prochnow, H. V. ed. Dilemmas facing the nation p222-37

The second managerial revolution: the shift of economic decision-making from business to government. *In* Planning, politics, and the public interest p45-69

Weidlé, Wladimir

The poison of modernism. *In* Gibian, G. and Tjalsma, H. W. eds. Russian modernism p18-30

About

Stacy, R. H. Reaction. *In* Stacy, R. H. Russian literary criticism p231-55

Weigand, Hermann John

"Wandrers Sturmlied": once more with obiter dicta. *In* Creative encounter p105-16

Weiger, John George
Teaching foreign language and literature. *In* Cahn, S. M. ed. Scholars who teach p163-91

Weight (Physics)
Hahm, D. E. Weight and lightness in Aristotle and his predecessors. *In* Motion and time, space and matter p56-82

Weights and measures. See Balance; Weight (Physics)

Weigley, Russell Frank
Dissent in wars. *In* Encyclopedia of American foreign policy p253-67

Weil, Andrew T.
The marriage of the sun and moon. *In* Alternate states of consciousness p37-52

Weil, Judith

About individual works
Christopher Marlowe
Alexander, N. English drama, edited by Marie Axton and Raymond Williams and Judith Weil's Christopher Marlowe. *In* Drama and society p279-89

Weil, Simone

About
Miłosz, C. The importance of Simone Weil. *In* Miłosz, C. Emperor of the earth p85-98

About individual works
The Iliad, or, The poem of force
Chiaromonte, N. Simone Weil's Iliad. *In* Chiaromonte, N. The worm of consciousness, and other essays p183-90

Weimann, Robert
Past significance and present meaning in literary history. *In* Cohen, R. ed. New directions in literary history p43-61
Shakespeare and the popular tradition in the theater: studies in the social dimension of dramatic form and function

Contents
The Elizabethan drama
The folk play and social custom
The mimus
Moralities and interludes
The mystery cycles
Shakespeare's theater: tradition and experiment

Weimar

Intellectual life
Krumpelmann, J. T. Charles Sealsfield and Weimar. *In* The German contribution to the building of the Americas p173-80

Weinberg, Julius Rudolph
Ockham, Descartes, and Hume
Contents
The argument of Anselm and some medieval critics
Descartes on the distinction of mind and body
Fourteenth- and twentieth-century positivism
Gregory of Rimini's critique of Anselm
Hume's theory of causal belief
Kenny, Hume, and causal necessity
Logic and the laws of nature
The novelty of Hume's philosophy
Ockham's theory of scientific method
The problem of sensory cognition
Relation and qualities
The sources and nature of Descartes' cogito
Two recent criticisms of Hume
The universal affirmative

Weinberg, Kurt
The impact of ancient Greece and of French classicism on Nietzsche's concept of tragedy. *In* O'Flaherty, J. C.; Sellner, T. F. and Helm, R. M. eds. Studies in Nietzsche and the classical tradition p89-108

Weinberg, Louise
A new judicial federalism? *In* A New America? p129-41

Weinberg, Martha Wagner. See Heymann, P. B. jt. auth.

Weinberg, Samuel Kirson
Shaw-McKay theories of delinquency in cross-cultural context. *In* Delinquency, crime, and society p167-85

Weinberger, Caspar Willard
Creativity and collaboration in government—the budget process. *In* The Frontiers of knowledge p235-66

Weiner, Dora B.
Three champions of the handicapped in Revolutionary France. *In* From Parnassus p161-76

Weiner, Joseph Sidney
Physiological variation. *In* Racial variation in man p65-69

Weingartner, Charles. See Postman, N. jt. auth.

Weinreich, Max
About
Dawidowicz, L. S. Max Weinreich: scholarship of Yiddish. *In* Dawidowicz, L. S. The Jewish presence p163-76

Weinrib, Ernest Joseph
The family connections of M. Livius Drusus Libo. *In* Harvard Studies in classical philology v72 p247-78

Weinryb, Bernard D. See Weinryb, Sucher Berek

Weinryb, Sucher Berek
Reappraisals in Jewish history. *In* Salo Wittmayer Baron v2 p939-74

Weinsheimer, Joel
Jane Austen's anthropocentrism. *In* Weinsheimer, J. ed. Jane Austen today p128-41

Weinstein, Allen
About individual works
Perjury: the Hiss-Chambers case
Galbraith, J. K. Last word on the Hiss case? *In* Galbraith, J. K. Annals of an abiding liberal p303-10

Weinstein, Brian
The French West Indies: dualism from 1848 to the present. *In* Kilson, M. L. and Rotberg, R. I. eds. The African diaspora p237-79

Weinstein, Lois. See Atchley, M. W. jt. auth.

Weinstein, Marcia Esther
Menander Epitrepontes 44 and 139. *In* Harvard Studies in classical philology v75 p135-38
An unpublished papyrus fragment of new comedy. *In* Harvard Studies in classical philology v75 p131-34

Weinstein, Michael A.
C. B. Macpherson: the roots of democracy and liberalism. *In* De Crespigny, A. and Minogue, K. R. eds. Contemporary political philosophy p253-71

Weinstein, W. L.
The academic and the political. *In* Montefiore, A. ed. Neutrality and impartiality p165-95

Weintraub, Stanley
Bernard Shaw. *In* Finneran, R. J. ed. Anglo-Irish literature p167-215
Three views of the nineties. *In* Review, v 1 1979 p301-08

Weintraub, Wiktor. See Part 2 under title: For Wiktor Weintraub

Weir, Robert M.
Rebelliousness: personality development and the American Revolution in the Southern colonies. *In* The Southern experience in hte American Revolution p25-54

Weisband, Edward, and Roguly, Damir
Palestinian terrorism: violence, verbal strategy, and legitimacy. *In* International terrorism p258-319

Weisfelder, Richard F.
Lesotho: changing patterns of dependence. *In* Carter, G. M. and O'Meara, P. eds. Southern Africa: the continuing crisis p249-68

Weisheipl, James A.
The nature, scope, and classification of the sciences. *In* Lindberg, D. C. ed. Science in the Middle Ages p461-82

Weisman, Avery Danto
Is mourning necessary? *In* Anticipatory grief p14-18
The psychiatrist and the inexorable. *In* Feifel, H. [ed.] New meanings of death p107-22

Weiss, Abner
Ethics as transcendence and the contemporary world: a response to Emmanuel Levinas. *In* Modern Jewish ethics p139-52

Weiss, Michael
The castellan: the early career of Hubert De Burgh. *In* Viator: medieval and Renaissance studies v5 p235-52

Weiss, Peter

About individual works
The persecution and assassination of Jean-Paul Marat as performed by the inmates of the asylum at Charenton under the direction of the Marquis de Sade

Kauffmann, S Peter Brook. *In* Kauffmann, S. Persons of the drama p51-62
Schlueter, J. Weiss's inmates at Charenton. *In* Schlueter, J. Metafictional characters in modern drama p71-78
Simon, J. I. Madness as theater. *In* Simon, J. I. Singularities p188-91

Characters
Schlueter, J. Weiss's inmates at Charenton. *In* Schlueter, J. Metafictional characters in modern drama p71-78

Weiss, Robert Stuart
A new marital form: the marriage of uncertain duration. *In* On the making of Americans p221-33

Weiss, Seymour
Is Brezhnev a man of peace? *In* Decline of the West? George Kennan and his critics p75-78

Weiss, Theodore
QRL: hallelujah on a straw. *In* Anderson, E. and Kinzie, M. eds. The little magazine in America: a modern documentary history p164-83

Weissenberger, Klaus
Poetic rhythm and the exile situation. *In* Strelka, J. P.; Bell, R. F. and Dobson, E. eds. Protest—form—tradition p133-44

Weisskopf, Victor F.
The impact of quantum theory on modern physics. *In* Neyman, J. ed. The heritage of Copernicus: theories "pleasing to the mind" p311-31

Weissman, Ernest
Rethinking a framework for settlement planning. *In* Strategies for human settlements: habitat and environment p15-18

Weitz, Morris
Literature without philosophy: 'Antony and Cleopatra.' *In* Shakespeare survey 28 p29-36

About individual works
The role of theory in aesthetics

Binkley, T. Deciding about art. *In* Aagaard-Mogensen, L. ed. Culture and art p90-109

Weitzman, Arthur J.
Dr. Johnson's philurbanism. *In* Aeolian harps p95-109

Weitzman, Lenore J.
Legal requirements, structures, and strategies for eliminating sex discrimination in academe. *In* Women in academia p45-81

Weitzman, Martin L. See Cohen, J. S. jt. auth.

Weitzmann, Kurt
A group of early twelfth-century Sinai icons attributed to Cyprus. *In* Studies in memory of David Talbot Rice p47-63
The study of Byzantine book illumination, past, present, and future. *In* The Place of book illumination in Byzantine art p 1-60

Weizmann, Chaim, President, Israel
The Jewish people and Palestine; excerpts. *In* The Palestinians p46-50

Weizsäcker, Carl Friedrich, Freiherr von
A sceptical contribution. *In* On the creation of a just world order p111-50

Welch, Claude Emerson
The OAU and international recognition: lessons from Uganda. *In* El-Ayouty, Y. ed. The Organization of African Unity after ten years p103-17

Welch, Colin
Intellectuals have consequences. *In* Tyrrell, R. E. ed. The future that doesn't work p42-63

Welch, Holmes
Buddhism in China today. *In* Dumoulin, H. ed. Buddhism in the modern world p164-78
The fate of religion. *In* Terrill, R. ed. The China difference p117-37

Welch, James

About individual works
Winter in the blood

Larson, C. R. Survivors of the relocation. *In* Larson, C. R. American Indian fiction p133-64

Welch, Richard E.
Revolution and foreign policy. *In* Encyclopedia of American foreign policy p914-23

Welch, William Henry

About

Harvey, A. M. Teacher and distinguished pupil: William Henry Welch and George Hoyt Whipple. *In* Harvey, A. M. Adventures in medical research p39-48

Temkin, O. The European background of the young Dr Welch. *In* Temkin, O. The double face of Janus p252-60

Weldon, Roberta F.

Hawthorne's "Foot-prints on the seashore" and the literature of walking. *In* Kagle, S. E. ed. America: exploration and travel p127-35

Welfare (Economics) See Welfare economics

Welfare economics

Buchanan, J. M. The political economy of franchise in the welfare state. *In* Capitalism and freedom p52-77

Buchanan, J. M. Public goods and natural liberty. *In* The Market and the state p271-86

Lenkowsky, L. Welfare in the welfare state. *In* Tyrrell, R. E. ed. The future that doesn't work p144-66

Self, P. Techniques and values in policy decisions. *In* Royal Institute of Philosophy. Nature and conduct p298-312

Welfare work. See Public welfare

Welland, Dennis Sydney Reginald, and Walker, Ian Malcolm

American literature to 1900. *In* English Association. The year's work in English studies v53 p410-33

American literature to 1900 [another essay] *In* English Association. The year's work in English studies v54 p406-24

Wellek, René

Cleanth Brooks, critic of critics. *In* Simpson, L. P. ed. The possibilities of order: Cleanth Brooks and his work p196-229

The fall of literary history. *In* Amacher, R. E. and Lange, V. eds. New perspectives in German literary criticism p418-31

James Marshall Osborn (1906-1976) *In* Evidence in literary scholarship pv-xv

A map of contemporary criticism in Europe. *In* The Frontiers of literary criticism p11-24

The parallelism between literature and the arts. *In* Wimsatt, W. K. ed. Literary criticism: idea and act p44-65

Russian formalism. *In* Gibian, G. and Tjalsma, H. W. eds. Russian modernism p31-48

What is literature? *In* Hernadi, P. ed. What is literature? p16-23

About

Sale, R. H. René Wellek. *In* Sale, R. H. On not being good enough p129-36

Weller family

Paroissien, D. H. Charles Dickens and the Weller family. *In* Dickens Studies Annual v2 p 1-38

Welles, Chris

The eclipse of Sun Myung Moon. *In* Horowitz, I. L. ed. Science, sin, and scholarship p242-58

Welles, Orson

About

Henderson, B. The long take. *In* Nichols, B. ed. Movies and methods p314-24

About individual works

Citizen Kane

Bordwell, D. Citizen Kane. *In* Nichols, B. ed. Movies and methods p273-90

Murray, E. Citizen Kane. *In* Murray, E. Ten film classics p18-32

Truffaut, F. Orson Welles: Citizen Kane: the fragile giant. *In* Truffaut, F. The films in my life p278-85

Falstaff

Jorgens, J. J. Orson Welles's Chimes at midnight (Falstaff) *In* Jorgens, J. J. Shakespeare on film p106-21

Macbeth

Jorgens, J. J. Defining Macbeth: Schaefer, Welles, and Kurosawa. *In* Jorgens, J. J. Shakespeare on film p148-60

Mr Arkadin

Truffaut, F. Orson Welles: Confidential report. *In* Truffaut, F. The films in my life p285-87

Othello

Jorgens, J. J. Orson Welles's Othello. *In* Jorgens, J. J. Shakespeare on film p175-90

Touch of evil

Truffaut, F. Orson Welles: Touch of evil. *In* Truffaut, F. The films in my life p288-91

Wellman, Carl

A new conception of human rights. *In* Human rights p48-58

Wellmer, Albrecht

Communications and emancipation: reflections on the linguistic turn in critical theory. *In* O'Neill, J. ed. On critical theory p231-63

Wells, A. P. See Palmer, J. J. N. jt. auth.

Wells, Elizabeth J.

A statistical analysis of the prose style of Ernest Hemingway: "Big two-hearted river." *In* Benson, J. J. ed. The short stories of Ernest Hemingway: critical essays p129-35

Wells, Herbert George

About

Chernysheva, T. The folktale, Welles, and modern science fiction. *In* H. G. Wells and modern science fiction p35-47

Colmer, J. Utopian fantasy. *In* Colmer, J. Coleridge to Catch-22 p162-76

Gillie, C. The early twentieth-century novel: James, Wells and Conrad. *In* Gillie, C. Movements in English literature, 1900-1940 p24-46

Hughes, D. Y. The garden in Wells's early science fiction. *In* H. G. Wells and modern science fiction p48-69

Mudford, P. H. G. Wells. *In* Mudford, P. schafft der wilden/nacketen/grimmigen menschfresser Lauthen": the German image The art of celebration p165-79

Mullen, R. D. "I told you so": Wells's last decade, 1936-1945. *In* H. G. Wells and modern science fiction p116-25

Shepperson, G. H. G. Wells. *In* Abroad in America: Visitors to the new Nation, 1776-1914 p293-301

Suvin, D. Introduction. *In* H. G. Wells and modern science fiction p9-32

Suvin, D. Wells as the turning point of the SF tradition. *In* Suvin, D. Metamorphoses of science fiction p208-21

Vernier, J. P. Evolution as a literary theme in H. G. Wells's science fiction. *In* H. G. Wells and modern science fiction p70-89

Wells, Herbert G.—*Continued*

About individual works

Ann Veronica

Kennard, J. E. Her transitory self. *In* Kennard, J. E. Victims of convention p136-57

Men like gods

Fink, H. The shadow of Men like gods: Orwell's Coming up for air as parody. *In* H. G. Wells and modern science fiction p144-58

The time machine

Suvin, D. A grammar of form and a criticism of fact: The time machine as a structural model for science fiction. *In* H. G. Wells and modern science fiction p90-115

Suvin, D. The time machine versus Utopia as structural models for SF. *In* Suvin, D. Metamorphoses of science fiction p222-42

Tono-Bungay

Colmer, J. The modern 'condition of England' novel. *In* Colmer, J. Coleridge to Catch-22 p139-61

Influence

Komatsu, S. H. G. Wells and Japanese science fiction. *In* H. G. Wells and modern science fiction p179-90

Influence—Borges

Philmus, R. M. Borges and Wells and the labyrinths of time. *In* H. G. Wells and modern science fiction p159-78

Influence—Zamíatin

Parrinder, P. Imagining the future: Wells and Zamyatin. *In* H. G. Wells and modern science fiction p126-43

Wells, James M.
Imprint on history. *In* Review, v 1 1979 p309-19

Wells, Peter H.
Applying to college: bulldog bibs and potency myths. *In* Hurdles 48-75

Wells, Rulon S.
Criteria for semiosis. *In* Sebeok, T. A. ed. A perfusion of signs p 1-21

Metonymy and misunderstanding: an aspect of language change. *In* Current issues in linguistic theory p195-214

Wells, Stanley W.
The revenger's tragedy revived. *In* The Elizabethan theatre, VI p105-33

Shakespeare in Max Beerbohm's theatre criticism. *In* Shakespeare survey v29 p133-41

Welser family
Smith, D. ". . . beschreibung eyner Landtschafft der wilden/nacketen/grimmigen menschfresser Lauthen": the German image of America in the sixteenth century. *In* The German contribution to the building of the Americas p 1-19

Welsh, Andrew
Heritage in Pericles. *In* Shakespeare's late plays p89-113

Welsh, David
The political economy of Afrikaner nationalism. *In* Leftwich, A. ed. South Africa: economic growth and political change p249-85

The politics of white supremacy. *In* Thompson, L. M. and Butler, J. eds. Change in contemporary South Africa p51-78

Welsh, Paul
Osborne on the art of appreciation. *In* Fact, value, and perception p123-37

Welsh, Robert P.
Mondrian and theosophy. *In* Kaplan, P. and Manso, S. eds. Major European art movements, 1900-1945 p250-74

Welsh language
Jones, D. A London artist looks at contemporary Wales. *In* Jones, D. The dying Gaul, and other writings p35-40

Welsh literature (English). See English literature—Welsh authors

Welter, Rush
On studying the national mind. *In* Higham, J. and Conkin, P. K. eds. New directions in American intellectual history p64-82

Welton, Donn Curtis
Structure and genesis in Husserl's phenomenology. *In* Elliston, F. A. and McCormick, P. eds. Husserl p54-69

Welton, John M. See Alcock, A. E. jt. auth.

Welty, Eudora
The eye of the story

Contents

Arthur Mizener's The saddest story: a biography of Ford Madox Ford
E.B. White's Charlotte's web
E. M. Forster's Marianne Thornton
E. M. Forster's The life to come, and other stories
Elizabeth Bowen's Pictures and conversations
Fairy tale of the Natchez Trace
The flavor of Jackson
George R. Stewart's Names on the land
Henry Green: novelist of the imagination
The house of Willa Cather

Also in The art of Willa Cather p3-20

Ida M'Toy
"Is Phoenix Jackson's grandson really dead?"
Isak Dinesen's Last tales
Katherine Anne Porter: the eye of the story
The letters of Virginia Woolf, volume II
The little store
Looking at short stories
Must the novelist crusade?
One time, one place; excerpt
A pageant of birds
Patrick White's The cockatoos
Place in fiction
The radiance of Jane Austen
Reality in Chekhov's stories
Ross Macdonald's The underground man
S. J. Perelman's The most of S. J. Perelman; Baby, it's cold inside
Selected letters of William Faulkner
Some notes on river country
Some notes on time in fiction
A sweet devouring
Virginia Woolf's Granite and rainbow
The Western journals of Washington Irving
William Faulkner's Intruder in the dust
Words into fiction
Writing and analyzing a story

of Willa Cather p3-20

Introduction to Hanging by a thread ed. by Joan Kahn. *In* Praise from famous men: an anthology of introductions p162-68

The reading and writing of short stories. *In* May, C. E. ed. Short story theories p159-77

West Indian literature (English)

History and criticism

Le Page, R. B. Dialect in West Indian literature. *In* Baugh, E. ed. Critics on Caribbean literature p123-29

Rohlehr, G. The folk in Caribbean literature. *In* Baugh, E. ed. Critics on Caribbean literature p27-30

Walcott, D. The muse of history; excerpt from "Is Massa Day dead?" *In* Baugh, E. ed. Critics on Caribbean literature p38-43

West Indian poetry (English)

History and criticism

Moore, G. The language of West Indian poetry. *In* Baugh, E. ed. Critics on Caribbean literature p130-36

Rohlehr, G. Blues and rebellion: Edward Brathwaite's Rights of passage. *In* Baugh, E. ed. Critics on Caribbean literature p63-74

West Indies

Religion

Smith, R. T. Religion in the formation of West Indian society: Guyana and Jamaica. *In* Kilson, M. L. and Rotberg, R. I. eds. The African diaspora p312-41

West Indies, French

Social conditions

Weinstein, B. The French West Indies: dualism from 1848 to the present. *In* Kilson, M. L. and Rotberg, R. I. eds. The African diaspora p237-79

West Kootenays. See Kootenay, Canada

West Point. See United States. Military Academy, West Point

Westall, Richard

About

Bentley, G. E. A jewel in an Ethiop's ear. *In* Essick, R. N. and Pearce, D. R. eds. Blake in his time p213-40

Westbrook, Perry Dickie

Abandonment and desertion in the poetry of Robert Frost. *In* Frost: centennial essays II p291-304

Westen, Peter, and Drubel, Richard

Toward a general theory of double jeopardy. *In* The Supreme Court review, 1978 p81-169

Western Academy of Natural Sciences, Cincinnati

Shapiro, H. D. The Western Academy of Natural Sciences of Cincinnati and the structure of science in the Ohio Valley 1810-1850. *In* Oleson, A. and Brown, S. C. eds. The pursuit of knowledge in the early American Republic p219-47

Western civilization. See Civilization, Occidental

Western Europe. See Europe

Western films

History and criticism

Bazin, A. The evolution of the Western. *In* Nichols, B. ed. Movies and methods p150-57

Cawelti, J. G. The Western: a look at the evolution of a formula. *In* Cawelti, J. G. Adventure, mystery, and romance p192-259

Collins, R. Genre: a reply to Ed Buscombe. *In* Nichols, B. ed. Movies and methods p157-63

Lovell, A. The Western. *In* Nichols, B. ed. Movies and methods p164-75

Marsden, M. T. Iconology of the Western romance. *In* Browne, R. B. and Fishwick, M. W. eds. Icons of America p284-91

Warshow, R. The Westerner. *In* Denby, D. ed. Awake in the dark p248-63

Western Germany. See Germany, West

Western stories

History and criticism

Cawelti, J. G. The Western: a look at the evolution of a formula. *In* Cawelti, J. G. Adventure, mystery, and romance p192-259

Homans, P. The uses and limits of psychobiography as an approach to popular culture: the case of 'the Western.' *In* Reynolds, F. E. and Capps, D. eds. The biographical process p297-316

Marsden, M. T. Iconology of the Western romance. *In* Browne, R. B. and Fishwick, M. W. eds. Icons of America p284-91

Westfall, Carroll William

Chivalric declaration: the Palazzo Ducale in Urbino as a political statement. *In* Millon, H. A. and Nochlin, L. eds. Art and architecture in the service of politics p20-45

Westfall, Richard Samuel

The role of alchemy in Newton's career. *In* Bonelli, M. L. R. and Shea, W. R. eds. Reason, experiment, and mysticism in the scientific revolution p189-232

Westmacott, Mary, pseud. See Christie, Dame Agatha (Miller)

Westman, Robert S.

Three responses to the Copernican theory: Johannes Praetorius, Tycho Brahe, and Michael Maestlin. *In* The Copernican achievement p285-345

The Wittenberg interpretation of the Copernican theory. *In* The Nature of scientific discovery p393-429

About individual works

Three responses to the Copernican theory: Johannes Praetorius, Tycho Brahe, and Michael Maestlin

Machamer, P. K. Commentary: fictionalism and realism in 16th century astronomy. *In* The Copernican achievement p346-53

Weston, Jessie Laidlay

About

Hyman, S. E. Jessie Weston and the Forest of Broceliande. *In* Hyman, S. E. The critic's credentials p284-97

Wet-nurses

Radbill, S. X. The role of animals in infant feeding. *In* American folk medicine p21-30

The wet parade (Motion picture)

Mansfield, J. Que viva prohibition? *In* Peary, G. and Shatzkin, R. eds. The modern American novel and the movies p308-16

Wetbacks. See Mexicans in the United States

Wetherbee, Winthrop

The theme of imagination in medieval poetry and the allegorical figure "Genius." *In* Medievalia et humanistica no. 7 p45-64

Wetherell, Charles

'For these or such like reasons': John Holt's attack on Benjamin Franklin. *In* American Antiquarian Society. Proceedings v88 pt2 p251-75

Wetherill, Elizabeth, pseud. See Warner, Susan

Wexford Rebellion, 1798. See Ireland—History—Rebellion of 1798

Whalen, Philip

About

Thurley, G. The development of the new language: Wieners, Jones, McClure, Whalen, Corso. *In* Thurley, G. The American moment p187-209

Whales. See Sperm whale

Whalley, George

Jane Austen: poet. *In* Jane Austen's achievement p106-33

Picking up the thread. *In* Gold, J. ed. In the name of language! p46-70

Where are English studies going? *In* Gold, J. ed. In the name of language! p131-60

Whalum, Wendell; Baker, David Nathaniel, and Long, Richard A.

Afro-American music. *In* The Black American reference book p791-826

Wharton, Edith Newbold (Jones)

About

Howard, M. Editor's note on Edith Wharton and Gertrude Stein. *In* Howard, M. ed. Seven American women writers of the twentieth century p28-34

Milne, G. Edith Wharton. *In* Milne, G. The sense of society p116-49

Widmer, E. R. Edith Wharton: the nostalgia for innocence. *In* French, W. G. ed. The twenties p27-38

About individual works
The age of innocence

Coxe, L. O. What Edith Wharton saw in Innocence. *In* Coxe, L. O. Enabling acts p62-69

Ethan Frome

Trilling, L. The morality of inertia. *In* Trilling, L. A gathering of fugitives p34-44

The house of mirth

Stineback, D. C. "The whirling surface of existence": Edith Wharton's The house of mirth. *In* Stineback, D. C. Shifting world p87-100

What's up, doc? (Motion picture)

Kauffmann, S. What's up, doc? *In* Kauffmann, S. Living images p106-07

Wheatley, Dennis

About

Barclay, G. S. The Devil and Dennis Wheatley. *In* Barclay, G. S. Anatomy of horror: the masters of occult fiction p111-25

Wheatley, James Melville Owen

Knowledge, empiricism and ESP. *In* Wheatley, J. M. O. and Edge, H. L. eds. Philosophical dimensions of parapsychology p142-53

Notes on guessing. *In* Ludwig, J. K. ed. Philosophy and parapsychology p 245-54

The question of survival: some logical reflections. *In* Wheatley, J. M. O. and Edge, H. L. eds. Philosophical dimensions of parapsychology p252-61

Wheatley, Paul

Analecta Sino-Africana recensa. *In* Chittick, H. N. and Rotberg, R. I. eds. East Africa and the Orient p76-114

Satyānrta in Suvarṇadvīpa: from reciprocity to redistribution in ancient Southeast Asia. *In* Ancient civilization and trade p227-83

Wheatley, Phillis

About

Bell, B. W. African-American writers. *In* Emerson, E. H. ed. American literature, 1764-1789 p171-93

Bibliography

Klinkowitz, J. Early writers: Jupiter Hammon, Phillis Wheatley, and Benjamin Banneker. *In* Inge, M. T.; Duke, J. M. and Bryer, J. R. eds. Black American writers v 1 p 1-20

Wheaton, Bruce R.

Philipp Lenard and the photoelectric effect, 1889-1911. *In* Historical studies in the physical sciences v9 p299-322

Wheaton, Michael A.

Political parties and government decision-making. *In* Hayward, J. E. S. and Berki, R. N. eds. State and society in contemporary Europe p42-57

Wheeler, Douglas L.

Rebels and rebellions in Angola, 1672-1892. *In* African dimensions p81-93

Wheeler, Gerald E.

National security. *In* Encyclopedia of American foreign policy p623-34

Wheeler, Hugh

About individual works
Candide

Kauffmann, S. Candide. *In* Kauffmann, S. Persons of the drama p263-66

Wheeler, John Archibald

Man's view of the cosmos in America, 1776-1976. *In* A Time to hear and answer: essays for the Bicentennial season p59-101

Memoir. *In* Einstein p21-22

The universe as home for man. *In* The Nature of scientific discovery p261-96

Wheeler, Judith P. See Morrison, P. A. jt. auth.

Wheeler, Obadiah

About

Slater, J. A. and Caulfield, E. J. The colonial gravestone carvings of Obadiah Wheeler. *In* American Antiquarian Society. Proceedings v84 pt 1 p73-103

Wheeler, Robert A.

The county court in colonial Virginia. *In* Daniels, B. C. ed. Town and county p111-33

Wheelis, Samuel Millard

Ulrich von Hutten: representative of patriotic humanism. *In* Hoffmeister, G. ed. The Renaissance and Reformation in Germany p 111-27

Wheelwright, Philip Ellis

Mimesis and katharsis: an archetypal consideration. *In* Wimsatt, W. K. ed. Literary criticism: idea and act p110-27

Wheldon, Huw Pyrs

Creativity and collaboration in television programs. *In* The Frontiers of knowledge p177-99

Whetmore, Edward, and Hibbard, Don J.

Paradox in paradise: the icons of Waikiki. *In* Browne, R. B. and Fishwick, M. W. eds. Icons of America p241-52

Whig Party

Massachusetts

Goodman, P The politics of industrialism: Massachusetts, 1830-1870. *In* Uprooted Americans p161-207

Whig Party (Great Britain)

Kenyon, J. P. The Revolution of 1688: resistance and contract. *In* Historical perspectives p43-69

Skinner, Q. The principles and practice of opposition: the case of Bolingbroke versus Walpole. *In* Historical perspectives p93-128

Whilde, Anthony

A note on the storm petrel and corncrake. *In* Harmon, M. ed. Richard Murphy: poet of two traditions p70-72

Whipple, Fred Lawrence

Perspectives: past, present, and future. *In* Man and cosmos p169-79

Whipple, George Hoyt

About

Harvey, A. M. Teacher and distinguished pupil: William Henry Welch and George Hoyt Whipple. *In* Harvey, A. M. Adventures in medical research p39-48

Whisenand, Paul, and Ferguson, R. Fred

Controlling: the use of authority, power, and influence; excerpt from "The managing of police organizations." *In* Armstrong, T. R. and Cinnamon, K. M. eds. Power and authority in law enforcement p56-74

Whistler, James Abbott McNeill

About

Williamson, A. Whistler, Wilde and the aesthetic influence. *In* Williamson, A. Artists and writers in revolt p182-96

Whitaker, Benjamin Charles George

Minority rights and self-determination. *In* Kommers, D. P. and Loescher, G. D. eds. Human rights and American foreign policy p63-76

Whitaker, Haiganoosh, and Whitaker, Harry

Language disorders. *In* Wardhaugh, R. and Brown, H. D. eds. A survey of applied linquistics p250-74

Whitaker, Harry. See Whitaker, Haiganoosh, jt. auth.

Whitaker, Virgil Keeble

Still another source for Troilus and Cressida. *In* English Renaissance drama p100-07

Whitbeck, Caroline

Theories of sex difference. *In* Gould, C. C. and Wartofsky, M. W. eds. Women and philosophy p54-80

White, Charles Matthew Newton

The material culture of the Lunda-Lovale peoples. *In* The Occasional papers of the Rhodes-Livingstone Museum p53-70

White, Dan. See Pollock, J. C. jt. auth.

White, Diana Gould

Ovid, Heroides 16.45-46. *In* Harvard Studies in classical philology v74 p187-91

White, Elizabeth H.

Legal reform as an indicator of women's status in Muslim nations. *In* Beck, L. and Keddie, N. R. eds. Women in the Muslim world p52-68

White, Elwyn Brooks

Essays of E. B. White

Contents

Afternoon of an American boy
Bedfellows
Coon tree
Death of a pig
Don Marquis
The eye of Edna
Farewell, my lovely!
The geese
Good-bye to forty-eighth street
Here is New York
Home-coming
Letter from the East
Mr Forbush's friends
On a Florida key
Once more to the lake
The railroad
A report in January
A report in spring
The ring of time
Riposte
The St Nicholas League
The sea and the wind that blows
A slight sound at evening
Some remarks on humor
Sootfall and fallout
Unity
What do our hearts treasure?
Will Strunk
The winter of the great snows
The World of Tomorrow
The years of wonder

About

White, E. B. Afternoon of an American boy. *In* White, E. B. Essays of E. B. White p157-61

White, E. B. Once more to the lake. *In* White, E. B. Essays of E. B. White p197-202

White, E. B. The years of wonder. *In* White, E. B. Essays of E. B. White p169-96

About individual works

Charlotte's web

Cameron, E. McLuhan, youth, and literature. *In* Horn Book Magazine. Crosscurrents of criticism p98-120

Welty, E. E. B. White's Charlotte's web. *In* Welty, E. The eye of the story p203-06

The letters of E. B. White

Sheed, W. Letters of E. B. White. *In* Sheed, W. The good word & other words p248-53

White, G. Edward

The American judicial tradition

Contents

Cardozo, Learned Hand, and Frank: the dialectic of freedom and constraint
The Four Horsemen: the sources of judicial notoriety
Holmes, Brandeis, and the origins of judicial liberalism
Hughes and Stone: ironies of the Chief Justiceship
John Marshall and the genesis of tradition
John Marshall Harlan I: the precursor
Kent, Story, and Shaw: the judicial function and property rights
Miller, Bradley, Field and the reconstructed Constitution
The mosaic of the Warren Court: Frankfurter, Black, Warren, and Harlan

White, Patrick—About individual works
—*Continued*

The season at Sarsaparilla

Douglas, D. Influence and individuality: the indebtedness of Patrick White's The ham funeral and The season at Sarsaparilla to Strindberg and the German expressionist movement. *In* Bards, bohemians, and bookmen p266-80

White, Peter

The friends of Martial, Statius, and Pliny, and the dispersal of patronage. *In* Harvard Studies in classical philology v79 p265-300

White, Ray Lewis

Sherwood Anderson: fugitive pamphlets and broadsides, 1918-1940. *In* Virginia. University. Bibliographical Society. Studies in bibliography v31 p257-63

The warmth of desire: sex in Anderson's novels. *In* Anderson, D. D. ed. Sherwood Anderson: dimensions of his literary art p24-40

White, Roger M.

Can whether one proposition makes sense depend on the truth of another? (Tractatus 2.0211-2). *In* Royal Institute of Philosophy. Understanding Wittgenstein p14-29

White, Stephen

The USSR: patterns of autocracy and industrialism. *In* Brown, A. H. and Gray, J. eds. Political culture and political change in Communist states p25-65

White, William Hale

About

Cunningham, V. Was there a revolution in Tanner's Lane? *In* Cunningham, V. Everywhere spoken against p249-77

Lucas, W. J. William Hale White and the problems of deliverance. *In* Lucas, W. J. The literature of change p57-118

White collar crimes

United States

Cressey, D. R. Restraint of trade, recidivism, and delinquent neighborhoods. *In* Delinquency, crime, and society p209-38

Whitecotton, Joseph W. See Pailes, R. A. jt. auth.

Whitehall Palace

Gordon, D. J. Rubens and the Whitehall ceiling. *In* Gordon, D. J. The Renaissance imagination p24-50

Whitehead, Alfred North

About individual works

Process and reality

Kraus, E. M. Individual and society: a Whiteheadian critique of B. F. Skinner. *In* Roth, R. J. ed. Person and community p103-32

Whitehead, Alfred North, and Russell, Bertrand Russell, 3d Earl

About individual works

Principia mathematica

Fitch, F. B. Towards proving the consistency of Principia mathematica. *In* Nakhnikian, G. ed. Bertrand Russell's philosophy p 1-17

Myhill, J. The undefinability of the set of natural numbers in the ramified Principia. *In* Nakhnikian, G. ed. Bertrand Russell's philosophy p19-27

Whitehead, Evelyn Eaton

Religious images of aging: an examination of themes in contemporary Christian thought. *In* Spicker, S. F.; Woodward, K. M. and Van Tassel, D. D. eds. Aging and the elderly p37-48

Whitehead, Harriet

Reasonably fantastic: some perspectives on scientology, science fiction, and occultism. *In* Zaretsky, I. I. and Leone, M. P. eds. Religious movements in contemporary America p547-87

Whitehill, Walter Muir

Early learned societies in Boston and vicinity. *In* Oleson, A. and Brown, S. C. eds. The pursuit of knowledge in the early American Republic p151-73

Whitehurst, Robert N.

Violently jealous husbands. *In* Gross, L. ed. Sexual issues in marriage p75-84

Whiteley, Jon

Homer abandoned: a French neo-classical theme. *In* The Artist and the writer in France p40-51

Whitfield, John Humphreys

Livy>Tacitus. *In* Classical influences on European culture A.D. 1500-1700 p281-93

Whitfield, Marylin A.

Euripides, Alcestis 1092-1098. *In* Harvard Studies in classical philology v73 p105-08

Whitfield, Stephen J.

"Totalitarianism" in eclipse: the recent fate of an idea. *In* Images and ideas in American culture p60-95

Whiting, Allen Suess

Mao, China, and the Cold war. *In* The Origins of the Cold war in Asia p252-76

Whiting, Bartlett Jere

About

Staines, D. Bartlett Jere Whiting. *In* The Learned and the lewed p 1-9

Whiting, Beatrice Blyth

Changing life styles in Kenya. *In* Rossi, A. S.; Kagan, J. and Hareven, T. K. eds. The family p211-26

Contributions of anthropology to the study of gender identity, gender role, and sexual behavior. *In* Katchadourian, H. A. ed. Human sexuality p320-31

The dependency hang-up and experiments in alternative life styles. *In* Major social issues p217-26

See also Whiting, J. W. M. jt. auth.

Whiting, John

About individual works

The devils

Kauffmann, S. The devils. *In* Kauffmann, S. Persons of the drama p163-65

Whiting, John Wesley Mayhew, and Whiting, Beatrice Blyth

Aloofness and intimacy of husbands and wives: a cross-cultural study. *In* Schwartz, T. ed. Socialization as cultural communication p91-115

A strategy for psychocultural research. *In* Spindler, G. D. ed. The making of psychological anthropology p41-61

Whitman, Cedric Hubbell

ΑΗΚΥΘΙΟΝ ΑΠΩΛΕΣΕΝ. *In* Harvard Studies in classical philology v73 p109-12

Hera's anvils. *In* Harvard Studies in classical philology v74 p37-42

Sophocles: Ajax, 815-824. *In* Harvard Studies in classical philology v78 p67-69

Whitman, Cedric, H.—*Continued*

About individual works
ΑΗΚΥΘΙΟΝ ΑΠΩΛΕΣΕΝ

Henderson, J. The lekythos and Frogs 1200-1248. *In* Harvard Studies in classical philology v76 p133-43

Whitman, Walt
About
Allen, G W. Walt Whitman and Stoicism. *In* The Stoic strain in American literature p43-60

Couser, G. T. Walt Whitman: vision and revision. *In* Couser, G. T. American autobiography p80-100

Diggory, T. Armored women, naked men: Dickinson, Whitman, and their successors. *In* Gilbert, S. M. and Gubar, S. eds. Shakespeare's sisters p135-50

Hobsbaum, P. Eliot, Whitman and American tradition. *In* Hobsbaum, P. Tradition and experiment in English poetry p255-88

Kaplan, J. The "real life". *In* Studies in biography p 1-8

Kinkead-Weekes, M. Walt Whitman passes the full-stop by ... *In* An English miscellany p163-78

Morris, W. Whitman. *In* Morris, W. Earthly delights, unearthly adornments p25-32

Richardson, R. D. Whitman. *In* Richardson, R. D. Myth and literature in the American renaissance p138-64

Shapiro, K. J. The first white aboriginal. *In* Shapiro, K. J. The poetry wreck p156-74

Tanner, T. Walt Whitman's ecstatic first step. *In* Tanner, T. The reign of wonder p64-86

Tichi, C. Walt Whitman, the literatus of the new earth. *In* Tichi, C. New World, new earth p206-49

Wilbur, R. The present state of Whitman. *In* Wilbur, R. Responses p146-51

About individual works
Leaves of grass

Miller, J. E. She's here, install'd amid the kitchen ware: Walt Whitman's epic creation. *In* Miller, J. E. The American quest for a supreme fiction p30-49

Out of the cradle endlessly rocking

Trilling, L. Walt Whitman: Out of the cradle endlessly rocking. *In* Trilling, L. Prefaces to The experience of literature p254-60

Song of myself

Berryman, J. "Song of myself": intention and substance. *In* Berryman, J. The freedom of the poet p227-41

Blasing, M. K. "Walt Whitman, a kosmos, of Manhattan the son." *In* Blasing, M. K. The art of life p25-53

Bloom, H. Emerson and Whitman: the American sublime. *In* Bloom, H. Poetry and repression p235-66

Bibliography
Buckingham, W. J. Whitman and Dickinson. *in* American literary scholarship, 1977 p65-97

Fisher, M. and Buckingham, W. J. Whitman and Dickinson. *In* American literary scholarship, 1975 p83-102

Fisher, M. and Buckingham, W. J. Whitman and Dickinson [another essay] *In* American literary scholarship, 1976 p61-78

Slote, B. Whitman and Dickinson. *In* American literary scholarship, 1973 p85-98

Slote B. Whitman and Dickinson [another essay] *In* American literary scholarship, 1974 p61-74

Criticism, Textual
Bowers, F. T. The facsimile of Whitman's blue book. *In* Bowers, F. T. Essays in bibliography, text, and editing p440-46

Influence
Miller, J. E. Bards of the great idea: seekers of the supreme fiction. *In* Miller, J. E. The American quest for a supreme fiction p318-32

Miller, J. E. The care & feeding of long poems: the American epic from Barlow to Berryman. *In* Miller, J. E. The American quest for a supreme fiction p12-29

Miller, J. E. Poetic metamorphoses: Lowell and Berryman (a prologue). *In* Miller, J. E. The American quest for a supreme fiction p2-11

Influence—Berryman
Miller, J. E. The American bard/embarrassed Henry heard himself a-being: John Berryman's "Dream songs." *In* Miller, J. E. The American quest for a supreme fiction p234-75

Influence—Crane
Miller, J. E. An epic of modern consciousness: Hart Crane's "Bridge." *In* Miller, J. E. The American quest for a supreme fiction p162-99

Influence—Eliot
Miller, J. E. Personal mood transmuted into epic: T. S. Eliot's "Waste land." *In* Miller, J. E. The American quest for a supreme fiction p100-25

Influence—Ginsberg
Miller, J. E. Dreaming of the lost America of love: Allen Ginsberg's "Fall of America." *In* Miller, J. E. The American quest for a supreme fiction p276-316

Influence—Olson
Miller, J. E. Making a mappermunde to include my being: Charles Olson's Maximus poems. *In* Miller, J. E. The American quest for a supreme fiction p202-32

Influence—Pound
Miller, J. E. An epic is a poem containing history: Ezra Pound's "Cantos." *In* Miller, J. E. The American quest for a supreme fiction p68-98

Influence—Stevens
Miller, J. E. Meditations on a recipe for a modern American epic: Wallace Stevens's "Notes toward a supreme fiction." *In* Miller, J. E. The American quest for a supreme fiction p50-66

Influence—Williams
Miller, J. E. How shall I be mirror to this modernity? William Carlos Williams's "Paterson." *In* Miller, J. E. The American quest for a supreme fiction p126-61

Whitney, Geoffrey
About individual works
A choice of emblemes

Gordon, D. J. Veritas filia temporis: Hadrianus Junius and Geoffrey Whitney. *In* Gordon, D. J. The Renaissance imagination p220-32

Whitney, Geoffrey—About individual works
—A choice of emblemes—*Continued*

Tung, M. Whitney's A choice of emblemes revisited: a comparative study of the manuscript and the printed versions. *In* Virginia. University. Bibliographical Society. Studies in bibliography v29 p32-101

Whitrow, Gerald James

The role of time in cosmology. *In* Cosmology, history, and theology p159-77

Whittemore, Reed

On editing Furioso. *In* Anderson, E. and Kinzie, M. eds. The little magazine in America: a modern documentary history p100-10

Whitten, Phillip

The changing world of college textbook publishing. *In* Altbach, P. G. and McVey, S. eds. Perspectives on publishing p247-58

Whitworth, John Mckelvie

Communitarian groups and the world. *In* Wallis, R. ed. Sectarianism p117-37

Whole and parts (Philosophy)

Sacksteder, W. Spinoza on part and whole: the worm's eye view. *In* Shahan, R. W. and Biro, J. I. eds. Spinoza: new perspectives p139-59

Weiss, A. Ethics as transcendence and the contemporary world: a response to Emmanuel Levinas. *In* Modern Jewish ethics p139-52

See also Holism; Individuation; Structuralism

Whole and parts (Psychology)

Kennedy, J. M. Perception, pictures, and the etcetera principle. *In* Perception p209-26

Wholeness (Philosophy) See Whole and parts (Philosophy)

Wholeness (Psychology) See Whole and parts (Psychology)

Whorf, Benjamin Lee

An American Indian model of the universe. *In* Tedlock, D. E. and Tedlock, B. eds. Teachings from the American earth p121-29

About individual works
Language, thought and reality

Steiner, G. Whorf, Chomsky, and the student of literature. *In* Steiner, G. On difficulty and other essays p137-63

Also in Wimsatt, W. K. ed. Literary criticism: idea and act p242-62

Who's Who in America

Nevins, A. A new horizon for Who's Who: a proposal. *In* Nevins, A. Allan Nevins on history p294-301

Why (Motion picture)

Kauffmann, S. Why? *In* Kauffmann, S. Living images p155-56

Whyte, Lancelot Law

Reminiscences of Einstein; excerpt from "Focus and diversions." *In* Einstein p18-20

Whyte, William Foote

Organizational behavior research—where do we go from here? *In* Eddy, E. M. and Partridge, W. L. eds. Applied anthropology in America p129-43

Wiatt, William E.
About

Robertson, J. I. Chaplain Wiliam E. Wiatt: soldier of the cloth. *In* Rank and file p113-36

Wickens, George Michael

Introduction to the Middle East. *In* Savory, R. M. ed. Introduction to Islamic civilisation p 1-13

Khātimah. *In* Savory, R. M. ed. Introduction to Islamic civilisation p189-94

The Middle East as a world centre of science and medicine. *In* Savory, R. M. ed. Introduction to Islamic civilisation p111-19

Persian literature: an affirmation of identity. *In* Savory, R. M. ed. Introduction to Islamic civilisation p71-77

What the West borrowed from the Middle East. *In* Savory, R. M. ed. Introduction to Islamic civilisation p120-25

Wickens, James F.

Depression and the New Deal in Colorado. *In* Braeman, J.; Bremner, R. H. and Brody, D. eds. The New Deal v2 p269-310

Wicker, Brian

The story-shaped world
Contents

Beckett and the death of the God-narrator
Joyce and the sense of an ending
Lawrence and the unseen presences
Mailer and the big plot being hatched by nature
Metaphor and 'analogy'
Metaphor and 'fiction'
Metaphor and 'God'
Metaphor and 'nature'
Robbe-Grillet and the one-dimensional novel
Waugh and the narrator as dandy

Wickham, Glynne William Gladstone

From tragedy to tragi-comedy: 'King Lear' as prologue. *In* Shakespeare survey 26 p33-48

Masque and anti-masque in 'The tempest.' *In* English Association. Essays and studies, 1975 p 1-14

Medieval comic traditions and the beginnings of English comedy. *In* Howarth, W. D. ed. Comic drama p40-62

Wickramasinghe, Malalazama Martin. See Wickramasinghe, Martin

Wickramasinghe, Martin

About individual works
Gamperaliya

Gunawardana, A. J. From the village to the city: The song of the road. *In* Narasimhaiah, C. D. ed. Awakened conscience p206-15

Wickremasinghe, Martin. See Wickramasinghe, Martin

Wiclif, John. See Wycliffe, John

Wiclifites. See Lollards

Wide World Magazine

Hillier, B. The Victorian Crusoe. *In* The Saturday book 34 p135-47

Widmer, Eleanor Rackow

Edith Wharton: the nostalgia for innocence. *In* French, W. G. ed. The twenties p27-38

Widmer, Ellen

Qu Qiubai and Russian literature. *In* Modern Chinese literature in the May Fourth era p103-25

Widmer, Kingsley

The waste land and the American breakdown. *In* French, W. G. ed. The twenties p475-96

Widows

Silverman, P. R. Anticipatory grief from the perspective of widowhood. *In* Anticipatory grief p320-30

United States—Sexual behavior

Gossett, R. R. Black widows. *In* Gochros, H. L. and Gochros, J. S. eds The sexually oppressed p84-95

Widows in literature

Runte, R. The Matron of Ephesus in eighteenth-century France: the lady and the legend. *In* Studies in eighteenth-century culture v6 p361-75

Ure, P. The Widow of Ephesus: some reflections on an international comic theme. *In* Ure, P. Elizabethan and Jacobean drama p221-36

Widsið

Creed, R. P. Widsith's journey through Germanic tradition. *In* Anglo-Saxon poetry: essays in appreciation p376-87

Wiebe, Robert H.

White attitudes and Black rights from Brown to Bakke. *In* Have we overcome? Race relations since Brown p147-71

Wiechert, Ernst Emil

About individual works

Jederman, Geschichte eines Namenlosen

Klein, H. M. Projections of Everyman: the common soldier in Franconi, Wiechert and Williamson. *In* Klein, H. M. ed. The First World War in fiction p84-100

Wieland, Christoph Martin

About

Kurth-Voigt, L. E. Wieland and the French Revolution: the writings of the first year. *In* Studies in eighteenth-century culture v7 p79-103

About individual works

Agathon

Swales, M. Wieland: Agathon (1767). *In* Swales, M. The German Bildungsroman from Wieland to Hesse p38-56

Sämmtliche Werke; ed. by J. G. Gruber v47 p180-84

McCarthy, J. A. Shaftesbury and Wieland: the question of enthusiasm. *In* Studies in eighteenth-century culture v6 p79-95

Appreciation—United States

Kurth-Voight, L. E. The reception of C. M. Wieland in America. *In* The German contribution to the building of the Americas p97-133

Wieland, G. R. See Rigg, A. G. jt. auth.

Wiener, Frederick Bernays

American law for the coffee table—an impossible dream. *In* The Supreme Court review, 1975 p423-42

Wieners, John

About

Thurley, G. The development of the new language: Wieners, Jones, McClure, Whalen, Corso. *In* Thurley, G. The American moment p187-209

Wieruszowski, Helene

Jacob Burckhardt (1818-1897) and Vespasiano da Bisticci (1422-1489). *In* Philosophy and humanism p387-405

Wierzynski, Kazimierz

About

Terlecki, T. The Dionysian and Apollinian antinomy in Kazimierz Wierzyński's early poetry. *In* For Wiktor Weintraub p515-38

Wiesel, Elie

Why I write. *In* Rosenfeld, A. H. and Greenberg, I. eds. Confronting the Holocaust p200-06

About

Berenbaum, M. The additional covenant. *In* Rosenfeld, A. H. and Greenberg, I. eds. Confronting the Holocaust p169-85

Des Pres, T. The authority of silence in Elie Wiesel's art. *In* Rosenfeld, A. H. and Greenberg, I. eds. Confronting the Holocaust p49-57

Eckardt, A. R. The recantation of the covenant? *In* Rosenfeld, A. H. and Greenberg, I. eds. Confronting the Holocaust p159-68

Eitinger, L. On being a psychiatrist and a survivor. *In* Rosenfeld, A. H. and Greenberg, I. eds. Confronting the Holocaust p186-99

Fackenheim, E. L. Midrashic existence after the Holocaust: reflections occasioned by the work of Elie Wiesel. *In* Rosenfeld, A. H. and Greenberg, I. eds. Confronting the Holocaust p99-116

Lamont, R. C. Elie Wiesel: in search of a tongue. *In* Rosenfeld, A. H. and Greenberg, I. eds. Confronting the Holocaust p80-98

Langer, L. L. The divided voice: Elie Wiesel and the challenge of the Holocaust. *In* Rosenfeld, A. H. and Greenberg, I. eds. Confronting the Holocaust p31-48

Rosenfeld, A. H. The problematics of Holocaust literature. *In* Rosenfeld, A. H. and Greenberg, I. eds. Confronting the Holocaust p 1-30

Roth, J. K. Telling a tale that cannot be told: reflections on the authorship of Elie Wiesel. *In* Rosenfeld, A. H. and Greenberg, I. eds. Confronting the Holocaust p58-79

Sherwin, B. L. Wiesel's Midrash: the writings of Elie Wiesel and their relationship to Jewish tradition. *In* Rosenfeld, A. H. and Greenberg, I. eds. Confronting the Holocaust p117-32

Wiesenfarth, Joseph

Austen and Apollo. *In* Weinsheimer, J. ed. Jane Austen today p46-63

Emma: point counter point. *In* Halperin, J. ed. Jane Austen p207-20

Wife and husband. See Husband and wife

The wife's complaint. See The wife's lament (Anglo-Saxon poem)

The wife's lament (Anglo-Saxon poem)

Renoir, A. A reading context for The wife's lament. *In* Anglo-Saxon poetry: essays in appreciation p224-41

Wiggins, David

The De re 'must': a note on the logical form of essentialist claims. *In* Evans, G. L. and McDowell, J. H. eds. Truth and meaning p285-312

Locke, Butler and the stream of consciousness: and men as a natural kind. *In* Rorty, A. O. ed. The identities of persons p139-73

Wiggins, James Russell

Charting cultural priorities. *In* American Antiquarian Society. Proceedings v87 pt2 p291-97

Wigglesworth, Michael

About

Daly, R. J. Gnostics and naturalists. *In* Daly, R. J. God's altar p128-61

Wight, Willard Eugene

Colonel Cyrus B. Harkie: a troubled military career. *In* Rank and file p79-91

Wightman, Gordon. See Brown, A. H. jt. auth.

Wightman, William Persehouse Delisle

Adam Smith and the history of ideas. *In* Skinner, A. S. and Wilson, T. eds. Essays on Adam Smith p44-67

Cosmological and technological trends in the French Renaissance. *In* French Renaissance studies, 1540-70 p70-80

Wigner, Eugene Paul

Memoir. *In* Einstein p33

The scope and promise of science. *In* Hook, S.; Kurtz, P. and Todorovich, M. eds. The ethics of teaching and scientific research p131-33

Wiingaard, Jytte

Dom Juan, a reassessment in view of modern existentialism. *In* Johnson, R. B.; Neumann, E. S. and Trail, G. T. eds. Molière and the commonwealth of letters: patrimony and posterity p639-44

Wilamowitz-Moellendorff, Ulrich von

About

Calder, W. M. The correspondence of Ulrich von Wilamowitz-Moellendorff with Werner Jaeger. *in* Harvard Studies in classical philology v82 p303-07

Calder, W. M. Seventeen letters of Ulrich von Wilamowitz-Moellendorff to Eduard Fraenkel. *In* Harvard Studies in classical philology v81 p275-97

Calder, W. M. Ulrich von Wilamowitz-Moellendorff to James Loeb: two unpublished letters. *In* Illinois classical studies v2 1977 p315-32

Wilbur, Richard

Responses

Contents

The bottles become new, too
Edgar Allan Poe
Explaining the obvious
Introductions to Molière
"The narrative of Arthur Gordon Pym"
On my own work
On Robert Frost's "The gum-gatherer"
The Poe mystery case
Poetry and happiness
Poetry's debt to poetry
The present state of Whitman
Regarding places
Round about a poem of Housman's
Shakespeare's poems
A speech at a ceremony
"Sumptuous destitution"

About

Thurley, G. Benign diaspora: the landscape of Richard Wilbur. *In* Thurley, G. The American moment p35-50

Wilbur, R. On my own work. *In* Wilbur, R. Responses p115-26

About individual works
Candide

Kauffmann, S. Candide. *In* Kauffmann, S. Persons of the drama p263-66

Wilbur, Richard, tr.

About individual works
The misanthrope

Simon, J. I. Translation or adaptation? *In* From Parnassus p147-57

Wilcoxon, Reba

Rochester's sexual politics. *In* Studies in eighteenth-century culture v8 p137-49

Wild, J. P.

Textiles. *In* Strong, D. E. and Brown, D. eds. Roman crafts p167-77

Wild, Jonathan

About

Ousby, I. Thief-taking and thief-making. *In* Ousby, I. Bloodhounds of heaven p3-18

The wild child (Motion picture)

Kauffmann, S. The wild child. *In* Kauffmann, S. Living images p15-17

Wild men

White, H. V. The forms of wildness: archaeology of an idea. *In* White, H. V. Tropics of discourse p150-82

Wild strawberries (Motion picture)

Erikson, E. H. Reflections on Dr Borg's life cycle. *In* Erikson, E. H. ed. Adulthood p 1-31

Murray, E. Wild strawberries. *In* Murray, E. Ten film classics p102-20

Wildavsky, Aaron B.

Doing better and feeling worse: the political pathology of health policy. *In* Knowles, J. H. ed. Doing better and feeling worse p105-23

Wildavsky, Aaron B. and Knott, Jack

Jimmy Carter's theory of governing. *In* Burnham, W. D. and Weinberg, M. W. eds. American politics and public policy p55-76

Wilde, Alexander Wiley

Conversations among gentlemen: oligarchical democracy in Colombia. *In* The Breakdown of democratic regimes pt3 p28-81

Wilde, Oscar

About

Skilton, D. Late-Victorian choices: James, Wilde, Gissing and Moore. *In* Skilton, D. The Engish novel p178-91

Williamson, A. Whistler, Wilde and the aesthetic influence. *In* Williamson, A. Artists and writers in revolt p182-96

About individual works
The artist as critic

Connolly, C. Oscar Wilde. *In* Connolly, C. The evening colonnade p167-70

The ballad of Reading Gaol

Lodge, D. Oscar Wilde: 'The ballad of Reading Gaol.' *In* Lodge, D. The modes of modern writing p17-22

De profundis

Farrell, J. T. On Oscar Wilde's De profundis. *In* Farrell, J. T. Literary essays, 1954-1974 p16-22

Wiley, William Leon
Mary, Queen of Scots, in France. *In* Studies in the continental background of Renaissance English literature: essays presented to John L. Lievsay p133-54

Wilgus, D. K.
Irish traditional narrative songs in English: 1800-1916. *In* Casey, D. J. and Rhodes, R. E, eds. Views of the Irish peasantry, 1800-1916 p107-28

Wilhelm, James J.
Arnaut Daniel's legacy to Dante and to Pound. *In* Italian literature: roots and branches p67-83

Wilhelmsen, Frederick D.
Christianity and political philosophy
Contents
Cicero and the politics of the public orthodoxy
Donoso Cortés and the meaning of political power
Jaffa, the school of Strauss, and the Christian tradition
The limits of natural law
The natural law tradition and the American political experience
The problem of political power and the forces of darkness
Professor Voegelin and the Christian tradition
Sir John Fortescue and the English tradition

Wilhelmsen, Frederick D. and Kendall, Willmoore
Cicero and the politics of the public orthodoxy. *In* A Public philosophy reader p112-41

Wilken, Robert Louis
Wisdom and philosophy in early Christianity. *In* Aspects of wisdom in Judaism and early Christianity p143-68

Wilkes, John

About individual works
An essay on woman
Winton, C. John Wilkes and "An essay on woman." *In* A Provision of human nature p121-32

Wilkes, John William
The transformation of dissent: a review of the change from the seventeenth to the eighteenth centuries. *In* The Dissenting tradition p108-22

Wilkie, Sir David

About
Walling, W. More than sufficient room: Sir David Wilkie and the Scottish literary tradition. *In* Kroeber, K. and Walling, W. eds. Images of romanticism p107-31

Wilkins, David
The meaning of space in fourteenth-century Tuscan painting. *In* Jeffrey, D. L. ed. By things seen: reference and recognition in medieval thought p109-21

Wilkins, George

About
Prior, R. George Wilkins and the young heir. *In* Shakespeare survey v29 p33-39

About individual works
The painfull adventures of Pericles Prince of Tyre
Michael, N. C. The relationship between the 1609 quarto of Pericles and Wilkins' painful adventures. *In* Tulane studies in English v22 p51-68

Wilkins, Kay
Attitudes toward women in two eighteenth-century French periodicals. *In* Studies in eighteenth-century culture v6 p393-406

Wilkins, Mira
The oil companies in perspective. *In* Vernon, R. ed. The oil crisis p159-78

Wilkinson, Catherine
The new professionalism in the Renaissance. *In* Kostof, S. ed. The architect p124-60

Wilkinson, G. N.
Carving a social message: the Malanggans of Tabar. *In* Greenhalgh, M. and Megaw, J. V. S. eds. Art in society p227-41

Wilkinson, J. Harvie
Goss v. Lopez. *In* The Supreme Court review, 1975 p25-75

Wilkinson, Nick
The novel and a vision of the land. *In* Narasimhaiah, C. D. ed. Awakened conscience p185-94

Wilks, Ivor
Dissidence in Asante politics: two tracts from the late nineteenth century. *In* African themes p47-63

Will
Arendt, H. Conclusions. *In* Arendt, H. The life of the mind v2 p147-217
Arendt, H. The philosophers and the will. *In* Arendt, H. The life of the mind v2 p11-51
Arendt, H. Quaestio mihi factus sum: the discovery of the inner man. *In* Arendt, H. The life of the mind v2 p53-110
Arendt, H. Will and intellect. *In* Arendt, H. The life of the mind v2 p111-46
Eberhart, R. Will and psyche in poetry. *In* Eberhart, R. Of poetry and poets p59-75
See also Desire; Free will and determinism; Self

Will in literature
Cooke, M. G. The extremes of self and system. *In* Cooke, M. G. The romantic will p52-56
Cooke, M. G. The extremes of self and system: Blake's Jerusalem: a self without selfhood, a system against system. *In* Cooke, M. G. The romantic will p118-44
Cooke, M. G. The extremes of self and system: Fruitful failure and incidental cause: the will in The prelude. *In* Cooke, M. G. The romantic will p84-118
Cooke, M. G. The will in English romanticism: The question of the will. *In* Cooke, M. G. The romantic will p5-29
Cooke, M. G. The will in English romanticism: The will in romantic poetry. *In* Cooke, M. G. The romantic will p29-51
Spilka, M. On Lawrence's hostility to wilful women: the Chatterley solution. *In* Smith, A. ed. Lawrence and women p189-211
Trilling, L. Art, will, and necessity. *In* Trilling, L. The last decade p129-47

Willard, Archibald M.

About individual works
The spirit of '76
Pauly, T. H. In search of "The spirit of '76." *In* Zenderland, L. ed. Recycling the past p29-49

Willard, Barbara
The thorny paradise. *In* Blishen, E. ed. The thorny paradise p158-62

Willard, Dallas Albert
The paradox of logical psychologism: Husserl's way out. *In* Elliston, F. A. and McCormick, P. eds. Husserl p10-17

Willcock, Malcolm M.
Ad hoc invention in the Iliad. *In* Harvard Studies in classical philology v81 p41-53
Some aspects of the gods in the Iliad. *In* Wright, J. H. ed. Essays on the Iliad p58-69

Willems, Emilio
Social change on the Latin American taine frontier. *In* Miller, D. H. and Steffen, J. O. eds. The frontier p259-73

Willer, David. See Hingers, R. H. jt. auth.

Willett, Frank
African arts and the future: decay or development? *In* African themes p213-26

Willetts, Harry Taylor
Soviet Russia. *In* Auty, R. and Obolensky, D. eds. An introduction to Russian history p272-314

Willey, Basil
Arnold and religion. *In* Allott, K. ed. Matthew Arnold p236-58

Willey, Edward P.
A late-century Spectatorial essayist and his personae. *In* The Dress of words p209-18

Willey, Gordon Randolph
The classic Maya hiatus: a rehearsal for the collapse? *In* Mesoamerican archaeology p417-30
The rise of Classic Maya civilization: a Pasión Valley perspective. *In* The Origins of Maya civilization p133-57
The rise of Maya civilization: a summary view. *In* The Origins of Maya civilization p383-423

William V, called the Great, Duke of Aquitaine. See Guillaume V le Grand, comte de Poitiers et duc d'Aquitaine

William V, the Great, Duke of Aquitaine. See Guillaume V le Grand, comte de Poitiers et duc d'Aquitaine

William IX, Duke of Aquitaine, Count of Poitiers. See Guillaume IX, Duke of Aquitaine

William of Auvergne. See Guilelmus Arvernus, Bp. of Paris

William of Malmesbury

About
Thomson, R. M. William of Malmesbury and some other Western writers on Islam. *In* Medievalia et humanistica no. 6 p179-87
Thomson, R. M. William of Malmesbury and the letters of Alcuin. *In* Medievalia et humanistica no. 8 p147-61

William of Ockham. See Ockham, William

Williams, Alden. See Williams, Timothy Alden

Williams, Aubrey L.
What Pope did to Donne. *In* A Provision of human nature p111-19

About individual works
Pope's Dunciad
Connolly, C. Pope: 2. *In* Connolly, C. The evening colonnade p115-17

Williams, Aubrey Willis, 1890-

About
Salmond, J. A. Aubrey Williams: atypical New Dealer. *In* Braeman, J.; Bremner, R. H. and Brody, D. eds. The New Deal v 1 p218-45

Williams, Bernard Arthur Owen
The Makropulos case: reflections on the tedium of immortality; excerpt from "Problems of the self." *In* Donnelly, J. P. ed. Language, metaphysics, and death p228-42
Persons, character and morality. *In* Rorty, A. O. ed. The identities of persons p197-216
Politics and moral character. *In* Hampshire, S. ed. Public and private morality p55-73
Wittgenstein and idealism. *In* Royal Institute of Philosophy. Understanding Wittgenstein p76-95

Williams, Beryl J. See Epstein, Beryl (Williams)

Williams, Charles, 1886-1945

About
Barclay, G. S. Orthodox horrors: Charles Williams and William P. Blatty. *In* Barclay, G. S. Anatomy of horror: the masters of occult fiction p97-110
Sayers, D. L. Dante and Charles Williams; excerpt from "The poetry of search and the poetry of statement and other posthumous essays on literature, religion, and language." *In* Sayers, D. L. The whimsical Christian p180-204

Williams, Charles G. S.
(comp.) A bibliography of the writings of George R. Havens. *In* Literature and history in the age of ideas p387-98
The diamond of courtoisie and the dragonnades of 1681: Valincour's Vie de François de Lorraine. *In* Literature and history in the age of ideas p31-56

Williams, D. J. See Allen, R. jt. auth.; Davenport, W. A. jt. auth; McTurk, R. W. jt. auth.

Williams, David
Condorcet, feminism, and the egalitarian principle. *In* Studies in eighteenth-century culture v5 p151-63

Williams, David Anthony
G. Flaubert: Sentimental education. *In* Williams, D. A. ed. The monster in the mirror p75-101
The practice of realism. *In* Williams, D. A. ed. The monster in the mirror p257-79

Williams, David G. T.
Prosecution, discretion and the accountability of the police. *In* Crime, criminology and public policy p161-95

Williams, Douglass Price-. See Price-Williams, Douglass

Williams, Drid
The Brides of Christ. *In* Ardener, S. G. ed. Perceiving women p105-25

Williams, E. K. Duncan-. See Duncan-Williams, E. K.

Williams, George Huntston
Justin glimpsed as martyr among his Roman contemporaries. *In* The Context of contemporary theology p99-126
The Sarmatian myth sublimated in the Historia Reformationis Polonicae (1664/1685) of Stanislas Lubieniecki and related documents. *In* For Wiktor Weintraub p571-83

Williams, George Huntston, and Petersen, Rodney L.
Evangelicals: society, the state, the nation. *In* Wells, D. F. and Woodbridge, J. D. eds. The evangelicals p211-48

Williams, George Walton
Textual studies. *In* Shakespeare survey v31 p191-98

Williams, Glanmor
External influences and the upper Rio-Verde drainage basin at Los Altos, West Mexico. *In* Mesoamerican archaeology p21-50

Williams, Glanville Llewelyn
The concept of legal liberty. *In* Summers, R. S. ed. Essays in legal philosophy p121-45
Euthanasia and the physician. *In* Kohl, M. ed. Beneficent euthanasia p145-68

Williams, Glyn. See Williams, Glanmor

Williams, Gordon Willis
A version of pastoral: Virgil, Eclogue 4. *In* Woodman, T. and West, D. eds. Quality and pleasure in Latin poetry p31-46

Williams, Howard R.
Some ingredients of a national oil and gas policy. *In* Stanford legal essays p445-60

Williams, James Robert

About individual works
Cowboys out our way
Dobie, J. F. Jim Williams and "Out our way." *In* Dobie, J. F. Prefaces p112-18

Williams, John, 1664-1729

About individual works
The redeemed captive returning to Zion
Seelye, J. Providential passages: wherein a matron, a minister, a militiaman, and a madam display the cardinal points of the Puritan compass. *In* Seelye, J. Prophetic waters p279-309

Williams, John
Marcialis Pincerna and the provincial in Spanish medieval art. *In* Enggass, R. C. and Stokstad, M. eds. Hortus imaginum p29-36

Williams, John Alfred

About individual works
Captain Blackman
Sale, R. H. Williams, Weesner, Drabble. *In* Sale, R. H. On not being good enough p42-53

Son in the afternoon
Freese, P. John A. Williams, Son in the afternoon. *In* Bruck, P. ed. The Black American short story in the 20th century p141-55

Williams, John Edward

About individual works
Stoner, a novel
Howe, I. A fine novel of academic life. *In* Howe, I. Celebrations and attacks p109-11

Williams, John Whitridge

About
Harvey, A. M. John Whitridge Williams —his contributions to obstetrics. *In* Harvey, A. M. Adventures in medical research p188-94

Williams, Jonathan
Out of sight, out of conscience. *In* Morgan, R. G. ed. Kenneth Patchen: a collection of essays p59-80

Williams, Kathleen
Milton, greatest Spenserian. *In* Wittreich, J. A. ed. Milton and the line of vision p25-55

The moralized song: some Renaissance themes in Pope. *In* ELH essays for Earl R. Wasserman p285-308

Williams, Leslie Pearce
A comparative study of two nineteenth-century educational systems. *In* Science and society: past, present, and future p211-16

Williams, Lorna Valerie
The African presence in the poetry of Nicolás Guillén. *In* Crahan, M. E. and Knight, F. W. eds. Africa and the Caribbean p124-45

Williams, P. and Smith, Michael H.
The conduct of foreign policy in democratic and authoritarian states. *In* The Year book of world affairs, 1976 p205-22

Williams, Patrick Sims- See Sims-Williams, Patrick

Williams, Raymond
Communications as cultural science. *In* Bigsby, C. W. E. ed. Approaches to popular culture p27-38
The knowable community in George Eliot's novels. *In* Spilka, M. ed. Towards a poetics of fiction p225-38
Literature in society. *In* Contemporary approaches to English studies p24-37
Social environment and theatrical environment: the case of English naturalism. *In* English drama: forms and development p203-23

About
Watkins, E. Raymond Williams and Marxist criticism. *In* Watkins, E. The critical act p141-57

Williams, Raymond L.
The narrative art of Mario Vargas Llosa: two organizing principles in Pantaleón y las visitadoras. *In* Rossman, C. R. and Friedman, A. W. eds. Mario Vargas Llosa p76-87

Williams, Robin Murphy
Competing models of multiethnic and multiracial societies: an appraisal of possibilities. *In* Major social issues p50-65
Prejudice: Prejudice and society. *In* The Black American reference book p528-36
Relative deprivation. *In* The Idea of social structure p355-78

Williams, Roger
The multinational enterprise: a 1977 perspective. *In* Hayward, J. E. S. and Berki, R. N. eds. State and society in contemporary Europe p237-52
Science, technology, and the future of warfare. *In* Beaumont, R. A. and Edmonds, M. ed. War in the next decade p157-79

About
Daly, R. J. Gnostics and naturalists. *In* Daly, R. J. God's altar p128-61

Williams, Roger John, and others
A renaissance of nutritional science. *In* Sobel, D. S. ed. Ways of health p459-77

Williams, Sherley Anne
The blues roots of contemporary Afro-American poetry. *In* Fisher, D. and Stepto, R. B. eds. Afro-American literature p72-87

Williams, Stephen West

About individual works
American medical biography
Bell, W. J. Lives in medicine: the biographical dictionaries of Thacher, Williams, and Gross. *In* Bell, W. J. The colonial physician & other essays p149-68

Williams, Tennessee—About individual works—*Continued*

The milk train doesn't stop here anymore

McBride, M. Prisoners of illusion: surrealistic escape in The milk train doesn't stop here anymore. *In* Tennessee Williams: a tribute p341-48

The night of the iguana

Embrey, G. The subterranean world of The night of the iguana. *In* Tennessee Williams: a tribute p325-40

Moorman, C. The night of the iguana: a long introduction, a general essay, and no explication at all. *In* Tennessee Williams: a tribute p318-24

Orpheus descending

Matthew, D. C. C. "Towards Bethlehem": Battle of angels and Orpheus descending. *In* Tennessee Williams: a tribute p172-91

Period of adjustment

Goldfarb, A. Period of adjustment and the new Tennessee Williams. *In* Tennessee Williams: a tribute p310-17

The Red Devil battery sign

Kahn, S. M. The Red Devil battery sign: Williams' Gotterdämmerung in Vienna. *In* Tennessee Williams: a tribute p362-71

The rose tattoo

Kolin, P. C. "Sentiment and humor in equal measure": comic forms in The rose tattoo. *In* Tennessee Williams: a tribute p214-31

A streetcar named Desire

Berlin, N. Complementarity in A streetcar named Desire. *In* Tennessee Williams: a tribute p97-103

Cardullo, B. Drama of intimacy and tragedy of incomprehension: A streetcar named Desire reconsidered. *In* Tennessee Williams: a tribute p137-53

Dickson, V. A streetcar named Desire: its development through the manuscripts. *In* Tennessee Williams: a tribute p154-71

Ehrlich, A. A streetcar named Desire under the elms: a study of dramatic space in A streetcar named Desire and Desire under the elms. *In* Tennessee Williams: a tribute p126-36

Harwood, B. J. Tragedy as habit: A streetcar named Desire. *In* Tennessee Williams: a tribute p104-15

Quirino, L. The cards indicate a voyage on A streetcar named Desire. *In* Tennessee Williams: a tribute p77-96

Roderick, J. M. From "Tarantula Arms" to "Della Robbia blue": the Tennessee Williams tragicomic transit authority. *In* Tennessee Williams: a tribute p116-25

Summer and smoke

Adler, J. H. Tennessee Williams' South: the culture and the power. *In* Tennessee Williams: a tribute p30-52

The two-character play

Stamper, R. The two-character play: psychic individuation. *In* Tennessee Williams: a tribute p354-61

Characters—Brick Pollitt

May, C. E. Brick Pollitt as homo ludens: "three players of a summer game" and Cat on a hot tin roof. *In* Tennessee Williams: a tribute p277-91

Characters—Women

McGlinn, J. M. Tennessee Williams' women: illusion and reality, sexuality and love. *In* Tennessee Williams: a tribute p510-24

Tischler, N. M. A gallery of witches. *In* Tennessee Williams: a tribute p494-509

Language

Hafley, J. Abstraction and order in the language of Tennessee Williams. *In* Tennessee Williams: a tribute p735-62

Style

See Williams, Tennessee—Language

Technique

Fedder, N. J. Tennessee Williams' dramatic technique. *In* Tennessee Williams: a tribute p795-812

Williams, Terry. See Kornblum, W. S. jt. auth.

Williams, Timothy Alden

Youthful officer retirement: matrix for political action. *In* Beaumont, R. A. and Edmonds, M. eds. War in the next decade p69-88

Williams, Walter L.

Patterns in the history of the remaining Southeastern Indians, 1840-1975. *In* Williams, W. L. ed. Southeastern Indians since the removal era p193-207

Southeastern Indians before removal: prehistory, contact, decline. *In* Williams, W. L. ed. Southeastern Indians since the removal era p3-24

Williams, Walter L. and French, Thomas R.

Bibliographic essay. *In* Williams, W. L. ed. Southeastern Indians since the removal era p212-41

Williams, William Appleman

Open Door interpretation. *In* Encyclopedia of American foreign policy p703-10

About

Reintz, R. Niebuhrian irony and historical interpretation: the relationship between consensus and New Left history. *In* Canary, R. H. and Kozicki, H. J. eds. The writing of history p93-128

Williams, William Carlos

A counsel of madness. *In* Morgan, R. G. ed. Kenneth Patchen: a collection of essays p3-9

About

Johnson, K. Eliot as enemy: William Carlos Williams and The waste land. *In* French, W. G. ed. The twenties p377-86

Kenner, H. Something to say. *In* Kenner, H. A homemade world p50-90

Nemerov, H. What was modern poetry? Three lectures: Image and metaphor. *In* Nemerov, H. Figures of thought p149-66

Ober, W. B. William Carlos Williams, M.D.: physician as poet. *In* Ober, W. B. Boswell's clap and other essays p206-32

Paul, S. An introduction to William Carlos Williams. *In* Paul, S. Repossessing and renewing p179-94

Williams, William C.—About—*Continued*

Salomon, R. B. The mock-heroics of desire: some stoic personae in the work of William Carlos Williams. *In* The Stoic strain in American literature p97-112

Shapiro, K. J. William Carlos Williams: the true contemporary. *In* Shapiro, K. J. The poetry wreck p111-38

Tashjian, D. L. The Soil and Contact. *In* Tashjian, D. L. Skyscraper primitives p71-90

Tashjian, D. L. William Carlos Williams. *In* Tashjian, D. L. Skyscraper primitives p91-115

About individual works
The autobiography of William Carlos Williams

Connolly, C. William Carlos Williams: 2. *In* Connolly, C. The evening colonnade p289-92

In the American grain

Bollier, E. P. Against the American grain: William Carlos Williams between Whitman and Poe. *In* Tulane Studies in English v23 p123-42

Paterson

Blasing, M. K. Paterson: notes toward an American revolution. *In* Blasing, M. K. The art of life p117-39

Miller, J. E. How shall I be mirror to this modernity? William Carlos Williams's "Paterson." *In* Miller, J. E. The American quest for a supreme fiction p126-61

Paterson: Books I-V

Connolly, C. William Carlos Williams: 1. *In* Connolly, C. The evening colonnade p285-88

Williams, William David

Nietzsche's masks. *In* Pasley, J. M. S. ed. Nietzsche: imagery and thought p83-103

Williams, William Hayes

The significance of Jansenism in the history of the French Catholic clergy in the pre-Revolutionary era. *In* Studies in eighteenth-century culture v7 p289-306

Williams, William Proctor

Chetwin, Crooke, and the Jonson folios. *In* Virginia. University. Bibliographical Society. Studies in bibliography v30 p75-95

The revised STC. *In* Review, v 1 1979 p249-54

Williams & Wilkins Co. v. United States. *In* The Supreme Court review, 1975 p355-417

Williamsburg, Va.

Noël Hume, I. Material culture with the dirt on it: a Virginia perspective. *In* Material culture and the study of American life p21-40

Williamson, Audrey

Artists and writers in revolt

Contents

Burne-Jones: the stained-glass influence
Hunt and Millais: retreat to respectability
Industrial change and the artist
Morris: craft and saga
Rossetti and Pre-Raphaelitism
Ruskin: art and the critic
Ruskin and Morris: the Socialist legacy
Swinburne: poet and Enfant Terrible
Whistler, Wilde and the aesthetic influence

Williamson, Eugene

Guiding principles in Fielding's criticism of the critics. *In* A Provision of human nature p 1-24

Williamson, Henry

About

Cavaliero, G. The land of lost content: Henry Williamson, Llewelyn Powys. *In* Cavaliero, G. The rural tradition in the English novel, 1900-1939 p118-32

About individual works
The patriot's progress

Klein, H. M. Projections of Everyman: the common soldier in Franconi, Wiechert and Williamson. *In* Klein, H. M. ed. The First World War in fiction p84-100

Williamson, Jack

About

Stewart, A. D. Jack Williamson: the comedy of cosmic evolution. *In* Clareson, T. D. ed. Voices for the future: essays on major science fiction writers v 1 p14-43

Williamson, Jerry W.

Thackeray's mirror. *In* Tennessee Studies in literature v22 p133-53

Williamson, Joel

W. E. B. DuBois as a Hegelian. *In* What was freedom's price? p21-49

Williamson, Nancy E. See Warwick, D. P. jt. auth.

Williamson, René de Visme

British and European commentaries on the American political experience. *In* Havard, W. C. and Bernd, J. L. eds. 200 years of the Republic in retrospect p101-09

Willingham, Warren W.

Free-access colleges: where they are and whom they serve. *In* Murphy, T. P. ed. Universities in the urban crisis p197-213

Willis, Edward David

Rhetoric and responsibility in Calvin's theology. *In* The Context of contemporary theology p43-63

Willis, James Alfred

The multiples of the as. *In* Harvard Studies in classical philology v76 p233-44

Willis, Peter

The visual arts. *In* Rogers, P. ed. The eighteenth century p208-39

Willis, William Hailey

Two literary papyri in an archive from Panopolis. *In* Illinois classical studies v3, 1978 p140-51

Wills, John Elliot

Maritime China from Wang Chih to Shih Lang: themes in peripheral history. *In* Spence, J. D. and Wills, J. E. eds. From Ming to Ch'ing p201-38

Wills, Morris W.

The California-Victoria irrigation frontiers, 1880-1900. *In* The Frontier v2 p235-49

Wills

Great Britain

Phelps, W. H. Some sixteenth-century stationers' wills. *In* Virginia. University. Bibliographical Society. Studies in bibliography v32 p48-59

London

Miskimin, H. A. The legacies of London: 1259-1330. *In* The Medieval city p209-27

Wills—*Continued*

Venice

Gilbert, F. The last will of a Venetian Grand Chancellor. *In* Philosophy and humanism p502-17

Labalme, P. H. The last will of a Venetian patrician (1489) *In* Philosophy and humanism p483-501

Willson, Robert F.
Brabantio seduced: the opening scene of Othello. *In* Tennessee Studies in literature v22 p28-36

Wilmot, John, 2d Earl of Rochester. See Rochester, John Wilmot, 2d Earl of

Wilmurt, Arthur
Post-war drama in the U.S.A. *In* Nicoll, A. World drama p797-805

Wilson, Alexander
The suffrage movement. *In* Hollis, P. ed. Pressure from without p80-104

Wilson, Angus

About individual works
Émile Zola, an introductory study of his novels

Trilling, L. In defense of Zola. *In* Trilling, L. A gathering of fugitives p14-22

The neighborhood of Tombuctoo

Mudrick, M. Jane Austen. *In* Mudrick, M. The man in the machine p61-78

Wilson, Augusta Jane

About

Baym, N. Z. Augusta Evans and the waning of woman's fiction. *In* Baym, N. Z. Woman's fiction p276-99

Wilson, Bryan R.
American religious sects in Europe. *In* Bigsby, C. W. E. Superculture p107-22

Wilson, Carroll Louis
A plan for energy independence. *In* Bundy, W. P. ed. The world economic crisis p50-68

Wilson, Charles Henry
Keynes and economic history. *In* Keynes, M. ed. Essays on John Maynard Keynes p230-36

Multinationals, management, and world markets: a historical view. *In* Evolution of international management structures p193-216

Wilson, Colin
A personal response to Wuthering Heights. *In* Smith, A. ed. The art of Emily Brontë p223-37

Wilson, Constance M.
Toward a bibliography of the life and times of Mongkut, King of Thailand, 1851-1868. *In* Southeast Asian history and historiography p164-89

Wilson, Curtis A.
Rheticus, Ravetz, and the "necessity" of Copernicus' innovation. *In* The Copernican achievement p17-39

About individual works
Rheticus, Ravetz and the "necessity" of Copernicus' innovation

Bochner, S. Commentary [on Rheticus, Ravetz and the "necessity" of Copernicus' innovation]. *In* The Copernican achievement p40-48

Wilson, David B.
Concepts of physical nature: John Herschel to Karl Pearson. *In* Knoepflmacher, U. C. and Tennyson, G. B. eds. Nature and the Victorian imagination p201-15

Wilson, David Scofield
In the presence of nature

Contents

Epilogue
John Bartram, a Pennsylvania farmer
Jonathan Carver, a Connecticut Yankee
Mark Catesby, a Georgian reporter
The nature reporter in colonial American culture
The nature reporter in the presence of nature and culture

Wilson, Dudley Butler
The quadrivium in the scientific poetry of Guy Lefèvre de la Boderie. *In* French Renaissance studies, 1540-70 p95-108

Wilson, Sir Duncan
Yugoslavia and Soviet policy. *In* Kirk, G. L. and Wessell, N. H. eds. The Soviet threat p77-87

Wilson, Edmund
An analysis of Max Beerbohm; excerpt from "Classics and commercials". *In* Riewald, J. G. ed. The surprise of excellence p38-46

Introduction to In our time: stories by Ernest Hemingway. *In* Praise from famous men: an anthology of introductions p169-74

A miscellany of Max Beerbohm; excerpt from "The bit between my teeth". *In* Riewald, J. G. ed. The surprise of excellence p138-51

Mr Hemingway's dry-points. *In* Wagner, L. W. ed. Ernest Hemingway p222-23

About

Mudrick, M. Issues and answers; or, If you've tried it don't knock it. *In* Mudrick, M. Books are not life but then what is? p143-56

Sheed, W. Edmund Wilson, 1895-1972. *In* Sheed, W. The good word & other words p3-7

Trilling, L. Edmund Wilson: a backward glance. *In* Trilling, L. A gathering of fugitives p53-60

About individual works
Letters in literature and politics, 1912-1972

Howe, I. A man of letters. *In* Howe, I. Celebrations and attacks p221-24

Mudrick, M. Issues and answers; or, If you've tried it don't knock it. *In* Mudrick, M. Books are not life but then what is? p143-56

The shores of light

Trilling, L. Edmund Wilson: a backward glance. *In* Trilling, L. A gathering of fugitives p53-60

Wilson, Edward Osborne
Introduction: what is sociobiology? *In* Sociobiology and human nature p1-12

About individual works
Sociobiology: the new synthesis

Hardin, G. J. Nice guys finish last. *In* Sociobiology and human nature p183-94

Wilson, Francis
The political implications for Blacks of economic changes now taking place in South Africa. *In* Thompson, L. M. and Butler, J. eds. Change in contemporary South Africa p168-200

Wilson, H. T.
Science, critique, and criticism: the "open society" revisited. *In* O'Neill, J. ed. On critical theory p205-30

Wilson, Henry S.
Edward Wilmot Blyden. *In* Abroad in America: Visitors to the new Nation, 1776-1914 p157-66

Wilson, James Quinn
Crime and punishment in England. *In* Tyrrell, R. E. ed. The future that doesn't work p64-94
The politics of regulation. *In* McKie, J. W. ed. Social responsibility and the business predicament p135-68

Wilson, Joan Hoff
Economic foreign policy. *In* Encyclopedia of American foreign policy p281-91

Wilson, John, 1627?-1696

About individual works

Belphegor

Lesko, K. M. A rare Restoration manuscript prompt-book: John Wilson's Belphegor, corrected by the author. *In* Virginia. University. Bibliographical Society. Studies in bibliography p215-19

Manuscripts

Lesko, K. M. A rare Restoration manuscript prompt-book: John Wilson's Belphegore, corrected by the author. *In* Virginia. University. Bibliographical Society. Studies in bibliography p215-19

Wilson, John, 1785-1854

About

Hart, F. R. The other Blackwoodians. *In* Hart, F. R. The Scottish novel p53-84

Wilson, John Anthony Burgess

About

Kennard, J. E. Anthony Burgess: double vision. *In* Kennard, J. E. Number and nightmare p131-54

About individual works

A clockwork orange

Colmer, J. Science fiction. *In* Colmer, J. Coleridge to Catch-22 p 197-209
Tilton, J. W. A clockwork orange: awareness is all. *In* Tilton, J. W. Cosmic satire in the contemporary novel p21-42

Wilson, John Frederick
The historical study of marginal American religious movements. *In* Zaretsky, I. I. and Leone, M. P. eds. Religious movements in contemporary America p596-611

Wilson, John R.
ΚΑΙ ΚΕ ΤΙΣ ΩΔ' ΕΡΕΕΙ: an Homeric device in Greek literature. *In* Illinois classical studies v4, 1979 p 1-15

Wilson, Leonard G.
Science by candlelight. *In* Altholz, J. L. ed. The mind and art of Victorian England p94-106

Wilson, Leslie Nelson
La poesia negra: its background, themes and significance. *In* DeCosta, M. ed. Blacks in Hispanic literature p90-104

Wilson, Margaret Dauler
Cartesian dualism. *In* Hooker, M. ed. Descartes p197-211
Leibniz's dynamics and contingency in nature. *In* Motion and time, space and matter p264-89

Wilson, Marie G. and Sugrue, Regina
Senior companion program. *In* Home care p178-84

Wilson, Milton Thomas
Poet without a muse: Earle Birney. *In* Woodcock, G. ed. Poets and critics p26-32

Wilson, Monica
Strangers in Africa: reflections on Nyakyusa, Nguni, and Sotho evidence. *In* Shack, W. A. and Skinner, E. P. eds. Strangers in African society p51-66

Wilson, Neil Leslie
Notes on the form of certain elementary facts. *In* Fact, value, and perception p43-51

Wilson, Prince E.
Discrimination against Blacks in education: an historical perspective. *In* Social justice & preferential treatment p161-75

Wilson, Richard Bartley Joseph
The rhetoric of Patrick White's "Down at the dump." *In* Bards, bohemians, and bookmen p281-88
"The splinters of a mind make a whole piece": Patrick White's The eye of the storm. *In* Hamilton, K. G. ed. Studies in the recent Australian novel p61-83

Wilson, Robert Henry
Malory and the ballad "King Arthur's death." *In* Medievalia et humanistica no. 6 p139-49

Wilson, Robert M.

About

Kauffmann, S. Robert Wilson. *In* Kauffmann, S. Persons of the drama p41-47

About individual works

The life and times of Joseph Stalin

Simon, J. I. How many ostriches can dance on a pinhead? *In* Simon, J. I. Singularities p137-44

Wilson, Robert O. See Black, K. jt. auth.

Wilson, Theodore A.
Summit conferences. *In* Encyclopedia of American foreign policy p936-44

Wilson, Thomas
Sympathy and self-interest. *In* The Market and the state p73-99

Wilson, Woodrow, President U.S.

About

Corwin, E. S. Wilson and the Senate. *In* Corwin, E. S. Presidential power and the Constitution p28-31
Corwin, E. S. Woodrow Wilson and the Presidency. *In* Corwin, E. S. Presidential power and the Constitution p32-53
George, A. L. and George, J. L. Woodrow Wilson and Colonel House: research note; excerpt from "Woodrow Wilson and Colonel House, a personality study." *In* Kren, G. M. and Rappoport, L. H. eds. Varieties of psychohistory p111-19
Smith, D. M. The Fourteen Points. *In* Encyclopedia of American foreign policy p380-86
Trask, R. R. Missionary diplomacy. *In* Encyclopedia of American foreign policy p575-83

Wilson (Motion picture)
Knock, T. J. "History with lightning": the forgotten film Wilson. *In* Zenderland, L. ed. Recycling the past p95-115

Wilt, Judith

Frankenstein as Mystery play. *In* Levine, G. L. and Knoepflmacher, U. C. eds. The endurance of Frankenstein p31-48

Wilton-Ely, John

The rise of the professional architect in England. *In* Kostof, S. ed. The architect p180-208

Wiltz, John Edward

The Korean War and American society. *In* The Korean War p112-58

Wimbush, S. Enders. See Bennigsen, A. A. jt. auth.

Wimsatt, James I.

Chaucer and French poetry. *In* Brewer, D. S. ed. Geoffrey Chaucer p109-36

The mirror as metaphor for literature. *In* Hernadi, P. ed. What is literature? p127-40

Wimsatt, William Kurtz

Day of the leopards

Contents

Battering the object
Belinda ludens
Day of the leopards
Genesis: an argument resumed

Same as: Wimsatt, W. K. Genesis: a fallacy revisited. *In* On literary intention p116-38

I.A.R.: what to say about a poem
Imitation as freedom—1717-1798

Also in Wimsatt, W. K. ed. Literary criticism: idea and act p463-82

In praise of Rasselas: four notes (converging)

In search of verbal mimesis (supplement to "Laokoon: an oracle reconsulted")

Johnson's Dictionary
Laokoon: an oracle reconsulted
Northrop Frye: criticism as myth
Organic form: some questions about a metaphor

Genesis: a fallacy revisited. *In* On literary intention p116-38

Same as: Wimsatt, W. K. Genesis: an argument resumed. *In* Wimsatt, W. K. Day of the leopards p11-39

Images of Samuel Johnson. *In* ELH essays for Earl R. Wasserman p69-84

Rhetoric and poems: the example of Swift. *In* Martz, L. L. and Williams, A. L. eds. The author in his work p229-44

See also Riely, J. C. jt. auth

Wimsatt, William Kurtz, and Beardsley, Monroe Curtis

The concept of meter: an exercise in abstraction; excerpt from "Hateful contraries, studies in literature and criticism." *In* Gross, H. S. ed. The structure of verse p147-72

The intentional fallacy; excerpt from "The verbal icon." *In* On literary intention p 1-13

About individual works

The intentional fallacy

Cioffi, F. Intention and interpretation in criticism. *In* Margolis, J. Z. ed. Philosophy looks at the arts p307-24

Also in On literary intention p55-73

Peckham, M. The intentional? Fallacy? *In* On literary intention p139-57

Roma, E. The scope of the intentional fallacy. *In* On literary intention p74-86

Wimsatt, W. K. Genesis: a fallacy revisited. *In* On literary intention p116-38

Same as: Wimsatt, W. K. Genesis: an argument resumed. *In* Wimsatt, W. K. Day of the leopards p11-39

Winberg, Alan R.

Resource politics: the future of international markets for raw materials. *In* Orr, D. W. and Soroos, M. S. eds. The global predicament p178-94

Winch, Peter

Meaning and religious language. *In* Reason and religion p193-221

About individual works

The idea of a social science

Gellner, E. A. The new idealism—cause and meaning in the social sciences. *In* Giddens, A. ed. Positivism and sociology p129-56

Meaning and religious language

Brown, S. C. Religion and the limits of language. *In* Reason and religion p233-55

Durrant, M. Some comments on "Meaning and religious language." *In* Reason and religion p222-32

Winchilsea, Anne (Kingsmill) Finch, Countess of

About

Rogers, K. Anne Finch, Countess of Winchilsea: an Augustan woman poet. *In* Gilbert, S. M. and Gubar, S. eds. Shakespeare's sisters p32-46

Winckelmann, Johann Joachim

About

Baeumer, M. L. Simplicity and grandeur: Winckelmann, French classicism, and Jefferson. *In* Studies in eighteenth-century culture v7 p63-78

Wind from the East (Motion picture)

MacBean, J. R. Vent d'Est or Godard and Rocha at the crossroads. *In* Nichols, B. ed. Movies and methods p91-106

Windeatt, Barry

Gesture in Chaucer. *In* Medievalia et humanistica. new ser. no. 9 p143-61

Wine, Martin L.

Thomas Dekker. *In* Logan, T. P. and Smith, D. S. eds. The popular school p3-50

Wineke, Donald Richard

Hieronimo's garden and "the fall of Babylon": culture and anarchy in The Spanish tragedy. *In* Aeolian harps p65-79

Wingler, Hedwig

Aristotle in the thought of Nietzsche and Thomas Aquinas. *In* O'Flaherty, J. C.; Sellner, T. F. and Helm, R. M. eds. Studies in Nietzsche and the classical tradition p33-54

Winifred Wagner (Motion picture)

Craft, R. "Winnie" and "Uncle Wolf." *In* Craft, R. Current convictions p92-104

Winkler, J. T.

The coming corporatism. *In* Skidelsky, R. J. A. ed. The end of the Keynesian era p78-87

Winks, Robin W.

Cliché and the Canadian-American relationship. *In* Perspectives on revolution and evolution p12-21

Winner, Anthony

Character and knowledge in Dickens: the enigma of Jaggers. *In* Dickens Studies Annual v2 p100-21

Winnington-Ingram, Reginald Pepys
The musical art of Richard Brome's comedies. *In* Renaissance drama [1976] p219-42

Septem contra Thebas. *In* Yale classical studies v25 p 1-45

"To find the players and all that longeth therto": notes on the production of medieval drama in Conventry. *In* The Elizabethan theatre, V p17-4

Winsey, Valentine Rossilli
The Italian immigrant women who arrived in the United States before World War I. *In* Studies in Italian American social history p199-210

Winslow, David John
Tollgate lore from upstate New York. *In* Yoder, D. ed. American folklife p209-38

Winsor, Charlotte B.
Early Progressive schools—II. *In* Roots of open education in America p135-47

Winsor, Mary Pickard
Louis Agassiz and the species question. *In* Studies in history of biology v3 p89-117

Winstanley, Gerrard

About

George, C. H. Gerrard Winstanley: a critical retrospect. *In* The Dissenting tradition p191-225

Winter, J. M.
Introduction: The economic and social history of war. *In* War and economic development p 1-10

Select bibliography of works on war and economic development. *In* War and economic development p257-92

Winter, John Anthony
Le Corbusier's technological dilemma. *In* Walden, R. ed. The open hand p322-47

Winter

Maine

White, E. B. The winter of the great snows. *In* White, E. B. Essays of E. B. White p53-59

Winterbottom, Michael
Aldhelm's prose style and its origins. *In* Anglo-Saxon England 6 p39-76

Winternitz, Emanuel
Musical instruments and their symbolism in Western art

Contents

Appendix: images as records for the history of music
Bagpipes and hurdy-gurdies in their social setting
Bagpipes for the Lord
The curse of Pallas Athena
Early violins in paintings by Gaudenzio Ferrari and his school
The golden harpsichord and Todini's Galleria Armonica
The importance of quattrocento intarsias for the history of musical instruments
The inspired musician: a 16th-century musical pastiche
The knowledge of musical instruments as an aid to the art historian
The lira da braccio
Muses and music in a burial chapel: an interpretation of Filippino Lippi's window wall in the Cappella Strozzi
Musical archaeology of the Renaissance in Raphael's Parnassus

Musical instruments for the stage in paintings by Filippino Lippi, Piero di Cosimo, and Lorenzo Costa
On angel concerts in the 15th century: a critical approach to realism and symbolism in sacred painting
Quattrocento science in the Gubbio study
The survival of the kithara and the evolution of the English cittern: a study in morphology
The visual arts as a source for the historian of music
Peter H. Von Blanckenhagen. *In* Studies in classical art and archaeology pxi-xiv

Winters, Francis Xavier
Ethics, diplomacy, and defense. *In* Ethics and nuclear strategy? p14-50

The nuclear arms race: machine versus man. *In* Ethics and nuclear strategy? p144-55

Winters. Warrington W.
Dickens' Hard times: the lost childhood. *In* Dickens Studies Annual v2 p217-36

Winters, Yvor
The audible reading of poetry; excerpt from "The function of criticism." *In* Gross, H. S. ed. The structure of verse p129-46

Winthrop, John 1588-1649

About

Seelye, J. Return, Alpheus: Taylor, Sewall, Wolcott, and Company: some poetic fabrics from the linsey-woolsey loom. *In* Seelye, J. Prophetic waters p311-39

Winthrop, John, 1606-1676

About

Seelye, J. Glorious enterprise: Governor John Winthrop's wonderful wall. *In* Seelye, J. Prophetic waters p131-58

Seelye, J. Womb of nature: Thomas Morton and the call of the wild. *In* Seelye, J. Prophetic waters p159-85

Winton, Calhoun
John Wilkes and "An essay on woman." *In* A Provision of human nature p121-23

The theater and drama. *In* Emerson, E. H. ed. American literature, 1764-1789 p87-104

Wintun Indians
Lee, D. D. Linguistic reflection of Wintu thought; excerpt from "Freedom and culture." *In* Tedlock, D. E. and Tedlock, B. eds. Teachings from the American earth p130-40

Winwick, England

Church history

Curtis, M. H. The trials of a Puritan in Jacobean Lancashire. *In* The Dissenting tradition p78-99

Wireless telephone. See Telephone, Wireless

Wirt, William

About

Granger, B. I. William Wirt. *In* Granger, B. I. American essay serials from Franklin to Irving p182-202

Wirth, Andrzej
Brecht: writer between ideology and politics. *In* Mews, S. and Knust, H. eds. Essays on Brecht p199-208

Wisdom

Bateson, M. C. Daddy, can a scientist be wise? *In* About Bateson p57-73

Kerferd, G. B. What does the wise man know? *In* Rist, J. M. ed. The Stoics p125-36

Nemerov, H. The first county of places. *In* Images and ideas in American culture p158-68

See also Judgment

Wisdom literature

Criticism, interpretation, etc.

Fiorenza, E. S. Wisdom mythology and the Christological hymns of the New Testament. *In* Aspects of wisdom in Judaism and early Christianity p17-41

Fischel, H. A. The transformation of wisdom in the world of Midrash. *In* Aspects of wisdom in Judaism and early Christianity p67-101

Laporte, J. Philo in the tradition of Biblical wisdom literature. *In* Aspects of wisdom in Judaism and early Christianity p103-41

Pearson, B. A. Hellenistic-Jewish wisdom speculation and Paul. *In* Aspects of wisdom in Judaism and early Christianity p43-66

Robinson, J. M. Jesus as Sophos and Sophia: wisdom tradition and the Gospels. *In* Aspects of wisdom in Judaism and early Christianity p 1-16

Schoedel, W. R. Jewish wisdom and the formation of the Christian ascetic. *In* Aspects of wisdom in Judaism and early Christianity p169-99

Wilken, R. L. Wisdom and philosophy in early Christianity. *In* Aspects of wisdom in Judaism and early Christianity p143-68

Wise, David

Covert operations abroad: an overview. *In* Borosage, R. L. and Marks, J. D. eds. The CIA file p3-27

Wise, Isaac Mayer

About

Dawidowicz, L. S. When Reform was young. *In* Dawidowicz, L. S. The Jewish presence p92-104

Wise, Matthew Norton

William Thomson's mathematical route to energy conservation: a case study of the role of mathematics in concept formation. *In* Historical studies in the physical sciences v10 p49-83

Wiseberg, Laurie S. and Scoble, Harry M.

Monitoring human rights violations: the role of nongovernmental organizations. *In* Kommers, D. P. and Loescher, G. D. eds. Human rights and American foreign policy p179-208

Wiseman, Nicholas Patrick Stephen, Cardinal

About individual works

Fabiola

Sanders, A. The argument from tradition: Hypatia, Fabiola and Callista. *In* Sanders, A. The Victorian historical novel, 1840-1880 p120-48

Wiseman, Timothy Peter

Pulcher Claudius. *In* Harvard Studies in classical philology v74 p207-21

Wishart, David J.

The fur trade of the West, 1807-1840: a geographic synthesis. *In* Miller, D. H. and Steffen, J. O. eds The frontier p161-200

Wissel, Peter. See Fiorina, M. P. jt. auth.

Wister, Owen

About individual works

The Virginian

Cawelti, J. G. The Western: a look at the evolution of a formula. *In* Cawelti, J. G. Adventure, mystery, and romance p192-259

Wit and humor

Koestler, A. Humour and wit. *In* Koestler, A. Janus p109-30

See also Comedy; Comic, The; Nonsenseverses; Satire; Indian wit and humor; and similar headings

History and criticism

Gilman, E. B. Conclusion: the witness as rational amphibian. *In* Gilman, E. B. The curious perspective p232-38

Gilman, E. B. Tesauro on visual and verbal wit. *In* Gilman, E. B. The curious perspective p67-87

Juvenile literature

See Wit and humor, Juvenile

Philosophy

Chiaromonte, N. Pirandello and humor. *In* Chiaromonte, N. The worm of consciousness, and other essays p80-93

Psychology

Koestler, A. Humour and wit. *In* Koestler, A. Janus p109-30

Korsmeyer, C. W. The hidden joke: generic uses of masculine terminology. *In* Feminism and philosophy p138-53

Weber, S. The divaricator: remarks on Freud's Witz. *In* Glyph I p 1-27

White, E. B. Some remarks on humor. *In* White, E. B. Essays of E. B. White p243-49

Wit and humor, Juvenile

History and criticism

Fleischman, A. S. Laughter and children's literature. *In* Horn Book Magazine. Crosscurrents of criticism p199-204

Schwartz, A. Children, humor, and folklore. *In* Horn Book Magazine. Crosscurrents of criticism p205-16

Wit and humor, Pictorial

Gilman, E. B. The curious perspective in England. *In* Gilman, E. B. The curious perspective p50-66

Gilman, E. B. Tesauro on visual and verbal wit. *In* Gilman, E. B. The curious perspective p67-87

See also Caricature and cartoons, Comic books, strips, etc.; Italian wit and humor, Pictorial; and similar headings

Wit and social status

Garrett, G. P. Ladies in Boston have their hats: notes on WASP humor. *In* Cohen, S .B. ed. Comic relief p207-37

Witchcraft

Truzzi, M. Towards a sociology of the occult: notes on modern witchcraft. *In* Zaretsky, I. I. and Leone, M. P. eds. Religious movements in contemporary America p628-45

See also Demonology; Evil eye; Voodooism

History

Currie, E. P. Crimes without criminals: witchcraft and its control in Renaissance Europe. *In* Davis, F. J. and Stivers, R. eds. The collective definition of deviance p296-316

Witchcraft—History—*Continued*

Szasz, T. S. Society's internal enemies and protectors; excerpt from "The manufacture of madness". *In* Davis, F. J. and Stivers, R. eds. The collective definition of deviance p177-96

Africa

Brain, J. L. Witchcraft in Africa: a hardy perennial. *In* Colonialism and change p179-201

Greece

Dionisopoulas-Mass, R. The evil eye and bewitchment in a peasant village. *In* The Evil eye p42-62

New England

Demos, J. Underlying themes in the witchcraft of seventeenth century New England. *In* Mulder, J. M. and Wilson, J. F. eds. Religion in American history p86-104

Also in Vaughan, A. T. and Bremer, F. J. eds. Puritan New England p250-66

New Hampshire—Hampton

Demos, J. Witchcraft and local culture in Hampton, New Hampshire. *In* Uprooted Americans p9-42

United States

Fogelson, R. D. An analysis of Cherokee sorcery and witchcraft. *In* Hudson, C. M. ed. Four centuries of Southern Indians p113-31

Witemeyer, Hugh

Walter Savage Landor and Ezra Pound. *In* Bornstein, G. ed. Romantic and modern p147-63

Witherspoon, John

About

Meyer, D. H. John Witherspoon and the education of the public conscience. *In* Meyer, D. H. The democratic Enlightenment p182-98

Witke, Charles

Aspects of Roman poetic technique in a Carolingian Latin satiric text. *In* Illinois classical studies v4, 1979 p220-31

Witke, Roxane

The performing arts. *In* Terrill, R. ed. The China difference p263-83

Witkiewicz, Stanisław Ignacy

About

Miłosz, C. Stanisław Ignacy Witkiewicz: a writer for today? *In* Miłosz, C. Emperor of the earth p32-49

Nicoll, A. The American advent and dramatic revolution in Poland. *In* Nicoll, A. World drama p647-53

Witnesses. See Evidence, Expert; Self-incrimination

Witsen, Nicolaas Corneliszoon

About

Sebeok, T. A. The seventeenth century Cheremis: the evidence from Witsen. *In* On language, culture, and religion: in honor of Eugene A. Nida p301-14

Wittenberg, Diana

Art therapy for adolescent drug abusers. *In* Ulman, E. and Dachinger, P. eds. Art therapy p150-58

Wittenberg. Universität

History

Westman, R. S. Three responses to the Copernican theory: Johannes Praetorius, Tycho Brahe, and Michael Maestlin. *In* The Copernican achievement p285-345

Westman, R. S. The Wittenberg interpretation of the Copernican theory. *In* The Nature of scientific discovery p393-429

Wittfogel, Karl August

About

Steward, J. H. Wittfogel's irrigation hypothesis. *In* Steward, J. H. Evolution and ecology p87-99

Wittgenstein, Ludwig

About

Abrams, M. H. A note on Wittgenstein and literary criticism. *In* ELH essays for Earl R. Wasserman p248-61

Bambrough, R. How to read Wittgenstein. *In* Royal Institute of Philosophy. Understanding Wittgenstein p117-32

Cavell, S. The availability of Wittgenstein's later philosophy. *In* Cavell, S. Must we mean what we say? p44-72

Chihara, C. S. and Fodor, J. A. Operationalism and ordinary language: a critique of Wittgenstein. *In* Dunlop, C. E. M. ed. Philosophical essays on dreaming p174-204

Dilman, I. Wittgenstein on the soul. *In* Royal Institute of Philosophy. Understanding Wittgenstein p162-92

Grene, M. G. Life, death, and language: some thoughts on Wittgenstein and Derrida. *In* Grene, M. G. Philosophy in and out of Europe p142-54

Hanfling, O. Hume and Wittgenstein. *In* Royal Institute of Philosophy. Impressions of empiricism p47-65

Hughes, H. S. Philosophical prologue in England. *In* Hughes, H. S. The sea change p35-69

Jones, P. Strains in Hume and Wittgenstein. *In* Livingston, D. W. and King, J. T. eds. Hume p191-209

McGuinness, B. The Grundgedanke of the Tractatus. *In* Royal Institute of Philosophy. Understanding Wittgenstein p49-61

Riverso, E. Vico and Wittgenstein. *In* Giambattista Vico's science of humanity p263-73

Teichman, J. Wittgenstein on persons and human beings. *In* Royal Institute of Philosophy. Understanding Wittgenstein p133-48

Vesey, G. N. A. Other minds. *In* Royal Institute of Philosophy. Understanding Wittgenstein p149-61

Warnock, M. The nature of the mental image: phenomenology, Sartre and Wittgenstein. *In* Warnock, M. Imagination p131-95

Williams, B. A. O. Wittgenstein and idealism. *In* Royal Institute of Philosophy. Understanding Wittgenstein p76-95

About individual works
On certainty

Ayer, Sir A. J. Wittgenstein on certainty. *In* Royal Institute of Philosophy. Understanding Wittgenstein p226-45

Philosophical investigations

Chappell, V. C. The concept of dreaming *In* Dunlop, C. E. M. ed. Philosophical essays on dreaming p280-308

Wittgenstein Ludwig—About individual works—Philosophical investigations—*Cont.*

Chihara, C. S. What dreams are made on. *In* Dunlop, C. E. M. ed. Philosophical essays on dreaming p251-64

Curley, E. M. Dreaming and conceptual revision. *In* Dunlop, C. E. M. ed. Philosophical essays on dreaming p317-46

Lewis, P. B. Wittgenstein on seeing and interpreting. *In* Royal Institute of Philosophy. Impressions of empiricism p93-108

Mandel, R. Heidegger and Wittgenstein: a second Kantian revolution. *In* Murray, M. E. ed. Heidegger and modern philosophy p259-70

Tractatus logico-philosophicus

Kenny, A. The ghost of the Tractatus. *In* Royal Institute of Philosophy. Understanding Wittgenstein p 1-13

McGuinness, B. The Grundgedanke of the Tractatus. *In* Royal Institute of Philosophy. Understanding Wittgenstein p49-61

Morris, W. A. The centrality of language. *In* Morris, W. A. Friday's footprint p84-146

Stock, G. Wittgenstein on Russell's theory of judgment. *In* Royal Institute of Philosophy. Understanding Wittgenstein p62-75

Tractatus logico-philosophicus (2.0211-2)

White, R. M. Can whether one proposition makes sense depend on the truth of another? (Tractatus 2.0211-2). *In* Royal Institute of Philosophy. Understanding Wittgenstein p14-29

Zettel

Holborow, L. The 'prejudice in favour of psychophysical parallelism'. *In* Royal Institute of Philosophy. Understanding Wittgenstein p193-207

Ethics

Griffiths, A. P. Wittgenstein, Schopenhauer, and ethics. *In* Royal Institute of Philosophy. Understanding Wittgenstein p96-116

Influence

Grene, M. G. Philosophy in and out of Europe: The European sources of recent Anglo-American philosophy. *In* Grene, M. G. Philosophy in and out of Europe p11-23

Knowledge, Theory of

Coope, C. Wittgenstein's theory of knowledge. *In* Royal Institute of Philosophy. Understanding Wittgenstein p246-67

Logic

Rhees, R. Questions on logical inference. *In* Royal Institute of Philosophy. Understanding Wittgenstein p30-48

Wittig, Joseph Sylvester
Figural narrative in Cynewulf's Juliana. *In* Anglo-Saxon England 4 p37-55

Wittkower, Rudolf
Studies in the Italian baroque
Contents

Carlo Rainaldi and the architecture of the High Baroque in Rome
A counter-project to Bernini's Piazza S. Pietro
Francesco Borromini, his character and life
Guarini the man
Pietro da Cortona's project for reconstructing the Temple of Palestrina

Piranesi and eighteenth-century Egyptomania
Piranesi as architect
Piranesi's architectural creed
The role of classical models in Bernini's and Poussin's preparatory work
Santa Maria della Salute
A sketchbook of Filippo Juvarra at Chatsworth
The third arm of Bernini's Piazza S. Pietro
The vicissitudes of a dynastic monument: Bernini's equestrian statue of Louis XIV
Vittone's domes
Vittone's drawings in the Musée des Arts Décoratifs

Wittreich, Joseph Anthony
The new Milton criticism. *In* Review, v 1 1979 p123-64

Painted prophecies: the tradition of Blake's illuminated books. *In* Essick, R. N. and Pearce, D. R. eds. Blake in his time p101-15

"A poet amongst poets": Milton and the tradition of prophecy. *In* Wittreich, J. A. ed. Milton and the line of vision p97-142

Wives. See Diplomats' wives

Wlosok, Antonie
Amor and Cupid. *In* Harvard Studies in classical philology v79 p165-79

Wodehouse, Pelham Grenville

About

Medcalf, S. The innocence of P. G. Wodehouse. *In* Josipovici, G. ed. The modern English novel: the reader, the writer and the work p186-205

About individual works
Leave it to Psmith

Sheed, W. P. G. Wodehouse: Leave it to Psmith. *In* Sheed, W. The good word & other words p215-22

Wohl, Anthony S.
Sex and the single room: incest among the Victorian working classes. *In* Wohl, A. S. ed. The Victorian family p197-216

Wohlfahrt, Jürgen
The European Economic Community: expectations and realities of integration. *In* Hayward, J. E. A. and Berki, R. N. eds. State and society in contemporary Europe p203-17

Wohlfarth, Irving
On the messianic structure of Walter Benjamin's last reflections. *In* Glyph 3 p148-212

Wohlstetter, Albert
Nuclear threats and Allied responses in an era of negotiation. *In* The New Atlantic challenge p235-60

Wojciechowski, Jerzy A.
The ecology of knowledge. *In* Science and society: past, present, and future p258-302

Wojick, David
The structure of technological revolutions. *In* Bugliarello, G. and Doner, D. B. eds. The history and philosophy of technology p238-61

Wolcott, Roger

About individual works
Poetical meditations

Seelye, J. Return, Alpheus: Taylor, Sewall, Wolcott, and Company: some poetic fabrics from the linsey-woolsey loom. *In* Seelye, J. Prophetic waters p311-39

Wolf, Arthur Paul

Childhood association, sexual attraction, and fertility in Taiwan. *In* Zubrow, E. B. W. ed. Demographic anthropology p227-44

Marriage and adoption in northern Taiwan. *In* Social organization and the applications of anthropology p128-60

Wolf, Edwin

More books from the library of the Byrds of Westover. *In* American Antiquarian Society. Proceedings v88 pt 1 p51-82

Wolf, Eleanor P.

Northern school desegregation and residential choice. *In* The Supreme Court review, 1977 p63-85

Wolf, Ernest S.

The disconnected self. *In* Roland, A. ed. Psychoanalysis, creativity, and literature p103-14

'Irrationality' in a psychoanalytic psychology of the self. *In* Mischel, T. ed. The self p203-23

Wolf, Morris Philip

Casanova's portmanteau: Camino Real and recurring communication patterns of Tennessee Williams. *In* Tennessee Williams: a tribute p252-76

Wolf, Richard B.

The publication of Shaftesbury's Letter concerning enthusiasm. *In* Virginia. University. Bibliographical Society. Studies in bibliography v32 p237-41

Wolfe, Gary K.

The known and the unknown: structure and image in science fiction. *In* Clareson, T. D. ed. Many futures, many worlds p94-116

Wolfe, George H.

Lessons in evil: Fielding's ethics in The Champion essays. *In* A Provision of human nature p65-81

Wolfe, James

Three congregations. *In* The New religious consciousness p227-44

Wolfe, Thomas

About

Donald, M. The traditional novel. *In* Donald, M. The American novel in the twentieth century p13-72

Gray, R. J. The good farmer: some variations on a historical theme. *In* Gray, R. J. The literature of memory p106-49

Holman, C. H. The dwarf on Wolfe's shoulder. *In* Holman, C. H. Windows on the world p144-57

Holman, C. H. The Southern provincial in metropolis. *In* Holman, C. H. Windows on the world p158-67

Rubin, L. D. Thomas Wolfe once again. *In* Rubin, L. D. William Elliott shoots a bear p164-94

Wolfe, Thomas P.

The inward vocation: an essay on George Eliot's Daniel Deronda. *In* Literary monographs v8 p 1-46

Wolfe, Tom

About

Sheed, W. A fun-house mirror. *In* Sheed, W. The good word & other words p105-09

Wolff, Christian

On Euripides' Helen. *In* Harvard Studies in classical philology v77 p61-84

Wolff, Egon

About

Peden, M. S. The theater of Egon Wolff. *In* Lyday, L. F. and Woodyard, G. W. eds. Dramatists in revolt p190-201

Wolff, Gerald William

Party and section: the Senate and the Kansas-Nebraska bill. *In* Swierenga, R. P. ed. Beyond the Civil War synthesis p165-83

Wolff, John U.

Malay borrowings in Tagalog. *In* Southeast Asian history and historiography p345-67

Wolff, Philippe

The significance of the "feudal period" in the monetary history of Europe. *In* Order and innovation in the Middle Ages p77-85

Wolff, Robert Lee

Some erring children in children's literature: the world of Victorian religious strife in miniature. *In* The Worlds of Victorian fiction p295-318

Wolff, Robert Paul

The concept of social injustice. *In* Dallmayr, F. R. ed. From contract to community p65-79

There's nobody here but us persons. *In* Gould, C. C. and Wartofsky, M. W. eds. Women and philosophy p128-44

Wolfgang, Marvin E.

Crime in a birth cohort. *In* Crime, criminology and public policy p80-92

Real and perceived changes of crime and punishment. *In* A New America? p143-57

Seriousness of crime and a policy of juvenile justice. *In* Delinquency, crime, and society p267-86

Wolfle, Dael Lee

The university's compact with society. *In* Smith, B. L. R. ed. The new political economy: the public use of the private sector p109-48

Wolfram von Eschenbach

About individual works

Parzival

Tax, P. W. The Grail kingdom and Parzival's first visit: intrigue, minne, despair. *In* Medieval and Renaissance studies [1975] p20-36

Wolfskill, George

The Webb "Great Frontier" hypothesis and international law. *In* Essays on Walter Prescott Webb p73-93

Wolfson, Harry Austryn

Saadia on the semantic aspect of the problem of attribute. *In* Salo Wittmayer Baron v2 p1009-22

Wolin, Sheldon S.

Hume and conservatism. *In* Livingston, D. W. and King, J. T. eds. Hume p239-56

Wollaston, William

About

Rocke, A. J. Atoms and equivalents: the early development of the chemical atomic theory. *In* Historical studies in the physical sciences v9 p225-63

Wollaston, Mass. See Quincy, Mass.

Women—*Continued*

Legal status, laws, etc.
(Islamic law)

Coulson, N. J. and Hinchcliffe, D. Women and law reform in contemporary Islam. *In* Beck, L. and Keddie, N. R. eds. Women in the Muslim world p37-51

Mohsen, S. K. The Egyptian woman: between modernity and tradition. *In* Matthiasson, C. J. ed. Many sisters p37-58

White, E. H. Legal reform as an indicator of women's status in Muslim nations. *In* Beck, L. and Keddie, N. R. eds. Women in the Muslim world p52-68

Mental health

Gilbert, S. M. and Gubar, S. Infection in the sentence: the woman writer and the anxiety of authorship. *In* Gilbert, S. M. and Gubar, S. The madwoman in the attic p45-92

Mortality

Johansson, S. R. Sex and death in Victorian England: an examination of age-and sex-specific death rates, 1840-1910. *In* Vicinus, M. ed. A widening sphere p163-81

Occupations

See Women—Employment

Physical education

See Physical education for women

Political activity

See Women in politics

Professional education

See Professional education of women

Psychology

Adams, R. M. Religion of man, religion of woman. *In* Art, politics, and will p173-90

Blum, L. and others. Altruism and women's oppression. *In* Gould, C. C. and Wartofsky, M. W. eds. Women and philosophy p222-47

Simon, B. Hysteria and social issues. *In* Simon, B. Mind and madness in ancient Greece p238-68

Suter, B. Suicide and women. *In* Wolman, B. B. ed. Between survival and suicide p129-61

See also Femininity (Psychology)

Religious life

See Women and religion

Rights of women

See Women's rights

Sexual behavior

Gochros, J. S. Women—minority in transition. *In* Gochros, H. L. and Gochros, J. S. eds. The sexually oppressed p71-83

Johnson, M. T. Asexual and autoerotic women: two invisible groups. *In* Gochros, H. L. and Gochros, J. S. eds. The sexually oppressed p96-109

Salutin, M. Stripper morality. *In* Henslin, J. M. ed. Deviant life-styles p191-208

See also Lesbianism

Social conditions

Bettelheim, B. Growing up female. *In* Bettelheim, B. Surviving, and other essays p221-38

Blum, L. and others. Altruism and women's oppression. *In* Gould, C. C. and Wartofsky, M. W. eds. Women and philosophy p222-47

Brown, J. K. Iroquois women: an ethnohistoric note. *In* Reiter, R. R. ed. Toward an anthropology of women p235-51

Diamond, N. Collectivization, kinship, and the status of women in rural China. *In* Reiter, R. R. ed. Toward an anthropology of women p372-95

Dunn, C. M. The changing image of woman in Renaissance society and literature. *In* Springer, M. A. ed. What manner of woman p15-38

Giele, J. Z. Introduction: The status of women in comparative perspective. *In* Giele, J. Z. and Smock, A. C. eds. Women: roles and status in eight countries p 1-31

Gould, C. C. The woman question: philosophy of liberation and the liberation of philosophy. *In* Gould, C. C. and Wartofsky, M. W. eds. Women and philosophy p5-44

Greene, M. The lived world. *In* Greene, M. Landscapes of learning p213-24

Held, V. Marx, sex, and the transformation of society. *In* Gould, C. C. and Wartofsky, M. W. eds. Women and philosophy p168-84

Latt, D. J. Praising virtuous ladies: the literary image and historical reality of women in seventeenth-century England. *In* Springer, M. A. ed. What manner of woman p39-64

Marković, M. Women's liberation and human emancipation. *In* Gould, C. C. and Wartofsky, M. W. eds. Women and philosophy p145-67

Matthiasson, C. J. Conclusion. *In* Matthiasson, C. J. ed. Many sisters p421-37

Morgan, E. Women and the future. *In* Bundy, R. F. ed. Images of the future: the twenty-first century and beyond p143-51

Piliavin, J. A. On feminine self-presentation in groups. *In* Roberts, J. I. ed. Beyond intellectual sexism p138-59

Rich, A. C. The antifeminist woman. *In* Rich, A. C. On lies, secrets, and silence p69-84

Rubin, G. The traffic in women: notes on the "political economy" of sex. *In* Reiter, R. R. ed. Toward an anthropology of women p157-210

Sacks, K. Engels revisited: women, the organization of production, and private property. *In* Reiter, R. R. ed. Toward an anthropology of women p211-34

Schlegel, A. E. An overview. *In* Schlegel, A. E. ed. Sexual stratification p344-57

Schlegel, A. E. Toward a theory of sexual stratification. *In* Schlegel, A. E. ed. Sexual stratification p 1-40

Shapiro, J. Cross-cultural perspectives on sexual differentiation. *In* Katchadourian, H. A. ed. Human sexuality p269-308

Smock, A. C. Conclusion: Determinants of women's role and status. *In* Giele, J. Z. and Smock, A. C. eds. Women: roles and status in eight countries p383-421

Springer, M. A. Angels and other women in Victorian literature. *In* Springer, M. A. ed. What manner of woman p124-59

Stycos, J. M. Some minority opinions on birth control. *In* Population policy and ethics p169-96

Trilling, D. Women's liberation: Female biology in a male culture. *In* Trilling, D. We must march my darlings p189-98

Wolff, R. P. There's nobody here but us persons. *In* Gould, C. C. and Wartofsky, M. W. eds. Women and philosophy p128-44

See also Women—Legal status, laws, etc.

Women—*Continued*

Study and teaching
See Women's studies

Suffrage—Great Britain
Harper, P. H. Votes for women? A graphic episode in the battle of the sexes. *In* Millon, H. A. and Nochlin, L. eds. Art and architecture in the service of politics p150-61

Morgan, D. Women suffrage in Britain and America in the early twentieth century. *In* Allen, H. C. and Thompson, R. eds. Contrast and connection p272-95

Showalter, E. Women writers and the suffrage movement. *In* Showalter, E. A literature of their own p216-39

Suffrage—United States
Harper, P. H. Votes for women? A graphic episode in the battle of the sexes. *In* Millon, H. A. and Nochlin, L. eds. Art and architecture in the service of politics p150-61

Morgan, D. Woman suffrage in Britain and America in the early twentieth century. *In* Allen, H. C. and Thompson, R. eds. Contrast and connection p272-95

Young, L. M. Women's place in American politics: the historical perspective. *In* Havard, W. C. and Bernd, J. L. eds. 200 years of the Republic in retrospect p295-335

Suicidal behavior
Suter, B. Suicide and women. *In* Wolman, B. B. ed. Between survival and suicide p129-61

Africa
Sacks, K. Engels revisited: women, the organization of production, and private property. *In* Reiter, R. R. ed. Toward an anthropology of women p211-34

Algeria—Social conditions
Minces, J. Women in Algeria. *In* Beck, L. and Keddie, N. R. eds. Women in the Muslim world p159-71

Bangladesh
Smock, A. C. Bangladesh: a struggle with tradition and poverty. *In* Giele, J. Z. and Smock, A. C. eds. Women: roles and status in eight countries p81-126

Barbados—Social conditions
Sutton, C. and Makiesky-Barrow, S. Social inequality and sexual status in Barbados. *In* Schlegel, A. E. ed. Sexual stratification p292-325

Cambodia
Ebihara, M. M. Khmer village women in Cambodia: a happy balance. *In* Matthiasson, C. J. ed. Many sisters p305-47

Cameroon—Social conditions
Ardener, S. G. Sexual insult and female militancy. *In* Ardener, S. G. ed. Perceiving women p29-53

China
Collins, L. E. Death-profit, "evil," and the Chinese feminist movement. *In* Kren, G. M. and Rappoport, L. H. eds. Varieties of psychohistory p264-81

Diamond, N. Collectivization, kinship, and the status of women in rural China. *In* Reiter, R. R. ed. Toward an anthropology of women p372-95

Johnson, K. A. Women in China: problems of sex inequality and socioeconomic change. *In* Roberts, J. I. ed. Beyond intellectual sexism p286-319

Pillsbury, B. L. K. Being female in a Muslim minority in China. *In* Beck, L. and Keddie, N. R. eds. Women in the Muslim world p651-73

Wong, A. K. Women in China: past and present. *In* Matthiasson, C. J. ed. Many sisters p229-59

Colombia
Rubbo, A. The spread of capitalism in rural Colombia: effects on poor women. *In* Reiter, R. R. ed. Toward an anthropology of women p333-57

Dominican Republic
Brown, S. E. Love unites and hunger separates them: poor women in the Dominican Republic. *In* Reiter, R. R. ed. Toward an anthropology of women p322-32

Egypt
Mohsen, S. K. The Egyptian woman: between modernity and tradition. *In* Matthiasson, C. J. ed. Many sisters p37-58

Smock, A. C. and Youssef, N. H. Egypt: from seclusion to limited participation. *In* Giele, J. Z. and Smock, A. C. eds. Women: roles and status in eight countries p33-79

Egypt—Social conditions
al-Sayyid Marsot, A. L. The revolutionary gentlewomen in Egypt. *In* Beck, L. and Keddie, N. R. eds. Women in the Muslim world p261-76

Egypt—Cairo
el-Messiri, S. Self-images of traditional urban women in Cairo. *In* Beck, L. and Keddie, N. R. eds. Women in the Muslim world p522-40

Egypt—Fateha
Morsy, S. A. Sex differences and folk illness in an Egyptian village. *In* Beck, L. and Keddie, N. R. eds. Women in the Muslim world p599-616

England
Johansson, S. R. Sex and death in Victorian England: an examination of age-and sex-specific death rates, 1840-1910. *In* Vicinus, M. ed. A widening sphere p163-81

England—Historiography
Casey, K. Women in Norman and Plantagenet England. *In* Kanner, B. ed. The women of England p83-123

Ferguson, N. A. Women in twentieth-century England. *In* Kanner, B. ed. The women of England p345-87

Johansson, S. R. Demographic contributions to the history of Victorian women. *In* Kanner, B. ed. The women of England p259-95

Masek, R. Women in an age of transition, 1485-1714. *In* Kanner, B. ed. The women of England p138-82

Otto, P. C. Women in the mirror: using novels to study Victorian women. *In* Kanner, B. ed. The women of England p296-344

Schnorrenberg, B. B. The eighteenth-century Englishwoman. *In* Kanner, B. ed. The women of England p183-228

England—History—Sources
Dietrich, S. C. An introduction to women in Anglo-Saxon society. *In* Kanner, B. ed. The women of England p32-56

Women—*Continued*

Spain

Harding, S. Women and words in a Spanish village. *In* Reiter, R. R. ed. Toward an anthropology of women p283-308

Spain—Social conditions

Dillard, H. Women in reconquest Castile: the fueros of Sepúlveda and Cuenca. *In* Stuard, S. M. ed. Women in medieval society p71-94

Sudan—Social conditions

Fluehr-Lobban, C. Agitation for change in the Sudan. *In* Schlegel, A. E. ed. Sexual stratification p127-43

Sweden

Camerini, I. The ideal and the reality: women in Sweden. *In* Roberts, J. I. ed. Beyond intellectual sexism p277-85

Syria

Chatty, D. Changing sex roles in Bedouin society in Syria and Lebanon. *In* Beck, L. and Keddie, N. R. eds. Women in the Muslim world p399-415

Sweet, L. E. In reality: some Middle Eastern women. *In* Matthiasson, C. J. ed. Many sisters p379-97

Tunisia—Social conditions

Tessler, M. A. Women's emancipation in Tunisia. *In* Beck, L. and Keddie, N. R. eds. Women in the Muslim world p141-58

Turkey—History

Bates, U. U. Women as patrons of architecture in Turkey. *In* Beck, L. and Keddie, N. R. eds. Women in the Muslim world p245-60

Turkey—Social conditions

Cosar, F. M. Women in Turkish society. *In* Beck, L. and Keddie, N. R. eds. Women in the Muslim world p124-40

Dengler, I. C. Turkish women in the Ottoman Empire: the classical age. *In* Beck, L. and Keddie, N. R. eds. Women in the Muslim world p229-44

Good, M. J. D. A comparative perspective on women in provincial Iran and Turkey. *In* Beck, L. and Keddie, N. R. eds. Women in the Muslim world p482-500

Turkey—Hatay

Aswad, B. C. Women, class, and power: examples from the Hatay, Turkey. *In* Beck, L. and Keddie, N. R. eds. Women in the Muslim world p473-81

United States

Chmaj, B. E. Some paradox! Some irony! Changing images of American woman, 1930-1974. *In* Luedtke, L. S. ed. The study of American culture p121-76

Giele, J. Z. United States: a prolonged search for equal rights. *In* Giele, J. Z. and Smock, A. C. eds. Women: roles and status in eight countries p301-45

Mead, M. Styles of American womanhood through 200 years of history. *In* The American Revolution: a continuing commitment p55-65

United States—Economic conditions

Galbraith, J. K. The higher economic purpose of women. *In* Galbraith, J. K. Annals of an abiding liberal p36-46

United States—History

Scott, A. F. Self-portraits: three women. *In* Uprooted Americans p43-76

Ulrich, L. T. Vertuous women found: New England ministerial literature, 1668-1735. *In* Vaughan, A. T. and Bremer, F. J. eds. Puritan New England p215-31

United States—Social conditions

Schreiber, A. P. The status of women in the United States and the Scandinavian countries. *In* Claude, R. P. ed. Comparative human rights p251-66

West Africa—Economic conditions

Lewis, B. C. Economic activity and marriage among Ivoirian urban women. *In* Schlegel, A. E. ed. Sexual stratification p161-91

West Africa—Social conditions

Lewis, B. C. Economic activity and marriage among Ivoirian urban women. *In* Schlegel, A. E. ed. Sexual stratification p161-91

Yugoslavia—Social conditions

Denich, B. Women, work, and power in modern Yugoslavia. *In* Schlegel, A. E. ed. Sexual stratification p215-44

Women (in religion, folklore, etc.)

Fife, A. E. Birthmarks and psychic imprinting of babies in Utah folk medicine. *In* American folk medicine p273-83

Friedl, E. Women in contemporary Persian folktales. *In* Beck, L. and Keddie, N. R. eds. Women in the Muslim world p629-50

Women, Afro-American. See Afro-American women

Women, Bakwiri

Ardener, E. Belief and the problem of women. *In* Ardener, S. G. ed. Perceiving women p 1-17

Women, Discrimination against. See Sex discrimination against women

Women, Gypsy

Okely, J. Gypsy women: models in conflict. *In* Ardener, S. G. ed. Perceiving women p55-86

Women, Islamic. See Women, Muslim

Women, Jewish

See also Women in Judaism

Religious life

Dawidowicz, L. S. On being a woman in shul. *In* Dawidowicz, L. S. The Jewish presence p46-57

Women, Mexican American. See Mexican American women

Women, Muslim

Bates, U. U. Women as patrons of architecture in Turkey. *In* Beck, L. and Keddie, N. R. eds. Women in the Muslim world p245-60

Beck, L. Women among Qashqa'i nomadic pastoralists in Iran. *In* Beck, L. and Keddie, N. R. eds. Women in the Muslim world p351-73

Cosar, F. M. Women in Turkish society. *In* Beck, L. and Keddie, N. R. eds. Women in the Muslim world p124-40

Coulson, N. J. and Hinchcliffe, D. Women and law reform in contemporary Islam. *In* Beck, L. and Keddie, N. R. eds. Women in the Muslim world p37-51

Women authors—*Continued*

Rich, A. C. When we dead awaken: writing as re-vision. *in* Rich, A. C. On lies, secrets, and silence p33-49

Sheed, W. Men's women, women's men. *In* Sheed, W. The good word & other words p137-41

Women authors, American

Howard, M. Introduction. *In* Howard, M. ed. Seven American women writers of the twentieth century p3-27

Register, C. American feminist literary criticism: a bibliographical introduction. *In* Donovan, J. C. ed. Feminist literary criticism p 1-28

Stanford, A. Images of women in early American literature. *In* Springer, M. A. ed. What manner of woman p184-210

Women authors, English

Otto, P. C. Women in the mirror: using novels to study Victorian women. *In* Kanner, B. ed. The women of England p296-344

Spacks, P. A. M. Female identities. *In* Spacks, P. A. M. Imagining a self p57-91

Women authors, French

Brée, G. French women writers: a problematic perspective. *In* Roberts, J. I. ed. Beyond intellectual sexism p196-209

Women authors, Swedish

Ørvig, M. A collage: eight women who write books in Swedish for children. *In* Horn Book Magazine. Crosscurrents of criticism p248-60

Women college students

Rich, A. C. Taking women students seriously. *In* Rich, A. C. On lies, secrets, and silence p237-45

United States

Trilling, D. We must march my darlings: A return to the past. *In* Trilling, D. We must march my darlings p213-50

Trilling, D. We must march my darlings: Daughters of the middle class. *In* Trilling, D. We must march my darlings p272-91

Women college teachers

Rich, A. C. Claiming an education. *In* Rich, A. C. On lies, secrets, and silence p231-35

United States

Barasch, F. K. HEW, the university, and women. *In* Gross, B. R. ed. Reverse discrimination p54-65

Beach, R. I. A case history of affirmative action. *In* Women in academia p128-38

Cook, A. H. Sex discrimination at universities: an ombudsman's view. *In* Women in academia p120-27

Hochschild, A. R. Inside the clockwork of male careers. *In* Women and the power to change p47-80

Hornig, L. S. Affirmative action through affirmative attitudes. *In* Women in academia p8-19

Martin, M. L. Pedagogical arguments for preferential hiring and tenuring of women teachers in the university. *In* Gould, C. C. and Wartofsky, M. W. eds. Women and philosophy p325-33

Weitzman, L. J. Legal requirements, structures, and strategies for eliminating sex discrimination in academe. *In* Women in academia p45-81

Women criminals. See Female offenders

Women graduate students

Onat, E. S. Gladly would she learn and gladly teach: the femal graduate student. *In* Hurdles p288-317

Women in art

Chmaj, B. E. Some paradox! Some irony! Changing images of American woman, 1930-1974. *In* Luedtke, L. S. ed. The study of American culture p121-76

Fabricant, C. Binding and dressing nature's loose tresses: the ideology of Augustan landscape design. *In* Studies in eighteenth-century culture v8 p109-35

Women in Christianity

Neal, M. A. Women in religious symbolism and organization. *In* Johnson, H. M. ed. Religious change and continuity p218-50

Women in drama. See Women in literature

Women in fiction. See Women in literature

Women in Islam

Dwyer, D. H. Women, sufism, and decision-making in Moroccan Islam. *In* Beck, L. and Keddie, N. R. eds. Women in the Muslim world p585-98

Women in Judaism

Dawidowicz, L. S. On being a woman in shul. *In* Dawidowicz, L. S. The Jewish presence p46-57

Neal, M. A. Women in religious symbolism and organization. *In* Johnson, H. M. ed. Religious change and continuity p218-50

Women in literature

Accad, E. The theme of sexual oppression in the North African novel. *In* Beck, L. and Keddie, N. R. eds. Women in the Muslim world p617-28

Allen, M. Conclusion. *In* Allen, M. The necessary blankness p179-85

Allen, M. John Updike's love of "dull bovine beauty." *In* Allen, M. The necessary blankness p97-132

Allen, M. Philip Roth: when she was good she was horrid. *In* Allen, M. The necessary blankness p70-96

Allen, M. Sylvia Plath's defiance: The bell jar. *In* Allen, M. The necessary blankness p160-78

Allen, M. The terrified women of Joyce Carol Oates. *In* Allen, M. The necessary blankness p133-59

Allen, M. Women of the fabulators: Barth, Pynchon, Purdy, Kesey. *In* Allen, M. The necessary blankness p14-69

Apter, T. E. Let's hear what the male chauvinist is saying: The plumed serpent. *In* Smith, A. ed. Lawrence and women p156-77

Auerbach, N. Austen and Alcott on matriarchy: new women or new wives? *In* Spilka, M. ed. Towards a poetics of fiction p266-86

Auerbach, N. Beyond the family: idyll and inferno. *In* Auerbach, N. Communities of women p75-113

Auerbach, N. Beyond the self: the spectacle of history and a new religion. *In* Auerbach, N. Communities of women p115-57

Auerbach, N. Introduction: the communal eye. *In* Auerbach, N. Communities of women p 1-32

Auerbach, N. Waiting together: two families. *In* Auerbach, N. Communities of women p33-73

Auerbach, N. A world at war: one big Miss Brodie. *In* Auerbach, N. Communities of women p159-91

Women in literature—*Continued*

Backscheider, P. R. Defoe's women: snares and prey. *In* Studies in eighteenth-century culture v5 p103-20

Balakian, N. Bitches and sad ladies. *In* Balakian, N. Critical encounters p159-61

Balakian, N. The prophetic vogue of the anti-heroine. *In* Balakian, N. Critical encounters p36-47

Banta, M. They shall have faces, minds, and (one day) flesh: women in late nineteenth-century and early twentieth-century American literature. *In* Springer, M. A. ed. What manner of woman p235-70

Barber, P. What if Bartleby were a woman? *In* Diamond, A. and Edwards, L. R. eds. The authority of experience p212-23

Barnes, A. Female criticism: a prologue. *In* Diamond, A. and Edwards, L. R. eds. The authority of experience p 1-15

Baym, N. Z. Ann Stephens, Mary Jane Holmes, and Marion Harland. *In* Baym, N. Z. Woman's fiction p175-207

Baym, N. Z. Augusta Evans and the waning of woman's fiction. *In* Baym, N. Z. Woman's fiction p276-99

Baym, N. Z. Caroline Chesebro'. *In* Baym, N. Z. Woman's fiction p208-30

Baym, N. Z. Catharine Sedgwick and other early novelists. *In* Baym, N. Z. Woman's fiction p31-85

Baym, N. Z. E. D. E. N. Southworth and Caroline Lee Hentz. *In* Baym, N. Z. Woman's fiction p110-39

Baym, N. Z. Introduction and conclusions. *In* Baym, N. Z. Woman's fiction p11-21

Baym, N. Z. Maria McIntosh. *In* Baym, N. Z. Woman's fiction p86-109

Baym, N. Z. Other novelists of the fifties. *In* Baym, N. Z. Woman's fiction p231-75

Baym, N. Z. Portrayal of women in American literature, 1790-1870. *In* Springer, M. A. ed. What manner of woman p211-34

Baym N. Z. Susan Warner, Anna Warner, and Maria Cummins. *In* Baym, N. Z. Woman's fiction p140-74

Blau Duplessis, R. The critique of consciousness and myth in Levertov, Rich, and Rukeyser. *In* Gilbert, S. M. and Gubar, S. eds. Shakespeare's sisters p280-300

Brooks, R. A. Rousseau's antifeminism in the Lettre à d' Alembert and Emile. *In* Literature and history in the age of ideas p209-27

Carson, B. H. Winning: Katherine Anne Porter's women. *In* Diamond, A. and Edwards, L. R. eds. The authority of experience p239-56

Castile, P. Women and myth in Faulkner's first novel. *In* Tulane Studies in English, v23 p175-86

Chmaj, B. E. Some paradox! Some irony! Changing images of American woman, 1930-1974. *In* Luedtke, L. S. ed. The study of American culture p121-76

Clubb, L. G. Woman as wonder: a generic figure in Italian and Shakespearean comedy. *In* Studies in the continental background of Renaissance English literature: essays presented to John L. Lievsay p109-32

Cohen, S. B. The Jewish literary comediennes. *In* Cohen, S. B. ed. Comic relief p172-86

Collins, M. L. and Pierce, C. Holes and slime: sexism in Sartre's psychoanalysis. *In* Gould, C. C. and Wartofsky, M. W. eds. Women and philosophy p112-27

Colmer, J. Sex, the family and the new woman. *In* Colmer, J. Coleridge to Catch-22 p105-21

Crabbe, J. K. The harmony of her mind: Peacock's emancipated women. *In* Tennessee Studies in literature v23 p75-86

Dash, I. G. A penchant for Perdita on the eighteenth-century English stage. *In* Studies in eighteenth-century culture v6 p331-46

Davis, S. D. The Bostonians reconsidered. *In* Tulane Studies in English v23 p39-60

Diamond, A. Chaucer's women and woman's Chaucer. *In* Diamond, A. and Edwards, L. R. eds. The authority of experience p60-83

Donaldson, S. and Massa, A. Freedom and repression. *In* Donaldson, S. and Massa, A. American literature: nineteenth and early twentieth centuries p152-89

Dunn, C. M. The changing image of woman in Renaissance society and literature. *In* Springer, M. A. ed. What manner of woman p15-38

Dyhouse, C. The role of women: from self-sacrifice to self-awareness. *In* Lerner, L. ed. The Victorians p174-92

Eakin, P. J. Henry James and the New England consciousness: Roderick Hudson, The Europeans, Hawthorne. *In* Eakin, P. J. The New England girl p131-67

Eakin, P. J. The Howells heroine: from The lady of the Aroostook to April hopes. *In* Eakin, P. J. The New England girl p83-130

Eakin, P. J. Introduction: History and the heroines of fiction. *In* Eakin, P. J. The New England girl p3-24

Eakin, P. J. New England in extremis: The Bostonians. *In* Eakin, P. J. The New England girl p195-217

Eakin, P. J. Renunciation in New England: Harriet Beecher Stowe and The minister's wooing. *In* Eakin, P. J. The New England girl p27-48

Eakin, P. J. Self-culture: Margaret Fuller and Hawthorne's heroines. *In* Eakin, P. J. The New England girl p49-79

Eakin, P. J. The tragedy of self-culture: The portrait of a lady. *In* Eakin, P. J. The New England girl p168-94

Fabricant, C. Binding and dressing nature's loose tresses: the ideology of Augustan landscape design. *In* Studies in eighteenth-century culture v8 p109-35

Ferrante, J. M. Allegory. *In* Ferrante, J. M. Woman as image in medieval literature p37-64

Ferrante, J. M. Dante. *In* Ferrante, J. M. Woman as image in medieval literature p129-52

Ferrante, J. M. In the thirteenth century. *In* Ferrante, J. M. Woman as image in medieval literature p99-127

Fetterley, J. An American dream: "Hula, hula," said the witches. *In* Fetterley, J. The resisting reader p154-89

Fetterley, J. The Bostonians. Henry James's eternal triangle. *In* Fetterley, J. The resisting reader p101-53

Fetterley, J. A farewell to arms: Hemingway's "resentful cryptogram." *In* Fetterley, J. The resisting reader p46-71

Fetterley, J. The Great Gatsby: Fitzgerald's droit de seigneur. *In* Fetterley, J. The resisting reader p72-100

Women in literature—*Continued*

Fetterley, J. Introduction: On the politics of literature. *in* Fetterley, J. The resisting reader pxi-xxvi

Fetterley, J. Palpable designs: four American short stories: An American dream: "Rip Van Winkle." *In* Fetterley, J. The resisting reader p 1-11

Fetterley, J. Palpable designs: four American short stories: A rose for "A rose for Emily." *In* Fetterley, J. The resisting reader p34-45

Fetterley, J. Palpable designs: four American short stories: Women beware science: "The birthmark." *In* Fetterley, J. The resisting reader p22-33

Fowles, J. Hardy and the hag. *In* Butler, L. S. ed. Thomas Hardy after fifty years p28-42

Frazee, M. P. Ellen Glasgow as feminist. *In* Ellen Glasgow p167-87

Friend, B. Virgin territory: the bonds and boundaries of women in science fiction. *In* Clareson, T. D. ed. Many futures, many worlds p140-63

Fryer, J. The Great Mother: The mother-surrogates. *In* Fryer, J. The faces of Eve p153-73

Fryer, J. The Great Mother: The neglecters. *In* Fryer, J. The faces of Eve p173-82

Fryer, J. The Great Mother: The real witch-bitches. *In* Fryer, J. The faces of Eve p182-202

Fryer, J. The myth of America as New World Garden of Eden: The American Eve. *In* Fryer, J. The faces of Eve p8-26

Fryer, J. The new woman: The new myth of Atalanta. *In* Fryer, J. The faces of Eve p203-08

Fryer, J. The new woman: The unnatural lady reformers of Boston. *In* Fryer, J. The faces of Eve p220-34

Gasiorowska, X. Solzhenitsyn's women. *In* Dunlop, J. B.; Haugh, R. and Klimoff, A. eds. Aleksandr Solzhenitsyn: critical essays and documentary materials 2d ed. p117-28

Gelpi A. Emily Dickinson and the Deerslayer: the dilemma of the women poet in America. *In* Gilbert, S. M. and Gubar, S. eds. Shakespeare's sisters p122-34

Gilbert, S. M. and Gubar, S. Infection in the sentence: the woman writer and the anxiety of authorship. *In* Gilbert, S. M. and Gubar, S. The madwoman in the attic p45-92

Gilbert, S. M. and Gubar, S. The queen's looking glass: female creativity, male images of women, and the metaphor of literary paternity. *In* Gilbert, S. M. and Gubar, S. The madwoman in the attic p3-44

Gottlieb, L. C. and Keitner, W. Colonialism as metaphor and experience in 'The grass is singing' and 'Surfacing.' *In* Narasimhaiah, C. D. ed. Awakened conscience p307-14

Hail, S. J. Henry James and the bluestockings: satire and morality in The Bostonians. *In* Aeolian harps p207-25

Hawkins, H. 'The victim's side': Webster's Duchess of Malfi and Chaucer's Clerk's tale. *In* Hawkins, H. Poetic freedom and poetic truth p26-54

Heilbrun, C. G. Axiothea's grief: the disability of the female imagination. *In* From Parnassus p227-36

Holder, A. The other Hemingway. *In* Wagner, L. W. ed. Ernest Hemingway p103-09

Holly, M. Consciousness and authenticity: toward a feminist aesthetic. *In* Donovan, J. C. ed. Feminist literary criticism p38-47

Jung, U. O. H. Jean Toomer, Fern. *In* Bruck, P. ed. The Black American short story in the 20th century p53-69

Kennard, J. E. Capital punishment. *In* Kennard, J. E. Victims of convention p63-79

Kennard, J. E. Conclusion. *In* Kennard, J. E. Victims of convention p158-67

Kennard, J. E. Her transitory self. *In* Kennard, J. E. Victims of convention p136-57

Kennard, J. E. Introduction. *In* Kennard, J. E. Victims of convention p9-20

Kennard, J. E. Jane Austen: the establishment. *In* **Kennard, J. E. Victims of convention** p21-45

Kennard, J. E. A question of mastery: the novels of Charlotte Brontë. *In* Kennard, J. E. Victims of convention p80-107

Kennard, J. E. A wife who waddles: the novels of George Eliot. *In* Kennard, J. E. Victims of convention p108-35

Lander, D. Eve among the Indians. *In* Diamond, A. and Edwards, L. R. eds. The authority of experience p194-211

Landy, M. The silent woman: towards a feminist critique. *In* Diamond, A. and Edwards, L. R. eds. The authority of experience p16-27

Latt, D. J. Praising virtuous ladies: the literary image and historical reality of women in seventeenth-century England. *In* Springer, M. A. ed. What manner of woman p39-64

Lerenbaum, M. Moll Flanders: "a woman on her own account." *In* Diamond, A. and Edwards, L. R. eds. The authority of experience p101-17

Lucas, W. J. Hardy's women. *In* Lucas, W. J. The literature of change p119-91

Luck, G. The woman's role in Latin love poetry. *In* Perspectives of Roman poetry p15-31

McGlinn, J. M. Tennessee Williams' women: illusion and reality, sexuality and love. *In* Tennessee Williams: a tribute p510-24

Masinton, M. and Masinton, C. G. Second-class citizenship: the status of women in contemporary American fiction. *In* Springer, M. A. ed. What manner of woman p297-315

Matlack, C. S. "Spectatress of the mischief which she made": tragic woman perceived and perceiver. *In* Studies in eighteenth-century culture v6 p317-30

Meyer, V. J. The images of women in contemporary Mexican literature. *In* Roberts, J. I. ed. Beyond intellectual sexism p210-28

Mickelson, A. Z. Erica Jong: flying or grounded? *In* Mickelson, A. Z. Reaching out: sensitivity and order in recent American fiction by women p35-48

Mickelson, A. Z. Gail Godwin: order and accommodation. *In* Mickelson, A. Z. Reaching out: sensitivity and order in recent American fiction by women p68-86

Mickelson, A. Z. Introduction. *In* Mickelson, A. Z. Reaching out: sensitivity and order in recent American fiction by women p 1-14

Mickelson, A. Z. Joan Didion: the hurting woman. *In* Mickelson, A. Z. Reaching out: sensitivity and order in recent American fiction by women p87-111

Women in literature—*Continued*

Mickelson, A. Z. Lois Gould: the musical chairs of power. *In* Mickelson, A. Z. Reaching out: sensitivity and order in recent American fiction by women p49-67

Mitchell, S. The forgotten woman of the period: penny weekly family magazines of the 1840's and 1850's. *In* Vicinus, M. ed. A widening sphere p29-51

Moers, E. Performing heroinism: the myth of Corinne. *In* The Worlds of Victorian fiction p319-50

Moynahan, J. Lawrence, woman and the Celtic fringe. *In* Smith, A. ed. Lawrence and women p122-35

North, H. F. The mare, the vixen, and the bee: sophrosyne as the virtue of women in antiquity. *In* Illinois classical studies v2 1977 p35-48

Otto, P. C. Women in the mirror: using novels to study Victorian women. *In* Kanner, B. ed. The women of England p296-344

Parrill, A. S. Portraits of ladies. *In* Tennessee Studies in literature v20 p92-99

Pratt, A. V. The new feminist criticisms: exploring the history of the new space. *In* Roberts, J. I. ed. Beyond intellectual sexism p175-95

Pullin, F. Lawrence's treatment of women in Sons and lovers. *In* Smith, A. ed. Lawrence and women p49-74

Renoir, A. A reading context for The wife's lament. *In* Anglo-Saxon poetry: essays in appreciation p224-41

Rich, A. C. When we dead awaken: writing as re-vision. *In* Rich, A. C. On lies, secrets, and silence p33-49

Richetti, J. J. The portrayal of women in Restoration and eighteenth-century English literature. *In* Springer, M. A. ed. What manner of woman p65-97

Rogers, K. Richardson's empathy with women. *In* Diamond, A. and Edwards, L. R. eds. The authority of experience p118-36

Salinger, L. 'The changeling' and the drama of domestic life. *In* English Association. Essays and studies, 1979 p80-96

Schultz, E. A. "Free in fact and at last": the image of the Black woman in Black contemporary women novelists. *In* Showalter, E. A literature of their own p298-319

Showalter, E. Beyond the female aesthetic: American fiction. *In* Springer, M. A. ed. What manner of woman p316-44

Showalter, E. The female aesthetic. *In* Showalter, E. A literature of their own p240-62

Showalter, E. The female tradition. *In* Showalter, E. A literature of their own p3-36

Showalter, E. Feminine heroines: Charlotte Brontë and George Eliot. *In* Showalter, E. A literature of their own p100-32

Showalter, E. The feminine novelists and the will to write. *In* Showalter, E. A literature of their own p37-72

Showalter, E. The feminist novelists. *In* Showalter, E. A literature of their own p182-215

Showalter, E. Subverting the feminine novel: sensationalism and feminine protest. *In* Showalter, E. A literature of their own p153-81

Showalter, E. Virginia Woolf and the flight into androgyny. *In* Showalter, E. A literature of their own p263-97

Showalter, E. Women writers and the suffrage movement. *In* Showalter, E. A literature of their own p216-39

Sjogren, C. O. The status of women in several of Lessing's dramas. *In* Studies in eighteenth-century culture v6 p347-59

Solomon, M. "To steal a hint was never known": the Sodom apple motif and Swift's "A beautiful young nymph going to bed." *In* Tennessee Studies in literature v22 p105-16

Spacks, P. A. M. Female identities. *In* Spacks, P. A. M. Imagining a self p57-91

Spilka, M. On Lawrence's hostility to wilful women: the Chatterley solution. *In* Smith, A. ed. Lawrence and women p189-211

Springer, M. A. Angels and other women in Victorian literature. *In* Springer, M. A. ed. What manner of woman p124-59

Stanbrough, J. Edna St. Vincent Millay and the language of vulnerability. *In* Gilbert, S. M. and Gubar, S. eds. Shakespeare's sisters p183-99

Stanford, A. Images of women in early American literature. *In* Springer, M. A. ed. What manner of woman p184-210

Steadman, J. M. The wife of Bath's Prologue: book-burning and the Veda of women's wiles. *In* Steadman, J. M. Nature into myth p95-103

Steeves, E. L. "No time for fainting"; the frontier woman in some early American novels. *In* Kagle, S. E. ed. America: exploration and travel p191-205

Sukenick, L. Feeling and reason in Doris Lessing's fiction. *In* Pratt, A. V. and Dembo, L. S. eds. Doris Lessing p98-118

Tayler, I. B. S. and Luria, G. Gender and genre: women in British romantic literature. *In* Springer, M. A. ed. What manner of woman p98-123

Thomas, D. A. Dickens' Mrs Lirriper and the evolution of a feminine stereotype. *In* Dickens Studies Annual v6 p154-66

Thomas, J. R. Old worlds and new: antifeminism in "Watership Down." *In* Horn Book Magazine. Crosscurrents of criticism p311-14

Tischler, N. M. A gallery of witches. *In* Tennessee Williams: a tribute p494-509

Tristram, P. Eros and death (Lawrence, Freud and women). *In* Smith, A. ed. Lawrence and women p136-55

Tuttleton, J. W. "Combat in the erogenous zone": women in the American novel between the two world wars. *In* Springer, M. A. ed. What manner of woman p271-96

Wagner, L. W. Faulkner and (Southern) women. *In* The South and Faulkner's Yoknapatawpha p128-46

Wallace, P. The "estranged point of view": the thematics of imagination in Frost's poetry. *In* Frost: centennial essays II p177-95

Young, A. V. The Black woman in Afro-Caribbean poetry. *In* DeCosta, M. ed. Blacks in Hispanic literature p137-42

Women in mass media

United States

Chmaj, B. E. Some paradox! Some irony! Changing images of American woman, 1930-1974. *In* Luedtke, L. S. ed. The study of American culture p121-76

Women in moving-pictures

French, B. The amiable spouse. *In* French, B. On the verge of revolt p35-47

French, B. Androgyny, anyone? *In* French, B. On the verge of revolt p137-54

Women's education. See Education of women

Women's employment. See Women—Employment

Women's etiquette. See Etiquette for women

Women's liberation movement. See Feminism; Women's rights

Women's rights

Giele, J. Z. Introduction: The status of women in comparative perspective. *In* Giele, J. Z. and Smock, A. C. eds. Women: roles and status in eight countries p 1-31

Jaggar, A. M. Abortion and a woman's right to decide. *In* Gould, C. C. and Wartofsky, M. W. eds. Women and philosophy p347-60

Marković, M. Women's liberation and human emancipation. *In* Gould, C. C. and Wartofsky, M. W. eds. Women and philosophy p145-67

Smock, A. C. Conclusion: Determinants of women's roles and status. *In* Giele, J. Z. and Smock, A. C. eds. Women: roles and status in eight countries p383-421

See also Sex discrimination against women; Women—Legal status, laws, etc.; Women—Suffrage

Egypt

Philipp, T. Feminism and nationalist politics in Egypt. *In* Beck, L. and Keddie, N. R. eds. Women in the Muslim world p277-94

France

Rosenfield, L. D. C. The rights of women in the French Revolution. *In* Studies in eighteenth-century culture v7 p117-37

Scandinavia

Schreiber, A. P. The status of women in the United States and the Scandinavian countries. *In* Claude, R. P. ed. Comparative human rights p251-66

Tunisia

Tessler, M. A. Women's emancipation in Tunisia. *In* Beck, L. and Keddie, N. R. eds. Women in the Muslim world p141-58

United States

Schreiber, A. P. The status of women in the United States and the Scandinavian countries. *In* Claude, R. P. ed. Comparative human rights p251-66

Women's studies

Rich, A. C. Toward a woman-centered university. *In* Rich, A. C. On lies, secrets, and silence p125-55

United States

Roberts, J. I. The ramifications of the study of women. *In* Roberts, J. I. ed. Beyond intellectual sexism p3-13

Wonder

Cunningham, J. V. Wonder. *In* Cunningham, J. V. The collected essays of J. V. Cunningham p53-96

Wong, Aline K.

Women in China: past and present. *In* Matthiasson, C. J. ed. Many sisters p229-59

Wong, Kam-ming

Point of view, norms, and structure: Hung-lou meng and lyrical fiction. *In* Chinese narrative p203-26

Wong, Siu-Kit

Ch'ing and ching in the critical writings of Wang Fu-chih. *In* Chinese approaches to literature from Confucius to Liang Ch'i-ch'ao p121-50

Wood, A. J. R. Russell- See Russell-Wood, A. J. R.

Wood, Bryce

Human rights and the inter-American system. *In* Farer, T. J. ed. The future of the inter-American system p119-52

The Organisation of American States. *In* The Year book of world affairs, 1979 p148-66

Wood, Charles T.

Queens, queans, and kingship: an inquiry into theories of royal legitimacy in late medieval England and France. *In* Order and innovation in the Middle Ages p385-400

Wood, Gordon S.

The democratization of mind in the American Revolution. *In* Library of Congress Symposia on the American Revolution, 3d, 1974. Leadership in the American Revolution p63-89

Also in The moral foundation of the American Republic p102-28

Intellectual history and the social sciences. *In* Higham J. and Conkin, P. K. eds. New directions in American intellectual history p27-41

Revolution and the political integration of the enslaved and disenfranchised. *In* America's continuing revolution p99-116

Wood, Herbert John

Nelson Trusler Johnson: the diplomacy of benevolent pragmatism. *In* Burns, R. D. and Bennett, E. M. eds. Diplomats in crisis p7-26

Wood, John A.

The moon. *In* Man and cosmos p50-62

Wood, Peter H.

"Taking care of business" in Revolutionary South Carolina: Republicanism and the slave society. *In* The Southern experience in the American Revolution p268-93

Television as dream. *In* Television as a cultural force p17-35

Wood, Robert, 1717?-1771

About

Simonsuuri, K. Poetry is original 'imitation': Robert Wood's theory of the Homeric epic. *In* Simonsuuri, K. Homer's original genius p133-42

Wood, Robin

Charles Laughton on Grubb Street. *In* Peary, G. and Shatzkin, R. eds. The modern American novel and the movies p204-14

To have (written) and have not (directed) *In* Nichols, B. ed. Movies and methods p297-305

Wood, Susan

Discovering worlds: the fiction of Ursula K. Le Guin. *In* Clareson, T. D. ed. Voices for the future: essays on major science fiction writers v2 p154-79

Wood, W. Barry

About

Harvey, A. M. More bright stars in the Johns Hopkins galaxy. *In* Harvey, A. M. Adventures in medical research p333-63

Wood, William, ca. 1580-1639
About individual works
New Englands prospect
Seelye, J. Glorious enterprise: Governor John Winthrop's wonderful wall. *In* Seelye, J. Prophetic waters p131-58

Wood. See Woodwork

Wood-carving
See also Kilenge (Melanesian people)—Wood-carving
New Guinea
Wilkinson, G. N. Carving a social message: the Malanggans of Tabar. *In* Greenhalgh, M. and Megaw, J. V. S. eds. Art in society p227-41

Woodall, Guy R.
Letters by Ellen Glasgow and others on first editions of three of her novels. *In* Tennessee Studies in literature v 21 p43-48

Woodard, Charles R.
Wordsworth and The romantic agony. *In* Tennessee Studies in literature v20 p 1-10

Woodard, Kim
People's China and the world energy crisis: the Chinese attitude toward global resource. *In* China's changing role in the world economy p114-42

Woodbridge, Frederick James Eugene
About
Wilder, T. N. Frederick J. E. Woodbridge, 1867-1940. *In* Wilder, T. N. American characteristics, and other essays p225-28

Woodcock, George
A grab at Proteus: notes on Irving Layton. *In* Woodcock, G. ed. Poets and critics p53-70

Possessing the land: notes on Canadian fiction. *In* Staines, D. ed. The Canadian imagination p69-96

Woodcuts. See Wood-engravings

Wood-engraving
History
Woodward, D. A. The woodcut technique. *In* Woodward, D. A. ed. Five centuries of map printing p25-50

Woodham Smith, Cecil Blanche (Fitz Gerald)
About individual works
The great hunger
Marcus, S. Hunger and ideology. *In* Marcus, S. Representations p3-16

Woodman, Tony
Exegi monumentum: Horace, Odes 3.30. *In* Woodman, T. and West, D. eds. Quality and pleasure in Latin poetry p115-28

Woodress, James Leslie
Willa Cather: American experience and European tradition. *In* The Art of Willa Cather p43-64

Woodring, Carl Ray
Virginia Woolf. *In* Stade, G. ed. Six modern British novelists p175-217

What Coleridge thought of pictures. *In* Kroeber, K. and Walling, W. eds. Images of romanticism p91-106

Woodring, Sally
Hospice pilot project in an acute-care general hospital 1975-1976. *In* Home care p159-64

Woods, Michael John
Existence and tense. *In* Evans, G. L. and McDowell, J. H. eds. Truth and meaning p248-62
About individual works
Reasons for actions and desires
Foot, P. Reasons for action and desires. *In* Foot, P. Virtues and vices, and other essays in moral philosophy p148-56

Woodson, Carter Godwin
Attitudes of the Iberian Peninsula (in literature) *In* DeCosta, M. ed. Blacks in Hispanic literature p36-46

Woodson, William C.
The printer's copy for the 1785 Variorum Shakespeare. *In* Virginia. University. Bibliographical Society. Studies in bibliography v31 p208-10

The 1785 Variorum Shakespeare. *In* Virginia. University. Bibliographical Society. Studies in bibliography v28 p318-20

Woodward, Comer Vann
The future of Southern history. *In* The Future of history p135-49

The price of freedom. *In* What was freedom's price? p93-113
About individual works
Origins of the new South, 1877-1913
Downs, R. B. Reconstruction to the new freedom. *In* Downs, R. B. Books that changed the South p259-69

Woodward, David Alfred
The woodcut technique. *In* Woodward, D. A. ed. Five centuries of map printing p25-50

Woodward, George Washington
About
Shankman, A. M. For the Union as it was and the Constitution as it is: a Copperhead views the Civil War. *In* Rank and file p93-111

Woodward, Kathleen M.
Master songs of meditation: the late poems of Eliot, Pound, Stevens, and Williams. *In* Spicker, S. F.; Woodward, K. M. and Van Tassel, D. D. eds. Aging and the elderly p181-202

Woodward, Vann. See Woodward, Comer Vann

Woodwork
England—History
Hewett, C. A. Anglo-Saxon carpentry. *In* Anglo-Saxon England 7 p205-29
Rome
Liversidge, J. E. A. Woodwork. *In* Strong, D. E. and Brown, D. eds. Roman crafts p155-65

Woodyard, George W.
Jorge Diaz and the liturgy of violence. *In* Lyday, L. F. and Woodyard, G. W. eds. Dramatists in revolt p59-76

Wool trade and industry
Europe—History
Baker, R. L. The government of Calais in 1363. *In* Order and innovation in the Middle Ages p207-14

Munro, J. H. A. Industrial protectionism in medieval Flanders: urban or national? *In* The Medieval city p229-67

Wool trade and industry in literature

Feingold, R. Two worlds of work: John Dyer's The fleece. *In* Feingold, R. Nature and society p83-119

Woolf, Leonard Sidney

Preface to A writer's diary by Virginia Woolf. *In* Praise from famous men: an anthology of introductions p175-81

Woolf, Rosemary

English imitations of the Homelia Origenis de Maria Magdalena. *In* Chaucer and Middle English studies in honour of Rossell Hope Robbins p384-91

The ideal of men dying with their lord in the Germania and in The Battle of Maldon. *In* Anglo-Saxon England 5 p63-81

The influence of the mystery plays upon the popular tragedies of the 1560's. *In* Renaissance drama [1973] p89-105

The wanderer, The seafarer, and the genre of planctus. *In* Anglo-Saxon poetry: essays in appreciation p192-207

Woolf, Virginia (Stephen)

About

Adams, R. M. Woolf and Faulkner: streams of consciousness. *In* Adams, R. M. Afterjoyce p65-89

Bell, B. C. and Ohmann, C. B. Virginia Woolf's criticism: a polemical preface. *In* Donovan, J. C. ed. Feminist literary criticism p48-60

Fleishman, A. Virginia Woolf: tradition and modernity. *In* Forms of modern British fiction p133-63

Gillie, C. Diversification of the novel, 1920-1930. *In* Gillie, C. Movements in English literature 1900-1940 p90-121

Hynes, S. The whole contention between Mr Bennett and Mrs Woolf. *In* Spilka, M. ed. Towards a poetics of fiction p179-89

Lewis, W. Virginia Woolf; excerpt from "Men without art." *In* Lewis, W. Enemy salvoes p93-98

Lodge, D. Virginia Woolf. *In* Lodge, D. The modes of modern writing p177-88

Oates, J. C. The art of relationships: Henry James and Virginia Woolf. *In* Oates, J. C. New heaven, new earth: the visionary experience in literature p9-35

Rahv, P. Mrs Woolf and Mrs Brown. *In* Rahv, P. Essays on literature and politics, 1932-1972 p247-50

Schneider, D. J. "Orts, scraps, fragments" and the circle of wholeness: the symbolism of Virginia Woolf. *In* Schneider, D. J. Symbolism: the Manichean vision p118-53

Showalter, E. Virginia Woolf and the flight into androgyny. *In* Showalter, E. A literature of their own p263-97

Woodring, C. R. Virginia Woolf. *In* Stade, G. ed. Six modern British novelists p175-217

About individual works

Granite and rainbow

Welty, E. Virginia Woolf's Granite and rainbow. *In* Welty, E. The eye of the story p190-92

The letters of Virginia Woolf, v.II (ed. by Nigel Nicolson and Joann Trautmann)

Welty, E. The letters of Virginia Woolf, volume II. *In* Welty, E. The eye of the story p193-202

Mrs Dalloway

Edwards, L. R. War and roses: the politics of Mrs Dalloway. *In* Diamond, A. and Edwards, L. R. eds. The authority of experience p160-77

Rigney, B. H. "The sane and the insane": psychosis and mysticism in Mrs. Dalloway. *In* Rigney, B. H. Madness and sexual politics in the feminist novel p39-63

Orlando

Philipson, W. H. Virginia Woolf's Orlando: biography as a work of fiction. *In* From Parnassus p237-48

To the lighthouse

Gregor, I. Spaces: To the lighthouse. *In* Martz, L. L. and Williams, A. L. eds. The author in his work p375-89

Hardy, B. N. Good stories, good listeners. *In* Hardy, B. N. Tellers and listeners p131-62

Mepham, J. Figures of desire: narration and fiction in To the lighthouse. *In* Josipovici, G. ed. The modern English novel: the reader, the writer and the work p149-85

Pritchard, W. H. Some 1920s fiction: Ford, Forster, Woolf. *In* Pritchard, W. H. Seeing through everything p90-113

The waves

McConnell, F. D. "Death among the apple trees": The waves and the world of things. *In* Garvin, H. R. ed. Makers of the twentieth-century novel p49-61

May, K. M. The search for identity. *In* May, K. M. Out of the maelstrom p62-77

A writer's diary

Woolf, L. S. Preface to A writer's diary by Virginia Woolf. *In* Praise from famous men: an anthology of introductions p175-81

The years

Marder, H. Beyond the lighthouse: The years. *In* Garvin, H. R. ed. Makers of the twentieth-centry novel p62-69

Schneider, D. J. "Orts, scraps, fragments" and the circle of wholeness: the symbolism of Virginia Woolf. *In* Schneider, D. J. Symbolism: the Manichean vision p118-53

Characters—Clarissa Dalloway

Edwards, L. R. War and roses: the politics of Mrs Dalloway. *In* Diamond, A. and Edwards, L. R. eds. The authority of experience p160-77

Characters—Septimus Warren Smith

Edwards, L. R. War and roses: the politics of Mrs Dalloway. *In* Diamond, A. and Edwards, L. R. eds. The authority of experience p160-77

Characters—Women

Kaplan, S. J. Virginia Woolf. *In* Kaplan, S. J. Feminine consciousness in the modern British novel p76-109

Plots

Caserio, R. L. The family plot: Conrad, Joyce Lawrence, Woolf, and Faulkner. *In* Caserio, R. L. Plot, story and the novel p232-79

Woolford, John

Sources and resources in Browning's early reading. *In* Armstrong, I. ed. Robert Browning p 1-46

Woolhouse, Roger Stuart

The empiricist account of dispositions. *In* Royal Institute of Philosophy. Impressions of empiricism p184-99

Woolley, James

Friends and enemies in Verses on the death of Dr Swift. *In* Studies in eighteenth-century culture v8 p205-32

Woolman, John

About individual works

The journal of John Woolman

Couser, G. T. John Woolman: a prophet among prophets. *In* Couser, G. T. American autobiography p28-40

Medeiros, P. M. Three travelers: Carver, Bartram, and Woolman. *In* Emerson, E. H. ed. American literature, 1764-1789 p195-211

Woolsey, R. James

Chipping away at the bargains. *In* Long, F. A. and Rathjens, G. W. eds. Arms, defense policy, and arms control p175-85

Woolsey, Suzanne Haley

Pied Piper politics and the child-care debate. *In* Rossi, A. S.; Kagan, J. and Hareven, T. K. eds. The family p127-46

Wooster, Warren Scriver

Conditions for ocean research. *In* Borgese, E. M. and Krieger, D. eds. The tides of change p310-17

Worcester, Donald E.

The significance of the Spanish borderlands to the United States. *In* Weber, D. J. ed. New Spain's far northern frontier p 1-14

Worcester, England

History

Dyer, C. A redistribution of incomes in fifteenth-century England? *In* Peasants, knights and heretics p192-215

Worcester, Mass.

Genealogy

Chudacoff, H. P. New branches on the tree: household structure in early stages of the family cycle in Worcester, Massachusetts, 1860-1880. *In* American Antiquarian Society. Proceedings v86 pt2 p303-20

Word (Linguistics)

Miller, G. A. Semantic relations among words. *In* Linguistic theory and psychological reality p60-118

Richards, I. A. The interinanimations of words. *In* Richards, I. A. Poetries p71-84

Word history. See Language and languages —Etymology

Worde, Wynkyn de

About

Garbáty, T. J. Wynkyn de Worde's "Sir Thopas" and other tales. *In* Virginia. University. Bibliographical Society. Studies in bibliography v31 p57-67

Words, Coinage of. See Words, New

Words, New

English

Burchfield, R. W. Further aspects of short-term historical lexicography. *In* James B. McMillan: essays in linguistics by his friends and colleagues p115-31

Words, Obscene

English

Lawrence, B. Four-letter words can hurt you. *In* Baker, R. and Elliston, F. A. eds. Philosophy & sex p31-33

French

Pearcy, R. J. Modes of signification and the humor of obscene diction in the fabliaux. *In* Cooke, T. D. and Honeycutt, B. L. eds. The humor of the fabliaux p163-96

Words for colors. See Colors, Words for

Wordsworth, William

About

Brisman, L. Wordsworth: how shall I seek the origin? *In* Brisman, L. Romantic origins p276-361

Cooke, M. G. The will in English romanticism: The will in romantic poetry. *In* Cooke, M. G. The romantic will p29-51

Cooke, M. G. The will to art: Wordsworth and the stoical resolution of art. *In* Cooke, M. G. The romantic will p201-16

Dawson, C. "The lamp of memory": Wordsworth and Dickens. *In* Dawson, C. Victorian noon p123-43

Donoghue, D. The eye and the mind's eye. *In* Donoghue, D. The sovereign ghost p128-82

Foakes, R. A. "The power of prospect": Wordsworth's visionary poetry. *In* Martz, L. L. and Williams, A. L. eds. The author in his work p103-21

Hartman, G. H. Evening star and evening land. *In* Hartman, G. H. The fate of reading p147-78

Hobsbaum, P. The essential Wordsworth. *In* Hobsbaum, P. Tradition and experiment in English poetry p180-205

Langbaum, R. W. Wordsworth: the self as process. *In* Langbaum, R. W. The mysteries of identity p25-47

Morgan, E. Wordsworth in 1970. *In* Morgan, E. Essays p130-34

Nalbantian, S. The stylistic alchemy. *In* Nalbantian, S. The symbol of the soul from Hölderlin to Yeats p100-18

Nalbantian, S. Wordsworth, Hölderlin and their contemporaries: the imperial soul. *In* Nalbantian, S. The symbol of the soul from Hölderlin to Yeats p13-37

Newey, V. The steadfast self: an aspect of Wordsworth. *In* Davies, R. T. and Beatty, B. G. eds. Literature of the romantic period, 1750-1850 p36-55

Prickett, S. Wordsworth and the language of nature. *In* Prickett, S. Romanticism and religion p70-90

Ragussis, M. Epilogue: the word. *In* Ragussis, M. The subterfuge of art p226-29

Ragussis, M. Wordsworth: the Arab dream: the language behind nature and art. *In* Ragussis, M. The subterfuge of art p17-34

Rieger, J. Wordsworth unalarm'd. *In* Wittreich, J. A. ed. Milton and the line of vision p185-208

Schneidau, H. N. Pound and Wordsworth on poetry and prose. *In* Bornstein, G. ed. Romantic and modern p133-45

Tave, S. M. Jane Austen and one of her contemporaries. *In* Halperin, J. ed. Jane Austen p61-74

Taylor, A. Wordsworth's arguments against magical words. *In* Taylor, A. Magic and English romanticism p134-83

Trilling, L. The fate of pleasure: Wordsworth to Dostoevski; excerpt from "Beyond culture". *In* Wimsatt, W. K. ed. Literary criticism: idea and act p189-211

Work—*Continued*

Ryan, J. J. Humanistic work: its philosophical and cultural implications. *In* Heisler, W. J. and Houck, J. W. eds. A matter of dignity p11-22

Psychological aspects

Clayre, A. Habits and customs of working people. *In* Clayre, A. Work and play p113-29

Clayre, A. The search for golden ages of labour. *In* Clayre, A. Work and play p151-68

Coles, R. Work and self-respect. *In* Erikson, E. H. ed. Adulthood p217-26

Heisler, W. J. Worker alienation: 1900-1975. *In* Heisler, W. J. and Houck, J. W. eds. A matter of dignity p65-84

Kanter, R. M. Work in a new America. *In* A New America? p47-78

Kasl, S. V. Work and mental health: contemporary research evidence. *In* Heisler, W. J. and Houck, J. W. eds. A matter of dignity p85-110

Plaut, W. G. The Sabbath as protest: thoughts on work and leisure in the automated society. *In* Tradition and change in Jewish experience p169-83

Rich, A. C. Conditions for work: the common world of women. *In* Rich, A. C. On lies, secrets, and silence p203-14

Sexton, W. P. Work humanization in practice: what should business do? *In* Heisler, W. J. and Houck, J. W. eds. A matter of dignity p131-45

Work (Theology)

Fiorenza, F. S. Work and critical theology. *In* Heisler, W. J. and Houck, J. W. eds. A matter of dignity p23-44

Work, Method of. See Work

Work, Psychology of. See Work—Psychological aspects

Work in literature

Clayre, A Levin in the fields. *In* Clayre, A. Work and play p147-50

Work-songs

Clayre, A. Songs in oral tradition. *In* Clayre, A. Work and play p130-46

Workers. See Labor and laboring classes

Working-classes. See Labor and laboring classes

Working-men. See Labor and laboring classes

Working-men's dwellings. See Labor and laboring classes—Dwellings

Working mothers. See Mothers—Employment

Working women. See Women—Employment

World and the church. See Church and the world

World Council of Churches

About individual works

The programme to combat racism

Hudson, D. The World Council of Churches and racism. *In* The Year book of world affairs, 1975 p155-72

World Council of Churches. Commission of the Churches on International affairs. See Commission of the Churches on International Affairs

World economics. See Commercial policy

World Health Organization

Waldheim, K. Health in a world perspective. *In* Cahill, K. M. ed. Health and development p 1-3

World history

Aron, R. The dawn of universal history. *In* Politics and history p212-33

Mink, L. O. Narrative form as a cognitive instrument. *In* Canary, R. H. and Kozicki, H. J. eds. The writing of history p129-49

Chronology

See Chronology, Historical

Study and teaching

See History—Study and teaching

World literature. See Literature

World news. See Foreign news

World organization. See International organization

World politics

Buchan, A. Mothers and daughters (Or Greeks and Romans) *In* Two hundred years of American foreign policy p20-66

Claude, I. L. Domestic jurisdiction and colonialism. *In* Kilson, M. ed. New states in the modern world p121-35

Hoffmann, S. Regulating the new international system. *In* Kilson, M. ed. New states in the modern world p171-99

Rostow, E. V. Future world systems. *In* The New Atlantic challenge p285-99

Seton-Watson, H. How right the old Kennan was! *In* Decline of the West? p39-48

See also Detente; Geopolitics; Great powers; International organization; International relations

Congresses

Wilson, T. A. Summit conferences. *In* Encyclopedia of American foreign policy p936-44

To 1900

Gilbert, F. The "new diplomacy" of the eighteenth century. *In* Gilbert, F. History p323-49

20th century

French, A. P. Einstein and world affairs. *In* Einstein p185-97

Hoffmann, S. The international system and U.S. policy toward Latin America. *In* The Americas in a changing world p78-94

Morgenthau, H. J. World politics and the politics of oil. *In* Eppen, G. D. ed. Energy: the policy issues p43-51

1933-1945

Garson, R. The Atlantic alliance, Eastern Europe and the origins of the Cold war: from Pearl Harbor to Yalta. *In* Allen, H. C. and Thompson, R. eds. Contrast and connection p296-320

Itō, T. The genesis of the Cold war: confrontation over Poland, 1941-44. *In* The Origins of the Cold war in Asia p147-202

Spender, S. Background to the forties. *In* Spender, S. The thirties and after p63-76

1945-

Aruga, T. The United States and the Cold war: the Cold war era in American history. *In* The Origins of the Cold war in Asia p66-88

Auty, P. Yugoslavia and the Cold war. *In* Siracusa, J. M. and Barclay, G. S. eds. The impact of the Cold war p125-43

World politics—1945- —*Continued*

Barclay, G. S. Australia and the Cold war. *In* Siracusa, J. M. and Barclay, G. S. eds. The impact of the Cold war p3-25

Buchan, A. An expedition to the poles. *In* The Year book of world affairs, 1975 p4-21

Bundy, W. M. The avoidance of nuclear war since 1945. *In* Griffiths, F. and Polanyi, J. C. eds. The dangers of nuclear war p27-33

DeSantis, V. P. Italy and the Cold war. *In* Siracusa, J. M. and Barclay, G. S. eds. The impact of the Cold war p26-39

Freedman, L. Whose crisis?: Britain as an international problem. *In* Kramnick, I. ed. Is Britain dying? p203-14

Govaerts, F. Belgium and the Cold war. *In* Siracusa, J. M. and Barclay, G. S. eds. The impact of the Cold war p40-63

Gregory, R. The domino theory. *In* Encyclopedia of American foreign policy p275-80

Heath, E. R. G. A Tory view. *In* Kramnick, I. ed. Is Britain dying? p31-44

Herring, G. C. The Cold War. *In* Encyclopedia of American foreign policy p111-23

Iriye, A. The United States in Chinese foreign policy. *In* China and America p11-52

Kaplan, M. A. The international political system and the U.S. system of alliances. *In* Isolation or interdependence? p13-23

Kennan, G. F. Western decadence and Soviet moderation. *In* Decline of the West? George Kennan and his critics p3-9

Mahajani, U. Sino-American rapprochement and the new configurations in Southeast Asia. *In* The Year book of world affairs, 1975 p106-20

Moneta Testa, C. Argentine foreign policy in the Cold war. *In* Siracusa, J. M. and Barclay, G. S. eds. The impact of the Cold war p101-24

Moses, J. A. Germany and the Cold war: historiographical consequences. *In* Siracusa, J. M. and Barclay, G. S. eds. The impact of the Cold war p64-83

Nagai, Y. The roots of Cold war doctrine: the esoteric and the exoteric. *In* The Origins of the Cold war in Asia p15-42

Nicholas, H. G. The wartime alliance and after; the Cold war alliance; excerpt from "Britain and the U.S.A." *In* Burton, D. H. ed. American history—British historians p93-124

Nicolson, I. F. Nigeria: wars cold and hot, and lukewarm ideas. *In* Siracusa, J. M. and Barclay, G. S. eds. The impact of the Cold war p84-100

Okabe, T. The Cold war and China. *In* The Origins of the Cold war in Asia p224-51

Pasti, N. The military balance between East and West in Europe. *In* International terrorism and world security p189-233

Said, A. A. and Simmons, L. R. The ethnic factor in world politics. *In* Said, A. A. and Simmons, L. R. eds. Ethnicity in an international context p15-47

Seton-Watson, H. How right the old Kennan was! *In* Decline of the West? George Kennan and his critics p39-48

Siracusa, J. M. FDR, Truman, and Indochina, 1941-1952: the forgotten years. *In* Siracusa, J. M. and Barclay, G. S. eds. The impact of the Cold war p163-83

Steinbruner, J. An assessment of nuclear crises. *In* Griffiths, F. and Polyani, J. C. eds. The dangers of nuclear war p34-49

Strausz-Hupé, R. America and the defense of the West. *In* Prochnow, H. V. ed. Dilemmas facing the nation p271-93

Warner, G. America, Russia, China and the origins of the Cold war, 1945-1950. *In* Siracusa, J. M. and Barclay, G. S. eds. The impact of the Cold war p144-62

Watt, D. C. Britain and the Cold war in the Far East, 1945-58. *In* The Origins of the Cold war in Asia p89-122

Watt, D. C. Introduction: The historian's tasks and responsibilities. *In* The Origins of the Cold war in Asia p3-14

Whiting, A. S. Mao, China, and the Cold war. *In* The Origins of the Cold war in Asia p252-76

Yamamoto, M. The Cold war and U.S.-Japan economic cooperation. *In* The Origins of the Cold war in Asia p408-25

Yano, T. Who set the stage for the Cold war in Southeast Asia? *In* The Origins of the Cold war in Asia p321-37

Yergin, D. Order and survival. *In* A New America? p263-87

See also Underdeveloped areas—Foreign relations

1945-1955

LaFeber, W. American policy-makers, public opinion, and the outbreak of the Cold war, 1945-50. *In* The Origins of the Cold war in Asia p43-65

1955-

Brown, N. Threats to security in Europe. *In* The New Atlantic challenge p219-28

1965-1975

Bock, F. The impact of international economic factors on the conduct of foreign policy. *In* The Interaction of economics and foreign policy p130-50

Donaldson, R. H. Global power relationships in the seventies: the view from the Kremlin. *In* Cocks, P.; Daniels, R. V. and Heer, N. W. eds. The dynamics of Soviet politics p309-33

Legum, C. International rivalries in the Southern African conflict. *In* Carter, G. M. and O'Meara, P. eds. Southern Africa: the continuing crisis p3-17

Morse, E. L. The Atlantic economy in crisis. *In* Atlantis lost p149-82

1975-1985

Birnbaum, N. On the possibility of a new politics in the West. *In* Beyond the crisis p201-32

Legum, C. International rivalries in the Southern African conflict. *In* Carter, G. M. and O'Meara, P. eds. Southern Africa: the continuing crisis p3-17

Rosecrance, R. N. New directions? *In* Rosecrance, R. N. ed. America as an ordinary country p245-66

World Theatre season, London

Brustein, R. S. Window on the world: the World Theatre Festival. *In* Brustein, R. S. The culture watch p102-07

World War, 1939-1945

Aerial operations

Watt, D. C. Restraints on war in the air before 1945. *In* Howard, M. ed. Restraints on war p57-77

Atrocities

See Holocaust, Jewish (1939-1945)

World War, 1939-1945—*Continued*

Concentration camps

Eitinger, L. On being a psychiatrist and a survivor. *In* Rosenfeld, A. H. and Greenberg, I. eds. Confronting the Holocaust p186-99

Diplomatic history

See Russo-German treaty, 1939

Economic aspects

Moggridge, D. E. Economic policy in the Second World War. *In* Keynes, M. ed. Essays on John Maynard Keynes p 177-201

Economic aspects—United States

Brody, D. The New Deal and World War II. *In* Braeman, J.; Bremner, R. H. and Brody, D. eds. The New Deal v 1 p267-309

Fiction

Krzyzanowski, J. R. Men at work: the Polish version. *In* For Wiktor Weintraub p239-50

Historiography

Watt, D. C. The historiography of appeasement. *In* Crisis and controversy p110-29

Music and the war

Sessions, R. No more business-as-usual. *In* Sessions, R. Roger Sessions on music p304-12

Poetry

Scannell, V. Alan Ross and Charles Causley. *In* Scannell, V. Not without glory p113-33

Scannell, V. Alun Lewis. *In* Scannell, V. Not without glory p52-73

Scannell, V. American poets of the Second World War. *In* Scannell, V. Not without glory p172-237

Scannell, V. Henry Reed and others. *In* Scannell, V. Not without glory p134-71

Scannell, V. Keith Douglas. *In* Scannell, V. Not without glory p23-51

Scannell, V. Roy Fuller. *In* Scannell, V. Not without glory p95-112

Scannell, V. Setting the scene. *In* Scannell, V. Not without glory p7-22

Scannell, V. Sidney Keyes. *In* Scannell, V. Not without glory p74-94

Reconstruction

See Reconstruction (1939-1951)

Treaties

See Russo-German treaty, 1939

Underground movements—Jews

Dawidowicz, L. S. Resistance: a doomed struggle. *In* Dawidowicz, L. S. The Jewish presence p280-88

Afro-Americans

McCoy, D. R. and Ruetten, R. T. Towards equality: Blacks in the United States during the Second World War. *In* Hepburn, A. C. ed. Minorities in history p135-53

Jews

See Holocaust, Jewish (1939-1945)

Great Britain

Marwick, A. People's War and top People's Peace? British society and the Second World War. *In* Crisis and controversy p148-64

Japan

Nish, I. H. Japan and the outbreak of war in 1941. *In* Crisis and controversy p130-47

World's fairs. See Exhibitions

Worms, Jean-Pierre. See Grémion, P. jt. auth.

The Wormwood Review
Malone, M. The gall of Wormwood in printing over 66 issues and still continuing. *In* Anderson, E. and Kinzie, M. eds. The little magazine in America: a modern documentary history p389-404

Woronoff, Jon
The OAU and sub-Saharan regional bodies. *In* El-Ayouty, Y. ed. The Organization of African Unity after ten years p62-78

Worry
Thomas, L. On transcendental metaworry (TMW) *In* Thomas, L. The medusa and the snail p82-87

Worship. See Idols and images—Worship; Liturgics; Sacrifice

Worship (Judaism)
Werner, E. Two types of ritual and their music. *In* Salo Wittmayer Baron v2 p975-1008

Worship of Christian martyrs. See Christian martyrs—Cult

Worsthorne, Peregrine
The trade unions: new lads on top. *In* Tyrrell, R. E. ed. The future that doesn't work p5-21

Worth, Katharine Joyce
The Irish drama of Europe from Yeats to Beckett

Contents
Beckett
Maeterlinck
O'Casey
Salomé and A full moon in March
Synge
The syntax achieved
Towards modernism: a new theatrical syntax
The vitality of the Yeatsian theatre
Yeats, Maeterlinck and Synge
Yeat's drama of the interior: a technique for the modern theatre

Worth. See Values

Wortham, Thomas Richard
19-century literature. *In* American literary scholarship, 1977 p207-43

Wounded Knee Creek, Battle of, 1890
Seymour, F. W. A look back at Wounded Knee. *In* American Antiquarian Society. Proceedings v84 pt 1 p33-42

Wozniak, Robert H.
Dialecticism and structuralism: the philosophical foundation of Soviet psychology and Piagetian cognitive developmental theory. *In* Riegel, K. F. and Rosenwald, G. C. eds. Structure and transformation p25-45

Wrabetz, James F.
A new Serenus stamping from Sardis and the origins of the Eastern Sigillata B ware. *In* Harvard Studies in classical philology v81 p195-97

Wren, Robert M.
'Mister Johnson' and the complexity of 'Arrow of God.' *In* Narasimhaiah, C. D. ed. Awakened conscience p50-62

Wren, Thomas E.
John Macmurray's search for reality: introduction. *In* The Personal universe p 1-6

Wright, Andrew H.
Jane Austen abroad. *In* Halperin, J. ed. Jane Austen p298-317

Wright, Charles Robert
Social structure and mass communications behavior: exploring patterns through constructional analysis. *In* The Idea of social structure p379-413

Wright, Christopher. See Long, T. D. jt. auth.

Wright, Crispin
Language-mastery and the Sorites paradox. *In* Evans, G. L. and McDowell, J. H. eds. Truth and meaning p223-47

Wright, Esmond
Lincoln before his election. *In* Burton, D. H. ed. American history—British historians p221-37

The loyalists. *In* Allen, H. C. and Thompson, R. eds. Contrast and connection p113-48

William Howard Russell and Edward Dicey. *In* Abroad in America: Visitors to the new Nation, 1776-1914 p145-56

Wright, Frank Lloyd

About

Paul, S. Louis Sullivan and organic architecture. *In* Paul, S. Repossessing and renewing p111-30

About individual works
An autobiography

Couser, G. T. Two prophetic architects: Louis Sullivan and Frank Lloyd Wright. *In* Couser, G. T. American autobiography p120-47

Influence

Pevsner, N. Frank Lloyd Wright's peaceful penetration of Europe. *In* Sharp, D. ed. The rationalists p35-41

Wright, Gordon
Contemporary history in the contemporary age. *In* The Future of history p219-30

Wright, Gwendolyn
On the fringe of the profession: women in American architecture. *In* Kostof, S. ed. The architect p280-308

Wright, Henry Tutwiler
Toward an explanation of the origin of the state. *In* Explanation of prehistoric change p215-30

Wright, Herbert E.
Glacial fluctuations, sea-level changes, and catastrophic floods. *In* Ramage, E. S. ed. Atlantis, fact or fiction? p161-74

Wright, James

About

Lieberman, L. James Wright: words of grass. *In* Lieberman, L. Unassigned frequencies p182-89

Molesworth, C. James Wright and the dissolving self. *In* Boyers, R. ed. Contemporary poetry in America p267-78

Wright, John Kirtland. See Part 2 under title: Geographies of the mind

Wright, Judith

About individual works
Nigger's Leap: New England

Healy, J. J. The absolute and the image of man in Australia: Judith Wright and Patrick White. *In* Narasimhaiah, C. D. ed. Awakened conscience p3-13

Wright, M. A.

About individual works
The assault on private enterprise

Galbraith, J. K. Defenders of the faith, III: Wright and Slick. *In* Galbraith, J. K. Annals of an abiding liberal p118-22

Wright, Madeleine
Nathalie Sarraute: alienated or alienator? *In* Garvin, H. R. ed. Makers of the twentieth-century novel p253-58

Wright, Maurice Gordon, and Young, Stephen
Regional planning in Britain. *In* Planning, politics and public policy p237-68

Wright, N. A. R.
The tree of battles of Honoré Bouvet and the laws of war. *In* War, literature, and politics in the late Middle Ages p12-31

Wright, Nathalia
Roderick Usher: Poe's turn-of-the-century artist. *In* Artful thunder p55-67

Wright, Nathan
Afro-American religion: Non-establishment Black religion. *In* The Black American reference book p506-14

Wright, Orville

About

Stever, H. G. Man takes wings. *In* Neyman, J. ed. The heritage of Copernicus: theories "pleasing to the mind" p467-86

Wright, Richard

About

Feuser, W. F. The men who lived underground: Richard Wright and Ralph Ellison. *In* King, B. A. and Ogungbesan, K. eds. A celebration of Black and African writing p87-101

Howe, I. Richard Wright: a word of farewell. *In* Howe, I. Celebrations and attacks p89-92

Hyman, S. E. Richard Wright reappraised. *In* Hyman, S. E. The critic's credentials p58-68

Jackson, B. Richard Wright: Black boy from America's Black belt and urban ghettos. *In* Jackson, B. The waiting years p103-28

About individual works
Big Boy leaves home

Jackson, B. Richard Wright in a moment of truth. *In* Jackson, B. The waiting years p129-45

Fire and cloud

Karrer, W. Richard Wright, Fire and cloud. *In* Bruck, P. ed. The Black American short story in the 20th century p99-110

Native son

Brunette, P. Two Wrights, one wrong. *In* Peary, G. and Shatzkin, R. eds. The modern American novel and the movies p131-42

Reed, I. Native son lives! *In* Reed, I. Shrovetide in old New Orleans p44-49

Bibliography

Reilly, J. M. Richard Wright. *In* Inge, M. T.; Duke, J. M. and Bryer, J. R. eds. Black American writers v2 p 1-46

Style

Morris, W. Richard Wright: real and imagined Black voices. *In* Morris, W. Earthly delights, unearthly adornments p147-57

Wright, Sarah E.

About individual works
This child's gonna live

Mickelson, A. Z. Winging upward: Black women: Sarah E. Wright, Toni Morrison, Alice Walker. *In* Mickelson, A. Z. Reaching out: sensitivity and order in recent American fiction by women p112-74

Wright, Terence. See Roberts, P. jt. auth.

Wright, Thomas

About

Hoskin, M. A. The English background to the cosmology of Wright and Herschel. *In* Cosmology, history, and theology p219-31

Wright, Wilbur

About

Stever, H. G. Man takes wings. *In* Neyman, J. ed. The heritage of Copernicus: theories "pleasing to the mind" p467-86

Wright, Winthrop R.

Elitist attitudes toward race in twentieth-century Venezuela. *In* Toplin, R. B. ed. Slavery and race relations in Latin America p325-47

Wrightsman, Amos Bruce

Andreas Osiander's contribution to the Copernican achievement. *In* The Copernican achievement p213-43

Wrightsman, Bruce. See Wrightsman, Amos Bruce

Wrigley, Edward Anthony

Parasite or stimulus: the town in a pre-industrial economy. *In* Towns in societies p295-309

Reflections on the history of the family. *In* Rossi, A. S.; Kagan, J. and Hareven, T. K. eds. The family p71-86

A simple model of London's importance in changing English society and economy, 1650-1750. *In* Towns in societies p215-43

Writers. See Authors; also special classses of writers, e.g. Novelists

Writing

Britton, J. N. Teaching writing. *In* Davies, A. ed. Problems of language and learning p113-33

Derrida, J. Freud and the scene of writing. *In* Derrida, J. Writing and difference p196-231

See also Indians of Central America [Mexico, etc.]—Writing

Writing (Authorship) See Authorship

Writing as a profession. See Authorship

Written on the wind (Motion picture)

Truffaut, F. Douglas Sirk: Written on the wind. *In* Truffaut, F. The films in my life p148-50

Wrocław. See Breslau

Wrong, Dennis Hume

Competent authority: reality and legitimating model. *In* The Uses of controversy in sociology p262-72

Wrong, George Mackinnon

About

Berger, C. The founders of critical history: George M. Wrong and Adam Shortt. *In* Berger, C. The writing of Canadian history p 1-31

The wrong man (Motion picture)

Truffaut, F. Alfred Hitchcock: The wrong man. *In* Truffaut, F. The films in my life p83-86

Wroth, William Henry

The flowering and decline of the New Mexican santero: 1780-1900. *In* Weber, D. J. ed. New Spain's far northern frontier p273-82

Wu, Ch'êng-ên

About individual works
Monkey

Plaks, A. H. Allegory in Hsi-yu chi and Hung-lou meng. *In* Chinese narrative p163-202

Wu, Ching-tzu

About individual works
The scholars

Kao, Yu-kung. Lyric vision in Chinese narrative tradition: a reading of Hung-lou meng and Ju-lin wai-shih. *In* Chinese narrative p227-43

Lin, Shuen-fu. Ritual and narrative structure in Ju-lin wai-shih. *In* Chinese narrative p244-65

Wu, Pei-yi

The spiritual autobiography of Te-ch'ing. *In* The Unfolding of Neo-Confucianism p67-92

Wu, Wen-ying

About

Chao, Chia-ying Yeh. Wu Wen-ying's Tz'u: a modern view. *In* Birch, C. ed. Studies in Chinese literary genres p154-91

Wu, Yuan-li

Economic trends in the future of the western Pacific. *In* Pacific Asia and U.S. policies: a political-economic-strategic assessment p95-107

Wuellenkemper, Theodor

Innovative transport technologies: the airship. *In* Strategies for human settlements: habitat and environment p164-69

Wulfstan II, Abp. of York

About

Scragg, D. G. Napier's 'Wulfstan' homily xxx: its sources, its relationship to the Vercelli Book and its style. *In* Anglo-Saxon England 6 p197-211

About individual works
Sermo Lupi ad Anglos

Hollis, S. The thematic structure of the Sermo Lupi. *In* Anglo-Saxon England 6 p175-95

Wunderlich, Carl August. See Wunderlich, Karl Reinhold August

Wunderlich, Karl Reinhold August

About

Temkin, O. Wunderlich, Schelling and the history of medicine. *In* Temkin, O. The double face of Janus p246-51

Wundt, Wilhelm Max

About

Fancher, R. E. Psychology in the university: Wilhelm Wundt and William James. *In* Fancher, R. E. Pioneers of psychology p126-69

Wurtzel, Alan H. and Turner, Colin

Latent functions of the telephone: what missing the extension means. *In* The Social impact of the telephone p246-61

Wuthnow, Robert
The new religions in social context. *In* The New religious consciousness p267-93

Religious movements and the transition in world order. *In* Needleman, J. and Baker, G. eds. Understanding the new religions p63-79

Wyandot Indians. See Huron Indians

Wyatt, David K.
Chronicle traditions in Thai historiography. *In* Southeast Asian history and historiography p107-22

Education and the modernization of Thai society. *In* Change and persistence in Thai society p125-49

Wyatt, David M.
Choosing in Frost. *In* Frost: centennial essays II p129-40

Wyatt, Sir Thomas, 1503-1542

About

Hannen, T. A. The humanism of Sir Thomas Wyatt. *In* Sloan, T. O. and Waddington, R. S. eds. The rhetoric of Renaissance poetry p37-57

About individual works
They flee from me

Trilling, L. Sir Thomas Wyatt: They flee from me. *In* Trilling, L. Prefaces to The experience of literature p182-87

Wyatt-Brown, Bertram
William Lloyd Garrison and antislavery unity: a reappraisal. *In* Swierenga, R. P. ed. Beyond the Civil War synthesis p309-28

Wycherley, William

Sources

Kearful, F. J. Molière among the English, 1660-1737. *In* Johnson, R. B.; Neumann, E. S. and Trail, G. T. eds. Molière and the commonwealth of letters: patrimony and posterity p199-217

Wyclif, John. See Wycliffe, John

Wycliffe, John

About

Aston, M. E. Lollardy and sedition, 1381-1431. *In* Peasants, knights and heretics p273-318

Breck, A. D. John Wyclyf on time. *In* Cosmology, history, and theology p211-18

Shepherd, G. Religion and philosophy in Chaucer. *In* Brewer, D. S. ed. Geoffrey Chaucer p262-89

Wyclifites. See Lollards

Wyclyf, John. See Wycliffe, John

Wylie, Harold A.
Alain Robbe-Grillet: scientific humanist. *In* Garvin, H. R. ed. Makers of the twentieth-century novel p245-52

Wymer, Thomas L.
Philip José Farmer: the trickster as artist. *In* Clareson, T. D. ed. Voices for the future: essays on major science fiction writers v2 p34-55

The Swiftian satire of Kurt Vonnegut, Jr. *In* Clareson, T. D. ed. Voices for the future: essays on major science fiction writers v 1 p238-62

Wynne, Brian
Physics and psychics: science, symbolic action, and social control in late Victorian England. *In* Barnes, B. and Shapin, S. eds. Natural order p167-86

Wynter, Sylvia
The eye of the other: images of the Black in Spanish literature. *In* DeCosta, M. ed. Blacks in Hispanic literature p8-19

'The necessary background.' *In* Baugh, E. ed. Critics on Caribbean literature p19-23

Wyoming

Politics and government

Coombs, F. A. The impact of the New Deal on Wyoming politics. *In* Braeman, J.; Bremner, R. H. and Brody, D. eds. The New Deal v2 p198-239

Wyzanski, Charles E.
The rights of man. *In* Warner, S. B. ed. The American experiment p39-52

X

X-ray spectroscopy
Kragh, H. Niels Bohr's second atomic theory. *In* Historical studies in the physical sciences v10 p123-86

X-rays. See X-ray spectroscopy

Xenophon

About

Markovic, M. Xenophanes on drinking-parties and Olympic Games. *In* Illinois classical studies v3, 1978 p 1-26

About individual works
Cyropaedia

Heiserman, A. R. Erotic suffering. *In* Heiserman, A. R. The novel before the novel p3-10

Hellenica

Rice, D. G. Xenophon, Diodorus and the year 379/378 B.C. Reconstruction and reappraisal. *In* Yale classical studies v24 p95-130

Xenophon of Ephesus

About individual works
Ephesian history; or, The love-adventures of Abrocomas and Anthis

Heiserman, A. R. Bits and epitomes. *In* Heiserman, A. R. The novel before the novel p41-63

Xiques, Donez
John Muir's My first summer in the Sierra. *In* Kagle, S. E. ed. America: exploration and travel p102-12

Xodasevic, V. F. See Khodasevich, Vladislav Felitsianovich

Xodasevič, Vladislav Felitsianovich. See Khodasevich, Vladislav Felitsianovich

!Xü (African people) See !Kung (African people)

Xun, Lu. See Chow, Shu-jên

Y

Yahweh. See God (Judaism)—Name

Yakemtchouk, Romain
The OAU and international law. *In* El-Ayouty, Y. ed. The Organization of African Unity after ten years p79-102

Yakobson, Sergius
Richard Cobden's sojourn in Russia, 1847. *In* Oxford Slavonic papers, new ser. v7 p60-74

Yakubovich, M. P.
From the history of ideas. *In* Medvedev, R. A. ed. The Samizdat register p147-202

Yale Repertory Theatre
Brustein, R. S. No more masterpieces revisited: a speech to the Shakespeare '74 Convention at Brooklyn College. *In* Brustein, R. S. The culture watch p131-37
Brustein, R. S. The Yale idea: an address to students at the School of Drama. *In* Brustein, R. S. The culture watch p7-13

Yale University

School of Drama

Brustein, R. S. A Dean's goodbye: a speech to the graduates of the School of Drama. *In* Brustein, R. S. The culture watch p138-42
Brustein, R. S. The Yale idea: an address to students at the School of Drama. *In* Brustein, R. S. The culture watch p7-13

Yalem, Ronald J.
The concept of world order. *In* The Year book of world affairs, 1975 p320-36
The decline of international relations theory. *In* The Year book of world affairs, 1976 p292-306
The level-of-analysis problem reconsidered. *In* The Year book of world affairs, 1977 p306-26
Regional security communities and world order. *In* The Year book of world affairs, 1979 p217-42
Transnational politics versus international politics. *In* The Year book of world affairs, 1978 p237-50

Yamacraw Indians. See Creek Indians

Yamagawa, Kenjiro

About

Koizumi, K. The emergence of Japan's first physicists: 1868-1900. *In* Historical studies in the physical sciences v6 p3-108

Yamamoto, Mitsuru
The Cold war and U.S.-Japan economic cooperation. *In* The Origins of the Cold war in Asia p408-25

Yamamura, Kozo
A compromise with culture: the historical evolution of the managerial structure of large Japanese firms. *In* Evolution of international management structures p159-85

Yamanouchi, Hisaaki
Abe Kōbō and Oe Kenzaburō: the search for identity in contemporary Japanese literature. *In* Modern Japan p166-86
The search for authenticity in modern Japanese literature
Contents
The agonies of individualism: Natsume Soseki
The eternal womanhood: Tanizaki Jun'ichiro and Kawabata Yasunari
From romanticism to naturalism: Kitamura Tōkoku and Shimazaki Tōson
In search of identity: Abé Kōbō and Ōe Kenzaburō
A phantasy world: Mishima Yukio
The rivals: Shiga Naoya and Akutagawa Ryūnosuke
Two precursors: Tsubouchi Shōyō and Futabatei Shimei

Yandell, Keith E.
Hume on religious belief. *In* Livingston, D. W. and King, J. T. eds. Hume p109-25

Yang, C. K. See Yang, Ch'ing-K'un

Yang, Ch'ing-K'un
Some preliminary statistical patterns of mass actions in nineteenth-century China. *In* Conflict and control in late imperial China p174-210

Yannella, Donald J.
"Seeing the elephant" in Mardi. *In* Artful thunder p105-17

Yano, Tōru
Who set the stage for the Cold war in Southeast Asia? *In* The Origins of the Cold war in Asia p321-37

Yans-McLaughlin, Virginia
A flexible tradition: South Italian immigrants confront a new work experience. *In* Immigrants in industrial America, 1850-1920 p67-84

Yap, Caroline Islands

Population

Schneider, D. M. Depopulation and the Yap tabinau. *In* Social organization and the applications of anthropology p94-113

Yapp, Malcolm E.
The modernization of Middle Eastern armies in the nineteenth century: a comparative view. *In* War, technology and society in the Middle East p330-66

Yardley, David Charles Miller
The effectiveness of the Westminster model of constitution. *In* The Year book of world affairs, 1977 p342-51

Yarker, P. M.
Byron and the satiric temper. *In* Jump, J. D. ed. Byron p76-93

Yarmolinsky, Adam
What future for the professional in American society? *In* A New America? p159-74

Yaron, Zvi
Religion and morality in Israel and in the Dispersion. *In* Modern Jewish ethics p228-42

About individual works
Religion and morality in Israel and in the Dispersion

Herman, S. N. A response to Zvi Yaron. *In* Modern Jewish ethics p243-47

Yarrow, C. H.
Quaker efforts toward conciliation in the India-Pakistan War of 1965. *In* Unofficial diplomats p89-110

Yarrow, Mike. See Yarrow, C. H.

Yates, Douglas
The roots of American leadership: political style and policy consequences. *In* Burnham, W. D. and Weinberg, M. W. eds. American politics and public policy p140-68

Yates, Peter
Patchen's poetry and jazz. *In* Morgan, R. G. ed. Kenneth Patchen: a collection of essays p208-17

Yates, W. E.
Cultural life in early nineteenth-century Vienna. *In* Branscombe, P. ed. Austrian life and literature, 1780-1938 p12-25

Yavetz, Zvi
Existimatio, fama, and the ides of March. *In* Harvard Studies in classical philology v78 p35-65

Yeats, Jack Butler
About

Berger, J. Jack Yeats. *In* Berger, J. The look of things p54-60

Rose, M. G. Jack B. Yeats's picture of the peasant. *In* Casey, D. J. and Rhodes, R. E. eds. Views of the Irish peasantry, 1800-1916 p192-202

Yeats, John Butler
About

Donoghue, D. John Butler Yeats. *In* Abroad in America: Visitors to the new Nation, 1776-1914 p260-69

About individual works
Early memories: some chapters of autobiography

Bornstein, G. The antinomial structure of John Butler Yeats's early memories: some chapters of autobiography. *In* Landow, G. P. ed. Approaches to Victorian autobiography p200-11

Yeats, William Butler
Preface to the first edition of The well of the saints by J. M. Synge. *In* Praise from famous men: an anthology of introductions p182-89

About

Bloom, H. Yeats, Gnosticism, and the sacred void. *In* Bloom, H. Poetry and repression p205-34

Bornstein, G. Yeats and the greater romantic lyric. *In* Bornstein, G. ed. Romantic and modern p91-110

Brooks. C. William Faulkner and William Butler Yeats: parallels and affinities. *In* Faulkner: fifty years after The marble faun p139-58

Clarke, A. Reminiscences of Yeats: glimpses of W. B. Yeats. *In* Yeats, Joyce, and Beckett p46-51

Eliot, T. S. Yeats. *In* Eliot, T. S. Selected prose of T. S. Eliot p248-57

Fraser, G. S. Seven poems by Yeats. *In* Fraser, G. S. Essays on twentieth-century poems p29-44

Fraser, G. S. W. B. Yeats. *In* Fraser, G. S. Essays on twentieth-century poets p11-28

Fraser, G. S. Yeats and the ballad style. *In* Essays on twentieth-century poets p45-60

Fraser, G. S. Yeats: two dream poems. *In* Fraser, G. S. Essay on twentieth-century poets p61-79

Gillie, C. Yeats and Eliot: the climax. *In* Gillie, C. Movements in English literature, 1900-1940 p150-63

Hardy, B. N. Passion and contemplation in Yeats's love poetry. *In* Hardy, B. N. The advantage of lyric p67-83

Henn, T. R. The centenary Yeats. *In* Henn, T. R. Last essays p65-80

Henn, T. R. Choice and chance. *In* Henn, T. R. Last essays p51-64

Henn, T. R. 'The place of shells.' *In* Henn, T. R. Last essays p13-25

Henn, T. R. Yeats and the poetry of war. *In* Henn, T. R. Last essays p81-97

Hough, G. G. W. B. Yeats: a study in poetic integration. *In* Hough, G. G. Selected essays p144-72

Langbaum, R. W. Exteriority of self. *In* Langbaum, R. W. The mysteries of identity p147-74

Langbaum, R. W. The self as a work of art. *In* Langbaum, R. W. The mysteries of identity p175-219

Langbaum, R. W. The self as God. *In* Langbaum, R. W. The mysteries of identity p220-47

Lenson, D. R. Toward lyric tragedy: W. B. Yeats. *In* Lenson, D. R. Achilles' choice p65-97

O'Donnell, W. H. Yeats as adept and artist: The speckled bird, The secret rose, and The wind among the reeds. *In* Yeats and the occult p55-79

Olney, J. L. The esoteric flower: Yeats and Jung. *In* Yeats and the occult p27-54

Orel, H. The Irishry of William Butler Yeats. *In* Orel, H. ed. Irish history and culture p291-307

Ragussis, M. W. B. Yeats: "Her vision in the wood" as tragic art: a "hollow image of fulfilled desire." *In* Ragussis, M. The subterfuge of art p109-32

Shapiro, K. J. W. B. Yeats: trial by culture. *In* Shapiro, K. J. The poetry wreck p55-82

Sidnell, M. J. Mr Yeats, Michael Robartes and their circle. *In* Yeats and the occult p225-54

Stauffer, D. A. The modern myth of the modern myth. *In* Wimsatt, W. K. ed. Literary criticism: idea and act p66-82

Unterecker, J. E. Countryman, peasant and servant in the poetry of W. B. Yeats. *In* Casey, D. J. and Rhodes, R. E. eds. Views of the Irish peasantry, 1800-1916 p178-91

Webb, E. The one and the many: the ambiguous challenge of Being in the poetry of Yeats and Rilke. *In* Webb, E. The dark dove p88-110

Worth, K. J. The syntax achieved. *In* Worth, K. J. The Irish drama of Europe from Yeats to Beckett p48-71

Worth, K. J. Towards modernism: a new theatrical syntax. *In* Worth, K. J. The Irish drama of Europe from Yeats to Beckett p11-47

Worth, K. J. Yeats, Maeterlinck and Synge. *In* Worth, K. J. The Irish drama of Europe from Yeats to Beckett p140-57

Worth, K. J. Yeats's drama of the interior: a technique for the modern theatre. *In* Worth, K. J. The Irish drama of Europe from Yeats to Beckett p158-93

About individual works
Among school children

Holbrook, D. What can creativity do? W. B. Yeats's Among school children. *In* Holbrook, D. Lost bearings in English poetry p194-203

Byzantium

Brooke, N. Crazy Jane and 'Byzantium.' *In* English Association. Essays and studies, 1974 p68-83

Collected plays

Berryman, J. The ritual of W. B. Yeats. *In* Berryman, J. The freedom of the poet p245-52'

Collected works in verse and prose

Mulryne, J. R. Printer's copy for part of volume seven of the W. B. Yeats Collected works in verse and prose (1908). *In* Virginia. University. Bibliographical Society. Studies in bibliography v30 p235-40

Yeats, William B.—*Continued*

Knowledge—Occult sciences

Goldman, A. Yeats, spiritualism, and psychical research. *In* Yeats and the occult p108-29

Harper, G. M. "A subject of investigation": miracle at Mirebeau. *In* Yeats and the occult p172-89

Harper, G. M. Yeats's occult papers. *In* Yeats and the occult p 1-10

Harper, G. M. and Kelly, J. S. Preliminary examination of the script of E[lizabeth] R[adcliffe]. *In* Yeats and the occult p130-71

O'Donnell, W. H. Yeats as adept and artist: The speckled bird, The secret rose, and The wind among the reeds. *In* Yeats and the occult p55-79

Raine, K. J. Hades wrapped in cloud. *In* Yeats and the occult p80-107

Watkins, G. M. Yeats and Mr Watkins' Bookshop. *In* Yeats and the occult p307-10

Library

Harper, G. W. Yeats's occult papers. *In* Yeats and the occult p 1-10

Manuscripts

Hood, W. K. Michael Robartes: two occult manuscripts. *In* Yeats and the occult p204-24

Mysticism

See Yeats, William Butler—Religion and ethics

Philosophy

Henn, T. R. Towards the values. *In* Henn, T. R. Last essays p240-53

See also Yeats, William Butler—Religion and ethics

Political and social views

Henn, T. R. Towards the values. *In* Henn, T. R. Last essays p240-53

Henn, T. R. The weasel's tooth. *In* Henn, T. R. Last essays p26-50

Religion and ethics

Henn, T. R. 'The property of the dead.' *In* Henn, T. R. Last essays p221-39

Supernatural element

See Yeats, William Butler—Knowledge—Occult sciences

Technique

Henn, T. R. The rhetoric of Yeats. *In* Henn, T. R. Last essays p98-118

Yeats family

Murphy, W. M. Psychic daughter, mystic son, sceptic father. *In* Yeats and the occult p11-26

Yefremov, Ivan Antonovich. See Efremov, Ivan Antonovich

Yeh, Chia-ying

The Ch'ang-chou school of Tzu' criticism. *In* Chinese approaches to literature from Confucius to Liang Ch'i-ch'ao p151-88

Yehoshua, Abraham B.

About

Alter, R. Fiction in a state of siege. *In* Alter, R. Defenses of the imagination p213-31

Yehovah. See God (Judaism)—Name

The Yellow Emperor's classic of internal medicine. See Huang-ti nei ching su wên

Yen, Fu

About

Hsia, Chih-tsing. Yen Fu and Liang Ch'i-ch'ao as advocates of new fiction. *In* Chinese approaches to literature from Confucius to Liang Ch'i-ch'ao p221-57

Yen, Yüan

About

Tu, Wei-ming. Yen Yüan: from inner experience to lived concreteness. *In* The Unfolding of Neo-Confucianism p511-41

Yergin, Daniel

Order and survival. *In* A New America? p263-87

Yerkes, David

The text of the Canterbury fragment of Werferth's translation of Gregory's Dialogues and its relation to the other manuscripts. *In* Anglo-Saxon England 6 p121-35

Yermakov, Ivan. See Ermakov, Ivan Dmitrievich

Yerushalmi, Yosef Hayim

Professing Jews in post-expulsion Spain and Portugal. *In* Salo Wittmayer Baron v2 p1009-22

Yerusholayim de-Lita (Jerusalem of Lithuania)

Dawidowicz, L. S. Picturing the past. *In* Dawidowicz, L. S. The Jewish presence p177-90

Yesenin-Volpin, Alexander Sergeevich. See Esenin-Vol'pin, Aleksandr Sergeevich

Yeshivot. See Rabbinical seminaries

Yetiv, Isaac

Alienation in the modern novel of French North Africa before independence. *In* Exile and tradition p85-97

Yetman, Norman R.

The Irish experience in America. *In* Orel, H. ed Irish history and culture p347-76

Yevreinov, Nikolai Nikolayevich. See Evreinov, Nikolai Nikolaevich

Yiddish language

Dawidowicz, L. S. Yiddish and its translation. *In* Dawidowicz, L. S. The Jewish presence p154-62

Dawidowicz, L. S. Yiddish: past, present, and perfected. *In* Dawidowicz, L. S. The Jewish presence p133-53

Dictionaries

Dawidowicz, L. S. Yiddish: past, present, and perfected. *In* Dawidowicz, L. S. The Jewish presence p133-53

Yiddish language in the United States

Dawidowicz, L. S. Yiddish: past, present, and perfected. *In* Dawidowicz, L. S. The Jewish presence p133-53

Yinger, John Milton

Countercultures and social change. *In* Major social issues p476-97

Ethnicity in complex societies: structural, cultural, and characterological factors. *In* The Uses of controversy in sociology p197-216

Yoder, Don

Folklife studies in American scholarship. *In* Yoder, D. ed. American folklife p3-18

Hohman and Romanus: origins and diffusion of the Pennsylvania German powwow manual. *In* American folk medicine p235-48

Yoga

De Ropp, R. S. Drugs, yoga, and psychotransformism. *In* Needleman, J. and Lewis, D. eds. On the way to self knowledge p148-69

Psychology

Chaudhuri, H. Yoga psychology. *In* Tart, C. T. ed. Transpersonal psychologies p231-80

Therapeutic use

Kuvalayananda, S. and Vinekar, S. L. Principles of yogic therapy; excerpt from "Yogi therapy: its basic principles and methods." *In* Sobel, D. S. ed. Ways of health p319-29

Yogic therapy. See Yoga—Therapeutic use

Yom Kippur War, 1973. See Israel-Arab War, 1973

Yombe (African people)

Religion and mythology

Bond, G. Minor prophets and Yombe cultural dynamics. *In* Colonialism and change p145-62

Yonge, Charlotte Mary

About

Brownell, D. B. The two worlds of Charlotte Yonge. *In* The Worlds of Victorian fiction p165-78

York, Ernest Charles

Isolt's trial in Béroul and La Folie Tristan d'Oxford. *In* Medievalia et humanistica no. 6 p157-61

York, Herbert Frank

The origins of MIRV. *In* The Dynamics of the arms race p23-35

An outline history of nuclear proliferation. *In* International terrorism and world security p105-17

Reconnaissance satellites and the arms race. *In* Arms control and technological innovation p224-31

Yoruba art. See Art, Yoruba

Yoruba gods. See Gods, Yoruba

Yoruba mythology. See Mythology, Yoruba

Yoruba women. See Women, Yoruba

Yorubas

Eades, J. S. Kinship and entrepreneurship among Yoruba in northern Ghana. *In* Shack, W. A. and Skinner, E. P. eds. Strangers in African societies p169-82

Sudarkasa, N. From stranger to alien: the socio-political history of the Nigerian Yoruba in Ghana, 1900-1970. *In* Shack, W. A. and Skinner, E. P. eds. Strangers in African societies p141-67

Religion

Booth, N. S. God and the gods in West Africa. *In* African religions: a symposium p159-81

Women

See Women, Yoruba

Yoshioka, Yoshitoyo

Taoist monastic life. *In* Welch, H. and Seidel, A. K. eds. Facets of Taoism p229-52

Yost, Robert Morris, and Kalish, Donald

Miss MacDonald on sleeping and waking. *In* Dunlop, C. E. M. ed. Philosophical essays on dreaming p81-102

Young, Al

About

Reed, I. The song turning back into itself. *In* Reed, I. Shrovetide in old New Orleans p118-19

Young, Albert James. See Young, Al

Young, Ann Venture

The Black woman in Afro-Caribbean poetry. *In* DeCosta, M. ed. Blacks in Hispanic literature p137-42

Young, Arthur

About

Feingold, R. Bucolic tradition and virtuous work: Arthur Young and Adam Smith. *In* Feingold, R. Nature and society p51-82

Young, Crawford

Nationalism and separatism in Africa. *In* Kilson, M. ed. New states in the modern world p57-74

Young, David P.

"The living world for text": life and art in The wild swans at Coole. *In* Martz, L. L. and Williams, A. L. eds. The author in his work p143-60

Where the bee sucks: A triangular study of Doctor Faustus, The alchemist, and The tempest. *In* Shakespeare's romances reconsidered p149-66

Young, Elizabeth

Arms control in the oceans: active and passive. *In* Borgese, E. M. and Krieger, D. eds. The tides of change p110-20

Young, Emily Hilda

About

Cavaliero, G. Romantic landscapes: Mary Webb, E. H. Young. *In* Cavaliero, G. The rural tradition in the English novel, 1900-1939 p133-56

Young, Ernest Paddock

The Hung-hsien emperor as a modernizing conservative. *In* The Limits of change p171-90

Young, Francis Brett

About

Cavaliero, G. Town and country: Francis Brett Young, Winifred Holtby. *In* Cavaliero, G. The rural tradition in the English novel, 1900-1939 p81-100

Young, Gloria L.

"The fountainhead of all forms": poetry and the unconscious in Emerson and Howard Nemerov. *In* Artful thunder p241-67

Young, Hugh Hampton

About

Harvey, A. M. Early contributions to the surgery of cancer: William S. Halsted, Hugh H. Young, and John G. Clark. *In* Harvey, A. M. Adventures in medical research p69-83

Young, James Harvey

Euclid + Lincoln = Kent. *In* From Parnassus p271-82

Young, Louise Merwin

Women's place in American politics: the historical perspective. *In* Havard, W. C. and Bernd, J. L. eds. 200 years of the Republic in retrospect p295-335

Young, M. Crawford. See Young, Crawford

Young, Melanie

Distorted expectations: Pip and the problems of language. *In* Dickens Studies Annual v7 p203-20

Young, Philip

"Big world out there": The Nick Adams stories. *In* Benson, J. J. ed. The short stories of Ernest Hemingway: critical essays p29-45

Young, Stephen

A comparison of the industrial experiences. *In* Planning, politics and public policy p141-54

See also Wright, M. G. jt. auth.

Young, Thomas Daniel

The evolution of Ransom's critical theory: image and idea. *In* Young, T. D. ed. The New Criticism and after p22-35

Introduction. *In* Young, T. D. ed. The New Criticism and after p xv-xxi

A little divergence: the critical theories of John Crowe Ransom and Cleanth Brooks. *In* Simpson, L. P. ed. The possibilities of order: Cleanth Brooks and his work p168-95

Narration as creative act: the role of Quentin Compson in Absalom, Absalom! *In* Faulkner, modernism, and film: Faulkner and Yoknapatawpha, 1978 p82-101

Our two worthies: Robert Frost and John Crowe Ransom. *In* Frost: centennial essays II p281-90

Pioneering on principle; or how a traditional society may be dissolved. *In* Faulkner, modernism, and film: Faulkner and Yoknapatawpha, 1978 p34-48

Social form and social order: an examination of The optimist's daughter. *In* Prenshaw, P. W. ed. Eudora Welty p367-85

Young, Vernon

About

Murray, E. Vernon Young, ethnological-aesthetic critic. *In* Murray, E. Nine American film critics p172-204

Young-Bruehl, Elisabeth

From the pariah's point of view: reflections on Hannah Arendt's life and work. *In* Hannah Arendt: the recovery of the public world p3-26

Young men. See Youth

Young Mr Lincoln (Motion picture)

John Ford's Young Mr Lincoln. *In* Nichols, B. ed. Movies and methods p493-529

Nichols, B. Style, grammar, and the movies. *In* Nichols, B. ed. Movies and methods p607-28

Young nations. See States, New

Young Turkish Party

Kedourie, É. The impact of the Young Turk revolution on the Arabic-speaking provinces of the Ottoman Empire. *In* Kedourie, É. Arabic political memoirs and other studies p124-61

Young women

See also Youth

United States—Conduct of life

Critoph, G. E. The flapper and her critics. *In* "Remember the ladies": new perspectives on women in American history p145-60

Youngs, Frederick J.

The Tudor governments and dissident religious books. *In* The dissenting tradition p167-90

Your show of shows (Television program)

Sarris, A. Your show of shows revisited. *In* Sarris, A. Politics and cinema p172-80

Yourgrau, Wolfgang

On some cosmological theories and constants. *In* Cosmology, history, and theology p179-210

Youssef, Nadia Haggag

The status and fertility patterns of Muslim women. *In* Beck, L. and Keddie, N. R. eds. Women in the Muslim world p69-99

See also Smock, A. C. jt. auth.

Youth

Eisenstadt, S. N. Cultural settings and adolescence and youth around the year 2000. *In* Adolescence and youth in prospect p114-24

Faessler, M. Youth in the year 2000: the problem of values. *In* Adolescence and youth in prospect p125-36

Hill, J. P. and Mönks, F. J. Overview and outcomes. *In* Adolescence and youth in prospect p 1-12

Rosenmayr, H. and Rosenmayr, L. The social plasticity of youth. *In* Adolescence and youth in prospect p95-113

See also Adolescence; Boys; Children; Sexual ethics for youth; Youth movement

Attitudes

Gallatin, J. E. The conceptualization of rights: psychological development and cross-national perspectives. *In* Claude, R. P. ed. Comparative human rights p302-25

Books and reading

See Books and reading for youth

Conduct of life

Prince, R. H. Cocoon work: an interpretation of the concern of contemporary youth with the mysical. *In* Zaretsky, I. I. and Leone, M. P. eds. Religious movements in contemporary America p255-71

Schafer, W. E. Sport and youth counter-culture: contrasting socialization themes. *In* Social problems in athletics p183-200

Employment—United States

Coleman, J. S. Needed: new routes to adulthood. *In* Gross, B. and Gross, R. eds. The children's rights movement p244-50

Levine, J. A. Three in enterprise. *In* Gross, B. and Gross, R. eds. The children's rights movement p283-86

Political activity

See Students—Political activity

Psychology

See Adolescent psychology

Religious life

Anthony, D. and Robbins, T. The Meher Baba movement: its affect [sic!] on post-adolescent social alienation. *In* Zaretsky, I. I. and Leone, M. P. eds. Religious movements in contemporary America p479-511

Bellah, R. N. New religious consciousness and the crisis in modernity. *In* The New religious consciousness p333-52

Judah, J. S. The Hare Krishna movement. *In* Zaretsky, I. I. and Leone, M. P. eds. Religious movements in contemporary America p463-78

See also Christian World Liberation Front; Jesus people

Sexual behavior

Bettelheim, B. About the sexual revolution. *In* Bettelheim, B. Surviving, and other essays p370-86

New York (City)

Cole, L. Kill each other, be killed, kill yourself; excerpt from "Street kids." *In* Gross, B. and Gross, R. eds. The children's rights movement p74-78

Yucatan Peninsula

Antiquities

Ball, J. W. The rise of the northern Maya chiefdoms: a socioprocessual analysis. *In* The Origins of Maya civilization p101-32

Sabloff, J. A. and others. Trade and power in postclassic Yucatan: initial observations. *In* Mesoamerican archaeology p397-416

Yugoslavia

Foreign relations

Auty, P. Yugoslavia and the Cold war. *In* Siracusa, J. M. and Barclay, G. S. eds. The impact of the Cold war p125-43

Popvic, N. D. Yugoslavia's crucial place in world politics. *In* Kaplan, M. A. ed. The many faces of communism p266-78

Foreign relations—Russia

Wilson, Sir D. Yugoslavia and Soviet policy. *In* Kirk, G. L. and Wessell, N. H. eds. The Soviet threat p77-87

Politics and government

Bridge, S. Some causes of political change in modern Yugoslavia. *In* Esman, M. J. ed. Ethnic conflict in the Western world p343-68

Politics and government—1945-

Auty, P. Yugoslavia and the Cold war. *In* Siracusa, J. M. and Barclay, G. S. eds. The impact of the Cold war p125-43

Dyker, D. A. Yugoslavia: unity out of diversity? *In* Brown, A. H. and Gray, J. eds. Political culture and political change in Communist states p66-100

Furtak, R. K. Yugoslavia: a special case. *In* Hayward, J. E. S. and Berki, R. N. eds. State and society in contemporary Europe p158-78

Yügrüm, Güldem. See Mitten, D. G. jt. auth.

Yurieff, Zoya

Prishedshy: A. Bely and A. Chekhov. *In* Janecek, G. ed. Andrey Bely p44-55

Z

Zabeeh, Farhang

Hume's problem of induction: an appraisal. *In* Livingston, D. W. and King, J. T. eds. Hume p69-90

Zabinski, Zbigniew

The biological index of the buying power of money. *In* Biology of man in history p179-90

Zabolotskiĭ, Nikolaĭ Alekseevich

About

Slonim, M. L. Posthumous revivals: Bulgakov, Platonov, Zabolotsky. *In* Slonim, M. L. Soviet Russian literature p352-62

Zacharias Lisieux. See Zacharie de Lisieux, père

Zacharie de Lisieux, père

About individual works

La philosophie Chrestienne

Grant, P. Richard Crashaw and the Capucins: images and the force of belief. *In* Grant, P. Images and ideas in literature of the English Renaissance p89-128

Zacher, Christian K.

Curiosity and pilgrimage

Contents

The bibliophile as curious pilgrim: Richard De Bury's Philobiblon

Curiositas

Curiosity and the instability of pilgrimage: Chaucer's Canterbury tales

A new sense of the world

The pilgrim as curious traveler: Mandeville's Travels

Pilgrimage

Zaddikim

Bosk, C. The routinization of charisma: the case of the zaddik. *In* Johnson, H. M. ed. Religious change and continuity p150-67

Zadikim. See Zaddikim

Zadkine, Ossip

About

Berger, J. Zadkine. *In* Berger, J. The look of things p66-69

Zaghlul, Sa'd

About

Smith, R. Y. The British and Sa'd Zaghlul, 1906-1912. *In* Nationalism in a non-national state p195-206

Zago, Marcello

Buddhism in contemporary Laos. *In* Dumoulin, H. ed. Buddhism in the modern world p120-29

Contemporary Khmer Buddhism. *In* Dumoulin, H. ed. Buddhism in the modern world p109-19

Zagoria, Donald S.

Stability in Asia—can it last? *In* Pacific Asia and U.S. policies: a political-economic-strategic assessment p63-66

Zahar, Elie

About

Lakatos, I. and Zahar, E. Why did Copernicus' research program supersede Ptolemy's? *In* The Copernican achievement p354-83

See also Lakatos, I. jt. auth.

Zahniser, Marvin R.

The continental system. *In* Encyclopedia of American foreign policy p204-11

Zaid, Gabriel

About

Forster, M. H. Four contemporary Mexican poets: Marco Antonio Montes de Oca, Gabriel Zaid, José Emilio Pacheco, Homero Aridjis. *In* Forster, M. H. ed. Tradition and renewal p139-56

Zaire

Foreign relations

Kanza, T. R. Zaire's foreign policy. *In* Aluko, O. ed. The foreign policies of African states p235-43

Religion

Janzen, J. M. The tradition of renewal in Kongo religion. *In* African religions: a symposium p69-115

Zak, Michele Wender

The grass is singing: a little novel about the emotions. *In* Pratt, A. V. and Dembo, L. S. eds. Doris Lessing p64-73

Żale Matki Boskiej pod krzyżem

Pietrkiewicz, J. Simultaneity in a sequence: the time pattern of a mediaeval poem. *In* For Wiktor Weintraub p333-44

Zelazny, Roger
About
Sanders, J. Zelazny: unfinished business. *In* Clareson, T. D. ed. Voices for the future: essays on major science fiction writers v2 p180-96

Zeldin, Theodore
France. *In* Spring, D. ed. European landed elites in the nineteenth century p127-39

Zelinsky, Wilbur
Unearthly delights: cemetery names and the map of the changing American afterworld. *In* Geographies of the mind p171-95

Zeller, Hans
A new approach to the critical constitution of literary texts. *In* Virginia. University. Bibliographical Society. Studies in bibliography v28 p231-64

Zeller, Nancy Anne
The spiral of time in Ada. *In* A Book of things about Vladimir Nabokov p280-90

Zellner, Arnold
The quality of quantitative economic policy-making when targets and costs of change are mis-specified. *In* Econometrics and economic theory p147-64

Zeman, J. Jay
Peirce's theory of signs. *In* Sebeok, T. A. ed. A perfusion of signs p22-39

Zen, E-tu. See Sun, E-tu (Zên)

Zen. See Zen Buddhism

Zen Buddhism
Owens, C. M. Zen Buddhism. *In* Tart, C. T. ed. Transpersonal psychologies p153-202

Psychology
Owens, C. M. Zen Buddhism. *In* Tart, C. T. ed. Transpersonal psychologies p153-202

United States
Ellwood, R. S. Zen journeys to the West. *In* Ellwood, R. S. Alternative altars p136-63

Tipton, S. M. New religious movements and the problem of a modern ethic. *In* Johnson, H. M. ed. Religious change and continuity p286-312

Zen Buddhism in literature
Dauenhauer, R. Some notes on Zen Buddhist tendencies in modern Finnish poetry. *In* Dauenhauer, R. and Binham P. eds. Snow in May p60-66

Zender, Karl Francis
Faulkner. *In* American literary scholarship, 1974 p123-38

Faulkner [another essay] *In* American literary scholarship, 1975 p143-65

Zenith Radio Corp. v. United States. *In* The Supreme Court review, 1978 p297-312

Zeno
Aesthetics
Sparshott, F. E. Zeno on art: anatomy of a definition. *In* Rist, J. M. ed. The Stoics p273-90

Zenobia, Queen of Palmyra
Art
Shapley, F. R. Tiepolo's Zenobia cycle. *In* Enggass, R. C. and Stokstad, M. eds. Hortus imaginum p193-98

Zeppenfeld, Werner
The economics and structure of the record and tape industry: the example of West Germany. *In* Fischer, H. D. and Melnik, S. R. eds. Entertainment: a cross-cultural examination p248-57

Zero (The number)
Coomeraswamy, A. K. Kha and other words denoting "zero," in connection with the Indian metaphysics of space. *In* Coomaraswamy, A. K. Selected papers v2 p220-30

Zetzel, James E. G.
Cicero and the Scipionic Circle. *In* Harvard Studies in classical philology v76 p173-79

Emendavi ad tironem: some notes on scholarship in the second century A.D. *In* Harvard Studies in classical philology v77 p225-43

On the history of Latin scholia. *In* Harvard Studies in classical philology v79 p335-54

Zeus. See Jupiter

Zevi, Bruno
The Italian rationalists. *In* Sharp, D. ed. The rationalists p118-29

Zeyl, Donald John
Plato and talk of a world in flux: Timaeus. *In* Harvard Studies in classical philology v79 p125-48

Zhandova, Ivanka Akrabova- See Akrabova-Zhandova, Ivanka

Zhirmunskiĭ, Viktor Maksimovich
The passion of Aleksandr Blok. *In* Erlich, V. ed. Twentieth-century Russian literary criticism p117-37

About
Beyer, T. R. The Bely-Zhirmunsky polemic. *In* Janecek, G. ed. Andrey Bely p205-13

Zhirmunskij, Viktor. See Zhirmunskiĭ, Viktor Maksimovich

Zhou, Shuren. See Chow, Shu-jên

Zhü/wäsi (African people) See !Kung (African people)

Zhukovskiĭ, Vasilii Andreevich
About
Katz, M. R. The epithet in Zhukovsky's literary ballads. *In* Katz, M. R. The literary ballad in early nineteenth-century Russian literature p76-100

Katz, M. R. Polemics. *In* Katz, M. R. The literary ballad in early nineteenth-century Russian literature p101-20

Katz, M. R. Zhukovsky's literary ballads. *In* Katz, M. R. The literary ballad in early nineteenth-century Russian literature p37-75

Influence
Katz, M. R. Zhukovsky's imitators. *In* Katz, M. R. The literary ballad in early nineteenth-century Russian literature p121-38

Ziff, Larzer
Shakespeare and Melville's America. *In* Pullin, F. ed. New perspectives on Melville p54-67

Zilversmit, Arthur
The failure of progressive education, 1920-1940. *In* Schooling and society p252-63

Zilversmit, Arthur—*Continued*

Politics and government

O'Meara, P. Rhodesia: from white rule to independent Zimbabwe. *In* Carter, G. M. and O'Meara, P. eds. Southern Africa in crisis p15-47

O'Meara, P. Rhodesia/Zimbabwe: guerrilla warfare or political settlement? *In* Carter, G. M. and O'Meara, P. eds. Southern Africa: the continuing crisis p18-56

Race relations

O'Meara, P. Rhodesia: from white rule to independent Zimbabwe. *In* Carter, G. M. and O'Meara, P. eds. Southern Africa in crisis p15-47

Zimin, A.

On the question of the place in history of the social structure of the Soviet Union. *In* Medvedev, R. A. ed. The Samizdat register p116-46

Zimmer, Basil George

The urban centrifugal drift. *In* Hawley, A. H. and Rock, V. P. eds. Metropolitan America in contemporary perspective p23-91

Zimmerman, Donald H.

Ethnomethodology. *In* McNall, S. G. ed. Theoretical perspectives in sociology p381-96

Zimmerman, Everett

Admiring Pope no more than is proper: Sense and sensibility. *In* Halperin, J. ed. Jane Austen p112-22

Zimmerman, Joseph Francis

The patchwork approach: adaptive responses to increasing urbanization. *In* Hawley, A. H. and Rock, V. P. eds. Metropolitan America in contemporary perspective p431-73

Zimmerman, Marvin

Objectivity in education. *In* Hook, S.; Kurtz, P. and Todorovich, M. eds. The ethics of teaching and scientific research p49-51

Zimmerman, Michael E.

Some important themes in current Heidegger research. *In* Radical phenomenology p259-81

Zimmermann, Johann Georg, Ritter von

About individual works

On experience in the medical art

Temkin, O. Zimmermann's philosophy of the physician. *In* Temkin, O. The double face of Janus p239-45

Zinberg, Cecile

The usable dissenting past: John Strype and Elizabethan Puritanism. *In* The Dissenting tradition p123-39

Zinberg, Norman Earl

The study of consciousness states: problems and progress. *In* Alternate states of consciousness p 1-36

Zinn, Grover A.

Hugh of Saint Victor and the art of memory. *In* Viator: medieval and Renaissance studies v5 p211-34

Ziolkowski, Theodore

Some features of religious figuralism in twentieth-century literature. *In* Miner, E. R. ed. Literary uses of typology p345-69

Zionism

Arendt, H. Herzl and Lazare. *In* Arendt, H. The Jew as pariah: Jewish identity and politics in the modern age p125-30

Arendt, H. The Jewish state: fifty years after. *In* Arendt, H. The Jew as pariah: Jewish identity and politics in the modern age p164-77

Arendt, H. Peace or armistice in the Near East. *In* Arendt, H. The Jew as pariah: Jewish identity and politics in the modern age p193-222

Arendt, H. To save the Jewish homeland. *In* Arendt, H. The Jew as pariah: Jewish identity and politics in the modern age p178-92

Arendt, H. Zionism reconsidered. *In* Arendt, H. The Jew as pariah: Jewish identity and politics in the modern age p131-63

Avineri, S. Political and social aspects of Israeli and Arab nationalism. *In* The Palestinians p97-111

Deutsch, D. The Palestine question: domestic pressures on the President for intervention, 1944-1948. *In* Higham, R. D. ed. Intervention or abstention: the dilemma of American foreign policy p79-94

Green, L. C. Jewish isues on the human-rights agenda in the first half of the twentieth century. *In* Sidorsky, D. ed. Essays on human rights p297-308

Halpern, B. Jewish nationalism: self-determination as a human right. *In* Sidorsky D. ed. Essays on human rights p307-35

Moynihan, D. P. The significance of the Zionism-as-racism resolution for international human rights. *In* Sidorsky, D. ed. Essays on human rights p37-45

Tauber, G. E. Einstein and Zionism. *In* Einstein p199-207

Weizmann, C. The Jewish people and Palestine; excerpts. *In* The Palestinians p46-50

See also Jewish question

Zionist movement. See Zionism

Zither. See Cithern

Zlataric, Bogdan

History of international terrorism and its legal control. *In* International terrorism and political crimes p474-84

Zoffer, H. Jerome

The road ahead for management: evolution or obsolescence. *In* Benton, L. R. ed. Management for the future p317-29

Zogby, Edward G.

Triadic patterns in Lewis's life and thought. *In* Schakel, P. J. ed. The longing for a form p20-39

Zola, Émile

About

Adhémar, J. Emile Zola, photographer. *In* One hundred years of photographic history p 1-6

Farrell, J. T. On Zola. *In* Farrell, J. T. Literary essays, 1954-1974 p39-43

Larkin, M. La bête humaine. *In* Larkin, M. Man and society in nineteenth-century realism p123-33

Larkin, M. The dismal science: economic man. *In* Larkin, M. Man and society in nineteenth-century realism p139-51

Larkin, M. Hope and despair. *In* Larkin, M. Man and society in nineteenth-century realism p163-74

Zola, Émile—About—*Continued*

Palamari, D. The shark who swallowed his epoch: family, nature and society in the novels of Emile Zola. *In* Tufte, V. and Myerhoff, B. G. eds. Changing images of the family p155-72

Pascal, R. The French masters: Emile Zola—use and abuse. *In* Pascal, R. The dual voice p112-22

Pritchett, V. S. Emile Zola: Zola's life. *In* Pritchett, V. S. The myth makers p108-14

Robinson, C. Science, reason and the material world. *In* Robinson, C. French literature in the nineteenth century p50-107

Trilling, L. In defense of Zola. *In* Trilling, L. A gathering of fugitives p14-22

About individual works
The ladies paradise

Niess, R. J. Zola's Au bonheur des dames: the making of a symbol. *In* Symbolism and modern literature p130-50

Zolberg, Aristide R.

International migration policies in a changing world system. *In* Human migration p241-86

Splitting the difference: federalization without federalization in Belgium. *In* Esman, M. J. ed. Ethnic conflict in the Western world p103-42

Zonabend, Françoise Flis. See Jolas, T. jt. auth.

Zonis, Marvin

Oil and politics in the Middle East. *In* Eppen, G. D. ed. Energy: the policy issues p52-68

The political elite of Iran: a second stratum? *In* Political elites and political development in the Middle East p193-216

Zonn, Wlodzimierz

Explosive events in the universe. *In* Neyman, J. ed. The heritage of Copernicus: theories "pleasing to the mind" p95-115

Zoo animals

Behavior

Berger, J. Through the bars. *In* Berger, J. The look of things p28-31

Zoology. See Animals, Habits and behavior of

Zoppo, Ciro E.

Arms control in the Mediterranean and European security. *In* International terrorism and world security p248-76

Zoque Indians

Lowe, G. W. The Mixe-Zoque as competing neighbors of the early Lowland Maya. *In* The Origins of Maya civilization p197-248

Zosimus

About individual works
The new history of Count Zosimus, sometime advocate of the treasury of the Roman empire

Cameron, A. Theodosius the Great and the regency of Stilico. *In* Harvard Studies in classical philology v73 p247-80

Zotzil Indians. See Tzotzil Indians

Zuber, Frédéric

About

Leuilliot, P. Frédéric Zuber's visits to England, 1834-41. *In* Great Britain and her world, 1750-1914 p87-98

Zubin, Joseph

A biometric approach to diagnosis and evaluation of therapeutic intervention in schizophrenia. *In* Overview of the psychotherapies p153-204

Zubkowski, Ludwik Kos-Rabcewicz- See Kos-Rabcewicz-Zubkowski, Ludwik

Zubrow, Ezra B. W.

Demographic anthropology: an introductory analysis. *In* Zubrow, E. B. W. ed. Demographic anthropology p 1-25

Stability and instability: a problem in long-term regional growth. *In* Zubrow, E. B. W. ed. Demographic anthropology p245-74

Zuckerman, Arthur J.

Unpublished materials on the relationship of early fifteenth century Jewry to the central government. *In* Salo Wittmayer Baron v2 p1059-95

Zuckerman, Harriet Anne

Theory choice and problem choice in science. *In* Gaston, J. ed. Sociology of science p65-95

See also Cole, J. R. jt. auth.

Zuckerman, Michael

Dr Spock: the confidence man. *In* Rosenberg, C. E. ed. The family in history p179-207

Zuckmayer, Carl

About individual works
Kiktahan or the backwoodsmen; Pankraz awakens

Mews, S. and English, R. The Jungle transcended: Brecht and Zuckmayer. *In* Mews, S. and Knust, H. eds. Essays on Brecht p79-98

Zukofsky, Louis

About

Kenner, H. Classroom accuracies. *In* Kenner, H. A homemade world p158-93

Zulu literature

Kunene, M. South African oral traditions. *In* Heywood, C. ed. Aspects of South African literature p24-41

Zululand

Schlemmer, L. and Muil, T. J. Social and political change in the African areas: a case study of ZwaZulu. *In* Thompson, L. M. and Butler, J. eds. Change in contemporary South Africa p107-37

Zulus

Religion

M'Timkulu, D. Some aspects of Zulu religion. *In* African religions: a symposium p13-30

Zumthor, Paul

About individual works
Style and expressive register in medieval poetry

Nichols, S. G. Toward an aesthetic of the Provençal lyric II: Marcabru's Dire vos vuoill ses doptansa (BdT 293, 18). *In* Italian literature: roots and branches p15-37

Zumwalt, Elmo Russell

Soviet strategy and U.S. counter-strategy *In* Grand strategy for the 1980s p37-55

Zupnick, Irving L.

Saint Sebastian. *In* Concepts of the hero in the Middle Ages and the Renaissance p239-67

Zur, Benjamin
Controlled irrigation. *In* Strategies for human settlements: habitat and environment p84-90

Zurbarán, Francisco de

About

Brown, J. Zurbarán's paintings in the sacristy of the monastery of Guadalupe. *In* Brown, J. Images and ideas in seventeenth-century Spanish painting p111-27

Zurif, Edgar B. and Blumstein, Sheila Ellen
Language and the brain. *In* Linguistic theory and psychological reality p229-45

Zvobgo, Eddison Jonas Mudadirwa
A Third World view. *In* Kommers, D. P. and Loescher, G. D. eds. Human rights and American foreign policy p90-106

Zweig, Arnold

About individual works

The case of Sergeant Grischa

Sebald, W. G. Humanitarianism and law: Arnold Zweig. Der Streit um den Sergeanten Grischa. *In* Klein, H. M. ed. The First World War in fiction p126-35

Zweig, Paul
The new surrealism. *In* Boyers, R. ed. Contemporary poetry in America p314-29

Zweig, Stefan

About individual works

The world of yesterday, an autobiography

Arendt, H. Portrait of a period. *In* Arendt, H. The Jew as pariah: Jewish identity and politics in the modern age p112-21

Zwicker, Steven N.
Politics and panegyric: the figural mode from Marvell to Pope. *In* Miner, E. R. ed. Literary uses of typology p115-46

Zwicky, Fay
Essay 11. *In* Fitzgerald, R. ed. What it means to be human p209-20

Zwinger, Theodore, 1533-1588

About individual works

Theatrum humanae vitae

Ong, W. J. Commonplace rhapsody: Ravisius Textor, Zwinger and Shakespeare. *In* Classical influences on European culture A.D. 1500-1700 p91-126
Same as Ong, W. J. Typographic rhapsody: Ravisius Textor, Zwinger, and Shakespeare. *In* Ong, W. J. Interfaces of the word p147-88

Zwinger, Theodore (the elder) See Zwinger, Theodore, 1533-1588

Zysberg, André
Galley rowers in the mid-eighteenth century. *In* Deviants and the abandoned in French society p83-110

List of Books Indexed

The list, arranged in one alphabet, includes both works by various authors and works by individual authors. Full information is given in the main entry for a book, with cross references from the title and the editor. For a collection of essays published in honor of a particular individual, a reference is made from the latter to the main entry. Generally, only American publishers are given. The English publisher is given when the book in question is obtainable only in an English edition.

Aagaard-Morgensen, Lars (ed.) Culture and art; an anthology. Humanities Press 1976 211p ISBN 0-391-00539-1 LC 75-45455
"Eclipse books"

Aaron, Daniel (ed.) Studies in biography. *See* Studies in biography

Abadie, Ann J. See Dollarhide, L. jt. ed.

Abbs, Peter (ed.) The black rainbow; essays on the present breakdown of culture. Heinemann Educ. [distributed by Rowman & Littlefield] 1975 247p ISBN 0-435-18025-8

The **Abdication** of philosophy: philosophy and the public good; essays in honor of Paul Arthur Schilpp. Ed. by Eugene Freeman. Open Ct. 1976 328p ISBN 0-87548-274-0 LC 72-93357

About Bateson; essays on Gregory Bateson by: Mary Catherine Bateson [and others]. Ed. by John Brockman; afterword by Gregory Bateson. Dutton 1977 250p ISBN 0-525-47469-2 LC 77-4971
"A Dutton paperback"

Abrams, Phillip (ed.) Towns in societies. *See* Towns in societies

Abramsky, Chimen (ed.) Essays in honour of E. H. Carr. *See* Essays in honour of E. H. Carr

Abroad in America: Visitors to the new Nation, 1776-1914. Ed. and with an introduction by Marc Pachter. Co-ed. by Frances Wein. Published in association with the National Portrait Gallery, Smithsonian Institution by Addison-Wesley 1976 347p ISBN 0-201-00031-8 LC 75-39542
Essays written to accompany the exhibition at the National Portrait Gallery, Smithsonian Institution

Abstraction and artifice in twentieth-century art. See Osborne, H.

Abu-Lughod, Ibrahim Ali (ed.) African themes. *See* African themes

Achebe, Chinua. Morning yet on creation day; essays. Anchor Press 1975 175p ISBN 0-385-01703-0. LC 74-33603

The **achievement** of William Styron. See Morris, R. K. and Malin, I. eds.

Achilles' choice. See Lenson, D. R.

Action and interpretation. See Hookway, C. and Pettit, P. eds.

Action theory and the human condition. See Parsons, T.

Adam Smith and The wealth of nations. See Glahe, F. R. ed.

Adams, Charles J. (ed.) A reader's guide to the great religions. 2d ed. Free Press 1977 521p ISBN 0-02-900240-0 LC 76-10496
Previous edition analyzed in 1965-1969 cumulation

Adams, Percy Guy. Graces of harmony; alliteration, assonance, and consonance in eighteenth-century British poetry. Univ. of Ga. Press 1977 253p ISBN 0-8203-0399-2 LC 76-1144

Adams, Richard E. W. The origins of Maya civilization. *See* The Origins of Maya civilization

Adams, Richard P. See entry under title: Tulane Studies in English

Adams, Robert Martin. Afterjoyce; studies in fiction after Ulysses. Oxford 1977 201p ISBN 0-19-502168-1 LC 76-51707

Adam's dream. See Belitt, B.

The **added** dimension. See Friedman, M. J. and Lawson, L. A. eds.

Adolescence and youth in prospect; ed. by John P. Hill and Franz J. Mönks. Humanities Press 1977 217p ISBN 0-391-00715-7 LC 77-3431

Adulthood. See Erikson, E. H. ed.

The **advantage** of lyric. See Hardy, B. N.

Adventure, mystery, and romance. See Cawelti, J. G.

Adventures in medical research. See Harvey, A. M.

The **adventurous** muse. See Spengemann, W. C.

The **adversary** literature. See Karl, F. R.

Aeolian harps; essays in literature in honor of Maurice Browning Cramer. Ed. by Donna G. Fricke and Douglas C. Fricke. Bowling Green Univ. Press 1976 293p   LC 76-353
Partially analyzed

Africa. See Martin, P. M. and O'Meara, P. eds.

Africa and the Caribbean. See Crahan, M. and Knight, F. W. eds.

The **African** diaspora. See Kilson, M. L. and Rotberg, R. I. eds.

African dimensions; essays in honor of William O. Brown; ed. by Mark Karp. Boston Univ, African Studies Center 1975 [distributed by] Africana Pub. Co. 213p ISBN 0-915118-05-X. LC 74-84802

African folklore in the New World. See Crowley, D. J. ed.

African images; essays in African iconology. Ed. by Daniel F. McCall [and] Edna G. Bay. [Published] for The African Studies Center [by] Africana Pub. Co. 1975 326p (Boston University Papers on Africa, v6) ISBN 0-8419-0147-3. LC 74-12204

African literature today no. 7: Focus on criticism. A review; ed. by Eldred Durosimi Jones. Africana Pub. Co. 1975 169p ISBN 0-8419-0168-6. LC 72-75254
Partially analyzed
Previous volumes analyzed in 1970-74 cumulation

African literature today no. 8: Drama in Africa. A review; ed. by Eldred Durosimi Jones. Africana Pub. Co. 1976 152p ISBN 0-8419-0261-5 LC 72-75254
Partially analyzed

African literature today no. 9: Africa, America and the Caribbean. A review; ed. by Eldred Durosimi Jones. Africana Pub. Co. 1978 118p ISBN 0-8419-0335-2 LC 72-75254
Partially analyzed

African literatures: an introduction. See Owomoyela, O.

African religions: a symposium; ed .by Newell S. Booth, Jr. NOK Pubs. 1977 390p ISBN 0-88357-012-2 LC 73-88062

African studies since 1945; a tribute to Basil Davidson. Ed. by Christopher Fyfe. Proceedings of a seminar in honour of Basil Davidson's sixtieth birthday at the Centre of African Studies, University of Edinburgh under the chairmanship of George Shepperson. Holmes & Meier Pub. 1976 255p ISBN 0-582-64207-8

African themes; Northwestern University Studies in honor of **Gwendolen M. Carter. Ed. by Ibrahim Ali Abu-Lughod. Program of African Studies. Northwestern Univ. Press 1975 234p LC 74-29355**

Afro-American literature. See Fisher, D. and Stepto, R. B. eds.

The **Afro-American** woman. See Harley, S. and Terborg-Penn, R. eds.

Afterjoyce. See Adams, R. M.

Aftermath of empire; in honor of Max Salvadori. Smith College Lib. 1975 159p (Studies in history v47) LC 75-1728

Against pollution and hunger; [sponsored by] Society for Social Responsibility in Science. Alice Mary Hilton (ed.) Wiley 1974 309p ISBN 0-470-39771-6. LC 73-17751
"A Halsted Press book"
Partially analyzed

Agatha Christie: first lady of crime. Ed. by H. R. F. Keating. Holt 1977 224p ISBN 0-03-018251-4 LC 76-29907
Partially analyzed

The **age** of atrocity. See Langer, L. L.

The **age** of partnership. See Kling, B. B. and Pearson, M. N. eds.

The **Age** of segregation: race relations in the South, 1890-1945. Ed. by Robert Haws; essays by Derrick Bell [and others]. Univ. Press of Miss. 1978 156p ISBN 0-87805-087-6 LC 78-14233
"Essays from the Third Chancellor's Symposium on Southern History held at the University of Mississippi in October 1977"

Aging and the elderly. See Spicker, S. F.; Woodward, K. M. and Van Tassel, D. D. eds.

Aging into the 21st century. See Jarvik, L. F. ed.

Aging: the process and the people. Ed. by Gene Usdin and Charles K. Hofling. Brunner/Mazel 1978 248p ISBN 0-87630-178-2 LC 78-16777

Aiken, William, and La Follette, Hugh (eds.) World hunger and moral obligation. Prentice-Hall 1977 195p ISBN 0-13-967968-5 LC 76-56381

Albrecht, William Price. The sublime pleasures of tragedy; a study of critical theory from Dennis to Keats. Univ. Press of Kan. 1975 205p ISBN 0-7006-0135-X LC 75-11896

Alcock, Antony Evelyn; Taylor Brian K. and Welton, John M. (eds.) The future of cultural minorities. St Martins 1979 221p ISBN 0-312-31470-1 LC 78-13725
"Based on a seminar held at the Richardson Institute for Peace and Conflict Research in May 1977"

Alcorn, John. The nature novel from Hardy to Lawrence. Columbia Univ. Press 1977 139p ISBN 0-231-04122-5 LC 76-17552

Alderson, William Thomas (ed.) American issues; understanding who we are. Am. Assn. for State & Local Hist. 1976 144p ISBN 0-910050-25-2

Aleksandr Solzhenitsyn: critical essays and documentary materials. 2d. ed. See Dunlop, J. B.; Haugh, R. and Klimoff, A. eds.

Alexander, Yonah (ed.) International terrorism. *See* International terrorism

Allan Nevins on history. See Nevins, A.

Allegories of history, allegories of love. See Barney, S. A.

Allen, Harry Cranbrook, and Thompson, Roger (eds.) Contrast and connection; Bicentennial essays in Anglo-American history. Ohio Univ. Press 1976 373p ISBN 0-8214-0355-9 LC 76-7095

Allen, Mary. The necessary blankness; women in major American fiction of the sixties. Univ. of Ill. Press 1976 226p ISBN 0-252-00519-8 LC 75-38780

Allende's Chile. See O'Brien, P. ed.

Allmand, C. T. (ed.) War, literature, and politics in the late Middle Ages. *See* War, literature, and politics in the late Middle Ages

Allott, Kenneth (ed.) Matthew Arnold. Ohio Univ. Press 1976 353p (Writers and their background) ISBN 0-8214-0197-1 LC 75-15339

An **Almost** chosen people; the moral aspirations of Americans. Editors: Walter Nicgorski [and] Ronald Weber. Univ. of Notre Dame Press 1976 160p ISBN 0-268-00581-9 LC 76-41343

Altbach, Philip G. and McVey, Sheila (eds.) Perspectives on publishing. Lexington Bks. 1976 283p ISBN 0-669-99564-9 LC 75-3516

Alter, Robert. Defenses of the imagination; Jewish writers and modern historical crisis. Jewish Publication Soc. of Am. [1978] c1977 262p ISBN 0-8276-0097-6 LC 77-87244

Alter, Robert. Partial magic; the novel as a self-conscious genre. Univ. of Calif. Press 1975 248p ISBN 0-520-02755-8 LC 74-77725

Alternate states of consciousness. Ed. by Norman E. Zinberg. Free Press 1977 294p ISBN 0-02-935770-5 LC 76-46722

Alternative altars. See Ellwood, R. S.

Altholz, Josef Lewis (ed.) The mind and art of Victorian England. Univ. of Minn. Press 1976 206p ISBN 0-8166-0772-9 LC 75-22686

Altieri, Charles F. Enlarging the temple; new directions in American poetry during the 1960s. Bucknell Univ. Press 1979 258p ISBN 0-8387-2127-3 LC 77-89773

Altman, Joel Barrett. The Tudor play of mind; rhetorical inquiry and the development of Elizabethan drama. Univ. of Calif. Press 1978 406p ISBN 0-520-03427-9 LC 76-52022

Altschule, Mark David. Origins of concepts in human behavior; social and cultural factors. Hemisphere Pub. Corp. [ditsributed by Halsted Press, a division of John Wiley & Sons, Inc.] 1977 204p ISBN 0-470-99001-5 LC 76-46320 "A Halsted Press book"

Aluko, Olajide (ed.) The foreign policies of African states. Hodder [distributed by Humanities Press] 1977 243p ISBN 0-340-21030-3

Amacher, Richard E. and Lange, Victor (eds.) New perspectives in German literary criticism; a collection of essays. Tr. by David Henry Wilson and others. Princeton Univ. Press 1979 480p ISBN 0-691-06380-X LC 78-12472

America as an ordinary country. See Rosecrance, R. N. ed.

America: exploration and travel. See Kagle, S. E. ed.

America in an interdependent world. See Baldwin, D. A. ed.

America in theological perspective; the annual publication of the College Theology Society; ed. by Thomas M. McFadden. Seabury 1976 248p ISBN 0-8164-0294-9 LC 75-45201 "A Crossroad book"

American Academic Association for Peace in the Middle East. The Palestinians. *See* The Palestinians

American Antiquarian Society, Worcester, Mass. Proceedings of the American Antiquarian Society . . . 1974-1978, v84-88. The Society 1974-1978 10 parts ISSN 0044-751X LC 5-13654

The **American** as anarchist. See DeLeon, D.

American autobiography. See Couser, G. T.

American characteristics, and other essays. See Wilder, T. N.

American Enterprise Institute for Public Policy Research. America's continuing revolution. *See* America's continuing revolution

American Enterprise Institute for Public Policy Research. Arab and American cultures. *See* Arab and American cultures

American essay serials from Franklin to Irving. See Granger, B. I.

The **American** experiment. See Warner, S. B. ed.

American folk medicine; a symposium; ed. with an introduction, by Wayland D. Hand. Univ. of Calif. Press 1976 347p (Publication of the UCLA Center for the Study of Comparative Folklore and Mythology) ISBN 0-520-02941-0 LC 74-30522
Published under the auspices of the Center for the Study of Comparative Folklore and Mythology, University of California, Los Angeles

American folklife. See Yoder, D. ed.

American history/American film. See O'Connor, J. E. and Jackson, M. A. eds.

American history—British historians. See Burton, D. H. ed.

The **American** Indian; ed. by Norris Hundley, Jr. Foreword by Vine Deloria, Jr. Essays from the Pacific Historical Review by Robert F. Berkhofer, Jr. [and others] ABC-CLIO [1975 c1974] 151p ISBN 0-87436-139-7. LC 74-76443

American Indian fiction. See Larson, C. R.

American issues. See Alderson, W. T. ed.

The **American** judicial tradition. See White, G. E.

American lawyers in a changing society, 1776-1876. See Bloomfield, M. H.

American Library Association. Libraries and the life of the mind in America. *See* Libraries and the life of the mind in America

American literary scholarship, 1973-1977; an annual. Duke Univ. Press 1975-1979 5v ISBN 1973 0-8223-0338-8; 1974 0-8223-0362-0; 1975 0-8223-0384-1; 1976 0-8223-0406-6; 1977 0-8223-0423-6 LC 65-19450
Volumes for 1973, 1974, 1975, and 1977 ed. by James Woodress; volume for 1976 ed. by J. Albert Robbins

American literature: nineteenth and early twentieth centuries. See Donaldson, S. and Massa, A. auths.

American literature, 1764-1789. See Emerson, E. H. ed.

The **American** moment. See Thurley, G.

The **American** novel in the twentieth century. See Donald, M.

The **American** party systems; stages of political development. Ed. by William Nisbet Chambers and Walter Dean Burnham. Contributors: Frank J. Sorauf [and others]. 2d ed. Oxford 1975 374p ISBN 0-19-501917-2 LC 74-22876
Previous editions analyzed in 1965-1969 cumulation. This edition analyzed for new material only

American Philosophical Society. Aspects of American liberty. *See* Aspects of American liberty

American politics and public policy. See Burnham, W. D. and Weinberg, M. W. eds.

American psychiatry: past, present, and future; papers presented on the occasion of the 200th anniversary of the establishment of the first state-supported mental hospital in America. George Kriegman; Robert D. Gardner, and D. Wilfred Abse, editors. Univ. Press of Va. 1975 205p ISBN 0-8139-0571-0 LC 75-8962
Partially analyzed

The **American** quest for a supreme fiction. See Miller, J. E.

The **American** Revolution: a continuing commitment. Papers presented at the fifth symposium, May 6 and 7, 1976. Lib. of Congress 1976 88p (Library of Congress Symposia on the American Revolution) ISBN 0-8444-0196-X LC 76-608237

The **American** Revolution and "a candid world." Ed. by Lawrence S. Kaplan. Kent State Univ. Press 1977 169p ISBN 0-87338-205-6 LC 77-6671

American Society for Psychical Research. Parapsychology: its relation to physics, biology, psychology, and psychiatry. *See* Parapsychology: its relation to physics, biology, psychology, and psychiatry

Les **américanistes.** See Johnson, I. D. and Johnson, C. eds.

America's continuing revolution; an act of conservation [by] Irving Kristol [and others]; with an introduction by Stephen J. Tonsor. Am. Enterprise Inst. for Public Policy Res. 1975 398p (Distinguished lecture ser. on the Bicentennial) ISBN 0-8447-1317-1. LC 74-31866

The **Americas** in a changing world; a report of the Commission on United States-Latin American relations, with a preface by Sol M. Linowitz. Selected papers by Kalman H. Silvert [and others]. Quadrangle/The N.Y. Times Bk. Co. 1975 248p ISBN 0-8129-0561-X. LC 74-26014
Partially analyzed

Américo Castro and the meaning of Spanish civilization; ed. by José Rubia Barcia with the assistance of Selma Margaretten. Univ. of Calif. Press 1976 336p ISBN 0-520-02920-8 LC 74-27282

Amos, Dan Ben- See Ben-Amos, Dan

The **anatomy** of Communist takeovers. See Hammond, T. T. ed.

Anatomy of horror: the masters of occult fiction. See Barclay, G. S.

Ancient civilization and trade; ed. by Jeremy A. Sabloff and C. C. Lamberg-Karlovsky. Univ. of N. Mex. Press 1975 485p (School of American Research book) ISBN 0-8263-0345-5. LC 74-83382

—And I worked at the writer's trade. See Cowley, M.

Anderson, Charles B. (ed.) Bookselling in America and the world. *See* Bookselling in America and the world

Anderson, David D. (ed.) Sherwood Anderson: dimensions of his literary art; a collection of critical essays. Mich. State Univ. Press 1976 141p ISBN 0-87013-204-0 LC 76-25796

Anderson, Elliott, and Kinzie, Mary (eds.) The little magazine in America: a modern documentary history. Pushcart Press 1978 770p ISBN 0-916366-04-9 LC 78-69929
Partially analyzed

Anderson, George Lester (ed.) Land-grant universities and their continuing challenge. *See* Land-grant universities and their continuing challenge

Anderson, Quentin (ed.) Art, politics, and will. *See* Art, politics, and will

Andrew Marvell; essays on the tercentenary of his death. Ed. by R. L. Brett. Published for the University of Hull by Oxford 1979 (University of Hull Publications) 128p ISBN 0-19-713435-1 LC 78-41136

Andrey Bely. See Janecek, G. ed.

Anglo-Irish literature. See Finneran, R. J. ed.

Anglo-Saxon England 3-7; ed. by Peter Clemoes [and others]. Cambridge 1974-1978 5v ISBN 1974 0-521-20574-3; 1975 0-521-20868-8; 1976 0-521-21270-7; 1977 0-521-21701-6; 1978 0-521-22164-1 LC 1974 74-79139; 1975-1978 78-190423

Anglo-Saxon poetry: essays in appreciation; for John C. McGalliard. Ed. by Lewis E. Nicholson [and] Dolores Warwick Frese. Univ. of Notre Dame Press 1975 387p ISBN 0-268-00575-3 LC 74-27893

The **angry** young men of the thirties. See Smith, E. E.

Annales, économies, sociétés, civilisations. Biology of man in history. *See* Biology of man in history

Annales, économies, sociétés, civilisations. Deviants and the abandoned in French society. *See* Deviants and the abandoned in French society

Annales, économies, sociétés, civilisations. Family and society. *See* Family and society

Annales, économies, sociétés, civilisations. Food and drink in history. *See* Food and drink in history

Annales, économies, sociétés, civilisations. Rural society in France. *See* Rural society in France

Annals of an abiding liberal. See Galbraith, J. K.

Antebellum Charleston dramatists. See Watson, C. S.

Anticipatory grief. Ed. by Bernard Schoenberg [and others] with the editorial assistance of Lillian G. Kutscher. Columbia Univ. Press 1974 381p. ISBN 0-231-03770-8. LC 74-1252

Applied anthropology in America. See Eddy, E. M. and Partridge, W. L. eds.

Approaches to Joyce's Portrait. See Staley, T. F. and Benstock, B. eds.

Approaches to popular culture. See Bigsby, C. W. E. ed.

Approaches to the study of social structure. See Blau, P. M. ed.

Approaches to Victorian autobiography. See Landow, G. P. ed.

Arab and American cultures; ed. by George N. Atiyeh. Am. Enterprise Inst. for Public Policy Res. 1977 236p ISBN 0-8447-2116-6 LC 77-94069
Partially analyzed

Arab-Israeli Research and Relations Project. The elusive peace in the Middle East. *See* The Elusive peace in the Middle East

Arabic political memoirs and other studies. See Kedourie, E.

The **architect.** See Kostof, S. ed.

Ardener, Shirley G. (ed.) Perceiving women. Wiley 1975 xxiii, 167p ISBN 0-470-03309-6 LC 75-12662
"A Halsted Press book"

Arendt, Hannah. The Jew as pariah: Jewish identity and politics in the modern age. Ed. and with an introduction by Ron H. Feldman. Grove Press [distributed by Random House] 1978 288p ISBN 0-394-50160-8 LC 77-18342
Partially analyzed

Arendt, Hannah. The life of the mind. 2v Harcourt 1978 ISBN v 1 0-15-151895-5; v2 0-15-151896-3 LC v 1 77-1181; LC v2 77-74801
v 1 Thinking, v2 Willing

Arendt, Hannah. *See also* entry under title Hannah Arendt: the recovery of the public world

Ariotti, Piero E. (ed.) A sense of the future. *See* Bronowski, J. A sense of the future

Ariotti, Piero E. (ed.) The visionary eye. *See* Bronowski, J. The visionary eye

Arms control and technological innovation; [Sixth Course of the International School on Disarmament and Research on Conflicts] ed. by David Carlton and Carlo Schaerf. Wiley [1978 c1976] 366p ISBN 0-470-99274-3 LC 77-8790
"A Halsted Press Book"

Arms, defense policy, and arms control. See Long, F. A. and Rathjens, G. W. eds.

Armstrong, Isobel (ed.) Robert Browning. Ohio Univ. Press 1975 [c1974] 365p (Writers and their background) ISBN 0-8214-0131-9. LC 72-96846

Armstrong, Terry R. and **Cinnamon, Kenneth M.** (eds.) Power and authority in law enforcement; with a foreword by Donald Kreps. Thomas, C. C. 1976 190p ISBN 0-398-03571-7 LC 76-7384

Arndt, John Richard. See entry under title: The German contribution to the building of the Americas

Arnold, Matthew. The last word; ed. by R. H. Super. Univ. of Mich. Press 1977 598p (The Complete prose works of Matthew Arnold v11) ISBN 0-472-11661-4 LC 60-5018
Partially analyzed

Aron, Raymond. Politics and history; selected essays. Collected, tr. and ed. by Miriam Bernheim Conant. Free Press 1978 xxx, 274p ISBN 0-02-901000-4 LC 78-54122

Art and architecture in the service of politics. See Millon, H. A and Nochlin, L. eds.

Art as second nature. See Hamburger, M.

Art in society. See Greenhalgh, M. and Megaw, J. V. S. eds.

The **art** of celebration. See Mudford, P.

The **art** of Emily Brontë. See Smith, A. ed.

The **art** of life. See Blasing, M. K.

The **Art** of Willa Cather; ed. by Bernice Slote and Virginia Faulkner. Univ. of Neb. Press 1974 267p ISBN 0-8032-0841-3 LC 74-78479
Partially analyzed

Art on the edge. See Rosenberg, H.

Art, politics, and will; essays in honor of Lionel Trilling. Ed. by Quentin Anderson; Stephen Donadio, [and] Steven Marcus. Basic Bks. 1977 295p ISBN 0-465-00448-2 LC 76-48881

Art therapy. See Ulman, E. and Dachinger, P. eds.

Artful thunder; versions of the romantic tradition in American literature, in honor of Howard P. Vincent. Ed. by Robert J. DeMott and Sanford E. Marovitz. Kent State Univ. Press 1975 312p ISBN 0-87338-172-6. LC 74-21886

The **Artist** and the writer in France; essays in honour of Jean Seznec. Ed. by Francis Haskell, Anthony Levi, and Robert Shackleton. Oxford [1975 c1974] 184p ISBN 0-19-817187-0
Partially analyzed

"An **artist** is his own fault." See O'Hara, J.

Artists and traditions; uses of the past in Chinese culture. Ed. by Christian F. Murck. The Art Museum, Princeton University; distributed by Princeton Univ. Press [1977 c1976] 230p ISBN 0-691-03909-7 LC 74-77300

Artists and writers in revolt. See Williamson, A.

The **arts** and cognition. See Perkins, D. and Leondar, B. eds.

The **arts** in a democratic society. See Mann, D. A. ed.

As her whimsey took her. See Hannay, M. P. ed.

As much to learn as to teach; essays in honor of Lester Asheim. Ed. by Joel M. Lee and Beth A. Hamilton. Linnet Bks. 1979 273p ISBN 0-208-01751-4 LC 78-11313
Partially analyzed

Asheim, Lester Eugene. See entry under title: As much to learn as to teach

Ashley-Montagu, Montague Francis. See Montagu, Ashley

The **Asian** American: the historical experience; ed. by Norris Hundley, Jr. Introduction by Akira Iriye. Essays by Roger Daniels [and others] ABC-CLIO 1976 186p (Clio Books/Pacific Historical Review ser) ISBN 0-87436-219-9 LC 75-2354

Awake in the dark. See Denby, D. ed.

Awakkened conscience. See Narasimhaiah, C. D. ed.

Axton, Marie (ed.) English drama: forms and development. *See* English drama: forms and development

Ayala, Francisco Jose, and Dobzhansky, Theodosius Grigorievich (eds.) Studies in the philosophy of biology; reduction and related problems. Univ. of Calif. Press 1974 390p ISBN 0-520-02649-7. LC 73-90656

el-Ayouty, Yassin (ed.) The Organization of African Unity after ten years; comparative perspectives. Praeger 1975 262p (Praeger Special studies in international politics and government) ISBN 0-275-09910-5. LC 74-15421

Ayres, Clarence Edwin. See entry under title: Science and ceremony

Azmon, Yael. See Eisenstadt, S. N. jt. ed.

B

Babcock, Barbara Allen (ed.) The reversible world; symbolic inversion in art and society. Ed. and with an introduction. Cornell Univ. Press 1978 302p (Symbol, myth, and ritual ser) ISBN 0-8014-1112-2 LC 77-3113

Background to the English Renaissance; introductory lectures [by] A. G. Dickens [and others]. Grey-Mills [distributed by Int. Scholarly Bk. Services] 1974 108p ISBN 0-85641-022-5

Backgrounds to Augustan poetry: Gallus, elegy and Rome. See Ross, D. O.

Badeau, John Stothoff. The genius of Arab civilization. *See* The Genius of Arab civilization

Baker, Derek, (ed.) Church, society and politics. *See* Church, society and politics

Baker, George. See Needleman, J. jt. ed.

Baker, Robert, and Elliston, Frederick A. (eds.) Philosophy & sex. Prometheus Bks. 1975 397p ISBN 0-87975-050-2. LC 75-21670

Balakian, Nona. Critical encounters; literary views and reviews, 1953-1977. Bobbs 1978 250p ISBN 0-672-52341-8 LC 77-15421

Baldwin, David Allen (ed.) America in an interdependent world; problems of United States foreign policy. Foreword by Gene M. Lyons. Contributions by Louis Morton [and others]. Published for Dartmouth College by the Univ. Press of New England 1976 352p ISBN 0-87451-124-0 LC 75-41909

Baldwin, Kenneth H. and Kirby, David K. (eds.) Individual and community; variations on a theme in American fiction. Duke Univ. Press 1975 222p ISBN 0-8223-0319-1. LC 74-75476

Ball, Patricia M. The heart's events; the Victorian poetry of relationships. Athlone Press [of the] Univ. of London [distributed by Humanities Press] 1976 227p ISBN 0-485-11163-2

Ball, Terence (ed.) Political theory and praxis. *See* Political theory and praxis

Ballad studies; ed. by E. B. Lyle. Published for The Folklore Society by D. S. Brewer Ltd and Rowman and Littlefield. Rowman & Littlefield 1976 212p (The Folklore Society Mistletoe ser) ISBN 0-87471-898-8

Banks, Robert J. (ed.) Reconciliation and hope. *See* Reconciliation and hope

Barcia, José, Rubia. See Rubia Barcia, José

Baym, Nina Zippin. Woman's fiction; a guide to novels by and about women in America, 1820-1870. Cornell Univ. Press 1978 320p ISBN 0-8014-1128-9 LC 77-90897

Beasley, William G. (ed.) Modern Japan. *See* Modern Japan

Beast or angel? See Dubos, R. J.

Beattie, John Hugh Marshall (ed.) Studies in social anthropology. *See* Studies in social anthropology

Beatty, Bernard G. See Davies, R. T. jt. ed.

Beaumont, Roger A. and Edmonds, Martin (eds.) War in the next decade. Univ. Press of Ky. 1974 217p ISBN 0-8131-1291-5. LC 73-77251

Beck, Lois, and Keddie, Nikki R. eds. Women in the Muslim world. Harvard Univ. Press 1978 698p ISBN 0-674-95480-7 LC 78-3633

Behavior modification and families. Ed. by Eric J. Mash; Leo A. Hamerlynck and Lee C. Handy. Brunner/Mazel 1976 362p ISBN 0-87630-118-9 LC 75-37733

Belitt, Ben. Adam's dream; a preface to translation. Grove Press [distributed by Random House] 186p ISBN 0-394-50288-4 LC 78-51399

Bell, Gwen (ed.) Strategies for human settlements: habitat and environment. *See* Strategies for human settlements: habitat and environment

Bell, Robert F. See Strelka, J. P. jt. ed.

Bell, Whitfield Jenks. The colonial physician & other essays [by] Whitfield J. Bell, Jr. Science Hist. Pubs. 1975 229p ISBN 0-88202-024-2. LC 75-6652

Belsley, David A. (ed.) Inflation, trade and taxes. *See* Inflation, trade and taxes

Ben-Amos, Dan (ed.) Folklore genres. *See* Folklore genres

Ben-David, Joseph (ed.) Culture and its creators. *See* Culture and its creators

Beneficent euthanasia. See Kohl, M. ed.

The benevolence of laughter: comic poetry of the Commonwealth and Restoration. See Farley-Hills, D.

Benjamin, Walter. Reflections; essays, aphorisms, autobiographical writings. Ed. and with an introduction by Peter Demetz. Tr. by Edmund Jephcott. Harcourt 1978 348p ISBN 0-15-176189-2 LC 77-92529
"A Helen and Kurt Wolff book"
Partially analyzed

Bennett, Edward M. See Burns, R. D. jt. ed.

Benson, Jackson J. (ed.) The short stories of Ernest Hemingway: critical essays. Ed. with an overview and checklist. Duke Univ. Press 1975 375p ISBN 0-8223-0320-5. LC 74-75815

Benson, Larry Dean. (ed.) The learned and the lewed. *See* The Learned and the lewed

Benstock, Bernard. See Staley, G. F. jt. ed.

Benton, Lewis R. (ed.) Management for the future. McGraw 1978 355p ISBN 0-07-004818-5 LC 77-22862

Bentsi-Enchill, Kwamena. See Smock, D. R. jt. ed.

Berger, Carl. The writing of Canadian history; aspects of English-Canadian historical writing: 1900-1970. Oxford 1976 300p ISBN 19-5402529 C76-017066-5

Berger, John. The look of things; essays. Ed. with an introduction by Nikos Stangos. Viking [1975 c1974] 251p ISBN 0-670-43987-8. LC 74-12428
"A Richard Seaver book"

Biosocial anthropology; ed. by Robin Fox. Wiley 1975 169p (ASA studies 1) ISBN 0-470-270330-0 LC 75-4110
"A Halsted Press book"

Birch, Cyril. (ed.) Studies in Chinese literary genres. Univ. of Calif. Press 1974 398p. ISBN 0-520-02037-5. LC 77-157825

Birnbaum, Norman (ed.) Beyond the crisis. *See* Beyond the crisis

Biro, John Ivan. See Shahan, R. W. jt. ed.

Bishirjian, Richard J. (ed.) A public philosophy reader. *See* A Public philosophy reader

Bishop, Donald Harold (ed.) Indian thought; an introduction. Wiley 1975 427p ISBN 0-470-07580-5 LC 73-13206
"A Halsted Press book"

The **Bitter** air of exile: Russian writers in the West, 1922-1972. Ed. by Simon Karlinsky and Alfred Appel, Jr. Univ. of Calif. Press 1977 473p ISBN 0-520-02846-5 LC 74-84147
Partially analyzed

Bjornson, Richard. The picaresque hero in European fiction. Univ. of Wis. Press 1977 308p ISBN 0-299-07100-6 LC 76-11312
Title on spine: The picaresque hero

Black, Matthew. (ed.) On language, culture, and religion: in honor of Eugene A. Nida. *See* On language, culture, and religion: in honor of Eugene A. Nida

The **Black** American reference book; ed. by Mabel M. Smythe; sponsored by the Phelps-Stokes Fund. Prentice-Hall 1976 xxviii,1026p ISBN 0-13-077586-X LC 75-26511
Earlier edition, entitled The American Negro reference book, edited by John Preston Davis, analyzed in 1965-1969 cumulation

The **Black** American short story in the 20th century. See Bruck, P. ed.

Black American writers. See Inge, M. T.; Duke, J. M. and Bryer, J. R. eds.

The **black** rainbow. See Abbs, P. ed.

Blacks in Hispanic literature. See DeCosta, M. ed.

Blackstone, William T. (ed.) Philosophy & environmental crisis. *See* Philosophy & environmental crisis

Blackstone, William T. (ed.) Social justice & preferential treatment. *See* Social justice & preferential treatment

Blake, Nelson Manfred. See entry under title: "Remember the ladies": new perspectives on women in American history

Blake in his time. See Essick, R. N. and Pearce, D. R. eds.

Blanckenhagen, Peter Heinrich von. See entry under title: Studies in classical art and archaeology

Blasier, Cole (ed.) Cuba in the world. *See* Cuba in the world

Blasing, Mutlu Konuk. The art of life; studies in American autobiographical literature. Univ. of Tex. Press 1977 xxviii, 193p ISBN 0-292-70315-5 LC 76-20760

Blau, Peter Michael (ed.) Approaches to the study of social structure. A publication of The American Sociological Association. Free Press 1975 294p ISBN 0-02-903651-8. LC 75-2809

Blishen, Edward (ed.) The thorny paradise; writers on writing for children. [Penguin distributed by Horn Bk] 1975 176p ISBN 0-7226-5463-4
"Kestrel book"

Blom-Cooper, Louis Jacques (ed.) Progress in penal reform. *See* Progress in penal reform

Bloodhounds of heaven. See Ousby, I.

Bruner, Jerome Seymour. On knowing; essays for the left hand; expanded edition. Belknap Press [of] Harvard Univ. Press 1979 189p ISBN 0-674-63475-6 LC 78-66286

Original edition analyzed in 1960-1964 cumulation. This edition has been analyzed for one new essay added, entitled Psychology and the image of man

Bruss, Elizabeth W. Autobiographical acts; the changing situation of a literary genre. Johns Hopkins Univ. Press 1976 184p ISBN 0-8018-1821-4 LC 76-13460

Brustein, Robert Sanford. The culture watch; essays on theatre and society, 1969-1974. Knopf 1975 197p ISBN 0-394-49814-3. LC 75-8227

Bryant, Donald Cross. See entry under title: Rhetoric: a tradition in transition

Bryer, Jackson R. See Inge, M. T. jt. ed.

Buckley, Jerome Hamilton (ed.) The worlds of Victorian fiction. *See* The Worlds of Victorian fiction

Buddhism in the modern world. See Dumoulin, H. ed.

Buergenthal, Thomas (ed.) Human rights, international law and the Helsinki Accord. *See* Human rights, international law and the Helsinki Accord

Bugliarello, George, and Doner, Dean B. (eds.) The history and philosophy of technology; with an introduction by Melvin Kranzberg. Univ. of Ill. Press 1979 384p ISBN 0-252-00462-0 LC 78-26846

Papers presented at the Symposium on the history and philosophy of technology, Chicago, 1973 sponsored by the College of Engineering and the College of Liberal Arts and Sciences of the University of Illinois at Chicago Circle

Bundy, Robert Franklin (ed.) Images of the future: the twenty-first century and beyond. Prometheus Bks. 1976 239p ISBN 0-87975-048-0 LC 75-32697

Partially analyzed

Bundy, William P. (ed.) Two hundred years of American foreign policy. *See* Two hundred years of American foreign policy

Bundy, William P. (ed.) The world economic crisis. Ed. with an introduction. Norton 1975 252p ISBN 0-393-05545-0. LC 74-32279

"A Foreign Affairs book"

Burbank, John (ed.) Structure, sign, and function. *See* Mukařovský, J. Structure, sign, and function

Burks, Don Marvin (ed.) Rhetoric, philosophy, and literature: an exploration. Purdue Univ. Press 1978 115p ISBN 0-911198-52-0 LC 77-92712

"This collection of essays grew out of an interdisciplinary seminar held at Purdue University during the spring semester of 1974 . . . entitled Seminar in rhetoric, philosophy, and literature."

Burnham, Walter Dean, and Weinberg, Martha Wagner (eds.) American politics and public policy. MIT Press 1978 418p (MIT Studies in American politics and public policy;4) ISBN 0-262-02132-3 LC 78-17304

Burns, Norman T. (ed.) Concepts of the hero in the Middle Ages and the Renaissance. *See* Concepts of the hero in the Middle Ages and the Renaissance

Burns, Richard Dean, and Bennett, Edward M. (eds.) Diplomats in crisis; United States-Chinese-Japanese relations, 1919-1941. ABC-Clio 1974 346p ISBN 0-87436-135-4. LC 74-76444

Burton, David Henry (ed.) American history—British historians; a cross-cultural approach to the American experience. Nelson-Hall 1976 xxii, 322p ISBN 0-88229-280-3 LC 76-8458

Bushman, Richard L. (ed.) Uprooted Americans. *See* Uprooted Americans.

Butler, Jeffrey. See Thompson, L. M. jt. ed.

Butler, Lance St John (ed.) Thomas Hardy after fifty years. Rowman & Littlefield 1977 153p ISBN 0-87471-980-1 LC 77-3057

Butler, Marilyn. Jane Austen and the war of ideas. Clarendon Press 1975 310p ISBN 0-19-812068-0

Butscher, Edward (ed.) Sylvia Plath; the woman and the work. Ed. with an introduction. Dodd 1977 242p ISBN 0-396-07497-9 LC 77-24700
Partially analyzed

Buxton, Thomas H. and Prichard, Keith W. (eds.) Excellence in university teaching; new essays. Comp. and ed. by Thomas H. Buxton and Keith W. Prichard; foreword by Thomas F. Jones. Univ. of S.C. Press 1975 291p ISBN 0-87249-321-0 LC 74-19340

By things seen: reference and recognition in medieval thought. See Jeffrey, D. L. ed.

Byars, Robert S. (ed.) Quantitative social science research on Latin America. *See* Quantitative social science research on Latin America

Byron. See Jump, J. D. ed.

C

The CIA file. See Borosage, R. L. and Marks, J. D. eds.

Cafferty, Pastora San Juan (ed.) The Diverse society: implications for social policy. *See* The Diverse society: implications for social policy

Cahill, Kevin M. (ed.) Health and development; ed. and presented by Kevin M. Cahill. Orbis Bks. 1976 101p ISBN 0-88344-178-0 LC 75-29504

Cahn, Steven M. (ed.) New studies in the philosophy of John Dewey. Published for the University of Vermont by the Univ. Press of New England 1977 213p ISBN 0-87451-140-2 LC 76-62914

Cahn, Steven M. (ed.) Scholars who teach; the art of college teaching. Nelson-Hall 1978 246p ISBN 0-88229-373-7 LC 78-944

Cairns, Christopher. Italian literature; the dominant themes. Barnes & Noble 1977 189p (Comparative literature ser) ISBN 0-06-490921-2 LC 76-24070

Calder, Angus. Russia discovered; nineteenth-century fiction from Pushkin to Chekhov. Barnes & Noble 1976 302p ISBN 0-06-490924-7

Calderone, Mary S. (ed.) Sexuality and human values. *See* Sexuality and human values

California Slavic studies v8-10. Editors: Nicholas V. Riasanovsky; Gleb Struve [and] Thomas Eekman. Univ. of Calif. Press 1975-1977 3v ISBN v8 0-520-09519-7; v9 0-520-09485-9; v10 0-520-09564-2 LC 61-1041
Gleb Struve [and] Thomas Eekman. Univ. of Calif. Press

Callahan, William James, and Higgs, David (eds.) Church and society in Catholic Europe of the eighteenth century. Cambridge 1979 168p ISBN 0-521-22424-1 LC 78-12165
"This [expanded] collection of essays on the Catholic Church in eighteenth-century Europe arose from a conference on the topic held at the University of Toronto in November 1974"

The Canadian imagination. See Staines, D. ed.

Canary, Robert H. and Kozicki, Henry James (eds.) The writing of history; literary form and historical understanding. Univ. of Wis. Press 1978 165p ISBN 0-299-07570-2 LC 78-4590

Canetti, Elias. The conscience of words. Tr. from the German by Joachim Neugroschel. Seabury 1979 246p ISBN 0-8164-9334-0 LC 78-15377
"A Continuum book"

Cantrell, Leon (ed.) Bards, bohemians, and bookmen. *See* Bards, bohemians, and bookmen

Capitalism and freedom; problems and prospects. Proceedings of a conference in honor of Milton Friedman. Ed. by Richard T. Selden. Univ. Press of Va. 1975 331p ISBN 0-8139-0555-9. LC 74-5333

Capps, Donald. See Reynolds, F. E. jt. ed.

Capps, Walter Holden (ed.) Seeing with a native eye. *See* Seeing with a native eye

Cardinal, Roger (ed.) Sensibility and creation; studies in twentieth-century French poetry. Barnes & Noble 1977 252p ISBN 0-06-490957-3 LC 76-40876

Carlson, Leland Henry. See entry under title: The Dissenting tradition

Carlton, David (ed.) Arms control and technological innovation. *See* Arms control and technological innovation

Carlton, David (ed.) The dynamics of the arms race. *See* The Dynamics of the arms race

Carlton, David (ed.) International terrorism and world security. *See* International terrorism and world security

Carlyle and his contemporaries; essays in honor of Charles Richard Sanders. Ed. by John Clubbe. Duke Univ. Press 1976 xxiii,371p ISBN 0-8223-0340-X LC 74-31830

Carlyle past and present. See Felding, K. J. and Tarr, R. L. eds.

Carlyle's friendships, and other studies. See Sanders, C. R.

Carnegie Commission on Higher Education. Women and the power to change. *See* Women and the power to change

Carpenter, Andrew (ed.) Place, personality and the Irish writer. *See* Place, personality and the Irish writer

Carr, Edward Hallett. See entry under title: Essays in honour of E. H. Carr

Carter, Gwendolen Margaret. See entry under title: African themes

Carter, Gwendolen Margaret, and O'Meara, Patrick (eds.) Southern Africa in crisis. Ind. Univ. Press 1977 279p ISBN 0-253-35399-8 LC 76-48534

Carter, Gwendolen Margaret, and O'Meara, Patrick (eds.) Southern Africa: the continuing crisis. Ind. Univ. Press 1979 404p ISBN 0-253-31181-0 LC 78-20280
A revised expanded version of the editors' Southern Africa in crisis, listed above

Caserio, Robert L. Plot, story, and the novel; from Dickens and Poe to the modern period. Princeton Univ. Press 1979 304p ISBN 0-691-06382-6 LC 79-4321

Casey, Daniel Joseph, and Rhodes, Robert E. (eds.) Views of the Irish peasantry, 1800-1916. Archon Bks. 1977 225p ISBN 0-208-1630-9 LC 76-39913

Cassirer, Ernst. Symbol, myth, and culture; essays and lectures of Ernst Cassirer, 1935-1945. Ed. by Donald Phillip Verene. Yale Univ. Press 1979 304p ISBN 0-300-02306-5 LC 78-9887

Cater, Douglass (ed.) Television as a cultural force. *See* Television as a cultural force

Cater, Douglass (ed.) Television as a social force: new approaches to TV criticism. *See* Television as a social force: new approaches to TV criticism

Cavaliero, Glen. The rural tradition in the English novel, 1900-1939. Rowman & Littlefield 1977 240p ISBN 0-87471-952-6 LC 76-30536

The child and society. See Elkind, D.

Childhood and selfhood. See Homans, P. ed.

The children's rights movement. See Gross, B. and Gross, R. eds.

China and America; the search for a new relationship. Ed. by William J. Barnds. N.Y. Univ. Press 1977 254p ISBN 0-8147-0989-3 LC 76-46694
"A Council on Foreign Relations book"

The China difference. See Terrill, R. ed.

China's changing role in the world economy; ed. by Bryant G. Garth and the editors of the Stanford Journal of International Studies. Published in cooperation with the National Council on U.S.-China Trade [by] Praeger 1975 222p (Praeger Special studies in international economics and development) ISBN 0-275-01280-8 LC 75-22250

Chinese approaches to literature from Confucius to Liang Ch'i-ch'ao. Ed. with an introduction by Adele Austin Rickett; with contributions by Chia-ying Yeh Chao [and others]. Princeton Univ. Press 1978 267p ISBN 0-691-06343-5 LC 77-7311

Chinese narrative: critical and theoretical essays. Andrew H. Plaks, editor; with a foreword by Cyril Birch. Contributors: Kenneth J. DeWoskin [and others]. Princeton Univ. Press 1977 365p ISBN 0-691-06328-1 LC 76-45907

Chittick, H. Neville, and Rotberg, Robert I. (eds.) East Africa and the Orient; cultural syntheses in pre-colonial times. Africana Pub Co. 1975 343p ISBN 0-8419-0142-2 LC 73-89568

Christian faith in a religiously plural world. Ed. by Donald G. Dawe and John B. Carman. Orbis Bks. 1978 195p ISBN 0-88344-083-0 LC 78-50927

Christian letters to a post-Christian world. See Sayers, D. L. The whimsical Christian

Christianity and political philosophy. See Wilhelmsen, F. D.

Chu, Godwin Chien (ed.) Popular media in China; shaping new cultural patterns. Foreword by A. Doak Barnett. Published for the East-West Center by The Univ. Press of Hawaii 1978 263p ISBN 0-8248-0622-0 LC 78-13282
"An East-West Center book"

Church and government in the Middle Ages. Essays presented to C. R. Cheney on his 70th birthday and ed. by C. N. L. Brooke [and others]. Cambridge [1977 c1976] 312p ISBN 0-521-21172-7 LC 75-41614

Church and society in Catholic Europe of the eighteenth century. See Callahan, W. J. and Higgs, D. eds.

Church, society and politics; papers read at the 13th summer meeting and the 14th winter meeting of the Ecclesiastical History Society. Ed. by Derek Baker. Published for the Ecclesiastical History Society by Blackwell 1975 440p (Studies in church history v12) ISBN 0-631-16970-9 LC 73-82131

Cinnamon, Kenneth M. See Armstrong, T. R. jt. ed.

The city in comparative perspective. See Walton, J. and Masotti, L. H. eds.

The city in Russian history. See Hamm, M. F. ed.

The city in Southern history. See Brownell, B. A. and Goldfield, D. R. eds.

Clapp, Priscilla, and Halperin, Morton H. (eds.) United States-Japanese relations, the 1970's. Harvard Univ. Press 1974 234p ISBN 0-674-92571-8. LC 74-80441

Clareson, Thomas D. (ed.) Many futures, many worlds; theme and form in science fiction. Kent State Univ. Press 1977 303p ISBN 0-87338-199-8 LC 76-42448

Clareson, Thomas D. (ed.) Voices for the future: essays on major science fiction writers. Bowling Green Univ. Pop. Press 1976-1979 2v ISBN v 1 0-87972-119-7; v2 0-87972-135-9 LC v 1 76-10939; v2 78-61202

Clark, Andrew Hill. See entry under title: European settlement and development in North America: essays on geographical change in honour and memory of Andrew Hill Clark

Clark, Harry Hayden. See entry under title: Literature and ideas in America

Clarke, Mary Washington. See LeMaster, J. R. jt. ed.

Classical influences on European culture, A.D. 1500-1700. Proceedings of an international conference held at King's College, Cambridge, April 1974. Ed. by R. R. Bolgar. Cambridge 1976 383p ISBN 0-521-20840-8
Partially analyzed

Claude, Richard P. (ed.) Comparative human rights. Johns Hopkins Univ. Press 1976 410p ISBN 0-8018-1784-6 LC 76-7043

Clausen, Wendell Vernon. (ed.) Harvard Studies in classical philology. See Harvard Studies in classical philology

Clayre, Alasdair. Work and play; ideas and experience of work and leisure. Harper [1975 c1974] 217p ISBN 0-06-01833-9. LC 75-4267

Clemoes Peter (ed.) Anglo-Saxon England. See Anglo-Saxon England

Clogan, Paul Maurice (ed.) Medievalia et humanistica. See Medievalia et humanistica

Clubbe, John, (ed.) Carlyle and his contemporaries See Carlyle and his contemporaries

Coale, Ansley J. (ed.) Economic factors in population growth. See Economic factors in population growth

Cocks, Paul; Daniels, Robert Vincent, and Heer, Nancy Whittier (eds.) The dynamics of Soviet politics. Harvard Univ. Press 1976 427p (Russian Research Center studies 76) ISBN 0-674-21881-7 LC 76-21667

Cockshut, A. O. J. Man and woman: a study of love and the novel, 1740-1940. Oxford 1978 221p ISBN 0-19-520040-3 LC 77-18142

Coffey, John W. Political realism in American thought. Bucknell Univ. Press 1977 217p ISBN 0-8387-1903-1 LC 76-760

Cohen, Ralph. (ed.) New directions in literary history. Johns Hopkins Univ. Press 1974 263p ISBN 0-8018-1549-5. LC 73-8115

Cohen, Sarah Blacher (ed.) Comic relief; humor in contemporary American literature. Univ. of Ill. Press 1978 339p ISBN 0-252-00576-7 LC 78-16510

Coke, F. Van Deren (ed.) One hundred years of photographic history. See One hundred years of photographic history

Cole, C. Robert (ed.) The Dissenting tradition. See The Dissenting tradition

Cole, Robert Taylor. See Cole, Taylor

Cole, Roger William (ed.) Current issues in linguistic theory. See Current issues in linguistic theory

Cole, Taylor. See entry under title: Prospects for constitutional democracy

Coleman, James Samuel. Parents, teachers, and children: prospects for choice in American education. See Parents, teachers, and children: prospects for choice in American education

Coleman, William (ed.) Studies in history of biology. See Studies in history of biology

Coleridge to Catch-22. See Colmer, J.

Collaboration in Italian Renaissance art. Ed. by Wendy Stedman Sheard and John T. Paoletti. Yale Univ. Press 1978 268p ISBN 0-300-02175-5 LC 77-91068
Festschrift in honor of Charles Seymour

The **collected** essays of J. V. Cunningham. See Cunningham, J. V.

The **collective** definition of deviance. See Davis, F. J. and Stivers, R. eds.

Colmer, John. Coleridge to Catch-22; images of society. St Martins 1978 239p ISBN 0-312-14720-1 LC 77-25948

The **colonial** physician & other essays. See Bell, W. J.

Colonialism and change; essays presented to Lucy Mair. Ed. (with introduction) by Maxwell Owusu. Foreword by Meyer Fortes. Mouton 1975 264p (Studies in anthropology 4) LC 74-83128

Colorado State University, Fort Collins. Red men and hat-wearers. *See* Red men and hat-wearers

Comic drama. See Howarth, W. D. ed.

The **comic** hero. See Torrance, R. M.

Comic relief. See Cohen, S. B. ed.

The **comic** spirit of eighteenth-century novels. See Auty, S. G.

The **comic** theatre of Greece and Rome. See Sandbach, F. H.

Commission on United States-Latin American relations. The Americas in a changing world. *See* The Americas in a changing world

Communication and understanding. See Royal Institute of Philosophy

Communication arts in the ancient world. See Havelock, E. A. and Hershbell, J. P. eds.

Communication research—a half-century appraisal. See Lerner, D. and Nelson, L. M. eds.

Communities of women. See Auerbach, N.

Comparative human rights. See Claude, R. P. ed.

Complementarities. See Richards, I. A.

Conant, Miriam Bernheim (ed.) Politics and history. *See* Aron, R. Politics and history

The **Concept** of academic freedom. Ed. by Edmund L. Pincoffs. Univ. of Tex Press 1975 272p ISBN 0-292-71016-X. LC 74-20852
Partially analyzed

Concepts and categories. See Berlin, Sir I.

Concepts of the hero in the Middle Ages and the Renaissance. Papers of the fourth and fifth annual conferences of the Center for Medieval and Early Renaissance Studies, State University of New York at Binghamton 2-3 May 1970, 1-2 May 1971. Ed. by Norman T. Burns & Christopher J. Reagan. Contributors: Bernard F. Huppé [and others]. State Univ. of N.Y. Press 1975 293p ISBN 0-87395-276-6. LC 74-34081

Concerning contemporary art; The Power lectures, 1968-1973. Ed. by Bernard Smith. Oxford 1975 [c1974] 185p ISN 0-19-920062-9

The **conditioned** imagination from Shakespeare to Conrad. See Echeruo, M. J. C.

Cone, Edward T. (ed.) Roger Sessions on music. *See* Sessions, R. Roger Sessions on music

Conference on the Concept of Academic Freedom, University of Texas at Austin, 1972. The concept of academic freedom. *See* The Concept of academic freedom

Coppa, Frank John (ed.) The immigrant experience in America. *See* The Immigrant experience in America

Cordasco, Francesco (ed.) Studies in Italian American social history. *See* Studies in Italian American social history

Cornell, James (ed.) Man and cosmos. *See* Man and cosmos

Cornforth, Maurice Campbell (ed.) Rebels and thier causes. *See* Rebels and their causes

Corwin, Edward Samuel. Presidential power and the Constitution; essays. Ed. with an introduction by Richard Loss. Cornell Univ. Press 1976 xx,185p ISBN 0-8014-0982-9 LC 75-38000

Coser, Lewis Alfred (ed.) The idea of social structure. *See* The Idea of social structure

Coser, Lewis Alfred (ed.) The uses of controversy in sociology. *See* The Uses of controversy in sociology

Cosmic satire in the contemporary novel. See Tilton, J. W.

Cosmology, history, and theology. Ed. by Wolfgang Yourgrau and Allen D. Breck. Contributors: Hannes O. Alfvén [and others]. Plenum Press 1977 416p ISBN 0-306-30940-8 LC 76-54269

Courcel, Martine Hallade de (ed.) Malraux; life and work. Harcourt 1976 284p ISBN 0-15-156280-6
Partially analyzed

Couser, G. Thomas. American autobiography; the prophetic mode. Univ. of Mass. Press 1979 222p ISBN 0-87023-263-0 LC 78-11835

Covello, Leonard. See entry under title: Studies in Italian American social history

Cowan, Charles Donald (ed.) Southeast Asian history and historiography. *See* Southeast Asian history and historiography

Cowley, Malcolm. —And I worked at the writer's trade; chapters of literary history, 1918-1978. Viking 1978 276p ISBN 0-670-12291-2 LC 77-28713

Coxe, Louis Osborne. Enabling acts; selected essays in criticism. Univ. of Mo. Press 1976 164p ISBN 0-8262-0200-4 LC 76-4485

Craft, Robert. Current convictions; views and reviews. Knopf 1977 338p ISBN 0-394-41367-9 LC 77-74991
Partially analyzed

Crahan, Margaret Ellen, and Knight, Franklin W. (eds.) Africa and the Caribbean; the legacies of a link. Johns Hopkins Univ. Press 1979 159p (Johns Hopkins Studies in Atlantic history and culture) ISBN 0-8018-2186-X LC 78-20531

Cramer, Maurice Browning. See entry under title: Aeolian harps

Creative encounter; festschrift for Herman Salinger. Ed. by Leland R. Phelps with the assistance of A. Tilo Alt. Univ. of N.C. Press 1978 182p (University of North Carolina Studies in the Germanic languages and literatures 1978) ISBN 0-8078-8091-4 LC 77-27603
Partially analyzed

Crew, Louie (ed.) The gay academic. Written by Ellen M. Barrett [and others]. ETC Publications 1978 444p ISBN 0-88280-036-1 LC 75-37780

Crews, Frederick C. Out of my system; psychoanalysis, ideology, and critical method. Oxford 1975 214p ISBN 0-19-501974-4. LC 75-7361

Crime, criminology and public policy; essays in honour of Sir Leon Radzinowicz. Ed. by Roger Hood; editorial advisers: F. H. McClintock and Marvin E. Wolfgang. Free Press [1975 c1974] 650p LC 75-2813

Crisis and controversy; essays in honour of A. J. P. Taylor. Ed. by Alan Sked and Chris Cook. St Martins 1976 198p LC 75-42863

The **critical** act. See Watkins, E.

Critical encounters. See Balakian, N.

Critical perspectives on The Decameron. See Dombroski, R. S. ed.

The **critic's** credentials. See Hyman, S. E.

Critics on Caribbean literature. See Baugh, E. ed.

Crosscurrents of criticism. See Horn Book Magazine. Crosscurrents of criticism

Crouch, Colin (ed.) State and economy in contemporary capitalism. St Martins 1979 264p ISBN 0-312-75601-1 LC 78-26539

Crow, Charles R. See entry under title: Shakespeare's late plays

Crow, Jeffrey J. ed. The Southern experience in the American Revolution. *See* The Southern experience in the American Revolution

Crowley, Daniel J. (ed.) African folklore in the New World. Univ. of Tex. Press 1977 91p ISBN 0-292-70326-0 LC 76-050962

Crunden, Robert Morse (ed.) The superfluous men; conservative critics of American culture, 1900-1945. Univ. of Tex. Press 1977 289p ISBN 0-292-77527-X LC 76-18060
Partially analyzed

Cry of the human. See Mills, R. J.

Cuba in the world. Cole Blasier [and] Carmelo Mesa-Lago, editors. Univ. of Pittsburgh Press 1979 343p ISBN 0-8229-3383-7 LC 78-53598
"Early versions of many of the chapters in this book were first presented at an international conference, 'The Role of Cuba in World Affairs,' at the University of Pittsburgh, November 15-17, 1976."

The **cultural** drama. See Smithsonian Institution

Cultural revolution in Russia, 1928-1931. Ed. by Sheila Fitzpatrick. Ind. Univ. Press 1978 309p (Columbia Univ. Russian Inst. Studies) ISBN 0-253-31591-3 LC 77-74439

Culture and art. See Aagaard, Morgensen, L. ed.

Culture and its creators; essays in honor of Edward Shils. Ed. by Joseph Ben-David and Terry Nichols Clark. Contributors: Raymond Aron [and others]. Univ. of Chicago Press 1977 325p ISBN 0-226-04222-7 LC 76-610

Culture and the Nigerian novel. See Taiwo, O.

The **Culture** watch. See Brustein, R. S.

Cunningham, James Vincent. The collected essays of J. V. Cunningham. Swallow Press [1977 c1976] 463p ISBN 0-8040-0670-9 LC 75-21800

Cunningham, Valentine. Everywhere spoken against; dissent in the Victorian novel. Oxford 1975 311p ISBN 0-19-812066-4

Curiosity and pilgrimage. See Zacher, C. K.

The **curious** perspective. See Gilman, E. B.

Current convictions. See Craft, R.

Current issues in Biblical and patristic interpretation; studies in honor of Merrill C. Tenney presented by his former students. Ed. by Gerald F. Hawthorne. Eerdmans 1975 377p ISBN 0-8028-3442-6. LC 74-19326

Current issues in linguistic theory; ed. by Roger W. Cole. Ind. Univ. Press 1977 303p ISBN 0-253-31608-1 LC 76-26427

Current thought in musicology; ed. by John W. Grubbs with the assistance of Rebecca A. Baltzer, Gilbert L. Blount, and Leeman Perkins Univ. of Tex. Press 1976 313p (Symposia in the arts and the humanities no.4) ISBN 0-292-71017-8 LC 75-29245

Currents in the contemporary Argentine novel: Arlt, Mallea, Sabato, and Cortázar. See Foster, D. W.

Curtis, Michael Raymond (ed.) The Palestinians. *See* The Palestinians

Czudnowski, Moshe M. See Eulau, H. jt. ed.

D

Dachinger, Penny. See Ulman, E. jt. ed.

Daedalus. Language as a human problem. *See* Bloomfield, M. W. and Haugen, E. I. eds. Language as a human problem

Daedalus. A New America? *See* A New America?

Dahl, Norman C. (ed.) World change and world security. *See* World change and world security

Dallmayr, Fred R. (ed.) From contract to community; political theory at the crossroads. Dekker, M. 1978 172p (Publications in political science: 4) ISBN 0-8247-6680-6 LC 78-884

Daly, Robert James. God's altar; the world and the flesh in Puritan poetry. Univ. of Calif. Press 1978 253p ISBN 0-520-03480-5 LC 77-76182

The **dangerous** edge. See Lambert, G.

The **dangers** of nuclear war. See Griffiths, F. and Polanyi, J. C. eds.

Daniels, Bruce Colin (ed.) Town and county; essays on the structure of local government in the American colonies. Wesleyan Univ. Press 1978 279p   ISBN 0-8195-5020-5 LC 77-14834

Daniels, Robert Vincent. See Cocks, P. jt. ed.

The **dark** dove. See Webb, E.

Dark prophets of hope. See Kellogg, G.

The **Darker** vision of the Renaissance; beyond the fields of reason. Ed. with introduction by Robert S. Kinsman. Univ. of Calif. Press 1974 320p (UCLA Center for Medieval and Renaissance Studies contributions: 6). ISBN 0-520-02259-9. LC 72-78939

Dauenhauer, Richard, and Binham, Philip (eds.) Snow in May; an anthology of Finnish writing, 1945-1972. Fairleigh Dickinson Univ. Press 1978 389p ISBN 0-8386-1583-X LC 77-24549
Partially analyzed

David Hume; bicentenary papers. Ed. by G. P. Morice. Univ. of Tex. at Austin Press 1977 232p ISBN O-292-71515-3 LC 77-81915
Partially analyzed

Davidson, Basil. See entry under title: African studies since 1945

Davidson, Hilda Roderick Ellis (ed.) Symbols of power. *See* Symbols of power

Davie, Donald. A gathered Church; the literature of the English dissenting interest, 1700-1930. Oxford 1978 152p (The Clark lectures, 1976) ISBN 0-19-519999-5 LC 77-12110

Davies, Alan (ed.) Problems of language and learning. Heinemann [distributed by Humanities Press] 1975 154p ISBN 0-435-10190-0

Davies, Reginald Thorne, and Beatty, Bernard G. (eds.) Literature of the romantic period, 1750-1850. Barnes & Noble 1976 212p (English texts and studies) ISBN 0-06-491614-6

Davis, Floyd James, and Stivers, Richard (eds.) The collective definition of deviance. Free Press 1975 420p ISBN 0-02-907260-3. LC 74-10138

Davis, Kenneth Culp. Discretionary justice in Europe and America; [by] Kenneth Culp Davis and European Associates; Lars Busck [and others]. Univ. of Ill. Press 1976 203p ISBN 0-252-00579-1 LC 75-38842

Dawe, Donald G. (ed.) Christian faith in a religiously plural world. *See* Christian faith in a religiously plural world

Dawidowicz, Lucy S. The Jewish presence; essays on identity and history. Holt 1977 308p ISBN 0-03-016676-4 LC 76-54229

The **Dawn** of modern banking. Center for Medieval and Renaissance Studies, University of California, Los Angeles. Yale Univ. Press 1979 321p ISBN 0-300-02318-9 LC 78-14022
Selected papers delivered at a conference held at UCLA Sept. 23-25, 1977

Dawson, Carl. Victorian noon; English literature in 1850. Johns Hopkins Univ. Press 1979 268p ISBN 0-8018-2110-X LC 78-13939

Day of the leopards. See Wimsatt, W. K.

Dean, Winton (ed.) The rise of romantic opera. *See* Dent, E. J. The rise of romantic opera

Death in America; ed. with an introduction by David E. Stannard. [Contributors] Philippe Ariés [and others] Univ. of Pa. Press 1975 158p ISBN 0-8122-7695-7. LC 75-10124

Death inside out; The Hastings Center report. Ed. by Peter Steinfels and Robert M. Veatch. Harper 1975 149p ISBN 0-06-067576-4 LC 74-25706
Partially analyzed

De Bary, William Theodore (ed.) The unfolding of Neo-Confucianism. *See* The Unfolding of Neo-Confucianism

De Breffny, Brian (ed.) The Irish world; the art and culture of the Irish people. Texts by E. Estyn Evans [and others]. Abrams 1977 296p ISBN 0-8109-1120-5 LC 77-6659

Decline of the West? George Kennan and his critics. Ed. by Martin F. Herz. [Contributors] George F. Kennan [and others]. Ethics and Public Policy Center Georgetown Univ. Press 1978 173p ISBN 0-89633-018-4 LC 78-20038
Partially analyzed

DeCosta, Miriam (ed.) Blacks in Hispanic literature; critical essays. Kennikat 1977 157p (National University Publications. Literary criticism ser) ISBN 0-8046-9140-1 LC 76-45192

DeConde, Alexander (ed.) Encyclopedia of American foreign policy. *See* Encyclopedia of American foreign policy

De Courcel, Martine Hallade. See Courcel, Martine Hallade de

De Crespigny, Anthony, and Minogue Kenneth R. (eds.) Contemporary political philosophers. Dodd 1975 296p ISBN 0-396-07095-7. LC 74-26158

Defenses of the imagination. See Alter R.

De Gracia, Juan José Linz Storch. See Linz Storch de Gracia, Juan José

DeLeon, David. The American as anarchist; reflections on indigenous radicalism. Johns Hopkins Univ. Press 1978 242p ISBN 0-8018-2126-6 LC 78-58290

Delinquency, crime, and society. Ed. by James F. Short, Jr. Contributors: Daniel J. Abbott [and others]. Univ. of Chicago Press 1976 325p ISBN 0-226-75468-5 LC 75-27895
Festschrift in honor of Henry Donald McKay and Clifford Robe Shaw

Delzell, Charles F. (ed.) The future of history. *See* The Future of history

DeMause, Lloyd (ed.) The new psychohistory. Psychohistory Press 1975 313p ISBN 0-914434-01-2. LC 75-14687

DeMause, Lloyd, and Ebel, Henry, 1938- (eds.) Jimmy Carter and American fantasy; psychohistorical explorations. Two Continents/Psychohistory Press 1977 136p ISBN 0-8467-9363-7 LC 77-9146

Dembo, L. S. See Krieger, M. jt. ed.; Pratt, A. V. jt. ed.

Demetz, Peter, ed. Reflections. See Benjamin, W. Reflections

Democracy and the novel. See Smith, H. N.

The democratic Enlightenment. See Meyer, D. H.

Demographic anthropology. See Zubrow, E. B. W. ed.

DeMolen, Richard L. (ed.) Essays on the works of Erasmus. See Essays on the works of Erasmus

De Molina, David Newton- See Newton-De Molina, David

Demonic vision. See Rose, A. H.

DeMott, Robert J. (ed.) Artful thunder. See Artful thunder

Denby, David (ed.) Awake in the dark; an anthology of American film criticism, 1915 to the present. Random House 1977 xxii, 395p ISBN 0-394-72194-2 LC 76-62494
"Vintage books"

Dent, Edward Joseph. The rise of romantic opera. Ed. by Winton Dean. Cambridge 1976 198p ISBN 0-521-213371 LC 76-14029

De Romilly, Jacqueline. See Romilly, Jacqueline de

Derrida, Jacques. Writing and difference. Tr. with an introduction and additional notes, by Alan Bass. Univ. of Chicago Press 1978 342p ISBN 0-226-14328-7 LC 77-25933

Descartes. See Hooker, M. ed.

De Sola Pool, Ithiel. See Pool, Ithiel de Sola

Dessen, Alan C. (ed.) Renaissance drama [1973]. See Renaissance drama [1973]

Developing countries in British fiction. See Goonetilleke, D. C. R. A.

Deviant life-styles. See Henslin, J. M. ed.

Deviants and the abandoned in French society; selections from the Annales, économies, sociétés, civilisations v4. Ed. by Robert Forster and Orest Ranum; tr. by Elborg Forster and Patricia M. Ranum. Johns Hopkins Univ. Press 1978 245p ISBN 0-8018-1991-1 LC 77-17253

De Vogel, Cornelia J. See entry under title: Kephalaion

De Vos, George. Ethnic identity. See Ethnic identity

Dialectical criticism and Renaissance literature. See McCanles, M.

The dialectics of isolation. See Terdiman, R.

Diamond, Arlyn, and Edwards, Lee R. (eds.) The authority of experience; essays in feminist criticism. Univ. of Mass. Press 1977 304p ISBN 0-87023-220-7 LC 76-8755

Dickens, Arthur Geoffrey. Background to the English Renaissance. See Background to the English Renaissance

Dickens Studies Annual v 1-7. Ed. by Robert B. Partlow, Jr. Southern Ill. Univ. Press, 1970, 1972, 1974-1978 7v ISBN v 1 0-8093-0473-2; v2 0-8093-0535-6; v3 0-8093-0570-4; v4 0-8093-0733-2; v5 0-8093-0765-0; v6 0-8093-0806-1; v7 0-8093-0867-3 LC 78-123048

Dickinson, Donald C. (ed.) Voices from the Southwest. See Voices from the Southwest

Dilemmas facing the nation. See Prochnow, H. V. ed.

Dillon, Wilton S. (ed.) The cultural drama. See Smithsonian Institution. The cultural drama

Diplomatic studies in Latin and Greek documents from the Carolingian age. See Wallach, L.

Diplomats in crisis. See Burns, R. D. and Bennett, E. M. eds.

Directions for criticism. See Krieger, M. and Dembo, L. S. eds.

Directors and directions. See Taylor, J. R.

Discretionary justice in Europe and America. See Davis, K. C.

Disguises of the demonic; contemporary perspectives on the power of evil; ed. by Alan M. Olson. Assn. Press 1975 159p ISBN 0-8096-1896-6. LC 74-31321
Partially analyzed

Dissent in the USSR. See Tokes, R. L. ed.

The **Dissenting** tradition; essays for Leland H. Carlson. Ed. by C. Robert Cole and Michael E. Moody. Ohio Univ. Press 1975 xxiii, 272p ISBN 8214-0176-9 LC 74-27706

The **dissimulating** harmony. See Jacobs, C.

The **Diverse** society: implications for social policy. Pastora San Juan Cafferty and Leon Chestang, editors. Natl. Assn. of Social Workers 1976 176p ISBN 0-87101-072-0 LC 76-43633

Dobie, James Frank. Prefaces. Little 1975 204p ISBN 0-316-18788-7 LC 74-34092

Dobson, Eugene. See Strelka, J. P. jt. ed.

Dobzhansky, Theodosius Grigorievich. See Ayala, F. J. jt. ed.

Doing better and feeling worse. See Knowles, J. H. ed.

Doing good; the limits of benevolence. [Contributors]: Willard Gaylin [and others]. Pantheon Bks. 1978 171p ISBN 0-394-41133-1 LC 77-88776

Dolan, Paul J. Of war and war's alarms; fiction and politics in the modern world. Free Press 1976 192p ISBN 0-02-907500-9 LC 75-11287

Dollarhide, Louis, and Abadie, Ann J. (eds.) Eudora Welty: a form of thanks. Essays by Cleanth Brooks [and others]. Univ. Press of Miss. 1979 138p ISBN 0-87805-089-2 LC 78-13285
"Papers delivered at a symposium held at the University of Mississippi on November 10-12, 1977"

Dombroski, Robert Stanley (ed.) Critical perspectives on The Decameron. Barnes & Noble [1977 c1976] 148p ISBN 0-06-491735-5 LC 76-24068

Donald, Miles. The American novel in the twentieth century. Barnes & Noble 1978 215p (Comparative literature ser) ISBN 0-06-491742-8

Donaldson, Ethelbert Talbot (ed.) Essays and studies, 1976. See English Association. Essays and studies, 1976

Donaldson, Scott, and Massa, Ann. American literature: nineteenth and early twentieth centuries. Barnes & Noble 1978 240p (Comparative literature ser) ISBN 0-06-491741-X LC 78-52628

Doner, Dean B. See Bugliarello, G. jt. ed.

Donnelly, John Patrick (ed.) Language, metaphysics, and death. Fordham Univ. Press 1978 244p ISBN 0-8232-1016-2 LC 76-18463

Donoghue, Denis (ed.) Seven American poets from MacLeish to Nemerov; an introduction. Univ. of Minn. Press 1975 329p ISBN 0-8166-0739-7. LC 74-22560

Donoghue, Denis. The sovereign ghost; studies in imagination. Univ. of Calif. Press 1976 229p ISBN 0-520-03134-2 LC 75-27923

Donovan, Josephine Campbell (ed.) Feminist literary criticism; explorations in theory. Univ. Press of Ky. 1975 81p ISBN 0-8131-1334-2 LC 75-12081

Doran, Madeleine. See entry under title: English Renaissance drama

Doris Lessing. See Pratt, A. V. and Dembo, L. S. eds.

The **double** face of Janus. See Temkin, O.

Doubleday, Neal Frank. Variety of attempt; British and American fiction in the early nineteenth century. Univ. of Neb. Press 1976 218p ISBN 0-8032-0876-6 LC 75-38057

Douglas, Jack D. and Johnson, John M. [eds.] Existential sociology; with [contributions by] David L. Altheide [and others] Cambridge 1977 327p ISBN 0-521-21515-3 LC 76-47198

Down home. See Bone, R. A.

Downs, Robert Bingham. Books that changed the South. Littlefield, Adams & Co. 1977 292p ISBN 0-8078-1286-2 LC 76-13181

Downs, Robert Bingham. Books that changed the world. 2d ed. ALA 1978 400p   ISBN 0-8389-0270-7 LC 78-13371
First edition analyzed in 1955-1959 cumulation

Drabble, Margaret (ed.) The genius of Thomas Hardy. Knopf 1976 191p ISBN 0-394-49556-X LC 75-24525

Drama and society; [ed. by James Redmond] Cambridge 1979 321p (Themes in drama, no. 1) ISBN 0-521-22076-9 LC 78-54723

Dramatic identities and cultural tradition. See Hunter, G. K.

Dramatists in revolt. See Lyday, L. F. and Woodyard, G. W. eds.

The **Dress** of words; essays on Restoration and eighteenth century literature in honor of Richmond P. Bond. Ed. by Robert B. White, Jr. Univ. of Kan. 1978 220p (University of Kansas Publications library ser. 42)

Dropkin, Ruth (ed.) Roots of open education in America. *See* Roots of open education in America

The **dual** voice. See Pascal, R.

Dubos, René Jules. Beast or angel? Choices that make us human. Scribner 1974 226p ISBN 0-684-13901-4. LC 74-10737

Duggan, Joseph J. (ed.) Oral literature; seven essays. Barnes & Noble 1975 107p ISBN 0-06-491819-X. LC 74-33851

Duke, Jean Maurice. See Inge, M. T. jt. ed.

Dumoulin, Heinrich (ed.) Buddhism in the modern world. John C. Maraldo, associate editor. Macmillan Pub. Co. 1976 368p ISBN 0-02-533790-4 LC 75-42342

Dunlop, Charles E. M. (ed.) Philosophical essays on dreaming. Cornell Univ. Press 1977 352p ISBN 0-8014-1015-0 LC 77-4582

Dunlop, John B.; Haugh, Richard, and **Klimoff, Alexis** (eds.) Aleksandr Solzhenitsyn: critical essays and documentary materials. 2d. ed. Contributors: Dorothy Atkinson [and others]. Collier Bks. [1975 c1973] 666p ISBN 0-02-050550-7. LC 75-1359 1359
Earlier edition published by Nordland in 1973, analyzed in 1969-1974 cumulation
Partially analyzed

The **dying** Gaul, and other writings. See Jones, D.

The **dynamics** of Soviet politics. See Cocks, P.; Daniels, R. V. and Heer, N. W. eds.

The **Dynamics** of the arms race; ed. by David Carlton and Carlo Schaerf. Wiley 1975 244p ISBN 0-470-13480-1. LC 74-20106
"A Halsted Press book"

Dyson, Anthony Edward, and **Lovelock, Julian.** Masterful images; English poetry from metaphysicals to romantics. Barnes & Noble 1976 254p ISBN 0-06-491863-7 LC 75-39324

E

ELH essays for Earl R. Wasserman; ed. by Ronald Paulson and Arnold Stein. Johns Hopkins Univ. Press 1976 402p ISBN 0-8018-1815-X LC 75-36934

Eakin, Paul John. The New England girl; cultural ideals in Hawthorne, Stowe, Howells and James. Univ. of Ga. Press [1977 c1976] 252p ISBN 0-8203-0398-4 LC 74-18583

Earthly delights, unearthly adornments. See Morris, W.

East Africa and the Orient. See Chittick, H. N. and Rotberg, R. I. eds.

Eaton, Trevor (ed.) Poetries, their media and ends. See Richards, I. A. Poetries, their media and ends

Ebel, Henry. See DeMause, L. jt. ed.

Eberhart, Richard. Of poetry and poets. Univ. of Ill. Press 1979 312p ISBN 0-252-00630-5 LC 78-11597

Ebling, Francis John Govier (ed.) Racial variation in man. See Racial variation in man

Eccles, Mark. See entry under title: English Renaissance drama

Echeruo, Michael J. C. The conditioned imagination from Shakespeare to Conrad. Holmes & Meier Pubs. 1978 135p ISBN 0-8419-0330-1 LC 77-11081

Econometrics and economic theory; essays in honour of Jan Tinbergen. Ed. by Willy Sellekaerts. Int. Arts & Sciences Press [1975 c1974]. 298p ISBN 0-87332-056-5. LC 73-92709
Companion volume to: International trade and finance, analyzed in 1970-74 cumulation

Economic development and planning; essays in honour of Jan Tinbergen. Ed. by Willy Sellekaerts. Int. Arts & Science Press 1974 xxiv, 266p ISBN 0-87332-055-7 LC 73-92712
Companion volumes, International trade and finance and Econometrics and economic theory, analyzed in 1970-1974 cumulation and entered above respectively

Economic factors in population growth; proceedings of a conference held by the International Economic Association at Valescure, France. Ed. by Ansley J. Coale. Wiley 1976 600p ISBN 0-470-16147-7 LC 74-17375
"A Halsted Press book"
Partially analyzed

Economic issues and national security. See Knorr, K. E. and Trager, F. N. eds.

The economy of literature. See Shell, M.

Eddy, Elizabeth M. and Partridge, William L. (eds.) Applied anthropology in America. Columbia Univ. Press 1978 484p ISBN 0-231-04466-6 LC 78-6386

Edelman, Nathan. The eye of the beholder; essays in French literature. Ed. by Jules Brody. Johns Hopkins Univ. Press 1974 210p ISBN 0-8018-1621-1. LC 74-6813

Edelstein, Arthur (ed.) Images and ideas in American culture. See Images and ideas in American culture

Edelstein, Joel C. See Chilcote, R. H. jt. ed.

Edge, Hoyt Littleton. See Wheatley, J. M. O. jt. ed.

Edmonds, Martin. See Beaumont, R. A. jt. ed.

Educated lives: the rise of modern autobiography in America. See Cooley, T.

Edward Gibbon and The decline and fall of the Roman Empire; ed. by G. W. Bowersock; John Clive [and] Stephen R. Graubard. Harvard Univ. Press 1977 257p ISBN 0-674-23940-7 LC 76-48192

Edwards, Lee R. See Diamond, A. jt. ed.

Egoff, Sheila A. (ed.) One ocean touching; papers from the first Pacific Rim Conference on Children's Literature. Scarecrow 1979 252p ISBN 0-8108-1199-5 LC 78-31308
Papers presented at "Pacific Rim Conference on Children's Literature, 1st, University of British Columbia, 1976."

Ehrenberg, Ralph E. (ed.) Pattern and process. *See* Pattern and process

Ehrlich, Richard L. (ed.) Immigrants in industrial America, 1850-1920. *See* Immigrants in industrial America, 1850-1920

The **eighteenth** century. See Rogers, P. ed.

Einstein; a centenary volume; ed. by A. P. French. Harvard Univ. Press 1979 332p ISBN 0-674-24230-0 LC 78-25968
Partially analyzed

Eisenstadt, Shmuel Noah, and **Azmon, Yael** (eds.) Socialism and tradition. Humanities Press 1975 262p (The Van Leer Jerusalem Foundation ser.) ISBN 0-391-00375-5 LC 73-85036

El-Ayouty, Yassin (ed.) The Organization of African Unity after ten years; comparative perspectives. Praeger 1975 262p (Praeger Special studies in international politics and government) ISBN 0-275-09910-5. LC 74-15421

Elegant nightmares. See Sullivan, J.

Eliot, Thomas Stearns. Selected prose of T. S. Eliot. Ed. with an introduction by Frank Kermode. Harcourt [and] Farrar, Straus 1975 320p
Partially analyzed

Elite recruitment in democratic polities. See Eulau, H. and Czudnowski, M. M. eds.

Elizabethan and Jacobean drama. See Ure, P.

The **Elizabethan** prodigals. See Helgerson, R.

The **Elizabethan theatre, V;** papers given at the Fifth International Conference on Elizabethan Theatre held at the University of Waterloo, Ontario, in July 1973. Ed. and with an introduction by G. R. Hibbard. Published in collaboration with the University of Waterloo. Archon Bks. 1974 158p ISBN 0-208-01515-9. LC 75-14300
Previous volumes analyzed in 1970-1974 cumulation

The **Elizabethan theatre, VI;** papers given at the Sixth International Conference on Elizabethan Theatre held at the University of Waterloo, Ontario, in July 1975. Ed. and with an introduction by G. R. Hibbard. Published in collaboration with the University of Waterloo. Archon Bks. [1978] 161p ISBN 0-208-01636-8 LC 77-7123

Elkin, Adolphus Peter (ed.) *See* Grafton Elliot Smith

Elkind, David. The child and society; essays in applied child development. Oxford 1979 304p ISBN 0-19-502371-4 LC 78-2758

Ellen Glasgow; centennial essays. Ed. by M. Thomas Inge. Univ. Press of Va. 1976 232p ISBN 0-8139-0620-2 LC 75-15976

Elliston, Frederick A. See Baker, R. jt. ed.

Elliston, Frederick A. and **McCormick, Peter** (eds.) Husserl; expositions and appraisals. Ed. with introductions. Univ. of Notre Dame Press 1977 378p ISBN 0-268-01063-3 LC 75-19882

Ellrodt, Robert (ed.) Essays and studies, 1975. *See* English Association. Essays and studies, 1975

Ellwood, Robert S. Alternative altars; unconventional and Eastern spirituality in America [by] Robert S. Ellwood, Jr. Univ. of Chicago Press 1979 192p (Chicago History of American religion ser) ISBN 0-226-20618-1 LC 78-15089

The **Elusive** peace in the Middle East; ed. by Malcolm H. Kerr. Published under the auspices of the Arab-Israeli Research and Relations Project, a program of the International Peace Academy. State Univ. of N.Y. Press 1975 347p ISBN 0-87395-305-3. LC 75-15581

The **emergence** of the Latin American novel. See Brotherston, G.

The **Emergent** gospel; theology from the underside of history. Papers from the Ecumenical Dialogue of Third World Theologians, Dar es Salaam, August 5-12, 1976. Ed. by Sergio Torres and Virginia Fabella. Orbis Bks. 1978 274p ISBN 0-88344-112-8 LC 77-22134

Emerson, Everett H. (ed.) American literature, 1764-1789; the Revolutionary years. Univ. of Wis. Press 1977 301p ISBN 0-299-07270-3 LC 75-32073

Emerson, Rupert. See entry under Kilson, M. ed. New states in the modern world

Emerson: prophecy, metamorphosis, and influence. See Levin, D. ed.

Emperor of the earth. See Miłosz, C.

Empey, LaMar Taylor (ed.) Juvenile justice; the Progressive legacy and current reforms. Contributors: LaMar T. Empey [and others] Univ. Press of Va. 1979 ISBN 0-8139-0799-3 LC 78-17536
Essays presented at a Kenyon Public Affairs Forum held Sept. 16-19, 1976, as well as commissioned additional essays

Enabling acts. See Coxe, L. O.

Enchill, Kwamena Bentsi. See Bentsi-Enchill, Kwamena

Encyclopedia of American foreign policy; studies of the principal movements and ideas. Alexander DeConde, editor. Scribner 1978 3v (1201p) ISBN 0-684-155036-6 LC 78-5453

The **end** of the Keynesian era. See Skidelsky, R. J. A. ed.

The **endurance** of Frankenstein. See Levine, G. L. and Knoepflmacher, U. C. eds.

Enemy salvoes. See Lewis, W.

Energy supply and government policy. See Kalter, R. J. and Vogely, W. A. eds.

Energy: the policy issues. See Eppen, G. D. ed.

Enggass, Robert Clarence and Stokstad, Marilyn (eds.) Hortus imaginum; essays in Western art. Univ. of Kansas 1974 211p LC 74-620191

English Association. Contemporary approaches to English studies. *See* Contemporary approaches to English studies

English Association. Essays and studies, 1974; being volume 27 of the new series of essays and studies collected for the English Association by Kenneth Muir. Humanities Press 1974 113p ISBN 391-00279-1

English Association. Essays and studies, 1975; being volume 28 of the new series of essays and studies collected for the English **Association by Robert Ellrodt. Humanities Press** 1975 122p ISBN 0-391-00372-0
Earlier volumes cumulated in previous volumes

English Association. Essays and studies, 1976; being volume 29 of the new series of essays and studies collected for the English Association by E. Talbot Donaldson. Published by the English Association by Humanities Press 1976 121p ISBN 0-391-00535-9

English Association. Essays and studies, 1977; being volume 30 of the new series of essays and studies collected for the English Association by W. Moelwyn Merchant. [Published for the English Association by] Humanities Press 1977 109p ISBN 0-391-00701-7

English Association. Essays and studies, 1978; being volume 31 of the new series of essays and studies collected for the English Association by W. W. Robson [Published for the English Association by] Humanities Press 1978 130p ISBN 0-391-00838-2

English Association. Essays and studies, 1979; being volume 32 of the new series of essays and studies collected for the English Association by Dieter Mehl. [Published for the English Association] by Humanities Press 1979 114p ISBN 0-391-01035-2

English Association. The year's work in English studies v53-57; ed. by James Redmond [and others]. Published for the English Association by Humanities Press 1974-1979 5v ISBN v53 0-391-00363-1; v54 0-391-00606-1; v55 0-391-00648-7; v56 0-391-00748-3; v57 0-391-00917-6

English drama: forms and development. Essays in honour of Muriel Clara Bradbrook. Ed. by Marie Axton and Raymond Williams; with an introduction by Raymond Williams. Cambridge 1977 263p ISBN 0-521-21588-9 LC 76-57099

English Institute. Emerson: prophecy, metamorphosis, and influence. *See* Levin, D. ed. Emerson: prophecy, metamorphosis, and influence

English Institute. The literature of fact. *See* Fletcher, A. J. S. ed. The literature of fact

English Institute. Literary criticism: idea and act. *See* Wimsatt, W. K. ed. Literary criticism: idea and act

English Institute. New approaches to eighteenth-century literature. *See* Harth, J. P. ed. New approaches to eighteenth-century literature

English Institute. Two Renaissance mythmakers. *See* Kernan, A. B. ed. Two Renaissance mythmakers

The **English** Jacobin novel, 1780-1805. See Kelly, G.

English literature in the age of disguise; ed. by Maximillan E. Novak. Univ. of Calif. Press 1977 316p (California. University. University at Los Angeles. William Andrews Clark Memorial Library. Clark Library Professorship. Publications, 4) ISBN 0-520-03342-6 LC 76-48031

The **English** middle-class novel. See Tomlinson, T. B.

An **English** miscellany; presented to W. S. Mackie. Ed. by Brian S. Lee. Oxford 1977 218p ISBN 0-19-570101-1
Partially analyzed

The **English** novel. See Skilton, D.

English poetic diction from Chaucer to Wordsworth. See Sherbo, A.

English Renaissance drama; essays in honor of Madeleine Doran & Mark Eccles. Ed. by Standish Henning, Robert Kimbrough [and] Richard Knowles. Southern Ill. Univ. Press 1976 186p ISBN 0-8093-0777-4 LC 76-18907

English romanticism and the French tradition. See Sabin, M.

Enlarging the temple. See Altieri, C. F.

Ensor, Allison Rash (ed.) Tennessee Studies in literature. *See* Tennessee Studies in literature

Entertainment: a cross-cultural examination. See Fischer, H. D. and Melnik, S. R. eds.

Epic to novel. See Maresca, T. E.

Eppen, Gary Dean (ed.) Energy: the policy issues; with a foreword by Harold S. Geneen. Univ. of Chicago Press 1975 121p ISBN 0-226-21175-4 LC 75-14800

Essays on modern European revolutionary history, by Stanley H. Palmer [and others]. Introduction by Charles Tilly. Ed. by Bede K. Lackner and Kenneth Roy Philp. Univ. of Tex. at Austin Press 1977 132p (The Walter Prescott Webb Memorial lectures v11) ISBN 0-292-72021-1 LC 76-43976

Essays on poetry. See Mill, J. S.

Essays on the Constitution of the United States. [Contributors]: Henry J. Abraham [and others]. Ed. by M. Judd Harmon. Kennikat 1978 202p (National University publications. Multidisciplinary studies in the law) ISBN 0-8046-9210-6 LC 78-6445

Essays on the Iliad. See Wright, J. H. ed.

Essays on the works of Erasmus; ed. by Richard L. DeMolen. Yale Univ. Press 1978 282p ISBN 0-300-02177-1 LC 78-3481 Festschrift in honor of Craig R. Thompson

Essays on twentieth-century poets. See Fraser, G. S.

Essays on urban America; by Robert F. Oaks [and others]; introductions by Constance McLaughlin Green. Ed. by Margaret **Francine Morris and Elliott West.** Univ. of Tex. Press 1975 147p (The Walter Prescott Webb Memorial lectures v9) ISBN 0-292-72011-4. LC 74-31058

Essays on Walter Prescott Webb; by Joe B. Frantz [and others]. Foreword by Jubal R. Parten; introduction by Ray Allen Billington. Ed. by Kenneth R. Philp and Elliott West. Univ. of Tex. Press 1976 123p (The Walter Prescott Webb Memorial lectures v10) ISBN 0-292-72016-5 LC 75-37672

Essential articles for the study of John Donne's poetry. See Roberts, J. R. ed.

Essick, Robert N. and Pearce, Donald R. (eds.) Blake in his time. Ind. Univ. Press 1978 253p ISBN 0-253-31207-8 LC 77-15759

Ethical issues in death and dying. See Weir, R. F. ed.

Ethical patterns in early Christian thought. See Osborn, E. F.

Ethics and nuclear strategy? Ed. by Harold P. Ford and Francis X. Winters. Published by Orbis Books in collaboration with the Woodstock Theological Center, Washington, D.C., and the Institute for the Study of Ethics and International Affairs, School of Foreign Service, Georgetown University. Orbis Bks. 1977 246p ISBN 0-88344-117-9 LC 77-5129

The **ethics** of teaching and scientific research. See Hook, S.; Kurtz, P. and Todorovich, M. eds.

Ethnic conflict in the Western world. See Esman, M. J. ed.

Ethnic identity; cultural continuities and change. Ed. by George De Vos and Lola Romanucci-Ross. Sponsored by the Wenner-Gren Foundation for Anthropological Research. Mayfield Pubs. 1975 395p ISBN 0-87484-298-0. LC 73-93341

Ethnic leadership in America; ed. by John Higham. Johns Hopkins Univ. Press 1978 214p (The Johns Hopkins Symposia in comparative history, no. 9) ISBN 0-8018-2036-7 LC 77-17257

Ethnicity. See Glazer, N. and Moynihan, D. P. eds.

Ethnicity in an international context. See Said, A. A. and Simmons, L. R. eds.

Eudora Welty. See Prenshaw, P. W. ed.

Eudora Welty: a form of thanks. See Dollarhide, L. and Abadie, A. J. eds.

Eulau, Heinz, and Czudnowski, Moshe M. (eds.) Elite recruitment in democratic polities; comparative studies across nations. Sage Publications [distributed by Halsted Press, a division of John Wiley & Sons, Inc.] 1976 299p ISBN 0-470-15056-4 LC 76-2698

Europe and the world. See Twitchett, K. J. ed.

European landed elites in the nineteenth century. See Spring, D. ed.

European peasants and their markets. See Parker, W. N. and Jones, E. L. eds.

European settlement and development in North America: essays on geographical change in honour and memory of Andrew Hill Clark. Ed. by James R. Gibson. Univ. of Toronto Press 1978 230p ISBN 0-8020-5415-3 LC 78-8335

The evangelicals. See Wells, D. F. and Woodbridge, J. D. eds.

Evans, G. B. (ed.) Shakespeare: aspects of influence. *See* Shakespeare: aspects of influence

Evans, Gareth Lloyd, and McDowell, John Henry (eds.) Truth and meaning; essays in semantics. Oxford 1976 419p ISBN 0-19-824517-3

Evans-Pritchard, Edward Evan. See entry under title: Studies in social anthropology

The evening colonnade. See Connolly, C.

Everywhere spoken against. See Cunningham, V.

Evidence in literary scholarship. Essays in memory of James Marshall Osborn. Ed. by René Wellek and Alvaro Ribeiro. Clarendon 1979 417p ISBN 0-19-812612-3 LC 78-40240

The Evil eye. Clarence Maloney, editor. Columbia Univ. Press 1976 335p ISBN 0-231-04006-7 LC 76-16861

Evolution and ecology. See Steward, J. H.

Evolution of consciousness; studies in polarity. Ed. by Shirley Sugerman. Wesleyan Univ. Press 1976 239p ISBN 0-8195-4094-3 LC 75-37592
"In honor of Owen Barfield"
Partially analyzed

Evolution of international management structures; ed. by Harold F. Williamson. A joint publication of the University of Delaware and the Eleutherian Mills-Hagley Foundation. Univ. of Delaware Press [distributed by Temple Univ. Press] 1975 254p ISBN 0-87722-101-4. LC 74-83671
Partially analyzed

Excellence in university teaching. See Buxton, T. H. and Prichard, K. W. eds.

Excursions. See Boyers, R.

Exile and tradition; studies in African and Caribbean literature. Ed. by Rowland Smith. African Pub. 1976 190p (Dalhousie African Studies ser) ISBN 0-8419-0263-1 LC 76-2379

Existential sociology. See Douglas, J. D. and Johnson, J. M. [eds.]

Explanation of prehistoric change. Ed. by James N. Hill. Univ. of N.Mex. Press 1977 356p (School of American Research advanced seminar ser) ISBN 0-8263-0451-6 LC 76-57541
"A School of American Research book"

Explorations in psychohistory; the Wellfleet papers. Ed. by Robert Jay Lifton with Eric Olson. Simon & Schuster 1974 372p ISBN 0-671-21848-4 LC 74-13758
Partially analyzed

Explorations 3. See Knights, L. C.

Explorers of humankind. See Hanna, T. ed.

The eye of the beholder. See Edelman, N.

The eye of the story. See Welty, E.

F

Fable's end. See Richter, D. H.

Fabulation and metafication. See Scholes, R. E.

The **faces** of Eve. See Fryer, J.

Facets of Taoism. See Welch, H. and Seidel, A. K. eds.

Fact, value, and perception; essays in honor of Charles Baylis. Paul Welsh, editor. Duke Univ. Press 1975 174p ISBN 0-8223-0321-3. LC 74-75987
Partially analyzed

The **failure** of criticism. See Goodheart, E.

Fair forms. See Røstvig, M. S. ed.

'A **faire** and easie way to heaven.' See Stoever, W. K. B.

Fairfield, Roy P. (ed.) Humanistic frontiers in American education. [2d ed] Prometheus Bks. [1975 c1971] 333p ISBN 0-87975-054-5. LC 79-166138
First published 1971 by Prentice-Hall
Partially analyzed

Falk, Robert P. (ed.) Literature and ideas in America. *See* Literature and ideas in America

The **family.** See Rossi, A. S.; Kagan, J. and Hareven, T. K. eds.

Family and inheritance; rural society in Western Europe, 1200-1800. Ed. by Jack Goody; Joan Thirsk [and] E. P. Thompson. Cambridge 1976 421p (Past and Present Publications) ISBN 0-521-21246-4 LC 76-10402

Family and society; selections from the Annales, économies, sociétés, civilisations v2. Ed. by Robert Forster and Orest Ranum. tr. by Elborg Forster and Patricia M. Ranum. Johns Hopkins Univ. Press 1976 261p ISBN 0-8018-1780-3 LC 76-17299

The **family** in history. See Rosenberg, C. E. ed.

Family policy. See Kamerman, S. B. and Kahn, A. J. eds.

Fancher, Raymond E. Pioneers of psychology. Norton 1979 397p ISBN 0-393-01161-5 LC 78-10845

Farer, Tom J. (ed.) The future of the inter-American system. Praeger 1979 290p (Prager Special studies) ISBN 0-03-047391-8 LC 78-31153
Published under the auspices of The American Society of International Law

Farley-Hills, David. The benevolence of laughter; comic poetry of the Commonwealth and Restoration. Rowman & Littlefield 1974 212p ISBN 0-87471-502-4. LC 73-22229

Farrell, James Thomas. Literary essays, 1954-1974. Collected and ed. by Jack Alan Robbins. Kennikat 1976 147p (National University Publications; Literary criticism ser.) ISBN 0-8046-9125-8 LC 76-17588
Partially analyzed

Fascism: a reader's guide. See Laqueur, W. Z. ed.

The **fate** of reading. See Hartman, G. H.

Faulkner: fifty years after The marble faun. Ed. by George H. Wolfe. Univ. of Ala. Press 1976 188p ISBN 0-8173-7609-7 LC 75-40380

Filler, Louis (ed.) A question of quality: popularity and value in modern creative writing. Bowling Green Univ. Pop. Press 1976 264p ISBN 0-87972-077-8 LC 76-20958

Film propaganda. See Taylor, R.

The **films** in my life. See Truffaut, F.

Finger, Seymour Maxwell (ed.) The new world balance and peace in the Middle East: reality or mirage? *See* The New world balance and peace in the Middle East: reality or mirage?

Finneran, Richard J. (ed.) Anglo-Irish literature; a review of research. Modern Lang. Assn of Am. 1976 596p ISBN 0-87352-252-4 LC 74-31959

Fiorenza, Elisabeth Schüssler (ed.) Aspects of religious propaganda in Judaism and early Christianity. *See* Aspects of religious propaganda in Judaism and early Christianity

First images of America; the impact of the New World on the Old. Ed. by Fredi Chiappelli; co-editors: Michael J. B. Allen & Robert L. Benson. Univ. of Calif. Press 1976 2v xxii,(957p) ISBN 0-520-03010-9 LC 75-7191
Published under the auspices of the Center for Medieval and Renaissance Studies, University of California, Los Angeles

The **first** World War in fiction. See Klein, H. M. ed.

Fischer, Heinz-Dietrich, and Melnik, Stefan Reinhard (eds.) Entertainment: a cross-cultural examination. Ed. with an introduction and a select bibliography. Hastings House 1979 330p (Humanistic studies in the communication arts) ISBN 0-8038-1945-5 LC 79-66
"Communication arts books"

Fischer, Heinz-Dietrich, and Merrill, John Calhoun (eds.) International and intercultural communication. Ed. with introductory notes and suggested readings. [2d ed. rev and enl] Hastings House 1976 524p (Humanistic Studies in the communication arts) ISBN 0-8083-3402-0 LC 76-17806
"Communicaton arts books"
First published in 1970 under title: International communication

Fisher, Dexter (ed.) Minority language and literature. *See* Minority language and literature

Fisher, Dexter, and Stepto, Robert B. (eds.) Afro-American literature; the reconstruction of instruction; [edited] for the Commission on the Literatures and Languages of America. Modern Lang. Assn. of Am. 1979 256p ISBN 0-87352-351-2 LC 78-62061
This volume is the result of a seminar entitled "Afro-American literature: from critical approach to course design," held at Yale University in June, 1977
Partially analyzed

Fisher, Sydney Nettleton. See entry under title: Nationalism in a non-national state

Fisher, Walter R. (ed.) Rhetoric: a tradition in transition. *See* Rhetoric: a tradition in transition

Fishkin, James. See Laslett, P. jt. ed.

Fishwick, Marshall William. See Browne, R. B. jt. ed.

Fitzgerald, Ross (ed.) Human needs and politics. Pergamon 1977 278p ISBN 0-08-21402-9

Fitzgerald, Ross (ed.) What it means to be human; essays in philosophical anthropology, political philosophy and social psychology. Pergamon Press 1978 251p ISBN 0-08-023356-2
Partially analyzed

Fitzpatrick, Sheila (ed.) Cultural revolution in Russia, 1928-1931. *See* Cultural revolution in Russia, 1928-1931

Five centuries of map printing. See Woodward, D. A. ed.

Five temperaments. See Kalstone, D.

Foucault, Michel. Language, counter-memory, practice; selected essays and interviews. Ed. with an introduction by Donald F. Bouchard; tr. from the French by Donald F. Bouchard and Sherry Simon. Cornell Univ. Press 1977 240p ISBN 0-8014-0979-9 LC 77-4561
Partially analyzed

Founding principles of American government. See Graham, G. J. and Graham, S. G. eds.

Four centuries of Southern Indians. See Hudson, C. M. ed.

Fowler, Roger (ed.) Style and structure in literature; essays in the new stylistics. Cornell Univ. Press 1975 262p ISBN 0-8014-0949-7. LC 74-24277

Fowlie, Wallace. See entry under title: Symbolism and modern literature

Fox, Cyril James (ed.) Enemy salvoes. *See* Lewis, W. Enemy salvoes

Fox, Marvin (ed.) Modern Jewish ethics. *See* Modern Jewish ethics

Fox, Robin (ed.) Biosocial anthropology. *See* Biosocial anthropology

Francis Warner. See Prentki, T. ed.

Fraser, George Sutherland. Essays on twentieth-century poets. Rowman & Littlefield 1977 255p ISBN 0-87471-876-7 LC 77-9959

Freeborn, Richard (ed.) Russian literary attitudes from Pushkin to Solzhenitsyn; by Richard Freeborn; Georgette Donchin [and] N. J. Anning. Barnes & Noble 1976 158p ISBN 0-06-492260-X LC 76-15796

The freedom of the poet. See Berryman, J.

Freeman, Eugene (ed.) The Abdication of philosophy: philosophy and the public good. *See* The Abdication of philosophy: philosophy and the public good

Freeman, Eugene, and Mandelbaum, Maurice H. (eds.) Spinoza; essays in interpretation. Open Ct. 1975 323p ISBN 0-87548-079-9. LC 72-84079

French, Anthony Philip (ed.) Einstein. *See* Einstein

French, Brandon. On the verge of revolt; women in American films of the fifties. Ungar 1978 xxiv, 165p (Ungar film library) ISBN 0-8044-2220-6 LC 78-4294

French, Warren G. (ed.) The twenties; fiction, poetry, drama. Everett/Edwards 1975 532p ISBN 0-912112-05-0 LC 74-24534
Partially analyzed

French and Scandinavian sculpture in the nineteenth century. See Wennberg, B. G.

French comic drama. See Brereton, G.

French literary imagination and Dostoevsky, and other essays. See Peyre, H.

French literature in the nineteenth century. See Robinson, C.

French poets and the English Renaissance. See Prescott, A. L.

French Renaissance studies, 1540-70; humanism and the encyclopedia; editor: Peter Sharratt. Edinburgh Univ. Press 1976 276p ISBN 0-85224-276-X
Partially analyzed

French society and the Revolution. Ed. by Douglas Johnson. Cambridge 1976 321p (Past and Present Publications) ISBN 0-521-21275-8 LC 76-1136

Fricke, Donna G. (ed) Aeolian harps. *See* Aeolian harps

Friday's footprint. See Morris, W. A.

Frost: centennial essays III. Ed. by Jac Tharpe. Univ. Press of Miss. 1978 407p ISBN 0-87805-047-7 LC 72-3548
Companion volume to Frost: centennial essays [v 1] analyzed in 1970-1974 cumulation; and to Frost: centennial essays II entered above

Frye, Herman Northrop. See Frye, Northrop

Frye, Northrop. Northrop Frye on culture and literature; a collection of review essays. Ed. and with an introduction by Robert D. Denham. Univ. of Chicago Press 1978 264p ISBN 0-226-26647-8 LC 77-12917

Frye, Northrop. Spiritus mundi; essays on literature, myth, and society. Ind. Univ. Press 1976 296p ISBN 0-253-35432-3 LC 76-12364

Fryer, Judith. The faces of Eve; women in the nineteenth century American novel. Oxford 1976 294p ISBN 0-19-502025-1 LC 75-32345

Furth, Charlotte (ed.) The limits of change. *See* The Limits of change

A **future** for Astyanax. See Bersani, L.

The **future** of cultural minorities. See Alcock, A. E.; Taylor, B. K. and Welton, J. M. eds.

The **Future** of history; essays in the Vanderbilt University Centennial Symposium. Ed. by Charles F. Delzell. Vanderbilt Univ. Press 1977 263p ISBN 0-8265-1205-4 LC 76-48199

The **Future** of science. 1975 Nobel Conference organized by Gustavus Adolphus College. Ed. by Timothy C. L. Robinson. Contributors: John C. Eccles [and others]. Wiley 1977 xxii, 145p ISBN 0-471-01524-5 LC 76-49607
"A Wiley-Interscience publication"
Festschrift in honor of Edward Lawrie Tatum
Partially analyzed

The **future** of the inter-American system. See Farer, T. J. ed.

The **future** that doesn't work. See Tyrrell, R. E. ed.

Fyfe, Christopher (ed.) African studies since 1945. *See* African studies since 1945

G

Gakwandi, Shatto Arthur. The novel and contemporary experience in Africa. Africana Pub. Co. 1977 136p ISBN 0-8419-0306-9 LC 77-1273

Galbraith, John Kenneth. Annals of an abiding liberal. Ed. by Andrea D. Williams. Houghton 1979 384p ISBN 0-395-27617-9 LC 79-15782
Partially analyzed

Galinsky, Gotthard Karl (ed.) Perspectives of Roman poetry. *See* Perspectives of Roman poetry

Gallie, W. B. Philosophers of peace and war; Kant, Clausewitz, Marx, Engels and Tolstoy. Cambridge 1978 147p (The Wiles lectures) ISBN 0-521-21779-2 LC 77-23553

Gallup, Donald (ed.) American characteristics and other essays. *See* Wilder, T. N. American characteristics, and other essays

Galnoor, Itzhak (ed.) Government secrecy in democracies. N.Y. Univ. Press 1977 317p ISBN 0-8147-2964-9 LC 76-49772

Gans, Herbert J. (ed.) On the making of Americans. *See* On the making of Americans

The **gaping** pig. See Massey, I.

Garth, Bryant G. (ed.) China's changing role in the world economy. *See* China's changing role in the world economy

Gibson, James Jerome. See entry under title: Perception

Gibson, James R. (ed). European settlement and development in North America: essays on geographical change in honour and memory of Andrew Hill Clark. *See* European settlement and development in North America: essays on geographical change in honour and memory of Andrew Hill Clark

Giddens, Anthony (ed.) Positivism and sociology; ed. with an introduction. Heinemann distributed by Humanities Press 1974 244p ISBN 0-435-82340-X

Giele, Janet Zollinger [and] **Smock, Audrey Chapman** (eds.) Women: roles and status in eight countries. Wiley 1977 443p ISBN 0-471-01504-0 LC 76-39950
"A Wiley-Interscience Publication"

Gilbert, Felix. History; choice and commitment. Harvard Univ. Press 1977 549p ISBN 0-674-39656-1 LC 76-27352

Gilbert, Sandra M. and Gubar, Susan. The madwoman in the attic; the woman writer and the nineteenth-century literary imagination. Yale Univ. Press 1979 719p ISBN 0-300-02286-7 LC 78-20792

Gilbert, Sandra M. and Gubar, Susan (eds.) Shakespeare's sisters; feminist essays on women poets. Ed. with an introduction. Ind. Univ. Press 1979 xxvi, 337p ISBN 0-253-11258-3 LC 78-9510

Gillie, Christopher. Movements in English literature, 1900-1940. Cambridge 1975 207p ISBN 0-521-20655-3. LC 74-16993

Gilman, Ernest B. The curious perspective; literary and pictorial wit in the seventeenth century. Yale Univ. Press 1978 267p ISBN 0-300-02222-0 LC 78-6075

Gingerich, Owen (ed.) The nature of scientific discovery. *See* The nature of scientific discovery

Girard, René. "To double business bound"; essays on literature, mimesis, and anthropology. Johns Hopkins Univ. Press 1978 229p ISBN 0-8018-2114-2 LC 78-8418
Partially analyzed

Glahe, Fred R. (ed.) Adam Smith and The wealth of nations; 1776-1976 bicentennial essays; ed. and with an introduction. Colo. Associated Univ. Press 1978 172p ISBN 0-87081-108-8 LC 77-91609

Glazer, Nathan, and Moynihan, Daniel Patrick (eds.) Ethnicity; theory and experience. With the assistance of Corinne Saposs Schelling. Harvard Univ. Press 1975 531p ISBN 0-674-26855-5. LC 74-21230

Glicksberg, Charles Irving. The literature of commitment. Bucknell Univ. Press [1977 c1976] 467p ISBN 0-8387-1685-7 LC 75-5148

Glicksberg, Charles Irving. The literature of nihilism. Bucknell Univ. Press 1975 354p ISBN 0-8387-1520-6 LC 74-203

Glimpses of Germanic-Slavic relations from Pushkin to Heinrich Mann. See Kostka, E. K.

The **global** predicament. See Orr, D. W. and Soroos, M. S. eds.

Glock, Charles Y. (ed.) The New religious consciousness. *See* The New religious consciousness

Glyph 1-5; Johns Hopkins Textual studies. Editors: Samuel Weber and Henry Sussman. Johns Hopkins Univ. Press 1977-1979 5v ISBN v 1 0-8018-1930-X LC 76-47370; v2 0-8018-1993-8 LC 77-4536; v3 0-8018-2082-0 LC 76-47370; v4 0-8018-2143-6 LC 76-47370; v5 0-8018-2192-4 LC 76-47370
V 1 partially analyzed

Gochros, Harvey L. and Gochros, Jean S. (eds.) The sexually oppressed; ed. and with introductions. Association Press 1977 xxiii, 296p ISBN 0-8096-1915-6 LC 76-49051

Gochros, Jean S. See Gochros, H. L. jt. ed.

God's altar. See Daly, R. J.

Goedicke, Hans (ed.) Unity and diversity. *See* Unity and diversity

Gogol from the twentieth century. See Maguire, R. A. ed.

Going, William Thornbury. Essays on Alabama literature. Univ. of Ala. Press 1975 176p (Studies in the humanities: Literature no. 4) ISBN 0-8173-7318-7. LC 73-22586

Goist, Park Dixon. From Main Street to State Street; town, city, and community in America. Kennikat 1977 180p (Interdisciplinary urban ser. National University Pubs) ISBN 0-8046-9185-1 LC 77-2923

Gold, Joseph (ed.) In the name of language! Maclean-Hunter Press 1975 209p ISBN 0-7705-1355-7

Goldfield, David R. See Brownell, B. A. jt. ed.

Goldman, Merle (ed.) Modern Chinese literature in the May Fourth era. *See* Modern Chinese literature in the May Fourth era

Goldsmith, Donald (ed.) Scientists confront Velikovsky; with a foreword by Isaac Asimov. Cornell Univ. Press 1977 183p ISBN 0-8014-0961-6 LC 77-2457

Goldstein, Walter (ed.) Planning, politics, and the public interest. *See* Planning, politics and the public interest

Gombrich, Sir Ernst Hans Josef. See Gregory, R. L. jt. ed.

The good word & other words. See Sheed, W.

Goodall, Vanne Morris (ed.) The quest for man. With contributions by Barbara Bender [and others]. With a preface by Sir Julian Huxley. Praeger 1975 240p ISBN 0-275-49770-4. LC 72-79550

Goodheart, Eugene. The failure of criticism. Harvard Univ. Press 1978 203p ISBN 0-674-29115-8 LC 77-29055

Goodwin, Geoffrey L. (ed.) New dimensions of world politics. *See* New dimensions of world politics

Goody, John Rankine (ed.) Family and inheritance. *See* Family and inheritance

Goold, G. P. (ed.) Harvard Studies in classical philology. *See* Harvard Studies n classical philology

Goonetilleke, D. C. R. A. Developing countries in British fiction. Rowman & Littlefield 1977 282p ISBN 0-87471-908-9 LC 76-40275

Gordon, Donald James. The Renaissance imagination; essays and lectures by D. J. Gordon. Collected and ed. by Stephen Orgel. Univ. of Calif. Press 1975 ISBN 0-520-02817-1 LC 74-81432

The gorgon's head. See Brashear, W. R.

The Gothic visionary perspective. See Nolan, B.

Gould, Carol C. and Wartofsky, Marx W. (eds.) Women and philosophy; toward a theory of liberation. Putnam 1976 364p SBN 399-11652-4 LC 75-33604
"Capricorn books"

Gould, Thomas Fauss (ed.) Yale classical studies v25. *See* Yale classical studies v25

Gove, Walter R. (ed.) The labelling of deviance; evaluating a perspective. Sage Publications [distributed by Halsted Press, a division of John Wiley & Sons, inc] 1975 313p ISBN 0-470-31930-5 LC 75-14102

Government secrecy in democracies. See Galnoor, I. ed.

Graces of harmony. See Adams, P. G.

Gracia, Juan José Linz Storch de. See Linz Storch de Gracia, Juan José

Graff, Gerald. Literature against itself; literary ideas in modern society. Univ. of Chicago Press 1979 260p ISBN 0-226-30600-3 LC 78-9879

Grafton Elliot Smith; the man and his work; ed. by A. P. Elkin and N. W. G. Macintosh. Sydney Univ. Press [distributed by Int. Univs. Press] 1974 232p ISBN 0-424-06790-0. LC 73-84903
In honor of Grafton Elliot Smith
Partially analyzed

Graham, George J. and Graham, Scarlett G. (eds.) Founding principles of American government; two hundred years of democracy on trial. Ed. by George J. Graham, Jr. and Scarlett G. Graham. Contributors: Joseph M. Bessette [and others]. Ind. Univ. Press 1977 395p ISBN 0-253-32415-7 LC 76-12380

Graham, Scarlett G. See Graham, G. J. jt. ed.

Grand strategy for the 1980s. [Contributors:] Bruce K. Holloway [and others]. Ed. by Bruce Palmer, Jr. Am. Enterprise Inst. for Public Policy Res. 1978 113p ISBN 0-8447-3294-X LC 78-57065

Granger, Bruce Ingham. American essay serials from Franklin to Irving. Univ. of Tenn. Press 1978 277p ISBN 0-87049-221-7 LC 78-4120

Grant, Patrick. Images and ideas in literature of the English Renaissance. Univ. of Mass. Press 1979 243p ISBN 0-87023-163-4 LC 78-53176

Grantham, Dewey W. The regional imagination; the South and recent American history. Vanderbilt Univ. Press 1979 269p ISBN 0-8265-1207-0 LC 78-26556

Graubard, Stephen Richards (ed.) A New America? See A New America?

Graver, Lawrence Stanley, ed. Mastering the film, and other essays. See Samuels, C. T. Mastering the film, and other essays

Gray, Jack. See Brown, A. H. jt. ed.

Gray, Richard J. The literature of memory; modern writers of the American South. Johns Hopkins Univ. Press 1977 377p ISBN 0-8018-1803-6 LC 76-18941

Great Britain and her world, 1750-1914; essays in honour of W. O. Henderson; ed. by Barrie M. Ratcliffe. Manchester Univ. Press [distributed by Rowman & Littlefield] 1975 358p ISBN 0-87471-709-4

The Greek concept of justice. See Havelock, E. A.

Green, Mark J. See Nader, R. jt. ed.

Greenberg, Irving. See Rosenfeld, A. H. jt. ed.

Greene, Maxine. Landscapes of learning. Teachers College Press 1978 255p ISBN 0-8077-2534-X LC 78-6571

Greene, Robert W. Six French poets of our time; a critical and historical study. Princeton Univ. Press 1979 200p (Princeton Essays in literature) ISBN 0-691-06390-7 LC 78-70297

Greenfield, Harry I. (ed.) Theory for economic efficiency: essays in honor of Abba P. Lerner. See Theory for economic efficiency: essays in honor of Abba P. Lerner

Greenhalgh, Michael, and Megaw, J. Vincent S. (eds.) Art in society; studies in style, culture and aesthetics. St Martins 1978 350p ISBN 0-312-05267-7 LC 78-69954
This volume originated in a symposium held under the auspices of the Research Seminar in Archaeology and Related Subjects held at Leicester University in January, 1975

H

H. G. Wells and modern science fiction; ed. by Darko Suvin with Robert M. Philmus, associate editor. Bucknell Univ Press 1977 279p ISBN 0-8387-1773-X LC 75-18696
Partially analyzed

Haddad, William Woodrow (ed.) Nationalism in a non-national state. *See* Nationalism in a non-national state

Hadfield, John (ed.) The Saturday book 34. *See* The Saturday book 34

Hadgraft, Cecil. See entry under title: Bards, bohemians, and bookmen

Haley, Bruce. The healthy body and Victorian culture. Harvard Univ. Press 1978 296p ISBN 0-674-38610-8 LC 78-6933

Hall, Daniel George Edward. See entry under title: Southeast Asian history and historiography

Halle, Morris, (ed.) Linguistic theory and psychological reality. *See* Linguistic theory and psychological reality

Hallowell, John Hamilton (ed.) Prospects for constitutional democracy. *See* Prospects for constitutional democracy

Halperin, John (ed.) Jane Austen; bicentenary essays. Cambridge 1975 334p ISBN 0-521-20709-6 LC 74-25640

Halperin, Morton H. See Clapp, P. jt. ed.

Hamburger, Michael. Art as second nature; occasional pieces, 1950-74. Carcanet New Press distributed by Dufour 1975 156p ISBN 0-85635-973-7

Hamilton, Kenneth Gordon (ed.) Studies in the recent Australian novel; from the Australian Studies Centre, University of Queensland. Univ. of Queensland Press 1979 [c1978] [distributed by Technical Impex Corp.] 257p ISBN 0-7022-1247-4

Hamm, Michael Franklin (ed.) The city in Russian history. Univ. Press of Ky. 1976 349p ISBN 0-8131-1328-8 LC 75-3544

Hammond, Norman (ed.) Mesoamerican archaeology. *See* Mesoamerican archaeology

Hammond, Thomas Taylor (ed.) The anatomy of Communist takeovers. Associate editor: Robert Farrell; foreword by Cyril E. Black. Yale Univ. Press 1975 664p ISBN 0-300-01727-8. LC 74-79975

Hampshire, Stuart (ed.) Public and private morality. Cambridge 1978 ISBN 0-521-22084-X LC 78-2839

Hampshire, Stuart Newton. See Hampshire, Stuart

Hand, Wayland Debs (ed.) American folk medicine. *See* American folk medicine

Handbook of contemporary developments in world sociology. See Mohan, R. P. and Martindale, D. A. eds.

Handbook of contemporary urban life [by] David Street and associates. Jossey-Bass 1978 741p (The Jossey-Bass Social and behavioral science ser. ISBN 0-87589-372-4 LC 78-1155

Handlin, Oscar. See entry under title: Uprooted Americans

Hanfmann, George Maxim Anossov. From Croesus to Constantine; the cities of Western Asia Minor and their arts in Greek and Roman times. Univ. of Mich. Press 1975 127p illus. (Jerome lectures, 10th ser) ISBN 0-472-08420-8. LC 73-80574

Hanna, Thomas (ed.) Explorers of humankind. Ed. with introduction and biographical notes. [Contributors]: Moshe Feldenkrais [and others]. Harper 1979 147p ISBN 0-06-250375-8 LC 78-65664

Hannah Arendt: the recovery of the public world. Ed. by Melvyn A. Hill. St Martins 1979 362p ISBN 0-312-36071-1 LC 78-19393
Festschrift in memory of Hannah Arendt
Partially analyzed

Hannay, Margaret Patterson (ed.) As her whimsey took her; critical essays on the work of Dorothy L. Sayers. Kent State Univ. Press 1979 301p ISBN 0-87338-227-7 LC 79-10933
Partially analyzed

Hanning, Robert W. The individual in twelfth-century romance. Yale Univ. Press 1977 303p ISBN 0-300-02101-1 LC 77-75378

Hardy, Barbara (Nathan) The advantage of lyric; essays on feeling in poetry. Ind. Univ. Press 1977 142p ISBN 0-253-30130-0 LC 76-47167

Hardy, Barbara (Nathan) Tellers and listeners; the narrative imagination. The Athlone Press distributed by Humanities Press 1975 279p ISBN 0-485-11153-5

Hardy, Henry (ed.) Concepts and categories. *See* Berlin, I. Concepts and categories

Hardy, Henry (ed.) Russian thinkers. *See* Berlin, I. Russian thinkers

Hareven, Tamara K. See Rossi, A. S. jt. ed.

Harley, Sharon, and Terborg-Penn, Rosalyn (eds.) The Afro-American woman; struggles and images. Kennikat 1978 137p (National University Publications Series in American Studies) ISBN 0-8046-9209-2 LC 78-9821

Harman, Gilbert (ed.) On Noam Chomsky; critical essays. Anchor Bks. 1974 348p (Modern studies in philosophy). ISBN 0-385-03765-1. LC 74-3558
"A Doubleday Anchor original"
Partially analyzed

Harmon, M. Judd (ed.) Essays on the Constitution of the United States. *See* Essays on the Constitution of the United States

Harmon, Maurice (ed.) Richard Murphy: poet of two traditions; interdisciplinary studies. Wolfhound Press [distributed by Humanities Press] 1978 128p ISBN 0-905473-17-5
Partially analyzed

Harper, George Mills (ed.) Yeats and the occult. *See* Yeats and the occult

Harré, Rom. See Harré, Romano

Harré, Romano (ed.) Problems of scientific revolution; progress and obstacles to progress in the sciences. Oxford 1975 104p (The Herbert Spencer Lectures, 1973) ISBN 0-19-58211-0

Harrington, Evans (ed.) Faulkner, modernism, and film: Faulkner and Yoknapatawpha, 1978. *See* Faulkner, modernism, and film: Faulkner and Yoknapatawpha, 1978

Harrington, Evans (ed.) The Maker and the myth: Faulkner and Yoknapatawpha, 1977. *See* The Maker and the myth: Faulkner and Yoknapatawpha, 1977

Harrington, Evans (ed.) The South and Faulkner's Yoknapatawpha. *See* The South and Faulkner's Yoknapatawpha

Harris, Harold Arthur (ed.) Astride the two cultures; Arthur Koestler at 70. Random House 1976 219p ISBN 0-394-40063-1 LC 75-29459

Harry S. Truman Library, Independence, Mo. Institute for National and International Affairs. The Korean War. *See* The Korean War

Hart, Francis Russell. The Scottish novel; from Smollett to Spark. Harvard Univ. Press 1978 442p ISBN 0-674-79584-9 LC 77-20680

Harth, John Phillip (ed.) New approaches to eighteenth-century literature; selected papers from the English Institute. Ed. with a foreword by Phillip Harth. Columbia Univ. Press 1974 217p ISBN 0-231-03928-X. LC 74-13808

Harth, Phillip. See Harth, John Phillip

Hartman, Geoffrey H. The fate of reading; and other essays. Univ. of Chicago Press 1975 352p ISBN 0-226-31844-3. LC 74-11624

Hartman, Geoffrey H. (ed.) Psychoanalysis and the question of the text. Ed. with a preface. Johns Hopkins Univ. Press 1978 182p (Selected papers from the English Institute, 1976-77, new ser. no 2) ISBN 0-8018-2128-2 LC 78-7656

Harvard Studies in classical philology v71-82. Harvard Univ. Press 1967-1978 12v ISBN v74 0-674-37920-9; v75 0-674-37921-7; v76 0-674-37922-5; v77 0-674-37923-3; v78 0-674-37924-1; v79 0-674-37926-8; v80 0-674-37927-6; v81 0-674-37928-4; v82 0-674-37929-2 LC 44-32100
v71 ed. by Wendell V. Clausen and others; v72-74 ed. by G. P. Gold and others; v75-76 ed. by G. P. Goold; v77-78 ed. by Wendell V. Clausen; v79-82 ed. by Albert Henrichs
v71, 81 and 82 Partially analyzed; v76 Festschrift in honor of Walton Brooks McDaniel

Harvey, Abner McGehee. Adventures in medical research; a century of discovery at Johns Hopkins. Johns Hopkins Univ. Press 1976 464p ISBN 0-8018-1785-4 LC 75-36955
Supplement to the Johns Hopkins Medical Journal

Haskell, Francis (ed.) The artist and the writer in France. *See* The Artist and the writer in France

Hassan, Ihab Habib. Paracriticisms; seven speculations of the times. Univ. of Ill. Press 1975 184p ISBN 0-252-00469-8. LC 74-19108

Hastings Center. Death inside out. *See* Death inside out

Haugen, Einar Ingvald. See Bloomfield, M. W. jt. ed.

Haugh, Richard. See Dunlop, J. B. jt. ed.

Havard, William C. and Bernd, Joseph L. (eds.) 200 years of the Republic in retrospect. Univ. Press of Va. 1976 348p ISBN 0-8139-0690-3 LC 76-45777

Have we overcome? Race relations since Brown. Ed. by Michael V. Namorato; essays by C. Eric Lincoln [and others]. Univ. Press of Miss. 1979 232p ISBN 0-87805-099-X LC 78-31357
"The papers in this volume were presented at the Fourth Chancellor's Symposium on Southern History, held on October 2, 3, and 4 1978, at the University of Mississippi in Oxford."

Havelock, Eric Alfred. The Greek concept of justice; from its shadow in Homer to its substance in Plato. Harvard Univ. Press 1978 382p ISBN 0-674-36220-9 LC 78-6064

Havelock, Eric Alfred, and Hershbell, Jackson P. (eds.) Communication arts in the ancient world. Hastings House 1978 162p (Humanistic Studies in the communication arts) ISBN 0-8038-1252-3 LC 78-17482
"Communications arts books"

Havens, George Remington. See entry under title: **Literature and history in the age of ideas**

Hawkins, Harriet. Poetic freedom and poetic truth; Chaucer, Shakespeare, Marlowe, Milton. Oxford 1976 135p ISBN 0-19-8120710 LC 76-380606

Hawley, Amos Henry, and Rock, Vincent P. (eds.) Metropolitan America in contemporary perspective. Prepared for the Social Science Panel on the Significance of Community in the Metropolitan Environment of the Advisory Committee to the Department of Housing and Urban Development [and the] National Academy of Sciences. Sage Publications [distributed by Halsted Press, a division of John Wiley & Sons] 1975 504p ISBN 0-470-36305-3 LC 75-8613

Hepburn, Anthony C. (ed.) Minorities in history. St Martins 1979 251p (Historical studies 12) ISBN 0-312-53423-X LC 78-23410
"This volume of essays has its origin in the Thirteenth Irish Conference of Historians, held at the New University of Ulster, Coleraine. . . . on 25-28 May 1977."

The **heritage** of Copernicus: theories "pleasing to the mind". See Neyman, J. ed.

Hermassi, Karen Chagi. Polity and theater in historical perspective. Univ. of Calif. Press 1977 222p ISBN 0-520-03294-2 LC 76-19971

Hermeneutics and social science. See Bauman, Z.

Hernadi, Paul (ed.) What is literature? Ed. with an introduction. Ind. Univ. Press 1978 ISBN 0-253-36505-8 LC 77-23640

The **Hero** in Scandinavian literature; from Peer Gynt to the present. Ed. by John M. Weinstock and Robert T. Rovinsky. Univ. of Tex. Press 1975 226p (The Germanic languages symposia ser) ISBN 0-292-73001-2. LC 74-26815

Heroic epic and saga. See Oinas, F. J. ed.

Hershbell, Jackson P. See Havelock, E. A. jt. ed.

Herz, Martin Florian (ed.) Decline of the West? George Kennan and his critics. *See* Decline of the West? George Kennan and his critics

Hesburgh, Theodore Martin. The Hesburgh papers; higher values in higher education. Andrews & McMeel 1979 206p ISBN 0-8362-5908-4 LC 79-10408

The **Hesburgh** papers. See Hesburgh, T. M.

Hexter, Jack H. On historians; reappraisals of some of the makers of modern history. Harvard Univ. Press 1979 310p ISBN 0-674-63426-8 LC 78-16635

Heywood, Christopher (ed.) Aspects of South African literature. Africana Pub. Co. 1976 192p ISBN 0-8419-0292-5 LC 76-25033

Hibbard, George Richard (ed.) The Elizabethan theatre. *See* The Elizabethan theatre

Higgs, David. See Callahan, W. J. jt. ed.

Higham, John (ed.) Ethnic leadership in America. *See* Ethnic leadership in America

Higham, John, and Conkin, Paul Keith (eds.) New directions in American intellectual history. Johns Hopkins Univ. Press 1979 245p ISBN 0-8018-2183-5 LC 78-21563
"This book results from the Wingspread Conference on New Directions in American Intellectual History held at Racine, Wisconsin, in December 1977"

Higham, Robin D. (ed.) Intervention or abstention: the dilemma of American foreign policy. Univ. Press of Ky. 1975 221p ISBN 0-8131-1317-2. LC 74-18934

Highet, Gilbert. The immortal profession; the joys of teaching and learning. Weybright 1976 223p ISBN 0-679-40130-X LC 76-5515

Hill, Archibald A. Constituent and pattern in poetry. Univ. of Tex. Press 1976 157p ISBN 0-292-72010-6 LC 75-32582

Hill, James Newlin (ed.) Explanation of prehistoric change. *See* Explanation of prehistoric change

Hill, John P. (ed.) Adolescence and youth in prospect. *See* Adolescence and youth in prospect

Hill, Melvyn A. (ed.) Hannah Arendt: the recovery of the public world. *See* Hannah Arendt: the recovery of the public world

Hills, David Farley-. See Farley-Hills, David

Homer's original genius. See Simonsuri, K.

Homosexuality and literature, 1890-1930. See Meyers, J.

Honeycutt, Benjamin L. See Cooke, T. D. jt. ed.

Hood, Roger G. (ed.) Crime, criminology and public policy. *See* Crime, criminology and public policy

Hook, Sidney; Kurtz, Paul W. and Todorovich, Miro (eds.) The ethics of teaching and scientific research. Prometheus Bks. 1977 212p ISBN 0-87975-068-5 LC 76-569-2

Hook, Sidney; Kurtz, Paul W. and Todorovich, Miro (eds.) The philosophy of the curriculum: the need for general education. Prometheus Bks. 1975 281p ISBN 0-87975-051-0. LC 75-3921
Partially analyzed

Hook, Sidney; Kurtz, Paul W. and Todorovich, Miro, (eds.) The university and the state: what role for government in higher education? Prometheus Bks. 1978 296p ISBN 0-87975-098-7 LC 77-26375
"Essays delivered at the Fourth General Meeting of University Centers for Rational Alternatives held at George Washington University, Washington, D.C. in December 1976"

Hooker, Michael (ed.) Descartes; critical and interpretive essays. Johns Hopkins Univ. Press 1978 322p ISBN 0-8018-2111-8 LC 78-8419

Hookway, Christopher, and Pettit, Philip (eds.) Action and interpretation; studies in the philosophy of the social sciences. Cambridge 1978 178p ISBN 0-521-21740-7 LC 77-7875

Horn Book Magazine. Crosscurrents of criticism; Horn Book essays, 1968-1977. Selected and ed. by Paul Heins. Horn Bk. 1977 359p ISBN 0-87675-034-X LC 77-2456
Partially analyzed

Horowitz, Irving Louis (ed.) Science, sin, and scholarship; the politics of Reverend Moon and the Unification Church. MIT Press 1978 290p ISBN 0-262-08100-8 LC 78-9021

Horowitz, Louise K. Love and language; a study of the classical French moralist writers. Ohio State Univ. Press 1977 169p ISBN 0-8142-0233-0 LC 76-57232

Horton, Philip C. (ed.) The Third World and press freedom; foreword by John Chancellor. Praeger 1978 252p ISBN 0-03-045551-0 LC 78-17072

Hortus imaginum. See Enggass, R. C. and Stokstad, M. eds.

Horwitz, Robert Henry (ed.) The Moral foundations of the American Republic. *See* The Moral foundations of the American Republic

Houck, John W. See Heisler, W. J. jt. ed.

Hough, Graham Goulden. Selected essays. Cambridge 1978 247p ISBN 0-521-21901-9 LC 77-85692

Hourani, George Fadlo (ed.) Essays on Islamic philosophy and science. *See* Essays on Islamic philosophy and science

Howard, Maureen (ed.) Seven American women writers of the twentieth century; an introduction. Univ. of Minn. Press 1977 380p (The Minnesota Library on American Writers) ISBN 0-8166-0796-6 LC 77-072905

Howard, Michael (ed.) Restraints on war; studies in the limitation of armed conflict. Oxford 1979 173p ISBN 0-19-822545-8

Howarth, William Driver (ed.) Comic drama; the European heritage. St. Martins [1979 c1978] 194p ISBN 0-312-15091-1 LC 78-9848

Howe, Daniel Walker (ed.) Victorian America; ed. with an introductory essay. [Contributors]: Geoffrey Blodgett [and others]. Univ. of Pa. Press 1976 184p ISBN 0-8122-7713-9 LC 76-20155

Hundley, Norris (ed.) The Asian American: the historical experience. *See* The Asian American: the historical experience

Hunsinger, George (ed.) Karl Barth and radical politics. Ed. and tr. by George Hunsinger. Westminster Press 1976 233p ISBN 0-664-24797-0 LC 76-976

Hunter, George Kirkpatrick. Dramatic identities and cultural tradition; studies in Shakespeare and his contemporaries; critical essays. Barnes & Noble 1978 362p (Liverpool English texts and studies)   ISBN 0-06-493062-9

Hurdles; the admissions dilemma in American higher education [by] Herbert S. Sacks, and associates. Atheneum Pubs. 1978 364p ISBN 0-689-10857-5 LC 77-15350

Husserl. See Elliston, F. A. and McCormick, P. eds.

Hutton, James. See entry under title: Poetry and poetics from ancient Greece to the Renaissance

Huxley, Aldous Leonard. The human situation; lectures at Santa Barbara, 1959. Ed. by Piero Ferrucci. Harper 1977 261p   ISBN 0-06-012091-6 LC 76-5131

Hyman, Stanley Edgar. The critic's credentials; essays & reviews. Ed. by Phoebe Pettingell. Atheneum Pubs. 1978 325p ISBN 0-689-10847-8 LC 77-88902

I

Icons of America. See Browne, R. B. and Fishwick, M. W. eds.

The **Idea** of social structure; papers in honor of Robert K. Merton. Ed. by Lewis A. Coser. Harcourt 1975 547p ISBN 0-15-540548-9 LC 75-13881

The **idea** of the American South, 1920-1941. See O'Brien, M.

The **idea** of the clerisy in the nineteenth century. See Knights, B.

The **identities** of persons. See Rorty, A. O. ed.

Illinois classical studies, v 1-4, 1976-1979. Miroslav Marcovich, editor. Univ. of Ill. Press 1976-1979 4v ISBN v 1 0-252-00516-3; v2 0-252-00629-1; v3 0-252-00654-2; v4 0-252-00694-1

Illinois. University at Urbana-Champaign. Center for Latin American and Caribbean Studies. Quantitative social science research on Latin America. *See* Quantitative social science research on Latin America

Illusion in nature and art. See Gregory, R. L. and Gombrich, Sir E. H. J. eds.

Illustrious evidence; approaches to English literature of the early seventeenth century; ed. with an introduction, by Earl Miner. [Published under the auspices of the William Andrews Clark Memorial Library] Univ. of Calif. Press 1975 xxiii, 135p ISBN 0-520-02782-5. LC 74-79768

Image, music, text. See Barthes, R.

Images and ideas in American culture. the functions of criticism. Essays in memory of Philip Rahv; Arthur Edelstein, editor. Published by Brandeis Univ. Press 1979; distributed by the Univ. Press of New England 222p ISBN 0-87451-164-X LC 78-63584

Images and ideas in literature of the English Renaissance. See Grant, P.

Images and ideas in seventeenth-century Spanish painting. See Brown, J.

Images of romanticism. See Kroeber, K. and Walling, W. eds.

Images of the future: the twenty-first century and beyond. See Bundy, R. F. ed.

Imagination. See Warnock, M.

Imagining a self. See Spacks, P. A. M.

The **Immigrant** experience in America; ed. by Frank J. Coppa [and] Thomas J. Curran. Twayne [1977 c1976] 232p (The Immigrant heritage of America ser) ISBN 0-8057-8406-3 LC 76-8439

Immigrants in industrial America, 1850-1920. Ed. by Richard L. Ehrlich. Published for the Eleutherian Mills-Hagley Foundation and the Balch Institute by the Univ. Press of Va. 1977 218p ISBN 0-8139-0678-4 LC 76-56376

The **immortal** profession. See Highet, G.

The **Impact** of the American Revolution abroad. Papers presented at the fourth symposium, May 8 and 9, 1975. Lib. of Congress 1976 171p (Library of Congress Symposia on the American Revolution) ISBN 0-8444-0182-X LC 76-8163 Partially analyzed

The **impact** of the Cold war. See Siracusa, J. M. and Barclay, G. S. eds.

Impressions of empiricism. See Royal Institute of Philosophy

In pursuit of perfection; courtly love in medieval literature. A collaborative study by the editors Joan M. Ferrante [and others]. Kennikat 1975 266p (National University Pubs. ser in literary criticism). ISBN 0-8046-9092-8. LC 74-80596

In radical pursuit. See Snodgrass, W. D.

In the name of language! See Gold, J. ed.

In the presence of nature. See Wilson, D. S.

In time and place. See Watkins, F. C.

Indian novel in English. See Singh, R. S.

Indian thought. See Bishop, D. H. ed.

Individual and community. See Baldwin, K. H. and Kirby, D. K. eds.

Individual and state in ancient China. See Rubin, V. A.

The **individual** in twelfth-century romance. See Hanning, R. W.

Inescapable romance. See Parker, P. A.

Infernal paradise. See Walker, R. G.

Infinite jest: wit and humor in Italian Renaissance art. See Barolsky, P.

Inflation, trade and taxes; essays in honor of Alice Bourneuf. Ed. by David A. Belsley [and others]. Ohio State Univ. Press 1976 252p ISBN 0-8142-0194-6 LC 75-19099

The **influence** of East Europe and the Soviet West on the USSR. See Szporluk, R. ed.

Influx. See Primeau, R. ed.

Inge, M. Thomas (ed.) Ellen Glasgow. *See* Ellen Glasgow

Inge, M. Thomas (ed.) The frontier humorists; critical views. Archon Bks. 1975. 331p ISBN 0-208-01509-4 LC 75-12698

Inge, M. Thomas; Duke, Jean Maurice, and Bryer, Jackson, R. (eds.) Black American writers; bibliographical essays v 1-2. St Martins 1978 ISBN: v 1 0-312-08260-6; v2 0-312-08295-9 LC 77-85987
v 1 The beginnings through the Harlem Renaissance and Langston Hughes; v2 Richard Wright, Ralph Ellison, James Baldwin and Amiri Baraka

Innocence and arsenic. See Borowitz, A.

Institute for Judaism and Contemporary Thought. Modern Jewish ethics. *See* Modern Jewish ethics

Institute for Mediterranean Affairs. The New world balance and peace in the Middle East: reality or mirage? *See* The New world balance and peace in the Middle East: reality or mirage?

The **Interaction** of economics and foreign policy; ed. by Robert A. Bauer. Contributors: Richard J. Trethewey [and others]. Univ. Press of Va. 1975 154p ISBN 0-8139-0639-3. LC 75-2243

Interfaces of the word. See Ong, W. J.

International and intercultural communication. **See Fischer, H. D.** and Merrill, J. C. eds.

International Colloquium on Interpretation of Narrative, University of Toronto, 1976. Interpretation of narrative. *See* Valdés, M. J. and Miller, O. J. eds. Interpretation of narrative

The **International Commission on Physics Education.** Einstein. *See* Einstein

International Conference on Conrad, Canterbury, England, 1974. Joseph Conrad: a commemoration. *See* Joseph Conrad: a commemoration

International Council for Science Policy Studies. Science, technology and society. *See* Science, technology and society

International Institute for Advanced Criminal Science and Conference on Terrorism and Political Crimes, 3d. International terrorism and political crimes. *See* International terrorism and political crimes

International terrorism and political crimes; ed. by M. Cherif Bassiouni. Thomas, C.C. 1975 594p ISBN 0-398-03257-2. LC 74-12120

International terrorism and world security. [Ed. by David Carlton and Carlo Schaerf]. Wiley 1975 332p ISBN 0-470-13503-4 LC 75-16273
"A Halsted Press book"

International terrorism; national, regional, and global perspectives. Ed. by Yonah Alexander; foreword by Arthur J. Goldberg. Published in cooperation with the Ralph Bunche Institute on the United Nations, the City University of New York. Praeger 1976 xx, 390p (Praeger Special studies in international politics and government) ISBN 0-275-09480-4 LC 75-8396

International trade and finance. See Kenen, P. B. ed.

Interpretation of narrative. See Valdés, M. J. and Miller, O. J. eds.

Interpreting Blake. See Phillips, M. C. ed.

Intervention or abstention: the dilemma of American foreign policy. See Higham, R. D. ed.

Introduction to Islamic civilisation. See Savory, R. M. ed.

An **introduction** to Russian art and architecture. See Auty, R. and Obolensky, D. eds.

An **introduction** to Russian history. See Auty, R. and Obolensky, D. eds.

An **introduction** to Russian language and literature. See Auty, R. and Obolensky, D. eds.

The **invention** of the self. See Lyons, J. O.

The **Irish** drama of Europe from Yeats to Beckett. See Worth, K. J.

Irish history and culture. See Orel, H. ed.

The **Irish** world. See De Breffny, B. ed.

Iriye, Akira (ed.) Mutual images; essays in American-Japanese relations. Contributions by: Priscilla A. Clapp [and others]. Harvard Univ. Press 1975 304p (Harvard Studies in American-East Asia Relations 7) ISBN 0-674-59550-5 LC 75-4625

The ironic harvest. See Thurley, G.

Is Britain dying? See Kramnick, I. ed.

Islam and the Arab world. See Lewis, B. ed.

Isolation or interdependence? Today's choices for tomorrow's world; ed. by Morton A. Kaplan. Free Press 1975 254p LC 74-32547

Issues in criminal justice: planning and evaluation. See Riedel, M. and Chappell, D. eds.

Italian literature. See Cairns, C.

Italian literature: roots and branches; essays in honor of Thomas Goodard Bergin. Ed. by Giose Rimanelli and Kenneth John Atchity. Yale Univ. Press 1976 455p ISBN 0-300-01885-1 LC 75-18182

Ives, Eric William (ed.) Wealth and power in Tudor England. *See* Wealth and power in Tudor England

J

Jackson, Blyden. The waiting years; essays on American Negro literature. La. State Univ. Press 1976 216p ISBN 0-8071-0173-7 LC 74-82001

Jackson, Martin A. See O'Connor, J. E. jt. ed.

Jacobs, Carol. The dissimulating harmony; the image of interpretation in Nietzsche, Rilke, Artaud, and Benjamin. Johns Hopkins Univ Press 1978 ISBN 0-8018-2040-5 LC 77-18392

Jacobs, Glenn. See Gerstl, J. E. jt. ed.

Jahn, Egbert (ed.) Soviet foreign policy; its social and economic conditions. St Martins 1978 160p ISBN 0-312-74836-1 LC 77-18229

James B. McMillan: essays in linguistics by his friends and colleagues. Ed. by James C. Raymond and I. Willis Russell. Univ. of Ala. Press [1978 c1977] ISBN 0-8173-0503-3 LC 77-7169

Jamison, Albert Leland (ed.) Tradition and change in Jewish experience. See Tradition and change in Jewish experience

Jane Austen. See Halperin, J. ed.

Jane Austen and the war of ideas. See Butler, M.

Jane Austen Bicentennial Conference, University of Alberta, 1975. Jane Austen's achievement. *See* Jane Austen's achievement

Jane Austen today. See Weinsheimer, J. ed.

Jane Austen's achievement. Papers delivered at the Jane Austen Bicentennial Conference at the University of Alberta. Ed. by Juliet McMaster. Barnes & Noble 1976 139p ISBN 0-06-494734-3 LC 76-28821

Janecek, Gerald (ed.) Andrey Bely; a critical review. Univ. Press of Ky. 1978 222p ISBN 0-8131-1368-7 LC 77-77-75449

Janus. See Koestler, A.

Jarvik, Lissy F. (ed.) Aging into the 21st century; middle-agers today. Helene Kratz, assistant editor. Gardner Press Inc. distributed by Halsted Press [a] division of John Wiley & Sons, Inc. 1978 214p ISBN 0-470-99370-7 LC 77-25837

Jeffrey, David L. (ed.) By things seen: reference and recognition in medieval thought. Univ. of Ottawa Press 1979 270p ISBN 2-7603-4825-3

Jesse Stuart. See LeMaster, J. R. and Clarke, M. W. eds.

The Jew as pariah: Jewish identity and politics in the modern age. See Arendt, H.

The **Jewish** presence. See Dawidowicz, L. S.

Jimmy Carter and American fantasy. See DeMause, L. and Ebel, H. eds.

Johnson, Christiane. See Johnson, I. D. [jt. ed.]

Johnson, Douglas William John (ed.) French society and the Revolution. *See* French society and the Revolution

Johnson, Harry Alleyn (ed.) Negotiating the mainstream; a survey of the Afro-American experience. A.L.A. 1978 231p ISBN 0-8389-0254-5 LC 77-29041

Johnson, Harry Morton (ed.) Religious change and continuity. Jossey-Bass 1979 359p (The Jossey-Bass Social and behavioral science ser) ISBN 0-87589-408-9 LC 79-83574

Johnson, Ira D. and Johnson, Christiane [eds.] Les américanistes; new French criticism on modern American fiction. Kennikat 1978 (National University Publications. Literary criticism ser.) 238p ISBN 0-8046-9176-2 LC 76-58512

Johnson, John M. See Douglas, J. D. [jt. ed.]

Johnson, Roger Barton; Neumann, Editha S. and Trail, Guy T. (eds.) Molière and the commonwealth of letters: patrimony and posterity. Ed. by Roger Johnson, Jr.; Editha S. Neumann, and Guy T. Trail. Univ. Press of Miss. 1975 873p ISBN 0-87805-059-0 LC 74-77454
Partially analyzed

Johnson, Wendell Stacy. Sex and marriage in Victorian poetry. Cornell Univ. Press 1975 266p ISBN 0-8014-0845-8. LC 74-25370

Joint Committee on African Studies of the Social Science Research Council and the American Council of Learned Societies. Strangers in African societies. *See* Shack, W. A. and Skinner, E. P. eds. Strangers in African societies

Jones, David, 1895-1974. The dying Gaul, and other writings. Ed. with an introduction by Harman Grisewood. Faber & Faber 1978 230p ISBN 0-571-11067-3

Jones, Eldred Durosimi (ed.) African literature today. *See* African literature today

Jones, Eric L. See Parker, W. N. jt. ed.

Jones, Peter. Philosophy and the novel; philosophical aspects of Middlemarch, Anna Karenina, The brothers Karamazov, A la recherche du temps perdu, and of the methods of criticism. Oxford 1975 216p ISBN 0-19-824526-2

Jones, Thora Burnley, and Nicol, Bernard de Bear. Neo-classical dramatic criticism, 1560-1770. Cambridge 1976 188p ISBN 0-521-20857-2 LC 75-16873

Jones, William McKendry (ed.) The present state of scholarship in sixteenth-century literature. Univ. of Mo. Press 1978 257p ISBN 0-8262-0253-5 LC 78-50810
Originally presented as lectures at the University of Missouri, Columbia. 1976-1977

Jones, Wyndraeth Humphreys Morris- See Morris-Jones, Wyndraeth Humphreys

Jordan, William C. (ed.) Order and innovation in the Middle Ages. *See* Order and innovation in the Middle Ages

Jorgens, Jack J. Shakespeare on film. Ind. Univ. Press 1977 337p ISBN 0-253-35196-0 LC 76-12365

Joseph Conrad: a commemoration; papers from the 1974 International Conference on Conrad. Ed. by Norman Sherry. Barnes & Noble 1977 224p ISBN 0-06-496233-4 LC 76-24069

Josipovici, Gabriel. The lessons of modernism; and other essays. Rowman & Littlefield 1977 208p ISBN 0-87471-957-7 LC 76-58862

Karl Barth and radical politics. See Hunsinger, G. ed.

Karlinsky, Simon (ed.) The Bitter air of exile. *See* The Bitter air of exile

Karp, Mark (ed.) African dimensions. *See* African dimensions

Kaser, Michael. See Brown, A. H. jt. ed.

Katchadourian, Herant A. (ed.) Human sexuality; a comparative and developmental perspective. Univ. of Calif. Press 1979 358p ISBN 0-520-03654-9 LC 77-93458

Katz, Michael R. The literary ballad in early nineteenth-century Russian literature. Oxford 1976 248p ISBN 0-19-815528-X

Kauffmann, Stanley. Living images; film comment and criticism. Harper 1975 404p ISBN 0-06-012269-2. LC 74-1822
Partially analyzed

Kauffmann, Stanley. Persons of the drama; theater criticism and comment. Harper 1976 397p ISBN 0-06-012278-1 LC 75-30371
Partially analyzed

Kaufman, William E. Contemporary Jewish philosophies. Reconstructionist Press and Behrman 1976 276p ISBN 0-87441-239-0 LC 75-30761

Kay, Carol McGinnis, (ed.) Shakespeare's romances reconsidered. *See* Shakespeare's romances reconsidered

Kay, Donald (ed.) A provision of human nature. *See* A Provision of human nature

Kearney, Robert N. (ed.) Politics and modernization in South and Southeast Asia. Schenkman Pub. Co. 1975 277p (States and societies of the Third World ser) ISBN 0-470-46232-9. LC 74-13637

Keating, Henry Raymond Fitzwalter (ed.) Agatha Christie: first lady of crime. *See* Agatha Christie: first lady of crime

Keddie, Nikki R. See Beck, L. jt. ed.

Kedourie, Elie. Arabic political memoirs and other studies. Cass 1974 [distributed by Int. Scholarly Bk. Services] 327p ISBN 0-7146-3041-1. LC 73-93193

Keeton, George William (ed.) The Year book of world affairs. *See* The Year book of world affairs

Kellogg, Gene. Dark prophets of hope; Dostoevsky, Sartre, Camus, Faulkner. Loyola Univ. Press 1975 200p ISBN 0-8294-0234-9. LC 75-5697

Kelly, Douglas. Medieval imagination; rhetoric and the poetry of courtly love. Univ. of Wis. Press 1978 330p ISBN 0-299-07610-5 LC 78-3522

Kelly, Gary. The English Jacobin novel, 1780-1805. Oxford 1976 291p ISBN 0-19-812062-1

Kelly, Richard M. (ed.) Tennessee Studies in literature. *See* Tennessee Studies in literature

Kenen, Peter B. (ed.) International trade and finance; frontiers for research. Cambridge [1976 c1975] 539p ISBN 0-521-20719-3 LC 75-2717

Kennard, Jean E. Number and nightmare; forms of fantasy in contemporary fiction. Archon Bks. 1975 244p ISBN 0-208-01486-1. LC 74-28448

Kennard, Jean E. Victims of convention. Archon Bks. 1978 195p ISBN 0-208-01659-7 LC 77-17194

Kennedy, Alan. Meaning and signs in fiction. St Martins 1979 148p ISBN 0-312-52380-7 LC 78-24284

Kennedy, Alan. The protean self; dramatic action in contemporary fiction. Columbia Univ. Press 1974 304p ISBN 0-231-03922-0. LC 74-9792

Kirkwood, Gordon MacDonald (ed.) Poetry and poetics from ancient Greece to the Renaissance. *See* Poetry and poetics from ancient Greece to the Renaissance

Klein, Holger Michael (ed.) The First World War in fiction; a collection of critical essays. Barnes & Noble [1977 c1976] 246p ISBN 0-06-493792-5 LC 76-28822

Klimoff, Alexis. See Dunlop, J. B. jt. ed.

Kling, Blair B. and Pearson, Michael Naylor (eds.) The age of partnership; Europeans in Asia before Dominion . . . Univ. Press of Hawaii 1979 250p ISBN 0-8248-0495-3 LC 78-31650
"Published with the support of the Maurice J. Sullivan & Family Fund in The University of Hawaii Foundation"

Klinkowitz, Jerome, and Lawler, Donald L. (eds.) Vonnegut in America; an introduction to the life and work of Kurt Vonnegut. Original essays. Delacorte Press/Seymour Lawrence 1977 304p ISBN 0-440-09343-0 LC 77-9939
Partially analyzed

Knickerbocker, Kenneth Leslie. See entry under title: Tennessee Studies in literature v20-24

Knight, Damon Francis (ed.) Turning points; essays on the art of science fiction. Harper 1977 303p ISBN 0-06-012432-6 LC 75-5135
Partially analyzed

Knight, Franklin W. See Crahan, M. E. jt. ed.

Knights, Ben. The idea of the clerisy in the nineteenth century. Cambridge 1978 274p ISBN 0-521-21798-9 LC 77-80840

Knights, Lionel Charles. Explorations 3. Univ. of Pittsburgh Press 1976 196p ISBN 0-8229-1125-6 LC 75-29654

Knoche, Ulrich. Roman satire; tr. by Edwin S. Ramage. Ind. Univ. Press 1975 243p ISBN 0-253-35020-4 LC 74-25014
Partially analyzed

Knoepflmacher, Ulrich Camillus. See Levine, G. L. jt. ed.

Knoepflmacher, Ulrich Camillus, and Tennyson, Georg Bernhard (eds.) Nature and the Victorian imagination. Univ. of Calif. Press 1977 xxiii, 519p ISBN 0-520-03229-2 LC 76-7761
Partially analyzed

Knorr, Klaus Eugene, and Trager, Frank Newton (eds.) Economic issues and national security. Published for the National Security Education Program by the Regents Press of Kan. [1978 c1977] 330p (National Security Studies ser) ISBN 0-7006-167-8 LC 77-91836

Knowles, John Hilton (ed.) Doing better and feeling worse; health in the United States. Essays by Ivan L. Bennett, Jr. [and others]. Norton 1977 287p ISBN 0-393-06419-0 LC 77-3382

Knust, Herbert. See Mews, S. jt. ed.

Koestler, Arthur. The heel of Achilles; essays, 1968-1973. Random House 1975 [1974] 273p ISBN 0-394-49596-9 LC 74-17251
Partially analyzed

Koestler, Arthur. Janus; a summing up. Random House 1978 354p ISBN 0-394-50052-0 LC 77-90255

Kohl, Marvin (ed.) Beneficent euthanasia. Prometheus Bks. 1975 255p ISBN 0-87975-047-2. LC 74-84281

Kommers, Donald P. and Loescher, Gilburt D. (eds.) Human rights and American foreign policy. Univ. of Notre Dame Press 1979 333p ISBN 0-268-01071-4 LC 78-62966
This is a collection of papers presented at an "international symposium 'American Foreign Policy and Human Rights' held by the Law School Center for Civil Rights at the University of Notre Dame"

Konvitz, Milton Ridvas. Judaism and the American idea. Cornell Univ. Press 1978 223p ISBN 0-8014-1181-5 LC 78-58028

Kurz, Paul Konrad. On modern German literature. English translation by Sister Mary Frances McCarthy. Univ. of Ala. Press 1970-1971, 1973, 1977 4v ISBN v 1 0-8173-8000-0; v2 0-8173-8001-9; v3 0-8173-8002-7; v4 0-8173-8003-5 LC 73-96419

Kuttner, Stephen George. See entry under title: Law, church, and society

L

The **labelling** of deviance. See Gove, W. R. ed.

Lackner, Bede Karl (ed.) Essays on medieval civilization. *See* Essays on medieval civilization

Lackner, Bebe Karl (ed.) Essays on modern European revolutionary history. *See* Essays on modern European revolutionary history

Ladurie, Emmanuel Le Roy. See Le Roy Ladurie, Emmanuel

La Follette, Hugh. See Aiken, W. jt. ed.

LaFrance, Marston. See entry under title: The Stoic strain in American literature

Lambert, Gavin. The dangerous edge. Grossman Pubs. 1976 [c1975] 271p ISBN 0-670-25581-5 LC 76-2377

Land-grant universities and their continuing challenge; ed. by G. Lester Anderson. Mich. State Univ. Press 1976 354p ISBN 0-87013-198-2 LC 75-44530

Lander, Ernest McPherson (ed.) Two decades of change. *See* Two decades of change

Landers, Daniel M. (ed.) Social problems in athletics. *See* Social problems in athletics

Landmarks; a collection of essays on the Russian intelligentsia, 1909. Ed. by Boris Shragin [and] Albert Todd; tr. by Marian Schwartz. [Contributors]: Berdyaev [and others]. Karz Howard 1977 lvii, 210p ISBN 0-918294-00-2 LC 77-880

Landow, George P. (ed.) Approaches to Victorian autobiography. Ohio Univ. Press 1979 359p ISBN 0-8214-0400-8 LC 77-91505

Landscapes of learning. See Greene, M.

Lane, Gary (ed.) Sylvia Plath; new views on the poetry. Johns Hopkins Univ. Press 1979 264p ISBN 0-8018-2179-7 LC 78-20515

Langbaum, Robert Woodrow. The mysteries of identity; a theme in modern literature. Oxford 1977 383p ISBN 0-19-502189-4 LC 76-42657

Lange, Victor. See Amacher, R. E. jt. ed.

Langer, Lawrence L. The age of atrocity; death in modern literature. Beacon Press 1978 256p ISBN 0-8070-6369-X LC 77-88335

Language as a human problem. See Bloomfield, M. W. and Haugen, E. I. eds.

Language, counter-memory, practice. See Foucault, M.

Language, metaphysics, and death. See Donnelly, J. P. ed.

Lanham, Richard A. The motives of eloquence; literary rhetoric in the Renaissance. Yale Univ. Press 1976 234p ISBN 0-300-02002-3 LC 75-43323

Laqueur, Walter Ze'ev (ed.) Fascism: a reader's guide; analyses, interpretations, bibliography. Univ. of Calif. Press 1976 478p ISBN 0-520-03033-8 LC 75-13158

The **legacy** of Reinhold Niebuhr. See Scott, N. A. ed.

Lehmann, Paul Louis. See entry under title: The Context of contemporary theology

Leigh, Johanna, pseud. See Sayers, Dorothy Leigh

LeMaster, J. R. and Clarke, Mary Washington (eds.) Jesse Stuart; essays on his work. Univ. Press of Ky. 1977 165p ISBN 0-8131-1352-0 LC 76-46032

Lemay, Joseph A. Leo (ed.) The oldest revolutionary; essays on Benjamin Franklin. [Contributors]: Percy G. Adams [and others]. Univ. of Pa. Press 1976 165p ISBN 0-8122-7707-4 LC 75-41618

Lemert, Charles C. Sociology and the twilight of man; homocentrism and discourse in sociological theory. Southern Ill. Univ. Press 1979 260p ISBN 0-8093-0851-7 LC 78-17146

Lenson, David R. Achilles' choice; examples of modern tragedy. Princeton Univ. Press 1975 178p (Princeton Essays in literature) ISBN 0-691-06292-7 LC 75-2996

Leondar, Barbara. See Perkins, D. jt. ed.

Leone, Mark P. See Zaretsky, I. I. jt. ed.

Lerner, Abba P. Tachya. See entry under title: Theory for economic efficiency: essays in honor of Abba P. Lerner

Lerner, Daniel, and Nelson, Lyle M. (eds.) Communication research—a half-century appraisal. Published for the East-West Center by the Univ. Press of Hawaii 1977 348p ISBN 0-8248-0566-6 LC 77-89616
"An East-West Center book"

Lerner, Laurence (ed.) The Victorians. Holmes & Meier 1978 (The Context of English literature) 228p ISBN 0-8419-0419-7 LC 78-15642

Le Roy Ladurie, Emmanuel. The territory of the historian. Tr. from the French by Ben and Siân Reynolds. Univ. of Chicago Press 1979 345p ISBN 0-226-47327-9 LC 78-31362

Lesser, Simon O. The whispered meanings; selected essays. Ed by Robert Sprich and Richard W. Noland. Univ. of Mass. Press 1977 237p ISBN 0-87023-243-6 LC 77-73480

Lessing, Doris May. A small personal voice; essays, reviews, interviews. Ed. and introduced by Paul Schlueter. Knopf 1974 171p ISBN 0-394-49329-X. LC 74-7724
Partially analyzed

The **lessons** of modernism. See Josipovici, G.

Levenson, Joseph Richmond. See entry under: Meisner, M. J. and Murphey, R. eds. The Mozartian historian

Levin, David (ed.) Emerson: prophecy, metamorphosis, and influence; selected papers from the English Institute; ed. with a foreword. Columbia Univ. Press 1975 181p ISBN 0-231-04000-8 LC 75-17704

Levine, George Lewis, and Knoepflmacher, Ulrich Camillus (eds.) The endurance of Frankenstein; essays on Mary Shelley's novel. Univ. of Calif. Press 1979 341p ISBN 0-520-03612-3 LC 77-20325

Levine, Richard A. The Victorian experience: the novelists. Ohio Univ. Press 1976 273p ISBN 0-8214-0190-4 LC 75-15358

Levith, Murray Jay (ed.) Renaissance and modern. *See* Renaissance and modern

Lewalski, Barbara Kiefer. Protestant poetics and the seventeenth-century religious lyric. Princeton Univ. Press 1979 536p ISBN 0-691-06395-8 LC 78-70305

Lewis, Bernard (ed.) Islam and the Arab world; faith, people, culture. Texts by Bernard Lewis [and others]. 490 illus. 160 in colour, 330 photographs, drawings and maps. Knopf in association with Am. Heritage 1976 360p

Lewis, Dennis. See Needleman, J. jt. ed.

Lewis, Walter David, and Griessman, Benjamin Eugene (eds.)
The Southern mystique; the impact of technology on human
values in a changing region. Published for Auburn University
by Univ. of Ala. Press 1977 xxi, 131p ISBN 0-8173-5317-8 LC
76-55011
Partially analyzed

Lewis, Wyndham. Enemy salvoes; selected literary criticism.
Ed. with sectional introductions and notes by C. J. Fox. Gen-
eral introduction by C. H. Sisson. Barnes & Noble 1976 272p
ISBN 0-06-494258-9 LC 75-39325

Libraries and the life of the mind in America. Addresses delivered at the centennial celebration of the American Library
Association. ALA 1977 130p ISBN 0-8389-0238-3 LC 77-3288

Library of Congress Symposia on the American Revolution, 3d,
1974. Leadership in the American Revolution; papers presented
at the third symposium, May 9 and 10, 1974. Lib. of Congress
1974 135p ISBN 0-8444-0149-8. LC 74-30110

Lieberman, Laurence. Unassigned frequencies; American poetry
in review, 1964-77. Univ. of Ill. Press 1977 296p ISBN 0-252-
00477-9 LC 77-10072
Partially analyzed

Lieberman, Saul (ed.) Salo Wittmayer Baron. *See* Salo Wittmayer Baron

Lievsay, John Leon. See entry under title: Studies in the continental background of Renaissance English literature: essays
presented to John L. Lievsay

Lievsay, John Leon (ed.) Medieval and Renaissance studies. *See*
Medieval and Renaissance studies

Life after death [by] Arnold Toynbee, Arthur Koestler and
others. McGraw 1976 272p ISBN 0-07-065124-8 LC 76-16175

Life, law and letters. See Auchincloss, L.

The **life** of the mind. See Arendt, H.

Lifeboat ethics. See Lucas, G. R. and Ogletree, T. W. eds.

Lifton, Robert Jay (ed.) Explorations in psychohistory. *See* Explorations in psychohistory

Like a brother, like a lover. See Sarotte, G. M.

The **Limits** of change; essays on conservative alternatives in
Republican China. Ed. by Charlotte Furth; contributions by
Guy Alitto [and others]. Harvard Univ. Press 1976 426p
(Harvard Univ. East Asian ser 84) ISBN 0-674-53423-9 LC 75-
23490
"This book was sponsored by the Joint Committee on Con-
temporary China of the Social Science Research Council and the
American Council of Learned Societies"

Limits of scientific inquiry. See Holton, G. J. and Morison,
R. S. eds.

The **limits** to power. See Ro'i, Y. ed.

Lindberg, David C. (ed.) Science in the Middle Ages. Univ. of
Chicago Press 1978 549p (Chicago History of science and
medicine ser) ISBN 0-226-48232-4 LC 78-5367

Lines of enquiry. See Rudd, N.

The **linguist** and the English language. See Quirk, R.

Linguistic theory and psychological reality. Ed. by Morris Halle;
Joan Bresnan, [and] George A. Miller. Contributors: Joan
Bresnan [and others] MIT Press 1978 329p (MIT Bicenten-
nial studies, 3) ISBN 0-262-08095-8 LC 77-29054

Linz, Juan J. See Linz Storch de Gracia, Juan José

Linz Storch de Gracia, Juan José (ed.) The Breakdown of
democratic regimes. *See* The Breakdown of democratic regimes

The literary ballad in early nineteenth-century Russian literature. See Katz, M. R.

The Literary criticism of T. S. Eliot; new essays collected and ed. by David Newton-De Molina. Athlone Press [distributed by Humanities Press] 1977 216p ISBN 0-485-11167-5

Literary criticism: idea and act. See Wimsatt, W. K. ed.

Literary diseases. See Biasin, G. P.

Literary essays, 1954-1974. See Farrell, J. T.

Literary landmarks. See Fergusson, F.

Literary monographs, v6-9. Published for the Department of English by Univ. of Wis. Press 1975-1978 4v ISBN v6 0-299-066610-X; v7 0-299-06620-7; v8 0-299-06950-8; v9 0-299-07510-9 LC 66-25869
V6: Medieval & Renaissance literature; v7 Thackeray, Hawthorne, and Melville, and Dreiser; v8 Midnineteenth century writers: Eliot, De Quincey, Emerson; v9 Measuring Old English rhythm; an application of the principles of Gregorian chant rhythm to the meter of Beowulf [by] Jane-Marie Luecke
V6-9 edited by Eric Rothstein and Joseph Anthony Wittreich, Jr.; v9 edited by Eric Rothstein

Literary uses of typology. See Miner, E. R. ed.

Literature against itself. See Graff, G.

Literature and history in the age of ideas; essays on the French Enlightenment presented to George R. Havens. Ed. by Charles G. S. Williams. Ohio State Univ. Press 1975 414p ISBN 0-8142-0193-8. LC 74-23240
Partially analyzed

Literature and ideas in America; essays in memory of Harry Hayden Clark; ed. by Robert Falk. Ohio Univ. Press 1975 243p ISBN 0-8214-0180-7. LC 74-27708

Literature and reality, 1600-1800. See Manlove. C. N.

Literature as opera. See Schmidgall, G.

The literature of change. See Lucas, W. J.

The literature of commitment. See Glicksberg, C. I.

The literature of fact. See Fletcher, A. J. S. ed.

The literature of memory. See Gray, R. J.

The literature of nihilism. See Glicksberg, C. I.

Literature of the romantic period, 1750-1850. See Davies, R. T. and Beatty, B. G. eds.

A literature of their own. See Showalter, E.

The literature of war. See Rutherford, A.

The little magazine in America: a modern documentary history. See Anderson, E. and Kinzie, M. eds.

Living images. See Kauffmann, S.

Livingston, Donald Wilson, and King, James T. (eds.) Hume; a re-evaluation. Fordham Univ. Press 1976 421p ISBN 0-8232-1007-3 LC 76-13968

Locke, Miriam Austin. See entry under title: A Provision of human nature

Lodge, David. The modes of modern writing; metaphor, metonymy, and the typology of modern literature. Cornell Univ. Press 1977 279p ISBN 0-8014-1046-0 LC 76-51544

Loescher, Gilburt D. See Kommers, D. P. jt. ed.

Lyle, Guy Redvers (ed.) Praise from famous men: an anthology of introductions. *See* Praise from famous men: an anthology of introductions

Lyman, Stanford Morris. See Brown, R. H. jt. ed.

Lyons, John O. The invention of the self; the hinge of consciousness in the eighteenth century. Southern Ill. Univ. Press 1978 268p ISBN 0-8093-0815-0 LC 77-27103

M

MacAdam, Alfred J. Modern Latin American narratives; the dreams of reason. Univ. of Chicago Press 1977 150p ISBN 0-226-49993-6 LC 76-8098

McCall, Daniel Francis (ed.) African images. *See* African images

McCall, Morgan W. ed. Leadership. *See* Leadership

McCanles, Michael. Dialectical criticism and Renaissance literature. Univ. of Calif. Press 1975 278p ISBN 0-520-02694-2 LC 73-93056

McCormick, Peter. See Elliston, F. A. jt. ed.

McCormmach, Russell (ed.) Historical studies in the physical sciences. *See* Historical studies in the physical sciences

McDaniel, Walton Brooks. See entry under title: Harvard Studies in classical philology v76

McDowell, John Henry. See Evans, G. L. jt. ed.

McFadden, Thomas More (ed.) America in theological perspective. *See* America in theological perspective

McGalliard, John Calvin. See entry under title: Anglo-Saxon poetry: essays in appreciation

McGrory, Kathleen (ed.) Yeats, Joyce, and Beckett. *See* Yeats, Joyce, and Beckett

Machamer, Peter K. (ed.) Motion and time, space and matter. *See* Motion and time, space and matter

Machamer, Peter K. (ed.) Studies in perception. *See* Studies in perception

Machlup, Fritz (ed.) Essays on Hayek. *See* Essays on Hayek

McKay, Henry Donald. See entry under title: Delinquency, crime, and society

McKelway, Alexander J. (ed.) The context of contemporary theology. *See* The Context of contemporary theology

McKendrick, Neil (ed.) Historical perspectives. *See* Historical perspectives

McKenzie, Robert E. (ed.) The Rising South v2. See The Rising South v2

McKie, James W. (ed.) Social responsibility and the business predicament. Essays by James W. McKie [and others]. Brookings Inst. [1975 c1974] 361p (Studies in the regulation of economic activity) ISBN 0-8157-5608-9 LC 74-23967

Mackie, William Soutar. See entry under title: An English miscellany

MacLeish, Archibald. Riders on the earth; essays and recollections. Houghton 1978 162p ISBN 0-395-26382-4 LC 77-27015

MacLeod, Robert Brodie (ed.) Perception. *See* Perception

McMaster, Juliet (ed.) Jane Austen's achievement. *See* Jane Austen's achievement

McMillan, Dougald, 1937-. Transition; the history of a literary era, 1927-1938. Braziller 1975 303p ISBN 0-8076-0780-0 LC 74-25293

MacMillan, Duane Johnson (ed.) The Stoic strain in American literature. *See* The Stoic strain in American literature

McMillan, James Benjamin. See entry under title: James B. McMillan: essays in linguistics by his friends and colleagues

Macmurray, John. See entry under title: The Personal universe

McMurrin, Sterling M. (ed.) On the meaning of the university; ed. and with an introductory essay. [Contributors]: Eric Ashby [and others]. Univ. of Utah Press 1976 123p ISBN 0-87480-097-8 LC 74-22637

McNall, Scott G. (ed.) Theoretical perspectives in sociology. St Martins 1979 562p ISBN 0-312-79634-X LC 78-71724

McNeill, William Hardy (ed.) Human migration. *See* Human migration

McVey, Sheila. See Altbach, P. G. jt. ed.

Madness and sexual politics in the feminist novel. See Rigney, B. H.

The madwoman in the attic. See Gilbert, S. M. and Gubar, S. auths.

Magic and English romanticism. See Taylor, A.

Magic and rhetoric in ancient Greece. See Romilly, J. de

Maguire, Robert A. (ed.) Gogol from the twentieth century; eleven essays. Selected, edited, translated, and introduced by Robert A. Maguire. Princeton Univ. Press [1975 c1974] 415p ISBN 0-691-06268-4. LC 73-16750

Mahoney, Edward P. (ed.) Philosophy and humanism. *See* Philosophy and humanism

Mair, Lucy Philips. See entry under title: Colonialism and change

Major European art movements, 1900-1945. See Kaplan, P. and Manso, S. eds.

Major social issues; a multidisciplinary view. Ed. by J. Milton Yinger and Stephen J. Cutler. Free Press 1978 575p ISBN 0-02-935840-X LC 78-50846
A publication of the American Sociological Association

The Maker and the myth: Faulkner and Yoknapatawpha, 1977. Ed. by Evans Harrington and Ann J. Abadie. Univ. Press of Miss. 1978 169p ISBN 0-87805-049-3 LC 78-60158
Papers presented at a conference held at the University of Mississippi in 1977
A collection of essays from the 1976 conference, entitled The South & Faulkner's Yoknapatawpha, as well as another collection, from the 1978 conference, entitled Faulkner, modernism and film: Faulkner and Yoknapatawpha, are also indexed in this cumulation

Makers of American thought. See Ross, R. G. ed.

Makers of the twentieth-century novel. See Garvin, H. R. ed.

The Making of politicians: studies from Africa and Asia. Ed. by W. H. Morris-Jones. Published for the Institute of Commonwealth Studies, University of London. Athlone Press [distributed by Humanities Press] [1977 c1976] 249p (Univ. of London. Inst. of Commonwealth Studies. Commonwealth papers 20) ISBN 0-485-17620-3

The making of psychological anthropology. See Spindler, G. D. ed.

Malin, Irving. See Morris, R. K. jt. ed.

Malone, David H. (ed.) The frontiers of literary criticism. *See* The Frontiers of literary criticism

Maloney, Clarence (ed.) The evil eye. *See* The Evil eye

Malraux. See Courcel, M. H. de

Man and cosmos; nine Guggenheim lectures on the solar system. Sponsored by the Smithsonian Institution. Ed. by James Cornell and E. Nelson Hayes; with an introduction by Thornton Page. Norton 1975 191p ISBN 0-393-06402-6 LC 75-6687 "A Smithsonian Special publication"

Man and society in nineteenth-century realism. See Larkin, M.

Man and woman: a study of love and the novel, 1740-1940. See Cockshut, A. O. J.

The man in the machine. See Mudrick, M.

Management for the future. See Benton, L. R. ed.

Managing nonprofit organizations. Ed. by Diane Borst [and] Patrick J. Montana. AMACOM 1977 328p ISBN 0-8144-5437-2 LC 77-23169

Mandelbaum, Maurice H. See Freeman, E. jt. ed.

Mandel'shtam, Osip Emil'evich. Selected essays. Tr. by Sidney Monas. Univ. of Tex. Press 1977 245p (The Dan Danciger Publication ser.) ISBN 0-202-76006-X LC 76-22456

Manlove, Colin Nicholas. Literature and reality, 1600-1800. St Martins 1978 238p ISBN 0-312-48747-9 LC 78-6934

Manlove, Colin Nicholas. Modern fantasy; five studies. Cambridge 1975 308p ISBN 0-521-20746-0 LC 74-31798

Mann, Dennis Alan (ed.) The arts in a democratic society. Popular Press 1977 153p ISBN 0-87972-087-5 LC 77-84919

Mansfeld, Jaap (ed.) Kephalaion. *See* Kephalaion

Manso, Susan. See Kaplan, P. jt. ed.

The many faces of communism. See Kaplan, M. A. ed.

Many futures, many worlds. See Clareson, T. D. ed.

Many sisters. See Matthiasson, C. J. ed.

Mao Tse-tung in the scales of history. See Wilson, R. G. ed.

Marcovich, Miroslav. See Marković, Miroslav

Marcus, Steven. Representations; essays on literature and society. Random House 1975 331p ISBN 0-394-49559-4 LC 75-10252

Maresca, Thomas E. Epic to novel. Ohio State Univ. Press [1975 c1974] 238p ISBN 0-8142-0216-0. LC 74-19109

Margolis, Joseph Zalman. (ed.) Philosophy looks at the arts; contemporary readings in aesthetics. Rev. ed. Temple Univ. Press 1978 473p ISBN 0-87722-123-5 LC 77-95028
First edition analyzed in 1960-1964 cumulation. This edition analyzed for new material only
Partially analyzed

Mario Vargas Llosa. See Rossman, C. R. and Friedman, A. W. eds.

The mark and the knowledge. See Pryse, M.

The Market and the state; essays in honour of Adam Smith. Ed. by Thomas Wilson and Andrew S. Skinner. Oxford [1977 c1976] 359p ISBN 0-19-828406-3

Marković, Miroslav (ed.) Illinois classical studies. *See* Illinois classical studies

Marks, John D. See Borosage, R. L. jt. ed.

Martin, Phyllis M. and O'Meara, Patrick (eds.) Africa. Maps and charts by Cathryn L. Lombardi; photographic selection by Mary Joy Pigozzi. Ind. Univ. Press 1977 482p ISBN 0-253-30210-2 LC 77-74450

Martindale, Don Albert. See Mohan, R. P. jt. ed.

Martz, Louis Lohr, and Williams, Aubrey L. (eds.) The author in his work; essays on a problem in criticism. Introduction by Patricia Meyer Spacks. Yale Univ. Press 1978 407p ISBN 0-300-02179-8 LC 77-16309

Mash, Eric J. (ed.) Behavior modification and families. *See* Behavior modification and families

Masotti, Louis H. See Walton, J. jt. ed.

Mass media policies in changing cultures. See Gerbner, G. ed.

Massa, Ann. See Donaldson, S. jt. auth.

Massey, Irving. The gaping pig; literature and metamorphosis. Univ. of Calif. Press 1976 236p ISBN 0-520-02887-2 LC 74-22967

Masterful images: English poetry from metaphysicals to romantics. See Dyson, A. E. and Lovelock, J.

Mastering the film, and other essays. See Samuels, C. T.

Matejka, Ladislav, and Titunik, Irwin Robert (eds.) Semiotics of art; Prague School contributions. MIT Press 1976 298p ISBN 0-262-13117-X LC 75-32405

Material culture and the study of American life. Ed. by Ian M. G. Quimby. Published for The Henry Francis du Pont Winterthur Museum [by] Norton 1978 250p ISBN 0-393-05661-9 LC 77-10894

Mathewson, Rufus W. The positive hero in Russian literature. 2d ed. Stanford Univ. Press 1975 369p ISBN 0-8047-0836-3 LC 72-97207
1958 edition analyzed in 1955-1959 cumulation

A **matter** of dignity. See Heisler, W. J. and Houck, J. W. eds.

Matters of fact and of fiction. See Vidal, G.

Matthew Arnold. See Allott, K. ed.

Matthiasson, Carolyn J. (ed.) Many sisters; women in cross-cultural perspective. Free Press 1974 443p ISBN 0-02-920330-9 LC 74-2654

May, Charles E. ed. Short story theories. Ohio Univ. Press 1976 251p ISBN 0-8214-0189-0 LC 75-36982
Partially analyzed

May, Keith M. Out of the maelstrom; psychology and the novel in the twentieth century. St Martins 1977 135p ISBN 0-312-59115-2 LC 76-44599

May, Rollo. Psychology and the human dilemma. Norton [1978 c1979] 221p ISBN 0-393-01195-X LC 78-12027

Mayne, Richard (ed.) The new Atlantic challenge. *See* The New Atlantic challenge

Mayr, Ernst. See entry under title: Studies in history of biology v3

Mazzeo, Joseph Anthony. Varieties of interpretation. Univ. of Notre Dame Press 1978 178p ISBN 0-268-00589-3 LC 78-51518

Meaning and signs in fiction. See Kennedy, A.

Meaning in anthropology. See Basso, K. H. and Selby, H. A. eds.

The **medicine** show. See Branca, P. ed.

Medieval and Renaissance studies; proceedings of the Southeastern Institute of Medieval and Renaissance Studies, Summer, 1974; ed. by Dale B. J. Randall. Duke Univ. Press 1976 127p (Medieval and Renaissance ser. no.6) ISBN 0-8223-0379-5 LC 66-25361

Medieval and Renaissance studies; proceedings of the Southeastern Institute of Medieval and Renaissance Studies, Summer 1975; ed. by Siegfried Wenzel. Univ. of N.C. Press 1978 133p (Medieval and Renaissance ser. no.7) ISBN 0-8078-1311-7 LC 66-25361

Medieval and Renaissance studies; proceedings of the Southeastern Institute of Medieval and Renaissance Studies, Summer; 1976; ed. by Dale B. J. Randall. Duke Univ. Press 1979 166p (Medieval and Renaissance ser. no. 8) ISBN 0-8223-0419-8 LC 66-25361

The Medieval city. Ed. by Harry A. Miskimin; David Herlihy [and] A. L. Udovitch. Yale Univ. Press 1977 345p ISBN 0-300-02081-3 LC 77-76302
Festschrift in honor of Robert S. Lopez

Medieval eloquence. See Murphy, J. J. ed.

Medieval imagination. See Kelly, D.

Medieval studies. See Powell, J. M. ed.

Medievalia et humanistica; studies in medieval & Renaissance culture; new ser. no. 5; ed. by Paul Maurice Clogan. N. Tex. State Univ. 1974 266p (Medieval historiography). ISBN 0-913904-01-5. LC 70-99227

Medievalia et humanistica; studies in medieval & Renaissance culture; new ser. no. 6; ed. by Paul Maurice Clogan. Cambridge [1976] c1975 223p (Medieval hagiography and romance) ISBN 0-521-20999-4 LC 75-16872

Medievalia et humanistica; studies in medieval & Renaissance culture; new ser. no. 7; ed. by Paul Maurice Clogan. Cambridge 1976 209p (Medieval poetics) ISBN 0-521-21331-2 LC 75-32451

Medievalia et humanistica; studies in medieval & Renaissance culture; new ser. no. 8; ed. by Paul Maurice Clogan. Cambridge 1977 261p (Transformation and continuity) ISBN 0-521-21783-0 LC 75-16872

Medievalia et humanistica; studies in medieval & Renaissance culture; new ser. no. 9; ed. by Paul Maurice Clogan. Cambridge 1979 253p (Transformation and continuity) ISBN 0-521-22446-2 LC 75-32451

The medusa and the snail. See Thomas, L.

Medvedev, Roi Aleksandrovich (ed.) The Samizdat register; ed. by Roy A. Medvedev. Norton 1977 314p ISBN 0-393-05652-X LC 77-24984
Partially analyzed

Medvedev, Roy A. See Medvedev, Roi Aleksandrovich

Megaw, J. Vincent S. See Greenhalgh, M. jt. ed.

Megaw, Vincent. See Megaw, J. Vincent S.

Mehl, Dieter (ed.) Essays and studies, 1979. *See* English Association. Essays and studies, 1979

Meisner, Maurice J. and Murphey, Rhoads (eds.) The Mozartian historian; essays on the works of Joseph R. Levenson. Univ. of Calif. Press 1976 203p ISBN 0-520-02826-0 LC 74-82849

Melnik, Stefan Reinhard. See Fischer, H. D. jt. ed.

Memoirs and opinions, 1926-1974. See Tate, A.

Mendelson, Edward. See Seidel, M. A. jt. ed.

Mendlovitz, Saul H. (ed.) On the creation of a just world order. *See* On the creation of a just world order

Merchant, William Moelwyn (ed.) Essays and studies, 1977. *See* English Association. Essays and studies, 1977

Merrill, John Calhoun. See Fischer, H. D. jt. ed.

Millon, Henry A. and Nochlin, Linda (eds.) Art and architecture in the service of politics. MIT Press 1978 381p ISBN 0-262-13137-4 LC 78-1311

Mills, Ralph J. Cry of the human; essays on contemporary American poetry [by] Ralph J. Mills, Jr. Univ. of Ill. Press 1975 275p ISBN 0-252-00459-0   LC 74-14507

Milne, Gordon. The sense of society; a history of the American novel of manners. Fairleigh Dickinson Univ. Press 1977 305p ISBN 0-8386-1927-4 LC 76-748

Milne, William Gordon. See Milne, Gordon

Miłosz, Czesław. Emperor of the earth; modes of eccentric vision. Univ. of Calif. Press 1977 253p ISBN 0-520-03302-7 LC 76-20005

Milton and the art of sacred song. See Patrick, J. M. and Sundell, R. H. eds.

Milton and the line of vision. See Wittreich, J. A. ed.

The mind and art of Victorian England. See Altholz, J. L. ed.

Mind and language. See Guttenplan, S. D. ed.

Mind and madness in ancient Greece. See Simon, B.

Miner, Earl Roy (ed.) Illustrious evidence. See Illustrious evidence

Miner, Earl Roy (ed.) Literary uses of typology; from the late Middle Ages to the present. Princeton Univ. Press 1977 403p ISBN 0-691-06327-3 LC 76-45904

Minogue, Kenneth R. See De Crespigny, A. jt. ed.

Minorities in history. See Hepburn, A. C. ed.

Minority language and literature; retrospective and perspective. Ed. by Dexter Fisher. Modern Lang. Assn. of Am. 1977 160p ISBN 0-87352-350-4

Mintz, Sidney Wilfred (ed.) Slavery, colonialism, and racism. Essays by: J. F. Ade·Ajayi [and others]. Norton 1974 213p ISBN 0-393-01115-1

Mirror on mirror. See Brower, R. A.

Mirrors of man in existentialism. See Scott, N. A.

Mischel, Theodore (ed.) The self; psychological and philosophical issues. Rowman & Littlefield 1977 359p ISBN 0-87471-969-0 LC 77-1508

Miskimin, Harry A. (ed.) The Medieval city. See The Medieval city

The modern American novel and the movies. See Peary, G. and Shatzkin, R. eds.

Modern Chinese literature in the May Fourth era. Ed. by Merle Goldman. Contributors: John Berninghausen [and others]. Harvard Univ. Press 1977 464p (Harvard East Asian ser. 89) ISBN 0-674-57910-0 LC 76-47652

The modern English novel: the reader, the writer and the work. See Josipovici, G. ed.

Modern fantasy. See Manlove, C. N.

The modern Italian novel: from Capuana to Tozzi. See Pacifici, S.

The modern Italian novel: from Pea to Moravia. See Pacifici, S.

Modern Japan; aspects of history, literature and society. Ed. by William G. Beasley. Univ. of Calif. Press 1975 296p ISBN 0-520-02972-0 LC 74-29802

Modern Japanese fiction and its traditions. See Rimer, J. T.

Modern Japanese writers. See Ueda, M.

Modern Jewish ethics; theory and practice. Ed. by Marvin Fox. Ohio State Univ. Press 1975 262p ISBN 0-8142-0192-X LC 74-28395
Partially analyzed

Modern Language Association of America. Commission on Minority Groups and the Study of Language and Literature. Minority language and literature. *See* Minority language and literature

Modern Latin American narratives. See MacAdam, A. J.

Modern Russian poets on poetry. See Proffer, C. R. ed.

The **modes** of modern writing. See Lodge, D.

Mogensen, Lars Aagaard- See Aagaard-Mogensen, Lars

Mohan, Raj Pal, and Martindale, Don Albert (eds.) Handbook of contemporary developments in world sociology. Greenwood Press 1975 493p (Contributions in sociology no. 17) ISBN 0-8371-7961-0 LC 75-70

Momigliano, Arnaldo. Essays in ancient and modern historiography. Wesleyan Univ. Press 1977 387p ISBN 0-8195-5010-8 LC 76-41484

Monaco, James. The new wave; Truffaut, Godard, Chabrol, Rohmer, Rivette. Oxford 1976 372p ISBN 0-19-501992-X LC 75-38099

The **monster** in the mirror. See Williams, D. A. ed.

Montagu, Ashley (ed.) Learning non-aggression; the experience of non-literate societies. Oxford 1978 235p ISBN 0-19-502342-0 LC 77-11675

Montagu, Ashley (ed.) Race and IQ. Oxford 1975 322p ISBN 0-19-501884-2. LC 74-22881

Montagu, Montague Francis Ashley- See Montagu, Ashley

Montefiore, Alan (ed.) Neutrality and impartiality; the university and political commitment. Cambridge 1975 292p ISBN 0-521-20664-2
Partially analyzed

Moody, Anthony David (ed.) The waste land in different voices. *See* The Waste land in different voices

Moody, Ernest Addison. Studies in medieval philosophy, science and logic; collected papers, 1933-1969. [Published under the auspices of the Center for Medieval and Renaissance Studies by] Univ. of Calif. Press 1975 453p ISBN 0-520-02668-3 LC 73-91661

Mooney, Michael (ed.) Small comforts for hard times. *See* Small comforts for hard times

The **Moral** foundations of the American Republic. Ed. by Robert H. Horwitz. Contributors: Robert A. Goldwin [and others]. Univ. Press of Va. 1977 245p ISBN 0-8139-0723-3 LC 76-52991

The **moral** tradition in English fiction, 1785-1850. See Pickering, S.

Morality and architecture. See Watkin, D.

Morgan, Edwin. Essays. Carcanet [distributed by Dufour] [1975 c1974] 299p ISBN 0-85653-072-9
Partially analyzed

Morgan, Richard G. (ed.) Kenneth Patchen: a collection of essays. Ed. and with an introduction. Foreword by Miriam Patchen. AMS Press 1977 262p ISBN 0-404-16005-0 LC 77-78319
Partially analyzed

Morgenthau, Hans Joachim. See entry under title: [Truth and tragedy]: a tribute to Hans Morgenthau

Morice, G. P. (ed.) David Hume. *See* David Hume

Morison, Robert Swain. See Holton, G. J. jt. ed.

Morning yet on creation day. See Achebe, C.

Morris, Leon Lamb. See entry under title: Reconciliation and hope

Morris, Margaret Francine (ed.) Essays on urban America. *See* Essays on urban America

Morris, Robert K. and Malin, Irving (eds.) The achievement of William Styron. Univ. of Ga. Press 1975 280p ISBN 0-8203-0351-8 LC 74-75942
Partially analyzed

Morris, Wesley Abram. Friday's footprint; structuralism and the articulated text. Ohio State Univ. Press 1979 253p ISBN 0-8142-0302-7 LC 79-14147

Morris, Wright. Earthly delights, unearthly adornments; American writers as image-makers. Harper 1978 193p ISBN 0-06-013107-1 LC 78-2154

Morris-Jones, Wyndraeth Humphreys (ed.) The Making of politicians: studies from Africa and Asia. *See* The Making of politicians: studies from Africa and Asia

Mortal questions. See Nagel, T.

Morton, Arthur Leslie. See entry under title: Rebels and their causes

Moseley, Edwin M. See entry under title: Renaissance and modern

Motion and time, space and matter; interrelations in the history of philosophy and science. Ed. by Peter K. Machamer and Robert G. Turnbull. Ohio State Univ. Press 1976 559p ISBN 0-8142-0207-1 LC 75-26517

The motives of eloquence. See Lanham, R. A.

Movements in English literature, 1900-1940. See Gillie, C.

Movies and methods. See Nichols, B. ed.

Moynihan, Daniel Patrick. See Glazer, N. jt. ed.

The Mozartian historian. See Meisner, M. J. and Murphey, R. eds.

Mudford, Peter. The art of celebration. Faber & Faber 1979 199p ISBN 0-571-10852-0

Mudrick, Marvin. Books are not life but then what is? Oxford 1979 348p ISBN 0-19-502508-3 LC 78-9939

Mudrick, Marvin. The man in the machine. Horizon Press 1977 191p ISBN 0-8180-1164-5 LC 75-5994

Muir, Kenneth (ed.) Essays and studies, 1974. *See* English Association. Essays and studies, 1974

Muir, Kenneth (ed.) Shakespeare survey. *See* Shakespeare survey

Muir, Kenneth. The singularity of Shakespeare, and other essays. Barnes & Noble 1977 235p (Liverpool English texts and studies) ISBN 0-06-495018-2 LC 77-72251

Mukařovský, Jan. Structure, sign, and function; selected essays; tr. and ed. by John Burbank and Peter Steiner. Yale Univ. Press 1978 [c1977] xxxix, 269p (Yale Russian and East European studies, 14) ISBN 0-300-02108-9 LC 77-76310

Mulder, John M. and Wilson, John Frederick (eds.) Religion in American history; interpretive essays. Prentice-Hall 1978 459p ISBN 0-13-771998-1 LC 77-2883

Murck, Christian F. (ed.) Artists and traditions. *See* Artists and traditions

National Portrait Gallery, Smithsonian Institution. Abroad in America. *See* Abroad in America

The **National** purpose reconsidered; Dona Baron, editor. Columbia Univ. Press 1978 139p ISBN 0-231-04472-0 LC 78-6103
Symposia held at Columbia University, 1976

National Research Council. Social Science Panel on the Significance of Community in the Metropolitan Environment. Metropolitan America in contemporary perspective. *See* Hawley, A. H. and Rock, V. P. eds. Metropolitan America in contemporary perspective

Nationalism in a non-national state; the dissolution of the Ottoman Empire. Ed. by William W. Haddad and William Ochsenwald. Ohio State Univ. Press 1977 297p ISBN 0-8142-0191-1 LC 77-1253
Festschrift in honor of Sydney Nettleton Fisher

Nationalist movements. See Smith, A. D. ed.

Native languages of the Americas. See Sebeok, T. A. ed.

Natural order.See Barnes, B. and Shapin, S. eds.

Nature and conduct. See Royal Institute of Philosophy

Nature and society. See Feingold, R.

Nature and the Victorian imagination. See Knoepflmacher, U. C. and Tennyson, G. B. eds.

Nature, community, & will. See West, T. R.

Nature into myth. See Steadman, J. M.

The **nature** novel from Hardy to Lawrence. See Alcorn, J.

The **Nature** of scientific discovery; a symposium commemorating the 500th anniversary of the birth of Nicolaus Copernicus. Ed. by Owen Gingerich. Smithsonian Inst. Press 1975 616p (Smithsonian international symposia series, 5) ISBN 0-87474-148-3 LC 74-18374
Partially analyzed

Neale, Ronald Stanley. See Kamenka, E. jt. ed.

The **necessary** blankness. See Allen, M.

Needleman, Jacob, and Baker, George (eds.) Understanding the new religions. Seabury 1978 314p ISBN 0-8164-0403-8 LC 78-14997
"A Crossroad book"

Needleman, Jacob, and Lewis, Dennis (eds.) On the way to self knowledge. Knopf 1976 241p ISBN 0-394-49753-8 LC 76-13706
Partially analyzed

Negotiating the mainstream. See Johnson, H. A. ed.

Nelson, Lyle M. See Lerner, D. jt. ed.

Nemerov, Howard. Figures of thought; speculations on the meaning of poetry & other essays. Godine 1978 199p ISBN 0-87923-212-9 LC 77-78361

Neo-classical dramatic criticism, 1560-1770. See Jones, T. B. and Nicol, B. de Bear

Neumann, Editha S. See Johnson, R. B. jt. ed.

Neutrality and impartiality. See Montefiore, A. ed.

Nevins, Allan. Allan Nevins on history; comp. and introduced by Ray Allen Billington. Scribner 1975 xxvii,420p ISBN 0-684-14320-8 LC 75-4870

A **New** America? Ed. by Stephen R. Graubard. Essays by Elizabeth Hardwick [and others]. Norton 1979 [c1978] 350p ISBN 0-393-01197-6 LC 78-12423
Originally published as the Winter 1978 issue of Daedalus

Neyman, Jerzy (ed.) The heritage of Copernicus: theories "pleasing to the mind". MIT Press 1974 542p (The Copernican volume of the National Academy of Sciences). ISBN 0-262-14021-7. LC 74-6415

Niblett, William Roy (ed.) The sciences, the humanities and the technological threat. Wiley 1975 168p ISBN 0-470-63655-6 LC 74-11838
"A Halsted Press book"

Nicgorski, Walter (ed.) An almost chosen people. *See* An Almost chosen people

Nicholls, Peter (ed.) Science fiction at large; a collection of essays, by various hands, about the interface between science fiction and reality. Contributors: Ursula K. Le Guin [and others] Harper 1976 224p ISBN 0-06-013198-5 LC 76-50161

Nichols, Bill (ed.) Movies and methods; anthology. Univ. of Calif. Press 1976 640p ISBN 0-520-02890-2 LC 74-22968
Partially analyzed

Nicholson, Lewis E. (ed.) Anglo-Saxon poetry: essays in appreciation. *See* Anglo-Saxon poetry: essays in appreciation

Nicol, Bernard de Bear. See Jones, T. B. jt. auth.

Nicoll, Allardyce. World drama; from Aeschylus to Anouilh; with contributions by Arthur Wilmurt [and others]; with fifty-six plates in half-tone. Rev. enl. and completely reset. Barnes & Noble 1976 1965p ISBN 0-06-495157-X
Original 1949 edition analyzed in 1948-1954 cumulation

Nicoll, John Ramsay Allardyce. See Nicoll, Allardyce

Nida, Eugene Albert. See entry under title: On language, culture, and religion: in honor of Eugene A. Nida

Nietzsche: imagery and thought. See Pasley, J. M. S. ed.

Night visitors. See Briggs, J.

Nine American film critics. See Murray, E.

1975 Nobel Conference. The future of science. *See* The Future of science

Noble, Donald Robert (ed.) The rising South v 1. *See* The Rising South v 1

Nochlin, Linda. See Millon, H. A. jt. ed.

Noel, Thomas. Theories of the fable in the eighteenth century. Columbia Univ. Press 1975 177p ISBN 0-231-03858-5 LC 74-23251

Nolan, Barbara. The Gothic visionary perspective. Princeton Univ. Press 1977 268p ISBN 0-691-06337-0 LC 76-56241

Northrop Frye on culture and literature. See Frye, N.

Northwest perspectives. See Bingham, E. R. and Love, G. A. eds.

Not without glory. See Scannell, V.

Novak, Maximillian E. (ed.) English literature in the age of disguise. *See* English literature in the age of disguise

The novel and contemporary experience in Africa. See Gakwandi, S. A.

The novel before the novel. See Heiserman, A. R.

The novels of Thomas Hardy. See Smith, A. ed.

Number and nightmare. See Kennard, J. E.

Nye, Russel Blaine. See entry under title: Essays in honor of Russel B. Nye

O

Oakeshott, Michael Joseph. Rationalism in politics; and other essays. Barnes & Noble [1974 c1962] 333p. ISBN 0-06-475215-1

The **oaten** flute. See Poggioli, R.

Oates, Joyce Carol. New heaven, new earth: the visionary experience in literature. Vanguard 1974 307p. ISBN 0-8149-0743-1. LC 74-76438

Ober, William B. Boswell's clap and other essays; medical analyses of literary's men's afflictions. Southern Ill. Univ. Press 1979 291p ISBN 0-8093-0889-4 LC 78-16018

Obolensky, Dimitri. See Auty, R. jt. ed.

O'Brien, Michael. The idea of the American South, 1920-1941. Johns Hopkins Univ. Press 1979 273p ISBN 0-8018-2166-5 LC 78-12250

O'Brien, Philip J. (ed.) Allende's Chile. Praeger 1976 296p (Praeger Special studies in international politics and government) ISBN 0-275-55750-2 LC 75-23987

The **Occasional** papers of the Rhodes-Livingstone Museum, nos. 1-16; in one volume; reprinted on behalf of The Institute for African Studies, University of Zambia by Manchester Univ. Press; distributed by Humanities Press 1974 826p ISBN 0-7190-1273-2

Ockham, Descartes, and Hume. See Weinberg, J. R.

O'Connor, John E. and Jackson, Martin A. (eds.) American history/American film; interpreting the Hollywood image. Foreword by Arthur M. Schlesinger, Jr. Ungar 1979 xxix, 290p (Ungar Film library) ISBN 0-8044-2263-5 LC 78-4295

Of poetry and poets. See Eberhart, R.

Of war and war's alarms. See Dolan, P. J.

O'Flaherty, James C.; Sellner, Timothy F. and Helm, Robert Meredith (eds.) Studies in Nietzsche and the classical tradition. Univ. of N.C. Press 1976 278p (Univ. of N.C. Studies in the Germanic languages and literatures (85) ISBN 0-8078-8085-X LC 75-22444

Ogletree, Thomas W. See Lucas, G. R. jt. ed.

Ogungbesan, Kolawole. See King, B. A. jt. ed.

O'Hara, John. "An artist is his own fault;" John O'Hara on writers and writing. Ed. with an introduction by Matthew J. Bruccoli. Southern Ill. Univ. Press 1977 226p ISBN 0-8093-0796-0 LC 76-43279
Partially analyzed

The **oil** crisis. See Vernon, R. ed.

Oinas, Felix J. (ed.) Heroic epic and saga; an introduction to the world's great folk epics. Ind. Univ. Press 1978 373p ISBN 0-253-32738-5 LC 77-9637

The **oldest** revolutionary. See Lemay, J. A. L. ed.

Oleson, Alexandra, and Brown, Sanborn C. (eds.) The pursuit of knowledge in the early American Republic; American scientific and learned societies from Colonial times to the Civil War. Johns Hopkins Univ. Press 1976 xxv,372p ISBN 0-8018-1679-3 LC 75-36941

Oleson, Alexandra, and Voss, John (eds.) The organization of knowledge in modern America, 1860-1920. Johns Hopkins Univ. Press 1979 xxi, 478p ISBN 0-8018-2108-8 LC 78-20521
This is "a companion volume to The pursuit of knowledge in the early American Republic: American scientific and learned societies from colonial times to the Civil War, ed. by Alexandra Oleson, and Sanborn C Brown" entered above

Olson, Alan M. (ed.) Disguises of the demonic. *See* Disguises of the demonic

Olson, Elder. On value judgments in the arts, and other essays. Univ. of Chicago Press 1976 365p ISBN 0-226-62895-7 LC 75-9057

O'Meara, Patrick. See Carter, G. M. jt. ed.; Martin, P. M. jt. ed.

On aesthetics in science. See Wechsler, J. ed.

On critical theory. See O'Neill, J. ed.

On difficulty and other essays. See Steiner, G.

On historians. See Hexter, J. H.

On knowing. See Bruner, J. S.

On language, culture, and religion: in honor of Eugene A. Nida. Ed. by Matthew Black [and] William A. Smalley. Mouton 1974 386p (Approaches to semiotics). ISBN 0-90-279-3011-2

On lies, secrets, and silence. See Rich, A. C.

On literary intention; critical essays selected and introduced by David Newton-De Molina. Edinburgh Univ. Press 1976 275p ISBN 0-85224-275-1

On modern German literature. See Kurz, P. K.

On Noam Chomsky. See Harman, G. ed.

On not being good enough. See Sale, R. H.

On the creation of a just world order; preferred worlds for the 1990's. Ed. by Saul H. Mendlovitz. Free Press 1975 (Preferred worlds for the 1990's) 302p ISBN 0-02-920900-5 LC 74-28937

On the making of Americans; essays in honor of David Riesman. Ed. by Herbert J. Gans [and others]. Univ. of Pa. Press 1979 350p ISBN 0-8122-7754-6 LC 78-65118

On the meaning of the university. See McMurrin, S. M. ed.

On the verge of revolt. See French, B.

On the way to self knowledge. See Needleman, J. and Lewis, D. jt. eds.

On value judgments in the arts, and other essays. See Olson, E.

One hundred years of photographic history; essays in honor of Beaumont Newhall. Ed. by Van Deren Coke. Univ. of N.Mex. Press 1975 180p ISBN 0-8263-0344-7 LC 74-83381

One ocean touching. See Egoff, S. A. ed.

O'Neill, John (ed.) On critical theory. Seabury 1976 265p ISBN 0-8164-9297-2 LC 76-21229
"A Continuum book"

Ong, Walter Jackson. Interfaces of the word; studies in the evolution of consciousness and culture. Cornell Univ. Press 1977 352p ISBN 0-8014-1105-X LC 77-3124

The open hand. See Walden, R. ed.

Oral literature. See Duggan, J. J. ed.

Order and innovation in the Middle Ages; essays in honor of Joseph R. Strayer. Ed. by William C. Jordan; Bruce McNab [and] Teofilo F. Ruiz. Princeton Univ. Press 1976 582p

Orel, Harold (ed.) Irish history and culture; aspects of a people's heritage. Univ. Press of Kan. 1976 387p ISBN 0-7006-0136-8 LC 75-35532

The Organization of African Unity after ten years. See El-Ayouty, Y. ed.

Pacific Historical Review. The American Indian. *See* The American Indian

Pacifici, Sergio. The modern Italian novel: from Capuana to Tozzi; with a preface by Harry T. Moore. Southern Ill. Univ. Press 1979 188p (Crosscurrents: modern critiques) ISBN 0-8093-0614-X LC 75-156786
Companion volume to The modern Italian novel: from Manzoni to Svevo, analyzed in 1965-1969 cumulation, and to: The modern Italian novel: from Pea to Moravia, entered below

Pacifici, Sergio. The modern Italian novel: from Pea to Moravia; with a preface by Harry T. Moore. Southern Ill. Univ. Press 1979 273p (Crosscurrents: modern critiques) ISBN 0-8093-0873-8 LC 67-13047
Companion volume to: The modern Italian novel: from Manzoni to Svevo, entered in 1965-1969 cumulation, and to: The modern Italian novel: from Capuana to Tozzi, entered above

Pagliaro, Harold E. (ed.) Studies in eighteenth-century culture. *See* Studies in eighteenth-century culture

Painting and the novel. See Meyers, J.

The **Palestinians;** people, history, politics. Ed. by Michael Curtis [and others]. Prepared under the auspices of the American Academic Association for Peace in the Middle East. Transaction Bks. 1975 277p. ISBN 0-87855-112-3. LC 74-32601
Partially analyzed

Palmer, Bruce (ed.) Grand strategy for the 1980s. *See* Grand strategy for the 1980s

Panek, LeRoy Lad. Watteau's shepherds: the detective novel in Britain, 1914-1940. Bowling Green Univ. Pop. Press 1979 232p ISBN 0-87972-131-6 LC 79-83887

Paracriticisms. See Hassan, I. H.

The **paradox** of cause, and other essays. See Miller, J. W.

Parapsychology: its relation to physics, biology, psychology, and psychiatry. Ed. by Gertrude R. Schmeidler. Scarecrow 1976 278p ISBN 0-8108-0909-5 LC 76-916

Parents, teachers, and children: prospects for choice in American education [by] James S. Coleman [and others]. Inst. for Contemporary Studies 1977 336p ISBN 0-917616-18-9 LC 77-79164

Parker, Kenneth (ed.) The South African novel in English; essays in criticism and society. Africana Pub. Co. 1978 202p ISBN 0-8419-0425-1 LC 78-18343

Parker, Patricia A. Inescapable romance; studies in the poetics of a mode. Princeton Univ. Press 1979 289p ISBN 0-691-06398-2 LC 78-70312

Parker, William Nelson, and Jones, Eric L. (eds.) European peasants and their markets; essays in agrarian economic history. Princeton Univ. Press [1976 c1975] 366p ISBN 0-691-05230-1 LC 75-15281

Parry, Adam Milman. See entry under title: Yale classical studies v24

Parry, Albert. Terrorism: from Robespierre to Arafat. Vanguard 1976 624p ISBN 0-8149-0746-6 LC 76-12006

Parry, Vernon J. (ed.) War, technology and society in the Middle East. *See* War, technology and society in the Middle East

Parsons, Talcott. Action theory and the human condition. Free Press 1978 464p ISBN 0-02-923990-7 LC 77-94084

Parsons, Talcott. Social systems and the evolution of action theory. Free Press 1977 420p ISBN 0-02-924800-0 LC 76-55100

Partial magic. See Alter, R.

Partlow, Robert B. (ed.) Dickens Studies Annual. *See* Dickens Studies Annual

Perception; essays in honor of James J. Gibson. Ed. by Robert B. MacLeod and Herbert L. Pick, Jr. Cornell Univ. Press 1974 317p ISBN 0-8014-0835-0 LC 74-1547

Percy, Walker. The message in the bottle; how queer man is, how queer language is, and what one has to do with the other. Farrar, Straus 1975 335p LC 75-5846

Perella, Nicolas James. Midday in Italian literature; variations on an archetypal theme. Princeton Univ. Press 1979 336 ISBN 0-691-06389-3 LC 78-70313

A perfusion of signs. See Sebeok, T. A. ed.

Perkins, David, and Leondar, Barbara (eds). The arts and cognition. Johns Hopkins Univ. Press 1977 341p ISBN 0-8018-1843-5 LC 76-17237

Person and community. See Roth, R. J. ed.

The Personal universe; essays in honor of John Macmurray. Ed. by Thomas E. Wren. Humanities Press 1975 113p ISBN 0-391-00398-4 LC 75-20225

Persons of the drama. See Kauffmann, S.

Perspectives of Roman poetry; a classics symposium. Essays by Georg Luck [and others]. Ed. and prefaced by G. Karl Galinsky. Published for the College of Humanities and the College of Fine Arts of The University of Texas at Austin by Univ. of Tex. Press 1974 160p (Symposia in the arts and the humanities no 1) ISBN 0-292-76420-0 LC 74-5314
Partially analyzed

Perspectives on justice. [Contributors] Telford Taylor; Constance Baker Motley [and] James Kern Feibleman. Northwestern Univ. Press 1975 135p (1973 Rosenthal lectures. Northwestern University School of Law) ISBN 0-8101-0453-9 LC 74-14309

Perspectives on publishing. See Altbach, P. G. and McVey, S. eds.

Perspectives on revolution and evolution. [Contributors]: Henry S. Albinski [and others]. Ed. by Richard A. Preston. 300p (Duke Univ. Center for Commonwealth and Comparative Studies, 46) ISBN 0-8223-0425-2 LC 78-74448
Papers presented at a Bicentennial Conference of American and Canadian scholars held October 14-16, 1976 in Durham, North Carolina

Perspectives on the American Revolution. See Suggs, G. G. ed.

Peters, Richard Stanley (ed.) Nature and conduct. See Royal Institute of Philosophy. Nature and conduct

Pettit, Philip. See Hookway, C. jt. ed.

Peyre, Henri. French literary imagination and Dostoevsky, and other essays. Univ. of Ala. Press 1975 164p (Studies in the humanities no.10; Literature) ISBN 0-8173-7324-1 LC 74-28294

Phelps, Leland R. (ed.) Creative encounter. See Creative encounter

Phelps-Stokes Fund. The Black American reference book. See The Black American reference book

Phenomenology and philosophical understanding. See Pivčević, E. ed.

Phillips, Michael Curtis (ed.) Interpreting Blake; essays. Cambridge 1978 269p ISBN 0-521-22176-5 LC 78-8322

Philosophers and philosophies. See Copeleston, F. C.

Philosophers discuss education. Ed. by S. C. Brown. Rowman & Littlefield 1975 260p ISBN 0-87471-774-4
Partially analyzed

Philosophers of peace and war. See Gallie, W. B.

Philosophical aspects of the mind-body problem; ed. and with an introduction by Chung-ying Cheng. Univ. Press of Hawaii 1975 221p ISBN 0-8248-0342-6 LC 75-17914

Philosophical dimensions of parapsychology. See Wheatley, J. M. O. and Edge, H. L. eds.

Philosophical essays on dreaming. See Dunlop, C. E. M. ed.

Philosophy & environmental crisis; ed. by William T. Blackstone. Univ. of Ga. Press 1974 140p. ISBN 0-8203-0343-7. LC 73-90842

Philosophy and humanism; Renaissance essays in honor of Paul Oskar Kristeller. Ed. by Edward P. Mahoney. Columbia Univ. Press 1976 xxiv, 624p ISBN 0-231-03904-2 LC 75-42285

Philosophy and parapsychology. See Ludwig, J. K. ed.

Philosophy and psychical research. See Thakur, S. C. ed.

Philosophy & sex. See Baker, R. and Elliston, F. A. eds.

Philosophy and the civilizing arts; essays presented to Herbert W. Schneider. Ed. by Craig Walton and John P. Anton. Ohio Univ. Press [1975 c1974] xxii, 508p ISBN 0-8214-0145-9 LC 73-92907

Philosophy and the novel. See Jones, P.

Philosophy Conference, 4th. University of Georgia, 1971. Philosophy & environmental crisis. *See* Philosophy & environmental crisis

Philosophy East/philosophy West; a critical comparison of Indian, Chinese, Islamic, and European philosophy. [Contributors:] Ben-Ami Scharfstein [and others]. Oxford 1978 359p ISBN 0-19-520064-0 LC 78-18473

Philosophy in and out of Europe. See Grene, M. G.

Philosophy looks at the arts. See Margolis, J. Z. ed.

The **philosophy** of the curriculum. See Hook, S.; Kurtz, P. W. and Todorovich, M. eds.

Philosophy, politics and society. See Laslett, P. and Fishkin, J. eds.

Philp, Kenneth R. (ed.) Essays on Walter Prescott Webb. *See* Essays on Walter Prescott Webb

The **picaresque** hero in European fiction. See Bjornson, R.

Pickering, Samuel. The moral tradition in English fiction, 1785-1850, by Samuel Pickering, Jr. Published for Dartmouth College by Univ. Press of New England 1976 184p ISBN 0-87451-109-7 LC 74-12540

Pincoffs, Edmund L. (ed.) The concept of academic freedom. *See* The Concept of academic freedom

Pioneers of psychology. See Fancher, R. E.

Pivčević, Edo (ed.) Phenomenology and philosophical understanding. Cambridge 1975 288p ISBN 0-521-20637-5 LC 74-19533

Pizer, Donald (ed.) Tulane Studies in English. *See* Tulane Studies in English

The **Place** of book illumination in Byzantine art. [Contributors]: Kurt Weitzmann [and others]. Princeton University, Art Museum. Distributed by Princeton Univ. Press [1976 c1975] 184p ISBN 0-691-03910-0 LC 74-84574 "A tribute to Kurt Weitzmann"

Place, personality and the Irish writer; ed. by Andrew Carpenter. Barnes & Noble 1977 199p (Irish literary studies 1) ISBN 0-06-490727-9

Plaks, Andrew H. (ed.) Chinese narrative. *See* Chinese narrative

Planning, politics and public policy; the British, French and Italian experience; ed. by Jack Hayward and Michael Watson. Cambridge 1975 496p ISBN 0-521-20570-0 LC 74-82587

Planning, politics, and the public interest. Ed. by Walter Goldstein. Columbia Univ. Press 1978 202p ISBN 0-231-04538-7 LC 78-1720

Plot, story, and the novel. See Caserio, R. L.

Plumb, John Harold. See entry under title: Historical perspectives

Poetic freedom and poetic truth. See Hawkins, H.

Poetics, rhetoric, and logic. See Howell, W. S.

Poetries. See Richards, I. A.

Poetry and poetics from ancient Greece to the Renaissance: studies in honor of James Hutton. Ed. by G. M. Kirkwood. Cornell Univ. Press 1975 (Cornell Studies in classical philology, 38) 236p ISBN 0-8014-0847-4 LC 74-10410

Poetry and repression. See Bloom, H.

The **poetry** wreck. See Shapiro, K. J.

Poets and critics. See Woodcock, G. ed.

Poets' riddles. See Le Comte, E. S.

The **poet's** self and the poem. See Heller, E.

The **poet's** work: 29 masters of 20th century poetry on the origins and practice of their art. See Gibbons, R. ed.

Poggioli, Renato. The oaten flute; essays on pastoral poetry and the pastoral ideal. Harvard Univ. Press 1975 340p ISBN 0-674-62950-7 LC 74-16540

Polanyi, John Charles. See Griffiths, F. jt. ed.

Political and social essays. See Ricoeur, P.

Political culture and political change in Communist states. See Brown, A. H. and Gray, J. eds.

The **Political** economy of inflation. Ed. by Fred Hirsch and John H. Goldthorpe. Harvard Univ. Press 1978 307p ISBN 0-674-68583-0 LC 77-26195

Political elites and political development in the Middle East; ed. by Frank Tachau. Halstead Press 1975 310p (States and societies of the Third World) ISBN 0-470-84314-4 LC 74-20507

Political realism in American thought. See Coffey, J. W.

Political theory and praxis; new perspectives; ed. by Terence Ball. Univ. of Minn. Press 1977 281p ISBN 0-8166-0816-4 LC 77-073320

Politics and cinema. See Sarris, A.

Politics and history. See Aron, R.

Politics and literature in modern Britain. See Watson, G.

Politics and modernization in South and Southeast Asia. See Kearney, R. N. ed.

The **politics** of reappraisal, 1918-1939. See Peele, G. and Cook, C. eds.

Polity and theater in historical perspective. See Hermassi, K. C.

Pool, Ithiel de Sola (ed.) The social impact of the telephone. *See* The Social impact of the telephone

Popular media in China. See Chu, G. C. ed.

The **popular** school. See Logan, T. P. and Smith, D. S. eds.

Population policy and ethics; the American experience. Ed. by Robert M. Veatch. A Project of The Research Group on Ethics and Population of The Institute of Society, Ethics and the Life Sciences. Irvington Pubs. [distributed by] Halsted Press 1977 501p (Irvington Population and demographic ser) ISBN 0-470-15170-6 LC 76-18887

Porter, Arabel J. (ed.) Essays on literature and politics, 1932-1972. *See* Rahv, P. Essays on literature and politics, 1932-1972

The **positive** hero in Russian literature. See Mathewson, R. W.

Positivism and sociology. See Giddens, A. ed.

The **possibilities** of order: Cleanth Brooks and his work. *See* Simpson, L. P. ed.

Postwar trends in Japan; studies in commemoration of Rev. Aloysius Miller S. J. Ed. by Shunichi Takayanagi and Kimitada Miwa. Univ. of Tokyo Press [distributed by Int. Scholarly Bk. Services] 1975 272p ISBN 0-86008-129-X

Powell, James Matthew (ed.) Medieval studies; an introduction. Syracuse Univ. Press 1976 389p ISBN 0-8156-2175-2 LC 76-8870

Powell, Lawrence Clark. See entry under title: Voices from the Southwest

Power and authority in law enforcement. See Armstrong, T. R. and Cinnamon, K. M. eds.

Praise from famous men: an anthology of introductions. Selected and ed. by Guy R. Lyle; with a preface on prefaces by Kevin Guinagh. Scarecrow 1977 194p ISBN 0-8108-1002-6 LC 76-55402

Pratt, Annis Vilas, and Dembo, L. S. (eds.) Doris Lessing; critical studies. Univ. of Wis. Press 1974 172p ISBN 0-299-06560-X LC 74-5909
Partially analyzed

Prefaces. See Dobie, J. F.

Prefaces to The experience of literature. See Trilling, L.

Prenshaw, Peggy Whitman (ed.) Eudora Welty; critical essays. Univ. Press of Miss. 1979 446p ISBN 0-87805-093-0 LC 79-4124

Prentki, Tim (ed.) Francis Warner; poet and dramatist. Sceptre Press [distributed by Humanities Press 1978 c1977] 154p ISBN 0-7068-0378-7

Pre-Raphaelitism. See Sambrook, J. ed.

Prescott, Anne Lake. French poets and the English Renaissance; studies in fame and transformation. Yale Univ. Press 1978 290p ISBN 0-300-02140-2 LC 77-5482

The **present** state of scholarship in sixteenth-century literature. See Jones, W. M. ed.

Presidential power and the Constitution. See Corwin, E. S.

Press, John (ed.) Essays by divers hands. *See* Royal Society of Literature of the United Kingdom, London. Essays by divers hands

Pressure from without. See Hollis, P. ed.

Preston, Paul (ed.) Spain in crisis; the evolution and decline of the Franco regime. Barnes & Noble 1976 341p ISBN 0-06-495711-X LC 75-41577

Preston, Richard Arthur (ed.) Perspectives on revolution and evolution. *See* Perspectives on revolution and evolution

Prichard, Elizabeth R. ed. Home care. *See* Home care

Prichard, Keith W. See Buxton, T. H. jt. ed.

Prickett, Stephen. Romanticism and religion; the tradition of Coleridge and Wordsworth in the Victorian Church. Cambridge 1976 295p ISBN 0-521-21072-0 LC 75-22554

Prickett, Stephen. Victorian fantasy. Indiana Univ. Press 1979 257p ISBN 0-253-17461-9 LC 78-21751

Primeau, Ronald (ed.) Influx; essays on literary influence. Kennikat 1977 186p (National University Publications. Literary criticism ser.) ISBN 0-8046-9151-7 LC 76-44836

Princes and artists. See Trevor-Roper, H. R.

Pritchard, Edward Evan Evans-. See Evans-Pritchard, Edward Evan

Pritchard, James Bennett (ed.) Solomon & Sheba. [Contributors]: Gus W. van Beek [and others]. Phaidon [distributed by Praeger] 1974 160p ISBN 0-7148-1613-2 LC 72-79551

Pritchard, William H. Seeing through everything; English writers, 1918-1940. Oxford 1977 234p ISBN 0-19-519951-0 LC 76-47434

Pritchett, Victor Sawdon. The myth makers; literary essays. Random House 1979 190p ISBN 0-394-50472-O LC 78-21801

Problems of language and learning. See Davies, A. ed.

Problems of scientific revolution. See Harré, R. ed.

Proceedings of the American Antiquarian Society. See American Antiquarian Society

Prochnow, Herbert Victor (ed.) Dilemmas facing the nation. Harper 1979 302p ISBN 0-06-013448-8 LC 78-2157

Professing poetry. See Wain, J.

Professions for the people. See Gerstl, J. E. and Jacobs, G. eds.

Proffer, Carl R. (ed.). A book of things about Vladimir Nabokov. See A Book of things about Vladimir Nabokov

Proffer, Carl R. (ed.) Modern Russian poets on poetry; selected and introduced by Joseph Brodsky. Tr. by Alexander Golubov [and others]. Ardis Pubs. 1976 203p ISBN 0-88233-102-7 Title on spine: Russian poets on poetry

Progress in penal reform; ed. by Louis Blom-Cooper. Oxford 1974 288p ISBN 0-19-825325-7 LC 75-311466

Prophetic waters. See Seelye, J.

Prospects for constitutional democracy; essays in honor of R. Taylor Cole; ed. by John H. Hallowell. Duke Univ. Press 1976 197p ISBN 0-8223-0368-X LC 76-4220

The protean self. See Kennedy, A.

Protest—form—tradition. See Strelka, J. P.; Bell, R. F. and Dobson, E. eds.

Protestant poetics and the seventeenth-century religious lyric. See Lewalski, B. K.

A Provision of human nature; essays on Fielding and others. In honor of Miriam Austin Locke. Ed. by Donald Kay. Univ. of Ala. Press 1977 207p ISBN 0-8173-7425-6 LC 76-40469

Pryse, Marjorie. The mark and the knowledge; social stigma in classic American fiction. Ohio State Univ. Press 1979 179p ISBN 0-8142-0296-9 LC 78-23229

Psychiatry and the humanities v 1. Editor: Joseph H. Smith. Published under the auspices of the Forum on Psychiatry and the Humanities, The Washington School of Psychiatry. Yale Univ. Press 1976 247p ISBN 0-300-01982-3 LC 75-32283

Psychoanalysis and Catholicism. See Wolman, B. B. ed.

Psychoanalysis and language. Editor: Joseph H. Smith; Assistant editor: Gloria H. Parloff. Published under the auspices of the Forum on Psychiatry and the Humanities, The Washington School of Psychiatry. Yale Univ. Press 1978 xxx,402p (Psychiatry and the humanities v3) ISBN 0-300-02249-2 LC 78-9156

Psychoanalysis and the question of the text. See Hartman, G. H. ed.

Psychoanalysis, creativity, and literature. See Roland, A. ed.

Psychology and the human dilemma. See May, R.

Public and private morality. See Hampshire, S. ed.

A Public philosophy reader; [ed. by] Richard J. Bishirjian. Arlington House 1978 336p ISBN 0-87000-435-2 LC 78-23415

Published in Paris. See Ford, H. D.

Pullin, Faith (ed.) New perspectives on Melville. Kent State Univ. Press 1978 314p ISBN 0-87338-226-9 LC 78-16505

The Pulse of freedom; American liberties: 1920-1970s. Ed. by Alan Reitman; foreword by Ramsey Clark. Norton 1975 352p. ISBN 0-393-05527-2. LC 74-14613

Puritan New England. See Vaughan, A. T. and Bremer, F. J. eds.

The pursuit of knowledge in the early American Republic. See Oleson, A. and Brown, S. C. eds.

Q

Quality and pleasure in Latin poetry. See Woodman, T. & West, D. eds.

Quantitative social science research on Latin America; ed. by Robert S. Byars and Joseph LeRoy Love. Published in conjunction with the Office of International Programs and Studies. Univ. of Ill. Press 1973 272p (Center for Latin American and Caribbean Studies, no 1) ISBN 0-252-00335-7   LC 72-95001

The quest for man. See Goodall, V. M. G. ed.

A question of quality: popularity and value in modern creative writing. See Filler, L. ed.

Quimby, Ian M. G. (ed.) Material culture and the study of American life. See Material culture and the study of American life

Quine, Willard Van Orman. The ways of paradox, and other essays; rev. and enl. ed. Harvard Univ. Press 1976 335p ISBN 0-674-94835-1 LC 76-4200

Quirk, Randolph. The linguist and the English language. St Martins 1974 181p LC 74-78938

R

Race and IQ. See Montagu, A. ed.

Race, science and society. See United Nations Educational, Scientific and Cultural Organization

Racial variation in man (Proceedings of a symposium held at the Royal Geographical Society, London, on 19 and 20 September, 1974). Ed. by F. J. Ebling; published by the Institute of Biology. Wiley 1975 245p (Symposia of the Institute of Biology no.22) ISBN 0-470-22955-1 LC 75-12803
"A Halsted Press book"
Partially analyzed

Radical education. See Barrow, R.

Radical phenomenology; essays in honor of Martin Heidegger. Ed. by John Sallis. Humanities Press 1978 318p ISBN 0-391-00928-1 LC 78-12763
Partially analyzed
Reprinted from v7 of Research in phenomenology

Radicalism in the contemporary age. Seweryn Bialer, editor; Sophia Sluzar, associate editor. Preface by Zbigniew Brzezinski. 3v Westview Press 1977 (Columbia Univ. Res. Inst. on Int. Change. Studies) ISBN v1 0-89158-217-7; v2 0-89158-131-6; v3 0-89158-129-4: LC v 1 76-39891; v2 76-52453; v3 76-39890
v 1 Sources of contemporary radicalism; v2 Radical visions of the future; v3 Strategies and impact of contemporary radicalism

Radosh, Ronald (ed.) The new Cuba: paradoxes and potentials. Morrow 1976 [c1975] 248p ISBN 0-688-02965-5 LC 75-19266

Radzinowicz, Sir Leon. See entry under title: Crime, criminology and public policy

Ragusa, Olga. Narrative and drama; essays in modern Italian literature from Verga to Pasolini. Mouton 1976 166p (De proprietatibus litterarum: Ser. practica, 110) ISBN 0-90-279-3474-6

Ragussis, Michael. The subterfuge of art; language and the romantic tradition. Johns Hopkins Univ. Press 1978 243p ISBN 0-8018-2059-6 LC 78-5845

Rahv, Philip. Essays on literature and politics, 1932-1972. Ed. by Arabel J. Porter and Andrew J. Dvosin; with a memoir by Mary McCarthy. Houghton 1978 366p ISBN 0-395-27270-X LC 78-13373
Partially analyzed

Rahv, Philip. See entry under title: Images and ideas in American culture

Ramage, Edwin Stephen (ed.) Atlantis, fact or fiction? Contributors: J. Rufus Fears [and others]. Indiana Univ. Press 1978 210p ISBN 0-253-10482-3 LC 77-23264
"This collection of essays developed out of a panel discussion, 'Atlantis: Fact or Fiction?' sponsored by the Department of Classical Studies at Indiana University in April 1975."

Ramage, Edwin Stephen. Roman satirists and their satire. See Roman satirists and their satire

Rance, Nicholas. The historical novel and popular politics in nineteenth-century England. Barnes & Noble 1975 176p (Barnes & Noble Critical studies). ISBN 0-06-495805-1

Randall, Dale B. J. (ed.) Medieval and Renaissance studies. See Medieval and Renaissance studies

Randall, Dale B. J. (ed.) Studies in the continental background of Renaissance English literature: essays presented to John L. Lievsay. See Studies in the continental background of Renaissance English literature: essays presented to John L. Lievsay

Rank and file; Civil War essays in honor of Bell Irvin Wiley. Ed. by James I. Robertson, Jr. and Richard M. McMurry. Presidio Press [1977 c1976] 164p ISBN 0-89141-011-2 LC 76-48787
Partially analyzed

Ranum, Orest (ed.) National consciousness, history, and political culture in early-modern Europe. See National consciousness, history, and political culture in early-modern Europe

Rappoport, Leon H. See Kren, G. M. jt. ed.

Ratcliffe, Barrie M. (ed.) Great Britain and her world, 1750-1914. See Great Britain and her world, 1750-1914

Rathjens, George W. See Long, F. A. jt. ed.

A **rational** animal. See Flew, A. G. N.

Rationalism in politics. See Oakeshott, M. J.

The **rationalists.** See Sharp, D. ed.

Raymond, James C. (ed.) James B. McMillan: essays in linguistics by his friends and colleagues. See James B. McMillan: essays in linguistics by his friends and colleagues

Renaissance drama [1973]; essays on dramatic antecedents; ed. by Alan C. Dessen. New ser. 6. Northwestern Univ. Press 1973 [c1975] 250p. ISBN 0-8101-0454-7. LC 67-29872

Renaissance drama [1976]; drama and the other arts; ed. by Joel H. Kaplan. New ser. 7. Northwestern Univ. Press 1976 [c1977] 288p ISBN 0-8101-0406-1 LC 67-29872

The **Renaissance** imagination. See Gordon, D. J.

Repossessing and renewing. See Paul, S.

Representations. See Marcus, S.

The **resisting** reader. See Fetterley, J.

Responses. See Wilbur, R.

Restraints on war. See Howard, M. ed.

Reverse discrimination. See Gross, B. R. ed.

The **reversible** world. See Babcock, B. A. ed.

Review, v 1 1979. Ed. by James O. Hoge and James L. W. West III. Univ. Press of Va. 1979 345p ISBN 0-8139-0760-8

A **revolution** in taste. See Simpson, L.

Reynolds, Frank E. and Capps, Donald (eds.) The biographical process; studies in the history and psychology of religion. Mouton 1976 436p (Religion and reason 11; Method and theory in the study and interpretation of religion) ISBN 90-279-7522-1

Rhetoric: a tradition in transition; in honor of Donald C. Bryant with a reprinting of his "Rhetoric: its functions and scope" and "'Rhetoric its functions and scope' rediviva." Ed. by Walter R. Fisher. Mich. State Univ. Press 1974 315p ISBN 0-87013-18-5 LC 74-80391
Partially analyzed

The **rhetoric** of Renaissance poetry. See Sloan, T. O. and Waddington, R. B. eds.

Rhetoric, philosophy, and literature: an exploration. See Burks, D. M. ed.

Rhetorical norms in Renaissance literature. See Kennedy, W. J.

Rhodes, Robert E. See Casey, D. J. jt. ed.

Rhodes-Livingstone Museum. The occasional papers of the Rhodes-Livingstone Museum. *See* The Occasional papers of the Rhodes-Livingstone Museum

Riasanovsky, Nicholas Valentine (ed.) California Slavic studies. See California Slavic studies

Rice, David Talbot. See entry under title: Studies in memory of David Talbot Rice

Rich, Adrienne Cecile. On lies, secrets, and silence; selected prose, 1966-1978. Norton 1979 310p ISBN 0-393-01233-6 LC 78-26432

Richard Murphy: poet of two traditions. See Harmon, M. ed.

Richards, Ivor Armstrong. Complementarities; uncollected essays. Ed. by John Paul Russo. Harvard Univ. Press 1976 xxiv, 293p ISBN 0-674-15520-3 LC 76-19044
Partially analyzed

Richards, Ivor Armstrong. Poetries; their media and ends; a collection of essays by I. A. Richards published to celebrate his 80th birthday. Ed. by Trevor Eaton. Mouton 1974 256p (De proprietatibus litterarum: ser. maior, 30) LC 73-93947

Richardson, Robert D. Myth and literature in the American renaissance. Ind. Univ. Press 1978 309p ISBN 0-253-33965-0 LC 77-22638

Roberts, Joan I. (ed.) Beyond intellectual sexism; a new woman, a new reality. McKay 1976 386p ISBN 0-679-50631-4 LC 76-4905

Roberts, John R. (ed.) Essential articles for the study of John Donne's poetry. Archon Bks. 1975 558p (The Essential article ser) ISBN 0-208-01447-0 LC 75-20059
Title on spine: Essential articles: John Donne's poetry

Robertson, Giles (ed.) Studies in memory of David Talbot Rice. *See* Studies in memory of David Talbot Rice

Robertson, James I. (ed.) Rank and file. *See* Rank and file

Robinson, Christopher. French literature in the nineteenth century. Barnes & Noble 1978 216p (Comparative literature ser) ISBN 0-06-495943-0 LC 77-79571

Robinson, Timothy C. L. (ed.) The future of science. *See* The Future of science

Robson, W. W. (ed.) Essays and studies, 1978. *See* English Association. Essays and studies, 1978

Rock, Vincent P. See Hawley, A. H. jt. ed.

Roger Sessions on music. See Sessions, R.

Rogers, Pat (ed.) The eighteenth century. Holmes & Meier 1978 (The Context of English literature) 246p ISBN 0-8419-0421-9 LC 78-15568

Ro'i, Yaacov (ed.) The limits to power; Soviet policy in the Middle East. St Martins 1979 376p ISBN 0-312-48695-2 LC 78-10555

Roland, Alan (ed.) Psychoanalysis, creativity, and literature; a French-American inquiry. Columbia Univ. Press 1978 368p ISBN 0-231-04324-4 LC 77-26613
Papers delivered at a series of symposia co-sponsored by the National Psychological Association for Psychoanalysis and New York University entitled "A Franco-American dialogue: Self and culture today," held at New York University in May, 1976

Rollin, Roger B. and Patrick, John Max (eds.) "Trust to good verses": Herrick tercentenary essays. Univ. of Pittsburgh Press 1978 291p ISBN 0-8229-3353-5 LC 77-74547
"The essays collected in this volume were originally presented at the Robert Herrick Memorial Conference at the University of Michigan on October 11-13, 1974"

Roman crafts. See Strong, D. E. and Brown, D. eds.

Roman satire. See Knoche, U.

Roman satirists and their satire; the fine art of criticism in ancient Rome [by] Edwin S. Ramage; David L. Sigsbee [and] Sigmund C. Fredericks. Noyes Press [1975 c1974] 212p ISBN 0-8155-5028-6. LC 74-81538

Romantic and modern. See Bornstein, G. ed.

Romantic origins. See Brisman, L.

The **romantic** prison. See Brombert, V. H.

The **romantic** will. See Cooke, M. G.

Romanticism and behavior. See Peckham, M.

Romanticism and religion. See Prickett, S.

Romilly, Jacqueline de. Magic and rhetoric in ancient Greece. Harvard Univ. Press 1975 108p (The Carl Newell Jackson Lectures, 1974) ISBN 0-674-54152-9 LC 75-29535

Roots of open education in America; reminiscences and reflections. Editors: Ruth Dropkin and Arthur Tobier. City College Workshop Center for Open Education 1976 201p ISBN 0-918374-01-4 LC 76-531-46
Partially analyzed

Rorty, Amélie Oksenberg (ed.) The identities of persons. Univ. of Calif. Press 1976 333p (Topics in philosophy 3) ISBN 0-520-03030-3 LC 75-13156

Rosbottom, Ronald C. (ed.) Studies in eighteenth-century culture. *See* Studies in eighteenth-century culture

Rose, Alan Henry. Demonic vision; racial fantasy and Southern fiction. Archon Bks. 1976 168p ISBN 0-208-01582-5 LC 76-12088

Rosecrance, Richard N. (ed.) America as an ordinary country; U.S. foreign policy and the future. Cornell Univ. Press 1976 276p ISBN 0-8014-1010-X LC 75-38427

Rosemont, Henry. See Feinberg, W. jt. auth.

Rosenberg, Charles E. (ed.) The family in history. [Contributors]: Charles E. Rosenberg [and others]. Univ. of Pa. Press 1975 210p (Haney Foundation ser. 17) ISBN 0-8122-7703-3 LC 75-14962

Rosenberg, Harold. Art on the edge; creators and situations. Macmillan Pub. Co. 1975 303p ISBN 0-02-604900-7 LC 75-16128

Rosenfeld, Alvin Hirsch, and Greenberg, Irving (eds.) Comfronting the Holocaust; the impact of Elie Wiesel. Ind. Univ. Press 1978 239p ISBN 0-253-11290-7 LC 78-15821

Rosenwald, George C. See Riegel, K. F. jt. ed.

Rösing, Ina Susanne Spiegel- See Spiegel-Rösing, Ina Susanne

Ross, David O. Backgrounds to Augustan poetry: Gallus, elegy and Rome. Cambridge 1975 176p ISBN 0-521-20704-5 LC 74-31782

Ross, Ralph Gilbert (ed.) Makers of American thought; an introduction to seven American writers. Univ. of Minn. Press 1974 301p (The Minnesota Lib. on American Writers). ISBN 0-8166-0712-5. LC 74-78993

Ross, Ralph Gilbert; Schneider, Herbert Wallace, and Waldman, Theodore (eds.) Thomas Hobbes in his time. Univ. of Minn. Press [1975 c1974] 150p. ISBN 0-8166-0727-3. LC 74-83134

Rossi, Alice S.; Kagan, Jerome, and Hareven, Tamara K. (eds.) The family. Essays by Alice S. Rossi [and others]. Norton 1978 267p ISBN 0-393-01167-4 LC 77-16798

Rossman, Charles Raymond, and Friedman, Alan Warren (eds.) Mario Vargas Llosa; a collection of critical essays. Univ. of Tex. at Austin Press 1978 186p ISBN 0-292-75039-0 LC 78-50821 Partially analyzed

Røstvig, Maren-Sofie (ed.) Fair forms; essays in English literature from Spenser to June Austen. Rowman & Littlefield 1975 248p ISBN 0-87471-598-9 LC 74-17472

Rotberg, Robert I. See Chittick, H. N. jt. ed.; Kilson, M. L. jt. ed.

Roth, Philip. Reading myself and others. Farrar, Straus 1975 269p ISBN 0-374-24753-6 LC 75-2475 Partially analyzed

Roth, Robert J. (ed.) Person and community; a philosophical exploration. Fordham Univ. Press 1975 175p. ISBN 0-8232-0975-X. LC 73-93143

Rothstein, Eric (ed.) Literary monographs. *See* Literary monographs

Rothstein, Eric. Systems of order and inquiry in later eighteenth-century fiction. Univ. of Calif. Press 1975 274p ISBN 0-520-02862-7 LC 74-16716

Rowe, William Woodin. Nabokov & others: patterns in Russian literature. Ardis 1979 185p ISBN 0-88233-335-6 LC 79-51639

Rowland, Beryl (ed.) Chaucer and Middle English studies in honour of Rossell Hope Robbins. *See* Chaucer and Middle English studies in honour of Rossell Hope Robbins

Royal Institute of Philosophy. Communication and understanding; ed. by Godfrey Vesey. Harvester Press [distributed by Humanities Press] 1978 [c1977] xxxiii, 235p (Royal Institute of Philosophy lectures v10, 1975-1976) ISBN 0-391-00746-7 LC 77-23095

Royal Institute of Philosophy. Human values; ed. by Godfrey Vesey. Harvester Press [distributed by] Humanities Press 1978 231p (Royal Institute of Philosophy lectures v11, 1976-77) ISBN 0-391-00746-7 LC 77-28237

Royal Institute of Philosophy. Impressions of empiricism; ed. by Godfrey Vesey. St Martins 1976 xxi, 237p (Royal Institute of Philosophy lectures v9, 1974-1975) LC 75-29964

Royal Institute of Philosophy. Nature and conduct. Ed. by R. S. Peters. St Martins 1975 315p (Royal Institute of Philosophy lectures v8, 1973-1974) LC 75-21703

Royal Institute of Philosophy. Understanding Wittgenstein. St Martins 1974 285p (Royal Institute of Philosophy lectures v7, 1972-1973). LC 74-78895

Royal Society of Literature of the United Kingdom, London. Essays by divers hands; being the transactions of the Society. New ser. v38-39 Oxford 1975-1977 2v ISBN v38 0-19-711223-4; v39 0-19-711224-2
V38 edited by John Guest; v39 by John Press

Rubia Barcia, José, ed. Américo Castro and the meaning of Spanish civilization. *See* Américo Castro and the meaning of Spanish civilization

Rubin, Louis Decimus. William Elliott shoots a bear; essays on the Southern literary imagination. La. State Univ. Press [1976 c1975] 279p ISBN 0-8071-0160-5 LC 75-5352

Rubin, Vitaly Aronovich. Individual and state in ancient China; essays on four Chinese philosophers. Tr. by Steven I. Levine. Columbia Univ. Press 1976 ISBN 0-231-04064-4 LC 76-4516

Rudd, Niall. Lines of enquiry; studies in Latin poetry. Cambridge 1976 215p ISBN 0-521-20993-5 LC 75-12467

Ruggiers, Paul G. (ed.) Versions of medieval comedy; ed. and with an introduction. Univ. of Okla. Press 1977 252p ISBN 0-8061-1425-8 LC 77-6384

Runte, Roseann, (ed.) Studies in eighteenth-century culture. *See* Studies in eighteenth-century culture

Rural society in France; selections from the Annales, économies, sociétés, civilisations v3. Ed. by Robert Forster and Orest Ranum; tr. by Elborg Forster and Patricia M. Ranum. Johns Hopkins Univ. Press 1977 180p ISBN 0-8018-1916-4 LC 76-47373

The rural tradition in the English novel, 1900-1939. See Cavaliero, G.

Russell, John David. Style in modern British fiction; studies in Joyce, Lawrence, Forster, Lewis, and Green. Johns Hopkins Univ. Press 1978 196p ISBN 0-8018-2029-4 LC 77-22477

Russell-Wood, A. J. R. (ed.) From colony to nation. *See* From colony to nation

Russia discovered. See Calder, A.

Russian literary attitudes from Pushkin to Solzhenitsyn. See Freeborn, R. ed.

Russian literary criticism. See Stacy, R. H.

Russian modernism. See Gibian, G. and Tjalsma, H. W. eds.

Sarris, Andrew. Politics and cinema. Columbia Univ. Press 1978 215p ISBN 0-231-04034-2 LC 78-16334

The Saturday book 34; ed. by John Hadfield. Potter, C.N. distributed by Crown 1975 237p LC 42-51009
Partially analyzed

Savage, William W. (ed.) The Frontier v2. *See* The Frontier v2

Savory, Roger Mervyn (ed.) Introduction to Islamic civilisation; Cambridge 1976 204p ISBN 0-521-20777-0 LC 74-25662

Sayers, Dorothy Leigh. The whimsical Christian; 18 essays. Macmillan Pub. Co. 1978 275p ISBN 0-02-606930-X LC 78-5613
First published 1969 by Eerdmans with title: Christian letters to a post-Christian world

Sayre, Robert F. Solitude in society; a sociological study in French literature. Harvard Univ. Press 1978 237p ISBN 0-674-81761-3 LC 77-16265

Scannell, Vernon. Not without glory; poets of the Second World War. Woburn Press 1976 245p ISBN 0-7130-0094-5 LC 76-366174

Schakel, Peter J. (ed.) The longing for a form; essays on the fiction of C. S. Lewis. Kent State Univ. Press 1977 234p ISBN 0-87338-204-8 LC 77-2586

Schapiro, Meyer. Selected papers. 2v Braziller 1977-1978 ISBN v 1 0-8076-0853-X; v2 0-8076-0899-8 LC v 1 76-11842; v2 78-6831
V 1 Romanesque art v2 Modern art, 19th & 20th centuries

Scharfstein, Ben-Ami. Philosophy East/philosophy West. *See* Philosophy East/philosophy West

Schiff, Hilda, (ed.) Contemporary approaches to English studies. *See* Contemporary approaches to English studies

Schilpp, Paul Arthur. See entry under title: The Abdication of philosophy: philosophy and the public good

Schlegel, Alice Elizabeth (ed.) Sexual stratification; a cross-cultural view. Columbia Univ. Press 1977 371p ISBN 0-231-04214-0 LC 77-2742

Schlueter, June. Metafictional characters in modern drama. Columbia Univ. Press 1979 143p ISBN 0-231-04752-5 LC 79-4207

Schmeidler, Gertrude R. (ed.) Parapsychology: its relation to physics, biology, psychology, and psychiatry. *See* Parapsychology: its relation to physics, biology, psychology, and psychiatry

Schmidgall, Gary. Literature as opera. Oxford 1977 431p ISBN 0-19-502213-0 LC 76-57264
Partially analyzed

Schneider, Daniel John. Symbolism: the Manichean vision; a study in the art of James, Conrad, Woolf & Stevens. Univ. of Neb. Press 1975 235p ISBN 0-8032-0847-2 LC 74-12841

Schneider, Herbert Wallace. See entry under title: Philosophy and the civilizing arts
See also Ross, R. G. jt. ed.

Schoenberg, Bernard (ed.) Anticipatory grief. *See* Anticipatory grief

Scholars who teach. See Cahn, S. M. ed.

Scholes, Robert E. Fabulation and metafiction. Univ. of Ill. Press 1979 222p ISBN 0-252-00704-2 LC 78-10776

Schooling and society; studies in the history of education. Ed. by Lawrence Stone. Johns Hopkins Univ. Press 1976 263p ISBN 0-8018-1749-8 LC 76-15005
Published under the auspices of the Shelby Cullom Davis Center for Historical Studies, Princeton University

Schutte, Thomas F. (ed.) The uneasy coalition: design in corporate America. *See* The Uneasy coalition: design in corporate America

Schwartz, David C. and Schwartz, Sandra Kenyon (eds.) New directions in political socialization. Free Press 1975 340p. ISBN 0-02-928180-6. LC 74-2653
Partially analyzed

Schwartz, Robert George (ed.) Shakespeare and the popular tradition in the theater: studies in the social dimension of dramatic form and function. *See* Weimann, R. Shakespeare and the popular tradition in the theater: studies in the social dimension of dramatic form and function

Schwartz, Ronald. Spain's New Wave novelists, 1950-1974; studies in Spanish realism. Scarecrow 1976 417p ISBN 0-8108-0854-4 LC 75-44366

Schwartz, Sandra Kenyon. See Schwartz, D. C. jt. ed.

Schwartz, Theodore (ed.) Socialization as cultural communication; development of a theme in the work of Margaret Mead. Univ. of Calif. Press 1976 250p ISBN 0-520-03061-3 LC 75-17282

Schwarz, Alfred. From Büchner to Beckett; dramatic theory and the modes of tragic drama. Ohio Univ. Press 1978 360p ISBN 0-8214-0391-5 LC 77-92255

Science and ceremony; the institutional economics of C. E. Ayres. Ed. by William Breit and William Patton Culbertson, Jr. Foreword by John Kenneth Galbraith. Univ. of Tex. Press 1976 210p (The Dan Danciger Publication ser) ISBN 0-292-77523-7 LC 76-8238

Science and society: past, present, and future. Ed. by Nicholas Hans Steneck. Univ. of Mich. Press 1975 412p ISBN 0-472-08800-9 LC 73-90887
Partially analyzed

Science fiction at large. See Nicholls, P. ed.

Science in the Middle Ages. See Lindberg, D. C. ed.

Science policies of industrial nations; case studies of the United States, Soviet Union, United Kingdom, France, Japan, and Sweden. Ed. by T. Dixon Long and Christopher Wright. Praeger 1975 232p (Praeger Special studies in international politics and government) ISBN 0-275-05600-7 LC 74-13616

Science, sin, and scholarship. See Horowitz, I. L. ed.

Science, technology and society; a cross-disciplinary perspective. Ed. by Ina Spiegel-Rösing and Derek de Solla Price; under the aegis of the International Council for Science Policy Studies. Sage 1977 607p ISBN 0-8039-9858-9 LC 76-55928

The sciences, the humanities and the technological threat. See Niblett, W. R. ed.

Scientists confront Velikovsky. See Goldsmith, D. ed.

Scott, Nathan A. (ed.) The legacy of Reinhold Niebuhr; ed. by Nathan A. Scott, Jr. Univ. of Chicago Press 1975 xxiv, 124p ISBN 0-226-74297-0 LC 74-30714

Scott, Nathan A. Mirrors of man in existentialism [by] Nathan A. Scott, Jr. Collins + World 1978 248p ISBN 0-529-05641-0 LC 78-69971

The Scottish novel. See Hart, F. R.

Scottish society in the fifteenth century. See Brown, J. M. ed.

The sea change. See Hughes, H. S.

Seabury, Paul (ed.) Universities in the Western world. *See* Universities in the Western world

The search for authenticity in modern Japanese literature. See Yamanouchi, H.

The search for national integration in Africa. See Smock, D. R. and Bentsi-Enchill, K.

Sebeok, Thomas Albert. (ed.) Native languages of the Americas. Plenum Press 1976-1977 2v ISBN v 1 0-306-37157-X; v2 0-306-37158-8 LC 76-28216

Sebeok, Thomas Albert (ed.) A perfusion of signs. Ind. Univ. Press 1977 212p (Advances in semiotics) ISBN 0-253-34352-6 LC 76-29318

Companion volume to: Sight, sound, and sense, entered below

The essays included were delivered as lectures at the First North American Semiotics Colloquium, held at the University of South Florida in 1975

Sebeok, Thomas Albert (ed.) Sight, sound, and sense. Ind. Univ. Press 1978 289p (Advances in semiotics) ISBN 0-253-35230-4 LC 77-21520

Companion volume to: A perfusion of signs, entered above

The essays included are the outcome of a pilot program in semiotics in the humanities held at Indiana University during the 1975-76 academic year

Sectarianism. See Wallis, R. ed.

The secularization of the European mind in the nineteenth century. See Chadwick, O.

Seeing through everything. See Pritchard, W. H.

Seeing with a native eye; essays on native American religion; by Åke Hultkrantz [and others]. Ed. by Walter Holden Capps; assisted by Ernst F. Tonsing. Harper 1976 132p ISBN 0-06-061312 LC 76-9980

"A Harper Forum book"

Seelye, John. Prophetic waters; the river in early American life and literature. Oxford 1977 423p ISBN 0-19-502047-2 LC 75-46353

Segerstedt, Torgny Torgnysson (ed.) The frontiers of human knowledge. See The Frontiers of human knowledge

Segre, Cesare. Structures and time; narration, poetry, models. Tr. by John Meddemmen. Univ. of Chicago Press 1979 271p ISBN 0-226-74476-0 LC 79-68

Seidel, Anna K. (eds.) See Welch, H. jt. ed.

Seidel, Michael A. and Mendelson, Edward (eds.) Homer to Brecht; the European epic and dramatic traditions. Yale Univ. Press 1977 352p ISBN 0-300-02028-7 LC 76-25014

Selby, Henry A. See Basso, K. H. jt. ed.

Selden, Richard T. (ed.) Capitalism and freedom. See Capitalism and freedom

Selected essays. See Hough, G. G.

Selected essays. See Mandel'shtam, O. E.

Selected papers. See Schapiro, M.

Selected papers v 1-2. See Coomaraswamy, A. K.

Selected prose of T. S. Eliot. See Eliot, T. S.

The self. See Mischel, T. ed.

Sellekaerts, Willy (ed.) Econometrics and economic theory. See Econometrics and economic theory

Sellekaerts, Willy (ed.) Economic development and planning. See Economic development and planning

Sellner, Timothy F. See O'Flaherty, J. C. jt. ed.

Semiotics of art. See Matejka, L. and Titunik, I. R. eds.

The sense of society. See Milne, G.

A sense of the future. See Bronowski, J.

Sensibility and creation. See Cardinal, R. ed.

Shapin, Steven. See Barnes, B. jt. ed.

Shapiro, Karl Jay. The poetry wreck; selected essays: 1950-1970. Random House 1975 365p ISBN 0-394-49373-7 LC 74-22205

Sharp, Dennis (ed.) The rationalists; theory and design in the modern movement. Architectural Bk. Pub. Co. [1979 c1978] 232p ISBN 0-8038-0219-6
Sequel to: James Maude Richards' and Nikolaus Pevsner's The anti-rationalists, analyzed in 1970-1974 cumulation

Sharp, Lauriston. See entry under title: Change and persistence in Thai society

Sharp, Lauriston. See entry under title: Social organization and the applications of anthropology

Sharpless, Francis Parvin (ed.) Essays on poetry. See Mill, J. S. Essays on poetry

Sharratt, Peter (ed.) French Renaissance studies, 1540-70. See French Renaissance studies, 1540-70

Shatzkin, Roger. See Peary, G. jt. ed.

Shaw, Clifford Robe. See entry under title: Delinquency, crime, and society

Shaw, Donald Leslie. The generation of 1898 in Spain. Barnes & Noble 1975 246p ISBN 0-06-496208-3

Shea, William R. See Bonelli, M. L. R. jt. ed.

Sheard, Wendy Stedman (ed.) Collaboration in Italian Renaissance art. See Collaboration in Italian Renaissance art

Sheed, Wilfrid. The good word & other words. Dutton 1978 300p ISBN 0-525-11592-7 LC 78-15338
"A Henry Robbins book"

Shell, Marc. The economy of literature. Johns Hopkins Univ. Press 1978 176p ISBN 0-8018-2030-8 LC 77-21640

Sherbo, Arthur. English poetic diction from Chaucer to Wordsworth. Mich. State Univ. Press 1975 214p ISBN 0-8713-192-3 LC 75-2705

Sherrard, Philip. The wound of Greece; studies in neo-Hellenism. St Martins 1979 128p ISBN 0-312-8900-0 LC 78-27758

Sherry, Norman (ed.) Joseph Conrad: a commemoration. See Joseph Conrad: a commemoration

Sherwood Anderson: dimensions of his literary art. See Anderson, D. D. ed.

Shifting world. See Stineback, D. C.

Shils, Edward Albert. See entry under title: Culture and its creators

Shimahara, Nobuo Kenneth. Social forces and schooling. See Social forces and schooling

Short, James F. (ed.) Delinquency, crime and society. See Delinquency, crime, and society

The short stories of Ernest Hemingway: critical essays. See Benson, J. J. ed.

Short story theories. See May, C. E. ed.

Showalter, Elaine. A literature of their own; British women novelists from Brontë to Lessing. Princeton Univ. Press 1977 378p ISBN 0-691-06318-4 LC 76-3018

Shragin, Boris (ed.) Landmarks. See Landmarks

Shrovetide in old New Orleans. See Reed, I.

Shy, John Willard. A people numerous and armed; reflections on the military struggle for American independence. Oxford 1976 304p ISBN 0-19-502013-8 LC 75-32353

Sidorsky, David (ed.) Essays on human rights; contemporary issues and Jewish perspectives. in collaboration with Sidney Liskofsky and Jerome J. Shestack. [Contributors]: Salo W. Baron [and others]. Jewish Publications Soc. of Am. 1979 359p ISBN 0-8276-0107-7 LC 78-1170

This book had its origin in the "McGill International Colloquium on Judaism and Human Rights, sponsored by the Jacob Blaustein Institute for the Advancement of Human Rights of the American Jewish Committee, the Canadian Jewish Congress, the Consultative Council of Jewish Organizations, and the International Institute for Human Rights (Cassin Foundation)"

Sight, sound, and sense. See Sebeok, T. A. ed.

Silvert, Kalman H. The Americas in a changing world. *See* The Americas in a changing world

Simmons, Luiz R. See Said, A. A. jt. ed.

Simon, Bennett. Mind and madness in ancient Greece; the classical roots of modern psychiatry. Cornell Univ. Press 1978 336p ISBN 0-8014-0859-8 LC 77-90911

Simon, John Ivan. Singularities; essays on the theater/1964-1973. Random House 1975 239p ISBN 0-394-49804-6 LC 75-10260

Simonsuuri, Kirsti. Homer's original genius; eighteenth-century notions of the early Greek epic (1688-1798). Cambridge 1979 219p ISBN 0-521-22198-6 LC 78-56758

Simpson, Lewis Pearson (ed.) The possibilities of order: Cleanth Brooks and his work. La. State Univ. Press 1976 xxiv,254p ISBN 0-8071-0165-6 LC 75-18046
Partially analyzed

Simpson, Louis. A revolution in taste. Macmillan Pub. Co. 1978 198p ISBN 0-02-611320-1 LC 78-9370

Singh, Ram Sewak. Indian novel in English; a critical study. Humanities Press 1978 206p

Singularities. See Simon, J. I.

The **singularity** of Shakespeare, and other essays. See Muir, K.

Siracusa, Joseph M. and Barclay, Glen St John (eds.) The impact of the Cold war; reconsiderations. Kennikat 1977 208p (National University Publications. Series in American studies) ISBN 0-8046-9158-4 LC 76-18721

The **siren** & the seashell, and other essays on poets and poetry. See Paz, O.

Six contemporary British novelists. See Stade, G. ed.

Six dramatists in search of a language. See Kennedy, A.

Six French poets of our time. See Greene, R. W.

Six modern British novelists. See Stade, G. ed.

Sked, Alan (ed.) Crisis and controversy. *See* Crisis and controversy

Skidelsky, Robert Jacob Alexander (ed.) The end of the Keynesian era; essays on the disintegration of the Keynesian political economy. Contributors: Robert Skidelsky [and others]. Holmes & Meier Pubs. 1977 114p ISBN 0-8419-0329-8 LC 77-8878

Skilton, David. The English novel; Defoe to the Victorians. Barnes & Noble 1977 200p (Comparative literature ser.) ISBN 0-06-496250-4 LC 76-57108

Skinner, Andrew S. and Wilson, Thomas (eds.) Essays on Adam Smith. Oxford [1976] c1975 647p (The Glasgow edition of the works and correspondence of Adam Smith) ISBN 0-19-828191-9

Skinner, Elliott Percival. See Shack, W. A. jt. ed.

Skinner, George William (ed.) Change and persistence in Thai society. *See* Change and persistence in Thai society

Skyscraper primitives. See Tashjian, D. L.

Slavery and race relations in Latin America. See Toplin, R. B. ed.

Slavery, colonialism, and racism. See Mintz, S. A. ed.

Sloan, Thomas O. and Waddington, Raymond Bruce (eds.) The rhetoric of Renaissance poetry; from Wyatt to Milton. Univ. of Calif. Press 1974 247p. ISBN 0-520-02501-6. LC 73-80824

Slonim, Marc L'vovich. Soviet Russian literature; writers and problems, 1917-1977. 2d rev. ed. Oxford 1977 437p ISBN 0-19-502151-7 LC 76-426661
Previous edition analyzed in 1965-1969 cumulation. This edition analyzed for new material only

Slote, Bernice (ed.) The art of Willa Cather. *See* The Art of Willa Cather

Small comforts for hard times; humanists on public policy. Michael Mooney and Florian Stuber, editors; introduced by Florian Stuber; with a foreword by James Gutmann. Columbia Univ. Press 1977 402p ISBN 0-231-04042-3 LC 77-5851

A small personal voice. See Lessing, D. M.

Smalley, William Allen (ed.) On language, culture, and religion: in honor of Eugene A. Nida. *See* On language, culture, and religion

Smith, Anne (ed.) The art of Emily Brontë. Barnes & Noble 1976 246p (Barnes & Noble Critical studies) ISBN 0-06-496376-4 LC 76-19859

Smith, Anne (ed.) Lawrence and women. Barnes & Noble 1978 217p (Barnes & Noble Critical studies) ISBN 0-06-496377-2 LC 78-110886

Smith, Anne (ed.) The novels of Thomas Hardy. Barnes & Noble 1979 196p ISBN 0-06-496379-9 LC 79-111738

Smith, Anthony Douglas (ed.) Nationalist movements. St Martins [1977 c1976] 185p ISBN 0-312-56012-5 LC 77-75680

Smith, Bernard (ed.) Concerning contemporary art. *See* Concerning contemporary art

Smith, Bruce L. R. (ed.) The new political economy: the public use of the private sector. Wiley 1975 344p ISBN 0-470-80377-0 LC 74-7430
"A Halstead Press book"

Smith, Denzell Stewart. See Logan, T. P. jt. ed.

Smith, Elton Edward. The angry young men of the thirties. With a preface by Harry T. Moore. Southern Ill. Univ. Press 1975 172p (Crosscurrents/Modern critiques). ISBN 0-8093-0698-0. LC 74-20731

Smith, Sir Grafton Elliot. See entry under title: Grafton Elliot Smith

Smith, Henry Nash. Democracy and the novel; popular resistance to classic American writers. Oxford 1978 204p ISBN 0-19-502397-8 LC 78-1290

Smith, Joseph H. (ed.) Psychiatry and the humanities v 1. *See* Psychiatry and the humanities, v 1

Smith, Joseph H. (ed.) Psychoanalysis and language. *See* Psychoanalysis and language

Smith, Joseph H. (ed.) Thought, consciousness, and reality. *See* Thought, consciousness, and reality

Smith, Paul (ed.) The historian and film. Cambridge 1976 208p ISBN 0-521-20992-7 LC 75-19577

Smith, Robert Jerome (ed.) Social organization and the applications of anthropology. *See* Social organization and the applications of anthropology

Sociobiology and human nature. Michael S. Gregory, Anita Silvers & Diane Sutch, editors. Jossey-Bass 1978 326p (The Jossey-Bass Social and behavioral science ser) ISBN 0-87589-384-8 LC 78-62559

Sociology and the twilight of man. See Lemert, C. C.

Sociology of science. See Gaston, J. ed.

Solitude in society. See Sayre, R. F.

Solomon & Sheba. See Pritchard, J. B. ed.

Solzhenitsyn, Alexander. See Solzhenifŝyn, Aleksandr Isaevich

Solzhenifŝyn, Aleksandr Isaevich. From under the rubble. *See* From under the rubble

Soroos, Marvin S. See Orr, D. W. jt. ed.

Soundings. See Leary, L. G.

South Africa: economic growth and political change. **See** Leftwich, A. ed.

The **South** African novel in English. See Parker, K. ed.

The **South** and Faulkner's Yoknapatawpha; the actual and the apocryphal; ed. by Evans Harrington and Ann J. Abadie. Univ. Press of Miss. 1977 212p ISBN 0-87805-035-3 LC 77-8741
Papers presented at the 1976 Faulkner and Yoknapatawpha Conference at the University of Mississippi
Partially analyzed
A collection of essays from the 1977 conference; entitled The Maker and the myth: Faulkner and Yoknapatawpha, as well as another collection from the 1978 conference, entitled Faulkner, modernism and film: Faulkner and Yoknapatawpha, are also indexed in this cumulation

Southeast Asian history and historiography; essays presented to D G. E. Hall. Ed. by C. D. Cowan and O. W. Wolters; with a foreword by John M. Echols. Cornell Univ. Press 1976 436p ISBN 0-8014-0841-5 LC 75-18726

Southeastern Indians since the removal era. See Williams, W. L. ed.

Southern Africa in crisis. See Carter, G. M. and O'Meara, P. eds.

Southern Africa: the continuing crisis. See Carter, G. M. and O'Meara, P. eds.

The **Southern** experience in the American Revolution. Ed. by Jeffrey J. Crow and Larry E. Tise. Univ. of N.C. Press 1978 310p ISBN 0-8078-1313-3 LC 77-21519
"Based on lectures given at the University of North Carolina at Chapel Hill, Duke University, and North Carolina State University, in the fall of 1975, and sponsored by the North Carolina Bicentennial Committee and others."

The **Southern** mystique. See Lewis, W. D. and Griessman, B. E. eds.

The **sovereign** ghost. See Donoghue, D.

Soviet foreign policy. See Jahn, E. ed.

Soviet Russian literature. See Slonim, M. L.

Soviet Russian literature since Stalin. See Brown, D. B.

The **Soviet** threat. See Kirk, G. L. and Wessell, N. H. eds.

The **Soviet** Union since the fall of Khrushchev. See Brown, A. H. and Kaser, M. eds.

Spacks, Patricia Ann (Meyer). Imagining a self; autobiography and novel in eighteenth-century England. Harvard Univ. Press 1976 342p ISBN 0-674-44005-6 LC 76-22460

Spain in crisis. See Preston, P ed.

Spain's New Wave novelists, 1950-1974. See Schwartz, R.

Staley, Thomas F. and Benstock, Bernard (eds.) Approaches to Joyce's Portrait; ten essays. Univ. of Pittsburgh Press 1977 241p ISBN 0-8229-3331-4 LC 76-6670

Stalinism: essays in historical interpretation. Ed. by Robert C. Tucker; with contributions by Włodzimierz Brus [and others]. Norton 1977 xx, 332p ISBN 0-393-05608-2 LC 76-56110

Stanage, Sherman Miller (ed.) Reason and violence; philosophical investigations. Contributors: Robert Audi [and others]. Rowman & Littlefield 1975 [c1974] 253p. ISBN 0-87471-603-9. LC 72-85273

Stanford Journal of International Studies. China's changing role in the world economy. *See* China's changing role in the world economy

Stanford legal essays. Ed. by John Henry Merryman. Printed and distributed by Stanford Univ. Press 1975 467p ISBN 0-8047-0884-3 LC 75-182

Stannard, David E. (ed.) Death in America. *See* Death in America

State and economy in contemporary capitalism. See Crouch, C. ed.

State and society in contemporary Europe. See Hayward, J. E. S. and Berki, R. N. eds.

Stave, Bruce M. (ed.) Socialism and the cities; with an appendix "On municipal socialism, 1903" from the correspondence of the late Walter Lippmann. Kennikat 1975 212p (National University Publications. Interdisciplinary urban ser) ISBN 0-8046-9133-9 LC 75-34435

Steadman, John M. Nature into myth; medieval and Renaissance moral symbols. Duquesne Univ. Press 1979 308p ISBN 0-391-00752-1 LC 77-25397

Steffen, Jerome O. See Miller, D. H. jt. ed.

Steiner, George. On difficulty and other essays. Oxford 1978 209p ISBN 0-19-212208-8 LC 78-40280

Steinfels, Peter (ed.) Death inside out. *See* Death inside out

Steneck, Nicholas Hans (ed.) Science and society: past, present, and future. *See* Science and society: past, present, and future

Stepto, Robert B. See Fisher, D. jt. ed.

Steward, Jane C. (ed.) Evolution and ecology. *See* Steward, J. H. Evolution and ecology

Steward, Julian Haynes. Evolution and ecology; essays on social transformation. Ed. by Jane C. Steward and Robert F. Murphy. Univ. of Ill. Press 1977 406p ISBN 0-252-00612-7 LC 76-46341

Stilling, Roger. Love and death in Renaissance tragedy. La. State Univ. Press 1976 303p ISBN 0-8071-0188-5 LC 74-27193

Stineback, David C. Shifting world; social change and nostalgia in the American novel. Bucknell Univ. Press 1976 192p ISBN 0-8387-1686-5 LC 74-31510

Stivers, Richard. See Davis, F. J. jt. ed.

Stoever, William Kenneth Bristow. 'A faire and easie way to heaven'; covenant theology and antinomianism in early Massachusetts. Wesleyan Univ. Press 1978 251p ISBN 0-8195-5024-8 LC 77-14851

The Stoic strain in American literature; essays in honour of Marston LaFrance. Ed. by Duane J. MacMillan. Univ. of Toronto Press 1979 224p ISBN 0-8020-5441-2 LC 79-523 Partially analyzed

The Stoics. See Rist, J. M. ed.

Stokstad, Marilyn. See Enggass, R. C. jt. ed.

Stone, Lawrence Joseph (ed.) Schooling and society. *See* Schooling and society

Stone, Lawrence Joseph (ed.) The University in society. *See* The University in society

Storch de Gracia, Juan José Linz. See Linz Storch de Gracia, Juan José

The story-shaped world. See Wicker, B.

Strangers in African societies. See Shack, W. A. and Skinner, E. P. eds.

Strategies for human settlements: habitat and environment. Ed. by Gwen Bell. Univ. Press of Hawaii 1976 xxiii,172p ISBN 0-8248-0414-7 LC 76-5416
"An East-West Center Book from the East-West Technology and Development Institute"

Strayer, Joseph Reese. See entry under title: Order and innovation in the Middle Ages

Street, David. Handbook of contemporary urban life. *See* Handbook of contemporary urban life

Strelka, Joseph P.; Bell, Robert F. and Dobson, Eugene (eds.) Protest—form—tradition; essays on German exile literature. Univ. of Ala. Press 1979 144p ISBN 0-8173-8008-6 LC 78-18190
"Based on a symposium held at the University of Alabama in March, 1975"

Strong, Donald Emrys, and Brown, David (eds.) Roman crafts. N.Y. Univ. Press 1976 256p ISBN 0-8147-7801-1 LC 76-28589

Structure and transformation. See Riegel, K. F. and Rosenwald, G. C. eds.

Structure, consciousness, and history. See Brown, R. H. and Lyman, S. M. eds.

The structure of scientific theories. See Suppe, F. R. ed.

The structure of verse. See Gross, H. S. ed.

Structure, sign, and function. See Mukařovský, J.

Structures and time. See Segre, C.

Stuard, Susan Mosher (ed.) Women in medieval society; ed. with an introduction. [Contributors]: Brenda H. Bolton [and others]. Univ. of Pa. Press 1976 219p (The Middle Ages) ISBN 0-8122-7708-2 LC 75-41617

Studies in bibliography. See Virginia. University. Bibliographical Society

Studies in biography; ed. by Daniel Aaron. Harvard Univ. Press 1978 200p (Harvard English studies 8) ISBN 0-674-84651-6 LC 77-18033

Studies in Chinese literary genres. See Birch, C. ed.

Studies in classical art and archaeology; a tribute to Peter Heinrich von Blanckenhagen. Ed. by Günter Kopcke and Mary B. Moore. Augustin 1979 344p ISBN 0-0071-3287 LC 79-50203
Partially analyzed

Studies in eighteenth-century culture v4-8. Published for the American Society for Eighteenth-Century Studies by Univ. of Wis. Press 1975-1978 5v ISBN v4 0-299-06700-9; v5 0-299-06930-3; v6 0-299-07130-8; v7 0-299-07400-5; v8 0-299-07740-3 LC 74-25572
Volume 4 edited by Harold E. Pagliaro; volumes 5 and 6 by Ronald C. Rosbottom; volumes 7 and 8 by Roseann Runte
Volumes 5,6,7, and 8 partially analyzed. Volume 8 To the memory of Roy McKeen Wiles, 1903-1974

Studies in history of biology, v 1-3. William Coleman and Camille Limoges, editors. Johns Hopkins Univ. Press 1977-1979 3v ISBN v 1 0-8018-1862-1; v2 0-8018-2034-0; v3 0-8010-2215-7 LC 76-47139
V3 Essays in honor of Ernst Mayr

Studies in Italian American social history; essays in honor of Leonard Covello. Ed. by Francesco Cordasco. Rowman & Littlefield 1975 264p ISBN 0-87471-705-1 LC 75-14462

Studies in Italian Renaissance architecture. See Lotz, W.

Studies in medieval philosophy, science, and logic. See Moody, E. A.

Studies in memory of David Talbot Rice. Giles Robertson and George Henderson, editors. Edinburgh Univ. Press [1976 c1975]· 334p ISBN 0-85224-253-0
Partially analyzed

Studies in Nietzsche and the classical tradition. See O'Flaherty, J. C.; Sellner, T. F. and Helm, R. M. eds.

Studies in perception; interrelations in the history of philosophy and science. Ed. by Peter K. Machamer and Robert G. Turnbull. Ohio State Univ. Press 1978 567p ISBN 0-8142-0244-6 LC 77-10857

Studies in social anthropology; essays in memory of E. E. Evans-Pritchard by his former Oxford colleagues. Ed. by J. H. M. Beattie and R. G. Lienhardt. Oxford 1975 394p ISBN 0-19-823183-0

Studies in the continental background of Renaissance English literature; essays presented to John L. Lievsay. Ed. by Dale B. J. Randall and George Walton Williams. Duke Univ. Press 1977 235p ISBN 0-8223-0388-4 LC 77-78523

Studies in the Greek historians. See Yale classical studies v24

Studies in the Italian baroque. See Wittkower, R.

Studies in the philosophy of biology. See Ayala, F. J. and Dobzhansky, T. G. eds.

Studies in the recent Australian novel. See Hamilton, K. G. ed.

Studies in twentieth century Russian literature. See Barnes, C. J. ed.

The study of American culture. See Luedtke, L. S. ed.

Style and structure in literature. See Fowler, R. ed.

Style in modern British fiction. See Russell, J. D.

The sublime pleasures of tragedy. See Albrecht, W. P.

The subterfuge of art. See Ragussis, M.

Sugerman, Shirley Greene (ed.) Evolution of consciousness. See Evolution of consciousness

Suggs, George Graham (ed.) Perspectives on the American Revolution; a Bicentennial contribution. Ed. by George G. Suggs, Jr. Published for Southeast Missouri State University [by] Southern Ill. Univ. Press 1977 141p ISBN 0-8093-0827-4 LC 77-5737

Sullivan, Jack. Elegant nightmares; the English ghost story from Le Fanu to Blackwod. Ohio Univ. Press 1978 155p ISBN 0-8214-0374-5 LC 77-92258

Summers, Robert S. (ed.) Essays in legal philosophy; selected and ed. by Robert S. Summers. Univ. of Calif. Press [1976 c1968] 307p (California Lib. reprint ser) ISBN 0-520-03213-6 LC 68-31075
First published 1968 by Blackwell

Sundell, Roger H. See Patrick, J. M. jt. ed.

Super, Robert Henry (ed.) The last word. See Arnold, M. The last word

Super realism. See Battcock, G. ed.

Superculture. See Bigsby, C. W. E. ed.

T

Tachau, Frank (ed.) Political elites and political development in the Middle East. *See* Political elites and political development in the Middle East

Tagliacozzo, Giorgio (ed.) Giambattista Vico's science of humanity. *See* Giambattista Vico's science of humanity

Taiwo, Oladele. Culture and the Nigerian novel. St Martins 1976 235p LC 76-11278

Takayanagi, Shunichi (ed.) Postwar trends in Japan. *See* Postwar trends in Japan

Tanner, Tony. The reign of wonder; naivety and reality in American literature. Cambridge 1965 388p ISBN 0-521-06599-2 LC 65-15304

Tarr, Rodger LeRoy. See Fielding, K. J. jt. ed.

Tart, Charles T. (ed.) Transpersonal psychologies. Harper 1975 502p ISBN 0-06-067823-2 LC 73-18672

Tashjian, Dickran Levon. Skyscraper primitives; Dada and the American avant-garde, 1910-1925. Wesleyan Univ. Press 1975 283p ISBN 0-8195-4081-1 LC 74-21925

Tatar, Maria Magdalene. Spellbound; studies on mesmerism and literature. Princeton Univ. Press 1978 293p ISBN 0-691-06377-X LC 78-51199

Tate, Allen. Memoirs and opinions, 1926-1974. Swallow Press 1975 225p ISBN 0-8040-0662-8 LC 75-10757

Tatum, Edward Lawrie. See entry under title: The Future of science

Taylor, Alan John Percival. See entry under title: Crisis and controversy

Taylor, Anya. Magic and English romanticism. Univ. of Ga. Press 1979 278p ISBN 0-8203-0453-0 LC 78-5590

Taylor, Brian K. See Alcock, A. E. jt. ed.

Taylor, John Russell. Directors and directions; cinema for the seventies. Hill & Wang 1975 327p ISBN 0-8090-3901-X LC 75-2129

Taylor, Richard, 1946- Film propaganda; Soviet Russia and Nazi Germany. Barnes & Noble 1979 265p ISBN 0-06-496778-6 LC 79-318345

Taylor, Telford. Perspectives on justice. *See* Perspectives on justice

Teachings from the American earth. See Tedlock, D. E. and Tedlock, B. eds.

Technology and the frontiers of knowledge. Foreword: Daniel J. Boorstin. [Contributors; Saul Bellow [and others]. Doubleday 1975 134p (The Frank Nelson Doubleday Lectures—1972-73). ISBN 0-385-09942-8. LC 73-14077

Tedlock, Barbara. See Tedlock, D. E. jt. ed.

Tedlock, Dennis Ernest, and Tedlock, Barbara (eds.) Teachings from the American earth; Indian religion and philosophy. Liveright 1975 279p ISBN 0-87140-599-7 LC 74-34146

Television as a cultural force. Douglass Cater, editor; Richard Adler, project editor. Published with the Aspen Institute Program on Communications and Society. Praeger 1976 189p (Praeger Special studies in U.S. economic social and political issues) ISBN 0-275-23180-1 LC 76-10714

Television as a social force: new approaches to TV criticism. Douglass Cater, editor; Richard Adler, project editor. Sponsored by the Aspen Institute on Communications and Society. Praeger 1975 171p (Praeger Special studies in U.S. economic, social, and political issues) ISBN 0-275-01190-9 LC 75-6835

Thomas Hobbes in his time. See Ross, R. G.; Schneider, H. W. and Waldman, T. eds.

Thompson, Craig Reingwalt. See entry under title: Essays on the works of Erasmus

Thompson, Denys. The uses of poetry. Cambridge 1978 238p ISBN 0-521-21804-7 LC 77-82517

Thompson, Kenneth Winfred (ed.) [Truth and tragedy]: a tribute to Hans Morgenthau. *See* [Truth and tragedy]: a tribute to Hans Morgenthau

Thompson, Leonard Monteath, and Butler, Jeffrey (eds.) Change in contemporary South Africa. Univ. of Calif. Press 1975 447p (Perspectives on Southern Africa 17) ISBN 0-520-02839-2 LC 74-82851

Thompson, Roger. See Allen, H. C. jt. ed.

Thomson, Boris. Lot's wife and the Venus of Milo; conflicting attitudes to the cultural heritage in modern Russia. Cambridge 1978 171p ISBN 0-521-21677-X LC 77-77703

The thorny paradise. See Blishen, E. ed.

Thought, consciousness, and reality. Editor: Joseph H. Smith. Published under the auspices of the Forum on Psychiatry and the Humanities. The Washington School of Psychiatry. Yale Univ. Press 1977 316p (Psychiatry and the humanities v2) ISBN 0-300-02138-0 LC 76-640132

Thrupp, Sylvia Lettice. Society and history; essays. Ed. by Raymond Grew and Nicholas H. Steneck. Univ. of Mich. Press 1977 363p ISBN O-472-08880-7 LC 75-31056

Thurley, Geoffrey. The American moment; American poetry in the mid-century. St Martins [1978 c1977] 249p ISBN 0-312-02884-9 LC 77-91071

Thurley, Geoffrey. The ironic harvest: English poetry in the twentieth century. St Martins 1974 215p. LC 74-82269

Tichi, Cecelia. New World, new earth; environmental reform in American literature from the Puritans through Whitman. Yale Univ. Press 1979 290p ISBN 0-300-02287-5 LC 78-15809

The tides of change. See Borgese, E. M. and Krieger, D. eds.

Tillotson, Geoffrey. A view of Victorian literature. Oxford 1978 396p ISBN 0-19-812044-3 LC 77-30178

Tilly, Charles (ed.) The formation of national states in Western Europe. Contributors: Gabriel Ardant [and others]. Princeton Univ. Press 1975 711p (Studies in political development 8) ISBN 0-691-05219-0 LC 74-20941

Tilton, John Wightman. Cosmic satire in the contemporary novel. Bucknell Univ. Press 1977 108p ISBN 0-8387-1378-5 LC 75-18240

Time and the novel. See Tobin, P. D.

A Time to hear and answer: essays for the Bicentennial season. [Contributors]: Robert Penn Warren [and others]. Preface by Taylor Littleton. Published for Auburn University by the Univ. of Ala. Press 1977 218p (The Franklin lectures in the sciences & humanities; 4th ser) ISBN 0-8173-6644-X LC 75-31774

Time was away; the world of Louis MacNeice. Ed. by Terence Brown & Alec Reid. Dolmen [distributed by Humanities Press] 1974 151p ISBN 0-85105-237-1
Partially analyzed

Tinbergen, Jan. See entry under title: Econometrics and economic theory

Tinbergen, Jan. See entry under title: Economic development and planning

Tindall, William York. See entry under title: Yeats, Joyce, and Beckett

The **Tricentennial** people; human applications of the new genetics. Iowa State Univ. Press 1978 102p ISBN 0-8138-1650-5 LC 78-8420

Trilling, Diana (ed.) The last decade. *See* Trilling, L. The last decade

Trilling, Diana. We must march my darlings; a critical decade. Harcourt 1977 315p ISBN 0-15-195599-9 LC 76-54566
Partially analyzed

Trilling, Lionel. A gathering of fugitives. Harcourt [1978 c1956] 179p (The works of Lionel Trilling; Uniform edition) ISBN 0-15-134582-1 LC 77-17318
Originally published 1956 in paper by Beacon Press. Not previously analyzed in Essay Index

Trilling, Lionel. The last decade; essays and reviews, 1965-75. Ed. by Diana Trilling. Harcourt 1979 241p (The works of Lionel Trilling. Uniform edition) ISBN 0-15-148421-X LC 79-1849

Trilling, Lionel. Prefaces to The experience of literature. Harcourt 1979 302p (The works of Lionel Trilling. Uniform edition) ISBN 0-15-173915-3 LC 79-1850

Trilling, Lionel. *See also* entry under title Art, politcs, and will

Tropics of discourse. See White, H. V.

Troubadours and love. See Topsfield, L. T.

Trowbridge, Frederick Hoyt. From Dryden to Jane Austen; essays on English critics and writers, 1660-1818. Univ. of N. Mex. Press 1977 300p ISBN 0-8263-0430-3 LC 76-21490

Trowbridge, Hoyt. See Trowbridge, Frederick Hoyt

Truffaut, François. The films in my life; tr. by Leonard Mayhew. Simon & Schuster 1978 358p ISBN 0-671-22919-2 LC 77-29036
Partially analyzed

"**Trust** to good verses": Herrick tercentenary essays. See Rollin, R. B. and Patrick, J. M. eds.

Truth and meaning. See Evans, G. L. and McDowell, J. H. eds.

[**Truth** and tragedy]: a tribute to Hans Morgenthau; with an intellectual autobiography by Hans J. Morgenthau. Ed. by Kenneth Thompson and Robert J. Myers; with the assistance of Robert Osgood and Tang Tsou. New Republic 1977 336p ISBN 0-915220-21-0 LC 76-56206

Tucker, Robert C. (ed.) Stalinism. *See* Stalinism

The **Tudor** play of mind. See Altman, J. B.

Tufte, Virginia, and Myerhoff, Barbara G. (eds.) Changing images of the family. Yale Univ. Press 1979 403p ISBN 0-300-02361-8 LC 79-537

Tulane Studies in English, v21-23. Tulane Univ. 1975-1978 3v
Volume 23, subtitled Essays in American literature in memory of Richard P. Adams, edited by Donald Pizer

Turnell, Martin. The rise of the French novel; Marivaux [and others]. New Directions 1978 309p ISBN 0-8112-0688-2 LC 77-26792
"A New Directions book"

Turning points. See Knight, D. F. ed.

The **twenties.** See French, W. G. ed.

Twentieth-century Russian literary criticism. See Erlich, V. ed.

Twitchett, Kenneth Joseph (ed.) Europe and the world; the external relations of the Common Market. Published for the David Davies Memorial Institute of International Studies by St Martins 1976 210p LC 75-45817

Unity and diversity; essays in the history, literature, and religion of the ancient Near East. Ed. by Hans Goedicke and J. J. M. Roberts. Johns Hopkins Univ. Press 1975 225p (The Johns Hopkins Near Eastern studies) ISBN 0-8018-1638-6 LC 74-24376

Universities in the urban crisis. See Murphy, T. P. ed.

Universities in the Western world; ed. by Paul Seabury. Published in cooperation with the International Council on the Future of the University. Free Press 1975 303p ISBN 0-02-928340-X LC 75-5235

The **university** and the state. See Hook, S.; Kurtz, P. W. and Todorovich, M. eds.

The **University** in society. Ed. by Lawrence Stone. Princeton Univ. Press 1974 2v (642p). ISBN 0-691-05213-1; 0-691-05214-X. LC 72-14033
Written under the auspices of the Shelby Cullom Davis Center for Historical Studies, Princeton University
Contents: v 1 Oxford and Cambridge from the 14th to the early 19th century; [contributors]: Lawrence Stone [and others]; v2 Europe, Scotland, and the United States from the 16th to the 20th century; [contributors]: Richard L. Kagan [and others]

Unofficial diplomats. Maureen R. Berman and Joseph E. Johnson, editors. Columbia Univ. Press 1977 268p ISBN 0-231-04396-1 LC 77-9376
Prepared and published with the support of the Academy for Educational Development and the Charles F. Kettering Foundation
Partially analyzed

Uppsala. Universitet. The frontiers of human knowledge. *See* The Frontiers of human knowledge

Uprooted Americans; essays to honor Oscar Handlin; ed. by Richard L. Bushman [and others]. Little 1979 366p ISBN 0-316-11810-9 LC 79-11095

Ure, Peter. Elizabethan and Jacobean drama; critical essays. Ed. by J. C. Maxwell. Barnes & Noble 1974 258p (English texts and studies) ISBN 0-06-497113-9 LC 74-6718

Usdin, Gene Leonard (ed.) Aging: the process and the people. *See* Aging: the process and the people

Usdin, Gene L. (ed.) Overview of the psychotherapies. *See* Overview of the psychotherapies

The **Uses** of controversy in sociology. Ed. by Lewis A. Coser and Otto N. Larsen. Free Press 1976 398p ISBN 0-02-906830-4 LC 76-7177
"A publication of the American Sociological Association"

The **uses** of division. See Bayley, J.

The **uses** of poetry. See Thompson, D.

V

Valdés, Mario J. and Miller, Owen J. (eds.) Interpretation of narrative. Univ. of Toronto Press 1978 202p ISBN 0-8020-5443-9 LC 78-23683
"This volume contains an edited selection of the papers read at the International Colloquium on Interpretation of Narrative held at the University of Toronto, 24 to 27 March 1976 by the Graduate Programme in Comparative Literature."

Van Tassel, David D. See Spicker, S. F. jt. ed.

Varieties of interpretation. See Mazzeo, J. A.

Varieties of psychohistory. See Kren, G. M. and Rappoport, L. H. eds.

Variety of attempt. See Doubleday, N. F.

Virtues and vices, and other essays in moral philosophy. See Foot, P.

The **visionary** eye. See Bronowski, J.

Viva Vivas! Essays in honor of Eliseo Vivas on the occasion of his seventy-fifth birthday, July 13, 1976. Henry Regnery, editor. Liberty Press 1976 379p ISBN 0-913966-08-8 LC 76-9432

Vivas, Eliseo. See entry under title: Viva Vivas!

Voegelin, Eric. From Enlightenment to revolution. Ed. by John H. Hallowell. Duke Univ. Press 1975 302p. ISBN 0-8223-0326-4. LC 74-81864

Vogely, William A. See Kalter, R. J. jt. ed.

Voices for the future: essays on major science fiction writers. See Clareson, T. D. ed.

Voices from the Southwest; a gathering in honor of Lawrence Clark Powell. Gathered by Donald C. Dickinson, W. David Laird [and] Margaret F. Maxwell. Northland Press 1976 159p ISBN 0-87358-157-1 LC 76-26769
Partially analyzed

Vonnegut in America. See Klinkowitz, J. and Lawler, D. L. eds.

Voss, John. See Oleson, A. jt. ed.

W

Waddington, Raymond B. See Sloan, T. O. jt. ed.

Wagner, Linda Welshimer (ed.) Ernest Hemingway; five decades of criticism. Mich. State Univ. Press 1974 328p. ISBN 0-87013-182-6. LC 73-91870
Partially analyzed

Wagschal, Peter H. (ed.) Learning tomorrows; commentaries on the future of education. Praeger 1979 164p ISBN 0-03-046716-0 LC 78-19763

Wain, John. Professing poetry. Viking 1978 275p ISBN 0-670-38015-6 LC 77-25952
Partially analyzed

The **waiting** years. See Jackson, B.

Wakeman, Frederic E. (ed.) Conflict and control in late imperial China. *See* Conflict and control in late imperial China

Walcutt, Charles Child (ed.) Seven novelists in the American naturalist tradition; an introduction. Univ. of Minn. Press 1974 331p (The Minn. Lib. on American writers). ISBN 0-8166-0730-3. LC 74-14209

Walden, Russell (ed.) The open hand; essays on Le Corbusier. MIT Press 1977 484p ISBN 0-262-23074-7 LC 76-40046

Waldman, Theodore. See Ross, R. G. jt. ed.

Waldmeir, Joseph J. (ed.) Essays in honor of Russel B. Nye. *See* Essays in honor of Russel B. Nye

Walker, Ronald G. Infernal paradise; Mexico and the modern English novel. Univ. of Calif. Press 1978 391p ISBN 0-520-03197-0 LC 75-46046

Wallace, Ronald H. The last laugh; form and affirmation in the contemporary American comic novel. Univ. of Mo. Press 1979 159p ISBN 0-8262-0274-8 LC 78-21376

Wallach, Luitpold. Diplomatic studies in Latin and Greek documents from the Carolingian age. Cornell Univ. Press 1977 396p ISBN 0-8014-1019-3 LC 76-28027

Walling, William. See Kroeber, K. jt. ed.

Wallis, Roy (ed.) Sectarianism; analyses of religious and non-religious sects. Wiley 1975 212p (Contemporary issues ser) ISBN 0-470-91910-8 LC 75-9715
"A Halsted Press book"

Walton, Craig (ed.) Philosophy and the civilizing arts. *See* Philosophy and the civilizing arts

Walton, John, and Masotti, Louis H. (eds.) The city in comparative perspective; cross-national research and new directions in theory. Sage Publications [distributed by Halsted Press, a division of John Wiley & Sons, Inc] 1976 317p ISBN 0-470-15217-6 LC 76-7040

War and economic development; essays in memory of David Joslin. Ed. by J. M. Winter. Cambridge 1975 297p ISBN 0-521-20535-2 LC 74-82219

The **War** generation; veterans of the First World War. Stephen R. Ward, Editor. [Contributors]: James M. Diehl [and others] Kennikat 1975 192p (National University Publications ser. in American studies) ISBN 0-8046-9101-0 LC 75-15596

War in the next decade. See Beaumont, R. A. and Edmonds, M. eds.

War, literature, and politics in the late Middle Ages. Ed. by C. T. Allmand. Barnes & Noble 1976 202p ISBN 0-06-490159-9 LC 75-40530

War, technology and society in the Middle East; ed. by Vernon J. Parry and M. E. Yapp. Oxford 1975 448p ISBN 0-19-713581-1
Partially analyzed

Ward, Stephen R. (ed.) The War generation. *See* The War generation

Wardhaugh, Ronald, and Brown, H. Douglas (eds.) A survey of applied linguistics. Univ. of Mich. Press 1976 308p ISBN 0-472-08958-7 LC 75-31053

Warner, Sam Bass (ed.) The American experiment; perspectives on 200 years; ed. by Sam Bass Warner, Jr. Houghton 1976 ISBN 0-395-24008-5

Warnock, Mary. Imagination. Univ. of Calif. Press 1976 213p ISBN 0-520-03115-6 LC 75-22663

Warren, Robert Penn. A time to hear and answer: essays for the Bicentennial season. *See* A Time to hear and answer: essays for the Bicentennial season

Wartofsky, Marx W. See Gould, C. C. jt. ed.

Wasserman, Earl Reeves. See entry under title: ELH essays for Earl R. Wasserman

Wasserman, Elga Ruth (ed.) Women in academia. *See* Women in academia

The **Waste** land in different voices; the revised versions of lectures given at the University of York in the fiftieth year of The waste land, by A. C. Charity [and others]. Ed. by A. D. Moody. St Martins [1975 c1974] 237p LC 74-19953

Watkin, David. Morality and architecture; the devolpment of a theme in architectural history and theory from the Gothic Revival to the modern movement. Oxford [1978 c1977] 126p ISBN 0-19-817350-4

Watkins, Evan. The critical act; criticism and community. Yale Univ. Press 1978 251p ISBN 0-300-02221-2 LC 78-3426

Watkins, Floyd C. In time and place; some origins of American fiction. Univ. of Ga. Press 1977 250p ISBN 0-8203-0415-8 LC 76-12682

Watson, Charles Sullivan. Antebellum Charleston dramatists. Univ. of Ala. Press 1976 183p ISBN 0-8173-6001-8 LC 75-30635

Watson, George. Politics and literature in modern Britain. Rowman & Littlefield 1977 190p ISBN 0-87471-987-9 LC 77-4664

Watteau's shepherds: the detective novel in Britain, 1914-1940. See Panek, L. L.

Ways of health. See Sobel, D. S. ed.

The ways of paradox, and other essays. See Quine, W. V.

We must march my darlings. See Trilling, D.

Wealth and power in Tudor England; essays presented to S. T. Bindoff. Ed. by E. W. Ives; R. J. Knecht [and] J. J. Scarisbrick. Athlone Press distributed by Humanities Press 1978 248p ISBN 0-485-11176-4

Webb, Eugene. The dark dove; the sacred and secular in modern literature. Univ. of Wash. Press 1975 280p ISBN 0-295-95377-2 LC 74-28210

Weber, David J. (ed.) New Spain's far northern frontier; essays on Spain in the American West, 1540-1821. Univ. of New Mexico Press 1979 321p ISBN 0-8263-0498-2 LC 78-21428

Weber, Samuel (ed.) Glyph. See Glyph

Wechsler, Judith (ed.) On aesthetics in science. MIT Press 1978 180p ISBN 0-262-23088-7 LC 77-26175

Weimann, Robert. Shakespeare and the popular tradition in the theater: studies in the social dimension of dramatic form and function. Ed. by Robert Schwartz. Johns Hopkins Univ. Press 1978 325p ISBN 0-8018-1985-7 LC 77-13673

Weinberg, Julius Rudolph. Ockham, Descartes, and Hume; self-knowledge, substance, and causality. Univ. of Wis. Press 1977 179p ISBN 0-299-072120-0 LC 76-11315

Weinberg, Martha Wagner. See Burnham, W. D. jt. ed.

Weiner, Dora B. (ed.) From Parnassus. See From Parnassus

Weinsheimer, Joel (ed.) Jane Austen today. Univ. of Ga. Press 1975 178p ISBN 0-8203-0382-8 LC 75-11447

Weinstock, John M. (ed.) The hero in Scandinavian literature. See The Hero in Scandinavian literature

Weintraub, Wiktor. See entry under title: For Wiktor Weintraub

Weir, Robert F. (ed.) Ethical issues in death and dying. Columbia Univ. Press 1977 xxi, 405p ISBN 0-231-04306-6 LC 77-24707

Welch, Holmes, and Seidel, Anna K. (eds.) Facets of Taoism; essays in Chinese religion. Yale Univ. Press 1979 302p ISBN 0-300-01695-6 LC 77-28034
"Most of these papers were presented originally at the International Conference of Taoist Studies, 2nd, China, Japan, 1972."

Wellek, René (ed.) Evidence in literary scholarship. See Evidence in literary scholarship

Wells, David F. and Woodbridge, John D. (eds.) The evangelicals; what they believe, who they are, where they are changing. Abingdon 1975 304p ISBN 0-687-12181-7 LC 75-15574

Welsh, Paul (ed.) Fact, value, and perception. See Fact, value, and perception

Welton, John M. See Alcock, A. E. jt. ed.

Welty, Eudora. The eye of the story; selected essays and reviews. Random House [1978 c1977] 355p ISBN 0-394-42506-5 LC 78-103296

Wennberg, Bo Göte. French and Scandinavian sculpture in the nineteenth century; a study of trends and innovations. Humanities Press [1979 c1978] 213p

Wenner-Gren Foundation for Anthropological Research. Ethnic identity. See Ethnic identity

Williams, Charles G. S. (ed.) Literature and history in the age of ideas. *See* Literature and history in the age of ideas

Williams, David Anthony (ed.) The monster in the mirror; studies in nineteenth-century realism. Published for the University of Hull by Oxford 1978 300p ISBN 0-19-713433-5 LC 78-40261
This book originated in a series of lectures given in the University of Hull in 1974

Williams, Walter L. (ed.) Southeastern Indians since the removal era. Univ. of Ga. Press 1979 253p ISBN 0-8203-0464-6 LC 78-10490

Williamson, Audrey. Artists and writers in revolt; the pre-Raphaelites. Art Alliance Press 1976 208p ISBN 0-87982-022-5 LC 76-40504

Williamson, Harold Francis (ed.) Evolution of international management structures. *See* Evolution of international management structures

Wills, John Elliot. See Spence, J. D. jt. ed.

Wilson, David Scofield. In the presence of nature. Univ. of Mass. Press 1978 234p ISBN 0-87023-020-4 LC 77-90733

Wilson, Dick. See Wilson, Richard Garrat

Wilson, John Frederick. See Mulder, J. M. jt. ed.

Wilson, Richard Garrat (ed.) Mao Tse-tung in the scales of history; a preliminary assessment organized by the China Quarterly. Cambridge 1977 331p (Contemporary China Institute Pubs.) ISBN 0-521-215583-8 LC 76-57100

Wilson, Thomas (ed.) The market and the state. *See* The Market and the state
See also Skinner, A. S. jt. ed.

Wimsatt, William Kurtz. Day of the leopards; essays in defense of poems. Yale Univ. Press 1976 258p ISBN 0-300-01960-2 LC 75-27762

Wimsatt, William Kurtz (ed.) Literary criticism: idea and act. The English Institute, 1939-1972; selected essays. Ed. with an introduction. Univ. of Calif. Press 1974 650p ISBN 0-520-02585-7 LC 73-85797

Windows on the world. See Holman, C. H.

Winter, J. M. (ed.) War and economic development. *See* War and economic development

Winternitz, Emanuel. Musical instruments and their symbolism in Western art; studies in musical iconology. Yale Univ. Press 1979 253p ISBN 0-300-02324-3 LC 78-65482

Wittkower, Rudolf. Studies in the Italian baroque; with 357 illustrations. Westview Press 1975 304p (The collected essays of Rudolf Wittkower) ISBN 0-89158-506-0 LC 75-22083

Wittreich, Joseph Anthony (ed.) Milton and the line of vision, by Joseph Anthony Wittreich, Jr. Univ. of Wis. Press 1975 xxi, 278p ISBN 0-299-06910-9 LC 75-12215

Wohl, Anthony S. (ed.) The Victorian family; structure and stresses. St Martins 1978 224p ISBN 0-312-84276-7 LC 77-9234

Wolf masks. See Ries, L. R.

Wolfe, George Herbert (ed.) Faulkner: fifty years after The marble faun. *See* Faulkner: fifty years after The marble faun

Wolman, Benjamin B. (ed.) Between survival and suicide. Consulting editor: Herbert H. Krauss. Gardner Press distributed by Halsted Press [a] division of John Wiley & Sons, Inc. 1976 195p ISBN 0-470-95944-4 LC 75-17706

Wolman, Benjamin B. (ed.) Psychoanalysis and Catholicism. Gardner Press distributed by Halsted Press, a division of John Wiley & Sons, inc. 1976 219p ISBN 0-470-15079-3 LC 76-10765

Worth, Katharine Joyce. The Irish drama of Europe from Yeats to Beckett. Humanities Press 1978 276p ISBN 0-391-00891-9 LC 78-18909

The wound of Greece. See Sherrard, P.

Wren, Thomas E. (ed.) The personal universe. *See* The Personal universe

Wright, John Henry. (ed.) Essays on the Iliad; selected modern criticism. Ind. Univ. Press 1978 150p ISBN 0-253-31990-0 LC 77-23634

Wright, John Kirtland. See entry under title: Geographies of the mind

Writing and difference. See Derrida, J.

The writing of Canadian history. See Berger, C.

The writing of history. See Canary, R. H. and Kozicki, H. J. eds.

Y

Yale classical studies v24. Studies in the Greek historians; in memory of Adam Parry. Ed. for the Department of Classics by Donald Kagan. Cambridge 1975 236p ISBN 0-521-20587-5 LC 74-12982

Yale classical studies v25; Greek tragedy. Ed. for the Department of Classics by T. F. Gould ad C. J. Herington. Cambridge 1977 350p ISBN 0-521-21112-3 LC 76-8156

Yamanouchi, Hisaaki. The search for authenticity in modern Japanese literature. Cambridge 1978 214p ISBN 0-521-21856-X LC 77-84815

The Year book of world affairs, 1975. Editors: George W. Keeton and Georg Schwarzenberger. Published under the auspices of The London Institute of World Affairs [v29]. Praeger 1975 ISBN 0-275-33500-3

The Year book of world affairs, 1976-1979. Editors: George W. Keeton and Georg Schwarzenberger. Published under the auspices of The London Institute of World Affairs [v30-33] Westview Press 1976-1979 4v ISBN v30 0-89158-529-X; v31 0-89158-529; v32 0-89158-824-8; v33 0-89158-5551-6 LC 47-29156

The year's work in English studies. See English Association.

Yeats and the occult. Ed. by George Mills Harper. Maclean-Hunter Press 1975 322p (Yeats Studies ser) ISBN 0-7705-1308-5

Yeats, Joyce, and Beckett; new light on three modern Irish writers. Ed. by Kathleen McGrory and John Unterecker. Bucknell Univ. Press 1976 184p ISBN 0-8387-1465-X LC 74-4983
Festschrift in honor of William York Tindall
Partially analyzed

Yinger, John Milton (ed.) Major social issues. *See* Major social issues

Yoder, Don (ed.) American folklife. Univ. of Tex. Press 1976 304p ISBN 0-292-70308-2 LC 75-16073

Young, Thomas Daniel (ed.) The New Criticism and after. John Crowe Ransom Memorial lectures 1975, delivered at Kenyon College on April 3-5. Univ. Press of Va. [1977 c1976] 90p ISBN 0-8139-0672-5 LC 76-6165

Yourgrau, Wolfgang (ed.) Cosmology, history, and theology. *See* Cosmology, history, and theology

Z

Directory of Publishers and Distributors

ABC-Clio. American Bibliographical Center —Clio Press, Inc. Riviera Campus, P.O. Box 4397, 2040 Alameda Padre Serra, Santa Barbara, Calif. 93103

A.L.A. American Library Association, 50 E Huron St, Chicago, Ill. 60611

AMACOM. (Division of American Management Assn) 135 W 50th St, New York, N. Y. 10020

AMS Press. AMS Press, 56 E 13th St, New York, N.Y. 10003

Abingdon. Abingdon Press, 201 8th Av, S, Nashville, Tenn. 37202

Abrams. Harry N. Abrams, Inc, 110 E 59th St, New York, N.Y. 10022

Addison-Wesley. Addison-Wesley Publishing Company, Inc, Reading, Mass. 01867

Africana Pub. Co. See Holmes & Meier Pubs.

Allanheld, Osmun/Universe Bks. Allanheld, Osmun & Company, 19 Brunswick Rd, Montclair, N.J. 07042

Allen, G. George Allen & Unwin Ltd, 40 Museum St, London WC1A 1LU, England

Am. Antiquarian Soc. American Antiquarian Society, 185 Salisbury St, Worcester, Mass. 01609

Am. Assn. for State & Local Hist. American Association for State & Local History, 1400 8th Av, S, Nashville, Tenn. 37203

Am. Enterprise Inst. for Public Policy Res. American Enterprise Institute for Public Policy Research, 1150 17th St, N.W., Washington, D.C. 20036

Am. Heritage. American Heritage Publishing Company, Inc, 10 Rockefeller Plaza, New York, N.Y. 10020

Am. Philosophical Soc. American Philosophical Society, 104 S. 5th St, Philadelphia, Pa. 19106

Anchor Press. See Doubleday

Andrews & McMeel. Andrews & McMeel, 6700 Squibb Rd, Mission, Kan. 66202

Architectural Bk. Pub. Co. Architectural Book Publishing Co, Inc, 10 E 40th St, New York, N.Y. 10016

Archon Bks. See Shoe String

Ardis. Ardis Publishers, 2901 Heatherway, Ann Arbor, Mich. 48104

Ardis Pubs. Ardis Publishers, 2901 Heatherway, Ann Arbor, Mich. 48104

Arlington House. Arlington House, Inc, 165 Huguenot St, New Rochelle, N.Y. 10801

Art Alliance Press. Art Alliance Press, c/o Associated University Presses, Inc, Box 421, Cranbury, N.J. 08512

Association Press. See Follett Pub.

Atheneum Pubs. Atheneum Publishers, 122 E 42nd St, New York, N.Y. 10017

Athlone Press of the Univ. of London. See Humanities Press

Augustin. J. J. Augustin, Inc.—Publisher, Locust Valley, N.Y. 11560

Barnes & Noble. See Harper

Basic Bks. Basic Books, Inc, Publishers, 10 E 53rd St, New York, N.Y. 10022

Beacon Press. Beacon Press, 25 Beacon St, Boston, Mass. 02108

Behrman. Behrman House, Inc, 1261 Broadway, New York, N.Y. 10001

Belknap Press. See Harvard Univ. Press

Blackwell. Basil Blackwell, 5 Alfred St, Oxford OX1 4HB, England

Bobbs, The Bobbs-Merrill Company, Inc, 4300 W 62d St, Indianapolis, Ind. 46206

Bowling Green Univ. Pop. Press. Bowling Green University Popular Press, 100 University Hall, Bowling Green, Ohio 43403

Bowling Green Univ. Press. Bowling Green University Press, Donna G. Fricke, Center for Bibliography, Dept. of English, Bowling Green State University, Bowling Green, Ohio 43403

Branden Press. Branden Press, 221 Columbus Av, Boston, Mass. 02116

Braziller. George Braziller, Inc, 1 Park Av, New York, N.Y. 10016

Brookings. Brookings Institution, Publications Division, 1775 Massachusetts Av, N.W., Washington, D.C. 20036

Brunner/Mazel. Brunner/Mazel, Inc, 19 Union Sq, W. New York, N.Y. 10003

Bucknell Univ. Press. Bucknell University Press, Lewisburg, Pa. 17837

Cambridge. Cambridge University Press, 32 E 57th St, New York, N.Y. 10022

Change Mag Press. Change Magazine Press, NBW Tower, New Rochelle, N.Y. 10801

City College Workshop Center for Open Education. Room 6, Shepard Hall, City College, Convent Av. and 140th St, New York, N.Y. 10031

Clarendon Press. See Oxford

Collier Bks. See Macmillan Pub. Co.

Collins. William Collins Publishers, Inc, 2080 W 117th St, Cleveland, Ohio 44111

Collins + World. See Collins

Colo. Associated Univ. Press. Colorado Associated University Press, University of Colorado, 1424 15th St, Boulder, Colo. 80309

Columbia Univ. Press. Columbia University Press, 136 S Broadway, Irvington, N.Y. 10533

Cornell Univ. Press. Cornell University Press, 124 Roberts Pl, Ithaca, N.Y. 14850

Crossroads Press. Crossroads Press, Epstein Bldg, Brandeis University, Waltham, Mass. 02154

Crowell. Thomas Y. Crowell Company, 10 E 53rd St, New York, N.Y. 10022

Crown. Crown Publishers, 1 Park Av, New York, N.Y. 10016

Dekker, M. Marcel Dekker, Inc, 270 Madison Av, New York, N.Y. 10016

Delacorte Press. Delacorte Press, 1 Dag Hammarskjold Plaza, New York, N.Y. 10017

Dodd. Dodd, Mead & Company, Inc, 79 Madison Av, New York, N.Y. 10016

Doubleday. Doubleday & Company, Inc, 245 Park Av, New York, N.Y. 10017

Dufour. Dufour Editions, Chester Springs, Pa. 19425

Duke Univ. Press. Duke University Press, College Station, Box 6697, Durham, N.C. 27708

Duquesne Univ. Press. Duquesne University Press, University Hall, Pittsburgh, Pa. 15219

Dutton. E. P. Dutton & Company, 2 Park Av, New York, N.Y. 10016

ETC Publications. ETC Publications, Drawer 1627-A, Palm Springs, Calif. 92262

Ecco Press. The Ecco Press, 1 W 30th St, New York, N.Y. 10001

Edinburgh Univ. Press. Edinburgh University Press, c/o Biblio Distribution Center, 81 Adams Dr, Totowa, N.J. 07512

Eerdmans. William B. Eerdmans Publishing Company, 255 Jefferson Av, S.E., Grand Rapids, Mich. 49502

Everett/Edwards. Everett/Edwards, Inc, Box 1060, Deland, Fla. 32720

Faber & Faber. Faber and Faber, 22 S. Broadway, Salem, N.H. 03079

Fairleigh Dickinson Univ. Press. Fairleigh Dickinson University Press, Madison, N.J. 07940

Farrar, Straus. Farrar, Straus & Giroux, Inc, 19 Union Sq, W, New York, N.Y. 10003

Follett, Pub. Follett Publishing Company, 1010 Washington Blvd, Chicago, Ill. 60607

Fordham Univ. Press. Fordham University Press, University Box L, Bronx, N.Y. 10458

Free Press. See Macmillan Pub. Co.

Georgetown Univ. Press. Georgetown University Press, Washington, D.C 20057

Godine. The Godine Press, Inc. 306 Dartmouth St, Boston, Mass. 02116

Greenwood Press. Greenwood Press, Inc, 51 Riverside Av, Westport, Conn. 06880

Grossman Pubs. See Viking

Hall, G.K.&Co. G. K. Hall & Company, 70 Lincoln St, Boston, Mass. 02111

Halsted Press. See Wiley

Harcourt. Harcourt Brace Jovanovich, Inc, 757 3d Av, New York, N.Y. 10017

Harper. Harper & Row, Publishers, 10 E 53d St, New York, N.Y. 10022

Harvard Univ. Press. Harvard University Press, 79 Garden St, Cambridge, Mass. 02138

Hastings House. Hastings House, Publishers, Inc, 10 E 40th St, New York, N.Y. 10016

Heath. D.C. Heath & Company, 125 Spring St, Lexington, Mass. 02173

Hennessey & Ingalls. Hennessey & Ingalls, Inc, 11833 Wilshire Blvd, Los Angeles, Calif. 90025

Hill & Wang. See Farrar, Straus

Holmes & Meier Pubs. Holmes & Meier Publishers, 101 5th Av, New York, N.Y. 10003

Holt. Holt, Rinehart and Winston, 383 Madison Av, New York, N.Y. 10017

Horizon Press. Horizon Press, 156 5th Av, New York, N.Y. 10010

Horn Bk. The Horn Book, Inc, Dept. W, Park Sq. Bldg, 31, St James Av, Boston, Mass. 02116

Houghton. Houghton Mifflin Company, 1 Beacon St, Boston, Mass. 02107

Howard Univ. Press. Howard University Press, 2935 Upton St, N.W., Washington, D.C. 20008

Humanities Press. Humanities Press, Atlantic Highlands, N.J. 07716

Ind. Univ. Press. Indiana University Press, 10th and Morton Sts, Bloomington, Ind. 47401

Inst. for Contemporary Studies. Institute for Contemporary Studies, 260 California St, Suite 811, San Francisco, Calif. 94111

Int. Arts & Sciences Press. International Arts & Sciences Press, 901 N Broadway, White Plains, N.Y. 10603

Int. Scholarly Bk. Services. International Scholarly Book Services, Inc, 2130 Pacific Av, Forest Grove, Ore. 97116

Int. Univs. Press. International Universities Press, Inc, 315 5th Av, New York, N.Y. 10016

Iowa State Univ. Press. Iowa State University Press, South State Av, Ames, Iowa 50010

Jewish Pub. Soc. of Am. Jewish Publication Society of America, 117 S 17th St, Philadelphia, Pa. 19103

John Knox Press. John Knox Press, 341 Ponce de Leon Av, N.E., Atlanta, Ga. 30308

Johns Hopkins Univ. Press. The Johns Hopkins University Press, Baltimore, Md. 21218

Jossey-Bass. Jossey-Bass, Inc, Publishers, 615 Montgomery St, San Francisco, Calif. 94111

Karz. Karz Publishers, 320 W 105th St, New York, N.Y. 10025

Kennikat. Kennikat Press Corporation, 90 S Bayles Av, Port Washington, N.Y. 11050

Kent State Univ. Press. Kent State University Press, Kent, Ohio 44242

Knopf. Alfred E. Knopf, Inc, 201 E 50th St, New York, N.Y. 10022

La. State Univ. Press. Louisiana State University Press, Baton Rouge, La. 70803

Lawrence, S. Seymour Lawrence, Inc, 90 Beacon St, Boston, Mass. 02108

Lexington Bks. See Heath

Lib. of Congress. See Supt. of Docs.

Liberty Press. Liberty Fund, Inc, 7440 N Shadeland, Indianapolis, Ind. 46250

Linnet Bks. See Shoe String

Little. Little, Brown & Company, 34 Beacon St, Boston, Mass. 02106

Littlefield, Adams & Company, 81 Adams Dr, Totowa, N.J. 07512

Liveright. See Norton

Loyola Univ. Press. Loyola University Press, 3441 N Ashland Av, Chicago, Ill. 60657

MIT Press. The MIT Press, 28 Carleton St, Cambridge, Mass. 02142

McGill-Queens Univ. Press. McGill-Queen's University Press, 1020 Pine Av, W, Montreal, Quebec, Canada H3A 1A2

McGraw. McGraw-Hill Book Company, Inc, 1221 Av. of the Americas, New York, N.Y. 10020

McKay. David McKay Company, Inc, 750 3d Av, New York, N.Y. 10017

Maclean-Hunter Press. See Macmillan Co. of Canada

Macmillan Co. of Canada. Macmillan Company of Canada, Ltd, 70 Bond St, Toronto, Ont. M5B 1X3, Can.

Macmillan Pub. Co. The Macmillan Publishing Company, 866 3d Av, New York, N.Y. 10022

Mason/Charter. Mason/Charter Publishers, 641 Lexington Av, New York, N.Y. 10022

Mayfield Pubs. Mayfield Publishing Co, 285 Hamilton Av, Palo Alto, Calif. 94301

Mich. State Univ. Press. Michigan State University Press, 1405 S. Harrison Rd, Lansing, Mich. 48824

Modern Lang. Assn. of Am. Modern Language Association of America, 62 5th Av, New York, N.Y. 10011

Monthly Review Press. Monthly Review Press, 62 W 14th St, New York, N.Y. 10011

Morrow. William Morrow & Company, Inc, 105 Madison Av, New York, N.Y. 10016

Mouton. Mouton & Company, NV, Publishers, 5 Henderstratt, The Hague, 2076 Netherlands

N.Y. Univ. Press. New York University Press, Washington Sq, New York, N.Y. 10003

NOK Pubs. N O K Publishers, Ltd, 150 5th Av, New York, N.Y. 10011

Natl. Assn. of Social Workers. National Association of Social Workers, Inc, 1425 H St, N.W, Washington, D.C. 20005

Neale Watson Acad. Publs. Neale Watson Academy Publications, 156 5th Av, New York, N.Y. 10010

Nelson-Hall. Nelson-Hall Company, 111 N. Canal St, Chicago, Ill. 60606

New Directions. New Directions Publishing Corporation, 333 Av. of the Americas, New York, N.Y. 10014

New Republic. The New Republic Book Company, Inc, 1220 19th St, N.W, Washington, D.C. 20036

N. Texas State Univ. North Texas State University, Box 13647, Denton, Tex. 76203

Northland Press. Northland Press, Box N, Flagstaff, Arizona 86001

Northwestern Univ. Press. Northwestern University Press, 1735 Benson Av, Box 1093X, Evanston, Ill. 60201

Norton. W. W. Norton & Company, Inc. 500 5th Av, New York, N.Y. 10036

Ohio State Univ. Press. Ohio State University Press, Hitchock Hall, Rm 316, 2070 Neil Av, Columbus, Ohio 43210

Ohio Univ. Press. Ohio University Press, Scott Quadrangle, Athens, Ohio 45701

Open Ct. Open Court Publishing Company, Box 599, 1039 8th St, LaSalle, Ill. 61301

Orbis Bks. Orbis Books, Maryknoll, N.Y. 10545

Oxford. Oxford University Press, Inc, 200 Madison Av, New York, N.Y. 10016

Pa. State Univ. Press. The Pennsylvania State University Press, 215 Wagner Bldg, University Park, Pa. 16802

Pantheon Bks. See Random House

Pergamon. Pergamon Press, Inc, Maxwell House, Fairview Park, Elmsford, N.Y. 10523

Plenum Press. Plenum Publishing Corporation, 227 W 17th St, New York, N.Y. 10011

Popular Press. The Popular Press Culture Center, Bowling Green State University, Bowling Green, Ohio 43403

Praeger. Praeger Publishers, Inc, 521 5th Av, New York, N.Y. 10017

Prentice-Hall. Prentice-Hall International, Inc, Englewood Cliffs, N.J. 07632

Presidio Press. Presidio Press, 1114 Irwin St, San Rafael, Calif. 94901

Princeton Univ. Press. Princeton University Press, Princton, N.J. 08540

Prometheus Bks. Prometheus Books, 923 Kensington Av, Buffalo, N.Y. 14215

Pruett Pub. Pruett Publishing Company, 3235 Prairie Av, Boulder, Colo. 80301

Psychohistory Press. The Psychohistory Press, 2315 Broadway, New York, N.Y. 10024

Purdue Univ. Press. Purdue University Press, S Campus Courts-D, West, Lafayette, Ind. 47907

Pushcart Press. Pushcart Press, Box 845, Yonkers, N.Y. 10701

Putnam. See Rowman & Littlefield

Quadrangle/The N.Y. Times Bk. Co. See Times Bks.

Random House. Random House, Inc, 201 E 50th St, New York, N.Y. 10022

Reconstructionist Press. Reconstructionist Press, 432 Park Av, S. New York, N.Y. 10016

Regents Press of Kan. The Regents Press of Kansas, 366 Watson Library, Lawrence, Kan. 66045

Rowman & Littlefield. Rowman & Littlefield, 81 Adams Dr, Totowa, N.J. 07512

Rutgers Univ. Press. Rutgers University Press, 30 College Av, New Brunswick, N.J. 08903

Sage. Sage Publications, Inc, 275 S Beverly Dr, Beverly Hills, Calif. 90212

St Martins. St Martin's Press, Inc, 175 5th Av, New York, N.Y. 10010

Scarecrow. Scarecrow Press, Inc, 52 Liberty St, Metuchen, N.J. 08840

Schenkman Pub. Co. Schenkman Publishing Company, Inc, 3 Mt Auburn Pl, Harvard Sq, Cambridge, Mass. 02138

Schocken. Schocken Books, Inc, 200 Madison Av, New York, N.Y. 10016

Science Hist. Pubs. See Neale Watson Acad. Publs.

Scottish Acad. Press. See Columbia Publs. Univ. Press

Scribner. Charles Scribner's Sons, 597 5th Av, New York, N.Y. 10017

Seabury. The Seabury Press, Inc, 815 2d Av, New York, N.Y. 10017

Sheed, Andrews and McMeel, Inc. See Andrews & McMeel

Shoe String. The Shoe String Press Inc, Shoe String. The Shoe String Press, Inc, Box 4327, 995 Sherman Av, Hamden, Conn. 06514

Simon & Schuster. Simon & Schuster, Inc, Publishers, 630 5th Av, New York, N.Y. 10020

Smith College Lib. Smith College Library, Order Department, Northampton, Mass. 01060

Smithsonian Inst. Press. Smithsonian Institution Press. 111 N Capitol St, Washington, D.C. 20002

Southern Ill. Univ. Press. Southern Illinois University Press, Box 3697, Carbondale, Ill. 62901

Springer Pub. Co. Springer Publishing Company, Inc, 200 Park Av S, New York, N.Y. 10003

Stanford Univ. Press. Stanford University Press, Stanford, Calif. 94305

State Univ. of N.Y. Press. State University of New York Press, 99 Washington Av, Albany, N.Y. 12246

Supt. of Docs. Superintendent of Documents, Government Printing Office, Washington, D.C. 20402

Swallow Press. The Swallow Press, 811 W Junior Terr, Chicago, Ill. 60613

Syracuse Univ. Press. Syracuse University Press, 1011 E Water St, Syracuse, N.Y. 13210

Teachers College Press. Teachers College Press, 1234 Amsterdam Av, New York, N.Y. 10027

Technical Impex Corp. Technical Impex Corp, 5 S. Union St, Lawrence, Mass. 01843

Temple Univ. Press. Temple University Press, Broad & Oxford Sts, Philadelphia, Pa. 19122

Thomas, C.C. Charles C. Thomas, Publisher, 301-27 E. Lawrence Av, Springfield, Ill. 62717

Times Bks. Times Books, 3 Park Av, New York, N.Y. 10016

Transaction Bks. Transaction Books, Rutgers University, New Brunswick, N.J. 08903

Tulane Univ. Tulane University, New Orleans, La. 70118

Twayne. See Hall, G.K.&Co.

Two Continents. The Two Continents Publishing Group, Ltd, 171 Madison Av, New York, N.Y. 10017

Ungar. Frederick Ungar Publishing Company, 250 Park Av, S, New York, N.Y. 10003

Univ. of Ala. Press. University of Alabama Press, Drawer 2877, University, Ala. 35486

Univ. of Ariz. Press. University of Arizona Press, Box 3398, Tucson, Ariz. 85722

Univ. of Calif. Press. University of California Press, 2223 Fulton St, Berkeley, Calif. 94720

Univ. of Chicago Press. University of Chicago Press, 5801 Ellis Av, Chicago, Ill. 60637

Univ. of Ga. Press. University of Georgia Press, Athens, Ga. 30602

Univ. of Ill. Press. University of Illinois Press, Urbana, Ill. 61801

Univ. of Kan. University of Kansas, Lawrence, Kansas 66045

Univ. of Mass. Press. University of Massachusetts Press, Box 429, Amherst, Mass. 01002

Univ. of Mich. Press. University of Michigan Press, 615 E University Av, Ann Arbor, Mich. 48106

Univ. of Minn. Press. University of Minnesota Press, 2037 University Av, SE, Minneapolis, Minn. 55455

Univ. of Mo. Press. University of Missouri Press, 107 Swallow Hall, Columbia, Mo. 65201

Univ. of N.Mex. Press. University of New Mexico Press, Albuquerque, N.M. 87131

Univ. of Neb. Press. University of Nebraska Press, 901 N 17th St, Lincoln, Nebr. 68508

Univ. of N.C. Press. University of North Carolina Press, Box 2288, Chapel Hill, N.C. 27514

Univ. of Notre Dame Press. University of Notre Dame Press, Notre Dame, Ind. 46556

Univ. of Okla. Press. University of Oklahoma Press, 1005 Asp Av, Norman, Okla. 73069

Univ. of Ore. University of Oregon, Eugene, Ore. 97403

Univ. of Ottawa Press. University of Ottawa Press, 65 Hastey Av, Ottawa, Ont. KIN 6N5, Canada

Univ. of Pa. Press. University of Pennsylvania Press, 3933 Walnut St, Philadelphia, Pa. 19104

Univ. of Pittsburgh Press. University of Pittsburgh Press, Pittsburgh, Pa. 15260

Univ. of Queensland Press. University of Queensland Press, 5 South Union St, Lawrence, Mass. 01843

Univ. of S.C. Press. University of South Carolina Press, Columbia, S.C. 29208

Univ. of Tenn. Press. University of Tennessee Press, 293 Communication Bldg, Knoxville, Tenn. 37916

Univ. of Tex. at Austin Press. University of Texas at Austin Press, Box 7819, Austin, Tex. 78712

Univ. of Toronto Press. University of Toronto Press, St George Campus, Toronto, Ont. M5S 1A6 Canada

Univ. of Wash. Press. University of Washington Press, Seattle, Wash. 98105

Univ. of Wis. Press. University of Wisconsin Press, Box 1379, Madison, Wis. 53701

Univ. Press of Hawaii. University Press of Hawaii, 2840 Kolowalu St, Honolulu, Hawaii 96822

Univ. Press of Kan. See Regents Press of Kan.

Univ. Press of Ky. University Press of Kentucky, Lexington, Ky. 40506

Univ. Press of Miss. University Press of Mississippi, 3825 Ridgewood Rd, Jackson, Miss. 39211

Univ. Press of New England. The University Press of New England, Box 979, Hanover, N.H. 03755

Univ. Press of Va. University Press of Virginia, Box 3608, University Sta, Charlottesville, Va. 22903

Vanderbilt Univ. Press. Vanderbilt University Press, 2505 (Rear) West End Av, Nashville, Tenn. 37203

Vanguard. The Vanguard Press, 424 Madison Av, New York, N.Y. 10017

Viking. The Viking Press, 625 Madison Av, New York, N.Y. 10022

Wesleyan Univ. Press. Wesleyan University Press, 55 High St, Middletown, Conn. 06457

Westminster Press. The Westminster Press, Witherspoon Bldg, Philadelphia, Pa. 19107 19107

Westview Press. Westview Press, 1898 Flatiron Ct, Boulder, Colo. 80301

Weybright. Weybright & Talley, Inc, 750 3d Av, New York, N.Y. 10017

Wiley. John Wiley & Sons, Inc, 605 3d Av, New York, N.Y. 10016

Woburn Press. The Woburn Press, c/o Center Biblio Distribution, 81 Adams Dr, Totowa, N.J. 07512

Yale Univ. Press. Yale University Press, 92A Yale Station, New Haven, Conn. 06520

NOTES

NOTES

NOTES

NOTES

NOTES

NOTES

NOTES

NOTES